standard catalog of

4x4's

A COMPREHENSIVE GUIDE TO FOUR-WHEEL DRIVE VEHICLES INCLUDING TRUCKS, VANS AND SPORTS SEDANS AND SPORT UTILITY VEHICLES

1945-1993

Published by:

Krause Publications, Inc.
700 E. State Street
Iola, WI 54990-0001

Library of Congress Number: 92-71443

ISBN: 0-87341-203-6

Printed in the United States of America

TABLE OF CONTENTS

HOW TO USE THIS CATALOG

APPEARANCE AND EQUIPMENT: Word descriptions help identify 4x4 vehicles down to details such as styling features, trim and interior appointments. Standard equipment lists usually begin with low-priced base models. Then, subsequent data blocks cover higher-priced lines of the same year.

VEHICLE I.D. NUMBERS: This edition features expanded data explaining the basic serial numbering system used by each postwar vehicle manufacturer. This data reveals where, when and in what order your vehicle was built. There is much more information on assembly plant, body style and original engine codes.

SPECIFICATIONS CHART: The first chart column gives series or model numbers for 4x4 vehicles. The second column gives body type. The third column tells factory price. The fourth column gives GVW. The fifth column gives the vehicle's original shipping weight. The sixth column provides model year production totals (if available) or makes reference to additional notes found below the specifications chart. When the same vehicle came with different engines or trim levels at different prices and weights, slashes (/) are used to separate the low price or weight from the high one. In some cases, model numbers are also presented this way. In rare cases where data is non-applicable or not available the abbreviation "N.A." appears.

BASE ENGINE DATA: According to make of vehicle, engine data will be found either below the data block for each series or immediately following the specifications chart for the last vehicle-line. Displacement, bore and stroke and horsepower ratings are listed, plus a lot more data where available. This edition has more complete engine listings for many models. In other cases, extra-cost engines are listed in the "options" section.

VEHICLE DIMENSIONS: The main data compiled here consists of wheelbase, overall length and tire size. Front and rear tread widths are given for most 4x4 vehicles through the early 1960s and some later models. Overall width and height appears in some cases, too.

OPTIONAL EQUIPMENT LISTS: This section includes data blocks listing all types of options and accessories. A great deal of attention has been focused on cataloging both the availability and the original factory retail prices of optional equipment. Because of size and space limitations, a degree of selectivity has been applied by concentrating on those optional features of greatest interest to collectors. Important option packages have been covered and detailed as accurately as possible in the given amount of space. When available, options prices are listed.

HISTORICAL FOOTNOTES: 4x4 vehicles are already recognized as an important part of America's automotive heritage. Revealing statistics; important dates and places; personality profiles; performance milestones; and other historical facts are highlighted in this "automotive trivia" section.

New for 1990 were three-point lap and shoulder belts for all out-board passengers (front and rear). Redesigned for 1990 was the Cherokee's optional exterior-mounted swing-away spare tire carrier. For 1990 it was entirely bumper-mounted to reduce the potential for body corrosion. The Cherokee Limited and Wagoneer Limited had a new standard overhead console housing holders for garage door opener and sun glasses, outside temperature display, compass, lights for front and rear seating areas, and remote-control door lock receiver. This feature was optional for the Cherokee Laredo. All Cherokees for 1990 had a standard AM/FM electronically tuned radio with four speakers. The exterior color selection for the 1990 Cherokee models consisted of bright white, black, Colorado red, black cherry pearlcoat, sand metallic, midnight blue metallic, sterling metallic, dover grey metallic, dark baltic metallic and spinnaker blue metallic. All paints were clearcoat except for black cherry. The metallic paints were extra cost. The color selection for the Wagoneer Limited was restricted to bright white, black, black cherry pearlcoat, midnight blue metallic, and dover grey metallic. As with the Cherokee models, the metallic paints were extra-cost items for the Wagoneer Limited. The Grand Wagoneer's color selection consisted of bright white, black, black cherry pearlcoat, sand metallic, sterling metallic, dover grey metallic, and dark baltic metallic. The interiors of the Wagoneer Limited and Grand Wagoneer were upholstered in leather/Country cord fabric and offered in either cordovan or sand.

I.D. DATA: The serial number was located on the left-hand hinge pillar. The V.I.N. had 17 symbols. The first three entries identified the manufacturer, make and type of vehicle. The fourth unit, a letter, designated the engine (C-4.2 liter 6-cyl., H-2.5 liter 4-cyl., M-4.0 liter 6-cyl., N-5.9 liter V-8). The fifth character, a letter, identified the transmission. The sixth and seventh characters identified the series and body style. The eighth character identified the GVW rating. Next followed a check digit. The eleventh character was the manufacturing plant identification. The final six digits were the sequential production number. The vehicle identification indicated the model as follows: Grand Wagoneer: ( )J4( )S587( )L( )000001 and up. Wagoneer (6-cyl.): ( )J4( )N78L( )L( )000001 and up, Cherokee (4-cyl.): ( )J4( )(model)E( )L000001 and up, Cherokee (6-cyl.): ( )J4( )(model)L( )L( )000001 and up. Vehicle identification was as follows: S58: Grand Wagoneer station wagon, N78: Wagoneer, J27: Two-door Cherokee, J28: Four-door Cherokee, J77:Two-door Cherokee Limited, J78: Four-door Cherokee Limited.

Model Number	Body Type & Seating	Factory Price	GVW	Shipping Weight	Prod. Total
Grand Wagoneer Station Wagon V-8					
S58	4-dr.	$27,795	5980	4499	6449*

* Calendar year production.

Model Number	Body Type & Seating	Factory Price	GVW	Shipping Weight	Prod. Total
Wagoneer Station Wagon 6-cyl.					
N78	4-dr. Limited	$24,795	4900	3453	3888*

* Calendar year production

Model Number	Body Type & Seating	Factory Price	GVW	Shipping Weight	Prod. Total
Cherokee Station Wagon 4-cyl.					
J27	2-dr.	$14,695	4850	3033	151,230*
J28	4-dr.	$15,545	4900	3076	—
Cherokee Station Wagon 6-cyl.					
J27	2-dr.	$15,295	4850	3157	—
J28	4-dr.	$16,145	4900	3200	—
J77	2-dr. Limited	$24,650	4850	—	—
J78	4-dr. Limited	$25,775	4900	—	—

* Calendar year production-includes all Cherokee models.

STANDARD ENGINE: Grand Wagoneer: Engine Type: OHV, V-8. Cast iron block and cylinder head. Bore x Stroke: 4.08 in. x 3.44 in. Lifters: Hydraulic. Number of main bearings-5. Fuel Induction: 2-bbl. carburetor. Compression Ratio: 8.25:1. Displacement: 360 cu. in. (5.89 liters). Horsepower: Net: 144 @ 3200 rpm. Torque: Net: 280 lb.-ft. @ 1500 rpm. Oil refill capacity: 5 qt. with filter change. Fuel Requirements: Unleaded.

STANDARD ENGINE: Cherokee: Engine Type: OHV, In-line-4. Cast iron block and cylinder head. Bore x Stroke: 3.88 in. x 3.19 in. Lifters: Hydraulic. Number of main bearings-5. Fuel Induction: Throttle body single point fuel injection. Compression Ratio: 9.2:1. Displacement: 150.45 cu. in. (2.4 liters). Horsepower: Net: 121 @ 5000 rpm. Torque: Net: 141 lb.-ft. @ 3500 rpm. Oil refill capacity: 5 qt. with filter change. Fuel Requirements: Unleaded.

OPTIONAL ENGINE: Cherokee: Standard for Cherokee Limited and Wagoneer Limited. Engine Type: OHV, 6-cyl. Cast iron block and cylinder head. Bore x Stroke: 3.88 in. x 3.14 in. Lifters: Hydraulic. Number of main bearings-7. Fuel Induction: Multi-point, electronic fuel injection. Compression Ratio: 9.2:1. Displacement: 241.6 cu. in. (3.96 liters). Horsepower: Net: 177 @ 4500 rpm. Torque: Net: 224 lb.-ft. @ 2500 rpm. Oil refill capacity: 5 qt. with filter change. Fuel Requirements: Unleaded.

VEHICLE DIMENSIONS: Wagoneer and Cherokee. Wheelbase: 101.4 in. Overall Length: 165.3 in. Front/Rear Tread: 57.0 in./57.0 in. Overall Height: 63.33 in. Width: 70.5 in. Front/Rear Overhang: 27.5 in./36.4 in. Approach/Departure Degrees: 39.7/31.0. Ground Clearance: Minimum clearance: 7.4 in. (rear axle to ground). Minimum Running Clearance: 8.8 in. Maximum capacity: 71.8 cu. ft. (with rear seat folded). Front headroom: 38.3 in. Front legroom: 39.9 in. Front shoulder room: 55.3 in. Front hip room: 55.3 in. Rear headroom: 38.0 in. Rear legroom: 35.3 in. Rear shoulder room: 55.3 in. Rear hip room: 44.5 in. Grand Wagoneer.

OPTIONS: 4.0 liter engine: Anti-lock brakes (Cherokee Laredo and Limited, Wagoneer Limited). Automatic transmission. Selec-Trac (requires 4.0 liter engine and auto. trans.). Rear Trac-Lok differential (requires 4.0 liter engine and conventional spare. Air conditioning. Pioneer Package. Laredo Package. Sport Package (two-door Cherokee). Includes 4.0 liter engine, carpeting, body side stripes, exterior body moldings, 225/75R15 OWL tires, aluminum wheels. Sport Option Group (two-door Cherokee). Includes Sport Package content plus console with armrest, Gauge Group with tachometer, AM/FM electronically tuned stereo radio, spare tire cover. Option Group 1 (base two-door Cherokee). Includes floor carpeting, spare tire cover, 205/75R15 tires, and wheel trim rings. Option Group 1 (base four-door Cherokee). Includes floor carpeting, spare tire cover, 205/75R15 tires, wheel trim rings, air conditioning, console with armrest, AM/FM electronically tuned stereo radio, roof rack and rear window wiper and washer. Pioneer Package Option Group 1 (two-door Cherokee only). Includes content of Pioneer Package plus air conditioning, console with armrest, extra-quiet insulation, Protection Group, roof rack, tilt steering column, remote control exterior mirrors, intermittent windshield wipers and rear defogger. Pioneer Package Option Group 2 (two-door Cherokee only). Includes content of Group 1 plus cruise control, power windows and locks, keyless entry system, AM/FM/ET radio and cassette player. Laredo Package Option Group. Contains Laredo Package, air conditioning, cruise control, fog lamps, power windows and locks, keyless entry system, AM/FM/ET radio and cassette player. Fabric bucket seats (base and Sport Cherokee. Carpeting (base Cherokee). Console with armrest (requires carpeting option). Cruise control (requires Visibility Group, not available with 4-cyl. engine and manual transmission). Deep tinted glass (Cherokee base and Sport two-door). Deep tinted glass (Cherokee Pioneer). Rear window defogger. Heavy-duty alternator and battery. Extra-Quiet Insulation Package. Gauge Package (Cherokee Sport).

HISTORICAL FOOTNOTES: In 1990, as in earlier years, the Jeep Cherokee's production exceeded the previous year's total.

INTRODUCTION

Nearly six years ago, John Gunnell wrote in his introduction to the *Standard Catalog of American Light-Duty Trucks* that "creating this catalog was more challenging, frustrating and nerve-wracking than any other book we've ever worked on. But it's been exciting to venture where no one has gone before; to create something significantly new."

Long before I finished the final section of this book, I had begun to recognize John, on the strength of these words, as a prophet-of-sorts; maybe even the patron saint of writers who had accepted a similar challenge. Perhaps such an assertion is a bit too bold, possibly even bordering on extremism. But John's words about challenge, frustration and wracking of one's nerves remain valid. A research foray into new and uncharted territory soon encounters discrepancies that resist nearly every effort at resolution; errors caused by the human condition and dark holes of nothingness left unwittingly by writers who decades ago went about their assigned duties unaware that years later their efforts would emerge as primary sources for transportation historians.

But these formidable obstacles notwithstanding, the field of historical data concerning four-wheel-drive vehicles proved rich, varied and fertile. If some questions remain unanswered and some doubts linger about the absolute accuracy of some material, there remains little doubt in my mind that this book represents a major step forward in the chronicling of the history of four-wheel drive vehicles.

This standard catalog is organized alphabetically by marque. Within each marque's section the various models are examined in chronological order. Our goal was to present to the reader a detailed and lively account of American 4x4 vehicles. Major attention was given to their historical development, annual model revisions, technical data, options and prices.

This area of research also proved to be an area populated by many fine people who combined an extensive knowledge base with an unstinting eagerness to assist the author. Paul Politis was an invaluable source of early sales literature and data books. Among the members of the various public relations departments, special thanks is extended to Ed Lechtzin of Pontiac, Kari St. Antoine of Chevrolet, Paul Preuss of Ford, Rita McKay of Chrysler and Jeep, Jill Witzenburg at Oldsmobile, and Craig MacNab at AM General Corporation. A note of appreciation goes to John Barlow for the extended use of his 4x4 magazine collection. As always, my friend Dick Wood was a source of support. Special thanks for his assistance is extended to Bill Davis, president of Country Club Chevrolet in Oneonta, New York. Both the members of my family — my wife, Grace, and daughters Cindy, Lynn and Susan — and my editors at Krause Publications — Pat Klug and Mary Sieber — are worthy of special medals cast in recognition of their patience and understanding.

On a very personal note I would like to dedicate this book to the memory of my very dear friend and loyal companion, "Pup." He was present at its beginning, and although he did not live to see its completion, his spirit, companionship and especially his courage in his final days won't be forgotten.

Robert C. Ackerson
Schenevus, New York
November 1992

ABBREVIATIONS

A.A.A. .... American Automobile Assoc.
Adj. .... Adjustable
AMC .... American Motors Corp.
Approx. .... Approximate
Auto. .... Automatic
Auxil. .... Auxiliary
Avg. .... Average
B.H.P. .... Brake horsepower
BSW .... Black sidewall
Calif. .... California
Carb. .... Carburetor
Chas. .... Chassis
Ch.-Cab .... Chassis & Cab
CJ .... Civilian Jeep
Comm. .... Commercial
C.R. .... Compression ratio
CST .... Custom Sport Truck (Chevy)
Cu. In, ... Cubic Inch(es)
Cust. .... Custom
Cyl. .... Cylinder
Del. .... Deluxe
Dely. .... Delivery
Dia. .... Diameter
Dif. .... Differential
Div. .... Division
Dr. (2-dr.) .... Door (two-door)
DRW .... Dual rear wheels
EFI .... Electronic fuel injection
Endgt. .... End-Gate
Equip. .... Equipment
Exp. .... Express
E-Z-Eye .... Tinted glass
FC .... Forward control
F-head .... Valves in head and block
Flare .... Flareside pickup (Ford)
Fleet .... Fleetside pickup (Chevy)
"Four" .... Four-cylinder
4x4 .... Four-Wheel Drive
4x2 .... Two-Wheel Drive
4-spd .... Four-speed

Frt. .... Front
FS .... Fender-side pickup
4V .... Four-barrel carburetor
Gal. .... Gallon
GM .... General Motors
GMC ... General Motors Corporation, GM
Truck & Bus, GM Truck & Coach
GVW .... Gross Vehicle Weight
H-D .... Heavy-duty
H.P. .... Horsepower
Hr. .... Hour
Hwy. .... Highway
ICC .... Type of emergency flasher
I.D. .... Identification
In(s). .... Inch(es)
Int. .... Interior
L (L-head) .... Side-valve engine
Lb(s). .... Pound(s)
Lbs.-Ft. .... Pounds-feet
L-head .... Side-valve engine
LUV .... Light Utility Vehicle
LWB .... Long Wheelbase
Max. .... Maximum
M.P.G. .... Miles Per Gallon
M.P.H. .... Miles Per Hour
N/A .... Not Available
N.A. .... Not Available
NC .... No charge
NADA .... National Automobile
Dealers Assoc.
No. .... Number
OHC .... Overhead camshaft
OHV .... Overhead valves
Opt. .... Optional
OSRV .... Outside rearview mirror
PR .... Ply-rated (tires)
Prod. .... Production
P.T.O. .... Power Take-Off
P.U. .... Pickup
Pwr. .... Power (power-assist)

Quad .... Four (quad shocks on 4x4)
Rad. .... Radio
Reg. .... Regular
R.P.M. .... Revolutions per minute
R.P.O. .... Regular Production Option
RWL .... Raised White Letter
SBR .... Steel-belted Radial Tires
SE .... Special Edition
"Six" .... Six-cylinder
Spd. .... Speed
Spec. .... Special
Spl. .... Special
Spt. .... Sport
Sq. In. .... Square Inch(es)
SRW .... Single Rear Wheel
Sta. Wag. .... Station Wagon
Std. .... Standard
Step. .... Stepside pickup (Chevy)
Style. .... Styleside pickup (Ford)
Sub. .... Suburban
SWB .... Short wheelbase
Tach. .... Tachometer
TBI .... Throttle-Body Injection
THM ...... Turbo-Hydramatic transmission
Trans. .... Transmission
2V .... Two-barrel (carburetor)
2WD .... Two-Wheel Drive
U.S.A. .... United States of America
Util. .... Utility
V .... Venturi (carburetor)
V-6/8 .... Vee-block engines 6- /8-cyl.
VIN .... Vehicle identification number
V.P. .... Vice-president
Wag. .... Wagon
W.B. .... Wheelbase
W/O .... Without
WS .... Wide-Side pickup (GMC)
WSW .... White sidewall (tires)

1992-1993 HUMMER

The history of the HUMMER began in 1979 when AM General entered the competition to win a major government contract for a new High Mobility Multi-Purpose Wheeled Vehicle (HMMWV). At that time both Teledyne and Chrysler Defense had HMMWV designs under development. The proposed Chrysler design was based upon a vehicle identified as the Saluki desert design. Teledyne used as the basic for its model a vehicle known as the Cheetah. Although AM General appeared to be well behind its competitors, it moved into this field with no preconceived notions.

AM General's first prototype HUMMER went to test in the Nevada desert in July, 1980, just eleven months after its development had started. The U.S. Army's formal procurement of test vehicles began in February, 1981. Six proposals were evaluated against the Army's HMMWV specifications and the three most responsive designs were selected. In June, 1981 contracts were awarded to General Dynamics, Teledyne and AM General. The test vehicles to be acquired from each company included Tow Carriers, Cargo Troop Carriers and Mini and Maxi Ambulance variant.

Army specifications were extremely stringent with demands for light armor, deep water fording capability, reliability, durability and maintainability. AM General was the first company to complete its test vehicles. Prototype HUMMERs were delivered to Army testing grounds at Aberdeen and Yuma, and to a test site at Fort Hunter-Liggett in April, 1982.

The Army's test phase took place over a five month period after which a call for production proposals from the competing contractors was scheduled. The HUMMERs were the first vehicles to complete durability testing. They also had the lightest weight and high performance ratings.

In March, 1983, following AM General's production proposal, the initial production contract for the HUMMER was awarded. It called for 55,000 vehicles to be delivered over a five year period.

The HUMMER proved its mettle during the Gulf War and in October, 1992 AM General, while continuing to provide HUMMERs for the U.S. Army began production of a civilian version. These models were offered through a network of charter dealers who worked with AM General to establish a market niche for the HUMMER.

The civilian HUMMER was offered in five models — 2 passenger hardtop, 4 passenger hardtop, 4 passenger open canvas top, 2 passenger industrial/fleet hardtop and a four-door wagon. The civilian HUMMER used the same drive train, chassis, engine and body as the military version. AM General provided the civilian model with numerous safety and luxury upgrades including steel safety doors and steel roof, more comfortable seating, padded instrument panels and interior padded door panels, a commercially compatible 12-volt system and conventional lighting.

The HUMMER used a full-time four-wheel drive and all-independent suspension. It was powered by a General Motors 6.2 liter diesel V-8 and used a General Motors 3-speed automatic transmission. Torque biasing differentials delivered power to all four wheels through half shafts that entered the HUMMER's wheel-mounted gear hub 4 inches above the center of the wheel. This design raised the center line of the entire drive train and was a major contributor to the HUMMER's 16 in. ground clearance. The hubs had a two to one gear reduction that doubled torque at the wheel. The HUMMER could also be fitted with an optional runflat assembly that allowed it to operate with completely flat tires for distances up to 30 miles. Other unique options included a Central Tire Inflation System (CTIS) which allowed the driver to adjust tire pressure according to terrain conditions.

The Civilian HUMMER had a 36-month/36,000 mile bumper-to-bumper warranty. Exterior colors were tan, black, red and white. A special polyurethane chemical agent resistant coating (CARC) used on all military HUMMERS was available in Military green or Camouflage.

Standard equipment included power steering, power disc brakes, aluminum body, molded fiberglass hood, high-back bucket seats, 3-point seat belts, padded interior, heat and sound insulation, and halogen headlights.

1993 HUMMER four passenger hardtop

Body Type	Factory Price	GVW	Curb Weight	Prod. Total
HUMMER				
2-pass. Hardtop	$46,550	10,300	5800	—
4-pass. Open Canvas Top	$48,500	10,300	5700	—
4-pass. Hardtop	$49,950	10,300	6200	—
4-pass. Wagon	$52,950	10.300	6400	—

STANDARD ENGINE: Engine Type: General Motors OHV 6.2 liter V-8 diesel. Bore x Stroke: 3.98 in. x 3.82 in. Fuel Induction: Fuel injection. Compression Ratio: 21.3:1. Displacement: 379.4 cu. in. (6.2 liters). Horsepower: 150 @ 3600 rpm. Torque: 250 lb.-ft. @ 2000 rpm. Fuel Requirements: Diesel.

CHASSIS FEATURES: Steel box with 5 cross members.

SUSPENSION AND RUNNING GEAR: Front and Rear Suspension: Independent double A-frame with open end coil springs and hydraulic shock absorbers. Front and Rear Axle: Hypoid with 2.73:1 ratio. Geared hubs have 1.92:1 ratio. Transfer Case: New Venture Gear Model 242, 2-speed: 2.721, 1.00:1. Brakes: Type: Hydraulic activated four wheel inboard mounted power discs with dual reservoir master cylinder. Rotor dia.: 10.5 in. Tires: 37 x 12.5 OR-16.5, load range D Goodyear MT-2A radial with beadlock and optional runflat device. Steering: Power-assisted. Ratio: 13:1-16:1. Turning Circle: 50 ft. Transmission: GM 3L80 3-speed automatic. Transmission Ratios: 2.48, 1.48, 1.00:1. Reverse: 2.08:1 Torque converter ratio: 1.96:1.

VEHICLE DIMENSIONS: Wheelbase: 130.0 in. Overall Length: 184.5 in. Front/Rear Tread: 72 in./72 in. Overall Height: 72 in. Width: 86.5 in. Approach/Departure Degrees: 73/37.5. Ground Clearance: 16 in.

CAPACITIES: Fuel Tank: 25 gal.

ACCOMMODATIONS: Seating Capacity: 2 or 4 passenger depending upon body type.

OPTIONS: Air conditioning. Central Tire Inflation System. 12,000 lb. winch. Runflats. Sliding rear window. Swing-away spare tire carrier. Rocker panel protection. Lighting Package. Deluxe Interior Package. Includes upgraded trim and premium sound system. 124 amp alternator. Trailer Towing Unit. Spare tire with wheel. Cargo and canvas covers. Driveline protection. Brush and headlight guard.

HISTORICAL FOOTNOTES: Two civilian HUMMER prototypes took part in the Great 1990 London to Peking Motoring Challenge. This was a 55 day venture covering nine countries, two continents and over 9,000 miles.

AMC EAGLE

1980-1987

In many ways it seemed almost preordained that AMC would break new ground with the Eagle in 1980. Throughout its short life span (1953-1987) AMC was the struggling, last-of-the-independents underdog in an automotive market where if the competition from the American Big Three wasn't enough to keep AMC in an almost continuous state of precarious health, the advent of a global market left little doubt that the days of a relatively small company like AMC were numbered.

But AMC did not give up easily. In the years following the end of the World War II, when the parched automobile market eagerly absorbed every new car coming off the assembly line regardless of its design and/or appearance, George Mason the head of Nash-Kelvinator, foresaw the day when the sellers' market would end and an age of intense neo-cutthroat competition would commence. Then, Mason reasoned, would be the time for the remaining independents to have already consolidated their resources. Only such a union would make possible the survival of firms like Nash, Hudson, Studebaker and Packard.

History leaves no doubt that Mason was correct. The Independents were able to do reasonably well until the early fifties when the predicted era of high-level competition began. Aggressive marketing and rapid-fire product development by Ford, GM and Chrysler left the small marques almost totally outflanked and outmaneuvered. Consolidation did take place, but in the case of Studebaker and Packard the obstacles were just too great to overcome in spite of the often-underrated efforts of Jim Nance to revive Packard as the Grand Marque of American automobiles. Nash and Hudson, which Mason successfully joined together in 1954, was in slightly better shape. But Mason's death in October 1954 seemed to leave the company's future in doubt. This dismal prognosis failed to take into account the Messianic nature and business savvy of Mason's successor, George Romney. Years earlier Romney had been courted by Packard to begin an internship-of-sorts leading to Packard's presidency. But Romney chose instead, to cast his lot with Mason and upon his death became the president of AMC. What Romney headed was a company hampered by some obsolete products but endowed with a spirit of innovation that was arguably Mason's greatest legacy. For years Mason had encouraged his team to seek new paradigms, to consider alternatives to the status quo and to venture into fresh territory. Some results had been the Nash-Healey sports car which predated both the Ford Thunderbird and Chevrolet Corvette; the Nash Metropolitan. (Veteran Nash employees must muse over the current use of the Metro name for Chevrolet's Japanese-built small car) and perhaps most importantly, the Nash Rambler which arrived in 1950 almost a decade before the Big Three introduced their first generation compacts.

Romney took his clue from the Rambler's popularity and phased out the big Nash and Hudson models in favor of new Rambler models. The result was one of the greatest come-from-behind stories of American industrial history. In 1958, the original Rambler was returned to production as the Rambler American joining the slightly larger, but decidedly compact Ramblers that had bowed in 1956.

AMC's success was short-lived. After Romney left to pursue a political career, its management seemed to lose the nerve needed to keep American Motors on the profit track. Sales slowed as the market shifted to a youth-orientation. Sales slogans as "The Sensible Spectators" failed to ignite much excitement. A major opportunity provided by the popular Tarpon show car for AMC to establish a position in the emerging sporty car market was irreparably flawed when management decreed the production Marlin version should be a full-sized 6 passenger sedan. AMC did score a major success with the Javelin and AMX but stumbled badly with the ill-fated Pacer. Here again, the story was full of might-have-beens since original plans called for a trimmer Pacer powered by a Wankel engine and available in a sporty convertible form.

Faced with the need for a very large infusion of capital and the technology needed to develop a new generation of front-wheel drive compact cars, AMC first signed manufacturing and financing agreements with Renault in late 1979. This lead to more and more influence by Renault since it eventually owned nearly half of AMC's common stock. But there was one final burst of AMC's genetic creativity, the Eagle. Bowing in 1980, the Eagle quickly captured the attention of many American drivers who found its unique union of four-wheel drive safety and security with the comfort of a traditional domestic sedan an appealing combination. But the Eagle suffered from three maladies that collectively combined to cause its demise. First was its appearance. Although purposeful and pleasing to the eye of AMC loyalists, the Eagle's exterior was already dated by 1980 since it had first been seen in the guise of the 1970 Hornet and Gremlin. Secondly was the impact of a severe economic downturn in union with the rising fuel prices. AMC responded with smaller engines and new part-time four-wheel drive systems but with only limited success. Finally, it was inevitable that AMC would place primary emphasis upon the Renault Alliance, which proved to be a false hope. AMC and Renault also invested heavily in what was to emerge as the Renault Premier. But in 1987, faced with mounting political and economic pressures at home, Renault decided to leave the American market and accept an offer from Chrysler to purchase AMC. Clearly, the crown jewels of AMC were the Jeep division and the new Canadian plant built to produce the Premier. In that context prospects were almost nonexistent that Chrysler would fund a modernized Eagle, so production ended after the 1987 model year.

Even today aging but still serviceable four-wheel drive Eagles are seen in operation. And in the case of one owner of a 1980 model who, one summer evening, happened to come upon this writer working on the Eagle section in the Chief Schenevus Coffee Shop, there was that almost poignant question: "Can I still buy a new one?"

1980 EAGLE

The 1980 AMC Eagle was, as the first U.S. mass-produced four-wheel drive automobile, a major automotive development. The basic styling/body format of the Eagle was based upon the AMC Concord, which, in turn, was a derivative of the Hornet, which had debuted as a 1970 model. This close similarity to an existing model that was, if generally pleasing to the eye, getting a bit long in the tooth took some of the edge off the Eagle's debut. But the Eagle, beneath its familiar exterior was, in most respects, a totally new automobile with a sophisticated four-wheel drive drivetrain. Available in two-door, four-door and station wagon form, the Eagle had a full-time four-wheel drive system based upon the design developed by FF Developments in England. This firm, aside from its involvement with tractors and Henry Ford many years earlier, attracted international attention with the development of this four-wheel drive system in the early 1960s. Interest was further enhanced by the appearance of a Ferguson Formula One racing car that was evaluated by Stirling Moss. This system didn't gain acceptance among the manufacturers of Formula One cars who were at that time making the transition to a rear-engine format. Eventually the manufacturing rights were acquired by the New Process Gear Division of Chrysler Corporation. The single speed model 119 New Process case supplied to AMC by Chrysler used a viscous coupling consisting of a liquid silicone-based material to link the front and rear differentials. The only transmission initially available was a 3-speed Chrysler model 998 automatic. At midyear AMC announced a 4-speed manual transmission as the Eagle's standard transmission except for California where the automatic continued to be standard. Compared to the Concord, the Eagle was 3 inches higher. Also setting it apart from the Concord was the Eagle's injection-molded plastic fender flares and lower body skirting. Under Clear Air Federal Regulations, the Eagle was classified as a light-duty truck and thus was not equipped with impact-type bumpers.

1980 AMC Eagle station wagon

In addition to the automatic transmission, the Eagle's standard equipment consisted of power steering, power brakes, Landau roof (two-door), full vinyl roof (four-door), individual reclining seats with Sport vinyl trim, transfer case skid plate, 12 oz. carpeting, electronic quartz clock, color-coordinated wheel flares and rocker panel moldings, styled steel wheels, exterior molding for belt (not available for two-door), lower body side, drip rail, hood front edge, windshield, rear window liftgate and hood windsplit; opera windows (not available for station wagon), pinstriping, front stabilizer bar, extra-quiet insulation, high level ventilation, rear door and quarter window blackout treatment (station wagon), blackout windshield wipers, woodgrain instrument panel overlay, custom door trim panels, custom steering wheel with woodgrain accents, folding rear seat back (station wagon), trunk carpeting, cargo area carpeting and skid plates (station wagon), high pressure compact spare tire, courtesy lights, 10 in. interior day/night mirror, cigarette lighter, front lighted ashtray, dual rear seat ashtrays, parking brake warning light, color-keyed seat belts, inside hood release, and dual note horns.

The luxury-oriented Eagle Limited models had in addition to or in place of the standard equipment these items: Individual reclining seats in Chelsea leather or St. Lauren deep plush fabric, 18 oz. carpeting, carpeted cargo area side panels (station wagon), AM radio, Luxury woodgrain tilt steering wheel, power door locks, front armrest woodgrain overlays, lockable cargo area stowage compartment (station wagon), rear overhead passenger assist straps, Light Group, Visibility Group, Convenience Group, Protection Group, instrument panel parcel shelf, cloth sun visors, door frame inner moldings and Limited medallions and nameplates.

1980 AMC Eagle four-door sedan

An Eagle Sport Package was offered for the two-door sedan and station wagon. Its content was as follows: Durham plaid fabric seat trim, leather-wrapped Sport steering wheel, high beam halogen headlights, Sport fog lamps, dual black remote mirrors, P195/75R15 Tiempo steel belted radial black sidewall tires, black opera window insert (sedan), blackout taillamp paint treatment, black bumpers with nerf strips, blackout grille, blackout lower body moldings with 4x4 graphics, blackout moldings including windshield, rear window or liftgate, door frames and B pillar, and Sport medallions (body pinstriping was deleted).

1980 AMC Eagle two-door sedan with Sport Package

Fifteen exterior colors were available for the Eagle: Classic black, olympic white, cameo blue, medium blue metallic, cameo tan, medium brown metallic, dark brown metallic, quick silver metallic, russet metallic, smoke gray metallic, navy blue, dark green metallic, cardinal red, Saxon yellow, and Bordeaux metallic.

I.D. DATA: The V.I.N. consisted of 13 elements. The first entry, a letter, identified the manufacturer, the second entry, a number, designated the model year. The third symbol was a letter indicating the transmission and drivetrain, the fourth and fifth entries, both numbers, identified the body type. The sixth unit, a letter, was the GVW rating identification. The seventh unit, a letter identified the engine. The final six digits were the plant sequential production number.

Model Number	Body Type & Seating	Factory Price	GVW	Shipping Weight	Prod. Total
Eagle					
355	4-door Sedan	$7418	4463[1]	3450	10,616[2]
365	2-door Sedan	$7168	4463	3382	9956
385	4-door St. Wag.	$7718	4463	3470	25,807
Eagle Limited					
357	4-door Sedan	$7815	4463	3465	—
367	2-door Sedan	$7565	4463	3397	—
387	4-door St. Wag.	$8115	4463	3491	—

NOTE 1: 4463 and 4657 lb. GVW optional for all models.
NOTE 2: All production figures include Limited models.

STANDARD ENGINE: Engine Type: OHV, Cast iron block. In-line 6-cyl. Bore x Stroke: 3.75 in. x 3.90 in. Lifters: Hydraulic. Number of main bearings-7. Fuel Induction: 2-barrel carburetor. Compression Ratio: 8.3:1. Displacement: 258 cu. in. (4.22 liter). Horsepower: Net: 114 @ 3200 rpm. (108 @ 3000 rpm also reported). Torque: Net: 218 lb.-ft. @ 1800 rpm. (200 lb.-ft. @ 1800 rpm also reported). Oil capacity: 5 qt. with filter change. Fuel Requirements: 91 octane unleaded.

CHASSIS FEATURES: Welded steel unitized.

SUSPENSION AND RUNNING GEAR: Front Suspension: Independent with unequal length A-arms, coil springs, tubular shock absorbers, stabilizer bar. Rear Suspension: Beam axle, tubular shock absorbers and 4-leaf springs. Front Axle. Capacity: 2377 lb. Rear Axle. Capacity: 2500 lb. Final Drive Ratio: 3.08:1. Optional: 3.54:1 (not available for California). High altitude and medium duty trailer package, not available for California: 3.54:1. Transfer Case: New Process model 119, single speed. Brakes: Type: Hydraulic, power assisted. Front: Discs. Rear: Drums. Dimensions: Front: 11.00 in. x 0.88 in. rotor. Rear: 10.0 in. x 1.75 in. Total brake swept area: 329 sq. in. Wheels: 15 x 6.00 in. Tires: P195/75R15 glass belted radial white sidewall. Optional: P195/75R15 Tiempo steel belted radial black sidewall. Steering: Power assisted recirculated ball. Ratio: 17:1. Turning diameter: 35.45 ft. Transmission: Initially: Chrysler model 998 3-speed automatic. Floor-mounted T-handle shifter. Ratios: 2.45, 1.45, 1.00:1. At midyear a 4-speed manual became the Eagle's standard transmission except for California. Optional: Chrysler model 998 3-speed automatic after midyear.

VEHICLE DIMENSIONS: Wheelbase: 109.3 in. Overall Length: 186.2 in. Overhang Front/Rear: 34.2 in./42.8 in. Front/rear tread: 59.9 in./57.6 in. Overall Height: Two-door: 55.8 in.; four-door: 55.4 in.; station wagon: 55.0 in. Width: 71.9 in. Headroom: Front: 38.1 in. Rear: 37.5 in. (37.9 in. for station wagon). Legroom: Front: 40.8 in. Rear: 36.1 in. Shoulder room: Front: 54.0 in. Rear: 53.2 in. (two-door sedan), 54.4 in. all others. Hip room: Front: 54.3 in. (two-door sedan), 54.4 in. all others. Rear: 52.5 in. (two-door sedan), 53.6 in. all others. Ground Clearance: Front axle: 6.5 in. Rear axle: 7.25 in. Oil pan: 8.5 in. Transfer case skid plate: 7.0 in. Fuel tank: 12.0 in. Exhaust system: 8.0 in. Load space (length x width x height): With seats in place: 37.5 in. x 41.0 in. x 24.25 in. With rear seat folded or removed: 58.25 in. x 41.0 in. x 24.25 in. Tailgate: 43.5 in. x 22.5 in.

CAPACITIES: Fuel Tank: 22 gal. tank. Coolant system: 14 qts.

ACCOMMODATIONS: Seating Capacity: Standard: 5, Optional: none.

INSTRUMENTATION: Speedometer, 99,999.9 mi. odometer, fuel gauge, engine coolant temperature gauge, warning lights for ammeter, oil pressure, and emergency brake, hazard warning lights, and directional lights.

OPTIONS AND PRICES: Power windows. Power door locks: $124. Power deck lid release. AM radio. AM/FM radio: $219. AM/FM radio with cassette tape player. AM/FM/CB stereo radio. Premium audio system with power amplifier, 4 high-fidelity speakers, and fader control: $95. Air conditioning: $560. Visibility Group. Includes remote left and right side mirrors. Light Group. Includes dome-map light, engine compartment light, rear door light switches, trunk light, lighted dome light: $43. Convenience Group. Includes lighted passenger visor mirror, lights-on buzzer, intermittent windshield wipers: $63 Protection Group. Includes front and rear nerf strips, door edge guards, front and rear floor mats. Cold Climate Group. Includes engine block heater, heavy-duty battery, heavy-duty alternator, coolant protection to -34 degrees. Extra-Duty Suspension Package. Includes rear sway bar, heavy-duty shock absorbers, heavy-duty springs: $65. Tachometer: $54. Tinted glass: $70. Rear window defogger: $95. Rear window wiper/washer (station wagon): $79. Popup sun roof (sedans): $299. Cruise Control. Tilt steering wheel: $78. Leather-wrapped Sport steering wheel. Roof rack (station wagon). Halogen headlights. Fog lamps. Woodgrain body side panels (station wagon). Light-Duty

Trailer Towing Package. Medium-Duty Towing Package. Protective inner coat. Locking gas cap. Scuff molding. Front suspension skid plate: $05. Automatic load leveling air shock absorbers. Heavy-duty battery: $19. Sport Package: $299.00.

HISTORICAL FOOTNOTES: The Eagle has three warranties: The AMC Full 12-month/ 12,000 New Automobile Warranty; the 1980 AMC Buyer Protection Plan and the Ziebart factory Rust Protection and Full Five Year Perforation from Corrosion Warranty. The Eagle was selected as four-wheel drive of the year for 1980 by *Pickup Van & Four-Wheel Drive* magazine. Introduction of the 1980 Eagle took place on September 27, 1979.

1981 EAGLE

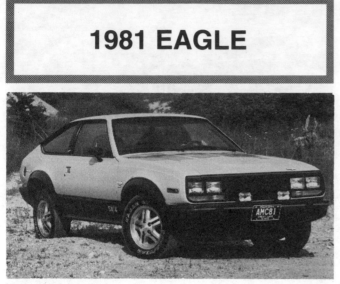

1981 AMC Eagle SX/4

American Motors added two new models, the SX/4 and Kammback, to the range of Eagles for 1981. All Eagles for 1981 incorporated a number of significant changes. Most important was the use of a 2.5 liter 4-cylinder engine (purchased from General Motors) as standard across the line. A 4-speed manual transmission was also standard on all Eagle models. A 3-speed automatic transmission was optional for the SX/4 and Kammback models with either the 4-cylinder or 6-cylinder engines. The automatic transmission on other Eagle models (two-door, four-door and station wagon) was available only with the 6-cylinder engine. The chassis and drivetrain were virtually common to all Eagle models. Because of their shorter (97.2 in. as compared to the 109.3 in. wheelbase used on other models) wheelbase the driveshaft and rear suspension of the SX/4 and Kammback was modified. The overall length of the larger Eagles was reduced from 186.2 in. to 183.2 in. due to the integration of front and rear bumper extensions with color-keyed Krayton lower body side moldings and wheel opening flares. The SX/4 and Kammback also had this feature. The Eagles also received a new rectangular-shaped grille for 1981 as well as a lockup torque converter with 6-cylinder engines and automatic transmissions. As in 1980 the sedans and station wagon were offered in either Standard or Limited trim form. The SX/4 and Kammback were available in base or upscale DL trim. All models (Base, Standard or DL) could be ordered with the Sport Package. The primary Base/Standard exterior and operational equipment for 1980 consisted of these features: 4-cylinder engine, 4-speed manual transmission, automatic four-wheel drive transfer case with skid plate, extra-quiet insulation (sedan and station wagon), high-level ventilation, heater/ defroster, front stabilizer bar, compact spare tire, dual horns (sedans and station wagon), landau vinyl roof (two-door sedans), full vinyl roof (four-door sedans), integrated lower body Krayton treatment, black lower body side scuff moldings, bumper nerf strips, quad rectangular headlights, styled wheelcovers (sedans and station wagon), custom wheelcovers (SX/4 and Kammback), dual Sport chrome mirrors (sedan and station wagon), left exterior rearview mirror (SX/4 and Kammback), moldings: Drip, backlight surrounds and windshield surround, bright belt moldings (four-door sedan and station wagon), color-keyed backlight moldings (sedans), dual body side striping, special body accent pinstriping (four-door sedan and station wagon), hood ornament (sedans and station wagon), four-wheel drive identification and Eagle medallions.

1981 AMC Eagle Kammback

Primary interior features included individual reclining front seats in deluxe grain vinyl (sedans and station wagon), bucket seat in deluxe grain vinyl (SX/4 and Kammback), fold-down rear seat (station wagon, SX/4 and Kammback), premium door panels with woodgrain accents (sedans and station wagon), custom door trim panels (SX/4 and Kammback), quartz digital clock (sedans and station wagon), custom color-keyed steering wheel (woodgrain accented on sedans and station wagon), woodgrain instrument panel overlay (sedans and station wagon), color-keyed 12 oz. carpeting in passenger and cargo areas, trunk carpeting (sedans), carpeted spare tire cover (SX/4 and Kammback), cigarette lighter, lighted front ashtray, rear seat ashtrays (sedans and station wagon), cargo skid strips (station wagon), inside hood

release, dome light, key warning buzzer (SX/4 and Kammback), parking brake warning light, glove box lock, 10 in. day/night mirror (sedans and station wagon), and 8 in. rearview mirror (SX/4 and Kammback).

The Eagle SX/4 and Kammback DL models had the following equipment in addition to or in place of Base model equipment: White sidewall tires, extra quiet insulation, dual horns, styled wheelcovers, dual remote chrome mirrors, quarter panel blackout (SX/4), bright belt moldings (SX/4), premium reclining bucket seats, split folding rear seat, premium door panels with woodgrain accents, woodgrain instrument panel overlay, quartz digital clock, custom steering wheel with woodgrain overlay, and 10 in. day/night mirror.

The Limited two- and four-door sedans and station wagon models had the following equipment in addition to or in place of Base model equipment: Limited exterior identification, bright door frame accent moldings, individual reclining seats in Chelsea leather, premium door panels with Limited identification, luxury woodgrain steering wheel, 18 oz. carpeting in passenger area and under dash parcel panel.

1981 AMC Eagle station wagon

The Sport Package, for the Eagle two-door, station wagon and SX/4 included a low gloss black finish for the black Krayton lower body side moldings, bumpers and bumper guards, grille, taillamp lens, windshield moldings, door frames, B pillar, wheel flares and flare trap moldings, color-coordinated inserts on body side moldings, and dual remote control sports mirrors. Other features included rectangular fog lights mounted on the front bumper, P195/75R15 black sidewall steel belted radial All-Season Goodyear Arriva tires, silver 4x4 graphics on doors (not used for SX/4 which had SX/4 door graphics), Sport nameplates and a black quarter window insert for the two-door Eagle. A color-keyed leather Sport steering wheel with a woodgrain hub was installed on the sedan and station wagon with a color-keyed Sport steering wheel specified for the SX/4. A rear spoiler was available for SX/4 models with the Sport Package.

The Eagle's 258 cu. in. 6-cylinder engine weighed 90 pounds less than its predecessor. This weight reduction was achieved through the redesigning of primary componentry and the use of alternate materials-mainly aluminum. Highlights of the revamped 6-cylinder included a 12 pound lighter cylinder head, aluminum housings for the oil and water pump and an aluminum intake manifold. The rocker arm cover was fabricated of glass-filled nylon and replaced a stamped steel cover.

1981 Eagle two-door sedan

A re-profiled camshaft reduced valve overlap without a loss of maximum horsepower output. The new cam specifications also allowed a lower idle speed and increased low speed torque output. California versions of the 258 engine had a new front accessory drive system with a single belt routed through and around all engine pulleys. The 1981 engine weighed 445 lbs., compared to 535 lbs. for the earlier version.

All Eagles had 100 percent galvanized steel in all exterior body panels. Specific galvanized steel components included front fenders, roof panels, body pillars, door frames, roof rails and structural drip, quarter window fillers, tail lamp mounting panels and (two-side) deck upper panels. These panels were in addition to existing one and two-side galvanized components — hood cowl top panel, door panels, rear quarter panels, deck and liftgate panels, rocker panels, front modesty panels, rear body cross member and rear floor extensions. The fifteen exterior colors for 1981 Eagles were classic black, olympic white, quick silver metallic, steel gray metallic, medium blue metallic, moonlight blue, autumn gold, Sherwood green metallic, cameo tan, copper brown metallic, medium brown metallic, dark brown metallic, Oriental red, vintage red metallic and deep maroon metallic.

At midyear AMC introduced an optional Select-Drive four-wheel drive system for Eagles with all engine/transmission combinations. This system allowed the driver to select between two-wheel drive and full-time four-wheel drive by the movement of a dashboard mounted switch located to the left of the steering wheel. The system required the vehicle to be stopped. The driver then pulled a safety switch downward and moved a horizontal control to either the two-wheel drive or four-wheel drive position. The four-wheel drive system remained fully automatic. No other two-wheel drive/four-wheel drive system had this feature. Other new options for 1981 included 6-way power seats, aluminum wheels, floor shift console and Gauge Package.

1981 AMC Eagle four-door sedan

I.D. DATA: The V.I.N. consisted of 13 elements. The first entry, a letter, identified the manufacturer, the second entry, a number, designated the model year. The third symbol was a letter indicating the transmission and drivetrain, the fourth and fifth entries, both numbers, identified the body type. The sixth unit, a letter, was the GVW rating identification. The seventh unit, a letter identified the engine. The final six digits were the plant sequential production number.

Model Number	Body Type & Seating	Factory Price	GVW	Shipping Weight	Prod. Total
Eagle 4-cyl.					
530	Liftback SX/4	$6966	—	2967	17,340
560	Kammback 2-dr.	$6144	—	2919	5603
Eagle DL 4-cyl.					
535	Liftback SX/4	$7418	—	3040	—
565	Kammback 2-dr.	$6714	—	2990	—
Eagle 6-cyl.					
530	Liftback SX/4	$7102	—	3123	—
560	Kammback 2-dr.	$6280	—	3075	—
Eagle DL 6-cyl.					
535	Liftback SX/4	$7554	—	3196	—
565	Kammback 2-dr.	$6850	—	3146	—
Eagle 4-cyl.					
355	4-door Sedan	$8357	4463[1]	3172	1737
365	2-door Sedan	$8107	4463	3104	2378
385	4-door St. Wag.	$8761	4463	3184	10,371[2]
Eagle Limited 4-cyl.					
357	4-door Sedan	$8804	4463	3180	—
367	2-door Sedan	$8554	4463	3114	—
387	4-door St. Wag.	$9208	4463	3198	—
Eagle 6-cyl.					
355	4-door Sedan	$8493	4463[1]	3328	—
365	2-door Sedan	$8243	4463	3260	—
385	4-door St. Wag.	$8897	4463	3340	—
Eagle Limited 6-cyl.					
357	4-door Sedan	$8940	4463	3336	—
367	2-door Sedan	$8690	4463	3270	—
387	4-door St. Wag.	$9344	4463	3354	—

NOTE 1: 4463 and 4657 lb. GVW optional for all models.
NOTE 2: All production figures are the totals for each body style regardless of trim level or engine.

STANDARD ENGINE: Engine Type: OHV, Cast iron block. In-line 4-cyl. Bore x Stroke: 4.00 in. x 3.00 in. Lifters: Hydraulic. Number of main bearings-5. Fuel Induction: Rochester staged 2-barrel carburetor. Compression Ratio: 8.2:1. Displacement: 151 cu. in. (2.5 liter). Horsepower: Net: 82 @ 4000 rpm. Torque: Net: 125 lb.-ft. @ 2600 rpm. Oil capacity: 5 qt. with filter change. Fuel Requirements: 91 octane unleaded.

OPTIONAL ENGINE: (Required for sedans and station wagons with automatic transmission): Engine Type: OHV, Cast iron block. In-line 6-cyl. Bore x Stroke: 3.75 in. x 3.90 in. Lifters: Hydraulic. Number of main bearings-7. Fuel Induction: 2-barrel carburetor. Compression Ratio: 8.3:1. Displacement: 258 cu. in. (4.22 liter). Horsepower: Net: 115 @ 3200 rpm. Torque: Net: 210 lb.-ft. @ 1800 rpm. Oil capacity: 5 qt. with filter change. Fuel Requirements: 91 octane unleaded.

CHASSIS FEATURES: Welded steel unitized.

SUSPENSION AND RUNNING GEAR: Front Suspension: Independent with unequal length A-arms, coil springs, tubular shock absorbers, stabilizer bar. Rear Suspension: Beam axle, tubular shock absorbers and 4-leaf springs. Front Axle. Capacity: 2377 lb. Rear Axle. Capacity: 2500 lb. Final Drive Ratio: 2.5 liter engine: 3.54:1. 4.2 liter: Optional: 4.2 liter engine: 3.08, 3.31:1. High Altitude: 4.2 liter engine with automatic transmission: 3.31:1. AMC recommended the 3.08:1 ratio for Eagles with the 6-cylinder engine operated primarily in hilly terrain. Transfer Case: New Process model 119, single speed. Brakes: Type: Hydraulic, power assisted. Front: Discs. Rear: Drums. Dimensions: Front: 11.00 in. x 0.88 in. rotor. Rear: 10.0 in. x 1.75 in. Total brake swept area: 329 sq. in. Wheels: 15 x 6.00 in. Tires: P195/75R15 glass belted radial (Sedan and station wagon: White sidewall, SX/4 and Kammback: Black sidewall). Optional: P195/75R15 glass belted radial white sidewall (Base model SX/4 and Kammback), P195/75R15 Arriva steel belted black sidewall, P195/75R15 Arriva steel belted radial white sidewall, P215/75R15 Eagle GT steel belted radial outline white letters. Steering: Power assisted recirculated ball. Ratio: 17:1. Turns Lock-to-Lock: 3.0. Turning diameter: Sedans and station wagon: 35.45 ft. SX/4 and Kammback: 32.5-ft. Transmission: 4-speed manual. Optional: Chrysler model 998 3-speed automatic. Ratios: 2.45, 1.45, 1.00:1.

VEHICLE DIMENSIONS: Wheelbase: Sedans and station wagon: 109.3 in. SX/4 and Kammback: 97.2 in. Overall Length: Sedans and station wagon: 183.2 in. SX/4 and Kammback: 166.6 in. Overhang Front/Rear: Sedans and station wagon: 34.2 in./42.8 in. SX/4 and Kammback: 34.2 in./35.2 in. Front/rear tread: All models: 59.6 in./57.6 in. Approach/Departure angle in degrees: Sedans and station wagon: 29.4/25.5. SX/4 and Kammback: 29.4/30.9. Overall Height: Sedans and station wagon: Two-door: 55.8 in.; four-door: 55.4 in.; station wagon: 55.0 in. SX/4 and Kammback: 52.5 in. Width: Sedans and station wagon: 72.3 in. SX/4 and Kammback: 73.0 in. Headroom: Sedans and station

wagon: Front: 38.1 in. Rear: 37.5 in. (37.9 in. for station wagon). Legroom: Sedans and station wagon: Front: 40.8 in. Rear: 36.1 in. SX/4 and Kammback: Front: 40.8 in. Rear: 26.2 in. Shoulder Room: Sedans and station wagon: Front: 54.0 in. Rear: 53.2 in. (two-door sedan), 54.4 in. all others. SX/4 and Kammback: 53.9 in. Rear: SX/4: 53.2 in. Kammback: 53.0 in. Hip Room: Sedans and station wagon: Front: 54.3 in. (2-door sedan), 54.4 in. all others. Rear: 52.5 in. (two-door sedan), 53.6 in. all others. SX/4 and Kammback: Front: 54.3 in. Rear: SX/4: 40.3 in. Kammback: 43.5 in. Ground Clearance: Sedans and station wagon: Front axle: 6.5 in. Rear axle: 7.25 in. Oil pan: 8.5 in. Transfer case skid plate: 7.0 in. Fuel tank: 12.0 in. Exhaust system: 8.0 in. SX/4 and Kammback: Front and rear differential: 7.7 in. Load space station wagon: (length x width x height): With seats in place: 37.5 in. x 41.0 in. x 24.25 in. With rear seat folded or removed: 58.25 in. x 41.0 in. x 24.25 in. Tailgate: Station wagon: 43.5 in. x 22.5 in.

CAPACITIES: Fuel Tank: Sedans and station wagon: 22 gal. tank. SX/4 and Kammback: 21 gal. Coolant system: 6-cyl.: 14 qts.

ACCOMMODATIONS: Seating Capacity: Sedans and station wagon: Standard: 5, Optional: None. SX/4 and Kammback: 4. Optional: None.

INSTRUMENTATION: Speedometer, 99,999.9 mi. odometer, fuel gauge, engine coolant temperature gauge, warning lights for ammeter, oil pressure, and emergency brake, hazard warning lights, and directional lights.

OPTIONS AND PRICES: Power windows. Power door locks: $130. Power deck lid release. Retractable cargo area cover (station wagon): $62. AM radio. AM/FM radio. AM/FM radio with MPX cassette tape player: $356. AM/FM/CB stereo radio. Premium audio system with power amplifier, 4 high-fidelity speakers, and fader control. Power antenna: $53. Air conditioning: $585. Visibility Group. Includes remote left and right side mirrors. Light Group. Includes dome-map light, engine compartment light, rear door light switches, trunk light, liftgate dome light: $46. Convenience Group. Includes lighted passenger visor mirror, lights-on buzzer, intermittent windshield wipers: $67. Protection Group. Includes front and rear nerf strips, door edge guards, front and rear floor mats: $36. Cold Climate Group. Includes engine block heater, heavy-duty battery, heavy-duty alternator, coolant protection to -34 degrees. Extra-duty Suspension Package. Includes rear sway bar, heavy-duty shock absorbers, heavy-duty springs. Tachometer. Tinted glass: $75. Rear window defroster: $107. Rear window wiper/washer (station wagon): $99. Popup sun roof (sedans). Cruise control. Tilt steering wheel: $82. Leather-wrapped Sport steering wheel. Roof rack (station wagon): $98. Halogen headlights. Fog lamps. Woodgrain body side panels (station wagon). Light-Duty Trailer Towing Package. Medium-Duty Towing Package. Protective inner coat. Locking gas cap. Scuff molding: $44. Front suspension skid plate. Automatic load leveling air shock absorbers. Heavy-duty battery. Sport Package: $314.00. Select Drive: $149. 6-way power seats: $262. Aluminum wheels. Floor shift console: $52. Gauge Package: $81. Aluminum wheels: $310.

HISTORICAL FOOTNOTES: The 1981 Eagle was introduced on August 21, 1980.

1982 EAGLE

For 1982 the Select Drive system was standard for all Eagles. The Eagle was again offered in five separate body styles: SX/4, three-door hatchback; Kammback; two-door sedan; four-door sedan and station wagon. In addition to the use of Select Drive as standard equipment, the Eagles received other significant powertrain and functional changes. A new Warner Gear 5-speed manual transmission was optional while a new Warner Gear 4-speed manual transmission was standard. The optional 258 engine had a new microprocessor-controlled fuel system. A new serpentine accessory system was standard for all California cars and those equipped with air conditioning. A new wide-ratio automatic transmission with higher numerical ratios in low and second gears was offered for the 6-cylinder engines. A low drag front disc brake system was introduced which reduced rolling resistance. This system had increased clearances between the brake pads and the rotor. A lightweight master cylinder was also part of this new system. A new option for all Eagles was an electronically-tuned AM/FM stereo cassette tape player and radio. The 2.5 liter engine continued to be standard across the Eagle line. The automatic transmission was optional for the SX/4 and Kammback models. Automatic transmission on other Eagle models was available only with the 6-cylinder engine. The SX/4 and Kammback were again offered in base and DL form. The SX/4 and the two-door sedan and station wagon models were available with the Sport Package. The two- and four-door sedans and station wagon Eagles were available in DL trim (standard) or Limited form. A new slate blue interior was offered for 1982. Exterior colors were more extensively revised by the availability of five new colors: Deep night blue, mist silver metallic, slate blue metallic, Jamaican beige and topaz gold metallic. Offered for the SX/4 and Kammback models was a new sun yellow color.

1982 AMC Eagle station wagon

I.D. DATA: The V.I.N. consisted of 13 elements. The first entry, a letter, identified the manufacturer, the second entry, a number, designated the model year. The third symbol was a letter indicating the transmission and drivetrain, the fourth and fifth entries, both numbers, identified the body type. The sixth unit, a letter, was the GVW rating identification. The seventh unit, a letter identified the engine. The final six digits were the plant sequential production number.

1982 AMC Eagle two-door sedan

Model Number	Body Type & Seating	Factory Price	GVW	Shipping Weight	Prod. Total
Eagle 4-cyl.					
530	Liftback SX/4	$7451	—	2972	10,445[2]
560	Kammback 2-dr.	$6799	—	2933	520
Eagle DL 4-cyl.					
535	Liftback SX/4	$7903	—	3041	—
565	Kammback 2-dr.	$7369	—	3000	—
Eagle 6-cyl.					
530	Liftback SX/4	$7601	—	3100	—
560	Kammback 2-dr.	$6949	—	3061	—
Eagle DL 6-cyl.					
535	Liftback SX/4	$8053	—	3169	—
565	Kammback 2-dr.	$7519	—	3128	—
Eagle 4-cyl.					
355	4-door Sedan	$8869	4463[1]	3172	4091
365	2-door Sedan	$8719	4463	3107	1968
385	4-door St. Wag.	$9566	4463	3299	20,899
Eagle Limited 4-cyl.					
357	4-door Sedan	$9316	4463	3180	—
367	2-door Sedan	$9166	4463	3115	—
387	4-door St. Wag.	$10,013	4463	3213	—
Eagle 6-cyl.					
355	4-door Sedan	$9019	4463[1]	3310	—
365	2-door Sedan	$8869	4463	3235	—
385	4-door St. Wag.	$9716	4463	3327	—
Eagle Limited 6-cyl.					
357	4-door Sedan	$9466	4463	3308	—
367	2-door Sedan	$9316	4463	3235	—
387	4-door St. Wag.	$10,163	4463	3341	—

NOTE 1: 4463 and 4657 lb. GVW optional for all models.
NOTE 2: All production figures are the totals for each body style regardless of trim level or engine.

1982 AMC Eagle Kammback

STANDARD ENGINE: Engine Type: OHV, Cast iron block. In-line 4-cyl. Bore x Stroke: 4.00 in. x 3.00 in. Lifters: Hydraulic. Number of main bearings-5. Fuel Induction: Rochester staged 2-barrel carburetor. Compression Ratio: 8.2:1. Displacement: 151 cu. in. (2.5 liter). Horsepower: Net: 82 @ 4000 rpm. Torque: Net: 125 lb.-ft. @ 2600 rpm. Oil capacity: 5 qt. with filter change. Fuel Requirements: 91 octane unleaded.

OPTIONAL ENGINE: (Required for sedans and station wagons with automatic transmission): Engine Type: OHV, Cast iron block. In-line 6-cyl. Bore x Stroke: 3.75 in. x 3.90 in. Lifters: Hydraulic. Number of main bearings-7. Fuel Induction: 2-barrel carburetor. Compression Ratio: 8.3:1. Displacement: 258 cu. in. (4.22 liter). Horsepower: Net: 115 @ 3200 rpm. Torque: Net: 210 lb.-ft. @ 1800 rpm. Oil capacity: 5 qt. with filter change. Fuel Requirements: 91 octane unleaded.

CHASSIS FEATURES: Welded steel unitized.

SUSPENSION AND RUNNING GEAR: Front Suspension: Independent with unequal length A-arms, coil springs, tubular shock absorbers, 0.81 in. stabilizer bar. Spring rates: 4-cyl.: 98 lb./in. 6-cyl.: 108 lb./in. Rear Suspension: Beam axle, tubular shock absorbers and 4-leaf semi-elliptical springs. Spring rate: Station wagon: 107 lb./in. All other models: 95 lb./in. Optional 0.62 in. stabilizer bar. Front Axle. Capacity: 2377 lb. Rear Axle. Hypoid. Capacity: 2500 lb. Final Drive Ratio: 2.5 liter engine: 3.54:1. 4.2 liter: manual transmissions: 2.73:1, automatic transmission: 2.35:1. Optional: 4.2 liter engine with Trailer Towing Package only: 3.08:1. Transfer Case: New Process model 119, single speed. Brakes: Type: Hydraulic, power assisted. Front: Discs. Rear: Drums. Dimensions: Front: 11.00 in. x 0.88 in. rotor. Rear: 10.0 in. x 1.75 in. Total brake swept area: 329 sq. in. Wheels: 15 x 6.00 in. Tires: P195/75R15 glass belted radial (Sedan and station wagon: White sidewall, SX/4 and Kammback: Black sidewall). Optional: P195/75R15 glass belted radial white sidewall (Base model SX/4 and Kammback),

1982 AMC Eagle SX/4

P195/75R15 Arriva steel belted radial black sidewall, P195/75R15 Arriva steel belted radial white sidewall, P215/75R15 Eagle GT steel belted radial outline white letters. Steering: Power assisted recirculated ball. Ratio: 17:1. Turns Lock-to-Lock: 3.4. Turning diameter: Sedans and station wagon: 35.45 ft. SX/4 and Kammback: 31.5-ft. Transmission: Warner gear T-4 four-speed manual. Ratios: 4.03, 2.37, 1.50. 1.00:1. Reverse: 3.76:1. Optional: Warner T5 five-speed manual. Ratios: 4.03, 2.37, 1.50. 1.00:1, 0.76:1(6-cylinder) or 0.86:1 (4-cylinder) Reverse: 3.76:1. Optional: 3-speed automatic with lock up converter. Ratios: 2.74, 1.55, 1.00:1. Reverse: 2.20:1.

VEHICLE DIMENSIONS: Wheelbase: Sedans and station wagon: 109.3 in. SX/4 and Kammback: 97.2 in. Overall Length: Sedans and station wagon: 183.2 in. SX/4 and Kammback: 166.6 in. Overhang Front/Rear: Sedans and station wagon: 34.2 in./42.8 in. SX/4 and Kammback: 34.2 in./35.2 in. Front/rear tread: All models: 59.6 in./57.6 in. Approach/Departure angle in degrees: Sedans and station wagon: 29.4/25.5. SX/4 and Kammback: 29.4/30.9. Overall Height: Sedans and station wagon: Two-door: 55.8 in.; four-door: 55.4 in.; station wagon: 55.0 in. SX/4 and Kammback: 5.2 in. Width: Sedans and station wagon: 72.3 in. SX/4 and Kammback: 73.0 in. Headroom: Sedans and station wagon: Front: 38.1 in. Rear: 37.5 in. (37.9 in. for station wagon). Legroom: Sedans and station wagon: Front:40.8 in. Rear: 36.1 in. SX/4 and Kammback: Front: 40.8 in. Rear: 26.2 in. Shoulder room: Sedans and station wagon: Front: 54.0 in. Rear: 53.2 in. (two-door sedan), 54.4 in. all others. SX/4 and Kammback: 53.9 in. Rear: SX/4: 53.2 in. Kammback: 53.0 in. Hip room: Sedans and station wagon: Front: 54.3 in. (2-door sedan), 54.4 in. all others. Rear: 52.5 in. (two-door sedan), 53.6 in. all others. SX/4 and Kammback: Front: 54.3 in. Rear: SX/4: 40.3 in. Kammback: 43.5 in. Ground Clearance: Sedans and station wagon: Front axle: 6.5 in. Rear axle: 7.25 in. Oil pan: 8.5 in. Transfer case skid plate: 7.0 in. Fuel tank: 12.0 in. Exhaust system: 8.0 in. SX/4 and Kammback: Front and rear differential: 7.7 in. Load space station wagon: (length x width x height): With seats in place: 37.5 in. x 41.0 in. x 24.25 in. With rear seat folded or removed: 58.25 in. x 41.0 in. x 24.25 in. Tailgate: Station wagon: 43.5 in. x 22.5 in.

CAPACITIES: Fuel Tank: Sedans and station wagon: 22 gal. tank. SX/4 and Kammback: 21 gal. Coolant system: 6-cyl.: 14 qts.

ACCOMMODATIONS: Seating Capacity: Sedans and station wagon: Standard: 5, Optional: None. SX/4 and Kammback: 4. Optional: None.

INSTRUMENTATION: Speedometer, 99,999.9 mi. odometer, fuel gauge, engine coolant temperature gauge, warning lights for ammeter, oil pressure, and emergency brake, hazard warning lights, and directional lights.

OPTIONS AND PRICES: Power windows: $169. Power door locks. Power deck lid release. Retractable cargo area cover (station wagon). AM radio. AM/FM radio. AM/FM radio with MPX cassette tape player. AM/FM/CB stereo radio: $208. Premium audio system with power amplifier, 4 high-fidelity speakers, and fader control. Power antenna. Air conditioning. Visibility Group. Includes remote left and right side mirrors. Light Group. Includes dome-map light, engine compartment light, rear door light switches, trunk light, liftgate dome light. Convenience Group. Includes lighted passenger visor mirror, lights-on buzzer, intermittent windshield wipers. Protection Group. Includes front and rear nerf strips, door edge guards, front and rear floor mats. Cold Climate Group. Includes engine block heater, heavy-duty battery, heavy-duty alternator, coolant protection to -34 degrees. Extra-duty Suspension Package. Includes rear sway bar, heavy-duty shock absorbers, heavy-duty springs. Tachometer. Tinted glass. Rear window defroster. Rear window wiper/washer (station wagon): $99. Popup sun roof (sedans): $279. Cruise control: $159. Tilt steering wheel. Leather-wrapped sport steering wheel. Roof rack (station wagon). Halogen headlights. Fog lamps. Woodgrain body side panels (station wagon). Light-Duty Trailer Towing Package. Medium-Duty Towing Package. Protective inner coat. Locking gas cap. Scuff molding. Front suspension skid plate. Automatic load leveling air shock absorbers. Heavy-duty battery. Sport Package. 6-way power seats: $262. Aluminum wheels. Floor shift console. Gauge Package. Aluminum wheels.

HISTORICAL FOOTNOTES: The five-speed manual transmission offered for the Eagle was the first such gearbox offered by AMC in its 27 year history.

1983 EAGLE

Several technical refinements plus additional standard equipment content highlighted the 1983 Eagle models. Only three body styles were offered for 1983 — the four-door sedan, station wagon and SX/4 liftback. The SX/4 was available in base, DL and Sport versions. The four-door sedan was produced only as a DL model. The station wagon was available in DL, Sport and Limited model forms. The 2.5 liter 4-cylinder engine and 4-speed manual transmission were the standard Eagle engine/transmission combination. The 3-speed automatic transmission was available on the SX/4 with either the standard engine or the optional 4.2 liter 6-cylinder engine. As in 1982, automatic transmission was available on the other Eagles only with the 6-cylinder engine. The 4.2 liter's compression ratio was increased from 8.2:1 to 9.2:1. A fuel feedback system and knock sensor were added for increased engine efficiency.

Interior deluxe grain vinyl trim colors for 1983 were black, slate blue, beige and, except for the base model, nutmeg. The optional Durham plaid fabric was offered in black, beige, nutmeg, wine or blue. The Coventry check fabric interior was available in black, beige, blue or nutmeg. The genuine leather interior was offered in nutmeg.

The SX/4 was available in 14 exterior color combinations: Dark brown metallic, deep night blue, copper brown metallic, classic black/Low gloss black, vintage red/Deep maroon Metallic, olympic white/Deep night blue, mist silver metallic/Deep night blue, slate blue metallic/Deep night blue, olympic white/Dark brown metallic, olympic white/Copper brown metallic, Jamaican beige/Dark brown metallic, and copper brown metallic/Dark brown metallic. The SX/4 Sport Package was offered in classic black, olympic white, mist silver metallic, slate blue metallic, Topaz gold metallic, Jamaican beige, vintage red metallic, Sebring red, and copper brown metallic. The Eagle four-door sedan and four-door station wagon were available in the same colors as the SX/4, with an additional deep maroon metallic color available.

1983 AMC Eagle SX/4

I.D. DATA: The V.I.N. consisted of 13 elements. The first entry, a letter, identified the manufacturer, the second entry, a number, designated the model year. The third symbol was a letter indicating the transmission and drivetrain, the fourth and fifth entries, both numbers, identified the body type. The sixth unit, a letter, was the GVW rating identification. The seventh unit, a letter identified the engine. The final six digits were the plant sequential production number.

Model Number	Body Type & Seating	Factory Price	GVW	Shipping Weight	Prod. Total
Eagle 4-cyl.					
530	Liftback SX/4	$7697	—	3034	2259
Eagle DL 4-cyl.					
535	Liftback SX/4	$8164	—	3094	—
Eagle 6-cyl.					
530	Liftback SX/4	$7852	—	3165	—
Eagle DL 6-cyl.					
535	Liftback SX/4	$8319	—	3225	—
Eagle 4-cyl.					
355	4-door Sedan	$9162	4463[1]	3265	3093
385	4-door St. Wag.	$9882	4463	3285	12,378[2]
Eagle Limited 4-cyl.					
387	4-door St. Wag.	$10,343	4463[1]	3301	—
Eagle 6-cyl.					
355	4-door Sedan	$9317	4463	3396	—
385	4-door St. Wag.	$10,037	4463	3416	—
Eagle Limited 6-cyl.					
387	4-door St. Wag.	$10,498	4463	3432	—

NOTE 1: 4463 and 4657 lb. GVW optional for all models.
NOTE 2: All production figures are the totals for each body style regardless of trim level or engine.

STANDARD ENGINE: Engine Type: OHV, Cast iron block. In-line 4-cyl. Bore x Stroke: 4.00 in. x 3.00 in. Lifters: Hydraulic. Number of main bearings-5. Fuel Induction: Rochester staged 2-barrel carburetor. Compression Ratio: 8.2:1. Displacement: 151 cu. in. (2.5 liter). Horsepower: Net: 82 @ 4000 rpm. Torque: Net: 125 lb.-ft. @ 2600 rpm. Oil capacity: 5 qt. with filter change. Fuel Requirements: 91 octane unleaded.

OPTIONAL ENGINE: (Required for sedans and station wagons with automatic transmission): Engine Type: OHV, Cast iron block. In-line 6-cyl. Bore x Stroke: 3.75 in. x 3.90 in. Lifters: Hydraulic. Number of main bearings-7. Fuel Induction: 2-barrel carburetor. Compression Ratio: 9.2:1. Displacement: 258 cu. in. (4.22 liter). Horsepower: Net: 110 @ 3200 rpm. Torque: Net: 210 lb.-ft. @ 1800 rpm. Oil capacity: 5 qt. with filter change. Fuel Requirements: 91 octane unleaded.

1983 Eagle station wagon

CHASSIS FEATURES: Welded steel unitized.

SUSPENSION AND RUNNING GEAR: Front Suspension: Independent with unequal length A-arms, coil springs, tubular shock absorbers, 0.81 in. stabilizer bar. Spring rates: 4-cyl.: 98 lb./in. 6-cyl.: 108 lb./in. Rear Suspension: Beam axle, tubular shock absorbers and 4-leaf

semi-elliptical springs. Spring rate: Station wagon: 107 lb./in. All other models: 95 lb./in. Optional 0.62 in. stabilizer bar. Front Axle. Capacity: 2377 lb. Rear Axle. Hypoid. Capacity: 2500 lb. Final Drive Ratio: Sedan and station wagon: 3.54:1 with 4-cylinder engine and 4 or 5-speed manual transmissions; 2.73:1 with 6-cylinder and 4 or 5-speed manual trans.; 2.35:1 with automatic transmission (2.73:1 high altitude); 3.08:1 for trailer applications with 6-cylinder and automatic trans. SX/4: 3.54:1 with 4-cylinder and all available transmissions (not available for high altitude with automatic transmission); 2.35:1 with 6-cylinder engine and standard or automatic transmission (2.73:1 high altitude). Transfer Case: New Process model 119, single speed. Brakes: Type: Hydraulic, power assisted. Front: Discs. Rear: Drums. Dimensions: Front: 11.00 in. x 0.88 in. rotor. Rear: 10.0 in. x 1.75 in. Total brake swept area: 329 sq. in. Wheels: 15 x 6.00 in. Tires: P195/75R15 glass belted radial (sedan and station wagon: White sidewall, SX/4: Black sidewall). Optional: P195/75R15 glass belted radial white sidewall (Base model SX/4), P195/75R15 Arriva steel belted radial black sidewall, P195/75R15 Arriva steel belted radial white sidewall, P215/75R15 Eagle GT steel belted radial outline white letters. Steering: Power assisted recirculated ball. Ratio: 17:1. Turns Lock-to-Lock: 3.4. Turning diameter: Sedans and station wagon: 35.45 ft. SX/4:31.5-ft. Transmission: Warner Gear T-4 four-speed manual. Ratios: 4.03, 2.37, 1.50. 1.00:1. Reverse: 3.76:1. Optional: Warner Gear T5 five-speed manual. Ratios: 4.03, 2.37, 1.50. 1.00:1, 0.76:1(6-cylinder) or 0.86:1 (4-cylinder) Reverse: 3.76:1. Optional: 3-speed automatic with lock up converter. Ratios: 2.74, 1.55, 1.00:1. Reverse: 2.20:1.

VEHICLE DIMENSIONS: Wheelbase: Sedans and station wagon: 109.3 in. SX/4: 97.2 in. Overall Length: Sedans and station wagon: 183.2 in. SX/4: 166.6 in. Overhang Front/Rear: Sedans and station wagon: 34.2 in./42.8 in. SX/4: 34.2 in./35.2 in. Front/rear tread: All models: 59.6 in./57.6 in. Approach/Departure angle in degrees: Sedans and station wagon: 29.4/25.5. SX/4: 29.4/30.9. Overall Height: Sedans and station wagon: Two-door: 55.8 in.; four-door: 55.4 in.; station wagon: 55.0 in. SX/4: 5.2 in. Width: Sedans and station wagon: 72.3 in. SX/4: 73.0 in. Headroom: Sedans and station wagon: Front: 38.1 in. Rear: 37.5 in. (37.9 in. for station wagon). Legroom: Sedans and station wagon: Front: 40.8 in. Rear: 36.1 in. SX/4: Front: 40.8 in. Rear: 26.2 in. Shoulder Room: Sedans and station wagon: Front: 54.0 in. Rear: 53.2 in. (two-door sedan), 54.4 in. all others. SX/4: 53.9 in. Rear: 53.2 in. Kammback: 53.0 in. Hip Room: Sedans and station wagon: Front: 54.3 in. (two-door sedan), 54.4 in. all others. Rear: 52.5 in. (two-door sedan), 53.6 in. all others. SX/4: Front: 54.3 in. Rear: SX/4: 40.3 in. Kammback: 43.5 in. Ground Clearance: Sedans and station wagon: Front axle: 6.5 in. Rear axle: 7.25 in. Oil pan: 8.5 in. Transfer case skidplate: 7.0 in. Fuel tank: 12.0 in. Exhaust system: 8.0 in. SX/4: Front and rear differential: 7.7 in. Load space station wagon: (length x width x height): With seats in place: 37.5 in. x 41.0 in. x 24.25 in. With rear seat folded or removed: 58.25 in. x 41.0 in. x 24.25 in. Tailgate: Station wagon: 43.5 in. x 22.5 in.

CAPACITIES: Fuel Tank: Sedans and station wagon: 22 gal. tank. SX/4: 21 gal. Coolant system: 6-cyl.: 14 qts.

ACCOMMODATIONS: Seating Capacity: Sedans and station wagon: Standard: 5, Optional: none. SX/4: 4. Optional: None.

INSTRUMENTATION: Speedometer, 99,999.9 mi. odometer, fuel gauge, engine coolant temperature gauge, warning lights for ammeter, oil pressure, and emergency brake, hazard warning lights, and directional lights.

OPTIONS AND PRICES: Power windows: $255 (sedan and station wagon), $180 (SX/4). Power door locks: $170. Power deck lid release. Retractable cargo area cover (station wagon). AM radio. AM/FM stereo radio: $199. AM/FM radio with MPX cassette tape player. AM/FM/CB stereo radio: $329 Premium audio system with power amplifier, 4 high-fidelity speakers, and fader control. Power antenna. Air conditioning. Visibility Group. Includes remote left and right side mirrors. Light Group. Includes dome-map light, engine compartment light, rear door light switches, trunk light, liftgate dome light. Convenience Group. Includes lighted passenger visor mirror, lights-on buzzer, intermittent windshield wipers. Protection Group. Includes front and rear nerf strips, door edge guards, front and rear floor mats. Cold Climate Group. Includes engine block heater, heavy-duty battery, heavy-duty alternator, coolant protection to -34 degrees. Extra-Duty Suspension Package. Includes rear sway bar, heavy-duty shock absorbers, heavy-duty springs. Tachometer. Tinted glass. Rear window defroster: $130 (SX/4). Rear window wiper/washer (station wagon). Popup sun roof (sedans): $295. Cruise control: $170. Tilt steering wheel. Leather-wrapped Sport steering wheel. Roof rack (station wagon). Halogen headlights. Fog lamps. Woodgrain body side panels (station wagon). Light-Duty Trailer Towing Package. Medium-Duty Towing Package. Protective inner coat. Locking gas cap. Scuff molding. Front suspension skid plate. Automatic load leveling air shock absorbers. Heavy-duty battery. Sport Package: $344 (sedan and station wagon), $516 (SX/4). 6-way power seats: $302 Aluminum wheels: $346 (sedan and station wagon), $400 (SX/4). Floor shift console. Gauge Package.

HISTORICAL FOOTNOTES: The Eagle was the official vehicle of the National Ski Patrol.

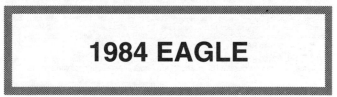

1984 EAGLE

The Eagle was marketed in just two body styles for 1984 — the four-door sedan and the four-door station wagon. The four-door sedan was available in a DL model only while the station wagon was available in DL, Sport and Limited models. The standard engine for all Eagles was the new AMC 2.5 liter 4-cylinder. Full details of this engine are found in the 1984 Jeep Cherokee section. The 258 cu. in. 6-cylinder remained optional as did the 5-speed manual and 3-speed automatic transmissions. New for 1984 were the Eagle's wheelcover design and an upshift indicator light.

I.D. DATA: The V.I.N. consisted of 13 elements. The first entry, a letter, identified the manufacturer, the second entry, a number, designated the model year. The third symbol was a letter indicating the transmission and drivetrain, the fourth and fifth entries, both numbers, identified the body type. The sixth unit, a letter, was the GVW rating identification. The seventh unit, a letter identified the engine. The final six digits were the plant sequential production number.

Model Number	Body Type & Seating	Factory Price	GVW	Shipping Weight	Prod. Total
Eagle 4-cyl.					
355	4-door Sedan	$9495	4463[1]	3273	4241
385	4-door St. Wag.	$10,225	4463	3304	21,294[2]
Eagle Limited 4-cyl.					
387	4-door St. Wag.	$10,695	4463	3320	—
Eagle 6-cyl.					
355	4-door Sedan	$9966	4463[1]	3391	—
385	4-door St. Wag.	$10,396	4463	3422	—

Eagle Limited 6-cyl.

387	4-door St. Wag.	$10,866	4463	3438	

NOTE 1: 4463 and 4657 lb. GVW optional for all models.
NOTE 2: All production figures are the totals for each body style regardless of trim level or engine.

STANDARD ENGINE: Engine Type: OHV, Cast iron block. In-line 4-cyl. Bore x Stroke: 3.875 in. x 3.188 in. Lifters: Hydraulic. Number of main bearings-5. Fuel Induction: 1-barrel carburetor. Compression Ratio: 9.2:1. Displacement: 150.4 cu. in. (2.465 liter). Horsepower: Net: 105 @ 5000 rpm. Torque: Net: 132 lb.-ft. @ 2800 rpm. Oil capacity: 5 qt. with filter change. Fuel Requirements: 91 octane unleaded.

OPTIONAL ENGINE: Engine Type: OHV, Cast iron block. In-line 6-cyl. Bore x Stroke: 3.75 in. x 3.90 in. Lifters: Hydraulic. Number of main bearings-7. Fuel Induction: 2-barrel carburetor. Compression Ratio: 9.2:1. Displacement: 258 cu. in. (4.22 liter). Horsepower: Net: 110 @ 3200 rpm. Torque: Net: 210 lb.-ft. @ 1800 rpm. Oil capacity: 5 qt. with filter change. Fuel Requirements: 91 octane unleaded.

CHASSIS FEATURES: Welded steel unitized.

SUSPENSION AND RUNNING GEAR: Front Suspension: Independent with unequal length A-arms, coil springs, tubular shock absorbers, 0.81 in. stabilizer bar. Spring rates: 4-cyl.: 98 lb./in. 6-cyl.: 108 lb./in. Rear Suspension: Beam axle, tubular shock absorbers and 4-leaf semi-elliptical springs. Spring rate: Station wagon: 107 lb./in. All other models: 95 lb./in. Optional 0.62 in. stabilizer bar. Front Axle. Capacity: 2377 lb. Rear Axle. Hypoid. Capacity: 2500 lb. Final Drive Ratio: Sedan and station wagon: 3.54:1 with 4-cylinder engine and 4 or 5-speed manual transmissions; 2.73:1 with 6-cylinder and 4 or 5-speed manual trans.; 2.35:1 with automatic transmission (2.73:1 high altitude); 3.08:1 for trailer applications with 6-cylinder and automatic trans. Transfer Case: New Process model 119, single speed. Brakes: Type: Hydraulic, power assisted. Front: Discs. Rear: Drums. Dimensions: Front: 11.00 in. x 0.88 in. rotor. Rear: 10.0 in. x 1.75 in. Total brake swept area: 329 sq. in. Wheels: 15 x 6.00 in. Tires: P195/75R15 glass belted radial white sidewall. Optional: P195/75R15 Arriva steel belted radial black sidewall, P195/75R15 Arriva steel belted radial white sidewall, P215/75R15 Eagle GT steel belted radial outline white letters. Steering: Power assisted recirculated ball. Ratio: 17:1. Turns Lock-to-Lock: 3.4. Turning diameter: 35.45 ft. Transmission: Warner Gear T-4 four-speed manual. Ratios: 4.03, 2.37, 1.50. 1.00:1. Reverse: 3.76:1. Optional: Warner Gear T5 five-speed manual. Ratios: 4.03, 2.37, 1.50. 1.00:1, 0.76:1(6-cylinder) or 0.86:1 (4-cylinder) Reverse: 3.76:1. Optional: 3-speed automatic with lock up converter. Ratios: 2.74, 1.55, 1.00:1. Reverse: 2.20:1.

VEHICLE DIMENSIONS: Wheelbase: 109.3 in. Overall Length: 183.2 in. Overhang Front/Rear: 34.2 in./42.8 in. Front/rear tread: All models: 59.6 in./57.6 in. Approach/Departure angle in degrees: 29.4/25.5. Overall Height: Four-door sedan: 55.4 in.; station wagon: 55.0 in. Width: 72.3 in. Headroom: Front: 38.1 in. Rear: 37.5 in. (37.9 in. for station wagon). Legroom: Front: 40.8 in. Rear: 36.1 in. Shoulder Front: 54.0 in. Rear: 54.4 in. Hip room: Front: 54.4 in. Rear: 53.6 in. Ground Clearance: Front axle: 6.5 in. Rear axle: 7.25 in. Oil pan: 8.5 in. Transfer case skid plate: 7.0 in. Fuel tank: 12.0 in. Exhaust system: 8.0 in. SX/4: Front and rear differential: 7.7 in. Load space station wagon: (length x width x height): With seats in place: 37.5 in. x 41.0 in. x 24.25 in. With rear seat folded or removed: 58.25 in. x 41.0 in. x 24.25 in. Tailgate: Station wagon: 43.5 in. x 22.5 in.

CAPACITIES: Fuel Tank: 22 gal. tank. Coolant system: 6-cyl.: 14 qts.

ACCOMMODATIONS: Seating Capacity: 5, Optional: none.

INSTRUMENTATION: Speedometer, 99,999.9 mi. odometer, fuel gauge, engine coolant temperature gauge, warning lights for ammeter, oil pressure, and emergency brake, hazard warning lights, and directional lights.

OPTIONS AND PRICES: Power windows: $264. Power door locks: $176. Power deck lid release: $41. Retractable cargo area cover (station wagon). AM radio: $86. AM/FM stereo radio: $206. AM/FM radio with MPX cassette tape player: $340. AM/FM/CB stereo radio. Premium audio system with power amplifier, 4 high-fidelity speakers, and fader control. Power antenna. Air conditioning. Visibility Group. Includes remote left and right side mirrors. Light Group. Includes dome-map light, engine compartment light, rear door light switches, trunk light, liftgate dome light. Convenience Group. Includes lighted passenger visor mirror, lights-on buzzer, intermittent windshield wipers. Protection Group. Includes front and rear nerf strips, door edge guards, front and rear floor mats. Cold Climate Group. Includes engine block heater, heavy-duty battery, heavy-duty alternator, coolant protection to -34 degrees. Extra-Duty Suspension Package. Includes rear sway bar, heavy-duty shock absorbers, heavy-duty springs. Tachometer. Tinted glass. Rear window defroster: $140. Rear window wiper/washer (station wagon). Popup sun roof (sedans). Cruise control: $176. Tilt steering wheel. Leather-wrapped Sport steering wheel. Roof rack (station wagon): $119. Halogen headlights. Fog lamps. Woodgrain body side panels (station wagon): $149. Light-Duty Trailer Towing Package. Medium-Duty Towing Package. Protective inner coat. Locking gas cap. Scuff molding. Front suspension skid plate. Automatic load leveling air shock absorbers. Heavy-duty battery. Sport Package: $356. Power seats: $196. Aluminum wheels: $358 Floor shift console: $67. Gauge Package: $94.

HISTORICAL FOOTNOTES: AMC reported that the "Eagle for 1984 is designed and built with rugged four-wheel drive capacity to go almost anywhere in passenger comfort and style."

1985 EAGLE

The 1985 Eagle was again available in just two body styles — the four-door sedan and the four-door station wagon. The DL identification was not used for 1985. The base four-door sedan and station wagon were listed simply as Eagle Sedan and Eagle Wagon. The station wagon was available in Sport and Limited form. A major technical development was the inclusion of a shift on the fly capability for the Eagle's standard Select Drive system. All that was now needed to shift between two-wheel drive and four-wheel drive was the movement of the instrument panel selector to the desired position. The only engine offered for the Eagle was the familiar 258 cu. in. 6-cylinder. The standard transmission was the 5-speed manual overdrive unit with a 3-speed automatic optional. Exterior color choices for 1985 were almond beige, mist silver metallic, autumn brown metallic, mocha dark brown metallic, olympic white, classic black, medium blue metallic, garnet metallic and dark brown metallic. The standard Eagle and sedan interior was offered in a choice of deluxe grain vinyl or Highland Check fabric in garnet, almond, honey, or blue. The Eagle Limited station wagon had a standard leather interior in a honey hue. The standard equipment level of the Eagles was of a high order. Among the major features were front and rear armrests, front and rear ashtrays, (front unit was illuminated), Alpine fabric headliner sun visors, key-in-ignition warning chimes, front and rear bumper nerf strips, argent styled wheelcovers, extra-quiet insulation, transfer case skid plate, and 2-speed windshield wipers and washer. The Sport Wagon's standard equipment was highlighted by its leather-wrapped steering wheel, black grille, black left-side remote control sport mirror, and blackout moldings and accents. The Limited version of the station wagon had chrome dual remote exterior mirrors, luxury woodgrain steering wheel, bright inner door frame, and, the-new-for-1985 wire wheelcovers. These wheelcovers were also optional for other Eagle models. A new standard feature for all Eagles was a full-face radio with four speakers. A new option was a keyless entry system which provided a remote lock unlock control for the doors.

1985 AMC Eagle station wagon

I.D. DATA: The V.I.N. consisted of 13 elements. The first entry, a letter, identified the manufacturer, the second entry, a number, designated the model year. The third symbol was a letter indicating the transmission and drivetrain, the fourth and fifth entries, both numbers, identified the body type. The sixth unit, a letter, was the GVW rating identification. The seventh unit, a letter identified the engine. The final six digits were the plant sequential production number.

Model Number	Body Type & Seating	Factory Price	GVW	Shipping Weight	Prod. Total
Eagle 6-cyl.					
355	4-door Sedan	$10,457	4463[1]	3390	2655
385	4-door St. Wag.	$11,217	4463	3421	13,535[2]
Eagle Limited 6-cyl.					
387	4-door St. Wag.	$11,893	4463	3452	—

NOTE 1: 4463 and 4657 lb. GVW optional for all models.
NOTE 2: All production figures are the totals for each body style regardless of trim level.

STANDARD ENGINE: Engine Type: OHV, Cast iron block. In-line 6-cyl. Bore x Stroke: 3.75 in. x 3.90 in. Lifters: Hydraulic. Number of main bearings-7. Fuel Induction: 2-barrel carburetor. Compression Ratio: 9.2:1. Displacement: 258 cu. in. (4.22 liter). Horsepower: Net: 110 @ 3200 rpm. Torque: Net: 210 lb.-ft. @ 1800 rpm. Oil capacity: 5 qt. with filter change. Fuel Requirements: 91 octane unleaded.

CHASSIS FEATURES: Welded steel unitized.

SUSPENSION AND RUNNING GEAR: Front Suspension: Independent with unequal length A-arms, coil springs, tubular shock absorbers, 0.81 in. stabilizer bar. Spring rates: 4-cyl.: 98 lb./in. 6-cyl.: 108 lb./in. Rear Suspension: Beam axle, tubular shock absorbers and 4-leaf semi-elliptical springs. Spring rate: Station wagon: 107 lb./in. All other models: 95 lb./in. Optional 0.62 in. stabilizer bar. Front Axle. Capacity: 2377 lb. Rear Axle. Hypoid. Capacity: 2500 lb. Final Drive Ratio: 2.73:1 with 5-speed manual transmission, 2.35:1 with automatic transmission, (high altitude with automatic transmission: 2.73:1), 3.08:1 for trailer applications with automatic transmission. Transfer Case: New Process model 119, single speed. Brakes: Type: Hydraulic, power assisted. Front: Discs. Rear: Drums. Dimensions: Front: 11.00 in. x 0.88 in. rotor. Rear: 10.0 in. x 1.75 in. Total brake swept area: 329 sq. in. Wheels: 15 x 6.00 in. Tires: Base sedan and station wagon, and Limited station wagon: P195/75R15 white sidewall glass belted radial. Sport station wagon: P195/75R15 black sidewall steel belted radial. Optional: P195/75R15 black sidewall steel belted radial, P195/75R15 white sidewall steel belted radial, P215/65R15 outline white letters, steel belted radial. Steering: Power assisted recirculated ball. Ratio: 17:1. Turns Lock-to-Lock: 3.4. Turning diameter: 35.45 ft. Transmission: Warner Gear T5 five-speed manual. Ratios: 4.03, 2.37, 1.50. 1.00:1, 0.76:1(6-cylinder) or 0.86:1 (4-cylinder) Reverse: 3.76:1. Optional: 3-speed automatic with lock up converter. Ratios: 2.74, 1.55, 1.00:1. Reverse: 2.20:1.

VEHICLE DIMENSIONS: Wheelbase: 109.3 in. Overall Length: 183.2 in. Overhang Front/Rear: 34.2 in./42.8 in. Front/rear tread: All models: 59.6 in./57.6 in. Approach/Departure angle in degrees: 29.4/25.5. Overall Height: Four-door sedan: 55.4 in.; station wagon: 55.0 in. Width: 72.3 in. Headroom: Front: 38.1 in. Rear: 37.5 in. (37.9 in. for station wagon). Legroom: Front: 40.8 in. Rear: 36.1 in. Shoulder Front: 54.0 in. Rear: 54.4 in. Hip room: Front: 54.4 in. Rear: 53.6 in. Ground Clearance: Front axle: 6.5 in. Rear axle: 7.25 in. Oil pan: 8.5 in. Transfer case skid plate: 7.0 in. Fuel tank: 12.0 in. Exhaust system: 8.0 in. SX/4: Front and rear differential: 7.7 in. Load space station wagon: (length x width x height): With seats in place: 37.5 in. x 41.0 in. x 24.25 in. With rear seat folded or removed: 58.25 in. x 41.0 in. x 24.25 in. Tailgate: Station wagon: 43.5 in. x 22.5 in.

1985 AMC Eagle four-door sedan

CAPACITIES: Fuel Tank: 22 gal. tank. Coolant system: 14 qts.

ACCOMMODATIONS: Seating Capacity: 5, Optional: none.

INSTRUMENTATION: Speedometer, 99,999.9 mi. odometer, fuel gauge, engine coolant temperature gauge, warning lights for ammeter, oil pressure, and emergency brake, hazard warning lights, and directional lights.

OPTIONS AND PRICES: Sport Package: $416. Tilt steering wheel: $115. Floor shift console. Convenience Group: $79. Gauge Package. Includes electric clock, tachometer, oil, volt and vacuum gauges: $98. Tinted glass-all windows. Light Group: $66. Individual reclining front seats. Parcel shelf. Leather-wrapped steering wheel (standard with Sport Package). Front and rear bumper guards (standard with Sport Package). Halogen high and low beam headlights (standard with Sport Package): $16 Left and right remote chrome mirrors. Right remote control chrome mirror. Right remote control sport mirror (standard with Sport Package). Left and right electric remote control chrome mirrors (not available with Sport Package). Black color-keyed with woodgrain scuff plates. Roof rack (not available for sedan): $124. Woodgrain side panels for station wagon: $155. Wire wheelcovers: $156. Aluminum wheels: $373. Air conditioning: $781. Heavy-duty battery: $28. Cold Climate Group. Maximum Cooling System. Cruise control (for automatic transmission only): $183. California emissions system. High altitude emissions system. Halogen fog lamps. Not available for sedan, standard with Sport Package. Keyless entry system. Requires power door locks: $101. Power station wagon deck lid release: $43. Power door locks: $183. Power door locks and windows. Six-way power driver seat. Six-way power driver and passenger seats: $326. Protection Group. Includes stainless steel door edge guards, front and rear bumper guards and floor mats. AM radio. AM/FM stereo radio with 4 speakers. AM/FM/ cassette tape player stereo radio with 4 speakers. Electronically tuned AM/FM cassette tape player with built-in power amplifier, and 4 coaxial speakers. Front suspension skid plate. Extra-duty Suspension Package with rear sway bar, heavy-duty front and rear shock absorbers, and front and rear heavy-duty springs. Load leveling automatic air shock absorbers (not available with Extra-Duty Suspension Package). Trailer Towing Packages. Rear station wagon window washer/wiper. Rear window electric defroster: $146.

HISTORICAL FOOTNOTES: Joseph E. Cappy, group vice-president sales and marketing for American Motors reported that "our AMC Eagle is the only four-wheel drive passenger car-like automobile built in North America, and it has been a favorite with women drivers since its introduction in 1980. Our most recent study showed that women accounted for 41 percent of all Eagle purchases."

1986 EAGLE

The Eagle was unchanged for 1986. It continued to offer the only full-time four-wheel drive system available on a domestic automobile. The 4.2 liter 6-cylinder was the only engine available for the Eagle. Two body styles were available — the four-door sedan and the four-door station wagon.

I.D. DATA: The V.I.N. consisted of 13 elements. The first entry, a letter, identified the manufacturer, the second entry, a number, designated the model year. The third symbol was a letter indicating the transmission and drivetrain, the fourth and fifth entries, both numbers, identified the body type. The sixth unit, a letter, was the GVW rating identification. The seventh unit, a letter identified the engine. The final six digits were the plant sequential production number.

Model Number	Body Type & Seating	Factory Price	GVW	Shipping Weight	Prod. Total
Eagle 6-cyl.					
355	4-door Sedan	$10,615	4463[1]	3391	1274
385	4-door St. Wag.	$11,385	4463	3425	6943[2]
Eagle Limited 6-cyl.					
387	4-door St. Wag.	$12,075	4463	3456	—

NOTE 1: 4463 and 4657 lb. GVW optional for all models.
NOTE 2: All production figures are the totals for each body style regardless of trim level.

STANDARD ENGINE: Engine Type: OHV, Cast iron block. In-line 6-cyl. Bore x Stroke: 3.75 in. x 3.90 in. Lifters: Hydraulic. Number of main bearings-7. Fuel Induction: 2-barrel carburetor. Compression Ratio: 9.2:1. Displacement: 258 cu. in. (4.22 liter). Horsepower: Net: 110 @ 3200 rpm. Torque: Net: 210 lb.-ft. @ 1800 rpm. Oil capacity: 5 qt. with filter change. Fuel Requirements: 91 octane unleaded.

CHASSIS FEATURES: Welded steel unitized.

SUSPENSION AND RUNNING GEAR: Front Suspension: Independent with unequal length A-arms, coil springs, tubular shock absorbers, 0.81 in. stabilizer bar. Spring rates: 4-cyl.: 98 lb./in. 6-cyl.: 108 lb./in. Rear Suspension: Beam axle, tubular shock absorbers and 4-leaf semi-elliptical springs. Spring rate: Station wagon: 107 lb./in. All other models: 95 lb./in. Optional 0.62 in. stabilizer bar. Front Axle. Capacity: 2377 lb. Rear Axle. Hypoid. Capacity: 2500 lb. Final Drive Ratio: 2.73:1 with 5-speed manual transmission, 2.35:1 with automatic transmission, (high altitude with automatic transmission: 2.73:1), 3.08:1 for trailer applications with automatic transmission. Transfer Case: New Process model 119, single speed. Brakes: Type: Hydraulic, power assisted. Front: Discs. Rear: Drums. Dimensions: Front: 11.00 in. x 0.88 in. rotor. Rear: 10.0 in. x 1.75 in. Total brake swept area: 329 sq. in. Wheels: 15 x 6.00 in. Tires: Base sedan and station wagon, and Limited station wagon: P195/75R15 white sidewall glass belted radial. Sport station wagon: P195/75R15 black sidewall steel belted radial. Optional: P195/75R15 black sidewall steel belted radial, P195/75R15 white sidewall steel belted radial, P215/65R15 outline white letters, steel belted radial. Steering: Power assisted recirculated ball. Ratio: 17:1. Turns Lock-to-Lock: 3.4. Turning diameter: 35.45 ft. Transmission: Warner Gear T5 five-speed manual. Ratios: 4.03, 2.37, 1.50. 1.00:1, 0.76:1(6-cylinder) or 0.86:1 (4-cylinder) Reverse: 3.76:1. Optional: 3-speed automatic with lock up converter. Ratios: 2.74, 1.55, 1.00:1. Reverse: 2.20:1.

VEHICLE DIMENSIONS: Wheelbase: 109.3 in. Overall Length: 183.2 in. Overhang Front/ Rear: 34.2 in./42.8 in. Front/rear tread: All models: 59.6 in./57.6 in. Approach/Departure angle in degrees: 29.4/25.5. Overall Height: Four-door sedan: 55.4 in.; station wagon: 55.0 in. Width: 72.3 in. Headroom: Front: 38.1 in. Rear: 37.5 in. (37.9 in. for station wagon). Legroom: Front: 40.8 in. Rear: 36.1 in. Shoulder Front: 54.0 in. Rear: 54.4 in. Hip room: Front: 54.4 in. Rear: 53.6 in. Ground Clearance: Front axle: 6.5 in. Rear axle: 7.25 in. Oil pan: 8.5 in. Transfer case skid plate: 7.0 in. Fuel tank: 12.0 in. Exhaust system: 8.0 in. SX/4: Front and rear differential: 7.7 in. Load space station wagon: (length x width x height): With seats in place: 37.5 in. x 41.0 in. x 24.25 in. With rear seat folded or removed: 58.25 in. x 41.0 in. x 24.25 in. Tailgate: Station wagon: 43.5 in. x 22.5 in.

CAPACITIES: Fuel Tank: 22 gal. tank. Coolant system: 14 qts.

ACCOMMODATIONS: Seating Capacity: 5, Optional: None.

INSTRUMENTATION: Speedometer, 99,999.9 mi. odometer, fuel gauge, engine coolant temperature gauge, warning lights for ammeter, oil pressure, and emergency brake, hazard warning lights, and directional lights.

OPTIONS AND PRICES: Sport Package: $431. Tilt steering wheel. Floor shift console. Convenience Group.: $82 Gauge Package. Includes electric clock, tachometer, oil, volt and vacuum gauges: $101 Tinted glass-all windows. Light Group: $68. Individual reclining front seats. Parcel shelf. Leather-wrapped steering wheel (standard with Sport Package). Front and rear bumper guards (standard with Sport Package). Halogen high and low beam headlights (standard with Sport Package). Left and right remote chrome mirrors. Right remote control chrome mirror. Right remote control Sport mirror (standard with Sport Package). Left and right electric remote control chrome mirrors (not available with Sport Package). Black color-keyed with woodgrain scuff plates. Roof rack (not available for sedan). Woodgrain side panels for station wagon. Wire wheelcovers. Aluminum wheels. Air conditioning: $795. Heavy-duty battery. Cold Climate Group. Maximum cooling system. Cruise control (for automatic transmission only). California emissions system. High altitude emissions system. Halogen fog lamps. Not available for sedan, standard with Sport Package. Keyless entry system. Requires power door locks. Power station wagon deck lid release. Power door locks. Power door locks and windows. Power windows: $285. Six-way power driver seat: $211. Six-way power driver and passenger seats: $337. Protection Group. Includes stainless steel door edge guards, front and rear bumper guards and floor mats: $84. AM radio. AM/FM stereo radio with 4 speakers: $186. AM/FM/cassette tape player stereo radio with 4 speakers. Electronically tuned AM/FM cassette tape player with built-in power amplifier, and 4 coaxial speakers. Front suspension skid plate: $86. Extra-Duty Suspension Package with rear sway bar, heavy-duty front and rear shock absorbers, and front and rear heavy-duty springs. Load leveling automatic air shock absorbers (not available with Extra-Duty Suspension Package). Trailer Towing Packages. Rear station wagon window washer/wiper: $138. Rear window electric defroster: $151.

HISTORICAL FOOTNOTES: AMC reported the 1986 Eagle had 50-State Fuel Economy estimates of 17 mpg city and 21 mpg highway with the standard 5-speed manual transmission. With the automatic transmission the respective estimates were 16 mpg and 19 mpg. Introduction of the 1986 Eagle took place on October 1, 1985.

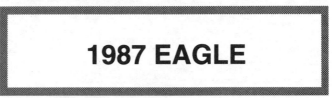

1987 EAGLE

The Eagle was unchanged for the 1987 model year.

I.D. DATA: The V.I.N. consisted of 13 elements. The first entry, a letter, identified the manufacturer, the second entry, a number, designated the model year. The third symbol was a letter indicating the transmission and drivetrain, the fourth and fifth entries, both numbers, identified the body type. The sixth unit, a letter, was the GVW rating identification. The seventh unit, a letter, identified the engine. The final six digits were the plant sequential production number.

Model Number	Body Type & Seating	Factory Price	GVW	Shipping Weight	Prod. Total
Eagle 6-cyl.					
355	4-door Sedan	$11,150	4463[1]	3383	—
385	4-door St. Wag.	$11,943	4463	3417	—
Eagle Limited 6-cyl.					
387	4-door St. Wag.	$12,653	4463	3431	—

NOTE 1: 4463 and 4657 lb. GVW optional for all models.

STANDARD ENGINE: Engine Type: OHV, Cast iron block. In-line 6-cyl. Bore x Stroke: 3.75 in. x 3.90 in. Lifters: Hydraulic. Number of main bearings-7. Fuel Induction: 2-barrel carburetor. Compression Ratio: 9.2:1. Displacement: 258 cu. in. (4.22 liter). Horsepower: Net: 112 @ 3000 rpm. Torque: Net: 210 lb.-ft. @ 2000 rpm. Oil capacity: 5 qt. with filter change. Fuel Requirements: 91 octane unleaded.

CHASSIS FEATURES: Welded steel unitized.

SUSPENSION AND RUNNING GEAR: Front Suspension: Independent with unequal length A-arms, coil springs, tubular shock absorbers, 0.81 in. stabilizer bar. Spring rates: 4-cyl.: 98 lb./in. 6-cyl.: 108 lb./in. Rear Suspension: Beam axle, tubular shock absorbers and 4-leaf semi-elliptical springs. Spring rate: Station wagon: 107 lb./in. All other models: 95 lb./in. Optional 0.62 in. stabilizer bar. Front Axle. Capacity: 2377 lb. Rear Axle. Hypoid. Capacity: 2500 lb. Final Drive Ratio: 2.73:1 with 5-speed manual transmission, 2.35:1 with automatic transmission, (high altitude with automatic transmission: 2.73:1), 3.08:1 for trailer applications with automatic transmission. Transfer Case: New Process model 119, single speed. Brakes: Type: Hydraulic, power assisted. Front: Discs. Rear: Drums. Dimensions: Front: 11.00 in. x 0.88 in. rotor. Rear: 10.0 in. x 1.75 in. Total brake swept area: 329 sq. in. Wheels: 15 x 6.00 in. Tires: Base sedan and station wagon, and Limited station wagon: P195/75R15 white sidewall glass belted radial. Sport station wagon: P195/75R15 black sidewall steel belted radial. Optional: P195/75R15 black sidewall steel belted radial, P195/75R15 white sidewall steel belted radial, P215/65R15 outline white letters, steel belted radial. Steering: Power assisted recirculated ball. Ratio: 17:1. Turns Lock-to-Lock: 3.4. Turning diameter: 35.45 ft. Transmission: Warner Gear T5 five speed manual. Ratios: 4.03, 2.37, 1.50. 1.00:1, 0.76:1(6-cylinder) or 0.86:1 (4-cylinder) Reverse: 3.76:1. Optional: 3-speed automatic with lock up converter. Ratios: 2.74, 1.55, 1.00:1. Reverse: 2.20:1.

VEHICLE DIMENSIONS: Wheelbase: 109.3 in. Overall Length: 183.2 in. Overhang Front/ Rear: 34.2 in./42.8 in. Front/rear tread: All models: 59.6 in./57.6 in. Approach/Departure angle in degrees: 29.4/25.5. Overall Height: Four-door sedan: 55.4 in.; station wagon: 55.0 in. Width: 72.3 in. Headroom: Front: 38.1 in. Rear: 37.5 in. (37.9 in. for station wagon). Legroom: Front: 40.8 in. Rear: 36.1 in. Shoulder Front: 54.0 in. Rear: 54.4 in. Hip room: Front: 54.4 in. Rear: 53.6 in. Ground Clearance: Front axle: 6.5 in. Rear axle: 7.25 in. Oil pan: 8.5 in. Transfer case skid plate: 7.0 in. Fuel tank: 12.0 in. Exhaust system: 8.0 in. SX/4: Front and rear differential: 7.7 in. Load space station wagon: (length x width x height): With seats in place: 37.5 in. x 41.0 in. x 24.25 in. With rear seat folded or removed: 58.25 in. x 41.0 in. x 24.25 in. Tailgate: Station wagon: 43.5 in. x 22.5 in.

CAPACITIES: Fuel Tank: 22 gal. tank. Coolant system: 14 qts.

ACCOMMODATIONS: Seating Capacity: 5, Optional: none.

INSTRUMENTATION: Speedometer, 99,999.9 mi. odometer, fuel gauge, engine coolant temperature gauge, warning lights for ammeter, oil pressure, and emergency brake, hazard warning lights, and directional lights.

OPTIONS AND PRICES: Sport Package: $456. Tilt steering wheel. Floor shift console. Convenience Group. Gauge Package. Includes electric clock, tachometer, oil, volt and vacuum gauges. Tinted glass-all windows. Light Group. Individual reclining front seats. Parcel shelf. Leather-wrapped steering wheel (standard with Sport Package). Front and rear bumper guards (standard with Sport Package). Halogen high and low beam headlights (standard with Sport Package). Left and right remote chrome mirrors. Right remote control chrome mirror. Right remote control Sport mirror (standard with Sport Package). Left and right electric remote control chrome mirrors (not available with Sport Package). Black color-keyed with woodgrain scuff plates. Roof rack (not available for sedan). Woodgrain side panels for station wagon. Wire wheelcovers. Aluminum wheels. Air conditioning. Heavy-duty battery. Cold Climate Group. Maximum cooling system. Cruise control (for automatic transmission only). California emissions system. High altitude emissions system. Halogen fog lamps. Not available for sedan, standard with Sport Package. Keyless entry system. Requires power door locks. Power station wagon deck lid release. Power door locks. Power door locks and windows. Power windows: $303. Six-way power driver seat. Six-way power driver and passenger seats.

Protection group. Includes stainless steel door edge guards, front and rear bumper guards and floor mats. AM radio. AM/FM stereo radio with 4 speakers. AM/FM/cassette tape player stereo radio with 4 speakers. Electronically tuned AM/FM cassette tape player with built-in power amplifier, and 4 coaxial speakers. Front suspension skid plate. Extra-Duty Suspension Package with rear sway bar, heavy-duty front and rear shock absorbers, and front and rear heavy-duty springs. Load leveling automatic air shock absorbers (not available with Extra-Duty Suspension Package). Trailer Towing Packages. Rear station wagon window washer/wiper. Rear window electric defroster.

HISTORICAL FOOTNOTES: This was the final year of Eagle production. The acquisition of AMC by Chrysler Corporation and plans to use the Eagle name for a new range of vehicles left the original Eagle with little corporate support for its continuation.

CHEVROLET PICKUPS

1957-1993

Chevrolet's history as a truck manufacturer dates back to 1918. By following the same philosophy that guided the development of its passenger cars — the offering of vehicles providing a solid, reliable mode of transportation that, if not the least expensive vehicle of their type were recognized as offering good value for the price — Chevrolet's truck models soon were major players in the light truck field. Both in terms of technical competence and design innovation, the Chevrolet trucks made substantial and consistent improvements throughout the 1920s and 1930s. Shortly after the availability in 1929 of a 6-cylinder engine came such improvements as standard hydraulic shock absorbers, electric fuel gauges, vacuum windshield wipers, and exterior mirrors. Keeping pace with these developments was a steady flow of useful body-chassis combinations, including vans, canopy models, open-pickups, platforms and stake bodies.

In 1930, Chevrolet's truck sales exceeded 188,000 units. In 1933 it out-produced Ford for the first time. Ford regained the lead in 1935 and 1937. After that point Chevrolet was at the top until 1969. In recent years the battle between Chevrolet's pickups and their Ford counterparts have been one of the highlights of the American industrial scene.

The modern era of Chevrolet truck development is considered to be 1937 when dramatic new styling that broke away from that of past models was adopted. The Chevrolet's "steel stream styling" was not an empty sales department inspired slogan. The new trucks had flowing fenders, a steel current roof and an overall look that gave them a coherent, contemporary appearance. Technically, the 1937 models were distinguished by Chevrolet's use of a modernized 216.5 cu. in. overhead valve 6-cylinder engine that was destined for a long and useful production life. Although styling refinements took place on a regular basis, the light-duty Chevrolets retained their basic format during the remaining years of the decade. In 1940 a major development was the introduction of the Sedan Delivery model which was styled along the lines of Chevrolet's passenger cars.

The immediate postwar Chevrolet trucks were essentially carryover models from 1942 but in the summer of 1947 the new "Advance Design" models debuted. These trucks possessed a style and charm that was destined to make them prime examples of the old truck hobby several years later. But their model run was relatively short by truck standards. In 1955 came their successors, with wraparound windshields and a distinctly automotive styling theme. Moreover, the new Chevrolets were offered with a V-8 engine. If anyone still harbored a belief that light-duty trucks were intended only for the farm and hauling industry, they were sent into full retreat by the dazzling Cameo pickup.

The age of factory-built four-wheel drive models began in 1957. These trucks, like most other four-wheel drive models were originally envisioned as strictly utilitarian vehicles, intended for a life of work in back-country, rough terrain environments. But this virtue quickly became just one facet of their market strength as the concept of recreational vehicles took hold in the early sixties. In a fashion not very dissimilar to the explosion of the ponycar market, a new spectrum of four-wheel drive models appeared, in the midst of which were vehicles such as Chevrolet's Blazer.

The Chevrolet four-wheel drive trucks were, of course, dependent upon the mainstream development of conventional two-wheel drive models for most of their styling and body arrangements. Thus, all-new models were introduced in 1973 that also served as the basis for the subsequent introduction of extended cab and crew cab body styles. Technical highlights of these K series pickups included a full-time four-wheel drive system with V-8 engines in 1974 and the introduction of K30 one-ton models in 1977. The decade of the 1980s saw the arrival of the 6.2 liter diesel V-8 and the use of fuel injected V-6 and V-8 gasoline engines. But the highlight of the decade was the introduction of the new generation pickups in 1988.

The Chevrolet Blazers, which adopted this new platform for the 1992 model year, were originally introduced in 1969. Based upon the K series trucks they shared many of the features of those four-wheel drive models including the 6.2 liter V-8 diesel and a steady flow of anti-corrosion improvements. But the Blazer was a distinct model in its own right as evident by its evolutionary development. In 1973, for example, it not only was available with full-time four-wheel drive, but also offered a tailgate with a roll-down window. In 1975 the practice of producing the Blazer with a removable hardtop was abandoned. In 1980 the Blazer was offered in the upscale Silverado trim form.

The Blazer's alter-ego of sorts, the Suburban, dates back to 1936. Its career as a four-wheel drive model began in 1957. The popularity of the Suburban, both as two or four-wheel drive models is demonstrated by the position of sales leadership it enjoyed in 1991. In that year, sales in the truck-wagon segment of the market totalled 76,000 units. Of that amount, the Suburban was the top seller with well over a 50 percent share of the market.

Following the introduction of the Blazer in 1969, the next major inroad into the four-wheel drive market by Chevrolet took place in 1983 when both the S-10 pickup and S-10 Blazer models were announced. These new compact-size pickup and utility vehicles was joined by yet another variation on the four-wheel drive theme in the form of the Astro in 1990.

1957 PICKUP

Chevrolet introduced its first factory four-wheel drive models in 1957. They were offered in Chevrolet's "Task Force" trucks in Series 3100 (1/2 ton-114 in. wheelbase), Series 3600 (3/4 ton-123.25 in. wheelbase) and Series 3800 (1 ton, 135 in. wheelbase) trucks. The four-wheel drive system was offered for all chassis cab, pickup, panel, Carryall and Stake models in the three series. The four-wheel drive system was listed as an option (RPO 690) and included a 4-speed transmission (RPO 318) and the 2-speed transfer case. It was available only with the Thiftmaster 6-cylinder engine. For the 3100 and 3600 series it also included RPO 254 (heavy-duty 8-leaf rear springs). For the 3800 series RPO 200 (rear shock absorbers) and RPO 254 (a heavy-duty rear spring) were included.

In addition to a power take-off opening located on the left side of the transmission there were two additional power take-off opening on the transfer case-one at the rear and one on the left side. Power could be taken from either or both of these openings when the truck was in motion or when stationary if the transfer case control lever was in the neutral position. The front axle of the four-wheel drive unit used the same pinion ring and differential gears that were used in the rear axle. The front wheels were driven through Rzeppa constant velocity universal joints which delivered an even flow of power for all positions of the front wheels, and kept driving forces from being transmitted to the steering wheel. To allow sufficient ground clearance for the four-wheel drive mechanism, truck height was increased approximately 7 inches as compared to a conventional two-wheel drive Chevrolet truck. All series were available in either "Flite-Ride Deluxe" or "Flite-Ride Custom" cabs. The Custom cabs had foam rubber seats, dual sun visors, cigarette lighter, driver-side arm rests and chrome-plated control knobs. Standard equipment content for the pickups included the following items: Under slung spare tire holder, 54-plate, 53 amp-hr.12-volt battery, 25 amp generator, oil-bath air cleaner, front painted bumper, key-locked dispatch box, dome light, left side exterior mirror with short fixed bracket, left-side adjustable sun visor and dual vacuum windshield wipers. The Suburban had the same equipment except that only a driver's side seat was standard. Exterior colors for 1957 consisted of the following: Brewster green, ocean green, cardinal red, Indian turquoise, Royal blue, alpine blue, sand beige, golden yellow, granite gray, jet black, Omaha orange, Yukon yellow, pure white and sandstone beige. Chevrolet also offered this wide range of extra cost two-tone color combinations: Ocean green/Brewster green, Bombay ivory/Ocean green, Bombay ivory/Cardinal red, Bombay ivory/Indian turquoise, Alpine blue/Royal blue, Bombay ivory/Alpine blue, Bombay ivory/sand beige, jet black/golden yellow, Bombay Ivory/Granite gray, Bombay ivory/Jet black, Bombay ivory/Omaha orange, Bombay ivory/Yukon yellow, and Bombay ivory/Sandstone beige.

I.D. DATA: The truck identification plate was located on the left side body hinge panel. The first numeral and letter designated the series: 3A-3100, 3E-3600 and 3G-3800. The next numerical group-57, indicated the model year. The next entry, a letter, indicated the assembly plant as follows: A-Atlanta, B-Baltimore, F-Flint, J-Janesville, K-Kansas City, L-Los Angeles, N-Norwood, O-Oakland, S-St. Louis, T-Tarrytown and W-Willow Run. The next six digits-10001, designated the truck number by plant. For example a truck with the truck identification of 3E57F100092 was a Series 3600, 1957 model that was the 92nd truck to be built at Flint.

Model Number	Body Type & Seating	Factory Price	GVW	Shipping Weight	Prod. Total
Series 3100 1/2 ton 6-cyl.114 in. wheelbase					
3153	Chassis and Cab	$2444	5400	3271	—
3154	Pickup Stepside	$2549	5400	3615	—
3155	Panel	$2829	5400	3860	—
3156	Suburban, pnl. Dr.	$3139	5400	4140	—
3166	Suburban, Endgate	$3169	5400	4150	—
Series 3600 3/4 ton 6-cyl. 123.25 in. wheelbase					
3653	Chassis and Cab	$2505	7300	3650	—
3654	Pickup Stepside	$2810	7300	4030	—
3659	Stake	$2895	7300	4275	—
Series 3800 1 ton, 135 in. wheelbase					
3853	Chassis and Cab	$2890	7400	3895	—
3854	Pickup Stepside	$3015	7400	4340	—
3855	Panel	$3320	7400	4645	—
3859	Stake	$3120	7400	4685	—

STANDARD ENGINE: All models: Thriftmaster Six. Engine Type: OHV, In-line 6-cylinder. Cast iron block and cylinder head. Bore x Stroke: 3.5625 in. x 3.9375 in. Lifters: Hydraulic. Number of main bearings-4. Fuel Induction: Single Rochester 1-bbl. carburetor, model 7007181. Compression Ratio: 8.0:1. Displacement: 235.5 cu. in. (3.85 liters). Horsepower: Gross: 140 @ 4200 rpm. Net: 123 @ 4000 rpm. Torque: Gross: 210 lb.-ft. @ 2000 rpm. Net: 195 lb.-ft. @ 2000 rpm. Oil refill capacity: 5 qt. without filter change; 1 and 2 quart filters were optional. Fuel Requirements: Regular.

OPTIONAL ENGINE: None.

CHASSIS FEATURES: Series 3100: Separate body and frame with channel side rails measuring 6 in. x 2.25 in. x 0.1406 in. and five cross members. Section modules: 2.54 in. Series 3600: Separate body and frame with channel side rails measuring 6.093 in. x 2.25 in. x 0.1875 in. and five cross members. Section modules: 3.37 in. Series 3800: Separate body and frame with channel side rails measuring 7.25 in. x 2.75 in. x 0.2187 in. and five cross members. Section modules: 5.70 in.

SUSPENSION AND RUNNING GEAR: Series 3100: Front Suspension: 44 in. x 2.0 in. 7-leaf, semi-elliptical springs, 1.0 in. dia. absorbers. 1360 lb. rating (at ground). Series 3600: Front Suspension: Semi-elliptical 7-leaf, 44.0 in. x 2.0 in. springs, direct double acting 1.0 in. dia. shock absorbers. 1430 lb. rating (at ground), Optional: None. Optional rating: None. Series 3800: Semi-elliptical 7-leaf, 44.0 in. x 2.0 in. springs, direct double acting 1.0 in. dia. shock absorbers. 1430 lb. rating (at ground), Optional: None. Rear Suspension: Series 3100: 52 in. x 2.0 in. Single-stage, 8-leaf, semi-elliptical springs, 1.0 in. dia. shock absorbers. 1570 lb. rating (at ground). Series 3600: Semi-elliptical 8-leaf, single-stage, 52 in. x 2.0 in. springs, 2430 lb. rating (at ground). Series 3800: Semi-elliptical leaf, single-stage, 52 in. x 2.0 in. springs, 2400 lb. rating (at ground). Optional Rating: None. Optional Rating: None. Front Axle Type and Capacity: Series 3100: Semi-floating, 3000 lb. capacity. Series 3600: Semi-floating, 3300 lb. capacity. Optional: None. Series 3800: Semi-floating, 3500 lb. capacity. Optional: None. Rear Axle Type and Capacity: Series 3100: Semi-floating, 3300 lb. capacity. Optional: None. Series 3600: Semi-floating, 5000 lb. capacity. Optional: None. Series 3800: Semi-floating, 7200 lb. capacity. Optional: None. Final Drive Ratio: Series 3100: 3.90:1. Series 3600: 5.14:1. Series 3800: 4.57:1. Transfer Case: Single lever, two-speed: 1.87, 1.00:1. Brakes: Type: Hydraulic, front and rear drums. Dimensions: Series 3100: Front: 11.0 in. x 2.0 in. Rear: 11.0 in. x 1.75 in. Effective lining area: 157 sq. in. Series 3600: Front: 12.0 in. x 2.0 in. Rear: 12.0 in. x 2.0 in. Effective lining area: 184 sq. in. Series 3800: 12.0 in. x 2.0 in. Rear: 14.0 in. x 2.50 in. Effective lining area: 228 sq. in. Wheels. Series 3100. 16 x 5.5K 5-stud disc. Series 3600: 17.5 in. x 5.25 in. disc. Series 3800: 17.5 in. x 5.25 in. disc. Tires: Series 3100: Either RPO 6.50 x 16 6-ply rating or 7 x 17.5 6-ply rating had to be ordered. The latter tires required 17.5 x 5.25 in. wheels. Series 3600: 8-19.5 6-ply rating. Series 380: 8-19.5 6-ply rating. Steering: Recirculating ball gear. Ratio: Series 3100 and 3600: 21.30:1. Series 3800: 23.30:1. Steering wheel diameter: 18.0 in. Optional: None. Transmission: 4-speed, synchromesh manual. Transmission Ratios: 7.05, 6.69, 3.19, 1.00:1 reverse: 12.60:1. Optional: None. Clutch: Diaphragm, spring. Clutch diameter: 10 in. Total lining area: 100.5 sq. in. Optional: None.

VEHICLE DIMENSIONS: Series 3100. Wheelbase: 114 in. Overall Length: Pickup: 185.6875 in. Panel: 197.875 in. Overall Height: Panel: 79.6875 in. Width: Pickup: 76.0 in. Panel: 76.375 in. Front/Rear Overhang: Pickup: 30.6875 in./41 in. Tailgate: Width and Height: 50 in. x 17.56 in. Ground Clearance: Front axle: 8.625 in. Rear axle: 8.625 in. Load space: Pickup box dimensions: 78.125 in. x 50.0 in. x 17.56 in. Series 3600. Wheelbase: 123.25 in. Overall Length: Pickup: 205.5625. Stake: 204.9375 in. Width: Pickup: 76.0 in. Stake: 79.56 in. Front/ Rear Overhang: Pickup: 30.6875 in./51.625 in. Stake: 30.6875 in./50.625 in. Tailgate: Width and Height: 50 in. x 17.56 in. Load space: Pickup box dimensions: 98 in. x 50.0 in. x 17.56 in. Series 3800. Wheelbase: 135 in. Overall Length: Pickup and chassis & cab: 215.8125 in. Panel: 228.875 in. Stake: 222.5625 in. Width: Pickup: 76.0 in. Panel: 786.625 in. Stake: 91.5625 in. Front/Rear Overhang: Pickup: 30.6875 in./50.125 in. Stake: 30.6875 in./56.875 in. Tailgate: Width and Height: 50 in. x 17.56 in. Load space: Pickup box dimensions: 108.25 in. x 50.0 in. x 17.56 in.

CAPACITIES: Fuel Tank: 17.5 gal. Optional: None. Engine coolant system: 17 qt.

ACCOMMODATIONS: Seating Capacity: 3 passenger. Optional: None.

INSTRUMENTATION: Speedometer, odometer, gauges for oil pressure, engine coolant temperature, battery charge and fuel level.

OPTIONS AND PRICES: Right side exterior mirror with long or short bracket (RPO 210): $4.85. Rear shock absorber shields (RPO 21): $2.15. Oil bath air cleaner, 1 qt. capacity (RPO 216): $4.35. Positive crankcase ventilation, includes RPO 216 (RPO 217): $13.45. Painted rear bumper (RPO 218): $21.55. Chrome rear bumper (RPO 218): 26.90. Heavy-duty, 11 in. clutch (RPO 227): $5.40. Oil filter, 1 qt. capacity (RPO 237): $8.65. Oil filter, 2 qt. capacity (RPO 237): $11.85. Heavy-duty radiator (RPO 256): $16.15. Foam rubber seat for Deluxe cab only (RPO 258): $14.00. Auxiliary seat for Suburban (RPO 263): $40.90. Electric windshield wipers (RPO 320): $12.95. 30 amp generator (RPO 326): $7.55. 40 amp generator with low cut-in rate (RPO 326): $80.70. Heavy-duty generator (RPO 326): $80.70. Side-mount spare tire carrier for pickups with painted bumper (RPO 341): $14.00. Side-mount spare tire carrier for pickups with chrome bumper (RPO 341): $15.10. Heavy-duty 66 amp battery (RPO 345): $7.55. Chrome trim for Suburban models only (RPO 393): $50.60. Full view rear window for pickups (RPO 394): $43.05. Left side door lock for Deluxe cab only (RPO 395): $1.65. Side-mount spare tire lock for Deluxe cab only (RPO 395): $6.50. Left side door and side-mount spare tire lock for Deluxe cab only (RPO 395): $.55. Pickup running boards for model 3153 only (RPO 423): $7.00. Custom cab, includes foam rubber seat (RPO 431): $86.10. Custom dash panel (RPO 434): $69.95. Two-tone paint combinations for Deluxe cab only (RPO 443): $10.80. Two-tone color combinations for Custom cab (RPO 444): $16.15. Two-tone color combinations for Panels (RPO 445): $26.90.

HISTORICAL FOOTNOTES: The first year of Chevrolet factory-installed four-wheel drive marked the start of an ever-increasing presence by Chevrolet in what was to be a major growth segment of the light-duty truck market.

1958 PICKUP

The 1958 models were modernized by the use of dual headlights, a revamped grille with two narrow horizontal bars just below the hood and a more massive lower bar that extended out and under the headlamps. This element carried Chevrolet lettering. New Fleetside pickup bodies were introduced for 1958. New exterior colors for 1958 were dawn blue, marine blue, kodiak brown, glade green, oriental green, polar green and tartan turquoise.

I.D. DATA: The truck identification plate was located on the left side body hinge panel. The first numeral and letter designated the series: 3A-3100, 3E-3600 and 3G-3800. The next numerical group-58, indicated the model year. The next entry, a letter, indicated the assembly plant as follows: A-Atlanta, B-Baltimore, F-Flint, J-Janesville, K-Kansas City, L-Los Angeles, N-Norwood, O-Oakland, S-St. Louis, T-Tarrytown and W-Willow Run. The next six digits-10001, designated the truck number by plant. For example a truck with the truck identification of 3E58F100092 was a Series 3600, 1958 model that was the 92nd truck to be built at Flint.

Model Number	Body Type & Seating	Factory Price	GVW	Shipping Weight	Prod. Total
Series 3100 1/2 ton 6-cyl.114 in. wheelbase					
3153	Chassis and Cab	$2528	5400	3271	—
3154	Pickup Stepside	$2569	5400	3615	—
3184	Pickup Fleetside	$2664	5400	N.A.	—
3155	Panel	$2913	5400	3860	—
3156	Suburban, pnl. Dr.	$3223	5400	4140	—
3166	Suburban, Endgate	$3253	5400	4150	—
Series 3600 3/4 ton 6-cyl. 123.25 in. wheelbase					
3653	Chassis and Cab	$2589	7300	3650	—
3654	Pickup Stepside	$2894	7300	4030	—
3684	Pickup Fleetside	$2909	7300	N.A.	—
3659	Stake	$3063	7300	4275	—
Series 3800 1 ton, 135 in. wheelbase					
3853	Chassis and Cab	$2974	7400	3895	—
3854	Pickup Stepside	$3099	7400	4340	—
3855	Panel	$3404	7400	4645	—
3859	Stake	$3204	7400	4685	—

STANDARD ENGINE: All models: Thriftmaster Six. Engine Type: OHV, In-line 6-cylinder. Cast iron block and cylinder head. Bore x Stroke: 3.5625 in. x 3.9375 in. Lifters: Hydraulic. Number of main bearings-4. Fuel Induction: Single Rochester 1-bbl. carburetor, model 7007181. Compression Ratio: 8.0:1. Displacement: 235.5 cu. in. (3.85 liters). Horsepower: Gross: 140 @ 4200 rpm. Net: 123 @ 4000 rpm. Torque: Gross: 210 lb.-ft. @ 2000 rpm. Net: 195 lb.-ft. @ 2000 rpm. Oil refill capacity: 5 qt. without filter change 1 and 2 quart filters were optional. Fuel Requirements: Regular.

OPTIONAL ENGINE: None.

CHASSIS FEATURES: Series 3100: Separate body and frame with channel side rails measuring 6 in. x 2.25 in. x 0.1406 in. and five cross members. Section modules: 2.54 in. Series 3600: Separate body and frame with channel side rails measuring 6.093 in. x 2.25 in. x 0.1875 in. and five cross members. Section modules: 3.37 in. Series 3800: Separate body and frame with channel side rails measuring 7.25 in. x 2.75 in. x 0.2187 in. and five cross members. Section modules: 5.70 in.

SUSPENSION AND RUNNING GEAR: Series 3100: Front Suspension: 44 in. x 2.0 in. 7-leaf, semi-elliptical springs, 1.0 in. dia. absorbers. 1360 lb. rating (at ground). Series 3600: Front Suspension: Semi-elliptical 7-leaf, 44.0 in. x 2.0 in. springs, direct double acting 1.0 in. dia. shock absorbers. 1430 lb. rating (at ground), Optional: None. Optional rating: None. Series 3800: Semi-elliptical 7-leaf, 44.0 in. x 2.0 in. springs, direct double acting 1.0 in. dia. shock absorbers. 1430 lb. rating (at ground), Optional: None. Rear Suspension: Series 3100: 52 in. x 2.0 in. Single-stage, 8-leaf, semi-elliptical springs, 1.0 in. dia. shock absorbers. 1570 lb. rating (at ground). Series 3600: Semi-elliptical 8-leaf, single-stage, 52 in. x 2.0 in. springs, 2430 lb. rating (at ground). Series 3800: Semi-elliptical leaf, single-stage, 52 in. x 2.0 in. springs, 2400 lb. rating (at ground). Optional Rating: None. Optional Rating: None. Front Axle Type and Capacity: Series 3100: Semi-floating, 3000 lb. capacity. Series 3600: Semi-floating, 3300 lb. capacity. Optional: None. Series 3800: Semi-floating, 3500 lb. capacity. Optional: None. Rear Axle Type and Capacity: Series 3100: Semi-floating, 3300 lb. capacity. Optional: None. Series 3600: Semi-floating, 5000 lb. capacity. Optional: None. Series 3800: Semi-floating, 7200 lb. capacity. Optional: None. Final Drive Ratio: Series 3100: 3.90:1. Series 3600: 5.14:1. Series 3800: 4.57:1. Transfer Case: Single lever, two-speed: 1.87, 1.00:1. Brakes: Type: Hydraulic, front and rear drums. Dimensions: Series 3100: Front: 11.0 in. x 2.0 in. Rear: 11.0 in. x 1.75 in. Effective lining area: 157 sq. in. Series 3600: Front: 12.0 in. x 2.0 in. Rear: 12.0 in. x 2.0 in. Effective lining area: 184 sq. in. Series 3800: 12.0 in. x 2.0 in. Rear: 14.0 in. x 2.50 in. Effective lining area: 228 sq. in. Wheels: Series 3100: 16 x 5.5K 5-stud disc. Series 3600: 17.5 in. x 5.25 in. disc. Series 3800: 17.5 in. x 5.25 in. disc. Tires: Series 3100: Either RPO 6.50 x 16 6-ply rating or 7 x 17.5 6-ply rating had to be ordered. The latter tires required 17.5 x 5.25 in. wheels. Series 3600: 8-19.5 6-ply rating. Series 380: 8-19.5 6-ply rating. Steering: Recirculating ball gear. Ratio: Series 3100 and 3600: 21.30:1. Series 3800: 23.30:1. Steering wheel diameter: 18.0 in. Optional: None. Transmission: 4-speed, synchromesh manual. Transmission Ratios: 7.05, 6.69, 3.19, 1.00:1 reverse: 12.60:1. Optional: None. Clutch: Diaphragm, spring. Clutch diameter: 10 in. Total lining area: 100.5 sq. in. Optional: None.

VEHICLE DIMENSIONS: Series 3100: Wheelbase: 114 in. Overall Length: Pickup: 185.6875 in. Panel: 197.875 in. Overall Height: Panel: 79.6875 in. Width: Pickup: 76.0 in. Panel: 76.375 in. Front/Rear Overhang: Pickup: 30.6875 in./41 in. Tailgate: Width and Height: 50 in. x 17.56 in. Ground Clearance: Front axle: 8.625 in. Rear axle: 8.625 in. Load space: Pickup box dimensions: 78.125 in. x 50.0 in. x 17.56 in. Series 3600. Wheelbase: 123.25 in. Overall Length: Pickup: 205.5625. Stake: 204.9375 in. Width: Pickup: 76.0 in. Stake: 79.56 in. Front/Rear Overhang: Pickup: 30.6875 in./51.625 in. Stake: 30.6875 in./50.625 in. Tailgate: Width and Height: 50 in. x 17.56 in. Load space: Pickup box dimensions: 98 in. x 50.0 in. x 17.56 in. Series 3800. Wheelbase: 135 in. Overall Length: Pickup and chassis & cab: 215.8125 in. Panel: 228.875 in. Stake: 222.5625 in. Width: Pickup: 76.0 in. Panel: 786.625 in. Stake: 91.5625 in. Front/Rear Overhang: Pickup: 30.6875 in./50.125 in. Stake: 30.6875 in./56.875 in. Tailgate: Width and Height: 50 in. x 17.56 in. Load space: Pickup box dimensions: 108.25 in. x 50.0 in. x 17.56 in.

CAPACITIES: Fuel Tank: 17.5 gal. Optional: None. Engine coolant system: 17 qt.

ACCOMMODATIONS: Seating Capacity: 3 passenger. Optional: None.

INSTRUMENTATION: Speedometer, odometer, gauges for oil pressure, engine coolant temperature, battery charge and fuel level.

OPTIONS AND PRICES: Right side exterior mirror with long or short bracket (RPO 210): $4.85. Rear shock absorber shields (RPO 21): $2.15. Oil bath air cleaner, 1 qt. capacity (RPO 216): $4.35. Positive crankcase ventilation, includes RPO 216 (RPO 217): $13.45. Painted rear bumper (RPO 218): $21.55. Chrome rear bumper (RPO 218): 26.90. Heavy-duty, 11 in. clutch (RPO 227): $5.40. Oil filter, 1 qt. capacity (RPO 237): $8.65. Oil filter, 2 qt. capacity (RPO 237): $11.85. Heavy-duty radiator (RPO 256): $16.15. Foam rubber seat for Deluxe cab only (RPO 258): $14.00. Auxiliary seat for Suburban (RPO 263): $40.90. Electric windshield wipers (RPO 320): $12.95. 30 amp generator (RPO 326): $7.55. 40 amp generator with low cut-in rate (RPO 326): $80.70. Heavy-duty generator (RPO 326): $80.70. Side-mount spare tire carrier for pickups with painted bumper (RPO 341): $14.00. Side-mount spare tire carrier for pickups with chrome bumper (RPO 341): $15.10. Heavy-duty 66 amp battery (RPO 345): $7.55. Chrome trim for Suburban models only (RPO 393): $50.60. Full view rear window for pickups (RPO 394): $43.05. Left side door lock for Deluxe cab only (RPO 395): $1.65. Side-mount spare tire lock for Deluxe cab only (RPO 395): $6.50. Left side door and side mount spare tire lock for Deluxe cab only (RPO 395): $.55. Pickup running boards for Model 3153 only (RPO 423): $7.00. Custom cab, includes foam rubber seat (RPO 431): $86.10. Custom dash panel (RPO 434): $69.95. Two-tone paint combinations for Deluxe cab only (RPO 443): $10.80. Two-tone color combinations for Custom cab (RPO 444): $16.15. Two-tone color combinations for Panels (RPO 445): $26.90.

HISTORICAL FOOTNOTES: The 1958 models were announced in October, 1957. The new Fleetside pickup body featured double-wall construction and reflected the influence of the Cameo model of 1957.

1959 PICKUP

The 1959 models carried restyled front fender series identification and a revamped hood ornament. The uppermost horizontal grille bar was also reshaped. Standard equipment included a 12-volt battery, 1 pint oil bath air cleaner, front bumper, painted Bombay White; Deluxe cab, left side 8 in. fixed bracket exterior mirror, single tail and stop light, and positive-action vacuum windshield wipers. The Deluxe cab was finished in charcoal and silver-beige. The upholstery was vinyl. The interior surfaces were painted and a rubber floor mat was installed. The instrument panel was finished in charcoal and silver-beige enamel. The crown of the panel had a glare-proof crinkle finish. For cab models the Custom cab was finished in charcoal and silver-beige, blue or green to harmonize with the exterior color. A foam rubber seat was upholstered in nylon fabric and trimmed with vinyl. The Custom Panels retained the charcoal and silver-beige decor of the Deluxe panel. Interior surfaces were painted, except for the fabric insert panel on the doors. A rubber floor mat was included. Exterior colors for 1959 were frontier beige, jet black, Baltic blue, dawn blue, cadet gray, Galway green, Sherwood green, Omaha orange, cardinal red, tartan turquoise, pure white, golden yellow and Yukon yellow.

1959 Chevrolet Model 3154 Stepside pickup, 114 inch wheelbase

I.D. DATA: The truck identification plate was located on the left side body hinge panel. The first numeral and letter designated the series: 3A-3100, 3E-3600 and 3G-3800. The next numerical group-59, indicated the model year. The next entry, a letter, indicated the assembly plant as follows: A-Atlanta, B-Baltimore, F-Flint, J-Janesville, K-Kansas City, L-Los Angeles, N-Norwood, O-Oakland, S-St. Louis, T-Tarrytown and W-Willow Run. The next six digits-10001, designated the truck number by plant. For example a truck with the truck identification of 3E59F100092 was a Series 3600, 1959 model that was the 92nd truck to be built at Flint.

Model Number	Body Type & Seating	Factory Price	GVW	Shipping Weight	Prod. Total
Series 3100 1/2 ton 6-cyl. 114 in. wheelbase					
3153	Chassis and Cab	$2608	5400	3271	—
3154	Pickup Stepside	$2713	5400	3615	—
3184	Pickup Fleetside	$2728	5400	N.A.	—
3155	Panel	$2993	5400	3860	—
3156	Suburban, pnl. Dr.	$3303	5400	4140	—
3166	Suburban, Endgate	$3333	5400	4150	—
Series 3600 3/4 ton 6-cyl. 123.25 in. wheelbase					
3653	Chassis and Cab	$2853	7300	3650	—
3654	Pickup Stepside	$2958	7300	4030	—
3684	Pickup Fleetside	$2973	7300	N.A.	—
3659	Stake	$3043	7300	4275	—
Series 3800 1 ton, 135 in. wheelbase					
3853	Chassis and Cab	$3038	7400	3895	—
3854	Pickup Stepside	$3163	7400	4340	—
3855	Panel	$3468	7400	4645	—
3859	Stake	$3268	7400	4685	—

STANDARD ENGINE: All models: Thriftmaster Six. Engine Type: OHV, In-line 6-cylinder. Cast iron block and cylinder head. Bore x Stroke: 3.5625 in. x 3.9375 in. Lifters: Hydraulic. Number of main bearings-4. Fuel Induction: Single Rochester 1-bbl. carburetor, model 7007181. Compression Ratio: 8.0:1. Displacement: 235.5 cu. in. (3.85 liters). Horsepower: Gross: 135 @ 4200 rpm. Net: 115 @ 4000 rpm. Torque: Gross: 217 lb.-ft. @ 2000 rpm. Net: 195 lb.-ft. @ 2000 rpm. Oil refill capacity: 5 qt. without filter change; 1 and 2 quart filters were optional. Fuel Requirements: Regular.

OPTIONAL ENGINE: None.

CHASSIS FEATURES: Series 3100: Separate body and frame with channel side rails measuring 6 in. x 2.25 in. x 0.1406 in. and five cross members. Section modules: 2.54 in. Series 3600: Separate body and frame with channel side rails measuring 6.093 in. x 2.25 in. x 0.1875 in. and five cross members. Section modules: 3.37 in. Series 3800: Separate body and frame with channel side rails measuring 7.25 in. x 2.75 in. x 0.2187 in. and five cross members. Section modules: 5.70 in.

1959 Chevrolet Model 3184 Fleetside pickup, 114 inch wheelbase

SUSPENSION AND RUNNING GEAR: Series 3100: Front Suspension: 44 in. x 2.0 in. 7-leaf, semi-elliptical springs, 1.0 in. dia. absorbers. 1360 lb. rating (at ground). Series 3600: Front Suspension: Semi-elliptical 7-leaf, 44.0 in. x 2.0 in. springs, direct double acting 1.0 in. dia. shock absorbers. 1430 lb. rating (at ground), Optional: None. Optional rating: None. Series 3800: Semi-elliptical 7-leaf, 44.0 in. x 2.0 in. springs, direct double acting 1.0 in. dia. shock absorbers. 1430 lb. rating (at ground), Optional: None. Rear Suspension: Series 3100: 52 in. x 2.0 in. Single-stage, 8-leaf, semi-elliptical springs, 1.0 in. dia. shock absorbers. 1570 lb. rating (at ground). Series 3600: Semi-elliptical 8-leaf, single-stage, 52 in. x 2.0 in. springs, 2430 lb. rating (at ground). Series 3800: Semi-elliptical leaf, single-stage, 52 in. x 2.0 in. springs, 2400 lb. rating (at ground). Optional Rating: None. Optional Rating: None. Front Axle Type and Capacity: Series 3100: Semi-floating, 3000 lb. capacity. Series 3600: Semi-floating, 3300 lb. capacity. Optional: None. Series 3800: Semi-floating, 3500 lb. capacity. Optional: None. Rear Axle Type and Capacity: Series 3100: Semi-floating, 3300 lb. capacity. Optional: None. Series 3600: Semi-floating, 5000 lb. capacity. Optional: None. Series 3800: Semi-floating, 7200 lb. capacity. Optional: None. Final Drive Ratio: Series 3100: 3.90:1. Series 3600: 5.14:1. Series 3800: 4.57:1. Transfer Case: Single lever, two-speed: 1.87, 1.00:1.

Brakes: Type: Hydraulic, front and rear drums. Dimensions: Series 3100: Front: 11.0 in. x 2.0 in. Rear: 11.0 in. x 1.75 in. Effective lining area: 157 sq. in. Series 3600: Front: 12.0 in. x 2.0 in. Rear: 12.0 in. x 2.0 in. Effective lining area: 184 sq. in. Series 3800: 12.0 in. x 2.0 in. Rear: 14.0 in. x 2.50 in. Effective lining area: 228 sq. in. Wheels: Series 3100: 16 x 5.5K 5-stud disc. Series 3600: 17.5 in. x 5.25 in. disc. Series 3800: 17.5 in. x 5.25 in. disc. Tires: Series 3100: Either RPO 6.50 x 16 6-ply rating or 7 x 17.5 6-ply rating had to be ordered. The latter tires required 17.5 x 5.25 in. wheels. Series 3600: 8-19.5 6-ply rating. Series 380: 8-19.5 6-ply rating. Steering: Recirculating ball gear. Ratio: Series 3100 and 3600: 21.30:1. Series 3800: 23.30:1. Steering wheel diameter: 18.0 in. Optional: None. Transmission: 4-speed, synchromesh manual. Transmission Ratios: 7.05, 6.69, 3.19, 1.00:1 reverse: 12.60:1. Optional: None. Clutch: Diaphragm, spring. Clutch diameter: 10 in. Total lining area: 100.5 sq. in. Optional: None.

1959 Chevrolet model 3654 Stepside pickup, 123.25 inch wheelbase

VEHICLE DIMENSIONS: Series 3100: Wheelbase: 114 in. Overall Length: Pickup: 185.6875 in. Panel: 197.875 in. Overall Height: Panel: 79.6875 in. Width: Pickup: 76.0 in. Panel: 76.375 in. Front/Rear Overhang: Pickup: 30.6875 in./41 in. Tailgate: Width and Height: 50 in. x 17.56 in. Ground Clearance: Front axle: 8.625 in. Rear axle: 8.625 in. Load space: Pickup box dimensions: 78.125 in. x 50.0 in. x 17.56 in. Series 3600. Wheelbase: 123.25 in. Overall Length: Pickup: 205.5625 in. Stake: 204.9375 in. Width: Pickup: 76.0 in. Stake: 79.56 in. Front/ Rear Overhang: Pickup: 30.6875 in./51.625 in. Stake: 30.6875 in./50.625 in. Tailgate: Width and Height: 50 in. x 17.56 in. Load space: Pickup box dimensions: 98 in. x 50.0 in. x 17.56 in. Series 3800. Wheelbase: 135 in. Overall Length: Pickup and chassis & cab: 215.8125 in. Panel: 228.875 in. Stake: 222.5625 in. Width: Pickup: 76.0 in. Panel: 786.625 in. Stake: 91.5625 in. Front/Rear Overhang: Pickup: 30.6875 in./50.125 in. Stake: 30.6875 in./56.875 in. Tailgate: Width and Height: 50 in. x 17.56 in. Load space: Pickup box dimensions: 108.25 in. x 50.0 in. x 17.56 in.

CAPACITIES: Fuel Tank: 17.5 gal. Optional: None. Engine coolant system: 17 qt.

ACCOMMODATIONS: Seating Capacity: 3 passenger. Optional: None.

1959 Chevrolet model 3684 Fleetside pickup, 123.25 inch wheelbase

INSTRUMENTATION: Speedometer, odometer, gauges for oil pressure, engine coolant temperature, battery charge and fuel level.

1959 Chevrolet model 3854 pickup, 135 inch wheelbase

OPTIONS AND PRICES: Rear shock absorber shields (RPO 21): $2.20. Oil bath air cleaner, 1 qt. capacity (RPO 216): $4.35. Heavy-duty 12-volt, 70 amp-hr. battery: $7.35. 35 amp generator: $7.55. Custom cab: $86.10, for Fleetside models: $102.25. Painted rear bumper for Deluxe cab (RPO 218): $21.55. Chrome rear bumper for Custom cab (RPO 218): $32.30. Heavy-duty, 11 in. clutch (RPO 227): $5.40. Engine governor: $10.80. Deluxe heater and defroster: $73.85. Recirculating heater and defroster: $53. Free-wheeling manual-control front hubs: $78.55. Exterior left-side mirror, 17.5 in. swinging arm: $2.20. Exterior right side mirror, 17.5 in. swinging arm: $4.85. Exterior right side 8.0 in. fixed bracket mirror: $4.85. Oil filter, 1 qt. capacity (RPO 237): $9.15. Oil filter, 2 qt. capacity (RPO 237): $12.95. Custom Panel interior: $69.95. Two-tone paint: $106.15 (all pickups except Fleetside) $37.70 (Fleetsides); $26.90 (Panels). Heavy-duty radiator (RPO 256): $16.15. Auxiliary seat for Panel models:

$40.90. Foam rubber seat for Deluxe cab only (RPO 258): $17.25. Full-view rear window: $43.05. Electric windshield wipers (RPO 320): $7.55. Side-mount spare tire carrier for pickups with painted bumper (RPO 341): $14.00. Side-mount spare tire carrier for Fleetside pickups (RPO 341): $14.00. Side-mount-spare tire carrier for Stepside pickups with Deluxe cab and painted hubcaps (RPO 341): $15.10, with Custom Cab: $16.15.

HISTORICAL FOOTNOTES: The 1958 models were announced in October, 1958. Chevrolet reported that official registration figures showed 631,628 Chevrolet trucks ten years old or older were still in use.

1959 Chevrolet model 3855 panel, 135 inch wheelbase

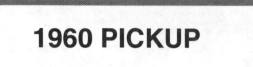

1960 PICKUP

1960 Chevrolet model K1404 Stepside pickup, 115 inch wheelbase

The 1960 Chevrolet trucks were totally restyled. They continued to use a wraparound windshield but the overall impression of the models was that they were extremely contemporary-appearing vehicles. The front end was dominated by two large pods containing the secondary lights. The headlights were positioned in a large lower section that included a grille consisting of horizontal bars. Chevrolet lettering was placed along the lower portion of the grille panel. In profile, the new models were characterized by a high beltline and a mid-body crease line. Chevrolet trucks were identified by model designations consisting of a letter followed by four digits. The letter K represented four-wheel drive. The first two digits in the model designation identified the truck series in order of increasing GVW designations. The last two digits in the model designation identified the body or truck type as follows: 03-chassis cab, 04-Stepside pickup, 05-Panel, 06-Carryall with Panel rear doors, 09-Stake, 16-Carryall with endgate, 34-Fleetside pickup. The exterior color selection for 1959 consisted of these colors: jet black, hemlock, tartan turquoise, brigade blue, Neptune green, pure white, marlin blue, Omaha orange, golden yellow, Klondike gold, cardinal red, Yukon yellow, Garrison gray, and grenadier red. Bombay ivory was available for trim and two-toning only.

1960 Chevrolet model K1434 Fleetside pickup, 115 inch wheelbase

I.D. DATA: The serial number was stamped on a plate mounted on the upper left hinge pillar The first entry, a letter S, denoted a truck with an optional 7800 lb. GVW plate. Next came a 0 for the 1960 model year. The truck code followed, consisting of two numbers: 03-Chassis & cab, 04-Stepside pickup, 05-Panel, 06-Carryall (panel rear doors), 16-Carryall (tail and liftgate), 34-Fleetside pickup. The series number followed. The assembly plant code, a letter was next. The last six digits were the unit number, beginning at 100,001 at each truck plant, regardless of truck series. The engine number for the 6-cyl. was stamped on the right side of the block next to the distributor. On V-8 engines it was stamped on the forward edge of the block protruding from under the right cylinder head. The engine number for 6-cylinder engines was stamped on the right side of the cylinder block next to the distributor. The V-8 engine number was stamped on the right-hand side of the block, protruding from under the right cylinder head.

Model Number	Body Type & Seating	Factory Price	GVW	Shipping Weight	Prod. Total
Series K10 1/2 ton 6-cyl.115 in. wheelbase					
K1453	Chassis & Cab	$2640[1]	4900[2]	—	—
K1454	Pickup Stepside	$2754	4900	—	—
K1455	Panel Dlx.	$3071	4900	—	—
K1456	Carryall Pnl. Dr.	$3453	4900	—	—
K1466	Carryall Endgate	$3486	4900	—	—
K1484	Pickup Fleetside	$2770	4900	—	—
Series K20 3/4 ton 6-cyl.127 in. wheelbase					
K2553	Chassis & Cab	$2849	5700*	—	—
K2554	Pickup Stepside	$2963	5700	—	—
K2584	Pickup Fleetside	$2979	5700	—	—

NOTE 1: Unlike previous price listings, these prices include factory delivery and preparation, and factory suggested dealer delivery and preparation.
NOTE 2: All K10 models: 5300 lb. GVW available with 6.50 x 16 6-ply rated tires. 5600 lb. GVW available with 7 x 17.5 6-ply rated tires.
* All K20 models: 6100 lb. GVW available with 3150 lb. rear springs and 8 x 17.5 6-ply rated tires. 6800 lb. GVW available with 3150 lb. rear springs and 8 x 17.5 8-ply rated tires. 7200 lb. GVW available with 3150 lb. rear springs and 8 x 19.5 6-ply rated tires. 7600 lb. GVW available with 3150 lb. rear springs and 8 x 19.5 8-ply rated tires.

EL K1403 CHASSIS-CAB—4-Wheel Drive

tings up to 5600 lb
se: 115"

1960 Chevrolet model K1403 chassis cab, 115 inch wheelbase

STANDARD ENGINE: All models: Thriftmaster Six. Engine Type: OHV, In-line 6-cylinder. Cast iron block and cylinder head. Bore x Stroke: 3.5625 in. x 3.9375 in. Lifters: Mechanical. Fuel Induction: Single downdraft Rochester. 2.134 in. venturi. Compression Ratio: 8.25:1. Displacement: 235.5 cu. in. (3.86 liters). Number of main bearing: 4. Horsepower: Gross: 135 @ 4000 rpm. Net: 110 @ 3600 rpm. Torque: Gross: 217 lb.-ft. @ 2000 rpm. Net: 195 lb.-ft. @ 2000 rpm. Fuel Requirements: Regular. Oil capacity: 5 qt.

OPTIONAL ENGINE: All models: Trademaster V-8. Engine type: OHV V-8, cast iron block and cylinder heads. Bore x Stroke: 3.875 in. x 3.0 in. Lifters: Hydraulic. Number of main bearings: 5. Fuel Induction: Single Rochester 2-bbl. carburetor. Venturi dia.: 1.09 in. Displacement: 336.1 cu. in. (5.50 liters). Horsepower: Gross: 160 @ 4200 rpm. Net: 137 @ 4000 rpm. Torque: Gross: 270 lb.-ft. @ 2000 rpm. Net: 250 lb.-ft. @ 2000 rpm. Compression ratio: 8.5:1. Fuel Requirements: Regular. Oil capacity: 5 qt.

CHASSIS FEATURES: Separate body and frame. Ladder type. Drop-center frame. K10: 115 in. wheelbase: 7.1875 in. x 2.75 in. x 0.1875 in. Section modules: 5.09. K20: 127 in. wheelbase: 7.1875 in. x 2.75 in. x 0.1875 in. Section modules: 5.09.

tings up to 5600 lb
se: 115"

1960 Chevrolet models K1406 and K1416 Carryalls, 115 inch wheelbase

SUSPENSION AND RUNNING GEAR: Front Suspension: K10: 44 in. x 2.0 in. 10-leaf semi-elliptical springs. Capacity: 1650 lb. at ground. K20: 44 in. x 2.0 in. 10-leaf semi-elliptical springs. Capacity: 1750 lb. at ground. Optional rating. Rear Suspension: K10: 52 in. x 2.5 in. 6-leaf semi-elliptical springs. Capacity: 1900 lb. rating (at ground). K20: 52 in. x 2.5 in. 6-leaf semi-elliptical springs. Capacity: 1900 lb. rating (at ground). Optional Rating: K20: Rear 8-leaf springs, 3150 lb. capacity. Deflection rate: 497 lb./in. Front Axle Type and Capacity: K10: Hypoid, 3300 lb. capacity. K20: Hypoid, 3500 lb. capacity. Rear Axle Type and Capacity: K10: Hypoid, semi-floating, 3300 lb. K20: Full-floating, hypoid, 5200 lb. capacity. Optional: None. Final Drive Ratio: K10: Front: 3.92:1, rear: 3.90:1. K20: Front: 4.55:1. Rear: 4.57:1. Transfer Case: Timken Model T-221. Single lever, 4-position, 2-speed: 1.94, 1.00:1. Brakes: Type: Hydraulic, front and rear drums. Dimensions: K10: Front: 11.0 in. x 2.0 in. Rear: 11.0 in. x 2.0 in. Effective drum area: 276 sq. in. Effective lining area: 167 sq. in. K20: Front and Rear: 12 in. x 2.0 in. Effective drum area: 300 sq. in. Effective lining area: 190 sq. in. Wheels: Ventilated steel disc. K10: 15 x 5K, 6-stud on 5.5 in. circle. K20: 17.5 x 5.25 in. 8-stud on 6.5 in. circle. Tires: K10: 6.70 x 15, 6-ply rating, tubeless. K20: 7 x 17.5 in., 6-ply rating, tubeless. Steering: Ball-gear, 17 in. steering wheel. Ratio: 24.0:1. Optional: None. Transmission: 4-speed synchromesh. Transmission Ratios: 7.06, 3.58, 1.71, 1.00:1 reverse: 6.78:1. Optional: None. Clutch: Hydraulic control, coil-spring. Clutch diameter: 11 in. dia. Total lining area: 124.5 sq. in.

VEHICLE DIMENSIONS: 115 in. wheelbase models: Overall Length: Pickup: 186.625 in. Panel: 201 in. Front Tread: 63.125 in. Overall Height: Pickup: 77.125 in. Panel: 80.5 in. Width: 78.75 in. Front/Rear Overhang: Pickup: 31.75./39.875 in. Panel: 31.75 in./54.25 in. Tailgate: Width and Height: 50 in. x 17.50 in. Load space: Pickup box dimensions: 78.125 in. x 50.0 in. x 17.56 in. 127 in. wheelbase models. Overall Length: 206 in. Front Tread: 63.125 in. Overall Height: 78.25 in. Width: 78.75 in. Front/Rear Overhang: 31.75 in./47.25 in.

CAPACITIES: Fuel Tank: Pickup: 17.5 gal. Panel: 17.0 gal.

L K1405 PANEL (7½-Ft)

ngs up to 5600 lb
115"

1960 Chevrolet model K1405 panel, 115 inch wheelbase

ACCOMMODATIONS: Seating Capacity: Pickup and Panel: 3 passenger. Carryall: 6. Optional.

INSTRUMENTATION: Speedometer, odometer, gauges for oil pressure, fuel level, engine coolant temperature, battery charge.

L K2534 PICKUP (8-Ft Fleetside)

ings up to 7600 lb
e: 127"

1960 Chevrolet model K2534 Fleetside pickup, 127 inch wheelbase

OPTIONS AND PRICES: K-10 tires: 6.50 x 15 6-ply rated tires: $27.65. 7 x 17.5 6-ply rated tires: $103.35. K-20 tires: 8 x 17.5 6-ply rated: $34.90. 8 x 17.5 8-ply rated: $69.30. 8 x 19.5 6-ply rated: $67.70. 8 x 18.5 8-ply rated: $112.25. Oil bath air cleaner: $2.20 (for use with governor), $6.50 (for use without governor). Heavy-duty 70 amp-hr. battery: $7.55. Chrome front bumper (except Panel and Carryall): $10.80. Chrome front and rear bumper (Panel and Carryall only): $21.55. Custom cab. Includes Custom seat and left door lock): $91.50 (Fleetside pickups), $80.70 (all other models). Spare wheel carrier: $14.00 (Fleetside pickups), $15.10 (Stepside pickups). Directional signals: $26.90 (chassis and cab), $21.55 (all others). Trademaster V-8, includes full-flow oil filter: $118.40. 35 amp generator: $7.55. 40 amp generator: $29.10. 50 amp, low cut-in generator: $98.85. Governor (for 6-cyl. engine with synchromesh trans. 1800-3000 rpm or 2600-3600 rpm range available): $15.10. Deluxe heater and defroster $68.35. Recirculating, inside air heater and Defroster: $47.90. Free wheeling manual front hubs: $78.55. Left door lock (Deluxe cab, panel or Carryall): $1.65. Lock for side wheel carrier: $6.50. Lock for left door and side wheel carrier (Deluxe pickups): $7.65. Exterior left 17.5 in. swinging arm mirror (pickups, chassis and cab): $2.20. Exterior right 17.5 in. swinging arm mirror (pickups, chassis and cab): $4.85. Exterior right 8.0 in. fixed bracket: $4.85. Oil filter for 6-cyl. engine: $9.15 (1 qt. capacity), $12.95 (2 qt. capacity). Two-tone paint: $16.15 (chassis and cab, Stepside pickups), $32.30 (Fleetside pickups), $26.90 (Panels and Carryalls). Heavy-duty radiator: $21.55. Auxiliary rear seat for Panel: $40.90. Custom seat (for Deluxe cab only): $17.25. 20 gal. fuel tank (chassis and cab and pickups only): $8.10. Full-view rear window (cabs only): $43.05. Windshield washers: $11.30.

HISTORICAL FOOTNOTES: The 1960 models were announced in the fall of 1959.

tings up to 7600 lb
se: 127"

1960 Chevrolet Model 2504 Stepside pickup, 127 inch wheelbase

1961 PICKUP

The latest Chevrolet four-wheel drive trucks had a new K series identification for 1961. Physical changes included a revised front end design with bow tie inserts in the cat's eye parking light nacelles. The primary grille section now contained Chevrolet lettering. The front fender model identification was mounted higher on the front fender than in 1960. Three new long-wheelbase models in the 5600 lb. GVW, K15 series expanded Chevrolet's lineup of four-wheel drive models to a total of twelve. The new versions consisted of a 8 ft. Fleetside and Stepside pickups plus a chassis-cab model. all models featured an extra-capacity, fully enclosed front axle, a two-speed transfer case with a single lever drive selection and dual power take-off openings. The standard "Comfort-King" cab could be upgraded by the Custom Comfort Equipment option which featured a seat with a 6 in. foam cushion.

1961 Chevrolet model K1534 Fleetside pickup

I.D. DATA: The serial number was stamped on a plate mounted on the upper left hinge pillar The first entry, a letter S, denoted a truck with an optional 7800 lb. GVW plate. Next came a 1 for the 1961 model year. The truck code followed, consisting of two numbers: 03-Chassis & cab, 04-Stepside pickup, 05-Panel, 06-Carryall (panel rear doors), 16-Carryall (tail and liftgate), 34-Fleetside pickup. The series number followed. The assembly plant code, a letter was next. The last six digits were the unit number, beginning at 100,001 at each truck plant, regardless of truck series. The engine number for the 6-cyl. engine was stamped on the right side of the block next to the distributor. On V-8 engines it was stamped on the forward edge of the block protruding from under the right cylinder head. The engine number for the 6-cyl. engine was stamped on the right side of the block next to the distributor. On V-8 engines it was stamped on the forward edge of the block protruding from under the right cylinder head.

Model Number	Body Type & Seating	Factory Price	GVW	Shipping Weight	Prod. Total
Series K14 1/2 ton 6-cyl. 115 in. wheelbase					
K1403	Chassis and Cab	$2554	5600	3430	—
K1404	78 in. Stepside Pickup	$2668	5600	3790	—
K1434	78 in. Fleetside Pickup	$2684	5600	3825	—
K1405	7.5 ft. Panel	$2985	5600	4065	—
K1406	Suburban Pnl. Dr.	$3346	5600	4370	—
K1416	Suburban Endgate	$3379	5600	4400	—
Series K15 1/2 ton 6-cyl. 127 in. wheelbase					
K1503	Chassis and Cab	$2554	5600	3430	—
K1504	98 in. Stepside Pickup	$2668	5600	3790	—
K1534	98 in. Fleetside Pickup	$2684	5600	3825	—
Series K25 3/4 ton, 1127 in. wheelbase					
K2503	Chassis and Cab	$2736	7200	3795	—
K2504	98 in. Stepside Pickup	$2850	7200	4210	—
K2534	98 in. Fleetside Pickup	$2866	7200	4255	—
3809	Stake	$2911	7400	4685	—

STANDARD ENGINE: All models: Thriftmaster Six. Engine Type: OHV, In-line 6-cylinder. Cast iron block and cylinder head. Bore x Stroke: 3.5625 in. x 3.9375 in. Lifters: Hydraulic. Number of main bearings-4. Fuel Induction: Single Rochester 1-bbl. carburetor, model B7015011. Compression Ratio: 8.0:1. Displacement: 235.5 cu. in. (3.85 liters). Horsepower: Gross: 135 @ 4000 rpm. Torque: Gross: 217 lb.-ft. @ 2000 rpm. Oil refill capacity: 5 qt. without filter change. Fuel Requirements: Regular.

OPTIONAL ENGINE: Trademaster V-8. Engine Type: OHV, V-8. Cast iron block and cylinder head. Bore x Stroke: 3.875 in. x 3.00 in. Lifters: Hydraulic. Number of main bearings-5. Fuel Induction: Single Rochester 2-bbl. carburetor, model 2G7015017. Compression Ratio: 8.5:1. Displacement: 283 cu. in. (4.63 liters). Horsepower: Gross: 160 @ 4200 rpm. Torque: Gross: 270 lb.-ft. @ 2000 rpm. Oil refill capacity: 5 qt. with filter change. Fuel Requirements: Regular.

CHASSIS FEATURES: Series K14 and K15: Separate body and frame with channel side rails measuring 7.1875 in. x 2.75 in. x 0.1875 in. Section modules: 5.09 in. Series K25: Separate body and frame with channel side rails measuring 7.1875 in. x 2.75 in. x 0.1875 in. Section modules: 5.09 in.

SUSPENSION AND RUNNING GEAR: Series K14 and K15: Front Suspension: 44 in. x 2.0 in. 10-leaf, semi-elliptical springs, shock absorbers. 1650 lb. rating (at ground). Optional rating: None. Series K25: Semi-elliptical 10-leaf, 44.0 in. x 2.0 in. springs, shock absorbers. 1750 lb. rating (at ground). Optional: None. Rear Suspension: Series K10 and K15: 52 in. x 2.5 in. Single-stage, 6-leaf, semi-elliptical springs, shock absorbers. 1900 lb. rating (at ground). Optional Rating: None. Series K25: Semi-elliptical 6-leaf, single-stage, 52 in. x 2.50 in. springs, 1900 lb. rating (at ground). Front Axle Type and Capacity: Series K10 and K15: Semi-floating, 3300 lb. capacity. Optional: None. Series K25: Semi-floating, 3500 lb. capacity. Optional: None. Rear Axle Type and Capacity: Series K10 and K15: Semi-floating, 3300 lb. capacity. Optional: None. Series K25: Semi-floating, 5200 lb. capacity. Optional: None. Final Drive Ratio: Series K10 and K15: Front: 3.92:1. Rear; 3.90:1. Series K25: Front: 4.55:1. Rear: 4.57:1. Transfer Case: Single lever, two-speed: 1.87, 1.00:1. Brakes: Type: Hydraulic, front and rear drums. Dimensions: Series K10

and K15: Front: 11.0 in. x 2.0 in. Rear: 11.0 in. x 2.0 in. Total lining area: 167 sq. in. Series K25: 12.0 in. x 2.0 in. Rear: 12.0 in. x 2.0 in. Total lining area: 190 sq. in. Wheels: Series K10 and K15: 15 x 5.0K 5-stud disc. Optional: 15 x 5.25 in. Series K25: 5.25 in. 8-stud disc. Maximum rim size optional: 5.25 in. Tires: Series K10 and K15: 7.10 x 15 4-ply. Maximum size optional: 7-17.5 6-ply. Series K25: 7-17.5 6-ply rating. Maximum size optional: 8-19.5 8-ply rating. Steering: Recirculating ball gear. Ratio: 24:1. 17.0 in. Optional: None. Transmission: 3-speed, synchromesh manual. Transmission Ratios: 2.94, 1.68. 1.00:1. Reverse: 3.14:1. Optional: 4-speed heavy-duty manual synchromesh. Transmission ratios: 7.06, 3.58, 1.71, 1.00:1. Reverse: 6.78:1. Clutch: Diaphragm, spring. Clutch diameter: 10 in. dia. Total lining area: 100.5 sq. in. Optional: Heavy-duty, 11.0 in. dia. for 235 engine only.

VEHICLE DIMENSIONS: Series K14 and K15: Wheelbase: K14: 115 in. K15: 127 in. Overall Length: 115 in. Fleetside pickups: 186.75 in. 127 in. Fleetside pickups: 206.25 in. 115 in. Stepside pickups: 186.875 in. 127 in. Stepside pickups: 206.25 in. Front/Rear Overhang: Pickup: 31.75 in./40 in. Series K25. Wheelbase: 127 in. Overall Length: Fleetside and Stepside: 206.25 in. Front/Rear Overhang: 31.75 in./40 in.

CAPACITIES: Fuel Tank: 18.5 gal. except for Panel models which had 17.0 gal. tanks. Optional: 20.5 gal. Engine coolant system: 6-cyl.: 17 qt. V-8: 17.5 qt.

ACCOMMODATIONS: Seating Capacity: Pickup and chassis cab models: 3 passenger. Optional: None. Suburban: 3 passenger. Optional: 6 or 9 passenger.

INSTRUMENTATION: Speedometer, odometer, gauges for oil pressure, engine coolant temperature, fuel level, and battery charge

OPTIONS AND PRICES: Trademaster V-8: $118. Custom Comfort equipment (interior). Custom Appearance equipment (exterior). Custom Chrome equipment (exterior). Custom side molding equipment (Fleetside pickups only). Rear bumper. Radio. Heater. Clock. Cigarette lighter. Radio antenna. Seat covers.

HISTORICAL FOOTNOTES: The 1961 models were available starting in the fall of 1960.

1961 Chevrolet model K1406 Carryall

1962 PICKUP

1962 Chevrolet model K1404 Stepside pickup, 115 inch wheelbase

The 1962 models had a new revamped, less extreme-appearing front end design. It featured single headlights, a small center insert with two horizontal and two vertical dividers and Chevrolet lettering positioned along its lower edge. The hood's leading edge was sharp-edged and the parking/directional lights were positioned in its outer edges. Two air-intakes were positioned in the center of this panel. Standard equipment included front painted bumper, front and rear directional signals, hand choke, left side, 8.0 in. fixed arm exterior mirror, and electric windshield wipers. The panoramic windshield had an area of approximately 1260 sq. in. The electric windshield wipers had 13.0 in. blades and a wiping speed of 110 strokes per minute. The full-view rear window was available as an option and had an area of 761 sq. in. as compared to the standard window's area of 330 sq. in. All cab had left-door key-operated locks standard with right door locks optional. The standard cab had a beige color theme. Body cab metal was painted fawn beige. An accent color, cameo white, was used for the steering wheel, turn signal housing, instrument cluster bezel and lower face of the instrument panel beneath the cluster. The steering column was white. Control knobs on the instrument panel were finished in charcoal plastic. The sunshade (standard on the driver's side) was beige in a leather-grain finish. The floor was covered by a black rubber mat. A dome light was standard. It was centered above the rear window and was operated by the main light switch on the instrument panel.

Ratings up to 5600 lb
[whee]lbase: 115"

1962 Chevrolet model K1434 Fleetside pickup, 115 inch wheelbase

The Custom Comfort cab option included the following: Left armrest, right sunshade, right door lock, chromed cigarette lighter, full-depth foam seat and special insulation. The left armrest was covered with red or beige vinyl on the top half and was made of white plastic on the bottom. A matching armrest for the right side was available as a dealer-installed custom feature. The special insulation included undercoating, perforated dash pad, and an asphalt-impregnated pad applied to the rear cab panel. With the Custom Comfort option, both seat and backrest were upholstered in nylon-faced cloth with a muted beige pattern. Red vinyl was used for the facings with red, white or gray exteriors. Beige vinyl facings were used with all other exterior colors.

Ratings up to 5600 lb
[whee]lbase: 127"

1962 Chevrolet model K1504 Stepside pickup, 127 inch wheelbase

The Custom Appearance exterior option consisted of the following equipment: Bright metal (silver anodized aluminum) grille, bright metal windshield molding, steering wheel with horn ring, chrome-trimmed instrument panel knobs, two-tone dispatch box and interior door panels. The steering wheel was painted cameo white. The instrument panel knobs had chrome-plated metal rims. The body of each knob was black plastic.

[R]atings up to 5600 lb
[wheelb]ase: 127"

1962 Chevrolet model K1534 Fleetside pickup, 127 inch wheelbase

The Custom Chrome option consisted of a chrome-plated front bumper. The exterior colors for 1962 were these: Desert beige, seamist jade, crystal turquoise, jet black, Glenwood green, cameo white, Balboa blue, Woodland green, pure white, Brigade blue, Omaha orange, Yuma yellow, Georgian gray and cardinal red.

[Ratin]gs up to 7600 lb
[wheelbase]: 127"

1962 Chevrolet model K2504 Stepside pickup, 127 inch wheelbase

I.D. DATA: The serial number was stamped on a plate mounted on the upper left hinge pillar. The first entry, a letter S, denoted a truck with an optional 7800 lb. GVW plate. Next came a 2 for the 1962 model year. The truck code followed, consisting of two numbers: 03-Chassis & cab, 04-Stepside pickup, 05-Panel, 06-Carryall (panel rear doors), 16-Carryall (tail and liftgate), 34-Fleetside pickup. The series number followed. The assembly plant code, a letter was next. The last six digits were the unit number, beginning at 100,001 at each truck plant, regardless of truck series. The engine number for the 6-cyl. engine was stamped on the right side of the block next to the distributor. On V-8 engines it was stamped on the forward edge

of the block protruding from under the right cylinder head. The engine number for the 6-cyl. engine was stamped on the right side of the block next to the distributor. On V-8 engines it was stamped on the forward edge of the block protruding from under the right cylinder head.

Model Number	Body Type & Seating	Factory Price	GVW	Shipping Weight	Prod. Total
Series K10 1/2 ton 6-cyl. 115 in. wheelbase					
K1403	Chassis and Cab	$2548	5600	3430	—
K1404	78 in. Stepside Pickup	$2662	5600	3790	—
K1434	78 in. Fleetside Pickup	$2678	5600	3825	—
K1405	7.5 ft. Panel	$2979	5600	4065	—
K1406	Suburban Pnl. Dr.	$3273	5600	4370	—
K1416	Suburban Endgate	$3306	5600	4400	—
Series K10 1/2 ton 6-cyl. 127 in. wheelbase					
K1503	Chassis and Cab	$2585	5600	3430	—
K1504	98 in. Stepside Pickup	$2699	5600	3790	—
K1534	98 in. Fleetside Pickup	$2715	5600	3825	—
Series K20 3/4 ton, 1127 in. wheelbase					
K2503	Chassis and Cab	$2757	7200	3795	—
K2504	98 in. Stepside Pickup	$2871	7200	4210	—
K2534	98 in. Fleetside Pickup	$2887	7200	4255	—

[R]atings up to 7600 lb
[wheelb]ase: 127"

1962 Chevrolet model K2534 pickup, 127 inch wheelbase

STANDARD ENGINE: All models: Thriftmaster Six. Engine Type: OHV, In-line 6-cylinder. Cast iron block and cylinder head. Bore x Stroke: 3.5625 in. x 3.9375 in. Lifters: Hydraulic. Number of main bearings-4. Fuel Induction: Single Rochester 1-bbl. carburetor, model B7015011. Compression Ratio: 8.0:1. Displacement: 235.5 cu. in. (3.85 liters). Horsepower: Gross: 135 @ 4000 rpm. Torque: Gross: 217 lb.-ft. @ 2000 rpm. Oil refill capacity: 5 qt. without filter change. Fuel Requirements: Regular.

OPTIONAL ENGINE: All models: High Torque Six. Engine Type: OHV, In-line 6-cylinder. Cast iron block and cylinder head. Bore x Stroke: 3.759375 in. x 3.9375 in. Lifters: Hydraulic. Number of main bearings-4. Fuel Induction: Single downdraft Rochester 1-bbl. carburetor, 1.46 in. venturi. Compression Ratio: 8.0:1. Displacement: 261 cu. in. (4.27 liters). Horsepower: Gross: 150 @ 4000 rpm. Net: 130 @ 3800 rpm. Torque: Gross: 235 lb.-ft. @ 2000 rpm. Net: 218 lb.-ft. @ 2000 rpm. Oil refill capacity: 6 qt. without filter change. Fuel Requirements: Regular.

OPTIONAL ENGINE: All models: High Torque 283 V-8. Engine Type: OHV, V-8. Cast iron block and cylinder head. Bore x Stroke: 3.875 in. x 3.00 in. Lifters: Hydraulic. Number of main bearings-5. Fuel Induction: Single Rochester 2-bbl. carburetor, model 2G7015017. Compression Ratio: 8.5:1. Displacement: 283 cu. in. (4.63 liters). Horsepower: Gross: 160 @ 4200 rpm. Net: 137 @ 4000 rpm. Torque: Gross: 270 lb.-ft. @ 2000 rpm. Net: 250 lb.-ft. @ 2000 rpm. Oil refill capacity: 5 qt. with filter change. Fuel Requirements: Regular.

Ratings up to 5600 lb
[wheel]base: 115"

1962 Chevrolet model K1405 panel, 115 inch wheelbase

CHASSIS FEATURES: Series K10, K20: Separate body and frame with channel side rails measuring 7.1875 in. x 2.75 in. x 0.1875 in. Section modules: 5.09 in.

SUSPENSION AND RUNNING GEAR: Series K10 and K20: Front Suspension: 44 in. x 2.0 in. 5-leaf, semi-elliptical springs, shock absorbers. K10: 1650 lb. rating (at ground). K20: 1750 lb. capacity at ground. Rear Suspension: Series K10 and K20: 52 in. x 2.5 in. Single-stage, 6-leaf, semi-elliptical springs, shock absorbers, 1900 lb. rating (at ground). Front Axle Type and Capacity: Series K10 and K20: Hypoid, K10: 3300 lb. capacity, K20: 3500 lb. Optional: None. Rear Axle Type and Capacity: Series K10: Semi-floating, 3300 lb. capacity. K20: Full-floating, 5200 lb. capacity. Optional: None. Final Drive Ratio: Series K10: Front: 3.92:1. Rear; 3.90:1. Series K20: Front: 4.55:1. Rear: 4.57:1. Transfer Case: Timken T-221. Single lever, two-speed: 1.94, 1.00:1. Brakes: Type: Hydraulic, front and rear drums. Dimensions: Series K10: Front: 11.0 in. x 2.0 in. Rear: 11.0 in. x 2.0 in. Total lining area: 167 sq. in. Series K20: 12.0 in. x 2.0 in. Rear: 12.0 in. x 2.0 in. Total lining area: 190 sq. in. Wheels: Series K10: 15 x 5.0 K 6-stud disc. Optional: 15 x 5.25 in. Series K20: 17.5 x 5.25 in. 8-stud disc. Tires: Series K10: Tubeless 6.70 x 15 4-ply. Series K20: Tubeless 7-17.5 6-ply rating. Steering: Recirculating ball gear. Ratio: 24:1. 17.0 in. Optional: None. Transmission: 3-speed, synchromesh manual. Transmission Ratios: 2.94, 1.68. 1.00:1. Reverse: 3.14:1. Optional: 4-speed heavy-duty manual synchromesh. Transmission ratios: 7.06, 3.58, 1.71, 1.00:1. Reverse: 6.78:1. Clutch: Diaphragm, spring. Clutch diameter: 10 in. dia. Total lining area: 100.5 sq. in. Optional: Heavy-duty, 11.0 in. dia. for 235 engine only.

VEHICLE DIMENSIONS: Series K10 and K20: Wheelbase: 115 in. 127 in. Overall Length: 115 in. Fleetside pickups: 186.75 in. 127 in. Fleetside pickups: 206.25 In. 115 in. Stepside pickups: 186.875 in. 127 in. Stepside pickups: 206.25 in. Front/Rear Overhang: Pickup: 31.75 in./40 in.

CAPACITIES: Fuel Tank: 18.5 gal. except for Panel models which had 17.0 gal. tanks. Optional: 20.5 gal. Engine coolant system: 6-cyl.: 17 qt. V-8: 17.5 qt.

ACCOMMODATIONS: Seating Capacity: Pickup and chassis cab models: 3 passenger. Optional: None. Suburban: 3 passenger. Optional: 6 or 9 passenger.

1962 Chevrolet models K1406 and K1416 Carryalls, 115 inch wheelbase

INSTRUMENTATION: Speedometer, odometer, fuel level gauge, warning lights for oil pressure, engine coolant temperature, and battery charge.

OPTIONS AND PRICES: Oil bath air cleaner: $2.20. Heavy-duty 70 amp battery: $7.55. Side-mounted spare tire carrier: Fleetside: $14.00; Stepside: $15.10. Heavy-duty 11.0 in. clutch: $5.40. Custom Appearance option: $43.05-$51.65 depending upon body type. Custom Chrome option: Chassis & cab and pickups: $10.80; Panels and Carryalls: $21.55. Custom side molding (Fleetside only): $21.55. 261 6-cyl. Includes 11.0 in. clutch and heavy-duty radiator: $64.60. 283 V-8. Includes 11.0 in. clutch: $118.40. Temperature-controlled radiator fan: $21.55. Gauges for oil pressure, engine coolant temperature and ammeter: $7.55. Increased capacity generator: $7.55-$96.85. Laminated side window glass: $5.40. Soft-Ray glass: Windshield only: $12.95; all windows (except Carryalls): $15.10; Carryalls: $19.40. Engine governor: $10.80-$21.55 depending upon engine. Deluxe heater and defroster: $68.35. Recirculating air heater and defroster: $47.90. Two front towing hooks: $12.95. Free wheeling front hubs, manual control: $78.55. Side spare wheel lock: $6.50. Right door lock: $1.65. Exterior left side 17.25 in. mirror with swinging arm: $2.20. Exterior right side 17.25 in. mirror with swinging arm: $4.85. Exterior right side 6.25 in. mirror with fixed arm: $4.85. Two quart oil filter (235 engine): $3.80. Two-tone exterior paint (chassis & cabs and pickups): $16.15. Two-tone exterior paint (Panels and Carryalls): $26.90. Heavy-duty radiator: $21.55. Manual control radio: $47.90. Short running board: $8.65 (model K1403); $12.95 (model K1503). Auxiliary seat for Panel: $40.90. Full-depth foam seat: $32.30. Third seat for Carryalls. Includes sliding rear windows: $66.75. Tachometer for 283 engine: $48.45. 20.5 gal. fuel tank for cab models: $8.10. Heavy-duty 4-speed transmission: $86.10. Full-view rear window: $43.05. Electric 2-speed windshield wipers and washers: $16.15.

HISTORICAL FOOTNOTES: The 1962 models were available starting in the fall of 1961. Calendar year production of all Chevrolet models was 396,819.

1962 Chevrolet model K1403 chassis cab, 115 inch wheelbase

1963 PICKUP

1963 Chevrolet model K1404 Stepside pickup, 115 inch wheelbase

The K series trucks had several appearance revisions for 1963. These included a relocated I.D. badge now found on the fender side instead of just above the front fender feature line as in 1962, a new front grille with a mesh design, and headlights moved outward from their 1962 locations. Standard equipment included front painted bumper, front and rear directional signals, hand choke, left side, 8.0 in. fixed arm exterior mirror, and electric windshield wipers. The panoramic windshield had an area of approximately 1260 sq. in. The electric windshield wipers had 13.0 in. blades and a wiping speed of 110 strokes per minute. The full-view rear window was available as an option and had an area of 761 sq. in. as compared to the standard window's area of 330 sq. in. All cab had left-door key-operated locks standard with right door locks optional. The standard cab had a beige color theme. Body cab metal was painted fawn beige. An accent color, cameo white, was used for the steering wheel, turn signal housing, instrument cluster bezel and lower face of the instrument panel beneath the cluster. The steering column was white. Control knobs on the instrument panel was finished in charcoal plastic. The sunshade (standard on the driver's side) was beige in a leather-grain finish. The floor was covered by a black rubber mat. A dome light was standard. It was centered above the rear window and was operated by the main light switch on the instrument panel.

1963 Chevrolet model K 1434 Fleetside pickup, 115 inch wheelbase

The Custom Comfort cab option included the following: Left armrest, right sunshade, right door lock, chromed cigarette lighter, full-depth foam seat and special insulation. The left armrest was covered with red or beige vinyl on the top half and was made of white plastic on the bottom. A matching armrest for the right side was available as a dealer-installed custom feature. The special insulation included undercoating, perforated dash pad, and an asphalt-impregnated pad applied to the rear cab panel. With the Custom Comfort option, both seat and backrest were upholstered in nylon-faced cloth with a muted beige pattern. Red vinyl was used for the facings with red, white or gray exteriors. Beige vinyl facings were used with all other exterior colors.

1963 Chevrolet model K1504 Stepside pickup, 127 inch wheelbase

The Custom Appearance exterior option consisted of the following equipment: Bright metal (silver anodized aluminum) grille, bright metal windshield molding, steering wheel with horn ring, chrome-trimmed instrument panel knobs, two-tone dispatch box and interior door panels. The steering wheeler was painted cameo white. The instrument panel knobs had chrome-plated metal rims. The body of each knob was black plastic.

1963 Chevrolet model K 1534 Fleetside pickup, 127 inch wheelbase

The Custom chrome option consisted of a chrome-plated front bumper. The exterior colors for 1963 were unchanged from 1962: Desert beige, seamist jade, crystal turquoise, jet black, Glenwood green, cameo white, Balboa blue, Woodland green, pure white, brigade blue, Omaha orange, Yuma yellow, Georgian gray and cardinal red.

I.D. DATA: The serial number was stamped on a plate mounted on the upper left hinge pillar The first entry, a letter S, denoted a truck with an optional 7800 lb. GVW plate. Next came a 3 for the 1963 model year. The truck code followed, consisting of two numbers: 03-Chassis & cab, 04-Stepside pickup, 05-Panel, 06-Carryall (panel rear doors), 16-Carryall (tail and liftgate), 34-Fleetside pickup. The series number followed. The assembly plant code, a letter was next. The last six digits were the unit number, beginning at 100,001 at each truck plant, regardless of truck series. The engine number for the 6-cyl. engine was stamped on the right side of the block next to the distributor. On V-8 engines it was stamped on the forward edge of the block protruding from under the right cylinder head. The engine number for the 6-cyl. engine was stamped on the right side of the block next to the distributor. On V-8 engines it was stamped on the forward edge of the block protruding from under the right cylinder head.

Model Number	Body Type & Seating	Factory Price	GVW	Shipping Weight	Prod. Total
Series K10 1/2 ton 6-cyl. 115 in. wheelbase					
K1403	Chassis and Cab	$2546	5600	3430	—
K1404	78 in. Stepside Pickup	$2660	5600	3790	—
K1434	78 in. Fleetside Pickup	$2676	5600	3825	—
K1405	7.5 ft. Panel	$2977	5600	4065	—
K1406	Suburban Pnl. Dr.	$3271	5600	4370	—
K1416	Suburban Endgate	$3304	5600	4400	—
Series K10 1/2 ton 6-cyl. 127 in. wheelbase					
K1503	Chassis and Cab	$2584	5600	3430	—
K1504	98 in. Stepside Pickup	$2697	5600	3790	—
K1534	98 in. Fleetside Pickup	$2713	5600	3825	—
Series K20 3/4 ton, 1127 in. wheelbase					
K2503	Chassis and Cab	$2757	7200	3795	—
K2504	98 in. Stepside Pickup	$2869	7200	4210	—
K2534	98 in. Fleetside Pickup	$2885	7200	4255	—

1963 Chevrolet model K2504 Stepside pickup, 127 inch wheelbase

STANDARD ENGINE: All models: High Torque 230 Six. Engine Type: OHV, In-line 6-cylinder. Cast iron block and cylinder head. Bore x Stroke: 3.875 in. x 3.25 in. Lifters: Hydraulic. Number of main bearings-7. Fuel Induction: Single Rochester 1-bbl. downdraft carburetor, 1.29 in. venturi. Compression Ratio: 8.50:1. Displacement: 230 cu. in. (3.76 liters). Horsepower: Gross: 140 @ 4400 rpm. Net: 120 @ 3600 rpm. Torque: Gross: 220 lb.-ft. @ 1600 rpm. Net: 205 lb-ft. @ 1600 rpm. Oil refill capacity: 5 qt. without filter change. Fuel Requirements: Regular.

OPTIONAL ENGINE: All models: High Torque 292 Six. Engine Type: OHV, In-line 6-cylinder. Cast iron block and cylinder head. Bore x Stroke: 3.875 in. x 4.125 in. Lifters: Hydraulic. Number of main bearings-7. Fuel Induction: Single downdraft Rochester 1-bbl. carburetor, 1.34 in. venturi. Compression Ratio: 8.0:1. Displacement: 292 cu. in. (4.78 liters). Horsepower: Gross: 165 @ 3800 rpm. Net: 147 @ 3600 rpm. Torque: Gross: 280 lb.-ft. @ 1600 rpm. Net: 262 lb.-ft. @ 2000 rpm. Oil refill capacity: 6 qt. without filter change. Fuel Requirements: Regular.

OPTIONAL ENGINE: All models: High Torque 283 V-8. Engine Type: OHV, V-8. Cast iron block and cylinder head. Bore x Stroke: 3.875 in. x 3.00 in. Lifters: Hydraulic. Number of main bearings-5. Fuel Induction: Single Rochester 2-bbl. downdraft carburetor, 1.09 in. venturi. Compression Ratio: 9.01. Displacement: 283 cu. in. (4.63 liters). Horsepower: Gross: 175 @ 4400 rpm. Net: 145 @ 4200 rpm. Torque: Gross: 275 lb.-ft. @ 2400 rpm. Net: 245 lb.-ft. @ 2000 rpm. Oil refill capacity: 5 qt. with filter change. Fuel Requirements: Regular.

CHASSIS FEATURES: Series K10, K20: Separate body and frame with channel side rails measuring 7.1875 in. x 2.75 in. x 0.1875 in. Section modules: 5.09 in.

1963 Chevrolet model K1405 panel, 115 inch wheelbase

SUSPENSION AND RUNNING GEAR: Series K10 and K20: Front Suspension: 44 in. x 2.0 in. 5-leaf, semi-elliptical springs, shock absorbers. K10: 1650 lb. rating (at ground). K20: 1750 lb. capacity at ground. Rear Suspension: Series K10 and K20: 52 in. x 2.5 in. Single-stage, 6-leaf, semi-elliptical springs, shock absorbers, 1900 lb. rating (at ground). Front Axle Type and Capacity: Series K10 and K20: Hypoid, K10: 3300 lb. capacity, K20: 3500 lb. capacity. Optional: None. Rear Axle Type and Capacity: Series K10: Semi-floating, 3300 lb. capacity. K20: Full-floating, 5200 lb. capacity. Optional: None. Final Drive Ratio: Series K10: Front: 3.92:1. Rear: 3.90:1. Series K20: Front: 4.55:1. Rear: 4.57:1. Transfer Case: Timken T-221. Single lever, two-speed: 1.94, 1.00:1. Brakes: Type: Hydraulic, front and rear drums. Dimensions: Series K10: Front: 11.0 in. x 2.0 in. Rear: 11.0 in. x 2.0 in. Total lining area: 167 sq. in. Series K20: 12.0 in. x 2.0 in. Rear: 12.0 in. x 2.0 in. Total lining area: 190 sq. in. Wheels: Series K10: 15 x

5.0 K 6-stud disc. Optional: 15 x 5.25 in. Series K20: 17.5 x 5.25 in. 8-stud disc. Tires: Series K10: Tubeless 6.70 x 15 4-ply. Series K20: Tubeless 7-17.5 6-ply rating. Steering: Recirculating ball gear. Ratio: 24:1. 17.0 in. Optional: None. Transmission: 3-speed, synchromesh manual. Transmission Ratios: 2.94, 1.68. 1.00:1. Reverse: 3.14:1. Optional: 4-speed heavy-duty manual synchromesh. Transmission ratios: 7.06, 3.58, 1.71, 1.00:1. Reverse: 6.78:1. Clutch: Diaphragm, spring. Clutch diameter:10 in. dia. Total lining area: 100.5 sq. in. Optional: heavy-duty, 11.0 in. dia. for 230 engine only.

VEHICLE DIMENSIONS: Series K10 and K20: Wheelbase: 115 in. 127 in. Overall Length: 115 in. Fleetside pickups: 186.75 in. 127 in. Fleetside pickups: 206.25 in. 115 in. Stepside pickups: 186.875 in. 127 in. Stepside pickups: 206.25 in. Front/Rear Overhang: Pickup: 31.75 in./40 in.

CAPACITIES: Fuel Tank: 18.5 gal. except for Panel models which had 17.0 gal. tanks. Optional: 20.5 gal. Engine coolant system: 6-cyl: 17 qt. V-8: 17.5 qt.

ACCOMMODATIONS: Seating Capacity: Pickup and chassis cab models: 3 passenger. Optional: None. Suburban: 3 passenger. Optional: 6 or 9 passenger.

INSTRUMENTATION: Speedometer, odometer, fuel level gauge, warning lights for oil pressure, engine coolant temperature, and battery charge.

1963 Chevrolet models K1406 and K1416 Carryalls, 115 inch wheelbase

OPTIONS AND PRICES: Oil bath air cleaner: $2.20. Heavy-duty 70 amp battery: $7.55. Side-mounted spare tire carrier: Fleetside: $14.00; Stepside: $15.10. Heavy-duty 11.0 in. clutch: $5.40. Custom Appearance option: $43.05-$51.65 depending upon body type. Custom Chrome option: Chassis & cab and pickups: $10.80; Panels and Carryalls: $21.55. Custom side molding (Fleetside only): $21.55. 292 6-cyl. Includes 11.0 in. clutch and heavy-duty radiator: $64.60. 283 V-8. Includes 11.0 in. clutch: $118.40. Temperature-controlled radiator fan: $21.55. Gauges for oil pressure, engine coolant temperature and ammeter: $7.55. Increased capacity generator: $7.55-$96.85. Laminated side window glass: $5.40. Soft-Ray glass: Windshield only: $12.95; all windows (except Carryalls): $15.10; Carryalls: $19.40. Engine governor: $10.80-$21.55 depending upon engine. Deluxe heater and defroster: $68.35. Recirculating air heater and defroster: $47.90. Two front towing hooks: $12.95. Free wheeling front hubs, manual control: $78.55. Side spare wheel lock: $6.50. Right door lock: $1.65. Exterior left side 17.25 in. mirror with swinging arm: $2.20. Exterior right side 17.25 in. mirror with swinging arm: $4.85. Exterior right 6.25 in. mirror with fixed arm: $4.85. Two quart oil filter (235 engine): $3.80. Two-tone exterior paint (chassis & cabs and pickups): $16.15. Two-tone exterior paint (Panels and Carryalls): $26.90. Heavy-duty radiator: $21.55. Manual control radio: $47.90. Short running board: $8.65 (model K1403); $12.95 (model K1503). Auxiliary seat for Panel: $40.90. Full-depth foam seat: $32.30. Third seat for Carryalls. Includes sliding rear windows: $66.75. Tachometer for 283 engine: $48.45. 20.5 gal. fuel tank for cab models: $8.10. Heavy-duty 4-speed transmission: $86.10. Full-view rear window: $43.05. Electric 2-speed windshield wipers and washers: $16.15.

HISTORICAL FOOTNOTES: The 1963 models were introduced on September 28, 1962. As it had done since 1938, Chevrolet lead all its competition in overall truck registrations in 1963.

1963 Chevrolet model K1403 chassis cab, 115 inch wheelbase

1964 PICKUP

The K series trucks were little changed for 1964. They were identified by their new grille with two large horizontal bars and a thin mesh inset. Chevrolet lettering was located on the top grille edge. The headlight nacelles were square-shaped.

Standard interior appointments included a driver's sunshade, left-door lock, rubber floor mat, dome light, and hooded non-glare instrument panel. The Custom interior option featured a full-foam cushion seat upholstered in nylon fabric and trimmed with vinyl in red or beige, depending upon exterior truck color. Other features included a driver's armrest, right door lock, chrome-trimmed control knobs, cigarette lighter, passenger's sunshade, horn ring and white trim on doors and trim plate for dispatch box.

I.D. DATA: The serial number was stamped on a plate mounted on the upper left hinge pillar. The first entry, a letter S, denoted a truck with an optional 7800 lb. GVW plate. Next came a 4 for the 1964 model year. The truck code followed, consisting of two numbers: 03-Chassis & cab, 04-Stepside pickup, 05-Panel, 06-Carryall (panel rear doors), 16-Carryall (tail and liftgate), 34-Fleetside pickup. The series number followed. The assembly plant code, a letter was next. The last six digits were the unit number, beginning at 100,001 at each truck plant, regardless of truck series. The engine number for the 6-cyl. engine was stamped on the right side of the block next to the distributor. On V-8 engines it was stamped on the forward edge of the block protruding from under the right cylinder head.

Model Number	Body Type & Seating	Factory Price	GVW	Shipping Weight	Prod. Total
Series K10 1/2 ton 6-cyl. 115 in. wheelbase					
K1403	Chassis and Cab	$2544	5600	3430	—
K1404	78 in. Stepside Pickup	$2658	5600	3790	—
K1434	78 in. Fleetside Pickup	$2674	5600	3825	—
K1405	7.5 ft. Panel	$2975	5600	4065	—
K1406	Suburban Pnl. Dr.	$3269	5600	4370	—
K1416	Suburban Endgate	$3302	5600	4400	—
Series K10 1/2 ton 6-cyl. 127 in. wheelbase					
K1503	Chassis and Cab	$2582	5600	3430	—
K1504	98 in. Stepside Pickup	$2695	5600	3790	—
K1534	98 in. Fleetside Pickup	$2711	5600	3825	—
Series K20 3/4 ton, 1127 in. wheelbase					
K2503	Chassis and Cab	$2756	7200	3795	—
K2504	98 in. Stepside Pickup	$2869	7200	4210	—
K2534	98 in. Fleetside Pickup	$2885	7200	4255	—

STANDARD ENGINE: All models: High Torque 230 Six. Engine Type: OHV, In-line 6-cylinder. Cast iron block and cylinder head. Bore x Stroke: 3.875 in. x 3.25 in. Lifters: Hydraulic. Number of main bearings-7. Fuel Induction: Single Rochester 1-bbl. downdraft carburetor, 1.29 in. venturi. Compression Ratio: 8.50:1. Displacement: 230 cu. in. (3.76 liters). Horsepower: Gross: 140 @ 4400 rpm. Net: 120 @ 3600 rpm. Torque: Gross: 220 lb.-ft. @ 1600 rpm. Net: 205 lb-ft. @ 1600 rpm. Oil refill capacity: 5 qt. without filter change. Fuel Requirements: Regular.

OPTIONAL ENGINE: All models: High Torque 292 Six. Engine Type: OHV, In-line 6-cylinder. Cast iron block and cylinder head. Bore x Stroke: 3.875 in. x 4.125 in. Lifters: Hydraulic. Number of main bearings-7. Fuel Induction: Single downdraft Rochester 1-bbl. carburetor, 1.34 in. venturi. Compression Ratio: 8.0:1. Displacement: 292 cu. in. (4.78 liters). Horsepower: Gross: 165 @ 3800 rpm. Net: 147 @ 3600 rpm. Torque: Gross: 280 lb.-ft. @ 1600 rpm. Net: 262 lb.-ft. @ 2000 rpm. Oil refill capacity: 6 qt. without filter change. Fuel Requirements: Regular.

OPTIONAL ENGINE: All models: High Torque 283 V-8. Engine Type: OHV, V-8. Cast iron block and cylinder head. Bore x Stroke: 3.875 in. x 3.00 in. Lifters: Hydraulic. Number of main bearings-5. Fuel Induction: Single Rochester 2-bbl. downdraft carburetor, 1.09 in. venturi. Compression Ratio: 9.01. Displacement: 283 cu. in. (4.63 liters). Horsepower: Gross: 175 @ 4400 rpm. Net: 145 @ 4200 rpm. Torque: Gross: 275 lb.-ft. @ 2400 rpm. Net: 245 lb.-ft. @ 2000 rpm. Oil refill capacity: 5 qt. with filter change. Fuel Requirements: Regular.

CHASSIS FEATURES: Series K10, K20: Separate body and frame with channel side rails measuring 7.1875 in. x 2.75 in. x 0.1875 in. Section modules: 5.09 in.

SUSPENSION AND RUNNING GEAR: Series K10 and K20: Front Suspension: 44 in. x 2.0 in. 5-leaf, semi-elliptical springs, shock absorbers. K10: 1650 lb. rating (at ground). K20: 1750 lb. capacity at ground. Rear Suspension: Series K10 and K20: 52 in. x 2.5 in. Single-stage, 6-leaf, semi-elliptical springs, shock absorbers, 1900 lb. rating (at ground). Front Axle Type and Capacity: Series K10 and K20: Hypoid, K10: 3300 lb. capacity, K20: 3500 lb. Optional: None. Rear Axle Type and Capacity: Series K10: Semi-floating, 3300 lb. capacity. K20: Full-floating, 5200 lb. capacity. Optional: None. Final Drive Ratio: Series K10: Front: 3.92:1. Rear; 3.90:1. Series K20: Front: 4.55:1. Rear: 4.57:1. Transfer Case: Timken T-221. Single lever, two-speed: 1.94, 1.00:1. Brakes: Type: Hydraulic, front and rear drums. Dimensions: Series K10: Front: 11.0 in. x 2.0 in. Rear: 11.0 in. x 2.0 in. Total lining area: 167 sq. in. Series K20: 12.0 in. x 2.0 in. Rear: 12.0 in. x 2.0 in. Total lining area: 190 sq. in. Wheels: Series K10: 15 x 5.0 K 6-stud disc. Optional: 15 x 5.25 in. Series K20: 17.5 x 5.25 in. 8-stud disc. Tires: Series K10: tubeless 6.70 x 15 4-ply. Series K20: tubeless 7-17.5 6-ply rating. Steering: Recirculating ball gear. Ratio: 24:1. 17.0 in. Optional: None. Transmission: 3-speed, synchromesh manual. Transmission Ratios: 2.94, 1.68. 1.00:1. Reverse: 3.14:1. Optional: 4-speed heavy-duty manual synchromesh. Transmission ratios: 7.06, 3.58, 1.71, 1.00:1. Reverse: 6.78:1. Clutch: Diaphragm, spring. Clutch diameter: 10 in. dia. Total lining area: 100.5 sq. in. Optional: Heavy-duty, 11.0 in. dia. for 230 engine only.

VEHICLE DIMENSIONS: Series K10 and K20: Wheelbase: 115 in. 127 in. Overall Length: 115 in. Fleetside pickups: 186.75 in. 127 in. Fleetside pickups: 206.25 in. 115 in. Stepside pickups: 186.875 in. 127 in. Stepside pickups: 206.25 in. Front/Rear Overhang: Pickup: 31.75 in./40 in.

CAPACITIES: Fuel Tank: 18.5 gal. except for Panel models which had 17.0 gal. tanks. Optional: 20.5 gal. Engine coolant system: 6-cyl.: 17 qt. V-8: 17.5 qt.

ACCOMMODATIONS: Seating Capacity: Pickup and chassis cab models: 3 passenger. Optional: None. Suburban: 3 passenger. Optional: 6 or 9 passenger.

INSTRUMENTATION: Speedometer, odometer, fuel level gauge, warning lights for oil pressure, engine coolant temperature, and battery charge.

OPTIONS AND PRICES: Oil bath air cleaner: $2.20. Heavy-duty 70 amp battery: $7.55. Side-mounted spare tire carrier: Fleetside: $14.00; Stepside: $15.10. Heavy-duty 11.0 in. clutch: $5.40. Custom Appearance option: $43.05-$51.65 depending upon body type. Custom Chrome option: Chassis & Cab and pickups: $10.80; Panels and Carryalls: $21.55. Custom side molding (Fleetside only): $21.55. 292 6-cyl. Includes 11.0 in. clutch and heavy-duty radiator: $64.60. 283 V-8. Includes 11.0 in. clutch: $118.40. Temperature-controlled radiator fan: $21.55. Gauges for oil pressure, engine coolant temperature and ammeter: $7.55. Increased capacity generator: $7.55-$96.85. Laminated side window glass: $5.40. Soft-Ray glass: Windshield only: $12.95; all windows (except Carryalls): $15.10; Carryalls: $19.40. Engine governor: $10.80-$21.55 depending upon engine. Deluxe heater and defroster: $68.35. Recirculating air heater and defroster: $47.90. Two front towing hooks: $12.95. Free wheeling front hubs, manual control: $78.55. Side spare wheel lock: $6.50. Right door lock: $1.65. Exterior left side 17.25 in. mirror with swinging arm: $2.20. Exterior right side 17.25 in. mirror with swinging arm: $4.85. Exterior right side 6.25 in. mirror with fixed arm: $4.85. Two quart oil filter (235 engine): $3.80. Two-tone exterior paint (chassis & cabs and pickups): $16.15. Two-tone exterior paint (Panels and Carryalls): $26.90. Heavy-duty radiator: $21.55. Manual control radio: $47.90. Short running board: $8.65 (model K1403); $12.95 (model K1503). Auxiliary seat for Panel: $40.90. Full-depth foam seat: $32.30. Third seat for Carryalls. Includes sliding rear windows: $66.75. Tachometer for 283 engine: $48.45. 20.5 gal. fuel tank for cab models: $8.10. Heavy-duty 4-speed transmission: $86.10. Full-view rear window: $43.05. Electric 2-speed windshield wipers and washers: $16.15.

HISTORICAL FOOTNOTES: The 1964 models were introduced on September 29, 1963. Model year production of all Chevrolet trucks was 483,853.

1965 PICKUP

The1965 K series trucks had their series identification plaques mounted higher on the body sides than in 1964. Suburbans could be ordered with a new optional hot-water rear compartment heater.

Standard interior appointments included a driver's sunshade, left-door lock, rubber floor mat, dome light, and hooded non-glare instrument panel. The Custom interior option featured a full-foam cushion seat upholstered in nylon fabric and trimmed with vinyl in red or beige, depending upon exterior truck color. Other features included a driver's armrest, right door lock, chrome-trimmed control knobs, cigarette lighter, passenger's sunshade, horn ring and white trim on doors and trim plate for dispatch box.

I.D. DATA: The serial number was stamped on a plate mounted on the upper left hinge pillar The first entry, a letter K, denoted a four-wheel drive truck. Next came two digits representing the series designation. The body or chassis type was next identified by a single digit. The model year was represented by the number 5. The assembly plant code in the form of a letter followed. The last six entries were numbers indicating the unit number build which began at 100,001 at each assembly plant regardless of series. The engine number for the 6-cyl. engine was stamped on the right side of the block next to the distributor. On V-8 engines it was stamped on the forward edge of the block protruding from under the right cylinder head.

Model Number	Body Type & Seating	Factory Price	GVW	Shipping Weight	Prod. Total
Series K10 1/2 ton 6-cyl. 115 in. wheelbase					
K1403	Chassis and Cab	$2546	5600	3450	—
K1404	78 in. Stepside Pickup	$2659	5600	3805	—
K1434	78 in. Fleetside Pickup	$2675	5600	3825	—
K1405	7.5 ft. Panel	$2976	5600	4080	—
K1406	Suburban Pnl. Dr.	$3270	5600	4385	—
K1416	Suburban Endgate	$3303	5600	4415	—
Series K10 1/2 ton 6-cyl. 127 in. wheelbase					
K1503	Chassis and Cab	$2584	5600	3445	—
K1504	98 in. Stepside Pickup	$2697	5600	3805	—
K1534	98 in. Fleetside Pickup	$2713	5600	3840	—
Series K20 3/4 ton, 1127 in. wheelbase					
K2503	Chassis and Cab	$2756	7200	3805	—
K2504	98 in. Stepside Pickup	$2869	7200	4225	—
K2534	98 in. Fleetside Pickup	$2885	7200	4270	—

STANDARD ENGINE: All models: High Torque 230 Six. Engine Type: OHV, In-line 6-cylinder. Cast iron block and cylinder head. Bore x Stroke: 3.875 in. x 3.25 in. Lifters: Hydraulic. Number of main bearings-7. Fuel Induction: Single Rochester 1-bbl. downdraft carburetor, 1.29 in. venturi. Compression Ratio: 8.50:1. Displacement: 230 cu. in. (3.76 liters). Horsepower: Gross: 140 @ 4400 rpm. Net: 120 @ 3600 rpm. Torque: Gross: 220 lb.-ft. @ 1600 rpm. Net: 205 lb-ft. @ 1600 rpm. Oil refill capacity: 5 qt. without filter change. Fuel Requirements: Regular.

OPTIONAL ENGINE: All models: High Torque 292 Six. Engine Type: OHV, In-line 6-cylinder. Cast iron block and cylinder head. Bore x Stroke: 3.875 in. x 4.125 in. Lifters: Hydraulic. Number of main bearings-7. Fuel Induction: Single downdraft Rochester 1-bbl. carburetor, 1.34 in. venturi. Compression Ratio: 8.0:1. Displacement: 292 cu. in. (4.78 liters). Horsepower: Gross: 165 @ 3800 rpm. Net: 147 @ 3600 rpm. Torque: Gross: 280 lb.-ft. @ 1600 rpm. Net: 262 lb.-ft. @ 2000 rpm. Oil refill capacity: 6 qt. without filter change. Fuel Requirements: Regular.

OPTIONAL ENGINE: All models: High Torque 283 V-8. Engine Type: OHV, V-8. Cast iron block and cylinder head. Bore x Stroke: 3.875 in. x 3.00 in. Lifters: Hydraulic. Number of main bearings-5. Fuel Induction: Single Rochester 2-bbl. downdraft carburetor, 1.09 in. venturi. Compression Ratio: 9.01. Displacement: 283 cu. in. (4.63 liters). Horsepower: Gross: 175 @ 4400 rpm. Net: 145 @ 4200 rpm. Torque: Gross: 275 lb.-ft. @ 2400 rpm. Net: 245 lb.-ft. @ 2000 rpm. Oil refill capacity: 5 qt. with filter change. Fuel Requirements: Regular.

CHASSIS FEATURES: Series K10, K20: Separate body and frame with channel side rails measuring 7.1875 in. x 2.75 in. x 0.1875 in. Section modules: 5.09 in.

SUSPENSION AND RUNNING GEAR: Series K10 and K20: Front Suspension: 44 in. x 2.0 in. 5-leaf, semi-elliptical springs, shock absorbers. K10: 1650 lb. rating (at ground). K20: 1750 lb. capacity at ground. Rear Suspension: Series K10 and K20: 52 in. x 2.5 in. Single-stage, 6-leaf, semi-elliptical springs, shock absorbers, 1900 lb. rating (at ground). Front Axle Type and Capacity: Series K10 and K20: Hypoid, K10: 3300 lb. capacity, K20: 3500 lb. Optional: None. Rear Axle Type and Capacity: Series K10: Semi-floating, 3300 lb. capacity. K20: Full-floating, 5200 lb. capacity. Optional: None. Final Drive Ratio: Series K10: Front: 3.92:1. Rear; 3.90:1. Series K20: Front: 4.55:1. Rear: 4.57:1. Transfer Case: Timken T-221. Single lever, two-speed: 1.94, 1.00:1. Brakes: Type: Hydraulic, front and rear drums. Dimensions: Series K10: Front: 11.0 in. x 2.0 in. Rear: 11.0 in. x 2.0 in. Total lining area: 167 sq. in. Series K20: 12.0 in. x 2.0 in. Rear: 12.0 in. x 2.0 in. Total lining area: 190 sq. in. Wheels: Series K10: 15 x 5.0 K 6-stud disc. Optional: 15 x 5.25 in. Series K20: 17.5 x 5.25 in. 8-stud disc. Tires: Series K10: Tubeless 6.70 x 15 4-ply. Series K20: tubeless 7-17.5 6-ply rating. Steering: Recirculating ball gear. Ratio: 24:1. 17.0 in. Optional: None. Transmission: 3-speed, synchromesh manual. Transmission Ratios: 2.94, 1.68. 1.00:1. Reverse: 3.14:1. Optional: 4-speed heavy-duty manual synchromesh. Transmission ratios: 7.06, 3.58, 1.71, 1.00:1. Reverse: 6.78:1. Clutch: Diaphragm, spring. Clutch diameter: 10 in. dia. Total lining area: 100.5 sq. in. Optional: Heavy-duty, 11.0 in. dia. for 230 engine only.

VEHICLE DIMENSIONS: Series K10 and K20: Wheelbase: 115 in. 127 in. Overall Length: 115 in. Fleetside pickups: 186.75 in. 127 in. Fleetside pickups: 206.25 in. 115 in. Stepside pickups: 186.875 in. 127 in. Stepside pickups: 206.25 in. Front/Rear Overhang: Pickup: 31.75 in./40 in.

CAPACITIES: Fuel Tank: 18.5 gal. except for Panel models which had 17.0 gal. tanks. Optional: 20.5 gal. Engine coolant system: 6-cyl.: 17 qt. V-8: 17.5 qt.

ACCOMMODATIONS: Seating Capacity: Pickup and chassis cab models: 3 passenger. Optional: None. Suburban: 3 passenger. Optional: 6 or 9 passenger.

INSTRUMENTATION: Speedometer, odometer, fuel level gauge, warning lights for oil pressure, engine coolant temperature, and battery charge.

OPTIONS AND PRICES: Oil bath air cleaner: $2.20. Heavy-duty 70 amp battery: $7.55. Side-mounted spare tire carrier: Fleetside: $14.00; Stepside: $15.10. Heavy-duty 11.0 in. clutch: $5.40. Custom Appearance option: $43.05-$51.65 depending upon body type. Custom Chrome option: Chassis & cab and pickups: $10.80; Panels and Carryalls: $21.55. Custom side molding (Fleetside only): $21.55. 292 6-cyl. Includes 11.0 in. clutch and heavy-duty radiator: $64.60. 283 V-8. Includes 11.0 in. clutch: $118.40. Temperature-controlled radiator fan: $21.55. Gauges for oil pressure, engine coolant temperature and ammeter: $7.55. Increased capacity generator: $7.55-$96.85. Laminated side window glass: $5.40. Soft-Ray glass: Windshield only: $12.95; all windows (except Carryalls): $15.10; Carryalls: $19.40. Engine governor: $10.80-$21.55 depending upon engine. Deluxe heater and defroster: $68.35. Recirculating air heater and defroster: $47.90. Two front towing hooks: $12.95. Free wheeling front hubs, manual control: $78.55. Side spare wheel lock: $6.50. Right door lock: $1.65. Exterior left side 17.25 in. mirror with swinging arm: $2.20. Exterior right side 17.25 in. mirror with swinging arm: $4.85. Exterior right side 6.25 in. mirror with fixed arm: $4.85. Two quart oil filter (235 engine): $3.80. Two-tone exterior paint (chassis & cabs and pickups): $16.15. Two-tone exterior paint (Panels and Carryalls): $26.90. Heavy-duty radiator: $21.55. Manual control radio: $47.90. Short running board: $8.65 (model K1403); $12.95 (model K1503). Auxiliary seat for Panel: $40.90. Full-depth foam seat: $32.30. Third seat for Carryalls. Includes sliding rear windows: $66.75. Tachometer for 283 engine: $48.45. 20.5 gal. fuel tank for cab models: $8.10. Heavy-duty 4-speed transmission: $86.10. Full-View rear window: $43.05. Electric 2-speed windshield wipers and washers: $16.15.

HISTORICAL FOOTNOTES: The 1965 models were introduced on September 24, 1964. Model year production of all Chevrolet trucks was 619,685.

1966 PICKUP

The latest models had their series identification located lower on the body side for 1966. Standard equipment highlights for 1966 included front painted bumper, front and rear on 05, 06 and 16 models, front and rear directional signals, left and right-hand 6.25 in. exterior mirrors on 03 and 05 models; 04, 06, 16 and 34 models; left hand exterior 6.25 in. fixed arm mirror and inside non-glare, shatterproof mirror. Seat belts were installed as follows: Driver and passenger on models K1403, 04, 34 and K1503, 04 and 34. For models K1406-16 four seat belts, two front and two rear, were installed. A single driver seat belt was installed on model K1405. all models had two-speed electric windshield wipers. The standard cab had a medium fawn textured vinyl upholstery for all facings, bolsters and coverings. The surface had an embossed appearance. Fawn seat belts were provided for the driver and passenger. The fawn color theme was continued in the cab interior. All body metal was painted medium fawn while a non-glare dark fawn was used for the instrument panel and related components. The instrument cluster bezel was painted silver. Cluster faces and gauge dials were charcoal with light green markings. The steering column was medium fawn. A silver gray glove box door nameplate with Chevrolet in black lettering was also featured. The standard driver's sunshade was medium fawn in a textured-vinyl finish. The dome light was operated by the main light switch. A black rubber floor mat was installed.

The Custom Comfort interior option included a left side armrest covered in medium fawn vinyl. A matching armrest for the right side was a dealer-installed option. Also included was a right side sunshade in matching medium fawn, a chromed cigarette lighter, full-depth foam seat, special insulation, and a right door lock. Both the seat and backrest in the Custom Comfort option were upholstered in nylon-faced cloth having a medium and dark fawn pattern. Medium fawn vinyl facings and bolsters were used with all exterior colors. The backrest insert was white vinyl. The Custom Appearance option included a bright metal windshield molding, embossed stainless steel cab trim plate with the word "Custom" in the center, silver anodized aluminum grille, steering wheel finished in medium fawn with a chromed half-circle horn ring, chrome-trimmed instrument panel knobs and a two-tone trim for the interior door panels. A chrome front bumper was available through the Custom Chrome option. A silver anodized aluminum side trim molding was offered for the Fleetside pickups. The area between the double chromed moldings was off-white or white with white exterior paint.

The exterior color selection for 1966 included these colors: Dark aqua metallic, black, dark blue, light blue, gray metallic, dark green, light green, orange, red, saddle metallic, silver metallic, turquoise metallic, white, and off-white. A School Bus yellow was also offered.

I.D. DATA: The serial number was stamped on a plate mounted on the upper left hinge pillar The first entry, a letter K, denoted a four-wheel drive truck. Next came two digits representing the series designation. The body or chassis type was next identified by a single digit. The model year was represented by the number 6. The assembly plant code in the form of a letter followed. The last six entries were numbers indicating the unit number build which began at 100,001 at each assembly plant regardless of series. The engine number for the 6-cyl. engine was stamped on the right side of the block next to the distributor. On V-8 engines it was stamped on the forward edge of the block protruding from under the right cylinder head.

Model Number	Body Type & Seating	Factory Price	GVW	Shipping Weight	Prod. Total
Series K10 1/2 ton 6-cyl. 115 in. wheelbase					
K1403	Chassis and Cab	$2578	5600	3450	1
K1404	78 in. Stepside Pickup	$2702	5600	3805	—
K1434	78 in. Fleetside Pickup	$2718	5600	3825	—
K1405	7.5 ft. Panel	$3012	5600	4080	—
Series K10 1/2 ton 6-cyl. 127 in. wheelbase					
K1503	Chassis and Cab	$2615	5600	3445	—
K1504	98 in. Stepside Pickup	$2739	5600	3805	—
K1534	98 in. Fleetside Pickup	$2755	5600	3840	—

NOTE 1: Total production of four-wheel drive models with 115 in. wheelbase was 2,959.

Model Number	Body Type & Seating	Factory Price	GVW	Shipping Weight	Prod. Total
Series K20 3/4 ton, 1127 in. wheelbase					
K2503	Chassis and Cab	$2791	7200	3805	2
K2504	98 in. Stepside Pickup	$2913	7200	4225	—
K2534	98 in. Fleetside Pickup	$2929	7200	4270	—

NOTE 2: Total production of four-wheel drive models with 127 in. wheelbase was 2,463.

STANDARD ENGINE: All models: High Torque 250 Six. Engine Type: OHV, In-line 6-cylinder. Cast iron block and cylinder head. Bore x Stroke: 3.875 in. x 3.53 in. Lifters: Hydraulic. Number of main bearings-7. Fuel Induction: Single Rochester 1-bbl. downdraft carburetor, 1.343 in. venturi. Compression Ratio: 8.50:1. Displacement: 250 cu. in. (4.09 liters). Horsepower: Gross: 155 @ 4200 rpm. Net: 125 @ 3800 rpm. Torque: Gross: 235 lb.-ft. @ 1600 rpm. Net: 220 lb-ft. @ 1600 rpm. Oil refill capacity: 5 qt. without filter change. Fuel Requirements: Regular.

OPTIONAL ENGINE: All models: High Torque 292 Six. Engine Type: OHV, In-line 6-cylinder. Cast iron block and cylinder head. Bore x Stroke: 3.875 in. x 4.125 in. Lifters: Hydraulic. Number of main bearings-7. Fuel Induction: Single downdraft Rochester 1-bbl. carburetor, 1.625 in. venturi. Compression Ratio: 8.0:1. Displacement: 292 cu. in. (4.78 liters). Horsepower: Gross: 170 @ 4000 rpm. Net: 153 @ 3600 rpm. Torque: Gross: 275 lb.-ft. @ 1600 rpm. Net: 255 lb.-ft. @ 2400 rpm. Oil refill capacity: 6 qt. without filter change. Fuel Requirements: Regular.

OPTIONAL ENGINE: All models: High Torque 283 V-8. Engine Type: OHV, V-8. Cast iron block and cylinder head. Bore x Stroke: 3.875 in. x 3.00 in. Lifters: Hydraulic. Number of main bearings-5. Fuel Induction: Single Rochester 2-bbl. downdraft carburetor, 1.09 in. venturi. Compression Ratio: 9.01. Displacement: 283 cu. in. (4.63 liters). Horsepower: Gross: 175 @ 4400 rpm. Net: 145 @ 4200 rpm. Torque: Gross: 275 lb.-ft. @ 2400 rpm. Net: 245 lb.-ft. @ 2000 rpm. Oil refill capacity: 5 qt. with filter change. Fuel Requirements: Regular.

CHASSIS FEATURES: Series K10, K20: Separate body and frame with channel side rails measuring 7.1875 in. x 2.75 in. x 0.1875 in. Section modules: 5.09 in.

SUSPENSION AND RUNNING GEAR: Series K10 and K20: Front Suspension: 44 in. x 2.0 in. 5-leaf, semi-elliptical springs, shock absorbers. K10: 1650 lb. rating (at ground). K20: 1750 lb. capacity at ground. Rear Suspension: Series K10 and K20: 52 in. x 2.5 in. Single-stage, 6-leaf, semi-elliptical springs, shock absorbers, 1900 lb. rating (at ground). Front Axle Type and Capacity: Series K10 and K20: Hypoid, K10: 3300 lb. capacity, K20: 3500 lb. Optional: None. Rear Axle Type and Capacity: Series K10: Semi-floating, 3300 lb. capacity. K20: Full-floating, 5200 lb. capacity. Optional: None. Final Drive Ratio: Series K10: Front: 3.92:1. Rear; 3.90:1. Series K20: Front: 4.55:1. Rear: 4.57:1. Transfer Case: Timken T-221. Single lever, two-speed: 1.94, 1.00:1. Brakes: Type: Hydraulic, front and rear drums. Dimensions: Series K10: Front: 11.0 in. x 2.0 in. Rear: 11.0 in. x 2.0 in. Total lining area: 167 sq. in. Series K20: 12.0 in. x 2.0 in. Rear: 12.0 in. x 2.0 in. Total lining area: 190 sq. in. Wheels: Series K10: 15 x 5.0 K 6-stud disc. Optional: 15 x 5.25 in. Series K20: 17.5 x 5.25 in. 8-stud disc. Tires: Series K10: tubeless 7-17.5 x 15 4-ply. (K1406-16: 8.15 x 15 4-ply). Series K20: Tubeless 7-17.5 6-ply rating. Steering: Recirculating ball gear. Ratio: 24:1. 17.0 in. Optional: None. Transmission: 3-speed, synchromesh manual. Transmission Ratios: 2.94, 1.68. 1.00:1. Reverse: 3.14:1. Optional: 4-speed heavy-duty manual synchromesh. Transmission ratios: 7.06, 3.58, 1.71, 1.00:1. Reverse: 6.78:1. Clutch: Diaphragm, spring. Clutch diameter:10 in. dia. Total lining area: 100.5 sq. in. Optional: Heavy-duty, 11.0 in. dia. for 230 engine only.

VEHICLE DIMENSIONS: Series K10 and K20: Wheelbase: 115 in. 127 in. Overall Length: 115 in. Fleetside pickups: 186.75 in. 127 in. Fleetside pickups: 206.25 in. 115 in. Stepside pickups: 186.875 in. 127 in. Stepside pickups: 206.25 in. Front/Rear Overhang: Pickup: 31.75 in./40 in.

CAPACITIES: Fuel Tank: 18.5 gal. except for Panel models which had 17.0 gal. tanks. Optional: 20.5 gal. Engine coolant system: 6-cyl.: 17 qt. V-8: 17.5 qt.

ACCOMMODATIONS: Seating Capacity: Pickup and chassis cab models: 3 passenger. Optional: None. Suburban: 3 passenger. Optional: 6 or 9 passenger.

INSTRUMENTATION: Speedometer, odometer, fuel level gauge, warning lights for oil pressure, engine coolant temperature, and battery charge.

OPTIONS AND PRICES: Oil bath air cleaner: $2.20-$6.50 depending upon engine. Heavy-duty air cleaner: $63.80. Heavy-duty 70 amp battery: $7.55. Rear step bumper: $45.20. Side-mounted spare tire carrier: Fleetside: $14.00; Stepside: $15.10. Heavy-duty 11.0 in. clutch: $5.40. Heavy-duty cooling system: $30.15. Custom Appearance option: $43.05-$51.65 depending upon body type. Custom Comfort option: Chassis and Cab: $54.90, panel: $11.85. Custom Chrome option: Chassis & cab and pickups: $10.80; Panels and Carryalls: $21.55. Custom side molding (Fleetside only): $21.55. Custom side molding: $37.70. 292 6-cyl. Includes 11.0 in. clutch and heavy-duty radiator: $96.85. 283 V-8. Includes 11.0 in. clutch: $118.40. Fuel filter equipment: $7.55. Temperature-controlled radiator fan: $21.55. Gauges for oil pressure, engine coolant temperature and ammeter: $10.80. Increased capacity generator: $7.55-$96.85. Soft-Ray glass: Windshield only: $14.00; all windows (except Carryalls): $15.10; Carryalls: $19.40. Engine governor: $10.80-$21.55 depending upon engine. Deluxe air heater and defroster: $68.35. Thrift-Air heater and defroster: $53.80. Two front towing hooks: $16.15. Free wheeling front hubs, manual control, K10 only: $78.55. Hazard and marker lights: $37.70. Side spare wheel lock: $6.50. Right door lock: $1.65. Exterior mirrors; various sizes and styles ranging in price from $2.20 to 33.40. Two-tone exterior paint (chassis & cabs and pickups): $16.15. Two-tone exterior paint (Panels and Carryalls): $26.90. Heavy-duty radiator: $21.55. Manual control radio: $47.90. Auxiliary seat for Panel: $48.45. Full-depth foam seat: $21.55. Heavy-duty starting motor: $21.55. Tachometer for 283 engine: $48.45. 21.0 gal. fuel tank for Cab models: $8.10. Heavy-duty 4-speed transmission: $96.85. Full-view rear window: $43.05. Electric 2-speed windshield wipers and washers: $16.15.

HISTORICAL FOOTNOTES: Model Year production of all Chevrolet trucks was 621,354.

1967 PICKUP

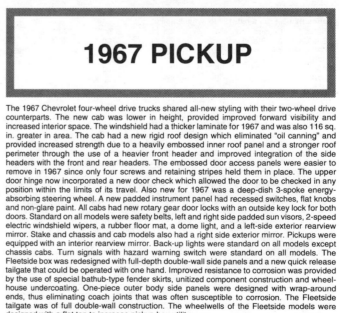

The 1967 Chevrolet four-wheel drive trucks shared all-new styling with their two-wheel drive counterparts. The new cab was lower in height, provided improved forward visibility and increased interior space. The windshield had a thicker laminate for 1967 and was also 116 sq. in. greater in area. The cab had a new rigid roof design which eliminated "oil canning" and provided increased strength due to a heavily embossed inner roof panel and a stronger roof perimeter through the use of a heavier front header and improved integration of the side headers with the front and rear headers. The embossed door access panels were easier to remove in 1967 since only four screws and retaining stripes held them in place. The upper door hinge now incorporated a new door check which allowed the door to be checked in any position within the limits of its travel. Also new for 1967 was a deep-dish 3-spoke energy-absorbing steering wheel. A new padded instrument panel had recessed switches, flat knobs and non-glare paint. All cabs had new rotary gear door locks with an outside key lock for both doors. Standard on all models were safety belts, left and right side padded sun visors, 2-speed electric windshield wipers, a rubber floor mat, a dome light, and a left-side exterior rearview mirror. Stake and chassis and cab models also had a right side exterior mirror. Pickups were equipped with an interior rearview mirror. Back-up lights were standard on all models except chassis cabs. Turn signals with hazard warning switch were standard on all models. The Fleetside box was redesigned with full-depth double-wall side panels and a new quick release tailgate that could be operated with one hand. Improved resistance to corrosion was provided by the use of special bathub-type fender skirts, unitized component construction and wheel-house undercoating. One-piece outer body side panels were designed with wrap-around ends, thus eliminating coach joints that was often susceptible to corrosion. The Fleetside tailgate was of full double-wall construction. The wheelwells of the Fleetside models were designed with a flat top to increase pickup box utility.

The use of a redesigned powertrain configuration on the four-wheel drive models resulted in a reduction of five inches in their overall height. No reduction was made in the ground clearance of the transfer case which remained at 12.5 in. The major revision in the four-wheel drive setup was the relocation of the transfer case to a higher position where it was attached directly to the transmission. The four-wheel drive frame continued to be of a heavier gauge than that used on two-wheel drive models. Both the front and rear leaf springs were of a new weight-saving tapered leaf design which also reduced inter-leaf friction and provided a smoother ride. For the first time the 327 cu. in. V-8 engine was offered as an option. The standard 6-cylinder engine had a new camshaft and valve springs as well as improved oil delivery. A new dual brakes system was installed on all models. The brakes operated through two master cylinders during normal braking. Damage to a hydraulic line was isolated by a pressure valve and stopping power was maintained at front or rear wheels. A caution light on the instrument panel indicated low pressure during this situation.

1967 Chevrolet Stepside and Fleetside pickups

The standard cab interior was fitted with a color-keyed bench seat upholstered in vinyl with foam cushions over a steel spring base. The Custom cab equipment included a full-depth foam seat with color-keyed woven fabric and vinyl trim, left and right hand armrest, right-hand padded sun visor, cigarette lighter, cowl insulation, underbody coating and embossed vinyl door trim panels with bright retainer. Bucket seats were available for all conventional models. This option consisted of bucket-type seats for the driver and right-hand passenger and a console-type seat for the center passenger. The console seat was a padded cushion which could be raised to reach a storage console. The padded backrest provided for the center passenger could be folded down to provide an armrest for the driver and passenger. The seats were covered in textured vinyl. The seat backs were fixed, with the driver's seat adjustable fore and aft. Available for all Fleetside and Stepside pickups as well as the chassis and cab models was a new Custom Sport Truck (CST) option. This included use of bright metal trim for the grille opening, headlights and windshield. A CST emblem was installed on the doors just below the window sill. The CST interior featured bucket seats and a center console seat, The floor and fuel tank were carpeted. Additional CST content included a chrome front bumper, bright metal frames for the clutch, brake and accelerator pedals, chrome-trimmed instrument knobs and horn button, right-hand padded sun visor and underbody coating.

I.D. DATA: The serial number was stamped on a plate mounted on the upper left hinge pillar The first entry, a letter K, denoted a four-wheel drive truck. Next came two digits representing the series designation. The body or chassis type was next identified by a single digit. The model year was represented by the number 6. The assembly plant code in the form of a letter followed. The last six entries were numbers indicating the unit number build which began at 100,001 at each assembly plant regardless of series. The engine number for the 6-cyl. engine was stamped on the right side of the block next to the distributor. On V-8 engines it was stamped on the forward edge of the block protruding from under the right cylinder head.

Model Number	Body Type & Seating	Factory Price	GVW	Shipping Weight	Prod. Total
Series K10-1/2 ton 6-cyl. 115 in. wheelbase					
KS10703	Chassis and Cab	$2718	4600*	3195	—
KS10704	6.5 ft. Stepside Pickup	$2834	4600	3540	1046
KS10734	6.5 ft. Fleetside Pickup	$2872	4600	3605	—
KS10904	8 ft. Stepside Pickup	$2872	4600	3620	—
KS10934	8 ft. Fleetside Pickup	$2909	4600	3710	2715
KS10905	Panel, 127 in. wb.	$3290	4600	—	—
KS10906	Suburb.127 in. wb.	$3523	4600	—	—

* 5600 lb. GVW optional.

Model Number	Body Type & Seating	Factory Price	GVW	Shipping Weight	Prod. Total
Series K20-3/4 ton 6-cyl. 127 in. wheelbase					
KS20903	Chassis and Cab	$2911	5700*	3540	—
KS20904	8 ft. Stepside Pickup	$3076	5700	3940	872
KS20934	8 ft. Fleetside Pickup	$3074	5700	4030	2773
KS20909	8 ft. Stake	$3126	5700	4165	—
KS20905	Panel	$3455	5700	—	—
KS20906	Suburban	$3685	5700	—	—

* 7600 lb. GVW optional.

STANDARD ENGINE: All models: 250 Six. Engine Type: OHV, In-line 6-cylinder. Cast iron block and cylinder head. Key features include 12-counterweight crankshaft and torsional damper, and molybdenum-filled top piston rings. Bore x Stroke: 3./875 in. x 3.53 in. Lifters: Hydraulic. Number of main bearings-7. Fuel Induction: Single Rochester 1-bbl. carburetor, model 7028007/7028011. Compression Ratio: 8.5:1. Displacement: 250 cu. in. (4.09 liters). Horsepower: Gross: 155 @ 4000 rpm. Net: 125 @ 3800 rpm. Torque: Gross: 235 lb.-ft. @ 2000 rpm. Net: 220 lb.-ft. @ 1600 rpm. Oil refill capacity: 5 qt. with filter change. Fuel Requirements: Regular.

STANDARD ENGINE: V-8 models: 283 V-8. Engine Type: OHV, V-8. Cast iron block and cylinder head. Key features include aerotype valve mechanism, and steel-backed babbitt bearings. Bore x Stroke: 3.875 in. x 3.00 in. Lifters: Hydraulic. Number of main bearings-5. Fuel Induction: Single Rochester 2-bbl. carburetor. Compression Ratio: 9.0:1. Displacement: 283 cu. in. (4.63 liters). Horsepower: Gross: 175 @ 4400 rpm. Net: 145 @ 4200 rpm. Torque: Gross: 275 lb.-ft. @ 2400 rpm. Net: 245 lb.-ft. @ 2000 rpm. Oil refill capacity: 5 qt. with filter change. Fuel Requirements: Regular.

OPTIONAL ENGINE: 6-cyl. models: 292 Six. Engine Type: OHV, 6-cyl. Cast iron block and cylinder head. Key features include aluminized intake valves, automatic rotors on exhaust valves, full-chromed top piston rings, and premium aluminum bearings. Bore x Stroke: 3.875 in. x 4.125 in. Lifters: Hydraulic. Number of main bearings-7. Fuel Induction: Single Rochester 1-bbl. carburetor. Model 7028001/7028011. Compression Ratio: 8.0:1. Displacement: 292 cu. in. (4.78 liters). Horsepower: Gross: 170 @ 4200 rpm. Net: 153 @ 3600 rpm. Torque: Gross: 275 lb.-ft. @ 1600 rpm. Net: 255 lb.-ft. @ 2400 rpm. Oil refill capacity: 6 qt. Fuel Requirements: Regular.

OPTIONAL ENGINE: V-8 models: 327 V-8. Engine Type: OHV, V-8. Cast iron block and alloy iron cylinder head. Key features include chain drive camshaft, molybdenum-filed top piston rings, premium aluminum main bearings. Bore x Stroke: 4.0 in. x 3.25 in. Lifters: Hydraulic. Number of main bearings-5. Fuel Induction: Single Rochester 4-bbl. carburetor. Model 4G. Compression Ratio: 8.5:1. Displacement: 327 cu. in. (5.35 liters). Horsepower: Gross: 220 @ 4400 rpm. Net: 177 @ 4000 rpm. Torque: Gross: 320 lb.-ft. @ 2800 rpm. Net: 283 lb.-ft. @ 2400 rpm. Oil refill capacity: 5 qt. with filter change. Fuel Requirements: Regular.

CHASSIS FEATURES: Series K10 and K20: Separate body and frame. Section modules: K10: 3.62 in. Optional: 4.85 in. K20: 4.85 in.

SUSPENSION AND RUNNING GEAR: Front Suspension: Tapered shot-peened leaf springs, hydraulic shock absorbers. K10: 1450 lb. rating (at ground). K20: 1510 lb. rating (at ground). Rear Suspension: Tapered leaf springs, hydraulic shock absorbers. K10: 1800 lb. rating (at ground). K20: 1900 lb. Optional Rating: K10 and K20: 2500 lb. Front Axle Type and Capacity: K10: Full-floating, 3300 lb. capacity. Optional: None. K20: Full-floating, 3500 lb. capacity. Rear Axle Type and Capacity: K10: Semi-floating, 3300 lb. capacity. Optional: None. K20: Full-floating, 5200 lb. Final Drive Ratio: K10: Front: 3.73:1. Rear: 3.73:1. K20: 4.55:1. Rear: 4.75:1. Transfer Case: Single lever, two-speed: 1.94, 1.00:1. Brakes: Type: Hydraulic, front and rear drums. Optional: Power assisted. Wheels: K10: 15 x 5.5 6-stud disc. Optional: 16 x 5.50 and 16 x 5.0. K20: 7-17.5 x 5.25. Optional: 8-17.5 x 5.0, 8-17.5 x 5.5, 8-17.5 x 6.0. Tires: K10: 8.15 x 15. tubeless. Optional: Tubeless: 6.50 x 15, 7-17.5. Tube-type: 8.15 x 15, 7.00 x 15, 6.50 x 16. K20: Tubeless: 7-17.5. Optional: Tubeless: 8-17.5, 8-19.5. Tube-type: 7.50 x 16, 7.00 x 17, 7.50 x 17. Steering: Recirculating ball gear. Transmission: 3-speed, synchromesh manual. Optional: 4-speed manual synchromesh and close-ratio 4-speed manual synchromesh. Clutch: Diaphragm, spring. Clutch diameter: 6-cyl.: 10 in. dia. Total lining area: 100.0 sq. in. V-8: 11 in. dia. Total lining area: 124 sq. in. Optional: 6-cyl.: 11 in. dia. Total lining area: 124.0 sq. in. V-8: 12 in. dia. Total lining area: 150 sq. in.

VEHICLE DIMENSIONS: Series K10 and K20: Wheelbase: K10: 115 in. 127 in. K20: 127 in. All Suburbans and Panels: 127 in. Overall Length: 115 in. Fleetside pickups: 188.75 in. 127 in. Fleetside pickups: 208.0 in. 115 in. Stepside pickups: 188.125 in. 127 in. Stepside pickups: 208.0 in. Front/Rear Overhang: 115 in. wheelbase. pickups: 33.25 in./40.0 in. 127 in. wheelbase. pickups: 33.25 in./47.75 in.

CAPACITIES: Fuel Tank: Series K10 and K20 pickups: 20.0 gal. Optional: None.

ACCOMMODATIONS: Seating Capacity: Pickup and chassis cab models: 3 passenger. Optional: None. Suburban: 3 passenger. Optional: 6 or 9 passenger.

INSTRUMENTATION: Speedometer, odometer, fuel level gauge, warning lights for engine coolant temperature, oil pressure, battery charge.

OPTIONS: Most options were continued from 1966. A representative sampling follows. 292 cu. in. 6-cyl. engine. 327 cu. in. V-8. Power brakes. 70 amp-hr. alternator. 42, 61 or 62 amp batteries. Wooden bed floor for Fleetside models. Heavy-duty front and rear shock absorbers. Front stabilizer bar. Custom Sport Package.

HISTORICAL FOOTNOTES: The 1967 models were introduced on September 11, 1966.

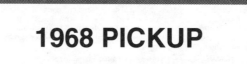

1968 PICKUP

After the introduction of all-new styling in 1967, the new model Chevrolet trucks were only modestly changed for 1968. The most apparent exterior change was the placement of safety side marker lamps on the truck's front fenders. Exterior colors for 1968 were the following: Black, dark blue, light blue, medium blue, dark green, orange, red, saddle, silver, vermillion, white, off-white, dark yellow and light yellow. Interior were offered in a choice of white or black. Basic standard equipment included painted front bumper, directional signals, Deluxe air heater and defroster, backup lights, exterior left and right side mirrors, vinyl trim full-width seat, driver and passenger seat belts with retractors, electric 2-speed windshield wipers and washer.

I.D. DATA: The 1968 model identification system consisted of 7 characters: Two letters followed by five numbers. The first letter identified the chassis type: K-4x4. The second letter identified the engine type: S-6-cylinder engine, E-V-8 engine. The first number identified the GVW designation: 1-3600-5600 lb.; 2-5600-8100 lb.; 3-6700-10,000 lb. The second and third numbers identified the cab-to-axle dimension. The last two numbers identified the body and brake type. A combination GVW and serial plate was attached to the left-hand door pillar. The first letter was the chassis designation: K-4x4. The next letter was the engine designation: S-6-cyl. E-V-8. The third entry, a number was the GVW range. The next entry, a number was the model code: 3-chassis cab, 4-Pickup, 5-Panel, 6-Carryall. The assembly plant code followed: A-Atlanta, B-Baltimore, F-Flint, Z-Fremont, J-Janesville, N-Norwood, p-Pontiac, S-St. Louis, T-Tarrytown and 1-Oshawa. The last six numbers were the vehicle number.

Models with the standard 6-cylinder engine had a KS prefix. Those with the standard V-8 engine had a KE prefix.

Model Number	Body Type & Seating	Factory Price	GVW	Shipping Weight[2]	Prod. Total
Series K10-1/2 ton 6-cyl. wheelbase					
KS10703	Chassis & Cab	$2874	4600[1]	3435	—
KS10903	Chassis & Cab, 127 in. wb.	$2911	4600	3512	—
KS10704	6.5 ft. S.S Pickup	$2985	4600	3771	—
KS10734	6.5 ft. F.S Pickup	$3022	4600	3851	—
KS10904	8 ft. Stepside Pickup	$3022	4600	3916	—
KS10934	8 ft. Fleetside Pickup	$3060	4600	4024	—
KS10905	Panel, 127 in. wb.	$3393	4600	N.A.	—

Add $97 for V-8 models with KE identification.
NOTE 1: 5600 lb. GVW optional.
NOTE 2: Curb weights.

Model Number	Body Type & Seating	Factory Price	GVW	Shipping Weight	Prod. Total
Series K20-3/4 ton 6-cyl. 127 in. wheelbase					
KS20903	Chassis and Cab	$3054	5700*	3540	—
KS20904	8 ft. Stepside Pickup	$3163	5700	3940	—
KS20934	8 ft. Fleetside Pickup	$3201	5700	4030	—
KS20905	Panel	$3534	5700	—	—

Add $96 for V-8 models with KE identification.
* 7600 lb. GVW optional.

STANDARD ENGINE: All models: 250 Six. Engine Type: OHV, In-line 6-cylinder. Cast iron block and cylinder head. Key features include 12-counterweight crankshaft and torsional damper, and molybdenum-filled top piston rings. Bore x Stroke: 3.875 in. x 3.53 in. Lifters:

Hydraulic. Number of main bearings-7. Fuel Induction: Single Rochester 1-bbl. carburetor, model 7028007/7028011. Compression Ratio: 8.5:1. Displacement: 250 cu. in. (4.09 liters). Horsepower: Gross: 155 @ 4200 rpm. Net: 125 @ 3800 rpm. Torque: Gross: 235 lb.-ft. @ 1600 rpm. Net: 215 lb.-ft. @ 2000 rpm. Oil refill capacity: 5 qt. with filter change. Fuel Requirements: Regular.

STANDARD ENGINE: KE models: 307 V-8. Engine Type: OHV, V-8. Cast iron block and cylinder head. Key features include aerotype valve mechanism, and steel-backed babbitt bearings. Bore x Stroke: 3.875 in. x 3.25 in. Lifters: Hydraulic. Number of main bearings-5. Fuel Induction: Single Rochester 2-bbl. carburetor. Compression Ratio: 9.0:1. Displacement: 307 cu. in. (5.03 liters). Horsepower: Gross: 200 @ 4600 rpm. Net: 150 @ 4000 rpm. Torque: Gross: 300 lb.-ft. @ 2400 rpm. Net: 255 lb.-ft. @ 2000 rpm. Oil refill capacity: 5 qt. with filter change. Fuel Requirements: Regular.

OPTIONAL ENGINE: KS models: 292 Six. Engine Type: OHV, 6-cyl. Cast iron block and cylinder head. Key features include aluminized intake valves, automatic rotors on exhaust valves, full-chromed top piston rings, and premium aluminum bearings. Bore x Stroke: 3.875 in. x 4.125 in. Lifters: Hydraulic. Number of main bearings-7. Fuel Induction: Single Rochester 1-bbl. carburetor. Model 7028001/7028011. Compression Ratio: 8.0:1. Displacement: 292 cu. in. (4.78 liters). Horsepower: Gross: 170 @ 4000 rpm. Net: 153 @ 3600 rpm. Torque: Gross: 275 lb.-ft. @ 1600 rpm. Net: 255 lb.-ft. @ 2400 rpm. Oil refill capacity: 6 qt. Fuel Requirements: Regular.

OPTIONAL ENGINE: KE models: 327 V-8. Engine Type: OHV, V-8. Cast iron block and alloy iron cylinder head. Key features include chain drive camshaft, molybdenum-filed top piston rings, premium aluminum main bearings. Bore x Stroke: 4.0 in. x 3.25 in. Lifters: Hydraulic. Number of main bearings-5. Fuel Induction: Single Rochester 4-bbl. carburetor. Model 4G. Compression Ratio: 8.5:1. Displacement: 327 cu. in. (5.35 liters). Horsepower: Gross: 220 @ 4400 rpm. Net: 177 @ 4000 rpm. Torque: Gross: 320 lb.-ft. @ 2800 rpm. Net: 283 lb.-ft. @ 2400 rpm. Oil refill capacity: 5 qt. with filter change. Fuel Requirements: Regular.

CHASSIS FEATURES: Separate body and frame with channel side rails K10, 115 in. wheelbase: 2.57 in. x 5.98 in. x 0.151 in. Section modules: 2.70 K10, 127 in. wheelbase: 2.57 in. x 5.98 in. x 0.186 in. Section modules: 3.48. K20, 2.57 in. x 6.98 in. x 0.186 in. Section modules: 3.48.

SUSPENSION AND RUNNING GEAR: Front Suspension: K10: 2-leaf tapered shot-peened springs. Capacity: 1450 lb. Hydraulic direct action 1.0 in. dia. shock absorbers. K20: 2-leaf tapered shot-peened springs. Capacity: 1600 lb. Hydraulic direct action 1.0 in. dia. shock absorbers. Optional rating: K10 and K20: 3-leaf tapered shot-peened springs. Capacity: 1750 lb. Rear Suspension: K10: 5-leaf tapered leaf springs, 52 in. x 2.5 in. Capacity: 1800 lb. at ground. Deflection rate: 280/420 lb./in. shock absorbers. K10: 1800 lb. rating (at ground). K20: 5-leaf tapered leaf springs, 52 in. x 2.5 in. Capacity: 1900 lb. at ground. Deflection rate: 280/420 lb./in. Hydraulic direct action 1.0 in. dia. shock absorbers. Optional Rating: K20: 2500 lb. capacity, 365/420 lb./in. deflection rate. Front Axle Type and Capacity: K10: Spicer 44, Semi-floating, 3300 lb. capacity. K20: Spicer 44, Full-floating, 3500 lb. capacity. Rear Axle Type and Capacity: K10: Semi-floating, 3300 lb. capacity. Optional: None. K20: Full-floating, 5200 lb. Final Drive Ratio: K10: Front: 3.73:1. Rear: 3.73:1. K20: 4.55:1. Rear: 4.75:1. Transfer Case: Timken Model T-221. Single lever, two-speed: 1.94, 1.00:1. Brakes: Type: Hydraulic, front and rear drums. Dimensions: K10: Front: 11.0 in. x 2.0 in. Rear: 11.0 in. x 2.0 in. Total lining area: 167 sq. in. K20: Front: 12.0 in. x 2.0 in. Rear: 12.0 in. x 2.0 in. Total lining area: 185.2 sq. in. Optional: Power assisted. Wheels: K10: 15 x 5.5 6-stud disc. Optional: 16 x 5.50 and 16 x 5.0. K20: 17.5 x 5.25 8-stud disc. Optional: 17.5 x 5.0, 17.5 x 5.5, 17.5 x 6.0. Tires: K10: 8.25 x 15 tubeless. Optional: Tubeless: 7.75 x 15, 6.50 x 16, 8.00 x 16.5. Tube-type: 7.75 x 15, 8.25 x 15, 7.77 x 15, 6.50 x 16. K20: Tubeless: 8.00 x 16.5 Optional: Tubeless: 8.75 x 16.5, 9.50 x 16.5, 10.00 x 16.5 Tube-type: 7.50 x 16. Steering: Saginaw recirculating ball gear. Steering wheel diameter: 17.5 in. Ratio: 29.9:1. Optional: Power-assisted. Transmission: Chevrolet 3-speed, heavy-duty fully-synchromesh manual. Transmission Ratios: 3.03, 1.75, 1.00:1. Reverse: 3.02:1. Optional: Chevrolet CH465 4-speed manual synchromesh. Ratios: 6.55, 3.58, 1.70, 1.00:1. Reverse: 6.09:1. Clutch: Diaphragm, spring. Clutch diameter: 6-cyl.: 10 in. dia. (11.0 in. with 292 6-cyl.) Total lining area: 100.0 sq. in. (11.0 in.-124 sq. in.). Total plate pressure: 1875 lb. V-8: 12 in. dia. Total lining area: 150 sq. in. Total plate pressure: 1877 lb.

VEHICLE DIMENSIONS: Wheelbase: K10: 115 in. 127 in. K20: 127 in. All Suburbans and Panels: 127 in. Overall Length: 115 in. Fleetside pickups: 188.75 in. 127 in. Fleetside pickups: 208.0 in. 115 in. Stepside pickups: 188.125 in. 127 in. Stepside pickups: 208.0 in. Overall Height: K10: 72.5 in. K20: 73.25 in. K10 Panel: 74.5 in. Width: Pickup: 79 in. Panel. Front/Rear Overhang: 115 in. wheelbase pickups: 33.25 in./40.25 in. 127 in. wheelbase. pickups: 33.25 in./47.50 in. Tailgate: Width and Height: 50 in. x 19.25 in. Ground Clearance: Lowest point: K10 Stepside: Front axle: 7.25 in. Rear axle: 7.5 in. K10 Fleetside: Front axle: 7.25 in. Rear axle: 7.0 in. K20 Stepside and Fleetside: Front axle: 8.75 in. Rear axle: 7.75 in. Load space: Pickup box dimensions: Stepside115 in. wheelbase: 78 in. x 50 in. x 17.5 in. Fleetside 115 in. wheelbase: 78 in. x 60 in. x 17.5 in. Stepside 127 in. wheelbase: 98 in. x 50 in. x 17.5 in. Fleetside 127 in. wheelbase: 98 in. x 66 in. x 17.5 in. Capacity: 115 in. wheelbase: 39.7 cu. ft. 127 in. wheelbase: 49.8 cu. ft. Front headroom: 40 in. Front legroom: 40.75 in. Front shoulder room: 58 in. Front hip room: 64.75 in. Steering wheel to seat back (max.): 14.7 in.

CAPACITIES: Fuel Tank: pickups: 21.0 gal. Panels: 23.5 gal. Optional: None.

ACCOMMODATIONS: Seating Capacity: 3 passenger. Seat Dimensions: 58.75 in.

INSTRUMENTATION: Speedometer, odometer, fuel gauge. Warning lights for generator, oil pressure, engine coolant temperature, brake system.

OPTIONS AND PRICES: 292 6-cyl. engine (KS10 only): $96.85. 327 V-8 (KE10 only): $43.05. 4-spd. manual trans.: $96.85. Oil-bath, 1 qt. air cleaner: $10.80. Heavy-duty air cleaner: $53.80. All-Weather air conditioning: $378.25. Heavy-duty front axle (K20): $161.40. Driver and passenger armrests: $8.65. Driver side armrest (Panel only): $4.35. Auxiliary battery: 43.05. Heavy-duty 66 amp-hr. battery: $7.55. Seat belt for third passenger: $6.50. Power brakes: $45.20. Painted rear bumper: $23.70. Rear step painted bumper: $45.20. Chromed front and rear bumpers: $49.50 (Pickups), $25.85. (Panel). Front chromed bumper: $12.95. Rear chromed bumper: $36.60. Side-mounted spare wheel carrier: $14 (Fleetside), $16.15-21.55 depending on wheelcover and hubcap format. Heavy-duty, 11.0 in. clutch for 250 engine): $5.40. Heavy-duty radiator: $21.55. Heavy-duty radiator and extra-heavy-duty cooling: $46.30. Custom Comfort and Appearance Package: $31.25 (Panels), $86.10, (pickups and cab models). Custom side molding: $26.90 (chassis & cab and Stepside), $43.05 (Fleetside, also includes pickup box moldings), $43.05 (Panels). Custom Sport Truck Package: $161.40. Fuel filter: $7.55. Gauge Package. Includes ammeter, oil pressure and engine coolant temperature: $10.80. Gauge Package. Includes ammeter, oil pressure tachometer and engine coolant temperature: $48.45. 42 amp Delcotron: $21.55. 61 amp Delcotron: $30.15 62 amp Delcotron: $89.35. Soft-Ray glass: $15 (all windows), $14 (windshield only). Governor: $17.25. Door edge guards: $3.25. Camper body wiring: $16.15. Shoulder harness: $26.90. Heater and Defroster Deletion: $68.35 credit. Two front towing hooks: $16.15. Free-wheeling hubs (K10 only): $78.55. Marker lamps: $26.90. Side wheel carrier lock: $6.50. Swing arm exterior mirrors: $6.50. West Coast type, 6 in. x 11 in.: $18.30. West Coast type, 7 in. x 16 in.: $31.25. Non-glare interior mirror: $8.65. Two-tone paint: $16.15 (pickups), $26.90 (Panels). Two-tone anniversary gold with off-white secondary color: $49.50 (Fleetside), $31.25 (Stepside). Push-button radio: $58.65. Bucket seats: $113 (with Custom Sport truck), $139 (without Custom Sport truck). Speed warning indicator: $12.95. Heavy-duty front springs (K10): $32.30. Heavy-duty starter motor: $14 (without air conditioning), $29.10 (with air conditioning). Body side paint stripes: $7.55 (Stepside), $10.80 (Fleetside).

HISTORICAL FOOTNOTES: Chevrolet established an all-time sales and production record in 1968. Calendar year production of all models was 680,499.

1969 PICKUP

The 1969 four-wheel drive Chevrolets had a revised front end appearance dominated by a large blue Bow Tie in the leading edge of the hood. A wide aluminum center grille bar carried large CHEVROLET lettering. The headlights were positioned within nacelles that were integrated into the center grille bar. A new low-profile steering wheel was standard for all models. Also debuting in 1969 was a new foot-operated parking brake and a reconstructed seat back construction with wire springs and a four inch thick foam pad intended to lessen driver fatigue. Contributing to a reduced noise level within the cab were improvements in body sealing and new body mounts. Chevrolet replaced the 327 V-8 was the 350 cu. in. V-8. Power steering was now optional for four-wheel drive models. Standard equipment content of the 1969 four-wheel drive trucks included dome light, rubber floor mat, dual sun visors, back-up lights and directional signals, panoramic rear window, side marker reflectors, left-hand and right-hand outside rearview mirrors, heater and defroster, and self-adjusting brakes. The standard interior of embossed vinyl was available in one of these colors: Saddle, blue, green, red, black and turquoise. Exterior colors for 1969 were maroon, black, dark blue, light blue, olive green, dark green, light green, orange, red, yellow metallic, silver, saddle metallic, white, turquoise metallic and dark yellow. The Custom Comfort and Appearance option contained the following exterior items: Bright metal around the windshield, rear window and ventiplanes, Custom nameplates on front fenders, color-keyed vinyl-coated rubber floor mat, full-depth foam seat with color-keyed fabric and vinyl trim, vinyl trim door panels with bright upper retainers, cigarette lighter, Chevrolet custom nameplate on dispatch box door, bright metal control knob inserts, cowl insulation and full-depth armrests. The Custom Sport Truck option had in addition to, or in place of the contents of the Custom Comfort and Appearance option, these items: Chrome front bumper, CST nameplate on front fenders, full-vinyl seats, full-width vinyl seats, bright frames for clutch, brake and accelerator, bright roof trim moldings and extra insulation. The matching floor carpet also extended into the toeboard region. Bucket seats with a center console were also optional for the CST models. The standard interior of embossed vinyl as well as the optional interiors was available in one of these colors: Saddle, blue, green, red, black and turquoise. A total of twelve pickup and six chassis-cab models as well as eight Suburban models were available. A new standard 3-speed synchromesh manual transmission with a steering column-mounted shift lever was standard. A 4-speed manual transmission with a floor-mounted shift lever was optional.

1969 Chevrolet Series 10 Fleetside pickup

I.D. DATA: Unchanged from 1968. The final six digits served as the production sequence, beginning with 100001. The engine number for the 6-cyl. engine was stamped on the right side of the block next to the distributor. On V-8 engines it was stamped on the forward edge of the block protruding from under the right cylinder head. Models with the standard 6-cylinder engine had a KS prefix. Those with the standard V-8 engine had a KE prefix.

Model Number	Body Type & Seating	Factory Price	GVW	Shipping Weight	Prod. Total
Series K10-1/2 ton 6-cyl. 115 in. wheelbase					
KS10703	Chassis and Cab	$2936	4600*	3316	—
KS10704	6.5 ft. Stepside Pickup	$3047	4600	3652	1698
KS10734	6.5 ft. Fleetside Pickup	$3085	4600	3732	1649
KS10904	8 ft. Stepside Pickup	$3085	4600	3651	521
KS10934	8 ft. Fleetside Pickup	$3123	4600	3836	4937
KS10905	Panel, 127 in. wb.	$3513	4600	3935	—
KS10906	Suburb.127 in. wb.	$3749	4600	4024	—

* 5800 lb. GVW optional.

Model Number	Body Type & Seating	Factory Price	GVW	Shipping Weight	Prod. Total
Series K20-3/4 ton 6-cyl. 127 in. wheelbase					
KS20903	Chassis and Cab	$3205	6400*	3626	—
KS20904	8 ft. Stepside Pickup	$3315	6400	4025	1071
KS20934	8 ft. Fleetside Pickup	$3353	6400	4131	6124
KS20909	8 ft. Stake	$3423	6400	4165	—
KS20905	Panel	$3763	6400	4212	—
KS20906	Suburban	$4040	6400	4316	545

* 7500 lb. GVW optional.

STANDARD ENGINE: KS models: 250 Six. Engine Type: OHV, In-line 6-cylinder. Cast iron block and cylinder head. Key features include 12-counterweight crankshaft and torsional damper, and molybdenum-filled top piston rings. Bore x Stroke: 3.875 in. x 3.53 in. Lifters: Hydraulic. Number of main bearings-7. Fuel Induction: Single Rochester 1-bbl. carburetor, model 7028007/7028011. Compression Ratio: 8.5:1. Displacement: 250 cu. in. (4.09 liters).

Horsepower: Gross: 155 @ 4200 rpm. Net: 125 @ 3800 rpm. Torque: Gross: 235 lb.-ft. @ 1600 rpm. Net: 215 lb.-ft. @ 2000 rpm. Oil refill capacity: 5 qt. with filter change. Fuel Requirements: Regular.

STANDARD ENGINE: KE models: 307 V-8. Engine Type: OHV, V-8. Cast iron block and cylinder head. Key features include aerotype valve mechanism, and steel-backed babbitt bearings. Bore x Stroke: 3.875 in. x 3.25 in. Lifters: Hydraulic. Number of main bearings-5. Fuel Induction: Single Rochester 2-bbl. carburetor. Compression Ratio: 9.0:1. Displacement: 307 cu. in. (5.03 liters). Horsepower: Gross: 200 @ 4600 rpm. Net: 157 @ 4000 rpm. Torque: Gross: 300 lb.-ft. @ 2400 rpm. Net: 260 lb.-ft. @ 2000 rpm. Oil refill capacity: 5 qt. with filter change. Fuel Requirements: Regular.

OPTIONAL ENGINE: KS models: 292 Six. Engine Type: OHV, 6-cyl. Cast iron block and cylinder head. Key features include aluminized intake valves, automatic rotors on exhaust valves, full-chromed top piston rings, and premium aluminum bearings. Bore x Stroke: 3.875 in. x 4.125 in. Lifters: Hydraulic. Number of main bearings-7. Fuel Induction: Single Rochester 1-bbl. carburetor. Model 7028001/7028011. Compression Ratio: 8.0:1. Displacement: 292 cu. in. (4.78 liters). Horsepower: Gross: 170 @ 4000 rpm. Net: 153 @ 3600 rpm. Torque: Gross: 275 lb.-ft. @ 1600 rpm. Net: 255 lb.-ft. @ 2400 rpm. Oil refill capacity: 6 qt. Fuel Requirements: Regular.

OPTIONAL ENGINE: KE models: 350 V-8. Engine Type: OHV, V-8. Cast iron block and alloy iron cylinder head. Key features include chain drive camshaft, "Rotocoil" exhaust valve rotators, special coating applied to exhaust valves to reduce deposit formation, molybdenum-filed top piston rings, premium aluminum main bearings. Bore x Stroke: 4.0 in. x 3.50 in. Lifters: Hydraulic. Number of main bearings-5. Fuel Induction: Single Rochester 4-bbl. carburetor. Compression Ratio: 9.0:1. Displacement: 350 cu. in. (5.73 liters). Horsepower: Gross: 255 @ 4600 rpm. Net: 200 @ 4000 rpm. Torque: Gross: 355 lb.-ft. @ 3000 rpm. Net: 315 lb.-ft. @ 2400 rpm. Oil refill capacity: 5 qt. with filter change. Fuel Requirements: Regular.

CHASSIS FEATURES: Separate body and frame with channel side rails K10, 115 in. wheelbase: 2.57 in. x 5.98 in. x 0.151 in. Section modules: 2.70 K10, 127 in. wheelbase: 2.57 in. x 5.98 in. x 0.186 in. Section modules: 3.48. K20, 2.57 in. x 6.98 in. x 0.186 in. Section modules: 3.48.

SUSPENSION AND RUNNING GEAR: Front Suspension: K10: 2-leaf tapered shot-peened springs. Capacity: 1450 lb. Hydraulic direct action 1.0 in. dia. shock absorbers. K20: 2-leaf tapered shot-peened springs. Capacity: 1600 lb. Hydraulic direct action 1.0 in. dia. shock absorbers. Optional rating: K10 and K20: 3-leaf tapered shot-peened springs. Capacity: 1750 lb. Rear Suspension: K10: 5-leaf tapered leaf springs, 52 in. x 2.5 in. Capacity: 1800 lb. at ground. Deflection rate: 280/420 lb./in. shock absorbers. K10: 1800 lb. rating (at ground). K20: 5-leaf tapered leaf springs, 52 in. x 2.5 in. Capacity: 1900 lb. at ground. Deflection rate: 280/420 lb./in. Hydraulic direct action 1.0 in. dia. shock absorbers. Optional Rating: K20: 2500 lb. capacity, 365/420 lb./in. deflection rate. Front Axle Type and Capacity: K10: Spicer 44, Semi-floating, 3300 lb. capacity. K20: Spicer 44, Full-floating, 3500 lb. capacity. Rear Axle Type and Capacity: K10: Semi-floating, 3300 lb. capacity. Optional: None. K20: Full-floating, 5200 lb. Final Drive Ratio: K10: Front: 3.73:1. Rear: 3.73:1. K20: 4.55:1. Rear: 4.75:1. Transfer Case: Timken Model T-221. Single lever, two-speed: 1.94, 1.00:1. Brakes: Type: Hydraulic, front and rear drums. Dimensions: K10: Front: 11.0 in. x 2.0 in. Rear: 11.0 in. x 2.0 in. Total lining area: 167 sq. in. K20: Front: 12.0 in. x 2.0 in. Rear: 12.0 in. x 2.0 in. Total lining area: 185.2 sq. in. Optional: Power assisted. Wheels: K10: 15 x 5.5 6-stud disc. Optional: 16 x 5.50 and 16 x 5.0. K20: 17.5 x 5.25 8-stud disc. Optional: 17.5 x 5.0, 17.5 x 5.5, 17.5 x 6.0. Tires: K10: 8.25 x 15 tubeless. Optional: Tubeless: 7.75 x 15, 6.50 x 16, 8.00 x 16.5. Tube-type: 7.75 x 15, 8.25 x 15, 7.77 x 15, 6.50 x 16. K20: Tubeless: 8.00 x 16.5 Optional: Tubeless: 8.75 x 16.5, 9.50 x 16.5, 10.00 x 16.5 Tube-type: 7.50 x 16. Steering: Saginaw recirculating ball gear. Steering wheel diameter: 17.5 in. Ratio: 29.9:1. Optional: Power-assisted. Transmission: Chevrolet 3-speed, heavy-duty fully-synchromesh manual. Transmission Ratios: 3.03, 1.75, 1.00:1. Reverse: 3.02:1. Optional: Chevrolet CH465 4-speed manual synchromesh. Ratios: 6.55, 3.58, 1.70, 1.00:1. Reverse: 6.09:1. Clutch: Diaphragm, spring. Clutch diameter: 6-cyl.: 10 in. dia. (11.0 in. with 292 6-cyl.) Total lining area: 100.0 sq. in. (11.0 in.-124 sq. in.) Total plate pressure: 1875 lb. V-8: 12 in. dia. Total lining area: 150 sq. in. Total plate pressure: 1877 lb.

VEHICLE DIMENSIONS: Wheelbase: K10: 115 in. 127 in. K20: 127 in. All Suburbans and Panels: 127 in. Overall Length: 115 in. Fleetside pickups: 188.75 in. 127 in. Fleetside pickups: 208.0 in. 115 in. Stepside pickups: 188.125 in. 127 in. Stepside pickups: 208.0 in. Overall Height: K10: 72.5 in. K20: 73.25 in. K10 Panel: 74.5 in. Width: Pickup: 79 in. Panel. Front/Rear Overhang: 115 in. wheelbase pickups: 33.25 in./40.25 in. 127 in. wheelbase. pickups: 33.25 in./47.50 in. Tailgate: Width and Height: 50 in. x 19.25 in. Ground Clearance: Lowest point: K10 Stepside: Front axle: 7.25 in. Rear axle: 7.5 in. K10 Fleetside: Front axle: 7.25 in. Rear axle: 7.0 in. K20 Stepside and Fleetside: Front axle: 8.75 in. Rear axle: 7.75 in. Load space: Pickup box dimensions: Stepside115 in. wheelbase: 78 in. x 50 in. x 17.5 in. Fleetside 115 in. wheelbase: 78 in. x 60 in. x 17.5 in. Stepside 127 in. wheelbase: 98 in. x 50 in. x 17.5 in. Fleetside 127 in. wheelbase: 98 in. x 66 in. x 17.5 in. Capacity: 115 in. wheelbase: 39.7 cu. ft. 127 in. wheelbase: 49.8 cu. ft. Front headroom: 40 in. Front legroom: 40.75 in. Front shoulder room: 58 in. Front hip room: 64.75 in. Steering wheel to seat back (max.): 14.7 in.

CAPACITIES: Fuel Tank: pickups: 21.0 gal. Panels: 23.5 gal. Optional: None.

ACCOMMODATIONS: Seating Capacity: 3 passenger. Seat Dimensions: 58.75 in.

INSTRUMENTATION: Speedometer, odometer, fuel gauge. Warning lights for generator, oil pressure, engine coolant temperature, brake system.

OPTIONS AND PRICES: With the exception of the addition of power steering, and the replacement of the 327 V-8 cu. in. with the 350 cu. in. V-8, the options offered were unchanged from 1968.

HISTORICAL FOOTNOTES: The 1969 models debuted in the fall of 1968. The 350 cu. in. V-8 was introduced. Total model year production of all Chevrolet trucks was 684,748.

1970 PICKUP

The exterior of the 1970 Chevrolet was set apart from that of the1969 model by its use of a modified grille insert of two sets (one above the grille divider, the second, below) of rectangular finned segments. Half-ton models had new bias ply, glass-belted tires. Chevrolet noted that the lower profile and wider tread of the advantage of these tires offered increased traction and improved handling. In addition, they ran cooler and had a longer service life. The 3/4 ton models were fitted with larger 8.75 x 16.5 highway nylon cord tires. Introduced as an option for the 3/4 ton Fleetside pickups was an auxiliary frame-mounted fuel tank positioned just behind the rear axle. Trucks with this option had their spare tire carrier moved towards the rear on frame extension supports. The flow of fuel from either tank was controlled by a manually-operated valve on the floor next to the left side of the driver's seat. Depending on the position of a dash-mounted toggle switch, the fuel level in each tank was read on the same fuel gauge.

Another new option for Fleetside models was a storage compartment located just ahead of the right rear wheel housing. It measured 7 in. x 28 in. x 127 in. It was fitted with a lockable flush-mounted steel door of double-panel construction.

1970 Chevrolet K20 Fleetside with 292 engine (and incorrect C/20 id)

Also added to the option list for 1970 was an adjustable tilting steering column that locked into seven different positions and an AM/FM radio with built-in 8-track tape player. For the first time Turbo Hydra-Matic was available for four-wheel drive models. It was used along with a new type transfer case designed to offer quieter operation and easier shifting into four-wheel drive. Four wheel drive models were also equipped with a new 40 degree steer front axle that reduced the turning radius. A maximum traction rear axle was also introduced as an option. Both 1/2 ton and 3/4 ton models had revised standard axle ratios. The 1/2 ton models with the 350 cu. in. V-8 had a 3.07:1 ratio in place of the 3.73:1 used in 1969. The 3/4 ton standard axle with the 350-V-8 now was 4.10:1 instead of 4.57:1. As in 1969 a total of twelve pickup and six chassis-cab models were offered with four wheel drive. Standard equipment for the pickup models included self-adjusting brakes, dual master cylinder brake system with warning light, back-up lights, directional signals and four-way flasher, side marker and reflectors, left-hand and right-hand exterior rearview mirrors, non-glare interior rearview mirror and heater and defroster. Among the safety related standard equipment found on all models were the following: Energy-absorbing padded instrument panel and sun visors, thick-laminate windshield, non-glare finish on top of dash and instrument panel insert, safety door locks and hinges, low-profile steering wheel, windshield washers and defrosters and 2-speed electric windshield wipers. The standard interior had a 3 passenger bench seat with foam padding, dome light, rubber floor mat and dual armrests. Exterior elements of the Custom Comfort and Appearance option included bright metal around the front and rear windows plus bright ventipane frames and custom nameplates on front fenders. Interior items included color-keyed rubber floor mat, full-depth foam seat with color-keyed fabric and vinyl trim, vinyl trim door panels, cigarette lighter, Custom nameplate on glove box door and cowl insulation. The Custom Sport Truck option included a chrome front bumper, CST nameplate on front fenders, full-width vinyl seats, bright frames for clutch, brake and accelerator pedals, extra insulation, carpeting and cargo light. The CST option was also available with new two-tone color combinations. All interiors were available in a choice of any one of six colors: Saddle, blue, green, red, black, and turquoise. Among the exterior colors offered were black, white, yellow, medium bronze metallic, medium red, medium olive metallic, dark olive, metallic, ochre and red orange.

I.D. DATA: Unchanged from 1969. Models with the standard 6-cylinder engine had a KS prefix. Those with the standard V-8 engine had a KE prefix.

Model Number	Body Type & Seating	Factory Price	GVW	Shipping Weight	Prod. Total
Series K10-1/2 ton 6-cyl. 115 in. wheelbase					
KS10703	Chassis and Cab	$2975	5200*	3295	—
KS10704	6.5 ft. Stepside Pickup	$3090	5200	3631	1629
KS10734	6.5 ft. Fleetside Pickup	$3158	5200	3711	2554
KS10904	8 ft. Stepside Pickup	$3158	5200	3715	464
KS10934	8 ft. Fleetside Pickup	$3165	5200	3810	7348
KS10905	Panel, 127 in. wb.	$3641	5200	3923	—
KS10906	Suburb.127 in. wb.	$3849	5200	4055	—

* 5600 lb. GVW optional.

Model Number	Body Type & Seating	Factory Price	GVW	Shipping Weight	Prod. Total
Series K20-3/4 ton 6-cyl. 127 in. wheelbase					
KS20903	Chassis and Cab	$3402	6400*	3606	—
KS20904	8 ft. Stepside Pickup	$3502	6400	4006	—
KS20934	8 ft. Fleetside Pickup	$3540	6400	4101	—
KS20905	Panel	$4019	6400	4221	—
KS20906	Suburban	$4190	6400	4343	541

* 7500 lb. GVW optional.

STANDARD ENGINE: KS series: 250 Six. Engine Type: OHV, In-line 6-cylinder. Cast iron block and cylinder head. Key features include 12-counterweight crankshaft and torsional damper, and molybdenum-filled top piston rings. Bore x Stroke: 3.875 in. x 3.53 in. Lifters: Hydraulic. Number of main bearings-7. Fuel Induction: Single Rochester 1-bbl. carburetor, model 7028007/7028011. Compression Ratio: 8.5:1. Displacement: 250 cu. in. (4.09 liters). Horsepower: Gross: 155 @ 4000 rpm. Net: 120 @ 3800 rpm. Torque: Gross: 235 lb.-ft. @ 2000 rpm. Net: 210 lb.-ft. @ 2000 rpm. Oil refill capacity: 5 qt. with filter change. Fuel Requirements: Regular.

OPTIONAL ENGINE: KS series: 292 Six. Engine Type: OHV, 6-cyl. Cast iron block and cylinder head. Key features include aluminized intake valves, automatic "Rotocoil" rotors on exhaust valves, special coating applied to exhaust valves to reduce deposit formation, full-chromed top piston rings, and premium aluminum bearings. Bore x Stroke: 3.875 in. x 4.125 in. Lifters: Hydraulic. Number of main bearings-7. Fuel Induction: Single Rochester 1-bbl. carburetor. Model 7028001/7028011. Compression Ratio: 8.5:1. Displacement: 292 cu. in. (4.78 liters). Horsepower: Gross: 170 @ 4000 rpm. Net: 153 @ 3600 rpm. Torque: Gross: 275 lb.-ft. @ 1600 rpm. Net: 240 lb.-ft. @ 1800 rpm. Oil refill capacity: 6 qt. Fuel Requirements: Regular.

STANDARD ENGINE: KE models: 307 V-8. Engine Type: OHV, V-8. Cast iron block and cylinder head. Key features include aerotype valve mechanism, and steel-backed babbitt bearings. Bore x Stroke: 3.875 in. x 3.25 in. Lifters: Hydraulic. Number of main bearings-5. Fuel Induction: Single Rochester 2-bbl. carburetor. Compression Ratio: 9.0:1. Displacement: 307 cu. in. (5.03 liters). Horsepower: Gross: 200 @ 4600 rpm. Net: 157 @ 4000 rpm. Torque: Gross: 300 lb.-ft. @ 2400 rpm. Net: 260 lb.-ft. @ 2000 rpm. Oil refill capacity: 5 qt. with filter change. Fuel Requirements: Regular.

OPTIONAL ENGINE: KE models: 350 V-8. Engine Type: OHV, V-8. Cast iron block and alloy iron cylinder head. Key features include chain drive camshaft, "Rotocoil" exhaust valve rotators, special coating applied to exhaust valves to reduce deposit formation, molybdenum-filed top piston rings, premium aluminum main bearings. Bore x Stroke: 4.0 in. x 3.50 in.

Lifters: Hydraulic. Number of main bearings-5. Fuel Induction: Single Rochester 4-bbl. carburetor. Compression Ratio: 9.0:1. Displacement: 350 cu. in. (5.73 liters). Horsepower: Gross: 255 @ 4600 rpm. Net: 200 @ 4000 rpm. Torque: Gross: 355 lb.-ft. @ 3000 rpm. Net: 315 lb.-ft. @ 2400 rpm. Oil refill capacity: 5 qt. with filter change. Fuel Requirements: Regular.

CHASSIS FEATURES: Separate body and frame with channel side rails KE-1500, 115 in. wheelbase: 2.57 in. x 5.98 in. x 0.151 in. Section modules: 2.70 KE-1500, 127 in. wheelbase: 2.57 in. x 5.98 in. x 0.186 in. Section modules: 3.48. K20, 2.57 in. x 6.98 in. x 0.186 in. Section modules: 3.48.

SUSPENSION AND RUNNING GEAR: Front Suspension: K10: 2-leaf tapered shot-peened springs. Capacity: 1450 lb. Hydraulic direct action 1.0 in. dia. shock absorbers. K20: 2-leaf tapered shot-peened springs. Capacity: 1600 lb. Hydraulic direct action 1.0 in. dia. shock absorbers. Optional rating: K10 and K20: 3-leaf tapered shot-peened springs. Capacity: 1750 lb. Rear Suspension: K10: 5-leaf tapered leaf springs, 52 in. x 2.5 in. Capacity: 1800 lb. at ground. Deflection rate: 280/420 lb./in. shock absorbers. K20: 5-leaf tapered leaf springs, 52 in. x 2.5 in. Capacity: 1900 lb. at ground. Deflection rate: 280/420 lb./in. Hydraulic direct action 1.0 in. dia. shock absorbers. Optional Rating: K20: 2500 lb. capacity, 365/420 lb./in. deflection rate. Front Axle Type and Capacity: K10: Spicer 44, Semi-floating, 3300 lb. capacity. K20: Spicer 44, Full-floating, 3500 lb. capacity. Rear Axle Type and Capacity: K10: Semi-floating, 3300 lb. capacity. Optional: None. K20: Full-floating, 5200 lb. Final Drive Ratio: K10: Front: 3.73:1. Rear: 3.73:1. K20: 4.55:1. Rear: 4.75:1. K10 with 350 cu. in. V-8: 3.07:1. K20 with 350-V-8: 4.10:1. Transfer Case: New Process 205. Single lever, two-speed: 1.96, 1.00:1. Brakes: Type: Hydraulic, front and rear drums. Dimensions: K10: Front: 11.0 in. x 2.0 in. Rear: 11.0 in. x 2.0 in. Total lining area: 167 sq. in. K20: Front: 12.0 in. x 2.0 in. Rear: 12.0 in. x 2.0 in. Total lining area: 185.2 sq. in. Optional: Power assisted. Wheels: K10: 15 x 5.5 6-stud disc. Optional: 16 x 5.50 and 16 x 5.0. K20: 17.5 x 5.25 8-stud disc. Optional: 17.5 x 5.0, 17.5 x 5.5, 17.5 x 6.0. Tires: K1500: G78 x 15B tubeless. Optional: Tubeless: H78 x 15B. Tube-type: G78 x 15B, 7.00 x 15, 6.50 x 16. K2500: Tubeless: 8.75 x 16.5 Optional: Tubeless: 10.00 x 16.5, 9.50 x 16.5, Tube-type: 7.50 x 16, 6.50 x 16. Steering: Saginaw recirculating ball gear. Steering wheel diameter: 17.5 in. Ratio: 24:1. Optional: Power-assisted. Transmission: SM-330 3-speed, heavy-duty fully-synchromesh manual. Transmission Ratios: 3.03, 1.75, 1.00:1. Reverse: 3.02:1. Optional: SM465 4-speed manual synchromesh. Ratios: 6.55, 3.58, 1.70, 1.00:1. Reverse: 6.09:1. Optional: Hydra-Matic automatic 3-speed automatic. Clutch: Diaphragm, spring. Clutch diameter: 6-cyl.: 10 in. dia. (11.0 in. with 292 6-cyl.) Total lining area: 100.0 sq. in. (11.0 in.-124 sq. in.) Total plate pressure: 1875 lb. V-8: 12 in. dia. Total lining area: 150 sq. in. Total plate pressure: 1877 lb.

VEHICLE DIMENSIONS: Wheelbase: K10: 115 in. 127 in. K20: 127 in. All Suburbans and Panels: 127 in. Overall Length: 115 in. Fleetside pickups: 188.75 in. 127 in. Fleetside pickups: 208.0 in. 115 in. Stepside pickups: 188.125 in. 127 in. Stepside pickups: 208.0 in. Overall Height: K10: 72.5 in. K20: 73.25 in. K10 Panel: 74.5 in. Width: Pickup: 79 in. Panel. Front/Rear Overhang: 115 in. wheelbase pickups: 33.25 in./40.25 in. 127 in. wheelbase. pickups: 33.25 in./47.50 in. Tailgate: Width and Height: 50 in. x 17.5 in. Ground Clearance: Lowest point: K10 Stepside: Front axle: 7.25 in. Rear axle: 7.5 in. K10 Fleetside: Front axle: 7.25 in. Rear axle: 7.0 in. K20 Stepside and Fleetside: Front axle: 8.75 in. Rear axle: 7.75 in. Suburban Carryall: Front axle: 7.25 in. Rear axle: 7.5 in. Load space: Pickup box dimensions: Fleetside 115 in. wheelbase: 78 in. x 60 in. x 17.5 in. Stepside 127 in. wheelbase: 98 in. x 50 in. x 17.5 in. Fleetside 127 in. wheelbase: 98 in. x 66 in. x 17.5 in. Capacity: 115 in. wheelbase: 39.7 cu. ft. 127 in. wheelbase: 49.8 cu. ft. Front headroom: 40 in. Front legroom: 40.75 in. Front shoulder room: 58 in. Front hip room: 64.75 in. Steering wheel to seat back (max.): 14.7 in.

CAPACITIES: Fuel Tank: pickups: 20.0 gal. Panels and Suburbans: 21.0 gal. Optional: None.

ACCOMMODATIONS: Seating Capacity: Pickup: 3 passenger. Suburban: Up to 9 passengers. Seat Dimensions: 58.75 in.

INSTRUMENTATION: Speedometer, odometer, fuel gauge. Warning lights for generator, oil pressure, engine coolant temperature, brake system.

OPTIONS AND PRICES: 292 cu. in. 6-cyl. engine. 350 cu. in. V-8. Power brakes. Power steering. Wooden bed floor for Fleetside models. Tachometer. AM radio. Air conditioning. Heavy-duty front and rear shock absorbers. Front stabilizer bar. Chrome below eye-level mirror. Armrests. Engine block heater. Cab clearance lights. Pickup side step. Front bumper guards. Chrome front bumper. Painted rear bumper. Door edge guards. Heavy-duty air cleaner. Heavy-duty battery. Heavy-duty clutch. Heavy-duty cooling. Heavy-duty generator, Heavy-duty front and rear springs. Heavy-duty starter. Tinted glass. Two-tone paint. Bucket seats and console. Bright pickup box hand rails. Super Custom Package. Adjustable tilting steering column. AM/FM radio with 8-track tape player.

HISTORICAL FOOTNOTES: Model year output of all versions of Chevrolet's truck line was 492,607.

1971 PICKUP

Chevrolet endowed its 1971 four-wheel drive trucks with a handsome new front end highlighted by a grille treatment reminiscent of that introduced on the 1955 Chevrolet passenger cars. Naturally, it therefore had a simple, yet elegant egg-crate insert that was well-suited to the businesslike and rugged character of the four-wheel drive truck. Other changes for1971 included the repositioning of the Chevrolet bow-tie from the leading edge of the hood to a location in the grille center. The parking/directional lights were moved to the lower portion of the bumper. They were now amber instead of white. A total of 14 pickup and chassis-cab four-wheel drive models were offered along with the Suburban models. The standard Custom interior/exterior provided a 3 passenger bench seat with foam padding. It was vinyl covered and available in a choice of black, blue, green or parchment. The vinyl-covered instrument panel and low-profile steering wheel were color-keyed to the interior/exterior. All interior hardware had a bright metal finish. Exterior elements included front and rear side marker lights and reflectors, left-and right-hand chrome-plated rearview mirrors, bright series and disc brake designation, and painted front bumper. The optional Custom Deluxe trim level contained a 3 passenger bench seat in a patterned cloth and vinyl upholstery offered in black, blue, parchment or olive. A vinyl-coated, color-keyed floor mat was included along with a cigarette lighter, dual horns, special insulation and door-operated dome light switches. The Custom Deluxe exterior included all Custom trim items plus bright metal windshield and rear window moldings, and bright ventipane frames. New for 1971 was the Cheyenne package which, said Chevrolet, was "the one you could drive to the Met and hold your head high." It consisted of a 3 passenger bench seat with full-depth foam padding trimmed in deluxe all-vinyl. The door panels were finished in the same material. The interior color selection was black, blue, saddle, parchment or olive. The floor was carpeted and a color-keyed headliner with a bright metal frame was installed. Other elements were dual horns, cigarette lighter, bright pedal trim, special insulation and door-operated dome light switches. The Cheyenne was also available with bucket seats and a center console at extra cost. The Cheyenne exterior included all items from the Custom and Custom Deluxe packages plus Cheyenne nameplates, chrome front bumper, and a cargo compartment light. Fleetside pickups with the Cheyenne option also had bright lower body side moldings, fuel filler cap and tailgate trim.

1971 Chevrolet K20 Fleetside pickup

Additional standard equipment on all models included a sealed side-terminal battery (54 plate/2350 watts for 250 L-6 and 307 V-8; 66 plate/2900 watts for 292 L-6 and 350 V-8 engines), dual brake system with warning light, high-intensity Power-Beam headlights, back-up lights, directional signals with 4-way flasher, "panoramic" rear window, 2-speed electric windshield wipers, windshield washer, right-hand coat hook and heater/defroster. A major development was the use of front disc brakes as standard equipment. New rear finned brake drums were standard for the K10.

A total of 15 exterior colors were offered for 1971 as follows: Black, white, yellow, medium bronze metallic, medium red, medium olive metallic, dark olive metallic, ochre, red orange, orange, dark yellow, medium green, dark green, medium blue and dark blue. The last six listed were new for 1971.

I.D. DATA: A vehicle identification number was stamped on a combination vehicle identification number and rating plate located on the left door pillar. It contained 12 units. The first, a letter K, identified the truck as a four-wheel drive. The second entry, also a letter, identified the engine type. A letter S designated a 6-cyl. engine; an E identified a V-8 engine. Next followed a letter which identified the GVW range. A number 1 represented a 1/2 ton truck; a number 2 represented a 3/4 ton truck. Another number was next in the sequence. It provided information about the body type as follows: 3-Cab-chassis; 4-Cab and pickup box. The 1971 model year was next represented by a number 1. A letter or a number, according to the following scheme, next identified the assembly plant: A-Lakewood, B-Baltimore, C-Southgate, D-Doraville, F-Flint, G-Framingham, J-Janesville, K-Leeds, L-Van Nuys, N-Norwood, p-GM Truck-Pontiac, R-Arlington, S-St. Louis. T-Tarrytown. U-Lordstown, W-Willow Run, Y-Wilmington, Z-Fremont, 1-Oshawa, 2-Ste. Therese. The final six entries were the unit number. The starting unit number was 600001 or 800001 at each assembly plant regardless of series. The engine number for the 6-cyl. engine was stamped on a boss on the right side of the engine block to the rear of the distributor. On V-8 engines it was stamped on a boss on the right front of the engine block.

Model Number	Body Type & Seating	Factory Price	GVW	Shipping Weight	Prod. Total
Series K10-1/2 ton 6-cyl. 115 in. wheelbase					
KS10704	6.5 ft. Stepside Pickup	$3414	5200	3739	—
KS10734	6.5 ft. Fleetside Pickup	$3414	5200	3824	3068[2]
KS10904	8 ft. Stepside Pickup	$3451	5200	3832	—
KS10934	8 ft. Fleetside Pickup	$3351	5200	3927	9417
KS10906	Suburban Panl. Doors	$4226	5200	4191	—
KS10916	Suburban Endgate	$4256	5200	4191	—

NOTE 1: 5600 lb. GVW optional.
NOTE 2: Production figures are for KE models.

Models with the standard 6-cylinder engine had a KS prefix. Those with the standard V-8 engine had a KE prefix. The price of an equivalent KE with a 307 V-8 is $121 above that of the respective KS in the K10 series and $124 for the K20 series.

Model Number	Body Type & Seating	Factory Price	GVW	Shipping Weight	Prod. Total
Series K20-3/4 ton 6-cyl. 127 in. wheelbase					
KS20903	Chassis and Cab	$3641	6400*	3659	—
KS20904	8 ft. Stepside Pickup	$3804	6400	4061	—
KS20934	8 ft. Fleetside Pickup	$3804	6400	4156	—
KS20906	Suburban Pnl. Doors	$4530	6400	4414	—
KS20916	Suburban End gate	$4538	6400	4414	—

* 7500 lb. GVW optional.

STANDARD ENGINE: KS models: 250 Six. Engine Type: OHV, In-line 6-cylinder. Cast iron block and cylinder head. Key features include 12-counterweight crankshaft and torsional damper, and molybdenum-filled top piston rings. Bore x Stroke: 3.875 in. x 3.53 in. Lifters: Hydraulic. Number of main bearings-7. Fuel Induction: Single Rochester 1-bbl. carburetor. Compression Ratio: 8.5:1. Displacement: 250 cu. in. (4.09 liters). Horsepower: Gross: 145 @ 4200 rpm. Net: 110 @ 4000 rpm. Torque: Gross: 230 lb.-ft. @ 1600 rpm. Net: 185 lb.-ft. @ 1600 rpm. Oil refill capacity: 5 qt. with filter change. Fuel Requirements: Regular or reduced lead content fuel.

STANDARD ENGINE: KE models: 307 V-8. Engine Type: OHV, V-8. Cast iron block and cylinder head. Key features include aerotype valve mechanism, and steel-backed babbitt bearings. Bore x Stroke: 3.875 in. x 3.25 in. Lifters: Hydraulic. Number of main bearings-5. Fuel Induction: Single Rochester 2-bbl. carburetor. Compression Ratio: 8.5:1. Displacement: 307 cu. in. (5.03 liters). Horsepower: Series 10: Gross: 200 @ 4600 rpm. Net: 135 @ 4000 rpm. Series 20: Gross: 215 @ 4800 rpm. Net: 135 @ 4000 rpm. Torque: Series 10: Gross: 300 lb.-ft. @ 2400 rpm. Net: 235 lb.-ft. @ 2400 rpm. Series 20: 305 lb.-ft. @ 2800 rpm. Net: 230 lb.-ft. @ 2000 rpm. Oil refill capacity: 5 qt. with filter change. Fuel Requirements: Regular or reduced lead content fuel.

OPTIONAL ENGINE: KS models: 292 Six. Engine Type: OHV, 6-cyl. Cast iron block and cylinder head. Key features include aluminized intake valves, automatic "Rotocoil" rotors on exhaust valves, special coating applied to exhaust valves to reduce deposit formation, full-chromed top piston rings, and premium aluminum bearings. Bore x Stroke: 3.875 in. x 4.125 in. Lifters: Hydraulic. Number of main bearings-7. Fuel Induction: Single Rochester 1-bbl. carburetor. Compression Ratio: 8.0:1. Displacement: 292 cu. in. (4.78 liters). Horsepower: Gross: 165 @ 4000 rpm. Net: 130 @ 4400 rpm. Torque: Gross: 270 lb.-ft. @ 1600 rpm. Net: 225 lb.-ft. @ 1800 rpm. Oil refill capacity: 6 qt. Fuel Requirements: Regular or reduced lead content fuel.

OPTIONAL ENGINE: KS models: 350 V-8. Engine Type: OHV, V-8. Cast iron block and alloy iron cylinder head. Key features include chain drive camshaft, "Rotocoil" exhaust valve rotators, special coating applied to exhaust valves to reduce deposit formation, molybdenum-filed top piston rings, premium aluminum main bearings. Bore x Stroke: 4.0 in. x 3.50 in.

Lifters: Hydraulic. Number of main bearings-5. Fuel Induction: Single Rochester 4-bbl. carburetor. Compression Ratio: 8.5:1. Displacement: 350 cu. in. (5.73 liters). Horsepower: Gross: 250 @ 4600 rpm. Net: 190 @ 4000 rpm. Torque: Gross: 350 lb.-ft. @ 3000 rpm. Net: 310 lb.-ft. @ 2400 rpm. Oil refill capacity: 5 qt. with filter change. Fuel Requirements: Regular or reduced lead content fuel.

CHASSIS FEATURES: Separate body and frame with channel side rails K10, 115 in. wheelbase: 2.57 in. x 5.98 in. x 0.151 in. Section modules: 2.70 K10, 127 in. wheelbase: 2.57 in. x 5.98 in. x 0.186 in. Section modules: 3.48. K20, 2.57 in. x 6.98 in. x 0.186 in. Section modules: 3.48.

SUSPENSION AND RUNNING GEAR: Front Suspension: K10: 2-leaf tapered shot-peened springs. Capacity: 1450 lb. Hydraulic direct action 1.0 in. dia. shock absorbers. K20: 2-leaf tapered shot-peened springs. Capacity: 1600 lb. Hydraulic direct action 1.0 in. dia. shock absorbers. Optional rating: K10 and K20: 3-leaf tapered shot-peened springs. Capacity: 1750 lb. Rear Suspension: K10: 5-leaf tapered leaf springs, 52 in. x 2.5 in. Capacity: 1800 lb. at ground. Deflection rate: 280/420 lb./in. shock absorbers. K20: 5-leaf tapered leaf springs, 52 in. x 2.5 in. Capacity: 1900 lb. at ground. Deflection rate: 280/420 lb./in. Hydraulic direct action 1.0 in. dia. shock absorbers. Optional Rating: K20: 2500 lb. capacity, 365/420 lb./in. deflection rate. Front Axle Type and Capacity: K10: Spicer 44, Semi-floating, 3300 lb. capacity. K20: Spicer 44, Full-floating, 3500 lb. capacity. Rear Axle Type and Capacity: K10: Semi-floating, 3300 lb. capacity. Optional: None. K20: Full-floating, 5200 lb. Final Drive Ratio: K10: Front and rear: 3.73:1. K20: Front: 4.55:1, Rear: 4.57:1. Transfer Case: Single lever, two-speed: 1.94, 1.00:1. Brakes: Type: Hydraulic, front disc and rear drums. Dimensions: K10: Front: 11.86 in. rotor. Rear: 11.0 in. x 2.0 in. Rear brake area: 138.2 sq. in. Lining area: 84.4 sq. in. K20: Front: 12.50 in. rotor. Rear: 12.0 in. x 2.0 in. Rear brake area: 150.8 sq. in. Lining area: 89.0 sq. in. Optional: Power assisted. Wheels: K10: 15 x 6.0 6-stud disc. K20: 16.5 x 5.25 8-stud disc. Tires: K10: G78 x 15B tubeless. Optional: Tube-type tires: G78 x 15B, 6.50 x 16C. Tubeless: H78 x 15B, G78 x 15B, 10.00 x 16.5C. K20: Tubeless: 8.75 x 16.5 Optional: Tubeless: 10.00 x 16.5, 9.50 x 16.5, Tube-type: 7.50 x 16, 6.50 x 16, plus numerous other sizes. Steering: Saginaw recirculating ball gear. Steering wheel diameter: 17.5 in. Ratio: 24:1. Optional: Power-assisted. Transmission: SM-330 3-speed, heavy-duty fully-synchromesh manual. Transmission Ratios: 3.03, 1.75, 1.00:1. Reverse: 3.02:1. Optional: SM465 4-speed manual synchromesh. Ratios: 6.55, 3.58, 1.70, 1.00:1. Reverse: 6.09:1. Optional: Turbo Hydra-Matic automatic 3-speed automatic. Clutch: Diaphragm, spring. Clutch diameter: 6-cyl.: 10 in. dia. (11.0 in. with 292 6-cyl.) Total lining area: 100.0 sq. in. (11.0 in.-124 sq. in.) Total plate pressure: 1875 lb. V-8: 12 in. dia. Total lining area: 150 sq. in. Total plate pressure: 1877 lb.

VEHICLE DIMENSIONS: Wheelbase: K10: 115 in. 127 in. K20: 127 in. All Suburbans and Panels: 127 in. Overall Length: 115 in. Fleetside pickups: 188.75 in. 127 in. Fleetside pickups: 208.0 in. 115 in. Stepside pickups: 188.125 in. 127 in. Stepside pickups: 208.0 in. Overall Height: K10: 72.5 in. K20: 73.25 in. K10 Suburban Carryall: 75.25 in. Width: Pickup: 79 in. Suburban Carryall: 78.75 in. Front/Rear Overhang: 115 in. wheelbase pickups: 33.25 in./40.25 in. 127 in. wheelbase. pickups: 33.25 in./47.50 in. Suburban Carryall: 33.25 in./55.25 in. Tailgate: Width and Height: 50 in. x 17.5 in. Ground Clearance: Lowest point: K10 Stepside: Front axle: 7.25 in. Rear axle: 7.5 in. K10 Fleetside: Front axle: 7.25 in. Rear axle: 7.0 in. K20 Stepside and Fleetside: Front axle: 8.75 in. Rear axle: 7.75 in. Suburban Carryall: Front axle: 7.25 in. Rear axle: 7.5 in. Load space: Pickup box dimensions: Fleetside 115 in. wheelbase: 78 in. x 60 in. x 17.5 in. Stepside 127 in. wheelbase: 98 in. x 50 in. x 17.5 in. Fleetside 127 in. wheelbase: 98 in. x 66 in. x 17.5 in. Capacity: 115 in. wheelbase: 39.7 cu. ft. 127 in. wheelbase: 49.8 cu. ft. Front headroom: 40 in. Front legroom: 40.75 in. Front shoulder room: 58 in. Front hip room: 64.75 in. Steering wheel to seat back (max.): 14.7 in.

CAPACITIES: Fuel Tank: pickups: 20.0 gal. Panels and Suburbans: 21.0 gal. Optional: 20.5 gal. auxiliary fuel tank for 3/4 ton Fleetsides.

ACCOMMODATIONS: Seating Capacity: 3 passenger. Seat Dimensions: 58.75 in.

INSTRUMENTATION: Speedometer, odometer, fuel gauge. Warning lights for generator, oil pressure, engine coolant temperature, brake system.

OPTIONS AND PRICES: 292 cu. in. 6-cyl. engine: $95. 307 cu. in. V-8. 350 cu. in. V-8: $45 above price of model with 307 V-8. Custom Deluxe Package: $107.60. Cheyenne Package: $210.90 (chassis and cab and Stepside), $253.95 (Fleetside). Cheyenne Super Package. Turbo Hydra-Matic: $247.50. 4-speed manual trans.: $113. Optional axle ratios: 12.95. Oil bath air cleaner: $10.80. All-Weather air conditioner (V-8 only): $430.40. Auxiliary battery: $48.45. Heavy-duty 80 amp-hr. battery: $17.25. Seat belts for third passenger: $7.00. Painted rear bumper: $23.70. Rear step bumper: $51.65. Chromed front and rear bumper: $53.80. Chromed front bumper: $16.15. Chromed rear bumper: $37.70. Chromed hubcap (K10 only): $14. Side-mounted spare wheel carrier: $15.10 (Fleetside), $17.25 (Stepside), additional cost for use with chromed wheels and covers. Heavy-duty cooling: $26.90. Wood pickup box floor for Fleetside: $20.45. Gauge Package. Includes ammeter, engine coolant temperature and oil pressure gauges: $12.95. Gauge Package. Includes tachometer, ammeter, engine coolant temperature and oil pressure gauges: $59.20. 42 amp Delcotron generator: $23.70. 61 amp Delcotron generator: $32.30. Soft-Ray tinted glass, all windows: $19.40. Door edge guards: $6.50. Camper body wire harness: $16.15. Two front towing hooks: $19.40. Front free-wheeling hubs: $78.55. Cargo area lamp: 20.45. Roof marker lamps: $26.90. Exterior below eye-level painted mirrors: $21. Exterior below eye-level stainless steel mirrors: $37.70. Camper style painted mirrors: $21. Camper style stainless steel mirrors: $52.75. Two-tone paint with white secondary color: $26.90. Custom two-tone paint: $26.90. Deluxe two-tone paint: $123.75, $80.70 (with Cheyenne and Cheyenne Super). AM radio: $69.95. AM/FM radio: $151.75. Front bucket seats: $148.50, $121.60 (with Cheyenne). Full depth foam seat: 30.15. Front and rear heavy-duty shock absorbers: $16.15. Front 1750 lb. springs: $33.40. Rear 2500 lb. springs (K20): $19.40. Power steering: $150.65. ComforTilt steering wheel: $59.20. Body side paint stripes: $14. Door operated dome lamp switch: $4.35. Manual throttle control: $15.10. Sliding rear window: 53.80.

HISTORICAL FOOTNOTES: Chevrolet produced 48,993 four-wheel drive recreational vehicles in 1971.

1972 PICKUP

With its all-new series ready for introduction in1973, Chevrolet made only minor changes in the exterior appearance of its four-wheel drive models for 1972. The most apparent revision was the elimination of the black finish of the grille surround. The interior of the1972 models had new molded door trim panels incorporating integral armrests with foam padding. A fair number of technical developments were, however, offered for the 1972 model year. Both the 307 and 350 cu. in. V-8 engines now had exhaust valve rotators. The exhaust valves used in the 350 V-8 were now Stellite plated. The 250 cu. in. 6-cylinder engine was fitted with an improved automatic choke as well as higher quality spark plug leads. Replacing the 3300 lb.-rated rear axle on the K10 models was a 3500 lb.-rated unit. Rear brakes on the 3/4 ton models had revised measurements of 11 in. x 2.75 in. instead of 12 in. x 2.0 in. as used in 1971. This change yielded a net increase of 25 sq. in. of brake swept area. A number of new dealer-installed items were added to the list of available options. These included a coolant recovery system and a wrap-around electric blanket for the battery. This item plugged into a 110-volt outlet.

The 1972 Suburban was no longer available with the 292 cu. in. 6-cylinder engine. A new vinyl side body trim was offered for the Suburban models. The Suburban's optional air conditioning system was modified to include a front-mounted condenser and blower in conjunction with corresponding revised rear units. The front system, which also served as the Suburban's heating system, could be ordered separately or with the rear system. If the latter arrangement was chosen, there were individually-controlled front and rear outlets. The rear outlets were integral, unlike the older system in which they were routed to the back along with the full length ceiling duct.

I.D. DATA: A vehicle identification number was stamped on a combination vehicle identification number and rating plate located on the left door pillar. It contained 12 units. The first, a letter K, identified the truck as a four-wheel drive. The second entry, also a letter, identified the engine type. A letter S designated a 6-cyl. engine; an E identified a V-8 engine. Next followed a letter which identified the GVW range. A number 1 represented a 1/2 ton truck; a number 2 represented a 3/4 ton truck. Another number was next in the sequence. It provided information about the body type as follows: 3-Cab-chassis; 4-Cab and pickup box. The 1972 model year was next represented by a number 2. A letter or a number, according to the following scheme, next identified the assembly plant: A-Lakewood, B-Baltimore, C-Southgate, D-Doraville, F-Flint, G-Framingham, J-Janesville, K-Leeds, L-Van Nuys, N-Norwood, p-GM Truck-Pontiac, R-Arlington, S-St. Louis. T-Tarrytown. U-Lordstown, W-Willow Run, Y-Wilmington, Z-Fremont, 1-Oshawa, 2-Ste. Therese. The final six entries were the unit number. The starting unit number was 600001 or 800001 at each assembly plant regardless of series. The engine number for the 6-cyl. engine was stamped on a boss on the right side of the engine block to the rear of the distributor. On V-8 engines it was stamped on a boss on the right front of the engine block.

Model Number	Body Type & Seating	Factory Price	GVW	Shipping Weight	Prod. Total
Series K10-1/2 ton 6-cyl. 115 in. wheelbase					
KS10704	6.5 ft. Stepside Pickup	$3251	5200	3766	—
KS10734	6.5 ft. Fleetside Pickup	$3251	5200	3836	3068
KS10904	8 ft. Stepside Pickup	$3287	5200	3846	—
KS10934	8 ft. Fleetside Pickup	$3287	5200	3926	9417
KS10906	Suburban Pnl. Doors	$4273	5200	4206	—
KS10916	Suburban Endgate	$4305	5200	4206	—

* 5600 lb. GVW optional.

Model Number	Body Type & Seating	Factory Price	GVW	Shipping Weight	Prod. Total
Series K20-3/4 ton 6-cyl. 127 in. wheelbase					
KS20903	Chassis and Cab	$3415	6400*	3651	676
KS20904	8 ft. Stepside Pickup	$3567	6400	4051	—
KS20934	8 ft. Fleetside Pickup	$3567	6400	4141	—
KS20906	Suburban Pnl. Doors	$4275	6400	4141	—
KS20916	Suburban Endgate	$4307	6400	4585	—

* 7500 lb. GVW optional.

Models with the standard 6-cylinder engine had a KS prefix. Those with the standard V-8 engine had a KE prefix. The price of an equivalent K10 model with a 307 V-8 is $120 above that of the 6-cyl. model. The price differential for K20 is $124.

STANDARD ENGINE: KS models: 250 Six. Engine Type: OHV, In-line 6-cylinder. Cast iron block and cylinder head. Key features include 12-counterweight crankshaft and torsional damper, and molybdenum-filled top piston rings. Bore x Stroke: 3.875 in. x 3.53 in. Lifters: Hydraulic. Number of main bearings-7. Fuel Induction: Single Rochester 1-bbl. carburetor. Compression Ratio: 8.5:1. Displacement: 250 cu. in. (4.09 liters). Horsepower: Gross: 145 @ 4200 rpm. Net: 110 @ 4000 rpm. Torque: Gross: 230 lb.-ft. @ 1600 rpm. Net: 185 lb.-ft. @ 1600 rpm. Oil refill capacity: 5 qt. with filter change. Fuel Requirements: Regular or reduced lead content fuel.

STANDARD ENGINE: KE models: 307 V-8. Engine Type: OHV, V-8. Cast iron block and cylinder head. Key features include aerotype valve mechanism, and steel-backed babbitt bearings. Bore x Stroke: 3.875 in. x 3.25 in. Lifters: Hydraulic. Number of main bearings-5. Fuel Induction: Single Rochester 2-bbl. carburetor. Compression Ratio: 8.5:1. Displacement: 307 cu. in. (5.03 liters). Horsepower: Series 10: Gross: 200 @ 4600 rpm. Net: 135 @ 4000 rpm. Series 20: Gross: 215 @ 4800 rpm. Net: 135 @ 4000 rpm. Torque: Series 10: Gross: 300 lb.-ft. @ 2400 rpm. Net: 235 lb.-ft. @ 2400 rpm. Series 20: 305 lb.-ft. @ 2800 rpm. Net: 230 lb.-ft. @ 2000 rpm. Oil refill capacity: 5 qt. with filter change. Fuel Requirements: Regular or reduced lead content fuel.

OPTIONAL ENGINE: KS models: 292 Six. Engine Type: OHV, 6-cyl. Cast iron block and cylinder head. Key features include aluminized intake valves, automatic "Rotocoil" rotors on exhaust valves, special coating applied to exhaust valves to reduce deposit formation, full-chromed top piston rings, and premium aluminum bearings. Bore x Stroke: 3.875 in. x 4.125 in. Lifters: Hydraulic. Number of main bearings-7. Fuel Induction: Single Rochester 1-bbl. carburetor. Compression Ratio: 8.0:1. Displacement: 292 cu. in. (4.78 liters). Horsepower: Gross: 165 @ 4000 rpm. Net: 130 @ 4400 rpm. Torque: Gross: 270 lb.-ft. @ 1600 rpm. Net: 225 lb.-ft. @ 1800 rpm. Oil refill capacity: 6 qt. with filter change. Fuel Requirements: Regular or reduced lead content fuel.

OPTIONAL ENGINE: KS models: 350 V-8. Engine Type: OHV, V-8. Cast iron block and alloy iron cylinder head. Key features include chain drive camshaft, "Rotocoil" exhaust valve rotators, special coating applied to exhaust valves to reduce deposit formation, molybdenum-filed top piston rings, premium aluminum main bearings. Bore x Stroke: 4.0 in. x 3.50 in. Lifters: Hydraulic. Number of main bearings-5. Fuel Induction: Single Rochester 4-bbl. carburetor. Compression Ratio: 8.5:1. Displacement: 350 cu. in. (5.73 liters). Horsepower: Gross: 250 @ 4600 rpm. Net: 190 @ 4000 rpm. Torque: Gross: 350 lb.-ft. @ 3000 rpm. Net: 310 lb.-ft. @ 2400 rpm. Oil refill capacity: 5 qt. with filter change. Fuel Requirements: Regular or reduced lead content fuel.

CHASSIS FEATURES: Separate body and frame with channel side rails K10, 115 in. wheelbase: 2.57 in. x 5.98 in. x 0.151 in. Section modules: 2.70. K10, 127 in. wheelbase: 2.57 in. x 5.98 in. x 0.186 in. Section modules: 3.48. K20, 2.57 in. x 6.98 in. x 0.186 in. Section modules: 3.48.

SUSPENSION AND RUNNING GEAR: Front Suspension: K10: 2-leaf tapered shot-peened springs. Capacity: 1450 lb. Hydraulic direct action 1.0 in. dia. shock absorbers. K20: 2-leaf tapered shot-peened springs. Capacity: 1600 lb. Hydraulic direct action 1.0 in. dia. shock absorbers. Optional rating: K10 and K20: 3-leaf tapered shot-peened springs. Capacity: 1750 lb. Rear Suspension: K10: 5-leaf tapered leaf springs, 52 in. x 2.5 in. Capacity: 1800 lb. at ground. Deflection rate: 280/420 lb./in. shock absorbers. K20: 5-leaf tapered leaf springs, 52 in. x 2.5 in. Capacity: 1900 lb. at ground. Deflection rate: 280/420 lb./in. Hydraulic direct action 1.0 in. dia. shock absorbers. Optional Rating: K20: 2500 lb. capacity, 365/420 lb./in. deflection rate. Front Axle Type and Capacity: K10: Spicer 44, Semi-floating, 3500 lb. capacity. K20: Spicer 44, Full-floating, 3500 lb. capacity. Rear Axle Type and Capacity: K10: Semi-floating, 3300 lb. capacity. Optional: None. K20: Full-floating, 5200 lb. Final Drive Ratio: K10: Front and rear: 3.73:1. K20: Front: 4.55:1, Rear: 4.57:1. Transfer Case: Single lever, two-speed: 1.94, 1.00:1. Brakes: Type: Hydraulic, front disc and rear drums. Dimensions: K10: Front: 11.86 in. rotor. Rear: 11.0 in. x 2.0 in. Rear brake area: 138.2 sq. in. Lining area: 84.4 sq. in. K20: Front: 12.50 in. rotor. Rear: 11.0 in. x 2.75 in. Rear brake area: 175.8 sq. in. Lining area: 89.0 sq. in. Optional: Power assisted. Wheels: K10: 15 x 6.0 6-stud disc. K20: 16.5 x 5.25 8-stud disc. Tires: K10: G78 x 15B tubeless. Optional: Tube-type tires: G78 x 15B, 6.50 x 16C. Tubeless: H78 x 15B, G78 x 15B, 10.00 x 16.5C. K20: Tubeless: 8.75 x 16.5 Optional: Tubeless: 10.00 x 16.5, 9.50 x 16.5, Tube-type: 7.50 x 16, 6.50 x 16, plus numerous other sizes. Steering: Saginaw recirculating ball gear. Steering wheel diameter: 17.5 in. Ratio: 24:1. Optional: Power-assisted. Transmission: SM-330 3-speed, heavy-duty fully-synchromesh manual. Transmission Ratios: 3.03, 1.75, 1.00:1. Reverse: 3.02:1. Optional: SM465 4-speed manual synchromesh. Ratios: 6.55, 3.58, 1.70, 1.00:1. Reverse: 6.09:1. Optional: Turbo Hydra-Matic automatic 3-speed automatic. Clutch: Diaphragm, spring. Clutch diameter: 6-cyl.: 10 in. dia. (11.0 in. with 292 6-cyl.) Total lining area: 100.0 sq. in. (11.0 in.-124 sq. in.) Total plate pressure: 1875 lb. V-8: 12 in. dia. Total lining area: 150 sq. in. Total plate pressure: 1877 lb.

VEHICLE DIMENSIONS: Wheelbase: K10: 115 in. 127 in. K20: 127 in. All Suburbans and Panels: 127 in. Overall Length: 115 in. Fleetside pickups: 188.75 in. 127 in. Fleetside pickups: 208.0 in. 115 in. Stepside pickups: 188.125 in. 127 in. Stepside pickups: 208.0 in. Overall Height: K10: 72.5 in. K20: 73.25 in. K10 Suburban Carryall: 75.25 in. Width: Pickup: 79 in. Suburban Carryall: 78.75 in. Front/Rear Overhang: 115 in. wheelbase pickups: 33.25 in./40.25 in. 127 in. wheelbase. pickups: 33.25 in./47.50 in. Suburban Carryall: 33.25 in./55.25 in. Tailgate: Width and Height: 50 in. x 17.5 in. Ground Clearance: Lowest point: K10 Stepside: Front axle: 7.25 in. Rear axle: 7.5 in. K10 Fleetside: Front axle: 7.25 in. Rear axle: 7.0 in. K20 Stepside and Fleetside: Front axle: 8.75 in. Rear axle: 7.75 in. Suburban Carryall: Front axle: 7.25 in. Rear axle: 7.5 in. Load space: Pickup box dimensions: Fleetside 115 in. wheelbase: 78 in. x 60 in. x 17.5 in. Stepside 127 in. wheelbase: 98 in. x 50 in. x 17.5 in. Fleetside 127 in. wheelbase: 98 in. x 66 in. x 17.5 in. Capacity: 115 in. wheelbase: 39.7 cu. ft. 127 in. wheelbase: 49.8 cu. ft. Front headroom: 40 in. Front legroom: 40.75 in. Front shoulder room: 58 in. Front hip room: 64.75 in. Steering wheel to seat back (max.): 14.7 in.

CAPACITIES: Fuel Tank: pickups: 20.0 gal. Panels and Suburbans: 21.0 gal. Optional: 20.5 gal. auxiliary fuel tank for 3/4 ton Fleetsides.

ACCOMMODATIONS: Seating Capacity: Pickup: 3 passenger. Suburban: 3-9 passenger. Seat Dimensions: 58.75 in.

INSTRUMENTATION: Speedometer, odometer, fuel gauge. Warning lights for generator, oil pressure, engine coolant temperature, brake system.

OPTIONS AND PRICES: Pickup models: 292 cu. in. 6-cyl. engine: $90. 307 cu. in. V-8: $120 above price of base 6-cyl. model. 350 cu. in. V-8: $49 above price of model with 307 V-8. Power steering: $140. Free-wheeling front hubs: $73. Wooden bed floor for Fleetside models: $19. Sliding rear window: $50. Limited slip rear differential: K10: $67; K20: $135. Cheyenne Super Trim Package: $265. Bucket seats and console (Cheyenne-equipped models only): $115. Turbo Hydra-Matic: $230. Special Instrumentation. Includes ammeter, oil pressure and temperature needle gauges. Available with or without tachometer. Tachometer: $43. AM radio: $65. AM/FM radio. Air conditioning: $400. Heavy-duty front and rear shock absorbers: $15. Heavy-duty front springs (K20): $6. Heavy-duty rear springs (K20): $18. Front stabilizer bar. Chrome below eye-level mirror. Armrests. Engine block heater. Cab clearance lights. Cargo compartment light. ComforTilt steering wheel: $55. Auxiliary battery: $45. Heavy-duty battery: $16. Auxiliary fuel tank: $75. Door edge guards: $6. Dual exterior camper-type rearview mirrors: $49. Camper wiring: $15. Two-tone paint: $25. Tinted glass: $18. Pickup side step. Front bumper guards. Chrome front bumper. Painted rear bumper. Rear step bumper: $48. Door edge guards. Heavy-duty air cleaner. Heavy-duty battery. Heavy-duty clutch. Heavy-duty cooling. Heavy-duty generator. Heavy-duty front and rear springs. Heavy-duty starter. Tinted glass. Bright pickup box hand rails. Tool and storage compartment. 10-16.5 tires and wheels 10-16.5 spare tire and wheel: $137. (K20): $263. Suburban: 350 V-8: $45 above price of 307-V-8 equipped models. Turbo Hydra-Matic: $242. Air conditioning: $648. Power steering: $147. Free-running front hubs: $7. Limited slip rear differential: K10: $65; K20: $132. Custom Deluxe Trim Package (with standard front seat): $186. Center seat.

HISTORICAL FOOTNOTES: The 1972 models were announced on Sept. 21, 1971.

1973 PICKUP

The Chevrolet four-wheel drive pickups were, by the standards of the day, completely new vehicles. The exterior form of the new models was extremely clean with sculptured sides, curved side windows and yet another successful rendition of the ever-green egg-crate grille format. No drip moldings were used. This change plus the new form of the cab resulted in a noticeable reduction in both wind resistance and noise. The wheel opening were now oblong rather than round as in 1972. The wheel openings were also flared to accommodate larger tires and wheels. Total glass area was increased by 528 sq. in. Total windshield area measured 1447 sq. in. The rear window area was 790 sq. in. The side door window area, including the ventipane was 546 sq. in. If a radio was ordered the radio antenna was imbedded in the windshield. The instrument panel was of a new one-piece design which was welded in place to reduce shake and vibration. Additional structural changes included a new hood fabricated from two pieces of steel that were welded together to provide improved torsional rigidity. New all-steel, one-piece inner fenders were attached to the inner front fenders for structural integrity. The Fleetside pickup box side panel/load floor assembly was redesigned to eliminate exposed flanges and bolt heads. Changes to the exhaust system involved the use of compression-positioned hangers that provided secondary support and lessened the intrusion of exhaust noise into the cab interior. The rear shock absorbers were positioned in a staggered for/aft fashion to reduce axle hop under severe acceleration and deceleration. High capacity 2-speed windshield wipers with 16 in. blades were standard as were new dual-orifice windshield washers. A new energy-absorbing/telescoping steering column provided additional protection for the driver in case of an accident.

Pickup frames were completely redesigned for 1973. The side rail thickness was increased and a new cross member design was used to allow for an increased wheelbase, frame-mounted fuel tank (the tank was located outside the cab on the right frame rail) and a new cab mounting system. The front disc brakes were now fitted with a road splash shield. At the rear wheels new finned cast iron-steel brakes were used.

The four-wheel drive models had new wide front springs with lower ride rates and a new front stabilizer bar that Chevrolet reported made a significant improvement in ride and handling. Specific changes involved the movement of the front wheels forward by 2.5 inches, which made it possible to use the longer, tapered springs while providing easier oil pan removal. Both the front and rear spring eyes were now rubber bushed. K20 models had a new Salisbury type rear axle with a rigid cast differential carrier and steel shaft tubes that were pressed and anchored in the carrier.

The new cab provided added leg, hip, head and shoulder room. A new flow-through power ventilation system provided the interior with a steady supply of outside air. This system used larger inlet valves and a larger plenum chamber. An electric fan directed the air flow through the cab to outlet valves at the bottom of each door. This system also provided for pressure relief when the doors were closed.

1973 Chevrolet K10 Fleetside pickup with Cheyenne trim

The standard Custom interior was equipped with a 3 passenger bench seat with ladder-embossed vinyl upholstery with grained vinyl bolsters and foam padding. It was offered in pearl, slate blue, saddle and slate green. Additional standard interior equipment consisted of right and left side individually controlled air vents, right and left side armrests integral with door trim panel, dash-mounted ashtray, right-side mounted coat hook, inside push-button door locks, color-keyed, embossed molded plastic door trim panels, embossed black rubber floor mat, trim rings on gauges and warning lights, white graphic instrumentation identification, soft black knobs for all controls except heater and air conditioner, color-keyed instrument panel with Custom nameplate and hardboard top, deluxe air heater and defroster, instrument cluster and courtesy/map lights operated by main switch, 10 in. vinyl edged primatic rearview mirror, three seat belts with push-button release, retractor for driver and right-side passenger, 17 in. dia. steering wheel with black finish and padded two-spoke design, right and left side padded, color-keyed sun visors and door opening scuff plates.

The Custom standard model was equipped with the following exterior items: A center-grille mounted Chevrolet emblem with bright outer edge and ochre paint fill, Custom nameplates with series designation located on the upper portion of the front fenders near the door opening, bright steel outer grille area with inner plastic grid in silver color, front white-painted bumper, back-up lights (integral with taillights on Fleetside models), side markers and reflectors, right and left side exterior mirrors with chrome fixed arms and 5.25 in. x 4.00 in. heads, single electric horn, white "CHEVROLET" lettering on tailgate (painted black on trucks with Frost White color), under frame spare tire carrier, mechanical jack, undercoating under wheel-housings and white painted wheels.

The Custom Deluxe model option (RPOI Z62) included all standard items plus the following additions or substitutions: Custom Deluxe nameplates with series designations on front fenders, rear window reveal moldings, windshield reveal moldings, door handles with black plastic insets, additional electric horn with high note, Custom Deluxe nameplate on instrument panel, dome light bezel, full length doorsill scuff plates, color-keyed molded plastic door trim panels with woodgrain insert and bright trim, color panel insulation, color-keyed rubber floor mat, full-depth foam seat cushion seat with multi-striped nylon cloth/vinyl trim in choice of pearl gray, charcoal, slate blue, saddle or avocado, special all-vinyl trim in choice of pearl gray, charcoal, slate blue, saddle or slate green also available.

The Cheyenne option (RPO Z84) included all Custom Deluxe items plus the following additions or substitutions: Cheyenne nameplates with series designations on front fenders, Chevrolet nameplate on tailgate panel, chrome front bumper, front side marker lamp moldings, front turn signal lamp moldings, cab back panel molding and applique, hubcaps (except K10 with 10.00 x 16.5 tires), upper body side trim moldings (Fleetside only), rear lamp molding (Fleetside only), tailgate upper and lower moldings with bright finish applique panel insert and nameplate (Fleetside only), cab-to-fender seal, hood insulator, Cheyenne nameplate on instrument panel, chrome transmission and transfer case levers on models with 4-speed transmission, color-keyed carpeting, color-keyed molded plastic door trim panels with storage pockets, teakwood grain inserts with chrome bead and black plastic border, color-keyed plastic headliner with retainer moldings, foam instrument panel pad with color-keyed grained vinyl cover, color-keyed molded plastic trim on windshield pillars, and all-vinyl trim bench seat in choice of pearl gray, slate blue, saddle, charcoal or slate green. A Herringbone striped nylon cloth/vinyl trimmed seat in a choice of pearl gray, charcoal, slate blue, saddle or avocado was also available.

The Cheyenne Super option (RPO YE9) included all items in the Cheyenne option plus the following additions or substitutions: Cheyenne Super nameplates with series designation on front fenders, lower body side moldings (on Fleetside only), wheel opening lip molding (Fleetside only), Cheyenne Super nameplate on instrument panel, color-keyed molded plastic trim on cowl side panels, gauges for battery, engine coolant temperature and oil pressure, bench seat with special herringbone nylon cloth and vinyl trim in a choice of pearl gray, charcoal, slate blue, saddle or avocado. A special-vinyl trim was offered in a choice of pearl gray, charcoal, slate blue, saddle or slate green.

A total of fifteen exterior colors were offered for 1973. Ten colors were new and five were carried over from 1972. The available colors were: Skyline blue, Glenwood green, Sport silver metallic, Catalina blue metallic, frost white, Hawaiian blue, Spanish gold, crimson red, burnt orange metallic, lime green metallic, sunset gold, desert sand, Mojave tan, moss olive, and Marine turquoise metallic. Chevrolet also offered three fleet colors (black, Omaha orange and Schoolbus yellow) on a no-charge COPO basis. They previously had been available as regular production colors. The fifteen primary colors were available as main body colors in association with white as a secondary color in three different two-tone paint schemes. The conventional two-tone style required RPO BX6 moldings. The Special two-tone option was offered for Fleetside models with RPO YG1 moldings. A Deluxe version was available for Fleetside models with RPO BX6 and RPO YG1.

I.D. DATA: The vehicle identification number was stamped on a plate mounted on the windshield corner post. The first entry, the letter C represented the Chevrolet division, The second entry, the letter K identified the chassis type as a four-wheel drive. The third entry, a letter, designated the engine: Q-250-6-cyl. T-292 6-cyl. V-350 V-8, Y-350 4-bbl. V-8. The Series identification, by a number, followed: 1-1/2 ton. 2-3/4 ton. The body style was next identified by a number: 3-Cab and Chassis, 4-Cab and Pickup box, 6-Suburban. The model year, 1973, was then identified by the number 3. The assembly plant identification, a letter, followed. The final six entries, numbers, were the sequential production number.

Model Number	Body Type & Seating	Factory Price	GVW	Shipping Weight	Prod. Total
Series K10-1/2 ton 350 V-8 117.5 in. 131.5 in. (Suburb.: 129.5 in. wheelbase)					
CK10703	Chassis and Cab	$3324	5200[1]	3663	—
CK10703	6.5 ft. Stepside Pickup	$3510	5200	3989	—
CK10703	6.5 ft. Fleetside Pickup	$3510	5200	4108	—
CK 10903	8 ft. Stepside Pickup	$3546	5200	4085	—
CK10903	8 ft. Fleetside Pickup	$3546	5200	4210	—
CK10906	Suburban[2]	$4338	5200	5034	—

NOTE 1: 5600 lb. and 6000 lb. GVW optional.
NOTE 2: Suburban (both K10 and K20) available with panel rear doors (ZW9) or end gate (E55).

Model Number	Body Type & Seating	Factory Price	GVW	Shipping Weight	Prod. Total
Series K20-3/4 ton 307 V-8. (Suburb.: 129.5 in. 131.5 in. wheelbase)					
CK20903	Chassis and Cab	$3562	6800[3]	4119	—
CK20903	8 ft. Stepside Pickup	$3747	6800	4514	—
CK20903	8 ft. Fleetside Pickup	$3747	6800	4640	—
CK20906	Suburb.129.5 in. wb.	$4668	6800	5136	—

NOTE 3: 7500 lb. and 8200 lb. GVW optional.

A base engine code was added to the model identification for 1973. Models with the standard 6-cylinder engine had an LD4 designation. Those with a standard 350 V-8 (K20 models) had a LG8 identification.

STANDARD ENGINE: K10, K20: 250 Six (LD4 ordering code). Engine Type: OHV, In-line 6-cylinder. Cast iron block and cylinder head. Key features include 12-counterweight crankshaft and torsional damper, and molybdenum-filled top piston rings. Bore x Stroke: 3.875 in. x 3.53 in. Lifters: Hydraulic. Number of main bearings-7. Fuel Induction: Single Rochester 1-bbl. carburetor. Compression Ratio: 8.5:1. Displacement: 250 cu. in. (4.09 liters). Horsepower: Net: 100 @ 4000 rpm. Torque: Net: 175 lb.-ft. @ 1600 rpm. Oil refill capacity: 5 qt. with filter change. Fuel Requirements: Regular.

STANDARD ENGINE: K20 V-8 models: 307 V-8 (LG8 Ordering Code). Not available in California. Engine Type: OHV, V-8. Cast iron block and cylinder head. Key features include aerotype valve mechanism, and steel-backed babbitt bearings. Bore x Stroke: 3.875 in. x 3.25 in. Lifters: Hydraulic. Number of main bearings-5. Fuel Induction: Single Rochester 2-bbl. carburetor. Compression Ratio: 8.5:1. Displacement: 307 cu. in. (5.03 liters). Horsepower: Net: 130 @ 4000 rpm. Torque: Net: 220 lb.-ft. @ 2200 rpm. Oil refill capacity: 5 qt. with filter change. Fuel Requirements: Regular.

OPTIONAL ENGINE: Available only for 6-cyl. K20 pickup models: 292 Six Ordering Code: L25. Engine Type: OHV, 6-cyl. Cast iron block and cylinder head. Key features include aluminized intake valves, automatic "Rotocoil" rotors on exhaust valves, special coating applied to exhaust valves to reduce deposit formation, full-chromed top piston rings, and premium aluminum bearings. Bore x Stroke: 3.875 in. x 4.125 in. Lifters: Hydraulic. Number of main bearings-7. Fuel Induction: Single Rochester 1-bbl. carburetor. Compression Ratio: 8.0:1. Displacement: 292 cu. in. (4.78 liters). Horsepower: Net: 120 @ 3600 rpm. Torque: Net: 215 lb.-ft. @ 2000 rpm. Oil refill capacity: 6 qt. Fuel Requirements: Regular.

OPTIONAL ENGINE: K20 V-8 models; standard for K10 V-8 models: 350 V-8. Ordering Code: LS9: 350 V-8 Engine Type: OHV, V-8. Cast iron block and alloy iron cylinder head. Key features include chain drive camshaft, "Rotocoil" exhaust valve rotators, special coating applied to exhaust valves to reduce deposit formation, molybdenum-filled top piston rings, premium aluminum main bearings. Bore x Stroke: 4.0 in. x 3.50 in. Lifters: Hydraulic. Number of main bearings-5. Fuel Induction: Single Rochester 4-bbl. carburetor. Compression Ratio: 8.5:1. Displacement: 350 cu. in. (5.73 liters). Horsepower: Net: 155 @ 4000 rpm. Torque: Net: 255 lb.-ft. @ 2400 rpm. Oil refill capacity: 5 qt. with filter change. Fuel Requirements: Regular.

CHASSIS FEATURES: Separate body and frame with channel side rails. Carbon-Steel, 39,000 psi. Section modules: 117.5 in. wheelbase: 3.06. 131.5 in. wheelbase: 3.84. Optional: None.

SUSPENSION AND RUNNING GEAR: Front Suspension: 2-leaf, tapered leaf springs 1.0 in. dia. shock absorbers. K10: 1850 lb. rating (at ground). K20: 1950 lb. rating (at ground). Optional rating: 1900 lb. (both series). Rear Suspension: 52 in. x 2.25 in. Two-stage, 5-leaf. 1.0 in. dia. shock absorbers. K10: 1700 lb. rating (at ground). K20: 2800 lb. Optional Rating: K10: 2000 lb. Front Axle Type and Capacity: K10: Spicer 44F Semi-floating. 3400 lb. capacity. Optional: None. K20: Full-floating, 3500 lb. capacity. Optional: None. Rear Axle Type and Capacity: K10: Chevrolet, Semi-floating, 3750 lb. capacity. Optional: None. K20: Chevrolet, Full-floating, 5700 lb. Final Drive Ratio: K10: Front: 6-cyl.: 4.11:1; V-8: 3.73:1. (The V-8 ratio was subsequently changed to 3.07:1. Rear: 6-cyl.: 4.11:1. V-8: 3.73:1. K20: Front: 6-cyl. and V-8: 4.56:1; V-8. Rear: 6-cyl. and V-8: 4.56:1. Optional K10: Rear: 3.73:1, 4.1:1. K20: Rear: 4.10:1, 4.56:1. Transfer Case: New Process 205. Single lever, two-speed: 1.94, 1.00:1. Brakes: Type: Hydraulic, power assisted. Dimensions: K10: Front: Disc: 11.86 in. dia. Rear: Drums: 11.0 in. x 2.0 in. K20: Front: Disc: 12.5 in. dia. Rear: Drums: 11.0 in. x 2.75 in. Optional: None. Wheels: K10: 15 x 6.0 6-stud disc. K20: 16.5 x 6.0 in. 8-stud disc. Tires: K10: G78 x 15B 4-ply rating, tubeless or tube-type. K20: 8.75 x 16.5C 6-ply rating, tubeless. Optional: K10: G78 x 15B, white stripe; H78 x 15B, tubeless, black sidewall or white stripe; L78 x 15B black sidewall or white stripe, tubeless; 10.00 x 16.5C tubeless; G78 x 15B tube-type; 7.00 x 15C tube-type; 6.50 x 16C tube-type. The following tires were specified for K10 models with the 5600 lb. GVW package which included a front heavy-duty stabilizer bar: H78 x 15B 4-ply rating, tubeless; 6.50 x 16C 6-ply rating, tube-type, truck type. The following tires were specified for K10 models with the 6000 lb. GVW Package which included a front heavy-duty stabilizer bar and heavy-duty rear springs: L78 x 15B 4-ply rating, tubeless. Optional K20: 8.75 x 16.5D tubeless; 9.50 x 16.5D tubeless; 10.00 x 16.5C tubeless (not available for Stepside models); 7.50 x 16C 6-ply rating, tube-type; 7.50 x 16D tube-type; 7.50 x 16E tube-type. The following tires were specified for K20 models with the 7500 lb. GVW Package which included a front heavy-duty stabilizer bar: 8.75 x 16.5 C 6-ply rating, tubeless; 7.50 x 16C 6-ply rating, tubeless. The following tires were specified for K20 models with the 8200 lb. GVW Package which included a front heavy-duty stabilizer bar: 9.50 x 16.5D 8-ply rating, tubeless; 7.50 x 16C 6-ply rating, tube type. Steering: Recirculating ball gear. Ratio: 20:1, turns Lock-to-Lock: 3.4. Turning Circle: 47 ft. Steering wheel diameter: 17.5 in. Optional: Power-assisted. Ratio: 16.4:1. Transmission: 3-speed, synchromesh manual (ZW4 Ordering Code). Transmission Ratios: 2.85, 1.68, 1.00:1. Optional: Chevrolet CH465. 4-speed manual synchromesh (RPO M20). Ratios: 6.55, 3.58, 1.70, 1.00:1. Optional: 3-speed Turbo Hydra-Matic (RPO M49). Ratios: 2.52, 1.52, 1.00:1. Clutch: Diaphragm, spring. Clutch diameter: K10: 6-cyl.: 10 in. dia. Total lining area: 100.0 sq. in. V-8: 12 in. dia. Total lining area: 150 sq. in. K20: 10 in. dia. Total lining area: 100.0 sq. in. V-8: 11 in. dia. Total lining area: 124.0 sq. in. K20 with 350 V-8: 12 in. dia. Total lining area: 150 sq. in. Optional: K20 6-cyl.: 11 in. dia. Total lining area: 124.0 sq. in. 307 V-8: 12 in. dia. Total lining area: 150 sq. in.

VEHICLE DIMENSIONS: Wheelbase: K10: 117.5 in. 131.5 in. K20: 131.5 in. All Suburbans and Panels: 129.5 in. Overall Length: 117.5 in. Fleetside pickups: 191.25 in. 131.5 in. Fleetside pickups: 211.25. 117.5 in. Stepside pickups: 190.5 in. 131.5 in. Stepside pickups: 210.25. Front/Rear Tread: 67.4 in./65.8 in. Overall Height: K10 Pickup and Suburban: 72.25 in. K20 Pickup and Suburban: 73.9 in. Width: Pickup: 79.5 in. Front/Rear Overhang: pickups: 33 in./41 in. Tailgate: Width and Height: 72 in. x 19.25 in. Approach/Departure Degrees: 30/21. Ground Clearance: Front axle: 7.25 in. Rear axle: 7.0 in. Oil pan: 16.5 in. Transfer case: 12.0 in. Fuel tank: 16.6 in. Load space: Pickup box dimensions: 117.5 in. wheelbase Fleetside: 78.25 in. x 50 in. x 19.25 in. 131.5 in. wheelbase Fleetside: 98 in. x 50 in. x 19.25 in. Capacity: 117.5 in. wheelbase: 58.4 cu. ft. 131.5 in. wheelbase: 74.3 cu. ft. 117.5 in. wheelbase Stepside: 78.5 in. x 50 in. x 17.5 in. 131.5 in. wheelbase Stepside: 96.25 in. x 50 in. x 17.5 in. Front headroom: 38.5 in. (seat to top of cab). Front hip room: 67.25 in. Pedal to seat back (max.): 43.5 in. Steering wheel to seat back (max.): 17.3 in. Seat to ground: 35.0 in. Floor to ground: 23.0 in.

CAPACITIES: Fuel Tank: K10: 117.5 in. wheelbase: 160 gal. 131.5 in. wheelbase: 20.0: gal. Optional: 16 gal. auxiliary for 117.5 in. wheelbase; 20 gal. for 131.5 in. wheelbase. K20: 20 gal. Optional: 20 gal. auxiliary. Coolant System Capacity: 250 6-cyl.: 14.8 qt. 292 6-cyl.: 13.6 qt. 350 V-8: 17.6 qt. (All figures for vehicles with manual transmission and without air conditioning).

ACCOMMODATIONS: Seating Capacity: Pickup and chassis cab models: 3 passenger. Optional: None. Suburban: K10: 3 passenger. K20: 6 passenger. Optional: 6 passenger (K10), 9 passenger (K10 and K20).

INSTRUMENTATION: Speedometer, odometer, fuel level gauge. Warning lights for battery, oil pressure, generator, brake system warning, directional/hazard lights, high beam, and engine coolant temperature.

OPTIONS AND PRICES: Pickup models: 292 cu. in. 6-cyl. engine-RPO L25 (K20 only). 307 cu. in. V-8-RPO LG8: $120 above price of base 6-cyl. model. 350 cu. in. V-8-RPO LS9: $161 above price of model with 307 V-8. Turbo Hydra-Matic-RPO M49. Includes extra heavy-duty cooling: $236. 4-speed manual transmission-RPO M20: $108. Positraction rear axle-RPO G80 (available for K10 only): $64. NoSPIN rear axle-RPO G86 (available for K20 only). Custom Deluxe Package. With cloth bench seat-RPO Z62/YJ4; with custom vinyl bench seat-RPO Z62/YJ5. Cheyenne Package. With Custom cloth bench seat-RPO Z84/YJ6; with custom vinyl bench seat-RPO Z84/YJ5: $213. Cheyenne Super Package. With Custom cloth bench seat-RPO YE9/YJ6; with Custom vinyl bench seat-RPO YE9/YJ5: $252. Custom Camper chassis equipment-Basic Camper Group-RPO Z81. Available with K20 V-8 models with 8200 lb. GVW and either 4-spd. manual trans. or Turbo Hydra-Matic. Requires 9.50 x 16.5D tubeless or 7.50 x 16E tube type rear tires only. Includes heavy-duty front and rear shock absorbers, heavy-duty front springs, heavy-duty front stabilizer, Custom Camper nameplate and camper body wiring harness. Deluxe Camper Group for Cab-Over Camper Bodies-RPO Z83. Available with K20 V-8 models with 8200 lb. GVW and either 4-spd. manual trans. or Turbo Hydra-Matic Requires 9.50 x 16.5D tubeless or 7.50 x 16E tube type rear tires and Fleetside body. Not available with wooden floor. Includes Basic Camper Group plus camper body tie-down brackets mounted to pickup box under body, spring loaded turn-buckles shipped loose, horizontal shock absorbers mounted between cab rear panel and pickup box side panels and vertical shock absorber brackets mounted on front fenders. Camper body wiring harness-RPO UY1. Included when Custom Camper chassis equipment is ordered. Camper-type stainless steel mirrors: RPO DF2. Poly-wrap air cleaner-RPO K43. All-Weather air conditioning-RPO C60. Auxiliary 61 amp battery-RPO TP2. Heavy-duty 80 amp battery-RPO T60. Painted rear bumper-RPO V38. Painted rear step bumper-RPO V43.Chromed front and rear bumper-RPO V37. Front chromed bumper (not available if painted rear bumper is ordered)-RPO V46. Chromed rear bumper (available only with Cheyenne or Cheyenne Super is ordered)-RPO VF1. California Assembly Line Emission Test-RPO YF5. Bright metal hubcaps (not available for K10 models with 10.00 x 16.5 tires)-RPO PO3. Side-mounted spare tire carrier-RPO P13. Electric clock (available only with gauge package, not available if tachometer is ordered)-RPO U35: $18. Heavy-duty clutch (available only for models with 250 engine and 3-spd. manual trans.)-RPO MO1. Exterior tool stowage (available for Fleetside only. Not available if auxiliary fuel tank is ordered)-RPO VK4. Coolant recovery system-RPO VQ1. Heavy-duty radiator (requires RPO VQ1)-RPO VO1. Wood 8 ft. Fleetside pickup box-RPO E81. Gauge Package-Z53: $12. Tachometer (V-8 models only, not available if electric clock is ordered)-RPO U16: $56. 42 amp Delcotron generator (not available if air conditioning is ordered)-RPO K79.61 amp Delcotron generator (included with air conditioning)-RPO K76. Soft-Ray tinted glass, all windows-RPO V22: $18. Chromed grille-RPO V22. Door edge guards (not available with woodgrained exterior trim)-RPO B93. Free-wheeling front hubs-RP F76. Cargo area lamp-RPO UF2: $19. Dome light-RPO C91. Roof marker lights-RPO U01. Cigarette lighter-RPO U37. Exterior below eye-level 7.5 in. x 10.5 in. painted mirrors-RPO D29. Exterior below eye-level 7.5 in. x 10.5 in. stainless steel mirrors-RPO DG4. Cab backpanel applique-RPO BX6. Upper body moldings. For Fleetside only. Includes fender, door cab panel, tailgate and pickup box moldings pus bright front turn signal, side marker and taillight trim-RPO B85. Upper and lower body molding (adds lower body side, tailgate and wheel opening moldings to RPO B85)-RPO YG1. Painted roof drip molding-RPO BX5. Soft instrument panel pad-RPO B70. Fuel tank shield-RPO NY1. AM radio-RPO U63: $67. AM/FM radio-RPO U69: $145. Vinyl roof cover-RPO CO8: $36. Bucket seats-RPO A50/YJ5: $135. Full-depth foam bench seat-RPO Z52. Heavy-duty front and rear shock absorbers-RPO F51: $15. Heavy-duty rear shock absorbers-RPO G68. Heavy-duty front springs-RPO F60. Heavy-duty rear springs (K10 only)-RPO G50. Heavy-duty front stabilizer-RPO F58. Power steering-RPO N40. ComforTilt steering wheel (not available with 3-spd. manual trans.)-RPO N33: $56. Custom steering wheel (available only with power steering, includes 16 in. steering wheel)-RPO N31. Auxiliary fuel tank (not avail. with K10 with 250 engine)-RPO NL2: $77. Manual throttle control (not available with air conditioning)-RPO K31. Front towing hooks-RPO V76. Bright metal wheelcovers (K10 only; not avail. with 6.50 x 16 or 10.00 x 16.5 tires)-RPO PO1. Wheel trim rings (not avail. with 10.00 x 16.5 tires on K10 or with 7.50 x 16 tires)-RPO PO6. Sliding rear window-RPO A28: $51. Exterior woodgrained trim (avail. only with Fleetside models with custom upper and lower moldings or Cheyenne Super only. Not avail. with special or deluxe two-tone paint)-RPO YG2. Suburban: 350 V-8: $45 above price of 307 V-8 equipped models. Turbo Hydra-Matic: $242. Air conditioning: $648.Power steering: $147. Free-running front hubs: $7. Limited slip rear differential: K10: $65; K20: $132. Custom Deluxe Trim Package (with standard front seat): $186.

HISTORICAL FOOTNOTES: Chevrolet took a bold step towards contemporary concepts of transportation quality by declaring "Our goal: Produce an all-new truck with zero defects."

1974 PICKUP

After introducing full-time four-wheel drive in the 1973 Blazer, Chevrolet extended this system to its four-wheel drive pickup trucks. Initially, all four-wheel drive models were equipped with the New Process 203 system, but during the model year Chevrolet reintroduced the New Process 205 part-time system for 6-cylinder models. Due to emissions controls, no 6-cylinder trucks were available for California delivery. The 307 cu. in. V-8 was not offered for the K series trucks. A brake wearing sensor was a new feature for 1974. The K10 models were now available with a 15 in. rally-styled wheel option which included a center hub and bright trim ring. Steel-belted, LR78 x 15C white sidewall radial ply tires were introduced for the K10 pickup. Added to the list of options oriented towards the camping enthusiast was a telescoping step-type bumper.

The same three trim packages Chevrolet offered in 1973-Custom, Custom Deluxe, Cheyenne and Cheyenne Super were carried over into 1974.

1974 Chevrolet K20 Fleetside pickup with Cheyenne trim

I.D. DATA: The Light Duty model series identification introduced in 1973 was continued for 1974. The number 4 represented the 1974 model year

Model Number	Body Type & Seating	Factory Price	GVW	Shipping Weight	Prod. Total
Series K10-1/2 ton 350 V-8 117.5 in. 131.5 in. (Suburb.: 129.5 in. wheelbase)					
CK10703	6.5 ft. Stepside Pickup	$3937	5200*	4020	—
CK10703	6.5 ft. Fleetside Pickup	$3937	5200	4124	—
CK10903	8 ft. Stepside Pickup	$3973	5200	4128	—
CK10903	8 ft. Fleetside Pickup	$3973	5200	4238	—
CK10906	Suburb.129.5 in wb.	$4846	5200	4578	—

* 5600 lb. and 6000 lb. GVW optional.

Model Number	Body Type & Seating	Factory Price	GVW	Shipping Weight	Prod. Total
Series K20-3/4 ton 350 V-8. 127 in. wheelbase					
CK20903	Chassis and Cab	$4087	6800*	4183	—
CK20903	8 ft. Stepside Pickup	$4254	6800	4578	—
CK20903	8 ft. Fleetside Pickup	$4254	6800	4688	—
CK20906	Suburb.129.5 in. wb.	$5753	6800	5415	—

* 7500-lb. and 8200 lb. GVW optional.

STANDARD ENGINE: K10, K20: 250 Six (LD4 ordering code). Engine Type: OHV, In-line 6-cylinder. Cast iron block and cylinder head. Key features include 12-counterweight crankshaft and torsional damper, and molybdenum-filled top piston rings. Bore x Stroke: 3.875 in. x 3.53 in. Lifters: Hydraulic. Number of main bearings-7. Fuel Induction: Single Rochester 1-bbl. carburetor. Compression Ratio: 8.5:1. Displacement: 250 cu. in. (4.09 liters). Horsepower: Net: 100 @ 4000 rpm. Torque: Net: 175 lb.-ft. @ 1600 rpm. Oil refill capacity: 5 qt. with filter change. Fuel Requirements: 91 octane.

OPTIONAL ENGINE: Available only for 6-cyl. K20 pickup models: 292 Six Ordering Code: L25. Engine Type: OHV, 6-cyl. Cast iron block and cylinder head. Key features include aluminized intake valves, automatic "Rotocoil" rotors on exhaust valves, special coating applied to exhaust valves to reduce deposit formation, full-chromed top piston rings, and premium aluminum bearings. Bore x Stroke: 3.875 in. x 4.125 in. Lifters: Hydraulic. Number of main bearings-7. Fuel Induction: Single Rochester 1-bbl. carburetor. Compression Ratio: 8.0:1. Displacement: 292 cu. in. (4.78 liters). Horsepower: Net: 120 @ 3600 rpm. Torque: Net: 215 lb.-ft. @ 2000 rpm. Oil refill capacity: 6 qt. Fuel Requirements: 91 octane.

STANDARD ENGINE: K20 V-8 models; standard for K10 V-8 models: 350 V-8. Ordering Code: LS9: 350 V-8 Engine Type: OHV, V-8. Cast iron block and alloy iron cylinder head. Key features include chain drive camshaft, "Rotocoil" exhaust valve rotators, special coating applied to exhaust valves to reduce deposit formation, molybdenum-filled top piston rings, premium aluminum main bearings. Bore x Stroke: 4.0 in. x 3.50 in. Lifters: Hydraulic. Number of main bearings-5. Fuel Induction: Single Rochester 4-bbl. carburetor. Compression Ratio: 8.5:1. Displacement: 350 cu. in. (5.73 liters). Horsepower: Net: 155 @ 4000 rpm. Torque: Net: 255 lb.-ft. @ 2400 rpm. Oil refill capacity: 5 qt. with filter change. Fuel Requirements: 91 octane.

CHASSIS FEATURES: Separate body and frame with channel side rails. Carbon-Steel, 39,000 psi. Section modules: 117.5 in. wheelbase: 3.06. 131.5 in. wheelbase: 3.84. Optional: None.

SUSPENSION AND RUNNING GEAR: Front Suspension: 2-leaf, tapered leaf springs 1.0 in. dia. shock absorbers. K10: 1850 lb. rating (at ground). K20: 1950 lb. rating (at ground). Optional rating: 1900 lb. (both series). Rear Suspension: 52 in. x 2.25 in. Two-stage, 5-leaf. 1.0 in. dia. shock absorbers. K10: 1700 lb. rating (at ground). K20: 2800 lb. Optional Rating: K10: 2000 lb. Front Axle Type and Capacity: K10: Spicer 44F Semi-floating. 3400 lb. capacity. Optional: None. K20: Full-floating, 3500 lb. capacity. Optional: None. Rear Axle Type and Capacity: K10: Chevrolet, Semi-floating, 3750 lb. capacity. Optional: None. K20: Chevrolet, Full-floating, 5700 lb. Final Drive Ratio: K10: Front: 6-cyl.: 4.11:1; V-8: 3.73:1. (The V-8 ratio was subsequently changed to 3.07:1. Rear: 6-cyl.: 4.11:1. V-8: 3.73:1. K20: Front: 6-cyl. and V-8: 4.56:1; V-8. Rear: 6-cyl. and V-8: 4.56:1. Optional K10: Rear: 3.73:1, 4.1:1. K20: Rear: 4.10:1, 4.56:1. Transfer Case: New Process 205. Single lever, two-speed: 1.94, 1.00:1. Brakes: Type: Hydraulic, power assisted. Dimensions: K10: Front: Disc: 11.86 in. dia. Rear: Drums: 11.0 in. x 2.0 in. K20: Front: Disc: 12.5 in. dia. Rear: Drums: 11.0 in. x 2.75 in. Optional: None. Wheels: K10: 15 x 6.0 6-stud disc. K20: 16.5 x 6.0 in. 8-stud disc. Tires: K10: G78 x 15B 4-ply rating, tubeless or tube-type. K20: 8.75 x 16.5C 6-ply rating, tubeless. Optional: K10: G78 x 15B, white stripe; H78 x 15B, tubeless, black sidewall or white stripe; L78 x 15B black sidewall or white stripe, tubeless; 10.00 x 16.5C tubeless; G78 x 15B tube-type; 7.00 x 15C tube-type; 6.50 x 16C tube-type and LR78 x 15C white sidewall radial ply. The following tires were specified for K10 models with the 5600 lb. GVW package which included a front heavy-duty stabilizer bar: H78 x 15B 4-ply rating, tubeless; 6.50 x 16C 6-ply rating, tube-type, truck type. The following tires were specified for K10 models with the 6000 lb. GVW Package which included a front heavy-duty stabilizer bar and heavy-duty rear springs: L78 x 15B 4-ply rating, tubeless. Optional K20: 8.75 x 16.5D tubeless; 9.50 x 16.5D tubeless; 10.00 x 16.5C tubeless (not available for Stepside models); 7.50 x 16C 6-ply rating, tube-type; 7.50 x 16D tube-type; 7.50 x 16E tube-type. The following tires were specified for K20 models with the 7500 lb. GVW Package which included a front heavy-duty stabilizer bar: 8.75 x 16.5 C 6-ply rating, tubeless; 7.50 x 16C 6-ply rating, tubeless. The following tires were specified for K20 models with the 8200 lb. GVW Package which included a front heavy-duty stabilizer bar: 9.50 x 16.5D 8-ply rating, tubeless; 7.50 x 16C 6-ply rating, tube type. Steering: Recirculating ball gear. Ratio: 20:1, turns Lock-to-Lock: 3.4. Turning Circle: 47 ft. Steering wheel diameter: 17.5 in. Optional: Power-assisted. Ratio: 16.4:1. Transmission: 3-speed, synchromesh manual (ZW4 Ordering Code). Transmission Ratios: 2.85, 1.68, 1.00:1. Optional: Chevrolet CH465. 4-speed manual synchromesh (RPO M20). Ratios: 6.55, 3.58, 1.70, 1.00:1. Optional: 3-speed Turbo Hydra-Matic (RPO M49). Ratios: 2.52, 1.52, 1.00:1. Clutch: Diaphragm, spring. Clutch diameter: K10: 6-cyl.: 10 in. dia. Total lining area: 100.0 sq. in. V-8: 12 in. dia. Total lining area: 150 sq. in. K20: 10 in. dia. Total lining area: 100.0 sq. in. V-8: 11 in. dia. Total lining area: 124.0 sq. in. K20 with 350 V-8: 12 in. dia. Total lining area: 150 sq. in. Optional: K20 6-cyl.: 11 in. dia. Total lining area: 124.0 sq. in. 307 V-8: 12 in. dia. Total lining area: 150 sq. in.

VEHICLE DIMENSIONS: Wheelbase: K10: 117.5 in. 131.5 in. K20: 131.5 in. All Suburbans and Panels: 131.5 in. Overall Length: 117.5 in. Fleetside pickups: 191.25 in. 131.5 in. Fleetside pickups: 211.25. 117.5 in. Stepside pickups: 190.5 in. 131.5 in. Stepside pickups: 210.25. Front/Rear Tread: 67.4 in./65.8 in. Overall Height: K10 Pickup and Suburban: 72.25 in. K20 Pickup and Suburban: 73.9 in. Width: Pickup: 79.5 in. Front/Rear Overhang: pickups: 33 in./41 in. Tailgate: Width and Height: 72 in. x 19.25 in. Approach/Departure Degrees: 30/21. Ground Clearance: Front axle: 7.25 in. Rear axle: 7.0 in. Oil pan: 16.5 in. Transfer case: 12.0 in. Fuel tank: 16.6 in. Load space: Pickup box dimensions: 117.5 in. wheelbase Fleetside: 78.25 in. x 50 in. x 19.25 in. 131.5 in. wheelbase Fleetside: 98 in. x 50 in. x 19.25 in. Capacity: 117.5 in. wheelbase: 58.4 cu. ft. 131.5 in. wheelbase: 74.3 cu. ft. 117.5 in. wheelbase Stepside: 78.5 in. x 50 in. x 17.5 in. 131.5 in. wheelbase Stepside: 96.25 in. x 50 in. x 17.5 in. Front headroom: 38.5 in. (seat to top of cab). Front hip room: 67.25 in. Pedal to seat back (max.): 43.5 in. Steering wheel to seat back (max.): 17.3 in. Seat to ground: 35.0 in. Floor to ground: 23.0 in.

1974 Chevrolet K10 Suburban with Cheyenne trim. This vehicle lacks its grille engine id plaque

CAPACITIES: Fuel Tank: K10: 117.5 in. wheelbase: 160 gal. 131.5 in. wheelbase: 20.0: gal. Optional: 16 gal. auxiliary for 117.5 in. wheelbase; 20 gal. for 131.5 in. wheelbase. K20: 20 gal. Optional: 20 gal. auxiliary. Coolant System Capacity: 250 6-cyl.: 14.8 qt. 292 6-cyl.: 13.6 qt. 350 V-8: 17.6 qt. (All figures for vehicles with manual transmission and without air conditioning).

ACCOMMODATIONS: Seating Capacity: Pickup and chassis cab models: 3 passenger. Optional: None. Suburban: K10: 3 passenger. K20: 6 passenger. Optional: 6 passenger (K10), 9 passenger (K10 and K20).

INSTRUMENTATION: Speedometer, odometer, fuel level gauge. Warning lights for battery, oil pressure, generator, brake system warning, directional/hazard lights, high beam, and engine coolant temperature.

OPTIONS AND PRICES: Most 1973 model year options were carried over into 1972. What follows is a representative sampling. Pickup models: Tinted glass: $21. Sliding rear window: $53. Roof drip molding: $16. Air conditioning: $437. Heavy-duty front stabilizer bar: $6. Heavy-duty brakes: $37. Turbo Hydra-Matic: $250. Four-speed manual transmission: $108. Auxiliary fuel tank: $82. Fuel tank skid plate: $101. Bucket seats: $135. Full-depth foam bench seat: $29. Custom steering wheel, 16 in. dia.: $10. Tilt steering wheel: $58. Variable ratio power steering: $152. Tachometer and gauges: $47. Tachometer: $56. Gauge Package (engine coolant temperature, ammeter and oil pressure): $12. AM/FM radio: $145. Chrome rear bumper: $39. 10.00 x 15 tires: $235.44. Cheyenne Super Package: $277. Suburban models: 350 V-8: $45 above price of 307-V-8 equipped models. Turbo Hydra-Matic: $242. Air conditioning: $648. Power steering: $147. Free-running front hubs: $7. Limited slip rear differential: K10: $65; K20: $132. Custom Deluxe Trim Package (with standard front seat): $186. Center seat.

HISTORICAL FOOTNOTES: Calendar year production of all Chevrolet trucks was 923,189.

1975 PICKUP

Minor front end revisions characterized the 1975 K series trucks. A thicker grille gridwork was employed as were clear-lenses parking/directional lights. As in previous years, the grille was easily removable from the front. The grille-mounted engine displacement designation had a yellow, rather than white finish. The form of the front-fender-mounted model/series identification was revised. All Fleetside models had a new quick-release tailgate that could be quickly and easily removed or re-installed.

Available as an alternative to the 350 V-8 engine standard in V-8 models was a 400 cu. in. version of Chevrolet's small-block V-8. This engine was only available on models with a GVW of 6001 and above. Use of the 250 6-cylinder engine was restricted on K10 models with GVW ratings of 5200 and 5800 lb. The K10 models under 6001 GVW along with all other K10, K20 and K30 models with a GVW above 6000 lb. destined for California had a new ducted carburetor air intake system that drew exterior air from outside the engine compartment. The intake was positioned at the side of the radiator. The purpose of this arrangement was to improve both engine performance and fuel economy. Replacing the 250 cu. in. engine as the standard 6-cylinder engine for the K20 models was the 292 cu. in. engine. Standard on all engines was a new transistorized high energy ignition system that delivered up to 35,000 volts to each spark plug. Chevrolet promised quicker starting, longer mileage between tune-ups and improved performance as a result. Chevrolet also announced new extended maintenance schedules. For example, pickups rated at 6000 lbs. GVW or below had engine oil changes and chassis lubrication mileage intervals of 7500 mile. Previously the recommended mileage had been 6000 miles. The base 250 6-cyl. engine was redesigned to produce more horsepower and torque as well as improved gasoline mileage. Among the major changes found in this engine was a new integrally cast intake manifold with more uniform length passages. A new heat sump positioned below the carburetor improved fuel vaporization. All pickups with a GVW below 6001 lb. were equipped with a catalytic converter. All K series trucks used unleaded fuel exclusively and thus were equipped with the new narrow fuel nozzles required for dispensing unleaded fuel. Both V-8 engines had new Mod-Quad 4-barrel carburetors with an integral hot-air choke, a larger primary venturi, larger fuel filter area and additional Teflon coated parts. Also adopted for 1975 were new fully aluminized mufflers with thicker interior baffles and outer shell.

1975 Chevrolet K10 Fleetside pickup

Standard for all four-wheel drive pickups with a V-8 engine and Turbo Hydra-Matic was Chevrolet's full-time four-wheel drive system. A conventional four-wheel drive system with locking front hubs was found on models with a V-8 engine and manual transmission. All trucks with a 6-cylinder engine and either manual or automatic transmissions also had this system. At the start of the 1975 model year Chevrolet had limited availability of the conventional four-wheel drive system to just those trucks powered by a 6-cylinder engine. During the model year Chevrolet introduced an improved and modified suspension intended to improve the riding quality of these 4x4 trucks. Also coming on-line during the 1975 model year was the availability of All-Weather air conditioning for vehicles equipped with either the 250 or 292 6-cylinder engines. Previously, air conditioning was available only with V-8 engines. Series 10 models with the 250 6-cylinder engine now had a standard 11 in. dia. clutch rather than the 10 in. dia. unit previously used. A new 7-lead, heavy-duty trailer-towing wiring harness was now available both for Suburbans and Conventional Cab models. Also new-for-1975 was an optional headlights-on warning buzzer.

Chevrolet eliminated the base Custom trim level for 1975, replacing it with the Custom Deluxe trim package. It included a full-width foam-padded bench seat upholstered in a plaid pattern vinyl offered in blue, green, saddle or red. The steel roof panel was painted to match the exterior color. Other amenities consisted of a black rubber floor mat that extended to the firewall, padded armrests and sun visors, courtesy lamp, prismatic rearview mirror, and a foam-padded instrument panel pad. The Custom Deluxe exterior featured bright upper and lower grille outline moldings, bright headlight bezels, silver plastic grille insert, bright outside rearview mirrors, bright door handles, white-painted front bumper, hubcaps and wheels and bright Custom Deluxe nameplates. Next step up from the base model was the Scottsdale. Its interior was fitted with a full-depth padded cushion bench seat, door trim panels with simulated woodgrain inserts, ashtray-mounted lighter, door or manually-operated dome and courtesy lights, color-keyed rubber floor mat, full-length bright doorsill plates and a high-note horn. The seat upholstery was a grid-patterned nylon cloth with vinyl bolsters and facings. Four color choices were available. The Scottsdale exterior included all the bright items in the Custom Deluxe trim plus chromed front bumper, chromed hubcaps, spear-type upper body side moldings on Fleetsides, bright windshield and rear window trim, bright-trimmed parking and side marker lights, bright-trimmed Fleetside taillights and Scottsdale nameplates.

The Cheyenne's bench seat was fitted with a full-depth foam cushion and was upholstered with either custom-grained vinyl or nylon cloth and vinyl. Vinyl-covered bucket seats were optional. Also included in the Cheyenne interior were these items: Ashtray-mounted cigarette lighter, simulated woodgrain instrument panel insert, door or manually operated courtesy and dome lights and additional cab insulation. The Cheyenne exterior included all bright items found in the Scottsdale and Custom Deluxe options plus these additions or substitutions: Bright metal cab back panel applique and moldings, bright upper body side and tailgate moldings and central tailgate appliques for Fleetsides, and Cheyenne nameplates.

The new Silverado was depicted as the "most luxurious Chevrolet pickup". Its full-width bench seat had a foam cushion nearly 7 inches thick. The Silverado upholstery was a basketweave-patterned nylon cloth with vinyl bolsters and facings. It was available in a choice of five colors. Also offered was a buffalo-hide vinyl in any of six colors. Custom vinyl bucket sears with a center console were also offered. Also included in the Silverado interior was full-gauge instrumentation set in a simulated woodgrain panel with bright trim, simulated woodgrain inserts with bright accent trim and storage pockets on both doors, deep-twist nylon carpeting, insulated headliner and insulation for the floor, cowl, hood and back panel.

The Silverado exterior consisted of all bright items from the Cheyenne, Scottsdale and Custom Deluxe models, except that Silverado nameplates were substituted. In addition, the Silverado had bright lower body side and tailgate moldings, wheel-opening moldings and a full tailgate applique on Fleetside models.

The basic standard equipment from the 1974 models was carried over into 1975.

The color selection for 1975 consisted of these fifteen colors: Skyline blue, Hawaiian blue, Catalina blue, Grecian bronze, buckskin, Yuba gold, willoway green, spring Green, Glenwood green, crimson red, rosedale red, Saratoga silver, Santa Fe tan and frost white. The conventional two-tone style required RPO BX6 moldings. The Special two-tone option was offered for Fleetside models with RPO YG1 moldings. A Deluxe version was available for Fleetside models with RPO BX6 and RPO YG1.

1975 Chevrolet K10 Suburban

I.D. DATA: Unchanged from 1974 except the number 5 represented the 1975 model year. The letter M identified trucks with the 400 cu. in. V-8.

Model Number	Body Type & Seating	Factory Price	GVW	Shipping Weight	Prod. Total
Series K10-1/2 ton 350 V-8 117.5 in. 131.5 in. wheelbase					
CK10703	Chassis and Cab	$4765	6200	3685	—
CK10703	6.5 ft. Stepside Pickup	$4698	6200	4013	—
CK10703	6.5 ft. Fleetside Pickup	$4698	6200	4083	—
CK10903	8 ft. Stepside Pickup	$4741	6200	4141	—
CK10903	8 ft. Fleetside Pickup	$4741	6200	4211	—
CK10906	Suburb.131.5 in wb.	$5796	6200	4703	—
Series K20-3/4 ton 350 V-8. 131.5 in. wheelbase. (Suburban-129.5 in. wheelbase)					
CK20903	Chassis and Cab	$4872	6800*	4206	—
CK20903	8 ft. Stepside Pickup	$5039	6800	4606	—
CK20903	8 ft. Fleetside Pickup	$5039	6800	4676	—
CK20906	Suburban	$6054	6800	5133	—

* 7500 lb. and 8200 lb. GVW optional.

STANDARD ENGINE: All K-10 6-cyl. models: 250 Six (LD4 ordering code). Engine Type: OHV, In-line 6-cylinder. Cast iron block and cylinder head. Key features include 12-counter-weight crankshaft and torsional damper, and molybdenum-filled top piston rings. Bore x Stroke: 3.875 in. x 3.53 in. Lifters: Hydraulic. Number of main bearings-7. Fuel Induction: Single Rochester 1-bbl. carburetor. Compression Ratio: 8.25:1. Displacement: 250 cu. in. (4.09 liters). Horsepower: Net: 105 @ 3800 rpm. Torque: Net: 185 lb.-ft. @ 1200 rpm. Oil refill capacity: 5 qt. with filter change. Fuel Requirements: Regular.

STANDARD ENGINE: K20 6-cyl. models: 292 Six. Ordering Code: L25. Not available in California. Engine Type: OHV, 6-cyl. Cast iron block and cylinder head. Key features include aluminized intake valves, automatic "Rotocoil" rotors on exhaust valves, special coating applied to exhaust valves to reduce deposit formation, full-chromed top piston rings, and premium aluminum bearings. Bore x Stroke: 3.875 in. x 4.125 in. Lifters: Hydraulic. Number of main bearings-7. Fuel Induction: Single Rochester 1-bbl. carburetor. Compression Ratio: 8.0:1. Displacement: 292 cu. in. (4.78 liters). Horsepower: Net: 120 @ 3600 rpm. Torque: Net: 215 lb.-ft. @ 2000 rpm. Oil refill capacity: 6 qt. Fuel Requirements: Regular.

STANDARD ENGINE: V-8 models. Ordering Code: LS9. 350 V-8. Engine Type: OHV, V-8. Cast iron block and alloy iron cylinder head. Key features include chain drive camshaft, "Rotocoil" exhaust valve rotators, special coating applied to exhaust valves to reduce deposit formation, molybdenum-filled top piston rings, premium aluminum main bearings. Bore x Stroke: 4.0 in. x 3.50 in. Lifters: Hydraulic. Number of main bearings-5. Fuel Induction: Single Rochester 4-bbl. carburetor. Compression Ratio: 8.5:1. Displacement: 350 cu. in. (5.73 liters). Horsepower: Net: 160 @ 3800 rpm. Torque: Net: 250 lb.-ft. @ 2400 rpm. Oil refill capacity: 5 qt. with filter change. Fuel Requirements: Regular.

OPTIONAL ENGINE: V-8 models. 400 V-8. Available only with heavy-duty emissions for models of 6001 lb. GVW and above. Engine Type: OHV, V-8. Cast iron block and alloy iron cylinder head. Bore x Stroke: 4.125 in. x 4.0 in. Lifters: Hydraulic. Number of main bearings-5. Fuel Induction: Single Rochester 4-bbl. carburetor. Compression Ratio: 8.5:1. Displacement: 400 cu. in. (6.55 liters). Horsepower: Net: 175 @ 3600 rpm. Torque: Net: 290 lb.-ft. @ 2800 rpm. Oil refill capacity: 5 qt. with filter change. Fuel Requirements: Regular.

CHASSIS FEATURES: Separate body and frame with channel side rails. Carbon-Steel, 39,000 psi. Section modules: 117.5 in. wheelbase: 3.06. 131.5 in. wheelbase: 3.84. Optional: None.

SUSPENSION AND RUNNING GEAR: Front Suspension: 2-leaf, tapered leaf springs 1.0 in. dia. shock absorbers. K10: 1850 lb. rating (at ground). K20:1950 lb. rating (at ground). Optional rating: 1900 lb. (both series). Rear Suspension: 52 in. x 2.25 in. Two-stage, 5-leaf. 1.0 in. dia. shock absorbers. K10: 1700 lb. rating (at ground). K20: 2800 lb. Optional Rating: K10: 2000 lb. Front Axle Type and Capacity: K10: Spicer 44F Semi-floating. 3400 lb. capacity. Optional: None. K20: Full-floating, 3500 lb. capacity. Optional: None. Rear Axle Type and Capacity: K10: Chevrolet, Semi-floating, 3750 lb. capacity. Optional: None. K20: Chevrolet, Full-floating, 5700 lb. Final Drive Ratio: K10: Front: 6-cyl.: 4.11:1; V-8: 3.07:1. Rear: 6-cyl.: 4.11:1. V-8: 3.07:1. K20: Front: 6-cyl. 4.56:1; V-8: 4.10:1. Rear: 6-cyl.: 4.56:1; V-8: 4.101. Optional K10: 3.07,3.73:1, 4.11:1. K20: None. Transfer Case: 6-cylinder models: New Process 205. Single lever, two-speed: 1.94, 1.00:1. V-8 models: New Process 203. Ratios: 2.0:1, 1.0:1. Tires: K10: G78 x 15B 4-ply rating, tubeless or tube-type. K20: 8.75 x 16.5C 6-ply rating, tubeless. Optional: K10: G78 x 15B, white stripe; H78 x 15B, tubeless, black sidewall or white stripe; L78 x 15B black sidewall or white stripe, tubeless; 10.00 x 16.5C tubeless; G78 x 15B tube-type; 7.00 x 15C tube-type; 6.50 x 16C tube-type and LR78 x 15C white sidewall radial ply. The following tires were specified for K10 models with the 5600 lb. GVW package which included a front heavy-duty stabilizer bar: H78 x 15B 4-ply rating, tubeless; 6.50 x 16C 6-ply rating, tube-type, truck type. The following tires were specified for K10 models with the 6000 lb. GVW Package which included a front heavy-duty stabilizer bar and heavy-duty rear springs: L78 x 15B 4-ply rating, tubeless. Optional K20: 8.75 x 16.5D tubeless; 9.50 x 16.5D tubeless; 10.00 x 16.5C tubeless (not available for Stepside models); 7.50 x 16C 6-ply rating, tube-type; 7.50 x 16D tube-type; 7.50 x 16E tube-type. The following tires were specified for K20 models with the 7500 lb. GVW Package which included a front heavy-duty stabilizer bar: 8.75 x 16.5 C 6-ply rating, tubeless; 7.50 x 16C 6-ply rating, tubeless. The following tires were specified for K20 models with the 8200 lb. GVW Package which included a front heavy-duty stabilizer bar: 9.50 x 16.5D 8-ply rating, tubeless; 7.50 x 16E tube type. Steering: Recirculating ball gear. Ratio: 20:1. Turning Circle: 47 ft. Steering wheel diameter: 17.5 in. Optional: Power-assisted. Ratio: 16.4:1. Transmission: 3-speed, synchromesh manual (ZW4 Ordering Code). Transmission Ratios: 3.03, 1.75, 1.00:1. Optional: Chevrolet CH465. 4-speed manual synchromesh (RPO M20). Ratios: 2.52, 1.52, 1.00:1. Clutch: Diaphragm, spring. Clutch diameter: K10: 6-cyl.: 10 in. dia. Total lining area: 100.0 sq. in. V-8: 12 in. dia. Total lining area: 150 sq. in. K20: 10 in. dia. Total lining area: 100.0 sq. in. V-8: 11 in. dia. Total lining area: 124.0 sq. in. K20 with 350 V-8: 12 in. dia. Total lining area: 150 sq. in. Optional: K20 6-cyl.: 11 in. dia. Total lining area: 124.0 sq. in. 307 V-8: 12 in. dia. Total lining area: 150 sq. in.

VEHICLE DIMENSIONS: Wheelbase: K10: 117.5 in. 131.5 in. K20: 131.5 in. All Suburbans and Panels: 129.5 in. Overall Length: 117.5 in. Fleetside pickups: 191.25 in. 131.5 in. Fleetside pickups: 211.25. 117.5 in. Stepside pickups: 190.5 in. 131.5 in. Stepside pickups: 210.25. Front/Rear Tread: 67.4 in./65.8 in. Overall Height: K10 Pickup and Suburban: 72.25 in. K20 Pickup and Suburban: 73.9 in. Width: Pickup: 79.5 in. Front/Rear Overhang: pickups:33 in./41 in. Tailgate: Width and Height: 72 in. x 19.25 in. Approach/Departure Degrees: 30/21. Ground Clearance: Front axle: 7.25 in. Rear axle: 7.0 in. Oil pan: 16.5 in. Transfer case: 12.0 in. Fuel tank: 16.6 in. Load space: Pickup box dimensions: 117.5 in. wheelbase Fleetside: 78.25 in. x 50 in. x 19.25 in. 131.5 in. wheelbase Fleetside: 90 in. x 50 in. x 19.25 in. Capacity: 117.5 in. wheelbase: 58.4 cu. ft. 131.5 in. wheelbase: 74.3 cu. ft. 117.5 in. wheelbase Stepside: 78.5 in. x 50 in. x 17.5 in. 131.5 in. wheelbase Stepside: 96.25 in. x 50 in. x 17.5 in. Front headroom: 38.5 in. (seat to top of cab). Front hip room: 67.25 in. Pedal to seat back (max.): 43.5 in. Steering wheel to seat back (max.): 17.3 in. Seat to ground: 35.0 in. Floor to ground: 23.0 in.

CAPACITIES: Fuel Tank: K10: 117.5 in. wheelbase: 16.0 gal. 131.5 in. wheelbase: 20.0: gal. Optional: 16 gal. auxiliary for 117.5 in. wheelbase; 20 gal. for 131.5 in. wheelbase. K20: 20 gal. Optional: 20 gal. auxiliary. Coolant System Capacity: 250 6-cyl.: 14.8 qt. 292 6-cyl.: 13.6 qt. 350 V-8: 17.6 qt. (All figures for vehicles with manual transmission and without air conditioning).

ACCOMMODATIONS: Seating Capacity: Pickup and chassis cab models: 3 passenger. Optional: None. Suburban: K10: 3 passenger. K20: 6 passenger. Optional: 6 passenger (K10), 9 passenger (K10 and K20).

INSTRUMENTATION: Speedometer, odometer, fuel level gauge. Warning lights for battery, oil pressure, generator, brake system warning, directional/hazard lights, high beam, and engine coolant temperature.

OPTIONS AND PRICES: Positraction rear axle-RPO G80 (available for K10 only). NoSPIN rear axle-RPO G86 (available for K20 only). Custom Deluxe Package. With cloth bench seat-RPO Z62/YJ4; with custom vinyl bench seat-RPO Z62/YJ5. Cheyenne Package. With custom cloth bench seat-RPO Z84/YJ5. Cheyenne Super Package. With custom cloth bench seat-RPO YE9/YJ6; with custom vinyl bench seat-RPO YE9/YJ5. Custom Camper Chassis Equipment-Basic Camper Group-RPO Z81. Available with K20 V-8 models with 8200 lb. GVW and either 4-spd. manual trans. or Turbo Hydra-Matic. Requires 9.50 x 16.5D tubeless or 7.50 x 16E tube type rear tires only. Includes heavy-duty front and rear shock absorbers, heavy-duty front springs, heavy-duty clutch, Custom Camper nameplate and camper body wiring harness. Deluxe Camper Group for Cab-Over Camper Bodies-RPO Z83. Available with K20 V-8 models with 8200 lb. GVW and either 4-spd. manual trans. or Turbo Hydra-Matic Requires 9.50 x 16.5D tubeless or 7.50 x 16E tube type rear tires and Fleetside body. Not available with wooden floor. Includes Basic Camper Group plus camper body tie-down brackets mounted to pickup box under body, spring loaded turnbuckles shipped loose, horizontal shock absorbers mounted between cab rear panel and pickup box side panels, and vertical shock absorber brackets mounted on front fenders. Camper body wiring harness-RPO UY1. Available when Custom Camper Chassis equipment is ordered. Camper-type stainless steel mirrors: RPO DF2. Poly-wrap air cleaner-RPO K43. All-Weather air conditioning-RPO C60. Auxiliary 61 amp battery-RPO TP2. Heavy-duty 80 amp battery-RPO T60. Painted rear bumper-RPO V38. Painted rear step bumper-RPO V43.Chromed front and rear bumper-RPO V37. Front chromed bumper (not available if painted rear bumper is ordered)-RPO V46. Chromed rear bumper (available only with Cheyenne or Cheyenne Super is ordered)-RPO VF1. California Assembly Line Emission Test-RPO YF5. Bright metal hubcaps (not available for K10 models with 10.00 x 16.5 tires)-RPO PO3. Side-mounted spare tire carrier-RPO P13. Electric clock (available only with gauge package, not available if tachometer is ordered)-RPO U35. Heavy-duty clutch (available only for models with 250 engine and 3-spd. manual trans.)-RPO MO1. Exterior tool stowage (available for Fleetside only. Not available if auxiliary fuel tank is ordered)-RPO VK4. Coolant recovery system-RPO U35. Heavy-duty radiator (requires RPO VQ1)-RPO VO1. Wood 8 ft. Fleetside pickup box-RPO E81. Gauge Package-Z53: $12. Tachometer (V-8 models only, not available if electric clock is ordered)-RPO U16: $56. 42 amp Delcotron generator (not available if air conditioning is ordered)-RPO K79. 61 amp Delcotron generator (included with air conditioning)-RPO K76. Soft-Ray tinted glass, all windows-RPO V22: $18. Chromed grille-RPO V22. Door edge guards (not available with woodgrained exterior trim)-RPO B93. Free-wheeling front hubs-RP F76. Cargo area lamp-RPO UF2. Dome light-RPO C91. Roof marker lights-RPO U01. Cigarette lighter-RPO U37. Exterior below eye-level 7.5 in. x 10.5 in. painted mirrors-RPO D29. Exterior below eye-level 7.5 in. x 10.5 in. stainless steel mirrors-RPO DG4. Cab back panel applique-RPO BX6. Upper body moldings. For Fleetside only. Includes fender, door cab panel, tailgate and pickup box moldings plus bright front turn signal, side marker and taillight trim-RPO B85. Upper and lower body molding (adds lower body side, tailgate and wheel opening moldings to RPO B85)-RPO YG1. Painted roof drip molding-RPO BX5. Soft instrument panel pad-RPO B70. Fuel tank shield-RPO NY1. AM radio-RPO U63. AM/FM radio-RPO U69. Vinyl roof cover-RPO CO8. Bucket seats-RPO A50/YJ5: $135. Full-depth foam bench seat-RPO Z52: $29. Heavy-duty front and rear shock absorbers-RPO F51. Heavy-duty rear shock absorbers-RPO G68. Heavy-duty front springs-RPO F60. Heavy-duty rear springs (K10 only)-RPO G50. Heavy-duty front stabilizer-RPO F58. Power steering-RPO N40. ComfortTilt steering wheel (not available with 3-spd. manual trans.)-RPO N33. Custom steering wheel (available only with power steering, includes 16 in. steering wheel)-RPO N31. Auxiliary fuel tank (not avail. with K10 with 250 engine)-RPO NL2: $77. Manual throttle control (not available with air conditioning)-RPO K31: $410. Front towing hooks-RPO V76. Bright metal wheelcovers (K10 only; not avail. with 6.50 x 16 or 10.00 x 16.5 tires)-RPO PO1. Wheel trim rings (not avail. with 10.00 x 16.5 tires on K10 or with 7.50 x 16 tires)-RPO PO6. Sliding rear window-RPO A28. Exterior woodgrained trim (avail. only with Fleetside models with custom and deluxe two-tone paint. Not avail. with special or deluxe two-tone paint)-RPO YG2. Suburban: 350 V-8 $45 above price of 307 V-8 equipped models. Turbo Hydra-Matic: $242. Air conditioning: $648. Power steering: $147. Free-running front hubs. Limited slip rear differential: K10: $65; K20: $132. Custom Deluxe Trim Package (with standard front seat): $186.

HISTORICAL FOOTNOTES: The 1975 Chevrolet models were introduced on September 1, 1974.

1976 PICKUP

Chevrolet eliminated the engine displacement identification from the grillework of its 1976 K series trucks. A slight revision of the texture of the grille insert also distinguished the new model from the 1975 version. The full-time four-wheel drive system was used in conjunction with all models equipped with Turbo Hydra-Matic transmission for 1976. A conventional four-wheel drive system was used with manual transmissions. A heavy-duty stabilizer bar was now standard for the K10 and K20, previously it had been an option. The 400 cu in. version of the Chevrolet "Big Block" V-8 was replaced by a 400 cu. in. version of the "Small Block V-8." The air conditioning option had a new 7-position control with an "Economy" setting. Added to the list of available options was a new rear chromed step bumper with a skid resistent top surface and a recessed step for Fleetside models. It was pre-drilled for a trailer hitch ball and was offered in either 1.875 in. or 2.0 in. sizes. A painted version was available for all pickups. A new exterior appearance format was offered in the form of a two-tone paint scheme employing selected secondary colors in combination with the main body color. This option included upper and lower body side and tailgate moldings on Fleetside with Special or Deluxe two-tone treatments. A new trim package was offered for Stepside pickups with the 6.5 ft. box. It included special striping, chromed front and rear bumpers, Rallye wheels, white lettered tires, and Scottsdale trim including a Custom vinyl bench seat. A choice of four exterior colors were offered: Blue, orange, red or black. The Custom Deluxe trim level was unchanged. The Scottsdale level has several changes for 1976. Among them was the use of simulated tigerwood inserts for the door trim panels and a ribbed-patterned velour cloth with grained vinyl facings or buffalo-hide embossed vinyl. The Cheyenne package was also revised to include the use of ribbed-pattern velour cloth or buffalo-hide vinyl. The seat back folded forward to make the stowage area behind the seat more accessible. Vinyl-upholstered bucket seats with a center console were also available (they were also available for all regular cabs with all trim levels). The door-trim panels and instrument panel had simulated tigerwood inserts. The latest Silverado format included new ribbed-pattern velour cloth with grained vinyl facings and bolsters available in a choice of four colors. A buffalo-hide vinyl, with a selection of five colors, was an alternative. The seat back also tilted forward on the Silverado. Simulated tigerwood grain inserts were used for the instrumentation panel and door inserts. A cut-pile floor carpeting was installed. Both the basic standard equipment from the 1975 models and the exterior color selection were carried over into 1976.

1976 Chevrolet Fleetside pickup

I.D. DATA: Unchanged from 1975 except the number 6 represented the 1975 model year. The letter U identified trucks with the 400 cu. in. V-8.

Model Number	Body Type & Seating	Factory Price	GVW	Shipping Weight	Prod. Total
Series K10-1/2 ton 350 V-8 117.5 in. 131.5 in. wheelbase					
CK10703	Chassis and Cab	$5104	5200*	3816	—
CK10703	6.5 ft. Stepside Pickup	$5010	5200	4147	—
CK10703	6.5 ft. Fleetside Pickup	$5010	5200	4215	—
CK10903	8 ft. Stepside Pickup	$5055	5200	4244	—
CK10903	8 ft. Fleetside Pickup	$5055	5200	4320	—
CK10906	Suburb.131.5 in. wb.	$6234	5200	4702	—

* 5600 lb. and 6400 lb. GVW optional.

Model Number	Body Type & Seating	Factory Price	GVW	Shipping Weight	Prod. Total
Series K20-3/4 ton 350 V-8. 131.5 in. wheelbase. (Suburban-129.5 in. wheelbase)					
CK20903	Chassis and Cab	$5205	6800*	4206	—
CK20903	8 ft. Stepside Pickup	$5372	6800	4606	—
CK20903	8 ft. Fleetside Pickup	$5372	6800	4676	—
CK20906	Suburban	$6441	6800	5133	—

* 7500 lb. and 8200 lb. GVW optional.

STANDARD ENGINE: All K-10 6-cyl. models: 250 Six (LD4 ordering code). Engine Type: OHV, In-line 6-cylinder. Cast iron block and cylinder head. Key features include 12-counterweight crankshaft and torsional damper, and molybdenum-filled top piston rings. Bore x Stroke: 3.875 in. x 3.53 in. Lifters: Hydraulic. Number of main bearings-7. Fuel Induction: Single Rochester 1-bbl. carburetor. Compression Ratio: 8.25:1. Displacement: 250 cu. in. (4.09 liters). Horsepower: Net: 105 @ 3800 rpm. Torque: Net: 185 lb.-ft. @ 1200 rpm. Oil refill capacity: 5 qt. with filter change. Fuel Requirements: No-lead, Low lead or Regular fuel, 91 octane or higher.

STANDARD ENGINE: K20 6-cyl. models: 292 Six. Ordering Code: L25. Not available in California. Engine Type: OHV, 6-cyl. Cast iron block and cylinder head. Key features include aluminized intake valves, automatic "Rotocoil" rotors on exhaust valves, special coating applied to exhaust valves to reduce deposit formation, full-chromed top piston rings, and premium aluminum bearings. Bore x Stroke: 3.875 in. x 4.125 in. Lifters: Hydraulic. Number of main bearings-7. Fuel Induction: Single Rochester 1-bbl. carburetor. Compression Ratio:

8.0:1. Displacement: 292 cu. in. (4.78 liters). Horsepower: Net: 120 @ 3600 rpm. Torque: Net: 215 lb.-ft. @ 2000 rpm. Oil refill capacity: 6 qt. Fuel Requirements: No-lead, Low lead or Regular fuel, 91 octane or higher.

STANDARD ENGINE: V-8 models: Ordering Code: LS9: 350 V-8 Engine Type: OHV, V-8. Cast iron block and alloy iron cylinder head. Key features include chain drive camshaft, "Rotocoil" exhaust valve rotators, special coating applied to exhaust valves to reduce deposit formation, molybdenum-filled top piston rings, premium aluminum main bearings. Bore x Stroke: 4.0 in. x 3.50 in. Lifters: Hydraulic. Number of main bearings-5. Fuel Induction: Single Rochester 4-bbl. carburetor. Compression Ratio: 8.5:1. Displacement: 350 cu. in. (5.73 liters). Horsepower: Net: 165 @ 3800 rpm. Torque: Net: 260 lb.-ft. @ 2400 rpm. (255 lb.-ft. @ 2800 rpm for models with heavy-duty emissions and 6001 lb. GVW and above). Oil refill capacity: 5 qt. with filter change. Fuel Requirements: No-lead, Low lead or Regular fuel, 91 octane or higher.

OPTIONAL ENGINE: V-8 models: 400 V-8. Available only with heavy-duty emissions for models of 6001 lb. GVW and above. Engine Type: OHV, V-8. Cast iron block and alloy iron cylinder head. Bore x Stroke: 4.10 in. x 3.8 in. Lifters: Hydraulic. Number of main bearings-5. Fuel Induction: Single Rochester 4-bbl. carburetor. Compression Ratio: 8.5:1. Displacement: 400 cu. in. (6.55 liters). Horsepower: Net: 175 @ 3600 rpm. Torque: Net: 290 lb.-ft. @ 2800 rpm. Oil refill capacity: 5 qt. with filter change. Fuel Requirements: No-lead, Low lead or Regular fuel, 91 octane or higher.

CHASSIS FEATURES: Separate body and frame with channel side rails. Carbon-Steel, 39,000 psi. Section modules: 117.5 in. wheelbase: 3.06 in. 131.5 in. wheelbase: 3.84 in. Optional: None.

SUSPENSION AND RUNNING GEAR: Front Suspension: 2-leaf, tapered. 1.0 in. dia. shock absorbers. K10: 1850 lb. rating (at ground). K20:1900 lb. rating (at ground). Optional rating: K10:1900 lb. Rear Suspension: 52 in. x 2.25 in. Two-stage, 5-leaf. 1.0 in. dia. shock absorbers. K10: 2000 lb. rating (at ground), K20: 2800 lb. Optional Rating: None. Front Axle Type and Capacity: K10: Semi-floating. 3600 lb. capacity. Optional: None. K20: Full-floating, 3800 lb. capacity. Optional: None. Rear Axle Type and Capacity: K10: Chevrolet, Semi-floating, 3750 lb. capacity. Optional: None. K20: Chevrolet, Full-floating, 5700 lb. Final Drive Ratio: K10: Front: 6-cyl.: 4.11:1; V-8: 3.07:1. Rear: 6-cyl.: 4.11:1. V-8: 3.07:1. K20: Front: 6-cyl. 4.56:1; V-8: 4.10:1. Rear: 6-cyl.: 4.56:1; V-8: 4.101. Optional K10: 3.07,3.73:1, 4.1:1. K20: None. Transfer Case: 6-cylinder models: New Process 205. Single lever, two-speed: 1.94, 1.00:1. V-8 models: New Process 203. Ratios: 2.0:1, 1.0:1. Brakes: Type: Hydraulic, power assisted. Dimensions: K10: Front: Disc: 11.86 in. dia. Rear: Drums: 11.0 in. x 2.0 in. K20: Front: Disc: 12.5 in. dia. Rear: Drums: 11.0 in. x 2.75 in. Optional: K10 and K20: Heavy-duty. Wheels: K10: 15 x 6.0 6-stud disc. K20: 16.5 x 6.0 in. 8-stud disc. Tires: K10: L78 x 15B. K20: 8.75 x 16.5C 6-ply rating, tubeless. Optional: K10: G78 x 15B, white stripe; H78 x 15B, tubeless, black sidewall or white stripe; L78 x 15B black sidewall or white stripe, tubeless; 10.00 x 16.5C tubeless; G78 x 15B tube-type; 7.00 x 15C tube-type; 6.50 x 16C tube-type and LR78 x 15C white sidewall radial ply. The following tires were specified for K10 models with the 5600 lb. GVW package which included a front heavy-duty stabilizer bar: H78 x 15B 4-ply rating, tubeless; 6.50 x 16C 6-ply rating, tube-type, truck type. The following tires were specified for K10 models with the 6000 lb. GVW Package which included a front heavy-duty stabilizer bar and heavy-duty rear springs: L78 x 15B 4-ply rating, tubeless. Optional K20: 8.75 x 16.5D tubeless; 9.50 x 16.5D tubeless; 10.00 x 16.5C tubeless (not available for Stepside models); 7.50 x 16C 6-ply rating, tube-type; 7.50 x 16D tube-type; 7.50 x 16E tube-type. The following tires were specified for K20 models with the 7500 lb. GVW Package which included a front heavy-duty stabilizer bar: 8.75 x 16.5 C 6-ply rating, tubeless; 7.50 x 16C 6-ply rating, tubeless. The following tires were specified for K20 models with the 8200 lb. GVW Package which included a front heavy-duty stabilizer bar: 9.50 x 16.5D 8-ply rating, tubeless; 7.50 x 16C 6-ply rating, tube type. Steering: Recirculating ball gear. Ratio: 20:1. Turning Circle: 47 ft. Steering wheel diameter: 17.5 in. Optional: Power-assisted. Ratio: 16.4:1. In late 1976 as a rolling model change, the power steering gear imput shaft diameter was reduced to provide a common coupling size for all GM vehicles. Transmission: 3-speed, synchromesh manual (ZW4 Ordering Code). Transmission Ratios: 3.03, 1.75, 1.00:1. Optional: Chevrolet CH465. 4-speed manual synchromesh (RPO M20). Ratios: 6.55, 3.58, 1.70, 1.00:1. Optional: 3-speed Turbo Hydra-Matic (RPO M49). Ratios: 2.52, 1.52, 1.00:1. Clutch: Diaphragm, spring. Clutch diameter: K10: 6-cyl.: 10 in. dia. Total lining area: 100.0 sq. in. V-8: 12 in. dia. Total lining area: 150 sq. in. K20: 10 in. dia. Total lining area: 100.0 sq. in. V-8: 11 in. dia. Total lining area: 124.0 sq. in. K20 with 350 V-8: 12 in. dia. Total lining area: 150 sq. in. Optional: K20 6-cyl.: 11 in. dia. Total lining area: 124.0 sq. in. 307 V-8: 12 in. dia. Total lining area: 150 sq. in.

VEHICLE DIMENSIONS: Wheelbase: K10: 117.5 in. 131.5 in. K20: 131.5 in. All Suburbans and Panels: 129.5 in. Overall Length: 117.5 in. Fleetside pickups: 191.25 in. 131.5 in. Fleetside pickups: 211.25. 117.5 in. Stepside pickups: 190.5 in. 131.5 in. Stepside pickups: 210.25. 117.5 in. Front/Rear Tread: 67.4 in./65.8 in. Overall Height: K10 pickup: 72.0 in. K20 pickup: 74.0 in. K10 and K20 Suburban: 73.5 in. Width: Pickup: 79.5 in. Front/Rear Overhang: pickups: 33 in./41 in. Tailgate: Width and Height: 72 in. x 19.25 in. Approach/Departure Degrees: K10 117.5 in. Fleetside and Stepside: 33/19. K10 131.5 in. Fleetside: 33/15. K10 131.5 in. wheelbase Stepside: 33/16. K20 131.5 in. wheelbase Fleetside: 35/20. K20 131.5 in. wheelbase Stepside: 35/21. Ground Clearance: Front axle: 7.25 in. Rear axle: 7.0 in. Oil pan: 16.5 in. Transfer case: 12.0 in. Fuel tank: 16.6 in. Load space: Pickup box dimensions: 117.5 in. wheelbase Fleetside: 78.25 in. x 50 in. x 19.25 in. 131.5 in. wheelbase. Fleetside: 98 in. x 50 in. x 19.25 in. Capacity: 117.5 wheelbase: 58.4 cu. ft. 131.5 in. wheelbase: 74.3 cu. ft. 117.5 in. wheelbase. Stepside: 78.5 in. x 50 in. x 17.5 in. 131.5 in. wheelbase Stepside: 96.25 in. x 50 in. x 17.5 in. Front headroom: 38.5 in. (seat to top of cab). Front hip room: 67.25 in. Pedal to seat back (max.): 43.5 in. Steering wheel to seat back (max.): 17.3 in. Seat to ground: 35.0 in. Floor to ground: 23.0 in.

CAPACITIES: Fuel Tank: 117.5 in. wheelbase: 16.0 gal. 131.5 in. wheelbase: 20.0: gal. Optional: 17 gal. auxiliary tank. for 117.5 in.; 20 gal. auxiliary for 131.5 in. wheelbase. Coolant System Capacity: 250 6-cyl.: 14.8 qt. 292 6-cyl.: 13.6 qt. 350 V-8: 17.6 qt. (All figures for vehicles with manual transmission and without air conditioning).

ACCOMMODATIONS: Seating Capacity: Pickup and chassis cab models: 3 passenger. Optional: None. Suburban: 3 passenger. Optional: 6 or 9 passenger.

INSTRUMENTATION: Speedometer, odometer, fuel level gauge. Warning lights for battery, oil pressure, generator, brake system warning, directional/hazard lights, high beam, and engine coolant temperature.

OPTIONS AND PRICES: Gauge Package. Includes voltmeter, oil pressure and engine coolant temperature. AM radio. AM/FM radio. Turbo Hydra-Matic. ComforTilt steering wheel. Tachometer (V-8only). Delco Freedom battery. Sliding rear window. Air conditioning. Speed and cruise control. Requires V-8 engine and Turbo Hydra-Matic. Cargo area lamp. Below eye-level mirrors. Bucket seats. Two-tone paint. Pickup box side rails. Rear chromed step bumper. Deluxe chrome bumpers (available for front only or front and rear). Chromed front bumper guards with rubber impact stripes. Glide-out spare tire carrier. Stainless steel wheelcovers. Bright hubcaps. Fuel tank skid plate. Transfer case skid plate. Soft-Ray tinted glass. Rallye wheels. Engine oil cooler. Heavy-duty alternator. Weight-equalizing hitch platform. Trailer Special Package. Includes power steering, heavy-duty battery, and Trailer Special nameplate. Camper Special Package. Includes camper body wiring, heavy-duty front springs, heavy-duty front and rear shock absorbers, added capacity rear springs and Camper Special nameplate. Available only for K20 and requires V-8 engine and either 4-spd. manual or Turbo Hydra-Matic transmission. Deluxe Camper Special Package. Includes all Camper Special equipment plus Camper Tie-Down Package, Elimi-Pitch Package (includes two horizontal shock absorbers mounted between cab rear panel and pickup box, and two vertical shock absorber mounted between camper overhang and front fenders and rear stabilizer (available for cab over campers on Fleetside models only).

HISTORICAL FOOTNOTES: Chevrolet introduced its 1976 trucks on October 2, 1975.

1976 Chevrolet K20 Suburban

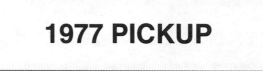

1977 PICKUP

A revamped grille made it easy to identify the 1977 K series trucks. The new grille consisted of two horizontal and four vertical dividers. This arrangement helped accent the new inner gridwork. The headlight bezel color was changed from argent to dark gray metallic. The body side moldings for the Cheyenne, Silverado and RPO B85 and RPO YG1 molding packages had ochre paint in place of the black paint used in 1976. K10 models were available with newly styled RPO PO1 black and chrome wheelcovers in a spoked wheel design. Another new option, RPO PA6, white painted wheels also had a spoke-type design.

1977 Chevrolet K10 Stepside pickup

Extending the market range of the Chevrolet four-wheel drive models was the introduction of new K30 one ton four-wheel drive models available in two-door chassis cab, two-door Fleetside, bonus cab and crew cab Fleetside, bonus cab and crew cab chassis cab. All were equipped with a 4500 lb. Dana-Spicer front axle which utilized a spring loaded king pin rather than a conventional ball joint. A 7500 lb. rear axle was used. The GVWRs for these trucks ranged from 6600 to 9200 lbs. for single rear-wheel models and 9200 to 10,000 lbs. on dual rear wheel models. All K30 pickup boxes were 8 ft. long. Power steering was standard for the K30 range. All K series pickups and Suburban models equipped with either the RPO M20 4-speed manual transmission or RPO MC1 3-speed manual transmission and GT4 (3.73:1), HO4 (4.11:1), GT5 or HC4 rear axles had a new two-piece prop shaft. The exhaust systems on the K series trucks incorporated new exhaust hanger assemblies. The exhaust system were also modified to accommodate the new 2-piece propeller shafts on the K pickups and Suburbans. K10 and K20 models with RPO LS9 350 V-8 engine had a new, quieter muffler. The tail, stop and back-up light assemblies for the Stepside and chassis cab models were now combined into a single unit which also included the turn signal function.

Added to the list of K series optional equipment were power windows and power door locks. A new Exterior Package (RPO ZY5) also debuted for 1977. It was available for Fleetside pickups and consisted of a choice of six special two-tone paint treatments in which the secondary color was used on the hood, cab roof and between the RPO YG1 body side and rear moldings. This package also included color-coordinated hood stripes (decals) and a bright stand-up hood emblem. Also offered were Sport Packages for both the Fleetside and Stepside pickups. They included special hood and side striping and a choice of new styled or Rallye wheels.

The standard Custom Deluxe interior consisted of a full-width foam-padded front bench seat upholstered in a new plaid-pattern embossed vinyl offered in a selection of four colors. A matching rear seat was standard for crew cab models. Black rubber floor mats were included as were new larger door trim panels, padded armrests, padded sun visors, courtesy lamp, prismatic inside rearview mirror, foam-padded instrument panel with Custom Deluxe nameplate and simulated chestnut woodgrain insert.

The Custom Deluxe exterior included bright upper and lower grille outline moldings, bright headlight bezels, silver plastic grille insert, bright outside rearview mirrors, bright door handles, white-painted front bumper, hubcaps and wheels, bright drip rails over doors and bright Custom Deluxe nameplates.

The Scottsdale trim level included all Custom Deluxe elements plus front bench seat with bright trim for regular cabs, door or manually-operated dome light, full-length bright doorsill plates, high-note horn (and more). The regular cab front seat folded forward for access to the inside stowage area. The upholstery for the regular cabs was a new Custom-ribbed-pattern velour cloth with grained vinyl facings and bolsters or a Custom buffalo-hide embossed vinyl. A striped knit vinyl trim was also available. Standard trim on the crew cabs and bonus cabs was a plaid-pattern vinyl with Custom buffalo-hide vinyl also available. The rubber floor mat was color-keyed. On the bonus cab the front mat was also color-keyed but the rear was black. The Scottsdale exterior included all items from the Custom Deluxe plus chromed front bumper, bright hubcaps, spear-type side moldings on Fleetsides, bright windshield and rear window trim, bright-trimmed parking and side-marker lamps, bright-trimmed Fleetside taillights and Scottsdale nameplates. Models with dual-rear wheels had clearance lamps.

The Cheyenne option was available for regular cab models only. Its interior included all trim items from the Scottsdale plus door trim panels with simulated chestnut woodgrain inserts and storage pockets, color-keyed carpeting headliner and garnish moldings, added floor insulation, Cheyenne nameplate on instrument panel (and More). The Cheyenne exterior added these items to the Scottsdale level: Bright cab back panel molding, bright upper body side and tailgate moldings on Fleetsides, Fleetside tailgate applique and Cheyenne nameplates.

The top-of-the-line Silverado package included all Cheyenne items when ordered for a regular cab. When specified for crew cab and bonus cab models it began with items from the Scottsdale package. In addition, these items were included: Full-gauge instrumentation in a simulated chestnut woodgrain panel, full-door trim panels with bright trim and color-keyed carpeting on lower section, full cowl trim panels and Silverado instrument panel nameplate. crew cabs and bonus cab versions were offered in a choice of Custom cloth-and-vinyl or Custom all-vinyl seat trim and cut-pile carpeting. The Silverado exterior incorporated Cheyenne items for the regular cabs or the Scottsdale package for crew and bonus cabs plus bright upper and lower body side and tailgate moldings, wheel opening moldings, full tailgate applique, bright cab back panel applique molding and Silverado nameplates.

1977 Chevrolet Suburban

The color selection for 1977 consisted of fifteen choices: Mariner blue, cordova brown, Saratoga silver, light blue, cardinal red, buckskin, Holy green, russet metallic, Hawaiian blue, Santa Fe tan, mahogany, red metallic, Colonial yellow, frost white and seamist green.

I.D. DATA: Unchanged from 1976 except the number 7 represented the 1977 model year. The letter U identified trucks with the 400 cu. in. V-8.

Model Number	Body Type & Seating	Factory Price	GVW	Shipping Weight	Prod. Total
Series K10-1/2 ton 250 6-cyl. 117.5 in. 131.5 in. wheelbase (Suburban: 129.5 in. wheelbase and standard 305 V-8)					
CK10703	Chassis and Cab	$5216	6200	3618[1]	—
CK10703	6.5 ft. Stepside Pickup	$5222	6200	3952	—
CK10703	6.5 ft. Fleetside Pickup	$5222	6200	4012	—
CK10903	8 ft. Stepside Pickup	$5272	6200	4539	—
CK10903	8 ft. Fleetside Pickup	$5272	6200	4539	—
CK10906	Suburban Panel Drs.	$N.A.	6200	4682	—
CK10906	Suburban Endgate	$6348	6200	—	—

NOTE 1: Weights are for models with V-8 engines.

Series K20-3/4 ton 350 V-8. 131.5 in. wheelbase. (Suburban-129.5 in. wheelbase. Crew and bonus cab: 164.5 in. wheelbase, Suburban weight with standard 305 V-8)					
CK20903	Chassis and Cab	$5475	6800*	4131	—
CK20903	8 ft. Stepside Pickup	$5700	6800	4520	—
CK20903	8 ft. Fleetside Pickup	$5700	6800	4611	—
CK20943	Chassis & Bonus Cab	$6122	6800	4633	—
CK20943	Fleetside Bonus Cab	$6347	6800	5740	—
CK20943	Chassis & Crew Cab	$6496	6800	5889	—
CK20943	Fleetside Crew Cab	$6721	6800	5349	—
CK20906	Suburban Panel Drs.	$N.A.	6800	5140	—
CK20906	Suburban Endgate	$6851	—	—	—

NOTE 1: Weights are for models with V-8 engines.
* Up to 8400 lb. GVW optional.

Series K30-1 ton 350 V-8. 131.5 in. wheelbase. Crew and bonus cab: 164.5 in. wheelbase					
CK30903	Chassis & Cab	$6657	6600*	3803	—
CK30903	8 ft. Stepside Pickup	$6882	6600	4192	—
CK30903	8 ft. Fleetside Pickup	$6882	6600	4283	—
CK30943	Chassis & Bonus Cab	$7588	6600	4444	—
CK30943	Fleetside Bonus Cab	$7813	6600	4924	—
CK30943	Chassis & Crew Cab	$7698	6600	5475	—
CK30943	Fleetside Crew Cab	$7923	6600	5015	—

* GVW up to 10,000 lb. optional.

STANDARD ENGINE: All K-10 6-cyl. models: 250 Six (LD4 ordering code). Not available for California where a 350 V-8 is installed. Engine Type: OHV, In-line 6-cylinder. Cast iron block and cylinder head. Key features induction hardened exhaust valve seats, and timing tabs.

Bore x Stroke: 3.875 in. x 3.53 in. Lifters: Hydraulic. Number of main bearings-7. Fuel Induction: Single Rochester 1-bbl. carburetor. Compression Ratio: 8.0:1. Displacement: 250 cu. in. (4.09 liters). Horsepower: Net: 100 @ 3600 rpm. Torque: Net: 175 lb.-ft. @ 1800 rpm. Oil refill capacity: 5 qt. with filter change. Fuel Requirements: Regular.

STANDARD ENGINE: K20 and K30 6-cyl. models: 292 Six. Ordering Code: L25. Engine Type: OHV, 6-cyl. Cast iron block and cylinder head. Key features include cast iron intake manifold, aluminized-face intake valves, stellite-faced exhaust valves with hardened faces. Bore x Stroke: 3.875 in. x 4.125 in. Lifters: Hydraulic. Number of main bearings-7. Fuel Induction: Single Rochester 1-bbl. carburetor. Compression Ratio: 8.0:1. Displacement: 292 cu. in. (4.78 liters). Horsepower: Net: 120 @ 3600 rpm. Torque: Net: 215 lb.-ft. @ 2000 rpm. Oil refill capacity: 6 qt. Fuel Requirements: Regular.

STANDARD ENGINE: K20 and K30 V-8 models: Ordering Code: LS9: 350 V-8 Engine Type: OHV, V-8. Cast iron block and alloy iron cylinder head. Key features include chain drive camshaft and forged steel connecting rods. Bore x Stroke: 4.0 in. x 3.50 in. Lifters: Hydraulic. Number of main bearings-5. Fuel Induction: Single Rochester 4-bbl. carburetor. Compression Ratio: 8.5:1. Displacement: 350 cu. in. (5.73 liters). Horsepower: Net: 165 @ 3800 rpm. Torque: Net: 255 lb.-ft. @ 2800 rpm. Oil refill capacity: 5 qt. with filter change. Fuel Requirements: Regular.

OPTIONAL ENGINE: K20 and K30 V-8 models: Ordering Code: LF4: 400 V-8. Key features include induction-hardened valve seats and cast iron camshaft. Engine Type: OHV, V-8. Cast iron block and alloy iron cylinder head. Bore x Stroke: 4.10 in. x 3.8 in. Lifters: Hydraulic. Number of main bearings-5. Fuel Induction: Single Rochester 4-bbl. carburetor. Compression Ratio: 8.5:1. Displacement: 400 cu. in. (6.55 liters). Horsepower: Net: 175 @ 3600 rpm. Torque: Net: 290 lb.-ft. @ 2800 rpm. Oil refill capacity: 5 qt. with filter change. Fuel Requirements: Regular.

STANDARD ENGINE: K10 and K20 V-8 Suburban models: Ordering Code: LG9 305 V-8. Not available in California. Engine Type: OHV, V-8. Cast iron block and alloy iron cylinder head. Bore x Stroke: 3.74 in. x 3.48 in. Lifters: Hydraulic. Number of main bearings-5. Fuel Induction: Single Rochester 2-bbl. carburetor. Compression Ratio: 8.5:1. Displacement: 305 cu. in. (4.997 liters). Horsepower: Net: 145 @ 3800 rpm. Torque: Net: 245 lb.-ft. @ 2400 rpm. Oil refill capacity: 5 qt. with filter change. Fuel Requirements: Regular.

CHASSIS FEATURES: Separate body and frame with channel side rails. Carbon-Steel, 39,000 psi. 117.5 in. wheelbase: 2.30 in. x 5.92 in. x 0.156 in. Section modules: 3.06 in. 129.5 in.: 2.30 in. x 5.92 in. x 0.194. Section modules: 3.93. 135.5 in. wheelbase: 2.78 in. x 7.74 in. 0.194 in. Section modules: 6.20. 164.5 in. wheelbase: 2.78 in. x 7.74 in. x 0.224 in. Section modules: 7.33. 131.5 in. wheelbase: 2.30 in. x 5.92 in. x 0.194 in. Section modules: 3.84 in. Optional: None.

SUSPENSION AND RUNNING GEAR: Front Suspension: K10: Tapered 2-leaf springs. Capacity: 1650 lb. (16), 1850 lb. (03,06). K15: Tapered 2-leaf springs. Capacity: 1850-lb. K35: Tapered 3-leaf springs. Capacity: 2250 lb. Optional rating: K10 and K20: 2250 lb. Rear Suspension: K10 and K-20: 52 in. x 2.25 in. Two-stage, 7-leaf. K30: 56 in. x 2.50 in. Capacity: K10: 2075 lb. K20: 2800 lb. K30: 3500 lb. 1.0 in. dia. shock absorbers. Optional: K30: 3750 lb. capacity. Front Axle Type and Capacity: K10 and K20: GMC or Spicer. K35: Spicer. K10: Semi-floating. 3600 lb. capacity. Optional: None. K20: Full-floating, 3800 lb. capacity. K30: Full-floating, 4500 lb. Optional: None. Rear Axle Type and Capacity: K10: Chevrolet, Semi-floating, 3750 lb. capacity. K20: Chevrolet, Full-floating, 5700 lb. K30: 7500 lb. Optional: None. Final Drive Ratio: Standard: K10: 4.11:1; K20 and K30: 4.10:1. Optional: K10: 2.76, 3.07, 3.73, 4.11:1. Transfer Case: Manual Transmission models: New Process 205. Single lever, two-speed: 1.96, 1.00:1. Automatic transmission models: New Process 203. Ratios: 2.01:1, 1.0:1. Brakes: Hydraulic, power assisted. Dimensions: K10: Front: Disc: 11.86 in. x 1.28 in. Rear: Drums: 11.15 x 2.75 in. K20: Front: Disc: 12.5 in. x 1.28 in. Rear: Drums: 11.15 in. x 2.75 in. Optional: K20 (all models including Suburban) (standard with 7500-8400 GVW): Heavy-duty brakes: Front: Disc: 12.50 in. x 1.28 in. Rear: Drums: 13.00 in. x 2.50 in. K30: Front: Disc: 121.50 in. x 1.53 in. Rear: Drum: 13.00 in. x 3.50 in. Wheels: K10: 15 x 6.0JJ 6-stud disc. Optional: 15 x 8JJ. K20: 16.5 x 6.00 in. 8-stud disc. Optional: 16.5 x 6.75. K30: 16.5 x 6.75 in. Tires: K10: L78 x 15B. K20: 8.75 x 16.5C K30: 9.50 x 16.5D. Optional: K10: G78 x 15B, white stripe; H78 x 15B, tubeless, black sidewall or white stripe; L78 x 15B black sidewall or white stripe, tubeless; 10.00 x 16.5C tubeless; G78 x 15B tube-type; 7.00 x 15C tube-type; 6.50 x 16C tube-type and LR78 x 15C white sidewall radial ply. The following tires were specified for K10 models with the 5600 lb. GVW package which included a front heavy-duty stabilizer bar: H78 x 15B 4-ply rating, tubeless; 6.50 x 16C 6-ply rating, tube-type, truck type. The following tires were specified for K10 models with the 6000 lb. GVW Package which included a front heavy-duty stabilizer bar and heavy-duty rear springs: L78 x 15B 4-ply rating, tubeless. Optional K20: 8.75 x 16.5D tubeless; 10.00 x 16.5C tubeless (not available for Stepside models); 7.50 x 16C 6-ply rating, tube-type; 7.50 x 16D tube-type; 7.50 x 16E tube-type. The following tires were specified for K20 models with the 7500 lb. GVW Package which included a front heavy-duty stabilizer bar: 8.75 x 16.5 C 6-ply rating, tubeless; 7.50 x 16C 6-ply rating, tubeless. The following tires were specified for K20 models with the 8200 lb. GVW Package which included a front heavy-duty stabilizer bar: 9.50 x 16.5D 8-ply rating, tubeless; 7.50 x 16C 6-ply rating, tube type. Steering: Recirculating ball gear. Ratio: 20:1. Turning Circle: 47 ft. Steering wheel diameter: 17.5 in. Optional: Power-assisted. Ratio: 16.4:1. Transmission: K10 and K20: 3-speed, synchromesh manual (RPO M15). Transmission Ratios: 2.85, 1.68, 1.00:1. Optional: Chevrolet CH465. 4-speed manual synchromesh (RPO M20). Ratios: 6.55, 3.58, 1.70, 1.00:1. Reverse: 6.09:1. The K20 crew cab and all K30 models had this transmission as standard equipment. Optional: 3-speed Turbo Hydra-Matic 400 (RPO M40). Ratios: 2.1 x 2.48, 1.48, 1.00:1. Reverse: 2.10:1. The 400 cu. in. V-8 was available only with this transmission. Clutch: Diaphragm, spring. Clutch diameter: 6-cyl.: 11 in. dia. Total lining area: 123.5 sq. in. Total plate pressure: 2075 lb. V-8: 12 in. dia. Total lining area: 149.2 sq. in. Total plate pressure: 2060 lb. Optional: K20 6-cyl.: 11 in. dia. Total lining area: 124.0 sq. in. V-8: 307 V-8: 12 in. dia. Total lining area: 150 sq. in.

VEHICLE DIMENSIONS: Series K10 and K20. Wheelbase: K10: 117.5 in. 131.5 in. K20: 131.5 in. All Suburbans and Panels: 129.5 in. K30: 131.5 in. 164.5 in. Overall Length: 117.5 in. Fleetside pickups: 191.30 in. 131.5 in. Fleetside pickups: 212.00. 117.5 in. Stepside pickups: 190.5 in. 131.5 in. Stepside pickups: 210.25. 117.5 in. Chassis cab: 186.05 in. K30 data: 164.5 in. wheelbase: 244.43 in. Front/Rear Tread: 67.4 in./65.8 in. Overall Height: K10 Fleetside pickup: 72.0 in. K20 Fleetside pickup: 74.0 in. K30 Fleetside pickup: 74.0 in. K10 crew cab: 75.0 in. K10 Suburban: 73.5 in. K20 Suburban: 75.5 in. Width: Pickup: 79.5 in. Front/Rear Overhang: pickups: 33 in./41 in. Tailgate: Width and Height: 72 in. x 19.25 in. Approach/Departure Degrees: K10 117.5 in. Fleetside Stepside: 33/19. K10 131.5 in. Fleetside: 33/15. K10 131.5 in. wheelbase Stepside: 33/16. K20 131.5 in. wheelbase Fleetside: 35/20. K20 131.5 in. wheelbase Stepside: 35/21. K30 Fleetside pickup: 41/19. K30 crew cab Pickup: 38/18. Ground Clearance: Front axle: 7.25 in. Rear axle: 7.0 in. Oil pan: 16.5 in. Transfer case: 12.0 in. Fuel tank: 16.6 in. Load space: Pickup box dimensions: 117.5 in. wheelbase Fleetside: 78.25 in. x 50 in. x 19.25 in. 131.5 in. wheelbase Fleetside: 98 in. x 50 in. x 19.25 in. Capacity: 117.5 in. wheelbase Fleetside: 58.4 cu. ft. 131.5 in. wheelbase Fleetside: 74.3 cu. ft. 117.5 in. wheelbase Stepside: 78.5 in. x 50 in. x 17.5 in. 131.5 in. wheelbase Stepside: 96.25 in. x 50 in. x 17.5 in. Front headroom: 38.5 in. (seat to top of cab). Front hip room: 67.25 in. Pedal to seat back (max.): 43.5 in. Steering wheel to seat back (max.): 17.3 in. Seat to ground: 35.0 in. Floor to ground: 23.0 in.

CAPACITIES: Fuel Tank: 117.5 in. wheelbase: 16.0 gal. 131.5 in. wheelbase: 20.0: gal. 164.5 in.: 20 gal. Optional: 17 gal. auxiliary tank. for 117.5 in.; 20 gal. auxiliary for 131.5 in. and 164.5 in. wheelbase. Engine Coolant System: 250 6-cyl.: 14.8 qt. 305 V-8: 17.6 qt. 350 V-8: 17.6 qt. 400 V-8: 19.6 qt. (20 qt. on K20 and K30).

ACCOMMODATIONS: Seating Capacity: Pickup and chassis cab models: 3 passenger. Optional: None. Suburban: 3 passenger. Optional: 6 or 9 passenger.

INSTRUMENTATION: Speedometer, odometer, fuel level gauge. Warning lights for battery, oil pressure, generator, brake system warning, directional/hazard lights, high beam, and engine coolant temperature.

OPTIONS AND PRICES: 350 V-8: $210 above base 250 engine. Variable ratio power steering: $188. Heavy-duty vacuum power brakes (K20 only): $53. ComforTilt steering wheel. Turbo Hydra-Matic: $315. Below eye-level mirrors. Gauge Package. Includes voltmeter, oil pressure and engine coolant temperature gauges; available with either tachometer or clock. All-Weather air conditioning: $509. Deluxe chromed bumpers. Chrome front bumper guards with impact stripes. Delco Freedom battery. Heavy-duty battery: $31. Auxiliary battery: $88. Heavy-duty radiator: $34.Stainless steel wheelcovers (K10 only). Bright metal hubcaps (K10 only). Exterior Decor Package. Cold Climate Package: $120 for K10, K20 picks with base trim. Prices for vehicles with other trim levels and equipment range from $89 to $129. Speed and cruise control: $80. Scottsdale Package: $236 (for Stepside pickups with base equipment). Other prices depend upon model, dual or single rear wheels and installation of bucket seats. Silverado Package: $431 (for Stepside pickups with base equipment). Other prices depend upon model, dual or single rear wheels and installation of bucket seats. Cheyenne Package: $350 (for Stepside pickups with base equipment). Other prices depend upon model, dual or single rear wheels and installation of bucket seats. Operating Convenience Group: $206. Knit vinyl bench seat: $38. Custom vinyl bench seat bonus cab: $38; Crew cab: $76. Fuel tank shield plate. Transfer case shield plate. Extra capacity fuel tank. Soft-Ray tinted glass: pickups: $27, bonus and crew cab: $34. Special Custom cloth bench seat: Bonus cab with Scottsdale: $38; Crew cab with Scottsdale: $76. Full depth foam seat: $36. Rallye wheels. Electric clock. Two-tone paint. 61 amp alternator. Pickup box side rails. Bucket seats. Glide-out spare tire carrier. Sliding rear window: $62. Cargo area lamp. AM radio: $79. AM/FM radio: $155. Engine oil cooler. Heavy-duty front springs and shock absorbers. Heavy-duty rear springs. Heavy-duty alternator. Weight-equalizing hitch platform. Power door locks. Power windows. Color-keyed front compartment floor mats. Intermittent windshield wipers. Inside hood release. Trailer Special Package (for K10 and K20, except for Chassis and Cab): $219. Includes power steering, heavy-duty battery, trailer wiring harness, rear step bumper, weight-distributing trailer hitch or ball hitch for step bumper. Camper Special Package. Specific equipment content varied with body weight. General content included camper body wiring, heavy-duty front and rear springs, heavy-duty front and rear shock absorbers, and Camper Special nameplate. Available only for K20 and K30; requires V-8 engine and either 4-spd. manual or Turbo Hydra-Matic transmission. Deluxe Camper Special Package. Includes all Camper Special equipment plus Camper Tie-Down Package, Elimi-Pitch Package (includes two horizontal shock absorbers mounted between cab rear panel and pickup box, and two vertical shock absorber mounted between camper overhang and front fenders and rear stabilizer (standard on K30 with dual rear wheels). Fleetside Sport Package. Stepside Sport Package. Scottsdale Package. Cheyenne Package. Silverado Package.

HISTORICAL FOOTNOTES: Calendar year registration of all Chevrolet trucks for 1977 was 1,113, 201.

1978 PICKUP

Numerous detail refinements, revisions and improvements highlighted the 1978 K series trucks from Chevrolet. Interior changes began with the instrument pad applique. For the Custom Deluxe and Scottsdale models a black diamond-textured applique was used. A silver-applique was used for the Cheyenne. A bright brush-finished treatment was used for the Silverado. A new brush-finished instrument cluster bezel and instrument panel applique along with a gauge-type instrument cluster comprised the new Deluxe instrument panel option, RPO BC3. It replaced RPO BC2. The windshield wiper/washer system for 1978 had an improved performance wiper motor with an integral washer pump. Because of this motor, the intermittent windshield wiper system, RPO CD4, was all new.

1978 Chevrolet K10 Suburban

All front seat safety belts systems now used a single emergency locking retractor for both the lap and shoulder belt. The rear seat lap belt retractors on crew cab models were also changed to this type.

A new hood assembly was used to meet new impact requirements. Replacing the old one-piece hood insulation was a two-piece version. In order to comply with new windshield retention requirements, a new bonded-in urethane rubber strip was used. all models also were equipped with new insulators and deadeners to reduce noise. A new drip gutter over the rear door was added as base equipment for Suburban models. Chevrolet also announced major improvements in corrosion protection for 1978. Galvanized steel was used in such areas as the radiator grille lower panel and all door glass channels. In addition, use of pre-coated steel was extended to the side outer panels and the tailgate of Fleetside and Stepside pickup boxes. The side inner panel extension on those models was redesigned to minimize entry of water and other material between the inner and outer panels. For 1978 front and rear wheel openings were available as separate options. Previously they had been part of other options. The full wheelcovers, RPO PO1, that had been available only for the K10 were now offered for the K20. The Rallye wheel option had a newly styled chromed plastic center hub. The rear

hub of both the Rallye and styled wheels carried four-wheel drive identification. Optional bright metal hubcaps for the K10 and K30 were revised with the addition of extensions to the front caps which concealed the sides of the axle hub units. Door hardware for all trim levels now featured a bright brushed finish instead of the former pewter finish. The Custom Deluxe vinyl bench and bucket seat trims featured a new cover material with an oxen hide grain with a smoother texture than the former buffalo hide grain. The Custom Deluxe vinyl trim for bench-type seats also was restyled. The Custom Deluxe cloth trim for bench-type seats had new styling and new ribbed velour cloth covers. The color selection and general interior format were unchanged. The vinyl seat trim for the Scottsdale was restyled. Also, the cover material was changed from knit to porous vinyl. The Scottsdale color choices were unchanged.

CHEVY STEPSIDE SPORT, FOREGROUND; PICKUP AT REAR HICKEY EQUIPPED.

1978 Chevrolet K10 Stepside pickup

Minor changes were made in the K series frames to accommodate a new catalytic converter exhaust system required in California. The California K series trucks with the 5.7 liter RPO LS9 and 6.6 liter RPO LF4 engines had a single exhaust system with larger diameter pipes and larger muffler, rather than a dual exhaust system. RPO dual exhausts were not available in California. All converter-equipped vehicles had new transmission supports. All two-piece propeller shafts were revised to increase center bearing cushion durability. K20 and K30 models had new rear spring U-bolts. On all models with V-8 engine and full-time four-wheel drive, struts were added between the engine and transmission, and between the transmission and transfer case to lessen the chance of driveshaft boom. Locking front hubs were not available on the K30 series with manual transmission. All steering column assemblies were new to incorporate metric attachments. A newly styled soft vinyl steering wheel and horn button. This wheel had a 16.0 in. diameter and replaced the 17.5 in. diameter unit previously used on K10 and K20 models. Minor instrument cluster changes involved a lens change for the PRNDL portion on automatic transmission models, and the use of an electric oil pressure gauge for RPO Z53, the gauge package option.

The Fleetside and Stepside Sport Packages were available after January, 1978. They were offered for K10 models only. Their content included multi-tone sport decal striping (either red or gold) down the body sides, hood and tailgate, RPO V22 black painted grille with chrome trim, RPO Z62 Scottsdale trim (without side moldings), RPO B32 color-keyed floor mats, BC3 Deluxe instrument panel, RPO U35 clock, rear bumper painted body color (stepside only), front bumper painted body color with impact strip, rear bumper painted body color with impact strip (Fleetside only), "Chevy Sport" hood ornament, RPO N67 Rallye wheels, and 10.00 x 15B white-lettered on-off highway tires Also available as options were RPO PA6 white-spoked styled wheels, low-profile white-lettered radial LR60-15B tires and RPO PH7 15 x 7 in. aluminum wheels. The Chevy Sport was available in midnight black, cardinal red, frost white or Colonial yellow. All except the last color had interior trim colors of buckskin and red. The Colonial white exterior had a buckskin interior trim. All fifteen exterior color choices were carried over unchanged from 1977.

1978 Chevrolet K30 "Big Dooley" crew cab

I.D. DATA: Unchanged from 1976 except the number 7 represented the 1977 model year. The letter U identified trucks with the 400 cu. in. V-8.

Model Number	Body Type & Seating	Factory Price	GVW	Shipping Weight	Prod. Total

Series K10-1/2 ton 250 6-cyl. 117.5 in. 131.5 in. wheelbase (Suburban: 129.5 in. wheelbase and standard 305 V-8)

Model Number	Body Type & Seating	Factory Price	GVW	Shipping Weight	Prod. Total
CK10703	117.5 in. Chassis & Cab	$5006	6200	4143	—
CK10903	131.5 in. Chassis & Cab	$N.A.	6200	4250	—
CK10703	6.5 ft. Stepside Pickup	$5006	6200	4477	—
CK10703	6.5 ft. Fleetside Pickup	$5006	6200	4537	—
CK10903	8 ft. Stepside Pickup	$5062	6200	4639	—
CK10903	8 ft. Fleetside Pickup	$5062	6200	4720	—
CK10906	Suburban Endgate	$6348	6200	5273	—
CK10906	Suburban Panl. Drs.	$N.A.	6200	5235	—

Series K20-3/4 ton 292 V-8[1]. 131.5 in. wheelbase. (Suburban-129.5 in. wheelbase). Crew and bonus cab: 164.5 in. wheelbase, Suburban weight with standard 305 V-8

Model Number	Body Type & Seating	Factory Price	GVW	Shipping Weight	Prod. Total
CK20903	Chassis and Cab	$5209	6800*	4485	—
CK20903	8 ft. Stepside Pickup	$5434	6800	4874	—
CK20903	8 ft. Fleetside Pickup	$5434	6800	4955	—
CK20906	Suburban Endgate	$6795	6800	5472	—
CK20906	Suburban Panl. Drs.	$N.A.	6800	5434	—

NOTE 1: Not available in California where the 350 engine is base.
* 7500 and 8400 lb. GVW optional.

Series K30-1 ton 350 V-8. 131.5 in. wheelbase. Crew and bonus cab: 164.5 in. wheelbase

Model Number	Body Type & Seating	Factory Price	GVW	Shipping Weight	Prod. Total
CK31003	Chassis & Cab[1]	$5589	8400*	4956	—
CK31403	Chassis & Cab[2]	$N.A.	8490	5243	—
CK30903	8 ft. Fleetside Pickup	$5814	8400	5426	—
CK30943	Chassis & Bonus Cab	$6520	8400	5370	—
CK30943	Fleetside Bonus Cab	$6745	8400	5840	—
CK30943	Chassis & Crew Cab	$6630	8400	5370	—
CK30943	Fleetside Crew Cab	$6855	8400	5840	—

NOTE 1: 135.5 in. wheelbase.
NOTE 2: 159.9 in. wheelbase.
* 9200 and 10,000 lb. GVW optional.

STANDARD ENGINE: All K-10 6-cyl. models: 250 Six (LD4 ordering code). Not available for California where a 350 V-8 is installed. Engine Type: OHV, In-line 6-cylinder. Cast iron block and cylinder head. Key features induction hardened exhaust valve seats, and timing tabs. Bore x Stroke: 3.875 in. x 3.53 in. Lifters: Hydraulic. Number of main bearings-7. Fuel Induction: Single Rochester 1-bbl. carburetor. Compression Ratio: 8.0:1. Displacement: 250 cu. in. (4.09 liters). Horsepower: Net: 100 @ 3600 rpm. Torque: Net: 175 lb.-ft. @ 1800 rpm. Oil refill capacity: 5 qt. with filter change. Fuel Requirements: Regular.

STANDARD ENGINE: K20 and K30 6-cyl. models: 292 Six. Ordering Code: L25. Engine Type: OHV, 6-cyl. Cast iron block and cylinder head. Key features include cast iron intake manifold, aluminized-face intake valves, stellite-faced exhaust valves with hardened faces. Bore x Stroke: 3.875 in. x 4.125 in. Lifters: Hydraulic. Number of main bearings-7. Fuel Induction: Single Rochester 1-bbl. carburetor. Compression Ratio: 8.0:1. Displacement: 292 cu. in. (4.78 liters). Horsepower: Net: 120 @ 3600 rpm. Torque: Net: 215 lb.-ft. @ 2000 rpm. Oil refill capacity: 6 qt. Fuel Requirements: Regular.

STANDARD ENGINE: K20 and K30 V-8 models: Ordering Code: LS9: 350 V-8 Engine Type: OHV, V-8. Cast iron block and alloy iron cylinder head. Key features include chain drive camshaft and forged steel connecting rods. Bore x Stroke: 4.0 in. x 3.50 in. Lifters: Hydraulic. Number of main bearings-5. Fuel Induction: Single Rochester 4-bbl. carburetor. Compression Ratio: 8.5:1. Displacement: 350 cu. in. (5.73 liters). Horsepower: Net: 165 @ 3800 rpm. Torque: Net: 255 lb.-ft. @ 2800 rpm. Oil refill capacity: 5 qt. with filter change. Fuel Requirements: Regular.

OPTIONAL ENGINE: K20 and K30 V-8 models: Ordering Code: LF4: 400 V-8. Key features include induction-hardened valve seats and cast iron camshaft. Engine Type: OHV, V-8. Cast iron block and alloy iron cylinder head. Bore x Stroke: 4.10 in. x 3.8 in. Lifters: Hydraulic. Number of main bearings-5. Fuel Induction: Single Rochester 4-bbl. carburetor. Compression Ratio: 8.5:1. Displacement: 400 cu. in. (6.55 liters). Horsepower: Net: 175 @ 3600 rpm. Torque: Net: 290 lb.-ft. @ 2800 rpm. Oil refill capacity: 5 qt. with filter change. Fuel Requirements: Regular.

STANDARD ENGINE: K10 and K20 V-8 Suburban models: Ordering Code: LG9 305 V-8. Not available in California. Engine Type: OHV, V-8. Cast iron block and alloy iron cylinder head. Bore x Stroke: 3.74 in. x 3.48 in. Lifters: Hydraulic. Number of main bearings-5. Fuel Induction: Single Rochester 2-bbl. carburetor. Compression Ratio: 8.5:1. Displacement: 305 cu. in. (4.997 liters). Horsepower: Net: 145 @ 3800 rpm. Torque: Net: 245 lb.-ft. @ 2400 rpm. Oil refill capacity: 5 qt. with filter change. Fuel Requirements: Regular.

CHASSIS FEATURES: Separate body and frame with channel side rails. Carbon-Steel, 39,000 psi. 117.5 in. wheelbase: 2.30 in. x 5.92 in. x 0.156 in. Section modules: 3.06 in. 129.5 in.: 2.30 in. x 5.92 in x 0.194. Section modules: 3.93. 135.5 in. wheelbase: 2.78 in. x 7.74 in. 0.194 in. Section modules: 6.20. 164.5 in. wheelbase: 2.78 in. x 7.74 in. x 0.224 in. Section modules: 7.33. 131.5 in. wheelbase: 2.30 in. x 5.92 in. x 0.194 in. Section modules: 3.84 in. Optional: None.

SUSPENSION AND RUNNING GEAR: Front Suspension: K10: Tapered 2-leaf springs. Capacity: 1650 lb. (16), 1850 lb. (03,06). K15: Tapered 2-leaf springs. Capacity: 1850 lb. K35: Tapered 3-leaf springs. Capacity: 2250 lb. Rear Suspension: K10 and K-20: 52 in. x 2.25 in. Two-stage, 7-leaf. K30: 56 in. x 2.50 in. Capacity: K10: 2075 lb. K20: 2800 lb. K30: 3500 lb. 1.0 in. dia. shock absorbers. Optional: K30: 3750 lb. capacity. Front Axle Type and Capacity: K10 and K20: GMC or Spicer, K35: Spicer. K10: Semi-floating. 3600 lb. capacity. Optional: None. K30: Full-floating, 3800 lb. K30: Full-floating, 4500 lb. Optional: None. Rear Axle Type and Capacity: K10: Chevrolet, Semi-floating, 3750 lb. K20: Chevrolet, Full-floating, 5700 lb. K30: 7500 lb. Optional: None. Final Drive Ratio: Standard: K10: 4.11:1; K20 and K30: 4.10:1. Optional: K10: 2.76, 3.07, 3.73, 4.11:1. Transfer Case: Manual transmission models: New Process 205. Single lever, two-speed: 1.96, 1.00:1. Automatic transmission models: New Process 203. Ratios: 2.01:1, 1.0:1. Brakes: Type: Hydraulic, power assisted. Dimensions: K10: Front: Disc: 11.86 in. x 1.28 in. Rear: Drums: 11.15 x 2.75 in. K20: Front: Disc: 12.5 in. x 1.28 in. Rear: Drums: 11.15 in. x 2.75 in. Optional: K20 (all models including Suburban) (standard with 7500-8400 GVW): Heavy-duty brakes: Front: Disc: 12.50 in. x 1.28 in. Rear: Drums: 13.00 in. x 2.50 in. K30: Front: Disc: 121.50 in. x 1.53 in. Rear: Drum: 13.00 in. x 3.50 in. Wheels: K10: 15 x 6.0JJ 6-stud disc. Optional: 15 x 8JJ. K20: 16.5 x 6.00 in. 8-stud disc. Optional: 16.5 x 6.75. K30: 16.5 x 6.75. Tires: K10: L78 x 15B. K20: 8.75 x 16.5C K30: 9.50 x 16.5D. Optional: K10: G78 x 15B, white stripe; H78 x 15B, tubeless, black

---

sidewall or white stripe; L78 x 15B black sidewall or white stripe, tubeless; 10.00 x 16.5C tubeless; G78 x 15B tube-type; 7.00 x 15C tube-type; 6.50 x 16C tube-type and LR78 x 15C white sidewall radial ply. The following tires were specified for K10 models with the 5600 lb. GVW package which included a front heavy-duty stabilizer bar: H78 x 15B 4-ply rating, tubeless; 6.50 x 16C 6-ply rating, tube-type, truck type. The following tires were specified for K10 models with the 6000 lb. GVW Package which included a front heavy-duty stabilizer bar and heavy-duty rear springs: L78 x 15B 4-ply rating, tubeless. Optional K20: 8.75 x 16.5D tubeless; 9.50 x 16.5D tubeless; 10.00 x 16.5C tubeless (not available for Stepside models); 7.50 x 16C 6-ply rating, tube-type; 7.50 x 16D tube-type; 7.50 x 16E tube-type. The following tires were specified for K20 models with the 7500 lb. GVW Package which included a front heavy-duty stabilizer bar: 8.75 x 16.5 C 6-ply rating, tubeless; 7.50 x 16C 6-ply rating, tubeless. The following tires were specified for K20 models with the 8200 lb. GVW Package which included a front heavy-duty stabilizer bar: 9.50 x 16.5D 8-ply rating, tubeless; 7.50 x 16C 6-ply rating, tube type. Steering: Recirculating ball gear. Ratio: 20:1. Turning Circle: 47 ft. Steering wheel diameter: 17.5 in. Optional: Power-assisted. Ratio: 16.4:1. Transmission: K10 and K20: 3-speed, synchromesh manual (RPO M15). Transmission Ratios: 2.85, 1.68, 1.00:1. Optional: Chevrolet CH465. 4-speed manual synchromesh (RPO M20). Ratios: 6.55, 3.58, 1.70, 1.00:1. Reverse: 6.09:1. The K20 crew cab and all K30 models had this transmission as standard equipment. Optional: 3-speed Turbo Hydra-Matic 400 (RPO M40). Ratios: 2.1 x 2.48, 1.48, 1.00:1. Reverse: 2.10:1. The 400 cu. in. V-8 was available only with this transmission. Clutch: Diaphragm, spring. Clutch diameter: 6-cyl.: 11 in. dia. Total lining area: 123.5 sq. in. Total plate pressure: 2075 lb. V-8: 12 in. dia. Total lining area: 149.2 sq. in. Total plate pressure: 2060 lb. K20 6-cyl.: 11 in. dia. Total lining area: 124.0 sq. in. 307 V-8: 12 in. dia. Total lining area: 150 sq. in.

VEHICLE DIMENSIONS: Series K10 and K20: Wheelbase: K10: 117.5 in. 131.5 in. K20: 131.5 in. All Suburbans and Panels: 129.5 in. K30: 131.5 in. 164.5 in. Overall Length: 117.5 in. Fleetside pickups: 191.30 in. 131.5 in. Fleetside pickups: 212.00. 117.5 in. Stepside pickups: 190.5 in. 131.5 in. Stepside pickups: 210.25. 117.5 in. Chassis cab: 186.05 in. K30 data: 164.5 in. wheelbase: 244.43 in. Front/Rear Tread: 67.4 in./65.8 in. Overall Height: K10 Fleetside pickup: 72.0 in. K20 Fleetside pickup: 74.0 in. K30 Fleetside pickup: 74.0 in. K30 crew cab: 75.0 in. K10 Suburban: 73.5 in. K20 Suburban: 75.5 in. Width: 79.5 in. Front/Rear Overhang: pickups: 33 in./41 in. Tailgate: Width and Height: 72 in. x 19.25 in. Approach/Departure Degrees: K10 117.5 in. Fleetside and Stepside: 33/19. K10 131.5 in. Fleetside: 33/15. K10 131.5 in. wheelbase Stepside: 33/16. K20 131.5 in. wheelbase Fleetside: 35/20. K20 131.5 in. wheelbase Stepside: 35/21. K30 Fleetside pickup: 41/19. K30 crew cab Pickup: 38/18. Ground Clearance: Front axle: 7.25 in. Rear axle: 7.0 in. Oil pan: 16.5 in. Transfer case: 12.0 in. Fuel tank: 16.6 in. Load space: Pickup box dimensions: 117.5 in. wheelbase Fleetside: 78.25 in. x 50 in. x 19.25 in. 131.5 in. wheelbase Fleetside: 98 in. x 50 in. x 19.25 in. Capacity: 117.5 wheelbase: 58.4 cu. ft. 131.5 in. wheelbase: 74.3 cu. ft. 117.5 in. wheelbase Stepside: 78.5 in. x 50 in. x 17.5 in. 131.5 in. wheelbase Stepside: 96.25 in. x 50 in. x 17.5 in. Front headroom: 38.5 in. (seat to top of cab). Front hip room: 67.25 in. Pedal to seat back (max.): 43.5 in. Steering wheel to seat back (max.): 17.3 in. Seat to ground: 35.0 in. Floor to ground: 23.0 in.

CAPACITIES: Fuel Tank: 117.5 in. wheelbase: 16.0 gal. 131.5 in. wheelbase: 20.0: gal. 164.5 in.: 20 gal. Optional: 17 gal. auxiliary tank. for 117.5 in.; 20 gal. auxiliary for 131.5 in. and 164.5 in. wheelbase. Engine Coolant System: 250 6-cyl.: 14.8 qt. 305 V-8: 17.6 qt. 350 V-8: 17.6 qt. 400 V-8: 19.6 qt. (20 qt. on K20 and K30).

ACCOMMODATIONS: Seating Capacity: Pickup and chassis cab models: 3 passenger. Optional: None. Suburban: 3 passenger. Optional: 6 or 9 passenger.

INSTRUMENTATION: Speedometer, odometer, fuel level gauge. Warning lights for battery, oil pressure, generator, brake system warning, directional/hazard lights, high beam, and engine coolant temperature.

OPTIONS AND PRICES: Power steering (RPO N41): $207. 350 V-8 (RPO LS9): $300. 400 V-8 (RPO LF4): $465. 4-speed manual synchromesh (RPO MM4): $152. Turbo Hydra-Matic (RPO MX1): $345. Poly-Wrap air cleaner (RPO K43). Air conditioning (RPO C60). Locking rear differential (RPO G80): $175. Auxiliary 3500 watt Delco Freedom battery (RPO TP2). Heavy-duty 4000 watt Delco freedom battery (RPO UA1). Painted rear bumper (RPO V38). Rear step bumper (RPO V43). Front and rear chromed bumpers (RPO V37). Front chrome bumper (RPO V46). Rear chrome bumper (RPO VF1). Rear step bumper-Fleetside only, (RPO V42). Front and rear deluxe chromed bumpers-Fleetside only (RPO VE5). Front deluxe chromed bumper (RPO VG3). Chromed front bumper guards (RPO V31). Glide-out spare wheel carrier (RPO P11). Side-mounted spare wheel carrier (RPO P13). Chevy Sport Package (RPO Z77). Electric clock (RPO U35). Cold Climate Package. Includes UA1 battery and K76 generator. (RPO Z56). Engine oil cooler. Available for V-8 engines only (RPO KC4). Transmission oil cooler. Available for V-8 engines and auto. trans. only. (RPO VO2). Heavy-duty radiator (RPO VO1). Power door locks (RPO AU3). California emission system (RPO YF5). Dual exhaust system. Requires LS9 (RPO N10). Color-keyed floor mats (RPO B32). Wood pickup box, CK10903 Fleetside only (RPO E81). Gauge Package. Includes voltmeter, engine coolant temperature and oil pressure (RPO Z53). Tachometer. Requires V-8 engine. (RPO U16): $87, with Silverado option: $60. 61 amp Delcotron alternator (RPO K76). Soft-Ray tinted glass, all windows (RPO AO1). Chrome grille (RPO V22). Camper body wiring harness (RPO UY1). Headlight warning buzzer (RPO T63). Inside hood lock release (RPO T44). Deluxe instrument panel (RPO BC3). Cargo area lamp (RPO UF2). Dome lamp (RPO C91). Roof marker lights (RPO UO1). Cigarette lighter (RPO U37). Below eye-level painted 7.5 in. x 10.5 in. mirrors (RPO D29). Below eye-level stainless steel 7.5 in. x 10.5 in. mirrors (RPO DG4). Camper-type below eye-level mirrors (RPO DFG4). Body side spear molding, Fleetside only (RPO B84). Body upper moldings, Fleetside only (RPO B85). Body side upper and lower moldings, Fleetside only (RPO YG1). Door edge guard (RPO B93). Wheel opening moldings, Fleetside only (RPO B96). Operating Convenience Package. Includes AU3 door locks and A31 windows. (RPO ZQ2). Fuel tank shield (RPO NY1). AM push-button radio (RPO U63). AM/FM push-button radio (RPO U69). Folding seat back (RPO AN1). Full-depth foam seat (RPO Z52). Pickup box side rails (RPO D73). Speed and cruise control (RPO K30). Heavy-duty front springs. Includes heavy-duty front and rear shock absorbers. Recommended for snowplow type usage only on K10. (RPO F60): $67. ComforTilt steering wheel (RPO N33). Custom steering wheel (RPO N31). Red exterior stripe (RPO 71A). Auxiliary fuel tank (RPO NL2): $150. Two front towing hooks (RPO V76). Weight distributing platform type trailer hitch (RPO VR4). Trailering Special Package. Includes UA1 battery and K76 generator. (RPO Z82). Bright metal hubcaps (RPO PO3). Trim rings (RPO PO6). Wheelcovers (RPO PO1). Special wheelcovers (RPO PA1). Spare dual wheel, K30 only (RPO QE2 or QE6 depending upon tire size). Dual rear wheels, K30 only (RPO RO5). Single rear wheels, K30 only (RPO ZW3). Aluminum wheels, K10 only. (RPO PH7). Rallye wheels, K10 only (RPO N67). Styled wheels, K10 only. (RPO PA6). Power windows (RPO A31). Sliding rear window (RPO A28). Intermittent windshield wipers (RPO CD4). Heavy-duty vacuum brakes, K30 only. (RPO JA5). Basic Camper Group, K20 and K30 only. Includes F60 springs and UY1 harness. (RPO Z81). Deluxe Camper Group, K20 and K30 only. (RPO Z83). Frame-mounted spare wheel carrier,

K30 only (RPO P10). Senior West Coast type painted mirrors, K30 only (RPO DG5). Heavy-duty front and rear shock absorbers (RPO F51). Conventional two-tone paint ZY2). Special two-tone paint, Fleetside only (RPO ZY3). Deluxe two-tone paint, Fleetside only (RPO XY4). Exterior Decor Package, Fleetside only. Includes YG1 and B96 moldings, hood ornament and hood accent stripes (RPO ZY5).

HISTORICAL FOOTNOTES: Chevrolet reported its sales of 1.34 million trucks in 1978 was an all-time division record.

1978 Chevrolet K30 chassis cab with wrecker body

1979 PICKUP

For 1979 the Chevrolet trucks had a new front end with new integral head/parking lamps, a new bright metal lower grille outline molding and a new grille paint scheme for the grille. Additional new features included new exterior and interior colors, and a new concealed fuel filler. The 250 6-cylinder engine had a new staged 2-barrel carburetor, new cylinder head with improved porting, and a new dual takedown exhaust system. These changes improved the engine's horsepower output. The 1979 exterior color selection consisted of white, silver metallic, dark bright blue, medium blue, dark blue, medium green metallic, bright green metallic, dark green, yellow, neutral, camel metallic, dark carmine, bright red, russet metallic, dark brown metallic, dark yellow, charcoal and black.

I.D. DATA: The vehicle identification number was located on a plate in the lower left side of the windshield. It had 13 units. The first, the letter C represented the Chevrolet Division Code. The second digit, K, indicated 4-wheel drive. The third digit represented the engine: D-250 6-cyl. L-350 V-8, R-400 V-8, T-292 6-cyl. The fourth digit indicated the Series: 1-Chev. 10, 2-Chev 20, 3-Chev 30. The fifth digit identified the body type: 3-Chassis and cab, 4-Pickup, 6-Suburban. The sixth digit, a 9 indicated the1979 model year. The seventh digit represented the assembly plant. The eighth through thirteenth digit was the assembly sequence number.

Model Number	Body Type & Seating	Factory Price	GVW	Shipping Weight	Prod. Total
Series K10-1/2 ton 250 6-cyl. 117.5 in. 131.5 in. wheelbase (Suburban: 129.5 in. wheelbase and standard 305 V-8)					
CK10703	117.5 in. Chassis & Cab	$6043	6200	4143	—
CK10903	131.5 in. Chassis & Cab	$6123	6200	4250	—
CK10703	6.5 ft. F-S Pickup	$6191	6200	4477	—
CK10703	6.5 ft. Wideside Pickup	$6191	6200	4537	—
CK10903	8 ft. Fenderside Pickup	$6271	6200	4639	—
CK10903	8 ft. Wideside Pickup	$6271	6200	4720	—
CK10906	Suburban Endgate	$7714	6200	5273	—
CK10906	Suburban Panl. Drs.	$N.A.	6200	5235	—

Series K20-3/4 ton 292 V-8[1]. 131.5 in. wheelbase. (Suburban-129.5 in. wheelbase). Crew and bonus cab: 164.5 in. wheelbase, Suburban weight with standard 305 V-8

CK20903	Chassis and Cab	$6557	6800*	4485	—
CK20903	8 ft. Fenderside Pickup	$6818	6800	4874	—
CK20903	8 ft. Wideside Pickup	$6818	6800	4955	—
CK20906	Suburban Endgate	$8151	6800	5472	—
CK20906	Suburban Panl. Drs.	$N.A.	6800	5434	—

NOTE 1: Not available in California where the 350 engine is base.
* 7500 and 8400 lb. GVW optional.

Series K30-1 ton 350 V-8. 131.5 in. wheelbase. Crew and bonus cab: 164.5 in. wheelbase

CK31003	Chassis & Cab[1]	$8059	8400*	4956	—
CK31403	Chassis & Cab[2]	$N.A.	8400	5243	—
CK30903	8 ft. Wideside Pickup	$8355	8400	5426	—
CK30943	Chassis & Bonus Cab	$8858	8400	5370	—
CK30943	Wideside Bonus Cab	$9141	8400	5840	—
CK30943	Chassis & Crew Cab	$9018	8400	5370	—
CK30943	Wideside Crew Cab	$9301	8400	5840	—

NOTE 1: 135.5 in. wheelbase.
NOTE 2: 159.9 in. wheelbase.
* 9200 and 10,000 lb. GVW optional.

STANDARD ENGINE: All K10 6-cyl. models: 250 Six (LE3 ordering code). Engine Type: OHV, In-line 6-cylinder. Cast iron block and cylinder head. Key features induction hardened exhaust valve seats, and timing tabs. Not available for California delivery where 350 engine is standard. Bore x Stroke: 3.875 in. x 3.53 in. Lifters: Hydraulic. Number of main bearings-7. Fuel Induction: Single Rochester staged 2-bbl. carburetor. Compression Ratio: 8.3:1. Displacement: 250 cu. in. (4.09 liters). Horsepower: Net: 130 @ 4000 rpm. Torque: Net: 210 lb.-ft. @ 2000 rpm. Oil refill capacity: 5 qt. with filter change. Fuel Requirements: Regular.

STANDARD ENGINE: K30 6-cyl. models: 292 Six. Ordering Code: L25. Engine Type: OHV, 6-cyl. Cast iron block and cylinder head. Key features include cast iron intake manifold, aluminized-face intake valves, stellite-faced exhaust valves with hardened faces. Bore x Stroke: 3.875 in. x 4.125 in. Lifters: Hydraulic. Number of main bearings-7. Fuel Induction: Single Rochester 1-bbl. carburetor. Compression Ratio: 7.8:1. Displacement: 292 cu. in. (4.78 liters). Horsepower: Net: @ 3400 rpm. Torque: Net: 215 lb.-ft. @ 1600 rpm. Oil refill capacity: 6 qt. Fuel Requirements: Regular.

STANDARD ENGINE: K20 and K30 V-8 models: Standard for K20 Suburban. Ordering Code: LS9: 350 V-8 Engine Type: OHV, V-8. Cast iron block and alloy iron cylinder head. Key features include chain drive camshaft and forged steel connecting rods. Bore x Stroke: 4.0 in. x 3.50 in. Lifters: Hydraulic. Number of main bearings-5. Fuel Induction: Single Rochester 4-bbl. carburetor. Compression Ratio: 8.2:1. (8500 lb. GVW and below), 8501 lb. and up GVW: 8.3:1. Displacement: 350 cu. in. (5.73 liters). Horsepower: Net: 165 @ 3800 rpm. California and GVW below 8500 lb. GVW: 155 @ 3600 rpm. 8501 lb. and up GVW: 165 @ 3800 rpm. Torque: Net: 8500 lb. and below, except California: 270 lb.-ft. @ 2000 rpm. 8500 lb. and below, for California: 260 lb.-ft.@ 2000 rpm.8501 lb. and up GVW: 255 lb.-ft. @ 2800 rpm. Oil refill capacity: 5 qt. with filter change. Fuel Requirements: Regular.

OPTIONAL ENGINE: K20 and K30 V-8 models: Ordering Code: LF4: 400 V-8. Key features include induction-hardened valve seats and cast iron camshaft. Engine Type: OHV, V-8. Cast iron block and alloy iron cylinder head. Bore x Stroke: 4.10 in. x 3.8 in. Lifters: Hydraulic. Number of main bearings-5. Fuel Induction: Single Rochester 4-bbl. carburetor. Compression Ratio: 8.5:1. Displacement: 400 cu. in. (6.55 liters). Horsepower: Net: 185 @ 3600 rpm. California and GVW below 8500 lb. GVW: 170 @ 3600 rpm. 8501 lb. and up GVW: 180 @ 3600 rpm. Torque: Net: 8500 lb. and below, except California: 300 lb.-ft. @ 2400 rpm. 8500 lb. and below, for California: 305 lb.-ft. @ 1600 rpm. 8501 lb. and up GVW: 310 lb.-ft. @ 2400 rpm. Oil refill capacity: 5 qt. with filter change. Fuel Requirements: Regular.

STANDARD ENGINE: K10 Suburban models: Ordering Code: LG9 305 V-8. Not available in California. Engine Type: OHV, V-8. Cast iron block and alloy iron cylinder head. Bore x Stroke: 3.74 in. x 3.48 in. Lifters: Hydraulic. Number of main bearings-5. Fuel Induction: Single Rochester 2-bbl. carburetor. Compression Ratio: 8.4:1. Displacement: 305 cu. in. (4.997 liters). Horsepower: Net: 140 @ 4000 rpm. Torque: Net: 240 lb.-ft. @ 2000 rpm. Oil refill capacity: 5 qt. with filter change. Fuel Requirements: Regular.

CHASSIS FEATURES: Separate body and frame with channel side rails. Carbon-Steel, 39,000 psi. 117.5 in. wheelbase: 2.30 in. x 5.92 in. x 0.156 in. Section modules: 3.06 in. 129.5 in.: 2.30 in. x 5.92 in. x 0.194. Section modules: 3.93. 135.5 in. wheelbase: 2.78 in. x 7.74 in. 0.194 in. Section modules: 6.20. 164.5 in. wheelbase: 2.78 in. x 7.74 in. x 0.224 in. Section modules: 7.33. 131.5 in. wheelbase: 2.30 in. x 5.92 in. x 0.194 in. Section modules: 3.84 in. Optional: None.

SUSPENSION AND RUNNING GEAR: Front Suspension: K10: Tapered 2-leaf springs. Capacity: 1650 lb. (16), 1850 lb. (03,06). K15: Tapered 2-leaf springs. Capacity: 1850 lb. K35: Tapered 3-leaf springs. Capacity: 2250 lb. Rear Suspension: K10 and K-20: 52 in. x 2.25 in. Two-stage, 7-leaf. K30: 56 in. x 2.50 in. Capacity: K10: 2075 lb. K20: 2800 lb. K30: 3500 lb. 1.0 in. dia. shock absorbers. Optional: K30: 3750 lb. capacity. Front Axle Type and Capacity: K10 and K20: GM or Spicer, K35: Spicer. K10: Semi-floating. 3600 lb. capacity. Optional: None. K20: Full-floating, 3800 lb. capacity. K30: Full-floating, 4500 lb. Optional: None. Rear Axle Type and Capacity: K10: Chevrolet, Semi-floating, 3750 lb. capacity. K20: Chevrolet, Full-floating, 5700 lb. K30: 7500 lb. Optional: None. Final Drive Ratio: Standard: K10: 4.11:1; K20 and K30: 4.10:1. Optional: K10: 2.76, 3.07, 3.73, 4.11:1. Transfer Case: Manual Transmission models: New Process 205. Single lever, two-speed: 1.96, 1.00:1. Automatic transmission models: New Process 203. Ratios: 2.01:1, 1.0:1. Brakes: Type: Hydraulic, power assisted. Dimensions: K10: Front: Disc. 11.86 in. x 1.28 in. Rear: Drums: 11.15 x 2.75 in. K20: Front: Disc. 12.5 in. x 1.28 in. Rear: Drums: 11.15 in. x 2.75 in. Optional: K20 (all models including Suburban) (standard with 7500-8400 GVW): Heavy-duty brakes: Front: Disc: 12.50 in. x 1.28 in. Rear: Drums: 13.00 in. x 2.50 in. K30: Front: Disc: 121.50 in. x 1.53 in. Rear: Drum: 13.00 in. x 3.50 in. Wheels: K10: 15 x 6.0JJ 6-stud disc. Optional: 15 x 8JJ. K20: 16.5 x 6.00 in. 8-stud disc. Optional: 16.5 x 6.75. K30: 16.5 x 6.75. Tires: K10: L78 x 15B. K20: 8.75 x 16.5C K30: 9.50 x 16.5D. Optional: K10: G78 x 15B, white stripe; H78 x 15B, tubeless, black sidewall or white stripe; L78 x 15B black sidewall or white stripe, tubeless; 10.00 x 16.5C tubeless; G78 x 15B tube-type; 7.00 x 15C tube-type; 6.50 x 16C tube-type and LR78 x 15C white sidewall radial ply. The following tires were specified for K10 models with the 5600 lb. GVW package which included a front heavy-duty stabilizer bar: H78 x 15B 4-ply rating, tubeless; 6.50 x 16C 6-ply rating, tube-type, truck type. The following tires were specified for K10 models with the 6000 lb. GVW Package which included a front heavy-duty stabilizer bar and heavy-duty rear springs: L78 x 15B 4-ply rating, tubeless. Optional K20: 8.75 x 16.5D tubeless; 9.50 x 16.5D tubeless; 10.00 x 16.5C tubeless (not available for Stepside models); 7.50 x 16C 6-ply rating, tube-type; 7.50 x 16D tube-type; 7.50 x 16E tube-type. The following tires were specified for K20 models with the 7500 lb. GVW Package which included a front heavy-duty stabilizer bar: 8.75 x 16.5 C 6-ply rating, tubeless; 7.50 x 16C 6-ply rating, tubeless. The following tires were specified for K20 models with the 8200 lb. GVW Package which included a front heavy-duty stabilizer bar: 9.50 x 16.5D 8-ply rating, tubeless; 7.50 x 16C 6-ply rating, tube type. Steering: Recirculating ball gear. Ratio: 20:1. Turning Circle: 47 ft. Steering wheel diameter: 17.5 in. Optional: Power-assisted. Ratio: 16.4:1. Transmission: K10 and K20: 3-speed, synchromesh manual (RPO M15). Transmission Ratios: 2.85, 1.68, 1.00:1. Optional: Chevrolet CH465. 4-speed manual synchromesh (RPO M20). Ratios: 6.55, 3.58, 1.70, 1.00:1. Reverse: 6.09:1. The K20 crew cab and all K30 models had this transmission as standard equipment. Optional: 3-speed Turbo Hydra-Matic 400 (RPO M40). Ratios: 2.1 x 2.48, 1.48, 1.00:1. Reverse: 2.10:1. The 400 cu. in. V-8 was available only with this transmission. Clutch: Diaphragm, spring. Clutch diameter: 6-cyl.: 11 in. dia. Total lining area: 123.5 sq. in. Total plate pressure: 2075 lb. V-8: 12 in. dia. Total lining area: 149.2 sq. in. Total plate pressure: 2060 lb. Optional: K20 6-cyl.: 11 in. dia. Total lining area: 124.0 sq. in. 307 V-8: 12 in. dia. Total lining area: 150 sq. in.

VEHICLE DIMENSIONS: Series K10 and K20: Wheelbase: K10: 117.5 in. 131.5 in. K20: 131.5 in. All Suburbans and Panels: 129.5 in. K30: 131.5 in. 164.5 in. Overall Length: 117.5 in. Fleetside pickups: 191.30 in. 131.5 in. Fleetside pickups: 212.00. 117.5 in. Stepside pickups: 190.5 in. 131.5 in. Stepside pickups: 210.25. 117.5 in. Chassis cab: 186.05 in. K30 data: 164.5 in. wheelbase. 244.43 in. Front/Rear Tread: 67.4 in./65.8 in. Overall Height: K10 Fleetside pickup: 72.0 in. K20 Fleetside pickup: 74.0 in. K30 Fleetside pickup: 74.0 in. K30 crew cab: 75.0 in. K10 Suburban: 73.5 in. K20 Suburban: 79.5 in. Front/Rear Overhang: pickups: 33 in./41 in. Tailgate: Width and Height: 72 in. x 19.25 in. Approach/Departure Degrees: K10 117.5 in. Fleetside and Stepside: 33/19. K10 131.5 in. Fleetside: 33/15. K10 131.5 in. wheelbase Stepside: 35/20. K20 131.5 in. wheelbase Fleetside: 35/20. K20 131.5 in. wheelbase Stepside: 35/21. K30 Fleetside pickup: 41/19. K30 crew cab Pickup: 38/18. Ground Clearance: Front axle: 7.25 in. Rear axle: 7.0 in. Oil pan: 16.5 in. Transfer case: 12.0 in. Fuel tank: 16.6 in. Load space: Pickup box dimensions: 117.5 in. wheelbase Fleetside: 78.25 in. x 50 in. x 19.25 in. 131.5 in. wheelbase Fleetside: 98 in. x 50 in. x 19.25 in. Capacity:

117.5 wheelbase: 58.4 cu. ft. 131.5 in. wheelbase: 74.3 cu. ft. 117.5 in. wheelbase Stepside: 78.5 in. x 50 in. x 17.5 in. 131.5 in. wheelbase Stepside: 96.25 in. x 50 in. x 17.5 in. Front headroom: 38.5 in. (seat to top of cab). Front hip room: 67.25 in. Pedal to seat back (max.): 43.5 in. Steering wheel to seat back (max.): 17.3 in. Seat to ground: 35.0 in. Floor to ground: 23.0 in.

CAPACITIES: Fuel Tank: 117.5 in. wheelbase: 16.0 gal. 131.5 in. wheelbase: 20.0: gal. 164.5 in.: 20 gal. Optional: 17 gal. auxiliary tank. for 117.5 in.; 20 gal. auxiliary for 131.5 in. and 164.5 in. wheelbase. Engine Coolant System: 250 6-cyl.: 14.8 qt. 305 V-8: 17.6 qt. 350 V-8: 17.6 qt. 400 V-8: 19.6 qt. (20 qt. on K20 and K30).

ACCOMMODATIONS: Seating Capacity: Pickup and chassis cab models: 3 passenger. Optional: None. Suburban: 3 passenger. Optional: 6 or 9 passenger.

INSTRUMENTATION: Speedometer, odometer, fuel level gauge. Warning lights for battery, oil pressure, generator, brake system warning, directional/hazard lights, high beam, and engine coolant temperature.

OPTIONS AND PRICES: Power steering (RPO N41): $207. 350 V-8 (RPO LS9): $300. 400 V-8 (RPO LF4): $465. 4-speed manual synchromesh (RPO MM4): $152. Turbo Hydra-Matic (RPO MX1): $345. Poly-Wrap air cleaner (RPO K43). Air conditioning (RPO C60). Locking rear differential (RPO G80): $175. Auxiliary 3500 watt Delco Freedom battery (RPO TP2). Heavy-duty 4000 watt Delco Freedom battery (RPO UA1). Painted rear bumper (RPO V38). Rear step bumper (RPO V43). Front and rear chromed bumpers (RPO V37). Front chrome bumper (RPO V46). Rear chrome bumper (RPO VF1). Rear step bumper-Fleetside only, (RPO V42). Front and rear deluxe chromed bumpers-Fleetside only (RPO VE5). Front deluxe chromed bumper (RPO VG3). Chromed front bumper guards (RPO VV1). Glide-out spare wheel carrier (RPO P11). Side-mounted spare wheel carrier (RPO P13). Chevy Sport Package (RPO Z77). Electric clock (RPO U35). Cold Climate Package. Includes UA1 battery and K76 generator. (RPO Z56). Engine oil cooler. Available for V-8 engines only (RPO KC4). Transmission oil cooler. Available for V-8 engines and auto. trans. only. (RPO VO2). Heavy-duty radiator (RPO VO1). Power door locks (RPO AU3). California emission system (RPO YF5). Dual exhaust system. Requires LS9 (RPO N10). Color-keyed floor mats (RPO B32). Wood pickup box, CK10903 Fleetside only (RPO E81). Gauge Package. Includes voltmeter, engine coolant temperature and oil pressure (RPO Z53): $27. Tachometer. Requires V-8 engine. (RPO U16): $87, with Silverado option: $60. 61 amp Delcotron alternator (RPO K76). Soft-Ray tinted glass, all windows (RPO AO1). Chrome grille (RPO V22). Camper body wiring harness (RPO UY1). Headlight warning buzzer (RPO T63). Inside hood lock release (RPO T44). Deluxe instrument panel (RPO BC3). Cargo area lamp (RPO UF2). Dome lamp (RPO C91). Roof marker lights (RPO UO1). Cigarette lighter (RPO U37). Below eye-level painted 7.5 in. x 10.5 in. mirrors (RPO D29). Below eye-level stainless steel 7.5 in. x 10.5 in. mirrors (RPO DG4). Camper-type below eye-level mirrors (RPO DFG4). Body side spear molding, Fleetside only (RPO B84). Body upper moldings, Fleetside only (RPO B85). Body side upper and lower moldings, Fleetside only (RPO YG1). Wheel opening guard (RPO B93). Wheel opening moldings, Fleetside only (RPO B96). Operating Convenience Package. Includes AU3 door locks and A31 windows. (RPO ZQ2). Fuel tank shield (RPO NY1). AM push-button radio (RPO U63). AM/FM push-button radio (RPO U69). Folding seat back (RPO AN1). Full-depth foam seat (RPO Z52). Pickup box side rails (RPO D73). Speed and cruise control (RPO K30). Heavy-duty front springs. Includes heavy-duty front and rear shock absorbers. Recommended for snowplow type usage only on K10. (RPO F60): $67. Custom steering wheel (RPO N33). Custom steering wheel (RPO N31). Red exterior stripe (RPO 71A). Auxiliary fuel tank (RPO NL2): $150. Two front towing hooks (RPO V76). Weight distributing platform type trailer hitch (RPO VR4). Trailering Special Package. Includes UA1 battery and K76 generator. (RPO Z82). Bright metal hubcaps (RPO PO3). Trim rings (RPO PO6). Wheelcovers (RPO PO1). Special wheelcovers (RPO PA1). Spare dual wheel, K30 only (RPO QE2 or QE6 depending upon tire size). Dual rear wheels, K30 only (RPO RO5). Single rear wheels, K30 only (RPO ZW3). Aluminum wheels, K10 only. (RPO PH7). Rallye wheels, K10 only (RPO N67). Styled wheels, K10 only (RPO PA6). Power window (RPO A31). Sliding rear window (RPO A28). Intermittent windshield wipers (RPO CD4). Heavy-duty vacuum brakes, K20 only (RPO J55). Basic Camper Group, K20 and K30 only. Includes F60 springs and UY1 harness. (RPO Z81). Deluxe Camper Group, K20 and K30 only. (RPO Z83). Frame-mounted spare wheel carrier, K30 only (RPO P10). Senior West Coast type painted mirrors, K30 only (RPO DG5). Heavy-duty front and rear shock absorbers (RPO F51). Conventional two-tone paint ZY2. Special two-tone paint, Fleetside only (RPO ZY3). Deluxe two-tone paint, Fleetside only (RPO XY4). Exterior Decor Package, Fleetside only. Includes YG1 and B96 moldings, hood ornament and hood accent stripes (RPO ZY5).

HISTORICAL FOOTNOTES: The 1979 models debuted in the fall of 1978.

1980 PICKUP

All K series trucks had a new argent colored grille treatment with smaller grid dividers for 1980. Models equipped with the Silverado option had rectangular headlights. all models has a new front end full-width air dam. Except for the inclusion of international symbols for the gauges, there were no changes in the instrument panel for 1980. The seat back angle was increased from 3.0 to 3.5 degrees in order to improve seating comfort. Numerous revisions and changes intended primarily to improve the operating efficiency of the K trucks were incorporated into their design for 1980. The most important of these was the abandonment of the New Process 203 full-time four-wheel drive system. For 1980 the transfer of engine or transmission had a New Process 205 2-speed part-time four-wheel drive system. The 400 cu. in. V-8 was not available for the K10 in 1980. The K30 models were carried over into 1980 with the same choice of engines and gear ratios. Major revisions took place in the K20 model lineup. In effect, Chevrolet, in order to break away from the use of catalytic converters on the K20 that had reduced its performance, used the 1979 K30 models with an 8600 lb. GVW as the basis for three new 1980 K20 models with 8600 lb. GVW ratings that operated on regular fuel and were not fitted with catalytic converters. Whereas the 6800 lb. GVW K20 was offered with only the 350 V-8, the three new 8600 lb. GVW K20 models were available with either a standard 292 6-cyl. or optional 350 and 400 V-8 engines. Chevrolet also introduced a new engine fan clutch operation that operated the fan only when conditions merited. Contributing to improved fuel efficiency was the use of a new single inlet, dual exhaust system on 350 V-8 engines which reduced exhaust back pressure. New P215/75R15P radial tires were standard for K10 models.

New exterior graphics were offered for 1980 as were eight new two-tone color combinations.

I.D. DATA: The vehicle identification number, located on a plate in the lower left side of the windshield. It had 13 units. The first, the letter C represented the Chevrolet Division Unit. The second digit, K, indicated four-wheel drive. The third digit represented the engine: D-250 6-cyl. L-350 V-8, R-400 V-8, T-292 6-cyl. The fourth digit indicated the Series: 1-Chev. 10, 2-Chev. 20, 3-Chev 30. The fifth digit identified the body type: 3-Chassis and cab, 4-Pickup,

6-Suburban. The sixth entry, the letter A, indicated the 1980 model year. The seventh digit represented the assembly plant. The eighth through the thirteenth digit was the assembly sequence number.

Model Number	Body Type & Seating	Factory Price	GVW	Shipping Weight	Prod. Total
Series K10-1/2 ton 250 6-cyl. 117.5 in. 131.5 in. wheelbase (Suburban: 129.5 in. wheelbase and standard 305 V-8)					
CK10703	117.5 in. Chassis & Cab	$6965	6200	4143	—
CK10903	131.5 in. Chassis & Cab	$N.A.	6200	4250	—
CK10703	6.5 ft. Stepside Pickup	$6685	6200	4477	—
CK10703	6.5 ft. Fleetside Pickup	$6685	6200	4537	—
CK10903	8 ft. Stepside Pickup	$6770	6200	4639	—
CK10903	8 ft. Fleetside Pickup	$6770	6200	4720	—
CK10906	Suburban Endgate	$8636	6200	5273	—
CK10906	Suburban Panl. Drs.	$N.A.	6200[1]	5235	—

NOTE 1: Suburban available with optional 6800 and 730 lb. GVW packages.

Series K20-3/4 ton 292 V-8[1]. 131.5 in. wheelbase. (Suburban-129.5 in. wheelbase. Crew and bonus cab: 164.5 in. wheelbase, Suburban weight with standard 350 V-8

Model Number	Body Type & Seating	Factory Price	GVW	Shipping Weight	Prod. Total
CK20903	Chassis and Cab	$7404	6800*	4485	—
CK20903	8 ft. Stepside Pickup	$7514	6800	4874	—
CK20903	8 ft. Fleetside Pickup	$7414	6800	4955	—
CK20906	Suburban Endgate	$9111	6800	5472	—
CK20906	Suburban Panl. Drs.	$N.A.	6800	5434	—

NOTE 1: Not available in California where the 350 engine is base.

* 8600 lb. GVW optional.

Series K30-1 ton 350 V-8. 131.5 in. wheelbase. Crew and bonus cab: 164.5 in. wheelbase

Model Number	Body Type & Seating	Factory Price	GVW	Shipping Weight	Prod. Total
CK31003	Chassis & Cab[1]	$8629	8400*	4956	—
CK31403	Chassis & Cab[2]	$N.A.	8490	5243	—
CK30903	8 ft. Fleetside Pickup	$8917	8400	5426	—
CK30903	8 ft. Stepside Pickup	$8917	8400	5501	—
CK30943	Chassis & Bonus Cab	$9350	8400	5370	—
CK30943	Fleetside Bonus Cab	$9627	8400	5840	—
CK30943	Chassis & Crew Cab	$9604	8400	5370	—
CK30943	Fleetside Crew Cab	$9881	8400	5840	—

NOTE 1: 135.5 in. wheelbase.
NOTE 2: 159.9 in. wheelbase.
* 9200 and 10,000 lb. GVW optional.

STANDARD ENGINE: All K10 6-cyl. models: 250 Six (LE3 ordering code). Engine Type: OHV, In-line 6-cylinder. Cast iron block and cylinder head. Key features induction hardened exhaust valve seats, and timing tabs. Not available for California delivery where 350 engine is standard. Bore x Stroke: 3.875 in. x 3.53 in. Lifters: Hydraulic. Number of main bearings-7. Fuel Induction: Single Rochester staged 2-bbl. carburetor. Compression Ratio: 8.3:1. Displacement: 250 cu. in. (4.09 liters). Horsepower: Net: 130 @ 4000 rpm. Torque: Net: 210 lb.-ft. @ 2000 rpm. Oil refill capacity: 5 qt. with filter change. Fuel Requirements: Regular.

STANDARD ENGINE: K30 6-cyl. models: 292 Six. Ordering Code: L25. Engine Type: OHV, 6-cyl. Cast iron block and cylinder head. Key features include cast iron intake manifold, aluminized-face intake valves, stellite-faced exhaust valves with hardened faces. Bore x Stroke: 3.875 in. x 4.125 in. Lifters: Hydraulic. Number of main bearings-7. Fuel Induction: Single Rochester 1-bbl. carburetor. Compression Ratio: 7.8:1. Displacement: 292 cu. in. (4.78 liters). Horsepower: Net: 115 @ 3400 rpm. Torque: Net: 215 lb.-ft. @ 1600 rpm. Oil refill capacity: 6 qt. Fuel Requirements: Regular.

STANDARD ENGINE: K20 and K30 V-8 models: Standard for K20 Suburban. Ordering Code: LS9: 350 V-8 Engine Type: OHV, V-8. Cast iron block and alloy iron cylinder head. Key features include chain drive camshaft and forged steel connecting rods. Bore x Stroke: 4.0 in. x 3.50 in. Lifters: Hydraulic. Number of main bearings-5. Fuel Induction: Single Rochester 4-bbl. carburetor. Compression Ratio: 8.2:1. (8500 lb. GVW and below), 8501 lb. and up GVW: 8.3:1. Displacement: 350 cu. in. (5.73 liters). Horsepower: Net: 175 @ 3800 rpm. California and GVW below 8500 lb. GVW: 170 @ 3600 rpm. 8501 lb. and up GVW: 165 @ 3800 rpm. Torque: Net: 8500 lb. and below, except California: 275 lb.-ft. @ 2400 rpm. 8500 lb. and below, for California: 275 lb.-ft. @ 2400 rpm. 8501 lb. and up GVW: 255 lb.-ft. @ 2800 rpm. Oil refill capacity: 5 qt. with filter change. Fuel Requirements: Regular.

OPTIONAL ENGINE: K20 and K30 V-8 models: Ordering Code: LF4: 400 V-8. Key features include induction hardened valve seats and cast iron camshaft. Engine Type: OHV, V-8. Cast iron block and alloy iron cylinder head. Bore x Stroke: 4.10 in. x 3.8 in. Lifters: Hydraulic. Number of main bearings-5. Fuel Induction: Single Rochester 4-bbl. carburetor. Compression Ratio: 8.5:1. Displacement: 400 cu. in. (6.55 liters). Horsepower: Net: 185 @ 3600 rpm. California and GVW below 8500 lb. GVW: 170 @ 3600 rpm. 8501 lb. and up GVW: 180 @ 3600 rpm. Torque: Net: 8500 lb. and below, except California: 300 lb.-ft. @ 2400 rpm. 8500 lb. and below, for California: 305 lb.-ft. @ 1600 rpm. 8501 lb. and up GVW: 310 lb.-ft. @ 2400 rpm. Oil refill capacity: 5 qt. with filter change. Fuel Requirements: Regular.

STANDARD ENGINE: K10 Suburban models: Ordering Code: LG9 305 V-8. Not available in California. Engine Type: OHV, V-8. Cast iron block and alloy iron cylinder head. Bore x Stroke: 3.74 in. x 3.48 in. Lifters: Hydraulic. Number of main bearings-5. Fuel Induction: Single Rochester 2-bbl. carburetor. Compression Ratio: 8.4:1. Displacement: 305 cu. in. (4.997 liters). Horsepower: Net: 140 @ 4000 rpm. Torque: Net: 240 lb.-ft. @ 2000 rpm. Oil refill capacity: 5 qt. with filter change. Fuel Requirements: Regular.

CHASSIS FEATURES: Separate body and frame with channel side rails. Carbon-Steel, 39,000 psi. 117.5 in. wheelbase: 2.30 in. x 5.92 in. x 0.156 in. Section modules: 3.06 in. 129.5 in.: 2.30 in. x 5.92 in. x 0.194. Section modules: 3.93. 135.5 in. wheelbase: 2.78 in. x 7.74 in. 0.194 in. Section modules: 6.20. 164.5 in.: 2.78 in. x 7.74 in. x 0.224 in. Section modules: 7.33. 131.5 in. wheelbase: 2.30 in. x 5.92 in. x 0.194 in. Section modules: 3.84 in. Optional: None.

SUSPENSION AND RUNNING GEAR: Front Suspension: K10: Tapered 2-leaf springs. Capacity: 1650 lb. (16), 1850 lb. (03,06). K15: Tapered 2-leaf springs. Capacity: 1850 lb. K30: Tapered 3-leaf springs. Capacity: 2250 lb. Rear Suspension: K10 and K-20: 52 in. x 2.25 in. Two-stage, 7-leaf. K30: 56 in. x 2.50 in. Capacity: K10: 2075 lb. K30: 3500 lb. 1.0 in. dia. shock absorbers. Optional: K30: 3750 lb. capacity. Front Axle Type and Capacity: K10 and K20: GMC or Spicer, K35: Spicer. K10: Semi-floating. 3600 lb. capacity. Optional: None. K20: Full-floating, 3800 lb. capacity. Optional: None. Rear Axle Type and Capacity: K10: Chevrolet, Semi-floating, 3750 lb. capacity. K20: Chevrolet, Full-floating, K30: 7500 lb. capacity. Optional: None. Final Drive Ratio: Standard: K10: 6-cyl.: 3.42:1; 350 V-8: 2.76:1. K20 and K30: 292 6-cyl: 4.10:1; 350 and 400 V-8: 4.10:1. K10 Suburban: 350 V-8: 3.08:1. K20 Suburban. Optional: 250 6-cyl.: 3.73:1; 350 V-8: 3.08:1. Optional: K20 and K30: 292 6-cyl: 4.56:1; 350 V-8: 4.56:1. Transfer Case: New Process 205. Single lever, two-speed: 1.96, 1.00:1. Brakes: Type: Hydraulic, power assisted. Dimensions: K10: Front: Disc: 11.86 in. x 1.28 in. Rear: Drums: 11.15 in. x 2.75 in. K20: Front: Disc: 12.5 in. x 1.28 in. Rear: Drums: 11.15 in. x 2.75 in. K20 and K30: Front: Disc: 12.50 in. x 1.53 in. Rear:

Drum: 13.00 in. x 3.50 in. Wheels: K10: 15 x 6.0JJ 6-stud disc. Optional: 15 x 8JJ. K20: 16.5 x 6.00 in. 8-stud disc. Optional: 16.5 x 6.75. K30: 16.5 x 6.75. Tires: K10: P215/75R15-P metric radial. K20: 8.75 x 16.5C K30: 9.50 x 16.5D. Optional: K10: G78 x 15B, white stripe; H78 x 15B, tubeless, black sidewall or white stripe; L78 x 15B black sidewall or white stripe, tubeless; 10.00 x 16.5C tubeless; G78 x 15B tube-type; 7.00 x 15C tube-type; 6.50 x 16C tube-type and LR78 x 15C white sidewall radial ply. The following tires were specified for K10 models with the 5600 lb. GVW package which included a front heavy-duty stabilizer bar: H78 x 15B 4-ply rating, tubeless; 6.50 x 16C 6-ply rating, tube-type, truck type. The following tires were specified for K10 models with the 6000 lb. GVW Package which included a front heavy-duty stabilizer bar and heavy-duty rear springs: L78 x 15B 4-ply rating, tubeless. Optional K20: 9.50 x 16.5E Firestone Town and Country, 8.75 x 16.5D tubeless; 9.50 x 16.5D tubeless; 10.00 x 16.5C tubeless (not available for Stepside models); 7.50 x 16C 6-ply rating, tube-type; 7.50 x 16D tube-type; 7.50 x 16E tube-type. The following tires were specified for K20 models with the 7500 lb. GVW Package which included a front heavy-duty stabilizer bar: 8.75 x 16.5 C 6-ply rating, tubeless; 7.50 x 16C 6-ply rating, tubeless. The following tires were specified for K20 models with the 8200 lb. GVW Package which included a front heavy-duty stabilizer bar: 9.50 x 16.5D 8-ply rating, tubeless; 7.50 x 16C 6-ply rating, tube type. Steering: Recirculating ball gear. Ratio: 20:1. Turning Circle: 47 ft. Steering wheel diameter: 17.5 in. Optional: Power-assisted. Ratio: 16.4:1. Transmission: K10 and K20: 3-speed, synchromesh manual (RPO M15). Transmission Ratios: 2.85, 1.68, 1.00:1. Optional: Chevrolet CH465. 4-speed manual synchromesh (RPO M20). Ratios: 6.55, 3.58, 1.70, 1.00:1. Reverse: 6.09:1. The K20 crew cab and all K30 models had this transmission as standard equipment. Optional: 3-speed Turbo Hydra-Matic 400 (RPO M40). Ratios: 2.1 x 2.48, 1.48, 1.00:1. Reverse: 2.10:1. The 400 cu. in. V-8 was available only with this transmission. Clutch: Diaphragm, spring. Clutch diameter: 6-cyl.: 11 in. dia. Total lining area: 123.5 sq. in. Total plate pressure: 2075 lb. V-8: 12 in. dia. Total lining area: 149.2 sq. in. Total plate pressure: 2060 lb. Optional: K20 6-cyl.: 11 in. dia. Total lining area: 124.0 sq. in. 307 V-8: 12 in. dia. Total lining area: 150 sq. in.

VEHICLE DIMENSIONS: Series K10 and K20: Wheelbase: K10: 117.5 in. 131.5 in. K20: 131.5 in. All Suburbans and Panels: 129.5 in. K30: 131.5 in. 164.5 in. Overall Length: 117.5 in. Fleetside pickups: 191.30 in. 131.5 in. Fleetside pickups: 212.00. 117.5 in. Stepside pickups: 190.5 in. 131.5 in. Stepside pickups: 210.25. 117.5 in. Chassis cab: 186.05 in. K30 data: 164.5 in. wheelbase: 244.43 in. Front/Rear Tread: 67.4 in./65.8 in. Overall Height: K10 Fleetside pickup: 72.0 in. K20 Fleetside pickup: 74.0 in. K30 Fleetside pickup: 74.0 in. K30 crew cab: 75.0 in. K10 Suburban: 73.5 in. K20 Suburban: 75.5 in. Width: Pickup: 79.5 in. Front/Rear Overhang: pickups: 33 in./41 in. Tailgate: Width and Height: 72 in. x 19.25 in. Approach/Departure Degrees: K10 117.5 in. Fleetside and Stepside: 33/19. K10 131.5 in. Fleetside: 33/15. K10 131.5 in. wheelbase Stepside: 33/16. K20 131.5 in. wheelbase Fleetside: 35/20. K20 131.5 in. wheelbase Stepside: 35/21. K30 Fleetside pickup: 41/19. K30 crew cab pickup: 38/18. Ground Clearance: Front axle: 7.25 in. Rear axle: 7.0 in. Oil pan: 16.5 in. Transfer case: 12.0 in. Fuel tank: 16.6 in. Load space: Pickup box dimensions: 117.5 in. wheelbase Fleetside: 78.25 in. x 50 in. x 19.25 in. 131.5 in. wheelbase Fleetside: 98 in. x 50 in. x 19.25 in. Capacity: 117.5 wheelbase: 58.4 cu. ft. 131.5 in. wheelbase: 74.3 cu. ft. 117.5 in. wheelbase Stepside: 78.5 in. x 50 in. x 17.5 in. 131.5 in. wheelbase Stepside: 96.25 in. x 50 in. x 17.5 in. Front headroom: 38.5 in. (seat to top of cab). Front hip room: 67.25 in. Pedal to seat back (max.): 43.5 in. Steering wheel to seat back (max.): 17.3 in. Seat to ground: 35.0 in. Floor to ground: 23.0 in.

CAPACITIES: Fuel Tank: 117.5 in. wheelbase: 16.0 gal. 131.5 in. wheelbase: 20.0: gal. 164.5 in.: 20 gal. Optional: 17 gal. auxiliary tank for 117.5 in.; 20 gal. auxiliary for 131.5 in. and 164.5 in. wheelbase. Engine Coolant System: 250 6-cyl.: 14.8 qt. 305 V-8: 17.6 qt. 350 V-8: 17.6 qt. 400 V-8: 19.6 qt. (20 qt. on K20 and K30).

ACCOMMODATIONS: Seating Capacity: Pickup and chassis cab models: 3 passenger. Optional: None. Suburban: 3 passenger. Optional: 6 or 9 passenger.

INSTRUMENTATION: Speedometer, odometer, fuel level gauge. Warning lights for battery, oil pressure, generator, brake system warning, directional/hazard lights, high beam, and engine coolant temperature.

OPTIONS AND PRICES: Options were essentially unchanged from 1979. This is a representative sampling of options and prices. Tinted glass: $36. Sliding rear window: $90. Power windows: $148. Color-keyed floor mats: $12. Pulse windshield wipers: $35. Air conditioning: $607. Locking rear differential: $197. 400 V-8: $575. Turbo Hydra-Matic: $411. Auxiliary fuel tank: $182. Fuel tank and differential skid plates: $139. Tilt steering wheel: $83. Glide-out spare tire carrier: $34. Tachometer: $62. AM/FM radio: $153. Chrome front bumper: $19. Chrome rear step bumper: $156. Silverado Trim Package: $645. Exterior Decor Package: $236. Vinyl bucket seats: $230. 9.50 x 16.5E tires: $331.46.

HISTORICAL FOOTNOTES: Calendar year registration of all Chevrolet trucks was 737,788, of which 403,487 were pickup models and 19,518 were Suburbans.

1981 PICKUP

Significant changes that Chevrolet regarded as manifesting "New technology for the eighties and beyond" characterized the 1981 K series trucks. The front-end sheet metal was new from the cowl forward. The front fenders were restyled for improved aerodynamics and occupant visibility. Also new were the radiator grille, painted plastic headlight bezels, front bumper, Fleetside rear bumper and the parking lights which were now located in the front bumper. New front bumper braces and an 8-point attachment improved bumper stiffness. The use of HSLA steel for all bumpers except the Stepside conventional bumper contributed to the vehicle's overall weight reduction. The weight of the K series trucks was reduced from 115 to 309 pounds, depending upon the model. New front fender skirts with attached shields helped reduce engine compartment splash. Standard on all K series models with GVW ratings up to 8500 lb. (except for chassis cab models) was a front air deflector. Single rectangular headlights were now standard. Other changes included a restyled Fleetside pickup tailgate and front fender name and series designation plates. All windows had new, thinner glass for weight reduction. Numerous interior changes accompanied these developments. The standard front bench seat was redesigned. The full-foam-type seat cushion (previously RPO AQ1) was now standard on both two-door and four-door cabs. The folding seat back (formerly RPO AN1) was now standard for two-door cabs and for the crew cab rear seat. Also restyled for 1981 were the interior side door trim panels, door lock and window control handles. The revised instrument panel now had provision at the top for new stereo radio speakers. The old speaker position had been in the front door trim panels. Other interior changes included a new instrument panel pad, new instrument panel appliques and name plates, new instrument panel cluster bezels and revised graphics for the windshield wiper-washer switch. A new steering wheel column upper cover matched the new instrument panel bezel. The K10 and K20 models had a new floor-mounted illuminated transfer case indicator console. The K30 retained the shift range graphics on the control lever knob. All K10 and K20 models under 8500 lb. GVW ratings had drag-free front disc brake calipers with a new quick take-up master cylinder. All K20 models had a new standard 6000 lb. capacity, semi-floating rear axle with a 9.5 in. ring gear. Adding incrementally to improved fuel mileage was the deletion of the constant "on" status of the heater blower. A new "off" position was provided.

As might be expected, Chevrolet made major revisions in its powertrain availability for 1981. RPO LE4, the 6.6 liter, 400 cu. in. V-8 was no longer available. A new optional 5.0 liter, 305 V-8 (RPO LE9) with Electronic Spark Control (ESC) was available for K10 models. This engine was intended to provide the fuel economy of a 5.0 liter V-8 while delivering performance competitive with a 1980 model year 5.7 liter V-8. This engine's 9.2:1 compression ratio was the highest ever offered in a light-duty Chevrolet truck. The RPO LE9 V-8 was designed to operate on regular unleaded fuel and its ESC system provided protection from audible engine detonation. Other refinements included a camshaft modified to provide less valve overlap, a staged 4-barrel carburetor and larger exhaust passages. Internal dimensions were similar to other 5.0 liter Chevrolet V-8 engines except for the combustion chamber volume, which was reduced by approximately 10 percent. This engine was not available in California where a 4-barrel 305 V-8 similar except for the higher compression ratio and ESC system was offered. Also refined for 1981 was the LE3, 4.1 liter 6-cylinder which had a carburetor recalibrated to provide smoother operation at cruising speeds. The lift profile of the cam was also modified for improved engine idle operation. The EPA fuel mileage of this engine improved by approximately 1 mpg over the1980 level. All engines were cooled by new high-efficiency radiators with more cooling fins in their cores than those used in 1980.

1981 Chevrolet K10 Stepside pickup with Sport Package

The K10 and K20 models had a new New Process 208 transfer case which used an aluminum case and included synchronizers for easier shifting. No provision for power take-off was provided in this transfer case. The K30 series retained the New Process 205 transfer case which included a power take-off opening. This system was also improved by the inclusion of shifting synchronizers. All four-wheel drive models had automatic locking front hubs. These hubs would freewheel until the vehicle was placed in four-wheel drive and torque was applied to the front wheels. The front hubs were returned to their freewheeling mode when the transfer case was shifted to two-wheel drive and the vehicle was backed up approximately three feet.

Included among the body and chassis changes for 1981 was the relocation of the standard fuel tank from the right-hand frame rail to the left-hand frame rail. The filler pipe and access door were now located on the driver's side. Chevrolet also introduced several significant anti-corrosion features for 1981. The front wheelhousing-to-frame seals were new and the use of corrosion-resistent steel in the pickup boxes was increased. On the Fleetside boxes, new urethane stone shields were added ahead of the wheel openings. On the brake and fuel lines of all models, zinc-rich paint was applied over the existing anti-corrosion exterior coating. The Fleetside tailgate also had a new hemmed construction for improved anti-corrosion. The standard rear springs on K10 and K20 models with a GVW rating under 8500 lb. were new and featured greater durability and improved corrosion protection.

Numerous revisions, changes, additions and deletions took place in the K series option list for 1981. The introduction of new exterior colors produced two new exterior two-tone color combinations. The RPO ZY3 Special and RPO ZY4 Deluxe two-tone paint options were limited to single rear wheel Fleetside pickups. Two-tone interiors were discontinued.

All body side and rear moldings, except wheel opening moldings, were new for 1981. They continued to be available only for Fleetside Pickups and Suburbans. Trim moldings were located low on the body and ran between the wheel openings and continued around the side panels and across the rear of the vehicle. RPO B84 moldings were black and trimmed in black plastic. They were included in the Scottsdale Trim Package and were available for both the Custom Deluxe and Cheyenne trim levels. The RPO B85 moldings were bright plastic with black paint trim and included bright trimmed front side marker lights and tail lights. They were available for the Custom Deluxe, Scottsdale and Cheyenne trim levels. RPO B96 was a carry-over option from 1980. It consisted of bright front and rear opening moldings with black paint trim. These were included in the Cheyenne trim package and were available for the Custom Deluxe and Scottsdale trim levels.

A new chromed grille option, RPO V22, added a chrome finish on the leading edges of the grille insert. The center bar had a brushed chrome treatment. This finish was also used on the headlight bezels. Also included in this option were dual rectangular head lights. These high-intensity, high-beam halogen lights, listed as RPO TT5 were not available separately. A new RPO K35, automatic speed control, included a resume feature. It was available for 6-cyl. and V-8 models with automatic transmission. New RPO Z75 front quad shock absorbers for K10 and K20 models included an extra pair of shock absorbers on the front axle, heavy-duty rear shock absorbers, and a front axle pinion nose snubber to limit front axle windup. The electric clock option, RPO U35, had a new solid-state quartz mechanism for improved performance. A new center console in the RPO AV5 bucket seat option was redesigned for a new appearance as well as reduced weight.

The cab back beltline molding was newly styled for 1981 and was available for all pickup and chassis-cab models. It continued to be included in the Cheyenne and Silverado trim packages and in conventional two-tone and deluxe two-tone paint schemes.

The RPO YG1 molding package had new content for 1981. As previously, it was available for Fleetside pickups and Suburbans. It consisted of bright trimmed black plastic body side and rear molding, the RPO B84 moldings and the RPO B96 moldings. This package was available for the Custom Deluxe, RPO Z62 Scottsdale or RPO Z84, Cheyenne trim levels. It was not available for models with the Silverado trim or with dual rear wheels.

RPO YG3 introduced a new-for-1981 molding package for single rear wheel Fleetside pickups and Suburbans. It consisted of bright plastic body side and rear moldings with black paint trim, RPO B85 and RPO B96 moldings. It was included with the RPO YE9, Silverado trim and was available for all other trim levels. The RPO ZY5 Exterior Decor Package for both the pickups

and Suburban was restyled for 1981. It was offered in a choice of eight colors and included the RPO YG1 and RPO B96 moldings. In addition, it included dual-tone body side and rear tape decal striping keyed to the exterior body color. This striping was applied to the front fenders, side doors and pickup box/body sides and tailgate several inches above the styling crease line. The areas above the striping and below the moldings were painted the primary paint color. The secondary color choice was used between the striping and the molding. A bright, spring-loaded, stand-up type hood emblem was also included.

The RPO Z77, Chevy Sport Package available only for the K10 Fleetside and Stepside pickups was also modified for 1981. The front bumper in this option was painted the primary body color with resilient black impact stripes. The rear bumper was painted the secondary body color. Impact stripes were fitted on Fleetsides only. Also included was the Deluxe Front End Appearance Package with left-and right-hand dual rectangular head lights. The grille and head light bezels were painted dark gray with a brushed chrome finish applied to the center bar. The hood ornament was chromed and carried "CHEVY SPORT" lettering. Also included was the new Special two-tone paint RPO ZY6 feature, and RPO Z62, the Scottsdale exterior trim items (except for the body side and rear moldings and chromed front bumper). New Sport Striping of this option involved multi-toned decal striping on the front fenders and Stepside rear fenders, cab and Fleetside pickup body sides, and tailgate with "CHEVY SPORT" lettering over the rear wheel openings. A bright tailgate applique and Chevrolet nameplate were installed on Fleetside models. The interior contained the Scottsdale interior trim items and color-keyed carpeting.

Due to the fuel tank location change and low demand in1980, the RPO P13 side-mounted spare tire carrier for the Stepside pickups was cancelled for 1981. Also no longer available was RPO E81, the wood floor for the 8 foot Fleetside pickup box.

1981 Chevrolet K10 Suburban Silverado

The standard Custom Deluxe trim, in addition to the new standard features previously mentioned also included large padded armrests, padded sun shades, cab interior light, prismatic inside rear view mirror, and a nameplate on the new instrument pad panel. Exterior items included bright drip rails over the doors, bright rearview mirrors, and a white painted front bumper.

Both the Scottsdale interior and exterior trim included the items from the base trim plus these additions or changes: A choice of either a new Custom cloth or Custom vinyl seat covering in a selection of five colors with grained vinyl facings; a new black crackle finish insert and bright trim in door panels; color-keyed floormat, door or manual operated dome light; cigarette lighter and ashtray lamp; and a new Scottsdale nameplate on the instrument panel. The Scottsdale exterior for regular pickup cabs began with the Custom Deluxe elements and included these major changes or additions: Chromed front bumper, bright-trimmed Fleetside tail lamps and dual rear wheel clearance lamps, bright-trimmed black moldings on body sides and tailgate of Fleetside pickups, bright windshield/rear window trim, new Scottsdale front fender-mounted nameplates and dual horns.

Both the Cheyenne's interior and exterior trim included all the Scottsdale items plus numerous additions or changes The Cheyenne interior included a silver instrument cluster bezel, instrument panel pad applique and door trim panels; color-keyed vinyl insert on door trim panels; door storage pockets, perforated, color-keyed headliner; Custom steering wheel, extra-thick floor insulation, headliner insulation and new Cheyenne nameplate on instrument panel. Additional Cheyenne exterior features for regular cabs included bright front/rear wheel opening moldings with black paint trim on the Fleetside Pickup only; hood and cab-to-fender sound insulators, new bright cab-back panel moldings, bright tailgate panel with Chevrolet lettering on Fleetside pickup only, secondary door weather strips and new Cheyenne front fender mounted nameplates.

The Silverado interior trim contained all items in the Cheyenne package for regular cabs and all items in the Scottsdale package for crew and bonus cabs plus full cowl side trim panels, new door-closing assist strap, new carpet trim below door panel, new Silverado nameplate on instrument panel, bright brushed-finish stainless steel instrument cluster frame and matching insert on the instrument panel pad and door trim panels, needle-type and full-gauge instrumentation. The crew cab and bonus cab models were fitted with custom steering wheel, color-keyed carpeting (except for the rear compartment of the bonus cab), and a choice of Custom cloth or Custom vinyl seats, and extra-thick floor insulation. The Silverado exterior was based on the Cheyenne trim and added these additions or changes: New bright-trimmed grille, headlight bezels and dual rectangular headlights, and new Silverado front fender-mounted nameplates.

Four new exterior colors were added for 1981: Light silver metallic, charcoal metallic, Colonial yellow and dark chestnut. Also available for 1981 were these colors: Frost white, Nordic blue metallic, carmine red, light blue metallic, medium blue, Santa Fe tan, midnight black, cardinal red, dark carmine red, Emerald green and burnt orange metallic.

Five interior colors, including three carryovers: Carmine, blue and green were available.

I.D. DATA: The V.I.N. plate was mounted on the lower left side windshield corner. The V.I.N. consisted of 17 elements. The first, the number 1 identified the U.S. as the nation of origin. The letter G followed, for the manufacturer, General Motors. The third entry, the letter C represented the make as Chevrolet. The GVWR brake system identification followed. Next came the truck line and chassis type; the letter K indicated four-wheel drive. The truck series was identified by a number: 1-1/2 ton; 2-3/4 ton 3-one ton. The truck body type identification was next: 3-four-door cab; 4-two-door cab; 6-Suburban. The engine code followed according to this scheme: D-250 6-cyl.; E-350 V-8; T-292 6-cyl.; W-454 V-8. A check digit followed. The model year was identified by the letter B. The assembly plant code followed. The final six digits were the plant sequential production number.

Model Number	Body Type & Seating	Factory Price	GVW	Shipping Weight	Prod. Total
Series K10-1/2 ton 250 6-cyl. 117.5 in. 131.5 in. wheelbase (Suburban: 129.5 in.) wheelbase and standard 305 V-8					
CK10703	6.5 ft. Stepside Pickup	$7762	6200	4442	—
CK10703	6.5 ft. Fleetside Pickup	$7762	6200	4485	—
CK10903	8 ft. Stepside Pickup	$7849	6200	4807	—
CK10903	8 ft. Fleetside Pickup	$7849	6200	4686	—
CK10906	Suburban Endgate	$10,267	6200	5273	—
CK10906	Suburban Panl. Drs.	$N.A.	6200[1]	5250	—

NOTE 1: Suburban available with optional 6800 and 7300 lb. GVW packages.

Series K20-3/4 ton 292 6-cyl.[1] 131.5 in. wheelbase. (Suburban-129.5 in. wheelbase). Crew and bonus cab: 164.5 in. wheelbase, Suburban weight with standard 350 V-8

CK20903	Chassis and Cab	$7975	6800*	—	—
CK20903	8 ft. Stepside Pickup	$8479	6800	4807	—
CK20903	8 ft. Fleetside Pickup	$8479	6800	4878	—
CK20906	Suburban Endgate	$10,141	6800	5472	—
CK20906	Suburban Panl. Drs.	$N.A.	6800	5434	—

NOTE 1: Not available in California where the 350 engine is base.
* 8600 lb. GVW optional.

Series K30-1 ton 350 V-8. 131.5 in. wheelbase. Crew and bonus cab: 164.5 in. wheelbase

CK30903	Chassis & Cab[1]	$9064	8400*	4956	—
CK30903	Chassis & Cab[2]	$N.A.	8400	5243	—
CK30903	8 ft. Fleetside Pickup	$9558	8400	5318	—
CK30903	8 ft. Stepside Pickup	$9558	8400	5330	—
CK30943	Ch & Bonus Cab	$9969	8400	5370	—
CK30943	Fleetside Bonus Cab	$10,458	8400	5743	—
CK30943	Chassis & Crew Cab	$10,259	8400	5370	—
CK30943	Fleetside Crew Cab	$10,748	8400	5840	—

NOTE 1: 135.5 in. wheelbase.
NOTE 2: 159.9 in. wheelbase.
* 9200 and 10,000 lb. GVW optional.

STANDARD ENGINE: All K-10 6-cyl. models: 250 Six (LE3 ordering code). Not available for California where a 305 V-8 with 4-bbl. carburetor is installed. Engine Type: OHV, In-line 6-cylinder. Cast iron block and cylinder head. Key features include a staged 2-bbl. carburetor that uses only one barrel for normal operation. The second barrel is used when more power is needed. The emissions control uses engine vacuum pulses instead of an air pump, pulley, and belt. This systems saves about 15 lbs. in weight as compared to the older system. This engine was produced by GM-Chevrolet Motor Division. Bore x Stroke: 3.875 in. x 3.53 in. Lifters: Hydraulic. Number of main bearings-7. Fuel Induction: Single Rochester 2-bbl. carburetor. Compression Ratio: 8.3:1. Displacement: 250 cu. in. (4.1 liters). Horsepower: Net: 115 @ 3600 rpm. Torque: Net: 200 lb.-ft. @ 1800 rpm. Oil refill capacity: 5 qt. with filter change. Fuel Requirements: Regular unleaded.

STANDARD ENGINE: K20 with RPO CH6 and K30 models: 292 Six. Ordering Code: L25. This engine was produced by GM de Mexico. Engine Type: OHV, 6-cyl. Cast iron block and cylinder head. Key features include cast iron intake manifold, aluminized-face intake valves, stellite-faced exhaust valves with hardened faces. Bore x Stroke: 3.875 in. x 4.125 in. Lifters: Hydraulic. Number of main bearings-7. Fuel Induction: Single Rochester 1-bbl. carburetor. Compression Ratio: 7.8:1. Displacement: 292 cu. in. (4.8 liters). Horsepower: Net: 115 @ 3400 rpm. Torque: Net: 215 lb.-ft. @ 1600 rpm. Oil refill capacity: 6 qt. Fuel Requirements: Regular unleaded.

STANDARD ENGINE: K20: Optional for K20 with HP6 and all K30 models. Ordering Code: LS9: 350 V-8 Engine Type: OHV, V-8. Cast iron block and alloy iron cylinder head. Key features include chain drive camshaft and forged steel connecting rods. This engine was produced by GM-Chevrolet Motor Division. Bore x Stroke: 4.0 in. x 3.50 in. Lifters: Hydraulic. Number of main bearings-5. Fuel Induction: Single Rochester 4-bbl. carburetor. Compression Ratio: 8.2:1. Displacement: 350 cu. in. (5.7 liters). Horsepower: Net: 165 @ 3800 rpm. Torque: Net: 275 lb.-ft. @ 1600 rpm. Oil refill capacity: 5 qt. with filter change. Fuel Requirements: Regular unleaded.

STANDARD ENGINE: K20: Optional for K20 with HP6 and all K30 models with GVW of 8500 lb. and above. Ordering Code: LT9: 350 V-8 Engine Type: OHV, V-8. Cast iron block and alloy iron cylinder head. Key features include chain drive camshaft and forged steel connecting rods. This engine was produced by GM-Chevrolet Motor Division. Bore x Stroke: 4.0 in. x 3.50 in. Lifters: Hydraulic. Number of main bearings-5. Fuel Induction: Single Rochester 4-bbl. carburetor. Compression Ratio: 8.3:1. Displacement: 350 cu. in. (5.7 liters). Horsepower: Net: 160 @ 3800 rpm. (California rating: 155 @ 3600 rpm). Torque: Net: 260 lb.-ft. @ 2800 rpm. (California rating: 240 lb.-ft. @ 2800 rpm). Oil refill capacity: 5 qt. with filter change. Fuel Requirements: Regular unleaded.

OPTIONAL ENGINE: K10 models: Ordering Code: LE9: 305 V-8. Key features include Electronic Spark Control, new staged 4-barrel carburetor, camshaft and free-flow exhaust system. Not available for California. This engine was produced by GM-Chevrolet Motor Division and GM of Canada. Engine Type: OHV. Cast iron block and alloy iron cylinder head. Bore x Stroke: 3.74 in. x 3.48 in. Lifters: Hydraulic. Number of main bearings-5. Fuel Induction: Single Rochester 4-bbl. staged carburetor. Compression Ratio: 9.2:1. Displacement: 305 cu. in. (5.0 liters). Horsepower: 160 @ 4400 rpm. Torque: 235 lb.-ft. @ 2000 rpm. Oil refill capacity: 5 qt. with filter change. Fuel Requirements: Regular unleaded.

OPTIONAL ENGINE: K10 models: Ordering Code: LG9: 305 V-8. Key features include 2-barrel carburetor. This engine was produced by GM-Chevrolet Motor Division and GM of Canada. Engine Type: OHV, V-8. Cast iron block and alloy iron cylinder head. Bore x Stroke: 3.74 in. x 3.48 in. Lifters: Hydraulic. Number of main bearings-5. Fuel Induction: Single Rochester 4-bbl. staged carburetor. Compression Ratio: 8.5:1. Displacement: 305 cu. in. (5.0 liters). Horsepower: 130 @ 4000 rpm. Torque: 240 lb.-ft. @ 2000 rpm. Oil refill capacity: 5 qt. with filter change. Fuel Requirements: Regular unleaded.

OPTIONAL ENGINE: K10 models for California: Ordering Code: LF3: 305 V-8. Key features include 4-barrel carburetor, camshaft and free-flow exhaust system. This engine was produced by GM-Chevrolet Motor Division and GM of Canada. Engine Type: OHV, V-8. Cast iron block and alloy iron cylinder head. Bore x Stroke: 3.74 in. x 3.48 in. Lifters: Hydraulic. Number of main bearings-5. Fuel Induction: Single Rochester 4-bbl. carburetor. Compression Ratio: 8.6:1. Displacement: 305 cu. in. (5.0 liters). Horsepower: 150 @ 4200 rpm. Torque: 240 lb.-ft. @ 2000 rpm. Oil refill capacity: 5 qt. with filter change. Fuel Requirements: Regular unleaded.

OPTIONAL ENGINE: K30 Pickup and Chassis and Cab models: Ordering Code: LE9: 454 V-8. Engine Type: OHV, V-8. Cast iron block and alloy iron cylinder head. Bore x Stroke: 4.25 in. x 4.00 in. Lifters: Hydraulic. Number of main bearings-5. Fuel Induction: Single Rochester 4-bbl. carburetor. Compression Ratio: 7.9:1. Displacement: 454 cu. in. (7.4 liters). Horsepower: 210 @ 3800 rpm. Torque: 340 lb.-ft. @ 2800 rpm. Oil refill capacity: 7 qt. with filter change. Fuel Requirements: Regular unleaded.

CHASSIS FEATURES: Separate body and frame with channel side rails. Carbon-Steel, 39,000 psi. 117.5 in. wheelbase: 2.30 in. x 5.92 in. x 0.156 in. Section modules: 3.06 in. 129.5 in.: 2.30 in. x 5.92 in. x 0.194. Section modules: 3.93. 135.5 in. wheelbase: 2.78 in. x 7.74 in. 0.194 in. Section modules: 6.20. 164.5 in. wheelbase: 2.78 in. x 7.74 in. x 0.224 in. Section modules: 7.33. 131.5 in. wheelbase: 2.30 in. x 5.92 in. x 0.194 in. Section modules: 3.84 in. Optional: None.

SUSPENSION AND RUNNING GEAR: Front Suspension: K10: Tapered 2-leaf springs. Capacity: 1650 lb.-1850 lb. K20: Tapered 2-leaf springs. Capacity: 1850 lb. K30: Tapered 3-leaf springs. Capacity: 2250 lb. Rear Suspension: K10 and K20: 52 in. x 2.25 in. Two-stage, 7-leaf. K30: 56 in. x 2.50 in. Capacity: K10: 2075 lb. K20: 2800 lb. K30: 3500 lb. 1.0 in. dia. shock absorbers. Optional Rating: K20: 3000 lb. rating at ground. Capacity: 6000 lb. with RPO CP6 K30: RPO RO5 (Dual rear wheels): 3750 lb. rating at ground. Capacity: 7500 lb. Front Axle Type and Capacity: K10 and K20: GMC or Spicer, K35: Spicer. K10: Semi-floating. 3600 lb. capacity. Optional: None. K20: Full-floating, 3800 lb. capacity. K30: Full-floating, 4500 lb. Optional: None. Rear Axle Type and Capacity: K10: Chevrolet, Semi-floating, 3750 lb. capacity. K20: Chevrolet, Full-floating, 5700 lb. K30: 7500 lb. Optional: None. Final Drive Ratio: Standard: K10: 6-cyl. and 3-spd. man. trans.3.73:1; with 4-spd. man. trans. or 3-spd. auto. trans.: 3.42:1. LE9-305 V-8 and 3-spd. man. trans.: 3.08:1; with 4-spd. man. trans.: 2.73:1; with 3-spd. auto. trans.: 2.56:1. California only: LS9-350 V-8 3-spd. auto. trans.: 2.73:1. Optional K10. K10: 6-cyl. with 4-spd. man. trans. or 3-spd. auto. trans.: 3.73:1. LE9-305 V-8 and 4-spd. man. trans.: 3.08:1; with 3-spd. auto. trans.: 2.73:1, 3.73:1 (requires RPO Z82, Trailering Special Package). California only: LS9-350 V-8 3-spd. auto. trans.: 3.08:1. Standard: K20 with GVW up to 8500 lb.: LS9 350 V-8 and 3-spd. man. trans.: 3.42:1, with 4-spd. man. trans. or 3-spd. auto. trans.: 3.23:1 (not avail. with locking rear differential). California only: LS9 350 V-8 and 3-spd. auto. trans: 3.23:1. K20 with GVW over 8500 lb.: L25 6-cyl.: With 4-spd. man. trans. or 3-spd. auto. trans.: 4.10:1; with LT9 350 V-8: 4-spd. man. trans.: 3.73:1; 3-spd. auto. trans.: 4.10:1. K20 with GVW over 8500 lb. L25 292 6-cyl.: 4.10:1 (4-spd. man. and auto. trans.); LT9 350 V-8: 4-spd. man. trans.: 3.73:1; 3-spd. auto. trans.: 4.10:1. Optional: LT9 350 V-8: 4-spd. man. trans.: 4.10:1. Standard K30: L25, 6-cyl, 4-spd. man. and auto. trans.: 4.56:1; LT9, 350 V-8, 4-spd. man. and auto. trans. and 9200 lb. GVW: 4.10:1; LT9, 350 V-8, 4-spd. man. and auto. trans. and 10,000 lb. GVW: 4.56:1. Optional K30: LT9, 350 V-8, 4-spd. man. and auto. trans. and 9200 lb. GVW: 4.56:1; LT9, 350 V-8, 4-spd. man. and auto. trans. and 10,000 lb. GVW: 4.10:1. Transfer Case: K10 and K20: New Process 208. Single lever, 2.61, 1.00:1. K30: New Process 205, two-speed: 1.96, 1.00:1. Brakes: Type: Hydraulic, power assisted. Dimensions: K10: Front: Disc: 11.86 in. x 1.28 in. Rear: Drums: 11.15 x 2.75 in. K20: Front: Disc: 12.5 in. x 1.28 in. Rear: Drums: 11.15 in. x 2.75 in. K20 and K30: Front: Disc: 12.50 in. x 1.53 in. Rear: Drum: 13.00 in. x 3.50 in. Wheels: K10: 15 x 6.0JJ 6-stud disc. Optional: 15 x 8JJ. K20: 16.5 x 6.00 in. 8-stud disc. Optional: 16.5 x 6.75. K30: 16.5 x 6.75. Tires: K10: P215/75R15-P metric radial. K20: 8.75 x 16.5C K30: 9.50 x 16.5D. Optional: K10: G78 x 15B, white stripe; H78 x 15B, tubeless, black sidewall or white stripe; L78 x 15B black sidewall or white stripe, tubeless; 10.00 x 16.5C tubeless; G78 x 15B tube-type; 7.00 x 15C tube-type; 6.50 x 16C tube-type and LR78 x 15C white sidewall radial ply. The following tires were specified for K10 models with the 5600 lb. GVW package which included a front heavy-duty stabilizer bar: H78 x 15B 4-ply rating, tubeless; 6.50 x 16C 6-ply rating, tube-type, truck type. The following tires were specified for K10 models with the 6000 lb. GVW Package which included a front heavy-duty stabilizer bar and heavy-duty rear springs: L78 x 15B 4-ply rating, tubeless. Optional K20: 9.50 x 16.5E Firestone Town and Country, 8.75 x 16.5D tubeless; 9.50 x 16.5D tubeless; 10.00 x 16.5C tubeless (not available for Stepside models); 7.50 x 16C 6-ply rating, tube-type; 7.50 x 16D tube-type; 7.50 x 16E tube-type. The following tires were specified for K20 models with the 7500 lb. GVW Package which included a front heavy-duty stabilizer bar: 8.75 x 16.5C 6-ply rating, tubeless; 7.50 x 16C 6-ply rating, tubeless. The following tires were specified for K20 models with the 8200 lb. GVW Package which included a front heavy-duty stabilizer bar: 9.50 x 16.5D 8-ply rating, tubeless; 7.50 x 16C 6-ply rating, tube type. Steering: Recirculating ball gear. Ratio: 20:1. Turning Circle: 47 ft. Steering wheel diameter: 17.5 in. Optional: Power-assisted. Ratio: 16.4:1. Transmission: K10 and K20: 3-speed GMC, synchromesh manual (RPO M15). Transmission Ratios: 5.7 liter V-8: 2.85, 1.68, 1.00:1. Reverse: 2.95:1. 5.0 liter V-8: 3.11, 1.84, 1.0:1 Reverse: 3.22:1. 4.1 liter 6-cyl.: 3.50, 1.89, 1.00:1. Reverse: 3.62:1. Optional: SM465. 4-speed manual synchromesh (RPO M20). Ratios: 6.56, 3.58, 1.70, 1.00:1. Reverse: 6.09:1. The K20 crew cab and all K30 models had this transmission as standard equipment. Optional: 3-speed Turbo Hydra-Matic 400 (RPO M40). Ratios: 2.1 x 2.48, 1.48, 1.00:1. Reverse: 2.10:1. The 400 cu. in. V-8 was available only with this transmission. Clutch: Diaphragm, spring. Clutch diameter: 6-cyl.: 11 in. dia. Total lining area: 123.5 sq. in. Total plate pressure: 2075 lb. V-8: 12 in. dia. Total lining area: 149.2 sq. in. Total plate pressure: 2060 lb. Optional: K20 6-cyl.: 11 in. dia. Total lining area: 124.0 sq. in. 307 V-8: 12 in. dia. Total lining area: 150 sq. in.

VEHICLE DIMENSIONS: Wheelbase: K10: 117.5 in. 131.5 in. K20: 131.5 in. All Suburbans and Panels: 129.5 in. K30: 131.5 in. 164.5 in. Overall Length: 117.5 in. Fleetside pickups: 191.30 in. 131.5 in. Fleetside pickups: 212.00. 117.5 in. Stepside pickups: 190.5 in. 131.5 in. Stepside pickups: 210.25. 117.5 in. Chassis cab: 186.05 in. K30: 164.5 in. wheelbase: 244.43 in. Front/Rear Tread: 67.4 in./65.8 in. Overall Height: K10 Fleetside pickup: 72.0 in. K20 Fleetside pickup: 74.0 in. K30 Fleetside pickup: 74.0 in. K30 crew cab: 75.0 in. K10 Suburban: 73.5 in. K20 Suburban: 75.5 in. Width: Pickup: 79.5 in. Front/Rear Overhang: pickups: 33 in./41 in. Tailgate: Width and Height: 72 in. x 19.25 in. Approach/Departure Degrees: K10 117.5 in. Fleetside and Stepside: 33/19. K10 131.5 in. Fleetside: 33/15. K10 131.5 in. wheelbase Stepside: 33/16. K20 131.5 in. wheelbase Fleetside: 35/20. K20 131.5 in. wheelbase Stepside: 35/21. K30 Fleetside pickup: 41/19. K30 crew cab pickup: 38/18. Ground Clearance: Front axle: 7.25 in. Rear axle: 7.0 in. Oil pan: 16.5 in. Transfer case: 12.0 in. Fuel tank: 16.6 in. Load space: Pickup box dimensions: 117.5 in. wheelbase Fleetside: 78.25 in. x 50 in. x 19.25 in. 131.5 in. wheelbase Fleetside: 98 in. x 50 in. x 19.25 in. Capacity: 117.5 wheelbase: 58.4 cu. ft. 131.5 in. wheelbase: 74.3 cu. ft. 117.5 in. wheelbase Stepside: 78.5 in. x 50 in. x 17.5 in. 131.5 in. wheelbase Stepside: 96.25 in. x 50 in. x 17.5 in. Front headroom: 38.5 in. (seat to top of cab). Front hip room: 67.25 in. Pedal to seat back (max.): 43.5 in. Steering wheel to seat back (max.): 17.3 in. Seat to ground: 35.0 in. Floor to ground: 23.0 in.

CAPACITIES: Fuel Tank: 117.5 in. wheelbase: 16.0 gal. 131.5 in. wheelbase, 135.5 in. wheelbase and 164.5 in. wheelbase: 20 gal. Optional: 16 gal. auxiliary tank. for 117.5 in.; 20 gal. auxiliary for 131.5 in., 135.5 in. and 164.5 in. wheelbase. Engine Coolant System: 250 6-cyl.: 14.8 qt. 305 V-8: 17.6 qt. 350 V-8: 17.6 qt.

ACCOMMODATIONS: Seating Capacity: Pickup and chassis cab models: 3 passenger. Optional: None. Crew cab: 6 passenger. Suburban: 3 passenger. Optional: 6 or 9 passenger.

INSTRUMENTATION: Speedometer, odometer, fuel level gauge. Warning lights for battery, oil pressure, generator, brake system warning, directional/hazard lights, high beam, and engine coolant temperature.

OPTIONS AND PRICES: 305 V-8 (RPO LE9): $345.00. 305 V-8 (RPO LG9). 350 V-8 (RPO LS9). Air conditioning (RPO C60): $563.00. GU2, 2.73:1 axle ratio (RPO GU2): $25.00. Chrome grille (RPO V22). Automatic transmission (RPO MX1): $366.00. Four-speed manual transmission. Chrome front bumper. Chrome front bumper guards. Chrome rear bumper. Chrome rear step bumper. Deluxe front bumper. Deluxe rear bumper. Painted rear step bumper. Cargo area lamp. Cigarette lighter. Color-keyed floor mats (RPO B32): $11.00. ComforTilt steering wheel. Deluxe Front End Appearance Package. Deluxe instrument panel. Dome lamp. Electric clock. Gauge Package. Includes voltmeter, engine coolant temperature and oil pressure gauges. Headlamp warning buzzer. Halogen high-beam headlamps, available with Deluxe Front Appearance Package only (RPO TT5): $25.00. Intermittent windshield wipers (RPO CD4): $32.00. Painted below eye-level mirrors (RPO D44). Stainless steel below eye-level mirrors (RPO D45). Stainless steel camper mirror (RPO DF2). Painted steel below eye-level mirrors (RPO DF1). Visor mirror. Black body moldings. Bright body moldings. Custom Molding Package-Black. Deluxe Molding Package-Bright. Door edge guards. Wheel opening moldings. Cruise control (RPO K35): 122.00. Power door locks (two-door models only). Power windows. Rear bench seat (K30 bonus/crew cab). Painted West Coast mirrors (K30 bonus/crew cab only), (RPO DG5). Conventional two-tone paint. Deluxe two-tone paint (RPO ZY4). Exterior Decor Package (RPO ZY5). Special two-tone paint (RPO ZY3). Pickup box side rails. AM radio. AM/FM radio. Operating Convenience Package (RPO ZQ2): $230.00. AM/FM radio with cassette player (RPO UN3): $325.00. AM/FM radio with CB and antenna. Windshield antenna. Roof marker lamps. Sliding rear window (RPO A28): $84.00. Glide-out spare tire carrier (RPO P11): $31.00. Side-mounted spare tire carrier. Tachometer (RPO U16): $86.00. Tinted glass. (RPO AO1): $33.00. Auxiliary fuel tank (RPO NL2): $169.00. Auxiliary battery. Locking rear differential (RPO G80): $182.00. Cold Climate Package. Engine oil cooler (RPO KC4): $90.00. 10R-15B tires white letter, on-off road tires available for K10 only (RPO XXN): $170.48. 10R-15B spare tire, available for K10 only (RPO ZNX): $85.74. Transmission oil cooler (RPO VO2): $45.00. 55 amp generator. 63 amp generator. Heavy-duty battery. Heavy-duty front and rear shock absorbers. Heavy-duty radiator. Trailering special. Camper body wiring harness. Dual exhaust system (K30 only). Dual rear wheels (K30 only). Front tow hooks. Front quad shock absorbers, available for K10 and K20 only (RPO Z75): $102.00. Fuel tank shield, not available for K30 bonus/crew cab (RPO NY1): $129.00. Heavy-duty front springs (K20 only.) Extra capacity rear springs (K20 and K30 bonus/crew cab). Extra capacity rear springs (K30 bonus/crew cab only). Main and auxiliary rear springs (K30 models only). Special camper chassis equipment-Basic (K20 HD, and K30 models only). Special camper chassis equipment-Deluxe (K20 HD, and K30 models only). Chevy Sport option (RPO Z77): $868.00. Wheelcovers, available for K10 and K20 only (RPO PO1). Wheel trim rings (RPO PO6). Aluminum wheels, available for K10 only (RPO PA6). Rallye wheels, available for K10 only (RPO N67).

HISTORICAL FOOTNOTES: Calendar year registrations of all Chevrolet trucks was 650,460, of which 403,487 were pickups and 19,518 were Suburbans.

1982 PICKUP

As an encore to the introduction of the lighter, more fuel efficient models of 1981, Chevrolet offered a new, 379 cu. in. 6.2 liter diesel V-8 (a 5.7 liter diesel had offered for the C10, two-wheel drive pickup in 1981) for all its K series trucks for 1982. The factory in which this engine was built in Moraine, Ohio was depicted as one of the world's most technologically advanced engine assembly plants in the world. This plant had a computer network with 400 programmable controllers — at that time this was more than any other manufacturing facility possessed in the United States. Employees at this plant received 80 hours of classroom training on the diesel engine that was intended to provide them with a total understanding of the assembly process and their role in its operation. This engine's major design features included a cast alloy iron block with webbed areas in the lower end for rigidity, a nodular iron crankshaft with deep rolled fillets, four-bolt five main bearing caps, induction-hardened valve seats, intake valves constructed of Silchrome No. 1 steel, roller-type hydraulic lifters, carburized forged steel camshaft and cast-aluminum pistons. Also introduced and exclusive to this engine was a new 4-speed manual overdrive transmission. K10 and K20 gasoline models and the K10 diesel were available with a new 4-speed overdrive automatic transmission. The K20 heavy-duty model (equipped with RPO HD6) and the K30 trucks with GVW ratings over 8500 lb. were fitted with a standard 3-speed automatic transmission if ordered with the diesel. The K30 transfer case was now equipped with synchronized gearings. This placed the K30 models on a par with the K10 and K20 models in that it was now possible for them to be shifted into four-wheel drive at speeds under 25 mph. To revert to two-wheel drive the vehicle had only to be brought to a stop, the transfer case shifted into two-wheel drive and the vehicle driven in reverse slowly for about 10 feet.

The exterior of the K series trucks was a virtual carbon-copy of the 1981 models, but there were some changes. For example, a chrome front bumper was now standard on all models. Improved anti-corrosion methods were also now employed.

With the elimination of the Cheyenne level, the number of trim packages was reduced to three. The standard Custom Deluxe interior consisted of a full-foam front seat with a new dual-tone leather-grain vinyl trim, an inertia latch seat back that folded forward for access to the cab storage area, color-keyed door trim panels with large padded arm rests, padded sunshades, cab interior light, prismatic day/night rearview mirror and a foam-padded instrument panel pad with a Custom Deluxe nameplate.

The Scottsdale trim included these changes or additions to the base level's content: A choice of Custom Cloth or Vinyl seats, black crackle insert and bright trim on door panels, color-keyed floormat, door or manually operated dome light, extra insulation, cigarette lighter and Scottsdale nameplate on instrument panel. The Silverado trim included all Scottsdale items plus the following changes or additions: Full cowl side trim panels, door-closing assist strap, door area carpet trim on lower portion of door panel, nameplate on instrument panel, bright brushed-finished aluminum trim on instrument cluster and door trim panels, needle-type full-gauge instrumentation, right-hand visor mirror, custom steering wheel, color-keyed carpeting, door storage pockets and (except for bonus cab rear compartment), extra-thick floor insulation.

All interior trim offering were available in a choice of two carry over colors: Blue and carmine, or three new colors: Charcoal, mahogany and medium almond. Charcoal and mahogany were limited to application on two-door cab models only.

Four exterior colors were carried over from 1981: Midnight black, frost white, Colonial yellow and Carmine red. Six new colors debuted for the 1982 models: Silver metallic, light blue metallic, mahogany metallic, almond, midnight blue and light bronze metallic.

1982 Chevrolet K10 Scottsdale diesel pickup

I.D. DATA: Unchanged from 1981 except the letter C designated the 1982 model year.

Model Number	Body Type & Seating	Factory Price	GVW	Shipping Weight	Prod. Total
Series K10-1/2 ton 250 6-cyl. 117.5 in. 131.5 in. wheelbase and standard 305 V-8 (Suburban: 129.5 in. wheelbase)					
CK10703	6.5 ft. F-S Pickup	$8874	6200	4442	—
CK10703	6.5 ft. Fleetside Pickup	$8749	6200	4485	—
CK10903	8 ft. Fleetside Pickup	$8899	6200	4686	—
CK10906	Suburban Endgate	$10,656	6200	5273	—
CK10906	Suburban Panl. Drs.	$10,622	6200[1]	5250	—

NOTE 1: Suburban available with optional 6800 and 730 lb. GVW packages.

Series K20-3/4 ton 292 6-cyl.1. 131.5 in. wheelbase. (Suburban-129.5 in. wheelbase). Crew and bonus cab: 164.5 in. wheelbase, Suburban weight with standard 350 V-8

CK20903	8 ft. Stepside Pickup	$9815	6800	4807	—
CK20903	8 ft. Fleetside Pickup	$9690	6800	4878	—
CK20906	Suburban Endgate	$11,584	6800	5472	—
CK20906	Suburban Panl. Drs.	$11,550	6800	5434	—

NOTE 1: Not available in California where the 350 engine is base.

* 8600 lb. GVW optional.

Series K30-1 ton 350 V-8. 131.5 in. wheelbase. Crew and bonus cab: 164.5 in. wheelbase

CK30903	Chassis & Cab[1]	$10,435	8400*	4956	—
CK30903	8 ft. Fleetside Pickup	$10,793	8400	5318	—
CK30943	Chassis & Bonus Cab	$11,274	8400	5370	—
CK30943	W-S Bonus Cab	$11,617	8400	5743	—
CK30943	Chassis & Crew Cab	$10,259	8400	5370	—

NOTE 1: 135.5 in. wheelbase.
NOTE 2: 164.5 in. wheelbase.
* 9200 and 10,000 lb. GVW optional.

STANDARD ENGINE: All K10 6-cyl. models: 250 Six (LE3 ordering code). Not available for California where a 305 V-8 with 4-bbl. carburetor is installed. Engine Type: OHV, In-line 6-cylinder. Cast iron block and cylinder head. Key features include a staged 2-bbl. carburetor that uses only one barrel for normal operation. The second barrel is used when more power is needed. The emissions control uses engine vacuum pulses instead of an air pump, pulley, and belt. This systems saves about 15 lbs. in weight as compared to the older system. This engine was produced by GM-Chevrolet Motor Division. Bore x Stroke: 3.875 in. x 3.53 in. Lifters: Hydraulic. Number of main bearings-7. Fuel Induction: Single Rochester 2-bbl. carburetor. Compression Ratio: 8.3:1. Displacement: 250 cu. in. (4.1 liters). Horsepower: Net: 120 @ 3600 rpm. (California: 110 @ 360 rpm). Torque: Net: 200 lb.-ft. @ 2000 rpm. (California: 195 lb.-ft. @ 2000 rpm). Oil refill capacity: 5 qt. with filter change. Fuel Requirements: Regular unleaded.

STANDARD ENGINE: K20 with RPO CH6 and K30 models: 292 Six. Ordering Code: L25. This engine was produced by GM de Mexico. Engine Type: OHV, 6-cyl. Cast iron block and cylinder head. Key features include cast iron intake manifold, aluminized-face intake valves, stellite-faced exhaust valves with hardened faces. Bore x Stroke: 3.875 in. x 4.125 in. Lifters: Hydraulic. Number of main bearings-7. Fuel Induction: Single Rochester 1-bbl. carburetor. Compression Ratio: 7.8:1. Displacement: 292 cu. in. (4.8 liters). Horsepower: Net: 115 @ 3400 rpm. Torque: Net: 215 lb.-ft. @ 1600 rpm. Oil refill capacity: 6 qt. Fuel Requirements: Regular unleaded.

STANDARD ENGINE: K20: Optional for K-20 with HP6 and all K30 models. Ordering Code: LS9: 350 V-8 Engine Type: OHV, V-8. Cast iron block and alloy iron cylinder head. Key features include chain drive camshaft and forged steel connecting rods. This engine was produced by GM-Chevrolet Motor Division. Bore x Stroke: 4.00 in. x 3.50 in. Lifters: Hydraulic. Number of main bearings-5. Fuel Induction: Single Rochester 4-bbl. carburetor. Compression Ratio: 8.2:1. Displacement: 350 cu. in. (5.7 liters). Horsepower: Net: 165 @ 3800 rpm. Torque: Net: 275 lb.-ft. @ 1600 rpm. Oil refill capacity: 5 qt. with filter change. Fuel Requirements: Regular unleaded.

STANDARD ENGINE: K20: Optional for K20 with HP6 and all K30 models with GVW of 8500 lb. and above. Ordering Code: LT9: 350 V-8 Engine Type: OHV, V-8. Cast iron block and alloy iron cylinder head. Key features include chain drive camshaft and forged steel connecting rods. This engine was produced by GM-Chevrolet Motor Division. Bore x Stroke: 4.0 in. x 3.50 in. Lifters: Hydraulic. Number of main bearings-5. Fuel Induction: Single Rochester 4-bbl. carburetor. Compression Ratio: 8.3:1. Displacement: 350 cu. in. (5.7 liters). Horsepower: Net: 160 @ 3800 rpm. (California rating: 155 @ 3600 rpm). Torque: Net: 260 lb.-ft. @ 2800 rpm. (California rating: 240 lb.-ft. @ 2800 rpm). Oil refill capacity: 5 qt. with filter change. Fuel Requirements: Regular unleaded.

OPTIONAL ENGINE: K10 models: Ordering Code: LE9: 305 V-8. Key features include Electronic Spark Control, new staged 4-barrel carburetor, camshaft and free-flow exhaust system. Not available for California. This engine was produced by GM-Chevrolet Motor Division and GM of Canada. Engine Type: OHV, V-8. Cast iron block and alloy iron cylinder head. Bore x Stroke: 3.74 in. x 3.48 in. Lifters: Hydraulic. Number of main bearings-5. Fuel Induction: Single Rochester 4-bbl. staged carburetor. Compression Ratio: 9.2:1. Displacement: 305 cu. in. (5.0 liters). Horsepower: 160 @ 4400 rpm. Torque: 235 lb.-ft. @ 2000 rpm. Oil refill capacity: 5 qt. with filter change. Fuel Requirements: Regular unleaded.

OPTIONAL ENGINE: K10 models for California: Ordering Code: LF3: 305 V-8. Key features include 4-barrel carburetor, camshaft and free-flow exhaust system. This engine was produced by GM-Chevrolet Motor Division and GM of Canada. Engine Type: OHV, V-8. Cast iron block and alloy iron cylinder head. Bore x Stroke: 3.74 in. x 3.48 in. Lifters: Hydraulic. Number of main bearings-5. Fuel Induction: Single Rochester 4-bbl. carburetor. Compression Ratio: 8.6:1. Displacement: 305 cu. in. (5.0 liters). Horsepower: 150 @ 4200 rpm. Torque: 240 lb.-ft. @ 2000 rpm. Oil refill capacity: 5 qt. with filter change. Fuel Requirements: Regular unleaded.

OPTIONAL ENGINE: K30 pickup and chassis and cab models: Ordering Code: LE9: 454 V-8. Engine Type: OHV, V-8. Cast iron block and alloy iron cylinder head. Bore x Stroke: 4.25 in. x 4.00 in. Lifters: Hydraulic. Number of main bearings-5. Fuel Induction: Single Rochester 4-bbl. carburetor. Compression Ratio: 7.9:1. Displacement: 454 cu. in. (7.4 liters). Horsepower: 210 @ 3800 rpm. Torque: 340 lb.-ft. @ 2800 rpm. Oil refill capacity: 5 qt. with filter change. Fuel Requirements: Regular unleaded.

OPTIONAL ENGINE: All models: Ordering Code: LH4: 379 diesel V-8. Engine Type: OHV, V-8. Cast iron block and alloy iron cylinder head. Bore x Stroke: 3.98 in. x 3.80 in. Lifters: Hydraulic. Number of main bearings-5. Fuel Induction: Fuel injection. Compression Ratio: 21.5:1. Displacement: 379 cu. in. (6.2 liters). Horsepower: 130 @ 3600 rpm. (LL4 for K20 with C6P has 135 up @ 3600 rpm.) Torque: 240 lb.-ft. @ 2000 rpm. Oil refill capacity: 7 qt. with filter change. Fuel Requirements: Diesel.

CHASSIS FEATURES: Separate body and frame with channel side rails. Carbon-Steel, 39,000 psi. 117.5 in. wheelbase: 2.30 in. x 5.92 in. x 0.156 in. Section modules: 3.06 in. 129.5 in.: 2.30 in. x 5.92 in. x 0.194. Section modules: 3.93. 135.5 in. wheelbase: 2.78 in. x 7.74 in. 0.194. Section modules: 6.20. 164.5 in. wheelbase: 2.78 in. x 7.74 in. x 0.224 in. Section modules: 7.33. 131.5 in. wheelbase: 2.30 in. x 5.92 in. x 0.194. Section modules: 3.84 in. Optional: None.

SUSPENSION AND RUNNING GEAR: Front Suspension: K10: Tapered 2-leaf springs. Capacity: 1650 lb.-1850 lb. K20: Tapered 2-leaf springs. Capacity: 1850 lb. K30: Tapered 3-leaf springs. Capacity: 2250 lb. Rear Suspension: K10 and K20: 52 in. x 2.25 in. Two-stage, 7-leaf. K30: 56 in. x 2.50 in. Capacity: K10: 2075 lb. K20: 2800 lb. K30: 3500 lb. 1.0 in. dia. shock absorbers. Optional Rating: K20: 3000 lb. rating at ground. Capacity: 6000 lb. with RPO CP6 RPO RO5 (Dual rear wheels). K30: 3750 lb. rating at ground. Capacity: 7500 lb. Front Axle Type and Capacity: K10 and K20: GMC or Spicer; K35: Spicer. K10: Semi-floating. 3600 lb. capacity. Optional: None. K20: Full-floating, 3800 lb. capacity. K30: Full-floating, 4500 lb. Optional: None. Rear Axle Type and Capacity: K10: Chevrolet, Semi-floating, 3750 lb. capacity. K20: Chevrolet, Full-floating, 5700 lb. K30: 7500 lb. Optional: None. Final Drive Ratio: Standard: K10: 6-cyl. and 3-spd. man. trans.: 3.73:1; with 4-spd. man. trans. or 3-spd. auto. trans.: 3.42:1. LE9-305 V-8 and 4-spd. man. trans.: 3.08:1; with 4-spd. man. trans.: 2.73:1; with 3-spd. auto. trans.: 2.56:1. California only: LS9-350 V-8 3-spd. auto. trans.: 2.73:1. Optional K10: 6-cyl. with 4-spd. man. trans. or 3-spd. auto. trans.: 3.73:1. LE9-305 V-8 and 4-spd. man. trans.: 3.08:1; with 3-spd. auto. trans.: 2.73:1, 3.73:1 (requires RPO Z82, Trailering Special Package). California only: LS9-350 V-8 3-spd. auto. trans.: 3.08:1. Standard: K20 with GVW up to 8500 lb.: LS9 350 V-8 and 3-spd. man. trans.: 3.42:1,with 4-spd. man. trans. or 3-spd. auto. trans.: 3.23:1 (not avail. with locking rear differential). California only: LS9 350 V-8 and 3-spd. auto. trans. 3.23:1; K20 with GVW over 8500 lb.: L25 6-cyl.: With 4-spd. man. trans. or 3-spd. auto. trans.: 4.10:1; with LT9 350 V-8 4-spd. man. trans.: 3.73:1; 3-spd. auto. trans.: 4.10:1. K20 with GVW over 8500 lb. L25 292 6-cyl.: 4.10:1 (4-spd. man. and auto. trans.); LT9 350 V-8: 4-spd. man. trans.: 3.73:1; 3-spd. auto. trans.: 4.10:1. Optional: LT9 350 V-8: 4-spd. man. trans.: 4.10:1. Standard K30: L25, 6-cyl. 4-spd. man. and auto. trans.: 4.56:1; LT9, 350 V-8, 4-spd. man. and auto. trans. and 9200 lb. GVW: 4.10:1; LT9, 350 V-8, 4-spd. man. and auto. trans. and 10,000 lb. GVW: 4.56:1. Optional K30: LT9, 350 V-8, 4-spd. man. and auto. trans. and 9200 lb. GVW: 4.56:1; LT9, 350 V-8, 4-spd. man. and auto. trans. and 10,000 lb. GVW: 4.10:1. Optional: K10 and K20: 700R4 4-speed automatic overdrive. Ratios: 3.06, 1.36, 1.00, 0.70. Reverse: 2.29:1. Transfer Case: K10 and K20: New Process 208. Single lever, 2.61, 1.00:1. K30: New Process 205, two-speed: 1.96, 1.00:1. Brakes: Type: Hydraulic, power assisted. Dimensions: K10: Front: Disc: 11.86 in. x 1.28 in. Rear: Drums: 11.15 in. x 2.75 in. K20: Front: Disc: 12.5 in. x 1.28 in. Rear: Drums: 11.15 in. x 2.75 in. K20 and K30: Front: Disc: 12.50 in. x 1.53 in. Rear: Drum: 13.00 in. x 3.50 in. Wheels: K10: 15 x 6.0JJ 6-stud disc. Optional: 15 x 8JJ. K20: 16.5 x 6.00 in. 8-stud disc. Optional: 16.5 x 6.75. K30: 16.5 x 6.75. Tires: K10: P215/75R15-P metric radial. K20: 8.75 x 16.5C K30: 9.50 x 16.5D. Optional: G78 x 15B, white stripe; H78 x 15B, tubeless, black sidewall or white stripe; L78 x 15B black sidewall or white stripe, tubeless. 10.00 x 16.5C tubeless; G78 x 15B tube-type; 7.00 x 15C tube-type; 6.50 x 16C tube-type and LR78 x 15C white sidewall radial ply. The following tires were specified for K10 models with the 5600 lb. GVW package which included a front heavy-duty stabilizer bar: H78 x 15B 4-ply rating, tubeless; 6.50 x 16C 6-ply rating, tube-type, truck type. The following tires were specified for K10 models with the 6000 lb. GVW Package which included a front heavy-duty stabilizer bar and heavy-duty rear springs: L78 x 15B 4-ply rating, tubeless. Optional K20: 9.50 x 16.5E Firestone Town and Country, 8.75 x 16.5D tubeless; 9.50 x 16.5C tubeless (not available for Stepside models); 7.50 x 16C 6-ply rating, tube-type; 7.50 x 16D tube-type; 7.50 x 16E tube-type. The following tires were specified for K20 models with the 7500 lb. GVW Package which included a front heavy-duty stabilizer bar: 8.75 x 16.5 C 6-ply rating, tubeless; 7.50 x 16C 6-ply rating, tubeless. The following tires were specified for K20 models with the 8200 lb. GVW Package which included a front heavy-duty stabilizer bar: 9.50 x 16.5D 8-ply rating, tubeless; 7.50 x 16C 6-ply rating, tube type. Steering: Recirculating ball gear. Ratio: 20:1. Turning Circle: 47 ft. Steering wheel diameter: 17.5 in. Optional: Power-assisted. Ratio: 16.4:1. Transmission: K10 and K20: 3-speed GMC, synchromesh manual (RPO M15). Transmission Ratios: 5.7 liter V-8: 2.85, 1.68, 1.00:1. Reverse: 2.95:1. 5.0 liter V-8: 3.11, 1.84, 1.0:1 Reverse: 3.22:1. 4.1 liter 6-cyl.: 3.50, 1.89, 1.00:1. Reverse: 3.62:1. Optional: SM465. 4-speed manual synchromesh (RPO M20). Ratios: 6.56, 3.58, 1.70, 1.00:1. Reverse: 6.09:1. The K20 crew cab and all K30 models had this transmission as standard equipment. Optional: 3-speed Turbo Hydra-Matic 400 (RPO M40). Ratios: 2.1 x 2.48, 1.48, 1.00:1. Reverse: 2.10:1. The 400 cu. in. V-8 was available only with this transmission. Clutch: Diaphragm, spring. Clutch diameter: 6-cyl.: 11 in. dia. Total lining area: 123.5 sq. in. Total plate pressure: 2075 lb. V-8: 12 in. dia. Total lining area: 149.2 sq. in. Total plate pressure: 2060 lb. Optional: K20 6-cyl.: 11 in. dia. Total lining area: 124.0 sq. in. 307 V-8: 12 in. dia. Total lining area: 150 sq. in.

VEHICLE DIMENSIONS: Series K10 and K20: Wheelbase: K10: 117.5 in. 131.5 in. K20: 131.5 in. All Suburbans and Panels: 129.5 in. K30: 131.5 in. 164.5 in. Overall Length: 117.5 in. Fleetside pickups: 191.30 in. 131.5 in. Fleetside pickups: 212.00. 117.5 in. Stepside pickups: 190.5 in. 131.5 in. Stepside pickups: 210.25 in. 117.5 in. Chassis cab: 186.05 in. K30 data: 164.5 in. wheelbase: 244.43 in. Front/Rear Tread: 67.4 in./65.8 in. Overall Height: K10 Fleetside pickup: 72.0 in. K20 Fleetside pickup: 74.0 in. K30 Fleetside pickup: 74.0 in. K10 crew cab: 75.0 in. K10 Suburban: 73.5 in. K20 Suburban: 75.5 in. Width: Pickup: 79.5 in. Front/Rear Overhang: pickups 33 in./41 in. Tailgate: Width and Height: 72 in. x 19.25 in. Approach/Departure Degrees: K10 117.5 in. Fleetside and Stepside: 33/19. Fleetside: 33/15. K10 131.5 in. wheelbase Stepside: 33/16. K20 131.5 in. wheelbase Stepside: 35/21. K30 Fleetside pickup: 41/19. K30 crew cab Fleetside: 38/18. Ground Clearance: Front axle: 7.25 in. Rear axle: 7.0 in. Oil pan: 16.5 in. Transfer case: 12.0 in. Fuel tank: 16.6 in. Load space: Pickup box dimensions: 117.5 in. wheelbase Fleetside: 78.25 in. x 50 in. x 19.25 in. 131.5 in. wheelbase Fleetside: 98 in. x 50 in. x 19.25 in. Capacity: 117.5 wheelbase: 58.4 cu. ft. 131.5 in. wheelbase: 74.3 cu. ft. 117.5 in. wheelbase Stepside: 78.5 in. x 50 in. x 17.5 in. 131.5 in. wheelbase Stepside: 96.25 in. x 50 in. x 17.5 in. Front headroom: 38.5 in. (seat to top of cab). Front hip room: 67.25 in. Pedal to seat back (max.): 43.5 in. Steering wheel to seat back (max.): 17.3 in. Seat to ground: 35.0 in. Floor to ground: 23.0 in.

CAPACITIES: Fuel Tank: 117.5 in. wheelbase: 16.0 gal. 131.5 in. wheelbase, 135.5 in. wheelbase and 164.5 in. wheelbase: 20 gal. Optional: 16 gal. auxiliary tank. for 117.5 in.; 20 gal. auxiliary for 131.5 in., 135.5 in. and 164.5 in. wheelbase. Engine Coolant System: 250 6-cyl.: 14.8 qt. 305 V-8: 17.6 qt. 350 V-8: 17.6 qt. 400 V-8: 19.6 qt. (20 qt. on K20 and K30).

ACCOMMODATIONS: Seating Capacity: Pickup and chassis cab models: 3 passenger. Optional: None. Crew cab: 6 passenger. Suburban: 3 passenger. Optional: 6 or 9 passenger.

INSTRUMENTATION: Speedometer, odometer, fuel level gauge. Warning lights for battery, oil pressure, generator, brake system warning, directional/hazard lights, high beam, and engine coolant temperature.

OPTIONS AND PRICES: 5 liter V-8: $170. California emissions: $90. 5.7 liter V-8: $345. 379 cu. in. diesel engine: $1334. 4-speed manual trans.: $198. 4-speed manual with overdrive: $75. 3-speed automatic trans.: $438. 4-speed automatic with overdrive: $637. Optional axle ratios: $35. Rear step painted bumper: $106. Chromed rear bumper: $97. Rear step chromed bumper: $177. Front bumper guards: $39. Glide-out spare tire carrier: $39. Side-mounted spare tire carrier: $27. Quartz analog electric clock: $70, without Silverado, $36 with Silverado. Cold Climate Package: $184, without Trailering Package, $126 with Trailering Package. $172 with Scottsdale or Silverado and without Trailering Package, $114 with Scottsdale or Silverado and with Trailering Package. Engine oil cooler: $112. Heavy-duty transmission oil cooler: $55. Heavy-duty cooling system: $48. Power door locks: $115. Color-keyed floor mats: $14. Gauges Package. Includes voltmeter, engine coolant temperature and oil pressure: $34. 62 amp Delcotron generator: $58. Tinted glass: $40. Halogen high beam headlights: $15. Halogen high and low beam headlights: $20. Cargo area lamp: $56, with Scottsdale or Silverado: $32, without Scottsdale or Silverado: $56.Dome light: $24. Cigarette lighter: $28. Below eye-level painted mirrors: $44. Below eye-level stainless steel mirrors: $72. Camper style painted mirrors: $86. Black body side moldings: $105. Bright body side moldings: $131, without Scottsdale $13 with Scottsdale. Custom Package: $144 without Scottsdale, $26 with Scottsdale. Deluxe Package: $157 without Scottsdale, $39 with Scottsdale. Door edge guard: $13. Pickup box side rails: $88. Operating Convenience Package: $281. Am radio: $92. AM/FM radio: $143. AM/FM stereo radio: $226. AM/FM stereo radio with 8-track tape player: $322. AM/FM stereo radio with cassette tape player: $327. AM/FM stereo radio with CB radio and triband antenna: $559. Windshield antenna: $31. Fuel tank shield: $84. without NL2 tank, $154 with NL tank. Front quad shock absorbers: $117. Speed control: $159 with automatic transmission, $169 with manual trans. Heavy-duty front springs: $84 without quad shocks, $53 with quad shocks. ComforTilt steering wheel: $95. Auxiliary 16 gal. fuel tank: $208. Two front towing hooks: $34. Bright wheelcovers: $38. Aluminum forged wheels: $411. Rallye wheels: $103. Styled wheels: $201. Power windows: $166. Sliding rear window: $100. Intermittent windshield wipers: $45. Scottsdale Package: $208, Stepside, $318, Fleetside. Silverado: $614, Stepside, $780 without Exterior Decor Package, $753 with Exterior Decor Package. Seat trim: $48. Conventional two-tone paint: $69 with Silverado, $42 without Silverado. Special two-tone paint: $291 without Silverado or Scottsdale, $173 with Scottsdale, $147 with Silverado. Deluxe two-tone paint: $328 without Scottsdale, or Silverado, $210 with Scottsdale, $157 with Silverado. Dual rear wheels for K30: $664 to $677. Exterior Decor Package: $503, without Scottsdale or Silverado, $385 with Scottsdale, $359 with Silverado. Additional Suburban options: Center folding seat: $343. Center and rear folding seats: $640.31 gal. fuel tank: $39. 40 gal. fuel tank: $91. Heavy-duty trailering special: $354-$619 depending upon vehicle option content. Scottsdale trim: $379. Silverado: $1135. Diesel equipment: $1041. Includes heavy-duty generator, dual batteries, engine oil cooler, engine block heater, sound insulation, water-in-fuel detection and drain system, dual exhaust and In-line fuel heater.

HISTORICAL FOOTNOTES: Calendar registrations of all types of Chevrolet trucks was 758,107, of which 105,741 were full-sized pickups. Suburban registrations were 34,846.

1983 PICKUP

Chevrolet's pickups and Suburbans were mildly restyled for 1983. Indeed, the changes were so minor that the front cover of the 1982 sales brochure was used for the 1983 edition, with the proper amount of air brushing of course! For 1983 the parking/directionals were moved from the grille to the bumpers, the primary grille insert was blacked out, and the center grille dividing bar was available in the truck's body color. The standard Custom interior was unchanged for 1983.

The Scottsdale trim included these changes or additions to the base level's content: A choice of Custom Cloth or Vinyl seats, black crackle insert and bright trim on door panels, color-keyed floormat, door or manually operated dome light, extra insulation, cigarette lighter and Scottsdale nameplate on instrument panel. Improved corrosion protection was provided by the use of a new Zincrometal hood inner panel and a new galvanized, high-strength-steel front-end cargo box on Fleetside models.

1983 Chevrolet K20 Scottsdale pickup

The optional Silverado trim was little changed from 1982. It still offered a choice of cut-pile velour cloth seats or a leather-grained Custom vinyl. Also included was a new pewter-toned brushed aluminum instrument panel, and fiber optic ashtray illumination. The top-ranked Silverado trim option was unchanged as was the color selection for all three versions.

All ten exterior colors were carried over from 1982.

I.D. DATA: Unchanged from 1981 except the letter D designated the 1983 model year.

Model Number	Body Type & Seating	Factory Price	GVW	Shipping Weight	Prod. Total
Series K10-1/2 ton 250 6-cyl. 117.5 in. 131.5 in. wheelbase (Suburban: 129.5 in. wheelbase and standard 305 V-8)					
CK10703	6.5 ft. F-S Pickup	$9020	6200	4442	—
CK10703	6.5 ft. Fleetside Pickup	$8895	6200	4485	—
CK10903	8 ft. Fleetside Pickup	$9045	6200	4686	—
CK10906	Suburban Endgate	$10,802	6200	5273	—
CK10906	Suburban Panl. Drs.	$10,768	6200[1]	5250	—

NOTE 1: Suburban available with optional 6800 and 7300 lb. GVW packages.

Series K20-3/4 ton 292 6-cyl.[1]. 131.5 in. wheelbase. (Suburban-129.5 in. wheelbase). Crew and bonus cab: 164.5 in. wheelbase, Suburban weight with standard 350 V-8

CK20903	8 ft. Stepside Pickup	$9980	6800	4807	—
CK20903	8 ft. Fleetside Pickup	$9855	6800	4878	—
CK20906	Suburban Endgate	$11,749	6800	5472	—
CK20906	Suburban Panl. Drs.	$11,715	6800	5434	—

NOTE 1: Not available in California where the 350 engine is base.
* 8600 lb. GVW optional.

Series K30-1 ton 350 V-8. 131.5 in. wheelbase. Crew and bonus cab: 164.5 in. wheelbase

CK30903	Chassis & Cab[1]	$10,605	8400*	4956	—
CK30903	8 ft. Fleetside Pickup	$10,963	8400	5318	—
CK30943	Chassis & Bonus Cab	$11,444	8400	5370	—
CK30943	W-S Bonus Cab	$11,787	8400	5743	—
CK30943	Chassis & Crew Cab	$10,429	8400	5370	—

NOTE 1: 135.5 in. wheelbase.
NOTE 2: 164.5 in. wheelbase.
* 9200 and 10,000 lb. GVW optional.

STANDARD ENGINE: All K-10 6-cyl. models: 250 Six (LE3 ordering code). Engine Type: OHV, In-line 6-cylinder. Cast iron block and cylinder head. Bore x Stroke: 3.875 in. x 3.53 in. Lifters: Hydraulic. Number of main bearings-7. Fuel Induction: Single Rochester 2-bbl. carburetor. Compression Ratio: 8.3:1. Displacement: 250 cu. in. (4.1 liters). Horsepower: Net: 115 @ 3600 rpm. (California Rating: 110 @ 3600 rpm). Torque: Net: 200 lb.-ft. @ 2000 rpm. (California Rating: 200 lb.-ft. @ 1600 rpm). Oil refill capacity: 5 qt. with filter change. Fuel Requirements: Regular unleaded.

STANDARD ENGINE: K20 with RPO CH6 and K30 models: 292 Six. Ordering Code: L25. This engine was produced by GM de Mexico. Not available in California with under 8500 lb. GVW rating. Engine Type: OHV, 6-cyl. Cast iron block and cylinder head. Key features include cast iron intake manifold, aluminized-face intake valves, stellite-faced exhaust valves with hardened faces. Bore x Stroke: 3.875 in. x 4.125 in. Lifters: Hydraulic. Number of main bearings-7. Fuel Induction: Single Rochester 1-bbl. carburetor. Compression Ratio: 7.8:1. Displacement: 292 cu. in. (4.8 liters). Horsepower: Net: 115 @ 3400 rpm. Torque: Net: 215 lb.-ft. @ 1600 rpm. Oil refill capacity: 6 qt. Fuel Requirements: Regular unleaded.

STANDARD ENGINE: K20: Optional for K10 (California only), K20 with HP6 and all K30 models. Ordering Code: LS9: 350 V-8 Engine Type: OHV, V-8. Cast iron block and alloy iron cylinder head. Key features include chain drive camshaft and forged steel connecting rods. This engine was produced by GM-Chevrolet Motor Division. Bore x Stroke: 4.0 in. x 3.50 in. Lifters: Hydraulic. Number of main bearings-5. Fuel Induction: Single Rochester 4-bbl. carburetor. Compression Ratio: 8.2:1. Displacement: 350 cu. in. (5.7 liters). Horsepower: Net: 165 @ 3800 rpm. Torque: Net: 275 lb.-ft. @ 1600 rpm. Oil refill capacity: 5 qt. with filter change. Fuel Requirements: Regular unleaded.

OPTIONAL ENGINE: K20 with HP6 and all K30 models: Ordering Code: LT9: 350 V-8 Engine Type: OHV, V-8. Cast iron block and alloy iron cylinder head. Key features include chain drive camshaft and forged steel connecting rods. This engine was produced by GM-Chevrolet Motor Division. Bore x Stroke: 4.0 in. x 3.50 in. Lifters: Hydraulic. Number of main bearings-5. Fuel Induction: Single Rochester 4-bbl. carburetor. Compression Ratio: 8.3:1. Displacement: 350 cu. in. (5.7 liters). Horsepower: Net: 160 @ 3800 rpm. (California rating: 155 @ 3600 rpm). Torque: Net: 260 lb.-ft. @ 2800 rpm. (California rating: 240 lb.-ft. @ 2800 rpm). Oil refill capacity: 5 qt. with filter change. Fuel Requirements: Regular unleaded.

OPTIONAL ENGINE: K10 models: Ordering Code: LE9: 305 V-8. Key features include Electronic Spark Control, new staged 4-barrel carburetor, camshaft and free-flow exhaust system. Not available for California. This engine was produced by GM-Chevrolet Motor Division and GM of Canada. Engine Type: OHV, V-8. Cast iron block and alloy iron cylinder head. Bore x Stroke: 3.74 in. x 3.48 in. Lifters: Hydraulic. Number of main bearings-5. Fuel Induction: Single Rochester 4-bbl. staged carburetor. Compression Ratio: 9.2:1. Displacement: 305 cu. in. (5.0 liters). Horsepower: 160 @ 4400 rpm. Torque: 235 lb.-ft. @ 2000 rpm. Oil refill capacity: 5 qt. with filter change. Fuel Requirements: Regular unleaded.

OPTIONAL ENGINE: K10 models for California: Ordering Code: LF3: 305 V-8. Key features include 4-barrel carburetor, camshaft and free-flow exhaust system. This engine was produced by GM-Chevrolet Motor Division and GM of Canada. Engine Type: OHV, V-8. Cast iron block and alloy iron cylinder head. Bore x Stroke: 3.74 in. x 3.48 in. Lifters: Hydraulic. Number of main bearings-5. Fuel Induction: Single Rochester 4-bbl. carburetor. Compression Ratio: 8.6:1. Displacement: 305 cu. in. (5.0 liters). Horsepower: 155 @ 4200 rpm. Torque: 240 lb.-ft. @ 1600 rpm. Oil refill capacity: 5 qt. with filter change. Fuel Requirements: Regular unleaded.

OPTIONAL ENGINE: K30 models: Ordering Code: LE8: 454 V-8. This engine was produced by GM-Chevrolet Motor Division. a. Engine Type: OHV, V-8. Cast iron block and alloy iron cylinder head. Bore x Stroke: 4.3 in. x 4.0 in. Lifters: Hydraulic. Number of main bearings-5. Fuel Induction: Single Rochester 4-bbl. carburetor. Compression Ratio: 7.9:1. Displacement: 454 cu. in. (7.4 liters). Horsepower: 230 @ 3800 rpm. Torque: 360 lb.-ft. @ 2800 rpm. Oil refill capacity: 5 qt. with filter change. Fuel Requirements: Regular unleaded.

OPTIONAL ENGINE: All models: Ordering Code: LH6: 6.2 liter V-8. This engine was produced by GM-Detroit Diesel Allison Division. Engine Type: OHV, diesel V-8. Bore x Stroke: 3.98 in. x 3.80 in. Lifters: Hydraulic. Number of main bearings-5. Fuel Induction: Fuel injection. Compression Ratio: 21.3:1. Displacement: 379.4 cu. in. (6.2 liters). Horsepower: 135 @ 3600 rpm. Torque: 240 lb.-ft. @ 2000 rpm. Oil refill capacity: 7 qt. with filter change. Fuel Requirements: Diesel. An LL4 version of this engine for models with GVW of 8500 lb. and above was also available. its power ratings were 135 hp. @ 3600 rpm and 240 lb.-ft. of torque @ 2000 rpm.

CHASSIS FEATURES: Separate body and frame with channel side rails. Carbon-Steel, 39,000 psi. 117.5 in. wheelbase: 2.30 in. x 5.92 in. x 0.156 in. Section modules: 3.06 in. 129.5 in.: 2.30 in. x 5.92 in. x 0.194. Section modules: 117.5 in. wheelbase: 3.14 in. 131.5 in. wheelbase: 3.88 in. K20 with CP6: 4.53 in. Optional: None.

SUSPENSION AND RUNNING GEAR: Front Suspension: K10: Tapered 2-leaf springs. Capacity: 1650 lb.-1850 lb. K20: Tapered 2-leaf springs. Capacity: 1850 lb. K30: Tapered 3-leaf springs. Capacity: 2250 lb. Rear Suspension: K10 and K20: 52 in. x 2.25 in. Two-stage, 5-leaf. K30: 56 in. x 2.50 in. Rating: K10: 2075 lb. K20: 2800 lb. K30: 3500 lb. K10: 22mm. dia. shock absorbers. K30: 32mm shock absorbers. Capacity: K10: 3750 lb. K20: 5700 lb. K30: 7000 lb. (7500 lb. for 159.9 in. wheelbase Chassis and Cab). 000. Optional Rating: K20: 3000 lb. rating at ground. Capacity: 6000 lb. with RPO CP6 K30: RPO RO5 (Dual rear wheels): 3750 lb. rating at ground. Capacity: 7500 lb. Front Axle Type and Capacity: K10 and K20: GMC or Spicer, K35: Spicer. K10: Semi-floating. 3600 lb. capacity. Optional: None. K20: Full-floating, 3800 lb. capacity. K30: Full-floating, 4500 lb. Optional: None. Rear Axle Type and Capacity: K10: Chevrolet, Semi-floating, 3750 lb. capacity. K20: Chevrolet, Full-floating, 5700 lb. K30: 7500 lb. Optional: None. Final Drive Ratio: Standard: K10: 6-cyl. and 3-spd. man. trans.3.73:1; with 4-spd. man. trans. or 3-spd. auto. trans.: 3.42:1. LE9-305 V-8 and 3-spd. man. trans.: 3.08:1; with 4-spd. man. trans.: 2.73:1; with 3-spd. auto. trans.: 2.56:1. California only: LS9-350 V-8 3-spd. auto. trans.: 2.73:1. Optional K10: 6-cyl. with 4-spd. man. trans. or 3-spd. auto. trans.: 3.73:1. LE9-305 V-8 and 4-spd. man. trans.: 3.08:1; with 3-spd. auto. trans.: 2.73:1, 3.73:1 (requires RPO Z82, Trailering Special Package). California only: LS9-350 V-8 3-spd. auto. trans.: 3.08:1. Standard: K20 with GVW up to 8500 lb.: LS9 350 V-8 and 3-spd. man. trans.: 3.42:1, with 4-spd. man. trans. or 3-spd. auto. trans.: 3.23:1 (not avail. with locking rear differential). California only: LS9 350 V-8 and 3-spd. auto. trans: 3.23:1. K20 with GVW over 8500 lb.: L25 6-cyl.: With 4-spd. man. trans. or 3-spd. auto. trans.: 4.10:1; with LT9 350 V-8: 4-spd. man. trans.: 3.73:1; 3-spd. auto. trans.: 4.10:1. K20 with GVW over 8500 lb. L25 292 6-cyl.: 4.10:1 (4-spd. man. and auto. trans.); LT9 350 V-8: 4-spd. man. trans.: 3.73:1; 3-spd. auto. trans.: 4.10:1. Optional: LT9 350 V-8: 4-spd. man. trans.: 4.10:1. Standard K30: L25, 6-cyl, 4-spd. man. and auto. trans.: 4.56:1; LT9, 350 V-8, 4-spd. man. and auto. trans. and 9200 lb. GVW: 4.10:1; LT9, 350 V-8, 4-spd. man. and auto. trans. and 10,000 lb. GVW: 4.56:1. Optional K30: LT9, 350 V-8, 4-spd. man. and auto. trans. and 9200 lb. GVW: 4.56:1; LT9, 350 V-8, 4-spd. man. and auto. trans. and 10,000 lb. GVW: 4.10:1. Optional: K10 and K20: 700R4 4-speed automatic overdrive. Ratios: 3.06, 1.36, 1.00, 0.70. Reverse: 2.29:1. Transfer Case: K10 and K20: New Process 208. Single lever, 2.61, 1.00:1. K30: New Process 205, two-speed: 1.96, 1.00:1. Brakes: Type: Hydraulic, power assisted. Dimensions: K10: Front: Disc: 11.86 in. x 1.28 in. Rear: Drums: 11.15 x 2.75 in. K20: Front: Disc: 12.5 in. x 1.28 in. Rear: Drums: 11.15 in. x 2.75 in. K20 and K30: Front: Disc: 12.50 in. x 1.53 in. Rear: Drum: 13.00 in. x 3.50 in. Wheels: K10: 15 x 6.0JJ 6-stud disc. Optional: 15 x 8JJ. K20: 16.5 x 6.00 in. 8-stud disc. Optional: 16.5 x 6.75. K30: 16.5 x 6.75. Tires: K10: P215/75R15-P metric radial. K20: 8.75 x 16.5C K30: 9.50 x 16.5D. Optional: K10: G78 x 15B, white stripe; H78 x 15B, tubeless, black sidewall or white stripe; L78 x 15B black sidewall or white stripe, tubeless; 10.00 x 16.5C tubeless; G78 x 15B tube-type; 7.00 x 15C tube-type; 6.50 x 16C tube-type and LR78 x 15C white sidewall radial ply. The following tires were specified for K10 models with the 5600 lb. GVW package which included a front heavy-duty stabilizer bar: H78 x 15B 4-ply rating, tubeless; 6.50 x 16C 6-ply rating, tube-type, truck type. The following tires were specified for K10 models with the 6000 lb. GVW Package which included a front heavy-duty stabilizer bar and heavy-duty rear springs: L78 x 15B 4-ply rating, tubeless. Optional K20: 9.50 x 16.5E Firestone Town and Country, 8.75 x 16.5D tubeless; 9.50 x 16.5D tubeless; 10.00 x 16.5C tubeless (not available for Stepside models); 7.50 x 16C 6-ply rating, tube-type; 7.50 x 16D tube-type; 7.50 x 16E tube-type. The following tires were specified for K20 models with the 7500 lb. GVW Package which included a front heavy-duty stabilizer bar: 8.75 x 16.5 C 6-ply rating, tubeless; 7.50 x 16C 6-ply rating, tubeless. The following tires were specified for K20 models with the 8200 lb. GVW Package which included a front heavy-duty stabilizer bar: 9.50 x 16.5D 8-ply rating, tubeless; 7.50 x 16C 6-ply rating, tube type. Steering: Recirculating ball gear. Ratio: 20:1. Turning Circle: 47 ft. Steering wheel diameter: 17.5 in. Optional: Power-assisted. Ratio: 16.4:1. Transmission: K10 and K20: 3-speed GMC, synchromesh manual (RPO M15). Transmission Ratios: 5.7 liter V-8: 2.85, 1.68, 1.00:1. Reverse: 2.95:1. 5.0 liter V-8: 3.11, 1.84, 1.0:1 Reverse: 3.22:1. 4.1 liter 6-cyl.: 3.50, 1.89, 1.00:1. Reverse: 3.62:1. Optional: SM465. 4-speed manual synchromesh (RPO M20). Ratios: 6.56, 3.58, 1.70, 1.00:1. Reverse: 6.09:1. The K20 crew cab and all K30 models had this transmission as standard equipment. Optional: 3-speed Turbo Hydra-Matic 400 (RPO M40). Ratios: 2.1 x 2.48, 1.48, 1.00:1. Reverse: 2.10:1. The 400 cu. in. V-8 was available only with this transmission. Clutch: Diaphragm, spring. Clutch diameter: 6-cyl.: 11 in. dia. Total lining area: 123.5 sq. in. Total plate pressure: 2075 lb. V-8: 12 in. dia. Total lining area: 149.2 sq. in. Total plate pressure: 2060 lb. Optional: K20 6-cyl.: 11 in. dia. Total lining area: 124.0 sq. in. 307 V-8: 12 in. dia. Total lining area: 150 sq. in.

VEHICLE DIMENSIONS: Series K10 and K20: Wheelbase: K10: 117.5 in. 131.5 in. K20: 131.5 in. All Suburbans and Panels: 129.5 in. K30: 131.5 in. 164.5 in. Overall Length: 117.5 in. Fleetside pickups: 191.30 in. 131.5 in. Fleetside pickups: 212.00. 117.5 in. Stepside pickups: 190.5 in. 131.5 in. Stepside pickups: 210.25. 117.5 in. Chassis cab: 186.05 in. K30 data: 164.5 in. wheelbase: 244.43 in. Front/Rear Tread: 67.4 in./65.8 in. Overall Height: K10 Fleetside pickup: 72.0 in. K20 Fleetside pickup: 74.0 in. K30 Fleetside pickup: 74.0 in. K30 crew cab: 75.0 in. K10 Suburban: 73.5 in. K20 Suburban: 75.5 in. Width: Pickup: 79.5 in. Front/Rear Overhang: pickups: 33 in./41 in. Tailgate: Width and Height: 72 in. x 19.25 in. Approach/Departure Degrees: K10 117.5 in. Fleetside and Stepside: 33/19. K10 131.5 in. Fleetside: 33/15. K10 131.5 in. wheelbase Stepside: 33/16. K20 131.5 in. wheelbase Fleetside: 35/20. K20 131.5 in. wheelbase Stepside: 35/21. K30 Fleetside pickup: 41/19. K30 crew cab pickup: 38/18. Ground Clearance: Fleetside models: K10 pickups: Front: 74 in.; rear: 7.1 in. K20 pickups: Front: 8.8 in.; rear: 7.2 in. K30 pickups: Front: 8.3 in.; rear: 7.8 in. Step side models: K10 pickups: Front: 7.2 in.; rear: 7.1 in. K20 pickups: Front: 8.8 in.; rear: 7.2 in. K30 pickups: K30 chassis cab (131.5 in. 135.5 in. and 159.5 in. wheelbase): Front: 8.3 in.; rear: 7.7 in. K30 bonus/crew cab: Front: 8.3 in.; rear: 7.7 in. Load space: Pickup box dimensions: 117.5 in. wheelbase Fleetside: 78.25 in. x 50 in. x 19.25 in. 131.5 in. wheelbase Fleetside: 98 in. x 50 in. x 19.25 in. Capacity: 117.5 wheelbase: 58.4 cu. ft. 131.5 in. wheelbase: 74.3 cu. ft. 117.5 in. wheelbase Stepside: 78.5 in. x 50 in. x 17.5 in. 131.5 in. wheelbase Stepside: 96.25 in. x 50 in. x 17.5 in. Front headroom: 38.5 in. (seat to top of cab). Front hip room: 67.25 in. Pedal to seat back (max.): 43.5 in. Steering wheel to seat back (max.): 17.3 in. Seat to ground: 35.0 in. Floor to ground: 23.0 in.

CAPACITIES: Fuel Tank: 117.5 in. wheelbase: 16.0 gal. 131.5 in. wheelbase, 135.5 in. wheelbase and 164.5 in. wheelbase: 20 gal. Optional: 16 gal. auxiliary tank. for 117.5 in.; 20 gal. auxiliary for 131.5 in., 135.5 in. and 164.5 in. wheelbase. Engine Coolant System: 250 6-cyl.: 14.8 qt. 305 V-8: 17.6 qt. 350 V-8: 17.6 qt. 400 V-8: 19.6 qt. (20 qt. on K20 and K30).

ACCOMMODATIONS: Seating Capacity: Pickup and chassis cab models: 3 passenger. Optional: None. Crew cab: 6 passenger. Suburban: 3 passenger. Optional: 6 or 9 passenger.

INSTRUMENTATION: Speedometer, odometer, fuel level gauge. Warning lights for battery, oil pressure, generator, brake system warning, directional/hazard lights, high beam, and engine coolant temperature.

OPTIONS AND PRICES: 292 6-cyl. (RPO L25), 305 V-8 (RPO LE9). 305 V-8 (RPO LF3). 350 V-8 (RPO LS9). 350 V-8 (RPO LT9). 454 V-8 (RPO LE8). 379 Diesel V-8 (RPO LH6). 379 Diesel V-8 (RPO LL4). Air conditioning (RPO C60). Automatic transmission. Chromed front bumper guards. Chromed rear bumper. Chromed rear step bumper (Fleetside only). Painted rear step bumper. Cargo area lamp. Cigarette lighter. Color-keyed floor mats. ComforTilt steering wheel. Deluxe Front End Appearance Package. Dome light. Quartz electric clock. Gauge Package. Includes voltmeter, engine coolant temperature and oil pressure gauges. Halogen headlights. Painted below eye-level mirrors. Stainless steel below eye-level mirrors. Stainless steel camper mirrors. Black body moldings (Fleetside only). Bright body moldings (Fleetside only). Custom Molding Package-Black (Fleetside only). Door edge guards. Conventional two-tone paint. Deluxe two-tone paint (Fleetside only). Exterior Decor Package (Fleetside only). Special two-tone paint (Fleetside only). AM radio. AM/FM radio. AM stereo radio. AM/FM stereo radio. AM/FM stereo radio with cassette tape. AM/FM stereo radio with 8-track tape. AM/FM stereo radio with CB. Note: Stereo radios not available for K30 bonus/crew cab models. Operating Convenience Package. Pickup box side rails. Power door locks. Power windows. Painted West Coast mirrors. Roof marker lights. Frame-mounted spare tire carrier. Aluminum wheels (for K10 only). Rallye wheels (for K10 only). Styled wheels (for K10 only). Bright metal wheelcovers (not available for K30 bonus/crew cab). Bright metal wheel trim rings. (available for K30 pickup only). Windshield antenna. Sliding rear window. Glide-out spare tire carrier. Side-mounted spare tire carrier (Fleetside only). Tinted glass. Pre-cleaner air cleaner (for diesels only). Auxiliary fuel tank. Rear locking differential. Cold Climate Package (not available for diesels). Cruise control. Engine oil cooler (not available for diesels). Fuel tank shield. 63 amp generator (standard on (K30). Heavy-duty automatic transmission cooler (not available for diesels). Heavy-duty battery (not available for diesels). Front and rear heavy-duty shock absorbers (standard on K20 with HP6 and all K30 models). Heavy-duty radiator (not available for diesels). Auxiliary battery (not available for diesels). Camper wiring harness. Dual rear wheels (available for K30 only). Front tow hooks. Front quad shocks (K10 and K20 models only). Heavy-duty front springs (available for K10 and K20 only). Main and auxiliary rear springs (available for K30 only). Special camper chassis equipment-Basic (available for K20 and K30 only). Special camper chassis equipment-Deluxe (available for K20 and K30 only). Heavy-duty trailering special.

HISTORICAL FOOTNOTES: Chevrolet received an order for nearly 30,000 diesel-powered four-wheel drive pickups and chassis cabs from the U.S. Government for use by the military. Except for several specialized military adaptations like a special electrical system, these were regular production models.

1984 PICKUP

Refinement of the basic format of the K series trucks was Chevrolet's theme for 1984. New for 1984 were two-sided galvanized steel interior door panels for improved corrosion protection. Also introduced for 1984 were semi-metallic front brake linings on K10 and K20 models. Most K10 and K20 trucks also had new non-asbestos rear brake linings. All K series pickups and chassis-cabs had new plastic fuel tank stone shields.

The standard Custom interior had a full-foam front seat with a new dual-tone leather-grain vinyl trim. New dual-tone woven Deluxe cloth or Custom vinyl were available at extra cost. The seat, as in 1983, folded forward to provide access to the cab storage area. The base interior also included color-keyed door trim panels with padded armrests and a foam-padded instrument panel.

Based on the standard trim, the Scottsdale trim offered the customer a choice of either new dual-tone woven Deluxe cloth seats or a new leather-grain vinyl. Scottsdale items carried over from 1983 included a pewter-toned brushed aluminum instrument panel, a door-operated dome light, cab back insulation, dual horns, color-keyed vinyl coated floor mats, a cigarette lighter, instrument panel nameplate, plastic door trim panels and fiber optic ashtray illumination. Exterior items consisted of bright rear window and windshield moldings, bright side marker lamp bezels and nameplates on front fenders. Fleetside models also had bright taillight trim.

The Silverado trim option included a choice of Custom cloth or Custom vinyl seats, full cowl side trim panels, a custom steering wheel, door-closing assist straps, color-keyed carpeting for front seat area, plastic door trim panels with storage pockets and bright brushed-finish accents, carpet trim on lower portion of the door panels and needle-type, full-gauge (voltmeter, engine coolant temperature and oil pressure gauges) instrumentation, nameplate on deluxe instrument panel, visor vanity mirror, headliner. Exterior Silverado features consisted of bright side marker lamp bezels, front fender nameplates and Deluxe Front End Appearance Package. Fleetside models also had bright taillight trim and cab back panel applique molding, Deluxe Molding Package and tailgate applique.

1984 Chevrolet K20 Fleetside diesel pickup

Power door locks and power windows were now available for bonus and crew cab models. The electronic speed control now had a feature allowing for the set speed to be increased in one-mph increments.

Three exterior paint options for the Fleetside pickups with single rear wheels were offered for 1984. The Special two-tone version included body side/wheel opening moldings and bright trim for the standard marker and taillights. The secondary body color was installed below the side and rear moldings. The Exterior Decor Package included dual-tone body side/rear tape striping keyed to the body colors and a hood ornament. The secondary color was positioned between the decal stripes and body side moldings. The Deluxe two-tone option included a special two-tone paint option with the secondary color on the roof and cab back panel down to the bright beltline moldings.

Ten exterior colors were offered for 1984: Doeskin tan, desert sand metallic, apple red, frost white, silver metallic, midnight black, light blue metallic, midnight blue and Colonial yellow.

I.D. DATA: Unchanged from 1983 except the letter E designated the 1984 model year.

Series K10-1/2 ton 250 6-cyl. 117.5 in. 131.5 in. wheelbase (Suburban: 129.5 in. wheelbase and standard 350 V-8)

Model Number	Body Type & Seating	Factory Price	GVW	Shipping Weight	Prod. Total
CK10703	6.5 ft. Stepside Pickup	$9197	6100	4453	—
CK10703	6.5 ft. Fleetside Pickup	$9063	6100	4500	—
CK10903	8 ft. Fleetside Pickup	$9321	6100	4686	—
CK10906	Suburban Endgate	$11,356	6100	5195	—
CK10906	Suburban Panl. Drs.	$11,116	6100[1]	5161	—

NOTE 1: Suburban available with optional 6600 GVW package.

Series K20-3/4 ton 292 V-8. 131.5 in. wheelbase. (Suburban-129.5 in. wheelbase). Crew and bonus cab: 164.5 in. wheelbase, Suburban weight with standard 350 V-8. K20 Pickup prices include C6P heavy-duty chassis

Model Number	Body Type & Seating	Factory Price	GVW	Shipping Weight	Prod. Total
CK20903	8 ft. Stepside Pickup	$11,817	6600*	4883	—
CK20903	8 ft. Fleetside Pickup	$11,770	6600	4945	—
CK20906	Suburban Endgate	$12,824	6600	5579	—
CK20906	Suburban Panl. Drs.	$12,831	6600	5545	—

* 8600 lb. GVW optional.

Series K30-1 ton 350 V-8. 131.5 in. wheelbase. Crew and bonus cab: 164.5 in. wheelbase

Model Number	Body Type & Seating	Factory Price	GVW	Shipping Weight	Prod. Total
CK 30903	Chassis & Cab[1]	$11,814	9200*	4992	—
CK31003	Chassis & Cab[2]	$11,826	9200	5002	—
CK31403	Chassis & Cab[3]	$12,549	9200	5275	—
CK30903	8 ft. Fleetside Pickup	$12,009	9200	5414	—
CK30943	Chassis & Bonus Cab	$12,524	9200	5393	—
CK30943	Fleetside Bonus Cab	$12,888	9200	5816	—
CK30943	Chassis & Crew Cab	$12,861	9200	5905	—
CK30943	Fleetside Crew Cab	$13,226	9200	5816	—

NOTE 1: 131.5 in. wheelbase.
NOTE 2: 135.5 in. wheelbase.
NOTE 3: 159.5 in. wheelbase.
* 10,000 lb. GVW optional.

Diesel engine adds 454 lb. to weights of gasoline-engined models in all series.

STANDARD ENGINE: All K-10 6-cyl. models: 250 Six (LE3 ordering code). Engine Type: OHV, In-line 6-cylinder. Cast iron block and cylinder head. Bore x Stroke: 3.875 in. x 3.53 in. Lifters: Hydraulic. Number of main bearings-7. Fuel Induction: Single Rochester 2-bbl. carburetor. Compression Ratio: 8.3:1. Displacement: 250 cu. in. (4.1 liters). Horsepower: Net: 115 @ 3600 rpm. (California Rating: 110 @ 3600 rpm). Torque: Net: 200 lb.-ft. @ 2000 rpm. (California Rating: 200 lb.-ft. @ 1600 rpm). Oil refill capacity: 5 qt. with filter change. Fuel Requirements: Regular unleaded.

STANDARD ENGINE: K20 with RPO CH6 and K30 models: 292 Six. Ordering Code: L25. This engine was produced by GM de Mexico. Not available in California with under 8500 lb. GVW rating. Engine Type: OHV, 6-cyl. Cast iron block and cylinder head. Key features include cast iron intake manifold, aluminized-face intake valves, stellite-faced exhaust valves with hardened faces. Bore x Stroke: 3.875 in. x 4.125 in. Lifters: Hydraulic. Number of main bearings-7. Fuel Induction: Single Rochester 1-bbl. carburetor. Compression Ratio: 7.8:1. Displacement: 292 cu. in. (4.8 liters). Horsepower: Net: 115 @ 3400 rpm. Torque: Net: 215 lb.-ft. @ 1600 rpm. Oil refill capacity: 6 qt. Fuel Requirements: Regular unleaded.

STANDARD ENGINE: K20: Optional for K10 (California only), K20 with HP6 and all K30 models. Ordering Code: LS9: 350 V-8 Engine Type: OHV, V-8. Cast iron block and alloy iron cylinder head. Key features include chain drive camshaft and forged steel connecting rods. This engine was produced by GM-Chevrolet Motor Division. Bore x Stroke: 4.0 in. x 3.50 in. Lifters: Hydraulic. Number of main bearings-5. Fuel Induction: Single Rochester 4-bbl. carburetor. Compression Ratio: 8.2:1. Displacement: 350 cu. in. (5.7 liters). Horsepower: Net: 165 @ 3800 rpm. Torque: Net: 275 lb.-ft. @ 1600 rpm. Oil refill capacity: 5 qt. with filter change. Fuel Requirements: Regular unleaded.

OPTIONAL ENGINE: K20 with HP6 and all K30 models: Ordering Code: LT9: 350 V-8 Engine Type: OHV, V-8. Cast iron block and alloy iron cylinder head. Key features include chain drive camshaft and forged steel connecting rods. This engine was produced by GM-Chevrolet Motor Division. Bore x Stroke: 4.0 in. x 3.50 in. Lifters: Hydraulic. Number of main bearings-5. Fuel Induction: Single Rochester 4-bbl. carburetor. Compression Ratio: 8.3:1. Displacement: 350 cu. in. (5.7 liters). Horsepower: Net: 160 @ 3800 rpm. (California rating: 155 @ 3600 rpm). Torque: Net: 260 lb.-ft. @ 2800 rpm. (California rating: 240 lb.-ft. @ 2800 rpm). Oil refill capacity: 5 qt. with filter change. Fuel Requirements: Regular unleaded.

OPTIONAL ENGINE: K10 models: Ordering Code: LE9: 305 V-8. Key features include Electronic Spark Control, new staged 4-barrel carburetor, camshaft and free-flow exhaust system. Not available for California. This engine was produced by GM-Chevrolet Motor Division and GM of Canada. Engine Type: OHV, V-8. Cast iron block and alloy iron cylinder head. Bore x Stroke: 3.74 in. x 3.48 in. Lifters: Hydraulic. Number of main bearings-5. Fuel Induction: Single Rochester 4-bbl. staged carburetor. Compression Ratio: 9.2:1. Displacement: 305 cu. in. (5.0 liters). Horsepower: 160 @ 4400 rpm. Torque: 235 lb.-ft. @ 2000 rpm. Oil refill capacity: 5 qt. with filter change. Fuel Requirements: Regular unleaded.

OPTIONAL ENGINE: K10 models for California: Ordering Code: LF3: 305 V-8. Key features include 4-barrel carburetor, camshaft and free-flow exhaust system. This engine was produced by GM-Chevrolet Motor Division and GM of Canada. Engine Type: OHV, V-8. Cast iron block and alloy iron cylinder head. Bore x Stroke: 3.74 in. x 3.48 in. Lifters: Hydraulic. Number of main bearings-5. Fuel Induction: Single Rochester 4-bbl. carburetor. Compression Ratio: 8.6:1. Displacement: 305 cu. in. (5.0 liters). Horsepower: 155 @ 4200 rpm. Torque: 240 lb.-ft. @ 1600 rpm. Oil refill capacity: 5 qt. with filter change. Fuel Requirements: Regular unleaded.

OPTIONAL ENGINE: K30 models: Ordering Code: LE8: 454 V-8. This engine was produced by GM-Chevrolet Motor Division. a. Engine Type: OHV, V-8. Cast iron block and alloy iron cylinder head. Bore x Stroke: 4.3 in. x 4.0 in. Lifters: Hydraulic. Number of main bearings-5. Fuel Induction: Single Rochester 4-bbl. carburetor. Compression Ratio: 7.9:1. Displacement: 454 cu. in. (7.4 liters). Horsepower: 230 @ 3800 rpm. Torque: 360 lb.-ft. @ 2800 rpm. Oil refill capacity: 5 qt. with filter change. Fuel Requirements: Regular unleaded.

OPTIONAL ENGINE: All models: Ordering Code: LH6: 6.2 liter V-8. This engine was produced by GM-Detroit Diesel Allison Division. Engine Type: OHV, diesel V-8. Bore x Stroke: 3.98 in. x 3.80 in. Lifters: Hydraulic. Number of main bearings-5. Fuel Induction: Fuel injection. Compression Ratio: 21.3:1. Displacement: 379.4 cu. in. (6.2 liters). Horsepower: 135 @ 3600 rpm. Torque: 240 lb.-ft. @ 2000 rpm. Oil refill capacity: 7 qt. with filter change. Fuel Requirements: Diesel. An LL4 version of this engine for models with GVW of 8500 lb. and above was also available. its power ratings were 135 hp. @ 3600 rpm and 240 lb.-ft. of torque @ 2000 rpm.

CHASSIS FEATURES: Separate body and frame with channel side rails. Carbon-Steel, 39,000 psi. 117.5 in. wheelbase: 2.30 In. x 5.92 In. x 0.156 in. Section modules: 3.06 in. 129.5 in.: 2.30 in. x 5.92 in. x 0.194. Section modules: 117.5 in. wheelbase: 3.14 in. 131.5 in. wheelbase: 3.88 in. K20 with CP6: 4.53 in. Optional: None.

SUSPENSION AND RUNNING GEAR: Front Suspension: K10: Tapered 2-leaf springs. Capacity: 1650 lb.-1850 lb. K20: Tapered 2-leaf springs. Capacity: 1850-lb. K30: Tapered 3-leaf springs. Capacity: 2250 lb. Rear Suspension: K10 and K20: 52 in. x 2.25 in. Two-stage, 5-leaf. K30: 56 in. x 2.50 in. Rating: K10: 2075 lb. K20: 2800 lb. K30: 3500 lb. K10: 22mm. dia. shock absorbers. K30: 32mm shock absorbers. Capacity: K10: 3750 lb. K20: 5700 lb. K30: 7000 lb. (7500 lb. for 159.9 in. wheelbase chassis and cab). Optional Rating: K20: 3000 lb. rating at ground. Capacity: 6000 lb. with RPO CP6 K30: RPO RO5 (Dual rear wheels): 3750 lb. rating at ground. Capacity: 7500 lb. Front Axle Type and Capacity: K10: Semi-floating. 3700 lb. capacity. Optional: None. K20: Full-floating, 3800 lb. capacity. K30: Full-floating, 4500 lb. Optional: None. Rear Axle Type and Capacity: K10: Chevrolet, Semi-floating, 3750 lb. capacity. K20: Semi-floating, 5700 lb. capacity. K30: Full-floating, 7500 lb. Optional Rating: K20: 3000 lb. rating at ground. Capacity: 6000 lb. with RPO CP6 K30: RPO RO5 (dual rear wheels): 3750 lb. rating at ground. Capacity: 7500 lb. Final Drive Ratio: The following transmission designations were used by Chevrolet: MM3: 3-spd. manual; MM4: 4-spd. manual; MM7: 4-spd. manual with overdrive; MXO: 4-spd. auto. with Overdrive; MX1: 3-spd. automatic. All ratios are with standard emission equipment. Standard: K10: LB1 engine/MM4, MXO: 3.42:1; LB1/MM7: 3.73:1 (requires engine oil cooler); LS9/MM7: 3.42:1, LS9/M4: 2.73:1, LS9/MXO: 3.08:1, LH6/MM4, MXO: 3.08:1; LH6/MM7: 3.42:1. Optional: LB1/MM4, MXO: 3.73:1 (requires RPO KC4, engine oil cooler), LE9/MM7: 3.73:1, LE9/MM4: 3.08:1, LH6/MM4, MXO: 3.42:1. Standard: K20: L25/MM4: 4.10:1, LS9/MM4MXO: 3.23:1, LT9/MM4: 3.42:1, LT9/MX1: 4.10:1; LH6/MM4: 3.73:1, LH6/MXO: 3.42:1, LL4/M4: 3.73:1, LL4/MX1: 4.10:1. Optional: LS9/MM4: 3.42:1, LS9/MXO: 3.42:1, 3.73:1; LT9/MM4: 3.73:1, 4.10:1; LH6/MM4: 4.10:1, LH6/MXO: 3.73:1; LL4/MM4: 4.10:1. Standard K30: K25/MM4, MX1: 4.56:1; LT9/MM4: 3.73:1; LT9/MX1: 4.10:1; LE8/MM4, MX1: 3.73:1, LL4/MM4, MX1: 4.10:1. Optional: LT9/MM4: 4.10:1, 4.56:1; LT9/MX1: 4.56:1; LE8/MM4, MX1: 4.10:1, 4.56:1; LL4/MM4, MX1: 4.56:1. Transfer Case: K10 and K20: New Process 208. Single lever, 2.61, 1.00:1. K30: New Process 205, two-speed: 1.96, 1.00:1. Brakes: Type: Hydraulic, power assisted. Dimensions: K10: Front: Disc: 11.86 in. x 1.28 in. Rear: Drums: 11.15 x 2.75 in. K20: Front: Disc: 12.5 in. x 1.28 in. Rear: Drums: 11.15 in. x 2.75 in. K20 and K30: Front: Disc: 12.50 in. x 1.53 in. Rear: Drum: 13.00 in. x 3.50 in. Wheels: K10: 15 x 6.0JJ 6-stud disc. Optional: 15 x 8JJ. K20: 16.5 x 6.00 in. 8-stud disc. Optional: 16.5 x 6.75. K30: 16.5 x 6.75. Tires: K10: P235/75R15 steel belted radial. K20: LT215/85R16C. K20 with RPO CP6: Front: LT235/85R16D, 8-ply rating; rear: LT235/85R16E, 10-ply rating. K30: Front: LT235/85R16D, 8-ply rating; rear: LT235/85R16E, 10-ply rating. Optional: K10: P235/75R15 white sidewall; P235/75R15R white letters; 31 x 10.50R/15B black wall or white letters (both require RPO N67, N90 or PA6 wheels). Optional K20: Tubeless steel belted radials 7.50R/16D, LT215/85R16C, LT215/85R16D, LT235/85R16D, LT235/85R16E. Optional: K30: Tube-type, nylon: 7.50-16D. Tubeless steel belted radial: LT215/85R16D, LT235/85R16E. Steering: Recirculating ball gear. Ratio: 20:1. Turning Circle: 47 ft. Steering wheel diameter: 17.5 in. Optional: Power-assisted. Ratio: 16.4:1. Transmission: K10, K20, K30: 4-speed, synchromesh manual. Transmission Ratios: 6.55, 3.58, 1.70, 1.00:1. Optional: K10: 4-spd. manual overdrive, 4-spd. automatic overdrive; K20: 4-spd. automatic overdrive; K30: 3-spd. automatic. Diesel models: K10: 4-spd. manual overdrive, 4-spd. automatic overdrive; K20: 4-spd. automatic overdrive; K20 HD (with RPO C6P) and K30: 3-spd. automatic. Clutch: Diaphragm, spring. Clutch diameter: 6-cyl.: 11 in. dia. Total lining area: 123.5 sq. in. Total plate pressure: 2075 lb. V-8: 12 in. dia. Total lining area: 149.2 sq. in. Total plate pressure: 2060 lb. Optional: K20 6-cyl.: 11 in. dia. Total lining area: 124.0 sq. in. 307 V-8: 12 in. dia. Total lining area: 150 sq. in.

VEHICLE DIMENSIONS: Wheelbase: K10: 117.5 in. 131.5 in. K20: 131.5 in. All Suburbans and Panels: 129.5 in. K30: 131.5 in. 135.5 in. 164.5 in. Overall Length: 117.5 in. Fleetside pickups: 192.60 in. 131.5 in. Fleetside pickups: 212.50. 117.5 in. Stepside pickups: 191.1 in. 131.5 in. Stepside pickups: 211.00 in. K30: 131.5 in. Chassis cab: 206.20 in.; 135.5 in. wheelbase: 215.6 in.; 159.5 in. wheelbase: 239.7 in.; 164.5 in. wheelbase (bonus/crew cab): 239.3 in. Approach/Departure Degrees: K10 117.5 in. Fleetside and Stepside: 33/19. K10 131.5 in. Fleetside: 33/15. K10 131.5 in. wheelbase Stepside: 33/16. K20 131.5 in. wheelbase Fleetside: 35/20. K20 131.5 in. wheelbase Stepside: 35/21. K30 Fleetside pickup: 41/19. K30 crew cab Pickup: 38/18. Ground Clearance: Fleetside models: K10 pickups: Front: 74 in.; rear: 7.1 in. K20 pickups: Front: 8.8 in.; rear: 7.2 in. K30 pickups: Front: 8.3 in.; rear: 7.8 in. Stepside models: K10 pickups: Front: 7.2 in.; rear: 7.1 in. K20 pickups: Front: 8.8 in.; rear: 7.2 in. K30 pickups: K30 chassis cab (131.5 in. 135.5 in. and 159.5 in. wheelbase): Front: 8.3 in.; rear: 7.7 in. K30 bonus/crew cab: Front: 8.3 in.; rear: 7.7 in. Load space: Pickup box dimensions: 117.5 in. wheelbase Fleetside: 78.25 in. x 50 in. x 19.25 in. 131.5 in. wheelbase Fleetside: 98 in. x 50 in. x 19.25 in. Capacity: 117.5 wheelbase: 58.4 cu. ft. 131.5 in. wheelbase: 74.3 cu. ft. 117.5 in. wheelbase Stepside: 78.5 in. x 50 in. x 17.5 in. 131.5 in. wheelbase Stepside: 96.25 in. x 50 in. x 17.5 in. Front headroom: 38.5 in. (seat to top of cab). Front hip room: 67.25 in. Pedal to seat back (max.): 43.5 in. Steering wheel to seat back (max.): 17.3 in. Seat to ground: 35.0 in. Floor to ground: 23.0 in.

CAPACITIES: Fuel Tank: 117.5 in. wheelbase: 16.0 gal. 131.5 in. wheelbase, 135.5 in. wheelbase and 164.5 in. wheelbase: 20 gal. Optional: 16 gal. auxiliary tank. for 117.5 in.; 20 gal. auxiliary for 131.5 in., 135.5 in. and 164.5 in. wheelbase. Engine Coolant System: 250 6-cyl.: 14.8 qt. 305 V-8: 17.6 qt. 350 V-8: 17.6 qt. 400 V-8: 19.6 qt. (20 qt. on K20 and K30).

ACCOMMODATIONS: Seating Capacity: Pickup and chassis cab models: 3 passenger. Optional: None. Crew cab: 6 passenger. Suburban: 3 passenger. Optional: 6 or 9 passenger.

INSTRUMENTATION: Speedometer, odometer, fuel level gauge. Warning lights for battery, oil pressure, generator, brake system warning, directional/hazard lights, high beam, and engine coolant temperature.

OPTIONS AND PRICES: 292 6-cyl. 305 V-8. 350 V-8. 454 V-8. 379 diesel V-8. Air conditioning. Automatic transmission. Chromed front bumper guards. Chromed rear bumper. Chromed rear step bumper (Fleetside only). Painted rear step bumper. Cargo area lamp. Cigarette lighter. Color-keyed floor mats. ComforTilt steering wheel. Deluxe Front End Appearance Package. Dome light. Quartz electric clock. Gauge Package. Includes voltmeter, engine coolant temperature and oil pressure gauges. Halogen headlights. Painted below eye-level mirrors. Stainless steel below eye-level mirrors. Stainless steel camper mirrors. Black body moldings (Fleetside only). Bright body moldings (Fleetside only). Custom Molding Package-Black (Fleetside only). Door edge guards. Conventional two-tone paint. Deluxe two-tone paint (Fleetside only). Exterior Decor Package (Fleetside only). Special two-tone paint (Fleetside only). AM radio. AM/FM radio. AM stereo radio. AM/FM stereo radio. AM/FM stereo radio with cassette tape. AM/FM stereo radio with 8-track tape. AM/FM stereo radio with CB. Note: Stereo radios not available for K30 bonus/Crew cab models. Operating Convenience Package. Pickup box side rails. Power door locks. Power windows. Painted West Coast mirrors. Roof marker lights. Frame-mounted spare tire carrier. Aluminum wheels (for K10 only). Rallye wheels (for K10 only). Styled wheels (for K10 only). Bright metal wheelcovers (not available for K30 bonus/crew cab). Bright metal wheel trim rings. (available for K30 pickup only). Windshield antenna. Sliding rear window. Glide-out spare tire carrier. Side-mounted spare tire carrier (Fleetside only). Tinted glass. Pre-cleaner air cleaner (for diesels only). Auxiliary fuel tank. Rear locking differential. Cold Climate Package (not available for diesels). Cruise control. Engine oil cooler (not available for diesels). Fuel tank shield. 63 amp generator (standard on K30). Heavy-duty automatic transmission cooler (not available for diesels). Heavy-duty battery (not available for diesels). Front and rear heavy-duty shock absorbers (standard on K20 with HP6 and all K30 models). Heavy-duty radiator (not available for diesels). Auxiliary battery (not available for diesels). Camper wiring harness. Dual rear wheels (available for K30 only). Front tow hooks. Front quad shocks (K10 and K20 models only). Heavy-duty front springs (available for K10 and K20 only). Main and auxiliary rear springs (available for K30 only). Special camper chassis equipment-Basic (available for K20 and K30 only). Special camper chassis equipment-Deluxe (available for K20 and K30 only). Heavy-duty trailering special.

HISTORICAL FOOTNOTES: Calendar year sales of all Chevrolet truck models was 1,111,839. Calendar year full-size pickup production (all types) was 332,404. Suburban production totaled 57,286.

1985 PICKUP

The latest full-size four-wheel drive trucks from Chevrolet had a new front grille with a wider grid network and a thicker center divider. Of greater significance was the new 4.3 liter Vortex V-6 engine that was standard for the K10 models. This engine, which was the most powerful 6-cylinder ever offered in a Chevrolet pickup, featured a cast iron cylinder block, 4-barrel carburetion, centralized spark plugs and swirl-port cylinder heads. It was linked to a standard 4-speed manual transmission (except for California) and was available with a 4-speed overdrive automatic transmission. Also new for the K10 were All-Season steel-belted radial tires designed for year-round use. all models were equipped with a new wet-arm windshield system in which the washer fluid was piped up the wiper arms and squirted along the path of the wiper blades. This system reduced waste and improved driver vision under adverse conditions. Models with manual transmission now had a hydraulic clutch which provided a smoother operation and improved driveability. The K10 was offered with optional automatic hubs and a synchronized transfer case which allowed for nonstop shifting from two-wheel drive into four-wheel drive high at speeds up to 25 mph.

The content of three trim levels-Custom Deluxe, Scottsdale and Silverado were carried over unchanged into 1985. The exterior colors available for 1985 were as follows: Frost white, silver metallic, midnight black, light blue metallic, Colonial yellow, doeskin tan, desert sand metallic, Indian bronze metallic and apple red.

1985 Chevrolet K20 Fleetside Custom Deluxe pickup

I.D. DATA: Unchanged from 1984 except the letter F designated the 1985 model year.

Model Number	Body Type & Seating	Factory Price	GVW	Shipping Weight	Prod. Total
Series K10-1/2 ton 250 6-cyl. 117.5 in. 131.5 in. wheelbase (Suburban: 129.5 in. wheelbase and standard 350 V-8)					
CK10703	6.5 ft. Stepside Pickup	$9854	6100	4453	—
CK10703	6.5 ft. Fleetside Pickup	$9719	6100	4500	—
CK10903	8 ft. Fleetside Pickup	$9888	6100	4686	—
CK10906	Suburban Endgate	$11,813	6100	5195	—
CK10906	Suburban Panl. Drs.	$11,776	6100[1]	5161	—

NOTE 1: Suburban available with optional 6600 GVW package.

Series K20-3/4 ton 292 V-8. 131.5 in. wheelbase. (Suburban-129.5 in. wheelbase). Crew and bonus cab: 164.5 in. wheelbase, Suburban weight with standard 350 V-8.K20 Pickup prices include C6P heavy-duty chassis

CK20903	8 ft. Stepside Pickup	$11,277	6600*	4883	—
CK20903	8 ft. Fleetside Pickup	$11,143	6600	4945	—
CK20906	Suburban Endgate	$13,298	6600	5579	—
CK20906	Suburban Panl. Drs.	$13,335	6600	5545	—

* 8600 lb. GVW optional.

Series K30-1 ton 350 V-8. 131.5 in. wheelbase. Crew and bonus cab: 164.5 in. wheelbase

CK 30903	Chassis & Cab[1]	$11,900	9200*	4992	—
CK31003	Chassis & Cab[2]	$12,112	9200	5002	—
CK31403	Chassis & Cab[3]	$12,635	9200	5275	—
CK30903	8 ft. Fleetside Pickup	$12,283	9200	5414	—
CK30943	Chassis & Bonus Cab	$12,796	9200	5393	—
CK 30943	Fleetside Bonus Cab	$13,162	9200	5816	—
CK 30943	Chassis & Crew Cab	$13,135	9200	5905	—
CK30943	Fleetside Crew Cab	$13,500	9200	5816	—

NOTE 1: 131.5 in. wheelbase.
NOTE 2: 135.5 in. wheelbase.
NOTE 3: 159.5 in. wheelbase.
* 10,000 lb. GVW optional.

Diesel engine adds 454 lb. to weights of gasoline-engined models in all series.

STANDARD ENGINE: All K-10 6-cyl. models: 262 V-6 (LB1 ordering code). Engine Type: Vortex OHV, V-6-cylinder. Cast iron block. Key features include a 4-bbl. carburetor. Bore x Stroke: 4.0 in. x 3.48 in. Lifters: Hydraulic. Fuel Induction: Single Rochester 4-bbl. carburetor. Compression Ratio: 9.3:1. Displacement: 262 cu. in. (4.3 liters). Horsepower: Net: 155 @ 4000 rpm. Torque: Net: 230 lb.-ft. @ 2400 rpm. Oil refill capacity: 5 qt. with filter change. Fuel Requirements: Regular unleaded.

STANDARD ENGINE: K20 with RPO CH6 and K30 models: 292 Six. Ordering Code: L25. This engine was produced by GM de Mexico. Not available in California with under 8500 lb. GVW rating. Engine Type: OHV, 6-cyl. Cast iron block and cylinder head. Key features include cast iron intake manifold, aluminized-face intake valves, stellite-faced exhaust valves with hardened faces. Bore x Stroke: 3.875 in. x 4.125 in. Lifters: Hydraulic. Number of main bearings-7. Fuel Induction: Single Rochester 1-bbl. carburetor. Compression Ratio: 7.8:1. Displacement: 292 cu. in. (4.8 liters). Horsepower: Net: 115 @ 3400 rpm. Torque: Net: 215 lb.-ft. @ 1600 rpm. Oil refill capacity: 6 qt. Fuel Requirements: Regular unleaded.

STANDARD ENGINE: K20: Optional for K10 (California only), K20 with HP6 and all K30 models. Ordering Code: LS9: 350 V-8 Engine Type: OHV, V-8. Cast iron block and alloy iron cylinder head. Key features include chain drive camshaft and forged steel connecting rods. This engine was produced by GM-Chevrolet Motor Division. Bore x Stroke: 4.0 in. x 3.50 in. Lifters: Hydraulic. Number of main bearings-5. Fuel Induction: Single Rochester 4-bbl. carburetor. Compression Ratio: 8.2:1. Displacement: 350 cu. in. (5.7 liters). Horsepower: Net: 165 @ 3800 rpm. Torque: Net: 275 lb.-ft. @ 1600 rpm. Oil refill capacity: 5 qt. with filter change. Fuel Requirements: Regular unleaded.

OPTIONAL ENGINE: K20 with HP6 and all K30 models: Ordering Code: LT9: 350 V-8 Engine Type: OHV, V-8. Cast iron block and alloy iron cylinder head. Key features include chain drive camshaft and forged steel connecting rods. This engine was produced by GM-Chevrolet Motor Division. Bore x Stroke: 4.0 in. x 3.50 in. Lifters: Hydraulic. Number of main bearings-5. Fuel Induction: Single Rochester 4-bbl. carburetor. Compression Ratio: 8.3:1. Displacement: 350 cu. in. (5.7 liters). Horsepower: Net: 160 @ 3800 rpm. (California rating: 155 @ 3600 rpm). Torque: Net: 260 lb.-ft. @ 2800 rpm. (California rating: 240 lb.-ft. @ 2800 rpm). Oil refill capacity: 5 qt. with filter change. Fuel Requirements: Regular unleaded.

OPTIONAL ENGINE: K10 models: Ordering Code: LE9: 305 V-8. Key features include Electronic Spark Control, new staged 4-barrel carburetor, camshaft and free-flow exhaust system. Not available for California. This engine was produced by GM-Chevrolet Motor Division and GM of Canada. Engine Type: OHV, V-8. Cast iron block and alloy iron cylinder head. Bore x Stroke: 3.74 in. x 3.48 in. Lifters: Hydraulic. Number of main bearings-5. Fuel Induction: Single Rochester 4-bbl. staged carburetor. Compression Ratio: 9.2:1. Displacement: 305 cu. in. (5.0 liters). Horsepower: 160 @ 4400 rpm. Torque: 235 lb.-ft. @ 2000 rpm. Oil refill capacity: 5 qt. with filter change. Fuel Requirements: Regular unleaded.

OPTIONAL ENGINE: K10 models for California: Ordering Code: LF3: 305 V-8. Key features include 4-barrel carburetor, camshaft and free-flow exhaust system. This engine was produced by GM-Chevrolet Motor Division and GM of Canada. Engine Type: OHV, V-8. Cast iron block and alloy iron cylinder head. Bore x Stroke: 3.74 in. x 3.48 in. Lifters: Hydraulic. Number of main bearings-5. Fuel Induction: Single Rochester 4-bbl. carburetor. Compression Ratio: 8.6:1. Displacement: 305 cu. in. (5.0 liters). Horsepower: 155 @ 4200 rpm. Torque: 240 lb.-ft. @ 1600 rpm. Oil refill capacity: 5 qt. with filter change. Fuel Requirements: Regular unleaded.

OPTIONAL ENGINE: K30 models: Ordering Code: LE8: 454 V-8. This engine was produced by GM-Chevrolet Motor Division. Engine Type: OHV, V-8. Cast iron block and alloy iron cylinder head. Bore x Stroke: 4.3 in. x 4.0 in. Lifters: Hydraulic. Number of main bearings-5. Fuel Induction: Single Rochester 4-bbl. carburetor. Compression Ratio: 7.9:1. Displacement: 454 cu. in. (7.4 liters). Horsepower: 230 @ 3800 rpm. Torque: 360 lb.-ft. @ 2800 rpm. Oil refill capacity: 5 qt. with filter change. Fuel Requirements: Regular unleaded.

OPTIONAL ENGINE: All models: Ordering Code: LH6: 6.2 liter V-8. This engine was produced by GM-Detroit Diesel Allison Division. Engine Type: OHV, diesel V-8. Bore x Stroke: 3.98 in. x 3.80 in. Lifters: Hydraulic. Number of main bearings-5. Fuel Induction: Fuel injection. Compression Ratio: 21.3:1. Displacement: 379.4 cu. in. (6.2 liters). Horsepower: 135 @ 3600 rpm. Torque: 240 lb.-ft. @ 2000 rpm. Oil refill capacity: 7 qt. with filter change. Fuel Requirements: Diesel. An LL4 version of this engine for models with GVW of 8500 lb. and above was also available. its power ratings were 135 hp. @ 3600 rpm and 240 lb.-ft. of torque @ 2000 rpm.

CHASSIS FEATURES: Separate body and frame with channel side rails. Carbon-Steel, 39,000 psi. 117.5 in. wheelbase: 2.30 in. x 5.92 in. x 0.156 in. Section modules: 3.06 in. 129.5 in.: 2.30 in. x 5.92 in. x 0.194. Section modules: 117.5 in. wheelbase: 3.14 in. 131.5 in. wheelbase: 3.88 in. K20 with CP6: 4.53 in. Optional: None.

SUSPENSION AND RUNNING GEAR: Front Suspension: K10: Tapered 2-leaf springs. Capacity: 1650 lb-1850 lb. K20: Tapered 2-leaf springs. Capacity: 1850-lb. K30: Tapered 3-leaf springs. Capacity: 2250 lb. Rear Suspension: K10 and K20: 52 in. x 2.25 in. Two-stage, 5-leaf. K30: 56 in. x 2.50 in. Rating: K10: 2075 lb. K20: 2800 lb. K30: 3500 lb. K10: 22mm. dia. shock absorbers. K30: 32mm shock absorbers. Capacity: K10: 3750 lb. K20: 5700 lb. K30: 7000 lb. (7500 lb. for 159.9 in. wheelbase Chassis and Cab). 000. Optional Rating: K20: 3000 lb. rating at ground. Capacity: 6000 lb. with RPO CP6 K30: RPO RO5 (Dual rear wheels): 3750 lb. rating at ground. Capacity: 7500 lb. Front Axle Type and Capacity: K10: Semi-floating. 3700 lb. capacity. Optional: None. K20: Full-floating, 3800 lb. capacity. K30: Full-floating, 4500 lb. Optional: None. Rear Axle Type and Capacity: K10: Chevrolet, Semi-floating, 3750 lb. capacity. K20: Semi-floating, 5700 lb. capacity. K30: Full-floating, 7500 lb. Optional Rating: K20: 3000 lb. rating at ground. Capacity: 6000 lb. with RPO CP6 K30: RPO RO5 (Dual rear wheels): 3750 lb. rating at ground. Capacity: 7500 lb. Final Drive Ratio: The following transmission designations were used by Chevrolet: MM3: 3-spd. manual; MM4: 4-spd. manual; MM7: 4-spd. manual with Overdrive; MXO: 4-spd. auto. with Overdrive; MX1: 3-spd. automatic. All ratios are with standard emission equipment. Standard: K10: LB1 engine/MM4, MXO: 3.42:1; LB1/MM7: 3.73:1 (requires engine oil cooler); LS9/MM7: 3.42:1, LS9/M4: 2.73:1 LS9/MXO: 3.08:1; LH6/MM4, MXO: 3.08:1; LH6/MM7: 3.42:1. Optional: LB1/MM4, MXO: 3.73:1 (requires RPO KC4, engine oil cooler); LE9/MM7: 3.73:1, LE9/M4: 3.08:1; LH6/ MM4, MXO: 3.42:1. Standard: K20: L25/MM4: 4.10:1, LS9/MM4MXO: 3.23:1, LT9/MM4: 3.42:1, LT9/MX1: 4.10:1; LH6/MM4: 3.73:1, LH6/MXO: 3.42:1, LL4/M4: 3.73:1, LL4/MX1: 4.10:1. Optional: K20: L25/MM4: 3.42:1, LS9/MXO: 3.42:1; LT9/MM4: 3.73:1, 4.10:1; LH6/ MM4: 4.10:1, LH6/MXO: 3.73:1; LL4/MM4: 4.10:1. Standard K30: K25/MM4, MX1: 4.56:1; LT9/MM4: 3.73:1; LT9/MX1: 4.10:1; LE8/MM4, MX1: 3.73:1, LL4/MM4, MX1: 4.10:1. Optional: LT9/MM4: 4.10:1, 4.56:1; LT9/MX1: 4.56:1; LE8/MM4, MX1: 4.10:1, 4.56:1; LL4/MM4, MX1: 4.56:1. Transfer Case: K10 and K20: New Process 208. Single lever, 2.61, 1.00:1. K30: New Process 205, two-speed: 1.96, 1.00:1. Brakes: Type: Hydraulic, power assisted. Dimensions: K10: Front: Disc: 11.86 in. x 1.28 in. Rear: Drums: 11.15 x 2.75 in. K20: Front: Disc: 12.5 in. x 1.28 in. Rear: Drums: 11.15 in. x 2.75 in. K20 and K30: Front: Disc: 12.50 in. x 1.53 in. Rear: Drum: 13.00 in. x 3.50 in. Wheels: K10: 15 x 6.0JJ 6-stud disc. Optional: 15 x 8JJ. K20: 16.5 x 6.00 in. 8-stud disc. Optional: 16.5 x 6.75. K30: 16.5 x 6.75. Tires: K10: P235/75R15 steel belted radial. K20: LT215/85R16C. K20 with RPO CP6: Front: LT235/85R16D, 8-ply rating; rear: LT235/85R16E, 10-ply rating.; K30: Front: LT235/85R16D, 8-ply rating; rear: LT235/85R16D, 10-ply rating. Optional: K10: P235/75R15 white sidewall; P235/75R15R White letters; 31 x 10.50R/15B blackwall or white letters (both require RPO N67, N90 or PA6 wheels). K20: Tubeless steel belted radials 7.50R/16D, LT215/85R16D, LT235/85R16E. Optional: K30: Tube-type, nylon: 7.50-16D. Tubeless steel belted radial: LT215/85R16D, LT235/85R16E. Steering: Recirculating ball gear. Ratio: 20:1. Turning Circle: 47 ft. Steering wheel diameter: 17.5 in. Optional: Power-assisted. Ratio: 16.4:1. Transmission: K10, K20, K30: 4-speed, synchromesh manual. Transmission Ratios: 6.55, 3.58, 1.70, 1.00:1. Optional: K10: 4-spd. manual overdrive, 4-spd. automatic overdrive; K20: 4-spd. manual overdrive; K30: 3-spd. automatic. Diesel models: K10: 4-spd. manual overdrive, 4-spd. automatic overdrive; K20: 4-spd. automatic overdrive; K20 HD (with RPO C6P) and K30: 3-spd. automatic. Clutch: Diaphragm, spring. Clutch diameter: 6-cyl.: 11 in. dia. Total lining area: 123.5 sq. in. Total plate pressure: 2075 lb. V-8: 12 in. dia. Total lining area: 149.2 sq. in. Total plate pressure: 2060 lb. Optional: K20 6-cyl.: 11 in. dia. Total lining area: 124.0 sq. in. 307 V-8: 12 in. dia. Total lining area: 150 sq. in.

VEHICLE DIMENSIONS: Wheelbase: K10: 117.5 in. 131.5 in. K20: 131.5 in. All Suburbans and Panels: 129.5 in. K30: 131.5 in. 135.5 in. 164.5 in. Overall Length: 117.5 in. Fleetside pickups: 192.60 in. 131.5 in. Fleetside pickups: 212.50. 117.5 in. Stepside pickups: 191.1 in. 131.5 in. Stepside pickups: 211.00 in. K30: 131.5 in. Chassis cab: 206.20 in.; 135.5 in. wheelbase: 215.6 in.; 159.5 in. wheelbase: 239.7 in.; 164.5 in. wheelbase (bonus/crew cab): 239.3 in. Approach/Departure Degrees: Fleetside pickups: K10 117.5 in. Fleetside and Stepside: K10 131.5 in. Fleetside: 33/15. K10 131.5 in. wheelbase Stepside: 33/16. K20 131.5 in. wheelbase Fleetside: 35/20. K20 131.5 in. wheelbase Stepside: 35/21. K30 Fleetside pickup: 41/19. K30 crew cab pickup: 38/18. Ground Clearance: Fleetside models: K10 pickups: Front: 74 in.; rear: 7.1 in. K20 pickups: Front: 8.8 in.; rear: 7.2 in. K30 pickups: Front: 8.3 in.; rear: 7.8 in. Step side models: K10 pickups: Front: 7.2 in.; rear: 7.1 in. K20 pickups: Front: 8.8 in.; rear: 7.2 in. K30 pickups: K30 chassis cab (131.5 in. 135.5 in. and 159.5 in. wheelbase): Front: 8.3 in.; rear: 7.7 in. K30 bonus/crew cab: Front: 8.3 in.; rear: 7.7 in. Load space: Pickup box dimensions: 117.5 in. wheelbase Fleetside: 78.25 in. x 50 in. x 19.25 in. 131.5 in. wheelbase Fleetside: 98 in. x 50 in. x 19.25 in. Capacity: 117.5 wheelbase: 58.4 cu. ft. 131.5 in. wheelbase: 74.3 cu. ft. 117.5 in. wheelbase Stepside: 78.5 in. x 50 in. x 17.5 in. 131.5 in. wheelbase Stepside: 96.25 in. x 50 in. x 17.5 in. Front headroom: 38.5 in. (seat to top of cab). Front hip room: 67.25 in. Pedal to seat back (max.): 43.5 in. Steering wheel to seat back (max.): 17.3 in. Seat to ground: 35.0 in. Floor to ground: 23.0 in.

CAPACITIES: Fuel Tank: 117.5 in. wheelbase: 16.0 gal. 131.5 in. wheelbase, 135.5 in. wheelbase and 164.5 in. wheelbase: 20 gal. 16 gal. auxiliary tank. for 117.5 in.; 20 gal. auxiliary for 131.5 in., 135.5 in. and 164.5 in. wheelbase. Engine Coolant System: 250 6-cyl.: 14.8 qt. 305 V-8: 17.6 qt. 350 V-8: 17.6 qt. 400 V-8: 19.6 qt. (20 qt. on K20 and K30).

ACCOMMODATIONS: Seating Capacity: Pickup and chassis cab models: 3 passenger. Optional: None. Crew cab: 6 passenger. Suburban: 3 passenger. Optional: 6 or 9 passenger.

INSTRUMENTATION: Speedometer, odometer, fuel level gauge. Warning lights for battery, oil pressure, generator, brake system warning, directional/hazard lights, high beam, and engine coolant temperature.

OPTIONS AND PRICES: Silverado Package (RPO YE9): $671-$1016, depending on body and additional packages installed. Deluxe bench seat: $17 with Scottsdale Package: $62 without Scottsdale Package (RPO Z62). Bonus cab Custom bench seat: $50 with RPO Z62. crew cab bonus seat: $100 with RPO Z62. Regular cab and bonus cab Custom vinyl bench seat: $50 without RPO Z62 or RPO YE9. Crew cab Custom vinyl bench seat: $$100 with RPO YE9. Conventional two-tone paint (RPO ZY2): $43 to $89 depending on body and additional options. Exterior Decor Package (RPO ZY5): $418-$575 depending on body and additional options. Special Big Dooley two-tone paint (RPO ZY9): $444 without RPO Z62; $426 with RPO Z62. California emissions requirement (RPO YF5): $235. 5.0 liter V-8 (RPO LE9 or RPO LF3): $465. 5.7 liter V-8 (RPO LT9): $650. 5.7 liter V-8 (ROP LT9): $620. 7.4 liter V-8 (RPO LE8): $790. 6.2 liter diesel V-8. 3-spd. automatic trans. (RPO MX1): $510. 4-spd. manual overdrive trans.: $80. 4-spd. automatic trans. with overdrive (RPO MXO): $670. Optional axle ratios: $36. Locking rear differential (RPO G80): $238. Heavy-duty power brakes for K10 and K20 (RPO J55): $104. Chrome rear bumper (RPO VF1): $103. Chromed rear step bumper for Fleetside only (RPO V42): $189. Painted rear step bumper (RPO V43): $120. Chromed front bumper guards (RPO V31): $41. Camper Special chassis equipment (RPO Z81): $108 for K20 with required C6H chassis: $49 for K30 with required RPO RO5 dual rear wheels. Glide-Out spare tire carrier (RPO P11): $41. Side-mounted spare tire carrier for Fleetside only (RPO P13): $29. Quartz electric clock (RPO U35). Not available when UM6 radio is specified: $79 without RPO YE9. Includes RPO Z53 voltmeter, temperature and oil pressure gauges; $39 with RPO YE9. Cold Climate Package. Not available when RPO C60 air conditioning or RPO B3J diesel equipment is specified. Includes special insulation, RPO K81 66 amp generator, special heater and defroster, RP0 KO5 engine block heater, anti-freeze protection to -32 degrees and RPO UA1 heavy-duty battery (RPO V10): $126 to $200 depending upon additional options and series applications. Engine oil cooling system (RPO KC4). Not avail. with RPO L25E engine or RPO B3J: $120. Heavy-duty radiator (RPO VO1): $53. Heavy-duty radiator and transmission oil (RPO VO2). Avail. only with RPO MX1 or RPO MXO transmission are specified. Not avail. with RPO L25 engine or RPO VO1 are specified: $59. Decor Value Package. Includes black-painted radiator grille and headlight bezels, and special body stripe located between body feature lines on fenders, pickup box and across the tailgate. Not avail. on bonus cab, crew cab and Stepside models. Not available with the following options: RPO YE9, RO5, V22, pA6, N90, B84 or B85. Requires RPO ZY1 solid paint and blackwall or white lettered tires (RPO YJ6): $256 for K10; $141 for K20 and K30. Power door lock system (RPO AU3): $135 for regular cab; $198 for bonus and crew cab. Color-keyed front floor mats (RPO B32). Requires RPO YE9: $15. Gauge Package. Includes voltmeter, engine coolant temperature and oil pressure (RPO Z53): $40. 66 amp Delcotron generator. Standard on K30 except when RPO LE8 engine is ordered (RPO K81): $62. 94 amp Delcotron generator. Included with LE8 engine on K30 models (RPO K22): $62. Tinted glass-all windows (RPO AO1): $46 for regular cab; $56 for bonus or crew cab. Halogen high-beam headlamps. Avail. only when RPO V22 or RPO YE9 is specified (RPO TT5): $17. 60. 0 watts engine block heater. Not avail. when RPO BK3 or RPO LF3 engine is specified (RPO KO5): $31. Heavy-duty front heater (RPO C42). Avail. only with RPO B3J is specified. Not avail. with RPO C60 air conditioning: $43. Automatic front locking hubs. Avail. only for K10 (RPO X6Z): $40. Cargo lamp (RPO UF2): $60 without RPO Z62 or RPO YE9 (includes RPO C91 dome lamp). Dome lamp (RPO C91): 26. Roof marker lamps. Avail. for K20 only. Standard for K30 (RPO UO1): $50. Cigarette lighter. Included when RPO Z62 or YE9 is specified (RPO U37): $30. Exterior left and right side below eye-level mirrors: Painted (RPO D44): $50.; stainless steel (RPO D45): $83. Camper type stainless steel left and right side exterior mirrors (RPO DF2): $94. Senior West Coast type painted exterior left and right side mirrors (RPO DG5): $65. Black body side molding. Avail. for Fleetside only (RPO B84): $115. Bright body side molding. Avail. for Fleetside only (RPO B85): $144 without RPO Z62; $15 with RPO Z62. Custom Package (RPO YG1). Avail. for Fleetside only. Includes wheel opening moldings, RPO B84, RPO B96 and bright trim for front sidemarker lamps and taillights: $157 without RPO Z62; $29 with RPO Z62. Deluxe Package (RPO YG3). Avail. for Fleetside only. Not avail. with RPO YG1 or RPO RO5. Includes bright trim for front side marker lamps and taillights, RPO B85 and RPO B96: $173 without RPO Z62, RPO ZY3, RPO ZY4 or ZY5; $44 with RPO Z62; $16 with RPO ZY3, RPO ZY4 or RPO ZY5. Wheel opening molding (RPO B96). Avail. only with RPO ZY6: $29. Door edge guards (RPO B93): $17 for regular cab; $22 for bonus or crew cab. Operating Convenience Package (RPO ZQ2). Includes RPO AU3 power door locks and RPO A31 power windows: $325 for regular cab; $488 for bonus and crew cab. AM radio (RPO U63): $112. AM/FM radio (RPO U69): 171. AM/FM stereo radio (RPO U58): $198. AM/FM stereo radio with stereo cassette tape player (RPO UN3): $298. Electronically tuned AM/FM stereo radio with Seek-Scan, stereo cassette player and clock (RPO UM6): $419. Windshield antenna (RPO U76): $32. Pickup box side rails (RPO D73): $94. Transfer case shield (RPO NY7): $41. Front quad shock absorbers (RPO Z75): $128 for K10 and K20 without C6P heavy-duty chassis; $94 for K20 with C6P. Electronic speed control (RPO K34). Not avail. for K10 with MM7 trans. or K20 and K30 with LS9, LT9 and LE8 with MM4 trans.: $195. Heavy-duty front springs (RPO F60). Not avail. for K30. For K10 and K20 series includes heavy-duty front and rear shock absorbers. Recommended for snowplow use for K10: $92 without RPO Z75 front quad shock absorbers; $59 with RPO Z75. Main and auxiliary rear springs (RPO Q46): $97. ComforTilt steering wheel (RPO N33). Not avail. when RPO MM3 was specified: $115. Auxiliary fuel tank (RPO NL2): $260-$270 depending on model. Two front towing hooks (RPO V76): $36. Bright

metal wheelcovers, for K10 only (RPO PO1): $40. Special wheelcovers, for K20 only (RPO PA1): $118. Rallye wheels, K10 only (RPO N67): $115. Styled wheels (RPO PA6): $174. Aluminum cast wheels (RPO N90): $299. Dual rear wheels for K30 only (RPO RO5): $678-740 depending on options and transmission specified. Power windows (RPO A31): $190 for regular cab; $290 for bonus and crew cab. Sliding rear window (RPO A28): $107. Intermittent windshield wiper system (RPO CD4): $55.

HISTORICAL FOOTNOTES: The 1985 Chevrolet trucks were introduced on September 21, 1984. Calendar year production of all Chevrolet truck models was 1,325,491.

1985 Chevrolet K10 Stepside Silverado short box pickup

1986 PICKUP

The 1986 K series were virtually unchanged in both appearance and design from 1985. All gasoline engines now had new generator drive belts that increased friction due to their greater area of contact with pulleys. All V-type engines except for the 7.4 liter V-8 had new crankshaft seals and oil pan gaskets. All three interior trim levels were available in blue, burgundy or tan. The exterior color selection for 1986 consisted of frost white, steel gray metallic, midnight black, light blue metallic, midnight blue, canyon copper metallic, doeskin tan, Nevada gold metallic, Indian bronze metallic and apple red.

1986 Chevrolet K20 Fleetside Custom deluxe pickup

I.D. DATA: Unchanged from 1985 except the letter G designated the 1986 model year.

Model Number	Body Type & Seating	Factory Price	GVW	Shipping Weight	Prod. Total
Series K10-1/2 ton 250 6-cyl. 117.5 in. 131.5 in. wheelbase (Suburban: 129.5 in. wheelbase and standard 350 V-8)					
CK10703	6.5 ft. Stepside Pickup	$10,374	6100	4403	—
CK10703	6.5 ft. Fleetside Pickup	$10,239	6100	4450	—
CK10903	8 ft. Fleetside Pickup	$10,408	6100	4636	—
CK10906	Suburban Endgate	$12,333	6100	5145	—
CK10906	Suburban Panl. Drs.	$12,296	6100	5111	—

NOTE 1: Suburban available with optional 6600 GVW package.

Series K20-3/4 ton 292 V-8. 131.5 in. wheelbase. (Suburban-129.5 in. wheelbase). Crew and bonus cab: 164.5 in. wheelbase, Suburban weight with standard 350 V-8. K20 Pickup prices include C6P heavy-duty chassis

CK20903	8 ft. Stepside Pickup	$11,897	6600*	4863	—
CK20903	8 ft. Fleetside Pickup	$11,763	6600	4985	—
CK20906	Suburban Endgate	$13,918	6600	5519	—
CK20906	Suburban Panl. Drs.	$13,955	6600	5585	—

* 8600 lb. GVW optional.

Series K30-1 ton 350 V-8. 131.5 in. wheelbase. Crew and bonus cab: 164.5 in. wheelbase

CK30903	Chassis & Cab[1]	$13,110	9200*	4512	—
CK31003	Chassis & Cab[2]	$13,322	9200	5022	—
CK31403	Chassis & Cab[3]	$13,845	9200	5295	—
CK30903	8 ft. Fleetside Pickup	$13,493	9200	5434	—
CK30943	Chassis & Bonus Cab	$14,006	9200	5417	—
CK30943	Fleetside Bonus Cab	$14,372	9200	5836	—
CK30943	Chassis & Crew Cab	$14,345	9200	5925	—
CK30943	Fleetside Crew Cab	$14,710	9200	5836	—

NOTE 1: 131.5 in. wheelbase.
NOTE 2: 135.5 in. wheelbase.
NOTE 3: 159.5 in. wheelbase.
* 10,000 lb. GVW optional.

Diesel engine adds 454 lb. to weights of gasoline-engined models in all series.

STANDARD ENGINE: All K-10 6-cyl. models: 262 V-6 (LB1 ordering code). Engine Type: Vortex OHV, V-6-cylinder. Cast iron block. Key features include a 4-bbl. carburetor. Bore x Stroke: 4.0 in. x 3.48 in. Lifters: Hydraulic. Fuel Induction: Single Rochester 4-bbl. carburetor. Compression Ratio: 9.3:1. Displacement: 262 cu. in. (4.3 liters). Horsepower: Net: 155 @ 4000 rpm. Torque: 230 lb.-ft. @ 2400 rpm. Oil refill capacity: 5 qt. with filter change. Fuel Requirements: Regular unleaded.

STANDARD ENGINE: K20 with RPO CH6 and K30 models: 292 Six. Ordering Code: L25. This engine was produced by GM de Mexico. Not available in California with under 8500 lb. GVW rating. Engine Type: OHV, 6-cyl. Cast iron block and cylinder head. Key features include cast iron intake manifold, aluminized-face intake valves, stellite-faced exhaust valves with hardened faces. Bore x Stroke: 3.875 in. x 4.125 in. Lifters: Hydraulic. Number of main bearings-7. Fuel Induction: Single Rochester 1-bbl. carburetor. Compression Ratio: 7.8:1. Displacement: 292 cu. in. (4.8 liters). Horsepower: Net: 115 @ 3400 rpm. Torque: Net: 215 lb.-ft. @ 1600 rpm. Oil refill capacity: 6 qt. Fuel Requirements: Regular unleaded.

STANDARD ENGINE: K20: Optional for K10 (California only), K20 with HP6 and all K30 models. Ordering Code: LS9: 350 V-8 Engine Type: OHV, V-8. Cast iron block and alloy iron cylinder head. Key features include chain drive camshaft and forged steel connecting rods. This engine was produced by GM-Chevrolet Motor Division. Bore x Stroke: 4.0 in. x 3.50 in. Lifters: Hydraulic. Number of main bearings-5. Fuel Induction: Single Rochester 4-bbl. carburetor. Compression Ratio: 8.2:1. Displacement: 350 cu. in. (5.7 liters). Horsepower: Net: 165 @ 3800 rpm. Torque: 275 lb.-ft. @ 1600 rpm. Oil refill capacity: 5 qt. with filter change. Fuel Requirements: Regular unleaded.

OPTIONAL ENGINE: K20 with HP6 and all K30 models: Ordering Code: LT9: 350 V-8 Engine Type: OHV, V-8. Cast iron block and alloy iron cylinder head. Key features include chain drive camshaft and forged steel connecting rods. This engine was produced by GM-Chevrolet Motor Division. Bore x Stroke: 4.0 in. x 3.50 in. Lifters: Hydraulic. Number of main bearings-5. Fuel Induction: Single Rochester 4-bbl. carburetor. Compression Ratio: 8.3:1. Displacement: 350 cu. in. (5.7 liters). Horsepower: Net: 160 @ 3800 rpm. (California rating: 155 @ 3600 rpm). Torque: Net: 260 lb.-ft. @ 2800 rpm. (California rating: 240 lb.-ft. @ 2800 rpm). Oil refill capacity: 5 qt. with filter change. Fuel Requirements: Regular unleaded.

OPTIONAL ENGINE: K10 models: Ordering Code: LE9: 305 V-8. Key features include Electronic Spark Control, new staged 4-barrel carburetor, camshaft and free-flow exhaust system. Not available for California. This engine was produced by GM-Chevrolet Motor Division and GM of Canada. Engine Type: OHV. Cast iron block and alloy iron cylinder head. Bore x Stroke: 3.74 in. x 3.48 in. Lifters: Hydraulic. Number of main bearings-5. Fuel Induction: Single Rochester 4-bbl. staged carburetor. Compression Ratio: 9.2:1. Displacement: 305 cu. in. (5.0 liters). Horsepower: 160 @ 4400 rpm. Torque: 235 lb.-ft. @ 2000 rpm. Oil refill capacity: 5 qt. with filter change. Fuel Requirements: Regular unleaded.

OPTIONAL ENGINE: K10 models for California: Ordering Code: LF3: 305 V-8. Key features include 4-barrel carburetor, camshaft and free-flow exhaust system. This engine was produced by GM-Chevrolet Motor Division and GM of Canada. Engine Type: OHV. Cast iron block and alloy iron cylinder head. Bore x Stroke: 3.74 in. x 3.48 in. Lifters: Hydraulic. Number of main bearings-5. Fuel Induction: Single Rochester 4-bbl. carburetor. Compression Ratio: 8.6:1. Displacement: 305 cu. in. (5.0 liters). Horsepower: 155 @ 4200 rpm. Torque: 240 lb.-ft. @ 1600 rpm. Oil refill capacity: 5 qt. with filter change. Fuel Requirements: Regular unleaded.

OPTIONAL ENGINE: K30 models: Ordering Code: LE8: 454 V-8. This engine was produced by GM-Chevrolet Motor Division. a. Engine Type: OHV, V-8. Cast iron block and alloy iron cylinder head. Bore x Stroke: 4.3 in. x 4.0 in. Lifters: Hydraulic. Number of main bearings-5. Fuel Induction: Single Rochester 4-bbl. carburetor. Compression Ratio: 7.9:1. Displacement: 454 cu. in. (7.4 liters). Horsepower: 230 @ 3800 rpm. Torque: 360 lb.-ft. @ 2800 rpm. Oil refill capacity: 5 qt. with filter change. Fuel Requirements: Regular unleaded.

OPTIONAL ENGINE: All models: Ordering Code: LH6: 6.2 liter V-8. This engine was produced by GM-Detroit Diesel Allison Division. Engine Type: OHV, diesel V-8. Bore x Stroke: 3.98 in. x 3.80 in. Lifters: Hydraulic. Number of main bearings-5. Fuel Induction: Fuel injection. Compression Ratio: 21.3:1. Displacement: 379.4 cu. in. (6.2 liters). Horsepower: 135 @ 3600 rpm. Torque: 240 lb.-ft. @ 2000 rpm. Oil refill capacity: 7 qt. with filter change. Fuel Requirements: Diesel. An LL4 version of this engine for models with GVW of 8500 lb. and above was also available. Its power ratings were 135 hp. @ 3600 rpm and 240 lb.-ft. of torque at 2000 rpm.

CHASSIS FEATURES: Separate body and frame with channel side rails. Carbon-Steel, 39,000 psi. 117.5 in. wheelbase: 2.30 in. x 5.92 in. x 0.156 in. Section modules: 3.06 in. 129.5 in.: 2.30 in. x 5.92 in. x 0.194. Section modules: 117.5 in. wheelbase: 3.14 in. 131.5 in. wheelbase: 3.88 in. K20 with CP6: 4.53 in. Optional: None.

1986 Chevrolet K10 Stepside Custom Deluxe pickup

SUSPENSION AND RUNNING GEAR: Front Suspension: K10: Tapered 2-leaf springs. Capacity: 1650 lb.-1850 lb. K20: Tapered 2-leaf springs. Capacity: 1850 lb. K30: Tapered 3-leaf springs. Capacity: 2250 lb. Rear Suspension: K10 and K20: 52 in. x 2.25 in. Two-stage, 5-leaf. K30: 56 in. x 2.50 in. Rating: K10: 2075 lb. K20: 2800 lb. K30: 3500 lb. K10: 22mm. dia. shock absorbers. K30: 32mm shock absorbers. Capacity: K10: 3750 lb. K20: 5700 lb. K30: 7000 lb. (7500 lb. for 159.9 in. wheelbase chassis and cab). Front Axle Type: K10: 3000 lb. rating at ground. Capacity: 6000 lb. with RPO CP6 K30: RPO RO5 (Dual rear wheels): 3750 lb. rating at ground. Capacity: 7500 lb. Front Axle Type and Capacity: K10: Semi-floating 3700 lb. capacity. Optional: None. K20: Full-floating, 3800 lb. K30: Full-floating, 4500 lb. Rear Axle Type and Capacity: K10: Chevrolet, Semi-floating, 3750 lb. capacity. K20: Semi-floating, 5700 lb. capacity. K30: Full-floating, 7500 lb. Optional Rating: K20: 3000 lb. rating at ground. Capacity: 6000 lb. with RPO CP6 K30: RPO RO5 (Dual rear

wheels): 3750 lb. rating at ground. Capacity: 7500 lb. Final Drive Ratio: The following transmission designations were used by Chevrolet: MM3: 3-spd. manual; MM4: 4-spd. manual; MM7: 4-spd. manual with Overdrive; MXO: 4-spd. auto. with Overdrive; MX1: 3-spd. automatic. All ratios are with standard emission equipment. Standard: K10: LB1 engine/MM4, MXO: 3.42:1; LB1/MM7: 3.73:1 (requires engine oil cooler); LS9/MM7: 3.42:1, LS9/MX: 2.73:1, LS9/MXO: 3.08:1; LH6/MM4, MXO: 3.08:1; LH6/MM7: 3.42:1. Optional: LB1/MM4, MXO: 3.73:1 (requires RPO KC4, engine oil cooler); LE9/MM7: 3.73:1, LE9/MM4: 3.08:1, LH6/MM4, MXO: 3.42:1; LT9/MM4: 3.73:1, LT9/MX1: 4.10:1; LH6/MM4: 3.73:1, LH6/MXO: 3.42:1; LL4/MM4: 3.73:1, LL4/MX1: 4.10:1. Optional: LS9/MM4: 3.42:1, LS9/MM4MX0: 3.23:1; LT9/MM4: 3.42:1; LT9/MX1: 4.10:1; LH6/MM4: 3.73:1, LH6/MXO: 3.42:1; LL4/MM4: 4.10:1. Standard K30: K25/MM4, MX1: 4.56:1; LT9/MM4: 3.73:1; LT9/MX1: 4.10:1; LE8/MM4, MX1: 3.73:1, LL4/MM4, MX1: 4.10:1. Optional: LT9/MM4: 4.10:1, 4.56:1; LT9/MX1: 4.56:1; LE8/MM4, MX1: 4.10:1, 4.56:1; LL4/MM4, MX1: 4.56:1. Transfer Case: K10 and K20: New Process 208. Single lever, 2.61, 1.00:1. K30: New Process 205, two-speed: 1.96, 1.00:1. Brakes: Type: Hydraulic, power assisted. Dimensions: K10: Disc: 11.86 in. x 1.28 in. Rear: Drums: 11.15 x 2.75 in. K20: Front: Disc: 12.5 in. x 1.28 in. Rear: Drums: 11.15 in. x 2.75 in. K20 and K30: Front: Disc: 12.50 in. x 1.53 in. Rear: Drum: 13.00 in. x 3.50 in. Wheels: K10: 15 x 6.0JJ 6-stud disc. Optional: 15 x 8JJ. K20: 16.5 x 6.00 in. 8-stud disc. Optional: 16.5 x 6.75. K30: 16.5 x 6.75. Tires: K10: P235/75R15 steel belted radial. K20: LT215/85R16C. K20 with RPO CP6: Front: LT235/85R16D, 8-ply rating; rear: LT235/85R16E, 10-ply rating.; K30: Front: LT235/85R16D, 8-ply rating; rear: LT235/85R16E, 10-ply rating. Optional: K10: P235/75R15 white sidewall; P235/75R15R white letters; 31 x 10.50R/15B blackwall or white letters (both require RPO N67, N90 or PA6 wheels). Optional K20: Tubeless steel belted radials 7.50R/16D, LT215/85R16C, LT215/85R16D, LT235/85R16D, LT235/85R16E. Optional: K30: Tube-type, nylon: 7.50-16D. Tubeless steel belted radial: LT215/85R16D, LT235/85R16E. Steering: Recirculating ball gear. Ratio: 20:1. Turning Circle: 47 ft. Steering wheel diameter: 17.5 in. Optional: Power-assisted. Ratio: 16.4:1. Transmission: K10, K20, K30: 4-speed, synchromesh manual. Transmission Ratios: 6.55, 3.58, 1.70, 1.00:1. Optional: K10: 4-spd. manual overdrive, 4-spd. automatic overdrive; K20: 4-spd. automatic overdrive; K30: 3-spd. automatic. Diesel models: K10: 4-spd. manual overdrive, 4-spd. automatic overdrive; K20: 4-spd. automatic overdrive; K20 HD (with RPO C6P) and K30: 3-spd. automatic. Clutch: Diaphragm, spring. Clutch diameter: 6-cyl.: 11 in. dia. Total lining area: 123.5 sq. in. Total plate pressure: 2075 lb. V-8: 12 in. dia. Total lining area: 149.2 sq. in. Total plate pressure: 2060 lb. Optional: K20 6-cyl.: 11 in. dia. Total lining area: 124.0 sq. in. 307 V-8: 12 in. dia. Total lining area: 150 sq. in.

VEHICLE DIMENSIONS: Wheelbase: K10: 117.5 in. 131.5 in. K20: 131.5 in. All Suburbans and Panels: 129.5 in. K30: 131.5 in. 135.5 in. 164.5 in. Overall Length: 117.5 in. Fleetside pickups: 192.60 in. 131.5 in. Fleetside pickups: 212.50. 117.5 in. Stepside pickups: 191.1 in. 131.5 in. Stepside pickups: 211.00 in. K30: 131.5 in. Chassis cab: 206.20 in.; 135.5 in. wheelbase: 215.6 in.; 159.5 in. wheelbase: 239.7 in.; 164.5 in. wheelbase (bonus/crew cab): 239.3 in. Approach/Departure Degrees: K10 117.5 in. Fleetside and Stepside: 33/19. K10 131.5 in. Stepside: 33/16. K20 131.5 in. Fleetside and Stepside: 35/20. K20 131.5 in. wheelbase Stepside: 35/21. K30 Fleetside pickup: 41/19. K30 crew cab Pickup: 38/18. Ground Clearance: Fleetside models: K10 pickups: Front: 7.4 in.; rear: 7.1 in. K20 pickups: Front: 8.8 in.; rear: 7.2 in. K30 pickups: Front: 7.2 in.; rear: 7.8 in. Stepside models: K10 pickups: Front: 7.2 in.; rear: 7.1 in. K20 pickups: Front: 8.8 in.; rear: 7.8 in. K30 pickups: K30 chassis cab (131.5 in. 135.5 in. and 159.5 in. wheelbase): Front: 8.3 in.; rear: 7.7 in. K30 bonus/crew cab: Front: 8.3 in.; rear: 7.7 in. Load space: Pickup box dimensions: 117.5 in. wheelbase Fleetside: 78.25 in. x 50 in. x 19.25 in. 131.5 in. wheelbase Fleetside: 98 in. x 50 in. x 19.25 in. Capacity: 117.5 wheelbase: 58.4 cu. ft. 131.5 in. wheelbase: 74.3 cu. ft. 117.5 in. wheelbase Stepside: 78.5 in. x 50 in. x 17.5 in. 131.5 in. wheelbase Stepside: 96.25 in. x 50 in. x 17.5 in. Front headroom: 38.5 in. (seat to top of cab). Front hip room: 67.25 in. Pedal to seat back (max.): 43.5 in. Steering wheel to seat back (max.): 17.3 in. Seat to ground: 35.0 in. Floor to ground: 23.0 in.

CAPACITIES: Fuel Tank: 117.5 in. wheelbase: 16.0 gal. 131.5 in. wheelbase, 135.5 in. wheelbase and 164.5 in. wheelbase: 20 gal. Optional: 16 gal. auxiliary tank for 117.5 in.; 20 gal. auxiliary for 131.5 in., 135.5 in. and 164.5 in. wheelbase. Engine Coolant System: 250 6-cyl.: 14.8 qt. 305 V-8: 17.6 qt. 350 V-8: 17.6 qt. 400 V-8: 19.6 qt. (20 qt. on K20 and K30).

ACCOMMODATIONS: Seating Capacity: Pickup and chassis cab models: 3 passenger. Optional: None. Crew cab: 6 passenger. Suburban: 3 passenger. Optional: 6 or 9 passenger.

INSTRUMENTATION: Speedometer, odometer, fuel level gauge. Warning lights for battery, oil pressure, generator, brake system warning, directional/hazard lights, high beam, and engine coolant temperature.

OPTIONS AND PRICES: Silverado Package (RPO YE9) $671-$1016, depending on body and additional packages installed. Deluxe bench seat: $17 with Scottsdale Package; $62 without Scottsdale Package (RPO Z62). Bonus cab Custom bench seat: $50 with RPO Z62. Crew cab bonus seat: $100 with RPO Z62. Regular cab and bonus cab Custom vinyl bench seat: $50 without RPO Z62 or RPO YE9. Crew cab Custom vinyl bench seat: $100 with RPO YE9. Conventional two-tone Paint (RPO ZY2): $43 to $89 depending on body and additional options. Exterior Decor Package (RPO ZY5): $418-$575 depending on body and additional options. Special Big Dooley two-tone paint (RPO ZY9): $444 without RPO Z62; $426 with RPO Z62. California emissions requirement (RPO YF5): $235. 5.0 liter V-8 (RPO LE9 or RPO LF3): $465. 5.7 liter V-8 (RPO LT9): $650. 5.7 liter V-8 (ROP LT9): $620. 7.4 liter V-8 (RPO LE8): $790. 6.2 liter diesel V-8. 3-spd. automatic trans. (RPO MX1): $510. 4-spd. manual overdrive trans.: $80. 4-spd. automatic trans. with overdrive (RPO MXO): $670. Optional axle ratios: $36. Locking rear differential (RPO G80): $238. Heavy-duty power brakes for K10 and K20 (RPO J55): $104. Chrome rear bumper (RPO VF1): $103. Chromed rear step bumper for Fleetside only (RPO V42): $189. Painted rear step bumper (RPO V43): $120. Chromed front bumper guards (RPO V31): $41. Camper Special chassis equipment (RPO Z81): $108 (for K20 with required C6H chassis). $49 for K30 with required RPO RO5 dual rear wheels. Glide-Out spare tire carrier for Fleetside only (RPO P11): $41. Side-mounted spare tire carrier for Fleetside only (RPO P13): $29. Quartz electric clock (RPO U35). Not available when UM6 radio is specified: $79 without RPO YE9. Includes RPO Z53 voltmeter, temperature and oil pressure gauges; $39 with RPO YE9. Cold Climate Package. Not available when RPO C60 air conditioning or RPO B3J diesel equipment is specified. Includes special insulation, RPO K81 66 amp generator, special heater and defroster, RPO KO5 engine block heater, anti-freeze protection to -32 degrees and RPO UA1 heavy-duty battery (RPO V10): $126 to $200 depending on additional options and series applications. Engine oil cooling system (RPO KC4). Not avail. with RPO L25 engine or RPO B3J: $43. Heavy-duty radiator and transmission oil (RPO VO2). Avail. only with RPO MX1 or RPO MXO transmission are specified. Not avail. with RPO L25 engine or RPO VO1 are specified: $59. Decor Value Package. Includes black painted radiator grille and headlight bezels, and special body stripe located between body feature lines on front fenders, pickup box and across the tailgate. Not avail. on bonus cab, crew cab and Stepside models. Not available with the following options: RPO YE9, RO5, V22, pA6, N90, B84 or B85. Requires RPO ZY1 solid paint and blackwall or white lettered tires are specified (RPO YJ6): $256 for K10; $141 for K20 and K30. Power door lock system (RPO AU3): $135 for regular cab; $198 for bonus and crew cab. Color-keyed front floor mats (RPO B32). Requires RPO YE9: $15. Gauge Package. Includes voltmeter, engine coolant temperature and oil pressure (RPO Z53): $40. 66 amp Delcotron generator. Standard on K30 except when RPO LE8 engine is ordered (RPO K81): $62. 94 amp Delcrotron generator. Included with LE8 engine on K30 models (RPO K22): $62. Tinted glass-all windows (RPO AO1): $46 for regular cab; $56 for bonus or crew cab. Halogen high-beam headlamps. Avail. only when RPO V22 or RPO YE9 is specified (RPO TT5): $17. 600

watts engine block heater. Not avail. when RPO BK3 or RPO LF3 engine is specified (RPO K05): $31. Heavy-duty front heater (RPO C42). Avail. only with RPO B3J is specified. Not avail. with RPO C60 air conditioning: $43. Automatic front locking hubs. Avail. only for K10 (RPO X6Z): $40. Cargo lamp (RPO UF2): $60 without RPO Z62 or YE9 (includes RPO C91 dome lamp). Dome lamp (RPO C91): 26. Roof marker lamps. Avail. for K20 only. Standard for K30 (RPO UO1): $50. Cigarette lighter. Included when RPO Z62 or YE9 is specified (RPO U37): $30. Exterior left and right side below eye-level mirrors: Painted (RPO D44): $50.; stainless steel (RPO D45): $83. Camper type stainless steel left and right side exterior mirrors (RPO DF2): $94. Senior West Coast type painted exterior left and right side mirrors (RPO DG5): $65. Black body side molding. Avail. for Fleetside only (RPO B84): $115. Bright body side molding. Avail. for Fleetside only (RPO B85): $144 without RPO Z62; $15 with RPO Z62. Custom Package (RPO YG1). Avail. for Fleetside only. Includes wheel opening moldings, RPO B84, RPO B96 and bright trim for front sidemarker lamps and taillights: $157 without RPO Z62; $29 with RPO Z62. Deluxe Package (RPO YG3). Avail. for Fleetside only. Not avail. with RPO YG1 or RPO RO5. Includes bright trim for front side marker lamps and taillights, RPO B85 and RPO B96: $173 without RPO Z62, RPO ZY3, RPO ZY4 or ZY5; $44 with RPO Z62; $16 with RPO ZY3, RPO ZY4 or RPO ZY5. Wheel opening molding (RPO B96). Avail. only with RPO ZY6: $29. Door edge guards (RPO B93): $17 for regular cab; $22 for bonus or crew cab. Operating Convenience Package (RPO ZQ2). Includes RPO AU3 Power door locks and RPO A31 Power windows: $325 for regular cab; $488 for bonus and crew cab. AM radio (RPO U63): $112. AM/FM radio (RPO U69): 171. AM/FM stereo radio (RPO U58): $198. AM/FM stereo radio with stereo cassette tape player (RPO UN3): $298. Electronically tuned AM/FM stereo radio with Seek-Scan, stereo cassette player and clock (RPO UM6): $419. Windshield antenna (RPO U76): $32. Pickup box side rails (RPO D73): $94. Transfer case shield (RPO NY7): $41. Front quad shock absorbers (RPO Z75): $128 for K10 and K20 without C6P heavy-duty chassis; $94 for K20 with C6P. Electronic speed control (RPO K34). Not avail. for K10 with MM7 trans. or K20 and K30 with LS9, LT9 and LE8 with MM4 trans.: $195. Heavy-duty front springs (RPO F60). Not avail. for K30. For K10 and K20 series includes heavy-duty front and rear shock absorbers. Recommended for snowplow use for K10: $92 without RPO Z75 front quad shock absorbers; $59 with RPO Z75. Main and auxiliary rear springs (RPO G60): $97. ComforTilt steering wheel (RPO N33). Not avail. when RPO MM3 was specified: $115. Auxiliary fuel tank (RPO NL2): $260-$270 depending on model. Two front towing hooks (RPO V76): $36. Bright metal wheelcovers, for K10 only (RPO PO1): $40. Special wheelcovers, for K20 only (RPO PA1): $118. Rallye wheels, K10 only (RPO N67): $115. Styled wheels (RPO PA6): $174. Aluminum cast wheels (RPO N90): $299. Dual rear wheels for K30 only (RPO RO5): $678-740 depending on options and transmission specified. Power windows (RPO A31): $190 for regular cab; $290 for bonus and crew cab. Sliding rear window (RPO A28): $107. Intermittent windshield wiper system (RPO CD4): $55.

HISTORICAL FOOTNOTES: The 1986 Chevrolet trucks were introduced in the fall of 1985. Total sales of all Chevrolet truck models from Nov.1985 through Nov. 1986 was 1,174,217. Of this total pickup sales were 438,422. Suburbans sales were 53,842.

1986 Chevrolet K30 Fleetside Big Dooley pickup

1987 PICKUP

Chevrolet used a new V designation for its 1987 four-wheel drive trucks. All V-6 and V-8 engines had engines equipped with throttle body electronic fuel injection. This system replaced the carburetor and allowed for higher compression ratios and greater horsepower. As the engine section indicates both the 305 and 350 cu. in. V-8 engines were significantly more powerful for 1987. Computer controls were incorporated into the spark advance fuel to air ratio, idle speed and fuel cutoff, enhancing driveability and performance. For 1987 the engine-mounted mechanical fuel pump was replaced by an electric unit mounted in the fuel tank. This pump along with a fuel pressure regulator provided instant and constant fuel pressure for more precise fuel control during engine starting and driving. No longer offered was the 292 cu. in. 6-cylinder. The 262 cu. in. Vortex V-6 was now the standard base engine. For 1987 it was equipped with low friction roller hydraulic valve lifters. This increased engine efficiency while proving a three percent fuel economy increase. Chevrolet offered new lower-weight Delco batteries with higher cold cranking current for all gasoline engine applications. Cold cranking amps were increased from 500 to 525 amps on the 4.3 liter V-6; from 405 to 525 on 5-liter V-8s with automatic transmission and all 5.7 liter applications, and from 540 to 630 amps on the 7.4 liter gasoline engine.

The 6.2 liter diesel for 1987 continued to use two batteries, each with 540 cold cranking amps. The RPO UA1 heavy-duty battery option for the 5.0 and 5.7 liter V-8 engines was revised to include an increased performance cranking motor for 1987. Alternator changes for 1987 involved replacement of the standard 37 amp output alternator with a 66 amp alternator as standard equipment. The 66 amp alternator had been an option in 1986.

Suburban models shared the above technical revisions for 1987. The latest versions of the Suburbans were fitted with a new seat belt system providing reduced belt effort on both front seat positions. This arrangement also incorporated a dual mode operation to secure a child safety seat. Under full extension, the belt had an automatic lock feature that override the inertia locking mechanism and provided positive child seat retention. Suburban models with either the RPO C69 rear air conditioning or the combination of RPO C36 auxiliary heater and RPO C49 rear defogger had a 78 amp alternator with the diesel engine or a 105 amp unit with gasoline engines. Also new for 1987 was the use of a 94 amp alternator on Suburbans equipped with the combination of RPO C60 air conditioner, RPO C36 auxiliary heater, or RPO C40 rear defogger.

The content of three trim levels — Custom Deluxe, Scottsdale and Silverado were carried over unchanged into 1987. The exterior and interior color selections were also unchanged from 1986.

I.D. DATA: Unchanged from 1986 except the letter H designated the 1987 model year.

Model Number	Body Type & Seating	Factory Price	GVW	Shipping Weight	Prod. Total
Series V10-1/2 ton 250 6-cyl. 117.5 in. 131.5 in. wheelbase (Suburban: 129.5 in. wheelbase and standard 350 V-8)					
CV10703	6.5 ft. Stepside Pickup	$11,114	6100	4383	—
CV10703	6.5 ft. Fleetside Pickup	$10,979	6100	4420	—
CV10903	8 ft. Fleetside Pickup	$11,148	6100	4616	—
CV10906	Suburban Endgate	$13,073	6100	5125	—
CV10906	Suburban Panl. Drs.	$13,036	6100[1]	5179	—

NOTE 1: Suburban available with optional 6600 GVW package.

Series V20-3/4 ton 350 V-8. 131.5 in. wheelbase. (Suburban-129.5 in. wheelbase). Crew and bonus cab: 164.5 in. wheelbase. Suburban weight with standard 350 V-8.V20 Pickup prices include C6P heavy-duty chassis.

CV20903	8 ft. Stepside Pickup	$12,847	6600*	4848	—
CV20903	8 ft. Fleetside Pickup	$12,603	6600	4960	—
CV20906	Suburban Endgate	$14,768	6600	5496	—
CV20906	Suburban Panl. Drs.	$14,805	6600	5560	—

* 8600 lb. GVW optional.

Series V30-1 ton 350 V-8. 131.5 in. wheelbase. Crew and bonus cab: 164.5 in. wheelbase CV

CV30903	Chassis & Cab[1]	$14,410	9200*	4512	—
CV31003	Chassis & Cab[2]	$14,622	9200	5022	—
CV31403	Chassis & Cab[3]	$15,175	9200	5295	—
CV30903	8 ft. Fleetside Pickup	$14,823	9200	5434	—
CV30943	Chassis & Bonus Cab	$15,336	9200	5417	—
CV30943	Fleetside Bonus Cab	$15,702	9200	5836	—
CV30943	Chassis & Crew Cab	$15,675	9200	5925	—
CV30943	Fleetside Crew Cab	$16,040	9200	5836	—

NOTE 1: 131.5 in. wheelbase.
NOTE 2: 135.5 in. wheelbase.
NOTE 3: 159.5 in. wheelbase.
* 10,000 lb. GVW optional.

Diesel engine adds 454 lb. to weights of gasoline-engined models in all series.

STANDARD ENGINE: All V10 6-cyl. models: 262 V-6 (LB4 ordering code). Engine Type: Vortex OHV, V-6-cylinder. Cast iron block. Bore x Stroke: 4.0 in. x 3.48 in. Lifters: Hydraulic. Fuel Induction: Electronic fuel injection. Compression Ratio: 9.3:1. Displacement: 262 cu. in. (4.3 liters). Horsepower: Net: 155 @ 4000 rpm. Torque: Net: 230 lb.-ft. @ 2400 rpm. Oil refill capacity: 5 qt. with filter change. Fuel Requirements: Regular unleaded. Standard engine: V20, V30 series, optional for V10. Ordering Code: LO5. Engine Type: OHV, V-8. 350 V-8. Cast iron block and alloy iron cylinder head. Key features include chain drive camshaft and forged steel connecting rods. This engine was produced by GM-Chevrolet Motor Division. Bore x Stroke: 4.0 in. x 3.50 in. Lifters: Hydraulic. Number of main bearings-5. Fuel Induction: Electronic fuel injection. Compression Ratio: 8.2:1. Displacement: 350 cu. in. (5.7 liters). Horsepower: Net: 210 @ 4000 rpm. Torque: Net: 300 lb.-ft. @ 2800 rpm. Oil refill capacity: 5 qt. with filter change. Fuel Requirements: Regular unleaded.

OPTIONAL ENGINE: V10 models: Ordering Code: LO3: 305 V-8. This engine was produced by GM-Chevrolet Motor Division and GM of Canada. Engine Type: OHV, V-8. Cast iron block and alloy iron cylinder head. Bore x Stroke: 3.74 in. x 3.48 in. Lifters: Hydraulic. Number of main bearings-5. Fuel Induction: Electronic fuel injection. Compression Ratio: 9.2:1. Displacement: 305 cu. in. (5.0 liters). Horsepower: 170 @ 4000 rpm. Torque: 260 lb.-ft. @ 2400 rpm. Oil refill capacity: 5 qt. with filter change. Fuel Requirements: Regular unleaded.

OPTIONAL ENGINE: V30 models: Ordering Code: L19 454 V-8. This engine was produced by GM-Chevrolet Motor Division. Engine Type: OHV, V-8. Cast iron block and alloy iron cylinder head. Bore x Stroke: 4.3 in. x 4.0 in. Lifters: Hydraulic. Number of main bearings-5. Fuel Induction: Electronic fuel injection. Compression Ratio: 7.9:1. Displacement: 454 cu. in. (7.4 liters). Horsepower: 230 @ 3600 rpm. Torque: 385 lb.-ft. @ 1600 rpm. Oil refill capacity: 5 qt. with filter change. Fuel Requirements: Regular unleaded.

OPTIONAL ENGINE: All V10 and V20 models: Ordering Code: LH6: 6.2 liter V-8. This engine was produced by GM-Detroit Diesel Allison Division. Engine Type: OHV, diesel V-8. Bore x Stroke: 3.98 in. x 3.80 in. Lifters: Hydraulic. Number of main bearings-5. Fuel Induction: Fuel injection. Compression Ratio: 21.3:1. Displacement: 379.4 cu. in. (6.2 liters). Horsepower: 130 @ 3600 rpm. Torque: 240 lb.-ft. @ 2000 rpm. Oil refill capacity: 5 qt. with filter change. Fuel Requirements: Regular unleaded. An LL4 version of this engine for V20 and V30 models with GVW of 8600 lb. and above was also available. Use in the V20 regular cab required the C6P heavy-duty chassis. Its power ratings were 148 hp. @ 3600 rpm and 246 lb.-ft. of torque @ 2000 rpm.

CHASSIS FEATURES: Separate body and frame with channel side rails. Carbon-Steel, 39,000 psi. 117.5 in. wheelbase: 2.30 in. x 5.92 in. x 0.156 in. Section modules: 3.06 in. 129.5 in.: 2.30 in. x 5.92 in. x 0.194. Section modules: 117.5 in. wheelbase: 3.14 in. 131.5 in. wheelbase: 3.88 in. x 0.194 with CP6: 4.53 in. Optional: None.

SUSPENSION AND RUNNING GEAR: Front Suspension: V10: Tapered 2-leaf springs. Capacity: 1650 lb.-1850 lb. V20: Tapered 2-leaf springs. Capacity: 1850 lb. V30: Tapered 3-leaf springs. Capacity: 2250 lb. Rear Suspension: V10 and V20: 52 in. x 2.25 in. Two-stage, 5-leaf. V30: 56 in. x 2.50 in. Rating: V10: 2075 lb. V20: 2800 lb. V30: 3500 lb. V10: 22mm. dia. shock absorbers. V30: 32mm shock absorbers. Capacity: V10: 3750 lb. V20: 5700 lb. V30: 7000 lb. (7500 lb. for 159.9 in. wheelbase Chassis and Cab). Optional Rating: V20: 3000 lb. rating at ground. Capacity: 6000 lb. with RPO CP6 V30: RPO RO5 (Dual rear wheels): 3750 lb. rating at ground. Capacity: 7500 lb. Front Axle Type and Capacity: V10: Semi-floating. 3700 lb. capacity. Optional: None. V20: Full-floating, 3800 lb capacity. V30: Full-floating, 4500 lb. Optional: None. Rear Axle Type and Capacity: V10: Chevrolet, Semi-floating, 3750 lb. capacity. V20: Semi-floating, 5700 lb. capacity. V30: Full-floating, 7500 lb. Optional Rating: V20: 3000 lb. rating at ground. Capacity: 6000 lb. with RPO CP6 V30: RPO RO5 (Dual rear wheels): 3750 lb. rating at ground. Capacity: 7500 lb. Final Drive Ratio: The following transmission designations were used by Chevrolet: MM3: 3-spd. manual; MM4: 4-spd. manual; MM7: 4-spd. manual with Overdrive; MXO: 4-spd. auto. with Overdrive; MX1: 3-spd. automatic. All ratios are with standard emission equipment. Standard: V10: LB1 engine/MM4, MXO: 3.42:1. LB1/MM7: 3.73:1 (requires engine oil cooler); LS9/MM7: 3.42:1, LS9/MXO: 2.73:1. LS9/MXO: 3.08:1, LH6/MM4, MXO: 3.08:1; LH6/MM7: 3.42:1. Optional: LB1/MM4, MXO: 3.73:1 (requires RPO KC4, engine oil cooler), LH6/MM4, MXO: 3.42:1. Standard: V20: L25/MM4, MX1: 4.10:1, LS9/MM4/MXO: 3.23:1, LT9/MM4: 3.42:1, LH6/MX1: 4.10:1; LH6/MM4: 3.73:1, LH6/MXO: 3.42:1. LL4/MM4: 3.73:1, LL4/MX1: 4.10:1. Optional: LS9/MM4: 3.42:1, LS9/MXO: 3.42:1, 3.73:1; and V20 with Overdrive: LT9/MM4: 3.73:1, 4.10:1; LH6/MM4: 4.10:1, LH6/MXO: 3.73:1; LL4/MM4: 4.10:1. Standard V30: K25/MM4, MX1: 4.56:1; LT9/MM4: 3.73:1; LT9/MX1: 4.10:1;

LE8/MM4, MX1: 3.73:1, LL4/MM4, MX1: 4.10:1. Optional: LT9/MM4: 4.10:1, 4.56:1; LT9/MX1: 4.56:1; LE8/MM4, MX1: 4.10:1, 4.56:1; LL4/MM4, MX1: 4.56:1. Transfer Case: V10 and V20: New Process 208. Single lever, 2.61, 1.00:1. V30: New Process 205, two-speed: 1.96, 1.00:1. Brakes: Type: Hydraulic, power assisted. Dimensions: V10: Front: Disc: 11.86 in. x 1.28 in. Rear: Drums: 11.15 x 2.75 in. V20: Front: Disc: 12.5 in. x 1.28 in. Rear: Drums: 11.15 in. x 2.75 in. V20 and V30: Front: Disc: 12.50 in. x 1.53 in. Rear: Drum: 13.00 in. x 3.50 in. Wheels: V10: 15 x 6.0JJ 6-stud disc. Optional: 15 x 8JJ. V20: 16.5 x 6.00 in. 8-stud disc. Optional: 16.5 x 6.75. V30: 16.5 x 6.75. Tires: V10: P235/75R15 steel belted radial. V20: LT215/85R16C. V20 with RPO CP6: Front: LT235/85R16D, 8-ply rating; rear: LT235/85R16E, 10-ply rating.; V30: Front: LT235/85R16D, 8-ply rating; rear: LT235/85R16E, 10-ply rating. Optional: V10: P235/75R15 white sidewall; P235/75R15R white letters; 31 x 10.50R/15B blackwall or white letters (both require RPO N67, N90 or PA6 wheels). Optional V20: Tubeless steel belted radials 7.50R/16D, LT215/85R16C, LT215/85R16D, LT235/85R16D, LT235/85R16E. Optional: V30: Tube-type, nylon: 7.50-16D. Tubeless steel belted radial: LT215/85R16D, LT235/85R16E. Steering: Recirculating ball gear. Ratio: 20:1. Turning Circle: 47 ft. Steering wheel diameter: 17.5 in. Optional: Power-assisted. Ratio: 16.4:1. Transmission: V10, V20, V30: 4-speed, synchromesh manual. Transmission Ratios: 6.55, 3.58, 1.70, 1.00:1. Optional: V10: 4-spd. manual overdrive, 4-spd. automatic overdrive; V20: 4-spd. automatic overdrive; V30: 3-spd. automatic. Diesel models: V10: 4-spd. manual overdrive, 4-spd. automatic overdrive; V20: 4-spd. automatic overdrive; V20 HD (with RPO C6P) and V30: 3-spd. automatic. Clutch: Diaphragm, spring. Clutch diameter: 6-cyl.: 11 in. dia. Total lining area: 123.5 sq. in. Total plate pressure: 2075 lb. V-8: 12 in. dia. Total lining area: 149.2 sq. in. Total plate pressure: 2060 lb. Optional: V20 6-cyl.: 11 in. dia. Total lining area: 124.0 sq. in. 307 V-8: 12 in. dia. Total lining area: 150 sq. in.

VEHICLE DIMENSIONS: Wheelbase: V10: 117.5 in. 131.5 in. V20: 131.5 in. All Suburbans and Panels: 129.5 in. V30: 131.5 in. 135.5 in. 164.5 in. Overall Length: 117.5 in. Fleetside pickups: 192.60 in. 131.5 in. Fleetside pickups: 212.50. 117.5 in. Stepside pickups: 191.1 in. 131.5 in. Stepside pickups: 211.00 in. V30: 131.5 in. Chassis cab: 206.20 in.; 135.5 in. wheelbase: 215.6 in.; 159.5 in. wheelbase: 239.7 in.; 164.5 in. wheelbase (bonus/crew cab): 239.3 in. Approach/Departure Degrees: V10 117.5 in. Fleetside and Stepside: 33/19. V10 131.5 in. Fleetside: 33/15. V10 131.5 in. wheelbase Stepside: 33/16. V20 131.5 in. wheelbase Fleetside: 35/20. V20 131.5 in. wheelbase Stepside: 35/21. V30 Fleetside pickup: 41/19. V30 crew cab Pickup: 38/18. Ground Clearance: Fleetside models: V10 pickups: Front: 74 in.; rear: 7.1 in. V20 pickups: Front: 8.8 in.; rear: 7.2 in.V30 pickups: Front: 8.3 in.; rear: 7.8 in. Step side models: V10 pickups: Front: 7.2 in.; rear: 7.1 in. V20 pickups: Front: 8.8 in.; rear: 7.2 in. V30 pickups: V30 chassis cab (131.5 in. 135.5 in. and 159.5 in. wheelbase): Front: 8.3 in.; rear: 7.7 in. V30 bonus/crew cab: Front: 8.3 in.; rear: 7.7 in. Load space: Pickup box dimensions: 117.5 in. wheelbase Fleetside: 78.25 in. x 50 in. x 19.25 in. 131.5 in. wheelbase Fleetside: 98 in. x 50 in. x 19.25 in. Capacity: 117.5 wheelbase: 58.4 cu. ft. 131.5 in. wheelbase: 74.3 cu. ft. 117.5 in. wheelbase Stepside: 78.5 in. x 50 in. x 17.5 in. 131.5 in. wheelbase Stepside: 96.25 in. x 50 in. x 17.5 in. Front headroom: 38.5 in. (seat to top of cab). Front hip room: 67.25 in. Pedal to seat back (max.): 43.5 in. Steering wheel to seat back (max.): 17.3 in. Seat to ground: 35.0 in. Floor to ground: 23.0 in.

CAPACITIES: Fuel Tank: 117.5 in. wheelbase: 16.0 gal. 131.5 in. wheelbase, 135.5 in. wheelbase and 164.5 in. wheelbase: 20 gal. Optional: 16 gal. auxiliary tank. for 117.5 in.; 20 gal. auxiliary for 131.5 in., 135.5 in. and 164.5 in. wheelbase. Engine Coolant System: 250 6-cyl.: 14.8 qt. 305 V-8: 17.6 qt. 350 V-8: 17.6 qt. 400 V-8: 19.6 qt. (20 qt. on V20 and V30).

ACCOMMODATIONS: Seating Capacity: Pickup and chassis cab models: 3 passenger. Optional: None. Crew cab: 6 passenger. Suburban: 3 passenger. Optional: 6 or 9 passenger.

INSTRUMENTATION: Speedometer, odometer, fuel level gauge. Warning lights for battery, oil pressure, generator, brake system warning, directional/hazard lights, high beam, and engine coolant temperature.

OPTIONS AND PRICES: Silverado Package (RPO YE9). Deluxe bench seat. Bonus cab Custom bench seat crew cab bonus seats. regular cab and bonus cab Custom vinyl bench seat. Crew cab Custom vinyl bench seat. Conventional two-tone paint. Exterior Decor Package (RPO ZY5). Special Big Dooley two-tone paint. California emissions requirement. 5.0 liter V-8 (RPO LE9 or RPO LF3). 5.7 liter V-8 (RPO L05). 7.4 liter V-8 (RPO LE8). 6.2 liter diesel V-8. 3-spd. automatic trans. (RPO MX1). 4-spd. manual overdrive trans. 4-spd. automatic trans. with overdrive (RPO MXO). Optional axle ratios. Locking rear differential (RPO G80). Heavy-duty power brakes for V10 and V20 (RPO J55). Chromed rear bumper (RPO VF1). Chromed rear step bumper for Fleetside only (RPO V42). Painted rear step bumper (RPO V43). Chromed front bumper guards (RPO V31). Camper Special chassis equipment (RPO Z81). Glide-Out spare tire carrier (RPO P11). Side-mounted spare tire carrier for Fleetside only (RPO P13). Quartz electric clock (RPO U35). Not available when UM6 radio is specified. Includes RPO Z53 voltmeter, temperature and oil pressure gauges. Cold Climate Package. Not available when RPO C60 air conditioning or RPO B3J diesel equipment is specified. Includes special insulation, RPO K81 66 amp generator, special heater and defroster, RP0 KO5 engine block heater, anti-freeze protection to -32 degrees and RPO UA1 heavy-duty battery (RPO V10). Engine oil cooling system (RPO KC4). Not avail. with RPO L25E engine or RPO B3J. Heavy-duty radiator (RPO VO1). Heavy-duty radiator and transmission oil (RPO VO2). Avail. only with RPO MX1 or RPO MXO transmission are specified. Not avail. with RPO L25 engine or RPO VO1 are specified. Decor Value Package. Includes blacked painted radiator grille and headlight bezels, and special body stripe located between body feature lines on front fenders, pickup box and across the tailgate. Not avail. on bonus cab, crew cab and Stepside models. Not available with the following options: RPO YE9, RO5, V22, PA6, N90, B84 or B85. Requires RPO ZY1 solid paint and blackwall or white lettered tires are specified (RPO YJ6). Power door lock system (RPO AU3). Color-keyed front floor mats (RPO B32). Requires RPO YE9. Gauge Package. Includes voltmeter, engine coolant temperature and oil pressure (RPO Z53). 66 amp Delcotron generator. Standard on V30 except when RPO LE8 engine is ordered (RPO K81). 94 amp Delcotron generator. Included with LE8 engine on V30 models (RPO K22). Tinted glass-all windows (RPO AO1). Halogen high-beam headlamps. Avail. only when RPO V22 or RPO YE9 is specified (RPO TT5). 600 watts engine block heater. Not avail. when RPO BK3 or RPO LF3 engine is specified (RPO KO5). Heavy-duty front heater (RPO C42). Avail. only with RPO B3J is specified. Not avail. with RPO C60 air conditioning. Automatic front locking hubs. Avail. only for V10 (RPO X6Z). Cargo lamp (RPO UF2). Dome lamp (RPO C91). Roof marker lamps. Avail. for V20 only. Standard for V30 (RPO UO1). Cigarette lighter. Included when RPO Z62 or YE9 is specified (RPO U37); Exterior left and right side below eye-level mirrors: Painted (RPO D44), stainless steel (RPO D45). Camper type stainless steel left and right side exterior mirrors (RPO DF2). Senior West Coast type painted exterior left and right side mirrors (RPO DG5). Black body side molding. Avail. for Fleetside only (RPO B84). Bright body side molding. Avail. for Fleetside only (RPO B85). Custom Package (RPO YG1). Avail. for Fleetside only. Includes wheel opening moldings, RPO B84, RPO B96 and bright trim for front sidemarker lamps and taillights. Deluxe Package (RPO YG3). Avail. for Fleetside only. Not avail. with RPO YG1 or RPO RO5. Includes bright trim for front side marker lamps and taillights. Wheel opening molding (RPO B96). Avail. only with RPO ZY6. Door edge guards (RPO B93). Operating Convenience Package (RPO ZQ2). Includes RPO AU3 Power door locks and RPO A31 Power windows. AM radio (RPO U63). AM/FM radio (RPO U69). AM/FM stereo radio (RPO U58). AM/FM stereo radio with stereo cassette tape player (RPO UN3). Electronically tuned AM/FM stereo radio with Seek-Scan, stereo cassette player and clock (RPO UM6). Windshield antenna (RPO U76). Pickup box side rails (RPO D73). Transfer case shield (RPO NY7). Front quad shock absorbers (RPO Z75). Electronic speed control (RPO K34). Not avail. for V10 with MM7 trans. or V20 and V30 with LS9, LT9 and LE8 with MM4 trans. Heavy-duty front springs (RPO F60). Not avail. for V30. For V10 and V20 series includes heavy-duty front and rear shock absorbers. Recommended for snowplow use for V10. ComforTilt steering wheel (RPO N33). Not avail. when RPO MM3 was specified. Auxiliary fuel tank (RPO NL2). Two front towing hooks (RPO V76). Bright metal wheelcovers, for V10 only (RPO PO1). Special wheelcovers, for V20 only (RPO PA1). Rallye wheels, V10 only (RPO N67). Styled wheels (RPO PA6). Aluminum cast wheels (RPO N90). Dual rear wheels for V30 only (RPO RO5). Power windows (RPO A31). Sliding rear window (RPO A28). Intermittent windshield wiper system (RPO CD4).

HISTORICAL FOOTNOTES: The 1987 full-size pickup was the most popular truck produced by Chevrolet.

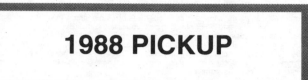

1988 PICKUP

Chevrolet introduced its new range of full-size four-wheel drive pickups on April 23, 1987 as 1988 models. The new trucks were produced at three assembly plants — Fort Wayne, Ind.; Pontiac, Mich. and Oshawa, Ont. Adding sales appeal as well as representing a new avenue of versatility were the extended cab models with optional 6 passenger seating. While the wheelbases of the new models were unchanged, they were longer and wider than the older models. The exterior was 3.5 inches narrower but the interior had more leg and shoulder room as well as more seat travel. The new model's doors were larger and extended upward into the roof line and downward nearly to the bottom of the rocker. The new doors along with a low step-up height and high headroom made for ease of entry and exit. The Fleetside box measured 49.15 inches between the wheel wells and 63.8 inches between the side panels. Numerous features such as flush side glass, modular-assembled bonded-flush windshield, single-piece door frames, and robotic welding marked the latest four-wheel drive Chevrolet trucks as very advanced vehicles. Chevrolet went to great lengths to improve the fit and finish of its 1988 models. The use of hidden roof pillar and built-in drip rails eliminated matching problems on door cuts. The back of the cab and the front of the pickup box were both mounted on a single, one-piece fixture. This bracket eliminated mismatch of the two sections, especially when the box was loaded.

The new model's front end was fitted with a single-piece grille which eliminated potential molding mismatch with single headlamps at each corner. The Silverado was equipped with dual halogen headlamps. Structural rigidity was improved with double panel construction for roof, hood, fenders, doors and pickup box. One of the most apparent features of the new generation Chevrolet truck was its greatly increased glass area which, at 4,256 sq. in. was one-third larger than the older model's. The use of a bonded, angled and curved backlite was credited with reducing glare. To improve visibility in poor weather, the wiper pattern was enlarged.

Improved anti-corrosion protection was a high priority for designers of the Chevrolet. The all-welded pickup box had a seamless floor without bolts for enhanced corrosion resistance. Two-sided galvanized steel was used for all major exterior panels except the roof. All exterior sheet metal was primer dipped and anti-stone protection was applied to the lower fenders, door and pickup box. Both the windshield and backlite was constructed without mitered corners. The front bumper was devoid of attaching bolts. This had the dual result of improving appearance while also removing another source of potential corrosion. Prior to painting, all sheet metal panels were immersion-washed to remove contaminants for better paint adhesion. A uniprime ELPO dip treatment drew the protective primer into recessed areas. The color coat/clear coat paint provided a hard, high-luster finish. The color selection for 1988 consisted of brandywine metallic, sandstone metallic, pacific blue metallic, Adobe gold metallic, Sable black metallic, quicksilver metallic, spice brown metallic, Summit white, flame red and iced blue metallic. Three optional exterior two-tone schemes were offered. The Conventional two-tone placed the accent color below the lower styling line. The Special two-tone included a multi-stripe decal at the upper styling line and the accent color below. The Deluxe two-tone featured a multi-stripe decal at the upper styling line and the accent color between the decal and the lower feature line.

1988 Chevrolet K10 Suburban Scottsdale

In place of the former K10, K20 and K30 designations (and the short-lived V prefix), the 1988 four-wheel drive designations for Chevrolet's 1/2 ton, 3/4 ton and one ton models were K1500, K2500 and K3500. No Stepside models were offered.

Chevrolet used three well-known names for the trim packages available for 1988. The base package was the Cheyenne, which was depicted as "a new value standard in full-size work trucks." The mid-range Scottsdale was described as "a big step up in a sensible blend of function and form." The Silverado, regarded as "the finest expression of the new '88 Chevy full-size pickup", remained the top-of-the line trim package. Standard interior features on all models were the following items: Right and left hand armrests, instrument panel-mounted ashtray, right-side coat hook (also a left-hand unit on extended cabs), painted areas in the same color as the exterior primary color; interior trim identical to seat trim, color-keyed molded plastic door trim panels, left-door jam switch operated dome light, tinted glass in all windows on extended cab models, heater and defroster with side window defoggers, inside-operated hood lock release, speedometer, odometer and fuel gauges, warning lights for generator, oil pressure, engine coolant temperature, safety belt, service/parking brake, direction/hazard signal and high beams; insulation and sound-deadening material installed on firewall, under floor mats and on extended cab-rear quarter and cab back panels; storage box located on right side of instrument panel with beverage holder on inside of door, instrument cluster and cab interior lights, shift point indicator light with manual transmission and gasoline engine, 4x4 lighted display, 10 in. inside day/night rearview mirror, foam-padded, full-width bench seat and folding back rear with vinyl trim, safety belts for all seating positions, 15.25 in. soft black plastic 4-spoke steering wheel. Energy-absorbing steering column, left and right side padded vinyl sunshades, front chrome bumper, molded plastic argent painted grille, single electric low-tone horn, black plastic hubcaps with 4x4 identification, backup lights integral with tail lamps, two rectangular headlights, front and rear directional and parking lamps, front side marker lamps, removable tailgate with embossed Chevrolet lettering, mechanical jack and wheel wrench, painted silver wheels and electric two-speed windshield wipers and washers. all models were fitted with new anti-theft door locks in the form of sliding levers integrated into the door trim panels.

Contents of the Cheyenne included Cheyenne designation on rear cab side pillars and a choice of five interior colors: Gray, blue, saddle, beige or garnet.

The Scottsdale Package (RPO Z62) had the following equipment in addition to or replacing that of the Cheyenne level: Dual electric high-note and low-note horn, Scottsdale nameplates on rear cab side pillars, chrome front bumper with black rub strip, Chevrolet block lettering decal on tailgate, standard bench seat with cloth upholstery and folding backrest in same color selection as Scottsdale, grained plastic interior door panels with soft-vinyl upper trim, integral armrests, map products and Scottsdale identification, color-keyed door-sill plates, color-keyed rubber floor mats (front compartment only on bonus cab), full-length mystic-colored insulated cloth headliner with matching retainer moldings, left and right-side coat hooks, and Scottsdale identification on door trim panels.

The Silverado Package (RPO YE9), included all Scottsdale features plus the following: Hood and cab-to-fender insulators, Deluxe front end appearance with dark argent grille and quad rectangular halogen headlamps, Deluxe bright-accented front bumper rub strip, bright accent body side moldings, bright accent wheel-opening molding (Fleetside single rear wheel models only), deluxe tailgate trim with Chevrolet lettering over bright aluminum applique, Silverado identification on cab back pillars, Custom Vinyl seat trim in gray, blue, beige, garnet or saddle (or at no extra cost-Custom Cloth seat trim), soft-vinyl two-tone door trim panels with integral armrests, map pockets, door closing assist straps and Silverado identification, color-keyed full-length carpeting, carpeted cowl/kick panel with insulator, carpeted cab back panels, color-keyed headliner, cloth-covered sunshades with left-hand storage strap and right-hand vanity mirror, Custom four-spoke steering wheel and cigarette lighter in ashtray.

The 4x4 Chevrolets were fitted with a new independent front suspension utilizing a new wire-form design for the upper control arms that were lighter and stronger than the components previously used. Torsion bar springs and jounce bumpers were connected to the lower control arms. The torsion bars were computer selected to correspond with the truck's GVW rating and balance with the rear springs. The frame used on 4x4 trucks had an additional front cross member located under the transmission case. The 4x4 trucks also had a new "Shift-On-The-Fly Instra-Trac" transfer case system allowing for shifting from two-wheel drive to four-wheel drive high and back without stopping at any speed. The front axle disconnect system locked the front hubs automatically when the single lever operated the four-wheel drive system was pulled backward. This shifter was located in the center of the cab floor and was connected directly to the transfer case rather than using cables. In two-wheel drive the front-axle disconnect allowed the front wheels to turn freely. In four-wheel drive the transfer case split the power and directed it equally to the front and rear wheels. The K1500 was available with an optional Off-Road Chassis Package consisting of a front differential carrier, engine and transfer case shields, front stabilizer bar, Delco/Bilstein high-pressure gas shock absorbers and heavier front and rear jounce bumpers. The standard V-6 engine for the K1500 and K2500 series had a new one-piece rubber oil pan gasket to help prevent oil leakage. As a mid-year treat Chevrolet introduced a new K1500 Sportside model on the 117.5 in. wheelbase chassis with a 6.5 ft. box, fiberglass rear fenders (side panels) flanked by functional steps to aid in loading and unloading. The Sportside was available with any trim level and most appearance, convenience and performance options offered for other 4x4 models. This truck body style identification was E62. Also introduced during the latter part of the 1988 year was a new instrument cluster featuring enhanced cluster graphics that increased clarity of instrument readings at all light levels.

I.D. DATA: Unchanged from 1987. The tenth entry, the letter J represented the 1988 model year.

Series K1500-1/2 ton 262 V-6-cyl. 117.5 in. 131.5 in. wheelbase. Suburban: 129.5 in. wheelbase and standard 305 V-8

Model	Body Type	MSRP
CK10703	6.5 ft. Sportside Pickup	$11,906
CK10703	6.5 ft. Fleetside Pickup	$11,755
CK10903	8.0 ft. Fleetside Pickup	$12,040
CK10753	6.5 ft. Extended Pickup	$12,881*
CK10953	8 ft. Extended Pickup	$13,081
CV 10906	Suburban Panl. Drs.	$14,955
CV10906	Suburban Tailgate	$14,995

* Add $2322 for diesel engine and equipment on CK10903
Add $2518 for diesel equipment on CK10953.
Add $3108 for diesel equipment on Suburbans.

Series K2500-3/4 ton 262 V-61. 131.5 in. wheelbase. (Suburban-129.5 in. wheelbase). Crew and bonus cab: 164.5 in. wheelbase, Suburban weight with standard 350 V-8

Model	Body Type	MSRP
CK20903	Chassis and Cab	$13,433
CK20953	Chassis & Ext. Cab	$11,948
CK20903	8 ft. Fleetside Pickup E63	$12,204[1]
CK20753	6.5 ft. Extended Cab	$13,321[2]
CK20953	8.0 ft. Extended Cab	$13,521
CK20906	Suburban Panl. Drs.	$16,389[3]
CV20906	Suburban Tailgate	$16,429

NOTE 1: Add $1719.88 to price of E63 for RPO C6P.
Add $1077 to price of chassis & cab for B3J.
Add $1209 to price of E63 with C6P for B3J diesel equipment.
Add $2684 to price of E63 for B3J diesel equipment.

NOTE 2: Add $1450 to price of CK20953 for C6P.
Add $2423 to price of CK20753 and CK20953 for B3J.
Add $1209 to price of CK20953 with C6P for B3J.

NOTE 3: Add $2283 to price of Suburbans for B3J diesel equipment.

Series K3500-1 ton 350 V-8. 131.5 in. wheelbase. Crew and bonus cab: 164.5 in. wheelbase

Model	Body Type	MSRP
CK30903	Chassis & Cab	$13,533[1]
CK30903	8 ft. Fltside Pickup	$13,957
CV30943	Chassis & Cab Bonus Cab	$15,600
CV30943	Chassis & Cab Crew	$16,114
CV30943	HD Chassis & Cab Bonus	$16,000
CV30943	HD Chassis & Cab Crew	$16,508

NOTE 1: Add $1811.12 for B3J diesel equipment.

STANDARD ENGINE: All K1500, K2500 models: 262 V-6 (LB4 ordering code). Engine Type: Vortex OHV, V-6-cylinder. Cast iron block. Bore x Stroke: 4.0 in. x 3.48 in. Lifters: Hydraulic. Fuel Induction: Electronic fuel injection. Compression Ratio: 9.3:1. Displacement: 262 cu. in. (4.3 liters). Horsepower: Net: 160 @ 4000 rpm. Torque: Net: 235 lb.-ft. @ 2400 rpm. Oil refill capacity: 5 qt. with filter change. Fuel Requirements: Regular unleaded.

STANDARD ENGINE: K2500 with C6P and V3500 and K3500 models: Optional for K1500 and K2500 models: 350 V-8 (LO5 ordering code). Engine Type: OHV, V-8. Cast iron block and cylinder head. Bore x Stroke: 4.0 in. x 3.48 in. Lifters: Hydraulic. Number of main bearings-5. Fuel Induction: Electronic fuel injection. Compression Ratio: 8.6:1. K1500 and K2500: 9.3:1. Displacement: 350 cu. in. (5.7 liters). Horsepower: K3500: Net: 185 @ 4000 rpm. K1500 and K2500: 210 @ 4000 rpm. Torque: K3500: Net 295 lb.-ft. @ 2400 rpm. K1500 and K2500: 300 lb.-ft. @ 2800 rpm. Oil refill capacity: 5 qt. with filter change. Fuel Requirements: Regular unleaded. Optional: K1500 and K2500: 305 V-8, Ordering Code: LO3. Engine Type: OHV, V-8. Cast iron block and alloy iron cylinder head. Key features include chain drive camshaft and forged steel connecting rods. This engine was produced in U.S. or Canada. Bore x Stroke: 3.74 in. x 3.48 in. Lifters: Hydraulic. Number of main bearings-5. Fuel Induction: Electronic fuel injection. Compression Ratio: 9.2:1. Displacement: 305 cu. in. (5.0 liters). Horsepower: Net: 175 @ 4000 rpm. Torque: Net: 270 lb.-ft. @ 2400 rpm. Oil refill capacity: 5 qt. with filter change. Fuel Requirements: Regular unleaded.

OPTIONAL ENGINE: K3500 models: Ordering Code: L19: 454 V-8. Engine Type: OHV, V-8. Cast iron block and alloy iron cylinder head. Bore x Stroke: 4.30 in. x 4.0 in. Lifters: Hydraulic. Number of main bearings-5. Fuel Induction: Electronic fuel injection. Compression Ratio: 7.9:1. Displacement: 454 cu. in. (7.4 liters). Horsepower: 230 @ 3600 rpm. Torque: 385 lb.-ft. @ 1600 rpm. Oil refill capacity: 5 qt. with filter change. Fuel Requirements: Regular unleaded.

OPTIONAL ENGINE: K2500: Ordering Code LH6. Not available for in California. This engine was produced by GM-Detroit Diesel Allison Division. Engine Type: OHV, diesel V-8. Bore x Stroke: 3.98 in. x 3.80 in. Lifters: Hydraulic. Number of main bearings-5. Fuel Induction: Gear driven mechanical pump. Compression Ratio: 21.3:1. Displacement: 379.4 cu. in. (6.2 liters). Horsepower: 126 @ 3600 rpm. (140 @ 3600 rpm with automatic transmission). Torque: 240 @ 2000 rpm. (247 lb.-ft. @ 2000 rpm with automatic transmission). Oil refill capacity: 7 qt. with filter change. Fuel Requirements: Diesel.

OPTIONAL ENGINE: K3500 and V3500 models: Ordering Code LL4. This engine was produced by GM-Detroit Diesel Allison Division. Engine Type: OHV, diesel V-8. Bore x Stroke: 3.98 in. x 3.80 in. Lifters: Hydraulic. Number of main bearings-5. Fuel Induction: Fuel injection. Compression Ratio: 21.3:1. Displacement: 379.4 cu. in. (6.2 liters). Horsepower: 143 @ 3600 rpm. Torque: 257 lb.-ft. @ 2000 rpm. Oil refill capacity: 7 qt. with filter change. Fuel Requirements: Diesel.

CHASSIS FEATURES: Semi-perimeter design, all-welded channel beam frame with boxed front end. Dimensions: K1500 and K2500 regular cab: 2.18 x 7.48 x 0.134 in. K1500 extended cab: 2.18 x 7.48 x 0.165 in. K2500 regular cab with C6P: 2.18 x 7.48 x 0.213 in. K2500 extended cab: 2.31 x 7.48 x 0.165 in. K2500 extended cab with C6P: 2.18 x 7.48 x 0.244 in. K3500 regular cab: 2.18 x 7.48 x 0.213 in. K3500 extended cab: 2.18 x 7.48 x 0.244 in. V3500 models: 2.788 x 7.74 x 0.244 in. Section modules: K1500 regular cab: 3.46; K1500 extended cab: 4.30; K2500: 4.30; K2500 with C6P: 6.48; K3500 regular cab: 5.61; K3500 extended cab: 6.48, V3500: 7.33.

SUSPENSION AND RUNNING GEAR: Front Suspension: Torsion bar springs. K1500 Capacity: 3860 lb. K2500 and K3500 capacity: 3750 lb. V3500: Tapered leaf springs. Capacity: 4500 lb. Shock absorber dia.: K1500; 25mm; K2500, K3500 and V3500: 32mm. 32mm optional for K1500. 1.00 in. stabilizer optional for all series except V3500 which had a standard 1.25 in. bar standard. Optional rating: K1500: RPO F44/F60: 6100 lb. K2500: 8600 lb. GVW. K3500: 10,000 lb. GVW. Rear Suspension: Semi-elliptical 2-stage, 4-leaf for K1500; 6-leaf for K2500; 6-leaf plus 1-leaf auxiliary for K3500. K1500 capacity: 3750 K2500 capacity: 4800 K3500 capacity: 7500 lb. V3500: Semi-elliptical 2-stage, 9-leaf. Capacity: 7000 lb. Shock absorber dia.: K1500: 25mm; K2500, K3500 and V3500: 32mm. 32mm optional for K1500. Optional Rating: See above for GVW ratings. Front Axle Type and Capacity: Independent, GM or K1500; Spicer on K2500 and K3500. Capacity: K1500 regular cab: 3925; K1500 extended cab: 4800; K2500 and K3500: 4250 V3500: Spicer full-floating. Capacity: 4500, manual hub locks. Optional: K1500: 3925 capacity; K1500 extended cab: 4800 lb.; All other K series: 4250 lb. Rear Axle Type: Semi-floating for K1500; Full-floating for K2500, K3500 and V3500. GM manufacture for all series. Capacity: K1500: 3750, K2500: 6000; K3500, V3500: 7500 lb. Optional: K2500: Regular cab: 4800 lb.; K250 extended cab: 6000; K3500: 7500. Final Drive Ratio: The following transmission designations were used by Chevrolet: MM4: 4-spd. manual; MM5: 5-spd. manual overdrive; MX1: 3-spd. automatic; MXO: 4-spd. automatic. All ratios are with standard emission equipment. Standard: K1500, K2500: 3.42:1. Optional: 3.73:1. All engine/transmission combinations except K2500 with LL4 diesel engine which had standard 3.73:1 ratio and optional 4.10:1 ratio, and K2500 with 5.7 liter V-8 and C6P which also had an optional 4.56:1 ratio. Standard: K3500: 4.10:1 with 5.7 liter V-8 with 4.56:1 optional; 3.42:1 standard for 7.4 liter V-8 with 3.73 and 4.10:1 optional; 6.2 liter diesel (LL4) had standard 4.10:1 ratio with 4.56:1 optional. Standard for V3500: 3.73:1 with 5.7 liter and manual 4-spd. trans.; 4.10:1 with 3-spd. auto. trans.; with 7.4 liter V-8; 4.10:1 with LL4 diesel. Optional: 4.10 and 4.56:1 for 5.7 liter V-8 with man. 4-spd.; 4.56:1 with 5.7 liter V-8 with 3-spd. auto. trans.; 4.10 and 4.56:1 for 7.4 liter V-8; 4.56:1 for LL4 diesel. Transfer Case: K1500, K2500, K3500: New Process 241. Single lever. Ratios: 2.72:1, 1.00:1. K3500 with RPO RO5: Borg Warner 1370: Ratios: 2.69:1, 1.00:1. The Borg Warner unit has a right hand side power take-off. Brakes: Type: Hydraulic, power assisted. Dimensions: K1500: Front: Disc: 11.86 in. x 1.00 in. Rear: Drums: 10.0 x 2.25 in. K1500 regular cab with RPO F44/F60 had 11.57 in. x 1.25 in. front disc brakes. K2500 regular cab: Front: Disc: 11.57 in. x 1.20 in. Rear: Drums: 11.15 in. x 2.75 in. K2500 extended cab: Front Disc: 11.57 in. x 1.25 in. Rear: 10.0 in. x 2.25 in. drums. All K2500 with 8600 lb. GVW Package had 12.50 in. x 1.26 in. front disc brakes and 13.0 in. x 2.5 in. rear drum brakes. K3500 all models: Front: Disc: 12.50 in. x 1.26 in. Rear: Drum: 13.00 in. x 2.50 in. V3500 all models: Front Disc: 12.54 in. x 1.54 in. Rear: Drums: 13.0 in. x 3.5 in. Wheels: K1500 and K2500: 16 x 6.5, 6-stud disc. K3500 and V3500: 16.0 x 6.0. Tires: K1500 Sportside and regular cab: LT225/75R-16C steel belted radial. K1500 extended cab: LT245/75R-16C. K2500 all models: LT245/75R-16E. K3500: LT225/75RD. V3500 all models: 7.50-16D tubeless nylon. Optional: K1500: LT225/75R16C, blackwall, LT225/75R16C on-off road; blackwall, white stripe or white lettered. Available for K10903 only with the following engines: LB4, LO3 and LH6 and RPO GVT4 axle; and K10703 with LB4 or LO3 engine with RPO GT4 axle. LT265/75R16C blackwall or white letter, on-off road. Optional K2500: LTR225/75R16D steel belted radial blackwall or white stripe, LT245/75R16E highway or on-off road, LT225/75R16D blackwall, on-off road, LT245/75R16E blackwall (K20903 only). Optional: K3500: LT225/75R16D, blackwall, LT245/75R16E blackwall, LT245/75R16E on-off road blackwall, LT245/75R16E blackwall, 7.50 x 16D highway and on-off road. Optional: V3500: 7.50x 16D tubeless nylon, dual rear, LT215/85R16D dual rear tubeless steel belted radial, LT235/85R16E. Steering: Integral power. Ratio: K1500 regular cab Sportside and Fleetside: 17.44:1. K1500 extended cab model K10753: 18.8:1, model K10953: 17.44:1. K2500 regular cab: 17.44:1. K2500 extended cab: K20753: 18.88:1; model K20953: 17.44:1. K3500 regular cab: 127.44:1. K3500 extended cab: 17.44:1. V3500: 13.5:1. Turning Diameter (curb-to-curb): K1500 regular cab Sportside: 40.3 ft. K1500 regular cab Fleetside: 44.4 ft. K1500 extended cab Model K10753: 47.9 ft. Model K10953: 52.2 ft. K2500 regular cab: 44.4 ft. (with C6P: 45.1 ft.). K2500 extended cab: Model K20753: 47.9 ft. Model K20953: 52.2 ft. K3500 regular cab: 52.2 ft. V3500: 54.5 ft. Transmission: Standard K1500/2500: With gasoline engines: RPO MM5-spd. manual with overdrive fully-synchronized. Transmission Ratios: 4.02, 2.32, 1.40, 1.00.

0.73:1; reverse: 3.74:1. Standard: K3500, V3500 and K2500 with C6P, and K1500 and K2500 with diesel engine: RPO MM4 4-spd. SM465 manual, synchromesh on top three gears (optional: K1500/2500). Transmission ratios: 6.55, 3.58, 1.70, 1.00:1, reverse: 6.09:1. Optional: All series: RPO MX1-3-spd. 400 automatic. Transmission ratios: 2.48, 1.48, 1.0:1, reverse: 2.08:1. Optional: K1500/2500, (except K2500 regular cab and extended cab chassis cab, and all V3500 models): RPO MXO-4-spd. automatic overdrive 700R4: 3.06, 1.63, 1.0, 0.70:1, Reverse: 2.29:1.

VEHICLE DIMENSIONS: Wheelbase: All series regular cab: 117.5 in. 131.5 in. extended cab: 6.5 ft. box models: 141.5 in.; 8.0 ft. box models: 155.5 in.; V3500 models: 164.5 in. Overall Length (without rear bumper): K1500 Sportside: 194.0 in. K1500 regular cab: 194.1 in. K1500 extended cab: Model K10753 (6.5 ft. box): 223.0 in. K10953 (8.0 ft. box): 237.0 in. K2500 regular cab: 212.6 in. K2500 extended cab: Model K20753: 223.0 in. Model K20953: 237.0 in. K3500 Regular cab: 212.6 in. V3500: 246.4 in. Front/Rear Tread: 74 in./74 in. Overall Height: K1500 all models: 73.8 in. K2500 regular cab: 74.3 in. (75.8 in. if equipped with C6P). K2500 extended cab: 74.4 in. (75.8 in. if equipped with C6P). K3500 75.8 in. V3500: 76.3 in. Width: All models except V3500 and those equipped with RO5: 76.8 in. V3500: 79.6 in. V3500 and K3500 with RO5: 107.3 in. Front/Rear Overhang: 117.5 in. wheelbase. pickups: 34.9 in./41.6 in. 131.5 in. wheelbase pickups: 34.9 in./46.5 in. extended cab: 34.9/46.5 in. Chassis cab models: 34.9/41.8 in. Tailgate: Width and Height: K1500 Sportside: 50.9 x 19.3 in. All others: 62.0 in. x 19.3 in. Approach/Departure Degrees: K1500 117.5 in.: 22/28. Ground Clearance (Front/Rear in inches): K1500 Sportside and Fleetside: 8.6/9.0. K1500 extended cab: 9.2/9.6. K2500 regular cab: 8.7/7.7 (with C6P: 7.8/8.1). K2500 extended cab: Model K20753: 9.2/8.2, model K20953: 9.2/8.1. K3500 Regular and extended cab: 9.2/8.1 (with RO5 dual rear wheels: 7.2/7.4). V3500: 8.3/7.8. Front headroom, all models: 40.0 in. Front legroom, all models: 41.7 in. Front shoulder room, all models: 66.0 in.

CAPACITIES: Fuel Tank: All K series: 25.0 gal. All V3500 models: 20 gal. Optional: Models K10903, K10753, K10953, K20903, K20953, K30903: 34 gal. V3500 models: 20 gal.

ACCOMMODATIONS: Seating Capacity: Pickup, extended cab and chassis cab models: 3 passenger. Optional: Extended cab: 6 passenger. Suburban: 6 passenger. Optional: 9 passenger.

INSTRUMENTATION: Speedometer, odometer, fuel level gauge. Warning lights for battery, oil pressure, generator, brake system warning, directional/hazard lights, high beam, and engine coolant temperature.

OPTIONS AND PRICES: Pre-cleaner air cleaner (RPO K46). Air conditioning (RPO C60). Deluxe front appearance (RPO V22). Optional axle ratio. Locking rear differential (RPO G80). Heavy-duty Delco Freedom auxiliary battery with 540 cold cranking amps. Not avail. with B3J diesel equipment. (RPO TP2). Heavy-duty Delco Freedom battery with 630 cold cranking amps (RPO UA1). Painted rear step bumper (RPO V43). Chromed front Deluxe bumper with rub strip. Included with RPO Z62 and RPO YE9. (RPO VB3). Rear step bumper with rub strip (RPO VB3). Black front bumper guards. Requires RPO VG3. (RPO V 27). Spare tire and wheel carrier. Not avail. with K10753. (RPO P13): No charge. Heavy-duty chassis. Included with B3J diesel equip. (RPO F44). Cold Climate Package. Not avail. with RPO C60. Includes UA1 battery, KO5 block heater and C42 heater. (RPO V10). Console. Requires bucket seats. (RPO D55). Engine oil cooling system. Not available with B3J diesel equip. with RPO MXO transmission requires VO2 cooling, included with Z82 trailering option. (RPO KC4). Heavy-duty radiator. Not avail. with RPO VO2. (RPO VO1). Heavy-duty radiator and transmission oil cooler. Requires RPO MXO transmission. Included with RPO Z823. (RPO VO2). Scottsdale Trim Package. (RPO Z62). Silverado Trim Package (RPO YE). Rear window defogger. Requires RPO YE9 or RPO Z62. Not avail. with RPO A28 window or RPO AJ1 glass. (RPO C49). 5.0 liter V-8 (RPO LO3). 5.7 liter V-8 (RPO LO5). Locking fuel filler cap (RPO NO5). Front color-keyed floor mats. Requires RPO YE9 (RPO B32). Rear color-keyed floor mats. Requires RPO AM7 seat and RPO B32. (RPO B33). Gauge Package. Includes voltmeter, engine coolant temperature and oil pressure gauges. Included with RPO YE9. (RPO Z53). Deep tinted glass with light tinted rear window. Not avail. with RPO AJ1. Includes RPO A20 window. (RPO AA3). Deep, tinted glass. Not avail. with RPO C49 defogger. Includes A20 window. (RPO AJ1). Heavy-duty trailering wiring harness. Included with RPO Z82. (RPO UY7). Halogen headlights. Not avail. with RPO V22 or RPO YE9. (RPO TT4). Engine block heater. Included with RPO V10. (RPO KO5). Front heavy-duty heater. Included with V10; not avail. with RPO C60. (RPO C42). Cargo area lamp (RPO UF2). Roof marker lamps. Not avail. with Calif. emissions. (RPO UO1). Dome and reading lamps. Included with RPO TR9. (RPO C95). Cigarette lighter (RPO U37). Auxiliary lighting (RPO TR9). Below eye-level black painted exterior mirrors (RPO D44). Below eye-level stainless steel exterior mirrors (RPO D45). Camper-type exterior mirrors (RPO DF2). Black body side moldings (RPO B84). Bright body side moldings (RPO B85). Black wheel opening moldings (RPO B74). Bright wheel opening moldings (RPO B96): No charge. Operating Convenience Package. Includes power door locks and power windows. (RPO ZQ2). Conventional two-tone paint (RPO YZ2). Special two-tone paint (RPO YZ3). Deluxe two-tone paint (RPO 243.00. AM radio (RPO U63). Electronically tuned AM/FM stereo radio with Seek-Scan. Electronically tuned AM/FM stereo radio with Seek-Scan and digital clock (RPO UM7). Electronically tuned AM/FM stereo radio with Seek-Scan and stereo cassette tape player (RPO UK5). Electronically tuned AM/FM stereo radio with Seek-Scan, stereo cassette tape player and digital clock (RPO UM6). Electronically tuned AM/FM stereo radio with Seek-Scan, stereo cassette tape player with Search and Repeat, graphic equalizer and digital clock (RPO UX1). Fixed mast antenna. Included with RPO U63, UK4, UK5, UM6, or UX1 radio. (RPO U73). Rear folding seat. Requires bucket or split front seat. (RPO AM7). Heavy-duty front and rear shock absorbers (RPO F51). Off-road skid plate. Avail. for K1500 only. (RPO NZZ). Electronic speed control (RPO K34). 4x4 Sports Graphic Package (RPO BQ4). Heavy-duty front springs. Not avail. with B3J diesel equip. (RPO F60). Front stabilizer bar (RPO F59). ComforTilt steering wheel (RPO N33). Custom steering wheel (RPO N31). Sport steering wheel (RPO NKJ3). Striping (RPO D85). Fuel tank with approx. 34 gal. total vehicle capacity. Not avail. with K10753. (RPO NJ8). Two front towing hooks (RPO B76). Weight distributing platform trailer hitch (RPO VR4). Heavy-duty trailering special equipment (RPO Z82). 4-speed manual trans. (RPO MM4). 4-spd. auto. with overdrive trans (RPO MXO). Wheelcovers (RPO PO1). Rallye wheels (RPO N67). Swing-out quarter windows (RPO A20). Sliding rear window (RPO A28). Intermittent windshield wipers (RPO CD4).

HISTORICAL FOOTNOTES: Total sales of Chevrolet's light duty trucks for 1988 totalled 1,336,407. Total pickup sales were 515,637. Suburban sales totalled 66,637.

1989 PICKUP

The "New Generation" full-size Chevrolet 4x4 pickups, along with their two-wheel drive counterparts, entered the 1989 model year as the best-selling vehicles in General Motors' lineup. To meet consumer demand second shifts and overtime were added to production schedules. Also a good sign of the times for Chevrolet was the news from GM surveys that the C/K trucks had the highest customer satisfaction of any full-size pickup.

Numerous changes were found in the1989 models, in terms of their engineering as well as option availability and content. The regular cab and extended cab models had a new optional 4x4 sport graphic package that, said Chevrolet, "makes a bold statement for performance enthusiasts." Complementing the Sportside 4x4 was a new Fleetside Sport with a 6.5 foot pickup box that was available as an interim 1989 model. The 4x4 Sport models featured blackout wheel opening flares. bumpers, mirrors and front air dam with tow hooks.

1989 Chevrolet K1500 Suburban

A new Borg-Warner Model 1370 transfer case with an electrically actuated synchronizer was offered for K3500 models with dual rear wheels. This allowed RPO RO5 dual rear wheels to be ordered on one-ton pickups and chassis cabs. This development also increased the available GVW on the K3500 to 10,000 lbs.

Extensive changes took place in the brake system used on the K series trucks. The parking brake cable was given increased protection form rocks and road debris by revised routing and the addition of a shield. To reduce brake noise a new molded, semi-metallic brake lining material was used. A new 28MT starter motor and revised engine dipstick lettering was used on 6.2 liter diesel engine-equipped models.

The following exterior colors were carried over from 1988: Brandywine metallic, sandstone metallic, Adobe gold metallic, sable black metallic, quicksilver metallic, summit white, and flame red. They were joined by three new colors: Smoke blue metallic, caramel brown metallic and midnight blue metallic. Initially, a new dark cognac replaced saddle in the interior color offering. But in January, 1989 saddle rejoined beige, blue, garnet and grey as available interior colors. Beige and gray were not available for the extended cab models. Three optional exterior two-tone schemes were again offered. The Conventional two-tone (RPO ZY2) was available only on single rear wheel Fleetside Pickup models. The primary color was applied to the areas above the lower side body styling crease line (including the roof) with the secondary color below the crease line. Outlined block "Chevrolet" decal lettering was applied to the tailgate. A bright trim panel with lettering was applied when the Silverado option was ordered. The Special two-tone (RPO ZY3) also available only on single rear wheel Fleetside pickup models, included a multi-stripe decal applied over the paint break at the beltline. One color paint was applied to the areas above the decal (including the roof) with the second color applied to the areas below. The Deluxe two-tone (RPO ZY4) also featured a multi-stripe decal at the upper styling line and the accent color between the decal and the lower feature line. Outlined block "Chevrolet" decal lettering was applied to the tailgate. A bright trim panel with lettering was applied when the Silverado option was ordered.

The base Cheyenne, mid-range Scottsdale and top-ranked Silverado trim levels were carried into 1989 with minor changes. Features of the Cheyenne were as follows: Single electric low-note horn, power steering, rear brake drums with anti-lock brake system (operated in two-wheel drive only), front chromed bumper, molded plastic grille painted light argent with dark argent air intake areas, single rectangular headlights, silver painted wheels with black hub ornament, All-Season steel-belted radial tires (steel-belted radials on RPO RO5), winch-type spare tire carrier mounted under frame (K1500 models only), right and left side fixed arm mirrors with adjustable heads and black finish, right and right hand padded armrests integral with door panels with grained molded plastic finish, 3 passenger all-vinyl trim bench seat with folding backrest, right hand coat hook, left hand coat hook on extended cab models, dark gray doorsill plate, dome light with switch in left hand door jamb, embossed black rubber floor mats, tinted glass in all windows on extended cab models, padded, color-keyed left and right side sunshades, 4-spoke steering wheel, 10 in. rearview mirror, vinyl headliner (same color as retainer moldings, extended cab models had cab upper, lower and side trim panels and a molded cloth color-keyed headliner with matching retainer moldings), insulation on dash panel, cowl top and sides and doors, extended cab rear quarter and back panels and on floor covering, extra insulation for models with diesel engines.

The Scottsdale trim (RPO Z62) contained the following equipment in addition to or in place of that of the Cheyenne trim level: Front chromed bumper with bumper rub stripes, black plastic body side moldings, black wheel opening lip moldings (except on K2500 C6P models, dual rear wheel models and Sportside models), color-keyed door panels with grained molded plastic finish with soft vinyl trim, map pocket and Scottsdale emblem, left and right hand coat hooks, color-keyed doorsill plate, dome light with switches in left and right side door jambs, color-keyed embossed rubber floor mats, full width storage tray behind seat on floor, color-keyed cloth headliner; regular cab and extended cab models had matching retainer moldings, color-keyed door pillar and roof side panels, additional insulation on headliner.

The Silverado trim package (RPO YE9), had this equipment in addition to or replacing that of the Scottsdale trim level: Additional electric high-note horn, Silverado exterior nameplates, dual rectangular halogen headlights, black plastic body side moldings with bright trim, hood and cab-to-fender insulators, door panels with two-toned soft vinyl over plastic trim with map pocket and door closing assist straps and Silverado emblem, color-keyed floor carpeting, padded, color-keyed left and right hand sunshades with cloth covering, storage strap on left side unit and visor mirror on right side unit, gauges for voltmeter, engine coolant temperature and oil pressure (replacing warning lights), cigarette lighter in ashtray, color-keyed carpet on cab back panel and insulation on regular cab back panels. The content of the V3500 Crew and bonus cab models differed slightly from the other four-wheel drive Chevrolets. The Cheyenne package had white painted wheels, bright metal hubcaps with black trim (on single rear wheel models) exterior below eye-level mirrors, an AM radio, 2-spoke steering wheel and a heavy-duty heater/defogger.

The primary differences in the Scottsdale Package for the V3500 models included a full-width front bench seat in a choice of dual-woven cloth vinyl trim or all-vinyl pigskin trim, door-operated dome lamp with bright trim, color-keyed rubber floor mats (for front compartment only of bonus cab), full-length, Mystic-colored insulated headliner with matching retainer moldings and insulation under cowl panel or headliner and on cab back panel. The V3500 Silverado Package differed from the content for other 4x4 Chevrolets in having bright body side and rear moldings with black trim plus bright wheel opening (Fleetside single rear wheel models only), under hood reel-type lamp, bright tailgate applique, bright trim for front marker lights and taillights, special color-keyed plastic door panels with cloth inserts, vinyl stowage pockets, plus carpeting and bright trim strips on lower portions, right hand visor mirror, headlamp warning buzzer, 2-spoke steering wheel with bright trim on horn buttons, mystic-colored full-length cloth headliner and extra-thick insulation on floor panels.

1989 Chevrolet K1500 pickup with optional 4x4 Sport graphics

I.D. DATA: Unchanged from 1988. The tenth entry, the letter K represented the 1989 model year.

The 1989 prices listed are those revised in January, 1989

Series K1500-1/2 ton 262 V-6-cyl. 117.5 in. 131.5 in. wheelbase. Suburban: 129.5 in. wheelbase and standard 305 V-8

Model	Body Type	MSRP
CK10703	6.5 ft. Sportside Pickup	$12,516
CK10703	6.5 ft. Fleetside Pickup	$12,365
CK10903	8.0 ft. Fleetside Pickup	$12,560*
CK10753	6.5 ft. Extended Pickup	$13,491
CK10953	8 ft. Extended Pickup	$13,691
CV10906	Suburban Panl. Drs.	$15,565
CV10906	Suburban Tailgate	$15,605

* Add $2322 for diesel engine and equipment on CK10903
Add $2518 for diesel equipment on CK10953.
Add $3108 for diesel equipment on Suburbans.

Series K2500-3/4 ton 262 V-61. 131.5 in. wheelbase. (Suburban-129.5 in. wheelbase). Crew and bonus cab: 164.5 in. wheelbase, Suburban weight with standard 350 V-8

Model	Body Type	MSRP
CK20903	Chassis and Cab	$14,428.00
CK20953	Chassis & Ext. Cab	$12,558.00
CK20903	8 ft. Fleetside Pickup E63	$12,814.00
CK20753	6.5 ft. Extended Cab	$13,931.00
CK20953	8.0 ft. Extended Cab	$14,131.00
CK20906	Suburban Panl. Drs.	$16,998.76
CV20906	Suburban Tailgate	$17,038.76

Add $1719.88 to price of E63 for RPO C6P.
Add $1077 to price of chassis & cab for B3J.
Add $1209 to price of E63 with C6P for B3J diesel equipment.
Add $2684 to price of E63 for B3J diesel equipment.
Add $1450 to price of CK20953 for C6P.
Add $2423 to price of CK20753 and CK20953 for B3J.
Add $1209 to price of CK20953 with C6P for B3J.
Add $2283 to price of Suburbans for B3J diesel equipment.

Series K3500-1 ton 350 V-8. 131.5 in. wheelbase. Crew and bonus cab: 164.5 in. wheelbase

Model	Body Type	MSRP
CK30903	Chassis & Cab	$14,442.88[1]
CK30903	8 ft. Fleetside Pickup	$14,442.88[1]
CV30943	Chassis & Cab Bonus Cab	$16,509.76
CV30943	Chassis & Cab Crew	$17,023.76
CV30943	HD Chassis & Cab Bonus	$16,905.00
CV30943	HD Chassis & Cab Crew	$17,418.00

NOTE 1: Add $1811.12 for B3J diesel equipment.

STANDARD ENGINE: All K1500, K2500 models: 262 V-6 (LB4 ordering code). Engine Type: Vortex OHV, V-6-cylinder. Cast iron block. Bore x Stroke: 4.0 in. x 3.48 in. Lifters: Hydraulic. Fuel Induction: Electronic fuel injection. Compression Ratio: 9.3:1. Displacement: 262 cu. in. (4.3 liters). Horsepower: Net 160 @ 4000 rpm. Torque: Net 235 lb.-ft. @ 2400 rpm. Oil refill capacity: 5 qt. with filter change. Fuel Requirements: Regular unleaded.

STANDARD ENGINE: K2500 with C6P and V3500 and K3500 models: Optional for K150 and K2500 models: 350 V-8 (LO5 ordering code). Engine Type: OHV, V-8. Cast iron block and cylinder head. Bore x Stroke: 4.0 in. x 3.48 in. Lifters: Hydraulic. Number of main bearings-5. Fuel Induction: Electronic fuel injection. Compression Ratio: K3500: 8.6:1. K1500 and K2500: 9.3:1. Displacement: 350 cu. in. (5.7 liters). Horsepower: Net: 190 @ 4400 rpm. K1500 and K2500: 210 @ 4000 rpm. Torque: Net 300 lb.-ft. @ 2400 rpm. K1500 and K2500: 300 lb.-ft. @ 2800 rpm. Oil refill capacity: 5 qt. with filter change. Fuel Requirements: Regular unleaded. Optional: K1500 and K2500: 305 V-8, Ordering Code: LO3. Engine Type: OHV, V-8. Cast iron block and alloy iron cylinder head. Key features include chain drive camshaft and forged steel connecting rods. This engine was produced in U.S. or Canada. Bore x Stroke: 3.74 in. x 3.48 in. Lifters: Hydraulic. Number of main bearings-5. Fuel Induction: Electronic fuel injection. Compression Ratio: 9.2:1. Displacement: 305 cu. in. (5.0 liters). Horsepower: Net: 175 @ 4000 rpm. Torque: Net: 270 lb.-ft. @ 2400 rpm. Oil refill capacity: 5 qt. with filter change. Fuel Requirements: Regular unleaded.

STANDARD ENGINE: K3500 models with rear wheels. Optional: other K3500 models. Ordering Code: L19: 454 V-8. Engine Type: OHV, V-8. Cast iron block and alloy iron cylinder head. Bore x Stroke: 4.00 in. x 4.0 in. Lifters: Hydraulic. Number of main bearings-5. Fuel Induction: Electronic fuel injection. Compression Ratio: 7.9:1. Displacement: 454 cu. in. (7.4 liters). Horsepower: 230 @ 3600 rpm. Torque: 385 lb.-ft. @ 1600 rpm. Oil refill capacity: 5 qt. with filter change. Fuel Requirements: Regular unleaded.

OPTIONAL ENGINE: K1500 and K2500. Ordering Code LH6. Not available in California for K2500. This engine was produced by GM-Detroit Diesel Allison Division. Engine Type: OHV, diesel V-8. Bore x Stroke: 3.98 in. x 3.80 in. Lifters: Hydraulic. Number of main bearings-5. Fuel Induction: Gear driven mechanical fuel injection. Compression Ratio: 21.3:1. Displacement: 379.4 cu. in. (6.2 liters). Horsepower: 126 @ 3600 rpm. (140 @ 3600 rpm with automatic transmission). Torque: 240 lb.-ft. @ 2000 rpm. (247 lb.-ft. @ 2000 rpm with automatic transmission). Oil refill capacity: 7 qt. with filter change. Fuel Requirements: Diesel.

OPTIONAL ENGINE: K3500 and V3500 models. Ordering Code LL4. This engine was produced by GM-Detroit Diesel Allison Division. Engine Type: OHV, diesel V-8. Bore x Stroke: 3.98 in. x 3.80 in. Lifters: Hydraulic. Number of main bearings-5. Fuel Induction: Fuel injection. Compression Ratio: 21.3:1. Displacement: 379.4 cu. in. (6.2 liters). Horsepower: 143 @ 3600 rpm. Torque: 257 lb.-ft. @ 2000 rpm. Oil refill capacity: 7 qt. with filter change. Fuel Requirements: Diesel.

CHASSIS FEATURES: Semi-perimeter design, all-welded channel beam frame with boxed front end. Dimensions: K1500 and K2500 regular cab: 2.18 x 7.48 x 0.134 in. K1500 extended cab: 2.18 x 7.48 x 0.165 in. K2500 regular cab with C6P: 2.18 x 7.48 x 0.213 in. K2500 extended cab: 2.31 x 7.48 x 0.165 in. K2500 extended cab with C6P: 2.18 x 7.48 x 0.244 in. K3500 regular cab: 2.18 x 7.48 x 0.213 in. K3500 extended cab: 2.18 x 7.48 x 0.244 in. V3500 models: 2.788 x 7.74 x 0.244 in. Section modules: K1500 regular cab: 3.46; K1500 extended cab: 4.30; K2500: 4.30; K2500 with C6P: 6.48; K3500 regular cab: 5.61; K3500 extended cab: 6.48, V3500: 7.33.

SUSPENSION AND RUNNING GEAR: Front Suspension: Torsion bar springs. K1500 Capacity: 3860 lb. K2500 and K3500 capacity: 3750 lb. V3500: Tapered leaf springs. Capacity: 4500 lb. Shock absorber dia.: K1500: 25mm; K2500, K3500: 32mm. 32mm optional for K1500. 1.00 in. stabilizer optional for all series except V3500 which had a standard 1.25 in. bar. Optional rating: K1500: RPO F44/F60: 6100 lb. GVW. K2500: 8600 lb. GVW. K3500: 10,000 lb. GVW. Rear Suspension: Semi-elliptical 2-stage, 4-leaf for K1500; 6-leaf for K2500; 6-leaf plus 1-leaf auxiliary for K3500. K1500 capacity: 3750 lb. K2500 capacity: 4800 lb. K3500 capacity: 7500 lb. V3500: Semi-elliptical 2-stage, 9-leaf. Capacity: 7000 lb. Shock absorber dia.: K1500: 25mm; K2500, K3500 and V3500: 32mm. 32mm optional for K1500. Optional Rating: See above for GVW ratings. Front Axle Type and Capacity: Independent, GM or K1500; Spicer on K2500 and K3500. Capacity: K1500 regular cab: 3925; K1500 extended cab: 4800; K2500 and K3500: 4250 V3500: Spicer full-floating. Capacity: 4500, manual hub locks. Optional: K1500: 3925 lb. capacity; K1500 extended cab: 4800 lb. All other K series: 4250 lb. Rear Axle Type: Semi-floating for K1500; Full-floating for K2500, K3500 and V3500. GM manufacture for all series. Capacity: K1500: 3750 lb.; K2500: 6000 lb.; K3500, V3500: 7500 lb. Optional: K2500: Regular cab: 4800 lb.; K250 extended cab: 6000; K3500: 7500 lb. Final Drive Ratio: The following transmission designations were used by Chevrolet: MM4: 4-spd. manual; MM5: 5-spd. manual overdrive; MX1: 3-spd. automatic; MXO: 4-spd. automatic: All ratios are with standard emission equipment. Standard: K1500, K2500: 3.42:1. Optional: 3.73:1. All engine/transmission combinations except LL4 diesel engine which had standard 3.73:1 ratio and optional 4.10:1 ratio, and K2500 with 5.7 liter V-8 and C6P which also had an optional 4.56:1 ratio. Standard: K3500: 4.10:1 with 5.7 liter V-8 with 4.56:1 optional; 3.42:1 standard for 7.4 liter V-8 with 3.73 and 4.10:1 optional; 6.2 liter diesel (LL4) had standard 4.10:1 ratio with 4.56:1 optional. Standard for V3500: 3.73:1 with 5.7 liter and manual 4-spd. trans.; 4.10:1 with 3-spd. auto. trans.; 3.73:1 with 7.4 liter V-8; 4.10:1 with 6.2 liter diesel. Optional: 4.10 and 4.56:1 for 5.7 liter V-8 with man. 4-spd.; 4.56:1 for 5.7 liter V-8 with 3-spd. auto. trans.; 4.10 and 4.56:1 for 7.4 liter V-8; 4.56:1 for LL4 diesel. Transfer Case: K1500, K2500, K3500: New Process 241. Single lever. Ratios: 2.72:1, 1.00:1. K3500 with RPO RO5: Borg Warner 1370: Ratios: 2.69:1, 1.00:1. The Borg Warner unit has a right hand side power take-off. Brakes: Type: Hydraulic, power assisted. Dimensions: K1500: Front: Disc: 11.86 in. x 1.00 in. Rear: 10.0 x 2.25 in. K1500 regular cab with RPO F44/F60 had 11.57 in. x 1.25 in. front disc brakes. K2500 regular cab: Front: Disc: 11.57 in. x 1.20 in. Rear: Drums: 11.15 in. x 2.75 in. K2500 extended cab: Front Disc: 11.57 in. x 1.25 in. Rear: 10.0 in. x 2.25 in. drums. All K2500 with 8600 lb. GVW Package had 12.50 in. x 1.26 in. front disc brakes and 13.0 in. x 2.5 in. rear drum brakes. K3500 all models: Front: Disc: 12.50 in. x 1.26 in. Rear: Drum: 13.00 in. x 2.50 in. V3500 all models: Front Disc: 12.54 in. x 1.54 in. Rear: Drums: 13.0 in. x 3.5 in. Wheels: K1500 and K2500: 16 x 6.5, 6-stud disc. K3500 and V3500: 16.0 x 6.0. Tires: K1500 Sportside and regular cab: LT225/75R-16C steel belted radial. K1500 extended cab: LT245/75R16C. K2500 all models: LT245/75R-16E. K3500: LT225/75RD. V3500 all models: 7.50-16D tubeless nylon. Optional: K1500: LT225/75R16C, blackwall, LT225/75R16C on-off road; blackwall, white stripe or white lettered. Available for K10903 only with the following engines: LB4, LO3 and LH6 and RPO GVT4 axle; and K10703 with LB4 or LO3 engine with RPO GT4 axle. LT265/75R16C blackwall or white letter, on-off road. Optional K2500: LTR225/75R16D steel belted radial blackwall or white stripe, LT245/75R16E highway or on-off road, LT225/75R16D blackwall, on-off road, LT245/75R16E blackwall (K20903 only). Optional: K3500: LT225/75R16D, blackwall, LT245/75R16E blackwall, LT245/75R16E on-off road blackwall, LT245/75R16E blackwall, 7.50 x 16D highway and on-off road. Optional: V3500: V30943 only: 7.50x 16D tubeless nylon, dual rear, LT215/85R16D dual rear tubeless steel belted radial; LT235/85R16E. Steering: Integral power. Ratio: K1500 regular cab Sportside and Fleetside: 17.44:1. K1500 extended cab model K10753: 18.8:1; model K10953: 17.44:1. K2500 regular cab: 17.44:1. K2500 extended cab: 17.44:1. V3500: 13.5:1. Turning Diameter (curb-to-curb): K1500 regular cab Sportside: 40.3 ft. K1500 regular cab Fleetside: 40.3 ft. K1500 extended cab Model K10753: 47.9 ft. Model K10953: 52.2 ft. K2500 regular cab: 44.4 ft. (with C6P: 45.1 ft.). K2500 extended cab: Model K20753: 47.9 ft. Model 52.2 ft. K3500 regular cab: 45.1 ft. K3500 extended cab: 52.2 ft. V3500: 54.5 ft. Transmission: Standard K1500/2500: With gasoline engines: RPO MM5-5-spd. manual with overdrive fully-synchronized. Transmission Ratios: 4.02, 2.32, 1.40, 1.00. 0.73:1; reverse: 3.74:1. Standard: K3500, V3500 and K2500 with C6P, and K1500 and K2500 with diesel engine: RPO MM4 4-spd. manual. SM465 manual, synchromesh on top three gears (optional: K1500/2500). Transmission ratios: 6.55, 3.58, 1.70, 1.00:1; reverse: 6.09:1. Optional: All series: RPO MX1-3-spd. 400 automatic. Transmission ratios: 2.48, 1.48, 1.0:1, reverse: 2.08:1. Optional: K1500/2500, (except K2500 regular cab and extended cab chassis cab, and all V3500 models): RPO MXO-4-spd. automatic overdrive 700R4: 3.06, 1.63, 1.0, 0.70:1, Reverse: 2.29:1.

VEHICLE DIMENSIONS: Wheelbase: All series regular cab: 117.5 in. 131.5 in. extended cab: 6.5 ft. box models: 141.5 in.; 8.0 ft. box models: 155.5 in.; V3500 models: 164.5 in. Overall Length (without rear bumper): K1500 Sportside: 194.0 in. K1500 regular cab: 194.1 in. K1500 extended cab: Model K10753 (6.5 ft. box): 223.0 in. K10953 (8.0 ft. box): 237.0 in. K2500 regular cab: 212.6 in. K2500 extended cab: Model K20753: 223.0 in. Model K20953: 237.0 in. K3500 Regular cab: 212.6 in. V3500: 246.4 in. Front/Rear Tread: 74 in./74 in. Overall Height: K1500 all models: 73.8 in. K2500 regular cab: 74.3 in. (75.8 in. if equipped with C6P). K2500 extended cab: 74.4 in. (75.8 in. if equipped with C6P). K3500 75.8 in. V3500: 76.3 in. Width: All models except V3500 and those equipped with RO5: 76.8 in. V3500: 79.6 in. V3500 and K3500 with RO5: 107.3 in. Front/Rear Overhang: 117.5 in. wheelbase. pickups: 34.9 in./41.6 in. 131.5 in. wheelbase pickups: 34.9 in./46.5 in. extended cab: 34.9/46.5 in. Chassis cab models: 34.9/41.8 in. Tailgate: Width and Height: K1500 Sportside: 50.9 x 19.3 in. All others: 62.0 in. x 19.3 in. Approach/Departure Degrees: K1500 117.5 in.: 22/28. Ground Clearance (Front/Rear in inches): K1500 Sportside and Fleetside: 8.6/9.0. K1500 extended cab: 9.2/9.6. K2500 regular cab: 8.7/7.7 (with C6P: 7.8/8.1). K2500 extended cab: Model K20753: 9.2/8.2, model K20953: 9.2/8.1. K3500 Regular and extended cab: 9.2/8.1 (with RO5 dual rear wheels: 7.2/7.4). V3500: 8.3/7.8. Front headroom, all models: 40.0 in. Front legroom, all models: 41.7 in. Front shoulder room, all models: 66.0 in.

CAPACITIES: Fuel Tank: All K series: 25.0 gal. All V3500 models: 20 gal. Optional: Models K10903, K10753, K10953, K20903, K20953, K30903: 34 gal. V3500 models: 20 gal.

ACCOMMODATIONS: Seating Capacity: Pickup, extended cab and chassis cab models: 3 passenger. Optional: Extended cab: 6 passenger. Suburban: 6 passenger. Optional: 9 passenger.

INSTRUMENTATION: Speedometer, odometer, fuel level gauge. Warning lights for battery, oil pressure, generator, brake system warning, directional/hazard lights, high beam, and engine coolant temperature.

OPTIONS AND PRICES: Pre-cleaner air cleaner (RPO K46): $44.00. Air conditioning (RPO C60): $781.00. Deluxe front appearance (RPO V22): $145.00. Optional axle ratio: $38. Locking rear differential (RPO G80): $252. Heavy-duty Delco Freedom auxiliary battery with 540 cold cranking amps. Not avail. with B3J diesel equipment. (RPO TP2): $134.00. Heavy-duty Delco Freedom battery with 630 cold cranking amps RPO UA1: $56.00 Painted rear step bumper (RPO V43): $130.00. Chromed front Deluxe bumper with rub strip. Included with RPO Z62 and RPO YE9. (RPO VB3): $229.00. Rear step bumper with rub strip (RPO VB3): $229.00. Black front bumper guards. Requires RPO VG3. (RPO V27): $32.00. Spare tire and wheel carrier. Not avail. with K10753. (RPO P13): No charge. Heavy-duty chassis. Included with B3J diesel equip. (RPO F44): $230.00. Cold Climate Package. Not avail. with RPO C60. Includes UA1 battery, KO5 block heater and C42 heater. (RPO V10): $134.00. Console. requires bucket seats. (RPO D55): $114.00. Engine oil cooling system. Not available with B3J diesel equip. with RPO MXO transmission requires VO2 cooling, included with Z82 trailering option. (RPO KC4): $126.00. Heavy-duty radiator. Not avail. with RPO VO2. (RPO VO1): $56.00. Heavy-duty radiator and transmission oil cooler. Requires RPO MXO transmission. Included with RPO Z823. (RPO VO2): $63.00. Scottsdale Trim Package. (RPO Z62): $223. Silverado Trim Package (RPO YE9): $665.00. Rear window defogger. Requires RPO YE9 or RPO Z62. Not avail. with RPO A28 window or RPO AJ1 glass. (RPO C49): $1564.00. 5.0 liter V-8 (RPO LO3): $555.00. 5.7 liter V-8 (RPO LO5): $755.00. Locking fuel filler cap (RPO NO5): $18.00. Front color-keyed floor mats. Requires RPO YE9. (RPO B32): $16.00. Rear color-keyed floor mats. Requires RPO AM7 seat and RPO B32. (RPO B33): $12.00. Gauge Package. Includes voltmeter, engine coolant temperature and oil pressure gauges. Included with RPO YE9. (RPO Z53): $42.00. Deep tinted glass with light tinted rear window. Not avail. with RPO AJ1. Includes RPO A20 window. (RPO AA3): $98.00. Deep, tinted glass. Not avail. with RPO C49 defogger. Includes A20 window. (RPO AJ1): $144.00. Heavy-duty trailering wiring harness. Included with RPO Z82. (RPO UY7): $46.00. Halogen headlights. Not avail. with RPO V22 or RPO YE9. (RPO TT4): $24.00. Engine block heater. Included with RPO V10 (RPO KO5): $33.00. Front heavy-duty heater. Included with V10; not avail. with RPO C60. (RPO C42): $45.00. Cargo area lamp (RPO UF2): $36.00. Roof marker lamps. Not avail. with Calif. emissions. (RPO UO1): $52.00. Dome and reading lamps. Included with RPO TR9. (RPO C95): $33.00. Cigarette lighter (RPO U37): $25.00. Auxiliary lighting (RPO TR9): $90.00. Below eye-level black painted exterior mirrors (RPO D44): $52.00. Below eye-level stainless steel exterior mirrors (RPO D45): $87.00. Camper-type exterior mirrors (RPO DF2): $100.00. Black body side moldings (RPO B84): $59.00. Bright body side moldings (RPO B85): $17.0. Black wheel opening moldings (RPO B74): $31.00. Bright wheel opening moldings (RPO B96): No charge. Operating Convenience Package. Includes power door locks and power windows. (RPO ZQ2): $344.00. Conventional two-tone paint (RPO YZ2): $132.00. Special two-tone paint (RPO YZ3): $215.00. Deluxe two-tone paint (RPO 243.00. AM radio (RPO U63): $122.00. Electronically tuned AM/FM stereo radio with Seek-Scan (RPO *K4): $268.00. Electronically tuned AM/FM stereo radio with Seek-Scan and digital clock (RPO UM7): $333.00. Electronically tuned AM/FM stereo radio with Seek-Scan and stereo cassette tape player (RPO UK5): $390.00. Electronically tuned AM/FM stereo radio with Seek-Scan, stereo cassette tape player and digital clock (RPO UM6): $454.00. Electronically tuned AM/FM stereo radio with Seek-Scan, stereo cassette tape player with Search and Repeat, graphic equalizer and digital clock (RPO UX1): $604.00. Fixed mast antenna. Included with RPO U63, UK4, UK5, UM6, or UX1 radio. (RPO U73): $41.00. Rear folding seat. Requires bucket or split front seat. (RPO AM7): $385.00. Heavy-duty front and rear shock absorbers (RPO F51): $36.00. Off-road skid plate. Avail. for K1500 only. (RPO NZZ): $95.00. Electronic speed control (RPO K34): $205.00. 4x4 Sports Graphic Package (RPO BQ4): $110.00. Heavy-duty front springs. Not avail. with B3J diesel equip. (RPO F60): $63.00. Front stabilizer bar (RPO F59): $40.00. ComforTilt steering wheel (RPO N33): $121.00. Custom steering wheel (RPO N31): $28.00. Sport steering wheel (RPO NKJ3): $7.0 with RPO YE9; $35.0 with RPO Z62. Striping (RPO D85): $69.00. Fuel tank with approx. 34 gal. total vehicle capacity. Not avail. with K10753. (RPO NJ8): $56.00. Two front towing hooks (RPO B76): $38.00. Weight distributing platform trailer hitch (RPO VR4): $164.00. Heavy-duty trailering special equipment (RPO Z82): $435.00 without B3J diesel equip.; $273.00 with B3J. 4-speed manual trans. (RPO MM4): $98.00 without B3J. 4-spd. auto. with overdrive trans (RPO MXO): $795.00. Wheelcovers (RPO PO1): $42.00. Rallye wheels (RPO N67): $75.00. Swing-out quarter windows (RPO A20): $43.00. Sliding rear window (RPO A28): $113.00. Intermittent windshield wipers (RPO CD4): $59.00.

HISTORICAL FOOTNOTES: Total production of Chevrolet's light duty trucks for 1989 totalled 1,309,837.

1990 PICKUP

The full-size K Pickup models, in conjunction with their two-wheel drive counterparts continued to be the best-selling vehicles in the GM lineup, accounting for three out of every ten light trucks sold by General Motors. Efforts by General Motors to simplify the production, ordering and sales of light-duty trucks resulted in a "deproliferation" of optional equipment. Many previously optional items were now either standard equipment on the 1990 models or included in larger option packages. The following low volume options were eliminated for 1990: RPO B84-Black body side molding, RPO B85-Bright body side molding, RPO K46-Pre-cleaner air cleaner, RPO PA6-Styled wheels, RPO UK4-AM/FM stereo radio with Seek-Scan, RPO UK5-AM/FM stereo radio with Seek-Scan and stereo cassette tape, RPO VDA-Headliner and color-keyed floor mats, RPO XHV, YHV and ZHV tires-LT225/75R16C, RPO XHO, XBL, YHO, YBL, ZHO, ZBL tires-LT245/75R16C, RPO XEU, YEU, ZEU tires-P25/75R15.

A heavy-duty version of the 4.3 liter V-6 with electronic fuel injection was standard on K2500 series pickups with C6P. It was also available as a credit option on the K3500 pickups. The primary features of this engine that set it apart from the standard V-6 included a lower 8.6:1 compression ratio and a larger, 3.0 in. low restriction exhaust system for improved performance in heavy-duty applications. The 7.4 liter V-8 now had electronic spark control to control spark knock. The standard and heavy-duty 6.2 liter diesel engines had different horsepower and torque ratings for 1990-actual engine output was not changed, however. Both the RPO LO3, 5.0 liter V-8 and the RPO LO5, 5.7 liter V-8 were upgraded for 1990 by the use of improved oil control rings, a redesigned rear crankshaft seal, a new camshaft sprocket design, the use of a non-asbestos intake manifold gasket and the adoption of heavy-duty intake valves.

The content of the base Cheyenne trim was substantially increased for 1990 by the addition of the following items (RPO numbers are included for reference purposes): RPO AO1-Tinted glass in all windows, RPO C42-Deluxe heater, RPO F59-1.00 in. dia. front stabilizer bar, RPO NJ8-34 gal. (approx.) fuel tank, standard for all models except K10703 and K10753, RPO TT4-Halogen headlights, RPO CCA heavy-duty, 630 cold cranking amps battery, standard for all gasoline engine models, RPO U37-Cigarette lighter, RPO U63-AM radio, RPO U73-Fixed mast radio antenna, RPO V76-Two front towing hooks, RPO Z53-Voltmeter, temperature and oil pressure gauges, and RPO CD4-Intermittent windshield wiper system.

Equipment added to the content of the Scottsdale trim level consisted of RPO B84-Black body side moldings, RPO N31-Custom steering wheel, RPO N67-Rallye wheels, standard on all models except those with RPO RO5 (dual rear wheels), RPO V22-Deluxe Front Appearance containing dark argent grille with bright trim, composite halogen headlights and a dual note horn; and RPO V27-front bumper guards with rub strip.

New standard features of the Silverado package were as follows: RPO A20-Swing-out rear quarter windows on extended cab models, RPO B32-Front removable color-keyed floor mats, RPO B33-Rear removable color-keyed floor mats on extended cab models, RPO NK3-Sport steering wheel and RPO UM7-Electronically-tuned AM/FM stereo radio with Seek-Scan and digital clock.

1990 Chevrolet K2500 extended cab short bed

Also included in the list of 1989 model year options that were part of other options for 1990 were these: RPO N33-ComforTilt steering wheel and RPO K34-Electronic speed control (now included in RPO ZQ3-Convenience Package), RPO D55-Console (now included in RPO A55 low back or RPO A95 bucket seats, RPO KO5-Engine block heater (now included in RPO V10-Cold Climate Package), RPO VR4-Weight distributing platform type trailer hitch (now included in RPO Z82-Heavy-duty trailering equipment), and RPO UF2-Cargo area light (now included in RPO TR9-Auxiliary lighting).

Following the lead of the previously released S-10 EL truck was a new K1500 "WT" Work Truck offering a specific level of features and limited option availability. The Work Truck was offered only in K10903/E63 form and had the Cheyenne trim except for a number of items specific to the Work Truck. These consisted of a dark charcoal painted front bumper, air deflector and bumper filler, blackout grille and special "W/T1500" body side decals with integrated Chevrolet Bowtie. This truck was available only in blue, red, silver or white. The only powerteam initially offered was the 4.3 liter Vortex V-6 and a 5-spd. manual transmission (MM5) with a 3.08:1 axle ratio. Effective December 8, 1989 the Work Truck was also offered with RPO MX1, the 3-speed automatic transmission. The following items comprised the Work Truck's standard equipment: Power steering, power brakes, rear-wheel anti-lock brake system (operative in two-wheel drive mode only), power front disc/rear drum brakes, double wall construction in cargo boxsides, tailgate, fenders and doors, All-Season steel-belted radial ply tires, electric speedometer, dome light, glove compartment with latched door and two-side galvanized exterior sheet metal surfaces (except for roof). Options for the Work Truck were limited to a single Preferred Equipment Group 2 Package consisting of the RPO F4 heavy-duty chassis, RPO F51 heavy-duty shock absorbers and RPO D44 painted below eye-level mirrors and the following individual items in addition to those previously mentioned: Air conditioning, optional axle ratio, locking differential, heavy-duty auxiliary battery, painted rear step bumper, heavy-duty chassis, Cold Climate Package, engine oil cooler, heavy-duty engine and transmission cooler, black painted below eye-level mirrors, AM radio, AM/FM stereo radio with

Seek-Scan, stereo cassette tape and digital clock, AM stereo/FM stereo radio and Seek-Scan, stereo cassette tape with search and repeat, graphic equalizer and digital clock; heavy-duty front and rear shock absorbers, wheelcovers and sliding rear window.

The content of the trim levels for the V3500 crew and bonus cab models was also revised for 1990. Added to the Cheyenne trim package were: RPO C91-Dome Light, RPO C91-Pulse windshield wiper system, RPO T63-Headlight warning buzzer, RPO UA1-Heavy-duty battery with 630 CCA, RPO UT5-AM radio (this item replaced RPO U63), RPO U37-Cigarette lighter and RPO NL2-Auxiliary fuel tank.

Three additional items were now included in the Silverado Package: RPO TR9-Auxiliary lighting, RPO V22-Deluxe Front Appearance Package and RPO YG3-Deluxe Molding Package. Several options for the V3500 that carried over for 1990 were revised. RPO K34-Electronic Speed Control and RPO N33-ComforTilt steering wheel was now part of RPO ZQ3, the Convenience Package. RPO B85-Body side molding was incorporated into RPO YG3, the Deluxe Molding Package which, in turn, was now included in the Silverado Package. The RPO V22, Deluxe Front Appearance Package now required the Silverado Package. Three options were no longer available for the V3500 models: RPO K46-Pre-cleaner air cleaner, RPO B93-door edge molding guards and RPO UU9-Electronically-tuned AM/FM stereo radio with clock.

Three new exterior colors were offered for 1990. Replacing Sable black metallic was mlack onyx, replacing midnight blue metallic was Catalina blue metallic, and replacing brandywine metallic was crimson red metallic. Carried over from 1989 were blue smoke metallic, caramel brown metallic, Adobe gold metallic and quicksilver metallic. A new garnet interior color was available for 1990. Both the Scottsdale and Silverado interiors had all-new molded seats. The regular cab models were now available with 60/40 seats.

Once again available were the three optional exterior two-tone schemes Conventional two-tone (RPO ZY2), Special two-tone (RPO ZY3) and the Deluxe two-tone (RPO ZY4). Their format and content were unchanged from those of 1989.

I.D. DATA: Unchanged from 1989. The tenth entry, the letter L represented the 1990 model year.

Model	Body Type	MSRP

Series K1500-1/2 ton 262 V-6-cyl. 117.5 in. 131.5 in. wheelbase (Suburban: 129.5 in. wheelbase and standard 350 V-8)

CK10903	8.0 ft. Worktruck	$13,020
CK10703	6.5 ft. Sportside Pickup	$14,300
CK10703	6.5 ft. Fleetside Pickup	$13,980
CK10903	8.0 ft. Fleetside Pickup	$14,255
CK10753	6.5 ft. Ext. Cab Fleetside	$14,929
CK10953	8.0 ft. Ext. Cab Fleetside	$15,204
CV10906	Suburban Panl. Drs.	$17,255
CV10906	Suburban Tailgate	$17,405
CV10906	Suburban Panl. Drs.	$15,565
CV10906	Suburban Tailgate	$15,605

The above prices were placed in effect on December 8, 1989. Subsequently these prices were effective with vehicles produced on and after April 2, 1990:

CK10903	8.0 ft. Worktruck	$12,470
CK10703	6.5 ft. Sportside Pickup	$13,750
CK10703	6.5 ft. Fleetside Pickup	$13,430
CK10903	8.0 ft. Fleetside Pickup	$13,705
CK10753	6.5 ft. Ext. Cab Fleetside	$14,379
CK10953	8.0 ft. Ext. Cab Fleetside	$14,654

Add $2335 for diesel equipment B3J on extended cab CK10953, $2530 on extended cab CK10753.
Add $3100 for B3J on Suburban tailgate and $3105 on Suburban panel doors.

K2500-3/4 ton 262 V-6. 131.5 in. wheelbase. (Suburban-129.5 in. wheelbase). Crew and bonus cab: 164.5 in. wheelbase, Suburban weight with standard 350 V-8

CK20903	Chassis & Cab	$15,234
CK20953	Ext. Cab Chassis & Cab	$16,264
CK20903	8.0 ft. Fleetside Pickup	$14,455
CK20903	8.0 ft. C6P Fleetside Pickup	$15,571
CK20753	6.5 ft. Extended Cab Pickup	$15,483
CK20953	8.0 ft. Extended Cab Pickup	$15,763
CK20953	8.0 ft. C6P Ext. Cab Pickup	$16,608

Add $1050 for B3J for CK20903 Chg. & Cab and CK20903 extended cab chassis & cab.
Add $1830 for B3J for CK20903 with C6P, add $2710 for B3J on CK20903.
Add $1835 for B3J for CK20953 with C6P, add $2435 for B3J for CK20953 add $2440 for CK20753 with C6P.

The above prices were placed in effect on December 8, 1989. Subsequently these prices were effective with vehicles produced on and after April 2, 1990:

CK20903	8.0 ft. Fleetside Pickup	$13,905
CK20903	8.0 ft. C6P Fleetside Pickup	$15,029
CK20753	6.5 ft. Extended Cab Pickup	$14,933
CK20953	8.0 ft. Extended Cab Pickup	$15,213
CK20953	8.0 ft. C6P Ext. Cab Pickup	$16,059

Series K3500-1 ton 350 V-8. 131.5 in. wheelbase. Crew and bonus cab: 164.5 in. wheelbase

CK30903	8.0 ft. Fleetside Pickup	$16,584
CK30953	8.0 ft. Ext. Cab Fleetside Pickup	$17,609
CK30903	Chassis & Cab, 131.5 in. wb.	$16,133
CK31003	Chassis & Cab, 135.5 in. wb.	$16,560*
CK31403	Chassis & Cab, 159.9 in. wb.	$16,675*
CK30953	Ext. Cab Chassis & Cab	$17,167

* Prices for these models were not available on December 8, 1989. These prices are those effective April 2, 1990.

Add $1868 for B3J for CK30953.
Add $2281 for B3J for CK30903.
Add $2287 for B3J for CK31003.
Add $1871 to CK30903 for B3J.
Add $1621 for B3J to price of CK31003.

CK30903 price was subsequently changed to $16,033 on vehicles produced on or after April 1, 1990.

The revised price for CK30953 was $17,059.
The revised price for CK30903 was $15,584.
The revised price for CK30953 was $16,619.

STANDARD ENGINE: All K1500, K2500 models: 262 V-6 (LB4 ordering code). Engine Type: Vortex OHV, V-6-cylinder. Cast iron block. Bore x Stroke: 4.0 in. x 3.48 in. Lifters: Hydraulic. Fuel Induction: Electronic fuel injection. Compression Ratio: For models under 8500 GVWR: 9.3:1. For models over 8500 lb. GVWR: 8.6:1. Displacement: 262 cu. in. (4.3 liters). Horsepower: Net: For models under 8500 lb. GVWR: 160 @ 4000 rpm. For models over 85900 lb. GVWR: 155 @ 4000 rpm. Torque: Net: For models under 8500 lb. GVWR: 235 lb.-ft. @ 2400 rpm. For models over 85900 lb. GVWR: 230 lb.-ft. @ 2400 rpm. Oil refill capacity: 5 qt. with filter change. Fuel Requirements: Regular unleaded.

OPTIONAL ENGINE: K1500, K2500, Standard:V3500 and K3500 models: Optional for K150 and K2500 models: 350 V-8 (LO5 ordering code). Engine Type: OHV, V-8. Cast iron block and cylinder head. Bore x Stroke: 4.0 in. x 3.48 in. Lifters: Hydraulic. Number of main bearings-5. Fuel Induction: Electronic fuel injection. Compression Ratio: K3500: 8.6:1. K1500 and K2500: 9.3:1. Displacement: 350 cu. in. (5.7 liters). Horsepower: K3500: Net: 190 @ 4000 rpm. K1500 and K2500: 210 @ 4000 rpm. Torque: Net 300 lb.-ft. @ 2400 rpm. K1500 and K2500: 300 lb.-ft. @ 2800 rpm. Oil refill capacity: 5 qt. with filter change. Fuel Requirements: Regular unleaded. Optional: K1500 and K2500: 305 V-8, Ordering Code: LO3. Engine Type: OHV, V-8. Cast iron block and alloy iron cylinder head. Key features was chain drive camshaft and forged steel connecting rods. This engine was produced in U.S. or Canada. Bore x Stroke: 3.74 in. x 3.48 in. Lifters: Hydraulic. Number of main bearings-5. Fuel Induction: Electronic fuel injection. Compression Ratio: 9.2:1. Displacement: 305 cu. in. (5.0 liters). Horsepower: Net: 175 @ 4000 rpm. Torque: Net: 270 lb.-ft. @ 2400 rpm. Oil refill capacity: 5 qt. with filter change. Fuel Requirements: Regular unleaded.

STANDARD ENGINE: K3500 models with dual rear wheels: Optional: other K3500 models. Ordering Code: L19: 454 V-8. Engine Type: OHV, V-8. Cast iron block and alloy iron cylinder head. Bore x Stroke: 4.30 in. x 4.0 in. Lifters: Hydraulic. Number of main bearings-5. Fuel Induction: Electronic fuel injection. Compression Ratio: 7.9:1. Displacement: 454 cu. in. (7.4 liters). Horsepower: 230 @ 3600 rpm. Torque: 385 lb.-ft. @ 1600 rpm. Oil refill capacity: 5 qt. with filter change. Fuel Requirements: Regular unleaded.

OPTIONAL ENGINE: K1500 and K2500: Ordering Code LH6. Not available in California for K2500. This engine was produced by GM-Detroit Diesel Allison Division. Engine Type: OHV, diesel V-8. Bore x Stroke: 3.98 in. x 3.80 in. Lifters: Hydraulic. Number of main bearings-5. Fuel Induction: Gear driven mechanical fuel injection. Compression Ratio: 21.3:1. Displacement: 379.4 cu. in. (6.2 liters). Horsepower: 126 @ 3600 rpm (140 @ 3600 rpm with automatic transmission). Torque: 240 lb.-ft. @ 2000 rpm. (247 lb.-ft. @ 2000 rpm with automatic transmission). Oil refill capacity: 7 qt. with filter change. Fuel Requirements: Diesel.

OPTIONAL ENGINE: K3500 and V3500 models: Ordering Code LL4. This engine was produced by GM-Detroit Diesel Allison Division. Engine Type: OHV, diesel V-8. Bore x Stroke: 3.98 in. x 3.80 in. Lifters: Hydraulic. Number of main bearings-5. Fuel Induction: Fuel injection. Compression Ratio: 21.3:1. Displacement: 379.4 cu. in. (6.2 liters). Horsepower: 143 @ 3600 rpm. Torque: 257 lb.-ft. @ 2000 rpm. Oil refill capacity: 7 qt. with filter change. Fuel Requirements: Diesel.

CHASSIS FEATURES: Semi-perimeter design, all-welded channel beam frame with boxed front end. Dimensions: K1500 and K2500 regular cab: 2.18 x 7.48 x 0.134 in. K1500 extended cab: 2.18 x 7.48 x 0.165 in. K2500 regular cab with C6P: 2.18 x 7.48 x 0.213 in. K2500 extended cab: 2.31 x 7.48 x 0.165 in. K2500 extended cab with C6P: 2.18 x 7.48 x 0.244 in. K3500 regular cab: 2.18 x 7.48 x 0.213 in. K3500 extended cab: 2.18 x 7.48 x 0.244 in. V3500 models: 2.788 x 7.74 x 0.244 in. Section modules: K1500 regular cab: 3.46; K1500 extended cab: 4.30; K2500: 4.30; K2500 with C6P: 6.48; K3500 regular cab: 5.61; K3500 extended cab: 6.48, V3500: 7.33.

SUSPENSION AND RUNNING GEAR: Front Suspension: Torsion bar springs. K1500 Capacity: 3860 lb. K2500 and K3500 capacity: 3750 lb. V3500: Tapered leaf springs. Capacity: 4500 lb. Shock absorber dia.: K1500: 25mm; K2500, K3500 and V3500: 32mm. 32mm optional for K1500. 1.00 in. stabilizer optional for all series except V3500 which had a standard 1.25 in. bar standard. Optional rating: K1500: RPO F44/F60: 6100 lb. GVW. K2500: 8600 lb. GVW. K3500: 10,000 lb. GVW. Rear Suspension: Semi-elliptical 2-stage, 4-leaf for K1500; 6-leaf for K2500; 6-leaf plus 1-leaf auxiliary for K3500. K1500 capacity: 3750 K2500 capacity: 4800 K3500 capacity: 7500 lb. V3500: Semi-elliptical 2-stage, 9-leaf. Capacity: 7000. Shock absorber dia.: K1500: 25mm; K2500, K3500 and V3500: 32mm. 32mm optional for K1500. Optional Rating: See above for GVW ratings. Front Axle Type and Capacity: Independent, GM or K1500; Spicer on K2500 and K3500. Capacity: K1500 regular cab: 3925; K1500 extended cab: 4800; K2500 and K3500: 4250 V3500: Spicer full-floating. Capacity: 4500, manual hub locks. Optional: K1500: 3925 capacity; K1500 extended cab: 4800 lb.; All other K series: 4250. Rear Axle Type: Semi-floating for K1500; Full-floating for K2500, K3500 and V3500. GM manufacture for all series. Capacity: K1500: 3750, K2500: 6000; K3500, V3500: 7500 lb. Optional: K2500: Regular cab: 4800 lb.; K250 extended cab: 6000; K3500: 7500. Final Drive Ratio: The following transmission designations were used by Chevrolet: MM4: 4-spd. manual; MM5: 5-spd. manual overdrive; MX1: 3-spd. automatic; MXO: 4-spd. automatic: All ratios are with standard emission equipment. Standard: K1500, K2500: 3.42:1. Optional: 3.73:1. All engine/transmission combinations except K2500 with LL4 diesel engine which had 3.73:1 ratio and optional 4.10:1 ratio, and 6.2 liter diesel (LL4) which also had an optional 4.56:1 ratio. Standard: K3500: 4.10:1 with 5.7 liter V-8 with 4.56:1 optional; 3.42:1 standard for 7.4 liter V-8 with 3.73 and 4.10:1 optional; 6.2 liter diesel (LL4) had standard 4.10:1 ratio with 4.56:1 optional. Standard for V3500: 3.73:1 with 5.7 liter and manual 4-spd. trans.; 4.10:1 with 3-spd. auto. trans.; 3.73:1 with 7.4 liter V-8; 4.10:1 with LL4 diesel. Optional: 4.10 and 4.56:1 for 5.7 liter V-8 with man. 4-spd.; 4.56:1 for 5.7 liter V-8 with 3-spd. auto. trans.; 4.10 and 4.56:1 for 7.4 liter V-8; 4.56:1 for LL4 diesel. Transfer Case: K1500, K2500, K3500: New Process 241. Single lever. Ratios: 2.72:1, 1.00:1. K3500 with RPO RO5: Borg Warner 1370: Ratios: 2.69:1, 1.00:1. The Borg Warner unit has a right hand side power take-off. Brakes: Type: Hydraulic, power assisted. Dimensions: K1500: Front: Disc: 11.86 in. x 1.00 in. Rear: Drums: 10.0 x 2.25 in. K1500 regular cab with RPO F44/F60 had 11.57 in. x 1.25 in. front disc brakes. K2500 regular cab: Front: Disc: 11.57 in. x 1.20 in. Rear: Drums: 11.15 in. x 2.75 in. K2500 extended cab: Front Disc: 11.57 in. x 1.25 in. Rear: 10.0 in. x 2.25 in. drums. All K2500 with 8600 lb. GVW Package had 12.50 in. x 1.26 in. front disc brakes and 13.0 in. x 2.5 in. rear drum brakes. K3500 and models: Front Disc: 12.50 in. x 1.26 in. Rear: Drum: 13.00 in. x 2.50 in. V3500 all models: Front Disc: 12.54 in. x 1.54 in. Rear: Drums: 13.0 in. x 3.5 in. Wheels: K1500 and K2500: 16 x 6.5, 6-stud disc. K3500 and V3500: 16.0 x 6.0. Tires: K1500 Sportside and regular cab: LT225/75R16C steel belted radial. K1500 extended cab: LT245/75R16C. K2500 all models: LT245/75R16-E. K3500: LT225/75RD, V3500 all models: 7.50-16D tubeless nylon. Optional: K1500: LT225/75R16C, blackwall, LT245/75R16C on-off road; blackwall, white stripe or white letter. Available for K10903 only with the following engines: LB4, LO3 and LH6 and RPO GVT4 axle; and K10703 with LB4 or LO3 engine with RPO GT4 axle. LT265/75R16C blackwall or white letter, on-off road. K2500: LTR225/75R16D steel belted radial blackwall or white stripe; LT245/75R16E highway or on-off road, LT225/75R16D blackwall, on-off road, LT245/75R16E blackwall (K20903 only). Optional: K3500: LT225/75R16D, LT245/75R16E blackwall, LT245/75R16E on-off road blackwall, LT245/75R16E blackwall, 7.50 x 16D highway and on-off road. Optional: V3500: V30943 only: 7.50x 16D tubeless nylon, dual rear, LT215/85R16D dual rear tubeless steel belted radial. Steering: Integral power. Ratio: K1500 regular cab Sportside and Fleetside: 17.44:1. K1500 extended cab model K10753: 18.8:1, model K10953: 17.44:1. K2500 regular cab: 17.44:1. K2500 extended cab: K20753: 18.88:1; model K20953: 17.44:1. K3500 regular cab: 17.44:1. K3500 extended cab: 17.44:1. Turning Diameter (curb-to-curb): K1500 regular cab Sportside: 40.3 ft. K1500 regular cab Fleetside: 44.4 ft. K1500 extended cab Model K10753: 47.9 ft. Model K10953: 52.2 ft. K2500 regular cab: 44.4 ft. (with C6P: 45.1 ft.). K2500 extended cab: Model K20753: 47.9 ft. Model 52.2 ft. K3500 regular cab: 45.1 ft. K3500 extended cab: 52.2 ft. K3500 54.5 ft. Transmission: Standard K1500/2500: With gasoline engines: RPO MM5-5-spd. manual with overdrive fully-synchronized. Transmission Ratios: 4.02, 2.32, 1.40, 1.00. 0.73:1; reverse: 3.74:1. Standard: K3500, V3500 and K2500 with C6P, and K1500 and K2500 with diesel engine: RPO MM4 4-spd. SM465 manual, synchromesh on top three gears (optional K1500/2500). Transmission ratios: 6.55, 3.58, 1.70, 1.00:1, reverse: 6.09:1. Optional: All series: RPO MX1-3-spd. 400 automatic. Transmission ratios: 2.48, 1.48, 1.0:1, reverse: 2.08:1. Optional: K1500/2500, (except K2500 regular cab and extended cab chassis cab, and all V3500 models): RPO MXO-4-spd. automatic overdrive 700R4: 3.06, 1.63, 1.0, 0.70:1, Reverse: 2.29:1.

VEHICLE DIMENSIONS: Wheelbase: All series regular cab: 117.5 in. 131.5 in. extended cab: 6.5 ft. box models: 141.5 in.; 8.0 ft. box models: 155.5 in.; V3500 models: 164.5 in. Overall Length (without rear bumper): K1500 Sportside: 194.0 in. K1500 regular cab: 194.1 in. K1500 extended cab K10753 (6.5 ft. box): 223.0 in. K10953 (8.0 ft. box): 237.0 in. K2500 regular cab: 212.6 in. K2500 extended cab: Model K20753: 223.0 in. Model K20953: 237.0 in. K3500 Regular cab: 212.6 in. V3500: 246.4 in. Front/Rear Tread: .74 in./74 in. Overall Height: K1500 all models: 73.8 in. K2500 regular cab: 74.3 in. (75.8 in. if equipped with C6P) K2500 extended cab: 74.4 in. (75.8 in. if equipped with C6P). K3500 75.8 in. V3500: 76.3 in. Width: All models except V3500 and those equipped with RO5: 76.8 in. V3500: 79.6 in. V3500 and K3500 with RO5: 107.3 in. Front/Rear Overhang: 117.5 in. wheelbase: pickups: 34.9 in./41.6 in. 131.5 in. wheelbase pickups: 34.9 in./46.5 in. extended cab: 34.9/46.5 in. Chassis cab models: 34.9/41.8 in. Tailgate: Width and Height: K1500 Sportside: 50.9 x 19.3 in. All others: 62.0 in. x 19.3 in. Approach/Departure Degrees: K1500 117.5 in.: 22/28. Ground Clearance (Front/Rear in inches): K1500 Sportside and Fleetside: 8.6/9.0. K1500 extended cab: 9.2/9.6. K2500 regular cab: 8.7/7.7 (with C6P: 7.8/8.1). K2500 extended cab: Model K20753: 9.2/8.2, model K20953: 9.2/8.1. K3500 Regular and extended cab: 9.2/8.1 (with RO5 dual rear wheels: 7.2/7.4). V3500: 8.3/7.8. Front headroom, all models: 40.0 in. Front legroom, all models: 41.7 in. Front shoulder room, all models: 66.0 in.

CAPACITIES: Fuel Tank: All K series: 25.0 gal. All V3500 models: 20 gal. Optional: Models K10903, K10753, K10953, K20903, K20953, K30903: 34 gal. V3500 models: 20 gal.

ACCOMMODATIONS: Seating Capacity: Pickup, extended cab and chassis cab models: 3 passenger. Optional: Extended cab: 6 passenger. Suburban: 6 passenger. Optional: 9 passenger.

INSTRUMENTATION: Speedometer, odometer, fuel level gauge. Warning lights for battery, oil pressure, generator, brake system warning, directional/hazard lights, high beam, and engine coolant temperature.

OPTIONS AND PRICES: Air conditioning (RPO C60): $780, $820 for V350 without B3J, $758 for V3500 with B3J. Optional axle ratios: $38. Locking differential (RPO G80): $252. Auxiliary heavy-duty battery, not avail. with B3J (RPO TP2): $134. Painted rear step bumper, requires E63 body (RPO V43): $130. Front Deluxe chromed bumper with rub strip, K10703 only (RPO VG3): $26. Chromed rear step bumper with rub strip (RPO VB3): $229. Front black bumper guards (RPO V27): $32. Heavy-duty chassis equipment, K1500 only (RPO F44): $38. Off-Road Package, avail. for K1500 only. Includes skid plate and Bilstein shock absorbers (RPO Z71): $270. Cold Climate Package, not avail. with B3J. Includes engine block heater (RPO V10): $33. Convenience Group. Includes power door locks and windows (RPO ZQ2): $344. Convenience Group. Includes tilt wheel and speed control (RPO ZQ3): $346. Engine Oil Cooling System (RPO KC4): $135. Heavy-duty radiator (RPO VO1): $56. Heavy-duty radiator and transmission oil cooler (RPO VO2): $63. Rear window defogger (RPO C49): $154. 5.0 liter V-8 (RPO LO3): $555. 5.7 liter V-8 (RPO LO5): $800. 6.2 liter diesel V-8 (RPO LH6): $. Locking fuel filler cap (RPO NO5): $18. Cargo area lamp (RPO UF2): $36. Dome and reading lamp (RPO C95): $33. Roof marker lamps, not avail. with Calif. emissions (RPO UO1): $52. Auxiliary lighting. Includes dome and reading lamps and ashtray, glove box and under hood lamps (RPO TR9): $125. Below eye-level type painted mirrors (RPO D44): $52. Below eye-level type stainless steel mirrors (RPO D45): $92. Camper-type stainless steel mirrors (RPO DF2): $100. Black exterior moldings (RPO B84): $90. Exterior bright moldings (RPO B85): $17. Conventional two-tone exterior paint (RPO ZY2): $132. Special two-tone exterior paint (RPO ZY3): $215. Deluxe two-tone exterior paint (RPO ZY4): $243. Electronically tuned AM/FM stereo radio with Seek-Scan and digital clock (RPO UM7): $210. Electronically tuned AM/FM Stereo Radio with Seek-Scan, stereo cassette tape and digital clock (RPO UM6): $332. Electronically Tuned AM/FM stereo radio with Seek-Scan, stereo cassette player with Search and Repeat, graphic equalizer and digital clock (RPO UX1): $482. Radio delete option (RPO UL5): $77. Scottsdale Trim Package (RPO Z62): K series pickups: E62: $601 without RPO ZQB, $526 with RPO ZQB. E63: $632 without RPO ZQB, $557 with RPO ZQB, $235 for K1500 Sport Pickup. K series chassis & cab: $452 for regular cab with RPO RO5, $527 without RO5, $337 for extended cab with RO5, $412 without RO5. Heavy-duty front and rear shock absorbers (RPO F51): $40. Silverado Trim Package (RPO YE9): K1500 regular cab Pickup E62: $1009. E63: $1040 without RPO ZQB, $934 with RPO ZQB. Silverado Trim Package for K1500 and K2500 extended cab Pickup: $1056 without RPO ZQB, $950 with ZQB, $1056 for K2500 extended cab without C6P, $1025 for K2500 extended cab with C6P, $883 for K2500 regular cab chassis & cab, $1025 for K3500 extended cab pickup, $899 for K2500 extended cab chassis & cab, $942 for V3500 bonus cab pickup, $976 for V3500 crew cab pickup, $734 for V3500 bonus cab pickup with RPO RO5, $768 for V3500 crew cab with RPO RO5. Off-road skid plate, K1500 only (RPO NZZ): $95. Heavy-duty front springs K1500 only, requires F44 heavy-duty chassis, not avail. with B3J or RPO Z71 off-road chassis (RPO F60): $63. Body striping (RPO D85): $69. Tow hooks, standard on K1500 (RPO V76): $38. Heavy-duty Trailering Special Equipment (RPO Z82): $408 with RPO Z71 or XQ8, $448 without RPO Z71 or ZQ8. Four-speed manual trans. (RPO MM4): $98. Four-speed auto. trans. with overdrive (RPO MXO): $860. Four-speed auto. trans. (RPO MX1): $625. Wheel-covers (RPO PO1): $42. Aluminum wheels, K1500 only (RPO PF4): $295. Sliding rear window (RPO A28): $113. Camper Special chassis equipment K2500 and K3500 only (RPO Z81): $280 without B2J, $148 with B3J. Deep tinted glass, (RPO AJ1): $150. Sport Equipment Package (Sport Truck), K10703 only. Includes V43 black bumpers, black wheel flares, deluxe front appearance, black mirrors, GL LT265/75R16 blackwall tires, pF4 aluminum wheels with special hubcaps and 4x4 sport decal (RPO BPY): $1140.20. Sport steering wheel (RPO NK3): $7.00. Rear-mounted fuel tank, avail for K2500 and K3500 chassis & cab models, approximate capacity of 31 gal. (RPO NK7): $63. Special chassis camper equipment. Includes TP2 auxiliary battery without B3J equipment, camper wiring harness and DF2 mirrors (RPO Z81): $280 for K series pickups, $1436 with B3J, $81 for V3500. Dual rear wheels, available for 3500 models only. Includes plastic rear fender extensions with side marker lamps on front and rear siders and dual rear chassis provisions (RPO RO5): $1038, $1101 with MX1 trans. Includes VO2 heavy-duty radiator and trans. oil cooler, $785 for V3500. The following options and prices applied to the V3500 models: Glide-out spare tire carrier (RPO P11): $43. Side-mounted spare tire carrier (RPO P13): $31. Door edge guards (RPO B93): $24.

HISTORICAL FOOTNOTES: In the full-size, light-duty truck market Ford was the best-seller, followed by Chevrolet which projected its share of this market as 46.4 percent

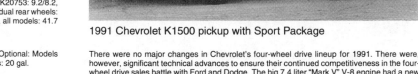

1991 PICKUP

1991 Chevrolet K1500 pickup with Sport Package

There were no major changes in Chevrolet's four-wheel drive lineup for 1991. There were, however, significant technical advances to ensure their continued competitiveness in the four-wheel drive sales battle with Ford and Dodge. The big 7.4 liter "Mark V" V-8 engine had a new one-piece intake manifold with a relocated throttle body injector, thus eliminating the previous TYBI mounting adaptors. Other new features included improved piston-to-cylinder tolerances, improved oil pan gaskets to help eliminate oil leaks, rigid cast iron rocker covers and new engine oil cooler lines with improved bracketing. This engine also benefited from a new manufacturing process and updated tooling. that Chevrolet noted was intended to improve the engine's overall reliability. General Motors' all-new 4L80-E heavy-duty electronic control (for enhanced shifting precision and smoothness) 4-speed automatic overdrive transmission (RPO MXO) was available for all models rated at or above 8600 lb. GVWR. The 4L80-E nomenclature had the following significance: 4-4 forward speeds, L-Longitudinal type, 80-transmission gears based on relative torque capacity. This transmission could handle 885 lbs.-ft. of gearbox torque which represented 440 lb.-ft. of imput torque, E-electronic controls. Aside from its 4-speed overdrive configuration this transmission also featured an aluminum case and a Powertrain Control Module (PCM) which combined engine and transmission functions on all gasoline engines and compensated for variations in temperature, altitude and engine performance. A Transmission Control Module (TCM) was used with the diesel V-8. A new dual stator 310mm torque converter was also included for increased low-speed torque. The 4L80-E was touted by Chevrolet as "one of the most technologically advanced transmissions ever offered in a Chevrolet truck."

1991 Chevrolet K2500 pickup

Powertrain improvements on all K series trucks included a new 220 series throttle body injection system. A new SD 260 starter motor was used for the 4.3 liter V-6 and the 5.0 liter V-8. It was lighter in weight and more durable and reliable than the SD300 motor it replaced. The new TBI system was used on the 4.3 liter V-6, 5.0 liter V-8, 5.7 liter V-8 and the 7.4 liter V-8 engines. It incorporated longer throttle shaft bearings, new throttle return springs and improved fuel mixture distribution. The 4.3 liter V-6 was also improved by the use of a revised air cleaner system and a processing changes in manufacturing spark plugs. Both the 5.0 liter V-8 and 5.7 liter V-8 were upgrade with heavy-duty intake valves, powdered metal camshaft sprockets and improved oil pan baffling on the heavy-duty 5.7 liter engine. Replacing the 12-SI-100 alternator was a lighter weight, more reliable CS130 alternator. A 100 amp alternator was now standard on the V3500 pickup and chassis cab models.

1991 Chevrolet K1500 Suburban

The Work Truck continued as Chevrolet's no-frills, basic four-wheel drive pickup. Changes for 1991 included a new four spoke steering wheel and larger outside rear view mirrors. A Custom urethane 4-spoke steering wheel was standard. Below eye-level exterior mirrors were now standard on the K series pickups and chassis & cab models. These mirrors had adjustable heads in a black finish and measured 9.0 in. x 6.5 in. The standard AM/FM stereo radio in the V series pickups and chassis & cab were improved by increasing signal sensitivity and reducing signal interference and signal tracking. The RPO C60 air conditioning option for the K series models included a HVAC climate control incorporating new controls allowing for manual selection of the recirculation air inlet mode. In addition, revised display graphics provided clear readings in a dark cab. A software change provided an indication that the system required refrigerant servicing.

New options for 1991 included a bed liner for Fleetside and extended cab models, high-back reclining front bucket seats and gauge cluster with tachometer. The Cheyenne trim package had a new impact-resistant metal grille for 991. Two new metallic colors, brilliant blue and slate brought the total number of exterior colors to ten. A light gray color was added to the list of available interior colors.

I.D. DATA: Unchanged from 1990. The letter M represented the 1991 model year.

Model	Body Type	Price

Series K1500-1/2 ton 262 V-6-cyl. 117.5 in. 131.5 in. wheelbase (Suburban: 129.5 in. wheelbase and standard 350 V-8)

Model	Body Type	Price
CK10903	8.0 ft. Worktruck	$12,625.00
CK10703	6.5 ft. Sportside Pickup	$14,665.00
CK10703	6.5 ft. Fleetside Pickup	$14,335.00
CK10903	8.0 ft. Fleetside Pickup	$14,615.00
CK10753	6.5 ft. Ext. Cab Fleetside	$18,059.05
CK10953	8.0 ft. Ext. Cab Fleetside	$18,349.05
CV10906	Suburban Panl. Drs.	$18,540.00
CV10906	Suburban Tailgate	$18,690.00

Add $2540 for Fleetside CK 10753 with LH6 diesel engine. The diesel engine is not available on K10703 models.
Add $2740 for CK10753 with diesel engine.
Add $2174 for CK10953 with LH6 diesel engine.
Add $2440 for LH6 diesel on CV10906 models.

K2500-3/4 ton 262 V-6l. 131.5 in. wheelbase. (V2500 Suburban-129.5 in. wheelbase). Crew and bonus cab: 164.5 in. wheelbase, Suburban with standard 350 V-8

Model	Body Type	Price
CK20903	Chassis & Cab	$15,234.00
CK20953	Ext. Cab Chassis & Cab	$17,278.80
CK20903	8.0 ft. Fleetside Pickup	$14,825.00
CK20903	8.0 ft. C6P Fleetside Pickup	$15,988.00
CK20753	6.5 ft. Extended Cab Pickup	$15,888.24
CK20953	8.0 ft. Extended Cab Pickup	$16,188.24
CK20953	8.0 ft. C6P Ext. Cab Pickup	$17,058.80
CV20906	Suburban Panl. Drs.	$ 2,003.08
CV20906	Suburban Tailgate	$20,188.08

Add $2940 to CK20903 for LH6 diesel engine.
Add $2030 to CK20903 C6P for LL4 diesel engine.
Add $2660 to CK20753 for LH6 diesel engine.
Add $2640 to CK20953 for diesel engine.
Add $2030 to CK20953 with C6P for LL4 diesel engine.
Add $1210 to CK20953 extended cab chassis & cab for LL4 diesel engine.
Add $1855 for LH6 diesel on Suburban models.

Series K3500-1 ton 350 V-8. 131.5 in. wheelbase. Extended cab: 155.5 in. wheelbase. Crew and bonus cab: 164.5 in. wheelbase

Model	Body Type	Price
CK30903	8.0 ft. Fleetside Pickup	$18,120
CK30953	8.0 ft. Ext. Cab F-S Pickup	$19,180
CK30903	Chassis & Cab, 131.5 in. wb.	$16,133
CK31003	Chassis & Cab, 135.5 in. wb.	$16,560
CK31403	Chassis & Cab, 159.9 in. wb.	$16,675
CK30953	Ext. Cab Chassis & Cab	$19,040

Add $1405 for LL4 diesel engine with CK30903.
Add $1415 for LL4 diesel engine with CK30953.
Add $1260 to CK30953, Ext. Cab chassis & cab for LL4 diesel engine.

Series V3500-1 ton 350 V-8. 164.5 in. wheelbase. Fleetside crew and bonus cab: 164.5 in. wheelbase

Model	Body Type	Price
CV30943	Bonus Cab	$19,068.08
CV30943	Crew Cab	$19,168.08
CV30943	Bonus Cab Chassis & Cab	$18,598.08
CV30943	Crew Cab Chassis & Cab	$19,148.08
CV30943	H-D Bonus Cab Chassis & Cab	$19,025.00
CV30943	H-D Crew Cab Chassis & Cab	$19,565.00

Add $1140 for all bonus and crew cab with LL4 diesel engine.
Add $1510 for LL4 diesel engine for H-D chassis & cab bonus cab models.
Add $1520 for LL4 diesel engine for H-D chassis & cab crew cab models.

STANDARD ENGINE: All K1500, K2500 models: 262 V-6 (LB4 ordering code). Engine Type: Vortex OHV, V-6-cylinder. Cast iron block. Bore x Stroke: 4.0 in. x 3.48 in. Lifters: Hydraulic. Fuel Induction: Electronic fuel injection. Compression Ratio: For models under 8500 GVWR: 9.3:1. For models over 8500 lb. GVWR: 8.6:1. Displacement: 262 cu. in. (4.3 liters). Horsepower: Net: For models under 8500 lb. GVWR: 160 @ 4000 rpm. For models over 8590 lb. GVWR: 155 @ 4000 rpm. Torque: Net: For models under 8500 lb. GVWR: 235 lb.-ft. @ 2400 rpm. For models over 85900 lb. GVWR: 230 lb.-ft. @ 2400 rpm. Oil refill capacity: 5 qt. with filter change. Fuel Requirements: Regular unleaded.

OPTIONAL ENGINE: K1500, K2500, Standard:V3500 and K3500 models: Optional for K150 and K2500 models. 350 V-8 (LO5 ordering code). Engine Type: OHV, V-8. Cast iron block and cylinder head. Bore x Stroke: 4.0 in. x 3.48 in. Lifters: Hydraulic. Number of main bearings-5. Fuel Induction: Electronic fuel injection. Compression Ratio: K3500: 8.6:1. K1500 and K2500: 9.3:1. Displacement: 350 cu. in. (5.7 liters). Horsepower: K3500: Net: 190 @ 4000 rpm. K1500 and K2500: 210 @ 4000 rpm. Torque: K3500: Net 300 lb.-ft. @ 2400 rpm. K1500 and K2500: 300 lb.-ft. @ 2800 rpm. Oil refill capacity: 5 qt. with filter change. Fuel Requirements: Regular unleaded. Optional: K1500 and K2500: 305 V-8, Ordering Code LO3. Engine Type: OHV, V-8. Cast iron block and alloy iron cylinder head. Key features include chain drive camshaft and forged steel connecting rods. This engine was produced in U.S. or Canada. Bore x Stroke: 3.74 in. x 3.48 in. Lifters: Hydraulic. Number of main bearings-5. Fuel Induction: Electronic fuel injection. Compression Ratio: 9.2:1. Displacement: 305 cu. in. (5.0 liters). Horsepower: Net: 175 @ 4000 rpm. Torque: Net 270 lb.-ft. @ 2400 rpm. Oil refill capacity: 5 qt. with filter change. Fuel Requirements: Regular unleaded.

STANDARD ENGINE: K3500 models with rear wheels: Optional: Other K3500 models. Ordering Code: L19. 454 V-8 Engine Type: OHV, V-8. Cast iron block and alloy iron cylinder head. Bore x Stroke: 4.30 in. x 4.0 in. Lifters: Hydraulic. Number of main bearings-5. Fuel Induction: Electronic fuel injection. Compression Ratio: 7.9:1. Displacement: 454 cu. in. (7.4 liters). Horsepower: 230 @ 3600 rpm. Torque: 385 lb.-ft. @ 1600 rpm. Oil refill capacity: 5 qt. with filter change. Fuel Requirements: Regular unleaded.

OPTIONAL ENGINE: K1500 and K2500: Ordering Code LH6. Not available in California for K2500. This engine was produced by GM-Detroit Diesel Allison Division. Engine Type: OHV, diesel V-8. Bore x Stroke: 3.98 in. x 3.80 in. Lifters: Hydraulic. Number of main bearings-5. Fuel Induction: Gear driven mechanical fuel injection. Compression Ratio: 21.3:1. Displacement: 379.4 cu. in. (6.2 liters). Horsepower: 126 @ 3600 rpm. (140 @ 3600 rpm with automatic transmission). Torque: 240 lb.-ft. @ 2000 rpm. (247 lb.-ft. @ 2000 rpm with automatic transmission). Oil refill capacity: 7 qt. with filter change. Fuel Requirements: Diesel.

OPTIONAL ENGINE: K3500 and V3500 models: Ordering Code LL4. This engine was produced by GM-Detroit Diesel Allison Division. Engine Type: OHV, diesel V-8. Bore x Stroke: 3.98 in. x 3.80 in. Lifters: Hydraulic. Number of main bearings-5. Fuel Induction: Fuel injection. Compression Ratio: 21.3:1. Displacement: 379.4 cu. in. (6.2 liters). Horsepower: 143 @ 3600 rpm. Torque: 257 lb.-ft. @ 2000 rpm. Oil refill capacity: 7 qt. with filter change. Fuel Requirements: Diesel.

CHASSIS FEATURES: Semi-perimeter design, all-welded channel beam frame with boxed front end. Dimensions: K1500 and K2500 regular cab: 2.18 x 7.48 x 0.134 in. K1500 extended cab: 2.18 x 7.48 x 0.165 in. K2500 regular cab with C6P: 2.18 x 7.48 x 0.213 in. K2500 extended cab: 2.31 x 7.48 x 0.165 in. K2500 extended cab with C6P: 2.18 x 7.48 x 0.244 in. K3500 regular cab: 2.18 x 7.48 x 0.213 in. K3500 extended cab: 2.18 x 7.48 x 0.244 in. V3500 models: 2.788 x 7.74 x 0.244 in. Section modules: K1500 regular cab: 3.46; K1500 extended cab: 4.30; K2500: 4.30; K2500 with C6P: 6.48; K3500 regular cab: 5.61; K3500 extended cab: 6.48, V3500: 7.33.

1991 Chevrolet K2500 extended cab short bed pickup

SUSPENSION AND RUNNING GEAR: Front Suspension: Torsion bar springs. K1500 Capacity: 3860 lb. K2500 and K3500 capacity: 3750 lb. V3500: Tapered leaf springs. Capacity: 4500 lb. Shock absorber dia.: K1500; 25mm; K2500, K3500 and V3500: 32mm. 32mm optional for K1500. 1.00 in. stabilizer optional for all series except V3500 which had a standard 1.25 in. bar standard. Optional rating: K1500: RPO F44/F60: 6100 lb. GVW. K2500: 8600 lb. GVW. K3500: 10,000 lb. GVW. Rear Suspension: Semi-elliptical 2-stage, 4-leaf for K1500; 6-leaf for K2500; 6-leaf plus 1-leaf auxiliary for K3500. K1500 capacity: 3750 lb.K2500 capacity: 4800 lb. K3500 capacity: 7500 lb. V3500: Semi-elliptical 2-stage, 9-leaf. Capacity: 7000 lb. Shock absorber dia.: K1500: 25mm; K2500, K3500 and V3500: 32mm. 32mm optional for K1500. Optional Rating: See above for GVW ratings. Front Axle Type and Capacity: Independent, GM or K1500; Spicer on K2500 and K3500. Capacity: K1500 regular cab: 3925 lb.; K1500 extended cab: 4800 lb.; K2500 and K3500: 4250 lb. V3500: Spicer full-floating. Capacity: 4500 lb., manual hub locks. Optional: K1500: 3925 capacity; K1500 extended cab: 4800 lb. All other K series: 4250 lb. Rear Axle Type: Semi-floating for K1500; Full-floating for K2500, K3500 and V3500. GM manufacture for all series. Capacity: K1500: 3750 lb. K2500: 6000 lb.; K3500, V3500: 7500 lb. Optional: K2500: Regular cab: 4800 lb.; K250 extended cab: 6000 lb.; K3500: 7500 lb. Final Drive Ratio: The following transmission designations were used by Chevrolet: MM4: 4-spd. manual; MM5: 5-spd. manual overdrive; MX1: 3-spd. automatic; MXO: 4-spd. automatic. All ratios with standard emission equipment. Standard: K1500, K2500: 3.42:1. Optional: 3.73:1. All engine/transmission combinations except K2500 with LL4 diesel engine which had standard 3.73:1 ratio and optional 4.10:1 ratio, and K2500 with 5.7 liter V-8 and C6P which also had an optional 4.56:1 ratio. Standard: K3500: 4.10:1 with 5.7 liter V-8 with 4.56:1 optional; 3.42:1 standard for 7.4 liter V-8 with 3.73 and 4.10:1 optional; 6.2 liter diesel (LL4) had standard 4.10:1 ratio with 4.56:1 optional. Standard for V3500: 3.73:1 with 5.7 liter and manual 4-spd. trans.; 4.10:1 with 3-spd. auto. trans.; 3.73:1 with 7.4 liter V-8; 4.10:1 with LL4 diesel. Optional: 4.10 and 4.56:1 for 5.7 liter V-8 with man. 4-spd.; 4.56:1 for 5.7 liter V-8 with 3-spd. auto. trans.; 4.10 and 4.56:1 for 7.4 liter V-8; 4.56:1 for LL4 diesel. Transfer Case: K1500, K2500, K3500: New Process 241. Single lever. Ratios: 2.72:1, 1.00:1. K3500 with RPO RO5: Borg Warner 1370: Ratios: 2.69:1, 1.00:1. The Borg Warner unit has a right hand side power take-off. Brakes: Type: Hydraulic, power assisted. Dimensions: K1500: Front: Disc. 11.86 in x 1.00 in. Rear: Drums: 10.0 x 2.25 in. K1500 regular cab with RPO F44/F60 had 11.57 in. x 1.25 in. front disc brakes. K2500 regular cab: Front: Disc: 11.57 in. x 1.20 in. Rear: Drums: 11.15 in. x 2.75 in. K2500 extended cab: Front Disc: 11.57 in. x 1.25 in. Rear: 10.0 in. x 2.25 in. drums. All K2500 with 8600 lb. GVW Package had 12.50 in. x 1.26 in. front disc brakes and 13.0 in. x 2.5 in. rear drum brakes. K3500 all models: Front: Disc: 12.50 in. x 1.26 in. Rear: Drum: 13.00 in. x 2.50 in. V3500 all models: Front Disc: 12.54 in. x 1.54 in. Rear: Drums: 13.0 in. x 3.5 in. Wheels: K1500 and K2500: 16 x 6.5, 6-stud disc. K3500 and V3500: 16.0 x 6.0. Tires: K1500 Sportside and regular cab: LT225/75-R-16C steel belted radial. K1500 extended cab: LT245/75R. K2500 all models: LT245/75R-16E. K3500: LT225/75RD. V3500 all models: 7.50-16D tubeless nylon. Optional: K1500: LT225/75R16C, blackwall, LT245/75R16C on-off road; blackwall, white stripe or white lettered. Available for K10903 only with the following engines: LB4, LO3 and LH6 and RPO GVT4 axle; and K10703 with LB4 or LO3 engine with RPO GT4 axle. LT265/75R16C blackwall or white letter, on-off road. Optional K2500: LTR225/75R16D steel belted radial blackwall or white stripe, LT245/75R16E highway or on-off road; LT225/75R16D blackwall, on-off road, LT245/75R16E blackwall (K20903 only). Optional: K3500: LT225/75R16D, blackwall, LT245/75R16E blackwall, LT245/75R16E on-off road blackwall, 7.50 x 16D highway and on-off road. Optional: V3500: V30943 only: 7.50 x 16D tubeless nylon, dual rear, LT215/75R16D dual rear tubeless steel belted radial; LT235/85R16E. Steering: Integral power. Ratio: K1500 regular cab Sportside and Fleetside: 17.44:1. K1500 extended cab model K10753: 18.8:1, model K10953: 17.44:1. K2500 regular cab: 17.44:1. K2500 extended cab: model K20753: 18.88:1; model K20953: 17.44:1. K3500 regular cab: 127.44:1. K3500 extended cab: 17.44:1. V3500: 13.5:1. Turning Diameter (curb-to-curb): K1500 regular cab Sportside: 40.3 ft. K1500 regular cab Fleetside: 44.4 ft. K1500 extended cab Model K10753: 47.9 ft K10953: 52.2 ft K2500 regular cab: 44.4 in. (with C6P: 45.1 ft.). K2500 extended cab: Model K20753: 47.9 ft. Model 52.2 ft. K3500 regular cab: 45.1 ft. K3500 extended cab: 52.2 ft. V3500: 54.5 ft. Transmission: Standard K1500/2500: With gasoline engines: RPO MM5-5-spd. manual with overdrive fully-synchronized. Transmission Ratios: 4.02, 2.32, 1.40, 1.00. 0.73:1; reverse: 3.74:1. Standard: K3500, V3500 and K2500 with C6P, and K1500 and K2500 with diesel engine: RPO MM4 4-spd. SM465 manual, synchromesh on top three gears (optional: K1500/2500). Transmission ratios: 6.55, 3.58, 1.70, 1.00:1, reverse: 6.09:1. Optional: All series: RPO MX1-3-spd. 400 automatic. Transmission ratios: 2.48, 1.48, 1.0:1, reverse: 2.08:1. Optional: K1500/2500, (except K2500 regular cab and extended cab chassis cab, and all V3500 models): RPO MXO-4-spd. automatic overdrive 700R4: 3.06, 1.63, 1.0, 0.70:1, Reverse: 2.29:1.

VEHICLE DIMENSIONS: Wheelbase: All series regular cab: 117.5 in. 131.5 in. extended cab: 6.5 ft. box models: 141.5 in.; 8.0 ft. box models: 155.5 in.; V3500 models: 164.5 in. Overall Length (without rear bumper): K1500 Sportside: 194.0 in. K1500 regular cab: 194.1 in. K1500 extended cab: Model K10753 (6.5 ft. box): 223.0 in. K10953 (8.0 ft. box): 237.0 in. K2500 regular cab: 212.6 in. K2500 extended cab: Model K20753: 223.0 in. Model K20953: 237.0 in. K3500 regular cab: 212.6 in. V3500: 246.4 in. Front/Rear Tread: 74 in./74 in. Overall Height: K1500 all models: 73.8 in. K2500 regular cab: 74.3 in. (75.8 in. if equipped with C6P). K2500 extended cab: 74.4 in. (75.8 in. if equipped with C6P). K3500 75.8 in. V3500: 76.3 in. Width: All models except V3500 and those equipped with RO5: 76.8 in. V3500: 79.6 in. V3500 and K3500 with RO5: 107.3 in. Front/Rear Overhang: 117.5 in. wheelbase. pickups: 34.9 in./41.6 in. 131.5 in. wheelbase pickups: 34.9 in./46.5 in. extended cab: 34.9/46.5 in. Chassis cab models: 34.9/41.8 in. Tailgate: Width and Height: K1500 Sportside: 50.9 x 19.3 in. All others: 62.0 in. x 19.3 in. Approach/Departure Degrees: K1500 117.5 in.: 22/28. Ground Clearance (Front/Rear in inches): K1500 Sportside and Fleetside: 8.6/9.0. K1500 extended cab: 9.2/9.6. K2500 regular cab: 8.7/7.7 (with C6P: 7.8/8.1). K2500 extended cab: Model K20753: 9.2/8.2, model K20953: 9.2/8.1. K3500 regular and extended cab: 9.2/8.1 (with RO5 dual rear wheels: 7.2/7.4). V3500: 8.3/7.8. Front headroom, all models: 40.0 in. Front legroom, all models: 41.7 in. Front shoulder room, all models: 66.0 in.

CAPACITIES: Fuel Tank: All K series: 25.0 gal. All V3500 models: 20 gal. Optional: Models K10903, K10753, K10953, K20903, K20953, K30903: 34 gal. V3500 models: 20 gal.

ACCOMMODATIONS: Seating Capacity: Pickup, extended cab and chassis cab models: 3 passenger. Optional: Extended cab: 6 passenger. Suburban: 6 passenger. Optional: 9 passenger.

INSTRUMENTATION: Speedometer, odometer, fuel level gauge. Warning lights for battery, oil pressure, generator, brake system warning, directional/hazard lights, high beam, and engine coolant temperature.

OPTIONS AND PRICES: All K series: Air conditioning (RPO C60): $705, Optional axle ratios: $44. Locking differential (RPO G80): $252. Auxiliary heavy-duty battery, not avail. with B3J (RPO TP2): $134. Painted rear step bumper, requires E63 body (RPO V43): $130. Front Deluxe chromed bumper with rub strip, K10703 only (RPO VG3): $26. Chromed rear step bumper with rub strip (RPO VB3): $229. Front black bumper guards (RPO V27): $32. Heavy-duty chassis equipment, K1500 only (RPO F44): $38. Off-Road Package, avail. for K1500 only. Includes skid plate and Bilstein shock absorbers (RPO Z71: $270. Cold Climate Package, not avail. with B3J. Includes engine block heater (RPO V10): $33. Convenience Group. Includes power door locks and windows (RPO ZQ2): $367. Convenience Group. Includes tilt wheel and speed control (RPO ZQ3): $383. Engine Oil Cooling System (RPO KC4): $135. Heavy-duty radiator (RPO VO1): $56. Heavy-duty radiator and transmission oil cooler (RPO VO2): $63. Rear window defogger (RPO C49): $154. 5.0 liter V-8 (RPO LO3): $575. 5.7 liter V-8 (RPO LO5): $840. 6.2 liter diesel V-8 (RPO LH6): $. Locking fuel filler cap (RPO NO5): $18. Cargo area lamp (RPO UF2): $36. Dome and reading lamp (RPO C95): $33. Roof marker lamps, not avail. with Calif. emissions (RPO UO1): $52. Auxiliary lighting. Includes dome and reading lamps and ashtray, glove box and under hood lamps (RPO TR9): $94. Below eye-level type stainless steel mirrors (RPO D45): $45. Camper-type stainless steel mirrors (RPO DF2): $53. Black exterior moldings (RPO B84): $90. Exterior bright moldings (RPO B85): $17. Conventional two-tone exterior paint (RPO ZY2): $132. Special two-tone exterior paint (RPO ZY3): $215. Deluxe two-tone exterior paint (RPO ZY4): $243. Electronically tuned AM/FM stereo radio with Seek-Scan and digital clock (RPO UM7): $210. Electronically tuned AM/FM stereo radio with Seek-Scan, stereo cassette tape and digital clock (RPO UM6): $332. Electronically tuned AM/FM stereo radio with Seek-Scan, stereo cassette player with Search and Repeat, graphic equalizer and digital clock (RPO UX1): $482. Radio delete option (RPO UL5): $77. Scottsdale Trim Package (RPO Z62): K series pickups: $573 to $604. Heavy-duty front and rear shock absorbers (RPO F51): $40. Silverado Trim Package (RPO YE9): K1500 regular cab pickup: $981 to $1012. Off-road skid plate, K1500 only (RPO NZZ): $95. Heavy-duty front springs K1500 only, requires F44 heavy-duty chassis, not avail. with B3J or RPO Z71 off-road chassis (RPO F60): $63. Body striping (RPO D85): $69. Tow hooks, standard on K1500 (RPO V76): $38. Heavy-duty trailering special equipment (RPO Z82): $408 with RPO Z71 or XQ8, $448 without RPO Z71 or ZQ8. Four-speed manual trans. (RPO MM4): $98. Four-speed auto. trans. with overdrive (RPO MXO): $860. Three-speed auto. trans. (RPO MX1): $625. Wheelcovers (RPO PO1): $42. Aluminum wheels, K1500 only (RPO PF4): $295. Sliding rear window (RPO A28): $113. Camper Special chassis equipment K2500 and K3500 only (RPO Z81): $280 without B2J, $148 with B3J. Deep tinted glass, (RPO AJ1): $150. Sport Equipment Package (Sport Truck), K10703 only. Includes V43 black bumpers, black wheel flares, deluxe front appearance, black mirrors, GL LT265/75R16 blackwall tires, pF4 aluminum wheels with special hubcaps and 4x4 sport decal (RPO BPY): $1140.20. Sport steering wheel (RPO NK3): $7.00. Rear-mounted fuel tank, avail for K2500 and K3500 chassis & cab models, approximate capacity of 31 gal. (RPO NK7): $63. Special chassis camper equipment. Includes TP2 auxiliary battery without B3J equipment, camper wiring harness and DF2 mirrors (RPO Z81): $280 for K series pickups, $1436 with B3J, $81 for V3500. Dual rear wheels, available for 3500 models only. Includes plastic rear fender extensions with side marker lamps on front and rear siders and dual rear chassis provisions (RPO RO5): $1038, $1101 with MX1 trans. Includes VO2 heavy-duty radiator and trans. oil cooler, $785 for V3500

HISTORICAL FOOTNOTES: Total registration of Chevrolet trucks for 1991 was 1,058,547. Total Pickup production for 1991 was 291,404. Suburban production total was 25,000.

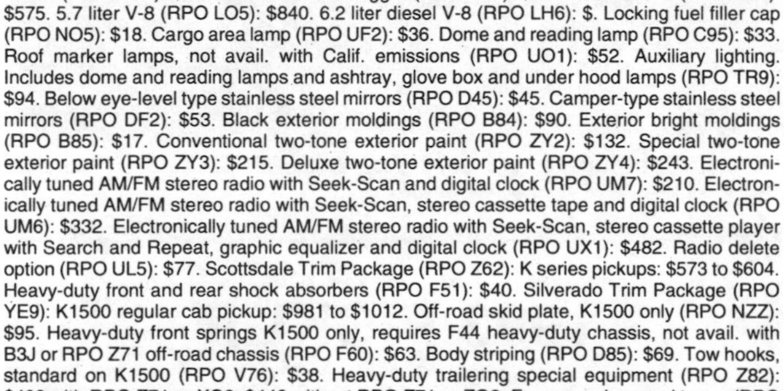

1991 Chevrolet K3500 extended cab pickup with dual rear wheels

1992 PICKUP

Changes for 1992 in the Chevrolet trucks were lead by major developments in the Suburban and the four-door crew cab pickup. The Suburban adopted the styling and full frame construction of the full-size Chevrolet pickup. The Suburban had decreased step-in height and load floor height. It also had increased towing capacity, load space, and front and rear leg, shoulder and hip room. Anti-lock brakes were standard for all Suburbans. A modified version of the full-size pickup's suspension was used for the Suburban. The front suspension was independent with upper and lower control arms and a stabilizer bar. The rear suspension was of semi-elliptical, two-stage, multi-leaf design. A 5.7 liter fuel injected V-8 was standard. Suburbans with a GVW over 8500 lbs. used a heavy-duty version of the 5.7 liter V-8. The 7.4 liter V-8 was optional for Suburbans with GVW over 8600 lb. Standard Suburban equipment included seats with additional foam support, head restraints for the front outboard seat position (all Chevrolet pickups had new front seats with this feature), a full gauge cluster, All-Season radial tires and an extended-range AM radio. A lift-glass/drop gate was optional.

Along with the Blazer and Suburban, the crew cab K3500 pickup was the last Chevrolet truck to adopt the styling adopted in 1988. The crew cab had a 4 in. longer wheelbase, nearly 7 inches more rear-seat legroom and increased front leg and shoulder room. The crew cab also had anti-lock brakes. The standard crew cab engine-transmission was a 5.7 liter V-8 with a 5-speed heavy-duty manual transmission with "deep low" and overdrive. Available for all trucks with a GVW rating of 8600 lb. and up was a new 6.5 liter turbo diesel. This engine, built at the General Motors Moraine Engine Plant in Dayton, Ohio had a special warranty of five years or 100,00 miles. Among its features were an all-new cylinder case design, and an optimized combustion chamber for totally smokeless performance. Added to the interior color availability for 1992 was beige. New exterior colors were bright red and beige metallic.

I.D. DATA: Unchanged for 1992. The letter N represented the 1992 model year.

Model	Body Type	Price
Series K1500-1/2 ton 262 V-6-cyl. 117.5 in. 131.5 in. wheelbase (Suburban: 129.5 in. wheelbase and standard 350 V-8)		
CK10903	8.0 ft. Worktruck	$13,615
CK10703	6.5 ft. Sportside Pickup	$15,745
CK10703	6.5 ft. Fleetside Pickup	$15,345
CK10903	8.0 ft. Fleetside Pickup	$15,635
CK10753	6.5 ft. Ext. Cab Fleetside	$16,297
CK10953	8.0 ft. Ext. Cab Fleetside	$16,587
CV10906	Suburban Panl. Drs.	$20,593
CV10906	Suburban Tailgate	$20,743
K2500-3/4 ton 262 V-61. 131.5 in. wheelbase. (V2500 Suburban-129.5 in. wheelbase). Crew and bonus cab: 164.5 in. wheelbase, Suburban with standard 350 V-8		
CK20903	8.0 ft. Fleetside Pickup	$15,805
CK20753	6.5 ft. Extended Cab Pickup	$16,867
CK20953	8.0 ft. Extended Cab Pickup	$17,167
CV20906	Suburban Panl. Drs.	$21,797
CV20906	Suburban Tailgate	$20,373
Series K3500-1 ton 350 V-8. 131.5 in. wheelbase. Extended cab: 155.5 in. wheelbase. Crew and bonus cab: 164.5 in. wheelbase		
CK30903	8.0 ft. Fleetside Pickup	$17,888
CK30953	8.0 ft. Ext. Cab F-S Pickup	$18,948
Series V3500-1 ton 350 V-8. 164.5 in. wheelbase. Fleetside crew and bonus cab: 164.5 in. wheelbase		
CV30943	Bonus Cab	$N.A.
CV30943	Crew Cab	$N.A.
CV30943	Bonus Cab Chassis & Cab	$N.A
CV30943	Crew Cab Chassis & Cab	$N.A.
CV30943	H-D Bonus Cab Chassis & Cab	$N.A.
CV30943	H-D Crew Cab Chassis & Cab	$19,565

STANDARD ENGINE: All K1500, K2500 models: 262 V-6 (LB4 ordering code). Engine Type: Vortex OHV, V-6-cylinder. Cast iron block. Bore x Stroke: 4.0 in. x 3.48 in. Lifters: Hydraulic. Fuel Induction: Electronic fuel injection. Compression Ratio: 9.3:1. Displacement: 262 cu. in. (4.3 liters). Horsepower: Net: 160 @ 4000 rpm. Torque: Net: 235 lb.-ft. @ 2400 rpm. Oil refill capacity: 5 qt. with filter change. Fuel Requirements: Regular unleaded.

OPTIONAL ENGINE: K1500, K2500-305 V-8 (LO3 ordering code). Engine Type: OHV, V-8. Cast iron block and cylinder head. Bore x Stroke: 3.74 in. x 3.48 in. Lifters: Hydraulic. Number of main bearings-5. Fuel Induction: Electronic fuel injection. Compression Ratio: 9.1:1. Displacement: 350 cu. in. (5.7 liters). Horsepower: Net: 175 @ 4000 rpm. Torque: Net 270 lb.-ft. @ 2400 rpm. Oil refill capacity: 5 qt. with filter change. Fuel Requirements: Regular unleaded.

OPTIONAL ENGINE: K1500, K2500, Standard: V3500 and K3500 models: Optional for K150 and K2500 models. 350 V-8 (LO5 ordering code). Engine Type: OHV, V-8. Cast iron block and cylinder head. Bore x Stroke: 4.0 in. x 3.48 in. Lifters: Hydraulic. Number of main bearings-5. Fuel Induction: Electronic fuel injection. Compression Ratio: K3500: 8.6:1. K1500 and K2500: 9.3:1. Displacement: 350 cu. in. (5.7 liters). Horsepower: K3500: Net: 190 @ 4000 rpm. K1500 and K2500: 210 @ 4000 rpm. Torque: K3500: Net 300 lb.-ft. @ 2400 rpm. K1500 and K2500: 300 lb.-ft. @ 2800 rpm. Oil refill capacity: 5 qt. with filter change. Fuel Requirements: Regular unleaded.

STANDARD ENGINE: K3500 models with dual rear wheels: Optional: other K3500 models. Ordering Code: L19: 454 V-8. Engine Type: OHV, V-8. Cast iron block and alloy iron cylinder head. Bore x Stroke: 4.30 in. x 4.0 in. Lifters: Hydraulic. Number of main bearings-5. Fuel Induction: Electronic fuel injection. Compression Ratio: 7.9:1. Displacement: 454 cu. in. (7.4 liters). Horsepower: 230 @ 3600 rpm. Torque: 385 lb.-ft. @ 1600 rpm. Oil refill capacity: 5 qt. with filter change. Fuel Requirements: Regular unleaded.

OPTIONAL ENGINE: K1500 and K2500: Ordering Code LH6. Not available in California for K2500. This engine was produced by GM-Detroit Diesel Allison Division. Engine Type: OHV, diesel V-8. Bore x Stroke: 3.98 in. x 3.80 in. Lifters: Hydraulic. Number of main bearings-5. Fuel Induction: Gear driven mechanical fuel injection. Compression Ratio: 21.3:1. Displacement: 379.4 cu. in. (6.2 liters). Horsepower: 126 @ 3600 rpm. (140 @ 3600 rpm with automatic transmission). Torque: 240 lb.-ft. @ 2000 rpm. (247 lb.-ft. @ 2000 rpm with automatic transmission). Oil refill capacity: 7 qt. with filter change. Fuel Requirements: Diesel.

OPTIONAL ENGINE: K3500 and V3500 models: Ordering Code LL4. This engine was produced by GM-Detroit Diesel Allison Division. Engine Type: OHV, diesel V-8. Bore x Stroke: 3.98 in. x 3.80 in. Lifters: Hydraulic. Number of main bearings-5. Fuel Induction: Fuel injection. Compression Ratio: 21.3:1. Displacement: 379.4 cu. in. (6.2 liters). Horsepower: 143 @ 3600 rpm. Torque: 257 lb.-ft. @ 2000 rpm. Oil refill capacity: 7 qt. with filter change. Fuel Requirements: Diesel.

OPTIONAL ENGINE: All 8600 lb. and up GVWR models: Ordering Code L65. This engine was produced by GM-Detroit Diesel Allison Division. Engine Type: OHV, diesel V-8. Bore x Stroke: 4.52 in. x 3.82 in. Lifters: Hydraulic. Number of main bearings-5. Fuel Induction: Fuel injection. Compression Ratio: 21.5:1. Displacement: 396.67 cu. in. (6.5 liters). Horsepower: 190 @ 3400 rpm. Torque: 380 lb.-ft. @ 1700 rpm. Oil refill capacity: 7 qt. with filter change. Fuel Requirements: Diesel.

CHASSIS FEATURES: Semi-perimeter design, all-welded channel beam frame with boxed front end. Dimensions: K1500 and K2500 regular cab: 2.18 x 7.48 x 0.134 in. K1500 extended cab: 2.18 x 7.48 x 0.165 in. K2500 regular cab with C6P: 2.18 x 7.48 x 0.213 in. K2500 extended cab: 2.31 x 7.48 x 0.165 in. K2500 extended cab with C6P: 2.18 x 7.48 x 0.244 in. K3500 regular cab: 2.18 x 7.48 x 0.213 in. K3500 extended cab: 2.18 x 7.48 x 0.244 in. V3500 models: 2.788 x 7.74 x 0.244 in. Section modules: K1500 regular cab: 3.46; K1500 extended cab: 4.30; K2500: 4.30; K2500 with C6P: 6.48; K3500 regular cab: 5.61; K3500 extended cab: 6.48, V3500: 7.33.

SUSPENSION AND RUNNING GEAR: Front Suspension: Torsion bar springs. K1500 Capacity: 3860 lb. K2500 and K3500 capacity: 3750 lb. V3500: Tapered leaf springs. Capacity: 4500 lb. Shock absorber dia.: K1500; 25mm; K2500, K3500 and V3500: 32mm. 32mm optional for K1500. 1.00 in. stabilizer optional for all series except V3500 which had a standard 1.25 in. bar standard. Optional rating: K1500: RPO F44/F60: 6100 lb. GVW. K2500: 8600 lb. GVW. K3500: 10,000 lb. GVW. Rear Suspension: Semi-elliptical 2-stage, 4-leaf for K1500; 6-leaf for K2500; 6-leaf plus 1-leaf auxiliary for K3500. K1500 capacity: 3750 lb. K2500 capacity: 4800 lb. K3500 capacity: 7500 lb. V3500: Semi-elliptical 2-stage, 9-leaf. Capacity: 7000 lb. Shock absorber dia.: K1500: 25mm; K2500, K3500 and V3500: 32mm. 32mm optional for K1500. Optional Rating: See above for GVW ratings. Front Axle Type and Capacity: Independent, GM or K1500; Spicer on K2500 and K3500. Capacity: K1500 regular cab: 3925 lb.; K1500 extended cab: 4800 lb.; K2500 and K3500: 4250 lb. V3500: Spicer full-floating. Capacity: 4500 lb. manual hub locks. Optional: K1500: 3925 lb. capacity; K1500 extended cab: 4800 lb. All other K series: 4250 lb. Rear Axle Type: Semi-floating for K1500; Full-floating for K2500, K3500 and V3500. GM manufacture for all series. Capacity: K1500: 3750 lb.; K2500: 6000 lb.; K3500, V3500: 7500 lb. Optional: K2500: Regular cab: 4800 lb.; K250 extended cab: 6000 lb.; K3500: 7500 lb. Final Drive Ratio: The following transmission designations were used by Chevrolet: MM4: 4-spd. manual; MM5: 5-spd. manual overdrive; MX1: 3-spd. automatic; MXO: 4-spd. automatic. All ratios are with standard emission equipment. Standard: K1500, K2500: 3.42:1. Optional: 3.73:1. All engine/transmission combinations except K2500 with LL4 diesel engine which had standard 3.73:1 ratio and optional 4.10:1 ratio, and K2500 with 5.7 liter V-8 and C6P which also had an optional 4.56:1 ratio. Standard: K3500: 4.10:1 with 5.7 liter V-8 with 4.56:1 optional; 3.42:1 standard for 7.4 liter V-8 with 3.73 and 4.10:1 optional; 6.2 liter diesel (LL4) had standard 4.10:1 ratio with 4.56:1 optional. Standard for V3500: 3.73:1 with 5.7 liter and manual 4-spd. trans.; 4.10:1 with 3-spd. auto. trans.; 3.73:1 with 7.4 liter V-8; 4.10:1 with LL4 diesel. Optional: 4.10 and 4.56:1 for 5.7 liter V-8 with man. 4-spd.; 4.56:1 for 5.7 liter V-8 with 3-spd. auto. trans.; 4.10 and 4.56:1 for 7.4 liter V-8; 4.56:1 for LL4 diesel. Transfer Case: K1500, K2500, K3500: New Process 241. Single lever. Ratios: 2.72:1, 1.00:1. K3500 with RPO RO5: Borg Warner 1370: Ratios: 2.69:1, 1.00:1. The Borg Warner unit has a right hand side power take-off. Brakes: Type: Hydraulic, power assisted. Dimensions: K1500: Front: Disc: 11.86 in. x 1.00 in. Rear: Drums: 10.0 x 2.25 in. K1500 regular cab with RPO F44/F60 had 11.57 in. x 1.25 in. front disc brakes. K2500 regular cab: Front: Disc: 11.57 in. x 1.20 in. Rear: Drums: 11.15 in. x 2.75 in. K2500 extended cab: Front Disc: 11.57 in. x 1.25 in. Rear: 10.0 in. x 2.25 in. drums. All K2500 with 8600 lb. GVW Package had 12.50 in. x 1.26 in. front disc brakes and 13.0 in. x 2.5 in. rear drum brakes. K3500 all models: Front: Disc: 12.50 in. x 1.26 in. Rear: Drum: 13.00 in. x 2.50 in. V3500 all models: Front Disc: 12.54 in. x 1.54 in. Rear: Drums: 13.0 in. x 3.5 in. Wheels: K1500 and K2500: 16 x 6.5, 6-stud disc. K3500 and V3500: 16.0 x 6.0. Tires: K1500 Sportside and regular cab: LT225/75R-16C steel belted radial. K1500 extended cab: LT245/75R16C. K2500 all models: LT245/75R-16E. K3500: LT225/75RD. V3500 all models: 7.50-16D tubeless nylon. Optional: K1500: LT225/75R16C, blackwall, LT225/75R16C on-off road; blackwall, white stripe or white lettered. Available for K10903 only with the following engines: LB4, LO3 and LH6 and RPO GVT4 axle; and K10703 with LB4 or LO3 engine with RPO GT4 axle. LT265/75R16C blackwall or white letter, on-off road. Optional K2500: LTR225/75R16D steel belted radial blackwall or white stripe, LT245/75R16E highway or on-off road, LT225/75R16D blackwall, on-off road, LT245/75R16E blackwall (K20903 only). Optional: K3500: LT225/75R16D, blackwall, LT245/75R16E blackwall, LT245/75R16E on-off road blackwall, LT245/75R16E blackwall, 7.50 x 16D highway and on-off road. Optional: V3500: V30943 only: 7.50x 16D tubeless nylon, dual rear, LT215/85R16D dual rear tubeless steel belted radial; LT235/85R16E. Steering: Integral power. Ratio: K1500 regular cab Sportside and Fleetside: 17.44:1. K1500 extended cab model K10753: 18.8:1, model K10953: 17.44:1. K2500 regular cab: 17.44:1. K2500 extended cab: K20753: 18.88:1; model K20953: 17.44:1. K3500 regular cab: 127.44:1. K3500 extended cab: 17.44:1. V3500: 13.5:1. Turning Diameter (curb-to-curb): K1500 regular cab Sportside: 40.3 ft. K1500 regular cab Fleetside: 44.4 ft. K1500 extended cab Model K10753: 47.9 ft. Model K10953: 52.2 ft. K2500 regular cab: 44.4 ft. (with C6P: 45.1 ft.). K2500 extended cab: Model K20753: 47.9 ft. Model 52.2 ft. K3500 regular cab: 45.1 ft. K3500 extended cab: 52.2 ft. V3500: 54.5 ft. Transmission: Standard K1500/2500: With gasoline engines: RPO MM5-5-spd. manual with overdrive fully-synchronized. Transmission Ratios: 4.02, 2.32, 1.40, 1.00. 0.73:1; reverse: 3.74:1. Standard: K3500, V3500 and K2500 with C6P, and K1500 and K2500 with diesel engine: RPO MM4 4-spd. SM465 manual, synchromesh on top three gears (optional: K1500/2500). Transmission ratios: 6.55, 3.58, 1.70, 1.00:1, reverse: 6.09:1. Optional: All series: RPO MX1-3-spd. 400 automatic. Transmission ratios: 2.48, 1.48, 1.0:1, reverse: 2.08:1. Optional: K1500/2500, (except K2500 regular cab and extended cab chassis cab, and all V3500 models): RPO MXO-4-spd. automatic overdrive 700R4: 3.06, 1.63, 1.0, 0.70:1, Reverse: 2.29:1.

VEHICLE DIMENSIONS: Wheelbase: All series regular cab: 117.5 in. 131.5 in. extended cab: 6.5 ft. box models: 141.5 in.; 8.0 ft. box models: 155.5 in.; V3500 models: 164.5 in. Overall Length (without rear bumper): K1500 Sportside: 194.0 in. K1500 regular cab: 194.1 in. K1500 extended cab: Model K10753 (6.5 ft. box): 223.0 in. K10953 (8.0 ft. box): 237.0 in. K2500 regular cab: 212.6 in. K2500 extended cab: Model K20753: 223.0 in. Model K20953: 237.0 in. K3500 regular cab: 212.6 in. V3500: 246.4 in. Front/Rear Tread: 74 in./74 in. Overall Height: K1500 all models: 73.8 in. K2500 regular cab: 74.3 in. (75.8 in. if equipped with C6P). K2500 extended cab: 74.4 in. (75.8 in. if equipped with C6P). K3500 75.8 in. V3500: 76.3 in. Width: All models except V3500 and those equipped with RO5: 76.8 in. V3500: 79.6 in. V3500 and K3500 with RO5: 107.3 in. Front/Rear Overhang: 117.5 in. wheelbase. pickups: 34.9 in./41.6 in. 131.5 in. wheelbase pickups: 34.9 in./46.5 in. extended cab: 34.9/46.5 in. Chassis cab models: 34.9/41.8 in. Tailgate: Width and Height: K1500 Sportside: 50.9 x 19.3 in. All others: 62.0 in. x 19.3 in. Approach/Departure Degrees: K1500 117.5 in.: 22/28. Ground Clearance (Front/Rear in inches): K1500 Sportside and Fleetside: 8.6/9.0. K1500 extended cab: 9.2/9.6. K2500 regular cab: 8.7/7.7 (with C6P: 7.8/8.1). K2500 extended cab: Model K20753: 9.2/8.2, model K20953: 9.2/8.1. K3500 Regular and extended cab: 9.2/8.1 (with RO5 dual rear wheels: 7.2/7.4). V3500: 8.3/7.8. Front headroom, all models: 40.0 in. Front legroom, all models: 41.7 in. Front shoulder room, all models: 66.0 in.

CAPACITIES: Fuel Tank: All K series: 25.0 gal. All V3500 models: 20 gal. Optional: Models K10903, K10753, K10953, K20903, K20953, K30903: 34 gal. V3500 models: 20 gal.

ACCOMMODATIONS: Seating Capacity: Pickup, extended cab and chassis cab models: 3 passenger. Optional: Extended cab: 6 passenger. Suburban: 6 passenger. Optional: 9 passenger.

INSTRUMENTATION: Speedometer, odometer, fuel level gauge. Warning lights for battery, oil pressure, generator, brake system warning, directional/hazard lights, high beam, and engine coolant temperature.

OPTIONS AND PRICES: All K series: Air conditioning (RPO C60): $705, optional axle ratios: $44. Locking differential (RPO G80): $252. Auxiliary heavy-duty battery, not avail. with B3J (RPO TP2): $134. Painted rear step bumper, requires E63 body (RPO V43): $130. Front Deluxe chromed bumper with rub strip, K10703 only (RPO VG3): $26. Chromed rear step bumper with rub strip (RPO VB3): $229. Front black bumper guards (RPO V27): $32. Heavy-duty chassis equipment, K1500 only (RPO F44): $38. Off-Road Package, avail. for K1500 only. Includes skid plate and Bilstein shock absorbers (RPO Z71: $270. Cold Climate Package, not avail. with B3J. Includes engine block heater (RPO V10): $33. Convenience Group. Includes power door locks and windows (RPO ZQ2): $367. Convenience Group. Includes tilt wheel and speed control (RPO ZQ3): $383. Engine oil cooling system (RPO KC4): $135. Heavy-duty radiator (RPO VO1): $56. Heavy-duty radiator and transmission oil cooler (RPO VO2): $63. Rear window defogger (RPO C49): $154. 5.0 liter V-8 (RPO LO3): $575. 5.7 liter V-8 (RPO LO5): $840. 6.2 liter diesel V-8 (RPO LH6): $. Locking fuel filler cap (RPO NO5): $18. Cargo area lamp (RPO UF2): $36. Dome and reading lamp (RPO C95): $33. Roof marker lamps, not avail. with Calif. emissions (RPO UO1): $52. Auxiliary lighting. Includes dome and reading lamps and ashtray, glove box and under hood lamps (RPO TR9): $94. Below eye-level type stainless steel mirrors (RPO D45): $45. Camper-type stainless steel mirrors (RPO DF2): $53. Black exterior moldings (RPO B84): $90. Exterior bright moldings (RPO B85): $17. Conventional two-tone exterior paint (RPO ZY2): $132. Special two-tone exterior paint (RPO ZY3): $215. Deluxe two-tone exterior paint (RPO ZY4): $243. Electronically tuned AM/FM stereo radio with Seek-Scan and digital clock (RPO UM7): $210. Electronically tuned AM/FM stereo radio with Seek-Scan, stereo cassette tape and digital clock (RPO UM6): $332. Electronically tuned AM/FM stereo radio with Seek-Scan, stereo cassette player with Search and Repeat, graphic equalizer and digital clock (RPO UX1): $482. Radio delete option (RPO UL5): $77. Scottsdale Trim Package (RPO Z62): K series pickups: $573 to $604. Heavy-duty front and rear shock absorbers (RPO F51): $40. Silverado Trim Package (RPO YE9): K1500 regular cab Pickup: $981 to $1012. Off-road skid plate, K1500 only (RPO NZZ): $95. Heavy-duty front springs K1500 only, requires F44 heavy-duty chassis, not avail. with B3J or RPO Z71 off-road chassis (RPO F60): $63. Body striping (RPO D85): $69. Tow hooks, standard on K1500 (RPO V76): $38. Heavy-duty trailering special equipment (RPO Z82): $408 with RPO Z71 or XQ8, $448 without RPO Z71 or ZQ8. Four-speed manual trans. (RPO MM4): $98. Four-speed auto. trans. with overdrive (RPO MXO): $860. Three-speed auto. trans. (RPO MX1): $625. Wheelcovers (RPO PO1): $42. Aluminum wheels, K1500 only (RPO PF4): $295. Sliding rear window (RPO A28): $113. Camper Special chassis equipment K2500 and K3500 only (RPO Z81): $280 without B2J, $148 with B3J. Deep tinted glass, (RPO AJ1): $150. Sport Equipment Package (Sport Truck), K10703 only. Includes V43 black bumpers, black wheel flares, deluxe front appearance, black mirrors, GL LT265/75R16 blackwall tires, PF4 aluminum wheels with special hubcaps and 4x4 sport decal (RPO BPY): $1140.20. Sport steering wheel (RPO NK3): $7.00. Rear-mounted fuel tank, avail for K2500 and K3500 chassis & cab models, approximate capacity of 31 gal. (RPO NK7): $63. Special chassis camper equipment. Includes TP2 auxiliary battery without B3J equipment, camper wiring harness and DF2 mirrors (RPO Z81): $280 for K series pickups, $1436 with B3J, $81 for V3500. Dual rear wheels, available for 3500 models only. Includes plastic rear fender extensions with side marker lamps on front and rear siders and dual rear chassis provisions (RPO RO5): $1038, $1101 with MX1 trans. Includes VO2 heavy-duty radiator and trans. oil cooler, $785 for V3500

HISTORICAL FOOTNOTES: As of July 1, 1992, sales of the full size Chevrolet pickups totalled 199,602. Suburban sales were 19,840.

1993 PICKUP

1993 Chevrolet K3500 extended cab Dooley pickup

Powertrain changes were the major developments for 1993. The 6.5 liter turbo diesel was now offered for crew cabs and extended cab pickups with GVWR over 8500 lb. The 4.3 liter V-6 was upgraded with a new balance shaft intended to dampen vibrations in high rpm ranges. Other developments involved revised cylinder heads with improved flow characteristics, revised throttle-body injection unit for smoother idle, a new quiet fan drive that reduced engine noise, especially during cold starts, a new thermostat, revised oil filter and a new dual-stud air cleaner. Both the 5.0 liter and 5.7 liter V-8 engines were improved in several areas. The induction system was modified to reduce interior noise. Its throttle-body injection unit was also revised for smoother idle operation. They also had a new quiet fan drive and a dual-stud air cleaner and revised oil filter. The 5.0 V-8 also had new low tension piston pins for 1993. Beginning in 1993, a modified version of the 5.7 liter V-8 was available for conversion to compressed natural gas, propane or to dual fuel capability with gasoline. As with the other V-8 engines, the 7.4 liter V-8 had a modified throttle-body injection unit, and a larger radiator (mid-year release). Other improvements included a one-piece dip stick, new spark plug shields, revised intake manifold and machined water pump outlet, and a quiet fan drive.

A new electronic 4-speed automatic Hydra-Matic 4L60-E was available for trucks under 8500 lb. GVRW.

A new Sportside Sport Pickup for the 1500 series regular cab included Silverado trim, Sport decals, body-color Dura-Grille™, Sportside box, cast aluminum wheels, painted exterior mirrors, and color-keyed front and rear bumpers. The Sportside Sport pickup was offered in summit white, onyx or victory red. all models had a new "Leading Edge" anti-chip coating applied to the leading edges of the hood, roof and A pillars. Solar-Ray™ tinted glass was standard in all windows. Scotchgard™ fabric protector was applied to all cloth seat and door trim panels. The extended cab was now available with 2 passenger seating, giving customers a choice of 2, 3, 5 or 6 passenger seating. A 40/6-split-bench seat in cloth or vinyl, and low-back bucket seats in cloth or vinyl were available with the Cheyenne option. It previously required the Scottsdale trim. A seat-back recliner was added to the passenger side on the 40/60 split-bench seat and low-back bucket seats. Dual cupholders were now mounted on the instrument panel (this feature was not available with bucket seat). A steel sleeve steering column was used with the ComforTilt steering wheel for improved security. The sun visors were now cloth-covered. The radio controls were revised with a new control panel and improved button operation. A full-cloth headliner was now optional for regular cab pickups. A cloth headliner continued as standard for the Silverado decor on pickups and extended cab models. A new electronic fuel shut-off automatically limited maximum engine speed to less than tire speed rating. A Deluxe front appearance (RPO V22) was available as an option with Cheyenne models. The Cheyenne K3500 chassis cab with crew cab was available with a new Auxiliary Lighting option. Four new 1993 exterior colors were introduced: Light Quasar blue metallic, teal green metallic, Indigo blue metallic and dark garnet red metallic. They replaced brilliant blue metallic, smoke blue metallic, Catalina blue metallic and crimson red metallic. The only new color offered for the crew cab chassis cab and Suburban models was Indigo blue metallic. The Scottsdale decor was cancelled for 1993. Phased out during 1992 and not offered for 1993 was the Special two-tone paint option.

1993 Chevrolet K1500 regular cab longbox pickup

I.D. DATA: Unchanged for 1992. The letter O represented the 1993 model year.

Model	Body Type	Price

Series K1500-1/2 ton 262 V-6-cyl. 117.5 in. 131.5 in. wheelbase (Suburban: 129.5 in. wheelbase and standard 350 V-8)

Prices of 1993 models were not available at press time

Model	Body Type	Price
CK10903	8.0 ft. Worktruck	N.A.
CK10703	6.5 ft. Sportside Pickup	N.A.
CK10703	6.5 ft. Fleetside Pickup	N.A.
CK10903	8.0 ft. Fleetside Pickup	N.A.
CK10753	6.5 ft. Ext. Cab Fleetside	N.A.
CK10953	8.0 ft. Ext. Cab Fleetside	N.A.
CV10906	Suburban Panl. Drs.	N.A.
CV10906	Suburban Tailgate	N.A.

K2500-3/4 ton 262 V-6l. 131.5 in. wheelbase. (V2500 Suburban-129.5 in. wheelbase). Crew and bonus cab: 164.5 in. wheelbase, Suburban with standard 350 V-8

Model	Body Type	Price
CK20903	8.0 ft. Fleetside Pickup	N.A.
CK20753	6.5 ft. Extended Cab Pickup	N.A.
CK20953	8.0 ft. Extended Cab Pickup	N.A.
CV20906	Suburban Panl. Drs.	N.A.
CV20906	Suburban Tailgate	N.A.

Series K3500-1 ton 350 V-8. 131.5 in. wheelbase. Extended Cab: 155.5 in. wheelbase Crew and bonus cab: 164.5 in. wheelbase

Model	Body Type	Price
CK30903	8.0 ft. Fleetside Pickup	N.A.
CK30953	8.0 ft. Ext. Cab F-S Pickup	N.A.

Series V3500-1 ton 350 V-8. 164.5 in. wheelbase Fleetside Crew and bonus cab: 164.5 in. wheelbase

Model	Body Type	Price
CV30943	Bonus Cab	N.A.
CV30943	Crew Cab	N.A.
CV30943	Bonus Cab Chassis & Cab	N.A.
CV30943	Crew Cab Chassis & Cab	N.A.
CV30943	H-D Bonus Cab Chassis & Cab	N.A.
CV30943	H-D Crew Cab Chassis & Cab	N.A.

STANDARD ENGINE: All K1500, K2500 models: 262 V-6 (LB4 ordering code). Engine Type: Vortex OHV, V-6-cylinder. Cast iron block. Bore x Stroke: 4.0 in. x 3.48 in. Lifters: Hydraulic. Fuel Induction: Electronic fuel injection. Compression Ratio: 9.1:1. Displacement: 262 cu. in. (4.3 liters). Horsepower: Net 165 @ 4000 rpm. Torque: Net 235 lb.-ft. @ 2400 rpm. Oil refill capacity: 5 qt. with filter change. Fuel Requirements: Regular 87 octane unleaded.

OPTIONAL ENGINE: K1500, K2500-305 V-8 (LO3 ordering code). Engine Type: OHV, V-8. Cast iron block and cylinder head. Bore x Stroke: 3.74 in. x 3.48 in. Lifters: Hydraulic. Number of main bearings-5. Fuel Induction: Electronic fuel injection. Compression Ratio: 9.1:1. Displacement: 305 cu. in. (5.0 liters). Horsepower: Net 175 @ 4000 rpm. Torque: Net 270 lb.-ft. @ 2400 rpm. Oil refill capacity: 5 qt. with filter change. Fuel Requirements: Regular unleaded.

OPTIONAL ENGINE: K1500, K2500, Standard: Suburban under 8500 lb. GVRW, V3500 and K3500 models: Optional for K150 and K2500 models. 350 V-8 (LO5 ordering code). Engine Type: OHV, V-8. Cast iron block and cylinder head. Bore x Stroke: 4.0 in. x 3.48 in. Lifters: Hydraulic. Number of main bearings-5. Fuel Induction: Electronic fuel injection. Compression Ratio: 9.1:1. Displacement: 350 cu. in. (5.7 liters). Horsepower: GVWR over 8500 (LO5 HD): Net: 190 @ 4000 rpm. GVWR under 8500 lb.: 210 @ 4000 rpm. Torque: GVWR over 8500 (LO5 HD): Net 300 lb.-ft. @ 2400 rpm. GVWR under 8500 lb.: 300 lb.-ft. @ 2800 rpm. Oil refill capacity: 5 qt. with filter change. Fuel Requirements: Regular unleaded.

STANDARD ENGINE: K3500 models with dual rear wheels" Optional: Other K3500 models and Suburban over 8500 lb. GVWR: Ordering Code: L19: 454 V-8. Engine Type: OHV, V-8. Cast iron block and alloy iron cylinder head. Bore x Stroke: 4.30 in. x 4.0 in. Lifters: Hydraulic. Number of main bearings-5. Fuel Induction: Electronic fuel injection. Compression Ratio: 7.9:1. Displacement: 454 cu. in. (7.4 liters). Horsepower: 230 @ 3600 rpm. Torque: 385 lb.-ft. @ 1600 rpm. Oil refill capacity: 5 qt. with filter change. Fuel Requirements: Regular unleaded.

OPTIONAL ENGINE: K1500 and K2500: Ordering Code LH6. Not available in California for K2500. This engine was produced by GM-Detroit Diesel Allison Division. Engine Type: OHV, diesel V-8. Bore x Stroke: 3.98 in. x 3.80 in. Lifters: Hydraulic. Number of main bearings-5. Fuel Induction: Gear driven mechanical fuel injection. Compression Ratio: 21.3:1. Displacement: 379.4 cu. in. (6.2 liters). Horsepower: 126 @ 3600 rpm. (140 @ 3600 rpm with automatic transmission). Torque: 240 lb.-ft. @ 2000 rpm. (247 lb.-ft. @ 2000 rpm with automatic transmission). Oil refill capacity: 7 qt. with filter change. Fuel Requirements: Diesel.

OPTIONAL ENGINE: K3500 and V3500 models: Ordering Code LL4. This engine was produced by GM-Detroit Diesel Allison Division. Engine Type: OHV, diesel V-8. Bore x Stroke: 3.98 in. x 3.80 in. Lifters: Hydraulic. Number of main bearings-5. Fuel Induction: Fuel injection. Compression Ratio: 21.3:1. Displacement: 379.4 cu. in. (6.2 liters). Horsepower: 143 @ 3600 rpm. Torque: 257 lb.-ft. @ 2000 rpm. Oil refill capacity: 7 qt. with filter change. Fuel Requirements: Diesel.

OPTIONAL ENGINE: All 8600 lb. and up GVWR models: Ordering Code L65. This engine was produced by GM-Detroit Diesel Allison Division. Engine Type: OHV, diesel V-8. Bore x Stroke: 4.52 in. x 3.82 in. Lifters: Hydraulic. Number of main bearings-5. Fuel Induction: Fuel injection. Compression Ratio: 21.5:1. Displacement: 396.67 cu. in. (6.5 liters). Horsepower: 190 @ 3400 rpm. Torque: 380 lb.-ft. @ 1700 rpm. Oil refill capacity: 7 qt. with filter change. Fuel Requirements: Diesel.

CHASSIS FEATURES: Semi-perimeter design, all-welded channel beam frame with boxed front end. Dimensions: K1500 and K2500 regular cab: 2.18 x 7.48 x 0.134 in. K1500 extended cab: 2.18 x 7.48 x 0.165 in. K2500 regular cab with C6P: 2.18 x 7.48 x 0.213 in. K2500 extended cab: 2.31 x 7.48 x 0.165 in. K2500 extended cab with C6P: 2.18 x 7.48 x 0.244 in. K3500 regular cab: 2.18 x 7.48 x 0.213 in. K3500 extended cab: 2.18 x 7.48 x 0.244 in. V3500 models: 2.788 x 7.74 x 0.244 in. Section modules: K1500 regular cab: 3.46; K1500 extended cab: 4.30; K2500: 4.30; K2500 with C6P: 6.48; K3500 regular cab: 5.61; K3500 extended cab: 6.48, V3500: 7.33.

SUSPENSION AND RUNNING GEAR: Front Suspension: Torsion bar springs. K1500 Capacity: 3860 lb. K2500 and K3500 capacity: 3750 lb. V3500: Tapered leaf springs. Capacity: 4500 lb. Shock absorber dia.: K1500: 1.18 in.; K2500, K3500 and V3500: 32mm. 32mm optional for K1500. 1.00 in. stabilizer optional for all series except V3500 which had a standard 1.25 in. bar standard. Optional rating: K1500: RPO F44/F60: 6100 lb. GVW. K2500: 8600 lb. K3500: 10,000 lb. GVW. Rear Suspension: Semi-elliptical 2-stage, 4-leaf for K1500; 6-leaf for K2500; 6-leaf plus 1-leaf auxiliary for K3500. K1500 capacity: 3750 lb. K2500 capacity: 4800 lb. K3500 capacity: 7500 lb. V3500: Semi-elliptical 2-stage, 9-leaf. Capacity: 7000 lb. Shock absorber dia.: K1500: 25mm; K2500, K3500 and V3500: 32mm. 32mm optional for K1500. Optional Rating: See above for GVW ratings. Front Axle Type and Capacity: Independent, GM or K1500; Spicer on K2500 and K3500. Capacity: K1500 regular cab: 3925 lb.; K1500 extended cab: 4800 lb.; K2500 and K3500: 4250 lb. K1500 full-floating. Capacity: 4500 lb. manual hub locks. Optional: K1500: 3925 lb. capacity; K1500 extended cab: 4800 lb. All other K series: 4250 lb. Rear Axle Type: Semi-floating for K1500; Full-floating for K2500, K3500 and V3500. GM manufacture for all series. Capacity: K1500: 3750 lb., K2500: 6000 lb.; K3500, V3500: 7500 lb. Optional: K2500: Regular cab: 4800 lb.; K250 extended cab: 6000 lb.; K3500, V3500: 7500 lb. Final Drive Ratio: The following transmission designations were used by Chevrolet: MM4: 4-spd. manual; MM5: 5-spd. manual overdrive; MX1: 3-spd. automatic; MXO: 4-spd. automatic. All ratios are with standard emission equipment. Standard: K1500, K2500: 3.42:1. Optional: 3.73:1. All engine/transmission combinations except K2500 with LL4 diesel engine which had standard 3.73:1 ratio and optional 4.10:1 ratio, and K2500 with 5.7 liter V-8 and C6P which also had an optional 4.56:1 ratio. Standard: K3500: 4.10:1 with 5.7 liter V-8 and 4.56:1 optional; 3.42:1 standard for 7.4 liter V-8 with 3.73 and 4.10:1 optional; 6.2 liter diesel (LL4) had standard 4.10:1 ratio with 4.56:1 optional. Standard for V3500: 3.73:1 with 5.7 liter and manual 4-spd. trans.; 4.10:1 with 3-spd. auto. trans.; 3.73:1 with 7.4 liter V-8; 4.10:1 with LL4 diesel. Optional: 4.10 and 4.56:1 for 5.7 liter V-8 with man. 4-spd.; 4.56:1 for 5.7 liter V-8 with 3-spd. auto. trans.; 4.10 and 4.56:1 for 7.4 liter V-8; 4.56:1 for LL4 diesel. Transfer Case: K1500, K2500, K3500: New Process 241. Single lever. Ratios: 2.72:1, 1.00:1. K3500 with RPO RO5: Borg Warner 1370: Ratios: 2.69:1, 1.00:1. The Borg Warner unit has a right hand side power take-off. Brakes: Type: Hydraulic, power assisted. Dimensions: K1500: Front: Disc 11.57 in. x 1.00 in. Rear: Drums: 10.0 x 2.25 in. K1500 regular cab with RPO F44/F60 had 11.57 in. x 1.25 in. front disc brakes. K2500 regular cab: Front: Disc 11.57 in. x 1.20 in. Rear: Drums: 11.15 in. x 2.75 in. K2500 extended cab: Front Disc: 11.57 in. x 1.25 in. Rear: 10.0 in. x 2.25 in. drums. All K2500 with 8600 lb. GVW Package had 12.50 in. x 1.26 in. front disc brakes and 13.0 in. x 2.5 in. rear drum brakes. K3500 all models: Front: Disc: 12.50 in. x 1.26 in. Rear: Drum: 13.00 in. x 2.50 in. V3500 all models: Front: Disc: 12.50 in. x 1.54 in. Rear: Drums: 13.0 in. x 3.5 in. Wheels: K1500 and K2500: 16 x 6.5, 6-stud disc. K3500 and V3500: 16.0 x 6.0. Tires: K1500 Sportside and regular cab: LT225/75R-16C steel belted radial. K1500 extended cab: LT245/75R16C. K2500 all models: LT245/75R-16E. K3500: LT225/75RD. V3500 all models: 7.50-16D tubeless nylon. Optional: K1500: LT225/75R16C, blackwall, LT225/75R16C on-off road; blackwall, white stripe or white lettered. Available for K10903 only with the following engines: LB4, LO3 and LH6 and RPO GVT4 axle; and K10703 with LB4 or LO3 engine with RPO GT4 axle. LT225/75R16C blackwall or white letter, on-off road. Optional K2500: LTR225/75R16D steel belted radial blackwall or white stripe, LT245/75R16E highway or on-off road, LT225/75R16D blackwall, on-off road, LT245/75R16E blackwall (K20903 only). Optional: K3500: LT225/75R16D, blackwall, LT245/75R16E blackwall, LT245/75R16E on-off road blackwall, LT245/75R16E blackwall, 7.50 x 16D highway and on-off road. Optional: V3500: V30943 only: 7.50x 16D tubeless nylon, dual rear, LT215/85R16D dual rear tubeless steel belted radial; LT235/85R16E. Steering: Integral power. Ratio: K1500 regular cab Sportside and Fleetside: 17.44:1. K1500 extended cab model K10753: 18.8:1, model K10953: 17.44:1. K2500 regular cab: 17.44:1. K2500 extended cab: K20753: 18.88:1; model K20953: 17.44:1. K3500 regular cab: 127.44:1. K3500 extended cab: 17.44:1. V3500: 13.5:1. Turning Diameter (curb-to-curb): K1500 regular cab Sportside: 40.3 ft. K1500 regular cab Fleetside: 44.4 ft. K1500 regular cab Model K10753: 47.9 ft. K10953: 52.2 ft. K2500 regular cab: 44.4 ft. (with C6P): 45.1 ft.). K2500 extended cab: Model K20753: 47.9 ft. Model 52.2 ft. K3500 regular cab: 45.1 ft. K3500 extended cab: 52.2 ft. V3500: 54.5 ft. Transmission: Standard K1500/2500: With gasoline engines: RPO MM5-5-spd. manual with overdrive fully-synchronized. Transmission Ratios: 4.02, 2.32, 1.40, 1.00. 0.73:1; reverse: 3.74:1. Standard: K3500, V3500 and K2500 with C6P, and K1500 and K2500 with diesel engine: RPO MM4 4-spd. manual. SM465 manual, synchromesh on top three gears (optional: K1500/2500). Transmission ratios: 6.34, 3.44, 1.71, 1.00:1, reverse: 6.34:1. Optional: All models: 4-speed electronic Hydra-Matic 4L80-E automatic with overdrive. Transmission ratios: 2.48, 1.48, 1.0:1, reverse: 2.08:1. Optional: All models: 4-spd. automatic overdrive electronic Hydra-Matic 4L60-E. Ratios: 3.06, 1.63, 1.0, 0.70:1, Reverse: 2.29:1.

VEHICLE DIMENSIONS: Wheelbase: All series regular cab: 117.5 in. 131.5 in. extended cab: 6.5 ft. box models: 141.5 in.; 8.0 ft. box models: 155.5 in.; V3500 models: 164.5 in. Overall Length (without rear bumper): K1500 Sportside: 194.0 in. K1500 regular cab: 194.1 in. K1500 extended cab: Model K10753 (6.5 ft. box): 223.0 in. K10953 (8.0 ft. box): 237.0 in. K2500 regular cab: 212.6 in. K2500 extended cab: Model K20753: 223.0 in. Model K20953: 237.0 in.

K3500 regular cab: 212.6 in. V3500: 246.4 in. Front/Rear Tread: 74 in./74. Overall Height: K1500 all models: 73.8 in. K2500 regular cab: 74.3 in. (75.8 in. if equipped with C6P). K2500 extended cab: 74.4 in. (75.8 in. if equipped with C6P). K3500 75.8 in. V3500: 76.3 in. Width: All models except V3500 and those equipped with RO5: 76.8 in. V3500: 79.6 in. V3500 and K3500 with RO5: 107.3 in. Front/Rear Overhang: 117.5 in. wheelbase pickups: 34.9 in./41.6 in. 131.5 in. wheelbase pickups: 34.9 in./46.5 in. extended cab: 34.9/46.5 in. Chassis cab models: 34.9/41.8 in. Tailgate: Width and Height: K1500 Sportside: 50.9 x 19.3 in. All others: 62.0 in. x 19.3 in. Approach/Departure Degrees: K1500 117.5 in.: 22/28. Ground Clearance (Front/Rear in inches): K1500 Sportside and Fleetside: 8.6/9.0. K1500 extended cab: 9.2/9.6. K2500 regular cab: 8.7/7.7 (with C6P: 7.8/8.1). K2500 extended cab: Model K20753: 9.2/8.2, model K20953: 9.2/8.1. K3500 regular and extended cab: 9.2/8.1 (with RO5 dual rear wheels: 7.2/7.4). V3500: 8.3/7.8. Front headroom, all models: 40.0 in. Front legroom, all models: 41.7 in. Front shoulder room, all models: 66.0 in.

CAPACITIES: Fuel Tank: All K series: 25.0 gal. All V3500 models: 20 gal. Optional: Models K10903, K10753, K10953, K20903, K20953, K30903: 34 gal. V3500 models: 20 gal.

ACCOMMODATIONS: Seating Capacity: Pickup, extended cab and chassis cab models: 3 passenger. Optional: Extended cab: 6 passenger. Suburban: 6 passenger. Optional: 9 passenger.

INSTRUMENTATION: Speedometer, odometer, fuel level gauge. Warning lights for battery, oil pressure, generator, brake system warning, directional/hazard lights, high beam, and engine coolant temperature. Option: Except as noted above, the options for 1993 were unchanged from 1992.

HISTORICAL FOOTNOTES: It was expected that the market mix of the 1993 K series pickup and crew cab models would be 80 percent-K1500, 15 percent-K2500 and 5 percent-K3500. The Suburban model mix was expected to be 85 percent-K1500 and 15 percent-K2500.

CHEVROLET BLAZER
1969-1993

1969 BLAZER

The Blazer originated as a design that shared its basic configuration with the K10 four-wheel drive pickups. Both vehicles had the same front end sheet metal, the same basic running gear and suspension, and identical powerplants and trim options. In essence the Blazer was a short wheelbase version of the K10 available with a full-length, removable roof.

As a result, the Blazer was considerably larger than many of its competitors. For example, it was almost a foot wider and over two feet longer than a Ford Bronco. This provided the Blazer owner with much more interior space but with less agility and maneuverability than smaller off-road vehicles. An important by-product of the Blazer's close association with the K10 was the steady flow of improvements made in the high-volume Chevrolet pickup truck line that were shared with the Blazer. Other four-wheel drive vehicles, because of their low production runs were often committed to a particular design for extended periods of time. In its base form the Blazer was an open model with a single seat for the driver. A passenger seat and a bench type rear seat could be ordered separately or collectively. The Blazer's optional fiberglass top was available in either a black or white textured paint finish. It was equipped with a lockable lift gate. Fifteen body colors were offered. Standard Blazer equipment included heater and defroster, two-speed windshield wipers, side marker reflectors, hazard warning switch, directional signals, dual hydraulic brake system, back-up lights, driver's seat belt, padded sun visors, inside mirror, left and right-side exterior mirrors and water-proofed horn button, ignition switch and instrument cluster.

1969 Chevrolet K10 Blazer

I.D. DATA: The Blazer's V.I.N. consisted of 12 symbols. The first (a letter) identified the chassis. The second (a letter) identified the engine. The third (a digit) indicated the GVW range. The fourth entry (a digit) identified the model type. The fifth (a digit) identified the model year. The sixth (a letter) identified the assembly plant. The last six elements (all digits) served as the sequential production numbers. The combination V.I.N./GVW number was located on the left door pillar. The engine number indicated the manufacturing plant, day of manufacture and transmission type. It was located on a pad positioned on the right-hand side of the cylinder block at the rear of the distributor on V-8 engines and on a pad located at the front right hand side of the cylinder block of 6-cylinder engines.

Model Number	Body Type & Seating	Factory Price	GVW	Shipping Weight	Prod. Total
Blazer K10					
KS10514	Utility	$2852	5000	3552	4935

STANDARD ENGINE: High Torque 250 Six. (KS prefix). Engine Type: OHV, In-line 6-cylinder. Bore x Stroke: 3.875 in. x 3.50 in. Lifters: Hydraulic. Number of main bearings-7. Carburetion: Single barrel Rochester downdraft. Compression Ratio: 8.5:1. Displacement: 250 cu. in. (4.09 liters). Horsepower: Gross: 155 @ 4200 rpm. Net: 125 @ 3800 rpm. Torque: Gross: 235 lb.-ft. @ 1600 rpm. Net: 215 @ 2000 rpm. Oil capacity: 5 qt. with filter change. Fuel Requirements: Regular.

STANDARD ENGINE: Turbo-Fire V-8, V-8 models (KE prefix): Engine Type: OHV, V-8. Bore x Stroke: 3.875 in. x 3.25 in. Lifters: Hydraulic. Number of main bearings-5. Carburetion: 2-barrel Rochester. Compression Ratio: 9.0:1. Displacement: 307 cu. in. (5.03 liters). Horsepower: Gross: 200 @ 4600 rpm. Net: 157 @ 4000 rpm. Torque: Gross: 300 lb.-ft. @ 2400 rpm. Net: 260 @ 2000 rpm. Oil capacity: 5 qt. with filter change. Fuel Requirements: Regular.

OPTIONAL ENGINE: Turbo-Fire V-8: V-8 models: Engine Type: OHV V-8. Bore x Stroke: 4.00 in. x 3.50 in. Lifters: Hydraulic. Number of main bearings-5. Displacement: 350 cu. in. (5.73 liters). Carburetion: Single 4-barrel Rochester. Compression Ratio: 9.0:1. Horsepower: Gross: 255 @ 4600 rpm. Net: 200 @ 4000 rpm. Torque: Gross: 355 lb.-ft. @ 3000 rpm. Net: 310 @ 2400 rpm. Fuel Requirements: Regular.

CHASSIS FEATURES: Ladder-type, heavy-gauge channel side members, alligator-jaw cross members. Section modules: 2.70 in.

SUSPENSION AND RUNNING GEAR: Front Suspension: Tapered single leaf. Capacity: 2900 lb. Optional: 3500 lb. capacity. Rear Suspension: Two-stage tapered and multi-leaf (four-conventional leaves, one tapered leaf). Capacity: 3600 lb. Optional: None. Front Axle. Type: Hypoid, tubular driving. Capacity: 3300 lb. Rear Axle. Type: Hypoid, semi-floating. Capacity: 3300 lb. Final Drive Ratio: 3.73:1 (3.07:1 with 350 V-8). Optional: 3.07:1. Transfer Case: Type: Manual transmission: Dana 20. Ratios: 2.03:1, 1.00:1. Automatic transmission: New Process 205. Ratios: 1.96:1, 1.00:1. Brakes: Type: Hydraulic, drums. Optional: Power. Dimensions: Front and rear: 11.0 in. x 2.00 in. Total lining area: 167 sq. in. Wheels: 6-stud, 5.5 in. Optional: 6-stud, 5.0 in. and 6.0 in. Tires: 8.25 x 15 4-ply rating. Optional: various sizes. Steering: Manual recirculating ball. Ratio: 24.0:1. Optional: Power-assisted. Transmission: Type: Saginaw 3-speed manual, fully synchronized. Steering column-mounted shifter. Transmission Ratios: 2.85, 1.68, 1.0:1. Reverse: 2.95:1. Optional: Chevrolet CH465 4-speed manual. Floor-mounted shift lever. Optional: Turbo Hydra-Matic 3-speed automatic. Clutch: Six-cylinder: 10.0 in. dia., 100 sq. in. area. V-8: Type: 11.0 in. dia., 124 sq. in. area. Optional: V-8-cylinder: 12.0 in., 150 sq. in.

VEHICLE DIMENSIONS: Wheelbase: 104 in. Overall Length: 177.5 in. Front/Rear Tread 64.0 in./61.0 in. Overall Height: 68.5 in. With optional hardtop; 72.75 in. Width: 79.0 in. Front/Rear Overhang: 33.25 in./40.25 in. Tailgate: Width and Height: 65.0 in. x 19.25 in. Approach/Departure Degrees: 35.2/25.0. Ground Clearance: Front axle: 8.0 in. Rear axle: 8.0 in. Load space: With rear seat removed or folded: 70.0 in. x 65.0 in. x 19.25 in.

CAPACITIES: Fuel Tank: 23.5 gal. Optional: None. Coolant system: 250 6-cyl.: 12.2 qt. 307 V-8: 18.5 qt. 350 V-8: 17.1 qt.

ACCOMMODATIONS: Seating Capacity: Standard: Driver. Optional: Driver and front passenger and/or 3 passenger rear bench seat.

INSTRUMENTATION: Speedometer, odometer, fuel level gauge; warning lights for generator, engine coolant temperature and oil pressure. Brake warning light. Hazard warning switch.

OPTIONS AND PRICES: Fiberglass top. 11 in. clutch for 6-cyl. Front passenger seat. Rear bench seat. 307 cu. in. V-8. 350 cu. in. V-8. various tire sizes. 3.07:1 axle ratio (350 and 307 engines only). Oil bath air cleaner (not available with 350 V-8 and automatic transmission). Engine governor (not available with 350 V-8 and automatic transmission). Power steering. Power brakes. Front bucket seats. Carpeting. Radio. Soft-Ray tinted glass. Air conditioning. Bright exterior trim. Bright wheelcovers. Chrome hubcaps. Chrome front and rear bumpers. Chrome shift lever. Heavy-duty shock absorbers. Heavy-duty clutch. Heavy-duty radiator (standard with 350 V-8). Fuel filter. Heavy-duty shock absorbers. Heavy-duty starter. Shoulder harnesses. Custom Sport Truck: $358. Includes special exterior trim, front bucket seas, right-hand armrest and color-keyed floor coverings. Towing hooks. Free-wheeling front hubs. Courtesy lights. Spare tire lock.

HISTORICAL FOOTNOTES: The introduction of the Blazer moved Chevrolet into the mainstream of off-road four-wheel drive activities.

1970 BLAZER

The 1970 Blazer had a mildly restyled front end format highlighted by a grille insert containing a dozen sets of horizontal bright bars. They were equally positioned above and below the aluminum center pieces that contained CHEVROLET lettering. Chevrolet's blue "Bow Tie" emblem was once again positioned on the leading edge of the hood.

1970 Chevrolet K10 Blazer

I.D. DATA: The Blazer's V.I.N. consisted of 12 symbols. The first (a letter) identified the chassis. The second (a letter) identified the engine. The third (a digit) indicated the GVW range. The fourth entry (a digit) identified the model type. The fifth (a digit) identified the model year. The sixth (a letter) identified the assembly plant. The last six elements (all digits) served as the sequential production numbers. The combination V.I.N./GVW number was located on the left door pillar. The engine number indicated the manufacturing plant, day of manufacture and transmission type. It was located on a pad positioned on the right-hand side of the cylinder block at the rear of the distributor on V-8 engines and on a pad located at the front right hand side of the cylinder block of 6-cylinder engines.

Model Number	Body Type & Seating	Factory Price	GVW	Shipping Weight	Prod. Total
Blazer K10					
KS10514	Utility	$2956	4600*	3552	11,527

* 5000 lb. GVW package optional.

STANDARD ENGINE: High Torque 250 Six. (KS prefix): Engine Type: OHV, In-line 6-cylinder. Bore x Stroke: 3.875 in. x 3.50 in. Lifters: Hydraulic. Number of main bearings-7. Carburetion: Rochester downdraft one-barrel, Model M7028007 or M7028011. Compression Ratio: 8.5:1. Displacement: 250 cu. in. (4.09 liters). Horsepower: Gross: 155 @ 4200 rpm. Net: 125 @ 3800 rpm. Torque: Gross: 235 lb.-ft. @ 1600 rpm. Net: 215 @ 2000 rpm. Oil capacity: 5 qt. with filter change. Fuel Requirements: Regular.

STANDARD ENGINE: Turbo-Fire V-8, V-8 models (KE prefix): Engine Type: OHV, V-8. Bore x Stroke: 3.875 in. x 3.25 in. Lifters: Hydraulic. Number of main bearings-5. Carburetion: 2-barrel Rochester. Compression Ratio: 9.0:1. Displacement: 307 cu. in. (5.03 liters). Horsepower: Gross: 200 @ 4600 rpm. Net: 157 @ 4000 rpm. Torque: Gross: 300 lb.-ft. @ 2400 rpm. Net: 260 @ 2000 rpm. Oil capacity: 5 qt. with filter change. Fuel Requirements: Regular.

OPTIONAL ENGINE: Turbo-Fire V-8: V-8 models: Engine Type: OHV V-8. Bore x Stroke: 4.00 in. x 3.50 in. Lifters: Hydraulic. Number of main bearings-5. Displacement: 350 cu. in. (5.73 liters). Carburetion: Single 4-barrel Rochester. Compression Ratio: 9.0:1. Horsepower: Gross: 255 @ 4600 rpm. Net: 200 @ 4000 rpm. Torque: Gross: 355 lb.-ft. @ 3000 rpm. Net: 310 @ 2400 rpm. Fuel Requirements: Regular.

CHASSIS FEATURES: Ladder-type, heavy-gauge channel side members, alligator-jaw cross members. Section modules: 2.70 in.

SUSPENSION AND RUNNING GEAR: Front Suspension: Tapered single leaf. Capacity: 2900 lb. Optional: 3500 lb. capacity springs and heavy-duty shock absorbers. Rear Suspension: Two-stage tapered and multi-leaf (four-conventional leaves, one tapered leaf). Capacity: 3600 lb. Optional: None. Front Axle. Type: Hypoid, tubular driving. Capacity: 3300 lb. Rear Axle. Type: Hypoid, semi-floating. Capacity: 3300 lb. Final Drive Ratio: 3.73:1 (3.07:1 with 350 V-8). Optional: 3.07:1. Transfer Case: Type: Manual transmission: Dana 20. Ratios: 2.03:1, 1.00:1. Automatic transmission: New Process 205. Ratios: 1.96:1, 1.00:1. Brakes: Type: Hydraulic, drums. Optional: Power. Dimensions: Front and rear: 11.0 in. x 2.00 in. Total lining area: 167 sq. in. Wheels: 6-stud, 5.5 in. Optional: 6-stud, 5.0 in. and 6.0 in. Tires: E78 x 15B. Optional: G78 x 15B, H78 x 15B, 8.75 x 16.5, 10.00 x 16.5, G78 x 15B, 6.50 x 16, 7.0 x 15. Steering: Manual recirculating ball. Ratio: 24.0:1. Optional: Power-assisted. Transmission: Type: Saginaw 3-speed manual, fully synchronized. Steering column-mounted shifter. Transmission Ratios: 2.85, 1.68, 1.0:1. Reverse: 2.95:1. Optional: Chevrolet CH465 4-speed manual. Floor-mounted shift lever. Optional: Turbo Hydra-Matic 3-speed automatic. Clutch: Six-cylinder: 10.0 in. dia., 100 sq. in. area. V-8: Type: 11.0 in. dia., 124 sq. in. area. Optional: V-8-cylinder: 12.0 in., 150 sq. in.

VEHICLE DIMENSIONS: Wheelbase: 104 in. Overall Length: 177.5 in. Front/Rear Tread 64.0 in./61.0 in. Overall Height: 68.5 in. With optional hardtop; 72.75 in. Width: 79.0 in. Front/Rear Overhang: 33.25 in./40.25 in. Tailgate: Width and Height: 65.0 in. x 19.25 in. Approach/Departure Degrees: 35.2/25.0. Ground Clearance: Front axle: 8.0 in. Rear axle: 8.0 in. Load space: With rear seat removed or folded: 70.0 in. x 65.0 in. x 19.25 in.

CAPACITIES: Fuel Tank: 23.5 gal. Optional: None. Coolant system: 250 6-cyl.: 12.2 qt. 307 V-8: 18.5 qt. 350 V-8: 17.1 qt.

ACCOMMODATIONS: Seating Capacity: Standard: Driver. Optional: Driver and front passenger and/or 3 passenger rear bench seat.

INSTRUMENTATION: Speedometer, odometer, fuel level gauge; warning lights for generator, engine coolant temperature and oil pressure. Brake warning light. Hazard warning switch.

OPTIONS AND PRICES: Fiberglass top. 11 in. clutch for 6-cyl. Front passenger seat. Rear bench seat. 307 cu. in. V-8. 350 cu. in. V-8. various tire sizes. 3.07:1 axle ratio (350 and 307 engines only). Oil bath air cleaner (not available with 350 V-8 and automatic transmission). Engine governor (not available with 350 V-8 and automatic transmission). Power steering. Power brakes. Front bucket seats. Carpeting. Radio. Soft-Ray tinted glass. Air conditioning. Bright exterior trim. Bright wheelcovers. Chrome hubcaps. Chrome front and rear bumpers. Chrome shift lever. Heavy-duty shock absorbers. Heavy-duty clutch. Heavy-duty radiator (standard with 350 V-8). Fuel filter. Heavy-duty shock absorbers. Heavy-duty starter. Shoulder harnesses. Custom Sport Truck: $358. Includes special exterior trim, front bucket seas, right-hand armrest and color-keyed floor coverings. Towing hooks. Free-wheeling front hubs. Courtesy lights. Spare tire lock.

HISTORICAL FOOTNOTES: The four-wheel drive Blazer outsold the two-wheel drive version by approximately ten-to-one in 1970.

1971 BLAZER

The 1971 Blazer had a revamped front end appearance highlighted by an attractive version of Chevrolet's familiar egg-crate format. The blue "Bow Tie" emblem was now positioned in the grille center.

I.D. DATA: The Blazer's V.I.N. consisted of 12 symbols. The first (a letter) identified the chassis. The second (a letter) identified the engine. The third (a digit) indicated the GVW range. The fourth entry (a digit) identified the model type. The fifth (a digit) identified the model year. The sixth (a letter) identified the assembly plant. The last six elements (all digits) served as the sequential production numbers. The combination V.I.N./GVW number was located on the left door pillar. The engine number indicated the manufacturing plant, day of manufacture and transmission type. It was located on a pad positioned on the right-hand side of the cylinder block at the rear of the distributor on V-8 engines and on a pad located at the front right hand side of the cylinder block of 6-cylinder engines.

Model Number	Body Type & Seating	Factory Price	GVW	Shipping Weight	Prod. Total
KS10514	Util. (6-cyl.)	$3237	4600*	3624	17,220[1]
KE10514	Util. (V-8)	$3358	4600	3719	—

* 5000 GVW package optional.
NOTE 1: Total Blazer production.

STANDARD ENGINE: High Torque 250 Six (KS prefix): Engine Type: OHV, In-line 6-cylinder. Bore x Stroke: 3.875 in. x 3.50 in. Lifters: Hydraulic. Number of main bearings-7. Carburetion: Rochester downdraft one-barrel, Model M7028007 or M7028011. Compression Ratio: 8.5:1. Displacement: 250 cu. in. (4.09 liters). Horsepower: Gross: 145 @ 4200 rpm. Net: 110 @ 4000 rpm. Torque: Gross: 230 lb.-ft. @ 1600 rpm. Net: 185 @ 1600 rpm. Oil capacity: 5 qt. with filter change. Fuel Requirements: Regular.

STANDARD ENGINE: High Torque V-8, V-8 models (KE prefix): Engine Type: OHV, V-8. Bore x Stroke: 3.875 in. x 3.25 in. Lifters: Hydraulic. Number of main bearings-5. Carburetion: 2-barrel Rochester. Compression Ratio: 8.5:1. Displacement: 307 cu. in. (5.03 liters). Horsepower: Gross: 200 @ 4600 rpm. Net: 135 @ 4000 rpm. Torque: Gross: 300 lb.-ft. @ 2400 rpm. Net: 235 @ 2000 rpm. Oil capacity: 5 qt. with filter change. Fuel Requirements: Regular.

OPTIONAL ENGINE: Turbo-Fire V-8: V-8 models: Engine Type: OHV V-8. Bore x Stroke: 4.00 in. x 3.50 in. Lifters: Hydraulic. Number of main bearings-5. Displacement: 350 cu. in. (5.73 liters). Carburetion: Single 4-barrel Rochester. Compression Ratio: 8.5:1. Horsepower: Gross: 250 @ 4600 rpm. Net: 170 @ 3600 rpm. Torque: Gross: 350 lb.-ft. @ 3000 rpm. Net: 310 @ 2400 rpm. Fuel Requirements: Regular.

CHASSIS FEATURES: Ladder-type, heavy-gauge channel side members, alligator-jaw cross members. Section modules: 2.70 in.

SUSPENSION AND RUNNING GEAR: Front Suspension: Tapered single leaf. Capacity: 2900 lb. Optional: 3500 lb. capacity springs and heavy-duty shock absorbers. Rear Suspension: Two-stage tapered and multi-leaf (four-conventional leaves, one tapered leaf). Capacity: 3600 lb. Optional: None. Front Axle. Type: Hypoid, tubular driving. Capacity: 3300 lb. Rear Axle. Type: Hypoid, semi-floating. Capacity: 3300 lb. Final Drive Ratio: 6-cyl.: 3.73:1. 307 V-8: 3.73:1 with 3-speed manual and CH465 4-speed manual; 3.07:1 with Turbo Hydra-Matic. 350 V-8: 3.07:1. Optional: 3.73:1, for 350 V-8 only. Transfer Case: Type: Manual transmission: Dana 20. Ratios: 2.03:1, 1.00:1. Automatic transmission: New Process 205. Ratios: 1.96:1, 1.00:1. Brakes: Type: Hydraulic, Front: Disc, Rear: Drums. Optional: Power. Dimensions: Front disc: 11.86 in. rotor. Rear: 11.0 in. x 2.00 in. Rear brake area: 138.2 sq. in. Wheels: 6-stud, 15 x 6.0 in. Tires: E78 x 15B. Optional: Steering: Manual recirculating ball. Ratio: 24.0:1. Optional: Power-assisted. Transmission: Type: Saginaw 3-speed manual, fully synchronized. Steering column-mounted shifter. Transmission Ratios: 2.85, 1.68, 1.0:1. Reverse: 2.95:1. Optional: Chevrolet CH465 4-speed manual. Floor-mounted shift lever. Optional: Turbo Hydra-Matic 3-speed automatic. 350 V-8 available only with CH465 or Turbo Hydra-Matic. Clutch: Six-cylinder: 10.0 in. dia., 100 sq. in. area. 307 V-8: Type: 11.0 in. dia., 124 sq. in. area. 350 V-8: 12 in. clutch, 150 sq. in. area. Optional: 11.0 in. heavy-duty. Available for standard 3-speed only; included when 4-speed manual transmission is ordered.

VEHICLE DIMENSIONS: Wheelbase: 104 in. Overall Length: 177.5 in. Front/Rear Tread 64.0 in./61.0 in. Overall Height: 68.5 in. With optional hardtop; 72.75 in. Width: 79.0 in. Front/Rear Overhang: 33.25 in./40.25 in. Tailgate: Width and Height: 65.0 in. x 19.25 in. Approach/Departure Degrees: 35.2/25.0. Ground Clearance: Front axle: 8.0 in. Rear axle: 8.0 in. Load space: With rear seat removed or folded: 70.0 in. x 65.0 in. x 19.25 in.

CAPACITIES: Fuel Tank: 21.0 gal. Optional: None. Coolant system: 250 6-cyl.: 12.2 qt. 307 V-8: 18.5 qt. 350 V-8: 17.1 qt.

ACCOMMODATIONS: Seating Capacity: Standard: Driver. Optional: Driver and front passenger and/or 3 passenger rear bench seat.

INSTRUMENTATION: Speedometer, odometer, fuel level gauge; warning lights for generator, engine coolant temperature and oil pressure. Brake warning light. Hazard warning switch.

OPTIONS AND PRICES: CST Package. Includes bucket seats, console, right hand sunshade and armrest, cigarette lighter, nameplates, special insulation, undercoating, chromed bumpers, bright control knob and pedal trim, bright windshield, body side, tailgate, taillight and back-up light molding, bright fuel filler cap, side marker reflectors and bright transfer case shift lever: $364.45 (with auxiliary top), $301.25 (without auxiliary top). The auxiliary top version also includes bright vent window molding, door and body trim panels with bright upper retainers, spare tire cover and front color-keyed carpeting. The version without auxiliary top. includes front color-keyed vinyl coated rubber floor mat. 350 V-8. Turbo Hydra-Matic: $242.25. 4-speed manual transmission: $110.60. 3.07:1 rear axle: $12.65 with 3-spd. trans.; $19.00 with 4-spd. or Turbo Hydra-Matic 3.73:1 axle ratio. Available only when 350 engine is ordered with 4-spd. or Turbo Hydra-Matic is ordered with 307 V-8: $12.65. Positraction: $65.30. Oil bath air cleaner. Not available with 350 engine: $10.55. All-Weather air conditioning, V-8 models only: $421.30. Auxiliary battery: $47.40. Heavy-duty 80 amp-hr. battery: $16.90. Rear seat belts: $6.85. Chrome front and rear bumpers: $31.60. Chrome hubcaps: $13.70. Heavy-duty 11 in. clutch. Available only for KS10 with 3-spd. trans.: $6.85. Heavy-duty radiator: $26.35. Ammeter, engine coolant temperature and oil pressure gauges: $12.65. Tachometer, ammeter, engine coolant temperature and oil pressure gauges: $57.95. 402 amp Delcotron generator: $23.20. 61 amp Delcotron generator: $31.60. Door glass (frameless drop glass windows and framed vent window glass). Included when auxiliary top is ordered: $42.15 without CST; $52.70 with CST. Also includes chromed vent window moldings. Soft-Ray glass. Available only when auxiliary top or door glass is ordered: $19.00 with door glass: $30.55 with auxiliary top. Door edge guards: $6.35. Two front towing hooks. Not available when chromed bumpers or CST are ordered: $19.

HISTORICAL FOOTNOTES: Introduction of the 1971 Blazer took place on September 29, 1970.

1972 BLAZER

Identifying the 1972 Blazer was its bright front grille border. It had previously been painted black. A new Highlander interior package was introduced for Blazers equipped with the CST option. New exterior decal packages, with names such as "Featherfoot," were now available. Both the 307 and 350 cu. in. V-8 engines now were fitted with exhaust valve rotators. For 1972 all Chevrolet engines were designed to operate on no-lead or low-lead gasoline. If neither type was available, any leaded regular gasoline with a Research Octane rating number of 91 or higher could be used.

I.D. DATA: The Blazer's V.I.N. consisted of 13 symbols. The first symbol (a letter) identified the Chevrolet Motor Division. The second symbol (a letter) indicated vehicle type. The third symbol (a letter) indicated engine type. The fourth symbol (a number) identified the tonnage. The fifth symbol indicated model type. The sixth symbol identified the model year. The seventh symbol (a letter) indicated the assembly plant. The remaining six digits served as the sequential production numbers. The V.I.N. number was located on the left door pillar. The engine number indicated the manufacturing plant, day of manufacture and transmission type.

It was located on a pad positioned on the right-hand side of the cylinder block at the rear of the distributor on V-8 engines and on a pad located at the front right hand side of the cylinder block of 6-cylinder engines.

Model Number	Body Type & Seating	Factory Price	GVW	Shipping Weight	Prod. Total
Blazer K10. With 307 V-8: Model KE10514. With 6-cyl.: Model KS10514					
KE10514	Utility	$3258	4600*	3790	44,266

* 5600 GVW package optional.

STANDARD ENGINE: High Torque 250 Six. (KS prefix): Engine Type: OHV, In-line 6-cylinder. Bore x Stroke: 3.875 in. x 3.50 in. Lifters: Hydraulic. Number of main bearings-7. Carburetion: Rochester downdraft one-barrel, Model M7028007 or M7028011. Compression Ratio: 8.5:1. Displacement: 250 cu. in. (4.09 liters). Horsepower: Net: 110 @ 3800 rpm. Torque: Gross: Net: 185 @ 1600 rpm. Oil capacity: 5 qt. with filter change. Fuel Requirements: No-lead or low-lead gasoline.

STANDARD ENGINE: High Torque V-8, V-8 models (KE prefix): Engine Type: OHV, V-8. Bore x Stroke: 3.875 in. x 3.25 in. Lifters: Hydraulic. Number of main bearings-5. Carburetion: 2-barrel Rochester. Compression Ratio: 8.5:1. Displacement: 307 cu. in. (5.03 liters). Horsepower: Net: 135 @ 4000 rpm. Torque: Gross: Net: 230 @ 2400 rpm. Oil capacity: 5 qt. with filter change. Fuel Requirements: No-lead or low-lead gasoline.

OPTIONAL ENGINE: Turbo-Fire V-8: V-8 models: Engine Type: OHV V-8. Bore x Stroke: 4.00 in. x 3.50 in. Lifters: Hydraulic. Number of main bearings-5. Displacement: 350 cu. in. (5.73 liters). Carburetion: Single 4-barrel Rochester. Compression Ratio: 8.5:1. Horsepower: Net: 175 @ 4000 rpm. Torque: Net: 290 @ 2400 rpm. Fuel Requirements: No-lead or low-lead gasoline.

CHASSIS FEATURES: Ladder-type, heavy-gauge channel side members, alligator-jaw cross members. Section modules: 2.70 in.

SUSPENSION AND RUNNING GEAR: Front Suspension: Tapered single leaf. Capacity: 2900 lb. Optional: 3500 lb. capacity springs and heavy-duty shock absorbers. Rear Suspension: Two-stage tapered and multi-leaf (four-conventional leaves, one tapered leaf). Capacity: 3600 lb. Optional: None. Front Axle. Type: Hypoid, tubular driving. Capacity: 3300 lb. Rear Axle. Type: Hypoid, semi-floating. Capacity: 3300 lb. Final Drive Ratio: 6-cyl.: 3.73:1. 307 V-8: 3.73:1 with 3-speed manual and CH465 4-speed manual; 3.07:1 with Turbo Hydra-Matic. 350 V-8: 3.07:1. Optional: 3.73:1, for 350 V-8 only. Transfer Case: Type: Manual transmission: Dana 20. Ratios: 2.03:1, 1.00:1. Automatic transmission: New Process 205. Ratios: 1.96:1, 1.00:1. Brakes: Type: Hydraulic, Front: Disc, Rear: Drums. Optional: Power. Dimensions: Front disc: 11.86 in. rotor. Rear: 11.0 in. x 2.00 in. Rear brake area: 138.2 sq. in. Wheels: 6-stud, 15 x 6.0 in. Tires: E78 x 15B. Optional: Steering: Manual recirculating ball. Ratio: 24.0:1. Optional: Power-assisted. Transmission: Type: Saginaw 3-speed manual, fully synchronized. Steering column-mounted shifter. Transmission Ratios: 2.85, 1.68, 1.0:1. Reverse: 2.95:1. Optional: Chevrolet CH465 4-speed manual, floor-mounted shift lever. Optional: Turbo Hydra-Matic 3-speed automatic. 350 V-8 available only with CH465 or Turbo Hydra-Matic. Clutch: Six-cylinder: 10.0 in. dia., 100 sq. in. area. 307 V-8: Type: 11.0 in. dia., 124 sq. in. area. 350 V-8: 12 in. clutch, 150 sq. in. area. Optional: 11.0 in. heavy-duty, available for standard 3-speed only; included when 4-speed manual transmission is ordered.

VEHICLE DIMENSIONS: Wheelbase: 104 in. Overall Length: 177.5 in. Front/Rear Tread 64.0 in./61.0 in. Overall Height: 68.5 in. With optional hardtop; 72.75 in. Width: 79.0 in. Front/Rear Overhang: 33.25 in./40.25 in. Tailgate: Width and Height: 65.0 in. x 19.25 in. Approach/Departure Degrees: 35.2/25.0. Ground Clearance: Front axle: 8.0 in. Rear axle: 8.0 in. Load space: With rear seat removed or folded: 70.0 in. x 65.0 in. x 19.25 in.

CAPACITIES: Fuel Tank: 21.0 gal. Optional: None. Coolant system: 250 6-cyl.: 12.2 qt. 307 V-8: 18.5 qt. 350 V-8: 17.1 qt.

ACCOMMODATIONS: Seating Capacity: Standard: Driver. Optional: Driver and front passenger and/or 3 passenger rear bench seat.

INSTRUMENTATION: Speedometer, odometer, fuel level gauge; warning lights for generator, engine coolant temperature and oil pressure. Brake warning light. Hazard warning switch.

OPTIONS AND PRICES: Fiberglass top. 10 in., 11 in. and 12 in. clutches. Front passenger seat. Rear bench seat. 307 cu. in. V-8. 350 cu. in. V-8. various tire sizes. 3.07:1 axle ratio (350 and 307 engines only). Oil bath air cleaner (not available with 350 V-8 and automatic transmission). Engine governor (not available with 350 V-8 and automatic transmission). Power steering. Power brakes. Auxiliary battery. Front bucket seats. Carpeting. Radio. Soft-Ray tinted glass. Air conditioning. Bright exterior trim. Bright wheelcovers. Chrome hubcaps. Chrome front and rear bumpers. Chrome shift lever. Heavy-duty shock absorbers. Heavy-duty clutch. Heavy-duty radiator (standard with 350 V-8). Fuel filter. Heavy-duty shock absorbers. Heavy-duty starter. Shoulder harnesses. Custom Sport Truck: $364. Includes: Special exterior trim, front bucket seats, right-hand armrest and color-keyed floor coverings. Towing hooks. Free-wheeling front hubs. Courtesy lights. Spare tire lock.

HISTORICAL FOOTNOTES: The 1972 Blazer was introduced on September 21, 1971.

1973 BLAZER

The 1973 Blazer had all-new sheet metal, a substantially revised front suspension and, for Blazers with automatic transmission and V-8 engines, a full-time four-wheel drive system. The full-time transfer case was a New Process Model 203 2-speed unit which used an inter-axle differential to compensate for speed differences between the two axles. A Hurst shifter was used for the transfer case. The latest Blazer was slighter larger than the original model. Its wheelbase was increased by 2.5 inches and overall length was extended 4 inches. The primary reason for the longer 106.5 in. wheelbase was the movement of the front wheels forward to provide easier access to the engine oil pan. The 1973 Blazer, also benefited from an improved cooling system. The older tube and center type radiator core was replaced by a multi-louver unit with increased surface area to more efficiently transfer engine heat. A larger water pump was installed with V-8 engines and all units were of a more durable design.

The completely new front suspension now incorporated a standard stabilizer bar. Both the length and width of the front springs were increased. The rear springs were now canted outward. The front spring rates were lowered for 1973 while those at the rear were stiffer. Among the Blazer's new exterior parts that gave it a contemporary appearance were its grille, fenders and hood. Curved glass was now used for the Blazer's door and rear quarter windows. Glass area was also substantially increased. In place of the liftgate used on the older model was a crank up or down rear window. Particularly noticeable when the new Blazer was viewed in profile were its rectangular-shaped wheel cutouts. These contrasted with the circular shape used on the original Blazer body shell. They were also flared for 1973 to accommodate larger tires. At the rear functional wraparound taillights were used. A new design was used for the Blazer's fiberglass top which now had thicker side sections and a thinner top. Also incorporated into its structure were stiffening ribs in the roof for increased rigidity. The Blazer interior was also modernized to incorporate a cockpit-type instrument panel format. All the controls and instruments were located in a partial oval located directly in front of the driver. It included an integral automatic transmission indicator dial, courtesy light, labeled control knobs and, if factory air conditioning was installed, four (three were provided in 1972) air outlets. The air conditioning system was also upgraded for 1973 with an improved condenser and increased air flow. An energy absorbing steering column was introduced for 1973. The Blazer's front doors were equipped with interior push-button locks that, if depressed while closing the door, locked the doors automatically. The front bucket seats and optional rear bench seat were carried over for 1973 but new vinyl covered door panels were used incorporating elastic topped pockets useful for storage of small items. The 1973 Blazer's factory installed radio used an antenna embedded in the windshield. The Blazer was offered in either standard Custom or optional Cheyenne trim. The standard trim included bright grille work, chrome finished left and right hand exterior mirrors, front and rear white painted bumpers and white painted wheels. Except for slightly lower power ratings the same three engines offered in 1972 were available for the 1973 Blazer. The 1973 exterior color selection consisted of light skyline blue, medium Hawaiian blue, dark Catalina blue, lime green, moss green, dark Glenwood green, Spanish gold, sunset gold, burnt orange, crimson red, desert sand, sport silver, Mojave tan, Marine turquoise and frost white.

I.D. DATA: The Blazer's V.I.N. consisted of 13 symbols. The first symbol (a letter) identified the Chevrolet Motor Division. The second symbol (a letter) indicated vehicle type. The third symbol (a letter) indicated engine type. The fourth symbol (a number) identified the tonnage. The fifth symbol indicated model type. The sixth symbol identified the model year. The seventh symbol (a letter) indicated the assembly plant. The remaining six digits served as the sequential production numbers. The V.I.N. number was located on the left door pillar. The engine number indicated the manufacturing plant, day of manufacture and transmission type. It was located on a pad positioned on the right-hand side of the cylinder block at the rear of the distributor on V-8 engines and on a pad located at the front right hand side of the cylinder block of 6-cylinder engines. Chevrolet adopted a new Light-Duty model series identification for 1973. The first symbol (a letter-C) identified the Chevrolet Motor Division. The second symbol (a letter-K) indicated vehicle type-four-wheel drive. The third symbol (a number) indicated Series-1 (Series 10). The next two entries (digits) indicated CA dimensions-05. The next two components (digits) identified body style; Blazer-14. Finally, three entries (a letter followed by two numbers) served as the body code, Blazer-ZW9.

Model Number	Body Type & Seating	Factory Price	GVW	Shipping Weight	Prod. Total
Blazer K10 (with 307 V-8)					
CK10514	Utility	$3319	4600*	3892	44,841

* 4900, 5350, 5800, 6200 lb. GVW package optional.

STANDARD ENGINE: 250 Six: Ordering Code: LD4. Engine Type: OHV, In-line 6-cylinder. Bore x Stroke: 3.875 in. x 3.50 in. Lifters: Hydraulic. Number of main bearings-7. Carburetion: Rochester downdraft one-barrel, Model M7028007 or M7028011. Compression Ratio: 8.5:1. Displacement: 250 cu. in. (4.09 liters). Horsepower: Net: 100 @ 3600 rpm. Torque: Net: 175 lb.-ft. @ 1600 rpm. Oil capacity: 5 qt. with filter change. Fuel Requirements: No-lead or low-lead gasoline.

STANDARD ENGINE: High Torque V-8, V-8 models: Ordering Code: LG8. Engine Type: OHV, V-8. Bore x Stroke: 3.875 in. x 3.25 in. Lifters: Hydraulic. Number of main bearings-5. Carburetion: 2-barrel Rochester. Compression Ratio: 8.5:1. Displacement: 307 cu. in. (5.03 liters). Horsepower: Net: 115 @ 3600 rpm. Torque: Gross: Net: 205 lb.-ft. @ 2000 rpm. Oil capacity: 5 qt. with filter change. Fuel Requirements: No-lead or low-lead gasoline.

OPTIONAL ENGINE: V-8 models: Ordering Code: LS9. Engine Type: OHV V-8. Bore x Stroke: 4.00 in. x 3.50 in. Lifters: Hydraulic. Number of main bearings-5. Displacement: 350 cu. in. (5.73 liters). Carburetion: Single 4-barrel Rochester. Compression Ratio: 8.5:1. Horsepower: Net: 155 @ 4000 rpm. Torque: Net: 225 lb.-ft. @ 2400 rpm. Fuel Requirements: No-lead or low-lead gasoline.

CHASSIS FEATURES: Ladder-type. Carbon steel, 39,000 psi. Heavy-gauge channel side members, alligator-jaw cross members. Section modules: 3.06 in.

SUSPENSION AND RUNNING GEAR: Front Suspension: Tapered leaf springs. Capacity: 1650 lb. Rating: 340 lb./in. Optional: 1900 lb. capacity. Rear Suspension: Two-stage tapered and multi-leaf (four-conventional leaves, one tapered leaf). Capacity: 1700 lb. Rating: 386/632 lb./in. Optional: None. Front Axle. Type: Hypoid, tubular driving. Capacity: 3400 lb. Rear Axle. Type: Hypoid, semi-floating. Capacity: 3750 lb. Final Drive Ratio: 4.11:1 (3.73:1 with 307 V-8). Optional: 3.07, 3.73, 4.11:1. Transfer Case: Type: Manual transmission: Dana 20. Ratios: 2.03:1, 1.00:1. New Process 203 (automatic transmission-full time). Ratios: 1.96:1, 1.00:1. New Process 205 (conventional). Ratios: 2.01, 1.00:1. Brakes: Type: Hydraulic, self-adjusting. Front: Discs. Rear: Drums. Optional: Power. Dimensions: Front: 11.86 in. dia. rotor. Rear: 11.0 in. x 2.0 in. Wheels: 6-stud, 15 x 6.0 in. Optional: 16 x 5.0, 16 x 5.5, 15 x 8.0. Tires: E78 x 15B, 4-ply rating. Optional: G78 x 15B, 6.50 x 16C, 7.00 x 16C, H78 x 15B, L78 x 15C, LR78 x 15C and 10.00 x 15C. Steering: Manual recirculating ball. Ratio: 24.0:1. Turns Lock-to-Lock: 3.4. Optional: Power-assisted. ratio. Turning circle: 37.6 ft. Transmission: Type: Saginaw 3-speed manual, fully synchronized. Steering column-mounted shifter. The Muncie 4-speed manual is the only manual transmission available for the 350 cu. in. V-8. Transmission Ratios: 2.85, 1.68, 1.0:1. Optional: Muncie 4-speed manual, synchromesh on to three gears, floor-mounted shift lever. Ratios: 6.55, 3.58, 1.70, 1.00:1. Optional: Turbo Hydra-Matic 3-speed automatic. Ratios: 2.52, 1.52, 1.00:1. Clutch: Six-cylinder: 10.0 in. dia., 100 sq. in. area. 307 V-8: 11.0 in. dia., 124 sq. in. area. 350 V-8: 12.0 in. dia., 150 sq. in. area. Optional: 6-cylinder: 11.0 in.

VEHICLE DIMENSIONS: Wheelbase: 106.5 in. Overall Length: 184.5 in. Front/Rear Tread 65.75 in./62.75 in. Overall Height: 69.5 in. With optional hardtop; 71.50 in. Width: 79.5 in. Front/Rear Overhang: 33.5 in./44.5 in. Tailgate: Width and Height: 66.8 in. x 22.0 in. Approach/Departure Degrees: 31/24. Ground Clearance: Front axle: 7.7 in. Rear axle: 8.0 in. Oil pan: 15.5 in. Transfer case: 10.0 in. Fuel tank: 14.3 in. Load space: With rear seat installed: 33 in. x 50 in. x 41.6 in. With rear seat removed or folded: 76.5 in. x 50 in. x 41.6 in.

CAPACITIES: Fuel Tank: 24.0 gal. Coolant system: 250 6-cyl.: 12.2 qt. 307 V-8: 18.5 qt. 350 V-8: 17.1 qt.

ACCOMMODATIONS: Seating Capacity: Standard: Driver. Optional: Driver and front passenger and/or 3 passenger rear bench seat. Headroom: 38.8 in. Maximum steering wheel to seat back: 18.3 in. Seat to ground: 35.0 in. Floor to ground: 20.2 in.

INSTRUMENTATION: 0-100 mph speedometer, 99,999.9 mi. odometer, fuel gauge, warning lights for alternator, oil pressure, engine coolant temperature, brake operating system, hazard warning lights, directional lights.

OPTIONS AND PRICES: Cheyenne Package. Includes tachometer, temperature, fuel level, and oil pressure instrumentation. Tinted glass. Custom instrument panel. Includes tachometer, temperature, fuel level, and oil pressure instrumentation. Air conditioning. Camper mirrors. Heavy-duty rear spring. Positraction rear axle. Heavy-duty rear springs. 61

amp alternator. 32 gal. fuel tank. Custom steering wheel. Tilt steering wheel. Power steering. Chrome hubcaps. Heavy-duty battery. Tachometer. AM/FM radio. Chrome front and rear bumpers. Dual front tow hooks.

HISTORICAL FOOTNOTES: The Blazer's new design and appearance marked the start of the second generation of Blazer history.

1974 BLAZER

Externally, the Blazer was virtually unchanged for 1974 but there were numerous refinements and improvements. The 1974 Blazer was available with a factory-installed padded roll bar. Previously it had been available only as a dealer-installed option. Also available for 1974 was a new factory-installed swing-away tire carrier. The limited-slip rear differential could now be ordered with the full-time four-wheel drive system. Blazers with optional GVW ratings above the 5600 lb. level were equipped with larger 11.15 in. x 2.75 in. rear drum brakes. The rear drums were finned for improved cooling. Steel belted radial tires as well as a new trailer weight distributing hitch platform were added to the Blazer's option list. The base level Custom interior and exterior included a foam-cushioned driver's side bucket trimmed in vinyl in a choice of four colors, driver's side sun visor, one-piece molded door trim panels, rubber front floor matting, padded sun visors, courtesy lamp, prismatic rearview mirror, 2-speed electric windshield wipers, windshield washers, back-up lights, power brakes, heater/defroster, chrome finished left and right exterior mirrors and white painted front and rear bumpers. The Blazer Cheyenne was fitted with an exterior woodgrain trim for 1974. The Blazer brake system was fitted with a brake lining wear sensor for 1974 which emitted a warning sound just before the lining rivets contacted the front disc brake rotor. The 307 cu. in. V-8 was not offered for the 1974 Blazer. Blazers with the 6-cylinder engine were not available in California. A dealer installed convertible top was available. The Blazer's removable top was available in either black or white. Color choices for 1974 consisted of skyline blue, Spanish gold, sunset gold, Glenwood green, crimson red, desert sand, Grecian bronze, rosedale red, Granada beige, Catalina blue, lime green, moss olive, Hawaiian blue, frost white and Killarney green.

1974 Chevrolet K10 Blazer with top removed

I.D. DATA: The Blazer's V.I.N. consisted of 13 symbols. The first symbol (a letter-C) identified the Chevrolet Motor Division. The second symbol (a letter-K) indicated vehicle type. The third symbol (a letter) indicated engine type: Q-250 cu. in. L-6, X-307 cu. in. V-8, Y-350 cu. in. V-8. The fourth symbol (a number) identified the tonnage. The fifth symbol indicated model type. The sixth symbol, a number 4, identified the 1974 model year. The seventh symbol (a letter) indicated the assembly plant. The remaining six digits served as the sequential production numbers beginning with 100083. The V.I.N. number was located on the left door pillar. The engine number indicated the manufacturing plant, day of manufacture and transmission type. It was located on a pad positioned on the right-hand side of the cylinder block at the rear of the distributor on V-8 engines and on a pad located at the front right hand side of the cylinder block of 6-cylinder engines.

Model Number	Body Type & Seating	Factory Price	GVW	Shipping Weight	Prod. Total
Blazer K10 (with 307 V-8)					
CK10514	Utility	$3798[a]	4600*	3854	56,798[1]

a Deduct $216.00 for 250 cu. in. 6-cyl. engine.
* 6200 GVW package optional.
NOTE 1: Includes both two-wheel drive and four-wheel drive models.

STANDARD ENGINE: 250 Six: Ordering Code: LD4. Engine Type: OHV, In-line 6-cylinder. Bore x Stroke: 3.875 in. x 3.50 in. Lifters: Hydraulic. Number of main bearings-7. Carburetion: Rochester downdraft one-barrel, Model M7028007 or M7028011. Compression Ratio: 8.5:1. Displacement: 250 cu. in. (4.09 liters). Horsepower: Net: 100 @ 3600 rpm. Torque: Net: 175 lb.-ft. @ 1600 rpm. Oil capacity: 5 qt. with filter change. Fuel Requirements: Unleaded or low-lead gasoline of at least 91 Research Octane.

STANDARD ENGINE: V-8 models: Engine Type: Cast iron block. OHV, V-8. Bore x Stroke: 4.0 in. x 3.50 in. Lifters: Hydraulic. Number of main bearings-5. Carburetion: Rochester two-barrel. Compression Ratio: 8.51. Displacement: 350 cu. in. Horsepower: Net: 145 @ 3800 rpm. Torque: Gross: Net: 250 lb.-ft. @ 2200 rpm. Oil capacity: 5 qt. with filter change. Fuel Requirements: Unleaded or low-lead gasoline of at least 91 Research Octane.

OPTIONAL ENGINE: V-8 models: Engine Type: OHV V-8. Bore x Stroke: 4.00 in. x 3.50 in. Lifters: Hydraulic. Number of main bearings-5. Displacement: 350 cu. in. (5.73 liters). Carburetion: Single 4-barrel Rochester. Compression Ratio: 8.5:1. Horsepower: Net: 160 @ 3800 rpm. Torque: Net: 250 lb.-ft. @ 2400 rpm. Fuel Requirements: No-lead or low-lead gasoline.

CHASSIS FEATURES: Ladder-type. Carbon steel, 39,000 psi. Heavy-gauge channel side members, alligator-jaw cross members. Section modules: 3.06 in.

SUSPENSION AND RUNNING GEAR: Front Suspension: Tapered leaf springs. Capacity: 1650 lb. Rating: 340 lb./in. Optional: 1900 lb. Rear Suspension: Two-stage tapered and multi-leaf (four-conventional leaves, one tapered leaf). Capacity: 1700 lb. Rating: 386/632 lb./in. Optional: None. Front Axle. Type: Hypoid, tubular driving. Capacity: 3400 lb. Rear Axle. Type:

Hypoid, semi-floating. Capacity: 3750 lb. Final Drive Ratio: 4.11:1 (3.73:1 with 307 V-8). Optional: 3.07, 3.73, 4.11:1. Transfer Case: Type: Manual transmission: Dana 20. Ratios: 2.03:1, 1.00:1. New Process 203 (automatic transmission-full time). Ratios: 1.96:1, 1.00:1. New Process 205 (conventional). Ratios: 2.01, 1.00:1. Brakes: Type: Hydraulic, self-adjusting. Front: Discs. Rear: Drums. Optional: Power. Dimensions: Front: 11.86 in. dia. rotor. Rear: 11.0 in. x 2.0 in. Wheels: 6-stud, 15 x 6.0 in. Optional: 16 x 5.0, 16 x 5.5, 15 x 8.0. Tires: E78 x 15B, 4-ply rating. Optional: G78 x 15B, 6.50 x 16C, 7.00 x 16C, H78 x 15B, L78 x 15C, LR78 x 15C and 10.00 x 15C. Steering: Manual recirculating ball. Ratio: 24.0:1. Turns Lock-to-Lock: 3.4. Optional: Power-assisted. Turning circle: 37.6 ft. Transmission: Type: Saginaw 3-speed manual, fully synchronized. Steering column-mounted shifter. Saginaw 3-speed manual, fully synchronized. Steering column-mounted shifter. This transmission is not available for the 2-bbl. 350 cu. in. V-8. The Muncie 4-speed manual is the only manual transmission available for the 350 cu. in. V-8. Transmission Ratios: 2.85, 1.68, 1.0:1. Optional: Muncie 4-speed manual, synchromesh on to three gears, floor-mounted shift lever. Ratios: 6.55, 3.58, 1.70, 1.00:1. Optional: Turbo Hydra-Matic 3-speed automatic. Ratios: 2.52, 1.52, 1.00:1. Clutch: Six-cylinder: 10.0 in. dia., 100 sq. in. area. 307 V-8: 11.0 in. dia., 124 sq. in. area. 350 V-8: 12.0 in. dia., 150 sq. in. area. Optional: 6-cylinder: 11.0 in.

VEHICLE DIMENSIONS: Wheelbase: 106.5 in. Overall Length: 184.5 in. Front/Rear Tread 65.75 in./62.75 in. Overall Height: 69.5 in. With optional hardtop: 71.50 in. Width: 79.5 in. Front/Rear Overhang: 33.5 in./44.5 in. Tailgate: Width and Height: 66.8 in. x 22.0 in. Approach/Departure Degrees: 31/24. Ground Clearance: Front axle: 7.7 in. Rear axle: 8.0 in. Oil pan: 15.5 in. Transfer case: 10.0 in. Fuel tank: 14.3 in. Load space: With rear seat installed: 33 in. x 50 in. x 41.6 in. With rear seat removed or folded: 76.5 in. x 50 in. x 41.6 in.

CAPACITIES: Fuel Tank: 24.0 gal. Coolant system: 250 6-cyl.: 12.2 qt. 307 V-8: 18.5 qt. 350 V-8: 17.1 qt.

ACCOMMODATIONS: Seating Capacity: Standard: Driver. Optional: Driver and front passenger and/or 3 passenger rear bench seat. Headroom: 38.8 in. Maximum steering wheel to seat back: 18.3 in. Seat to ground: 35.0 in. Floor to ground: 20.2 in.

INSTRUMENTATION: 0-100 mph speedometer, 99,999.9 mi. odometer, fuel gauge, warning lights for alternator, oil pressure, engine coolant temperature, brake operating system, hazard warning lights, directional lights.

OPTIONS AND PRICES: Cheyenne Package. Includes tachometer, temperature, fuel level, and oil pressure instrumentation. Tinted glass. Custom instrument panel. Includes tachometer, temperature, fuel level, and oil pressure instrumentation. Air conditioning. Camper mirrors. Heavy-duty rear spring. Positraction rear axle. Heavy-duty rear springs. 61 amp alternator. 32 gal. fuel tank. Custom steering wheel. Tilt steering wheel. Power steering. Chrome hubcaps. Heavy-duty battery. Tachometer. AM/FM radio. Chrome front and rear bumpers. Dual front tow hooks.

HISTORICAL FOOTNOTES: The 1974 Blazer was introduced on September 2, 1973.

1975 BLAZER

The 1975 Blazer was unchanged in appearance. A new optional, "Soft Ride" front suspension was offered with recambered springs, revalved shock absorbers and a change in suspension geometry from four to eight degrees of caster. This suspension was not recommended by Chevrolet for use in vocational applications such as snowplowing. At mid-year the Blazer was available with Chevrolet's 400 cu. in. V-8. This was not a new engine, having been used in Chevrolet passenger cars since 1970. It was based upon the 350 cu. in. V-8 and had the same block and exterior dimensions as that engine. Its larger bore was accomplished by the use of siamesed cylinders. All Blazer engines were fitted with a new transistorized ignition system that delivered up to 35,000 volts to the sparkplugs. The Blazer's hardtop was now available with optional sliding side glass windows. Open Blazer models had a restyled tailgate with a quick release feature. The hardtop model had a tailgate and a manually operated drop window. The 1975 Blazer's front passenger seat was of a new counterbalanced design making for easier exit by rear compartment occupants. The optional Cheyenne package had new styled front bucket seats in a new leather grain. New fabric and vinyl trim was also available for the hardtop Blazer with the Cheyenne option. The standard Custom Deluxe interior included foam-cushioned bucket driver's seat trimmed in vinyl (available in four new-for-1975 colors), one-piece molded door trim panels, rubber front floor covering, padded sun visor, prismatic rearview mirror, bright grille surround, chrome left and right side exterior mirrors, White painted front and rear bumpers. Fifteen colors were offered for the 1975 Blazer: Skyline blue, Hawaiian blue, Catalina blue, Grecian bronze, buckskin, Yuba gold, moss gold, willoway green, spring green, Glenwood green, crimson red, rosedale red, Saratoga Silver, Santa Fe tan and frost white.

1975 Chevrolet K10 Blazer

I.D. DATA: The Blazer's V.I.N. consisted of 13 symbols. The first symbol (a letter-C) identified the Chevrolet Motor Division. The second symbol (a letter-K) indicated vehicle type. The third symbol (a letter) indicated engine type: Q-250 cu. in. L-6, M-4-bbl. 400 cu. in V-8Y-4-bbl. 350 cu. in. V-8. The fourth symbol (a number) identified the tonnage. The fifth symbol indicated model type. The sixth symbol identified the model year. The seventh symbol (a letter) indicated the assembly plant. The remaining six digits served as the sequential production numbers. The V.I.N. number was located on the left door pillar. The engine number indicated the manufacturing plant, day of manufacture and transmission type. It was located on a pad positioned on the right-hand side of the cylinder block at the rear of the distributor on V-8 engines and on a pad located at the front right hand side of the cylinder block of 6-cylinder engines.

Model Number	Body Type & Seating	Factory	GVW Price	Shipping Weight	Prod. Total
Blazer K10 (with 350 V-8)					
CK10514	Util. (no top)	$4569	4900*	4026	50,548[1]
CK10516	Util. (top)	$4998	4900	4313	—

* 6300 GVW package optional.
NOTE 1: Includes both two-wheel drive and four-wheel drive models.

STANDARD ENGINE: 250 Six: Ordering Code: LD4. Engine Type: OHV, In-line 6-cylinder. Bore x Stroke: 3.875 in. x 3.50 in. Lifters: Hydraulic. Number of main bearings-7. Carburetion: Rochester downdraft one-barrel, Model M7028007 or M7028011. Compression Ratio: 8.5:1. Displacement: 250 cu. in. (4.09 liters). Horsepower: Net: 100 @ 3800 rpm. Torque: Net: 175 lb.-ft. @ 1800 rpm. Oil capacity: 5 qt. with filter change. Fuel Requirements: Unleaded or low-lead gasoline of at least 91 Research Octane.

STANDARD ENGINE: V-8 models: Engine Type: Cast iron block. OHV, V-8. Bore x Stroke: 4.0 in. x 3.50 in. Lifters: Hydraulic. Number of main bearings-5. Carburetion: Rochester four-barrel. Compression Ratio: 8.51. Displacement: 350 cu. in. Horsepower: Net: 160 @ 3800 rpm. Torque: Gross: Net: 250 lb.-ft. @ 2400 rpm. Oil capacity: 5 qt. with filter change. Fuel Requirements: Unleaded or low-lead gasoline of at least 91 Research Octane.

OPTIONAL ENGINE: V-8 models: Engine Type: Cast Iron block. OHV V-8. Bore x Stroke: 4.125 in. x 4.75 in. Lifters: Hydraulic. Number of main bearings-5. Displacement: 400 cu. in. (6.55 liters). Carburetion: Single Rochester 4-barrel. Compression Ratio: 8.5:1. Horsepower: Net: 175 @ 3600 rpm. Torque: Net: 290 lb.-ft. @ 2800 rpm. Fuel Requirements: Unleaded or low-lead gasoline of at least 91 Research Octane.

CHASSIS FEATURES: Ladder-type. Carbon steel, 39,000 psi. Heavy-gauge channel side members, alligator-jaw cross members. Section modules: 3.06 in.

SUSPENSION AND RUNNING GEAR: Front Suspension: Four tapered leaf springs. Capacity: 1650 lb. Rating: Standard: 380 lb./in. Soft Ride: 250 lb./in. Optional Capacity: 1900 lb. Rear Suspension: Two-stage tapered and multi-leaf (four-conventional leaves, one tapered leaf). Capacity: 1700 lb. Rating: Standard: 386/632 lb. in. Soft Ride: 270/510 lb./in. Optional: None. Front Axle. Type: Hypoid, tubular driving. Capacity: 3600 lb. Rear Axle. Type: Hypoid, semi-floating. Capacity: 3750 lb. Final Drive Ratio: 6-cyl.: 4.11:1; V-8: 3.07:1. Optional: 3.07, 3.73, 4.11:1. Transfer Case: Type: Manual transmission: New Process 205. Ratios: 1.96:1, 1.00:1. Automatic transmission: New Process 203. Ratios: 2.00:1, 1.00:1. Brakes: Type: Hydraulic, self-adjusting. Front: Discs. Rear: Drums. Optional: Power. Dimensions: Front: 11.86 in. dia. rotor. Rear: 11.15 in. x 2.75 in. Wheels: 6-stud, 15 x 6JJ. Optional: 15 x 7JJ Rallye, 15 x 8JJ, 15 x 8JJ Rallye, 16 x 5K. Tires: H78 x 15B, 4-ply rating. Optional: L78 x 15B, LR78 x 15B, 6.50 x 16C, 7.00 x 15C, 7.00 x 16C, 10 x 15B. Steering: Manual recirculating ball. Ratio: 24.0:1. Turns Lock-to-Lock: 3.4. Turning Circle: 37.6 ft. Optional: Power-assisted. Ratio: 20/16.4:1. Turning circle: 37.58 ft. Transmission: Type: Saginaw 3-speed manual, fully synchronized. Steering column-mounted shifter. This transmission was not available for the 350 and 400 cu. in. V-8 engine with 4-bbl. carburetor. Transmission Ratios: 2.85, 1.68, 1.0:1. Optional: Muncie 4-speed manual, synchromesh on top three gears, floor-mounted shift lever. Ratios: 6.55, 3.58, 1.70, 1.00:1. Optional: Turbo Hydra-Matic 3-speed automatic. Ratios: 2.52, 1.52, 1.00:1. Clutch: Six-cylinder: 11.0 in. dia., 124 sq. in. area. V-8 engines: 12.0 in. dia., 150 sq. in. area. Optional: None.

VEHICLE DIMENSIONS: Wheelbase: 106.5 in. Overall Length: 184.5 in. Front/Rear Tread 65.75 in./62.75 in. Overall Height: 69.0 in. With optional hardtop; 71.0 in. Width: 79.5 in. Tailgate: Width and Height: 66.8 in. x 22.0 in. Approach/Departure Degrees: 34/22. Ground Clearance: Front axle: 8.9 in. Rear axle: 8.5 in. Oil pan: 17.2 in. Transfer case: 11.5 in. Fuel tank: 14.0 in. Load space: With rear seat installed: 38.8 in. x 50 in. x 42.3 in. With rear seat removed or folded: 76.0 in. x 50 in. x 42.3 in.

CAPACITIES: Fuel Tank: 25.0 gal. Optional: Replacement 30 gal. tank. Coolant system: 250 6-cyl.: 12.2 qt. 350 V-8: 17.1 qt.

ACCOMMODATIONS: Seating Capacity: Standard: Driver. Optional: Driver and front passenger and/or 3 passenger rear bench seat. Headroom: 38.3 in. Maximum steering wheel to seat back: 18.5 in. Seat to ground: 36.3 in. Floor to ground: 21.9 in.

INSTRUMENTATION: 0-100 mph speedometer, 99,999.9 mi. odometer, fuel gauge, warning lights for alternator, oil pressure, engine coolant temperature, brake operating system, hazard warning lights, directional lights.

OPTIONS AND PRICES: Heavy-duty rear shock absorbers. Instrumentation Package. Includes ammeter, oil pressure gauge, and engine coolant temperature gauges: $17. Clock. Tachometer: $67. Cheyenne Package. Includes front and rear chrome bumpers, bright upper and lower body side and rear moldings, bright hubcaps, bright accents, Cheyenne nameplate, front bucket seats, front console, gauge instrumentation with simulated woodgrain trim and added insulation. Hardtop version was fitted with color-keyed carpeting, special front door and rear sidewall trim panels with bright accents and simulated woodgrain trim. Map pockets were included in front door trim panels. Special two-tone exterior paint treatment. ComforTilt steering wheel (available with 4-speed manual or Hydra-Matic transmissions only). Air conditioning (an increased capacity engine cooling system plus a 61 amp Delcotron are included). Passenger-side bucket seat (for Custom Deluxe Blazer): $87. Full-width rear bench seat: $153. Skid plates for fuel tank and transfer case. Sliding side glass windows. Below eye-level mirrors. Rear window air deflector, Heavy-duty 80 amp battery. Heavy-duty 42 or 61 amp generator (37 amp is standard). Heavy-duty radiator. Heavy-duty front shock absorbers: $18. Heavy-duty rear shock absorber: $10. Heavy-duty front springs: $36. Replacement 30 gal. fuel tank: $21. Soft-Ray tinted glass. Free-wheeling front hubs. Locking differential rear axle: $145. Power steering: $170. Various rear axle ratios. Front tow hooks. Trailer weight-distributing hitch. Woodgrain vinyl exterior trim. Rallye wheels. Special tires. Rooftop luggage carrier. AM radio. AM/FM radio. 400 cu. in. V-8: $144. 4-speed manual transmission: $123. Hydra-Matic transmission: $286.

HISTORICAL FOOTNOTES: The Blazer was introduced on September 1, 1974. *Four Wheeler* magazine recognized the Blazer as its "Four Wheeler of the Year" for 1975.

1976 BLAZER

The major development in the Blazer for 1976 was the use of a new roof design that involved a permanent steel front "half-cab" portion and a removable rear fiberglass-reinforced plastic portion that was attached to the Blazer by 16 bolts. The front section incorporated the roll bar. The "Soft Ride" suspension was now standard on the Blazer.

1976 Chevrolet Blazer Cheyenne

I.D. DATA: The Blazer's V.I.N. consisted of 13 symbols. The first symbol (a letter-C) identified the Chevrolet Motor Division. The second symbol (a letter-K) indicated vehicle type. The third symbol (a letter) indicated engine type: Q-250 cu. in. L-6, M-4-bbl. 400 cu. in V-8, Y-4-bbl. 350 cu. in. V-8. The fourth symbol (a number) identified the tonnage. The fifth symbol indicated model type. The sixth symbol identified the model year. The seventh symbol (a letter) indicated the assembly plant. The remaining six digits served as the sequential production numbers. The V.I.N. number was located on the left door pillar. The engine number indicated the manufacturing plant, day of manufacture and transmission type. It was located on a pad positioned on the right-hand side of the cylinder block at the rear of the distributor on V-8 engines and on a pad located at the front right hand side of the cylinder block of 6-cylinder engines.

Model Number	Body Type & Seating	Factory	GVW Price	Shipping Weight	Prod. Total
Blazer K10 (with 350 V-8)					
CK10516	Util. (with top)	$5365	6200	4017	74,389[1]

NOTE 1: Includes both two-wheel drive and four-wheel drive models.

STANDARD ENGINE: 250 Six: Ordering Code: LD4. Engine Type: OHV, In-line 6-cylinder. Bore x Stroke: 3.875 in. x 3.50 in. Lifters: Hydraulic. Number of main bearings-7. Carburetion: Rochester downdraft one-barrel, Model M7028007 or M7028011. Compression Ratio: 8.5:1. Displacement: 250 cu. in. (4.09 liters). Horsepower: Net: 100 @ 3800 rpm. Torque: Net: 175 lb.-ft. @ 1800 rpm. Oil capacity: 5 qt. with filter change. Fuel Requirements: Unleaded or low-lead gasoline of at least 91 Research Octane.

STANDARD ENGINE: V-8 models: Engine Type: Cast iron block. OHV, V-8. Bore x Stroke: 4.0 in. x 3.50 in. Lifters: Hydraulic. Number of main bearings-5. Carburetion: Rochester four-barrel. Compression Ratio: 8.51. Displacement: 350 cu. in. Horsepower: Net: 160 @ 3800 rpm. Torque: Gross: Net: 250 lb.-ft. @ 2400 rpm. Oil capacity: 5 qt. with filter change. Fuel Requirements: Unleaded or low-lead gasoline of at least 91 Research Octane.

OPTIONAL ENGINE: V-8 models: Engine Type: Cast Iron block. OHV V-8. Bore x Stroke: 4.125 in. x 4.75 in. Lifters: Hydraulic. Number of main bearings-5. Displacement: 400 cu. in. (6.55 liters). Carburetion: Single Rochester 4-barrel. Compression Ratio: 8.5:1. Horsepower: Net: 175 @ 3600 rpm. Torque: Net: 290 lb.-ft. @ 2800 rpm. Fuel Requirements: Unleaded or low-lead gasoline of at least 91 Research Octane.

CHASSIS FEATURES: Ladder-type. Carbon steel, 39,000 psi. Heavy-gauge channel side members, alligator-jaw cross members. Section modules: 3.06 in.

SUSPENSION AND RUNNING GEAR: Front Suspension: Four tapered leaf springs. Capacity: 1650 lb. Rating: Standard: 380 lb./in. Soft Ride: 250 lb./in. Optional Capacity: 1900 lb. Rear Suspension: Two-stage tapered and multi-leaf (four-conventional leaves, one tapered leaf). Capacity: 1700 lb. Rating: Standard: 386/632 lb. in. Soft Ride: 270/510 lb./in. Optional: None. Front Axle. Type: Hypoid, tubular driving. Capacity: 3600 lb. Rear Axle. Type: Hypoid, semi-floating. Capacity: 3750 lb. Final Drive Ratio: 6-cyl.: 4.11:1; V-8: 3.07:1. Optional: 3.07, 3.73, 4.11:1. Transfer Case: Type: Manual transmission: New Process 205. Ratios: 1.96:1, 1.00:1. Automatic transmission: New Process 203. Ratios: 2.00:1, 1.00:1. Brakes: Type: Hydraulic, self-adjusting. Front: Discs. Rear: Drums. Optional: Power. Dimensions: Front: 11.86 in. dia. rotor. Rear: 11.15 in. x 2.75 in. Wheels: 6-stud, 15 x 6JJ. Optional: 15 x 7JJ Rallye, 15 x 8JJ, 15 x 8JJ Rallye, 16 x 5K. Tires: H78 x 15B, 4-ply rating. Optional: L78 x 15B, LR78 x 15B, 6.50 x 16C, 7.00 x 15C, 7.00 x 16C, 10 x 15B. Steering: Manual recirculating ball. Ratio: 24.0:1. Turns Lock-to-Lock: 3.4. Turning Circle: 37.6 ft. Optional: Power-assisted. Ratio: 20/16.4:1. Turns Lock-to-Lock. Turning circle: 37.58 ft. Transmission: Type: Saginaw 3-speed manual, fully synchronized. Steering column-mounted shifter. This transmission was not available for the 350 and 400 cu. in. V-8 engine with 4-bbl. carburetor. Transmission Ratios: 2.85, 1.68, 1.0:1. Optional: Muncie 4-speed manual, synchromesh on top three gears, floor-mounted shift lever. Ratios: 6.55, 3.58, 1.70, 1.00:1. Optional: Turbo Hydra-Matic 3-speed automatic. Ratios: 2.52, 1.52, 1.00:1. Clutch: Six-cylinder: 11.0 in. dia., 124 sq. in. area. V-8 engines: 12.0 in. dia., 150 sq. in. area. Optional: None.

VEHICLE DIMENSIONS: Wheelbase: 106.5 in. Overall Length: 184.5 in. Front/Rear Tread 65.75 in./62.75 in. Overall Height: 69.0 in. With optional hardtop; 71.0 in. Width: 79.5 in. Tailgate: Width and Height: 66.8 in. x 22.0 in. Approach/Departure Degrees: 34/22. Ground Clearance: Front axle: 8.9 in. Rear axle: 8.5 in. Oil pan: 17.2 in. Transfer case: 11.5 in. Fuel tank: 14.0 in. Load space: With rear seat installed: 38.8 in. x 50 in. x 42.3 in. With rear seat removed or folded: 76.0 in. x 50 in. x 42.3 in.

CAPACITIES: Fuel Tank: 25.0 gal. Optional: Replacement 30 gal. tank. Coolant system: 250 6-cyl.: 12.2 qt. 350 V-8: 17.1 qt.

ACCOMMODATIONS: Seating Capacity: Standard: Driver. Optional: Driver and front passenger and/or 3 passenger rear bench seat. Headroom: 38.3 in. Maximum steering wheel to seat back: 18.5 in. Seat to ground: 36.3 in. Floor to ground: 21.9 in.

INSTRUMENTATION: 0-100 mph speedometer, 99,999.9 mi. odometer, fuel gauge, warning lights for alternator, oil pressure, engine coolant temperature, brake operating system, hazard warning lights, directional lights.

OPTIONS AND PRICES: Heavy-duty rear shock absorbers. Instrumentation Package. Includes ammeter, oil pressure gauge, and engine coolant temperature gauges. Clock. Tachometer. Cheyenne Package: $626. Includes front and rear chrome bumpers, bright upper and lower body side and rear moldings, bright hubcaps, bright accents, Cheyenne nameplate, front bucket seats, front console, gauge instrumentation with simulated woodgrain trim and added insulation. Hardtop version was fitted with color-keyed carpeting, special front door and rear sidewall trim panels with bright accents and simulated woodgrain trim. Map pockets were included in front door trim panels. Special two-tone exterior paint treatment. ComforTilt steering wheel (available with 4-speed manual or Hydra-Matic transmissions only). Air conditioning (an increased capacity engine cooling system plus a 61 amp Delcotron are included). Passenger-side bucket seat (for Custom Deluxe Blazer). Full-width rear bench seat skid plates for fuel tank and transfer case. Sliding side glass windows. Below eye-level mirrors. Rear window air deflector. Heavy-duty 80 amp battery. Heavy-duty 42 or 61 amp generator (37 amp is standard). Heavy-duty radiator. Heavy-duty front shock absorbers. Heavy-duty rear shock absorber. Heavy-duty front springs. Replacement 30 gal. fuel tank. Soft-Ray tinted glass. Free-wheeling front hubs. Locking differential rear axle. Power steering. Various rear axle ratios. Front tow hooks. Trailer weight-distributing hitch. Woodgrain vinyl exterior trim. Rallye wheels. Special tires. Rooftop luggage carrier. AM radio. AM/FM radio. 400 cu. in. V-8. 4-speed manual transmission. Hydra-Matic transmission. California emission certification: $75.

HISTORICAL FOOTNOTES: The latest Chevrolet Blazer was introduced in the fall of 1975.

1977 BLAZER

The 1977 K10 Blazer had a redesigned grille in which the headlight bezel paint color was changed from argent to dark gray metallic. Larger door trim panels of molded plastic were used. New seat trim colors and fabrics were also introduced. The Cheyenne option package had an ochre paint in place of the black trim color used in 1976.

Offered as an alternative to Blazers with the full or partial tops was a factory soft rear top option available in a choice of four colors: White, black, blue or buckskin. A hardboard-backed foam rubber front compartment headliner with perforated light fawn vinyl skin (RPO BB5) was introduced for 1977. The interior color of the standard hardtop headliner was changed from white to light fawn. The Blazer was now available with a new rear speaker (RPO U80) located in the right-hand rear trim panel. It was only available on Blazers equipped with RPO Z84, the Cheyenne equipment package. Also debuting was RPO ZY5, an Exterior Decor Package, consisting of a special two-tone paint treatment using a secondary color on the hood and between body side moldings. A bright stand-up spring-loaded hood ornament was also included as were color-coordinated hood stripes. Six two-tone choices were offered for this package which was not available on Blazers with black tops. Other new-for-1977 options included an inside hood lock release and intermittent windshield wipers. Both the optional styled steel wheels and bright metal wheelcovers were of new designs. Joining the 250 cu. in. L-6 and the 350 and 400 cu. in. V-8 engines in the Blazer engine line was a new 305 cu. in. V-8. Neither this engine nor the 250 L-6 were available in California. The 250 engine was equipped with a new electric carburetor choke. A new accelerator pedal and rod that were relocated further inboard towards the tunnel hump for improved right foot riding comfort were adopted for 1973. A new Chalet camper option consisted of a self-contained camper unit with a fiberglass-reinforced plastic body over a steel frame that was built by the Chinook Mobilodge Company. The camper that was permanently attached to the Blazer. This arrangement was promoted as "the Blazer you can live in." When the Blazer was parked the top could be extended to provide over six feet of headroom. The length of a Blazer with this package was extended 26 inches beyond the rear tailgate. The Chalet Blazer had a 6700 lb. GVWR (Gross Vehicle Weight rating) and had a list price of $9444 which included a 350 cu. in. V-8, 3-speed manual transmission, front bucket seats, chromed bumpers, front-mounted spare tire carrier and power steering. Chevrolet offered the following colors for the 1977 Blazer: Frost white, Mariner blue, buckskin, mahogany, Hawaiian blue, Santa Fe tan, red metallic, light blue, Colonial yellow, cardinal red, midnight black, Saratoga silver, seamist green, russet metallic and Cordova brown.

1977 Chevrolet K10 Blazer with Exterior Decor Package

I.D. DATA: The Blazer's V.I.N. consisted of 13 symbols. The first symbol (a letter-C) identified the Chevrolet Motor Division. The second symbol (a letter-K) indicated vehicle type. The third symbol (a letter) indicated engine type: D-250 cu. in. L-6, U-305 V-8, R-4-bbl. 400 cu. in V-8, L-4-bbl. 350 cu. in. V-8. The fourth symbol (a number) identified the tonnage. The fifth symbol indicated model type. The sixth symbol identified the model year. The seventh symbol (a letter) indicated the assembly plant. The remaining six digits served as the sequential production numbers. The V.I.N. number was located on the left door pillar. The engine number indicated the manufacturing plant, day of manufacture and transmission type. It was located on a pad positioned on the right-hand side of the cylinder block at the rear of the distributor on V-8 engines and on a pad located at the front right hand side of the cylinder block of 6-cylinder engines.

Model Number	Body Type & Seating	Factory Price	GVW	Shipping Weight	Prod. Total
Blazer K10 (with 305 V-8)					
CK10516	Util. (Hardtop)	$5603	6050*	4268	—
CK10516	Util. (folding top)	$5503	6050	N.A.	—

* 6200 lb GVW optional

STANDARD ENGINE: 250 Six: Ordering Code: LD4. Engine Type: OHV, In-line 6-cylinder. Bore x Stroke: 3.875 in. x 3.50 in. Lifters: Hydraulic. Number of main bearings-7. Carburetion: Rochester downdraft one-barrel, Model M7028007 or M7028011. Compression Ratio: 8.5:1. Displacement: 250 cu. in. (4.09 liters). Horsepower: Net: 100 @ 3800 rpm. Torque: Net: 175 lb.-ft. @ 1800 rpm. Oil capacity: 5 qt. with filter change. Fuel Requirements: Unleaded or low-lead gasoline of at least 91 Research Octane.

STANDARD ENGINE: V-8 models: Available in all states except California. Engine Type: Cast iron block. OHV, V-8. Bore x Stroke: 3.74 in. x 3.48 in. Lifters: Hydraulic. Number of main bearings-5. Carburetion: Rochester two-barrel. Compression Ratio: 8.5:1. Displacement: 305 cu. in. Horsepower: 140 @ 3800 rpm. Torque: Gross: 235 lb.-ft. @ 2000 rpm. Oil capacity: 5 qt. with filter change. Fuel Requirements: Unleaded or low-lead gasoline of at least 91 Research Octane.

OPTIONAL ENGINE: V-8 models: Engine Type: Cast iron block. OHV, V-8. Bore x Stroke: 4.0 in. x 3.50 in. Lifters: Hydraulic. Number of main bearings-5. Carburetion: Rochester four-barrel. Compression Ratio: 8.51. Displacement: 350 cu. in. Horsepower: Net: 160 @ 3800 rpm. Torque: Gross: Net: 250 lb.-ft. @ 2400 rpm. Oil capacity: 5 qt. with filter change. Fuel Requirements: Unleaded or low-lead gasoline of at least 91 Research Octane.

OPTIONAL ENGINE: V-8 models: Option LF4. Engine Type: Cast Iron block. OHV V-8. Bore x Stroke: 4.125 in. x 4.75 in. Lifters: Hydraulic. Number of main bearings-5. Displacement: 400 cu. in. (6.55 liters). Carburetion: Single Rochester 4-barrel. Compression Ratio: 8.5:1. Horsepower: Net: 175 @ 3600 rpm. Torque: Net: 290 lb.-ft. @ 2800 rpm. Fuel Requirements: Unleaded or low-lead gasoline of at least 91 Research Octane.

CHASSIS FEATURES: Ladder-type. Carbon steel, 39,000 psi. Heavy-gauge channel side members, alligator-jaw cross members. Section modules: 3.06 in.

SUSPENSION AND RUNNING GEAR: Front Suspension: Two tapered semi-elliptical leaf springs. Capacity: 1650 lb. Rating: 250 lb./in. 1.0 in. shock absorbers, 1.25 in. stabilizer bar. Optional Capacity: 2250 lb. 32mm shock absorbers (available with RPO F60 heavy-duty springs only). Rear Suspension: Two-stage tapered and multi-leaf (six-conventional leaves, one tapered leaf). Capacity: 1700 lb. Rating: 270/510 lb./in. Optional: None. Front Axle. Type: Hypoid, tubular driving. Capacity: 3600 lb. Rear Axle. Type: Hypoid, semi-floating. Capacity: 3750 lb. Final Drive Ratio: 6-cyl.: 4.11:1; 305 V-8: 3.73:1; 350 V-8: 3.07:1, 400 V-8: 2.77:1 (initial production), 3.07:1 (interim 1977). Optional: 6-cyl.: 3.73:1; 305 V-8: 2.76, 3.07, 4.11:1; 350 V-8: 2.76, 3.73, 4.11:1, 400 V-8: 3.07, 3.73, 4.11:1. Transfer Case: Type: Manual transmission: New Process 205. Ratios: 1.96:1, 1.00:1. Automatic transmission: New Process 203. Ratios: 2.00:1, 1.00:1. Brakes: Type: Hydraulic, self-adjusting. Front: Discs. Rear: Drums. Optional: Power. Dimensions: Front: 11.86 in. dia. rotor. Rear: 11.15 in. x 2.75 in. Wheels: 6-stud, 15 x 6JJ. Optional: 15 x 7JJ Rallye, 15 x 8JJ, 15 x 8JJ Rallye, 16 x 5K. Tires: H78 x 15B, 4-ply rating. Optional: L78 x 15B, LR78 x 15B, 6.50 x 16C, 7.00 x 15C, 7.00 x 16C, 10 x 15B. Steering: Manual recirculating ball. Ratio: 24.0:1. Turns Lock-to-Lock: 3.4. Turning Circle: 37.6 ft. Optional: Power-assisted. Ratio: 20/16.4:1. Turns Lock-to-Lock. Turning circle: 37.58 ft. Transmission: Type: Saginaw 3-speed manual, fully synchronized. Steering column-mounted shifter. This transmission was not available for the 350 and 400 cu. in. V-8 engine with 4-bbl. carburetor. Transmission Ratios: 2.85, 1.68, 1.0:1. Optional: Muncie 4-speed manual, synchromesh on top three gears, floor-mounted shift lever. Ratios: 6.55, 3.58, 1.70, 1.00:1. Optional: Turbo Hydra-Matic 3-speed automatic. Ratios: 2.52, 1.52, 1.00:1. Clutch: Six-cylinder: 11.0 in. dia., 124 sq. in. area. V-8 engines: 12.0 in. dia., 150 sq. in. area. Optional: None.

VEHICLE DIMENSIONS: Wheelbase: 106.5 in. Overall Length: 184.5 in. Front/Rear Tread 65.75 in./62.75 in. Overall Height: 69.0 in. With optional hardtop; 71.0 in. Width: 79.5 in. Tailgate: Width and Height: 66.8 in. x 22.0 in. Approach/Departure Degrees: 34/22. Ground Clearance: Front axle: 8.9 in. Rear axle: 8.5 in. Oil pan: 17.2 in. Transfer case: 11.5 in. Fuel tank: 14.0 in. Load space: With rear seat installed: 38.8 in. x 50 in. x 42.3 in. With rear seat removed or folded: 76.0 in. x 50 in. x 42.3 in.

CAPACITIES: Fuel Tank: 25.0 gal. Optional: Replacement 30 gal. tank. Coolant system: 250 6-cyl.: 12.2 qt.350 V-8: 17.1 qt.

ACCOMMODATIONS: Seating Capacity: Standard: Driver. Optional: Driver and front passenger and/or 3 passenger rear bench seat. Headroom: 38.3 in. Maximum steering wheel to seat back: 18.5 in. Seat to ground: 36.3 in. Floor to ground: 21.9 in.

INSTRUMENTATION: 0-100 mph speedometer, 99,999.9 mi. odometer, fuel gauge, warning lights for alternator, oil pressure, engine coolant temperature, brake operating system, hazard warning lights, directional lights.

OPTIONS AND PRICES: 305 cu. in. V-8 (RPO LG9): $150. 350 cu. in. V-8 (RPO LS9). 400 cu. in V-8 (RPO LF4): $160. Four-speed manual transmission (RPO MM4): $142. Front passenger bucket seat (RPO RPO A57). Full-width rear bench seat (RPO AM7): $. Three-speed automatic transmission (RPO MX1): $300. Power steering (RPO N41): $188. Gauge instrumentation (RPO Z53): $21. Tachometer (RPO U16): $76. Cheyenne interior (RPO Z84). Includes front bucket seats in leather-grained Custom vinyl in a selection of four colors (Custom cloth upholstery in buckskin and blue also available), center console, gauge instrumentation, simulated woodgrain trim, additional insulation, color-keyed carpeting (carpeting covers rear floor if rear bench seat is ordered), and rear sidewall trim panels with bright accents and simulated woodgrain trim. Custom Deluxe interior. Includes foam-cushioned driver's bucket seat trimmed in plaid-pattern vinyl in a choice of four colors (matching auxiliary front bucket seat and rear bench seat available), one-piece molded door trim panels, foam-cushioned instrument panel pad, padded sun visors, rubber floor covering and driver combination lap-shoulder belt. Exterior Decor Package (RPO ZY5). Inside hood release. (RPO T44). AM radio (RPO U63): $80. AM/FM radio (RPO U69): $130. Windshield antenna (RPO U76). Auxiliary rear radio speaker (RPO U80). Deluxe front and rear chrome bumpers with impact strips (RPO V37): $75. Deluxe front and rear bumpers (RPO VE5). Stainless steel camper-type exterior mirrors (RPO DF2). Stainless steel below eye-level type exterior mirrors (RPO DG4). Painted below eye-level type exterior mirrors (RPO D29). Soft-Ray tinted glass (RPO AO1). Front stabilizer bar (RPO F59). Engine oil cooler (RPO KC4). Dual exhaust system (RPO N10). Simulated woodgrained exterior trim (RPO YG2). Special two-tone paint (RPO ZY3). Styled steel wheels (PA6). Bright metal wheelcovers (RPO PO1): $35. Rallye wheels (RPO N67). Wheel trim rings (RPO PO6). Speed and cruise control (RPO K30). Intermittent windshield wipers (RPO CD4). Chromed bumper guards (RPO V31: $50. Luggage carrier. Replacement 31 gal. fuel tank (RPO NK7): $25. Rear window air deflector. 61 amp Delcotron generator (RPO K76). Heavy-duty radiator (RPO VO1). Transmission oil cooler (RPO VO2).

Towing device (RPO V76). Special tires. Custom steering wheel (RPO N31). Cigarette lighter (RPO U37): $15. Swing-away spare tire carrier: $100. Locking differential rear axle (RPO G80): $155. Special Trailering Equipment Package (RPO Z82). Includes power steering, heavy-duty battery, Trailering Special nameplate with GVW rating. Heavy-duty trailer wiring harness (RPO UY7). Auxiliary battery (RPO TP2). Heavy-duty front and rear shock absorbers (F51): $20. Heavy-duty front springs (F60): $36. Weight-distributing hitch platform (RPO VR4). Deadweight trailer hitch (RPO VR2). Fuel tank shield plates (RPO NY1). Convertible top (RPO C1A-White, RPO C1B-Black, C1C-Blue, RPO C1D-Buckskin). ComforTilt steering wheel (RPO N33). Air conditioning (RPO C60). Sliding rear side windows (RPO AD5): $156. Color-keyed front floor mats (RPO B32). Rear roll bar (RPO E50). Spare tire cover (RPO P17).

HISTORICAL FOOTNOTES: The latest Chevrolet Blazer was introduced in the fall of 1976.

1978 BLAZER

The Blazer instrument panel pad applique and instrument cluster bezel were changed for 1978. A bright brush-finished treatment was used for the bezel and applique. A new Deluxe instrument panel option (RPO BC3) was available with a black diamond-textured plastic center section on Custom Deluxe models and a bright brush-finish insert on the Cheyenne. The windshield wiper/washer system had an improved performance wiper motor. The intermittent wiper option (RPO CD4) was also of all-new design. The front seat belt system now used one emergency locking retractor for both the lap and shoulder belt. The Blazer's lap and shoulder belt retractor was now mounted on the door lock pillar instead of the floor as on the1977 model. This improved rear compartment exit and entry. Blazer models with a folding rear seat also have new seat belts similar in design to those used on 1977 Blazers with the 3 passenger rear seat. Enabling the Blazer to comply with new windshield retention requirements, a new bonded-in urethane rubber strip was used. New insulators and sound deadeners were incorporated into the Blazer's manufacture. All Blazer side outer panels and, on Blazers with the optional folding seat, the tailgate panel, were now constructed of pre-coated steel. The Blazer's side inner panel extension was redesigned to minimize entry of water and other matter between the inner and outer panels. The 1978 Blazer could be fitted with front and rear wheel opening moldings as a separate option (RPO B96). Previously, they had been tied in with other optional equipment. Bright plastic decorative molding was added to the hood's rear edge. The optional Rallye wheels had a new style center hub of chromed plastic. These hubcaps were also used in conjunction with the optional styled wheels. The rear hubs of both the Rallye and styled wheels carried a new four-wheel drive center insert identification. Replacing the previous woodgrain door trim appliques on Cheyenne Blazers were new bright brush-finished appliques. This change was also made to the rear quarter trim panel appliques for Cheyenne Blazer models which also had a new bright molding. Door hardware inserts for all Blazer trim levels now had a bright brushed finish instead of the former pewter finish. The Custom vinyl bench and bucket seat trims had a new cover material with an oxen hide grain which had a smoother texture than the former buffalo hide grain. Basic vinyl seat trims were unchanged, except that the mandarin orange color was no longer offered. A new red color was added to the blue and buckskin choices for the Blazer's Custom cloth trim. The front immediately behind the Blazer's front seat was now depressed to the same level as the front compartment. This change provided a major increase in rear legroom.

1978 Chevrolet K10 Blazer Cheyenne

The Blazer was also available with a new folding rear seat (RPO AM7) which replaced the older rear bench seat (RPO AS3). The new seat could be folded forward by first unlatching the backrest, which then folded forward and down to the cushion. The cushion was then unlatched to allow the entire assembly to swing up and forward against the front seat. The entire assembly could be removed by unbolting four bolts. On some early 1978 model Blazers a 3-bolt attachment may be found. A new latch mechanism facilitated the folding of the auxiliary front seat (RPO A57) out of the way for easier rear seat access. New standard high-back bucket seats were also introduced for the Blazer. The Blazer was now offered with power front door locks (RPO AU3), power front door windows (RPO A31) and a power tailgate (RPO A33). The power front door locks and power windows were also included in a new Operating Convenience Package (RPO ZQ2). Replacing the 17.5 in. diameter steering wheel used on earlier Blazers was a smaller 16.0 in. diameter soft vinyl steering wheel with a soft vinyl horn button cap. The Custom steering wheel (RPO N31) had a bright trimmed horn button cap. Both the Blazer's engine lineup and its exterior color selections were carried over from 1977.

I.D. DATA: The Blazer's V.I.N. consisted of 13 symbols. The first symbol (a letter-C) identified the Chevrolet Motor Division. The second symbol (a letter-K) indicated vehicle type. The third symbol (a letter) indicated engine type: D-250 cu. in. L-6, U-305 V-8, R-4-bbl. 400 cu. in V-8, L-4-bbl. 350 cu. in. V-8. The fourth symbol (a number) identified the tonnage. The fifth symbol indicated model type. The sixth symbol identified the model year. The seventh symbol (a letter) indicated the assembly plant. The remaining six digits served as the sequential production numbers. The V.I.N. number was located on the left door pillar. The engine number indicated the manufacturing plant, day of manufacture and transmission type. It was located on a pad positioned on the right-hand side of the cylinder block at the rear of the distributor on V-8 engines and on a pad located at the front right hand side of the cylinder block of 6-cylinder engines.

Model Number	Body Type & Seating	Factory Price	GVW	Shipping Weight	Prod. Total
Blazer K10 (with 250 6-cyl.)					
CK10516	Util. (Hardtop)	$6193.40	6050	4268	—
CK10516	Uti. (folding top)	$6093.40	6050*	N.A.	—

* 6200 lb GVW optional
Prices listed are for vehicles produced on or after February 6, 1978.

STANDARD ENGINE: 250 Six: Ordering Code: LD4. Engine Type: OHV, In-line 6-cylinder. Bore x Stroke: 3.875 in. x 3.50 in. Lifters: Hydraulic. Number of main bearings-7. Carburetion: Rochester downdraft one-barrel, Model M7028007 or M7028011. Compression Ratio: 8.5:1. Displacement: 250 cu. in. (4.09 liters). Horsepower: Net: 100 @ 3800 rpm. Torque: Net: 175 lb.-ft. @ 1800 rpm. Oil capacity: 5 qt. with filter change. Fuel Requirements: Unleaded or low-lead gasoline of at least 91 Research Octane.

STANDARD ENGINE: V-8 models: Available in all states except California. Ordering Code: LG9. Engine Type: Cast iron block. OHV, V-8. Bore x Stroke: 3.74 in. x 3.48 in. Lifters: Hydraulic. Number of main bearings-5. Carburetion: Rochester two-barrel. Compression Ratio: 8.5:1. Displacement: 305 cu. in. Horsepower: 140 @ 3800 rpm. Torque: Gross: 235 lb.-ft. @ 2000 rpm. Oil capacity: 5 qt. with filter change. Fuel Requirements: Unleaded or low-lead gasoline of at least 91 Research Octane.

OPTIONAL ENGINE: V-8 models: Ordering Code: LS9. Engine Type: Cast iron block. OHV, V-8. Bore x Stroke: 4.0 in. x 3.50 in. Lifters: Hydraulic. Number of main bearings-5. Carburetion: Rochester four-barrel. Compression Ratio: 8.51. Displacement: 350 cu. in. Horsepower: Net: 160 @ 3800 rpm. Torque: Gross: Net: 250 lb.-ft. @ 2400 rpm. Oil capacity: 5 qt. with filter change. Fuel Requirements: Unleaded or low-lead gasoline of at least 91 Research Octane.

OPTIONAL ENGINE: V-8 models: Option LF4. Engine Type: Cast Iron block. OHV V-8. Bore x Stroke: 4.125 in. x 4.75 in. Lifters: Hydraulic. Number of main bearings-5. Displacement: 400 cu. in. (6.55 liters). Carburetion: Single Rochester 4-barrel. Compression Ratio: 8.5:1. Horsepower: Net: 175 @ 3600 rpm. Torque: Net: 290 lb.-ft. @ 2800 rpm. Fuel Requirements: Unleaded or low-lead gasoline of at least 91 Research Octane.

CHASSIS FEATURES: Ladder-type. Carbon steel, 39,000 psi. Heavy-gauge channel side members, alligator-jaw cross members. Section modules: 3.06 in.

SUSPENSION AND RUNNING GEAR: Front Suspension: Two tapered semi-elliptical leaf springs. Capacity: 1650 lb. Rating: 250 lb./in. 1.0 in. shock absorbers, 1.25 in. stabilizer bar. Optional Capacity: 2250 lb. 32mm shock absorbers (available with RPO F60 heavy-duty springs only). Rear Suspension: Two-stage tapered and multi-leaf (six-conventional leaves, one tapered leaf). Capacity: 1700 lb. Rating: 270/510 lb./in. Optional: None. Front Axle. Type: Hypoid, tubular driving. Capacity: 3600 lb. Rear Axle. Type: Hypoid, semi-floating. Capacity: 3750 lb. Final Drive Ratio: 6-cyl.: 4.11:1; 305 V-8: 3.40:1; 350 and V-8: 3.07:1. Optional: 6-cyl.: 3.40:1; 305 V-8: 2.76, 3.07, 3.73:1; 350 and 400 V-8: 2.76, 3.40, 3.73:1. Transfer Case: Type: Manual transmission: New Process 205. Ratios: 1.96:1, 1.00:1. Automatic transmission: New Process 203. Ratios: 2.00:1, 1.00:1. Brakes: Type: Hydraulic, self-adjusting. Front: Discs. Rear: Drums. Optional: Power. Dimensions: Front: 11.86 in. dia. rotor. Rear: 11.15 in. x 2.75 in. Wheels: 6-stud, 15 x 6JJ. Optional: 15 x 7JJ Rallye, 15 x 8JJ, 15 x 8JJ Rallye, 16 x 5K. Tires: H78 x 15B, 4-ply rating. Optional: LR78 x 15C (highway steel belted radial white stripe), H78 x 15B (highway), H78 x 15B (highway, white stripe), H78 x 15B (on-off road), L78 x 15B (highway), L78 x15B (on-off road), L78 x 15B (highway, white stripe), 6.50 x 16C (highway), 7.00 x 15C (highway), 10.00 x 15B (polyester), 10.00 x 15B (polyester white lettered). Steering: Manual recirculating ball. Ratio: 24.0:1. Turns Lock-to-Lock: 3.4. Turning Circle: 37.6 ft. Optional: Power-assisted. Ratio: 20/16.4:1. Turning circle: 37.58 ft. Transmission: Type: Saginaw 3-speed manual, fully synchronized. Steering column-mounted shifter. This transmission was not available for the 350 and 400 cu. in. V-8 engine with 4-bbl. carburetor. Transmission Ratios: 2.85, 1.68, 1.0:1. Optional: Muncie 4-speed manual, synchromesh on top three gears, floor-mounted shift lever. Ratios: 6.55, 3.58, 1.70, 1.00:1. Optional: Turbo Hydra-Matic 3-speed automatic. Ratios: 2.52, 1.52, 1.00:1. Clutch: Six-cylinder: 11.0 in. dia., 124 sq. in. area. V-8 engines: 12.0 in. dia., 150 sq. in. area. Optional: None.

VEHICLE DIMENSIONS: Wheelbase: 106.5 in. Overall Length: 184.5 in. Front/Rear Tread 65.75 in./62.75 in. Overall Height: 69.0 in. With optional hardtop; 71.0 in. Width: 79.5 in. Tailgate: Width and Height: 66.8 in. x 22.0 in. Approach/Departure Degrees: 34/22. Ground Clearance: Front axle: 8.9 in. Rear axle: 8.5 in. Oil pan: 17.2 in. Transfer case: 11.5 in. Fuel tank: 14.0 in. Load space: With rear seat installed: 38.8 in. x 50 in. x 42.3 in. With rear seat removed or folded: 76.0 in. x 50 in. x 42.3 in.

CAPACITIES: Fuel Tank: 25.0 gal. Optional: Replacement 30 gal. tank. Coolant system: 250 6-cyl.: 12.2 qt. 350 V-8: 17.1 qt.

ACCOMMODATIONS: Seating Capacity: Standard: Driver. Optional: Driver and front passenger and/or 3 passenger rear bench seat. Headroom: 38.3 in. Maximum steering wheel to seat back: 18.5 in. Seat to ground: 36.3 in. Floor to ground: 21.9 in.

INSTRUMENTATION: 0-100 mph speedometer, 99,999.9 mi. odometer, fuel gauge, warning lights for alternator, oil pressure, engine coolant temperature, brake operating system, hazard warning lights, directional lights.

OPTIONS AND PRICES: Prices shown were in effect on or after February 6, 1978. 305 cu. in. V-8 (RPO LG9): $185. 350 cu. in. V-8 (RPO LS9): $300. 400 cu. in V-8 (RPO LF4): $485. Automatic transmission (RPO MX1): $345. Four-speed manual transmission (RPO MM4): $152. Cheyenne Package (RPO Z84): $758-$781 depending upon tire selection. Poly Wrap air cleaner (RPO K43): $15. All-Weather air conditioning: (RPOC60): $550. Auxiliary battery (RPO TP2): $92. Heavy-duty battery (RPO UA1): $36. Chromed front and rear bumpers (RPO VE5): $84, without Cheyenne, $32 with Cheyenne. Chromed front bumper guards: $31. California emissions requirements (RPO YF5): $93. Electric clock (RPO YF5): $52 without Cheyenne, $25 with Cheyenne. Cold Climate Package (RPO Z56): $97-$133. Engine oil cooler (RPO KC4): $86. Transmission oil cooler (RPO VO2): $42. Heavy-duty radiator (RPO VO1): $39. Spare tire cover (RPO P17): $23. Power door lock system (RPO AU3): $90. Dual exhaust system (RPO N10): $37. Color-keyed front floor mats (RPOB32): $10. Gauge Package. Includes voltmeter, oil pressure and engine coolant temperature (RPO Z53): $27. Tachometer. Available only with V-8 engine (RPO U16) $87. 61 amp Delcotron generator (RPO K76): $45. Sliding side window (RPO AD5): $163. Tinted glass (RPO AO1): $46. Chromed grille (RPO V22): $26. Heavy-duty trailer wiring harness (RPO UY7): $31. Headlight warning buzzer (RPO T63): $7. Full length interior headliner (RPO BB5): $59. Inside hood release (RPO T44): $21. Deluxe instrument panel (RPO BC3): $35. Cigarette lighter (RPO U37): $17. Exterior below eye-level painted mirrors (RPO D29): $28. Exterior below eye-level stainless steel mirrors (RPO DG4): $52. Camper style stainless steel mirrors (RPO DF2): $67. Body spear molding (RPO B84): $59. Body side upper molding (RPO 85): $61. Upper and lower body side moldings (RPO YG1): $150. Door edge guards (RPO B93): $10. Wheel opening moldings (RPO B96): $21. Operating Convenience Group. Includes power door locks and power windows (RPO ZQ2): $221. Special two-tone exterior paint (RPO YZ3): $244, without Cheyenne, $94 with Cheyenne. Exterior Decor Package (RPO ZY5): $349 without Cheyenne, $199 with Cheyenne. Fuel tank and transfer case skid plates (RPO NY1): $123. AM radio: $86. AM/FM radio: $167. Rear seat speaker. (RPO U80): $38. Windshield antenna. Included when AM or AM/FM radio is ordered (RPO U76): $24. Rear roll bar (RPO E50): $9. Front passenger seat (RPO A57): $13. Rear 3 passenger seat (RPOAM7): $243, without

Custom trim, $264 with Custom trim. High-back bucket seats $74 to $284 depending on seat trim and seat options. Speed and cruise control, V-8 only (RPO K30): $90. Heavy-duty front springs (RPO F60): $67. Tilt-type steering wheel (RPO N33): $72. Custom steering wheel (RPO N31): $14. 31 gal. fuel tank (RPO K7O: $31. Two front towing hooks (RPO V76): $28. Deadweight towing hitch (RPO VR2): $41. Platform type towing hitch (RPO VR4): $115. Trailering Special Package (RPO Z82): $36-$81. Bright metal hubcaps (RPO PO3): $19. Bright wheel trim rings (RPO PO6): $41. Bright wheelcovers (RPO PO1): $20 without Cheyenne, $29 with Cheyenne. Rallye wheels (RPO N67): $93. Styled wheels (RPO PA6): $108. Power side door windows (RPO A31): $131. Power tailgate (RPO A33): $62. Intermittent windshield wiper system (RPO CD4 Woodgrained exterior trim (RPO YG2): $279 without Cheyenne, $129 with Cheyenne.

HISTORICAL FOOTNOTES: The 1978 Chevrolet Blazer was introduced in the fall of 1977.

1979 BLAZER

The 1979 Blazer had a smoother and more aerodynamic hood leading edge. New integral headlight/parking light bezels were used as was a new concealed fuel filler door. Improved anti-corrosion protection was provided by extending the use of zinc-rich precoated metal to the side door hinges and door panels, front fender and hood inner panels, front fender outer panels, standard tailgate, and radiator grille upper panel. The standard Custom Deluxe interior had high-back bucket seats (the passenger seat was included in both the Custom vinyl trim and Cheyenne options) in a choice of blue or camel tan houndstooth pattern vinyl. Also included was a padded instrument panel with bright-trimmed applique and nameplate. The full floor covering was black embossed rubber. The door trim panels were color-keyed plastic with right-hand and left-hand integral armrests. Hardtop models had two dome lights with door-activated switches. Optional was a Custom vinyl seat trim in blue or camel tan. This option also included color-keyed carpeting for the front compartment and color-keyed plastic console between the seats. A matching floor covering was included if the optional rear bench seat was ordered.

The Cheyenne interior included all the standard features plus these additions or substitutions: Custom vinyl seat trim in blue, carmine or camel tan or Custom cloth seat trim in Ccarmine or camel tan. Also included was bright trim and color-keyed carpeting for the front compartment and a color-keyed plastic console. Matching floor covering for the rear compartment was included when the optional rear bench seat was ordered. New for 1979 was the inclusion of a Custom steering wheel plus available two-tone interior in a choice of blue, carmine or camel tan in combination with Mystic Custom vinyl or cloth seat trim or cloth seat trim, door trim panels and sunshades. The Cheyenne instrument panel cluster had a bright finish and gauges for engine coolant temperature, voltmeter and oil pressure. Also part of the Cheyenne's interior was special front door trim and rear sidewall trim panels with ashtrays.

I.D. DATA: The Blazer's V.I.N. consisted of 13 symbols. The first symbol (a letter-C) identified the Chevrolet Motor Division. The second symbol (a letter-K) indicated vehicle type. The third symbol (a letter) indicated engine type: D-250 cu. in. L-6, U-305 V-8, R-4-bbl. 400 cu. in V-8, L-4-bbl. 350 cu. in. V-8. The fourth symbol (a number) identified the tonnage. The fifth symbol indicated model type. The sixth symbol identified the model year. The seventh symbol (a letter) indicated the assembly plant. The remaining six digits served as the sequential production numbers. The V.I.N. number was located on the left door pillar. The engine number indicated the manufacturing plant, day of manufacture and transmission type. It was located on a pad positioned on the right-hand side of the cylinder block at the rear of the distributor on V-8 engines and on a pad located at the front right hand side of the cylinder block of 6-cylinder engines.

Model Number	Body Type & Seating	Factory Price	GVW	Shipping Weight	Prod. Total
Blazer K10 (with 305 V-8)					
CK10516	Util. (hardtop)	$7373	6200	4490[1]	57,734[2]
CK10516	Util. (folding top)	$7273	6200	4342[1]	—

NOTE 1: With 6-cyl. engine.
NOTE 2: Includes all two-wheel drive and four-wheel drive models.

STANDARD ENGINE: 250 Six: Ordering Code: LD4. Engine Type: OHV, In-line 6-cylinder. Bore x Stroke: 3.875 in. x 3.50 in. Lifters: Hydraulic. Number of main bearings-7. Carburetion: Rochester downdraft one-barrel, Model M7028007 or M7028011. Compression Ratio: 8.5:1. Displacement: 250 cu. in. (4.09 liters). Horsepower: Net: 100 @ 3800 rpm. Torque: Net: 175 lb.-ft. @ 1800 rpm. Oil capacity: 5 qt. with filter change. Fuel Requirements: Unleaded or low-lead gasoline of at least 91 Research Octane.

STANDARD ENGINE: V-8 models: Available in all states except California. Ordering Code: LG9. Engine Type: Cast iron block. OHV, V-8. Bore x Stroke: 3.74 in. x 3.48 in. Lifters: Hydraulic. Number of main bearings-5. Carburetion: Rochester two-barrel. Compression Ratio: 8.5:1. Displacement: 305 cu. in. Horsepower: 140 @ 3800 rpm. Torque: Gross: 235 lb.-ft. @ 2000 rpm. Oil capacity: 5 qt. with filter change. Fuel Requirements: Unleaded or low-lead gasoline of at least 91 Research Octane.

OPTIONAL ENGINE: V-8 models: Ordering Code: LS9. Engine Type: Cast iron block. OHV, V-8. Bore x Stroke: 4.0 in. x 3.50 in. Lifters: Hydraulic. Number of main bearings-5. Carburetion: Rochester four-barrel. Compression Ratio: 8.5:1. Displacement: 350 cu. in. Horsepower: Net: 160 @ 3800 rpm. Torque: Gross: Net: 250 lb.-ft. @ 2400 rpm. Oil capacity: 5 qt. with filter change. Fuel Requirements: Unleaded or low-lead gasoline of at least 91 Research Octane.

OPTIONAL ENGINE: V-8 models: Option LF4. Engine Type: Cast Iron block. OHV V-8. Bore x Stroke: 4.125 in. x 4.75 in. Lifters: Hydraulic. Number of main bearings-5. Displacement: 400 cu. in. (6.55 liters). Carburetion: Single Rochester 4-barrel. Compression Ratio: 8.5:1. (California rating: 8.2:1). Horsepower: 175 @ 3600 rpm. (California rating: 170 @ 3600 rpm). Torque: 290 lb.-ft. @ 2800 rpm. Fuel Requirements: Unleaded or low-lead gasoline of at least 91 Research Octane.

CHASSIS FEATURES: Ladder-type. Carbon steel, 39,000 psi. Heavy-gauge channel side members, alligator-jaw cross members. Section modules: 3.06 in.

SUSPENSION AND RUNNING GEAR: Front Suspension: Two tapered semi-elliptical leaf springs. Capacity: 1650 lb. Rating: 250 lb./in. 1.0 in. shock absorbers, 1.25 in. stabilizer bar. Optional Capacity: 2250 lb. 32mm shock absorbers (available with RPO F60 heavy-duty springs only). Rear Suspension: Two-stage tapered and multi-leaf (six-conventional leaves, one tapered leaf). Capacity: 1700 lb. Rating: 270/510 lb./in. Optional: None. Front Axle. Type: Hypoid, tubular driving. Capacity: 3600 lb. Rear Axle. Type: Hypoid, semi-floating. Capacity: 3750 lb. Final Drive Ratio: 250 cu. in. 6-cyl.: 3.40:1. 305 V-8: 3.40:1; 350 and 400 cu. in. V-8 engines: 3.07:1. Optional: 250 cu. in. 6-cyl.: 3.40:1; 305, 350 V-8: and 400 cu. in. V-8 engines: 2.76, 3.40, 3.73:1. Transfer Case: Type: Manual transmission: New Process 205. Ratios: 1.96:1, 1.00:1. Automatic transmission: New Process 203. Ratios. 2.00:1, 1.00:1. Brakes: Type: Hydraulic, self-adjusting. Front: Discs. Rear: Drums. Optional: Power. Dimensions: Front: 11.86 in. dia. rotor. Rear: 11.15 in. x 2.75 in. Wheels: 6-stud, 15 x 6JJ. Optional: 15 x 7JJ Rallye, 15 x 8JJ, 15 x 8JJ Rallye, 16 x 5K. Tires: H78 x 15B, 4-ply rating. Optional: LR78 x 15C (highway steel belted radial white stripe), H78 x 15B (highway), H78 x 15B (highway, white stripe), H78 x 15B (on-off road), L78 x 15B (highway), L78 x15B (on-off road), L78 x 15B (highway, white stripe), 6.50 x 16C (highway), 7.00 x 15C (highway), 10.00 x 15B (polyester), 10.00 x 15B (polyester white lettered). Steering: Power assisted recirculating ball. Ratio: 20/16.4:1. Turning circle: 37.58 ft. Transmission: Type: Saginaw 3-speed manual, fully synchronized. Steering column-mounted shifter. This transmission was not available for the 350 and 400 cu. in. V-8 engine with 4-bbl. carburetor. Transmission Ratios: 2.85, 1.68, 1.0:1. Optional: Muncie 4-speed manual, synchromesh on top three gears, floor-mounted shift lever. Ratios: 6.55, 3.58, 1.70, 1.00:1. Optional: Turbo Hydra-Matic 3-speed automatic. Ratios: 2.52, 1.52, 1.00:1. Clutch: Six-cylinder: 11.0 in. dia., 124 sq. in. area. V-8 engines: 12.0 in. dia., 150 sq. in. area. Optional: None.

VEHICLE DIMENSIONS: Wheelbase: 106.5 in. Overall Length: 184.5 in. Front/Rear Tread 65.75 in./62.75 in. Overall Height: 69.0 in. With optional hardtop; 71.0 in. Width: 79.5 in. Tailgate: Width and Height: 66.8 in. x 22.0 in. Approach/Departure Degrees: 34/22. Ground Clearance: Front axle: 8.9 in. Rear axle: 8.5 in. Oil pan: 17.2 in. Transfer case: 11.5 in. Fuel tank: 14.0 in. Load space: With rear seat installed: 38.8 in. x 50 in. x 42.3 in. With rear seat removed or folded: 76.0 in. x 50 in. x 42.3 in.

CAPACITIES: Fuel Tank: 25.0 gal. Optional: Replacement 30 gal. tank. Coolant system: 250 6-cyl.: 12.2 qt. 350 V-8: 17.1 qt. 400 V-8: 20 qt.

ACCOMMODATIONS: Seating Capacity: Standard: Driver and front passenger bucket seats. Optional: 3 passenger rear bench seat. Headroom: 38.3 in. Maximum steering wheel to seat back: 18.5 in. Seat to ground: 36.3 in. Floor to ground: 21.9 in.

INSTRUMENTATION: 0-100 mph speedometer, 99,999.9 mi. odometer, fuel gauge, warning lights for alternator, oil pressure, engine coolant temperature, brake operating system, hazard warning lights, directional lights.

OPTIONS AND PRICES: 305 cu. in. V-8 (RPO LG9). 350 cu. in. V-8 (RPO LS9). 400 cu. in V-8 (RPO LF4). Automatic transmission (RPO MX1). Four-speed manual transmission (RPO MM4). Cheyenne Package (RPO Z84). Poly Wrap air cleaner (RPO K43). All-Weather air conditioning. (RPO C60). Auxiliary battery (RPO TP2). Heavy-duty battery (RPO UA1). Chromed front and rear bumpers (RPO VE5). Chromed front bumper guards. California emissions requirements (RPO YF5). Electric clock (RPO YF5). Cold Climate Package (RPO Z56). Engine oil cooler (RPO KC4). Transmission oil cooler (RPO VO2). Heavy-duty radiator (RPO VO1). Spare tire cover (RPO P17). Power door lock system (RPO AU3). Dual exhaust system, K1500 only (RPO N10). Color-keyed front floor mats (RPO B32). Gauge Package. Includes voltmeter, oil pressure and engine coolant temperature (RPO Z53). Tachometer. Available only with V-8 engine (RPO U16). 61 amp Delcotron generator (RPO K76). Sliding side window (RPO AD5). Tinted glass (RPO AO1). Chromed grille (RPO V22). Heavy-duty trailer wiring harness (RPO UY7). Headlight warning buzzer (RPO T63). Full length interior headliner (RPO BB5). Inside hood release (RPO T44). Deluxe instrument panel (RPO BC3). Cigarette lighter (RPO U37). Exterior below eye-level painted mirrors (RPO D29). Exterior below eye-level stainless steel mirrors (RPO DG4). Camper style stainless steel mirrors (RPO DF2). Body spear molding (RPO B84). Body side upper molding (RPO B85). Upper and lower body side moldings (RPO YG1). Door edge guards (RPO B93). Wheel opening moldings (RPO B96). Operating Convenience Group. Includes power door locks and power windows (RPO ZQ2). Special two-tone exterior paint (RPO YZ3). Exterior Decor Package (RPO ZY5). Fuel tank and transfer case skid plates (RPO NY1). AM radio. AM/FM radio. Rear seat speaker. (RPO U80). Windshield antenna. Included when AM or AM/FM radio is ordered (RPO U76). Rear roll bar (RPOE50). Front passenger seat (RPO A57). Rear 3 passenger seat (RPO AM7). High-back bucket seats. Speed and cruise control, V-8 only (RPO K30). Heavy-duty front springs, K1500 only (RPO F60). Tilt-type steering wheel (RPO N33). Custom steering wheel (RPO N31) 31 gal. fuel tank (RPO NK7). Two front towing hooks (RPO V76). Deadweight towing hitch (RPO VR2). Platform type towing hitch (RPO VR4). Trailering Special Package (RPO Z82). Bright metal hubcaps (RPO PO3). Bright wheel trim rings (RPO PO6). Bright wheelcovers (RPO PO1). Rallye wheels (RPO N67). Styled wheels (RPO PA6). Power side door windows (RPO A31). Power tailgate (RPO A33). Intermittent windshield wiper system (RPO CD4). Woodgrained exterior trim (RPO YG2).

HISTORICAL FOOTNOTES: The 1979 Chevrolet Blazer was introduced in the fall of 1978.

1980 BLAZER

The 1980 Blazer was identified by a new grille with a small "ice cube" gridwork and a new front air dam. The grille insert was finished in argent silver. Except for the addition of International symbols for the gauges, the1980 Blazer dash was unchanged from 1979. The Silverado trim package was now available for the Blazer. Among its exterior features were rectangular headlights, a chromed grille and larger parking lights. Interior features of the Silverado included new Custom cloth or Brahman-grain vinyl seat trim in blue (vinyl only), carmine or camel tan, new visor mirror, new interior nameplates, trimmed cowl side panels, and new front door trim panels with assist straps and carpet trim. The Silverado two-tone interior (seat trim, door trim panels and sunshades) was available with blue, carmine or camel tan in combination with Mystic custom vinyl (all colors) or Custom cloth in either blue or carmine. The Silverado option also included a Custom steering wheel, Mystic headliner, color-keyed center console and carpeting, bright trim instrument cluster gauges for speedometer, odometer, fuel level, voltmeter, engine coolant temperature and oil pressure. A new part-time New Process transfer case was used for 1980. A dash-mounted light operated when the Blazer was in four-wheel drive. The 350 cu. in. V-8 had a new single inlet, dual outlet exhaust system designed to reduce back pressure. A new engine fan clutch allowed the fan to operate only when it was needed. Both the 305 and 400 cu. in. engines were dropped for 1980. Other changes made for 1980 in order to improve the Blazer's fuel economy included the use of radial tires. The Blazer's front seat back angle was increased by 3.0 to 3.5 degrees. A new four speaker system for the Blazer with the front speakers mounted high in the door panels and the rear speakers positioned in the sidewalls ahead of the wheelhousings was introduced. Also joining the option list were new forged aluminum wheels. The 1980 Blazer color selection consisted of frost white, medium blue, light blue metallic, Nordic blue metallic, Emerald green, Santa Fe tan, carmine red, cardinal red, midnight black and burnt orange metallic.

I.D. DATA: The Blazer's V.I.N. consisted of 13 symbols. The first symbol (a letter-C) identified the Chevrolet Motor Division. The second symbol (a letter-K) indicated vehicle type. The third symbol (a letter) indicated engine type: D-250 cu. in. L-6, L-4-bbl. 350 cu. in. V-8. The fourth symbol (a number) identified the tonnage. The fifth symbol indicated model type. The sixth symbol identified the model year. The seventh symbol (a letter) indicated the assembly plant.

The remaining six digits served as the sequential production numbers. The V.I.N. number was located on the left door pillar. The engine number indicated the manufacturing plant, day of manufacture and transmission type. It was located on a pad positioned on the right-hand side of the cylinder block at the rear of the distributor on V-8 engines and on a pad located at the front right hand side of the cylinder block of 6-cylinder engines.

Model Number	Body Type & Seating	Factory Price	GVW	Shipping Weight	Prod. Total
Blazer K10 (with 350 V-8)					
CK10516	Util. (hardtop)	$8233	6200	4429	21,399*
CK10516	Util. (folding top)	$8130	6200	N.A.	—

* Calendar year sales: Two-wheel drive and four-wheel drive Blazers.

STANDARD ENGINE: All states except California: Order Code LE3. Engine Type: OHV, Cast iron block. In-line 6-cylinder. Bore x Stroke: 3.875 in. x 3.50 in. Lifters: Mechanical. Number of main bearings-7. Carburetion: Rochester Staged two-barrel. Compression Ratio: 8.3:1. Displacement: 250 cu. in. (4.09 liters). Horsepower: Net: 130 @ 4000 rpm. Torque: Net: 210 lb.-ft. @ 2000 rpm. Oil capacity: 5 qt. with filter change. Fuel Requirements: Leaded or unleaded.

OPTIONAL ENGINE: 350 V-8: Order Code LG9. Engine Type: Cast iron block. OHV, V-8. Bore x Stroke: 4.0 in. x 3.50 in. Lifters: Hydraulic. Number of main bearings-5. Carburetion: Rochester four-barrel. Compression Ratio: 8.2:1. Displacement: 350 cu. in. Horsepower: 170 @ 4000 rpm. Torque: Gross: 270 lb.-ft. @ 2400 rpm. (California: 275 lb.-ft. @ 2400 rpm. Available in California only with 4-speed manual or automatic transmission). Oil capacity: 5 qt. with filter change. Fuel Requirements: Unleaded.

CHASSIS FEATURES: Ladder-type. Carbon steel, 39,000 psi. Heavy-gauge channel side members, alligator-jaw cross members. Section modules: 3.06 in.

SUSPENSION AND RUNNING GEAR: Front Suspension: Two tapered semi-elliptical leaf springs. Capacity: 1650 lb. Rating: 250 lb./in. 1.0 in. shock absorbers, 1.25 in. stabilizer bar. Optional Capacity: 2250 lb. 32mm shock absorbers (available with RPO F60 heavy-duty springs only). Rear Suspension: Two-stage tapered and multi-leaf (six-conventional leaves, one tapered leaf). Capacity: 1700 lb. Rating: 270/510 lb./in. Optional: None. Front Axle. Type: Hypoid, tubular driving. Capacity: 3600 lb. Rear Axle. Type: Hypoid, semi-floating. Capacity: 3750 lb. Final Drive Ratio: 6-cyl.: 3.73:1, 350 V-8: 2.76:1. Optional: 6-cyl.: 3.42. V-8: 3.08:1. Transfer Case: 2-speed. Brakes: Type: Hydraulic, self-adjusting. Front: Discs. Rear: Drums. Optional: Power. Dimensions: Front: 11.86 in. dia. rotor. Rear: 11.15 in. x 2.75 in. Wheels: 6-stud, 15 x 6JJ. Optional: 15 x 7JJ Rallye, 15 x 8JJ, 15 x 8JJ Rallye, 16 x 5K. Tires: P215/75R15 steel belted radial. Optional: P215/75R15 steel belted radial whitewall, P235/75R15 steel belted radial, P235/75R15 steel belted radial whitewall, P235/75R15 white lettered steel belted radial, 10R-15B steel belted radial, 10R-15B white lettered steel belted radial. Steering: Power assisted recirculating ball, variable ratio. Ratio: 17.6/13.1. Turns Lock-to-Lock: 3.4. Turning Circle: 37.6 ft. Transmission: Type: Saginaw 3-speed manual, fully synchronized. Steering column-mounted shifter. This transmission was not available for the state of California. Transmission Ratios: 2.85, 1.68, 1.0:1. Optional: Muncie 4-speed manual, synchromesh on top three gears, floor-mounted shift lever. Ratios: 6.55, 3.58, 1.70, 1.00:1. Optional: Turbo Hydra-Matic 3-speed automatic. Ratios: 2.52, 1.52, 1.00:1. Clutch: 11.0 in. dia., 124 sq. in. area. 12 in. clutch included with 350 V-8 engines.

VEHICLE DIMENSIONS: Wheelbase: 106.5 in. Overall Length: 184.4 in. Front/Rear Tread 66.70 in./63.70 in. Overall Height: 72.0 in. Width: 79.5 in. Tailgate: Width and Height: 66.8 in. x 22.0 in. Approach/Departure Degrees: 27/23. Ground Clearance: Front axle: 7.4 in. Rear axle: 7.0 in. Oil pan: 17.2 in. Transfer case: 11.5 in. Fuel tank: 14.0 in. Load space: With rear seat installed: 38.8 in. x 50 in. x 42.3 in. With rear seat removed or folded: 76.0 in. x 50 in. x 42.3 in.

CAPACITIES: Fuel Tank: 25.0 gal. Optional: Replacement 31 gal. tank. Coolant system: 250 6-cyl.: 12.2 qt. 350 V-8: 17.1 qt.

ACCOMMODATIONS: Seating Capacity: Standard: Driver and front passenger bucket seats. Optional: 3 passenger rear bench seat. Headroom: 38.3 in. Maximum steering wheel to seat back: 18.5 in. Seat to ground: 36.3 in. Floor to ground: 21. in.

INSTRUMENTATION: 0-100 mph speedometer, 99,999.9 mi. odometer, fuel gauge, warning lights for alternator, oil pressure, engine coolant temperature, brake operating system, hazard warning lights, directional lights, seat belt warning.

OPTIONS AND PRICES: Most options were carried over from 1979; this is a representative sampling. 350 cu. in. V-8: $470. Sliding rear windows: $18. Folding rear seat: $300. Tinted window glass (RPO AO1): $52. Woodgrain trim (RPO YG2). Electric tailgate window: $69. Intermittent windshield wipers: $35. Air conditioning: $607. Rear roll bar: $112. Locking rear differential: $197. 3.07:1 rear axle: $27. Engine oil cooler: $97. 4-speed manual transmission: $175. 31 gal. replacement fuel tank: $35. Fuel tank skid plate: $139. Tilt steering wheel: $83. 3500 watt Delco auxiliary battery: $103. 4000 watt Delco Freedom battery: $41. AM/FM cassette 351. Silverado Package (RPO YE9): $895. Operating Convenience Package: $248. Inside hood lock release: $25. Power windows. Power door locks. Four AM/FM/Tape/CB options were available.

HISTORICAL FOOTNOTES: The 1980 Blazer was introduced in the fall of 1979.

1981 BLAZER

The Blazer was extensively restyled and redesigned for 1981. New aerodynamic styling highlighted the Blazer's front end appearance. The wind tunnel-tested front-end sheet metal was new from the cowl forward. The front fenders and hood were restyled. The result improved both the Blazer's aerodynamics and driver visibility. New front fender skirts with attached shields was used to help reduce engine compartment splash. Other new elements consisted of the radiator grille, front and rear bumpers, use of a HSLA-type steel for the bumpers that reduced weight, an 8-point front bumper attachment for improved bumper stiffness, parking lamps in the front bumper, side marker lights, single rectangular headlights with painted plastic bezels, a front-bumper-mounted air dam for improved aerodynamics and restyled front fender nameplates.

The Blazer body had improved anti-corrosion features for 1981. Two-sided galvanized steel was used for the side inner panels and the rear wheel housings. Urethane stone shields were added forward of the rear wheel openings. A zinc-rich paint was added to the anti-corrosion coating of the brake and fuel lines. Drag-free front disc brakes and a new quick take-up master cylinder also helped improve fuel economy. Four new colors were added for 1981. They were: Light silver metallic, charcoal metallic, Colonial yellow and dark chestnut metallic. They joined these colors carried over from 1980: Frost white, medium blue, light blue metallic, Nordic blue Mmetallic, Emerald green, Santa Fe tan, carmine red, cardinal red, midnight black and burnt orange metallic. Four interior colors were available for 1981. Continued from 1980 were carmine and blue. New for 1981 were doeskin and slate. All of the Blazer's interior trim panels were new for 1981. In addition, new chromed diecast hardware was used. All models had a color-keyed plastic door trim panel with an integrated armrest. Two-tone interiors were discontinued. The driver's seat adjuster was modified for improved stability and greater seat travel. A new bucket seat center console, designed to reduced weight, had a positive-type latch with key lock and a torsion bar hinge which permitted the cover, after being released, to pop up for easy access to the interior. The cover could be lifted to a 110 degree position and was held in place by a check strap. If the check strap was released, the cover could be rotated to a 180 degree position to be used a a tray for rear seat occupants. The console also had two beverage pockets and a loose article storage pocket for the driver and front seat passenger. Helping to lower overall vehicle weight was reduced-thickness glass used in all the Blazer's windows. In place of the old RPO AO1 option, the Blazer now had tinted glass in all windows. The Blazer instrument panel was revised to accommodate a new stereo radio speaker. Changing the appearance of the dash panel were new instrument panel cluster bezels and a new instrument panel pad with new appliques and nameplate. There were new international operating symbols for the windshield wiper-washer control. A new illuminated transfer case range indicator was also installed. In place of the constant "on" function of the heater blower was a new "off" position. A number of changes took place in the Blazer's seat trim. The standard vinyl seats now had a striped design available in either blue or doeskin. The Custom vinyl bucket seats had a leather-grained vinyl seat trim material. If the Silverado package was ordered the seats were available in any of four colors: Blue, carmine, doeskin or slate. Colors for the Custom Deluxe interior were blue or doeskin. The Custom cloth bucket seats had a carryover houndstooth-patterned cloth cover available in carmine, doeskin or slate.

1981 Chevrolet K10 Blazer Silverado

The primary changes of the Blazer's engine changes for 1981 were intended to improve its fuel economy. The 4.1 liter 6-cylinder engine had a recalibrated carburetor as well as a redesigned cam. The 5.7 liter 350 cu. in. V-8 continued to be available only in California. The 5.0 liter 305 cu. in. V-8 was available in all states but California. It was equipped with a staged four-barrel carburetor with a large dual-element air filter and electronic spark control. This system had a sensor that retarded spark advance under engine knock conditions. This allowed the higher compression engine to operate at the highest spark curve possible for increased performance with unleaded fuel. A modified cam that provided less valve overlap was also used as were larger diameter exhaust ports. This engine, (RPO LE9) has the highest compression ratio (9.2:1) of any Chevrolet V-8 in the past ten years. It was also used in Chevrolet four-wheel drive pickup trucks and aspects of its design are found in that section.

The transfer case was a new New Process 208 unit with an aluminum case and synchronizers for smoother shifting. This system also featured automatic front locking hubs that free wheeled until the vehicle was placed in four-wheel drive and torque was applied to the front wheels. The hubs returned to their freewheeling mode when the transfer case was shifted back to two-wheel drive and the Blazer was driven in reverse for approximately three feet. The Blazer was also equipped with a lighter rear axle with 9.5 in. ring gears. The Blazer's axle ratios were also changed to improve fuel economy. The standard rear springs had a higher capacity for 1981. They were also of a more durable, lighter weight design and had improved corrosion protection. A new jack with a larger base, more suitable for off-road use was standard Blazer equipment.

A number of changes took place in the Blazer's optional equipment content and availability. All the body side and rear moldings were new except for the wheel openings. The Bright trimmed black plastic RPO B84 moldings were available for Blazers with the Custom Deluxe trim package. The Custom Deluxe Blazer could also be fitted with RPO B85 moldings of bright plastic with black paint trim and bright trimmed front side marker lights and tail lights. Another molding package available for the Custom Deluxe Blazer was RPO B96. This provided bright front and rear front and rear wheel opening moldings with black paint trim. The RPO YG1 molding package had new content for 1981. Available for the Custom Blazer, it consisted of bright trimmed black plastic body side and rear molding, RPO B84 and RPO B96. Included in the RPO YE9 Silverado package and available for all other trim levels was RPO YG3. This introduced a new molding package for the Blazer consisting of bright plastic body side and rear moldings with black paint trim, RPO B96, plus bright trimmed front side marker lights and tail lights. Included in the Silverado trim level was a new tailgate trim panel of bright anodized aluminum. Additional aspects of the 1981 Silverado package began with full foam front bucket seats in either Custom vinyl (in any of four colors) or Custom cloth, also offered in four colors. The Silverado instrument panel had brushed stainless steel accents on cluster and pad, and cluster gauges. Other features included a new console, Custom steering wheel, visor mirror, color-keyed front carpeting, full door trim panels with brushed stainless steel inserts, a soft vinyl insert in the armrest area, carpet trim below the trim panel, a door-closing assist strap and storage pockets. The Silverado exterior was highlighted by a chrome-trimmed grille with stacked dual rectangular headlights and a bright anodized aluminum tailgate trim panel. The Silverado grille was also available as RPO V22. It featured a chrome finish on the leading edge of the grille insert. Both its center bar and head light bezels had a brushed chrome finish. It could also be ordered with RPO TT5, high-intensity, high-beam halogen headlights. A new one-way glass, RPO AJ1 option for the side and rear windows back of the driver was introduced for hardtop model Blazers. A new automatic speed control, RPO K35, included a resume feature and was available on 6-cylinder models. The RPO U35 electric clock now had a solid-state quartz mechanism. The RPO YG2 exterior woodgrain trim was discontinued. A new Front Quad Shock Package, RPO Z75, was introduced which included an extra pair of 25mm shock absorbers on the front axle, heavy-duty 32mm rear shock absorbers and a front axle pinion nose snubber to limit front axle windup to help improve off-road handling.

I.D. DATA: The V.I.N. plate was mounted on the lower left side windshield corner. The V.I.N. consisted of 17 elements. The first, the number 1 identified the U.S. as the nation of origin. The letter G followed, for the manufacturer: General Motors. The third entry, the letter C represented the make as Chevrolet. The GVWR brake system identification followed. Next came the truck line and chassis type; the letter K indicated four-wheel drive. The truck series was identified by a number: 1-1/2 ton. The truck body type identification was next: 8-Utility. The engine code was next, followed by a check digit. The model year was identified by the letter B. The assembly plant code followed. The final six digits were the plant sequential production number.

Model Number	Body Type & Seating	Factory Price	GVW	Shipping Weight	Prod. Total
Blazer K10 (with 250 6-cyl.)					
CK10516	Util. (hardtop)	$8856	6100	4087	—
CK10516	Util. (folding top)	$8750	6100	N.A.	—

STANDARD ENGINE: All states except California: Order Code LE3. Engine Type: OHV, Cast iron block. In-line 6-cylinder. Bore x Stroke: 3.875 in. x 3.50 in. Lifters: Mechanical. Number of main bearings-7. Carburetion: Rochester Staged two-barrel. Compression Ratio: 8.30:1. Displacement: 250 cu. in. Horsepower: Net: 115 @ 3600 rpm. Torque: Net: 200 lb.-ft. @ 1800 rpm. Oil capacity: 5 qt. with filter change. Fuel Requirements: Unleaded. Optional: Engine Type: OHV, Cast iron block. V-8. Order Code LE9 with Electronic Spark Control. Not available for California. Bore x Stroke: 3.74 in. x 3.48 in. Lifters: Hydraulic. Number of main bearings-5. Carburetion: Four-barrel. Compression Ratio: 9.2:1. Displacement: 305 cu. in. Horsepower: Net: 165 @ 4400 rpm. Torque: Net: 240 lb.-ft. @ 2000 rpm. Oil capacity: 5 qt. with filter change. Fuel Requirements: Unleaded. Optional: Engine Type: OHV, Cast iron block. V-8. Order Code LS9. Required for California. Bore x Stroke: 4.0 in. x 3.50 in. Lifters: Hydraulic. Number of main bearings-5. Carburetion: Four-barrel. Compression Ratio: 8.2:1. Displacement: 350 cu. in. Horsepower: Net: 150 @ 3600 rpm. Torque: Net: 255 lb.-ft. @ 1600 rpm. Oil capacity: 5 qt. with filter change. Fuel Requirements: Unleaded.

CHASSIS FEATURES: Ladder-type. Carbon steel, 39,000 psi. Heavy-gauge channel side members, alligator-jaw cross members. Section modules: 3.06 in.

SUSPENSION AND RUNNING GEAR: Front Suspension: Two tapered semi-elliptical leaf springs. Capacity: 1650 lb. Rating: 250 lb./in. 1.0 in. shock absorbers, 1.25 in. stabilizer bar. Optional Capacity: 2250 lb. 32mm shock absorbers (available with RPO F60 heavy-duty springs only). Rear Suspension: Two-stage tapered and multi-leaf (six-conventional leaves, one tapered leaf). Capacity: 1700 lb. Rating: 270/510 lb./in. Optional: None. Front Axle. Type: Hypoid, tubular driving. Capacity: 3600 lb. Rear Axle. Type: Hypoid, semi-floating. Capacity: 3750 lb. Final Drive Ratio: 6-cyl.: 3.73:1, 305 V-8: 2.73:1, 350 V-8: 2.73:1. Optional: 6-cyl.: 3.42; 305 V-8: 2.56, 3.08, 3.73:1; 350 V-8: 3.08:1. Transfer Case: New Process 208. Ratios: 2.61, 1.00:1. Brakes: Type: Hydraulic, self-adjusting. Front: Discs. Rear: Drums. Optional: Power. Dimensions: Front: 11.86 in. dia. rotor. Rear: 11.15 in. x 2.75 in. Wheels: 6-stud, 15 x 6JJ. Optional: 15 x 7JJ Rallye, 15 x 8JJ, 15 x 8JJ Rallye, 16 x 5K. Tires: P215/75R15 steel belted radial. Optional: P215/75R15 steel belted radial whitewall, P235/75R15 steel belted radial, P235/75R15 steel belted radial whitewall, P235/75R15 white lettered steel belted radial, 10R-15B steel belted radial, 10R-15B white lettered steel belted radial. Steering: Power assisted recirculating ball, variable ratio. Ratio: 17.6/13.1. Turns Lock-to-Lock: 3.4. Turning Circle: 37.6 ft. Transmission: Type: Saginaw 3-speed manual, fully synchronized. Steering column-mounted shifter. This transmission was not available for the state of California. Transmission Ratios: 2.85, 1.68, 1.0:1. Optional: Muncie 4-speed manual, synchromesh on top three gears, floor-mounted shift lever. Ratios: 6.55, 3.58, 1.70, 1.00:1. Optional: Turbo Hydra-Matic 3-speed automatic. Ratios: 2.52, 1.52, 1.00:1. Clutch: 11.0 in. dia., 124 sq. in. area. 12 in. clutch included with 350 V-8 engines.

VEHICLE DIMENSIONS: Wheelbase: 106.5 in. Overall Length: 184.8 in. Front/Rear Tread 66.10 in./63.0 in. Overall Height: 73.40 in. Width: 79.6 in. Tailgate: Width and Height: 66.8 in. x 22.0 in. Approach/Departure Degrees: 34/25. Ground Clearance: Front axle: 7.4 in. Rear axle: 6.7 in. Oil pan: 17.2 in. Transfer case: 11.5 in. Fuel tank: 14.0 in. Load space: With rear seat installed: 38.8 in. x 50 in. x 42.3 in. With rear seat removed or folded: 76.0 in. x 50 in. x 42.3 in.

CAPACITIES: Fuel Tank: 25.0 gal. Optional: Replacement 31 gal. tank. Coolant system: 250 6-cyl.: 12.2 qt. 305 V-8: 17.6 qt. 350 V-8: 17.6 qt.

ACCOMMODATIONS: Seating Capacity: Standard: Driver and front passenger bucket seats. Optional: 3 passenger rear bench seat. Headroom: 38.3 in. Maximum steering wheel to seat back: 18.5 in. Seat to ground: 36.3 in. Floor to ground: 21. in.

INSTRUMENTATION: 0-100 mph speedometer, 99,999.9 mi. odometer, fuel gauge, warning lights for alternator, oil pressure, engine coolant temperature, brake operating system, hazard warning lights, directional lights, seat belt warning.

OPTIONS AND PRICES: Air conditioning. Bright metal wheelcovers. Bright metal wheel trim rings. Chromed front and rear bumpers. Chromed front bumper guards. Deluxe front and rear bumpers. Cigarette lighter. Color-keyed floor mats. ComforTilt steering wheel. Custom steering wheel. Chromed grille (RPO V22). Deluxe instrument panel. Electric clock (RPO U35). Folding top (available in either black or white). One-way glass (RPO AJ1). Sliding glass rear side windows. Halogen headlights (RPO TT5). Headlight warning buzzer. Intermittent windshield wipers. Painted below eye-level mirrors (RPO D44). Stainless steel below eye-level mirrors (RPO D45). Stainless steel camper mirrors (RPO DF2). Black body side moldings (RPO B84). Bright body side moldings (RPOB85). Black molding package. Bright molding package. Operating Convenience Package. Power door locks. Power windows. Special two-tone paint. Exterior decor package. AM radio. AM/FM radio. AM/FM radio with 8-track tape player. AM/FM radio with cassette tape player. AM/FM stereo radio with cassette tape player. AM/FM radio with CB and antenna. Rear auxiliary speaker. Windshield antenna. Rear roll bar. Spare tire carrier. Folding rear seat. Tachometer. Electric tailgate window. Aluminum wheels (RPO PH7). Rallye wheels (RPO N67). Styled wheels (RPO PA6). Silverado Trim Package (RPO YE9): $881. Auxiliary battery. Cold Climate Package. Engine oil cooler. Transmission oil cooler. Cruise Control. Deadweight trailer hitch. Front Quad shock absorbers (RPO Z75). Front tow hooks. 31 gal. fuel tank. Fuel tank shield plate. Gauge Package (includes voltmeter, engine coolant temperature and oil pressure gauges. 55 amp generator. 61 amp generator. Heavy-duty battery. Heavy-duty front and rear shock absorbers. Heavy-duty front springs. Heavy-duty radiator. Locking rear differential. Trailering special equipment. Trailer wiring harness. Weight-distributing hitch platform.

HISTORICAL FOOTNOTES: Chevrolet reported that 94.4% of its light, medium and heavy-duty trucks and commercial vans in the ten most recent years recorded were still "on the job."

1982 BLAZER

The 1982 Blazer was offered only in hardtop form. A major development was the availability of the General Motors' 6.2 liter diesel V-8 engine. This engine was paired with a new optional 4-speed automatic overdrive transmission. The required diesel equipment option included two heavy-duty Freedom batteries, 63 amp Delcotron generator, hydraulic power brakes, heavy-duty radiator, engine oil cooler, dual exhaust system, heavy-duty front springs, special sound insulation package, warning lights for glow plugs, water-in-fuel and low coolant, 6.2 LITRE DIESEL hood emblem, and fender and tailgate identification nameplates. The standard Blazer engine continued to be the 4.1 liter 6-cylinder. For California the 5.7 liter V-8 was specified for the Blazer. The standard transmission, (except for the LS9 and LH6 engines which both had the 4-speed automatic overdrive transmission as standard) was an all-synchromesh 4-speed manual. Other developments for 1982 included new two-tone paint combinations, new permanent magnet motors for the optional power windows, single rectangular headlights for the Custom Deluxe model, automatic speed control for both manual and automatic transmission, and a new AM/FM/CB stereo radio with antenna.

I.D. DATA: The V.I.N. plate was mounted on the lower left side windshield corner. The V.I.N. consisted of 17 elements. The first, the number 1 identified the U.S. as the nation of origin. The letter G followed, for the manufacturer: General Motors. The third entry, the letter C represented the make as Chevrolet. The GVWR brake system identification followed. Next came the truck line and chassis type; the letter K indicated four-wheel drive. The truck series was identified by a number: 1-1/2 ton. The truck body type identification was next: 8-Utility. The engine code was next, followed by a check digit. The model year was identified by the letter C. The assembly plant code followed. The final six digits were the plant sequential production number.

Model Number	Body Type & Seating	Factory Price	GVW	Shipping Weight	Prod. Total
Blazer K10. (with 250 6-cyl.)					
CK10516	Util. (hardtop)	$9874.20[1]	6100	4294	24,004[2]

NOTE 1: Add $1334 for diesel engine and $1125 for diesel equipment RPO B3J.
NOTE 2: Included both two-wheel drive and four-wheel drive Blazers.

STANDARD ENGINE: All states except California: Order Code LE3. Engine Type: OHV, Cast iron block. In-line 6-cylinder. Bore x Stroke: 3.875 in. x 3.50 in. Lifters: Mechanical. Number of main bearings-7. Carburetion: Rochester Staged two-barrel. Compression Ratio: 8.30:1. Displacement: 250 cu. in. Horsepower: Net: 120 @ 3600 rpm. Torque: Net: 200 lb.-ft. @ 1800 rpm. Oil capacity: 5 qt. with filter change. Fuel Requirements: Unleaded. Optional: Engine Type: OHV, Cast iron block. V-8. Order Code LE9 with Electronic Spark Control. Not available for California. Bore x Stroke: 3.74 in. x 3.48 in. Lifters: Hydraulic. Number of main bearings-5. Carburetion: Four-barrel. Compression Ratio: 9.2:1. Displacement: 305 cu. in. Horsepower: Net: 165 @ 4400 rpm. Torque: Net: 240 lb.-ft. @ 2000 rpm. Oil capacity: 5 qt. with filter change. Fuel Requirements: Unleaded. Optional: Engine Type: OHV, Cast iron block. V-8. Order Code LS9. Required for California. Bore x Stroke: 4.0 in. x 3.50 in. Lifters: Hydraulic. Number of main bearings-5. Carburetion: Four-barrel. Compression Ratio: 8.2:1. Displacement: 350 cu. in. Horsepower: Net: 165 @ 3800 rpm. Torque: Net: 275 lb.-ft. @ 1600 rpm. Oil capacity: 5 qt. with filter change. Fuel Requirements: Unleaded. Optional: Engine Type: OHV, Cast iron block. Diesel V-8. Order Code LH6. Bore x Stroke: 3.98 in. x3.80 in. Lifters: Hydraulic. Number of main bearings-5. Carburetion: Fuel injection. Compression Ratio: 21.5:1. Displacement: 379 cu. in. (6.2 liter). Horsepower: Net: 130 @ 3600 rpm. Torque: Net: 240 lb.-ft. @ 2000 rpm. Oil capacity: 7 qt. with filter change. Fuel Requirements: Diesel.

CHASSIS FEATURES: Ladder-type. Carbon steel, 39,000 psi. Heavy-gauge channel side members, alligator-jaw cross members. Section modules: 3.06 in.

SUSPENSION AND RUNNING GEAR: Front Suspension: Two tapered semi-elliptical leaf springs. Capacity: 1650 lb. Rating: 250 lb./in. 1.0 in. shock absorbers, 1.25 in. stabilizer bar. Optional Capacity: 2250 lb. 32mm shock absorbers (available with RPO F60 heavy-duty springs only). Front quad shock absorbers. Rear Suspension: Two-stage tapered and multi-leaf (six-conventional leaves, one tapered leaf). Capacity: 1700 lb. Rating: 270/510 lb./in. Optional: None. Front Axle. Type: Hypoid, tubular driving. Capacity: 3600 lb. Rear Axle. Type: Hypoid, semi-floating. Capacity: 3750 lb. Final Drive Ratio: 6-cyl.: 3.42:1; 305 V-8 with ESC: 2.73:1; 350 V-8: 2.73:1; 379 diesel V-8: 3.08:1. Optional: 6-cyl.: 3.73; 305 V-8: 3.08, 3.73:1; 350 V-8: 3.08:1; 379 diesel V-8: 3.42, 3.73:1. Transfer Case: New Process 208. Ratios: 2.61, 1.00:1. Brakes: Type: Hydraulic, self-adjusting. Front: Discs. Rear: Drums. Optional: Power. Dimensions: Front: 11.86 in. dia. rotor. Rear: 11.15 in. x 2.75 in. Wheels: 6-stud, 15 x 6JJ. Optional: 15 x 7JJ Rallye, 15 x 8JJ, 15 x 8JJ Rallye, 16 x 5K. Tires: P215/75R15 steel belted radial. Optional: P215/75R15 steel belted radial whitewall, P235/75R15 steel belted radial, P235/75R15 steel belted radial whitewall, P235/75R15 white lettered steel belted radial, 10R-15B steel belted radial, 10R-15B white lettered steel belted radial. Steering: Power assisted recirculating ball, variable ratio. Ratio: 17.6/13.1. Turns Lock-to-Lock: 3.4. Turning Circle: 37.6 ft. Transmission: No standard manual transmissions were available in California. Type: Muncie 4-speed manual, synchromesh on top three gears, floor-mounted shift lever. Ratios: 6.55, 3.58, 1.70, 1.00:1. Optional: 700R4 4-speed automatic with overdrive. Ratios: 3.06, 1.36, 1.00, 0.70:1. R2.29:1. Reverse. Clutch: 11.0 in. dia., 124 sq. in. area. 12 in. clutch included with 350 V-8 engines.

VEHICLE DIMENSIONS: Wheelbase: 106.5 in. Overall Length: 184.8 in. Front/Rear Tread 66.10 in./63.0 in. Overall Height: 73.40 in. Width: 79.6 in. Tailgate: Width and Height: 66.8 in. x 22.0 in. Approach/Departure Degrees: 34/25. Ground Clearance: Front axle: 7.4 in. Rear axle: 6.7 in. Oil pan: 17.2 in. Transfer case: 11.5 in. Fuel tank: 14.0 in. Load space: With rear seat installed: 38.8 in. x 50 in. x 42.3 in. With rear seat removed or folded: 76.0 in. x 50 in. x 42.3 in.

CAPACITIES: Fuel Tank: 25.0 gal. Optional: Replacement 31 gal. tank. Coolant system: 250 6-cyl.: 12.2 qt. 305 V-8: 17.6 qt. 350 V-8: 17.6 qt.

ACCOMMODATIONS: Seating Capacity: Standard: Driver and front passenger bucket seats. Optional: 3 passenger rear bench seat. Headroom: 38.3 in. Maximum steering wheel to seat back: 18.5 in. Seat to ground: 36.3 in. Floor to ground: 21. in.

INSTRUMENTATION: 0-100 mph speedometer, 99,999.9 mi. odometer, fuel gauge, warning lights for alternator, oil pressure, engine coolant temperature, brake operating system, hazard warning lights, directional lights, seat belt warning.

OPTIONS AND PRICES: Air conditioning: $677. Deluxe front appearance: $100. Locking rear differential: $217. Heavy-duty battery: $45. Deluxe chromed front and rear bumpers: $44. Front chromed bumper guards: $39. Quartz analog electric clock: $36 without YE9 trim; $70 without YE9 trim. Cold Climate Package: $114-$172. Engine oil cooler: $112. Engine transmission oil cooler: $55. Heavy-duty radiator: $48. Power door locks: $115. Color-keyed front floor mats: $14. Gauges: voltmeter, engine coolant temperature and oil pressure: $34. 63 amp generator: $58. Deep tinted glass with tinted rear window: $119. Deep tinted glass with deep tinted rear window: $168. Sliding side windows with air deflectors: $216. Halogen high-beam headlamps: $15. High and low-beam halogen headlamps: $20. Trailer wiring harness: $42. Headlight warning buzzer: $11. Headliner interior: $74. Cigarette lighter: $28. Exterior below eye-level painted mirrors: $44. Exterior below eye-level stainless steel mirrors: $72. Black body side moldings: $105. Bright body side moldings: 131. Custom Package moldings: $144. Deluxe Package moldings: $157. Door edge guards: $15. Operating Convenience Package: $281. AM radio: $92. AM/FM radio: $143. AM/FM stereo radio: $226. AM/FM stereo radio with 8-track stereo tape player: $322. AM/FM stereo radio with cassette stereo tape player: $327. AM/FM stereo radio and CB radio: $559. Rear roll bar: $123. Folding rear seat: $308. Fuel tank and transfer case shield: $84. Front quad shock absorbers: $117. Speed control: $159 with auto. trans., $169 with manual trans. Heavy-duty front shock absorbers: $53. ComforTilt steering wheel: $234. 31 gal. fuel tank: $39. Two front towing hooks: $34. Deadweight trailer hitch: $53. Platform type trailer hitch: $145. Trailering Special Package: $354-$619. Bright metal wheelcovers: $38. Aluminum forged wheels: $411. Rallye wheels: $103. Styled wheels: $201. Power side door windows: $166. Power tailgate: $79. Intermittent windshield wipers: $45. Silverado Package: $931. Special two-tone paint: $147-$291. Exterior Decor Package: $279-$423.

HISTORICAL FOOTNOTES: The 1982 Blazers debuted in the fall of 1981.

1983 BLAZER

The 1983 Blazer carried most of its interior and exterior appearance features over from 1982. Changes were made in its grille treatment and parking light placement. Extra corrosion protection was provided by the use of galvanized HSLA steel in the front panel of the pickup box and the use of a Zincrometal hood inner liner. The standard Blazer engine was the 5.0 liter, 305 cu. in. V-8. Standard exterior colors for 1983 were almond, midnight black, light blue metallic, midnight blue, light bronze metallic, mahogany metallic, carmine red, silver metallic, frost white and Colonial white. The removable hardtop was available in black or white, coordinated to the body color selected.

1983 Chevrolet K10 Blazer with S-10 Blazer

I.D. DATA: The V.I.N. plate was mounted on the lower left side windshield corner. The V.I.N. consisted of 17 elements. The first, the number 1 identified the U.S. as the nation of origin. The letter G followed, for the manufacturer: General Motors. The third entry, the letter C represented the make as Chevrolet. The GVWR brake system identification followed. Next came the truck line and chassis type; the letter K indicated four-wheel drive. The truck series was identified by a number: 1-1/2 ton. The truck body type identification was next: 8-Utility. The engine code was next, followed by a check digit. The model year was identified by the letter D. The assembly plant code followed. The final six digits were the plant sequential production number.

Model Number	Body Type & Seating	Factory Price	GVW	Shipping Weight	Prod. Total
Blazer K10 (with 305 V-8)					
CK10516	Util. (with top)	$10,287	6100*	4426	31,282

* 6250 GVW Package available.
NOTE 1: Includes both two-wheel drive and four-wheel drive models.

STANDARD ENGINE: All states except California: Engine Type: Cast iron block. OHV, V-8 with Electronic Spark Control. Ordering Code: LE9. Produced by GM-Chevrolet Motor Division and GM of Canada. Bore x Stroke: 3.74 in. x 3.48 in. Lifters: Hydraulic. Number of main bearings-5. Carburetion: Rochester 2-barrel. Compression Ratio: 9.2:1. Displacement: 305 cu. in. Horsepower: Net: 160 @ 4000 rpm. Torque: Net: 235 lb.-ft. @ 2000 rpm. Oil capacity: 5 qt. with filter change. Fuel Requirements: Unleaded.

STANDARD ENGINE: California only: Engine Type: Cast iron block. OHV, V-8. Ordering Code: LS9. Produced by GM-Chevrolet Motor Division. Bore x Stroke: 4.0 in. x 3.48 in. Lifters: Hydraulic. Number of main bearings-5. Carburetion: Rochester 4-barrel. Compression Ratio: 8.2:1. Displacement: 350 cu. in. (5.7 liters). Horsepower: Net: 165 @ 3800 rpm. Torque: Net: 275 lb.-ft. @ 1600 rpm. Oil capacity: 5 qt. with filter change. Fuel Requirements: Unleaded.

OPTIONAL ENGINE: 50 states: Engine Type: OHV, Cast iron block. Diesel V-8. Order Code LH6. Produced by GM-Detroit Diesel Allison Division. Requires B3J Diesel Equipment Package which consists of dual batteries, hydraulic power-assisted brakes, engine block heater, heavy-duty radiator, K81 alternator, engine oil cooler and additional insulation. Bore x Stroke: 3.98 in. x 3.80 in. Lifters: Hydraulic. Number of main bearings-5. Carburetion: Fuel injection. Compression Ratio: 21.5:1. Displacement: 379 cu. in. (6.2 liter). Horsepower: Net: 130 @ 3600 rpm. Torque: Net: 240 lb.-ft. @ 2000 rpm. Oil capacity: 7 qt. with filter change. Fuel Requirements: Diesel.

CHASSIS FEATURES: Ladder-type. Carbon steel, 36,000-39,000 psi. Heavy-gauge channel side members, alligator-jaw cross members. Section modules: 3.14 in.

SUSPENSION AND RUNNING GEAR: Front Suspension: Two tapered semi-elliptical leaf springs. Capacity: Gasoline engines: 1650 lb. Optional Capacity: 2250 lb. Diesel engine: 1850 lb. Optional: 2250 lb. Standard 1.25 in. stabilizer bar and 25mm shock absorbers. Optional: 32mm shock absorbers. Rear Suspension: Two-stage tapered and multi-leaf (six-conventional leaves, one tapered leaf). Capacity: 1875 lb. Optional: None. Front Axle. Type: Hypoid, tubular driving. Capacity: 3600 lb. Rear Axle. Type: Hypoid, semi-floating. Capacity: 3750 lb. Final Drive Ratio: Gasoline engines: 2.73:1. Diesel engine: 3.08:1. Optional: Gasoline engines: 3.08:1, 3.73:1 (not available for California). Diesel engine: 3.42, 3.73:1. Transfer Case: Type: New Process 208. Ratios: 2.61, 1.00:1. Brakes: Type: Hydraulic, self-adjusting. Front: Discs. Rear: Drums. Optional: Power. Dimensions: Front: 11.86 in. dia. rotor. Rear: 11.15 in. x 2.75 in. Wheels: 6-stud, 15 x 6JJ. Optional: 15 x 7JJ Rallye, 15 x 8JJ, 15 x 8JJ Rallye, 16 x 5K. Tires: P215/75R15 steel belted radial. Optional: P215/75R15 steel belted radial whitewall, P235/75R15 steel belted radial, P235/75R15 steel belted radial whitewall, p235/75R15 white lettered steel belted radial, 10R-15B steel belted radial, 10R-15B white lettered steel belted radial. Steering: Power assisted recirculating ball, variable ratio. Ratio: 17.6/13.1. Turns Lock-to-Lock: 4.0. Turning Circle: 37.6 ft. Optional: None. Transmission: Gasoline engines: Muncie 4-speed manual, synchromesh on top three gears, floor-mounted shift lever. Ratios: 6.55, 3.58, 1.70, 1.00:1 Interim 1983. Not available in California. Standard: Diesel, optional gasoline engines: 700R4 4-speed automatic with overdrive. Ratios: 3.06, 1.36, 1.00, 0.70:1. Reverse: 2.29:1. Clutch: 11.0 in. dia., 124 sq. in. area. 12 in. clutch included with 350 V-8 engines).

VEHICLE DIMENSIONS: Wheelbase: 106.5 in. Overall Length: 184.8 in. Front/Rear Tread 66.10 in./63.00 in. Overall Height: 73.4 in. Width: 79.6 in. Tailgate: Width and Height: 66.8 in. x 22.0 in. Approach/Departure Degrees: 34/25. Ground Clearance: Front axle: 7.4 in. Rear axle: 7.0 in. Oil pan: 17.2 in. Transfer case: 11.5 in. Fuel tank: 14.0 in. Load space: With rear seat installed: 38.8 in. x 50 in. x 42.3 in. With rear seat removed or folded: 76.0 in. x 50 in. x 42.3 in.

CAPACITIES: Fuel Tank: 25.0 gal. Optional: Replacement 31 gal. tank. Coolant system: 305 V-8: 17.6 qt. 350 V-8: 17.6 qt.

ACCOMMODATIONS: Seating Capacity: Standard: Driver and passenger front high-back bucket sets. Optional: 3 passenger rear bench seat. Headroom: 38.3 in. Maximum steering wheel to seat back: 18.5 in. Seat to ground: 36.3 in. Floor to ground: 21.9 in.

INSTRUMENTATION: 0-100 mph speedometer, 99,999.9 mi. odometer, fuel gauge, warning lights for alternator, oil pressure, engine coolant temperature, brake operating system, hazard warning lights, directional lights, seat belt warning.

OPTIONS AND PRICES: Tinted glass: $177. Air conditioning: $725. Bright metal wheelcovers. Bright metal wheel trim rings. Deluxe front and rear bumpers: $47. Chromed front bumper guards. Deluxe front and rear bumpers. Cigarette lighter. Color-keyed floor mats. ComforTilt steering wheel: $105. Custom steering wheel. Chromed grille (RPO V22). Deluxe instrument panel. Electric clock (RPO U35). One-way glass (RPO AJ1). Sliding glass rear side windows. Halogen high-beam headlights (RPO TT5): $16. Headlight warning buzzer: $11. Intermittent windshield wipers/washer: $49. Painted below eye-level mirrors (RPO D44). Stainless steel below eye-level mirrors (RPO D45): $76. Stainless steel camper mirrors (RPO DF2). Black body side moldings (RPO B84). Bright body side moldings (RPO B85). Black molding package. Bright molding package. Operating Convenience Package. Power door locks. Power windows. Special two-tone paint. Exterior decor package. AM radio. AM/FM radio. AM/FM radio with 8-track tape player. AM/FM radio with cassette tape player. AM/FM stereo radio with cassette tape player: $298. AM/FM radio with CB and antenna. Rear auxiliary speaker. Windshield antenna. Quartz electric clock: $38. Rear roll bar. Spare tire carrier. Folding rear seat: $353. Tachometer. Electric tailgate window: $85. Aluminum wheels (RPO PH7). Rallye wheels (RPO N67). Styled wheels (RPO PA6): $208. Silverado Package (RPO YE9): $983. Operating Convenience Package: $300. Exterior Decor Package: $294. Auxiliary battery. Cold Climate Package. Engine oil cooler. Transmission oil cooler: $57. Cruise Control: $185. Deadweight trailer hitch: $56. Heavy-duty front springs: $57. Front quad shock absorbers: $123. Front tow hooks. 31 gal. fuel tank. Fuel tank shield plate. Gauge Package (includes voltmeter, engine coolant temperature and oil pressure gauges. 55 amp generator. 61 amp generator. Heavy-duty battery. Heavy-duty radiator. Locking rear differential. Trailering special equipment. Trailer wiring harness. Weight-distributing hitch platform. Automatic 4-speed overdrive transmission: $650.10-15LT radial tires: $728.45.

HISTORICAL FOOTNOTES: The 1983 Blazer was introduced on September 14, 1982. Calendar year production was 31,282.

1984 BLAZER

The 1984 Blazer was unchanged in appearance from 1983. Chevrolet reported that a Blazer with the 6.2 liter diesel engine and 4-speed automatic transmission with overdrive had ratings of 28 mpg est. highway and 20 mpg EPA. The standard Custom Deluxe interior provided full-foam-padded front bucket vinyl seats, color-keyed door trim panels, integrated armrest, and instrument panel pad. The Silverado trim option included full-foam front bucket seats in a choice of either Custom vinyl or Custom cloth upholstery. New for the Silverado interior were saddle tan, burgundy or slate gray color choices in addition to the blue color from 1983. A new neutral-colored cloth-covered headliner was also included. The Blazer exterior featured a new anti-chip coating on lower fender and body areas. The optional diesel engine had a new integral fuel/water separator. Carried over from 1983 was the optional Exterior Decor Package. It included moldings and lamp trim in a special two-tone scheme, plus dual-tone decal striping on body sides and across the rear of the vehicle. The accent color was applied on the body sides and rear between the striping and molding. Also included was a stand-up hood emblem on gasoline models. A total of ten two-tone color combinations were offered for this package. The 1984 Blazer exterior color selection consisted of frost white, silver metallic, midnight black, light blue metallic, midnight blue, Colonial yellow, doeskin tan, desert sand metallic, Indian bronze metallic and apple red.

1984 Chevrolet K10 Blazer

I.D. DATA: The V.I.N. plate was mounted on the lower left side windshield corner. The V.I.N. consisted of 17 elements. The first, the number 1 identified the U.S. as the nation of origin The letter G followed, for the manufacturer: General Motors. The third entry, the letter C represented the make as Chevrolet. The GVWR brake system identification followed. Next came the truck line and chassis type; the letter K indicated four-wheel drive. The truck series was identified by a number: 1-1/2 ton. The truck body type identification was next: 8-Utility. The engine code was next, followed by a check digit. The model year was identified by the letter E. The assembly plant code followed. The final six digits were the plant sequential production number.

Model Number	Body Type & Seating	Factory Price	GVW	Shipping Weight	Prod. Total
Blazer K10. (with 305 V-8)					
CK10516	Util. (with top)	$10,819	6100*	4409	46,919[1]

* 6250 GVW Package available.
NOTE 1: Calendar year sales, all models.

STANDARD ENGINE: All states except California: Engine Type: Cast iron block. OHV, V-8 with Electronic Spark Control. Ordering Code: LE9. Produced by GM-Chevrolet Motor Division and GM of Canada. Bore x Stroke: 3.74 in. x 3.48 in. Lifters: Hydraulic. Number of main bearings-5. Carburetion: Rochester 2-barrel. Compression Ratio: 9.2:1. Displacement: 305 cu. in. Horsepower: Net: 160 @ 4000 rpm. Torque: Net: 235 lb.-ft. @ 2000 rpm. Oil capacity: 5 qt. with filter change. Fuel Requirements: Unleaded.

STANDARD ENGINE: California only: Engine Type: Cast iron block. OHV, V-8. Ordering Code: LS9. Produced by GM-Chevrolet Motor Division. Bore x Stroke: 4.0 in. x 3.48 in. Lifters: Hydraulic. Number of main bearings-5. Carburetion: Rochester 4-barrel. Compression Ratio: 8.2:1. Displacement: 350 cu. in. (5.7 liters). Horsepower: Net: 165 @ 3800 rpm. Torque: Net: 275 lb.-ft. @ 1600 rpm. Oil capacity: 5 qt. with filter change. Fuel Requirements: Unleaded.

OPTIONAL ENGINE: 50 states: Engine Type: OHV, Cast iron block. Diesel V-8. Order Code LH6. Produced by GM-Detroit Diesel Allison Division. Requires B3J Diesel Equipment Package which consists of dual batteries, hydraulic power-assisted brakes, engine block heater, heavy-duty radiator, K81 alternator, engine oil cooler and additional insulation. Bore x Stroke: 3.98 in. x 3.80 in. Lifters: Hydraulic. Number of main bearings-5. Carburetion: Fuel injection. Compression Ratio: 21.5:1. Displacement: 379 cu. in. (6.2 liter). Horsepower: Net: 130 @ 3600 rpm. Torque: Net: 240 lb.-ft. @ 2000 rpm. Oil capacity: 7 qt. with filter change. Fuel Requirements: Diesel.

CHASSIS FEATURES: Ladder-type. Carbon steel, 36,000-39,000 psi. Heavy-gauge channel side members, alligator-jaw cross members. Section modules: 3.14 in.

SUSPENSION AND RUNNING GEAR: Front Suspension: Two tapered semi-elliptical leaf springs. Capacity: Gasoline engines: 1650 lb. Optional Capacity: 2250 lb. Diesel engine: 1850 lb. Optional: 2250 lb. Standard 1.25 in. stabilizer bar and 25mm shock absorbers. Optional: 32mm shock absorbers. Rear Suspension: Two-stage tapered and multi-leaf (six-conventional leaves, one tapered leaf). Capacity: 1875 lb. Optional: None. Front Axle. Type: Hypoid, tubular driving. Capacity: 3600 lb. Rear Axle. Type: Hypoid, semi-floating. Capacity: 3750 lb. Final Drive Ratio: Gasoline engines: 2.73:1. Diesel engine: 3.08:1. Optional: Gasoline engines: 3.08:1, 3.73:1 (not available for California). Diesel engine: 3.42, 3.73:1. Transfer Case: Type: New Process 208. Ratios: 2.61, 1.00:1. Brakes: Type: Hydraulic, self-adjusting. Front: Discs. Rear: Drums. Optional: Power. Dimensions: Front: 11.86 in. dia. rotor. Rear: 11.15 in. x 2.75 in. Wheels: 6-stud, 15 x 6JJ. Optional: 15 x 7JJ Rallye, 15 x 8JJ, 15 x 8JJ Rallye, 16 x 5K. Tires: P215/75R15 steel belted radial. Optional: P215/75R15 steel belted radial whitewall, P235/75R15 steel belted radial, P235/75R15 steel belted radial whitewall, p235/75R15 white lettered steel belted radial, 10R-15B steel belted radial, 10R-15B white lettered steel belted radial. Steering: Power assisted recirculating ball, variable ratio. Ratio: 17.6/13.1. Turns Lock-to-Lock: 4.0. Turning Circle: 37.6 ft. Optional: None. Transmission: Gasoline engines: Muncie 4-speed manual, synchromesh on top three gears, floor-mounted shift lever. Ratios: 6.55, 3.58, 1.70, 1.00:1. Not available in California. Standard: Diesel, optional gasoline engines: 700R4 4-speed automatic with overdrive. Ratios: 3.06, 1.36, 1.00, 0.70:1. Reverse: 2.29:1. Clutch: 11.0 in. dia., 124 sq. in. area. 12 in. clutch included with 350 V-8 engines.

VEHICLE DIMENSIONS: Wheelbase: 106.5 in. Overall Length: 184.8 in. Front/Rear Tread 66.10 in./63.00 in. Overall Height: 73.4 in. Width: 79.6 in. Tailgate: Width and Height: 66.8 in. x 22.0 in. Approach/Departure Degrees: 34/25. Ground Clearance: Front axle: 7.4 in. Rear axle: 7.0 in. Oil pan: 17.2 in. Transfer case: 11.5 in. Fuel tank: 14.0 in. Load space: With rear seat installed: 38.8 in. x 50 in. x 42.3 in. With rear seat removed or folded: 76.0 in. x 50 in. x 42.3 in.

CAPACITIES: Fuel Tank: 25.0 gal. Optional: Replacement 31 gal. tank. Coolant system: 305 V-8: 17.6 qt. 350 V-8: 17.6 qt.

ACCOMMODATIONS: Seating Capacity: Standard: Driver and passenger front high-back bucket sets. Optional: 3 passenger rear bench seat. Headroom: 38.3 in. Maximum steering wheel to seat back: 18.5 in. Seat to ground: 36.3 in. Floor to ground: 21.9 in.

INSTRUMENTATION: 0-100 mph speedometer, 99,999.9 mi. odometer, fuel gauge, warning lights for alternator, oil pressure, engine coolant temperature, brake operating system, hazard warning lights, directional lights, seat belt warning.

OPTIONS: Tinted glass. Air conditioning. Bright metal wheelcovers. Bright metal wheel trim rings. Deluxe front and rear bumpers. Chromed front bumper guards. Deluxe front and rear bumpers. Cigarette lighter. Color-keyed floor mats. ComforTilt steering wheel. Custom steering wheel. Chromed grille (RPO V22). Deluxe instrument panel. Electric clock (RPO U35). One-way glass (RPO AJ1). Sliding glass rear side windows. Halogen high-beam headlights (RPO TT5). Headlight warning buzzer. Intermittent windshield wipers/washer. Painted below eye-level mirrors (RPO D44). Stainless steel below eye-level mirrors (RPO D45). Stainless steel camper mirrors (RPO DF2). Black body side moldings (RPO B84). Bright body side moldings (RPO B85). Black molding package. Bright molding package. Operating Convenience Package. Power door locks. Power windows. Special two-tone paint. Exterior decor package. AM radio. AM/FM radio. AM/FM radio with 8-track tape player. AM/FM radio with cassette tape player. AM/FM stereo radio with cassette tape player. AM/FM radio with CB and antenna. Rear auxiliary speaker. Windshield antenna. Quartz electric clock. Rear roll bar. Spare tire carrier. Folding rear seat. Tachometer. Electric tailgate window. Aluminum wheels (RPO PH7). Rallye wheels (RPO N67). Styled wheels (RPO PA6). Silverado Package (RPO YE9). Operating Convenience Package. Exterior Decor Package. Auxiliary battery. Cold Climate Package. Engine oil cooler. Transmission oil cooler. Cruise control. Deadweight trailer hitch. Heavy-duty front springs. Front quad shock absorbers. Front tow hooks. 31 gal. fuel tank. Fuel tank shield plate. Gauge Package (includes voltmeter, engine coolant temperature and oil pressure gauges. 55 amp generator. 61 amp generator. Heavy-duty battery. Heavy-duty radiator. Locking rear differential. Trailering special equipment. Trailer wiring harness. Weight-distributing hitch platform. Automatic 4-speed overdrive transmission.10-15LT radial tires.

HISTORICAL FOOTNOTES: By the 1984 model year, Chevrolet had received a military contract for over 23,000 Blazers equipped with the 6.2 liter diesel engine.

1985 BLAZER

The Blazer's front grille was slightly altered by the use of a wider center dividing bar which was painted the primary body color. A color-keyed hardtop in a choice of midnight black, blue, bronze, silver, tan or frost white was offered. The special two-tone paint treatment included black vinyl body side and rear moldings, with a secondary body color applied below. The Exterior Decor Package included black vinyl body side and rear moldings with side and rear decal striping. The secondary body color was applied between the moldings and the decal striping. The Silverado's standard front bucket seats were now available in a choice of new Custom vinyl or new Custom cloth trim as well as pewter-toned brushed aluminum instrument panel trim, color-keyed front carpeting and a Custom steering wheel. The exterior colors offered for 1985 consisted of frost white, silver metallic, midnight black, light blue metallic, midnight blue, doeskin tan, Indian bronze metallic and apple red.

1985 Chevrolet K10 Blazer Silverado

I.D. DATA: The V.I.N. plate was mounted on the lower left side windshield corner. The V.I.N. consisted of 17 elements. The first, the number 1 identified the U.S. as the nation of origin. The letter G followed, for the manufacturer: General Motors. The third entry, the letter C represented the make as Chevrolet. The GVWR brake system identification followed. Next came the truck line and chassis type; the letter K indicated four-wheel drive. The truck series was identified by a number: 1-1/2 ton. The truck body type identification was next: 8-Utility. The engine code was next, followed by a check digit. The model year was identified by the letter F. The assembly plant code followed. The final six digits were the plant sequential production number.

Model Number	Body Type & Seating	Factory Price	GVW	Shipping Weight	Prod. Total
Blazer K10 (with 305 V-8)					
CK10516	Util. ZW9	$11,340[1]	6100[2]	4462	—

NOTE 1: $14,070 with 379 cu. in. diesel V-8 and B3J Diesel Equipment Package consisting of dual batteries, hydraulic power-assisted brakes, engine block heater, heavy-duty radiator, K81 alternator, engine oil cooler and additional insulation.
NOTE 2: 6250 GVW Package available. Its content, compared to the standard GVW follows:

GVW Rating	GVWR (lbs.) Front/Rear	Tire Capacities Front/Rear	Chassis Equip.
6100	3166/3166	1583/1583	None
6250	3550/3550	1775/1775	Requires B3J

STANDARD ENGINE: All states except California: Engine Type: Cast iron block. OHV, V-8 with Electronic Spark Control. Ordering Code: LE9. Produced by GM-Chevrolet Motor Division and GM of Canada. Bore x Stroke: 3.74 in. x 3.48 in. Lifters: Hydraulic. Number of main bearings-5. Carburetion: Rochester 2-barrel. Compression Ratio: 9.2:1. Displacement: 305 cu. in. Horsepower: Net: 160 @ 4000 rpm. Torque: Net: 235 lb.-ft. @ 2000 rpm. Oil capacity: 5 qt. with filter change. Fuel Requirements: Unleaded.

STANDARD ENGINE: California only: Engine Type: Cast iron block. OHV, V-8. Ordering Code: LS9. Produced by GM-Chevrolet Motor Division. Bore x Stroke: 4.0 in. x 3.48 in. Lifters: Hydraulic. Number of main bearings-5. Carburetion: Rochester 4-barrel. Compression Ratio: 8.2:1. Displacement: 350 cu. in. (5.7 liters). Horsepower: Net: 165 @ 3800 rpm. Torque: Net: 275 lb.-ft. @ 1600 rpm. Oil capacity: 5 qt. with filter change. Fuel Requirements: Unleaded.

OPTIONAL ENGINE: 50 states: Engine Type: OHV, Cast iron block. Diesel V-8. Order Code LH6. Produced by GM-Detroit Diesel Allison Division. Requires B3J Diesel Equipment Package which consists of dual batteries, hydraulic power-assisted brakes, engine block heater, heavy-duty radiator, K81 alternator, engine oil cooler and additional insulation. Bore x Stroke: 3.98 in. x 3.80 in. Lifters: Hydraulic. Number of main bearings-5. Carburetion: Fuel injection. Compression Ratio: 21.5:1. Displacement: 379 cu. in. (6.2 liter). Horsepower: Net: 130 @ 3600 rpm. Torque: Net: 240 lb.-ft. @ 2000 rpm. Oil capacity: 7 qt. with filter change. Fuel Requirements: Diesel.

CHASSIS FEATURES: Ladder-type. Carbon steel, 36,000-39,000 psi. Heavy-gauge channel side members, alligator-jaw cross members. Section modules: 3.14 in.

SUSPENSION AND RUNNING GEAR: Front Suspension: Two tapered semi-elliptical leaf springs. Capacity: Gasoline engines: 1650 lb. Optional Capacity: 2250 lb. Diesel engine: 1850 lb. Optional: 2250 lb. Standard 1.25 in. stabilizer bar and 25mm shock absorbers. Optional: 32mm shock absorbers. Rear Suspension: Two-stage tapered and multi-leaf (six-conventional leaves, one tapered leaf). Capacity: 1875 lb. Optional: None. Front Axle. Type: Hypoid, tubular driving. Capacity: 3600 lb. Rear Axle. Type: Hypoid, semi-floating. Capacity: 3750 lb. Final Drive Ratio: Gasoline engines: 2.73:1. Diesel engine: 3.08:1. Optional: Gasoline engines: 3.08:1, 3.73:1 (not available for California). Diesel engine: 3.42, 3.73:1. Transfer Case: Type: New Process 208. Ratios: 2.61, 1.00:1. Brakes: Type: Hydraulic, self-adjusting. Front: Discs. Rear: Drums. Optional: Power. Dimensions: Front: 11.86 in. dia. rotor. Rear: 11.15 in. x 2.75 in. Wheels: 6-stud, 15 x 6JJ. Optional: 15 x 7JJ Rallye, 15 x 8JJ, 15 x 8JJ Rallye, 16 x 5K. Tires: P215/75R15 steel belted radial. Optional: P215/75R15 steel belted radial whitewall, P235/75R15 steel belted radial, P235/75R15 steel belted radial whitewall, p235/75R15 white lettered steel belted radial, 10R-15B steel belted radial, 10R-15B white lettered steel belted radial. Steering: Power assisted recirculating ball, variable ratio. Ratio: 17.6/13.1. Turns Lock-to-Lock: 4.0. Turning Circle: 37.6 ft. Optional: None. Transmission: Gasoline engines: Muncie 4-speed manual, synchromesh on top three gears, floor-mounted shift lever. Ratios: 6.55, 3.58, 1.70, 1.00:1. Not available in California. Standard: Diesel, optional gasoline engines: 700R4 4-speed automatic with overdrive. Ratios: 3.06, 1.36, 1.00, 0.70:1. Reverse: 2.29:1. Clutch: 11.0 in. dia., 124 sq. in. area. 12 in. clutch included with 350 V-8 engines).

VEHICLE DIMENSIONS: Wheelbase: 106.5 in. Overall Length: 184.8 in. Front/Rear Tread 66.10 in./63.00 in. Overall Height: 73.4 in. Width: 79.6 in. Tailgate: Width and Height: 66.8 in. x 22.0 in. Approach/Departure Degrees: 34/25. Ground Clearance: Front axle: 7.4 in. Rear axle: 7.0 in. Oil pan: 17.2 in. Transfer case: 11.5 in. Fuel tank: 14.0 in. Load space: With rear seat installed: 38.8 in. x 50 in. x 42.3 in. With rear seat removed or folded: 76.0 in. x 50 in. x 42.3 in.

CAPACITIES: Fuel Tank: 25.0 gal. Optional: Replacement 31 gal. tank. Coolant system: 305 V-8: 17.6 qt. 350 V-8: 17.6 qt.

ACCOMMODATIONS: Seating Capacity: Standard: Driver and passenger front high-back bucket sets. Optional: 3 passenger rear bench seat. Headroom: 38.3 in. Maximum steering wheel to seat back: 18.5 in. Seat to ground: 36.3 in. Floor to ground: 21.9 in.

INSTRUMENTATION: 0-100 mph speedometer, 99,999.9 mi. odometer, fuel gauge, warning lights for alternator, oil pressure, engine coolant temperature, brake operating system, hazard warning lights, directional lights, seat belt warning.

OPTIONS AND PRICES: Silverado Package (RPO YE9): $1015. Includes either Custom cloth or Custom vinyl seats, Custom steering wheel, Deluxe Molding Package, taillight and rear door or tailgate moldings, bright front turn signal and front side marker lamp bezels, fender nameplates, bright windshield and side rear window moldings, color-keyed carpeting with bright sill plates, plastic door trim panels with storage pockets, and bright brushed finish accents, visor vanity mirror, Deluxe Front Appearance Package, dual horns, nameplate on instrument panel, cigarette lighter, headliner, wheel opening moldings, special insulation, bright body side moldings, pillar trim panels, storage console between front seats, floor and wheelwell carpeting, spare tire cover and voltmeter, engine coolant temperature and oil pressure gauges. Custom vinyl bucket seats (without YE9): $200 (without rear seat), $250 (with rear seat). Custom vinyl seats (with YE9): $50 (with rear seat). No extra charge without rear seat. Special two-tone paint: $327 (without YE9), $170 (with YE9). Includes Custom Molding Package and wheel opening moldings. Exterior Decor: $471 (without YE9), $414 (with YE9). Includes hood ornament. California emission systems (RPO YF5): $235. 5.7 liter V-8 (available only with YF5): $290. 4-speed with overdrive automatic transmission (standard on B3J diesel): $670. Optional axle ratio: $36. Locking rear differential (RPO G80): $238. P215/75R15 All-Season steel belted radial blackwall: $70. P215/75R15 highway steel belted radial blackwall: $125. P235/75R15 highway steel belted radial whitewall: $210. P235/75R15 highway steel belted radial white lettered: $240. P235/75R15 All-Season steel belted radial blackwall: $125. P235/75R15 on-off road steel belted radial blackwall: $175. P235/75R15 All-Season steel belted radial whitewall: $210. P235/75R15 All-Season steel belted radial white lettered: $240. 31 x 10.50R/15LTB on-off road steel belted radial blackwall (available only if N67, N90 or PA6 wheels are specified): $564. 31 x 10.50R/15LTB (available only if N67, N90 or PA6 wheels are specified): $720. Pre-cleaner air cleaner (RPO K46): $42. Air conditioning (not available with Cold Climate Package): $740. Deluxe Front Appearance (RPO V22). Includes dark argent grille with bright trim and dual rectangular headlights): $109. Heavy-duty battery: $53. Deluxe chromed front and rear bumpers (RPO VE5): $49. Chromed front bumper guards (RPO V31): $41. Quartz electric clock (RPO U35). Not available with UM6 radio: $79 (without YE9. Includes Z53 gauge package). With YE9: $39. Cold Climate Package (RPO V10). Includes special insulation, special heater and defroster, engine block heater, anti-freeze protection to -31 degrees, heavy-duty battery. $188 (without Trailering Special Package. Also includes 66 amp generator). With Trailering Special Package: $126. Engine oil cooling system (RPO KC4): $120. Heavy-duty radiator (RPO VO1): $53. Heavy-duty radiator and transmission oil cooler (RPO VO2): $59. Power door locks (RPO AU3): $135. Color-keyed front floor mats (RPO B32): $15. Gauge Package (RPO Z54). Includes voltmeter, engine coolant temperature and oil pressure gauges: $40. 66 amp generator (RPO K81): $62. Deep tinted glass (RPO AJ1). Includes dark laminated glass on side windows and rear tailgate glass: $194. Deep tinted glass with light tinted rear window (RPO AA3). Includes tinted glass on rear tailgate glass, passenger and driver's side door and dark laminated glass on side windows: $140. Heavy-duty, 7-lead wiring harness (RPO UY7): $44. Halogen high-beam headlights (RPO TT5). Available only with V22 or YE9 was ordered: $17. Headlight warning buzzer (RPO T63): $11. Interior headliner (RPO BB5): $80. 600 watt engine block heater (RPO KO5). Not available for diesel engine: $31. Heavy-duty front heater (RPO C42). Available only with diesel engine: $43. Automatic locking hubs (RPO X6Z): $40. Cigarette lighter (RPO U37): $30. Painted exterior below eye-level mirrors (RPO D45): $83. Black body side molding (RPO B84). Includes lower side and rear moldings of black plastic with bright trim: $115. Bright body side molding (RPO B85). Includes bright plastic body side and rear lower moldings with black paint trim, plus bright trim for front side marker lamps and taillights, fender, door, rear side panel and tailgate moldings: $144. Custom Molding Package (RPO YG1). Includes B84 black body side moldings, wheel opening moldings and bright trim for front side marker lights and taillight trim. Included with ZY3 or ZY5 Packages: $157. Deluxe Molding Package (RPO YG3). Includes bright trim for front side marker lamps and taillight trim, wheel opening molding and B85 bright body side moldings: $173 (without ZY3 or ZY5). With ZY3 or ZY5: $16. Door edge guards (RPO B93): $17. Operating Convenience Package (RPO ZQ2). Includes power door locks and power windows: $325. AM radio (RPO U63): $112. AM/FM radio (RPO U69): $171. AM/FM stereo radio (RPO U58), available only with YE9: $198. AM/FM electronically tuned stereo radio with Seek-Scan, stereo cassette tape player and clock: $419. Windshield antenna (RPO U76), included with radio: $32. Rear seat (RPO AM7). With Custom trim: $369. Without Custom trim: $341. Fuel tank shield (RPO NY1): $164. Front quad shock absorbers (RPO Z75). Includes dual left and right hand shock absorbers on front axle, heavy-duty shock absorbers on rear axle and a front axle nose bumper to limit axle windup: $128. Electronic speed control (RPO K34): $195. Front heavy-duty 2250 lb. capacity springs with heavy-duty front and rear shock absorbers. Recommended with snowplow-type usage only: $92 (with Z75). Without Z75: $59. ComforTilt steering wheel (RPO N33): $115. 31 gal. replacement fuel tank (RPO NK7): $43. Two front towing hooks (RPO V76): $36. Deadweight type trailer hitch (RPO VR2). Not available with Z82: $58. Weight distributing platform trailer hitch (RPO VR4). Included with Z82: $155. Trailering special equipment (RPO Z82). Available only with 3.24 or 3.73:1 rear axle ratio and MXO automatic transmission when ordered. Not available with 5.7 liter LS9 engine. Includes VR4, UY7 and V02 options: $440. With B3J diesel equipment: $258. With C80 air conditioning: $378. Bright metal wheelcovers (RPO P01): $40. Rallye 15 x 8 wheels (RPO N67). Not available with P215 tires: $115. Styled 15 x 8 wheels (RPO PA6). Not available with P215 tires: $174. Cast aluminum 15 x 7 wheels with special hubcaps (RPO N90). Not available with P215 tires: $299. Power side door electric windows (RPO A31): $10. Power tailgate electric window (RPO A33): $95. Sliding side quarter windows (RPO AD5): $243. Intermittent windshield wipers (RPO CD4): $55.

HISTORICAL FOOTNOTES: The 1985 Blazer, when delivered in the United States by a Chevrolet dealer, came with a one-year, $10,000 seat belt insurance certificate from MIC General Insurance Corporation at no additional charge. It paid $10,000 to the estate of any occupant who suffered fatal injuries as a result of an accident involving that vehicle while wearing a GM seat belt.

1986 BLAZER

New design front bucket seats standard for the 1986 Blazer provided more rear legroom. The front seats had folding back rests. The front passenger seat slid forward for easier access to the rear. All gasoline engines had new-design generator drive belts that provided greater drive friction than the older versions. Also found on the latest engines were new crankshaft seals and oil pan gaskets. The Silverado option was continued. Exterior colors for 1986 were frost white, steel gray metallic, midnight black, midnight blue, doeskin tan, Indian bronze metallic, apple red and light blue metallic.

I.D. DATA: The V.I.N. plate was mounted on the lower left side windshield corner. The V.I.N. consisted of 17 elements. The first, the number 1 identified the U.S. as the nation of origin. The letter G followed, for the manufacturer: General Motors. The third entry, the letter C represented the make as Chevrolet. The GVWR brake system identification followed. Next came the truck line and chassis type; the letter K indicated four-wheel drive. The truck series was identified by a number: 1-1/2 ton. The truck body type identification was next: 8-Utility. The engine code was next, followed by a check digit. The model year was identified by the letter G. The assembly plant code followed. The final six digits were the plant sequential production number.

Model Number	Body Type & Seating	Factory Price	GVW	Shipping Weight	Prod. Total
Blazer K10 Body Code: ZW9 (with 305 V-8)					
CK10516	Util.	$12,034	6100[1]	4444	41,866[2]

NOTE 1: 6250 GVW Package available. Its content was unchanged from 1985.
NOTE 2: Sales of all models from Nov. 1985-Nov. 1986.

STANDARD ENGINE: All states except California: Engine Type: Cast iron block. OHV, V-8 with Electronic Spark Control. Ordering Code: LE9. Produced by GM-Chevrolet Motor Division and GM of Canada. Bore x Stroke: 3.74 in. x 3.48 in. Lifters: Hydraulic. Number of main bearings-5. Carburetion: Rochester 2-barrel. Compression Ratio: 9.2:1. Displacement: 305 cu. in. Horsepower: Net: 160 @ 4000 rpm. Torque: Net: 235 lb.-ft. @ 2000 rpm. Oil capacity: 5 qt. with filter change. Fuel Requirements: Unleaded.

STANDARD ENGINE: California only: Engine Type: Cast iron block. OHV, V-8. Ordering Code: LS9. Produced by GM-Chevrolet Motor Division. Bore x Stroke: 4.0 in. x 3.48 in. Lifters: Hydraulic. Number of main bearings-5. Carburetion: Rochester 4-barrel. Compression Ratio: 8.2:1. Displacement: 350 cu. in. (5.7 liters). Horsepower: Net: 165 @ 3800 rpm. Torque: Net: 275 lb.-ft. @ 1600 rpm. Oil capacity: 5 qt. with filter change. Fuel Requirements: Unleaded.

OPTIONAL ENGINE: 50 states: Engine Type: OHV, Cast iron block. Diesel V-8. Order Code LH6. Produced by GM-Detroit Diesel Allison Division. Requires B3J Diesel Equipment Package which consists of dual batteries, hydraulic power-assisted brakes, engine block heater, heavy-duty radiator, K81 alternator, engine oil cooler and additional insulation. Bore x Stroke: 3.98 in. x 3.80 in. Lifters: Hydraulic. Number of main bearings-5. Carburetion: Fuel injection. Compression Ratio: 21.5:1. Displacement: 379 cu. in. (6.2 liter). Horsepower: Net: 130 @ 3600 rpm. Torque: Net: 240 lb.-ft. @ 2000 rpm. Oil capacity: 7 qt. with filter change. Fuel Requirements: Diesel.

CHASSIS FEATURES: Ladder-type. Carbon steel, 36,000-39,000 psi. Heavy-gauge channel side members, alligator-jaw cross members. Section modules: 3.14 in.

SUSPENSION AND RUNNING GEAR: Front Suspension: Two tapered semi-elliptical leaf springs. Capacity: Gasoline engines: 1650 lb. Optional Capacity: 2250 lb. Diesel engine: 1850 lb. Optional: 2250 lb. Standard 1.25 in. stabilizer bar and 25mm shock absorbers. Optional: 32mm shock absorbers. Rear Suspension: Two-stage tapered and multi-leaf (six-conventional leaves, one tapered leaf). Capacity: 1875 lb. Optional: None. Front Axle. Type: Hypoid, tubular driving. Capacity: 3600 lb. Rear Axle. Type: Hypoid, semi-floating. Capacity: 3750 lb. Final Drive Ratio: Gasoline engines: 2.73:1. Diesel engine: 3.08:1. Optional: Gasoline engines: 3.08:1, 3.73:1 (not available for California). Diesel engine: 3.42, 3.73:1. Transfer Case: Type: New Process 208. Ratios: 2.61, 1.00:1. Brakes: Type: Hydraulic, self-adjusting. Front: Discs. Rear: Drums. Optional: Power. Dimensions: Front: 11.86 in. dia. rotor. Rear: 11.15 in. x 2.75 in. Wheels: 6-stud, 15 x 6JJ. Optional: 15 x 7JJ Rallye, 15 x 8JJ, 15 x 8JJ Rallye, 16 x 5K. Tires: P215/75R15 steel belted radial. Optional: P215/75R15 steel belted radial whitewall, P235/75R15 steel belted radial, P235/75R15 steel belted radial whitewall, p235/75R15 white lettered steel belted radial, 10R-15B steel belted radial, 10R-15B white lettered steel belted radial. Steering: Power assisted recirculating ball, variable ratio. Ratio: 17.6/13.1. Turns Lock-to-Lock: 4.0. Turning Circle: 37.6 ft. Optional: None. Transmission: Gasoline engines: Muncie 4-speed manual, synchromesh on top three gears, floor-mounted shift lever. Ratios: 6.55, 3.58, 1.70, 1.00:1. Not available in California. Standard: Diesel, optional gasoline engines: 700R4 4-speed automatic with overdrive. Ratios: 3.06, 1.36, 1.00, 0.70:1. Reverse: 2.29:1. Clutch: 11.0 in. dia., 124 sq. in. area. 12 in. clutch included with 350 V-8 engines.

VEHICLE DIMENSIONS: Wheelbase: 106.5 in. Overall Length: 184.8 in. Front/Rear Tread 66.10 in./63.00 in. Overall Height: 73.4 in. Width: 79.6 in. Tailgate: Width and Height: 66.8 in. x 22.0 in. Approach/Departure Degrees: 34/25. Ground Clearance: Front axle: 7.4 in. Rear axle: 7.0 in. Oil pan: 17.2 in. Transfer case: 11.5 in. Fuel tank: 14.0 in. Load space: With rear seat installed: 38.8 in. x 50 in. x 42.3 in. With rear seat removed or folded: 76.0 in. x 50 in. x 42.3 in.

CAPACITIES: Fuel Tank: 25.0 gal. Optional: Replacement 31 gal. tank. Coolant system: 305 V-8: 17.6 qt. 350 V-8: 17.6 qt.

ACCOMMODATIONS: Seating Capacity: Standard: Driver and passenger front high-back bucket sets. Optional: 3 passenger rear bench seat. Headroom: 38.3 in. Maximum steering wheel to seat back: 18.5 in. Seat to ground: 36.3 in. Floor to ground: 21.9 in.

INSTRUMENTATION: 0-100 mph speedometer, 99,999.9 mi. odometer, fuel gauge, warning lights for alternator, oil pressure, engine coolant temperature, brake operating system, hazard warning lights, directional lights, seat belt warning.

OPTIONS AND PRICES: Silverado Package (RPO YE9): $1050. Includes either Custom cloth or Custom vinyl seats, Custom steering wheel, Deluxe Molding Package, taillight and rear door or tailgate moldings, bright front turn signal and front side marker lamp bezels, fender nameplates, bright windshield and side rear window moldings, color-keyed carpeting with bright sill plates, plastic door trim panels with storage pockets, and bright brushed finish accents, visor vanity mirror, Deluxe Front Appearance Package, dual horns, nameplate on instrument panel, cigarette lighter, headliner, wheel opening moldings, special insulation, bright body side moldings, pillar trim panels, storage console between front seats, floor and wheelwell carpeting, spare tire cover and voltmeter, engine coolant temperature and oil pressure gauges. Custom vinyl bucket seats (without YE9): $200 (without rear seat), $250 (with rear seat). Custom vinyl seats (with YE9): $50 (with rear seat). No extra charge without rear seat. Special two-tone paint: $327 (without YE9), $170 (with YE9). Includes Custom Molding Package and wheel opening moldings. Exterior Decor: $471 (without YE9), $414 (with YE9). Includes hood ornament. California emission systems (RPO YF5): $235. 5.7 liter V-8 (available only with YF5): $290. 4-speed with overdrive automatic transmission (standard on B3J diesel): $670. Optional axle ratio: $36. Locking rear differential (RPO G80): $238. P215/75R15 All-Season steel belted radial blackwall: $70. P215/75R15 highway steel belted radial blackwall: $125. P235/75R15 highway steel belted radial whitewall: $210. P235/75R15 highway steel belted radial white lettered: $240. P235/75R15 All-Season steel belted radial blackwall: $125. P235/75R15 on-off road steel belted radial blackwall: $175. P235/75R15 All-Season steel belted radial whitewall: $210. P235/75R15 All-Season steel belted radial white lettered: $240. 31 x 10.50R/15LTB on-off road steel belted radial blackwall (available only if N67, N90 or PA6 wheels are specified): $564. 31 x 10.50R/15LTB (available only if N67, N90 or PA6 wheels are specified): $720. Pre-cleaner air cleaner (RPO K46): $42. Air conditioning (not available with Cold Climate Package): $740. Deluxe Front Appearance (RPO V22). Includes dark argent grille with bright trim and dual rectangular headlights): $109. Heavy-duty battery (RPO UA1): $53. Deluxe chromed front and rear bumpers (RPO VE5): $49. Chromed front bumper guards (RPO V31): $41. Quartz electric clock (RPO U35). Not available with UM6 radio: $79 (without YE9. Includes Z53 gauge package). With YE9: $39. Cold Climate Package (RPO V10). Includes special insulation, special heater and defroster, engine block heater, anti-freeze protection to -31 degrees, heavy-duty battery. $188 (without Trailering Special Package. Also includes 66 amp generator). With Trailering Special Package: $126. Engine oil cooling system (RPO KC4): $120. Heavy-duty radiator (RPO VO1): $53. Heavy-duty radiator and transmission oil cooler (RPO VO2): $59. Power door locks (RPO AU3): $135. Color-keyed front floor mats (RPO B32): $15. Gauge Package (RPO Z54). Includes voltmeter, engine coolant temperature and oil pressure gauges: $40. 66 amp generator (RPO K81): $62. Deep tinted glass (RPO AJ1). Includes dark laminated glass on side windows and rear tailgate glass: $194. Deep tinted glass with light tinted rear window (RPO AA3). Includes tinted glass on rear tailgate glass, passenger and driver's side door and dark laminated glass on side windows: $140. Heavy-duty, 7-lead wiring harness (RPO UY7): $44. Halogen high-beam headlights (RPO TT5). Available only when V22 or YE9 was ordered: $17. Headlight warning buzzer (RPO T63): $11. Interior headliner (RPO BB5): $80. 600 watt engine block heater (RPO KO5). Not available for diesel engine: $31. Heavy-duty front heater (RPO C42). Available only with diesel engine: $43. Automatic locking hubs (RPO X6Z): $40. Cigarette lighter (RPO U37): $30. Painted exterior below eye-level mirrors (RPO D44): $50. Stainless steel exterior below eye-level mirrors (RPO D45): $83. Black body side molding (RPO B84). Includes lower side and rear moldings of black plastic with bright trim: $115. Bright body side molding (RPO B85). Includes bright plastic body side and rear lower moldings with black paint trim, plus bright trim for front side marker lamps and taillights, fender, door, rear side panel and tailgate moldings: $144. Custom Molding Package (RPO YG1). Includes B84 black body side moldings, wheel opening moldings and bright trim for front side marker lights and taillight trim. Included with ZY3 or ZY5 Packages: $157. Deluxe Molding Package (RPO YG3). Includes bright trim for front side marker lamps and taillight trim wheel opening molding and B85 bright body side moldings: $173 (without ZY3 or ZY5). With ZY3 or ZY5: $16. Door edge guards (RPO B93): $17. Operating Convenience Package (RPO ZQ2). Includes power door locks and power windows: $325. AM radio (RPO U63): $112. AM/FM radio (RPO U69): $171. AM/FM stereo radio (RPO U58), available only with YE9: $198. AM/FM electronically tuned stereo radio with Seek-Scan, stereo cassette tape player and clock: $419. Windshield antenna (RPO U76), included with radio: $32. Rear seat (RPO AM7). With Custom trim: $369. Without Custom trim: $341. Fuel tank shield (RPO NY1): $164. Front quad shock absorbers (RPO Z75). Includes dual left and right hand shock absorbers on front axle, heavy-duty shock absorbers on rear axle and a front axle nose bumper to limit axle windup: $128. Electronic speed control (RPO K34): $195. Front heavy-duty 2250 lb. capacity springs with heavy-duty front and rear shock absorbers. Recommended for snowplow-type usage only: $92 (with ZY5). Without Z75: $59. ComforTilt steering wheel (RPO N33): $115. 31 gal. replacement fuel tank (RPO NK7): $43. Two front towing hooks (RPO V76): $36. Deadweight type trailer hitch (RPO VR2). Not available with Z82: $58. Weight distributing platform trailer hitch (RPO VR4). Included with Z82: $155. Trailering Special Equipment (RPO Z82). Available only with 3.24 or 3.73:1 rear axle ratio and MXO automatic transmission when ordered. Not available with 5.7 liter LS9 engine. Includes VR4, UY7 and V02 options: $440. With B3J diesel equipment: $258. With C80 air conditioning: $378. Bright metal wheelcovers (RPO P01): $40. Rallye 15 x 8 wheels (RPO N67). Not available with P215 tires: $115. Styled 15 x 8 wheels (RPO PA6). Not available with P215 tires: $174. Cast aluminum 15 x 7 wheels with special hubcaps (RPO N90). Not available with P215 tires: $299. Power side door electric windows (RPO A31): $10. Power tailgate electric window (RPO A33): $95. Sliding side quarter windows (RPO AD5). Intermittent windshield wipers (RPO CD4): $55.

HISTORICAL FOOTNOTES: The 1986 Blazer was introduced in the fall of 1985.

1987 BLAZER

All Blazer engines for 1987 had electronic fuel injection. The results included improved cold starting performance, enhanced cold weather operation, better driveability and increased power output. Lighter-weight Delco batteries with increased cranking power were used for the 5.0 and 5.7 liter engine. Blazers with the 5.7 liter V-8 and those with the 5.0 liter V-8 and automatic transmission had batteries with 525 cold cranking amps. The previous rating had been 405. The previously optional 66 amp alternator was now standard. It replaced a 37 amp unit. The heavy-duty battery option now included an increased performance cranking motor on Blazers with the 5.7 liter V-8. The exterior colors for 1987 were carry-over 1986 colors: Midnight black, light blue metallic, midnight blue, Indian bronze metallic, steel gray metallic, apple red, doeskin tan, and frost white.

I.D. DATA: The V.I.N. plate was mounted on the lower left side windshield corner. The V.I.N. consisted of 17 elements. The first, the number 1 identified the U.S. as the nation of origin. The letter G followed, for the manufacturer: General Motors. The third entry, the letter C represented the make as Chevrolet. The GVWR brake system identification followed. Next came the truck line and chassis type; the letter K indicated four-wheel drive. The truck series was identified by a number: 1-1/2 ton. The truck body type identification was next: 8-Utility. The engine code was next, followed by a check digit. The model year was identified by the letter H. The assembly plant code followed. The final six digits were the plant sequential production number.

Model Number	Body Type & Seating	Factory Price	GVW	Shipping Weight	Prod. Total
Blazer V10 Body Code: ZW9 (with 305 V-8)					
CV10516	Util.	$13,066	6100*	4379	—

NOTE 1: 6250 GVW Package available. Its content was unchanged from 1986.

STANDARD ENGINE: All states: Engine Type: Cast iron block. OHV, V-8 with Electronic Spark Control. Ordering Code: L03 Produced by GM-Chevrolet Motor Division and GM of Canada. Bore x Stroke: 3.74 in. x 3.48 in. Lifters: Hydraulic. Number of main bearings-5. Carburetion: Electronic fuel injection. Compression Ratio: 9.3:1. Displacement: 305 cu. in. Horsepower: Net: 170 @ 4400 rpm. Torque: Net: 260 lb.-ft. @ 2400 rpm. Oil capacity: 5 qt. with filter change. Fuel Requirements: Unleaded.

OPTIONAL ENGINE: All states: Engine Type: Cast iron block. OHV, V-8. Ordering Code: L05. Produced by GM-Chevrolet Motor Division. Bore x Stroke: 4.0 in. x 3.48 in. Lifters: Hydraulic. Number of main bearings-5. Carburetion: Electronic fuel injection. Compression Ratio: 9.2:1. Displacement: 350 cu. in. (5.7 liters). Horsepower: Net: 210 @ 4000 rpm. Torque: Net: 300 lb.-ft. @ 2800 rpm. Oil capacity: 5 qt. with filter change. Fuel Requirements: Unleaded.

OPTIONAL ENGINE: Not available for California: Engine Type: OHV, Cast iron block. Diesel V-8. Order Code LH6. Produced by GM-Detroit Diesel Allison Division. Requires B3J Diesel Equipment Package which consists of dual batteries, hydraulic power-assisted brakes, engine block heater, heavy-duty radiator, K81 alternator, engine oil cooler and additional insulation. Bore x Stroke: 3.98 in. x 3.80 in. Lifters: Hydraulic. Number of main bearings-5. Carburetion: Fuel injection. Compression Ratio: 21.5:1. Displacement: 379 cu. in. (6.2 liter). Horsepower: Net: 130 @ 3600 rpm. Torque: Net: 240 lb.-ft. @ 2000 rpm. Oil capacity: 7 qt. with filter change. Fuel Requirements: Diesel.

CHASSIS FEATURES: Ladder-type. Carbon steel, 36,000-39,000 psi. Heavy-gauge channel side members, alligator-jaw cross members. Section modules: 3.14 in.

SUSPENSION AND RUNNING GEAR: Front Suspension: Two tapered semi-elliptical leaf springs. Capacity: Gasoline engines: 1650 lb. Optional Capacity: 2250 lb. Diesel engine: 1850 lb. Optional: 2250 lb. Standard 1.25 in. stabilizer bar and 25mm shock absorbers. Optional: 32mm shock absorbers. Rear Suspension: Two-stage tapered and multi-leaf (six-conventional leaves, one tapered leaf). Capacity: 1875 lb. Optional: None. Front Axle. Type: Hypoid, tubular driving. Capacity: 3600 lb. Rear Axle. Type: Hypoid, semi-floating. Capacity: 3750 lb. Final Drive Ratio: 305 V-8: 3.08:1; 350 V-8: 3.42:1; diesel engine: 3.73:1. Optional: Gasoline engines: 3.73:1; diesel engine: 3.42, 3.73:1. Transfer Case: Type: New Process 208. Ratios: 2.61, 1.00:1. Brakes: Type: Hydraulic, self-adjusting. Front: Discs. Rear: Drums. Optional: Power. Dimensions: Front: 11.86 in. dia. rotor. Rear: 11.15 in. x 2.75 in. Wheels: 6-stud, 15 x 6JJ. Optional: 15 x 7JJ Rallye, 15 x 8JJ, 15 x 8JJ Rallye, 16 x 5K. Tires: P215/75R15 steel belted radial. Optional: P215/75R15 steel belted radial whitewall, P235/75R15 steel belted radial, P235/75R15 steel belted radial whitewall, p235/75R15 white lettered steel belted radial, 10R-15B steel belted radial, 10R-15B white lettered steel belted radial. Steering: Power assisted recirculating ball, variable ratio. Ratio: 17.6/13.1. Turns Lock-to-Lock: 4.0. Turning Circle: 37.6 ft. Optional: None. Transmission: Gasoline engines: Muncie 4-speed manual, synchromesh on top three gears, floor-mounted shift lever. Ratios: 6.55, 3.58, 1.70, 1.00:1 Not available in California. Standard: Diesel, optional gasoline engines: 700R4 4-speed automatic with overdrive. Ratios: 3.06, 1.36, 1.00, 0.70:1. Reverse: 2.29:1. Clutch: 11.0 in. dia., 124 sq. in. area. 12 in. clutch included with 350 V-8 engines).

VEHICLE DIMENSIONS: Wheelbase: 106.5 in. Overall Length: 184.8 in. Front/Rear Tread 66.10 in./63.00 in. Overall Height: 73.4 in. Width: 79.6 in. Tailgate: Width and Height: 66.8 in. x 22.0 in. Approach/Departure Degrees: 34/25. Ground Clearance: Front axle: 7.4 in. Rear axle: 7.0 in. Oil pan: 17.2 in. Transfer case: 11.5 in. Fuel tank: 14.0 in. Load space: With rear seat installed: 38.8 in. x 50 in. x 42.3 in. With rear seat removed or folded: 76.0 in. x 50 in. x 42.3 in.

CAPACITIES: Fuel Tank: 25.0 gal. Optional: Replacement 31 gal. tank. Coolant system: 305 V-8: 17.6 qt. 350 V-8: 17.6 qt.

ACCOMMODATIONS: Seating Capacity: Standard: Driver and passenger front high-back bucket sets. Optional: 3 passenger rear bench seat. Headroom: 38.3 in. Maximum steering wheel to seat back: 18.5 in. Seat to ground: 36.3 in. Floor to ground: 21.9 in.

INSTRUMENTATION: 0-100 mph speedometer, 99,999.9 mi. odometer, fuel gauge, warning lights for alternator, oil pressure, engine coolant temperature, brake operating system, hazard warning lights, directional lights, seat belt warning.

OPTIONS AND PRICES: Silverado Package (RPO YE9): $1073. Includes either Custom cloth or Custom vinyl seats, Custom steering wheel, Deluxe Molding Package, taillight and rear door or tailgate moldings, bright front turn signal and front side marker lamp bezels, fender nameplates, bright windshield and side rear window moldings, color-keyed carpeting with bright sill plates, plastic door trim panels with storage pockets, and bright brushed finish accents, visor vanity mirror, Deluxe Front Appearance Package, dual horns, nameplate on instrument panel, cigarette lighter, headliner, wheel opening moldings, special insulation, bright body side moldings, pillar trim panels, storage console between front seats, floor and wheelwell carpeting, spare tire cover and voltmeter, engine coolant temperature and oil pressure gauges. Custom vinyl bucket seats Custom vinyl seats. Special two-tone paint. Includes Custom Molding Package and wheel opening moldings. Exterior Decor. Includes hood ornament. California emission systems (RPO YF5). 5.7 liter V-8. 4-speed with overdrive automatic transmission (standard on B3J diesel). Optional axle ratio. Locking rear differential (RPO G80). P215/75R15 All-Season steel belted radial blackwall. P215/75R15 highway steel belted radial blackwall. P235/75R15 highway steel belted radial whitewall. P235/75R15 highway steel belted radial white lettered. P235/75R15 All-Season steel belted radial blackwall. P235/75R15 on-off road steel belted radial blackwall. P235/75R15 All-Season steel belted radial whitewall. P235/75R15 All-Season steel belted radial white lettered 31 x 10.50R/15LTB on-off road steel belted radial blackwall. 31 x 10.50R/15LTB (available only if N67, N90 or PA6 wheels are specified). Pre-cleaner air cleaner (RPO K46). Air conditioning (not available with Cold Climate Package). Deluxe Front Appearance (RPO V22). Includes dark argent grille with bright trim and dual rectangular headlights). Heavy-duty battery (RPO UA1). Deluxe chromed front and rear bumpers (RPO VE5). Chromed front bumper guards (RPO V31). Quartz electric clock (RPO U35). Not available with UM6 radio. Includes Z53 gauge package). Cold Climate Package (RPO V10). Includes special insulation, special heater and defroster, engine block heater, anti-freeze protection to -31 degrees, heavy-duty battery. Engine oil cooling system (RPO KC4). Heavy-duty radiator (RPO VO1). Heavy-duty radiator and transmission oil cooler (RPO VO2). Power door locks (RPO AU3). Color-keyed front floor mats (RPO B32). Gauge Package (RPO Z54). Includes voltmeter, engine coolant temperature and oil pressure gauges. 66 amp generator (RPO K81). Deep tinted glass (RPO AJ1). Includes dark laminated glass on side windows and rear tailgate glass. Deep tinted glass with light tinted rear window (RPO AA3). Includes tinted glass on rear tailgate glass, passenger and driver's side door and dark laminated glass on side windows. Heavy-duty, 7-lead wiring harness (RPO UY7). Halogen high-beam headlights (RPO TT5). Available only with V22 or when YE9 was ordered. Headlight warning buzzer (RPO T63). Interior headliner (RPO BB5). 600 watt engine block heater (RPO KO5). Not available for diesel engine. Heavy-duty front heater (RPO C42). Available only with diesel engine. Automatic locking hubs (RPO X6Z). Cigarette lighter (RPO U37). Painted exterior below eye-level mirrors (RPO D44). Stainless steel exterior below eye-level mirrors (RPO D45). Black body side molding (RPO B84). Includes lower side and rear moldings of black plastic with bright trim. Bright body side molding (RPO B85). Includes bright plastic body side and rear lower moldings with black paint trim, plus bright trim for front side marker lamps and taillights, fender, door, rear side panel and tailgate moldings. Custom Molding Package (RPO YG1). Includes B84 black body side moldings, wheel opening moldings and bright trim for front side marker lights and taillight trim. Included with ZY3 or ZY5 packages. Deluxe Molding Package (RPO YG3). Includes bright trim for front side marker lamps and taillight trim wheel opening molding and B85 bright body side moldings. Door edge guards (RPO B93). Operating Convenience Package (RPO ZQ2). Includes power door locks and power windows. AM radio (RPO U63). AM/FM radio (RPO U69). AM/FM stereo radio (RPO U58), available only with YE9. AM/FM electronically tuned stereo radio with Seek-Scan, stereo cassette tape player and clock. Windshield antenna (RPO U76), included with radio. Rear seat (RPO AM7). Fuel tank shield (RPO NY1). Front quad shock absorbers (RPO Z75). Includes dual left and right hand shock absorbers on front axle, heavy-duty shock absorbers on rear axle and a front axle note bumper to limit axle windup. Electronic speed control (RPO K34). Front heavy-duty 2250 lb. capacity springs with heavy-duty front and rear shock absorbers. Recommended for snowplow-type usage only. ComforTilt steering wheel (RPO N33). 31 gal. replacement fuel tank (RPO NK7). Two front towing hooks (RPO V76). Deadweight type trailer hitch (RPO VR2). Not available with Z82. Weight distributing platform trailer hitch (RPO VR4). Included with Z82. Trailering special equipment (RPO Z82). Available only with 3.24 or 3.73:1 rear axle ratio and MXO automatic transmission when ordered. Not available with 5.7 liter LS9 engine. Includes VR4, UY7 and V02 options. Bright metal wheelcovers (RPO P01): $40. Rallye 15 x 8 wheels (RPO N67). Not available with P215 tires. Styled 15 x 8 wheels (RPO PS6). Not available with P215 tires. Cast aluminum 15 x 7 wheels with special hubcaps (RPO A31). Power tailgate electric window (RPO A33). Sliding side quarter windows (RPO AD5). Intermittent windshield wipers (RPO CD4).

HISTORICAL FOOTNOTES: The use of fuel injection for all Blazer engines was an historic first for Chevrolet.

1988 BLAZER

The 1988 Blazer was offered with either the standard 5.7 liter electronic fuel injected V-8 or the 6.2 liter diesel, also with electronic fuel injection. Four new colors were introduced for 1988: Bright blue metallic, forest green metallic, light Mesa brown metallic and dark Mesa brown metallic. New features for 1988 include a fixed mast antenna in place of the old windshield antenna, a trip odometer as part of the gauge package cluster and an improved pulse windshield wiper control. Helping to reduce air leaks in the Blazer doors was a new door handle seal. Brake noise was lowered due to new front lining noise insulators. The Blazer's fuel tank corrosion was upgraded to be more tolerant of methanol fuel.

1988 Chevrolet Blazer

I.D. DATA: The V.I.N. plate was mounted on the lower left side windshield corner. The V.I.N. consisted of 17 elements. The first, the number 1 identified the U.S. as the nation of origin. The letter G followed, for the manufacturer: General Motors. The third entry, the letter C represented the make as Chevrolet. The GVWR brake system identification followed. Next came the truck line and chassis type; the letter K indicated four-wheel drive. The truck series was identified by a number: 1-1/2 ton. The truck body type identification was next: 8-Utility. The engine code was next, followed by a check digit. The model year was identified by the letter J. The assembly plant code followed. The final six digits were the plant sequential production number.

Model Number	Body Type & Seating	Factory Price	GVW	Shipping Weight	Prod. Total
Blazer V10 Body Code: ZW9 (with 350 V-8)					
CV10516	Util.	$14,509	6100*	4676	26,314

NOTE 1: 6250 GVW Package available. Its content was unchanged from 1987.

STANDARD ENGINE: All states: Engine Type: Cast iron block. OHV, V-8. Ordering Code: L05. Produced by GM-Chevrolet Motor Division. Bore x Stroke: 4.0 in. x 3.48 in. Lifters: Hydraulic. Number of main bearings-5. Carburetion: Electronic fuel injection. Compression Ratio: 9.2:1. Displacement: 350 cu. in. (5.7 liters). Horsepower: Net: 210 @ 4000 rpm. Torque: Net: 300 lb.-ft. @ 2800 rpm. Oil capacity: 5 qt. with filter change. Fuel Requirements: Unleaded.

OPTIONAL ENGINE: Engine Type: OHV, Cast iron block. Diesel V-8. Order Code LH6. Produced by GM-Detroit Diesel Allison Division. Requires B3J Diesel Equipment Package which consists of dual batteries, hydraulic power-assisted brakes, engine block heater, heavy-duty radiator, K81 alternator, engine oil cooler and additional insulation. Bore x Stroke: 3.98 in. x 3.80 in. Lifters: Hydraulic. Number of main bearings-5. Carburetion: Fuel injection. Compression Ratio: 21.5:1. Displacement: 379 cu. in. (6.2 liter). Horsepower: Net: 130 @ 3600 rpm. Torque: Net: 240 lb.-ft. @ 2000 rpm. Oil capacity: 7 qt. with filter change. Fuel Requirements: Diesel.

CHASSIS FEATURES: Ladder-type. Carbon steel, 36,000-39,000 psi. Heavy-gauge channel side members, alligator-jaw cross members. Section modules: 3.14 in.

SUSPENSION AND RUNNING GEAR: Front Suspension: Two tapered semi-elliptical leaf springs. Capacity: Gasoline engines: 1650 lb. Optional Capacity: 2250 lb. Diesel engine: 1850 lb. Optional: 2250 lb. Standard 1.25 in. stabilizer bar and 25mm shock absorbers. Optional: 32mm shock absorbers. Rear Suspension: Two-stage tapered and multi-leaf (six-conventional leaves, one tapered leaf). Capacity: 1875 lb. Optional: None. Front Axle. Type: Hypoid, tubular driving. Capacity: 3600 lb. Rear Axle. Type: Hypoid, semi-floating. Capacity: 3750 lb. Final Drive Ratio: 305 V-8: 3.08:1; 350 V-8: 3.42:1; diesel engine: 3.73:1. Optional: Gasoline engines: 3.73:1; diesel engine: 3.42, 3.73:1. Transfer Case: Type: New Process 208. Ratios: 2.61, 1.00:1. Brakes: Type: Hydraulic, self-adjusting. Front: Discs. Rear: Drums. Optional: Power. Dimensions: Front: 11.86 in. dia. rotor. Rear: 11.15 in. x 2.75 in. Wheels: 6-stud, 15 x 6JJ. Optional: 15 x 7JJ Rallye, 15 x 8JJ, 15 x 8JJ Rallye, 16 x 5K. Tires: P215/75R15 steel belted radial. Optional: P215/75R15 steel belted radial whitewall, P235/75R15 steel belted radial, P235/75R15 steel belted radial whitewall, p235/75R15 white lettered steel belted radial, 10R-15B steel belted radial, 10R-15B white lettered steel belted radial. Steering: Power assisted recirculating ball, variable ratio. Ratio: 17.6/13.1. Turns Lock-to-Lock: 4.0. Turning Circle: 37.6 ft. Optional: None. Transmission: Type: SM465, RPO MM4. 4-speed manual, fully synchronized. Floor-mounted shifter. Standard transmission with diesel V-8: 4-speed automatic overdrive. Optional (gasoline engined models, and models with California emissions): 4-speed automatic overdrive. Transmission Ratios: SM465. Synchromesh on top three gears, floor-mounted shift lever. Ratios: 6.55, 3.58, 1.70, 1.00:1. Reverse: 6.09:1. 700R4 Automatic: 3.06, 1.63, 1.00, 0.70. Reverse: 2.29:1. Clutch: 12.0 in. dia.

VEHICLE DIMENSIONS: Wheelbase: 106.5 in. Overall Length: 184.8 in. Front/Rear Tread 66.10 in./63.00 in. Overall Height: 73.4 in. Width: 79.6 in. Tailgate: Width and Height: 66.8 in. x 22.0 in. Approach/Departure Degrees: 34/25. Ground Clearance: Front axle: 7.4 in. Rear axle: 7.0 in. Oil pan: 17.2 in. Transfer case: 11.5 in. Fuel tank: 14.0 in. Load space: With rear seat installed: 38.8 in. x 50 in. x 42.3 in. With rear seat removed or folded: 76.0 in. x 50 in. x 42.3 in.

CAPACITIES: Fuel Tank: 25.0 gal. Optional: Replacement 31 gal. tank. Coolant system: 305 V-8: 17.6 qt. 350 V-8: 17.6 qt.

ACCOMMODATIONS: Seating Capacity: Standard: Driver and passenger front high-back bucket seats. Optional: 3 passenger rear bench seat. Headroom: 38.3 in. Maximum steering wheel to seat back: 18.5 in. Seat to ground: 36.3 in. Floor to ground: 21.9 in.

INSTRUMENTATION: 0-100 mph speedometer, 99,999.9 mi. odometer, fuel gauge, warning lights for alternator, oil pressure, engine coolant temperature, brake operating system, hazard warning lights, directional lights, seat belt warning.

OPTIONS AND PRICES: Silverado Package (RPO YE9): $1249. Includes either Custom cloth or Custom vinyl seats, Custom steering wheel, Deluxe Molding Package, taillight and rear door or tailgate moldings, bright front turn signal and front side marker lamp bezels, fender nameplates, bright windshield and side rear window moldings, color-keyed carpeting with bright sill plates, plastic door trim panels with storage pockets, and bright brushed finish accents, visor vanity mirror, Deluxe Front Appearance Package, dual horns, nameplate on instrument panel, cigarette lighter, headliner, wheel opening moldings, special insulation, bright body side moldings, pillar trim panels, storage console between front seats, floor and wheelwell carpeting, spare tire cover and voltmeter, engine coolant temperature and oil pressure gauges. Custom vinyl bucket seats. Custom vinyl seats. Special two-tone paint. Includes Custom Molding Package and wheel opening moldings. Exterior Decor. Includes hood ornament. California emission systems (RPO YF5). 5.7 liter V-8. 4-speed with overdrive automatic transmission (standard on B3J diesel). Optional axle ratio. Locking rear differential (RPO G80). P215/75R15 All-Season steel belted radial blackwall. P215/75R15 highway steel belted radial blackwall. P235/75R15 highway steel belted radial whitewall. P235/75R15 highway steel belted radial white lettered. P235/75R15 All-Season steel belted radial blackwall. P235/75R15 on-off road steel belted radial blackwall. P235/75R15 All-Season steel belted radial whitewall. P235/75R15 All-Season steel belted radial white lettered 31 x 10.50R/15LTB on-off road steel belted radial blackwall. 31 x 10.50R/15LTB (available only if N67, N90 or PA6 wheels are specified). Pre-cleaner air cleaner (RPO K46). Air conditioning (not available with Cold Climate Package). Deluxe Front Appearance (RPO V22). Includes dark argent grille with bright trim and dual rectangular headlights). Heavy-duty battery (RPO UA1). Deluxe chromed front and rear bumpers (RPO VE5). Chromed front bumper guards (RPO V31). Quartz electric clock (RPO U35). Not available with UM6 radio. Includes Z53 gauge package). Cold Climate Package (RPO V10). Includes special insulation, special heater and defroster, engine block heater, anti-freeze protection to -31 degrees, heavy-duty battery. Engine oil cooling system (RPO KC4). Heavy-duty radiator (RPO VO1). Heavy-duty radiator and transmission oil cooler (RPO VO2). Power door locks (RPO AU3). Color-keyed front floor mats (RPO B32). Gauge Package (RPO Z54). Includes voltmeter, engine coolant temperature and oil pressure gauges. 66 amp generator (RPO K81). Deep tinted glass (RPO AJ1). Includes dark laminated glass on side windows and rear tailgate glass. Deep tinted glass with light tinted rear window (RPO AA3). Includes tinted glass on rear tailgate glass, passenger and driver's side door and dark laminated glass on side windows. Heavy-duty, 7-lead wiring harness (RPO UY7). Halogen high-beam headlights (RPO TT5). Available only with V22 or when YE9 was ordered. Headlight warning buzzer (RPO T63). Interior headliner (RPO BB5). 600 watt engine block heater (RPO KO5). Not available for diesel engine. Heavy-duty front heater (RPO C42). Available only with diesel engine. Automatic locking hubs (RPO X6Z). Cigarette lighter (RPO U37). Painted exterior below eye-level mirrors (RPO D44). Stainless steel exterior below eye-level mirrors (RPO D45). Black body side molding (RPO B84). Includes lower side and rear moldings of black plastic with bright trim. Bright body side molding (RPO B85). Includes bright plastic body side and rear lower moldings with black paint trim, plus bright trim for front sidemarker lamps and taillights, fender, door, rear side panel and tailgate moldings. Custom Molding Package (RP0 YG1). Includes B84 black body side moldings, wheel opening moldings and bright trim for front side marker lights and taillight trim. Included with ZY3 or ZY5 packages. Deluxe Molding Package (RPO YG3). Includes bright trim for front side marker lamps and taillight trim wheel opening molding and B85 bright body side moldings. Door edge guards (RPO B93). Operating Convenience Package (RPO ZQ2). Includes power door locks and power windows. AM radio (RPO U63). AM/FM radio (RPO U69). AM/FM stereo radio (RPO U58), available only with YE9. AM/FM electronically tuned stereo radio with Seek-Scan, stereo cassette tape player and clock. Windshield antenna (RPO U76), included with radio. Rear seat (RPO AM7). Fuel tank shield (RPO NY1). Front quad shock absorbers (RPO Z75). Includes dual left and right hand shock absorbers on front axle, heavy-duty shock absorbers on rear axle and a front axle nose bumper to limit axle windup. Electronic speed control (RPO K34). Front heavy-duty 2250 lb. capacity springs with heavy-duty front and rear shock absorbers. Recommended for snowplow-type usage only. ComforTilt steering wheel (RPO N33). 31 gal. replacement fuel tank (RPO NK7). Two front towing hooks (RPO V76). Deadweight type trailer hitch (RPO VR2). Not available with Z82. Weight distributing platform trailer hitch (RPO VR4). Included with Z82. Trailer special equipment (RPO Z82). Available only with 3.24 or 3.73:1 rear axle ratio and MXO automatic transmission when ordered. Not available with 5.7 liter LS9 engine. Includes VR4, UY7 and V02 options. Bright metal wheelcovers (RPO P01): $40. Rallye 15 x 8 wheels (RPO N67). Not available with P215 tires. Styled 15 x 8 wheels (RPO PA6). Not available with P215 tires. Cast aluminum 15 x 7 wheels with special hubcaps (RPO N90). Not available with P215 tires. Power side door electric windows (RPO A31). Power tailgate electric window (RPO A33). Sliding side quarter windows (RPO AD5). Intermittent windshield wipers (RPO CD4).

HISTORICAL FOOTNOTES: At the start of 1988, Chevrolet had 4,910 dealers who sold Chevrolet trucks.

1989 BLAZER

The 1989 Blazer had both a new base and uplevel grille as well as new headlight bezels. The Blazer's body nameplate and emblems were identical to those used on the four-wheel drive K series pickups. Also shared with the K models were the Blazer's new body side moldings and bumper rub strips. The Blazer exterior had a new "wet-look" shine that was credited to the replacement of the older high solid enamel paint with an all-new base coat/clear coat paint. Ten solid colors were offered: Onyx black, smoke blue metallic, Mojave beige, sunset gold metallic, wintergreen metallic, summit white, fire red, gray metallic, quicksilver metallic and midnight blue metallic. In addition, the Blazer could be ordered in 114 different two-tone combinations with new colors breaks for 1989. The Blazer's new styling was enhanced by its new body-color side door drip moldings and newly styled full wheelcovers. Other changes for 1989 included new black below eye-level mirrors, standard sun visors on the Silverado that were color-keyed and fitted with plastic extenders. The driver's side visor had a map strap and the passenger's side had a lighted vanity mirror. Vehicle corrosion protection was upgraded by extending the use of additional body and front end metal components with two-sided galvanized coatings. Ride characteristics of the Blazer were improved by adding five new spring assemblies and 16 new front and rear shock absorber assemblies. The LO5 5.7 liter V-8 now had serpentine accessory drive belts in place of the older multi-belt accessory drive. New combination lap/shoulder belts were now standard for the Blazer. The auxiliary lighting package now included a glove box light and an underhood reel lamp. The new series of Delco 2000 electronic tuned radios were offered for the Blazer. Standard Blazer trim was Scottsdale. Optional was Silverado. Standard equipment for the Blazer consisted of the following chassis items: Dual electric high-note and low-tone horns, front stabilizer bar, 2-speed transfer case and manual-locking front hubs, and power steering and brakes. Standard exterior features included front and rear chromed bumpers, molded plastic grille and front lamp bezels painted light and dark argent, bright metal hubcaps with black trim, argent painted wheels, All-Season steel belted radial tires, full-size spare and wheel, tool kit (includes mechanical jack and wheel wrench), Scottsdale nameplates, black below eye-level exterior mirrors and roll-down rear tailgate glass window.

The standard Scottsdale interior consisted of right and left side padded armrests, high-back front bucket seats with Custom vinyl pigskin-grained trim in any of four colors: Dark blue, burgundy, saddle or slate gray; easy rear entry passenger seat front sliding mechanism, two coat hooks on left side, full-length bright sill plates at front doors and rear of rear compartment floor, map light, two dome lamps with door-operated switches, floor covering of embossed black rubber mats in front and rear, insulation on dash panel, floor panel and between double-wall cab roof, tinted glass on all windows, padded, color-keyed left and right side sunshades, gauges for fuel level, voltmeter, oil pressure and engine pressure, trip odometer, heavy-duty heater and defogger, AM radio with fixed mast antenna, 2-spoke steering wheel and anti-theft locking feature on steering column, 10 in. rearview mirror, color-keyed, molded plastic door trim panels, cigarette lighter with ashtray illumination and spare tire carrier on right hand rear panel.

Chevrolet described the RPO YE9 Silverado trim level as "designed to offer buyers an increased level of comfort and convenience features compared to the standard Scottsdale level."

1989 Chevrolet Blazer

I.D. DATA: The V.I.N. plate was mounted on the lower left side windshield corner. The V.I.N. consisted of 17 elements. The first, the number 1 identified the U.S. as the nation of origin. The letter G followed, for the manufacturer: General Motors. The third entry, the letter C represented the make as Chevrolet. The GVWR brake system identification followed. Next came the truck line and chassis type; the letter K indicated four-wheel drive. The truck series was identified by a number: 1-1/2 ton. The truck body type identification was next: 8-Utility. The engine code was next, followed by a check digit. The model year was identified by the letter K. The assembly plant code followed. The final six digits were the plant sequential production number.

Model Number	Body Type & Seating	Factory Price	GVW	Shipping Weight	Prod. Total
Blazer V10 Body Code: ZW9 (with 350 V-8)					
CV10516	Util.	$15,355	6100	4797	—
CV10516	(w/Diesel V-8)	$18,088	6250	N.A.	—

STANDARD ENGINE: All states: Engine Type: Cast iron block. OHV, V-8. Ordering Code: L05. Produced by GM-Chevrolet Motor Division. Bore x Stroke: 4.0 in. x 3.48 in. Lifters: Hydraulic. Number of main bearings-5. Carburetion: Electronic fuel injection. Compression Ratio: 9.2:1. Displacement: 350 cu. in. (5.7 liters). Horsepower: Net: 210 @ 4000 rpm. Torque: Net: 300 lb.-ft. @ 2800 rpm. Oil capacity: 5 qt. with filter change. Fuel Requirements: Unleaded.

OPTIONAL ENGINE: Not available for California: Engine Type: OHV, Cast iron block. Diesel V-8. Order Code LH6. Produced by GM-Detroit Diesel Allison Division. Requires B3J Diesel Equipment Package which consists of dual batteries, hydraulic power-assisted brakes, engine block heater, heavy-duty radiator, K81 alternator, engine oil cooler and additional insulation. Bore x Stroke: 3.98 in. x 3.80 in. Lifters: Hydraulic. Number of main bearings-5. Carburetion: Fuel injection. Compression Ratio: 21.5:1. Displacement: 379 cu. in. (6.2 liter). Horsepower: Net: 130 @ 3600 rpm. Torque: Net: 240 lb.-ft. @ 2000 rpm. Oil capacity: 7 qt. with filter change. Fuel Requirements: Diesel.

CHASSIS FEATURES: Ladder-type. Carbon steel, 36,000-39,000 psi. Heavy-gauge channel side members, alligator-jaw cross members. Section modules: 3.14 in.

SUSPENSION AND RUNNING GEAR: Front Suspension: Two tapered semi-elliptical leaf springs. Capacity: Gasoline engines: 1650 lb. Optional Capacity: 2250 lb. Diesel engine: 1850 lb. Optional: 2250 lb. Standard 1.25 in. stabilizer bar and 25mm shock absorbers. Optional: 32mm shock absorbers. Rear Suspension: Two-stage tapered and multi-leaf (six-conventional leaves, one tapered leaf). Capacity: 1875 lb. Optional: None. Front Axle. Type: Hypoid, tubular driving. Capacity: 3600 lb. Rear Axle. Type: Hypoid, semi-floating. Capacity: 3750 lb. Final Drive Ratio: 350 V-8: 3.42:1; diesel engine: 3.73:1. Optional: Gasoline engines: 3.73:1; diesel engine: 3.42, 3.73:1. Transfer Case: Type: New Process 208. Ratios: 2.61, 1.00:1. Brakes: Type: Hydraulic, self-adjusting. Front: Discs. Rear: Drums. Optional: Power. Dimensions: Front: 11.86 in. dia. rotor. Rear: 11.15 in. x 2.75 in. Wheels: 6-stud, 15 x 6JJ. Optional: 15 x 7JJ Rallye, 15 x 8JJ, 15 x 8JJ Rallye, 16 x 5K. Tires: P215/75R15 steel belted radial. Optional: P215/75R15 steel belted radial whitewall, P235/75R15 steel belted radial, P235/75R15 steel belted radial whitewall, P235/75R15 white lettered steel belted radial, 10R-15B steel belted radial, 10R-15B white lettered steel belted radial. Steering: Power assisted recirculating ball, variable ratio. Ratio: 17.6/13.1. Turns Lock-to-Lock: 4.0. Turning Circle: 37.6 ft. Optional: None. Transmission: Type: SM465, RPO MM4. 4-speed manual, fully synchronized. Floor-mounted shifter. Standard transmission with diesel V-8: 4-speed automatic overdrive. Optional (gasoline engined models, and models with California emissions): 4-speed automatic overdrive. Transmission Ratios: SM465. Synchromesh on top three gears, floor-mounted shift lever. Ratios: 6.55, 3.58, 1.70, 1.00:1. Reverse: 6.09:1. 700R4 Automatic: 3.06, 1.63, 1.00, 0.70. Reverse: 2.29:1. Clutch: 12.0 in. dia.

VEHICLE DIMENSIONS: Wheelbase: 106.5 in. Overall Length: 184.8 in. Front/Rear Tread 66.10 in./63.00 in. Overall Height: 73.4 in. Width: 79.6 in. Tailgate: Width and Height: 66.8 in. x 22.0 in. Approach/Departure Degrees: 34/25. Ground Clearance: Front axle: 7.4 in. Rear axle: 7.0 in. Oil pan: 17.2 in. Transfer case: 11.5 in. Fuel tank: 14.0 in. Load space: With rear seat installed: 38.8 in. x 50 in. x 42.3 in. With rear seat removed or folded: 76.0 in. x 50 in. x 42.3 in.

CAPACITIES: Fuel Tank: 350 V-8: 31.0 gal. Diesel: 32 gal. Coolant system: 350 V-8: 17.6 qt.

ACCOMMODATIONS: Seating Capacity: Standard: Driver and passenger front high-back bucket sets. Optional: 3 passenger rear bench seat. Headroom: 38.3 in. Maximum steering wheel to seat back: 18.5 in. Seat to ground: 36.3 in. Floor to ground: 21.9 in.

INSTRUMENTATION: 0-100 mph speedometer, 99,999.9 mi. odometer, fuel gauge, warning lights for alternator, oil pressure, engine coolant temperature, brake operating system, hazard warning lights, directional lights, seat belt warning.

OPTIONS AND PRICES: Silverado Package (RPO YE9): $1340. Exterior features in addition to, or in place of Scottsdale items consisted of front and rear chromed bumpers with black rub stripes (front rub strip has bright trim), Silverado nameplates, molded plastic grille and front lamp bezels painted dark argent with chrome trim, rectangular dual halogen headlamps, body side and rear black moldings with bright trim, bright wheel opening moldings, bright metal wheelcovers, cab-to-fender and hood insulators, underhood reel-type lamp and electric power rear tailgate window and bright applique. The Silverado interior had, in addition to, or in place of the standard items the following: High-back reclining front bucket seats with choice of Custom vinyl pigskin-grained trim (available in either dark blue or saddle) or textured velour Custom cloth trim (in a choice of dark blue, burgundy, saddle or slate gray), right side front and left and right side rear assist straps, glove box light, floor covering of color-keyed front compartment carpeting (matching rear compartment floor covering including wheelhousings, was also provided with optional rear seat), insulation on dash panel, between double-wall cab roof, on floor panel (extras thick at front, extra-thick at rear when rear seat was ordered), under cowl panel, on headliner and on body side trim panels, extra insulation on diesel engine models, sunshades with flexible outboard ends and sliding extenders at inboard ends, storage strap on left side sunshade, illuminated mirror on right sunshade, brushed pewter-toned instrument panel trim, 4-spoke Sport steering wheel with simulated stitched leather appearance, front compartment foam-backed cloth headliner with matching retainer moldings, special door trim panels, including door closing assist strips, decorative inserts, map pockets and carpet trim, rear sidewall trim panels with ashtrays and carpet trim, cigarette lighter with ashtray illumination, black vinyl spare tire cover, headlight warning buzzer, and color-keyed molded plastic console with storage and beverage pockets. Air cleaner pre-cleaner (RPO K46): $44. Air conditioning (RPO C60): $781 (without B3J); $719 (with B3J). Deluxe front end appearance (RPO V22). Includes dark argent grille with chrome trim and quad halogen headlamps. Included with Silverado: $145. Optional rear axle ratios: $38. Locking rear differential (RPO G80): $252. Heavy-duty Delco Freedom battery with 630 cold cranking amps (RPO UA1), included with V10 Cold Climate Package: $56. Chromed front bumper guards (RPO V31): $43. Cold Climate Package (RPO V10). Includes UA1 battery and KO5 engine block heater: $104. Engine oil cooler (RPO KC4): $126. Heavy-duty radiator (RPO VO1): $56. Heavy-duty radiator and transmission oil cooler (RPO VO2): $63. Front floor mats (RPO B32): $16. Rear floor mats (RPO B33): $22. Deep tinted glass with light tinted rear glass (RPO AA3): $149. Deep tinted glass (RPO AJ1): $205. Wiring harness (RPO UY7): $46. Headlamp warning buzzer (RPO T63): $12. Engine block heater (RPO KO5): $33. Locking front hubs (RPO X6Z): $60. Auxiliary lighting (RPO TR9) Includes glove box and underhood lights: $26. Below eye-level stainless steel exterior mirrors (RPO D45): 35. Deluxe Molding Package (RPO YG3). Includes deluxe front and rear chrome bumpers with rub strips, bright trim for front side marker lights and taillights, bright wheel opening moldings and black body side and rear moldings with bright trim: $234. Operating Convenience Package (RPO ZQ2). Includes power door locks and front door power windows: $344. Conventional two-tone exterior paint (RPO ZY2): $413 (without YE9), $180 (with YE9). Special two-tone exterior paint (RPO ZY3): $464 (without YE9), $450 (with YE9). Deluxe two-tone exterior paint (RPO ZY4): $566 (without YE9), $332 (with YE9). Puncture sealant tires (RPO P42): $230. Electronically tuned AM/FM stereo radio (RPO UU9): $148. Electronically tuned AM/FM stereo radio with Seek-Scan and digital clock (RPO UM7): $208. Electronically tuned AM/FM stereo radio with Seek-Scan, stereo cassette tape player and digital clock (RPO UM6): $329. Electronically tuned AM/FM stereo radio with Seek-Scan, stereo cassette tape player with Search and Repeat, graphic equalizer and digital clock (RPO UX1): $504. Radio delete (RPO UL5): -$77. Fuel tank shield (RPO NY1). Includes protective shield on transfer case: $175. Rear folding 3 passenger seat (AM7): $411. Rear seat not desired (RPO YG4): No charge. Electronic speed control (RPO K34): $205. Heavy-duty 2250 lb. front springs (F60). Includes heavy-duty front and rear shock absorbers. Recommended for front mounted accessory applications only: $62. ComforTilt steering wheel (RPO N33): $121. Two front towing hooks (RPO V76): $38. Deadweight type trailer hitch (RPO VR2): $62. Weight distributing platform type trailer hitch (RPO VR4): $164. Trailering special equipment (RPO Z82). Includes VR4 hitch, UY7 wiring and VO2 trans. oil cooler; without BJ3 includes KC4 engine oil cooler: $398. 4-speed automatic with overdrive (RPO MXO): $795 — no charge with B3J equipment. Wheelcovers (RPO PO1): $42. Rallye wheels (RPO N67): $121 (without YE9), $278 (with YE9). Power electric tailgate window (RPO A33): $103. Sliding rear quarter windows (AD5): $257. Intermittent windshield wipers (RPO CD4): $59.

HISTORICAL FOOTNOTES: The 1989 Blazer had a new-truck warranty which included 6-year/100,000 mile rust-through protection. The Blazer celebrated its 20th anniversary in 1989.

1990 BLAZER

There were no major changes in the Blazer's external appearance for 1990. All Blazers now had a standard rear wheel anti-lock braking system. A new electronic speedometer was also introduced for 1990 along with non-asbestos brake linings. The Blazer body also used two-side galvanized exterior sheet metal. The 5.7 liter V-8 (LO5) engine was upgraded for 1990 with the addition of the following: Improved oil control rings, redesigned rear crankshaft seal, new camshaft sprocket design, non-asbestos intake manifold gasket and heavy-duty intake valves. The 6.2 liter diesel had new horsepower and torque ratings for 1990 but these were due to changes in the horsepower and torque rating methodology and did not affect actual engine performance.

The Blazer benefited from General Motors' efforts to simplify the production ordering and sales of its light-duty trucks. One example of this program was the deproliferation of optional equipment for the Blazer. Many options of 1989 became standard for 1990. Many other items that had proven to be low volume options were eliminated. These consisted of deep tinted glass with light tinted rear window (RPO AA3), pre-cleaner air cleaner (RPO K46), electronically-tuned AM/FM stereo radio with clock (RPO UU9), front bumper guards (RPO V31), puncture proof tires (RPO P42) and the auxiliary battery (RPO TP2). Options that were previously available separately now were combined into packages with other options. Added to the standard Scottsdale package was a power-operated tailgate window, pulse windshield wiper system, headlight warning buzzer and front towhooks. A heavy-duty battery with 630 CCA was also standard on the Scottsdale model. An AM radio (RPO UT5) replaced the RPO U63 version. The full range of Scottsdale exterior features consisted of the following: Front and rear chromed bumpers, Scottsdale nameplates, molded plastic grille and front lamp bezels painted light and dark argent, bright metal hubcaps with black trim, argent painted 15 x 6.0 wheels, four All-Season steel belted radial ply tires, tools, including a mechanical jack and wheel wrench, intermittent windshield wipers, left and right side below eye-level 6.5 in. x 9.0 in. black painted exterior bumpers, power-operated tailgate and front tow hooks.

The standard Scottsdale interior consisted of right and left side padded armrests, high-back front bucket seats with Custom vinyl pigskin-grained trim in any of four colors: Dark blue, garnet, saddle or slate gray; easy rear entry passenger seat front sliding mechanism, two coat hooks on left side, full-length bright sill plates at front doors and rear of rear compartment floor, map light, two dome lamps with door-operated switches, floor covering of embossed black rubber mats in front and rear, insulation on dash panel, floor panel and between double-wall cab roof, tinted glass on all windows, padded, color-keyed left and right side sunshades, gauges for fuel level, voltmeter, oil pressure and engine pressure, trip odometer, heavy-duty heater and defogger, AM radio with fixed mast antenna, 2-spoke steering wheel and anti-theft locking feature on steering column, 10 in. rearview mirror, color-keyed, molded plastic door trim panels, cigarette lighter with ashtray illumination and spare tire carrier on right hand rear panel. Now included in the Silverado option was auxiliary lighting (RPO TR9), Deluxe Front Appearance Package (RPO V22) and a Deluxe Molding Package (RPO YG3). The electronic speed control was now included in the Convenience Package (RPO ZQ3). New options for 1990 were an outside electric mirror (RPO D48), rear seat shoulder belts (RPO AK9) and the Convenience Package (RO ZQ3). The Blazer's exterior colors were carried over from 1989. Garnet replaced burgundy in the Blazer's interior trim color selection.

1990 Chevrolet Blazer Silverado

I.D. DATA: The V.I.N. plate was mounted on the lower left side windshield corner. The V.I.N. consisted of 17 elements. The first, the number 1 identified the U.S. as the nation of origin. The letter G followed, for the manufacturer: General Motors. The third entry, the letter C represented the make as Chevrolet. The GVWR brake system identification followed. Next came the truck line and chassis type; the letter K indicated four-wheel drive. The truck series was identified by a number: 1-1/2 ton. The truck body type identification was next: 8-Utility. The engine code was next, followed by a check digit. The model year was identified by the letter L. The assembly plant code followed. The final six digits were the plant sequential production number.

Model Number	Body Type & Seating	Factory Price	GVW	Shipping Weight	Prod. Total
Blazer V10 Body Code: ZW9 (with 350 V-8)					
CV10516	Util.	$17,035	6100	4797	15,352*
CV10516	(w/Diesel V-8/B3J)	$19,790	6250	N.A.	—

* Production of all models.

STANDARD ENGINE: All states: Engine Type: Cast iron block. OHV, V-8. Ordering Code: L05. Produced by GM-Chevrolet Motor Division. Bore x Stroke: 4.0 in. x 3.48 in. Lifters: Hydraulic. Number of main bearings-5. Carburetion: Electronic fuel injection. Compression Ratio: 9.2:1. Displacement: 350 cu. in. (5.7 liters). Horsepower: Net: 210 @ 4000 rpm. Torque: Net: 300 lb.-ft. @ 2800 rpm. Oil capacity: 5 qt. with filter change. Fuel Requirements: Unleaded.

OPTIONAL ENGINE: Not available for California: Engine Type: OHV, Cast iron block. Diesel V-8. Order Code LH6. Produced by GM-Detroit Diesel Allison Division. Requires B3J Diesel Equipment Package which consists of dual batteries, hydraulic power-assisted brakes, engine block heater, heavy-duty radiator, K81 alternator, engine oil cooler and additional insulation. Bore x Stroke: 3.98 in. x 3.80 in. Lifters: Hydraulic. Number of main bearings-5. Carburetion: Fuel injection. Compression Ratio: 21.5:1. Displacement: 379 cu. in. (6.2 liter). Horsepower: Net: 130 @ 3600 rpm. Torque: Net: 240 lb.-ft. @ 2000 rpm. Oil capacity: 7 qt. with filter change. Fuel Requirements: Diesel.

CHASSIS FEATURES: Ladder-type. Carbon steel, 36,000-39,000 psi. Heavy-gauge channel side members, alligator-jaw cross members. Section modules: 3.14 in.

SUSPENSION AND RUNNING GEAR: Front Suspension: Two tapered semi-elliptical leaf springs. Capacity: Gasoline engines: 1650 lb. Optional Capacity: 2250 lb. Diesel engine: 1850 lb. Optional: 2250 lb. Standard 1.25 in. stabilizer bar and 25mm shock absorbers. Optional: 32mm shock absorbers. Rear Suspension: Two-stage tapered and multi-leaf (six-conventional leaves, one tapered leaf). Capacity: 1875 lb. Optional: None. Front Axle. Type: Hypoid, tubular driving. Capacity: 3600 lb. Rear Axle. Type: Hypoid, semi-floating. Capacity: 3750 lb. Final Drive Ratio: 5.7 liter V-8 with manual 4-spd. trans.: 3.08:1. Optional: 3.42:1. 5.7 liter V-8 with 4-spd. auto. trans.: 2.73:1. Optional: 3.08, 3.42, 3.73[1], [2]. [1]-Requires Z82 Trailering without California emissions. With California emissions requires KC4 engine oil cooler. [2]-Requires Z82 Trailering Special or High Altitude emissions. Final Drive Ratio: 6.2 liter diesel V-8: 3.08:1. Optional: 3, 42, 3.73:1[1]. [1]-Requires Z82 Trailering Special or High Altitude emissions. Transfer Case: Type: New Process 208. Ratios: 2.61, 1.00:1. Brakes: Type: Hydraulic, self-adjusting. Front: Discs. Rear: Drums. Optional: Power. Dimensions: Front: 11.86 in. dia. rotor. Rear: 11.15 in. x 2.75 in. Wheels: 6-stud, 15 x 6.00JJ. Optional: 15 x 7JJ Rallye, 15 x 8JJ, 15 x 8JJ Rallye, 16 x 5K. Tires: P235/75R15 steel belted radial. Optional: P235/75R15 steel belted radial on-off road, P235/75R15 steel belted radial whitewall, P235/75R15 steel belted radial white letters, P235/75R15 steel belted radial whitewall XL (requires N67 or N90 wheels), 31 x 10.50R15B white letters steel belted radial on-off road. Steering: Power assisted recirculating ball, variable ratio. Ratio: 17.6/13.1. Turns Lock-to-Lock: 4.0. Turning Circle: 37.6 ft. Optional: None. Transmission: Type: SM465, RPO MM4. 4-speed manual, fully synchronized. Floor-mounted shifter. Standard transmission with diesel V-8: 4-speed automatic overdrive. Optional (gasoline engined models, and models with California emissions): 4-speed automatic overdrive. Transmission Ratios: SM465. Synchromesh on top three gears, floor-mounted shift lever. Ratios: 6.55, 3.58, 1.70, 1.00:1. Reverse: 6.09:1. 700R4 Automatic: 3.06, 1.63, 1.00, 0.70. Reverse: 2.29. Clutch: 12.0 in. dia.

VEHICLE DIMENSIONS: Wheelbase: 106.5 in. Overall Length: 184.8 in. Front/Rear Tread 66.10 in./63.00 in. Overall Height: 73.4 in. Width: 79.6 in. Tailgate: Width and Height: 66.8 in. x 22.0 in. Approach/Departure Degrees: 34/25. Ground Clearance: Front axle: 7.4 in. Rear axle: 7.0 in. Oil pan: 17.2 in. Transfer case: 11.5 in. Fuel tank: 14.0 in. Load space: With rear seat installed: 38.8 in. x 50 in. x 42.3 in. With rear seat removed or folded: 76.0 in. x 50 in. x 42.3 in.

CAPACITIES: Fuel Tank: 350 V-8: 31.0 gal. Diesel: 32 gal. Coolant system: 350 V-8: 17.6 qt.

ACCOMMODATIONS: Seating Capacity: Standard: Driver and passenger front high-back bucket sets. Optional: 3 passenger rear bench seat. Headroom: 38.3 in. Maximum steering wheel to seat back: 18.5 in. Seat to ground: 36.3 in. Floor to ground: 21.9 in.

INSTRUMENTATION: 0-100 mph speedometer, 99,999.9 mi. odometer, fuel gauge, warning lights for alternator, oil pressure, engine coolant temperature, brake operating system, hazard warning lights, directional lights, seat belt warning.

OPTIONS AND PRICES: Silverado Package (RPO YE9): $1281. Exterior features in addition to, or in place of Scottsdale items consisted of front and rear chromed bumpers with black rub stripes (front rub strip has bright trim), Silverado nameplates, molded plastic grille and front lamp bezels painted dark argent with chrome trim, rectangular dual halogen headlamps, body side and rear black moldings with bright trim, bright wheel opening moldings, bright metal wheelcovers, cab-to-fender and hood insulators, underhood reel-type lamp and electric power rear tailgate window and bright applique. The Silverado interior had, in addition to, or in place of the standard items the following: High-back reclining front bucket seats with choice of Custom vinyl pigskin-grained trim (available in either dark blue, garnet, slate gray or saddle) or textured velour Custom cloth trim (in a choice of dark blue, garnet, saddle or slate gray), right side front and left and right side rear assist straps, glove box light, auxiliary lighting, floor covering of color-keyed front compartment carpeting (matching rear compartment floor covering including wheelhousings, was also provided with optional rear seat), insulation on dash panel, between double-wall cab roof, on floor panel (extra thick at front, extra-thick at rear when rear seat was ordered), under cowl panel, on headliner and on body side trim panels, extra insulation on diesel engine models, sunshades with flexible outboard ends and sliding extenders at inboard ends, storage strap on left side sunshade, illuminated mirror on right sunshade, brushed pewter-toned instrument panel trim, 4-spoke Sport steering wheel with simulated stitched leather appearance, front compartment foam-backed cloth headliner with matching retainer moldings, special door trim panels, including door closing assist strips, decorative inserts, map pockets and carpet trim, rear sidewall trim panels with ashtrays and carpet trim, cigarette lighter with ashtray illumination, black vinyl spare tire cover, and color-keyed molded plastic console with storage and beverage pockets. Air conditioning (RPO C60) $820 (without B3J); $758 (with B3J). Optional rear axle ratios: $38. Locking rear differential (RPO G80): $252. Cold Climate Package (RPO V10). Includes special insulation, special heater and defroster, engine block heater, anti-freeze protection to -32 degrees and heavy-duty battery: $48. Engine oil cooler (RPO KC4): $135 Heavy-duty radiator (RPO VO1): $56. Heavy-duty radiator and transmission oil cooler (RPO VO2): $63. Deep tinted glass (RPO AJ1): $215. Locking front hubs (RPO X6Z): $60. Below eye-level stainless steel exterior mirrors (RPO D45): $40. Operating Convenience Package (RPO ZQ2). Includes power door locks and front door power windows: $344. Operating Convenience Package (RPO ZQ3). Includes tilt wheel and speed control: $346. Conventional two-tone exterior paint (RPO ZY2): $413 (without YE9), $180 (with YE9). Special two-tone exterior paint (RPO ZY3): $464 (without YE9), $450 (with YE9). Deluxe two-tone exterior paint (RPO ZY4): $566 (without YE9), $332 (with YE9). Electronically tuned AM/FM stereo radio with Seek-Scan and digital clock (RPO UM7): $131. Electronically tuned AM/FM stereo radio with Seek-Scan, stereo cassette tape player and digital clock (RPO UM6): $253. Electronically tuned AM/FM stereo radio with Seek-Scan, stereo cassette tape player with Search and Repeat, graphic equalizer and digital clock (RPO UX1): $403. Radio delete (RPO UL5): $95. Fuel tank shield (RPO NY1). Includes protective shield on transfer case: $175. Rear folding 3 passenger seat (AM7): $411 (without shoulder harness), $461 (with shoulder harness). Rear seat not desired (RPO YG4): No charge. Heavy-duty 2250 lb. front springs (F60). Includes heavy-duty front and rear shock absorbers. Recommended for front mounted accessory applications only: $62. Trailering special equipment (RPO Z82). Includes trailer hitch platform and hitch, wiring harness and transmission oil cooler. Requires either 3.42 or 3.73 rear axle, without B3J includes engine oil cooler: $407 (without B3J diesel equipment) $272 (with B3J diesel equipment). 4-speed automatic with overdrive (RPO MXO): $879 — standard with B3J equipment. Wheelcovers (RPO PO1): $42. Rallye wheels (RPO N67): $121 (without YE9),

$79 (with YE9). Aluminum cast wheels (RPO N90): $318 (without YE9), $276 (with YE9). Sliding rear quarter windows (AD5): $257. Electric remote exterior mirror (RPO D48): $98. California emission system (RPO YF5): $100. P235/75R15 steel belted radial on-off road blackwall tires: $55. P235/75R15 steel belted All-Season radial whitewall: $90. P235/75R15 steel belted radial All-Season white letters: $125. 31 x 10.50R15B white letters steel belted radial on-off road: $630.40.

HISTORICAL FOOTNOTES: The Chevrolet Blazer was now built at the General Motors assembly plant in Flint, Michigan.

1991 BLAZER

Powertrain refinements characterized the 1991 Blazer. The 200 series throttle body fuel injection system used on the Blazer's standard 5.7 liter V-8 had longer throttle shaft bearings, new throttle return springs and improved fuel mixture distribution. The 5.7 liter V-8 also had new heavy-duty intake valves and powdered metal camshaft sprockets. Standard on all engines was a lighter and more powerful 100 amp CS130 alternator. Two new exterior colors brilliant blue and slate metallic were offered. A new light gray joined the four interior colors for 1991. The AM/FM radios had improved reception.

1991 Chevrolet K1500 Blazer

I.D. DATA: The V.I.N. plate was mounted on the lower left side windshield corner. The V.I.N. consisted of 17 elements. The first, the number 1 identified the U.S. as the nation of origin. The letter G followed, for the manufacturer: General Motors. The third entry, the letter C represented the make as Chevrolet. The GVWR brake system identification followed. Next came the truck line and chassis type; the letter K indicated four-wheel drive. The truck series was identified by a number: 1-1/2 ton; The truck body type identification was next: 8-Utility. The engine code was next, followed by a check digit. The model year was identified by the letter M. The assembly plant code followed. The final six digits were the plant sequential production number.

Model Number	Body Type & Seating	Factory Price	GVW	Shipping Weight	Prod. Total
Blazer V10 Body Code: ZW9 (with 350 V-8)					
CV10516	Util.	$18,185	6100	4797	15,352*
CV10516	(w/Diesel V-8/B3J)	$21,175	6250	N.A.	—

* Production of all models.

STANDARD ENGINE: All states: Engine Type: Cast iron block. OHV, V-8. Ordering Code: L05. Produced by GM-Chevrolet Motor Division. Bore x Stroke: 4.0 in. x 3.48 in. Lifters: Hydraulic. Number of main bearings-5. Carburetion: Electronic fuel injection. Compression Ratio: 9.2:1. Displacement: 350 cu. in. (5.7 liters). Horsepower: Net: 210 @ 4000 rpm. Torque: Net: 300 lb.-ft. @ 2800 rpm. Oil capacity: 5 qt. with filter change. Fuel Requirements: Unleaded.

OPTIONAL ENGINE: Not available for California: Engine Type: OHV, Cast iron block. Diesel V-8. Order Code LH6. Produced by GM-Detroit Diesel Allison Division. Requires B3J Diesel Equipment Package which consists of dual batteries, hydraulic power-assisted brakes, engine block heater, heavy-duty radiator, K81 alternator, engine oil cooler and additional insulation. Bore x Stroke: 3.98 in. x 3.80 in. Lifters: Hydraulic. Number of main bearings-5. Carburetion: Fuel injection. Compression Ratio: 21.5:1. Displacement: 379 cu. in. (6.2 liter). Horsepower: Net: 130 @ 3600 rpm. Torque: Net: 240 lb.-ft. @ 2000 rpm. Oil capacity: 7 qt. with filter change. Fuel Requirements: Diesel.

CHASSIS FEATURES: Ladder-type. Carbon steel, 36,000-39,000 psi. Heavy-gauge channel side members, alligator-jaw cross members. Section modules: 3.14 in.

SUSPENSION AND RUNNING GEAR: Front Suspension: Two tapered semi-elliptical leaf springs. Capacity: Gasoline engines: 1650 lb. Optional Capacity: 2250 lb. Diesel engine: 1850 lb. Optional: 2250 lb. Standard 1.25 in. stabilizer bar and 25mm shock absorbers. Optional: 32mm shock absorbers. Rear Suspension: Two-stage tapered and multi-leaf (six-conventional leaves, one tapered leaf). Capacity: 1875 lb. Optional: None. Front Axle. Type: Hypoid, tubular driving. Capacity: 3600 lb. Rear Axle. Type: Hypoid, semi-floating. Capacity: 3750 lb. Final Drive Ratio: 5.7 liter V-8 with manual 4-spd. trans.: 3.08:1. Optional: 3.42:1. 5.7 liter V-8 with 4-spd. auto. trans.: 2.73:1. Optional: 3.08, 3.42, 3.73[1], [2]. [1]-Requires Z82 Trailering without California emissions. With California emissions requires KC4 engine oil cooler. [2]-Requires Z82 Trailering Special or High Altitude emissions. Final Drive Ratio: 6.2 liter diesel V-8: 3.08:1. Optional: 3,42, 3.73:1[1]. [1]-Requires Z82 Trailering Special or High Altitude emissions. Transfer Case: Type: New Process 208. Ratios: 2.61, 1.00:1. Brakes: Type: Hydraulic, self-adjusting. Front: Discs. Rear: Drums. Optional: Power. Dimensions: Front: 11.86 in. dia. rotor. Rear: 11.15 in. x 2.75 in. Wheels: 6-stud, 15 x 6.00JJ. Optional: 15 x 7JJ Rallye, 15 x 8JJ, 15 x 8JJ Rallye, 16 x 5K. Tires: P235/75R15 steel belted radial. Optional: P235/75R15 steel belted radial on-off road, P235/75R15 steel belted radial whitewall, P235/75R15 steel belted radial white letters, P235/75R15 steel belted radial whitewall XL (requires N67 or N90 wheels), 31 x 10.50R15B white letters steel belted radial on-off road. Steering: Power assisted recirculating ball, variable ratio. Ratio: 17.6/13.1. Turns Lock-to-Lock: 4.0. Turning Circle: 37.6 ft. Optional: None. Transmission: Type: SM465, RPO MM4. 4-speed manual, fully synchronized. Floor-mounted shifter. Standard transmission with diesel V-8: 4-speed automatic overdrive. Optional (gasoline engined models, and models with California emissions): 4-speed automatic overdrive. Transmission Ratios: SM465. Synchromesh on top three gears, floor-mounted shift lever. Ratios: 6.55, 3.58, 1.70, 1.00:1. Reverse: 6.09:1. 700R4 Automatic: 3.06, 1.63, 1.00, 0.70. Reverse: 2.29. Clutch: 12.0 in. dia.

VEHICLE DIMENSIONS: Wheelbase: 106.5 in. Overall Length: 184.8 in. Front/Rear Tread 66.10 in./63.00 in. Overall Height: 73.4 in. Width: 79.6 in. Tailgate: Width and Height: 66.8 in. x 22.0 in. Approach/Departure Degrees: 34/25. Ground Clearance: Front axle: 7.4 in. Rear axle: 7.0 in. Oil pan: 17.2 in. Transfer case: 11.5 in. Fuel tank: 14.0 in. Load space: With rear seat installed: 38.8 in. x 50 in. x 42.3 in. With rear seat removed or folded: 76.0 in. x 50 in. x 42.3 in.

CAPACITIES: Fuel Tank: 350 V-8: 31.0 gal. Diesel: 32 gal. Coolant system: 350 V-8: 17.6 qt.

ACCOMMODATIONS: Seating Capacity: Standard: Driver and passenger front high-back bucket sets. Optional: 3 passenger rear bench seat. Headroom: 38.3 in. Maximum steering wheel to seat back: 18.5 in. Seat to ground: 36.3 in. Floor to ground: 21.9 in.

INSTRUMENTATION: 0-100 mph speedometer, 99,999.9 mi. odometer, fuel gauge, warning lights for alternator, oil pressure, engine coolant temperature, brake operating system, hazard warning lights, directional lights, seat belt warning.

OPTIONS AND PRICES: Silverado Package (RPO YE9): $1298. Air conditioning (RPO C60) $845 (without B3J); $783 (with B3J). Optional rear axle ratios: $38. Locking rear differential (RPO G80): $252. Cold Climate Package (RPO V10). Includes special insulation, special heater and defroster, engine block heater, anti-freeze protection to -32 degrees and heavy-duty battery: $48. Engine oil cooler (RPO KC4): $135 Heavy-duty radiator (RPO VO1): $56. Heavy-duty radiator and transmission oil cooler (RPO VO2): $63. Deep tinted glass (RPO AJ1): $215. Locking front hubs (RPO X6Z): $60. Below eye-level stainless steel exterior mirrors (RPO D45): $45. Below eye-level electric remote painted mirrors: $58-$98 depending upon other options selected. Operating Convenience Package (RPO ZQ2). Includes power door locks and front door power windows: $367. Operating Convenience Package (RPO ZQ3). Includes tilt wheel and speed control: $383. Conventional two-tone exterior paint (RPO ZY2): $413 (without YE9), $180 (with YE9). Special two-tone exterior paint (RPO ZY3): $464 (without YE9), $450 (with YE9). Deluxe two-tone exterior paint (RPO ZY4): $566 (without YE9), $332 (with YE9). Electronically tuned AM/FM stereo radio with Seek-Scan and digital clock (RPO UM7): $131. Electronically tuned AM/FM stereo radio with Seek-Scan, stereo cassette tape player and digital clock (RPO UM6): $253. Electronically tuned AM/FM stereo radio with Seek-Scan, stereo cassette tape player with Search and Repeat, graphic equalizer and digital clock (RPO UX1): $403. Radio delete (RPO UL5): $95. Fuel tank shield (RPO NY1). Includes protective shield on transfer case: $175. Rear folding 3 passenger seat (AM7): $411 (without shoulder harness), $461 (with shoulder harness). Rear seat not desired (RPO YG4): No charge. Heavy-duty 2250 lb. front springs (F60). Includes heavy-duty front and rear shock absorbers. Recommended for front mounted accessory applications only: $62. Front quad shock absorbers: $100. Trailering Special Equipment (RPO Z82). Includes trailer hitch platform and hitch, wiring harness and transmission oil cooler. Requires either 3.42 or 3.73 rear axle, without B3J includes engine oil cooler: $407 (without B3J diesel equipment), $272 (with B3J diesel equipment). 4-speed automatic with overdrive (RPO MXO): $890-(standard with B3J equipment). Wheelcovers (RPO PO1): $42. Rallye wheels (RPO N67): $121 (without YE9), $79 (with YE9). Aluminum cast wheels (RPO N90): $212-$333 (without YE9 and depending upon other options selected.), $291 (with YE9). Sliding rear quarter windows (AD5): $257. P235/75R15 steel belted radial on-off road blackwall tires: $55 P235/75R15 steel belted All-Season radial whitewall: $90. P235/75R15 steel belted radial All-Season white letters: $125. 31 x 10.50R15B white letters steel belted radial on-off road: $631.10.

HISTORICAL FOOTNOTES: The 1991 Chevrolet Blazer was announced on September 1, 1990.

1992 BLAZER

The 1992 Blazer was completely restyled and was based upon Chevrolet's K pickup. The 1992 Blazer had a 6 passenger capacity and could tow 7,000 lbs; 1,000 lbs. more than its predecessor. Compared to the 1991 Blazer, the 1992 model had a 5 in. longer wheelbase, a higher gross vehicle weight rating and increased front and rear legroom and rear hip room. A good deal of the Blazer's exterior sheetmetal was shared with the Chevrolet pickup. New standard features included anti-lock brakes and Chevrolet's patented Insta-Trac four-wheel drive shift-on-the-fly system. The 5.7 liter Electronic Fuel Injection (EFI) V-8 was standard as was a 5-speed manual transmission with overdrive. The diesel engine was not offered. A 4-speed automatic with locking torque converter and overdrive was optional. New exterior and interior appointments for the Blazer included improved seats with head restraints for the front outboard positions, a standard full gauge cluster and an extended range AM radio. An optional new Sport Appearance Package provided an up-level sport look with two-tone paint, special grille and bumpers and wheel flares. New safety enhancements included a self-aligning steering wheel that aligned parallel to the driver's body to distribute force more equally in the event of a crash. Added to the interior color selection was beige. Bright red and beige metallic were new exterior colors. Major standard features of the base Cheyenne model included LT225 All-Season steel belted radial tires, power steering, power brakes, tinted glass, black below eye-level dual outside rearview mirrors, base-coat/clear coat paint, chrome front and black rear bumpers, high-back front bucket seats with Custom vinyl trim and matching rear vinyl seat, inside spare tire carrier on left rear panel, full-coverage, intermittent wet-arm windshield wiper/washer system, electronically tuned AM radio, dual horns, glove box with beverage wells on door back, heavy-duty battery, dual dome lights, headlights-on reminder, voltmeter, oil pressure and engine coolant temperature gauges, trip odometer, lift glass/drop tailgate system with electric tailgate release. The Silverado Package added these items: Custom cloth 40/60 split front bench seat and matching rear cloth seat with armrests, chrome front and rear bumpers with rub strips, body side and wheel-opening moldings, dark argent grille with quad halogen headlights, deluxe bumper guards, Rallye wheel trim, bright, below eye-level dual outside rearview mirrors, electronically-tuned AM/FM stereo radio with Seek-

Scan, spare wheel carpet cover, full-length color-keyed cloth headliner, color-keyed carpeting, front and rear color-keyed floormats, interior assist straps, front and rear map lights, illuminated mirror on passenger's side sun visor, vinyl storage pockets and assist straps on doors.

1992 Chevrolet K1500 Blazer

I.D. DATA: The V.I.N. plate was mounted on the lower left side windshield corner. The V.I.N. consisted of 17 elements. The first, the number 1 identified the U.S. as the nation of origin. The letter G followed, for the manufacturer: General Motors. The third entry, the letter C represented the make as Chevrolet. The GVWR brake system identification followed. Next came the truck line and chassis type; the letter K indicated four-wheel drive. The truck series was identified by a number: 1-1/2 ton. The truck body type identification was next: 8-Utility. The engine code was next, followed by a check digit. The model year was identified by the letter N. The assembly plant code followed. The final six digits were the plant sequential production number.

Model Number	Body Type & Seating	Factory Price	GVW	Shipping Weight	Prod. Total
K1500 Blazer					
K10516	Util.	$19,280	6250	N.A.	5,451*

* Sales through June 10, 1992.

STANDARD ENGINE: All states: Engine Type: Cast iron block. OHV, V-8. Ordering Code: L05. Produced by GM-Chevrolet Motor Division. Bore x Stroke: 4.0 in. x 3.48 in. Lifters: Hydraulic. Number of main bearings-5. Carburetion: Electronic fuel injection. Compression Ratio: 9.3:1. Displacement: 350 cu. in. (5.7 liters). Horsepower: Net: 210 @ 4000 rpm. Torque: Net: 300 lb.-ft. @ 2800 rpm. Oil capacity: 5 qt. with filter change. Fuel Requirements: 87 octane minimum, unleaded.

CHASSIS FEATURES: Ladder-type. All-welded, ladder-type channel-design with boxed front end.

SUSPENSION AND RUNNING GEAR: Front Suspension: Independent with torsion bars, 1.25 in. anti-roll bar, steel upper and lower control arms. Capacity: 1900 lb. each. Optional: 2500 lb. capacity. 32mm shock absorbers. Rear Suspension: Variable-rate, two-stage, multi-leaf semi-elliptical springs. Capacity: 1875 lb. each. 32mm shock absorbers. Front Axle: Type: Hypoid, tubular driving. Capacity: 3600 lb. Rear Axle. Type: Hypoid, semi-floating. Capacity: 3750 lb. Final Drive Ratio: 3.42:1. Optional: 3.73:1 (manual transmission only). Transfer Case: New Process 241. Part-time, two-speed. Ratios: 2.72:1, 1.00:1. Brakes: Type: Hydraulic, self-adjusting. Front: Discs. Rear: Drums. Optional: Power. Dimensions: Front: 11.50 in. x 1.25 in. rotor. Rear: 10.0 in. x 2.25 in. Wheels: 16 x 6.50. Tires: LT225/75R16C. Optional: Various sizes available. Steering: Power assisted recirculating ball, variable ratio. Ratio: 13:1. Turning Circle: 41.5 ft. Optional: None. Transmission: 5-speed manual with overdrive. Transmission Ratios: 4.02, 2.32, 1.40, 1.00, 0.73:1. Reverse: 3.75:1. Clutch: 12.0 in. dia. Optional: Automatic 4-speed with overdrive.

VEHICLE DIMENSIONS: Wheelbase: 111.5 in. Overall Length: 187.7 in. Front/rear overhang: 34.9 in./41.2 in. Front/Rear Tread 64.1 in./63.50 in. Overall Height: 71.0 in. Width: 76.4 in. Approach/departure angle: 13/27. Ground Clearance: Minimum Front: 6.9 in. Minimum Rear axle: 7.1 in. Rear door opening: 61.4 in. width, 53.5 in. height. Load space: With rear seat installed: 38.9 in. x 61.4 in. x 41.7 in. Without rear seat: 74.0 in. x 61.4 in. x 41.7 in.

CAPACITIES: Fuel Tank: 30.0 gal. Coolant system: 15.6 qt.

ACCOMMODATIONS: Seating Capacity: 6. Front headroom: 40.2 in. Rear headroom: 38.0 in. Front legroom: 41.7 in. Rear legroom: 37.6 in. Front shoulder room: 66.0 in. Rear shoulder room: 63.2 in. Front hip room: 60.5 in. Rear hip room: 53.1 in.

INSTRUMENTATION: 0-100 mph speedometer, 99,999.9 mi. odometer, gauges for fuel level, voltmeter, oil pressure, and engine coolant temperature; warning lights for brake operating system, hazard warning lights, directional lights, seat belt warning.

OPTIONS: Most options were continued from 1992. They included the following: Silverado Package. Sport Appearance Package. Air conditioning. Operating Convenience Package. Driver's Convenience Package.

HISTORICAL FOOTNOTES: The 1992 Chevrolet Blazer was announced on September 1, 1991.

1993 BLAZER

After adopting the styling, chassis and powertrain of the full-size K pickup in 1992, the Blazer entered 1993 in the envious position of having its production facilities unable to keep pace with demand. New for 1993 was the optional electronic 4-speed Hydra-Matic automatic transmission. This transmission was the first General Motors rear-wheel electronic transmission to interface with the cruise control. The 4L60-E weighed seven pounds less than its non-electric predecessor (the 4L60). This new transmission monitored such items as the fuel injection rate, ignition timing, internal transmission temperature, idle speed and exhaust gas recirculation several times a second. It then determined the proper shift points and shift smoothness. The transmission also had a built-in learning feature that allowed the system to

adapt to its environment and make subtle adjustments in clutch pressure to match it. The 4L60 also had fail-safe controls that defaulted to operable gear ratios should a problem develop, allowing the driver to maintain vehicle control and reach a safe location. A second safety feature permitted second-gear starts when increased wheel traction was desired.

A new single-rail shift control improved both reliability and durability. The 5.7 liter EFI V-8 and 5-speed manual transmission remained the standard powertrain. The fan was not engaged upon engine start to reduce noise. Other standard features included 4-wheel anti-lock brakes (4WAL) and the shift-on the fly Insta-Trac system. The tilt steering column had a new steel sleeve for 1993 to reduce theft. Specific details included three steel shields, revised lock cylinder and a new lock bolt spring. An electronic fuel shut-off automatically limited maximum vehicle speed to less than the tire speed rating. A Deluxe front appearance option (RPO V22) was now available with the Cheyenne decor.

Indigo blue metallic was a new exterior color for 1993. It replaced brilliant blue metallic. The other exterior colors for 1993 were black, olympic white, ultra silver metallic, dark gray metallic, victory red, dark garnet red metallic, light French blue metallic, medium dark teal metallic and beige metallic. Both a Sport appearance package and new coordinated striping colors were also available. The Special two-tone paint feature (RPO ZY3) was not offered for 1993. It had been phased out during the 1992 model run. Anti-chip paint coating was more widely used for 1993. It was installed on the leading edges of the hood, roof, and the A-pillars. Four interior colors were available for 1993: Beige, blue, garnet and gray. Blazers with the standard Cheyenne trim had vinyl seating; the uplevel Silverado trim had custom cloth trim.

The passenger side of the optional Silverado 40/60 split bench seats and the standard Cheyenne low back bench seats reclined for 1993. Other changes included Scotchgard™ protection for seats and door fabric and the use of Solar-Ray™ glass for a cooler interior. Also new for 1993 was a dual stud air cleaner, a more durable oil filter, improved cruise control and user-friendly radio controls. The cruise control improvement included increased reliability of the circuit board component, and a "soft pedal off" feature to eliminate the pedal slapping the sole of the driver's foot when the cruise was turned off at the column switch. Installed, interim 1993, was an improved brake hose material that provided reduced moisture ingression, improved heat resistance, sealability, ozone resistance, hot/cold fatigue resistance and flex fatigue resistance.

1993 Chevrolet K1500 Blazer

I.D. DATA: The V.I.N. plate was mounted on the lower left side windshield corner. The V.I.N. consisted of 17 elements. The first, the number 1 identified the U.S. as the nation of origin. The letter G followed, for the manufacturer: General Motors. The third entry, the letter C represented the make as Chevrolet. The GVWR brake system identification followed. Next came the truck line and chassis type; the letter K indicated four-wheel drive. The truck series was identified by a number: 1-1/2 ton. The truck body type identification was next: 8-Utility. The engine code was next, followed by a check digit. The model year was identified by the letter O. The assembly plant code followed. The final six digits were the plant sequential production number.

Model Number	Body Type & Seating	Factory Price	GVW	Shipping Weight	Prod. Total
K1500 Blazer					
K10516	Util.	$*	6250	N.A.	—

* 1993 prices were not available at press time.

STANDARD ENGINE: All states: Engine Type: Cast iron block. OHV, V-8. Ordering Code: L05. Produced by GM-Chevrolet Motor Division. Bore x Stroke: 4.0 in. x 3.48 in. Lifters: Hydraulic. Number of main bearings-5. Carburetion: Electronic fuel injection. Compression Ratio: 9.3:1. Displacement: 350 cu. in. (5.7 liters). Horsepower: Net: 210 @ 4000 rpm. Torque: Net: 300 lb.-ft. @ 2800 rpm. Oil capacity: 5 qt. with filter change. Fuel Requirements: 87 octane minimum, unleaded.

CHASSIS FEATURES: Ladder-type. All-welded, ladder-type channel-design with boxed front end.

SUSPENSION AND RUNNING GEAR: Front Suspension: Independent with torsion bars, 1.25 in. anti-roll bar, steel upper and lower control arms. Capacity: 1900 lb. each. Optional: 2500 lb. capacity. 32mm shock absorbers. Rear Suspension: Variable-rate, two-stage, multi-leaf semi-elliptical springs. Capacity: 1875 lb. each. 32mm shock absorbers. Front Axle: Type: Hypoid, tubular driving. Capacity: 3600 lb. Rear Axle. Type: Hypoid, semi-floating. Capacity: 3750 lb. Final Drive Ratio: 3.42:1. Optional: 3.73:1 (manual transmission only). Transfer Case: New Process 241. Part-time, two-speed. Ratios: 2.721, 1.00:1. Brakes: Type: Hydraulic, self-adjusting. Front: Discs. Rear: Drums. Optional: Power. Dimensions: Front: 11.50 in. x 1.25 in. rotor. Rear: 10.0 in. x 2.25 in. Wheels: 16 x 6.50. Tires: LT225/75R16C. Optional: Various sizes available. Steering: Power assisted recirculating ball, variable ratio. Ratio: 13:1. Turning Circle: 41.5 ft. Optional: None. Transmission: 5-speed manual with overdrive. Transmission Ratios: 4.02, 2.32, 1.40, 1.00, 0.73:1. Reverse: 3.75:1. Clutch: 12.0 in. dia. Optional: Automatic 4-speed Hydra-Matic 4L60-E with overdrive. Ratios: 3.06, 1.63, 1.00, 0.70:1. Reverse: 2.29:1.

VEHICLE DIMENSIONS: Wheelbase: 111.5 in. Overall Length: 187.7 in. Front/rear overhang: 34.9 in./41.2 in. Front/Rear Tread 64.1 in./63.50 in. Overall Height: 71.0 in. Width: 76.4 in. Approach/departure angle: 13/27. Ground Clearance: Minimum Front: 6.9 in. Minimum Rear axle: 7.1 in. Rear door opening: 61.4 in. width, 53.5 in. height. Load space: With rear seat installed: 38.9 in. x 61.4 in. x 41.7 in. With out rear seat: 74.0 in. x 61.4 in. x 41.7 in.

CAPACITIES: Fuel Tank: 30.0 gal. Coolant system: 15.6 qt.

ACCOMMODATIONS: Seating Capacity: 6. Front headroom: 40.2 in. Rear headroom: 38.0 in. Front legroom: 41.7 in. Rear legroom: 37.6 in. Front shoulder room: 66.0 in. Rear shoulder room: 63.2 in. Front hip room: 60.5 in. Rear hip room: 53.1 in.

INSTRUMENTATION: 0-100 mph speedometer, 99,999.9 mi. odometer, gauges for fuel level, voltmeter, oil pressure, and engine coolant temperature; warning lights for brake operating system, hazard warning lights, directional lights, seat belt warning.

OPTIONS: Silverado Package. Sport Appearance Package. Air conditioning. Operating Convenience Package. Driver's Convenience Package. Hydra-Matic 4L60-E automatic transmission. Various AM/FM, stereo radio and tape player systems.

HISTORICAL FOOTNOTES: The 1993 Chevrolet Blazer was announced on September 24, 1992. Blazers were built at a GM assembly plant in Janesville, Wisconsin.

CHEVROLET LUV
1979-1982

Chevrolet first introduced the LUV (Light Utility Vehicle) in March, 1972. The LUV was manufactured by Isuzu Motors in Japan and functioned as Chevrolet's entry into the mini-truck market until the arrival of the S10 in mid-1981 as a 1982 model. After the 1982 model year the LUV was withdrawn from the market.

The first four-wheel drive LUV models were introduced in 1979 as part of the Series 9 LUV trucks. It was fitted with a 4-speed, fully synchronized manual transmission. The transfer case was combined with the transmission in a single unit and each was operated by a separate shift lever. Manual locking front hubs were standard. The LUV 4x4 had a minimum ground clearance of 7.5 in., but was only 1.5 inches higher than the two-wheel drive version. The front suspension was independent, with upper and lower control arms, ball-type joints and torsion bar springs. Also included were direct double-acting shock absorbers and a stabilizer bar. The rear suspension consisted of semi-elliptical, rubber-bushed leaf springs and direct double-acting shock absorbers. Other standard features included 14 in. x 5.5 in. styled wheels and white-lettered F70 x14B bias-belted tires. Exterior identification included a 4x4 decal on the tailgate. A new assist grip was mounted above the door on the right interior. The standard interior had a vinyl-covered bench seat available in blue or saddle. The available exterior colors were crimson red, jasmine yellow, light blue, stato white and black.

1979 LUV

I.D. DATA: The LUV's V.I.N. consisted of 13 symbols. The first symbol identified the Chevrolet Motor Division. The second symbol indicated vehicle type. The third symbol (a letter) indicated engine type. The fourth symbol (a number) identified the tonnage. The fifth symbol indicated body type. The sixth symbol (a number) identified the series. The seventh symbol (a letter) indicated the assembly plant. The remaining six digits served as the sequential production numbers. The V.I.N. number was located on the left door pillar.

Model Number	Body Type & Seating	Factory Price	GVW	Shipping Weight	Prod. Total
LUV					
L14	Pickup	$6247	3750	2585	33,843

STANDARD ENGINE: OHC 4-cyl: Engine Type: OHV, In-line 4-cylinder, cast iron block and aluminum cylinder head. Bore x Stroke: 3.31 in. x 3.23 in. Lifters: Hydraulic. Number of main bearings-5. Carburetion: Hitachi two-barrel. Compression Ratio: 8.5:1. Displacement: 110.8 cu. in. (1.817 liters). Horsepower: Net: 80 @ 4800 rpm. Torque: Net: 95 lb.-ft. @ 3000 rpm. Oil capacity: 5.7 qt. with filter change. Fuel Requirements: Unleaded or low-lead gasoline of at least 91 Research Octane.

CHASSIS FEATURES: Ladder-type.

1979 Chevy LUV Series 9 with optional decal

SUSPENSION AND RUNNING GEAR: Front Suspension: Independent, torsion bars, stabilizer bar, 1.0 in. direct, double-acting shock absorbers. Rear Suspension: Semi-elliptical leaf springs, 1.0 in. direct, double-acting shock absorbers. Front Axle. Type: Solid with constant velocity U-joints. Rear Axle. Type: Hypoid, solid. Capacity: 3500 lb. Final Drive Ratio: 4.10:1. Transfer Case: Two-speed. Ratios: 1.86, 1.00:1. Transmission: Type: Manual 4-speed transmission. Ratios: 3.79, 2.18, 1.42, 1.00:1. Brakes: Type: Hydraulic, power-assisted. Front: Discs. Rear: Drums. Dimensions: Front: 9.84 in. dia. rotor. Rear: 10.00 in. x 1.8 in. drums. Wheels: 5.5 x 14 in. Tires: F70 x 14B, bias-belted All-Terrain white-lettered. Steering: Variable ratio, recirculating ball. Turning circle: 36.7 ft. Turns Lock-to-Lock: 4.5.

VEHICLE DIMENSIONS: Wheelbase: 102.4 in. Overall Length: 173.8 in. Front/Rear Tread 54.4 in./ 52.5 in. Overall Height: 60.8 in. Width: 63.0 in. Tailgate: Width: 57.5 in. Ground Clearance: 7.5 in. Load space: 73.0 in. x 57.5 in., 38 cu. ft. capacity.

CAPACITIES: Fuel Tank: 13 gal. Coolant system: 6.4 qt.

ACCOMMODATIONS: Seating Capacity: Standard: 2 passenger bench seat. Optional: 2 bucket seats. Headroom: 34.2 in. Maximum Steering wheel to seat back: 19.9 in. Accelerator to seat back: 43.5 in. Seat to ground: 25.5 in. Floor to ground: 14.5 in.

INSTRUMENTATION: Speedometer, odometer, gauges for fuel gauge and engine coolant temperature, warning lights for alternator, oil pressure, parking brake, hazard warning lights, directional lights.

OPTIONS AND PRICES: Chrome or painted rear step bumper: $100 (chrome). Skid Plate Package. Includes skid plates for fuel tank, and transfer case. 4x4 Decal Package. LUV Sport Decal Package: $107. Decor Package. Includes bright beltline moldings, bright roof drip moldings, bright windshield and rear window moldings, and chromed wheel discs: $86. Air conditioning: $525. Sliding rear window: $81. AM push-button radio. AM/FM push-button radio: $155. E78-14B bias-belted whitewall tires. Front bumper guards: $33. Mud flaps (dealer installed). Below eye-level mirrors: $53. Right-hand exterior mirror (dealer installed). Mikado Package. Includes full-width seats in blue, saddle or red cloth. Matching door inserts, carpeted floor, Mikado nameplate on glove door box and a leather-like vinyl-covered 3-spoke steering wheel and gearshift knob: $199. Bucket seats in red Mikado cloth with red, black or white exterior color.

HISTORICAL FOOTNOTES: The LUV was introduced in September, 1979.

1980 LUV

The Series 10 LUV was fitted with a new heavy-duty 8.5 in. clutch. The exterior colors were basically carried over for 1980 except that the yellow, white and red colors were slightly changed, due to the discontinuation of lead in their formulation. For 1980 they were renamed marigold yellow, frost white, and scarlet red. Light blue and midnight black were carried over from 1979. The bright side marker light bezels were replaced by black rubber-type seals around the perimeter of the side marker light lenses. The instrument panel now included an indicator light that operated when the transfer case was in four-wheel drive. The basic vinyl seat trim and the Mikado cloth seat trim was new in both color and sew pattern. All body fasteners were changed to stainless steel to improve corrosion protection. Other added corrosion protection features included ELPO-dipped cowl vent grille strainer, one-side galvanized drip rail and cowl vent grille and the addition of an aluminum coating to the steel engine heat shield. A new 50 amp alternator was now standard for the four-wheel drive LUV. Both the Standard and Mikado interiors were offered in blue, red or daddle. The 4x4 decal color combinations were red/orange black or Light blue/Dark blue/black. The Sport Package decal colors were light orange/orange/red and light blue metallic/Medium blue/Dark blue.

I.D. DATA: The LUV's V.I.N. consisted of 13 symbols. The first symbol identified the Chevrolet Motor Division. The second symbol indicated vehicle type. The third symbol (a letter) indicated engine type. The fourth symbol (a number) identified the tonnage. The fifth symbol indicated body type. The sixth symbol (a number) identified the series. The seventh symbol (a letter) indicated the assembly plant. The remaining six digits serve as the sequential production numbers. The V.I.N. number was located on the left door pillar.

Model Number	Body Type & Seating	Factory Price	GVW	Shipping Weight	Prod. Total
LUV					
L14	Pickup	$6583	3750	2585	33,859

STANDARD ENGINE: OHC 4-cyl. Engine Type: OHV, In-line 4-cylinder, cast iron block and aluminum cylinder head. Bore x Stroke: 3.31 in. x 3.23 in. Lifters: Hydraulic. Number of main bearings-5. Carburetion: Hitachi two-barrel. Compression Ratio: 8.5:1. Displacement: 110.8 cu. in. (1.817 liters). Horsepower: Net: 80 @ 4800 rpm. Torque: Net: 95 lb.-ft. @ 3000 rpm. Oil capacity: 5.7 qt. with filter change. Fuel Requirements: Unleaded or low-lead gasoline of at least 91 Research Octane.

CHASSIS FEATURES: Ladder-type.

SUSPENSION AND RUNNING GEAR: Front Suspension: Independent, torsion bars, stabilizer bar, 1.0 in. direct, double-acting shock absorbers. Rear Suspension: Semi-elliptical leaf springs, 1.0 in. direct, double-acting shock absorbers. Front Axle. Type: Solid with constant velocity U-joints. Rear Axle. Type: Hypoid, solid. Capacity: 3600 lb. Final Drive Ratio: 4.10:1. Transfer Case: Two-speed. Ratios: 1.86, 1.00:1. Transmission: Type: Manual 4-speed transmission: Ratios: 3.79, 2.18, 1.42, 1.00:1. Clutch: 8.5 in., heavy-duty. Brakes: Type: Hydraulic, power-assisted. Front: Discs. Rear: Drums. Dimensions: Front: 9.84 in. dia. rotor. Rear: 10.00 in. x 1.8 in. drums. Wheels: 5.5 x 14 in. Tires: F70 x 14B, bias-belted All-Terrain white-lettered. Steering: Variable ratio, recirculating ball. Turning circle: 36.7 ft. Turns Lock-to-Lock: 4.5.

VEHICLE DIMENSIONS: Wheelbase: 102.4 in. Overall Length: 173.8 in. Front/Rear Tread 54.4 in./ 52.5 in. Overall Height: 60.8 in. Width: 63.0 in. Tailgate: Width: 57.5 in. Ground Clearance: 7.5 in. Load space: 73.0 in. x 57.5 in., 38 cu. ft. capacity.

CAPACITIES: Fuel Tank: 13 gal. Coolant system: 6.4 qt.

ACCOMMODATIONS: Seating Capacity: Standard: 2 passenger bench seat. Optional: 2 bucket seats. Headroom: 34.2 in. Maximum steering wheel to seat back: 19.9 in. Accelerator to seat back: 43.5 in. Seat to ground: 25.5 in. Floor to ground: 14.5 in.

INSTRUMENTATION: Speedometer, odometer, gauges for fuel gauge and engine coolant temperature, warning lights for alternator, oil pressure, parking brake, hazard warning lights, directional lights.

OPTIONS AND PRICES: Chrome or painted rear step bumper. Skid Plate Package. Includes skid plates for fuel tank, and transfer case. 4x4 Decal Package. LUV Sport Decal Package. Decor Package. Includes bright beltline moldings, bright roof drip moldings, bright windshield and rear window moldings, and chromed wheel discs. Air conditioning. Sliding rear window. AM push-button radio. AM/FM push-button radio. E78-14B bias-belted whitewall tires. Front bumper guards. Mud flaps (dealer installed). Below eye-level mirrors. Right-hand exterior mirror (dealer installed). Mikado Package. Includes full-width seats in blue, saddle or red cloth.

Matching door inserts, carpeted floor, Mikado nameplate on glove door box and a leather-like vinyl-covered 3-spoke steering wheel and gearshift knob. Bucket seats in red Mikado cloth with red, black or white exterior color.

HISTORICAL FOOTNOTES: The LUV was introduced in the Autumn of 1979.

The Series 11 LUV featured new aerodynamic styling and weight reduction designed for fuel economy improvements. The curb weight of the four-wheel drive model was reduced by 27 pounds. The new aerodynamic appearance resulted from redesigned sheet metal in the hood and cab. The glass area was increased while the windshield and window glass weight was reduced. The curved rear window was designed to reduce glare and reflection. Functional changes in the interior added about 2.5 inches to interior legroom and approximately an inch to shoulder room. Realignment of the door opening provided easier exit and entry. The tailgate now was operated by a center pull release. This arrangement replaced the old style hooks on each side of the tailgate. A new wraparound front bumper incorporated the parking and turn signals. A new style step bumper was now available. The front braking area was increased while the rear brake area was reduced to improve brake balance and durability. The power brakes had increased booster diameter. The heater and ventilation system had improved temperature control. A new side window defroster was standard. The engine was fitted with a new electronic ignition system which eliminated the points and condenser. The spark plug maintenance recommendation was extended from 15,000 to 30,000 miles.

The interiors featured a restyled, color-keyed instrument panel and pad, new instrument cluster, color-keyed steering wheel, new seat trim material, door and window regulator handles, headliner, door trim panel material, and redesigned steering column. The new glove box was fitted with a lock. A new "Smart Switch", a combination windshield wiper, turn indicator and headlight dimmer switch was located on the steering column. The Mikado Package was redesigned with new blue or red Mikado cloth seat trim, door trim panels, Deluxe steering wheel, stitched-urethane, leather-grained gearshift knob and instrument panel trim. Wall-to-wall carpeting was installed. The standard LUV interior was all vinyl. It featured a foam-padded bench seat and interior trim in a choice of either blue or saddle. Color-keyed, molded floor mats, color-keyed seat belts and embossed door trim panels were also standard. The Sport stripe option provided dual-color stripes installed the length of both body sides, across the front of the hood and across the bottom of the tailgate. The available colors were blue/green or dark orange/light orange. Six exterior colors were offered. Metallic silver was added and metallic blue replaced the light blue option. Other colors were midnight black, scarlet red, frost white and marigold yellow.

I.D. DATA: The LUV's V.I.N. consisted of 13 symbols. The first symbol identified the Chevrolet Motor Division. The second symbol indicated vehicle type. The third symbol (a letter) indicated engine type. The fourth symbol (a number) identified the tonnage. The fifth symbol indicated body type. The sixth symbol (a number) identified the series. The seventh symbol (a letter) indicated the assembly plant. The remaining six digits served as the sequential production numbers. The V.I.N. number was located on the left door pillar.

Model Number	Body Type & Seating	Factory Price	GVW	Shipping Weight	Prod. Total
LUV					
L14	Pickup	$7865	3750	2558	15,045

STANDARD ENGINE: OHC 4-cyl: Type L10. Engine Type: OHV, In-line 4-cylinder, cast iron block and aluminum cylinder head. Bore x Stroke: 3.31 in. x 3.23 in. Lifters: Hydraulic. Number of main bearings-5. Carburetion: Hitachi Model DCP-340 two-barrel. Compression Ratio: 8.5:1. Displacement: 110.8 cu. in. (1.817 liters). Horsepower: Net: 80 @ 4800 rpm. Torque: Net: 95 lb.-ft. @ 3000 rpm. Oil capacity: 5.7 qt. with filter change. Fuel Requirements: Unleaded or low-lead gasoline of at least 91 Research Octane.

CHASSIS FEATURES: Ladder-type.

1981 Chevy LUV Light Utility Vehicle

SUSPENSION AND RUNNING GEAR: Front Suspension: Independent, torsion bars, stabilizer bar, 1.0 in. direct, double-acting shock absorbers. Rear Suspension: Semi-elliptical leaf springs, 1.0 in. direct, double-acting shock absorbers. Front Axle. Type: Solid with constant velocity U-joints. Rear Axle. Type: Hypoid, solid. Capacity: 3500 lb. Final Drive Ratio: 4.10:1. Transfer Case: Two-speed. Ratios: 1.86, 1.00:1. Transmission: Type: Manual 4-speed transmission: Ratios: 3.79, 2.18, 1.42, 1.00:1. Clutch: 8.5 in., heavy-duty. Brakes: Type: Hydraulic, power-assisted. Front: Discs. Rear: Drums. Dimensions: Front: 10.16 in. dia. rotor. Rear: 10.00 in. drums. Wheels: 5.5 x 14 in. Tires: F70 x 14B, bias-belted All-Terrain white-lettered. Steering: Variable ratio, recirculating ball. Turning circle: 36.1 ft. Turns Lock-to-Lock: 4.5.

VEHICLE DIMENSIONS: Wheelbase: 104.3 in. Overall Length: 174.5 in. Front/Rear Tread 54.2 in./ 52.7 in. Overall Height: 61.0 in. Width: 63.1 in. Tailgate: Width: 57.5 in. Ground Clearance: 7.5 in. Load space: 73.0 in. x 57.5 in., 38 cu. ft. capacity.

CAPACITIES: Fuel Tank: 13.2 gal. Coolant system: 6.4 qt.

ACCOMMODATIONS: Seating Capacity: Standard: 2 passenger bench seat. Optional: 2 bucket seats. Headroom: 34.2 in. Maximum steering wheel to seat back: 19.9 in. Accelerator to seat back: 43.5 in. Seat to ground: 25.5 in. Floor to ground: 14.5 in.

INSTRUMENTATION: Speedometer, odometer, gauges for fuel gauge and engine coolant temperature, warning lights for alternator, oil pressure, parking brake, hazard warning lights, directional lights.

OPTIONS AND PRICES: Air conditioning: $603. Below eye-level mirrors: $61. Front bumper guards. Painted rear step bumper. Chromed rear step bumper: $98. Exterior Decor Package (requires Mikado Package). High-back bucket seats (requires Mikado Package). Mikado Trim Package: $354. AM push-button radio. AM/FM push-button radio; $176. Sliding rear window: $92. Sport stripe decals. 4x4 decals.

HISTORICAL FOOTNOTES: The Series 11 LUV was introduced in November, 1980.

The major development for the Series 12 LUV was the availability of an optional diesel engine. The Series 12 diesel LUV trucks were not available in California until May, 1982. Aside from this change, The basic design of the LUV was retained for 1982. The standard vinyl and optional Mikado cloth/vinyl interiors were offered in a choice of blue or saddle colors. Exterior colors were frost white, midnight black, metallic silver, scarlet red, metallic blue and marigold yellow.

I.D. DATA: The LUV's V.I.N. consisted of 13 symbols. The first symbol identified the Chevrolet Motor Division. The second symbol indicated vehicle type. The third symbol (a letter) indicated engine type. The fourth symbol (a number) identified the tonnage. The fifth symbol indicated body type. The sixth symbol (a number) identified the series. The seventh symbol (a letter) indicated the assembly plant. The remaining six digits served as the sequential production numbers. The V.I.N. number was located on the left door pillar.

Model Number	Body Type & Seating	Factory Price	GVW	Shipping Weight	Prod. Total
LUV					
L14	Pickup	$7535	3750	2558	10,367

STANDARD ENGINE: OHC 4-cyl. Type L10. Engine Type: OHV, In-line 4-cylinder, cast iron block and aluminum cylinder head. Bore x Stroke: 3.31 in. x 3.23 in. Lifters: Hydraulic. Number of main bearings-5. Carburetion: Hitachi Model DCP-340 two-barrel. Compression Ratio: 8.5:1. Displacement: 110.8 cu. in. (1.817 liters). Horsepower: Net: 80 @ 4800 rpm. Torque: Net: 95 lb.-ft. @ 3000 rpm. Oil capacity: 5.7 qt. with filter change. Fuel Requirements: Unleaded or low-lead gasoline of at least 91 Research Octane.

OPTIONAL ENGINE: OHC 4-cyl. Type LQ7. Engine Type: OHV, In-line 4-cylinder, cast iron block. Bore x Stroke: 3.46 in. x 3.62 in. Lifters: Hydraulic. Number of main bearings-5. Compression Ratio: 21:1. Displacement: 136.6 cu. in. (2.2 liters). Horsepower: Net: 58 @ 4300 rpm. Torque: Net: 93 lb.-ft. @ 2200 rpm. Fuel Requirements: Diesel.

CHASSIS FEATURES: Ladder-type.

SUSPENSION AND RUNNING GEAR: Front Suspension: Independent, torsion bars, stabilizer bar, 1.0 in. direct, double-acting shock absorbers. Rear Suspension: Semi-elliptical leaf springs, 1.0 in. direct, double-acting shock absorbers. Front Axle. Type: Solid with constant velocity U-joints. Rear Axle. Type: Hypoid, solid. Capacity: 3500 lb. Final Drive Ratio: 4.10:1. Transfer Case: Two-speed. Ratios: 1.86, 1.00:1. Transmission: Type: Manual 4-speed transmission. Ratios: 3.79, 2.18, 1.42, 1.00:1. Clutch: 8.5 in., heavy-duty. Brakes: Type: Hydraulic, power-assisted. Front: Discs. Rear: Drums. Dimensions: Front: 10.16 in. dia. rotor. Rear: 10.00 in. drums. Wheels: 5.5 x 14 in. Tires: F70 x 14B, bias-belted All-Terrain white-lettered. Steering: Variable ratio, recirculating ball. Turning circle: 36.1 ft. Turns Lock-to-Lock: 4.5.

1982 Chevy LUV with optional 4x4 decals

VEHICLE DIMENSIONS: Wheelbase: 104.3 in. Overall Length: 174.5 in. Front/Rear Tread 54.2 in./ 52.7 in. Overall Height: 61.0 in. Width: 63.1 in. Tailgate: Width: 57.5 in. Ground Clearance: 7.5 in. Load space: 73.0 in. x 57.5 in., 38 cu. ft. capacity.

CAPACITIES: Fuel Tank: 13.2 gal. Coolant system: 6.4 qt.

ACCOMMODATIONS: Seating Capacity: Standard: 2 passenger bench seat. Optional: 2 bucket seats. Headroom: 34.2 in. Maximum steering wheel to seat back: 19.9 in. Accelerator to seat back: 43.5 in. Seat to ground: 25.5 in. Floor to ground: 14.5 in.

INSTRUMENTATION: Speedometer, odometer, gauges for fuel gauge and engine coolant temperature, warning lights for alternator, oil pressure, parking brake, hazard warning lights, directional lights.

OPTIONS AND PRICES: Diesel engine. Air conditioning. Below eye-level mirrors. Front bumper guards. Painted rear step bumper. Chromed rear step bumper. Exterior Decor Package (requires Mikado Package). High-back bucket seats (requires Mikado Package). Mikado Trim Package. AM push-button radio. AM/FM push-button radio. Sliding rear window. Sport stripe decals. 4x4 decals.

HISTORICAL FOOTNOTES: The LUV was not offered by Chevrolet after the 1982 model year. However, quite a few models remained in Chevrolet dealer inventories. As a result, 2,445 four-wheel drive models were sold in 1983. In 1984 another 166 were sold.

CHEVROLET S-10 BLAZER
1983-1992

1983 S-10 BLAZER

The regular-size Blazer was joined by the smaller S-10 model for 1983. Based on the S-10 pickup models, the new Blazer had a 1000 lb. payload capacity, 4 passenger seating with front bucket seats and an optional rear bench seat. It was offered in three trim levels and had a full-length steel top, 15 in. wheels, tinted glass and a fold-down tailgate with lift glass. Its 100.5 in. wheelbase was 6 inches less than that of the full-size Blazer. A new 2.0 liter 4-cylinder engine was standard for the Blazer except in California where a 1.9 liter 4-cylinder was standard. A 110 hp. V-6 was a Blazer option. The standard trim level included chrome and black grille, headlight and parking lamp bezels with chrome finish and black trim, chromed front and rear bumpers with rub strips, black windshield and rear window moldings, left and right black outside mirrors, radial ply ties and 15 in. argent wheels with hubcaps. The standard interior provided front bucket seats, in vinyl trim in a choice of four colors, and color-keyed instrument panel, sun shades, headliner and windshield pillars. Also included were these items: Front and rear passenger assist handles, headlights-on warning buzzer, rubber floor covering, interior light, door/roof sound deadener, and front floor insulation. The optional Tahoe package included a chromed grille, cigarette lighter, right hand sun visor, body side and wheel opening moldings, spare tie cover, and gauges for voltmeter, engine coolant temperature, oil pressure and trip odometer. Other Tahoe features included bucket seats in Custom vinyl or Special Custom cloth, side window defoggers, deluxe color-keyed steering wheel and zippered rear armrest pockets.

The Sport Package added to or replaced the Tahoe features with the following: Painted color-keyed front bumper (required Sport two-tone paint), center floor-mounted console, reclining front bucket seats in Sport cloth in two color choices, a locking front console, color-keyed carpeting, Sport steering wheel, special interior trim, fiberglass hood blanket and cab/floor insulation. Available exterior colors for the S-10 Blazer were midnight blue, silver metallic, midnight black, light blue metallic, frost white, sunshine yellow, almond, nugget gold metallic, cinnamon red, apple red and, as a secondary color only, satin black.

The Blazer's Insta-Trac four-wheel drive system was the first 4x4 system to have a lighted action display of the gear position. To shift from rear-wheel drive into four wheel-drive the driver moved the 4 wheel shift lever on the lighted shift console from 2 Wheel to 4 High. When the lever is moved from 2 Wheel to 4 High the transfer case divides the torque. At the same time a locking sleeve in the front axle engaged the central disconnect to provide power to both front axle shafts. Shifting from 4x4 to rear wheel-drive was accomplished by shifting from 4 High to 2 Wheel. The locking sleeve then disengaged the central disconnect, allowing the front axle to freewheel. The Truck had to be stopped only when shifting into and out of four wheel-drive low.

1983 Chevrolet S-10 Blazer

I.D. DATA: The V.I.N. plate was mounted on the lower left side windshield corner. The V.I.N. consisted of 17 elements. The first, the number 1 identified the U.S. as the nation of origin. The letter G followed, for the manufacturer: General Motors. The third entry, the letter C represented the make as Chevrolet. The GVWR brake system identification followed. Next came the truck line and chassis type; the letter K indicated four-wheel drive. The truck series was identified by a number: 1-1/2 ton. The truck body type identification was next: 8-Utility. The engine code was next: Y-2.0 liter, A-1.9 liter, B-2.8 liter V-6, followed by a check digit. The model year was identified by the letter D. The assembly plant code followed. The final six digits were the plant sequential production number.

Model Number	Body Type & Seating	Factory Price	GVW	Shipping Weight	Prod. Total
Blazer S-10					
CT10516	Util. (with top)	$9433	4075[1]	3106	106,214[2]

NOTE 1: 4850 lb. GVW optional.
NOTE 2: Calendar year sales, includes both two-wheel drive and four-wheel drive models.

STANDARD ENGINE: All states except California: Ordering Code LQ2. Produced by GM-Chevrolet Motor Division. Engine Type: Cast iron block. OHV, In-line 4. Bore x Stroke: 3.50 in. x 3.15 in. Lifters: Hydraulic. Number of main bearings-5. Carburetion: Two barrel. Compression Ratio: 9.3:1. Displacement: 121 cu. in. (2.0 liter). Horsepower: Net: 83 @ 4600 rpm. Torque: Net: 108 lb.-ft. @ 2400 rpm. Oil capacity: 5 qt. with filter change. Fuel Requirements: Unleaded.

STANDARD ENGINE: California only: Engine Type: Cast iron block. OHV, In-line 4. Ordering Code: LR1. Produced by Isuzu Motors Limited, Japan. Bore x Stroke: 3.42 in. x 3.23 in. Lifters: Hydraulic. Carburetion: Two barrel. Compression Ratio: 8.4:1. Displacement: 119 cu. in. (1.9 liters). Horsepower: Net: 82 @ 4600 rpm. Torque: Net: 101 lb.-ft. @ 3000 rpm. Fuel Requirements: Unleaded.

OPTIONAL ENGINE: 50 states: Engine Type: OHV, Cast iron block. V-6. Order Code LR2. Produced by GM-Chevrolet Motor Division. Bore x Stroke: 3.50 in. x 2.99 in. Lifters: Hydraulic. Number of main bearings-5. Carburetion: 2-barrel. Compression Ratio: 8.5. Displacement: 173 cu. in. (2.8 liter). Horsepower: Net: 110 @ 4800 rpm. Torque: Net: 145 lb.-ft. @ 2100 rpm. Oil capacity: 5 qt. with filter change. Fuel Requirements: Unleaded.

CHASSIS FEATURES: Carbon steel, welded front box section and open channel rear section.

SUSPENSION AND RUNNING GEAR: Front Suspension: Independent with torsion bar springs, 25mm dia. shock absorbers. 32mm stabilizer bar. Capacity: 1150 lbs. each at ground. Optional: 32mm shock absorbers. Rear Suspension: Two-stage multi-leaf shot-peened springs. Capacity: 1350 lbs. each at ground. 25mm shock absorbers. Optional: 32mm shock absorbers. Front Axle. Type: Hypoid, tubular driving. Capacity: 2300 lb. Rear Axle. Type: Salisbury, hypoid. Capacity: 2700 lb. Final Drive Ratio: Standard 4-spd. manual transmission and optional 5-spd. manual overdrive: 3.73:1 (3.08:1 for high altitude emission system). Automatic transmission: 3.42:1 (3.73:1 for high altitude emission system). Optional: Standard 4-spd. manual transmission and optional 5-spd. manual overdrive: 4.11:1 (3.73:1 for high altitude emission system). Automatic transmission: 3.73:1. Transfer Case: New Process 207. Brakes: Type: Hydraulic, power assisted self-adjusting. Front: Discs. Rear: Drums. Dimensions: Front: 9.5 in. x 2.0 in. rotor. Rear: 9.5 in. x 2.0 in. Wheels: 15 in. Tires: P195/75R15 glass belted radial black sidewall. Optional: P195/75R15 black sidewall, P205/75R15 black sidewall, P205/75R15 white sidewall, P205/75R15 white letters, P205/75R15 on-off road black sidewall. Steering: Manual. Optional: Power. Transmission: 4-speed manual. Optional: 5-speed manual with overdrive, 4-speed automatic with overdrive (with V-6 engine only). Clutch: 4-cyl. engine: 9.12 in. dia., V-6: 9.76 in. dia.

VEHICLE DIMENSIONS: Wheelbase: 100.5 in. Overall Length: 170.3 in. Front/Rear Tread 55.6 in./54.1 in. Overall Height: 64.9 in. Width: 64.7 in. Approach/Departure Degrees: 28° 17'/ 25.5° 30'. Ground Clearance: Front axle: 8.1 in. Rear axle: 6.9 in.

CAPACITIES: Fuel Tank: 13.2 gal. Optional: Replacement 20 gal. tank.

ACCOMMODATIONS: Seating Capacity: Standard: Driver and passenger front high back bucket sets. Optional: 3 passenger rear bench seat.

INSTRUMENTATION: 0-100 mph speedometer, 99,999.9 mi. odometer, fuel gauge, warning lights for alternator, oil pressure, engine coolant temperature, brake operating system, hazard warning lights, directional lights, seat belt warning.

OPTIONS: Tahoe Package: $576. Air conditioning. Automatic speed control. ComforTilt steering wheel. Power steering. Gauges for oil pressure, engine coolant temperature and voltmeter with trip odometer. Tachometer with gauges. Digital clock (with radio only). Delco radios. Premium rear speakers. Below eye-level mirrors. Styled wheels with special hub ornament and bright trim rings. Operating Convenience Package. Includes power windows and door locks. Dome/reading light. Halogen headlamps. 66 amp Delcotron generator. Heavy-duty Freedom battery. Reclining bucket seat backs. Center console. Color-keyed floor mats. Visor mirror. Door edge guards. Body striping. Spare tire cover. Body side/wheel-opening moldings. Color-keyed front/rear bumpers. Black front bumper guards. Rear air deflector. Front tow hooks. Black or bright wheel-opening moldings. Cast aluminum wheels. Bright wheel trim rings. Full-size spare tire. Heavy-duty radiator. Heavy-duty radiator with transmission or engine cooler with V-6 and automatic transmission. Locking differential rear axle. Heavy-duty front and rear shock absorbers. Off-Road Chassis Package. Stone shield for transfer case and differential carrier. Intermittent windshield wipers. Engine block heater. Deadweight trailer hitch. Trailering Package (either 4,000 or 5,000 lb).

HISTORICAL FOOTNOTES: The new-size Blazer was introduced on September 14, 1982. *4-Wheel & Off-Road* magazine recognized the S-10 Blazer as "4x4 of the Year." *Four Wheeler* magazine gave the S-10 Blazer its "4-Wheeler of the Year" award.

1984 S-10 BLAZER

Changes for 1984 were limited to detail refinements. Models with the V-6 engine had "2.8 liter V-6" identification below the driver's side headlight. A small V6 emblem mounted on the front fender had been used in 1983. A new Off-Road Package was introduced, with availability beginning in October, 1983, featuring Delco Bilstein gas-pressure shock absorbers, transfer case shield, fuel tank shield, front tow hooks and jounce bumpers. This option requires the optional 1500 lb. payload package and P235 steel belted, on/off-road white lettered tires, including full-size spare. Front and axle clearance with this feature are respectively, 7.1 in. and 8.2 in. A new hydraulic clutch was standard for 1984 with an automatic adjustment feature. The 1984 interior color selection consisted of clue, carmine, charcoal or Saddle tan. Exterior colors were: Silver metallic, frost white, midnight black, light blue metallic, galaxy blue metallic, doeskin tan, Indian bronze metallic, desert sand metallic, apple red, cinnamon red and, as a secondary color only, satin black. As in 1983, the front passenger seat slid forward on rails when the back rest was tilted forward. When the back rest was returned to its normal position, the seat returned to its preset position when pushed to the rear. The Sport interior was available with optional High Country Sheepskin in saddle tan. The optional rear seat in this arrangement was trimmed in Sport cloth. A new speed adjustment was included in the optional electronic speed control. It allowed the driver to increase or decrease speed in increments of 1 mph.

1984 Chevrolet S-10 Blazer Sport

I.D. DATA: The V.I.N. plate was mounted on the lower left side windshield corner. The V.I.N. consisted of 17 elements. The first, the number 1 identified the U.S. as the nation of origin. The letter G followed, for the manufacturer: General Motors. The third entry, the letter C represented the make as Chevrolet. The GVWR brake system identification followed. Next came the truck line and chassis type; the letter K indicated four-wheel drive. The truck series was identified by a number: 1-1/2 ton. The truck body type identification was next: 8-Utility. The engine code was next: Y-2.0 liter, A-1.9 liter, B-2.8 liter V-6, followed by a check digit. The model year was identified by the letter E. The assembly plant code followed. The final six digits were the plant sequential production number.

Model Number	Body Type & Seating	Factory Price	GVW	Shipping Weight	Prod. Total
Blazer S-10					
CT10516	Util. (with top)	$9685	4075[1]	3146	150,599[2]

NOTE 1: 4850 lb. GVW optional.
NOTE 2: Calendar year sales, both two-wheel drive and four-wheel drive.

STANDARD ENGINE: All states except California: Ordering Code LQ2. Produced by GM-Chevrolet Motor Division. Engine Type: Cast iron block. OHV, In-line 4. Bore x Stroke: 3.50 in. x 3.15 in. Lifters: Hydraulic. Number of main bearings-5. Carburetion: Two barrel. Compression Ratio: 9.3:1. Displacement: 121 cu. in. (2.0 liter). Horsepower: Net: 83 @ 4600 rpm. Torque: Net: 108 lb.-ft. @ 2400 rpm. Oil capacity: 5 qt. with filter change. Fuel Requirements: Unleaded.

STANDARD ENGINE: California only: Engine Type: Cast iron block. OHV, In-line 4. Ordering Code: LR1. Produced by Isuzu Motors Limited, Japan. Bore x Stroke: 3.42 in. x 3.23 in. Lifters: Hydraulic. Carburetion: Two barrel. Compression Ratio: 8.4:1. Displacement: 119 cu. in. (1.9 liters). Horsepower: Net: 82 @ 4600 rpm. Torque: Net: 101 lb.-ft. @ 3000 rpm. Fuel Requirements: Unleaded.

OPTIONAL ENGINE: 50 states. Engine Type: OHV, Cast iron block. V-6. Order Code LR2. Produced by GM-Chevrolet Motor Division. Bore x Stroke: 3.50 in. x 2.99 in. Lifters: Hydraulic. Number of main bearings-5. Carburetion: 2-barrel. Compression Ratio: 8.5:1. Displacement: 173 cu. in. (2.8 liter). Horsepower: Net: 110 @ 4800 rpm. Torque: Net: 145 lb.-ft. @ 2100 rpm. Oil capacity: 5 qt. with filter change. Fuel Requirements: Unleaded.

CHASSIS FEATURES: Carbon steel, welded front box section and open channel rear section.

SUSPENSION AND RUNNING GEAR: Front Suspension: Independent with torsion bar springs, 25mm dia. shock absorbers. 32mm stabilizer bar. Capacity: 1200 lbs. each at ground. Optional: 32mm shock absorbers. Rear Suspension: Two-stage multi-leaf shot-peened springs. Capacity: 1350 lbs. each at ground. 25mm shock absorbers. Optional: 32mm shock absorbers. Front Axle. Type: Hypoid, tubular driving. Capacity: 2400 lb. Rear Axle. Type: Salisbury, hypoid. Capacity: 2700 lb. Final Drive Ratio: Standard 4-spd. manual transmission and optional 5-spd. manual overdrive: 3.73:1 (3.08:1 for high altitude emission system). Automatic transmission: 3.42:1 (3.73:1 for high altitude emission system). Optional: Standard 4-spd. manual transmission and optional 5-spd. manual overdrive: 4.11:1 (3.73:1 for high altitude emission system). Automatic transmission: 3.73:1. Transfer Case: New Process 207. Brakes: Type: Hydraulic, power assisted self-adjusting. Front: Discs. Rear: Drums. Dimensions: Front: 9.5 in. x 2.0 in. rotor. Rear: 9.5 in. x 2.0 in. Wheels: 15 in. Tires: P195/75R15 glass belted radial black sidewall. Optional: P195/75R15 black sidewall, P205/75R15 black sidewall, P205/75R15 white sidewall, P205/75R15 white letters, P205/75R15 on-off road black sidewall. Steering: Manual. Optional: Power. Transmission: 4-speed manual. Optional: 5-speed manual with overdrive, 4-speed automatic with overdrive (with V-6 engine only). Clutch: 4-cyl. engine: 9.12 in. dia., V-6: 9.76 in. dia.

VEHICLE DIMENSIONS: Wheelbase: 100.5 in. Overall Length: 170.3 in. Front/Rear Tread 55.6 in./54.1 in. Overall Height: 64.9 in. Width: 64.7 in. Approach/Departure Degrees: 28° 17'/ 25.5° 30'. Ground Clearance: Front axle: 8.1 in. Rear axle: 6.9 in.

CAPACITIES: Fuel Tank: 13.2 gal. Optional: Replacement 20 gal. tank.

ACCOMMODATIONS: Seating Capacity: Standard: Driver and passenger front high back bucket sets. Optional: 3 passenger rear bench seat.

INSTRUMENTATION: 0-100 mph speedometer, 99,999.9 mi. odometer, fuel gauge, warning lights for alternator, oil pressure, engine coolant temperature, brake operating system, hazard warning lights, directional lights, seat belt warning.

OPTIONS: Tahoe Package: $576. Air conditioning. Automatic speed control. ComforTilt steering wheel. Power steering. Gauges for oil pressure, engine coolant temperature and voltmeter with trip odometer. Tachometer with gauges. Digital clock (with radio only). Delco radios. Premium rear speakers. Below eye-level mirrors. Styled wheels with special hub ornament and bright trim rings. Operating Convenience Package. Includes power windows and door locks. Dome/reading light. Halogen headlamps. 66 amp Delcotron generator. Heavy-duty Freedom battery. Reclining bucket seat backs. Center console. Color-keyed floor mats. Visor mirror. Door edge guards. Body striping. Spare tire cover. Body side/wheel opening moldings. Color-keyed front/rear bumpers. Black front bumper guards. Rear air deflector. Front tow hooks. Black or bright wheel opening moldings. Cast aluminum wheels. Bright wheel trim rings. Full-size spare tire. Heavy-duty radiator. Heavy-duty radiator with transmission or

engine cooler with V-6 and automatic transmission. Locking differential rear axle. Heavy-duty front and rear shock absorbers. Off-Road Chassis Package. Stone shield for transfer case and differential carrier. Intermittent windshield wipers. Engine block heater. Deadweight trailer hitch. Trailering Package (either 4,000 or 5,000 lb).

HISTORICAL FOOTNOTES: The 1984 Blazer was introduced in the fall of 1983. Combined sales of the four-wheel drive S-10 Blazer and its GMC counterpart for 1984 were 129,264.

1985 S-10 BLAZER

The Blazer had a new Tech IV, 2.5 liter, 4-cylinder, electronically fuel injected standard engine for 1985. This engine provided a 10 percent increase in horsepower and a 22 percent increase in torque over the previous standard engine. The Tahoe option was now available with a new Custom vinyl or extra cost Special Custom cloth upholstery. It also included color-keyed door handle inserts, body side and bright wheel opening moldings, black quarter window moldings, special tailgate applique, wheel trim rings, Tahoe nameplate on instrument panel, special door trim with coin holder in left hand door panel, deluxe armrests and map pockets, special color-keyed carpeting, visor mirror, special body insulation, gauge package with trip odometer, and spare tire cover (if spare tire and wheel carrier were not ordered). The Sport Equipment Package included reclining seat backs, console, color-keyed front and rear bumpers, black door handle inserts, body side and black wheel opening moldings, black quarter window moldings, special tailgate applique, Sport nameplate on instrument panel, special door trim with coin holder in left hand door panel, deluxe armrests and map pockets, color-keyed carpeting, visor mirror, special body insulation, gauge package with trip odometer and spare tire cover (if spare tire and wheel carrier are not ordered). Both the interior and exterior color selections of 1984 were carried over into 1985.

1985 Chevrolet S-10 Blazer

I.D. DATA: The V.I.N. plate was mounted on the lower left side windshield corner. The V.I.N. consisted of 17 elements. The first, the number 1 identified the U.S. as the nation of origin. The letter G followed, for the manufacturer: General Motors. The third entry, the letter C represented the make as Chevrolet. The GVWR brake system identification followed. Next came the truck line and chassis type; the letter K indicated four-wheel drive. The truck series was identified by a number: 1-1/2 ton. The truck body type identification was next: 8-Utility. The engine code was next: E-2.5 liter, B-2.8 liter V-6, followed by a check digit. The model year was identified by the letter E. The assembly plant code followed. The final six digits were the plant sequential production number.

Model Number	Body Type & Seating	Factory Price	GVW	Shipping Weight	Prod. Total
Blazer S-10					
CT10516	Util. (with top)	$10,134[1]	4075[2]	3156	150,599[3]

NOTE 1: Price effective with vehicles produced after January 2, 1985. Earlier price sources indicate a price of $9994.
NOTE 2: 4850 lb. GVW optional.
NOTE 3: Calendar year sales, both two-wheel drive and four-wheel drive.

STANDARD ENGINE: Ordering Code LN8. Produced by Pontiac Motor Division. Engine Type: Cast iron block. OHV, In-line 4. Bore x Stroke: 4.0 in. x 3.0 in. Lifters: Hydraulic. Number of main bearings-5. Compression Ratio: 9.0:1. Displacement: 151 cu. in. (2.5 liter). Horsepower: Net: 92 @ 4400 rpm. Torque: Net: 134 lb.-ft. @ 2800 rpm. Oil capacity: 5 qt. with filter change. Fuel Requirements: Unleaded.

OPTIONAL ENGINE: Engine Type: OHV, Cast iron block. V-6. Order Code LR2. Produced by GM-Chevrolet Motor Division. Bore x Stroke: 3.50 in. x 2.99 in. Lifters: Hydraulic. Number of main bearings-5. Carburetion: 2-barrel. Compression Ratio: 8.5:1. Displacement: 173 cu. in. (2.8 liter). Horsepower: Net: 115 @ 4800 rpm. Torque: Net: 150 lb.-ft. @ 2100 rpm. Oil capacity: 5 qt. with filter change. Fuel Requirements: Unleaded.

CHASSIS FEATURES: Carbon steel, welded front box section and open channel rear section.

SUSPENSION AND RUNNING GEAR: Front Suspension: Independent with torsion bar springs, 25mm dia. shock absorbers. 32mm stabilizer bar. Capacity: 1200 lbs. each at ground. Optional: 32mm shock absorbers. Rear Suspension: Two-stage multi-leaf shot-peened springs. Capacity: 1350 lbs. each at ground. 25mm shock absorbers. Optional: 32mm shock absorbers. Front Axle. Type: Hypoid, tubular driving. Capacity: 2400 lb. Rear Axle. Type: Salisbury, hypoid. Capacity: 2700 lb. Final Drive Ratio: Standard 4-spd. manual transmission and optional 5-spd. manual overdrive: 3.73:1 (3.08:1 for high altitude emission system). Automatic transmission: 3.42:1 (3.73:1 for high altitude emission system). Optional: Standard 4-spd. manual transmission and optional 5-spd. manual overdrive: 4.11:1 (3.73:1 for high altitude emission system). Automatic transmission: 3.73:1. Transfer Case: New Process 207. Brakes: Type: Hydraulic, power assisted self-adjusting. Front: Discs. Rear: Drums. Dimensions: Front: 9.5 in. x 2.0 in. rotor. Rear: 9.5 in. x 2.0 in. Wheels: 15 in. Tires: P195/75R15 glass belted radial black sidewall. Optional: P195/75R15 black sidewall, P205/75R15 black sidewall, P205/75R15 white sidewall, P205/75R15 white letters, P205/75R15 on-off road black sidewall. Steering: Manual. Optional: Power. Transmission: 4-speed manual. Optional: 5-speed manual with overdrive, 4-speed automatic with overdrive. Clutch: 4-cyl. engine: 9.12 in. dia., V-6: 9.76 in. dia.

VEHICLE DIMENSIONS: Wheelbase: 100.5 in. Overall Length: 170.3 in. Front/Rear Tread 55.6 in./54.1 in. Overall Height: 64.9 in. Width: 64.7 in. Approach/Departure Degrees: 28° 17'/ 25.5° 30'. Ground Clearance: Front axle: 8.1 in. Rear axle: 6.9 in.

CAPACITIES: Fuel Tank: 13.2 gal. Optional: Replacement 20 gal. tank.

ACCOMMODATIONS: Seating Capacity: Standard: Driver and passenger front high back bucket sets. Optional: 3 passenger rear bench seat.

INSTRUMENTATION: 0-100 mph speedometer, 99,999.9 mi. odometer, fuel gauge, warning lights for alternator, oil pressure, engine coolant temperature, brake operating system, hazard warning lights, directional lights, seat belt warning.

OPTIONS: Tahoe Package: $595. Sport Package: $940. Sport cloth vinyl high-back bucket seat trim: $24. High Country Sheepskin high-back bucket seats: $295. Custom two-tone paint: $200. Special two-tone paint: $167-$311 depending upon trim package. Sport two-tone paint: $162-$227 depending upon trim package. California emissions system: $99. 2.6 liter V-6 engine: $225. 4-speed overdrive automatic transmission: $670. Optional axle ratio: $36. Locking rear differential: $238. Pre-cleaner air cleaner: 49. 5-speed manual overdrive transmission: $175. All-Weather air conditioning: $705. Heavy-duty battery: $53. Front black bumper guards: $30. Luggage carrier, black or bright finish: $120. Spare wheel and tire carrier: $118-$150 depending upon trim package. Off-Road Package: $602-$658 depending upon trim package. Cold Climate Package: $107-$179 depending upon trim package. Front compartment console: $108. Engine oil cooling system: $120. Heavy-duty radiator: $53. Heavy-duty radiator and transmission oil cooler: $59 with air conditioning, $112 without air conditioning. Spare tire cover: $32. Air deflector: $41. Rear window defogger: $114 with air conditioning, $145 without air conditioning. Power door locks: $135. Color-keyed floor mats: Front: $15, Rear: $11. Gauge Package. Includes voltmeter, engine coolant temperature, oil pressure: $58. Gauge Package plus tachometer: $55-$113 depending upon trim package. 66 amp Delcotron generator: $31. Deep tinted glass: $190. Deep tinted glass with light tinted rear window: $135. Halogen headlights: $22. Engine block heater: $31. Engine compartment light: $15. Exterior left and right side painted mirrors: $50. Exterior left and right side bright mirrors: $83. Body side and wheel opening moldings: $17-$144 depending upon trim package. Door edge guards: $17. Bright wheel opening moldings: $28. Black wheel opening moldings: $12-$41 depending upon trim package. Operating Convenience Package: $325. AM radio: $112. AM/FM radio: $171. AM/FM radio with clock: $210. AM/FM stereo radio with electronic tuning: $238. AM/FM stereo radio and clock with electronic tuning: 277. AM/FM stereo radio with Seek-Scan, stereo cassette tape, clock and graphic equalizer and electronic tuning and premium rear speakers: $594. Premium rear speakers: $25. Folding rear bench seat: $341. Reclining front seat backs: $70. Transfer case shield: $67. Heavy-duty front and rear shock absorbers: $34. Full size spare tire: $46-90 depending upon size. Electronic speed control: $260. ComforTilt steering wheel: $115. Striping: $65. Heavy-duty suspension equipment: $59. Power release tailgate window: $41. 20 gal. fuel tank: $49. Two front towing hooks: $36. Dead weight trailer hitch: $64. Heavy-Duty Trailering Special: $199. Light-Duty Trailering Special: $103. Wheel trim rings: $56. Rallye wheels: $32-$88 depending upon trim package. Styled wheels: $32-$88 depending upon trim package. Cast aluminum wheels: $238-$294 depending upon trim package. Power side door windows: $190. Intermittent windshield wiper system: $55.

HISTORICAL FOOTNOTES: The 1985 Blazer was introduced on September 21, 1984.

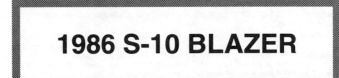

1986 S-10 BLAZER

The 1986 S-10 Blazer had a new instrument panel with a revamped instrument cluster, and a tray at the panel bottom. The gauge cluster now included tell-tale lights in addition to the voltmeter, oil pressure and engine coolant temperature gauges. The door trim panels were restyled and the switches for the optional power windows were relocated on the door panels. A new black molded urethane steering wheel was installed on all models. The Sport steering wheel now had a simulated leather look. Also new for the Sport Package was tweed-pattern cloth seat trim. The standard 2.5 liter engine had lighter-weight high silicon pistons. The 2.8 liter V-6 was fitted with electronic fuel injection. Its exterior front body identification now read "2.8 Fuel Injection." Models with the V-6 had a higher-capacity Delco Freedom III battery. The optional heavy-duty battery offered for both engines had a higher capacity for 1986. Also new for 1986 was a lighter-weight radiator with a standard copper-brass core arranged for crossflow coolant movement and plastic side tanks. The exterior color selection for 1986 consisted of midnight black, steel gray metallic, light blue metallic, galaxy blue metallic, doeskin tan, Indian bronze metallic, cinnamon red, apple red, Nevada gold and silver metallic (used as a secondary color only).

I.D. DATA: The V.I.N. plate was mounted on the lower left side windshield corner. The V.I.N. consisted of 17 elements. The first, the number 1 identified the U.S. as the nation of origin. The letter G followed, for the manufacturer: General Motors. The third entry, the letter C represented the make as Chevrolet. The GVWR brake system identification followed. Next came the truck line and chassis type; the letter K indicated four-wheel drive. The truck series was identified by a number: 1-1/2 ton. The truck body type identification was next: 8-Utility. The engine code was next: E-2.5 liter, B-2.8 liter V-6, followed by a check digit. The model year was identified by the letter G. The assembly plant code followed. The final six digits were the plant sequential production number.

Model Number	Body Type & Seating	Factory Price	GVW	Shipping Weight	Prod. Total
Blazer S-10					
CT10516	Util. (with top)	$10,698	4075[1]	3152	170,742[2]

NOTE 1: 4850 lb. GVW optional.
NOTE 2: Nov., 1985-Nov., 1986 sales, both two-wheel drive and four-wheel drive.

STANDARD ENGINE: Ordering Code LN8. Produced by Pontiac Motor Division. Engine Type: Cast iron block. OHV, In-line 4. Bore x Stroke: 4.0 in. x 3.0 in. Lifters: Hydraulic. Number of main bearings-5. Fuel induction: Electronic fuel injection. Compression Ratio: 9.0:1. Displacement: 151 cu. in. (2.5 liter). Horsepower: Net: 92 @ 4400 rpm. Torque: Net: 134 lb.-ft. @ 2800 rpm. Oil capacity: 5 qt. with filter change. Fuel Requirements: Unleaded.

OPTIONAL ENGINE: Engine Type: OHV, Cast iron block. V-6. Order Code LR2. Produced by GM-Chevrolet Motor Division. Bore x Stroke: 3.50 in. x 2.99 in. Lifters: Hydraulic. Number of main bearings-5. Fuel Induction: Electronic fuel injection. Compression Ratio: 8.9:1. Displacement: 173 cu. in. (2.8 liter). Horsepower: Net: 125 @ 4800 rpm. Torque: Net: 150 lb.-ft. @ 2200 rpm. Oil capacity: 5 qt. with filter change. Fuel Requirements: Unleaded.

CHASSIS FEATURES: Carbon steel, welded front box section and open channel rear section.

SUSPENSION AND RUNNING GEAR: Front Suspension: Independent with torsion bar springs, 25mm dia. shock absorbers. 32mm stabilizer bar. Capacity: 1200 lbs. each at ground. Optional: 32mm shock absorbers. Rear Suspension: Two-stage multi-leaf shot-peened springs. Capacity: 1350 lbs. each at ground. 25mm shock absorbers. Optional: 32mm shock absorbers. Front Axle. Type: Hypoid, tubular driving. Capacity: 2400 lb. Rear Axle. Type: Salisbury, hypoid. Capacity: 2700 lb. Final Drive Ratio: Standard 4-spd. manual transmission and optional 5-spd. manual overdrive: 3.73:1 (3.08:1 for high altitude emission system). Automatic transmission: 3.42:1 (3.73:1 for high altitude emission system). Optional: Standard 4-spd. manual transmission and optional 5-spd. manual overdrive: 4.11:1 (3.73:1 for high altitude emission system). Automatic transmission: 3.73:1. Transfer Case: New Process 207. Brakes: Type: Hydraulic, power assisted self-adjusting. Front: Discs. Rear: Drums. Dimensions: Front: 9.5 in. x 2.0 in. rotor. Rear: 9.5 in. x 2.0 in. Wheels: 15 in. Tires: P195/75R15 glass belted radial black sidewall. Optional: P195/75R15 black sidewall, P205/75R15 black sidewall, P205/75R15 white sidewall, P205/75R15 white letters, P205/75R15 on-off road black sidewall. Steering: Manual. Optional: Power. Transmission: 4-speed manual. Optional: 5-speed manual with overdrive, 4-speed automatic with overdrive. Clutch: 4-cyl. engine: 9.12 in. dia., V-6: 9.76 in. dia.

VEHICLE DIMENSIONS: Wheelbase: 100.5 in. Overall Length: 170.3 in. Front/Rear Tread 55.6 in./54.1 in. Overall Height: 64.9 in. Width: 64.7 in. Approach/Departure Degrees: 28° 17'/ 25.5° 30'. Ground Clearance: Front axle: 8.1 in. Rear axle: 6.9 in.

CAPACITIES: Fuel Tank: 13.2 gal., Optional: Replacement 20 gal. tank.

ACCOMMODATIONS: Seating Capacity: Standard: Driver and passenger front high back bucket sets. Optional: 3 passenger rear bench seat.

INSTRUMENTATION: 0-100 mph speedometer, 99,999.9 mi. odometer, fuel gauge, warning lights for alternator, oil pressure, engine coolant temperature, brake operating system, hazard warning lights, directional lights, seat belt warning.

OPTIONS: Tahoe Package: $595. Sport Package: $940. Sport cloth vinyl high-back bucket seat trim: $24. High Country Sheepskin high-back bucket seats: $295. Custom two-tone paint: $200. Special two-tone paint: $167-$311 depending upon trim package. Sport two-tone paint: $162-$227 depending upon trim package. California emissions system: $99. 2.6 liter V-6 engine: $225. 4-speed overdrive automatic transmission: $670. Optional axle ratio: $36. Locking rear differential: $238. Pre-cleaner air cleaner: 49. 5-speed manual overdrive transmission: $175. All-Weather air conditioning: $705. Heavy-duty battery: $53. Front black bumper guards: $30. Luggage carrier, black or bright finish: $120. Spare wheel and tire carrier: $118-$150 depending upon trim package. Off-Road Package: $602-$658 depending upon trim package. Cold Climate Package: $107-$179 depending upon trim package. Front compartment console: $108. Engine oil cooling system: $120. Heavy-duty radiator: $53. Heavy-duty radiator and transmission oil cooler: $59 with air conditioning, $112 without air conditioning. Spare tire cover: $32. Air deflector: $41. Rear window defogger: $114 with air conditioning, $145 without air conditioning. Power door locks: $135. Color-keyed floor mats: Front: $15, Rear: $11. Gauge Package. Includes voltmeter, engine coolant temperature, oil pressure and tell-tale lights: $58. Gauge Package plus tachometer: $55-$113 depending upon trim package. 66 amp Delcotron generator: $31. Deep tinted glass: $190. Deep tinted glass with light tinted rear window: $135. Halogen headlights: $22. Engine block heater: $31. Engine compartment light: $15. Exterior left and right side painted mirrors: $50. Exterior left and right side bright mirrors: $83. Body side and wheel opening moldings: $17-$144 depending upon trim package. Door edge guards: $17. Bright wheel opening moldings: $28. Black wheel opening moldings: $12-$41 depending upon trim package. Operating Convenience Package: $325. AM radio: $112. AM/FM radio: $171. AM/FM radio with clock: $210. AM/FM stereo radio with electronic tuning: $238 AM/FM stereo radio and clock with electronic tuning: 277. AM/FM stereo radio with Seek-Scan, stereo cassette tape, clock and graphic equalizer and electronic tuning and premium rear speakers: $594. Premium rear speakers: $25. Folding rear bench seat: $341. Reclining front seat backs: $70. Transfer case shield: $67. Heavy-duty front and rear shock absorbers: $34. Full size spare tire: $46-90 depending upon size. Electronic speed control: $260. ComforTilt steering wheel: $115. Striping: $65. Heavy-duty suspension equipment: $59. Power release tailgate window: $41. 20 gal. fuel tank: $49. Two front towing hooks: $36. Dead weight trailer hitch: $64. Heavy-Duty Trailering Special: $199. Light-Duty Trailering Special: $103. Wheel trim rings: $56. Rallye wheels: $32-$88 depending upon trim package. Styled wheels: $32-$88 depending upon trim package. Cast aluminum wheels: $238-$294 depending upon trim package. Power side door windows: $190. Intermittent windshield wiper system: $55.

HISTORICAL FOOTNOTES: The 1986 Blazer was introduced in the fall of 1985.

1987 S-10 BLAZER

Introduced as a mid-year option for the 1987 S-10 Blazer, which was the most popular vehicle of its kind in the U.S., was a new "High Country" Package. It featured a gold lower paint color that gradually blended into the black upper body color. It also included special gold color aluminum wheels, gold color key bumpers with rub strips, gold fender name plates, black grille, black exterior mirrors, black body side moldings, and black wheel opening moldings. The standard 2.5 liter engine had a redesigned intake manifold and high flow ports in the cylinder head. A single belt accessory "serpentine" drive replaced the conventional multiple V belts on both the 2.5 and 2.8 liter engines. This system featured automatic belt tensioning that eliminated the need for adjustments throughout the life of the truck. The expected belt life was 100,000 miles. Both the standard Delcotron generator and all batteries had higher capacities for 1987. The tailgate applique for the Tahoe and Sport models was restyled. The cinnamon red color of 1986 was not offered for 1987. A new color added to the remaining colors carried over from 1986 was Emerald metallic. The interior color selections were unchanged from 1986.

1987 Chevrolet S-10 "High Country" Blazer

I.D. DATA: The V.I.N. plate was mounted on the lower left side windshield corner. The V.I.N. consisted of 17 elements. The first, the number 1 identified the U.S. as the nation of origin. The letter G followed, for the manufacturer: General Motors. The third entry, the letter C represented the make as Chevrolet. The GVWR brake system identification followed. Next came the truck line and chassis type; the letter K indicated four-wheel drive. The truck series was identified by a number: 1-1/2 ton. The truck body type identification was next: 8-Utility. The engine code was next: E-2.5 liter, B-2.8 liter V-6, followed by a check digit. The model year was identified by the letter H. The assembly plant code followed. The final six digits were the plant sequential production number.

Model Number	Body Type & Seating	Factory Price	GVW	Shipping Weight	Prod. Total
Blazer S-10					
CT10516	Util. (with top)	$11,588	4075[1]	3140	—

NOTE 1: 4850 lb. GVW optional.

STANDARD ENGINE: Ordering Code LN8. Produced by Pontiac Motor Division. Engine Type: Cast iron block. OHV, In-line 4. Bore x Stroke: 4.0 in. x 3.0 in. Lifters: Hydraulic. Number of main bearings-5. Fuel induction: Electronic fuel injection. Compression Ratio: 9.0:1. Displacement: 151 cu. in. (2.5 liter). Horsepower: Net: 92 @ 4400 rpm. Torque: Net: 134 lb.-ft. @ 2800 rpm. Oil capacity: 5 qt. with filter change. Fuel Requirements: Unleaded.

OPTIONAL ENGINE: Engine Type: OHV, Cast iron block. V-6. Order Code LR2. Produced by GM-Chevrolet Motor Division. Bore x Stroke: 3.50 in. x 2.99 in. Lifters: Hydraulic. Number of main bearings-5. Fuel Induction: Electronic fuel injection. Compression Ratio: 8.9:1. Displacement: 173 cu. in. (2.8 liter). Horsepower: Net: 125 @ 4800 rpm. Torque: Net: 150 lb.-ft. @ 2200 rpm. Oil capacity: 5 qt. with filter change. Fuel Requirements: Unleaded.

CHASSIS FEATURES: Carbon steel, welded front box section and open channel rear section.

SUSPENSION AND RUNNING GEAR: Front Suspension: Independent with torsion bar springs, 25mm dia. shock absorbers. 32mm stabilizer bar. Capacity: 1200 lbs. each at ground. Optional: 32mm shock absorbers. Rear Suspension: Two-stage multi-leaf shot-peened springs. Capacity: 1350 lbs. each at ground. 25mm shock absorbers. Optional: 32mm shock absorbers. Front Axle. Type: Hypoid, tubular driving. Capacity: 2400 lb. Rear Axle. Type: Salisbury, hypoid. Capacity: 2700 lb. Final Drive Ratio: Standard 4-spd. manual transmission and optional 5-spd. manual overdrive: 3.73:1 (3.08:1 for high altitude emission system). Automatic transmission: 3.42:1 (3.73:1 for high altitude emission system). Optional: Standard 4-spd. manual transmission and optional 5-spd. manual overdrive: 4.11:1 (3.73:1 for high altitude emission system). Automatic transmission: 3.73:1. Transfer Case: New Process 207. Brakes: Type: Hydraulic, power assisted self-adjusting. Front: Discs. Rear: Drums. Dimensions: Front: 9.5 in. x 2.0 in. rotor. Rear: 9.5 in. x 2.0 in. Wheels: 15 in. Tires: P195/75R15 glass belted radial black sidewall. Optional: P195/75R15 black sidewall, P205/75R15 black sidewall, P205/75R15 white sidewall, P205/75R15 white letters, P205/75R15 on-off road black sidewall. Steering: Manual. Optional: Power. Transmission: 4-speed manual. Optional: 5-speed manual with overdrive, 4-speed automatic with overdrive. Clutch: 4-cyl. engine: 9.12 in. dia., V-6: 9.76 in. dia.

VEHICLE DIMENSIONS: Wheelbase: 100.5 in. Overall Length: 170.3 in. Front/Rear Tread 55.6 in./54.1 in. Overall Height: 64.9 in. Width: 64.7 in. Approach/Departure Degrees: 28° 17'/ 25.5° 30'. Ground Clearance: Front axle: 8.1 in. Rear axle: 6.9 in.

CAPACITIES: Fuel Tank: 13.2 gal., Optional: Replacement 20 gal. tank.

ACCOMMODATIONS: Seating Capacity: Standard: Driver and passenger front high back bucket sets. Optional: 3 passenger rear bench seat.

INSTRUMENTATION: 0-100 mph speedometer, 99,999.9 mi. odometer, fuel gauge, warning lights for alternator, oil pressure, engine coolant temperature, brake operating system, hazard warning lights, directional lights, seat belt warning.

OPTIONS: Tahoe Package. Sport Package. High Country Package. Sport cloth vinyl high-back bucket seat trim. High Country Sheepskin high-back bucket seats. Custom two-tone paint. Special two-tone paint. Sport two-tone paint. California emissions system. 2.8 liter V-6 engine. 4-speed overdrive automatic transmission. Optional axle ratio. Locking rear differential. Pre-cleaner air cleaner. 5-speed manual overdrive transmission. All-Weather air conditioning. Heavy-duty battery. Front black bumper guards. Luggage carrier, black or bright finish. Spare wheel and tire carrier. Off-Road Package. Cold Climate Package. Front compartment console. Engine oil cooling system. Heavy-duty radiator. Heavy-duty radiator and transmission oil cooler. Spare tire cover. Air deflector. Rear window defogger. Power door locks: $135. Color-keyed floor mats. Gauge Package. Includes voltmeter, engine coolant temperature, oil pressure. Gauge Package plus tachometer. 66 amp Delcotron generator. Deep tinted glass. Deep tinted glass with light tinted rear window. Halogen headlights. Engine block heater. Engine compartment light. Exterior left and right side painted mirrors. Exterior left and right side bright mirrors. Body side and wheel opening moldings. Door edge guards. Bright wheel opening moldings. Black wheel opening moldings. Operating Convenience Package. AM radio. AM/FM radio. AM/FM radio with clock. AM/FM stereo radio with electronic tuning. AM/FM stereo radio and clock with electronic tuning. AM/FM stereo radio with Seek-Scan, stereo cassette tape, clock and graphic equalizer and electronic tuning and premium rear speakers. Premium rear speakers. Folding rear bench seat. Reclining front seat backs. Transfer case shield. Heavy-duty front and rear shock absorbers. Full size spare tire. Electronic speed control. ComforTilt steering wheel. Striping. Heavy-duty suspension equipment. Power release tailgate window. 20 gal. fuel tank. Two front towing hooks. Deadweight trailer hitch: $64. Heavy-Duty Trailering Special: $199. Light-Duty Trailering Special. Wheel trim rings. Rallye wheels. Styled wheels. Cast aluminum wheels. Power side door windows. Intermittent windshield wiper system.

HISTORICAL FOOTNOTES: The 1987 Blazer was introduced on September 7, 1986.

1988 S-10 BLAZER

The 1988 Blazer's standard engine was the 2.8 liter V-6. Additional changes for 1988 were very limited. Models with rear seats were fitted with rear seat shoulder belts midway into the model year. Re-developed All-Season tires were available for the 1988 S-10 Blazer. Installed on all front brakes were new "SAS II" brake lining insulators that reduced brake noise. For 1988 the Blazer was available with a new optional factory-installed tinted sun roof. It was manually operated with five different opening positions and was non-removable. The S-10 Blazer's instrument panel was revised with gray accents on the trim plates. The knobs and switches remained black. L.E.D. displays on stereo radios were replaced by vacuum florescent lights. During the model year Blazers with air conditioning were equipped with illuminated blue heating, ventilation, and air-conditioning control lighting for improved indication of knob locations. Map lights were added to the inside rearview mirror. Four new exterior colors were added for 1988: Light Mesa brown, bright blue metallic, light Mesa brown metallic and dark Mesa brown metallic. Replacing saddle tan as an interior color was cognac. Beginning in April, 1988, the new 4.3 liter Vortex V-6 became an option for the S-10 Blazer.

1988 Chevrolet S-10 Blazer with Sport Package

I.D. DATA: The V.I.N. plate was mounted on the lower left side windshield corner. The V.I.N. consisted of 17 elements. The first, the number 1 identified the U.S. as the nation of origin. The letter G followed, for the manufacturer: General Motors. The third entry, the letter C represented the make as Chevrolet. The GVWR brake system identification followed. Next came the truck line and chassis type; the letter K indicated four-wheel drive. The truck series was identified by a number: 1-1/2 ton. The truck body type identification was next: 8-Utility. The engine code was next: B-2.8 liter V-6, N-4.3 liter V-6 followed by a check digit. The model year was identified by the letter H. The assembly plant code followed. The final six digits were the plant sequential production number.

Model Number	Body Type & Seating	Factory Price	GVW	Shipping Weight	Prod. Total
Blazer S-10					
T18	Util. (with top)	$12,737	4075[1]	3217	—

NOTE 1: 4850 lb. GVW optional.

STANDARD ENGINE: Engine Type: OHV, Cast iron block. V-6. Order Code LL2. Produced by GM-Chevrolet Motor Division in Canada and Mexico. Bore x Stroke: 3.50 in. x 2.99 in. Lifters: Hydraulic. Number of main bearings-5. Fuel Induction: Electronic fuel injection. Compression Ratio: 8.9:1. Displacement: 173 cu. in. (2.8 liter). Horsepower: Net: 125 @ 4800 rpm. Torque: Net: 150 lb.-ft. @ 2200 rpm. Oil capacity: 5 qt. with filter change. Fuel Requirements: Unleaded.

OPTIONAL ENGINE: Engine Type: OHV, Cast iron block. V-6. Order Code LB4. Bore x Stroke: 4.00 in. x 3.48 in. Lifters: Hydraulic. Number of main bearings-5. Fuel Induction: Electronic fuel injection. Compression Ratio: 9.3:1. Displacement: 262 cu. in. (4.3 liter). Horsepower: Net: 160 @ 4000 rpm. Torque: Net: 230 lb.-ft. @ 2400 rpm. Oil capacity: 5 qt. with filter change. Fuel Requirements: Unleaded.

CHASSIS FEATURES: Carbon steel, welded front box section and open channel rear section.

SUSPENSION AND RUNNING GEAR: Front Suspension: Independent with torsion bar springs, 25mm dia. shock absorbers. 32mm stabilizer bar. Capacity: 1200 lbs. each at ground. Optional: 32mm shock absorbers. Rear Suspension: Two-stage multi-leaf shot-peened springs. Capacity: 1350 lbs. each at ground. 25mm shock absorbers. Optional: 32mm shock absorbers. Front Axle. Type: Hypoid, tubular driving. Capacity: 2400 lb. Rear Axle. Type: Salisbury, hypoid. Capacity: 2700 lb. Final Drive Ratio: Standard 4-spd. manual transmission and optional 5-spd. manual overdrive: 3.73:1 (3.08:1 for high altitude emission system). Automatic transmission: 3.42:1 (3.73:1 for high altitude emission system). Optional: Standard 4-spd. manual transmission and optional 5-spd. manual overdrive: 4.11:1 (3.73:1 for high altitude emission system). Automatic transmission: 3.73:1. Transfer Case: New Process 207. Brakes: Type: Hydraulic, power assisted self-adjusting. Front: Discs. Rear: Drums. Dimensions: Front: 9.5 in. x 2.0 in. rotor. Rear: 9.5 in. x 2.0 in. Wheels: 15 in. Tires: P195/75R15 glass belted radial black sidewall. Optional: P195/75R15 black sidewall, P205/75R15 black sidewall, P205/75R15 white sidewall, P205/75R15 white letters, P205/75R15 on-off road black sidewall. Steering: Manual. Optional: Power. Transmission: 2.8 liter V-6: 5-speed manual with overdrive. 4.2 liter V-6: 4-speed automatic with overdrive. Optional: 2.8 liter V-6: 4-speed automatic with overdrive. Clutch: 9.76 in. dia.

VEHICLE DIMENSIONS: Wheelbase: 100.5 in. Overall Length: 170.3 in. Front/Rear Tread 54.1 in./54.1 in. Overall Height: 64.3 in. Width: 65.4 in. Approach/Departure Degrees: 28° 17'/ 25.5° 30'. Ground Clearance: Front axle: 6.3 in. Rear axle: 7.2 in.

CAPACITIES: Fuel Tank: 20 gal. tank.

ACCOMMODATIONS: Seating Capacity: Standard: Driver and passenger front high back bucket sets. Optional: 3 passenger rear bench seat.

INSTRUMENTATION: 0-100 mph speedometer, 99,999.9 mi. odometer, fuel gauge, warning lights for alternator, oil pressure, engine coolant temperature, brake operating system, hazard warning lights, directional lights, seat belt warning.

OPTIONS: Tahoe Package. Sport Package. High Country Package. Sport cloth vinyl high-back bucket seat trim. High Country Sheepskin high-back bucket seats. Custom two-tone paint. Special two-tone paint. Sport two-tone paint. California Emissions System. 4.3 liter V-6 engine. 4-speed overdrive automatic transmission. Optional axle ratio. Locking rear differential. Pre-cleaner air cleaner. 5-speed manual overdrive transmission. All-Weather air conditioning. Heavy-duty battery. Front black bumper guards. Luggage carrier, black or bright finish. Spare wheel and tire carrier. Off-Road Package. Cold Climate Package. Front compartment console. Engine oil cooling system. Heavy-duty radiator. Heavy-duty radiator and transmission oil cooler. Spare tire cover. Air deflector. Rear window defogger. Power door locks. Color-keyed floor mats. Gauge Package. Includes voltmeter, engine coolant temperature, oil pressure. Gauge Package plus tachometer. 66 amp Delcotron generator. Deep tinted glass. Deep tinted glass with light tinted rear window. Halogen headlights. Engine block heater. Engine compartment light. Exterior left and right side painted mirrors. Exterior left and right side bright mirrors. Body side and wheel opening moldings. Door edge guards. Bright wheel opening moldings. Black wheel opening moldings. Operating Convenience Package. AM radio. AM/FM radio. AM/FM radio with clock. AM/FM stereo radio with electronic tuning. AM/FM stereo radio and clock with electronic tuning. AM/FM stereo radio with Seek-Scan, stereo cassette tape, clock and graphic equalizer and electronic tuning and premium rear speakers. Premium rear speakers. Folding rear bench seat. Reclining front seat backs. Transfer case shield. Heavy-duty front and rear shock absorbers. Full size spare tire. Electronic speed control. ComforTilt steering wheel. Striping. Heavy-duty suspension equipment. Power release tailgate window. 20 gal. fuel tank. Two front towing hooks. Deadweight trailer hitch. Heavy-Duty Trailering Special. Light-Duty Trailering Special. Wheel trim rings. Rallye wheels. Styled wheels. Cast aluminum wheels. Power side door windows. Intermittent windshield wiper system.

HISTORICAL FOOTNOTES: The S-10 Blazer was produced at three assembly plants — Pontiac, Michigan; Moraine, Ohio and Shreveport, Louisiana. The 4.3 liter V-6 quickly became a high-demand option. Shortly after its availability, the V-6 was being installed in over 60 percent of all new S-10 Blazers. The S-10 Blazer continued to be the best-selling sport utility vehicle. In the first ten months of the 1988 model year, through April, 1988, Blazer sales (all models) totalled 80,335.

1989 S-10 BLAZER

The S-10 Blazer was fitted with standard rear-wheel anti-lock (RWAL) brakes for 1989. This system controlled the rear brake line pressure through a control valve located between the master cylinder and the rear brakes. By modulating rear brake pressure, RWAL improved directional stability by preventing rear-wheel skid under varying road and rear loading factors. A new standard electric speedometer generated the speed signal necessary for RWAL. In addition to RWAL all 1989 Blazers had standard power steering. An optional electronic instrument panel cluster was also new for 1989. It included speedometer, tachometer, voltmeter and fuel, oil pressure and engine coolant temperature gauges. The gauges utilized high-brightness vacuum fluorescent display tubes. All models had standard rear seat shoulder belts. Models with the standard 2.8 liter engine had a new transfer case with redesigned gear sets for reduced noise and smoother operation. This development also included new controls, a longer shift lever, a new vacuum switch and a relocated vent tube. A new option for 1989 was a rear window wiper/washer system attached to the rear window in the upper right corner. This system used a glass-mounted motor and wet arm nozzle. Incorporated into this system was a single-bottle reservoir and two high-pressure pumps-one for the front and one for the rear. One new exterior color — Woodlands brown metallic was offered. Dark blue replaced medium blue in the choice of interior colors. Premium rear speakers were now included with all optional stereo radios. The base model included these exterior features: Single electric horn, power brakes, power steering, front and rear chromed bumpers with black rub strips, chrome and black molded plastic grille and headlamp/side marker lamp bezels, black hubcaps, bright finish door handles/lock cylinders, bright taillight trim, All-Season steel belted radial tires, and right and left side fixed arm black finish mirrors. Interior features consisted of right and left handle padded armrests integral with door panels, color-keyed plastic door panels with map pockets and gray housing for the door latch release area, high-back bucket seats with folding seat backs and leather-grained custom vinyl, right and left side coat hooks, black plastic door sill plate, color-keyed plastic endgate scuff plate, door-operated courtesy and front and rear dome lights with bright trim, color-keyed rubber mat floor-covering, tinted glass for all windows, convenience tray, front and rear passenger grab handles, deluxe heater with side window defoggers, cigarette lighter with ashtray illumination, padded, color-keyed left and right side sunshades, gauges for speedometer, odometer and fuel level, deluxe color-keyed 2-spoke steering wheel, headlamp warning buzzer, 10 in. rearview mirror and full-foam headliner with color-keyed cloth cover.

The Tahoe trim level (RPO YC2) had the following items in addition to or replacing the base trim level: Bright wheel opening moldings, black body side moldings with bright insert plus rear quarter window moldings, hood insulators and cowl to fender seals, wheel trim rings, body color door handle inserts, and black tailgate applique. Tahoe interior features consisted of door panels with custom cloth upper insert, carpeted lower insert with map pocket and coin holder in left hand door, color-keyed floor carpeting, right side sunshade with mirror, trip odometer, gauges for voltmeter, oil pressure and engine coolant temperature (replace warning lamps), dual reading lamps, spare tire cover, color-keyed cowl kick panels and carpeted lower rear quarter and endgate panels.

1989 Chevrolet S-10 Blazer with High Country Appearance Package

The Sport trim level had the following items in addition to or replacing the Tahoe trim level: Bumpers color-keyed to lower accent color with black rub strips, black chrome grille with matching headlamp bezels, black finish for door handles and lock cylinders, two-tone paint (Conventional or Special), and black chrome taillamp trims. Interior features consisted of reclining bucket seats with folding seat backs and deluxe cloth, floor console, sport steering wheel with simulated leather look and Deluxe cloth trim panel inserts.

I.D. DATA: The V.I.N. plate was mounted on the lower left side windshield corner. The V.I.N. consisted of 17 elements. The first, the number 1 identified the U.S. as the nation of origin. The letter G followed, for the manufacturer: General Motors. The third entry, the letter C represented the make as Chevrolet. The GVWR brake system identification followed. Next came the truck line and chassis type; the letter K indicated four-wheel drive. The truck series was identified by a number: 1-1/2 ton. The truck body type identification was next: 8-Utility. The engine code was next: B-2.8 liter V-6, N-4.3 liter V-6 followed by a check digit. The model year was identified by the letter H. The assembly plant code followed. The final six digits were the plant sequential production number.

Model Number	Body Type & Seating	Factory Price	GVW	Shipping Weight	Prod. Total
Blazer S-10					
T18	Util. (with top)	$13,313	4075[1]	3295	—

NOTE 1: 4850 lb. GVW optional.

STANDARD ENGINE: Engine Type: OHV, Cast iron block. V-6. Order Code LL2. Produced by GM-Chevrolet Motor Division in Canada and Mexico. Bore x Stroke: 3.50 in. x 2.99 in. Lifters: Hydraulic. Number of main bearings-5. Fuel Induction: Electronic fuel injection. Compression Ratio: 9:13:1. Displacement: 173 cu. in. (2.8 liter). Horsepower: Net: 125 @ 4800 rpm. Torque: Net: 150 lb.-ft. @ 2400 rpm. Oil capacity: 5 qt. with filter change. Fuel Requirements: Unleaded.

OPTIONAL ENGINE: Engine Type: OHV, Cast iron block. V-6. Order Code LB4. Bore x Stroke: 4.00 in. x3.48 in. Lifters: Hydraulic. Number of main bearings-5. Fuel Induction: Electronic fuel injection. Compression Ratio: 9.3:1. Displacement: 262 cu. in. (4.3 liter). Horsepower: Net: 160 @ 4000 rpm. Torque: Net: 230 lb.-ft. @ 2800 rpm. Oil capacity: 5 qt. with filter change. Fuel Requirements: Unleaded.

CHASSIS FEATURES: Carbon steel, welded front box section and open channel rear section. Side rail dimensions: 2.28 in. (width) x 5.00 in. (depth) x 0.118 in. (thickness). Overall length: 162.46 in. Side rail section modules: 1.78.

SUSPENSION AND RUNNING GEAR: Front Suspension: Independent with torsion bar springs, 25mm dia. shock absorbers. 32mm stabilizer bar. Capacity: 1350 lbs. each at ground. Optional: 32mm shock absorbers. Rear Suspension: Two-stage 4-leaf shot-peened springs. Capacity: 1350 lbs. each at ground. 25mm shock absorbers. Optional: 32mm shock absorbers. Front Axle. Type: Hypoid, tubular driving. Capacity: 2400 lb. Rear Axle. Type: Salisbury, hypoid. Capacity: 2700 lb. Final Drive Ratio: 2.8 V-6 with manual trans.: 3.73:1. 4.3 liter V-6 with 4-speed automatic: 3.08:1. Optional: 2.8 V-6 with manual trans.: 4.11:1. 4.3 liter V-6 with 4-speed automatic: 3.42:1. Transfer Case: New Process 231. Ratios: 2.72, 1.00:1. Brakes: Type: Hydraulic, power assisted self-adjusting. Front: Discs. Rear: Drums. Dimensions: Front: 10.5 in. x 1.03 in. rotor. Rear: 9.5 in. x 2.0 in. Wheels: 15 x 6.00 in. Tires: P195/75R15 steel belted radial All-Season black sidewall. Optional: P20575R15 black sidewall, All-Season steel belted radial, P205/75R15 white letter All-Season steel belted radial, P205/75R15 black or white sidewall front highway and rear on-off road All-Season steel belted radial, P205/75R15 black or white sidewall Front/Rear on-off road All-Season steel belted radial, All-Season steel belted radial, P205/75R15 white letter Front/Rear on-off road All-Season steel belted radial, P235/75R15 white letter Front/Rear on-off road All-Season steel belted radial. Steering: Power assisted. Ratio: 17.5:1. Turning diameter: 35.4 ft. Transmission: 2.8 liter V-6: 5-speed manual with overdrive. 4.2 liter V-6: 4-speed automatic with overdrive. Ratios: 5-speed manual: 4.02, 2.32, 1.40, 1.00, 0.83:1. Reverse: 3.74:1. 4-speed automatic: 3.06, 1.63, 1.0, 0.70:1. reverse: 2.29:1.

VEHICLE DIMENSIONS: Wheelbase: 100.5 in. Overall Length: 170.3 in. Front/Rear Tread 54.1 in./54.1 in. Overall Height: 64.3 in. Width: 65.4 in. Approach/Departure Degrees: 28^{0} 17'/ 25.5^{0} 30'. Ground Clearance: Front axle: 6.1 in. Rear axle: 7.2 in. Load space: With rear seat installed: 35.5 in. x 53.4 in. x 35.0 in. With rear seat removed or folded: 68.6 in. x 53.4 in. x 35.0 in.

CAPACITIES: Fuel Tank: 20 gal. tank. Coolant System Capacity: 2.8 Liter V-6: 11.6 qt., 4.2 liter V-6: 12.0 qt.

ACCOMMODATIONS: Seating Capacity: Standard: Driver and passenger front high back bucket sets. Optional: 3 passenger rear bench seat. Front headroom: 39.1 in. Rear headroom: 38.1 in. Front Legroom: 42.5 in. Rear Legroom: 35.5 in. Front hip room: 50.5 in. Rear hip room: 37.6 in.

INSTRUMENTATION: 0-100 mph speedometer, 99,999.9 mi. odometer, fuel gauge, warning lights for alternator, oil pressure, engine coolant temperature, brake operating system, hazard warning lights, directional lights, seat belt warning.

OPTIONS: Air conditioning: $736 without LL2 engine, $680 with LL2 engine. Optional axle ratio: $38. Locking rear differential: $252. Heavy-duty battery: 56. Luggage carrier: $126. Spare tire and wheel carrier: $159-$192 depending upon trim option. Cold Climate Package: $113-$156 depending upon trim option. Center console: $114. Engine oil cooler: $126. Heavy-duty radiator: $56. Heavy-duty radiator and engine oil cooler: $63, with air conditioning, $118 without air conditioning. Spare tire cover: $33. Sport Package: $1038 without High Country Option, $671 with High Country Option. Tahoe Package: $683 without High Country Option, $473 with High Country Option. Air deflector: $43. Driver Convenience Package. Includes ComforTilt steering wheel and intermittent wiper system: $180. Rear Window Convenience Package. Includes electric tailgate release and rear window defogger: $197. 4.3 liter V-6: $255. Color-keyed front floor mats: $16. Color-keyed rear floor mats: $12. Gauge Package: $62. Deep tinted glass with light tinted rear window: $56-$200 depending on trim package. Halogen headlights: $24. Engine block heater: $33. Electronic instrumentation: $296-$358 depending on trim package. Engine compartment light: $16. Interior visor mirror: $7. Exterior Below eye-level black mirrors: $52. Exterior below eye-level bright mirrors: $87. Interior rearview tilting mirror with dual reading lamps: $26. Body side and wheel opening moldings: $152. Black wheel opening molding: $13-$43 depending upon trim package. Bright wheel opening molding: 31. Operating Convenience Package. Includes power door locks and power windows: $344. Custom two-tone paint: $172-$344 depending upon trim package. Special two-tone paint: $163-$212 depending upon trim package. Deluxe two-tone paint: $177-$329 depending upon trim package. Electronically tuned AM/FM stereo radio: $275. Electronically tuned AM/FM stereo radio with Seek-Scan, stereo cassette tape player and digital clock: $454. Electronically tuned AM/FM stereo radio with Seek-Scan, stereo cassette tape player with Search and Repeat, graphic equalizer and digital clock: $604. Rear folding rear seat: $409. Reclining seat backs: $74. Transfer case and front differential skid plates and steering linkage shield: $75. Front and rear heavy-duty shock absorbers: $36. Electronic speed control: $205. Heavy-duty front springs: $63. Body striping: $49. Sunshine striping: $116. Manual sun roof: $250. Suspension Package: $160-$220 depending upon trim package. High Country Package: $925 with Sport Package, $1026 with Tahoe Package. Two front tow hooks: $38. Dead weight trailer hitch: $68. Light-Duty Trailering Package: $109. Heavy-Duty Trailering Special Package: $211. 4-speed automatic transmission: $795. Wheel trim rings: $60. Cast aluminum wheels: $252-$308 depending upon trim package. Sliding rear window: $257. Rear window wiper/washer: $125.

HISTORICAL FOOTNOTES: The 1989 S-10 Blazer was produced at Pontiac, Michigan and Shreveport, Louisiana.

1990 S-10 BLAZER

The S-10 Blazer had a more powerful standard engine, increased standard equipment content and a new gross vehicle weight rating system for 1990. Now standard was the 4.3 liter Vortex V-6. Its power ratings were unchanged from 1989. Three trim levels were again offered-standard, Tahoe and Sport — but their standard equipment content was significantly increased. All three trim levels had the following new-for-1990 items: Full-size spare tire, inside spare tire cover, P205/75R15 All-Season steel belted radial tires, Deluxe front appearance package, right and left-side exterior black finish mirrors, Halogen headlights, redesigned instrument cluster, voltmeter, engine coolant temperature and oil pressure gauges, electronically tuned AM radio, and front tow hooks. The Sport Package now included cast aluminum wheels. A new light dimming control was used for the four-wheel drive indicator. The Trailering Special Equipment Package was now available for models equipped with manual transmission. Previously, it had limited to Blazers with automatic transmission.

The new Gross Vehicle Weight Rating (GVWR) system for 1990 replaced the older net payload system in which trucks were assigned a net payload rating and were rated to carry that payload regardless of the factory option content or aftermarket accessories. With the new fixed system, ratings were done on an individual, truck-by-truck basis. The net cargo rating was more accurately calculated by subtracting the curb weight and the weight of the options, passengers and any aftermarket equipment. Two new exterior colors were offered for 1990. The total selection of exterior colors were frost white, silver metallic, midnight black, Aspen blue metallic, wheat, Woodlands brown metallic, royal blue metallic (which replaced Galaxy blue metallic), garnet, Nevada gold metallic, apple red and steel gray metallic. The Emerald exterior color was dropped for 1990. One new interior color was offered for 1990. The Custom vinyl and Custom cloth interiors were offered in blue, garnet (which replaced carmine), charcoal or saddle. The Deluxe cloth and Leather upholsteries were offered in either charcoal or saddle. The High Country Option was not offered for 1991.

I.D. DATA: The V.I.N. plate was mounted on the lower left side windshield corner. The V.I.N. consisted of 17 elements. The first, the number 1 identified the U.S. as the nation of origin. The letter G followed, for the manufacturer: General Motors. The third entry, the letter C represented the make as Chevrolet. The GVWR brake system identification followed. Next came the truck line and chassis type; the letter K indicated four-wheel drive. The truck series was identified by a number: 1-1/2 ton. The truck body type identification was next: 8-Utility. The engine code was next: N-4.3 liter V-6 followed by a check digit. The model year was identified by the letter L. The assembly plant code followed. The final six digits were the plant sequential production number.

Model Number	Body Type & Seating	Factory Price	GVW	Shipping Weight	Prod. Total
Blazer S-10					
CT10506	Util.	$14,595	4700	3295	—

STANDARD ENGINE: Engine Type: OHV, Cast iron block. V-6. Order Code LB4. Bore x Stroke: 4.00 in. x 3.48 in. Lifters: Hydraulic. Number of main bearings-5. Fuel Induction: Electronic fuel injection. Compression Ratio: 9.3:1. Displacement: 262 cu. in. (4.3 liter). Horsepower: Net: 160 @ 4000 rpm. Torque: Net: 230 lb.-ft. @ 2800 rpm. Oil capacity: 5 qt. with filter change. Fuel Requirements: Unleaded.

CHASSIS FEATURES: Carbon steel, welded front box section and open channel rear section. Side rail dimensions: 2.28 in. (width) x 5.00 in. (depth) x 0.118 in. (thickness). Overall length: 162.46 in. Side rail section modules: 1.78.

SUSPENSION AND RUNNING GEAR: Front Suspension: Independent with torsion bar springs, 25mm dia. shock absorbers. 32mm stabilizer bar. Capacity: 1200 lbs. each at ground. Optional: 32mm, 46mm shock absorbers. Rear Suspension: Two-stage 4-leaf shot-peened springs. Capacity: 1350 lbs. each at ground. 25mm shock absorbers. Optional: 32mm, 46mm shock absorbers. Front Axle. Type: Independent GM Hypoid, tubular driving. Capacity: 2400 lb. Rear Axle. Type: Semi-floating GM Hypoid Capacity: 2700 lb. Final Drive Ratio: 3.08:1. Optional: 3.42:1. Transfer Case: New Process 231. Ratios: 2.72, 1.00:1. Brakes: Type: Hydraulic, power assisted self-adjusting. Front: Discs. Rear: Drums. Dimensions: Front: 10.5 in. x 1.03 in. rotor. Rear: 9.5 in. x 2.0 in. Wheels: 15 x 6.00 in. Optional: 15 x 7.0 in. Rallye wheels, 15 x 7.0 in. Cast aluminum (RPO N90), 15 x 7.0 in. cast aluminum (RPO N60). Tires: P205/75R15 steel belted radial All-Season black sidewall. Optional: P205/75R15 black sidewall, All-Season steel belted radial, P205/75R15 on-off road steel belted radial, white letters, P205/75R15 All-Season steel belted radial, white letters, P205/75R15 on-off road steel belted radial black sidewall, P205/75R15 steel belted radial. Front: Highway, Rear: On-off road, P235/75R15 on-off road steel belted radial white letters. Steering: Variable ratio, integral power. Ratio: 17.5:1. Turning diameter: 35.4 ft. Transmission: 5-speed manual with overdrive (RPO MM5). Ratios: 4.02, 2.32, 1.40, 1.00, 0.83:1. Reverse: 3.74:1. Optional: 4-speed automatic with overdrive (RPO MXO): 3.06, 1.63, 1.0, 0.70:1. Reverse: 2.29:1.

VEHICLE DIMENSIONS: Wheelbase: 100.5 in. Overall Length: 170.3 in. Front/Rear Tread 54.1 in./54.1 in. Overall Height: 64.3 in. Width: 65.4 in. Front/Rear Overhang: 30.6/39.2 in. Approach/Departure Degrees: 28° 17'/25.5° 30'. Ground Clearance: Front axle: 6.1 in. Rear axle: 7.2 in. Load space: With rear seat installed: 35.5 in. x 53.4 in. x 35.0 in. With rear seat removed or folded: 68.6 in. x 53.4 in. x 35.0 in.

CAPACITIES: Fuel Tank: 20 gal. tank. Coolant System Capacity: 12.0 qt.

ACCOMMODATIONS: Seating Capacity: Standard: Driver and passenger front high back bucket sets. Optional: 3 passenger rear bench seat. Front headroom: 39.1 in. Rear headroom: 38.1 in. Front legroom: 42.5 in. Rear legroom: 35.5 in. Front hip room: 50.5 in. Rear hip room: 37.6 in.

INSTRUMENTATION: 0-100 mph speedometer, 99,999.9 mi. odometer, fuel gauge, gauges for voltmeter, oil pressure, engine coolant temperature. Warning lights for brake operating system, hazard warning lights, directional lights, seat belt warning.

OPTIONS: Air conditioning: $755. Optional axle ratio: $38. Locking rear differential: $252. Heavy-duty battery: $56. Luggage carrier: $169. Spare tire and wheel carrier: $159. Cold Climate Package: $146-$189 depending upon trim option. Center console: $135. Heavy-duty radiator: $56. Heavy-duty radiator and engine oil cooler: $63, with air conditioning, $118 without air conditioning. Sport Package: $1239. Tahoe Package: $809. Driver Convenience Package. Includes ComforTilt steering wheel and intermittent wiper system: $197. Color-keyed front floor mats: $20. Color-keyed rear floor mats: $16. Deep tinted glass with light tinted rear window: $225. Electronic instrumentation: $296. Lighted interior visor mirror: $68-$75 depending upon trim package. Body side and wheel opening moldings: $152. Black wheel opening molding: $13-$43 depending upon trim package. Bright wheel opening molding: $31. Operating Convenience Package. Includes power door locks and power windows: $344. Custom two-tone paint: $172-$344 depending upon trim package. Special two-tone paint: $163-$218 depending upon trim package. Deluxe two-tone paint: $177-$329 depending upon trim package. Electronically tuned AM/FM stereo radio with Seek-Scan, stereo cassette tape player and digital clock. $122. Electronically tuned AM/FM stereo radio with Seek Scan, stereo cassette tape player with Search and Repeat, graphic equalizer and digital clock: $272. Delete radio: $226 credit. Rear folding rear seat: $409. Transfer case and front differential skid plates and steering linkage shield: $75. Front and rear heavy-duty shock absorbers: $40. Electronic speed control: $225. Heavy-duty front springs. Includes heavy-duty shock absorbers: $63. Body striping: $49. Sunshine striping: $70 to $125 depending upon trim package. Manual sun roof: $250. Off-road suspension equipment: 122-$182 depending upon trim package. Light-Duty Trailering Package: $165. Heavy-Duty Trailering Special Package: $211. 4-speed automatic transmission: $860. Wheel trim rings: $60. Cast aluminum wheels: $269-$325 depending upon trim package. Gray aluminum wheels: $233-$325 depending upon trim option. Sliding rear window: $257. Rear window wiper/washer: $125.

HISTORICAL FOOTNOTES: The 1990 Blazer was introduced on September 1, 1989.

1991 S-10 BLAZER

Chevrolet added a four-door model to the Blazer lineup as a 1991 model early in 1990. The new model's rear doors provided easier access and exit from a standard 3 passenger rear seat. It also had as standard, the Tahoe level of interior trim, 4-wheel anti-lock brake system (ABS) and a 2900 lb. capacity rear axle. The two-door model had a standard rear-wheel anti-lock brake system that operated in two-wheel drive only. Both the two-door and four-door models for 1991 has a new grille design suggestive of that found on the Chevrolet pickups of 1967-1969. Also new for 1991 were the Blazer's exterior nameplates, emblems, bumper rub stripes, body side moldings, and body stripes and decals. New wheels and wheel trim designs were also introduced. High-back front bucket seats were standard. During the 1991 model year numerous changes were introduced. These included a 220 TBI (Throttle Body Injection) system, use of Hydra-Matic 5LM60 5-speed manual transmission in place of the 290 unit, revised Thermac III air cleaner, use of a revised accessory drive, a new Geolast PCV connector, and new Quantum spark plugs. Additional interim 1991 improvements involved front and rear suspension changes, accelerator pedal effort reduction, revised floor console latch, revised Rallye wheel center insert, use of a lever-type power door lock switch, improved AM/FM radio reception, availability of aluminum wheel colors, inclusion of a heavy-duty battery as standard equipment, improved front axle half-shaft, improved heating/ventilation and the introduction of a front bench seat for maximum 6 passenger capacity. All models were available with new RPO D48 electric OSRV mirrors with control on the instrument cluster. The two-door model had single-rate rear springs with revised rates for an improved ride. The Tahoe trim had new seat fabric, door panels and rear quarter panels. The front floor console had a revised catch for easy, keyless entry. Exterior colors for 1991 were midnight black, Aspen blue metallic, sky blue, royal blue metallic, garnet red, steel gray metallic, mint green, apple red, wheat, frost white and silver metallic. The two-door models were available in four interior colors: Blue, charcoal, garnet or saddle. Blue and charcoal were initially offered for four-door model interiors. By the fall of 1991 the standard Tahoe interior for the four-door was also available in blue, charcoal, garnet or saddle.

1991 Chevrolet S-10 four-door Blazer

A new Tahoe LT Package was available for both Blazer models. It included a new interior with Ultrasoft leather surfaces, available in three colors, on the front bucket seats and folding rear bench seat, color-keyed leather and carpeted door trim panels, full carpeting, front color-keyed floor mats, color-keyed cloth headliner, full instrumentation, an all-new two-tone exterior finish with multi-shaded stripe, chromed grille with new silver accents, new 15 x 7.0 in. cast-aluminum wheels, P205/75R16 All-Season white lettered tires, front and rear bumpers color-keyed to lower body color, black tail lamp bezels, optional electronically tuned AM/FM stereo radio with CD player, special exterior LT badge, and Tahoe LT badge on glove box door.

I.D. DATA: The V.I.N. plate was mounted on the lower left side windshield corner. The V.I.N. consisted of 17 elements. The first, the number 1 identified the U.S. as the nation of origin. The letter G followed, for the manufacturer: General Motors. The third entry, the letter C represented the make as Chevrolet. The GVWR brake system identification followed. Next came the truck line and chassis type; the letter K indicated four-wheel drive. The truck series was identified by a number: 1-1/2 ton. The truck body type identification was next: 8-Utility. The engine code was next: N-4.3 liter V-6 followed by a check digit. The model year was identified by the letter M. The assembly plant code followed. The final six digits were the plant sequential production number.

Model Number	Body Type & Seating	Factory Price	GVW	Shipping Weight	Prod. Total
Blazer S-10					
CT10506	2-dr.	Util.	$15,575[1]	4700	3295
CT10506	4-dr.	Util.	$17,215[1]	5100	—

NOTE 1: Price announced on January 28, 1991, the two-door price increased to $16,050 on February 25, 1991. That of the four-door Blazer moved up to $17,690.

STANDARD ENGINE: Engine Type: OHV, Cast iron block. V-6. Order Code LB4. Bore x Stroke: 4.00 in. x 3.48 in. Lifters: Hydraulic. Number of main bearings-5. Fuel Induction: Electronic fuel injection. Compression Ratio: 9.3:1. Displacement: 262 cu. in. (4.3 liter). Horsepower: Net: 160 @ 4000 rpm. Torque: Net: 230 lb.-ft. @ 2800 rpm. Oil capacity: 5 qt. with filter change. Fuel Requirements: Unleaded.

CHASSIS FEATURES: Carbon steel, welded front box section and open channel rear section. Dimensions: Two-door: Side rail dimensions: 2.28 in. (width) x 5.00 in. (depth) x 0.118 in. (thickness). Overall length: 162.46 in. Side rail section modules: 1.78. Dimensions: Four-door: Side rail dimensions: 2.28 in. (width) x 5.00 in. (depth) x 0.118 in. (thickness). Overall length: 168.96 in. Side rail section modules: 1.78.

SUSPENSION AND RUNNING GEAR: Front Suspension: Independent with torsion bar springs, 25mm dia. shock absorbers. 32mm stabilizer bar. Capacity: 1200 lbs. each at ground. Optional: 32mm, 46mm shock absorbers. Rear Suspension: Two-stage 4-leaf shot-peened springs. Capacity: Two-door: 1350 lbs. each at ground, four-door: 1450 lb. each at ground. 25mm shock absorbers. Optional: 32mm, 46mm shock absorbers. Front Axle. Type: Independent GM Hypoid, tubular driving. Capacity: 2400 lb. Rear Axle. Type: Semi-floating GM Hypoid Capacity: Two-door: 2700 lb. Four-door: 2900 lb. Final Drive Ratio: 3.08:1. Optional: 3.42:1. Transfer Case: New Process 231. Ratios: 2.72, 1.00:1. Brakes: Type: Hydraulic, power assisted self-adjusting. Front: Discs. Rear: Drums. Dimensions: Front: 10.5 in. x 1.03 in. rotor. Rear: 9.5 in. x 2.0 in. Wheels: 15 x 6.00 in. Optional: 15 x 7.0 in. Rallye wheels, 15 x 7.0 in. Cast aluminum (RPO N90), 15 x 7.0 in. cast aluminum (RPO N60). Tires: P205/75R15 steel belted radial All-Season black sidewall. Optional: P205/75R15 black sidewall, All-Season steel belted radial, P205/75R15 on-off road steel belted radial, white letters, P205/75R15 All-Season steel belted radial, white letters, P205/75R15 on-off road steel belted radial black sidewall, P205/75R15 steel belted radial, front: Highway, Rear: On-off road, P235/75R15 on-off road steel belted radial white letters. Steering: Variable ratio, integral power. Ratio: 17.5:1. Turning diameter: 35.4 ft. Transmission: 5-speed manual with overdrive (RPO MM5). Ratios: 4.02, 2.32, 1.40, 1.00, 0.83:1. Reverse: 3.74:1. Optional: 4-speed automatic with overdrive (RPO MXO): 3.06, 1.63, 1.0, 0.70:1. Reverse: 2.29:1.

VEHICLE DIMENSIONS: Wheelbase: Two-door/Four-door: 100.5 in./107.0-in. Overall Length: Two-door/Four-door: 170.3 in./176.8. Front/Rear Tread 54.1 in./54.1 in. Overall Height: 62.8 in. Width: 65.4 in. Front/Rear Overhang: 30.6/39.2 in. Approach/Departure Degrees: 28° 17'/25.5° 30'. Ground Clearance: Front axle: 8.5 in. Rear axle: 8.1 in. Load space: Two-door: With rear seat installed: 35.5 in. x 50.0 in. x 35.0 in. With rear seat removed or folded: 68.6 in. x 53.4 in. x 35.0 in. Four-door: With rear seat installed: 38.5 in. x 52.5 in. x 34.5 in. With rear seat removed or folded: 76.1 in. x 52.5 in. x 34.5 in. Maximum cargo space: Two-door: 67.3 cu. ft. Four-door: 74.3 cu. ft.

CAPACITIES: Fuel Tank: 20 gal. tank. Coolant System Capacity: 12.0 qt.

ACCOMMODATIONS: Seating Capacity: Standard: Two-door: Driver and passenger front high back bucket sets. Optional: 3 passenger rear bench seat. Four-door: 5 passenger with standard rear bench seat. Front headroom: 39.1 in. Rear headroom: 38.1 in. Front legroom: 42.5 in. Rear legroom: 35.5 in. Front hip room: 50.5 in. Rear hip room: 37.6 in.

INSTRUMENTATION: 0-100 mph speedometer, 99,999.9 mi. odometer, fuel gauge, gauges for voltmeter, oil pressure, engine coolant temperature. Warning lights for brake operating system, hazard warning lights, directional lights, seat belt warning.

OPTIONS: Air conditioning: $724 with engine oil cooler, $780 without engine oil cooler. Air dam with fog lamps: $115. Optional axle ratio: $44. Locking rear differential: $252. Heavy-duty battery: $56. Spare tire and wheel carrier: $159. Cold Climate Package: $146. Heavy-duty radiator: $56. Heavy-duty radiator and engine oil cooler: $63, with air conditioning, $118 without air conditioning. Driver Convenience Package (RPO ZM7). Includes ComforTilt steering wheel and Intermittent wiper system: $204. Driver Convenience Package (RPO ZM8). Includes rear window defroster and tailgate release: $197. California Emissions Package: $100. Color-keyed front floor mats (two-door only): $20. Rear color-keyed floor mays: $16. Deep tinted glass (RPO AJ1): $225. Deep tinted glass with light tinted rear window (RPO AA3): $144. Electronic instrumentation: $195. Black luggage carrier: $169. Exterior electric remote mirrors: $83. Visor mirrors, left and right side: $68. Black wheel opening molding: $13-$43 depending on trim package. Operating Convenience Package. Includes power door locks and power windows: $542, four-door, $367, two-door. Special two-tone paint: $218. Deluxe two-tone paint: $177. Electronically tuned AM/FM stereo radio with Seek-Scan, and digital clock: $131. Electronically tuned AM/FM stereo radio with Seek-Scan, stereo cassette tape player: $122-$253 depending upon other options selected. Electronically tuned AM/FM stereo radio with Seek-Scan, stereo cassette tape player with Search and Repeat, graphic equalizer and digital clock: $403. Delete radio: $95 credit. Special Custom cloth reclining high-back bucket seats: $345. Deluxe cloth reclining high-back bucket seats: $26 with rear seat. Folding rear bench seat: $409. Leather reclining high-back bucket seats, two-door only: $312 with folding rear bench seat, $412 without folding rear seat. Transfer case and front differential skid plates and steering linkage shield: $75. Front and rear heavy-duty shock absorbers: $40. Electronic speed control: $238. Sport Equipment: $714, four-door, $1082, two-door. Body striping: $55. Sunroof, manual, non-removable, two-door only: $250. Heavy-duty front springs: $63. Off-road suspension, two-door only: $122-$182 depending on other options selected. Light-Duty Trailering Package: $165 with oil cooler, $109 without oil cooler. Heavy-Duty Trailering Special Package: $211. Tahoe Package: Four-door: $600-$3020 depending upon Preferred Equipment Group selected; Two-door: $809. Sport Package: $3306-$4260 depending upon Preferred Equipment Group selected. 4-speed automatic transmission: $890. Rallye wheels: $92. Cast aluminum wheels: $284-$340 depending upon trim package. Gray aluminum wheels: $248-$340 depending upon trim option. Sliding rear side window, two-door only: $257. Rear window wiper/washer: $125.

HISTORICAL FOOTNOTES: The 1991 Blazer was introduced on September 1, 1990. The two-door Blazers were built at GM manufacturing facilities in Pontiac, Michigan and Moraine, Ohio. The four-door Blazer was built only at the Moraine plant.

1992 S-10 BLAZER

Changes for 1992 were limited primarily to minor mechanical and trim revisions. The Tahoe LT was offered for two-door models beginning in February, 1992. The latest Blazers had a new grille insert with a bold egg-crate format. A new 2-speed electronic shift transfer was optional. Other 1992 changes included new seats with integral head restraints for front bench seats in four-door models and high-back buckets with optional leather. A new compact disc player was optional.

1992 Chevrolet S-10 four-door Blazer

I.D. DATA: The V.I.N. plate was mounted on the lower left side windshield corner. The V.I.N. consisted of 17 elements. The first, the number 1 identified the U.S. as the nation of origin. The letter G followed, for the manufacturer: General Motors. The third entry, the letter C represented the make as Chevrolet. The GVWR brake system identification followed. Next came the truck line and chassis type; the letter K indicated four-wheel drive. The truck series was identified by a number: 1-1/2 ton. The truck body type identification was next: 8-Utility. The engine code was next: N-4.3 liter V-6 followed by a check digit. The model year was identified by the letter N. The assembly plant code followed. The final six digits were the plant sequential production number.

Model Number	Body Type & Seating	Factory Price	GVW	Shipping Weight	Prod. Total
Blazer S-10					
CT10506	2-dr. Util.	$16,583	4700	3295	—
CT10506	3-dr. Util.	$17,953	5100	—	—

STANDARD ENGINE: Engine Type: OHV, Cast iron block. V-6. Order Code LB4. Bore x Stroke: 4.00 in. x 3.48 in. Lifters: Hydraulic. Number of main bearings-5. Fuel Induction: Electronic fuel injection. Compression Ratio: 9.3:1. Displacement: 262 cu. in. (4.3 liter). Horsepower: Net: 160 @ 4000 rpm. Torque: Net: 230 lb.-ft. @ 2800 rpm. Oil capacity: 5 qt. with filter change. Fuel Requirements: Unleaded.

CHASSIS FEATURES: Carbon steel, welded front box section and open channel rear section. Dimensions: Two-door: Side rail dimensions: 2.28 in. (width) x 5.00 in. (depth) x 0.118 in. (thickness). Overall length: 162.46 in. Side rail section modules: 1.78. Dimensions: Four-door: Side rail dimensions: 2.28 in. (width) x 5.00 in. (depth) x 0.118 in. (thickness). Overall length: 168.96 in. Side rail section modules: 1.78.

SUSPENSION AND RUNNING GEAR: Front Suspension: Independent with torsion bar springs, 25mm dia. shock absorbers. 32mm stabilizer bar. Capacity: 1200 lbs. each at ground. Optional: 32mm, 46mm shock absorbers. Rear Suspension: Two-stage 4-leaf shot-peened springs. Capacity: Two-door: 1350 lbs. each at ground, four-door: 1450 lb. each at ground. 25mm shock absorbers. Optional: 32mm, 46mm shock absorbers. Front Axle. Type: Independent GM Hypoid, tubular driving. Capacity: 2400 lb. Rear Axle. Type: Semi-floating GM Hypoid Capacity: Two-door: 2700 lb. Four-door: 2900 lb. Final Drive Ratio: 3.08:1. Optional: 3.42:1. Transfer Case: New Process 231. Ratios: 2.72, 1.00:1. Brakes: Type: Hydraulic, power assisted self-adjusting. Front: Discs. Rear: Drums. Dimensions: Front: 10.5 in. x 1.03 in. rotor. Rear: 9.5 in. x 2.0 in. Wheels: 15 x 6.00 in. Optional: 15 x 7.0 in. Rallye wheels, 15 x 7.0 in. Cast aluminum (RPO N90), 15 x 7.0 in. cast aluminum (RPO N60). Tires: P205/75R15 steel belted radial All-Season black sidewall. Optional: P205/75R15 black sidewall, All-Season steel belted radial, P205/75R15 on-off road steel belted radial, white letters, P205/75R15 All-Season steel belted radial, white letters, P205/75R15 on-off road steel belted radial black sidewall, P205/75R15 steel belted radial. Front: Highway, Rear: On-off road, P235/75R15 on-off road steel belted radial white letters. Steering: Variable ratio, integral power. Ratio: 17.5:1. Turning diameter: 35.4 ft. Transmission: 5-speed manual with overdrive (RPO MM5). Ratios: 4.02, 2.32, 1.40, 1.00, 0.83:1. Reverse: 3.74:1. Optional: 4-speed automatic with overdrive (RPO MXO): 3.06, 1.63, 1.0, 0.70:1. Reverse: 2.29:1.

VEHICLE DIMENSIONS: Wheelbase: Two-door/Four-door: 100.5 in./107.0-in. Overall Length: Two-door/Four-door: 170.3 in./176.8. Front/Rear Tread 54.1 in./54.1 in. Overall Height: 62.8 in. Width: 65.4 in. Front/Rear Overhang: 30.6/39.2 in. Approach/Departure Degrees: 28° 17'/25.5° 30'. Ground Clearance: Front axle: 8.5 in. Rear axle: 8.1 in. Load space: Two-door: With rear seat installed: 35.5 in. x 50.0 in. x 35.0 in. With rear seat removed or folded: 68.6 in. x 53.4 in. x 35.0 in. Four-door: With rear seat installed: 38.5 in. x 52.5 in. x 34.5 in. With rear seat removed or folded: 76.1 in. x 52.5 in. x 34.5 in. Maximum cargo space: Two-door: 67.3 cu. ft. Four-door: 74.3 cu. ft.

CAPACITIES: Fuel Tank: 20 gal. tank. Coolant System Capacity: 12.0 qt.

ACCOMMODATIONS: Seating Capacity: Standard: Two-door: Driver and passenger front high back bucket sets. Optional: 3 passenger rear bench seat. Four-door: 5 passenger with standard rear bench seat. Front headroom: 39.1 in. Rear headroom: 38.1 in. Front legroom: 42.5 in. Rear legroom: 35.5 in. Front hip room: 50.5 in. Rear hip room: 37.6 in.

INSTRUMENTATION: 0-100 mph speedometer, 99,999.9 mi. odometer, fuel gauge, gauges for voltmeter, oil pressure, engine coolant temperature. Warning lights for brake operating system, hazard warning lights, directional lights, seat belt warning.

OPTIONS: Air conditioning: Air dam with fog lamps. Optional axle ratio. Locking rear differential. Heavy-duty battery. Spare tire and wheel carrier. Cold Climate Package. Heavy-duty radiator. Heavy-duty radiator and engine oil cooler. Driver Convenience Package (RPO ZM7). Includes ComforTilt steering wheel and Intermittent wiper system. Driver Convenience Package (RPO ZM8). Includes rear window defroster and tailgate release. California Emissions Package. Color-keyed front floor mats (two-door only). Rear color-keyed floor mats. Deep tinted glass (RPO AJ1). Deep tinted glass with light tinted rear window (RPO AA3). Electronic instrumentation. Black luggage carrier. Exterior electric remote mirrors. Visor mirrors, left and right side. Black wheel opening molding. Operating Convenience Package. Includes power door locks and power windows. Special two-tone paint. Deluxe two-tone paint. Electronically tuned AM/FM stereo radio with Seek-Scan, and digital clock. Electronically tuned AM/FM stereo radio with Seek-Scan, stereo cassette tape player. Electronically tuned AM/FM stereo radio with Seek-Scan, stereo cassette tape player with Search and Repeat, graphic equalizer and digital clock. Delete radio: $95 credit. Special Custom cloth reclining high-back bucket seats. Deluxe cloth reclining high-back bucket seats. Folding rear bench seat. Leather reclining high-back bucket seats, two-door. Transfer case and front differential skid plates and steering linkage shield. Front and rear heavy-duty shock absorbers. Electronic speed control. Sport Equipment. Body striping. Sunroof, manual, non-removable, two-door only. Heavy-duty front springs. Off-road suspension, two-door only. Light-Duty Trailering

Package. Heavy-Duty Trailering Special Package. Tahoe Package: Sport Package. 4-speed automatic transmission. Rallye wheels. Cast aluminum wheels. Gray aluminum wheels. Sliding rear side window, two-door only. Rear window wiper/washer.

HISTORICAL FOOTNOTES: *Consumers Digest* called the S-10 Blazer a "best buy" among vehicle of its type.

1993 S-10 BLAZER

For 1993, an enhanced 4.3 liter CPI V-6 was optional with 35 more horsepower than the standard engine. The standard 4.3 liter EFI V-6 had a five-horsepower increase for 1993. Compared to the1992 version it offered less noise, less vibration, and smoother performance. The enhanced V-6 was linked to a standard Hydra-Matic 4L60-E electronic 4-speed automatic transmission. This powertrain had been introduced interim 1992. The standard V-6 engine had a standard 5-speed manual transmission. An internal balance shaft was added to the V-6 engine for smoother performance by reducing vibration in the higher rpm ranges. Theft-deterring improvements were made to the S-10 Blazer's tilt steering column that increased the time required to bypass the steering column ignition key. Four-wheel anti-lock brakes continued as standard equipment. A new aluminum wheel was optional. New interior convenience features included an illuminated entry light under the inside rearview mirror, keyless entry and convenience net (with Tahoe and Tahoe LT trim packages), a floor console with a 12-volt power outlet (limited model availability), and an overhead console with lights and storage areas. Cupholders are included with the automatic transmission, and a stowage tray is fitted to vehicles with manual transmission. Solar-Ray™ tinted glass, optional sun visors and a redesigned luggage rack are also new for 1993. Coat hooks were now installed at both sides of the cargo compartment (in addition to coat hooks behind the front doors). The convenience tray now had a soft liner. A dual note horn was now used. Seating changes include manual lumbar adjusters and the former deluxe cloth in four colors, both as standard equipment. Identification of The 1993 base two-door Blazer was aided by its new black grille and body color front and rear bumpers. The grille of the S-10 Blazer two-door Tahoe and four-door Tahoe (base) was now chrome and gray. The black body-side moldings for these models was wider and had revised bright inserts. The black rub strips and bright inserts on the Tahoe chrome front and rear bumpers were also revised. A power driver's seat and recliner were new for the Tahoe LT package. Beige is a new interior color. New exterior colors for the S-10 Blazer were dove gray and khaki. They replaced aquamarine green and sky blue. The paint process now included primer surface with anti-chip protection extended to the entire vehicle. The Tahoe trim package on two-door models now had new optional two-tone paint and striping. The color-keyed front and rear floor mats for the Tahoe trim level Blazers were now carpeted.

All tailgates now had a Chevrolet nameplate which was bright and black. This was identical to that previously used on models with an outside spare tire carrier. Also found on the 1993 model were black taillight bezels, color-keyed door trim air conditioner and radio bezels.

Three trim options were offered for the two-door Blazer-standard, Tahoe and Tahoe LT. The four-door model had two trim levels — Tahoe (standard) and Tahoe LT.

1993 Chevrolet S-10 two-door Blazer

New or revised options included a new padded cover with Blazer lettering (without red underlines) for the outside spare tire carrier (RPO P16). The floor console (RPO D55) which was standard for the two-door Blazer Tahoe. was raised to match the height of the door armrest. The transfer case floor shifter console had a revised design. On the standard 4x4 version, the shifter tray is deeper on the right hand side. On models with an electronic shift transfer case, the console was similar but had a larger tray. A new overhead console option (RPO DK6) was offered. A new Heavy-Duty Cooling System Option (RPO VO8) included an engine oil cooler. Color-keyed, carpeted removable front (RPO B32) and rear (RPO B33) floor mats were now optional for the two-door Base Blazer. They were included with the Tahoe Package and standard for four-door models. Available as an interim 1993 option was a new Deluxe cloth 60/40 front split-bench seat.

I.D. DATA: The V.I.N. plate was mounted on the lower left side windshield corner. The V.I.N. consisted of 17 elements. The first, the number 1 identified the U.S. as the nation of origin. The letter G followed, for the manufacturer: General Motors. The third entry, the letter C represented the make as Chevrolet. The GVWR brake system identification followed. Next came the truck line and chassis type; the letter K indicated four-wheel drive. The truck series was identified by a number: 1-1/2 ton. The truck body type identification was next: 8-Utility. The engine code was next: N-4.3 liter V-6 followed by a check digit. The model year was identified by the letter O. The assembly plant code followed. The final six digits were the plant sequential production number.

Model Number	Body Type & Seating	Factory Price	GVW	Shipping Weight	Prod. Total
Blazer S-10					
T10506	2-dr. Util.	—	—	—	—
T10506	4-dr. Util.	—	—	—	—

1993 prices and weights were not available at press time.

STANDARD ENGINE: Engine Type: OHV, Cast iron block. V-6. Order Code LB4. Bore x Stroke: 4.00 in. x 3.48 in. Lifters: Hydraulic. Number of main bearings-5. Fuel Induction: Electronic fuel injection. Compression Ratio: 9.1:1. Displacement: 262 cu. in. (4.3 liter). Horsepower: Net: 165 @ 4000 rpm. Torque: Net: 235 lb.-ft. @ 2400 rpm. Oil capacity: 5 qt. with filter change. Fuel Requirements: 87 minimum octane.

OPTIONAL ENGINE: Engine Type: OHV, Cast iron block. V-6. Order Code L35 (Enhanced). Bore x Stroke: 4.00 in. x 3.48 in. Lifters: Hydraulic. Number of main bearings-5. Fuel Induction: Central-Port Electronic fuel injection. Compression Ratio: 9.1:1. Displacement: 262 cu. in. (4.3 liter). Horsepower: Net: 200 @ 4500 rpm. Torque: Net: 260 lb.-ft. @ 3600 rpm. Oil capacity: 5 qt. with filter change. Fuel Requirements: 87 minimum octane.

CHASSIS FEATURES: Carbon steel, welded front box section and open channel rear section. Dimensions: Two-door: Side rail dimensions: 2.28 in. (width) x 5.00 in. (depth) x 0.118 in. (thickness). Overall length: 162.46 in. Side rail section modules: 1.78. Dimensions: Four-door: Side rail dimensions: 2.28 in. (width) x 5.00 in. (depth) x 0.118 in. (thickness). Overall length: 168.96 in. Side rail section modules: 1.78.

SUSPENSION AND RUNNING GEAR: Front Suspension: Independent with torsion bar springs, 25mm dia. shock absorbers. 32mm stabilizer bar. Capacity: 1200 lbs. each at ground. Optional: 32mm, 46mm shock absorbers. Rear Suspension: Two-stage 4-leaf shot-peened springs. Capacity: Two-door: 1350 lbs. each at ground, four-door: 1450 lb. each at ground. 25mm shock absorbers. Optional: 32mm, 46mm shock absorbers. Front Axle. Type: Independent GM Hypoid, tubular driving. Capacity: 2400 lb. Rear Axle. Type: Semi-floating GM Hypoid Capacity: Two-door: 2700 lb. Four-door: 2900 lb. Final Drive Ratio: 3.08:1. Optional: 3.42:1. Transfer Case: New Process 231. Ratios: 2.72, 1.00:1. Brakes: Type: Hydraulic, power assisted self-adjusting. Front: Discs. Rear: Drums. Dimensions: Front: 10.5 in. x 1.03 in. rotor. Rear: 9.5 in. x 2.0 in. Wheels: 15 x 6.00 in. Optional: 15 x 7.0 in. Rallye wheels, 15 x 7.0 in. Cast aluminum (RPO N90), 15 x 7.0 in. cast aluminum (RPO N60). Tires: P205/75R15 steel belted radial All-Season black sidewall. Optional: P205/75R15 black sidewall, All-Season steel belted radial, P205/75R15 on-off road steel belted radial, white letters, P205/75R15 All-Season steel belted radial, white letters, P205/75R15 on-off road steel belted radial black sidewall, P205/75R15 steel belted radial. Front: Highway, Rear: On-off road, P235/75R15 on-off road steel belted radial white letters. Steering: Variable ratio, integral power. Ratio: 17.5:1. Turning diameter: 35.4 ft. Transmission: 5-speed manual with overdrive (RPO MM5). Ratios: 4.02, 2.32, 1.40, 1.00, 0.83:1. Reverse: 3.74:1. Optional: Hydra-Matic 4L60-E 4-speed automatic with overdrive. Ratios: 3.06, 1.63, 1.0, 0.70:1. Reverse: 2.29:1.

VEHICLE DIMENSIONS: Wheelbase: Two-door/Four-door: 100.5 in./107.0-in. Overall Length: Two-door/Four-door: 170.3 in./176.8. Front/Rear Tread 54.1 in./54.1 in. Overall Height: 62.8 in. Width: 65.4 in. Front/Rear Overhang: 30.6/39.2 in. Approach/Departure Degrees: 28° 17'/25.5° 30'. Ground Clearance: Front axle: 8.5 in. Rear axle: 8.1 in. Load space: Two-door: With rear seat installed: 35.5 in. x 50.0 in. x 35.0 in. With rear seat removed or folded: 68.6 in. x 53.4 in. x 35.0 in. Four-door: With rear seat installed: 38.5 in. x 52.5 in. x 34.5 in. With rear seat removed or folded: 76.1 in. x 52.5 in. x 34.5 in. Maximum cargo space: Two-door: 67.3 cu. ft. Four-door: 74.3 cu. ft.

CAPACITIES: Fuel Tank: 20 gal. tank. Coolant System Capacity: 12.0 qt.

ACCOMMODATIONS: Seating Capacity: Standard: Two-door: Driver and passenger front high back bucket sets. Optional: 3 passenger rear bench seat. Four-door: 5 passenger with standard rear bench seat. Front headroom: 39.1 in. Rear headroom: 38.1 in. Front legroom: 42.5 in. Rear legroom: 35.5 in. Front hip room: 50.5 in. Rear hip room: 37.6 in.

INSTRUMENTATION: 0-100 mph speedometer, 99,999.9 mi. odometer, fuel gauge, gauges for voltmeter, oil pressure, engine coolant temperature. Warning lights for brake operating system, hazard warning lights, directional lights, seat belt warning.

OPTIONS: In addition to the changes noted above, these options from 1992 were carried over into 1993. Air conditioning: Air dam with fog lamps. Optional axle ratio. Locking rear differential. Heavy-duty battery. Spare tire and wheel carrier. Cold Climate Package. Heavy-duty radiator. Heavy-duty radiator and engine oil cooler. Driver Convenience Package (RPO ZM7). Includes ComforTilt steering wheel and intermittent wiper system. Driver Convenience Package (RPO ZM8). Includes rear window defroster and tailgate release. California Emissions Package. Color-keyed front floor mats (two-door only). Rear color-keyed floor mats. Deep tinted glass (RPO AJ1). Deep tinted glass with light tinted rear window (RPO AA3). Electronic instrumentation. Black luggage carrier. Exterior electric remote mirrors. Visor mirrors, left and right side. Black wheel opening molding. Operating Convenience Package. Includes power door locks and power windows. Special two-tone paint. Deluxe two-tone paint. Electronically tuned AM/FM stereo radio with Seek-Scan, and digital clock. Electronically tuned AM/FM stereo radio with Seek-Scan, stereo cassette tape player. Electronically tuned AM/FM stereo radio with Seek-Scan, stereo cassette tape player with Search and Repeat, graphic equalizer and digital clock. Delete radio: $95 credit. Special Custom cloth reclining high-back bucket seats. Deluxe cloth reclining high-back bucket seats. Folding rear bench seat. Leather reclining high-back bucket seats, two-door. Transfer case and front differential skid plates and steering linkage shield. Front and rear heavy-duty shock absorbers. Electronic speed control. Sport equipment. Body striping. Sunroof, manual, non-removable, two-door only. Heavy-duty front springs. Off-road suspension, two-door only. Light-Duty Trailering Package. Heavy-Duty Trailering Special Package. Tahoe Package: Sport Package. 4-speed automatic transmission. Rallye wheels. Cast aluminum wheels. Gray aluminum wheels. Sliding rear side window, two-door only. Rear window wiper/washer.

HISTORICAL FOOTNOTES: The S-10 Blazer's sales were particularly strong in the northeast and central states. The S-10 Blazer was built in Moraine, Ohio and Pontiac, Michigan.

CHEVROLET S-10 PICKUPS
1983-1993

1983 S-10 PICKUP

After their introduction in 1982 as two-wheel drive vehicles the S-10 Chevrolet trucks were available as four-wheel drive models for 1983. The only S trucks not available as 4x4s were the chassis and utility cab models. Also joining the short and long wheelbase models was an extended cab version. The extension added 14.5 inches to cab length, sufficient for 18.8 cu. ft. of additional cargo room or two side-mounted jump seats. The extended cab model had a 73 in. pickup box and a 122.9 in. wheelbase. The right-front seat on extended cab models automatically moved forward on its track when folded.

The standard trim level included chrome and black grille, headlight and parking lamp bezels with chrome finish and black trim, chromed front and rear bumpers with rub strips, black windshield and rear window moldings, left and right black outside mirrors, radial ply tires and 15 in. argent wheels with hubcaps. The standard interior provided a front bench seat in vinyl trim in a choice of four colors, and color-keyed instrument panel, sun shades, headliner and windshield pillars. Also included were these items: Front and rear passenger assist handles, headlights-on warning buzzer, rubber floor covering, interior light, door/roof sound deadener, and front floor insulation. The optional Durango package replaced counterpart standard items or added these new items to the standard trim content: Deluxe chrome front end with rub strips, chrome grille, cigarette lighter, cargo area lamp, and bright wheel trim rings. The optional Tahoe package contained these items: Chromed grille, cigarette lighter, right hand sun visor, body side and wheel opening moldings, spare tire cover, and gauges for voltmeter, engine coolant temperature, oil pressure and trip odometer.

The Sport Package added to or replaced the Tahoe features with the following: Painted color-keyed front bumper, and Sport two-tone paint. Available exterior colors for the S-10 trucks were midnight blue, silver metallic, midnight black, light blue metallic, frost white, sunshine yellow, almond, nugget gold metallic, cinnamon red, apple red and, as a secondary color only, satin black.

The S-10's Insta-Trac four-wheel drive system was the first 4x4 system to have a lighted action display of the gear position. To shift from rear-wheel drive into four-wheel drive the driver moved the shift lever on the lighted shift console from 2 Wheel to 4 High. When the lever is moved from 2 Wheel to 4 High the transfer case divided the torque. At the same time a locking sleeve in the front axle engaged the central disconnect to provide power to both front axle shafts. Shifting from four-wheel drive to rear wheel-drive was accomplished by shifting from 4 High to 2 Wheel. The locking sleeve then disengaged the central disconnect, allowing the front axle to freewheel. The truck had to be stopped only when shifting into and out of four-wheel drive low.

1983 Chevrolet S-10 extended cap pickup

I.D. DATA: The V.I.N. plate was mounted on the lower left side windshield corner. The V.I.N. consisted of 17 elements. The first, the number 1 identified the U.S. as the nation of origin. The letter G followed, for the manufacturer: General Motors. The third entry, the letter C represented the make as Chevrolet. The GVWR brake system identification followed. Next came the truck line and chassis type; the letter K indicated four-wheel drive. The truck series was identified by a number: 1-1/2 ton. The truck body type identification was next: 4-Two-door cab. The engine code was next: Y-2.0 liter, A-1.9 liter, B-2.8 liter V-6, followed by a check digit. The model year was identified by the letter D. The assembly plant code followed. The final six digits were the plant sequential production number.

Model Number	Body Type & Seating	Factory Price	GVW	Shipping Weight	Prod. Total
S-10					
T10603	108.3 in. wb. Pickup	$7537	3825[1]	2886	—
T10803	117.9 in. wb. Pickup	$7690	3825[1]	2966	—
T10653	122.9 in. wb. Ext. Cab	$7919	3825[1]	3024	—

NOTE 1: 4650 lb. GVW optional for 1000 lb. payload, standard GVW for 1500 lb. payload is 4050 lb. with 4750 lb. optional.

STANDARD ENGINE: All states except California: Ordering Code LQ2. Produced by GM-Chevrolet Motor Division. Engine Type: Cast iron block. OHV, In-line 4. Bore x Stroke: 3.50 in. x 3.15 in. Lifters: Hydraulic. Number of main bearings-5. Carburetion: Two barrel. Compression Ratio: 9.3:1. Displacement: 121 cu. in. (2.0 liter). Horsepower: Net: 83 @ 4600 rpm. Torque: Net: 108 lb.-ft. @ 2400 rpm. Oil capacity: 5 qt. with filter change. Fuel Requirements: Unleaded.

STANDARD ENGINE: California only: Engine Type: Cast iron block. OHV, In-line 4. Ordering Code: LR1. Produced by Isuzu Motors Limited, Japan. Bore x Stroke: 3.42 in. x 3.23 in. Lifters: Hydraulic. Carburetion: Two barrel. Compression Ratio: 8.4:1. Displacement: 119 cu. in. (1.9 liters). Horsepower: Net: 82 @ 4600 rpm. Torque: Net: 101 lb.-ft. @ 3000 rpm. Oil capacity: qt. with filter change. Fuel Requirements: Unleaded.

OPTIONAL ENGINE: 50 states: Engine Type: OHV, Cast iron block. V-6. Order Code LR2. Produced by GM-Chevrolet Motor Division. Bore x Stroke: 3.50 in. x 2.99 in. Lifters: Hydraulic. Number of main bearings-5. Carburetion: 2-barrel. Compression Ratio: 8.5:1. Displacement: 173 cu. in. (2.8 liter). Horsepower: Net: 110 @ 4800 rpm. Torque: Net: 145 lb.-ft. @ 2100 rpm. Oil capacity: 5 qt. with filter change. Fuel Requirements: Unleaded.

CHASSIS FEATURES: Carbon steel, 39,000 psi., welded front box section and open channel rear section, section modules: 2.19.

SUSPENSION AND RUNNING GEAR: Front Suspension: Independent with torsion bar springs, 25mm dia. shock absorbers. 32mm stabilizer bar. Capacity: 1250 lbs. each at ground. Optional: 32mm shock absorbers. Rear Suspension: Two-stage multi-leaf shot-peened springs. Capacity: 1150 lbs. each at ground. 25mm shock absorbers. Optional: 32mm shock absorbers. Front Axle. Type: Hypoid, tubular driving. Capacity: 2300 lb. Rear Axle. Type: Salisbury, hypoid. Capacity: 2700 lb. Final Drive Ratio: Standard 4-spd. manual transmission and optional 5-spd. manual overdrive: 3.73:1 (3.08:1 for high altitude emission system). Automatic transmission: 3.42:1 (3.73:1 for high altitude emission system). Optional: Standard 4-spd. manual transmission and optional 5-spd. manual overdrive: 4.11:1 (3.73:1 for high altitude emission system). Automatic transmission: 3.73:1. Transfer Case: New Process 207. Brakes: Type: Hydraulic, power assisted self-adjusting. Front: Discs. Rear: Drums. Dimensions: Front: 10.51 in. x 2.0 in. rotor. Rear: 9.49 in. x 2.0 in. Wheels: 15 in. Tires: P195/75R15 glass belted radial black sidewall. Optional: P195/75R15 black sidewall, P205/75R15 black sidewall, P205/75R15 white sidewall, P205/75R15 white letters, P205/75R15 on-off road black sidewall. Steering: Manual. Optional: Power. Transmission: 4-speed manual. Optional: 5-speed manual with overdrive, 4-speed automatic with overdrive (with V-6 engine only). Clutch: 4-cyl. engine: 9.13 in. dia., V-6: 9.76 in. dia.

VEHICLE DIMENSIONS: Wheelbase: Short wheelbase/Long Wheelbase/Extended Cab: 108.5 in./117.9 in./122.9 in. Overall Length: Short wheelbase/Long Wheelbase/Extended Cab: 178.2 in./170.3 in./194.1 in. Overall Height: 61.2 in. Width: 64.8 in. Load space: Short wheelbase and extended cab: 73.1 in. x 16 in. Long wheelbase: 90.1 in. x 16.0 in.

CAPACITIES: Fuel Tank: 13.2 gal. Optional: Replacement 20 gal. tank.

ACCOMMODATIONS: Seating Capacity: Standard: 3. Headroom: 39.5 in. Legroom: 42.4 in.

INSTRUMENTATION: 0-100 mph speedometer, 99,999.9 mi. odometer, fuel gauge, warning lights for alternator, oil pressure, engine coolant temperature, brake operating system, hazard warning lights, directional lights, seat belt warning.

OPTIONS: Tahoe Package. Durango Package. Sport Package. Air conditioning. Automatic speed control. ComforTilt steering wheel. Power steering. Gauges for oil pressure, engine coolant temperature and voltmeter with trip odometer. Tachometer with gauges. Digital clock (with radio only). Delco radios. Below eye-level mirrors. Styled wheels with special hub ornament and bright trim rings. Operating Convenience Package. Includes power windows and door locks. Dome/reading light. Halogen headlamps. 66 amp Delcotron generator. Heavy-duty Freedom battery. Reclining bucket seat backs. Center console. Color-keyed floor mats. Visor mirror. Door edge guards. Body striping. Spare tire cover. Body side/wheel-opening moldings. Color-keyed front/rear bumpers. Black front bumper guards. Rear air deflector. Front tow hooks. Black or bright wheel-opening moldings. Cast aluminum wheels. Bright wheel trim rings. Full-size spare tire. Heavy-duty radiator. Heavy-duty radiator with transmission or engine cooler with V-6 and automatic transmission. Locking differential rear axle. Heavy-duty front and rear shock absorbers. Off-Road Chassis Package. Stone shield for transfer case and differential carrier. Intermittent windshield wipers. Engine block heater. Deadweight trailer hitch. Trailering Package (either 4,000 or 5,000 lb).

HISTORICAL FOOTNOTES: An S-10 was the only totally stock truck to enter and finish the Nov. 1982 Baja 1000.

1984 S-10 PICKUP

Only minor refinements identified the 1984 S-10 pickups. Trucks with the V-6 engine had "2.8 liter V-6" identification below the driver's side headlight. This replaced the small V6 emblem mounted on the front fender of 1983 S-10 trucks. A new Off-Road Package was introduced in October, 1983. Among its features were Delco Bilstein gas-pressure shock absorbers, transfer case shield, fuel tank shield, front tow hooks and jounce bumpers. This option requires the optional 1500 lb. payload package and P235 steel belted, on/off-road white lettered tires, including full-size spare. A new hydraulic clutch was standard for 1984 with an automatic adjustment feature. The 1984 interior color selection consisted of blue, carmine, charcoal or saddle tan. Exterior colors were: Silver metallic, frost white, midnight black, light blue metallic, galaxy blue metallic, doeskin tan, Indian bronze metallic, desert sand metallic, apple red, cinnamon red and, as a secondary color only, satin black. The Sport interior was available with optional High Country Sheepskin in saddle tan. A new speed adjustment with incremental 1 mph settings was included in the optional electronic speed control.

1984 Chevrolet S-10 pickup with Sport paint

I.D. DATA: The V.I.N. plate was mounted on the lower left side windshield corner. The V.I.N. consisted of 17 elements. The first, the number 1 identified the U.S. as the nation of origin. The letter G followed, for the manufacturer: General Motors. The third entry, the letter C represented the make as Chevrolet. The GVWR brake system identification followed. Next came the truck line and chassis type; the letter K indicated four-wheel drive. The truck series was identified by a number: 1-1/2 ton. The truck body type identification was next: 4-Two-door cab. The engine code was next: Y-2.0 liter, A-1.9 liter, B-2.8 liter V-6, followed by a check digit. The model year was identified by the letter E. The assembly plant code followed. The final six digits were the plant sequential production number.

Model Number	Body Type & Seating	Factory Price	GVW	Shipping Weight	Prod. Total
S-10					
T10603	108.3 in. wb. Pickup	$7592	3825[1]	2925	—
T10803	117.9 in. wb. Pickup	$7745	3825[1]	2997	—
T10653	122.9 in. wb. Ext. Cab	$7974	3825[1]	3066	—

NOTE 1: 4650 lb. GVW optional for 1000 lb. payload, standard GVW for 1500 lb. payload is 4050 lb. with 4750 lb. optional.

STANDARD ENGINE: All states except California: Ordering Code LQ2. Produced by GM-Chevrolet Motor Division. Engine Type: Cast iron block. OHV, In-line 4. Bore x Stroke: 3.50 in. x 3.15 in. Lifters: Hydraulic. Number of main bearings-5. Carburetion: Two barrel. Compression Ratio: 9.3:1. Displacement: 121 cu. in. (2.0 liter). Horsepower: Net: 83 @ 4600 rpm. Torque: Net: 108 lb.-ft. @ 2400 rpm. Oil capacity: 5 qt. with filter change. Fuel Requirements: Unleaded.

STANDARD ENGINE: California only and short wheel base regular cab models: Engine Type: Cast iron block. OHV, In-line 4. Ordering Code: LR1. Produced by Isuzu Motors Limited, Japan. Bore x Stroke: 3.42 in. x 3.23 in. Lifters: Hydraulic. Carburetion: Two barrel. Compression Ratio: 8.4:1. Displacement: 119 cu. in. (1.9 liters). Horsepower: Net: 82 @ 4600 rpm. Torque: Net: 101 lb.-ft. @ 3000 rpm. Fuel Requirements: Unleaded.

OPTIONAL ENGINE: 50 states: Engine Type: OHV, Cast iron block. V-6. Order Code LR2. Produced by GM-Chevrolet Motor Division. Bore x Stroke: 3.50 in. x 2.99 in. Lifters: Hydraulic. Number of main bearings-5. Carburetion: 2-barrel. Compression Ratio: 8.5:1. Displacement: 173 cu. in. (2.8 liter). Horsepower: Net: 110 @ 4800 rpm. Torque: Net 145 lb.-ft. @ 2100 rpm. Oil capacity: 5 qt. with filter change. Fuel Requirements: Unleaded.

CHASSIS FEATURES: Carbon steel, 39,000 psi., welded front box section and open channel rear section, section modules: 2.19.

SUSPENSION AND RUNNING GEAR: Front Suspension: Independent with torsion bar springs, 25mm dia. shock absorbers. 32mm stabilizer bar. Capacity: 1250 lbs. each at ground. Optional: 32mm shock absorbers. Rear Suspension: Two-stage multi-leaf shot-peened springs. Capacity: 1150 lbs. each at ground. 25mm shock absorbers. Optional: 32mm shock absorbers. Front Axle. Type: Hypoid, tubular driving. Capacity: 2300 lb. Rear Axle. Type: Salisbury, hypoid. Capacity: 2700 lb. Final Drive Ratio: Standard 4-spd. manual transmission and optional 5-spd. manual overdrive: 3.73:1 (3.08:1 for high altitude emission system). Automatic transmission: 3.42:1 (3.73:1 for high altitude emission system). Optional: Standard 4-spd. manual transmission and optional 5-spd. manual overdrive: 4.11:1 (3.73:1 for high altitude emission system). Automatic transmission: 3.73:1. Transfer Case: New Process 207. Brakes: Type: Hydraulic, power assisted self-adjusting. Front: Discs. Rear: Drums. Dimensions: Front: 10.51 in. x 2.0 in. rotor. Rear: 9.49 in. x 2.0 in. Wheels: 15 in. Tires: P195/75R15 glass belted radial black sidewall. Optional: P195/75R15 black sidewall, P205/75R15 black sidewall, P205/75R15 white sidewall, P205/75R15 white letters, P205/75R15 on-off road black sidewall. Steering: Manual. Optional: Power. Transmission: 4-speed manual. Optional: 5-speed manual with overdrive, 4-speed automatic with overdrive (with V-6 engine only). Clutch: 4-cyl. engine: 9.13 in. dia., V-6: 9.76 in. dia.

VEHICLE DIMENSIONS: Wheelbase: Short wheelbase/Long Wheelbase/Extended Cab: 108.5 in./117.9 in./122.9 in. Overall Length: Short wheelbase/Long Wheelbase/Extended Cab: 178.2 in./170.3 in./194.1 in./208.6 in. Overall Height: 61.2 in. Width: 64.8 in. Tailgate Height: 16.0 in. Load space: Short wheelbase and extended cab: 73.1 in. x 16 in. Long wheelbase: 90.1 in. x 16.0 in.

CAPACITIES: Fuel Tank: 13.2 gal. Optional: Replacement 20 gal. tank.

ACCOMMODATIONS: Seating Capacity: Standard: 3. Headroom: 39.5 in. Legroom: 42.4 in.

INSTRUMENTATION: 0-100 mph speedometer, 99,999.9 mi. odometer, fuel gauge, warning lights for alternator, oil pressure, engine coolant temperature, brake operating system, hazard warning lights, directional lights, seat belt warning.

OPTIONS: Tahoe Package. Durango Package. Sport Package. Air conditioning. Automatic speed control. ComforTilt steering wheel. Power steering. Gauges for oil pressure, engine coolant temperature and voltmeter with trip odometer. Tachometer with gauges. Digital clock (with radio only). Delco radios. Below eye-level mirrors. Styled wheels with special hub ornament and bright trim rings. Operating Convenience Package. Includes power windows

and door locks. Dome/reading light. Halogen headlamps. 66 amp Delcotron generator. Heavy-duty Freedom battery. Reclining bucket seat backs. Center console. Color-keyed floor mats. Visor mirror. Door edge guards. Body striping. Spare tire cover. Body side/wheel opening moldings. Color-keyed front/rear bumpers. Black front bumper guards. Rear air deflector. Front tow hooks. Black or bright wheel opening moldings. Cast aluminum wheels. Bright wheel trim rings. Full-size spare tire. Heavy-duty radiator. Heavy-duty radiator with transmission or engine cooler with V-6 and automatic transmission. Locking differential rear axle. Heavy-duty front and rear shock absorbers. Off-Road Chassis Package. Stone shield for transfer case and differential carrier. Intermittent windshield wipers. Engine block heater. Deadweight trailer hitch. Trailering Package (either 4,000 or 5,000 lb).

HISTORICAL FOOTNOTES: The 1984 S-10 was introduced in the fall of 1983.

1985 S-10 PICKUP

A new computer-controlled Tech IV, 2.5 liter, 4-cylinder, electronically fuel injected was the standard 4x4 S-10 engine for 1985. With 92 horsepower and 134 lb.-ft. of torque, this engine had 10 percent more horsepower and 22 percent more torque than the previous standard engine. Both the Durango and Tahoe trim offered a choice of new Custom vinyl or extra cost Custom cloth upholstery. The Tahoe option was now available with a new Custom vinyl or extra cost Special Custom cloth upholstery. The Tahoe Package also included full instrumentation in a brushed aluminum dash, color-keyed carpeting, trim panels and moldings. The Sport Equipment Package included high-back bucket seats in High Country Sheepskin, center locking console and Sport steering wheel. The interior colors for 1985 were blue, carmine, charcoal and saddle tan. Exterior colors were midnight black, galaxy blue metallic, Indian bronze metallic, apple red, cinnamon red, desert sand metallic, silver metallic, doeskin tan, and frost white.

1985 Chevrolet S-10 with special two-tone paint

I.D. DATA: The V.I.N. plate was mounted on the lower left side windshield corner. The V.I.N. consisted of 17 elements. The first, the number 1 identified the U.S. as the nation of origin. The letter G followed, for the manufacturer: General Motors. The third entry, the letter C represented the make as Chevrolet. The GVWR brake system identification followed. Next came the truck line and chassis type; the letter K indicated four-wheel drive. The truck series was identified by a number: 1-1/2 ton. The truck body type identification was next: 4-Two-door cab. The engine code was next: E-2.5 liter, B-2.8 liter V-6, followed by a check digit. The model year was identified by the letter F. The assembly plant code followed. The final six digits were the plant sequential production number.

Model Number	Body Type & Seating	Factory Price	GVW	Shipping Weight	Prod. Total
S-10 with 2.8 liter V-6					
T10603	108.3 in. wb. Pickup	$7802	3825[1]	2918	—
T10803	117.9 in. wb. Pickup	$7955	3825[1]	3004	—
T10653	122.9 in. wb. Ext. Cab	$8420	3825[1]	3072	—

NOTE 1: 4650 lb. GVW optional for 1000 lb. payload, standard GVW for 1500 lb. payload is 4050 lb. with 4750 lb. optional.

STANDARD ENGINE: Ordering Code LN8. Produced by Pontiac Motor Division. Engine Type: Cast iron block. OHV, In-line 4. Bore x Stroke: 4.0 in. x 3.0 in. Lifters: Hydraulic. Number of main bearings-5. Fuel Induction: Electronic fuel injection. Compression Ratio: 9.0:1. Displacement: 151 cu. in. (2.5 liter). Horsepower: Net: 92 @ 4400 rpm. Torque: Net: 134 lb.-ft. @ 2800 rpm. Oil capacity: 5 qt. with filter change. Fuel Requirements: Unleaded.

OPTIONAL ENGINE: Engine Type: OHV, Cast iron block. V-6. Order Code LR2. Produced by GM-Chevrolet Motor Division. Bore x Stroke: 3.50 in. x 2.99 in. Lifters: Hydraulic. Number of main bearings-5. Carburetion: 2-barrel. Compression Ratio: 8.5:1. Displacement: 173 cu. in. (2.8 liter). Horsepower: Net: 115 @ 4800 rpm. Torque: Net: 150 lb.-ft. @ 2100 rpm. Oil capacity: 5 qt. with filter change. Fuel Requirements: Unleaded.

CHASSIS FEATURES: Carbon steel, 39,000 psi., welded front box section and open channel rear section, section modules: 2.19.

SUSPENSION AND RUNNING GEAR: Front Suspension: Independent with torsion bar springs, 25mm dia. shock absorbers. 32mm stabilizer bar. Capacity: 1250 lbs. at ground. Optional: 32mm shock absorbers. Rear Suspension: Two-stage multi-leaf shot-peened springs. Capacity: 1150 lbs. each at ground. 25mm shock absorbers. Optional: 32mm shock absorbers. Front Axle. Type: Hypoid, tubular driving. Capacity: 2300 lb. Rear Axle. Type: Salisbury, hypoid. Capacity: 2700 lb. Final Drive Ratio: Standard 4-spd. manual transmission and optional 5-spd. manual overdrive: 3.73:1 (3.08:1 for high altitude emission system). Automatic transmission: 3.42:1 (3.73:1 for high altitude emission system). Optional: Standard 4-spd. manual transmission and optional 5-spd. manual overdrive: 4.11:1 (3.73:1 for high altitude emission system). Automatic transmission: 3.73:1. Transfer Case: New Process 207. Brakes: Type: Hydraulic, power assisted self-adjusting. Front: Discs. Rear: Drums. Dimensions: Front: 10.51 in. x 2.0 in. rotor. Rear: 9.49 in. x 2.0 in. Wheels: 15 in. Tires: P195/75R15 glass belted radial black sidewall. Optional: P195/75R15 black sidewall, P205/75R15 black sidewall, P205/75R15 white sidewall, P205/75R15 white letters, P205/75R15 on-off road black sidewall. Steering: Manual. Optional: Power. Transmission: 4-speed manual. Optional: 5-speed manual with overdrive, 4-speed automatic with overdrive (with V-6 engine only). Clutch: 4-cyl. engine: 9.13 in. dia., V-6: 9.76 in. dia.

VEHICLE DIMENSIONS: Wheelbase: Short wheelbase/Long Wheelbase/Extended Cab: 108.5 in./117.9 in./122.9 in. Overall Length: Short wheelbase/Long Wheelbase/Extended Cab: 178.2 in./170.3 in./194.1 in./208.6 in. Overall Height: 61.2 in. Width: 64.8 in. Tailgate Height: 16.0 in. Load space: Short wheelbase and extended cab: 73.1 in. x 16 in. Long wheelbase: 90.1 in. x 16.0 in.

CAPACITIES: Fuel Tank: 13.2 gal. Optional: Replacement 20 gal. tank.

ACCOMMODATIONS: Seating Capacity: Standard: 3. Headroom: 39.5 in. Legroom: 42.4 in.

INSTRUMENTATION: 0-100 mph speedometer, 99,999.9 mi. odometer, fuel gauge, warning lights for alternator, oil pressure, engine coolant temperature, brake operating system, hazard warning lights, directional lights, seat belt warning.

OPTIONS: Durango Package: $339. Tahoe Package: $442. Sport Package: $940. Custom vinyl bench seat: $50. Custom vinyl high-back bucket seats: $128-$178 depending upon trim package. Custom two-tone paint: $200. Special two-tone paint: $167-$311 depending upon trim package. Sport two-tone paint: $162-$227 depending upon trim package. California emissions system: $99. 2.6 liter V-6 engine: $225. 4-speed overdrive automatic transmission: $670. Optional axle ratio: $36. Locking rear differential: $238. Pre-cleaner air cleaner: 49. 5-speed manual overdrive transmission: $175. All-Weather air conditioning: 705. Heavy-duty battery: $53. Front black bumper guards: $30. Off-Road Package: $602-$658 depending upon trim package. Cold Climate Package: $107-$179 depending upon trim package. Front compartment console: $108. Engine oil cooling system: $120. Heavy-duty radiator: $53. Heavy-duty radiator and transmission oil cooler: $59 with air conditioning, $112 without air conditioning. Spare tire cover: $32. Air deflector: $41. Rear window defogger: $114 with air conditioning, $145 without air conditioning. Power door locks: $135. Color-keyed floor mats: $15. Gauge Package. Includes voltmeter, engine coolant temperature, oil pressure: $58. Gauge Package plus tachometer: $55-$113 depending upon trim package. 66 amp Delcotron generator: $31. Deep tinted back window glass with light tinted windshield and side door glass: $55. Tinted glass, all windows: $46. Halogen headlights: $22. Engine block heater: $31. Engine compartment light: $15. Exterior left and right side painted mirrors: $50. Exterior left and right side bright mirrors: $83. Body side and wheel opening moldings: $17-$144 depending upon trim package. Door edge guards: $17. Bright wheel opening moldings: $28. Black wheel opening moldings: $12-$41 depending upon trim package. Operating Convenience Package: $325. AM radio: $112. AM/FM radio: $171. AM/FM radio with clock: $210. AM/FM stereo radio with electronic tuning: $238 AM/FM stereo radio and clock with electronic tuning: $277. AM/FM stereo radio with Seek-Scan, stereo cassette tape, clock and graphic equalizer and electronic tuning and premium rear speakers: $594. Premium rear speakers: $25. Transfer case shield: $67. Heavy-duty front and rear shock absorbers: $34. Full-size spare tire: $46-90 depending upon size. Electronic speed control: $260. ComforTilt steering wheel: $115. Striping: $65. Heavy-duty suspension equipment: $59. 20 gal. fuel tank: $49. Two front towing hooks: $36. Deadweight trailer hitch: $64. Heavy-Duty Trailering Special: $199. Light-Duty Trailering Special: $103. Wheel trim rings: $56. Rallye wheels: $32-$88 depending upon trim package. Styled wheels: $32-$88 depending upon trim package. Cast aluminum wheels: $238-$294 depending upon trim package. Power side door windows: $190. Intermittent windshield wiper system: $55.

HISTORICAL FOOTNOTES: The 1985 S-10 models were introduced on September 21, 1984.

1986 S-10 PICKUP

The 1986 S-10 pickup instrument panel was revised to include a redesigned instrument cluster with tell-tale lights in addition to the voltmeter, oil pressure and engine coolant temperature gauges. Another new feature was a panel bottom-mounted tray. Door trim panels were restyled and the switches for the optional power windows were repositioned on the door panels. All models had a new black molded urethane steering wheel. The Sport steering wheel now had a simulated leather look. New tweed-pattern cloth seat trim was used for the Sport Package. The standard 2.5 liter engine had lighter-weight high silicon pistons. The 2.8 liter V-6 was fitted with electronic fuel injection. Exterior front body identification for models with this engine now read "2.8 Fuel Injection." Models with the V-6 had a higher-capacity Delco Freedom III battery. The optional heavy-duty battery offered for both engines had a higher capacity for 1986. Also new for 1986 was a lighter-weight radiator with a standard copper-brass core with crossflow coolant movement and plastic side tanks. The exterior color selection for 1986 consisted of midnight black, steel gray metallic, light blue metallic, galaxy blue metallic, doeskin tan, Indian bronze metallic, cinnamon red, apple red, Nevada gold and silver metallic (used as a secondary color only).

I.D. DATA: The V.I.N. plate was mounted on the lower left side windshield corner. The V.I.N. consisted of 17 elements. The first, the number 1 identified the U.S. as the nation of origin. The letter G followed, for the manufacturer: General Motors. The third entry, the letter C represented the make as Chevrolet. The GVWR brake system identification followed. Next came the truck line and chassis type; the letter K indicated four-wheel drive. The truck series was identified by a number: 1-1/2 ton. The truck body type identification was next: 4-Two-door cab. The engine code was next: E-2.5 liter, B-2.8 liter V-6, followed by a check digit. The model year was identified by the letter G. The assembly plant code followed. The final six digits were the plant sequential production number.

Model Number	Body Type & Seating	Factory Price	GVW	Shipping Weight	Prod. Total
S-10 with 2.8 liter V-6					
T10603	108.3 in. wb. Pickup	$8115	3825[1]	2918	195,620[2]
T10803	117.9 in. wb. Pickup	$8350	3825[1]	3004	—
T10653	122.9 in. wb. Ext. Cab	$8802	3825[1]	3072	—

NOTE 1: 4650 lb. GVW optional for 1000 lb. payload, standard GVW for 1500 lb. payload is 4050 lb. with 4750 lb. optional.
NOTE 2: Sales (Nov., 1985-Nov., 1986) all S-10 models.

STANDARD ENGINE: Ordering Code LN8. Produced by Pontiac Motor Division. Engine Type: Cast iron block. OHV, In-line 4. Bore x Stroke: 4.0 in. x 3.0 in. Lifters: Hydraulic. Number of main bearings-5. Fuel induction: Electronic fuel injection. Compression Ratio: 9.0:1. Displacement: 151 cu. in. (2.5 liter). Horsepower: Net: 92 @ 4400 rpm. Torque: Net: 134 lb.-ft. @ 2800 rpm. Oil capacity: 5 qt. with filter change. Fuel Requirements: Unleaded.

OPTIONAL ENGINE: Engine Type: OHV, Cast iron block. V-6. Order Code LR2. Produced by GM-Chevrolet Motor Division. Bore x Stroke: 3.50 in. x 2.99 in. Lifters: Hydraulic. Number of main bearings-5. Fuel Induction: Electronic fuel injection. Compression Ratio: 8.9:1. Displacement: 173 cu. in. (2.8 liter). Horsepower: Net: 125 @ 4800 rpm. Torque: Net: 150 lb.-ft. @ 2200 rpm. Oil capacity: 5 qt. with filter change. Fuel Requirements: Unleaded.

CHASSIS FEATURES: Carbon steel, 39,000 psi., welded front box section and open channel rear section, section modules: 2.19.

SUSPENSION AND RUNNING GEAR: Front Suspension: Independent with torsion bar springs, 25mm dia. shock absorbers. 32mm stabilizer bar. Capacity: 1250 lbs. each at ground. Optional: 32mm shock absorbers. Rear Suspension: Two-stage multi-leaf shot-peened springs. Capacity: 1150 lbs. each at ground. 25mm shock absorbers. Optional: 32mm shock absorbers. Front Axle. Type: Hypoid, tubular driving. Capacity: 2300 lb. Rear Axle. Type: Salisbury, hypoid. Capacity: 2700 lb. Final Drive Ratio: Standard 4-spd. manual transmission and optional 5-spd. manual overdrive: 3.73:1 (3.08:1 for high altitude emission system). Automatic transmission: 3.42:1 (3.73:1 for high altitude emission system). Optional: Standard 4-spd. manual transmission and optional 5-spd. manual overdrive: 4.11:1 (3.73:1 for high altitude emission system). Automatic transmission: 3.73:1. Transfer Case: New Process 207. Brakes: Type: Hydraulic, power assisted self-adjusting. Front: Discs. Rear: Drums. Dimensions: Front: 10.51 in. x 2.0 in. rotor. Rear: 9.49 in. x 2.0 in. Wheels: 15 in. Tires: P195/75R15 glass belted radial black sidewall. Optional: P195/75R15 black sidewall, P205/75R15 black sidewall, P205/75R15 white sidewall, P205/75R15 white letters, P205/75R15 on-off road black sidewall. Steering: Manual. Optional: Power. Transmission: 4-speed manual. Optional: 5-speed manual with overdrive, 4-speed automatic with overdrive (with V-6 engine only). Clutch: 4-cyl. engine: 9.13 in. dia., V-6: 9.76 in. dia.

VEHICLE DIMENSIONS: Wheelbase: Short wheelbase/Long Wheelbase/Extended Cab: 108.5 in./117.9 in./122.9 in. Overall Length: Short wheelbase/Long Wheelbase/Extended Cab: 178.2 in./170.3 in./194.1 in./208.6 in. Overall Height: 61.2 in. Width: 64.8 in. Tailgate Height: 16.0 in. Load space: Short wheelbase and extended cab: 73.1 in. x 16 in. Long wheelbase: 90.1 in. x 16.0 in.

CAPACITIES: Fuel Tank: 13.2 gal. Optional: Replacement 20 gal. tank.

ACCOMMODATIONS: Seating Capacity: Standard: 3. Headroom: 39.5 in. Legroom: 42.4 in.

INSTRUMENTATION: 0-100 mph speedometer, 99,999.9 mi. odometer, fuel gauge, warning lights for alternator, oil pressure, engine coolant temperature, brake operating system, hazard warning lights, directional lights, seat belt warning.

OPTIONS: Durango Package: $339. Tahoe Package: $442. Sport Package: $940. Custom vinyl bench seat: $50. Custom vinyl high-back bucket seats: $128-$178 depending upon trim package. Custom two-tone paint: $200. Special two-tone paint: $167-$311 depending upon trim package. Sport two-tone paint: $162-$227 depending upon trim package. California emissions system: $99. 2.6 liter V-6 engine: $225. 4-speed overdrive automatic transmission: $670. Optional axle ratio: $36. Locking rear differential: $238. Pre-cleaner air cleaner: $49. 5-speed manual overdrive transmission: $175. All-Weather air conditioning: 705. Heavy-duty battery: $53. Front black bumper guards: $30. Off-Road Package: $602-$658 depending upon trim package. Cold Climate Package: $107-$179 depending upon trim package. Front compartment console: $108. Engine oil cooling system: $120. Heavy-duty radiator: $53. Heavy-duty radiator and transmission oil cooler: $59 with air conditioning, $112 without air conditioning. Spare tire cover: $32. Air deflector: $41. Rear window defogger: $114 with air conditioning, $145 without air conditioning. Power door locks: $135. Color-keyed floor mats: $15. Gauge Package. Includes voltmeter, engine coolant temperature, oil pressure: $58. Gauge Package plus tachometer: $55-$113 depending upon trim package. 66 amp Delcotron generator: $31. Deep tinted back window glass with light tinted windshield and side door glass: $55. Tinted glass, all windows: $46. Halogen headlights: $22. Engine block heater: $31. Engine compartment light: $15. Exterior left and right side painted mirrors: $50. Exterior left and right side bright mirrors: $83. Body side and wheel opening moldings: $17-$144 depending upon trim package. Door edge guards: $17. Bright wheel opening moldings: $28. Black wheel opening moldings: $12-$41 depending upon trim package. Operating Convenience Package: $325. AM radio: $112. AM/FM radio: $171. AM/FM radio with clock: $210. AM/FM stereo radio with electronic tuning: $238 AM/FM stereo radio and clock with electronic tuning: $277. AM/FM stereo radio with Seek-Scan, stereo cassette tape, clock and graphic equalizer and electronic tuning and premium rear speakers: $594. Premium rear speakers: $25. Transfer case shield: $67. Heavy-duty front and rear shock absorbers: $34. Full-size spare tire: $46-90 depending upon size. Electronic speed control: $260. ComforTilt steering wheel: $115. Striping: $65. Heavy-duty suspension equipment: $59. 20 gal. fuel tank: $49. Two front towing hooks: $36. Dead weight trailer hitch: $64. Heavy-Duty Trailering Special: $199. Light-Duty Trailering Special: $103. Wheel trim rings: $56. Rallye wheels: $32-$88 depending upon trim package. Styled wheels: $32-$88 depending upon trim package. Cast aluminum wheels: $238-$294 depending upon trim package. Power side door windows: $190. Intermittent windshield wiper system: $55.

HISTORICAL FOOTNOTES: The 1986 S-10 models were introduced in the fall of 1985.

1987 S-10 PICKUP

The 1987 S-10's standard 2.5 liter engine featured new high flow ports in the cylinder head and a redesigned intake manifold. A single-belted accessory "serpentine" drive replaced the conventional multiple V belts on both the 2.5 and 2.8 liter engines. The automatic belt tensioning feature in this system eliminated the need for belt adjustment and provided an expected belt life of 100,000 miles. A new 85 amp Delcotron generator was standard, replacing the 78 amp unit used in 1986. The new unit was lighter and provided improved performance and durability. A new Delco battery increased cold cranking amps from 405 to 525. An optional heavy-duty Delco battery featured cold cranking amps from 540 to 630. The tailgate applique for the Tahoe and Sport models was restyled. The cinnamon red color of 1986 was not offered for 1987. A new color added to the remaining exterior colors carried over from 1986 was Emerald metallic. The interior color selection was unchanged from 1986.

I.D. DATA: The V.I.N. plate was mounted on the lower left side windshield corner. The V.I.N. consisted of 17 elements. The first, the number 1 identified the U.S. as the nation of origin. The letter G followed, for the manufacturer: General Motors. The third entry, the letter C represented the make as Chevrolet. The GVWR brake system identification followed. Next came the truck line and chassis type; the letter K indicated four-wheel drive. The truck series was identified by a number: 1-1/2 ton. The truck body type identification was next: 4-Two-door cab. The engine code was next: E-2.5 liter, B-2.8 liter V-6, followed by a check digit. The model year was identified by the letter H. The assembly plant code followed. The final six digits were the plant sequential production number.

Model Number	Body Type & Seating	Factory Price	GVW	Shipping Weight	Prod. Total
S-10 with 2.8 liter V-6					
T10603	108.3 in. wb. Pickup	$9551	3825[1]	2928	—
T10803	117.9 in. wb. Pickup	$9818	3825[1]	3014	—
T10653	122.9 in. wb. Ext. Cab	$10,283	3825[1]	3082	—

NOTE 1: 4650 lb. GVW optional for 1000 lb. payload, standard GVW for 1500 lb. payload is 4050 lb. with 4750 lb. optional.

STANDARD ENGINE: Ordering Code LN8. Produced by Pontiac Motor Division. Engine Type: Cast iron block. OHV, In-line 4. Bore x Stroke: 4.0 in. x 3.0 in. Lifters: Hydraulic. Number of main bearings-5. Fuel induction: Electronic fuel injection. Compression Ratio: 9.0:1. Displacement: 151 cu. in. (2.5 liter). Horsepower: Net: 92 @ 4400 rpm. Torque: Net: 134 lb.-ft. @ 2800 rpm. Oil capacity: 5 qt. with filter change. Fuel Requirements: Unleaded.

OPTIONAL ENGINE: Engine Type: OHV, Cast iron block. V-6. Order Code LR2. Produced by GM-Chevrolet Motor Division. Bore x Stroke: 3.50 in. x 2.99 in. Lifters: Hydraulic. Number of main bearings-5. Fuel Induction: Electronic fuel injection. Compression Ratio: 8.9:1. Displacement: 173 cu. in. (2.8 liter). Horsepower: Net: 125 @ 4800 rpm. Torque: Net: 150 lb.-ft. @ 2200 rpm. Oil capacity: 5 qt. with filter change. Fuel Requirements: Unleaded.

CHASSIS FEATURES: Carbon steel, 39,000 psi., welded front box section and open channel rear section, section modules: 2.19.

SUSPENSION AND RUNNING GEAR: Front Suspension: Independent with torsion bar springs, 25mm dia. shock absorbers. 32mm stabilizer bar. Capacity: 1250 lbs. each at ground. Optional: 32mm shock absorbers. Rear Suspension: Two-stage multi-leaf shot-peened springs. Capacity: 1150 lbs. each at ground. 25mm shock absorbers. Optional: 32mm shock absorbers. Front Axle. Type: Hypoid, tubular driving. Capacity: 2300 lb. Rear Axle. Type: Salisbury, hypoid. Capacity: 2700 lb. Final Drive Ratio: Standard 4-spd. manual transmission and optional 5-spd. manual overdrive: 3.73:1 (3.08:1 for high altitude emission system). Automatic transmission: 3.42:1 (3.73:1 for high altitude emission system). Optional: Standard 4-spd. manual transmission and optional 5-spd. manual overdrive: 4.11:1 (3.73:1 for high altitude emission system). Automatic transmission: 3.73:1. Transfer Case: New Process 207. Brakes: Type: Hydraulic, power assisted self-adjusting. Front: Discs. Rear: Drums. Dimensions: Front: 10.51 in. x 2.0 in. rotor. Rear: 9.49 in. x 2.0 in. Wheels: 15 in. Tires: P195/75R15 glass belted radial black sidewall. Optional: P195/75R15 black sidewall, P205/75R15 black sidewall, P205/75R15 white sidewall, P205/75R15 white letters, P205/75R15 on-off road black sidewall. Steering: Manual. Optional: Power. Transmission: 4-speed manual. Optional: 5-speed manual with overdrive, 4-speed automatic with overdrive (with V-6 engine only). Clutch: 4-cyl. engine: 9.13 in. dia., V-6: 9.76 in. dia.

VEHICLE DIMENSIONS: Wheelbase: Short wheelbase/Long Wheelbase/Extended Cab: 108.5 in./117.9 in./122.9 in. Overall Length: Short wheelbase/Long Wheelbase/Extended Cab: 178.2 in./170.3 in./194.1 in./208.6 in. Overall Height: 61.2 in. Width: 64.8 in. Tailgate Height: 16.0 in. Load space: Short wheelbase and extended cab: 73.1 in. x 16 in. Long wheelbase: 90.1 in. x 16.0 in.

CAPACITIES: Fuel Tank: 13.2 gal. Optional: Replacement 20 gal. tank.

ACCOMMODATIONS: Seating Capacity: Standard: 3. Headroom: 39.5 in. Legroom: 42.4 in.

INSTRUMENTATION: 0-100 mph speedometer, 99,999.9 mi. odometer, fuel gauge, warning lights for alternator, oil pressure, engine coolant temperature, brake operating system, hazard warning lights, directional lights, seat belt warning.

OPTIONS: Durango Package: $339. Tahoe Package: $442. Sport Package: $940. Custom vinyl bench seat: $50. Custom vinyl high-back bucket seats: $128-$178 depending upon trim package. Custom two-tone paint: $200. Special two-tone paint: $167-$311 depending upon trim package. Sport two-tone paint: $162-$227 depending upon trim package. California emissions system: $99. 2.6 liter V-6 engine: $225. 4-speed overdrive automatic transmission: $670. Optional axle ratio: $36. Locking rear differential: $238. Pre-cleaner air cleaner: 49. 5-speed manual overdrive transmission: $175. All-Weather air conditioning: 705. Heavy-duty battery: $53. Front black bumper guards: $30. Off-Road Package: $602-$658 depending upon trim package. Cold Climate Package: $107-$179 depending upon trim package. Front compartment console: $108. Engine oil cooling system: $120. Heavy-duty radiator: $53. Heavy-duty radiator and transmission oil cooler: $59 with air conditioning, $112 without air conditioning. Spare tire cover: $32. Air deflector: $41. Rear window defogger: $114 with air conditioning, $145 without air conditioning. Power door locks: $135. Color-keyed floor mats: $15. Gauge Package. Includes voltmeter, engine coolant temperature, oil pressure: $58. Gauge Package plus tachometer: $55-$113 depending upon trim package. 66 amp Delcotron generator: $31. Deep tinted back window glass with light tinted windshield and side door glass: $55. Tinted glass, all windows: $46. Halogen headlights: $22. Engine block heater: $31. Engine compartment light: $15. Exterior left and right side painted mirrors: $50. Exterior left and right side bright mirrors: $83. Body side and wheel opening moldings: $17-$144 depending upon trim package. Door edge guards: $17. Bright wheel opening moldings: $28. Black wheel opening moldings: $12-$41 depending upon trim package. Operating Convenience Package: $325. AM radio: $112. AM/FM radio: $171. AM/FM radio with clock: $210. AM/FM stereo radio with electronic tuning: $238 AM/FM stereo radio and clock with electronic tuning: $277. AM/FM stereo radio with Seek-Scan, stereo cassette tape, clock and graphic equalizer and electronic tuning and premium rear speakers: $594. Premium rear speakers: $25. Transfer case shield: $67. Heavy-duty front and rear shock absorbers: $34. Full-size spare tire: $46-90 depending upon size. Electronic speed control: $260. ComforTilt steering wheel: $115. Striping: $65. Heavy-duty suspension equipment: $59. 20 gal. fuel tank: $49. Two front towing hooks: $36. Dead weight trailer hitch: $64. Heavy-Duty Trailering Special: $199. Light-Duty Trailering Special: $103. Wheel trim rings: $56. Rallye wheels: $32-$88 depending upon trim package. Styled wheels: $32-$88 depending upon trim package. Cast aluminum wheels: $238-$294 depending upon trim package. Power side door windows: $190. Intermittent windshield wiper system: $55.

HISTORICAL FOOTNOTES: The 1987 S-10 models were introduced on the September 7, 1986.

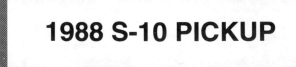

1988 S-10 PICKUP

Initially, the 1988 S-10 was offered with either the 2.5 liter or 2.8 liter engines. Beginning in April, 1988, Chevrolet's new 4.3 liter Vortex V-6 became an option. Redeveloped All-Season tires were available for the 1988 S-10. Front brakes had new noise reducing "SAS II" brake lining insulators. The S-10 instrument panel now had gray trim plate accents. The knobs and switches remained black. L.E.D. displays on stereo radios were replaced by vacuum fluorescent lights. During the 1988 model the optional air conditioning system was fitted with illuminated blue heating, ventilation, and air-conditioning control lighting for improved indication of knob locations. Map lights were added to the inside rearview mirror. For 1988 the S-10 was available with an optional factory-installed tinted sun roof. This non-removable roof had manual operation for its five different opening positions. Four new exterior colors were added for 1988: Light Mesa brown, bright blue metallic, light Mesa brown metallic and dark Mesa brown metallic. Replacing saddle tan as an interior color was cognac. The base model's standard equipment included a 3 passenger vinyl bench seat with folding back rest, sound insulation and sound-deadening material installed in dash, doors and roof, color-keyed door trim panels with padded armrests, embossed color-keyed headliner, and AM radio. The Durango stepped up the base interior equipment to include bright Durango nameplate on storage box door, choice of Custom vinyl or Special Custom cloth seat trim, color-keyed rubber matting for floor area, deluxe steering wheel, side window defoggers, bright dome lamp trim, cigarette lighter, headlamps-on warning buzzer and deluxe heater and defogger. The Durango exterior included bright Durango nameplates with series designation on front fenders, bright front bumper with black rub strips, bright trim on black grille, bright taillight trim bright wheel trim rings and reflectorized Chevrolet tailgate lettering. The Tahoe Package included all interior Durango items plus the following additions or substitutions: Bright Tahoe nameplate on stowage box, color-keyed carpeting for floor area and cab back panel, color-keyed cowl kick panels, visor mirror on right side sun visor, special Custom cloth inserts in door trim panels, carpeted lower door panel insert with storage pocket, plus coin holder in left side door, full-coverage molded styrene headliner of full foam, with color-keyed cloth (in regular cab) and an instrument panel cluster including voltmeter, oil pressure gauge, engine coolant temperature gauge and trip odometer. The Tahoe exterior had these features: Bright Tahoe nameplates with series designations on front fenders, black body-side moldings with bright trim, bright wheel opening lip moldings, black hub covers, body-color door handle inserts, black applique tailgate trim with Chevrolet lettering, and argent colored wheels.

The Sport Package included all interior Tahoe items plus the following additions or substitutions: Bright Sport nameplate on stowage box door, Sport cloth high-back front bucket seats, Sport steering wheel, door trim panels with Sport cloth inserts that matched the seat trim, and a color-keyed console with lockable storage compartment operated by door key. The Sport exterior featured these items: Sport nameplates with series designation on front fenders, Sport two-tone paint, bumper color-keyed to lower accent stripe of two-tone paint with black rib strips, base argent wheels with black ornamental hubs and bright trim rings, black chrome door handles, grille and headlamp bezels, and black wheel opening lip moldings.

Introduced during the 1987 model year and continued for 1988 was the Back Country option for Tahoe-equipped S-10 trucks. It featured a front grille guard with driving lamps and headlight brush hoops, light bridge with off-road lamps, tubular rear bumper, switches in instrument panel for driving/off-road lights, black chrome accent on wheels, headlight and taillight bezels and grille; and striping around wheel openings and front of grille. Required options for the Back Country Package included power steering, 1500 lb. load package, off-road chassis equipment and 2.8 liter V-6.

1988 Chevrolet S-10 extended cap pickup with Back Country equipment

I.D. DATA: The V.I.N. plate was mounted on the lower left side windshield corner. The V.I.N. consisted of 17 elements. The first, the number 1 identified the U.S. as the nation of origin. The letter G followed, for the manufacturer: General Motors. The third entry, the letter C represented the make as Chevrolet. The GVWR brake system identification followed. Next came the truck line and chassis type; the letter K indicated four-wheel drive. The truck series was identified by a number: 1-1/2 ton. The truck body type identification was next: 4-Two-door cab. The engine code was next: E-2.5 liter, B-2.8 liter V-6, N-4.3 liter V-6, followed by a check digit. The model year was identified by the letter I. The assembly plant code followed. The final six digits were the plant sequential production number.

Model Number	Body Type & Seating	Factory Price	GVW	Shipping Weight	Prod. Total
S-10 with 2.8 liter V-6					
T10603	108.3 in. wb. Pickup	$10,444	3825[1]	2974	296,308[2]
T10803	117.9 in. wb. Pickup	$10,528	3825[1]	3060	—
T10653	122.9 in. wb. Ext. Cab	$11,373	3825[1]	3128	—

NOTE 1: 4650 lb. GVW optional for 1000 lb. payload, standard GVW for 1500 lb. payload is 4050 lb. with 4750 lb. optional.
NOTE 2: 1988 calendar year production, both two-wheel drive and four-wheel drive models.

STANDARD ENGINE: Ordering Code LN8. Produced by Pontiac Motor Division. Engine Type: Cast iron block. OHV, In-line 4. Bore x Stroke: 4.0 in. x 3.0 in. Lifters: Hydraulic. Number of main bearings-5. Fuel induction: Electronic fuel injection. Compression Ratio: 9.0:1. Displacement: 151 cu. in. (2.5 liter). Horsepower: Net: 92 @ 4400 rpm. Torque: Net: 134 lb.-ft. @ 2800 rpm. Oil capacity: 5 qt. with filter change. Fuel Requirements: Unleaded.

OPTIONAL ENGINE: Engine Type: OHV, Cast iron block. V-6. Order Code LL2. Produced by GM-Chevrolet Motor Division in Canada and Mexico. Bore x Stroke: 3.50 in. x 2.99 in. Lifters: Hydraulic. Number of main bearings-5. Fuel Induction: Electronic fuel injection. Compression Ratio: 8.9:1. Displacement: 173 cu. in. (2.8 liter). Horsepower: Net: 125 @ 4800 rpm. Torque: Net: 150 lb.-ft. @ 2200 rpm. Oil capacity: 5 qt. with filter change. Fuel Requirements: Unleaded.

OPTIONAL ENGINE: Engine Type: OHV, Cast iron block. V-6. Order Code LB4. Bore x Stroke: 4.00 in. x 3.48 in. Lifters: Hydraulic. Number of main bearings-5. Fuel Induction: Electronic fuel injection. Compression Ratio: 9.3:1. Displacement: 262 cu. in. (4.3 liter). Horsepower: Net: 160 @ 4000 rpm. Torque: Net: 230 lb.-ft. @ 2400 rpm. Oil capacity: 5 qt. with filter change. Fuel Requirements: Unleaded.

CHASSIS FEATURES: Carbon steel, 39,000 psi., welded front box section and open channel rear section, section modules: 2.19.

SUSPENSION AND RUNNING GEAR: Front Suspension: Independent with torsion bar springs, 25mm dia. shock absorbers. 32mm stabilizer bar. Capacity: 1250 lbs. each at ground. Optional: 32mm shock absorbers. Rear Suspension: Two-stage multi-leaf shot-peened springs. Capacity: 1150 lbs. each at ground. 25mm shock absorbers. Optional: 32mm shock absorbers. Front Axle. Type: Hypoid, tubular driving. Capacity: 2300 lb. Rear Axle. Type: Salisbury, hypoid. Capacity: 2700 lb. Final Drive Ratio: Standard 4-spd. manual transmission and optional 5-spd. manual overdrive: 3.73:1 (3.08:1 for high altitude emission system). Automatic transmission: 3.42:1 (3.73:1 for high altitude emission system). Optional: Standard 4-spd. manual transmission and optional 5-spd. manual overdrive: 4.11:1 (3.73:1 for high altitude emission system). Automatic transmission: 3.73:1. Transfer Case: New Process 207. Brakes: Type: Hydraulic, power assisted self-adjusting. Front: Discs. Rear: Drums. Dimensions: Front: 10.51 in. x 2.0 in. rotor. Rear: 9.49 in. x 2.0 in. Wheels: 15 in. Tires: P195/75R15 glass belted radial black sidewall. Optional: P195/75R15 black sidewall, P205/75R15 black sidewall, P205/75R15 white sidewall, P205/75R15 white letters, P205/75R15 on-off road black sidewall. Steering: Manual. Optional: Power. Transmission: 4-speed manual. Optional: 5-speed manual with overdrive, 4-speed automatic with overdrive (with V-6 engine only). Clutch: 4-cyl. engine: 9.13 in. dia., V-6: 9.76 in. dia.

VEHICLE DIMENSIONS: Wheelbase: Short wheelbase/Long Wheelbase/Extended Cab: 108.5 in./117.9 in./122.9 in. Overall Length: Short wheelbase/Long Wheelbase/Extended Cab: 178.2 in./170.3 in./194.1 in./208.6 in. Overall Height: 61.2 in. Width: 64.8 in. Tailgate Height: 16.0 in. Load space: Short wheelbase and extended cab: 73.1 in. x 16 in. Long wheelbase: 90.1 in. x 16.0 in.

CAPACITIES: Fuel Tank: 20 gal. tank.

ACCOMMODATIONS: Seating Capacity: Standard: 3. Headroom: 39.5 in. Legroom: 42.4 in.

INSTRUMENTATION: 0-100 mph speedometer, 99,999.9 mi. odometer, fuel gauge, warning lights for alternator, oil pressure, engine coolant temperature, brake operating system, hazard warning lights, directional lights, seat belt warning.

OPTIONS: Durango Package. Tahoe Package. Sport Package. Custom two-tone paint. Special two-tone paint. Sport two-tone paint. California emissions system. 2.6 liter V-6 engine. 4-speed overdrive automatic transmission. Optional axle ratio. Locking rear differential. Pre-cleaner air cleaner. 5-speed manual overdrive transmission. All-Weather air conditioning. Heavy-duty battery. Front black bumper guards. Luggage carrier, black or bright finish. Off-Road Package. Cold Climate Package. Front console. Engine oil cooling system. Heavy-duty radiator. Heavy-duty radiator and transmission oil cooler. Air deflector. Power door locks. Color-keyed floor mats. Gauge Package. Includes voltmeter, engine coolant temperature, oil pressure. Gauge Package plus tachometer. 66 amp Delcotron generator. Deep tinted glass. Deep tinted glass with light tinted rear window. Halogen headlights. Engine block heater. Engine compartment light. Exterior left and right side painted mirrors. Exterior left and right side bright mirrors. Body side and wheel opening moldings. Door edge guards. Bright wheel opening moldings. Black wheel opening moldings. Operating Convenience Package. AM radio. AM/FM radio. AM/FM radio with clock. AM/FM stereo radio with electronic tuning. AM/FM stereo radio and clock with electronic tuning. AM/FM stereo radio with Seek-Scan, stereo cassette tape, clock and graphic equalizer and electronic tuning and premium rear speakers. Premium rear speakers. Transfer case shield. Heavy-duty front and rear shock absorbers. Full-size spare tire. Electronic speed control. ComforTilt steering wheel. Striping. Heavy-duty suspension equipment. 20 gal. fuel tank. Two front towing hooks. Deadweight trailer hitch: $64. Heavy-Duty Trailering Special: $199. Light-Duty Trailering Special. Wheel trim rings. Rallye wheels. Styled wheels. Cast aluminum wheels. Power side door windows. Intermittent windshield wiper system.

HISTORICAL FOOTNOTES: The 1988 S-10 models were introduced on August 24, 1987.

1989 S-10 PICKUP

The S-10 pickups had a new standard rear-wheel anti-lock (RWAL) system on all models. Also standard was a new electric speedometer. Added to the option list was an electronic instrument panel cluster with speedometer, tachometer, voltmeter and fuel, oil pressure and engine coolant temperature gauges. The gauges utilized high-brightness vacuum fluorescent tubes for sharper visibility. Models with the standard 2.8 liter V-6 had a new transfer case with redesigned gear sets for reduced noise and smoother operation. The new transfer case also had new controls, longer shift lever, new vacuum switch and relocated vent tube. For 1989 the standard models had an upgraded vinyl interior and a heavy-duty heater. A new exterior color was Woodlands brown. Dark blue replaced medium blue as an interior color. The 4.3 liter V-6 was in greater supply for 1989. It was available only with the overdrive automatic transmission. Models with the 4.3 liter were changed in a number of ways to accommodate this larger V-6. The steering column was moved to the left to provide additional clearance for the left exhaust manifold and the frame was changed to gain clearance in several locations on the right side. When the Maxi Cab was ordered with the optional jump seats, rear shoulder safety belts were installed.

1989 Chevrolet S-10 Maxi Cap pickup

I.D. DATA: The V.I.N. plate was mounted on the lower left side windshield corner. The V.I.N. consisted of 17 elements. The first, the number 1 identified the U.S. as the nation of origin. The letter G followed, for the manufacturer: General Motors. The third entry, the letter C represented the make as Chevrolet. The GVWR brake system identification followed. Next came the truck line and chassis type; the letter K indicated four-wheel drive. The truck series was identified by a number: 1-1/2 ton. The truck body type identification was next: 4-Two-door cab. The engine code was next: B-2.8 liter V-6, N-4.3 liter V-6, followed by a check digit. The model year was identified by the letter J. The assembly plant code followed. The final six digits were the plant sequential production number.

Model Number	Body Type & Seating	Factory Price	GVW	Shipping Weight	Prod. Total
S-10 with 2.8 liter V-6					
T10603	108.3 in wb. Pickup	$11,275	3570[1]	2974	242,430[2]
T10803	117.9 in. wb. Pickup	$11,455	3825[1]	3060	—
T10653	122.9 in. wb. Maxi Cab	$12,085	3825[1]	3128	—

NOTE 1: 4710 lb. optional.
NOTE 2: 1989 calendar year production, both two-wheel drive and four-wheel drive models.

STANDARD ENGINE: Engine Type: OHV, Cast iron block. V-6. Order Code LL2. Produced by GM-Chevrolet Motor Division in Canada and Mexico. Bore x Stroke: 3.50 in. x 2.99 in. Lifters: Hydraulic. Number of main bearings-5. Fuel Induction: Electronic fuel injection. Compression Ratio: 8.9:1. Displacement: 173 cu. in. (2.8 liter). Horsepower: Net: 125 @ 4800 rpm. Torque: Net: 150 lb.-ft. @ 2200 rpm. Oil capacity: 5 qt. with filter change. Fuel Requirements: Unleaded.

OPTIONAL ENGINE: Engine Type: OHV, Cast iron block. V-6. Order Code LB4. Bore x Stroke: 4.00 in. x 3.48 in. Lifters: Hydraulic. Number of main bearings-5. Fuel Induction: Electronic fuel injection. Compression Ratio: 9.3:1. Displacement: 262 cu. in. (4.3 liter). Horsepower: Net: 160 @ 4000 rpm. Torque: Net: 230 lb.-ft. @ 2400 rpm. Oil capacity: 5 qt. with filter change. Fuel Requirements: Unleaded.

CHASSIS FEATURES: Carbon steel, 39,000 psi., welded front box section and open channel rear section, section modules: 2.19.

SUSPENSION AND RUNNING GEAR: Front Suspension: Independent with torsion bar springs, 25mm dia. shock absorbers. 32mm stabilizer bar. Capacity: 1350 lbs. each at ground. Optional: 32mm shock absorbers. Rear Suspension: Two-stage multi-leaf shot-peened springs. Capacity: 1150 lbs. each at ground. 25mm shock absorbers. Optional: 32mm shock absorbers. Front Axle. Type: Hypoid, tubular driving. Capacity: 2700 lb. Rear Axle. Type: Salisbury, hypoid. Capacity: 2700 lb. Final Drive Ratio: Standard 5-spd. manual overdrive for 2.8 liter engine: 3.73:1; 4-speed automatic overdrive standard for 4.3 liter V-6: 3.08:1. Optional: Standard 5-spd. manual overdrive for 2.8 liter engine: 4.11:1 4-speed automatic overdrive standard for 4.3 liter V-6: 4.42:1. Transfer Case: New Process 207. Brakes: Type: Hydraulic, power assisted self-adjusting. Front: Discs. Rear: Drums. Dimensions: Front: 10.51 in. x 2.0 in. rotor. Rear: 9.49 in. x 2.0 in. Wheels: 15 in. Tires: P195/75R15 glass belted radial black sidewall. Optional: P195/75R15 black sidewall, P205/75R15 black sidewall, P205/75R15 white sidewall, P205/75R15 white letters, P205/75R15 on-off road black sidewall. Steering: Integral variable ratio power. Ratios; 13-16.0:1. Transmission: Standard 5-spd. manual overdrive for 2.8 liter engine; 4-speed automatic overdrive standard for 4.3 liter V-6. Clutch: 9.13 in. dia.

VEHICLE DIMENSIONS: Wheelbase: Short wheelbase/Long Wheelbase/Maxi Cab: 108.5 in./117.9 in./122.9 in. Overall Length: Short wheelbase/Long Wheelbase/Extended Cab: 178.2 in./170.3 in./194.1 in./208.6 in. Overall Height: 61.2 in. Width: 64.8 in. Tailgate Width: 16.0 in. Load space: Short wheelbase and extended cab: 73.1 in. x 16 in. Long wheelbase: 90.1 in. x 16.0 in.

CAPACITIES: Fuel Tank: 20 gal. tank.

ACCOMMODATIONS: Seating Capacity: Standard: 3. Headroom: 39.5 in. Legroom: 42.4 in.

INSTRUMENTATION: 0-100 mph speedometer, 99,999.9 mi. odometer, fuel gauge, warning lights for alternator, oil pressure, engine coolant temperature, brake operating system, hazard warning lights, directional lights, seat belt warning.

OPTIONS: Durango Package. Tahoe Package: $683. Sport Package: $1038. Air conditioning: $736 without LL2 engine, $680 with LL2 engine. Optional axle ratio: $38. Locking rear differential: $252. Heavy-duty battery: $56. Cold Climate Package: $113-$156 depending upon trim option. Center console: $114. Engine oil cooler: $126. Heavy-duty radiator: $56. Heavy-duty radiator and engine oil cooler: $63, with air conditioning, $118 without air conditioning. Spare tire cover: $33. Air deflector: $43. Driver Convenience Package. Includes ComforTilt steering wheel and intermittent wiper system: $180. Rear Window Convenience Package. Includes electric tailgate release and rear window defogger: $197. 4.3 liter V-6: $255. Color-keyed front floor mats: $16. Color-keyed rear floor mats: $12. Gauge Package: $62. Deep tinted glass with light tinted rear window: $56-$200 depending on trim package. Halogen headlights: $24. Engine block heater: $33. Electronic instrumentation: $296-$358 depending on trim package. Engine compartment light: $16. Interior visor mirror: $7. Exterior below eye-level black mirrors: $52. Exterior below eye-level bright mirrors: $87. Interior rearview tilting mirror with dual reading lamps: $26. Body side and wheel opening moldings: $152. Black wheel opening molding: $13-$43 depending upon trim package. Bright wheel opening molding: $31. Operating Convenience Package. Includes power door locks and power windows: $344. Custom two-tone paint: $172-$344 depending upon trim package. Special two-tone paint: $163-$212 depending upon trim package. Deluxe two-tone paint: $177-$329 depending upon trim package. Electronically tuned AM/FM stereo radio: $275. Electronically tuned AM/FM stereo radio with Seek-Scan, stereo cassette tape player and digital clock: $454. Electronically tuned AM/FM stereo radio with Seek-Scan, stereo cassette tape player with Search and Repeat, graphic equalizer and digital clock: $604. Reclining seat backs: $74. Transfer case and front differential skid plates and steering linkage shield: $75. Front and rear heavy-duty shock absorbers: $36. Electronic speed control: $205. Heavy-duty front springs: $63.Body striping: $49. Sunshine striping: $116. Manual sun roof: $250. Suspension Package: $160-$220 depending upon trim package. Two front tow hooks: $38. Deadweight trailer hitch: $68. Light-Duty Trailering Package: $109. Heavy-Duty Trailering Special Package: $211. 4-speed automatic transmission: $795. Wheel trim rings: $60. Cast aluminum wheels: $252-$308 depending upon trim package. Sliding rear window: $257. Rear window wiper/washer: $125.

HISTORICAL FOOTNOTES: The 1989 S-10 models were introduced on September 4, 1988.

1990 S-10 PICKUP

A new Getrag-designed, Hydra-Matic-built 5-speed manual transmission with fifth gear overdrive was available with the 4.3 liter V-6 for 1990. The 2.8 liter V-6 and 5-speed manual transmission were not available for the 4x4 S-10. A new fixed gross vehicle weight rating replaced the net payload system. All S-10 models had a redesigned instrument cluster with improved legibility. The panel now included voltmeter, engine coolant temperature and oil pressure gauges. Added to the standard S-10 equipment were front tow hooks, P205/75R15 All-Season steel belted tires, reclining sear back on maxi cab models and electronically tuned AM radio. New 1990 features of the Durango included swing-out quarter windows, right-hand visor mirror, deluxe front chromed bumper and chromed grille. New for the Tahoe were right and left-hand black exterior mirrors, color-keyed floor mats and engine compartment lamp. New exterior colors were royal blue metallic and garnet. The interior was now offered in garnet.

1990 Chevrolet S-10 Maxi Cap pickup

I.D. DATA: The V.I.N. plate was mounted on the lower left side windshield corner. The V.I.N. consisted of 17 elements. The first, the number 1 identified the U.S. as the nation of origin. The letter G followed, for the manufacturer: General Motors. The third entry, the letter C represented the make as Chevrolet. The GVWR brake system identification followed. Next came the truck line and chassis type; the letter K indicated four-wheel drive. The truck series was identified by a number: 1-1/2 ton. The truck body type identification was next: 4-Two-door cab. The engine code was next: N-4.3 liter V-6, followed by a check digit. The model year was identified by the letter L. The assembly plant code followed. The final six digits were the plant sequential production number.

Model Number	Body Type & Seating	Factory Price	GVW	Shipping Weight	Prod. Total
S-10 with 4.3 liter V-6					
T10603	108.3 in. wb. Pickup	$12,430	4650[1]	2974	243,060[2]
T10803	117.9 in. wb. Pickup	$12,615	4650[1]	3060	—
T10653	122.9 in. wb. Maxi Cab	$13,215	4650[1]	3128	—

NOTE 1: 5150 lb. optional.
NOTE 2: 1990 calendar year production, both two-wheel drive and four-wheel drive models.

STANDARD ENGINE: Engine Type: OHV, Cast iron block. V-6. Order Code LB4. Bore x Stroke: 4.00 in. x 3.48 in. Lifters: Hydraulic. Number of main bearings-5. Fuel Induction: Electronic fuel injection. Compression Ratio: 9.3:1. Displacement: 262 cu. in. (4.3 liter). Horsepower: Net: 160 @ 4000 rpm. Torque: Net: 230 lb.-ft. @ 2400 rpm. Oil capacity: 5 qt. with filter change. Fuel Requirements: Unleaded.

CHASSIS FEATURES: Carbon steel, 39,000 psi., welded front box section and open channel rear section, section modules: 2.19.

SUSPENSION AND RUNNING GEAR: Front Suspension: Independent with torsion bar springs, 25mm dia. shock absorbers. 32mm stabilizer bar. Capacity: 1350 lbs. each at ground. Optional: 32mm shock absorbers. Rear Suspension: Two-stage multi-leaf shot-peened springs. Capacity: 1150 lbs. each at ground. 25mm shock absorbers. Optional: 32mm shock absorbers. Front Axle. Type: Hypoid, tubular driving. Capacity: 2700 lb. Rear Axle. Type: Salisbury, hypoid. Capacity: 2700 lb. Final Drive Ratio: 3.08:1. Optional: 3.42:1. Transfer Case: New Process 231. Ratios: 2.72, 1.00:1. Brakes: Type: Hydraulic, power assisted self-adjusting. Front: Discs. Rear: Drums. Dimensions: Front: 10.51 in. x 2.0 in. rotor. Rear: 9.49 in. x 2.0 in. Wheels: 15 in. Tires: P205/75R15 steel belted radial All-Season black sidewall. Optional: P205/75R15 black sidewall, All-Season steel belted radial, P205/75R15 on-off road steel belted radial, white letters, P205/75R15 All-Season steel belted radial, white letters, P205/75R15 on-off road steel belted radial black sidewall, P205/75R15 steel belted radial. Front: Highway. Rear: On-off road, P235/75R15 on-off road steel belted radial white letters. Steering: Variable ratio, integral power. Ratio: 17.5:1. Turning diameter: 35.4 ft. Transmission: 5-speed manual with overdrive (RPO MM5). Ratios: 4.02, 2.32, 1.40, 1.00, 0.83:1. Reverse: 3.74:1. Optional: 4-speed automatic with overdrive (RPO MXO): 3.06, 1.63, 1.0, 0.70:1. Reverse: 2.29:1. Clutch: 9.13 in. dia.

VEHICLE DIMENSIONS: Wheelbase: Short wheelbase/Long Wheelbase/Maxi Cab: 108.5 in./117.9 in./122.9 in. Overall Length: Short wheelbase/Long Wheelbase/Extended Cab: 178.2 in./170.3 in./194.1 in./208.6 in. Overall Height: 61.2 in. Width: 64.8 in. Tailgate Height: 16.0 in. Load space: Short wheelbase and extended cab: 73.1 in. x 16 in. Long wheelbase: 90.1 in. x 16.0 in.

CAPACITIES: Fuel Tank: 20 gal. tank.

ACCOMMODATIONS: Seating Capacity: Standard: 3. Headroom: 39.5 in. Legroom: 42.4 in.

INSTRUMENTATION: 0-100 mph speedometer, 99,999.9 mi. odometer, fuel gauge, gauges for voltmeter, oil pressure, and engine coolant temperature; warning lights for brake operating system, hazard warning lights, directional lights, seat belt warning.

OPTIONS: Durango Package: $73 to $108 depending on body style and other options ordered. Tahoe Package: $184-$722 depending on body style and other options ordered. Air conditioning: $755. Air dam with fog lamps: $115. Optional axle ratio: $38. Locking rear differential: $252. Heavy-duty battery: $56. Spare tire carrier: $100. Cold Climate Package: $140-$243 depending upon trim option. Center console: $135. Heavy-duty radiator: $56. Heavy-duty radiator and engine oil cooler: $63, with air conditioning, $118 without air conditioning. Engine oil cooler: $135. Driver Convenience Package. Includes ComforTilt steering wheel and intermittent wiper system: $180. Color-keyed front floor mats: $20. Full floor carpeting: $40. Deep tinted glass: Extended Cab: $101-$140 depending upon option package; Regular Cab: $11. Electronic instrumentation: $296. Lighted interior visor mirror: $68-$75 depending upon trim package. Body side and wheel opening moldings: $152. Black wheel opening molding: $13-$43 depending upon trim package. Bright wheel opening molding: $31. Endgate net: $110. Operating Convenience Package. Includes power door locks and power windows:

$344. Custom two-tone paint: $172-$344 depending upon trim package. Special two-tone paint. Includes pin striping: $296. Deluxe two-tone paint: $177. Electronically tuned AM/FM stereo radio with Seek-Scan, stereo cassette tape player and digital clock: $122. Electronically tuned AM/FM stereo radio with Seek-Scan, stereo cassette tape player with Search and Repeat, graphic equalizer and digital clock: $272. Delete radio: $226 credit. Rear jump seats with vinyl trim: $240. Shield Package. Includes transfer case and front differential skid plates and steering linkage shield: $126. Front and rear heavy-duty shock absorbers: $40. Electronic speed control: $225. Heavy-duty rear springs: $64. Heavy-duty front suspension with heavy-duty front and rear shock absorbers: $63. Sport Suspension: $415. Body striping: $55. Manual sun roof: $250. Heavy-Duty Trailering Special Package: $211. 4-speed automatic transmission: $860. Wheel trim rings: $60. Cast aluminum wheels: $269-$325 depending upon trim package. Aluminum Special wheels: $395 without spare tire carrier, $495 with spare tire carrier. Sliding rear window: $113.

HISTORICAL FOOTNOTES: The 1990 S-10 models were introduced in September, 1989.

1991 S-10 PICKUP

The 1991 S-10 models were introduced early in 1990. The exterior appearance was revised with a new grille, nameplates, emblems, bumper rub strips and body side moldings. The body striping, decals, wheels and wheel trim were also new as were the optional aluminum wheels. Two new exterior colors — Sky blue and mint green were offered. Woodlands brown metallic and Nevada gold metallic were cancelled. A new Baja Off-Road Appearance Package was introduced. It was based on the Tahoe trim except for the following: Charcoal interior with red/charcoal high back bucket seats and charcoal door inserts, Baja name stitched just below the headrest, wider red body side stripe, redesigned Baja graphic on pickup box, and black decal surrounding front grille.

The 4.3 liter V-6 had an improved 220 series throttle body injection system with longer throttle shaft bearings, new throttle return springs and improved fuel mixture distribution. These changes were designed to improve engine starts, idle and overall engine reliability and durability. A new Thermac III modified air cleaner system and Quantum spark plugs were adopted to improve cold starts and overall engine reliability. A lighter, more durable starting motor was also new for 1991. A "hardened" 72mm distributor replaced the 89mm Hall-Effect distributor to make the ignition more impervious to electromagnetic induction interference from other electrical components. Suspension changes included revisions to the front stabilizer bar bushings and shock absorber valving. Single stage rear spring rates were revised and the rear shock absorbers were also revalved. The optional front compartment floor console for models equipped with bucket seats had a revised thumb operated catch for easier, keyless entry. Replacing the rocker type switch previously used to control the power door locks in the Operating Convenience Package was a more convenient, redesigned lever type switch. Reception for both the AM and FM radios was also improved. Other changes that were incorporated as interim 1991 changes included an improved front axle halfshaft, improved heating/ventilation, and adoption of a heavy-duty battery as standard equipment. Replacing the Moraine interior cloth was Breton cloth.

1991 Chevrolet S-10 Baja pickup

I.D. DATA: The V.I.N. plate was mounted on the lower left side windshield corner. The V.I.N. consisted of 17 elements. The first, the number 1 identified the U.S. as the nation of origin. The letter G followed, for the manufacturer: General Motors. The third entry, the letter T represented the make as Chevrolet. The GVWR brake system identification followed. Next came the truck line and chassis type; the letter K indicated four-wheel drive. The truck series was identified by a number: 1-1/2 ton. The truck body type identification was next: 4-Two-door cab. The engine code was next: N-4.3 liter V-6, followed by a check digit. The model year was identified by the letter M. The assembly plant code followed. The final six digits were the plant sequential production number.

Model Number	Body Type & Seating	Factory Price	GVW	Shipping Weight	Prod. Total
S-10 with 4.3 liter V-6					
CT10603	108.3 in. wb. Pickup	$12,190	4650[1]	2974	251,476[2]
CT10803	117.9 in. wb. Pickup	$13,210	4650[1]	3060	—
CT10653	122.9 in. wb. Maxi Cab	$13,830	4650[1]	3128	—
CT10603	108.3 in. wb. Baja	$13,020	4650[1]	N.A.	—

NOTE 1: 5150 lb. optional.
NOTE 2: 1991 calendar year production, both two-wheel drive and four-wheel drive models.

STANDARD ENGINE: Engine Type: OHV, Cast iron block. V-6. Order Code LB4. Bore x Stroke: 4.00 in. x 3.48 in. Lifters: Hydraulic. Number of main bearings-5. Fuel Induction: Electronic fuel injection. Compression Ratio: 9.3:1. Displacement: 262 cu. in. (4.3 liter). Horsepower: Net: 160 @ 4000 rpm. Torque: Net: 230 lb.-ft. @ 2400 rpm. Oil capacity: 5 qt. with filter change. Fuel Requirements: Unleaded.

CHASSIS FEATURES: Carbon steel, 39,000 psi., welded front box section and open channel rear section, section modules: 2.19. Dimensions: 108.3 in. wheelbase: 2.34 in. x 6.50 in. x 0.118 in. Overall length: 170.31 in. 117.9 in. wheelbase: 2.34 in. x 6.50 in. x 0.134 in. Overall length: 186.26 in. 122.9 in. wheelbase: 2.34 in. x 6.50 in. x 0.134 in. Overall length: 184.46 in.

SUSPENSION AND RUNNING GEAR: Front Suspension: Independent with torsion bar springs, 25mm dia. shock absorbers. 32mm stabilizer bar. Capacity: 1350 lbs. each at ground. Optional: 32mm shock absorbers. Rear Suspension: Two-stage multi-leaf shot-peened springs. Capacity: 1150 lbs. each at ground. 25mm shock absorbers. Optional: 32mm shock absorbers. Front Axle. Type: Hypoid, tubular driving. Capacity: 2700 lb. Rear Axle. Type: Salisbury, hypoid. Capacity: 2700 lb. Final Drive Ratio: 3.08:1. Optional: 3.42:1. Transfer Case: New Process 231. Ratios: 2.72, 1.00:1. Brakes: Type: Hydraulic, power assisted self-adjusting. Front: Discs. Rear: Drums. Dimensions: Front: 10.51 in. x 2.0 in. rotor. Rear: 9.49 in. x 2.0 in. Wheels: 15 in. x 6.00 in. Tires: P205/75R15 steel belted radial All-Season black sidewall. Optional: P205/75R15 black sidewall, All-Season steel belted radial, P205/75R15 on-off road steel belted radial, white letters, P205/75R15 All-Season steel belted radial, white letters, P205/75R15 on-off road steel belted radial black sidewall, P205/75R15 steel belted radial. Front: Highway. Rear: On-off road, P235/75R15 on-off road steel belted radial white letters. Steering: Variable ratio, integral power. Ratio: 17.5:1. Turning diameter: 35.4 ft. Transmission: 5-speed manual with overdrive (RPO MM5). Ratios: 4.02, 2.32, 1.40, 1.00, 0.83:1. Reverse: 3.74:1. Optional: 4-speed automatic with overdrive (RPO MXO): 3.06, 1.63, 1.0, 0.70:1. Reverse: 2.29:1. Clutch: 9.13 in. dia.

VEHICLE DIMENSIONS: Wheelbase: Short wheelbase/Long Wheelbase/Maxi Cab: 108.5 in./117.9 in./122.9 in. Overall Length: Short wheelbase/Long Wheelbase/Maxi Cab: 178.2 in./ 194.2 in./192.8 in. Overall Height: 61.2 in. Width: 64.8 in. Tailgate Height: 16.0 in. Load space: Short wheelbase and extended cab: 73.1 in. x 55.3 in. x 15.9 in. Long wheelbase: 90.1 in. x 55.3 in. x 16.0 in.

CAPACITIES: Fuel Tank: 20 gal. tank.

ACCOMMODATIONS: Seating Capacity: Standard: 3. Headroom: 39.5 in. Legroom: 42.4 in.

INSTRUMENTATION: 0-100 mph speedometer, 99,999.9 mi. odometer, fuel gauge, gauges for voltmeter, oil pressure, and engine coolant temperature; warning lights for brake operating system, hazard warning lights, directional lights, seat belt warning.

OPTIONS: Tahoe Package: 532-$587 depending upon other options ordered. Air conditioning: $780. Air dam with fog lamps: $115. Optional axle ratio: $44. Locking rear differential: $252. Heavy-duty battery: $56. Rear step bumper: $130-$229 depending upon paint option. Spare tire carrier: $110. Cold Climate Package: $140-$243 depending upon trim option. Center console: $135. Heavy-duty radiator: $56. Heavy-duty radiator and transmission oil cooler: $63, with air conditioning, $118 without air conditioning. Engine oil cooler: $135. Driver Convenience Package. Includes ComforTilt steering wheel and intermittent wiper system: $204. Full floor carpeting: $40. Deep tinted glass: Extended Cab: $101-$140 depending upon Option Package; Regular Cab: $11. Electronic instrumentation: $195. Auxiliary lighting: $44-$66 depending upon other options ordered. Exterior below eye-level painted mirrors: $52. Lighted interior visor mirror: $68-$75 depending upon trim package. Body side and wheel opening moldings: $152. Black wheel opening molding: $13-$43 depending upon trim package. Bright wheel opening molding: $31. Endgate net: $110. Operating Convenience Package. Includes power door locks and power windows: $367. Special two-tone paint. Includes pin striping: $296. Deluxe two-tone paint: $177. Electronically tuned AM/FM stereo radio with digital clock: $201. Electronically tuned AM/FM stereo radio with Seek-Scan, stereo cassette tape player and digital clock: $131. Electronically tuned AM/FM stereo radio with Seek-Scan, stereo cassette tape player with Search and Repeat, and digital clock: $253. Electronically tuned AM/FM stereo radio with Seek-Scan, stereo cassette tape player with Search and Repeat, graphic equalizer and digital clock: $150-$403 depending upon other options ordered. Delete radio: $95 credit. Rear jump seats with vinyl trim: $240. Shield Package. Includes transfer case and front differential skid plates and steering linkage shield: $126. Heavy-duty front springs: $63. Sport suspension: $252. Off-road suspension: $122 with Tahoe equipment, $182 without Tahoe equipment. Front and rear heavy-duty shock absorbers: $40. Electronic speed control: $238. Heavy-duty rear springs: $64. Heavy-duty front suspension with heavy-duty front and rear shock absorbers: $63. Body striping: $55. Manual sun roof: $250. Heavy-duty Trailering Special Package: $211. 4-speed automatic transmission: $890. Wheel trim rings: $60. Cast aluminum wheels: $284-$340 depending upon trim package. Sliding rear window: $113.

HISTORICAL FOOTNOTES: The 1991 S-10 models were introduced on September 1, 1990.

1992 S-10 PICKUP

New for 1992 was the availability of a four-wheel drive EL model. Previously, the EL, which was defined by Chevrolet as a "decontented standard trim level designed to be a price leader for the value-conscious truck buyer" had been available only in two-wheel drive form. It was equipped with a 160 hp. Vortex V-6 engine, 5-speed manual transmission, power steering, compact spare and wheel and a solid exterior color. A convenient new 2-speed electronic-shift transfer case was optional for all models except the EL. New appointments for 1992 included seats with integral head restraints for front bench seat positions and high-back buckets with optional leather (extended cabs) seating, a standard self-aligning steering wheel, an optional premium sound system with compact disc player and new exterior colors. These consisted of midnight black, Aspen blue metallic, royal blue metallic, sky blue, garnet red, steel gray metallic, aquamarine green, forest green metallic, apple red, frost white and as a secondary color only, silver metallic.

1992 Chevrolet S-10 Maxi Cab pickup

I.D. DATA: The V.I.N. plate was mounted on the lower left side windshield corner. The V.I.N. consisted of 17 elements. The first, the number 1 identified the U.S. as the nation of origin. The letter G followed, for the manufacturer: General Motors. The third entry, the letter C represented the make as Chevrolet. The GVWR brake system identification followed. Next came the truck line and chassis type; the letter K indicated four-wheel drive. The truck series was identified by a number: 1-1/2 ton. The truck body type identification was next: 4-Two-door cab. The engine code was next: N-4.3 liter V-6, followed by a check digit. The model year was identified by the letter N. The assembly plant code followed. The final six digits were the plant sequential production number.

Model Number	Body Type & Seating	Factory Price	GVW	Shipping Weight	Prod. Total
S-10 with 4.3 liter V-6					
CT10603	EL 108.3 in. wb. Pickup	$12,273	4650	N.A.	—
CT10603	108.3 in wb. Pickup	$13,424	4650[1]	2974	—
CT10803	117.9 in. wb. Pickup	$13,724	4650[1]	3060	—
CT10653	122.9 in. wb. Maxi Cab	$14,924	4650[1]	3128	—

NOTE 1: 5150 lb. optional.

STANDARD ENGINE: Engine Type: OHV, Cast iron block. V-6. Order Code LB4. Bore x Stroke: 4.00 in. x 3.48 in. Lifters: Hydraulic. Number of main bearings-5. Fuel Induction: Electronic fuel injection. Compression Ratio: 9.3:1. (EL: 9.1:1). Displacement: 262 cu. in. (4.3 liter). Horsepower: Net: 195 @ 4500 rpm. (EL: 160 @ 4000 rpm). Torque: Net: 260 lb.-ft. @ 3600 rpm. (EL: 230 lb.-ft. @ 2800 rpm). Oil capacity: 5 qt. with filter change. Fuel Requirements: Unleaded.

CHASSIS FEATURES: Carbon steel, 39,000 psi., welded front box section and open channel rear section, section modules: 2.19. Dimensions: 108.3 in. wheelbase: 2.34 in. x 6.50 in. x 0.118 in. Overall length: 170.31 in. 117.9 in. wheelbase: 2.34 in. x 6.50 in. x 0.134 in. Overall length: 186.26 in. 122.9 in. wheelbase: 2.34 in. x 6.50 in. x 0.134 in. Overall length: 184.46 in.

SUSPENSION AND RUNNING GEAR: Front Suspension: Independent with torsion bar springs, 25mm dia. shock absorbers. 32mm stabilizer bar. Capacity: 1350 lbs. each at ground. Optional: 32mm shock absorbers. Rear Suspension: Two-stage multi-leaf shot-peened springs. Capacity: 1150 lbs. each at ground. 25mm shock absorbers. Optional: 32mm shock absorbers. Front Axle. Type: Hypoid, tubular driving. Capacity: 2700 lb. Rear Axle. Type: Salisbury, hypoid. Capacity: 2700 lb. Final Drive Ratio: 3.08:1. Optional: 3.42:1. Transfer Case: New Process 231. Ratios: 2.72, 1.00:1. Brakes: Type: Hydraulic, power assisted self-adjusting. Front: Discs. Rear: Drums. Dimensions: Front: 10.51 in. x 2.0 in. rotor. Rear: 9.49 in. x 2.0 in. Wheels: 15 in. x 6.00 in. Tires: P205/75R15 steel belted radial All-Season black sidewall. Optional: P205/75R15 black sidewall, All-Season steel belted radial, P205/75R15 on-off road steel belted radial, white letters, P205/75R15 All-Season steel belted radial, white letters, P205/75R15 on-off road steel belted radial black sidewall, P205/75R15 steel belted radial. Front: Highway. Rear: On-off road, P235/75R15 on-off road steel belted radial white letters. Steering: Variable ratio, integral power. Ratio: 17.5:1. Turning diameter: 35.4 ft. Transmission: 5-speed manual with overdrive (RPO MM5). Ratios: 4.02, 2.32, 1.40, 1.00, 0.83:1. Reverse: 3.74:1. Optional: 4-speed automatic with overdrive (RPO MXO): 3.06, 1.63, 1.0, 0.70:1. Reverse: 2.29:1. Clutch: 9.13 in. dia.

VEHICLE DIMENSIONS: Wheelbase: Short wheelbase/Long Wheelbase/Maxi Cab: 108.5 in./117.9 in./122.9 in. Overall Length: Short wheelbase/Long Wheelbase/Maxi Cab: 178.2 in./ 194.2 in./192.8 in. Overall Height: 61.2 in. Width: 64.8 in. Tailgate: Width and Height: 53.6 in. x 16.0 in. Load space: Short wheelbase and extended cab: 73.1 in. x 55.3 in. x 15.9 in. Long wheelbase: 90.1 in. x 55.3 in. x 16.0 in.

CAPACITIES: Fuel Tank: 20 gal. tank.

ACCOMMODATIONS: Seating Capacity: Standard: 3. Headroom: 39.5 in. Legroom: 42.4 in.

INSTRUMENTATION: 0-100 mph speedometer, 99,999.9 mi. odometer, fuel gauge, gauges for voltmeter, oil pressure, and engine coolant temperature; warning lights for brake operating system, hazard warning lights, directional lights, seat belt warning.

OPTIONS: Tahoe Package. Air conditioning: Air dam with fog lamps. Optional axle ratio. Locking rear differential. Heavy-duty battery. Spare tire and wheel carrier. Cold Climate Package. Heavy-duty radiator. Heavy-duty radiator and engine oil cooler. Driver Convenience Package (RPO ZM7). Includes ComforTilt steering wheel and intermittent wiper system. Driver Convenience Package (RPO ZM8). Includes rear window defroster and tailgate release. California Emissions Package. Color-keyed front floor mats (two-door only). Rear color-keyed floor mats. Deep tinted glass (RPO AJ1). Deep tinted glass with light tinted rear window (RPO AA3). Electronic instrumentation. Exterior electric remote mirrors. Visor mirrors, left and right side. Black wheel opening molding. Operating Convenience Package. Includes power door locks and power windows. Special two-tone paint. Deluxe two-tone paint. Electronically tuned AM/FM stereo radio with Seek-Scan, and digital clock. Electronically tuned AM/FM stereo radio with Seek-Scan, stereo cassette tape player. Electronically tuned AM/FM stereo radio with Seek-Scan, stereo cassette tape player with Search and Repeat, graphic equalizer and digital clock. Delete radio. Special Custom cloth reclining high-back bucket seats. Deluxe cloth reclining high-back bucket seats. Leather reclining high-back bucket seats. Transfer case and front differential skid plates and steering linkage shield. Front and rear heavy-duty shock absorbers. Electronic speed control. Body striping. Sun roof, manual, non-removable. Heavy-duty front springs. Off-road suspension. Light-Duty Trailering Package. Heavy-Duty Trailering Special Package. 4-speed automatic transmission. Rallye wheels. Cast aluminum wheels. Gray aluminum wheels. Sliding rear side window.

HISTORICAL FOOTNOTES: The 1992 S-10 models were introduced on September 1, 1991.

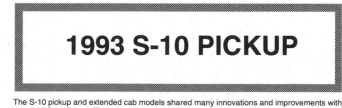

1993 S-10 PICKUP

The S-10 pickup and extended cab models shared many innovations and improvements with the 1993 S-10 Blazer. These included the addition of an internal balance shaft to the 4.3 liter V-6 and the use of Solar-Ray™ tinted glass in all windows. A single, more reliable controller was used for the engine, transmission and anti-lock brakes. An improved O ring seal on the intake manifold thermostat reduced coolant leaks. The V-6 engine also had revised spark plugs which improved engine idle quality. The 1993 S-10 also had new color-keyed door trim, air conditioning and radio bezels. A dual note horn was standard and the convenience tray now had a soft liner. Two new exterior colors — Dove gray and khaki replaced aquamarine green and sky blue. A revised high solids enamel painting process was used for 1993. It involved the use of corrosion-resistant steel, eight-stage zinc-phosphate coating, use of an E-coat (ELPO), a primer surface with anti-chip protection on body side panels and on the leading edges of the hood, front fenders, A-pillars and roof. The paint used was an acrylic enamel. A new beige color joined charcoal, blue and gray as interior colors choices for 1993. A paint treatment featuring a middle break line with a blended stripe was available for the first time in 1993.

The pickup and extended cab models with the Tahoe trim level had a redesigned chrome and gray grille. The taillight bezels were now black. The left and right side split-visors had lighted vanity mirrors and extenders. Door-activated reading lamps with a delay-off feature were installed. The extended cab had a parcel restraint net in the storage area behind the seat. The RPO D55 floor console was raised to match the height of the door armrest. The console used in conjunction with the manual transmission included a coin tray; that used with the automatic included a dual cupholder. The floor shifter console was revised with a deeper right-hand side shifter tray. A 12-volt outlet was also installed. A new RPO D48 electric dual remote mirror option was introduced for 1993. The new electronic 4L60-E Hydra-Matic 4-speed automatic overdrive transmission was available for the S-10. A new heavy-duty cooling system option (RPO V08) for trucks with the automatic transmission was introduced. It included an engine oil cooler as well as a transmission oil cooler. An anti-theft sleeve was added to the ComforTilt steering wheel/intermittent windshield wiper option (RPO ZM7). All-new Deluxe cloth reclining seats were available. They were fitted with manual 2-position lumbar adjustment. This option also included a floor console. The new Deluxe cloth 60/40 split-bench front seat option included an easy-entry passenger seat feature on the extended cab. This feature was listed in the "interim availability" category. A new RPO 5P2 15 in. aluminum five-spoke wheel option was also introduced for 1993. Options introduced late in the 1992 model year for the entry level EL model and continued for 1993 included: Automatic transmission, power steering, a heavy-duty battery, rear painted bumper, Cold Climate Package, two-tone paint, AM/FM stereo radio with cassette tape player and clock, shield package, heavy-duty shock absorbers, upper body stripe and P205/75R15 white lettered tires.

1993 Chevrolet S-10 Tahoe longbed pickup

I.D. DATA: The V.I.N. plate was mounted on the lower left side windshield corner. The V.I.N. consisted of 17 elements. The first, the number 1, identified the U.S. as the nation of origin. The letter G followed, for the manufacturer: General Motors. The third entry, the letter C represented the make as Chevrolet. The GVWR brake system identification followed. Next came the truck line and chassis type; the letter K indicated four-wheel drive. The truck series was identified by a number: 1-1/2 ton. The truck body type identification was next: 4-Two-door cab. The engine code was next: N-4.3 liter V-6, followed by a check digit. The model year was identified by the letter N. The assembly plant code followed. The final six digits were the plant sequential production number.

Model Number	Body Type & Seating	Factory Price	GVW	Shipping Weight	Prod. Total
S-10 with 4.3 liter V-6					
CT10603	EL 108.3 in. wb. Pickup	$[1]	4650[2]	N.A.	—
CT10603	108.3 in. wb. Pickup	$	4650[2]	2974	—
CT10803	117.9 in. wb. Pickup	$	4650[2]	3060	—
CT10653	122.9 in. wb. Ext. Cab	$	4650[2]	3128	—

NOTE 1: Prices of 1993 models were not available at press time.
NOTE 2: 5150 lb. optional.

STANDARD ENGINE: Engine Type: OHV, Cast iron block. V-6. Order Code LB4. Bore x Stroke: 4.00 in. x 3.48 in. Lifters: Hydraulic. Number of main bearings-5. Fuel Induction: Electronic fuel injection. Compression Ratio: 9.1:1. Displacement: 262 cu. in. (4.3 liter). Horsepower: Net: 165 @ 4500 rpm. Torque: Net: 235 lb.-ft. @ 2400 rpm. Oil capacity: 5 qt. with filter change. Fuel Requirements: Unleaded.

CHASSIS FEATURES: Carbon steel, 39,000 psi., welded front box section and open channel rear section, section modules: 2.19. Dimensions: 108.3 in. wheelbase: 2.34 in. x 6.50 in. x 0.118 in. Overall length: 170.31 in. 117.9 in. wheelbase: 2.34 in. x 6.50 in. x 0.134 in. Overall length: 186.26 in. 122.9 in. wheelbase: 2.34 in. x 6.50 in. x 0.134 in. Overall length: 184.46 in.

SUSPENSION AND RUNNING GEAR: Front Suspension: Independent with torsion bar springs, 25mm dia. shock absorbers. 32mm stabilizer bar. Capacity: 1350 lbs. each at ground. Optional: 32mm shock absorbers. Rear Suspension: Two-stage multi-leaf shot-peened springs. Capacity: 1150 lbs. each at ground. 25mm shock absorbers. Optional: 32mm shock absorbers. Front Axle. Type: Hypoid, tubular driving. Capacity: 2700 lb. Rear Axle. Type: Salisbury, hypoid. Capacity: 2700 lb. Final Drive Ratio: 3.08:1. Optional: 3.42:1. Transfer Case: New Process 231. Ratios: 2.72, 1.00:1. Brakes: Type: Hydraulic, power assisted self-adjusting. Front: Discs. Rear: Drums. Dimensions: Front: 10.51 in. x 2.0 in. rotor. Rear: 9.49 in. x 2.0 in. Wheels: 15 in. x 6.00 in. Tires: P205/75R15 steel belted radial All-Season black sidewall. Optional: P205/75R15 black sidewall, All-Season steel belted radial, P205/75R15 on-off road steel belted radial, white letters, P205/75R15 All-Season steel belted radial, white letters, P205/75R15 on-off road steel belted radial black sidewall, P205/75R15 steel belted radial. Front: Highway. Rear: On-off road, P235/75R15 on-off road steel belted radial white letters. Steering: Variable ratio, integral power. Ratio: 17.5:1. Turning diameter: 35.4 ft. Transmission: 5-speed manual with overdrive (RPO MM5). Ratios: 4.02, 2.32, 1.40, 1.00, 0.83:1. Reverse: 3.74:1. Optional: Electronic 4L60-E Hydra-Matic 4-speed automatic overdrive transmission 3.06, 1.63, 1.0, 0.70:1. Reverse: 2.29:1. Clutch: 9.13 in. dia.

VEHICLE DIMENSIONS: Wheelbase: Short wheelbase/Long Wheelbase/Maxi Cab: 108.5 in./117.9 in./122.9 in. Overall Length: Short wheelbase/Long Wheelbase/Maxi Cab: 178.2 in./ 194.2 in./192.8 in. Front/Rear Tread: 55.6 in./54.1 in. Overall Height: 63.4 in. Width: 64.7 in. Tailgate: Width and Height: 53.6 in. x 16.0 in. Ground Clearance: Minimum clearance: 8.1 in. Load space: Short wheelbase and extended cab: 73.1 in. x 55.3 in. x 15.9 in. Long wheelbase: 90.1 in. x 55.3 in. x 16.0 in.

CAPACITIES: Fuel Tank: 20 gal. tank. (16 gal. on EL model). Coolant system: 12 qt.

ACCOMMODATIONS: Seating Capacity: Standard: 3. Headroom: 39.5 in. Legroom: 42.4 in.

INSTRUMENTATION: 0-100 mph speedometer, 99,999.9 mi. odometer, fuel gauge, gauges for voltmeter, oil pressure, and engine coolant temperature; warning lights for brake operating system, hazard warning lights, directional lights, seat belt warning.

OPTIONS: With the exception of the changes noted above, the options were unchanged from 1993.

HISTORICAL FOOTNOTES: The 1993 S-10 models were introduced on September 24, 1992. The typical S-10 buyer was a 38-year old man with a $40,000 annual income, but a growing number of women were purchasers or purchase influencers.

CHEVROLET ASTRO

1985-1990

1990 ASTRO AWD

The Chevrolet Astro, originally introduced in 1985, became, in 1990, the first U.S.-built mini-van to offer full-time all-wheel-drive. Chevrolet reported that the all-wheel-drive (AWD) Astro or L-van required "no special driving skill or experience [since] it handles as easily as the existing two-wheel-drive (M-van) Astro." The AWD Astro had a higher axle ratio (3.34:1 versus 3.23:1) over the M-van to help compensate for the additional weight of the AWD system. Chevrolet noted that "drivers should notice an added responsiveness to steering inputs as the front wheels 'pull' around curves and corners, and the firm, low pedal travel of the hydro boost brakes." Power in the AWD system was transmitted to the rear through a planetary gear set in the transfer case to the standard open or optional limited-slip rear axle. At the front, the power moved via a random toothed-chain to an open differential front axle. Inside the transfer case was a viscous clutch connecting the front and rear through many closely spaced and heavily lubricated plates. When all the plates — alternately splined to the front or rear drive — rotated at the same rate, the viscous clutch was not active. When the front and rear wheel speed varied, the clutch transferred torque in proportion to the speed differential. The torque transfer was immediate, substantial and in direct proportion to need. The AWD Astro used the front suspension, steering and brake system of the K20 full-size pickup. The body, rear drivetrain and wheels were from the Astro M-van. The K-20 front axle and drive shafts were also used. Four-wheel anti-lock brakes were standard on the AWD Astro.

New components for the AWD Astro included new stub frame, single-speed transfer case, front stabilizer shaft, front prop shaft with constant velocity joints, and specific exhaust manifolds for frame clearance. The AWD Astro exterior was distinguished by its black bumper guards, acrylic emblems with "ALL WHEEL DRIVE" lettering on the rear, and side doors that ran the length of both lower sides. Chevrolet's 4.3 liter Vortex V-6 was standard as was a 4-speed automatic overdrive transmission. Initially, the AWD system was offered for the regular length Astro in either cargo or passenger configurations. Available interim 1990 was an extended model that increased cargo capacity by nearly 19 cubic feet by adding 10 inches behind the rear wheels. The extended model was available with an optional platform trailer hitch that fitted flush with the rear bumper. A new-for-1990 high-output (H.O.) version of the 4.3 liter V-6 was available at midyear. Its horsepower and torque ratings were 170 hp @ 4800 rpm and 235 lb.-ft. @ 3200 rpm respectively. The added power of the H.O. engine came from a low-restriction intake and exhaust system and a high-lift camshaft. The H.O. engine also featured a high-stall torque converter, performance calibrations for the automatic transmission, and a dual sport exhaust. As compared to the1989 V-6, the latest Vortex engine had improved durability and reliability due to the use of a closed-bottom charcoal canister, revised exhaust manifold heat stove and an improved piston pin.

The Astro AWD was offered in three trim levels — CS, CL and LT. Standard exterior features of the CS trim level were as follows: Front and rear bumpers painted lower body color, bright Astro nameplates, molded plastic black-painted grille, halogen headlights, bright metal hubcaps with black trim, 15 x 6.00 in. steel wheels painted argent, All-Season steel-belted tires, compact spare tire and wheel, intermittent windshield wiper system, right and left side black-painted mirrors with pivoting arm and adjustable 4.75 in. x 7.0 in. heads, hot melt wax on underbody, and front license plate bracket. Interior appointments consisted of right and left side armrests, color-keyed vinyl door trim panels with front door map pockets, front high-back adjustable bucket seats with all-vinyl trim plus center removable 3 passenger bench seat, two left and one right side coat hooks, latex foam rubber door seals, black plastic door sill plates, two dome lamps with front door-activated switches, headlight warning chimes, color-keyed carpeting on wheelhousings and floor, left and right side color-keyed sunshades with right side visor mirror, tinted glass in all windows, gauges for speedometer, odometer, fuel level, voltmeter, oil pressure, engine coolant temperature, and trip odometer, remote release for fuel filler door, black vinyl 4-spoke steering wheel with anti-theft device locking features, cigarette lighter and ashtray light, molded color-keyed plastic storage compartment in left side rear quarter area, full-length color-keyed, foam-backed cloth headliner, stowage box including beverage holder in front face of engine cover extension, swing-out glass on sliding side door, electronically-tuned AM radio with fixed mast antenna, and deluxe heater and defogger with side window defogger.

The CL trim level had the following interior and exterior equipment in addition to or replacing that of the CS trim — Exterior: front and rear bumpers with matching color-keyed end caps, rub strips and rear black combination top step surface, grille with argent paint on feature surfaces, black body side moldings and wheel opening moldings, 15 x 6.5 in. steel Rallye wheels, and air dam with fog lamps. Interior features were as follows: Expanded vinyl door trim panels with carpet inserts and insulation, choice of Custom vinyl trim or Custom cloth for seats, rear door and sliding door-actuated dome light switches as well as a door-jamb defeat switch, color-keyed floor mats, lighted right side visor mirror, Custom steering wheel, stowage box light, swing-out glass for rear door, convenience tray lamp, stepwell lamp, and storage compartment lamp.

The LT trim had in addition to or replacing equipment of the CL trim these items — Exterior: Special nameplates on front side door B pillars, wide, color-keyed, graduated-tone striping at beltline, and 15 x 6.5 in. Rallye wheels color-keyed to body. Interior features were: Special front bucket seats with reclining backs, folding integral armrests and full-width adjustable headrests, split-back center seat including fold-down center console with convenience tray and cup pockets, right side seat folded forward for access to rear, special velour fabric upholstery, deep tinted glass, special luxury sport-type leather-wrapped steering wheel, and storage pouch with zipper on left side trim panel of storage compartment in rear quarter area. Exterior colors for 1990 were ivory white, sterling silver metallic, onyx black, smoke blue metallic, Catalina blue metallic (available only for Astro LT), mojave beige, sunset gold metallic, caramel brown metallic (available only for Astro LT), deep red metallic, burnt red metallic, gray metallic and midnight blue metallic. Four colors were offered for the vinyl, Custom vinyl and Custom cloth interiors: Blue, garnet, saddle and slate gray. The velour option was offered in blue or saddle.

I.D. DATA: The V.I.N. plate was mounted on the lower left side windshield corner. The V.I.N. consisted of 17 elements. The first, the number 1 identified the U.S. as the nation of origin. The letter G followed, for the manufacturer: General Motors. The third entry, the letter C represented the make as Chevrolet. The GVWR brake system identification followed. Next came the truck line and chassis type; the letter K indicated four-wheel drive. The truck series was identified by a number: 1-1/2 ton. The truck body type identification was next. The engine code was next: N-4.3 liter V-6, followed by a check digit. The model year was identified by the letter L. The assembly plant code followed. The final six digits were the plant sequential production number.

Model Number	Body Type & Seating	Factory Price	GVW	Shipping Weight	Prod. Total
Astro Cargo Van					
CL10905	—	$14,950	5600	N.A.	197,979[1]
CL11005	Extended	$15,612	5850	N.A.	—
Astro Passenger Van					
CL10906	Astro Van-CS	$16,265	5800	N.A.	—
CL10906	Astro Van-CL	$17,305	5800	N.A.	—
CL10906	Astro Van-LT	$18,800	5800	N.A.	—
CL10908	Astro Van-CS	$16,427	6100	N.A.	—
CL10908	Astro Van-CL	$17,467	6100	N.A.	—
CL10908	Astro Van-LT	$18,962	6100	N.A.	—

NOTE 1: 1990 calendar year production, both two-wheel drive and four-wheel drive models.

STANDARD ENGINE: Engine Type: OHV, Cast iron block. V-6. Order Code LB4. Bore x Stroke: 4.00 in. x 3.48 in. Lifters: Hydraulic. Number of main bearings-5. Fuel Induction: Electronic fuel injection. Compression Ratio: 9.3:1. Displacement: 262 cu. in. (4.3 liter). Horsepower: Net: 150 @ 4000 rpm. Torque: Net: 230 lb.-ft. @ 2400 rpm. Oil capacity: 5 qt. with filter change. Fuel Requirements: Unleaded.

OPTIONAL ENGINE: 4.3 liter V-6 H.O. Order Code LU2. Engine Type: OHV, Cast iron block. V-6. Order Code LB4. Bore x Stroke: 4.00 in. x 3.48 in. Lifters: Hydraulic. Number of main bearings-5. Fuel Induction: Electronic fuel injection. Compression Ratio: 9.3:1. Displacement: 262 cu. in. (4.3 liter). Horsepower: Net: 175 @ 4600 rpm. Torque: Net: 235 lb-ft. @ 3200 rpm (early 1990 data quotes 230 lb.-ft. @ 2800 rpm). Oil capacity: 5 qt. with filter change. Fuel Requirements: Unleaded.

CHASSIS FEATURES: Integral body frame design with boxed section front stub frame.

SUSPENSION AND RUNNING GEAR: Front Suspension: Independent with torsion bar springs, 32mm dia. shock absorbers. 1.18 in. stabilizer bar. Capacity: 3050 lb. at ground. Rear Suspension: Composite leaf springs. Capacity: 3150 lb. at ground. 32mm shock absorbers. Front Axle. Type: Independent hypoid GM. Capacity: 3050 lb. Rear Axle. Type: GM, semi-floating, hypoid. Capacity: 3150 lb. Final Drive Ratio: LB4: 3.34:1 LU2: 4.10:1. Optional: 3.73, 4.10:1. Transfer Case: Single speed. Brakes: Type: Hydraulic, power assisted with 4-wheel Anti-Lock System. Front: Discs. Rear: Drums. Dimensions: Front: 11.57 in. x 1.25 in. rotor. Rear: 9.50 in. x 2.0 in. Wheels: 15 x 6.00 in. CL and LT: 15 x 6.5 in. Tires: P205/75R15 steel belted radial All-Season black sidewall. Optional: P205/75R15 black sidewall, All-Season steel-belted radial, P205/75R15 on-off road steel belted radial, white sidewall, P205/75R15 All-Season steel belted radial, black sidewall, P215/75R15 All-Season, steel belted radial black sidewall, P215/75R15 All-Season, steel belted radial, P245/60HR15, All-Season, steel belted radial, white outlined letters, GT. Steering: Integral power. Ratio: 16/13:1. Turning diameter: 40.5 ft. Transmission: Automatic 4-speed with overdrive (RPO MXO). Ratios: 3.06, 1.63, 1.00, 0.70:1. Reverse: 2.29:1.

VEHICLE DIMENSIONS: Wheelbase: 111.0 in. Overall Length: 176.8 in.; Extended Passenger/Cargo Van: 186.8 in. 178.2 in./170.3 in./194.1 in./208.6 in. Overall Height: 74.1 in. Width: 77.0 in. Headroom: Front/Middle/Rear: 39.2/37.9/38.3 in. Legroom: Front/Middle/Rear: 41.6/36.5/38.5 in. Shoulder Room: Front/Middle/Rear: 64.0/67.8/67.8 in. Hip Room: Front/Middle/Rear: 64.9/50.9/50.9 in. Ground Clearance: Front: 6.8 in. Rear: 7.7 in. Extended Passenger/Cargo Van: Front: 7.0 in. Rear: 7.8 in. Load space: 88.9.1 in. x 51.6 in. x 47.5 in. Extended Passenger/Cargo Van: 98.9 in. x 51.6 in. x 47.5 in.

CAPACITIES: Fuel Tank: 27 gal. tank. Coolant system: 13.6 gal.

ACCOMMODATIONS: Seating Capacity: Standard: 5, Optional: 8. Cargo Van: 1. 2.

INSTRUMENTATION: 0-85 mph speedometer, 99,999.9 mi. odometer, fuel gauge, gauges for voltmeter, oil pressure, and engine coolant temperature; warning lights for brake operating system, hazard warning lights, directional lights, seat belt warning.

OPTIONS AND PRICES: Air conditioning: Front: $820, Front and Rear: $1343. Optional axle ratio: $38. Locking rear differential: $252. Deluxe front and rear chromed bumpers: $76-$128 depending upon option packages, black luggage carrier: $126. Engine oil cooler: $135. Heavy-duty radiator: $56. Heavy-duty radiator and engine oil cooler: $63, with air conditioning, $118 without air conditioning. Power door locks: $211. Driver Convenience Package. Includes Comfortilt steering wheel and intermittent wiper system: $346. Operating Convenience Package. Includes power door locks and power windows: $411. Deep tinted glass: $161-$211 depending on body glass selected. Rear heater: $267. Electronic instrumentation: $88. Auxiliary Lighting: $96 with roof console; $129 without roof console. Black below eye-level exterior mirrors: $52. Exterior remote electric mirrors: $150. Special two-tone paint: $172. Deluxe two-tone paint: $172-$334 depending upon other options. Custom two-tone: $187 with SLE, $329 without SLE. Electronically tuned AM/FM stereo radio with Seek-Scan, digital clock, stereo cassette player and premium speakers: $122. Electronically tuned AM/FM stereo radio with Seek-Scan, stereo cassette tape player with Search and Repeat, graphic equalizer, digital clock and premium speakers: $272. Delete radio: $226 credit. Seven passenger seating: $878-$1069 depending upon other options. Eight passenger seating: $344-878 depending upon other options. Seat back recliner and dual armrests: $241. 6-way power seat: $240. Front and rear heavy-duty shock absorbers: $40. Heavy-Duty Trailering Equipment: $507-$564 depending upon other equipment ordered. Light-Duty Trailering Equipment: $109. Aluminum wheels: $233-$325, depending upon other options ordered. Rallye wheels: $92.

1991 ASTRO AWD

The Chevrolet Astro continued to be offered in three trim levels for 1991 — the standard CS, the mid-range CL and up-level LT. An improved version of the 4.3 liter Vortex V-6 was standard as was the 4-speed overdrive automatic transmission. Changes to the engine's 220 throttle body injection included longer throttle shaft bearings, new throttle return springs and improved fuel mixture distribution for better start and idle quality, reliability and performance. A Vortex III air cleaner system and "Quantum" spark plugs were added for improved cold sparks. A SD 260 starter motor replaced the SD300 to reduce overall weight and to increase starter motor reliability and lifespan. New options available on both the extended and standard Astro models included a storage tray located beneath the front passenger seat. Changes for 1991 found on all Astro models included swing-out glass with positive locking detents, and lap/shoulder belts for center right hand passenger seat. The grilles of the CS and CL models had the Chevrolet bow tie in black outlines in red. During the 1991 model year the extended vans received a unique sport graphic package as well as a complete body window package. Twelve exterior colors were available with the addition of Field Stone metallic. Slate, metallic red and a two-tone light gray metallic were new for the Astro LT. The caramel brown and gray metallic colors were discontinued. Four interior colors were offered including a new light gray. AM and FM radio reception was improved for 1990. Suspension components were carried over from 1990.

1991 Chevrolet AWD Extended Astro

I.D. DATA: The V.I.N. plate was mounted on the lower left side windshield corner. The V.I.N. consisted of 17 elements. The first, the number 1 identified the U.S. as the nation of origin. The letter G followed, for the manufacturer: General Motors. The third entry, the letter C represented the make as Chevrolet. The GVWR brake system identification followed. Next came the truck line and chassis type; the letter K indicated four-wheel drive. The truck series was identified by a number: 1-1/2 ton. The truck body type identification was next. The engine code was next: N-4.3 liter V-6, followed by a check digit. The model year was identified by the letter M. The assembly plant code followed. The final six digits were the plant sequential production number.

Model Number	Body Type & Seating	Factory Price	GVW	Shipping Weight	Prod. Total
Astro Cargo Van					
CL10905	—	$15,740	5600	N.A.	106,891[1]
CL11005	Extended	$16,430	5850	N.A.	—
Astro Passenger Van					
CL10906	Astro Van-CS	$16,590	5800	N.A.	—
CL10906	Astro Van-CL	$17,670	5800	N.A.	—
CL10906	Astro Van-LT	$19,220	5800	N.A.	—
CL10908	Astro Van-CS	$17,280	6100	N.A.	—
CL10908	Astro Van-CL	$18,360	6100	N.A.	—
CL10908	Astro Van-LT	$19,910	6100	N.A.	—

NOTE 1: 1991 calendar year production, both two-wheel drive and four-wheel drive models.

STANDARD ENGINE: Engine Type: OHV, Cast iron block. V-6. Order Code LB4. Bore x Stroke: 4.00 in. x 3.48 in. Lifters: Hydraulic. Number of main bearings: 5. Fuel Induction: Electronic fuel injection. Compression Ratio: 9.3:1. Displacement: 262 cu. in. (4.3 liter). Horsepower: Net: 150 @ 4000 rpm. Torque: Net: 230 lb.-ft. @ 2400 rpm. Oil capacity: 5 qt. with filter change. Fuel Requirements: Unleaded.

OPTIONAL ENGINE: 4.3 liter V-6 H.O. Order Code LU2. Engine Type: OHV, Cast iron block. V-6. Order Code LB4. Bore x Stroke: 4.00 in. x 3.48 in. Lifters: Hydraulic. Number of main bearings-5. Fuel Induction: Electronic fuel injection. Compression Ratio: 9.3:1. Displacement: 262 cu. in. (4.3 liter). Horsepower: Net: 175 @ 4600 rpm. Torque: Net: 235 lb-ft. @ 3200 rpm. Oil capacity: 5 qt. with filter change. Fuel Requirements: Unleaded.

CHASSIS FEATURES: Integral body frame design with boxed section front stub frame.

SUSPENSION AND RUNNING GEAR: Front Suspension: Independent with torsion bar springs, 32mm dia. shock absorbers. 1.18 in. stabilizer bar. Capacity: 3050 lb. at ground. Rear Suspension: Composite leaf springs. Capacity: 3150 lb. at ground. 32mm shock absorbers. Front Axle. Type: Independent hypoid GM. Capacity: 3050 lb. Rear Axle. Type: GM, semi-floating, hypoid. Capacity: 3150 lb. Final Drive Ratio: LB4: 3.34:1 LU2: 4.10:1. Optional: 3.73, 4.10:1. Transfer Case: Single speed. Brakes: Type: Hydraulic, power assisted with four-wheel Anti-Lock System. Front: Discs. Rear: Drums. Dimensions: Front: 11.57 in. x 1.25 in. rotor. Rear: 9.50 in. x 2.0 in. Wheels: 15 x 6.00 in. CL and LT: 15 x 6.5 in. Tires: P205/75R15 steel belted radial All-Season black sidewall. Optional: P205/75R15 black sidewall, All-Season steel-belted radial, P205/75R15 on-off road steel belted radial, white sidewall, P205/75R15 All-Season steel belted radial, black sidewall, P215/75R15 All-Season, steel belted radial black sidewall, P215/75R15 All-Season, steel belted radial, P245/60HR15, All-Season, steel belted radial, white outlined letters, GT. Steering: Integral power. Ratio: 16/13:1. Turning diameter: 40.5 ft. Transmission: Automatic 4-speed with overdrive (RPO MXO). Ratios: 3.06, 1.63, 1.00, 0.70:1. Reverse: 2.29:1.

VEHICLE DIMENSIONS: Wheelbase: 111.0 in. Overall Length: 176.8 in.; Extended Passenger/Cargo Van: 186.8 in. 178.2 in./170.3 in./194.1 in./208.6 in. Overall Height: 74.1 in. Width: 77.0 in. Headroom: Front/Middle/Rear: 39.2/37.9/38.3 in. Legroom: Front/Middle/Rear: 41.6/36.5/38.5 in. Shoulder Room: Front/Middle/Rear: 64.0/67.8/67.8 in. Hip Room: Front/

Middle/Rear: 64.9/50.9/50.9 in. Ground Clearance: Front: 6.8 in. Rear: 7.7 in. Extended Passenger/Cargo Van: Front: 7.0 in. Rear: 7.8 in. Load space: 88.9.1 in. x 51.6 in. x 47.5 in. Extended Passenger/Cargo Van: 98.9 in. x 51.6 in. x 47.5 in.

CAPACITIES: Fuel Tank: 27 gal. tank. Coolant system: 13.6 gal.

ACCOMMODATIONS: Seating Capacity: Standard: 5, Optional: 8. Cargo Van: 1, 2.

INSTRUMENTATION: 0-85 mph speedometer, 99,999.9 mi. odometer, fuel gauge, gauges for voltmeter, oil pressure, and engine coolant temperature; warning lights for brake operating system, hazard warning lights, directional lights, seat belt warning.

OPTIONS AND PRICES: Air conditioning: Front: $845, front and rear: $1368. Optional axle ratio: $44. Locking rear differential: $252. Deluxe front and rear chromed bumpers: $76-$128 depending upon option packages, black luggage carrier: $126. Cold Climate Package: $46. Console roof: $50-$83 depending upon other options. Engine oil cooler: $135. Heavy-duty radiator: $56. Heavy-duty radiator and engine oil cooler: $63, with air conditioning, $118 without air conditioning. Power door locks: $223. Driver Convenience Package. Includes Comfortilt steering wheel and speed control: $383. Operating Convenience Package. Includes power door locks and power windows: $434. Tinted glass, complete body: $157. Deep tinted glass: $161-$290 depending on body glass selected. Rear heater: $205. Electronic instrumentation: $195. Auxiliary lighting: $100 with roof console; $133 without roof console. Black below eye-level exterior mirrors: $52. Exterior remote electric mirrors: $150. Special two-tone paint: $172. Deluxe two-tone paint: $251-$476 depending upon other options. Custom two-tone: $104-$329 depending upon other options. Electronically tuned AM/FM stereo radio with Seek-Scan, digital clock, stereo cassette player and premium speakers: $151. Electronically tuned AM/FM stereo radio with Seek-Scan, stereo cassette tape player with Search and Repeat, graphic equalizer, digital clock and premium speakers: $273. Electronically tuned AM stereo and FM stereo radio with Seek-Scan, stereo cassette tape player with Search and Repeat, graphic equalizer, digital clock and premium speakers: $150-$423 depending upon other options ordered. Delete radio: $95 credit. Seven passenger seating: $878-$1069 depending upon other options. Eight passenger seating: $344-878 depending upon other options. Rear heater: $205. Seat back recliner and dual armrests: $241. 6-way power seat: $240. Front and rear heavy-duty shock absorbers: $40. Heavy-Duty Trailering Equipment: $507-$564 depending upon other equipment ordered. Light-Duty Trailering Equipment: $109. Aluminum wheels: $248-$340, depending upon other options ordered. Rallye wheels: $92.

HISTORICAL FOOTNOTES: The Astro AWD was built in Baltimore, Maryland.

1992 ASTRO AWD

The AWD Astro's standard V-6 was rated at 200 hp. for 1992. This increased output was due to the use of central port fuel injection. A new (interim 1992) option, a rear "Dutch Door," included a one-piece lift-gate with split panel doors below with an electronic release. New interior features included adjustable bench seats, an optional premium sound system with a compact disc player and a new beige interior color.

1992 Chevrolet AWD Extended Astro

I.D. DATA: The V.I.N. plate was mounted on the lower left side windshield corner. The V.I.N. consisted of 17 elements. The first, the number 1 identified the U.S. as the nation of origin. The letter G followed, for the manufacturer: General Motors. The third entry, the letter C represented the make as Chevrolet. The GVWR brake system identification followed. Next came the truck line and chassis type; the letter K indicated four-wheel drive. The truck series was identified by a number: 1-1/2 ton. The truck body type identification was next. The engine code was next: N-4.3 liter V-6, followed by a check digit. The model year was identified by the letter N. The assembly plant code followed. The final six digits were the plant sequential production number.

Model Number	Body Type & Seating	Factory Price	GVW	Shipping Weight	Prod. Total
Astro Cargo Van					
CL10905	—	$16,585	5600	N.A.	—
CL11005	Extended	$17,225	5850	N.A.	—
Astro Passenger Van (CL11006-Extended length models)					
CL10906	Astro Van-CS	$17,505	5800	N.A.	—
CL10906	Astro Van-CL	$18,585	5800	N.A.	—
CL10906	Astro Van-LT	$20,135	5800	N.A.	—
CL11006	Astro Van-CS	$18,145	6100	NA.	—
CL11006	Astro Van-CL	$19,230	6100	N.A.	—
CL11006	Astro Van-LT	$20,775	6100	N.A.	—

STANDARD ENGINE: Engine Type: OHV, Cast iron block. V-6. Order Code LB4. Bore x Stroke: 4.00 in. x 3.48 in. Lifters: Hydraulic. Number of main bearings-5. Fuel Induction: Electronic fuel injection. Compression Ratio: 9.3:1. Displacement: 262 cu. in. (4.3 liter). Horsepower: Net: 200 @ 4400 rpm. Torque: Net: 260 lb.-ft. @ 3600 rpm. Oil capacity: 5 qt. with filter change. Fuel Requirements: Unleaded.

CHASSIS FEATURES: Integral body frame design with boxed section front stub frame.

SUSPENSION AND RUNNING GEAR: Front Suspension: Independent with torsion bar springs, 32mm dia. shock absorbers. 1.18 in. stabilizer bar. Capacity: 3050 lb. at ground. Rear Suspension: Composite leaf springs. Capacity: 3150 lb. at ground. 32mm shock absorbers. Front Axle. Type: Independent hypoid GM. Capacity: 3050 lb. Rear Axle. Type: GM, semi-floating, hypoid. Capacity: 3150 lb. Final Drive Ratio: 3.42:1. Optional: 3.73:1. Transfer Case:

Single speed. Brakes: Type: Hydraulic, power assisted with four-wheel Anti-Lock System. Front: Discs. Rear: Drums. Dimensions: Front: 11.57 in. x 1.25 in. rotor. Rear: 9.50 in. x 2.0 in. Wheels: 15 x 6.00 in. Tires: Passenger and Cargo Van: P205/75R15 All-Weather steel belted radial. Extended Passenger and Cargo Van: P215/75R15 All-Weather steel belted radial. Optional: P205/75R15 black sidewall, All-Season steel-belted radial, P205/75R15 on-off road steel belted radial, white sidewall, P205/75R15 All-Season steel belted radial, black sidewall, P215/75R15 All-Season, steel belted radial black sidewall, P215/75R15 All-Season, steel belted radial, P245/60HR15, All-Season, steel belted radial, white outlined letters, GT. Steering: Integral power. Ratio: 16/13:1. Turning diameter: 40.5 ft. Transmission: Automatic 4-speed with overdrive (RPO MXO). Ratios: 3.06, 1.63, 1.00, 0.70:1. Reverse: 2.29:1.

VEHICLE DIMENSIONS: Wheelbase: 111.0 in. Overall Length: 176.8 in.; Extended Passenger/Cargo Van: 186.8 in. 178.2 in./170.3 in./194.1 in./208.6 in. Overall Height: 74.1 in. Width: 77.0 in. Headroom: Front/Middle/Rear: 39.2/37.9/38.3 in. Legroom: Front/Middle/Rear: 41.6/36.5/38.5 in. Shoulder Room: Front/Middle/Rear: 64.0/67.8/67.8 in. Hip Room: Front/Middle/Rear: 64.9/50.9/50.9 in. Ground Clearance: Front: 6.8 in. Rear: 7.7 in. Extended Passenger/Cargo Van: Front: 7.0 in. Rear: 7.8 in. Load space: 88.9.1 in. x 51.6 in. x 47.5 in. Extended Passenger/Cargo Van: 98.9 in. x 51.6 in. x 47.5 in.

CAPACITIES: Fuel Tank: 27 gal. tank. Coolant system: 13.6 qt.

ACCOMMODATIONS: Seating Capacity: Standard: 5, Optional: 8. Cargo Van: 1, 2.

INSTRUMENTATION: 0-85 mph speedometer, 99,999.9 mi. odometer, fuel gauge, gauges for voltmeter, oil pressure, and engine coolant temperature; warning lights for brake operating system, hazard warning lights, directional lights, seat belt warning.

OPTIONS: Air conditioning. Optional axle ratio. Locking rear differential. Deluxe front and rear chromed bumpers. Black luggage carrier. Cold Climate Package. Console Roof. Engine oil cooler. Heavy-duty radiator. Heavy-duty radiator and engine oil cooler. Power door locks. Driver Convenience Package. Includes Comfortilt steering wheel and speed control. Operating Convenience Package. Includes power door locks and power windows. Tinted glass, complete body. Deep tinted glass. Rear heater. Electronic instrumentation. Auxiliary Lighting. Black below eye-level exterior mirrors. Exterior remote electric mirrors. Special two-tone paint. Deluxe two-tone paint. Custom two-tone. Electronically tuned AM/FM stereo radio with Seek-Scan, digital clock, stereo cassette player and premium speakers. Electronically tuned AM/FM stereo radio with Seek-Scan, stereo cassette tape player with Search and Repeat, graphic equalizer, digital clock and premium speakers. Electronically tuned AM stereo and FM stereo radio with Seek-Scan, stereo cassette tape player with Search and Repeat, graphic equalizer, digital clock and premium speakers. Premium sound system with CD player. Delete radio. Seven passenger seating. Eight passenger seating. Seat back recliner and dual armrests. 6-way power seat. Front and rear heavy-duty shock absorbers. Heavy-Duty Trailering Equipment. Light-Duty Trailering Equipment. Aluminum wheels. Rallye wheels. Rear "Dutch Doors."

HISTORICAL FOOTNOTES: The most popular Astro color, based on 1992 model year production was ivory white.

1993 ASTRO AWD

The content and optional equipment of the AWD Astro was fine-tuned for 1993. The optional (RPO PF3) aluminum wheels had a new brushed appearance. All cloth interiors had Scotchgard™ protection on their seats, door and quarter trim panels. A new instrument panel cluster with analog gauges for improved appearance and readability was used for 1993. The speedometer graphics were revised from 85 mph to 100 mph. The instrument cluster also had an improved printed circuit design, increased talltale capacity and a new "flag in window" shift indicator system. The optional Heavy-Duty Cooling Package (RPO VO8) now included a heavy-duty radiator, engine oil cooler and transmission oil cooler. A new steel sleeve steering column with the Comfortilt steering wheel was designed for enhanced security. Improvements included three steel shields, revised lock cylinder and a new lock bolt spring. A new transmission/brake shift interlock required the driver to depress the brake pedal before shifting out of park. The standard Hydra-Matic 4L60-E 4-speed automatic overdrive transmission (RPO MXO) was now electronically controlled. Four-wheel anti-lock brakes (4WAL) was now standard for all models in 1993, including the Cargo Van and the Extended Cargo Van. The new-for-1993 4WAL system included three sensors and was less complex than in previous years. An improved brake hose material was used. The Astro Sport Package was cancelled for 1993.

1993 Chevrolet AWD EXT Astro with optional rear doors

Three new colors for 1993 were offered: Light Quasar blue metallic, indigo blue metallic and medium Quasar blue metallic. They replaced these colors: Smoke blue metallic, Catalina blue metallic and slate metallic. A color that had been previously limited to the 1992 LT model, teal blue, was now available for all Astros. The standard 200 horsepower V-6 had improved electronic spark control and new spark plugs for 1993.

The standard Custom vinyl interior and the optional Custom cloth interior were offered in beige, blue, garnet or gray. The LT trim was available in beige or gray. Cargo vans equipped with a driver's seat only were available in either blue or beige.

I.D. DATA: The V.I.N. plate was mounted on the lower left side windshield corner. The V.I.N. consisted of 17 elements. The first, the number 1 identified the U.S. as the nation of origin. The letter G followed, for the manufacturer: General Motors. The third entry, the letter C represented the make as Chevrolet. The GVWR brake system identification followed. Next came the truck line and chassis type; the letter K indicated four-wheel drive. The truck series was identified by a number: 1-1/2 ton; The truck body type identification was next. The engine code was next: N-4.3 liter V-6, followed by a check digit. The model year was identified by the letter O. The assembly plant code followed. The final six digits were the plant sequential production number.

Model Number	Body Type & Seating	Factory Price	GVW	Shipping Weight	Prod. Total
Astro Cargo Van					
CL10905	—	$*	5600	N.A.	—
CL11005	Extended	$	5850	N.A.	—
Astro Passenger Van (CL11006-Extended length models)					
CL10906	Astro Van-CS	$	5800	N.A.	—
CL10906	Astro Van-CL	$	5800	N.A.	—
CL10906	Astro Van-LT	$	5800	N.A.	—
CL11006	Astro Van-CS	$	6100	N.A.	—
CL11006	Astro Van-CL	$	6100	N.A.	—
CL11006	Astro Van-LT	$	6100	N.A.	—

* Prices were not available at press time.

STANDARD ENGINE: Engine Type: OHV, Cast iron block. V-6. Order Code LB4. Bore x Stroke: 4.00 in. x 3.48 in. Lifters: Hydraulic. Number of main bearings-5. Fuel Induction: Electronic fuel injection. Compression Ratio: 9.3:1. Displacement: 262 cu. in. (4.3 liter). Horsepower: Net: 200 @ 4400 rpm. Torque: Net: 260 lb.-ft. @ 3600 rpm. Oil capacity: 5 qt. with filter change. Fuel Requirements: Unleaded.

CHASSIS FEATURES: Integral body frame design with boxed section front stub frame.

SUSPENSION AND RUNNING GEAR: Front Suspension: Independent with torsion bar springs, 32mm dia. shock absorbers. 1.18 in. stabilizer bar. Capacity: 3050 lb. at ground. Rear Suspension: Composite leaf springs. Capacity: 3150 lb. at ground. 32mm shock absorbers. Front Axle. Type: Independent hypoid GM. Capacity: 3050 lb. Rear Axle. Type: GM, semi-floating, hypoid. Capacity: 3150 lb. Final Drive Ratio: 3.42:1. Optional: 3.73. Transfer Case: Single speed. Brakes: Type: Hydraulic, power assisted with four-wheel Anti-Lock System. Front: Discs. Rear: Drums. Dimensions: Front: 11.57 in. x 1.25 in. rotor. Rear: 9.50 in. x 2.0 in. Wheels: 15 x 6.00 in. CL and LT: 15 x 6.5 in. Tires: Passenger and Cargo Van: P205/75R15 All-Weather steel belted radial. Extended Passenger and Cargo Van: P215/75R15 All-Weather steel belted radial. Optional: P205/75R15 black sidewall, All-Season steel-belted radial, P205/75R15 on-off road steel belted radial, white sidewall, P205/75R15 All-Season steel belted radial, black sidewall, P215/75R15 All-Season, steel belted radial black sidewall, P215/75R15 All-Season, steel belted radial, P245/60HR15, All-Season, steel belted radial, white outlined letters, GT. Steering: Integral power. Ratio: 16/13:1. Turning diameter: 40.5 ft. Transmission: Hydra-Matic 4L60-E automatic 4-speed with overdrive (RPO MXO). Ratios: 3.06, 1.63, 1.00, 0.70:1. Reverse: 2.29:1.

VEHICLE DIMENSIONS: Wheelbase: 111.0 in. Overall Length: 176.8 in.; Extended Passenger/Cargo Van: 186.8 in. 178.2 in./170.3 in./194.1 in./208.6 in. Overall Height: 74.1 in. Width: 77.0 in. Headroom: Front/Middle/Rear: 39.2/37.9/38.3 in. Legroom: Front/Middle/Rear: 41.6/36.5/38.5 in. Shoulder Room: Front/Middle/Rear: 64.0/67.8/67.8 in. Hip Room: Front/Middle/Rear: 64.9/50.9/50.9 in. Ground Clearance: Front: 6.8 in. Rear: 7.7 in. Extended Passenger/Cargo Van: Front: 7.0 in. Rear: 7.8 in. Load space: 88.9.1 in. x 51.6 in. x 47.5 in. Extended Passenger/Cargo Van: 98.9 in. x 51.6 in. x 47.5 in.

CAPACITIES: Fuel Tank: 27 gal. tank. Coolant system: 13.6 qt.

ACCOMMODATIONS: Seating Capacity: Standard: 5, Optional: 8. Cargo Van: 1, 2.

INSTRUMENTATION: 0-85 mph speedometer, 99,999.9 mi. odometer, fuel gauge, gauges for voltmeter, oil pressure, and engine coolant temperature; warning lights for brake operating system, hazard warning lights, directional lights, seat belt warning.

OPTIONS: Air conditioning. Optional axle ratio. Locking rear differential. Deluxe front and rear chromed bumpers. Black luggage carrier. Cold Climate Package. Console Roof. Engine oil cooler. Heavy-duty radiator. Heavy-duty radiator and engine oil cooler. Power door locks. Driver Convenience Package. Includes Comfortilt steering wheel and speed control. Operating Convenience Package. Includes power door locks and power windows. Tinted glass, complete body. Deep tinted glass. Rear heater. Electronic instrumentation. Auxiliary Lighting. Black below eye-level exterior mirrors. Exterior remote electric mirrors. Special two-tone paint. Deluxe two-tone paint. Custom two-tone. Electronically tuned AM/FM stereo radio with Seek-Scan, digital clock, stereo cassette player and premium speakers. Electronically tuned AM/FM stereo radio with Seek-Scan, stereo cassette tape player with Search and Repeat, graphic equalizer, digital clock and premium speakers. Electronically tuned AM stereo and FM stereo radio with Seek-Scan, stereo cassette tape player with Search and Repeat, graphic equalizer, digital clock and premium speakers. Premium sound system with CD player. Delete radio. Seven passenger seating. Eight passenger seating. Seat back recliner and dual armrests. 6-way power seat. Front and rear heavy-duty shock absorbers. Heavy-Duty Trailering Equipment. Light-Duty Trailering Equipment. Aluminum wheels. Rallye wheels. Rear "Dutch Doors."

HISTORICAL FOOTNOTES: The AWD Astro accounted for approximately 12 percent of Astro retail sales. The announcement date for the 1993 models was September 24, 1992.

DODGE POWER WAGON

1946-1980

Dodge commercial vehicle production began in November, 1914. Just a day earlier, Dodge had commenced production of passenger cars. In both World War I and World War II Dodge provided vehicles for the United States military. The exploits of Dodge cars and trucks in World War I when they served as troop carriers, ambulances and light utility vehicles while significant, proved to be a prelude to a far more extensive tour of duty in World War II.

When Dodge began to convert for military production (the first Dodge military vehicles were produced in 1940) its civilian models were reaping the benefits of an all-new design introduced in 1939. These trucks represented many of the prevailing design and engineering concepts of the time — L-head 6-cylinder engines, divided windshields, headlights mounted upon fenders styled with just a hint of aerodynamics, grilles with horizontal bars, hydraulic brakes and 3-speed manual transmissions.

The 1939 model trucks were returned to active duty in 1946 with only minor changes. Not until 1948 would new models with an appearance designed for classic truck status arrive. But it was the pre-war TC series, updated to a WC postwar designation, in conjunction with the Dodge military trucks that provided the basis for the first Dodge civilian 4x4, the 1946 Power Wagon. Those trucks, with an appearance that seems to be the quintessential example of function determining form, were scaled to meet virtually any task that a light-duty truck could be assigned. Geared for true off-road high perfor-

mance use and constructed to withstand countless rigors, the Power Wagon joined the Willys Jeep as the prime driving forces of the embryonic 4x4 market in America. Not until 1968 was the Power Wagon finally withdrawn from the U.S. domestic market. By that time, the Power Wagon label had been applied to Dodge's conventionally-styled pickups. In what seemed to be a universal progression of the 4x4 market, these trucks gradually became more civilized and available with amenities that were no doubt inconceivable to many owners of the original Power Wagons.

One manifestation of this evolutionary process was the debut of the Dodge Ramcharger in 1974. Expanding upon this success venture, Dodge broadened its market coverage by introducing the Mitsubishi-built Power Ram 50 mini-pickup. This venture set the stage for another pair of 1980-vintage models provided by Mitsubishi, the Raider and the Colt Vista. As the decade closed Dodge's mid-sized Dakota pickup came on line in 4x4 form, followed in 1991 by an All-Wheel Drive version of the Caravan.

The full-size Dodge were destined for replacement in 1994. Their successors, the first all-new Dodge trucks of this type since 1972, will feature both radial styling and advanced technology. But perhaps their most important feature will be their heritage, best exemplified by the hundreds of old Power Wagons still earning their daily keep both on and off the road.

1946 POWER WAGON

Dodge introduced what was to become one of the great legends of the postwar four-wheel drive movement, the Power Wagon, in 1946. As a civilian derivative of the Dodge four-wheel drive military vehicles the Power Wagon arrived on the scene with an ironclad reputation. Its rugged no-nonsense styling, ability to carry a 3,000 pound load and versatility made it a popular heavy-duty work vehicle. Among its standard equipment was a front bumper, heavy-duty front shock absorbers, dual vacuum windshield wipers, one quart capacity oil bath air cleaner, driver's side sun visor and deluxe seat and back cushions. The Power Wagon's optional winch had a 7500 pound capacity and provided 250 ft. of 0.4375 in. steel cable. The optional power take-off was mounted on the left side of the transmission. Power was taken from the transmission countershafts and was transmitted to the winch drive shaft and tail shaft. It operated at 61 percent of engine speed when rotating in the direction of the engine or 47.5 percent of engine speed when rotating in opposite direction. The engagement and direction of rotation was controlled by a single lever inside the cab. The optional tail shaft consisted of two tubular drive shafts and one pillow block shaft inter-connected by cross and trunnion universal joints with cageless roller bearings. The Power Wagon was available in seawolf submarine green, red, dark blue or yellow.

I.D. DATA: The serial number was found on a plate mounted on the right front door hinge. The engine number was located on a pad on the left side of the cylinder block between cylinders one and two. Beginning serial number: Detroit: 83900001 to 83902665. Los Angeles: 8875001 to 88750225.

Body Type	Factory Price	GVW	Shipping Weight	Prod. Total
Model WDX				
Chassis and Cab	$1555	8700[1]	4475	2890[2]
Express Pickup	$1627	8700	4900	—

NOTE 1: With optional 9.00 x 16, 8-ply tires, 7600 lb. with 7.50 x 16, 8-ply tires.
NOTE 2: Based on serial numbers-both versions.

STANDARD ENGINE: Engine Type: L-head, In-line 6-cylinder. Cast iron block and cylinder head. Bore x Stroke: 3.25 in. x 4.625 in. Lifters: Mechanical. Number of main bearings-4. Fuel Induction: Stromberg carburetor. Compression Ratio: 6.7:1. Displacement: 230 cu. in. (3.76 liters). Horsepower: 94 @ 3200 rpm. Torque: 185 lb.-ft. @ 1200 rpm. The Power Wagon had a velocity type engine governor set at 3200 rpm. Oil refill capacity: 5 qt. Fuel Requirements: Regular.

OPTIONAL ENGINE: None.

CHASSIS FEATURES: Separate body and double-drop frame; side rail reinforcements (inside type). Frame dimensions: 122.45875 in. x 0.109375 in.

SUSPENSION AND RUNNING GEAR: Front Suspension: Eleven leaf, 39 in. x 1.75 in. semi-elliptical springs, heavy-duty, double-acting shock absorbers. Rear Suspension: Fourteen leaf, 52.25 in. x 1.75 in. semi-elliptical springs. Front Axle Type and Capacity: Full-floating, Hypoid-type. Rear Axle Type and Capacity: Full-floating, Hypoid-type. Final Drive Ratio: 4.89:1 with standard 7.50 x 16 8-ply tires; 5.83:1 with optional 9.00 x 16 8-ply tires. Transfer Case: Two-speed. Brakes: Hydraulic front and rear, centrifuse drums with cast iron braking surface. Dimensions: Front and rear: 14.125 in. x 1.75 in. Total lining area: 210 sq. in. Wheels: Five-stud ventilated disc. Tires: 7.50 x 16 8-ply. Optional: 9.00 x 16 8-ply. Steering: Worm and lever; 17.0 in. diameter steering wheel. Ratio: 23.2:1. Optional: None. Transmission: 4-speed manual. Transmission Ratios: Final drive ratios range from 4.89:1 to 73.12:1. Clutch: Single plate, Oilite bronze pilot bearing, 10.0 in. dia. Total lining area: 100.53 sq. in.

VEHICLE DIMENSIONS: Wheelbase: 126.0 in. Overall Length: Express body: 199.0 in. (without winch); 208.625 in. (with winch); chassis and cab: 191.156 in. (without winch); 201.093 in. (with winch). Front/Rear Tread: 64.75 in./64.75 in. Overall Height: 76 in. (loaded). Width: 79.25 in. Front/Rear Overhang: 33.0 in./47.35 in. Tailgate: Width and Height: 54.0 in. x 21.0 in. Ground Clearance: 8.8125 in.; with optional tires: 10.625 in. Load space: 96.0625 in. x 54.0 in. x 22.25 in.

CAPACITIES: Fuel Tank: 18 gal. Engine coolant system: 17 qt.

ACCOMMODATIONS: 3 passengers.

INSTRUMENTATION: Speedometer, odometer, gauges for oil pressure, fuel level, battery charge, engine coolant temperature.

OPTIONS: Deluxe Cab. Power take-off. Power winch. Tail shaft. Pulley drive. Mechanical governor. Drawbar. Pintle hook. Front tow hooks.

HISTORICAL FOOTNOTES: Dodge described the Power Wagon as a "Self-propelled power plant."

1947 POWER WAGON

The Power Wagon was unchanged for 1947. But the four-wheel drive Dodge remained a new type of truck for the American market. Dodge noted that it was a truck "designed to fill needs never before fully satisfied by any truck. Its tractive ability brings it through off-the-highway routes that would stall an ordinary truck. As a tractor it pulls a four-wheel trailer or other equipment with famed Dodge dependability. As a self-propelled power plant it powers a multitude of equipment...on location. The boys wrote home about it as an army truck. Now it has been redesigned for civilian service. It's a rough and ready mixer...Job-rated for work no the truck could be expected to do. No wonder owners by the thousands are saying 'It's the truck we've always needed.'"

1947 Dodge Power Wagon pickup

I.D. DATA: The serial number was found on a plate mounted on the right front door hinge. The engine number was located on a pad on the left side of the cylinder block between cylinders one and two. Beginning serial number: Detroit: 83902666 to 83906216. Los Angeles: 88750226 to 88750894.

Body Type	Factory Price	GVW	Shipping Weight	Prod. Total
Model WDX				
Chassis and Cab	$1679	8700[1]	4475	4220[2]
Express Pickup	$1764	8700	4900	—

NOTE 1: With optional 9.00 x 16, 8-ply tires, 7600 lb. with standard 7.50 x 16, 8-ply tires.
NOTE 2: Based on serial numbers-both versions.

STANDARD ENGINE: Engine Type: L-head, In-line 6-cylinder. Cast iron block and cylinder head. Bore x Stroke: 3.25 in. x 4.625 in. Lifters: Mechanical. Number of main bearings-4. Fuel Induction: Stromberg carburetor. Compression Ratio: 6.7:1. Displacement: 230 cu. in. (3.76 liters). Horsepower: 94 @ 3200 rpm. Torque: 185 lb.-ft. @ 1200 rpm. The Power Wagon had a velocity type engine governor set at 3200 rpm. Oil refill capacity: 5 qt. Fuel Requirements: Regular.

OPTIONAL ENGINE: None.

CHASSIS FEATURES: Separate body and double-drop frame; side rail reinforcements (inside type). Frame dimensions: 122.45875 in. x 0.109375 in.

SUSPENSION AND RUNNING GEAR: Front Suspension: Eleven leaf, 39 in. x 1.75 in. semi-elliptical springs, heavy-duty, double-acting shock absorbers. Rear Suspension: Fourteen leaf, 52.25 in. x 1.75 in. semi-elliptical springs. Front Axle Type and Capacity: Full-floating, Hypoid-type. Rear Axle Type and Capacity: Full-floating, Hypoid-type. Final Drive Ratio: 4.89:1 with standard 7.50 x 16 8-ply tires; 5.83:1 with optional 9.00 x 16 8-ply tires. Transfer Case: Two-speed. Brakes: Hydraulic front and rear, centrifuse drums with cast iron braking surface. Dimensions: Front and rear: 14.125 in. x 1.75 in. Total lining area: 210 sq. in. Wheels: Five-stud ventilated disc. Tires: 7.50 x 16 8-ply. Optional: 9.00 x 16 8-ply. Steering: Worm and lever; 17.0 in. diameter steering wheel. Ratio: 23.2:1. Optional: None. Transmission: 4-speed manual. Transmission Ratios: Final drive ratios range from 4.89:1 to 73.12:1. Clutch: Single plate, Oilite bronze pilot bearing, 10.0 in. dia. Total lining area: 100.53 sq. in.

VEHICLE DIMENSIONS: Wheelbase: 126.0 in. Overall Length: Express body: 199.0 in. (without winch); 208.625 in. (with winch); chassis and cab: 191.156 in. (without winch); 201.093 in. (with winch). Front/Rear Tread: 64.75 in./64.75 in. Overall Height: 76 in. (loaded). Width: 79.25 in. Front/Rear Overhang: 33.0 in./47.35 in. Tailgate: Width and Height: 54.0 in. x 21.0 in. Ground Clearance: 8.8125 in.; with optional tires: 10.625 in. Load space: 96.0625 in. x 54.0 in. x 22.25 in.

CAPACITIES: Fuel Tank: 18 gal. Engine coolant system: 17 qt.

ACCOMMODATIONS: 3 passengers.

INSTRUMENTATION: Speedometer, odometer, gauges for oil pressure, fuel level, battery charge, engine coolant temperature.

OPTIONS: Deluxe cab. Power take-off. Power winch. Tail shaft. Pulley drive. Mechanical governor. Drawbar. Pintle hook. Front tow hooks.

HISTORICAL FOOTNOTES: Dodge reported that the Power Wagon was "designed for jobs a conventional truck can't do."

1948 POWER WAGON

Except for a new model identification the Power Wagon was unchanged for 1948. For the first time it was offered in chassis-only form.

I.D. DATA: The serial number was found on a plate mounted on the right front door hinge. The engine number was located on a pad on the left side of the cylinder block between cylinders one and two. The Power Wagon serial numbers were carried over into 1949.

Body Type	Factory Price	GVW	Shipping Weight	Prod. Total
Model B-1-PW				
Chassis	$1790	8700[1]	4075	—
Chassis and Cab	$1950	8700	4550	—
Express Pickup	$2045	8700	4975	—

NOTE 1: With optional 9.00 x 16, 8-ply tires, 7600 lb. with standard 7.50 x 16, 8-ply tires.

STANDARD ENGINE: Engine Type: L-head, In-line 6-cylinder. Cast iron block and cylinder head. Bore x Stroke: 3.25 in. x 4.625 in. Lifters: Mechanical. Number of main bearings-4. Fuel Induction: Stromberg carburetor. Compression Ratio: 6.7:1. Displacement: 230 cu. in. (3.76

liters). Horsepower: 94 @ 3200 rpm. Torque: 185 lb.-ft. @ 1200 rpm. The Power Wagon had a velocity type engine governor set at 3200 rpm. Oil refill capacity: 5 qt. Fuel Requirements: Regular.

OPTIONAL ENGINE: None.

CHASSIS FEATURES: Separate body and double-drop frame; side rail reinforcements (inside type). Frame dimensions: 122.45875 in. x 0.109375 in.

SUSPENSION AND RUNNING GEAR: Front Suspension: Eleven leaf, 39 in. x 1.75 in. semi-elliptical springs, heavy-duty, double-acting shock absorbers. Rear Suspension: Fourteen leaf, 52.25 in. x 1.75 in. semi-elliptical springs. Front Axle Type and Capacity: Full-floating, Hypoid-type. Rear Axle Type and Capacity: Full-floating, Hypoid-type. Final Drive Ratio: 4.89:1 with standard 7.50 x 16 8-ply tires; 5.83:1 with optional 9.00 x 16 8-ply tires. Transfer Case: Two-speed. Brakes: Hydraulic front and rear, centrifuse drums with cast iron braking surface. Dimensions: Front and rear: 14.125 in. x 1.75 in. Total lining area: 210 sq. in. Wheels: Five-stud ventilated disc. Tires: 7.50 x 16 8-ply. Optional: 9.00 x 16 8-ply. Steering: Worm and lever; 17.0 in. diameter steering wheel. Ratio: 23.2:1. Optional: None. Transmission: 4-speed manual. Transmission Ratios: Final drive ratios range from 4.89:1 to 73.12:1. Clutch: Single plate, Oilite bronze pilot bearing, 10.0 in. dia. Total lining area: 100.53 sq. in.

VEHICLE DIMENSIONS: Wheelbase: 126.0 in. Overall Length: Express body: 199.0 in. (without winch); 208.625 in. (with winch); chassis and cab: 191.156 in. (without winch); 201.093 in. (with winch). Front/Rear Tread: 64.75 in./64.75 in. Overall Height: 76 in. (loaded). Width: 79.25 in. Front/Rear Overhang: 33.0 in./47.35 in. Tailgate: Width and Height: 54.0 in. x 21.0 in. Ground Clearance: 8.8125 in.; with optional tires: 10.625 in. Load space: 96.0625 in. x 54.0 in. x 22.25 in.

CAPACITIES: Fuel Tank: 18 gal. Engine coolant system: 17 qt.

ACCOMMODATIONS: 3 passengers.

INSTRUMENTATION: Speedometer, odometer, gauges for oil pressure, fuel level, battery charge, engine coolant temperature.

OPTIONS: Deluxe cab. Power take-off. Power winch. Tail shaft. Pulley drive. Mechanical governor. Drawbar. Pintle hook. Front tow hooks.

HISTORICAL FOOTNOTES: The 1948 Power Wagon was introduced in December, 1947.

1949 POWER WAGON

The Power Wagon was unchanged for 1949.

1949 Dodge Power Wagon pickup

I.D. DATA: The serial number was found on a plate mounted on the right front door hinge. The engine number was located on a pad on the left side of the cylinder block between cylinders one and two.

Body Type	Factory Price	GVW	Shipping Weight	Prod. Total
Model B-1-PW				
Chassis	$1750	8700[1]	4070	—
Chassis and Cab	$1940	8700	4550	—
Express Pickup	$2045	8700	4975	—

NOTE 1: With optional 9.00 x 16, 8-ply tires, 7600 lb. with standard 7.50 x 16, 8-ply tires.

STANDARD ENGINE: Engine Type: L-head, In-line 6-cylinder. Cast iron block and cylinder head. Bore x Stroke: 3.25 in. x 4.625 in. Lifters: Mechanical. Number of main bearings-4. Fuel Induction: Stromberg carburetor. Compression Ratio: 6.7:1. Displacement: 230 cu. in. (3.76 liters). Horsepower: 94 @ 3200 rpm. Torque: 185 lb.-ft. @ 1200 rpm. The Power Wagon had a velocity type engine governor set at 3200 rpm. Oil refill capacity: 5 qt. Fuel Requirements: Regular.

OPTIONAL ENGINE: None.

CHASSIS FEATURES: Separate body and double-drop frame; side rail reinforcements (inside type). Frame dimensions: 122.45875 in. x 0.109375 in.

SUSPENSION AND RUNNING GEAR: Front Suspension: Eleven leaf, 39 in. x 1.75 in. semi-elliptical springs, heavy-duty, double-acting shock absorbers. Rear Suspension: Fourteen leaf, 52.25 in. x 1.75 in. semi-elliptical springs. Front Axle Type and Capacity: Full-floating, Hypoid-type. Rear Axle Type and Capacity: Full-floating, Hypoid-type. Final Drive Ratio: 4.89:1 with standard 7.50 x 16 8-ply tires; 5.83:1 with optional 9.00 x 16 8-ply tires. Transfer Case: Two-speed. Brakes: Hydraulic front and rear, centrifuse drums with cast iron braking surface. Dimensions: Front and rear: 14.125 in. x 1.75 in. Total lining area: 210 sq. in. Wheels: Five-stud ventilated disc. Tires: 7.50 x 16 8-ply. Optional: 9.00 x 16 8-ply. Steering: Worm and lever; 17.0 in. diameter steering wheel. Ratio: 23.2:1. Optional: None. Transmission: 4-speed manual. Transmission Ratios: Final drive ratios range from 4.89:1 to 73.12:1. Clutch: Single plate, Oilite bronze pilot bearing, 10.0 in. dia. Total lining area: 100.53 sq. in.

VEHICLE DIMENSIONS: Wheelbase: 126.0 in. Overall Length: Express body: 199.0 in. (without winch); 208.625 in. (with winch); chassis and cab: 191.156 in. (without winch); 201.093 in. (with winch). Front/Rear Tread: 64.75 in./64.75 in. Overall Height: 76 in. (loaded).

Width: 79.25 in. Front/Rear Overhang: 33.0 in./47.35 in. Tailgate: Width and Height: 54.0 in. x 21.0 in. Ground Clearance: 8.8125 in.; with optional tires: 10.625 in. Load space: 96.0625 in. x 54.0 in. x 22.25 in.

CAPACITIES: Fuel Tank: 18 gal. Engine coolant system: 17 qt.

ACCOMMODATIONS: 3 passengers.

INSTRUMENTATION: Speedometer, odometer, gauges for oil pressure, fuel level, battery charge, engine coolant temperature.

OPTIONS: Deluxe cab (the Deluxe cab was installed on all cab and pickup models). Power take-off: $65. Power winch. Tail shaft. Pulley drive. Mechanical governor. Drawbar: $20. Pintle hook: $10. Front tow hooks: $5.

HISTORICAL FOOTNOTES: The 1949 Power Wagon was touted as "The four-wheel drive truck that's different."

1950 POWER WAGON

The Dodge Power Wagon was essentially unchanged for 1950. All new, unused and unregistered Power Wagons that were delivered to Dodge dealers on and after December 1, 1949 were regarded as 1950 models. The colors offered for the 1950 Power Wagon were red, dark blue, dark green, black, yellow and granite gray. A new option was a hydraulic lift that enabled the Power Wagon owner to operate rear-mounted implements. Most three-point hitch implements could be attached or detached from a Power Wagon in about 60 seconds.

1950 Dodge Power Wagon pickup

I.D. DATA: The serial number was found on a plate mounted on the right front door hinge. The engine number was located on a pad on the left side of the cylinder block between cylinders one and two. Beginning Power Wagon serial numbers were as follows: Detroit: 83917001X to 83921140. Los Angeles: 88766001 to 88766296. Starting engine number: T137-1001.

Body Type	Factory Price	GVW	Shipping Weight	Prod. Total
Model B-2-PW				
Chassis	$1750	8700	4075	—
Chassis and Cab	$1940	8700[1]	4575	—
Express Pickup	$2045	8700	5000	—

NOTE 1: With optional 9.00 x 16, 8-ply tires, 7600 lb. with standard 7.50 x 16, 8-ply tires.

STANDARD ENGINE: Engine Type: L-head, In-line 6-cylinder. Cast iron block and cylinder head. Bore x Stroke: 3.25 in. x 4.625 in. Lifters: Mechanical. Number of main bearings-4. Fuel Induction: Stromberg carburetor. Compression Ratio: 6.7:1. Displacement: 230 cu. in. (3.76 liters). Horsepower: 94 @ 3200 rpm. Torque: 185 lb.-ft. @ 1200 rpm. The Power Wagon had a velocity type engine governor set at 3200 rpm. Oil refill capacity: 5 qt. Fuel Requirements: Regular.

OPTIONAL ENGINE: None.

CHASSIS FEATURES: Separate body and double-drop frame; side rail reinforcements (inside type). Frame dimensions: 122.45875 in. x 0.109375 in.

SUSPENSION AND RUNNING GEAR: Front Suspension: Eleven leaf, 39 in. x 1.75 in. semi-elliptical springs, heavy-duty, double-acting shock absorbers. Rear Suspension: Fourteen leaf, 52.25 in. x 1.75 in. semi-elliptical springs. Front Axle Type and Capacity: Full-floating, Hypoid-type. Rear Axle Type and Capacity: Full-floating, Hypoid-type. Final Drive Ratio: 4.89:1 with standard 7.50 x 16 8-ply tires; 5.83:1 with optional 9.00 x 16 8-ply tires. Transfer Case: Two-speed. Brakes: Hydraulic front and rear, centrifuse drums with cast iron braking surface. Dimensions: Front and rear: 14.125 in. x 1.75 in. Total lining area: 210 sq. in. Wheels: Five-stud ventilated disc. Tires: 7.50 x 16 8-ply. Optional: 9.00 x 16 8-ply. Steering: Worm and lever; 17.0 in. diameter steering wheel. Ratio: 23.2:1. Optional: None. Transmission: 4-speed manual. Transmission Ratios: Final drive ratios range from 4.89:1 to 73.12:1. Clutch: Single plate, Oilite bronze pilot bearing, 10.0 in. dia. Total lining area: 100.53 sq. in.

VEHICLE DIMENSIONS: Wheelbase: 126.0 in. Overall Length: Express body: 199.0 in. (without winch); 208.625 in. (with winch); chassis and cab: 191.156 in. (without winch); 201.093 in. (with winch). Front/Rear Tread: 64.75 in./64.75 in. Overall Height: 76 in. (loaded). Width: 79.25 in. Front/Rear Overhang: 33.0 in./47.35 in. Tailgate: Width and Height: 54.0 in. x 21.0 in. Ground Clearance: 8.8125 in.; with optional tires: 10.625 in. Load space: 96.0625 in. x 54.0 in. x 22.25 in.

CAPACITIES: Fuel Tank: 18 gal. Engine coolant system: 17 qt.

ACCOMMODATIONS: 3 passengers.

INSTRUMENTATION: Speedometer, odometer, gauges for oil pressure, fuel level, battery charge, engine coolant temperature.

OPTIONS: Deluxe cab (the Deluxe cab was installed on all cab and pickup models). Power take-off. Power winch. Tail shaft. Pulley drive. Mechanical governor. Drawbar. Pintle hook. Front tow hooks. Hydraulic lift.

HISTORICAL FOOTNOTES: The 1950 Power Wagon, said Dodge, had "power for cities, towns, and a wide range of other uses." Many rural school districts used the Power Wagon as the basis for small school buses.

1951 POWER WAGON

Revisions to the Power Wagon for 1951 consisted of the use of a 3750 pound capacity front axle and a 6500 pound capacity rear axle. They replaced units rated at 3500 and 5500 pounds respectively. The dash panel that had been used since 1947 was replaced by a unit identical to that used in the conventional two-wheel drive Dodge trucks. A quieter 4 blade radiator fan replaced the older 6 blade unit. The Power Wagon engine now used "Floating Power" engine mounts.

I.D. DATA: The serial number was found on a plate mounted on the right front door hinge. The engine number was located on a pad on the left side of the cylinder block between cylinders one and two. Beginning Power Wagon serial numbers were as follows: Detroit: 83922501 to 83926471. Los Angeles: 88766501 to 88766833. Starting engine number: T137-1001.

Body Type	Factory Price	GVW	Shipping Weight	Prod. Total
Model B-3-PW				
Chassis	$1891	8700[1]	3750	—
Chassis and Cab	$2095	8700	4250	—
Express Pickup	$2209	8700	N.A.	—

NOTE 1: With optional 9.00 x 16, 8-ply tires, 7600 lb. with standard 7.50 x 16, 8-ply tires.

STANDARD ENGINE: Engine Type: L-head, In-line 6-cylinder. Cast iron block and cylinder head. Bore x Stroke: 3.25 in. x 4.625 in. Lifters: Mechanical. Number of main bearings-4. Fuel Induction: Stromberg carburetor. Compression Ratio: 6.7:1. Displacement: 230 cu. in. (3.76 liters). Horsepower: 94 @ 3200 rpm. Torque: 185 lb.-ft. @ 1200 rpm. The Power Wagon had a velocity type engine governor set at 3200 rpm. Oil refill capacity: 5 qt. Fuel Requirements: Regular.

OPTIONAL ENGINE: None.

CHASSIS FEATURES: Separate body and double-drop frame; side rail reinforcements (inside type). Frame dimensions: 122.45875 in. x 0.109375 in. Frame rail dimensions: 6.09 in. x 2.04 in. x 0.171 in.

SUSPENSION AND RUNNING GEAR: Front Suspension: Eleven leaf, 39 in. x 1.75 in. semi-elliptical springs, heavy-duty, double-acting shock absorbers. Rear Suspension: Fourteen leaf, 52.25 in. x 1.75 in. semi-elliptical springs. Front Axle Type and Capacity: Full-floating, Hypoid-type. Rear Axle Type and Capacity: Full-floating, Hypoid-type. Final Drive Ratio: 4.89:1 with standard 7.50 x 16 8-ply tires; 5.83:1 with optional 9.00 x 16 8-ply tires. Transfer Case: Two-speed. Ratios: 1.93:1, 1.00:1. Brakes: Hydraulic front and rear, centrifuse drums with cast iron braking surface. Dimensions: Front and rear: 14.125 in. x 1.75 in. Total lining area: 210 sq. in. Wheels: Five-stud ventilated disc. Tires: 7.50 x 16 8-ply. Optional: 9.00 x 16 8-ply. Steering: Worm and lever. 17.0 in. diameter steering wheel. Ratio: 23.2:1. Optional: None. Transmission: 4-speed manual. Transmission Ratios: Final drive ratios range from 4.89:1 to 73.12:1. Clutch: Single plate, Oilite bronze pilot bearing, 10.0 in. dia. Total lining area: 100.53 sq. in.

VEHICLE DIMENSIONS: Wheelbase: 126.0 in. Overall Length: Express body: 199.0 in. (without winch); 208.625 in. (with winch); chassis and cab: 191.156 in. (without winch); 201.093 in. (with winch). Front/Rear Tread: 64.75 in./64.75 in. Overall Height: 76 in. (loaded). Width: 79.25 in. Front/Rear Overhang: 33.0 in./47.35 in. Tailgate: Width and Height: 54.0 in. x 21.0 in. Ground Clearance: 8.8125 in.; with optional tires: 10.625 in. Load space: 96.0625 in. x 54.0 in. x 22.25 in.

CAPACITIES: Fuel Tank: 18 gal. Engine coolant system: 17 qt.

ACCOMMODATIONS: 3 passengers.

INSTRUMENTATION: Speedometer, odometer, gauges for oil pressure, fuel level, battery charge, engine coolant temperature.

OPTIONS: Deluxe cab (the Deluxe cab was installed on all cab and pickup models). Power take-off. Power winch. Tail shaft. Pulley drive. Mechanical governor. Drawbar. Pintle hook. Front tow hooks. Hydraulic lift.

HISTORICAL FOOTNOTES: The 1951 Power Wagon was announced in December, 1950.

1952 POWER WAGON

No changes took place in the Power Wagon for 1952.

I.D. DATA: The serial number was found on a plate mounted on the right front door hinge. The engine number was located on a pad on the left side of the cylinder block between cylinders one and two. Beginning Power Wagon serial numbers were as follows: Detroit: 83926501 to 83934000. Los Angeles: 88766901 to 887675000. Starting engine number: T137-1001.

Body Type	Factory Price	GVW	Shipping Weight	Prod. Total
Model B-3-PW				
Chassis	$2232	8700[1]	3750	—
Chassis and Cab	$2202	8700	4250	—
Express Pickup	$2321	8700	N.A.	—

NOTE 1: With optional 9.00 x 16, 8-ply tires, 7600 lb. with standard 7.50 x 16, 8-ply tires.

STANDARD ENGINE: Engine Type: L-head, In-line 6-cylinder. Cast iron block and cylinder head. Bore x Stroke: 3.25 in. x 4.625 in. Lifters: Mechanical. Number of main bearings-4. Fuel Induction: Stromberg carburetor. Compression Ratio: 6.7:1. Displacement: 230 cu. in. (3.76 liters). Horsepower: 94 @ 3200 rpm. Torque: 185 lb.-ft. @ 1200 rpm. The Power Wagon had a velocity type engine governor set at 3200 rpm. Oil refill capacity: 5 qt. Fuel Requirements: Regular.

OPTIONAL ENGINE: None.

CHASSIS FEATURES: Separate body and double-drop frame; side rail reinforcements (inside type). Frame dimensions: 122.45875 in. x 0.109375 in. Frame rail dimensions: 6.09 in. x 2.04 in. x 0.171 in.

SUSPENSION AND RUNNING GEAR: Front Suspension: Eleven leaf, 39 in. x 1.75 in. semi-elliptical springs, heavy-duty, double-acting shock absorbers. Rear Suspension: Fourteen leaf, 52.25 in. x 1.75 in. semi-elliptical springs. Front Axle Type and Capacity: Full-floating, Hypoid-type. Rear Axle Type and Capacity: Full-floating, Hypoid-type. Final Drive Ratio: 4.89:1 with standard 7.50 x 16 8-ply tires; 5.83:1 with optional 9.00 x 16 8-ply tires. Transfer Case: Two-speed. Ratios: 1.93:1, 1.00:1. Brakes: Hydraulic front and rear, centrifuse drums with cast iron braking surface. Dimensions: Front and rear: 14.125 in. x 1.75 in. Total lining area: 210 sq. in. Wheels: Five-stud ventilated disc. Tires: 7.50 x 16 8-ply. Optional: 9.00 x 16 8-ply. Steering: Worm and lever; 17.0 in. diameter steering wheel. Ratio: 23.2:1. Optional: None. Transmission: 4-speed manual. Transmission Ratios: Final drive ratios range from 4.89:1 to 73.12:1. Clutch: Single plate, Oilite bronze pilot bearing, 10.0 in. dia. Total lining area: 100.53 sq. in.

VEHICLE DIMENSIONS: Wheelbase: 126.0 in. Overall Length: Express body: 199.0 in. (without winch); 208.625 in. (with winch); chassis and cab: 191.156 in. (without winch); 201.093 in. (with winch). Front/Rear Tread: 64.75 in./64.75 in. Overall Height: 76 in. (loaded). Width: 79.25 in. Front/Rear Overhang: 33.0 in./47.35 in. Tailgate: Width and Height: 54.0 in. x 21.0 in. Ground Clearance: 8.8125 in.; with optional tires: 10.625 in. Load space: 96.0625 in. x 54.0 in. x 22.25 in.

CAPACITIES: Fuel Tank: 18 gal. Engine coolant system: 17 qt.

ACCOMMODATIONS: 3 passengers.

INSTRUMENTATION: Speedometer, odometer, gauges for oil pressure, fuel level, battery charge, engine coolant temperature.

OPTIONS: Deluxe cab (the Deluxe cab was installed on all cab and pickup models). Power take-off. Power winch. Tail shaft. Pulley drive. Mechanical governor. Drawbar. Pintle hook. Front tow hooks. Hydraulic lift.

HISTORICAL FOOTNOTES: The 1952 Power Wagon was announced on October 15, 1951.

1953 POWER WAGON

The Power Wagon engine's compression ratio was increased to 7.0:1 for 1953. Both its peak horsepower and torque were also increased.

I.D. DATA: The serial number was found on a plate mounted on the right front door hinge. The engine number was located on a pad on the left side of the cylinder block between cylinders one and two. Beginning Power Wagon serial numbers were as follows: Detroit: 83934001 to 83937729. Los Angeles: 88767501 to 887667693. Starting engine number: T137-1001.

Body Type	Factory Price	GVW	Shipping Weight	Prod. Total
Model B-4-PW				
Chassis	$N.A.	8700[1]	3750	—
Chassis and Cab	$2190	8700	4675	3996[2]
8 ft. Pickup	$2307	8700	5100	—

NOTE 1: With optional 9.00 x 16, 8-ply tires, 7600 lb. with standard 7.50 x 16, 8-ply tires.
NOTE 2: Production of all models.

STANDARD ENGINE: Engine Type: L-head, In-line 6-cylinder. Cast iron block and cylinder head. Bore x Stroke: 3.25 in. x 4.625 in. Lifters: Mechanical. Number of main bearings-4. Fuel Induction: Stromberg carburetor. Compression Ratio: 7.0:1. Displacement: 230 cu. in. (3.76 liters). Compression Ratio: 7.0:1. Horsepower: 99 @ 3600 rpm. Torque: 190 lb.-ft. @ 1200 rpm. The Power Wagon had a velocity type engine governor set at 3200 rpm. Oil refill capacity: 5 qt. Fuel Requirements: Regular.

OPTIONAL ENGINE: None.

CHASSIS FEATURES: Separate body and double-drop frame; side rail reinforcements (inside type). Frame dimensions: 122.45875 in. x 0.109375 in. Frame rail dimensions: 6.09 in. x 2.04 in. x 0.171 in.

SUSPENSION AND RUNNING GEAR: Front Suspension: Eleven leaf, 39 in. x 1.75 in. semi-elliptical springs, heavy-duty, double-acting shock absorbers. Rear Suspension: Fourteen leaf, 52.25 in. x 1.75 in. semi-elliptical springs. Front Axle Type and Capacity: Full-floating, Hypoid-type. Rear Axle Type and Capacity: Full-floating, Hypoid-type. Final Drive Ratio: 4.89:1 with standard 7.50 x 16 8-ply tires; 5.83:1 with optional 9.00 x 16 8-ply tires. Transfer Case: Two-speed. Ratios: 1.93:1, 1.00:1. Brakes: Hydraulic front and rear, centrifuse drums with cast iron braking surface. Dimensions: Front and rear: 14.125 in. x 1.75 in. Total lining area: 210 sq. in. Wheels: Five-stud ventilated disc. Tires: 7.50 x 16 8-ply. Optional: 9.00 x 16 8-ply. Steering: Worm and lever; 17.0 in. diameter steering wheel. Ratio: 23.2:1. Optional: None. Transmission: 4-speed manual. Transmission Ratios: Final drive ratios range from 4.89:1 to 73.12:1. Clutch: Single plate, Oilite bronze pilot bearing, 10.0 in. dia. Total lining area: 100.53 sq. in.

VEHICLE DIMENSIONS: Wheelbase: 126.0 in. Overall Length: Express body: 199.0 in. (without winch); 208.625 in. (with winch); chassis and cab: 191.156 in. (without winch); 201.093 in. (with winch). Front/Rear Tread: 64.75 in./64.75 in. Overall Height: 76 in. (loaded). Width: 79.25 in. Front/Rear Overhang: 33.0 in./47.35 in. Tailgate: Width and Height: 54.0 in. x 21.0 in. Ground Clearance: 8.8125 in.; with optional tires: 10.625 in. Load space: 96.0625 in. x 54.0 in. x 22.25 in.

CAPACITIES: Fuel Tank: 18 gal. Engine coolant system: 17 qt.

ACCOMMODATIONS: 3 passengers.

INSTRUMENTATION: Speedometer, odometer, gauges for oil pressure, fuel level, battery charge, engine coolant temperature.

OPTIONS: Deluxe cab (the Deluxe cab was installed on all cab and pickup models). Power take-off. Power winch. Tail shaft. Pulley drive. Mechanical governor. Drawbar. Pintle hook. Front tow hooks. Hydraulic lift.

HISTORICAL FOOTNOTES: The 1953 Power Wagon was announced on December 4, 1952.

1954 POWER WAGON

The Power Wagon was unchanged for 1954.

I.D. DATA: The serial number was found on a plate mounted on the right front door hinge. The engine number was located on a pad on the left side of the cylinder block between cylinders one and two. Beginning Power Wagon serial numbers were as follows: Detroit: 83938001 to 83943347. Los Angeles: 88768001 to 88768126. Starting engine number: T137-1001.

Body Type	Factory Price	GVW	Shipping Weight	Prod. Total
Model C-1-PW				
Chassis and Cowl	$1955	8700	4075	—
Chassis and Cab	$2190	8700[1]	4675	5601[2]
8 ft. Pickup	$2307	8700	5100	—

NOTE 1: With optional 9.00 x 16, 8-ply tires, 7600 lb. with standard 7.50 x 16, 8-ply tires.
NOTE 2: All versions.

STANDARD ENGINE: Engine Type: L-head, In-line 6-cylinder. Cast iron block and cylinder head. Bore x Stroke: 3.25 in. x 4.625 in. Lifters: Mechanical. Number of main bearings-4. Fuel Induction: Stromberg carburetor. Compression Ratio: 7.0:1. Displacement: 230 cu. in. (3.76 liters). Compression Ratio: 7.0:1. Horsepower: 99 @ 3600 rpm. Torque: 190 lb.-ft. @ 1200 rpm. The Power Wagon had a velocity type engine governor set at 3200 rpm. Oil refill capacity: 5 qt. Fuel Requirements: Regular.

OPTIONAL ENGINE: None.

CHASSIS FEATURES: Separate body and double-drop frame; side rail reinforcements (inside type). Frame dimensions: 122.45875 in. x 0.109375 in. Frame rail dimensions: 6.09 in. x 2.04 in. x 0.171 in.

SUSPENSION AND RUNNING GEAR: Front Suspension: Eleven leaf, 39 in. x 1.75 in. semi-elliptical springs, heavy-duty, double-acting shock absorbers. Rear Suspension: Fourteen leaf, 52.25 in. x 1.75 in. semi-elliptical springs. Front Axle Type and Capacity: Full-floating, Hypoid-type. Rear Axle Type and Capacity: Full-floating, Hypoid-type. Final Drive Ratio: 4.89:1 with standard 7.50 x 16 8-ply tires; 5.83:1 with optional 9.00 x 16 8-ply tires. Transfer Case: Two-speed. Ratios: 1.93:1, 1.00:1. Brakes: Hydraulic front and rear, centrifuse drums with cast iron braking surface. Dimensions: Front and rear: 14.125 in. x 1.75 in. Total lining area: 210 sq. in. Wheels: Five-stud ventilated disc. Tires: 7.50 x 16 8-ply. Optional: 9.00 x 16 8-ply. Steering: Worm and lever; 17.0 in. diameter steering wheel. Ratio: 23.2:1. Optional: None. Transmission: 4-speed manual. Transmission Ratios: Final drive ratios range from 4.89:1 to 73.12:1. Clutch: Single plate, Oilite bronze pilot bearing, 10.0 in. dia. Total lining area: 100.53 sq. in.

VEHICLE DIMENSIONS: Wheelbase: 126.0 in. Overall Length: Express body: 199.0 in. (without winch); 208.625 in. (with winch); chassis and cab: 191.156 in. (without winch); 201.093 in. (with winch). Front/Rear Tread: 64.75 in./64.75 in. Overall Height: 76 in. (loaded). Width: 79.25 in. Front/Rear Overhang: 33.0 in./47.35 in. Tailgate: Width and Height: 54.0 in. x 21.0 in. Ground Clearance: 8.8125 in.; with optional tires: 10.625 in. Load space: 96.0625 in. x 54.0 in. x 22.25 in.

CAPACITIES: Fuel Tank: 18 gal. Engine coolant system: 17 qt.

ACCOMMODATIONS: 3 passengers.

INSTRUMENTATION: Speedometer, odometer, gauges for oil pressure, fuel level, battery charge, engine coolant temperature.

OPTIONS: Deluxe cab (the Deluxe cab was installed on all cab and pickup models). Power take-off. Power winch. Tail shaft. Pulley drive. Mechanical governor. Drawbar. Pintle hook. Front tow hooks. Hydraulic lift.

HISTORICAL FOOTNOTES: The 1954 Power Wagon was announced in October, 1953.

1955 POWER WAGON

The Power Wagon's L-head engine was increased in both horsepower and torque for 1955. The compression ratio was also boosted to 7.6:1. Among the features of this engine were aluminum-alloy pistons, chrome-plated top piston rings, floating oil intake, and exhaust valve inserts. The Power Wagon was offered with an 8 foot express body or as a cab and chassis model ready for the installation of either standard or special bodies. Flat face-cowl models were also available.

1955 Dodge Power Wagon pickup

I.D. DATA: The serial number was found on a plate mounted on the right front door hinge. The engine number was located on a pad on the left side of the cylinder block between cylinders one and two. Beginning Power Wagon serial numbers were as follows: 83744001 to 83749000. The starting engine number was T137-1001.

Body Type	Factory Price	GVW	Shipping Weight	Prod. Total
Model C-3-PW				
Chassis and Cowl	$1965	9500	4075	—
Chassis and Cab	$2200	9500[1]	4675	5058[2]
8 ft. Pickup	$2317	9500	5100	—

NOTE 1: With optional 9.00 x 16, 8-ply tires, 7600 lb. with standard 7.50 x 16, 8-ply tires.
NOTE 2: All versions.

STANDARD ENGINE: Engine Type: L-head, In-line 6-cylinder. Cast iron block and cylinder head. Bore x Stroke: 3.25 in. x 4.625 in. Lifters: Mechanical. Number of main bearings-4. Fuel Induction: Stromberg carburetor. Compression Ratio: 7.0:1. Displacement: 230 cu. in. (3.76 liters). Compression Ratio: 7.6:1. Horsepower: Gross: 111 @ 3600 rpm. Net: 101 @ 3600 rpm. Torque: Gross: 198 lb.-ft. @ 1600 rpm. Net: 192 lb.-ft. @ 1300 rpm. The Power Wagon had a velocity type engine governor set at 3200 rpm. Oil refill capacity: 5 qt. Fuel Requirements: Regular.

OPTIONAL ENGINE: None.

CHASSIS FEATURES: Separate body and double-drop frame; side rail reinforcements (inside type). Frame dimensions: 122.45875 in. x 0.109375 in. Frame rail dimensions: 6.09 in. x 2.04 in. x 0.171 in.

SUSPENSION AND RUNNING GEAR: Front Suspension: Eleven leaf, 39 in. x 1.75 in. semi-elliptical springs, heavy-duty, double-acting shock absorbers. Capacity: 1,150 lb. (each). Rear Suspension: Fourteen leaf, 52.25 in. x 1.75 in. semi-elliptical springs. Capacity: 2,500 lb. (each). Optional: 3,000 lb. capacity. Front Axle Type and Capacity: Full-floating, Hypoid-type. Capacity: 3,750 lb. Rear Axle Type and Capacity: Full-floating, Hypoid-type. Capacity: 6,500 lb. Final Drive Ratio: 4.89:1 with standard 7.50 x 16 8-ply tires; 5.83:1 with optional 9.00 x 16 10-ply tires. Transfer Case: Two-speed. Ratios: 1.93:1, 1.00:1. Brakes: Hydraulic front and rear, centrifuse drums with cast iron braking surface. Dimensions: Front and rear: 14.125 in. x 1.75 in. Wheels: Five-stud ventilated disc. Tires: 7.50 x 16 8-ply. Optional: 9.00 x 16 10-ply. Steering: Worm and lever; 17.0 in. diameter steering wheel. Ratio: 23.2:1. Optional: None. Transmission: 4-speed manual. Transmission Ratios: Final drive ratios range from 4.89:1 to 73.12:1. Clutch: Single plate, Oilite bronze pilot bearing, 10.0 in. dia. Total lining area: 100.53 sq. in. Optional: 11.0 in. dia. with lining area of 123.7 sq. in.

VEHICLE DIMENSIONS: Wheelbase: 126.0 in. Overall Length: Express body: 199.0 in. (without winch); 208.625 in. (with winch); chassis and cab: 191.156 in. (without winch); 201.093 in. (with winch). Front/Rear Tread: 64.75 in./64.75 in. Overall Height: 76 in. (loaded). Width: 79.25 in. Front/Rear Overhang: 25.125 in./47.35 in. Tailgate: Width and Height: 54.0 in. x 19.9375 in. Ground Clearance: 8.8125 in.; with optional tires: 10.625 in. Load space: 96.0625 in. x 54.0 in. x 22.25 in.

CAPACITIES: Fuel Tank: 18 gal. Engine coolant system: 17 qt.

ACCOMMODATIONS: 3 passengers.

INSTRUMENTATION: Speedometer, odometer, gauges for oil pressure, fuel level, battery charge, engine coolant temperature.

OPTIONS: Pulley drive. Power winch. Pintle hook. Front end tow hooks. Brake booster. Deluxe cab equipment. Directional signals. Tinted glass. Heater. Rear vision mirror (interior and exterior). Oil filter. Paint (fenders painted to match cab and/or body). Windshield washers. Rear shock absorbers. Extra-duty springs (front: 1600 lb., rear: 3,000 lb.). Roof-mounted radio. Auxiliary taillamps. Heavy-duty battery. 11 in. clutch. Mechanical governor for use with rear drive shaft assembly. Fuel and vacuum pump. Radiator overflow tank.

HISTORICAL FOOTNOTES: The 1955 Power Wagon was depicted by Dodge as "the four-wheel drive performance leader in the low-tonnage field."

1956 POWER WAGON

No changes were made for 1956.

I.D. DATA: The serial number was found on a plate mounted on the right front door hinge. The engine number was located on a pad on the left side of the cylinder block between cylinders one and two. Beginning Power Wagon serial numbers were as follows: 83949001 to 83951794.

Body Type	Factory Price	GVW	Shipping Weight	Prod. Total
Model C-3-PW				
Chassis and Cowl	$2157	9500	3800	—
Chassis and Cab	$2393	9500[1]	4275	2730[2]
8 ft. Pickup	$2510	9500	5100	—

STANDARD ENGINE: Engine Type: L-head, In-line 6-cylinder. Cast iron block and cylinder head. Bore x Stroke: 3.25 in. x 4.625 in. Lifters: Mechanical. Number of main bearings-4. Fuel Induction: Stromberg carburetor. Compression Ratio: 7.0:1. Displacement: 230 cu. in. (3.76 liters). Compression Ratio: 7.6:1. Horsepower: Gross: 111 @ 3600 rpm. Net: 101 @ 3600 rpm. Torque: Gross: 198 lb.-ft. @ 1600 rpm. Net: 192 lb.-ft. @ 1300 rpm. The Power Wagon had a velocity type engine governor set at 3200 rpm. Oil refill capacity: 5 qt. Fuel Requirements: Regular.

OPTIONAL ENGINE: None.

CHASSIS FEATURES: Separate body and double-drop frame; side rail reinforcements (inside type). Frame dimensions: 122.45875 in. x 0.109375 in. Frame rail dimensions: 6.09 in. x 2.04 in. x 0.171 in.

SUSPENSION AND RUNNING GEAR: Front Suspension: Eleven leaf, 39 in. x 1.75 in. semi-elliptical springs, heavy-duty, double-acting shock absorbers. Capacity: 1,150 lb. (each). Rear Suspension: Fourteen leaf, 52.25 in. x 1.75 in. semi-elliptical springs. Capacity: 2,500 lb. (each). Optional: 3,000 lb. capacity. Front Axle Type and Capacity: Full-floating, Hypoid-type.

Capacity: 3,750 lb. Rear Axle Type and Capacity: Full-floating, Hypoid-type. Capacity: 6,500 lb. Final Drive Ratio: 4.89:1 with standard 7.50 x 16 8-ply tires; 5.83:1 with optional 9.00 x 16 10-ply tires. Transfer Case: Two-speed. Ratios: 1.93:1, 1.00:1. Brakes: Hydraulic front and rear, centrifuse drums with cast iron braking surface. Dimensions: Front and rear: 14.125 in. x 1.75 in. Total lining area: 210 sq. in. Wheels: Five-stud ventilated disc. Tires: 7.50 x 16 8-ply. Optional: 9.00 x 16 10-ply. Steering: Worm and lever; 17.0 in. diameter steering wheel. Ratio: 23.2:1. Optional: None. Transmission: 4-speed manual. Transmission Ratios: Final drive ratios range from 4.89:1 to 73.12:1. Clutch: Single plate, Oilite bronze pilot bearing, 10.0 in. dia. Total lining area: 100.53 sq. in. Optional: 11.0 in. dia. with lining area of 123.7 sq. in.

VEHICLE DIMENSIONS: Wheelbase: 126.0 in. Overall Length: Express body: 199.0 in. (without winch); 208.625 in. (with winch); chassis and cab: 191.156 in. (without winch); 201.093 in. (with winch). Front/Rear Tread: 64.75 in./64.75 in. Overall Height: 76 in. (loaded). Width: 79.25 in. Front/Rear Overhang: 25.125 in./47.35 in. Tailgate: Width and Height: 54.0 in. x 19.9375 in. Ground Clearance: 8.8125 in.; with optional tires: 10.625 in. Load space: 96.0625 in. x 54.0 in. x 22.25 in.

CAPACITIES: Fuel Tank: 18 gal. Engine coolant system: 17 qt.

ACCOMMODATIONS: 3 passengers.

INSTRUMENTATION: Speedometer, odometer, gauges for oil pressure, fuel level, battery charge, engine coolant temperature.

OPTIONS: Pulley drive. Power winch. Pintle hook. Front end tow hooks. Brake booster. Deluxe cab equipment. Directional signals. Draw bar. 40 amp generator. Tinted glass. Heater. Rear vision mirror (interior and exterior). Oil filter. Paint (fenders painted to match cab and/or body). Windshield washers. Rear shock absorbers. Extra-duty springs (front: 1600 lb., rear: 3,000 lb.). Roof-mounted radio. Auxiliary taillamps. Heavy-duty battery. 11 in. clutch. Mechanical governor for use with rear drive shaft assembly. Fuel and vacuum pump. Radiator overflow tank.

HISTORICAL FOOTNOTES: The 1956 Power Wagons was introduced in January, 1956.

1957 POWER WAGON

This was a year of major expansion of the Dodge four-wheel drive truck line. Joining the neo-classic Power Wagon were four-wheel drive models of Dodge's conventionally-styled 1/2 and 3/4 ton pickups. Dodge also introduced a new type of model designation for 1957 in which the 1/2 ton models were 100 models. The 3/4 ton models were 200 models and the 1 ton were 300 models. Four-wheel drive units had a W prefix. The original Power Wagon had a W300 designation. The Power Wagon for 1957 was unchanged in appearance. The Power Wagon engine had a higher, 7.9:1, compression ratio for 1957. Standard equipment for the W300 included a one quart oil-bath air cleaner, 12 volt, 50 amp-hr. battery, front black painted bumper; 12 volt, 450 watts, 30 amperes generator; exterior short arm stationary-type mirrors on left side, 1 quart oil filter, running boards, single taillight and ventilated disc wheels. Standard equipment for the W300 cab included vacuum controlled windshield wipers, right-side door key lock, vibrator-type horn, imitation leather seat covering and multi-material seat padding. The Deluxe cab for the W300 included a driver's side armrest, dome light, and right and left side sun visors.

1957 Dodge W100 pickup

The new "civilian-styled" models were styled in a fashion clearly influenced by the 1957 "Forward Look" Dodge sedans. Dodge referred to the 4x4 trucks as "Power Giants." At the front were forward canted fenders that gave the headlights a frenched appearance. Numerous other features included a full-opening alligator hood, new pull-type door handles, safety door locks, an adjustable, tilting seat back, and chrome grille bars. The standard cab was equipped with dual electric windshield wipers, ashtray, dome light, left side arm rest, sound-deadening door panels, locks on both doors, rubber floor mat, single air-note horn, left side outside mirror, 5-way adjustable seat, Saran seat covering, cotton and sisal seat back and seat-cushion padding, sound-deadener on floor and cab-back, driver's side sun visor, and two-tone interior trim. The custom cab had, in addition to (or replacing) standard cab items: Armrest on both sides, dash-panel liner, dispatch-box door lock, perforated, sound-deadening headlining, Saran and rayon seat covering, Latex-treated-hair seat back padding, foam rubber seat cushion, sun visors on both sides, wrap-around rear window, and two-speed dual electric windshield wipers.

1957 Dodge W100 Stake

The W100 pickup was offered with either a 6.5 ft. body and a 108 in. wheelbase or a 7.5 ft. box and a 116 in. wheelbase. The W200 pickup was offered in the latter form only. Both the W100 and W200 were also produced with 7.5 ft. stake and platform bodies. The W200 version was available with dual rear wheels and tires. Another new model for 1957 was the W100 Town Sedan, a multiple-use carryall-type truck with room for up to 8 passengers or a payload of up to 1575 lbs. Dodge noted that "the Town Wagon combines rugged truck construction with passenger-car beauty, comfort and driving ease." The Power Giant Dodge trucks were also offered in chassis and cab, chassis-only and flat-face cowl form. The exterior color selection for the W100 and W200 models consisted of Ecuador blue, Pacific blue, Dodge truck red, Bermuda coral, Pontchartrain green, Bayview green, stone gray, Omaha orange and Mojave beige.

1957 Dodge Town Wagon

I.D. DATA: The serial number was located on a ticket found in the glove box. W100, 6-cyl.: 8191001. W100, V-8: 82901001. W200, 6-cyl.: 82701001. W200 V-8: 83250001. W300: 83952001. Engine numbers: W100, 6-cyl.: T500-1001. W100 V-8: VT500-1001. W200, 6-cyl.: T502-1001. W300: T137-1001.

Body Type	Factory Price	GVW	Shipping Weight	Prod. Total
Model K6-W100, 1/2 ton 6-cyl.				
Chassis, 108 in. wb.	$1981	5700	2900	—
Ch. & Cab, 108 in. wb.	$2225	5700	3375	—
Pickup, 108 in. wb.	$2322	5700	3725	—
Town Wag., 108 in. wb.	$2865	5700	3950	—
Chassis, 116 in. wb.	$1997	5700	2925	—
Ch. & Cab, 116 in. wb.	$2241	5700	3400	—
Pickup, 116 in. wb.	$2348	5700	3775	—
Stake, 116 in. wb.	$2432	5700	3950	—
Model K6-W100, V-8				
Town Wag., 108 in. wb.	$2911	5700	4000	—
Model K6-W200, 3/4 ton, 6-cyl.				
Chassis, 116 in. wb.	$2028	8000	3100	—
Ch. & Cab, 116 in. wb.	$2273	8000	3575	—
Pickup, 116 in. wb.	$2379	8000	3950	—
Stake, 116 in. wb.	$2464	8000	4125	—
Model K6-W300				
Chassis, 126 in. wb.	$2299	7600*	3800	—
Ch. & Cab, 126 in. wb.	$2544	7600	4275	—
Pickup, 126 in. wb.	$2669	7600	4650	—

* 9500 lb. GVW package optional for all W300 models.

STANDARD ENGINE: W100 and W200: Engine Type: L-head, In-line 6-cylinder. Cast iron block and cylinder head. Bore x Stroke: 3.25 in. x 4.625 in. Lifters: Mechanical. Number of main bearings-4. Fuel Induction: Stromberg carburetor. Compression Ratio: 8.0:1. Displacement: 230 cu. in. (3.76 liters). Horsepower: 120 @ 3600 rpm. Torque: 202 lb.-ft. @ 1600 rpm. Oil refill capacity: 5 qt. Fuel Requirements: Regular.

STANDARD ENGINE: W300: Engine Type: L-head, In-line 6-cylinder. Cast iron block and cylinder head. Bore x Stroke. 3.25 in. x 4.625 in. Lifters: Mechanical. Number of main bearings-4. Fuel Induction: Stromberg downdraft carburetor. Compression Ratio: 7.9:1. Displacement: 230 cu. in. (3.76 liters). Horsepower: 113 @ 3600 rpm. Torque: 198 lb.-ft. @ 1200 rpm. Oil refill capacity: 5 qt. Fuel Requirements: Regular.

OPTIONAL ENGINE: W100 and W200: Engine Type: OHV, "Power-Dome V-8." Cast iron block and cylinder head. Bore x Stroke: 3.63 in. x 3.80 in. Lifters: Hydraulic. Number of main bearings-5. Fuel Induction: Downdraft carburetor. Compression Ratio: 8.5:1. Displacement: 341.6 cu. in. (5.597 liters). Horsepower: 204 @ 4400 rpm. Torque: 290 lb.-ft. @ 2400 rpm. Oil refill capacity: 5 qt. Fuel Requirements: Regular. W300:

CHASSIS FEATURES: Separate body and double-drop frame; side rail reinforcements (inside type). Frame dimensions: 122.45875 in. x 0.109375 in. Frame rail dimensions: 6.09 in. x 2.04 in. x 0.171 in.

SUSPENSION AND RUNNING GEAR: Front Suspension: Eleven leaf, 39 in. x 1.75 in. semi-elliptical springs, heavy-duty, double-acting shock absorbers. Capacity: 1,150 lb. (each). Rear Suspension: Fourteen leaf, 52.25 in. x 1.75 in. semi-elliptical springs. Capacity: 2,500 lb. (each). Optional: 3,000 lb. capacity. Front Axle Type and Capacity: Full-floating, Hypoid-type. Capacity: 3,750 lb. Rear Axle Type and Capacity: Full-floating, Hypoid-type. Capacity: 6,500 lb. Final Drive Ratio: 4.89:1 with standard 7.50 x 16 8-ply tires; 5.83:1 with optional 9.00 x 16 10-ply tires. Transfer Case: Two-speed. Ratios: 1.96:1, 1.00:1. Brakes: Hydraulic front and rear, centrifuse drums with cast iron braking surface. Dimensions: Front and rear: 14.125 in. x 1.75 in. Total lining area: 210 sq. in. Wheels: Five-stud ventilated disc. Tires: 7.50 x 16 8-ply. Optional: 9.00 x 16 8 or 10-ply tube-type tires with All-Service tread. Steering: Worm and lever; 17.0 in. diameter steering wheel. Ratio: 23.2:1. Optional: None. Transmission: New Process #420, 4-speed "Synchro-shift" manual. Transmission Ratios: 6.68, 3.10, 1.69, 1.00:1. Reverse: 8.25:1. Clutch: Single plate, Oilite bronze pilot bearing, 11.0 in. dia. with lining area of 123.7 sq. in.

VEHICLE DIMENSIONS: Wheelbase: 126.0 in. Overall Length: Express body: 199.0 in. (without winch); 208.625 in. (with winch); chassis and cab: 191.156 in. (without winch); 201.093 in. (with winch). Front/Rear Tread: 64.75 in./64.75 in. Overall Height: 76 in. (loaded). Width: 79.25 in. Front/Rear Overhang: 25.125 in./47.35 in. Tailgate: Width and Height: 54.0 in. x 19.9375 in. Ground Clearance: 8.8125 in.; with optional tires: 10.625 in. Load space: 96.0625 in. x 54.0 in. x 22.25 in.

CAPACITIES: Fuel Tank: 18 gal. Engine coolant system: 17 qt.

ACCOMMODATIONS: 3 passengers.

INSTRUMENTATION: Speedometer, odometer, gauges for oil pressure, fuel level, battery charge, engine coolant temperature.

W100 and W200:

CHASSIS FEATURES: Separate body and double-drop frame. Frame dimensions: 6.13 in. x 2.06 in. x 0.187 in. Section modulus: 3.197.

SUSPENSION AND RUNNING GEAR: Front Suspension: Semi-elliptical leaf springs. Capacity: 1,150 lb. Optional: 1,300 lb. Rear Suspension: Semi-elliptical leaf springs. Capacity: 1,750. Optional: W100: 1250 lb. ("Easy Ride", no extra cost). W200: 2,600 lb. Front Axle Type and Capacity: Full-floating, Hypoid-type. Capacity: 3,000 lb. Rear Axle Type and Capacity: W100: Semi-floating, Hypoid-type. Capacity: 3,600 lb. W200: Full-floating, Hypoid-type. Capacity: 6,500 lb. Final Drive Ratio: 4.89:1 or 4.89:1. Transfer Case: Two-speed. Ratios: 1.96:1, 1.00:1. Brakes: Hydraulic front and rear. Dimensions: Front and rear: W100: 12.125 in. x 1.75 in. Total lining area: 198.4 sq. in. W200: Front: 12.125 in. x 1.75 in. Rear: 13.0 in. x 2.5 in. Total lining area: 232.8 sq. in. Wheels: Six-stud ventilated disc. Tires: 7 x 17.5 6-ply, tubeless. Optional: W100: 7 x 17.5 8-ply. W200: 8 x 19.5 8-ply. Steering: Worm and roller. Ratio: 23.5:1. Optional: Power assisted. Transmission: 3-speed heavy-duty manual. Optional: New Process #420, 4-speed "Synchro-shift" manual. Transmission Ratios: 6.68, 3.10, 1.69, 1.00:1. Reverse: 8.25:1. Optional: 3-speed Loadflite automatic (available for V-8 models only). Clutch: Single plate, 11.0 in. with lining area of 123.7 sq. in.

VEHICLE DIMENSIONS: Wheelbase: W100: 108 in., 116 in. W200: 116 in. Overall Length: Town Wagon: 197 in., 108 in. wheelbase models: 185.25 in. 116 in. wheelbase models: 197.125 in. Width: Town Sedan: 75.125 in. W100 and W200: 79.75 in.

CAPACITIES: Fuel Tank: 17.4 gal. Engine coolant system: 6-cyl.: 14.5 qt. V-8: 20.5 qt.

ACCOMMODATIONS: 3 passengers. Town Wagon: Up to eight passengers.

INSTRUMENTATION: Speedometer, odometer, gauges for fuel level, oil pressure, battery charge and engine coolant temperature.

OPTIONS AND PRICES: W100, W200: Chrome front bumper: $13.20. Painted rear bumper: $19.20. Painted bumper guards: $5.30. Chrome bumper guards: $11.90. Directional signals: $23.10. Tinted glass: $17.20. Dual electric horns: $14.50. Horn ring: $3.00. Cigarette lighter: $4.70. Glove box lock: $4.00. Interior rearview mirror: $3.00. Grab handles: $8.50. Wraparound rear window: $29. Dual electric windshield wipers: $7.20. Windshield washer: $11.60. Heater: $46.10. W300: 60 amp-hr. battery. Pulley drive. Power winch: $243.45. Pintle hook: $12.50. Power take-off: $75.20. Front end tow hooks. Brake booster, 7.5 in. diaphragm: $42.50. Front bumper painted any standard truck color. Deluxe cab equipment: $19. Directional signals: $30.30. Drawbar: $23.10. 40 amp generator. Fenders painted to match body color: $13.20. Combined vacuum and fuel pump. Chrome grab handles (pair): $8.50. Tint glass: $17.20. Recirculating heater with defroster: $46.10. Hydraulic jack with 3 ton capacity: $7.90. Long arm left or right side exterior mirror: $2.40 (left side), $4.30 (right side). Interior mirror (in addition to standard): $3.00. Windshield washers: $11.60. Rear hydraulic telescopic shock absorbers. Power steering. Extra-duty springs (front: 1600 lb., rear: 3,000 lb.). Roof-mounted radio. Auxiliary taillamps. Heavy-duty battery. 11 in. clutch. Mechanical governor for use with rear drive shaft assembly. Fuel and vacuum pump. Radiator overflow tank.

HISTORICAL FOOTNOTES: The 1957 Dodge W300 four-wheel drive trucks were introduced on October 30, 1956. The W100 and W200 models followed in early 1957.

1958 POWER WAGON

Dodge added a new 1 ton W300 model to its four-wheel drive line for 1958 As a result, the original Power Wagon received a W300M designation for 1958. All 1958 models were identified as Power Wagons. A new front end design was introduced on the conventional four-wheel drive models. It featured dual headlights, a grille with three large horizontal bars, a new high-strength bumper, and a new optional chrome trim package. The contents of this package included chromed grille bars, bright-metal side moldings, a new chrome-plated hood ornament and anodized aluminum headlight trim plates. Also found on the conventional models was a new full-width hood that opened to a 90 degree angle. It also opened to a 45 degree angle for

routine oil and water checks. New vents were installed on the sides to improve the escape of engine heat. The W100 and W200 models were offered with the optional Power-Giant 315 V-8. The W300 was available with the Power-Giant H.D. V-8 equipped with double rocker shafts and exhaust valve inserts. All Power Wagons were available with the long-lived 230 cid 6-cylinder. Power ratings varied with the application.

1958 Dodge W1000 Town Wagon

The cab of the conventional models was fitted with a new steering wheel with a deep center. A new instrument panel had red warning lights for oil pressure and battery charge. A new option for the conventional models was a ceiling-mounted transistor radio with a sandalwood color exterior. This radio also used a roof-mounted antenna. New for 1958 was an optional Full-Traction rear differential for the W100 models. As in 1957, Dodge offered the Loadflite, push-button automatic transmission for the W100, W200 and W300 models powered by V-8 engines.

1958 Dodge W100 Power Wagon pickup

I.D. DATA: The serial number was located on a ticket found in the glove box. W100, 6-cyl.: L6W10-L01001. W100, V-8: L8W10-L01001. W200, 6-cyl.: L6W20-L01001. W200, V-8: L8W20-L01001. W300 6-cyl.: L6W30-L01001. W300 V-8: L8-W3-1001. W300M: L6-WM3-01001.

Body Type	Factory Price	GVW	Shipping Weight	Prod. Total
Model L6-W100, 1/2 ton 6-cyl.				
Chassis, 108 in. wb.	$2435	5100	2950	—
Ch. & Cab, 108 in. wb.	$2689	5100	3425	—
Pickup, 108 in. wb.	$2802	5100	3775	—
Town Panel, 108 in. wb.	$3093	5100	3800	—
Town Wag., 108 in. wb.	$3392	5100	4125	—
Chassis, 116 in. wb.	$2473	5100	2975	—
Ch. & Cab, 116 in. wb.	$2726	5100	3450	—
Pickup, 116 in. wb.	$2839	5100	3825	—
Platform, 116 in. wb.	$2873	5100	N.A.	—
Stake, 116 in. wb.	$2932	5100	4000	—
Model L6-W100, V-8				
Town Wag., 108 in. wb.	$3443	5100	4175	—
Model L6-W200, 3/4 ton, 6-cyl.				
Chassis, 116 in. wb.	$2590	6000*	3100	—
Ch. & Cab, 116 in. wb.	$2852	6000	3575	—
Pickup, 116 in. wb.	$2966	6000	3925	—
Stake, 116 in. wb.	$3058	6000	4125	—

* An 8000 lb. GVW package was optional for all models.

Body Type	Factory Price	GVW	Shipping Weight	Prod. Total
Model L6-W300, 1 ton, 6-cyl.				
Chassis, 129 in. wb.	$3027	8500*	3750	—
Ch. & Cab, 129 in. wb.	$3290	8500	4225	—
Pickup, 129 in. wb.	$3425	8500	4650	—
Platform, 129 in. wb.	$3469	8500	N.A.	—
Stake, 129 in. wb.	$3538	8500	4875	—

* A 10,000 lb. GVW package was available.

Body Type	Factory Price	GVW	Shipping Weight	Prod. Total
Model L6-W300M				
Chassis, 126 in. wb.	$2680	7600*	3800	—
Ch. & Cab, 126 in. wb.	$2943	7600	4275	—
Pickup, 126 in. wb.	$3077	7600	4650	—

* 9500 lb. GVW package optional for all W300M models.

STANDARD ENGINE: W100, W200: Engine Type: L-head, In-line 6-cylinder. Cast iron block and cylinder head. Bore x Stroke: 3.25 in. x 4.625 in. Lifters: Mechanical. Number of main bearings-4. Fuel Induction: Stromberg downdraft carburetor. Compression Ratio: 7.9:1. Displacement: 230 cu. in. (3.768 liters). Horsepower: 120 @ 3600 rpm. Torque: 202 lb.-ft. @ 1600 rpm. Oil refill capacity: 5 qt. Fuel Requirements: Regular.

STANDARD ENGINE: W300: Engine Type: L-head, In-line 6-cylinder. Cast iron block and cylinder head. Bore x Stroke: 3.437 in. x 4.50 in. Lifters: Mechanical. Number of main bearings-4. Fuel Induction: Stromberg downdraft carburetor. Compression Ratio: 7.1:1. Displacement: 250.6 cu. in. (4.1065 liters). Horsepower: 125 @ 3600 rpm. Torque: 216 lb.-ft. @ 1600 rpm. Oil refill capacity: 5 qt. Fuel Requirements: Regular.

STANDARD ENGINE: W300M: Engine Type: L-head, In-line 6-cylinder. Cast iron block and cylinder head. Bore x Stroke: 3.25 in. x 4.625 in. Lifters: Mechanical. Number of main bearings-4. Fuel Induction: Stromberg downdraft carburetor. Compression Ratio: 7.9:1. Displacement: 230 cu. in. (3.768 liters). Horsepower: 113 @ 3600 rpm. Torque: 198 lb.-ft. @ 1600 rpm. Oil refill capacity: 5 qt. Fuel Requirements: Regular.

OPTIONAL ENGINE: W100, W200 and W300: Engine Type: "Power Giant 315." OHV, V-8. Cast iron block and cylinder head. The heavy-duty version had identical specifications. Bore x Stroke: 3.63 in. x 3.80 in. Lifters: Hydraulic. Number of main bearings-5. Fuel Induction: Single 2-barrel downdraft carburetor. Compression Ratio: 8.1:1. Displacement: 314.61 cu. in. (5.155 liters). Horsepower: 204 @ 4400 rpm. Torque: 290 lb.-ft. @ 2400 rpm. Oil refill capacity: 5 qt. Fuel Requirements: Regular.

W300M:

CHASSIS FEATURES: Separate body and double-drop frame; side rail reinforcements (inside type). Frame dimensions: 122.45875 in. x 0.109375 in. Frame rail dimensions: 6.09 in. x 2.04 in. x 0.171 in.

SUSPENSION AND RUNNING GEAR: Front Suspension: Eleven leaf, 39 in. x 1.75 in. semi-elliptical springs, heavy-duty, double-acting shock absorbers. Capacity: 1,150 lb. (each). Rear Suspension: Fourteen leaf, 52.25 in. x 1.75 in. semi-elliptical springs. Capacity: 2,500 lb. (each). Optional: 3,000 lb. capacity. Front Axle Type and Capacity: Full-floating, Hypoid-type. Capacity: 3,750 lb. Rear Axle Type and Capacity: Full-floating, Hypoid-type. Capacity: 6,500 lb. Final Drive Ratio: 4.89:1 with standard 7.50 x 16 8-ply tires; 5.83:1 with optional 9.00 x 16 10-ply tires. Transfer Case: Two-speed, double-lever. Ratios: 1.96:1, 1.00:1. Brakes: Hydraulic front and rear, centrifuse drums with cast iron braking surface. Dimensions: Front and rear: 14.125 in. x 1.75 in. Total lining area: 215.18 sq. in. Wheels: Five-stud ventilated disc. Tires: 7.50 x 16 8-ply. Optional: 9.00 x 16 8 or 10-ply tube-type tires with All-Service tread. Steering: Worm and lever; 17.0 in. diameter steering wheel. Ratio: 23.2:1. Optional: None. Transmission: New Process #420, 4-speed "Synchro-shift" manual. Transmission Ratios: 6.68, 3.10, 1.69, 1.00:1. Reverse: 8.25:1. Clutch: Single plate, Oilite bronze pilot bearing, 11.0 in. dia. with lining area of 123.7 sq. in.

VEHICLE DIMENSIONS: Wheelbase: 126.0 in. Overall Length: Express body: 199.0 in. (without winch); 208.625 in. (with winch); chassis and cab: 191.156 in. (without winch); 201.093 in. (with winch). Front/Rear Tread: 64.75 in./64.75 in. Overall Height: 76 in. (loaded). Width: 79.25 in. Front/Rear Overhang: 25.125 in./47.35 in. Tailgate: Width and Height: 54.0 in. x 19.9375 in. Ground Clearance: 8.8125 in.; with optional tires: 10.625 in. Load space: 96.0625 in. x 54.0 in. x 22.25 in.

CAPACITIES: Fuel Tank: 18 gal. Engine coolant system: 17 qt.

ACCOMMODATIONS: 3 passengers.

INSTRUMENTATION: Speedometer, odometer, gauges for oil pressure, fuel level, battery charge, engine coolant temperature.

W100 and W200:

CHASSIS FEATURES: Separate body and double-drop frame. Frame dimensions: 6.13 in. x 2.06 in. x 0.187 in. Section modules: 3.197.

SUSPENSION AND RUNNING GEAR: Front Suspension: Semi-elliptical leaf springs. Capacity: 1,050 lb. Optional: 1,300 lb. Rear Suspension: Semi-elliptical leaf springs. Capacity: W100: 1250 lb. W200: 1,750. Optional: W100: 1750 lb. W200: 2,600 lb. Front Axle Type and Capacity: Full-floating, Hypoid-type. Capacity: 3,000 lb. Rear Axle Type and Capacity: W100: Semi-floating, Hypoid-type. Capacity: 3,600 lb. W200: Full-floating, Hypoid-type. Capacity: 6,500 lb. Final Drive Ratio: 4.89:1 or 4.89:1. Transfer Case: Two-speed. Ratios: 1.96:1, 1.00:1. Brakes: Hydraulic front and rear. Dimensions: Front and rear: W100: 12.125 in. x 1.75 in. Total lining area: 198.4 sq. in. W200: Front: 12.125 in. x 1.75 in. Rear: 13.0 in. x 2.5 in. Total lining area: 232.8 sq. in. Wheels: Six-stud ventilated disc. Tires: 7 x 17.5 6-ply, tubeless. Optional: W100: 7 x 17.5 8-ply. W200: 8 x 19.5 8-ply. Steering: Worm and roller. Ratio: 23.5:1. Optional: Power assisted. Transmission: 3-speed. Heavy-duty manual. Optional: 3-speed Loadflite automatic (available for V-8 models only). Clutch: Single plate, dry disc, 11.0 in. dia. with lining area of 123.7 sq. in.

VEHICLE DIMENSIONS: Wheelbase: W100: 108 in., 116 in. W200: 116 in. Overall Length: Town Wagon: 197 in., 108 in. wheelbase models: 185.25 in. 116 in. wheelbase models: 197.125 in. Width: Town Sedan: 75.125 in. W100 and W200: 79.75 in.

CAPACITIES: Fuel Tank: 18 gal. Engine coolant system: 6-cyl.: 12.0 qt. V-8: 19.0 qt.

ACCOMMODATIONS: 3 passengers. Town Wagon: Up to eight passengers.

INSTRUMENTATION: Speedometer, odometer, gauges for fuel level and engine coolant temperature. Warning lights for oil pressure and battery charge.

W300:

CHASSIS FEATURES: Separate body and double-drop frame. Frame dimensions: 8.09 in. x 2.78 in. x 0.210 in. Section modules: 6.44.

SUSPENSION AND RUNNING GEAR: Front Suspension: Semi-elliptical leaf springs. Capacity: 1,450 lb. Optional: 1,750 lb. Rear Suspension: Semi-elliptical leaf springs. Capacity: 2,450. Optional: 3,250, 4,050 lb. Front Axle Type and Capacity: Full-floating, Hypoid-type. Capacity: 4,500 lb. Rear Axle Type and Capacity: Full-floating, Hypoid-type. Capacity: 8,000 lb. Final Drive Ratio: 4.88:1 or 5.87:1. Transfer Case: Two-speed, single lever. Ratios: 1.96:1, 1.00:1. Brakes: Hydraulic front and rear. Dimensions: Front and rear: 13 in. x 2.5 in. Total lining area: 268.79 sq. in. Wheels: Six-stud ventilated disc. Tires: 8 x 195 6-ply, tubeless. Steering: Worm and roller. Ratio: 29.0:1. Optional: Power assisted. Transmission: 3-speed. Heavy-duty manual. Optional: 3-speed Loadflite automatic (available for V-8 models only). Clutch: Single plate, dry disc, 11.0 in. dia. with lining area of 123.7 sq. in.

VEHICLE DIMENSIONS: Wheelbase: 129 in. Overall Length: 204.5 in. Width: 79.75 in.

CAPACITIES: Fuel Tank: 25 gal. Engine coolant system: 6-cyl.: 12.0 qt. V-8: 19.0 qt.

ACCOMMODATIONS: 3 passengers.

INSTRUMENTATION: Speedometer, odometer, gauges for fuel level and engine coolant temperature. Warning lights for oil pressure and battery charge.

OPTIONS AND PRICES: W100, W200, W300: Chrome front bumper: $13.20. Painted rear bumper: $19.20. Painted bumper guards: $5.30. Chrome bumper guards: $11.90. Directional signals: $23.10. Tinted glass: $17.20. Dual electric horns: $14.50. Horn ring: $3.00. Cigarette lighter: $4.70. Glove box lock: $4.00. Interior rearview mirror: $3.00. Grab handles: $8.50. Wraparound rear window: $29. Dual electric windshield wipers: $7.20. Windshield washer: $11.60. Heater: $46.10. Roof-mounted transistor radio. W300M: 60 amp-hr. battery. Pulley drive. Power winch: $243.45. Pintle hook: $12.50. Power take-off: $75.20. Front end tow hooks. Brake booster, 7.5 in. diaphragm: $42.50. Front bumper painted any standard truck color. Deluxe cab equipment: $19. Directional signals: $30.30. Drawbar: $23.10. 40 amp generator. Fenders painted to match body color: $13.20. Combined vacuum and fuel pump. Chrome grab handles (pair): $8.50. Tint glass: $17.20. Recirculating heater with defroster: $46.10. Hydraulic jack with 3 ton capacity: $7.90. Long arm left or right side exterior mirror: $2.40 (left side), $4.30 (right side). Interior mirror (in addition to standard): $3.00. Windshield washers: $11.60. Rear hydraulic telescopic shock absorbers. Power steering. Extra-duty springs (front: 1600 lb., rear: 3,000 lb.). Roof-mounted radio. Auxiliary taillamps. Heavy-duty battery. 11 in. clutch. Mechanical governor for use with rear drive shaft assembly. Fuel and vacuum pump. Radiator overflow tank.

HISTORICAL FOOTNOTES: The 1958 Dodge four-wheel drive trucks were introduced on October 31, 1957. Dodge celebrated its 40th anniversary as a truck producer in 1958.

1958 Dodge W300M Power Wagon pickup

1959 POWER WAGON

The W100, W200 and W300 1959 Power Wagons had a new concave grille with two sets of rectangular openings. Dodge lettering remained on the leading surface of the hood, but it was now enclosed in a chrome panel. New features for the 1959 conventional models included an all-new instrument panel with a large circular speedometer and smaller circular gauges for the fuel level and engine coolant temperature. Installed just below these gauges and angled slightly inward were red warnings for oil pressure and generator charge. A new option was a heavy-duty-type all-gauge cluster that included a tachometer. New suspended brake and clutch pedals provided a draft-free floor. Additional new features consisted of built-in ashtrays, a new color-keyed decor and, for the W100 and W200 models, concealed steps that were protected from rain, snow and ice.

1959 Dodge W300 Power Wagon pickup

Additional standard cab interior features included pull-type door handles, driver-adjustable hand-brake levers, electric windshield wipers, safety door latches, fully adjustable seats, key locks for both doors, and embossed fiberboard door panels and headlining. The custom cab provided the following features in addition to (or in place of) standard items: A new cigarette lighter, roof-to-floor sound-deadening, dual sun visors, foam-rubber seat padding, variable-speed electric windshield wipers, and a upgraded decor. The W100 and W200 models were offered with a new optional extra heavy-duty 3-speed manual transmission.

Additional standard equipment included a front channel-type bumper painted sand dune white, a left-side exterior short arm stationary mirror, and a single taillight. The Town Wagon and Town Panel models also had a rear step-type bumper.

The Town Wagon had a standard Interior Lining Package consisting of perforated Masonite headlining in the driver and load compartment, Masonite side panels in the load compartment and Meadboard extending from the headliner to the side panels.

The original Power Wagon model had a new WM300 designation for 1959. It was unchanged in design and standard equipment content

1959 Dodge W100 Town Wagon

I.D. DATA: The serial number was found on a plate installed on the left lock pillar post. W100, 6-cyl.: M6W1-L01001. W100, V-8: M8W1-L01001. W200, 6-cyl.: M6W2-L01001. W200, V-8: M8W2-L01001. W300 6-cyl.: M6W3-L01001. W300 V-8: M8W3-1001. W300M: M6W3M-L01001. Starting engine numbers: W100, 6-cyl.: M6-W1-1001. W100, V-8: M8-W1-1001. W200, 6-cyl.: M6-W2-1001. W200, V-8: M8-W2-1001. W300, 6-cyl.; LM6-W3-01001. W300, V-8: M8-W3-1001. W300M: M6-W3M-1001.

Body Type	Factory Price	GVW	Shipping Weight	Prod. Total
Model M6-W100, 1/2 ton 6-cyl.				
Chassis, 108 in. wb.	$2429	6000	3050	—
Ch. & Cab, 108 in. wb.	$2682	6000	3525	—
Pickup, 108 in. wb.	$2796	6000	3825	—
Town Panel, 108 in. wb.	$3099	6000	4000	—
Town Wag., 108 in. wb.	$3393	6000	4225	—
Chassis, 116 in. wb.	$2467	6000	3075	—
Ch. & Cab, 116 in. wb.	$2721	6000	3550	—
Pickup, 116 in. wb.	$2834	6000	3900	—
Platform, 116 in. wb.	$2873	6000	N.A.	—
Stake, 116 in. wb.	$2926	6000	3950	—
Model M6-W100, V-8				
Town Wag., 108 in. wb.	$3443	6000	4250	—
Model M6-W200, 3/4 ton, 6-cyl.				
Chassis, 116 in. wb.	$2570	6000*	3250	—
Ch. & Cab, 116 in. wb.	$2834	6000	3725	—
Pickup, 116 in. wb.	$2947	6000	4075	—
Stake, 116 in. wb.	$3039	6000	4125	—
Platform, 116 in. wb.	$2986	6000	N.A.	—

* An 8000 lb. GVW package were optional for all models.

Body Type	Factory Price	GVW	Shipping Weight	Prod. Total
Model M6-W300, 1 ton, 6-cyl.				
Chassis, 129 in. wb.	$3165	8500*	3825	—
Ch. & Cab, 129 in. wb.	$3429	8500	4430	—
Pickup, 129 in. wb.	$3563	8500	4700	—
Platform, 129 in. wb.	$3613	8500	N.A.	—
Stake, 129 in. wb.	$3676	8500	4775	—

* GVW packages up to 10,000 lb. were available.

Body Type	Factory Price	GVW	Shipping Weight	Prod. Total
Model M6-W300M				
Chassis, 126 in. wb.	$3035	7600*	4200	—
Ch. & Cab, 126 in. wb.	$3299	7600	4675	—
Pickup, 126 in. wb.	$3450	7600	5050	—

* 9500 lb. GVW package optional for all W300M models.

STANDARD ENGINE: W100, W200: Engine Type: L-head, In-line 6-cylinder. Cast iron block and cylinder head. Bore x Stroke: 3.25 in. x 4.625 in. Lifters: Mechanical. Number of main bearings-4. Fuel Induction: Stromberg downdraft carburetor. Compression Ratio: 7.9:1. Displacement: 230 cu. in. (3.768 liters). Horsepower: 120 @ 3600 rpm. Torque: 202 lb.-ft. @ 1600 rpm. Oil refill capacity: 5 qt. Fuel Requirements: Regular.

STANDARD ENGINE: W300: Engine Type: L-head, In-line 6-cylinder. Cast iron block and cylinder head. Bore x Stroke: 3.437 in. x 4.50 in. Lifters: Mechanical. Number of main bearings-4. Fuel Induction: Stromberg downdraft carburetor. Compression Ratio: 7.1:1. Displacement: 250.6 cu. in. (4.1065 liters). Horsepower: 125 @ 3600 rpm. Torque: 216 lb.-ft. @ 1600 rpm. Oil refill capacity: 5 qt. Fuel Requirements: Regular.

STANDARD ENGINE: W300M: Engine Type: L-head, In-line 6-cylinder. Cast iron block and cylinder head. Bore x Stroke: 3.25 in. x 4.625 in. Lifters: Mechanical. Number of main bearings-4. Fuel Induction: Stromberg downdraft carburetor. Compression Ratio: 7.9:1. Displacement: 230 cu. in. (3.768 liters). Horsepower: 113 @ 3600 rpm. Torque: 198 lb.-ft. @ 1600 rpm. Oil refill capacity: 5 qt. Fuel Requirements: Regular.

OPTIONAL ENGINE: W100, W200 and W300: Engine Type: "Power Giant 315." OHV, V-8. Cast iron block and cylinder head. A heavy-duty version was offered for the W300. Bore x Stroke: 3.63 in. x 3.80 in. Lifters: Hydraulic. Number of main bearings-5. Fuel Induction: Single 2-barrel downdraft carburetor. Compression Ratio: 8.151. Displacement: 314.61 cu. in. (5.155 liters). Horsepower: 205 @ 4400 rpm. (Heavy-duty: 207 @ 4400 rpm). Torque: 290 lb.-ft. @ 2400 rpm. (Heavy-duty: 292 lb.-ft. @ 2400 rpm). Oil refill capacity: 5 qt. Fuel Requirements: Regular.

W300M:

CHASSIS FEATURES: Separate body and double-drop frame; side rail reinforcements (inside type). Frame dimensions: 122.45875 in. x 0.109375 in. Frame rail dimensions: 6.09 in. x 2.04 in. x 0.171 in.

SUSPENSION AND RUNNING GEAR: Front Suspension: Eleven leaf, 39 in. x 1.75 in. semi-elliptical springs, heavy-duty, double-acting shock absorbers. Capacity: 1,150 lb. (each). Rear Suspension: Fourteen leaf, 52.25 in. x 1.75 in. semi-elliptical springs. Capacity: 2,500 lb. (each). Optional: 3,000 lb. capacity. Front Axle Type and Capacity: Full-floating, Hypoid-type. Capacity: 3,750 lb. Rear Axle Type and Capacity: Full-floating, Hypoid-type. Capacity: 6,500 lb. Final Drive Ratio: 4.89:1 with standard 7.50 x 16 8-ply tires; 5.83:1 with optional 9.00 x 16 10-ply tires. Transfer Case: Two-speed, double-lever. Ratios: 1.96:1, 1.00:1. Brakes: Hydraulic front and rear, centrifuse drums with cast iron braking surface. Dimensions: Front and rear: 14.125 in. x 1.75 in. Total lining area: 215.18 sq. in. Wheels: Five-stud ventilated disc. Tires: 7.50 x 16 8-ply. Optional: 9.00 x 16 8 or 10-ply tube-type tires with All-Service tread. Steering: Worm and lever; 17.0 in. diameter steering wheel. Ratio: 23.2:1. Optional: None. Transmission: New Process #420, 4-speed "Synchro-shift" manual. Transmission Ratios: 6.68, 3.10, 1.69, 1.00:1. Reverse: 8.25:1. Clutch: Single plate, Oilite bronze pilot bearing, 11.0 in. dia. with lining area of 123.7 sq. in.

VEHICLE DIMENSIONS: Wheelbase: 126.0 in. Overall Length: Express body: 199.0 in. (without winch): 208.625 in. (with winch); chassis and cab: 191.156 in. (without winch); 201.093 in. (with winch). Front/Rear Tread: 64.75 in./64.75 in. Overall Height: 76 in. (loaded). Width: 79.25 in. Front/Rear Overhang: 25.125 in./47.35 in. Tailgate: Width and Height: 54.0 in. x 19.9375 in. Ground Clearance: 8.8125 in.; with optional tires: 10.625 in. Load space: 96.0625 in. x 54.0 in. x 22.25 in.

CAPACITIES: Fuel Tank: 18 gal. Engine coolant system: 17 qt.

ACCOMMODATIONS: 3 passengers.

INSTRUMENTATION: Speedometer, odometer, gauges for oil pressure, fuel level, battery charge, engine coolant temperature.

W100 and W200:

CHASSIS FEATURES: Separate body and double-drop frame. Frame dimensions: 6.13 in. x 2.06 in. x 0.187 in. Section modules: 3.197.

SUSPENSION AND RUNNING GEAR: Front Suspension: Semi-elliptical leaf springs. Capacity: 1,050 lb. Optional: 1,300 lb. Rear Suspension: Semi-elliptical leaf springs. Capacity: W100: 1250 lb. W200: 1,750. Optional: W100: 1750 lb. W200: 2,600 lb. Front Axle Type and Capacity: Full-floating, Hypoid-type. Capacity: 3,000 lb. Rear Axle Type and Capacity: W100: Semi-floating, Hypoid-type. Capacity: 3,600 lb. W200: Full-floating, Hypoid-type. Capacity: 6,500 lb. Final Drive Ratio: 4.89:1 or 4.89:1. Transfer Case: Two-speed. Ratios: 1.96:1, 1.00:1. Brakes: Hydraulic front and rear. Dimensions: Front and rear: W100: 12.125 in. x 1.75 in. Total lining area: 198.4 sq. in. W200: Front: 12.125 in. x 1.75 in. Rear: 13.0 in. x 2.5 in. Total lining area: 232.8 sq. in. Wheels: Six-stud ventilated disc. Tires: 7 x 17.5 6-ply, tubeless. Optional: W100: 7 x 17.5 8-ply. W200: 8 x 19.5 8-ply. Steering: Worm and roller. Ratio: 23.5:1. Optional: Power assisted. Transmission: 3-speed heavy-duty manual. Optional: New Process #420, 4-speed "Synchro-shift" manual. Transmission Ratios: 6.68, 3.10, 1.69, 1.00:1. Reverse: 8.25:1. Optional: 3-speed Loadflite automatic (available for V-8 models only). Clutch: Single plate, dry disc, 11.0 in. dia. with lining area of 123.7 sq. in.

VEHICLE DIMENSIONS: Wheelbase: W100: 108 in., 116 in. W200: 116 in. Overall Length: Town Wagon: 197 in., 108 in. wheelbase models: 185.25 in. 116 in. wheelbase models: 197.125 in. Width: Town Sedan: 75.125 in. W100 and W200: 79.75 in.

CAPACITIES: Fuel Tank: 18 gal. Engine coolant system: 6-cyl.: 12.0 qt. V-8: 19.0 qt.

ACCOMMODATIONS: 3 passengers. Town Wagon: Up to eight passengers.

INSTRUMENTATION: Speedometer, odometer, gauges for fuel level and engine coolant temperature. Warning lights for oil pressure and battery charge.

W300:

CHASSIS FEATURES: Separate body and double-drop frame. Frame dimensions: 8.09 in. x 2.78 in. x 0.210 in. Section modules: 6.44.

SUSPENSION AND RUNNING GEAR: Front Suspension: Semi-elliptical leaf springs. Capacity: 1,450 lb. Optional: 1,750 lb. Rear Suspension: Semi-elliptical leaf springs. Capacity: 2,450. Optional: 3,250, 4,050 lb. Front Axle Type and Capacity: Full-floating, Hypoid-type. Capacity: 4,500 lb. Rear Axle Type and Capacity: Full-floating, Hypoid-type. Capacity: 8,000 lb. Final Drive Ratio: 4.88:1 or 5.87:1. Transfer Case: Two-speed, single lever. Ratios: 1.96:1, 1.00:1. Brakes: Hydraulic front and rear. Dimensions: Front: 14.125 in. x 1.75 in. Rear: 13 in. x 2.5 in. Total lining area: 241.98 sq. in. Wheels: Six-stud ventilated disc. Tires: 8 x 19.5 6-ply, tubeless. Steering: Worm and roller. Ratio: 29.0:1. Optional: Power assisted. Transmission: 4-speed manual. Optional: 3-speed Loadflite automatic (available for V-8 models only). Clutch: Single plate, dry disc, 11.0 in. dia. with lining area of 123.7 sq. in.

VEHICLE DIMENSIONS: Wheelbase: 129 in. Overall Length: 204.5 in. Width: 79.75 in.

CAPACITIES: Fuel Tank: 25 gal. Engine coolant system: 6-cyl.: 12.0 qt. V-8: 19.0 qt.

ACCOMMODATIONS: 3 passengers.

INSTRUMENTATION: Speedometer, odometer, gauges for fuel level and engine coolant temperature. Warning lights for oil pressure and battery charge.

OPTIONS AND PRICES: W100, W200, W300: Chrome front bumper: $13.20. Painted rear bumper: $20.40. Chrome rear bumper: $33.60. Painted bumper guards: $5.30. Chrome bumper guards: $11.85. Directional signals: $23.10. Tinted glass: $17.20. Dual electric horns: $14.50. Horn ring: $3.00. Cigarette lighter: $4.70. Glove box lock: $3.95. Interior rearview mirror: $3.00. Grab handles: $8.50. Wraparound rear window: $40.15. Dual electric variable-speed electric windshield wipers: $7.15. Heavy-Duty Gauge Package: $52. Windshield washer: $11.85. Heater: $46.10. Deluxe heater: $63.20. Roof-mounted transistor radio: $55.30. Custom cab: $36.85. Loadflite automatic transmission: $221.10. 315 cu. in. V-8 engine: $120.75. W300M: 60 amp-hr. battery. Pulley drive. Power winch. Pintle hook. Power take-off. Front end tow hooks. Brake booster, 7.5 in. diaphragm. Front bumper painted any standard truck color. Deluxe cab equipment. Directional signals. Drawbar. 40 amp generator. Fenders painted to match body color. Combined vacuum and fuel pump. Chrome grab handles. Tinted glass. Recirculating heater with defroster. Hydraulic jack with 3 ton capacity. Long arm left or right side exterior mirror. Interior mirror (in addition to standard). Windshield washers. Rear hydraulic telescopic shock absorbers. Power steering. Extra-duty springs (front: 1600 lb., rear: 3,000 lb.). Auxiliary taillamps. Roof-mounted radio. Heavy-duty battery. 11 in. clutch. Mechanical governor for use with rear drive shaft assembly. Fuel and vacuum pump. Radiator overflow tank.

HISTORICAL FOOTNOTES: The 1959 Dodge four-wheel drive trucks were introduced on October 24, 1958.

1960 POWER WAGON

1960 Dodge Sweptline W100 Power Wagon pickup

The conventional body "Utiline" pickup in the W100 and W200 series was joined by a "Sweptline" model for 1960. This body style had been introduced for the two-wheel drive models in 1959 and featured a smooth-side profile. Dodge General Manager M.C. Patterson, explained this development by noting that "knowing that 63 percent of the 3 million trucks on American farms have pickup bodies, we are expanding our line in that area with the addition of such vehicles as these four-wheel drive units. Our stylish Sweptline pickups feature a larger payload capacity and bigger brakes than any other comparable models in the industry."

1960 Dodge Utiline W200 Power Wagon pickup

The W100, W200 and W300 Power Wagons had a moderately revised grille format with a center panel consisting of thin horizontal bars and a center star crest. The prominent "DODGE" lettering on the front of the hood was continued. The standard cab for all models except for the WM300 was equipped with suspended pedals, built-in ashtray, pull-type door handles, single-speed electric windshield wipers, safety door latches, embossed fiberboard door panels and headlining, dome light with manual switch, Saran seat upholstery with vinyl facings, seat and seat back padding of cotton sisal, rubber floor mat, driver's side sun visor, fully adjustable seat, concealed steps, key locks for both doors, outside-mounted mirror, driver-adjustable hand-brake lever, electric single-air-note-type horn, sound deadener on floor and a large dispatch box.

1960 Dodge W100 Town Wagon

The custom cab package included, in addition to, or replacing standard cab items, the following items: Driver's side armrest, variable-speed electric windshield wipers, insulated dash liner, sound-absorbent door panels, insulated headling, Saran and rayon seat upholstery with vinyl facings and bolsters, foam rubber seat and seat back padding, dual sun visors,

sound-deadener on cowl side panel, cab rear panel and underbody, and cigarette lighter. Both the standard and custom cabs were available with wrap-around rear windows. The WM300 cab featured vacuum windshield wipers, right door key lock, vibrator horn, imitation leather fabrics and a floor-mounted emergency brake control. The Deluxe cab available for the WM300 included a driver's side armrest, dome light and two sun visors. A new Power Wagon model for 1960 was the "Little Mo" fire engine on the W200 chassis. Powered by the 200 horsepower 318 cu. in. V-8, this vehicle was equipped by American LaFrance. The Town Wagon was again offered. It was described by Dodge as a "low-price station wagon-truck which carries up to eight passengers, or three passengers while providing 90 cubic feet of space for farm cargo." Fourteen exterior colors, five of them new, were offered for 1960. The color selection was as follows: Sand dune white, Klondike yellow, Nile green, Dodge truck red, mustang gray, pine green, Toreador red, Omaha orange, Indian turquoise, marlin blue, Arctic blue, bell green, angus black and school bus chrome yellow.

The Sweptline Pickup was painted a standard cab color both inside and out. If a two-tone color was selected, a sand dune white color was applied above the belt molding. The Utiline pickup was painted the cab color both inside and out, except for the body floor which was painted black. Stake and Platform models had their platforms painted black. Stake racks were the same color as the cab. The Town Panel and Town Wagon were painted any standard Dodge truck color. All conventional models had headlight panels painted sand dune white. Wheels and bumpers on light duty trucks were also painted sand dune white. On both the standard and custom cabs, the steering wheel, steering column and handbrake were painted black. The clutch and brake pedal shafts were painted body color.

When ordered in a standard truck color, the WM300 model had its radiator shell, hood, cowl, cab and wheels painted in that color. The fenders, bumpers and wheels were painted black. Fenders could be painted cab color at extra cost.

1960 Dodge WM300 Power Wagon pickup

I.D. DATA: The serial numbers were found on a plate located on the left door lock pillar. The first digit indicates the 1960 model year. The second digit indicated either six or eight cylinder engine. The next entry identified the nominal weight rating (1-1/2 ton, 2-3/4 ton and 3 for 1 ton). The next entry was a L for light duty. Then followed the six production sequence numbers. The serial numbers on 6-cylinder engines was located on the left side of the block at the front, below the cylinder head. The V-8 serial number was found on the left front of the block. Beginning in 1960 a new engine numbering system was used. The first two letters (T and P) represented "Truck" and "P" series. The next two digits indicated engine size (the exception was the 318 engine which had a third digit identification). The next two digits indicated month and date of manufacture. The final four digits were the production sequence numbers. The starting engine numbers for 1960 were as follows: 230 cu. in. 6-cyl.: TP-23-8-3-1001; 251 cu. in. 6-cyl.: TP-25-8-3-1001; 318 cu. in. V-8: TP-318-8-3-1001.

Body Type	Factory Price	GVW	Shipping Weight	Prod. Total
Model P6-W100, 1/2 ton 6-cyl.				
Chassis, 108 in. wb.	$2414	6000	3175	a
Ch. & Cab, 108 in. wb.	$2667	6000	3775	—
Pickup, Utiline, 108 in. wb.	$2782	6000	4085	—
Pickup, Sweptline, 108 in. wb.	$2796	6000	4085	—
Town Panel, 108 in. wb.	$3111	6000	4375	—
Town Wagon, 108 in. wb.	$3397	6000	4505	—

a Total model year production was 352 units with 6-cyl. engine and 165 with V-8 engine. (Includes Town Wagon listed below.)

Chassis, 116 in. wb.	$2452	6000	3200	b
Ch. & Cab, 116 in. wb.	$2704	6000	3800	—
Pickup, Utiline, 116 in. wb.	$2818	6000	4150	—
Pickup, Sweptline, 116 in. wb.	$2833	6000	4240	—
Platform, 116 in. wb.	$2857	6000	4190	—
Stake, 116 in. wb.	$2909	6000	4190	—

b Total model year production was 189 with 6-cyl. engine and 262 with V-8 engine.

Model P6-W100, V-8				
Town Wagon, 108 in. wb.	$3446	6000	4555	

Model P6-W200, 3/4 ton, 6-cyl.				
Chassis, 116 in. wb.	$2556	6000*	3350	c
Ch. & Cab, 116 in. wb.	$2818	6000	3950	—
Pickup, Utiline, 116 in. wb.	$2933	6000	4300	—
Pickup, Sweptline, 116 in. wb.	$2947	6000	4390	—
Stake, 116 in. wb.	$3024	6000	4340	—
Platform, 116 in. wb.	$2972	6000	4340	—

* An 8000 lb. GVW package was optional for all models.
c Total model year production was 262 units with 6-cyl. engine and 150 with V-8 engines.

Model P6-W300, 1 ton, 6-cyl.				
Chassis, 129 in. wb.	$3158	8500*	3950	d
Ch. & Cab, 129 in. wb.	$3420	8500	4550	—
Pickup, Utiline129 in. wb.	$3557	8500	4950	—
Platform, 129 in. wb.	$3607	8500	5415	—
Stake, 129 in. wb.	$3672	8500	5415	—

* GVW packages up to 10,000 lb. were available.
d Total model year production was 141 with 6-cyl. engine and 171 with V-8 engines.

Model P6-WM300

Chassis, 126 in. wb.	$3072	7600 lb.*	4375	e
Ch. & Cab, 126 in. wb.	$3339	7600 lb.	4975	—
Pickup, 126 in. wb.	$3492	7600 lb.	5445	—

* 9500 lb. GVW package optional for all WM300 models.
e Total model year production was 1517 units.

STANDARD ENGINE: W100, W200: Engine Type: L-head, In-line 6-cylinder. Cast iron block and cylinder head. Bore x Stroke: 3.25 in. x 4.625 in. Lifters: Mechanical. Number of main bearings-4. Fuel Induction: Stromberg downdraft carburetor. Compression Ratio: 7.9:1. Displacement: 230 cu. in. (3.768 liters). Horsepower: 120 @ 3600 rpm. Torque: 202 lb.-ft. @ 1600 rpm. Oil refill capacity: 5 qt. Fuel Requirements: Regular.

STANDARD ENGINE: W300: Engine Type: L-head, In-line 6-cylinder. Cast iron block and cylinder head. Bore x Stroke: 3.437 in. x 4.50 in. Lifters: Mechanical. Number of main bearings-4. Fuel Induction: Stromberg downdraft carburetor. Compression Ratio: 7.1:1. Displacement: 250.6 cu. in. (4.1065 liters). Horsepower: 125 @ 3600 rpm. Torque: 216 lb.-ft. @ 1600 rpm. Oil refill capacity: 5 qt. Fuel Requirements: Regular.

STANDARD ENGINE: W300M: Engine Type: L-head, In-line 6-cylinder. Cast iron block and cylinder head. Bore x Stroke: 3.25 in. x 4.625 in. Lifters: Mechanical. Number of main bearings-4. Fuel Induction: Stromberg downdraft carburetor. Compression Ratio: 7.9:1. Displacement: 230 cu. in. (3.768 liters). Horsepower: 113 @ 3600 rpm. Torque: 198 lb.-ft. @ 1600 rpm. Oil refill capacity: 5 qt. Fuel Requirements: Regular.

OPTIONAL ENGINE: W100, W200 and W300: Engine Type: "Power Giant 315." OHV, V-8. Cast iron block and cylinder head. A heavy-duty version was offered for the W300. Bore x Stroke: 3.63 in. x 3.80 in. Lifters: Hydraulic. Number of main bearings-5. Fuel Induction: Single 2-barrel downdraft carburetor. Compression Ratio: 8.151. Displacement: 314.61 cu. in. (5.155 liters). Horsepower: 205 @ 4400 rpm. (Heavy-duty: 207 @ 4400 rpm). Torque: 290 lb.-ft. @ 2400 rpm. (Heavy-duty: 292 lb.-ft. @ 2400 rpm). Oil refill capacity: 5 qt. Fuel Requirements: Regular.

W300M:

CHASSIS FEATURES: Separate body and double-drop frame; side rail reinforcements (inside type). Frame dimensions: 122.45875 in. x 0.109375 in. Frame rail dimensions: 6.09 in. x 2.04 in. x 0.171 in.

SUSPENSION AND RUNNING GEAR: Front Suspension: Eleven leaf, 39 in. x 1.75 in. semi-elliptical springs, heavy-duty, double-acting shock absorbers. Capacity: 1,150 lb. (each). Optional: 1600 lb. capacity, (included with rims). Rear Suspension: Fourteen leaf, 52.25 in. x 1.75 in. semi-elliptical springs. Capacity: 2,500 lb. (each). Optional: 3,000 lb. capacity. Front Axle Type and Capacity: Full-floating, Hypoid-type. Capacity: 3,750 lb. Rear Axle Type and Capacity: Full-floating, Hypoid-type. Capacity: 6,500 lb. Final Drive Ratio: 4.89:1 with standard 7.50 x 16 8-ply tires; 5.83:1 with optional 9.00 x 16 10-ply tires. Transfer Case: Two-speed, double-lever. Ratios: 1.96:1, 1.00:1. Brakes: Hydraulic front and rear, centrifuse drums with cast iron braking surface. Dimensions: Front and rear: 14.125 in. x 1.75 in. Total lining area: 215.18 sq. in. Wheels: Five-stud ventilated disc. Tires: 7.50 x 16 8-ply. Optional: 9.00 x 16 8 or 10-ply tube-type tires with All-Service tread. Steering: Worm and lever, 17.0 in. diameter steering wheel. Ratio: 23.2:1. Optional: None. Transmission: New Process #420, 4-speed "Synchro-shift" manual. Transmission Ratios: 6.68, 3.10, 1.69, 1.00:1. Reverse: 8.25:1. Clutch: Single plate, Oilite bronze pilot bearing, 11.0 in. dia. with lining area of 123.7 sq. in.

VEHICLE DIMENSIONS: Wheelbase: 126.0 in. Overall Length: Express body: 199.0 in. (without winch); 208.625 in. (with winch); chassis and cab: 191.156 in. (without winch); 201.093 in. (with winch). Front/Rear Tread: 64.75 in./64.75 in. Overall Height: 76 in. (loaded). Width: 79.25 in. Front/Rear Overhang: 25.125 in./47.35 in. Tailgate: Width and Height: 54.0 in. x 19.9375 in. Ground Clearance: 8.8125 in.; with optional tires: 10.625 in. Load space: 96.0625 in. x 54.0 in. x 22.25 in.

CAPACITIES: Fuel Tank: 18 gal. Engine coolant system: 17 qt.

ACCOMMODATIONS: 3 passengers.

INSTRUMENTATION: Speedometer, odometer, gauges for oil pressure, fuel level, battery charge, engine coolant temperature.

W100 and W200:

CHASSIS FEATURES: Separate body and double-drop frame. Frame dimensions: 6.13 in. x 2.06 in. x 0.187 in. Section modules: 3.197.

SUSPENSION AND RUNNING GEAR: Front Suspension: Semi-elliptical leaf springs. Capacity: 1,050 lb. Optional: 1,300 lb. Rear Suspension: Semi-elliptical leaf springs. Capacity: W100: 1250 lb. W200: 1,750. Optional: W100: 1750 lb. W200: 2,600 lb. Front Axle Type and Capacity: Full-floating, Hypoid-type. Capacity: 3,000 lb. Rear Axle Type and Capacity: W100: Semi-floating, Hypoid-type. W200: Full-floating, Hypoid-type. Capacity: 6,500 lb. Final Drive Ratio: 4.89:1 or 4.89:1. Transfer Case: Two-speed. Ratios: 1.96:1, 1.00:1. Brakes: Hydraulic front and rear. Dimensions: Front and rear: W100: 12.125 in. x 1.75 in. Total lining area: 198.4 sq. in. W200: Front: 12.125 in. x 1.75 in. Rear: 13.0 in. x 2.5 in. Total lining area: 232.8 sq. in. Wheels: Six-stud ventilated disc. Tires: 7 x 17.5 6-ply, tubeless. Optional: W100: 7 x 17.5 8-ply. W200: 8 x 19.5 8-ply. Steering: Worm and roller. Ratio: 23.5:1. Optional: Power assisted. Transmission: 3-speed heavy-duty manual. Optional: New Process #420, 4-speed "Synchro-shift" manual. Transmission Ratios: 6.68, 3.10, 1.69, 1.00:1. Reverse: 8.25:1. Clutch: Single plate, dry disc, 11.0 in. dia. with lining area of 123.7 sq. in.

VEHICLE DIMENSIONS: Wheelbase: W100: 108 in., 116 in. W200: 116 in. Overall Length: Town Wagon: 197 in., 108 in. wheelbase models: 185.25 in. 116 in. wheelbase models: 197.125 in. Width: Town Sedan: 75.125 in. W100 and W200: 79.75 in.

CAPACITIES: Fuel Tank: 18 gal. Engine coolant system: 6-cyl.: 12.0 qt. V-8: 19.0 qt.

ACCOMMODATIONS: 3 passengers. Town Wagon: Up to eight passengers.

INSTRUMENTATION: Speedometer, odometer, gauges for fuel level and engine coolant temperature. Warning lights for oil pressure and battery charge.

W300:

CHASSIS FEATURES: Separate body and double-drop frame. Frame dimensions: 8.09 in. x 2.78 in. x 0.210 in. Section modules: 6.44.

SUSPENSION AND RUNNING GEAR: Front Suspension: Semi-elliptical leaf springs. Capacity: 1,450 lb. Optional: 1,750 lb. Rear Suspension: Semi-elliptical leaf springs. Capacity: 2,450. Optional: 3,250, 4,050 lb. Front Axle Type and Capacity: Full-floating, Hypoid-type. Capacity: 4,500 lb. Rear Axle Type and Capacity: Full-floating, Hypoid-type. Capacity: 8,000 lb. Final Drive Ratios: 4.88:1 or 5.87:1. Transfer Case: Two-speed. Ratios: 1.96:1, 1.00:1. Brakes: Hydraulic front and rear. Dimensions: Front: 14.125 in. x 1.75 in. Rear: 13 in. x 2.5 in. Total lining area: 241.98 sq. in. Wheels: Six-stud ventilated disc. Tires: 8 x 19.5 6-ply, tubeless. Optional: 8 x 17.5 6-ply. Steering: Worm and roller. Ratio: 29.0:1. Optional: Power assisted. Transmission: 4-speed manual. Clutch: Single plate, dry disc, 11.0 in. dia. with lining area of 123.7 sq. in.

VEHICLE DIMENSIONS: Wheelbase: 129 in. Overall Length: 204.5 in. Width: 79.75 in.

CAPACITIES: Fuel Tank: 25 gal. Engine coolant system: 6-cyl.: 12.0 qt. V-8: 19.0 qt.

ACCOMMODATIONS: 3 passengers.

INSTRUMENTATION: Speedometer, odometer, gauges for fuel level and engine coolant temperature. Warning lights for oil pressure and battery charge.

OPTIONS AND PRICES: W100, W200, W300: Chrome front bumper: $13.20. Painted rear bumper: $20.40. Chrome rear bumper: $33.60. Painted bumper guards: $5.30. Chrome bumper guards: $11.85. Directional signals: $23.10. Tinted glass: $17.20. Dual electric horns: $14.50. Horn ring: $3.00. Cigarette lighter: $4.70. Glove box lock: $3.95. Interior rearview mirror: $3.00. Grab handles: $8.50. Wraparound rear window: $40.15. Dual electric variable-speed electric windshield wipers: $7.15. Heavy-Duty Gauge Package: $52. Windshield washer: $11.85. Heater: $46.10. Deluxe heater: $63.20. Roof-mounted transistor radio: $55.30. Custom cab: $36.85. Loadflite automatic transmission: $221.10. 315 cu. in V-8 engine: $120.75. W300M: 60 amp-hr. battery. Pulley drive. Power winch. Pintle hook. Power take-off. Front and tow hooks. Brake booster, 7.5 in. diaphragm: Front bumper painted any standard truck color. Deluxe cab equipment. Directional signals. Drawbar. 40 amp generator. Fenders painted to match body color. Combined vacuum and fuel pump. Chrome grab handles. Tinted glass. Recirculating heater with defroster. Hydraulic jack with 3 ton capacity. Long arm left or right side exterior mirror. Interior mirror (in addition to standard). Windshield washers. Rear hydraulic telescopic shock absorbers. Power steering. Extra-duty springs (front: 1600 lb., rear: 3,000 lb.). Roof-mounted radio. Auxiliary taillamps. Heavy-duty battery. 11 in. clutch. Mechanical governor for use with rear drive shaft assembly. Fuel and vacuum pump. Radiator overflow tank.

HISTORICAL FOOTNOTES: The 1960 Dodge four-wheel drive trucks were introduced on October 9, 1959.

1961 POWER WAGON

This was a year of significant changes for the four-wheel drive Dodge trucks. The conventional models received their first all-new bodies since 1954. The new body featured new sheet metal, new grilles, and new ornamentation. The doors of the new models were wider. All conventional cabs now had 60 in. wide seats, four inches wider than in 1960. The new models were lower and wider than those they replaced. The new body style also offered a larger by 41 sq. in. windshield and a standard rear window that was 86 sq. in. larger in area than its 1960 counterpart. All conventional models had improved rustproofing for 1961. The rocker panel sills were primed inside. After the primer was applied and cured, a rust-preventative was applied. Door interior surfaces were primed 12 inches up from the bottom.

1961 Dodge W100 Sweptline Power Wagon pickup

A new drop center frame for the W100 and W200 lowered the floor height by three inches. The Town Wagon retained its previous body shell. The W100 and W200 now had the Chrysler Corporation overhead valve slant-six as their standard engine. This engine was inclined 30 degrees and, said Dodge, would deliver up to 18 percent greater economy and up to 28 percent better acceleration than the previous engine. The old 230 cu. in. L-head 6-cylinder engine was retired. Both the W300 and WM300 now used the larger 251 cu. in. L-head 6-cylinder as their standard engines. This engine was equipped with a hardened crankshaft, tri-metal bearings, Silicrome XB sodium-filled exhaust valves, bronze exhaust-valve guides and a full-flow oil filter. A new heavy-duty New Process A745 transmission was standard for the W100 and W200 models. It had a low-gear ratio of 3.02:1.

1961 Dodge W300 Utiline Power Wagon pickup

The conventional model's cab had the following features: Pull-type door handles, single-speed electric windshield wipers, safety door latches, embossed metal door panels, woven fiber headlining, domelight with manual switch, Saran seat upholstery with vinyl facings, seat and seat back padding of cotton-sisal, rubber floor mat, sun visor-driver's side, fully adjustable seat, concealed steps (W100 and W200), key lock on right-hand door, outside-mounted mirror, driver-adjustable hand brake lever, electric single-air-note horn, sound-deadener on floor, and dispatch box.

1961 Dodge W100 Town Wagon

The Custom Cab Package included in addition to, or replacing standard cab items previously listed these features: Dual armrests, variable speed electric windshield wipers, foam-rubber seat pad, foam seat back, insulated floor mat, dash-panel liner, heat and noise insulation, seat material of patterned Saran interwoven with metallic threads, headlining of woven fiber backed with 0.25 in. amberlite, cigarette lighter, bright-metal cab moldings and chrome front bumper (W100 less winch). A 678 sq. in. rear window was available as an option.

1961 Dodge WM300 Power Wagon pickup

The WM300's standard deluxe cab featured electric windshield wipers, right door lock, vibrator lock, imitation-leather fabrics, floor-mounted emergency brake control, driver armrest, dome light and two sun visors. Standard on all models was a new 35 amp alternator. It was 43 percent more powerful than the old generator. Standard on all models except the WM300 was a new ammeter plus additional ignition circuit for improved cold weather starting.

1961 Dodge W100 Sweptline Power Wagon pickup with wrecker equipment

I.D. DATA: The serial numbers were found on a plate located on the left door lock pillar. The first digit indicated the 1961 model year. The second digit indicated either six or eight cylinder engine. The next entry identified the nominal weight rating (1-1/2 ton, 2-3/4 ton and 3 for 1 ton). The next entry was an L for light-duty. Then followed the six production sequence numbers. The serial numbers on 6-cylinder engines was located on the left side of the block at the front, below the cylinder head. The V-8 serial number was found on the left front of the block. The first two letters (T and P) represented "Truck" and "P" series. The next two digits indicated engine size (the exception was the 318 engine which had a third digit identification). The next two digits indicated month and date of manufacture. The final four digits were the production sequence numbers.

Standard Catalog of American Four-Wheel Drive Vehicles

Body Type	Factory Price	GVW	Shipping Weight	Prod. Total
Model R6-W100, 1/2 ton 6-cyl.				
Ch. & Cab, 114 in. wb.	$2620	5100*	3750	—
Pickup, Utiline, 114 in. wb.	$2735	5100	4060	—
Pickup, Sweptline, 114 in. wb.	$2749	5100	4160	—
Town Panel, 114 in. wb.	$3063	5100	4220	—
Town Wagon, 114 in. wb.	$3349	5100	4450	—

* 6000 lb. GVW optional.

Body Type	Factory Price	GVW	Shipping Weight	Prod. Total
Model R6-W100, V-8				
Town Wagon, 114 in. wb.	$3399	5100	4500	a

a Total model year production of all W100 trucks was 516 units with 6-cyl. engines and 281 with V-8 engines.

Body Type	Factory Price	GVW	Shipping Weight	Prod. Total
Model R6-W200, 3/4 ton, 6-cyl.				
Ch. & Cab, 122 in. wb.	$2675	6000*	3895	b
Pickup, Utiline, 122 in. wb.	$2790	6000	4245	—
Pickup, Sweptline, 122 in. wb.	$2804	6000	4375	—
Stake, 122 in. wb.	$2881	6000	4470	—
Platform, 116 in. wb.	$2829	6000	4270	—

* An 8000 lb. GVW package was optional for all models.
b Total model year production was 273 units with 6-cyl. engines and 258 with V-8 engines.

Body Type	Factory Price	GVW	Shipping Weight	Prod. Total
Model R6-W300, 1 ton, 6-cyl.				
Ch. & Cab, 133 in. wb.	$3427	8500*	4495	c
Pickup, Utiline, 133 in. wb.	$4562	8500	4895	—
Platform, 133 in. wb.	$3613	8500	5095	—
Stake, 133 in. wb.	$3677	8500	5395	—

* GVW packages up to 10,000 lb. were available.
c Total model year production was 239 units with 6-cyl. engines and 215 with V-8 engines.
Prices of the W100, W200 and W300 models with optional V-8 engine was an additional $130.00.

Body Type	Factory Price	GVW	Shipping Weight	Prod. Total
Model R6-WM300				
Ch. & Cab, 126 in. wb.	$3635	8700*	4875	d
Pickup, 126 in. wb.	$3789	8700	5275	—

* 9500 lb. GVW package optional for all WM300 models.
d Total model year production was 1367 units.

STANDARD ENGINE: W100, W200: Engine Type: OHV, In-line 6-cylinder. Cast iron block and cylinder head. Bore x Stroke: 3.40 in. x 4.125 in. Lifters: Mechanical. Number of main bearings 4. Fuel Induction: Single barrel carburetor. Compression Ratio: 8.2:1. Displacement: 224.7 cu. in. (3.68 liters). Horsepower: 140 @ 3900 rpm. Torque: 215 lb.-ft. @ 1600-2800 rpm. Oil refill capacity: 5 qt. with filter change.

STANDARD ENGINE: W300 and WM300: Engine Type: L-head, In-line 6-cylinder. Cast iron block and cylinder head. Bore x Stroke: 3.437 in. x 4.50 in. Lifters: Mechanical. Number of main bearings-4. Fuel Induction: Stromberg single barrel downdraft carburetor. Compression Ratio: 7.1:1. Displacement: 250.6 cu. in. (4.10 liters). Horsepower: 125 @ 3600 rpm. Torque: 216 lb.-ft. @ 1600 rpm. Oil refill capacity: 5 qt. Fuel Requirements: Regular.

OPTIONAL ENGINE: W100, W200, W300: Engine Type: OHV, Power Giant V-8. Cast iron block and cylinder head. Bore x Stroke: 3.91 in. x 3.3120 in. Lifters: Hydraulic. Number of main bearings-5. Fuel Induction: Single barrel carburetor. Compression Ratio: 8.25:1. Displacement: 318.14 cu. in. (5.21 liters). Horsepower: 200 @ 3900 rpm. Torque: 286 lb.-ft. @ 2400 rpm. Oil refill capacity: 5 qt. Fuel Requirements: Regular.

OPTIONAL ENGINE: W300: Engine Type: "Rugged Duty", Power Giant OHV, V-8. Cast iron block and cylinder head. This engine has the "Normal Duty" 318 V-8 features plus roller-chain drive, vibration damper, positive exhaust valve rotators and hydraulic valve lifters. Bore x Stroke: 3.63 in. x 3.80 in. Lifters: Hydraulic. Number of main bearings-5. Fuel Induction: 2-barrel carburetor. Compression Ratio: 8.25:1. Displacement: 318.14 cu. in. (5.21 liters). Horsepower: 202 @ 3900 rpm. Torque: 288 lb.-ft. @ 2400 rpm. Oil refill capacity: 5 qt. Fuel Requirements: Regular.

W300M:

CHASSIS FEATURES: Separate body and double-drop frame; side rail reinforcements (inside type). Frame dimensions: 122.45875 in. x 0.109375 in. Frame rail dimensions: 6.09 in. x 2.04 in. x 0.171 in.

SUSPENSION AND RUNNING GEAR: Front Suspension: Eleven leaf, 39 in. x 1.75 in. semi-elliptical springs, heavy-duty, double-acting shock absorbers. Capacity: 1,150 lb. (each). Optional: 1600 lb. capacity, (included with winch). Rear Suspension: Fourteen leaf, 52.25 in. x 1.75 in. semi-elliptical springs. Capacity: 2,500 lb. (each). Optional: 3,000 lb. capacity. Front Axle Type and Capacity: Full-floating, Hypoid-type. Capacity: 3,750 lb. Rear Axle Type and Capacity: Full-floating, Hypoid-type. Capacity: 6,500 lb. Final Drive Ratio: 5.83:1. Transfer Case: Two-speed, double-lever. Ratios: 1.96:1, 1.00:1. Brakes: Hydraulic front and rear, centrifuge drums with cast iron braking surface. Dimensions: Front and rear: 14.125 in. x 1.75 in. Total lining area: 215.18 sq. in. Wheels: Five-stud ventilated disc. Tires: 9.00 x 16 8-ply. Optional: 9.00 x 16 10-ply. Steering: Worm and lever; 17.0 in. diameter steering wheel. Ratio: 23.2:1. Optional: None. Transmission: New Process #420, 4-speed "Synchro-shift" manual. Transmission Ratios: 6.68, 3.10, 1.69, 1.00:1. Reverse: 8.25:1. Clutch: Single plate, Oilite bronze pilot bearing, 11.0 in. dia. with lining area of 123.7 sq. in.

VEHICLE DIMENSIONS: Wheelbase: 126.0 in. Overall Length: Pickup: 199.0 in. (without winch); 208.625 in. (with winch); chassis and cab: 191.156 in. (without winch) 201.093 in. (with winch). Front/Rear Tread: 64.75 in./64.75 in. Overall Height: 76 in. (loaded). Width: 79.25 in. Front/Rear Overhang: 25.125 in./47.35 in. Tailgate: Width and Height: 54.0 in. x 19.9375 in. Ground Clearance: 8.8125 in.; with optional tires: 10.625 in. Load space: 96.0625 in. x 54.0 in. x 22.25 in.

CAPACITIES: Fuel Tank: 18 gal. Engine coolant system: 17 qt.

ACCOMMODATIONS: 3 passengers.

INSTRUMENTATION: Speedometer, odometer, gauges for oil pressure, fuel level, battery charge, engine coolant temperature.

W100 and W200:

CHASSIS FEATURES: Separate body and drop-center frame. Section modulus: 3.43.

SUSPENSION AND RUNNING GEAR: Front Suspension: Semi-elliptical leaf springs. Capacity: 6-cyl.: 1, 100 lb. V-8: 1,350 lb. Optional: 6-cyl.: 1,350 lb. V-8: 1,550 lb. (both were standard with front-mounted winch). Rear Suspension: Semi-elliptical leaf springs. Capacity: W100: 1,350 lb. W200: 1,750 lb. Optional: W100: 1,750 lb. W200: 2,600 lb. Front Axle Type and Capacity: Full-floating, Hypoid-type. Capacity: 3,000 lb. Rear Axle Type and Capacity: W100: Semi-floating, Hypoid-type. Capacity: 4,500 lb. W200: Full-floating, Hypoid-type. Capacity: 5,500 lb. Final Drive Ratio: 4.1:1 or 4.88:1. Anti-slip differential available with 4.1:1

ratio. Transfer Case: Two-speed. Ratios: 1.96:1, 1.00:1. Brakes: Hydraulic front and rear. Dimensions: Front and rear: W100:12.125 in. x 1.75. Total lining area: 199.88 sq. in. Wheels: Eight-stud ventilated disc. Tires: W100: 6.50 x 16 6-ply. W200: 7 x 17.5 6-ply, tubeless. Optional: W100: 7.00 x 16 6-ply, 7 x 17.5 6-ply. W200: 8 x 19.5 8-ply. Steering: Recirculating ball. Transmission: 3-speed heavy-duty A745 manual. Optional: New Process #420, 4-speed "Synchro-shift" manual. Transmission Ratios: 6.68, 3.10, 1.69, 1.00:1. Reverse: 8.25:1. Clutch: Single plate, dry disc, 11.0 in. dia. with lining area of 123.7 sq. in.

VEHICLE DIMENSIONS: Wheelbase: W100: 114 in. W200: 122 in. Overall Length: Town Wagon: 197 in. Chassis cab: 114 in. wheelbase models: 185.6562 in. 122 in. wheelbase models: 205.9375 in. Height: W100: 75.218 in. W200: 73.5 in. Front/Rear tread: W100: 65.3125 in./63.3125 in. W200: 65.21875 in./63.3125 in.

CAPACITIES: Fuel Tank: 18 gal. Engine coolant system: 6-cyl.: 13.0 qt. V-8: 20.0 qt.

ACCOMMODATIONS: 3 passengers. Town Wagon: Up to eight passengers.

INSTRUMENTATION: Speedometer, odometer, gauges for fuel level, ammeter and engine coolant temperature.

W300:

CHASSIS FEATURES: Separate body and straight frame. Section modules: 5.70.

SUSPENSION AND RUNNING GEAR: Front Suspension: Semi-elliptical leaf springs. Capacity: 1,450 lb. Optional: 1,750 lb. (standard with front-mounted winch). Rear Suspension: Semi-elliptical leaf springs. Capacity: 2,450. Optional: 3,250, 4,050 lb. Front Axle Type and Capacity: Full-floating, Hypoid-type. Capacity: 4,500 lb. Rear Axle Type and Capacity: Full-floating, Hypoid-type. Capacity: 7,500 lb. Anti-slip differential optional. Final Drive Ratio: 4.88:1 or 5.87:1. Transfer Case: Two-speed, single lever. Ratios: 1.96:1, 1.00:1. Brakes: Hydraulic front and rear. Dimensions: Front: 14.125 in. x 1.75. Rear: 13 in. x 2.5 in. Total lining area: 241.98 sq. in. Wheels: Six-stud ventilated disc. Tires: 8 x 19.5 8-ply, tubeless. Optional: 9.00 x 16 10-ply. Steering: Worm and roller. Ratio: 29.0:1. Optional: Power assisted. Transmission: New Process #420, 4-speed "Synchro-shift" manual. Transmission Ratios: 6.68, 3.10, 1.69, 1.00:1. Reverse: 8.25:1. Clutch: Single plate, dry disc, 11.0 in. dia. with lining area of 123.7 sq. in.

VEHICLE DIMENSIONS: Wheelbase: 133 in. Overall Length: Chassis cab: 212.5 in. Width: 81.8125 in. Front/Rear tread: 62.5 in./64 in.

CAPACITIES: Fuel Tank: 18 gal. Engine coolant system: 6-cyl.: 20.0 qt. V-8: 24.0 qt.

ACCOMMODATIONS: 3 passengers.

INSTRUMENTATION: Speedometer, odometer, gauges for fuel level, ammeter and engine coolant temperature.

OPTIONS: W100, W200, W300: Chrome front bumper. Painted rear bumper. Chrome rear bumper. Painted bumper guards. Chrome bumper guards. Directional signals. Tinted glass. Dual electric horns. Horn ring. Cigarette lighter. Glove box lock. Interior rearview mirror. Grab handles. Wraparound rear window. Dual electric variable-speed electric windshield wipers. Windshield washer. Heater. Deluxe heater. Custom cab. 315 cu. in. V-8 engine. W300M: 60 amp-hr. battery. Pulley drive. Power winch. Pintle hook. Power take-off. Front end tow hooks. Brake booster, 7.5 in. diaphragm. Front bumper painted any standard truck color. Deluxe cab equipment. Directional signals. Drawbar. 40 amp generator. Fenders painted to match body color. Combined vacuum and fuel pump. Chrome grab handles. Tinted glass. Recirculating heater with defroster. Hydraulic jack with 3 ton capacity. Long arm left or right side exterior mirror. Interior mirror (in addition to standard). Windshield washers. Rear hydraulic telescopic shock absorbers. Power steering. Extra-duty springs (front: 1600 lb., rear: 3,000 lb.). Roof-mounted radio. Auxiliary taillamps. Heavy-duty battery. 11 in. clutch. Mechanical governor for use with rear drive shaft assembly. Fuel and vacuum pump. Radiator overflow tank.

HISTORICAL FOOTNOTES: The 1961 Dodge four-wheel drive trucks were introduced in October, 1960.

1962 POWER WAGON

The 1962 range of conventional four-wheel drive Dodge trucks had a revamped front grille with four chrome horizontal bars in place of the mesh-type insert used in 1961. Model identification was located in the grille center. Dodge lettering was positioned on the front fender just below the side character line. Power Wagon lettering was positioned just above the front wheel cutout. The WM300 fenders were now painted body color. They had previously been painted black regardless of body color. The W300 now used a premium heavy-duty version of Chrysler's 225 6-cyl. engine as its standard engine. It was fitted with a roller timing chain, bi-metal connecting rod bearings, heat-resistant Stellite-faced exhaust valves and valve stem seals. A premium heavy-duty 2-barrel 318 cu. in. V-8 was optional for the W300. It had a vibration damper, Roto-Caps valves, a roller timing chain and a one quart oil bath air cleaner.

1962 Dodge W200 Sweptline Power Wagon pickup

Standard cab equipment for the W100, 200 and 300 models included ashtray, dome light, woven fiber headlining with latex backing (Meadboard headlining on Town Wagon and Town Panel), embossed metal door panels, fiberboard door panels (Town Wagon and Town

Sedan), gray and black vinyl seat upholstery, cotton-sisal seat and seat back padding, rubber floor mat, driver's side sun visor, fully adjustable seat, concealed step, suspended clutch and brake pedals, pull-type exterior door handles, key locks in left and right side doors, safety door latches, exterior driver's side rearview mirror, dual, electric, single-speed windshield wipers (variable speed on Town Wagon and Town Panel), driver-adjustable handbrake lever, sound-deadener on cab floor and cowl sides, rustproofed body, hooded instrument cluster, deep-center steering wheel, dispatch box and high-level fresh air intake. Custom cab equipment that either replaced, or was in addition to standard cab features: Dual armrests, cigarette lighter, insulated dash liner, foam seat and seat back pads, roof insulation, under seat sound-deadener, insulated floor mat, bright-metal drip moldings (except for Town Wagon and Town Panel), chrome-plated grille, custom seat upholstery and custom cab emblem, except for Town Wagon. The Town Wagon was available only with custom cab equipment. The Town Panel was available only with standard cab equipment. The front parking/directional lights on the conventional models were now amber colored.

1962 Dodge W100 Town Wagon

I.D. DATA: The serial numbers were found on a plate located on the left door lock pillar. The first digit (2) indicated the 1962 model year. The second digit indicated either six or eight cylinder engine. The next entry identified the nominal weight rating (1-1/2 ton, 2-3/4 ton and 3 for 1 ton). The next entry was an L for light duty. Then followed the six production sequence numbers. The serial numbers on 6-cylinder engines were located on the left side of the block at the front, below the cylinder head. The V-8 serial number was found on the left front of the block. The first two letters (T and P) represented "Truck" and "P" series. The next two digits indicated engine size (the exception was the 318 engine which had a third digit identification). The next two digits indicated month and date of manufacture. The final four digits were the production sequence numbers.

Body Type	Factory Price	GVW	Shipping Weight	Prod. Total
Model S6-W100, 1/2 ton 6-cyl.				
Ch. & Cab, 114 in. wb.	$22558	5100*	3750	—
Pickup, Utiline, 114 in. wb.	$2673	5100	4060	—
Pickup, Sweptline, 114 in. wb.	$2687	5100	4160	—
Town Panel, 114 in. wb.	$3001	5100	4220	—
Town Wagon, 114 in. wb.	$3287	5100	4450	—

* 6000 lb. GVW optional.

Model S6-W100, V-8				
Town Wagon, 114 in. wb.	$3337	5100	4500	a

a Total model year production of all W100 trucks was 490 units with 6-cyl. engines and 297 with V-8 engines.

Model S6-W200, 3/4 ton, 6-cyl.				
Ch. & Cab, 122 in. wb.	$2613	6000*	3895	b
Pickup, Utiline, 122 in. wb.	$2728	6000	4245	—
Pickup, Sweptline, 122 in. wb.	$2742	6000	4375	—
Stake, 122 in. wb.	$2819	6000	4470	—
Platform, 122 in. wb.	$2767	6000	4270	—

* An 8000 lb. GVW package was optional for all models.
b Total model year production was 805 units with 6-cyl. engines and 375 with V-8 engines.

Model S6-W300, 1 ton, 6-cyl.				
Ch. & Cab, 133 in. wb.	$3431	8500*	4495	c
Pickup, Utiline, 133 in. wb.	$3566	8500	4895	—
Platform, 133 in. wb.	$3617	8500	5095	—
Stake, 133 in. wb.	$3681	8500	5395	—

* GVW packages up to 10,000 lb. were available.
c Total model year production was 221 units with 6-cyl. engines and 280 with V-8 engines.

Prices of the W100, W200 and W300 models with optional V-8 engine was an additional $120.00.

Model S6-WM300				
Ch. & Cowl, 126 in. wb.	$3124	8700	4095	—
Ch. & Cab, 126 in. wb.	$3642	8700*	4500	d
Pickup, 126 in. wb.	$3796	8700	4900	—

* 9500 lb. GVW package optional for all WM300 models.
d Total model year production was 2141 units.

STANDARD ENGINE: W100, W200: Engine Type: OHV, In-line 6-cylinder. Cast iron block and cylinder head. Bore x Stroke: 3.40 in. x 4.125 in. Lifters: Mechanical. Number of main bearings 4. Fuel Induction: Single barrel carburetor. Compression Ratio: 8.2:1. Displacement: 224.7 cu. in. (3.68 liters). Horsepower: 140 @ 3900 rpm. Torque: 215 lb.-ft. @ 1600-2800 rpm. Oil refill capacity: 5 qt. with filter change.

STANDARD ENGINE: W300: Engine Type: OHV, In-line 6-cylinder. Cast iron block and cylinder head. Bore x Stroke: 3.40 in. x 4.125 in. Lifters: Mechanical. Number of main bearings-5. Fuel Induction: Single barrel carburetor. Compression Ratio: 8.2:1. Displacement: 224.7 cu. in. (3.68 liters). Horsepower: 140 @ 3900 rpm. Torque: 215 lb.-ft. @ 1600-2800 rpm. Oil refill capacity: 5 qt. with filter change.

STANDARD ENGINE: WM300: Engine Type: L-head, In-line 6-cylinder. Cast iron block and cylinder head. Bore x Stroke: 3.437 in. x 4.50 in. Lifters: Mechanical. Number of main bearings-4. Fuel Induction: Stromberg single barrel downdraft carburetor. Compression Ratio: 7.1:1. Displacement: 250.6 cu. in. (4.10 liters). Horsepower: 125 @ 3600 rpm. Torque: 216 lb.-ft. @ 1600 rpm. Oil refill capacity: 5 qt. Fuel Requirements: Regular.

OPTIONAL ENGINE: W100, W200, W300: Engine Type: OHV, Power Giant V-8. Cast iron block and cylinder head. Bore x Stroke: 3.91 in. x 3.3120 in. Lifters: Hydraulic. Number of main bearings-5. Fuel Induction: Single barrel carburetor. Compression Ratio: 8.25:1. Displacement: 318.14 cu. in. (5.21 liters). Horsepower: 200 @ 3900 rpm. Torque: 286 lb.-ft. @ 2400 rpm. Oil refill capacity: 5 qt. Fuel Requirements: Regular.

OPTIONAL ENGINE: W300: Engine Type: "Rugged Duty", Power Giant OHV, V-8. Cast iron block and cylinder head. This engine has the "Normal Duty" 318 V-8 features plus roller-chain drive, vibration damper, positive exhaust valve rotators and hydraulic valve lifters. Bore x Stroke: 3.63 in. x 3.80 in. Lifters: Hydraulic. Number of main bearings-5. Fuel Induction: 2-barrel carburetor. Compression Ratio: 8.25:1. Displacement: 318.14 cu. in. (5.21 liters). Horsepower: 202 @ 3900 rpm. Torque: 288 lb.-ft. @ 2400 rpm. Oil refill capacity: 5 qt. Fuel Requirements: Regular.

W300M:

CHASSIS FEATURES: Separate body and double-drop frame; side rail reinforcements (inside type). Frame dimensions: 122.45875 in. x 0.109375 in. Frame rail dimensions: 6.09 in. x 2.04 in. x 0.171 in.

SUSPENSION AND RUNNING GEAR: Front Suspension: Eleven leaf, 39 in. x 1.75 in. semi-elliptical springs, heavy-duty, double-acting shock absorbers. Capacity: 1,150 lb. (each). Optional: 1600 lb. capacity, (included with winch). Rear Suspension: Fourteen leaf, 52.25 in. x 1.75 in. semi-elliptical springs. Capacity: 2,500 lb. (each). Optional: 3,000 lb. capacity. Front Axle Type and Capacity: Full-floating, Hypoid-type. Capacity: 3,750 lb. Rear Axle Type and Capacity: Full-floating, Hypoid-type. Capacity: 6,500 lb. Final Drive Ratio: 5.83:1. Transfer Case: Two-speed, double-lever. Ratios: 1.96:1, 1.00:1. Brakes: Hydraulic front and rear, centrifuse drums with cast iron braking surface. Dimensions: Front and rear: 14.125 in. x 1.75 in. Total lining area: 215.18 sq. in. Wheels: Five-stud ventilated disc. Tires: 9.00 x 16 8-ply. Optional: 9.00 x 16 10-ply. Steering: Worm and lever; 17.0 in. diameter steering wheel. Ratio: 23.2:1. Optional: None. Transmission: New Process #420, 4-speed "Synchro-shift" manual. Transmission Ratios: 6.68, 3.10, 1.69, 1.00:1. Reverse: 8.25:1. Clutch: Single plate, Oilite bronze pilot bearing, 11.0 in. dia. with lining area of 123.7 sq. in.

VEHICLE DIMENSIONS: Wheelbase: 126.0 in. Overall Length: Pickup: 199.0 in. (without winch); 208.625 in. (with winch); chassis and cab: 191.156 in. (without winch); 201.093 in. (with winch). Front/Rear Tread: 64.75 in./64.75 in. Overall Height: 76 in. (loaded). Width: 79.25 in. Front/Rear Overhang: 25.125 in./47.35 in. Tailgate: Width and Height: 54.0 in. x 19.9375 in. Ground Clearance: 8.8125 in.; with optional tires: 10.625 in. Load space: 96.0625 in. x 54.0 in. x 22.25 in.

CAPACITIES: Fuel Tank: 18 gal. Engine coolant system: 17 qt.

ACCOMMODATIONS: 3 passengers.

INSTRUMENTATION: Speedometer, odometer, gauges for oil pressure, fuel level, battery charge, engine coolant temperature.

W100 and W200:

CHASSIS FEATURES: Separate body and drop-center frame. Section modules: 3.43.

SUSPENSION AND RUNNING GEAR: Front Suspension: Semi-elliptical leaf springs. Capacity: 6-cyl.: 1, 100 lb. V-8: 1,350 lb. Optional: 6-cyl.: 1,350 lb. V-8: 1,550 lb. (both were standard with front-mounted winch). Rear Suspension: Semi-elliptical leaf springs. Capacity: W100: 1,350 lb. W200: 1,750 lb. Optional: W100: 1,750 lb. W200: 2,600 lb. Front Axle Type and Capacity: Full-floating, Hypoid-type. Capacity: 3,000 lb. Rear Axle Type and Capacity: W100: Semi-floating, Hypoid-type. Capacity: 4,500 lb. W200: Full-floating, Hypoid-type. Capacity: 5,500 lb. Final Drive Ratio: 4.1:1 or 4.88:1. Anti-slip differential available with 4.1:1 ratio. Transfer Case: Two-speed. Ratios: 1.96:1, 1.00:1. Brakes: Hydraulic front and rear. Dimensions: Front and rear: W100: 12.125 in. x 1.75 in. Total lining area: 199.88 sq. in. Wheels: Eight-stud ventilated disc. Tires: W100: 6.50 x 16 6-ply. W200: 7 x 17.5 6-ply, tubeless. Optional: W100: 7.00 x 16 6-ply, 7 x 17.5 6-ply. W200: 8 x 19.5 8-ply. Steering: Recirculating ball. Transmission: 3-speed heavy-duty A745 manual. Optional: New Process #420, 4-speed "Synchro-shift" manual. Transmission Ratios: 6.68, 3.10, 1.69, 1.00:1. Reverse: 8.25:1. Clutch: Single plate, dry disc, 11.0 in. dia. with lining area of 123.7 sq. in.

VEHICLE DIMENSIONS: Wheelbase: W100: 114 in., W200: 122 in. Overall Length: Town Wagon: 197 in. Chassis cab: 114 in. wheelbase models: 185.6562 in. 122 in. wheelbase models: 205.9375 in. Height: W100: 75.218 in. W200: 73.5 in. Front/Rear Tread: W100: 65.3125 in./63.3125 in. W200: 65.21875 in./63.3125 in. Load space: Town Panel: 65.25 in. x 50.125 in. x 52.75 in. Town Wagon: Center and rear seat removed: 94.06 in. x 50.125 in. x 52.75 in.; with rear seat only removed: 58.625 in. x 50.125 in. x 52.75 in. Capacity: Town Panel: 155 cu. ft. Seat Dimensions: Town Wagon: Driver's seat: 36.5 in., auxiliary folding passenger seat: 18 in.; center seat: 36.5 in., rear seat: 51 in.

CAPACITIES: Fuel Tank: 18 gal. Engine coolant system: 6-cyl.: 13.0 qt. V-8: 20.0 qt.

ACCOMMODATIONS: 3 passengers. Town Wagon: Up to eight passengers.

INSTRUMENTATION: Speedometer, odometer, gauges for fuel level, ammeter and engine coolant temperature.

W300:

CHASSIS FEATURES: Separate body and straight frame. Section modules: 5.70.

SUSPENSION AND RUNNING GEAR: Front Suspension: Semi-elliptical leaf springs. Capacity: 1,450 lb. Optional: 1,750 lb. (standard with front-mounted winch). Rear Suspension: Semi-elliptical leaf springs. Capacity: 2,450. Optional: 3,250, 4,050 lb. Front Axle Type and Capacity: Full-floating, Hypoid-type. Capacity: 4,500 lb. Rear Axle Type and Capacity: Full-floating, Hypoid-type. Capacity: 7,500 lb. Anti-slip differential optional. Final Drive Ratio: 4.88:1 or 5.87:1. Transfer Case: Two-speed, single lever. Ratios: 1.96:1, 1.00:1. Brakes: Hydraulic front and rear. Dimensions: Front: 14.125 in. x 1.75 in. Rear: 13 in. x 2.5 in. Total lining area: 241.98 sq. in. Wheels: Six-stud ventilated disc. Tires: 8 x 19.5 8-ply, tubeless. Optional: 9.00 x 16 10-ply. Steering: Worm and roller. Ratio: 29.0:1. Optional: Power assisted. Transmission: New Process #420, 4-speed "Synchro-shift" manual. Transmission Ratios: 6.68, 3.10, 1.69, 1.00:1. Reverse: 8.25:1. Clutch: Single plate, dry disc, 11.0 in. dia. with lining area of 123.7 sq. in.

VEHICLE DIMENSIONS: Wheelbase: 133 in. Overall Length: Chassis cab: 212.5 in. Width: 81.8125 in. Front/Rear tread: 62.5 in./64 in.

CAPACITIES: Fuel Tank: 18 gal. Engine coolant system: 6-cyl.: 20.0 qt. V-8: 24.0 qt.

ACCOMMODATIONS: 3 passengers.

INSTRUMENTATION: Speedometer, odometer, gauges for fuel level, ammeter and engine coolant temperature.

OPTIONS: W100, W200, W300: Chrome front bumper. Painted rear bumper. Chrome rear bumper. Painted bumper guards. Chrome bumper guards. Directional signals. Tinted glass. Dual electric horns. Horn ring. Cigarette lighter. Glove box lock. Interior rearview mirror. Grab handles. Wraparound rear window. Dual electric variable-speed electric windshield wipers. Windshield washer. Heater. Deluxe heater. Custom cab. 315 cu. in. V-8 engine. W300M: 60 amp-hr. battery. Pulley drive. Power winch. Pintle hook. Power take-off. Front end tow hooks. Brake booster, 7.5 in. diaphragm. Front bumper painted any standard truck color. Deluxe cab equipment. Directional signals. Drawbar. 40 amp generator. Fenders painted to match body color. Combined vacuum and fuel pump. Chrome grab handles. Tinted glass. Recirculating heater with defroster. Hydraulic jack with 3 ton capacity. Long arm left or right side exterior mirror. Interior mirror (in addition to standard). Windshield washers. Rear hydraulic telescopic shock absorbers. Power steering. Extra-duty springs (front: 1600 lb., rear: 3,000 lb.). Roof-mounted radio. Auxiliary taillamps. Heavy-duty battery. 11 in. clutch. Mechanical governor for use with rear drive shaft assembly. Fuel and vacuum pump. Radiator overflow tank.

HISTORICAL FOOTNOTES: The 1962 Dodge four-wheel drive trucks were introduced on September 28, 1961.

1962 Dodge WM300 Utiline

1963 POWER WAGON

No changes were made in the exterior appearance of the 1963 Power Wagons. Midway during the 1962 model year, Dodge had added a series of 6 passenger, crew cab models to its series of two-wheel drive models. This body style was offered in 1963 in the W200 line.

I.D. DATA: A new serial number coding system was introduced for 1963. The first two digits indicated the model code as follows: W100: 21; W200: 22; W300: 23; WM300: 24. The third digit indicated the number of cylinders. The last three digits were the production sequence number. The starting serial numbers were as follows: W100 (6-cyl.): 2161169185. W100 (V-8): 2181168067. W200 (6-cyl.): 2261173872. W200 (V-8): 2281175681. W300 (6-cyl.): 2361183710. W300 (V-8): 2381191367. WM300: 2461168692. The serial numbers on 6-cylinder OHV engines were located on the right side of the block on top of the boss directly behind the coil. The V-8 serial number was found on the left front of the block under the cylinder head. The L-head 6-cylinder engine serial number was found on the left front of block at the top. The first two letters indicated the series (TT, VT, AT, B, BT, C, CT). The next two digits indicated engine displacement. The third and fourth digits indicated month and date of manufacture.

Body Type	Factory Price	GVW	Shipping Weight	Prod. Total
Model T6-W100, 1/2 ton 6-cyl.				
Ch. & Cab, 114 in. wb.	$2571	5100*	3750	—
Pickup, Utiline, 114 in. wb.	$2686	5100	4060	—
Pickup, Sweptline, 114 in. wb.	$2700	5100	4160	—
Town Panel, 114 in. wb.	$3015	5100	4220	—
Town Wagon, 114 in. wb.	$3301	5100	4450	—

* 6000 lb. GVW optional.

Body Type	Factory Price	GVW	Shipping Weight	Prod. Total
Model T6-W100, V-8				
Town Wagon, 114 in. wb.	$3350	5100	4500	a

a Total model year production of all W100 trucks was 951 units with 6-cyl. engines and 445 with V-8 engines.

Model T6-W200, 3/4 ton, 6-cyl. (Crew cab models: 146 in. wheelbase)

Ch. & Cab, 122 in. wb.	$2626	6000*	3895	b
Pickup, Utiline, 122 in. wb.	$2741	6000	4245	—
Pickup, Sweptline, 122 in. wb.	$2755	6000	4375	—
Stake, 122 in. wb.	$2831	6000	4470	—
Platform, 122 in. wb.	$2779	6000	4270	—
Crew Cab, Ch.	$3149	6000	4259	—
Crew Cab, Utiline	$3256	6000	4569	—
Crew Cab, Sweptline	$3269	6000	4669	—

* An 8000 lb. GVW package was optional for all models.
b Total model year production, excluding crew cab models, was 2385 units with 6-cyl. engines and 764 with V-8 engines.

Model T6-W300, 1 ton, 6-cyl.

Ch. & Cab, 133 in. wb.	$3441	8500*	4495	c
Pickup, Utiline, 133 in. wb.	$3576	8500	4895	—
Platform, 133 in. wb.	$3626	8500	5095	—
Stake, 133 in. wb.	$3691	8500	5395	—

* GVW packages up to 10,000 lb. were available.
c Total model year production was 298 units with 6-cyl. engines and 335 with V-8 engines.

Prices of the W100, W200 and W300 models with optional V-8 engine was an additional $120.00.

Model T6-WM300

Ch. & Cowl, 126 in. wb.	$3140	8700*	4095	—
Ch. & Cab, 126 in. wb.	$3660	8700	4500	d
Pickup, 126 in. wb.	$3813	8700	4900	—

* 9500 lb. GVW package optional for all WM300 models.
d Total model year production was 3386 units.

STANDARD ENGINE: W100, W200: Engine Type: OHV, In-line 6-cylinder. Cast iron block and cylinder head. Bore x Stroke: 3.40 in. x 4.125 in. Lifters: Mechanical. Number of main bearings-4. Fuel Induction: Single barrel carburetor. Compression Ratio: 8.2:1. Displacement: 224.7 cu. in. (3.68 liters). Horsepower: 140 @ 3900 rpm. Torque: 215 lb.-ft. @ 1600-2800 rpm. Oil refill capacity: 5 qt. with filter change.

STANDARD ENGINE: W300: Engine Type: OHV, In-line 6-cylinder. Cast iron block and cylinder head. Bore x Stroke: 3.40 in. x 4.125 in. Lifters: Mechanical. Number of main bearings-4. Fuel Induction: Single barrel carburetor. Compression Ratio: 8.2:1. Displacement: 224.7 cu. in. (3.68 liters). Horsepower: 140 @ 3900 rpm. Torque: 215 lb.-ft. @ 1600-2800 rpm. Oil refill capacity: 5 qt. with filter change.

STANDARD ENGINE: WM300: Engine Type: L-head, In-line 6-cylinder. Cast iron block and cylinder head. Bore x Stroke: 3.437 in. x 4.50 in. Lifters: Mechanical. Number of main bearings-4. Fuel Induction: Stromberg single barrel downdraft carburetor. Compression Ratio: 7.1:1. Displacement: 250.6 cu. in. (4.10 liters). Horsepower: 125 @ 3600 rpm. Torque: 216 lb.-ft. @ 1600 rpm. Oil refill capacity: 5 qt. Fuel Requirements: Regular.

OPTIONAL ENGINE: W100, W200, W300: Engine Type: OHV, Power Giant V-8. Cast iron block and cylinder head. Bore x Stroke: 3.91 in. x 3.3120 in. Lifters: Hydraulic. Number of main bearings-5. Fuel Induction: SIngle barrel carburetor. Compression Ratio: 8.25:1. Displacement: 318.14 cu. in. (5.21 liters). Horsepower: 200 @ 3900 rpm. Torque: 286 lb.-ft. @ 2400 rpm. Oil refill capacity: 5 qt. Fuel Requirements: Regular.

OPTIONAL ENGINE: W300: Engine Type: "Rugged Duty", Power Giant OHV, V-8. Cast iron block and cylinder head. This engine has the "Normal Duty" 318 V-8 features plus roller-chain drive, vibration damper, positive exhaust valve rotators and hydraulic valve lifters. Bore x Stroke: 3.63 in. x 3.80 in. Lifters: Hydraulic. Number of main bearings-5. Fuel Induction: 2-barrel carburetor. Compression Ratio: 8.25:1. Displacement: 318.14 cu. in. (5.21 liters). Horsepower: 202 @ 3900 rpm. Torque: 288 lb.-ft. @ 2400 rpm. Oil refill capacity: 5 qt. Fuel Requirements: Regular.

W300M:

CHASSIS FEATURES: Separate body and double-drop frame; side rail reinforcements (inside type). Frame dimensions: 122.45875 in. x 0.109375 in. Frame rail dimensions: 6.09 in. x 2.04 in. x 0.171 in.

SUSPENSION AND RUNNING GEAR: Front Suspension: Eleven leaf, 39 in. x 1.75 in. semi-elliptical springs, heavy-duty, double-acting shock absorbers. Capacity: 1,150 lb. (each). Optional: 1600 lb. capacity, (included with winch). Rear Suspension: Fourteen leaf, 52.25 in. x 1.75 in. semi-elliptical springs. Capacity: 2,500 lb. (each). Optional: 3,000 lb. capacity. Front Axle Type and Capacity: Full-floating, Hypoid-type. Capacity: 3,750 lb. Rear Axle Type and Capacity: Full-floating, Hypoid-type. Capacity: 6,500 lb. Final Drive Ratio: 5.83:1. Transfer Case: Two-speed, double-lever. Ratios: 1.96:1, 1.00:1. Brakes: Hydraulic front and rear, centrifuse drums with cast iron braking surface. Dimensions: Front and rear: 14.125 in. x 1.75 in. Total lining area: 215.18 sq. in. Wheels: Five-stud ventilated disc. Tires: 9.00 x 16 8-ply. Optional: 9.00 x 16 10-ply. Steering: Worm and lever; 17.0 in. diameter steering wheel. Ratio: 23.2:1. Optional: None. Transmission: New Process #420, 4-speed "Synchro-shift" manual. Transmission Ratios: 6.68, 3.10, 1.69, 1.00:1. Reverse: 8.25:1. Clutch: Single plate, Oilite bronze pilot bearing, 11.0 in. dia. with lining area of 123.7 sq. in.

VEHICLE DIMENSIONS: Wheelbase: 126.0 in. Overall Length: Pickup: 199.0 in. (without winch); 208.625 in. (with winch); chassis and cab: 191.156 in. (without winch); 201.093 in. (with winch). Front/Rear Tread: 64.75 in./64.75 in. Overall Height: 76 in. (loaded). Width: 79.25 in. Front/Rear Overhang: 25.125 in./47.35 in. Tailgate: Width and Height: 54.0 in. x 19.9375 in. Ground Clearance: 8.8125 in.; with optional tires: 10.625 in. Load space: 96.0625 in. x 54.0 in. x 22.25 in.

CAPACITIES: Fuel Tank: 18 gal. Engine coolant system: 17 qt.

ACCOMMODATIONS: 3 passengers.

INSTRUMENTATION: Speedometer, odometer, gauges for oil pressure, fuel level, battery charge, engine coolant temperature.

W100 and W200:

CHASSIS FEATURES: Separate body and drop-center frame. Section modules: 3.43.

SUSPENSION AND RUNNING GEAR: Front Suspension: Semi-elliptical leaf springs. Capacity: 6-cyl.: 1,100 lb. V-8: 1,350 lb. Optional: 6-cyl.: 1,350 lb. V-8: 1,550 lb. (both were standard with front-mounted winch). Rear Suspension: Semi-elliptical leaf springs. Capacity: W100: 1,350 lb. W200: 1,750 lb. Optional: W100: 1,750 lb. W200: 2,600 lb. Front Axle Type and Capacity: Full-floating, Hypoid-type. Capacity: 3,000 lb. Rear Axle Type and Capacity: W100: Semi-floating, Hypoid-type. Capacity: 4,500 lb. W200: Full-floating, Hypoid-type. Capacity: 5,500 lb. Final Drive Ratio: 4.1:1 or 4.88:1. Anti-slip differential available with 4.1:1 ratio. Transfer Case: Two-speed. Ratios: 1.96:1, 1.00:1. Brakes: Hydraulic front and rear. Dimensions: Front and rear: W100: 12.125 in. x 1.75 in. Total lining area: 199.88 sq. in. Wheels: Eight-stud ventilated disc. Tires: W100: 6.50 x 16 6-ply. W200: 7 x 17.5 6-ply, tubeless. Optional: W100: 7.00 x 16 6-ply, 7 x 17.5 6-ply. W200: 8 x 19.5 8-ply. Steering: Recirculating ball. Transmission: 3-speed heavy-duty A745 manual. Optional: New Process #420, 4-speed "Synchro-shift" manual. Transmission Ratios: 6.68, 3.10, 1.69, 1.00:1. Reverse: 8.25:1. Clutch: Single plate, dry disc, 11.0 in. dia. with lining area of 123.7 sq. in.

VEHICLE DIMENSIONS: Wheelbase: W100: 114 in., W200: 122 in. Overall Length: Town Wagon: 197 in. Chassis cab: 114 in. wheelbase models: 185.6562 in. 122 in. wheelbase models: 205.9375 in. Height: W100: 75.218 in. W200: 73.5 in. Front/Rear tread: W100: 65.3125 in./63.3125 in. W200: 65.21875 in./63.3125 in. Load space: Town Panel: 65.25 in. x 50.125 in. x 52.75 in. Town Wagon: Center and rear seat removed: 94.06 in. x 50.125 in. x 52.75 in.; with rear seat only removed: 58.625 in. x 50.125 in. x 52.75 in. Capacity: Town Panel: 155 cu. ft. Seat Dimensions: Town Wagon: Driver's seat: 36.5 in., auxiliary folding passenger seat: 18 in., center seat: 36.5 in., rear seat: 51 in.

CAPACITIES: Fuel Tank: 18 gal. Engine coolant system: 6-cyl.: 13.0 qt. V-8: 20.0 qt.

ACCOMMODATIONS: 3 passengers. Town Wagon: Up to eight passengers.

INSTRUMENTATION: Speedometer, odometer, gauges for fuel level, ammeter and engine coolant temperature.

W300:

CHASSIS FEATURES: Separate body and straight frame. Section modules: 5.70.

SUSPENSION AND RUNNING GEAR: Front Suspension: Semi-elliptical leaf springs. Capacity: 1,450 lb. Optional: 1,750 lb. (standard with front-mounted winch). Rear Suspension: Semi-elliptical leaf springs. Capacity: 2,450. Optional: 3,250, 4,050 lb. Front Axle Type and Capacity: Full-floating, Hypoid-type. Capacity: 4,500 lb. Rear Axle Type and Capacity: Full-floating, Hypoid-type. Capacity: 7,500 lb. Anti-slip differential optional. Final Drive Ratio: 4.88:1 or 5.87:1. Transfer Case: Two-speed, single lever. Ratios: 1.96:1, 1.00:1. Brakes: Hydraulic front and rear. Dimensions: Front: 14.125 in. x 1.75 in. Rear: 13 in. x 2.5 in. Total lining area: 241.98 sq. in. Wheels: Six-stud ventilated disc. Tires: 8 x 19.5 8-ply, tubeless. Optional: 9.00 x 16 10-ply. Steering: Worm and roller. Ratio: 29.0:1. Optional: Power assisted. Transmission: New Process #420, 4-speed "Synchro-shift" manual. Transmission Ratios: 6.68, 3.10, 1.69, 1.00:1. Reverse: 8.25:1. Clutch: Single plate, dry disc, 11.0 in. dia. with lining area of 123.7 sq. in.

VEHICLE DIMENSIONS: Wheelbase: 133 in. Overall Length: Chassis cab: 212.5 in. Width: 81.8125 in. Front/Rear tread: 62.5 in./64 in.

CAPACITIES: Fuel Tank: 18 gal. Engine coolant system: 6-cyl.: 20.0 qt. V-8: 24.0 qt.

ACCOMMODATIONS: 3 passengers.

INSTRUMENTATION: Speedometer, odometer, gauges for fuel level, ammeter and engine coolant temperature.

OPTIONS: W100, W200, W300: Chrome front bumper. Painted rear bumper. Chrome rear bumper. Painted bumper guards. Chrome bumper guards. Directional signals. Tinted glass. Dual electric horns. Horn ring. Cigarette lighter. Glove box lock. Interior rearview mirror. Grab handles. Wraparound rear window. Dual electric variable-speed electric windshield wipers. Windshield washer. Heater. Deluxe heater. Custom cab. 315 cu. in. V-8 engine. W300M: 60 amp-hr. battery. Pulley drive. Power winch. Pintle hook. Power take-off. Front end tow hooks. Brake booster, 7.5 in. diaphragm. Front bumper painted any standard truck color. Deluxe cab equipment. Directional signals. Drawbar. 40 amp generator. Fenders painted to match body color. Combined vacuum and fuel pump. Chrome grab handles. Tinted glass. Recirculating heater with defroster. Hydraulic jack with 3 ton capacity. Long arm left or right side exterior mirror. Interior mirror (in addition to standard). Windshield washers. Rear hydraulic telescopic shock absorbers. Power steering. Extra-duty springs (front: 1600 lb., rear: 3,000 lb.). Roof-mounted radio. Auxiliary taillamps. Heavy-duty battery. 11 in. clutch. Mechanical governor for use with rear drive shaft assembly. Fuel and vacuum pump. Radiator overflow tank.

HISTORICAL FOOTNOTES: The 1963 Dodge four-wheel drive trucks were introduced in October, 1962.

1964 POWER WAGON

No changes were made in the exterior appearance of the 1964 Power Wagons. A new Custom Sports Package was available for the W100 and W200 Utiline and Sweptline pickups. It included bucket seats upholstered in black vinyl, carpeted floor area from the firewall to the top of the fuel tank behind the seat, dual armrests, a center console with cigarette lighter and map light, four hood stripes, chrome front bumper and grille, chrome hub caps, whitewall tires, twin sun visors, insulated headliner and added cab insulation.

1964 Dodge W200 Sweptline crew cab Power Wagon pickup

I.D. DATA: The first two digits of the serial number indicated the model code as follows: W100: 21; W200: 22; W300: 23; WM300: 24. The third digit indicated the number of cylinders. The last three digits were the production sequence number. The starting serial numbers were as follows: W100 (6-cyl.): 2161169185. W100 (V-8): 2181178067. W200 (6-cyl.): 2261191887. W200 (V-8): 2281175681. W300 (6-cyl.): 2361254254. W300 (V-8): 2381232619. WM300:

2461168692. The serial numbers on 6-cylinder OHV engines were located on the right side of the block on top of the boss directly behind the coil. The V-8 serial number was found on the left front of the block under the cylinder head. The L-head 6-cylinder engine serial number was found on the left front of the block at the top. The first two letters indicated the series. The next two digits indicated engine displacement. The third and fourth digits indicated month and date of manufacture.

Body Type	Factory Price	GVW	Shipping Weight	Prod. Total
Model V6-W100, 1/2 ton 6-cyl.				
Ch. & Cab, 114 in. wb.	$2571	5100*	3750	—
Pickup, Utiline, 114 in. wb.	$2686	5100	4060	—
Pickup, Sweptline, 114 in. wb.	$2700	5100	4160	—
Town Panel, 114 in. wb.	$3015	5100	4220	—
Town Wagon, 114 in. wb.	$3301	5100	4450	—

* 6000 lb. GVW optional.

Model V6-W100, V-8				
Town Wagon, 114 in. wb.	$3350	5100	4500	a

a Total model year production of all W100 trucks was 955 units with 6-cyl. engines and 504 with V-8 engines.

Model V6-W200, 3/4 ton, 6-cyl. Crew cab wheelbase: 146 in.				
Ch. & Cab, 122 in. wb.	$2625	6000*	3895	b
Pickup, Utiline, 122 in. wb.	$2741	6000	4245	—
Pickup, Sweptline, 122 in. wb.	$2755	6000	4375	—
Stake, 122 in. wb.	$2831	6000	4470	—
Platform, 122 in. wb.	$2779	6000	4270	—
Crew Cab, Ch.	$3399	6000	4335	—
Crew Cab, Utiline	$3514	6000	4745	—
Crew Cab, Sweptline	$3528	6000	4745	—

* An 8000 lb. GVW package was optional for all models.

b Total model year production, excluding crew cab models, was 2385 units with 6-cyl. engines and 764 with V-8 engines.

Model V6-W300, 1 ton, 6-cyl.				
Ch. & Cowl, 133 in. wb.	$2943	8500	4090	—
Ch. & Cab, 133 in. wb.	$3441	8500*	4495	c
Pickup, Utiline, 133 in. wb.	$3576	8500	4895	—
Platform, 133 in. wb.	$3626	8500	5095	—
Stake, 133 in. wb.	$3691	8500	5395	—

* GVW packages up to 10,000 lb. were available.

c Total model year production was 298 units with 6-cyl. engines and 335 with V-8 engines.

Prices of the W100, W200 and W300 models with optional V-8 engine was an additional $120.00.

Model V6-WM300				
Ch. & Cowl, 126 in. wb.	$3140	8700	4095	—
Ch. & Cab, 126 in. wb.	$3660	8700*	4500	d
Pickup, 126 in. wb.	$3813	8700	4900	—

* 9500 lb. GVW package optional for all WM300 models.

d Total model year production was 3386 units.

STANDARD ENGINE: W100, W200: Engine Type: OHV, In-line 6-cylinder. Cast iron block and cylinder head. Bore x Stroke: 3.40 in. x 4.125 in. Lifters: Mechanical. Number of main bearings-4. Fuel Induction: Single barrel carburetor. Compression Ratio: 8.2:1. Displacement: 224.7 cu. in. (3.68 liters). Horsepower: 140 @ 3900 rpm. Torque: 215 lb.-ft. @ 1600-2800 rpm. Oil refill capacity: 5 qt. with filter change.

STANDARD ENGINE: W300: Engine Type: OHV, In-line 6-cylinder. Cast iron block and cylinder head. Bore x Stroke: 3.40 in. x 4.125 in. Lifters: Mechanical. Number of main bearings-4. Fuel Induction: Single barrel carburetor. Compression Ratio: 8.2:1. Displacement: 224.7 cu. in. (3.68 liters). Horsepower: 140 @ 3900 rpm. Torque: 215 lb.-ft. @ 1600-2800 rpm. Oil refill capacity: 5 qt. with filter change.

STANDARD ENGINE: WM300: Engine Type: L-head, In-line 6-cylinder. Cast iron block and cylinder head. Bore x Stroke: 3.437 in. x 4.50 in. Lifters: Mechanical. Number of main bearings-4. Fuel Induction: Stromberg single barrel downdraft carburetor. Compression Ratio: 7.1:1. Displacement: 250.6 cu. in. (4.10 liters). Horsepower: 125 @ 3600 rpm. Torque: 216 lb.-ft. @ 1600 rpm. Oil refill capacity: 5 qt. Fuel Requirements: Regular.

OPTIONAL ENGINE: W100, W200, W300: Engine Type: OHV, Power Giant V-8. Cast iron block and cylinder head. Bore x Stroke: 3.91 in. x 3.3120 in. Lifters: Hydraulic. Number of main bearings-5. Fuel Induction: SIngle barrel carburetor. Compression Ratio: 8.25:1. Displacement: 318.14 cu. in. (5.21 liters). Horsepower: 200 @ 3900 rpm. Torque: 286 lb.-ft. @ 2400 rpm. Oil refill capacity: 5 qt. Fuel Requirements: Regular.

OPTIONAL ENGINE: W300: Engine Type: "Rugged Duty", Power Giant OHV, V-8. Cast iron block and cylinder head. This engine has the "Normal Duty" 318 V-8 features plus roller-chain drive, vibration damper, positive exhaust valve rotators and hydraulic valve lifters. Bore x Stroke: 3.63 in. x 3.80 in. Lifters: Hydraulic. Number of main bearings-5. Fuel Induction: 2-barrel carburetor. Compression Ratio: 8.25:1. Displacement: 318.14 cu. in. (5.21 liters). Horsepower: 202 @ 3900 rpm. Torque: 288 lb.-ft. @ 2400 rpm. Oil refill capacity: 5 qt. Fuel Requirements: Regular.

W300M:

CHASSIS FEATURES: Separate body and double-drop frame; side rail reinforcements (inside type). Frame dimensions: 122.45875 in. x 0.109375 in. Frame rail dimensions: 6.09 in. x 2.04 in. x 0.171 in.

SUSPENSION AND RUNNING GEAR: Front Suspension: Eleven leaf, 39 in. x 1.75 in. semi-elliptical springs, heavy-duty, double-acting shock absorbers. Capacity: 1,150 lb. (each). Optional: 1600 lb. capacity, (included with winch). Rear Suspension: Fourteen leaf, 52.25 in. x 1.75 in. semi-elliptical springs. Capacity: 2,500 lb. (each). Optional: 3,000 lb. capacity. Front Axle Type and Capacity: Full-floating, Hypoid-type. Capacity: 3,750 lb. Rear Axle Type and Capacity: Full-floating, Hypoid-type. Capacity: 6,500 lb. Final Drive Ratio: 5.83:1. Transfer Case: Two-speed, double-lever. Ratios: 1.96:1, 1.00:1. Brakes: Hydraulic front and rear. Dimensions: Front and rear: 14.125 in. x 1.75 in. Total lining area: 215.18 sq. in. Wheels: Five-stud ventilated disc. Tires: 9.00 x 16 8-ply. Optional: 9.00 x 16 10-ply. Steering: Worm and lever; 17.0 in. diameter steering wheel. Ratio: 23.2:1. Optional: None. Transmission: New Process #420, 4-speed "Synchro-shift" manual. Transmission Ratios: 6.68, 3.10, 1.69, 1.00:1. Reverse: 8.25:1. Clutch: Single plate, Oilite bronze pilot bearing, 11.0 in. dia. with lining area of 123.7 sq. in.

VEHICLE DIMENSIONS: Wheelbase: 126.0 in. Overall Length: Pickup: 199.0 in. (without winch); 208.625 in. (with winch); chassis and cab: 191.156 in. (without winch); 201.093 in. (with winch). Front/Rear Tread: 64.75 in./64.75 in. Overall Height: 76 in. (loaded). Width: 79.25 in. Front/Rear Overhang: 25.125 in./47.35 in. Tailgate: Width and Height: 54.0 in. x 19.9375 in. Ground Clearance: 8.8125 in.; with optional tires: 10.625 in. Load space: 96.0625 in. x 54.0 in. x 22.25 in.

CAPACITIES: Fuel Tank: 18 gal. Engine coolant system: 17 qt.

ACCOMMODATIONS: 3 passengers.

INSTRUMENTATION: Speedometer, odometer, gauges for oil pressure, fuel level, battery charge, engine coolant temperature.

W100 and W200:

CHASSIS FEATURES: Separate body and drop-center frame. Dimension: 6.12 in. x 2.30 in. x 0.188 in. Section modules: 3.43. W200 crew cab: 6.25 in. x 2.42 in. x 0.250 in. Section modules: 4.70.

SUSPENSION AND RUNNING GEAR: Front Suspension: Semi-elliptical leaf springs. Capacity: 6-cyl.: 1, 100 lb. V-8: 1,350 lb. W200 crew cab: 1,550 lb. Optional: 6-cyl.: 1,350 lb. V-8: 1,550 lb. (both were standard with front-mounted winch). Rear Suspension: Semi-elliptical leaf springs. Capacity: W100: 1,350 lb. W200: 1,750 lb. Optional: W100: 1,750 lb. W200: 2,600 lb. Front Axle Type and Capacity: Full-floating, Hypoid-type. Capacity: 3,000 lb. W200 Crew cab: 3,500 lb. Rear Axle Type and Capacity: W100: Semi-floating, Hypoid-type. Capacity: 4,500 lb. W200: Full-floating, Hypoid-type. Capacity: 5,500 lb. Final Drive Ratio: 4.1:1 or 4.88:1. Anti-slip differential available with 4.1:1 ratio. Transfer Case: Two-speed. Ratios: 1.96:1, 1.00:1. Brakes: Hydraulic front and rear. Dimensions: Front and rear: 12.125 in. x 1.75 in. Total lining area: 199.88 sq. in. Wheels: Eight-stud ventilated disc. Tires: W100: 6.50 x 16 6-ply. W200: 7 x 17.5 6-ply, tubeless. Optional: W100: 7.00 x 16 6-ply, 7 x 17.5 6-ply. W200: 8 x 19.5 8-ply. Steering: Recirculating ball. Transmission: 3-speed heavy-duty A745 manual. Optional: New Process #420, 4-speed "Synchro-shift" manual. Transmission Ratios: 6.68, 3.10, 1.69, 1.00:1. Reverse: 8.25:1. Clutch: Single plate, dry disc, 11.0 in. dia. with lining area of 123.7 sq. in.

VEHICLE DIMENSIONS: Wheelbase: W100: 114 in., W200: 122 in. Overall Length: Town Wagon: 197 in. Chassis cab: 114 in. wheelbase models: 185.6562 in. 122 in. wheelbase models: 205.9375 in. Height: W100: 75.218 in. W200: 73.5 in. Front/Rear tread: W100: 65.3125 in./63.3125 in. W200: 65.21875 in./63.3125 in. Load space: Town Panel: 65.25 in. x 50.125 in. x 52.75 in. Town Wagon: Center and rear seat removed: 94.06 in. x 50.125 in. x 52.75 in.; with rear seat only removed: 58.625 in. x 50.125 in. x 52.75 in. Capacity: Town Panel: 155 cu. ft. Seat Dimensions: Town Wagon: Driver's seat: 36.5 in., auxiliary folding passenger seat: 18 in., center seat: 36.5 in., rear seat: 51 in.

CAPACITIES: Fuel Tank: 18 gal. Engine coolant system: 6-cyl.: 13.0 qt. V-8: 20.0 qt.

ACCOMMODATIONS: 3 passengers. Town Wagon: Up to eight passengers.

INSTRUMENTATION: Speedometer, odometer, gauges for fuel level, ammeter and engine coolant temperature.

W300:

CHASSIS FEATURES: Separate body and straight frame. Dimensions: 7.25 in. x 2.75 in. x 0.2318 in. Section modules: 5.70.

SUSPENSION AND RUNNING GEAR: Front Suspension: Semi-elliptical leaf springs. Capacity: 1,450 lb. Optional: 1,750 lb. (standard with front-mounted winch). Rear Suspension: Semi-elliptical leaf springs. Capacity: 2,450. Optional: 3,250, 4,050 lb. Front Axle Type and Capacity: Full-floating, Hypoid-type. Capacity: 4,500 lb. Rear Axle Type and Capacity: Full-floating, Hypoid-type. Capacity: 7,500 lb. Anti-slip differential optional. Final Drive Ratio: 4.88:1 or 5.87:1. Transfer Case: Two-speed, single lever. Ratios: 1.96:1, 1.00:1. Brakes: Hydraulic front and rear. Dimensions: Front: 14.125 in. x 1.75 in. Rear: 13 in. x 2.5 in. Total lining area: 241.98 sq. in. Wheels: Six-stud ventilated disc. Tires: 8 x 19.5 8-ply, tubeless. Optional: 9.00 x 16 10-ply. Steering: Worm and roller. Ratio: 29.0:1. Optional: Power assisted. Transmission: New Process #420, 4-speed "Synchro-shift" manual. Transmission Ratios: 6.68, 3.10, 1.69, 1.00:1. Reverse: 8.25:1. Clutch: Single plate, dry disc, 11.0 in. dia. with lining area of 123.7 sq. in. 318 Premium V-8: 12 in. dia.; 150 sq. in. lining area.

VEHICLE DIMENSIONS: Wheelbase: 133 in. Overall Length: Chassis cab: 212.5 in. Width: 81.8125 in. Front/Rear tread: 62.5 in./64 in.

CAPACITIES: Fuel Tank: 18 gal. Engine coolant system: 6-cyl.: 20.0 qt. V-8: 24.0 qt.

ACCOMMODATIONS: 3 passengers.

INSTRUMENTATION: Speedometer, odometer, gauges for fuel level, ammeter and engine coolant temperature.

OPTIONS: W100, W200, W300: Chrome front bumper. Painted rear bumper. Chrome rear bumper. Painted bumper guards. Chrome bumper guards. Directional signals. Tinted glass. Dual electric horns. Horn ring. Cigarette lighter. Glove box lock. Interior rearview mirror. Grab handles. Wraparound rear window. Dual electric variable-speed electric windshield wipers. Windshield washer. Heater. Deluxe heater. Custom cab. 318 cu. in. V-8 engine. W300M: 60 amp-hr. battery. Pulley drive. Power winch. Pintle hook. Power take-off. Front end tow hooks. Brake booster, 7.5 in. diaphragm. Front bumper painted any standard truck color. Deluxe cab equipment. Directional signals. Drawbar. 40 amp generator. Fenders painted to match body color. Combined vacuum and fuel pump. Chrome grab handles. Tinted glass. Recirculating heater with defroster. Hydraulic jack with 3 ton capacity. Long arm left or right side exterior mirror. Interior mirror (in addition to standard). Windshield washers. Rear hydraulic telescopic shock absorbers. Power steering. Extra-duty springs (front: 1600 lb., rear: 3,000 lb.). Roof-mounted radio. Auxiliary taillamps. Heavy-duty battery. 11 in. clutch. Mechanical governor for use with rear drive shaft assembly. Fuel and vacuum pump. Radiator overflow tank.

HISTORICAL FOOTNOTES: The 1964 Dodge four-wheel drive trucks were introduced in October, 1963.

1965 POWER WAGON

At the start of the 1965 model year, the four-wheel drive Dodge trucks were unchanged in appearance from the 1964 models. In early 1965 revised styling was introduced for the W100, W200 and W300 models. These models were identified by a grille with three vertical dividers and four horizontal bars. The headlights (no longer dual) were now positioned in large circular shells. The amber directional/parking lights were positioned in the grille close to the headlights. Sweptline models were available with a full-length bright-metal body side molding with an insert of white or black paint. The series identification was now located on the front fenders just behind the wheel cutout. The tailgate on Sweptline models was redesigned and could be operated by one hand. The taillights were of a thin, vertical shape. The W200 chassis now had a 128 in. wheelbase.

Standard equipment for the W100, 200 and 300 models now included directional lights. Additional standard features included an engine oil filter, 35 amp alternator, self-adjusting brakes, painted front bumper, dual painted exterior mirrors, 6-way adjustable seat, variable-speed electric windshield wipers with non-glare arms and blades, and windshield washers. Prices for the second series of 1965 models were unchanged from those listed for the initial models. The standard pickup cab was equipped with a bench seat finished in a black and white vinyl upholstery, driver's side sun visor, dome light, ashtray, dispatch box, key lock on both doors, coat hook, rubber floor mat, high-level ventilation, and an adjustable Orscheln-lever hand brake. The optional Comfort Package added these items, or replaced items to the standard cab: A full-length foam rubber seat and foam-padded seat back, fabric and vinyl seat upholstery, driver's armrest, right side sun visor, cigarette lighter, and extra cab insulation. The fabric seat insert was available in red, beige, or dark green, depending on truck exterior color. The optional Appearance Package was a dress-up package with both interior and exterior elements. The exterior items included a chrome grille, bright drip moldings, Mylar trim for the windshield and rear window, "Custom" nameplates and delta emblems on the cab. The interior features consisted of a bright metal "face" for the instrument cluster and around the control knobs, a bright-finish dashboard molding, and textured metal trimpanels on the doors. The Custom Sports Special option was available for the W100 and W200 models in Sweptline, Utiline, Stake, or chassis cab form. Its features consisted of black bucket seats with seat belts, fully-carpeted cab floor, center console with cigarette lighter, ashtray, map light and storage compartment; chrome grille, front bumper and roof moldings; racing stripes on roof and hood, bright instrument panel, Mylar trim around windshield and rear window, custom nameplates and delta emblems on cab, and dual armrests and sun visors.

The W200 was available as a Camper Special model with the following components: 59 amp alternator, 70 amp-hr. battery, power brakes, additional engine cooling capacity, oil pressure gauge, dual, Western-style, bright-finish mirrors, front springs rated at 1550 lbs., rear springs rated at 2600 lbs., 7.50 x 16, 8-ply-rated tires, 16 x 5.50 in. wheels and "Camper Special" exterior emblems. A Deluxe Camper Package included these additional items: Comfort Package, custom Fresh-Air heater-defroster, traffic hazard warning lights and dual electric horns. The Sweptline W200 outfitted with the Camper Package was also available with the Custom Camper Package which included the Deluxe Camper Package plus the Appearance Package and exterior side moldings.

I.D. DATA: The first two digits of the serial number indicated the model code as follows: W100: 21; W200: 22; W300: 23; WM300: 24. The third digit indicated the number of cylinders. The last three digits were the production sequence number. The starting serial numbers for the A6 series were as follows: W100 (6-cyl.): 2161492000. W100 (V-8): 2181492000. W200 (6-cyl.): 2261492000. W200 (V-8): 2281492000. W300 (6-cyl.): 23611492000. W300 (V-8): 23811492000. WM300: 2461328341. The starting serial numbers for the V6 models that were initially produced for the 1965 model year were as follows: W100 (6-cyl.): 2161328341. W100 (V-8): 2181328341. W200 (6-cyl.): 2261328341. W200 (V-8): 2281328341. W300 (6-cyl.): 2361328341. W300 (V-8): 2381328341. The serial numbers on 6-cylinder OHV engines were located on the right side of the block on top of the boss directly behind the coil. The V-8 serial number was found on the left front of the block under the cylinder head. The L-head 6-cylinder engine serial number was found on the left front of the block at the top. The first two letters indicated the series (TT, VT, AT, B, BT, C, CT). The next two digits indicated engine displacement. The third and fourth digits indicated month and date of manufacture.

Body Type	Factory Price	GVW	Shipping Weight	Prod. Total
Model A6-W100, 1/2 ton 6-cyl.				
Ch. & Cab, 114 in. wb.	$2597	5100*	3750	—
Pickup, Utiline, 114 in. wb.	$2712	5100	4060	—
Pickup, Sweptline, 114 in. wb.	$2726	5100	4160	—
Town Panel, 114 in. wb.	$3037	5100	4220	—
Town Wagon, 114 in. wb.	$3323	5100	4450	—

* 6000 lb. GVW optional.

Model V6-W100, V-8				
Town Wagon, 114 in. wb.	$3373	5100	4500	a

a Total model year production of all W100 trucks was 843 units with 6-cyl. engines and 631 with V-8 engines.

Model A6-W200, 3/4 ton, 6-cyl. (Crew cab-146 in. wheelbase)				
Ch. & Cab, 128 in. wb.	$2652	6000*	3945	b
Pickup, Utiline, 128 in. wb.	$2767	6000	4385	—
Pickup, Sweptline, 128 in. wb.	$2781	6000	4475	—
Stake, 128 in. wb.	$2857	6000	4520	—
Platform, 128 in. wb.	$2805	6000	4320	—
Crew Cab, Ch.	$3424	6000	4385	—
Crew Cab, Utiline	$3539	6000	4745	—
Crew Cab, Sweptline	$3553	6000	4795	—

* An 8000 lb. GVW package was optional for all models.

b Total model year production, excluding crew cab models, was 607 units with 6-cyl. engines and 759 with V-8 engines. Production of the early 1965 model year 122 in. wheelbase models totalled 776 (6-cyl.) and 550 (V-8).

Model A6-W300, 1 ton, 6-cyl.				
Ch. & Cab, 133 in. wb.	$3466	8500*	4495	c
Pickup, Utiline, 133 in. wb.	$3602	8500	4895	—
Platform, 133 in. wb.	$3652	8500	5095	—
Stake, 133 in. wb.	$3717	8500	5395	—

* GVW packages up to 10,000 lb. were available.

c Total model year production was 223 units with 6-cyl. engines and 573 with V-8 engines.

Prices of the W100, W200 and W300 models with optional V-8 engine was an additional $120.00.

Model A6-WM300				
Ch. & Cowl, 126 in. wb.	$3154	8700	4095	—
Ch. & Cab, 126 in. wb.	$3685	8700*	4500	d
Pickup, 126 in. wb.	$3839	8700	4940	—

* 9500 lb. GVW package optional for all WM300 models.

d Total model year production was 2397 units.

STANDARD ENGINE: W100, W200: Engine Type: OHV, In-line 6-cylinder. Cast iron block and cylinder head. Bore x Stroke: 3.40 in. x 4.125 in. Lifters: Mechanical. Number of main bearings-4. Fuel Induction: Single barrel carburetor. Compression Ratio: 8.2:1. Displacement: 224.7 cu. in. (3.68 liters). Horsepower: 140 @ 3900 rpm. Torque: 215 lb.-ft. @ 1600-2800 rpm. Oil refill capacity: 5 qt. with filter change.

STANDARD ENGINE: W300: Engine Type: OHV, In-line "Premium Slant Six." Cast iron block and cylinder head, Premium components include roller timing chain, bimetal connecting rod bearings, heat-resistant Stellite-faced exhaust valves, and polyacrylic valve stem seals. Bore x Stroke: 3.40 in. x 4.125 in. Lifters: Mechanical. Number of main bearings-4. Fuel Induction: Single barrel carburetor. Compression Ratio: 8.2:1. Displacement: 224.7 cu. in. (3.68 liters). Horsepower: 140 @ 3900 rpm. Torque: 215 lb.-ft. @ 1600-2800 rpm. Oil refill capacity: 5 qt. with filter change.

STANDARD ENGINE: WM300: Engine Type: L-head, In-line 6-cylinder. Cast iron block and cylinder head. Bore x Stroke: 3.437 in. x 4.50 in. Lifters: Mechanical. Number of main bearings-4. Fuel Induction: Stromberg single barrel downdraft carburetor. Compression Ratio: 7.1:1. Displacement: 250.6 cu. in. (4.10 liters). Horsepower: 125 @ 3600 rpm. Torque: 216 lb.-ft. @ 1600 rpm. Oil refill capacity: 5 qt. Fuel Requirements: Regular.

OPTIONAL ENGINE: W100, W200, W300: Engine Type: OHV, Power Giant V-8. Cast iron block and cylinder head. Bore x Stroke: 3.91 in. x 3.3120 in. Lifters: Hydraulic. Number of main bearings-5. Fuel Induction: Single barrel carburetor. Compression Ratio: 8.25:1. Displacement: 318.14 cu. in. (5.21 liters). Horsepower: 200 @ 3900 rpm. Torque: 286 lb.-ft. @ 2400 rpm. Oil refill capacity: 5 qt. Fuel Requirements: Regular.

OPTIONAL ENGINE: W300: Engine Type: "Rugged Duty", Power Giant OHV, V-8. Cast iron block and cylinder head. This engine has the "Normal Duty" 318 V-8 features plus roller-chain drive, vibration damper, positive exhaust valve rotators and hydraulic valve lifters. Bore x Stroke: 3.63 in. x 3.80 in. Lifters: Hydraulic. Number of main bearings-5. Fuel Induction: 2-barrel carburetor. Compression Ratio: 8.25:1. Displacement: 318.14 cu. in. (5.21 liters). Horsepower: 202 @ 3900 rpm. Torque: 288 lb.-ft. @ 2400 rpm. Oil refill capacity: 5 qt. Fuel Requirements: Regular.

W300M:

CHASSIS FEATURES: Separate body and double-drop frame; side rail reinforcements (inside type). Frame dimensions: 122.45875 in. x 0.109375 in. Frame rail dimensions: 6.09 in. x 2.04 in. x 0.171 in.

SUSPENSION AND RUNNING GEAR: Front Suspension: Eleven leaf, 39 in. x 1.75 in. semi-elliptical springs, heavy-duty, double-acting shock absorbers. Capacity: 1,150 lb. (each). Optional: 1600 lb. capacity, (included with winch). Rear Suspension: Fourteen leaf, 52.25 in. x 1.75 in. semi-elliptical springs. Capacity: 2,500 lb. (each). Optional: 3,000 lb. capacity. Front Axle Type and Capacity: Full-floating, Hypoid-type. Capacity: 3,750 lb. Rear Axle Type and Capacity: Full-floating, Hypoid-type. Capacity: 6,500 lb. Final Drive Ratio: 5.83:1. Transfer Case: Two-speed, double-lever. Ratios: 1.96:1, 1.00:1. Brakes: Hydraulic front and rear. Dimensions: Front and rear: 14.125 in. x 1.75 in. Total lining area: 215.18 sq. in. Wheels: Five-stud ventilated disc. Tires: 9.00 x 16 8-ply. Optional: 9.00 x 16 10-ply. Steering: Worm and lever; 17.0 in. diameter steering wheel. Ratio: 23.2:1. Optional: None. Transmission: New Process #420, 4-speed "Synchro-shift" manual. Transmission Ratios: 6.68, 3.10, 1.69, 1.00:1. Reverse: 8.25:1. Clutch: Single plate, Oilite bronze pilot bearing, 11.0 in. dia. with lining area of 123.7 sq. in.

VEHICLE DIMENSIONS: Wheelbase: 126.0 in. Overall Length: Pickup: 199.0 in. (without winch); 208.625 in. (with winch); chassis and cab: 191.156 in. (without winch); 201.093 in. (with winch). Front/Rear Tread: 64.75 in./64.75 in. Overall Height: 76 in. (loaded). Width: 79.25 in. Front/Rear Overhang: 25.125 in./47.35 in. Tailgate: Width and Height: 54.0 in. x 19.9375 in. Ground Clearance: 8.8125 in.; with optional tires: 10.625 in. Load space: 96.0625 in. x 54.0 in. x 22.25 in.

CAPACITIES: Fuel Tank: 18 gal. Engine coolant system: 17 qt.

ACCOMMODATIONS: 3 passengers.

INSTRUMENTATION: Speedometer, odometer, gauges for oil pressure, fuel level, battery charge, engine coolant temperature.

W100 and W200:

CHASSIS FEATURES: Separate body and drop-center frame. Dimension: 6.12 in. x 2.30 in. x 0.188 in. Section modules: 3.43. W200 crew cab: 6.25 in. x 2.42 in. x 0.250 in. Section modules: 4.70.

SUSPENSION AND RUNNING GEAR: Front Suspension: Semi-elliptical leaf springs. Capacity: 6-cyl.: 1, 100 lb. V-8: 1,350 lb. W200 crew cab: 1,550 lb. Optional: 6-cyl.: 1,350 lb. V-8: 1,550 lb. (both were standard with front-mounted winch). Rear Suspension: Semi-elliptical leaf springs. Capacity: W100: 1,350 lb. W200: 1,750 lb. Optional: W100: 1,750 lb. W200: 2,600 lb. Front Axle Type and Capacity: Full-floating, Hypoid-type. Capacity: 3,000 lb. W200 Crew Cab: 3,500 lb. Rear Axle Type and Capacity: W100: Semi-floating, Hypoid-type. Capacity: 4,500 lb. W200: Full-floating, Hypoid-type. Capacity: 5,500 lb. Final Drive Ratio: 4.1:1 or 4.88:1. Anti-slip differential available with 4.1:1 ratio. Transfer Case: Two-speed. Ratios: 1.96:1, 1.00:1. Brakes: Hydraulic front and rear. Dimensions: Front and rear: 12.125 in. x 1.75 in. Total lining area: 199.88 sq. in. Wheels: Eight-stud ventilated disc. Tires: W100: 6.50 x 16 6-ply. W200: 7 x 17.5 6-ply, tubeless. Optional: W100: 7.00 x 16 6-ply, 7 x 17.5 6-ply. W200: 8 x 19.5 8-ply. Steering: Recirculating ball. Transmission: 3-speed heavy-duty A745 manual. Optional: New Process #420, 4-speed "Synchro-shift" manual. Transmission Ratios: 6.68, 3.10, 1.69, 1.00:1. Reverse: 8.25:1. Clutch: Single plate, dry disc, 11.0 in. dia. with lining area of 123.7 sq. in.

VEHICLE DIMENSIONS: W100: Wheelbase: 114 in. Overall Length: 181 in. (Add 15.125 in. for winch). Front/Rear Tread: 65.5 in./61.9375 in. Overall Height: 80.3125 in. Load space: Pickup box dimensions: Utiline body: 114 in. wheelbase: 78.125 in. x 49 in. x 20 in. Capacity: 47.25 cu. ft. Sweptline body: 114 in. wheelbase: 78.625 in. x 70 in. x 20 in. Capacity: 59.3 cu. ft. W200: Wheelbase: 128 in. Crew cab: 146 in. Overall Length: 192.75 in. (add 15.125 in. for winch). Front/Rear Tread: 65.0625 in./61.8125 in. Overall Height: 80.25 in. Load space: Pickup box dimensions: Utiline: 96 in. x 54 in. x 20 in. Capacity: 58.5 cu. ft. Sweptline: 98.875 in. x 70.75 in. x 20 in. Capacity: 75 cu. ft.

CAPACITIES: Fuel Tank: 18 gal. Engine coolant system: 6-cyl.: 13.0 qt. V-8: 20.0 qt.

ACCOMMODATIONS: 3 passengers. Town Wagon: Up to eight passengers.

INSTRUMENTATION: Speedometer, odometer, gauges for fuel level, ammeter and engine coolant temperature.

W300:

CHASSIS FEATURES: Separate body and straight frame. Dimensions: 7.25 in. x 2.75 in. x 0.2318 in. Section modules: 5.70.

SUSPENSION AND RUNNING GEAR: Front Suspension: Semi-elliptical leaf springs. Capacity: 1,450 lb. Optional: 1,750 lb. (standard with front-mounted winch). Rear Suspension: Semi-elliptical leaf springs. Capacity: 2,450. Optional: 3,250, 4,050 lb. Front Axle Type and Capacity: Full-floating, Hypoid-type. Capacity: 4,500 lb. Rear Axle Type and Capacity: Full-floating, Hypoid-type. Capacity: 7,500 lb. Anti-slip differential optional. Final Drive Ratio: 4.88:1 or 5.87:1. Transfer Case: Two-speed, single lever. Ratios: 1.96:1, 1.00:1. Brakes: Hydraulic front and rear. Dimensions: Front: 14.125 in. x 1.75 in. Rear: 13 in. x 2.5 in. Total lining area: 241.98 sq. in. Wheels: Six-stud ventilated disc. Tires: 8 x 19.5 8-ply, tubeless. Optional: 9.00 x 16 10-ply. Steering: Worm and roller. Ratio: 29.0:1. Optional: Power assisted. Transmission: New Process #420, 4-speed "Synchro-shift" manual. Transmission Ratios: 6.68, 3.10, 1.69, 1.00:1. Reverse: 8.25:1. Clutch: Single plate, dry disc, 11.0 in. dia. with lining area of 123.7 sq. in. 318 Premium V-8: 12 in. dia.; 150 sq. in. lining area.

VEHICLE DIMENSIONS: Wheelbase: 133 in. Overall Length: 204.5 in. (add 17.875 in. for winch). Width: 81.8125 in. Overall Height: 84.5 in. Front/Rear Tread: 64.5625 in./65.0 in.

CAPACITIES: Fuel Tank: 18 gal. Engine coolant system: 6-cyl.: 20.0 qt. V-8: 24.0 qt.

ACCOMMODATIONS: 3 passengers.

INSTRUMENTATION: Speedometer, odometer, gauges for fuel level, ammeter and engine coolant temperature.

OPTIONS: W100, W200, W300: Chrome front bumper. Painted rear bumper. Chrome rear bumper. Painted bumper guards. Chrome bumper guards. Directional signals. Tinted glass. Dual electric horns. Horn ring. Cigarette lighter. Glove box lock. Interior rearview mirror. Grab handles. Wraparound rear window. Dual electric variable-speed electric windshield wipers. Windshield washer. Heater. Deluxe heater. Custom cab. 318 cu. in. V-8 engine. W300M: 60 amp-hr. battery. Pulley drive. Power winch. Pintle hook. Power take-off. Front end tow hooks. Brake booster, 7.5 in. diaphragm. Front bumper painted any standard truck color. Deluxe cab equipment. Directional signals. Drawbar. 40 amp generator. Fenders painted to match body color. Combined vacuum and fuel pump. Chrome grab handles. Tinted glass. Recirculating heater with defroster. Hydraulic jack with 3 ton capacity. Long arm left or right side exterior mirror. Interior mirror (in addition to standard). Windshield washers. Rear hydraulic telescopic shock absorbers. Power steering. Extra-duty springs (front: 1600 lb., rear: 3,000 lb.). Roof-mounted radio. Auxiliary taillamps. Heavy-duty battery. 11 in. clutch. Mechanical governor for use with rear drive shaft assembly. Fuel and vacuum pump. Radiator overflow tank.

HISTORICAL FOOTNOTES: The 1965 Dodge four-wheel drive trucks were introduced in October, 1964.

1966 POWER WAGON

1966 Dodge W200 Sweptline Power Wagon pickup

The 383 cu. in. V-8 was offered as an option for the W100 and W200 models for 1966. All W100, W200 and W300 had the following standard equipment: Oil filter, 37 amp alternator, turn signals, 6-way adjustable seat, vinyl seat upholstery, painted left-side and inside rearview mirrors, back-up lights, 4-way emergency flashers, push-button door locks, variable-speed wipers, windshield washers, wheel wrench, two seat belts, dome light, keylock in both doors, coat hook, rubber mat for cab floor, ashtray, dispatch box, antifreeze and high-level ventilation.

1966 Dodge WM300 Utiline Power Wagon pickup

The standard pickup cab was also equipped with a bench seat finished in a black and white vinyl upholstery, and an adjustable Orscheln-lever hand brake. The optional Comfort Package added these items, or replaced items to the standard cab: A full-length foam rubber seat and foam-padded seat back, fabric and vinyl seat upholstery, driver's armrest, right side sun visor, cigarette lighter, and extra cab insulation. The fabric seat insert was available in red, beige, or dark green, depending on truck exterior color. The optional Appearance Package was a dress-up package with both interior and exterior elements. The exterior items included a chrome grille, bright trim moldings, mylar trim for the windshield and rear window, "Custom" nameplates and delta emblems on the cab. The interior features consisted of a bright metal "face" for the instrument cluster and around the control knobs, a bright-finish dashboard molding, and textured metal trimpanels on the doors. The Custom Sports Special option was available for the W100 and W200 models in Sweptline, Utiline, Stake, or chassis cab form. Its features consisted of black bucket seats with seat belts, fully-carpeted cab floor, center console with cigarette lighter, ashtray, map light and storage compartment; chrome grille, front bumper and roof moldings; racing stripes on roof and hood, bright instrument panel, Mylar trim around windshield and rear window, custom nameplates and delta emblems on cab, and dual armrests and sun visors.

1966 Dodge W300 Utiline Power Wagon pickup

The W200 was available as a Camper Special Model with the following components: 59 amp alternator, 70 amp-hr. battery, power brakes, additional engine cooling capacity, oil pressure gauge, dual, Western-style, bright-finish mirrors, front springs rated at 1550 lbs., rear springs rated at 2600 lbs., 7.50 x 16, 8-ply-rated tires, 16 x 5.50 in. wheels and "Camper Special" exterior emblems. A Deluxe Camper Package included these additional items: Comfort Package, custom Fresh-Air heater-defroster, traffic hazard warning lights and dual electric horns. The Sweptline W200 outfitted with the Camper Package was also available with the Custom Camper Package which included the Deluxe Camper Package plus the Appearance Package and exterior side moldings.

I.D. DATA: The first two digits of the serial number indicated the model code as follows: W100: 21; W200: 22; W300: 23; WM300: 24. The third digit indicated the number of cylinders. The last seven digits were the production sequence number. The serial numbers on 6-cylinder OHV engines were located on the right side of the block on top of the boss directly behind the coil. The V-8 serial number was found on the left front of the block under the cylinder head. The L-head 6-cylinder engine serial number was found on the left front of the block at the top. The first two letters indicated the series (TT, VT, AT, B, BT, C, CT). The next two digits indicated engine displacement. The third and fourth digits indicated month and date of manufacture.

Body Type	Factory Price	GVW	Shipping Weight	Prod. Total
Model B6-W100, 1/2 ton 6-cyl.				
Ch. & Cab, 114 in. wb.	$2638.25	5100*	3900	—
Pickup, Utiline, 114 in. wb.	$2751.25	5100	4210	—
Pickup, Sweptline, 114 in. wb.	$2765.25	5100	4310	—
Town Panel, 114 in. wb.	$3061.25	N.A.	N.A.	—
Town Wag. 6-P, 114 in. wb.	$3375.25	5100	4370	—
Town Wag. 8-P., 114 in. wb.	$3444.25	5100	4640	—

* 6000 lb. GVW optional.
a Total model year production of all W100 trucks was 1528 units with 6-cyl. engines and 820 with V-8 engines.

Body Type	Factory Price	GVW	Shipping Weight	Prod. Total
Model B6-W200, 3/4 ton, 6-cyl. (Crew cab-146 in. wheelbase)				
Ch. & Cab, 128 in. wb.	$2693.25	6000*	3945	—
Pickup, Utiline, 128 in. wb.	$2806.25	6000	4385	—
Pickup, Sweptline, 128 in. wb.	$2820.25	6000	4475	—
Stake, 128 in. wb.	$2898.25	6000	4520	—
Platform, 128 in. wb.	$2846.25	6000	4320	—
Crew Cab Ch.	$3560.25	6000	4259	—
Crew Cab, Utiline	$3672.25	6000	4569	—
Crew Cab, Sweptline	$3686.25	6000	4669	—

* An 8000 lb. GVW package was optional for all models.

Body Type	Factory Price	GVW	Shipping Weight	Prod. Total
Model B6-W300, 1 ton, 6-cyl.				
Ch. & Cowl, 133 in. wb.	$3205	8500	4090	—
Ch. & Cab, 133 in. wb.	$3507	8500*	4645	c
Pickup, Utiline, 133 in. wb.	$3641	8500	5045	—
Platform, 133 in. wb.	$3693	8500	5345	—
Stake, 133 in. wb.	$3758	8500	5545	—

* GVW packages up to 10,000 lb. were available.
c Total model year production of was 220 units with 6-cyl. engines and 625 with V-8 engines.

Prices of the W100, W200 and W300 models with optional V-8 engine was an additional $120.00.

Body Type	Factory Price	GVW	Shipping Weight	Prod. Total
Model B6-WM300				
Ch. & Cowl, 126 in. wb.	$3419.50	8700	4095	—
Ch. & Cab, 126 in. wb.	$3725.50	8700*	4500	d
Pickup, 126 in. wb.	$3872.50	8700	4940	—

* 9500 lb. GVW package optional for all WM300 models.
d Total model year production was 1245 units.

STANDARD ENGINE: W100, W200: Engine Type: OHV, In-line 6-cylinder. Cast iron block and cylinder head. Bore x Stroke: 3.40 in. x 4.125 in. Lifters: Mechanical. Number of main bearings-5. Fuel Induction: Single barrel carburetor. Compression Ratio: 8.4:1. Displacement: 224.7 cu. in. (3.68 liters). Horsepower: 140 @ 3900 rpm. Torque: 215 lb.-ft. @ 1600-2800 rpm. Oil refill capacity: 5 qt.

STANDARD ENGINE: W300: Engine Type: OHV, In-line "Premium Slant Six." Cast iron block and cylinder head, Premium components include roller timing chain, bimetal connecting rod bearings, heat-resistant Stellite-faced exhaust valves, and polyacrylic valve stem seals. Bore x Stroke: 3.40 in. x 4.125 in. Lifters: Mechanical. Number of main bearings-5. Fuel Induction: Single barrel carburetor. Compression Ratio: 8.4:1. Displacement: 224.7 cu. in. (3.68 liters). Horsepower: 140 @ 3900 rpm. Torque: 215 lb.-ft. @ 1600-2800 rpm. Oil refill capacity: 5 qt.

STANDARD ENGINE: WM300: Engine Type: L-head, In-line 6-cylinder. Cast iron block and cylinder head. Bore x Stroke: 3.437 in. x 4.50 in. Lifters: Mechanical. Number of main bearings-4. Fuel Induction: Stromberg single barrel downdraft carburetor. Compression Ratio: 7.1:1. Displacement: 250.6 cu. in. (4.10 liters). Horsepower: 125 @ 3600 rpm. Torque: 216 lb.-ft. @ 1600 rpm. Oil refill capacity: 5 qt. Fuel Requirements: Regular.

OPTIONAL ENGINE: W100, W200: Engine Type: OHV, V-8. Cast iron block and cylinder head. Bore x Stroke: 3.91 in. x 3.3120 in. Lifters: Hydraulic. Number of main bearings-5. Fuel Induction: Two barrel carburetor. Compression Ratio: 8.25:1. Displacement: 318.14 cu. in. (5.21 liters). Horsepower: 210 @ 4000 rpm. Torque: 318 lb.-ft. @ 2800 rpm. Oil refill capacity: 5 qt. Fuel Requirements: Regular.

OPTIONAL ENGINE: W300: Engine Type: OHV, Premium V-8. Cast iron block and cylinder head. This engine has the standard 318 V-8 features plus roller-chain drive, vibration damper, positive exhaust valve rotators and hydraulic valve lifters. Bore x Stroke: 3.63 in. x 3.80 in. Lifters: Hydraulic. Number of main bearings-5. Fuel Induction: 2-barrel carburetor. Compression Ratio: 7.5:1. Displacement: 318.14 cu. in. (5.21 liters). Horsepower: 202 @ 3900 rpm. Torque: 288 lb.-ft. @ 2400 rpm. Oil refill capacity: 5 qt. Fuel Requirements: Regular.

OPTIONAL ENGINE: W100, W200: Engine Type: OHV, V-8. Cast iron block and cylinder head. This engine has a vibraton damper, 18 in., 7 blade fan, and a drop-forged crankshaft. Bore x Stroke: 4.25 in. x 3.38 in. Lifters: Hydraulic. Number of main bearings-5. Fuel Induction: 2-barrel carburetor. Compression Ratio: 9.2:1. Displacement: 383 cu. in. (6.276 liters). Horsepower: 258 @ 4400 rpm. Torque: 375 lb.-ft. @ 2800 rpm. Oil refill capacity: 5 qt. Fuel Requirements: Regular.

W300M:

CHASSIS FEATURES: Separate body and double-drop frame; side rail reinforcements (inside type). Frame dimensions: 122.45875 in. x 0.109375 in. Frame rail dimensions: 6.09 in. x 2.04 in. x 0.171 in. Section modules: 4.51

SUSPENSION AND RUNNING GEAR: Front Suspension: Eleven leaf, 39 in. x 1.75 in. semi-elliptical springs, heavy-duty, double-acting shock absorbers. Capacity: 1,150 lb. (each). Optional: 1600 lb. capacity, (included with winch). Rear Suspension: Fourteen leaf, 52.25 in. x 1.75 in. semi-elliptical springs. Capacity: 2,500 lb. (each). Optional: 3,000 lb. capacity. Front Axle Type and Capacity: Full-floating, Hypoid-type. Capacity: 3,750 lb. Rear Axle Type and Capacity: Full-floating, Hypoid-type. Capacity: 6,500 lb. Final Drive Ratio: 5.83:1. Transfer Case: Two-speed, double-lever. Ratios: 1.96:1, 1.00:1. Brakes: Hydraulic front and rear. Dimensions: Front and rear: 14.125 in. x 1.75 in. Total lining area: 215.18 sq. in. Wheels: Five-stud ventilated disc. Tires: 9.00 x 16 8-ply. Optional: 9.00 x 16 10-ply. Steering: Worm and lever; 17.0 in. diameter steering wheel. Ratio: 23.2:1. Optional: None. Transmission: New Process #420, 4-speed "Synchro-shift" manual. Transmission Ratios: 6.68, 3.10, 1.69, 1.00:1. Reverse: 8.25:1. Clutch: Single plate, Oilite bronze pilot bearing, 11.0 in. dia. with lining area of 123.7 sq. in.

VEHICLE DIMENSIONS: Wheelbase: 126.0 in. Overall Length: Pickup: 199.0 in. (without winch); 208.625 in. (with winch); chassis and cab: 191.156 in. (without winch); 201.093 in. (with winch). Front/Rear Tread: 64.75 in./64.75 in. Overall Height: 76 in. (loaded). Width: 79.25 in. Front/Rear Overhang: 25.125 in./47.35 in. Tailgate: Width and Height: 54.0 in. x 19.9375 in. Ground Clearance: 8.8125 in.; with optional tires: 10.625 in. Load space: 96.0625 in. x 54.0 in. x 22.25 in.

CAPACITIES: Fuel Tank: 18 gal. Engine coolant system: 17 qt.

ACCOMMODATIONS: 3 passengers.

INSTRUMENTATION: Speedometer, odometer, gauges for oil pressure, fuel level, battery charge, engine coolant temperature.

W100 and W200:

CHASSIS FEATURES: Separate body and drop-center frame. Dimension: W100: 6.12 in. x 2.30 in. x 0.188 in. Section modules: W100: 3.43. W200: 3.88, W200 crew cab: 4.70. Dimension: W200: 6.25 in. x 2.42 in. x 0.250 in.

SUSPENSION AND RUNNING GEAR: Front Suspension: Semi-elliptical leaf springs. Capacity: 6-cyl.: 1, 100 lb. V-8: 1,350 lb. W200 crew cab: 1,550 lb. Optional: 6-cyl.: 1,350 lb. V-8: 1,550 lb. (both were standard with front-mounted winch). Rear Suspension: Semi-elliptical leaf springs. Capacity: W100: 1,350 lb. W200: 1,750 lb. Optional: W100: 1,750 lb. W200: 2,600 lb. Front Axle Type and Capacity: Full-floating, Hypoid-type. Capacity: 3,000 lb. W200 crew cab: 3,500 lb. Rear Axle Type and Capacity: W100: Full-floating, Hypoid-type. Capacity: 4,500 lb. W200: Full-floating, Hypoid-type. Capacity: 5,500 lb. Final Drive Ratio: 3.54:1 (with 383 engine only), 4.1:1 or 4.88:1 (not available with 383 V-8). Anti-slip differential available with 4.1:1 ratio. Transfer Case: Two-speed. Ratios: 1.96:1, 1.00:1. Brakes: Hydraulic front and rear. Dimensions: Front and rear: 12.125 in. x 2.0 in. Total lining area: 211.58 sq. in. Wheels: Eight-stud ventilated disc. Tires: W100: 6.50 x 16 6-ply. W200: 7 x 17.5 6-ply, tubeless. Optional: W100: 7.00 x 16 6-ply, 7 x 17.5 6-ply. W200: 8 x 19.5 8-ply. Steering: Recirculating ball. Transmission: 3-speed heavy-duty A745 manual. Optional: New Process #435, 4-speed manual. Clutch: Single plate, dry disc, 11.0 in. dia. with lining area of 123.7 sq. in. Standard with 383 V-8: 12 in. dia. and 150 sq. in. lining area.

VEHICLE DIMENSIONS: W100: Wheelbase: 114 in. Overall Length: 181 in. (Add 15.125 in. for winch). Front/Rear Tread: 65.5 in./61.9375 in. Overall Height: 80.3125 in. Load space: Pickup box dimensions: Utiline body: 114 in. wheelbase: 78.125 in. x 49 in. x 20 in. Capacity: 47.25 cu. ft. Sweptline body: 114 in. wheelbase: 78.625 in. x 70 in. x 20 in. Capacity: 59.3 cu. ft. W200: Wheelbase: 128 in. Crew cab: 146 in. Overall Length: 192.75 in. (add 15.125 in. for winch). Front/Rear Tread: 65.0625 in./61.8125 in. Overall Height: 80.25 in. Load space: Pickup box dimensions: Utiline: 96 in. x 54 in. x 20 in. Capacity: 58.5 cu. ft. Sweptline: 98.875 in. x 70.75 in. x 20 in. Capacity: 75 cu. ft.

CAPACITIES: Fuel Tank: 18 gal. Engine coolant system: 6-cyl.: 13.0 qt. V-8: 20.0 qt.

ACCOMMODATIONS: 3 passengers. Town Wagon: Up to eight passengers.

INSTRUMENTATION: Speedometer, odometer, gauges for fuel level, ammeter and engine coolant temperature.

W300:

CHASSIS FEATURES: Separate body and straight frame. Dimensions: 7.25 in. x 2.75 in. x 0.2318 in. Section modules: 5.70.

SUSPENSION AND RUNNING GEAR: Front Suspension: Semi-elliptical leaf springs. Capacity: 1,450 lb. Optional: 1,750 lb. (standard with front-mounted winch). Rear Suspension: Semi-elliptical leaf springs. Capacity: 3,250. Optional: 4,050 lb. Front Axle Type and Capacity: Full-floating, Hypoid-type. Capacity: 4,500 lb. Rear Axle Type and Capacity: Full-floating, Hypoid-type. Capacity: 7,500 lb. Anti-slip differential optional. Final Drive Ratio: 4.88:1 or 5.87:1. Transfer Case: Two-speed, single lever. Ratios: 1.96:1, 1.00:1. Brakes: Hydraulic front and rear. Dimensions: Front: 14.125 in. x 1.75 in. Rear: 13 in. x 2.5 in. Total lining area: 241.98 sq. in. Wheels: Six-stud ventilated disc. Tires: 8 x 19.5 8-ply, tubeless. Optional: 9.00 x 16 10-ply. Steering: Worm and roller. Ratio: 29.0:1. Optional: Power assisted. Transmission: New Process #435, 4-speed manual. Clutch: Single plate, dry disc, 11.0 in. dia. with lining area of 123.7 sq. in. 318 Premium V-8: 12 in. dia.; 150 sq. in. lining area.

VEHICLE DIMENSIONS: Wheelbase: 133 in. Overall Length: 204.5 in. (add 17.875 in. for winch). Width: 81.8125 in. Overall Height: 84.5 in. Front/Rear tread: 64.5625 in./65.0 in.

CAPACITIES: Fuel Tank: 18 gal. Engine coolant system: 6-cyl.: 20.0 qt. V-8: 24.0 qt.

ACCOMMODATIONS: 3 passengers.

INSTRUMENTATION: Speedometer, odometer, gauges for fuel level, ammeter and engine coolant temperature.

OPTIONS AND PRICES: W100, W200, W300: Full width rear window: $43.30. Appearance Package: $48.30. 318 V-8: $120.50. 4-speed NP435D manual transmission: $86.20. Oil-bath air cleaner: $6.60 (6-cyl. only). 46 amp alternator: $21.70. 59 amp alternator: $30.10. 70 amp-hr. battery: $7.90. Rear bumper painted Dodge truck white: $22. Left side armrest: $4.70. Inside body spare tire carrier for Sweptline: $15. Increased cooling system: $16.40. Oil pressure gauge: $10.10. Tinted glass for windshield and rear window: $18.10. Fresh-Air heater: $53.90. Transistor radio: $48.50. Custom Fresh-Air heater with defrosters: $68.10. Dual electric horns: $8.40. Front locking manual hubs: $79.40. Heavy-duty instrument cluster. Includes electric tachometer, oil pressure gauge: $63.90. Two-tone paint: $16.40 (cab models), $27 (panels and wagons). Undercoating: $12.90. W300M: 70 amp-hr. battery: $7.90. 46 amp alternator: $21.70. 59 amp alternator: $30.10. Traffic hazard warning switch: $11.50. Front locking manual hubs: $79.40. Pulley drive. Power winch: $417. Pintle hook. Power take-off: $148.80. Radiator overflow tank: $31.20. Front end tow hooks: $27. Brake booster: $45.50. Rear pintle hook: $28.50. Undercoating: $12.90. Recirculating heater with defroster: $48.90. Hydraulic jack with 3 ton capacity: $14.30.

HISTORICAL FOOTNOTES: The 1966 Dodge four-wheel drive trucks were introduced in October, 1965.

1967 POWER WAGON

No styling changes were made for 1967 in the four-wheel drive Dodge trucks. Both the Town Panel and Town Wagon were discontinued. The W100 and W200 were again offered in Sweptline pickup body form. The cargo box double-wall design was continued as was the Sweptline's all-steel floor and full-width tailgate that could be operated with one hand. The W200 was offered with a 128 in. wheelbase that Dodge noted would accept all popular camper units. The shorter, 114 in. wheelbase W100 with its 6.5 ft. box was depicted as a more suitable vehicle where maneuverability was important. The standard Sweptline cab had black and white vinyl upholstery. The seat had an extra-thick frame and 48 coil springs with cotton and foam pads. The Utiline pickups were again available in W100, W200 and W300 form. These placed the cargo box inside the rear wheels and featured running boards for easy side loading. The Utiline floor was again constructed of hardwood with steel skid strips for added service. The W100 Utiline had a 114 in. wheelbase and a 6.5 ft. box. The W200, on a 128 in. wheelbase had an 8 ft. box. The W300, with a 133 in. wheelbase had a 9 ft. box. The Utiline cab interior was identical to that used for the Sweptline models. The crew cab pickups were again available in both W200 Sweptline and Utiline form. The military type WM300 was described by Dodge as "the civilian version of the most famous military pickup in the world. When extremely rugged service is called for, you'll find the Dodge WM300 ready to answer the call." The WM300 wheelbase remained at 126 inches and its cargo box was unchanged at 8 feet in length. In addition to the pickup model, the WM300 was still offered in chassis-cab and chassis-cowl form for special bodies. The W200 Camper Special pickup was available as either a Sweptline or a Utiline model with an 8 foot pickup box. Optional for the Sweptline version was the Custom Camper Package. The Custom Sports Package was available for the W100 and W200 Sweptline or Utiline pickups as well as their stake or chassis-cab variations.

1967 Dodge W100 Sweptline Power Wagon pickup

Standard equipment for the W100, W200 and W300 models consisted of these items: Oil filter, 37 amp alternator, closed crankcase ventilation, directional signals, 6-way adjustable seat, painted left-side and inside rearview mirrors on pickups, dual long-arm exterior mirrors on stakes, chassis-cabs, back-up lights (pickups, stakes and platforms), 4-way emergency flashers, push-button door locks, variable-speed electric windshield wipers, windshield washers, wheel wrench, two seat belts, dome light, keylock in both doors, coat hook, cab floor rubber mat, ashtray, dispatch box, antifreeze and high-level ventilation. Standard equipment for the WM300 consisted of back-up lights (pickup), turn signals (pickup and chassis-cab), 4-way emergency flasher, padded instrument panel and sun visors, push-button door locks, vinyl seat upholstery, driver's side armrest, windshield washers and two seat belts.

1967 Dodge WM300 Utiline Power Wagon pickup

I.D. DATA: The first two digits of the serial number indicated the model code as follows: W100: 21; W200: 22; W300: 23; WM300: 24. The third digit indicated the number of cylinders. The last seven digits were the production sequence number. The serial numbers on 6-cylinder OHV engines were located on the right side of the block on top of the boss directly behind the coil. The V-8 serial number was found on the left front of the block under the cylinder head. The L-head 6-cylinder engine serial number was found on the left front of the block at the top. The first two letters indicated the series (TT, VT, AT, B, BT, C, CT). The next two digits indicated engine displacement. The third and fourth digits indicated month and date of manufacture.

Body Type	Factory Price	GVW	Shipping Weight	Prod. Total
Model W100, 1/2 ton 6-cyl.				
Ch. & Cab, 114 in. wb.	$2559	5100*	3900	—
Pickup, Utiline, 114 in. wb.	$2678	5100	4210	—
Pickup, Sweptline, 114 in. wb.	$2691	5100	4310	—

* 6000 lb. GVW optional.
a Total model year production of all W100 trucks was 570 units with 6-cyl. engines and 530 with V-8 engines.

Body Type	Factory Price	GVW	Shipping Weight	Prod. Total
Model W200, 3/4 ton, 6-cyl. (Crew cab-146 in. wheelbase)				
Ch. & Cab, 128 in. wb.	$2659	6000*	3945	b
Pickup, Utiline, 128 in. wb.	$2778	6000	4385	—
Pickup, Sweptline, 128 in. wb.	$2791	6000	4475	—
Stake, 128 in. wb.	$2865	6000	4520	—
Platform, 128 in. wb.	$2815	6000	4320	—
Crew Cab, Ch.	$3416	6000	4375	—
Crew Cab, Utiline	$3534	6000	4775	—
Crew Cab, Sweptline	$3547	6000	4785	—

* An 8000 lb. GVW package was optional for all models.
b Total model year production, excluding crew cab models, was 2099 units with 6-cyl. engines and 1997 with V-8 engines.

Body Type	Factory Price	GVW	Shipping Weight	Prod. Total
Model W300, 1 ton, 6-cyl.				
Ch. & Cowl, 133 in. wb.	$3011	8500	4090	—
Ch. & Cab, 133 in. wb.	$3395	8500*	4645	c
Pickup, Utiline, 133 in. wb.	$3534	8500	5045	—
Platform, 133 in. wb.	$3584	8500	5345	—
Stake, 133 in. wb.	$3644	8500	5545	—

* GVW packages up to 10,000 lb. were available.
c Total model year production was 214 units with 6-cyl. engines and 528 with V-8 engines.

Prices of the W100, W200 and W300 models with optional V-8 engine were an additional $120.00.

Body Type	Factory Price	GVW	Shipping Weight	Prod. Total
Model WM300				
Ch. & Cowl, 126 in. wb.	$3662	8700	4095	—
Ch. & Cab, 126 in. wb.	$4033	8700*	4520	d
Pickup, 126 in. wb.	$4184	8700	4920	—

* 9500 lb. GVW package optional for all WM300 models.
d Total model year production was 974 units.

STANDARD ENGINE: W100, W200: Engine Type: OHV, In-line 6-cylinder. Cast iron block and cylinder head. Bore x Stroke: 3.40 in. x 4.125 in. Lifters: Mechanical. Number of main bearings-5. Fuel Induction: Single barrel carburetor. Compression Ratio: 8.4:1. Displacement: 224.7 cu. in. (3.68 liters). Horsepower: 140 @ 3900 rpm. Torque: 215 lb.-ft. @ 1600-2800 rpm. Oil refill capacity: 5 qt.

STANDARD ENGINE: W300: Engine Type: OHV, In-line "Premium Slant Six." Cast iron block and cylinder head, Premium components include roller timing chain, bimetal connecting rod bearings, heat-resistant Stellite-faced exhaust valves, and polyacrylic valve stem seals. Bore x Stroke: 3.40 in. x 4.125 in. Lifters: Mechanical. Number of main bearings-5. Fuel Induction: Single barrel carburetor. Compression Ratio: 8.4:1. Displacement: 224.7 cu. in. (3.68 liters). Horsepower: 140 @ 3900 rpm. Torque: 215 lb.-ft. @ 1600-2800 rpm. Oil refill capacity: 5 qt.

STANDARD ENGINE: WM300: Engine Type: L-head, In-line 6-cylinder. Cast iron block and cylinder head. Bore x Stroke: 3.437 in. x 4.50 in. Lifters: Mechanical. Number of main bearings-4. Fuel Induction: Stromberg single barrel downdraft carburetor. Compression Ratio: 7.1:1. Displacement: 250.6 cu. in. (4.10 liters). Horsepower: 125 @ 3600 rpm. Torque: 216 lb.-ft. @ 1600 rpm. Oil refill capacity: 5 qt. Fuel Requirements: Regular.

OPTIONAL ENGINE: W100, W200: Engine Type: OHV, V-8. Cast iron block and cylinder head. Bore x Stroke: 3.91 in. x 3.3120 in. Lifters: Hydraulic. Number of main bearings-5. Fuel Induction: Two barrel carburetor. Compression Ratio: 8.25:1. Displacement: 318.14 cu. in. (5.21 liters). Horsepower: 210 @ 4000 rpm. Torque: 318 lb.-ft. @ 2800 rpm. Oil refill capacity: 5 qt. Fuel Requirements: Regular.

OPTIONAL ENGINE: W300: Engine Type: OHV, premium V-8. Cast iron block and cylinder head. This engine has the standard 318 V-8 features plus roller-chain drive, vibration damper, positive exhaust valve rotators and hydraulic valve lifters. Bore x Stroke: 3.63 in. x 3.80 in. Lifters: Hydraulic. Number of main bearings-5. Fuel Induction: 2-barrel carburetor. Compression Ratio: 7.5:1. Displacement: 318.14 cu. in. (5.21 liters). Horsepower: 202 @ 3900 rpm. Torque: 288 lb.-ft. @ 2400 rpm. Oil refill capacity: 5 qt. Fuel Requirements: Regular.

OPTIONAL ENGINE: W100, W200: Engine Type: OHV, V-8. Cast iron block and cylinder head. This engine has a vibraton damper, 18 in., 7 blade fan, and a drop-forged crankshaft. Bore x Stroke: 4.25 in. x 3.38 in. Lifters: Hydraulic. Number of main bearings-5. Fuel Induction: 2-barrel carburetor. Compression Ratio: 9.2:1. Displacement: 383 cu. in. (6.276 liters). Horsepower: 258 @ 4400 rpm. Torque: 375 lb.-ft. @ 2800 rpm. Oil refill capacity: 5 qt. Fuel Requirements: Regular.

W300M:

CHASSIS FEATURES: Separate body and double-drop frame; side rail reinforcements (inside type). Frame dimensions: 122.45875 in. x 0.109375 in. Frame rail dimensions: 6.09 in. x 2.04 in. x 0.171 in. Section modules: 4.51

SUSPENSION AND RUNNING GEAR: Front Suspension: Eleven leaf, 39 in. x 1.75 in. semi-elliptical springs, heavy-duty, double-acting shock absorbers. Capacity: 1,150 lb. (each). Optional: 1600 lb. capacity, (included with winch). Rear Suspension: Fourteen leaf, 52.25 in. x 1.75 in. semi-elliptical springs. Capacity: 2,500 lb. (each). Optional: 3,000 lb. capacity. Front Axle Type and Capacity: Full-floating, Hypoid-type. Capacity: 3,750 lb. Rear Axle Type and Capacity: Full-floating, Hypoid-type. Capacity: 6,500 lb. Final Drive Ratio: 5.83:1. Transfer Case: Two-speed, double-lever. Ratios: 1.96:1, 1.00:1. Brakes: Hydraulic front and rear. Dimensions: Front and rear: 14.125 in. x 1.75 in. Total lining area: 215.18 sq. in. Wheels: Five-stud ventilated disc. Tires: 9.00 x 16 8-ply. Optional: 9.00 x 16 10-ply. Steering: Worm and lever; 17.0 in. diameter steering wheel. Ratio: 23.2:1. Optional: None. Transmission: New Process #420, 4-speed "Synchro-shift" manual. Transmission Ratios: 6.68, 3.10, 1.69, 1.00:1. Reverse: 8.25:1. Clutch: Single plate, Oilite bronze pilot bearing, 11.0 in. dia. with lining area of 123.7 sq. in.

VEHICLE DIMENSIONS: Wheelbase: 126.0 in. Overall Length: Pickup: 199.0 in. (without winch); 208.625 in. (with winch); chassis and cab: 191.156 in. (without winch); 201.093 in. (with winch). Front/Rear Tread: 64.75 in./64.75 in. Overall Height: 76 in. (loaded). Width: 79.25 in. Front/Rear Overhang: 25.125 in./47.35 in. Tailgate: Width and Height: 54.0 in. x 19.9375 in. Ground Clearance: 8.8125 in.; with optional tires: 10.625 in. Load space: 96.0625 in. x 54.0 in. x 22.25 in.

CAPACITIES: Fuel Tank: 18 gal. Engine coolant system: 17 qt.

ACCOMMODATIONS: 3 passengers.

INSTRUMENTATION: Speedometer, odometer, gauges for oil pressure, fuel level, battery charge, engine coolant temperature.

W100 and W200:

CHASSIS FEATURES: Separate body and drop-center frame. Dimension: W100: 6.12 in. x 2.30 in. x 0.188 in. Section modules: W100: 3.43. W200: 3.88, W200 crew cab: 4.70. Dimension: W200: 6.25 in. x 2.42 in. x 0.250 in.

SUSPENSION AND RUNNING GEAR: Front Suspension: Semi-elliptical leaf springs. Capacity: 6-cyl.: 1, 100 lb. V-8: 1,350 lb. W200 crew cab: 1,550 lb. Optional: 6-cyl.: 1,350 lb. V-8: 1,550 lb. (both were standard with front-mounted winch). Rear Suspension: Semi-elliptical leaf springs. Capacity: W100: 1,350 lb. W200: 1,750 lb. Optional: W100: 1,750 lb. W200: 2,600 lb. Front Axle Type and Capacity: Full-floating, Hypoid-type. Capacity: 3,000 lb. W200 Crew Cab: 3,500 lb. Rear Axle Type and Capacity: W100: Full-floating, Hypoid-type. Capacity: 4,500 lb. W200: Full-floating, Hypoid-type. Capacity: 5,500 lb. Final Drive Ratio: 3.54:1 (with 383 engine only), 4.1:1 or 4.88:1 (not available with 383 V-8). Anti-slip differential available with 4.1:1 ratio. Transfer Case: Two-speed. Ratios: 1.96:1, 1.00:1. Brakes: Hydraulic front and rear. Dimensions: Front and rear: 12.125 in. x 2.0 in. Total lining area: 211.58 sq. in. Wheels: Eight-stud ventilated disc. Tires: W100: 6.50 x 16 6-ply. W200: 7 x 17.5 6-ply, tubeless. Optional: W100: 7.00 x 16 6-ply, 7 x 17.5 6-ply. W200: 8 x 19.5 8-ply. Steering: Recirculating ball. Transmission: 3-speed heavy-duty A745 manual. Optional: New Process #435, 4-speed manual. Clutch: Single plate, dry disc, 11.0 in. dia. with lining area of 123.7 sq. in. Standard with 383 V-8: 12 in. dia. and 150 sq. in. lining area.

VEHICLE DIMENSIONS: W100: Wheelbase: 114 in. Overall Length: 181 in. (Add 15.125 in. for winch). Front/Rear Tread: 65.5 in./61.9375 in. Overall Height: 80.3125 in. Load space: Pickup box dimensions: Utiline body: 114 in. wheelbase: 78.125 in. x 49 in. x 20 in. Capacity: 47.25 cu. ft. Sweptline body: 114 in. wheelbase: 78.625 in. x 70 in. x 20 in. Capacity: 59.3 cu. ft. W200: Wheelbase: 128 in. Crew cab: 146 in. Overall Length: 192.75 in. (add 15.125 in. for winch). Front/Rear Tread: 65.0625 in./61.8125 in. Overall Height: 80.25 in. Load space: Pickup box dimensions: Utiline: 96 in. x 54 in. x 20 in. Capacity: 58.5 cu. ft. Sweptline: 98.875 in. x 70.75 in. x 20 in. Capacity: 75 cu. ft.

CAPACITIES: Fuel Tank: 18 gal. Engine coolant system: 6-cyl.: 13.0 qt. V-8: 20.0 qt.

ACCOMMODATIONS: 3 passengers. Town Wagon: Up to eight passengers.

INSTRUMENTATION: Speedometer, odometer, gauges for fuel level, ammeter and engine coolant temperature.

W300:

CHASSIS FEATURES: Separate body and straight frame. Dimensions: 7.25 in. x 2.75 in. x 0.2318 in. Section modules: 5.70.

SUSPENSION AND RUNNING GEAR: Front Suspension: Semi-elliptical leaf springs. Capacity: 1,450 lb. Optional: 1,750 lb. (standard with front-mounted winch). Rear Suspension: Semi-elliptical leaf springs. Capacity: 3,250. Optional: 4,050 lb. Front Axle Type and Capacity: Full-floating, Hypoid-type. Capacity: 4,500 lb. Rear Axle Type and Capacity: Full-floating, Hypoid-type. Capacity: 7,500 lb. Anti-slip differential optional. Final Drive Ratio: 4.88:1 or 5.87:1. Transfer Case: Two-speed, single lever. Ratios: 1.96:1, 1.00:1. Brakes: Hydraulic front and rear. Dimensions: Front: 14.125 in. x 1.75 in. Rear: 13 in. x 2.5 in. Total lining area: 241.98 sq. in. Wheels: Six-stud ventilated disc. Tires: 8 x 19.5 8-ply, tubeless. Optional: 9.00 x 16 10-ply. Steering: Worm and roller. Ratio: 29.0:1. Optional: Power assisted. Transmission: New Process #435, 4-speed manual. Clutch: Single plate, dry disc, 11.0 in. dia. with lining area of 123.7 sq. in. 318 Premium V-8: 12 in. dia.; 150 sq. in. lining area.

VEHICLE DIMENSIONS: Wheelbase: 133 in. Overall Length: 204.5 in. (add 17.875 in. for winch). Width: 81.8125 in. Overall Height: 84.5n in. Front/Rear Tread: 64.5625 in./65.0 in.

CAPACITIES: Fuel Tank: 18 gal. Engine coolant system: 6-cyl.: 20.0 qt. V-8: 24.0 qt.

ACCOMMODATIONS: 3 passengers.

INSTRUMENTATION: Speedometer, odometer, gauges for fuel level, ammeter and engine coolant temperature.

OPTIONS: W100, W200, W300: Full width rear window. Appearance Package. 4-speed NP435D manual transmission. Oil-bath air cleaner (6-cyl. only). 46 amp alternator. 59 amp alternator. 70 amp-hr. battery. Rear bumper painted Dodge truck white. Left side armrest. Inside body spare tire carrier for Sweptline. Increased cooling system. Oil pressure gauge. Tinted glass for windshield and rear window. Fresh-Air heater. Transistor radio. Custom Fresh-Air heater with defrosters. Dual electric horns. Front locking manual hubs. Heavy-duty instrument cluster. Includes electric tachometer, oil pressure gauge. Two-tone paint. Undercoating. 318 cu. in. V-8. 383 cu. in. V-8. Front-mounted 8,000 lb. winch. Power take-off (transfer case). Anti-slip rear differential. Vacuum power brakes. Adjustable braced or Junior western-style mirrors. Sweptline side molding. Full-depth foam seat. Comfort Package. W300M: 70 amp-hr. battery. 46 amp alternator. 59 amp alternator. Traffic hazard warning switch. Front locking manual hubs. Pulley drive. Power winch. Power take-off. Radiator overflow tank. Front end tow hooks. Brake booster. Rear pintle hook. Undercoating. Recirculating heater with defroster. Hydraulic jack with 3 ton capacity.

HISTORICAL FOOTNOTES: The 1967 Dodge trucks were introduced in October, 1966. Model year production of all Dodge truck models was 128,732.

1968 POWER WAGON

The 1968 four-wheel drive Dodge W100, W200 and W300 truck models were distinguished by their new grille which consisted of a wide center bar and three vertical dividers. The headlights were carried in chrome nacelles that were less flamboyant than the units used in 1967. The Custom Sports Special was replaced by the new Adventurer model which was not available in four-wheel drive form. The standard cab for the conventional models was offered in vinyl with a choice of four colors: Blue, green, tan or black. The fabric and vinyl upholstery of the optional Comfort Package was available in blue, tan, green and black. Features of the standard cab included a dome light, ashtray, dispatch box, key lock for both doors, push-button door locks, dual armrests, coat hook, custom Fresh-Air heater-defroster, high-level fresh air intake, variable-speed windshield wipers, windshield washers, cab floor rubber mat, padded instrument panel and padded dual sun visors. A full-width rear window was standard for the conventional and crew cab pickups. A total of 13 exterior colors were offered. Color choices for 1968 consisted of white, black, medium green, dark green, grey, bright turquoise, light blue, dark blue, pale yellow, beige, tan, bright red and dark red.

1968 Dodge W200 Sweptline Power Wagon pickup

I.D. DATA: The first two digits of the serial number indicated the model code as follows: W100: 21; W200: 22; W300: 23; WM300: 24. The third digit indicated the number of cylinders. The last seven digits were the production sequence number. The serial numbers on 6-cylinder OHV engines were located on the right side of the block on top of the boss directly behind the coil. The V-8 serial number was found on the left front of the block under the cylinder head. The L-head 6-cylinder engine serial number was found on the left front of the block at the top. A new engine serial number format was used in 1968. The first two letters indicated the manufacturing plant as follows: PM (Mound Road), PT (Trenton), DW (Windsor). The next three digits indicated displacement as follows: 170 (170 cu. in.), 225 (225 cu. in.), 318 (318 cu. in.), etc. The next letter provided additional engine identification: R (regular gas), L (low compression), T (standard-duty), H (heavy-duty). The next four digits indicated the date of manufacture based on a 10,000 day calendar. The last four digits served as a sequence number for each day's production.

Body Type	Fact. Price	GVW	Shipping Weight	Prod. Total
Model W100, 1/2 ton 6-cyl.				
Ch. & Cab, 114 in. wb.	$2696	5100*	3735	a
Pickup, Utiline, 114 in. wb.	$2818	5100	4095	—
Pickup, Sweptline, 114 in. wb	$2831	5100	4145	—

* 6000 lb. GVW optional.
a Total model year production of all W100 trucks was 721 units with 6-cyl. engines and 752 with V-8 engines.

Body Type	Fact. Price	GVW	Shipping Weight	Prod. Total
Model W200, 3/4 ton, 6-cyl. (Crew cab-146 in. wb.).				
Ch. & Cab, 128 in. wb.	$2800	6000*	3945	b
Pickup, Utiline, 128 in. wb.	$2922	6000	4385	—
Pickup, Sweptline, 128 in. wb.	$2935	6000	4445	—
Stake, 128 in. wb.	$3011	6000	4520	—
Platform, 128 in. wb.	$2960	6000	4320	—
Crew Cab, Ch.	$3582	6000	4375	—
Crew Cab, Utiline	$3703	6000	4735	—
Crew Cab, Sweptline	$3716	6000	4785	—

* An 8000 lb. GVW package was optional for all models.
b Total model year production, excluding crew cab models, was 2759 units with 6-cyl. engines and 3178 with V-8 engines.

Body Type	Fact. Price	GVW	Shipping Weight	Prod. Total
Model W300, 1 ton, 6-cyl.				
Ch. & Cowl, 133 in. wb.	$3100	8500	4090	c
Ch. & Cab, 133 in. wb.	$3508	8500*	4645	—
Pickup, Utiline, 133 in. wb.	$3649	8500	5140	—
Platform, 133 in. wb.	$3700	8500	5345	—
Stake, 133 in. wb.	$3762	8500	5545	—

* GVW packages up to 10,000 lb. were available.
c Total model year production of was 175 units with 6-cyl. engines and 693 with V-8 engines.

Prices of the W100, W200 and W300 models with optional V-8 engine were an additional $120.00.

Body Type	Fact. Price	GVW	Shipping Weight	Prod. Total
Model WM300				
Ch. & Cowl, 126 in. wb.	$3662	8700	4095	d
Ch. & Cab, 126 in. wb.	$4033	8700*	4520	—
Pickup, 126 in. wb.	$4184	8700	4920	—

* 9500 lb. GVW package optional for all WM300 models.
d Total model year production was 974 units.

STANDARD ENGINE: W100, W200: Engine Type: OHV, In-line 6-cylinder. Cast iron block and cylinder head. Bore x Stroke: 3.40 in. x 4.125 in. Lifters: Mechanical. Number of main bearings-4. Fuel Induction: Single barrel carburetor. Compression Ratio: 8.4:1. Displacement: 224.7 cu. in. (3.68 liters). Horsepower: 140 @ 3900 rpm. Torque: 215 lb.-ft. @ 1600-2800 rpm. Oil refill capacity: 5 qt.

STANDARD ENGINE: W300: Engine Type: OHV, In-line "Premium Slant Six." Cast iron block and cylinder head, Premium components include roller timing chain, bimetal connecting rod bearings, heat-resistant Stellite-faced exhaust valves, and polyacrylic valve stem seals. Bore x Stroke: 3.40 in. x 4.125 in. Lifters: Mechanical. Number of main bearings-4. Fuel Induction: Single barrel carburetor. Compression Ratio: 8.4:1. Displacement: 224.7 cu. in. (3.68 liters). Horsepower: 140 @ 3900 rpm. Torque: 215 lb.-ft. @ 1600-2800 rpm. Oil refill capacity: 5 qt.

STANDARD ENGINE: WM300: Engine Type: L-head, In-line 6-cylinder. Cast iron block and cylinder head. Bore x Stroke: 3.437 in. x 4.50 in. Lifters: Mechanical. Number of main bearings-4. Fuel Induction: Stromberg single barrel downdraft carburetor. Compression Ratio: 7.1:1. Displacement: 250.6 cu. in. (4.10 liters). Horsepower: 125 @ 3600 rpm. Torque: 216 lb.-ft. @ 1600 rpm. Oil refill capacity: 5 qt. Fuel Requirements: Regular.

OPTIONAL ENGINE: W100, W200: Engine Type: OHV, V-8. Cast iron block and cylinder head. Bore x Stroke: 3.91 in. x 3.3120 in. Lifters: Hydraulic. Number of main bearings-5. Fuel Induction: Two barrel carburetor. Compression Ratio: 8.25:1. Displacement: 318.14 cu. in. (5.21 liters). Horsepower: 210 @ 4000 rpm. Torque: 318 lb.-ft. @ 2800 rpm. Oil refill capacity: 5 qt. Fuel Requirements: Regular.

OPTIONAL ENGINE: W300: Engine Type: OHV, Premium V-8. Cast iron block and cylinder head. This engine has the standard 318 V-8 features plus roller-chain drive, vibration damper, positive exhaust valve rotators and hydraulic valve lifters. Bore x Stroke: 3.63 in. x 3.80 in. Lifters: Hydraulic. Number of main bearings-5. Fuel Induction: 2-barrel carburetor. Compression Ratio: 7.5:1. Displacement: 318.14 cu. in. (5.21 liters). Horsepower: 202 @ 3900 rpm. Torque: 288 lb.-ft. @ 2400 rpm. Oil refill capacity: 5 qt. Fuel Requirements: Regular.

OPTIONAL ENGINE: W100, W200: Engine Type: OHV, V-8. Cast iron block and cylinder head. This engine has a vibraton damper, 18 in., 7-blade fan, and a drop-forged crankshaft. Bore x Stroke: 4.25 in. x 3.38 in. Lifters: Hydraulic. Number of main bearings-5. Fuel Induction: 2-barrel carburetor. Compression Ratio: 9.2:1. Displacement: 383 cu. in. (6.276 liters). Horsepower: 258 @ 4400 rpm. Torque: 375 lb.-ft. @ 2800 rpm. Oil refill capacity: 5 qt. Fuel Requirements: Regular.

W300M:

CHASSIS FEATURES: Separate body and double-drop frame; side rail reinforcements (inside type). Frame dimensions: 122.45875 in. x 0.109375 in. Frame rail dimensions: 6.09 in. x 2.04 in. x 0.171 in. Section modules: 4.51.

SUSPENSION AND RUNNING GEAR: Front Suspension: Eleven leaf, 39 in. x 1.75 in. semi-elliptical springs, heavy-duty, double-acting shock absorbers. Capacity: 1,150 lb. (each). Optional: 1600 lb. capacity, (included with winch). Rear Suspension: Fourteen leaf, 52.25 in. x 1.75 in. semi-elliptical springs. Capacity: 2,500 lb. (each). Optional: 3,000 lb. capacity. Front Axle Type and Capacity: Full-floating, Hypoid-type. Capacity: 3,750 lb. Rear Axle Type and Capacity: Full-floating, Hypoid-type. Capacity: 6,500 lb. Final Drive Ratio: 5.83:1. Transfer Case: Two-speed, double-lever. Ratios: 1.96:1, 1.00:1. Brakes: Hydraulic front and rear. Dimensions: Front and rear: 14.125 in. x 1.75 in. Total lining area: 215.18 sq. in. Wheels: Five-stud ventilated disc. Tires: 9.00 x 16 8-ply. Optional: 9.00 x 16 10-ply. Steering: Worm and lever; 17.0 in. diameter steering wheel. Ratio: 23.2:1. Optional: None. Transmission: New Process #420, 4-speed "Synchro-shift" manual. Transmission Ratios: 6.68, 3.10, 1.69, 1.00:1. Reverse: 8.25:1. Clutch: Single plate, Oilite bronze pilot bearing, 11.0 in, dia. with lining area of 123.7 sq. in.

VEHICLE DIMENSIONS: Wheelbase: 126.0 in. Overall Length: Pickup: 199.0 in. (without winch); 208.625 in. (with winch); Chassis and cab: 191.156 in. (without winch); 201.093 in. (with winch). Front/Rear Tread: 64.75 in./64.75 in. Overall Height: 76 in. (loaded). Width: 79.25 in. Front/Rear Overhang: 25.125 in./47.35 in. Tailgate: Width and Height: 54.0 in. x 19.9375 in. Ground Clearance: 8.8125 in.; with optional tires: 10.625 in. Load space: 96.0625 in. x 54.0 in. x 22.25 in.

CAPACITIES: Fuel Tank: 18 gal. Engine coolant system: 17 qt.

ACCOMMODATIONS: 3 passengers.

INSTRUMENTATION: Speedometer, odometer, gauges for oil pressure, fuel level, battery charge, engine coolant temperature.

W100 and W200:

CHASSIS FEATURES: Separate body and drop-center frame. Dimension: W100: 6.12 in. x 2.30 in. x 0.188 in. Section modules: W100: 3.43. W200: 3.88, W200 crew cab: 4.70. Dimension: W200: 6.25 in. x 2.42 in. x 0.250 in.

SUSPENSION AND RUNNING GEAR: Front Suspension: Semi-elliptical leaf springs. Capacity: 6-cyl.: 1,100 lb. V-8: 1,350 lb. W200 crew cab: 1,550 lb. Optional: 6-cyl.: 1,350 lb. V-8: 1,550 lb. (both were standard with front-mounted winch). Rear Suspension: Semi-elliptical leaf springs. Capacity: W100: 1,350 lb. W200: 1,750 lb. Optional: W100: 1,750 lb. W200: 2,600 lb. Front Axle Type and Capacity: Full-floating, Hypoid-type. Capacity: 3,000 lb. W200 crew cab: 3,500 lb. Rear Axle Type and Capacity: W100: Full-floating, Hypoid-type. Capacity: 4,500 lb. W200: Full-floating, Hypoid-type. Capacity: 5,500 lb. Final Drive Ratio: 3.54:1 (with 383 engine only), 4.1:1 or 4.88:1 (not available with 383 V-8). Anti-slip differential available with 4.1:1 ratio. Transfer Case: Two-speed. Ratios: 1.96:1, 1.00:1. Brakes: Hydraulic front and rear. Dimensions: Front and rear: 12.125 in. x 2.0 in. Total lining area: 211.58 sq. in. Wheels: Eight-stud ventilated disc. Tires: W100: 6.50 x 16 6-ply. W200: 7 x 17.5 6-ply, tubeless. Optional: W100: 7.00 x 16 6-ply, 7 x 17.5 6-ply. W200: 8 x 19.5 8-ply. Steering: Recirculating ball. Transmission: 3-speed heavy-duty A745 manual. Optional: New Process #435, 4-speed manual. Clutch: Single plate, dry disc, 11.0 in, dia. with lining area of 123.7 sq. in. Standard with 383 V-8: 12 in. dia. and 150 sq. in. lining area.

VEHICLE DIMENSIONS: W100: Wheelbase: 114 in. Overall Length: 181 in. (Add 15.125 in. for winch). Front/Rear Tread: 65.5 in./61.9375 in. Overall Height: 80.3125 in. Load space: Pickup box dimensions: Utiline body: 114 in. wheelbase: 78.125 in. x 49 in. x 20 in. Capacity: 47.25 cu. ft. Sweptline body: 114 in. wheelbase: 78.625 in. x 70 in. x 20 in. Capacity: 59.3 cu. ft. W200: Wheelbase: 128 in. Crew cab: 146 in. Overall Length: 192.75 in. (add 15.125 in. for winch). Front/Rear Tread: 65.0625 in./ 61.8125 in. Overall Height: 80.25 in. Load space: Pickup box dimensions: Utiline: 96 in. x 54 in. x 20 in. Capacity: 58.5 cu. ft. Sweptline: 98.875 in. x 70.75 in. x 20 in. Capacity: 75 cu. ft.

CAPACITIES: Fuel Tank: 18 gal. Engine coolant system: 6-cyl.: 13.0 qt. V-8: 20.0 qt.

ACCOMMODATIONS: 3 passengers. Town Wagon: Up to eight passengers.

INSTRUMENTATION: Speedometer, odometer, gauges for fuel level, ammeter and engine coolant temperature.

W300:

CHASSIS FEATURES: Separate body and straight frame. Dimensions: 7.25 in. x 2.75 in. x 0.2318 in. Section modules: 5.70.

SUSPENSION AND RUNNING GEAR: Front Suspension: Semi-elliptical leaf springs. Capacity: 1,450 lb. Optional: 1,750 lb. (standard with front-mounted winch). Rear Suspension: Semi-elliptical leaf springs. Capacity: 3,250. Optional: 4,050 lb. Front Axle Type and Capacity: Full-floating, Hypoid-type. Capacity: 4,500 lb. Rear Axle Type and Capacity: Full-floating, Hypoid-type. Capacity: 7,500 lb. Anti-slip differential optional. Final Drive Ratio: 4.88:1 or 5.87:1. Transfer Case: Two-speed, single lever. Ratios: 1.96:1, 1.00:1. Brakes: Hydraulic front and rear. Dimensions: Front: 14.125 in. x 1.75 in. Rear: 13 in. x 2.5 in. Total lining area: 241.98 sq. in. Wheels: Six-stud ventilated disc. Tires: 8 x 19.5 8-ply, tubeless. Optional: 9.00 x 16 10-ply. Steering: Worm and roller. Ratio: 29.0:1. Optional: Power assisted. Transmission: New Process #435, 4-speed manual. Clutch: Single plate, dry disc, 11.0 in. dia. with lining area of 123.7 sq. in. 318 Premium V-8: 12 in. dia.; 150 sq. in. lining area.

VEHICLE DIMENSIONS: Wheelbase: 133 in. Overall Length: 204.5 in. (add 17.875 in. for winch). Width: 81.8125 in. Overall Height: 84.5 in. Front/Rear tread: 64.5625 in./ 65.0 in.

CAPACITIES: Fuel Tank: 18 gal. Engine coolant system: 6-cyl.: 20.0 qt. V-8: 24.0 qt.

ACCOMMODATIONS: 3 passengers.

INSTRUMENTATION: Speedometer, odometer, gauges for fuel level, ammeter and engine coolant temperature.

OPTIONS: W100, W200, W300: Full width rear window. Appearance Package. 4-speed NP435D manual transmission. Oil-bath air cleaner (6-cyl. only). 46 amp alternator. 59 amp alternator. 70 amp-hr. battery. Rear bumper painted Dodge truck white. Left side armrest. Inside body spare tire carrier for Sweptline. Increased cooling system. Oil pressure gauge. Tinted glass for windshield and rear window. Fresh-Air heater. Transistor radio. Custom fresh-Air heater with defrosters. Dual electric horns. Front locking manual hubs. Heavy-duty instrument cluster. Includes electric tachometer, oil pressure gauge. Two-tone paint. Under-coating. 318 cu. in. V-8. 383 cu. in. V-8. Front-mounted 8,000 lb. winch. Power take-off (transfer case). Anti-slip rear differential. Vacuum power brakes. Adjustable braced or Junior Western-style mirrors. Sweptline side molding. Full-depth foam seat. Comfort Package. Outside body spare tire carrier, left side mounted with long stationary mirror with 5 in. head (Utiline body), directional signals: Class "A" flashing, self-cancelling type with steering column switch. Engine governor (high-speed velocity type with manual transmission). Auxiliary underseat heater. Dual electric horns. Cigarette lighter (for standard cabs). Comfort Package. Includes custom seat trim, roof headling insulation, full-foam seat cushion, foam pad seat back, color-keyed seat belts, color-keyed floor mat and cigarette lighter. Trim Molding Package (for Sweptline only). Includes straight rolled section molding with front and rear stamped sections extending along hood, cowl, cab door, cab, cab rear panel and Sweptline body. Two-tone paint. Instrument panel-mounted radio. Full-width seat assembly. Includes full-depth foam padding with foam topper on seat back and standard upholstery. Third seat belt for bench seat. Two shoulder belts. Power steering (for V-8 engine models only). Under-coating. Winch assembly. Camper Special Package (for W200). Includes power brakes, 60 amp alternator, 70 amp-hr. battery, increased engine cooling, oil pressure gauge, dual West Coast painted mirrors, "Camper Special" emblems. Camper Custom Package (for Sweptline W200) includes components of Camper Special Package plus Comfort Package, Appearance Package, dual electric horns and exterior side moldings. W300M: 70 amp.-hr. battery. 46 amp alternator. 59 amp alternator. Traffic hazard warning switch. Front locking manual hubs. Pulley drive. Power winch. Power take-off. Radiator overflow tank. Front end tow hooks. Brake booster. Rear pintle hook. Undercoating. Recirculating heater with defrost. Hydraulic jack with 3 ton capacity.

HISTORICAL FOOTNOTES: The Dodge four-wheel drive trucks were introduced in August, 1967. This was the last year the original Power Wagon was offered for domestic sale. It remained available for export.

1969 POWER WAGON

1969 Dodge W100 Sweptline Power Wagon pickup

The exterior appearance of the 1969 models was similar to that of the 1968 versions. The major change was the use of a revised hood design with a raised center section rather than the recessed surface found on the 1968 models. Numerous interior refinements were offered for 1969. A new instrument cluster and controls as well as a flip-up glove box, contoured padded dash and deep-dish, energy-absorbing steering wheel were among its highlights. A major development for 1969 was the introduction of a new single lever for the transfer case. This allowed the driver to chose four-wheel drive and then switch simply and quickly back to rear wheel drive with just a flip of the wrist. Compared to the older 2-lever system this new unit was lighter in weight, more durable and, due to its constant-mesh design, quieter running. The W100 had a lower profile resulting in easier entry and loading. Standard equipment for the W100, W200 and W300 consisted of self-adjusting brakes (W100 and W200), front and rear side marker lights and reflectors, and front and rear identification and clearance lights (stake and platform models plus W300 Utiline over 80 in. wide), full-width rear window, vinyl seat upholstery in choice of blue, green, beige or black; 6-way adjustable bench seat, dual armrests (four on crew cab), dispatch box, ashtray, high-level ventilation, Fresh-Air heater/

defroster, keylock in both doors, wheel wrench and jack, Cleaner Air system (W100), positive crankcase ventilation system (W200, W300), dual braking system with warning light, turn signals, back-up lights, 4-way emergency flashers, 2-speed windshield wipers, windshield washers, left and interior rearview mirrors (pickups), dual long-arm mirrors (stakes, platform and chassis-cab), push-button door locks, padded instrument panel, padded dual sun visors, recessed inside door-release handles, low profile window crank handles and vent latches, color-keyed seat belts, boots and retractors, and front and rear side marker reflectors (pickups, crew cabs, Stakes and Platforms).

1969 Dodge W300 Utiline Power Wagon pickup

I.D. DATA: The serial numbers were located on a plate on the left door lock pillar. A ten character identification system was used. The first two digits were the model code: 21-(W100), 22-(W200), 23-(W300), 24-(W300 for export). Next came a digit, either 6 or 8, identifying the number of cylinders. This was followed by another digit identifying the assembly plant as follows: 1-Warren Truck, 2-Warren Heavy duty, 6-Windsor, 7-Missouri. The remaining six digits were the production sequence numbers. The serial numbers on 6-cylinder engines were located on the right side of the block below the no. one spark plug. The 318 V-8 serial number was found on the left front of the block below the cylinder head. The 383 V-8 serial number was found on the right side of the block next to the distributor. The 225 6-cyl. and 318 V-8 used a system in which the first two letters indicated the manufacturing plant as follows: GM-Mound Road, GT-Trenton, NM-Maryland, GW-Windsor. The next three digits identified the engine's displacement, The next letter identified the engine type as follows: R-regular 318 V-8; T-standard 225 6-cyl; H-premium 225 6-cyl. The next four digits were the manufacturing date code base upon a 10,000 day calendar. The final four digits were the sequence production numbers beginning with 001 for each day. The 383 V-8 identification system used the following form: The first letter indicated the model year. The next letter identified the engine type (T-standard). The next three digits were the engine's displacement. The next digit identified the assembly plant shift. This was followed by four digits identifying the manufacturing date. The next two digits were used as a non-standard engine indicator. The last four digits were the production sequence production number.

Body Type	Factory Price	GVW	Shipping Weight	Prod. Total
Model W100, 1/2 ton 6-cyl.				
Ch. & Cab, 114 in. wb.	$2804	5100*	3735	a
Pickup, 114 in. wb.	$2931	5100	4095	—
Pickup, Sweptline, 114 in. wb.	$2967	5100	4145	—
Ch. & Cab, 128 in. wb.	$2840	5100	3735	—
Pickup, Utiline, 128 in. wb.	$2967	5100	4095	—
Pickup, Sweptline, 128 in. wb.	$3006	5100	N.A.	—

* 5600 lb. GVW optional.
Add $124.75 to all W100 prices for 318 V-8.
a Total model year production of all W100 trucks was 766 units with 6-cyl. engines and 1007 with V-8 engines.

Body Type	Factory Price	GVW	Shipping Weight	Prod. Total
Model W200, 3/4 ton, 6-cyl. (Crew cab-146 in. wheelbase)				
Ch. & Cab, 128 in. wb.	$3182	6000*	3945	b
Pickup, Utiline, 128 in. wb.	$3309	6000	4385	—
Pickup, Sweptline, 128 in. wb.	$3348	6000	4445	—
Crew Cab, Ch.	$3984.25	6000	4375	—
Crew Cab, Utiline	$4112.25	6000	4735	—
Crew Cab, Sweptline	$4130.25	6000	4785	—

* 6500 lb. and 8000 lb. GVW package was optional for all models.
Add $125.25 to all W100 prices for 318 V-8.
b Total model year production, excluding crew cab models, was 1091 units with 6-cyl. engines and 3427 with V-8 engines. Crew cab production was 698 units with 6-cyl. engine and 438 with V-8 engines.

Body Type	Factory Price	GVW	Shipping Weight	Prod. Total
Model W300, 1 ton, 6-cyl.				
Ch. & Cab, 133 in. wb.	$3884.25	8500*	4645	c
Pickup, Utiline, 133 in. wb.	$3969.25	8500	5140	—

Add $134.25 for 318 V-8.
* GVW packages up to 10,000 lb. were available.
c Total model year production of was 749 units with 6-cyl. engines and 901 with V-8 engines.

STANDARD ENGINE: W100, W200: Engine Type: OHV, In-line 6-cylinder. Cast iron block and cylinder head. Bore x Stroke: 3.40 in. x 4.125 in. Lifters: Mechanical. Number of main bearings-4. Fuel Induction: Single barrel carburetor. Compression Ratio: 8.4:1. Displacement: 224.7 cu. in. (3.68 liters). Horsepower: 140 @ 3900 rpm. Torque: 215 lb.-ft. @ 1600-2800 rpm. Oil refill capacity: 5 qt.

STANDARD ENGINE: W300: Engine Type: OHV, In-line "Premium Slant Six." Cast iron block and cylinder head, premium components include roller timing chain, bimetal connecting rod bearings, heat-resistant Stellite-faced exhaust valves, and polyacrylic valve stem seals. Bore x Stroke: 3.40 in. x 4.125 in. Lifters: Mechanical. Number of main bearings-4. Fuel Induction: Single barrel carburetor. Compression Ratio: 8.4:1. Displacement: 224.7 cu. in. (3.68 liters). Horsepower: 140 @ 3900 rpm. Torque: 215 lb.-ft. @ 1600-2800 rpm. Oil refill capacity: 5 qt.

OPTIONAL ENGINE: W100, W200: Engine Type: OHV, V-8. Cast iron block and cylinder head. Bore x Stroke: 3.91 in. x 3.3120 in. Lifters: Hydraulic. Number of main bearings-5. Fuel Induction: Two barrel carburetor. Compression Ratio: 8.25:1. Displacement: 318.14 cu. in. (5.21 liters). Horsepower: 210 @ 4000 rpm. Torque: 318 lb.-ft. @ 2800 rpm. Oil refill capacity: 5 qt. Fuel Requirements: Regular.

OPTIONAL ENGINE: W300: Engine Type: OHV, Premium V-8. Cast iron block and cylinder head. This engine has the standard 318 V-8 features plus roller-chain drive, vibration damper, positive exhaust valve rotators and hydraulic valve lifters. Bore x Stroke: 3.63 in. x 3.80 in. Lifters: Hydraulic. Number of main bearings-5. Fuel Induction: 2-barrel carburetor. Compression Ratio: 7.5:1. Displacement: 318.14 cu. in. (5.21 liters). Horsepower: 202 @ 3900 rpm. Torque: 288 lb.-ft. @ 2400 rpm. Oil refill capacity: 5 qt. Fuel Requirements: Regular.

OPTIONAL ENGINE: W100, W200: Engine Type: OHV, V-8. Cast iron block and cylinder head. This engine has a vibraton damper, 18 in., 7 blade fan, and a drop-forged crankshaft. Bore x Stroke: 4.25 in. x 3.38 in. Lifters: Hydraulic. Number of main bearings-5. Fuel Induction: 2-barrel carburetor. Compression Ratio: 9.2:1. Displacement: 383 cu. in. (6.276 liters). Horsepower: 258 @ 4400 rpm. Torque: 375 lb.-ft. @ 2800 rpm. Oil refill capacity: 5 qt. Fuel Requirements: Regular.

W100 and W200:

CHASSIS FEATURES: Separate body and drop-center frame. Dimension: W100: 6.12 in. x 2.30 in. x 0.188 in. Section modules: W100: 3.43. W200: 3.88, W200 crew cab: 4.70. Dimension: W200: 6.25 in. x 2.42 in. x 0.250 in.

SUSPENSION AND RUNNING GEAR: Front Suspension: Semi-elliptical leaf springs. Capacity: 1,200 lb., 1,350 lb. (standard for 128 in. wheelbase). Optional: 1,550 lb. Rear Suspension: Semi-elliptical leaf springs. Capacity: W100: 1,350 lb. W200: 1,750 lb. Optional: W100: 1,750 lb. W200: 2,600 lb. Front Axle Type and Capacity: Full-floating, Hypoid-type. Capacity: 3,000 lb. W200 crew cab: 3,500 lb. Rear Axle Type and Capacity: W100: Full-floating, Hypoid-type. Capacity: 4,500 lb. W200: Full-floating, Hypoid-type. Capacity: 5,500 lb. Final Drive Ratio: W100: 3.54:1, 4.1:1. W200: 3.54:1 (not available with 3,500 lb. axle), 4.1:1, 4.89:1 (not available with 383 V-8). Anti-slip rear differential available with 4.1:1 ratio. Transfer Case: Two-speed. Ratios: 1.96:1, 1.00:1. Brakes: Hydraulic front and rear. Dimensions: Front and rear: 12.125 in. x 2.0 in. Total lining area: 211.58 sq. in. Wheels: Eight-stud ventilated disc. Tires: W100: 6.50 x 16 6-ply. W200: 7 x 17.5 6-ply, tubeless. Optional: W100: 7.00 x 16 6-ply, 7 x 17.5 6-ply. W200: 8 x 19.5 8-ply. Steering: Recirculating ball. Transmission: 3-speed heavy-duty A745 manual. Optional: New Process #435, 4-speed manual. Clutch: Single plate, dry disc, 11.0 in. dia. with lining area of 123.7 sq. in. Standard with 383 V-8: 12 in. dia. and 150 sq. in. lining area.

VEHICLE DIMENSIONS: W100: Wheelbase: 114 in./128 in. Overall Length: 181 in. (114 in. wheelbase). (Add 15.125 in. for winch). Front/Rear Tread: 65.5 in./61.9375 in. Overall Height: 80.3125 in. Load space: Pickup box dimensions: Utiline body: 114 in. wheelbase: 78.125 in. x 49 in. x 20 in. Capacity: 47.25 cu. ft. Sweptline body: 114 in. wheelbase: 78.625 in. x 70 in. x 20 in. Capacity: 59.3 cu. ft. Utiline body: 128 in. wheelbase: 96 in. x 49 in. x 20 in. Sweptline body: 128 in. wheelbase: 98.875 in. x 70 in. x 20 in. W200: Wheelbase: 128 in. Crew cab: 146 in. Overall Length: 192.75 in. (add 15.125 in. for winch). Front/Rear Tread: 65.0625 in./ 61.8125 in. Overall Height: 80.25 in. Load space: Pickup box dimensions: Utiline body: 96 in. x 54 in. x 20 in. Capacity: 58.5 cu. ft. Sweptline body: 98.875 in. x 70.75 in. x 20 in. Capacity: 75 cu. ft.

CAPACITIES: Fuel Tank: 18 gal. Engine coolant system: 6-cyl.: 13.0 qt. V-8: 20.0 qt.

ACCOMMODATIONS: 3 passengers.

INSTRUMENTATION: Speedometer, odometer, gauges for fuel level, ammeter and engine coolant temperature.

W300:

CHASSIS FEATURES: Separate body and straight frame. Dimensions: 7.25 in. x 2.75 in. x 0.2318 in. Section modules: 5.70.

SUSPENSION AND RUNNING GEAR: Front Suspension: Semi-elliptical leaf springs. Capacity: 1,450 lb. Optional: 1,750 lb. (standard with front-mounted winch). Rear Suspension: Semi-elliptical leaf springs. Capacity: 3,250. Optional: 4,050 lb. Front Axle Type and Capacity: Full-floating, Hypoid-type. Capacity: 4,500 lb. Rear Axle Type and Capacity: Full-floating, Hypoid-type. Capacity: 7,500 lb. Anti-slip differential optional. Final Drive Ratio: 4.88:1 or 5.86:1. Transfer Case: Two-speed, single lever. Ratios: 1.96:1, 1.00:1. Brakes: Hydraulic front and rear. Dimensions: Front: 14.125 in. x 1.75 in. Rear: 13 in. x 2.5 in. Total lining area: 241.98 sq. in. Wheels: Six-stud ventilated disc. Tires: 8 x 19.5 8-ply, tubeless. Optional: 9.00 x 16 10-ply. Steering: Worm and roller. Ratio: 29.0:1. Optional: Power assisted. Transmission: New Process #435B 4-speed manual. Optional: New Process #435, 4-speed manual. Clutch: Single plate, dry disc, 11.0 in. dia. with lining area of 123.7 sq. in.

VEHICLE DIMENSIONS: Wheelbase: 133 in. Overall Length: 204.5 in. (add 17.875 in. for winch). Width: 81.8125 in. Overall Height: 84.5 in. Front/Rear tread: 64.5625 in./65.0 in.

CAPACITIES: Fuel Tank: 18 gal. Engine coolant system: 6-cyl.: 20.0 qt. V-8: 24.0 qt.

ACCOMMODATIONS: 3 passengers.

INSTRUMENTATION: Speedometer, odometer, gauges for fuel level, ammeter and engine coolant temperature.

OPTIONS AND PRICES: Air conditioning: $398.40. 46 amp alternator: $21.70. 60 amp alternator: $30.10. 70 amp-hr. battery (standard with 383 engine): $7.90. Platform body for 128 in. wheelbase): $160.50. Stake body (for 128 in. wheelbase): $213.50. Bright finish front bumper: $14.30. Rear white painted bumper: $23.90. Front and rear bright-finished bumpers: $51.80. Inside body spare tire carrier for Sweptline body: $15. Cigarette lighter: $5.10. Increased cooling capacity: $21.60. Directional signals: $15.90. 383 cu. in. V-8: $137.90. Oil pressure gauge: $7.80. Engine governor for 225 and 318 engines with manual transmission): $18.50. Heater delete credit: -$68. Dual electric horns: $6.60. Front locking manual hubs: $79.40. 3-ton hydraulic jack: $14.30. Light Package: $30.10. Custom Interior Package: $31.80. Custom Exterior Package: $68.20. Exterior Trim Body Side Molding Package (for Sweptline body): $32.30. Exterior Trim Wheel-Lip and Sill Molding Package (for Sweptline body): $41.90. Insulation Package: $7.20. Two-tone paint: $21.40. Pintle hook: $64.10. Power take-off assembly: $148.80. Undercoating: $12.90. Winch assembly: $417. Instrument panel cluster. Includes electric tachometer and oil pressure gauge: $63.90. Camper Special Package (for W200). Includes power brakes, 60 amp alternator, 70 amp-hr. battery, increased engine cooling, oil pressure gauge, dual West Coast painted mirrors, "Camper Special" emblems. Camper Custom Package (for Sweptline W200) includes components of Camper Special Package plus Comfort Package, Appearance Package, dual electric horns and exterior side moldings.

HISTORICAL FOOTNOTES: The 1969 Dodge four-wheel drive trucks were introduced in August, 1968.

1969 Dodge W200 Camper Special Power Wagon pickup

1970 POWER WAGON

A new grille of anodized aluminum and configured to include a divided upper portion and a narrow lower section identified the 1970 four-wheel drive Dodge models. Not immediately obvious was a thin mesh insert for the grille. A much higher front fender line was quite apparent. The grille for the W100 and W220 had a bright finish. The W300 used a painted grille surround. The W100 and W200 trucks were offered with Dodge's 3-speed Loadflite automatic transmission. The W100 and W200 models with 6-cylinder engines also had a new 3-speed all-synchromesh manual transmission. The W series interior had a new face plate for the instrument panel, flip-up glove box, contoured padded dash, deep-dish energy-absorbing steering wheel, and two-speed windshield wipers.

1970 Dodge W100 Sweptline Power Wagon pickup

I.D. DATA: The serial numbers were located on a plate on the left door lock pillar. A ten character identification system was used. The first two digits were the model code: 21-(W100), 22-(W200), 23-(W300), 24-(W300 for export). Next came a digit, either 6 or 8, identifying the number of cylinders. This was followed by another digit identifying the assembly plant as follows: 1-Warren Truck, 2-Warren Heavy-Duty, 6-Windsor, 7-Missouri. The remaining six digits were the production sequence numbers. The serial numbers on 6-cylinder engines were located on the right side of the block below the no. one spark plug. The 318 V-8 serial number was found on the left front of the block below the cylinder head. The 383 V-8 serial number was found on the right side of the block next to the distributor. The 225 6-cyl. and 318 V-8 used a system in which the first two letters indicated the manufacturing plant as follows: GM-Mound Road, GT-Trenton, NM-Maryland, GW-Windsor. The next three digits identified the engine's displacement. The next letter identified the engine type as follows: R-regular 318 V-8; T-standard 225 6-cyl; H-premium 225 6-cyl. The next four digits were the manufacturing date code base upon a 10,000 day calendar. The final four digits were the sequence production numbers beginning with 001 for each day. The 383 V-8 identification system used the following form: The first letter indicated the model year. The next letter identified the engine type (T-standard). The next three digits were the engine's displacement. The next digit identified the assembly plant. This was followed by four digits identifying the manufacturing date. The next two digits were used as a non-standard engine indicator. The last four digits were the production sequence production number.

Body Type	Factory Price	GVW	Shipping Weight	Prod. Total
Model W100, 1/2 ton 6-cyl.				
Ch. & Cab, 114 in. wb.	$2932	5100*	3735	a
Pickup, Utiline, 114 in. wb.	$3059	5100	4095	—
Pickup, Sweptline, 114 in. wb.	$3095	5100	4145	—
Ch. & Cab, 128 in. wb.	$2968	5100	3735	—
Pickup, Utiline, 128 in. wb.	$3095	5100	4095	—
Pickup, Sweptline, 128 in. wb.	$3134	5100	N.A.	—

* 5600 lb. GVW optional.
Add $124.75 to all W100 prices for 318 V-8.
a Total model year production of all W100 trucks was 1500.

Body Type	Factory Price	GVW	Shipping Weight	Prod. Total
Model W200, 3/4 ton, 6-cyl. (Crew cab-146 in. wheelbase)				
Ch. & Cab, 128 in. wb.	$3372	6000*	3945	b
Pickup, Utiline, 128 in. wb.	$3499	6000	4385	—
Pickup, Sweptline, 128 in. wb.	$3538	6000	4445	—
Crew Cab, Ch.	$4174	6000	4375	—
Crew Cab, Utiline	$4302	6000	4735	—
Crew Cab, Sweptline	$4320	6000	4785	—

* 6500 lb. and 8000 lb. GVW package was optional for all models.
Add $125.25 to all W100 prices for 318 V-8.
b Total W200 model year production, excluding crew cab models, was 5719. Crew cab production was 914.

Body Type	Factory Price	GVW	Shipping Weight	Prod. Total
Model W300, 1 ton, 6-cyl.				
Ch. & Cab, 133 in. wb.	$4036	8500*	4645	c
Pickup, Utiline, 133 in. wb.	$4121	8500	5140	—

Add $134.25 for 318 V-8.
* GVW packages up to 10,000 lb. were available.
c Total W300 model year production was 1053.

STANDARD ENGINE: W100, W200: Engine Type: OHV, In-line 6-cylinder. Cast iron block and cylinder head. Bore x Stroke: 3.40 in. x 4.125 in. Lifters: Mechanical. Number of main bearings-5. Fuel Induction: Single barrel carburetor. Compression Ratio: 8.4:1. Displacement: 224.7 cu. in. (3.68 liters). Horsepower: 140 @ 3900 rpm. Torque: 215 lb.-ft. @ 1600-2800 rpm. Oil capacity: 5 qt.

STANDARD ENGINE: W300: Engine Type: OHV, In-line "Premium Slant Six." Cast iron block and cylinder head. Premium components include roller timing chain, bimetal connecting rod bearings, heat-resistant Stellite-faced exhaust valves, and polyacrylic valve stem seals. Bore x Stroke: 3.40 in. x 4.125 in. Lifters: Mechanical. Number of main bearings-5. Fuel Induction: Single barrel carburetor. Compression Ratio: 8.4:1. Displacement: 224.7 cu. in. (3.68 liters). Horsepower: 140 @ 3900 rpm. Torque: 215 lb.-ft. @ 1600-2800 rpm. Oil refill capacity: 5 qt.

OPTIONAL ENGINE: W100, W200: Engine Type: OHV, V-8. Cast iron block and cylinder head. Bore x Stroke: 3.91 in. x 3.3120 in. Lifters: Hydraulic. Number of main bearings-5. Fuel Induction: Two barrel carburetor. Compression Ratio: 8.25:1. Displacement: 318.14 cu. in. (5.21 liters). Horsepower: 210 @ 4000 rpm. Torque: 318 lb.-ft. @ 2800 rpm. Oil refill capacity: 5 qt. Fuel Requirements: Regular.

OPTIONAL ENGINE: W300: Engine Type: OHV, Premium V-8. Cast iron block and cylinder head. This engine has the standard 318 V-8 features plus roller-chain drive, vibration damper, positive exhaust valve rotators and hydraulic valve lifters. Bore x Stroke: 3.63 in. x 3.80 in. Lifters: Hydraulic. Number of main bearings-5. Fuel Induction: 2-barrel carburetor. Compression Ratio: 7.5:1. Displacement: 318.14 cu. in. (5.21 liters). Horsepower: 202 @ 3900 rpm. Torque: 288 lb.-ft. @ 2400 rpm. Oil refill capacity: 5 qt. Fuel Requirements: Regular.

OPTIONAL ENGINE: W100, W200: Engine Type: OHV, V-8. Cast iron block and cylinder head. This engine has a vibraton damper, 18 in., 7 blade fan, and a drop-forged crankshaft. Bore x Stroke: 4.25 in. x 3.38 in. Lifters: Hydraulic. Number of main bearings-5. Fuel Induction: 2-barrel carburetor. Compression Ratio: 9.2:1. Displacement: 383 cu. in. (6.276 liters). Horsepower: 258 @ 4400 rpm. Torque: 375 lb.-ft. @ 2800 rpm. Oil refill capacity: 5 qt. Fuel Requirements: Regular.

W100 and W200:

CHASSIS FEATURES: Separate body and drop-center frame. Dimension: W100: 6.12 in. x 2.30 in. x 0.188 in. Section modules: W100: 3.43. W200: 3.88, W200 crew cab: 4.70. Dimension: W200: 6.25 in x 2.42 in. x 0.250 in.

SUSPENSION AND RUNNING GEAR: Front Suspension: Semi-elliptical leaf springs. Capacity: 1,200 lb., 1,350 lb. (standard for 128 in. wheelbase). Optional: 1,550 lb. Rear Suspension: Semi-elliptical leaf springs. Capacity: W100: 1,350 lb. W200: 1,750 lb. Optional: W100: 1,750 lb. W200: 2,600 lb. Front Axle Type and Capacity: Full-floating, Hypoid-type. Capacity: 3,000 lb. W200 crew cab: 3,500 lb. Rear Axle Type and Capacity: W100: Full-floating, Hypoid-type. Capacity: 4,500 lb. W200: Full-floating, Hypoid-type. Capacity: 5,500 lb. Final Drive Ratio: W100: 3.54:1, 4.1:1. W200: 3.54:1 (not available with 3,500 lb. axle), 4.1:1, 4.89:1 (not available with 383 V-8). Anti-slip rear differential available with 4.1:1 ratio. Transfer Case: Two-speed. Ratios: 1.96:1, 1.00:1. Brakes: Hydraulic front and rear. Dimensions: Front and rear: 12.125 in. x 2.0 in. Total lining area: 211.58 sq. in. Wheels: Eight-stud ventilated disc. Tires: W100: 6.50 x 16 6-ply. W200: 7 x 17.5 6-ply, tubeless. Optional: W100: 7.00 x 16 6-ply, 7 x 17.5 6-ply. W200: 8 x 19.5 8-ply. Steering: Recirculating ball. Transmission: 3-speed heavy-duty A745 manual. Optional: New Process #435, 4-speed manual. Clutch: Single plate, dry disc, 11.0 in. dia. with lining area of 123.7 sq. in. Standard with 383 V-8: 12 in. dia. and 150 sq. in. lining area.

VEHICLE DIMENSIONS: W100: Wheelbase: 114 in./128 in. Overall Length: 181 in. (114 in. wheelbase). (Add 15.125 in. for winch). Front/Rear Tread: 65.5 in./61.9375 in. Overall Height: 80.3125 in. Load space: Pickup box dimensions: Utiline body: 114 in. wheelbase: 78.125 in. x 49 in. x 20 in. Capacity: 47.25 cu. ft. Sweptline body: 114 in. wheelbase: 78.625 in. x 70 in. x 20 in. Capacity: 59.3 cu. ft. Utiline body: 128 in. wheelbase: 96 in. x 49 in. x 20 in. Sweptline body: 128 in. wheelbase: 98.875 in. x 70 in. x 20 in. W200: Wheelbase: 128 in. Crew cab: 146 in. Overall Length: 192.75 in. (add 15.125 in. for winch). Front/Rear Tread: 65.0625 in./61.8125 in. Overall Height: 80.25 in. Load space: Pickup box dimensions: Utiline body: 96 in. x 54 in. x 20 in. Capacity: 58.5 cu. ft. Sweptline body: 98.875 in. x 70.75 in. x 20 in. Capacity: 75 cu. ft.

CAPACITIES: Fuel Tank: 18 gal. Engine coolant system: 6-cyl.: 13.0 qt. V-8: 20.0 qt.

ACCOMMODATIONS: 3 passengers.

INSTRUMENTATION: Speedometer, odometer, gauges for fuel level, ammeter and engine coolant temperature.

W300:

CHASSIS FEATURES: Separate body and straight frame. Dimensions: 7.25 in. x 2.75 in. x 0.2318 in. Section modules: 5.70.

SUSPENSION AND RUNNING GEAR: Front Suspension: Semi-elliptical leaf springs. Capacity: 1,450 lb. Optional: 1,750 lb. (standard with front-mounted winch). Rear Suspension: Semi-elliptical leaf springs. Capacity: 3,250. Optional: 4,050 lb. Front Axle Type and Capacity: Full-floating, Hypoid-type. Capacity: 4,500 lb. Rear Axle Type and Capacity: Full-floating, Hypoid-type. Capacity: 7,500 lb. Anti-slip differential optional. Final Drive Ratio: 4.88:1 or 5.86:1. Transfer Case: Two-speed, single lever. Ratios: 1.96:1, 1.00:1. Brakes: Hydraulic front and rear. Dimensions: Front: 14.125 in. x 1.75 in. Rear: 13 in. x 2.5 in. Total lining area: 241.98 sq. in. Wheels: Six-stud ventilated disc. Tires: 8 x 19.5 8-ply, tubeless. Optional: 9.00 x 16 10-ply. Steering: Worm and roller. Ratio: 29.0:1. Optional: Power assisted. Transmission: New Process #435B 4-speed manual. Optional: New Process #435, 4-speed manual. Clutch: Single plate, dry disc, 11.0 in. dia. with lining area of 123.7 sq. in.

VEHICLE DIMENSIONS: Wheelbase: 133 in. Overall Length: 204.5 in. (add 17.875 in. for winch). Width: 81.8125 in. Overall Height: 84.5 in. Front/Rear tread: 64.5625 in./65.0 in.

CAPACITIES: Fuel Tank: 18 gal. Engine coolant system: 6-cyl.: 20.0 qt. V-8: 24.0 qt.

ACCOMMODATIONS: 3 passengers.

INSTRUMENTATION: Speedometer, odometer, gauges for fuel level, ammeter and engine coolant temperature.

OPTIONS: Four-speed synchro-shift transmission (standard on W300). Power take-off (transfer case). Heavy-duty instrument cluster. 383 cu. in. V-8. Oil-pressure gauge. Third seat belt. Two shoulder belts. Full-depth foam seat in standard cab. Wheel-lip and sill molding (Sweptline only). Dual electric horns. Dual long-arm adjustable braced or Junior West Coast mirrors. Double-face directional signals. Cab corner lights (standard on platform and stake). Identification lights (standard on platforms and stakes). Front-mounted 8,000 lb. winch. Locking front hubs. 3 ton hydraulic jack. Outboard fuel tanks (W300). Custom Interior Packages. Includes a full-depth foam rubber bench seat and foam-padded seat back, color-keyed metallic vinyl and nylon seat upholstery, color-keyed floor mats with jute backing, foam core headliner with bright-finish molding, floor sill molding, dash liner, glare-reducing trim around instrument cluster; cigarette lighter, color-keyed horn bar, "Dodge" nameplate on glove box door and additional cab insulation. Custom Exterior Package. Includes bright-finish grille, bright-finish drip moldings (not available with crew cab), bright Mylar trim for windshield and rear window and "Custom" nameplate on cab doors. Conventional Cab Exterior Molding Packages (available for W100 and W200 Sweptline pickups only). Incudes exterior side moldings and bright-finish taillight bezels or wheel-lip and sill moldings and bright-finish taillights. Neither molding was available with crew cab.

HISTORICAL FOOTNOTES: The 1970 Dodge four-wheel drive trucks were introduced in August, 1969.

1970 Dodge W200 Utiline Power Wagon pickup

1971 POWER WAGON

This was the last year the truck format introduced in 1961 was used. During the winter season Dodge introduced two Sno-Fiter packages. They were available with either a manual or power angling plow with power lift, and a three-way or seven-way control valve. The Sno-Fiter was delivered with a number of required options including heavy-duty springs, front clearance and identification lights and 6-ply rated Mud-Snow tread tires. The Sno-Fiter was offered with either the 225 cu. in. 6-cylinder or 318 cu. in. V-8 engines.

1971 Dodge W200 Sweptline Power Wagon pickup

I.D. DATA: The serial numbers were located on a plate on the left door lock pillar. A ten character identification system was used. The first two digits were the model code: 21-(W100), 22-(W200), 23-(W300), 24-(W300 for export). Next came a digit, either 6 or 8, identifying the number of cylinders. This was followed by another digit identifying the assembly plant as follows: 1-Warren Truck, 2-Warren Heavy-Duty, 6-Windsor, 7-Missouri. The remaining six digits were the production sequence numbers. The serial numbers on 6-cylinder engines were located on the right side of the block below the no. one spark plug. The 318 V-8 serial number was found on the left front of the block below the cylinder head. The 383 V-8 serial number was found on the right side of the block next to the distributor. The 225 6-cyl. and 318 V-8 used a system in which the first two letters indicated the manufacturing plant as follows: GM-Mound Road, GT-Trenton, NM-Maryland, GW-Windsor. The next three digits identified the engine's displacement. The next letter identified the engine type as follows: R-regular 318 V-8; T-standard 225 6-cyl; H-premium 225 6-cyl. The next four digits were the manufacturing date code base upon a 10,000 day calendar. The final four digits were the sequence production numbers beginning with 001 for each day. The 383 V-8 identification system used the following form: The first letter indicated the model year. The next letter identified the engine type (T-standard). The next three digits were the engine's displacement. The next digit identified the assembly plant shift. This was followed by four digits identifying the manufacturing date. The next two digits were used as a non-standard engine indicator. The last four digits were the production sequence production number.

Body Type	Factory Price	GVW	Shipping Weight	Prod. Total
Model W100, 1/2 ton 6-cyl.				
Ch. & Cab, 114 in. wb.	$3186	5100*	3735	a
Pickup, Utiline, 114 in. wb.	$3313	5100	4095	—
Pickup, Sweptline, 114 in. wb.	$3349	5100	4145	—
Ch. & Cab, 128 in. wb.	$3222	5100	3735	—
Pickup, Utiline, 128 in. wb.	$3349	5100	4095	—
Pickup, Sweptline, 128 in. wb.	$3388	5100	N.A.	—

* 5600 lb. GVW optional.

a Total model year production of 114 in. wheelbase and 128 in. wheelbase. W100 trucks was respectively 1626 and 2026.

Body Type	Factory Price	GVW	Shipping Weight	Prod. Total
Model W200, 3/4 ton, 6-cyl. (Crew cab-146 in. wheelbase)				
Ch. & Cab, 128 in. wb.	$3615	6000*	3945	b
Pickup, Utiline, 128 in. wb.	$3742	6000	4385	—
Pickup, Sweptline, 128 in. wb.	$3781	6000	4445	—
Crew Cab, Ch.	$4428	6000	4375	—
Crew Cab, Utiline.	$4556	6000	4735	—
Crew Cab, Sweptline	$4574	6000	4785	—

* 6500 lb. and 8000 lb. GVW package was optional for all models.

b Total W200 model year production, excluding crew cab models, was 4814. Crew cab production was 334.

Body Type	Factory Price	GVW	Shipping Weight	Prod. Total
Model W300, 1 ton, 6-cyl.				
Ch. & Cab, 133 in. wb.	$4279	8500*	4645	c
Pickup, Utiline, 133 in. wb.	$4363	8500	5140	—

* GVW packages up to 10,000 lb. were available.

c Total W300 model year production was 783.

STANDARD ENGINE: W100, W200: Engine Type: OHV, In-line 6-cylinder. Cast iron block and cylinder head. Bore x Stroke: 3.40 in. x 4.125 in. Lifters: Mechanical. Number of main bearings-5. Fuel Induction: Single barrel carburetor. Compression Ratio: 8.4:1. Displacement: 224.7 cu. in. (3.68 liters). Horsepower: 140 @ 3900 rpm. Torque: 215 lb.-ft. @ 1600-2800 rpm. Oil refill capacity: 5 qt.

STANDARD ENGINE: W300: Engine Type: OHV, In-line "Premium Slant Six." Cast iron block and cylinder head, Premium components include roller timing chain, bimetal connecting rod bearings, heat-resistant Stellite-faced exhaust valves, and polyacrylic valve stem seals. Bore x Stroke: 3.40 in. x 4.125 in. Lifters: Mechanical. Number of main bearings-5. Fuel Induction: Single barrel carburetor. Compression Ratio: 8.4:1. Displacement: 224.7 cu. in. (3.68 liters). Horsepower: 140 @ 3900 rpm. Torque: 215 lb.-ft. @ 1600-2800 rpm. Oil refill capacity: 5 qt.

OPTIONAL ENGINE: W100, W200: Engine Type: OHV, V-8. Cast iron block and cylinder head. Bore x Stroke: 3.91 in. x 3.3120 in. Lifters: Hydraulic. Number of main bearings-5. Fuel Induction: Two barrel carburetor. Compression Ratio: 8.25:1. Displacement: 318.14 cu. in. (5.21 liters). Horsepower: 210 @ 4000 rpm. Torque: 318 lb.-ft. @ 2800 rpm. Oil refill capacity: 5 qt. Fuel Requirements: Regular.

OPTIONAL ENGINE: W300: Engine Type: OHV, Premium V-8. Cast iron block and cylinder head. This engine has the standard 318 V-8 features plus roller-chain drive, vibration damper, positive exhaust valve rotators and hydraulic valve lifters. Bore x Stroke: 3.63 in. x 3.80 in. Lifters: Hydraulic. Number of main bearings-5. Fuel Induction: 2-barrel carburetor. Compression Ratio: 7.5:1. Displacement: 318.14 cu. in. (5.21 liters). Horsepower: 202 @ 3900 rpm. Torque: 288 lb.-ft. @ 2400 rpm. Oil refill capacity: 5 qt. Fuel Requirements: Regular.

OPTIONAL ENGINE: W200: Engine Type: OHV, V-8. Cast iron block and cylinder head. This engine has a vibraton damper, 18 in. 7 blade fan, and a drop-forged crankshaft. Bore x Stroke: 4.25 in. x 3.38 in. Lifters: Hydraulic. Number of main bearings-5. Fuel Induction: 2-barrel carburetor. Compression Ratio: 9.2:1. Displacement: 383 cu. in. (6.276 liters). Horsepower: 258 @ 4400 rpm. Torque: 375 lb.-ft. @ 2800 rpm. Oil refill capacity: 5 qt. Fuel Requirements: Regular.

W100 and W200:

CHASSIS FEATURES: Separate body and drop-center frame. Dimension: W100: 6.12 in. x 2.30 in. x 0.188 in. Section modules: W100: 3.43. W200: 3.88, W200 crew cab: 4.70. Dimension: W200: 6.25 in. x 2.42 in. x 0.250 in.

SUSPENSION AND RUNNING GEAR: Front Suspension: Semi-elliptical leaf springs. Capacity: 1,300 lb., 1,350 lb. (standard for 128 in. wheelbase). Optional: 1,550 lb. Rear Suspension: Semi-elliptical leaf springs. Capacity: W100: 1,350 lb. W200: 1,750 lb. Optional: W100: 1,750 lb. W200: 2,600 lb. Front Axle Type and Capacity: Full-floating, Hypoid-type. Capacity: 3,000 lb. W200 crew cab: 3,500 lb. Optional W200: 3,500 lb. Rear Axle Type and Capacity: W100: Full-floating, Hypoid-type. Capacity: 3,600 lb. W200: Full-floating, Hypoid-type. Capacity: 5,500 lb. Final Drive Ratio: W100: 3.54:1, 4.1:1. W200: 3.54:1, 4.1:1, 4.88:1. Transfer Case: Two-speed. Ratios: 1.96:1, 1.00:1. Brakes: Hydraulic front and rear. Dimensions: Front and rear: W100: 11 in. x 2.0 in. Total area: 170.2 sq. in. W200: 12.125 in. x 2.0 in. Total lining area: 209.4 sq. in. Wheels: Eight-stud ventilated disc. Tires: W100: G78 x 15B 4-ply rating. W200: 8.00 x 16.5D 8-ply rating. Optional: W100: 6.50 x 15C 6-ply rating (maximum size available). W200: 9.50 x 16.5D 8-ply rating (maximum size available). Steering: Recirculating ball. Transmission: 3-speed A230 manual. Optional: New Process 435 (close ratio) or New Process 445 (wide ratio), 4-speed manual. Chrysler 3-speed A-727 automatic. Clutch: Single plate, dry disc, 11.0 in. dia. with lining area of 123.7 sq. in. Standard with 383 V-8: 12 in. dia. and 150 sq. in. lining area.

VEHICLE DIMENSIONS: W100: Wheelbase: 114 in./128 in. Overall Length: 181 in. (114 in. wheelbase.) (Add 15.125 in. for winch). Front/Rear Tread: 65.5 in./61.9375 in. Overall Height: 80.3125 in. Load space: Pickup box dimensions: Utiline body: 114 in. wheelbase: 78.125 in. x 49 in. x 20 in. Capacity: 47.25 cu. ft. Sweptline body: 114 in. wheelbase: 78.625 in. x 70 in. x 20 in. Capacity: 59.3 cu. ft. Utiline body: 128 in. wheelbase: 96 in. x 49 in. x 20 in. Sweptline body: 128 in. wheelbase: 98.875 in. x 70 in. x 20 in. W200: Wheelbase: 128 in. Crew cab: 146 in. Overall Length: 192.75 in. (add 15.125 in. for winch). Front/Rear Tread: 65.0625 in./ 61.8125 in. Overall Height: 80.25 in. Load space: Pickup box dimensions: Utiline body: 96 in. x 54 in. x 20 in. Capacity: 58.5 cu. ft. Sweptline body: 98.875 in. x 70.75 in. x 20 in. Capacity: 75 cu. ft.

CAPACITIES: Fuel Tank: 25 gal. Optional 23 gal. auxiliary tank. Engine coolant system: 6-cyl.: 13.0 qt. V-8: 20.0 qt.

ACCOMMODATIONS: 3 passengers.

INSTRUMENTATION: Speedometer, odometer, gauges for fuel level, ammeter and engine coolant temperature.

W300:

CHASSIS FEATURES: Separate body and straight frame. Dimensions: 7.25 in. x 2.75 in. x 0.2318 in. Section modules: 5.70.

SUSPENSION AND RUNNING GEAR: Front Suspension: Semi-elliptical leaf springs. Capacity: 1,450 lb. Optional: 1,750 lb. (standard with front-mounted winch). Rear Suspension: Semi-elliptical leaf springs. Capacity: 3,250. Optional: 4,050 lb. Front Axle Type and Capacity: Full-floating, Hypoid-type. Capacity: 4,500 lb. Rear Axle Type and Capacity: Full-floating, Hypoid-type. Capacity: 7,500 lb. Anti-slip differential optional. Final Drive Ratio: 4.88:1 or 5.86:1. Transfer Case: Two-speed, single lever. Ratios: 1.96:1, 1.00:1. Brakes: Hydraulic front and rear. Dimensions: Front: 14.125 in. x 1.75 in. Rear: 13 in. x 2.5 in. Total lining area: 238.2 sq. in. Wheels: Six-stud ventilated disc. Tires: 8.75 x 16.5E 10-ply rating. Optional: 9.50 x 16.5D-ply rating, 7.50 x 16D 8-ply rating. Steering: Worm and roller. Ratio: 29.0:1. Optional: Power assisted. Transmission: New Process 435, 4-speed manual. Optional: New Process 445, 4-speed manual. Clutch: Single plate, dry disc, 11.0 in. dia. with lining area of 123.7 sq. in.

VEHICLE DIMENSIONS: Wheelbase: 133 in. Overall Length: 204.5 in. (add 17.875 in. for winch). Width: 81.8125 in. Overall Height: 84.5 in. Front/Rear tread: 64.5625 in./ 65.0 in.

CAPACITIES: Fuel Tank: 25 gal. Optional 23 gal. auxiliary tank. Engine coolant system: 6-cyl.: 20.0 qt. V-8: 24.0 qt.

ACCOMMODATIONS: 3 passengers.

INSTRUMENTATION: Speedometer, odometer, gauges for fuel level, ammeter and engine coolant temperature.

OPTIONS: Four-speed synchro-shift transmission (standard on W300). Power take-off (transfer case). Heavy-duty instrument cluster. 383 cu. in. V-8. Oil-pressure gauge. Third seat belt. Two shoulder belts. Full-depth foam seat in standard cab. Wheel-lip and sill molding (Sweptline only). Dual electric horns. Dual long-arm adjustable braced or Junior West Coast mirrors. Double-face directional signals. Cab corner lights (standard on platform and stake). Identification lights (standard on platform and stake). Front-mounted 8,000 lb. winch. Locking front hubs. 3-ton hydraulic jack. Outboard fuel tanks (W300). Custom Interior packages. Includes a full-depth foam rubber bench seat and foam-padded seat back, color-keyed metallic vinyl and nylon seat upholstery, color-keyed floor mats with jute backing, foam core headliner with bright-finish molding, floor sill molding, dash liner, glare-reducing trim around instrument cluster; cigarette lighter, color-keyed horn bar, "Dodge" nameplate on glove box door and additional cab insulation. Custom Exterior Package. Includes bright-finish grille, bright-finish drip moldings (not available with crew cab), bright Mylar trim for windshield and rear window and "Custom" nameplate on cab doors. Conventional Cab Exterior Molding Packages (available for W100 and W200 Sweptline pickups only). Incudes exterior side moldings and bright-finish taillight bezels or wheel-lip and sill moldings and bright-finish taillights. Neither molding was available with crew cab.

HISTORICAL FOOTNOTES: The 1971 Dodge four-wheel drive trucks were introduced in August, 1970.

1971 Dodge W100 Sweptline Sno-Fiter Power Wagon pickup

1972 POWER WAGON

Dodge spent $50 million to develop its new line of 1972 light-duty and recreational trucks. The total research and development time required to complete this project was nearly four years. The styling of the new four-wheel drive trucks retained a strong Dodge identity while also projecting a fresh new appearance. Glass area in both the windshield and rear window was greatly increased and for the first time in a pickup, curved side window glass was used. The front grille arrangement was very simple consisting of a broad opening divided into four sections within a larger bright surround. The single lamp headlights were positioned at the extremities of the grille. At the rear wraparound taillights were used that had built-in side markers and back-up lights.

The all-new interior had the most shoulder room (65.7 in.) of any American pickup due in part to the curved side glass. The door width was increased by two inches and the angle transversed by the door as it swung outward was increased. The color-coordinated interior was available in four levels of trim. In addition, it was more user friendly than in previous years. All the instruments were recessed to reduce reflections. It was also possible to service them without disturbing the steering column. The fuse box and flashers were located behind the padded glove box door. This door, of molded plastic, also functioned as a level tray. The combination of a repositioned steering wheel and a higher seating position improved overall visibility. A step-on parking brake was adopted. The ignition switch was mounted on the steering column. Additional enhancements included the use of increased insulation, quieter, caliper-type door latches and the positioning of the windshield wiper and heater motors under the hood. The standard heater had increased capacity.

Crew cab models had wider rear doors with concealed hinges. A full steel inner roof was also a new-for-1972 crew cab feature. The rear section of the crew cab was increased in length by two inches.

A new chassis, wider thread plus longer wheelbases also were used for the new Dodge trucks. Larger brake drums were fitted to all models. Extensive use was made of double-wall construction for the hood, fenders, roof, cargo box and tailgate. Improved corrosion protection resulted from the installation of inner shields for the front and rear wheel housings and the use of galvanized metal, zinc-rich primers and vinyl sealers. The standard fuel tank had a 25 gallon capacity (the largest available on a domestic pickup). In addition, an optional auxiliary 25 gallon tank was also offered for the 131 in. wheelbase models with the Sweptline body. Joining the engine lineup was a 360 cu. in. V-8. The 383 cu. in. V-8 was not available. At mid-year, the V-8 engines were available with electronic ignition at extra cost.

Dodge's efforts paid off handsomely in increased sales volume during the 1972 model year. Mr. George Butts, Dodge Truck Operations general manager noted that "Our policy of continual product evaluation and innovation is responsible for our rapidly improving sales picture. Through the1972 model year, Dodge Truck captured a much larger portion of the market." Specifically, while sales of the domestic truck industry increased approximately 40 percent in 1972, Dodge sales increased almost 70 percent.

I.D. DATA: The serial numbers were located on a plate on the left door lock pillar. A 13-character identification system was used. The first two characters were the model code: W1-(W100), W2-(W200), W3-(W300). The following digit identified the body code. The next entry, a letter, indicated the truck's GVW: A-6000 lbs. and under, B-6001 to 10,001 lbs., C-10,001 to 14,000 lbs. This was followed by a letter identifying engine displacement and a digit (2) identifying the 1972 model year. A letter followed identifying the assembly plant: J-Windsor, N-Burt Road, Detroit, S-Warren Truck No. 1, T-Warren Truck No. 2, U-St. Louis. The remaining six digits were the production sequence numbers. Each assembly plant began production with number 500001. The serial numbers on 6-cylinder engines were located on the right side of the block below the no. one spark plug. The 318 and 360 V-8 serial number was found on the left front of the block below the cylinder head. The 225 6-cyl. and 318 V-8 used a system in which the first two letters indicated the manufacturing plant as follows: GM-Mound Road, GT-Trenton, NM-Maryland, GW-Windsor. The next three digits identified the engine's displacement. The next letter identified the engine type as follows: R-regular 318 V-8; T-standard 225 6-cyl; H-premium 225 6-cyl. The next four digits were the manufacturing date code base upon a 10,000 day calendar. The final four digits were the sequence production numbers beginning with 0001 for each day.

Body Type	Factory Price	GVW	Shipping Weight	Prod. Total
Model W100, 1/2 ton 6-cyl.				
Ch. & Cab, 114 in. wb.	$3023	5100*	3510	a
Pickup, Utiline, 114 in. wb.	$3180	5100	3855	—
Pickup, Sweptline, 114 in. wb.	$3180	5100	3893	—
Ch. & Cab, 131 in. wb.	$3056	5100	3565	—
Pickup, Utiline, 131 in. wb.	$3217	5100	3994	—
Pickup, Sweptline, 131 in. wb.	$3217	5100	4023	—

* 5600 lb. GVW optional.

a Total model year production of all 115 in. wheelbase. W100 trucks was 2978. Output of models with a 131 in. wheelbase. was 4389.

Model W200, 3/4 ton, 6-cyl. (Crew cab models: 149 in. wheelbase)				
Ch. & Cab, 131 in. wb.	$3508	6500*	3810	b
Pickup, Utiline, 131 in. wb.	$3666	6500	4240	—
Pickup, Sweptline, 131 in. wb.	$3666	6500	4270	—
Crew Cab, Ch.	$4365	6500	4145	—
Crew Cab, Utiline	$4523	6500	4490	—
Crew Cab, Sweptline	$4523	6500	4530	—
Crew Cab, Sweptline	$3716	6500	4785	—

* 8000 lb. GVW package was optional for all models.

b Total model year production, excluding crew cab models, was 7886. Crew cab production was 1067.

Model W300, 1 ton, 6-cyl.				
Ch. & Cab, 135 in. wb.	$4227	8500	4320	c
Pickup, Utiline, 135 in. wb.	$4338	8500	4515	—
Platform, 133 in. wb.	$4640	8500	5325	—
Stake, 135 in. wb.	$4660	8500	5625	—

* GVW packages up to 10,000 lb. were available.

c Total model year production of W300 models was 943

STANDARD ENGINE: W100, W200, W300: Engine Type: OHV, In-line 6-cylinder. Cast iron block and cylinder head. Key components include a drop-forged, shot-peened crankshaft, roller timing chain, Stellite-faced exhaust valves, individually ported long-branch manifolds, aluminum parts and a large radiator. Bore x Stroke: 3.40 in. x 4.125 in. Lifters: Mechanical. Number of main bearings-4. Fuel Induction: Single 1-bbl. carburetor. Compression Ratio: 8.4:1. Displacement: 224.7 cu. in. (3.68 liters). Horsepower: Net: 110 @ 4000 rpm. (California rating: 97 hp.). Torque: Net: 185 lb.-ft. @ 2000 rpm. Oil refill capacity: 5 qt. with filter change. Fuel Requirements: Regular.

OPTIONAL ENGINE: W100, W200, W300: Features include a drop-forged five-bearing crankshaft, chain-driven camshaft, free-turning exhaust valves, drop-forged I-beam connecting rods and silent-chain camshaft. Engine Type: OHV, V-8. Cast iron block and cylinder head. Bore x Stroke: 3.91 in. x 3.312 in. Lifters: Hydraulic. Number of main bearings-5. Fuel Induction: Single 2-bbl. carburetor. Compression Ratio: 8.5:1. Displacement: 318 cu. in. (5.21 liters). Horsepower: Net: 160 @ 4000 rpm. Torque: Net: 265 lb.-ft. @ 1600 rpm. Oil refill capacity: 5 qt. with filter change. Fuel Requirements: Regular.

OPTIONAL ENGINE: W100, W200, W300: Features include vibration damper, 18 in. 4 blade fan and drop-forged crankshaft. Engine Type: OHV, V-8. Cast iron block and cylinder head. Bore x Stroke: 4.00 in. x 3.58 in. Lifters: Hydraulic. Number of main bearings-5. Fuel Induction: Single 2-bbl. carburetor. Compression Ratio: 9.2:1. Displacement: 360 cu. in. (5.89 liters). Horsepower: Net: 180 @ 4000 rpm. Torque: Net: 295 lb.-ft. @ 2400 rpm. Oil refill capacity: 5 qt. with filter change. Fuel Requirements: Regular.

CHASSIS FEATURES: W100: Separate body and channel-type, drop-center frame. Section 3.43 in.

SUSPENSION AND RUNNING GEAR: Front Suspension: Semi-elliptical springs, heavy-duty shock absorbers. Capacity: 1300 lb. Optional rating: 1550 lb. Rear Suspension: Semi-elliptical springs, heavy-duty shock absorbers. Capacity: 1350 lbs. Optional Rating: 1750 lb. Front Axle Type and Capacity: Full-floating, 3300 lb. capacity. Rear Axle Type and Capacity: Full-floating, 3300 lb. capacity. Final Drive Ratio: 3.9:1 (225 and 318 engines), 3.55:1 (360 engine). Optional: 3.55:1 for 225 and 318 engines. Transfer Case: Two-speed: 1.96, 1.00:1. Brakes: Type: Hydraulic drums (dual system with warning light) front and rear. Dimensions: Front and rear: 11.0 in. x 2.00 in. Total lining area: 171.5 sq. in. Wheels: 5-stud disc. Tires: G78 x 15B, 4-ply rating Optional (maximum available): 6.50 x 16, 6-ply rating. Steering: Recirculating ball. Transmission: 6-cyl.: A-250 3-speed manual. V-8: A-230 3-speed synchromesh manual. Transmission Ratios: 6-cyl.: 3.02, 1.76, 1.00:1. Optional: NP435, close-ratio 4-speed manual, NP445, close ratio 4-speed manual. 3-spd. Chrysler A-727 automatic. Clutch: Single dry plate disc, hydraulic actuation. Clutch diameter: 11 in. dia. Total lining area: 123.7 sq. in.

CHASSIS FEATURES: W200: Separate body and channel-type, drop-center frame. Section modulus 3.88 in. Crew cab: 4.70 in.

SUSPENSION AND RUNNING GEAR: Front Suspension: Semi-elliptical leaf, heavy-duty shock absorbers. Capacity: 1300 lb. Crew cab: 1550 lb. Optional rating: 1550 lb., 1750 lb. Rear Suspension: Semi-elliptical leaf. Capacity: 1750 lb. rating. Optional Rating: 2600 lb. Front Axle Type and Capacity: Full-floating, 3500 lb. capacity. Optional rating: 4000 lb. Rear Axle Type and Capacity: Full-floating, 5500 lb. capacity. Optional rating: None. Final Drive Ratio: 4.10:1, 4.56:1. Transfer Case: Two-speed: 1.96, 1.00:1. Brakes: Type: Hydraulic. Front: Rear: Dimensions: Front: 12.12 in. x 2.00. Rear: 12.12 in. x 2.50 in. Total lining area: 227.5 sq. in. Wheels: 17.5 in. x 5.25 in., 8-stud disc. Tires: 8.00 x 16.5D, 6-ply rating. Optional (max. size avail.): 9.50 x 19.5 in., 8-ply rating. Steering: Recirculating ball. Transmission: A-230 3-speed synchromesh manual. Transmission Ratios: 3.02, 1.76, 1.00:1. Optional: NP435, close-ratio 4-speed manua!, NP445, close ratio 4-speed manual. 3-spd. Chrysler A-727 automatic. Clutch: Single plate hydraulic actuation. Clutch diameter: 11.0 in. Total Area: 123.7 sq. in.

CHASSIS FEATURES: W300: Separate body and channel steel, straight frame, 5.70 in. Section modules.

SUSPENSION AND RUNNING GEAR: Front Suspension: Semi-elliptical springs, heavy-duty, absorbers. Capacity: 1550 lb. rating. Optional rating: 1750 lb. Rear Suspension: Semi-elliptical springs. Capacity: 3250 lbs. Optional Rating: 550 lb. auxiliary spring. Front Axle Type and Capacity: Full-floating. 4500 lb. capacity. Rear Axle Type and Capacity: 7500 lb. capacity. Final Drive Ratio: Front axle: 4.88, 5.86:1. Transfer Case: Two-speed: 1.96, 1.0:1. Brakes: Type: Hydraulic. Dimensions: Front: 12.0 in. x 3.0 in. Rear: 12.0 in. x 3.0 in. Total lining area: 294.8 sq. in. Wheels: 19.5 in. x 5.25 in., 6-stud disc. Tires: 8.75 x 16.5 in., 10-ply rating. Optional: 9.50 x 16.5D, 8-ply rating, 7.50 x 16.5D 8-ply rating. Steering: Worm and Roller. Transmission: NP435 4-speed synchromesh manual. Optional: NP445 4-spd. synchromesh manual, Chrysler A-727 3-spd. automatic. Clutch: Single plate dry disc, hydraulic actuation. Clutch diameter: 11.0 in. Total plate area: 123.7 sq. in.

VEHICLE DIMENSIONS: W100: Wheelbase: 115 in., 131 in. Overall Length: 131 in. wheelbase: 213.6 in. Front/Rear Tread: 62.5 in./62.5 in. Overall Height: 131 in. wheelbase: 74.0 in. Width: 79.5 in. Front/Rear Overhang: 30 in./47 in. Tailgate Height: 20 in. Approach/Departure Degrees: 131 in. wheelbase: 34/24. Ground Clearance: Front axle: 8.2 in. Rear axle: 8.5 in. Oil pan: 15.8 in. Transfer case: 10.4 in.

CAPACITIES: Fuel Tank: 25 gal.

ACCOMMODATIONS: Seating Capacity: 3 passenger.

INSTRUMENTATION: 0-100 mph speedometer, 99,999.9 mile odometer, gauges for fuel level, ammeter and engine coolant temperature. Warning lights for oil pressure, parking brake and hazard lights operation.

W200: Wheelbase: 131 in. Crew cab: 149 in. Overall Length: 131 in./149 in. wheelbase: 213.6 in./231.6 in. Front/Rear Tread: 62.5 in./62.5 in. Overall Height: 74.0 in. Width: 79.5 in. Front/Rear Overhang: 31 in./49 in. Tailgate: Width x Height: 66.5 in. x 19.3 in. Approach/Departure Degrees: 30/21 degrees. Ground Clearance: Front axle: 8.0 in. Rear axle: 7.8 in. Oil pan: 16.1 in. Transfer case: 10.7 in. Load space: Pickup box dimensions: Sweptline: 98.875 in. x 51.0 in. x 19.3 in.

CAPACITIES: Fuel Tank: 25 gal.

ACCOMMODATIONS: Seating Capacity: 3 passenger.

INSTRUMENTATION: 0-100 mph speedometer, 99,999.9 mile odometer, gauges for fuel level, ammeter and engine coolant temperature. Warning lights for oil pressure, parking brake and hazard lights operation.

W300: Wheelbase: 135 in. Load space: Pickup box dimensions: 108 in. x 54 in. x 20 in. Capacity: 66 cu. ft.

CAPACITIES: Fuel Tank: 25 gal.

ACCOMMODATIONS: Seating Capacity: 3 passenger.

INSTRUMENTATION: 0-100 mph speedometer, 99,999.9 mile odometer, gauges for fuel level, ammeter and engine coolant temperature. Warning lights for oil pressure, parking brake and hazard lights operation.

OPTIONS AND PRICES: 360 V-8: $209. Automatic transmission: $248. Air conditioning: $439. Power brakes: $151. Free-running front hubs: $79. Limited slip rear differential: $67 (W100), $135 (W200). Adventurer Sport Package: $245. AM radio: $73. Heavy-duty front and rear shock absorbers: $16. Heavy-duty springs: $26.

HISTORICAL FOOTNOTES: The 1972 Power Wagons were introduced in August, 1971.

1973 POWER WAGON

All six cylinder and V-8 engines had a standard electronic ignition for 1973. Also now standard for all four-wheel drive models was a power assisted drum brake system. The W series trucks were available in three levels of interior appointments and exterior trim for 1973. The standard custom interior featured a full-width bench seat in a color-keyed vinyl available in black, blue, green or beige. The steel door trim panel matched the body color. The armrest color was keyed to the interior. Both the instrument panel and steel inner roof were color-keyed to the interior. A black rubber floor mat was included. The custom exterior consisted of a bright grille, front bumper, 5 in. x 7 in. exterior left side mirror and bright "Custom" nameplates. The Adventurer interior included a full-width, full-foam bench seat. It had a pleated vinyl covering available in blue, beige, green or black. Both the fiberglass door trim and the rubber floor mat were color-keyed to the interior. A full horn bar was also fitted. The Adventurer exterior, offered for all models, had bright trim for the windshield moldings, vent window division bars, body side moldings, and, on the Sweptline bodies, the upper and lower tailgate moldings. Other features included bright "Adventurer" nameplates, and bright taillamp bezels on the Sweptline pickup. The top-of-the-line Adventurer Sport option was available for the 131 in. wheelbase Sweptline pickup and the 135 in. wheelbase chassis cab models. The Adventurer Sport interior had a full-width bench seat with square corners. Its vinyl fabric upholstery was offered in beige, blue, green or black. The color-keyed fiberglass door trim panel was equipped with a built-in armrest and flush door handles. A simulated woodgrained instrument finish was used for the door and instrument panel. A foam core headliner was credited with reducing in-cab noise as well as functioning as insulation against heat and cold.

DODGE CREW CAB POWER WAGON

1973 Dodge crew cab Power Wagon pickup

I.D. DATA: The serial numbers were located on a plate on the left door lock pillar. A 13-character identification system was used. The first two characters were the model code: W1-(W100), W2-(W200), W3-(W300). The following digit identified the body code. The next entry, a letter, indicated the truck's GVW: A-6000 lbs. and under, B-6001 to 10,001 lbs., C-10,001 to 14,000 lbs. This was followed by a letter identifying engine displacement and a digit (2) identifying the 1972 model year. A letter followed identifying the assembly plant: J-Windsor, N-Burt Road, Detroit, S-Warren Truck No. 1, T-Warren Truck No. 2, U-St. Louis. The remaining six digits were the production sequence numbers. Each assembly plant began production with number 500001. The serial numbers on 6-cylinder engines were located on the right side of the block below the no. one spark plug. The 318 and 360 V-8 serial number was found on the left front of the block below the cylinder head. The 225 6-cyl. and 318 V-8 used a system in which the first two letters indicated the manufacturing plant as follows: GM-Mound Road, GT-Trenton, NM-Maryland, GW-Windsor. The next three digits identified the engine's displacement. The next letter identified the engine type as follows: R-regular 318 V-8; T-standard 225 6-cyl; H-premium 225 6-cyl. The next four digits were the manufacturing date code base upon a 10,000 day calendar. The final four digits were the sequence production numbers beginning with 0001 for each day.

Body Type	Factory Price	GVW	Shipping Weight	Prod. Total
Model W100, 1/2 ton 6-cyl.				
Ch. & Cab, 115 in. wb.	$3257	5100*	3510	a
Pickup, Utiline, 115 in. wb.	$3414	5100	3855	—
Pickup, Sweptline, 115 in. wb.	$3414	5100	3893	—
Ch. & Cab, 131 in. wb.	$N.A.	5100	3565	—
Pickup, Utiline, 131 in. wb.	$N.A.	5100	3994	—
Pickup, Sweptline, 131 in. wb.	$N.A.	5100	4023	—

* 5600 lb. GVW optional.
a Total model year production of all 115 in. wheelbase. W100 trucks was 5889. Output of models with a 131 in. wheelbase was 10,310.

Model W200, 3/4 ton, 6-cyl. (Crew Cab models-149 in. wheelbase)				
Ch. & Cab, 131 in. wb.	$3760	6500*	3810	b
Pickup, Utiline, 131 in. wb.	$3914	6500	4240	—
Pickup, Sweptline, 131 in. wb.	$3914	6500	4270	—
Crew Cab, Ch.	$4554	6500	4145	—
Crew Cab, Utiline	$4707	6500	4490	—
Crew Cab, Sweptline	$4707	6500	4530	—

* 8000 lb. GVW package was optional for all models.
b Total model year production, excluding crew cab models, was 13,948. Crew cab production was 1023.

Model W300, 1 ton, 6-cyl.				
Ch. & Cab, 135 in. wb.	$4442	8500	4320	c
Pickup, Utiline, 135 in. wb.	$4553	8500	4515	—
Platform, 133 in. wb.	$4860	8500	4977	—
Stake, 135 in. wb.	$4879	8500	5275	—

* GVW packages up to 10,000 lb. were available.
c Total model year production of W300 models was 1243.

STANDARD ENGINE: W100, W200, W300: Engine Type: OHV, In-line 6-cylinder. Cast iron block and cylinder head. Key components include a drop-forged, shot-peened crankshaft, roller timing chain, Stellite-faced exhaust valves, individually ported long-branch manifolds, aluminum parts and a large radiator. Bore x Stroke: 3.40 in. x 4.125 in. Lifters: Mechanical. Number of main bearings-4. Fuel Induction: Single 1-bbl. carburetor. Compression Ratio: 8.4:1. Displacement: 224.7 cu. in. (3.68 liters). Horsepower: Gross: 140 @ 3900 rpm. Net: 110 @ 4000 rpm. Torque: 215 lb.-ft. @ 1600-2800 rpm. Net: 185 lb.-ft. @ 1600 rpm. Oil refill capacity: 5 qt. with filter change. Fuel Requirements: Regular.

OPTIONAL ENGINE: W100, W200, W300: Features include a drop-forged five-bearing crankshaft, chain-driven camshaft, free-turning exhaust valves, drop-forged I-beam connecting rods and silent-chain camshaft. Engine Type: OHV, V-8. Cast iron block and cylinder head. Bore x Stroke: 3.91 in. x 3.312 in. Lifters: Hydraulic. Number of main bearings-5. Fuel Induction: Single 2-bbl. carburetor. Compression Ratio: 8.5:1. Displacement: 318 cu. in. (5.21 liters). Horsepower: Net: 180 @ 4400 rpm. Torque: Net: 285 lb.-ft. @ 2400 rpm. Oil refill capacity: 5 qt. with filter change. Fuel Requirements: Regular.

OPTIONAL ENGINE: W100, W200, W300: Features include vibration damper, 18 in. 4 blade fan and drop-forged crankshaft. Engine Type: OHV, V-8. Cast iron block and cylinder head. Bore x Stroke: 4.00 in. x 3.58 in. Lifters: Hydraulic. Number of main bearings-5. Fuel Induction: Single 2-bbl. carburetor. Compression Ratio: 9.2:1. Displacement: 360 cu. in. (5.89 liters). Horsepower: Net: 180 @ 4000 rpm. Torque: Net: 295 lb.-ft. @ 2400 rpm. Oil refill capacity: 5 qt. with filter change. Fuel Requirements: Regular.

CHASSIS FEATURES: W100: Separate body and channel-type, drop-center frame. Section modulus 3.43 in.

SUSPENSION AND RUNNING GEAR: Front Suspension: Semi-elliptical springs, heavy-duty shock absorbers. Capacity: 1300 lb. Optional rating: 1550 lb. Rear Suspension: Semi-elliptical springs, heavy-duty shock absorbers. Capacity: 1350 lbs. Optional Rating: 1750 lb. Front Axle Type and Capacity: Full-floating, 3300 lb. capacity. Rear Axle Type and Capacity: Full-floating, 3300 lb. capacity. Final Drive Ratio: 3.9:1 (225 and 318 engines), 3.55:1 (360 engine). Optional: 3.55:1 for 225 and 318 engines. Transfer Case: Two-speed: 1.96, 1.00:1. Brakes: Type: Hydraulic drums (dual system with warning light) front and rear. Dimensions: Front and rear: 11.0 in. x 2.00 in. Total lining area: 171.5 sq. in. Wheels: 5-stud disc. Tires: G78 x 15B, 4-ply rating. Optional (maximum available): 6.50 x 16, 6-ply rating. Steering: Recirculating ball. Transmission: 6-cyl.: A-250 3-speed manual. V-8: A-230 3-speed synchromesh manual. Transmission Ratios: 6-cyl.: 3.02, 1.76, 1.00:1. Optional: NP435, close-ratio 4-speed manual, NP445, close ratio 4-speed manual. 3-spd. Chrysler A-727 automatic. Clutch: Single dry plate disc, hydraulic actuation. Clutch diameter: 11 in. dia. Total lining area: 123.7 sq. in.

CHASSIS FEATURES: W200: Separate body and channel-type, drop-center frame. Section modulus 3.88 in. Crew cab: 4.70 in.

SUSPENSION AND RUNNING GEAR: Front Suspension: Semi-elliptical leaf, heavy-duty shock absorbers. Capacity: 1300 lb. Crew cab: 1550 lb. Optional rating: 1550 lb., 1750 lb. Rear Suspension: Semi-elliptical leaf. Capacity: 1750 lb. rating. Optional Rating: 2600 lb. Front Axle Type and Capacity: Full-floating, 3500 lb. capacity. Optional rating: 4000 lb. Rear Axle Type and Capacity: Full-floating, 5500 lb. capacity. Optional rating: None. Final Drive Ratio: 4.10:1, 4.56:1. Transfer Case: Two-speed: 1.96, 1.00:1. Brakes: Type: Hydraulic. Front: Rear: Dimensions: Front: 12.12 in. x 2.00. Rear: 12.12 in. x 2.50 in. Total lining area: 227.5 sq. in. Wheels: 17.5 in. x 5.25 in., 8-stud disc. Tires: 8.00 x 16.5D, 6-ply rating. Optional (max. size avail.): 9.50 x 19.5 in., 8-ply rating. Steering: Recirculating ball. Transmission: A-230 3-speed synchromesh manual. Transmission Ratios: 3.02, 1.76, 1.00:1. Optional: NP435, close-ratio 4-speed manual, NP445, close ratio 4-speed manual. 3-spd. Chrysler A-727 automatic. Clutch: Single plate hydraulic actuation. Clutch diameter: 11.0 in. Total Area: 123.7 sq. in.

CHASSIS FEATURES: W300: Separate body and channel steel, straight frame, 5.70 in. Section modulus.

SUSPENSION AND RUNNING GEAR: Front Suspension: Semi-elliptical springs, heavy-duty, absorbers. Capacity: 1550 lb. rating. Optional rating: 1750 lb. Rear Suspension: Semi-elliptical springs. Capacity: 3250 lbs. Optional Rating: 550 lb. auxiliary spring. Front Axle Type and Capacity: Full-floating. 4500 lb. capacity. Rear Axle Type and Capacity: 7500 lb. capacity. Final Drive Ratio: Front axle: 4.88, 5.86:1. Transfer Case: Two-speed: 1.96, 1.0:1. Brakes: Type: Hydraulic. Dimensions: Front: 12.0 in. x 3.0 in. Rear: 12.0 in. x 3.0 in. Total lining area: 294.8 sq. in. Wheels: 19.5 in. x 5.25 in., 6-stud disc. Tires: 8.75 x 16.5 in., 10-ply rating. Optional: 9.50 x 16.5D, 8-ply rating, 7.50 x 16.5D 8-ply rating. Steering: Worm and Roller. Transmission: NP435 4-speed synchromesh manual. Optional: NP445 4-spd. synchromesh manual, Chrysler A-727 3-spd. automatic. Clutch: Single plate dry disc, hydraulic actuation. Clutch diameter: 11.0 in. Total plate area: 123.7 sq. in.

VEHICLE DIMENSIONS: W100: Wheelbase: 115 in./131 in. Overall Length: 190.2 in./213.6 in. Front/Rear Tread: 62.5 in./62.5 in. Overall Height: 74.0 in. Width: 79.5 in. Front/Rear Overhang: 30 in./47 in. Tailgate: Width and Height: 67 in. x 21.4 in. Approach/Departure Degrees: 34/24. Ground Clearance: Front axle: 8.2 in. Rear axle: 8.5 in. Oil pan: 15.8 in. Transfer case: 10.4 in. Load space: Pickup box dimensions: 131 in. wheelbase. Sweptline: 98 in. x 51 in. x 19.3 in. W200. Wheelbase: 131 in. Crew cab: 149 in. Overall Length: 131 in./149 in. wheelbase: 213.6 in./231.6 in. Front/Rear Tread: 62.5 in./62.5 in. Overall Height: 74.0 in. Width: 79.5 in. Front/Rear Overhang: 31 in./49 in. Tailgate: Width x Height: 66.5 in. x 19.3 in. Approach/Departure Degrees: 30/21 degrees. Ground Clearance: Front axle: 8.0 in. Rear axle: 7.8 in. Oil pan: 16.1 in. Transfer case: 10.7 in. Load space: Pickup box dimensions: Sweptline: 98.875 in. x 51.0 in. x 19.3 in. W300: Wheelbase: 135 in. Load space: Pickup box dimensions: 108 in. x 54 in. x 20 in. Capacity: 66 cu. ft.

CAPACITIES: Fuel Tank: 25 gal.

ACCOMMODATIONS: Seating Capacity: 3 passenger.

INSTRUMENTATION: 0-100 mph speedometer, 99,999.9 mile odometer, gauges for fuel level, ammeter and engine coolant temperature. Warning lights for oil pressure, parking brake and hazard lights operation.

OPTIONS AND PRICES: Adventurer Package. Adventurer Sport Package. Snow-Fiter Package. 318 V-8: W100: $132, W200: $167. 360 V-8: W100: $175, W200: $210. 4-spd. wide ratio manual transmission: $108-$143, depending on wheelbase. Loadflite automatic transmission: $237.10. Tinted glass; $21.20. Oil pressure gauge: $6.00. Tachometer; $44.00. Rear step bumper: $49. Electric clock: $18. AM radio: $69. AM/FM radio: $145.35. Limited slip rear differential: $63.95. Air conditioning: $420.45. Emission reduction control system: $27:90. 60 amp alternator: $8.15. 70 amp-hr. battery: $16.70. Heavy-duty front springs (W100): $6.40. Heavy-duty rear springs (W100): $18.75. Heavy-duty shock absorbers (W100): $15.65. Shoulder belts: $30.15. Oil pressure gauge: $6.20. Electric tachometer: $44.80. Dual short arm exterior mirrors: $5.05. Rear step bumper: $49.65. Front bumper guards: $16.50. Dual electric horns: $6.70. Front Light Package: $25.75. Front wheel locking hubs: $75.30. Power steering: $144.20. 7.00 x 15D 8-ply tires $162.80. Adventurer Package: $14.60. Convenience Package: $31.55. Camper Package. For W200.

HISTORICAL FOOTNOTES: The 1973 W series Dodge trucks were introduced in August, 1972.

1973 Dodge Utiline Power Wagon pickup

1974 POWER WAGON

The major news for 1974 was the availability of the club cab body style for either the 1/2 ton W100 or 3/4 ton W200 chassis. The club cab format, which was first offered for the D100 and D200 two-wheel drive models in 1973, was created by adding 18 inches of length to the standard cab. This additional 34 cubic feet of space was positioned behind the front seat and was available either for cargo use or as auxiliary seating for two passengers via optional jump seats that folded into depressions in the cab side trim panels when not in use. The seats faced inward when in use. Small windows on each side gave this area plenty of light and avoided any closed-in sensations on the part of its occupants. Access to the rear storage area was enhanced by the use of split-back seats. A safety-lever, located on the side of the seat back, was moved upward to unlock the seat back. Commenting on the extension of the club cab models for 1974, George Butts, general manager of Dodge Truck Operations, said "The success of this vehicle and the high demand for four-wheel drive applications had much to do with our decision to expand the club cab's availability in the 1974 model year.

The club cab is still a Dodge exclusive in the truck industry, and the addition of Power Wagon models will bolster the offerings from Dodge in 1974."

1974 Dodge Sweptline Power Wagon tow truck

The club cab was built on either a special 133 in. wheelbase chassis with a 6.5 foot box or the 149 in. wheelbase chassis with an 8 foot box. The club cab with the 8 foot box was suitable for use with a slide-in camper or a fifth-wheel trailer. A new anodized aluminum grille with a gridwork of rectangular openings gave the W series trucks a fresh appearance. Nine new exterior colors were offered for 1974: White, yellow, medium blue metallic, light gold, dark green metallic, light blue, avocado metallic, light green and medium gold metallic. The exterior paint was of a new non-aqueous dispersion enamel that resisted fading, chips and abrasions.

The W100 and W200 pickups were available with the Adventurer, Adventurer Sport and Adventurer SE (Special Edition) trim packages. The custom trim remained the base level for 1974. Both the Adventurer and Sport Adventurer packages included restyled vinyl seats. All conventional seats were now of full-foam construction. All W100, W200 and W300 Power Wagons had standard locking front hubs for 1974. A new option for 1974 was a coolant recovery system that allowed expanding coolant to flow to a reserve tank. As the temperature of the coolant decreased, the coolant in the reserve tank was drawn back into the radiator.

Except for the 115 in. wheelbase W100, all W models had a frame-mounted fuel tank. This new tank was of polyurethane construction and was located inside the frame rail just ahead of the driver's side rear wheel well. The filler cap and neck was located in the express box on the driver's side. The optional auxiliary tank was positioned inside the cab. Electronic ignition was standard for all engines for 1974.

DODGE POWER WAGON SNO-FITER

1974 Dodge Sweptline Power Wagon Sno-Fiter

I.D. DATA: The serial numbers were located on a plate on the left door lock pillar. A 13-character identification system was used. The first two characters were the model code: W1-(W100), W2-(W200), W3-(W300). The following digit identified the body code. The next entry, a letter, indicated the truck's GVW: A-6000 lbs. and under, B-6001 to 10,001 lbs., C-

10,001 to 14,000 lbs. This was followed by a letter identifying engine displacement and a digit (2) identifying the 1972 model year. A letter followed identifying the assembly plant: J-Windsor, N-Burt Road, Detroit, S-Warren Truck No. 1, T-Warren Truck No. 2, U-St. Louis. The remaining six digits were the production sequence numbers. Each assembly plant began production with number 500001. The serial numbers on 6-cylinder engines were located on the right side of the block below the no. one spark plug. The 318 and 360 V-8 serial number was found on the left front of the block below the cylinder head. The 225 6-cyl. and 318 V-8 used a system in which the first two letters indicated the manufacturing plant as follows: GM-Mound Road, GT-Trenton, NM-Maryland, GW-Windsor. The next three digits identified the engine's displacement. The next letter identified the engine type as follows: R-regular 318 V-8; T-standard 225 6-cyl; H-premium 225 6-cyl. The next four digits were the manufacturing date code base upon a 10,000 day calendar. The final four digits were the sequence production numbers beginning with 0001 for each day.

Body Type	Factory Price	GVW	Shipping Weight	Prod. Total
Model W100, 1/2 ton 6-cyl.				
Ch. & Cab, 115 in. wb.	$3588	5100*	3780	a
Pickup, Utiline, 115 in. wb.	$3745	5100	4125	—
Pickup, Sweptline, 115 in. wb.	$3745	5100	4150	—
Ch. & Cab, 131 in. wb.	$3621	5100	3790	—
Pickup, Utiline, 131 in. wb.	$3782	5100	4220	—
Pickup, Sweptline, 131 in. wb.	$3782	5100	4250	—
W100 Club Cab				
Pickup, Sweptline, 133 in. wb.	$3991	5100	N.A.	1830
Pickup, Sweptline, 149 in. wb.	$4028	5100	N.A.	3031

* 5600 lb. GVW optional.
a Total model year production of all 115 in. wheelbase. W100 trucks was 11,923. Output of models with a 131 in. wheelbase (not including club cab) was 11,923.

Body Type	Factory Price	GVW	Shipping Weight	Prod. Total
Model W200, 3/4 ton, 6-cyl. (Crew cab-149 in. wb.)				
Ch. & Cab, 131 in. wb.	$4083	6500*	3845	b
Pickup, Utiline, 131 in. wb.	$4237	6500	4275	—
Pickup, Sweptline, 131 in. wb.	$4237	6500	4305	—
Crew Cab, Ch.	$4952	6500	4245	—
Crew Cab, Utiline	$5105	6500	4590	—
Crew Cab, Sweptline	$5105	6500	4615	—

* 8000 lb. GVW package was optional for all models.
b Total model year production, excluding crew cab models, was 14,549. Production of crew cab and club cab models was 5895.

Body Type	Factory Price	GVW	Shipping Weight	Prod. Total
W200 Club Cab				
Pickup, Sweptline, 149 in. wb.	$4483	6500	4505	—

* 8000 lb. GVW package was optional for all models.

Body Type	Factory Price	GVW	Shipping Weight	Prod. Total
Model W300, 1 ton, 6-cyl.				
Ch. & Cab, 135 in. wb.	$4888	8500*	4380.	c
Pickup, Utiline, 135 in. wb.	$4999	8500	N.A.	—

* GVW packages up to 10,000 lb. were available.
c Total model year production of W300 models was 1867.

STANDARD ENGINE: W100, W200, W300: Engine Type: OHV, In-line 6-cylinder. Cast iron block and cylinder head. Key components include a drop-forged, shot-peened crankshaft, roller timing chain, Stellite-faced exhaust valves, individually ported long-branch manifolds, aluminum parts and a large radiator. Bore x Stroke: 3.40 in. x 4.125 in. Lifters: Mechanical. Number of main bearings-4. Fuel Induction: Single 1-bbl. carburetor. Compression Ratio: 8.4:1. Displacement: 224.7 cu. in. (3.68 liters). Horsepower: Net: 110 @ 4000 rpm. Torque: Net: 185 lb.-ft. @ 1600 rpm. Fuel Requirements: 91 octane. Oil refill capacity: 5 qt. with filter change. Fuel Requirements: Regular.

OPTIONAL ENGINE: W100, W200, W300: This engine is standard for the club cab. The 225 6-cyl. is available but it must be specified. The price of the club cab was reduced $162 if the 6-cylinder is ordered. Features include a drop-forged five-bearing crankshaft, chain-driven camshaft, free-turning exhaust valves, drop-forged I-beam connecting rods and silent-chain camshaft. Bore x Stroke: 3.91 in. x 3.312 in. Lifters: Hydraulic. Number of main bearings-5. Fuel Induction: Single 2-bbl. carburetor. Compression Ratio: 8.5:1. Displacement: 318 cu. in. (5.21 liters). Horsepower: Net: 180 @ 4000 rpm. Torque: Net: 285 lb.-ft. @ 2400 rpm. Oil refill capacity: 5 qt. with filter change. Fuel Requirements: 91 octane.

OPTIONAL ENGINE: W100, W200, W300: Features include vibration damper, 18 in. 4 blade fan and drop-forged crankshaft. Engine Type: OHV, V-8. Cast iron block and cylinder head. Bore x Stroke: 4.00 in. x 3.58 in. Lifters: Hydraulic. Number of main bearings-5. Fuel Induction: Single 2-bbl. carburetor. Compression Ratio: 9.2:1. Displacement: 360 cu. in. (5.89 liters). Horsepower: Net: 180 @ 4000 rpm. Torque: Net: 295 lb.-ft. @ 2400 rpm. Oil refill capacity: 5 qt. with filter change. Fuel Requirements: 91 octane.

CHASSIS FEATURES: W100: Separate body and channel-type, drop-center frame. Section modulus 3.43 in.

SUSPENSION AND RUNNING GEAR: Front Suspension: Semi-elliptical springs, heavy-duty shock absorbers. Capacity: 1300 lb. Optional rating: 1550 lb. Rear Suspension: Semi-elliptical springs, heavy-duty shock absorbers. Capacity: 1350 lbs. Optional Rating: 1750 lb. Front Axle Type and Capacity: Full-floating, 3300 lb. Rear Axle Type and Capacity: Full-floating, 3300 lb. capacity. Final Drive Ratio: 3.9:1 (225 and 318 engines), 3.55:1 (360 engine). Optional: 3.55:1 for 225 and 318 engines. Transfer Case: Two-speed: 1.96, 1.00:1. Brakes: Type: Hydraulic drums (dual system with warning light) front and rear. Dimensions: Front and rear: 11.0 in. x 2.00 in. Total lining area: 171.5 sq. in. Wheels: 5-stud disc. Tires: G78 x 15B, 4-ply rating. Optional (maximum available): 6.50 x 16, 6-ply rating. Steering: Recirculating ball. Ratio: 24:1, turns Lock-to-Lock: 3.5:1. Turning Circle: 43 ft. (131 in. wheelbase). Optional: Power assisted. Ratio: 17.8:1. Transmission: 6-cyl.: A-250 3-speed manual. V-8: A-230 3-speed synchromesh manual. Transmission Ratios: 6-cyl.: 3.02, 1.76, 1.00:1. Optional: NP435, wide-ratio 4-speed manual. Transmission ratios: 6.69, 3.34, 1.66, 1.00:1. Optional: NP445, close ratio 4-speed manual. Transmission ratios: 4.56, 2.28, 1.31, 1.00:1. Optional: 3-spd. Chrysler A-727 automatic. Transmission ratios: 2.45, 1.45., 1.00:1. Clutch: Single dry plate disc, hydraulic actuation. Clutch diameter: 11 in. dia. Total lining area: 123.7 sq. in.

CHASSIS FEATURES: W200: Separate body and channel-type, drop-center frame. Section modulus 3.88 in. Crew cab: 4.70 in.

SUSPENSION AND RUNNING GEAR: Front Suspension: Semi-elliptical leaf, heavy-duty shock absorbers. Capacity: 1300 lb. Crew cab: 1550 lb. Optional rating: 1550 lb., 1750 lb. Rear Suspension: Semi-elliptical leaf. Capacity: 1750 lb. rating. Optional Rating: 2600 lb. Front Axle Type and Capacity: Full-floating, 3500 lb. capacity. Optional rating: 4000 lb. Rear Axle Type and Capacity: Full-floating, 5500 lb. capacity. Optional rating: None. Final Drive Ratio: 4.10:1, 4.56:1. Transfer Case: Two-speed: 1.96, 1.00:1. Brakes: Type: Hydraulic. Rear: Dimensions: Front: 12.12 in. x 2.00. Rear: 12.12 in. x 2.50. Total lining area: 227.5

sq. in. Wheels: 17.5 in. x 5.25 in., 8-stud disc. Tires: 8.00 x 16.5D, 6-ply rating. Optional (max size avail.): 9.50 x 19.5 In., 8-ply rating. Steering: Recirculating ball. Transmission: A-230 3-speed synchromesh manual. Transmission Ratios: 3.02, 1.76, 1.00:1. Optional: NP435, close-ratio 4-speed manual, NP445, close ratio 4-speed manual. 3-spd. Chrysler A-727 automatic. Clutch: Single plate hydraulic actuation. Clutch diameter: 11.0 in. Total Area: 123.7 sq. in.

CHASSIS FEATURES: W300: Separate body and channel steel, straight frame, 5.70 in. Section modules.

SUSPENSION AND RUNNING GEAR: Front Suspension: Semi-elliptical springs, heavy-duty, absorbers. Capacity: 1550 lb. rating. Optional rating: 1750 lb. Rear Suspension: Semi-elliptical springs. Capacity: 3250 lbs. Optional Rating: 550 lb. auxiliary spring. Front Axle Type and Capacity: Full-floating. 4500 lb. capacity. Rear Axle Type and Capacity: 7500 lb. capacity. Final Drive Ratio: Front axle: 4.88, 5.86:1. Transfer Case: Two-speed: 1.96, 1.0:1. Brakes: Type: Hydraulic. Dimensions: Front: 12.0 in. x 3.0 in. Rear: 12.0 in. x 3.0 in. Total lining area: 294.8 sq. in. Wheels: 19.5 in. x 5.25 in., 6-stud disc. Tires: 8.75 x 16.5 in., 10-ply rating. Optional: 9.50 x 16.5D, 8-ply rating, 7.50 x 16.5D 8-ply rating. Steering: Worm and Roller. Transmission: NP435 4-speed synchromesh manual. Optional: NP445 4-spd. synchromesh manual, Chrysler A-727 3-spd. automatic. Clutch: Single plate dry disc, hydraulic actuation. Clutch diameter: 11.0 in. Total plate area: 123.7 sq. in.

VEHICLE DIMENSIONS: W100: Wheelbase: 115 in./131 in. Overall Length: 190.2 in./213.6 in. Front/Rear Tread: 62.5 in./62.5 in. Overall Height: 74.0 in. Width: 79.5 in. Front/Rear Overhang: 30 in./47 in. Tailgate: Width and Height: 67 in. x 21.4 in. Approach/Departure Degrees: 34/24. Ground Clearance: Front axle: 8.2 in. Rear axle: 8.5 in. Oil pan: 15.8 in. Transfer case: 10.4 in. Load space: Pickup box dimensions: 131 in. wheelbase Sweptline: 98 in. x 51 in. x 19.3 in. W200. Wheelbase: 131 in. Crew cab: 149 in. Overall Length: 131 in./149 in. wheelbase: 213.6 in./231.6 in. Front/Rear Tread: 62.5 in./62.5 in. Overall Height: 74.0 in. Width: 79.5 in. Front/Rear Overhang: 31 in./49 in. Tailgate: Width x Height: 66.5 in. x 19.3 in. Approach/Departure Degrees: 30/21 degrees. Ground Clearance: Front axle: 8.0 in. Rear axle: 7.8 in. Oil pan: 16.1 in. Transfer case: 10.7 in. Load space: Pickup box dimensions: Sweptline: 98.875 in. x 51.0 in. x 19.3 in. W300: Wheelbase: 135 in. Load space: Pickup box dimensions: 108 in. x 54 in. x 20 in. Capacity: 66 cu. ft.

CAPACITIES: Fuel Tank: 25 gal.

ACCOMMODATIONS: Seating Capacity: 3 passenger.

INSTRUMENTATION: 0-100 mph speedometer, 99,999.9 mile odometer, gauges for fuel level, ammeter and engine coolant temperature. Warning lights for oil pressure, parking brake and hazard lights operation.

OPTIONS AND PRICES: Sure-Grip, anti-spin rear differential: $139.45. 360 cu. in. V-8: $156.00. 360 V-8: $199. NP 435 4-spd. wide-ratio man. trans.: $105. NP 445 4-spd. close-ratio man. trans.: $130. A-727 Loadflite automatic transmission: $240. Tinted glass: $22.90. Sliding rear window: $55.60. Special Cooling Package: $26.00. Air conditioning: $455.30. 60 amp generator: $8.65 (W200), $31.65 (W100). 70 amp battery: $14.85. Flip-down rear seats (Club cab): $63.90. Shoulder belts: $32.50. Oil pressure gauge: $6.60. Tachometer: $44.00. Automatic speed control: $64.65. Electric clock: $19.45. AM/FM radio: $157.35. Chrome rear bumper: $39.15. Dual electric horns: $7.20. Grip rails: $64.65. Tool storage box: $50.30. Heavy-duty front and shock absorbers: $16.80 (W100, W200). Heavy-duty rear springs: $18.75 (W100). Heavy-duty front and rear springs (W200): $23. Heavy-duty front and rear shock absorbers: $16 (W100 and W200). Power steering: $145.95. 7.00 x 15D tires: $160 (W100). 9.50 x 16.5 tires: $115.76 (W200). Convenience Package: $34.05. Adventurer Sport Package: $285.25. 7.00 x 15D tires: $160 (W100). Auxiliary 24 gal. fuel tank: $69.00, club cab: $83.00.

HISTORICAL FOOTNOTES: The 1974 Dodge trucks were introduced in August, 1973.

1975 POWER WAGON

For 1975 the Dodge Power Wagons were equipped with a NP 203 full-time four-wheel drive and front wheel disc brakes. The four-wheel drive system had five settings: High lock, high, neutral, low and low lock. The suspension on the W100 and W200 was reworked for a smoother ride. The new suspension's geometry was similar to the of the Ramcharger. Longer front springs with reduced rates were used along with revalved shock absorbers. The new suspension reduced overall height by approximately one inch. Power Wagons were available with a new optional, front stabilizer bar. Other technical refinements involved the use of a Dana 44BJ front axle with a rating of 3500 lbs., a new steering linkage, and the use of 9.25 in. axles on the W100 in place of the 8.75 in. units used in 1974. The 440 cu. in. V-8 was added to the engine option list. The W100, W200 and W300 models were available in conventional cab, crew cab or club cab bodies. The club cab jump seats now had a new head-back rest.

A redesigned dash panel had a larger, wing-shaped instrument cluster with a reshaped hood to reduce glare. The standard interior had a matte black finish on the instrument cluster face plate. If either the Adventurer Sport or Adventurer SE options were installed, the plate had a simulated woodgrain finish. Both the AM and AM/FM radios were of an improved design by the Chrysler Space Division.

The selection of trim packages consisted of Custom, Adventurer, Sport Adventurer, and for the W100 only, the Adventurer SE package. Standard custom features included side "Custom" nameplate on Sweptline box, vinyl seats with full-depth foam cushion (the club cab seat had a spring back and foam-pad topper with molded full-foam in back), W100 or W200 nameplate on front fender, color-keyed padded instrument panel, color-keyed seat trim, color-keyed armrests, bright grille, bright front bumper, horn button, black rubber floor mat, 10 in. inside day/night rearview mirror, padded sun visors and bright exterior mirrors. The color selection consisted of blue, green, parchment and black. The Adventurer Package, in addition to the custom model features included exterior body side moldings along the fender, door and Sweptline box, side "Adventurer" nameplate, upper and lower tailgate moldings on Sweptline only, pleated vinyl seats with buttons and pad. A full-foam seat cushion and seat back were used. The club cab had a spring and foam-pad topper with molded full-foam in back. The seats were color-keyed on the conventional cab in a choice of parchment, blue, green and black. Color choices were parchment, black, gold, blue and green on club cab. Other items included fiberglass inner door trim panels with integral armrests, color-keyed with bright molding and "Adventurer" nameplate, bright grille, bright front bumper, bright vent window division bar, bright tail lamp bezels (Sweptline only), cigarette lighter, horn bar, deluxe front floor mat, color-keyed on conventional cab, black only on club cab, formed plastic rear side and back inner panel trim panels on club cab.

1975 Dodge W100 club coupe pickup with Adventurer Package

The Adventurer Sport package, had in addition to the custom features these items: Exterior paint-filled wide body side moldings, "Adventurer Sport" side body nameplate, bright paint-filled tailgate moldings (Sweptline only), bright and simulated woodgrained instrument panel trim molding, bright and simulated woodgrained instrument panel cluster face plate, color-keyed (the color selection consisted of parchment, blue, green or black), pleated vinyl seats with buttons and full-foam cushion and seat back (the club cab seat had a spring and foam-pad topper with molded full-foam back), inner door trim panels with integral armrests and simulated woodgrained applique, bright wheel-lip moldings (all models) and bright rear wheel-lip on Sweptline models, bright grille, bright front bumper, bright vent wing division bar, bright drip rails and bright windshield and rear window moldings, bright side window moldings (Sweptline only), parchment colored foam core headliner, cigarette lighter, horn bar, "Adventurer" nameplate on instrument panel, deluxe front floor mat, color-keyed on conventional cab, black only on club cab, formed plastic color-keyed rear side and back inner trim panels on club cab.

The W100 Adventurer SE Package added the following items to the Custom Package features: Exterior body side moldings with woodgrained vinyl inserts along the fender, door and body, "Adventurer SE" nameplate, tailgate moldings with woodgrained vinyl insert and nameplate (Sweptline pickup models only), bright and simulated woodgrained instrument panel trim molding, color-keyed pleated cloth and vinyl full-foam seats and back, inner door plastic trim panels with padded panel and integral armrests, nameplate, and vinyl lower door storage pockets, bright tread plates, bright trim around accelerator, brake, and clutch pedals, color-keyed carpeting, formed plastic rear side and lower inner panels on club cab, and Convenience Package.

The W100 and W200 club cab models with all trim packages were also available with a Bucket Seat Interior Package consisting of all-vinyl upholstery in a choice of parchment or black. Also included were a center console, carpeting and insulation. All models could be equipped for snowplowing. A new instrument panel for 1975 offered easier to read dials and gauges plus a new panel pad. However, the radio controls were still positioned directly behind the steering wheel. Three two-tone paint options were offered for 1975. All models were available with the main body color from the cab window sill down, and a secondary color from that line up. Sweptline models were available with the main body color on top and a secondary color on the bottom. Sweptline models were also available with the main body color in the middle with the secondary color on top and bottom. The exterior color selection for 1975 consisted of medium gold metallic, light green, avocado metallic, light gold, dark green metallic, bright red, white, light blue, medium blue metallic, yellow, medium gold, bronze metallic and silver cloud metallic. An extra cost paint choice was sunstone. The standard transmission for the W100 and W200 remained a 3-speed manual unit. The W300 was fitted with a standard 4-speed manual.

I.D. DATA: The vehicle identification number was located on a V.I.N. plate attached to the driver's side door body latch post. The V.I.N. consisted of 13 elements. The first two characters indicated the model code as follows: W1-W100, W2-W200, W3-W300. The next digit identified the body type as follows: 1-Conventional cab, 2-Crew cab, 3-Crew cab, 4-Utiline crew cab, 4-Sweptline conventional cab, 7-Sweptline club cab, 8-Club cab. The next entry, a letter, identified the GVW rating as follows: A-6,000 lb. or less, B-6001 to 10,000 lb., C-10,001 to 14,000 lb. The next unit, a letter, designated the engine type as follows: B-225-1 bbl., E-318-1 bbl., F-360, D-440. The next unit, the number 5 indicted the 1975 model year. Following this came a letter indicating the assembly plant as follows: J-Windsor, S-Warren Plant No.1, T-Warren Plant No. 2, X-Missouri. The V.I.N. ended with a six-digit production sequence number at the assembly plant. All models began with sequence number 000,001.

Body Type	Factory Price	GVW	Shipping Weight	Prod. Total
Model W100, 1/2 ton 6-cyl.				
Ch. & Cab, 115 in. wb.	$3588	5100*	3780	a
Pickup, Utiline, 115 in. wb.	$3745	5100	4125	—
Pickup, Sweptline, 115 in. wb.	$3745	5100	4150	—
Ch. & Cab, 131 in. wb.	$3621	5100	3790	—
Pickup, Utiline, 131 in. wb.	$3782	5100	4220	—
Pickup, Sweptline, 131 in. wb.	$3782	5100	4250	—
W100 Club Cab				
Pickup, Sweptline, 133 in. wb.	$3991	5100	N.A.	1830
Pickup, Sweptline, 149 in. wb.	$4028	5100	N.A.	3031

* 5600 lb. GVW optional.
a Total model year production of all 115 in. wheelbase. W100 trucks was 11,923. Output of models with a 131 in. wheelbase (not including club cab) was 11,923.

Body Type	Factory Price	GVW	Shipping Weight	Prod. Total
Model W200, 3/4 ton, 6-cyl. (Crew cab-149 in. wheelbase)				
Ch. & Cab, 131 in. wb.	$4083	6500*	3845	b
Pickup, Utiline, 131 in. wb.	$4237	6500	4275	—
Pickup, Sweptline, 131 in. wb.	$4237	6500	4305	—
Crew Cab, Ch.	$4952	6500	4245	—
Crew Cab, Utiline	$5105	6500	4590	—
Crew Cab, Sweptline	$5105	6500	4615	—

* 8000 lb. GVW package was optional for all models.
b Total model year production, excluding crew cab models, was 14,549. Production of crew cab and club cab models was 5895.

W200 Club Cab				
Pickup, Sweptline, 149 in. wb.	$4483	6500	4505	—
Model W300, 1 ton, 6-cyl.				
Ch. & Cab, 135 in. wb.	$4888	8500*	4380	c
Pickup, Utiline, 135 in. wb.	$4999	8500	N.A.	—

* GVW packages up to 10,000 lb. were available.
c Total model year production of W300 models was 1867.

STANDARD ENGINE: W100, W200, W300: Engine Type: OHV, In-line 6-cylinder. Cast iron block and cylinder head. Key components include a drop-forged, shot-peened crankshaft, roller timing chain, Stellite-faced exhaust valves, individually ported long-branch manifolds, aluminum parts and a large radiator. Bore x Stroke: 3.40 in. x 4.125 in. Lifters: Mechanical. Number of main bearings-4. Fuel Induction: Single 1-bbl. carburetor. Compression Ratio: 8.4:1. Displacement: 224.7 cu. in. (3.68 liters). Horsepower: Net: 110 @ 4000 rpm. Torque: Net: 185 lb.-ft. @ 1600 rpm. Fuel Requirements: 91 octane. Oil refill capacity: 5 qt. with filter change. Fuel Requirements: Regular.

OPTIONAL ENGINE: W100, W200, W300: This engine is standard for the club cab. The 225 6-cyl. is available but it must be specified. The price of the club cab was reduced $162 if the 6-cylinder is ordered. Features include a drop-forged five-bearing crankshaft, chain-driven camshaft, free-turning exhaust valves, drop-forged I-beam connecting rods and silent-chain camshaft. Bore x Stroke: 3.91 in. x 3.312 in. Lifters: Hydraulic. Number of main bearings-5. Fuel Induction: Single 2-bbl. carburetor. Compression Ratio: 8.5:1. Displacement: 318 cu. in. (5.21 liters). Horsepower: Net: 180 @ 4400 rpm. Torque: Net: 285 lb.-ft. @ 2400 rpm. Oil refill capacity: 5 qt. with filter change. Fuel Requirements: 91 octane.

OPTIONAL ENGINE: W100, W200, W300: Features include vibration damper, 18 in. 4 blade fan and drop-forged crankshaft. Engine Type: OHV, V-8. Cast iron block and cylinder head. Bore x Stroke: 4.00 in. x 3.58 in. Lifters: Hydraulic. Number of main bearings-5. Fuel Induction: Single 2-bbl. carburetor. Compression Ratio: 9.2:1. Displacement: 360 cu. in. (5.89 liters). Horsepower: Net: 185 @ 4000 rpm. Torque: Net: 295 lb.-ft. @ 2500 rpm. Oil refill capacity: 5 qt. with filter change. Fuel Requirements: 91 octane.

OPTIONAL ENGINE: W100, W200, W300: Engine Type: OHV, V-8. Cast iron block and cylinder head. Bore x Stroke: 4.32 in. x 3.75 in. Lifters: Hydraulic. Number of main bearings-5. Fuel Induction: Single 4-bbl. carburetor. Compression Ratio: 8.12:1. Displacement: 440 cu. in. (7.2 liters). Horsepower: 235 @ 4000 rpm. Torque: 340 lb.-ft. @ 2400 rpm. Oil refill capacity: 5.0 qt. with filter change. Fuel Requirements: 91 octane.

CHASSIS FEATURES: W100: Separate body and channel-type, drop-center frame. Section modulus 3.43 in.

SUSPENSION AND RUNNING GEAR: Front Suspension: Semi-elliptical springs, heavy-duty shock absorbers. Capacity: 1300 lb. Optional rating: 1550 lb. Rear Suspension: Semi-elliptical springs, heavy-duty shock absorbers. Capacity: 1350 lbs. Optional Rating: 1750 lb. Front Axle Type and Capacity: Full-floating, 3300 lb. capacity. Rear Axle Type and Capacity: Full-floating, 3300 lb. capacity. Final Drive Ratio: 3.9:1 (225 and 318 engines), 3.55:1 (360 engine). Optional: 3.55:1 for 225 and 318 engines. Transfer Case: Two-speed: 1.96, 1.00:1. Brakes: Type: Hydraulic drums (dual system with warning light) front and rear. Dimensions: Front and rear: 11.0 in. x 2.00 in. Total lining area: 171.5 sq. in. Wheels: 5-stud disc. Tires: G78 x 15B, 4-ply rating. Optional (maximum available): 6.50 x 16, 6-ply rating. Steering: Recirculating ball. Ratio: 24:1, turns Lock-to-Lock: 3.5:1. Turning Circle: 43 ft. (131 in. wheelbase). Optional: Power assisted. Ratio: 17.8:1. Transmission: 6-cyl.: A-250 3-speed manual. V-8: A-230 3-speed synchromesh manual. Transmission Ratios: 6-cyl.: 3.02, 1.76, 1.00:1. Optional: NP435, wide-ratio 4-speed manual. Transmission ratios: 6.69, 3.34, 1.66, 1.00:1. Optional: NP445, close ratio 4-speed manual. Transmission ratios: 4.56, 2.28, 1.31, 1.00:1. Optional: 3-spd. Chrysler A-727 automatic. Transmission ratios: 2.45, 1.45., 1.00:1. Clutch: Single dry plate disc, hydraulic actuation. Clutch diameter: 11 in. dia. Total lining area: 123.7 sq. in.

CHASSIS FEATURES: W200: Separate body and channel-type, drop-center frame. Section modulus 3.88 in. Crew cab: 4.70 in.

SUSPENSION AND RUNNING GEAR: Front Suspension: Semi-elliptical leaf, heavy-duty shock absorbers. Capacity: 1300 lb. Crew cab: 1550 lb. Optional rating: 1550 lb., 1750 lb. Rear Suspension: Semi-elliptical leaf. Capacity: 1750 lb. rating. Optional Rating: 2600 lb. Front Axle Type and Capacity: Full-floating, 3500 lb. capacity. Optional rating: 4000 lb. Rear Axle Type and Capacity: Full-floating, 5500 lb. capacity. Optional rating: None. Final Drive Ratio: 4.10:1, 4.56:1. Transfer Case: Two-speed: 1.96, 1.00:1. Brakes: Type: Hydraulic. Front: Rear: Dimensions: Front: 12.12 in. x 2.00. Rear: 12.12 in. x 2.50 in. Total lining area: 227.5 sq. in. Wheels: 17.5 in. x 5.25 in., 8-stud disc. Tires: 8.00 x 16.5D, 6-ply rating. Optional (max. size avail.): 9.50 x 19.5 in., 8-ply rating. Steering: Recirculating ball. Transmission: A-230 3-speed synchromesh manual. Transmission Ratios: 3.02, 1.76, 1.00:1. Optional: NP435, close-ratio 4-speed manual, NP445, close ratio 4-speed manual. 3-spd. Chrysler A-727 automatic. Clutch: Single plate hydraulic actuation. Clutch diameter: 11.0 in. Total Area: 123.7 sq. in.

CHASSIS FEATURES: W300: Separate body and channel steel, straight frame, 5.70 in. Section modulus.

SUSPENSION AND RUNNING GEAR: Front Suspension: Semi-elliptical springs, heavy-duty, absorbers. Capacity: 1550 lb. rating. Optional rating: 1750 lb. Rear Suspension: Semi-elliptical springs. Capacity: 3250 lbs. Optional Rating: 550 lb. auxiliary spring. Front Axle Type and Capacity: Full-floating. 4500 lb. capacity. Rear Axle Type and Capacity: 7500 lb. capacity. Final Drive Ratio: Front axle: 4.88, 5.86:1. Transfer Case: Two-speed: 1.96, 1.0:1. Brakes: Type: Hydraulic. Dimensions: Front: 12.0 in. x 3.0 in. Rear: 12.0 in. x 3.0 in. Total lining area: 294.8 sq. in. Wheels: 19.5 in. x 5.25 in., 6-stud disc. Tires: 8.75 x 16.5 in., 10-ply rating. Optional: 9.50 x 16.5D, 8-ply rating, 7.50 x 16.5D 8-ply rating. Steering: Worm and Roller. Transmission: NP435 4-speed synchromesh manual. Optional: NP445 4-spd. synchromesh manual, Chrysler A-727 3-spd. automatic. Clutch: Single plate dry disc, hydraulic actuation. Clutch diameter: 11.0 in. Total plate area: 123.7 sq. in.

VEHICLE DIMENSIONS: W100: Wheelbase: 115 in./131 in. Overall Length: 190.2 in./213.6 in. Front/Rear Tread: 62.5 in./62.5 in. Overall Height: 74.0 in. Width: 79.5 in. Front/Rear Overhang: 30 in./47 in. Tailgate: Width and Height: 67 in. x 21.4 in. Approach/Departure Degrees: 34/24. Ground Clearance: Front axle: 8.2 in. Rear axle: 8.5 in. Oil pan: 15.8 in. Transfer case: 10.4 in. Load space: Pickup box dimensions: 131 in. wheelbase Sweptline: 98 in. x 51 in. x 19.3 in. W200. Wheelbase: 131 in. Crew cab: 149 in. Overall Length: 131 in./149 in. wheelbase: 213.6 in./231.6 in. Front/Rear Tread: 62.5 in./62.5 in. Overall Height: 74.0 in. Width: 79.5 in. Front/Rear Overhang: 31 in./49 in. Tailgate: Width x Height: 66.5 in. x 19.3 in. Approach/Departure Degrees: 30/21 degrees. Ground Clearance: Front axle: 8.0 in. Rear axle: 7.8 in. Oil pan: 16.1 in. Transfer case: 10.7 in. Load space: Pickup box dimensions: Sweptline: 98.875 in. x 51.0 in. x 19.3 in. W300: Wheelbase: 135 in. Load space: Pickup box dimensions: 108 in. x 54 in. x 20 in. Capacity: 66 cu. ft.

CAPACITIES: Fuel Tank: 25 gal.

ACCOMMODATIONS: Seating Capacity: 3 passenger.

INSTRUMENTATION: 0-100 mph speedometer, 99,999.9 mile odometer, gauges for fuel level, ammeter and engine coolant temperature. Warning lights for oil pressure, parking brake and hazard lights operation.

OPTIONS AND PRICES: 4-spd. wide-ratio man. trans.: $108. 4-spd. close-ratio man. trans.: $134. Loadflite automatic transmission: $288.85. Air conditioning: $480.15. Power steering: $152.00. 440 engine: $256.15. Sliding rear window: $47.50. Auxiliary transmission oil cooler: $47.50. 72 amp alternator: $9.35. Oil pressure gauge: $7.20. Electric tachometer: $50.15. Automatic cruise control: $69.10. AM/FM radio: $159.50. Dual exterior mirrors: $42.20. Dual electric horns: $9.25. Rear step bumper: $57.50. Two-tone paint: $44.10. Power steering: $172.25. Skid plate: $31.00. Trailer Towing Package: $45.40. Convenience Package: $44.75. Adventurer Sport Package: $311.20. GVW 8,000 lb. Package: $113.08.

HISTORICAL FOOTNOTES: The 1975 Dodge trucks were introduced in August, 1974.

1976 POWER WAGON

Changes for 1976 were very limited. They included a repositioned fuel tank, which was now mounted higher between the frame rails, and raised tie rods for increased ground clearance.

I.D. DATA: The vehicle identification number was located on a V.I.N. plate attached to the driver's side door body latch post. The V.I.N. consisted of 13 elements. The first two characters indicated the model code as follows: W1-W100, W2-W200, W3-W300. The next digit identified the body type as follows: 1-Conventional cab, 2-Crew cab, 3-Crew cab, 4-Utiline crew cab, 4-Sweptline conventional cab, 7-Sweptline club cab, 8-Club cab. The next entry, a letter, identified the GVW rating as follows: A-6,000 lb. or less, B-6001 to 10,000 lb., C-10,001 to 14,000 lb. The next unit, a letter, designated the engine type as follows: B-225-1 bbl., E-318-1 bbl., F-360, D-440. The next unit, the number 6, indicted the 1976 model year. Following this came a letter indicating the assembly plant as follows: J-Windsor, S-Warren Plant No.1, T-Warren Plant No. 2, X-Missouri. The V.I.N. ended with a six-digit production sequence number at the assembly plant. All models began with sequence number 000,001.

Body Type	Factory Price	GVW	Shipping Weight	Prod. Total
Model W100, 1/2 ton 6-cyl.				
Ch. & Cab, 115 in. wb.	$4419	5100*	3780	a
Pickup, Utiline, 115 in. wb.	$4585	5100	4125	—
Pickup, Sweptline, 115 in. wb.	$4585	5100	4150	—
Ch. & Cab, 131 in. wb.	$4462	5100	3790	—
Pickup, Utiline, 131 in. wb.	$4628	5100	4220	—
Pickup, Sweptline, 131 in. wb.	$4628	5100	4250	—

* 5600 lb. GVW optional.
a Total model year production of all 115 in. wheelbase. W100 trucks was 10,580. Output of models with a 131 in. wheelbase (not including club cab) was 9,005.

W100 Club Cab				
Pickup, Sweptline, 133 in. wb.	$4879	5100	N.A.	1440
Pickup, Sweptline, 149 in. wb.	$4917	5100	N.A.	1921
Model W200, 3/4 ton, 6-cyl. (Crew cab-149 in. wheelbase)				
Ch. & Cab, 131 in. wb.	$5085	6500*	3845	b
Pickup, Utiline, 131 in. wb.	$5251	6500	4275	—
Pickup, Sweptline, 131 in. wb.	$5251	6500	4305	—
Crew Cab Ch., 149 in. wb.	$6078	6500	4245	—
Crew Cab, Utiline	$6244	6500	4590	—
Crew Cab, Sweptline	$6244	6500	4615	—

* 8000 lb. GVW package was optional for all models.
b Total model year production of 131 in. wheelbase models, was 20,507. Production of 149 in. wheelbase models was 3325.

W200 Club Cab				
Pickup, Sweptline, 149 in. wb.	$5661	6500	4605	—
Model W300, 1 ton, 6-cyl.				
Ch. & Cab, 135 in. wb.	$6039	8500	4380 lb.	1522

* GVW packages up to 10,000 lb. were available.

STANDARD ENGINE: W100, W200, W300: Engine Type: OHV, In-line 6-cylinder. Cast iron block and cylinder head. Key components include a drop-forged, shot-peened crankshaft, roller timing chain, Stellite-faced exhaust valves, individually ported long-branch manifolds, aluminum parts and a large radiator. Bore x Stroke: 3.40 in. x 4.125 in. Lifters: Mechanical. Number of main bearings-4. Fuel Induction: Single 1-bbl. carburetor. Compression Ratio: 8.4:1. Displacement: 224.7 cu. in. (3.68 liters). Horsepower: Net: 110 @ 4000 rpm. Torque: Net: 185 lb.-ft. @ 1600 rpm. Fuel Requirements: 91 octane. Oil refill capacity: 5 qt. with filter change. Fuel Requirements: Regular.

OPTIONAL ENGINE: W100, W200, W300: This engine is standard for the club cab. The 225 6-cyl. is available but it must be specified. Features include a drop-forged five-bearing crankshaft, chain-driven camshaft, free-turning exhaust valves, drop-forged I-beam connecting rods and silent-chain camshaft. Bore x Stroke: 3.91 in. x 3.312 in. Lifters: Hydraulic. Number of main bearings-5. Fuel Induction: Single 2-bbl. carburetor. Compression Ratio: 8.5:1. Displacement: 318 cu. in. (5.21 liters). Horsepower: Net: 180 @ 4400 rpm. Torque: Net: 285 lb.-ft. @ 2400 rpm. Oil refill capacity: 5 qt. with filter change. Fuel Requirements: 91 octane.

OPTIONAL ENGINE: W100, W200, W300: Features include vibration damper, 18 in. 4 blade fan and drop-forged crankshaft. Engine Type: OHV, V-8. Cast iron block and cylinder head. Bore x Stroke: 4.00 in. x 3.58 in. Lifters: Hydraulic. Number of main bearings-5. Fuel Induction: Single 2-bbl. carburetor. Compression Ratio: 9.2:1. Displacement: 360 cu. in. (5.89 liters). Horsepower: Net: 185 @ 4000 rpm. Torque: Net: 295 lb.-ft. @ 2500 rpm. Oil refill capacity: 5 qt. with filter change. Fuel Requirements: 91 octane.

OPTIONAL ENGINE: W100, W200, W300: Engine Type: OHV, V-8. Cast iron block and cylinder head. Bore x Stroke: 4.32 in. x 3.75 in. Lifters: Hydraulic. Number of main bearings-5. Fuel Induction: Single 4-bbl. carburetor. Compression Ratio: 8.12:1. Displacement: 440 cu. in. (7.2 liters). Horsepower: 235 @ 4000 rpm. Torque: 340 lb.-ft. @ 2400 rpm. Oil refill capacity: 5.0 qt. with filter change. Fuel Requirements: 91 octane.

CHASSIS FEATURES: W100: Separate body and channel-type, drop-center frame. Section 3.43 in.

SUSPENSION AND RUNNING GEAR: Front Suspension: Semi-elliptical springs, heavy-duty shock absorbers. Capacity: 1300 lb. Optional rating: 1550 lb. Rear Suspension: Semi-elliptical springs, heavy-duty shock absorbers. Capacity: 1350 lbs. Optional Rating: 1750 lb. Front Axle Type and Capacity: Full-floating, 3300 lb. capacity. Rear Axle Type and Capacity: Full-floating, 3300 lb. capacity. Final Drive Ratio: 3.9:1 (225 and 318 engines), 3.55:1 (360 engine). Optional: 3.55:1 for 225 and 318 engines. Transfer Case: Two-speed: 1.96, 1.00:1. Brakes:

Type: Hydraulic drums (dual system with warning light) front and rear. Dimensions: Front and rear: 11.0 in. x 2.00 in. Total lining area: 171.5 sq. in. Wheels: 5-stud disc. Tires: G78 x 15D, 4-ply rating. Optional (maximum available): 6.50 x 16, 6-ply rating. Steering: Recirculating ball. Ratio: 24:1, turns Lock-to-Lock: 3.5:1. Turning Circle: 43 ft. (131 in. wheelbase). Optional: Power assisted. Ratio: 17.8:1. Transmission: 6-cyl.: A-250 3-speed manual. V-8: A-230 3-speed synchromesh manual. Transmission Ratios: 6-cyl.: 3.02, 1.76, 1.00:1. Optional: NP435, wide-ratio 4-speed manual. Transmission ratios: 6.69, 3.34, 1.66, 1.00:1. Optional: NP445, close ratio 4-speed manual. Transmission ratios: 4.56, 2.28, 1.31, 1.00:1. Optional: 3-spd. Chrysler A-727 automatic. Clutch: Single dry plate disc, hydraulic actuation. Clutch diameter: 11 in. dia. Total lining area: 123.7 sq. in.

CHASSIS FEATURES: W200: Separate body and channel-type, drop-center frame. Section modules: 3.88 in. Crew cab: 4.70 in.

SUSPENSION AND RUNNING GEAR: Front Suspension: Semi-elliptical leaf, heavy-duty shock absorbers. Capacity: 1300 lb. Crew cab: 1550 lb. Optional rating: 1550 lb., 1750 lb. Rear Suspension: Semi-elliptical leaf. Capacity: 1750 lb. rating. Optional Rating: 2600 lb. Front Axle Type and Capacity: Full-floating, 3500 lb. capacity. Optional rating: 4000 lb. Rear Axle Type and Capacity: Full-floating, 5500 lb. capacity. Final Drive Ratio: 4.10:1, 4.56:1. Transfer Case: Two-speed: 1.96, 1.00:1. Brakes: Type: Hydraulic. Front: Disc. Rear: Drum. Dimensions: Front: 12.12 in. x 2.00. Rear: 12.12 in. x 2.50 in. Total lining area: 227.5 sq. in. Wheels.): 17.5 in. x 5.25 in., 8-stud disc. Tires: 8.00 x 16.5D, 6-ply rating. Optional (max. size avail.): 9.50 x 19.5 in., 8-ply rating. Steering: Recirculating ball. Transmission: A-230 3-speed synchromesh manual. Transmission Ratios: 3.02, 1.76, 1.00:1. Optional: NP435, close-ratio 4-speed manual, NP445, close ratio 4-speed manual. 3-spd. Chrysler A-727 automatic. Clutch: Single plate hydraulic actuation. Clutch diameter: 11.0 in. Total Area: 123.7 sq. in.

CHASSIS FEATURES: W300: Separate body and channel steel, straight frame, 5.70 in. Section modules.

SUSPENSION AND RUNNING GEAR: Front Suspension: Semi-elliptical springs, heavy-duty, absorbers. Capacity: 1550 lb. rating. Optional rating: 1750 lb. Rear Suspension: Semi-elliptical springs. Capacity: 3250 lbs. Optional Rating: 550 lb. auxiliary spring. Front Axle Type and Capacity: Full-floating, 4500 lb. capacity. Rear Axle Type and Capacity: 7500 lb. capacity. Final Drive Ratio: Front axle: 4.88, 5.86:1. Transfer Case: Two-speed: 1.96, 1.0:1. Brakes: Type: Hydraulic. Dimensions: Front: 12.0 in. x 3.0 in. Rear: 12.0 in. x 3.0 in. Total lining area: 294.8 sq. in. Wheels: 19.5 in. x 5.25 in., 6-stud disc. Tires: 8.75 x 16.5 in., 10-ply rating. Optional: 9.50 x 16.5D, 8-ply rating, 7.50 x 16.5D 8-ply rating. Steering: Worm and Roller. Transmission: NP435 4-speed synchromesh manual. Optional: NP445 4-spd. synchromesh manual, Chrysler A-727 3-spd. automatic. Clutch: Single plate dry disc, hydraulic actuation. Clutch diameter: 11.0 in. Total plate area: 123.7 sq. in.

VEHICLE DIMENSIONS: W100: Wheelbase: 115 in./131 in. Overall Length: 190.2 in./213.6 in. Front/Rear Tread: 62.5 in./62.5 in. Overall Height: 74.0 in. Width: 79.5 in. Front/Rear Overhang: 30 in./47 in. Tailgate: Width and Height: 67 in. x 21.4 in. Approach/Departure Degrees: 34/24. Ground Clearance: Front axle: 8.2 in. Rear axle: 8.5 in. Oil pan: 15.8 in. Transfer case: 10.4 in. Load space: Pickup box dimensions: 131 in. wheelbase. Sweptline: 98 in. x 51 in. x 19.3 in. W200: Wheelbase: 131 in. Crew cab: 149 in. Overall Length: 131 in./149 in. wheelbase. 213.6 in./231.6 in. Front/Rear Tread: 62.5 in./62.5 in. Overall Height: 74.0 in. Width: 79.5 in. Front/Rear Overhang: 31 in./49 in. Tailgate: Width x Height: 66.5 in. x 19.3 in. Approach/Departure Degrees: 30/21 degrees. Ground Clearance: Front axle: 8.0 in. Rear axle: 7.8 in. Oil pan: 16.1 in. Transfer case: 10.7 in. Load space: Pickup box dimensions: Sweptline: 98.875 in. x 51.0 in. x 19.3 in. W300: Wheelbase: 135 in. Load space: Pickup box dimensions: 108 in. x 54 in. x 20 in. Capacity: 66 cu. ft.

CAPACITIES: Fuel Tank: 25 gal.

ACCOMMODATIONS: Seating Capacity: 3 passenger.

INSTRUMENTATION: 0-100 mph speedometer, 99,999.9 mile odometer, gauges for fuel level, ammeter and engine coolant temperature. Warning lights for oil pressure, parking brake and hazard lights operation.

OPTIONS AND PRICES: Sure-Grip, anti-spin rear differential. 360 cu. in. V-8. 360 V-8. 4-spd. wide-ratio man. trans.: $108. 4-spd. close-ratio man. trans.: $134. Loadflite automatic transmission: $250. Tinted glass. Sliding rear window. Air conditioning: $443. 60 amp generator. 70 amp battery. Flip-down rear seats (club cab). Shoulder belts. Oil pressure gauge. Tachometer. Automatic speed control. Electric clock. AM/FM radio. Chrome rear bumper. Dual electric horns. Grip rails. Tool storage box. Heavy-duty front and shock absorbers (W100, W200). Heavy-duty rear springs (W100). Heavy-duty front and rear shock absorbers (W100). Power steering: $152.00. 7.00 x 15D tires (W100). 9.50 x 16.5 tires (W200). Convenience Package. Adventurer Sport Package. 7.00 x 15D tires (W100).

HISTORICAL FOOTNOTES: The 1976 Dodge trucks were introduced in August, 1975.

1977 POWER WAGON

1977 Dodge Power Wagon pickup with Macho Trim Package

The 1977 W series trucks from Dodge had a new grille similar to that used in 1976. The most apparent exterior change was the positioning of the parking/directional lights inboard from the headlights. The top section of the grille carried bold DODGE lettering. The side body trim was mounted higher on the body than in 1976. The base trim level remained the custom. Optional were Adventurer and Adventurer SE trim packages. A Warlock model was offered for the W100 line. This sport truck was available in exterior colors of bright red, medium green, sunfire metallic or black sunfire metallic. The Warlock was equipped with gold painted spoke wheels, gold pinstriping, chrome-plated mini running boards, oak sideboards and wide raised white letter tires. The Warlock interior was highlighted by black bucket seats and gold paint accents. Only the 115 in. wheelbase, Utiline, 6.5 ft. box pickup style was available for the Warlock. A 400 cu. in. V-8 was added to the engine option list for all W models. The 1977 Power Wagons also had new interior styling with new seat upholstery, door trim and instrument panel. Three new interior colors were available for 1977. Exterior color choices for 1977 consisted of medium blue metallic, yellow, light blue, russet sunfire metallic, medium green sunfire metallic, russet, light green metallic, bright red, bright tan metallic, white, light tan, black sunfire metallic, harvest gold and silver cloud metallic.

A new W150, heavy-duty half ton model was introduced at mid-year.

1977 Dodge Sweptline W100 Power Wagon pickup

I.D. DATA: The vehicle identification number was located on a V.I.N. plate attached to the driver's side door body latch post. The V.I.N. consisted of 13 elements. The first two characters indicated the model code as follows: W1-W100, W2-W200, W3-W300. The next digit identified the body type as follows: 1-Conventional cab, 2-Crew cab, 3-Crew cab, 4-Utiline crew cab, 4-Sweptline conventional cab, 7-Sweptline club cab, 8-Club cab. The next entry, a letter, identified the GVW rating as follows: A-6,000 lb. or less, B-6001 to 10,000 lb., C-10,001 to 14,000 lb. The next unit, a letter, designated the engine type as follows: B-225-1 bbl., E-318-1 bbl., F-360, D-440. The next unit, the number 7 indicted the 1977 model year. Following this came a letter indicating the assembly plant as follows: J-Windsor, S-Warren Plant No.1, T-Warren Plant No. 2, X-Missouri. The V.I.N. ended with a six-digit production sequence number at the assembly plant. All models began with sequence number 000,001.

Body Type	Factory Price	GVW	Shipping Weight	Prod. Total
Model W100, 1/2 ton 6-cyl.				
Ch. & Cab, 115 in. wb.	$5226	5100*	3780	a
Pickup, Utiline, 115 in. wb.	$5457	5100	4125	—
Pickup, Sweptline, 115 in. wb.	$5477	5100	4150	—
Ch. & Cab, 131 in. wb.	$5305	5100	3790	—
Pickup, Utiline, 131 in. wb.	$5525	5100	4220	—
Pickup, Sweptline, 131 in. wb.	$5525	5100	4250	—

* 5600 lb. GVW optional.
a Total model year production of all 115 in. wheelbase. W100 trucks was 17,523. Output of models with 131 in. wheelbase (not including club cab) was 13,339.

Body Type	Factory Price	GVW	Shipping Weight	Prod. Total
W100 Club Cab				
Pickup, Sweptline, 133 in. wb.	$N.A.	5100	N.A.	1956
Pickup, Sweptline, 149 in. wb.	$N.A.	5100	N.A.	2336
Model W150, heavy-duty 1/2 ton, 6-cyl.				
Ch. & Cab, 115 in. wb.	$5380	—	—	—
Pickup, Utiline, 115 in. wb.	$5601	—	—	—
Pickup, Sweptline, 115 in. wb.	$5649	—	—	—
Ch. & Cab, 131 in. wb.	$5429	—	—	—
Pickup Utiline, 131 in. wb.	$5649	—	—	—
Pickup Sweptline, 131 in. wb.	$5649	—	—	—
W150 Club Cab				
Pickup, Sweptline, 131in. wb.	$5848	—	—	—
Pickup, Sweptline, 149 in. wb.	$N.A.	—	—	—
Model W200, 3/4 ton, 6-cyl.				
Ch. & Cab, 131 in. wb.	$5713	6500*	3845	b
Pickup, Utiline, 131 in. wb.	$5970	6500	4275	—
Pickup, Sweptline, 131 in. wb.	$5970	6500	4305	—
Crew Cab Ch., 149 in. wb.	$6648	6500	4245	—
Crew Cab, Utiline, 149 in. wb.	$6900	6500	4590	—
Crew Cab, Sweptline, 149 in. wb.	$6900	6500	4615	—

* 8000 lb. GVW package was optional for all models.
b Total model year production of 131 in. wheelbase models, was 37,292. Production of 149 in. wheelbase models was 4322.

Body Type	Factory Price	GVW	Shipping Weight	Prod. Total
W200 Club Cab				
Pickup, Sweptline, 149 in. wb.	$6287	6500*	4605	
Model W300, 1 ton, 6-cyl.				
Ch. & Cab, 135 in. wb.	$N.A.	8500	4380	2365

* GVW packages up to 10,000 lb. were available.

STANDARD ENGINE: W100, W200, W300: Engine Type: OHV, In-line 6-cylinder. Cast iron block and cylinder head. Key components include a drop-forged, shot-peened crankshaft, roller timing chain, Stellite-faced exhaust valves, individually ported long-branch manifolds, aluminum parts and a large radiator. Bore x Stroke: 3.40 in. x 4.125 in. Lifters: Mechanical. Number of main bearings-4. Fuel Induction: Single 1-bbl. carburetor. Compression Ratio:

8.4:1. Displacement: 224.7 cu. in. (3.68 liters). 888. Net: 100 @ 3600 rpm. Torque: Net: 175 lb.-ft. @ 1600 rpm. Fuel Requirements: 91 octane. Oil refill capacity: 5 qt. with filter change. Fuel Requirements: Regular.

OPTIONAL ENGINE: W100, W200, W300: This engine is standard for the club cab. The 225 6-cyl. is available but it must be specified. Features include a drop-forged five-bearing crankshaft, chain-driven camshaft, free-turning exhaust valves, drop-forged I-beam connecting rods and silent-chain camshaft. Bore x Stroke: 3.91 in. x 3.312 in. Lifters: Hydraulic. Number of main bearings-5. Fuel Induction: Single 2-bbl. carburetor. Compression Ratio: 8.6:1. Displacement: 318 cu. in. (5.21 liters). Net: 150 @ 4000 rpm. Torque: Net: 230 lb.-ft. @ 2400 rpm. Oil refill capacity: 5 qt. with filter change. Fuel Requirements: 91 octane.

OPTIONAL ENGINE: W100, W200, W300: Features include vibration damper, 18 in. 4 blade fan and drop-forged crankshaft. Engine Type: OHV, V-8. Cast iron block and cylinder head. Bore x Stroke: 4.00 in. x 3.58 in. Lifters: Hydraulic. Number of main bearings-5. Fuel Induction: Single 2-bbl. carburetor. Compression Ratio: 8.4:1. Displacement: 360 cu. in. (5.89 liters). Net: 170 @ 4000 rpm. Torque: Net: 280 lb.-ft. @ 2400 rpm. Oil refill capacity: 5 qt. with filter change. Fuel Requirements: 91 octane.

OPTIONAL ENGINE: W100, W200, W300: Engine Type: OHV, V-8. Cast iron block and cylinder head. Bore x Stroke: 4.34 in. x 3.38 in. Lifters: Hydraulic. Number of main bearings-5. Fuel Induction: Single 2-bbl. carburetor. Compression Ratio: 8.2:1. Displacement: 400 cu. in. (6.55 liters). Horsepower: 165 @ 4000 rpm. Torque: 290 lb.-ft. @ 2400 rpm. Oil refill capacity: 5 qt. with filter change. Fuel Requirements: 91 octane.

OPTIONAL ENGINE: W100, W200, W300: Engine Type: OHV, V-8. Cast iron block and cylinder head. Bore x Stroke: 4.32 in. x 3.75 in. Lifters: Hydraulic. Number of main bearings-5. Fuel Induction: Single 4-bbl. carburetor. Compression Ratio: 8.2:1. Displacement: 440 cu. in. (7.2 liters). 220 @ 4000 rpm. Torque: 320 lb.-ft. @ 2400 rpm. Oil refill capacity: 5.0 qt. with filter change. Fuel Requirements: 91 octane.

1977 Dodge Utiline W100 Power Wagon pickup

CHASSIS FEATURES: W100: Front Suspension: Semi-elliptical springs, heavy-duty, absorbers. 1640 lb. rating. Optional rating: 1,800 lb. Available with Sno-Fiter Package only: 2,100 lbs. Rear Suspension: Semi-elliptical springs 1520 lbs. capacity for 115 and 131 in. wheelbase. 1,820 lb. capacity for 133 in. and 149 in. wheelbase. Optional Rating: 1,820 lbs. for 115 and 131 in. wheelbase. Front Axle Type and Capacity: Full-floating, 3500 lb. capacity. Optional: 4,000 lbs. Rear Axle Type and Capacity: Semi-floating, 3600 lb. capacity. Optional: None. Final Drive Ratio: 3.55:1-225, 318, 360, 400 cu. in. engines. 3.2:1-440 cu. in. engine. Optional: 3.2:1, 3.9:1-225, 318, 360, 400 cu. in. engines. 3.55:1-440 cu. in. engine. Transfer Case: Single lever, two-speed:1.96, 1.00:1. Brakes: Type: Power, hydraulic. Front: Discs. Rear: Drums. Dimensions: Front: 11.75 in. x 1.256 in. disc. Rear: 11 in. x 2.5 in. Rear lining area: 106.4 sq. in. Wheels: 15 x 5.5 5-stud disc. Optional: 15 x 8.0 (five-hole chrome disc or painted spoke). Tires: G78 x 15B, 4-ply rating 115 in. and 131 in. wheelbase. H78 x 15B all others. Optional: 10-15 LTB, maximum available: 7.00 x 15D, 8-ply; rating. Steering: Recirculating ball. Ratio: 24:1, turns Lock-to-Lock: 3.5:1. Turning Circle: 43 ft. (131 in. wheelbase). Optional: Power assisted. Ratio: 17.8:1. Transmission: A-230 3-speed, all-synchromesh manual. Transmission Ratios: 3.02, 1.76, 1.00:1. Reverse: Optional: NP435, wide-ratio 4-speed manual, synchromesh on top three gears. Transmission ratios: 6.69, 3.34, 1.66, 1.00:1. NP445, close ratio 4-speed manual, synchromesh on all forward gears. Transmission ratios: 4.56, 2.28, 1.31, 1.00:1. Chrysler A-727 3-speed automatic. Ratios: 2.45, 1.45., 1.00:1. Clutch: Single dry plate disc, hydraulic actuation. Clutch diameter: 11 in. dia. Total lining area: 123.7 sq. in. Optional: None. W200: Separate body and ladder-type frame. Section modules: 3.88 in. (131 in. wheelbase), 5.02 in. (149 in. wheelbase, crew cab), 5.47 in. (149 in. wheelbase, club cab). Front Suspension: Semi-elliptical leaf springs, heavy-duty shock absorbers. 1640 lb. capacity (131 in. wheelbase), 1,800 lb. capacity (149 in. wheelbase). Optional: 1,800 lb. capacity: 131 in. wheelbase, 2,250 lb. capacity: All wheelbases. Rear Suspension: Semi-elliptical leaf, 2,175 lb. capacity. Optional Rating: 2,725 lb., auxiliary springs: 585 lb. Front Axle Type and Capacity: Full-floating, 3500 lb. capacity. Optional rating: 4,000 lb. with Sno-Fiter package only, 4,500 lb. Rear Axle Type and Capacity: Full-floating, 5500 lb. capacity. Optional rating: None. Final Drive Ratio: 4.10:1. Transfer Case: Two-speed: 1.96, 1.00:1. Brakes: Type: Power, hydraulic. Front: Disc. Rear: Drum. Dimensions: Front: 12.82 in. x 1.19 in. disc. Rear: 12.0 in. x 2.50 in. Total rear lining area: 122.8 sq. in. Wheels: 6 in., 8-stud disc. Optional: None. Tires: 8.00 x 16.5D, 8-ply rating. Optional (max. size avail.): 9.50 x 16.5E, 8-ply rating. Steering: Recirculating ball. Ratio: 24:1. Optional: Power assisted. Ratio: 17.8:1. Transmission: A-230 3-speed, all-synchromesh manual. Transmission Ratios: 3.02, 1.76, 1.00:1. Optional: NP435, wide-ratio 4-speed manual, synchromesh on top three gears. Transmission ratios: 6.69, 3.34, 1.66, 1.00:1. NP445, close ratio 4-speed manual, synchromesh on all forward gears. Transmission ratios: 4.56, 2.28, 1.31, 1.00:1. Chrysler A-727 3-speed automatic. Ratios: 2.45, 1.45., 1.00:1. Clutch: Single dry plate disc, hydraulic actuation. Clutch diameter: 11 in. dia. Total lining area: 123.7 sq. in. W300: Separate body and channel steel, straight frame, 8 in. section modules, 36,000 psi. Front Suspension: Semi-elliptical springs, heavy-duty shock absorbers. 1940 lb. capacity. Optional rating: 2,250 lb. Rear Suspension: Semi-elliptical springs, 3650 lb. capacity. Optional Rating: 585 lb. and 900 lb. auxiliary springs. Front Axle Type and Capacity: Full-floating. 4500 lb. capacity. Rear Axle Type and Capacity: 7500 lb. capacity. Final Drive Ratio: 4.88:1. Transfer Case: Two-speed: 1.96, 1.0:1. Brakes: Type: Hydraulic. Front: Disc. Rear: Drum. Dimensions: Front: 12.88 in. x 1.19 in. disc. Rear: 12.0 in. x 3.0 in. Total rear lining area: 147.4 sq. in. Wheels: 6.75 in. rim, 8-stud disc. Tires: 8.75 x 16.5E, 10-ply. Optional: 8.00 x 16.5D, dual rear, 9.50 x 16.5E, 10-ply rating, 7.50 x 16.5D 8-ply rating. Transmission: NP435 4-speed synchromesh manual. Transmission Ratios: 6.69, 3.34, 1.66, 1.00:1. Optional: NP445, close ratio 4-speed manual. Transmission ratios: 4.56, 2.28, 1.31, 1.00:1. Chrysler Loadflite A-727 3-speed automatic. Transmission Ratios: 2.45, 1.45., 1.00:1. Clutch: Single plate dry disc, hydraulic actuation. Clutch diameter: 11.0 in. Total plate area: 123.7 sq. in. Optional: None.

VEHICLE DIMENSIONS: W100: Wheelbase: 115 in., 131 in., 133 in. (club cab), 149 in. (club cab). Overall Length: 115 in. wheelbase 193.6 in., 131 in. wheelbase: 213.6 in., 133 in. wheelbase 211.6 in., 149 in. wheelbase 231.6 in. wheelbase. All dimensions include optional rear bumper. Front/Rear Tread: 62.5 in./62.5 in. Overall Height: 74.0 in. Width: 79.5 in. Front/ Rear Overhang: 30 in./47 in. Tailgate: Width and Height: 67 in. x 21.4 in. Approach/Departure

Degrees: 34/24. Ground Clearance: Front axle: 8.2 in. Rear axle: 8.5 in. Oil pan: 15.8 in. Transfer case: 10.4 in. Load space: Pickup box dimensions: 115 in. wheelbase: 78 in. x 51 in. x 19.125 in. Capacity: 61.1 cu. ft. 131 in. wheelbase and 149 in. wheelbase. Sweptline: 98 in. x 51 in. x 19.3 in. Capacity: 76.6 cu. ft. W200: Wheelbase: 131 in. Crew cab: 149 in. Overall Length: 131 in./149 in. wheelbase 213.6 in./231.6 in. Front/Rear Tread: 62.5 in./62.5 in. Overall Height: 74.0 in. Width: 79.5 in. Front/Rear Overhang: 31 in./49 in. Tailgate: Width x Height: 66.5 in. x 19.3 in. Approach/Departure Degrees: 30/21 degrees. Ground Clearance: Front axle: 8.0 in. Rear axle: 7.8 in. Oil pan: 16.1 in. Transfer case: 10.7 in. Load space: Pickup box dimensions: Sweptline: 98.875 in. x 51.0 in. x 19.3 in. W300: Wheelbase: 135 in. Load space: Pickup box dimensions: 108 in. x 54 in. x 20 in. Capacity: 66 cu. ft.

CAPACITIES: Fuel Tank: 25 gal.

ACCOMMODATIONS: Seating Capacity: 3 passenger.

INSTRUMENTATION: 0-100 mph speedometer, 99,999.9 mile odometer, gauges for fuel level, ammeter and engine coolant temperature. Warning lights for oil pressure, parking brake and hazard lights operation.

OPTIONS AND PRICES: Sure-Grip, anti-spin rear differential. 360 cu. in. V-8: 360 V-8. 440 V-8: $271.45. 4-spd. wide-ratio man. trans.: $108. 4-spd. close-ratio man. trans.: $134. Loadflite automatic transmission: $3108.45. Tinted glass: $22.90. Sliding rear window: $55.60. Air conditioning: $515.18. Macho Package: $1407.40. 60 amp generator. 70 amp battery. Flip-down rear seats (club cab). Shoulder belts. Oil pressure gauge. Tachometer. Automatic speed control. Electric clock. AM/FM radio. Chrome rear bumper. Dual electric horns. Grip rails. Tool storage box. Heavy-duty front and shock absorbers (W100, W200). Heavy-duty rear springs (W100). Heavy-duty front and rear shock absorbers (W100). Power steering: $152.00. 7.00 x 15D tires. (W100). 9.50 x 16.5 tires (W200). Convenience Package. Adventurer Sport Package. 7.00 x 15D tires (W100).

HISTORICAL FOOTNOTES: The 1977 W series Dodge trucks were introduced in August, 1976. The W150 was announced in mid-year. *Four Wheeler* magazine declared the Dodge Power Wagon with the Macho Package its "Four Wheeler of the Year."

1977 Dodge W100 Adventurer club coupe Power Wagon pickup

1978 POWER WAGON

The major developments for 1978 centered around the use of the 225 cu. in. 6-cylinder engine with a single 2-barrel carburetor as the standard W series engine. This change added an additional ten horsepower to the engine's maximum output. For the first time the W100 and W200 Power Wagons were available with an optional 243 cu. in. 6-cylinder diesel engine. This engine had a 20:1 compression ratio, special starting and shutdown controls and two 70 amp-hr. batteries. It was offered with either a 4-speed manual or automatic transmission. Potential buyers were told that "if you plan to run your Dodge pickup long and hard in rugged work or recreational service, this could be your answer to lowest costs." This engine was a Chrysler-Mitsubishi 6DR 50A model that, in a slightly different form, had been used for many years in Mitsubishi trucks in Japan. Chrysler had conducted a two-year development program leading up to the diesel's introduction. Primary changes adopted for installation in the W models included a reduction in overall length, redesign of the intake and exhaust manifolds, modification of the rear portion of the engine to provide adaptability of Chrysler transmissions, revised accessory drives, the adaption of two American-type oil filters and the use of a new oil pan. All diesel-engined trucks were fitted with power steering. Production of diesel Power Wagons began on November 1, 1977. Projected output was 4,000 units. The diesel Power Wagon was not available in California and carried a one-year, unlimited mileage warranty.

1978 Dodge W150 Sweptline Power Wagon pickup

As in 1977, the Power Wagons were offered in numerous variations. The club cab continued to have an additional 18 inches of cab space as compared to the conventional cab. The crew cab had a second set of doors and was 28 inches longer than the standard cab. Pickup beds continued to be either the Utiline or Sweptline styles. The standard custom interior consisted of an all-vinyl upholstery and full-depth foam seat cushions. It was available in a choice of five colors: Blue, green, saddle, red and black. Red was a new interior for 1978. The custom interior also provided a color-keyed padded instrument panel and seat trim plus a 10 in. interior day/night mirror. The Adventurer interior had an all-vinyl seat with deep foam padding. It could also be matched with an optional patterned cloth and vinyl seat. It also included door trim and an instrument panel with argent-trimmed faceplate. The color selection was the same as that for the custom interior. The Adventurer SE interior had cloth and vinyl trim. An all-vinyl seat trim was optional. Other elements of the SE interior included color-keyed door trim with simulated rosewood insert and SE instrument panel with two-tone accent and nameplate. The color selection was the same as that for the custom and Adventurer.

Two new towing packages were available for the 1978 models. A light-duty version included a 7 in. section rear step bumper and a Class I hitch, 1.875 in. diameter ball. It was intended for use with trailers up to 2,000 pounds gross weight. The heavy-duty version had a Class IV load-equalizing hitch for trailers up to 7,000 pounds gross weight. A new tilt steering column was introduced with a 15 in. diameter steering wheel that could be locked in any of seven positions. This option was available only on trucks equipped with automatic transmission and power steering. New low-back bucket seats mounted on formed-steel risers that were color-coded to the interior trim color were available for the club cab models. The conventional cab models and the club cab were also available with the same bucket seat/center console as offered in 1977. The only color offered for this feature was black. No change was made in the design of the standard front bench seat. The front door vent window was now fitted with a positive locking device. The bed for the Sweptline models had a revised rear flange and improved wheelhousing sealing. The Utiline models had new taillamps that incorporated the tail, stop, directional and back-up light operations into a single unit.

1978 Dodge W150 Custom Utiline Power Wagon pickup

There were six radio options offered for 1978. All were panel-mounted and consisted of AM, AM/FM, AM/FM/MX stereo, AM/FM/MX stereo with 8-track stereo tape player, AM/40 channel CB and an AM/FM/Multiplex stereo 40-channel CB receiver. The Adventurer SE trim package was available for all models. Six new exterior colors were introduced for 1978: Mint green metallic, light silver metallic, canyon red sunfire metallic, citron green metallic, sunrise orange and black. Carried over from 1977 were light blue, medium blue metallic, medium green sunfire metallic, bright yellow, light tan, bright tan metallic, bright canyon red, and white. Making its debut as a Power Wagon option was a Sky Lite roof, which consisted of a removable tinted safety glass roof section. When removed, the glass panel could be stored in a vinyl container.

The W100 series was dropped for 1978, replaced by the W150 models. The most popular version of the W series continued to be the 3 passenger conventional cab. The Power Wagon pickups were equipped with a new Hurst transfer case shifter and boot. This shifter had positive range detents. The Warlock Utiline model was continued from 1977. It had gold tape stripes, oak side-boards, chrome-plated running boards, chrome five-slot disc wheels, wide tires, and bright bumpers. The Warlock was available in six exterior colors: Formal black, sunrise orange, bright canyon red, canyon red sunfire metallic, medium green sunfire metallic and citron green metallic. New for 1978 was the Macho pickup available in Sweptline shortbed form on either the 115 in. or 131 in. wheelbase chassis. Among its features were special decal body side, tailgate and hood trim, a unique exterior two-tone yellow-accented black paint scheme in combination with any one of nine colors, steel-spoke wide road wheels, 10-15LTB tires, 318 cu. in. V-8, bucket seats, power steering and tinted glass.

1978 Dodge W150 Sweptline Power Wagon pickup with Snowplow Package

I.D. DATA: The vehicle identification number was located on a V.I.N. plate attached to the driver's side door body latch post. The V.I.N. consisted of 13 elements. The first two characters indicated the model code as follows: W1-W150, W2-W200, W3-W300. The next digit identified the body type as follows: 1-Conventional cab/Chassis, 2-Crew cab/Chassis, 3-Utiline conventional cab, 4-Sweptline conventional cab, 5-Utiline crew cab, 6-Sweptline club cab, 7-Sweptline club cab, 8-Cowl/Windshield club cab, 9-Utiline club cab. The next entry, a letter, identified the GVW rating as follows: A-6,000 lb. or less, B-6001 to 10,000 lb., C-10,001 to 14,000 lb. The next unit, a letter, designated the engine type as follows: B-225-2 bbl., E-318-2 bbl., T-360-4 bbl., D-440-1, H-400-1, H-243-diesel. The next unit, the number 8, indicted the 1978 model year. Following this came a letter indicating the assembly plant as follows: C-Jefferson Assembly Plant, K-Pillette Road Truck, L-Lago Alberto Assembly Plant (Mexico), M-Toluca Assembly Plant (Mexico), N-Burt Road (KDX), S-Warren Truck #1, T-Warren Truck #2 (Sherwood), X-Missouri truck, V-Warren Truck #3 The V.I.N. ended with a six-digit production sequence number at the assembly plant as follows: 100001 at Warren Truck #1, Missouri Truck and Pillette Truck Plant. 500001 at Warren Truck #2. 700001 at Warren Truck Plant #3. All models began with sequence number 000,001. Engine numbers were in the same location as 1975-1977.

Body Type	Factory Price	GVW	Shipping Weight	Prod. Total
Model W150, 1/2 ton 6-cyl.				
Ch. & Cab, 115 in. wb.	$5292	5100*	3780	a
Pickup, Utiline, 115 in. wb.	$5514	5100	4125	—
Pickup, Sweptline, 115 in. wb.	$5514	5100	4150	—
Ch. & Cab, 131 in. wb.	$5366	5100	3790	—
Pickup, Utiline, 131 in. wb.	$5587	5100	4220	—
Pickup, Sweptline, 131 in. wb.	$5587	5100	4250	—

* 5600 lb. GVW optional.

a Total model production of 115 in. wheelbase models was 24,921. Production of 131 in. wheelbase models was 20,418.

Body Type	Factory Price	GVW	Shipping Weight	Prod. Total
W150 Club Cab				
Pickup, Sweptline, 133 in. wb.	$5805	5100	4285	2221
Pickup, Sweptline, 149 in. wb.	$5878	5100	4420	2283
Model W200, 3/4 ton, 6-cyl. (Crew Cab-149 in. wheelbase)				
Ch. & Cab, 131 in. wb.	$5705	6500*	3845	b
Pickup, Utiline, 131 in. wb.	$5927	6500	4275	—
Pickup, Sweptline, 131 in. wb.	$5927	6500	4305	—
Crew Cab, Ch.	$6503	6500	4345	—
Crew Cab, Sweptline	$6725	6500	4690	—

* 8000 lb. GVW package was optional for all models.

b Total model year production of 131 in. wheelbase models, was 13,413. Production of 149 in. wheelbase models was 1709.

Body Type	Factory Price	GVW	Shipping Weight	Prod. Total
W200 Club Cab				
Pickup, Sweptline, 149 in. wb.	$6218	6500	4605	—
Model W300, 1 ton, 6-cyl.				
Ch. & Cab, 135 in. wb.	$6872	8500	4480	1326

* GVW packages up to 10,000 lb. were available.

STANDARD ENGINE: W150, W200, W300: (Available in California only when installed in W150 with 115 in. wheelbase and automatic transmission). Engine Type: OHV, In-line 6-cylinder. Cast iron block and cylinder head. Key components include a drop-forged, shot-peened crankshaft, roller timing chain, Stellite-faced exhaust valves, individually ported long-branch manifolds, aluminum parts and a large radiator. Bore x Stroke: 3.40 in. x 4.125 in. Lifters: Mechanical. Number of main bearings-4. Fuel Induction: Single 2-bbl. carburetor. Compression Ratio: 8.4:1. Displacement: 224.7 cu. in. (3.68 liters). Horsepower: Net: 110 @ 3600 rpm. Torque: Net: 175 lb.-ft. @ 1600 rpm. Oil refill capacity: 5 qt. with filter change. Fuel Requirements: 91 octane.

OPTIONAL ENGINE: W150, W200: OHV 6-cylinder diesel. Not available in California. Engine Type: OHV, In-line 6-cyl. Cast iron block and cylinder head. Bore x Stroke: 3.62 in. x 3.94 in. Lifters: Hydraulic. Number of main bearings-7. Compression Ratio: 20.0:1. Displacement: 243 cu. in. (3.98 liters). Horsepower: 103 @ 3700 rpm. Torque: 168 lb.-ft. @ 2200 rpm. Fuel Requirements: Diesel.

OPTIONAL ENGINE: W100, W200, W300: This engine is standard for the club cab. The 225 6-cyl. is available but it must be specified. Features include a drop-forged five-bearing crankshaft, chain-driven camshaft, free-turning exhaust valves, drop-forged I-beam connecting rods and silent-chain camshaft. Bore x Stroke: 3.91 in. x 3.312 in. Lifters: Hydraulic. Number of main bearings-5. Fuel Induction: Single 2-bbl. carburetor. Compression Ratio: 8.6:1. Displacement: 318 cu. in. (5.21 liters). Horsepower: Net: 145 @ 4000 rpm. Torque: Net: 250 lb.-ft. @ 2000 rpm. Oil refill capacity: 5 qt. with filter change. Fuel Requirements: 91 octane.

OPTIONAL ENGINE: W100, W200, W300: Features include vibration damper, 18 in. 4 blade fan and drop-forged crankshaft. Engine Type: OHV, V-8. Cast iron block and cylinder head. Bore x Stroke: 4.00 in. x 3.58 in. Lifters: Hydraulic. Number of main bearings-5. Fuel Induction: Single 2-bbl. carburetor. Compression Ratio: 8.4:1. Displacement: 360 cu. in. (5.89 liters). Horsepower: Net: 160 @ 4000 rpm. Torque: Net: 280 lb.-ft. @ 2400 rpm. Oil refill capacity: 5 qt. with filter change. Fuel Requirements: 91 octane.

OPTIONAL ENGINE: W100, W200, W300: Engine Type: OHV, V-8. Cast iron block and cylinder head. Bore x Stroke: 4.34 in. x 3.38 in. Lifters: Hydraulic. Number of main bearings-5. Fuel Induction: Single 2-bbl. carburetor. Compression Ratio: 8.2:1. Displacement: 400 cu. in. (6.55 liters). Horsepower: 165 @ 4000 rpm. Torque: 290 lb.-ft. @ 2400 rpm. Oil refill capacity: 5 qt. with filter change. Fuel Requirements: 91 octane.

OPTIONAL ENGINE: W100, W200, W300: Engine Type: OHV, V-8. Cast iron block and cylinder head. Bore x Stroke: 4.32 in. x 3.75 in. Lifters: Hydraulic. Number of main bearings-5. Fuel Induction: Single 4-bbl. carburetor. Compression Ratio: 8.2:1. Displacement: 440 cu. in. (7.2 liters). Horsepower: 200 @ 4000 rpm. Torque: 330 lb.-ft. @ 2800 rpm. Oil refill capacity: 5.0 qt. with filter change. Fuel Requirements: 91 octane.

CHASSIS FEATURES: W150: Front Suspension: Semi-elliptical springs, heavy-duty, absorbers. 1640 lb. rating. Optional rating: 1,800 lb. Rear Suspension: Semi-elliptical springs 1820 lbs. capacity. Optional Rating: 1,820 lbs. for 115 and 131 in. wheelbase. Front Axle Type and Capacity: Full-floating, 3500 lb. capacity. Optional: 4,000 lbs. Rear Axle Type and Capacity: Semi-floating, 3600 lb. capacity. Optional: None. Final Drive Ratio: 3.55:1-225, 318, 360, 400 cu. in. engines. 3.2:1-440 cu. in. engine. Optional: 3.2:1, 3.9:1-225, 318, 360, 400 cu. in. engines. 3.55:1-440 cu. in. engine. Transfer Case: Single lever, two-speed:1.96, 1.00:1. Brakes: Type: Power, hydraulic. Front: Discs. Rear: Drums. Dimensions: Front: 11.75 in. x 1.256 in. disc. Rear: 11 in. x 2.5 in. Rear lining area: 106.4 sq. in. Wheels: 15 x 5.5 5-stud disc. Optional: 15 x 8.0 (five-hole chrome disc or painted spoke). Tires: L78 x 15B, 4-ply rating 115 in. and 131 in. wheelbase. H78 x 15B-all others. Optional: 10-15 LTB, maximum available: 7.00 x 15D, 8-ply; rating. Steering: Recirculating ball. Ratio: 24:1, turns Lock-to-Lock: 3.5:1. Turning Circle: 43 ft. (131 in. wheelbase). Optional: Power assisted. Ratio: 17.8:1. Transmission: A-230 3-speed, all-synchromesh manual. Transmission Ratios: 3.02, 1.76, 1.00:1. Reverse: Optional: NP435, wide-ratio 4-speed manual, synchromesh on top three gears. Transmission ratios: 6.69, 3.34, 1.66, 1.00:1. NP445, close ratio 4-speed manual, synchromesh on all forward gears. Transmission ratios: 4.56, 2.28, 1.31, 1.00:1. Chrysler A-727 3-speed automatic. Ratios: 2.45, 1.45., 1.00:1. Clutch: Single dry plate disc, hydraulic actuation. Clutch diameter: 11 in. dia. Total lining area: 123.7 sq. in. Optional: None. W200: Separate body and ladder-type frame. Section modulus: 3.88 in. (131 in. wheelbase), 5.02 in. (149. in. wheelbase, crew cab), 5.47 in. (149 in. wheelbase, club cab). Front Suspension: Semi-elliptical leaf springs, heavy-duty shock absorbers. 1640 lb. capacity (131 in. wheelbase), 1,800 lb. capacity (149 in. wheelbase). Optional: 1,800 lb. capacity: 131 in.

wheelbase), 2,250 lb. capacity: All wheelbases. Rear Suspension: Semi-elliptical leaf, 2,725 lb. capacity. Front Axle Type and Capacity: Full-floating, 3500 lb. capacity. Optional rating: 4,000 lb. with Sno-Fiter Package only, 4,500 lb. Rear Axle Type and Capacity: Full-floating, 5500 lb. capacity. Optional rating: None. Final Drive Ratio: 4.10:1. Transfer Case: Two-speed: 1.96, 1.00:1. Brakes: Type: Power, hydraulic. Front: Disc. Rear: Drum. Dimensions: Front: 12.82 in. x 1.19 in. disc. Rear: 12.0 in. x 2.50 in. Total rear lining area: 122.8 sq. in. Optional: None. Wheels: 6 in., 8-stud disc. Optional: None. Tires: 8.00 x 16.5D, 8-ply rating. Optional (max. size avail.): 9.50 x 16.5E, 8-ply rating. Steering: Recirculating ball. Ratio: 24:1. Optional: Power assisted. Ratio: 17.8:1. Transmission: A-230 3-speed, all-synchromesh manual. Transmission Ratios: 3.02, 1.76, 1.00:1. Optional: NP435, wide-ratio 4-speed manual, synchromesh on top three gears. Transmission ratios: 6.69, 3.34, 1.66, 1.00:1. NP445, close ratio 4-speed manual, synchromesh on all forward gears. Transmission ratios: 4.56, 2.28, 1.31, 1.00:1. Chrysler A-727 3-speed automatic. Ratios: 2.45, 1.45., 1.00:1. Clutch: Single dry plate disc, hydraulic actuation. Clutch diameter: 11 in. dia. Total lining area: 123.7 sq. in. W300: Separate body and channel steel, straight frame, 5.02 in. section modules, 36,000 psi. Front Suspension: Semi-elliptical springs, heavy-duty shock absorbers. 1940 in. capacity. Optional rating: 585 lb. and 900 lb. auxiliary springs. Front Axle Type and Capacity: Full-floating. 4500 lb. capacity. Rear Axle Type and Capacity: 7500 lb. capacity. Final Drive Ratio: 4.88:1. Transfer Case: Two-speed: 1.96, 1.0:1. Brakes: Type: Hydraulic. Front: Disc. Rear: Drum. Dimensions: Front: 12.88 in. x 1.19 in. disc. Rear: 12.0 in. x 3.0 in. Total rear lining area: 147.4 sq. in. Wheels: 6.75 in. rim, 8-stud disc. Tires: 8.75 x 16.5E., 10-ply. Optional: 8.00 x 16.5D, dual rear, 9.50 x 16.5E, 10-ply rating, 7.50 x 16.5D 8-ply rating. Transmission: NP435 4-speed synchromesh manual. Transmission Ratios: 6.69, 3.34, 1.66, 1.00:1. Optional: NP445, close ratio 4-speed manual. Transmission ratios: 4.56, 2.28, 1.31, 1.00:1. Chrysler Loadflite A-727 3-speed automatic. Transmission Ratios: 2.45, 1.45., 1.00:1. Clutch: Single plate dry disc, hydraulic actuation. Clutch diameter: 11.0 in. Total plate area: 123.7 sq. in. Optional: None.

VEHICLE DIMENSIONS: W150: Wheelbase: 115 in., 131 in., 133 in. (club cab), 149 in. (club cab). Overall Length: 115 in. wheelbase: 193.6 in., 131 in. wheelbase: 213.6 in., 133 in. wheelbase: 211.6 in., 149 in. wheelbase: 231.6 in. wheelbase. All dimensions include optional rear bumper. Front/Rear Tread: 62.5 in./62.5 in. Overall Height: 74.0 in. Width: 79.5 in. Front/Rear Overhang: 30 in./47 in. Tailgate: Width and Height: 67 in. x 21.4 in. Approach/Departure Degrees: 34/24. Ground Clearance: Front axle: 8.2 in. Rear axle: 8.5 in. Oil pan: 15.8 in. Transfer case: 10.4 in. Load space: Pickup box dimensions: 115 in. wheelbase: 78 in. x 51 in. x 19.125 in. Capacity: 61.1 cu. ft. 131 in. wheelbase and 149 in. wheelbase. Sweptline: 98 in. x 51 in. x 19.3 in. Capacity: 76.6 cu. ft. W200: Wheelbase: 131 in. Crew cab: 149 in. Overall Length: 131 in./149 in. wheelbase: 213.6 in./231.6 in. Front/Rear Tread: 62.5 in./62.5 in. Overall Height: 74.0 in. Width: 79.5 in. Front/Rear Overhang: 31 in./49 in. Tailgate: Width x Height: 66.5 in. x 19.3 in. Approach/Departure Degrees: 30/21 degrees. Ground Clearance: Front axle: 8.0 in. Rear axle: 7.8 in. Oil pan: 16.1 in. Transfer case: 10.7 in. Load space: Pickup box dimensions: Sweptline: 98.875 in. x 51.0 in. x 19.3 in. W300: Wheelbase: 135 in. Load space: Pickup box dimensions: 108 in. x 54 in. x 20 in. Capacity: 66 cu. ft.

CAPACITIES: Fuel Tank: 25 gal.

ACCOMMODATIONS: Seating Capacity: 3 passenger.

INSTRUMENTATION: 0-100 mph speedometer, 99,999.9 mile odometer, gauges for fuel level, ammeter and engine coolant temperature. Warning lights for oil pressure, parking brake and hazard lights operation.

OPTIONS: 318 cu. in. V-8. 360 cu. in V-8. 400 cu. in. V-8 (not available in California). 440 cu. in. V-8. 243 cu. in. diesel (not available in California). Sno-Commander Snowplow Package (for W150 and W200 only). Consists of factory-installed power angling plow, power blade lift, and seven-way control valve. Plow lights, clearance and identification lights are mandatory options. Trailer-towing Packages. Sky Lite roof. Air conditioning. AM radio. AM/FM radio. AM/FM/MX stereo radio. AM/FM/MX stereo radio with 8-track stereo tape player. AM/40 channel CB radio. AM/FM/Multiplex stereo radio and 40-channel CB receiver. Tilt steering column. Adventurer trim. Adventurer SE trim. Automatic transmission. 4-speed manual transmission. Wheelcovers.

HISTORICAL FOOTNOTES: Noting that it had enjoyed a 237 percent increase in sales, Dodge reported that it was the fastest growing truck company in America.

1979 POWER WAGON

1979 Dodge W200 Sweptline Power Wagon pickup

A new one-piece aluminum grille with a wide center bar separating two cross-hatched sections identified the 1979 Power Wagons. DODGE lettering was now mounted on the leading edge of the hood. If desired the standard 7 in. circular headlights could be replaced by optional dual vertically stacked rectangular headlights. These new lights were included in the Adventurer SE Package. In 1978 Dodge had used an "SE" nomenclature; in 1979 "S.E." was used. A more rigid hood panel was used for 1979 along with a new linkage-type hinge. New for 1979 were electric door locks. Also debuting in 1979 were flip-out rear quarter windows for the club cab. These were standard on the Adventurer S.E. club cab and optional for all other club cabs. The W200 models now had the 318 cu. in. V-8 as their standard engine. The W300 line had a standard 360 cu. in. V-8. Not available for 1979 were the 400 and 440 cu. in. V-8 engines. The

standard custom trim consisted of an all-vinyl bench seat with a new Timbuk insert. Optional was a new Trombley cloth insert. A color-keyed padded instrument panel with a "Custom" nameplate plus door trim and armrests were included. Five interior colors were offered for the custom level: Blue, green, cashmere, red or black. The custom exterior included bright grille and front bumper, bright-finish exterior mirrors, "Custom" nameplate on the front fenders, and painted hubcaps. The Adventurer option featured a deluxe vinyl bench seat, or, at extra cost, Trombley cloth inserts. The Adventurer interior also included a bright lower molding and woodgrain insert on the instrument panel and a bright door applique with wood grain. The color selection consisted of blue, green, cashmere, red and black. The Adventurer exterior included bright taillight bezels (Sweptline body only), bright moldings on the windshield, backlight and drip rail, and an upper body side molding. The Adventurer S.E. interior featured a bench seat with deluxe cloth and vinyl trim and deep-foam cushions. Optional was a deluxe vinyl bench seat with Winslow-grain vinyl. Additional standard S.E. items were soft-trimmed vinyl door trim panels with assist straps, an S.E. instrument panel with nameplate. Both the conventional and club cab models also had a color-coordinated full-interior trim as part of the S.E. Package that included the windshield header trim, A-pillar trim, door header trim and backlight trim. Four exterior colors were offered: Blue, green, cashmere and red. The Adventurer S.E. exterior featured the stacked rectangular dual headlights. All three trim levels were also available with optional low-back bucket seats finished in a black deluxe vinyl upholstery.

1979 Dodge W150 Sweptline Power Wagon pickup with Macho Package

Four optional exterior paint procedures were offered for 1979. Paint Procedure No. 1 consisted of a secondary color for the roof and cab back with the main color on the remaining portions of the truck. Paint Procedure No. 2 positioned the main color on the upper portion of the body with an Upper Molding Package providing a separation form the secondary color on the lower body section. Paint Procedure No. 3 combined the main body color on the upper body section with a secondary color on the tailgate and between the upper and lower body moldings. Both the Upper and Lower Molding Packages were included. The lower portion of the body was painted the main body color. Paint Procedure No. 4 also included the Upper and Lower Molding Packages. It consisted of the main color on the upper body section, the secondary color on the roof and cab back, the secondary color between the body moldings and the main color on the lower body section. Standard equipment for 1979 consisted of seat belts, 3 rear seat belts on the crew cab, insulated dash liner, directional signals, electronic ignition system, glove box with door, heater and defroster, black horn pad, padded instrument panel, axle-type jack, back-up lights, courtesy light switches, black floor mat with jute backing, dual bright finish short arm exterior mirrors, padded color-keyed sun visors, dual jet windshield washers and two-speed electric windshield wipers.

A total of fifteen exterior colors were available for 1979. The straight shades were formal black, white, cashmere, medium canyon red, sunburst orange and yellow flame. Metallic colors consisted of light silver, cadet blue, ensign blue, teal frost, citron green and medium tan, sunfire teal green, sunfire canyon red and sunfire sable brown.

The Macho Power Wagon for 1979 was available as either a 115 in. or 131 in. wheelbase, W-150 pickup. It featured striping on the body side, tailgate and hood, a special exterior two-tone paint scheme in a choice of six colors with low-luster black, 10-15LTB raised white letter tires, roll bar, low-luster painted bumpers and special painted spoke road wheels. The Warlock II Power Wagon, based on the W150 short bed Utiline pickup, was outfitted with gold tape stripes, oak sideboards, chrome-plated running boards, chrome-styled five-slot disc wide Sport road wheels, wide tires with raised white letters and bright bumpers. The Warlock II was offered in seven exterior colors: Medium canyon red, canyon red, sunfire metallic, teal green, sunfire metallic, formal black, sable brown, sunfire metallic, citron green metallic and sunburst orange.

1979 Dodge W150 Sweptline Power Wagon pickup with Warlock II Package

I.D. DATA: The vehicle identification number was located on a V.I.N. plate attached to the driver's side door body latch post. The V.I.N. consisted of 13 elements. The first two characters indicated the model code as follows: W1-W150, W2-W200, W3-W300. The next digit identified the body type as follows: 1-Conventional cab/Chassis, 2-Crew cab/Chassis, 3-Utiline conventional cab, 4-Sweptline conventional cab, 5-Utiline crew cab, 6-Sweptline club cab, 7-Sweptline club cab, 8-Cowl/Windshield club cab, 9-Utiline club cab. The next entry, a letter, identified the GVW rating as follows: A-6,000 lb. or less, B-6001 to 10,000 lb., C-10,001 to 14,000 lb. The next unit, a letter, designated the engine type as follows: B-225-2 bbl., E-318-

2 bbl., T-360-4 bbl., D-440-1., H-400-1, H-243-diesel. The next unit, the number 9, indicated the 1979 model year. Following this came a letter indicating the assembly plant as follows: C-Jefferson Assembly Plant, K-Pillette Road Truck, L-Lago Alberto Assembly Plant (Mexico), M-Toluca Assembly Plant (Mexico), N-Burt Road (KDX), S-Warren Truck #1, T-Warren Truck #2 (Sherwood), X-Missouri truck, V-Warren Truck #3 The V.I.N. ended with a six-digit production sequence number at the assembly plant as follows: 100001 at Warren Truck #1, Missouri Truck and Pillette Truck Plant. 500001 at Warren Truck #2. 700001 at Warren Truck Plant #3. All models began with sequence number 000,001. Engine numbers were in the same location as 1975-1978.

Body Type	Factory Price	GVW	Shipping Weight	Prod. Total
Model W150, 1/2 ton 6-cyl.				
Pickup, Utiline, 115 in. wb.	$5897	5100*	4125	—
Pickup, Sweptline, 115 in. wb.	$5897	5100	4150	—
Pickup, Utiline, 131 in. wb.	$5902	5100	4220	—
Pickup, Sweptline, 131 in. wb.	$5902	5100	4250	—
W150 Club Cab				
Pickup, Sweptline, 133 in. wb.	$6416	5100	4360	—
Pickup, Sweptline, 149 in. wb.	$6567	5100	4495	—
* 5600 lb. GVW optional.				
Model W200, 3/4 ton, V-8 (Crew cab-149 in. wheelbase)				
Pickup, Utiline, 131 in. wb.	$6565	6500*	4365	—
Pickup, Sweptline, 131 in. wb.	$6565	6500	4395	—
Crew Cab, Sweptline	$8235	6500	4785	—
* 8000 lb. GVW package was optional for all models.				
W200 Club Cab				
Pickup, Sweptline, 149 in. wb.	$6876	6500	4620	—
Model W300, 1 ton, V-8.				
Ch. & Cab, 135 in. wb.	$8237	8500*	4525	—

* GVW packages up to 10,000 lb. was available.

STANDARD ENGINE: W150: (Available in California only when installed in W150 with 115 in. wb and automatic transmission). Engine Type: OHV, In-line 6-cylinder. Cast iron block and cylinder head. Key components include a drop-forged, shot-peened crankshaft, roller timing chain, Stellite-faced exhaust valves, individually ported long-branch manifolds, aluminum parts and a large radiator. Bore x Stroke: 3.40 in. x 4.125 in. Lifters: Mechanical. Number of main bearings-4. Fuel Induction: Single 2-bbl. carburetor. Compression Ratio: 8.4:1. Displacement: 224.7 cu. in. (3.68 liters). Horsepower: Net: 110 @ 3600 rpm. Torque: Net: 175 lb.-ft. @ 1600 rpm. Oil refill capacity: 5 qt. with filter change. Fuel Requirements: 91 octane.

OPTIONAL ENGINE: W150, W200: OHV 6-cylinder diesel. Not available in California. Engine Type: OHV, In-line 6-cyl. Cast iron block and cylinder head. Bore x Stroke: 3.62 in. x 3.94 in. Lifters: Hydraulic. Number of main bearings-7. Compression Ratio: 20.0:1. Displacement: 243 cu. in. (3.98 liters). Horsepower: 103 @ 3700 rpm. Torque: 168 lb.-ft. @ 2200 rpm. Fuel Requirements: Diesel.

OPTIONAL ENGINE: W100, standard for W200: This engine is standard for the club cab. The 225 6-cyl. is available but it must be specified. Features include a drop-forged five-bearing crankshaft, chain-driven camshaft, free-turning exhaust valves, drop-forged I-beam connecting rods and silent-chain camshaft. Bore x Stroke: 3.91 in. x 3.312 in. Lifters: Hydraulic. Number of main bearings-5. Fuel Induction: Single 2-bbl. carburetor. Compression Ratio: 8.6:1. Displacement: 318 cu. in. (5.21 liters). Horsepower: Net: 145 @ 4000 rpm. Torque: Net: 250 lb.-ft. @ 2000 rpm. Oil refill capacity: 5 qt. with filter change. Fuel Requirements: 91 octane.

OPTIONAL ENGINE: W100, W200, standard for W300: Features include vibration damper, 18 in. 4 blade fan and drop-forged crankshaft. Engine Type: OHV, V-8. Cast iron block and cylinder head. Bore x Stroke: 4.00 in. x 3.58 in. Lifters: Hydraulic. Number of main bearings-5. Fuel Induction: Single 2-bbl. carburetor. Compression Ratio: 8.4:1. Displacement: 360 cu. in. (5.89 liters). Horsepower: Net: 160 @ 4000 rpm. Torque: Net: 280 lb.-ft. @ 2400 rpm. Oil refill capacity: 5 qt. with filter change. Fuel Requirements: 91 octane.

CHASSIS FEATURES: W150: Front Suspension: Semi-elliptical springs, heavy-duty, absorbers. 1640 lb. rating. Optional rating: 1,800 lb. Rear Suspension: Semi-elliptical springs 1820 lbs. capacity. Optional Rating: 1,820 lbs. for 115 and 131 in. wheelbase. Front Axle Type and Capacity: Full-floating, 3500 lb. capacity. Optional: 4,000 lbs. Rear Axle Type and Capacity: Semi-floating, 3600 lb. capacity. Optional: None. Final Drive Ratio: 3.55:1. 3.21:1. Transfer Case: Single lever, two-speed: 1.96, 1.00:1. Brakes: Type: Power, hydraulic. Front: Discs. Rear: Drums. Dimensions: Front: 11.75 in. x 1.256 in. disc. Rear: 11 in. x 2.5 in. Rear lining area: 106.4 sq. in. Wheels: 15 x 5.5 5-stud disc. Optional: 15 x 8.0 (five-hole chrome disc or painted spoke). Tires: L78 x 15B, 4-ply rating. Optional: 10-15 LTB, (maximum size optional). Steering: Recirculating ball. Ratio: 24:1, turns Lock-to-Lock: 3.5:1. Turning Circle: 43 ft. (131 in. wheelbase). Optional: Power assisted. Ratio: 17.8:1. Transmission: A-230 3-speed, all-synchromesh manual. Transmission Ratios: 3.02, 1.76, 1.00:1. Reverse: Optional: NP435, wide-ratio 4-speed manual, synchromesh on top three gears. Transmission ratios: 6.69, 3.34, 1.66, 1.00:1. NP445, close ratio 4-speed manual, synchromesh on all forward gears. Transmission ratios: 4.56, 2.28, 1.31, 1.00:1. Chrysler A-727 3-speed automatic. Ratios: 2.45, 1.45., 1.00:1. Clutch: Single dry plate disc, hydraulic actuation. Clutch diameter: 11 in. dia. Total lining area: 123.7 sq. in. Optional: None. W200: Separate body and ladder-type frame. Section modules: 3.88 in. (131 in. wheelbase), 5.02 in. (149 in. wheelbase, crew cab), 5.47 in. (149 in. wheelbase, club cab). Front Suspension: Semi-elliptical leaf springs, heavy-duty shock absorbers. 1640 lb. capacity (131 in. wheelbase), 1,800 lb. capacity (149 in. wheelbase). Optional: 1,800 lb. capacity: 131 in. wheelbase), 2,250 lb. capacity: All wheelbases. Rear Suspension: Semi-elliptical leaf, 2,725 lb. capacity. Front Axle Type and Capacity: Full-floating, 3500 lb. capacity. Optional rating: 4,000 lb. with Sno-Fiter package only, 4,500 lb. Rear Axle Type and Capacity: Full-floating, 5500 lb. capacity. Optional rating: None. Final Drive Ratio: 4.10:1. Transfer Case: Two-speed: 1.96, 1.00:1. Brakes: Type: Power, hydraulic. Front: Disc. Rear: Drum. Dimensions: Front: 12.82 in. x 1.19 in. disc. Rear: 12.0 in. x 2.50 in. Total rear lining area: 122.8 sq. in. Optional: None. Wheels: 6 in., 8-stud disc. Optional: None. Tires: 8.00 x 16.5D, 8-ply rating. Optional (max. size avail.): 9.50R x 16.5E, 8-ply rating. Steering: Recirculating ball. Ratio: 24:1. Optional: Power assisted. Ratio: 17.8:1. Transmission: A-230 3-speed, all-synchromesh manual. Transmission Ratios: 3.02, 1.76, 1.00:1. Optional: NP435, wide-ratio 4-speed manual, synchromesh on top three gears. Transmission ratios: 6.69, 3.34, 1.66, 1.00:1. NP445, close ratio 4-speed manual, synchromesh on all forward gears. Transmission ratios: 4.56, 2.28, 1.31, 1.00:1. Chrysler A-727 3-speed automatic. Ratios: 2.45, 1.45., 1.00:1. Clutch: Single dry plate disc, hydraulic actuation. Clutch diameter: 11 in. dia. Total lining area: 123.7 sq. in. W300: Separate body and channel steel, straight frame, 5.02 in. section modules, 36,000 psi. Front Suspension: Semi-elliptical springs, heavy-duty shock absorbers. 1940 lb. capacity. Optional rating: 2,250 lb. Rear Suspension: semi-elliptical springs, 3650 lb. capacity. Optional Rating: 585 lb. and 900 lb. auxiliary springs. Front Axle Type and Capacity: Full-floating. 4500 lb. capacity. Rear Axle Type and Capacity: 7500 lb. capacity. Final Drive Ratio: 4.88:1. Transfer Case: Two-speed: 1.96, 1.0:1. Brakes: Type: Hydraulic. Front: Disc. Rear: Drum. Dimensions: Front: 12.88 in. x 1.19 in. disc. Rear: 12.0 in. x 3.0 in. Total rear lining area: 147.4 sq. in. Wheels: 6.75 in. rim, 8-stud disc. Tires: 8.00 x 16.5D, 10-ply. Optional: 8.00R x 16.5E (maximum optional size). Transmission: NP435 4-speed synchromesh manual. Transmission Ratios: 6.69, 3.34, 1.66, 1.00:1. Optional: NP445, close ratio 4-speed manual. Transmission ratios: 4.56, 2.28, 1.31, 1.00:1. Chrysler Loadflite A-727 3-speed automatic. Transmission Ratios: 2.45, 1.45., 1.00:1. Clutch: Single plate dry disc, hydraulic actuation. Clutch diameter: 11.0 in. Total plate area: 123.7 sq. in. Optional: None.

VEHICLE DIMENSIONS: W150: Wheelbase: 115 in., 131 in., 133 in. (club cab), 149 in. (club cab). Overall Length: 115 in. wheelbase: 193.6 in., 131 in. wheelbase: 213.6 in., 133 in. wheelbase: 211.6 in., 149 in. wheelbase: 231.6 in. wheelbase. All dimensions include optional rear bumper. Front/Rear Tread: 62.5 in./62.5 in. Overall Height: 74.0 in. Width: 79.5 in. Front/Rear Overhang: 30 in./47 in. Tailgate: Width and Height: 67 in. x 21.4 in. Approach/Departure Degrees: 34/24. Ground Clearance: Front axle: 8.2 in. Rear axle: 8.5 in. Oil pan: 15.8 in. Transfer case: 10.4 in. Load space: Pickup box dimensions: 115 in. wheelbase: 78 in. x 51 in. x 19.125 in. Capacity: 61.1 cu. ft. 131 in. wheelbase and 149 in. wheelbase. Sweptline: 98 in. x 51 in. x 19.3 in. Capacity: 76.6 cu. ft. W200: Wheelbase: 131 in. Crew cab: 149 in. Overall Length: 131 in./149 in. wheelbase: 213.6 in./231.6 in. Front/Rear Tread: 62.5 in./62.5 in. Overall Height: 74.0 in. Width: 79.5 in. Front/Rear Overhang: 31 in./49 in. Tailgate: Width x Height: 66.5 in. x 19.3 in. Approach/Departure Degrees: 30/21 degrees. Ground Clearance: Front axle: 8.0 in. Rear axle: 7.8 in. Oil pan: 16.1 in. Transfer case: 10.7 in. Load space: Pickup box dimensions: Sweptline: 98.875 in. x 51.0 in. x 19.3 in. W300: Wheelbase: 135 in. Load space: Pickup box dimensions: 108 in. x 54 in. x 20 in. Capacity: 66 cu. ft.

CAPACITIES: Fuel Tank: 25 gal.

ACCOMMODATIONS: Seating Capacity: 3 passenger.

INSTRUMENTATION: 0-100 mph speedometer, 99,999.9 mile odometer, gauges for fuel level, ammeter and engine coolant temperature. Warning lights for oil pressure, parking brake and hazard lights operation.

OPTIONS: 318 cu. in. V-8 (W150). 360 cu. in. V-8. (W150, W200) 243 cu. in. diesel (W150 and W200). Sno-Commander Snowplow Package (for W150 and W200 only). Consists of factory-installed power angling plow, power blade lift, seven-way control valve and "Sno-Commander" body side decal. Plow lights, clearance and identification lights are mandatory options. Class I Trailer-Towing Package with 1.875 in. outside diameter ball hitch. Class IV Trailer-Towing Package with tow bar hitch. Sky Lite roof. Air conditioning. AM radio. AM/FM radio. AM/FM/MX stereo radio. AM/FM/MX stereo radio with 8-track stereo tape player. AM/40 channel CB radio. AM/FM/Multiplex stereo radio and 40-channel CB receiver. Tilt steering column. Skid plate. Sliding rear window. Chrome-styled road wheels. White-painted steel spoke wide Sport road wheels. 5-slot disc chrome-styled sport road wheels. Electric tachometer. Automatic speed control (W150 and W200). Quad rectangular headlights. Electric door locks. Adventurer trim. Adventurer SE trim. automatic transmission. 4-speed manual transmission. Wheelcovers.

HISTORICAL FOOTNOTES: The 1979 Dodge trucks were introduced in August, 1978.

1980 POWER WAGON

For 1980 Dodge offered a New Process 208 part time four-wheel drive system for the W150 and selected W200 truck models. The NP208 transfer case was used on the W150 and W200 pickups, except for crew cabs. The NP205 transfer case was used for the W200 crew cab and W300 models. Compared to the full-time New Process 203 transfer case used in 1979, the new unit was 111 pounds lighter due primarily to use of a die-cast aluminum housing. Use of the part-time system, which also featured a new planetary gear set for easier operation and less resistance, along with the Spicer front locking hubs resulted in an 11 percent improvement in fuel economy. By unlocking the manual front wheel hubs and putting the transfer case shift selector into "Two-Wheel-High" power was delivered to the rear wheels only. In this mode the front driving axles was disconnected and not in operation. The four-wheel drive mode was used by locking the front hubs and shifting the transfer case shift selector into "Four-Wheel-High" or Four-Wheel-Low" position.

1980 Dodge W150 Sweptline Power Wagon pickup

In order to further improve fuel economy Dodge used lighter-weight exhaust components on the 1980 models. In addition, both the 225 and 318 engines had lighter weight cylinder blocks and intake manifolds that reduced overall weight by 25 pounds. Standard axle ratios were also altered for better fuel mileage. All W series also had the New Process 435 wide-ratio 4-speed manual transmission as standard equipment. Most automatic transmissions now had a lock-up torque converter. Engine idle speeds were reduced by 100 rpm to further improve fuel economy. Externally, the 1980 models were identified by their grille which now had a black-finish mesh insert. The center divider retained its bright finish. Standard equipment included back-up lights, brake system warning light, electric windshield washers and wipers, energy-absorbing steering wheel, glare-reduction format for windshield wipers, instrument panel and steering wheel, ignition and steering column, interior (5 in. x 7 in.) and exterior (10 in.) rearview mirrors, instrument panel "four-wheel drive" light operative when transfer case is in four-wheel drive mode, padded instrument panel and sun visors, recessed inside door release handles, resilient window crank knobs, seat belts or Unibelt restraint system, side marker lights and reflectors, traffic hazard warning flasher system, directional signals, heater and defroster, back-up lights and courtesy light switches. Added to the list of standard features for 1980 was a rear step bumper with a trailer hitch and power steering. The standard custom trim level included a "Custom" nameplate on the front fenders and instrument panel. The custom interior specified a vinyl bench seat in a choice of four colors: Black, blue, cashmere or red. A cloth and vinyl bench seat was standard with the optional Adventurer Package. It was also available as an option for the custom model. On club cab models the seat back was split. It was offered in the same color selection as the custom seat. The Adventurer S.E. Package included a deluxe cloth and vinyl bench seat available in blue, green, cashmere and red. The club cab seat had a split back. This seat with its plaid cloth sections was also available at extra cost for the Adventurer Sport Package. Conversely, the standard vinyl bench seat for the new Adventurer Sport Package, which was offered in the above mentioned colors, was available as an option for the Adventurer S.E. and Adventurer Packages. An option exclusive to conventional cab pickups with the Adventurer S.E. Package was a leather bench seat with a bucket-seat-like cushions and thigh supports. This seat was available in either cashmere or red. The Adventurer S.E. instrument panel featured a woodtone faceplate with bright trim. The steering wheel had a woodtone insert. Both an oil pressure gauge and cigarette lighter were standard.

1980 Dodge W150 Utiline Power Wagon pickup

Other interior alternatives for 1980 included a Big Horn Package cloth and vinyl bench seat with Navajo body cloth. This package provided a cashmere colored interior and was available only for the W150 conventional cab Adventurer Sweptline pickup. The W150 was also the basis for a mid-year addition to the Power Wagon line; the Propector. This truck had a special "Prospector" body side nameplate, two-tone paint, bright rear bumper with nerf strips, bright low-mount exterior mirrors, quad rectangular headlights, Protection Package, air conditioning, AM/FM radio, headliner, steering wheel with insert in horn pad, cowl-side trim, woodgrain applique instrument cluster faceplate, oil pressure gauge, clock, Convenience Package, tinted glass, heavy-duty front springs, in-box tire carrier and auxiliary 21 gallon fuel tank. The Prospector was available either as a conventional or club cab model with a 6.5 or 8.0 ft. box.

The Macho Power Wagon was still available for 1980. It featured a two-tone exterior paint scheme (offered in a choice of eight colors with low-luster black), striping on the body side, tailgate and hood, yellow-painted spoke road wheels with 10-15 LTB outline white letter tires, 328 cu. in. V-8, "Sport" four-spoke steering wheel, roll bar, low-luster black painted bumpers and deluxe vinyl bench seat. The Macho Power Wagon was available either in 115 in. or 131 in. wheelbase W150 Sweptline pickup form.

Three optional exterior paint procedures were offered for 1980. One choice provided the roof in a secondary color with the rest of the body in the main color. The second choice consisted of the truck's midsection in the secondary color with the rest of the body in the main color. This scheme was offered only for pickups. The final choice had the roof and midsection in the secondary color with the rest of the body in the main color. It was also offered only for pickups.

Exterior colors for 1980 were white, cashmere, sunburst orange, impact yellow, ginger, black, impact red, impact blue, bright silver metallic, frost blue metallic, medium blue metallic, teal frost metallic, teal green sunfire, dark brown sunfire and medium red sunfire.

1980 Dodge W150 Utiline Power Wagon pickup with Macho Package

I.D. DATA: The vehicle identification number was located on a V.I.N. plate attached to the driver's side door body latch post. The V.I.N. consisted of 13 elements. The first two characters indicated the model code as follows: W1-W150, W2-W200, W3-W300. The next digit identified the body type as follows: 1-Conventional cab/Chassis, 2-Crew cab/Chassis, 3-Utiline conventional cab, 4-Sweptline conventional cab, 5-Utiline crew cab, 6-Sweptline club cab, 7-Sweptline club cab, 8-Cowl/Windshield club cab, 9-Utiline club cab. The next entry, a letter, identified the GVW rating as follows: A-6,000 lb. or less, B-6001 to 10,000 lb., C-10,001 to 14,000 lb. The next unit, a letter, designated the engine type as follows: B-225-2 bbl., E-318-1 bbl., F-360, The next unit, the letter A indicated the 1980 model year. Following this came a letter indicating the assembly plant as follows: C-Jefferson Ave., K-Windsor Pillette Road, N-Burt Road, KDX, S-Warren Truck No.1. T-Warren Truck No. 2, V-Warren Tuck No. 3, X-Missouri. The final entry was the six-digit production sequence number, according to the following schedule: 100001 for Warren Truck Plant No.1, Missouri Truck and Jefferson Truck. 500001 for Warren Truck No. 2, and 700001 for Warren Truck Plant No. 3. Engine numbers were in the same location as 1975-1979.

Body Type	Factory Price	GVW	Shipping Weight	Prod. Total
Model W150, 1/2 ton 6-cyl.				
Pickup, Utiline, 115 in. wb.	$7181	6050	3797	—
Pickup, Sweptline, 115 in. wb.	$7181	6050	3832	—
Pickup, Utiline, 131 in. wb.	$7266	6050	3947	—
Pickup, Sweptline, 131 in. wb.	$7266	6050	3947	—
W150 Club Cab				
Pickup, Sweptline, 133 in. wb.	$7837	6050	N.A.	—
Pickup, Sweptline, 149 in. wb.	$7990	6050	N.A.	—
Model W200, 3/4 ton, V-8 (Crew cab-149 in. wheelbase)				
Pickup, Utiline, 131 in. wb.	$7853	6900*	4120	—
Pickup, Sweptline, 131 in. wb.	$7853	6900	4155	—
Crew Cab, Sweptline	$9512	6900	4785	—

*7500 and 8550 lb. GVW package was optional for all models.

Body Type	Factory Price	GVW	Shipping Weight	Prod. Total
W200 Club Cab				
Pickup, Sweptline	$8503	6900	4842	—
Model W300, 1 ton, V-8				
Ch. & Cab, 135 in. wb.	$8869	8500*	4806	—

*GVW packages up to 10,000 lb. were available.

STANDARD ENGINE: 115 in. wheelbase and 131 in. wheelbase pickup W150 models. Engine Type: OHV, In-line 6-cylinder. Cast iron block and cylinder head. Key components include a drop-forged, shot-peened crankshaft, roller timing chain, Stellite-faced exhaust valves, individually ported long-branch manifolds, aluminum parts and a large radiator. Bore x Stroke: 3.40 in. x 4.125 in. Lifters: Mechanical. Number of main bearings-4. Fuel Induction: Single 2-bbl. carburetor. Compression Ratio: 8.4:1. Displacement: 224.7 cu. in. (3.68 liters). Horsepower: Net: 95 @ 3600 rpm. Torque: Net: 170 lb.-ft. @ 1600 rpm. Oil refill capacity: 5 qt. with filter change. Fuel Requirements: 91 octane.

STANDARD ENGINE: 133 in. and 149 in. wheelbase. W150 club cab pickups and 131 in. wheelbase. W200 conventional cab pickups; optional for other W150 models. Features include a drop-forged five-bearing crankshaft, chain-driven camshaft, free-turning exhaust valves, drop-forged I-beam connecting rods and silent-chain camshaft. Bore x Stroke: 3.91 in. x 3.312 in. Lifters: Hydraulic. Number of main bearings-5. Fuel Induction: Single 2-bbl. carburetor. Compression Ratio: 8.7:1. Displacement: 318 cu. in. (5.21 liters). Horsepower: 140 @ 4000 rpm. (155 hp. in vehicles over 8501 lb. GVWR). Torque: Net: 240 lb.-ft. @ 2000 rpm. Oil refill capacity: 5 qt. with filter change. Fuel Requirements: 91 octane.

OPTIONAL ENGINE: Standard Engine: W200 149 in. wheelbase. Club and crew cab models and 131 in. wheelbase. Conventional chassis cabs. Also standard for all W300 models. Optional for all W150 models and remaining W200 models. Features include vibration damper, 18 in. 4 blade fan and drop-forged crankshaft. Engine Type: OHV, V-8. Cast iron block and cylinder head. Bore x Stroke: 4.00 in. x 3.58 in. Lifters: Hydraulic. Number of main bearings-5. Fuel Induction: Single 2-bbl. carburetor. Compression Ratio: 8.4:1. Displacement: 360 cu. in. (5.89 liters). Horsepower: 170 @ 4000 rpm. (180 hp. for trucks over 8501 lb. GVWR). Torque: Net: 270 lb.-ft. @ 2000 rpm. Oil refill capacity: 5 qt. with filter change. Fuel Requirements: 91 octane.

CHASSIS FEATURES: W150: Front Suspension: Semi-elliptical springs, heavy-duty, absorbers. 1640 lb. rating. Optional rating: 1,800 lb. Rear Suspension: Semi-elliptical springs 1820 lbs. capacity. Optional Rating: 1,820 lbs. for 115 and 131 in. wheelbase. Front Axle Type and Capacity: Full-floating, 3500 lb. capacity. Optional: 4,000 lbs. Rear Axle Type and Capacity: Semi-floating, 3600 lb. capacity. Optional: None. Final Drive Ratio: 2.94, (225 engine) 3.21, 3.55:1 (318 and 360 engines). The 360 engine with automatic had a 2.94:1 axle ratio. Transfer Case: NP-208, single lever, two-speed: 2.61, 1.00:1. Brakes: Type: Power, hydraulic. Front: Disc. Rear: Drums. Dimensions: Front: 11.75 in. x 1.256 in. disc. Rear: 11 in. x 2.5 in. Rear lining area: 106.4 sq. in. Wheels: 15 x 6.5 5-stud disc. Optional: 15 x 7 in. cast aluminum with radial ribbed design. Available for W150 pickups only. These wheels weighed approximately four pounds less per unit than the standard wheels. Tires: P235/75R x 15B, 4-ply rating. Optional: P25570R x 15C, LR60 x 15B, 10-15 LTB, 7.00 x 15D. Steering: Recirculating ball. Ratio: 24:1, turns Lock-to-Lock: 3.5:1. Turning Circle: 43 ft. (131 in. wheelbase). Optional: Power assisted. Ratio: 17.8:1. Transmission: NP 435 wide ratio 4-speed manual. Transmission Ratios: 6.68, 3.34, 1.66, 1.00:1. Optional: Chrysler Loadflite A-727 3-speed automatic. Ratios: 2.45, 1.45., 1.00:1. Clutch: Single dry plate disc, hydraulic actuation. Clutch diameter: 11 in. dia. Total lining area: 123.7 sq. in. Optional: None. W200: Separate body and ladder-type frame. Section modules: 3.88 in. (131 in. wheelbase), 5.02 in. (149 in. wheelbase, crew cab), 5.47 in. (149 in. wheelbase, club cab). Front Suspension: Semi-elliptical leaf springs, heavy-duty shock absorbers. 1640 lb. capacity (131 in. wheelbase), 1,800 lb. capacity (149 in. wheelbase). Optional: 1,800 lb. capacity: 131 in. wheelbase, 2,250 lb. capacity: All wheelbases. Rear Suspension: Semi-elliptical leaf, 2,725 lb. capacity. Front Axle Type and Capacity: Full-floating, 3500 lb. capacity. Optional Rating: 4,000 lb. with Sno-Fiter Package only, 4,500 lb. Rear Axle Type and Capacity: Full-floating, 5500 lb. capacity. Optional rating: None. Final Drive Ratio: 3.54:1 (conventional cab); 4.10:1 (club cab and crew cab). Transfer Case: Conventional cab and club cab models: New Process 208, two-speed: 2.61, 1.00:1. Crew cab: New Process 205 two-speed. Brakes: Type: Power, hydraulic. Front: Disc. Rear: Drum. Dimensions: Front: 12.82 in. x 1.19 in. disc. Rear: 12.0 in. x 2.50 in. Total rear lining area: 122.8 sq. in. Optional: None. Wheels: 6 in., 8-stud disc. Optional: None. Tires: 8.00 x 16.5D, 8-ply rating. Optional (max. size avail.): 9.50R x 16.5E, 8-ply rating. Steering: Recirculating ball. Ratio: 24:1. Optional: Power assisted. Ratio: 17.8:1. Transmission: New Process 435, wide-ratio 4-speed manual. Transmission Ratios: 6.68, 3.34, 1.66, 1.00:1. Reverse. Optional: Chrysler A-727 Loadflite 3-speed automatic. Ratios: 2.45, 1.45., 1.00:1. Clutch: Single dry plate disc, hydraulic actuation. Clutch diameter: 11 in. dia. Total lining area: 123.7 sq. in. W300: Separate body and channel steel, straight frame, 5.02 in. section modules, 36,000 psi. Front Suspension: Semi-elliptical springs, heavy-duty shock absorbers. 1940 lb. capacity. Optional rating: 2,250 lb. Rear Suspension: Semi-elliptical springs, 3650 lb. capacity. Optional Rating: 585 lb. and 900 lb. auxiliary springs. Front Axle Type and Capacity: Full-floating. 4500 lb. capacity. Rear Axle Type and Capacity: 7500 lb. capacity. Final Drive Ratio: 4.56:1. Transfer Case: New Process 205 two-speed: 1.96, 1.0:1. Brakes: Type: Hydraulic. Front: Disc. Rear: Drum. Dimensions: Front: 12.88 in. x 1.19 in. disc. Rear: 12.0 in. x 3.0 in. Total rear lining area: 147.4 sq. in. Wheels: 6.75 in. rim, 8-stud disc. Tires: 8.00 x 16.5D, 10-ply. Optional: 8.00R x 16.5E (maximum optional size). Transmission: NP435 4-speed synchromesh manual. Transmission Ratios: 6.69, 3.34, 1.66, 1.00:1. Optional: Chrysler Loadflite A-727 3-speed automatic. Ratios: 2.45, 1.45., 1.00:1. Clutch: Single plate dry disc, hydraulic actuation. Clutch diameter: 11.0 in. Total plate area: 123.7 sq. in. Optional: None.

VEHICLE DIMENSIONS: W150. Wheelbase: 115 in., 131 in., 133 in. (club cab), 149 in. (club cab). Overall Length: 115 in. wheelbase: 193.6 in., 131 in. wheelbase: 213.6 in., 133 in. wheelbase: 211.6 in., 149 in. wheelbase: 231.6 in. wheelbase. All dimensions include optional rear bumper. Front/Rear Tread: 62.5 in./62.5 in. Overall Height: 74.0 in. Width: 79.5 in. Front/Rear Overhang: 30 in./47 in. Tailgate: Width and Height: 67 in. x 21.4 in. Approach/Departure Degrees: 34/24. Ground Clearance: Front axle: 8.2 in. Rear axle: 8.5 in. Oil pan: 15.8 in. Transfer case: 10.4 in. Load space: Pickup box dimensions: 115 in. wheelbase: 78 in. x 51 in. x 19.125 in. Capacity: 61.1 cu. ft. 131 in. wheelbase and 149 in. wheelbase. Sweptline: 98 in. x 51 in. x 19.3 in. Capacity: 76.6 cu. ft. W200: Wheelbase: 131 in. Crew cab: 149 in. Overall Length: 131 in./149 in. wheelbase: 213.6 in./231.6 in. Front/Rear Tread: 62.5 in./62.5 in. Overall Height: 74.0 in. Width: 79.5 in. Front/Rear Overhang: 31 in./49 in. Tailgate: Width x Height: 66.5 in. x 19.3 in. Approach/Departure Degrees: 30/21. Ground Clearance: Front axle: 8.0 in. Rear axle: 7.8 in. Oil pan: 16.1 in. Transfer case: 10.7 in. Load space: Pickup box dimensions: Sweptline: 98.875 in. x 51.0 in. x 19.3 in. W300: Wheelbase: 135 in. Load space: Pickup box dimensions: 108 in. x 54 in. x 20 in. Capacity: 66 cu. ft.

CAPACITIES: Fuel Tank: 25 gal.

ACCOMMODATIONS: Seating Capacity: 3 passenger.

INSTRUMENTATION: 0-100 mph speedometer, 99,999.9 mile odometer, gauges for fuel level, ammeter and engine coolant temperature. Warning lights for oil pressure, parking brake and hazard lights operation.

OPTIONS AND PRICES: 318 cu. in. V-8 (W150): $296. 360 cu. in. V-8 (W150, W200): $491. Loadflite automatic transmission: $233. Limited slip rear differential (3.91:1 ratio only): $197. Sno-Commander Snowplow Package: $1104. Includes 4,000 lb. front axle, power-angling blade, power lift, seven-way control, plow lights, Sno-Commander body side decals. Air conditioning. AM/FM stereo with Search-Tune: $192. AM/FM Stereo with cassette tape player. AM/FM stereo radio with 40-channel CB transreceiver. Automatic speed control (W150 and W200). Electric clock: $52. Sport steering wheel: $44. Transfer case skid plate: $41. Electric door locks: $100. Five-slot, 15 in. x 7 in. white painted disc road wheels (W150): $202. Five-slot, 15 in. x 7 in. chrome disc road wheels (W150). Aluminum, 15 in. x 7 in. radial-ribbed road wheels (W150). Tilt steering column (available with automatic transmission only). Quad rectangular headlights. Lockable sliding rear window. Bright hitch-type rear bumper with 2,000 lb. trailer capacity. Power Windows. Deluxe camper cap cover. Sky Lite sun roof. Light-Duty and Heavy-Duty Trailer Towing Packages. Adventurer S.E. Package: $547. Big Horn bench seat. Adventurer Package. Adventurer Sport Package. Adventurer S.E. leather bench seat.

HISTORICAL FOOTNOTES: The 1980 Dodge four-wheel drive trucks were introduced in August, 1979.

DODGE RAMCHARGER
1974-1993

1974 RAMCHARGER

The Ramcharger made its debut in March, 1974. Originally called the Rhino, a name that was rejected because of its associated connotations of sturdiness but somewhat ungainly motion, the Ramcharger was influenced by the changing nature of the four-wheel drive vehicle market. The director of market planning and research for Chrysler Motors Corp., Seymour Marshak, noted: "We are out there constantly studying the market, both our owners and those of competitive producers. We are interested in what they like about their vehicles and what they don't like." One market change that impacted upon the Ramcharger's design was the growing number of four-wheel drive vehicle owners who were opting for products with plenty of luxury and comfort combined with competent off-road performance. As first produced the Ramcharger made extensive use of existing components from Dodge trucks currently in production. For example, the front end sheet metal and dashboard were lifted virtually intact from the Dodge pickups. Similarly, the Ramcharger's engines, transmissions and transfer case were also shared with the W series trucks. Standard equipment included a 318 cu. in. V-8 engine, 3-spd. manual transmission, 2-spd. full-time transfer case, chrome front and rear bumpers, heater and defroster, 2-spd. electric windshield wipers, front driver's bucket seat, 2-spd. electric windshield wipers, windshield washers, dual exterior mirrors, power brakes.

I.D. DATA: The vehicle identification number was located on a V.I.N. plate attached to the driver's side door body latch post. The V.I.N. consisted of 13 elements. The first two characters indicated the model code. The next digit identified the body type. The next entry, a letter, identified the GVW rating. The next unit, a letter, designated the engine type. The next unit, the number 4, indicated the 1978 model year. Following this came a letter indicating the assembly plant. The V.I.N. ended with a six-digit production sequence number at the assembly plant as follows: 100001 at Warren Truck #1, Missouri Truck and Pillette Truck Plant. 500001 at Warren Truck #2. 700001 at Warren Truck Plant #3. All models began with sequence number 000,001.

Body Type	Factory Price	GVW	Shipping Weight	Prod. Total
AW100 Ramcharger				
AW100, Utility	$4096	4900*	3910	15,810

* 6000 GVW Package optional.

STANDARD ENGINE: OHV V-8. Features include a drop-forged five-bearing crankshaft, chain-driven camshaft, free-turning exhaust valves, drop-forged I-beam connecting rods and silent-chain camshaft. Not available in California. Engine Type: OHV, V-8. Cast iron block and cylinder head. Bore x Stroke: 3.9 in. x 3.312 in. Lifters: Hydraulic. Number of main bearings-5. Fuel Induction: Single 2-bbl. carburetor. Compression Ratio: 8.0:1. Displacement: 318 cu. in. (5.2 liters). Horsepower: 155 @ 4000 rpm. Torque: Net: 255 lb.-ft. @ 2400 rpm. Oil refill capacity: 5 qt. with filter change. Fuel Requirements: 91 octane.

OPTIONAL ENGINE: OHV V-8. Features include vibration damper, 18 in. 4-blade fan and drop-forged crankshaft. Available for California only. Engine Type: OHV, V-8. Cast iron block and cylinder head. Bore x Stroke: 4.00 in. x 3.58 in. Lifters: Hydraulic. Number of main bearings-5. Fuel Induction: Single 2-bbl. carburetor. Compression Ratio: 8.0:1. Displacement: 360 cu. in. (5.9 liters). Horsepower: 210 @ 4000 rpm. Torque: Net: 285 lb.-ft. @ 2400 rpm. Oil refill capacity: 5 qt. with filter change. Fuel Requirements: 91 octane.

OPTIONAL ENGINE: Not available for California. Engine Type: OHV, V-8. Cast iron block and cylinder head. Bore x Stroke: 4.34 in. x 3.38 in. Lifters: Hydraulic. Number of main bearings-5. Compression Ratio: 8.2:1. Displacement: 400 cu. in. (6.55 liters). Horsepower: 185 @ 4000 rpm. Torque: 305 lb.-ft. @ 2400 rpm. Oil refill capacity: 5 qt. with filter change. Fuel Requirements: 91 octane.

OPTIONAL ENGINE: Engine Type: OHV, V-8. Cast iron block and cylinder head. Bore x Stroke: 4.32 in. x 3.75 in. Lifters: Hydraulic. Number of main bearings-5. Fuel Induction: Single 4-bbl. carburetor. Compression Ratio: 8.12:1. Displacement: 440 cu. in. (7.2 liters). Horsepower: 230 @ 4000 rpm. (225 hp. in California). Torque: 350 lb.-ft. @ 3200 rpm. (345 lb.-ft. in California). Oil refill capacity: 5 qt. with filter change. Fuel Requirements: 91 octane.

CHASSIS FEATURES: Separate body and frame, ladder-type frame

SUSPENSION AND RUNNING GEAR: Front Suspension: Semi-elliptical leaf springs, stabilizer bar and tubular shock absorbers. Rear Suspension: Semi-elliptical leaf springs, and tubular shock absorbers. Front Axle Type and Capacity: Full-floating, 3500 lb. capacity. Rear Axle Type and Capacity: Semi-floating, hypoid-type 3600 lb. capacity. Final Drive Ratio: 3.23:1, 3.12:1, 3.90:1. Transfer Case: New Process 203 full-time, two-speed: 2.01, 1.00:1. Brakes: Power, hydraulic. Front: Discs. Rear: Drums. Dimensions: Front: 11.75 in. x 1.256 in. disc. Rear: 11 in. x 2.5 in. Rear lining area: 106.4 sq. in. Wheels: 15 x 5.5 5-stud disc. Optional: 15 x 6.0, 15 x 8, 16 x 5. Tires: E78 x 15B, 4-ply rating. Optional: F78 x 15B, 10 x 15B, 6.40 x 16C. Steering: Recirculating ball. Ratio: 24:1, turns Lock-to-Lock: 3.5:1. Turning Circle: 36.5 ft. Optional: Power assisted. Ratio: 17.8:1. Transmission: A-230 3-speed, all-synchromesh manual. No manual transmissions were available in California. Transmission Ratios: 3.02, 1.76, 1.00:1. Optional: NP435, wide-ratio 4-speed manual, synchromesh on top three gears. Transmission ratios: 6.69, 3.34, 1.66, 1.00:1. NP445, close ratio 4-speed manual, synchromesh on all forward gears. Transmission ratios: 4.56, 2.28, 1.31, 1.00:1. Chrysler A-727 3-speed automatic. Ratios: 2.45, 1.45., 1.00:1. Clutch: Single dry plate disc, hydraulic actuation. Clutch diameter: 11 in. dia. Total lining area: 123.7 sq. in.

VEHICLE DIMENSIONS: Wheelbase: 106.0 in. Overall Length: 184.6 in. Front/Rear Tread 65.75 in./63.15 in. Overall Height: 72.0 in. (with optional top). Width: 79.6 in. Front/Rear Overhang: 31.0 in./47 in. Tailgate: Width and Height: 67 in. x 19 in. Approach/Departure Degrees: 31/24. Ground Clearance: Front axle: 7.8 in. Rear axle: 7.3 in. Oil pan: 14.3 in. Transfer case: 10.3 in. Load space: With optional rear bench seat in place: 42.5 in. x 50.5 in.

x 41.3 in. With rear seat removed or folded: 78 in. x 50.5 in. x 41.3 in. Front headroom: 37.5 in. Pedal to seat back (max.): 42 in. Steering wheel to seat back (max.): 18.3 in. Seat to ground: 36 in. Floor to ground: 22.2 in.

CAPACITIES: Fuel Tank: 24 gal. Optional: 35 gal. replacement tank.

ACCOMMODATIONS: Seating Capacity: Driver with standard front bucket seat; driver and front seat occupant with optional front bucket seat. Five with optional rear bench seat.

INSTRUMENTATION: 0-100 mph speedometer, 99,999.9 mi. odometer, gauges for fuel level, engine coolant temperature, ammeter. Warning lights for oil pressure, brake system warning, hazard light operation.

OPTIONS AND PRICES: 360 cu. in. V-8: $89. 400 cu. in. V-8: $107. 440 cu. in. V-8: $214. 4-spd. manual wide ratio trans.: $108. 4-spd. close-ratio manual trans.: $134. 3-spd. auto. trans.: $250. Limited slip rear differential: $67. Power steering: $152. Tinted glass (windshield only): $16. Air conditioning: $443. Oil pressure gauge: $7. Tachometer: $47. Auxiliary 35 gal. replacement fuel tank: $24. Front passenger bucket seat. Rear bench seat. Center console. Steel top: $337. Roll bar. AM/FM radio. Automatic cruise control. Convenience Package. Heavy-duty front and rear springs. SE Package: $418. Soft top with side and rear roll-down windows (dealer-installed).

HISTORICAL FOOTNOTES: The Ramcharger was introduced in March, 1974. Plymouth offered the same vehicle as the Trail Duster. Except for minor trim changes and Plymouth styling clues, it was identical to the Dodge model.

1975 RAMCHARGER

The 1975 Ramcharger was fitted with a new dash panel with a standard matte black finish and a built-in fuse box. The instrument cluster was wing-shaped for improved visibility. It also was designed to accommodate the optional clock, tachometer and vacuum-voltmeter gauges. All units with a GVW under 6000 lb. were equipped with a catalytic converter. The optional steel top was offered in either white or black. A total of 14 exterior colors were available. The familiar Chrysler 225 cu. in. 6-cylinder engine was available for the Ramcharger. It was offered only with the 6100 GVW package. Standard equipment for 1975 included chrome front and rear bumpers, heater and defroster, front driver's bucket seat, 2-spd. electric windshield wipers, dual exterior mirrors and power brakes.

1975 Dodge Ramcharger SE

I.D. DATA: The vehicle identification number was located on a V.I.N. plate attached to the driver's side door body latch post. The V.I.N. consisted of 13 elements. The first two characters indicated the model code. The next digit identified the body type. The next entry, a letter, identified the GVW rating. The next unit, a letter, designated the engine type. The next unit, the number 5 indicated the 1975 model year. Following this came a letter indicating the assembly plant. The V.I.N. ended with a six-digit production sequence number at the assembly plant as follows: 100001 at Warren Truck #1, Missouri Truck and Pillette Truck Plant. 500001 at Warren Truck #2. 700001 at Warren Truck Plant #3. All models began with sequence number 000,001.

Body Type	Factory Price	GVW	Shipping Weight	Prod. Total
AW100 Ramcharger V-8				
AW100, Utility	$4546	4900*	3960	11,361

* 6000 GVW Package optional.

STANDARD ENGINE: OHV V-8. Features include a drop-forged five-bearing crankshaft, silent-chain camshaft, free-turning exhaust valves, drop-forged I-beam connecting rods and silent-chain camshaft. Not available in California. Engine Type: OHV, V-8. Cast iron block and cylinder head. Bore x Stroke: 3.9 in. x 3.312 in. Lifters: Hydraulic. Number of main bearings-5. Fuel Induction: Single 2-bbl. carburetor. Compression Ratio: 8.58:1. Displacement: 318 cu. in. (5.2 liters). Horsepower: 150 @ 4000 rpm. Torque: Net: 255 lb.-ft. @ 2000 rpm. Oil refill capacity: 5 qt. with filter change. Fuel Requirements: 91 octane.

OPTIONAL ENGINE: Requires 6001 GVW Package. OHV In-line 6-cyl. Cast iron block and cylinder head. Key components include a drop-forged, shot-peened crankshaft, roller timing chain, Stellite-faced exhaust valves, individually ported long-branch manifolds, aluminum parts and a large radiator. Bore x Stroke: 3.40 in. x 4.125 in. Lifters: Mechanical. Number of main bearings-4. Fuel Induction: Single 2-bbl. carburetor. Compression Ratio: 8.4:1. Displacement: 224.7 cu. in. (3.7 liters). Horsepower: Net: 105 @ 3600 rpm. Torque: Net: 175 lb.-ft. @ 2000 rpm. Oil refill capacity: 5 qt. with filter change. Fuel Requirements: Leaded or unleaded.

OPTIONAL ENGINE: OHV V-8. Features include vibration damper, 18 in. 4-blade fan and drop-forged crankshaft. Available for California only. Engine Type: OHV, V-8. Cast iron block and cylinder head. Bore x Stroke: 4.00 in. x 3.58 in. Lifters: Hydraulic. Number of main bearings-5. Fuel Induction: Single 2-bbl. carburetor. Compression Ratio: 8.4:1. Displacement: 360 cu. in. (5.9 liters). Horsepower: 175 @ 4000 rpm. Torque: Net: 285 lb.-ft. @ 2400 rpm. Oil refill capacity: 5 qt. with filter change. Fuel Requirements: 91 octane.

OPTIONAL ENGINE: Engine Type: OHV, V-8. Cast iron block and cylinder head. Bore x Stroke: 4.32 in. x 3.75 in. Lifters: Hydraulic. Number of main bearings-5. Fuel Induction: Single 4-bbl. carburetor. Compression Ratio: 8.2:1. Displacement: 440 cu. in. (7.2 liters). Horsepower: 235 @ 4000 rpm. Torque: 340 lb.-ft. @ 2400 rpm. Oil refill capacity: 5 qt. with filter change. Fuel Requirements: 91 octane.

CHASSIS FEATURES: Separate body and frame, ladder-type frame

SUSPENSION AND RUNNING GEAR: Front Suspension: Semi-elliptical leaf springs, stabilizer bar and tubular shock absorbers. Rear Suspension: Semi-elliptical leaf springs, and tubular shock absorbers. Front Axle Type and Capacity: Full-floating, 3500 lb. capacity. Rear Axle Type and Capacity: Semi-floating, hypoid-type 3600 lb. capacity. Final Drive Ratio: 3.2:1, 3.55:1, 3.90:1. Transfer Case: New Process 203 full-time, two-speed: 2.00, 1.00:1. Brakes: Power, hydraulic. Front: Discs. Rear: Drums. Dimensions: Front: 11.75 in. x 1.256 in. disc. Rear: 11 in. x 2.5 in. Rear lining area: 106.4 sq. in. Wheels: 15 x 5.5 5-stud disc. Optional: 15 x 6.5, 15 x 8, 16 x 5. Tires: E78 x 15B, 4-ply rating. Optional: F78 x 15B, G78 x 15B, G78 x 15D, H78 x 15B, HR78 x 15B, L78 x 15B, 6.50 x 16C, 7.00 x 15C, 7.00 x 15D, 10 x 15LTB. Steering: Recirculating ball. Ratio: 24:1, turns Lock-to-Lock: 3.5:1. Turning Circle: 36.5 ft. Optional: Power assisted. Ratio: 17.8:1. Transmission: A-230 3-speed, all-synchromesh manual. No manual transmissions were available in California. Transmission Ratios: 3.02, 1.76, 1.00:1. Optional: NP435, wide-ratio 4-speed manual, synchromesh on top three gears. Transmission ratios: 6.69, 3.34, 1.66, 1.00:1. NP445, close ratio 4-speed manual, synchromesh on all forward gears. Transmission ratios: 4.56, 2.28, 1.31, 1.00:1. Chrysler A-727 3-speed automatic. Ratios: 2.45, 1.45., 1.00:1. Clutch: Single dry plate disc, hydraulic actuation. Clutch diameter: 11 in. dia. Total lining area: 123.7 sq. in.

VEHICLE DIMENSIONS: Wheelbase: 106.0 in. Overall Length: 184.6 in. Front/Rear Tread 65.75 in./63.15 in. Overall Height: 72.0 in. (with optional top). Width: 79.6 in. Front/Rear Overhang: 31.0 in./47 in. Tailgate: Width and Height: 67 in. x 19 in. Approach/Departure Degrees: 31/24. Ground Clearance: Front axle: 7.8 in. Rear axle: 7.3 in. Oil pan: 14.3 in. Transfer case: 10.3 in. Load space: With optional rear bench seat in place: 42.5 in. x 50.5 in. x 41.3 in. With rear seat removed or folded: 78 in. x 50.5 in. x 41.3 in. Front headroom: 37.5 in. Pedal to seat back (max.): 42 in. Steering wheel to seat back (max.): 18.3 in. Seat to ground: 36 in. Floor to ground: 22.2 in.

CAPACITIES: Fuel Tank: 24 gal. Optional: 35 gal. replacement tank.

ACCOMMODATIONS: Seating Capacity: Driver with standard front bucket seat; driver and front seat occupant with optional front bucket seat. Five with optional rear bench seat.

INSTRUMENTATION: 0-100 mph speedometer, 99,999.9 mi. odometer, gauges for fuel level, engine coolant temperature, ammeter. Warning lights for oil pressure, brake system warning, hazard light operation.

OPTIONS AND PRICES: 360 cu. in. V-8: $52. 440 cu. in. V-8: $256. 4-spd. manual wide ratio trans.: $123. 4-spd. close-ratio manual trans.: $151. 3-spd. auto. trans.: $289. Limited slip rear differential: $75. Power steering: $170. Heavy-duty front springs: $8. Heavy-duty rear springs: $25. Heavy-duty front and rear shock absorbers: $20. Front passenger bucket seat: $86. Front passenger seat and full-width rear bench seat: $240. Oil pressure gauge: $7. Tachometer: $55. Auxiliary replacement 35 gal. fuel tank: $27. Console. Tinted glass. California emission certification. Cruise control. Steel top: $341. Air conditioning. 72 amp alternator. SE Package: $423. Roll bar. Shoulder belts. Clock. Dual horns. Fuel tank shield. Transfer case shield. Heavy-Duty Trailer Tow Package. Protection Package. Soft top with side and rear roll-down windows (dealer-installed).

HISTORICAL FOOTNOTES: The 1975 Ramcharger was introduced in August, 1974.

1976 RAMCHARGER

In reaction to complaints that the Ramcharger's suspension was overly-soft and tended to bottom-out even over slight road imperfections, the 1976 Ramcharger had a re-engineered front suspension that included stiffer springs and higher-mounted tie rods. The 225 cu. in. 6-cyl. engine was available only in California with the maximum 6100 lb. GVW package. The 360 cu. in. V-8 was available only in California while the 400 cu. in. V-8 was not available for California. The 440 cu. in. V-8 was available only with the 6100 lb. GVW suspension and automatic transmission. Standard equipment included chrome front and rear bumpers, heater and defroster, driver and passenger front bucket seats, 2-spd. electric windshield wipers and easy-off tailgate.

I.D. DATA: The vehicle identification number was located on a V.I.N. plate attached to the driver's side door body latch post. The V.I.N. consisted of 13 elements. The first two characters indicated the model code. The next digit identified the body type. The next entry, a letter, identified the GVW rating. The next unit, a letter, designated the engine type. The next unit, the number 6, indicated the 1976 model year. Following this came a letter indicating the assembly plant. The V.I.N. ended with a six-digit production sequence number at the assembly plant as follows: 100001 at Warren Truck #1, Missouri Truck and Pillette Truck Plant. 500001 at Warren Truck #2. 700001 at Warren Truck Plant #3. All models began with sequence number 000,001.

Body Type	Factory Price	GVW	Shipping Weight	Prod. Total
AW100 Ramcharger				
AW100, Utility, 6-cyl.	$4640	4900	—	—
AW100, Utility, 318 V-8	$4834	4900[1]	3980	12,101[2]

NOTE 1: 5200, 5600, 6100 GVW Packages optional.
NOTE 2: Production total for both models.

STANDARD 6-CYL. ENGINE: Cast iron block and cylinder head. Key components include a drop-forged, shot-peened crankshaft, roller timing chain, Stellite-faced exhaust valves, individually ported long-branch manifolds, aluminum parts and a large radiator. Bore x Stroke: 3.40 in. x 4.125 in. Lifters: Mechanical. Number of main bearings-4. Fuel Induction: Single 2-bbl. carburetor. Compression Ratio: 8.6:1. Displacement: 224.7 cu. in. (3.68 liters). Horsepower: Net: 100 @ 3600 rpm. For under 6000 lb. GVW. For 6100 GVW rating is 105 @ 3600 rpm. Torque: Net: 170 lb.-ft. @ 2000 rpm, for under 6000 lb. GVW. For 6100 GVW rating is 175 lb.-ft. @ 2000 rpm. Oil refill capacity: 5 qt. Fuel Requirements: Unleaded for 6000 lb. GVW, leaded for 6100 lb. GVW.

STANDARD V-8 ENGINE: Features include a drop-forged five-bearing crankshaft, chain-driven camshaft, free-turning exhaust valves, drop-forged I-beam connecting rods and silent-chain camshaft. Engine Type: OHV, V-8. Cast iron block and cylinder head. Bore x Stroke: 3.91 in. x 3.312 in. Lifters: Hydraulic. Number of main bearings-5. Fuel Induction: Single 2-bbl. carburetor. Compression Ratio: 8.6:1. Displacement: 318 cu. in. (5.2 liters). Horsepower: Net 150 @ 4000 rpm. California rating is 155 hp @ 4000 rpm. Torque: Net: 255 lb.-ft. @ 2000 rpm, for under 6000 lb. GVW. For 6100 GVW rating is 240 @ 2400 rpm. California rating is 245 lb.-ft. @ 2000 rpm. Oil refill capacity: 5 qt. Fuel Requirements: Unleaded. Leaded fuel with 6100 lb. GVW.

OPTIONAL ENGINE: OHV V-8. Features include vibration damper, 18 in. 4-blade fan and drop-forged crankshaft. Available only in California with 6200 lb. GVW and automatic transmission. Engine Type: OHV, V-8. Cast iron block and cylinder head. Bore x Stroke: 4.00 in. x 3.58 in. Lifters: Hydraulic. Number of main bearings-5. Fuel Induction: Single 2-bbl. carburetor. Compression Ratio: 8.4:1. Displacement: 360 cu. in. (5.9 liters). Horsepower: 185 @ 4000 rpm. Torque: Net: 290 lb.-ft. @ 2400 rpm. Oil refill capacity: 5 qt. Fuel Requirements: Leaded or unleaded.

OPTIONAL ENGINE: Available only with 6100 lb. GVW. Not available in California or with 3-spd. manual trans. Engine Type: OHV, V-8. Cast iron block and cylinder head. Bore x Stroke: 4.34 in. x 3.38 in. Lifters: Hydraulic. Number of main bearings-5. Fuel Induction: Single 2-bbl. carburetor. Compression Ratio: 8.2:1. Displacement: 400 cu. in. (6.55 liters). Horsepower: 165 @ 4000 rpm. Torque: 290 lb.-ft. @ 2400 rpm. Oil refill capacity: 5 qt. Fuel Requirements: Leaded or unleaded.

OPTIONAL ENGINE: Available only with automatic transmission. Engine Type: OHV, V-8. Cast iron block and cylinder head. Bore x Stroke: 4.32 in. x 3.75 in. Lifters: Hydraulic. Number of main bearings-5. Fuel Induction: Single 4-bbl. carburetor. Compression Ratio: 8.2:1. Displacement: 440 cu. in. (7.2 liters). Horsepower: 225 @ 4000 rpm. Torque: 330 lb.-ft. @ 2400 rpm. Oil refill capacity: 5 qt. Fuel Requirements: Leaded or unleaded.

CHASSIS FEATURES: Separate body and frame, ladder-type frame.

SUSPENSION AND RUNNING GEAR: Front Suspension: Semi-elliptical leaf springs, stabilizer bar and tubular shock absorbers. Rear Suspension: Semi-elliptical leaf springs, and tubular shock absorbers. Front Axle Type and Capacity: Full-floating, 3500 lb. capacity. Optional: 4000 lb. capacity. Rear Axle Type and Capacity: Semi-floating, hypoid-type 3600 lb. capacity. Final Drive Ratio: 3.2:1, 3.55:1, 3.90:1. Transfer Case: New Process 203 full-time, two-speed: 2.00, 1.00:1. Brakes: Power, hydraulic. Front: Discs. Rear: Drums. Dimensions: Front: 11.75 in. x 1.256 in. disc. Rear: 11 in. x 2.5 in. Rear lining area: 106.4 sq. in. Wheels: 15 x 5.5 5-stud disc. Optional: 15 x 6.0, 15 x 6.5, 15 x 8.0, 16 x 5.0. Tires: E78 x 15B, 4-ply rating. Optional: F78 x 15B, G78 x 15B, G78 x 15D, H78 x 15B, L78 x 15B, 6.50 x 16C, 7.00 x 15C, 7.00 x 15D, 10 x 15B. Steering: Recirculating ball. Ratio: 24:1, turns Lock-to-Lock: 3.5:1. Turning Circle: 36.5 ft. Optional: Power assisted. Ratio: 17.8:1. Transmission: A-230 3-speed, all-synchromesh manual. No manual transmissions were available in California. Transmission Ratios: 3.02, 1.76, 1.00:1. Optional: NP435, wide-ratio 4-speed manual, synchromesh on top three gears. Transmission ratios: 6.69, 3.34, 1.66, 1.00:1. NP445, close ratio 4-speed manual, synchromesh on all forward gears. Transmission ratios: 4.56, 2.28, 1.31, 1.00:1. Chrysler A-727 3-speed automatic. Ratios: 2.45, 1.45., 1.00:1. Clutch: Single dry plate disc, hydraulic actuation. Clutch diameter: 11 in. dia. Total lining area: 123.7 sq. in.

VEHICLE DIMENSIONS: Wheelbase: 106.0 in. Overall Length: 184.6 in. Front/Rear Tread 65.75 in./63.15 in. Overall Height: 72.0 in. (with optional top). Width: 79.6 in. Front/Rear Overhang: 31.0 in./47 in. Tailgate: Width and Height: 67 in. x 19 in. Approach/Departure Degrees: 31/24. Ground Clearance: Front axle: 7.8 in. Rear axle: 7.3 in. Oil pan: 14.3 in. Transfer case: 10.3 in. Load space: With optional rear bench seat in place: 42.5 in. x 50.5 in. x 41.3 in. With rear seat removed or folded: 78 in. x 50.5 in. x 41.3 in. Front headroom: 37.5 in. Pedal to seat back (max.): 42 in. Steering wheel to seat back (max.): 18.3 in. Seat to ground: 36 in. Floor to ground: 22.2 in.

CAPACITIES: Fuel Tank: 24 gal. Optional: 35 gal. replacement tank.

ACCOMMODATIONS: Seating Capacity: Driver and passenger with standard front bucket seats. Five with optional rear bench seat.

INSTRUMENTATION: 0-100 mph speedometer, 99,999.9 mi. odometer, gauges for fuel level, engine coolant temperature, ammeter. Warning lights for oil pressure, brake system warning, hazard light operation.

OPTIONS AND PRICES: 360 cu. in. V-8: $66. 400 cu. in. V-8: $66. 440 cu. in. V-8: $256. 4-spd. manual wide-ratio trans.: $135. 4-spd. manual close-ratio trans.: $169. 3-spd. auto. trans.: $305. Limited slip rear differential: $109. Power steering: $179. Heavy-duty front springs: $10. Heavy-duty rear springs: $21. Heavy-duty front and rear shock absorbers: $22. Heavy-duty front stabilizer bar: $20. Auxiliary replacement 35 gal. fuel tank: $27. Full-width rear bench seat: $170. Oil pressure gauge: $10. Vacuum and voltmeter gauge: $40. Tachometer: $53. Steel roof: $444. SE Package: $432. Exterior rear tire swing-out mount. Soft top with side and rear roll-down windows (dealer-installed).

HISTORICAL FOOTNOTES: The 1976 Ramcharger was introduced in August,1975.

1977 RAMCHARGER

The latest Ramcharger had a fresh appearance due to new two-tone paint and upper body moldings. A new grille with rectangular parking/directional lights mounted inward of the headlights and incorporating DODGE lettering made the 1977 Ramcharger easy to identify. Added to the SE Package were high-back swivel bucket seats with movable armrests.

1977 Dodge Ramcharger with Four By Four Package

I.D. DATA: The vehicle identification number was located on a V.I.N. plate attached to the driver's side door body latch post. The V.I.N. consisted of 13 elements. The first two characters indicated the model code. The next digit identified the body type. The next entry, a letter, identified the GVW rating. The next unit, a letter, designated the engine type. The next unit, the number 7, indicated the 1977 model year. Following this came a letter indicating the assembly plant. The V.I.N. ended with a six-digit production sequence number at the assembly plant as follows: 100001 at Warren Truck #1, Missouri Truck and Pillette Truck Plant. 500001 at Warren Truck #2. 700001 at Warren Truck Plant #3. All models began with sequence number 000,001.

Body Type	Factory Price	GVW	Shipping Weight	Prod. Total
AW100 Ramcharger				
AW100, Utility, 318 V-8	$5321	4900	3985	17,120[2]

NOTE 1: 5200, 5600, 6100 GVW Packages optional.
NOTE 2: Production total for all models.

STANDARD 6-CYL. ENGINE: Cast iron block and cylinder head. Key components include a drop-forged, shot-peened crankshaft, roller timing chain, Stellite-faced exhaust valves, individually ported long-branch manifolds, aluminum parts and a large radiator. Bore x Stroke: 3.40 in. x 4.125 in. Lifters: Mechanical. Number of main bearings-4. Fuel Induction: Single 2-bbl. carburetor. Compression Ratio: 8.6:1. Displacement: 224.7 cu. in. (3.68 liters). Horsepower: Net: 100 @ 3600 rpm. For under 6000 lb. GVW. For 6100 GVW rating is 105 @ 3600 rpm. Torque: Net: 170 lb.-ft. @ 2000 rpm. For 6100 GVW rating is 175 lb.-ft. @ 2000 rpm. Oil refill capacity: 5 qt. Fuel Requirements: Unleaded for 6000 lb. GVW, leaded for 6100 lb. GVW.

STANDARD V-8 ENGINE: Features include a drop-forged five-bearing crankshaft, chain-driven camshaft, free-turning exhaust valves, drop-forged I-beam connecting rods and silent-chain camshaft. Engine Type: OHV, V-8. Cast iron block and cylinder head. Bore x Stroke: 3.91 in. x 3.312 in. Lifters: Hydraulic. Number of main bearings-5. Fuel Induction: Single 2-bbl. carburetor. Compression Ratio: 8.6:1. Displacement: 318 cu. in. (5.2 liters). Horsepower: Net 150 @ 4000 rpm. California rating is 155 hp. @ 4000 rpm. Torque: Net: 255 lb.-ft. @ 2000 rpm, for under 6000 lb. GVW. For 6100 GVW rating is 240 @ 2400 rpm. California rating is 245 lb.-ft. @ 2000 rpm. Oil refill capacity: 5 qt. Fuel Requirements: Unleaded. Leaded fuel with 6100 lb. GVW.

OPTIONAL ENGINE: OHV V-8. Features include vibration damper, 18 in. 4-blade fan and drop-forged crankshaft. Available only in California with 6200 lb. GVW and automatic transmission. Engine Type: OHV, V-8. Cast iron block and cylinder head. Bore x Stroke: 4.00 in. x 3.58 in. Lifters: Hydraulic. Number of main bearings-5. Fuel Induction: Single 2-bbl. carburetor. Compression Ratio: 8.4:1. Displacement: 360 cu. in. (5.9 liters). Horsepower: 185 @ 4000 rpm. Torque: Net: 290 lb.-ft. @ 2400 rpm. Oil refill capacity: 5 qt. Fuel Requirements: Leaded or unleaded.

OPTIONAL ENGINE: Available only with 6100 lb. GVW. Not available in California or with 3-spd. manual trans. Engine Type: OHV, V-8. Cast iron block and cylinder head. Bore x Stroke: 4.34 in. x 3.38 in. Lifters: Hydraulic. Number of main bearings-5. Fuel Induction: Single 2-bbl. carburetor. Compression Ratio: 8.2:1. Displacement: 400 cu. in. (6.55 liters). Horsepower: 165 @ 4000 rpm. Torque: 290 lb.-ft. @ 2400 rpm. Oil refill capacity: 5 qt. Fuel Requirements: Leaded or unleaded.

OPTIONAL ENGINE: Available only with automatic transmission. Engine Type: OHV, V-8. Cast iron block and cylinder head. Bore x Stroke: 4.32 in. x 3.75 in. Lifters: Hydraulic. Number of main bearings-5. Fuel Induction: Single 4-bbl. carburetor. Compression Ratio: 8.2:1. Displacement: 440 cu. in. (7.2 liters). Horsepower: 225 @ 4000 rpm. Torque: 330 lb.-ft. @ 2400 rpm. Oil refill capacity: 5 qt. Fuel Requirements: Leaded or unleaded.

CHASSIS FEATURES: Separate body and frame, ladder-type frame.

SUSPENSION AND RUNNING GEAR: Front Suspension: Semi-elliptical leaf springs, stabilizer bar and tubular shock absorbers. Rear Suspension: Semi-elliptical leaf springs, and tubular shock absorbers. Front Axle Type and Capacity: Full-floating, 3500 lb. capacity. Rear Axle Type and Capacity: Semi-floating, hypoid-type 3600 lb. capacity. Final Drive Ratio: 3.2:1, 3.55:1, 3.90:1. Transfer Case: New Process 203 full-time,

two-speed: 2.00, 1.00:1. Brakes: Power, hydraulic. Front: Discs. Rear: Drums. Dimensions: Front: 11.75 in. x 1.256 in. disc. Rear: 11 in. x 2.5 in. Rear lining area: 106.4 sq. in. Wheels: 15 x 5.5 5-stud disc. Optional: 15 x 6.0, 15 x 6.5, 15 x 8.0, 16 x 5.0. Tires: E78 x 15B, 4-ply rating. Optional: F78 x 15B, G78 x 15B, G78 x 15D, H78 x 15B, L78 x 15B, 6.50 x 16C, 7.00 x 15C, 7.00 x 15D, 10 x 15B. Steering: Recirculating ball. Ratio: 24:1, turns Lock-to-Lock: 3.5:1. Turning Circle: 36.5 ft. Optional: Power assisted. Ratio: 17.8:1. Transmission: A-230 3-speed, all-synchromesh manual. No manual transmissions were available in California. Transmission Ratios: 3.02, 1.76, 1.00:1. Optional: NP435, wide-ratio 4-speed manual, synchromesh on top three gears. Transmission ratios: 6.69, 3.34, 1.66, 1.00:1. NP445, close ratio 4-speed manual, synchromesh on all forward gears. Transmission ratios: 4.56, 2.28, 1.31, 1.00:1. Chrysler A-727 3-speed automatic. Ratios: 2.45, 1.45., 1.00:1. Clutch: Single dry plate disc, hydraulic actuation. Clutch diameter: 11 in. dia. Total lining area: 123.7 sq. in.

VEHICLE DIMENSIONS: Wheelbase: 106.0 in. Overall Length: 184.6 in. Front/Rear Tread 65.75 in./63.15 in. Overall Height: 72.0 in. (with optional top). Width: 79.6 in. Front/Rear Overhang: 31.0 in./47 in. Tailgate: Width and Height: 67 in. x 19 in. Approach/Departure Degrees: 31/24. Ground Clearance: Front axle: 7.8 in. Rear axle: 7.3 in. Oil pan: 14.3 in. Transfer case: 10.3 in. Load space: With optional rear bench seat in place: 42.5 in. x 50.5 in. x 41.3 in. With rear seat removed or folded: 78 in. x 50.5 in. x 41.3 in. Front headroom: 37.5 in. Pedal to seat back (max.): 42 in. Steering wheel to seat back (max.): 18.3 in. Seat to ground: 36 in. Floor to ground: 22.2 in.

CAPACITIES: Fuel Tank: 24 gal. Optional: 35 gal. replacement tank.

ACCOMMODATIONS: Seating Capacity: Driver and passenger with standard front bucket seats. Five with optional rear bench seat.

INSTRUMENTATION: 0-100 mph speedometer, 99,999.9 mi. odometer, gauges for fuel level, engine coolant temperature, ammeter. Warning lights for oil pressure, brake system warning, hazard light operation.

OPTIONS AND PRICES: 360 cu. in. V-8: $72. 400 cu. in. V-8: $72. 440 cu. in. V-8: $271. Steel roof: $470. SE Package: $516. 4-spd. manual wide-ratio trans.4-spd. manual close-ratio trans. 3-spd. auto. trans. Limited slip rear differential. Power steering. Heavy-duty front springs. Heavy-duty rear springs. Heavy-duty front and rear shock absorbers. Heavy-duty front stabilizer bar. Auxiliary replacement 35 gal. fuel tank. Oil pressure gauge. Vacuum and voltmeter gauge. Tachometer. Exterior rear tire swing-out mount. Soft top with side and rear roll-down windows (dealer-installed).

HISTORICAL FOOTNOTES: The 1977 Ramcharger was introduced in August, 1976.

1978 RAMCHARGER

For 1978, the Ramcharger was available with a new optional three passenger split-back front seat. Also added to the Ramcharger's options were new light and heavy-duty trailer-towing packages. A new Hurst shift lever with positive position detents. Initially, the 225 cu. in. was not available for use in California. Later it was reinstated, albeit with reduced power ratings as compared to the 49 state version. Only a 6100 GVW rating was available for the Ramcharger. The 5200 and 5600 lb. packages of 1977 were not offered. New low-back, full-foam bucket seats were available in both standard and optional form. As an option for the standard interior, low-back deluxe cloth and vinyl seats with Trombley stripe cloth inserts were offered. Also introduced was a new three passenger vinyl bench front with a split-back. It was available in blue, green, red or saddle. Another new option for 1978 was a tilt steering wheel adjustable to seven different positions. Also adding to the Ramcharger's appeal were new radio/CB combinations. The standard Ramcharger interior included deluxe vinyl seats with Vanguard vinyl inserts for driver and passenger, color-keyed instrument panel, color-keyed door trim panels with armrests, color-keyed padded sun visors, black soft-touch vinyl steering wheel and horn pad, 10 in. day/night rearview mirror and a full-width black rubber driver compartment floor mat. Additional standard Ramcharger features consisted of seat belts, inside spare tire mounting, heater and defroster, dual armrests, bright-finish bumpers and grille, map and courtesy light, padded sun visors, electric two-speed windshield wipers and dual-jet windshield washer. The SE interior consisted of cloth and vinyl front bucket seats, fully soft-trimmed color-keyed doors with simulated rosewood insert, grab handle, and carpeting on lower portion; lockable center console with removable beverage chest (available with bucket seats only), bright instrument panel trim molding with woodgrained applique, front compartment color-keyed carpeting (available with optional hardtop only), horn pad with woodgrained insert, rear side inner trim panels with woodgrained trim and bright molding, bright door sill tread plate, color-keyed spare tire cover (not available with outside spare tire carrier), Convenience Package, 12 in. day/night rearview mirror, glove box lock and light, and inside hood release.

1978 Dodge AW100 Ramcharger

The Macho Package, which Dodge said "can turn a trip to the super market into an adventure" contained body and tailgate decals, painted spoke or chrome disc road wheels, 10-15LTB tires and power steering. A total of 14 exterior colors were offered for 1978 as follows: Light blue, medium blue metallic, mint green metallic, medium green sunfire metallic, bright yellow, citron green metallic, light tan, bright tan metallic, sunrise orange, bright canyon red, canyon red sunfire metallic, light silver metallic, white and formal black.

I.D. DATA: The vehicle identification number was located on a V.I.N. plate attached to the driver's side door body latch post. The V.I.N. consisted of 13 elements. The first two characters indicated the model code. The next digit identified the body type. The next entry, a letter, identified the GVW rating. The next unit, a letter, designated the engine type. The next unit, the number 8, indicated the 1978 model year. Following this came a letter indicating the assembly plant. The V.I.N. ended with a six-digit production sequence number at the assembly plant as follows: 100001 at Warren Truck #1, Missouri Truck and Pillette Truck Plant. 500001 at Warren Truck #2. 700001 at Warren Truck Plant #3. All models began with sequence number 000,001.

Body Type	Factory Price	GVW	Shipping Weight	Prod. Total
AW100 Ramcharger				
AW100, Utility, 318 V-8	$6002	6100	3990	19,123*

* Production total for all models.

STANDARD 6-CYL. ENGINE: Cast iron block and cylinder head. Key components include a drop-forged, shot-peened crankshaft, roller timing chain, Stellite-faced exhaust valves, individually ported long-branch manifolds, aluminum parts and a large radiator. Bore x Stroke: 3.40 in. x 4.125 in. Lifters: Mechanical. Number of main bearings-4. Fuel Induction: Single 2-bbl. carburetor. Displacement: 224.7 cu. in. (3.68 liters). Compression Ratio: 8.4:1. Horsepower: Net: 115 @ 3600 rpm. For California rating is 110 hp. @ 3600 rpm. Torque: Net: 175 lb.-ft. @ 1600 rpm. Oil refill capacity: 5 qt. Fuel Requirements: Unleaded.

OPTIONAL ENGINE: Features include a drop-forged five-bearing crankshaft, chain-driven camshaft, free-turning exhaust valves, drop-forged I-beam connecting rods and silent-chain camshaft. Engine Type: OHV, V-8. Cast iron block and cylinder head. Bore x Stroke: 3.91 in. x 3.312 in. Lifters: Hydraulic. Number of main bearings-5. Fuel Induction: Single 2-bbl. carburetor (not available in California, where a 4-bbl. version was offered). Compression Ratio: 8.6:1. Displacement: 318 cu. in. (5.2 liters). Horsepower: Net 145 @ 4000 rpm. California rating is 160 hp. @ 4000 rpm. Torque: Net: 250 lb.-ft. @ 2000 rpm. California rating is 250 lb.-ft. @ 2400 rpm. Oil refill capacity: 5 qt. Fuel Requirements: Unleaded.

OPTIONAL ENGINE: OHV V-8. Features include vibration damper, 18 in. 4-blade fan and drop-forged crankshaft. Engine Type: OHV, V-8. Cast iron block and cylinder head. Bore x Stroke: 4.00 in. x 3.58 in. Lifters: Hydraulic. Number of main bearings-5. Fuel Induction: Single 2-bbl. carburetor (not available in California, where a 4-bbl. version was offered). Compression Ratio: 8.2:1. Displacement: 360 cu. in. (5.9 liters). Horsepower: 160 @ 4000 rpm. California rating is 170 @ 3600 rpm. Torque: Net: 280 lb.-ft. @ 2000 rpm. California rating is 270 lb.-ft. @ 2000 rpm. Oil refill capacity: 5 qt. Fuel Requirements: Unleaded.

OPTIONAL ENGINE: Not available in California. Engine Type: OHV, V-8. Cast iron block and cylinder head. Bore x Stroke: 4.34 in. x 3.38 in. Lifters: Hydraulic. Number of main bearings-5. Fuel Induction: Single 2-bbl. carburetor. Compression Ratio: 8.2:1. Displacement: 400 cu. in. (6.55 liters). Horsepower: 165 @ 4000 rpm. Torque: 290 lb.-ft. @ 2400 rpm. Oil refill capacity: 5 qt. Fuel Requirements: Leaded.

OPTIONAL ENGINE: Engine Type: OHV, V-8. Cast iron block and cylinder head. Bore x Stroke: 4.32 in. x 3.75 in. Lifters: Hydraulic. Number of main bearings-5. Fuel Induction: Single 4-bbl. Thermo-Quad carburetor. Compression Ratio: 8.2:1. Displacement: 440 cu. in. (7.2 liters). Horsepower: 220 @ 4000 rpm. California rating is 200 @ 3600 rpm. Torque: 330 lb.-ft. @ 2400 rpm. California rating is 330 lb.-ft. @ 2800 rpm. Oil refill capacity: 5 qt. Fuel Requirements: Unleaded.

CHASSIS FEATURES: Separate body and frame, ladder-type, drop center frame, 36,000 psi, 2.86 in. modules.

SUSPENSION AND RUNNING GEAR: Front Suspension: 48 in. x 2.5 in. Semi-elliptical leaf springs, 1.0 in. stabilizer bar and tubular shock absorbers. 1640 lb. rating. Optional Rating: None. Rear Suspension: 52 in. x 2.5 in. Semi-elliptical leaf springs, and tubular shock absorbers. 1840 lb. rating. Optional Rating: None. Front Axle Type and Capacity: Spicer 44F-B-J full-floating, 3500 lb. capacity. Optional: None. Rear Axle Type and Capacity: Chrysler 9.25 in. Semi-floating, hypoid-type 3600 lb. capacity. Optional: None. Final Drive Ratio: 3.5:1. Optional: 3.20:1, 3.90:1 (3.90:1 not available in Calif.). Transfer Case: New Process 203 full-time, two-speed: 2.00, 1.00:1. Brakes: Type: Power, hydraulic. Front: Discs. Rear: Drums. Dimensions: Front: 11.75 in. x 1.256 in. disc. Rear: 11 in. x 2.5 in. Brake swept lining area: 404 sq. in. Wheels: 15 x 5.5 5-stud disc. Optional: 15 x 6.0 (chrome styled, road type), 15 x 8.0 (steel-spoke, white painted), 15 x 8.0 (slot, disc, chrome). Tires: H78 x 15B, 4-ply rating. Optional: G78-15D, L78-15B, LR78-15B, 7.00-15C, 7.00-15D, 10-15LTB. Steering: Recirculating ball. Ratio: 24:1, turns Lock-to-Lock: 3.5:1. Turning Circle: 36.9 ft. Optional: Power assisted. Ratio: 17.8:1. Transmission: A-230 3-speed, all-synchromesh manual. No manual transmissions were available in California. Transmission Ratios: 3.02, 1.76, 1.00:1. Optional: NP435, wide-ratio 4-speed manual, synchromesh on top three gears. Transmission ratios: 6.69, 3.34, 1.66, 1.00:1. NP445, close ratio 4-speed manual, synchromesh on all forward gears. Transmission ratios: 4.56, 2.28, 1.31, 1.00:1. Chrysler A-727 3-speed automatic. Ratios: 2.45, 1.45., 1.00:1. Clutch: Single dry plate disc, hydraulic actuation. Clutch diameter: 11 in. dia. Total lining area: 123.7 sq. in.

VEHICLE DIMENSIONS: Wheelbase: 106.0 in. Overall Length: 184.6 in. Front/Rear Tread 65.75 in./63.15 in. Overall Height: 72.0 in. (with optional top). Width: 79.6 in. Front/Rear Overhang: 31.0 in./47 in. Tailgate: Width and Height: 67 in. x 19 in. Approach/Departure Degrees: 31/24. Ground Clearance: Front axle: 7.8 in. Rear axle: 7.3 in. Oil pan: 14.3 in. Transfer case: 10.3 in. Load space: With optional rear bench seat in place: 42.5 in. x 50.5 in. x 41.3 in. With rear seat removed or folded: 78 in. x 50.5 in. x 41.3 in. Front headroom: 37.5 in. Pedal to seat back (max.): 42 in. Steering wheel to seat back (max.): 18.3 in. Seat to ground: 36 in. Floor to ground: 22.2 in.

CAPACITIES: Fuel Tank: 24 gal. Optional: 35 gal. replacement tank.

ACCOMMODATIONS: Seating Capacity: Driver and passenger with standard front bucket seats. Five with optional rear bench seat.

INSTRUMENTATION: 0-100 mph speedometer, 99,999.9 mi. odometer, gauges for fuel level, engine coolant temperature, ammeter. Warning lights for oil pressure, brake system warning, hazard light operation.

OPTIONS AND PRICES: Macho Package. Light-Duty Trailer-Towing Package. Includes 7 in. section rear bumper and 1.875 in. dia. hitch ball. Heavy-Duty Trailer-Towing Package. Includes load-equalizing hitch. Steel hardtop. Available in black or white vinyl-textured paint: $498. Sky Lite roof. Includes tinted safety glass, optional with steel roof. Soft top with roll-down side and rear windows, dealer-installed. SE Package: $530. Three passenger front seat. Three passenger rear seat. Tilt steering wheel. AM radio with CB. AM/FM stereo with CB. AM radio. AM/FM radio. AM/FM stereo radio. AM/FM stereo radio with eight-track tape. Clock or tachometer. Oil pressure gauge. Vacuum and voltmeter gauges. Inside hood release. Automatic speed control. Loadflite automatic transmission: $349. Close-ratio 4-speed manual trans.: $193. Wide ratio 4-spd. manual trans.: $152. 318 cu. in. V-8: $219 California version: $266. 360 cu. in. V-8: $287. California version: $334. 400 cu. in. V-8: $287. 440 cu. in. V-8: $511. Limited slip rear differential: $175. Tinted glass. Step-type rear bumper. Power steering: $211. Low-mount exterior rearview mirrors. Bright hubcaps. Chrome five-slot disc wheels. Eight spoke white-painted road wheels. Chrome styled wheels. Various tire sizes. Heavy-duty front and rear shock absorbers: $25. Heavy-duty front stabilizer bar: $25. Protection Package. Body Molding Package. Skid plates. 62 amp alternator. 117 amp alternator. 59 amp-hr. battery. 70 amp-hr. battery. 500 amp Long Life battery. Luxury Package. Easy Order Package. 35 gal. fuel tank: $31. Deluxe heater. Roll bar. Front bumper guards. Dual horns. Snowplow Package. Includes power angling blade and power blade lift.

HISTORICAL FOOTNOTES: The 1978 Ramcharger was introduced in August, 1977. Dodge reported that it was the fastest growing truck company in America by virtue of a 237% increase in sales from 1966 through 1976.

1979 RAMCHARGER

The Ramcharger was fitted with a new bright aluminum grille for 1979 that consisted of a broad center dividing bar separating two rectangular mesh sections. Provision was made for the installation of sacked dual rectangular headlights. The latest Ramcharger also had new front end sheet metal and carried DODGE lettering on the hood's leading edge. The standard engine for the AW100 Ramcharger was the 318 cu. in. V-8. The only engine option was the 360 cu. in. V-8. Neither the 400 cu. in. and 440 cu. in. engines were offered for 1979. The standard Ramcharger interior included low back deluxe vinyl front bucket seats, color-keyed instrument panel, color-keyed door trim panels with armrests, color-keyed padded sun visors, black soft-touch vinyl steering wheel and horn pad, 10 in. day/night rearview mirror and a full-width black rubber driver compartment floor mat. Additional standard Ramcharger features consisted of seat belts, inside spare tire mounting, heater and defroster, dual armrests, bright-finish bumpers and grille, map and courtesy light, padded sun visors, electric two-speed windshield wipers and dual-jet windshield washer. The SE Package consisted of cloth and vinyl low-back bucket seats that were available as a separate option for the standard Ramcharger interior. Other elements of the SE interior included color-keyed vinyl door trim panels with assist strap, locking console with removable beverage chest, woodgrain instrument panel face plate and bright trim. Optional for the SE Package were cloth and vinyl high-back Command bucket seats. A new option for 1979 was an electric door lock system. Color choices for 1979 consisted of the following straight shades: White, cashmere, medium canyon red, sunburst orange, yellow flame and formal black. Metallic colors for 1979 were light silver, cadet blue, ensign blue, teal frost, citron green and medium tan. The sunfire metallic selections were teal green, sable brown and canyon red.

1979 Dodge AW100 Ramcharger

I.D. DATA: The vehicle identification number was located on a V.I.N. plate attached to the driver's side door body latch post. The V.I.N. consisted of 13 elements. The first two characters indicated the model code as follows: A1-AW100. The next digit identified the body type as follows: 0-Sport Utility type vehicle. The next entry, a letter, identified the GVW rating as follows: B-6001 to 10,000 lb. The next unit, a letter, designated the engine type as follows: E-318-2 bbl. T-360-4 bbl. The next unit, the number 9, indicted the 1979 model year. Following this came a letter indicating the assembly plant as follows: C-Jefferson Assembly Plant, K-Pillette Road Truck, L-Lago Alberto Assembly Plant (Mexico), M-Toluca Assembly Plant (Mexico), N-Burt Road (KDX), S-Warren Truck #1, T-Warren Truck #2 (Sherwood), X-Missouri Truck, V-Warner Truck #3 (Comapcy). The V.I.N. ended with a six-digit production sequence number at the assembly plant as follows: 100001 at Warren Truck #1, Missouri Truck and Pillette Truck Plant. 500001 at Warren Truck #2. 700001 at Warren Truck Plant #3. All models began with sequence number 000,001.

Body Type	Factory Price	GVW	Shipping Weight	Prod. Total
AW100 Ramcharger				
AW100, Utility, 318 V-8	$7286	6050	3990	15,754*

* Production total for all models.

STANDARD ENGINE: Features include a drop-forged five-bearing crankshaft, chain-driven camshaft, free-turning exhaust valves, drop-forged I-beam connecting rods and silent-chain camshaft. Engine Type: OHV, V-8. Cast iron block and cylinder head. Bore x Stroke: 3.91 in. x 3.312 in. Lifters: Hydraulic. Number of main bearings-5. Fuel Induction: Single 2-bbl. carburetor. (not available in California, where a 4-bbl. version was offered). Compression Ratio: 8.6:1. Displacement: 318 cu. in. (5.2 liters). Horsepower: Net 145 @ 4000 rpm. California rating is 160 hp @ 4000 rpm. Torque: Net: 250 lb.-ft. @ 2000 rpm. California rating is 250 lb.-ft. @ 2400 rpm. Oil refill capacity: 5 qt. Fuel Requirements: Unleaded.

OPTIONAL ENGINE: OHV V-8. Features include vibration damper, 18 in. 4-blade fan and drop-forged crankshaft. Engine Type: OHV, V-8. Cast iron block and cylinder head. Bore x Stroke: 4.00 in. x 3.58 in. Lifters: Hydraulic. Number of main bearings-5. Fuel Induction: Single 2-bbl. carburetor. (not available in California, where a 4-bbl. version was offered). Compression Ratio: 8.2:1. Displacement: 360 cu. in. (5.9 liters). Horsepower: 160 @ 4000 rpm. California rating is 175 @ 4000 rpm. Torque: Net: 280 lb.-ft. @ 2000 rpm. California rating is 275 lb.-ft. @ 2400 rpm. Oil refill capacity: 5 qt. Fuel Requirements: Unleaded.

CHASSIS FEATURES: Separate body and frame, ladder-type, drop center frame, 36,000 psi, 2.86 in. modules.

SUSPENSION AND RUNNING GEAR: Front Suspension: 48 in. x 2.5 in. Semi-elliptical leaf springs, 1.0 in. stabilizer bar and 1.0 in. tubular shock absorbers. 1640 lb. rating. Optional: 1.1875 in. shock absorbers and 2100 b. capacity springs with Sno-Commander Package. Rear Suspension: 52 in. x 2.5 in. Semi-elliptical leaf springs, and 1.0 in. tubular shock absorbers. 1820 lbs. Optional: 1.1875 in. shock absorbers. Front Axle Type and Capacity: Spicer 44F-B-J full-floating, 3500 lb. capacity. Optional: 4000 lb. Rear Axle Type and Capacity: Chrysler 9.25 in. Semi-floating, hypoid-type 3600 lb. capacity. Optional: None. Final Drive Ratio: 3.55:1. Sno-Commander Package: 3.20:1. Transfer Case: New Process 203 full-time, two-speed: 2.00, 1.00:1. Brakes: Type: Power, hydraulic. Front: Discs. Rear: Drums. Dimensions: Front: 11.75 in. x 1.256 in. disc. Rear: 11 in. x 2.5 in. Brake swept lining area: 404 sq. in. Wheels: 15 x 65 5-stud disc. Optional: 15 x 6.0 (chrome styled, road type), 15 x 8.0 (steel-spoke, white painted), 15 x 8.0 (slot, disc, chrome). Tires: L78 x 15B, 4-ply rating. Optional: LR70-15B, LR60-15B, LR78-15B, 7.00-15B, 10-15LT-B, 7.00 15D. Steering: Recirculating ball. Ratio: 24:1, turns Lock-to-Lock: 3.5:1. Turning Circle: 36.9 ft. Optional: Power assisted. Ratio: 17.8:1. Transmission: A-230 3-speed, all-synchromesh manual. No manual transmissions were available in California. Transmission Ratios: 3.02, 1.76, 1.00:1. Optional: NP435, wide-ratio 4-speed manual, synchromesh on top three gears. Transmission ratios: 6.69, 3.34, 1.66, 1.00:1. NP445, close ratio 4-speed manual, synchromesh on all forward gears. Transmission ratios: 4.56, 2.28, 1.31, 1.00:1. Chrysler A-727 3-speed automatic. Ratios: 2.45, 1.45., 1.00:1. Clutch: Single dry plate disc, hydraulic actuation. Clutch diameter: 11 in. dia. Total lining area: 123.7 sq. in.

VEHICLE DIMENSIONS: Wheelbase: 106.0 in. Overall Length: 184.6 in. Front/Rear Tread 65.75 in./63.15 in. Overall Height: 72.0 in. (with optional top). Width: 79.6 in. Front/Rear Overhang: 31.0 in./47 in. Tailgate: Width and Height: 67 in. x 19 in. Approach/Departure Degrees: 31/24. Ground Clearance: Front axle: 7.8 in. Rear axle: 7.3 in. Oil pan: 14.3 in. Transfer case: 10.3 in. Load space: With optional rear bench seat in place: 42.5 in. x 50.5 in. x 41.3 in. With rear seat removed or folded: 78 in. x 50.5 in. x 41.3 in. Front headroom: 37.5 in. Pedal to seat back (max.): 42 in. Steering wheel to seat back (max.): 18.3 in. Seat to ground: 36 in. Floor to ground: 22.2 in.

CAPACITIES: Fuel Tank: 24 gal. Optional: 35 gal. replacement tank.

ACCOMMODATIONS: Seating Capacity: Driver and passenger with standard front bucket seats. Five with optional rear bench seat.

INSTRUMENTATION: 0-100 mph speedometer, 99,999.9 mi. odometer, gauges for fuel level, engine coolant temperature, ammeter. Warning lights for oil pressure, brake system warning, hazard light operation.

OPTIONS AND PRICES: Heavy-duty, 1.1875 in. front stabilizer bar: $26.20. SE Package: $647. 360 cu. in. V-8: $153.75. Tilt steering column. Sky Lite sun roof. AM radio with 40-channel CB. AM/FM/MX stereo with 40-channel CB. AM/FM: $199.50. AM. AM/FM/MX stereo with eight track tape. Chrome styled wheels. White-painted steel-spoke wide Sport wheels: $228.30. Goodyear 10 x 15LT polyester tires: $299.75. Five-slot chrome disc wide Sport road wheels. Electric door locks. Vinyl soft top (dealer-installed). Air conditioning: $578.20. Outside spare tire carrier. Trailer Towing Package: $145.90. Sno-Commander Package. Includes power angling blade, power lift and seven-way control valve. Automatic speed control: $106.80. Padded steering wheel: $42.40. Tilt steering column. Inside hood release. Transfer case skid plate: $65. 35 gal. fuel tank. Fuel tank skid plate: $65. Wide-ratio 4-spd. manual trans. Close-ratio 4-spd. manual trans. Loadflite 3-spd. automatic trans.: $381.35. Automatic transmission oil cooler: $65.40. 3 passenger rear bench seat: $246.20. Command bucket seats (available for SE only): $165.40. Shoulder belts: $49.80. Steel roof. Roll bar: $105. Exterior dual-mount side mirrors: $55. Rear step bumper: $80. Macho Package.

HISTORICAL FOOTNOTES: The 1979 Ramcharger was introduced in August, 1978.

1980 RAMCHARGER

The Ramcharger shared the harvest of Dodge's efforts to reduce overall vehicle weight and improve fuel efficiency with the W series trucks. These included a lighter, by 111 pounds, new part-time New Process 208 transfer case with a die-cast aluminum housing and improved internal operation. No full time four-wheel drive system was offered. The 318 cu. in. V-8 had a lighter cylinder block and intake manifold. These revisions resulted in another weight reduction of 25 pounds. A rear compartment floor mat and rear courtesy lamps were standard equipment on the 1980 Ramcharger. Additional standard features included 48 amp alternator, antifreeze (to -20° F), driver's compartment ashtray, front and rear bright bumpers, insulated dash liner, color-keyed door inner trim panels with armrests, glove box with door, bright/black finish grille, 7 in. round headlights, fresh air heater with defrosters, padded instrument panel, back-up lights, black floor mat with padded front compartment section, exterior dual bright-finish 5 in. x 7 in. mirrors, interior 10 in. mirror, power steering, inside spare tire mounting (located behind right rear wheelwell), driver and passenger color-keyed sun visors, dual jet windshield washers and two-speed windshield wipers. The standard Ramcharger interior included deluxe vinyl low-back bucket seats available in four colors. If desired, these seats could be ordered for the SE interior. The standard SE interior consisted of tilting high-back Command bucket seats in cloth and vinyl trim in a choice of five colors. Inboard folding armrests were also included as was a lockable console with a removable styrofoam beverage chest. Both the standard and interior and the SE version were also available with a deluxe vinyl split-back bench seat available in any of three colors. Additional features of the SE interior consisted of a woodtone applique on the door trim panels, assist straps, carpeting on lower door panel, perforated hardboard headliner (white only) with amberlite backing, color-keyed carpeting with underlayment throughout, color-keyed rear side inner trim panels, color-keyed cowl side trim panels, woodtone applique in instrument panel faceplate with bright trim, instrument panel faceplate with bright trim, instrument panel bright upper and lower molding with woodtone applique insert, Ramcharger SE nameplate on instrument panel, black horn pad with woodtone applique insert and black two-spoke 16.5 in. diameter steering wheel.

1980 Dodge AW100 Ramcharger with Macho Package

Exterior elements of the SE Package consisted of dual vertically stacked rectangular headlights with halogen high beam lamp, bright windshield molding, bright drip rail molding, bright taillamp bezels, bright quarter side window molding, bright liftgate window molding, SE medallion on front fenders, and tailgate surround molding with vinyl tape insert applique. The 1980 color selection consisted of 15 colors: White, cashmere, sunburst orange, Impact yellow, ginger, black, bright silver metallic, Frost blue metallic, medium blue metallic, teal frost metallic, teal green sunfire, dark brown sunfire, medium red sunfire, impact red and impact blue.

I.D. DATA. The vehicle identification number was located on a V.I.N. plate attached to the driver's side door body latch post. The V.I.N. consisted of 13 elements. The first two characters indicated the model code as follows: A1-AW100. The next digit identified the body type as follows: 0-Sport Utility type vehicle. The next entry, a letter, identified the GVW rating as follows: B-6001 to 10,000 lb. The next unit, a letter, designated the engine type as follows: E-318-2 bbl. T-360-4 bbl. The next unit, the letter A, indicted the 1980 model year. Following this came a letter indicating the assembly plant as follows: C-Jefferson Assembly Plant, K-Pillette Road Truck, L-Lago Alberto Assembly Plant (Mexico), M-Toluca Assembly Plant (Mexico), N-Burt Road (KDX), S-Warren Truck #1, T-Warren Truck #2 (Sherwood), X-Missouri Truck, V-Warner Truck #3 (Comapcy). The V.I.N. ended with a six-digit production sequence number at the assembly plant as follows: 100001 at Warren Truck #1, Missouri Truck and Pillette Truck Plant. 500001 at Warren Truck #2. 700001 at Warren Truck Plant #3. All models began with sequence number 000,001.

Body Type	Factory Price	GVW	Shipping Weight	Prod. Total
AW100 Ramcharger				
AW100, Utility, 318 V-8	$8298	5850[a]	4150	9411*

a 6050 lb. with Sno-Commander Package.
* Production total for all models.

STANDARD ENGINE: Features include a drop-forged five-bearing crankshaft, chain-driven camshaft, free-turning exhaust valves, drop-forged I-beam connecting rods and silent-chain camshaft. Engine Type: OHV, V-8. Cast iron block and cylinder head. Bore x Stroke: 3.91 in. x 3.312 in. Lifters: Hydraulic. Number of main bearings-5. Fuel Induction: Single 2-bbl. carburetor. (not available in California, where a 4-bbl. version was offered). Compression Ratio: 8.6:1. Displacement: 318 cu. in. (5.2 liters). Horsepower: Net 135 @ 4000 rpm. Torque: Net: 240 lb.-ft. @ 2000 rpm. Oil refill capacity: 5 qt. Fuel Requirements: Unleaded.

OPTIONAL ENGINE: OHV V-8. Features include vibration damper, 18 in. 4-blade fan and drop-forged crankshaft. Engine Type: OHV, V-8. Cast iron block and cylinder head. Bore x Stroke: 4.00 in. x 3.58 in. Lifters: Hydraulic. Number of main bearings-5. Fuel Induction: Single 2-bbl. carburetor. (not available in California, where a 4-bbl. version was offered). Compression Ratio: 8.2:1. Displacement: 360 cu. in. (5.9 liters). Horsepower: 160 @ 4000 rpm. California rating is 175 @ 4000 rpm. Torque: Net: 280 lb.-ft. @ 2000 rpm. California rating is 275 lb.-ft. @ 2400 rpm. Oil refill capacity: 5 qt. Fuel Requirements: Unleaded.

CHASSIS FEATURES: Separate body and frame, ladder-type, drop center frame, 36,000 psi, 2.86 in. modules.

SUSPENSION AND RUNNING GEAR: Front Suspension: 48 in. x 2.5 in. Semi-elliptical leaf springs, 1.0 in. stabilizer bar and 1.0 in. tubular shock absorbers. 1640 lb. rating. Optional: 1.1875 in. shock absorbers and 2100 b. capacity springs with Sno-Commander Package. Rear Suspension: 52 in. x 2.5 in. Semi-elliptical leaf springs, and 1.0 in. tubular shock absorbers. 1820 lbs. Optional: 1.1875 in. shock absorbers. Front Axle Type and Capacity: Spicer 44F-B-J full-floating, 3500 lb. capacity. Optional: 4000 lb. Rear Axle Type and Capacity: Chrysler 9.25 in. Semi-floating, hypoid-type 3600 lb. capacity. Optional: None. Final Drive Ratio: 3.21:1 with 4-spd. trans., 2.94:1 with auto. trans. Optional: 3.55:1. Transfer Case: New Process 208 part-time, two-speed: 2.61, 1.00:1. Brakes: Type: Power, hydraulic. Front: Discs. Rear: Drums. Dimensions: Front: 11.75 in. x 1.256 in. disc. Rear: 11 in. x 2.5 in. Brake swept lining area: 404 sq. in. Wheels: 15 x 6.5 in. 5-stud disc. Optional: 15 x 7.0 in. (aluminum radial ribbed), 15 x 7 in. (five-slot chrome disc), 15 x 7 in. (white painted steel spoke). Tires: P235/7515B BSW PBB. Optional: P235/75R15B BSW GBR, P235/75R15B WSW GBR, P235/7515C BSW PBB (standard with Sno-Commander package), P235/75R15C BSW GBR, P235/75R15B WSW XSBR, P255/70R15B OWL SBR, LR60-15B OWL ABR, 10-15LTB OWL PBB, 7.00-15D BSW NBB. Steering: Recirculating ball. Ratio: 24:1, turns Lock-to-Lock: 3.5:1. Turning Circle: 36.9 ft. Optional: Power assisted. Ratio: 17.8:1. Transmission: A-230 3-speed, all-synchromesh manual. No manual transmissions were available in California. Transmission Ratios: 3.02, 1.76, 1.00:1. Optional: NP435, wide-ratio 4-speed manual, synchromesh on top three gears. Transmission ratios: 6.69, 3.34, 1.66, 1.00:1. NP445, close ratio 4-speed manual, synchromesh on all forward gears. Transmission ratios: 4.56, 2.28, 1.31, 1.00:1. Chrysler A-727 3-speed automatic. Ratios: 2.45, 1.45., 1.00:1. Clutch: Single dry plate disc, hydraulic actuation. Clutch diameter: 11 in. dia. Total lining area: 123.7 sq. in.

VEHICLE DIMENSIONS: Wheelbase: 106.0 in. Overall Length: 184.6 in. Front/Rear Tread 65.75 in./63.15 in. Overall Height: 72.0 in. (with optional top). Width: 79.6 in. Front/Rear Overhang: 31.0 in./47 in. Tailgate: Width and Height: 67 in. x 19 in. Approach/Departure Degrees: 31/24. Ground Clearance: Front axle: 7.8 in. Rear axle: 7.3 in. Oil pan: 14.3 in. Transfer case: 10.3 in. Load space: With optional rear bench seat in place: 42.5 in. x 50.5 in. x 41.3 in. With rear seat removed or folded: 78 in. x 50.5 in. x 41.3 in. Front headroom: 37.5 in. Pedal to seat back (max.): 42 in. Steering wheel to seat back (max.): 18.3 in. Seat to ground: 36 in. Floor to ground: 22.2 in.

CAPACITIES: Fuel Tank: 24 gal. Optional: 35 gal. replacement tank.

ACCOMMODATIONS: Seating Capacity: Driver and passenger with standard front bucket seats. Five with optional rear bench seat.

INSTRUMENTATION: 0-100 mph speedometer, 99,999.9 mi. odometer, gauges for fuel level, engine coolant temperature, ammeter. Warning lights for oil pressure, brake system warning, hazard light operation.

OPTIONS AND PRICES: Anti-Spin rear differential: $197. Loadflite automatic trans.: $233. Power windows. Electric front door locks. AM/FM stereo radio with Search-Tune. AM/FM stereo radio with cassette tape player. Fold-up rear seat. Tilt steering column. Transfer case skid plate. Aluminum radial-ribbed road wheels. 5/50 Protection Plan. Air conditioning: $611. 63 amp alternator. 117 amp alternator. 59 amp-hr./375 amp cold crank battery. 70 amp-hr./ 430 amp cold crank maintenance-free battery. 85 amp-hr./500 amp cold crank Long Life battery. Black shoulder belts for driver and front seat passenger: $53. Painted rear step type bumper. Bright rear hitch type bumper. Cigarette lighter. Lockable console (standard on Ramcharger SE): $99. Auxiliary transmission oil to air cooler. Maximum engine cooling. 35 gal. fuel tank: $35. Rear bench seat: $246. Oil pressure gauge. Speedometer (kilometers/ miles) and odometer (kilometers). Privacy sunscreen glass. Tinted glass for all windows: $52. Quad rectangular headlights with halogen high beam (standard on SE). Deluxe heater. Engine block heater. Interior hood lock release. Dual electric horns. Two rubber, color-keyed floor mats for front floor). Low mount dual exterior 6 in. x 9 in bright mirrors: $65. Low mount extended 7.5 in. x 10.5 in bright mirrors. Lower exterior body moldings: $97. Upper exterior body moldings: $71. Upper and lower exterior body moldings. Power front door locks: $100. Power front door windows: $148. Two-tone paint: $159.30. AM radio. AM/FM radio. AM/FM stereo radio. AM/FM stereo radio with Search-Tune: $172. AM/FM stereo radio with eight-track tape player. AM/FM stereo radio with cassette tape player and Dolby noise reduction

system. AM/FM stereo radio with 40-channel CB transceiver. Roll bar: $112. Heavy-duty front and rear 1.1875 in. shock absorbers. Fuel tank skid plate: $66. Transfer case skid plate: $66. Sky Lite sun roof. Automatic speed control. Heavy-duty front stabilizer bar. Tilt type steering column: $83. Four-spoke "Sport" 15 in. steering wheel. Outside mounted swing out tire carrier. Bright wheelcovers. Aluminum radial finned road-type 15 in. x 7 in. wheels: $101. Chrome disc five slot road-type 15 in. x 7 in. wheels. Painted steel spoke white road-type 15 in. x 7 in. wheels. Ramcharger SE Package: $666. Convenience Package: $62. Includes day/night 10 in. rear vision mirror, glove box lock and light, ashtray, in-cab actuated hood lock release. Insulation Package (standard with SE). Includes perforated headboard headliner (white only) with amberlite backing, rear floor mat (black only) with underlayment. Protection Package. Includes door edge protectors, bright front bumper with guards and nerf strips, bright rear bumper with nerf strips. Macho Package: $511. Includes four 15 in. x 7.0 in. white painted steel spoke road wheels (with conventional steel spare wheel), "Sport" four-spoke steering wheel, low-luster black painted front and rear bumpers, special low-luster black paint treatment and black/orange tape stripes on lower portion of vehicle, tailgate decals "4WD" and "Dodge" in black with color accent and limited monotone exterior paint color selection. Required at extra cost with the Macho Package were five 10-15LT outline white letter tires priced at $335. Sno-Commander Package. Includes power angling 7.5 ft. plow, power lift, seven-way control valve, plow lights, 35 gal. fuel tank and larger capacity front leaf springs. Light-Duty Trailer Towing Package. Includes maximum engine cooling, heavy-duty variable load flasher, seven-wire harness, rear step type painted rear bumper, Class 1 1.875 in. ball hitch. Heavy-Duty Trailer Towing Package. Includes maximum engine cooling, 63 amp alternator, 70 amp hour/4530 amp cold crank battery, heavy-duty variable-load flasher, seven wire harness, heavy-duty front and rear shock absorbers, Class IV tow-bar hitch, heavy-duty front stabilizer bar and 35 gal. fuel tank.

HISTORICAL FOOTNOTES: The 1980 Ramcharger was introduced in August, 1979.

1981 RAMCHARGER

The Ramcharger shared its new-from-the-doors-forward sheetmetal with the Dodge pickup trucks. Although no exterior sheetmetal was carried over from 1980, the latest Ramcharger still looked like a Dodge product. Its more streamlined form and new front end dominated by a rectangular grille with larger grid dividers conveyed an image of continued rugged design along with a more contemporary design. This latter feature was further enhanced by the Ramcharger's new permanent integral roof and lightweight fiberglass liftgate. According to Chrysler research, only two percent of Ramcharger owners ever bothered to remove the roof. The new design also incorporated rear windows that wrapped upward into the roof section. These windows did not open but ventilation was provided by a standard pop-up rear roof vent. The side windows were also available with an optional dark tint that allowed a measured amount of light to enter the vehicle but kept most of the heat out. The interior featured a new dash and relocated radio with easy to use controls. Most of the major instruments were positioned in three circular pods located in a large, semi-rectangular bezel. The dash panel was constructed of a one-piece molded Noryl material and had built-in defroster vents and a graphic electronic display that registered the status of the front axle, the transfer case gear selected and an alert if the rear liftgate was open. The front suspension was slightly revised for improved riding comfort. New standard Borg Warner automatic front locking hubs were introduced for 1981. The hubs were engaged simply by shifting into four-wheel drive. To disengage the hubs the driver shifted the Ramcharger into two-wheel drive and backed up about ten feet. Additional revisions for 1981 included a more efficient and quieter heater, an improved air conditioning system, the use of the 35 gal. fuel tank and radial tires as standard equipment, and the availability of optional intermittent windshield wipers. Manual transmission models were now available with cruise control. Rear passenger legroom was extended by four inches due to a deeper floorpan. This change required the relocation of a frame cross member. A rear bench seat was now standard but it was also order to specify it as a delete option. Exterior colors for 1981 included bright silver metallic, medium seaspray green metallic, impact orange, daystar blue metallic, cashmere, impact red, nightwatch blue, ginger, medium crimson red, impact blue, coffee brown metallic, metallic black, light seaspray green metallic, graphic yellow and pearl white.

I.D. DATA: The vehicle identification number was located on a plate attached to the driver's side door body latch post. The V.I.N. consisted of 13 elements. The first two characters indicated the model code as follows: A1-AW100. The next digit identified the body type as follows: 0-Sport Utility type vehicle. The next entry, a letter, identified the GVW rating as follows: B-6001 to 10,000 lb. The next unit, a letter, designated the engine type as follows: E-318-2 bbl. P-318-4 bbl. T-360-4 bbl. The next unit, the letter B, indicated the 1981 model year. Following this came a letter indicating the assembly plant as follows: C-Jefferson Assembly Plant, K-Pillette Road Truck, L-Lago Alberto Assembly Plant (Mexico), M-Toluca Assembly Plant (Mexico), N-Burt Road (KDX), S-Warren Truck #1, T-Warren Truck #2 (Sherwood), X-Missouri Truck, V-Warner Truck #3 (Comapcy). The V.I.N. ended with a six-digit production sequence number at the assembly plant as follows: 100001 at Warren Truck #1, Missouri Truck and Pillette Truck Plant. 500001 at Warren Truck #2. 700001 at Warren Truck Plant #3. All models began with sequence number 000,001.

Body Type	Factory Price	GVW	Shipping Weight	Prod. Total
AW100 Ramcharger				
AW100, Utility, 318 V-8	$9466	5300[a]	4174	—

a 5850 lb. GVW optional.

STANDARD ENGINE: Features include a drop-forged five-bearing crankshaft, chain-driven camshaft, free-turning exhaust valves, drop-forged I-beam connecting rods and silent-chain camshaft. Engine Type: OHV, V-8. Cast iron block and cylinder head. Bore x Stroke: 3.91 in. x 3.312 in. Lifters: Hydraulic. Number of main bearings-5. Fuel Induction: Single Holley 2-bbl. carburetor. Compression Ratio: 8.7:1. Displacement: 318 cu. in. (5.2 liters). Horsepower: Net 140 @ 3600 rpm. Torque: Net: 240 lb.-ft. @ 2400 rpm. Oil refill capacity: 5 qt. with filter change. Fuel Requirements: Unleaded.

OPTIONAL ENGINE: Available only with automatic transmission. Features include a drop-forged five-bearing crankshaft, chain-driven camshaft, free-turning exhaust valves, drop-forged I-beam connecting rods and silent-chain camshaft. Engine Type: OHV, V-8. Cast iron block and cylinder head. Bore x Stroke: 3.91 in. x 3.312 in. Lifters: Hydraulic. Number of main bearings-5. Fuel Induction: Single Holley 4-bbl. carburetor. Compression Ratio: 8.7:1. Displacement: 318 cu. in. (5.2 liters). Oil refill capacity: 5 qt. with filter change. Fuel Requirements: Unleaded.

OPTIONAL ENGINE: OHV V-8. Available in 49 states with 4-spd. manual transmission only. In California available with automatic transmission only. Features include vibration damper, 18 in. 4-blade fan and drop-forged crankshaft. Engine Type: OHV, V-8. Cast iron block and cylinder head. Bore x Stroke: 4.00 in. x 3.58 in. Lifters: Hydraulic. Number of main bearings-5. Fuel Induction: Single 4-bbl. Holley carburetor. Compression Ratio: 8.6:1. Displacement: 360 cu. in. (5.9 liters). Horsepower: 175 @ 4000 rpm. Torque: Net: 260 lb.-ft. @ 2000 rpm. Oil refill capacity: 5 qt. Fuel Requirements: Unleaded.

CHASSIS FEATURES: Separate body and frame, ladder-type, drop center frame, 36,000 psi, 2.86 in. modules.

SUSPENSION AND RUNNING GEAR: Front Suspension: 48 in. x 2.5 in. Semi-elliptical leaf springs, 1.0 in. stabilizer bar and 1.0 in. tubular shock absorbers. 1640 lb. rating. Optional: 1.1875 in. shock absorbers. Optional Rating: 1800 lb. Rear Suspension: 52 in. x 2.5 in. Semi-elliptical leaf springs, and 1.0 in. tubular shock absorbers. 1820 lbs. Optional: 1.1875 in. shock absorbers. Optional Rating: None. Front Axle Type and Capacity: Spicer 44F-B-J full-floating, 3500 lb. capacity. Optional: None. Rear Axle Type and Capacity: Chrysler 9.25 in. Semi-floating, hypoid-type 3600 lb. capacity. Optional: None. Final Drive Ratio: 318 2-bbl. and 4-spd. trans.: 3.21:1. Optional: 3.21:1 with rear limited slip differential. 318 4-bbl. and auto. trans.: 3.21:1. Optional: 3.55:1. 360 4-bbl. and 4-spd. manual: 3.21:1. Optional 3.55:1. In California the 3128 engine was offered only with auto. trans. and 3.21:1. The 360 engine was available only with auto. trans. and either 3.21:1 or 3.55:1 ratios. Transfer Case: New Process 208 part-time, two-speed: 2.61, 1.00:1. Brakes: Type: Power, hydraulic. Front: Discs. Rear: Drums. Dimensions: Front: 11.75 in. x 1.256 in. disc. Rear: 10 in. x 2.5 in. Brake swept lining area: Sq. in. Wheels: 15 x 6.5 in. 5-stud disc. Optional: 15 x 7.0 in. (aluminum radial ribbed), 15 x 7 in. (five-slot chrome disc), 15 x 7 in. (white painted steel spoke). Tires: P235/75R15. Optional: P255/70R15, LR60 x 15B,10R x 15B, 7.00R x 15D. Steering: Saginaw integral power steering. Turning Circle: 36.9 ft. Optional: None. Transmission: NP435, wide-ratio 4-speed manual, synchromesh on top three gears. Transmission ratios: 6.69, 3.34, 1.66, 1.00:1. Optional: 3-speed automatic transmission: Ratios: 2.45, 1.45., 1.00:1. Clutch: Single dry plate disc, hydraulic actuation lining. Clutch diameter: 11 in. dia. Total lining area: 123.0 sq. in. Optional: None.

VEHICLE DIMENSIONS: Wheelbase: 106.0 in. Overall Length: 184.6 in. Front/Rear Tread: 65.7 in./63.4 in. Overall Height: 74.0 in. Width: 79.5 in. Front/Rear Overhang: 32.5 in./45.5 in. Tailgate: Width and Height: 37.5 in. x 50.5 in. Approach/Departure Degrees: 33/22.5. Ground Clearance: Front axle: 8.5 in. Rear axle: 8.0 in. Oil pan: 15.6 in. Transfer case: 11.0 in. Load space: With rear bench seat in place: 33 in. x 49.0 in. x 40.5 in. With rear seat removed or folded: 54 in. x 50 in. x 40.5 in. Front headroom: 37.75 in. Pedal to seat back (max.): 46 in. Steering wheel to seat back (max.): 19.25 in. Seat to ground: 37 in. Floor to ground: 23 in.

CAPACITIES: Fuel Tank: 35 gal.

ACCOMMODATIONS: Seating Capacity: Five with standard rear bench seat.

INSTRUMENTATION: 0-100 mph speedometer, 99,999.9 mi. odometer, gauges for fuel level and ammeter. Warning lights for oil pressure, engine coolant temperature, brake system warning, hazard light operation, liftgate ajar and 4x4 front hubs.

OPTIONS AND PRICES: 360 cu. in. V-8: $132. 318 cu. in. V-8 Performance Package (4-bbl. carburetor): $132. Anti-spin rear differential: $209. Automatic transmission: $234. Sunscreen glass: $154. Maximum engine cooling: $46. Air conditioning: $634. 117 amp alternator: $82. 85 amp battery: $43. Cruise control: $123. Tilt steering wheel: $88. Power windows: $157. Power door locks: $106. Digital clock: $55. AM/FM stereo radio with Dolby sound and cassette tape player: $241. Low mount bright exterior mirrors: $69. Rear step bumper: $68. Two-tone paint: $375. Aluminum wheels: $321. Spare aluminum wheel: $80. Heavy-duty shock absorbers: $30. Front heavy-duty stabilizer bar: $30. Fuel tank skid plate: $70. Transfer tank skid plate: $70. Goodyear Wrangler 10R x15 radial tires: $314. Convenience Package: $98. Royal SE Package: $1044. Macho Package: $2371. Towing Package: $303. Front winch: $355. Skylite sun roof: $355.

HISTORICAL FOOTNOTES: The 1981 Ramcharger was introduced in August, 1980.

1982 RAMCHARGER

There were no major changes in the Ramcharger for 1982.

I.D. DATA: The vehicle identification number was located on a plate attached to the driver's side door body latch post. The V.I.N. consisted of 13 elements. The first two characters indicated the model code as follows: A1-AW100. The next digit identified the body type as follows: 0-Sport Utility type vehicle. The next entry, a letter, identified the GVW rating as follows: B-6001 to 10,000 lb. The next unit, a letter, designated the engine type as follows: E-318-2 bbl. P-318-4 bbl. T-360-4 bbl. The next unit, the letter C, indicated the 1982 model year. Following this came a letter indicating the assembly plant as follows: C-Jefferson Assembly Plant, K-Pillette Road Truck, L-Lago Alberto Assembly Plant (Mexico), M-Toluca Assembly Plant (Mexico), N-Burt Road (KDX), S-Warren Truck #1, T-Warren Truck #2 (Sherwood), X-Missouri Truck, V-Warner Truck #3 (Comapcy). The V.I.N. ended with a six-digit production sequence number at the assembly plant as follows: 100001 at Warren Truck #1, Missouri Truck and Pillette Truck Plant. 500001 at Warren Truck #2. 700001 at Warren Truck Plant #3. All models began with sequence number 000,001.

Body Type	Factory Price	GVW	Shipping Weight	Prod. Total
AW100 Ramcharger				
AW100, Utility, 318 V-8	$10,095	5850	4163	—

STANDARD ENGINE: Features include a drop-forged five-bearing crankshaft, chain-driven camshaft, free-turning exhaust valves, drop-forged I-beam connecting rods and silent-chain camshaft. Engine Type: OHV, V-8. Cast iron block and cylinder head. Bore x Stroke: 3.91 in. x 3.312 in. Lifters: Hydraulic. Number of main bearings-5. Fuel Induction: Single Holley 2-bbl. carburetor. Compression Ratio: 8.7:1. Displacement: 318 cu. in. (5.2 liters). Horsepower: Net 140 @ 3600 rpm. Torque: Net: 240 lb.-ft. @ 2400 rpm. Oil refill capacity: 5 qt. with filter change. Fuel Requirements: Unleaded.

OPTIONAL ENGINE: Available only with automatic transmission. Features include a drop-forged five-bearing crankshaft, chain-driven camshaft, free-turning exhaust valves, drop-forged I-beam connecting rods and silent-chain camshaft. Engine Type: OHV, V-8. Cast iron block and cylinder head. Bore x Stroke: 3.91 in. x 3.312 in. Lifters: Hydraulic. Number of main bearings-5. Fuel Induction: Single Holley 4-bbl. carburetor. Compression Ratio: 8.7:1. Displacement: 318 cu. in. (5.2 liters). Oil refill capacity: 5 qt. with filter change. Fuel Requirements: Unleaded.

OPTIONAL ENGINE: OHV V-8. Available in 49 states with 4-spd. manual transmission only. In California available with automatic transmission only. Features include vibration damper, 18 in. 4-blade fan and drop-forged crankshaft. Engine Type: OHV, V-8. Cast iron block and cylinder head. Bore x Stroke: 4.00 in. x 3.58 in. Lifters: Hydraulic. Number of main bearings-5.

Fuel Induction: Single 4-bbl. Holley carburetor. Compression Ratio: 8.6:1. Displacement: 360 cu. in. (5.9 liters). Horsepower: 175 @ 4000 rpm. Torque: Net: 260 lb.-ft. @ 2000 rpm. Oil refill capacity: 5 qt. Fuel Requirements: Unleaded.

CHASSIS FEATURES: Separate body and frame, ladder-type, drop center frame, 36,000 psi, 2.86 in. modules.

SUSPENSION AND RUNNING GEAR: Front Suspension: 48 in. x 2.5 in. Semi-elliptical leaf springs, 1.0 in. stabilizer bar and 1.0 in. tubular shock absorbers. 1640 lb. rating. Optional: 1.1875 in. shock absorbers. Optional Rating: 1800 lb. Rear Suspension: 52 in. x 2.5 in. Semi-elliptical leaf springs, and 1.0 in. tubular shock absorbers. 1820 lbs. Optional: 1.1875 in. shock absorbers. Optional Rating: None. Front Axle Type and Capacity: Spicer 44F-B-J full-floating, 3500 lb. capacity. Optional: None. Rear Axle Type and Capacity: Chrysler 9.25 in. Semi-floating, hypoid-type 3600 lb. capacity. Optional: None. Final Drive Ratio: 318 2-bbl. and 4-spd. trans.: 3.21:1. Optional: 3.21:1 with rear limited slip differential. 318 4-bbl. and auto. trans.: 3.21:1. Optional: 3.55:1. 360 4-bbl. and 4-spd. manual: 3.21:1. Optional 3.55:1. In California the 3128 engine was offered only with auto. trans. and 3.21:1. The 360 engine was available only with auto. trans. and either 3.21:1 or 3.55:1 ratios. Transfer Case: New Process 208 part-time, two-speed: 2.61, 1.00:1. Brakes: Type: Power, hydraulic. Front: Discs. Rear: Drums. Dimensions: Front: 11.75 in. x 1.256 in. disc. Rear: 10 in. x 2.5 in. Brake swept lining area: Sq. in. Wheels: 15 x 6.5 in. 5-stud disc. Optional: 15 x 7.0 in. (aluminum radial ribbed), 15 x 7 in. (five-slot chrome disc), 15 x 7 in. (white painted steel spoke). Tires: P235/75R15. Optional: P255/70R15, LR60 x 15B,10R x 15B, 7.00R x 15D. Steering: Saginaw integral power steering. Turning Circle: 36.9 ft. Optional: None. Transmission: NP435, wide-ratio 4-speed manual, synchromesh on top three gears. Transmission ratios: 6.69, 3.34, 1.66, 1.00:1. Optional: 3-speed automatic transmission: Ratios: 2.45, 1.45., 1.00:1. Clutch: Single dry plate disc, hydraulic actuation lining. Clutch diameter: 11 in. dia. Total lining area: 123.0 sq. in. Optional: None.

VEHICLE DIMENSIONS: Wheelbase: 106.0 in. Overall Length: 184.6 in. Front/Rear Tread: 65.7 in./63.4 in. Overall Height: 74.0 in. Width: 79.5 in. Front/Rear Overhang: 32.5 in./45.5 in. Tailgate: Width and Height: 37.5 in. x 50.5 in. Approach/Departure Degrees: 33/22.5. Ground Clearance: Front axle: 8.5 in. Rear axle: 8.0 in. Oil pan: 15.6 in. Transfer case: 11.0 in. Load space: With rear bench seat in place: 33 in. x 49.0 in. x 40.5 in. With rear seat removed or folded: 54 in. x 50 in. x 40.5 in. Front headroom: 37.75 in. Pedal to seat back (max.): 46 in. Steering wheel to seat back (max.): 19.25 in. Seat to ground: 37 in. Floor to ground: 23 in.

CAPACITIES: Fuel Tank: 35 gal.

ACCOMMODATIONS: Seating Capacity: Five with standard (optional for Custom) Royal SE Package rear bench seat.

INSTRUMENTATION: 0-100 mph speedometer, 99,999.9 mi. odometer, gauges for fuel level and ammeter. Warning lights for oil pressure, engine coolant temperature, brake system warning, hazard light operation, liftgate ajar and 4x4 front hubs.

OPTIONS AND PRICES: 360 cu. in. V-8: 318 cu. in. V-8 Performance Package (4-bbl. carburetor). Anti-spin rear differential. Sunscreen glass: $156. Gold-filigree tape trim: $220. Maximum engine cooling. Air conditioning: $677. 117 amp alternator. 85 amp battery. Cruise control: $159. Tilt steering wheel. Power windows. Power door locks. Digital clock: $73. AM/FM radio: $88. AM/FM stereo radio with Dolby sound and cassette tape player. Low mount bright exterior mirrors. Rear step bumper. Two-tone paint. Aluminum wheels: $339. Spare aluminum wheel. Heavy-duty shock absorbers. Front heavy-duty stabilizer bar. Fuel tank skid plate. Transfer tank skid plate. Goodyear Wrangler 10R x 15 white letter radial tires: $666. Convenience Package: $85. Royal SE Package. Macho Package. Towing Package. Front winch. Skylite sun roof.

HISTORICAL FOOTNOTES: The latest Ramcharger was promoted as one of "America's Driving Machines" in 1982.

1983 RAMCHARGER

The Ramcharger was unchanged in appearance for 1983. Its standard equipment content was as follows: Ashtray, front and rear bright bumpers, cigarette lighter, insulated dash liner, color-keyed inner door trim panels with armrests and pull straps, black floormat for front compartment, tinted glass for all windows, glove box with door, aluminum grille with painted plastic insert and headlight doors, color-keyed soft headliner, fresh air hearer with defrosters, inner hood panel insulation, in-cab hood release, dual electric horns, bright hubcaps, combination map/courtesy light on instrument panel, rear compartment courtesy lights, exterior dual bright finish short arm 5 in. x 7 in. mirrors, interior 10 in. day/night mirror, bright moldings for windshield and quarter side windows, power steering, AM radio, rear roof vent, inside spare tire mount, driver and passenger sun visors, dual jet windshield wipers and 2-speed windshield wipers.

1983 Dodge AW150 Ramcharger

Deluxe vinyl high-back bucket seats were standard for the base Ramcharger Custom. They were available in red, beige or blue. The standard Royal SE Package seats were cloth and vinyl trimmed high-back bucket seats also offered in red, beige and blue. In addition, the package included inboard folding armrests, a locking center console and a rear three passenger folding bench seat. It was possible to order the SE interior fitted with the standard Custom bucket seats. Royal SE exterior features consisted of bright drip rail molding, bright taillamp housing, ram's head hood ornament, Leaping Ram ornament with "150 Royal SE" plaque on front fender, bright aluminum grille with chromed plastic insert and headlamp doors, liftgate upper and lower moldings with bright applique panel. Additional Royal SE interior elements included a woodtone trim door applique, assist strap, carpeting on lower door panel, color-keyed carpeting throughout with underlayment, color-keyed rear side and liftgate inner trim panels, woodtone instrument panel cluster faceplate, "Royal SE-Engineered Ram Tough" on instrument panel, Sport steering wheel, color-keyed spare tire cover (not available with 10RLT tires), bright front door sill scuff plate, oil pressure and engine coolant temperature gauges, trip odometer and color-keyed cowl inner trim panels.

The 1983 Ramcharger color choice consisted of these colors: Burnished silver metallic, beige sand, light blue metallic, pearl white, graphic red, crimson red, black, charcoal grey metallic, nightwatch blue, sable brown and spice metallic.

I.D. DATA: The vehicle identification number was located on a plate attached to the driver's side door body latch post. The V.I.N. consisted of 13 elements. The first two characters indicated the model code as follows: A1-AW100. The next digit identified the body type as follows: 0-Sport Utility type vehicle. The next entry, a letter, identified the GVW rating as follows: B-6001 to 10,000 lb. The next unit, a letter, designated the engine type as follows: E-318-2 bbl. P-318-4 bbl. T-360-4 bbl. The next unit, the letter D, indicated the 1983 model year. Following this came a letter indicating the assembly plant as follows: C-Jefferson Assembly Plant, K-Pillette Road Truck, L-Lago Alberto Assembly Plant (Mexico), M-Toluca Assembly Plant (Mexico), N-Burt Road (KDX), S-Warren Truck #1, T-Warren Truck #2 (Sherwood), X-Missouri Truck, V-Warner Truck #3 (Comapcy). The V.I.N. ended with a six-digit production sequence number at the assembly plant as follows: 100001 at Warren Truck #1, Missouri Truck and Pillette Truck Plant. 500001 at Warren Truck #2. 700001 at Warren Truck Plant #3. All models began with sequence number 000,001.

Body Type	Factory Price	GVW	Shipping Weight	Prod. Total
AW100 Ramcharger				
AW100, Utility, 318 V-8	$11,039	5850*	4065	—

* 6200 lb. GVW Package optional.

STANDARD ENGINE: Features include a drop-forged five-bearing crankshaft, chain-driven camshaft, free-turning exhaust valves, drop-forged I-beam connecting rods and silent-chain camshaft. Engine Type: OHV, V-8. Cast iron block and cylinder head. Bore x Stroke: 3.91 in. x 3.312 in. Lifters: Hydraulic. Number of main bearings-5. Fuel Induction: Single Holley 2-bbl. carburetor. Compression Ratio: 8.7:1. Displacement: 318 cu. in. (5.2 liters). Horsepower: Net 140 @ 3600 rpm. Torque: Net: 240 lb.-ft. @ 2400 rpm. Oil refill capacity: 5 qt. with filter change. Fuel Requirements: Unleaded.

OPTIONAL ENGINE: Available only with automatic transmission. Features include a drop-forged five-bearing crankshaft, chain-driven camshaft, free-turning exhaust valves, drop-forged I-beam connecting rods and silent-chain camshaft. Engine Type: OHV, V-8. Cast iron block and cylinder head. Bore x Stroke: 3.91 in. x 3.312 in. Lifters: Hydraulic. Number of main bearings-5. Fuel Induction: Single Holley 4-bbl. carburetor. Compression Ratio: 8.7:1. Displacement: 318 cu. in. (5.2 liters). Oil refill capacity: 5 qt. with filter change. Fuel Requirements: Unleaded.

OPTIONAL ENGINE: OHV V-8. Available in 49 states with 4-spd. manual transmission only. In California available with automatic transmission only. Features include vibration damper, 18 in. 4-blade fan and drop-forged crankshaft. Engine Type: OHV, V-8. Cast iron block and cylinder head. Bore x Stroke: 4.00 in. x 3.58 in. Lifters: Hydraulic. Number of main bearings-5. Fuel Induction: Single 4-bbl. Holley carburetor. Compression Ratio: 8.6:1. Displacement: 360 cu. in. (5.9 liters). Horsepower: 175 @ 4000 rpm. Torque: Net: 260 lb.-ft. @ 2000 rpm. Oil refill capacity: 5 qt. Fuel Requirements: Unleaded.

CHASSIS FEATURES: Separate body and frame, ladder-type, drop center frame, 36,000 psi, 2.86 in. modules.

SUSPENSION AND RUNNING GEAR: Front Suspension: 48 in. x 2.5 in. Semi-elliptical leaf springs, 1.0 in. stabilizer bar and 1.0 in. tubular shock absorbers. 1640 lb. rating. Optional: 1.1875 in. shock absorbers. Optional Rating: 1800 lb. Rear Suspension: 52 in. x 2.5 in. Semi-elliptical leaf springs, and 1.0 in. tubular shock absorbers. 1820 lbs. Optional: 1.1875 in. shock absorbers. Optional Rating: None. Front Axle Type and Capacity: Spicer 44F-B-J full-floating, 3500 lb. capacity. Optional: None. Rear Axle Type and Capacity: Chrysler 9.25 in. Semi-floating, hypoid-type 3600 lb. capacity. Optional: None. Final Drive Ratio: 318 2-bbl. and 4-spd. trans.: 3.21:1. Optional: 3.21:1 with rear limited slip differential. 318 4-bbl. and auto. trans.: 3.21:1. Optional: 3.55:1. 360 4-bbl. and 4-spd. manual: 3.21:1. Optional 3.55:1. In California the 3128 engine was offered only with auto. trans. and 3.21:1. The 360 engine was available only with auto. trans. and either 3.21:1 or 3.55:1 ratios. Transfer Case: New Process 208 part-time, two-speed: 2.61, 1.00:1. Brakes: Type: Power, hydraulic. Front: Discs. Rear: Drums. Dimensions: Front: 11.75 in. x 1.256 in. disc. Rear: 10 in. x 2.5 in. Brake swept lining area: Sq. in. Wheels: 15 x 6.5 in. 5-stud disc. Optional: 15 x 7.0 in. (aluminum radial ribbed), 15 x 7 in. (five-slot chrome disc), 15 x 7 in. (white painted steel spoke). Tires: P235/75R15. Optional: P255/70R15, LR60 x 15B,10R x 15B, 7.00R x 15D. Steering: Saginaw integral power steering. Turning Circle: 36.9 ft. Optional: None. Transmission: NP435, wide-ratio 4-speed manual, synchromesh on top three gears. Transmission ratios: 6.69, 3.34, 1.66, 1.00:1. Optional: 3-speed automatic transmission: Ratios: 2.45, 1.45., 1.00:1. Clutch: Single dry plate disc, hydraulic actuation lining. Clutch diameter: 11 in. dia. Total lining area: 123.0 sq. in. Optional: None.

VEHICLE DIMENSIONS: Wheelbase: 106.0 in. Overall Length: 184.6 in. Front/Rear Tread: 65.7 in./63.4 in. Overall Height: 74.0 in. Width: 79.5 in. Front/Rear Overhang: 32.5 in./45.5 in. Tailgate: Width and Height: 37.5 in. x 50.5 in. Approach/Departure Degrees: 33/22.5. Ground Clearance: Front axle: 8.5 in. Rear axle: 8.0 in. Oil pan: 15.6 in. Transfer case: 11.0 in. Load space: With rear bench seat in place: 33 in. x 49.0 in. x 40.5 in. With rear seat removed or folded: 54 in. x 50 in. x 40.5 in. Front headroom: 37.75 in. Pedal to seat back (max.): 46 in. Steering wheel to seat back (max.): 19.25 in. Seat to ground: 37 in. Floor to ground: 23 in.

CAPACITIES: Fuel Tank: 35 gal.

ACCOMMODATIONS: Seating Capacity: Five with standard (optional for Custom) Royal SE Package rear bench seat.

INSTRUMENTATION: 0-100 mph speedometer, 99,999.9 mi. odometer, gauges for fuel level and ammeter. Warning lights for oil pressure, engine coolant temperature, brake system warning, hazard light operation, liftgate ajar and 4x4 front hubs.

OPTIONS AND PRICES: Air conditioning.114 amp alternator. 500 amp maintenance-free, heavy-duty battery. Front bumper guards. Rear step type painted bumper. Electronic digital clock. Auxiliary transmission oil to air cooler. Gauges for oil pressure and engine coolant temperature; trip odometer. Bright grille insert and bright headlamp doors; also includes ram's head hood ornament. Engine block heater. Dual low mount 6 in. x 9 in. exterior mirrors. Lower body moldings. Upper body moldings. Upper and lower body moldings. Power front door locks. Front door power windows. AM/FM electronically tuned stereo radio. AM/FM electronically tuned stereo radio with cassette tape plater and Dolby noise reduction system. AM/FM stereo, manually tuned radio. Heavy-duty 1.1875 in. front and rear shock absorbers. Fuel tank skid plate. Transfer case skid plate. Automatic speed control. Sport bar. Heavy-duty front stabilizer bar. Tilt type steering column. Sport steering wheel. Sunscreen privacy glass. Bright wheelcovers. 15 in. x 7.0 in. road type wheels. Aluminum radial ribbed wheels. Two-speed windshield wipers with intermittent wipe. Royal SE Package: $1058. Convenience Package.

Includes halogen headlights, glove box lock and light, ashtray light and two-speed windshield wipers with intermittent wipe. Filigree Tape Stripe Package. Includes body side, wheel-lip and hood tape stripes, plus tape stripe decal with "Dodge Ram" on liftgate. Trailer Preparation Package. Requires, at extra cost: Transmission auxiliary oil cooler and 3.25 (3.21 in California) axle ratio. Includes maximum engine cooling, 500 amp maintenance-free heavy-duty battery, heavy-duty variable load flasher, heavy-duty front and rear shock absorbers and heavy-duty front stabilizer bar. Sno-Commander Package. Includes 6,200 lb. GVW Package, transmission auxiliary oil cooler with automatic transmission, power angling blade with blade markers, hydro/electric controls, power lift, plow lights, 114 amp alternator, 500 amp maintenance-free heavy-duty battery, maximum engine cooling, "Sno-Commander" decal and transmission oil temperature light with automatic transmission. Sno-Preparation Package. Requires at extra cost: 6,200 lb. GVW Package, transmission auxiliary oil cooler with automatic transmission, 114 amp alternator, 500 amp maintenance-free heavy-duty battery, maximum engine cooling and transmission oil temperature light with automatic transmission.

HISTORICAL FOOTNOTES: The 1983 Ramcharger was part of what was depicted as "The new Chrysler Corporation: Quality engineered to be the best."

1984 RAMCHARGER

Except for the availability of a new Prospector Package option, the Ramcharger was unchanged for 1984.

I.D. DATA: The vehicle identification number was located on a plate attached to the driver's side door body latch post. The V.I.N. consisted of 13 elements. The first two characters indicated the model code as follows: A1-AW100. The next digit identified the body type as follows: 0-Sport Utility type vehicle. The next entry, a letter, identified the GVW rating as follows: B-6001 to 10,000 lb. The next unit, a letter, designated the engine type as follows: E-318-2 bbl. P-318-4 bbl. T-360-4 bbl. The next unit, the letter E, indicated the 1984 model year. Following this came a letter indicating the assembly plant as follows: C-Jefferson Assembly Plant, K-Pillette Road Truck, L-Lago Alberto Assembly Plant (Mexico), M-Toluca Assembly Plant (Mexico), N-Burt Road (KDX), S-Warren Truck #1, T-Warren Truck #2 (Sherwood), X-Missouri Truck, V-Warner Truck #3 (Compact). The V.I.N. ended with a six-digit production sequence number at the assembly plant as follows: 100001 at Warren Truck #1, Missouri Truck and Pillette Truck Plant. 500001 at Warren Truck #2. 700001 at Warren Truck Plant #3. All models began with sequence number 000,001.

Body Type	Factory Price	GVW	Shipping Weight	Prod. Total
AW100 Ramcharger				
AW100, Utility, 318 V-8	$10,945	5850	4384	—

STANDARD ENGINE: Features include a drop-forged five-bearing crankshaft, chain-driven camshaft, free-turning exhaust valves, drop-forged I-beam connecting rods and silent-chain camshaft. Engine Type: OHV, V-8. Cast iron block and cylinder head. Bore x Stroke: 3.91 in. x 3.312 in. Lifters: Hydraulic. Number of main bearings-5. Fuel Induction: Single Holley 2-bbl. carburetor. Compression Ratio: 8.7:1. Displacement: 318 cu. in. (5.2 liters). Horsepower: Net 140 @ 3600 rpm. Torque: Net: 240 lb.-ft. @ 2400 rpm. Oil refill capacity: 5 qt. with filter change. Fuel Requirements: Unleaded.

OPTIONAL ENGINE: Available only with automatic transmission. Features include a drop-forged five-bearing crankshaft, chain-driven camshaft, free-turning exhaust valves, drop-forged I-beam connecting rods and silent-chain camshaft. Engine Type: OHV, V-8. Cast iron block and cylinder head. Bore x Stroke: 3.91 in. x 3.312 in. Lifters: Hydraulic. Number of main bearings-5. Fuel Induction: Single Holley 4-bbl. carburetor. Compression Ratio: 8.7:1. Displacement: 318 cu. in. (5.2 liters). Oil refill capacity: 5 qt. with filter change. Fuel Requirements: Unleaded.

OPTIONAL ENGINE: OHV V-8. Available in 49 states with 4-spd. manual transmission only. In California available with automatic transmission only. Features include vibration damper, 18 in. 4-blade fan and drop-forged crankshaft. Engine Type: OHV, V-8. Cast iron block and cylinder head. Bore x Stroke: 4.00 in. x 3.58 in. Lifters: Hydraulic. Number of main bearings-5. Fuel Induction: Single 4-bbl. Holley carburetor. Compression Ratio: 8.6:1. Displacement: 360 cu. in. (5.9 liters). Horsepower: 175 @ 4000 rpm. Torque: Net: 260 lb.-ft. @ 2000 rpm. Oil refill capacity: 5 qt. Fuel Requirements: Unleaded.

CHASSIS FEATURES: Separate body and frame, ladder-type, drop center frame, 36,000 psi, 2.86 in. modules.

SUSPENSION AND RUNNING GEAR: Front Suspension: 48 in. x 2.5 in. Semi-elliptical leaf springs, 1.0 in. stabilizer bar and 1.0 in. tubular shock absorbers. 1640 lb. rating. Optional: 1.1875 in. shock absorbers. Optional Rating: 1800 lb. Rear Suspension: 52 in. x 2.5 in. Semi-elliptical leaf springs, and 1.0 in. tubular shock absorbers. 1820 lbs. Optional: 1.1875 in. shock absorbers. Optional Rating: None. Front Axle Type and Capacity: Spicer 44F-B-J full-floating, 3500 lb. capacity. Optional: None. Rear Axle Type and Capacity: Chrysler 9.25 in. Semi-floating, hypoid-type 3600 lb. capacity. Optional: None. Final Drive Ratio: 318 2-bbl. and 4-spd. trans.: 3.21:1. Optional: 3.21:1 with rear limited slip differential. 318 4-bbl. and auto. trans.: 3.21:1. Optional: 3.55:1. 360 4-bbl. and 4-spd. manual: 3.21:1. Optional 3.55:1. In California the 3128 engine was offered only with auto. trans. and 3.21:1. The 360 engine was available only with auto. trans. and either 3.21:1 or 3.55:1 ratios. Transfer Case: New Process 208 part-time, two-speed: 2.61, 1.00:1. Brakes: Type: Power, hydraulic. Front: Discs. Rear: Drums. Dimensions: Front: 11.75 in. x 1.256 in. disc. Rear: 10 in. x 2.5 in. Brake swept lining area: Sq. in. Wheels: 15 x 6.5 in. 5-stud disc. Optional: 15 x 7.0 in. (aluminum radial ribbed), 15 x 7 in. (five-slot chrome disc), 15 x 7 in. (white painted steel spoke). Tires: P235/75R15. Optional: P255/70R15, LR60 x 15B,10R x 15B, 7.00R x 15D. Steering: Saginaw integral power steering. Turning Circle: 36.9 ft. Optional: None. Transmission: NP435, wide-ratio 4-speed manual, synchromesh on top three gears. Transmission ratios: 6.69, 3.34, 1.66, 1.00:1. Optional: 3-speed automatic transmission: Ratios: 2.45, 1.45., 1.00:1. Clutch: Single dry plate disc, hydraulic actuation lining. Clutch diameter: 11 in. dia. Total lining area: 123.0 sq. in. Optional: None.

VEHICLE DIMENSIONS: Wheelbase: 106.0 in. Overall Length: 184.6 in. Front/Rear Tread: 65.7 in./63.4 in. Overall Height: 74.0 in. Width: 79.5 in. Front/Rear Overhang: 32.5 in./45.5 in. Tailgate: Width and Height: 37.5 in. x 50.5 in. Approach/Departure Degrees: 33/22.5. Ground Clearance: Front axle: 8.5 in. Rear axle: 8.0 in. Oil pan: 15.6 in. Transfer case: 11.0 in. Load space: With rear bench seat in place: 33 in. x 49.0 in. x 40.5 in. With rear seat removed or folded: 54 in. x 50 in. x 40.5 in. Front headroom: 37.75 in. Pedal to seat back (max.): 46 in. Steering wheel to seat back (max.): 19.25 in. Seat to ground: 37 in. Floor to ground: 23 in.

CAPACITIES: Fuel Tank: 35 gal.

ACCOMMODATIONS: Seating Capacity: Five with standard (optional for Custom) Royal SE Package rear bench seat.

INSTRUMENTATION: 0-100 mph speedometer, 99,999.9 mi. odometer, gauges for fuel level and ammeter. Warning lights for oil pressure, engine coolant temperature, brake system warning, hazard light operation, liftgate ajar and 4x4 front hubs.

OPTIONS AND PRICES: Air conditioning.114 amp alternator. 500 amp maintenance-free, heavy-duty battery. Front bumper guards. Rear step type painted bumper. Electronic digital clock. Auxiliary transmission oil to air cooler. Gauges for oil pressure and engine coolant temperature; trip odometer. Bright grille insert and bright headlamp doors; also includes ram's head hood ornament. Engine block heater. Dual low mount 6 in. x 9 in. exterior mirrors. Lower body moldings. Upper body moldings. Upper and lower body moldings. Power front door locks. Front door power windows. AM/FM electronically tuned stereo radio. AM/FM electronically tuned stereo radio with cassette tape plater and Dolby noise reduction system. AM/FM stereo, manually tuned radio. Heavy-duty 1.1875 in. front and rear shock absorbers. Fuel tank skid plate. Transfer case skid plate. Automatic speed control. Sport bar. Heavy-duty front stabilizer bar. Tilt type steering column. Sport steering wheel. Sunscreen privacy glass. Bright wheelcovers. 15 in. x 7.0 in. road type wheels. Aluminum radial ribbed wheels. Two-speed windshield wipers with intermittent wipe. Royal SE Package: $1091. Prospector Package. Convenience Package. Includes halogen headlights, glove box lock and light, ashtray light and two-speed windshield wipers with intermittent wipe. Filigree Tape Stripe Package. Includes body side, wheel-lip and hood tape stripes, plus tape stripe decal with "Dodge Ram" on liftgate. Trailer Preparation Package. Requires, at extra cost: Transmission auxiliary oil cooler and 3.25 (3.21 in California) axle ratio. Includes maximum engine cooling, 500 amp maintenance-free heavy-duty battery, heavy-duty variable load flasher, heavy-duty front and rear shock absorbers and heavy-duty front stabilizer bar. Sno-Commander Package. Includes 6,200 lb. GVW Package, transmission auxiliary oil cooler with automatic transmission, power angling blade with blade markers, hydro/electric controls, power lift, plow lights, 114 amp alternator, 500 amp maintenance-free heavy-duty battery, maximum engine cooling, "Sno-Commander" decal and transmission oil temperature light with automatic transmission. Sno-Preparation Package. Requires at extra cost: 6,200 lb. GVW Package, transmission auxiliary oil cooler with automatic transmission, 114 amp alternator, 500 amp maintenance-free heavy-duty battery, maximum engine cooling and transmission oil temperature light with automatic transmission.

HISTORICAL FOOTNOTES: The 1984 Ramcharger was introduced in the fall of 1983.

1985 RAMCHARGER

The Ramcharger's styling was essentially unchanged for 1985. Standard for the Custom Ramcharger were deluxe vinyl high-back bucket seats available in red, blue or almond. The standard seats for the Royal SE were Tempo cloth high-back Command bucket seats in red, blue or almond. A rear three passenger bench seat was optional for the Custom Ramcharger and standard for the Royal SE The Royal SE Package also included these interior features: Bright door sill scuff plates, center console, color-keyed carpeting with underlayment, color-keyed cowl side trim panels, color-keyed rear side and liftgate inner panels with woodtone applique, color-keyed spare tire cover (not available with 31 x 10.5R15LT tires), color-keyed vinyl door trim panels with woodtone trim, assist strap, armrest, and carpeting on lower door, black Euro-style steering wheel, nameplate ("Royal SE-engineered Ram Tough") on instrument panel, woodtone applique on instrument panel and a bright trim storage box. Exterior Royal SE components consisted of bright aluminum grille with chromed plastic insert, headlight doors and halogen headlights, bright drip rail molding, Royal SE plaque on front fender, ram hood ornament, liftgate upper and lower moldings with bright applique panel and bright taillamp housing.

The Ramcharger's standard equipment for 1985 consisted of these items: Driver's compartment ashtray, front and rear bright bumpers, buzzer warning-key in ignition, headlights-on and fasten seat belts; cigarette lighter, coolant reserve system, insulated dash liner, color-keyed inner door trim panels, armrests and pull straps, electronic ignition system, exhaust emissions control system, black floor mat with padding (padding not available in rear compartment), 35 gallon fuel tank with tethered cap, tinted glass for all windows, glove box with door, aluminum grille with painted plastic insert and headlight doors, color-keyed soft cloth headliner, fresh air heater and defrosters, inner hood panel insulation, in-cab hood release, dual electric horns, bright hubcaps, back-up lights, dash-mounted combination map/courtesy lights, rear compartment courtesy lights, exterior dual 5 in. x 7 in. bright finish, short arm mirrors, interior 10 in. day/night rearview mirror, bright quarter side window and windshield moldings, power steering, electronically-tuned AM radio with digital clock, rear roof vent, inside spare tire mounting, driver and passenger sun visors, dual jet windshield washers and two-speed windshield wipers.

The Ramcharger color selection for 1985 provided the potential customer with these choices: Black, light blue metallic, Navy blue metallic, charcoal metallic, cream, forest green metallic, canyon red metallic, graphic red, silver metallic and white. Available only with the Prospector Package and two-tone paint procedure was golden brown metallic.

1985 Dodge AW150 Ramcharger Royal SE

I.D. DATA: The vehicle identification number was located on a plate attached to the driver's side door body latch post. The V.I.N. consisted of 17 elements. The first entry, indicated the nation of origin as follows: 1-U.S.A., 2-Canada. This was followed by a letter B identifying Dodge as the manufacturer. The number 7 then identified the vehicle type as a truck. The gross vehicle weight was next designated as follows: G-5001-6000 lb. The truck line was then identified as a 4x4 by the letter W. The next entry was a number 0 for the 100 truck series. A number 2 followed to identify the Ramcharger as a Sport Utility. This was then proceeded by the engine code according to the following: T-318-2-bbl. T-360-4 bbl. A check digit was then inserted, followed by the letter F for the 1985 model year. The next item, a letter, identified the assembly plant as follows: A-Lynch Road, C-Jefferson, D-Belvidere, F-Newark, G-St. Louis, K-Pillete, Canada, M-Lago Alberta, S-Warren #1, T-Warren #2, V-Warren #3 or X-Missouri. The final six numbers beginning with 10001 were the plant sequential number.

Body Type	Factory Price	GVW	Shipping Weight	Prod. Total
AW100 Ramcharger, Model W12				
AW100, Utility, 318 V-8	$11,581	5850	4315	—

STANDARD ENGINE: Features include a drop-forged five-bearing crankshaft, chain-driven camshaft, free-turning exhaust valves, drop-forged I-beam connecting rods and silent-chain camshaft. Engine Type: OHV, V-8. Cast iron block and cylinder head. Bore x Stroke: 3.91 in. x 3.312 in. Lifters: Hydraulic. Number of main bearings-5. Fuel Induction: Single Holley 2-bbl. carburetor. Compression Ratio: 8.7:1. Displacement: 318 cu. in. (5.2 liters). Horsepower: Net 140 @ 3600 rpm. Torque: Net: 240 lb.-ft. @ 2400 rpm. Oil refill capacity: 5 qt. with filter change. Fuel Requirements: Unleaded.

OPTIONAL ENGINE: Available only with automatic transmission. Features include a drop-forged five-bearing crankshaft, chain-driven camshaft, free-turning exhaust valves, drop-forged I-beam connecting rods and silent-chain camshaft. Engine Type: OHV, V-8. Cast iron block and cylinder head. Bore x Stroke: 3.91 in. x 3.312 in. Lifters: Hydraulic. Number of main bearings-5. Fuel Induction: Single Holley 4-bbl. carburetor. Compression Ratio: 8.7:1. Displacement: 318 cu. in. (5.2 liters). Oil refill capacity: 5 qt. with filter change. Fuel Requirements: Unleaded.

OPTIONAL ENGINE: OHV V-8. Available in 49 states with 4-spd. manual transmission only. In California available with automatic transmission only. Features include vibration damper, 18 in. 4-blade fan and drop-forged crankshaft. Engine Type: OHV, V-8. Cast iron block and cylinder head. Bore x Stroke: 4.00 in. x 3.58 in. Lifters: Hydraulic. Number of main bearings-5. Fuel Induction: Single 4-bbl. Holley carburetor. Compression Ratio: 8.6:1. Displacement: 360 cu. in. (5.9 liters). Horsepower: 175 @ 4000 rpm. Torque: Net: 260 lb.-ft. @ 2000 rpm. Oil refill capacity: 5 qt. Fuel Requirements: Unleaded.

CHASSIS FEATURES: Separate body and frame, ladder-type, drop center frame, 36,000 psi, 2.86 in. modules.

SUSPENSION AND RUNNING GEAR: Front Suspension: 48 in. x 2.5 in. Semi-elliptical leaf springs, 1.0 in. stabilizer bar and 1.0 in. tubular shock absorbers. 1640 lb. rating. Optional: 1.1875 in. shock absorbers. Optional Rating: 1800 lb. Rear Suspension: 52 in. x 2.5 in. Semi-elliptical leaf springs, and 1.0 in. tubular shock absorbers. 1820 lbs. Optional: 1.1875 in. shock absorbers. Optional Rating: None. Front Axle Type and Capacity: Spicer 44F-B-J full-floating, 3500 lb. capacity. Optional: None. Rear Axle Type and Capacity: Chrysler 9.25 in. Semi-floating, hypoid-type 3600 lb. capacity. Optional: None. Final Drive Ratio: 318 2-bbl. and 4-spd. trans.: 3.21:1. Optional: 3.21:1 with rear limited slip differential. 318 4-bbl. and auto. trans.: 3.21:1. Optional: 3.55:1. 360 4-bbl. and 4-spd. manual: 3.21:1. Optional 3.55:1. In California the 3128 engine was offered only with auto. trans. and 3.21:1. The 360 engine was available only with auto. trans. and either 3.21:1 or 3.55:1 ratios. Transfer Case: New Process 208 part-time, two-speed: 2.61, 1.00:1. Brakes: Type: Power, hydraulic. Front: Discs. Rear: Drums. Dimensions: Front: 11.75 in. x 1.256 in. disc. Rear: 10 in. x 2.5 in. Brake swept lining area: Sq. in. Wheels: 15 x 6.5 in. 5-stud disc. Optional: 15 x 7.0 in. (aluminum radial ribbed), 15 x 7 in. (five-slot chrome disc), 15 x 7 in. (white painted steel spoke). Tires: P235/75R15. Optional: P255/70R15, LR60 x 15B,10R x 15B, 7.00R x 15D. Steering: Saginaw integral power steering. Turning Circle: 36.9 ft. Optional: None. Transmission: NP435, wide-ratio 4-speed manual, synchromesh on top three gears. Transmission ratios: 6.69, 3.34, 1.66, 1.00:1. Optional: 3-speed automatic transmission: Ratios: 2.45, 1.45., 1.00:1. Clutch: Single dry plate disc, hydraulic actuation lining. Clutch diameter: 11 in. dia. Total lining area: 123.0 sq. in. Optional: None.

VEHICLE DIMENSIONS: Wheelbase: 106.0 in. Overall Length: 184.6 in. Front/Rear Tread: 65.7 in./63.4 in. Overall Height: 74.0 in. Width: 79.5 in. Front/Rear Overhang: 32.5 in./45.5 in. Tailgate: Width and Height: 37.5 in. x 50.5 in. Approach/Departure Degrees: 33/22.5. Ground Clearance: Front axle: 8.5 in. Rear axle: 8.0 in. Oil pan: 15.6 in. Transfer case: 11.0 in. Load space: With rear bench seat in place: 33 in. x 49.0 in. x 40.5 in. With rear seat removed or folded: 54 in. x 50 in. x 40.5 in. Front headroom: 37.75 in. Pedal to seat back (max.): 46 in. Steering wheel to seat back (max.): 19.25 in. Seat to ground: 37 in. Floor to ground: 23 in.

CAPACITIES: Fuel Tank: 35 gal.

ACCOMMODATIONS: Seating Capacity: Five with standard (optional for Custom) Royal SE Package rear bench seat.

INSTRUMENTATION: 0-100 mph speedometer, 99,999.9 mi. odometer, gauges for fuel level and ammeter. Warning lights for oil pressure, engine coolant temperature, brake system warning, hazard light operation, liftgate ajar and 4x4 front hubs.

OPTIONS AND PRICES: Air conditioning with bi-level ventilation.114 amp alternator. 500 amp maintenance-free, heavy-duty battery. Front bumper guards. Rear step-type painted bumper. Auxiliary transmission oil to air cooler. Maximum engine cooling. Gauges for oil pressure and engine coolant temperature; trip odometer. Privacy glass (sunscreen glass for rear quarter and liftgate only). Bright grille insert and bright headlamp doors; also includes ram's head hood ornament. Engine block heater. Dual low mount 6 in. x 9 in. exterior mirrors. Lower body moldings. Upper body moldings. Upper and lower body moldings. Power front door locks. Front door power windows. AM/FM electronically tuned stereo radio with integral digital clock. AM/FM radio electronically tuned stereo with Seek-Scan, cassette tape player with automatic reverse, Dynamic Noise Reduction, four speakers and integral digital clock. Fuel tank skid plate. Transfer case skid plate. Heavy-duty 1.1875 in. front and rear shock absorbers. Automatic speed control. Sport bar. Heavy-duty front stabilizer bar. Tilt type steering column. Sport steering wheel. Deluxe bright wheelcovers. 15 in. x 7.0 in. road type wheels. Aluminum radial ribbed wheels. Argent painted steel spoke wheels with bright trim ring. Two-speed windshield wipers with intermittent wipe. Royal SE Package: $1161. Prospector Package I. Includes Convenience Package, oil pressure and engine coolant temperature gauges, trip odometer, sunscreen privacy glass, bright grille with headlamp doors, halogen headlamps and ram's head hood ornament, bright front bumper guards, bright low mount exterior mirrors, deluxe wheelcovers and Prospector nameplates. Prospector Package II includes all items in Prospector I Package plus AM/FM electronically tuned stereo radio, Royal SE Decor Package and Power front door locks. Prospector II Package. Includes Royal SE Decor Package, Two-tone paint procedure, Convenience Package, air conditioning, sunscreen glass, power front windows, speed control, argent painted spoke steel road wheels with bright trim, 10R15LTB steel-belted radial outlined white letter tires and Prospector nameplate. Convenience Package. Includes ashtray light, glove box lock and light, and two-speed windshield wipers with intermittent wipe. Sno-Commander Package. Requires at extra cost: 6200 lb. GVW Package and transmission auxiliary oil cooler with automatic transmission. Includes power angling blade with blade markers, hydro/electric controls, power lift, 114 amp alternator, 500 amp maintenance-free heavy-duty battery, maximum engine cooling, Sno-Commander decal and transmission oil temperature light with automatic transmission. Sno-Preparation Package. Requires at extra cost: 6200 lb. GVW Package and transmission auxiliary oil cooler with automatic transmission. Includes 114 amp alternator, 500 amp maintenance-free heavy-duty battery, maximum engine cooling, and transmission oil temperature light with automatic transmission. Filigree Tape Stripe Package. Includes body side, wheel-lip and hood gold pin tape stripes, and tape stripe decal with "Dodge Ram" on liftgate. Convenience Package. Includes halogen headlights, glove box lock and light, ashtray light and two-speed windshield wipers with intermittent wipe. Filigree Tape Stripe Package. Includes body side, wheel-lip and hood tape stripes, plus tape stripe decal with "Dodge Ram" on liftgate. Trailer Preparation Package. Requires, at extra cost: Transmission auxiliary oil cooler and 3.25 (3.21 in California) axle ratio. Includes maximum engine cooling, 500 amp maintenance-free heavy-duty battery, heavy-duty variable load flasher, heavy-duty front and rear shock absorbers and heavy-duty front stabilizer bar. Sno-Commander Package. Includes 6,200 lb. GVW Package, transmission auxiliary oil cooler with automatic transmission, power angling blade with blade markers, hydro/electric controls, power lift, plow lights, 114 amp alternator, 500 amp maintenance heavy-duty battery, maximum engine cooling and transmission oil temperature light with automatic transmission.

HISTORICAL FOOTNOTES: Dodge said that the 1985 Ramcharger was "muscling into the future."

1986 RAMCHARGER

The 1986 Ramcharger featured a new grille with a bright divider separating the grille into four blacked out rectangular sections. The parking lights were also reshaped and the lower grille portion was no longer divided into two portions. Gauges for oil pressure and engine coolant temperature; trip odometer were made standard for the 1986 Ramcharger. Also standard for the Custom Ramcharger were deluxe vinyl high-back bucket seats available in red, blue or almond. The standard seats for the Royal SE were Tempo cloth high-back Command bucket seats in red, blue or almond. A rear three passenger bench seat was now standard for both the Custom Ramcharger and the Royal SE The Royal SE Package also included these interior features: Bright door sill scuff plates, center console, color-keyed carpeting with underlayment, color-keyed cowl side trim panels, color-keyed rear side and liftgate inner panels with woodtone applique, color-keyed spare tire cover (not available with 31 x 10.5R15LT tires), color-keyed vinyl door trim panels with woodtone trim, assist strap, armrest, and carpeting on lower door, black Euro-style steering wheel, nameplate ("Royal SE-engineered Ram Tough") on instrument panel, woodtone applique on instrument panel and a bright trim storage box. Exterior Royal SE components consisted of bright aluminum grille with chromed plastic insert, headlight doors and halogen headlights, bright drip rail molding, Leaping Ram plaque "150 Royal SE" on front fenders, ram's head hood ornament, bright liftgate upper and lower moldings, and bright taillamp housing.

The Ramcharger's standard equipment for 1986 consisted of these items: Driver's compartment ashtray, front and rear bright bumpers, buzzer warning-key in ignition, headlights-on and fasten seat belts; cigarette lighter, coolant reserve system, insulated dash liner, color-keyed inner door trim panels, armrests and pull straps, electronic ignition system, exhaust emissions control system, black floor mat with padding (padding not available in rear compartment), 35 gallon fuel tank with tethered cap, tinted glass for all windows, glove box with door, aluminum grille with painted plastic insert and headlight doors, color-keyed soft cloth headliner, fresh air heater and defrosters, inner hood panel insulation, in-cab hood release, dual electric horns, bright hubcaps, back-up lights, dash-mounted combination map/courtesy lights, rear compartment courtesy lights, exterior dual 5 in. x 7 in. bright finish, short arm mirrors, interior 10 in. day/night rearview mirror, bright quarter side window, rear window and windshield moldings, power steering, electronically-tuned AM radio with digital clock (could be deleted for credit on factory orders), rear roof vent, inside spare tire mounting, driver and passenger sun visors, dual jet windshield washers and two-speed windshield wipers.

For 1986, ten exterior colors were offered: Light cream, golden bronze pearlcoat, twilight blue pearlcoat, graphic red, gold dust, radiant silver, ice blue, white, black, charcoal pearlcoat.

1986 Dodge AW150 Ramcharger

I.D. DATA. The vehicle identification number was located on a plate attached to the driver's side door body latch post. The V.I.N. consisted of 17 elements. The first entry, indicated the nation of origin as follows: 1-U.S.A., 2-Canada. This was followed by a letter B identifying Dodge as the manufacturer. The number 7 then identified the vehicle type as a truck. The gross vehicle weight was next designated as follows: G-5001-6000 lb. The truck line was then identified as a 4x4 by the letter W. The next entry was a number 0 for the 100 truck series. A number 2 followed to identify the Ramcharger as a Sport Utility. This was then proceeded by the engine code according to the following: T-318-2-bbl. T-360-4 bbl. A check digit was then inserted, followed by the letter F for the 1985 model year. The next item, a letter, identified the assembly plant as follows: A-Lynch Road, C-Jefferson, D-Belvidere, F-Newark, G-St. Louis, K-Pillete, Canada, M-Lago Alberto, S-Warren #1, T-Warren #2, V-Warren #3 or X-Missouri. The final six numbers beginning with 10001 were the plant sequential number.

Body Type	Factory Price	GVW	Shipping Weight	Prod. Total
AW100 Ramcharger, Model W12				
AW100, Utility, 318 V-8	$12,763	6000*	4549	—

* 6400 lb. GVW Package optional.

STANDARD ENGINE: Features include a drop-forged five-bearing crankshaft, chain-driven camshaft, free-turning exhaust valves, drop-forged I-beam connecting rods and silent-chain camshaft. Engine Type: OHV, V-8. Cast iron block and cylinder head. Bore x Stroke: 3.91 in. x 3.312 in. Lifters: Hydraulic. Number of main bearings-5. Fuel Induction: Single Holley 2-bbl. carburetor. Compression Ratio: 8.7:1. Displacement: 318 cu. in. (5.2 liters). Horsepower: Net 140 @ 3600 rpm. Torque: Net: 240 lb.-ft. @ 2400 rpm. Oil refill capacity: 5 qt. with filter change. Fuel Requirements: Unleaded.

OPTIONAL ENGINE: Available only with automatic transmission. Features include a drop-forged five-bearing crankshaft, chain-driven camshaft, free-turning exhaust valves, drop-forged I-beam connecting rods and silent-chain camshaft. Engine Type: OHV, V-8. Cast iron block and cylinder head. Bore x Stroke: 3.91 in. x 3.312 in. Lifters: Hydraulic. Number of main bearings-5. Fuel Induction: Single Holley 4-bbl. carburetor. Compression Ratio: 8.7:1. Displacement: 318 cu. in. (5.2 liters). Oil refill capacity: 5 qt. with filter change. Fuel Requirements: Unleaded.

OPTIONAL ENGINE: OHV V-8. Available in 49 states with 4-spd. manual transmission only. In California available with automatic transmission only. Features include vibration damper, 18 in. 4-blade fan and drop-forged crankshaft. Engine Type: OHV, V-8. Cast iron block and cylinder head. Bore x Stroke: 4.00 in. x 3.58 in. Lifters: Hydraulic. Number of main bearings-5. Fuel Induction: Single 4-bbl. Holley carburetor. Compression Ratio: 8.6:1. Displacement: 360 cu. in. (5.9 liters). Horsepower: 175 @ 4000 rpm. Torque: Net: 260 lb.-ft. @ 2000 rpm. Oil refill capacity: 5 qt. Fuel Requirements: Unleaded.

CHASSIS FEATURES: Separate body and frame, ladder-type, drop center frame, 36,000 psi, 2.86 in. modules.

SUSPENSION AND RUNNING GEAR: Front Suspension: 48 in. x 2.5 in. Semi-elliptical leaf springs, 1.0 in. stabilizer bar and 1.0 in. tubular shock absorbers. 1640 lb. rating. Optional: 1.1875 in. shock absorbers. Optional Rating: 1800 lb. Rear Suspension: 52 in. x 2.5 in. Semi-elliptical leaf springs, and 1.0 in. tubular shock absorbers. 1820 lbs. Optional: 1.1875 in. shock absorbers. Optional Rating: None. Front Axle Type and Capacity: Spicer 44F-B-J full-floating, 3500 lb. capacity. Optional: None. Rear Axle Type and Capacity: Chrysler 9.25 in. Semi-floating, hypoid-type 3600 lb. capacity. Optional: None. Final Drive Ratio: 318 2-bbl. and 4-spd. trans.: 3.21:1. Optional: 3.21:1 with rear limited slip differential. 318 4-bbl. and auto. trans.: 3.21:1. Optional: 3.55:1. 360 4-bbl. and 4-spd. manual: 3.21:1. Optional 3.55:1. In California the 3128 engine was offered only with auto. trans. and 3.21:1. The 360 engine was available only with auto. trans. and either 3.21:1 or 3.55:1 ratios. Transfer Case: New Process 241 part-time, two-speed. Brakes: Type: Power, hydraulic. Front: Discs. Rear: Drums. Dimensions: Front: 11.75 in. x 1.256 in. disc. Rear: 10 in. x 2.5 in. Brake swept lining area: Sq. in. Wheels: 15 x 6.5 in. 5-stud disc. Optional: 15 x 7.0 in. (aluminum radial ribbed), 15 x 7 in. (five-slot chrome disc), 15 x 7 in. (white painted steel spoke). Tires: P235/75R15. Optional: P255/70R15, LR60 x 15B,10R x 15B, 7.00R x 15D. Steering: Saginaw integral power steering. Turning Circle: 36.9 ft. Optional: None. Transmission: NP435, wide-ratio 4-speed manual, synchromesh on top three gears. Transmission ratios: 6.69, 3.34, 1.66, 1.00:1. Optional: 3-speed automatic transmission: Ratios: 2.45, 1.45., 1.00:1. Clutch: Single dry plate disc, hydraulic actuation lining. Clutch diameter: 11 in. dia. Total lining area: 123.0 sq. in. Optional: None.

VEHICLE DIMENSIONS: Wheelbase: 106.0 in. Overall Length: 184.6 in. Front/Rear Tread: 65.7 in./63.4 in. Overall Height: 74.0 in. Width: 79.5 in. Front/Rear Overhang: 32.5 in./45.5 in. Tailgate: Width and Height: 37.5 in. x 50.5 in. Approach/Departure Degrees: 33/22.5. Ground Clearance: Front axle: 8.5 in. Rear axle: 8.0 in. Oil pan: 15.6 in. Transfer case: 11.0 in. Load space: With rear bench seat in place: 33 in. x 49.0 in. x 40.5 in. With rear seat removed or folded: 54 in. x 50 in. x 40.5 in. Front headroom: 37.75 in. Pedal to seat back (max.): 46 in. Steering wheel to seat back (max.): 19.25 in. Seat to ground: 37 in. Floor to ground: 23 in.

CAPACITIES: Fuel Tank: 35 gal.

ACCOMMODATIONS: Seating Capacity: Five with standard (optional for Custom) Royal SE Package rear bench seat.

INSTRUMENTATION: 0-100 mph speedometer, 99,999.9 mi. odometer, trip odometer, gauges for fuel level and ammeter, oil pressure and engine coolant temperature; trip odometer. Warning lights for brake system warning, hazard light operation, liftgate ajar and 4x4 front hubs.

OPTIONS AND PRICES: Air conditioning with bi-level ventilation. 114 amp alternator. 500 amp maintenance-free, heavy-duty battery. Front bumper guards. Rear step-type painted bumper. Anti-spin rear axle. Auxiliary transmission oil to air cooler. Maximum engine cooling. Privacy glass (sunscreen glass for rear quarter and liftgate only). Engine block heater. Dual low mount 6 in. x 9 in. exterior mirrors. Bright lower body moldings with black vinyl insert and partial wheel-lip. AM/FM electronically tuned stereo radio with integral digital clock. AM/FM radio electronically tuned stereo with Seek-Scan, cassette tape player with automatic reverse, Dynamic Noise Reduction and integral digital clock. Fuel tank skid plate. Transfer case skid plate. Automatic speed control (Royal SE Package required). Sport bar. Tilt type steering column. Requires Royal SE Package, intermittent windshield wipers and automatic transmission). Deluxe bright wheelcovers. 15 in. x 7.0 in. road type wheels. Aluminum radial ribbed wheels. Argent painted steel spoke wheels with bright trim ring. Two-speed windshield wipers with intermittent wipe. Royal SE Package. Prospector Package I. Includes Convenience Package, deluxe bright wheelcovers, grille with bright insert, headlight bezels, halogen headlights, ram's head hood ornament, Power Convenience Package, sunscreen glass (rear quarter and liftgate windows only). Prospector Package II includes all items in Prospector I Package except sunscreen glass plus dual 6 in. x 9 in. low mount exterior mirrors and Royal SE Decor Package. Prospector III Package. Includes air conditioning, aluminum ribbed road wheels, electronically tuned AM/FM stereo radio with integral clock, Convenience Package, P235/75R15XL raised white letter tires, Power Convenience Package, Royal SE Decor Package, speed control, sunscreen glass (rear quarter and liftgate only), and Two-Tone Paint Package. Power Convenience Package. Includes power front door locks and front door power windows. Heavy-Duty Package. Includes heavy-duty 1.1875 in. front and rear shock absorbers, and heavy-duty front stabilizer bar. Two-Tone Paint Package. Includes lower body side moldings with black vinyl insert and bright partial wheel-lip moldings, two-tone paint and upper side and rear quarter exterior moldings. Convenience Package. Includes halogen headlights, glove box lock and light, ashtray light and two-speed windshield wipers with intermittent wipe.

HISTORICAL FOOTNOTES: All North American-built 1986 Ramchargers were covered under Chrysler Corporation's 5-year/50,000 mile protection plan.

1987 RAMCHARGER

The Ramcharger's appearance and feature content were unchanged for 1987.

I.D. DATA. The vehicle identification number was located on a plate attached to the driver's side door body latch post. The V.I.N. consisted of 17 elements. The first entry, indicated the nation of origin as follows: 1-U.S.A., 2-Canada. This was followed by a letter B identifying Dodge as the manufacturer. The number 7 then identified the vehicle type as a truck. The gross vehicle weight was next designated as follows: G-5001-6000 lb. The truck line was then identified as a 4x4 by the letter W. The next entry was a number 0 for the 100 truck series. A number 2 followed to identify the Ramcharger as a Sport Utility. This was then proceeded by the engine code according to the following: T-318-2-bbl. T-360-4 bbl. A check digit was then inserted, followed by the letter H for the 1987 model year. The next item, a letter, identified the assembly plant as follows: A-Lynch Road, C-Jefferson, D-Belvidere, F-Newark, G-St. Louis, K-Pillete, Canada, M-Lago Alberto, S-Warren #1, T-Warren #2, V-Warren #3 or X-Missouri. The final six numbers beginning with 10001 were the plant sequential number.

Body Type	Factory Price	GVW	Shipping Weight	Prod. Total
AW100 Ramcharger, Model W12				
AW100, Utility, 318 V-8	$12,763	6000*	4549	—

* 6400 lb. GVW Package optional.

STANDARD ENGINE: Features include a drop-forged five-bearing crankshaft, chain-driven camshaft, free-turning exhaust valves, drop-forged I-beam connecting rods and silent-chain camshaft. Engine Type: OHV, V-8. Cast iron block and cylinder head. Bore x Stroke: 3.91 in. x 3.312 in. Lifters: Hydraulic. Number of main bearings-5. Fuel Induction: Single Holley 2-bbl. carburetor. Compression Ratio: 8.7:1. Displacement: 318 cu. in. (5.2 liters). Horsepower: 145 @ 4000 rpm. Torque: Net: 255 lb.-ft. @ 2000 rpm. Oil refill capacity: 5 qt. with filter change. Fuel Requirements: Unleaded.

OPTIONAL ENGINE: OHV V-8. Available in 49 states with 4-spd. manual transmission only. In California available with automatic transmission only. Features include vibration damper, 18 in. 4-blade fan and drop-forged crankshaft. Engine Type: OHV, V-8. Cast iron block and cylinder head. Bore x Stroke: 4.00 in. x 3.58 in. Lifters: Hydraulic. Number of main bearings-5. Fuel Induction: Single 4-bbl. Holley carburetor. Compression Ratio: 8.4:1. Displacement: 360 cu. in. (5.9 liters). 360-Horsepower: 190 @ 4000 rpm. Torque: Net: 255 lb.-ft. @ 1600 rpm. Oil refill capacity: 5 qt. Fuel Requirements: Unleaded.

CHASSIS FEATURES: Separate body and frame, ladder-type, drop center frame, 36,000 psi, 2.86 in. modules.

SUSPENSION AND RUNNING GEAR: Front Suspension: 48 in. x 2.5 in. Semi-elliptical leaf springs, 1.0 in. stabilizer bar and 1.0 in. tubular shock absorbers. 1640 lb. rating. Optional Rating: 2100 lb. (standard on AW150 with 6400 lb. GVW). Rear Suspension: 52 in. x 2.5 in. Semi-elliptical leaf springs, and 1.0 in. tubular shock absorbers. 1820 lb. capacity. Optional Rating: None. Front Axle Type and Capacity: Spicer 44F-B-J full-floating, 3500 lb. capacity. Optional: 4000 lb. (standard on AW150 with 6400 lb. GVW). Rear Axle Type and Capacity: Chrysler 9.25 in. Semi-floating, hypoid-type 3600 lb. capacity. Optional: None. Final Drive Ratio: 318 2-bbl. and 4-spd. trans.: 3.21:1. Optional with automatic transmission: 3.55:1. Transfer Case: New Process 241 part-time, two-speed. Brakes: Type: Power, hydraulic. Front: Discs. Rear: Drums. Dimensions: Front: 11.75 in. x 1.256 in. disc. Rear: 11 in. x 2.5 in. Wheels: 15 x 6.5 in. 5-stud disc. Optional: 15 x 7.0 in. heavy-duty, 15 x 7 in. argent painted steel spoke with bright trim ring and hub center, 15 x 7 in. aluminum radial ribbed. Tires: P325/75R15XL. Steering: Saginaw integral power steering. Turning Circle: 36.9 ft. Optional: None. Transmission: NP435, wide-ratio 4-speed manual, synchromesh on top three gears. Transmission ratios: 6.69, 3.34, 1.66, 1.00:1. Optional: 3-speed automatic transmission: Ratios: 2.45, 1.45., 1.00:1. Clutch: Single dry plate disc, hydraulic actuation lining. Clutch diameter: 11 in. dia. Total lining area: 123.0 sq. in. Optional: None.

VEHICLE DIMENSIONS: Wheelbase: 106.0 in. Overall Length: 184.6 in. Front/Rear Tread: 65.7 in./63.4 in. Overall Height: 74.0 in. Width: 79.5 in. Front/Rear Overhang: 32.5 in./45.5 in. Tailgate: Width and Height: 37.5 in. x 50.5 in. Approach/Departure Degrees: 33/22.5. Ground Clearance: Front axle: 8.5 in. Rear axle: 8.0 in. Oil pan: 15.6 in. Transfer case: 11.0 in. Load space: With rear bench seat in place: 33 in. x 49.0 in. x 40.5 in. With rear seat removed or folded: 54 in. x 50 in. x 40.5 in. Front headroom: 37.75 in. Pedal to seat back (max.): 46 in. Steering wheel to seat back (max.): 19.25 in. Seat to ground: 37 in. Floor to ground: 23 in.

CAPACITIES: Fuel Tank: 35 gal.

ACCOMMODATIONS: Seating Capacity: Five with standard (optional for Custom) Royal SE Package rear bench seat.

INSTRUMENTATION: 0-100 mph speedometer, 99,999.9 mi. odometer, trip odometer, gauges for fuel level and ammeter, oil pressure and engine coolant temperature; trip odometer. Warning lights for brake system warning, hazard light operation, liftgate ajar and 4x4 front hubs.

OPTIONS AND PRICES: Air conditioning with bi-level ventilation. 114 amp alternator. 500 amp maintenance-free, heavy-duty battery. Front bumper guards. Rear step-type painted bumper. Anti-spin rear axle. Auxiliary transmission oil to air cooler. Maximum engine cooling. Privacy glass (sunscreen glass for rear quarter and liftgate only). Engine block heater. Dual low mount 6 in. x 9 in. exterior mirrors. Bright lower body moldings with black vinyl insert and partial wheel-lip. AM/FM electronically tuned stereo radio with integral digital clock. AM/FM radio electronically tuned stereo with Seek-Scan, cassette tape player with automatic reverse, Dynamic Noise Reduction and integral digital clock. Fuel tank skid plate. Transfer case skid plate. Automatic spoed control (Royal SE Package required). Sport bar. Tilt type steering column. Requires Royal SE Package, intermittent windshield wipers and automatic transmission). Deluxe bright wheelcovers. 15 in. x 7.0 in. road type wheels. Aluminum radial ribbed wheels. Argent painted steel spoke wheels with bright trim ring. Two-speed windshield wipers with intermittent wipe. Royal SE Package. Prospector Package I. Includes Convenience Package, deluxe bright wheelcovers, grille with bright insert, headlight bezels, halogen headlights, ram's head hood ornament, Power Convenience Package, sunscreen glass (rear quarter and liftgate windows only). Prospector Package II includes all items in Prospector I Package except sunscreen glass plus dual 6 in. x 9 in. low mount exterior mirrors and Royal SE Decor Package. Prospector III Package. Includes air conditioning, aluminum ribbed road wheels, electronically tuned AM/FM stereo radio with integral clock, Convenience Package, P235/75R15XL raised white letter tires, Power Convenience Package, Royal SE Decor Package, speed control, sunscreen glass (rear quarter and liftgate only), and Two-Tone Paint

Package. Power Convenience Package. Includes power front door locks and front door power windows. Heavy-Duty Package. Includes heavy-duty 1.1875 in. front and rear shock absorbers, and heavy-duty front stabilizer bar. Two-Tone Paint Package. Includes lower body side moldings with black vinyl insert and bright partial wheel-lip moldings, two-tone paint and upper side and rear quarter exterior moldings. Convenience Package. Includes halogen headlights, glove box lock and light, ashtray light and two-speed windshield wipers with intermittent wipe.

HISTORICAL FOOTNOTES: Dodge dealers ranked third behind Ford and Chevrolet in truck registrations per outlet at the start of the 1987 model year.

1988 RAMCHARGER

Dodge extended the market potential of the Ramcharger by the introduction of the AW100 as a companion model to the AW150. In introducing the new model Dodge reported that the "new Dodge Ramcharger 100 has what it takes-high equipment level, low price, Ram Tough quality and overall ruggedness." In addition to the base equipment common to both Ramchargers, the AW100 was fitted with bright wheelcovers, front carpeting, scuff plates, rear rubber mat, front fender Leaping Ram plaque with "100" designation, Tempo cloth with vinyl trim high-back Commander bucket seats, lower body side molding, ram's head hood ornament and a woodtone faceplate instrument panel.

The standard 318 V-8 engine was now equipped with electronic fuel injection and roller-tappet camshaft followers. Its horsepower was increased by an impressive 17 percent. Also introduced for 1988 was a new passenger seat easy-entry system and new dual exterior low mount 6 in. x 9 in. bright finish rearview mirrors. The right hand mirror had convex glass.

Standard Ramcharger equipment for 1988 consisted of front and rear bright bumpers, stainless steel exhaust system, tinted glass for all windows, aluminum grille with painted plastic insert and headlight bezels, bright hubcaps, exterior dual short arm low mount 5 in. x 7 in. mirrors, bright molding for quarter side windows, rear window and windshield, electronic digital clock integral with AM electronically tuned radio, black floor mats with padding (padding not available for rear compartment, color-keyed soft cloth headliner, in-cab hood release, interior rear vision day/night 10 in. mirror, rear three passenger bench seat, inside spare tire mount, buzzer warning for fasten seat belts, headlights on and key in ignition, back-up lights, combination map/courtesy light on instrument panel, rear compartment courtesy light and two-speed windshield wipers. The standard interior trim for the AW100 Ramcharger featured front high-back Command bucket seats and a matching three passenger folding rear bench seat in Tempo cloth with vinyl trim. These seats were also included in the LE Decor Package. The standard AW150 seats were of the same design but upholstered in saddle grain all-vinyl. Available on all Ramchargers AW150 models as a no-charge option in place of the standard or LE decor was a saddle grain all-vinyl split-back front seat and a matching rear bench seat. All seats were offered in almond, red or blue. The LE package now included a new luxury steering wheel.

Nine exterior colors were offered for 1988: Medium suede (not available for AW100), twilight blue pearlcoat (extra cost), garnet red pearlcoat (extra cost), dark suede, radiant silver, glacier blue, white (not available for AW100), black, and charcoal pearlcoat. Chrysler Corporation protected the Ramcharger with the 7/70 Powertrain Limited Warranty and a 7/100 Anti-Corrosion Limited Warranty.

1988 Dodge AW150 Ramcharger

I.D. DATA: The vehicle identification number was located on a plate attached to the driver's side door body latch post. The V.I.N. consisted of 17 elements. The first entry, indicated the nation of origin as follows: 1-U.S.A., 2-Canada. This was followed by a letter B identifying Dodge as the manufacturer. The number 7 then identified the vehicle type as a truck. The gross vehicle weight was next designated as follows: G-5001-6000 lb. The truck line was then identified as a 4x4 by the letter W. The next entry was a number 0 for the 100 truck series. A number 2 followed to identify the Ramcharger as a Sport Utility. This was then proceeded by the engine code according to the following: T-318-2-bbl. T-360-4 bbl. A check digit was then inserted, followed by the letter J for the 1988 model year. The next item, a letter, identified the assembly plant as follows: A-Lynch Road, C-Jefferson, D-Belvidere, F-Newark, G-St. Louis, K-Pillete, Canada, M-Lago Alberta, S-Warren #1, T-Warren #2, V-Warren #3 or X-Missouri. The final six numbers beginning with 10001 were the plant sequential number.

Body Type	Factory Price	GVW	Shipping Weight	Prod. Total
Ramcharger, 318 V-8				
AW100, Utility, Model W02	$12,589	6000	4583	—
AW150, Utility, Model W12	$14,490	6000*	4597	—

* 6400 lb. GVW Package optional.

STANDARD ENGINE: Features include a drop-forged five-bearing crankshaft, chain-driven camshaft, free-turning exhaust valves, drop-forged I-beam connecting rods and silent-chain camshaft. Engine Type: OHV, V-8. Cast iron block and cylinder head. Bore x Stroke: 3.91 in. x 3.312 in. Lifters: Hydraulic. Number of main bearings-5. Fuel Induction: Electronic fuel injection. Compression Ratio: 8.7:1. Displacement: 318 cu. in. (5.2 liters). Horsepower: 170 @ 4000 rpm. Torque: Net: 260 lb.-ft. @ 2000 rpm. Oil refill capacity: 5 qt. with filter change. Fuel Requirements: Unleaded.

OPTIONAL ENGINE: OHV V-8. Available in 49 states with 4-spd. manual transmission only. In California available with automatic transmission only. Features include vibration damper, 18 in. 4-blade fan and drop-forged crankshaft. Engine Type: OHV, V-8. Cast iron block and cylinder head. Bore x Stroke: 4.00 in. x 3.58 in. Lifters: Hydraulic. Number of main bearings-5. Fuel Induction: Single 4-bbl. Holley carburetor. Compression Ratio: 8.4:1. Displacement: 360 cu. in. (5.9 liters). 360-Horsepower: 190 @ 4000 rpm. Torque: Net: 255 lb.-ft. @ 1600 rpm. Oil refill capacity: 5 qt. Fuel Requirements: Unleaded.

CHASSIS FEATURES: Separate body and frame, ladder-type, drop center frame, 36,000 psi, 2.86 in. modules.

SUSPENSION AND RUNNING GEAR: Front Suspension: 48 in. x 2.5 in. Semi-elliptical leaf springs, 1.0 in. stabilizer bar and 1.0 in. tubular shock absorbers. 1640 lb. rating. Optional Rating: 2100 lb. (standard on AW150 with 6400 lb. GVW). Rear Suspension: 52 in. x 2.5 in. Semi-elliptical leaf springs, and 1.0 in. tubular shock absorbers. 1820 lb. capacity. Optional Rating: None. Front Axle Type and Capacity: Spicer 44F-B-J full-floating, 3500 lb. capacity. Optional: 4000 lb. (standard on AW150 with 6400 lb. GVW). Rear Axle Type and Capacity: Chrysler 9.25 in. Semi-floating, hypoid-type 3600 lb. capacity. Optional: None. Final Drive Ratio: 318 2-bbl. and 4-spd. trans.: 3.21:1. Optional with automatic transmission: 3.55:1. Transfer Case: New Process 242 part-time, two-speed. Brakes: Type: Power, hydraulic. Front: Discs. Rear: Drums. Dimensions: Front: 11.75 in. x 1.256 in. disc. Rear: 11 in. x 2.5 in. Wheels: 15 x 6.5 in. 5-stud disc. Optional: 15 x 7.0 in. heavy-duty, 15 x 7 in. argent painted steel spoke with bright trim ring and hub center, 15 x 7 in. aluminum radial ribbed. Tires: P325/75R15XL. Steering: Saginaw integral power steering. Turning Circle: 36.9 ft. Optional: None. Transmission: NP435, wide-ratio 4-speed manual, synchromesh on top three gears. Transmission ratios: 6.69, 3.34, 1.66, 1.00:1. Optional: 3-speed automatic transmission: Ratios: 2.45, 1.45., 1.00:1. Clutch: Single dry plate disc, hydraulic actuation lining. Clutch diameter: 11 in. dia. Total lining area: 123.0 sq. in. Optional: None.

VEHICLE DIMENSIONS: Wheelbase: 106.0 in. Overall Length: 184.6 in. Front/Rear Tread: 65.7 in./63.4 in. Overall Height: 74.0 in. Width: 79.5 in. Front/Rear Overhang: 32.5 in./45.5 in. Tailgate: Width and Height: 37.5 in. x 50.5 in. Approach/Departure Degrees: 33/22.5. Ground Clearance: Front axle: 8.5 in. Rear axle: 8.0 in. Oil pan: 15.6 in. Transfer case: 11.0 in. Load space: With rear bench seat in place: 33 in. x 49.0 in. x 40.5 in. With rear seat removed or folded: 54 in. x 50 in. x 40.5 in. Front headroom: 37.75 in. Pedal to seat back (max.): 46 in. Steering wheel to seat back (max.): 19.25 in. Seat to ground: 37 in. Floor to ground: 23 in.

CAPACITIES: Fuel Tank: 35 gal.

ACCOMMODATIONS: Seating Capacity: Five with standard (optional for Custom) Royal SE Package rear bench seat.

INSTRUMENTATION: 0-100 mph speedometer, 99,999.9 mi. odometer, trip odometer, gauges for fuel level and ammeter, oil pressure and engine coolant temperature; trip odometer. Warning lights for brake system warning, hazard light operation, liftgate ajar and 4x4 front hubs.

OPTIONS AND PRICES: Air conditioning with bi-level ventilation. 114 amp alternator. 500 amp maintenance-free, heavy-duty battery. Front bumper guards. Rear step-type painted bumper. Anti-spin rear axle. Auxiliary transmission oil to air cooler. Maximum engine cooling. Privacy glass (sunscreen glass for rear quarter and liftgate only). Engine block heater. Dual low mount 6 in. x 9 in. exterior mirrors. Bright lower body moldings with black vinyl insert and partial wheel-lip. AM/FM electronically tuned stereo radio with integral digital clock. AM/FM radio electronically tuned stereo with Seek-Scan, cassette tape player with automatic reverse, Dynamic Noise Reduction and integral digital clock. Fuel tank skid plate. Transfer case skid plate. Automatic speed control (Royal SE Package required). Sport bar. Tilt type steering column. Requires Royal SE Package, intermittent windshield wipers and automatic transmission). Deluxe bright wheelcovers. 15 in. x 7.0 in. road type wheels. Aluminum radial ribbed wheels. Argent painted steel spoke wheels with bright trim ring. Two-speed windshield wipers with intermittent wipe. Royal SE Package. Prospector Package I. Includes Convenience Package, deluxe bright wheelcovers, grille with bright insert, headlight bezels, halogen headlights, ram's head hood ornament, Power Convenience Package, sunscreen glass (rear quarter and liftgate windows only). Prospector Package II includes all items in Prospector I Package except sunscreen glass plus dual 6 in. x 9 in. low mount exterior mirrors and Royal SE Decor Package. Prospector III Package. Includes air conditioning, aluminum ribbed road wheels, electronically tuned AM/FM stereo radio with integral clock, Convenience Package, P235/75R15XL raised white letter tires, Power Convenience Package, Royal SE Decor Package, speed control, sunscreen glass (rear quarter and liftgate only), and Two-Tone Paint Package. Power Convenience Package. Includes power front door locks and front door power windows. Heavy-Duty Package. Includes heavy-duty 1.1875 in. front and rear shock absorbers, and heavy-duty front stabilizer bar. Two-Tone Paint Package. Includes lower body side moldings with black vinyl insert and bright partial wheel-lip moldings, two-tone paint and upper side and rear quarter exterior moldings. Convenience Package. Includes halogen headlights, glove box lock and light, ashtray light and two-speed windshield wipers with intermittent wipe.

HISTORICAL FOOTNOTES: Manager of the Dodge Car and Truck Division was J.B. Damoose.

1989 RAMCHARGER

The design of the Ramcharger was unchanged for 1989. The Dodge Ram Trac 4x4 system allowed the driver to shift on the move into four-wheel drive and back to two-wheel drive. Power-assisted brakes and steering as well as the 5.2 liter EFI V-8 was once again standard.

1989 Dodge AW150 Ramcharger

I.D. DATA: The vehicle identification number was located on a plate attached to the driver's side door body latch post. The V.I.N. consisted of 17 elements. The first entry, indicated the nation of origin as follows: 1-U.S.A., 2-Canada. This was followed by a letter B identifying Dodge as the manufacturer. The number 7 then identified the vehicle type as a truck. The gross vehicle weight was next designated as follows: G-5001-6000 lb. The truck line was then identified as a 4x4 by the letter W. The next entry was a number 0 for the 100 truck series. A number 2 followed to identify the Ramcharger as a Sport Utility. This was then proceeded by the engine code according to the following: T-318-2-bbl. T-360-4 bbl. A check digit was then inserted, followed by the letter K for the 1989 model year. The next item, a letter, identified the assembly plant as follows: A-Lynch Road, C-Jefferson, D-Belvedere, F-Newark, G-St. Louis, K-Pillete, Canada, M-Lago Alberto, S-Warren #1, T-Warren #2, V-Warren #3 or X-Missouri. The final six numbers beginning with 10001 were the plant sequential number.

Body Type	Factory Price	GVW	Shipping Weight	Prod. Total
Ramcharger, 318 V-8				
AW100, Utility, Model W02	$14,043	6000	4583	18,309[2]
AW150, Utility, Model W12	$15,676	6000[1]	4597	—

NOTE 1: 6400 lb. GVW Package optional.
NOTE 2: 1998 model sales of all models.

STANDARD ENGINE: Features include a drop-forged five-bearing crankshaft, chain-driven camshaft, free-turning exhaust valves, drop-forged I-beam connecting rods and silent-chain camshaft. Engine Type: OHV, V-8. Cast iron block and cylinder head. Bore x Stroke: 3.91 in. x 3.312 in. Lifters: Hydraulic. Number of main bearings-5. Fuel Induction: Electronic fuel injection. Compression Ratio: 8.7:1. Displacement: 318 cu. in. (5.2 liters). Horsepower: 140. Oil refill capacity: 5 qt. with filter change. Fuel Requirements: Unleaded.

OPTIONAL ENGINE: OHV V-8. Features include vibration damper, 18 in. 4-blade fan and drop-forged crankshaft. Engine Type: OHV, V-8. Cast iron block and cylinder head. Bore x Stroke: 4.00 in. x 3.58 in. Lifters: Hydraulic. Number of main bearings-5. Fuel Induction: Throttle body fuel injection. Compression Ratio: 8.4:1. Displacement: 360 cu. in. (5.9 liters). 360-Horsepower: 190 @ 4000 rpm. Torque: Net: 255 lb.-ft. @ 1600 rpm. Oil refill capacity: 5 qt. Fuel Requirements: Unleaded.

CHASSIS FEATURES: Separate body and frame, ladder-type, drop center frame, 36,000 psi, 2.86 in. modules.

SUSPENSION AND RUNNING GEAR: Front Suspension: 48 in. x 2.5 in. Semi-elliptical leaf springs, 1.0 in. stabilizer bar and 1.0 in. tubular shock absorbers. 1640 lb. rating. Optional Rating: 2100 lb. (standard on AW150 with 6400 lb. GVW). Rear Suspension: 52 in. x 2.5 in. Semi-elliptical leaf springs, and 1.0 in. tubular shock absorbers. 1820 lb. capacity. Optional Rating: None. Front Axle Type and Capacity: Spicer 44F-B-J full-floating, 3500 lb. capacity. Optional: 4000 lb. (standard on AW150 with 6400 lb. GVW). Rear Axle Type and Capacity: Chrysler 9.25 in. Semi-floating, hypoid-type 3600 lb. capacity. Optional: None. Final Drive Ratio: 318 2-bbl. and 4-spd. trans.: 3.21:1. Optional with automatic transmission: 3.55:1. Transfer Case: New Process 241 part-time, two-speed. Brakes: Type: Power, hydraulic. Front: Discs. Rear: Drums. Dimensions: Front: 11.75 in. x 1.256 in. disc. Rear: 11 in. x 2.5 in. Wheels: 15 x 6.5 in. 5-stud disc. Optional: 15 x 7.0 in. heavy-duty, 15 x 7 in. argent painted steel spoke with bright trim ring and hub center, 15 x 7 in. aluminum radial ribbed. Tires: P325/75R15XL. Steering: Saginaw integral power steering. Turning Circle: 36.9 ft. Optional: None. Transmission: NP435, wide-ratio 4-speed manual, synchromesh on top three gears. Transmission ratios: 6.69, 3.34, 1.66, 1.00:1. Optional: 3-speed automatic transmission: Ratios: 2.45, 1.45., 1.00:1. Clutch: Single dry plate disc, hydraulic actuation lining. Clutch diameter: 11 in. dia. Total lining area: 123.0 sq. in. Optional: None.

VEHICLE DIMENSIONS: Wheelbase: 106.0 in. Overall Length: 184.6 in. Front/Rear Tread: 65.7 in./63.4 in. Overall Height: 74.0 in. Width: 79.5 in. Front/Rear Overhang: 32.5 in./45.5 in. Tailgate: Width and Height: 37.5 in. x 50.5 in. Approach/Departure Degrees: 33/22.5. Ground Clearance: Front axle: 8.5 in. Rear axle: 8.0 in. Oil pan: 15.6 in. Transfer case: 11.0 in. Load space: With rear bench seat in place: 33 in. x 49.0 in. x 40.5 in. With rear seat removed or folded: 54 in. x 50 in. x 40.5 in. Front headroom: 37.75 in. Pedal to seat back (max.): 46 in. Steering wheel to seat back (max.): 19.25 in. Seat to ground: 37 in. Floor to ground: 23 in.

CAPACITIES: Fuel Tank: 35 gal.

ACCOMMODATIONS: Seating Capacity: Five with standard (optional for Custom) Royal SE Package rear bench seat.

INSTRUMENTATION: 0-100 mph speedometer, 99,999.9 mi. odometer, trip odometer, gauges for fuel level and ammeter, oil pressure and engine coolant temperature; trip odometer. Warning lights for brake system warning, hazard light operation, liftgate ajar and 4x4 front hubs.

OPTIONS AND PRICES: Automatic transmission: $781. Air conditioning with bi-level ventilation: $781. 114 amp alternator. 500 amp maintenance-free, heavy-duty battery. Front bumper guards. Rear step-type painted bumper. Anti-spin rear axle. Auxiliary transmission oil to air cooler. Maximum engine cooling. Privacy glass (sunscreen glass for rear quarter and liftgate only). Engine block heater. Dual low mount 6 in. x 9 in. exterior mirrors. Bright lower body moldings with black vinyl insert and partial wheel-lip. AM/FM electronically tuned stereo radio with integral digital clock. AM/FM radio electronically tuned stereo with Seek-Scan, cassette tape player with automatic reverse, Dynamic Noise Reduction and integral digital clock. Fuel tank skid plate. Transfer case skid plate. Automatic speed control (Royal SE Package required). Sport bar. Tilt type steering column. Requires Royal SE Package, intermittent windshield wipers and automatic transmission). Deluxe bright wheelcovers. 15 in. x 7.0 in. road type wheels. Aluminum radial ribbed wheels. Argent painted steel spoke wheels with bright trim ring. Two-speed windshield wipers with intermittent wipe. Royal SE Package. Prospector Package I. Includes Convenience Package, deluxe bright wheelcovers, grille with bright insert, headlight bezels, halogen headlights, ram's head hood ornament, Power Convenience Package, sunscreen glass (rear quarter and liftgate windows only). Prospector Package II includes all items in Prospector I Package except sunscreen glass plus dual 6 in. x 9 in. low mount exterior mirrors and Royal SE Decor Package. Prospector III Package. Includes air conditioning, aluminum ribbed road wheels, electronically tuned AM/FM stereo radio with integral clock, Convenience Package, P235/75R15XL raised white letter tires, Power Convenience Package, Royal SE Decor Package, speed control, sunscreen glass (rear quarter and liftgate only), and Two-Tone Paint Package. Power Convenience Package. Includes power front door locks and front door power windows. Heavy-Duty Package. Includes heavy-duty 1.1875 in. front and rear shock absorbers, and heavy-duty front stabilizer bar. Two-Tone Paint Package. Includes lower body side moldings with black vinyl insert and bright partial wheel-lip moldings, two-tone paint and upper side and rear quarter exterior moldings. Convenience Package. Includes halogen headlights, glove box lock and light, ashtray light and two-speed windshield wipers with intermittent wipe.

HISTORICAL FOOTNOTES: For the 1989 model year, the Ramcharger ranked 13 in sales among the 25 Sport utility vehicles sold in the United States.

1990 RAMCHARGER

The Ramcharger was, once again, little changed for 1990. Its functional features now included standard anti-lock brakes.

I.D. DATA: The vehicle identification number was located on a plate attached to the driver's side door body latch post. The V.I.N. consisted of 17 elements. The first entry, indicated the nation of origin as follows: 1-U.S.A., 2-Canada. This was followed by a letter B identifying Dodge as the manufacturer. The number 7 then identified the vehicle type as a truck. The gross vehicle weight was next designated as follows: G-5001-6000 lb. The truck line was then identified as a 4x4 by the letter W. The next entry was a number 0 for the 100 truck series. A number 2 followed to identify the Ramcharger as a Sport Utility. This was then proceeded by the engine code according to the following: T-318-2-bbl. T-360-4 bbl. A check digit was then inserted, followed by the letter L for the 1990 model year. The next item, a letter, identified the assembly plant as follows: A-Lynch Road, C-Jefferson, D-Belvedere, F-Newark, G-St. Louis, K-Pillete, Canada, M-Lago Alberto, S-Warren #1, T-Warren #2, V-Warren #3 or X-Missouri. The final six numbers beginning with 10001 were the plant sequential number.

Body Type	Factory Price	GVW	Shipping Weight	Prod. Total
Ramcharger, 318 V-8				
AW100, Utility, Model W02	$15,575	6000	4638	10,346[2]
AW150, Utility, Model W12	$17,150	6000[1]	4598	—

NOTE 1: 6400 lb. GVW Package optional.
NOTE 2: 1990 model sales of all models.

STANDARD ENGINE: Features include a drop-forged five-bearing crankshaft, chain-driven camshaft, free-turning exhaust valves, drop-forged I-beam connecting rods and silent-chain camshaft. Engine Type: OHV, V-8. Cast iron block and cylinder head. Bore x Stroke: 3.91 in. x 3.312 in. Lifters: Hydraulic. Number of main bearings-5. Fuel Induction: Electronic fuel injection. Compression Ratio: 8.7:1. Displacement: 318 cu. in. (5.2 liters). Horsepower: 170. Oil refill capacity: 5 qt. with filter change. Fuel Requirements: Unleaded.

OPTIONAL ENGINE: OHV V-8. Features include vibration damper, 18 in. 4-blade fan and drop-forged crankshaft. Engine Type: OHV, V-8. Cast iron block and cylinder head. Bore x Stroke: 4.00 in. x 3.58 in. Lifters: Hydraulic. Number of main bearings-5. Fuel Induction: Fuel injection. Compression Ratio: 8.4:1. Displacement: 360 cu. in. (5.9 liters). 360-Horsepower: 190 @ 4000 rpm. Torque: Net: 255 lb.-ft. @ 1600 rpm. Oil refill capacity: 5 qt. Fuel Requirements: Unleaded.

CHASSIS FEATURES: Separate body and frame, ladder-type, drop center frame, 36,000 psi, 2.86 in. modules.

SUSPENSION AND RUNNING GEAR: Front Suspension: 48 in. x 2.5 in. Semi-elliptical leaf springs, 1.0 in. stabilizer bar and 1.0 in. tubular shock absorbers. 1640 lb. rating. Optional Rating: 2100 lb. (standard on AW150 with 6400 lb. GVW). Rear Suspension: 52 in. x 2.5 in. Semi-elliptical leaf springs, and 1.0 in. tubular shock absorbers. 1820 lb. capacity. Optional Rating: None. Front Axle Type and Capacity: Spicer 44F-B-J full-floating, 3500 lb. capacity. Optional: 4000 lb. (standard on AW150 with 6400 lb. GVW). Rear Axle Type and Capacity: Chrysler 9.25 in. Semi-floating, hypoid-type 3600 lb. capacity. Optional: None. Final Drive Ratio: 318 2-bbl. and 4-spd. trans.: 3.21:1. Optional with automatic transmission: 3.55:1. Transfer Case: New Process 241 part-time, two-speed. Brakes: Type: Power, hydraulic. Front: Discs. Rear: Drums. Dimensions: Front: 11.75 in. x 1.256 in. disc. Rear: 11 in. x 2.5 in. Wheels: 15 x 6.5 in. 5-stud disc. Optional: 15 x 7.0 in. heavy-duty, 15 x 7 in. argent painted steel spoke with bright trim ring and hub center, 15 x 7 in. aluminum radial ribbed. Tires: P325/75R15XL. Steering: Saginaw integral power steering. Turning Circle: 36.9 ft. Optional: None. Transmission: NP435, wide-ratio 4-speed manual, synchromesh on top three gears. Transmission ratios: 6.69, 3.34, 1.66, 1.00:1. Optional: 3-speed automatic transmission: Ratios: 2.45, 1.45., 1.00:1. Clutch: Single dry plate disc, hydraulic actuation lining. Clutch diameter: 11 in. dia. Total lining area: 123.0 sq. in. Optional: None.

VEHICLE DIMENSIONS: Wheelbase: 106.0 in. Overall Length: 184.6 in. Front/Rear Tread: 65.7 in./63.4 in. Overall Height: 74.0 in. Width: 79.5 in. Front/Rear Overhang: 32.5 in./45.5 in. Tailgate: Width and Height: 37.5 in. x 50.5 in. Approach/Departure Degrees: 33/22.5. Ground

Clearance: Front axle: 8.5 in. Rear axle: 8.0 in. Oil pan: 15.6 in. Transfer case: 11.0 in. Load space: With rear bench seat in place: 33 in. x 49.0 in. x 40.5 in. With rear seat removed or folded: 54 in. x 50 in. x 40.5 in. Front headroom: 37.75 in. Pedal to seat back (max.): 46 in. Steering wheel to seat back (max.): 19.25 in. Seat to ground: 37 in. Floor to ground: 23 in.

CAPACITIES: Fuel Tank: 35 gal.

ACCOMMODATIONS: Seating Capacity: Five with standard (optional for Custom) Royal SE Package rear bench seat.

INSTRUMENTATION: 0-100 mph speedometer, 99,999.9 mi. odometer, trip odometer, gauges for fuel level and ammeter, oil pressure and engine coolant temperature; trip odometer. Warning lights for brake system warning, hazard light operation, liftgate ajar and 4x4 front hubs.

OPTIONS AND PRICES: Automatic transmission: $860. Air conditioning with bi-level ventilation: $820. 114 amp alternator. 500 amp maintenance-free, heavy-duty battery. Front bumper guards. Rear step-type painted bumper. Anti-spin rear axle. Auxiliary transmission oil to air cooler. Maximum engine cooling. Privacy glass (sunscreen glass for rear quarter and liftgate only). Engine block heater. Dual low mount 6 in. x 9 in. exterior mirrors. Bright lower body moldings with black vinyl insert and partial wheel-lip. AM/FM electronically tuned stereo radio with integral digital clock: $239. AM/FM radio electronically tuned stereo with Seek-Scan, cassette tape player with automatic reverse, Dynamic Noise Reduction and integral digital clock. Fuel tank skid plate. Transfer case skid plate. Automatic speed control (Royal SE Package required). Sport bar. Tilt type steering column. Requires Royal SE Package, intermittent windshield wipers and automatic transmission). Deluxe bright wheelcovers. 15 in. x 7.0 in. road type wheels. Aluminum radial ribbed wheels. Argent painted steel spoke wheels with bright trim ring. Two-speed windshield wipers with intermittent wipe. Royal SE Package. Prospector Package I. Includes Convenience Package, deluxe bright wheelcovers, grille with bright insert, headlight bezels, halogen headlights, ram's head hood ornament, Power Convenience Package, sunscreen glass (rear quarter and liftgate windows only). Prospector Package II includes all items in Prospector I Package except sunscreen glass plus dual 6 in. x 9 in. low mount exterior mirrors and Royal SE Decor Package. Prospector III Package. Includes air conditioning, aluminum ribbed road wheels, electronically tuned AM/FM stereo radio with integral clock, Convenience Package, P235/75R15XL raised white letter tires, Power Convenience Package, Royal SE Decor Package, speed control, sunscreen glass (rear quarter and liftgate only), and Two-Tone Paint Package. Power Convenience Package. Includes power front door locks and front door power windows. Heavy-Duty Package. Includes heavy-duty 1.1875 in. front and rear shock absorbers, and heavy-duty front stabilizer bar. Two-Tone Paint Package. Includes lower body side moldings with black vinyl insert and bright partial wheel-lip moldings, two-tone paint and upper side and rear quarter exterior moldings. Convenience Package. Includes halogen headlights, glove box lock and light, ashtray light and two-speed windshield wipers with intermittent wipe.

HISTORICAL FOOTNOTES: The decline in Ramcharger sales for 1990 was indicative of the ground Dodge lost in the 1990 truck market. Whereas in 1989 it had 11.5 percent of that market, its 1990 share was 10.1 percent.

1991 RAMCHARGER

The 1991 Ramcharger was depicted by Dodge as a vehicle "targeted to outdoor enthusiasts who want a full-size, personal use off-road vehicle." Dodge also reported that the Ramcharger had "a lower base price than eight of its Ford or Chevrolet competitors. It has the highest standard towing rating for a 4x4 model."

1991 Dodge AW150 Ramcharger

For 1991 three new exterior colors were offered. Updating the Ramcharger's front-end appearance was a new grille with a massive looking perimeter frame and cross bars with vaned inserts mounted between the crossbars. Molded into the grille header was the Dodge name in block letters. Also giving the Ramcharger a contemporary appearance was the use of new clear "park and turn" lamp lenses. The front and rear bumpers received a new black full-width step pad on the top surface. These pads were intended to provide a bolder look as well as helping to protect the bumper top surface from scratches. A redesigned rear step bumper increased the Ramcharger's trailer tow rating to 5,000 pounds from 3,000 pounds. Also revised for 1991 were the lower body side and wheel-lip moldings. A new Ramcharger Canyon Sport Package was introduced at mid-year. It featured a body color grille with dark argent inserts accented by a lower sand-colored two-tone treatment which included sand-colored bumpers. Additional features included black trimmed mirrors, black window moldings and body side accents. This package was offered in red, black, white and hunter green exterior colors. A tundra interior was standard with the four colors. The 1991 Ramcharger interior featured a number of new comfort and convenience features. These included Unibelt three-point passenger restraints for the rear outboard seat positions, larger fabric-covered sun visors, bench seat restraints, seat back release lever and split-back rear bench seat. A tilt steering column was now available with all engines and transmissions. Standard equipment for 1991 consisted of front and rear bright finish bumpers, buzzer warning for key in ignition, headlamps on and fasten seat belts; cigarette lighter, console between front bucket seats, full floor covering, tinted glass for all windows, color-keyed soft cloth headliner, in-cab hood release, electric horn, insulation for dash and plenum liners and hood inner panel, interior 10 in. day/night mirror, exterior 6 in. x 9 in., low mount bright mirrors, bright moldings for windshield, quarter side and liftgate windows, power steering, rear roof vent, deluxe 15 in. dia., two-spoke black finish steering wheel, two vinyl sun visors, inside mounted spare tire carrier, rear compartment trim panels, bright hubcaps, and two-speed windshield wipers. Replacing the AW100 for 1991 was the AW150S model.

I.D. DATA. The vehicle identification number was located on a plate attached to the driver's side door body latch post. The V.I.N. consisted of 17 elements. The first entry, indicated the nation of origin as follows: 1-U.S.A., 2-Canada. This was followed by a letter B identifying Dodge as the manufacturer. The number 7 then identified the vehicle type as a truck. The gross vehicle weight was next designated as follows: G-5001-6000 lb. The truck line was then identified as a 4x4 by the letter W. The next entry was a number 0 for the 100 truck series. A number 2 followed to identify the Ramcharger as a Sport Utility. This was then proceeded by the engine code according to the following: T-318-2-bbl. T-360-4 bbl. A check digit was then inserted, followed by the letter M for the 1991 model year. The next item, a letter, identified the assembly plant as follows: A-Lynch Road, C-Jefferson, D-Belvedere, F-Newark, G-St. Louis, K-Pillete, Canada, M-Lago Alberto, S-Warren #1, T-Warren #2, V-Warren #3 or X-Missouri. The final six numbers beginning with 10001 were the plant sequential number.

Body Type	Factory Price	GVW	Shipping Weight	Prod. Total
Ramcharger, 318 V-8				
AW150S, Utility	$12,589	6000	4583	5606[2]
AW150, Utility	$14,490	6000[1]	4597	—

NOTE 1: 6400 lb. GVW Package optional.
NOTE 2: 1991 calendar sales, all models.

STANDARD ENGINE: Features include a drop-forged five-bearing crankshaft, chain-driven camshaft, free-turning exhaust valves, drop-forged I-beam connecting rods and silent-chain camshaft. Engine Type: OHV, V-8. Cast iron block and cylinder head. Bore x Stroke: 3.91 in. x 3.312 in. Lifters: Hydraulic. Number of main bearings-5. Fuel Induction: Electronic fuel injection. Compression Ratio: 9.2:1. Displacement: 318 cu. in. (5.2 liters). Horsepower: 170 @ 4000 rpm. Torque: Net: 260 lb.-ft. @ 2000 rpm. Oil refill capacity: 5 qt. with filter change. Fuel Requirements: Unleaded.

OPTIONAL ENGINE: OHV V-8. Features include vibration damper, 18 in. 4-blade fan and drop-forged crankshaft. Engine Type: OHV, V-8. Cast iron block and cylinder head. Bore x Stroke: 4.00 in. x 3.58 in. Lifters: Hydraulic. Number of main bearings-5. Fuel Induction: Fuel injection. Compression Ratio: 8.1:1. Displacement: 360 cu. in. (5.9 liters). Horsepower: 190 @ 4000 rpm. Torque: Net: 292 lb.-ft. @ 2400 rpm. Oil refill capacity: 5 qt. Fuel Requirements: Unleaded.

CHASSIS FEATURES: Separate body and frame, ladder-type, drop center frame, 36,000 psi, 2.86 in. modules.

SUSPENSION AND RUNNING GEAR: Front Suspension: 48 in. x 2.5 in. Semi-elliptical leaf springs, 1.0 in. stabilizer bar and 1.0 in. tubular shock absorbers. 1640 lb. rating. Optional Rating: 2100 lb. (standard on AW150 with 6400 lb. GVW). Rear Suspension: 52 in. x 2.5 in. Semi-elliptical leaf springs, and 1.0 in. tubular shock absorbers. 1820 lb. capacity. Optional Rating: None. Front Axle Type and Capacity: Spicer 44F-B-J full-floating, 3500 lb. capacity. Optional: 4000 lb. (standard on AW150 with 6400 lb. GVW). Rear Axle Type and Capacity: Chrysler 9.25 in. Semi-floating, hypoid-type 3600 lb. capacity. Optional: None. Final Drive Ratio: 318 2-bbl. and 4-spd. trans.: 3.21:1. Optional with automatic transmission: 3.55:1. Transfer Case: New Process 241 part-time, two-speed. Brakes: Type: Power, hydraulic. Front: Discs. Rear: Drums. Dimensions: Front: 11.75 in. x 1.256 in. disc. Rear: 11 in. x 2.5 in. Wheels: 15 x 6.5 in. 5-stud disc. Optional: 15 x 7.0 in. heavy-duty, 15 x 7 in. argent painted steel spoke with bright trim ring and hub center, 15 x 7 in. aluminum radial ribbed. Tires: P325/75R15XL. Steering: Saginaw integral power steering. Turning Circle: 36.9 ft. Optional: None. Transmission: NP435, wide-ratio 4-speed manual, synchromesh on top three gears. Transmission ratios: 6.69, 3.34, 1.66, 1.00:1. Optional: 3-speed automatic transmission: Ratios: 2.45, 1.45., 1.00:1. Clutch: Single dry plate disc, hydraulic actuation lining. Clutch diameter: 11 in. dia. Total lining area: 123.0 sq. in. Optional: None.

VEHICLE DIMENSIONS: Wheelbase: 106.0 in. Overall Length: 184.6 in. Front/Rear Tread: 65.7 in./63.4 in. Overall Height: 74.0 in. Width: 79.5 in. Front/Rear Overhang: 32.5 in./45.5 in. Tailgate: Width and Height: 37.5 in. x 50.5 in. Approach/Departure Degrees: 33/22.5. Ground Clearance: Front axle: 8.5 in. Rear axle: 8.0 in. Oil pan: 15.6 in. Transfer case: 11.0 in. Load space: With rear bench seat in place: 33 in. x 49.0 in. x 40.5 in. With rear seat removed or folded: 54 in. x 50 in. x 40.5 in. Front headroom: 37.75 in. Pedal to seat back (max.): 46 in. Steering wheel to seat back (max.): 19.25 in. Seat to ground: 37 in. Floor to ground: 23 in.

CAPACITIES: Fuel Tank: 34 gal.

ACCOMMODATIONS: Seating Capacity: Five with standard (optional for Custom) Royal SE Package rear bench seat.

INSTRUMENTATION: 0-100 mph speedometer, 99,999.9 mi. odometer, trip odometer, gauges for fuel level and ammeter, oil pressure and engine coolant temperature; trip odometer. Warning lights for brake system warning, hazard light operation, liftgate ajar and 4x4 front hubs.

OPTIONS AND PRICES: Automatic transmission: $860. Air conditioning with bi-level ventilation: $820. 114 amp alternator. 500 amp maintenance-free, heavy-duty battery. Front bumper guards. Rear step-type painted bumper. Anti-spin rear axle. Auxiliary transmission oil to air cooler. Maximum engine cooling. Privacy glass (sunscreen glass for rear quarter and liftgate only). Engine block heater. Dual low mount 6 in. x 9 in. exterior mirrors. Bright lower body moldings with black vinyl insert and partial wheel-lip. AM/FM electronically tuned stereo radio with integral digital clock: $239. AM/FM radio electronically tuned stereo with Seek-Scan, cassette tape player with automatic reverse, Dynamic Noise Reduction and integral digital clock. Fuel tank skid plate. Transfer case skid plate. Automatic speed control (Royal SE Package required). Sport bar. Tilt type steering column. Requires Royal SE Package, intermittent windshield wipers and automatic transmission). Deluxe bright wheelcovers. 15 in. x 7.0 in. road type wheels. Aluminum radial ribbed wheels. Argent painted steel spoke wheels with bright trim ring. Two-speed windshield wipers with intermittent wipe. Royal SE Package. Prospector Package I. Includes Convenience Package, deluxe bright wheelcovers, grille with bright insert, headlight bezels, halogen headlights, ram's head hood ornament, Power Convenience Package, sunscreen glass (rear quarter and liftgate windows only). Prospector Package II includes all items in Prospector I Package except sunscreen glass plus dual 6 in. x 9 in. low mount exterior mirrors and Royal SE Decor Package. Prospector III Package. Includes air conditioning, aluminum ribbed road wheels, electronically tuned AM/FM stereo radio with integral clock, Convenience Package, P235/75R15XL raised white letter tires, Power Convenience Package, Royal SE Decor Package, speed control, sunscreen glass (rear quarter and liftgate only), and Two-Tone Paint Package. Power Convenience Package. Includes power front door locks and front door power windows. Heavy-Duty Package. Includes heavy-duty 1.1875 in. front and rear shock absorbers, and heavy-duty front stabilizer bar. Two-Tone Paint Package. Includes lower body side moldings with black vinyl insert and bright partial wheel-lip moldings, two-tone paint and upper side and rear quarter exterior moldings. Convenience Package. Includes halogen headlights, glove box lock and light, ashtray light and two-speed windshield wipers with intermittent wipe.

HISTORICAL FOOTNOTES: The Ramcharger ranked fifth in sales for the 1991 calendar year among full-size Sport-utility vehicles.

1992 RAMCHARGER

The 1992 Ramcharger had the highest standard towing rating for a 4x4 model. New features for 1992 were highlighted by a updated 5.2 liter V-8 with a larger exhaust system. The Canyon Sport Package, introduced late in 1992 was strongly promoted by Dodge. It provided a premium "out-of-doors" look with a color-keyed grille and sand-colored lower two-tone and front and rear sand painted bumpers. A new heavy-duty 5-speed manual transmission was standard. A new heavy-duty 4-speed automatic was available with both the 5.2 and 5.9 liter V-8 engines. Three new exterior colors, dark copper, light champagne metallic and dark forest green metallic, were offered. One new interior color, spice/Dark spice, was also available.

1992 Dodge AW150 Ramcharger

I.D. DATA: The vehicle identification number was located on a plate attached to the driver's side door body latch post. The V.I.N. consisted of 17 elements. The first entry, indicated the nation of origin as follows: 1-U.S.A., 2-Canada. This was followed by a letter B identifying Dodge as the manufacturer. The number 7 then identified the vehicle type as a truck. The gross vehicle weight was next designated as follows: G-5001-6000 lb. The truck line was then identified as a 4x4 by the letter W. The next entry was a number 0 for the 100 truck series. A number 2 followed to identify the Ramcharger as a Sport Utility. This was then proceeded by the engine code according to the following: T-318-2-bbl. T-360-4 bbl. A check digit was then inserted, followed by the letter N for the 1992 model year. The next item, the letter M, identified the assembly plant as Lago Alberto, Mexico. The final six numbers beginning with 10001 were the plant sequential number.

Body Type	Factory Price	GVW	Shipping Weight	Prod. Total
Ramcharger, 318 V-8				
AW150S, Utility	$17,939	6000	4583	—
AW150, Utility	$19,595	6000[1]	4597	—

NOTE 1: 6400 lb. GVW Package optional. This package was required with Snowplow Preparation Package.

STANDARD ENGINE: Features include a drop-forged five-bearing crankshaft, chain-driven camshaft, free-turning exhaust valves, drop-forged I-beam connecting rods and silent-chain camshaft. Engine Type: OHV, V-8. Cast iron block and cylinder head. Bore x Stroke: 3.91 in. x 3.312 in. Lifters: Hydraulic. Number of main bearings-5. Fuel Induction: Electronic fuel injection. Compression Ratio: 9.2:1. Displacement: 318 cu. in. (5.2 liters). Horsepower: 230 @ 4800 rpm. Torque: Net: 280 lb.-ft. @ 3200 rpm. Oil refill capacity: 5 qt. with filter change. Fuel Requirements: Unleaded.

OPTIONAL ENGINE: OHV V-8. Features include vibration damper, 18 in. 4-blade fan and drop-forged crankshaft. Engine Type: OHV, V-8. Cast iron block and cylinder head. Bore x Stroke: 4.00 in. x 3.58 in. Lifters: Hydraulic. Number of main bearings-5. Fuel Induction: Electronic fuel injection. Compression Ratio: 8.1:1. Displacement: 360 cu. in. (5.9 liters). Horsepower: 190 @ 4000 rpm. Torque: Net: 292 lb.-ft. @ 2400 rpm. Oil refill capacity: 5 qt. Fuel Requirements: Unleaded.

CHASSIS FEATURES: Separate body and frame, ladder-type, drop center frame, 36,000 psi, 2.86 in. modules.

SUSPENSION AND RUNNING GEAR: Front Suspension: 48 in. x 2.5 in. single stage semi-elliptical 3-leaf springs, 1.0 in. stabilizer bar and gas-charged 30mm shock absorbers. 1640 lb. rating. Optional Rating: 2100 lb. (standard on AW150 with 6400 lb. GVW). Rear Suspension: 52 in. x 2.5 in. progressive 5-leaf springs, and gas-charged 30mm shock absorbers. 1820 lb. capacity. Optional Rating: None. Front Axle Type and Capacity: Spicer 44F-B-J full-floating, 3500 lb. capacity. Optional: 4000 lb. (standard on AW150 with 6400 lb. GVW). Rear Axle Type and Capacity: Chrysler 9.25 in. Semi-floating, hypoid-type 3600 lb. capacity. Optional: None. Final Drive Ratio: 3.55:1. Optional: 3.90:1. Transfer Case: New Process 241 part-time, two-speed. Brakes: Type: Power, hydraulic. Front: Discs. Rear: Drums. Dimensions: Front: 11.75 in. x 1.256 in. disc. Rear: 11 in. x 2.5 in. Wheels: 15 x 6.5 in. 5-stud disc. Tires: P325/75R15XL. Steering: Saginaw integral power steering. Turning Circle: 36.9 ft. Optional: None. Transmission: 5-speed manual. Optional: 4-speed automatic transmission. Clutch: Single dry plate disc, hydraulic actuation lining. Clutch diameter: 11 in. dia. Total lining area: 123.0 sq. in. Optional: None.

VEHICLE DIMENSIONS: Wheelbase: 106.0 in. Overall Length: 184.6 in. Front/Rear Tread: 65.6 in./63.4 in. Overall Height: 73.06 in. Width: 79.5 in. Front/Rear Overhang: 32.5 in./45.5 in. Tailgate: Width and Height: 37.5 in. x 50.5 in. Approach/Departure Degrees: 33/22.5. Ground Clearance: Front axle: 8.01 in. Rear axle: 8.41 in. Load space: With rear bench seat in place: 39 in. x 49.0 in. x 40.5 in. With rear seat removed or folded: 54 in. x 50 in. x 40.5 in. Front headroom: 37.75 in. Pedal to seat back (max.): 46 in. Steering wheel to seat back (max.): 19.25 in. Seat to ground: 37 in. Floor to ground: 23 in.

CAPACITIES: Fuel Tank: 34 gal.

ACCOMMODATIONS: Seating Capacity: Five with standard (optional for Custom) Royal SE Package rear bench seat.

INSTRUMENTATION: 0-100 mph speedometer, 99,999.9 mi. odometer, trip odometer, gauges for fuel level and ammeter, oil pressure and engine coolant temperature; trip odometer. Warning lights for brake system warning, hazard light operation, liftgate ajar and 4x4 front hubs.

OPTIONS AND PRICES: Automatic transmission: $887. Air conditioning with bi-level ventilation: $836. AM/FM radio with cassette tape player. AM/FM electronically tuned stereo radio with integral digital clock: $239 (standard for AW150). 120 amp alternator. 625 amp battery. Front bumper guards. Rear step bumper. Maximum engine cooling. Auxiliary automatic transmission oil cooler. Rear window defroster. Convenience Group. 5.9 liter V-8. Sunscreen glass. 6400 lb. GVW package. Engine block heater. Heavy-duty stabilizer bars. Dual power remote mirrors. Power Convenience Package. Fuel tank skid plate. Transfer case skid plate. Snowplow Preparation Package. Trailer Towing Preparation Package. Two-tone paint procedures. Argent styled steel wheels. Cast aluminum wheels. Deluxe windshield wipers with interim feature.

HISTORICAL FOOTNOTES: The basic format of the 1992 Ramcharger originated in the 1974 model year.

1993 RAMCHARGER

The leading edge of new-for-1993 developments for the Ramcharger was the availability of the more powerful 5.9 liter Magnum V-8. A 4-speed heavy-duty automatic transmission was standard for all models. Other developments included the use of modified styled steel wheels, two new exterior pearlcoat colors: Flame red and Emerald green, and a new optional AM/FM stereo radio with graphic equalizer and cassette tape player. The 5.9 liter Magnum engine had sequential multi-point fuel injection, a tuned intake manifold and a serpentine belt accessory drive.

1993 Dodge AW150 Ramcharger

I.D. DATA: The vehicle identification number was located on a plate attached to the driver's side door body latch post. The V.I.N. consisted of 17 elements. The first entry, indicated the nation of origin as follows: 1-U.S.A., 2-Canada. This was followed by a letter B identifying Dodge as the manufacturer. The number 7 then identified the vehicle type as a truck. The gross vehicle weight was next designated as follows: G-5001-6000 lb. The truck line was then identified as a 4x4 by the letter W. The next entry was a number 0 for the 100 truck series. A number 2 followed to identify the Ramcharger as a Sport Utility. This was then proceeded by the engine code according to the following: T-318 V-8 T-360 V-8. A check digit was then inserted, followed by the letter O for the 1993 model year. The next item, the letter M, identified the assembly plant as Lago Alberto, Mexico. The final six numbers beginning with 10001 were the plant sequential number.

Body Type	Factory Price	GVW	Shipping Weight	Prod. Total
Ramcharger, 318 V-8				
AW150S, Utility	$N.A.	6000	N.A.	—
AW150, Utility	$N.A.	6000[1]	N.A.	—

NOTE 1: 6400 lb. GVW Package optional. This package was required with Snowplow Preparation Package.

STANDARD ENGINE: Features include a drop-forged five-bearing crankshaft, chain-driven camshaft, free-turning exhaust valves, drop-forged I-beam connecting rods and silent-chain camshaft. Engine Type: OHV, V-8. Cast iron block and cylinder head. Bore x Stroke: 3.91 in. x 3.312 in. Lifters: Hydraulic. Number of main bearings-5. Fuel Induction: Electronic fuel injection. Compression Ratio: 9.1:1. Displacement: 318 cu. in. (5.2 liters). Horsepower: 230 @ 4800 rpm. Torque: Net: 280 lb.-ft. @ 3200 rpm. Oil refill capacity: 5 qt. with filter change. Fuel Requirements: Unleaded.

OPTIONAL ENGINE: OHV V-8. Features include vibration damper, 18 in. 4-blade fan and drop-forged crankshaft. Engine Type: OHV, V-8. Cast iron block and cylinder head. Bore x Stroke: 4.00 in. x 3.58 in. Lifters: Hydraulic. Number of main bearings-5. Fuel Induction: Sequential multi-point fuel injection. Compression Ratio: 8.9:1. Displacement: 360 cu. in. (5.9 liters). Horsepower: 230 @ 4000 rpm. Torque: Net: 325 lb.-ft. @ 3200 rpm. Oil refill capacity: 5 qt. Fuel Requirements: Unleaded.

CHASSIS FEATURES: Separate body and frame, ladder-type, drop center frame, 36,000 psi, 2.86 in. modules.

SUSPENSION AND RUNNING GEAR: Front Suspension: 48 in. x 2.5 in. single stage semi-elliptical 3-leaf springs, 1.0 in. stabilizer bar and gas-charged 30mm shock absorbers. 1640 lb. rating. Optional Rating: 2100 lb. (standard on AW150 with 6400 lb. GVW). Rear Suspension: 52 in. x 2.5 in. progressive 5-leaf springs, and gas-charged 30mm shock absorbers. 1820 lb. capacity. Optional Rating: None. Front Axle Type and Capacity: Spicer 44F-B-J full-floating, 3500 lb. capacity. Optional: 4000 lb. (standard on AW150 with 6400 lb. GVW). Rear Axle Type and Capacity: Chrysler 9.25 in. Semi-floating, hypoid-type 3600 lb.

capacity. Optional: None. Final Drive Ratio: 3.55:1. Optional: 3.90:1. Transfer Case: New Process 241 part-time, two-speed. Brakes: Type: Power, hydraulic. Front: Discs. Rear: Drums. Dimensions: Front: 11.75 in. x 1.256 in. disc. Rear: 11 in. x 2.5 in. Wheels: 15 x 6.5 in. 5-stud disc. Tires: P325/75R15XL. Steering: Saginaw integral power steering. Turning Circle: 36.9 ft. Transmission: 4-speed automatic transmission.

VEHICLE DIMENSIONS: Wheelbase: 106.0 in. Overall Length: 184.6 in. Front/Rear Tread: 65.6 in./63.4 in. Overall Height: 73.06 in. Width: 79.5 in. Front/Rear Overhang: 32.5 in./45.5 in. Tailgate: Width and Height: 37.5 in. x 50.5 in. Approach/Departure Degrees: 33/22.5. Ground Clearance: Front axle: 8.01 in. Rear axle: 8.41 in. Load space: With rear bench seat in place: 33 in. x 49.0 in. x 40.5 in. With rear seat removed or folded: 54 in. x 50 in. x 40.5 in. Front headroom: 37.75 in. Pedal to seat back (max.): 46 in. Steering wheel to seat back (max.): 19.25 in. Seat to ground: 37 in. Floor to ground: 23 in.

CAPACITIES: Fuel Tank: 34 gal.

ACCOMMODATIONS: Seating Capacity: Five with standard (optional for Custom) Royal SE Package rear bench seat.

INSTRUMENTATION: 0-100 mph speedometer, 99,999.9 mi. odometer, trip odometer, gauges for fuel level and ammeter, oil pressure and engine coolant temperature; trip odometer. Warning lights for brake system warning, hazard light operation, liftgate ajar and 4x4 front hubs.

OPTIONS AND PRICES: Air conditioning with bi-level ventilation: $836. AM/FM radio with cassette tape player. 120 amp alternator. 625 amp battery. Front bumper guards. Rear step bumper. Maximum engine cooling. Auxiliary automatic transmission oil cooler. Rear window defroster. Convenience Group. 5.9 liter V-8. Sunscreen glass. 6400 lb. GVW package. Engine block heater. Heavy-duty stabilizer bars. Dual power remote mirrors. Power Convenience Package. Fuel tank skid plate. Transfer case skid plate. Snowplow Preparation Package. Trailer Towing Preparation Package. Two-tone paint procedures. Argent styled steel wheels. Cast aluminum wheels. Deluxe windshield wipers with interim feature.

HISTORICAL FOOTNOTES: Dodge touted the Ramcharger's all-steel top, large fuel capacity and long-term anti-corrosion warranty as key sales advantages in its highly competitive market segment.

DODGE POWER RAM

1981-1993

1981 POWER RAM

The W series pickups were given new exterior sheet metal for 1981. Not the least of the resulting changes was the abandonment of the Power Wagon name and its replacement by Power Ram. Model designations for 1981 were W150, W250 and W350. The keynote of the resulting new appearance was a smooth aerodynamic shape. Chrysler reported that the new trucks had a three percent reduction in aerodynamic drag. This translated into a fuel improvement of 0.5 percent. The grille was similar to that used in 1980, but its mesh insert consisted of larger units. New front fenders were used and, on the Sweptline body, the rear side panels had a bolder horizontal highlight. A new tailgate with dual caliper locks was also used on Sweptline models. The Sweptline trucks could also be ordered with an optional upper body side molding. Dodge made a major effort to improvement the corrosion-resistance performance of its trucks for 1981. The rear corners of the Sweptline bodies were now integral with the sides, thus eliminating the flange joints where corrosion had been common. All Dodge trucks contained a higher percentage of galvanized steel than in 1980. The Sweptline, for example, had 340 sq. ft. of galvanized steel as compared to 160 sq. ft. in 1980.

Numerous refinements were also found in the 1981 models. These included lighter weight and more efficient air conditioning and heating systems, a redesigned instrument panel with an electronic four-wheel drive readout, nine new exterior colors and new blade-type fuses. Most four-wheel drive models had new automatic locking hubs developed by Borg Warner. In order to disengage the front hubs the transfer case was put into its two-wheel drive mode and the vehicles driven in reverse for several feet.

I.D. DATA: The vehicle identification number was located on a V.I.N. plate attached to the driver's side door body latch post. The V.I.N. consisted of 17 elements. The first entry, the number 1 or 2 identified the nation of origin as either the United States or Canada. The letter B followed identified Dodge as the manufacturer. The number 7 identified the vehicle type as a truck. The gross vehicle weight entry was next according to this format: G-5001-6000 lbs., H-6001-7000 lbs., J-7001-8000 lbs., K-8001-9000 lbs., L-9001-10,000 lbs. The Power Ram pickup 4x4 truck line was next identified by the letter W. The truck series was identified by one of the following numbers: 1-150, 2-250 or 3-350. The body style designation followed according to this nomenclature: 4-Conventional cab, 4-Club cab or 6-Crew cab. The engine code was the next entry. The following system was used: E-225-6-cyl.-1-bbl. carb. H-225-6-cyl.-2-bbl. S-318-V-8-4-bbl. T-318-V-8-2-bbl. T-360-V-8-4-bbl. U-360-V-8-4-bbl. H.D.1-360-V-8-4-bbl.-Calif.

Body Type	Factory Price	GVW	Shipping Weight	Prod. Total
Model W150, 1/2 ton 6-cyl.				
Pickup, Utiline,115 in. wb.	$7740	6050	3797	—
Pickup, Sweptline, 115 in. wb.	$7740	6050	3832	—
Pickup, Utiline,131 in. wb.	$7825	6050	3947	—
Pickup, Sweptline, 131 in. wb.	$7825	6050	3947	—
W150 Club Cab				
Pickup, Sweptline, 133 in. wb.	$8396	6050	N.A.	—
Pickup, Sweptline, 149 in. wb.	$8549	6050	N.A.	—
Model W250, 3/4 ton, V-8 (Crew cab-149 in. wheelbase)				
Pickup, Utiline, 131 in. wb.	$8425	6900*	4120	—
Pickup, Sweptline, 131 in. wb.	$8425	6900	4155	—
Crew Cab, Sweptline	$10,084	6900	4785	—
W250 Club Cab				
Pickup, Sweptline	$9075	6900	4842	—

* 7500 and 8550 lb. GVW package was optional for all models.

Body Type	Factory Price	GVW	Shipping Weight	Prod. Total
Model W350, 1 ton, V-8				
Ch. & Cab, 135 in. wb.	$10,227	8500*	4806	—

* GVW packages up to 10,000 lb. were available.

STANDARD ENGINE: 115 in. wheelbase and 131 in. wheelbase pickup W150 models. Engine Type: OHV, In-line 6-cylinder. Cast iron block and cylinder head. Key components include a drop-forged, shot-peened crankshaft, roller timing chain, Stellite-faced exhaust valves, individually ported long-branch manifolds, aluminum parts and a large radiator. Bore x Stroke: 3.40 in. x 4.125 in. Lifters: Mechanical. Number of main bearings-4. Fuel Induction: Single 2-bbl. carburetor. Compression Ratio: 8.4:1. Displacement: 224.7 cu. in. (3.68 liters). Horsepower: Net: 95 @ 3600 rpm. Torque: Net: 170 lb.-ft. @ 1600 rpm. Oil refill capacity: 5 qt. with filter change. Fuel Requirements: 91 octane.

STANDARD ENGINE: 133 in. and 149 in. wheelbase W150 club cab pickups and 131 in. wheelbase. W250 conventional cab pickups; optional for other W150 models. Features include a drop-forged five-bearing crankshaft, chain-driven camshaft, free-turning exhaust valves, drop-forged I-beam connecting rods and silent-chain camshaft. Bore x Stroke: 3.91 in. x 3.312 in. Lifters: Hydraulic. Number of main bearings-5. Fuel Induction: Single 2-bbl. carburetor. Compression Ratio: 8.7:1. Displacement: 318 cu. in. (5.21 liters). Horsepower: 140 @ 4000 rpm. (155 hp. in vehicles over 8,501 lb. GVWR). Torque: Net: 240 lb.-ft. @ 2000 rpm. Oil refill capacity: 5 qt. with filter change. Fuel Requirements: 91 octane.

OPTIONAL ENGINE: Standard Engine: W250 149 in. wheelbase. Club and crew cab models and 131 in. wheelbase. Conventional chassis-cabs. Also standard for all W300 models. Optional for all W150 models and remaining W250 models. Features include vibration damper, 18 in. 4-blade fan and drop-forged crankshaft. Engine Type: OHV, V-8. Cast iron block and cylinder head. Bore x Stroke: 4.00 in. x 3.58 in. Lifters: Hydraulic. Number of main bearings-5. Fuel Induction: Single 2-bbl. carburetor. Compression Ratio: 8.4:1. Displacement: 360 cu. in. (5.89 liters). Horsepower: 170 @ 4000 rpm. (180 hp. for trucks over 8501 lb. GVWR). Torque: Net: 270 lb.-ft. @ 2000 rpm. Oil refill capacity: 5 qt. with filter change. Fuel Requirements: 91 octane.

CHASSIS FEATURES: W150: Front Suspension: Semi-elliptical springs, heavy-duty, absorbers. 1,640 lb. rating. Optional rating: 1,800 lb. Rear Suspension: Semi-elliptical springs 1820 lbs. capacity. Optional Rating: 1,820 lbs. for 115 and 131 in. wheelbase. Front Axle Type and Capacity: Full-floating, 3,500 lb. capacity. Optional: 4,000 lbs. Rear Axle Type and Capacity: Semi-floating, 3,600 lb. capacity. Optional: None. Final Drive Ratio: 2.94, (225 engine) 3.21, 3.55:1 (318 and 360 engines). The 360 engine with automatic had a 2.94:1 axle ratio. Transfer Case: NP-208, single lever, two-speed: 2.61, 1.00:1. Brakes: Type: Power, hydraulic. Front: Disc. Rear: Drum. Dimensions: Front: 11.75 in. x 1.256 in. disc. Rear: 11 in. x 2.5 in. Rear lining area: 106.4 sq. in. Wheels: 15 x 6.5 5-stud disc. Optional: 15 x 7 in. cast aluminum with radial ribbed design. Available for W150 pickups only. These wheels weighed approximately four pounds less per unit than the standard wheels. Tires: P235/75R x 15B, 4-ply rating. Optional: P25570R x 15C, LR60 x 15B, 10-15 LTB, 7.00 x 15D. Steering: Recirculating ball. Ratio: 24:1, turns Lock-to-Lock: 3.5:1. Turning Circle: 43 ft. (131 in. wheelbase). Optional: Power assisted. Ratio: 17.8:1. Transmission: NP 435 wide ratio 4-speed manual. Transmission Ratios: 6.68, 3.34, 1.66, 1.00:1. Optional: Chrysler Loadflite A-727 3-speed automatic. Ratios: 2.45, 1.45, 1.00:1. Clutch: Single dry plate disc, hydraulic actuation. Clutch diameter: 11 in. dia. Total lining area: 123.7 sq. in. Optional: None. W250: Separate body and ladder-type frame. Section modules: 3.88 in. (131 in. wheelbase), 5.02 in. (149 in. wheelbase, crew cab), 5.47 in. (149 in. wheelbase, club cab). Front Suspension: Semi-elliptical leaf springs, heavy-duty shock absorbers. 1,640 lb. capacity (131 in. wheelbase), 1,800 lb. capacity (149 in. wheelbase). Optional: 1,800 lb. capacity: 131 in. wheelbase), 2,250 lb. capacity: All wheelbases. Rear Suspension: Semi-elliptical leaf, 2,725 lb. capacity. Front Axle Type and Capacity: Full-floating, 3,500 lb. capacity. Optional rating: 4,000 lb. with Sno-Fiter Package only, 4,500 lb. Rear Axle Type and Capacity: Full-floating, 5,500 lb. capacity. Optional rating: None. Final Drive Ratio: 3.54:1 (conventional cab); 4.10:1 (club cab and crew cab). Transfer Case: Conventional cab and club cab models: New Process 208, Two-speed: 2.61, 1.00:1. Crew cab: New Process 205 two-speed. Brakes: Type: Power, hydraulic. Front: Disc. Rear: Drum. Dimensions: Front: 12.82 in. x 1.19 in. disc. Rear: 12.0 in. x 2.50 in. Total rear lining area: 122.8 sq. in. Optional: None. Wheels: 6 in., 8-stud disc. Optional: None. Tires: 8.00 x 16.5D, 8-ply rating. Optional (max. size avail.): 9.50R x 16.5E, 8-ply rating. Steering: Recirculating ball. Ratio: 24:1. Optional: Power assisted. Ratio: 17.8:1. Transmission: New Process 435, wide-ratio 4-speed manual. Transmission Ratios: 6.68, 3.34, 1.66, 1.00:1 reverse. Optional: Chrysler A-727 Loadflite 3-speed automatic. Ratios: 2.45, 1.45, 1.00:1. Clutch: Single dry plate disc, hydraulic actuation. Clutch diameter: 11 in. dia. Total lining area: 123.7 sq. in. W350: Separate body and channel steel, straight frame, 5.02 in. section modules, 36,000 psi. Front Suspension: Semi-elliptical springs, heavy-duty shock absorbers. 1,940 lb. capacity. Optional rating: 2,250 lb. Rear Suspension: Semi-elliptical springs, 3,650 lb. capacity. Optional Rating: 585 lb. and 900 lb. auxiliary springs. Front Axle Type and Capacity: Full-floating. 4,500 lb. capacity. Rear Axle Type and Capacity: 7,500 lb. capacity. Final Drive Ratio: 4.56:1. Transfer Case: New Process 205 two-speed: 1.96, 1.0:1. Brakes: Type: Hydraulic. Front: Disc. Rear: Drum. Dimensions: Front: 12.88 in. x 1.19 in. disc. Rear: 12.0 in. x 3.0 in. Total rear lining area: 147.4 sq. in. Wheels: 6.75 in. rim, 8-stud disc. Tires: 8.00 x 16.5D, 10-ply. Optional: 8.00R x 16.5E (maximum optional size). Transmission: NP435 4-speed synchromesh manual. Transmission Ratios: 6.69, 3.34, 1.66, 1.00:1. Optional: Chrysler Loadflite A-727 3-speed automatic. Ratios: 2.45, 1.45, 1.00:1. Clutch: Single plate dry disc, hydraulic actuation. Clutch diameter: 11.0 in. Total plate area: 123.7 sq. in. Optional: None.

VEHICLE DIMENSIONS: W150: Wheelbase: 115 in., 131 in.,133 in. (club cab), 149 in. (club cab). Overall Length: 115 in. wheelbase: 193.6 in., 131 in. wheelbase: 213.6 in., 133 in. wheelbase: 211.6 in., 149 in. wheelbase: 231.6 in. wheelbase. All dimensions include optional rear bumper. Front/Rear Tread: 62.5 in./62.5 in. Overall Height: 74.0 in. Width: 79.5 in. Front/Rear Overhang: 30 in./47 in. Tailgate: Width and Height: 67 in. x 21.4 in. Approach/Departure Degrees: 34/24. Ground Clearance: Front axle: 8.2 in. Rear axle: 8.5 in. Oil pan: 15.8 in. Transfer case: 10.4 in. Load space: Pickup box dimensions: 115 in. wheelbase: 78 in. x 51 in. x 19.125 in. Capacity: 61.1 cu. ft. 131 in. wheelbase and 149 in. wheelbase. Sweptline: 98 in. x 51 in. x 19.3 in. Capacity: 76.6 cu. ft. W250: Wheelbase: 131 in. Crew cab: 149 in. Overall Length: 131 in./149 in. wheelbase: 213.6 in./231.6 in. Front/Rear Tread: 62.5 in./62.5 in. Overall Height: 74.0 in. Width: 79.5 in. Front/Rear Overhang: 31 in. /49 in. Tailgate: Width x Height: 66.5 in. x 19.3 in. Approach/Departure Degrees: 30/21. Ground Clearance: Front axle: 8.0 in. Rear axle: 7.8 in. Oil pan: 16.1 in. Transfer case: 10.7 in. Load space: Pickup box dimensions: Sweptline: 98.875 in. x 51.0 in. x 19.3 in. W350: Wheelbase: 135 in. Load space: Pickup box dimensions: 108 in. x 54 in. x 20 in. Capacity: 66 cu. ft.

CAPACITIES: Fuel Tank: 25 gal.

ACCOMMODATIONS: Seating Capacity: 3 passenger.

INSTRUMENTATION: 0-100 mph speedometer, 99,999.9 mile odometer, gauges for fuel level, ammeter and engine coolant temperature. Warning lights for oil pressure, parking brake and hazard lights operation.

OPTIONS AND PRICES: Automatic transmission: $214. AM/FM with cassette tape player: $211. Tinted glass: $35. 30 gallon fuel tank: $68. Convenience Package: $70. Light Package: $45. Gauge Package. Includes oil, temperature gauges and trip odometer: $35. Sport steering wheel: $43. Electric digital clock: $51. Side mirrors: $63. Rear bumper: $90. Bright grille insert: $49. Halogen headlights: $38. Front stabilizer bar (W150): $27. Heavy-duty front springs (W150): $44. Aluminum wheels (W150): $297. Goodyear Wrangler Radial tires: $549.

HISTORICAL FOOTNOTES: The abandonment of the Power Wagon name brought an end to the history of one of the most important vehicles in American trucking history.

1982 POWER RAM

The 1982 Dodge Power Rams were again offered in W150, W250 and W350 pickup versions and in W350 chassis-cab and pickup form. Standard equipment included antifreeze protection to -20° F, ashtray, front bright finish bumper on pickups, painted on cab and chassis models, cigarette lighter, coat hooks, dash and plenum liner, directional signals, parking lights, color-keyed door inner trim panels with pull straps and armrests, black floor mat with padding, glove box with door, aluminum grille with painted plastic insert, single rectangular headlights, front wheel automatic locking hubs, padded instrument panel, fresh-air heater with defrosters, in-cab hood release, dual electric horns, exterior dual bright finish short, 5 in. x 7 in. mirrors; dual painted West Coast type, 7 in. x 16 in. mirrors for cab and chassis models, 10 in. interior day/night rearview mirror, bright windshield molding, power steering, AM radio on pickup models, seat belts, color-keyed sun visors, rear quarter flip-out windows on club cab, and dual jet two-speed windshield wipers. The base level custom interior had a three-passenger all-vinyl available in black, blue or cashmere. Available as an option for the custom pickup interior, and included in the Royal Package was a cloth and vinyl bench seat offered in a choice of blue, cashmere or red. The Royal SE Package had a deluxe cloth and vinyl bench seat available in any of four colors: Blue, cashmere, red or silver. The Royal SE interior included a luxury steering wheel with woodtone insert around the rim. The instrument panel cluster featured gauges for oil pressure and engine coolant temperature plus a trip odometer. A woodtone panel faceplate and bright trim were also installed. Additional interior features of the Royal SE Package included a "Royal SE-Engineered Ram Tough" instrument panel nameplate, front door woodgrain applique, assist strap and carpeting on lower portion, color-keyed carpeting with underlayment, bright front door sill scuff plates, soft color-keyed headliner (not available for crew cab), color-keyed garnish molding over windshield, front pillar, door header, quarter trim panel upper and over backlight (not available for crew cab), color-keyed cowl side trim panels, dome light mounted in roof center (club cab only), rear side and back trim panels (Club Cab only), and insulation under hood panel. Exterior aspects of the Royal SE Package were as follows: Bright backlight molding, bright drip rail molding, plaque on front fenders with "Leaping Ram" and "Royal SE" name, ram's head hood ornament, "Dodge Ram" nameplate on Sweptline pickup tailgate, bright taillight bezels (Sweptline models), tailgate upper and lower moldings (Sweptline models), bright aluminum grille with chrome plastic insert and headlight doors, and bright tailgate applique (Sweptline models).

1982 Dodge W150 Sweptline Power Ram pickup

The Royal Package, which was not available for club cab or crew cab models, had these exterior features: Bright backlight molding, bright drip rail molding, plaque on front fenders with "Leaping Ram" and "Royal" name, bright taillight bezels (Sweptline models), and upper and lower tailgate moldings (Sweptline models). The Royal interior had a "Royal-Engineered Ram Tough" instrument panel nameplate, front door bright trim applique and pull straps, woodtone instrument panel applique, color-keyed carpeting with underlayment, insulation under hood panel, and a color-keyed hardboard headliner.

Exterior colors offered for 1982 were: Cashmere, spice tan metallic, charcoal gray metallic, medium seaspray green metallic, ginger, daystar blue metallic, manila cream, dark blue metallic, impact red, Morocco red, burnished silver metallic, pearl white and black.

I.D. DATA: The vehicle identification number was located on a V.I.N. plate attached to the driver's side door body latch post. The V.I.N. consisted of 17 elements. The first entry, the number 1 or 2 identified the nation of origin as either the United States or Canada. The letter B followed identified Dodge as the manufacturer. The number 7 identified the vehicle type as a truck. The gross vehicle weight entry was next according to this format: G-5001-6000 lbs., H-6001-7000 lbs., J-7001-8000 lbs., K-8001-9000 lbs., L-9001-10,000 lbs. The Power Ram pickup 4x4 truck line was next identified by the letter W. The truck series was identified by one of the following numbers: 1-150, 2-250 or 3-350. The body style designation followed according to this nomenclature: 4-Conventional cab, 4-Club cab or 6-Crew cab. The engine code was the next entry. The following system was used: E-225-6-cyl.-1-bbl. carb. H-225-6-cyl.-2-bbl. S-318-V-8-4-bbl. T-318-V-8-2-bbl. T-360-V-8-4-bbl. U-360-V-8-4-bbl. H.D.1-360-V-8-4-bbl.-Calif.

Body Type	Factory Price	GVW	Shipping Weight	Prod. Total
Model W150, 1/2 ton 6-cyl.				
Pickup, Utiline, 115 in. wb.	$8590	6050	3797	—
Pickup, Sweptline, 115 in. wb.	$8590	6050	3832	—
Pickup, Utiline, 131 in. wb.	$8675	6050	3947	—
Pickup, Sweptline, 131 in. wb.	$8675	6050	3947	—
W150 Club Cab				
Pickup, Sweptline, 133 in. wb.	$9246	6050	N.A.	—
Pickup, Sweptline, 149 in. wb.	$9399	6050	N.A.	—

Model W250, 3/4 ton, V-8 (Crew cab-149 in. wheelbase)				
Pickup, Utiline, 131 in. wb.	$9206	6900*	4120	—
Pickup, Sweptline, 131 in. wb.	$9206	6900	4155	—
Crew Cab, Sweptline	$10,865	6900	4785	
W250 Club Cab				
Pickup, Sweptline	$9856	6900	4842	—

* 7500 and 8550 lb. GVW package was optional for all models.

Model W350, 1 ton, V-8				
Ch. & Cab, 135 in. wb.	$11,629	8500*	4806	

* GVW packages up to 10,000 lb. were available.

STANDARD ENGINE: 115 in. wheelbase and 131 in. wheelbase pickup W150 models. Engine Type: OHV, In-line 6-cylinder. Cast iron block and cylinder head. Key components include a drop-forged, shot-peened crankshaft, roller timing chain, Stellite-faced exhaust valves, individually ported long-branch manifolds, aluminum parts and a large radiator. Bore x Stroke: 3.40 in. x 4.125 in. Lifters: Mechanical. Number of main bearings-4. Fuel Induction: Single 2-bbl. carburetor. Compression Ratio: 8.4:1. Displacement: 224.7 cu. in. (3.68 liters). Horsepower: Net: 95 @ 3600 rpm. (90 @ 3600 rpm for Calif.). Torque: Net: 170 lb.-ft. @ 1600 rpm. (165 lb.-ft.@ 1200 rpm for Calif.). Oil refill capacity: 5 qt. with filter change. Fuel Requirements: 91 octane.

STANDARD ENGINE: 133 in. and 149 in. wheelbase W150 club cab pickups and 131 in. wheelbase W250 conventional cab pickups; optional for other W150 models. Features include a drop-forged five-bearing crankshaft, chain-driven camshaft, free-turning exhaust valves, drop-forged I-beam connecting rods and silent-chain camshaft. Bore x Stroke: 3.91 in. x 3.312 in. Lifters: Hydraulic. Number of main bearings-5. Fuel Induction: Single 2-bbl. carburetor. Compression Ratio: 8.5:1. Displacement: 318 cu. in. (5.2 liters). Horsepower: 135 @ 4000 rpm. Torque: Net: 240 lb.-ft. @ 2000 rpm. Oil refill capacity: 5 qt. with filter change. Fuel Requirements: 91 octane.

OPTIONAL ENGINE: W150 and W250 conventional cab. Standard for W150 club cab, and W350 pickup and W350 131 in. wheelbase chassis-cab. Engine Type: OHV, V-8. Cast iron block and cylinder head. Bore x Stroke: 3.91 in. x 3.312 in. Lifters: Hydraulic. Number of main bearings-5. Fuel Induction: Single 4-bbl. carburetor. Compression Ratio: 8.5:1. (8.0:1 for W350). Displacement: 318 cu. in. (5.2 liters). Horsepower: 160 @ 4000 rpm. 160 @ 4000 rpm for over 8500 (GVWR). Torque: Net: 245 lb.-ft. @ 2000 rpm. (220 lb.-ft. @ 3200 lb.-ft. for W350). Oil refill capacity: 5 qt. with filter change. Fuel Requirements: 91 octane.

STANDARD ENGINE: W350 chassis-cab 135 in. wheelbase. Optional for W350 pickup models and 131 in. wheelbase chassis and cab. Features include vibration damper, 18 in. 4-blade fan and drop-forged crankshaft. Engine Type: OHV, V-8. Cast iron block and cylinder head. Bore x Stroke: 4.00 in. x 3.58 in. Lifters: Hydraulic. Number of main bearings-5. Fuel Induction: Single 4-bbl. carburetor. Compression Ratio: 8.6:1. Displacement: 360 cu. in. (5.9 liters). Horsepower: 180 @ 4000 rpm. (170 @ 4000 rpm for Calif.). Torque: Net: 270 lb.-ft. @ 2000 rpm. (265 lb.-ft. @ 2400 for Calif.). Oil refill capacity: 5 qt. with filter change. Fuel Requirements: 91 octane.

CHASSIS FEATURES: W150: Front Suspension: Semi-elliptical springs, heavy-duty, absorbers, 1,640 lb. rating. Optional rating: 1,800 lb. Rear Suspension: Semi-elliptical springs 1,820 lbs. capacity. Optional Rating: 1,820 lbs. for 115 and 131 in. wheelbase. Front Axle Type and Capacity: Full-floating, 3,500 lb. capacity. Optional: 4,000 lbs. Rear Axle Type and Capacity: Semi-floating, 3,600 lb. capacity. Optional: None. Final Drive Ratio: 2.94, (225 engine) 3.21, 3.55:1 (318 and 360 engines). The 360 engine with automatic had a 2.94:1 axle ratio. Transfer Case: NP-208, single lever, two-speed: 2.61, 1.00:1. Brakes: Type: Power, hydraulic. Front: Discs. Rear: Drums. Dimensions: Front: 11.75 in. x 1.256 in. disc. Rear: 11 in. x 2.5 in. Rear lining area: 106.4 sq. in. Wheels: 15 x 6.5 5-stud disc. Optional: 15 x 7 in. cast aluminum with radial ribbed design. Available for W150 pickups only. These wheels weighed approximately four pounds less per unit than the standard wheels. Tires: P235/75R x 15B, 4-ply rating. Optional: P25570R x 15C, LR60 x 15B, 10-15 LTB, 7.00 x 15D. Steering: Recirculating ball. Ratio: 24:1, turns Lock-to-Lock: 3.5:1. Turning Circle: 43 ft. (131 in. wheelbase). Optional: Power assisted. Ratio: 17.8:1. Transmission: NP 435 wide ratio 4-speed manual. Transmission Ratios: 6.68, 3.34, 1.66, 1.00:1. Optional: Chrysler Loadflite A-727 3-speed automatic. Ratios: 2.45, 1.45, 1.00:1. Clutch: Single dry plate disc, hydraulic actuation. Clutch diameter: 11 in. dia. Total lining area: 123.7 sq. in. Optional: None. W250: Separate body and ladder-type frame. Section modules: 3.88 in. (131 in. wheelbase), 5.02 in. (149 in. wheelbase, crew cab), 5.47 in. (149 in. wheelbase, club cab). Front Suspension: Semi-elliptical leaf springs, heavy-duty shock absorbers, 1,640 lb. capacity (131 in. wheelbase), 1,800 lb. capacity (149 in. wheelbase). Optional: 1,800 lb. capacity (131 in. wheelbase), 2,250 lb. capacity (149 in. wheelbases). Rear Suspension: Semi-elliptical leaf springs, 2,725 lb. capacity. Front Axle Type and Capacity: Full-floating, 3,500 lb. capacity. Optional rating: 4,000 lb. with Sno-Fiter package only, 4,500 lb. Rear Axle Type and Capacity: Full-floating, 5,500 lb. capacity. Optional rating: None. Final Drive Ratio: 3.54:1 (conventional cab), 4.10:1 (club cab and crew cab). Transfer Case: Conventional cab and club cab models: New Process 208, two-speed: 2.61, 1.00:1. Crew cab: New Process 205 two-speed. Brakes: Type: Power, hydraulic. Front: Disc. Rear: Drum. Dimensions: Front: 12.82 in. x 1.19 in. disc. Rear: 12.0 in. x 2.50 in. Total rear lining area: 122.8 sq. in. Optional: None. Wheels: 6 in., 8-stud disc. Optional: None. Tires: 8.00 x 16.5D, 8-ply rating. Optional (max. size avail.): 9.50R x 16.5E, 8-ply rating. Steering: Recirculating ball. Ratio: 24:1. Optional: Power assisted. Ratio: 17.8:1. Transmission: New Process 435, wide-ratio 4-speed manual. Transmission Ratios: 6.68, 3.34, 1.66, 1.00:1 reverse: Optional: Chrysler A-727 Loadflite 3-speed automatic. Ratios: 2.45, 1.45, 1.00:1. Clutch: Single dry plate disc, hydraulic actuation. Clutch diameter: 11 in. dia. Total lining area: 123.7 sq. in. W350: Separate body and channel steel, straight frame. 5.02 in. section modules, 36,000 psi. Front Suspension: Semi-elliptical springs, heavy-duty shock absorbers. 1,940 lb. capacity. Optional rating: 2,250 lb. Rear Suspension: Semi-elliptical springs, 3,650 lb. capacity. Optional Rating: 585 lb. and 900 lb. auxiliary springs. Front Axle Type and Capacity: Full-floating, 4,500 lb. capacity. Rear Axle Type and Capacity: 7,500 lb. capacity. Final Drive Ratio: 4.56:1. Transfer Case: New Process 205 Two-speed: 1.96, 1.0:1. Brakes: Type: Hydraulic. Front: Disc. Rear: Drum. Dimensions: Front: 12.88 in. x 1.19 in. disc. Rear: 12.0 in. x 3.0 in. Total rear lining area: 147.4 sq. in. Wheels: 6.75 in. rim, 8-stud disc. Tires: 8.00 x 16.5D., 10-ply. Optional: 8.00R x 16.5E (maximum size). Transmission: NP435 4-speed synchromesh manual. Transmission Ratios: 6.69, 3.34, 1.66, 1.00:1. Optional: Chrysler Loadflite A-727 3-speed automatic. Ratios: 2.45, 1.45, 1.00:1. Clutch: Single plate dry disc, hydraulic actuation. Clutch diameter: 11.0 in. Total plate area: 123.7 sq. in. Optional: None.

VEHICLE DIMENSIONS: W150: Wheelbase: 115 in., 131 in.,133 in. (club cab), 149 in. (club cab). Overall Length: 115 in. wheelbase: 193.6 in., 131 in. wheelbase: 213.6 in., 133 in. wheelbase: 211.6 in., 149 in. wheelbase: 231.6 in. All dimensions include optional rear bumper. Front/Rear Tread: 62.5 in./62.5 in. Overall Height: 74.0 in. Width: 79.5 in. Front/Rear Overhang: 30 in./47 in. Tailgate: Width and Height: 67 in. x 21.4 in. Approach/Departure Degrees: 34/24. Ground Clearance: Front axle: 8.2 in. Rear axle: 8.5 in. Oil pan: 15.8 in. Transfer case: 10.4 in. Load space: Pickup box dimensions: 115 in. wheelbase: 78 in. x 51 in. x 19.125 in. Capacity: 61.1 cu. ft. 131 in. wheelbase and 149 in. wheelbase Sweptline: 98 in. x 51 in. x 19.3 in. Capacity: 76.6 cu. ft. W250: Wheelbase: 131 in. Crew cab: 149 in. Overall Length: 131 in. wheelbase: 213.6 in. 231.6 in. Front/Rear Tread: 62.5 in./62.5 in. Overall Height: 74.0 in. Width: 79.5 in. Front/Rear Overhang: 31 in./49 in. Tailgate: Width x Height: 66.5 in. x 19.3 in. Approach/Departure Degrees: 30/21. Ground Clearance: Front axle:

8.0 in. Rear axle: 7.8 in. Oil pan: 16.1 in. Transfer case: 10.7 in. Load space: Pickup box dimensions: Sweptline: 98.875 in. x 51.0 in. x 19.3 in. W350: Wheelbase: 135 in. Load space: Pickup box dimensions: 108 in. x 54 in. x 20 in. Capacity: 66 cu. ft.

CAPACITIES: Fuel Tank: 25 gal.

ACCOMMODATIONS: Seating Capacity: 3 passenger.

INSTRUMENTATION: 0-100 mph speedometer, 99,999.9 mile odometer, gauges for fuel level, ammeter and engine coolant temperature. Warning lights for oil pressure, parking brake and hazard lights operation.

OPTIONS AND PRICES: Air conditioning. 60 amp and 114 amp alternators. 375 amp battery. 30 amp maintenance-free battery. 500 amp Long Life maintenance-free battery. Front and rear painted bumpers. Painted rear step type bumper. Bright finish rear bumper. Electric digital clock. Auxiliary transmission oil to air cooler. 30 gal. fuel tank. Gauges for oil pressure and engine coolant temperature; trip odometer. Tinted glass-all windows. Bright grille insert plus ram's head hood ornament. Deluxe bi-level heater. Engine block heater. Dual exterior low mount bright trim 6 in. x 9 in. extended mirrors. Dual exterior low mount extended bright trim 7.5 in. x 10.5 in. mirrors. Upper body moldings. Upper and lower body moldings. Power door locks. Power windows. AM/FM stereo radio. AM/FM stereo radio with electronic tuning and cassette tape player. AM/FM radio with eight-track tape player. AM/FM stereo radio with Search-Tune and electronic tuning. AM/FM stereo radio with 40-channel CB. Heavy-duty front and rear shock absorbers. Inside body spare tire carrier. Automatic speed control. Tilt type steering column. Luxury 15 in. diameter two-spoke steering wheel. Transfer case skid plate. Bright wheelcovers. Road type 15 in. x 7 in. aluminum ribbed wheels. Chrome disc five-slot wheels. Front stabilizer bar. Road type 15 in. x 7 in. five-slot white painted steel spoke wheels. Rear sliding window. Two-speed windshield wipers with intermittent wipe. Two-Tone Paint Procedure PXS. Filigree pin tape stripes. Includes gold or white thick-and-thin pinstripes on hood, body sides, wheel-lips and tailgate. Tailgate stripes, including Dodge Ram decal, were in reflective tape material. Royal Package. Royal SE Package. Light Package. Includes halogen headlamps, ashtray light, glove box lock and light, exterior cargo light and map light. Heavy-Duty Trailer Towing Package. Not available with 6-cyl. engine, underslung spare tire carrier. Requires V-8 engine, automatic transmission or NP435 manual transmission, transmission auxiliary oil cooler with automatic transmission. Includes 60 amp alternator, 430 amp battery, maximum engine cooling, heavy-duty variable load turn signal flasher, front stabilizer bar. Heavy-duty front and rear shock absorbers, seven-wire harness, heavy-duty harness and a Class IV heavy-duty tow bar hitch. Sno-Commander Package. Available for W150, W250 (all wheelbase models) and W350 131 in. wheelbase models. Includes a power angling blade with positive instrument panel-mounted fingertip controls, seven-way control valve, power lift and plow lights. Heavy-Duty Sno-Commander Package. Available only for W350 in. wheelbase pickup.

HISTORICAL FOOTNOTES: Dodge noted that "Dodge engineers didn't invent four-wheel drive, but they certainly improved upon the idea in the last 48 years."

1983 POWER RAM

For 1983 the Dodge Power Rams were visually unchanged. Of greater importance was the availability of the Miser model in four-wheel drive form on either the 115 in. or 131 in. wheelbase chassis. The Power Ram Miser pickup had among its standard equipment such items as carpeting, body side pin tape stripes, ram's head hood ornament, deluxe wheelcovers, and a woodtone instrument panel cluster. The Miser W150 joined the other W series models that were carried over from 1982. No longer offered was the club cab version. Unlike 1982 when the NP435 manual transmission was standard in all Power Rams, for 1983 it was standard only for the W150 models. Both the W250 and W350 had as standard equipment the three-speed TorqueFlite automatic transmission.

Standard equipment included antifreeze protection to -20^{0} F, ashtray, front bright finish bumper on pickups, painted on cab and chassis models, cigarette lighter, coat hooks, dash and plemun liner, directional signals, parking lights, color keyed door inner trim panels with pull straps and armrests, black floor mat with padding (color-keyed on Miser models), glove box with door, aluminum grille with painted plastic insert (bright finish on Miser models), single rectangular headlights, front wheel automatic locking hubs, padded instrument panel, fresh-air heater with defrosters, in-cab hood release, dual electric horns, exterior dual bright finish short, 5 in. x 7 in. mirrors; dual painted West Coast type, 7 in. x 16 in. mirrors for cab and chassis models, 10 in. interior day/night rearview mirror, bright windshield molding, power steering, seat belts, color-keyed sun visors, and dual jet two-speed windshield wipers. The base level custom interior had a three-passenger all-vinyl available in black, blue, beige or red. A Royal bench seat was standard for the Royal Package and optional for the custom pickup interior for conventional cab and crew cab models. A split-back bench seat was standard for the crew cab. The Royal bench seat was offered in blue, beige and red. The Royal SE bench seat was finished in cloth and vinyl. It was available in any one of four colors: Blue, beige, red and silver. A Deluxe vinyl bench seat was optional with both the Royal SE and Royal Package. A split-back version was standard on custom crew cab models. It was available in blue, beige, red or silver.

1983 Dodge W150 Sweptline Power Ram pickup

The Royal SE interior included a four-spoke luxury steering wheel with a black finish. The instrument panel cluster featured gauges for oil pressure and engine coolant temperature plus a trip odometer and a woodtone panel applique. A "Royal SE-Engineered Ram Tough" instrument panel nameplate was installed. Other features consisted of a front door woodgrain applique, assist strap and carpeting on lower portion, color-keyed carpeting with underlayment, bright front door sill scuff plates, soft color-keyed headliner (not available for crew cab), color-keyed garnish molding over windshield, front pillar, door header, quarter trim panel upper and over backlight (not available for crew cab), color-keyed cowl side trim panels, and insulation under hood panel. Exterior aspects of the Royal SE Package were as follows: Bright backlight molding, bright drip rail molding, plaque on front fenders with "Leaping Ram" and "Royal SE" name, ram's head hood ornament, "Dodge Ram" nameplate on Sweptline pickup tailgate, bright taillight bezels (Sweptline models), tailgate upper and lower moldings (Sweptline models), bright aluminum grille with chrome plastic insert and headlight doors, and bright tailgate applique panel (Sweptline models).

The Royal Package, which was not available for crew cab models, had these exterior features: Bright backlight molding, bright drip rail molding, plaque on front fenders with "Leaping Ram" and "Royal" name, bright taillight bezels (Sweptline models), and upper and lower tailgate moldings (Sweptline models). The Royal interior had a "Royal-Engineered Ram Tough" instrument panel nameplate, front door bright trim applique and pull straps, woodtone instrument panel applique, color-keyed carpeting with underlayment, insulation under hood panel, and a color-keyed hardboard headliner.

Exterior colors offered for 1983 were: Beige sand, graphic red, crimson red, spice metallic, nightwatch blue, pearl white and black. The following colors were also offered for all models except the Miser pickup: Burnished silver metallic, light blue metallic, charcoal gray metallic, sable brown.

I.D. DATA: The vehicle identification number was located on a V.I.N. plate attached to the driver's side door body latch post. The V.I.N. consisted of 17 elements. The first entry, the number 1 or 2 identified the nation of origin as either the United States or Canada. The letter B followed identified Dodge as the manufacturer. The number 7 identified the vehicle type as a truck. The gross vehicle weight entry was next according to this format: G-5001-6000 lbs., H-6001-7000 lbs., J-7001-8000 lbs., K-8001-9000 lbs., L-9001-10,000 lbs. The Power Ram pickup 4x4 truck line was next identified by the letter W. The truck series was identified by one of the following numbers: 1-150, 2-250 or 3-350. The body style designation followed according to this nomenclature: 4-Conventional cab, 4-Club cab or 6-Crew cab. The engine code was the next entry. The following system was used: E-225-6-cyl.-1-bbl. carb. H-225-6-cyl.-2-bbl. S-318-V-8-4-bbl. T-318-V-8-2-bbl. T-360-V-8-4-bbl. U-360-V-8-4-bbl. H.D.1-360-V-8-4-bbl.-Calif.

Body Type	Factory Price	GVW	Shipping Weight	Prod. Total
Model W150, 1/2 ton 6-cyl.				
Pickup, Utiline,115 in. wb.	$8658	6050	3797	—
Pickup, Sweptline, 115 in. wb.	$8658	6050	3832	—
Pickup, Utiline,131 in. wb.	$8743	6050	3947	—
Pickup, Sweptline, 131 in. wb.	$8743	6050	3947	—
W150 Club Cab				
Pickup, Sweptline, 133 in. wb.	$9314	6050	N.A.	—
Pickup, Sweptline, 149 in. wb.	$9467	6050	N.A.	—
Model W250, 3/4 ton, V-8 (Crew cab-149 in. wheelbase)				
Pickup, Utiline, 131 in. wb.	$9733	6900*	4120	—
Pickup, Sweptline, 131 in. wb.	$9733	6900	4155	—
Crew Cab, Sweptline	$11,392	6900	4785	—
W250 Club Cab				
Pickup, Sweptline	$10,383	6900	4842	—

* 7500 and 8550 lb. GVW package was optional for all models.

Body Type	Factory Price	GVW	Shipping Weight	Prod. Total
Model W350, 1 ton, V-8				
Ch. & Cab, 135 in. wb.	$11,948	8500*	4806	—

* GVW packages up to 10,000 lb. were available.

STANDARD ENGINE: 115 in. wheelbase and 131 in. wheelbase pickup W150 models. Engine Type: OHV, In-line 6-cylinder. Cast iron block and cylinder head. Key components include a drop-forged, shot-peened crankshaft, roller timing chain, Stellite-faced exhaust valves, individually ported long-branch manifolds, aluminum parts and a large radiator. Bore x Stroke: 3.40 in. x 4.125 in. Lifters: Mechanical. Number of main bearings-4. Fuel Induction: Single 1-bbl. carburetor or optional 2-bbl. carb. Compression Ratio: 8.4:1. Displacement: 224.7 cu. in. (3.68 liters). Horsepower: Net: 95 @ 3600 rpm. (California: 84 @ 3600 rpm, 2-bbl.: 100 @ 3600 rpm). Torque: Net: 170 lb.-ft. @ 1600 rpm. (California: 162 lb.-ft. @ 1600 rpm, 2-bbl.: 175 lb.-ft. @ 1600 rpm). Oil refill capacity: 5 qt. with filter change. Fuel Requirements: 91 octane.

STANDARD ENGINE: 133 in. and 149 in. wheelbase W150 club cab pickups and 131 in. wheelbase W250 and W350 conventional cab pickups; optional for other W150 models. Features include a drop-forged five-bearing crankshaft, chain-driven camshaft, free-turning exhaust valves, drop-forged I-beam connecting rods and silent-chain camshaft. Bore x Stroke: 3.91 in. x 3.312 in. Lifters: Hydraulic. Number of main bearings-5. Fuel Induction: Single 2-bbl. carburetor. Compression Ratio: 8.5:1. Displacement: 318 cu. in. (5.2 liters). Horsepower: 150 @ 4400 rpm. (California: 143 @3600 rpm. Over 8500 lb. GVWR: 158 @ 4000 rpm.). Torque: Net: 255 lb.-ft. @ 2000 rpm. (California: 253 lb.-ft. @ 1600 rpm. Over 8500 lb. GVWR 240 lb.-ft. @ 2000 rpm.). Oil refill capacity: 5 qt. with filter change. Fuel Requirements: 91 octane.

STANDARD ENGINE: W350 pickup: Features include vibration damper, 18 in. 4-blade fan and drop-forged crankshaft. Engine Type: OHV, V-8. Cast iron block and cylinder head. Bore x Stroke: 4.00 in. x 3.58 in. Lifters: Hydraulic. Number of main bearings-5. Fuel Induction: Single 4-bbl. carburetor. Compression Ratio: 8.6:1. (California: 8.2:1). Displacement: 360 cu. in. (5.9 liters). Horsepower: 190 @ 4000 rpm. (170 @ 4000 rpm for Calif.). Torque: Net: 265 lb.-ft. @ 3200 rpm. (265 lb.-ft. @ 3200 for Calif.). Oil refill capacity: 5 qt. with filter change. Fuel Requirements: 91 octane.

CHASSIS FEATURES: W150: Front Suspension: Semi-elliptical springs, heavy-duty, absorbers. 1,640 lb. rating. Optional rating: 1,800 lb. Rear Suspension: Semi-elliptical springs 1,820 lbs. capacity. Optional Rating: 1,820 lbs. for 115 and 131 in. wheelbase. Front Axle Type and Capacity: Full-floating, 3,500 lb. capacity. Optional: 4,000 lbs. Rear Axle Type and Capacity: Semi-floating, 3,600 lb. capacity. Optional: None. Final Drive Ratio: 2.94, (225 engine) 3.21, 3.55:1 (318 and 360 engines). The 360 engine with automatic had a 2.94:1 axle ratio. Transfer Case: NP-208, single lever, two-speed: 2.61, 1.00:1. Brakes: Type: Power, hydraulic. Front: Discs. Rear: Drums. Dimensions: Front: 11.75 in. x 1.256 in. disc. Rear: 11 in. x 2.5 in. Rear lining area: 106.4 sq. in. Wheels: 15 x 6.5 5-stud disc. Optional: 15 x 7 in. cast aluminum with radial ribbed design. Available for W150 pickups only. These wheels weighed approximately four pounds less per unit than the standard wheels. Tires: P235/75R x 15, 4-ply rating. Optional: P25570R x 15C, LR60 x 15B, 10-15 LTB, 7.00 x 15D. Steering: Recirculating ball. Ratio: 24:1, turns Lock-to-Lock: 3.5:1. Turning Circle: 43 ft. (131 in. wheelbase). Optional: Power assisted. Ratio: 17.8:1. Transmission: NP 435 wide ratio 4-speed manual. Transmission Ratios: 6.68, 3.34, 1.66, 1.00:1. Optional: Chrysler Loadflite

A-727 3-speed automatic. Ratios: 2.45, 1.45, 1.00:1. Clutch: Single dry plate disc, hydraulic actuation. Clutch diameter: 11 in. dia. Total lining area: 123.7 sq. in. Optional: None. W250: Separate body and ladder-type frame. Section modules: 3.88 in. (131 in. wheelbase), 5.02 in. (149 in. wheelbase, crew cab), 5.47 in. (149 in. wheelbase, club cab). Front Suspension: Semi-elliptical leaf springs, heavy-duty shock absorbers. 1,640 lb. capacity (131 in. wheelbase), 1,800 lb. capacity (149 in. wheelbase). Optional: 1,800 lb. capacity: 131 in. wheelbase), 2,250 lb. capacity: All wheelbases. Rear Suspension: Semi-elliptical leaf, 2,725 lb. capacity. Front Axle Type and Capacity: Full-floating, 3,500 lb. capacity. Optional rating: 4,000 lb. with Sno-Fiter package only, 4,500 lb. Rear Axle Type and Capacity: Full-floating, 5,500 lb. capacity. Optional rating: None. Final Drive Ratio: 3.54:1 (conventional cab); 4.10:1 (club cab and crew cab). Transfer Case: Conventional cab and club cab models: New Process 208, two-speed: 2.61, 1.00:1. Crew cab: New Process 205 two-speed. Brakes: Type: Power, hydraulic. Front: Disc. Rear; Drum. Dimensions: Front: 12.82 in. x 1.19 in. disc. Rear: 12.0 in. x 2.50 in. Total rear lining area: 122.8 sq. in. Optional: None. Wheels: 16.5 x 6.00 in., 8-stud disc. Optional: None. Tires: 8.00 x 16.5D, 8-ply rating. Optional (max. size avail.): 9.50R x 16.5E, 8-ply rating. Steering: Recirculating ball. Ratio: 24:1. Optional: Power assisted. Ratio: 17.8:1. Transmission: New Process 435, wide-ratio 4-speed manual. Transmission Ratios: 6.68, 3.34, 1.66, 1.00:1 reverse. Optional: Chrysler A-727 Loadflite 3-speed automatic. Ratios: 2.45, 1.45, 1.00:1. Clutch: Single dry plate disc, hydraulic actuation. Clutch diameter: 11 in. dia. Total lining area: 123.7 sq. in. W350: Separate body and channel steel, straight frame, 5.02 in. section modules, 36,000 psi. Front Suspension: Semi-elliptical springs, heavy-duty shock absorbers. 1,940 lb. capacity. Optional rating: 2,250 lb. Rear Suspension: Semi-elliptical springs, 3,650 lb. capacity. Optional Rating: 585 lb. and 900 lb. auxiliary springs. Front Axle Type and Capacity: Full-floating. 4,500 lb. capacity. Rear Axle Type and Capacity: 7,500 lb. capacity. Final Drive Ratio: 4.56:1. Transfer Case: New Process 205 two-speed: 1.96, 1.0:1. Brakes: Type: Hydraulic. Front: Disc. Rear: Drum. Dimensions: Front: 12.88 in. x 1.19 in. disc. Rear: 12.0 in. x 3.0 in. Total rear lining area: 147.4 sq. in. Wheels: 16.5 x 6.75 in. rim, 8-stud disc. Tires: 8.00 x 16.5 heavy-duty, 10-ply. Optional: 8.00R x 16.5E (maximum optional size). Transmission: NP435 4-speed synchromesh manual. Transmission Ratios: 6.69, 3.34, 1.66, 1.00:1. Optional: Chrysler Loadflite A-727 3-speed automatic. Ratios: 2.45, 1.45, 1.00:1. Clutch: Single plate dry disc, hydraulic actuation. Clutch diameter: 11.0 in. Total plate area: 123.7 sq. in. Optional: None.

VEHICLE DIMENSIONS: W150: Wheelbase: 115 in., 131 in.,133 in. (club cab), 149 in. (club cab). Overall Length: 115 in. wheelbase: 193.6 in., 131 in. wheelbase: 213.6 in., 133 in. wheelbase: 211.6 in., 149 in. wheelbase: 231.6 in. wheelbase. All dimensions include optional rear bumper. Front/Rear Tread: 62.5 in./62.5 in. Overall Height: 74.0 in. Width: 79.5 in. Front/Rear Overhang: 30 in./47 in. Tailgate: Width and Height: 67 in. x 21.4 in. Approach/Departure Degrees: 34/24. Ground Clearance: Front axle: 8.2 in. Rear axle: 8.5 in. Oil pan: 15.8 in. Transfer case: 10.4 in. Load space: Pickup box dimensions: 115 in. wheelbase: 78 in. x 51 in. x 19.125 in. Capacity: 61.1 cu. ft. 131 in. wheelbase and 149 in. wheelbase Sweptline: 98 in. x 51 in. x 19.3 in. Capacity: 76.6 cu. ft. W250: Wheelbase: 131 in. Crew cab: 149 in. Overall Length: 131 in./149 in. wheelbase: 213.6 in./231.6 in. Front/Rear Tread: 62.5 in./62.5 in. Overall Height: 74.0 in. Width: 79.5 in. Front/Rear Overhang: 31 in./49 in. Tailgate: Width x Height: 66.5 in. x 19.3 in. Approach/Departure Degrees: 30/21. Ground Clearance: Front axle: 8.0 in. Rear axle: 7.8 in. Oil pan: 16.1 in. Transfer case: 10.7 in. Load space: Pickup box dimensions: Sweptline: 98.875 in. x 51.0 in. x 19.3 in. W350: Wheelbase: 135 in. Load space: Pickup box dimensions: 108 in. x 54 in. x 20 in. Capacity: 66 cu. ft.

CAPACITIES: Fuel Tank: 25 gal.

ACCOMMODATIONS: Seating Capacity: 3 passenger.

INSTRUMENTATION: 0-100 mph speedometer, 99,999.9 mile odometer, gauges for fuel level, ammeter and engine coolant temperature. Warning lights for oil pressure, parking brake and hazard lights operation.

OPTIONS AND PRICES: Air conditioning. 60 amp and 114 amp alternators. 375 amp battery. 30 amp maintenance-free battery. 500 amp Long Life maintenance-free battery. Front and rear painted bumpers. Painted rear step type bumper. Bright finish rear bumper. Electric digital clock. Auxiliary transmission oil to air cooler. 30 gal. fuel tank. Gauges for oil pressure and engine coolant temperature; trip odometer. Tinted glass-all windows. Bright grille insert plus ram's head hood ornament. Deluxe bi-level heater. Engine block heater. Dual exterior low mount bright trim 6 in. x 9 in. extended mirrors. Dual exterior low mount extended bright trim 7.5 in. x 10.5 in. mirrors. Upper body moldings. Upper and lower body moldings. Power door locks. Power windows. AM/FM stereo radio. AM/FM stereo radio with electronic tuning and cassette tape player. AM/FM radio with eight-track tape player. AM/FM stereo radio with Search-Tune and electronic tuning. AM/FM stereo radio with 40-channel CB. Heavy-duty front and rear shock absorbers. Inside body spare tire carrier. Automatic speed control. Tilt type steering column. Luxury 15 in. diameter two-spoke steering wheel. Transfer case skid plate. Bright wheelcovers. Road type 15 in. x 7 in. aluminum ribbed wheels. Chrome disc five-slot wheels. Front stabilizer bar. Road type 15 in. x 7 in. five-slot white painted steel spoke wheels. Tear sliding window. Two-speed windshield wipers with intermittent wipe. Two-Tone Paint Procedure PXS. Filigree pin tape stripes. Includes gold or white thick-and-thin pinstripes on hood, body sides, wheel-lips and tailgate. Tailgate stripes, including Dodge Ram decal, were in reflective tape material. Royal Package. Royal SE Package. Light Package. Includes halogen headlamps, ashtray light, glove box lock and light, exterior cargo light and map light. Heavy-Duty trailer Towing Package. Not available with 6-cyl. engine, underslung spare tire carrier. Requires V-8 engine, automatic transmission or NP435 manual transmission, transmission auxiliary oil cooler with automatic transmission. Includes 60 amp alternator, 430 amp battery, maximum engine cooling, heavy-duty variable load turn signal flasher, front stabilizer bar. Heavy-duty front and rear shock absorbers, seven-wire harness, heavy-duty harness and a Class IV heavy-duty tow bar hitch. Sno-Commander Package. Available for W150, W250 (all wheelbase models) and W350 131 in. wheelbase models. Includes a power angling blade with positive instrument panel-mounted fingertip controls, seven-way control valve, power lift and plow lights. Heavy-Duty Sno-Commander Package. Available only for W350 in. wheelbase pickup.

HISTORICAL FOOTNOTES: Dodge told potential customers for its 1983 Power Ram trucks that "Whatever you have to carry, wherever you have to carry it, your best choice is Dodge."

1984 POWER RAM

The Dodge Power Rams were essentially unchanged for 1984.

I.D. DATA: The vehicle identification number was located on a V.I.N. plate attached to the driver's side door body latch post. The V.I.N. consisted of 17 elements. The first entry, the number 1 or 2 identified the nation of origin as either the United States or Canada. The letter B followed identified Dodge as the manufacturer. The number 7 identified the vehicle type as a truck. The gross vehicle weight entry was next according to this format: G-5001-6000 lbs., H-6001-7000 lbs., J-7001-8000 lbs., K-8001-9000 lbs., L-9001-10,000 lbs. The Power Ram pickup 4x4 truck line was next identified by the letter W. The truck series was identified by one of the following numbers: 1-150, 2-250 or 3-350. The body style designation followed according to this nomenclature: 4-Conventional cab, 4-Club cab or 6-Crew cab. The engine code was the next entry. The following system was used: E-225-6-cyl.-1-bbl. carb. H-225-6-cyl.-2-bbl. S-318-V-8-4-bbl. T-318-V-8-2-bbl. T-360-V-8-4-bbl. U-360-V-8-4-bbl. H.D.1-360-V-8-4-bbl.-Calif.

Body Type	Factory Price	GVW	Shipping Weight	Prod. Total
Model W150, 1/2 ton 6-cyl.				
Pickup, Utiline,115 in. wb.	$8997	6050	3797	—
Pickup, Sweptline, 115 in. wb.	$8969	6050	3832	—
Pickup, Utiline,131 in. wb.	$9054	6050	3947	—
Pickup, Sweptline, 131 in. wb.	$9054	6050	3947	—
W150 Club Cab				
Pickup, Sweptline, 133 in. wb.	$9625	6050	N.A.	—
Pickup, Sweptline, 149 in. wb.	$9778	6050	N.A.	—
Model W250, 3/4 ton, V-8 (Crew cab-149 in. wheelbase)				
Pickup, Utiline, 131 in. wb.	$10,049	6900*	4120	—
Pickup, Sweptline, 131 in. wb.	$10,049	6900	4155	—
Crew Cab, Sweptline	$11,708	6900	4785	—
W250 Club Cab				
Pickup, Sweptline	$10,699	6900	4842	—

* 7500 and 8550 lb. GVW package was optional for all models.

Body Type	Factory Price	GVW	Shipping Weight	Prod. Total
Model W350, 1 ton, V-8				
Ch. & Cab, 135 in. wb.	$12,287	8500*	4806	—
Pickup, Sweptline	$N.A.	8500	N.A.	—

* GVW packages up to 10,000 lb. were available.

STANDARD ENGINE: 115 in. wheelbase and 131 in. wheelbase pickup W150 models. Engine Type: OHV, In-line 6-cylinder. Cast iron block and cylinder head. Key components include a drop-forged, shot-peened crankshaft, roller timing chain, Stellite-faced exhaust valves, individually ported long-branch manifolds, aluminum parts and a large radiator. Bore x Stroke: 3.40 in. x 4.125 in. Lifters: Mechanical. Number of main bearings-4. Fuel Induction: Single 1-bbl. carburetor or optional 2-bbl. carb. Compression Ratio: 8.4:1. Displacement: 224.7 cu. in. (3.68 liters). Horsepower: Net: 95 @ 3600 rpm. (California: 84 @ 3600 rpm, 2-bbl.: 100 @ 3600 rpm). Torque: Net: 170 lb.-ft. @ 1600 rpm. (California: 162 lb.-ft. @ 1600 rpm, 2-bbl.: 175 lb.-ft. @ 1600 rpm). Oil refill capacity: 5 qt. with filter change. Fuel Requirements: 91 octane.

STANDARD ENGINE: 133 in. and 149 in. wheelbase W150 club cab pickups and 131 in. wheelbase W250 and W350 conventional cab pickups; optional for other W150 models. Features include a drop-forged five-bearing crankshaft, chain-driven camshaft, free-turning exhaust valves, drop-forged I-beam connecting rods and silent-chain camshaft. Bore x Stroke: 3.91 in. x 3.312 in. Lifters: Hydraulic. Number of main bearings-5. Fuel Induction: Single 2-bbl. carburetor. Compression Ratio: 8.5:1. Displacement: 318 cu. in. (5.2 liters). Horsepower: 150 @ 4400 rpm. (California: 143 @3600 rpm. Over 8500 lb. GVWR: 158 @ 4000 rpm.). Torque: Net: 255 lb.-ft. @ 2000 rpm. (California: 253 lb.-ft. @ 1600 rpm. Over 8500 lb. GVWR 240 lb.-ft. @ 2000 rpm.). Oil refill capacity: 5 qt. with filter change. Fuel Requirements: 91 octane.

STANDARD ENGINE: W350 pickup: Features include vibration damper, 18 in. 4-blade fan and drop-forged crankshaft. Engine Type: OHV, V-8. Cast iron block and cylinder head. Bore x Stroke: 4.00 in. x 3.58 in. Lifters: Hydraulic. Number of main bearings-5. Fuel Induction: Single 4-bbl. carburetor. Compression Ratio: 8.6:1. (California: 8.2:1). Displacement: 360 cu. in. (5.9 liters). Horsepower: 190 @ 4000 rpm. (170 @ 4000 rpm for Calif.). Torque: Net: 265 lb.-ft. @ 3200 rpm. (265 lb.-ft. @ 3200 for Calif.). Oil refill capacity: 5 qt. with filter change. Fuel Requirements: 91 octane.

CHASSIS FEATURES: W150: Front Suspension: Semi-elliptical springs, heavy-duty, absorbers. 1,640 lb. rating. Optional rating: 1,800 lb. Rear Suspension: Semi-elliptical springs 1,820 lbs. capacity. Optional Rating: 1,820 lbs. for 115 and 131 in. wheelbase. Front Axle Type and Capacity: Full-floating, 3,500 lb. capacity. Optional: 4,000 lbs. Rear Axle Type and Capacity: Semi-floating, 3,600 lb. capacity. Optional: None. Final Drive Ratio: 2.94, (225 engine) 3.21, 3.55:1 (318 and 360 engines). The 360 engine with automatic had a 2.94:1 axle ratio. Transfer Case: NP-208, single lever, two-speed: 2.61, 1.00:1. Brakes: Type: Power, hydraulic. Front: Discs. Rear: Drums. Dimensions: Front: 11.75 in. x 1.256 in. disc. Rear: 11 in. x 2.5 in. Rear lining area: 106.4 sq. in. Wheels: 15 x 6.5 5-stud disc. Optional: 15 x 7 in. cast aluminum with radial ribbed design. Available for W150 pickups only. These wheels weighed approximately four pounds less per unit than the standard wheels. Tires: P235/75R x 15, 4-ply rating. Optional: P25570R x 15C, LR60 x 15B, 10-15 LTB, 7.00 x 15D. Steering: Recirculating ball. Ratio: 24:1, turns Lock-to-Lock: 3.5:1. Turning Circle: 43 ft. (131 in. wheelbase). Optional: Power assisted. Ratio: 17.8:1. Transmission: NP 435 wide ratio 4-speed manual. Transmission Ratios: 6.68, 3.34, 1.66, 1.00:1. Optional: Chrysler Loadflite A-727 3-speed automatic. Ratios: 2.45, 1.45, 1.00:1. Clutch: Single dry plate disc, hydraulic actuation. Clutch diameter: 11 in. dia. Total lining area: 123.7 sq. in. Optional: None. W250: Separate body and ladder-type frame. Section modules: 3.88 in. (131 in. wheelbase), 5.02 in. (149 in. wheelbase, crew cab), 5.47 in. (149 in. wheelbase, club cab). Front Suspension: Semi-elliptical leaf springs, heavy-duty shock absorbers. 1,640 lb. capacity (131 in. wheelbase), 1,800 lb. capacity (149 in. wheelbase). Optional: 1,800 lb. capacity (131 in. wheelbase), 2,250 lb. capacity: All wheelbases. Rear Suspension: Semi-elliptical leaf, 2,725 lb. capacity. Front Axle Type and Capacity: Full-floating, 3,500 lb. capacity. Optional rating: 4,000 lb. with Sno-Fiter package only, 4,500 lb. Rear Axle Type and Capacity: Full-floating, 5,500 lb. capacity. Optional rating: None. Final Drive Ratio: 3.54:1 (Conventional Cab); 4.10:1 (club cab and crew cab). Transfer Case: Conventional cab and club cab models: New Process 208, two-speed: 2.61, 1.00:1. Crew cab: New Process 205 two-speed. Brakes: Type: Power, hydraulic, front disc, rear drum. Dimensions: Front: 12.82 in. x 1.19 in. disc. Rear: 12.0 in. x 2.50 in. Total rear lining area: 122.8 sq. in. Optional: None. Wheels: 16.5 x 6.00 in., 8-stud disc. Optional: None. Tires: 8.00 x 16.5D, 8-ply rating. Optional (max. size avail.): 9.50R x 16.5E, 8-ply rating. Steering: Recirculating ball. Ratio: 24:1. Optional: Power assisted. Ratio: 17.8:1. Transmission: New Process 435, wide-ratio 4-speed manual. Transmission Ratios: 6.68, 3.34, 1.66, 1.00:1 reverse. Optional: Chrysler A-727 Loadflite 3-speed automatic. Ratios: 2.45, 1.45, 1.00:1. Clutch: Single dry plate disc, hydraulic actuation. Clutch diameter: 11 in. dia. Total lining area: 123.7 sq. in. W350: Separate body and channel steel, straight frame, 5.02 in. section modules, 36,000 psi. Front Suspension: Semi-elliptical springs, heavy-duty shock absorbers. 1,940 lb. capacity. Optional rating: 2,250 lb. Rear Suspension: Semi-elliptical springs, 3,650 lb. capacity. Optional Rating: 585 lb. and 900 lb. auxiliary springs. Front Axle Type and Capacity: Full-floating. 4,500 lb. capacity. Rear Axle Type and Capacity: 7500 lb. capacity. Final Drive Ratio: 4.56:1. Transfer Case: New Process 205 two-speed: 1.96, 1.0:1. Brakes: Type: Hydraulic. Front: Disc. Rear: Drum. Dimensions: Front: 12.88 in. x 1.19 in. disc. Rear: 12.0 in. x 3.0 in. Total rear lining area: 147.4 sq. in. Wheels: 16.5 x 6.75 in. rim, 8-stud disc. Tires: 8.00 x 16.5 heavy-duty, 10-ply. Optional: 8.00R x 16.5E (maximum optional size). Transmission: NP435 4-speed synchromesh manual. Transmission Ratios: 6.69, 3.34, 1.66, 1.00:1. Optional: Chrysler Loadflite A-727 3-speed automatic. Ratios: 2.45, 1.45, 1.00:1. Clutch: Single plate dry disc, hydraulic actuation. Clutch diameter: 11.0 in. Total plate area: 123.7 sq. in. Optional: None.

VEHICLE DIMENSIONS: W150: Wheelbase: 115 in., 131 in.,133 in. (club cab), 149 in. (club cab). Overall Length: 115 in. wheelbase: 193.6 in., 131 in. wheelbase: 213.6 in., 133 in. wheelbase: 211.6 in., 149 in. wheelbase: 231.6 in. wheelbase. All dimensions include optional rear bumper. Front/Rear Tread: 62.5 in./62.5 in. Overall Height: 74.0 in. Width: 79.5 in. Front/Rear Overhang: 30 in./47 in. Tailgate: Width and Height: 67 in. x 21.4 in. Approach/Departure Degrees: 34/24. Ground Clearance: Front axle: 8.2 in. Rear axle: 8.5 in. Oil pan: 15.8 in. Transfer case: 10.4 in. Load space: Pickup box dimensions: 115 in. wheelbase: 78 in. x 51 in. x 19.125 in. Capacity: 61.1 cu. ft. 131 in. wheelbase and 149 in. wheelbase Sweptline: 98 in. x 51 in. x 19.3 in. Capacity: 76.6 cu. ft. W250: Wheelbase: 131 in. Crew cab: 149 in. Overall Length: 131 in./149 in. wheelbase: 213.6 in./231.6 in. Front/Rear Tread: 62.5 in./62.5 in. Overall Height: 74.0 in. Width: 79.5 in. Front/Rear Overhang: 31 in./49 in. Tailgate: Width & Height: 66.5 in. x 19.3 in. Approach/Departure Degrees: 30/21. Ground Clearance: Front axle: 8.0 in. Rear axle: 7.8 in. Oil pan: 16.1 in. Transfer case: 10.7 in. Load space: Pickup box dimensions: Sweptline: 98.875 in. x 51.0 in. x 19.3 in. W350: Wheelbase: 135 in. Load space: Pickup box dimensions: 108 in. x 54 in. x 20 in. Capacity: 66 cu. ft.

CAPACITIES: Fuel Tank: 25 gal.

ACCOMMODATIONS: Seating Capacity: 3 passenger.

INSTRUMENTATION: 0-100 mph speedometer, 99,999.9 mile odometer, gauges for fuel level, ammeter and engine coolant temperature. Warning lights for oil pressure, parking brake and hazard lights operation.

OPTIONS AND PRICES: Air conditioning. 60 amp and 114 amp alternators. 375 amp battery. 30 amp maintenance-free battery. 500 amp Long Life maintenance-free battery. Front and rear painted bumpers. Painted rear step type bumper. Bright finish rear bumper. Electric digital clock. Auxiliary transmission oil to air cooler. 30 gal. fuel tank. Gauges for oil pressure and engine coolant temperature; trip odometer. Tinted glass-all windows. Bright grille insert plus ram's head hood ornament. Deluxe bi-level heater. Engine block heater. Dual exterior low mount bright trim 6 in. x 9 in. extended mirrors. Dual exterior low mount extended bright trim 7.5 in. x 10.5 in. mirrors. Upper body moldings. Upper and lower body moldings. Power door locks. Power windows. AM/FM stereo radio. AM/FM stereo radio with electronic tuning and cassette tape player. AM/FM radio with eight-track tape player. AM/FM stereo radio with Search-Tune and electronic tuning. AM/FM stereo radio with 40-channel CB. Heavy-duty front and rear shock absorbers. Inside body spare tire carrier. Automatic speed control. Tilt type steering column. Luxury 15 in. diameter two-spoke steering wheel. Transfer case skid plate. Bright wheelcovers. Road type 15 in. x 7 in. aluminum ribbed wheels. Chrome disc five-slot wheels. Front stabilizer bar. Road type 15 in. x 7 in. five-slot white painted steel spoke wheels. Rear sliding window. Two-speed windshield wipers with intermittent wipe. Two-Tone Paint Procedure PXS. Filigree pin tape stripes. Includes gold or white thick-and-thin pinstripes on hood, body sides, wheel-lips and tailgate. Tailgate stripes, including Dodge Ram decal, are in reflective tape material. Royal Package. Royal SE Package. Light Package. Includes halogen headlamps, ashtray light, glove box lock and light, exterior cargo light and map light. Heavy-Duty Trailer Towing Package. Not available with 6-cyl. engine, underslung spare tire carrier. Requires V-8 engine, automatic transmission or NP435 manual transmission, transmission auxiliary oil cooler with automatic transmission. Includes 60 amp alternator, 430 amp battery, maximum mooling, heavy-duty variable load turn signal flasher, front stabilizer bar. Heavy-duty front and rear shock absorbers, seven-wire harness, heavy-duty harness and a Class IV heavy-duty tow bar hitch. Sno-Commander Package. Available for W150, W250 (all wheelbase models) and W350 131 in. wheelbase models. Includes a power angling blade with positive instrument panel-mounted fingertip controls, seven-way control valve, power lift and plow lights. Heavy-Duty Sno-Commander Package. Available only for W350 in. wheelbase pickup.

HISTORICAL FOOTNOTES: The 1984 Dodge trucks were introduced in the fall of 1983.

1985 POWER RAM

The 1985 Dodge models were unchanged in appearance from 1984. A new synchronized Ram Trac transfer case enabled the driver to shift form two-wheel drive to four-wheel drive and back when the vehicles was in motion up to speeds of 55 mph. A new Sport steering wheel was included in the Royal SE Package. Standard equipment for 1985 included the following items: Back-up lights, brake system warning light, directional signals, electric 2-speed windshield wipers and dual jet washers, interior and exterior rearview mirrors (exterior dual 5 in. x 7 in. bright finish short arm for pickups), exterior dual 7 in. x 16 in. painted West Coast type for cab and chassis models, padded instrument panel and sun visors, traffic hazard warning flasher system, front bumper with bright finish, cigarette lighter, black floor mat with backing (carpeting on W100), heater and defrosters, dual electric horns, interior dome light, bright windshield molding, power steering, driver and passenger sun visors. The standard custom interior consists of a saddle grain vinyl bench seat available in tan, charcoal, red or blue. Custom models were also available with a Tempo cloth bench seat in tan, red or blue. A split-back bench seat version was available on crew cab models. The optional Royal SE featured a bench seat of saddle grain vinyl in a choice of tan, red, silver or blue. A split-back version was standard on custom crew cab models. The Royal SE instrument panel included gauges for oil pressure and engine coolant temperature and a trip odometer. The top-ranked Premium Royal SE bench seat was upholstered in a Tribute cloth offered in four colors: Tan, red, silver or blue. This interior also featured a front door woodtone trim applique, assist strap and color-keyed carpeting. A trip odometer and a color-keyed soft headliner was also included. Crew cab models had a split-back bench seat. Optional gold filigree pin tapes strips for the hood, body sides, wheel-lips and tailgate were also available.

Color choices for 1985 consisted of black, light blue metallic, Navy blue metallic, charcoal metallic, cream, forest green metallic, canyon red metallic, graphic red, silver metallic, white and for trucks with the Prospector Package or with a two-tone paint procedure: Golden brown metallic.

1985 Dodge W150 Sweptline Power Ram pickup

I.D. DATA: The vehicle identification number was located on a V.I.N. plate attached to the driver's side door body latch post. The V.I.N. consisted of 17 elements. The first entry, the number 1 or 2 identified the nation of origin as either the United States or Canada. The letter B followed identified Dodge as the manufacturer. The number 7 identified the vehicle type as a truck. The gross vehicle weight entry was next according to this format: G-5001-6000 lbs., H-6001-7000 lbs., J-7001-8000 lbs., K-8001-9000 lbs., L-9001-10,000 lbs. The Power Ram Pickup 4x4 truck line was next identified by the letter W. The truck series was identified by one of the following numbers: 1-150, 2-250 or 3-350. The body style designation followed according to this nomenclature: 4-Conventional cab, 4-Club cab or 6-Crew cab. The engine code was the next entry. The following system was used: E-225-6-cyl.-1-bbl. carb. H-225-6-cyl.-2-bbl. S-318-V-8-4-bbl. T-318-V-8-2-bbl. T-360-V-8-4-bbl. U-360-V-8-4-bbl. H.D.1-360-V-8-4-bbl.-Calif.

Body Type	Factory Price	GVW	Shipping Weight	Prod. Total
Model W150, 1/2 ton 6-cyl.				
Pickup, Utiline,115 in. wb.	$9360	6050	3797	—
Pickup, Sweptline, 115 in. wb.	$9332	6050	3832	—
Pickup, Utiline,131 in. wb.	$9417	6050	3947	—
Pickup, Sweptline, 131 in. wb.	$9417	6050	3947	—
W150 Club Cab				
Pickup, Sweptline, 133 in. wb.	$9988	6050	N.A.	—
Pickup, Sweptline, 149 in. wb.	$10,141	6050	N.A.	—
Model W250, 3/4 ton, V-8 (Crew cab-149 in. wheelbase)				
Pickup, Utiline, 131 in. wb.	$10,439	6900*	4120	—
Pickup, Sweptline, 131 in. wb.	$10,439	6900	4155	—
Crew Cab, Sweptline	$12,096	6900	4785	—
W250 Club Cab				
Pickup, Sweptline	$11,089	6900	4842	—
Model W350, 1 ton, V-8				
Ch. & Cab, 135 in. wb.	$12,628	8500*	4806	—
Pickup, Sweptline	$N.A.	8500	N.A.	—

* 7500 and 8550 lb. GVW package was optional for all models.

* GVW packages up to 10,000 lb. were available.

STANDARD ENGINE: 115 in. wheelbase and 131 in. wheelbase pickup W150 models. Engine Type: OHV, In-line 6-cylinder. Cast iron block and cylinder head. Key components include a drop-forged, shot-peened crankshaft, roller timing chain, Stellite-faced exhaust valves, individually ported long-branch manifolds, aluminum parts and a large radiator. Bore x Stroke: 3.40 in. x 4.125 in. Lifters: Mechanical. Number of main bearings-4. Fuel Induction: Single 1-bbl. carburetor or optional 2-bbl. carb. Compression Ratio: 8.4:1. Displacement: 224.7 cu. in. (3.68 liters). Horsepower: Net: 95 @ 3600 rpm. (California: 84 @ 3600 rpm, 2-bbl.: 100 @ 3600 rpm). Torque: Net: 170 lb.-ft. @ 1600 rpm. (California: 162 lb.-ft. @ 1600 rpm, 2-bbl.: 175 lb.-ft. @ 1600 rpm). Oil refill capacity: 5 qt. with filter change. Fuel Requirements: 91 octane.

STANDARD ENGINE: 133 in. and 149 in. wheelbase W150 club cab pickups and 131 in. wheelbase W250 and W350 conventional cab pickups; optional for other W150 models. Features include a drop-forged five-bearing crankshaft, chain-driven camshaft, free-turning exhaust valves, drop-forged I-beam connecting rods and silent-chain camshaft. Bore x Stroke: 3.91 in. x 3.312 in. Lifters: Hydraulic. Number of main bearings-5. Fuel Induction: Single 2-bbl. carburetor. Compression Ratio: 8.5:1. Displacement: 318 cu. in. (5.2 liters). Horsepower: 150 @ 4400 rpm. (California: 143 @ 3600 rpm. Over 8500 lb. GVWR: 158 @ 4000 rpm.). Torque: Net: 255 lb.-ft. @ 2000 rpm. (California: 253 lb.-ft. @ 1600 rpm. Over 8500 lb. GVWR 240 lb.-ft. @ 2000 rpm.) Oil refill capacity: 5 qt. with filter change. Fuel Requirements: 91 octane.

STANDARD ENGINE: W350 pickup. Features include vibration damper, 18 in. 4-blade fan and drop-forged crankshaft. Engine Type: OHV, V-8. Cast iron block and cylinder head. Bore x Stroke: 4.00 in. x 3.58 in. Lifters: Hydraulic. Number of main bearings: 5. Fuel Induction: Single 4-bbl. carburetor. Compression Ratio: 8.6:1. (California: 8.2:1). Displacement: 360 cu. in. (5.9 liters). Horsepower: 190 @ 4000 rpm. (170 @ 4000 rpm for Calif.). Torque: Net: 265 lb.-ft. @ 3200 rpm. (265 lb.-ft. @ 3200 for Calif.). Oil refill capacity: 5 qt. with filter change. Fuel Requirements: 91 octane.

CHASSIS FEATURES: W150: Front Suspension: Semi-elliptical springs, heavy-duty, absorbers, 1,640 lb. rating. Optional rating: 1,800 lb. Rear Suspension: Semi-elliptical springs 1,820 lbs. capacity. for 115 and 131 in. wheelbase. Front Axle Type and Capacity: Full-floating, 3,500 lb. capacity. Optional: 4,000 lbs. Rear Axle Type and Capacity: Semi-floating, 3,600 lb. capacity. Optional: None. Final Drive Ratio: 2.94, (225 engine) 3.21, 3.55:1 (318 and 360 engines). The 360 engine with automatic had a 2.94:1 axle ratio. Transfer Case: NP-208, single lever, two-speed: 2.61, 1.00:1. Brakes: Type: Power, hydraulic. Front: Discs. Rear: Drums. Dimensions: Front: 11.75 in. x 1.256 in. disc. Rear: 11 in. x 2.5 in. Rear lining area: 106.4 sq. in. Wheels: 15 x 6.5 5-stud disc. Optional: 15 x 7 in. cast aluminum with radial ribbed design. Available for W150 pickups only. These wheels weighed approximately four pounds less per unit than the standard wheels. Tires: P235/75R x 15, 4-ply rating. Optional: P25570R x 15C, LR60 x 15B, 10-15 LTB, 7.00 x 15D. Steering: Recirculating ball. Ratio: 24:1, turns Lock-to-Lock: 3.5:1. Turning Circle: 43 ft. (131 in. wheelbase). Optional: Power assisted. Ratio: 17.8:1. Transmission: NP 435 wide ratio 4-speed manual. Transmission Ratios: 6.68, 3.34, 1.66, 1.00:1. Optional: Chrysler Loadflite A-727 3-speed automatic. Ratios: 2.45, 1.45, 1.00:1. Clutch: Single dry plate disc, hydraulic actuation. Clutch diameter: 11 in. dia. Total lining area: 123.7 sq. in. Optional: None. W250: Separate body and ladder-type frame. Section modules: 3.88 in. (131 in. wheelbase), 5.02 in. (149 in. wheelbase, crew cab), 5.47 in. (149 in. wheelbase, club cab). Front Suspension: Semi-elliptical leaf springs, heavy-duty shock absorbers, 1,640 lb. capacity (131 in. wheelbase), 1,800 lb. capacity (149 in. wheelbase). Optional: 1,800 lb. capacity (131 in. wheelbase), 2,250 lb. capacity: All wheelbases. Rear Suspension: Semi-elliptical leaf, 2,725 lb. capacity. Front Axle Type and Capacity: Full-floating, 3,500 lb. capacity. Optional rating: 4,000 lb. with Sno-Filter package only, 4,500 lb. Rear Axle Type and Capacity: Full-floating, 5,500 lb. capacity. Optional: None. Final Drive Ratio: 3.54:1 (conventional cab); 4.10:1 (club cab and crew cab). Transfer Case: Conventional cab and club cab models: New Process 208, two-speed: 2.61, 1.00:1. Crew cab: New Process 205 two-speed. Brakes: Type: Power, hydraulic. Front: Disc. Rear: Drum. Dimensions: Front: 12.82 in. x 1.19 in. disc. Rear: 12.0 in. x 2.50 in. Total rear lining area: 122.8 sq. in. Optional: None. Wheels: 16.5 x 6.00 in., 8-stud disc. Optional: None. Tires: 8.00 x 16.5D, 8-ply rating. Optional (max. size avail.): 9.50R x 16.5E, 8-ply rating. Steering: Recirculating ball. Ratio: 24:1. Optional: Power assisted. Ratio: 17.8:1. Transmission: New Process 435, wide-ratio 4-speed manual. Transmission Ratios: 6.68, 3.34, 1.66, 1.00:1 reverse. Optional: Chrysler A-727 Loadflite 3-speed automatic. Ratios: 2.45, 1.45, 1.00:1. Clutch: Single dry plate disc, hydraulic actuation. Clutch diameter: 11 in. dia. Total lining area: 123.7 sq. in. W350: Separate body and channel steel, straight frame. 5.02 in. section modules, 36,000 psi. Front Suspension: Semi-elliptical springs, heavy-duty shock absorbers, 1,940 lb. capacity. Optional Rating: 2,250 lb. Rear Suspension: Semi-elliptical springs, 3,650 lb. capacity. Optional Rating: 585 lb. and 900 lb. auxiliary springs. Front Axle Type and Capacity: Full-floating, 4,500 lb. capacity. Rear Axle Type and Capacity: Full-floating, 7,500 lb. capacity. Final Drive Ratio: 4.56:1. Transfer Case: New Process 205 two-speed: 1.96, 1.0:1. Brakes: Type: Hydraulic. Front: Disc. Rear: Drum. Dimensions: Front: 12.88 in. x 1.19

in. disc. Rear: 12.0 in. x 3.0 in. Total rear lining area: 147.4 sq. in. Wheels: 16.5 x 6.75 in. rim, 8-stud disc. Tires: 8.00 x 16.5 heavy-duty, 10-ply. Optional: 8.00R x 16.5E (maximum optional size). Transmission: NP435 4-speed synchromesh manual. Transmission Ratios: 6.69, 3.34, 1.66, 1.00:1. Optional: Chrysler Loadflite A-727 3-speed automatic. Ratios: 2.45, 1.45, 1.00:1. Clutch: Single plate dry disc, hydraulic actuation. Clutch diameter: 11.0 in. Total plate area: 123.7 sq. in. Optional: None.

VEHICLE DIMENSIONS: W150: Wheelbase: 115 in., 131 in.,133 in. (club cab), 149 in. (club cab). Overall Length: 115 in. wheelbase: 193.6 in., 131 in. wheelbase: 213.6 in. 133 in. wheelbase: 211.6 in., 149 in. wheelbase: 231.6 in. wheelbase. All dimensions include optional rear bumper. Front/Rear Tread: 62.5 in./62.5 in. Overall Height: 74.0 in. Width: 79.5 in. Front/Rear Overhang: 30 in./47 in. Tailgate: Width and Height: 67 in. x 21.4 in. Approach/Departure Degrees: 34/24. Ground Clearance: Front axle: 8.2 in. Rear axle: 8.5 in. Oil pan: 15.8 in. Transfer case: 10.4 in. Load space: Pickup box dimensions: 115 in. wheelbase: 78 in. x 51 in. x 19.125 in. Capacity: 61.1 cu. ft. 131 in. wheelbase and 149 in. wheelbase Sweptline: 98 in. x 51 in. x 19.3 in. Capacity: 76.6 cu. ft. W250: Wheelbase: 131 in. Crew cab: 149 in. Overall Length: 131 in./149 in. wheelbase: 213.6 in./231.6 in. Front/Rear Tread: 62.5 in./62.5 in. Overall Height: 74.0 in. Width: 79.5 in. Front/Rear Overhang: 31 in./49 in. Tailgate: Width x Height: 66.5 in. x 19.3 in. Approach/Departure Degrees: 30/21. Ground Clearance: Front axle: 8.0 in. Rear axle: 7.8 in. Oil pan: 16.1 in. Transfer case: 10.7 in. Load space: Pickup box dimensions: Sweptline: 98.875 in. x 51.0 in. x 19.3 in. W350: Wheelbase: 135 in. Load space: Pickup box dimensions: 108 in. x 54 in. x 20 in. Capacity: 66 cu. ft.

CAPACITIES: Fuel Tank: 25 gal.

ACCOMMODATIONS: Seating Capacity: 3 passenger.

INSTRUMENTATION: 0-100 mph speedometer, 99,999.9 mile odometer, gauges for fuel level, ammeter and engine coolant temperature. Warning lights for oil pressure, parking brake and hazard lights operation.

OPTIONS: Air conditioning with bi-level ventilation. 114 amp alternator. 500 amp maintenance-free battery. Front bumper guards. Rear step-type bumper. Painted rear bumper. Bright finish rear bumper. Auxiliary transmission cooler. Maximum cooling system. 30 gal. fuel tank. Gauge Package. Includes oil pressure, engine coolant temperature, trip odometer. Tinted glass (all windows). Bright grille insert. Includes halogen headlights, bright headlamp doors and ram's head front ornament. Engine block heater. Bright dual exterior low mounted mirrors. Body moldings: Upper and lower with partial wheel-lip. Electric door locks and power windows. AM radio. AM/FM stereo radio. AM/stereo/FM stereo with cassette player (all radios had electronic tuning and a digital clock). Heavy-duty front and rear shock absorbers. Inside body spare tire carrier. Automatic speed control. Front stabilizer bar. Tilt type steering column. 15 in. diameter Sport-type steering wheel. Road-type 15 in. x 7 in. aluminum radial ribbed or painted spoke wheels. Rear sliding window. Deluxe two-speed windshield wipers with intermittent wipe. Royal SE Package. Includes bright aluminum grille with chrome plastic insert, headlamp doors and halogen headlights, bright drip rail molding, bright rear window molding, bright tailgate housings (Sweptline pickup only), bright tailgate applique (Sweptline pickup only), bright upper and lower tailgate moldings (Sweptline pickup only), Dodge Ram nameplate on Sweptline pickup tailgate applique panel, plaque on front fender with "leaping ram" and Royal SE name, ram's head hood ornament, color-keyed carpeting with underlayment (a rubber floor mat was a no-charge option), color-keyed cowl side trim panels, color-keyed garnish trim over windshield, front pillar, door header, quarter trim panel and over backlight (not available on crew cab), Deluxe Tribune cloth bench seat (all vinyl was a no-charge option), front door woodtone trim applique with assist strap and carpeting on lower portion, bright sill scuff plates, insulation under hood panel, oil pressure and temperature gauges, trip odometer and woodtone instrument panel and bright trim. Light Package. Includes ash receiver light, exterior cargo light, glove box lock and light, and map light on instrument panel. Trailer Towing Preparation Package (not available with six-cylinder engine). Includes 500 amp maintenance-free battery, front stabilizer bar, heavy-duty front and rear shock absorbers, heavy-duty variable load flasher and maximum engine cooling. Job-Rated Package (for W250 only). Includes 114 amp alternator, 500 amp maintenance-free battery, argent painted rear step-type bumper, maximum engine cooling, 7500 lb. GVW Package, 30 gal. fuel tank, skid plate-transfer case shield and front stabilizer bar. The following Packages were offered for the W150 and W250 and W350 conventional cab Sweptline pickups: Prospector Package I. Includes bright front bumper guards, bright low mount exterior mirrors, bright wheelcovers, intermittent windshield wipers, Light Package, oil pressure and temperature gauges, trip odometer, Prospector nameplates, ram's head hood ornament, 30 gal. fuel tank and tinted glass. Prospector Package II. Includes all items in Package I plus the Royal SE Decor Package. Prospector Package III. Includes all the items in Package II plus air conditioning, electronically tuned AM radio with integral digital clock, power door locks and two-tone paint. The following Packages were offered for the W350 crew cab pickup: Prospector Package I. Includes bright front bumper guards, bright low mount exterior mirrors, intermittent windshield wipers, Light Package, oil pressure and temperature gauges, trip odometer, Prospector nameplates, ram's head hood ornament, 30 gal. fuel tank and tinted glass. Package II. Includes all items in Package I plus electronically tuned AM radio with integral digital clock, Royal SE Decor Package. The Prospector Package I for the W100 conventional cab pickup consisted of bright front bumper guard, bright low mount exterior mirrors, intermittent windshield wipers, Light Package, oil pressure and temperature gauges, trip odometer, Prospector nameplates, ram's head hood ornament, sliding rear window, 30 gal. fuel tank and tinted glass. Sno-Commander Package. Included specific GVW Packages. 5.2 liter 318 cid or 5.9 liter 360 cid engine and transmission auxiliary oil cooler with automatic transmission as required options. The Package included 500 amp maintenance-free battery, front clearance and identification lights, hydro/electric controls, maximum engine cooling, 114 amp alternator, plow lights, power angling blade with blade markers, power lift, Sno-Commander decal and transmission oil temperature light with automatic transmission. Sno-Preparation Package. Included specific GVW Packages. 5.2 liter 318 cid or 5.9 liter 360 cid engine and transmission auxiliary oil cooler with automatic transmission as required options. The Package included 114 amp alternator, 500 amp maintenance-free battery, maximum engine cooling and transmission oil temperature light with automatic transmission.

HISTORICAL FOOTNOTES: The 1985 Dodge trucks were introduced in the fall of 1984.

1986 POWER RAM

The 1986 W series trucks received a new grille with four rectangular subdivisions as well as a reshaped front bumper for 1986. Standard equipment for 1986 included antifreeze, ashtray, front bright-finish bumper, buzzer warning for seat belt fastening, headlights-on and key in ignition; cigarette lighter, gauges for engine coolant temperature, fuel level and oil pressure, insulated dash liner, color-keyed door armrest, inner trim panels and pull straps; black padded floor mats (carpeting on W100), tinted glass (all windows), glove box with door, aluminum grille with painted glass plastic insert and headlight doors, fresh air heater and defroster, dual note electric horns, 20 gal. fuel tank with tethered fuel cap, bright hubcaps (W100), back-up lights, interior day/night 10 in. rearview mirror, exterior dual West Coast type, 7 in. x 16 in. painted mirrors (chassis-cab models only), exterior dual short arm 5 in. x 7 in. bright trim mirrors (not available for chassis-cab), bright windshield molding, passenger and driver sun visors, body side tape stripe (W100 only), dual jet windshield washers and 2-speed windshield wipers with intermittent wipe. Dropped for the four-wheel drive lineup were the crew cab models.

The color selection for 1986 consisted of black, Navy blue metallic, cream, medium blue metallic, burnished silver metallic, light blue metallic, charcoal gray metallic, canyon red metallic, graphic red and white.

I.D. DATA: The vehicle identification number was located on a V.I.N. plate attached to the driver's side door body latch post. The V.I.N. consisted of 17 elements. The first entry, a number 1, identified the nation of origin as the United States. Vehicles built in Canada carried a number 2. The next element, the letter B, identified the manufacturer as Dodge. Then followed the number 7 signifying the vehicle type as a truck. The next element was a letter identifying the gross vehicle weight as follows: G-5001-6000 lb., H-6001-7000 lb., J-7001-8000 lb., K-8001-9000 lb., L-9001-10,000 lb., M-10,001-14,000 lb. The truck line was next identified by the letter W as a Power Ram pickup 4x4. The body style was the next element of the V.I.N. The number 4 identified a conventional cab; the number 5 identified a club cab and number 6 was a crew cab. The engine code was the next element according to this format: W-225-2-bbl., T-318-2-bbl. or 360-4-bbl. A check digit followed. The model year was then identified by the letter G. The assembly plant was identified by this scheme: A-Lynch Road, C-Jefferson, F-Newark, G-St. Louis, K-Pillete, Canada, M-Lago, Alberta, S-Warren Plant #1, T-Warren Plant #2, V-Warren Plant #3, X-Missouri. The final six digits, beginning with 100001 served as the plant sequential production number.

Body Type	Factory Price	GVW	Shipping Weight	Prod. Total
Model W150, 1/2 ton 6-cyl.				
Pickup, Utiline,115 in. wb.	$9781	6050	3797	—
Pickup, Sweptline, 115 in. wb.	$9753	6050	3832	—
Pickup, Utiline,131 in. wb.	$9838	6050	3947	—
Pickup, Sweptline, 131 in. wb.	$9838	6050	3947	—
W150 Club Cab				
Pickup, Sweptline, 133 in. wb.	$10,409	6050	N.A.	—
Pickup, Sweptline, 149 in. wb.	$10,562	6050	N.A.	—
Model W250, 3/4 ton, V-8 (Crew cab-149 in. wheelbase)				
Pickup, Utiline, 131 in. wb.	$11,383	6900*	4120	—
Pickup, Sweptline, 131 in. wb.	$11,383	6900	4155	—
Crew Cab, Sweptline	$13,050	6900	4785	—
W250 Club Cab				
Pickup, Sweptline	$12,033	6900	4842	—

* 7500 and 8550 lb. GVW package was optional for all models.

Body Type	Factory Price	GVW	Shipping Weight	Prod. Total
Model W350, 1 ton, V-8				
Ch. & Cab, 135 in. wb.	$14,608	8500*	4806	—
Pickup, Sweptline	$N.A.	8500	N.A.	—

* GVW packages up to 10,000 lb. were available.

STANDARD ENGINE: 115 in. wheelbase and 131 in. wheelbase pickup W150 models. Engine Type: OHV, In-line 6-cylinder. Cast iron block and cylinder head. Key components include a drop-forged, shot-peened crankshaft, roller timing chain, Stellite-faced exhaust valves, individually ported long-branch manifolds, aluminum parts and a large radiator. Bore x Stroke: 3.40 in. x 4.125 in. Lifters: Mechanical. Number of main bearings-4. Fuel Induction: Single 1-bbl. carburetor or optional 2-bbl. carb. Compression Ratio: 8.4:1. Displacement: 224.7 cu. in. (3.68 liters). Horsepower: Net: 95 @ 3600 rpm. (California: 84 @ 3600 rpm, 2-bbl.: 100 @ 3600 rpm). Torque: Net: 170 lb.-ft. @ 1600 rpm. (California: 162 lb.-ft. @ 1600 rpm, 2-bbl.: 175 lb.-ft. @ 1600 rpm). Oil refill capacity: 5 qt. with filter change. Fuel Requirements: 91 octane.

STANDARD ENGINE: 133 in. and 149 in. wheelbase W150 club cab pickups and 131 in. wheelbase W250 and W350 conventional cab pickups; optional for other W150 models. Features include a drop-forged five-bearing crankshaft, chain-driven camshaft, free-turning exhaust valves, drop-forged I-beam connecting rods and silent-chain camshaft. Bore x Stroke: 3.91 in. x 3.312 in. Lifters: Hydraulic. Number of main bearings-5. Fuel Induction: Single 2-bbl. carburetor. Compression Ratio: 8.5:1. Displacement: 318 cu. in. (5.2 liters). Horsepower: 150 @ 4400 rpm. (California: 143 @ 3600 rpm. Over 8500 lb. GVWR: 158 @ 4000 rpm.). Torque: Net: 255 lb.-ft. @ 2000 rpm. (California: 253 lb.-ft. @ 1600 rpm. Over 8,500 lb. GVWR 240 lb.-ft. @ 2000 rpm.). Oil refill capacity: 5 qt. with filter change. Fuel Requirements: 91 octane.

STANDARD ENGINE: W350 Pickup: Features include vibration damper, 18 in. 4-blade fan and drop-forged crankshaft. Engine Type: OHV, V-8. Cast iron block and cylinder head. Bore x Stroke: 4.00 in. x 3.58 in. Lifters: Hydraulic. Number of main bearings-5. Fuel Induction: Single 4-bbl. carburetor. Compression Ratio: 8.6:1. (California: 8.2:1). Displacement: 360 cu. in. (5.9 liters). Horsepower: 190 @ 4000 rpm. (170 @ 4000 rpm for Calif.). Torque: Net: 265 lb.-ft. @ 3200 rpm. (265 lb.-ft. @ 3200 for Calif.). Oil refill capacity: 5 qt. with filter change. Fuel Requirements: 91 octane.

CHASSIS FEATURES: W150: Front Suspension: Semi-elliptical springs, heavy-duty, absorbers. 1,640 lb. rating. Optional rating: 1,800 lb. Rear Suspension: Semi-elliptical springs 1,820 lbs. capacity. Optional Rating: 1,820 lbs. for 115 and 131 in. wheelbase. Front Axle Type and Capacity: Full-floating, 3,500 lb. capacity. Optional: 4,000 lbs. Rear Axle Type and Capacity: Semi-floating, 3,600 lb. capacity. Optional: None. Final Drive Ratio: 2.94, (225 engine) 3.21, 3.55:1 (318 and 360 engines). The 360 engine with automatic had a 2.94:1 axle ratio. Transfer Case: NP-208, single lever, two-speed: 2.61, 1.00:1. Brakes: Type: Power, hydraulic. Front: Disc. Rear: Drums. Dimensions: Front: 11.75 in. x 1.256 in. disc. Rear: 11 in. x 2.5 in. Rear lining area: 106.4 sq. in. Wheels: 15 x 6.5 5-stud disc. Optional: 15 x 7 in. cast aluminum with radial ribbed design. Available for W150 pickups only. These wheels weighed approximately four pounds less per unit than the standard wheels. Tires: P235/75R x 15, 4-ply rating. Optional: P25570R x 15C, LR60 x 15B, 10-15 LTB, 7.00 x 15D. Steering: Recirculating ball. Ratio: 24:1, turns Lock-to-Lock: 3.5:1. Turning Circle: 43 ft. (131 in. wheelbase). Optional: Power assisted. Ratio: 17.8:1. Transmission: NP 435 wide ratio 4-speed manual. Transmission Ratios: 6.68, 3.34, 1.66, 1.00:1. Optional: Chrysler Loadflite A-727 3-speed automatic. Ratios: 2.45, 1.45, 1.00:1. Clutch: Single dry plate disc, hydraulic actuation. Clutch diameter: 11 in. dia. Total lining area: 123.7 sq. in. Optional: None. W250: Separate body and ladder-type frame. Section modules: 3.88 in. (131 in. wheelbase), 5.02 in. (149 in. wheelbase, crew cab), 5.47 in. (149 in. wheelbase, club cab). Front Suspension: Semi-elliptical leaf springs, heavy-duty shock absorbers. 1,640 lb. capacity (131 in. wheelbase), 1,800 lb. capacity (149 in. wheelbase). Optional: 1,800 lb. capacity: 131 in. wheelbase), 2,250 lb. capacity: All wheelbases. Rear Suspension: Semi-elliptical leaf, 2,725 lb. capacity. Front Axle Type and Capacity: Full-floating, 3,500 lb. capacity. Optional rating: 4,000 lb. with Sno-Fiter package only, 4,500 lb. Rear Axle Type and Capacity: Full-floating, 5,500 lb. capacity. Optional rating: None. Final Drive Ratio: 3.54:1 (conventional cab); 4.10:1 (club cab and crew cab). Transfer Case: Conventional cab and club cab models: New Process 208, two-speed:

2.61, 1.00:1. Crew cab: New Process 205 two-speed. Brakes: Type: Power, hydraulic. Front: Disc. Rear: Drum. Dimensions: Front: 12.82 in. x 1.19 in. disc. Rear: 12.0 in. x 2.50 in. Total rear lining area: 122.8 sq. in. Optional: None. Wheels: 16.5 x 6.00 in., 8-stud disc. Optional: None. Tires: 8.00 x 16.5D, 8-ply rating. Optional (max. size avail.): 9.50R x 16.5E, 8-ply rating. Steering: Recirculating ball. Ratio: 24:1. Optional: Power assisted. Ratio: 17.8:1. Transmission: New Process 435, wide-ratio 4-speed manual. Transmission Ratios: 6.68, 3.34, 1.66, 1.00:1 reverse. Optional: Chrysler A-727 Loadflite 3-speed automatic. Ratios: 2.45, 1.45, 1.00:1. Clutch: Single dry plate disc, hydraulic actuation. Clutch diameter: 11 in. dia. Total lining area: 123.7 sq. in. W350: Separate body and channel steel, straight frame, 5.02 in. section modules, 36,000 psi. Front Suspension: Semi-elliptical springs, heavy-duty shock absorbers. 1,940 lb. capacity. Optional rating: 2,250 lb. Rear Suspension: Semi-elliptical springs, 3,650 lb. capacity. Optional Rating: 585 lb. and 900 lb. auxiliary springs. Front Axle Type and Capacity: Full-floating. 4,500 lb. capacity. Rear Axle Type and Capacity: 7,500 lb. capacity. Final Drive Ratio: 4.56:1. Transfer Case: New Process 205 two-speed: 1.96, 1.0:1. Brakes: Type: Hydraulic. Front: Disc. Rear: Drum. Dimensions: Front: 12.88 in. x 1.19 in. disc. Rear: 12.0 in. x 3.0 in. Total rear lining area: 147.4 sq. in. Wheels: 16.5 x 6.75 in. rim, 8-stud disc. Tires: 8.00 x 16.5 heavy-duty, 10-ply. Optional: 8.00R x 16.5E (maximum optional size). Transmission: NP435 4-speed synchromesh manual. Transmission Ratios: 6.69, 3.34, 1.66, 1.00:1. Optional: Chrysler Loadflite A-727 3-speed automatic. Ratios: 2.45, 1.45, 1.00:1. Clutch: Single plate dry disc, hydraulic actuation. Clutch diameter: 11.0 in. Total plate area: 123.7 sq. in. Optional: None.

VEHICLE DIMENSIONS: W150: Wheelbase: 115 in., 131 in.,133 in. (club cab), 149 in. (club cab). Overall Length: 115 in. wheelbase: 193.6 in., 131 in. wheelbase: 213.6 in., 133 in. wheelbase: 211.6 in., 149 in. wheelbase: 231.6 in. wheelbase. All dimensions include optional rear bumper. Front/Rear Tread: 62.5 in./62.5 in. Overall Height: 74.0 in. Width: 79.5 in. Front/Rear Overhang: 30 in./47 in. Tailgate: Width and Height: 67 in. x 21.4 in. Approach/Departure Degrees: 34/24. Ground Clearance: Front axle: 8.2 in. Rear axle: 8.5 in. Oil pan: 15.8 in. Transfer case: 10.4 in. Load space: Pickup box dimensions: 115 in. wheelbase: 78 in. x 51 in. x 19.125 in. Capacity: 61.1 cu. ft. 131 in. wheelbase and 149 in. wheelbase Sweptline: 98 in. x 51 in. x 19.3 in. Capacity: 76.6 cu. ft. W250: Wheelbase: 131 in. Crew cab: 149 in. Overall Length: 131 in./149 in. wheelbase: 213.6 in./231.6 in. Front/Rear Tread: 62.5 in./62.5 in. Overall Height: 74.0 in. Width: 79.5 in. Front/Rear Overhang: 31 in./49 in. Tailgate: Width x Height: 66.5 in. x 19.3 in. Approach/Departure Degrees: 30/21. Ground Clearance: Front axle: 8.0 in. Rear axle: 7.8 in. Oil pan: 16.1 in. Transfer case: 10.7 in. Load space: Pickup box dimensions: Sweptline: 98.875 in. x 51.0 in. x 19.3 in. W350: Wheelbase: 135 in. Load space: Pickup box dimensions: 108 in. x 54 in. x 20 in. Capacity: 66 cu. ft.

CAPACITIES: Fuel Tank: 25 gal.

ACCOMMODATIONS: Seating Capacity: 3 passenger.

INSTRUMENTATION: 0-100 mph speedometer, 99,999.9 mile odometer, gauges for fuel level, ammeter, engine coolant temperature, fuel level and oil pressure. Warning lights for parking brake and hazard lights operation.

OPTIONS: Air conditioning with bi-level ventilation. 114 amp alternator. 500 amp maintenance-free battery. Rear step-type bumper. Front bumper guards with black rub strip insert. Painted rear bumper. Bright finish rear bumper. Auxiliary transmission cooler. Maximum cooling system. 30 gal. fuel tank with tethered fuel cap. Bright dual exterior 6 in. x 9 in. low mounted mirrors (not available for chassis-cab). Bright dual exterior short arm, 5 in. x 7 in. mirrors (not available for chassis-cab). Exterior dual West Coast type 7 in. x 16 in. painted (available for chassis-cab only). Body moldings: Bright lower with partial wheel-lip (not available for chassis-cab). Electric door locks and power windows. AM radio. AM/FM stereo radio. (All radios had electronic tuning and a digital clock). Heavy-duty Package. Includes front stabilizer bar and front and rear heavy-duty shock absorbers. Inside body spare tire carrier. Automatic speed control (requires Royal SE Package). Tilt type steering column (requires Royal SE Package, automatic transmission, intermittent windshield wipers and power steering). Road-type 15 in. x 7 in. aluminum radial ribbed wheels (W150 only). Argent painted steel spoke wheels with bright trim ring and hubcbeter design. Deluxe bright wheelcovers (standard for W100). Rear sliding, lockable window. Two-speed windshield wipers with intermittent wipe. Royal SE Package. Exterior components. Include bright drip rail molding, bright grille with bright insert and headlight bezels, bright rear window molding, bright tailgate applique panel with Dodge Ram nameplate, bright taillight housing, bright tailgate upper and lower moldings, front fender Leaping Ram plaque "Royal SE", halogen headlights and ram's head hood ornament. Interior items consist of bright door sill scuff plate, color-keyed cowl side trim panels, color-keyed soft cloth headliner, color-keyed upper greenhouse garnish, color-keyed vinyl door trim panels with woodtone trim, assist strap with bright trim, armrest and carpeting on lower door, deluxe cloth with vinyl trim bench seat, electronically tuned AM radio with integral clock, Euro-sport steering wheel with black finish, hood inner panel insulation, "Royal SE-engineered Ram Tough" nameplate on instrument panel, and woodtone applique and bright trim on instrument panel. Trailer Towing Preparation Package (not available with six-cylinder engine). Includes 500 amp maintenance-free battery, front stabilizer bar, heavy-duty front and rear shock absorbers, heavy-duty variable load flasher and maximum engine cooling. Job-Rated Package (for W250 only). Includes 114 amp alternator, 500 amp maintenance-free battery, argent painted rear step-type bumper, maximum engine cooling, 7500 lb. GVW Package, 30 gal. fuel tank, skid plate-transfer case shield and front stabilizer bar. Heavy-Duty Package. Includes front stabilizer bar, and heavy-duty front and rear shock absorbers. Power Convenience Package. Includes ashtray light, exterior cargo light, glove box light and lock and map light. Two-Tone Paint Package (not available for chassis-cab models). Includes lower body side moldings with black vinyl insert and bright partial wheel-lip moldings, two-tone paint, upper side and rear exterior moldings. The following Packages were offered for the W150 and W250 Ram Sweptline pickups: Prospector Package I. Includes bright front bumper guards with black insert, AM radio with electronic tuning and integral clock, front bright bumper guards with black insert, bright deluxe wheelcovers, dual exterior low mount 6 in. x 9 in. mirrors, 30 gal. fuel tank, intermittent windshield wipers, Light Package and ram's head hood ornament. Prospector Package II. Includes all items in Package I plus the Royal SE Decor Package and Power Convenience Package. Prospector Package III. Includes all the items in Package II plus air conditioning and Two-Tone Paint Package. Light-Duty Sno-Commander Package (for W150 and W250 models). Includes front clearance and identification lights, hydroelectric controls, plow lights, power angling 90 in. blade, power lift with 7-way control valve, Sno-Commander decal on pickups, spare tires and wheel with 7500 lb. GVW Package (W250 pickup models only), and transmission oil temperature light with automatic transmission. Heavy-Duty Sno-Commander Package (for W250 and W350 models). Includes front clearance and identification lights, power angling 96 in. blade with blade markers, power lift with 7-way control valve, Sno-Commander decal on pickups, and transmission oil temperature light with automatic transmission. Job-Rated Package (not available with 6-cylinder engine or on chassis-cab models, available only for W250). Includes 114 amp alternator, 500 amp maintenance-free battery, front stabilizer bar, 30 gal. fuel tank, heavy-duty front and rear shock absorbers, maximum engine cooling, argent painted rear step bumper and transfer case skid plate.

HISTORICAL FOOTNOTES: The 1986 Dodge trucks were introduced in the fall of 1985.

1987 POWER RAM

The 1987 W series Dodge trucks had a new optional bright-finish rear step bumper. A twilight blue interior color was also introduced. The LE instrument panel now had a pecan wood finish applique. A flow-through ventilation system was standard. The radio speakers were molded into the trim panels. Trucks equipped with electric windows and door locks had new switches identifiable by their feel. Clear-coat paint plus a new anti-chip primer installed with a 2-stage paint system in which the base-coat primer was applied through a cathodic electro-coating process were also new features for the 1987 model year. A new hydraulically operated clutch was used in conjunction with 6-cylinder engines. It required fewer adjustments than the older unit and also reduced noise and vibration.

I.D. DATA: The vehicle identification number was located on a V.I.N. plate attached to the driver's side door body latch post. The V.I.N. consisted of 17 elements. The first entry, a number 1, identified the nation of origin as the United States. Vehicles built in Canada carried a number 2. The next element, the letter B, identified the manufacturer as Dodge. Then followed the number 7 signifying the vehicle type as a truck. The next element was a letter identifying the gross vehicle weight as follows: G-5001-6000 lb., H-6001-7000 lb., J-7001-8000 lb., K-8001-9000 lb., L-9001-10,000 lb., M-10,001-14,000 lb. The truck line was next identified by the letter W as a Power Ram pickup 4x4. The body style was the next element of the V.I.N. The number 4 identified a conventional cab; the number 5 identified a club cab and number 6 was a crew cab. The engine code was the next element according to this format: W-225-2-bbl., T-318-2-bbl. or 360-4-bbl. A check digit followed. The model year was then identified by the letter H. The assembly plant was identified by this scheme: A-Lynch Road, C-Jefferson, F-Newark, G-St. Louis, K-Pillete, Canada, M-Lago, Alberta, S-Warren Plant #1, T-Warren Plant #2, V-Warren Plant #3, X-Missouri. The final six digits, beginning with 100001 served as the plant sequential production number.

Body Type	Factory Price	GVW	Shipping Weight	Prod. Total
Model W150, 1/2 ton 6-cyl.				
Pickup, Utiline,115 in. wb.	$10,321	6050	3797	—
Pickup, Sweptline, 115 in. wb.	$10,293	6050	3832	—
Pickup, Utiline,131 in. wb.	$10,378	6050	3947	—
Pickup, Sweptline, 131 in. wb.	$10,378	6050	3947	—
W150 Club Cab				
Pickup, Sweptline, 133 in. wb.	$11,302	6050	N.A.	—
Pickup, Sweptline, 149 in. wb.	$11,455	6050	N.A.	—
Model W250, 3/4 ton, V-8 (Crew cab-149 in. wheelbase)				
Pickup, Utiline, 131 in. wb.	$12,276	6900*	4120	—
Pickup, Sweptline, 131 in. wb.	$12,276	6900	4155	—
Crew Cab, Sweptline	$13,943	6900	4785	—
W250 Club Cab				
Pickup, Sweptline	$12,926	6900	4842	—

* 7500 and 8550 lb. GVW package was optional for all models.

Body Type	Factory Price	GVW	Shipping Weight	Prod. Total
Model W350, 1 ton, V-8				
Ch. & Cab, 135 in. wb.	$15,350	8500*	4806	—
Pickup, Sweptline	$N.A.	8500	N.A.	—

* GVW packages up to 10,000 lb. were available.

STANDARD ENGINE: W100, W150: (Not available in California). Engine Type: OHV, In-line 6-cylinder. Cast iron block and cylinder head. Key components include a drop-forged, shot-peened crankshaft, roller timing chain, Stellite-faced exhaust valves, individually ported long-branch manifolds, aluminum parts and a large radiator. Bore x Stroke: 3.40 in. x 4.125 in. Lifters: Mechanical. Number of main bearings-4. Fuel Induction: Single 2-bbl. downdraft carburetor. Compression Ratio: 8.4:1. Displacement: 224.7 cu. in. (3.68 liters). Horsepower: Net: 90 @ 3600 rpm. Torque: Net: 170 lb.-ft. @ 1600 rpm. Oil refill capacity: 5 qt. without filter change. Fuel Requirements: Unleaded.

STANDARD ENGINE: W250, optional for W100 and W150, except for California where it is standard for W100 and W150. Features include a drop-forged five-bearing crankshaft, chain-driven camshaft, free-turning exhaust valves, drop-forged I-beam connecting rods and silent-chain camshaft. Engine Type: OHV, V-8. Cast iron block and cylinder head. Bore x Stroke: 3.91 in. x 3.312 in. Lifters: Hydraulic. Number of main bearings-5. Fuel Induction: Single 2-bbl. carburetor. Compression Ratio: 8.7:1. Displacement: 318 cu. in. (5.2 liters). Horsepower: 147 @ 4000 rpm. Torque: Net: 240 lb.-ft. @ 2000 rpm. Oil refill capacity: 5 qt. with filter change. Fuel Requirements: Unleaded.

STANDARD ENGINE: W350: Optional for all W100, W150 and W250 models. Features include vibration damper, 18 in. 4-blade fan and drop-forged crankshaft. Engine Type: OHV, V-8. Cast iron block and cylinder head. Bore x Stroke: 4.00 in. x 3.58 in. Lifters: Hydraulic. Number of main bearings-5. Fuel Induction: Single 4-bbl. carburetor. Compression Ratio: 8.4:1. Displacement: 360 cu. in. (5.9 liters). Horsepower: 175 @ 4000 rpm. Torque: Net: 280 lb.-ft. @ 2000 rpm. Oil refill capacity: 5 qt. with filter change. Fuel Requirements: Unleaded.

CHASSIS FEATURES: W150: Front Suspension: Semi-elliptical springs, heavy-duty, absorbers. 1,640 lb. rating. Optional rating: 1,800 lb. Rear Suspension: Semi-elliptical springs 1,820 lbs. capacity. Optional Rating: 1,820 lbs. for 115 and 131 in. wheelbase. Front Axle Type and Capacity: Full-floating, 3,500 lb. capacity. Optional: 4,000 lbs. Rear Axle Type and Capacity: Semi-floating, 3,600 lb. capacity. Optional: None. Final Drive Ratio: 2.94, (225 engine) 3.21, 3.55:1 (318 and 360 engines). The 360 engine with automatic had a 2.94:1 axle ratio. Transfer Case: NP-208, single lever, two-speed: 2.61, 1.00:1. Brakes: Type: Power, hydraulic. Front: Disc. Rear: Drum. Dimensions: Front: 11.75 in. x 1.256 in. disc. Rear: 11 in. x 2.5 in. Rear lining area: 106.4 sq. in. Wheels: 15 x 6.5 5-stud disc. Optional: 15 x 7 in. cast aluminum with radial ribbed design. Available for W150 pickups only. These wheels weighed approximately four pounds less per unit than the standard wheels. Tires: P235/75R x 15, 4-ply rating. Optional: P25570R x 15C, LR60 x 15B, 10-15 LTB, 7.00 x 15D. Steering: Recirculating ball. Ratio: 24:1, turns Lock-to-Lock: 3.5:1. Turning Circle: 43 ft. (131 in. wheelbase). Optional: Power assisted. Ratio: 17.8:1. Transmission: NP 435 wide ratio 4-speed manual. Transmission Ratios: 6.68, 3.34, 1.66, 1.00:1. Optional: Chrysler Loadflite A-727 3-speed automatic. Ratios: 2.45, 1.45, 1.00:1. Clutch: Single dry plate disc, hydraulic actuation. Clutch diameter: 11 in. dia. Total lining area: 123.7 sq. in. Optional: None. W250: Separate body and ladder-type frame. Section modules: 3.88 in. (131 in. wheelbase), 5.02 in. (149 in. wheelbase, crew cab), 5.47 in. (149 in. wheelbase, club cab). Front Suspension: Semi-elliptical leaf springs, heavy-duty shock absorbers. 1,640 lb. capacity (131 in. wheelbase), 1,800 lb. capacity (149 in. wheelbase). Optional: 1,800 lb. capacity: 131 in. wheelbase), 2,250 lb.

166 Standard Catalog of American Four-Wheel Drive Vehicles

capacity: All wheelbases. Rear Suspension: Semi-elliptical leaf, 2,725 lb. capacity. Front Axle Type and Capacity: Full-floating, 3,500 lb. capacity. Optional rating: 4,000 lb. with Sno-Fiter package only, 4,500 lb. Rear Axle Type and Capacity: Full-floating, 5,500 lb. capacity. Optional rating: None. Final Drive Ratio: 3.54:1 (conventional cab); 4.10:1 (club cab and crew cab). Transfer Case: Conventional cab and club cab models: New Process 208, two-speed: 2.61, 1.00:1. Crew cab: New Process 205 two-speed. Brakes: Type: Power, hydraulic. Front: Disc. Rear: Drum. Dimensions: Front: 12.82 in. x 1.19 in. disc. Rear: 12.0 in. x 2.50 in. Total rear lining area: 122.8 sq. in. Optional: None. Wheels: 16.5 x 6.00 in., 8-stud disc. Optional: None. Tires: 8.00 x 16.5D, 8-ply rating. Optional (max. size avail.): 9.50R x 16.5E, 8-ply rating. Steering: Recirculating ball. Ratio: 24:1. Optional: Power assisted. Ratio: 17.8:1. Transmission: New Process 435, wide-ratio 4-speed manual. Transmission Ratios: 6.68, 3.34, 1.66, 1.00:1 reverse: Optional: Chrysler A-727 Loadflite 3-speed automatic. Ratios: 2.45, 1.45, 1.00:1. Clutch: Single dry plate disc, hydraulic actuation. Clutch diameter: 11 in. dia. Total lining area: 123.7 sq. in. W350: Separate body and channel steel, straight frame, 5.02 in. section modules, 36,000 psi. Front Suspension: Semi-elliptical springs, heavy-duty shock absorbers. 1,940 lb. capacity. Optional rating: 2,250 lb. Rear Suspension: Semi-elliptical springs, 3,650 lb. capacity. Optional Rating: 585 lb. and 900 lb. auxiliary springs. Front Axle Type and Capacity: Full-floating. 4,500 lb. capacity. Rear Axle Type and Capacity: 7,500 lb. capacity. Final Drive Ratio: 4.56:1. Transfer Case: New Process 205 two-speed: 1.96, 1.0:1. Brakes: Type: Hydraulic. Front: Disc. Rear: Drum. Dimensions: Front: 12.88 in. x 1.19 in. disc. Rear: 12.0 in. x 3.0 in. Total rear lining area: 147.4 sq. in. Wheels: 16.5 x 6.75 in. rim, 8-stud disc. Tires: 8.00 x 16.5 heavy-duty, 10-ply. Optional: 8.00R x 16.5E (maximum optional size). Transmission: NP435 4-speed synchromesh manual. Transmission Ratios: 6.69, 3.34, 1.66, 1.00:1. Optional: Chrysler Loadflite A-727 3-speed automatic. Ratios: 2.45, 1.45, 1.00:1. Clutch: Single plate dry disc, hydraulic actuation. Clutch diameter: 11.0 in. Total plate area: 123.7 sq. in. Optional: None.

VEHICLE DIMENSIONS: W150: Wheelbase: 115 in., 131 in.,133 in. (club cab), 149 in. (club cab). Overall Length: 115 in. wheelbase: 193.6 in., 131 in. wheelbase: 213.6 in., 133 in. wheelbase: 211.6 in., 149 in. wheelbase: 231.6 in. wheelbase. All dimensions include optional rear bumper. Front/Rear Tread: 62.5 in./62.5 in. Overall Height: 74.0 in. Width: 79.5 in. Front/Rear Overhang: 30 in./47 in. Tailgate: Width and Height: 67 in. x 21.4 in. Approach/Departure Degrees: 34/24. Ground Clearance: Front axle: 8.2 in. Rear axle: 8.5 in. Oil pan: 15.8 in. Transfer case: 10.4 in. Load space: Pickup box dimensions: 115 in. wheelbase: 78 in. x 51 in. x 19.125 in. Capacity: 61.1 cu. ft. 131 in. wheelbase and 149 in. wheelbase Sweptline: 98 in. x 51 in. x 19.3 in. Capacity: 76.6 cu. ft. W250: Wheelbase: 131 in. Crew cab: 149 in. Overall Length: 131 in./149 in. wheelbase: 213.6 in./231.6 in. Front/Rear Tread: 62.5 in./62.5 in. Overall Height: 74.0 in. Width: 79.5 in. Front/Rear Overhang: 31 in./49 in. Tailgate: Width x Height: 66.5 in. x 19.3 in. Approach/Departure Degrees: 30/21. Ground Clearance: Front axle: 8.0 in. Rear axle: 7.8 in. Oil pan: 16.1 in. Transfer case: 10.7 in. Load space: Pickup box dimensions: Sweptline: 98.875 in. x 51.0 in. x 19.3 in. W350: Wheelbase: 135 in. Load space: Pickup box dimensions: 108 in. x 54 in. x 20 in. Capacity: 66 cu. ft.

CAPACITIES: Fuel Tank: 25 gal.

ACCOMMODATIONS: Seating Capacity: 3 passenger.

INSTRUMENTATION: 0-100 mph speedometer, 99,999.9 mile odometer, gauges for fuel level, ammeter, engine coolant temperature, fuel level and oil pressure. Warning lights for parking brake and hazard lights operation.

OPTIONS: Air conditioning with bi-level ventilation. 114 amp alternator. 500 amp maintenance-free battery. Rear step-type bumper. Front bumper guards with black rub strip insert. Painted rear bumper. Bright finish rear bumper. Auxiliary transmission cooler. Maximum cooling system. 30 gal. fuel tank with tethered fuel cap. Bright dual exterior 6 in. x 9 in. low mounted mirrors (not available for chassis-cab). Bright dual exterior short arm, 5 in. x 7 in. mirrors (not available for chassis-cab). Exterior dual West Coast type 7 in. x 16 in. painted (available for chassis-cab only). Body moldings: Bright lower with partial wheel-lip (not available for chassis-cab). Electric door locks and power windows. AM radio. AM/FM stereo radio. (All radios had electronic tuning and a digital clock). Heavy-Duty Package. Includes front stabilizer bar and front and rear heavy-duty shock absorbers. Inside body spare tire carrier. Automatic speed control (requires Royal SE Package). Tilt type steering column (requires Royal SE Package, automatic transmission, intermittent windshield wipers and power steering). Road-type 15 in. x 7 in. aluminum radial ribbed wheels (W150 only). Argent painted steel spoke wheels with bright trim ring and hubcbeter design. Deluxe bright wheelcovers (standard for W100). Rear sliding, lockable window. Two-speed windshield wipers with intermittent wipe. Royal SE Package. Exterior components Include bright drip rail molding, bright grille with bright insert and headlight bezels, bright rear window molding, bright tailgate applique panel with Dodge Ram nameplate, bright taillight housing, bright tailgate upper and lower moldings, front fender Leaping Ram plaque "Royal SE", halogen headlights and ram's head hood ornament. Interior items consist of bright door sill scuff plate, color-keyed cowl side trim panels, color-keyed soft cloth headliner, color-keyed upper greenhouse garnish, color-keyed vinyl door trim panels with woodtone trim, assist strap with bright trim, armrest and carpeting on lower door, deluxe cloth with vinyl trim bench seat, electronically tuned AM radio with integral clock, Euro-sport steering wheel with black finish, hood inner panel insulation, "Royal SE-engineered Ram Tough" nameplate on instrument panel, and woodtone applique and bright trim on instrument panel. Trailer Towing Preparation Package (not available with six-cylinder engine). Includes 500 amp maintenance-free battery, front stabilizer bar, heavy-duty front and rear shock absorbers, heavy-duty variable load flasher and maximum engine cooling. Job-Rated Package (for W250 only). Includes 114 amp alternator, 500 amp maintenance-free battery, argent painted rear step-type bumper, maximum engine cooling, 7500 lb. GVW Package, 30 gal. fuel tank, skid plate-transfer case shield and front stabilizer bar. Heavy-Duty Package. Includes front stabilizer bar, and heavy-duty front and rear shock absorbers. Power Convenience Package. Includes ashtray light, exterior cargo light, glove box light and lock and map light. Two-Tone Paint Package (not available for chassis-cab models). Includes lower body side moldings with black vinyl insert and bright partial wheel-lip moldings, two-tone paint, upper side and rear exterior moldings. The following Packages were offered for the W150 and W250 Ram Sweptline pickups: Prospector Package I. Includes bright front bumper guards with black insert, AM radio with electronic tuning and integral clock, front bright bumper guards with black insert, bright deluxe wheelcovers, dual exterior low mount 6 in. x 9 in. mirrors, 30 gal. fuel tank, intermittent windshield wipers, Light Package and ram's head hood ornament. Prospector Package II. Includes all items in Package I plus the Royal SE Decor Package and Power Convenience Package. Prospector Package III. Includes all the items in Package II plus air conditioning and Two-Tone Paint Package. Light-Duty Sno-Commander Package (for W150 and W250 models). Includes front clearance and identification lights, hydroelectric controls, plow lights, power angling 90 in. blade, power lift with 7-way control valve, Sno-Commander decal on pickups, spare tire and wheel with 7500 lb. GVW Package (W250 pickup models only), and transmission oil temperature light with automatic transmission. Heavy-Duty Sno-Commander Package (for W250 and W350 models). Includes front clearance and identification lights, power angling 96 in. blade with blade markers, power lift with 7-way control valve, Sno-Commander decal on pickups, and transmission oil temperature light with automatic transmission. Job-Rated Package (not available with 6-cylinder engine or on chassis-cab models, available only for W250). Includes 114 amp alternator, 500 amp maintenance-free battery, front stabilizer bar, 30 gal. fuel tank, heavy-duty front and rear shock absorbers, maximum engine cooling, argent painted rear step bumper and transfer case skid plate.

HISTORICAL FOOTNOTES: The 1987 Dodge trucks were introduced in the fall of 1986.

1988 POWER RAM

Dodge offered its four-wheel drive models for 1988 in W100, W150 W250 and W350 pickup form as well as W250 and W350 chassis-cab form. The pickups were available in conventional cab, Sweptline body form with either an 6.5 ft. box (61.0 cubic foot capacity) or an 8.0 ft. (76.60 cubic foot capacity) box. For the first time fuel injection was offered for Dodge trucks in 1988. It was standard on the 5.2 liter V-8 and offered improved driveability and 17 percent more horsepower than the engine it replaced. The 5.2 liter system included a throttle body-mounted fuel temperature sensor. Standard equipment content for 1988 consisted of these items: Front bright bumper, stainless steel exhaust system, 22 gal. fuel tank with tethered fuel cap, tinted glass for all windows, aluminum grille with painted plastic insert and headlight doors, single rectangular headlights, bright hubcaps, bright exterior, short arm 5 in. x 7 in. mirrors (not available for chassis-cab models), painted exterior dual West Coast type 7 in. x 16 in. mirrors (chassis-cab models only), bright windshield molding, insulated dash liner, two color-keyed armrests, black rubber floor mats with padding, glove box with door, fresh air heater with defroster, interior rearview 10 in. day/night mirror, driver and passenger sun visors, 75 amp alternator, 500 amp maintenance-free battery (625 amp on W350 and all chassis-cab models), warning buzzer for fasten seat belts, headlights-on and key in ignition, single note electric horns, instrumentation for all models: Ammeter, gauges for engine coolant temperature, fuel level and oil pressure, odometer, trip odometer, speedometer; back-up lights, power-assisted steering, duel jet windshield washers and two-speed windshield wipers.

The standard interior featured a saddle grain, all-vinyl bench seat available in almond, blue, charcoal or red. This seat was a no-cost option for the W100 which had, as its standard seat, a Tempo cloth and saddle grain vinyl bench seat available in almond, blue or red. This seat was optional for the standard interior or the other W series trucks. The LE Decor Package had a Sentry cloth with vinyl trim bench seat available in almond, blue or red. A no-charge option for the LE Decor Package was a Turin/Saddle grain all-vinyl bench seat available in almond, blue or red. The exterior color selection for 1988 consisted of black, twilight blue pearlcoat (extra cost), Light cream (not available for W100), dark suede, radiant silver, glacier blue, charcoal pearlcoat, medium suede (not available for W100), graphic red and bright white (not available for W100).

1988 Dodge W150 Sweptline Power Ram Sno-Commander

I.D. DATA: The vehicle identification number was located on a V.I.N. plate attached to the driver's side door body latch post. The V.I.N. consisted of 17 elements. The first entry, a number 1, identified the nation of origin as the United States. Vehicles built in Canada carried a number 2. The next element, the letter B, identified the manufacturer as Dodge. Then followed the number 7 signifying the vehicle type as a truck. The next element was a letter identifying the gross vehicle weight as follows: G-5001-6000 lb., H-6001-7000 lb., J-7001-8000 lb., K-8001-9000 lb., L-9001-10,000 lb., M-10,001-14,000 lb. The truck line was next identified by the letter W as a Power Ram pickup 4x4. The body style was the next element of the V.I.N. The number 4 identified a conventional cab; the number 5 identified a club cab and number 6 was a crew cab. The engine code was the next element according to this format: W-225-2-bbl., T-318-2-bbl. or 360-4-bbl. A check digit followed. The model year was then identified by the letter J. The assembly plant was identified by this scheme: A-Lynch Road, C-Jefferson, F-Newark, G-St. Louis, K-Pillete, Canada, M-Lago, Alberta, S-Warren Plant #1, T-Warren Plant #2, V-Warren Plant #3, X-Missouri. The final six digits, beginning with 100001 served as the plant sequential production number.

Body Type	Factory Price	GVW	Shipping Weight	Prod. Total
Model W150, 1/2 ton 6-cyl.				
Pickup, Utiline,115 in. wb.	$N.A.	6050	3797	—
Pickup, Sweptline, 115 in. wb.	$N.A.	6050	3832	—
Pickup, Utiline,131 in. wb.	$N.A.	6050	3947	—
Pickup, Sweptline, 131 in. wb.	$N.A.	6050	3947	—
W150 Club Cab				
Pickup, Sweptline, 133 in. wb.	$N.A.	6050	N.A.	—
Pickup, Sweptline, 149 in. wb.	$N.A.	6050	N.A.	—
Model W250, 3/4 ton, V-8 (Crew cab-149 in. wheelbase)				
Pickup, Utiline, 131 in. wb.	$N.A.	6900*	4120	—
Pickup, Sweptline, 131 in. wb.	$N.A.	6900	4155	—
Crew Cab, Sweptline	$N.A.	6900	4785	—
W250 Club Cab				
Pickup, Sweptline	$N.A.	6900	4842	—

* 7500 and 8550 lb. GVW package was optional for all models.

Body Type	Factory Price	GVW	Shipping Weight	Prod. Total
Model W350, 1 ton, V-8				
Ch. & Cab, 135 in. wb.	$N.A.	8500*	4806	—
Pickup, Sweptline	$N.A.	8500	N.A.	—

* GVW packages up to 10,000 lb. were available.

STANDARD ENGINE: W100, W150, W250 pickup models: Features include a drop-forged five-bearing crankshaft, chain-driven camshaft, free-turning exhaust valves, drop-forged I-beam connecting rods and silent-chain camshaft. Engine Type: OHV, V-8. Cast iron block and cylinder head. Bore x Stroke: 3.91 in. x 3.312 in. Lifters: Hydraulic. Number of main bearings-5. Fuel Induction: Electronic fuel injection. Displacement: 318 cu. in. (5.2 liters). Oil refill capacity: 5 qt. with filter change. Fuel Requirements: Unleaded.

STANDARD ENGINE: W350: Optional for all W100, W150 and W250 models. Not available in California for W100 and W150. Features include vibration damper, 18 in. 4-blade fan and drop-forged crankshaft. Engine Type: OHV, V-8. Cast iron block and cylinder head. Bore x Stroke: 4.00 in. x 3.58 in. Lifters: Hydraulic. Number of main bearings-5. Fuel Induction: Single 4-bbl. carburetor. Compression Ratio: 8.4:1. Displacement: 360 cu. in. (5.8 liters). Horse-power: 170 @ 4000 rpm. (180 hp. for trucks over 8501 GVWR). Torque: Net: 270 lb.-ft. @ 2000 rpm. Oil refill capacity: 5 qt. with filter change. Fuel Requirements: Unleaded.

CHASSIS FEATURES: W100, W150: Front Suspension: Semi-elliptical springs, heavy-duty, absorbers. 1,640 lb. rating. Optional rating: 1,800 lb. Rear Suspension: Semi-elliptical springs 1,820 lbs. capacity. Optional Rating: 1,820 lbs. for 115 and 131 in. wheelbase. Front Axle Type and Capacity: Full-floating, 3,500 lb. capacity. Optional: 4,000 lbs. Rear Axle Type and Capacity: Semi-floating, 3,600 lb. capacity. Optional: None. Final Drive Ratio: 2.94, (225 engine) 3.21, 3.55:1 (318 and 360 engines). The 360 engine with automatic had a 2.94:1 axle ratio. Transfer Case: NP-208, single lever, two-speed: 2.61, 1.00:1. Brakes: Type: Power, hydraulic. Front: Disc. Rear: Drum. Dimensions: Front: 11.75 in. x 1.256 in. disc. Rear: 11 in. x 2.5 in. Rear lining area: 106.4 sq. in. Wheels: 15 x 6.5 5-stud disc. Optional: 15 x 7 in. cast aluminum with radial ribbed design. Available for W150 pickups only. These wheels weighed approximately four pounds less per unit than the standard wheels. Tires: Steel belted radials. P235/75R15XL, Optional: 31 x 10.5R-15LTC (available in Mud and Snow tread only). Steering: Recirculating ball. Ratio: 24:1, turns Lock-to-Lock: 3.5:1. Turning Circle: 43 ft. (131 in. wheelbase). Optional: Power assisted. Ratio: 17.8:1. Transmission: NP 435 wide ratio 4-speed manual. Transmission Ratios: 6.68, 3.34, 1.66, 1.00:1. Optional: Chrysler Loadflite A-727 3-speed automatic. Ratios: 2.45, 1.45, 1.00:1. Clutch: Single dry plate disc, hydraulic actuation. Clutch diameter: 11 in. dia. Total lining area: 123.7 sq. in. Optional: None. W250: Separate body and ladder-type frame. Section modules: 3.88 in. (131 in. wheelbase), 5.02 in. (149 in. wheelbase, crew cab), 5.47 in. (149 in. wheelbase, club cab). Front Suspension: Semi-elliptical leaf springs, heavy-duty shock absorbers. 1,640 lb. capacity (131 in. wheelbase), 1,800 lb. capacity (149 in. wheelbase). Optional: 1,800 lb. capacity: 131 in. wheelbase), 2,250 lb. capacity: All wheelbases. Rear Suspension: Semi-elliptical leaf, 2,725 lb. capacity. Front Axle Type and Capacity: Full-floating, 3,500 lb. capacity. Optional rating: 4,000 lb. with Sno-Fiter Package only, 4,500 lb. Rear Axle Type and Capacity: Full-floating, 5,500 lb. capacity. Optional rating: None. Final Drive Ratio: 3.54:1 (conventional cab); 4.10:1 (club cab and crew cab). Transfer Case: Conventional cab and club cab models: New Process 208, two-speed: 2.61, 1.00:1. Crew cab: New Process 205 two-speed. Brakes: Type: Power, hydraulic. Front: Disc. Rear: Drum. Dimensions: Front: 12.82 in. x 1.19 in. disc. Rear: 12.0 in. x 2.50 in. Total rear lining area: 122.8 sq. in. Optional: None. Wheels: 16.5 x 6.00 in., 8-stud disc. Optional: None. Tires: 8.00 x 16.5D, 8-ply rating. Optional (max. size avail.): 9.50R x 16.5E, 8-ply rating. Steering: Recirculating ball. Ratio: 24:1. Optional: Power assisted. Ratio: 17.8:1. Transmission: New Process 435, wide-ratio 4-speed manual. Transmission Ratios: 6.68, 3.34, 1.66, 1.00:1. Reverse. Optional: Chrysler A-727 Loadflite 3-speed automatic. Ratios: 2.45, 1.45, 1.00:1. Clutch: Single dry plate disc, hydraulic actuation. Clutch diameter: 11 in. dia. Total lining area: 123.7 sq. in. W300: Separate body and channel steel, straight frame, 5.02 in. section modules, 36,000 psi. Front Suspension: Semi-elliptical springs, heavy-duty shock absorbers. 1,940 lb. capacity. Optional rating: 2,250 lb. Rear Suspension: Semi-elliptical springs, 3,650 lb. capacity. Optional Rating: 585 lb. and 900 lb. auxiliary springs. Front Axle Type and Capacity: Full-floating. 4,500 lb. capacity. Rear Axle Type and Capacity: 7,500 lb. capacity. Final Drive Ratio: 4.56:1. Transfer Case: New Process 205 Two-speed: 1.96, 1.0:1. Brakes: Type: Hydraulic. Front: Disc. Rear: Drum. Dimensions: Front: 12.88 in. x 1.19 in. disc. Rear: 12.0 in. x 3.0 in. Total rear lining area: 147.4 sq. in. Wheels: 16.5 x 6.75 in. rim, 8-stud disc. Tires: 8.00 x 16.5 heavy-duty, 10-ply. Optional: 8.00R x 16.5E (maximum optional size). Transmission: NP435 4-speed synchromesh manual. Transmission Ratios: 6.69, 3.34, 1.66, 1.00:1. Optional: Chrysler Loadflite A-727 3-speed automatic. Ratios: 2.45, 1.45, 1.00:1. Clutch: Single plate dry disc, hydraulic actuation. Clutch diameter: 11.0 in. Total plate area: 123.7 sq. in. Optional: None.

VEHICLE DIMENSIONS: W150: Wheelbase: 115 in., 131 in.,133 in. (club cab), 149 in. (club cab). Overall Length: 115 in. wheelbase: 193.6 in., 131 in. wheelbase: 213.6 in., 133 in. wheelbase: 211.6 in., 149 in. wheelbase: 231.6 in. wheelbase. All dimensions include optional rear bumper. Front/Rear Tread: 62.5 in./62.5 in. Overall Height: 74.0 in. Width: 79.5 in. Front/Rear Overhang: 30 in./47 in. Tailgate: Width and Height: 67 in. x 21.4 in. Approach/Departure Degrees: 34/24. Ground Clearance: Front axle: 8.2 in. Rear axle: 8.5 in. Oil pan: 15.8 in. Transfer case: 10.4 in. Load space: Pickup box dimensions: 115 in. wheelbase: 78 in. x 51 in. x 19.125 in. Capacity: 61.1 cu. ft. 131 in. wheelbase and 149 in. wheelbase Sweptline: 98 in. x 51 in. x 19.3 in. Capacity: 76.6 cu. ft. W250: Wheelbase: 131 in. Crew cab: 149 in. Overall Length: 131 in./149 in. wheelbase: 213.6 in./231.6 in. Front/Rear Tread: 62.5 in./62.5 in. Overall Height: 74.0 in. Width: 79.5 in. Front/Rear Overhang: 31 in./49 in. Tailgate: Width x Height: 66.5 in. x 19.3 in. Approach/Departure Degrees: 30/21. Ground Clearance: Front axle: 8.0 in. Rear axle: 7.8 in. Oil pan: 16.1 in. Transfer case: 10.7 in. Load space: Pickup box dimensions: Sweptline: 98.875 in. x 51.0 in. x 19.3 in. W350: Wheelbase: 135 in. Load space: Pickup box dimensions: 108 in. x 54 in. x 20 in. Capacity: 66 cu. ft.

CAPACITIES: Fuel Tank: 25 gal.

ACCOMMODATIONS: Seating Capacity: 3 passenger.

INSTRUMENTATION: 0-100 mph speedometer, 99,999.9 mile odometer, gauges for fuel level, ammeter, engine coolant temperature, fuel level and oil pressure. Warning lights for parking brake and hazard lights operation.

OPTIONS: Bright rear step bumper (not available for chassis-cab). Painted rear step bumper (not available for chassis-cab). Front bumper guards with black rub strip insert. Bright exterior dual low mount 6 in. x 9 in. mirrors (not available for chassis-cab models). Lower body side and partial wheel-lip moldings. Road 15 in. x 7 in. aluminum radial ribbed wheels (W150 only). Road 15 in. x 7 in. argent painted steel spoke wheels with bright trim ring and center (W150 only). Air conditioning. AM stereo radio with electronic tuning and integral digital clock. AM/FM stereo radio with electronic tuning, Seek-Scan, Dynamic Noise Reduction, cassette player with automatic reverse and integral digital clock. 120 amp alternator. Anti-slip rear axle. 625 amp maintenance-free battery. Auxiliary transmission oil cooler. Maximum engine cooling. Engine block heater. Transfer case shield. Rear sliding and lockable window. LE Package. Includes the following interior features: Bright sill scuff plates, color-keyed carpeting with underlayment, color-keyed door side trim panels with bolster and carpeting on lower door trim panel, color-keyed soft cloth headliner, color-keyed upper garnish moldings, deluxe Sentry cloth with vinyl trim bench seat, hood inner panel insulation, luxury black steering wheel, LE nameplate on instrument panel and a woodtone instrument panel applique. Exterior elements of the LE Package consisted of bright backlight molding, bright drip rail molding, bright grille insert and headlight bezels with halogen headlights, bright taillight applique with Dodge Ram nameplate, bright tailgate housing, bright taillight upper and lower molding and LE front fender nameplate. The LE package also included dual note electric horns. Prospector Package I. Contains bright deluxe wheelcovers, cigarette lighter, dual low mount 6 in. x 9 in. exterior mirrors, 30 gal. fuel tank (standard on W350), intermittent windshield wipers, Light Package, ram's head hood ornament and electronically tuned AM radio with integral digital clock (W100 only). Prospector Package II. Includes, in addition to contents of Package I, the following: Lower body side and wheel opening moldings, sliding rear window. Prospector Package III. Includes in addition to the contents of Package II, the following: Air conditioning, automatic speed control, bright backlight molding, bright drip rail molding, bright grille insert and headlight bezels with halogen headlights, bright sill scuff plate, bright tailgate housing, bright tailgate applique panel with Dodge Ram nameplate, bright taillight upper and lower molding, color-keyed carpeting with underlayment, color-keyed cowl side trim panels, color-keyed side door trim panels with bolster and carpeting on lower door trim panel, color-keyed soft cloth headliner, color-keyed upper garnish moldings, deluxe cloth with vinyl bench seat, hood inner panel insulation, dual note electric horns, intermittent windshield wipers, LE front fender nameplate, luxury black steering wheel, nameplate on instrument panel, woodtone instrument panel applique with bright trim. Power Convenience Package. Includes ignition key light time delay, power front door locks and front door power windows. Light Package (available only as part of Prospector Packages). Includes ashtray light, glove box lock and light, time delay ignition key light, map light and storage shelf behind seat. Heavy-Duty Package. Includes front and rear heavy-duty shock absorbers (standard on W350), and front stabilizer bar. Trailer Towing Preparation Package. Includes 120 amp alternator, 625 amp maintenance-free battery, auxiliary transmission cooling (with automatic transmission), Heavy-Duty Package, heavy-duty variable load flasher (dealer installed) and maximum engine cooling. APB Two-Tone Paint Package. Includes bright drip rail molding, bright lower body side molding with wide black vinyl insert and bright partial wheel opening molding, two-tone paint and upper body tape stripe. APC Two-Tone Paint Package (not available for chassis-cab models). Includes bright upper body side and rear moldings, bright lower body side and rear moldings with wide black vinyl insert and bright partial wheel opening moldings and two-tone paint. W150, W250 Light-Duty Sno-Commander Package. Includes front clearance and identification lights, hydroelectric controls, plow lights, 90 in. x 24 in. angling plow with blade markers, power lift with seven-way control valve, Sno-Commander decal and transmission oil temperature light with automatic transmission. W250, W350 Heavy-Duty Sno-Commander Package. Includes the same elements as the previous package except for a 96 in. x 27 in. plow. LE Package. Includes bright backlight molding, bright drip rail molding, bright grille insert and headlight bezels with halogen headlights, bright sill scuff plate, bright tailgate applique panel with Dodge Ram nameplate, bright tailgate housing, bright taillight upper and lower molding, color-keyed carpeting with underlayment, color-keyed cowl side trim panels, color-keyed side door trim panels with bolster and carpeting on lower door trim panel, color-keyed soft cloth headliner, color-keyed upper garnish moldings, deluxe cloth with vinyl bench seat, hood inner panel insulation, dual note electric horns, LE front fender nameplate, luxury black steering wheel, nameplate on instrument panel, woodtone instrument panel applique with bright trim.

HISTORICAL FOOTNOTES: Dodge depicted the Power Ram W150 as "Four-Wheel Drive Thunderfoot."

1989 POWER RAM

Dodge engineered a number of significant changes into the1989 Power Ram trucks. As in previous years, the four-wheel drive models were offered in W100, W150, W250 and W350 form with payloads of as much as 3,985 pounds. For 1989 the standard engine for the W100 and W150 was a 3.9 liter V-6 with electronic fuel injection (EFI). The W250 pickup had a standard 5.2 liter V-8 with EFI. New for 1989 was the 5.9 liter V-8 with EFI. This electronic fuel injection system with a low-pressure, throttle body was similar to the unit introduced in 1988 for the 5.2 liter V-8. Other modifications intended to improve engine durability and fuel efficiency included a redesigned cylinder head, a new exhaust port design and stronger pistons. The 5.9 liter with EFI had 17— more horsepower than the engine it replaced. Both the 5.2 liter and 5.9 liter V-8 engines as well as the 3.9 liter V-6 had new tubular push rods, revised rocker arms and hardened exhaust valve tips. The 5.9 liter V-8 was standard for the W350 pickup as well as the W250 and W350 chassis-cab models. All W250 and W350 trucks were also available with an optional 5.9 liter Cummins Turbo Diesel. This engine was originally introduced in July, 1983 and by the start of the 1989 model year over 140,000 had been produced. This 6-cylinder engine featured direct injection and a Holset-designed turbo-charger. The Holset Engineering Company, Limited was a Cummins subsidiary. The following items were also installed on diesel-engined trucks: 120 amp alternator, 1,025 amp maintenance-free battery, 30 gal. fuel tank, heavy-duty starter, heavy-duty air cleaner, maximum engine cooling, auxiliary transmission oil cooler (with automatic transmission), fuel shutoff, fuel and air heaters, warning lights for water in fuel, low fuel, low vacuum, engine block heater, Sound Insulation Package, transfer case skid plate, front bumper guards, underhood reel-type light and Cummins Turbo Diesel nameplates. All Dodge Ram pickups had a standard, computer-controlled rear-wheel anti-lock brake system for 1989.

The standard bench seat for the W-trucks was finished in a saddle grain vinyl. The choice of colors consisted of almond, twilight blue, medium quartz and Bordeaux. Optional for the standard interior was a Tempo cloth and saddle grain vinyl bench seat available in almond, twilight blue and Bordeaux. The LE Decor Package had a Sentry cloth with vinyl trim bench seat. It was offered in the same color selection as the standard seat. A no-charge LE Decor option was a Turin knit/Saddle grain all-vinyl bench seat available in the same three colors. Standard equipment content for 1989 was as follows: Bright front bumper, tinted glass for all windows, aluminum grille with painted plastic insert and headlight doors, bright hubcaps, electronic digital clock, integral with radio, color-keyed dual armrests with inner trim panels, black rubber floor mats with padding, fresh air heater with defroster, interior rear vision day/night mirror, AM/FM stereo radio with electronic tuning (may be deleted for credit on factory orders), buzzer warning system for fasten seat belts, headlights on, key in ignition; power steering, dual jet windshield washers and two-speed electric windshield wipers.

Standard exterior colors for 1989 were black, aquamarine blue (not available for W100), dark suede, diamond blue, dark quartz gray, medium suede (not available for W100), exotic red and bright white. Available at extra cost were twilight blue pearlcoat and platinum silver.

I.D. DATA: The vehicle identification number was located on a V.I.N. plate attached to the driver's side door body latch post. The V.I.N. consisted of 17 elements. The first entry, a number 1, identified the nation of origin as the United States. Vehicles built in Canada carried a number 2. The next element, the letter B, identified the manufacturer as Dodge. Then followed the number 7 signifying the vehicle type as a truck. The next element was a letter identifying the gross vehicle weight as follows: G-5001-6000 lb., H-6001-7000 lb., J-7001-8000 lb., K-8001-9000 lb., L-9001-10,000 lb., M-10,001-14,000 lb. The truck line was next identified by the letter W as a Power Ram pickup 4x4. The body style was the next element of the V.I.N. The number 4 identified a conventional cab; the number 5 identified a club cab and number 6 was a crew cab. The engine code was the next element according to this format: W-225-2-bbl., T-318-2-bbl. or 360-4-bbl. A check digit followed. The model year was then identified by the letter K. The assembly plant was identified by this scheme: A-Lynch Road, C-Jefferson, F-Newark, G-St. Louis, K-Pillete, Canada, M-Lago, Alberta, S-Warren Plant #1, T-Warren Plant #2, V-Warren Plant #3, X-Missouri. The final six digits, beginning with 100001 served as the plant sequential production number.

Body Type	Factory Price	GVW	Shipping Weight	Prod. Total
Model W100				
Pickup, Sweptline, 115 in. wb.	$11,776	6300*	N.A.	—

* 6400 lb. GVW optional.

1989 Dodge W150 LE Ram pickup

W150				
Pickup, Sweptline, 115 in. wb.	$12,898	6300*	N.A.	—
Pickup, Sweptline, 131 in. wb.	$13,099	6300	N.A.	—

* 6400 lb. GVW optional.

Model W250				
Pickup, Sweptline, 131 in. wb.	$13,807	6900*	N.A.	—

* 8510 lb. GVW optional.

Model W350				
Pickup, Sweptline,131 in. wb.	$14,904	8700	N.A.	—

STANDARD ENGINE: W100, W150, W250 pickup models. Features include a drop-forged five-bearing crankshaft, chain-driven camshaft, free-turning exhaust valves, drop-forged I-beam connecting rods and silent-chain camshaft. Engine Type: OHV, V-6. Bore x Stroke: 3.91 in. x 3.31 in. Lifters: Hydraulic. Fuel Induction: Electronic fuel injection. Compression Ratio: 9.2:1. Displacement: 239 cu. in. (3.9 liters). Horsepower: 125 @ 4000 rpm. Torque: Net: 195 lb.-ft. @ 2000 rpm. Fuel Requirements: Unleaded.

STANDARD ENGINE: W250: Optional for W100 and W150. Features include vibration damper, 18 in. 4-blade fan and drop-forged crankshaft. Engine Type: OHV, V-8. Cast iron block and cylinder head. Bore x Stroke: 3.91 in. x 3.31 in. Lifters: Hydraulic. Number of main bearings-5. Fuel Induction: Electronic fuel injection. Compression Ratio: 9.2:1. Displacement: 318 cu. in. (5.2 liters). Horsepower: 140. Oil refill capacity: 5 qt. with filter change. Fuel Requirements: Unleaded.

STANDARD ENGINE: W350: Optional for W250. Features include vibration damper, drop-forged crankshaft. Engine Type: OHV, V-8. Cast iron block and cylinder head. Bore x Stroke: 4.00 in. x 3.58 in. Lifters: Hydraulic. Number of main bearings-5. Fuel Induction: Electronic fuel injection. Displacement: 360 cu. in. (5.9 liters). Horsepower: 190. Oil refill capacity: 5 qt. with filter change. Fuel Requirements: Unleaded.

OPTIONAL ENGINE: W250 and W350: Engine Type: OHV, V-8. Cummins Turbocharged Diesel. Lifters: Hydraulic. Fuel Induction: Fuel injection. Displacement: 360 cu. in. (5.9 liters). Horsepower: 160 @ 2500 rpm. Torque: Net: 400 lb.-ft. @ 1700 rpm. Fuel Requirements: Diesel.

CHASSIS FEATURES: W100, W150: Front Suspension: Semi-elliptical springs, heavy-duty, absorbers. 1,640 lb. rating. Optional rating: 1,800 lb. Rear Suspension: Semi-elliptical springs 1,820 lbs. capacity. Optional Rating: 1,820 lbs. for 115 and 131 in. wheelbase. Front Axle Type and Capacity: Full-floating, 3,500 lb. capacity. Optional: 4,000 lbs. Rear Axle Type and Capacity: Semi-floating, 3,600 lb. capacity. Optional: None. Transfer Case: NP-208, single lever, two-speed: 2.61, 1.00:1. Brakes: Type: Power, hydraulic. Front: Disc. Rear: Drums. Dimensions: Front: 11.75 in. x 1.256 in. disc. Rear: 11 in. x 2.5 in. Rear lining area: 106.4 sq. in. Wheels: 15 x 6.5 5-stud disc. Optional: 15 x 7 in. cast aluminum with radial ribbed design. Available for W150 pickups only. These wheels weighed approximately four pounds less per unit than the standard wheels. Tires: Steel belted radials. P235/75R15XL, Optional: 31 x 10.5R-15LTC (available in Mud and Snow tread only). Steering: Recirculating ball. Ratio: 24:1, turns Lock-to-Lock: 3.5:1. Turning Circle: 43 ft. (131 in. wheelbase). Optional: Power assisted. Ratio: 17.8:1. Transmission: NP 435 wide ratio 4-speed manual. Transmission Ratios: 6.68, 3.34, 1.66, 1.00:1. Optional: Chrysler Loadflite A-727 3-speed automatic. Ratios: 2.45, 1.45, 1.00:1. Clutch: Single dry plate disc, hydraulic actuation. Clutch diameter: 11 in. dia. Total lining area: 123.7 sq. in. Optional: None. W250: Separate body and ladder-type frame. Section modules: 3.88 in. Front Suspension: Semi-elliptical leaf springs, heavy-duty shock absorbers. 1,640 lb. capacity. Rear Suspension: Semi-elliptical leaf, 3,650 lb. capacity. Front Axle Type and Capacity: Full-floating, 3,500 lb. capacity. Optional rating: 4,000 lb. with Sno-Fiter package only, 4,500 lb. Rear Axle Type and Capacity: Full-floating, 5,500 lb. capacity. Transfer Case: New Process 208, two-speed: 2.61, 1.00:1. Brakes: Type: Power, hydraulic. Front: Disc. Rear: Drum. Dimensions: Front: 12.82 in. x 1.19 in. disc. Rear: 12.0 in. x 2.50 in. Total rear lining area: 122.8 sq. in. Optional: None. Wheels: 16.0 x 6.00 in., 8-stud disc. Optional: None. Tires: LT215/85R16C. Steering: Recirculating ball. Ratio: 24:1. Optional: Power assisted. Ratio: 17.8:1. Transmission: New Process 435, wide-ratio 4-speed manual. Transmission Ratios: 6.68, 3.34, 1.66, 1.00:1. Optional: Getrag 5-speed manual overdrive. Clutch: Single dry plate disc, hydraulic actuation. Clutch diameter: 11 in. dia. Total lining area: 123.7 sq. in. W350: Separate body and channel steel, straight frame, 5.02 in. section modules, 36,000 psi. Front Suspension: Semi-elliptical springs, heavy-duty shock absorbers. 18,000 lb. capacity. Rear Suspension: Semi-elliptical springs, 3,650 lb. capacity. Front Axle Type and Capacity: Full-floating. 4,500 lb. capacity. Rear Axle Type and Capacity: 6,200 lb. capacity. Transfer Case: New Process 205 two-speed. Ratios: 1.96, 1.0:1. Brakes: Type: Hydraulic. Front: Disc. Rear: Drum. Dimensions: Front: 12.82 in. x 1.25 in. disc. Rear: 12.0 in. x 2.5 in. Wheels: 16.0 x 6.00 in. rim, 8-stud disc. Tires: LT235/85R16E. Transmission: NP435 4-speed synchromesh manual. Transmission Ratios: 6.69, 3.34, 1.66, 1.00:1. Optional: Chrysler Loadflite A-727 3-speed automatic. Ratios: 2.45, 1.45, 1.00:1. Optional: Getrag 5-speed manual overdrive. Clutch: Single plate dry disc, hydraulic actuation. Clutch diameter: 11.0 in. Total plate area: 123.7 sq. in. Optional: None.

VEHICLE DIMENSIONS: W100/W150: Wheelbase: 115 in., 131 in. Overall Length: 115 in. wheelbase: 190.78 in., 131 in. wheelbase: 210.78 in. Front/Rear Tread: 65.7 in./63.4 in. Overall Height: 73.1 in. Width: 79.5 in. Front/Rear Overhang: 29 in./43 in. Tailgate: Width and Height: 65 in. x 19.0 in. Approach/Departure Degrees: 34/28. Ground Clearance: Front axle: 8.5 in. Rear axle: 8.25 in. Oil pan: 15.25 in. Transfer case: 11.25 in. Load space: Pickup box dimensions: 115 in. wheelbase: 76.9 in. x 51 in. x 19.125 in. 131 in. wheelbase Sweptline: 96.9 in. x 51 in. x 19.3 in. Ground Clearance: Front axle: 8.2 in. Rear axle: 8.5 in. Oil pan: 15.8 in. Transfer case: 10.4 in. W250: Wheelbase: 131 in. Overall length: 210.78 in. Front/Rear Tread: 65.7 in./63.4 in. Overall Height: 73.1 in. Width: 79.5 in. Front/Rear Overhang: 29 in./43 in. Tailgate: Width and Height: 65 in. x 19.0 in. Approach/Departure Degrees: 34/28. Ground Clearance: Front axle: 8.5 in. Rear axle: 8.25 in. Oil pan: 15.25 in. Transfer case: 11.25 in. Load space: Pickup box dimensions: 96.9 in. x 51 in. x 19.3 in. W350: Wheelbase: 131 in. Load space: Pickup box dimensions: 96.9 in. x 51 in. x 19.3 in.

CAPACITIES: Fuel Tank: 22 gal. Optional: 30 gal.

ACCOMMODATIONS: Seating Capacity: 3 passenger.

INSTRUMENTATION: 0-100 mph speedometer, 99,999.9 mile odometer, gauges for fuel level, ammeter, engine coolant temperature, fuel level and oil pressure. Warning lights for parking brake and hazard lights operation.

OPTIONS: Bright rear step bumper. Painted rear step bumper. Front bumper guards with black rub strip insert. Bright exterior dual low mount 6 in. x 9 in. mirrors. Lower body side and partial wheel-lip moldings. Road 15 in. x 7 in. aluminum radial ribbed wheels (W150 only). Road 15 in. x 7 in. argent painted steel spoke wheels with bright trim ring and center (W150 only). Air conditioning. AM stereo radio with electronic tuning and integral digital clock. AM/FM stereo radio with electronic tuning, Seek-Scan, Dynamic Noise Reduction, cassette player with automatic reverse and integral digital clock. 120 amp alternator. Anti-slip rear axle. 625 amp maintenance-free battery. Auxiliary transmission oil cooler. Maximum engine cooling. Engine block heater. Transfer case shield. Rear sliding and lockable window. LE Package. Includes the following interior features: Bright sill scuff plates, color-keyed carpeting with underlayment, color-keyed door side trim panels with bolster and carpeting on lower door trim panel, color-keyed soft cloth headliner, color-keyed upper garnish moldings, deluxe Sentry cloth with vinyl trim bench seat, hood inner panel insulation, luxury black steering wheel, LE nameplate on instrument panel and a woodtone instrument panel applique. Exterior elements of the LE Package consisted of bright backlight molding, bright drip rail molding, bright grille insert and headlight bezels with halogen headlights, bright taillight applique with Dodge Ram nameplate, bright tailgate housing, bright taillight upper and lower molding and LE front fender nameplate. The LE package also included dual note electric horns. Prospector Package I. Contains bright deluxe wheelcovers, cigarette lighter, dual low mount 6 in. x 9 in. exterior mirrors, 30 gal. fuel tank (standard on W350), intermittent windshield wipers, Light Package, ram's head hood ornament and electronically tuned AM radio with integral digital clock (W100 only). Prospector Package II. Includes, in addition to contents of Package I, the following: Lower body side and wheel opening moldings, sliding rear window. Prospector Package III. Includes in addition to the contents of Package II, the following: Air conditioning, automatic speed control, bright backlight molding, bright drip rail molding, bright grille insert and headlight bezels with halogen headlights, bright sill scuff plate, bright tailgate housing, bright tailgate applique panel with Dodge Ram nameplate, bright taillight upper and lower molding, color-keyed carpeting with underlayment, color-keyed cowl side trim panels, color-keyed side door trim panels with bolster and carpeting on lower door trim panel, color-keyed soft cloth headliner, color-keyed upper garnish moldings, deluxe cloth with vinyl bench seat, hood inner panel insulation, dual note electric horns, intermittent windshield wipers, LE front fender nameplate, luxury black steering wheel, nameplate on instrument panel, woodtone instrument panel applique with bright trim. Power Convenience Package. Includes ignition key light time delay, power front door locks and front door power windows. Light Package (available only as part of Prospector Packages). Includes ashtray light, glove box lock and light, time delay ignition key light, map light and storage shelf behind seat. Heavy-Duty Package. Includes front and rear heavy-duty shock absorbers (standard on W350), and front stabilizer bar. Trailer Towing Preparation Package. Includes 120 amp alternator, 625 amp maintenance-free battery, auxiliary transmission cooling (with automatic transmission), Heavy-Duty Package, heavy-duty variable load flasher (dealer installed) and maximum engine cooling. APB Two-Tone Paint Package. Includes bright drip rail molding, bright lower body side molding with wide black vinyl insert and bright partial wheel opening molding, two-tone paint and upper body tape stripe. APC Two-Tone Paint Package (not available for chassis-cab models. Includes bright upper body side and rear moldings, bright lower body side and rear moldings with wide black vinyl insert and bright partial wheel opening moldings and two-tone paint. W150, W250 Light-Duty Sno-Commander Package. Includes front clearance and identification lights, hydroelectric controls, plow lights, 90 in. x 24 in. angling plow with blade markers, power lift with seven-way control valve, Sno-Commander decal and transmission oil temperature light with automatic transmission. W250, W350 Heavy-Duty Sno-Commander Package. Includes the same elements as the previous package except for a 96 in. x 27 in. plow. LE Package. Includes bright backlight molding, bright drip rail molding, bright grille insert and headlight bezels with halogen headlights, bright sill scuff plate, bright tailgate applique panel with Dodge Ram nameplate, bright tailgate housing, bright taillight upper and lower molding, color-keyed carpeting with underlayment, color-keyed cowl side trim panels, color-keyed side door trim panels with bolster and carpeting on lower door trim panel, color-keyed soft cloth headliner, color-keyed upper garnish moldings, deluxe cloth with vinyl bench seat, hood inner panel insulation, dual note electric horns, LE front fender nameplate, luxury black steering wheel, nameplate on instrument panel, woodtone instrument panel applique with bright trim.

HISTORICAL FOOTNOTES: On the basis of the construction by the Dodge Brothers of their first automobile in 1914, Dodge celebrated its 75th anniversary in 1989. The first Dodge trucks were subsequently produced in 1917.

1990 POWER RAM

Except for a doubling of the available number of diesel engines, and the replacement of the W100 line by W150 S models, the W series Dodge trucks were unchanged for 1990.

I.D. DATA: The vehicle identification number was located on a V.I.N. plate attached to the driver's side door body latch post. The V.I.N. consisted of 17 elements. The first entry, a number 1, identified the nation of origin as the United States. Vehicles built in Canada carried a number 2. The next element, the letter B, identified the manufacturer as Dodge. Then followed the number 7 signifying the vehicle type as a truck. The next element was a letter identifying the gross vehicle weight as follows: G-5001-6000 lb., H-6001-7000 lb., J-7001-8000 lb., K-8001-9000 lb., L-9001-10,000 lb., M-10,001-14,000 lb. The truck line was next identified by the letter W as a Power Ram pickup 4x4. The body style was the next element of the V.I.N. The number 4 identified a conventional cab; the number 5 identified a club cab and number 6 was a crew cab. The engine code was the next element according to this format: W-225-2-bbl., T-318-2-bbl. or 360-4-bbl. A check digit followed. The model year was then identified by the letter L. The assembly plant was identified by this scheme: A-Lynch Road, C-Jefferson, F-Newark, G-St. Louis, K-Pillete, Canada, M-Lago, Alberta, S-Warren Plant #1, T-Warren Plant #2, V-Warren Plant #3, X-Missouri. The final six digits, beginning with 100001 served as the plant sequential production number.

Body Type	Factory Price	GVW	Shipping Weight	Prod. Total
Model W150-S				
Pickup, Sweptline, 115 in. wb.	$12,425	6300*	N.A.	—
Pickup, Sweptline, 131 in. wb.	$12,625	6300	N.A.	—
* 6400 lb. GVW optional.				
W150				
Pickup, Sweptline, 115 in. wb.	$13,725	6300*	N.A.	—
Pickup, Sweptline, 131 in. wb.	$13,925	6300	N.A.	—
* 6400 lb. GVW optional.				

Body Type	Factory Price	GVW	Shipping Weight	Prod. Total
Model W250				
Pickup, Sweptline, 131 in. wb.	$16,675	6900*	N.A.	—
Pickup, Club Cab, 149 in. wb.	$16,525	6900	N.A.	—

* 8510 lb. GVW optional.

Model W350				
Pickup, Sweptline,131 in. wb.	$15,800	8700	NA	

STANDARD ENGINE: W150S, W150, W250 pickup models: Features include a drop-forged five-bearing crankshaft, chain-driven camshaft, free-turning exhaust valves, drop-forged I-beam connecting rods and silent-chain camshaft. Engine Type: OHV, V-6. Bore x Stroke: 3.91 in. x 3.31 in. Lifters: Hydraulic. Fuel Induction: Electronic fuel injection. Compression Ratio: 9.2:1. Displacement: 239 cu. in. (3.9 liters). Horsepower: 125 @ 4000 rpm. Torque: Net: 195 lb.-ft. @ 2000 rpm. Fuel Requirements: Unleaded.

STANDARD ENGINE: W250: Optional for W100 and W150. Features include vibration damper, 18 in. 4-blade fan and drop-forged crankshaft. Engine Type: OHV, V-8. Cast iron block and cylinder head. Bore x Stroke: 3.91 in. x 3.31 in. Lifters: Hydraulic. Number of main bearings-5. Fuel Induction: Electronic fuel injection. Compression Ratio: 9.2:1. Displacement: 318 cu. in. (5.2 liters). Horsepower: 140. Oil refill capacity: 5 qt. with filter change. Fuel Requirements: Unleaded.

STANDARD ENGINE: W350: Optional for W250. Features include vibration damper, drop-forged crankshaft. Engine Type: OHV, V-8. Cast iron block and cylinder head. Bore x Stroke: 4.00 in. x 3.58 in. Lifters: Hydraulic. Number of main bearings-5. Fuel Induction: Electronic fuel injection. Displacement: 360 cu. in. (5.9 liters). Horsepower: 190. Oil refill capacity: 5 qt. with filter change. Fuel Requirements: Unleaded.

OPTIONAL ENGINE: W250 and W350: Engine Type: OHV, V-8. Cummins Turbocharged Diesel. Lifters: Hydraulic. Fuel Induction: Fuel injection. Displacement: 360 cu. in. (5.9 liters). Horsepower: 160 @ 2500 rpm. Torque: Net: 400 lb.-ft. @ 1700 rpm. Fuel Requirements: Diesel.

CHASSIS FEATURES: W150S, W150: Front Suspension: Semi-elliptical springs, heavy-duty, absorbers. 1,640 lb. rating. Optional rating: 1,800 lb. Rear Suspension: Semi-elliptical springs 1,820 lbs. capacity. Optional Rating: 1,820 lbs. for 115 and 131 in. wheelbase. Front Axle Type and Capacity: Full-floating, 3,500 lb. capacity. Optional: 4,000 lbs. Rear Axle Type and Capacity: Semi-floating, 3,600 lb. capacity. Optional: None. Transfer Case: NP-208, single lever, two-speed: 2.61, 1.00:1. Brakes: Type: Power, hydraulic. Front: Discs. Rear: Drums. Dimensions: Front: 11.75 in. x 1.256 in. disc. Rear: 11 in. x 2.5 in. Rear lining area: 106.4 sq. in. Wheels: 15 x 6.5 5-stud disc. Optional: 15 x 7 in. cast aluminum with radial ribbed design. Available for W150 pickups only. These wheels weighed approximately four pounds less per unit than the standard wheels. Tires: Steel belted radials. P235/75R15XL, Optional: 31 x 10.5R-15LTC (available in Mud and Snow tread only). Steering: Recirculating ball. Ratio: 24:1, turns Lock-to-Lock: 3.5:1. Turning Circle: 43 ft. (131 in. wheelbase). Optional: Power assisted. Ratio: 17.8:1. Transmission: NP 435 wide ratio 4-speed manual. Transmission Ratios: 6.68, 3.34, 1.66, 1.00:1. Optional: Chrysler Loadflite A-727 3-speed automatic. Ratios: 2.45, 1.45, 1.00:1. Clutch: Single dry plate disc, hydraulic actuation. Clutch diameter: 11 in. dia. Total lining area: 123.7 sq. in. Optional: None. W250: Separate body and ladder-type frame. Section modules: 3.88 in. Front Suspension: Semi-elliptical leaf springs, heavy-duty shock absorbers. 1,640 lb. capacity. Rear Suspension: Semi-elliptical leaf, 3,650 lb. capacity. Front Axle Type and Capacity: Full-floating, 3,500 lb. capacity. Optional rating: 4,000 lb. with Sno-Fiter package only, 4,500 lb. Rear Axle Type and Capacity: Full-floating, 5,500 lb. capacity. Transfer Case: New Process 208, two-speed: 2.61, 1.00:1. Brakes: Type: Power, hydraulic. Front: Disc. Rear: Drum. Dimensions: Front: 12.82 in x 1.19 in. disc. Rear: 12.0 in. x 2.50 in. Total rear lining area: 122.8 sq. in. Optional: None. Wheels: 16.0 x 6.00 in., 8-stud disc. Optional: None. Tires: LT215/85R16C. Steering: Recirculating ball. Ratio: 24:1. Optional: Power assisted. Ratio: 17.8:1. Transmission: New Process 435, wide-ratio 4-speed manual. Transmission Ratios: 6.68, 3.34, 1.66, 1.00:1. Optional: Getrag 5-speed manual overdrive. Clutch: Single dry plate disc, hydraulic actuation. Clutch diameter: 11 in. dia. Total lining area: 123.7 sq. in. W350: Separate body and channel steel, straight frame, 5.02 in. section modules, 36,000 psi. Front Suspension: Semi elliptical springs, heavy-duty shock absorbers. 18,000 lb. capacity. Rear Suspension: Semi-elliptical springs, 3,650 lb. capacity. Front Axle Type and Capacity: Full-floating. 4,500 lb. capacity. Rear Axle Type and Capacity: 6,200 lb. capacity. Transfer Case: New Process 205 two-speed. Ratios: 1.96, 1.0:1. Brakes: Type: Hydraulic. Front: Disc. Rear: Drum. Dimensions: Front: 12.82 in. x 1.25 in. disc. Rear: 12.0 in. x 2.5 in. Wheels: 16.0 x 6.00 in. rim, 8-stud disc. Tires: LT235/85R16E. Transmission: NP435 4-speed synchromesh manual. Transmission Ratios: 6.69, 3.34, 1.66, 1.00:1. Optional: Chrysler Loadflite A-727 3-speed automatic. Ratios: 2.45, 1.45, 1.00:1. Optional: Getrag 5-speed manual overdrive. Clutch: Single plate dry disc, hydraulic actuation. Clutch diameter: 11.0 in. Total plate area: 123.7 sq. in. Optional: None.

VEHICLE DIMENSIONS: W150S/W150: Wheelbase: 115 in., 131 in. Overall Length: 115 in. wheelbase: 190.78 in., 131 in. wheelbase: 210.78 in. Front/Rear Tread: 65.7 in./63.4 in. Overall Height: 73.1 in. Width: 79.5 in. Front/Rear Overhang: 29 in./43 in. Tailgate: Width and Height: 65 in. x 19.0 in. Approach/Departure Degrees: 34/28. Ground Clearance: Front axle: 8.5 in. Rear axle: 8.25 in. Oil pan: 15.25 in. Transfer case: 11.25 in. Load space: Pickup box dimensions: 115 in. wheelbase: 76.9 in. x 51 in. x 19.125 in. 131 in. wheelbase Sweptline: 96.9 in. x 51 in. x 19.3 in. Ground Clearance: Front axle: 8.2 in. Rear axle: 8.5 in. Oil pan: 15.8 in. Transfer case: 10.4 in. W250: Wheelbase: 131 in. Overall length: 210.78 in. Front/Rear Tread: 65.7 in./63.4 in. Overall Height: 73.1 in. Width: 79.5 in. Front/Rear Overhang: 29 in./43 in. Tailgate: Width and Height: 65 in. x 19.0 in. Approach/Departure Degrees: 34/28. Ground Clearance: Front axle: 8.5 in. Rear axle: 8.25 in. Oil pan: 15.25 in. Transfer case: 11.25 in. Load space: Pickup box dimensions: 96.9 in. x 51 in. x 19.3 in. W350: Wheelbase: 131 in. Load space: Pickup box dimensions: 96.9 in. x 51 in. x 19.3 in.

CAPACITIES: Fuel Tank: 22 gal. Optional: 30 gal.

ACCOMMODATIONS: Seating Capacity: 3 passenger.

INSTRUMENTATION: 0-100 mph speedometer, 99,999.9 mile odometer, gauges for fuel level, ammeter, engine coolant temperature, fuel level and oil pressure. Warning lights for parking brake and hazard lights operation.

OPTIONS: Bright rear step bumper. Painted rear step bumper. Front bumper guards with black rub strip insert. Bright exterior dual low mount 6 in. x 9 in. mirrors. Lower body side and partial wheel-lip moldings. Road 15 in. x 7 in. aluminum radial ribbed wheels (W150 only). Road 15 in. x 7 in. argent painted steel spoke wheels with bright trim ring and center (W150 only). Air conditioning. AM stereo radio with electronic tuning and integral digital clock. AM/FM stereo radio with electronic tuning, Seek-Scan, Dynamic Noise Reduction, cassette player with automatic reverse and integral digital clock. 120 amp alternator. Anti-slip rear axle. 625 amp maintenance-free battery. Auxiliary transmission oil cooler. Maximum engine cooling. Engine block heater. Transfer case shield. Rear sliding and lockable window. LE Package. Includes the following interior features: Bright sill scuff plates, color-keyed carpeting with underlayment, color-keyed door side trim panels with bolster and carpeting on lower door trim panel, color-keyed soft cloth headliner, color-keyed upper garnish moldings, deluxe Sentry cloth with vinyl trim bench seat, hood inner panel insulation, luxury black steering wheel, LE nameplate on instrument panel and a woodtone instrument panel applique. Exterior elements of the LE Package consisted of bright backlight molding, bright drip rail molding, bright grille insert and headlight bezels with halogen headlights, bright taillight applique with Dodge Ram nameplate, bright tailgate housing, bright taillight upper and lower molding and LE front fender nameplate. The LE package also included dual note electric horns. Prospector Package I. Contains bright deluxe wheelcovers, cigarette lighter, dual low mount 6 in. x 9 in. exterior mirrors, 30 gal. fuel tank (standard on W350), intermittent windshield wipers, Light Package, Ram's head hood ornament and electronically tuned AM radio with integral digital clock (W100 only). Prospector Package II. Includes, in addition to contents of Package I, the following: lower body side and wheel opening moldings, sliding rear window. Prospector Package III. Includes in addition to the contents of Package II, the following: Air conditioning, automatic speed control, bright backlight molding, bright drip rail molding, bright grille insert and headlight bezels with halogen headlights, bright sill scuff plate, bright tailgate housing, bright tailgate applique panel with Dodge Ram nameplate, bright taillight upper and lower molding, color-keyed carpeting with underlayment, color-keyed cowl side trim panels, color-keyed side door trim panels with bolster and carpeting on lower door trim panel, color-keyed soft cloth headliner, color-keyed upper garnish moldings, deluxe cloth with vinyl bench seat, hood inner panel insulation, dual note electric horns, intermittent windshield wipers, LE front fender nameplate, luxury black steering wheel, nameplate on instrument panel, woodtone instrument panel applique with bright trim. Power Convenience Package. Includes ignition key light time delay, power front door locks and front door power windows. Light Package (available only as part of Prospector Packages). Includes ash tray light, glove box lock and light, time delay ignition key light, map light and storage shelf behind seat. Heavy-Duty Package. Includes front and rear heavy-duty shock absorbers (standard on W350), and front stabilizer bar. Trailer Towing Preparation Package. Includes 120 amp alternator, 625 amp maintenance-free battery, auxiliary transmission cooling (with automatic transmission), Heavy-Duty Package, heavy-duty variable load flasher (dealer installed) and maximum engine cooling. APB Two-Tone Paint Package. Includes bright drip rail molding, bright lower body side molding with wide black vinyl insert and bright partial wheel opening molding, two-tone paint and upper body tape stripe. APC Two-Tone Paint Package (not available for chassis-cab models). Includes bright upper body side and rear moldings, bright lower body side and rear moldings with wide black vinyl insert and bright partial wheel opening moldings and two-tone paint. W150, W250 Light-Duty Sno-Commander Package. Includes front clearance and identification lights, hydroelectric controls, plow lights, 90 in. x 24 in. angling plow with blade markers, power lift with seven-way control valve, Sno-Commander decal and transmission oil temperature light with automatic transmission. W250, W350 Heavy-Duty Sno-Commander Package. Includes the same elements as the previous package except for a 96 in. x 27 in. plow. LE Package. Includes bright backlight molding, bright drip rail molding, bright grille insert and headlight bezels with halogen headlights, bright sill scuff plate, bright tailgate applique panel with Dodge Ram nameplate, bright tailgate housing, bright taillight upper and lower molding, color-keyed carpeting with underlayment, color-keyed cowl side trim panels, color-keyed side door trim panels with bolster and carpeting on lower door trim panel, color-keyed soft cloth headliner, color-keyed upper garnish moldings, deluxe cloth with vinyl bench seat, hood inner panel insulation, dual note electric horns, LE front fender nameplate, luxury black steering wheel, nameplate on instrument panel, woodtone instrument panel applique with bright trim.

HISTORICAL FOOTNOTES: The full-size Dodge pickup had the highest customer satisfaction of any full-size pickup in 1990.

1991 POWER RAM

The 1991 W series Ram trucks received a new grille, lower body side and wheel-lip moldings, low mount extended arm mirrors, new wheel dress-up, new tailgate applique, new cloth interior trim, and three new exterior colors. In addition, the rear bumper was redesigned for increased towing capacity. The tilt steering and speed control options were now available with all engine combinations. A 750 amp battery was added to the option list. Standard equipment for 1991 consisted of these items: Front bright bumper (all except for W150S), argent painted front bumper (W150S only), digital clock (included in radio), cigarette lighter, door trim panels with arm rests, black floor mat with bright mat retainer (all except W1250, W250 club cab), gauges for voltmeter, oil pressure, engine coolant temperature, and trip odometer; tinted glass (all windows), single electric horn, dash and plenum liner insulation, power steering, AM/FM stereo radio with front door speakers, driver and passenger vinyl color-keyed sun visors, electric 2-speed windshield wipers.

1991 Dodge W250 Power Ram pickup

I.D. DATA: The vehicle identification number was located on a V.I.N. plate attached to the driver's side door body latch post. The V.I.N. consisted of 17 elements. The first entry, a number 1, identified the nation of origin as the United States. Vehicles built in Canada carried a number 2. The next element, the letter B, identified the manufacturer as Dodge. Then followed the number 7 signifying the vehicle type as a truck. The next element was a letter identifying the gross vehicle weight as follows: G-5001-6000 lb., H-6001-7000 lb., J-7001-8000 lb., K-8001-9000 lb., L-9001-10,000 lb., M-10,001-14,000 lb. The truck line was next identified by the letter W as a Power Ram pickup 4x4. The body style was the next element of the V.I.N. The number 4 identified a conventional cab; the number 5 identified a club cab and number 6 was a crew cab. The engine code was the next element according to this format: W-225-2-bbl., T-318-2-bbl. or 360-4-bbl. A check digit followed. The model year was then identified by the letter M. The assembly plant was identified by this scheme: A-Lynch Road, C-Jefferson, F-Newark, G-St. Louis, K-Pillete, Canada, M-Lago, Alberta, S-Warren Plant #1, T-Warren Plant #2, V-Warren Plant #3, X-Missouri. The final six digits, beginning with 100001 served as the plant sequential production number.

Body Type	Factory Price	GVW	Shipping Weight	Prod. Total
Model W150-S				
Pickup Sweptline, 115 in. wb.	$12,583	6300*	N.A.	—
Pickup Sweptline, 131 in. wb.	$12,792	6300	N.A.	—
* 6400 lb. GVW optional.				
W150				
Pickup Sweptline, 115 in. wb.	$14,523	6300*	N.A.	—
Pickup Sweptline, 131 in. wb.	$14,733	6300	N.A.	—
* 6400 lb. GVW optional.				
Model W250				
Pickup Sweptline, 131 in. wb.	$15,618	6900*	N.A.	—
Pickup Club Cab, 149 in. wb.	$17,655	6900	N.A.	—
* 8510 lb. GVW optional.				
Model W350				
Pickup Sweptline,131 in. wb.	$16,895	8700	N.A.	—

STANDARD ENGINE: W150S, W150, W250 pickup models: Features include a drop-forged five-bearing crankshaft, chain-driven camshaft, free-turning exhaust valves, drop-forged I-beam connecting rods and silent-chain camshaft. Engine Type: OHV, V-6. Bore x Stroke: 3.91 in. x 3.31 in. Lifters: Hydraulic. Fuel Induction: Electronic fuel injection. Compression Ratio: 9.2:1. Displacement: 239 cu. in. (3.9 liters). Horsepower: 125 @ 4000 rpm. Torque: Net: 195 lb.-ft. @ 2000 rpm. Fuel Requirements: Unleaded.

STANDARD ENGINE: W250: Optional for W100 and W150. Features include vibration damper, 18 in. 4-blade fan and drop-forged crankshaft. Engine Type: OHV, V-8. Cast iron block and cylinder head. Bore x Stroke: 3.91 in. x 3.31 in. Lifters: Hydraulic. Number of main bearings-5. Fuel Induction: Electronic fuel injection. Compression Ratio: 9.2:1. Displacement: 318 cu. in. (5.2 liters). Horsepower: 140. Oil refill capacity: 5 qt. with filter change. Fuel Requirements: Unleaded.

STANDARD ENGINE: W350: Optional for W250. Features include vibration damper, drop-forged crankshaft. Engine Type: OHV, V-8. Cast iron block and cylinder head. Bore x Stroke: 4.00 in. x 3.58 in. Lifters: Hydraulic. Number of main bearings-5. Fuel Induction: Electronic fuel injection. Displacement: 360 cu. in. (5.9 liters). Horsepower: 190. Oil refill capacity: 5 qt. with filter change. Fuel Requirements: Unleaded.

OPTIONAL ENGINE: W250 and W350: Engine Type: OHV, V-8. Cummins Turbocharged Diesel. Lifters: Hydraulic. Fuel Induction: Fuel injection. Displacement: 360 cu. in. (5.9 liters). Horsepower: 160 @ 2500 rpm. Torque: Net: 400 lb.-ft. @ 1700 rpm. Fuel Requirements: Diesel.

CHASSIS FEATURES: W150S, W150: Front Suspension: Semi-elliptical springs, heavy-duty, absorbers. 1,640 lb. rating. Optional rating: 1,800 lb. Rear Suspension: Semi-elliptical springs 1,820 lbs. capacity. Optional Rating: 1,820 lbs. for 115 and 131 in. wheelbase. Front Axle Type and Capacity: Full-floating, 3,500 lb. capacity. Optional: 4,000 lbs. Rear Axle Type and Capacity: Semi-floating, 3,600 lb. capacity. Optional: None. Transfer Case: NP-208, single lever, two-speed: 2.61, 1.00:1. Brakes: Type: Power, hydraulic. Front: Discs. Rear: Drums. Dimensions: Front: 11.75 in. x 1.256 in. disc. Rear: 11 in. x 2.5 in. Rear lining area: 106.4 sq. in. Wheels: 15 x 6.5 5-stud disc. Optional: 15 x 7 in. cast aluminum with radial ribbed design. Available for W150 pickups only. These wheels weighed approximately four pounds less per unit than the standard wheels. Tires: Steel belted radials. P235/75R15XL, Optional: 31 x 10.5R-15LTC (available in Mud and Snow tread only). Steering: Recirculating ball. Ratio: 24:1, turns Lock-to-Lock: 3.5:1. Turning Circle: 43 ft. (131 in. wheelbase). Optional: Power assisted. Ratio: 17.8:1. Transmission: NP 435 wide ratio 4-speed manual. Transmission Ratios: 6.68, 3.34, 1.66, 1.00:1. Optional: Chrysler Loadflite A-727 3-speed automatic. Ratios: 2.45, 1.45, 1.00:1. Clutch: Single dry plate disc, hydraulic actuation. Clutch diameter: 11 in. dia. Total lining area: 123.7 sq. in. Optional: None. W250: Separate body and ladder-type frame. Section modules: 3.88 in. Front Suspension: Semi-elliptical leaf springs, heavy-duty shock absorbers. 1,640 lb. capacity. Rear Suspension: Semi-elliptical leaf, 3,650 lb. capacity. Front Axle Type and Capacity: Full-floating, 3,500 lb. capacity. Optional rating: 4,000 lb. with Sno-Fiter package only, 4,500 lb. Rear Axle Type and Capacity: Full-floating, 5,500 lb. capacity. Transfer Case: New Process 208, two-speed: 2.61, 1.00:1. Brakes: Type: Power, hydraulic. Front: Disc. Rear: Drum. Dimensions: Front: 12.82 in. x 1.19 in. disc. Rear: 12.0 in. x 2.50 in. Total rear lining area: 122.8 sq. in. Optional: None. Wheels: 16.0 x 6.00 in., 8-stud disc. Optional: None. Tires: LT215/85R16C. Steering: Recirculating ball. Ratio: 24:1. Optional: Power assisted. Ratio: 17.8:1. Transmission: New Process 435, wide-ratio 4-speed manual. Transmission Ratios: 6.68, 3.34, 1.66, 1.00:1. Optional: Getrag 5-speed manual overdrive. Clutch: Single dry plate disc, hydraulic actuation. Clutch diameter: 11 in. dia. Total lining area: 123.7 sq. in. W350: Separate body and channel steel, straight frame, 5.02 in. section modules, 36,000 psi. Front Suspension: Semi-elliptical springs, heavy-duty shock absorbers. 18,000 lb. capacity. Rear Suspension: Semi-elliptical springs, 3,650 lb. capacity. Front Axle Type and Capacity: Full-floating, 4,500 lb. capacity. Rear Axle Type and Capacity: 6,200 lb. capacity. Transfer Case: New Process 205 two-speed. Ratios: 1.96, 1.0:1. Brakes: Type: Hydraulic. Front: Disc. Rear: Drum. Dimensions: Front: 12.82 in. x 1.25 in. disc. Rear: 12.0 in. x 2.5 in. Wheels: 16.0 x 6.00 in. rim, 8-stud disc. Tires: LT235/85R16E. Transmission: NP435 4-speed synchromesh manual. Transmission Ratios: 6.69, 3.34, 1.66, 1.00:1. Optional: Chrysler Loadflite A-727 3-speed automatic. Ratios: 2.45, 1.45, 1.00:1. Optional: Getrag 5-speed manual overdrive. Clutch: Single plate dry disc, hydraulic actuation. Clutch diameter: 11.0 in. Total plate area: 123.7 sq. in. Optional: None.

VEHICLE DIMENSIONS: W150S/W150: Wheelbase: 115 in., 131 in. Overall Length: 115 in. wheelbase: 190.78 in., 131 in. wheelbase: 210.78 in. Front/Rear Tread: 65.7 in./63.4 in. Overall Height: 73.1 in. Width: 79.5 in. Front/Rear Overhang: 29 in./43 in. Tailgate: Width and Height: 65 in. x 19.0 in. Approach/Departure Degrees: 34/28. Ground Clearance: Front axle: 8.5 in. Rear axle: 8.25 in. Oil pan: 15.25 in. Transfer case: 11.25 in. Load space: Pickup box dimensions: 115 in. wheelbase: 76.9 in. x 51 in. x 19.125 in. 131 in. wheelbase Sweptline: 96.9 in. x 51 in. x 19.3 in. Ground Clearance: Front axle: 8.2 in. Rear axle: 8.5 in. Oil pan: 15.8 in. Transfer case: 10.4 in. W250: Wheelbase: 131 in. Overall length: 210.78 in. Front/Rear Tread: 65.7 in./63.4 in. Overall Height: 73.1 in. Width: 79.5 in. Front/Rear Overhang: 29 in./43 in. Tailgate: Width and Height: 65 in. x 19.0 in. Approach/Departure Degrees: 34/28. Ground Clearance: Front axle: 8.5 in. Rear axle: 8.25 in. Oil pan: 15.25 in. Transfer case: 11.25 in. Load space: Pickup box dimensions: 96.9 in. x 51 in. x 19.3 in. W350: Wheelbase: 131 in. Load space: Pickup box dimensions: 96.9 in. x 51 in. x 19.3 in.

CAPACITIES: Fuel Tank: 22 gal. Optional: 30 gal.

ACCOMMODATIONS: Seating Capacity: 3 passenger.

INSTRUMENTATION: 0-100 mph speedometer, 99,999.9 mile odometer, gauges for fuel level, ammeter, engine coolant temperature, fuel level and oil pressure. Warning lights for parking brake and hazard lights operation.

OPTIONS: Bright rear step bumper. Painted rear step bumper. Front bumper guards with black rub strip insert. Bright exterior dual low mount 6 in. x 9 in. mirrors. Lower body side and partial wheel-lip moldings. Road 15 in. x 7 in. aluminum radial ribbed wheels (W150 only). Road 15 in. x 7 in. argent painted steel spoke wheels with bright trim ring and center (W150 only). Air conditioning. AM stereo radio with electronic tuning and integral digital clock. AM/FM stereo radio with electronic tuning, Seek-Scan, Dynamic Noise Reduction, cassette player with automatic reverse and integral digital clock. 120 amp alternator. Anti-slip rear axle. 625 amp maintenance-free battery. Auxiliary transmission oil cooler. Maximum engine cooling. Engine block heater. Transfer case shield. Rear sliding and lockable window. LE Package. Includes the following interior features: Bright sill scuff plates, color-keyed carpeting with underlayment, color-keyed door side trim panels with bolster and carpeting on lower door trim panel, color-keyed soft cloth headliner, color-keyed upper garnish moldings, deluxe Sentry cloth with vinyl trim bench seat, hood inner panel insulation, luxury black steering wheel, LE nameplate on instrument panel and a woodtone instrument panel applique. Exterior elements of the LE Package consisted of bright backlight molding, bright drip rail molding, bright grille insert and headlight bezels with halogen headlights, bright taillight applique with Dodge Ram nameplate, bright tailgate housing, bright taillight upper and lower molding and LE front fender nameplate. The LE package also included dual note electric horns. Prospector Package I. Contains bright deluxe wheelcovers, cigarette lighter, dual low mount 6 in. x 9 in. exterior mirrors, 30 gal. fuel tank (standard on W350), intermittent windshield wipers, Light Package, ram's head hood ornament and electronically tuned AM radio with integral digital clock (W100 only). Prospector Package II. Includes, in addition to contents of Package I, the following: Lower body side and wheel opening moldings, sliding rear window. Prospector Package III. Includes in addition to the contents of Package II, the following: Air conditioning, automatic speed control, bright backlight molding, bright drip rail molding, bright grille insert and headlight bezels with halogen headlights, bright sill scuff plate, bright tailgate housing, bright tailgate applique panel with Dodge Ram nameplate, bright taillight upper and lower molding, color-keyed carpeting with underlayment, color-keyed cowl side trim panels, color-keyed side door trim panels with bolster and carpeting on lower door trim panel, color-keyed soft cloth headliner, color-keyed upper garnish moldings, deluxe cloth with vinyl bench seat, hood inner panel insulation, dual note electric horns, intermittent windshield wipers, LE front fender nameplate, luxury black steering wheel, nameplate on instrument panel, woodtone instrument panel applique with bright trim. Power Convenience Package. Includes ignition key light time delay, power front door locks and front door power windows. Light Package (available only as part of Prospector Packages). Includes ashtray light, glove box lock and light, time delay ignition key light, map light and storage shelf behind seat. Heavy-Duty Package. Includes front and rear heavy-duty shock absorbers (standard on W350), and front stabilizer bar. Trailer Towing Preparation Package. Includes 120 amp alternator, 625 amp maintenance-free battery, auxiliary transmission cooling (with automatic transmission), Heavy-Duty Package, heavy-duty variable load flasher (dealer installed) and maximum engine cooling. APB Two-Tone Paint Package. Includes bright drip rail molding, bright lower body side molding with wide black vinyl insert and bright partial wheel opening molding, two-tone paint and upper body tape stripe. APC Two-Tone Paint Package (not available for chassis-cab models). Includes bright upper body side and rear moldings, bright lower body side and rear moldings with wide black vinyl insert and bright partial wheel opening moldings and two-tone paint. W150, W250 Light-Duty Sno-Commander Package. Includes front clearance and identification lights, hydroelectric controls, plow lights, 90 in. x 24 in. angling plow with blade markers, power lift with seven-way control valve, Sno-Commander decal and transmission oil temperature light with automatic transmission. W250, W350 Heavy-Duty Sno-Commander Package. Includes the same elements as the previous package except for a 96 in. x 27 in. plow. LE Package. Includes bright backlight molding, bright drip rail molding, bright grille insert and headlight bezels with halogen headlights, bright sill scuff plate, bright tailgate applique panel with Dodge Ram nameplate, bright tailgate housing, bright taillight upper and lower molding, color-keyed carpeting with underlayment, color-keyed cowl side trim panels, color-keyed side door trim panels with bolster and carpeting on lower door trim panel, color-keyed soft cloth headliner, color-keyed upper garnish moldings, deluxe cloth with vinyl bench seat, hood inner panel insulation, dual note electric horns, LE front fender nameplate, luxury black steering wheel, nameplate on instrument panel, woodtone instrument panel applique with bright trim.

HISTORICAL FOOTNOTES: The full-size Dodge pickup was built in Lago Alberto, Mexico and Warren, Michigan.

1992 POWER RAM

For 1992 the Power Ram pickups were set apart by new 3.9 liter V-6 and 5.2 liter V-8 multi-port fuel injected "Magnum" engines. A new W350 dual rear wheel model was also introduced. A new heavy-duty 5-speed manual transmission was now available. All gasoline engines were available with a heavy-duty 4-speed automatic transmission. The club cab model was now available with the diesel engine as well as a 30 gal. fuel tank. Trucks with the 5.9 liter diesel engine could now be ordered with a Heavy-Duty Snowplow Prep Package. Additional new features for 1992 included a larger exhaust system for the 3.9 liter and 5.2 liter engines, a 600 amp standard battery and the availability of speed control as an option for diesel engines.

Three new exterior colors were offered for 1992: Dark copper, light champagne metallic and dark forest green metallic. A new interior color — Spice/Dark spice was also offered.

1992 Dodge W250 LE Ram pickup with Cummins Turbo Diesel

I.D. DATA: The vehicle identification number was located on a V.I.N. plate attached to the driver's side door body latch post. The V.I.N. consisted of 17 elements. The first entry, a number 1, identified the nation of origin as the United States. Vehicles built in Canada carried a number 2. The next element, the letter B, identified the manufacturer as Dodge. Then followed the number 7 signifying the vehicle type as a truck. The next element was a letter identifying the gross vehicle weight as follows: G-5001-6000 lb., H-6001-7000 lb., J-7001-8000 lb., K-8001-9000 lb., L-9001-10,000 lb., M-10,001-14,000 lb. The truck line was next identified by the letter W as a Power Ram pickup 4x4. The body style was the next element of the V.I.N. The number 4 identified a conventional cab; the number 5 identified a club cab and number 6 was a crew cab. The engine code was the next element. A check digit followed. The model year was then identified by the letter M. The assembly plant was identified by this scheme: A-Lynch Road, C-Jefferson, F-Newark, G-St. Louis, K-Pillete, Canada, M-Lago, Alberta, S-Warren Plant #1, T-Warren Plant #2, V-Warren Plant #3, X-Missouri. The final six digits, beginning with 100001 served as the plant sequential production number.

Body Type	Factory Price	GVW	Shipping Weight	Prod. Total
W150S				
Pickup, Sweptline, 115 in. wb.	$N.A.	6300*	N.A.	—
Pickup, Sweptline, 131 in. wb.	$N.A.	6300	N.A.	—
W150				
Pickup, Sweptline, 115 in. wb.	$15,649	6300*	NA	
Pickup, Sweptline, 131 in. wb.	$15,869	6300	NA	

* 6400 lb. GVW optional.

Body Type	Factory Price	GVW	Shipping Weight	Prod. Total
Model W250				
Pickup, Sweptline, 131 in. wb.	$16,832	6900*	NA	—
Pickup, Club Cab, 149 in. wb.	$18,310	6900	N.A.	—

* 8510 lb. GVW optional.

Body Type	Factory Price	GVW	Shipping Weight	Prod. Total
Model W350				
Pickup, Sweptline,131 in. wb.	$17,733	8700	N.A.	—
Pickup, Club Cab, 149 in. wb.	$23,417	8700	N.A.	—

STANDARD ENGINE: W150, W250 pickup models: Features include a drop-forged five-bearing crankshaft, chain-driven camshaft, free-turning exhaust valves, drop-forged I-beam connecting rods and silent-chain camshaft. Engine Type: OHV, V-6. Bore x Stroke: 3.91 in. x 3.31 in. Lifters: Hydraulic. Fuel Induction: Electronic fuel injection. Compression Ratio: 9.2:1. Displacement: 239 cu. in. (3.9 liters). Horsepower: 180 @ 4800 rpm. Torque: Net: 225 lb.-ft. @ 3200 rpm. Fuel Requirements: Unleaded.

STANDARD ENGINE: W250: Optional for W150S and W150. Features include vibration damper, 18 in. 4-blade fan and drop-forged crankshaft. Engine Type: OHV, V-8. Cast iron block and cylinder head. Bore x Stroke: 3.91 in. x 3.31 in. Lifters: Hydraulic. Number of main bearings-5. Fuel Induction: Electronic fuel injection. Compression Ratio: 9.2:1. Displacement: 318 cu. in. (5.2 liters). Horsepower: 230 @ 4800 rpm. Torque: 280 lb.-ft. @ 3200 rpm. Oil refill capacity: 5 qt. with filter change. Fuel Requirements: Unleaded.

STANDARD ENGINE: W350: Optional for W250. Features include vibration damper, drop-forged crankshaft. Engine Type: OHV, V-8. Cast iron block and cylinder head. Bore x Stroke: 4.00 in. x 3.58 in. Lifters: Hydraulic. Number of main bearings-5. Fuel Induction: Electronic fuel injection. Compression ratio: 8.1:1. Displacement: 360 cu. in. (5.9 liters). Horsepower: 190 @ 4000 rpm. Torque: 292 lb.-ft. @ 2400 rpm. Oil refill capacity: 5 qt. with filter change. Fuel Requirements: Unleaded.

OPTIONAL ENGINE: W250 and W350: Engine Type: OHV, V-8. Cummins Turbocharged Diesel. Lifters: Hydraulic. Fuel Induction: Fuel injection. Compression ratio: 17.5:1. Displacement: 360 cu. in. (5.9 liters). Horsepower: 160 @ 2500 rpm. Torque: Net: 400 lb.-ft. @ 1700 rpm. Fuel Requirements: Diesel.

CHASSIS FEATURES: W150: Front Suspension: Semi-elliptical springs, heavy-duty, absorbers. 1,640 lb. rating. Optional rating: 1,800 lb. Rear Suspension: Semi-elliptical springs 1,820 lbs. capacity. Optional Rating: 1,820 lbs. for 115 and 131 in. wheelbase. Front Axle Type and Capacity: Full-floating, 3,500 lb. capacity. Optional: 4,000 lbs. Rear Axle Type and Capacity: Semi-floating, 3,600 lb. capacity. Optional: None. Transfer Case: NP-208, single lever, two-speed: 2.61, 1.00:1. Brakes: Type: Power, hydraulic. Front: Discs. Rear: Drums. Dimensions: Front: 11.75 in. x 1.256 in. disc. Rear: 11 in. x 2.5 in. Rear lining area: 106.4 sq. in. Wheels: 15 x 6.5 5-stud disc. Optional: 15 x 7 in. cast aluminum with radial ribbed design. Available for W150 pickups only. These wheels weighed approximately four pounds less per unit than the standard wheels. Tires: Steel belted radials. P235/75R15XL, Optional: 31 x 10.5R-15LTC (available in Mud and Snow tread only). Steering: Recirculating ball. Ratio: 24:1, turns Lock-to-Lock: 3.5:1. Turning Circle: 43 ft. (131 in. wheelbase). Optional: Power assisted. Ratio: 17.8:1. Transmission: 5-speed heavy-duty Getrag 360 manual. Optional: 4-speed automatic, heavy-duty 4-speed manual. Clutch: Single dry plate disc, hydraulic actuation. Clutch diameter: 11 in. dia. Total lining area: 123.7 sq. in. Optional: None. W250: Separate body and ladder-type frame. Section modules: 3.88 in. Front Suspension: Semi-elliptical leaf springs, heavy-duty shock absorbers. 1,640 lb. capacity. Rear Suspension: Semi-elliptical leaf, 3,650 lb. capacity. Front Axle Type and Capacity: Full-floating, 3,500 lb. capacity. Optional rating: 4,000 lb. with Sno-Fiter package only, 4,500 lb. Rear Axle Type and Capacity: Full-floating, 5,500 lb. capacity. Transfer Case: New Process 208, two-speed: 2.61, 1.00:1. Brakes: Type: Power, hydraulic, Front: Disc. Rear: Drum. Dimensions: Front: 12.82 in. x 1.19 in. disc. Rear: 12.0 in. x 2.50 in. Total rear lining area: 122.8 sq. in. Optional: None. Wheels: 16.0 x 6.00 in., 8-stud disc. Optional: None. Tires: LT215/85R16C. Steering: Recirculating ball. Ratio: 24:1. Optional: Power assisted. Ratio: 17.8:1. Transmission: New Process 435, wide-ratio 4-speed manual. (Vehicles with 8510 lb. GVW have the 5-speed heavy-duty Getrag 360 manual transmission as standard). Transmission Ratios: 6.68, 3.34, 1.66, 1.00:1. Optional: Getrag 5-speed manual overdrive, 4-spd. and 4-spd. automatic. Clutch: Single dry plate disc, hydraulic actuation. Clutch diameter: 11 in. dia. Total lining area: 123.7 sq. in. W350: Separate body and channel steel, straight frame, 5.02 in. section modules, 36,000 psi. Front Suspension: Semi-elliptical springs, heavy-duty shock absorbers. 18,000 lb. capacity. Rear Suspension: Semi-elliptical springs, 3,650 lb. capacity. Front Axle Type and Capacity: Full-floating. 4,500 lb. capacity. Rear Axle Type and Capacity: 6,200 lb. capacity. Transfer Case: New Process 205 two-speed. Ratios: 1.96, 1.0:1. Brakes: Type: Hydraulic. Front: Disc. Rear: Drum. Dimensions: Front: 12.82 in. x 1.25 in. disc. Rear: 12.0 in. x 2.5 in. Wheels: 16.0 x 6.00 in. rim, 8-stud disc. Tires: LT235/85R16E. Transmission: 5-speed heavy-duty Getrag 360 manual. Optional: 4-speed automatic. Ratios: 2.45, 1.45, 1.00:1. Optional: Getrag 5-speed manual overdrive. Clutch: Single plate dry disc, hydraulic actuation. Clutch diameter: 11.0 in. Total plate area: 123.7 sq. in. Optional: None.

VEHICLE DIMENSIONS: W150S/W150: Wheelbase: 115 in., 131 in. Overall Length: 115 in. wheelbase: 190.78 in., 131 in. wheelbase: 210.78 in. Front/Rear Tread: 65.7 in./63.4 in. Overall Height: 73.1 in. Width: 79.5 in. Front/Rear Overhang: 29 in./43 in. Tailgate: Width and Height: 65 in. x 19.0 in. Approach/Departure Degrees: 34/28. Ground Clearance: Front axle: 8.5 in. Rear axle: 8.25 in. Oil pan: 15.25 in. Transfer case: 11.25 in. Load space: Pickup box dimensions: 115 in. wheelbase: 76.9 in. x 51 in. x 19.125 in. 131 in. wheelbase Sweptline: 96.9 in. x 51 in. x 19.3 in. Ground Clearance: Front axle: 8.2 in. Rear axle: 8.5 in. Oil pan: 15.8 in. Transfer case: 10.4 in. W250: Wheelbase: 131 in. Overall length: 210.78 in. Front/Rear Tread: 65.7 in./63.4 in. Overall Height: 73.1 in. Width: 79.5 in. Front/Rear Overhang: 29 in./43 in. Tailgate: Width and Height: 65 in. x 19.0 in. Approach/Departure Degrees: 34/28. Ground Clearance: Front axle: 8.5 in. Rear axle: 8.25 in. Oil pan: 15.25 in. Transfer case: 11.25 in. Load space: Pickup box dimensions: 96.9 in. x 51 in. x 19.3 in. W350: Wheelbase: 131 in. Load space: Pickup box dimensions: 96.9 in. x 51 in. x 19.3 in.

CAPACITIES: Fuel Tank: 22 gal. Optional: 30 gal.

ACCOMMODATIONS: Seating Capacity: 3 passenger.

INSTRUMENTATION: 0-100 mph speedometer, 99,999.9 mile odometer, gauges for fuel level, ammeter, engine coolant temperature, fuel level and oil pressure. Warning lights for parking brake and hazard lights operation.

OPTIONS: Air conditioning. 120 amp alternator. 810 amp battery. Rear step bumper. Maximum engine cooling. Auxiliary automatic transmission oil cooler. Deluxe Convenience Group. 30 gal. fuel tank. Engine block heater. Heavy duty springs. Cab clearance lights. Exterior mirrors. Lower body side protective moldings. Power Convenience Group. Premium bucket seats with center storage console (club cabs). AM/FM cassette E.T. stereo radio. Skid plate. Snowplow Prep Group. Front stabilizer bar. Trailer Towing Prep Group. Two-tone paint. Argent steel-styled wheels. Cast aluminum wheels. Sliding rear window.

HISTORICAL FOOTNOTES: Three years after its introduction, the Dodge-Cummins diesel combination had over 30 percent of the light truck diesel truck market.

1993 POWER RAM

For 1993 the optional 30 gal. fuel tank was available for the 115 in. wheelbase W150 models with automatic transmission. It was now standard for the W250 and W350 models. The 5. liter engine was fitted with a sequential multi-point fuel injection and a serpentine belt accessory belt drive. Availability of the 5.9 liter V-8 was extended to the W150 models. A Super Duty transmission oil cooler was a new dealer-installed option for models with the 5.9 liter V-8 and automatic transmission. A new Work Special Package was offered for the W150 standard cab models. Two new exterior pearlcoat colors were introduced for 1993: Flame red and Emerald green.

1993 Dodge W250 Ram pickup with Cummins Turbo Diesel

I.D. DATA: The vehicle identification number was located on a V.I.N. plate attached to the driver's side door body latch post. The V.I.N. consisted of 17 elements. The first entry, a number 1, identified the nation of origin as the United States. Vehicles built in Canada carried a number 2. The next element, the letter B, identified the manufacturer as Dodge. Then followed the number 7 signifying the vehicle type as a truck. The next element was a letter identifying the gross vehicle weight as follows: G-5001-6000 lb., H-6001-7000 lb., J-7001-8000 lb., K-8001-9000 lb., L-9001-10,000 lb., M-10,001-14,000 lb. The truck line was next identified by the letter W as a Power Ram pickup 4 x4. The body style was the next element of the V.I.N. The number 4 identified a conventional cab; the number 5 identified a club cab and number 6 was a crew cab. The engine code was the next element. A check digit followed. The model year was then identified by the letter N. The assembly plant was identified by this scheme: A-Lynch Road, C-Jefferson, F-Newark, G-St. Louis, K-Pillete, Canada, M-Lago, Alberta, S-Warren Plant #1, T-Warren Plant #2, V-Warren Plant #3, X-Missouri. The final six digits, beginning with 100001 served as the plant sequential production number.

Body Type	Factory Price	GVW	Shipping Weight	Prod. Total
W150				
Pickup, Sweptline, 115 in. wb.	$N.A.	6400*	4149	—
Pickup, Sweptline, 131 in. wb.	$N.A.	6300	4332	—

* 6400 lb. GVW optional.

Body Type	Factory Price	GVW	Shipping Weight	Prod. Total
Model W250				
Ch. and Cab, 131 in. wb.	$N.A.	7500*	4347	—
Pickup, Sweptline, 131 in. wb.	$N.A.	7500	4582	—
Pickup, Club Cab, 149 in. wb.	$N.A.	7500	4812	—

* 8510 lb. GVW optional.

Body Type	Factory Price	GVW	Shipping Weight	Prod. Total
Model W350				
Ch. and Cab, 131 in. wb.	$N.A.	8700*	4578	—
Ch. and Cab,135 in. wb.	$N.A.	8700	4796	—
Pickup, Sweptline,131 in. wb.	$N.A.	8700	4881	—
Pickup, Club Cab, 149 in. wb.	$N.A.	8700	6025	—

* 10,100 lb. GVW optional.

STANDARD ENGINE: W150, pickup models: Features include a drop-forged five-bearing crankshaft, chain-driven camshaft, free-turning exhaust valves, drop-forged I-beam connecting rods and silent-chain camshaft. Engine Type: OHV, V-6. Bore x Stroke: 3.91 in. x 3.31 in. Lifters: Hydraulic. Fuel Induction: Electronic fuel injection. Compression Ratio: 9.2:1. Displacement: 239 cu. in. (3.9 liters). Horsepower: 180 @ 4800 rpm. Torque: Net: 225 lb.-ft. @ 3200 rpm. Fuel Requirements: Unleaded.

STANDARD ENGINE: W250: Optional for W150. Features include vibration damper, 18 in. 4-blade fan and drop-forged crankshaft. Engine Type: OHV, V-8. Cast iron block and cylinder head. Bore x Stroke: 3.91 in. x 3.31 in. Lifters: Hydraulic. Number of main bearings-5. Fuel Induction: Electronic fuel injection. Compression Ratio: 9.2:1. Displacement: 318 cu. in. (5.2 liters). Horsepower: 230 @ 4800 rpm. Torque: 280 lb.-ft. @ 3200 rpm. Oil refill capacity: 5 qt. with filter change. Fuel Requirements: Unleaded.

STANDARD ENGINE: W350: Optional for W150 and W250. Features include vibration damper, drop-forged crankshaft. Engine Type: OHV, V-8. Cast iron block and cylinder head. Bore x Stroke: 4.00 in. x 3.58 in. Lifters: Hydraulic. Number of main bearings-5. Fuel Induction: Electronic fuel injection. Compression ratio: 8.1:1. Displacement: 360 cu. in. (5.9 liters). Horsepower: 190 @ 4000 rpm. Torque: 292 lb.-ft. @ 2400 rpm. Oil refill capacity: 5 qt. with filter change. Fuel Requirements: Unleaded.

OPTIONAL ENGINE: W250 and W350: Engine Type: OHV, V-8. Cummins Turbocharged Diesel. Lifters: Hydraulic. Fuel Induction: Fuel injection. Compression ratio: 17.5:1. Displacement: 360 cu. in. (5.9 liters). Horsepower: 160 @ 2500 rpm. Torque: Net: 400 lb.-ft. @ 1700 rpm. Fuel Requirements: Diesel.

CHASSIS FEATURES: W150: Front Suspension: Semi-elliptical springs, heavy-duty, absorbers. 1,640 lb. rating. Optional rating: 1,800 lb. Rear Suspension: Semi-elliptical springs 1,820 lbs. capacity. Optional Rating: 1,820 lbs. for 115 and 131 in. wheelbase. Front Axle Type and Capacity: Full-floating, 3,500 lb. capacity. Optional: 4,000 lbs. Rear Axle Type and Capacity: Semi-floating, 3,600 lb. capacity. Optional: None. Transfer Case: NP-208, single lever, two-speed: 2.61, 1.00:1. Brakes: Type: Power, hydraulic. Front: Discs. Rear: Drums. Dimensions: Front: 11.75 in. x 1.256 in. disc. Rear: 11 in. x 2.5 in. Rear lining area: 106.4 sq. in. Wheels: 15 x 6.5 5-stud disc. Optional: 15 x 7 in. cast aluminum with radial ribbed design. Available for W150 pickups only. These wheels weighed approximately four pounds less per unit than the standard wheels. Tires: Steel belted radials. P235/75R15XL, Optional: 31 x 10.5R-15LTC (available in Mud and Snow tread only). Steering: Recirculating ball. Ratio: 24:1, turns Lock-to-Lock: 3.5:1. Turning Circle: 43 ft. (131 in. wheelbase). Optional: Power assisted. Ratio: 17.8:1. Transmission: 5-speed heavy-duty Getrag 360 manual. Optional: 4-speed automatic, heavy-duty 4-speed manual. Clutch: Single dry plate disc, hydraulic actuation. Clutch diameter: 11 in. dia. Total lining area: 123.7 sq. in. Optional: None. W250: Separate body and ladder-type frame. Section modules: 3.88 in. Front Suspension: Semi-elliptical leaf springs, heavy-duty shock absorbers. 1,640 lb. capacity. Rear Suspension: Semi-elliptical leaf, 3,650 lb. capacity. Front Axle Type and Capacity: Full-floating, 3,500 lb. capacity. Optional rating: 4,000 lb. with Sno-Fiter package only, 4,500 lb. Rear Axle Type and Capacity: Full-floating, 5,500 lb. capacity. Transfer Case: New Process 208, two-speed: 2.61, 1.00:1. Brakes: Type: Power, hydraulic. Front: Disc. Rear: Drum. Dimensions: Front: 12.82 in. x 1.19 in. disc. Rear: 12.0 in. x 2.50 in. Total rear lining area: 122.8 sq. in. Optional: None. Wheels: 16.0 x 6.00 in., 8-stud disc. Optional: None. Tires: LT215/85R16D. Steering: Recirculating ball. Ratio: 24:1. Optional: Power assisted. Ratio: 17.8:1. Transmission: New Process 435, wide-ratio 4-speed manual. (Vehicles with 8510 lb. GVW have the 5-speed heavy-duty Getrag 360 manual transmission as standard). Transmission Ratios: 6.68, 3.34, 1.66, 1.00:1. Optional: Getrag 5-speed manual overdrive, 4-spd. and 4-spd. automatic. Clutch: Single dry plate disc, hydraulic actuation. Clutch diameter: 11 in. dia. Total lining area: 123.7 sq. in.

W350: Separate body and channel steel, straight frame, 5.02 in. section modules, 36,000 psi. Front Suspension: semi-elliptical springs, heavy-duty shock absorbers. 18,000 lb. capacity. Rear Suspension: semi-elliptical springs, 3,650 lb. capacity. Front Axle Type and Capacity: Full-floating, 4,500 lb. capacity. Rear Axle Type and Capacity: 6,200 lb. capacity. Transfer Case: New Process 205 two-speed. Ratios: 1.96, 1.0:1. Brakes: Type: Hydraulic. Front: Disc. Rear: Drum. Dimensions: Front: 12.82 in. x 1.25 in. disc. Rear: 12.0 in. x 2.5 in. disc. Wheels: 16.0 x 6.00 in. rim, 8-stud disc. Tires: LT235/85R16E. Transmission: 5-speed heavy-duty Getrag 360 manual. Optional: None.

VEHICLE DIMENSIONS: W100/W150: Wheelbase: 115 in., 131 in. Overall Length: 115 in. wheelbase: 190.78 in., 131 in. wheelbase: 210.78 in. Front/Rear Tread: 65.7 in./63.4 in. Overall Height: 73.1 in. Width: 79.5 in. Front/Rear Overhang: 29 in./43 in. Tailgate: Width and Height: 65 in. x 19.0 in. Approach/Departure Degrees: 34/28. Ground Clearance: Front axle: 8.5 in. Rear axle: 8.25 in. Oil pan: 15.25 in. Transfer case: 11.25 in. Load space: Pickup box dimensions: 115 in. wheelbase: 76.9 in. x 51 in. x 19.125 in. 131 in. wheelbase Sweptline: 96.9 in. x 51 in. x 19.3 in. Ground Clearance: Front axle: 8.2 in. Rear axle: 8.5 in. Oil pan: 15.8 in. Transfer case: 10.4 in. W250: Wheelbase: 131 in. Overall length: 210.78 in. Front/Rear Tread: 65.7 in./63.4 in. Overall Height: 73.1 in. Width: 79.5 in. Front/Rear Overhang: 29 in./43 in. Tailgate: Width and Height: 65 in. x 19.0 in. Approach/Departure Degrees: 34/28. Ground Clearance: Front axle: 8.5 in. Rear axle: 8.25 in. Oil pan: 15.25 in. Transfer case: 11.25 in. Load space: Pickup box dimensions: 96.9 in. x 51 in. x 19.3 in. W350: Wheelbase: 131 in. Load space: Pickup box dimensions: 96.9 in. x 51 in. x 19.3 in.

CAPACITIES: Fuel Tank: 22 gal. Optional: 30 gal.

ACCOMMODATIONS: Seating Capacity: 3 passenger.

INSTRUMENTATION: 0-100 mph speedometer, 99,999.9 mile odometer, gauges for fuel level, ammeter, engine coolant temperature, fuel level and oil pressure. Warning lights for parking brake and hazard lights operation.

OPTIONS: Air conditioning. 120 amp alternator. 810 amp battery. Rear step bumper. Maximum engine cooling. Auxiliary automatic transmission oil cooler. Deluxe Convenience Group. 30 gal. fuel tank. Engine block heater. Heavy duty springs. Cab clearance lights. Exterior mirrors. Lower body side protective moldings. Power Convenience Group. Premium bucket seats with center storage console (club cabs). AM/FM cassette E.T. stereo radio. Skid plate. Snowplow Prep Group. Front stabilizer bar. Trailer Towing Prep Group. Two-tone paint. Argent steel-styled wheels. Cast aluminum wheels. Sliding rear window.

HISTORICAL HIGHLIGHTS: The platform for the 1993 Power Ram pickups dated back to 1972.

DODGE POWER RAM 50
1982-1993

1982 POWER RAM 50

The arrival of the D50 Dodge Power Ram 50 was preceded by intensive negotiations between its producer, Mitsubishi, and Dodge regarding Mitsubishi's long-term goal of establishing its own distribution system in the United States. The Ram pickup had been first introduced in two-wheel drive form for the U.S. market in 1979. The Power Ram D50 was offered with only one engine — a 2.6 liter 4-cylinder — and a 5-speed overdrive manual transmission. The front suspension utilized torsion bars and unequal length upper and lower A-arms. Rear suspension was by longitudinal leaf springs and bias-mounted shock absorbers. The Power Ram D50 was offered in two trim levels, the base custom and the Sport Package. Standard equipment content of the custom model included a bench seat, adjustable steering column, power steering, locking front hubs, and a 50 amp alternator. High-back bucket seats were standard with the Sport Package.

1982 Dodge Power Ram 50 pickup

Body Type	Factory Price	GVW	Shipping Weight	Prod. Total
Pickup, 109.8 in. wheelbase				
Custom	$8179	4120	N.A.	12,080*
Royal	$8663	4120	N.A.	—
Sport	$9245	4120	N.A.	—

* All models.

STANDARD ENGINE: Cast iron block, aluminum cylinder head, counter-rotating balance shafts and MCA Jet combustion system. Engine Type: In-line 4-cyl., OHV, OHC. Bore x Stroke: 3.58 in. x 3.85 in. Fuel Induction: Single 2-bbl. carburetor. Compression Ratio: 8.2:1. Displacement: 155 cu. in. (2.6 liters). Horsepower: 105 @ 5000 rpm. Torque: 139 lb.-ft. @ 2500 rpm. Fuel Requirements: Unleaded.

CHASSIS FEATURES: Welded steel body and ladder-type frame.

SUSPENSION AND RUNNING GEAR: Front Suspension: Independent, unequal length A-arms, torsion bars and Kayabar 1.0 in. tubular shock absorbers. Capacity: 1102 lb. Optional Rating: None. Rear Suspension: Semi-elliptical, longitudinal springs. Capacity: 1473 lb. Optional Rating: None. Front Axle Capacity: 2204 lb. Rear Axle Type and Capacity: Beam, 3600 lb. capacity. Final Drive Ratio: 3.909:1. Transfer Case: 2-speed; 1.944:1, 1.00:1. Brakes: Type: Power, hydraulic. Front: Discs. Rear: Drums. Dimensions: Front: 10.0 in. dia. disc. Rear: 9.5 in. x 2.0 in. Swept area: 314 sq. in. Wheels: 14 x 5.5 in. Tires: F70 x 14 Yokohama/B.F. Goodrich, All-Terrain. Steering: Power-assisted. Ratio: 18.5:1-22.5:1. Turning Circle: 20.3 ft. Optional: None. Transmission: 5-speed overdrive manual, all-synchromesh. Transmission Ratios: 0.856, 1.0, 1.360, 2.136, 3.740:1. 1.00:1. Optional: None. Clutch: Clutch diameter: 8.86 in. dia. Optional: None.

VEHICLE DIMENSIONS: Wheelbase: 109.8 in. Overall Length: 184.6 in. Front/Rear Tread: 54.7 in./53.7 in. Overall Height: 61 in. Width: 65 in. Front/Rear Overhang: 23.5 in./48 in. Tailgate: Width and Height: 51.25 in. x 15.5 in. Approach/Departure Degrees: 41.5/21.5. Ground Clearance: Front axle: 7.5 in. Rear axle: 7.3 in. Oil pan: 12.25 in. Transfer case: 9.0 in. Fuel Tank: 11.5 in. Load space: Pickup box dimensions: 81 in. x 40.25 in. x 15.5 in. Front headroom: 36.0 in. Front shoulder room: 42.5 in. Pedal to seat back (max.): 41 in. Steering wheel to seat back (max.): 17 in. Seat to ground: 26.25 in. Floor to ground: 16.25 in.

CAPACITIES: Fuel Tank: 18 gal. Optional: None.

ACCOMMODATIONS: Seating Capacity: Three passenger.

INSTRUMENTATION: Ammeter, fuel and temperature gauges, speedometer, odometer; warning lights for parking brake, seat belts, high beam, turn signals, oil pressure and ammeter.

HISTORICAL FOOTNOTES: *Pickup, Van & 4WD* magazine judged the Power Ram 50 as superior to other imported mini-trucks in 16 of 22 categories. Both *Four Wheeler* and *Off-Road* magazine named the Power Ram 50 their "Four Wheeler of the Year."

1983 POWER RAM 50

The 1983 Power Ram 50 was available with a new 2.0 liter (122 cu. in.) 4-cylinder engine and a new 2.3 liter (140 cu. in.) Turbo diesel. The 2.0 liter engine was standard for the Power Ram Custom. The Turbo diesel was standard for the new Power Ram 50 Royal and optional for the Power Ram 50 Sport which retained the 2.6 liter engine as its standard engine. Included with the diesel engine was an instrument panel readout for the glow-plug start assist, instrument panel warning light for the diesel fuel filter with its water separator, and a tachometer. The diesel was also equipped with engine block and fuel line heaters. Double wall pickup box construction was standard for the Royal and Sport models and optional for the custom. Standard custom equipment consisted of black painted front bumper with black rubber ends, cargo lamp, cigarette lighter, dome light with driver and passenger side door switches, engine splash pan, emergency flashers, flat black colored grille, color-keyed headliner, inside hood release, bright hubcaps, interior rearview mirror, exterior left and right side swing-away type black trimmed mirrors, bright drip rail molding, bright windshield molding, mud guards, power steering, AM radio, front suspension skid plate, transfer case skid plate, adjustable angle steering column, dual sun visors, tie-down bars (tubular low-mount on both interior sides of pickup box), front tow hook, trip odometer, and two-speed windshield wipers with washers. In addition to, or in place of items found on the custom model, the Power Ram 50 Royal was fitted with these items as standard equipment: Front chrome bumper with black rubber ends, double wall cargo box, carpeting, tinted glass and body side tape stripe. The Power Ram 50 Sport had the contents of the Royal in addition to these features: Center console with oil pressure gauge, ammeter, and transmission shift lever; AM/FM stereo radio, wide-spoke color-keyed road wheels, and variable speed windshield wipers.

1983 Dodge Power Ram 50 pickup

The standard Ram custom bench seat was vinyl covered. It was available in combinations of either dark/medium brown or dark/medium blue. Its seat back folded for access to 4.6 cu. ft. of storage space behind the seat. The Power Ram Royal standard seat was covered in cloth and vinyl and was offered in a single combination of dark/medium brown. The Royal interior also had full floor carpeting and matching door panels. The Power Ram 50 Sport interior was equipped with foam-padded full-face cloth high-back bucket seats. They were available only in red/black. Exterior colors for the Power Ram 50 custom consisted of polar white, silver metallic, bright red and light blue. The Power Ram 50 Royal was offered in bright metallic, medium brown and bright red. The Power Ram 50 Sport's color selection consisted of charcoal metallic, dark red and polar red.

Body Type	Factory Price	GVW	Shipping Weight	Prod. Total
Pickup, 109.8 in. wheelbase				
Custom	$8433	4120	N.A.	9297*
Royal	$8917	4120	N.A.	—
Sport	$9499	4120	N.A.	—

* All models.

STANDARD ENGINE: Power Ram 50 custom. Cast iron block, aluminum cylinder head, counter-rotating balance shafts and MCA Jet (12-valve) combustion system. Engine Type: In-line 4-cyl., OHV, OHC. Fuel Induction: Single 2-bbl. carburetor. Displacement: 2.0 liters. Horsepower: 90 @ 5000 rpm. (California: 88 @ 5000 rpm). Torque: 107 lb.-ft. @ 3500 rpm. Fuel Requirements: Unleaded.

STANDARD ENGINE: Power Ram 50 Royal. Cast iron block, aluminum cylinder head, counter-rotating balance shafts and MCA Jet combustion system. Engine Type: In-line 4-cyl., OHV, OHC. Bore x Stroke: 3.58 in. x 3.85 in. Fuel Induction: Single 2-bbl. carburetor. Compression Ratio: 8.2:1. Displacement: 155 cu. in. (2.6 liters). Horsepower: 105 @ 5000 rpm. (California: 103 @ 5000 rpm). Torque: 139 lb.-ft. @ 2500 rpm. Fuel Requirements: Unleaded.

STANDARD ENGINE: Power Ram 50 Sport. Optional: Power Ram 50 Royal. Cast iron block, aluminum cylinder head. Engine Type: In-line 4-cyl., OHV, OHC, turbo diesel. Displacement: 140 cu. in. (2.0 liters). Horsepower: 80 @ 4200 rpm. Torque: 125 lb.-ft. @ 2500 rpm. Fuel Requirements: Diesel.

CHASSIS FEATURES: Welded steel body and ladder-type frame.

SUSPENSION AND RUNNING GEAR: Front Suspension: Independent, unequal length A-arms, torsion bars and Kayabar 1.0 in. tubular shock absorbers. Capacity: 1102 lb. Optional Rating: None. Rear Suspension: Semi-elliptical, longitudinal springs. Capacity: 1473 lb. Optional Rating: None. Front Axle Capacity: 2204 lb. Rear Axle Type and Capacity: Beam, 3600 lb. capacity. Final Drive Ratio: 3.909:1. Transfer Case: 2-speed; 1.944:1, 1.00:1. Brakes: Type: Power, hydraulic. Front: Discs. Rear: Drums. Dimensions: Front: 10.0 in. dia. disc. Rear: 9.5 in. x 2.0 in. Swept area: 314 sq. in. Wheels: 14 x 5.5 in. Tires: F70 x 14 Yokohama/B.F. Goodrich, All-Terrain. Steering: Power-assisted. Ratio: 18.5:1-22.5:1. Turning Circle: 20.3 ft. Optional: None. Transmission: 5-speed overdrive manual, all-synchromesh. Transmission Ratios: 0.856, 1.0, 1.360, 2.136, 3.740:1. 1.00:1. Optional: For Power Ram 50 Sport with 2.3. liter engine only: 3-speed automatic transmission. Clutch: Clutch diameter: 2.0 liter engine: 8.46 in. dia.; 2.6 liter and 2.3 liter diesel engines: 8.86 in. dia. Optional: None.

VEHICLE DIMENSIONS: Wheelbase: 109.8 in. Overall Length: 184.6 in. Front/Rear Tread: 54.7 in./53.7 in. Overall Height: 61 in. Width: 65 in. Front/Rear Overhang: 23.5 in./48 in. Tailgate: Width and Height: 51.25 in. x 15.5 in. Approach/Departure Degrees: 41.5/21.5. Ground Clearance: Front axle: 7.5 in. Rear axle: 7.3 in. Oil pan: 12.25 in. Transfer case: 9.0 in. Fuel Tank: 11.5 in. Load space: Pickup box dimensions: 81 in. x 40.25 in. x 15.5 in. Front headroom: 36.0 in. Front shoulder room: 42.5 in. Pedal to seat back (max.): 41 in. Steering wheel to seat back (max.): 17 in. Seat to ground: 26.25 in. Floor to ground: 16.25 in.

CAPACITIES: Fuel Tank: 18 gal. Optional: None.

ACCOMMODATIONS: Seating Capacity: Three passenger.

INSTRUMENTATION: Ammeter, fuel and temperature gauges, speedometer, odometer; warning lights for parking brake, seat belts, high beam, turn signals, oil pressure and ammeter.

OPTIONS AND PRICES: Air conditioning. Rear step chrome bumper (not avail. for custom). Rear step low-luster black finish (avail. for custom only). Double wall cargo box (custom only). Electronic digital clock. High-Altitude Emissions Package. Front floor mats (not avail. for custom). Grille guard. Exterior low-mount chrome mirrors. Vinyl body side molding (not avail. for Sport). Vinyl pickup box top edge molding. Rear sliding window. Automatic speed control (not avail. for custom). Sport bar. Sky Lite sun roof. Body side tape stripe (avail. for custom only). Wheel trim rings (not avail. for Sport).

HISTORICAL FOOTNOTES: Dodge reported that the Power Ram 50 was designed to be "Best in Class."

1984 POWER RAM 50

Changes for 1984 included a new argent painted grille and standard automatic front locking hubs.

Body Type	Factory Price	GVW	Shipping Weight	Prod. Total
Pickup, 109.8 in. wheelbase				
Custom	$7597	4120	N.A.	12,726*
Royal	$8101	4120	N.A.	—
Sport	$8683	4120	N.A.	—

* All models.

STANDARD ENGINE: Power Ram 50 Custom. Cast iron block, aluminum cylinder head, counter-rotating balance shafts and MCA Jet (12-valve) combustion system. Engine Type: In-line 4-cyl., OHV, OHC. Fuel Induction: Single 2-bbl. carburetor. Displacement: 2.0 liters. Horsepower: 90 @ 5000 rpm. (California: 88 @ 5000 rpm). Torque: 107 lb.-ft. @ 3500 rpm. Fuel Requirements: Unleaded.

STANDARD ENGINE: Power Ram 50 Royal. Cast iron block, aluminum cylinder head, counter-rotating balance shafts and MCA Jet combustion system. Engine Type: In-line 4-cyl., OHV, OHC. Bore x Stroke: 3.58 in. x 3.85 in. Fuel Induction: Single 2-bbl. carburetor. Compression Ratio: 8.2:1. Displacement: 155 cu. in. (2.6 liters). Horsepower: 105 @ 5000 rpm. (California: 103 @ 5000 rpm). Torque: 139 lb.-ft. @ 2500 rpm. Fuel Requirements: Unleaded. Standard: Power Ram 50 Sport. Optional: Power Ram 50 Royal. Cast iron block, aluminum cylinder head. Engine Type: In-line 4-cyl., OHV, OHC, turbo diesel. Displacement: 140 cu. in. (2.0 liters). Horsepower: 80 @ 4200 rpm. Torque: 125 lb.-ft. @ 2500 rpm. Fuel Requirements: Diesel.

CHASSIS FEATURES: Welded steel body and ladder-type frame.

SUSPENSION AND RUNNING GEAR: Front Suspension: Independent, unequal length A-arms, torsion bars and Kayabar 1.0 in. tubular shock absorbers. Capacity: 1102 lb. Optional Rating: None. Rear Suspension: Semi-elliptical, longitudinal springs. Capacity: 1473 lb. Optional Rating: None. Front Axle Capacity: 2204 lb. Rear Axle Type and Capacity: Beam, 3600 lb. capacity. Final Drive Ratio: 3.909:1. Transfer Case: 2-speed; 1.944:1, 1.00:1. Brakes: Type: Power, hydraulic. Front: Discs. Rear: Drums. Dimensions: Front: 10.0 in. dia. disc. Rear: 9.5 in. x 2.0 in. Swept area: 314 sq. in. Wheels: 14 x 5.5 in. Tires: F70 x 14 Yokohama/B.F. Goodrich, All-Terrain. Steering: Power-assisted. Ratio: 18.5:1-22.5:1. Turning Circle: 20.3 ft. Optional: None. Transmission: 5-speed overdrive manual, all-synchromesh. Transmission Ratios: 0.856, 1.0, 1.360, 2.136, 3.740:1. 1.00:1. Optional: For Power Ram 50 Sport with 2.3. liter engine only: 3-speed automatic transmission. Clutch: Clutch diameter: 2.0 liter engine: 8.46 in. dia.; 2.6 liter and 2.3 liter diesel engines: 8.86 in. dia. Optional: None.

VEHICLE DIMENSIONS: Wheelbase: 109.8 in. Overall Length: 184.6 in. Front/Rear Tread: 54.7 in./53.7 in. Overall Height: 61 in. Width: 65 in. Front/Rear Overhang: 23.5 in./48 in. Tailgate: Width and Height: 51.25 in. x 15.5 in. Approach/Departure Degrees: 41.5/21.5. Ground Clearance: Front axle: 7.5 in. Rear axle: 7.3 in. Oil pan: 12.25 in. Transfer case: 9.0 in. Fuel Tank: 11.5 in. Load space: Pickup box dimensions: 81 in. x 40.25 in. x 15.5 in. Front headroom: 36.0 in. Front shoulder room: 42.5 in. Pedal to seat back (max.): 41 in. Steering wheel to seat back (max.): 17 in. Seat to ground: 26.25 in. Floor to ground: 16.25 in.

CAPACITIES: Fuel Tank: 18 gal. Optional: None.

ACCOMMODATIONS: Seating Capacity: Three passenger.

INSTRUMENTATION: Ammeter, fuel and temperature gauges, speedometer, odometer; warning lights for parking brake, seat belts, high beam, turn signals, oil pressure and ammeter.

OPTIONS AND PRICES: Air conditioning. Rear step chrome bumper (not avail. for custom). Rear step low-luster black finish (avail. for custom only). Double wall cargo box (custom only). Electronic digital clock. High-Altitude Emissions Package. Front floor mats (not avail. for custom). Grille guard. Exterior low-mount chrome mirrors. Vinyl body side molding (not avail. for Sport). Vinyl pickup box top edge molding. Rear sliding window. Automatic speed control (not avail. for custom). Sport bar. Sky Lite sun roof. Body side tape stripe (avail. for custom only). Wheel trim rings (not avail. for Sport).

HISTORICAL FOOTNOTES: The Power Ram 50 had record high sales in 1984.

1985 POWER RAM 50

The Power Ram 50 had a new grille with thin rectangular slots and large DODGE lettering for 1985.

Body Type	Factory Price	GVW	Shipping Weight	Prod. Total
Pickup, 109.8 in. wheelbase				
Custom	$7667	4120	N.A.	—
Royal	$8171	4120	N.A.	—
Sport	$8753	4120	N.A.	—

STANDARD ENGINE: Power Ram 50 Custom. Cast iron block, aluminum cylinder head, counter-rotating balance shafts and MCA Jet (12-valve) combustion system. Engine Type: In-line 4-cyl., OHV, OHC. Fuel Induction: Single 2-bbl. carburetor. Displacement: 2.0 liters. Horsepower: 90 @ 5000 rpm. (California: 88 @ 5000 rpm). Torque: 107 lb.-ft. @ 3500 rpm. Fuel Requirements: Unleaded.

STANDARD ENGINE: Power Ram 50 Royal. Cast iron block, aluminum cylinder head, counter-rotating balance shafts and MCA Jet combustion system. Engine Type: In-line 4-cyl., OHV, OHC. Bore x Stroke: 3.58 in. x 3.85 in. Fuel Induction: Single 2-bbl. carburetor. Compression Ratio: 8.2:1. Displacement: 155 cu. in. (2.6 liters). Horsepower: 105 @ 5000 rpm. (California: 103 @ 5000 rpm). Torque: 139 lb.-ft. @ 2500 rpm. Fuel Requirements: Unleaded.

STANDARD ENGINE: Power Ram 50 Sport. Optional: Power Ram 50 Royal. Cast iron block, aluminum cylinder head. Engine Type: In-line 4-cyl., OHV, OHC, turbo diesel. Displacement: 140 cu. in. (2.0 liters). Horsepower: 80 @ 4200 rpm. Torque: 125 lb.-ft. @ 2500 rpm. Fuel Requirements: Diesel.

CHASSIS FEATURES: Welded steel body and ladder-type frame.

SUSPENSION AND RUNNING GEAR: Front Suspension: Independent, unequal length A-arms, torsion bars and Kayabar 1.0 in. tubular shock absorbers. Capacity: 1102 lb. Optional Rating: None. Rear Suspension: Semi-elliptical, longitudinal springs. Capacity: 1473 lb. Optional Rating: None. Front Axle Capacity: 2204 lb. Rear Axle Type and Capacity: Beam, 3600 lb. capacity. Final Drive Ratio: 3.909:1. Transfer Case: 2-speed; 1.944:1, 1.00:1. Brakes: Type: Power, hydraulic. Front: Discs. Rear: Drums. Dimensions: Front: 10.0 in. dia. disc. Rear: 9.5 in. x 2.0 in. Swept area: 314 sq. in. Wheels: 14 x 5.5 in. Tires: F70 x 14 Yokohama/B.F. Goodrich, All-Terrain. Steering: Power-assisted. Ratio: 18.5:1-22.5:1. Turning Circle: 20.3 ft. Optional: None. Transmission: 5-speed overdrive manual, all-synchromesh. Transmission Ratios: 0.856, 1.0, 1.360, 2.136, 3.740:1. 1.00:1. Optional: For Power Ram 50 Sport with 2.3. liter engine only: 3-speed automatic transmission. Clutch: Clutch diameter: 2.0 liter engine: 8.46 in. dia.; 2.6 liter and 2.3 liter diesel engines: 8.86 in. dia. Optional: None.

VEHICLE DIMENSIONS: Wheelbase: 109.8 in. Overall Length: 184.6 in. Front/Rear Tread: 54.7 in./53.7 in. Overall Height: 61 in. Width: 65 in. Front/Rear Overhang: 23.5 in./48 in. Tailgate: Width and Height: 51.25 in. x 15.5 in. Approach/Departure Degrees: 41.5/21.5. Ground Clearance: Front axle: 7.5 in. Rear axle: 7.3 in. Oil pan: 12.25 in. Transfer case: 9.0 in. Fuel Tank: 11.5 in. Load space: Pickup box dimensions: 81 in. x 40.25 in. x 15.5 in. Front headroom: 36.0 in. Front shoulder room: 42.5 in. Pedal to seat back (max.): 41 in. Steering wheel to seat back (max.): 17 in. Seat to ground: 26.25 in. Floor to ground: 16.25 in.

CAPACITIES: Fuel Tank: 18 gal. Optional: None.

ACCOMMODATIONS: Seating Capacity: Three passenger.

INSTRUMENTATION: Ammeter, fuel and temperature gauges, speedometer, odometer; warning lights for parking brake, seat belts, high beam, turn signals, oil pressure and ammeter.

OPTIONS AND PRICES: Air conditioning. Rear step chrome bumper (not avail. for custom). Rear step low-luster black finish (avail. for custom only). Double wall cargo box (custom only). Electronic digital clock. High-Altitude Emissions Package. Front floor mats (not avail. for custom). Grille guard. Exterior low-mount chrome mirrors. Vinyl body side molding (not avail. for Sport). Vinyl pickup box top edge molding. Rear sliding window. Automatic speed control (not avail. for custom). Sport bar. Sky Lite sun roof. Body side tape stripe (avail. for custom only). Wheel trim rings (not avail. for Sport).

HISTORICAL FOOTNOTES: The Power Ram 50 continued to be offered in three trim levels for 1985.

1986 POWER RAM 50

The 1986 Power Ram 50 had a revamped front end appearance characterized by a grille with a narrower header section with DODGE letters that were of a smaller size than those found on the 1985 model. Another alteration for 1986 was the extension of the grille to include the region under the headlights. The grid work was of a finer mesh for 1986. The base Power Ram 50 was equipped with an all-vinyl bench seat. If the optional automatic transmission was ordered, vinyl bucket seats were installed. The standard seating for the Power Ram 50 Sport model consisted of cloth and vinyl bucket seats. If the optional Premium Package was specified for the Sport model, high-back cloth bucket seats were fitted. All interior were offered in a choice of gray or brown/beige. The 1986 exterior color selection consisted of medium blue, charcoal, bright red, bright silver, black, gold and white.

Standard equipment of the Power Ram 50 consisted of the following items: Cigarette lighter, short color-keyed door armrests, rubber mat floor covering, inside hood release, dome light, day/night rear view interior mirror, adjustable steering column, 2-spoke plastic steering wheel, trip odometer, 45 amp alternator, 45 amp-hr. maintenance-free battery, underbody protection skid plates, power-steering, front black painted bumper, double wall cargo box, tinted glass for all windows, argent color grille, argent colored hubcaps, cargo box light, outside left and right black swing-away mirrors, front and rear mud flaps and two-speed windshield wipers.

1986 Dodge Power Ram 50 pickup

The content of the Power Ram 50 Sport, in addition to, or in place of items found on the base model consisted of long color-keyed door armrests, floor carpeting, AM radio, electronic digital clock, 2-spoke soft-feel steering wheel, color-keyed scuff plate, chrome front bumper, chrome/black grille, vinyl body side molding, bright drip rail and windshield moldings, body side and tailgate tape stripes and 15 in. painted wide-spoke wheels.

Body	Factory	GVW	Shipping	Prod.
Type	Price		Weight	Total
Pickup, 109.8 in. wheelbase				
P24 Power Ram 50 Pickup	N.A.	4475	N.A.	—
P24 Power Ram 50 Sport Pickup	N.A.	4475	N.A.	—

STANDARD ENGINE: All models. Cast iron block, aluminum cylinder head, counter-rotating balance shafts and MCA Jet combustion system. Engine Type: In-line 4-cyl., OHV, OHC. Bore x Stroke: 3.58 in. x 3.85 in. Fuel Induction: Single 2-bbl. carburetor. Displacement: 155 cu. in. (2.6 liters). Horsepower: 106. Fuel Requirements: Unleaded.

CHASSIS FEATURES: Welded steel body and ladder-type frame.

SUSPENSION AND RUNNING GEAR: Front Suspension: Independent, unequal length A-arms, torsion bars and Kayabar 1.0 in. tubular shock absorbers. Capacity: 1102 lb. Optional Rating: None. Rear Suspension: Semi-elliptical, longitudinal springs. Capacity: 1473 lb. Optional Rating: None. Front Axle Capacity: 2204 lb. Rear Axle Type and Capacity: Beam, 3600 lb. capacity. Final Drive Ratio: 3.909:1. Transfer Case: 2-speed; 1.944:1, 1.00:1. Brakes: Type: Power, hydraulic. Front: Discs. Rear: Drums. Dimensions: Front: 10.0 in. dia. disc. Rear: 9.5 in. x 2.0 in. Swept area: 314 sq. in. Wheels: 15 in. painted wide spoke standard for Power Ram 50 Sport. Tires: F70 x 14 Yokohama/B.F. Goodrich, All-Terrain. Steering: Power-assisted. Ratio: 18.5:1-22.5:1. Turning Circle: 20.3 ft. Optional: None. Transmission: 5-speed overdrive manual, all-synchromesh. Transmission Ratios: 0.856, 1.0, 1.360, 2.136, 3.740:1. 1.00:1. Optional: For Power Ram 50 Sport with 2.3. liter engine only: 3-speed automatic transmission. Clutch: Clutch diameter: 2.0 liter engine: 8.46 in. dia.; 2.6 liter and 2.3 liter diesel engines: 8.86 in. dia. Optional: None.

VEHICLE DIMENSIONS: Wheelbase: 109.8 in. Overall Length: 184.6 in. Front/Rear Tread: 54.7 in./53.7 in. Overall Height: 61 in. Width: 65 in. Front/Rear Overhang: 23.5 in./48 in. Tailgate: Width and Height: 51.25 in. x 15.5 in. Approach/Departure Degrees: 41.5/21.5. Ground Clearance: Front axle: 7.5 in. Rear axle: 7.3 in. Oil pan: 12.25 in. Transfer case: 9.0 in. Fuel Tank: 11.5 in. Load space: Pickup box dimensions: 81 in. x 40.25 in. x 15.5 in. Front headroom: 36.0 in. Front shoulder room: 42.5 in. Pedal to seat back (max.): 41 in. Steering wheel to seat back (max.): 17 in. Seat to ground: 26.25 in. Floor to ground: 16.25 in.

CAPACITIES: Fuel Tank: 18 gal. Optional: None.

ACCOMMODATIONS: Seating Capacity: Three passenger.

INSTRUMENTATION: Ammeter, fuel and temperature gauges, speedometer, odometer; warning lights for parking brake, seat belts, high beam, turn signals, oil pressure and ammeter.

OPTIONS: Air conditioning. AM radio (Power Ram 50 only). Rear step black bumper (Power Ram 50 only). Rear step chrome bumper (Power Ram 50 Sport only). Low mount chrome outside left and right swing-away mirrors. Vinyl body side molding (Power Ram 50 only). Body side and tailgate tape stripes (Power Ram 50 only). Wheel trim rings (Power Ram 50 only). Rear sliding window. Premium Package. Includes tachometer, console with oil pressure gauge and ammeter, high-back premium cloth bucket seats, variable intermittent windshield wipers, AM/FM stereo radio, chrome wide spoke wheels and raised white letter tires.

HISTORICAL FOOTNOTES: The Power Ram 50 continued to be produced by Mitsubishi for Dodge.

1987 POWER RAM 50

Major changes took place in the format and design of the Dodge Power Ram for 1987. For the first time since their introduction in 1982 the Power Rams had all-new sheetmetal characterized by a more aerodynamic form. The hood now sloped downward at a greater angle than previously. Visibility was improved due to increased glass area. Single rectangular headlights, and a thick grille gridwork gave the new models a more substantial front end appearance. The

front parking/directions were, as in 1986, positioned in the bumper. For 1987 the Power Ram 50 was offered in either short bed/105.5 in. wheelbase or long bed/116.5 in. wheelbase versions. The standard 2.6 liter 4-cylinder continued to be equipped with dual Silent Shafts to reduce harshness and vibration. Peak horsepower was increased slightly to 109. Additional mechanical improvements included a wider front and rear track, and stronger frame side rails and cross members. Replacing the 3-speed automatic transmission as an option was a new 4-speed overdrive unit. The Power Ram 50 interior was roomier than in 1986 and was equipped with an all-new dash featuring a hooded instrument cluster and a tray.

Body	Factory	GVW	Shipping	Prod.
Type	Price		Weight	Total
Pickup, 109.8 in. wheelbase				
P24 Power Ram 50 Pickup	N.A.	4475	N.A.	—
P24 Power Ram 50 Sport Pickup	N.A.	4475	N.A.	—

STANDARD ENGINE: All models. Cast iron block, aluminum cylinder head, counter-rotating balance shafts and MCA Jet combustion system. Engine Type: In-line 4-cyl., OHV, OHC. Bore x Stroke: 3.58 in. x 3.85 in. Fuel Induction: Single 2-bbl. carburetor. Displacement: 155 cu. in. (2.6 liters). Horsepower: 109 @ 5000 rpm. Torque: 143 lb.-ft. @ 3000 rpm. Fuel Requirements: Unleaded.

CHASSIS FEATURES: Welded steel body and ladder-type frame.

SUSPENSION AND RUNNING GEAR: Front Suspension: Independent, unequal length A-arms, torsion bars and Kayabar 1.0 in. tubular shock absorbers. Capacity: 1102 lb. Optional Rating: None. Rear Suspension: Semi-elliptical, longitudinal springs. Capacity: 1473 lb. Optional Rating: None. Front Axle Capacity: 2204 lb. Rear Axle Type and Capacity: Beam, 3600 lb. capacity. Final Drive Ratio: 3.91:1. Transfer Case: 2-speed: 1.944:1, 1.00:1. Brakes: Type: Power, hydraulic. Front: Discs. Rear: Drums. Dimensions: Front: 10.0 in. dia. disc. Rear: 9.5 in. x 2.0 in. Swept area: 314 sq. in. Wheels: 15 in. painted wide spoke standard for Power Ram 50 Sport. Tires: P225/75R15 black sidewall. Steering: Power-assisted. Ratio: 18.5:1-22.5:1. Turning Circle: 20.3 ft. Optional: None. Transmission: 5-speed overdrive manual, all-synchromesh. Transmission Ratios: 0.856, 1.0, 1.360, 2.136, 3.740:1. 1.00:1. Optional: 4-speed automatic transmission, overdrive ratio: 0.69:1. Clutch: Clutch diameter: 8.86 in. dia. Optional: None.

VEHICLE DIMENSIONS: Wheelbase: 105.5 in./116.5 in. Overall Length: 176.9 in./193.5 in. Front/Rear Tread: 54.9 in./55.7 in. Overall Height: 63.4 in. Width: 65.9 in. Load space: Pickup box dimensions: 105.5 in. wheelbase: 72.0 in. x 55.7 in. inside at floor) x 15.8 in. 116.5 in. wheelbase: 88.3 in. x 72.0 in. (inside at floor) x 19.8 in.

CAPACITIES: Fuel Tank: 105.5 in. wheelbase: 15.7 gal., 116.5 in. wheelbase: 19.8 gal. Optional: None.

ACCOMMODATIONS: Seating Capacity: Three passenger.

INSTRUMENTATION: Ammeter, fuel and temperature gauges, speedometer, odometer; warning lights for parking brake, seat belts, high beam, turn signals, oil pressure and ammeter.

OPTIONS: Rear black bumper (not avail. for custom). Rear chrome bumper (avail. for custom only). Low mount outside left and right black trimmed mirrors. Wheel trim rings (avail. for Power Ram 50 only). Air conditioning. AM/FM stereo radio (avail. for Power Ram 50 and custom only). AM/FM stereo with cassette tape player and graphic equalizer.

HISTORICAL FOOTNOTES: The 1987 Power Ram 50 models were introduced in the fall of 1986.

1988 POWER RAM 50

Added to the Power Ram 50 lineup for 1988 was an extended cab Sports cab model. The additional space behind the seats was suitable for storing items out of the weather and hidden from sight. The extra space also allowed more room for a wider range of seat adjustments. Both the standard and custom Sports cab models had cloth and vinyl reclining bucket seats with sculptured headrests. The seat backs tilted forward for access to the rear storage area that was fitted with hidden storage and tire downs. The extended cab version of the Ram Power 50 had luxury cloth fully adjustable reclining bucket seats, a center armrest/console and cloth and carpet door trim panels. The Power Ram 50 conventional cab had an all-vinyl bench seat with adjustable headrests and matching door trim panels. Standard for the Power Ram 50 custom was a combination cloth-vinyl bench seat with two adjustable headrests. The Power Ram 50 Sport model was fitted with cloth reclining bucket seats with adjustable headrests and matching padded cloth and carpet door trim. If automatic transmission was ordered a bench seat was installed. All interiors were available in gray, blue or brown.

Exterior colors for 1988 consisted of black, dark blue, light blue, gold, dark gray, bright red, bright silver and white. A number of two-tone combinations were also available. Optional for the custom model was offered with these choices (the first color was specified for the upper and lower portions of the body; the second color was applied to the middle band): Black/dark gray, light blue/dark blue, bright red/silver and white/dark gray. The Sport model was offered with these colors for the upper and lower body portions respectively: Black/gold, dark blue/light blue, gold/dark gray, bright red/dark gray, silver/dark gray and white/dark gray.

1988 Dodge Power Ram 50 sports cab pickup

Standard equipment of the Power Ram 50 consisted of the following items: 45 amp alternator, 45 amp-hr. maintenance-free battery, underbody skid plates, stainless steel exhaust system, power-steering, black painted front bumper, double wall cargo box, cargo box tie down hooks, tinted glass in all windows except backlite, black finish grille, rectangular headlights, swing-away exterior left and right mirrors with black trim, front and rear mud flaps, front tow hook, argent painted styled steel wheels, carpeting, inside hood release, dome light, adjustable steering column, two-spoke steering wheel, and two-speed windshield wipers. The Power Ram 50 Custom had in place of, or in addition to the features of the Power Ram 50, these items: Front chrome bumper, chrome grille surround, cargo light box, vinyl body side moldings, body side and tailgate tape stripes, painted wide spoke wheels, two-spoke soft-feel steering wheel, and trip odometer. The Power Ram 50 Sport had these features either in place or in addition to those found on the custom: Painted black front bumper, black grille, and inter-mittent speed windshield wipers.

Body Type	Factory Price	GVW	Shipping Weight	Prod. Total
Pickup, 105.5 in. wheelbase, 116.5 in. wheelbase				
P24 Power Ram 50 Pickup	N.A.	4475	N.A.	—
P24 Power Ram 50 Sport Pickup	N.A.	4475	N.A.	—

STANDARD ENGINE: All models. Cast iron block, aluminum cylinder head, counter-rotating balance shafts and MCA Jet combustion system. Engine Type: In-line 4-cyl., OHV, OHC. Bore x Stroke: 3.58 in. x 3.85 in. Fuel Induction: Single 2-bbl. carburetor. Displacement: 155 cu. in. (2.6 liters). Horsepower: 109 @ 5000 rpm. Torque: 143 lb.-ft. @ 3000 rpm. Fuel Require-ments: Unleaded.

CHASSIS FEATURES: Welded steel body and ladder-type frame.

SUSPENSION AND RUNNING GEAR: Front Suspension: Independent, unequal length A-arms, torsion bars and Kayabar 1.0 in. tubular shock absorbers. Capacity: 1102 lb. Optional Rating: None. Rear Suspension: Semi-elliptical, longitudinal springs. Capacity: 1473 lb. Optional Rating: None. Front Axle Capacity: 2204 lb. Rear Axle Type and Capacity: Beam, 3600 lb. capacity. Final Drive Ratio: 3.91:1. Transfer Case: 2-speed; 1.944:1, 1.00:1. Brakes: Type: Power, hydraulic. Front: Discs. Rear: Drums. Dimensions: Front: 10.0 in. dia. disc. Rear: 9.5 in. x 2.0 in. Swept area: 314 sq. in. Wheels: 15 in. painted wide spoke standard for Power Ram 50 Sport. Tires: P225/75R15 black sidewall. P225/75R15-raised white letters optional for Custom and Sport models. Steering: Power-assisted. Ratio: 18.5:1-22.5:1. Turning Circle: 20.3 ft. Optional: None. Transmission: 5-speed overdrive manual, all-synchromesh. Trans-mission Ratios: 0.856, 1.0, 1.360, 2.136, 3.740:1. 1.00:1. Optional: 4-speed automatic trans-mission, overdrive ratio: 0.69:1. Clutch: Clutch diameter: 8.86 in. dia. Optional: None.

VEHICLE DIMENSIONS: Wheelbase: 105.5 in./116.5 in. Overall Length: 176.9 in./193.5 in. Front/Rear Tread: 54.9 in./55.7 in. Overall Height: 63.4 in. Width: 65.9 in.

CAPACITIES: Fuel Tank: 105.5 in. wheelbase: 15.7 gal., 116.5 in. wheelbase: 19.8 gal. Optional: None.

ACCOMMODATIONS: Seating Capacity: Three passenger.

INSTRUMENTATION: Ammeter, fuel and temperature gauges, speedometer, odometer; warning lights for parking brake, seat belts, high beam, turn signals, oil pressure and ammeter.

OPTIONS: Rear black bumper (not avail. for custom). Rear chrome bumper (avail. for custom only). Low mount outside left and right black trimmed mirrors. Wheel trim rings (avail. for Power Ram 50 only). Air conditioning. AM/FM stereo radio (avail. for Power Ram 50 and custom only). AM/FM stereo with cassette tape player and graphic equalizer. Optional Mopar accessories available for Dodge dealers included: Bed liner, sunshade louver for backlite, bed mat, door edge guards, off-road lights, fog lights, tool box, side rails, tonneau cover, side rails and running boards.

HISTORICAL FOOTNOTES: The Power Ram 50 trucks were used by off road racer Walker Evans in competition.

1989 POWER RAM 50

The Power Ram 50 trucks were essentially unchanged for 1989. The most significant changes was the availability of a monochromatic exterior of the Sport versions.

Body Type	Factory Price	GVW	Shipping Weight	Prod. Total
Power Ram 50				
Base Pickup, 105.1 in. wb.	$11,044	4475	N.A.	28,283*
Sport Pickup, 105.1 in. wb.	$12,169	4475	N.A.	—
Extended Cab, 116.1 in. wb.	$11,620	4475	N.A.	—
Ext. Cab Sport, 116.1 in. wb.	$13,089	4475	N.A.	—

* Sales of all models, both two-wheel drive and four-wheel drive.

STANDARD ENGINE: All models. Cast iron block, aluminum cylinder head, counter-rotating balance shafts and MCA Jet combustion system. Engine Type: In-line 4-cyl., OHV, OHC. Bore x Stroke: 3.58 in. x 3.85 in. Fuel Induction: Single 2-bbl. carburetor. Displacement: 155 cu. in. (2.6 liters). Horsepower: 109 @ 5000 rpm. Torque: 143 lb.-ft. @ 3000 rpm. Fuel Require-ments: Unleaded.

CHASSIS FEATURES: Welded steel body and ladder-type frame.

SUSPENSION AND RUNNING GEAR: Front Suspension: Independent, unequal length A-arms, torsion bars and Kayabar 1.0 in. tubular shock absorbers. Capacity: 1102 lb. Optional Rating: None. Rear Suspension: Semi-elliptical, longitudinal springs. Capacity: 1473 lb. Optional Rating: None. Front Axle Capacity: 2204 lb. Rear Axle Type and Capacity: Beam, 3600 lb. capacity. Final Drive Ratio: 3.91:1. Transfer Case: 2-speed; 1.944:1, 1.00:1. Brakes: Type: Power, hydraulic. Front: Discs. Rear: Drums. Dimensions: Front: 10.0 in. dia. disc. Rear: 9.5 in. x 2.0 in. Swept area: 314 sq. in. Wheels: 15 in. painted wide spoke standard for Power Ram 50 Sport. Tires: P225/75R15 black sidewall. P225/75R15-raised white letters optional for Custom and Sport models. Steering: Power-assisted. Ratio: 18.5:1-22.5:1. Turning Circle: 20.3 ft. Optional: None. Transmission: 5-speed overdrive manual, all-synchromesh. Trans-mission Ratios: 0.856, 1.0, 1.360, 2.136, 3.740:1. 1.00:1. Optional: 4-speed automatic trans-mission, overdrive ratio: 0.69:1. Clutch: Clutch diameter: 8.86 in. dia. Optional: None.

VEHICLE DIMENSIONS: Wheelbase: 105.5 in./116.5 in. Overall Length: 176.9 in./193.5 in. Front/Rear Tread: 54.9 in./55.7 in. Overall Height: 63.4 in. Width: 65.9 in.

CAPACITIES: Fuel Tank: 105.5 in. wheelbase: 15.7 gal., 116.5 in. wheelbase: 19.8 gal. Optional: None.

ACCOMMODATIONS: Seating Capacity: Three passenger.

INSTRUMENTATION: Ammeter, fuel and temperature gauges, speedometer, odometer; warning lights for parking brake, seat belts, high beam, turn signals, oil pressure and ammeter.

OPTIONS: Rear black bumper (not avail. for custom). Rear chrome bumper (avail. for custom only). Low mount outside left and right black trimmed mirrors. Wheel trim rings (avail. for Power Ram 50 only). Air conditioning: $713. AM/FM stereo radio: $273 (base models): $424 (Sport models). AM/FM stereo with cassette tape player and graphic equalizer. Optional Mopar accessories available for Dodge dealers included: Bed liner, sunshade louver for backlite, bed mat, door edge guards, off-road lights, fog lights, tool box, side rails, tonneau cover, side rails and running boards. Automatic transmission: $690 ($555 for Sport model).

HISTORICAL FOOTNOTES: The Power Ram 50 trucks were used in competition by off-road racer Walker Evans.

1990 POWER RAM 50

The Power Ram 50 trucks were available with a new 1990cc V-6 engine for 1990. Also debuting for 1990 were new SE and LE trim levels.

Body Type	Factory Price	GVW	Shipping Weight	Prod. Total
Power Ram 50				
Base Pickup, 105.1 in. wb.	$10,577	4475	N.A.	87,978*
SE Pickup, 105.1 in. wb.	$12,385	4475	N.A.	—
Extended Cab, 116.1 in. wb.	$13,058	4475	N.A.	—
SE Ext. Cab, 116.1 in. wb.	$13,089	4475	N.A.	—
LE Ext. Cab, 116.1 in. wb.	$14,473	4475	—	—

* Sales of all models, both two-wheel drive and four-wheel drive.

STANDARD ENGINE: All models. Cast iron block, aluminum cylinder head, counter-rotating balance shafts and MCA Jet combustion system. Engine Type: In-line 4-cyl., OHV, OHC. Bore x Stroke: 3.58 in. x 3.85 in. Fuel Induction: Single 2-bbl. carburetor. Displacement: 155 cu. in. (2.6 liters). Horsepower: 109 @ 5000 rpm. Torque: 143 lb.-ft. @ 3000 rpm. Fuel Require-ments: Unleaded. Optional: 170 hp. V-6.

CHASSIS FEATURES: Welded steel body and ladder-type frame.

SUSPENSION AND RUNNING GEAR: Front Suspension: Independent, unequal length A-arms, torsion bars and Kayabar 1.0 in. tubular shock absorbers. Capacity: 1102 lb. Optional Rating: None. Rear Suspension: Semi-elliptical, longitudinal springs. Capacity: 1473 lb. Optional Rating: None. Front Axle Capacity: 2204 lb. Rear Axle Type and Capacity: Beam, 3600 lb. capacity. Final Drive Ratio: 3.91:1. Transfer Case: 2-speed; 1.944:1, 1.00:1. Brakes: Type: Power, hydraulic. Front: Discs. Rear: Drums. Dimensions: Front: 10.0 in. dia. disc. Rear: 9.5 in. x 2.0 in. Swept area: 314 sq. in. Wheels: 15 in. painted wide spoke standard for Power Ram 50 Sport. Tires: P225/75R15 black sidewall. P225/75R15-raised white letters optional for Custom and Sport models. Steering: Power-assisted. Ratio: 18.5:1-22.5:1. Turning Circle: 20.3 ft. Optional: None. Transmission: 5-speed overdrive manual, all-synchromesh. Trans-mission Ratios: 0.856, 1.0, 1.360, 2.136, 3.740:1. 1.00:1. Optional: 4-speed automatic trans-mission, overdrive ratio: 0.69:1. Clutch: Clutch diameter: 8.86 in. dia. Optional: None.

VEHICLE DIMENSIONS: Wheelbase: 105.5 in./116.5 in. Overall Length: 176.9 in./193.5 in. Front/Rear Tread: 54.9 in./55.7 in. Overall Height: 63.4 in. Width: 65.9 in.

CAPACITIES: Fuel Tank: 105.5 in. wheelbase: 15.7 gal., 116.5 in. wheelbase: 19.8 gal. Optional: None.

ACCOMMODATIONS: Seating Capacity: Three passenger.

INSTRUMENTATION: Ammeter, fuel and temperature gauges, speedometer, odometer; warning lights for parking brake, seat belts, high beam, turn signals, oil pressure and ammeter.

OPTIONS: Automatic transmission: $684. Air conditioning: $713. Rear black bumper. Rear chrome bumper. Low mount outside left and right black trimmed mirrors. Wheel trim rings. AM/FM stereo radio. AM/FM stereo with cassette tape player and graphic equalizer. Optional Mopar accessories available for Dodge dealers included: Bed liner, sunshade louver for backlite, bed mat, door edge guards, off-road lights, fog lights, tool box, side rails, tonneau cover, side rails and running boards.

HISTORICAL FOOTNOTES: As compared to 1989, sales of the Ram 50, in both two-wheel drive and four-wheel drive form, fell by over 60% in 1990.

1991 POWER RAM 50

The 1991 Power Ram 50 was available in five styles with a 105 in. or 116 in. wheelbase and either a 6 ft. cargo box or one that extended just over 7 ft. in length. Trim levels consisted of the base Power Ram and the SE and LE Packages. The standard engine in the base models was a 2.4 liter Multi-Port fuel injected (MFI) 4-cyl. engine. The remaining four models were powered by a 3.0 liter MPI V-6. The standard transmission was a five-speed manual overdrive unit with a 4-speed automatic optional. The extended Sport cab models had stationary side windows and storage space behind the front seats. A storage compartment was also located beneath the carpeting. Two storage pockets were also positioned on the cab's back panel. Conventional cab interiors were available in either a cloth and vinyl bench seat or optional high-back bucket seats with recliners. Sport cab interiors featured a cloth and vinyl split-back bench seat with recliners. Standard equipment consisted of long color-keyed armrests, passenger-side assist grip, black painted front bumper, tie-down hooks, cigarette lighter, dome light, black painted grille, dual rectangular headlights, full molded headliner, needled carpeting, heater, inside hood release, dual exterior black-trimmed mirrors, bright windshield molding, front and rear mudguards, skid plates, adjustable steering column, 2-spoke plastic steering wheel, power-assisted steering, tinted glass for all windows, full-size spare tire, front tow hook, and two-speed windshield wipers. Revisions for 1991 included two new interior colors, a new vinyl and fabric upholstery, and revised exterior nameplate and graphics. Added to the standard equipment content of the LE was a new rear-wheel anti-lock brake system.

1991 Dodge Power ram 50 extended cab pickup

Body Type	Factory Price	GVW	Shipping Weight	Prod. Total
Power Ram 50				
Base Pickup, 105.1 in. wb.	$10,577	4475	N.A.	87,978*
SE Pickup, 105.1 in. wb.	$12,385	4475	N.A.	—
Extended Cab, 116.1 in. wb.	$13,058	4475	N.A.	—
SE Ext. Cab, 116.1 in. wb.	$13,089	4475	N.A.	—
LE Ext. Cab, 116.1 in. wb.	$14,473	4475	—	—

* Sales of all models, both two-wheel drive and four-wheel drive.

STANDARD ENGINE: 105 in. wheelbase base model only. Engine Type: OHV, In-line 4-cylinder. Fuel Induction: Electronic multi port fuel injection. Compression Ratio: 8.5:1. Displacement: 143 cu. in. (2.4 liters). Horsepower: 116 @ 3500 rpm. Torque: 136 lb.-ft. @ 2500 rpm. Fuel Requirements: Unleaded.

STANDARD ENGINE: All other models. Engine Type: OHV, V-6. Fuel Induction: Multi port fuel injection. Compression Ratio: 8.9:1. Displacement: 181 cu. in. (3.0 liters). Horsepower: 143 @ 5000 rpm. Torque: 168 lb.-ft. @ 2500 rpm. Fuel Requirements: Unleaded.

CHASSIS FEATURES: Welded steel body and ladder-type frame.

SUSPENSION AND RUNNING GEAR: Front Suspension: Independent, unequal length A-arms, torsion bars and Kayabar 1.0 in. tubular shock absorbers. Capacity: 1102 lb. Optional Rating: None. Rear Suspension: Semi-elliptical, longitudinal springs. Capacity: 1473 lb. Optional Rating: None. Front Axle Capacity: 2204 lb. Rear Axle Type and Capacity: Beam, 3600 lb. capacity. Final Drive Ratio: 3.91:1. Transfer Case: 2-speed; 1.944:1, 1.00:1. Brakes: Type: Power, hydraulic. Front: Discs. Rear: Drums. Dimensions: Front: 10.0 in. dia. disc. Rear: 9.5 in. x 2.0 in. Swept area: 314 sq. in. Wheels: 15 in. Tires: P225/75R15 black sidewall. Steering: Power-assisted. Ratio: 18.5:1-22.5:1. Turning Circle: 20.3 ft. Optional: None. Transmission: 5-speed overdrive manual, all-synchromesh. Transmission Ratios: 0.856, 1.0, 1.360, 2.136, 3.740:1. 1.00:1. Optional: 4-speed automatic transmission, overdrive ratio: 0.69:1. Clutch: Clutch diameter: 8.86 in. dia. Optional: None.

VEHICLE DIMENSIONS: Wheelbase: 105.5 in./116.5 in. Overall Length: 176.9 in./193.5 in. Front/Rear Tread: 54.9 in./55.7 in. Overall Height: 63.4 in. Width: 65.9 in.

CAPACITIES: Fuel Tank: 105.5 in wheelbase: 15.7 gal., 116.5 in. wheelbase: 19.8 gal. Optional: None.

ACCOMMODATIONS: Seating Capacity: Three passenger.

INSTRUMENTATION: Ammeter, fuel and temperature gauges, speedometer, odometer; warning lights for parking brake, seat belts, high beam, turn signals, oil pressure and ammeter.

OPTIONS: Automatic transmission: $684. Air conditioning: $713. Rear black bumper. Rear chrome bumper. Low mount outside left and right black trimmed mirrors. Wheel trim rings. AM/FM stereo radio. AM/FM stereo with cassette tape player and graphic equalizer. Optional Mopar accessories available for Dodge dealers included: Bed liner, sunshade louver for backlite, bed mat, door edge guards, off-road lights, fog lights, tool box, side rails, tonneau cover, side rails and running boards.

HISTORICAL FOOTNOTES: The Power Ram 50 trucks were built in Okazaki, Japan.

1992 POWER RAM 50

The Power Ram 50 model lineup was simplified for 1992. All extended cab models on the 116 in. wheelbase were dropped as was the 3.0 liter V-6 engine. The only model offered was on the 105 in. wheelbase with a 72 in. box. One new exterior color — Emerald green was offered.

1992 Dodge Power Ram pickup

Body Type	Factory Price	GVW	Shipping Weight	Prod. Total
Power Ram 50				
Base Pickup, 105.1 in. wb.	$11,347	4475	N.A.	—

STANDARD ENGINE: Engine Type: OHV, In-line 4-cylinder. Fuel Induction: Electronic multi port fuel injection. Compression Ratio: 8.5:1. Displacement: 143 cu. in. (2.4 liters). Horsepower: 116 @ 3500 rpm. Torque: 136 lb.-ft. @ 2500 rpm. Fuel Requirements: Unleaded.

CHASSIS FEATURES: Welded steel body and ladder-type frame.

SUSPENSION AND RUNNING GEAR: Front Suspension: Independent, unequal length A-arms, torsion bars and Kayabar 1.0 in. tubular shock absorbers. Capacity: 1102 lb. Optional Rating: None. Rear Suspension: Semi-elliptical, longitudinal springs. Capacity: 1473 lb. Optional Rating: None. Front Axle Capacity: 2204 lb. Rear Axle Type and Capacity: Beam, 3600 lb. capacity. Final Drive Ratio: 3.91:1. Transfer Case: 2-speed; 1.944:1, 1.00:1. Brakes: Type: Power, hydraulic. Front: Discs. Rear: Drums. Dimensions: Front: 10.0 in. dia. disc. Rear: 9.5 in. x 2.0 in. Swept area: 314 sq. in. Wheels: 15 in. painted wide spoke. Tires: P225/75R15 black sidewall. Steering: Power-assisted. Ratio: 18.5:1-22.5:1. Turning Circle: 20.3 ft. Optional: None. Transmission: 5-speed overdrive manual, all-synchromesh. Transmission Ratios: 0.856, 1.0, 1.360, 2.136, 3.740:1. 1.00:1. Optional: 4-speed automatic transmission, overdrive ratio: 0.69:1. Clutch: Clutch diameter: 8.86 in. dia. Optional: None.

VEHICLE DIMENSIONS: Wheelbase: 105.5 in. Overall Length: 176.9 in. Front/Rear Tread: 54.9 in./55.7 in. Overall Height: 67.3 in. Width: 65.1 in.

CAPACITIES: Fuel Tank: 15.7 gal. Optional: None.

ACCOMMODATIONS: Seating Capacity: Three passenger.

INSTRUMENTATION: Ammeter, fuel and temperature gauges, speedometer, odometer; warning lights for parking brake, seat belts, high beam, turn signals, oil pressure and ammeter.

OPTIONS: Air conditioning: $713. Bucket Seat Package. Black rear step bumper. Black rear tube bumper. Chrome rear step bumper. Digital clock. Cruise control with intermittent windshield wipers. Limited slip rear differential. Low mount mirrors. Power door locks. Power windows. AM/FM/ET stereo radio with cassette tape player. Argent or chrome wheels. Automatic transmission: $707.

HISTORICAL FOOTNOTES: The Power Ram 50 trucks were aimed primarily at urban buyers seeking a fuel-efficient compact truck. The average age of a Power Ram 50 was 38.

1993 POWER RAM 50

Rear wheel anti-lock brakes were standard for the 1993 Power Ram 50 pickup. The front bumper was painted dark gray. Three new exterior colors were available: Pearlcoat blue, dark silver metallic and blue green.

Body Type	Factory Price	GVW	Shipping Weight	Prod. Total
Power Ram 50				
Base Pickup, 105.1 in. wb.	$N.A.	4800	N.A.	—

STANDARD ENGINE: Engine Type: OHV, OHC In-line 4-cylinder. Bore x Stroke: 3.41 in. x 3.94 in. Fuel Induction: Electronic multi port fuel injection. Compression Ratio: 8.5:1. Displacement: 143.5 cu. in. (2.4 liters). Horsepower: 116 @ 5000 rpm. Torque: 136 lb.-ft. @ 3500 rpm. Fuel Requirements: Unleaded.

CHASSIS FEATURES: Welded steel body and ladder-type frame.

SUSPENSION AND RUNNING GEAR: Front Suspension: Independent, unequal length A-arms, torsion bars and Kayabar 1.0 in. tubular shock absorbers, 0.79 in. stabilizer bar. Capacity: 1102 lb. Optional Rating: None. Rear Suspension: Semi-elliptical, longitudinal springs. Capacity: 1473 lb. Optional Rating: None. Front Axle Capacity: 2204 lb. Rear Axle Type and Capacity: Beam, 3600 lb. capacity. Final Drive Ratio: 3.91:1. Transfer Case: 2-speed; 1.944:1, 1.00:1. Brakes: Type: Power, hydraulic. Front: Discs. Rear: Drums. Dimensions: Front: 10.0 in. dia. disc. Rear: 9.5 in. x 2.0 in. Swept area: 314 sq. in. Wheels: 15 x 6.0 in. painted wide spoke. Tires: P225/75R15 black sidewall. Steering: Power-assisted. Turns lock-to-lock: 3.4. Ratio: 17.8. Turning Circle: 40.0 ft. Optional: None. Transmission: 5-speed overdrive manual, all-synchromesh. Transmission Ratios: 0.856, 1.0, 1.360, 2.136, 3.740:1. 1.00:1. Optional: 4-speed automatic transmission, overdrive ratio: 0.69:1. Clutch: Clutch diameter: 8.86 in. dia. Optional: None.

VEHICLE DIMENSIONS: Wheelbase: 105.5 in. Overall Length: 176.9 in. Front/Rear Tread: 54.9 in./55.7 in. Overall Height: 67.3 in. Width: 65.1 in.

CAPACITIES: Fuel Tank: 19.8 gal. Optional: None.

ACCOMMODATIONS: Seating Capacity: Three passenger.

INSTRUMENTATION: Ammeter, fuel and temperature gauges, speedometer, odometer; warning lights for parking brake, seat belts, high beam, turn signals, oil pressure and ammeter.

OPTIONS: Air conditioning. Floor mats. Sliding rear window. Bright windshield moldings. Lower body side protective moldings. Bucket Seat Package. Black rear step bumper. Black rear tube bumper. Chrome rear step bumper. Digital clock. Cruise control with intermittent windshield wipers. Limited slip rear differential. Low mount mirrors. Power door locks. Power windows. AM/FM stereo ET radio. AM/FM ET stereo radio with cassette tape player. Bright wide-spoke wheels. Automatic transmission:

HISTORICAL FOOTNOTES: Dodge reported that the Power Ram 50 had more interior room than comparative models from Nissan and Toyota.

DODGE COLT VISTA

1985-1991

1985 COLT VISTA

Dodge added the Mitsubishi-built Colt Vista in front wheel drive form to its line of captive imports in 1984. It was almost immediately recognized as an extremely space-efficient vehicle that was tailor-made for evolution into a four-wheel drive version. This took place during the 1985 model year. Depicted as a "multi-purpose vehicle", the four-wheel drive Vista was very similar in appearance to its four-wheel drive counterpart. It stood approximately 2.6 inches higher, had a larger 14 gal. fuel tank and carried its spare tire inside the cabin against the right rear wall.

I.D. DATA: The vehicle identification number was located on a V.I.N. plate attached to the driver's side door body latch post.

Body Type	Factory Price	GVW	Shipping Weight	Prod. Total
G49 Station Wagon	$9809	N.A.	2545	*

* Approximately 2000 four-wheel drive Vistas were imported during 1985. They were sold by both Plymouth and Dodge dealers.

STANDARD ENGINE: Cast iron block, aluminum cylinder head, MCA Jet combustion system. Engine Type: In-line 4-cyl., OHV, OHC. Fuel Induction: Single 2-bbl. Mikuni 32-35 DID carburetor. Compression Ratio: 8.5:1. Displacement: 122 cu. in. (1977 cc). Horsepower: 88 @ 5000 rpm. Torque: 108 lb.-ft. @ 3500 rpm. Fuel Requirements: Unleaded.

SUSPENSION AND RUNNING GEAR: Front Suspension: Independent. MacPherson struts, lower control arms, trailing links and stabilizer bar. Optional Rating: None. Rear Suspension: Semi-trailing arms and transverse torsion bars. Optional Rating: None. Final Drive Ratio: 3.19:1. Transfer Case: 2-speed. Ratios: 1.944:1, 1.00:1. Brakes: Type: Power, hydraulic. Front: Discs. Rear: Drums. Wheels: 14 x 6.5 in. steel. Tires: 185/70R14. Steering: Power-assisted rack and pinion. Optional: None. Transmission: 5-speed overdrive manual, all-synchromesh.

VEHICLE DIMENSIONS: Wheelbase: 103.5 in. Overall Length: 174.6 in. Overall Height: 59.4 in. Width: 64.6 in.

CAPACITIES: Fuel Tank: 14.5 gals. Optional: None.

ACCOMMODATIONS: Seating Capacity: Seven passengers.

OPTIONS AND PRICES: Air conditioning. Luggage rack. AM/FM stereo radio. AM/FM stereo radio with cassette tape player: $426. Power door locks: $125. Custom Package. Includes cloth upholstery and power accessories. Cruise control: $139. Two-tone paint. Aluminum wheels: $197.

HISTORICAL FOOTNOTES: A total of 2,960 Dodge dealers sold the Colt models.

1986 COLT VISTA

The Colt Vista was essentially unchanged for 1986. Standard equipment included tinted glass, intermittent and variable speed windshield wipers, cut pile carpeting for the passenger and cargo areas, front low-back bucket seats, dual glove box, map pockets, magazine pocket, front under-seat tray, and front and rear cupholders. Exterior color choices included medium red, medium blue, medium brown, light blue, bright silver, black, charcoal, bright red and a gold and cream two-tone combination.

1986 Dodge Colt Vista

I.D. DATA: The vehicle identification number was located on a V.I.N. plate attached to the driver's side door body latch post.

Body Type	Factory Price	GVW	Shipping Weight	Prod. Total
G49 Station Wagon	$9913	N.A.	2865	—

STANDARD ENGINE: Cast iron block, aluminum cylinder head, MCA Jet combustion system. Engine Type: In-line 4-cyl., OHV, OHC. Fuel Induction: Single 2-bbl. Mikuni 32-35 DID carburetor. Compression Ratio: 8.5:1. Displacement: 122 cu. in. (1977 cc). Horsepower: 88 @ 5000 rpm. Torque: 108 lb.-ft. @ 3500 rpm. Fuel Requirements: Unleaded.

SUSPENSION AND RUNNING GEAR: Front Suspension: Independent. MacPherson struts, lower control arms, trailing links and stabilizer bar. Optional Rating: None. Rear Suspension: Semi-trailing arms and transverse torsion bars. Optional Rating: None. Final Drive Ratio: 3.19:1. Transfer Case: 2-speed. Ratios: 1.944:1, 1.00:1. Brakes: Type: Power, hydraulic. Front: Discs. Rear: Drums. Wheels: 14 x 6.5 in. steel. Tires: 185/70R14. Steering: Power-assisted rack and pinion. Optional: None. Transmission: 5-speed overdrive manual, all-synchromesh.

VEHICLE DIMENSIONS: Wheelbase: 103.5 in. Overall Length: 174.6 in. Overall Height: 59.4 in. Width: 64.6 in. Load space: 72.5 in. (load space length from back of front seat to end of cargo door). Headroom: Front seat: 38.3 in. Middle Seat: 38.3 in. Rear seat: 34.9 in. Legroom: Front seat: 38.8 in. Middle Seat: 36.5 in. Rear seat: 29.3 in. Shoulder room: Front seat: 53.1 in. Middle Seat: 53.2 in. Rear seat: 44.7 in. Hip room: Front seat: 53.2 in. Middle Seat: 53.7 in. Rear seat: 39.1 in.

CAPACITIES: Fuel Tank: 14.5 gals. Optional: None.

ACCOMMODATIONS: Seating Capacity: Seven passengers.

OPTIONS AND PRICES: Air conditioning. Luggage rack. AM/FM stereo radio. AM/FM stereo radio with cassette tape player. AM/FM/MX electronically tuned stereo radio with cassette tape player. Power door locks: $125. Power windows: $176. Automatic speed control: $148. Two-tone paint. Rear window wiper/washer. Custom Package. Includes full-face velour seats.

HISTORICAL FOOTNOTES: The Colt Vistas was one of six Colt models offered by Dodge.

1987 COLT VISTA

The Colt Vista was unchanged for 1987. Standard equipment included tinted glass, intermittent and variable speed windshield wipers, cut pile carpeting for the passenger and cargo areas, front low-back bucket seats, dual glove box, map pockets, magazine pocket, front under-seat tray, and front and rear cupholders. Exterior color choices included medium red, medium blue, medium brown, light blue, bright silver, black, charcoal, bright red and a gold and cream two-tone combination.

I.D. DATA: The vehicle identification number was located on a V.I.N. plate attached to the driver's side door body latch post.

Body Type	Factory Price	GVW	Shipping Weight	Prod. Total
H31 Station Wagon	$11,371	N.A.	2888	—

STANDARD ENGINE: Cast iron block, aluminum cylinder head, MCA Jet combustion system. Engine Type: In-line 4-cyl., OHV, OHC. Fuel Induction: Single 2-bbl. Mikuni 32-35 DID carburetor. Compression Ratio: 8.5:1. Displacement: 122 cu. in. (1977 cc). Horsepower: 88 @ 5000 rpm. Torque: 108 lb.-ft. @ 3500 rpm. Fuel Requirements: Unleaded.

SUSPENSION AND RUNNING GEAR: Front Suspension: Independent. MacPherson struts, lower control arms, trailing links and stabilizer bar. Optional Rating: None. Rear Suspension: Semi-trailing arms and transverse torsion bars. Optional Rating: None. Final Drive Ratio: 3.19:1. Transfer Case: 2-speed. Ratios: 1.944:1, 1.00:1. Brakes: Type: Power, hydraulic. Front: Discs. Rear: Drums. Wheels: 14 x 6.5 in. steel. Tires: 185/70R14. Steering: Power-assisted rack and pinion. Optional: None. Transmission: 5-speed overdrive manual, all-synchromesh.

VEHICLE DIMENSIONS: Wheelbase: 103.5 in. Overall Length: 174.6 in. Overall Height: 59.4 in. Width: 64.6 in. Load space: 72.5 in. (load space length from back of front seat to end of cargo door). Headroom: Front seat: 38.3 in. Middle Seat: 38.3 in. Rear seat: 34.9 in. Legroom: Front seat: 38.8 in. Middle Seat: 36.5 in. Rear seat: 29.3 in. Shoulder room: Front seat: 53.1 in. Middle Seat: 53.2 in. Rear seat: 44.7 in. Hip room: Front seat: 53.2 in. Middle Seat: 53.7 in. Rear seat: 39.1 in.

CAPACITIES: Fuel Tank: 14.5 gals. Optional: None.

ACCOMMODATIONS: Seating Capacity: Seven passengers.

OPTIONS AND PRICES: Air conditioning. Luggage rack. AM/FM stereo radio. AM/FM stereo radio with cassette tape player. AM/FM/MX electronically tuned stereo radio with cassette tape player. Power door locks. Power windows. Automatic speed control. Two-tone paint. Rear window wiper/washer. Custom Package. Includes full-face velour seats.

HISTORICAL FOOTNOTES: The 1987 Colt Vista was introduced in August, 1986.

1988 COLT VISTA

The Vista was given a moderate facelift for 1988 focusing on improving its front end aerodynamics. As in previous years the Vista offered seating for up to seven passengers with front bucket seats, a center seat for three passengers and a rear seat suitable for two occupants. The center and rear seats folded down to provide a six foot long cargo space. These seats could also be lowered for use as a sleeping area. The standard seat upholstery was a cloth and vinyl combination. Standard features of the Vista consisted of 65 amp alternator, 420 amp-hr. maintenance-free battery, stainless steel exhaust system, front and rear armrests, cut pile carpeting for the passenger and cargo areas, child protection rear door locks, cigarette lighter, shift lever console, electric rear window defroster, side window demisters, remote cable release fuel filer door, automatic "headlights-off" system, inside hood release, dome light, inside day/night rearview mirror, multifunction steering column (left side lever controls for directional signals, headlights, headlight dimmer with daytime pass/flash feature; right side lever controls windshield wipers and washer), deluxe urethane two-spoke steering wheel with built-in horn buttons, dual glove compartments, map pockets, magazine pockets, front passenger underseat tray and front and rear cupholders; urethane charcoal gray bumpers with color-keyed fillers, tinted glass for all windows, aerodynamic style halogen headlights with replaceable bulb, outside left side manual mirror, black windshield, drip rail, belt and quarter window moldings, wide charcoal-color body side molding, variable intermittent windshield wipers, four-wheel drive indicator on instrument panel, front mud flaps, rear mud flaps with four-wheel drive logo and skid plate. The Vista interior was offered in red, blue or gray. Exterior colors for 1988 consisted of medium red, rosewood, white, medium blue, bright silver and light blue. The available optional two-tone colors were rosewood/dark red, light blue/medium blue and silver/charcoal.

1988 Dodge Colt Vista

I.D. DATA: The vehicle identification number was located on a V.I.N. plate attached to the driver's side door body latch post.

Body Type	Factory Price	GVW	Shipping Weight	Prod. Total
H31 Station Wagon	$12,405	N.A.	2943	—

STANDARD ENGINE: Cast iron block, aluminum cylinder head, MCA Jet combustion system. Engine Type: In-line 4-cyl., OHV, OHC. Fuel Induction: Multipoint fuel injection. Compression Ratio: 8.5:1. Displacement: 122 cu. in. (1977 cc). Horsepower: 96 @ 5000 rpm. Torque: 113 lb.-ft. @ 3500 rpm. Fuel Requirements: Unleaded.

SUSPENSION AND RUNNING GEAR: Front Suspension: Independent. MacPherson struts, lower control arms, trailing links and stabilizer bar. Optional Rating: None. Rear Suspension: Semi-trailing arms and transverse torsion bars. Optional Rating: None. Final Drive Ratio: 3.19:1. Transfer Case: 2-speed. Ratios: 1.944:1, 1.00:1. Brakes: Type: Power, hydraulic. Front: Discs. Rear: Drums. Wheels: 14 x 6.5 in. steel. Tires: 185/70R14. Steering: Power-assisted rack and pinion. Optional: None. Transmission: 5-speed overdrive manual, all-synchromesh.

VEHICLE DIMENSIONS: Wheelbase: 103.5 in. Overall Length: 174.6 in. Overall Height: 59.4 in. Width: 64.6 in. Load space: 72.5 in. (load space length from back of front seat to end of cargo door). Headroom: Front seat: 38.3 in. Middle Seat: 38.3 in. Rear seat: 34.9 in. Legroom: Front seat: 38.8 in. Middle Seat: 36.5 in. Rear seat: 29.3 in. Shoulder room: Front seat: 53.1 in. Middle Seat: 53.2 in. Rear seat: 44.7 in. Hip room: Front seat: 53.2 in. Middle Seat: 53.7 in. Rear seat: 39.1 in.

CAPACITIES: Fuel Tank: 14.5 gals. Optional: None.

ACCOMMODATIONS: Seating Capacity: Seven passengers.

OPTIONS AND PRICES: Adjustable luggage rack. Air conditioning. Floor protectors. Limited slip rear differential. Two-tone paint. Power door locks. Power windows (front and rear doors). AM/FM electronically tuned stereo radio. AM/FM electronically tuned stereo radio with cassette tape player. Rear window wiper and washer. Automatic speed control. Custom Package. Includes carpeted lower door trim panels, front and rear door courtesy lights, digital clock, dual electric outside mirrors, dual visor vanity mirrors, exterior accent tape stripes, fabric head restraints (front, rear and middle seats), full-face velour seats, dual map lights, remote electric liftgate lock release and tachometer.

HISTORICAL FOOTNOTES: The 1988 Colt Vista was introduced in September, 1987.

1989 COLT VISTA

The Vista was unchanged for 1989.

I.D. DATA: The vehicle identification number was located on a V.I.N. plate attached to the driver's side door body latch post.

Body Type	Factory Price	GVW	Shipping Weight	Prod. Total
H31 Station Wagon	$12,828	N.A.	2955	—

STANDARD ENGINE: Cast iron block, aluminum cylinder head, MCA Jet combustion system. Engine Type: In-line 4-cyl., OHV, OHC. Fuel Induction: Multipoint fuel injection. Compression Ratio: 8.5:1. Displacement: 122 cu. in. (1977 cc). Horsepower: 96 @ 5000 rpm. Torque: 113 lb.-ft. @ 3500 rpm. Fuel Requirements: Unleaded.

SUSPENSION AND RUNNING GEAR: Front Suspension: Independent. MacPherson struts, lower control arms, trailing links and stabilizer bar. Optional Rating: None. Rear Suspension: Semi-trailing arms and transverse torsion bars. Optional Rating: None. Final Drive Ratio: 3.19:1. Transfer Case: 2-speed. Ratios: 1.944:1, 1.00:1. Brakes: Type: Power, hydraulic. Front: Discs. Rear: Drums. Wheels: 14 x 6.5 in. steel. Tires: 185/70R14. Steering: Power-assisted rack and pinion. Optional: None. Transmission: 5-speed overdrive manual, all-synchromesh.

VEHICLE DIMENSIONS: Wheelbase: 103.5 in. Overall Length: 174.6 in. Overall Height: 59.4 in. Width: 64.6 in. Load space: 72.5 in. (load space length from back of front seat to end of cargo door). Headroom: Front seat: 38.3 in. Middle Seat: 38.3 in. Rear seat: 34.9 in. Legroom: Front seat: 38.8 in. Middle Seat: 36.5 in. Rear seat: 29.3 in. Shoulder room: Front seat: 53.1 in. Middle Seat: 53.2 in. Rear seat: 44.7 in. Hip room: Front seat: 53.2 in. Middle Seat: 53.7 in. Rear seat: 39.1 in.

CAPACITIES: Fuel Tank: 14.5 gals. Optional: None.

ACCOMMODATIONS: Seating Capacity: Seven passengers.

OPTIONS AND PRICES: Adjustable luggage rack. Air conditioning. Floor protectors. Limited slip rear differential. Two-tone paint. Power door locks. Power windows (front and rear doors). AM/FM electronically tuned stereo radio. AM/FM electronically tuned stereo radio with cassette tape player. Rear window wiper and washer. Automatic speed control. Custom Package. Includes carpeted lower door trim panels, front and rear door courtesy lights, digital clock, dual electric outside mirrors, dual visor vanity mirrors, exterior accent tape stripes, fabric head restraints (front, rear and middle seats), full-face velour seats, dual map lights, remote electric liftgate lock release and tachometer.

HISTORICAL FOOTNOTES: The 1989 Colt Vista was introduced in October, 1988.

1990 COLT VISTA

The Vista was continued for 1990 in essentially the same format as in 1989.

I.D. DATA. The vehicle identification number was located on a V.I.N. plate attached to the driver's side door body latch post.

Body Type	Factory Price	GVW	Shipping Weight	Prod. Total
H31 Station Wagon	$13,167	—	2955	—

STANDARD ENGINE: Cast iron block, aluminum cylinder head, MCA Jet combustion system. Engine Type: In-line 4-cyl., OHV, OHC. Fuel Induction: Multipoint fuel injection. Compression Ratio: 8.5:1. Displacement: 122 cu. in. (1977 cc). Horsepower: 96 @ 5000 rpm. Torque: 113 lb.-ft. @ 3500 rpm. Fuel Requirements: Unleaded.

SUSPENSION AND RUNNING GEAR: Front Suspension: Independent. MacPherson struts, lower control arms, trailing links and stabilizer bar. Optional Rating: None. Rear Suspension: Semi-trailing arms and transverse torsion bars. Optional Rating: None. Final Drive Ratio: 3.19:1. Transfer Case: 2-speed. Ratios: 1.944:1, 1.00:1. Brakes: Type: Power, hydraulic. Front: Discs. Rear: Drums. Wheels: 14 x 6.5 in. steel. Tires: 185/70R14. Steering: Power-assisted rack and pinion. Optional: None. Transmission: 5-speed overdrive manual, all-synchromesh.

VEHICLE DIMENSIONS: Wheelbase: 103.5 in. Overall Length: 174.6 in. Overall Height: 59.4 in. Width: 64.6 in. Load space: 72.5 in. (load space length from back of front seat to end of cargo door). Headroom: Front seat: 38.3 in. Middle Seat: 38.3 in. Rear seat: 34.9 in. Legroom: Front seat: 38.8 in. Middle Seat: 36.5 in. Rear seat: 29.3 in. Shoulder room: Front seat: 53.1 in. Middle Seat: 53.2 in. Rear seat: 44.7 in. Hip room: Front seat: 53.2 in. Middle Seat: 53.7 in. Rear seat: 39.1 in.

CAPACITIES: Fuel Tank: 14.5 gals. Optional: None.

ACCOMMODATIONS: Seating Capacity: Seven passengers.

OPTIONS AND PRICES: Adjustable luggage rack. Air conditioning. Floor protectors. Limited slip rear differential. Two-tone paint. Power door locks. Power windows (front and rear doors). AM/FM electronically tuned stereo radio. AM/FM electronically tuned stereo radio with cassette tape player. Rear window wiper and washer. Automatic speed control. Custom Package. Includes carpeted lower door trim panels, front and rear door courtesy lights, digital clock, dual electric outside mirrors, dual visor vanity mirrors, exterior accent tape stripes, fabric head restraints (front, rear and middle seats), full-face velour seats, dual map lights, remote electric liftgate lock release and tachometer.

HISTORICAL FOOTNOTES: The Colt Vista was produced by Mitsubishi in its Okazaki, Japan plant.

1991 COLT VISTA

This was the final year for the Vista. Its design was, not surprisingly, unchanged for 1991.

1991 Dodge Colt Vista

I.D. DATA: The vehicle identification number was located on a V.I.N. plate attached to the driver's side door body latch post.

Body Type	Factory Price	GVW	Shipping Weight	Prod. Total
H31 Station Wagon	$13,167	—	2955	—

STANDARD ENGINE: Cast iron block, aluminum cylinder head, MCA Jet combustion system. Engine Type: In-line 4-cyl., OHV, OHC. Fuel Induction: Multipoint fuel injection. Compression Ratio: 8.5:1. Displacement: 122 cu. in. (1977 cc). Horsepower: 96 @ 5000 rpm. Torque: 113 lb.-ft. @ 3500 rpm. Fuel Requirements: Unleaded.

SUSPENSION AND RUNNING GEAR: Front Suspension: Independent. MacPherson struts, lower control arms, trailing links and stabilizer bar. Optional Rating: None. Rear Suspension: Semi-trailing arms and transverse torsion bars. Optional Rating: None. Final Drive Ratio: 3.19:1. Transfer Case: 2-speed. Ratios: 1.944:1, 1.00:1. Brakes: Type: Power, hydraulic. Front: Discs. Rear: Drums. Wheels: 14 x 6.5 in. steel. Tires: 185/70R14. Steering: Power-assisted rack and pinion. Optional: None. Transmission: 5-speed overdrive manual, all-synchromesh.

VEHICLE DIMENSIONS: Wheelbase: 103.5 in. Overall Length: 174.6 in. Overall Height: 59.4 in. Width: 64.6 in. Load space: 72.5 in. (load space length from back of front seat to end of cargo door). Headroom: Front seat: 38.3 in. Middle Seat: 38.3 in. Rear seat: 34.9 in. Legroom: Front seat: 38.8 in, Middle Seat: 36.5 in. Rear seat: 29.3 in. Shoulder room: Front seat: 53.1 in. Middle Seat: 53.2 in. Rear seat: 44.7 in. Hip room: Front seat: 53.2 in. Middle Seat: 53.7 in. Rear seat: 39.1 in.

CAPACITIES: Fuel Tank: 14.5 gals. Optional: None.

ACCOMMODATIONS: Seating Capacity: Seven passengers.

OPTIONS AND PRICES: Adjustable luggage rack. Air conditioning. Floor protectors. Limited slip rear differential. Two-tone paint. Power door locks. Power windows (front and rear doors). AM/FM electronically tuned stereo radio. AM/FM electronically tuned stereo radio with cassette tape player. Rear window wiper and washer. Automatic speed control. Custom Package. Includes carpeted lower door trim panels, front and rear door courtesy lights, digital clock, dual electric outside mirrors, dual visor vanity mirrors, exterior accent tape stripes, fabric head restraints (front, rear and middle seats), full-face velour seats, dual map lights, remote electric liftgate lock release and tachometer.

HISTORICAL FOOTNOTES: This was the final year for the Colt Vista.

DODGE DAKOTA

1987-1993

1987 DAKOTA

Dodge entered a new niche in the four-wheel drive market in 1987 with its mid-size Dakota pickup. Positioned between the full-size W models and the imported from Mitsubishi Dodge Ram models, the Dakota was available in either 111.9 in. wheelbase/6.5 ft. box or 123.9 in. wheelbase/8.0 ft. box versions. Styling of the Dakota was attractive, bearing a close resemblance to the larger W models while avoiding any overtones of simply being a scaled-down clone of the larger trucks.

The standard Dakota engine was a 3.9 liter (239 cu. in.) V-6 derived from the well-proven 5.2 liter V-8. The Dakota's front torsion bar suspension was the first independent system used on a domestic Dodge four-wheel drive truck. Production of the Dakota took place in the Warren, Michigan Dodge plant, which, after a renovation costing $500 million was renamed Dodge City. It was considered by many industry authorities as among the most technologically advanced truck production facilities in the world. The Dakota's standard equipment consisted of these items: Bright front bumper, Corrosion Package (included use of galvanized steel, protective urethane coating on lower body sides, wax-dipped frame and Uniprime coating), stainless steel exhaust system, tinted glass in all windows, argent painted grille, halogen rectangular headlights, exterior dual flag-type mirrors, bright hubcaps, underslung winch type spare tire carrier, drawer type cupholder, black rubber floor covering with padding, cloth-covered headliner with insulation pad, bi-level heater/defroster with flow-through ventilation, in-cab hood release, interior roof-mounted dome light with door-operated switches, interior day/night 10 in. mirror, AM radio with electronic tuning and integral clock, side window demisters, and two-speed windshield wipers.

The base Dakota was fitted with an all-vinyl bench seat. Standard in the Dakota equipped with the SE Decor Package was a cloth with vinyl trim bench seat. It was available as an option for the base Dakota. A deluxe cloth with vinyl trim bench seat was standard with the LE Decor Package. This seat had a fold-down center armrest. All seats were available in almond, blue or silver/charcoal. The Dakota's exterior color selection consisted of light cream, dark suede, graphic red, medium suede, radiant silver, glacier blue, bright white, black, charcoal pearlcoat and twilight blue pearlcoat (extra cost).

I.D. DATA: The vehicle identification number was located on a V.I.N. plate attached to the driver's side door body latch post. The V.I.N. consisted of 17 elements. The first three entries identified the nation of origin, manufacturer and vehicle type. The fourth entry, a letter, identified the gross vehicle weight. This was followed by three characters identifying the series and body type. The eighth character identified the engine. A check digit followed. Next was a letter representing the model year. The eleventh character identified the assembly plant. The last six digits functioned as the sequential production number.

Body Type	Factory Price	GVW	Shipping Weight	Prod. Total
Dakota				
Sweptline, 6 ft.	N.A.	N.A.	N.A.	—
Sweptline, 8 ft.	N.A.	N.A.	N.A.	—

STANDARD ENGINE: Features include valve rotators, forged connecting rods, and vibration damper. Engine Type: OHV, V-6. Cast iron block and cylinder head. Bore x Stroke: 3.91 in. x 3.312 in. Lifters: Hydraulic. Number of main bearings-5. Fuel Induction: Single carburetor. Compression Ratio: 9.2:1. Displacement: 239 cu. in. (3.9 liters). Horsepower: 125 @ 4000 rpm. Torque: 195 lb.-ft. @ 2000 rpm. Fuel Requirements: Unleaded.

OPTIONAL ENGINE: None.

CHASSIS FEATURES: Separate body and frame.

SUSPENSION AND RUNNING GEAR: Front Suspension: Torsion bars. 2615 lb. capacity with standard 1450 lb. payload capacity. Optional Rating: None. Rear Suspension: Dual-stage semi-elliptical leaf springs, 3000 lbs. Optional with 2000 lb. payload package: 3700 lb. capacity. Front Axle Type and Capacity: 2575 lb. capacity. Optional: None. Rear Axle Type and Capacity: 3650 lb. capacity. Optional: None. Final Drive Ratio: 2.94:1 (with standard 1450 lb. payload package); 3.55:1 (with 2000 lb. payload package). Transfer Case: New Process 231 part-time, two-speed: 2.61, 1.00:1. Brakes: Type: Power, hydraulic. Front: Discs. Rear: Drums. Dimensions: Front: 11.4 in. x 0.87 in. disc. Rear: 9 in. x 2.5 in. (rear brakes for 2000 lb. payload package: 10 in. x 2.5 in. Wheels: 15 x 6.00. (15 x 6.00 heavy-duty for 2000 lb. payload package). Optional: 15 in. styled steel wheels with bright trim ring and black center cap with molded-on ram's head and argent painted spokes. Requires Prospector Package I and 15 in. tires.15 in. x 6 in. cast aluminum wheels. requires Prospector Package III, IV or V and 15 in. tires. Tires: P195/75R15 All-Season steel-belted radial. Optional for 1450 lb. payload only: P205/75R15, P235/75R15XL All-Season steel-belted radial. Standard for 2000 lb. payload package: P235/75R15XL. Steering: Integral power steering, recirculating-ball. Turning Circle: 39.6 ft. Optional: None. Standard: Transmission: 5-speed manual overdrive. Optional: 3-speed automatic transmission. Clutch: Single dry plate disc. Clutch diameter: 10.5 in. dia. Optional: None.

VEHICLE DIMENSIONS: Wheelbase: 112 in./124 in. Overall Length: 185.9 in./204.4 in. Front/Rear Tread: 57.9 in./58.9 in. Overall Height: 67.1 in. Width: 68.4 in. Front/Rear Overhang: 30.4 in./43.6 in. (50.1 in. for 124 in. wheelbase). Tailgate: Width and Height: 59.6 in. x 17.5 in.

CAPACITIES: Fuel Tank: 15.9 gal.

ACCOMMODATIONS: Seating Capacity: Three with standard front bench seat.

INSTRUMENTATION: Speedometer, odometer, electrical system voltage and fuel gauges, warning lights for brake system, emission maintenance reminder, engine coolant temperature, engine oil pressure, fasten seat belts, high beam headlights and turn signals.

OPTIONS: Bright rear step bumper with black step pads, 22 gal. fuel tank with tethered fuel cap, bright trim exterior dual low mount 6 in. x 9 in. mirrors, deluxe bright wheelcovers, bi-level air conditioning, electronically tuned AM/FM stereo radio with four speakers, premium electronically tuned AM/FM stereo radio with four speakers, 120 amp alternator, Sure-Grip rear axle and maximum engine cooling. SE Decor Package. Includes AM/FM electronically tuned radio, bright deluxe wheelcovers, bright full wheel-lip molding, bright grille and headlight bezels, bright taillight housings, brushed finish instrument panel trim bezels, illuminated cigarette lighter, cloth with vinyl trim bench seat (all-vinyl seats available at no extra cost), color-keyed floor carpeting, color-keyed deluxe steering wheel, color-keyed seat track covers, color-keyed steering column, deluxe windshield wipers with intermittent wipe, dual exterior remote control flag-type mirrors, garnish trim on "B" pillar and below rear window, "Leaping Ram" plaque with SE insert on front fenders, molded plastic jack cover, storage tray behind seat on floor and vinyl applique on front door trim. LE Decor Package. Includes AM/FM electronically tuned radio, bright deluxe wheelcovers, bright full wheel-lip molding, bright grille and headlight bezels, bright taillight housings, illuminated cigarette lighter, color-keyed floor carpeting, color-keyed seat track covers, color-keyed steering column, deluxe windshield wipers with intermittent wipe, dual exterior remote control flag-type mirrors, garnish trim on "B" pillar and below rear window, molded plastic jack cover, storage tray behind seat on floor, accessory-type carpeted floor mats, black/dark mist wheel-lip moldings, black sill moldings, color-keyed carpeting on cab back panel, color-keyed cloth-covered sun visors with storage pocket on left side, color-keyed deluxe cloth with vinyl trim bench seat with folding center armrest and hinged seat back (deluxe all-vinyl bench seat available at no extra charge), color-keyed luxury steering wheel, deluxe body sound insulation, black front bumper protective rub strip, front door trim with soft cloth applique and lower carpet insert, Gauge Package, hood insulation pad, Leaping Ram plaque with LE insert on front fenders, Light Package, vanity mirror on passenger side sun visor, black with dark mist trim vinyl lower body side and tailgate moldings with 4x4 stencil, and woodtone trim on instrument panel trim bezels. Prospector I Package. Includes bright deluxe wheelcovers, illuminated cigarette lighter, deluxe windshield wipers with intermittent wipe, Gauge Package, Light Package, 22 gal. fuel tank with tethered cap and sliding rear window, tinted and latchable. Prospector Package II. Includes all items found in the SE Decor Package plus Gauge Package, Light Package, 22 gal. fuel tank with tethered cap and sliding rear window, tinted and latchable. Prospector III Package. Includes all items in the Prospector II Package (except bright deluxe wheelcovers, which were replaced by styled steel 15 in. x 6 in. five-spoke argent painted road wheels. Prospector IV Package. Includes the content of Prospector III Package except for cloth and vinyl bench seat, Leaping Ram plaque with SE insert on front fenders and vinyl applique on front door trim. Additional components consisted of accessory-type carpeted floor mats, black/dark mist wheel-lip moldings, black sill moldings, color-keyed carpeting on cab back panel, color-keyed sun visors with storage pocket on left side, color-keyed deluxe cloth with vinyl trim bench seat with folding center armrest and hinged seat back (deluxe all-vinyl seat available at no extra cost), color-keyed luxury steering wheel, deluxe body sound insulation, black front bumper protective rub strip, front door trim with soft cloth applique and lower carpet insert, hood insulation pad, Leaping Ram plaque with LE insert on front fenders, vanity mirror on passenger side sun visor, vinyl lower body side and tailgate moldings, black with dark mist trim and "4x4" stencil on molding, woodtone trim on instrument panel trim bezels and Deluxe Convenience Package. Prospector V Package. Includes all items found Prospector IV Package plus bi-level air conditioning and Power Convenience Package. Deluxe Convenience Package. Available only with Prospector Packages I and II. Includes automatic speed control and tilt steering column. Light Package. Included in LE Decor Package and all Prospector Packages. Includes ashtray light, courtesy light under instrument panel, glove box light, ignition switch light with time delay, swivel-type dome reading/cargo light and underhood light. Snowplow Preparation Package. Includes heavy-duty 120 amp alternator, maximum engine cooling (auxiliary transmission oil to air cooler included with automatic transmission), P235/75R15 steel belted radial Mud and Snow tires (five), 2000 lb. Payload Package and transmission oil overheat warning light with automatic transmission. Two-Tone Paint Package I. Includes color-keyed upper body side and tailgate tape stripes, two-tone paint primary color above tape stripe on cab and box and inside box; secondary color above tape stripe. Two-Tone Paint Package II. Includes black vinyl lower body side and tailgate molding with bright insert along top edge, color-keyed upper body side and tailgate tape stripes, full bright wheel-lip moldings, two-tone paint; primary color above tape stripe on cab and box, inside box and below vinyl molding; secondary color between tape stripe and molding. Power Convenience Package. Available with Prospector Packages III and IV only. Includes power door locks and power windows. 4x4 Protection Package. Includes fuel tank skid plate and transfer case skid plate. Trailer Towing Preparation Package. Includes 120 amp alternator, 22 gal. fuel tank, heavy-duty variable load flasher, maximum engine cooling (transmission oil cooler included with automatic transmission), and five-lead trailer towing harness. Gauge Package. Includes engine coolant temperature gauge, engine oil pressure gauge, low fuel warning light, low washer fluid level warning light and trip odometer. Heavy-Duty Package. Includes 625 amp maintenance-free battery, and heavy-duty front and rear shock absorbers.

HISTORICAL FOOTNOTES: The 1987 Dakota was protected by a 7/70 power train limited warranty and a 7 yr./100,000 mile anti-corrosion warranty.

1988 DAKOTA

New this year was electronic fuel injection for 3.9 liter V-6 engine. A new mid-year offering was the Dakota Sport model. It was available in red, white and black. Standard features of the Dakota Sport included AM/FM stereo radio with cassette tape player, carpeted logo floor mats, center armrest bench seat, charcoal/silver interior, color-keyed leather-wrapped Sport steering wheel, deluxe windshield wipers, dual remote control exterior mirrors, floor carpet, Gauge Package, Mopar air dam with fog lights, Mopar light bar with off-road lights, unique body side tape stripes, and sliding rear window. The Dakota continued to be available in either 111.9 in. wheelbase/6.5 ft. box or 123.9 in. wheelbase/8.0 ft. box versions.

1988 Dodge Dakota Sport pickup

The Dakota's standard equipment consisted of these items: Bright front bumper, Corrosion Package (included use of galvanized steel, protective urethane coating on lower body sides, wax-dipped frame and Uniprime coating), stainless steel exhaust system, tinted glass in all windows, argent painted grille, halogen rectangular headlights, exterior dual flag-type mirrors, bright hubcaps, underslung winch type spare tire carrier, drawer-type cupholder, black rubber floor covering with padding, cloth-covered headliner with insulation pad, bi-level heater/defroster with flow-through ventilation, in-cab hood release, interior roof-mounted dome light with door-operated switches, interior day/night 10 in. mirror, AM radio with electronic tuning and integral clock, side window demisters, and two-speed windshield wipers. The base Dakota was fitted with an all-vinyl bench seat. Standard in the Dakota equipped with the SE Decor Package was a cloth with vinyl trim bench seat. It was available as an option for the base Dakota. A deluxe cloth with vinyl trim bench seat was standard with the LE Decor Package. This seat had a fold-down center armrest. All seats were available in almond, blue or silver/charcoal. The Dakota's exterior color selection consisted of light cream, dark suede, graphic red, medium suede, radiant silver, glacier blue, bright white, black, charcoal pearlcoat and twilight blue pearlcoat (extra cost).

I.D. DATA: The vehicle identification number was located on a V.I.N. plate attached to the driver's side door body latch post. The V.I.N. consisted of 17 elements. The first three entries identified the nation of origin, manufacturer and vehicle type. The fourth entry, a letter, identified the gross vehicle weight. This was followed by three characters identifying the series and body type. The eighth character identified the engine. A check digit followed. Next was a letter representing the model year. The eleventh character identified the assembly plant. The last six digits functioned as the sequential production number.

Body Type	Factory Price	GVW	Shipping Weight	Prod. Total
Dakota				
Sweptline, 6 ft.	N.A.	N.A.	N.A.	—
Sweptline, 8 ft.	N.A.	N.A.	N.A.	—

STANDARD ENGINE: Features include valve rotators, forged connecting rods, and vibration damper. Engine Type: OHV, V-6. Cast iron block and cylinder head. Bore x Stroke: 3.91 in. x 3.312 in. Lifters: Hydraulic. Number of main bearings-5. Fuel Induction: Fuel injection. Compression Ratio: 9.2:1. Displacement: 239 cu. in. (3.9 liters). Horsepower: 125 @ 4000 rpm. Torque: 195 lb.-ft. @ 2000 rpm. Fuel Requirements: Unleaded.

OPTIONAL ENGINE: None.

CHASSIS FEATURES: Separate body and frame.

SUSPENSION AND RUNNING GEAR: Front Suspension: Torsion bars. 2615 lb. capacity with standard 1450 lb. payload capacity. Optional Rating: None. Rear Suspension: Dual-stage semi-elliptical leaf springs, 3000 lbs. Optional with 2000 lb. payload package: 3700 lb. capacity. Front Axle Type and Capacity: 2575 lb. capacity. Optional: None. Rear Axle Type and Capacity: 3650 lb. capacity. Optional: None. Final Drive Ratio: 2.94:1 (with standard 1450 lb. payload package); 3.55:1 (with 2000 lb. payload package). Transfer Case: New Process 231 part-time, two-speed: 2.61, 1.00:1. Brakes: Type: Power, hydraulic. Front: Discs. Rear: Drums. Dimensions: Front: 11.4 in. x 0.87 in. disc. Rear: 9 in. x 2.5 in. (rear brakes for 2000 lb. payload package: 10 in. x 2.5 in. Wheels: 15 x 6.00 stamped steel, argent painted. (15 x 6.00 heavy-duty for 2000 lb. payload package). 15 x 6.00 in. cast aluminum for Dakota Sport. Optional: 15 in. styled steel wheels with bright trim ring and black center cap with molded-on ram's head and argent painted spokes. Requires Prospector Package I and 15 in. tires.15 in. x 6 in. cast aluminum wheels. requires Prospector Package III, IV or V and 15 in. tires. Tires: P195/75R15 All-Season steel-belted radial. Optional for 1450 lb. payload only: P205/75R15, P235/75R15XL All-Season steel-belted radial. Standard for 2000 lb. payload package: P235/75R15XL. Steering: Integral power steering, recirculating-ball. Turning Circle: 39.6 ft. Optional: None. Standard: Transmission: 5-speed manual overdrive. Optional: 3-speed automatic transmission. Clutch: Single dry plate disc. Clutch diameter: 10.5 in. dia. Optional: None.

VEHICLE DIMENSIONS: Wheelbase: 112 in./124 in. Overall Length: 185.9 in./204.4 in. Front/Rear Tread: 57.9 in./58.9 in. Overall Height: 67.1 in. Width: 68.4 in. Front/Rear Overhang: 30.4 in./43.6 in. (50.1 in. for 124 in. wheelbase). Tailgate: Width and Height: 59.6 in. x 17.5 in.

CAPACITIES: Fuel Tank: 15.9 gal.

ACCOMMODATIONS: Seating Capacity: Three with standard front bench seat.

INSTRUMENTATION: Speedometer, odometer, electrical system voltage and fuel gauges, warning lights for brake system, emission maintenance reminder, engine coolant temperature, engine oil pressure, fasten seat belts, high beam headlights and turn signals.

OPTIONS: Bright rear step bumper with black step pads, 22 gal. fuel tank with tethered fuel cap, bright trim exterior dual low mount 6 in. x 9 in. mirrors, deluxe bright wheelcovers, bi-level air conditioning, electronically tuned AM/FM stereo radio with four speakers, premium electronically tuned AM/FM stereo radio with four speakers, 120 amp alternator, Sure-Grip rear axle and maximum engine cooling. SE Decor Package. Includes AM/FM electronically tuned radio, bright deluxe wheelcovers, bright full wheel-lip molding, bright grille and headlight bezels, bright taillight housings, brushed finish instrument panel trim bezels, illuminated cigarette lighter, cloth with vinyl trim bench seat (all-vinyl seats available at no extra cost), color-keyed floor carpeting, color-keyed deluxe steering wheel, color-keyed seat track covers, color-keyed steering column, deluxe windshield wipers with intermittent wipe, dual exterior remote control flag-type mirrors, garnish trim on "B" pillar and below rear window, "Leaping Ram" plaque with SE insert on front fenders, molded plastic jack cover, storage tray behind seat on floor and vinyl applique on front door trim. LE Decor Package. Includes AM/FM electronically tuned radio, bright deluxe wheelcovers, bright full wheel-lip molding, bright grille and headlight bezels, bright taillight housings, illuminated cigarette lighter, color-keyed floor carpeting, color-keyed seat track covers, color-keyed steering column, deluxe windshield wipers with intermittent wipe, dual exterior remote control flag-type mirrors, garnish trim on "B" pillar and below rear window, molded plastic jack cover, storage tray behind seat on floor, accessory-type carpeted floor mats, black/dark mist wheel-lip moldings, black sill moldings, color-keyed carpeting on cab back panel, color-keyed cloth-covered sun visors with storage pocket on left side, color-keyed deluxe cloth with vinyl trim bench seat with folding center armrest and hinged seat back (deluxe all-vinyl bench seat available at no extra charge), color-keyed luxury steering wheel, deluxe body sound insulation, black front bumper protective rub strip, front door trim with soft cloth applique and lower carpet insert, Gauge Package, hood insulation pad, Leaping Ram plaque with LE insert on front fenders, Light Package, vanity mirror on passenger side sun visor, black with dark mist trim vinyl lower body side and tailgate moldings with 4x4 stencil, and woodtone trim on instrument panel trim bezels. Prospector I Package. Includes bright deluxe wheelcovers, illuminated cigarette lighter, deluxe windshield wipers with intermittent wipe, Gauge Package, Light Package, 22 gal. fuel tank with tethered cap and sliding rear window, tinted and latchable. Prospector Package II. Includes all items found in the SE Decor Package plus Gauge Package, Light Package, 22 gal. fuel tank with tethered cap and sliding rear window, tinted and latchable. Prospector III Package. Includes all items in the Prospector II Package (except bright deluxe wheelcovers, which were replaced by styled steel 15 in. x 6 in. five-spoke argent painted road wheels. Prospector IV Package. Includes the content of Prospector III Package except for cloth and vinyl bench seat, Leaping Ram plaque with SE insert on front fenders and vinyl applique on front door trim. Additional components consisted of accessory-type carpeted floor mats, black/dark mist wheel-lip moldings, black sill moldings, color-keyed carpeting on cab back panel, color-keyed sun visors with storage pocket on left side, color-keyed deluxe cloth with vinyl trim bench seat with folding center armrest and hinged seat back (deluxe all-vinyl seat available at no extra cost), color-keyed luxury steering wheel, deluxe body sound insulation, black front bumper protective rub strip, front door trim with soft cloth applique and lower carpet insert, hood insulation pad, Leaping Ram plaque with LE insert on front fenders, vanity mirror on passenger side sun visor, vinyl lower body side and tailgate moldings, black with dark mist trim and "4x4" stencil on molding, woodtone trim on instrument panel trim bezels and Deluxe Convenience Package. Prospector V Package. Includes all items found Prospector IV Package plus bi-level air conditioning and Power Convenience Package. Deluxe Convenience Package. Available only with Prospector Packages I and II. Includes automatic speed control and tilt steering column. Light Package. Included in LE Decor Package and all Prospector Packages. Includes ashtray light, courtesy light under instrument panel, glove box light, ignition switch light with time delay, swivel-type dome reading/cargo light and underhood light. Snowplow Preparation Package. Includes heavy-duty 120 amp alternator, maximum engine cooling (auxiliary transmission oil to air cooler included with automatic transmission), P235/75R15 steel belted radial Mud and Snow tires (five), 2000 lb. Payload Package and transmission oil overheat warning light with automatic transmission. Two-Tone Paint Package I. Includes color-keyed upper body side and tailgate tape stripes, two-tone paint primary color above tape stripe on cab and box and inside box; secondary color above tape stripe. Two-Tone Paint Package II. Includes black vinyl lower body side and tailgate molding with bright insert along top edge, color-keyed upper body side and tailgate tape stripes, full bright wheel-lip moldings, two-tone paint; primary color above tape stripe on cab and box, inside box and below vinyl molding; secondary color between tape stripe and molding. Power Convenience Package. Available with Prospector Packages III and IV only. Includes power door locks and power windows. 4x4 Protection Package. Includes fuel tank skid plate and transfer case skid plate. Trailer Towing Preparation Package. Includes 120 amp alternator, 22 gal. fuel tank, heavy-duty variable load flasher, maximum engine cooling (transmission oil cooler included with automatic transmission), and five-lead trailer towing harness. Gauge Package. Includes engine coolant temperature gauge, engine oil pressure gauge, low fuel warning light, low washer fluid level warning light and trip odometer. Heavy-Duty Package. Includes 625 amp maintenance-free battery, and heavy-duty front and rear shock absorbers.

HISTORICAL FOOTNOTES: The 1988 Dakota was depicted by Dodge as "not too big, not too small."

1989 DAKOTA

Dodge made numerous technical improvements in the Dakota for 1989. The 3.9 liter fuel injected V-6 had improved internal lubrication and a revised intake manifold providing for a larger, higher-flow capacity thermostat. All Dakotas were equipped with a new standard rear wheel anti-lock brake system. A new four-speed overdrive automatic transmission was also introduced. Added to the Dakota's standard equipment was a new deluxe two-spoke steering wheel and the Gauge Package which had previously been an option. The elements of the 1988 model's standard equipment content was carried over for 1989. The features of the Dakota Sport were altered to include a tachometer, a premium AM/FM stereo radio with cassette tape player and cast aluminum wheels. Added to the Dakota model lineup was the Sport Convertible. Based on the Dakota Sport the Sport Convertible was offered in red, black or white with a Bordeaux interior and a black manual convertible top. Its standard functional equipment included tachometer, intermittent windshield wipers, Heavy-Duty Electrical Package, and Light Package. A high level of Interior features were also found on the Sport Convertible, including AM/FM stereo radio with cassette tape player, power windows and door locks, C.A.R. bench seat in unique fabric with vinyl trim, vinyl door trim appliques, bright instrument panel bezels, floor carpet, carpeted floor mats with logo and a color-keyed leather-wrapped steering wheel. The Sport Convertible exterior featured these items: Black grille and headlight bezels, black front bumper, black wheel-lip moldings, black rear step bumper, black door and tailgate handles, ram's head hood ornament, black sill moldings, cast aluminum wheels, P235 OWL tires, tape graphics on body sides and tailgate, fog lights, top stack boot, and a folded top lock down and support. The Sport Convertible's factory installed options were limited to air conditioning, automatic transmission, electronic speed control/tilt steering column, 22 gal. fuel tank, 4x4 Protection Package, Trailer Tow Preparation Package, Emission Reduction Control System, high altitude emissions and maximum engine cooling. As in 1988, the Dakota Sport trucks were not available with the 2000 lb. Payload Package.

Standard equipment for 1989 comprised these elements: Painted front bumper, tinted glass for all windows, argent painted grille, halogen rectangular head lights, bright hubcaps, exterior dual flag-type mirrors, underslung winch-type spare tire carrier, stamped steel 15 in. argent painted wheels, cupholder drawer-type, black rubber floor covering with pad, cloth-covered headliner, bi-level heater/defroster with flow-through ventilation, in-cab hood release, interior roof-mounted dome light with door-operated switches, interior day/night 10 in. mirror, AM/FM electronically tuned stereo radio with integral digital clock (may be deleted for credit on factory orders), side window demisters, and two-speed windshield wipers. An all-vinyl bench seat was standard for the Dakota. It was also available as a no-charge option for Dakotas with the SE Decor trim. A cloth with vinyl trim bench seat was part of the SE Decor trim option. It was available as an option for the base Dakota. A deluxe cloth bench seat with vinyl trim was standard on Dakotas equipped with the LE Decor trim. All of the above seats were offered in almond, blue or Bordeaux. The Dakota Sport cloth bench seat had vinyl trim plus a center fold-down armrest and a net-type storage pocket in front of the seat cushion. It was offered only in Bordeaux. All exterior colors for 1989 were of a clear coat finish. The color selection was as follows: Diamond blue, dark suede, exotic red, medium suede, aquamarine blue, bright white, black and dark quartz gray. Two additional extra-cost colors were available: Twilight blue pearlcoat and platinum silver.

1989 Dodge Dakota Sports Convertible pickup

I.D. DATA: The vehicle identification number was located on a V.I.N. plate attached to the driver's side door body latch post. The V.I.N. consisted of 17 elements. The first three entries identified the nation of origin, manufacturer and vehicle type. The fourth entry, a letter, identified the gross vehicle weight. This was followed by three characters identifying the series and body type. The eighth character identified the engine. A check digit followed. Next was a letter representing the model year. The eleventh character identified the assembly plant. The last six digits functioned as the sequential production number.

Body Type	Factory Price	GVW	Shipping Weight	Prod. Total
Dakota				
Sweptline, 111.9 in. wb.	$12,032	N.A.	N.A.	—
Sweptline, 123.9 in. wb.	$12,212	N.A.	N.A.	—
Sport, 111.9 in. wb.	$13,559	N.A.	N.A.	—
Sport Conv., 111.9 in. wb.	$16,595	N.A.	N.A.	—

STANDARD ENGINE: Features include valve rotators, forged connecting rods, and vibration damper. Engine Type: OHV, V-6. Cast iron block and cylinder head. Bore x Stroke: 3.91 in. x 3.312 in. Lifters: Hydraulic. Number of main bearings-5. Fuel Induction: Fuel injection. Compression Ratio: 9.2:1. Displacement: 239 cu. in. (3.9 liters). Horsepower: 125 @ 4000 rpm. Torque: 195 lb.-ft. @ 2000 rpm. Fuel Requirements: Unleaded.

OPTIONAL ENGINE: None.

CHASSIS FEATURES: Separate body and frame.

SUSPENSION AND RUNNING GEAR: Front Suspension: Torsion bars. 2615 lb. capacity with standard 1450 lb. payload capacity. Optional Rating: None. Rear Suspension: Dual-stage semi-elliptical leaf springs, 3000 lbs. Optional with 2000 lb. payload package: 3700 lb. capacity. Front Axle Type and Capacity: 2575 lb. capacity. Optional: None. Rear Axle Type and Capacity: 3650 lb. capacity. Optional: None. Final Drive Ratio: 2.94:1 (with standard 1450 lb. payload package); 3.55:1 (with 2000 lb. payload package). Transfer Case: New Process 231 part-time, two-speed: 2.61, 1.00:1. Brakes: Type: Power, hydraulic. Front: Discs. Rear: Drums. Dimensions: Front: 11.4 in. x 0.87 in. disc. Rear: 9 in. x 2.5 in. (rear brakes for 2000 lb. payload package: 10 in. x 2.5 in. Wheels: 15 x 6.00 stamped steel, argent painted. (15 x 6.00 heavy-duty for 2000 lb. payload package). 15 x 6.00 in. cast aluminum for Dakota Sport. Optional: 15 in. styled steel wheels with bright trim ring and black center cap with molded-on ram's head and argent painted spokes. Requires Prospector Package I and II and 15 in. tires.15 in. x 6 in. cast aluminum wheels. Requires Prospector Package II or III and 15 in. tires. Tires: P195/75R15 All-Season steel-belted radial. Dakota Sport: P235/75R15XL outline white letter, Mud and Snow tread. Optional for 1450 lb. payload only: P205/75R15, P235/75R15XL All-Season or Mud and Snow tread steel-belted radial. Standard for 2000 lb. payload package: P235/75R15XL All-Season or Mud and Snow tread. Steering: Integral power steering, recirculating-ball. Turning Circle: 39.6 ft. Optional: None. Standard: Transmission: 5-speed manual overdrive. Optional: 3-speed automatic transmission. Clutch: Single dry plate disc. Clutch diameter: 10.5 in. dia. Optional: None.

VEHICLE DIMENSIONS: Wheelbase: 112 in./124 in. Overall Length: 185.9 in./204.4 in. Front/Rear Tread: 57.9 in./58.9 in. Overall Height: 67.1 in. Width: 68.4 in. Front/Rear Overhang: 30.4 in./43.6 in. (50.1 in. for 124 in. wheelbase). Tailgate: Width and Height: 59.6 in. x 17.5 in.

CAPACITIES: Fuel Tank: 15.9 gal.

ACCOMMODATIONS: Seating Capacity: Three with standard front bench seat.

INSTRUMENTATION: Speedometer, odometer, electrical system voltage and fuel gauges, warning lights for brake system, emission maintenance reminder, engine coolant temperature, engine oil pressure, fasten seat belts, high beam headlights and turn signals.

OPTIONS: Bright rear step bumper with black step pads, 22 gal. fuel tank with tethered fuel cap, bright trim exterior dual low mount 6 in. x 9 in. mirrors, deluxe bright wheelcovers, bi-level air conditioning, electronically tuned AM/FM stereo radio with four speakers, premium electronically tuned AM/FM stereo radio with four speakers, 120 amp alternator, Sure-Grip rear axle and maximum engine cooling. SE Decor Package. Includes AM/FM electronically tuned radio, bright deluxe wheelcovers, bright full wheel-lip molding, bright grille and headlight bezels, bright taillight housings, brushed finish instrument panel trim bezels, illuminated cigarette lighter, cloth with vinyl trim bench seat (all-vinyl seats available at no extra cost), color-keyed floor carpeting, color-keyed deluxe steering wheel, color-keyed seat track covers, color-keyed steering column, deluxe windshield wipers with intermittent wipe, dual exterior remote control flag-type mirrors, garnish trim on "B" pillar and below rear window, "Leaping Ram" plaque with SE insert on front fenders, molded plastic jack cover, storage tray behind seat on floor and vinyl applique on front door trim. LE Decor Package. Includes AM/FM electronically tuned radio, bright deluxe wheelcovers, bright full wheel-lip molding, bright grille and headlight bezels, bright taillight housings, illuminated cigarette lighter, color-keyed floor carpeting, color-keyed seat track covers, color-keyed steering column, deluxe windshield wipers with intermittent wipe, dual exterior remote control flag-type mirrors, garnish trim on "B" pillar and below rear window, molded plastic jack cover, storage tray behind seat on floor, accessory-type carpeted floor mats, black/dark mist wheel-lip moldings, black sill moldings, color-keyed carpeting on cab back panel, color-keyed cloth-covered sun visors with storage pocket on left side, color-keyed deluxe cloth with vinyl trim bench seat with folding center armrest and hinged seat back (deluxe all-vinyl bench seat available at no extra charge), color-keyed luxury steering wheel, deluxe body sound insulation, black front bumper protective rub

strip, front door trim with soft cloth applique and lower carpet insert, Gauge Package, hood insulation pad, Leaping Ram plaque with LE insert on front fenders, Light Package, vanity mirror on passenger side sun visor, black with dark mist trim vinyl lower body side and tailgate moldings with 4x4 stencil, and woodtone trim on instrument panel trim bezels. Prospector I Package. Includes bright deluxe wheelcovers, illuminated cigarette lighter, deluxe windshield wipers with intermittent wipe, Gauge Package, Light Package, 22 gal. fuel tank with tethered cap and sliding rear window, tinted and latchable. Prospector Package II. Includes all items found in the SE Decor Package plus Gauge Package, Light Package, 22 gal. fuel tank with tethered cap and sliding rear window, tinted and latchable. Prospector III Package. Includes all items in the Prospector II Package (except bright deluxe wheelcovers, which were replaced by styled steel 15 in. x 6 in. five-spoke argent painted road wheels. Prospector IV Package. Includes the content of Prospector III Package except for cloth and vinyl bench seat, Leaping Ram plaque with SE insert on front fenders and vinyl applique on front door trim. Additional components consisted of accessory-type carpeted floor mats, black/dark mist wheel-lip moldings, black sill moldings, color-keyed carpeting on cab back panel, color-keyed sun visors with storage pocket on left side, color-keyed deluxe cloth with vinyl trim bench seat with folding center armrest and hinged seat back (deluxe all-vinyl seat available at no extra cost), color-keyed luxury steering wheel, deluxe body sound insulation, black front bumper protective rub strip, front door trim with soft cloth applique and lower carpet insert, hood insulation pad, Leaping Ram plaque with LE insert on front fenders, vanity mirror on passenger side sun visor, black with dark mist trim vinyl lower body side and tailgate moldings with 4x4 stencil, and woodtone trim on instrument panel trim bezels. Prospector I Package. Includes bright deluxe wheel covers, illuminated cigarette lighter, deluxe windshield wipers with intermittent wipe, Gauge Package, Light Package, 22 gal. fuel tank with tethered cap and sliding rear window, tinted and latchable. Prospector Package II. Includes all items found in the SE Decor Package plus Gauge Package, Light Package, 22 gal. fuel tank with tethered cap and sliding rear window, tinted and latchable. Prospector III Package. Includes all items in the Prospector II Package (except bright deluxe wheelcovers, which were replaced by styled steel 15 in. x 6 in. five-spoke argent-painted road wheels. Prospector IV Package. Includes the content of Prospector III Package except for cloth and vinyl bench seat, Leaping Ram plaque with SE insert on front fenders and vinyl applique on front door trim. Additional components consisted of accessory-type carpeted floor mats, black/dark mist wheel-lip moldings, black sill moldings, color-keyed carpeting on cab back panel, color-keyed sun visors with storage pocket on left side, color-keyed deluxe cloth with vinyl trim bench seat with folding center armrest and hinged seat back (deluxe all-vinyl seat available at no extra cost), color-keyed luxury steering wheel, deluxe body sound insulation, black front bumper protective rub strip, front door trim with soft cloth applique and lower carpet insert, hood insulation pad, Leaping Ram plaque with LE insert on front fenders, vanity mirror on passenger side sun visor, vinyl lower body side and tailgate moldings, black with dark mist trim and "4x4" stencil on molding, woodtone trim on instrument panel trim bezels and Deluxe Convenience Package. Prospector V Package. Includes all items found Prospector IV Package plus bi-level air conditioning and Power Convenience Package. Deluxe Convenience Package. Available only with Prospector Packages I and II. Includes automatic speed control and tilt steering column. Light Package. Included in LE Decor Package and all Prospector Packages. Includes ashtray light, courtesy light under instrument panel, glove box light, ignition switch light with time delay, swivel-type dome reading/cargo light and underhood light. Snowplow Preparation Package. Includes heavy-duty 120 amp alternator, maximum engine cooling (auxiliary transmission oil to air cooler included with automatic transmission), P235/75R15 steel belted radial Mud and Snow tires (five), 2000 lb. Payload Package and transmission oil overheat warning light with automatic transmission. Two-Tone Paint Package I. Includes color-keyed upper body side and tailgate tape stripes, two-tone paint primary color above tape stripe on cab and box and inside box; secondary color above tape stripe. Two-Tone Paint Package II. Includes black vinyl lower body side and tailgate molding with bright insert along top edge, color-keyed upper body side and tailgate tape stripes, full bright wheel-lip moldings, two-tone paint; primary color above tape stripe on cab and box, inside box and below vinyl molding; secondary color between tape stripe and molding. Power Convenience Package. Available with Prospector Packages III and IV only. Includes power door locks and power windows. 4x4 Protection Package. Includes fuel tank skid plate and transfer case skid plate. Trailer Towing Preparation Package. Includes 120 amp alternator, 22 gal. fuel tank, heavy-duty variable load flasher, maximum engine cooling (transmission oil cooler included with automatic transmission), and five-lead trailer towing harness. Gauge Package. Includes engine coolant temperature gauge, engine oil pressure gauge, low fuel warning light, low washer fluid level warning light and trip odometer. Heavy-Duty Package. Includes 625 amp maintenance-free battery, and heavy-duty front and rear shock absorbers.

HISTORICAL FOOTNOTES: The Dakota Sport Convertible was described as "the ultimate fun truck."

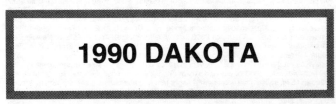

1990 DAKOTA

The Dodge Dakota continued to offer the only factory-built American convertible pickup in 1990.

I.D. DATA: The vehicle identification number was located on a V.I.N. plate attached to the driver's side door body latch post. The V.I.N. consisted of 17 elements. The first three entries identified the nation of origin, manufacturer and vehicle type. The fourth entry, a letter, identified the gross vehicle weight. This was followed by three characters identifying the series and body type. The eighth character identified the engine. A check digit followed. Next was a letter representing the model year. The eleventh character identified the assembly plant. The last six digits functioned as the sequential production number.

Body Type	Factory Price	GVW	Shipping Weight	Prod. Total
Dakota				
Sweptline, 111.9 in. wb.	$12,795	N.A.	N.A.	—
Sweptline, 123.9 in. wb.	$12,995	N.A.	N.A.	—
Sport, 111.9 in. wb.	$14,595	N.A.	N.A.	—
Sport Conv., 111.9 in. wb.	$17,700	N.A.	N.A.	—

STANDARD ENGINE: Features include valve rotators, forged connecting rods, and vibration damper. Engine Type: OHV, V-6. Cast iron block and cylinder head. Bore x Stroke: 3.91 in. x 3.312 in. Lifters: Hydraulic. Number of main bearings-5. Fuel Induction: Fuel injection. Compression Ratio: 9.2:1. Displacement: 239 cu. in. (3.9 liters). Horsepower: 125 @ 4000 rpm. Torque: 195 lb.-ft. @ 2000 rpm. Fuel Requirements: Unleaded.

OPTIONAL ENGINE: None.

CHASSIS FEATURES: Separate body and frame.

SUSPENSION AND RUNNING GEAR: Front Suspension: Torsion bars. 2615 lb. capacity with standard 1450 lb. payload capacity. Optional Rating: None. Rear Suspension: Dual-stage semi-elliptical leaf springs, 3000 lbs. Optional with 2000 lb. payload package: 3700 lb. capacity. Front Axle Type and Capacity: 2575 lb. capacity. Optional: None. Rear Axle Type and Capacity: 3650 lb. capacity. Optional: None. Final Drive Ratio: 2.94:1 (with standard 1450 lb. payload package); 3.55:1 (with 2000 lb. payload package). Transfer Case: New Process 231 part-time, two-speed: 2.61, 1.00:1. Brakes: Type: Power, hydraulic. Front: Discs. Rear: Drums. Dimensions: Front: 11.4 in. x 0.87 in. disc. Rear: 9 in. x 2.5 in. (rear brakes for 2000 lb. payload package: 10 in. x 2.5 in. Wheels: 15 x 6.00 stamped steel, argent painted. (15 x 6.00 heavy-duty for 2000 lb. payload package). 15 x 6.00 in. cast aluminum for Dakota Sport. Optional: 15 in. styled steel wheels with bright trim ring and black center cap with molded-on ram's head and argent painted spokes. Requires Prospector Package I and II and 15 in. tires.15 in. x 6 in. cast aluminum wheels. Requires Prospector Package II or III and 15 in. tires. Tires: P195/75R15 All-Season steel-belted radial. Dakota Sport: P235/75R15XL outline white letter, Mud and Snow tread. Optional for 1450 lb. payload only: P205/75R15, P235/75R15XL All-Season or Mud and Snow tread steel-belted radial. Standard for 2000 lb. payload package: P235/75R15XL All-Season or Mud and Snow tread. Steering: Integral power steering, recirculating-ball. Turning Circle: 39.6 ft. Optional: None. Standard: Transmission: 5-speed manual overdrive. Optional: 3-speed automatic transmission. Clutch: Single dry plate disc. Clutch diameter: 10.5 in. dia. Optional: None.

VEHICLE DIMENSIONS: Wheelbase: 112 in./124 in. Overall Length: 185.9 in./204.4 in. Front/Rear Tread: 57.9 in./58.9 in. Overall Height: 67.1 in. Width: 68.4 in. Front/Rear Overhang: 30.4 in./43.6 in. (50.1 in. for 124 in. wheelbase). Tailgate: Width and Height: 59.6 in. x 17.5 in.

CAPACITIES: Fuel Tank: 15.9 gal.

ACCOMMODATIONS: Seating Capacity: Three with standard front bench seat.

INSTRUMENTATION: Speedometer, odometer, electrical system voltage and fuel gauges, warning lights for brake system, emission maintenance reminder, engine coolant temperature, engine oil pressure, fasten seat belts, high beam headlights and turn signals.

OPTIONS: Bright rear step bumper with black step pads, 22 gal. fuel tank with tethered fuel cap, bright trim exterior dual low mount 6 in. x 9 in. mirrors, deluxe bright wheelcovers, bi-level air conditioning, electronically tuned AM/FM stereo radio with four speakers, premium electronically tuned AM/FM stereo radio with four speakers, 120 amp alternator, Sure-Grip rear axle and maximum engine cooling. SE Decor Package. Includes AM/FM electronically tuned radio, bright deluxe wheelcovers, bright full wheel-lip molding, bright grille and headlight bezels, bright taillight housings, brushed finish instrument panel trim bezels, illuminated cigarette lighter, cloth with vinyl trim bench seat (all-vinyl seats available at no extra cost), color-keyed floor carpeting, color-keyed deluxe steering wheel, color-keyed seat track covers, color-keyed steering column, deluxe windshield wipers with intermittent wipe, dual exterior remote control flag-type mirrors, garnish trim on "B" pillar and below rear window, "Leaping Ram" plaque with SE insert on front fenders, molded plastic jack cover, storage tray behind seat on floor and vinyl applique on front door trim. LE Decor Package. Includes AM/FM electronically tuned radio, bright deluxe wheelcovers, bright full wheel-lip molding, bright grille and headlight bezels, bright taillight housings, illuminated cigarette lighter, color-keyed floor carpeting, color-keyed seat track covers, color-keyed steering column, deluxe windshield wipers with intermittent wipe, dual exterior remote control flag-type mirrors, garnish trim on "B" pillar and below rear window, molded plastic jack cover, storage tray behind seat on floor, accessory-type carpeted floor mats, black/dark mist wheel-lip moldings, black sill moldings, color-keyed carpeting on cab back panel, color-keyed cloth-covered sun visors with storage pocket on left side, color-keyed deluxe cloth with vinyl trim bench seat with folding center armrest and hinged seat back (deluxe all-vinyl bench seat available at no extra charge), color-keyed luxury steering wheel, deluxe body sound insulation, black front bumper protective rub strip, front door trim with soft cloth applique and lower carpet insert, Gauge Package, hood insulation pad, Leaping Ram plaque with LE insert on front fenders, Light Package, vanity mirror on passenger side sun visor, black with dark mist trim vinyl lower body side and tailgate moldings with 4x4 stencil, and woodtone trim on instrument panel trim bezels. Prospector I Package. Includes bright deluxe wheelcovers, illuminated cigarette lighter, deluxe windshield wipers with intermittent wipe, Gauge Package, Light Package, 22 gal. fuel tank with tethered cap and sliding rear window, tinted and latchable. Prospector Package II. Includes all items found in the SE Decor Package plus Gauge Package, Light Package, 22 gal. fuel tank with tethered cap and sliding rear window, tinted and latchable. Prospector III Package. Includes all items in the Prospector II Package (except bright deluxe wheelcovers, which were replaced by styled steel 15 in. x 6 in. five-spoke argent painted road wheels. Prospector IV Package. Includes the content of Prospector III Package except for cloth and vinyl bench seat, Leaping Ram plaque with SE insert on front fenders and vinyl applique on front door trim. Additional components consisted of accessory-type carpeted floor mats, black/dark mist wheel-lip moldings, black sill moldings, color-keyed carpeting on cab back panel, color-keyed sun visors with storage pocket on left side, color-keyed deluxe cloth with vinyl trim bench seat with folding center armrest and hinged seat back (deluxe all-vinyl seat available at no extra cost), color-keyed luxury steering wheel, deluxe body sound insulation, black front bumper protective rub strip, front door trim with soft cloth applique and lower carpet insert, hood insulation pad, Leaping Ram plaque with LE insert on front fenders, vanity mirror on passenger side sun visor, vinyl lower body side and tailgate moldings, black with dark mist trim and "4x4" stencil on molding, woodtone trim on instrument panel trim bezels and Deluxe Convenience Package. Prospector V Package. Includes all items found Prospector IV Package plus bi-level air conditioning and Power Convenience Package. Deluxe Convenience Package. Available only with Prospector Packages I and II. Includes automatic speed control and tilt steering column. Light Package. Included in LE Decor Package and all Prospector Packages. Includes ashtray light, courtesy light under instrument panel, glove box light, ignition switch light with time delay, swivel-type dome reading/cargo light and underhood light. Snowplow Preparation Package. Includes heavy-duty 120 amp alternator, maximum engine cooling (auxiliary transmission oil to air cooler included with automatic transmission), P235/75R15 steel belted radial Mud and Snow tires (five), 2000 lb. Payload Package and transmission oil overheat warning light with automatic transmission. Two-Tone Paint Package I. Includes color-keyed upper body side and tailgate tape stripes, two-tone paint primary color above tape stripe on cab and box and inside box; secondary color above tape stripe. Two-Tone Paint Package II. Includes black vinyl lower body side and tailgate molding with bright insert along top edge, color-keyed upper body side and tailgate tape stripes, full bright wheel-lip moldings, two-tone paint; primary color above tape stripe on cab and box, inside box and below vinyl molding; secondary color between tape stripe and molding. Power Convenience Package. Available with Prospector Packages III and IV only. Includes power door locks and power windows. 4x4 Protection Package. Includes fuel tank skid plate and transfer case skid plate. Trailer Towing Preparation Package. Includes 120 amp alternator, 22 gal. fuel tank, heavy-duty variable load flasher, maximum engine cooling (transmission oil cooler included with automatic transmission), and five-lead trailer towing harness. Gauge Package. Includes engine coolant temperature gauge, engine oil pressure gauge, low fuel warning light, low washer fluid level warning light and trip odometer. Heavy-Duty Package. Includes 625 amp maintenance-free battery, and heavy-duty front and rear shock absorbers.

HISTORICAL FOOTNOTES: With sales of 74,812 for all variations, the Dakota's market share increased in 1990.

1991 DAKOTA

Dodge provided the four-wheel drive Dakota with added power in the form of the 318 cu. in. V-8 for 1991. Dodge didn't pretend that the 318 was on the cutting edge of technology, referring to it as "time-tested." But with 165 horsepower and 250 lb.-ft. of torque the V-8 provided the Dakota with plenty of power for heavy-duty hauling and trailer towing. The 318 V-8 was available only with automatic transmission. The 3.9 liter V-6 now had graphic-based cylinder head gaskets for better sealing. The Dakota's front end was revamped for 1991 by use of a bolder grille treatment, a new front bumper face bar and air dam. Aero headlamps were now used on the LE and Sport models. Sport models also had a new steel tube Sport bar in chrome with two off-road lights mounted on the top tube. Two new graphic tape treatments — A "whip" stripe and a "strobe" treatment were introduced for the Sport Dakota. All Dakotas had new exterior door handles of black, reinforced plastic that both reduced weight and improved corrosion protection.

Additional improvements included a new electrical power distribution center to provide better overload protection and better serviceability, larger front disc brake calipers for improved braking and non-asbestos brake pads. The Dakota now was fitted with new six-lug design wheels for added clamping force deemed desirable on larger payloads. In order to accommodate the V-8 engine the Dakota's hood was lengthened three inches. Additional changes included a new argent painted grille, on standard models. The Sport models used a body-painted grille. Both versions had the "Dodge" name molded into the header. The Dakota Sport treatment for 1991 included a body-color grille, a front air dam with integral fog lamps, a rear chrome tube bumper and a chrome light bar with two off-road lights. At mid-year a club cab model was added to the Dakota four-wheel drive lineup. The club cab was built on a 131 in. wheelbase and featured a 6.5 ft. pickup box, flip-open windows and two storage compartments beneath the rear seat. The club cab also had a 60/40 split bench seat. The back rest had a 40/20/40 split with the 20 percent split center section serving as a fold-down armrest. A new inertia sear back latch for split-back and bucket seats locked the seat back in place during severe braking conditions. Other changes for 1991 included the availability of three new exterior colors.

1991 Dodge Dakota club coupe Sport pickup

I.D. DATA: The vehicle identification number was located on a V.I.N. plate attached to the driver's side door body latch post. The V.I.N. consisted of 17 elements. The first three entries identified the nation of origin, manufacturer and vehicle type. The fourth entry, a letter, identified the gross vehicle weight. This was followed by three characters identifying the series and body type. The eighth character identified the engine. A check digit followed. Next was a letter representing the model year. The eleventh character identified the assembly plant. The last six digits functioned as the sequential production number.

Body Type	Factory Price	GVW	Shipping Weight	Prod. Total
Dakota				
Sweptline, 111.9 in. wb.	$13,449	N.A.	N.A.	—
Sweptline, 123.9 in. wb.	$13,656	N.A.	N.A.	—
Sport, 111.9 in. wb.	$15,522	N.A.	N.A.	—
Club Coupe, 130.9 in. wb.	$14,344	N.A.	N.A.	—
Spt. Club Coupe, 130.9 in. wb.	$15,522	N.A.	N.A.	—

STANDARD ENGINE: Features include valve rotators, forged connecting rods, and vibration damper. Engine Type: OHV, V-6. Cast iron block and cylinder head. Bore x Stroke: 3.91 in. x 3.312 in. Lifters: Hydraulic. Number of main bearings-5. Fuel Induction: Fuel injection. Compression Ratio: 9.2:1. Displacement: 239 cu. in. (3.9 liters). Horsepower: 125 @ 4000 rpm. Torque: 195 lb.-ft. @ 2000 rpm. Fuel Requirements: Unleaded.

OPTIONAL ENGINE: Engine Type: OHV, V-8. Cast iron block and cylinder head. Bore x Stroke: 3.91 in. x 3.312 in. Lifters: Hydraulic. Number of main bearings-5. Fuel Induction: Electronic fuel injection. Compression Ratio: 9.2:1. Displacement: 318 cu. in. (5.2 liters). Horsepower: 165 @ 4000 rpm. Torque: 250 lb.-ft. @ 2400 rpm. Oil refill capacity: 5 qt. with filter change. Fuel Requirements: Unleaded.

CHASSIS FEATURES: Separate body and frame.

SUSPENSION AND RUNNING GEAR: Front Suspension: Torsion bars. 2615 lb. capacity with standard 1450 lb. payload capacity. Optional Rating: None. Rear Suspension: Dual-stage semi-elliptical leaf springs, 3000 lbs. Optional with 2000 lb. payload package: 3700 lb. capacity. Front Axle Type and Capacity: 2575 lb. capacity. Optional: None. Rear Axle Type and Capacity: 3650 lb. capacity. Optional: None. Final Drive Ratio: 2.94:1 (with standard 1450 lb. payload package); 3.55:1 (with 2000 lb. payload package). Transfer Case: New Process 231 part-time, two-speed: 2.61, 1.00:1. Brakes: Type: Power, hydraulic. Front: Discs. Rear: Drums. Dimensions: Front: 11.4 in. x 0.87 in. disc. Rear: 9 in. x 2.5 in. (rear brakes for 2000 lb. payload package: 10 in. x 2.5 in. Wheels: 15 x 6.00 stamped steel, argent painted. (15 x 6.00 heavy-duty for 2000 lb. payload package). 15 x 6.00 in. cast aluminum for Dakota Sport. Optional: 15 in. styled steel wheels with bright trim ring and black center cap with molded-on ram's head and argent painted spokes. Requires Prospector Package I and II and 15 in. tires.15 in. x 6 in. cast aluminum wheels. requires Prospector Package II or III and 15 in. tires. Tires: P195/75R15 All-Season steel-belted radial. Dakota Sport: P235/75R15XL outline white letter, Mud and Snow tread. Optional for 1450 lb. payload only: P205/75R15, P235/75R15XL All-Season or Mud and Snow tread steel-belted radial. Standard for 2000 lb. payload package: P235/75R15XL All-Season or Mud and Snow tread. Steering: Integral power steering, recirculating-ball. Turning Circle: 39.6 ft. Optional: None. Standard: Transmission: 5-speed manual overdrive. Optional: 3-speed automatic transmission. Clutch: Single dry plate disc. Clutch diameter: 10.5 in. dia. Optional: None.

VEHICLE DIMENSIONS: Wheelbase: 112 in./124 in. (Dakota Sport available in 112 in. wheelbase form only.) Club cab: 131 in. Overall Length: 184.2 in./202.7 in. Club cab: 203.2 in. Front/Rear Tread: 59.5 in./60.8 in. Overall Height: 64.7 in. Width: 68.4 in. Front/Rear Overhang: 30.4 in./43.6 in. (50.1 for 124 in. wheelbase). Tailgate: Width and Height: 59.6 in. x 17.5 in. Front headroom: 39.5 in. Front shoulder room: 58.0 in. Front hip room: 56.0 in. Rear headroom: Club cab: 36.8 in. Rear shoulder room: Club cab: 58.0 in. Rear hip room: Club cab: 54.0 in. Steering wheel to seat back (max.): 13.3 in.

CAPACITIES: Fuel Tank: 15.9 gal. Optional: 22 gal.

ACCOMMODATIONS: Seating Capacity: Three with standard front bench seat.

INSTRUMENTATION: Speedometer, odometer, electrical system voltage and fuel gauges, warning lights for brake system, emission maintenance reminder, engine coolant temperature, engine oil pressure, fasten seat belts, high beam headlights and turn signals.

OPTIONS: Bright rear step bumper with black step pads, 22 gal. fuel tank with tethered fuel cap, bright trim exterior dual low mount 6 in. x 9 in. mirrors, deluxe bright wheelcovers, bi-level air conditioning, electronically tuned AM/FM stereo radio with four speakers, premium electronically tuned AM/FM stereo radio with four speakers, 120 amp alternator, Sure-Grip rear axle and maximum engine cooling. SE Decor Package. Includes AM/FM electronically tuned radio, bright deluxe wheelcovers, bright full wheel-lip molding, bright grille and headlight bezels, bright taillight housings, brushed finish instrument panel trim bezels, illuminated cigarette lighter, cloth with vinyl trim bench seat (all-vinyl seats available at no extra cost), color-keyed floor carpeting, color-keyed deluxe steering wheel, color-keyed seat track covers, color-keyed steering column, deluxe windshield wipers with intermittent wipe, dual exterior remote control flag-type mirrors, garnish trim on "B" pillar and below rear window, "Leaping Ram" plaque with SE insert on front fenders, molded plastic jack cover, storage tray behind seat on floor and vinyl applique on front door trim. LE Decor Package. Includes AM/FM electronically tuned radio, bright deluxe wheelcovers, bright full wheel-lip molding, bright grille and headlight bezels, bright taillight housings, illuminated cigarette lighter, color-keyed floor carpeting, color-keyed seat track covers, color-keyed steering column, deluxe windshield wipers with intermittent wipe, dual exterior remote control flag-type mirrors, garnish trim on "B" pillar and below rear window, molded plastic jack cover, storage tray behind seat on floor, accessory-type carpeted floor mats, black/dark mist wheel-lip moldings, black sill moldings, color-keyed carpeting on cab back panel, color-keyed cloth-covered sun visors with storage pocket on left side, color-keyed deluxe cloth with vinyl trim bench seat with folding center armrest and hinged seat back (deluxe all-vinyl bench seat available at no extra charge), color-keyed luxury steering wheel, deluxe body sound insulation, black front bumper protective rub strip, front door trim with soft cloth applique and lower carpet insert, Gauge Package, hood insulation pad, Leaping Ram plaque with LE insert on front fenders, Light Package, vanity mirror on passenger side sun visor, black with dark mist trim vinyl lower body side and tailgate moldings with 4x4 stencil, and woodtone trim on instrument panel trim bezels. Prospector I Package. Includes bright deluxe wheelcovers, illuminated cigarette lighter, deluxe windshield wipers with intermittent wipe, Gauge Package, Light Package, 22 gal. fuel tank with tethered cap and sliding rear window, tinted and latchable. Prospector Package II. Includes all items found in the SE Decor Package plus Gauge Package, Light Package, 22 gal. fuel tank with tethered cap and sliding rear window, tinted and latchable. Prospector III Package. Includes all items in the Prospector II Package (except bright deluxe wheelcovers, which were replaced by styled steel 15 in. x 6 in. five-spoke argent painted road wheels. Prospector IV Package. Includes the content of Prospector III Package except for cloth and vinyl bench seat, Leaping Ram plaque with SE insert on front fenders and vinyl applique on front door trim. Additional components consisted of accessory-type carpeted floor mats, black/dark mist wheel-lip moldings, black sill moldings, color-keyed carpeting on cab back panel, color-keyed sun visors with storage pocket on left side, color-keyed deluxe cloth with vinyl trim bench seat with folding center armrest and hinged seat back (deluxe all-vinyl seat available at no extra cost), color-keyed luxury steering wheel, deluxe body sound insulation, black front bumper protective rub strip, front door trim with soft cloth applique and lower carpet insert, hood insulation pad, Leaping Ram plaque with LE insert on front fenders, vanity mirror on passenger side sun visor, black with dark mist trim vinyl lower body side and tailgate moldings with 4x4 stencil, and woodtone trim on instrument panel trim bezels. Prospector I Package. Includes bright deluxe wheelcovers, illuminated cigarette lighter, deluxe windshield wipers with intermittent wipe, Gauge Package, Light Package, 22 gal. fuel tank with tethered cap and sliding rear window, tinted and latchable. Prospector Package II. Includes all items found in the SE Decor Package plus Gauge Package, Light Package, 22 gal. fuel tank with tethered cap and sliding rear window, tinted and latchable. Prospector III Package. Includes all items in the Prospector II Package (except bright deluxe wheelcovers, which were replaced by styled steel 15 in. x 6 in. five-spoke argent-painted road wheels. Prospector IV Package. Includes the content of Prospector III Package except for cloth and vinyl bench seat, Leaping Ram plaque with SE insert on front fenders and vinyl applique on front door trim. Additional components consisted of accessory-type carpeted floor mats, black/Dark mist wheel-lip moldings, black sill moldings, color-keyed carpeting on cab back panel, color-keyed sun visors with storage pocket on left side, color-keyed deluxe cloth with vinyl trim bench seat with folding center armrest and hinged seat back (deluxe all-vinyl seat available at no extra cost), color-keyed luxury steering wheel, deluxe body sound insulation, black front bumper protective rub strip, front door trim with soft cloth applique and lower carpet insert, hood insulation pad, Leaping Ram plaque with LE insert on front fenders, vanity mirror on passenger side sun visor, vinyl lower body side and tailgate moldings, black with dark mist trim and "4x4" stencil on molding, woodtone trim on instrument panel trim bezels and Deluxe Convenience Package. Prospector V Package. Includes all items found Prospector IV Package plus bi-level air conditioning and Power Convenience Package. Deluxe Convenience Package. Available only with Prospector Packages I and II. Includes automatic speed control and tilt steering column. Light Package. Included in LE Decor Package and all Prospector Packages. Includes ashtray light, courtesy light under instrument panel, glove box light, ignition switch light with time delay, swivel-type dome reading/cargo light and underhood light. Snowplow Preparation Package. Includes heavy-duty 120 amp alternator, maximum engine cooling (auxiliary transmission oil to air cooler included with automatic transmission), P235/75R15 steel belted radial Mud and Snow tires (five), 2000 lb. Payload Package and transmission oil overheat warning light with automatic transmission. Two-Tone Paint Package I. Includes color-keyed upper body side and tailgate tape stripes, two-tone paint primary color above tape stripe on cab and box and inside box; secondary color above tape stripe. Two-Tone Paint Package II. Includes black vinyl lower body side and tailgate molding with bright insert along top edge, color-keyed upper body side and tailgate tape stripes, full bright wheel-lip moldings, two-tone paint; primary color above tape stripe on cab and box, inside box and below vinyl molding; secondary color between tape stripe and molding. Power Convenience Package. Available with Prospector Packages III and IV only. Includes power door locks and power windows. 4x4 Protection Package. Includes fuel tank skid plate and transfer case skid plate. Trailer Towing Preparation Package. Includes 120 amp alternator, 22 gal. fuel tank, heavy-duty variable load flasher, maximum engine cooling (transmission oil cooler included with automatic transmission), and five-lead trailer towing harness. Gauge Package. Includes engine coolant temperature gauge, engine oil pressure gauge, low fuel warning light, low washer fluid level warning light and trip odometer. Heavy-Duty Package. Includes 625 amp maintenance-free battery, and heavy-duty front and rear shock absorbers.

HISTORICAL FOOTNOTES: Dodge reported that since its introduction in 1987, the Dakota had improved its share of the small pickup market segment each year. Dodge also noted that 95 percent of Dakota buyers were male, 81 percent were married and the primary use of the Dakota by owners was as a recreational vehicle.

1992 DAKOTA

New for 1992 features began with the availability of new Magnum series V-6 and V-8 engines with multipoint fuel injection. A new 5-speed manual transmission was linked to the V-6. A new heavy-duty 4-speed automatic transmission was standard for the 5.2 liter V-8. Replacing the Sport model was a new Sport Package. No changes were made in appearance of models with this features from that of their 1991 counterparts. A serpentine belt accessory drive with self adjustment was added to the 3.9 liter engine. The standard battery was upgraded to 600 amps. The optional battery was upgraded to 810 amps. Three new exterior colors were introduced: Copper metallic, light sand metallic and dark forest green metallic. A new interior color — Spice/Tan — replaced tundra.

1992 Dodge Dakota LE club coupe pickup

I.D. DATA: The vehicle identification number was located on a V.I.N. plate attached to the driver's side door body latch post. The V.I.N. consisted of 17 elements. The first three entries identified the nation of origin, manufacturer and vehicle type. The fourth entry, a letter, identified the gross vehicle weight. This was followed by three characters identifying the series and body type. The eighth character identified the engine. A check digit followed. Next was a letter representing the model year. The eleventh character identified the assembly plant. The last six digits functioned as the sequential production number.

Body Type	Factory Price	GVW	Shipping Weight	Prod. Total
Dakota				
Sweptline, 111.9 in. wb.	$14,284	N.A.	N.A.	—
Sweptline, 123.9 in. wb.	$14,498	N.A.	N.A.	—
Sport, 111.9 in. wb.	$13,472	N.A.	N.A.	—
Club Coupe, 130.9 in. wb.	$15,438	N.A.	N.A.	—

STANDARD ENGINE: Features include valve rotators, forged connecting rods, and vibration damper. Engine Type: OHV, V-6. Cast iron block and cylinder head. Bore x Stroke: 3.91 in. x 3.312 in. Lifters: Hydraulic. Number of main bearings-5. Fuel Induction: Multipoint Fuel injection. Compression Ratio: 9.2:1. Displacement: 239 cu. in. (3.9 liters). Horsepower: 180 @ 4800 rpm. Torque: 225 lb.-ft. @ 3200 rpm. Fuel Requirements: Unleaded.

OPTIONAL ENGINE: Engine Type: OHV, V-8. Cast iron block and cylinder head. Bore x Stroke: 3.91 in. x 3.312 in. Lifters: Hydraulic. Number of main bearings-5. Fuel Induction: Multipoint Fuel injection. Compression Ratio: 9.2:1. Displacement: 318 cu. in. (5.2 liters). Horsepower: 230 @ 4800 rpm. Torque: 280 lb.-ft. @ 3200 rpm. Oil refill capacity: 5 qt. with filter change. Fuel Requirements: Unleaded.

CHASSIS FEATURES: Separate body and frame.

SUSPENSION AND RUNNING GEAR: Front Suspension: Torsion bars. 2615 lb. capacity with standard 1450 lb. payload capacity. Optional Rating: None. Rear Suspension: Dual-stage semi-elliptical leaf springs, 3000 lbs. Optional with 2000 lb. payload package: 3700 lb. capacity. Front Axle Type and Capacity: 2575 lb. capacity. Optional: None. Rear Axle Type and Capacity: 3650 lb. capacity. Optional: None. Final Drive Ratio: 2.94:1 (with standard 1450 lb. payload package); 3.55:1 (with 2000 lb. payload package). Transfer Case: New Process 231 part-time, two-speed: 2.61, 1.00:1. Brakes: Type: Power, hydraulic. Front: Discs. Rear: Drums. Dimensions: Front: 11.4 in. x 0.87 in. disc. Rear: 9 in. x 2.5 in. (rear brakes for 2000 lb. payload package: 10 in. x 2.5 in. Wheels: 15 x 6.00 stamped steel. Optional: 15 x 6.00 in. Styled steel, 15 x 6.00 in. cast aluminum 6-bolt. Tires: Regular cab: P195/75R15. Club cab: P215/75R15. Optional: P205/75R15, P215/75R15, P235/75R15. Steering: Integral power steering, recirculating-ball. Turning Circle: 112 in. wheelbase: 38.5 ft., 124 in. wheelbase: 42.1 ft., club cab: 44.4 ft. Optional: None. Standard: Transmission: 5-speed manual overdrive. Optional: 3-speed automatic transmission. Clutch: Single dry plate disc. Clutch diameter: 10.5 in. dia. Optional: None.

VEHICLE DIMENSIONS: Wheelbase: 112 in./124 in. (Dakota Sport available in 112 in. wheelbase form only); club cab: 131 in. Overall Length: 184.2 in./202.7 in. Club cab: 203.2 in. Front/Rear Tread: 59.5 in./60.8 in. Overall Height: 64.7 in. Width: 68.4 in. Front/Rear Overhang: 30.4 in./43.6 in. (50.1 for 124 in. wheelbase). Tailgate: Width and Height: 59.6 in. x 17.5 in. Front headroom: 39.5 in. Front shoulder room: 58.0 in. Front hip room: 56.0 in. Rear headroom: Club cab: 36.8 in. Rear shoulder room: Club cab: 58.0 in. Rear hip room: Club cab: 54.0 in. Steering wheel to seat back (max.): 13.3 in.

CAPACITIES: Fuel Tank: 15.9 gal. Optional: 22 gal.

ACCOMMODATIONS: Seating Capacity: Three with standard front bench seat.

INSTRUMENTATION: Speedometer, odometer, electrical system voltage and fuel gauges, warning lights for brake system, emission maintenance reminder, engine coolant temperature, engine oil pressure, fasten seat belts, high beam headlights and turn signals.

OPTIONS: LE Decor Package. SE Decor Package. Air conditioning. Axle ratios. Rear step bumper. Maximum engine cooling. Custom Interior Group. 4x4 Protection Package (skid plates). Heavy-duty electrical system. Heavy-duty suspension. Light Group. Dual exterior 6.00 in. x 9.00 in. mirrors. Dual power remote 6.00 in. x 9.00 in. mirrors. Lower body side moldings.

Off-Road Appearance Group. Two-tone paint. Power door locks and windows. Premium bucket seats with reclining and lumbar features and center console. AM mono/FM stereo ET radio with cassette tape player. Speed control and tilt steering. Snowplow Preparation Package. Tachometer. Trailer Towing Preparation Package. Styled steel wheels. Cast aluminum wheels. Rear sliding window.

HISTORICAL FOOTNOTES: The Dakota was built in Warren, Michigan.

1993 DAKOTA

The 1993 Dakota was available with an optional four-wheel anti-lock brake system. Other changes and new features for 1993 included more comfortable bucket seats, a full stainless steel exhaust system, a new AM stereo/FM stereo radio with cassette tape player and graphic equalizer, more accessible power window and power lock switches, a more comfortable premium split bench seat, and outboard unibelt restraints with "Free Running" cinching tips. Two new exterior colors — Flame red and Emerald green were offered. Six two-tone color combinations were also offered.

1993 Dodge Dakota club coupe pickup

I.D. DATA: The vehicle identification number was located on a V.I.N. plate attached to the driver's side door body latch post. The V.I.N. consisted of 17 elements. The first three entries identified the nation of origin, manufacturer and vehicle type. The fourth entry, a letter, identified the gross vehicle weight. This was followed by three characters identifying the series and body type. The eighth character identified the engine. A check digit followed. Next was a letter representing the model year. The eleventh character identified the assembly plant. The last six digits functioned as the sequential production number.

Body Type	Factory Price	GVW	Shipping Weight	Prod. Total
Dakota				
Sweptline, 111.9 in. wb.	$N.A.	N.A.	N.A.	—
Sweptline, 123.9 in. wb.	$N.A.	N.A.	N.A.	—
Sport, 111.9 in. wb.	$N.A.	N.A.	N.A.	—
Club Coupe, 130.9 in. wb.	$N.A.	N.A.	N.A.	—

STANDARD ENGINE: Features include valve rotators, forged connecting rods, and vibration damper. Engine Type: OHV, V-6. Cast iron block and cylinder head. Bore x Stroke: 3.91 in. x 3.312 in. Lifters: Hydraulic. Number of main bearings-5. Fuel Induction: Multipoint Fuel injection. Compression Ratio: 9.1:1. Displacement: 239 cu. in. (3.9 liters). Horsepower: 180 @ 4800 rpm. Torque: 225 lb.-ft. @ 3200 rpm. Fuel Requirements: Unleaded.

OPTIONAL ENGINE: Engine Type: OHV, V-8. Cast iron block and cylinder head. Bore x Stroke: 3.91 in. x 3.312 in. Lifters: Hydraulic. Number of main bearings-5. Fuel Induction: Multipoint Fuel injection. Compression Ratio: 9.1:1. Displacement: 318 cu. in. (5.2 liters). Horsepower: 230 @ 4800 rpm. Torque: 280 lb.-ft. @ 3200 rpm. Oil refill capacity: 5 qt. with filter change. Fuel Requirements: Unleaded.

CHASSIS FEATURES: Separate body and frame.

SUSPENSION AND RUNNING GEAR: Front Suspension: Torsion bars. 2615 lb. capacity with standard 1450 lb. payload capacity, 0.9 in. dia. stabilizer bar. Optional Rating: None. Rear Suspension: Dual-stage semi-elliptical leaf springs, 3000 lbs. Optional with 2000 lb. payload package: 3700 lb. capacity. Front Axle Type and Capacity: 2575 lb. capacity. Optional: None. Rear Axle Type and Capacity: 3650 lb. capacity. Optional: None. Final Drive Ratio: 3.55:1. Optional: 3.90:1. Transfer Case: New Process 231 part-time, two-speed. 2.61, 1.00:1. Brakes: Type: Power, hydraulic. Front: Discs. Rear: Drums. Dimensions: Front: 11.3 in. x 0.9 in. disc. Rear: 9 in. x 2.5 in. (rear brakes for 2000 lb. payload package: 10 in. x 2.5 in. Wheels: 15 x 6.00 in. stamped steel. Optional: 15 x 6.00 in. Styled steel, 15 x 6.00 in. cast aluminum 6-bolt. Tires: Regular cab: P215/75R15. Optional: P235/75R15AT, P235/75R15XL, P235/75R15XL AT. Steering: Integral power steering, recirculating-ball. Ratio: 14:1. Turning Circle: 112 in. wheelbase: 38.5 ft., 124 in. wheelbase: 42.1 ft., club cab: 44.4 ft. Optional: None. Standard: Transmission: 5-speed manual overdrive. Optional: 4-speed automatic transmission. Clutch: Single dry plate disc. Clutch diameter: 10.5 in. dia. Optional: None.

VEHICLE DIMENSIONS: Wheelbase: 112 in./124 in. (Dakota Sport available in 112 in. wheelbase form only.) Club cab: 131 in. Overall Length: 184.2 in./202.7 in. Club cab: 203.2 in. Front/Rear Tread: 59.5 in./60.8 in. Overall Height: 64.7 in. Width: 68.4 in. Front/Rear Overhang: 30.4 in./43.6 in. (50.1 for 124 in. wheelbase). Tailgate: Width and Height: 59.6 in. x 17.5 in. Front headroom: 39.5 in. Front shoulder room: 58.0 in. Front hip room: 56.0 in. Rear headroom: Club cab: 36.8 in. Rear shoulder room: Club cab: 58.0 in. Rear hip room: Club cab: 54.0 in. Steering wheel to seat back (max.): 13.3 in.

CAPACITIES: Fuel Tank: 15.9 gal. Optional: 22 gal.

ACCOMMODATIONS: Seating Capacity: Three with standard front bench seat.

INSTRUMENTATION: Speedometer, odometer, electrical system voltage and fuel gauges, warning lights for brake system, emission maintenance reminder, engine coolant temperature, engine oil pressure, fasten seat belts, high beam headlights and turn signals.

OPTIONS: LE Decor Package. SE Decor Package. Air conditioning. Axle ratios. Rear step bumper. Maximum engine cooling. Custom Interior Group. 4x4 Protection Package (skid plates). Heavy-duty electrical system. Heavy-duty suspension. Light Group. Dual exterior 6.00 in. x 9.00 in. mirrors. Dual power remote 6.00 in. x 9.00 in. mirrors. Lower body side moldings. Off-Road Appearance Group. Two-tone paint. Power door locks and windows. Premium bucket seats with reclining and lumbar features and center console. AM stereo/FM stereo radio with cassette tape player and graphic equalizer. Speed control and tilt steering. Snowplow Preparation Package. Tachometer. Trailer Towing Preparation Package. Styled steel wheels. Cast aluminum wheels. Rear sliding window. Four-wheel anti-lock brake system.

HISTORICAL FOOTNOTES: The Dakota was built in Warren, Michigan.

DODGE RAIDER
1987-1989

1987 RAIDER

Dodge introduced its version of the Mitsubishi Montero in 1987 as the Dodge Raider. This vehicle with a short 92.5 in. wheelbase and a relatively larger 2.6 liter 4-cylinder engine was available in only one trim level and in a two-door body style.

Standard equipment for the Raider consisted of rear passenger assist grips, cut pile carpeting for the passenger and cargo area, cigarette lighter, electronic digital clock, floor shifter console, side windows demister, remote cable release fuel filler opener, color-keyed headliner, inside hood release, dome light, day/night rearview inside mirror, remote swing-gate lock, reclining cloth and vinyl seats, rear outside-mounted spare tire, adjustable steering column, two-spoke soft touch steering wheel, dual sun visors, 50 amp alternator, 45 amp maintenance-free battery, power steering, stainless steel exhaust system, black painted front bumper and black painted rear step bumper, tinted glass for all windows, cargo tie-down hooks, outside left and right mirrors, front and rear mud guards, skid plates for front differential, transfer case and fuel tank, left and right side sliding rear quarter windows, and intermittent, variable windshield wipers. The Raider's cloth and vinyl seats were available in blue, gray or brown. The exterior color selection consisted of light blue, dark blue, bright red, bright silver, black, gold and white. Available as optional two-tone upper and lower body color combinations were black/gold, dark blue/silver, red/silver and silver/black.

I.D. DATA: The vehicle identification number was located on a V.I.N. plate attached to the driver's side door body latch post.

Body Type	Factory Price	GVW	Shipping Weight	Prod. Total
J43 Utility	$10,165	4310	3219	—

STANDARD ENGINE: Cast iron block, aluminum cylinder head, drop-forged steel crankshaft and connecting rods, chain-driven camshaft, aluminum alloy pistons, counter-rotating balance shafts and MCA Jet combustion system. Engine Type: In-line 4-cyl., OHV, OHC. Bore x Stroke: 3.59 in. x 3.86 in. Compression Ratio: 8.7:1. Displacement: 156 cu. in. (2.6 liters). Horsepower: 109 @ 5000 rpm. Torque: 142 lb.-ft. @ 3000 rpm. Fuel Requirements: Unleaded.

CHASSIS FEATURES: Welded steel body and ladder-type frame.

SUSPENSION AND RUNNING GEAR: Front Suspension: Independent, unequal length A-arms, torsion bars, stabilizer bar. Optional Rating: None. Rear Suspension: Semi-elliptical, longitudinal springs. Optional Rating: None. Final Drive Ratio: 4.62:1. Transfer Case: 2-speed; 1.944:1, 1.00:1. Brakes: Type: Power, hydraulic. Front: Discs. Rear: Drums. Wheels: 15 in. painted wide spoke tires. Optional: 15 in. chrome plated, wide spoke steel wheels with raised white letter tires. Tires: P225/75R15. Steering: Power-assisted. Transmission: 5-speed overdrive manual, all-synchromesh.

VEHICLE DIMENSIONS: Wheelbase: 92.5 in. Overall Length: 157.3 in. Front/Rear Tread: 55.1 in./54.1 in. Overall Height: 72.8 in. Width: 66.1 in.

CAPACITIES: Fuel Tank: 15.9 gals. Optional: None.

ACCOMMODATIONS: Seating Capacity: Two passenger. Four with optional rear seat.

INSTRUMENTATION: Inclinometer, odometer, oil pressure gauge, tachometer, temperature gauge, trip odometer and voltmeter.

OPTIONS AND PRICES: Air conditioning. Rear window electric defroster. Low-mount exterior mirrors. Off-Road Package. Includes driver suspension seat, halogen headlights, headlight washer, and limited slip rear differential. Two-tone paint. AM/FM stereo radio (all radios have four speakers). AM/FM stereo radio with cassette tape player. AM/FM stereo radio with cassette tape player and graphic equalizer. Rear window washer/wiper. Fold-down rear seat. Spare tire cover.

HISTORICAL FOOTNOTES: The Dodge Raider was sold outside the U.S. market as the Mitsubishi Pajero.

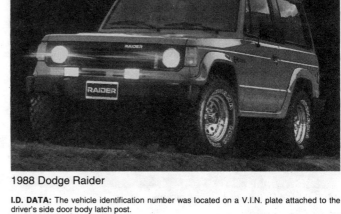

1988 Dodge Raider

I.D. DATA: The vehicle identification number was located on a V.I.N. plate attached to the driver's side door body latch post.

Body Type	Factory Price	GVW	Shipping Weight	Prod. Total
J43 Utility	$11,083	4310	3185	—

STANDARD ENGINE: Cast iron block, aluminum cylinder head, drop-forged steel crankshaft and connecting rods, chain-driven camshaft, aluminum alloy pistons, counter-rotating balance shafts and MCA Jet combustion system. Engine Type: In-line 4-cyl., OHV, OHC. Bore x Stroke: 3.59 in. x 3.86 in. Compression Ratio: 8.7:1. Displacement: 156 cu. in. (2.6 liters). Horsepower: 109 @ 5000 rpm. Torque: 142 lb.-ft. @ 3000 rpm. Fuel Requirements: Unleaded.

CHASSIS FEATURES: Welded steel body and ladder-type frame.

SUSPENSION AND RUNNING GEAR: Front Suspension: Independent, unequal length A-arms, torsion bars, stabilizer bar. Optional Rating: None. Rear Suspension: Semi-elliptical, longitudinal springs. Optional Rating: None. Final Drive Ratio: 4.62:1. Transfer Case: 2-speed; 1.944:1, 1.00:1. Brakes: Type: Power, hydraulic. Front: Discs. Rear: Drums. Wheels: 15 in. painted wide spoke tires. Optional: 15 in. chrome plated, wide spoke steel wheels with raised white letter tires. Tires: P225/75R15. Steering: Power-assisted. Transmission: 5-speed overdrive manual, all-synchromesh.

VEHICLE DIMENSIONS: Wheelbase: 92.5 in. Overall Length: 157.3 in. Front/Rear Tread: 55.1 in./54.1 in. Overall Height: 72.8 in. Width: 66.1 in.

CAPACITIES: Fuel Tank: 15.9 gals. Optional: None.

ACCOMMODATIONS: Seating Capacity: Two passenger. Four with optional rear seat.

INSTRUMENTATION: Inclinometer, odometer, oil pressure gauge, tachometer, temperature gauge, trip odometer and voltmeter.

OPTIONS AND PRICES: Air conditioning. Rear window electric defroster. Low-mount exterior mirrors. Off-Road Package. Includes driver suspension seat, halogen headlights, headlight washer, and limited slip rear differential. Two-tone paint. AM/FM stereo radio (all radios have four speakers). AM/FM stereo radio with cassette tape player. AM/FM stereo radio with cassette tape player and graphic equalizer. Rear window washer/wiper. Fold-down rear seat. Spare tire cover.

HISTORICAL FOOTNOTES: The Dodge Raider's counterpart, the Mitsubishi Pajero was a class winner in the Paris-Dakar endurance rally for five consecutive years.

1988 RAIDER

Standard equipment for the 1988 Raider consisted of rear passenger assist grips, cut pile carpeting for the passenger and cargo area, cigarette lighter, electronic digital clock, floor shifter console, side windows demister, remote cable release fuel filler opener, color-keyed headliner, inside hood release, dome light, day/night rearview inside mirror, remote swing-gate lock, reclining cloth and vinyl seats, rear outside-mounted spare tire, adjustable steering column, two-spoke soft touch steering wheel, dual sun visors, 50 amp alternator, 45 amp maintenance-free battery, power steering, stainless steel exhaust system, black painted front bumper and black painted rear step bumper, tinted glass for all windows, cargo tie-down hooks, outside left and right mirrors, front and rear mud guards, skid plates for front differential, transfer case and fuel tank, left and right side sliding rear quarter windows, and intermittent, variable windshield wipers. The Raider's cloth and vinyl seats were available in blue, gray or brown. The exterior color selection consisted of light blue, dark blue, bright red, bright silver, black, gold and white. Available as optional two-tone upper and lower body color combinations were black/gold, dark blue/silver, red/silver and silver/black.

1989 RAIDER

The Raider was available with a new optional 3.0 liter V-6 engine for 1989. The V-6 engine was included in a V-6 Engine Package that was also required if the Raider was to be equipped with power door locks and power windows with an automatic-down feature. Neither of these items had been available in 1988. Raiders with the V-6 engine carried chrome "V6" identification in the lower right corner of the grille which had a thicker grid band for 1989.

Standard equipment content for 1989 consisted of cut pile carpeting for the passenger and cargo areas, cigarette lighter, electronic digital clock, console and floor shifter, side window demisters, color-keyed headliner, remote cable release for the fuel filler door, heater with rear heat ducts, inside hood release, dome light, map light on right side sun visor, passenger side sun visor-mounted vanity mirror, remote swing-gate lock/release, reclining cloth and vinyl front bucket seats with passenger side walk-in device and see-through adjustable headrests, adjustable steering column, three-spoke, soft touch steering wheel, dual sun visors, 45 amp alternator, 45 amp-hr. maintenance-free battery, stainless steel exhaust system, front black-painted bumper with bumper guards, rear black-painted bumper with bright step, tinted glass for all windows, black-finish grille, cargo tie-down hooks, dual electric horns, exterior left and right black finish mirrors, front and rear mud guards, skid plates for front differential, transfer case and fuel tank; outside-mounted spare tire, spare tire lock, tow hooks-front and rear, left and right side sliding rear windows, intermittent and variable windshield wipers. The Raider's cloth and vinyl high-back and reclining bucket seats were available in these revised color choices for 1989: Light gray/dark gray or light buckskin/dark buckskin. Standard exterior colors for 1989 consisted of: Bright blue metallic, yellow, bright red, bright silver metallic, black, medium buckskin metallic and light buckskin metallic. Optional two-tone combinations (upper/lower body portions) were: Black/light buckskin, bright red/silver, light buckskin/medium buckskin and silver/black.

1989 Dodge Raider

I.D. DATA: The vehicle identification number was located on a V.I.N. plate attached to the driver's side door body latch post.

Body Type	Factory Price	GVW	Shipping Weight	Prod. Total
J43 Utility	$11,083	4310	3185	—

STANDARD ENGINE: Cast iron block, aluminum cylinder head, drop-forged steel crankshaft and connecting rods, chain-driven camshaft, aluminum alloy pistons, counter-rotating balance shafts and MCA Jet combustion system. Engine Type: In-line 4-cyl., OHV, OHC. Bore x Stroke: 3.59 in. x 3.86 in. Compression Ratio: 8.7:1. Displacement: 156 cu. in. (2.6 liters). Horsepower: 109 @ 5000 rpm. Torque: 142 lb.-ft. @ 3000 rpm. Fuel Requirements: Unleaded.

OPTIONAL ENGINE: (Included in V-6 Engine Package). Engine Type: V-6, OHV, OHC. Bore x Stroke: 3.61 in. x 2.99 in. Fuel Induction: Multi-port fuel injection. Compression Ratio: 8.9:1. Displacement: 181 cu. in. (3.0 liters). Horsepower: 143 @ 5000 rpm. Torque: 168 lb.-ft. @ 2500 rpm. Fuel Requirements: Unleaded.

CHASSIS FEATURES: Welded steel body and ladder-type frame.

SUSPENSION AND RUNNING GEAR: Front Suspension: Independent, unequal length A-arms, torsion bars, stabilizer bar. Optional Rating: None. Rear Suspension: Semi-elliptical, longitudinal springs. Optional Rating: None. Final Drive Ratio: 4.62:1. Transfer Case: 2-speed; 1.944:1, 1.00:1. Brakes: Type: Power, hydraulic. Front: Discs. Rear: Drums. Wheels: 15 in. painted wide spoke tires. Optional: 15 in. chrome plated, wide spoke steel wheels with P235/75R15 Mud and Snow raised white letter tires (requires V-6 Engine Package). 15 in. aluminum alloy wheels with P235/75R15 Mud and Snow raised white letter tires. Tires: P225/75R15 Mud-Snow steel-belted radial black sidewalls. Optional: P235/75R15 Mud and Snow. Steering: Power-assisted. Transmission: 5-speed overdrive manual, all-synchromesh. Optional: 4-speed overdrive automatic transmission.

VEHICLE DIMENSIONS: Wheelbase: 92.5 in. Overall Length: 157.3 in. Front/Rear Tread: 55.1 in./54.1 in. Overall Height: 72.8 in. Width: 66.1 in.

CAPACITIES: Fuel Tank: 15.9 gals. V-6 Engine Package includes a 19.8 gal. tank. Optional: None.

ACCOMMODATIONS: Seating Capacity: Two passenger. Four with optional rear seat.

INSTRUMENTATION: Inclinometer, odometer, oil pressure gauge, tachometer, temperature gauge, trip odometer and voltmeter.

OPTIONS: Air conditioning. Carpet protectors. Rear window electric defroster. Dual low-mount black-trimmed exterior mirrors. Two-tone paint. Power door locks (available in package only, requires V-6 Engine Package). Power windows with automatic-down feature on driver's side. (Available in package only, requires V-6 Engine Package). AM/FM stereo radio (available in package only). AM/FM stereo radio with cassette tape player (available in package only). Rear window washer/wiper (available in package only). Special suspension driver's seat (available in package only). Fold-down rear seat. Spare tire cover. Speed control (available in package only). V-6 Engine Package. Includes 3.0 liter V-6 engine, coil spring rear suspension, 19.8 gal. fuel tank, P235/75R15 Mud and Snow steel belted radial black sidewall tires and 'V-6' nameplate on grille. Off-Road Package. Includes driver suspension seat, halogen headlights, headlight washers and limited slip rear differential.

HISTORICAL HIGHLIGHTS: The Raider was not offered by Dodge after the 1989 model year.

DODGE CARAVAN
1991-1993

1991 CARAVAN

The Dodge Caravan, redesigned for 1991, was offered for the first time in an AWD (All-Wheel-Drive) form. Planning for the 1991 model began in 1986. This project drew on a variety of inputs, including consumer suggestion letters that represented the recommendations of the 2 million plus minivan owners. The interior was completely redesigned. Among its features was a new instrument panel with clusters and controls positioned for convenience. Switches were rounded, interior storage space was expanded and there was increased cupholder availability. A glove box was provided along with a storage bin located beneath the front passenger seat. A new quad seating arrangement was added with bucket sears for the second row. Extensive front suspension and steering revisions were implemented to improve the Caravan's handling.

New exterior sheet metal with lower hood and front fender lines, along with a new grille design, aero headlights and windshield treatments were key features of the new Caravan. Other new elements included increased glass area plus lower body facias. The AWD system was available with optional four-wheel anti-lock brakes. The AWD Caravan was offered in base, SE and LE trim levels.

1991 Dodge Caravan AWD

I.D. DATA: The vehicle identification number was located on a V.I.N. plate attached to the driver's side door body latch post. The V.I.N. consisted of 17 elements.

Body Type	Factory Price	GVW	Shipping Weight	Prod. Total
Dodge Caravan				
Caravan 112 in. wb.	$15,232	N.A.	N.A.	—
Grand Caravan 119 in. wb.	$15,831	N.A.	N.A.	—

STANDARD ENGINE: Engine Type: OHV, V-6. Bore x Stroke: 3.66 in. x 3.19 in. Lifters: Hydraulic. Fuel Induction: Electronic fuel injection. Compression Ratio: 8.9:1. Displacement: 201.5 cu. in. (3.3 liters). Horsepower: 150 @ 4800 rpm. Torque: 185 lb.-ft. @ 3600 rpm. Fuel Requirements: Unleaded.

CHASSIS FEATURES: Unibody.

SUSPENSION AND RUNNING GEAR: Front Suspension: Iso-Strut, coil springs, 1.06 in. stabilizer bar. Rear Suspension: Parallel 5-leaf springs with rigid beam axle, gas-charges shock absorbers. Brakes: Type: Power, hydraulic. Front: Discs. Rear: Drums. Dimensions: Front: 10.08 in. dia. disc. Rear: 8.95 in. Wheels: 14 x 5.5 in. Optional: Steel disc or cast aluminum 14 in. x 5.5 in., cast aluminum 15 in. x 6.0 in. Tires: P195/75R14. Optional: P195/75R15, P205/70R14, P205/70R15. Steering: Power, rack and pinion. Ratio: 18.3:1. Turns Lock-to-Lock: 2.96. Turning Circle: 41 ft. (Caravan), 43 ft. (Grand Caravan). Transmission: 4-speed automatic overdrive.

VEHICLE DIMENSIONS: Wheelbase: 112.3 in./119.3 in. Overall Length: 175.9 in./190.5 in. Front/Rear Tread: 59.9 in./62.1 in. Overall Height: 64.6 in./64.8 in. Width: 72.0 in.

CAPACITIES: Fuel Tank: 20.0 gal.

ACCOMMODATIONS: Seating Capacity: 5 passengers, 7 passengers with third seat.

INSTRUMENTATION: 0-100 mph speedometer, odometer, trip odometer, gauges for fuel level, and engine coolant temperature. Warning lights for low fuel, oil pressure, voltage, liftgate open and check engine.

OPTIONS: Front air conditioning. Rear heater/air conditioning (long wheelbase only). Front storage console. Overhead short console. Electric rear window defroster. Power door locks. California emissions. ES Decor Package. Includes silver fascia, conventional spare tire, body side and liftgate stripes, heavy-duty suspension, P205/70R15 tires, and cast aluminum 15 in. wheels. Sunscreen glass. Heavy-Duty Trailer Tow Package. Leather seat trim. Luggage rack. Two-tone paint. AM/FM stereo radio with cassette tape player. AM/FM stereo radio with cassette tape player and Seek-Scan with six Infinity speakers. AM/FM stereo radio with cassette tape player, Seek-Scan and graphic equalizer with Infinity II speakers. Power left seat. Speed control and tilt steering. Sport Roadwheel Package. Heavy-duty suspension. 205/

70R14 steel belted radial white sidewall tires. 195/70R15 steel belted radial white sidewall tires. 205/70R14 steel belted radial black sidewall tires. Conventional size spare tire. Cast aluminum wheels. Power front door locks.

HISTORICAL FOOTNOTES: The Dodge Caravan and its Plymouth counterpart were the top selling Chrysler Corporation vehicles. Two out of every three Chrysler minivans owners purchased another.

1992 CARAVAN

Numerous refinements were found in the 1992 AWD Dodge Caravan. A driver side airbag was now standard. Dual integrated child seats were optional. A new ES Decor Package was available on the Grand Caravan ES. A black finished luggage rack made its debut for 1992. Other new features included flush exterior door handles, new styled steel and a cast aluminum wheels, passenger assist handles on the roof rail for the ES Caravan, stalk-mounted wiper controls and two new exterior colors — Radiant red (short wheelbase) and teal blue.

I.D. DATA: The vehicle identification number was located on a V.I.N. plate attached to the driver's side door body latch post. The V.I.N. consisted of 17 elements.

Body Type	Factory Price	GVW	Shipping Weight	Prod. Total
Dodge Caravan, 112 in. wheelbase				
Caravan SE	$18,682	N.A.	N.A.	—
Caravan LE	$22,442	N.A.	N.A.	—
Caravan ES	$22,953	N.A.	N.A.	—
Caravan LE	$22, 442	N.A.	N.A.	—
Caravan ES	$22,953	N.A.	N.A.	—
Dodge Grand Caravan, 119 in. wheelbase				
Caravan SE	$19,606	N.A.	N.A.	—
Caravan LE	$23,060	N.A.	N.A.	—
Caravan ES	$23,571	N.A.	N.A.	—

STANDARD ENGINE: Engine Type: OHV, V-6. Bore x Stroke: 3.66 in. x 3.19 in. Lifters: Hydraulic. Fuel Induction: Electronic fuel injection. Compression Ratio: 8.9:1. Displacement: 201.5 cu. in. (3.3 liters). Horsepower: 150 @ 4800 rpm. Torque: 185 lb.-ft. @ 3600 rpm. Fuel Requirements: Unleaded.

CHASSIS FEATURES: Unibody.

SUSPENSION AND RUNNING GEAR: Front Suspension: Iso-Strut, coil springs, 1.06 in. stabilizer bar. Rear Suspension: Parallel 5-leaf springs with rigid beam axle, gas-charges shock absorbers. Brakes: Type: Power, hydraulic. Front: Discs. Rear: Drums. Dimensions: Front: 10.20 in. dia. disc. Rear: 8.98 in. Wheels: 14 x 5.5 in. Optional: Steel disc or cast aluminum 15 in. x 6.0 in. Tires: P195/75R14SL. Optional: P205/70R14, P205/70R15. Steering: Power, rack and pinion. Ratio: 18.3:1. Turns Lock-to-Lock: 2.96. Turning Circle: 41 ft. (Caravan), 43 ft. (Grand Caravan). Transmission: 4-speed automatic overdrive.

VEHICLE DIMENSIONS: Wheelbase: 112.3 in./119.3 in. Overall Length: 175.9 in./190.5 in. Front/Rear Tread: 59.9 in./62.1 in. Overall Height: 64.6 in./64.8 in. Width: 72.0 in.

CAPACITIES: Fuel Tank: 18.0 gal.

ACCOMMODATIONS: Seating Capacity: 5 passengers, 7 passengers with third seat.

INSTRUMENTATION: 0-100 mph speedometer, odometer, trip odometer, gauges for fuel level, and engine coolant temperature. Warning lights for low fuel, oil pressure, voltage, liftgate open and check engine.

OPTIONS: Front air conditioning. Rear heater/air conditioning (long wheelbase only). Front storage console. Overhead short console. Electric rear window defroster. Power door locks. California emissions. ES Decor Package. Includes body color fascia and body side chatting, P205/70R15 tires, Sport suspension, cast aluminum 15.0 in. wheels, fog lamps and sunscreen glass. Heavy-Duty Trailer Tow Package. Leather seat trim. Two-tone paint. AM/FM stereo radio with cassette tape player. AM/FM stereo radio with cassette tape player and Seek-Scan with six Infinity speakers. AM/FM stereo radio with cassette tape player Seek-Scan and graphic equalizer with Infinity II speakers. Power left seat. Speed control and tilt steering. Sport Roadwheel Package. Heavy-duty suspension. 205/70R14 steel belted radial white sidewall tires. 195/70R15 steel belted radial white sidewall tires. 205/70R14 steel belted radial black sidewall tires. Conventional size spare tire. Cast aluminum wheels. Power front door locks. Woodgrain Overlay Package.

HISTORICAL FOOTNOTES: The Dodge Caravan and its Plymouth counterpart were built in Windsor, Ontario, Canada and St. Louis, Missouri.

1993 CARAVAN

The Caravan entered 1993 as the number one selling nameplate in the minivan market and the number one selling nameplate for Chrysler Corporation. The new-for-1993 features began with a AWD Decor Package with five spoke aluminum wheels. Other first-time features included a Sport Suspension Package, Quad Command Seating with tilt feature, vertically-adjustable front shoulder belts, a quieter, higher-capacity heater-air conditioner fan, a premium AM/FM stereo radio with graphic equalizer and cassette tape or CD player, and a SE Gold Package with black/gold nerf insets. New exterior colors for 1993 were wildberry pearl-Coat, light driftwood satin glow, sky blue satin glow and flame red. Two new interior colors — slate blue and crimson red were offered.

1993 Dodge Grand Caravan ES AWD

I.D. DATA: The vehicle identification number was located on a V.I.N. plate attached to the driver's side door body latch post. The V.I.N. consisted of 17 elements.

Body Type	Factory Price	GVW	Shipping Weight	Prod. Total
Dodge Caravan, 112 in. wheelbase				
Caravan SE	$N.A.	N.A.	N.A.	—
Caravan LE	$N.A.	N.A.	N.A.	—
Caravan ES	$N.A.	N.A.	N.A.	—
Caravan LE	$N.A.	N.A.	N.A.	—
Caravan ES	$N.A.	N.A.	N.A.	—
Dodge Grand Caravan, 119 in. wheelbase				
Caravan SE	$N.A.	N.A.	N.A.	—
Caravan LE	$N.A.	N.A.	N.A.	—
Caravan ES	$N.A.	N.A.	N.A.	—

STANDARD ENGINE: Engine Type: OHV, V-6. Bore x Stroke: 3.66 in. x 3.19 in. Lifters: Hydraulic. Fuel Induction: Electronic fuel injection. Compression Ratio: 8.9:1. Displacement: 201.5 cu. in. (3.3 liters). Horsepower: 150 @ 4800 rpm. Torque: 185 lb.-ft. @ 3600 rpm. Fuel Requirements: Unleaded.

CHASSIS FEATURES: Unibody.

SUSPENSION AND RUNNING GEAR: Front Suspension: Iso-Strut, coil springs, 1.06 in. stabilizer bar. Rear Suspension: Parallel 5-leaf springs with rigid beam axle, gas-charges shock absorbers. Brakes: Type: Power, hydraulic. Front: Discs. Rear: Drums. Optional: ABS. Dimensions: Front: 11.1 in. dia. disc. Rear: 11.0 in. Wheels: 14 x 5.5 in. (15 x 6.0 in. Grand Caravan). Optional: Steel disc or cast aluminum 15 in. x 6.0 in. Tires: P195/70R14SL (P205/70R15 for Grand Caravan). Optional: P205/70R14, P205/70R15. Steering: Power, rack and pinion. Ratio: 18.3:1. Turns Lock-to-Lock: 2.96. Turning Circle: 41 ft. (Caravan), 43 ft. (Grand Caravan). Transmission: 4-speed automatic overdrive.

VEHICLE DIMENSIONS: Wheelbase: 112.3 in./119.3 in. Overall Length: 175.9 in./190.5 in. Front/Rear Tread: 59.9 in./62.1 in. Overall Height: 64.6 in./64.8 in. Width: 72.0 in.

CAPACITIES: Fuel Tank: 18.0 gal.

ACCOMMODATIONS: Seating Capacity: 5 passengers, 7 passengers with third seat.

INSTRUMENTATION: 0-100 mph speedometer, odometer, trip odometer, gauges for fuel level, and engine coolant temperature. Warning lights for low fuel, oil pressure, voltage, liftgate open and check engine.

OPTIONS: Front air conditioning. Premium AM/FM stereo radio with graphic equalizer and cassette tape or CD player. SE Gold Package. Rear heater/air conditioning (long wheelbase only). Front storage console. Overhead short console. Electric rear window defroster. Power door locks. California emissions. ES Decor Package. AWD Decor Package. Includes body color fascia and body side chatting, P205/70R15 tires, Sport suspension, cast aluminum 15.0 in. wheels, fog lamps and sunscreen glass. Heavy-Duty Trailer Tow Package. Leather seat trim. Luggage rack. Two-tone paint. Sport Suspension Package, Quad Command Seating. AM/FM stereo radio with cassette tape player. AM/FM stereo radio with cassette tape player and Seek-Scan with six Infinity speakers. AM/FM stereo radio with cassette tape player, Seek-Scan and graphic equalizer with Infinity II speakers. Power left seat. Speed control and tilt steering. Sport Roadwheel Package. Heavy-duty suspension. 205/70R14 steel belted radial white sidewall tires. 195/70R15 steel belted radial white sidewall tires. 205/70R14 steel belted radial black sidewall tires. Conventional size spare tire. Cast aluminum wheels. Power front door locks. Woodgrain Overlay Package.

HISTORICAL FOOTNOTES: The Dodge Caravan had the highest resale value in the minivan market.

FORD PICKUPS

1959-1993

1959 PICKUP

Ford introduced its first factory-built four-wheel drive models in 1959. They were available in either 1/2 ton, F-100, or 3/4 ton, F-250 form. Except for their obvious four-wheel drive underpinning (Ford told its service technicians that they "will recognize the distinguishing characteristics of the four wheel drive trucks by the increased road clearance, the transfer case lever in the cab floor, the adaptation of equipment operated by power take-offs, or by the optional cleat-type tires on all four wheels"). The new four-wheel drive Fords shared the mild restyling that distinguished the 1959 pickups from the 1958 models. A new hood featuring FORD lettering in a mesh insert superseded the Ford emblem found on 1958 models. Replacing the mesh grille design of 1958 was a grille format consisting of wide horizontal bars. The hood surface was now smooth rather than ribbed. The parking/directional lights were in the same location as 1958, directly below the dual headlights (which had been introduced on the 1958 models), but they were rectangular rather than round. The front fender series identification was revised to incorporate a Ford truck crest. A new custom cab was introduced with a two-tone instrument panel design that blended into new two-tone door panels. The seats were covered in a new candy-striped nylon-Saran fabric. The custom cab also included a chrome-trimmed instrument cluster and a white steering wheel with a chrome horn ring. Fords with the custom cab also had a front bumper with a center indent for the license plate. Ford offered the F-100 and F-250 four-wheel drive models on a 118 in. wheelbase in three forms: Chassis-cab, Styleside (flush side box with metal floor) or Flareside (with running boards between rear fender and cab, and wooden box with steel skid plates). Exterior colors for 1959 consisted of academy blue, goldenrod yellow, vermilion, April green, meadow green, Indian turquoise, wedgewood blue, colonial white, and raven black. Any color could be combined with colonial white for an extra-cost two-tone color scheme.

1959 Ford F-100 Styleside pickup

I.D. DATA: The V.I.N. consisted of series code, engine code, assembly plant code and sequential production numbers (starting at 100,001).

Body Type	Factory Price	GVW	Shipping Weight	Prod. Total
Series F-100, 118 in. wheelbase				
Chassis & Cab	$2418	5600	3138	—
Pickup, 8 ft. Flareside	$2537	5600	3563	—
Pickup, 8 ft. Styleside	$2553	5600	3573	—
Series F-250, 118 in. wheelbase				
Chassis & Cab	$2537	7400	3758	—
Pickup, 8 ft. Flareside	$2656	7400	3853	—
Pickup, 8 ft. Styleside	$2672	7400	3823	—

STANDARD ENGINE: F-100, F-250: Engine Type: OHV In-line 6-cylinder. Bore x Stroke: 3.62 in. x 3.60 in. Lifters: Hydraulic. Number of main bearings-4. Displacement: 223 cu. in. (3.65 liters). Fuel Induction: Holley 1-bbl. carburetor. Compression Ratio: 8.3:1. Horsepower: 139 @ 4200 rpm. Torque: 207 lb.-ft. @ 1800-2700 rpm. Fuel Requirements: Regular.

OPTIONAL ENGINE: F-100, F-250: Engine Type: OHV V-8. Bore x Stroke: 3.75 in. x 3.30 in. Lifters: Hydraulic. Displacement: 292 cu. in. (4.78 liters). Fuel Induction: 2-barrel downdraft carburetor. Compression Ratio: 8.0:1. Number of main bearings-5. Horsepower: 186 @ 4000 rpm. Torque: 269 lb.-ft. @ 2200-2700 rpm. Oil refill capacity: 5 qt., 6 with oil filter change. Fuel Requirements: Regular.

CHASSIS FEATURES: Separate body and frame. Frame side rail section: 6.0 in. x 2.25 in. x 0.19 in. (F-100 and F-250).

SUSPENSION AND RUNNING GEAR: Front Suspension: F-100: Wide-span semi-elliptical 7-leaf springs, 45 in. x 2.0 in., 950 lb. capacity. F-250: Wide-span semi-elliptical 7-leaf springs, 45 in. x 2.0 in., 1050 lb. capacity. Optional: 6-leaf, 1050 lb. rating for F-100; 7-leaf, 1200 lb. rating for F-250. Rear Suspension: F-100: Wide-span semi-elliptical 7-leaf springs, 52 in. x 2.25 in., 1025 lb. capacity. Optional: F-100: 7-leaf, 2-stage heavy-duty springs with 1350 lb. capacity, 9-leaf, single-stage extra heavy-duty with 1650 lb. capacity. Wide-span semi-elliptical 7-leaf springs, 52 in. x 2.25 in., 1200 lb. capacity. 10 leaf, heavy-duty springs with 1950 lb. capacity, 10 leaf, 2-stage, extra heavy-duty springs with 2400 lb. capacity. Front Axle Type and Capacity: F-100 and F-250: Spicer 55-4F, full-floating, 3000 lb. capacity. Rear Axle Type and Capacity: F-100: Hypoid, Ford-type, 3300 lb. capacity, ratio: 3.89:1. F-250 ratio: 4.56:1. F-250: Hypoid, Spicer, 5000 lb. capacity. Final Drive Ratio: Front: F-100: 3.98:1. F-250: 4.55:1. Rear: F-100: 3.89:1. F-250: 4.56:1. Transfer Case: Type: Constant mesh, 2-speed. Four-ranges : Two-wheel direct drive, four-wheel direct drive, neutral for operating PTO unit, four-wheel low range. Ratios: 1.86:1, 1.00:1. Brakes: Type: Hydraulic, drums front and rear, self-generating. Dimensions: F-100: Front: 11 in. x 2.0 in. Rear: 11.0 in. x 1.75 in. Total lining area: 179.5 sq. in. F-250: Front and Rear: 12.125 in. x 2.00 in. Total lining area: 197.8 sq. in. Wheels: F-100: 5-hole 4 PR, 15 in. x 5K, disc. F-250: 8-hole 6 PR, 16 x 6L, disc. Optional: 17.5 in x 5.25. Tires: F-100: 6.70 x 15, 4 PR. F-250: 6.50 x 16.6 6 PR. Optional: F-100: 6.70 x 15 6 PR, 7.10 x 15, 6 PR, 6.50 x 16, 6 PR, 7.17.5, 6 PR. F-250: 7 x 17.5, 6 PR, 8 x 17.5, 6 PR, 8 x 17.5, 8 PR, 8 x 19.5, 8 PR. Steering: F-100 and F-250: Worm and Roller. Ratio: 18.2:1. Optional: None. Transmission: Type: F-100 and F-250: "Synchro-Silent", helical gears, 3-speed, column-mounted shifter. Transmission Ratios: 6-cyl.: 2.79, 1.70, 1.0:1. Reverse: 2.87:1. V-8: 2.59, 1.58, 1.0:1. Reverse: 2.66:1. Clutch: "Gyro-Grip", semi-centrifugal, hydraulic. 10.5 in. dia. and 96.2 sq. in. with 223-6, 11.0 in. dia. and 123.7 sq. in. with 292 V-8. Optional: 11 in. clutch with 3-spd. 223 -6 (standard with 4-speed transmission). Optional: Three-speed, medium-duty and 4-speed transmission intended for extra-heavy type of service. The 4-speed had a floor-mounted gearshift.

VEHICLE DIMENSIONS: Wheelbase: 118 in.

CAPACITIES: Fuel Tank: 18 gal. Engine Coolant System: 233-6:17.5 qts. 292 V-8: 21 qts.

ACCOMMODATIONS: 3 occupants.

INSTRUMENTATION: Speedometer, odometer, gauges for oil pressure, engine coolant temperature and battery charge.

OPTIONS AND PRICES: Heater and defroster. 292 cu. in. V-8. Tow hooks, radio. Windshield washer. Clearance lights. Exterior rearview mirror with chrome finish. Front grille guard. Directional signals. Seat covers. Heavy-duty radiator. Side-mount for spare tire. Padded dash panel. Front and rear chrome bumper (Styleside body). Left and/or right side telescopic arm mirror. Cigarette lighter. Dome light. Custom cab.

HISTORICAL FOOTNOTES: Although the 1959 Fords were the first to be offered with factory four-wheel drive, the Marmon-Herrington Company of Indianapolis had converted Ford trucks and cars into four-wheel drive vehicles for several decades.

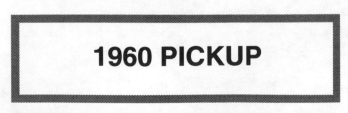

1959 Ford F-250 Styleside pickup with aftermarket wrecker equipment

1960 PICKUP

The 1960 four-wheel drive Fords were available in F-100 and F-250 form. A revamped front end appearance used a mesh lower section linked to a hood with twin vent slots and a Ford badge emblem. The headlamps were positioned in chrome receptacles with a pinched inner section. The front fender series identification was again revised to resemble an arrow.

Technical developments included the use of previously optional higher rate front and rear springs as well as an 11.0 in. clutch as standard equipment for the F-100 and F-250 models. The standard steering now had a 24:1 ratio. The four-wheel drive model body range was expanded to include a Stake and Platform F250. Exterior colors carried over from 1959 were goldenrod yellow, academy blue and raven black. New colors for 1960 were skymist blue, Caribbean turquoise, Adriatic green, Corinthian white, Monte Carlo red and holly green. No longer available were vermilion and meadow green.

1960 Ford F-250 Styleside pickup with aftermarket wrecker equipment

I.D. DATA: The V.I.N. consisted of series code, engine code, assembly plant code and sequential production numbers. (starting at 100,001).

Body Type	Factory Price	GVW	Shipping Weight	Prod. Total
Series F-100, 118 in. wheelbase				
Chassis & Cab	$2445	5600	3138	—
Pickup, 8 ft. Flareside	$2560	5600	3563	—
Pickup, 8 ft. Styleside	$2576	5600	3573	—
Series F-250, 118 in. wheelbase				
Chassis & Cab	$2564	7400	3758	—
Pickup, 8 ft. Flareside	$2681	7400	3853	—
Pickup, 8 ft. Styleside	$2697	7400	3823	—
Platform	$N.A.	7400	3743	—
Stake	$2774	7400	3928	—

STANDARD ENGINE: F-100, F-250: Engine Type: OHV In-line 6-cylinder. Bore x Stroke: 3.62 in. x 3.60 in. Lifters: Hydraulic. Number of main bearings-4. Displacement: 223 cu. in. (3.65 liters). Fuel Induction: Holley 1-bbl. carburetor. Compression Ratio: 8.3:1. Horsepower: 139 @ 4200 rpm. Torque: 207 lb.-ft.@ 1800-2700 rpm. Fuel Requirements: Regular.

OPTIONAL ENGINE: F-100, F-250: Engine Type: OHV V-8. Bore x Stroke: 3.75 in. x 3.30 in. Lifters: Hydraulic. Displacement: 292 cu. in. (4.78 liters). Fuel Induction: 2-barrel downdraft carburetor. Compression Ratio: 8.0:1. Number of main bearings-5. Horsepower: 172 @ 4000 rpm. Torque: 274 lb.-ft.@ 2200-2600 rpm. Oil refill capacity: 5 qt., 6 with oil filter change. Fuel Requirements: Regular.

CHASSIS FEATURES: Separate body and frame. Frame side rail section: 6.0 in. x 2.25 in. x 0.19 in. (F-100 and F-250).

SUSPENSION AND RUNNING GEAR: Front Suspension: F-100: Wide-span semi-elliptical 7-leaf springs, 45 in. x 2.0 in., 1050 lb. capacity. F-250: Wide-span semi-elliptical 7-leaf springs, 45 in. x 2.0 in., 1200 lb. capacity. Rear Suspension: F-100: Wide-span semi-elliptical 10-leaf springs, 52 in. x 2.25 in., 1350 lb. capacity. F-250: 10 leaf, heavy-duty springs with 1950 lb. capacity. Optional: F-100: 9-leaf, single-stage extra heavy-duty with 1650 lb. capacity. F-250: 10 leaf, 2-stage, extra heavy-duty springs with 2400 lb. capacity. Front Axle Type and Capacity: F-100 and F-250: Spicer 55-4F, full-floating, 3000 lb. capacity. Rear Axle Type and Capacity: F-100: Hypoid, Ford-type, 3300 lb. capacity, ratio: 3.89:1. F-250 ratio: 4.56:1. F-250: Hypoid, Spicer, 5000 lb. capacity. Final Drive Ratio: Front: F-100: 3.98:1. F-250: 4.55:1. Rear: F-100: 3.89:1. F-250: 4.56:1. Transfer Case: Type: Constant mesh, 2-speed. Four-ranges: Two-wheel direct drive, four-wheel direct drive, neutral for operating PTO unit, four-wheel low range. Ratios: 1.86:1, 1.00:1. Brakes: Type: Hydraulic, drums front and rear, self-generating. Dimensions: F-100: Front: 11 in. x 2.0 in. Rear: 11.0 in. x 1.75 in. Total lining area: 179.5 sq. in. F-250: Front and rear: 12.125 in. x 2.00 in. Total lining area: 197.8 sq. in. Wheels: F-100: 5-hole 4 PR, 15 in. x 5K, disc. F-250: 8-hole 6 PR, 16 x 6L, disc. Optional: 17.5 in. x 5.25. Tires: F-100: 6.70 x 15, 4 PR. F-250: 6.50 x 16.6 6 PR. Optional: F-100: 6.70 x 15 6 PR, 7.10 x 15, 6 PR, 6.50 x 16, 6 PR, 7.17.5, 6 PR. F-250: 7 x 17.5, 6 PR, 7 x 16, 6 PR, 8 x 17.5, 6 PR, 8 x 17.5, 8 PR, 8 x 19.5, 8 PR. Steering: F-100 and F-250: Worm and Roller. Ratio: 24.0:1. Optional: None. Transmission: Type: F-100 and F-250: "Synchro-Silent", helical gears, 3-speed, column-mounted shifter. Transmission Ratios: 6-cyl.: 2.79, 1.70, 1.0:1. Reverse: 2.87:1. V-8: 2.59, 1.58, 1.0:1. Reverse: 2.66:1. Clutch: "Gyro-Grip", semi-centrifugal, hydraulic. 11.0 in. dia. and 123.7 sq. in. Optional: Three-speed, medium-duty and 4-speed transmission intended for extra-heavy type of service. The 4-speed had a floor-mounted gearshift.

VEHICLE DIMENSIONS: Wheelbase: 118 in.

CAPACITIES: Fuel Tank: 18 gal. Engine Coolant System: 233-6:17.5 qts. 292 V-8: 21 qts.

ACCOMMODATIONS: 3 occupants.

INSTRUMENTATION: Speedometer, odometer, gauges for oil pressure, engine coolant temperature and battery charge.

OPTIONS AND PRICES: Heater and defroster. 292 cu. in. V-8. Tow hooks, radio. Windshield washer. Clearance lights. Exterior rearview mirror with chrome finish. Front grille guard. Directional signals. Seat covers. Heavy-duty radiator. Side-mount for spare tire. Padded dash panel. Front and rear chrome bumper (Styleside body). Left and/or right side telescopic arm mirror. Cigarette lighter. Dome light. Custom cab. Locking rear differential.

HISTORICAL FOOTNOTES: Total Ford light-duty production for 1960 was 255,538.

1961 PICKUP

The 1961 Ford F-100 and F-250 four-wheel drive pickups had a new grille with single seven inch headlights (for lower replacement cost), a new heater-defroster, improved electrical system including a moisture-proof wiring harness and a cab-mounted fuse box, 28 percent more glass area, and 50 percent more ventilation capability. The two-wheel drive F-100 and F-250 Styleside pickups had a new type integral cab and body which eliminated the separation between the cab and box. This resulted in a smoother, clean appearances and, said Ford, promises "greater rigidity and longer life." However, four-wheel drive was not available in this new body format. Instead, they retained the older Styleside and Flareside formats. A new frame was adopted for the four-wheel drive models which resulted in a 2.0 in. increase of the wheelbase of both the F-100 and F-250 models to 120 in. The 223 6-cylinder engine was improved via new oil seals. The 292 V-8 had new connecting rods. Both engines used a new 180 degree thermostat, improved oil bath cleaner, new fans and more durable radiators. The following exterior colors were offered for 1961: Monte Carlo red, goldenrod yellow, raven black, mint green, holly green, Caribbean turquoise, academy blue, starlight blue, and Corinthian white. Two-tone colors were again available by combining Corinthian white with any of the other listed colors.

I.D. DATA: The V.I.N. consisted of series code, engine code, assembly plant code and sequential production numbers (starting at 100,001).

Body Type	Factory Price	GVW	Shipping Weight	Prod. Total
Series F-100, 120 in. wheelbase				
Chassis & Cab	$2501	5600	3127	180
Pickup, 8 ft. Flareside	$2616	5600	3467	2468
Pickup, 8 ft. Styleside	$2631	5600	3429	255
Series F-250, 120 in. wheelbase				
Chassis & Cab	$2682	7400	3369	359
Pickup, 8 ft. Flareside	$2797	7400	3794	1671
Pickup, 8 ft. Styleside	$2811	7400	3799	149
Stake	$2888	7400	3894	—
Platform	$N.A.	7400	3709	—

STANDARD ENGINE: F-100, F-250: Engine Type: OHV In-line 6-cylinder. Bore x Stroke: 3.62 in. x 3.60 in. Lifters: Hydraulic. Number of main bearings-4. Displacement: 223 cu. in. (3.65 liters). Fuel Induction: Holley 1-bbl. carburetor. Compression Ratio: 8.3:1. Horsepower: 135 @ 4000 rpm. Torque: 200 lb.-ft.@ 1800-2400 rpm. Fuel Requirements: Regular.

OPTIONAL ENGINE: F-100, F-250: Engine Type: OHV V-8. Bore x Stroke: 3.75 in. x 3.30 in. Lifters: Hydraulic. Displacement: 292 cu. in. (4.78 liters). Fuel Induction: 2-barrel downdraft carburetor. Compression Ratio: 8.0:1. Number of main bearings-5. Horsepower: 160 @ 4000 rpm. Torque: 270 lb.-ft.@ 1800-2000 rpm. Oil refill capacity: 5 qt., 6 with oil filter change. Fuel Requirements: Regular.

CHASSIS FEATURES: Separate body and frame. Frame side rail section: 6.88 in. x 2.75 in. x 0.15 in.

SUSPENSION AND RUNNING GEAR: Front Suspension: F-100: Wide-span semi-elliptical 7-leaf springs, 45 in. x 2.0 in., 1050 lb. capacity. F-250: Wide-span semi-elliptical 7-leaf springs, 45 in. x 2.0 in., 1200 lb. capacity. Rear Suspension: F-100: Wide-span semi-elliptical 10-leaf springs, 52 in. x 2.25 in., 1350 lb. capacity. F-250: 10 leaf, heavy-duty springs with 1950 lb. capacity. Optional: F-100: 9-leaf, single-stage extra heavy-duty with 1650 lb. capacity. F-250: 10 leaf, 2-stage, extra heavy-duty springs with 2400 lb. capacity. Front Axle Type and Capacity: F-100 and F-250: Spicer 55-4F, full-floating, 3000 lb. capacity. Optional: F-250: heavy-duty 3500 lb. rated. Rear Axle Type and Capacity: F-100: Hypoid, Ford-type, 3300 lb. capacity, ratio: 3.89:1. F-250 ratio: 4.56:1. F-250: Hypoid, Spicer, 5000 lb. capacity. Final Drive Ratio: Front: F-100: 3.98:1. F-250: 4.55:1. Rear: F-100: 3.89:1. F-250: 4.56:1. Transfer Case: Type: Constant mesh, 2-speed. Four-ranges: Two-wheel direct drive, four-wheel direct drive, neutral for operating PTO unit, four-wheel low range. Ratios: 1.86:1, 1.00:1. Brakes: Type: Hydraulic, drums front and rear, self-generating. Dimensions: F-100: Front: 11 in. x 2.0 in. Rear: 11.0 in. x 1.75 in. Total lining area: 179.5 sq. in. F-250: Front and Rear: 12.125 in. x 2.00 in. Total lining area: 197.8 sq. in. Wheels: F-100: 5-hole 4 PR, 15 in. x 5K, disc. F-250: 8-hole 6 PR, 16 x 6L, disc. Optional: 17.5 in x 5.25. Tires: F-100: 6.70 x 15, 4 PR. F-250: 6.50 x 16.6 6 PR. Optional: F-100: 6.70 x 15 6 PR, 7.10 x 15, 6 PR, 6.50 x 16, 6 PR, 7.17.5, 6 PR. F-250: 7 x 17.5, 6 PR, 7 x 16, 6 PR, 8 x 17.5, 6 PR, 8 x 17.5, 8 PR, 8 x 19.5, 8 PR. Steering: F-100 and F-250: Worm and Roller. Ratio: 24.0:1. Optional: None. Transmission: Type: F-100 and F-250: "Synchro-Silent", helical gears, 3-speed, column-mounted shifter. Transmission Ratios: 6-cyl.: 2.79, 1.70, 1.0:1. Reverse: 2.87:1. V-8: 2.59, 1.58, 1.0:1. Reverse: 2.66:1. Clutch: "Gyro-Grip", semi-centrifugal, hydraulic. 11.0 in. dia. and 123.7 sq. in. Optional: Three-speed, medium-duty and 4-speed transmission intended for extra-heavy type of service. The 4-speed had a floor-mounted gearshift.

VEHICLE DIMENSIONS: Wheelbase: 120 in.

CAPACITIES: Fuel Tank: 18 gal. Engine Coolant System: 223-6:17.5 qts. 292 V-8: 21 qts.

ACCOMMODATIONS: 3 occupants.

INSTRUMENTATION: Speedometer, odometer, gauges for oil pressure, engine coolant temperature and battery charge.

OPTIONS AND PRICES: 292 V-8-$118. Tow hooks, radio. Passenger side armrest. Passenger side sun visor. Recirculating heater. Fresh-Air heater. Windshield washer. Clearance lights. Exterior rearview mirror with chrome finish. Front grille guard. Directional signals. Seat covers. Heavy-duty radiator. Side-mount for spare tire. Padded dash panel. Front and rear chrome bumper (Styleside body). Painted rear bumper. Tinted windshield. Left and/or right side telescopic arm mirror. Cigarette lighter. Dome light. Custom cab. Includes twill stripe woven plastic upholstery with brown woven-in bolster and brown Morocco-grain vinyl facings, chrome-trimmed instrument panel cluster, white steering wheel with chrome horn ring, foam rubber in seat cushion and seat back, bright grille and headlight assembly, bright metal windshield reveal molding, matched locks on both doors, and coat hook. Locking rear differential. Directional signals. Windshield washer. Rear wraparound window for Styleside cab.

HISTORICAL FOOTNOTES: Ford's 1961 truck line represented the greatest commercial vehicle expansion in Ford Motor Company's 58 year history. Wilbur Chase, truck marketing manager for Ford Division said the 1961 Ford truck line "exemplifies Ford's efforts to supply truck operators with durable, reliable tools, while incorporating the latest proven engineering advancements that will maintain Ford's historic leadership in truck economy."

1962 PICKUP

The F-100 and F-250 four-wheel drive pickups received a new front end look that repositioned the FORD lettering from the grille (where it had been in 1961) to a spot just above the grille. The block letter's size was also reduced for 1962. Ford recommended a 4000 mile engine oil change interval for vehicles operating in normal use conditions. Basic standard equipment included a driver-side sun visor, dome light, painted front bumper, electric windshield wipers, oil filter, dispatch box and rearview mirror.

I.D. DATA: The V.I.N. consisted of series code, engine code, assembly plant code and sequential production numbers. (starting at 100,0001).

Body Type	Factory Price	GVW	Shipping Weight	Prod. Total
Series F-100, 118 in. wheelbase				
Chassis & Cab	$2514	5600	3127	—
Pickup, 8 ft. Flareside	$2629	5600	3467	—
Pickup, 8 ft. Styleside	$2645	5600	3429	—
Series F-250, 120 in. wheelbase				
Chassis & Cab	$2706	6600[1]	3309	—
Pickup, 8 ft. Flareside	$2810	6600	3859	—
Pickup, 8 ft. Styleside	$2826	6600	3849	—
Platform	N.A.	6600	3749	—
Stake	$2875	6600	3934	—

NOTE 1: 7400 lb. GVW optional for all F-250 models, requires 4-speed manual transmission.

STANDARD ENGINE: F-100, F-250: Engine Type: OHV In-line 6-cylinder. Bore x Stroke: 3.62 in. x 3.60 in. Lifters: Hydraulic. Number of main bearings-4. Displacement: 223 cu. in. (3.65 liters). Fuel Induction: Holley 1-bbl. carburetor. Compression Ratio: 8.3:1. Horsepower: 135 @ 4000 rpm. Torque: 200 lb.-ft.@ 1800-2400 rpm. Fuel Requirements: Regular.

OPTIONAL ENGINE: F-100, F-250: Engine Type: OHV V-8. Bore x Stroke: 3.75 in. x 3.30 in. Lifters: Hydraulic. Displacement: 292 cu. in. (4.78 liters). Fuel Induction: 2-barrel downdraft carburetor. Compression Ratio: 8.0:1. Number of main bearings-5. Horsepower: 160 @ 4000 rpm. Torque: 270 lb.-ft.@ 1800-2000 rpm. Oil refill capacity: 5 qt., 6 with oil filter change. Fuel Requirements: Regular.

CHASSIS FEATURES: Separate body and frame. Frame side rail section: 6.88 in. x 2.75 in. x 0.15 in.

SUSPENSION AND RUNNING GEAR: Front Suspension: F-100: Wide-span semi-elliptical 7-leaf springs, 45 in. x 2.0 in., 1050 lb. capacity. F-250: Wide-span semi-elliptical 7-leaf springs, 45 in x 2.0 in., 1200 lb. capacity. Rear Suspension: F-100: Wide-span semi-elliptical 10-leaf springs, 52 in. x 2.25 in., 1350 lb. capacity. F-250: 10 leaf, heavy-duty springs with 1950 lb. capacity. Optional: 9-leaf, single-stage extra heavy-duty with 1650 lb. capacity. F-250: 10 leaf, 2-stage, extra heavy-duty springs with 2400 lb. capacity. Front Axle Type and Capacity: F-100 and F-250: Spicer 55-4F, full-floating, 3000 lb. capacity. Optional: F-250: heavy-duty 3500 lb. rated. Rear Axle Type and Capacity: F-100: Hypoid, Ford-type, 3300 lb. capacity, ratio: 3.89:1. F-250 ratio: 4.56:1. F-250: Hypoid, Spicer, 5000 lb. capacity. Final Drive Ratio: Front: F-100: 3.98:1. F-250: 4.55:1. Rear: F-100: 3.89:1. F-250: 4.56:1. Transfer Case: Type: Constant mesh, 2-speed. Four-ranges: Two-wheel direct drive, four-wheel direct drive, neutral for operating PTO unit, four-wheel low range. Ratios: 1.86:1, 1.00:1. Brakes: Type: Hydraulic, drums front and rear, self-generating. Dimensions: F-100: Front: 11 in. x 2.0 in. Rear: 11.0 in x 1.75 in. Total lining area: 179.5 sq. in. F-250: Front and Rear: 12.125 in. x 2.00 in. Total lining area: 197.8 sq. in. Wheels: F-100: 5-hole 4 PR, 15 in. x 5K, disc. F-250: 8-hole 6 PR, 16 x 6L, disc. Optional: 17.5 in x 5.25. Tires: F-100: 6.70 x 15, 4 PR. F-250: 6.50 x 16.6 6 PR. Optional: F-100: 6.70 x 15 6 PR, 7.10 x 15, 6 PR, 6.50 x 16, 6 PR, 7.17.5, 6 PR. F-250: 7 x 17.5, 6 PR, 7 x 16, 6 PR, 8 x 17.5, 6 PR, 8 x 17.5, 8 PR, 8 x 19.5, 8 PR. Steering: F-100 and F-250: Worm and Roller. Ratio: 24.0:1. Optional: None. Transmission: Type: F-100 and F-250: "Synchro-Silent", helical gears, 3-speed, column-mounted shifter. Transmission Ratios: 6-cyl.: 2.79, 1.70, 1.0:1. Reverse: 2.87:1. V-8: 2.59, 1.58, 1.0:1. Reverse: 2.66:1. Clutch: "Gyro-Grip", semi-centrifugal, hydraulic. 11.0 in. dia. and 123.7 sq. in. Optional: Three-speed, medium-duty and 4-speed transmission intended for extra-heavy type of service. The 4-speed had a floor-mounted gearshift.

VEHICLE DIMENSIONS: Wheelbase: 120 in.

CAPACITIES: Fuel Tank: 18 gal. Engine Coolant System: 233-6:17.5 qts. 292 V-8: 21 qts.

ACCOMMODATIONS: 3 occupants.

INSTRUMENTATION: Speedometer, odometer, gauges for oil pressure, engine coolant temperature and battery charge.

OPTIONS AND PRICES: 292 V-8-$118. Tow hooks, radio. Passenger side armrest. Passenger side sun visor. Recirculating heater. Fresh-Air heater. Windshield washer. Clearance lights. Exterior rearview mirror with chrome finish. Front grille guard. Directional signals. Seat covers. Heavy-duty radiator. Side-mount for spare tire. Padded dash panel. Front and rear chrome bumper (Styleside body). Painted rear bumper. Tinted windshield. Left and/or right side telescopic arm mirror. Cigarette lighter. Dome light. Custom cab. Includes twill stripe woven plastic upholstery with brown woven-in bolster and brown Morocco-grain vinyl facings, chrome-trimmed instrument panel cluster, white steering wheel with chrome horn ring, foam rubber in seat cushion and seat back, bright grille and headlight assembly, bright metal windshield reveal molding, matched locks on both doors, and coat hook. Locking rear differential. Directional signals. Windshield washer. Rear wraparound window for Styleside cab.

HISTORICAL FOOTNOTES: The 1962 four-wheel drive Ford models were announced in the fall of 1961.

1963 PICKUP

A new grille with four sets of horizontal slats was the primary exterior feature of the 1963 F-100 and F-250 four-wheel drive pickups. Interior changes included repositioned pedals that were now closer to the floor, a three-spoke steering wheel, seats filled with a new synthetic foam and standard locks on both doors.

I.D. DATA: The first letter and two digits represent the series. Next was the engine code for the engine, letter code for the assembly plant, then six digits which indicated sequential production numbers.

Body Type	Factory Price	GVW	Shipping Weight	Prod. Total
Series F-100, 120 in. wheelbase				
Chassis & Cab	$2539	5600	3437	179
Pickup, 8 ft. Flareside	$2653	5600	3804	967
Pickup, 8 ft. Styleside	$2681	5600	3854	2809
Series F-250, 120 in. wheelbase				
Chassis & Cab	$2720	7400	3504	348
Pickup, 8 ft. Flareside	$2835	7400	3954	865
Pickup, 8 ft. Styleside	$2861	7400	3949	1835

STANDARD ENGINE: F-100, F-250: Engine Type: OHV In-line 6-cylinder. Bore x Stroke: 3.62 in. x 3.60 in. Lifters: Hydraulic. Number of main bearings-4. Displacement: 223 cu. in. (3.65 liters). Fuel Induction: Holley 1-bbl. carburetor. Compression Ratio: 8.3:1. Horsepower: 135 @ 4000 rpm. Torque: 200 lb.-ft.@ 1800-2400 rpm. Fuel Requirements: Regular.

OPTIONAL ENGINE: F-100, F-250: Engine Type: OHV V-8. Bore x Stroke: 3.75 in. x 3.30 in. Lifters: Hydraulic. Displacement: 292 cu. in. (4.78 liters). Fuel Induction: 2-barrel downdraft carburetor. Compression Ratio: 8.0:1. Number of main bearings-5. Horsepower: 160 @ 4000 rpm. Torque: 270 lb.-ft.@ 1800-2000 rpm. Oil refill capacity: 5 qt., 6 with oil filter change. Fuel Requirements: Regular.

CHASSIS FEATURES: Separate body and frame. Frame side rail section: 6.88 in. x 2.75 in. x 0.15 in.

SUSPENSION AND RUNNING GEAR: Front Suspension: F-100: Wide-span semi-elliptical 7-leaf springs, 45 in. x 2.0 in., 1050 lb. capacity. F-250: Wide-span semi-elliptical 7-leaf springs, 45 in. x 2.0 in., 1200 lb. capacity. Rear Suspension: F-100: Wide-span semi-elliptical 10-leaf springs, 52 in. x 2.25 in., 1350 lb. capacity. F-250: 10 leaf, heavy-duty springs with 1950 lb. capacity. Optional: F-100: 9-leaf, single-stage extra heavy-duty with 1650 lb. capacity. F-250: 10 leaf, 2-stage, extra heavy-duty springs with 2400 lb. capacity. Front Axle Type and Capacity: F-100 and F-250: Spicer 55-4F, full-floating, 3000 lb. capacity. Optional: F-250: heavy-duty 3500 lb. rated. Rear Axle Type and Capacity: F-100: Hypoid, Ford-type, 3300 lb. capacity, ratio: 3.89:1. F-250 ratio: 4.56:1. F-250: Hypoid, Spicer, 5000 lb. capacity. Final Drive Ratio: F-100: 3.98:1. F-250: 4.55:1. Rear: F-100: 3.89:1. F-250: 4.56:1. Transfer Case: Type: Constant mesh, 2-speed. Four-ranges: Two-wheel direct drive, four-wheel direct drive, neutral for operating PTO unit, four-wheel low range. Ratios: 1.86:1, 1.00:1. Brakes: Type: Hydraulic, drums front and rear, self-generating. Dimensions: F-100: Front: 11 in. x 2.0 in. Rear: 11.0 in. x 1.75 in. Total lining area: 179.5 sq. in. F-250: Front and Rear: 12.125 in. x 2.00 in. Total lining area: 197.8 sq. in. Wheels: F-100: 5-hole 4 PR, 15 in. x 5K, disc. F-250: 8-hole 6 PR, 16 x 6L, disc. Optional: 17.5 in x 5.25. Tires: F-100: 6.70 x 15, 4 PR. F-250: 6.50 x 16.6 6 PR. Optional: F-100: 6.70 x 15 6 PR, 7.10 x 15, 6 PR, 6.50 x 16, 6 PR, 7.17.5, 6 PR. F-250: 7 x 17.5, 6 PR, 7 x 16, 6 PR, 8 x 17.5, 6 PR, 8 x 17.5, 8 PR, 8 x 19.5, 8 PR. Steering: F-100 and F-250: Worm and Roller. Ratio: 24.0:1. Optional: None. Transmission: Type: F-100 and F-250: "Synchro-Silent", helical gears, 3-speed, column-mounted shifter. Transmission Ratios: 6-cyl.: 2.79, 1.70, 1.0:1. Reverse: 2.87:1. V-8: 2.59, 1.58, 1.0:1. Reverse: 2.66:1. Clutch: "Gyro-Grip", semi-centrifugal, hydraulic. 11.0 in. dia. and 123.7 sq. in. Optional: Three-speed, medium-duty and 4-speed transmission intended for extra-heavy type of service. The 4-speed had a floor-mounted gearshift.

VEHICLE DIMENSIONS: Wheelbase: 120 in.

CAPACITIES: Fuel Tank: 18 gal. Engine coolant system: 233-6:17.5 qts. 292 V-8: 21 qts.

ACCOMMODATIONS: 3 occupants.

INSTRUMENTATION: Speedometer, odometer, gauges for oil pressure, engine coolant temperature and battery charge.

OPTIONS AND PRICES: 292 V-8-$118. 42 and 60 amp alternators. Tow hooks, radio. Passenger side armrest. Passenger side sun visor. Recirculating heater. Fresh-Air heater. Windshield washer. Clearance lights. Exterior rearview mirror with chrome finish. Front grille guard. Directional signals. Seat covers. Heavy-duty radiator. Side-mount for spare tire. Padded dash panel. Front and rear chrome bumper (Styleside body). Painted rear bumper. Tinted windshield. Left and/or right side telescopic arm mirror. Cigarette lighter. Dome light. Custom cab. Includes twill stripe woven plastic upholstery with brown woven-in bolster and brown Morocco-grain vinyl facings, chrome-trimmed instrument panel cluster, white steering wheel with chrome horn ring, foam rubber in seat cushion and seat back, bright grille and headlight assembly, bright metal windshield reveal molding, matched locks on both doors, and coat hook. Locking rear differential. Directional signals. Windshield washer. Rear wraparound window for Styleside cab.

HISTORICAL FOOTNOTES: Ford Motor Company celebrated its 60th anniversary in 1963. Calendar year production of all light truck models was 315,274.

1964 PICKUP

Yet another grille variation set the latest four-wheel drive Fords apart from their year-old counterparts. For 1964 the grille consisted of eight rectangular stamping placed in a a two-tier fashion. The parking/directionals were found in the same location as 1963. The FORD block letters above the grille were more widely spaced than in 1963. The cab roof was raised one inch. A three-spoke steering wheel was again used but it was now color-keyed to the truck color. Additional refinements for 1964 consisted of more thickly padded seat backs and the use of an additional four pounds of insulation. The standard exterior color selection for 1964 consisted of rangoon red, bengal tan, raven black, Navajo beige, holly green, Caribbean turquoise, academy blue, skylight blue, Wimbledon white, pure white and chrome yellow. Two-tone color combination of any of the standard colors, except pure white and chrome yellow with Wimbledon white on roof and around cab back panel above beltline. Standard equipment for the F-100 and F-250 included painted front bumper, under frame spare tire carrier, dome light, left and right side door locks, single electric horn, rear painted hubcaps, inside rearview mirror (pickups), left hand non-telescopic mirror (cabs), directional signals and single-speed electric windshield wipers.

1964 Ford F-250 Styleside pickup

I.D. DATA: The first letter and two digits represent the series. Next was the engine code for the engine, letter code for the assembly plant, then six digits which indicated sequential production numbers. Both the F-100 and F-250 Series began with a 445000 production number.

Body Type	Factory Price	GVW	Shipping Weight	Prod. Total
Series F-100, 120 in. wheelbase				
Chassis & Cab	$2539	5600	3455	330
Pickup, 8 ft. Flareside	$2653	5600	3820	802
Pickup, 8 ft. Styleside	$2681	5600	3820	2922
Series F-250, 120 in. wheelbase				
Chassis & Cab	$2627	7700	3540	410
Pickup, 8 ft. Flareside	$2739	7700	3995	1028
Pickup, 8 ft. Styleside	$2756	7700	4005	2232

STANDARD ENGINE: F-100, F-250: Engine Type: OHV In-line 6-cylinder. Bore x Stroke: 3.62 in. x 3.60 in. Lifters: Hydraulic. Number of main bearings-4. Displacement: 223 cu. in. (3.65 liters). Fuel Induction: Holley 1-bbl. downdraft carburetor. Compression Ratio: 8.1:1. Horsepower: Gross: 135 @ 4000 rpm. Net: 114 @ 3600 rpm. Torque: Gross: 200 lb.-ft.@ 1800-2400 rpm. Net: 186 lb.-ft. @ 1600-2200 rpm. Fuel Requirements: Regular.

OPTIONAL ENGINE: F-100, F-250: Engine Type: OHV V-8. Bore x Stroke: 3.75 in. x 3.30 in. Lifters: Hydraulic. Displacement: 292 cu. in. (4.78 liters). Fuel Induction: 2-barrel downdraft carburetor. Compression Ratio: 8.0:1. Number of main bearings-5. Horsepower: Gross: 160 @ 4000 rpm. Net: 135 @ 3800 rpm. Torque: Gross: 270 lb.-ft.@ 1800-2000 rpm. Net: 245 lb.-ft. @ 1800-2000 rpm. Oil refill capacity: 5 qt., 6 with oil filter change. Fuel Requirements: Regular.

CHASSIS FEATURES: Separate body and frame. Frame side rail section: 6.88 in. x 2.75 in. x 0.15 in. Section modulus: 4.74.

SUSPENSION AND RUNNING GEAR: Front Suspension: F-100: Wide-span semi-elliptical 6-leaf springs, 48 in. x 2.5 in. Capacity at pad: 1200 lb. Max. capacity at ground: 1445 lb. Deflection rate: 410 lb./in. F-250: Wide-span semi-elliptical 6-leaf springs, 48 in. x 2.5 in. Capacity at pad: 1350 lb. Max. capacity at ground: 1640 lb. Deflection rate: 450 lb./in. Optional: F-250: Semi-elliptical 6-leaf springs, 48 in. x 2.5 in. Capacity at pad: 1550 lb. Max. capacity at ground: 1890 lb. Deflection rate: 525 lb./in. Rear Suspension: F-100: Wide-span semi-elliptical 7-leaf springs, 52 in. x 2.25 in. Capacity at pad: 1450 lb. Max. capacity at ground: 1680 lb. Deflection rate: 225-340 lb./in. F-250: Semi-elliptical 10-leaf springs, 52 in. x 2.25 in. Capacity at pad: 1950 lb. Max. capacity at ground: 2200 lb. Deflection rate: 265-450 lb./in. Optional: F-100: Semi-elliptical 10-leaf springs, 52 in. x 2.25 in. Capacity at pad: 1950 lb. Max. capacity at ground: 2200 lb. Deflection rate: 265-450 lb./in. F-250: Semi-elliptical 10-leaf springs, 52 in. x 2.25 in. Capacity at pad: 2400 lb. Max. capacity at ground: 2680 lb. Deflection rate: 315-520 lb./in. Front Axle Type and Capacity: F-100 and F-250: Spicer model 2559, 3000 lb. capacity, full-floating, Hotchkiss. Ratio: F-100: 3.92:1, F-250: 4.55:1. Optional: F-100 and F-250: Spicer model 2558, 3500 lb. capacity, full-floating, Hotchkiss. Rear Axle Type and Capacity: F-100: Hypoid, Ford-3300, 3800 lb. capacity, semi-floating, Hotchkiss. F-250: Full-floating, Hotchkiss. Spicer model 60, 5200 lb. capacity. Final Drive Ratio: Front: F-100: 3.92:1. F-250: 4.55:1. Rear: F-100: 3.89:1. F-250: 4.56:1. Transfer Case: Type: Constant mesh, 2-speed. Spicer model 24. Ratios: 1.86:1, 1.00:1. Brakes: Type: Hydraulic, drums front and rear, self-generating. Dimensions: F-100: Front: 11 in. x 2.0 in. Rear: 11.0 in. x 1.75 in. Total lining area: 179.5 sq. in. F-250: Front and Rear: 12.125 in. x 2.00 in. Total lining area: 197.8 sq. in. Wheels: F-100: 5-hole stamped disc, 15 in. x 5.5K, disc. F-250: 8-hole stamped disc, 16 x 6L, disc. Optional: Tires: F-100: 6.70 x 15, 4 PR. F-250: 6.50 x 16.6 6 PR. Optional: F-100: Tubeless tires: 6.70 x 15 4 PR; 6.70 x 15 6 PR; 7.10 x 15,4 PR; 7.10 x 15, 6 PR; 6.50 x 16, 6 PR; 7.17.5, 6 PR. Tube-type tires: 6.50 x 16, 6 PR; 7.0 x 15, 6 PR. F-250: Tubeless tires: 6.50 x 16, 6 PR; 7.00 x 16, 6 PR; 7 x 17.5, 6 PR; 8 x 17.5, 6 PR; 8 x 17.5, 8 PR; 8 x 19.5, 8 PR. Tube-type tires: 6.50 x 16, 6 PR; 6.50 x 16, 6 PR, 7.00 x 16, 6 PR, 7.00 x 17, 8 PR; 7.50 x 16, 6 PR; 7.50 x 17, 8 PR. Steering: Type: Gemer #375, Worm and Roller, 18 in. dia. steering wheel. Turning circle: F-100: 49.1 ft. F-250: 48.9 ft. Ratio: 24.2:1. Optional: None. Transmission: Type: F-100 and F-250: "Synchro-Silent", helical gears, 3-speed, column-mounted shifter. Transmission Ratios: 6-cyl.: 2.79, 1.70, 1.0:1. Reverse: 2.87:1. V-8: 2.59, 1.58, 1.0:1. Reverse: 2.66:1. Clutch: "Gyro-Grip", semi-centrifugal, hydraulic. 11.0 in. dia. and 123.7 sq. in. Optional: Synchro-Silent Warner T-98A with floor-mounted gearshift. Ratios: 6.40, 3.09, 1.69, 1.00:1. Reverse: 7.82:1.

VEHICLE DIMENSIONS: Wheelbase: 120 in. Overall length: F-100 cab: 201.9 in., 8 ft. Flareside: 205.5 in., Styleside: 203.7 in. F-250: Cab: 201.9 in., 8 ft. Flareside: 205.5 in., Styleside: 205.0 in., Stake and Platform: 202.8 in. Front/Rear Overhang: 33.5 in./48.4 in. Height: 77.5 in. Width: 79.8 in. Front/Rear tread: 64.1 in./60.4-0 in.

CAPACITIES: Fuel Tank: 18 gal. Engine Coolant System: 233-6:13.5 qts. 292 V-8: 16.5 qts. (21.0 qt. optional).

ACCOMMODATIONS: 3 occupants.

INSTRUMENTATION: Speedometer, odometer, gauges for oil pressure, engine coolant temperature and battery charge.

OPTIONS AND PRICES: 292 V-8. Extra Cooling radiator. Closed crankcase ventilation (required for California). Velocity controlled governor. 42 amp alternator. 52 amp alternator. 60 amp alternator. Limited slip rear axle (3.92:1 ratio with 3-spd. trans.; 4.10:1 with V-8, includes 4.09:1 front axle ratio). 70 amp-hr. battery. Free-running front Spicer hubs. Two-stage 1950 lb. capacity rear springs. Warner T98A 4-speed trans (recommended for tow truck and snowplow applications). Driver's side armrest. Passenger side armrest. Cigarette lighter. Custom cab. Laminated sheet door glass. Tinted windshield glass. Fresh-Air heater and defroster. Recirculating-type heater and defroster. Inside safety mirror (standard for pickups). Exterior chrome left and right side mirrors. Non-telescopic 5 in. x 5 in. right side mirror. Non-telescopic 5 in. x 5 in. left side mirror. Telescopic 5 in. x 8 in. left and/or right side mirrors. Western-type 5 in. x 10.0 in. left and/or right side mirrors. Two-tone paint. Manual radio and antenna. Safety Package. Includes padded instrument panel and sun visors. Full foam seat cushion. Heavy-duty black vinyl seat trim. Door-located stowage compartment, left and right side for standard cab; right side for custom cab. Right side sun visor. Windshield washers. Two-speed electric windshield wipers. Chrome contour front bumper. Rear chrome contour bumper (Styleside pickups). Painted contour rear bumper (Styleside pickups). Painted channel rear bumper (Flareside pickups). Brush-type grille guard. Dual electric horns. ICC emergency lamp flasher. ICC cab clearance and marker lights (two or three corner lights). ICC rear reflectors. Front-mounted amber reflectors. Side-mounted spare tire carrier. Left side spare tire mount (Flareside and Styleside). Double-faced front and rear taillights directional signals.

HISTORICAL FOOTNOTES: Ford reported that the F-100 and F-250 four-wheel drive trucks were "built like the big trucks — with a big comfort bonus."

1965 PICKUP

A new grille format with thick dividers providing 18 openings plus an upper portion enclosing five air intakes and the FORD block lettering and the parking/directional lights was used on the 1965 F-100 and F-250 four-wheel drives. Of greater importance was the introduction of a larger 240 cu. in. In-line 6-cylinder as the standard engine for the F-100 and F-250. Two new optional engine choices were a 300 cu. in. In-line 6-cylinder or a 352 cu. in. V-8. The series identification was moved to a position lower on the front fenders.

1965 Ford F-250 Styleside pickup

I.D. DATA: The first letter and two digits represent the series. Next was the engine code for the engine, letter code for the assembly plant, then six digits which indicated sequential production numbers. Both the F-100 and F-250 Series began with a 580000 production number.

Body Type	Factory Price	GVW	Shipping Weight	Prod. Total
Series F-100, 120 in. wheelbase				
Chassis & Cab	$2548	5600	3320	—
Pickup, 8 ft. Flareside	$2662	5600	3640	—
Pickup, 8 ft. Styleside	$2677	5600	3705	—
Series F-250, 120 in. wheelbase				
Chassis & Cab	$2628	7700	3495	—
Pickup, 8 ft. Flareside	$2738	7700	3915	—
Pickup, 8 ft. Styleside	$2596	7700	3955	—

STANDARD ENGINE: F-100, F-250: Engine Type: OHV In-line 6-cylinder. Bore x Stroke: 4.00 in. x 3.18 in. Lifters: Hydraulic. Number of main bearings-7. Displacement: 240 cu. in. (3.93 liters). Induction system: Single venturi downdraft carburetor. Compression Ratio: 9.2:1. Horsepower: 150 @ 4000 rpm. Torque: 234 lb.-ft. @ 2200 rpm. Fuel Requirements: Regular.

OPTIONAL ENGINE: F-100, F-250: Engine Type: OHV In-line 6-cylinder. Bore x Stroke: 4.00 in. x 3.98 in. Displacement: 300 cu. in. Induction system: Single venturi downdraft carburetor. Compression Ratio: 8.0:1. Number of main bearings-7. Horsepower: 170 @ 3600 rpm. Torque: 283 lb.-ft. @ 2200 rpm. Fuel Requirements: Regular.

OPTIONAL ENGINE: F-100, F-250: Engine Type: OHV V-8. Bore x Stroke: 4.00 in. x 3.50 in. Displacement: 352 cu. in. (5.76 liters). Induction system: 2-barrel carburetor. Compression Ratio: 8.9:1. Number of main bearings-5. Horsepower: 208 @ 4400 rpm. Torque: 315 lb.-ft.@ 2400 rpm. Fuel Requirements: Regular.

CHASSIS FEATURES: Separate body and frame. Frame side rail section: 6.88 in. x 2.75 in. x 0.15 in. Section modulus: 4.74.

SUSPENSION AND RUNNING GEAR: Front Suspension: F-100: Wide-span semi-elliptical 6-leaf springs, 48 in. x 2.5 in. Capacity at pad: 1200 lb. Max. capacity at ground: 1445 lb. Deflection rate: 410 lb./in. F-250: Wide-span semi-elliptical 6-leaf springs, 48 in. x 2.5 in. Capacity at pad: 1350 lb. Max. capacity at ground: 1640 lb. Deflection rate: 450 lb./in. Optional: F-250: Semi-elliptical 6-leaf springs, 48 in. x 2.5 in. Capacity at pad: 1550 lb. Max. capacity at ground: 1890 lb. Deflection rate: 525 lb./in. Rear Suspension: F-100: Wide-span semi-elliptical 7-leaf springs, 52 in. x 2.25 in. Capacity at pad: 1450 lb. Max. capacity at ground: 1680 lb. Deflection rate: 225-340 lb./in. F-250: Semi-elliptical 10-leaf springs, 52 in. x 2.25 in. Capacity at pad: 1950 lb. Max. capacity at ground: 2200 lb. Deflection rate: 265-450 lb./in. Optional: F-100: Semi-elliptical 10-leaf springs, 52 in. x 2.25 in. Capacity at pad: 1950 lb. Max. capacity at ground: 2200 lb. Deflection rate: 265-450 lb./in. F-250: Semi-elliptical 10-leaf springs, 52 in. x 2.25 in. Capacity at pad: 2400 lb. Max. capacity at ground: 2680 lb. Deflection rate: 315-520 lb./in. Front Axle Type and Capacity: F-100 and F-250: Spicer model 2559, 3000 lb. capacity, full-floating, Hotchkiss. Ratio: F-100: 3.92:1, F-250: 4.55:1. Optional: F-100 and F-250: Spicer model 2558, 3500 lb. capacity, full-floating, Hotchkiss. Rear Axle Type and Capacity: F-100: Hypoid, Ford-3300, 3300 lb. capacity, semi-floating, Hotchkiss. F-250: Full-floating, Hotchkiss. Spicer model 60, 5200 lb. capacity. Final Drive Ratio: Front: F-100: 3.92:1. F-250: 4.55:1. Rear: F-100: 3.89:1. F-250: 4.56:1. Transfer Case: Type: Constant mesh, 2-speed. Spicer model 24. Ratios: 1.86:1, 1.00:1. Brakes: Type: Hydraulic, drums front and rear, self-generating. Dimensions: F-100: Front: 11 in. x 2.0 in. Rear: 11.0 in. x 1.75 in. Total lining area: 179.5 sq. in. F-250: Front and Rear: 12.125 in. x 2.00 in. Total lining area: 197.8 sq. in. Wheels: F-100: 5-hole stamped disc, 15 in. x 5.5K, disc. F-250: 8-hole, stamped disc, 16 x 6L, disc. Optional: Tires: F-100: 6.70 x 15, 4 PR. F-250: 6.50 x 16.6 6 PR. Optional: F-100: Tubeless tires: 6.70 x 15 4 PR; 6.70 x 15 6 PR; 7.10 x 15,4 PR; 7.10 x 15, 6 PR; 6.50 x 16, 6 PR; 7.17.5, 6 PR. Tube-type tires: 6.50 x 16, 6 PR; 7.0 x 15, 6 PR. F-250: Tubeless tires: 6.50 x 16, 6 PR; 7.00 x 16, 6 PR; 7 x 17.5, 6 PR; 8 x 17.5, 6 PR; 8 x 17.5, 8 PR; 8 x 19.5, 8 PR. Tube-type tires: 6.50 x 16, 6 PR; 6.50 x 16, 6 PR, 7.00 x 16, 6 PR, 7.00 x 17, 8 PR; 7.50 x 16, 6 PR; 7.50 x 17, 8 PR. Steering: F-100 and F-250: Gemer #375, Worm and Roller, 18 in. dia. steering wheel. Turning circle: F-100: 49.1 ft. F-250: 48.9 ft. Ratio: 24.2:1. Optional: None. Transmission: Type: F-100 and F-250: "Synchro-Silent", helical gears, 3-speed, column-mounted shifter. Transmission Ratios: 6-cyl.: 2.79, 1.70, 1.0:1. Reverse: 2.87:1. V-8: 2.59, 1.58, 1.0:1. Reverse: 2.66:1. Clutch: "Gyro-Grip", semi-centrifugal, hydraulic. 11.0 in. dia. and 123.7 sq. in. Optional: Synchro-Silent Warner T-98A with floor-mounted gearshift. Ratios: 6.40, 3.09, 1.69, 1.00:1. Reverse: 7.82:1.

VEHICLE DIMENSIONS: Wheelbase: 120 in. Overall length: F-100 Cab: 201.9 in., 8 ft. Flareside: 205.5 in., Styleside: 203.7 in. F-250: Cab: 201.9 in., 8 ft. Flareside: 205.5 in., Styleside: 205.0 in., Stake and Platform: 202.8 in. Front/Rear Overhang: 33.5 in./48.4 in. Height: 77.5 in. Width: 79.8 in. Front/Rear tread: 64.1 in./60.4-0 in.

CAPACITIES: Fuel Tank: 18 gal.

ACCOMMODATIONS: 3 occupants.

INSTRUMENTATION: Speedometer, odometer, fuel level and engine coolant temperature gauges, warning lights for oil pressure, and battery charge.

OPTIONS AND PRICES: 300 L-6. 352 V-8. Extra Cooling radiator. Closed crankcase ventilation (required for California). Velocity controlled governor. 42 amp alternator. 52 amp alternator. 60 amp alternator. Limited slip rear axle (3.92:1 ratio with 3-spd. trans.; 4.10:1 with V-8, includes 4.09:1 front axle ratio). 70 amp-hr. battery. Free-running front Spicer hubs. Two-stage 1950 lb. capacity rear springs. Warner T98A 4-speed trans (recommended for tow truck and snowplow applications). Driver-side armrest. Passenger side armrest. Cigarette lighter. Custom cab. Laminated sheet door glass. Tinted windshield glass. Fresh-Air heater and defroster. Recirculating-type heater and defroster. Inside safety mirror (standard for pickups). Exterior chrome left and right side mirrors. Non-telescopic 5 in. x 5 in. right side mirror. Non-telescopic 5 in. x 5 in. left side mirror. Telescopic 5 in. x 8 in. left and/or right side mirrors. Western-type 5 in. x 10.0 in. left and/or right side mirrors. Two-tone paint. Manual radio and antenna. Safety Package. Includes padded instrument panel and sun visors. Full foam seat cushion. Heavy-duty black vinyl seat trim. Door-located stowage compartment, left and right side for standard cab; right side for custom cab. Right side sun visor. Windshield washers. Two-speed electric windshield wipers. Chrome contour front bumper. Rear chrome contour bumper (Styleside pickups). Painted contour rear bumper (Styleside pickups). Painted channel rear bumper (Flareside pickups). Brush-type grille guard. Dual electric horns. ICC emergency lamp flasher. ICC cab clearance and marker lights (two or three corner lights). ICC rear reflectors. Front-mounted amber reflectors. Side-mounted spare tire carrier. Left side spare tire mount (Flareside and Styleside). Double-faced front and rear taillights directional signals.

HISTORICAL FOOTNOTES: The 1965 models were introduced in October, 1964. Philip Caldwell was Truck Operation manager. Production of the new 240 cu. in. 6-cylinder engine began in August, 1963. Its predecessor, the 223 cu. in. 6-cylinder had been a Ford mainstay for 12 years.

1966 PICKUP

For 1966 the front grille featured a narrow insert of 18 small rectangular slots below two narrow openings with pointed inner ends. For the first time the four-wheel drive models were offered in either 115 in. or 129 in. wheelbase form. The F-100 was fitted with a new Monobeam coil spring front suspension. Overall height of the F-100 four-wheel drive models was reduced by three inches. A single speed transfer case was also adopted for the F-100. Standard equipment for the F-100 and F-250 pickups included fresh-air heater and defroster, padded dash, windshield washers and emergency flashers. A new Sahara beige replaced Navajo beige for 1966. Other exterior colors for 1966 were rangoon red, raven black, holly green, Springtime yellow, Caribbean turquoise, marlin blue, Arcadian blue, Wimbledon white, pure white, and chrome yellow. A two-tone effect was available by combining any standard color except pure white and chrome yellow, with Wimbledon white on roof and around cab back panel above beltline. Both the standard and custom cabs were improved for 1966 by the inclusion of such features as a padded instrument panel, windshield washers, non-glare windshield wiper arms, left-side mirror on all models and a fresh-air heater and defroster.

1966 Ford F-100 Styleside pickup

I.D. DATA: The first letter and two digits represent the series. Next was the engine code for the engine, letter code for the assembly plant, then six digits which indicated sequential production numbers.

Body Type	Factory Price	GVW	Shipping Weight	Prod. Total
Series F-100, 115 in. wheelbase				
Pickup, 6.5 ft. Flareside	$2787	4600[1]	3615	—
Pickup, 6.5 ft. Styleside	$2803	4600	3680	—
Series F-100, 129 in. wheelbase				
Chassis & Cab	$2669	4600	3320	145
Pickup, 8 ft. Flareside	$2823	4600	3765	—
Pickup, 8 ft. Styleside	$2839	4600	3780	—

NOTE 1: 5600 lb. GVW optional.

F-100 Flareside production totalled 839 units in both wheelbases. Styleside output was 4493.

Body Type	Factory Price	GVW	Shipping Weight	Prod. Total
Series F-250, 129 in. wheelbase				
Chassis & Cab	$2729	4900[2]	3520	644
Pickup, 8 ft. Flareside	$2843	4900	3915	1595
Pickup, 8 ft. Styleside	$2861	4900	3930	3559
Platform, 7.5 ft.	$2880	4900	3925	29
Stake, 7.5 ft.	$2934	4900	4105	125

NOTE 2: 7700 lb. GVW optional.

STANDARD ENGINE: F-100, F-250: Engine Type: OHV In-line 6-cylinder. Bore x Stroke: 4.00 in. x 3.18 in. Lifters: Hydraulic. Number of main bearings-7. Displacement: 240 cu. in. (3.93 liters). Induction system: Single venturi downdraft carburetor. Compression Ratio: 9.2:1. Horsepower: Gross: 150 @ 4000 rpm. Net: 129 @ 400 rpm. Torque: Gross: 234 lb.-ft.@ 2200 rpm. Net: 218 lb.-ft. @ 2000 rpm. Fuel Requirements: Regular.

OPTIONAL ENGINE: F-100, F-250: Engine Type: OHV In-line 6-cylinder. Bore x Stroke: 4.00 in. x 3.98 in. Displacement: 300 cu. in. Induction system: Single venturi downdraft carburetor. Compression Ratio: 8.4:1. Number of main bearings-7. Horsepower: Net: 170 @ 3600 rpm. Gross: 150 @ 3600 rpm. Torque: Gross: 283 lb.-ft.@ 1400-2400 rpm. Net: 272 lb.-ft. @ 1400-210 rpm. Fuel Requirements: Regular.

OPTIONAL ENGINE: F-100, F-250: Engine Type: OHV V-8. Bore x Stroke: 4.00 in. x 3.50 in. Displacement: 352 cu. in. (5.76 liters). Induction system: 2-barrel carburetor. Compression Ratio: 8.9:1. Number of main bearings-5. Horsepower: Gross: 208 @ 4400 rpm. Net: 172 @ 4000 rpm. Torque: Gross: 315 lb.-ft.@ 2400 rpm. Net: 295 lb.-ft. @ 2000 rpm. Fuel Requirements: Regular.

CHASSIS FEATURES: Separate body and frame. Section modulus: F-100 with 115 in. wheelbase: 3.71; with 129 in. wheelbase: 4.14. F-250: 4.74.

SUSPENSION AND RUNNING GEAR: Front Suspension: F-100: 6-cyl. engines: 1000 lb. capacity; with V-8: 1125 lb. F-250: 1350 lb. capacity. Optional: F-100: 6-cyl. engines: 1125 lb. capacity; with V-8: 1250 lb. capacity. F-250: N.A. Rear Suspension: F-100: Progressive, 1250 lb. capacity. F-250: Progressive, 1950 lb. capacity. Optional: F-100: Single-stage, 1650 lb. capacity. F-250: Progressive, 2400 lb. capacity. Optional auxiliary spring for F-250 rated at 550 lb. Front Axle Type and Capacity: F-100 and F-250: Spicer model 2559, 3000 lb. capacity, full-floating, Hotchkiss. Optional: F-250: Spicer model 2558, 3500 lb. capacity, full-floating, Hotchkiss. Rear Axle Type and Capacity: F-100: Hypoid, Ford-3300, 3300 lb. capacity, semi-floating, Hotchkiss. F-250: Full-floating, Hotchkiss. Spicer model 60, 5200 lb. capacity. Final Drive Ratio: F-100: 6-cylinder engines: 3.70:1; V-8: 3.50:1 Optional: 4.11:1. Limited slip differential: 6-cylinders: 4.11:1; with V-8: 3.54:1. F-250: 4.56:1 with or without limited slip differential. Transfer Case: Type: F-100: Single-speed. F-250: 2-speed Spicer model 24. Ratios: 1.86:1, 1.00:1. Brakes: Type: Hydraulic, drums front and rear, self-generating. Dimensions: F-100: Front: 11 in. x 2.0 in. Rear: 11.0 in. x 1.75 in. Total lining area: 179.5 sq. in. F-250: Front and Rear: 12.125 in. x 2.00 in. Total lining area: 197.8 sq. in. Optional; F-250: Front and rear: 12.0 in. x 2.50 in. Heavy-duty. Wheels: F-100: 5-hole stamped disc, 15 in. x 5.5K, disc. F-250: 8-hole, stamped disc, 16 x 6L, disc. Tires: F-100: 7.75 x 15, 4 PR. F-250: 6.50 x 16.6 6 PR. Optional: F-100: Tubeless tires: 6.70 x 15 4 PR; 6.70 x 15 6 PR; 7.10 x 15,4 PR; 7.10 x 15, 6 PR; 6.50 x 16, 6 PR; 7.17.5, 6 PR. Tube-type tires: 6.50 x 16, 6 PR; 7.0 x 15, 6 PR. F-250: Tubeless tires: 6.50 x 16, 6 PR; 7.00 x 16, 6 PR; 7 x 17.5, 6 PR; 8 x 17.5, 6 PR; 8 x 17.5, 8 PR; 8 x 19.5, 8 PR. Tube-type tires: 6.50 x 16, 6 PR; 6.50 x 16, 6 PR, 7.00 x 16, 6 PR, 7.00 x 17, 8 PR; 7.50 x 16, 6 PR; 7.50 x 17, 8 PR. Steering: F-100 and F-250: Gemer #375, Worm and Roller, 18 in. dia. steering wheel. Ratio: 24.2:1. Optional: None. Transmission: Type: F-100: 4-speed New Process 435. F-250: Warner T89F 3-speed manual. Optional: F-250: 4-speed New Process 435. Ratios: New process 435: 6.69, 3.34, 1.66, 1.0:1. Reverse: 8.26:1. Clutch: Heavy-duty hydraulic. 11.0 in. dia. and 123.7 sq. in.

VEHICLE DIMENSIONS: Wheelbase: 115 in., 129 in. Overall length: F-100: 115 in. wheelbase: Pickup, 6.5 ft. Flareside: 188.9 in. Pickup, 6.5 ft. Styleside: 188.6 in. F-100: 129 in. wheelbase: Chassis & cab: 202.3 in. Pickup, 8 ft. Flareside: 206.5 in. Pickup, 8 ft. Styleside: 208.6 in. F-250: Chassis & cab: 203.3 in. Pickup, 8 ft. Flareside: 206.5 in. Pickup, 8 ft. Styleside: 208.6 in. Platform, 7.5 ft.: 203.8 in. Stake, 7.5 ft.: 203.8 in. Front/Rear Overhang: 33.5 in./48.4 in. Height: F-100: 75.0 in. F-250: 77.5 in. Width: 79.8 in. Front/Rear tread: 64.1 in./60.4 in.

CAPACITIES: Fuel Tank: 18 gal.

ACCOMMODATIONS: 3 occupants.

INSTRUMENTATION: Speedometer, odometer, fuel level and engine coolant temperature gauges, warning lights for oil pressure, and battery charge.

OPTIONS AND PRICES: 300 L-6. 352 V-8. Extra Cooling radiator. Closed crankcase ventilation (required for California). Velocity controlled governor. 42 amp alternator. 52 amp alternator. 60 amp alternator. Limited slip rear axle (3.92:1 ratio with 3-spd. trans.; 4.10:1 with V-8, includes 4.09:1 front axle ratio). 70 amp-hr. battery. Free-running front Spicer hubs. Two-stage 1950 lb. capacity rear springs. 4-speed New Process 435 manual transmission. Driver's side armrest. Passenger side armrest. Cigarette lighter. Custom cab. Laminated sheet door glass. Tinted windshield glass. Fresh-Air heater and defroster. Recirculating-type heater and defroster. Inside safety mirror (standard for Pickups). Exterior chrome left and right side mirrors. Non-telescopic 5 in. x 5 in. right side mirror. Non-telescopic 5 in. x 5 in. left side mirror. Telescopic 5 in. x 8 in. left and/or right side mirrors. Western-type 5 in. x 10.0 in. left and/or right side mirrors. Two-tone paint. Manual radio and antenna. Safety Package. Includes padded instrument panel and sun visors. Full foam seat cushion. Heavy-duty black vinyl seat trim. Door-located stowage compartment, left and right side for Standard cab; right side for Custom cab. Right side sun visor. Windshield washers. Two-speed electric windshield wipers. Chrome contour front bumper. Rear chrome contour bumper (Styleside pickups). Painted contour rear bumper (Styleside pickups). Painted channel rear bumper (Flareside pickups). Brush-type grille guard. Dual electric horns. ICC emergency lamp flasher. ICC cab clearance and marker lights (two or three corner lights). ICC rear reflectors. Front-mounted amber reflectors. Side-mounted spare tire carrier. Left side spare tire mount (Flareside and Styleside). Double-faced front and rear taillights directional signals.

HISTORICAL FOOTNOTES: The 1966 models were introduced on October 1, 1965.

1966 Ford F-250 Styleside pickup

1967 PICKUP

With new cabs and an extensive restyling the 1967 four-wheel drive Fords combined traditional four-wheel drive ruggedness with the growing trend towards trucks with a much more sophisticated level of ride and comfort. The 1967 Ford front end was characterized by a broad grille with four horizontal bars and three vertical dividers. The hood-mounted FORD lettering was especially prominent. The 8 ft. bed F-100 and all F-250 models had a longer, 131 in. wheelbase. All models were equipped with a new reversible ignition key and foot-operated parking brake. Expanded interior dimensions included increased headroom, legroom and shoulder room. A full-view, wide rear window was standard for all pickups. A new windshield was used along with curved side glass. Three trim levels were offered: Standard, custom and Ranger. The custom cab included woven-plastic seat trim in red, blue, green or beige, deep foam cushioned full-width seat, left and right side armrests, rubber floor mat, cigarette lighter, bright finish for horn ring, headlining retainer, instrument panel cluster; padded dash, bright metal grille and headlight assembly, bright windshield reveal molding and custom cab identification.

The Ranger Package included full-width deep-cushioned seat in vinyl with a soft cloth appearance, vinyl door trim panels, nylon carpeting with bright metal trim molding, bright-finish for the horn ring, instrument cluster, headliner and instrument panel padding; bright-finish front bumper, grille and headlight assembly, wheel-lips and rocker panel moldings.

The exterior colors for 1967 were rangoon red, pebble beige, raven black, Springtime yellow, holly green, frost turquoise, harbor blue, Wimbledon white, chrome yellow and pure white.

1967 Ford F-250 Styleside pickup

I.D. DATA: The first letter and two digits represent the series. Next was the engine code for the engine, letter code for the assembly plant, then six digits which indicated sequential production numbers.

Body Type	Factory Price	GVW	Shipping Weight	Prod. Total
Series F-100, 115 in., 131 in. wheelbase				
Chassis & Cab	$2723	4900[1]	3245	135
Pickup, 6.5 ft. Flareside	$2849	4900	3665	481[2]
Pickup, 6.5 ft. Styleside	$2888	4900	3610	3455[3]
Pickup, 8.0 ft. Flareside	$2888	4900	N.A.	—
Pickup, 8.0 ft. Styleside	$2924	4900	N.A.	—

NOTE 1: 5600 lb. GVW optional.
NOTE 2: Production figures include all F-100 Flareside models.
NOTE 3: Production figures include all F-100 Styleside models.

Series F-250, 131 in. wheelbase				
Chassis & Cab	$2887	6800[4]	3570	426
Pickup, 8 ft. Flareside	$3014	6800	3990	915[5]
Pickup, 8 ft. Styleside	$3051	6800	4005	3836[6]
Platform, 7.5 ft.	$3048	6800	3955	25
Stake, 7.5 ft.	$3103	6800	4165	89

NOTE 4: 7700 lb. GVW optional.
NOTE 5: Production figures include all F-250 Flareside models.
NOTE 6: Production figures include all F-250 Styleside models.

STANDARD ENGINE: F-100, F-250: Engine Type: OHV In-line 6-cylinder. Bore x Stroke: 4.00 in. x 3.18 in. Lifters: Hydraulic. Number of main bearings-7. Displacement: 240 cu. in. (3.93 liters). Induction system: Single venturi downdraft carburetor. Compression Ratio: 9.2:1. Horsepower: Gross: 150 @ 4000 rpm. Net: 129 @ 4000 rpm. Torque: Gross: 234 lb.-ft.@ 2200 rpm. Net: 218 lb.-ft. @ 2000 rpm. Fuel Requirements: Regular.

OPTIONAL ENGINE: F-100, F-250: Engine Type: OHV In-line 6-cylinder. Bore x Stroke: 4.00 in. x 3.98 in. Displacement: 300 cu. in. Induction system: Single venturi downdraft carburetor. Compression Ratio: 8.4:1. Number of main bearings-7. Horsepower: Net: 170 @ 3600 rpm. Gross: 150 @ 3600 rpm. Torque: Gross: 283 lb.-ft.@ 1400-2400 rpm. Net: 272 lb.-ft. @ 1400-2100 rpm. Fuel Requirements: Regular.

OPTIONAL ENGINE: F-100, F-250: Engine Type: OHV V-8. Bore x Stroke: 4.00 in. x 3.50 in. Displacement: 352 cu. in. (5.76 liters). Induction system: 2-barrel carburetor. Compression Ratio: 8.9:1. Number of main bearings-5. Horsepower: Gross: 208 @ 4400 rpm. Net: 172 @ 4000 rpm. Torque: Gross: 315 lb.-ft.@ 2400 rpm. Net: 295 lb.-ft. @ 2000 rpm. Fuel Requirements: Regular.

CHASSIS FEATURES: Separate body and frame.

SUSPENSION AND RUNNING GEAR: Front Suspension: F-100: 6-cyl. engines: 1000 lb. capacity; with V-8 1125 lb. F-250: 1200 lb. capacity. Optional: F-100: 6-cyl. engines: 1125 lb. capacity; with V-8: 1250 lb. capacity. F-250: N.A. Rear Suspension: F-100: Progressive, 1250 lb. capacity. F-250: Progressive, 1700 lb. capacity. Optional: F-100: Single-stage, 1650 lb. capacity. F-250: Progressive, 2400 lb. capacity. Optional auxiliary spring for F-250 rated at 550 lb. Front Axle Type and Capacity: F-100 and F-250: Spicer model 2559, 3000 lb. capacity, full-floating, Hotchkiss. Optional: F-250: Spicer model 2558, 3500 lb. capacity, full-floating, Hotchkiss. Rear Axle Type and Capacity: F-100: Hypoid, Ford-3300, 3300 lb. capacity, semi-floating, Hotchkiss. F-250: Full-floating, Hotchkiss. Spicer model 60, 5200 lb. capacity. Final Drive Ratio: F-100: 6-cylinder engines: 3.70:1; V-8: 3.50:1 Optional: 4.11:1. Limited slip differential: 6-cylinders: 4.11:1; with V-8: 3.54:1. F-250: 4.56:1 with or without limited slip differential. Transfer Case: Type: F-100: Single-speed. F-250: 2-speed Spicer model 24. Ratios: 1.86:1, 1.00:1. Brakes: Type: Hydraulic, drums front and rear, self-generating. Dimensions: F-100: Front: 11 in. x 2.0 in. Rear: 11.0 in. x 1.75 in. Total lining area: 179.5 sq. in. F-250: Front and Rear: 12.125 in. x 2.00 in. Total lining area: 197.8 sq. in. Optional: F-250: Front and rear: 12.0 in. x 2.50 in. Heavy-duty. Wheels: F-100: 5-hole stamped disc, 15 in. x 5.5K, disc. F-250: 8-hole, stamped disc, 16 x 6L, disc. Tires: F-100: 7.75 x 15, 4 PR. F-250: 6.50 x 16.6 6 PR. Optional: F-100: Tubeless tires: 6.70 x 15 4 PR; 6.70 x 15 6 PR; 7.10 x 15,4 PR; 7.10 x 15, 6 PR; 6.50 x 16, 6 PR; 7.17.5, 6 PR. Tube-type tires: 6.50 x 16, 6 PR; 7.0 x 15, 6 PR. F-250: Tubeless tires: 6.50 x 16, 6 PR; 7.00 x 16, 6 PR; 7 x 17.5, 6 PR; 8 x 17.5, 6 PR; 8 x 17.5, 8 PR; 8 x 19.5, 8 PR. Tube-type tires: 6.50 x 16, 6 PR; 6.50 x 16, 6 PR; 7.00 x 16, 6 PR; 7.00 x 17, 8 PR; 7.50 x 16, 8 PR; 7.50 x 17, 8 PR. Steering: F-100 and F-250: Gemer #375, Worm and Roller, 18 in. dia. steering wheel. Ratio: 24.2:1. Optional: None. Transmission: Type: F-100: 4-speed New Process 435. F-250: 4-speed New Process 435. Ratios: New Process 435: 6.69, 3.34, 1.66, 1.0:1. Reverse: 8.26:1. Clutch: Heavy-duty hydraulic. 11.0 in. dia. and 123.7 sq. in.

VEHICLE DIMENSIONS: Wheelbase: 115 in., 131 in. Overall length: F-100: 115 in. wheelbase: Pickup, 6.5 ft. Flareside: 188.9 in. Pickup, 6.5 ft. Styleside: 188.6 in. F-100: 131 in. wheelbase: Chassis & cab: 204.3 in. Pickup, 8 ft. Flareside: 208.5 in. Pickup, 8 ft. Styleside: 210.6 in. F-250: Chassis & cab: 2043 in. Pickup, 8 ft. Flareside: 208.5 in. Pickup, 8 ft. Styleside: 210.6 in. Platform, 7.5 ft.: 205.8 in. Stake, 7.5 ft.: 205.8 in. Front/Rear Overhang: 33.5 in./48.4 in. Height: F-100: 75.0 in. F-250: 77.5 in. Width: 79.8 in. Front/Rear tread: 64.1 in./60.4 in.

CAPACITIES: Fuel Tank: 18 gal.

ACCOMMODATIONS: 3 occupants.

INSTRUMENTATION: Speedometer, odometer, fuel level and engine coolant temperature gauges, warning lights for oil pressure, and battery charge.

OPTIONS AND PRICES: 300 L-6. 352 V-8. Extra Cooling radiator. Closed crankcase ventilation (required for California). Velocity controlled governor. 42 amp alternator. 52 amp alternator. 60 amp alternator. Limited slip rear axle (3.92:1 ratio with 3-spd. trans.; 4.10:1 with V-8, includes 4.09:1 front axle ratio). 70 amp-hr. battery. Free-running front Spicer hubs. Two-stage 1950 lb. capacity rear springs. 4-speed New Process 435 manual transmission. Driver's side armrest. Passenger side armrest. Cigarette lighter. Custom Package. Ranger Package. Laminated sheet door glass. Tinted windshield glass. Fresh-Air heater and defroster. Recirculating-type heater and defroster. Inside safety mirror (standard for Pickups). Exterior chrome left and right side mirrors. Non-telescopic 5 in. x 5 in. right side mirror. Non-telescopic 5 in. x 5 in. left side mirror. Telescopic 5 in. x 8 in. left and/or right side mirrors. Western-type 5 in. x 10.0 in. left and/or right side mirrors. Two-tone paint. Manual radio and antenna. Full foam seat cushion. Heavy-duty black vinyl seat trim. Right side sun visor. Windshield washers. Two-speed electric windshield wipers. Chrome contour front bumper. Rear chrome contour bumper (Styleside pickups). Painted contour rear bumper (Styleside pickups). Painted channel rear bumper (Flareside pickups). Brush-type grille guard. Dual electric horns. ICC emergency lamp flasher. ICC cab clearance and marker lights (two or three corner lights). ICC rear reflectors. Front-mounted amber reflectors. Side-mounted spare tire carrier. Left side spare tire mount (Flareside and Styleside). Double-faced front and rear taillights directional signals.

HISTORICAL FOOTNOTES: Ford offered a new 5 year or 50,000 mile warranty on powertrain and 2 year or 24,000 mile warranty on the entire truck for 1967.

1968 PICKUP

Replacing the optional 352 cu. in. V-8 was a 360 cu. in. V-8. The grille now had a wide horizontal divider and a new paint background for the insert which emphasized the remaining white or bright finished horizontal bars. The new front fender side marker lights were incorporated into the series identification. Those at the rear were positioned low on the rear fender. Standard equipment included padded sun visors, armrests with paddle-type door latch handles, domelight, double-grip door locks, Deluxe Fresh-Air heater and defroster, hardboard headliner, seat belts, floor mat and vinyl seat trim available in red, blue, beige or black.

The exterior colors for 1968 were rangoon red, pebble beige, raven black, meadowlark yellow, holly green, lunar green, sky view blue, harbor blue, Wimbledon white, chrome yellow and pure white. As in 1967, a two-tone paint option was offered for the Styleside pickups. It consisted of Wimbledon white, applied to the area below the side molding and lower tailgate section, with the remaining surfaces painted the selected color (except for chrome yellow and pure white).

1968 Ford F-250 Styleside pickup

I.D. DATA: The first letter and two digits represent the series. Next was the engine code for the engine, letter code for the assembly plant, then six digits which indicated sequential production numbers.

Body Type	Factory Price	GVW	Shipping Weight	Prod. Total
Series F-100, 115 in., 131 in. wheelbase				
Chassis & Cab	$2840	4600[1]	3335	—
Pickup, 6.5 ft. Flareside	$2965	4600	3655	—
Pickup, 6.5 ft. Styleside	$3004	4600	3700	—
Pickup, 8.0 ft. Flareside	$3004	4600	3790	—
Pickup, 8.0 ft. Styleside	$3040	4600	3805	—

NOTE 1: 5600 lb. GVW optional.

Body Type	Factory Price	GVW	Shipping Weight	Prod. Total
Series F-250, 131 in. wheelbase				
Chassis & Cab	$3059	6300[2]	3605	—
Pickup, 8 ft. Flareside	$3186	6300	4025	—
Pickup, 8 ft. Styleside	$3223	6300	4040	—
Platform, 7.5 ft.	$3220	6300	3985	—
Stake, 7.5 ft.	$3275	6300	4200	—

NOTE 2: 7700 lb. GVW optional.

STANDARD ENGINE: F-100, F-250: Engine Type: OHV In-line 6-cylinder. Bore x Stroke: 4.00 in. x 3.18 in. Lifters: Hydraulic. Number of main bearings-7. Displacement: 240 cu. in. (3.93 liters). Induction system: Single venturi downdraft carburetor. Compression Ratio: 9.2:1. Horsepower: Gross: 150 @ 4000 rpm. Net: 129 @ 4000 rpm. Torque: Gross: 234 lb.-ft.@ 2200 rpm. Net: 218 lb.-ft. @ 2000 rpm. Fuel Requirements: Regular.

OPTIONAL ENGINE: F-100, F-250: Engine Type: OHV In-line 6-cylinder. Bore x Stroke: 4.00 in. x 3.98 in. Displacement: 300 cu. in. Induction system: Single venturi downdraft carburetor. Compression Ratio: 8.8:1. Number of main bearings-7. Horsepower: Gross: 165 @ 3600 rpm. Torque: Gross: 294 lb.-ft. @ 2000 rpm. Fuel Requirements: Regular.

OPTIONAL ENGINE: F-100, F-250: Engine Type: OHV V-8. Bore x Stroke: 4.00 in. x 3.50 in. Displacement: 360 cu. in. (5.76 liters). Induction system: 2-barrel carburetor. Compression Ratio: 8.4:1. Number of main bearings-5. Horsepower: Gross: 215 @ 4400 rpm. Torque: Gross: 327 lb.-ft. @ 2600 rpm. Fuel Requirements: Regular.

CHASSIS FEATURES: Separate body and frame. Section modulus: F-100 (115 in. wheelbase): 3.71; F-100 (131 in. wheelbase): 4.14. F-250: 5.58.

SUSPENSION AND RUNNING GEAR: Front Suspension: F-100: 6-cyl. engines: 1250 lb. capacity; with V-8: 1250 lb. F-250: 1200 lb. capacity. Rear Suspension: F-100: Progressive, 1250 lb. capacity. F-250: Progressive, 1700 lb. capacity. Optional: F-100: Single-stage, 1650 lb. capacity. F-250: Progressive, 2400 lb. capacity. Optional auxiliary spring for F-250 rated at 550 lb. Front Axle Type and Capacity: F-100 and F-250: Spicer model 2559, 3000 lb. capacity, full-floating, Hotchkiss. Optional: F-250: Spicer model 2558, 3500 lb. capacity, full-floating, Hotchkiss. Rear Axle Type and Capacity: F-100: Hypoid, Ford-3300, 3300 lb. capacity, semi-floating, Hotchkiss. F-250: Full-floating, Hotchkiss. Spicer model 60, 5200 lb. capacity. Final Drive Ratio: F-100: 3.70:1. Optional: 3.50, 4.11:1. Limited slip differential with 3400 lb. capacity: 3.50, 4.09:1. F-250: 4.10:1. Optional: Limited slip differential with 5200 lb. capacity: 4.10:1. Transfer Case: Type: F-100: Single-speed. F-250: 2-speed Spicer model 24. Ratios: 1.86:1, 1.00:1. Brakes: Type: Hydraulic, drums front and rear, self-generating. Dimensions: F-100: Front: 11 in. x 2.0 in. Rear: 11.03 in. x 2.25 in. F-250: Front: 12.125 in. x 2.00 in. Rear: 12.0 in. x 2.50 in. Wheels: F-100: 5-hole stamped disc, 15 in. x 5.5K, disc. F-250: 8-hole, stamped disc, 16 x 6.0, disc. Tires: F-100: 6.50 x 16.6 6 PR. Optional: F-100: Tubeless tires: 6.70 x 15 4 PR; 6.70 x 15 6 PR; 7.10 x 15,4 PR; 7.10 x 15, 6 PR; 6.50 x 16, 6 PR; 7.17.5, 6 PR. Tube-type tires: 6.50 x 16, 6 PR; 7.0 x 15, 6 PR. F-250: Tubeless tires: 6.50 x 16, 6 PR; 7.00 x 16, 6 PR; 7 x 17.5, 6 PR; 8 x 17.5, 8 PR; 8 x 19.5, 8 PR. Tube-type tires: 6.50 x 16, 6 PR; 6.50 x 16, 6 PR; 7.00 x 16, 6 PR; 7.00 x 17, 8 PR; 7.50 x 16, 6 PR; 7.50 x 17, 8 PR. Steering: F-100 and F-250: Gemer #375, Worm and Roller, 18 in. dia. steering wheel. Ratio: 24.2:1. Optional: None. Transmission: Type: F-100: 4-speed New Process 435. F-250: Ford 3-speed manual. Optional: F-250: 4-speed New Process 435. Ratios: New Process 435: 6.69, 3.34, 1.66, 1.0:1. Reverse: 8.26:1. Clutch: Heavy-duty hydraulic. 11.0 in. dia. and 123.7 sq. in.

VEHICLE DIMENSIONS: Wheelbase: 115 in., 131 in. Overall length: F-100: 115 in. wheelbase: Pickup, 6.5 ft. Flareside: 188.9 in. Pickup, 6.5 ft. Styleside: 188.6 in. F-100: 131 in. wheelbase: Chassis & cab: 204.3 in. Pickup, 8 ft. Flareside: 208.5 in. Pickup, 8 ft. Styleside: 210.6 in. F-250: Chassis & cab: 202.3 in. Pickup, 8 ft. Flareside: 208.5 in. Pickup, 8 ft.

Styleside: 210.6 in. Platform, 7.5 ft.: 205.8 in. Stake, 7.5 ft.: 205.8 in. Front/Rear Overhang: 33.5 in./48.4 in. Height: F-100: 75.0 in. F-250: 77.5 in. Width: 79.8 in. Front/Rear tread: 64.1 in./60.4 in.

CAPACITIES: Fuel Tank: 18 gal.

ACCOMMODATIONS: 3 occupants.

INSTRUMENTATION: Speedometer, odometer, fuel level and engine coolant temperature gauges, warning lights for oil pressure, and battery charge.

OPTIONS AND PRICES: 300 L-6. 360 V-8. Extra Cooling radiator. Closed crankcase ventilation (required for California). Velocity controlled governor. 42 amp alternator. 52 amp alternator. 60 amp alternator. Limited slip rear axle (3.92:1 ratio with 3-spd. trans.; 4.10:1 with V-8, includes 4.09:1 front axle ratio). 70 amp-hr. battery. Free-running front Spicer hubs. Two-stage 1950 lb. capacity rear springs. 4-speed New Process 435 manual transmission. Driver-side armrest. Passenger side armrest. Cigarette lighter. Custom Package. Ranger Package: $238. Laminated sheet door glass. Tinted windshield glass. Fresh-Air heater and defroster. Recirculating-type heater and defroster. Inside safety mirror (standard for pickups). Exterior chrome left and right side mirrors. Non-telescopic 5 in. x 5 in. right side mirror. Non-telescopic 5 in. x 5 in. left side mirror. Telescopic 5 in. x 8 in. left and/or right side mirrors. Western-type 5 in. x 10.0 in. left and/or right side mirrors. Two-tone paint. Manual radio and antenna. Full foam seat cushion. Heavy-duty black vinyl seat trim. Right side sun visor. Windshield washers. Two-speed electric windshield wipers. Chrome contour front bumper. Rear chrome contour bumper (Styleside pickups). Painted contour rear bumper (Styleside pickups). Painted channel rear bumper (Flareside pickups). Brush-type grille guard. Dual electric horns. ICC emergency lamp flasher. ICC cab clearance and marker lights (two or three corner lights). ICC rear reflectors. Front-mounted amber reflectors. Side-mounted spare tire carrier. Left side spare tire mount (Flareside and Styleside). Double-faced front and rear taillights directional signals.

HISTORICAL FOOTNOTES: The 1968 models were introduced in the fall of 1967.

1969 PICKUP

The latest four-wheel drive Ford trucks were identified by their revamped grille work which no longer had the black painted vertical members used in 1968. At the start of the model year the base models retained their ivory painted grille headlight surround. Starting on February 10, 1969 all models had the chrome-trimmed front end previously limited to the up-scale models. The F-250 was now available on the 148.3 in. crew cab chassis.

The exterior colors for 1969 were raven black, Wimbledon white, Norway green, new lime, boxwood green, candyapple red, royal maroon, pebble beige, cordova copper, empire yellow, lunar green, reef aqua, sky view blue, harbor blue, chrome yellow and pure white. A choice of optional regular, Deluxe or combination two-tones were offered. Wimbledon white served as the accent color for all colors except for chrome yellow and pure white. In the regular format, the accent color was applied to the roof and upper back panel with a belt line molding from door to door around the back of the cab. In the Deluxe two-tone, available for Styleside pickups only, the accent color was applied to the area below the body side and lower tailgate moldings which were included in this option. The combination two-tone, again limited to the Styleside pickups, combined the regular and Deluxe two-tone options with the accent color applied as specified in those two options.

I.D. DATA: The first letter and two digits represent the series. Next was the engine code for the engine, letter code for the assembly plant, then six digits which indicated sequential production numbers.

Body Type	Factory Price	GVW	Shipping Weight	Prod. Total
Series F-100, 115 in., 131 in. wheelbase				
Chassis & Cab	$2874	4600[1]	3360	56
Pickup, 6.5 ft. Flareside	$2998	4600	3689	465[2]
Pickup, 6.5 ft. Styleside	$3037	4600	3725	7,940[3]
Pickup, 8.0 ft. Flareside	$3037	4600	3815	—
Pickup, 8.0 ft. Styleside	$3074	4600	3840	—

NOTE 1: 5600 lb. GVW optional.
NOTE 2: Includes all Flareside models.
NOTE 3: Includes all Styleside models.

Body Type	Factory Price	GVW	Shipping Weight	Prod. Total
Series F-250, 131 in. wheelbase				
Chassis & Cab	$3186	6300[4]	3620	641
Pickup, 8 ft. Flareside	$3313	6300	4040	973[5]
Pickup, 8 ft. Styleside	$3349	6300	4055	10,286[6]
Platform, 7.5 ft.	$3346	6300	4000	30
Stake, 7.5 ft.	$3402	6300	4215	102
Crew Cab, 148.3 in. wb.	$N.A.	N.A.	N.A.	—

NOTE 4: 7700 lb. GVW optional.
NOTE 5: Includes all Flareside models.
NOTE 6: Includes all Styleside models.

STANDARD ENGINE: F-100, F-250: Engine Type: OHV In-line 6-cylinder. Bore x Stroke: 4.00 in. x 3.18 in. Lifters: Hydraulic. Number of main bearings-7. Displacement: 240 cu. in. (3.93 liters). Induction system: Single venturi downdraft carburetor. Compression Ratio: 9.2:1. Horsepower: Gross: 150 @ 4000 rpm. Net: 129 @ 4000 rpm. Torque: Gross: 234 lb.-ft.@ 2200 rpm. Net: 218 lb.-ft. @ 2000 rpm. Fuel Requirements: Regular.

OPTIONAL ENGINE: F-100, F-250: Engine Type: OHV In-line 6-cylinder. Bore x Stroke: 4.00 in. x 3.98 in. Displacement: 300 cu. in. Induction system: Single venturi downdraft carburetor. Compression Ratio: 8.8:1. Number of main bearings-7. Horsepower: Gross: 165 @ 3600 rpm. Torque: Gross: 294 lb.-ft. @ 2000 rpm. Fuel Requirements: Regular.

OPTIONAL ENGINE: F-100, F-250: Engine Type: OHV V-8. Bore x Stroke: 4.00 in. x 3.50 in. Displacement: 360 cu. in. (5.76 liters). Induction system: 2-barrel carburetor. Compression Ratio: 8.4:1. Number of main bearings-5. Horsepower: Gross: 215 @ 4400 rpm. Torque: Gross: 327 lb.-ft. @ 2600 rpm. Fuel Requirements: Regular.

CHASSIS FEATURES: Separate body and frame. Section modulus: F-100 (115 in. wheelbase): 3.71; F-100 (131 in. wheelbase): 4.14. F-250: 5.58.

SUSPENSION AND RUNNING GEAR: Front Suspension: F-100: 6-cyl. engines: 1250 lb. capacity; with V-8: 1250 lb. F-250: 1200 lb. capacity. Rear Suspension: F-100: Progressive, 1250 lb. capacity. F-250: Progressive, 1700 lb. capacity. Optional: F-100: Single-stage, 1650 lb. capacity. F-250: Progressive, 2400 lb. capacity. Optional auxiliary spring for F-250 rated at 550 lb. Front Axle Type and Capacity: F-100 and F-250: Spicer model 2559, 3000 lb. capacity, full-floating, Hotchkiss. Optional: F-250: Spicer model 2558, 3500 lb. capacity, full-floating, Hotchkiss. Rear Axle Type and Capacity: F-100: Hypoid, Ford-3300, 3300 lb. capacity, semi-floating, Hotchkiss. F-250: Full-floating, Hotchkiss. Spicer model 60, 5200 lb. capacity. Final Drive Ratio: F-100: 3.70:1; Optional: 3.50, 4.11:1. Limited slip differential with 3600 lb. capacity: 3.50, 4.09:1. F-250: 4.10:1. Optional: Limited slip differential with 5200 lb. capacity: 4.10:1. Transfer Case: Type: F-100: Single-speed. F-250: 2-speed Spicer model 24. Ratios: 1.86:1, 1.00:1. Brakes: Type: Hydraulic, drums front and rear, self-generating. Dimensions: F-100: Front: 11 in. x 2.0 in. Rear: 11.03 in. x 2.25 in. F-250: Front: 12.125 in. x 2.00 in. Rear: 12.0 in. x 2.50 in. Wheels: F-100: 5-hole stamped disc, 15 in. x 5.5K, disc. F-250: 8-hole, stamped disc, 16 x 6.0, disc. Tires: F-100: 7.75 x 15, 4 PR. F-250: 6.50 x 16.6 6 PR. Optional: F-100: Tubeless tires: 6.70 x 15 4 PR; 6.70 x 15 6 PR; 7.10 x 15,4 PR; 7.10 x 15, 6 PR; 6.50 x 16, 6 PR; 7.17.5, 6 PR. Tube-type tires: 6.50 x 16, 6 PR; 7.0 x 15, 6 PR. F-250: Tubeless tires: 6.50 x 16, 6 PR; 7.00 x 16, 6 PR; 7 x 17.5, 6 PR; 8 x 17.5, 6 PR; 8 x 17.5, 8 PR; 8 x 19.5, 8 PR. Tube-type tires: 6.50 x 16, 6 PR; 6.50 x 16, 6 PR, 7.00 x 16, 6 PR, 7.00 x 17, 8 PR; 7.50 x 16, 6 PR; 7.50 x 17, 8 PR. Steering: F-100 and F-250: Gemer #375, Worm and Roller, 18 in. dia. steering wheel. Ratio: 24.2:1. Optional: None. Transmission: Type: F-100: 4-speed New Process 435. F-250: Ford 3-speed manual. Optional: F-250: 4-speed New Process 435. Ratios: New Process 435: 6.69, 3.34, 1.66, 1.0:1. Reverse: 8.26:1. Clutch: Heavy-duty hydraulic. 11.0 in. dia. and 123.7 sq. in.

VEHICLE DIMENSIONS: Wheelbase: 115 in., 131 in. Overall length: F-100: 115 in. wheelbase: Pickup, 6.5 ft. Flareside: 188.9 in. Pickup, 6.5 ft. Styleside: 188.6 in. F-100: 131 in. wheelbase: Chassis & cab: 204.3 in. Pickup, 8 ft. Flareside: 208.5 in. Pickup, 8 ft. Styleside: 210.6 in. F-250: Chassis & cab: 202.3 in. Pickup, 8 ft. Flareside: 208.5 in. Pickup, 8 ft. Styleside: 210.6 in. Platform, 7.5 ft.: 205.8 in. Stake, 7.5 ft.: 205.8 in. Front/Rear Overhang: 33.5 in./48.4 in. Height: F-100: 75.0 in. F-250: 77.5 in. Width: 79.8 in. Front/Rear tread: 64.1 in./60.4 in.

CAPACITIES: Fuel Tank: 18 gal.

ACCOMMODATIONS: 3 occupants.

INSTRUMENTATION: Speedometer, odometer, fuel level and engine coolant temperature gauges, warning lights for oil pressure, and battery charge.

OPTIONS AND PRICES: 300 L-6. 360 V-8. Extra Cooling radiator. Closed crankcase ventilation (required for California). Velocity controlled governor. 42 amp alternator. 52 amp alternator. 60 amp alternator. Limited slip rear axle (3.92:1 ratio with 3-spd. trans.; 4.10:1 with V-8, includes 4.09:1 front axle ratio). 70 amp-hr. battery. Free-running front Spicer hubs. Two-stage 1950 lb. capacity rear springs. 4-speed New Process 435 manual transmission. Driver-side armrest. Passenger side armrest. Cigarette lighter. Custom Package. Ranger Package: $238. Laminated sheet door glass. Tinted windshield glass. Fresh-Air heater and defroster. Recirculating-type heater and defroster. Inside safety mirror (standard for pickups). Exterior chrome left and right side mirrors. Non-telescopic 5 in. x 5 in. right side mirror. Non-telescopic 5 in. x 5 in. left side mirror. Telescopic 5 in. x 8 in. left and/or right side mirrors. Western-type 5 in. x 10.0 in. left and/or right side mirrors. Two-tone paint. Manual radio and antenna. Full foam seat cushion. Heavy-duty black vinyl seat trim. Right side sun visor. Windshield washers. Two-speed electric windshield wipers. Chrome contour front bumper. Rear chrome contour bumper (Styleside pickups). Painted contour rear bumper (Styleside pickups). Painted channel rear bumper (Flareside pickups). Brush-type grille guard. Dual electric horns. ICC emergency lamp flasher. ICC cab clearance and marker lights (two or three corner lights). ICC rear reflectors. Front-mounted amber reflectors. Side-mounted spare tire carrier. Left side spare tire mount (Flareside and Styleside). Double-faced front and rear taillights directional signals.

HISTORICAL FOOTNOTES: The 1969 models were introduced in the fall of 1968.

1970 PICKUP

A bold grille design with a wide center divider separating a bright gridwork identified the 1970 Ford F-10 and F-250 models. Four trim levels were available. The base custom trim consisted of deep-cushioned seats, a color-coordinated interior, "swept-away" instrument panel, energy-absorbing sun visors, and armrests (with squeeze door latch handles), seat belts, windshield washers, two-speed electric windshield wipers, day/night mirror, bright left side exterior mirror, turn signals, emergency flasher, Deluxe Fresh-Air heater with 3-speed fan, "hi-dri" all-weather ventilation, door courtesy light switches, ashtray, wedge-type vent window handles, glove compartment with push-button latch, hardboard headlining, black floor mats with heel pads, aluminum scuff plates, Deluxe instrument panel cluster bezel. Color-keyed, textured-steel door trim panels, black, blue, red, parchment or green vinyl seat trim with embossed patterned rib inserts, bright grille and chrome front bumper.

The Sport custom option had in addition to or in place of the custom items the following: Deep-foam seat cushion and foam padding in seat back, pleated basket-weave vinyl seat trim inserts, grained vinyl bolsters, color-keyed, pleated vinyl door panels with bright moldings, color-keyed floor mats, cigarette lighter, and horn ring. Exterior features of the Sport custom included bright moldings for the windshield, rocker panel and wheel-lip openings. The Styleside models had bright taillight bezels and tailgate appliques. The Ranger Styleside and chassis-cab model interiors included in addition to or in place of the Sport custom features, woodtone instrument panel, bright headlining retrainer molding, color-keyed pleated vinyl door panels with bright moldings and woodtone inserts, bright seat-pivot arm covers, and Ranger plaque on glove box door. The Ranger exterior had bright side, rear window and roof rail drip moldings. The Stylesides had a bright tailgate latch handle and full tailgate panel. Optional was a bright rocker panel and wheel-lip moldings. The new top-ranked Ranger XLT Styleside and chassis-cab models included in addition to or in place of the Ranger elements these items: Pleated cloth and vinyl seat upholstery, color-keyed wall-to-wall carpeting, special weather and sound insulation, Convenience Package (includes cargo end engine lights, glove box light and 12 in. day/night mirror), sound-absorbing perforated headliner, and bright instrument panel molding on right side and heater modesty panel with woodgrain insert. The Styleside exterior decor included bright side moldings with woodgrain inserts, bright rocker panel and wheel-lip moldings, and woodgrain tailgate panel.

The F-100 continued to use Ford's Mono-Beam front suspension with coil springs, forged radius rods and a steering linkage shock absorber. A single-speed transfer case and 4-speed manual transmission were standard. The F-250's front suspension retained leaf springs with lubrication-free shackles. It also had a standard 2-speed transfer case and 3-speed manual transmission.

1970 Ford F-100 Styleside pickup

Ford once again offered three Special Packages for the F-100 and F-250 8-foot Styleside pickups. The Contractor Special included a Contractor box with key-lock, and fold-down doors on both sides, rear step bumper, dual bright Western long arm exterior mirrors and a "Contractor Special" insignia. The Farm & Ranch Special included front and 9.0 in. high side cargo boards, rear step bumper, dual bright Western swing-lock exterior mirrors and a "Farm & Ranch" insignia. The Heavy-Duty Special consisted of heavy-duty front springs, heavy-duty battery, heavy-duty alternator, ammeter, oil pressure gauge, rear step bumper, dual bright Western swing-lock exterior mirrors and a "Heavy-Duty Special" insignia.

Standard exterior colors for 1970 were raven black, Wimbledon white, Norway green, new lime, boxwood green, candyapple red, royal maroon, Mojave tan, Yucatan gold, pinto yellow, diamond blue, reef aqua, sky view blue, harbor blue, chrome yellow and pure white. A total of 48 different regular, Deluxe or combination two-tones were offered. Wimbledon white served as the accent color for all colors except for chrome yellow and pure white. In the regular format, the accent color was applied to the roof and upper back panel with a belt line molding from door to door around the back of the cab. In the Deluxe two-tone, available for Styleside pickups only, the accent color was applied to the area below the body side and lower tailgate moldings which are included in this option. The combination two-tone, again limited to the Styleside pickups, combined the regular and Deluxe two-tone options with the accent color applied as specified in those two options.

I.D. DATA: The first letter and two digits represent the series. Next was the engine code for the engine, letter code for the assembly plant, then six digits which indicated sequential production numbers.

Body Type	Factory Price	GVW	Shipping Weight	Prod. Total
Series F-100, 115 in., 131 in. wheelbase				
Chassis & Cab	$3031	4600[1]	3340	—
Pickup, 6.5 ft. Flareside	$3155	4600	3655	—
Pickup, 6.5 ft. Styleside	$3194	4600	3720	—
Pickup, 8.0 ft. Flareside	$3194	4600	3770	—
Pickup, 8.0 ft. Styleside	$3231	4600	3785	—

NOTE 1: 5600 lb. GVW optional.

Body Type	Factory Price	GVW	Shipping Weight	Prod. Total
Series F-250, 131 in. wheelbase				
Chassis & Cab	$3379	6300[2]	3610	—
Pickup, 8 ft. Flareside	$3506	6300	4030	—
Pickup, 8 ft. Styleside	$3543	6300	4045	—
Platform, 7.5 ft.	$3540	6300	4020	—
Stake, 7.5 ft.	$3595	6300	4200	—
Crew Cab, 148.3 in. wb.	N.A.	N.A.	N.A.	—

NOTE 2: 7700 lb. GVW optional.

STANDARD ENGINE: F-100, F-250: Engine Type: OHV In-line 6-cylinder. Bore x Stroke: 4.00 in. x 3.18 in. Lifters: Hydraulic. Number of main bearings-7. Displacement: 240 cu. in. (3.93 liters). Induction system: Single venturi downdraft carburetor. Compression Ratio: 9.2:1. Horsepower: Gross: 150 @ 4000 rpm. Net: 129 @ 4000 rpm. Torque: Gross: 234 lb.-ft.@ 2200 rpm. Net: 218 lb.-ft. @ 2000 rpm. Fuel Requirements: Regular.

OPTIONAL ENGINE: F-100, F-250: Engine Type: OHV In-line 6-cylinder. Bore x Stroke: 4.00 in. x 3.98 in. Displacement: 300 cu. in. Induction system: Single venturi downdraft carburetor. Compression Ratio: 8.8:1. Number of main bearings-7. Horsepower: Gross: 165 @ 3600 rpm. Torque: Gross: 294 lb.-ft.@ 2000 rpm. Fuel Requirements: Regular.

OPTIONAL ENGINE: F-100, F-250: Engine Type: OHV V-8. Bore x Stroke: 4.00 in. x 3.50 in. Displacement: 360 cu. in. (5.76 liters). Induction system: 2-barrel carburetor. Compression Ratio: 8.4:1. Number of main bearings-5. Horsepower: Gross: 215 @ 4400 rpm. Torque: Gross: 327 lb.-ft. @ 2600 rpm. Fuel Requirements: Regular.

CHASSIS FEATURES: Separate body and frame. Section modulus: F-100 (115 in. wheelbase): 3.71; F-100 (131 in. wheelbase): 4.14. F-250: 5.58.

SUSPENSION AND RUNNING GEAR: Front Suspension: F-100: 6-cyl. engines: 1250 lb. capacity; with V-8: 1250 lb. F-250: 1200 lb. capacity. Rear Suspension: F-100: Progressive, 1250 lb. capacity. F-250: Progressive, 1700 lb. capacity. Optional: F-100: Single-stage, 1650 lb. capacity. F-250: Progressive, 2400 lb. capacity. Optional auxiliary spring for F-250 rated at 550 lb. Front Axle Type and Capacity: F-100 and F-250: Spicer model 2559, 3000 lb. capacity, full-floating, Hotchkiss. Optional: F-250: Spicer model 2558, 3500 lb. capacity, full-floating, Hotchkiss. Rear Axle Type and Capacity: F-100: Hypoid, Ford-3300, 3300 lb. capacity, semi-floating, Hotchkiss. F-250: Full-floating, Hotchkiss. Spicer model 60, 5200 lb. capacity. Final Drive Ratio: F-100: 3.70:1; Optional: 3.50, 4.11:1. Limited slip differential with 3600 lb. capacity: 3.50, 4.09:1. F-250: 4.10:1. Optional: Limited slip differential with 5200 lb. capacity: 4.10:1. Transfer Case: Type: F-100: Single-speed. F-250: 2-speed Spicer model 24. Ratios: 1.86:1, 1.00:1. Brakes: Type: Hydraulic, drums front and rear, self-generating. Dimensions: F-100: Front: 11 in. x 2.0 in. Rear: 11.03 in. x 2.25 in. F-250: Front: 12.125 in. x 2.00 in. Rear: 12.0 in. x 2.50 in. Wheels: F-100: 5-hole stamped disc, 15 in. x 5.5K, disc. F-250: 8-hole, stamped disc, 16 x 6.0, disc. Tires: F-100: G78 x 15 B 4 PR. F-250: 8.00 x 16.5 8 PR. Optional: F-100: Tubeless tires: 6.70 x 15 4 PR; 6.70 x 15 6 PR; 7.10 x 15,4 PR; 7.10 x 15, 6 PR; 6.50

x 16, 6 PR; 7.17.5, 6 PR. Tube-type tires: 6.50 x 16, 6 PR; 7.0 x 15, 6 PR. F-250: Tubeless tires: 6.50 x 16, 6 PR; 7.00 x 16, 6 PR; 7 x 17.5, 6 PR; 8 x 17.5, 6 PR; 8 x 17.5, 8 PR; 8 x 19.5, 8 PR. Tube-type tires: 6.50 x 16, 6 PR; 6.50 x 16, 6 PR, 7.00 x 16, 6 PR, 7.00 x 17, 8 PR; 7.50 x 16, 6 PR; 7.50 x 17, 8 PR. Steering: F-100 and F-250: Gemer #375, Worm and Roller, 18 in. dia. steering wheel. Ratio: 24.2:1. Optional: None. Transmission: Type: F-100: 4-speed New Process 435. F-250: Ford 3-speed manual. Optional: F-250: 4-speed New Process 435. Ratios: New Process 435: 6.69, 3.34, 1.66, 1.0:1. Reverse: 8.26:1. Clutch: Heavy-duty hydraulic. 11.0 in. dia. and 123.7 sq. in.

VEHICLE DIMENSIONS: Wheelbase: 115 in., 131 in. Overall length: F-100: 115 in. wheelbase: Pickup, 6.5 ft. Flareside: 188.9 in. Pickup, 6.5 ft. Styleside: 188.6 in. F-100: 131 in. wheelbase: Chassis & cab: 204.3 in. Pickup, 8 ft. Flareside: 208.5 in. Pickup, 8 ft. Styleside: 210.6 in. F-250: Chassis & cab: 202.3 in. Pickup, 8 ft. Flareside: 208.5 in. Pickup, 8 ft. Styleside: 210.6 in. Platform, 7.5 ft.: 205.8 in. Stake, 7.5 ft.: 205.8 in. Front/Rear Overhang: 33.5 in./48.4 in. Height: F-100: 75.0 in. F-250: 77.5 in. Width: 79.8 in. Front/Rear tread: 64.1 in./60.4 in. Pickup box (length x width x height): F-100 6.5 ft. Styleside: 78.2 in. x 49 in. x 19.3 in. F-250 and F-100 131 in. wheelbase. Styleside: 98.2 in. x 49 in. x 19.3 in. F-100 6.5 ft. Flareside: 77.9 in. x 49.0 in. x 20.3 in. F250 and F-100 131 in. wheelbase. Flaresides: 96.0 in. x 48.4 in. x 22.1 in. Tailgate: Styleside pickups: 65.0 in. x 19.3 in. Flareside pickups: 49.0 in. x 203 (F-100, 115 in. wheelbase); all others: 49.0 in. x 22.1 in.

CAPACITIES: Fuel Tank: 18 gal.

ACCOMMODATIONS: 3 occupants.

INSTRUMENTATION: Speedometer, odometer, warning lights for oil pressure, engine coolant temperature and battery charge.

OPTIONS AND PRICES: Ranger Package: $202. Ranger XLT Package: $328. 300 cu. in. 6-cylinder engine. 360 cu. in. V-8 engine. Convenience Group. Remote control outside mirror. Sliding rear window. Electric Power Pak. Bucket seats. Styleside spare tire carrier. Flareside spare tire carrier. Western-style mirrors. Auxiliary 25 gal. fuel tank. Rear step bumper. Lockable in-cab stowage compartment. Contractor boxes. Black textures painted roof. AM push-button radio. Air conditioning. Tool stowage box. Power front disc brakes. Ammeter and oil pressure gauges. Styleside body moldings. Chrome contour rear bumper for Stylesides. Painted channel rear bumper for Flaresides. Tinted glass for all windows. Shoulder harness. Dual electric horns. Heavy-duty black vinyl seat trim. Free-running front hubs. Oil-bath engine air cleaner. Velocity-type running governor.

HISTORICAL FOOTNOTES: Ford reported that its 1970 pickups, introduced on September 19, 1969, "work like trucks...ride like cars."

1971 PICKUP

The primary changes found in the 1971 models included a new, large rectangular pattern grille that, said Ford, "projects a strong, massive appearance", and new standard and optional features. A more comfortable two-spoke steering wheel that provided improved instrument visibility was standard for all models. Added to the base equipment level was a right-side coat hook. An AM/FM radio was now optional. The custom interior trim now had a chevron pattern. The Sport custom exterior trim had a revamped tailgate finish with a flat black applique with argent colored FORD letters. The 302 cu. in. V-8 was now available for the F-100 models.

Standard exterior colors for 1971 were revised to consist of these carry-over colors: Raven black, Wimbledon white, boxwood green, candyapple red, Mojave tan, diamond blue, sky view blue, chrome yellow and pure white along with seven new choices: Mallard green, seafoam green, calypso coral, regis red, prairie yellow, Swiss aqua, and Bahama blue. A total of 54 different regular, Deluxe or combination two-tones were offered. Wimbledon white served as the accent color for all colors except for chrome yellow and pure white. In the regular format, the accent color was applied to the roof and upper back panel with a belt line molding from door to door around the back of the cab. In the Deluxe two-tone, available for Styleside pickups only, the accent color was applied to the area below the body side and lower tailgate moldings which are included in this option. The combination two-tone, again limited to the Styleside pickups, combined the regular and Deluxe two-tone options with the accent color applied as specified in those two options.

1971 Ford F-100 Styleside pickup

I.D. DATA: The first letter and two digits represent the series. Next was the engine code for the engine, letter code for the assembly plant, then six digits which indicated sequential production numbers.

Body Type	Factory Price	GVW	Shipping Weight	Prod. Total
Series F-100, 115 in., 131 in. wheelbase				
Chassis & Cab	$3343	4600[1]	3340	96
Pickup, 6.5 ft. Flareside	$3506	4600	3660	591[2]
Pickup, 6.5 ft. Styleside	$3506	4600	3720	12,870[3]
Pickup, 8.0 ft. Flareside	$3543	4600	3805	—
Pickup, 8.0 ft. Styleside	$3543	4600	3820	—

NOTE 1: 5600 lb. GVW optional.
NOTE 2: Includes all Flareside models.
NOTE 3: Includes all Styleside models.

Series F-250, 131 in. wheelbase				
Chassis & Cab	$3793	6300[4]	3675	649
Pickup, 8 ft. Flareside	$3956	6300	4095	635[5]
Pickup, 8 ft. Styleside	$3956	6300	4110	16,164[6]
Platform, 7.5 ft.	$4069	6300	4090	23
Stake, 7.5 ft.	$4101	6300	4270	87
Crew Cab, 148.3 in. wb.	N.A.	N.A.	N.A.	N.A.

NOTE 4: 7700 lb. GVW optional.
NOTE 5: Includes all Flareside models.
NOTE 6: Includes all Styleside models.

STANDARD ENGINE: F-100, F-250: Engine Type: OHV In-line 6-cylinder. Bore x Stroke: 4.00 in. x 3.18 in. Lifters: Hydraulic. Number of main bearings-7. Displacement: 240 cu. in. (3.93 liters). Induction system: Single venturi downdraft carburetor. Compression Ratio: 9.2:1. Horsepower: Gross: 150 @ 4000 rpm. Net: 129 @ 4000 rpm. Torque: Gross: 234 lb. ft.@ 2200 rpm. Net: 218 lb.-ft. @ 2000 rpm. Fuel Requirements: Regular.

OPTIONAL ENGINE: F-100, F-250: Engine Type: OHV In-line 6-cylinder. Bore x Stroke: 4.00 in. x 3.98 in. Displacement: 300 cu. in. Induction system: Single venturi downdraft carburetor. Compression Ratio: 8.8:1. Number of main bearings-7. Horsepower: Gross: 165 @ 3600 rpm. Torque: Gross: 294 lb.-ft.@ 2000 rpm. Fuel Requirements: Regular.

OPTIONAL ENGINE: F-100, F-250: Engine Type: OHV V-8. Bore x Stroke: 4.00 in. x 3.50 in. Displacement: 360 cu. in. (5.76 liters). Induction system: 2-barrel carburetor. Compression Ratio: 8.4:1. Number of main bearings-5. Horsepower: Gross: 215 @ 4400 rpm. Torque: Gross: 327 lb.-ft. @ 2600 rpm. Fuel Requirements: Regular.

OPTIONAL ENGINE: F-100, F-250: Engine Type: OHV V-8. Bore x Stroke: 4.00 in. x 3.50 in. Displacement: 360 cu. in. (5.76 liters). Induction system: 2-barrel carburetor. Compression Ratio: 8.4:1. Number of main bearings-5. Horsepower: Gross: 215 @ 4400 rpm. Torque: Gross: 327 lb.-ft.@ 2600 rpm. Fuel Requirements: Regular.

CHASSIS FEATURES: Separate body and frame. Section modulus: F-100 (115 in. wheelbase): 3.71; F-100 (131 in. wheelbase): 4.14. F-250: 5.58.

SUSPENSION AND RUNNING GEAR: Front Suspension: F-100: 6-cyl. engines: 1250 lb. capacity; with V-8: 1250 lb. F-250: 1200 lb. capacity. Rear Suspension: F-100: Progressive, 1250 lb. capacity. F-250: Progressive, 1700 lb. capacity. Optional: F-100: Single-stage, 1650 lb. capacity. F-250: Progressive, 2400 lb. capacity. Optional auxiliary spring for F-250 rated at 550 lb. Front Axle Type and Capacity: F-100 and F-250: Spicer model 2559, 3000 lb. capacity, full-floating, Hotchkiss. Optional: F-250: Spicer model 2558, 3500 lb. capacity, full-floating, Hotchkiss. Rear Axle Type and Capacity: F-100: Hypoid, Ford-3300, 3300 lb. capacity, semi-floating, Hotchkiss. F-250: Full-floating, Hotchkiss. Spicer model 60, 5200 lb. capacity. Final Drive Ratio: F-100: 3.70:1; Optional: 3.50, 4.11:1. Limited slip differential with 3600 lb. capacity: 3.50, 4.09:1. F-250: 4.10:1. Optional: Limited slip differential with 5200 lb. capacity: 4.10:1. Transfer Case: Type: F-100: Single-speed. F-250: 2-speed Spicer model 24. Ratios: 1.86:1, 1.00:1. Brakes: Type: Hydraulic, drums front and rear, self-generating. Dimensions: F-100: Front: 11 in. x 2.0 in. Rear: 11.03 in. x 2.25 in. F-250: Front: 12.125 in. x 2.00 in. Rear: 12.0 in. x 2.50 in. Wheels: F-100: 5-hole stamped disc, 15 in. x 5.5K, disc. F-250: 8-hole, stamped disc, 16 x 6.0, disc. Tires: F-100: G78 x 15 B 4 PR. F-250: 8.00 x 16.5 8 PR. Optional: F-100: Tubeless tires: 6.70 x 15 4 PR; 6.70 x 15 6 PR; 7.10 x 15,4 PR; 7.10 x 15, 6 PR; 6.50 x 16, 6 PR; 7.17.5, 6 PR. Tube-type tires: 6.50 x 16, 6 PR; 7.0 x 15, 6 PR. F-250: Tubeless tires: 6.50 x 16, 6 PR; 7.00 x 16, 6 PR; 7 x 17.5, 6 PR; 8 x 17.5, 6 PR; 8 x 17.5, 8 PR; 8 x 19.5, 8 PR. Tube-type tires: 6.50 x 16, 6 PR; 6.50 x 16, 6 PR, 7.00 x 16, 6 PR, 7.00 x 17, 8 PR; 7.50 x 16, 6 PR; 7.50 x 17, 8 PR. Steering: F-100 and F-250: Gemer #375, Worm and Roller, 18 in. dia. steering wheel. Ratio: 24.2:1. Optional: None. Transmission: Type: F-100: 4-speed New Process 435. F-250: Ford 3-speed manual. Optional: F-250: 4-speed New Process 435. Ratios: New Process 435: 6.69, 3.34, 1.66, 1.0:1. Reverse: 8.26:1. Clutch: Heavy-duty hydraulic. 11.0 in. dia. and 123.7 sq. in.

VEHICLE DIMENSIONS: Wheelbase: 115 in., 131 in. Overall length: F-100: 115 in. wheelbase: Pickup, 6.5 ft. Flareside: 188.9 in. Pickup, 6.5 ft. Styleside: 188.6 in. F-100: 131 in. wheelbase: Chassis & cab: 204.3 in. Pickup, 8 ft. Flareside: 208.5 in. Pickup, 8 ft. Styleside: 210.6 in. F-250: Chassis & cab: 202.3 in. Pickup, 8 ft. Flareside: 208.5 in. Pickup, 8 ft. Styleside: 210.6 in. Platform, 7.5 ft.: 205.8 in. Stake, 7.5 ft.: 205.8 in. Front/Rear Overhang: 33.5 in./48.4 in. Height: F-100: 75.0 in. F-250: 77.5 in. Width: 79.8 in. Front/Rear tread: 64.1 in./60.4 in. Pickup box (length x width x height): F-100 6.5 ft. Styleside: 78.2 in. x 49 in. x 19.3 in. F-250 and F-100 131 in. wheelbase. Styleside: 98.2 in. x 49 in. x 19.3 in. F-100 6.5 ft. Flareside: 77.9 in. x 49.0 in. x 20.3 in. F250 and F-100 131 in. wheelbase. Flaresides: 96.0 in. x 48.4 in. x 22.1 in. Tailgate: Styleside pickups: 65.0 in. x 19.3 in. Flareside pickups: 49.0 in. x 203 (F-100, 115 in. wheelbase); all others: 49.0 in. x 22.1 in.

CAPACITIES: Fuel Tank: 18 gal.

ACCOMMODATIONS: 3 occupants.

INSTRUMENTATION: Speedometer, odometer, warning lights for oil pressure, engine coolant temperature and battery charge.

OPTIONS: 300 cu. in. 6-cylinder engine. 360 cu. in. V-8 engine. Convenience Group. Remote control outside mirror. Sliding rear window. Electric Power Pak. Bucket seats. Styleside spare tire carrier. Flareside spare tire carrier. Western-style mirrors. Auxiliary 25 gal. fuel tank. Rear step bumper. Lockable in-cab stowage compartment. Contractor boxes. Black textures painted roof. AM push-button radio. Air conditioning. Tool stowage box. Ammeter and oil pressure gauges. Styleside body moldings. Chrome contour rear bumper for Stylesides. Painted channel rear bumper for Flaresides. Tinted glass for all windows. Shoulder harness. Dual electric horns. Heavy-duty black vinyl seat trim. Free-running front hubs. Oil-bath engine air cleaner. Velocity-type engine governor.

HISTORICAL FOOTNOTES: The 1971 models were announced on August 20, 1970. John Naughton, Ford vice president and Ford Division general manager noted in regard to the new Fords: "A truck for almost every use, from heavy construction and interstate hauling to off-road fun and grocery-store shopping, is our summation of the 1971 Ford truck line."

1972 PICKUP

The 1972 Fords had the almost obligatory annual grille revision. For 1972 the grille consisted of a bright finish aluminum stamping with a vertical center divider with a black accent stripe separating argent colored plastic inserts with four divisions. The single headlights were recessed within black painted nacelles. The grille used combined the basic format of 1971 but with eight sub-sections rather than the twelve of 1971. The seat belts were now color-keyed to the interior. Most of the remaining changes for 1972 were technical in nature. The F-250 now had standard free-running front hubs, and a standard 4-speed transmission. Power brakes were now optional for both the F-100 and F-250 models. Both the F-100 and F-250 had a higher rated, 3300 lb. front axle. The 300 cu. in. 6-cylinder was now the standard F-250 engine.

New colors for 1972 included seapine green metallic, Winter green, royal maroon, Tampico yellow, wind blue, bay roc blue metallic, and sequoia brown.

I.D. DATA: The V.I.N. consisted of eleven entries. The first was a digit identifying the model year. The next was a letter identifying the assembly plant. The third and fourth, both digits, identified the product line and body style. The fifth symbol, a letter, designated the engine. The final six digits served as the sequential production number.

Body Type	Factory Price	GVW	Shipping Weight	Prod. Total
Series F-100, 115 in., 131 in. wheelbase				
Chassis & Cab	$3240	4600[1]	3230	96
Pickup, 6.5 ft. Flareside	$3403	4600	3550	5912
Pickup, 6.5 ft. Styleside	$3403	4600	3610	—
Pickup, 8.0 ft. Flareside	$3543	4600	3695	—
Pickup, 8.0 ft. Styleside	$3543	4600	3710	—
NOTE 1: 5600 lb. GVW optional.				
Series F-250, 131 in. wheelbase				
Chassis & Cab	$3678	6300[2]	3565	—
Pickup, 8 ft. Flareside	$3841	6300	3985	—
Pickup, 8 ft. Styleside	$3841	6300	4000	—
Platform, 7.5 ft.	$3954	6300	3980	—
Stake, 7.5 ft.	$3986	6300	4160	—
Crew Cab, 148.3 in. wb.	$N.A.	N.A.	N.A.	—

NOTE 2: 7700 lb. GVW optional.
NOTE 5: Includes all Flareside models.
NOTE 6: Includes all Styleside models.

STANDARD ENGINE: F-100: Engine Type: OHV In-line 6-cylinder. Bore x Stroke: 4.00 in. x 3.18 in. Lifters: Hydraulic. Number of main bearings-7. Displacement: 240 cu. in. (3.93 liters). Induction system: Single venturi downdraft carburetor. Compression Ratio: 9.2:1. Horsepower: N.A. Torque: Gross: N.A. Fuel Requirements: Regular.

STANDARD ENGINE: F-250, Optional for F-100: Engine Type: OHV In-line 6-cylinder. Bore x Stroke: 4.00 in. x 3.98 in. Displacement: 300 cu. in. Induction system: Single venturi downdraft carburetor. Compression Ratio: 8.8:1. Number of main bearings-7. Horsepower: Gross: 126 @ 3400 rpm, Net: 117 @ 3400 rpm. Torque: N.A. Fuel Requirements: Regular.

OPTIONAL ENGINE: F-100, F-250: Engine Type: OHV V-8. Bore x Stroke: 4.00 in. x 3.50 in. Displacement: 360 cu. in. (5.76 liters). Induction system: 2-barrel carburetor. Compression Ratio: 8.4:1. Number of main bearings-7. Horsepower: Gross: 196 @ 4600 rpm, Net: 156 @ 4600 rpm. Torque: N.A. Fuel Requirements: Regular.

CHASSIS FEATURES: Separate body and frame. Section modulus: F-100 (115 in. wheelbase): 3.71; F-100 (131 in. wheelbase): 4.14. F-250: 5.58.

SUSPENSION AND RUNNING GEAR: Front Suspension: F-100: 6-cyl. engines: 1150 lb. capacity; with V-8: 1250 lb. F-250: 1200 lb. capacity. Rear Suspension: F-100: Progressive, 1250 lb. capacity. F-250: Progressive, 1700 lb. capacity. Optional: F-100: Single-stage, 1650 lb. capacity. F-250: Progressive, 2400 lb. capacity. Optional auxiliary spring for F-250 rated at 550 lb. Front Axle Type and Capacity: F-100: Dana, 3300 lb. capacity, full-floating, Hotchkiss. F-250: Spicer model 6CF, 3300 lb. capacity, full-floating, Hotchkiss. Optional: F-250: Spicer model 2558, 3500 lb. capacity, full-floating, Hotchkiss. Rear Axle Type and Capacity: F-100: Hypoid, Ford-3300, 3300 lb. capacity, semi-floating, Hotchkiss. F-250: Full-floating, Hotchkiss. Spicer model 60, 5200 lb. capacity. Final Drive Ratio: F-100: 3.70:1; Optional: 3.50, 4.11:1. Limited slip differential with 3600 lb. capacity: 3.50, 4.09:1: F-250: 4.10:1. Optional: Limited slip differential with 5200 lb. capacity: 4.10:1. Transfer Case: F-100: Single-speed. F-250: 2-speed Spicer model 24. Ratios: 1.86:1, 1.00:1. Brakes: Type: Hydraulic, drums front and rear, self-generating. Dimensions: F-100: Front: 11 in. x 2.0 in. Rear: 11.03 in. x 2.25 in. F-250: Front: 12.125 in. x 2.00 in. Rear: 12.0 in. x 2.50 in. Wheels: F-100: 5-hole stamped disc, 15 in. x 5.5K, disc. F-250: 8-hole, stamped disc, 16 x 6.0, disc. Tires: F-100: G78 x 15 B 4 PR. F-250: 8.00 x 16.5 8 PR. Optional: F-100: Tubeless tires: 6.70 x 15 4 PR; 6.70 x 15 6 PR; 7.10 x 15,4 PR; 7.10 x 15, 6 PR; 6.50 x 16, 6 PR; 7.17.5, 6 PR. Tube-type tires: 6.50 x 16, 6 PR; 7.0 x 15, 6 PR. F-250: Tubeless tires: 6.50 x 16, 6 PR; 7.00 x 16, 6 PR; 7 x 17.5, 6 PR; 8 x 17.5, 6 PR; 8 x 17.5, 8 PR; 8 x 19.5, 8 PR. Tube-type tires: 6.50 x 16, 6 PR; 6.50 x 16, 6 PR, 7.00 x 16, 6 PR, 7.00 x 17, 8 PR; 7.50 x 16, 6 PR; 7.50 x 17, 8 PR. Steering: F-100 and F-250: Gemer #375, Worm and Roller, 18 in. dia. steering wheel. Ratio: 24.2:1. Optional: None. Transmission: Type: F-100 and F-250: 4-speed New Process 435. Ratios: New Process 435: 6.69, 3.34, 1.66, 1.0:1. Reverse: 8.26:1. Clutch: Heavy-duty hydraulic. 11.0 in. dia. and 123.7 sq. in.

VEHICLE DIMENSIONS: Wheelbase: 115 in., 131 in. Overall length: F-100: 115 in. wheelbase: Pickup, 6.5 ft. Flareside: 188.9 in. Pickup, 6.5 ft. Styleside: 188.6 in. F-100: 131 in. wheelbase: Chassis & cab: 204.3 in. Pickup, 8 ft. Flareside: 208.5 in. Pickup, 8 ft. Styleside: 210.6 in. F-250: Chassis & cab: 202.3 in. Pickup, 8 ft. Flareside: 208.5 in. Pickup, 8 ft. Styleside: 210.6 in. Platform, 7.5 ft.: 205.8 in. Stake, 7.5 ft.: 205.8 in. Front/Rear Overhang: 33.5 in./48.4 in. Height: F-100: 75.0 in. F-250: 77.5 in. Width: 79.8 in. Front/Rear tread: 64.1 in./60.4 in. Pickup box (length x width x height): F-100 6.5 ft. Styleside: 78.2 in. x 49 in. x 19.3 in. F-250 and F-100 131 in. wheelbase. Styleside: 98.2 in. x 49 in. x 19.3 in. F-100 6.5 ft. Flareside: 77.9 in. x 49.0 in. x 20.3 in. F250 and F-100 131 in. wheelbase. Flaresides: 96.0 in. x 48.4 in. x 22.1 in. Tailgate: Styleside pickups: 65.0 in. x 19.3 in. Flareside pickups: 49.0 in. x 203 (F-100, 115 in. wheelbase); all others: 49.0 in. x 22.1 in.

CAPACITIES: Fuel Tank: 18 gal.

ACCOMMODATIONS: 3 occupants.

INSTRUMENTATION: Speedometer, odometer, fuel level and engine coolant temperature gauges, warning lights for oil pressure and battery charge.

OPTIONS: 300 cu. in. 6-cylinder engine. 360 cu. in. V-8 engine. Convenience Group. Remote control outside mirror. Sliding rear window. Electric Power Pak. Styleside spare tire carrier. Flareside spare tire carrier. Western-style mirrors. Auxiliary 25 gal. fuel tank. Rear step bumper. Lockable in-cab stowage compartment. Contractor boxes. Black textures painted roof. AM push-button radio. AM/FM radio. Air conditioning. Tool stowage box. Ammeter and oil pressure gauges. Styleside body moldings. Chrome contour rear bumper for Stylesides. Painted channel rear bumper for Flaresides. Tinted glass for all windows. Shoulder harness. Dual electric horns. Heavy-duty black vinyl seat trim. Free-running front hubs. Oil-bath engine air cleaner. Velocity-type engine governor.

HISTORICAL FOOTNOTES: The 1972 models were introduced on September 24, 1971. Sales of the 1972 Ford trucks established a new record of 795,987 units.

1973 PICKUP

Ford's 1973 four-wheel drive trucks were generally regarded as all-new models with the most extensive changes in six years. Among the highlights of 1973 were longer wheelbases (the F-100 and F-250 wheelbases were increased to 117 and 133 inches), wide tracks, restyled sheet metal and new options. New features included a longer cab with behind-seat storage, the availability of automatic transmission and power steering, a redesigned instrument panel with integral optional air conditioning and a fiberglass pickup box cover designed specially for the Ford pickup. This cover for Styleside pickups with the 8 foot had a close tolerance fit with the box and the rear of the cab. It had a locking rear lift gate and tinted glass. The new air conditioning system had four outlets in the instrument panel, full-selection lighted controls, a four-speed fan, fresh air intake, and a blend-air reheat system for temperature control and maximum dehumidification. All instrument panel controls including the automatic transmission selector were illuminated. The panel format positioned all gauges within three rectangular segments. A bright molding surrounded the cluster area which was painted black. The control for the emergency flashers was located on the steering column. The steering wheel was redesigned to provide an improved grip. The glove box was 50 percent larger than in 1972. Full double-wall construction was used for the Styleside pickup box. A new metal forming procedure made it possible to use just two rather than the six sidewall stamping of previous years. The Styleside pickup tailgate had an improved latch that could be operated by one hand.

New options for 1973 included intermittent windshield wipers and low-profile swing lock mirrors. Beginning early in December, 1972 the SelectShift Cruise-O-Matic 3-speed automatic transmission was available for the F-100 and F-250 four-wheel drive trucks with the 133 in. wheelbase and the 360 cu. in. V-8 engine. F-100 models with this engine/transmission had a 2-speed transfer case. The power steering option required the 360 cu. in. V-8.

Highlighting the new exterior design for 1973 was a sculptured, full-length body side channel in which both the front and rear side marker lights were placed. New door handles were recessed and blended into the door sheet metal. The door locks now had a keyless locking feature. The hoods had new contours with full inner panels to resist shake. The full-width grille for 1973 had a bright metal design, vertical center divider bars and deep, bright and black plastic inserts. The side and rear glass area was increased by 2.21 sq. ft. The backlight sloped further forward to reduce glass in the mirror. Except for the F-250 Styleside model, the fuel tank was relocated to the outside of the cab, providing an inch more legroom and a larger storage area behind the seat. The seat back had an increased angle. Full foam cushioning was now standard with seven inches of foam installed on top of formed wire springs. The seat back had five inches of foam.

1973 Ford F-100 Custom Styleside pickup

The Custom model cabs had the following standard equipment: Deluxe Fresh-Air heater and defroster, energy-absorbing sun visors and instrument panel padding, color-keyed molded door panels with recessed squeeze-type door handle/armrests, seat belts, windshield washers, 2-speed electric windshield wipers, door courtesy switches, ashtray, sponge-grain headlining, black rubber floor mat, door scuff plates, vinyl seat trim in a choice of black, red, blue or green; day/night rearview mirror, and bright tailgate hand depression (Styleside models).

The Ranger models include in addition to or in place of custom features these interior items: Color-keyed pleated cloth seat upholstery with vinyl bolster, instrument panel molding with black accent, color-keyed door panels with bright moldings, additional insulation, perforated headlining with bright molding, color-keyed floor mat with vinyl-coated heel pads, and cigarette lighter. Exterior features included bright windshield, rear window and roof drip moldings, and bright rocker panel and wheel-lip moldings. The Styleside Ranger models had aluminum tailgate applique, bright tailgate moldings and taillight bezels.

The Ranger XLT models include in addition to or in place of Ranger features these interior items: Color-keyed quilted cloth with vinyl trim seat upholstery, color-keyed pleated vinyl upper door panels with woodtone accented moldings and map pocket lower panels, color-keyed wall-to-wall nylon carpeting, carpeted behind-seat storage area, black steering wheel with woodtone insert, bright instrument panel molding with woodtone accents, bright seat-pivot covers, additional insulation, Convenience Group, color-keyed vinyl headlining and sun visors. The Styleside pickup exterior decor includes bright cab and body side moldings with vinyl insert, and upper tailgate applique panel and molding. The 1973 colors were Wimbledon white, mallard green, limestone green metallic, seapine green metallic, Winter green, candy-apple red, royal maroon, Tampico yellow, Durango tan, raven black, wind blue, Bahama blue, midnight blue metallic, sequoia brown metallic, chrome yellow and pure white. Two-tone color choices were available by using all the standard colors except chrome yellow and pure white. Wimbledon white could be used as the accent color for any other color.

I.D. DATA: The V.I.N. consisted of eleven entries. The first was a digit identifying the model year. The next was a letter identifying the assembly plant. The third and fourth, both digits, identified the product line and body style. The fifth symbol, a letter, designated the engine. The final six digits served as the sequential production number.

Body Type	Factory Price	GVW	Shipping Weight	Prod. Total
Series F-100, 115 in., 133 in. wheelbase				
Chassis & Cab	$3316	5300[1]	3330	96
Pickup, 6.75 ft. Styleside	$3403	5300	3650	5912
Pickup, 8.0 ft. Flareside	$3479	5300	3710	—
Pickup, 8.0 ft. Styleside	$3619	5300	3795	—

NOTE 1: 5600 lb. GVW optional.

Series F-250, 133 in. wheelbase				
Chassis & Cab	$3773	6300[2]	3715	—
Pickup, 8 ft. Flareside	$3936	6300	4135	—
Pickup, 8 ft. Styleside	$3936	6300	4150	—
Platform, 7.5 ft.	$4049	6300	4130	—
Stake, 7.5 ft.	$4081	6300	4310	—
Crew Cab, 148.3 in. wb.	N.A.	N.A.	N.A.	N.A.

NOTE 2: 7100 lb. and 7700 lb. GVW optional.

STANDARD ENGINE: F-100: Engine Type: OHV In-line 6-cylinder. Bore x Stroke: 4.00 in. x 3.18 in. Lifters: Hydraulic. Number of main bearings-7. Displacement: 240 cu. in. (3.93 liters). Induction system: Single venturi downdraft carburetor. Compression Ratio: 9.2:1. Horsepower: N.A. Torque: Gross: N.A. Fuel Requirements: Regular.

STANDARD ENGINE: F-250: Engine Type: OHV In-line 6-cylinder. Bore x Stroke: 4.00 in. x 3.98 in. Displacement: 300 cu. in. Induction system: Single venturi downdraft carburetor. Compression Ratio: 8.8:1. Number of main bearings-7. Horsepower: Gross: 126 @ 3400 rpm, Net: 117 @ 3400 rpm. Torque: N.A. Fuel Requirements: Regular.

OPTIONAL ENGINE: F-100, F-250: Engine Type: OHV V-8. Bore x Stroke: 4.00 in. x 3.50 in. Displacement: 360 cu. in. (5.76 liters). Induction system: 2-barrel carburetor. Compression Ratio: 8.4:1. Number of main bearings-5. Horsepower: Gross: 196 @ 4600 rpm, Net: 156 @ 4600 rpm. Torque: N.A. Fuel Requirements: Regular.

CHASSIS FEATURES: Separate body and frame. Section modulus: F-100 (117 in. wheelbase): 3.92; F-100 (133 in. wheelbase): 4.14; F-250: 5.58.

SUSPENSION AND RUNNING GEAR: Front Suspension: F-100: 6-cyl. engines: 1365 lb. capacity; F-250: 1550 lb. capacity. Optional: F-100: 1600 lb. capacity. F-250: 1750 lb. capacity. Rear Suspension: F-100: Progressive, 1475 lb. capacity. F-250: Progressive, 1975 lb. capacity. Optional: F-100: Single-stage, 1875 lb. capacity. F-250: Progressive, 2700 lb. capacity. Optional auxiliary spring for F-250 rated at 550 lb. Front Axle Type and Capacity: F-100: Spicer model 2559, 3300 lb. capacity, full-floating, Hotchkiss. F-250: Spicer model 6CF, 3300 lb. capacity, full-floating, Hotchkiss. Optional: F-250: Spicer model 2558, 3500 lb. capacity, full-floating, Hotchkiss. Rear Axle Type and Capacity: F-100: Hypoid, Ford-3300, 3300 lb. capacity, semi-floating, Hotchkiss. F-250: Full-floating, Hotchkiss. Spicer model 60, 5300 lb. capacity. Final Drive Ratio: F-100: 3.70:1; Optional: 3.50, 4.11:1. F-250: 4.10:1. Limited slip differential with 3600 lb. capacity: 3.50, 4.09:1. F-250: 4.10:1. Optional: Limited slip differential with 5300 lb. capacity: 4.10:1. Transfer Case: Type: F-100: Single-speed. F-250: 2-speed Dana Model 24. Ratios: 1.86:1, 1.00:1 (F-100 with the 133 in. wheelbase and the 360 cu. in. V-8 engine has the 2-speed transfer case). Brakes: Type: Hydraulic, drums front and rear, self-generating. Dimensions: F-100: Front: 11 in. x 2.0 in. Rear: 11.03 in. x 2.25 in. F-250: Front: 12.125 in. x 2.00 in. Rear: 12.0 in. x 2.50 in. Wheels: F-100: 5-hole stamped disc, 15 in x 5.5K, disc. F-250: 8-hole, stamped disc, 16 x 6.0, disc. Tires: F-100: G78 x 15 B 4 PR. F-250: 8.00 x 16.5 8 PR. Optional: F-100: Tubeless tires: 6.70 x 15 4 PR; 6.70 x 15 6 PR; 7.10 x 15,4 PR; 7.10 x 15, 6 PR; 6.50 x 16, 6 PR; 7.17.5, 6 PR. Tube-type tires: 6.50 x 16, 6 PR; 7.0 x 15, 6 PR. F-250: Tubeless tires: 6.50 x 16, 6 PR; 7.00 x 16, 6 PR; 7 x 17.5, 6 PR; 8 x 17.5, 6 PR; 8 x 17.5, 8 PR; 8 x 19.5, 8 PR. Tube-type tires: 6.50 x 16, 6 PR; 7.00 x 16, 6 PR, 7.00 x 17, 8 PR; 7.50 x 16, 6 PR; 7.50 x 17, 8 PR. Steering: F-100 and F-250: Gemer #375, Worm and Roller, 18 in. dia. steering wheel. Ratio: 24.2:1. Optional: Linkage power. Transmission: Type: F-100 and F-250: 4-speed New Process 435. Ratios: New Process 435: 6.69, 3.34, 1.66, 1.0:1. Reverse: 8.26:1. Clutch: Heavy-duty hydraulic. 11.0 in. dia. and 123.7 sq. in. Optional: Cruise-O-Matic 3-speed automatic.

VEHICLE DIMENSIONS: Wheelbase: 117 in., 133 in. Overall length: F-100: 117 in. wheelbase: Pickup, 6.5 ft. Styleside: 195 in. Pickup, 6.5 ft. Styleside: 194.8 in. F-100: 133 in. wheelbase: Chassis & cab: 205.3 in. Pickup, 8 ft. Flareside: 208.5 in. Pickup, 8 ft. Styleside: 211 in. F-250: Chassis & cab: 205.3 in. Pickup, 8 ft. Flareside: 208.5 in. Pickup, 8 ft. Styleside: 211 in. Front/Rear Overhang: 28.0 in./48.0 in. Height: F-100 117 in. wheelbase: 72.9, 133 in. Styleside: 73.4 in. F-250 Styleside: 76.2 in. Width: 79.1 in. Front/Rear tread: F-100: 64.4 in./64.4 in. F-250: 64.2 in./65.0 in. Pickup box (length x width x height): F-100 6.5 ft. Styleside: 78.2 in. x 49 in. x 19.3 in. F-250 and F-100 131 in. wheelbase: 98.2 in. x 49 in. x 19.3 in. F-100 6.5 ft. Flareside: 77.9 in. x 49.0 in. x 20.3 in. F250 and F-100 131 in. wheelbase. Flaresides: 96.0 in. x 48.4 in. x 22.1 in. Tailgate: Styleside pickups: 65.0 in. x 19.3 in. Flareside pickups: 54.0 in. x 22.0.

CAPACITIES: Fuel Tank: F-100: 19.4 gal.; F-250: 19.5 gal (18.0 gal. for California).

ACCOMMODATIONS: 3 occupants.

INSTRUMENTATION: Speedometer, odometer, fuel level and engine coolant temperature gauges, warning lights for oil pressure and battery charge.

OPTIONS AND PRICES: Ranger Package. Ranger XLT Package: $349.98. 300 cu. in. 6-cylinder engine. 360 cu. in. V-8 engine: $153.68. Convenience Group. Dual exterior mirrors: $37.40. Knitted vinyl seat: $15.55. Remote control outside mirror. Sliding rear window: $51.33. Electric Power Pak. Power brakes: $48.46. Western-style mirrors. Auxiliary 24 gal. (20.2 gal. for F-100) fuel tank. 55 amp alternator: $6.00. Auxiliary 70 amp-hr. battery: $50. Rear step bumper: $49.24. Tie-down hooks: $27. AM radio: $72. AM/FM stereo radio: $218.92. Air conditioning. Special two-tone paint: $69. Ammeter and oil pressure gauges: $11.83. Automatic transmission: $236.09. Intermittent windshield wipers: $25.40. Power steering: $128.30. Dana limited slip rear axle: $128.30. Locking tool box: $46.37. Styleside body moldings. Cigarette lighter: $7.40. Chrome contour rear bumper for Stylesides. Painted channel rear bumper for Flaresides. Slideout spare tire carrier: $23.70. Tinted glass for all windows: $20.98. Shoulder harness. Dual electric horns: $6.69. Free-running front hubs. Heavy-duty radiator: $28.24. Oil-bath engine air cleaner. Velocity-type engine governor. Northland Special Package. Includes engine block heater, -35 degree antifreeze, 55 amp alternator and limited-slip rear axle. High-output engine heater. Shoulder harness. Dual paint stripe: $50. Grille guard push bar: $67.95. Roll bar with light track: $89.95.

HISTORICAL FOOTNOTES: The 1973 models were announced on September 10, 1972. Ford depicted these new trucks as "starting a new generation of better ideas."

1974 PICKUP

Beginning in February, 1974 a optional, full-time New Process 203 four-wheel drive system was introduced. It was limited to use with the 360 V-8 and automatic transmission. The custom, Ranger and Ranger XLT trim levels were carried over for 1974.

The 1974 colors were Wimbledon white, Samoa lime, pastel lime, limestone green metallic, village green, candyapple red, sandpiper yellow, burnt orange, raven black, wind blue, light grabber blue, midnight blue metallic, sequoia brown metallic, chrome yellow and pure white. New ivy glow and gold glow colors were optional. Two-tone color choices were available by using all the standard colors except chrome yellow and pure white. Wimbledon white could be used as the accent color for any other color.

1974 Ford F-250 Custom Styleside pickup

I.D. DATA: The V.I.N. consisted of eleven entries. The first was a digit identifying the model year. The next was a letter identifying the assembly plant. The third and fourth, both digits, identified the product line and body style. The fifth symbol, a letter, designated the engine. The final six digits served as the sequential production number.

Body Type	Factory Price	GVW	Shipping Weight	Prod. Total
Series F-100, 115 in., 133 in. wheelbase				
Chassis & Cab	$3672	5300[1]	3315	—
Pickup, 6.75 ft. Styleside	$3759	5300	3635	—
Pickup, 8.0 ft. Flareside	$3835	5300	3695	—
Pickup, 8.0 ft. Styleside	$3975	5300	3780	—

NOTE 1: 5600 lb. GVW optional.

Series F-250, 133 in. wheelbase				
Chassis & Cab	$4252	6300[2]	3680	—
Pickup, 8 ft. Flareside	$4435	6300	4115	—
Pickup, 8 ft. Styleside	$4415	6300	4135	—
Platform, 7.5 ft.	$4528	6300	4095	—
Stake, 7.5 ft.	$4560	6300	4295	—
Crew Cab, 148.3 in. wb.	$5156	N.A.	N.A.	—

NOTE 2: 7100 lb. and 7700 lb. GVW optional.

STANDARD ENGINE: F-100: Not available for California, where 300 cu. in. 6-cylinder was regarded as standard. Engine Type: OHV In-line 6-cylinder. Bore x Stroke: 4.00 in. x 3.18 in. Lifters: Hydraulic. Number of main bearings-7. Displacement: 240 cu. in. (3.93 liters). Induction system: Single venturi downdraft carburetor. Compression Ratio: 9.2:1. Horsepower: N.A. Torque: Gross: N.A. Fuel Requirements: Regular.

STANDARD ENGINE: F-250: Engine Type: OHV In-line 6-cylinder. Bore x Stroke: 4.00 in. x 3.98 in. Displacement: 300 cu. in. Induction system: Single venturi downdraft carburetor. Compression Ratio: 8.8:1. Number of main bearings-7. Horsepower: Gross: 126 @ 3400 rpm, Net: 117 @ 3400 rpm. Torque: N.A. Fuel Requirements: Regular.

OPTIONAL ENGINE: F-100, F-250: Engine Type: OHV V-8. Bore x Stroke: 4.00 in. x 3.50 in. Displacement: 360 cu. in. (5.76 liters). Induction system: 2-barrel Motorcraft carburetor. Compression Ratio: 8.4:1. Number of main bearings-5. Horsepower: Net: 148 @ 3800 rpm. Torque: 264 lb.-ft. @ 2200 rpm. Fuel Requirements: 91 octane.

CHASSIS FEATURES: Separate body and frame. Section modulus: F-100 (117 in. wheelbase): 3.92; F-100 (133 in. wheelbase): 4.14; F-250: 5.58.

SUSPENSION AND RUNNING GEAR: Front Suspension: F-100: 6-cyl. engines: 1365 lb. capacity; F-250: 1550 lb. capacity. Optional: F-100: 1600 lb. capacity. F-250: 1750 lb. capacity. Rear Suspension: F-100: Progressive, 1475 lb. capacity. F-250: Progressive, 1975 lb. capacity. Optional: F-100: Single-stage, 1875 lb. capacity. F-250: Progressive, 2700 lb. capacity. Optional auxiliary spring for F-250 rated at 550 lb. Front Axle Type and Capacity: F-100: Spicer model 2559, 3300 lb. capacity, full-floating, Hotchkiss. F-250: Spicer model 6CF, 3300 lb. capacity, full-floating, Hotchkiss. Optional: F-250: Spicer model 2558, 3500 lb. capacity, full-floating, Hotchkiss. Rear Axle Type and Capacity: F-100: Hypoid, Ford-3300, 3300 lb. capacity, semi-floating, Hotchkiss. F-250: Full-floating, Hotchkiss. Spicer model 60, 5300 lb. capacity. Final Drive Ratio: F-100: 3.70:1; Optional: 3.50, 4.09:1. F-250: 4.10:1. Limited slip differential with 3600 lb. capacity: 3.50, 4.09:1. F-250: 4.10:1. Optional: Limited slip differential with 5300 lb. capacity: 4.10:1. Transfer Case: Type: F-100: Single-speed. F-250: 2-speed Dana Model 24. Ratios: 1.86:1, 1.00:1 (F-100 with the 133 in. wheelbase and the 360 cu. in. V-8 engine has the 2-speed transfer case). Optional: New Process 203 full-time. Ratios: 2.01, 1.00:1. Brakes: Type: Hydraulic, drums front and rear, self-generating. Dimensions: F-100: Front: 11 in. x 2.0 in. Rear: 11.03 in. x 2.25 in. F-250: Front: 12.125 in. x 2.00 in. Rear: 12.0

in. x 2.50 in. Wheels: F-100: 5-hole stamped disc, 15 in. x 5.5K, disc. F-250: 8-hole, stamped disc, 16 x 6.0, disc. Tires: F-100: G78 x 15 B 4 PR. F-250: 8.00 x 16.5 8 PR. Optional: F-100: Tubeless tires: 6.70 x 15 4 PR; 6.70 x 15 6 PR; 7.10 x 15,4 PR; 7.10 x 15, 6 PR; 6.50 x 16, 6 PR; 7.17.5, 6 PR. Tube-type tires: 6.50 x 16, 6 PR; 7.0 x 15, 6 PR. F-250: Tubeless tires: 6.50 x 16, 6 PR; 7.00 x 16, 6 PR; 7 x 17.5, 6 PR; 8 x 17.5, 6 PR; 8 x 17.5, 8 PR; 8 x 19.5, 8 PR. Tube-type tires: 6.50 x 16, 6 PR; 6.50 x 16, 6 PR, 7.00 x 16, 6 PR, 7.00 x 17, 8 PR; 7.50 x 16, 6 PR; 7.50 x 17, 8 PR. Steering: F-100 and F-250: Gemer #375, Worm and Roller, 18 in. dia. steering wheel. Ratio: 24.2:1. Optional: Linkage power. Transmission: Type: F-100 and F-250: 4-speed New Process 435. Ratios: New Process 435: 6.69, 3.34, 1.66, 1.0:1. Reverse: 8.26:1. Clutch: Heavy-duty hydraulic. 11.0 in. dia. and 123.7 sq. in. Optional: Cruise-O-Matic 3-speed automatic.

VEHICLE DIMENSIONS: Wheelbase: 117 in., 133 in. Overall length: F-100: 117 in. wheelbase: Pickup, 6.5 ft. Flareside: 195 in. Pickup, 6.5 ft. Styleside: 194.8 in. F-100: 133 in. wheelbase: Chassis & cab: 205.3 in. Pickup, 8 ft. Flareside: 208.5 in. Pickup, 8 ft. Styleside: 211 in. F-250: Chassis & cab: 205.3 in. Pickup, 8 ft. Flareside: 208.5 in. Pickup, 8 ft. Styleside: 211 in. Front/Rear Overhang: 28.0 in./48.0 in. Height: F-100 117 in. Styleside: 72.9, 133 in. Styleside: 73.4 in. F-250 Styleside: 76.2 in. Width: 79.1 in. Front/Rear tread: F-100: 64.4 in./ 64.4 in. F-250: 64.2 in./65.0 in. Pickup box (length x width x height): F-100 6.5 ft. Styleside: 78.2 in. x 49 in. x 19.3 in. F-250 and F-100 131 in. wheelbase. Styleside: 98.2 in. x 49 in. x 19.3 in. F-100 6.5 ft. Flareside: 77.9 in. x 49.0 in. x 20.3 in. F250 and F-100 131 in. wheelbase. Flaresides: 96.0 in. x 48.4 in. x 22.1 in. Tailgate: Styleside pickups: 65.0 in. x 19.3 in. Flareside pickups: 54.0 in. x 22.0.

CAPACITIES: Fuel Tank: F-100: 19.4 gal.; F-250: 19.5 gal (18.0 gal. for California).

ACCOMMODATIONS: 3 occupants.

INSTRUMENTATION: Speedometer, odometer, fuel level and engine coolant temperature gauges, warning lights for oil pressure and battery charge.

OPTIONS AND PRICES: 300 cu. in. 6-cylinder engine. 360 cu. in. V-8 engine: F-100: $160, F-250: $70.40. Convenience Group. Dual exterior mirrors: $37.40. Remote control outside mirror. Sliding rear window. Electric Power Pak. Power brakes: $50.30. Styleside spare tire carrier. Flareside spare tire carrier. Western-style mirrors. Auxiliary 24 gal. (20.2 gal. for F-100) fuel tank. 55 amp alternator: $6.00. Auxiliary 70 amp-hr. battery: $17.30. Rear step bumper: $60. AM radio: $72. AM/FM radio. Air conditioning. Special two-tone paint: $69. Ammeter and oil pressure gauges: $12.30. Automatic transmission: $122.80. Power steering: $150. Styleside body moldings. Cigarette lighter: $7.40. Chrome contour rear bumper for Stylesides. Painted channel rear bumper for Flaresides. Tinted glass for all windows. Shoulder harness. Dual electric horns. Free-running front hubs. Oil-bath engine air cleaner. Velocity-type engine governor. Northland Special Package. Includes engine block heater, -35 degree antifreeze, 55 amp alternator and limited-slip rear axle. High-output heater. Shoulder harness. Dual paint stripe: $50. Grille guard push bar: $67.95. Roll bar with light track: $89.95.

HISTORICAL FOOTNOTES: The 1974 models were announced on September 21, 1973.

1975 PICKUP

Changes for the 1975 model year were extremely limited. The F-100 models were equipped with catalytic converters. Beginning on December 2, 1975 all engines for trucks with GVW over 6000 lbs. had a solid state ignition. All models with a GVW of less than 6000 lb. operated on unleaded fuel only. The optional auxiliary fuel tank now had an electric valving switch in place of the older manual valve unit. A new Custom Decor Group was introduced for the custom level models. It included knitted vinyl seat trim in black, red, blue, green or tan, color-keyed floor mats with insulation, bright moldings around the windshield and rear window, and bright drip railings. The Optional Instrument Package now included a fuel economy warning light. Exterior colors for 1975 included Wimbledon white, vineland gold, Viking red, baytree green, Hatteras green metallic, glen green, candyapple red, parrot orange, raven black, wind blue, Bahama blue, midnight blue metallic, sequoia brown metallic, and chrome yellow. Extra cost colors were ginger glow and medium green glow.

I.D. DATA: The V.I.N. consisted of eleven entries. The first was a digit identifying the model year. The next was a letter identifying the assembly plant. The third and fourth, both digits, identified the product line and body style. The fifth symbol, a letter, designated the engine. The final six digits served as the sequential production number.

Body Type	Factory Price	GVW	Shipping Weight	Prod. Total
Series F-100, 115 in., 133 in. wheelbase				
Chassis & Cab	$3749	5300[1]	3325	—
Pickup, 6.75 ft. Styleside	$3913	5300	3645	—
Pickup, 8.0 ft. Flareside	$3912	5300	3705	—
Pickup, 8.0 ft. Styleside	$4052	5300	3790	—

NOTE 1: 5600 lb. GVW optional.

Body Type	Factory Price	GVW	Shipping Weight	Prod. Total
Series F-250, 133 in. wheelbase				
Chassis & Cab	$4787	6300[2]	3695	—
Pickup, 8 ft. Flareside	$4970	6300	4130	—
Pickup, 8 ft. Styleside	$4950	6300	4150	—
Platform, 7.5 ft.	$5063	6300	4110	—
Stake, 7.5 ft.	$5095	6300	4305	—
Crew Cab, 148.3 in. wb.	$5691	N.A.	N.A.	—

NOTE 2: 7100 lb. and 7700 lb. GVW optional.

STANDARD ENGINE: F-100: Not available for California, where 300 cu. in. 6-cylinder was regarded as standard. Engine Type: OHV In-line 6-cylinder. Bore x Stroke: 4.00 in. x 3.18 in. Lifters: Hydraulic. Number of main bearings-7. Displacement: 240 cu. in. (3.93 liters). Induction system: Single venturi downdraft carburetor. Compression Ratio: 9.2:1. Horsepower: N.A. Torque: Gross: N.A. Fuel Requirements: Unleaded.

STANDARD ENGINE: F-250: Engine Type: OHV In-line 6-cylinder. Bore x Stroke: 4.00 in. x 3.98 in. Displacement: 300 cu. in. Induction system: Single venturi downdraft carburetor. Compression Ratio: 8.8:1. Number of main bearings-7. Horsepower: Gross: 126 @ 3400 rpm, Net: 117 @ 3400 rpm. Torque: N.A. Fuel Requirements: Regular.

OPTIONAL ENGINE: F-100, F-250: Engine Type: OHV V-8. Bore x Stroke: 4.00 in. x 3.50 in. Displacement: 360 cu. in. (5.76 liters). Induction system: 2-barrel Motorcraft carburetor. Compression Ratio: 8.4:1. Number of main bearings-5. Horsepower: Net: 148 @ 3800 rpm. Torque: 264 lb.-ft. @ 2200 rpm. Fuel Requirements: 91 octane.

CHASSIS FEATURES: Separate body and frame. Section modulus: F-100 (117 in. wheelbase): 3.92; F-100 (133 in. wheelbase): 4.14. F-250: 5.58.

SUSPENSION AND RUNNING GEAR: Front Suspension: F-100: 6-cyl. engines: 1365 lb. capacity; F-250: 1550 lb. capacity. Optional: F-100: 1600 lb. capacity. F-250: 1750 lb. capacity. Rear Suspension: F-100: Progressive, 1475 lb. capacity. F-250: Progressive, 1975 lb. capacity. Optional: F-100: Single-stage, 1875 lb. capacity. F-250: Progressive, 2700 lb. capacity. Optional auxiliary spring for F-250 rated at 550 lb. Front Axle Type and Capacity: F-100: Spicer model 2559, 3300 lb. capacity, full-floating, Hotchkiss. F-250: Spicer model 6CF, 3300 lb. capacity, full-floating, Hotchkiss. Optional: F-250: Spicer model 2558, 3500 lb. capacity, full-floating, Hotchkiss. Rear Axle Type and Capacity: F-100: Hypoid, Ford-3300, 3300 lb. capacity, semi-floating, Hotchkiss. F-250: Full-floating, Hotchkiss. Spicer model 60, 5300 lb. capacity. Final Drive Ratio: F-100: 3.70:1; Optional: 3.50, 4.11:1. Limited slip differential with 3600 lb. capacity: 3.50, 4.09:1. F-250: 4.10:1. Optional: Limited slip differential with 5300 lb. capacity: 4.10:1. Transfer Case: Type: F-100: Single-speed. F-250: 2-speed Dana Model 24. Ratios: 1.86:1, 1.00:1 (F-100 with the 133 in. wheelbase and the 360 cu. in. V-8 engine has the 2-speed transfer case). Optional: New Process 203 full-time. Ratios: 2.01, 1.00:1. Brakes: Type: Hydraulic, drums front and rear, self-generating. Dimensions: F-100: Front: 11 in. x 2.0 in. Rear: 11.03 in. x 2.25 in. F-250: Front: 12.125 in. x 2.00 in. Rear: 12.0 in. x 2.50 in. Wheels: F-100: 5-hole stamped disc, 15 in. x 5.5K, disc. F-250: 8-hole, stamped disc, 16 x 6.0, disc. Tires: F-100: G78 x 15 B 4 PR. F-250: 8.00 x 16.5 8 PR. Optional: F-100: Tubeless tires: 6.70 x 15 4 PR; 6.70 x 15 6 PR; 7.10 x 15,4 PR; 7.10 x 15, 6 PR; 6.50 x 16, 6 PR; 7.17.5, 6 PR. Tube-type tires: 6.50 x 16, 6 PR; 7.0 x 15, 6 PR. F-250: Tubeless tires: 6.50 x 16, 6 PR; 7.00 x 16, 6 PR; 7 x 17.5, 6 PR; 8 x 17.5, 6 PR; 8 x 17.5, 8 PR; 8 x 19.5, 8 PR. Tube-type tires: 6.50 x 16, 6 PR; 6.50 x 16, 6 PR, 7.00 x 16, 6 PR, 7.00 x 17, 8 PR; 7.50 x 16, 6 PR; 7.50 x 17, 8 PR. Steering: F-100 and F-250: Gemer #375, Worm and Roller, 18 in. dia. steering wheel. Ratio: 24.2:1. Optional: Linkage power. Transmission: Type: F-100 and F-250: 4-speed New Process 435. Ratios: New Process 435: 6.69, 3.34, 1.66, 1.0:1. Reverse: 8.26:1. Clutch: Heavy-duty hydraulic. 11.0 in. dia. and 123.7 sq. in. Optional: Cruise-O-Matic 3-speed automatic.

VEHICLE DIMENSIONS: Wheelbase: 117 in., 133 in. Overall length: F-100: 117 in. wheelbase: Pickup, 6.5 ft. Flareside: 195 in. Pickup, 6.5 ft. Styleside: 194.8 in. F-100: 133 in. wheelbase: Chassis & cab: 205.3 in. Pickup, 8 ft. Flareside: 208.5 in. Pickup, 8 ft. Styleside: 211 in. F-250: Chassis & cab: 205.3 in. Pickup, 8 ft. Flareside: 208.5 in. Pickup, 8 ft. Styleside: 211 in. Front/Rear Overhang: 28.0 in./48.0 in. Height: F-100 117 in. Styleside: 72.9, 133 in. Styleside: 73.4 in. F-250 Styleside: 76.2 in. Width: 79.1 in. Front/Rear tread: F-100: 64.4 in./ 64.4 in. F-250: 64.2 in./65.0 in. Pickup box (length x width x height): F-100 6.5 ft. Styleside: 78.2 in. x 49 in. x 19.3 in. F-250 and F-100 131 in. wheelbase. Styleside: 98.2 in. x 49 in. x 19.3 in. F-100 6.5 ft. Flareside: 77.9 in. x 49.0 in. x 20.3 in. F-250 and F-100 131 in. wheelbase. Flaresides: 96.0 in. x 48.4 in. x 22.1 in. Tailgate: Styleside pickups: 65.0 in. x 19.3 in. Flareside pickups: 54.0 in. x 22.0.

CAPACITIES: Fuel Tank: F-100: 19.4 gal.; F-250: 19.5 gal (18.0 gal. for California).

ACCOMMODATIONS: 3 occupants.

INSTRUMENTATION: Speedometer, odometer, fuel level and engine coolant temperature gauges, warning lights for oil pressure and battery charge.

OPTIONS: 300 cu. in. 6-cylinder engine. 360 cu. in. V-8 engine. Convenience Group. Dual exterior mirrors. Remote control outside mirror. Sliding rear window. Electric Power Pak. Power brakes. Styleside spare tire carrier. Flareside spare tire carrier. Western-style mirrors. Auxiliary 24 gal. (20.2 gal. for F-100) fuel tank. 55 amp alternator. Auxiliary 70 amp-hr. battery. Rear step bumper. AM radio. AM/FM radio. Air conditioning. Special two-tone paint. Ammeter and oil pressure gauges. Automatic transmission. Power steering. Styleside body moldings. Cigarette lighter. Chrome contour rear bumper for Stylesides. Painted channel rear bumper for Flaresides. Tinted glass for all windows. Shoulder harness. Dual electric horns. Free-running front hubs. Oil-bath engine air cleaner. Velocity-type engine governor. Northland Special Package. Includes engine block heater, -35 degree antifreeze, 55 amp alternator and limited slip rear axle. High-output heater. Shoulder harness. Dual paint stripe. Grille guard push bar. Roll bar with light track.

HISTORICAL FOOTNOTES: The 1975 models were the first to be fitted with catalytic converters.

1976 PICKUP

During the 1976 model year the shortbed, 6.5 foot, F-100 was returned to production. All models had a moderately revised grille. A major development was the introduction of the F-150, a heavy-duty 1/2 ton model in four-wheel drive form. Like the F-100, the F-150 had a Mono-Beam front suspension with coil springs, full-floating axle, forged-steel radius rods, and a track bar. The standard engine for the F-100 was now the 360 cu. in. V-8. Both the F-100 and F-150 had new integral power steering as an option. The F-250 retained the older link type. New power front disc brakes were standard on all models. Several minor revisions of Option Package content were made for 1977. The Convenience Group, which was standard for the Ranger XLT now contained intermittent windshield wipers, glove compartment door lock, door map pockets and a 12 in. day/night inside mirror. The Protection Group now consisted of door edge and front bumper guards, and a front bumper rub strip. A new Visibility Group option consisted of lights for cargo, engine, glove compartment, and ashtray, plus under instrument panel courtesy lights. At mid-year amber parking light lenses replaced the white units first used for the 1977 models. Ranger XLT models manufactured in the February to April time frame lacked both the Ranger XLT front grille bar divider and rear body identification found on other 1977 Ranger XLT models. A mid-year Pinstripe Accent Package for the Custom or Ranger shortbed Flareside models was carried over into 1977. It contained a black channel rear bumper, tape pin-striping in black, white or gold, and a blackout grille insert.

The three trim levels of previous years — Custom, Ranger and Ranger XLT were continued. The 1976 color selection consisted of Wimbledon white, Mecca gold, Indigo tan, Castillo red, copper metallic, Hatteras green metallic, glen green, candyapple red, raven black, Bali blue, Bahama blue, midnight blue metallic, sequoia brown metallic, and chrome yellow. Ginger glow and medium green glow were optional. The same two-tone combinations and restrictions of earlier years were used for 1976. A white body side accent tape panel was offered for Styleside models in the Ranger or XLT Ranger form. It was not available with Wimbledon white.

1976 Ford F-150 Ranger XLT Styleside pickup

I.D. DATA: The V.I.N. consisted of eleven entries. The first was a digit identifying the model year. The next was a letter identifying the assembly plant. The third and fourth, both digits, identified the product line and body style. The fifth symbol, a letter, designated the engine. The final six digits served as the sequential production number.

Body Type	Factory Price	GVW	Shipping Weight	Prod. Total
Series F-100, 117 in., 133 in. wheelbase				
Chassis & Cab	$4114	5300[1]	3325	—
Pickup, 6.75 ft. Styleside	$4278	5300	3645	—
Pickup, 8.0 ft. Flareside	$4277	5300	3705	—
Pickup, 8.0 ft. Styleside	$4417	5300	3790	—

NOTE 1: 5700 lb. GVW optional.

Body Type	Factory Price	GVW	Shipping Weight	Prod. Total
Series F-150, 117 in., 133 in. wheelbase				
Chassis & Cab	$4314	6050[2]	3610	—
Pickup, 8.0 ft. Flareside	$4577	6050	3990	—
Pickup, 8.0 ft. Styleside	$4717	6050	4075	—

NOTE 2: 6200 and 6400 lb. GVW optional.

Body Type	Factory Price	GVW	Shipping Weight	Prod. Total
Series F-250, 131 in. wheelbase				
Chassis & Cab	$5130	6300[3]	3695	—
Pickup, 8 ft. Flareside	$5313	6300	4130	—
Pickup, 8 ft. Styleside	$5293	6300	4150	–
Platform, 7.5 ft.	$5406	6300	4110	—
Stake, 7.5 ft.	$5438	6300	4305	–
Crew Cab, 148.3 in. wb.	$6034	N.A.	N.A.	—

NOTE 3: 7100 lb. and 7700 lb. GVW optional.

STANDARD ENGINE: F-150 and F-250: Engine Type: OHV In-line 6-cylinder. Bore x Stroke: 4.00 in. x 3.98 in. Displacement: 300 cu. in. Induction system: Single venturi downdraft carburetor. Compression Ratio: 8.3:1. Number of main bearings-7. Horsepower: Net: 114 @ 3400 rpm. Torque: 222 lb.-ft. @ 1600 rpm. Fuel Requirements: Leaded or unleaded.

STANDARD ENGINE: F-100: Optional for F-150 and F-250. Engine Type: OHV V-8. Bore x Stroke: 4.00 in. x 3.50 in. Displacement: 360 cu. in. (5.76 liters). Induction system: 2-barrel Motorcraft carburetor. Compression Ratio: 8.0:1. Number of main bearings-5. Horsepower: Net: 145 @ 3600 rpm. Torque: 263 lb.-ft. @ 2000 rpm. Fuel Requirements: Leaded or unleaded.

CHASSIS FEATURES: Separate body and frame. Section modulus: F-100 (117 in. wheelbase): 3.92; F-100 (133 in. wheelbase): 4.14. F-250: 5.58.

SUSPENSION AND RUNNING GEAR: Front Suspension: F-100 and F-150: Coil springs. F-250: Semi-elliptical leaf springs. All springs computer selected for GVW rating. Rear Suspension: All models: Semi-elliptical leaf springs. Front Axle Type and Capacity: F-100: Spicer model 2559, 3300 lb. capacity, full-floating, Hotchkiss. F-150 and F-250: 3550 lb. capacity, full-floating, Hotchkiss. Rear Axle Type and Capacity: F-100: Hypoid, Ford-3300, 3300 lb. capacity, semi-floating, Hotchkiss. F-150: 3750 lb. capacity. F-250: Full-floating, Hotchkiss. Spicer model 60, 5300 lb. capacity. Final Drive Ratio: F-100: 3.70:1; Optional: 3.50, 4.11:1. Limited slip differential with 3600 lb. capacity: 3.50, 4.09:1. F-250: 4.10:1. Optional: Limited slip differential with 5300 lb. capacity: 4.10:1. Transfer Case: Type: F-100: Single-speed. F-150 and F-250: 2-speed New Process 205. Ratios: 1.96:1, 1.00:1 (F-100 with the 133 in. wheelbase and the 360 cu. in. V-8 engine has the 2-speed transfer case). Optional: New Process 203 full-time. Ratios: 2.01, 1.00:1. Brakes: Type: Hydraulic, drums front and rear, self-generating. Dimensions: Front: Power disc on all models. F-250: 12.5 in. disc. Rear: F-100 and F-150: 11.03 in. x 2.25 in. F-250: Rear: 12.0 in. x 2.50 in. Wheels: F-100: 5-hole stamped disc, 15 in. x 5.5K, disc. F-250: 8-hole, stamped disc, 16 x 6.0, disc. Tires: F-100: G78 x 15 B 4 PR. F-150: L78 x 15B F-250: 8.00 x 16.5 8 PR. Optional: F-100: Tubeless tires: 6.70 x 15 4 PR; 6.70 x 15 6 PR; 7.10 x 15,4 PR; 7.10 x 15, 6 PR; 6.50 x 16, 6 PR; 7.17.5, 6 PR. Tube-type tires: 6.50 x 16, 6 PR; 7.0 x 15, 6 PR. F-250: 8.00 x 16.5E, 8.00R x 16.5E, 8.75 x 16.5E, 8.75R x 16.5E, 9.50 x 16.5D, 7.50 x 16C, 7.50 x 16D, 7.50 x 16F and 7.50 x 16E. Steering: Gemer #375, Worm and Roller, 18 in. dia. steering wheel. Ratio: 24.2:1. Optional: F-100 and F-150: Integral power. F-250: Linkage power. Transmission: 4-speed New Process 435. Ratios: New Process 435: 6.69, 3.34, 1.66, 1.0:1. Reverse: 8.26:1. Clutch: Heavy-duty hydraulic. 11.0 in. dia. and 123.7 sq. in. Optional: Cruise-O-Matic 3-speed automatic.

VEHICLE DIMENSIONS: Wheelbase: 117 in., 133 in. Overall length: F-100 and F-150: 117 in. wheelbase: Pickup, 6.5 ft. Flareside: 195 in. Pickup, 6.5 ft. Styleside: 194.8 in. F-100: 133 in. wheelbase: Chassis & cab: 205.3 in. Pickup, 8 ft. Flareside: 208.5 in. Pickup, 8 ft. Styleside: 211 in. F-250: Chassis & cab: 205.3 in. Pickup, 8 ft. Flareside: 208.5 in. Pickup, 8 ft. Styleside: 211 in. Front/Rear Overhang: 28.0 in./48.0 in. Height: F-100 and F-150: 117 in. Styleside: 72.9, 133 in. Styleside: 73.4 in. F-250 Styleside: 76.2 in. Width: 79.1 in. Front/Rear tread: F-100 and F-150: 64.4 in./64.4 in. F-250: 64.2 in./65.0 in. Pickup box (length x width x height): F-100 6.5 ft. Styleside: 78.2 in. x 49 in. x 19.3 in. F-100, F-150 and F-250: 131 in. wheelbase. Styleside: 98.2 in. x 49 in. x 19.3 in. F-100 6.5 ft. Flareside: 77.9 in. x 49.0 in. x 20.3 in. F-100, F-150 and F-250: 131 in. wheelbase. Flaresides: 96.0 in. x 48.4 in. x 22.1 in. Tailgate: Styleside pickups: 65.0 in. x 19.3 in. Flareside pickups: 54.0 in. x 22.0.

CAPACITIES: Fuel Tank: F-100, F-150: 19.4 gal.; F-250: 19.5 gal (18.0 gal. for California).

ACCOMMODATIONS: 3 occupants.

INSTRUMENTATION: Speedometer, odometer, fuel level and engine coolant temperature gauges, warning lights for oil pressure and battery charge.

OPTIONS: 360 cu. in. V-8 engine. Convenience Group. Dual exterior mirrors. Remote control outside mirror. Sliding rear window. Electric Power Pak. Power brakes. Styleside spare tire carrier. Flareside spare tire carrier. Western-style mirrors. Auxiliary 24 gal. (20.2 gal. for F-100) fuel tank. 55 amp alternator. Auxiliary 70 amp-hr. battery. Rear step bumper. AM radio. AM/FM radio. Air conditioning. Special two-tone paint. Ammeter and oil pressure gauges. Automatic transmission. Power steering. Styleside body moldings. Cigarette lighter. Chrome contour rear bumper for Stylesides. Painted channel rear bumper for Flaresides. Tinted glass for all windows. Shoulder harness. Dual electric horns. Free-running front hubs. Oil-bath engine air cleaner. Velocity-type engine governor. Northland Special Package. Includes engine block heater, -35 degree antifreeze, 55 amp alternator and limited slip rear axle. High-output heater. Shoulder harness. Dual paint stripe. Grille guard push bar. Roll bar with light track.

HISTORICAL FOOTNOTES: Total 1976 model year production of all Ford light-duty trucks was 663,537.

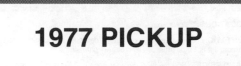

1977 PICKUP

For 1977 the F-100 was not offered in four-wheel drive form. Two new "High Efficiency" 351 and 400 cu. in. V-8 engines were available. The 300 cu. in. 6-cylinder was now standard for both the F-150 and F-250 models, except for California where one of the two V-8 engines were required. Numerous refinements were incorporated into the 1977 models. Among the highlights were the expanded use of precoated steel and galvanized steel, the adoption of front and rear fender plastic splash shields, extended oil and filter change intervals, and the use of a new DuraSpark ignition on all engines. Design changes included the availability of six new exterior colors and a new jade interior trim color; and a new custom seat sew style. New options included an electric rear window defroster for the regular cab, a new two-tone body side paint option outlined with bright moldings, a spare tie lock or padlock available with all spare tires, and a AM/FM monaural radio. Added to the Ranger XLT Package was a body side molding system. A new "Chain Mail" design vinyl upholstery was included in the Ranger option. Regular cab features included the following: Chrome front bumper, semi-flush door handles, bright grille, bright 4.25 in. x 5.5 in. left and right side door-mounted mirrors (bright finish on pickups, all others are painted), concealed tailgate handle, rope tie holes in corner stake pockets of Styleside pickups, and two-speed electric windshield wipers with 91 oz. capacity washer reservoir. Primary interior features included ashtray, courtesy light switches on both front doors, dome light, color-keyed plastic door trim panels with integral armrests (no armrest on crew cab models), black carpet grain rubber floor mats, glove box with push-button lock, heater and defroster with blend-air feature, white sponge grain hardwood headlining with painted moldings, color-keyed instrument panel with bright molding, windshield-mounted 10 in. rearview mirror, seven inch foam seat cushion with five inch foam seat back, three-point lap/shoulder belt system with retractors for outboard position, black 16.5 in. two-spoke steering wheel with black horn pad, behind-seat-stowage, and scuff plates for all doors. The crew cab also had these items: Full-width rear bench seat with fixed seat back, rear door pull straps, front and rear rubber floor mats, six sets of seat belts, rear door roll-down windows and push-button rear door locks without inside door handle override.

1977 Ford F-250 XLT Styleside pickup

The Ranger Package had these items in addition to or in place of standard features: Bright taillight bezels, Ranger side emblems, bright aluminum body side moldings with black vinyl inserts, and aluminum tailgate applique with stamped FORD lettering and bright moldings top and bottom. The Ranger interior had color-keyed 12 oz. loop carpeting extending to front of seat and floor pan sound insulation, color-keyed perforated hardboard headlining with bright molding and roof sound absorber, cigarette lighter, color-keyed plastic door trim panel with bright molding in upper half of panel and door sound insulation, bright molding with black paint on passenger side of instrument panel, color-keyed Chain Mail vinyl inserts in seats, color-keyed seat back cover, black steering wheel with simulated woodgrain applique, color-keyed sun visor retaining clip, and Ranger plaque on glove box.

The Ranger XLT Package had these items in addition to or in place of the Ranger features: Bright windshield, rear window and drip rail moldings (crew cab), XLT side body emblem, stamped aluminum applique covering upper tailgate depression; black center section on bright taillight applique, bright aluminum tailgate handle, and black paint filled bright molding on rear and along lower body side. The XLT Ranger interior had these appointments: Color-keyed 22 oz. cut-pile carpeting from front of floor pan up to back panel with insulation material and floor pan sound deadener, Convenience Group, padded vinyl insert door trim panel with bright molding and simulated woodgrain applique in bright molding groove, sound absorbing material in both doors, bright molding on instrument panel with simulated woodgrain applique in bright molding groove, color-keyed vinyl headlining, Ranger XLT instrument panel plaque, cloth and vinyl seat trim with vertical pleat sew style, color-keyed vinyl covered sun visors,

Deluxe color-keyed seat belts with bright mini-buckles (regular cab only), left and right center pillar-mounted ashtrays and front cigarette lighter (crew cab only), and bright seat pivot covers.

1977 Ford F-150 XLT Flareside pickup

The 1977 color selection consisting of the following: Raven black, Wimbledon white, candy-apple red, castillo red, silver metallic, midnight blue metallic, light blue, Bahama blue, light jade, dark jade metallic, chrome yellow, Indigo tan, medium copper, and copper metallic. New jade glow and dark cinnamon were optional. Wimbledon white could be used as the accent color for any exterior color except silver metallic. The pickup models were available in the regular, Deluxe or combination two-tone variations.

1977 Ford F-150 Ranger XLT Styleside pickup

I.D. DATA: The V.I.N. consisted of eleven entries. The first was a digit identifying the model year. Next was a letter identifying the assembly plant. The third and fourth, both digits, identified the product line and body style. The fifth symbol, a letter, designated the engine. The final six digits served as the sequential production number.

Body Type	Factory Price	GVW	Shipping Weight	Prod. Total
Series F-150, 117 in., 133 in. wheelbase				
Chassis & Cab	$5614	6050[1]	3615	—
Pickup, 8.0 ft. Flareside	$5877	6050	3995	—
Pickup, 8.0 ft. Styleside	$6117	6050	4080	—

NOTE 1: 6200 and 6400 lb. GVW optional.

Body Type	Factory Price	GVW	Shipping Weight	Prod. Total
Series F-250, 133 in. wheelbase				
Chassis & Cab	$6430	6300[2]	3700	—
Pickup, 8 ft. Flareside	$6613	6300	4135	—
Pickup, 8 ft. Styleside	$6593	6300	4155	—
Platform, 7.5 ft.	$6706	6300	4115	—
Stake, 7.5 ft.	$6738	6300	4310	—
Crew Cab, 148.3 in. wb.	$7334	N.A.	N.A.	—

NOTE 2: 7100 lb., 7700 lb., 8100 lb., 8400 lb. GVW optional.

STANDARD ENGINE: F-150 and F-250: Engine Type: OHV In-line 6-cylinder. Bore x Stroke: 4.00 in. x 3.98 in. Displacement: 300 cu. in. Induction system: Single venturi downdraft carburetor. Compression Ratio: 8.01. Number of main bearings-7. Horsepower: Net: 114 @ 3200 rpm. (California rating: 118 @ 3600 rpm). Torque: 227 lb.-ft. @ 1800 rpm. (California rating: 205 lb.-ft. @ 2200 rpm). Fuel Requirements: Leaded or unleaded. Optional: For F-150 and F-250. Standard for California. Engine Type: OHV V-8. Bore x Stroke: 4.00 in. x 3.50 in. Displacement: 351 cu. in. (5.75 liters). Induction system: 2-barrel Motorcraft carburetor. Compression Ratio: 8.0:1. Number of main bearings-5. Horsepower: Net: 163 @ 3800 rpm. (California rating: 161 @ 3800 rpm). Torque: Net: 267 lb.-ft. @ 2200 rpm. (California rating: 265 lb.-ft. @ 2200 rpm). Fuel Requirements: Leaded or unleaded. Optional: For F-150 and F-250. Engine Type: OHV V-8. Bore x Stroke: 4.00 in. x 4.00 in. Displacement: 400 cu. in. (6.55 liters). Induction system: 4-barrel carburetor. Compression Ratio: 8.0:1. Number of main bearings-5. Horsepower: Net: 169 @ 3600 rpm. (California rating: 167 @ 3600 rpm). Torque: Net: 303 lb.-ft. @ 2200 rpm. (California rating: 302 lb.-ft. @ 2200 rpm). Fuel Requirements: Leaded or unleaded.

CHASSIS FEATURES: Separate body and frame. Single channel, 36,000 psi. Section modulus: F-150 (117 in. wheelbase): 3.92; F-150 (133 in. wheelbase): 4.14. F-250: 5.58.

SUSPENSION AND RUNNING GEAR: Front Suspension: F-100 and F-150: Coil springs. F-250: Semi-elliptical leaf springs. All springs computer selected for GVW rating. Rear Suspension: All models: Semi-elliptical leaf springs. Front Axle Type and Capacity: F-150 and F-250: 3550 lb. capacity, full-floating, Hotchkiss. Rear Axle Type and Capacity: F-150: 3750 lb. capacity: F-250: Full-floating, Hotchkiss. Spicer model 60, 5300 lb. capacity. Transfer Case: Type: 2-speed New Process 205. Ratios: 1.96:1, 1.00:1. Optional: New Process 203 full-time. Ratios: 2.01, 1.00:1. Brakes: Type: Hydraulic, single-piston, floating caliper, Ford-designed disc front and drums rear, power assisted. Dimensions: Front: F-150: 11.54 in. disc, F-250: 12.5 in. disc on all models. Rear: F-150: 11.03 in. x 2.25 in. F-250: Rear: 12.0 in. x 2.50 in. Wheels: F-150: 5-hole stamped disc, 15 in. x 6.0, disc. F-250: 8-hole, stamped disc, 16 x 6.0, disc. Tires: F-150: L78 x 15D. F-250: 8.00 x 16.5D. Optional: F-250: 8.00 x 16.5E, 8.00R x 16.5E, 8.75 x 16.5E, 8.75R x 16.5E, 9.50 x 16.5D, 7.50 x 16C, 7.50 x 16D, 7.50 x 16F and 7.50 x 16E. Steering: Gemer #375, Worm and Roller, 18 in. dia. steering wheel. Ratio: F-150:

24.2:1. F-250: 27.6:1. Optional: F-100 and F-150: Integral power. F-250: Linkage power. Transmission: 4-speed New Process 435. Ratios: New Process 435: 6.69, 3.34, 1.66, 1.0:1. Reverse: 8.26:1. Clutch: Heavy-duty hydraulic. 11.0 in. dia. and 123.7 sq. in. Optional: Cruise-O-Matic 3-speed automatic.

VEHICLE DIMENSIONS: Wheelbase: 117 in., 133 in. Overall length: F-150: 117 in. wheelbase: Pickup, 6.5 ft. Flareside: 195 in. Pickup, 6.5 ft. Styleside: 194.8 in. F-150: 133 in. wheelbase: Chassis & cab: 205.3 in. Pickup, 8 ft. Flareside: 208.5 in. Pickup, 8 ft. Styleside: 211 in. F-250: Chassis & cab: 205.3 in. Pickup, 8 ft. Flareside: 208.5 in. Pickup, 8 ft. Styleside: 211 in. Front/Rear Overhang: 28.0 in./48.0 in. Height: F-150: 117 in. Styleside: 72.9 in., 133 in. Styleside: 73.4 in. F-250 Styleside: 76.2 in. Width: 79.1 in. Front/Rear tread: F-150: 64.4 in./64.4 in. F-250: 64.2 in./65.0 in.

CAPACITIES: Fuel Tank: F-150: 19.2 gal.; F-250: 19.3 gal.

ACCOMMODATIONS: 3 occupants. Crew cab: 6 occupants.

INSTRUMENTATION: Speedometer, odometer, fuel level and engine coolant temperature gauges, warning lights for oil pressure and battery charge.

OPTIONS: 351 cu. in. V-8 engine. 400 cu. in. V-8 engine. Convenience Group. AM/FM stereo radio. SelectShift Cruise-O-Matic. Speed control. Pickup box cover. Sliding front box cover window. Tool stowage box. Spare tire lock. Slide-out spare tire carrier. Auxiliary 12-volt 68 amp-hr. battery. Mag-type wheel 15 in. covers. Cargo tie-down hooks. Engine block heater. Electric rear window defroster. Auxiliary fuel tank for F-150. Locking fuel cap. Visibility Light Group. Northland Special. Pinstripe Accent Package (for Shorty Flaresides). Protection Package. Seat upholstery. Tinted glass (windshield only or all windows).

HISTORICAL FOOTNOTES: Total 1977 model year production of all Ford light-duty trucks was 723,925.

1978 PICKUP

The marketability of the Ford trucks was expanded by the introduction of new long wheelbase F-150 and F-250 SuperCab models. These models offered three seating variations. The standard format provided a front bench seat and 44 cubic feet of storage space behind the seat. The optional front-facing full-width rear seat offered total seating for six. The third choice, the optional dual center-facing jump seats provided a five passenger capacity. Both the F-150 and F-250 SuperCabs had new 2-leaf tapered front springs. Each leaf was thicker than the leaves in comparable multi-leaf springs and tapered to provide a constant stress distribution. Standard on all four-wheel drive models except for the F-150 regular cab, was integral power steering with a new hi-capacity pump. A new Handling Package was introduced for the F-150. It included a front stabilizer bar, quad front shock absorbers (F-150 regular cab only) and heavy-duty rear shock absorbers and heavy-duty front springs. Additional sound proofing was attained through the use of improved door and cowl seating and retuned body insulator mounts.

1978 Ford F-150 SuperCab pickup

Introduced in mid-1977 and continued into 1978 were the F-250 regular cab models with their overall height reduced by nearly 2.0 in. This change greatly improved ease of entry and exit while retaining sufficient clearance for off-road driving. The new F-250 also had a lower center of gravity which improved its handling. New for 1978 standard features for the Ford four-wheel drive F-150 and F-250 models included a newly designed front bumper, four new exterior colors for a total of 19, a new argent color egg-crate grille insert and grille surround, low-mounted front parking/turn signal lights, the replacement of tan and medium blue interior colors with saddle and bright blue, use of low-gloss color-keyed instrument panel paint, a new simulated woodgrain glove box door applique, a reduction of in-cab noise, modifications to the steering column to permit the installation of car-type steering wheels and tilt steering wheels and the incorporation of a lane-change feature into the turn-signal operating lever.

1978 Ford F-150 Shorty Flareside

Ford realigned its pickup trim levels for 1978. The base custom equipment level included a full-foam seat, two-speed windshield wipers, turn signal with lane change feature, dome light with door courtesy switches, glove compartment with woodgrain vinyl applique on door, black floor mat, door scuff plates, and a new patterned non-metallic Mohave vinyl seat trim in black, red, saddle, blue or jade green. A knitted vinyl and heavy-duty black vinyl were available as options. The next upgrade was the Ranger Package. It had new rectangular headlights, Chain Mail vinyl seat upholstery, color-keyed floor covering, sun visors, perforated hardboard headliner with bright moldings and seat-back covers. Additional sound insulation was also installed. The Ranger had more extensive brightwork than the custom. Some applications were the moldings for the windshield, backlight, roof, and rip and wheel-lip openings. The Ranger XLT featured new door trim panels with woodgrain vinyl inserts and bright trim moldings. The wall-to-wall 14 oz. carpeting now covered the cowl sides. Other elements of the Ranger XLT were body side moldings with black vinyl inserts, bright surround moldings on both the front and rear side marker lamps. Tailgate with stamped lower aluminum applique with black FORD letters with bright moldings, Westminister cloth seats, bright moldings and woodtone appliques for the instrument panel, Ranger XLT plaque mounted on woodtone glove box applique and a higher level of sound insulation than the Ranger. The top-of-the-line Ranger Lariat had Picton cloth seat upholstery trimmed in super-soft vinyl, door trim panels with padded inserts at top and map pockets beneath, headliner with button, quilted design and extra insulation. Additional features of what Ford called a "true 'designer series' pickup" were a Deluxe tu-tone paint equipment, wide black vinyl insert body side moldings and a bright body surround molding (for Styleside and chassis-cab models), and Ranger Lariat plaque mounted on the woodtone glove box applique. The Ranger Lariat was not available for crew cabs.

1978 Ford F-250 with Camper Special

Major changes took place in the availability of F series optional equipment. These included a 4500 lb. front axle (for the F-250 regular and SuperCab models only), chrome rear step bumper for Styleside models, carpeted cowl sides for the Ranger XLT and Duraweave Polyknit seat trim for regular cab models. A new Free Wheeling Styleside Package B was also offered. It contained a rainbow tape stripe, blackout grille, black front bumper, special interior, GT bar, and styled steel wheels. Other new options were a chrome-plated grille insert (standard on Ranger and above), GT bar, Handling Package (F-150 only), fog lights, rectangular headlights (standard on Ranger and above), inside locking hood release, Comfort Vent heater, Sport steering wheel, simulated leather-wrapped steering wheel, maintenance-free battery, rocker panel molding (custom models), wheel-lip molding (Custom models), low-mount Western 9 in. x 6.0 in. mirrors (black or bright), AM radio with LED digital clock, includes a digital display of radio frequency, 40-channel Citizens Band radio, radio flexibility option, Security Lock Group, Snowplow Preparation Package (F-250 regular and SuperCab), tilt steering wheel, vanity visor mirror, illuminated and color-keyed (except white only with custom), 10-hole web, polished 15 x 6.0 for F-150 only, styled steel, white painted for F-150 only (yellow painted wheels available with multi-color accent tape strips and "Free Wheeling" Package, and push bar.

The 1978 color selection consisting of these shades: Raven black, dark jade metallic, chrome yellow, dark brown metallic, Bahama blue, silver metallic, bright red, Wimbledon white, maroon, cinnamon glow, tangerine, light jade, midnight blue metallic, candyapple red, cream, silver metallic, jade glow, medium copper, bright yellow, tan, light blue and prime. Wimbledon white could be used as the accent color for any exterior color except silver metallic. The pickup models were again available in the regular, Deluxe or combination two-tone variations.

1978 Ford F-250 crew cab

I.D. DATA: The V.I.N. had 17 entries. The first three characters identified the manufacturer, make and type of vehicle. The next entry, a letter, designated the GVW rating. The next three characters identified the series and body style. The eighth character identified the engine. A check digit following, then an entry identifying the assembly plant. The final digits represented the sequential production number.

Body Type	Factory Price	GVW	Shipping Weight	Prod. Total
Series F-150, 117 in., 133 in. wheelbase. SuperCab-155 in. wheelbase				
Chassis & Cab	$5830	6050[1]	3585	—
Pickup, 8.0 ft. Flareside	$6093	6050	3955	—
Pickup, 8.0 ft. Styleside	$6093	6050	4040	—
SuperCab, Styleside	$6544	6050	3990	—
SuperCab, Chassis & Cab	$6312	6050	4263	—

NOTE 1: 6300 and 6400 lb. GVW optional.

Body Type	Factory Price	GVW	Shipping Weight	Prod. Total
Series F-250, 133 in. wheelbase SuperCab-155 in. wheelbase				
Chassis & Cab	$6848	6700[2]	3660	—
Pickup, 8 ft. Flareside	$7031	6700	4100	—
Pickup, 8 ft. Styleside	$7011	6700	4115	—
Crew Cab, 150 in. wb.	$7858	6700	4755	—
Crew Cab, Chassis & Cab	$7626	6700	4400	—
SuperCab, Styleside	$7425	6700	4388	—
SuperCab, Chassis & Cab	$7193	6700	4400	—

NOTE 2: 7300 lb., 8100 lb., 8400 lb. GVW optional.

STANDARD ENGINE: F-150 and F-250 regular cab and crew cab models: Engine Type: OHV In-line 6-cylinder. Bore x Stroke: 4.00 in. x 3.98 in. Displacement: 300 cu. in. Induction system: Single venturi downdraft carburetor. Compression Ratio: 8.01. Number of main bearings-7. Horsepower: Net: 114 @ 3200 rpm. (California rating: 118 @ 3600 rpm). Torque: 227 lb.-ft. @ 1800 rpm. (California rating: 205 lb.-ft. @ 2200 rpm). Fuel Requirements: Leaded or unleaded. Optional: For F-150 and F-250. Standard cab and crew cab models. Standard for F-150 and F-250 SuperCab models. Engine Type: OHV V-8. Bore x Stroke: 4.00 in. x 3.50 in. Displacement: 351 cu. in. (5.75 liters). Induction system: 2-barrel Motorcraft carburetor. Compression Ratio: 8.0:1. Number of main bearings-5. Horsepower: Net: 163 @ 3800 rpm. (California rating: 161 @ 3800 rpm). Torque: Net: 267 lb.-ft. @ 2200 rpm. (California rating: 265 lb.-ft. @ 2200 rpm). Fuel Requirements: Leaded or unleaded. Optional: For all F-150 and F-250. models. Engine Type: OHV V-8. Bore x Stroke: 4.00 in. x 4.00 in. Displacement: 400 cu. in. (6.55 liters). Induction system: 4-barrel carburetor. Compression Ratio: 8.0:1. Number of main bearings-5. Horsepower: Net: 169 @ 3600 rpm. (California rating: 167 @ 3600 rpm). Torque: Net: 303 lb.-ft. @ 2200 rpm. (California rating: 302 lb.-ft. @ 2200 rpm). Fuel Requirements: Leaded or unleaded.

CHASSIS FEATURES: Separate body and frame. Single channel, 36,000 psi. Section modulus: F-150 regular cab: (117 in. wheelbase): 3.95; F-150 regular cab (133 in. wheelbase): 4.33. F-250 (crew cab): 5.67. F-150 and F-250 (SuperCab): 6.67.

SUSPENSION AND RUNNING GEAR: Front Suspension: F-150 regular cab: Coil springs. F-150 SuperCab and all F-250: Semi-elliptical, tapered, constant rate 2-leaf springs. All springs computer selected for GVW rating. Rear Suspension: All models: Semi-elliptical leaf springs. F-150 regular cab and SuperCab: 5-leaf, 55.5 in. x 3.0 in. Capacity: 3750 lb. at ground. F-250 regular cab, crew cab and SuperCab: 5-leaf, 55.5 in. x 3.0 in. Capacity: 4000 lb. at ground. Optional: F-250: 4500 and 5480 lb. capacity at ground. Auxiliary spring, 34.5 in. x 3.0 in. with 710 lb. rating. Front Axle Type and Capacity: F-150 regular cab and SuperCab: 3550 lb. capacity, full-floating, Hotchkiss. F-250: 3800 lb. capacity, full-floating, Hotchkiss. Optional: F-250: 4500 lb. capacity. The F-250 front axle was of heavier construction than the F-150. It was of open knuckle design and used pen Cardan-type universal joints of alloy steel. Rear Axle Type and Capacity: F-150: Semi-floating, 3750 lb. capacity. F-250: Full-floating, Hotchkiss. Spicer model 60, 5300 lb. capacity. Ratios: F-150 regular cab: 3.50:1. Optional: 4.9 liter engine: 4.11:1; 5.8 liter V-8: 3.0:1 (not available with 117 in. wheelbase. and 4-speed trans.); 6.6 liter V-8: 4.11:1 (with part time four-wheel drive only). F-150 SuperCab: 3.50:1. Traction-Lok rear axle with 3.50:1 ratio also optional for all models. F-250 4.9 liter and 5.8 liter engines: 3.54:1. 6.6 liter engine: 4.10:1. (not available with Snowplow Preparation Package or 4500 lb. front axle with full-time four-wheel drive) Optional: 4.9 liter and 5.8 liter: Limited slip rear axle: 4.10:1 (not available with Snowplow Preparation Package or 4500 lb. front axle with full-time four-wheel drive). Transfer Case: Type: 2-speed New Process 205. Ratios: 1.96:1, 1.00:1. Optional: New Process 203 full-time. Ratios: 2.01, 1.00:1. Brakes: Type: Hydraulic, single-piston, floating caliper, Ford-designed disc front and drums rear, power assisted. Dimensions: Front: F-150: 11.54 in. disc, F-250: 12.5 in. disc on all models. Rear: F-150: 11.03 in. x 2.25 in. F-250: Rear: 12.0 in. x 2.50 in. Wheels: F-150: 5-hole stamped disc, 15 in. x 5.5K, disc. Optional: 6.0JK, 15 in. x 8JJ. F-250: 8-hole, stamped disc, 16 x 6.0, disc. Optional: 6.75, 6.0K. Tires: F-150: L78 x 15B. F-250: 8.00 x 16.5D. Optional: F-150: Tubeless: L78 x 15C, LR78 x 15C, 10 x 15C. Tube-type: 7.0 x 15D. F-250: Tubeless: 8.00 x 16.5E, 8.75 x 16.5E, 8.75 x 16.5E, 8.75R x 16.5E, 9.50 x 16.5D, 9.50 x 16.5E, 7.50 x 16C, 7.50 x 16D, 7.50 x 16E. Tube-type: 7.50 x 16D, 7.50 x 16E. Steering: Standard F-150 regular cab: Gemer #375, Worm and Roller. All others: Power assisted, recirculating ball (optional for F-150 regular cab). Transmission: 4-speed New Process 435. Ratios: New Process 435: 6.69, 3.34, 1.66, 1.0:1. Reverse: 8.26:1. Clutch: Heavy-duty hydraulic. 11.0 in. dia. and 123.7 sq. in. Optional: Cruise-O-Matic 3-speed automatic for 6.6 liter V-8 only.

VEHICLE DIMENSIONS: Styleside pickups: Wheelbase: 117 in./133 in. Overall length: 195.1 in./211.3 in. Flareside pickups: Wheelbase: 117 in./133 in. Overall length: 192.2 in./208.4 in. Chassis and cab: Wheelbase: 117 in./133 in./155 in. Overall length: 189.1 in./205.3 in./227.3 in. SuperCab: Wheelbase: 155 in. Overall length: 233.6 in. Front/Rear Overhang: 31.7.0 in./ 43.7 (Pickup) 40.6 in. (chassis and cab). Crew cab: Wheelbase: 150.3 in. Overall length: 75-75.8 in. depending upon model. Width: 79.1 in. Front/Rear tread: The tread width varies depending upon the tire size. Front treads average 64.3 in. and rear treads average 64.4 in. (F-150), and 65. in. (F-250).

CAPACITIES: Fuel Tank: 19.2 gal. Optional: Dual fuel tanks with total capacity of 38.7 to 46.2 gal. except for F-150 with 117 in. wheelbase.

ACCOMMODATIONS: 3 occupants. Crew cab and SuperCab: 6 occupants.

INSTRUMENTATION: Speedometer, odometer, fuel level and engine coolant temperature gauges, warning lights for oil pressure and battery charge.

OPTIONS:: In addition to the new options previously listed, these items were offered: 351 cu. in. V-8 engine. 400 cu. in. V-8. Convenience Group. AM/FM stereo radio. SelectShift Cruise-O-Matic. Speed control. Pickup box cover. Sliding front box cover window. Tool stowage box. Spare tire lock. Slide-out spare tire carrier. Auxiliary 12-volt 68 amp-hr. battery. Mag-type wheel 15 in. covers. Cargo tie-down hooks. Engine block heater. Electric rear window defroster. Auxiliary fuel tank for F-150. Locking fuel cap. Visibility Light Group. Northland Special. Pinstripe Accent Package (for Shorty Flaresides). Protection Package. Seat upholstery. Tinted glass (windshield only or all windows).

HISTORICAL FOOTNOTES: Total 1978 model year sales of all Ford light-duty trucks was 875,153.

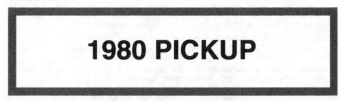

1979 PICKUP

Changes for the 1979 model year were limited. The most apparent visual development was the use of rectangular headlights in all models.

The 1979 color selection consisting of these shades: Raven black, Wimbledon white, dark brown metallic, coral, gold metallic, dark blue metallic, silver metallic, light sand, maroon metallic, light jade, candyapple red, dark jade metallic, medium copper, bright yellow, and light medium blue. Medium blue and walnut were optional glow colors. Wimbledon white could be used as the accent color for any exterior color except silver metallic. The pickup models were again available in the regular, Deluxe or combination two-tone variations.

I.D. DATA: The V.I.N. had 17 entries. The first three characters identified the manufacturer, make and type of vehicle. The next entry, a letter designated the GVW rating. The next three characters identified the series and body style. The eighth character identified the engine. A check digit following, then an entry identifying the assembly plant. The final digits represented the sequential production number.

Body Type	Factory Price	GVW	Shipping Weight	Prod. Total
Series F-150, 117 in., 133 in. wheelbase. SuperCab-155 in. wheelbase				
Chassis & Cab	$6300	6050[1]	3615	—
Pickup, 8.0 ft. Flareside	$6794	6050	3985	—
Pickup, 8.0 ft. Styleside	$6794	6050	4070	—
SuperCab, Styleside	$6544	6050	4025	—
SuperCab, Chassis & Cab	$6312	6050	4293	—

NOTE 1: 6300 and 6400 lb. GVW optional.

Body Type	Factory Price	GVW	Shipping Weight	Prod. Total
Series F-250, 133 in. wheelbase SuperCab-155 in. wheelbase				
Chassis & Cab	$7217	6700[2]	3660	—
Pickup, 8 ft. Flareside	$7732	6700	4100	—
Pickup, 8 ft. Styleside	$7732	6700	4115	—
Crew Cab, 150 in. wb.	$8728	6700	4755	—
Crew Cab, Chassis & Cab	$8494	6700	4400	—
SuperCab, Styleside	$8152	6700	4388	—
SuperCab, Chassis & Cab	$7984	6700	4400	-

NOTE 2: 7300 lb., 8100 lb., 8400 lb. GVW optional.

STANDARD ENGINE: F-150 and F-250 regular cab and crew cab models: Engine Type: OHV In-line 6-cylinder. Bore x Stroke: 4.00 in. x 3.98 in. Displacement: 300 cu. in. Induction system: Single venturi downdraft carburetor. Compression Ratio: 8.01. Number of main bearings-7. Horsepower: Net: 114 @ 3200 rpm. (California rating: 118 @ 3600 rpm). Torque: 227 lb.-ft. @ 1800 rpm. (California rating: 205 lb.-ft. @ 2200 rpm). Fuel Requirements: Leaded or unleaded. Optional: For F-150 and F-250. Standard cab and crew cab models. Standard for F-150 and F-250 SuperCab models. Engine Type: OHV V-8. Bore x Stroke: 4.00 in. x 3.50 in. Displacement: 351 cu. in. (5.75 liters). Induction system: 2-barrel Motorcraft carburetor. Compression Ratio: 8.0:1. Number of main bearings-5. Horsepower: Net: 163 @ 3800 rpm. (California rating: 161 @ 3800 rpm). Torque: Net: 267 lb.-ft. @ 2200 rpm. (California rating: 265 lb.-ft. @ 2200 rpm). Fuel Requirements: Leaded or unleaded. Optional: For all F-150 and F-250. models. Engine Type: OHV V-8. Bore x Stroke: 4.00 in. x 4.00 in. Displacement: 400 cu. in. (6.55 liters). Induction system: 4-barrel carburetor. Compression Ratio: 8.0:1. Number of main bearings-5. Horsepower: Net: 169 @ 3600 rpm. (California rating: 167 @ 3600 rpm). Torque: Net: 303 lb.-ft. @ 2200 rpm. (California rating: 302 lb.-ft. @ 2200 rpm). Fuel Requirements: Leaded or unleaded.

CHASSIS FEATURES: Separate body and frame. Single channel, 36,000 psi. Section modulus: F-150 regular cab: (117 in. wheelbase): 3.95; F-150 regular cab (133 in. wheelbase): 4.33. F-250 (crew cab): 5.67. F-150 and F-250 (SuperCab): 6.67.

SUSPENSION AND RUNNING GEAR: Front Suspension: F-150 regular cab: Coil springs. F-150 SuperCab and all F-250: Semi-elliptical, tapered, constant rate 2-leaf springs. All springs computer selected for GVW rating. Rear Suspension: All models: Semi-elliptical leaf springs. F-150 regular cab and SuperCab: 5-leaf, 55.5 in. x 3.0 in. Capacity: 3750 lb. at ground. F-250 regular cab, crew cab and SuperCab: 5-leaf, 55.5 in. x 3.0 in. Capacity: 4000 lb. at ground. Optional: F-250: 4500 and 5480 lb. capacity at ground. Auxiliary spring, 34.5 in. x 3.0 in. with 710 lb. rating. Front Axle Type and Capacity: F-150 regular cab and SuperCab: 3550 lb. capacity, full-floating, Hotchkiss. F-250: 3800 lb. capacity, full-floating, Hotchkiss. Optional: F-250: 4500 lb. capacity. The F-250 front axle was of heavier construction than the F-150. It was of open knuckle design and used pen Cardan-type universal joints of alloy steel. Rear Axle Type and Capacity: F-150: Semi-floating, 3750 lb. capacity. F-250: Full-floating, Hotchkiss. Spicer model 60, 5300 lb. capacity. Ratios: F-150 regular cab: 3.50:1. Optional: 4.9 liter engine: 4.11:1; 5.8 liter V-8: 3.0:1 (not available with 117 in. wheelbase. and 4-speed trans.); 6.6 liter V-8: 4.11:1 (with part time four-wheel drive only). F-150 SuperCab: 3.50:1. Traction-Lok rear axle with 3.50:1 ratio also optional for all models. F-250 4.9 liter and 5.8 liter engines: 3.54:1. 6.6 liter engine: 4.10:1. (not available with Snowplow Preparation Package or 4500 lb. front axle with full-time four-wheel drive) Optional: 4.9 liter and 5.8 liter: Limited slip rear axle: 4.10:1 (not available with Snowplow Preparation Package or 4500 lb. front axle with full-time four-wheel drive). Transfer Case: Type: 2-speed New Process 205. Ratios: 1.96:1, 1.00:1. Optional: New Process 203 full-time. Ratios: 2.01, 1.00:1. Brakes: Type: Hydraulic, single-piston, floating caliper, Ford-designed disc front and drums rear, power assisted. Dimensions: Front: F-150: 11.54 in. disc, F-250: 12.5 in. disc on all models. Rear: F-150: 11.03 in. x 2.25 in. F-250: Rear: 12.0 in. x 2.50 in. Wheels: F-150: 5-hole stamped disc, 15 in. x 5.5K, disc. Optional: 6.0JK, 15 in. x 8JJ. F-250: 8-hole, stamped disc, 16 x 6.0, disc. Optional: 6.75, 6.0K. Tires: F-150: L78 x 15B. F-250: 8.00 x 16.5D. Optional: F-150: Tubeless: L78 x 15C, LR78 x 15C, 10 x 15C. Tube-type: 7.0 x 15D. F-250: Tubeless: 8.00 x 16.5E, 8.75 x 16.5E, 8.75 x 16.5E, 8.75R x 16.5E, 9.50 x 16.5D, 9.50 x 16.5E, 7.50 x 16C, 7.50 x 16D, 7.50 x 16E. Tube-type: 7.50 x 16D, 7.50 x 16E. Steering: Standard F-150 regular cab: Gemer #375, Worm and Roller. All others: Power assisted, recirculating ball (optional for F-150 regular cab). Transmission: 4-speed New Process 435. Ratios: New Process 435: 6.69, 3.34, 1.66, 1.0:1. Reverse: 8.26:1. Clutch: Heavy-duty hydraulic. 11.0 in. dia. and 123.7 sq. in. Optional: Cruise-O-Matic 3-speed automatic for 6.6 liter V-8 only.

VEHICLE DIMENSIONS: Styleside pickups: Wheelbase: 117 in./133 in. Overall length: 195.1 in./211.3 in. Flareside pickups: Wheelbase: 117 in./133 in. Overall length: 192.2 in./208.4 in. Chassis and cab: Wheelbase: 117 in./133 in./155 in. Overall length: 189.1 in./205.3 in./227.3 in. SuperCab: Wheelbase: 155 in. Overall length: 233.6 in. Front/Rear Overhang: 31.7 in./43.7 (Pickup)-40.6 in. (chassis and cab). Crew cab: Wheelbase: 150.3 in. Overall length: 75-75.8 in. depending upon model. Width: 79.1 in. Front/Rear tread: The tread width varies depending upon the tire size. Front treads average 64.3 in. and rear treads average 64.4 in. (F-150), and 65. in. (F-250).

CAPACITIES: Fuel Tank: 19.2 gal. Optional: Dual fuel tanks with total capacity of 38.7 to 46.2 gal. except for F-150 with 117 in. wheelbase.

ACCOMMODATIONS: 3 occupants. Crew cab and SuperCab: 6 occupants.

INSTRUMENTATION: Speedometer, odometer, fuel level and engine coolant temperature gauges, warning lights for oil pressure and battery charge.

OPTIONS AND PRICES: In addition to the new options previously listed, these items were offered: 351 cu. in. V-8 engine. 400 cu. in. V-8. Convenience Group. AM/FM stereo radio. SelectShift Cruise-O-Matic. Speed control. Pickup box cover. Sliding front box cover window. Tool stowage box. Spare tire lock. Slide-out spare tire carrier. Auxiliary 12-volt 68 amp-hr. battery. Mag-type wheel 15 in. covers. Cargo tie-down hooks. Engine block heater. Electric rear window defroster. Auxiliary fuel tank for F-150. Locking fuel cap. Visibility Light Group. Northland Special. Pinstripe Accent Package (for Shorty Flaresides). Protection Package. Seat upholstery. Tinted glass (windshield only or all windows).

HISTORICAL FOOTNOTES: Total 1979 model year sales of all Ford light-duty trucks was 742,761. Total 1979 model year sales of all Ford four-wheel drive light-duty trucks was 196,104.

1980 PICKUP

Numerous engineering, convenience, styling and fuel-economy features were benchmarks of the new generation of Ford four-wheel drive trucks. Ford Division general manager Philip E. Benton, Jr. noted that "our new trucks retain the best of the past, but fresh styling, chassis innovations and powertrain advancements have been designed and engineered into the vehicles to give American pickup buyers a more fuel-efficient, yet full functional truck line." Among the most important developments was the introduction of independent front suspension, wind tunnel-tested aerodynamic styling, a specially designed driver-oriented instrument panel and fuel-efficient powertrains.

The new front suspension, designed and patented by Ford, utilized two high-strength steel axle carriers which permitted each front wheel to move up and down independently of the other. The F-150 continued to use coil springs with the F-250 retaining tapered leaf springs. A new 2-speed New Process 208 transfer case was also introduced.

Bolt-on fiberglass fenders highlighted the appearance of the F-150 Flareside model. A revised cab underbody design reduced mud-packing, while a revised rocker panel design reduced stone-pecking by preventing dirt and gravel from hitting the door.

Overall, the 1980 models were three inches shorter, two inches narrower and two inches lower. The use of a lower overall steering ratio improved ease of handling. Manual steering was improved two percent and power steering was improved by 13 percent. A maintenance-free battery, with a 33 percent longer service life was standard for all models. Another functional revision was the use of a dual-port windshield washer nozzle which provided a more efficient distribution of washer fluid. This feature also allowed for easier service to the fluid nozzle, wiper motor, linkage, arm and blade. An increased windshield wiper pattern provided 26.6 percent more visibility than the 1979 model. The F series trucks also had approximately nine percent (seven percent for SuperCab) more glass area than in 1979. Front legroom was increased by one inch to 41 inches. The seat-position control was relocated to the front of the bench seat for easier operation. An in-dash storage compartment for small items was now standard. The glove-box liner included two cup depressions and an integral coin/token slot. A squeeze-type latch was used. A new mini-fuse panel accessible under the dash panel used new shaped fuses for easy identification and replacement. International symbols were used for the instrument panel controls, gauges and warning lights. Major air conditioning components were relocated for easier servicing in the engine compartment. Tri-color temperature controls were included with air conditioning and heaters. For 1980, the windshields had Butyl-type mountings for improved protection against water leaks and wind noise. Color-keyed sun visors and bright windshield surround moldings were standard on all models. A new wrap-around taillamp design eliminated the need for separate side-marker lamps. The revised exterior styling reduced aerodynamic horsepower requirements by 15.3 percent for the F-150. The Free Wheeling Package was reformatted with pinstripes in place of the 1979 multi-color accent stripe. Ten new exterior colors as well as a new Victoria tu-tone paint treatment were offered.

Major new options included Captain's chairs and a console for SuperCab models, AM/FM stereo radios with eight-track or cassette tape players, an electronic digital clock and a Sports Instrumentation Package that included a tachometer and trip odometer. Another new option development was the inclusion of a "resume" feature for the speed control. An optional Light Group featured an underhood light with a built-in reel to permit its use as a trouble light. A new powertrain application was the addition of the 5.0 liter (302 cu. in.) V-8 for the F-150 and F-250 models, except for the SuperCab.

The 1980 color selection consisting of Raven black, Wimbledon white, candyapple red, silver metallic, light sand, maroon, dark chamois metallic, midnight blue metallic, medium blue, light caramel, dark pine metallic, medium grey metallic, dark silver blue metallic, light medium pine, medium copper and bright yellow. Optional "Glamour" colors were: Chamois glow, walnut glow and sand glow. Wimbledon white could be used as the accent color for any exterior color except silver metallic. The pickup models were again available in the regular, Deluxe or combination two-tone variations.

I.D. DATA: The V.I.N. had 17 entries. The first three characters identified the manufacturer, make and type of vehicle. The next entry, a letter, designated the GVW rating. The next three characters identified the series and body style. The eighth character identified the engine. A check digit following, then an entry identifying the assembly plant. The final digits represented the sequential production number.

Body Type	Factory Price	GVW	Shipping Weight	Prod. Total
Series F-150, 117 in., 133 in. wheelbase. SuperCab-155 in. wheelbase				
Pickup, 6.75 ft. Flareside	$6933	6050[1]	N.A.	—
Pickup, 6.75 ft. Styleside	$6933	6050	3885	—
Pickup, 8.0 ft. Styleside	$7018	6050	3970	—
SuperCab, Styleside	$7636	6050	3925	—

NOTE 1: 6300 and 6400 lb. GVW optional.

Body Type	Factory Price	GVW	Shipping Weight	Prod. Total
Series F-250, 133 in. wheelbase. SuperCab-155 in. wheelbase				
Pickup, 8 ft. Flareside	$N.A.	6700[2]	4000	—
Pickup, 8 ft. Styleside	$N.A.	6700	4015	—
SuperCab, Styleside	$N.A.	6700	4288	—

NOTE 2: 7300 lb., 8100 lb., 8400 lb. GVW optional.

Series F-350, 133 in. wheelbase				
Pickup, 8 ft. Styleside	$N.A.	8700[3]	4465	—

NOTE 3: 9100 lb. GVW optional.

STANDARD ENGINE: (All states except California where the 302 V-8 is standard): Engine Type: OHV In-line 6-cylinder. Bore x Stroke: 4.00 in. x 3.98 in. Displacement: 300 cu. in. Induction system: Single venturi downdraft carburetor. Number of main bearings-7. Carburetion: Single 1-barrel downdraft. Compression Ratio: 8.9:1. Horsepower: Net: 119 @ 3200 rpm. Torque: Net: 243 lb.-ft. @ 1200 rpm. Fuel Requirements: Unleaded.

OPTIONAL ENGINE: Engine type: OHV V-8. Cast-iron block and cylinder heads. Bore x Stroke: 4.00 in. x 3.00 in. Lifters: Hydraulic. Number of main bearings-5. Displacement: 302 cu. in. (5.0 liters). Lifters: Hydraulic. Carburetion: Single 2-barrel. Compression Ratio: 8.4:1. Horsepower: Net: 137 @ 3400 rpm. Torque: Net: 239 lb.-ft. @ 1800 rpm. Fuel Requirements: Unleaded. Optional: For standard cab and crew cab models. Standard for SuperCab models. Engine Type: OHV V-8. Bore x Stroke: 4.00 in. x 3.50 in. Displacement: 351 cu. in. (5.75 liters). Induction system: 2-barrel Motorcraft carburetor. Compression Ratio: 8.0:1. Number of main bearings-5. Horsepower: Net: 138 @ 3400 rpm. Torque: Net: 263 lb.-ft. @ 2000 rpm. Fuel Requirements: Unleaded. Optional: For all models. Engine Type: OHV V-8. Bore x Stroke: 4.00 in. x 4.00 in. Displacement: 400 cu. in. (6.55 liters). Induction system: 4-barrel carburetor. Compression Ratio: 8.0:1. Number of main bearings-5. Horsepower: Net: 136 @ 2800 rpm. Torque: Net: 310 lb.-ft. @ 1200 rpm. Fuel Requirements: Unleaded.

CHASSIS FEATURES: Separate body and frame. Single channel, 36,000 psi. Section modulus: F-150 regular cab: (117 in. wheelbase): 3.95; F-150 regular cab (133 in. wheelbase): 4.33. F-250 (crew cab): 5.67. F-150 and F-250 (SuperCab): 6.67.

SUSPENSION AND RUNNING GEAR: Front Suspension: F-150 regular cab: Coil springs. F-150 SuperCab and all F-250: Semi-elliptical, tapered, constant rate 2-leaf springs. All springs computer selected for GVW rating. Rear Suspension: All models: Semi-elliptical leaf springs. F-150 regular cab and SuperCab: 5-leaf, 55.5 in. x 3.0 in. Capacity: 3750 lb. at ground. F-250 regular cab, crew cab and SuperCab: 5-leaf, 55.5 in. x 3.0 in. Capacity: 4000 lb. at ground. Optional: F-250: 4500 and 5480 lb. capacity at ground. Auxiliary spring, 34.5 in. x 3.0 in. with 710 lb. rating. Front Axle Type and Capacity: F-150 regular cab and SuperCab: 3550 lb. capacity, full-floating, Hotchkiss. F-250: 3800 lb. capacity, full-floating, Hotchkiss. Optional: F-250: 4500 lb. capacity. The F-250 front axle was of heavier construction than the F-150. It was of open knuckle design and used pen Cardan-type universal joints of alloy steel. Rear Axle Type and Capacity: F-150: Semi-floating, 3750 lb. capacity. F-250: Full-floating, Hotchkiss. Spicer model 60, 5300 lb. capacity. Transfer Case: Type: 2-speed New Process 208. Ratios: 2.6:1, 1.00:1. Brakes: Type: Hydraulic, single-piston, floating caliper, Ford-designed disc front and drums rear, power assisted. Dimensions: Front: F-150: 11.54 in. disc, F-250: 12.5 in. disc on all models. Rear: F-150: 11.03 in. x 2.25 in. F-250: Rear: 12.0 in. x 2.50 in. Wheels: F-150: 5-hole stamped disc, 15 in. x 5.5K, disc. Optional: 6.0JK, 15 in. x 8JJ. F-250: 8-hole, stamped disc, 16 x 6.0, disc. Optional: 6.75, 6.0K. Tires: F-150: L78 x 15B. F-250: 8.00 x 16.5D. Optional: F-150: Tubeless: L78 x 15C, LR78 x 15C, 10 x 15C. Tube-type: 7.0 x 15D. F-250: Tubeless: 8.00 x 16.5E, 8.75 x 16.5E, 8.75 x 16.5E, 8.75R x 16.5E, 9.50 x 16.5D, 9.50 x 16.5E, 7.50 x 16C, 7.50 x 16D, 7.50 x 16E. Tube-type: 7.50 x 16D, 7.50 x 16E. Steering: Standard F-150 regular cab: Gemer #375, Worm and Roller. All others: Power assisted, recirculating ball (optional for F-150 regular cab). Ratio: 17:1. Transmission: 4-speed New Process 435. Ratios: New Process 435: 6.69, 3.34, 1.66, 1.0:1. Reverse: 8.26:1. Clutch: Heavy-duty hydraulic. 11.0 in. dia. and 123.7 sq. in. Optional: Cruise-O-Matic 3-speed automatic for 6.6 liter V-8 only.

VEHICLE DIMENSIONS: Styleside pickups: Wheelbase: 116.8 in./133 in. Overall length: 192.1 in./208.3 in. Flareside pickups: Wheelbase: 116.8 in. Overall length: 187.8.2 in. Overall width: 116.8 in. wheelbase. Styleside and Flareside: 69.3 in.; SuperCab. Wheelbase: 155 in. Overall length: 230.3 in. Width: 70.8 in.

CAPACITIES: Fuel Tank: 19.2 gal. Optional: Dual fuel tanks with total capacity of 38.7 to 46.2 gal. except for F-150 with 117 in. wheelbase.

ACCOMMODATIONS: 3 occupants. SuperCab: 6 occupants.

INSTRUMENTATION: Speedometer, odometer, fuel level and engine coolant temperature gauges, warning lights for oil pressure and battery charge.

OPTIONS AND PRICES: 302 V-8: $315. 351 V-8: $477. SelectShift automatic transmission: $233. Limited slip rear differential: $197. Chrome grille. Accent tape stripe. Tri-color tape stripe on hood and sides in Tri-Tone ted, orange/tan/creme, Tri-Tone yellow or Tri-Tone blue (with Free Wheeling options only). Lower body side molding with black vinyl insert (for custom only). Victoria Tu-tone paint: $195.00. Bright wheel-lip molding (for custom only). AM radio. AM/FM radio monaural (single speaker). AM/FM stereo (quad speakers): $242. AM/FM stereo with cassette tape player (quad speakers). 40-channel CB radio: $361. Air conditioning. High output heater. ComfortVent heater. Auxiliary heater. Western low-mount swing-away mirrors: $78. Bright low-mount swing-away recreational mirrors. GT roll bar: $112.00. Simulated leather-wrapped steering wheel (for custom only). Tilt steering wheel. Fingertip speed control with resume feature. Tinted glass for all windows. Electronic day/night digital clock: $52. Center console. Captain's chairs (reclining driver and passenger seats), front bench seat. Cloth seat trim inserts with Ranger XLT Package for front bucket seats. Automatic locking hubs (with SelectShift transmission only). SelectShift transmission. Quad heavy-duty front and rear shock absorbers. Heavy-duty rear shock absorbers. Heavy-duty air cleaner: $17.00. Sports instrumentation (0-6000 tachometer, ammeter, oil pressure gauge and trip odometer): $107. Gauges for oil pressure and ammeter. Engine block heater (single with 4.2 liter six and 5.0 liter V-8, dual with 5.8 liter V-8). Tool box (includes under hood light and locking inside hood release): $78. Tow hooks: $32. Auxiliary transmission oil cooler (with SelectShift automatic transmission). Skid plate: $78. Dual electric horns: $15. Fog lamps (includes plastic covers and bright front bumper guards. Front and/or rear chrome bumpers. Chrome rear step bumper. Argent rear step bumper. Styled steel painted white wheels (4 wheels with steel spare): $642 (with 10 x 15 tires). 10-hole polished forged aluminum with clear plastic coated wheels. (4 wheels with steel spare). Sport wheelcovers (4). 5-slot brushed forged aluminum wheels with clear plastic coating (4 wheels with steel spare). Ranger XLT Package. Includes, in addition to or in place of custom features, brushed aluminum tailgate applique with bright FORD and XLT plaque, chrome bumpers, bright lower body side molding with black vinyl insert, cloth trim or patterned vinyl, wall-to-wall cut-pile carpeting, bright accents on door trim panels with lower area carpeted, cargo lamp, vinyl headliner on foam padding, Deluxe seat belts, Ranger XLT dash plaque, courtesy lighting with passenger and driver's side door switches, simulated leather-wrapped steering wheel, cigar lighter, woodtone accent around steering wheel horn pad, polished woodtone applique on instrument panel with bright molding for instruments, added insulation. Tri-color tape stripe (in lieu of pinstripes on Free Wheeling Packages). Free Wheeling A Package. Includes body side, hood, tailgate and door windows pin-striping, Sport wheelcovers and bright bumpers (standard with Ranger XLT). Free Wheeling B Package. In addition to contents of the A Package includes Sports instrumentation, simulated leather-wrapped steering wheel (standard with Ranger XLT), foglamps with covers, bumper guards, Handling Package, GT roll bar, white styled wheels (five, in place of Sport wheelcovers). Exterior Protection Group. Includes bright door edge guards and rub strip. Security Lock Group. Includes locking gas cap and locks on inside hood release, glove box and spare tire. Trailer Towing Packages. Super Engine Cooling Package. Extra Engine Cooling Package. Sports Instrumentation Package. Includes 0-6000 rpm tachometer, ammeter, oil pressure gauge and trip odometer. Special Altitude Performance Package. Handling Package. Includes front stabilizer bar and quad heavy-duty hydraulic front and rear shock absorbers. Convenience Group. Includes intermediate windshield wipers, 12 in. day/night mirror, map box in doors, headlamp-on warning buzzer and right hand door courtesy light switch (custom only): $78. Light Group. Includes lights in glove box, ashtray, under instrument panel, dome light with map light (standard dome light only with optional front bucket seat), movable underhood worklight, and headlamp-on warning buzzer

HISTORICAL FOOTNOTES: Total 1980 model year sales of all Ford light-duty trucks were 537,476. Total 1980 model year sales of all Ford four-wheel drive light-duty trucks was 93,967.

1981 PICKUP

For the 1981 model year the F series Ford trucks were characterized by a large number of innovations and refinements. For 1981 a new tri-color tape stripe was offered with or without the Free Wheeling Package option. The tri-color stripes flowed back along the body, both above and below the chamfered character depression, to just behind the door. From the point the upper stripe swept up to the roof while the lower stripe continued back along the full length of the Styleside pickup box. The Ranger, Ranger XLT and Ranger Lariat were continued with new features. Among these was a new cloth covered cut-and-score headliner in place of the previous vinyl headlining. The Ranger Package was highlighted by such features as a folding and fully covered seat back, color-keyed seat belts, bright door accents, a color-keyed floor mat with additional insulation, and woodtone finish on the instrument panel. A passenger door courtesy light switch and cigarette lighter with light were also included. On the exterior a new upper body side trim molding system and rear window moldings were used.

The Ranger XLT featured such details as seats with cloth and vinyl upholstery, color-keyed carpeting, carpeted lower door, and color-keyed padded cloth covered headliner. The tailgate for the Styleside had a brushed aluminum applique. Flareside pickups with the Ranger XLT option had a special XLT tape treatment on the front fenders, body sides and the fiberglass rear fenders. The Ranger Lariat added to the XLT content a deeply cushioned seat with premium-level cloth and vinyl trim, door trim panels with a woodtone applique and a map box trimmed with carpet. On the exterior, there was a full-length lower body side molding with a black vinyl insert, and a special Lariat dual tape stripe that swept along the top of the front fenders, back under the side windows and then up and over the door window opening where it terminated at the windshield molding.

Seven new colors plus three new selections for interior color choices were offered. The new exterior standard colors included tan, dark spruce metallic, fawn and medium caramel metallic. The new interior colors were nutmeg, fawn and spruce green. Four two-tone paint combinations were available. The regular two-tone scheme applied an accent color to the roof and down the rear of the cab to the pickup box. The Deluxe two-tone applied an accent color to the center body side panels, and across the center of the tailgate. The accent color was framed with bright moldings. The combination two-tone combined the regular and Deluxe accent color patterns. In the Victoria two-tone an accent color was applied to the hood and upper fenders, forward roof pillars, and around the door windows. The accent color was also applied to the lower body sides.

For 1981 two new Snowplow Preparation Packages were available for all 4x4 pickups including the F-150 model for the first time. Previously only the F-250 and F-350 were available with Snowplow Packages. For 1981 the Snowplow Packages were supplied in two equipment levels — the "Base" Package and the "Plus" version. The base level included a heavy-duty alternator and upgraded chassis components. A higher rated front axle was included with the F-150 and F-250 models. The Plus Package added a heavy-duty battery, extra cooling, ammeter and oil pressure gauges and ICC-type roof clearance lights. New optional power door locks and power windows were now available as separate options for the F series trucks. The power door lock switches were mounted on the door trim panels at the front edge of the armrests and were labeled "Lock" and "Unlock". The power windows included a master control switch for both windows at the driver's position plus a single switch at the passenger's side window. Each switch was of bright metal with a woodtone applique.

Remote-control low-mount Western mirrors were another new option for 1981. This option provided quick adjustment of both mirrors from the driver's seat. New 10R-15C steel-belted radial-ply tires were introduced as an option for the F-150. They combined the advantages of radial-ply design with high flotation performance. They were available only in a Sport configuration with white outline raised letters in the sidewalls. They were supplied in sets of five and were mounted on white styled steel 15 x 7.0JJ wheels. Also new for 1981 were automatic locking front wheel hubs. With these hubs the driver no longer had to leave the cab and dial the hubs to lock each wheel and engage four-wheel drive. In two-wheel drive, the hubs automatically free-wheeled to permit the front axle, driveshaft and transfer case to remain stationary. The hubs engages automatically after the driver shifted the transfer case lever to a four-wheel drive position. As soon as the front axle shafts began to rotate in four-wheel drive, a cam in the hub lock sensed the motion and engaged the hub. Once engaged, the hubs remained engaged even when coasting downhill, thus helping to provide engine braking. To disengage the hubs, the driver had to shift back into two-wheel drive and reverse the vehicle direction for a few feet.

All F series trucks had halogen headlights and radial-ply tires for 1981. Joining Ford's four-wheel drive lineup was a new F-350 regular cab chassis-cab model. This vehicle had a 133 in. wheelbase and a standard 8700 lb. GVW rating. It was offered with optional 9100 lb. GVW rating. Its standard engine/transmission was the 351 cu. in. V-8 and a 4-speed manual transmission with a creeper first gear. A 3-speed automatic transmission with an external oil cooler was optional.

I.D. DATA: The V.I.N. had 17 entries. The first three characters identified the manufacturer, make and type of vehicle. The next entry, a letter designated the GVW rating. The next three characters identified the series and body style. The eighth character identified the engine. A check digit following, then an entry identifying the assembly plant. The final digits represented the sequential production number.

Body Type	Factory Price	GVW	Shipping Weight	Prod. Total
Series F-150, 117 in., 133 in. wheelbase. SuperCab-155 in. wheelbase				
Pickup, 6.75 ft. Flareside	$N.A.	6050[1]	N.A.	—
Pickup, 6.75 ft. Styleside	$N.A.	6050	3885	—
Pickup, 8.0 ft. Styleside	$N.A.	6050	3970	—
SuperCab, Styleside	$N.A.	6050	3925	—

NOTE 1: 6300 and 6400 lb. GVW optional.

Series F-250, 133 in. wheelbase SuperCab-155 in. wheelbase				
Pickup, 8 ft. Flareside	$N.A.	6700[2]	4000	—
Pickup, 8 ft. Styleside	$N.A.	6700	4015	—
SuperCab, Styleside	$7592	6700	4288	—

NOTE 2: 7300 lb., 8100 lb., 8400 lb. GVW optional.

Series F-350, 133 in. wheelbase				
Chassis and Cab	$N.A.	8700[3]	N.A.	—
Pickup, 8 ft. Styleside	$N.A.	8700	4465	—

NOTE 3: 9100 lb. GVW optional.

STANDARD ENGINE: All models except F-350 (not available for California where the 302 V-8 is standard): Engine Type: OHV In-line 6-cylinder. Bore x Stroke: 4.00 in. x 3.98 in. Displacement: 300 cu. in. Induction system: Single venturi downdraft carburetor. Number of main bearings-7. Carburetion: Single 1-barrel downdraft. Compression Ratio: 8.9:1. Horsepower: Net: 122 @ 3000 rpm. Torque: Net: 255 lb.-ft. @ 1400 rpm. Fuel Requirements: Unleaded.

OPTIONAL ENGINE: All models except F-150 and F-250 SuperCab and F-350: Engine type: OHV V-8. Cast-iron block and cylinder heads. Bore x Stroke: 4.00 in. x 3.00 in. Lifters: Hydraulic. Number of main bearings-5. Displacement: 302 cu. in. (5.0 liters). Lifters: Hydraulic. Carburetion: Single 2-barrel. Compression Ratio: 8.4:1. Horsepower: Net: 133 @ 3400 rpm. Torque: Net: 233 lb.-ft. @ 2000 rpm. Fuel Requirements: Unleaded. Optional: All models standard for F-350. Bore x Stroke: 4.00 in. x 3.50 in. Displacement: 351 cu. in. (5.75 liters). Induction system: 2-barrel Motorcraft carburetor. Compression Ratio: 8.0:1. Number of main bearings-5. Horsepower: Net: 136 @ 3000 rpm. Torque: Net: 262 lb.-ft. @ 1600 rpm. Fuel Requirements: Unleaded. Optional: For F-350 models. Engine Type: OHV V-8. Bore x Stroke: 4.00 in. x 4.00 in. Displacement: 400 cu. in. (6.55 liters). Induction system: 4-barrel carburetor. Compression Ratio: 8.0:1. Number of main bearings-5. Horsepower: Net: 136 @ 2800 rpm. Torque: Net: 310 lb.-ft. @ 1200 rpm. Fuel Requirements: Unleaded.

CHASSIS FEATURES: Separate body and frame. Single channel, 36,000 psi. Section modulus: F-150 regular cab: (117 in. wheelbase): 3.95; F-150 regular cab (133 in. wheelbase): 4.33. F-250 (crew cab): 5.67. F-150 and F-250 (SuperCab): 6.67.

SUSPENSION AND RUNNING GEAR: Front Suspension: F-150 regular cab: Coil springs. F-150 SuperCab and all F-250: Semi-elliptical, tapered, constant rate 2-leaf springs. All springs computer selected for GVW rating. Rear Suspension: All models: Semi-elliptical leaf springs. F-150 regular cab and SuperCab: 5-leaf, 55.5 in. x 3.0 in. Capacity: 3750 lb. at ground. F-250 regular cab, crew cab and SuperCab: 5-leaf, 55.5 in. x 3.0 in. Capacity: 4000 lb. at ground. Optional: F-250: 4500 and 5480 lb. capacity at ground. Auxiliary spring, 34.5 in. x 3.0 in. with 7100 lb. rating. Front Axle Type and Capacity: F-150 regular cab and SuperCab: 3550 lb. capacity, full-floating, Hotchkiss. F-250: 3800 lb. capacity, full-floating, Hotchkiss. Optional: F-250: 4500 lb. capacity. The F-250 front axle was of heavier construction than the F-150. It was of open knuckle design and used pen Cardan-type universal joints of alloy steel. Rear Axle Type and Capacity: F-150: Semi-floating, 3750 lb. capacity. F-250: Full-floating, Hotchkiss. Spicer model 60, 5300 lb. capacity. Transfer Case: Type: 2-speed New Process 208. Ratios: 2.6:1, 1.00:1. Brakes: Type: Hydraulic, single-piston, floating caliper, Ford-designed disc front and drums rear, power assisted. Dimensions: Front: F-150: 11.54 in. disc, F-250: 12.5 in. disc on all models. Rear: F-150: 11.03 in. x 2.25 in. F-250: Rear: 12.0 in. x 2.50 in. Wheels: F-150: 5-hole stamped disc, 15 in. x 5.5K, disc. Optional: 6.0JK, 15 in. x 8JJ. F-250: 8-hole, stamped disc, 16 x 6.0, disc. Optional: 6.75, 6.0K. Tires: F-150: L78 x 15B. F-250: 8.00 x 16.5D. Optional: F-150: Tubeless: L78 x 15C, LR78 x 15C, 10 x 15C. Tube-type: 7.0 x 15D. F-250: Tubeless: 8.00 x 16.5E, 8.75 x 16.5E, 8.75 x 16.5E, 8.75R x 16.5E, 9.50 x 16.5D, 9.50 x 16.5E, 7.50 x 16C, 7.50 x 16D, 7.50 x 16E. Tube-type: 7.50 x 16D, 7.50 x 16E. Steering: Standard F-150 regular cab: Gemer #375, Worm and Roller. All others: Power assisted, recirculating ball (optional for F-150 regular cab). Ratio: 17:1. Transmission: 4-speed New Process 435. Ratios: New Process 435: 6.69, 3.34, 1.66, 1.0:1. Reverse: 8.26:1. Clutch: Heavy-duty hydraulic. 11.0 in. dia. and 123.7 sq. in. Optional: Cruise-O-Matic 3-speed automatic for 6.6 liter V-8 only.

VEHICLE DIMENSIONS: Styleside pickups: Wheelbase: 116.8 in./133 in. Overall length: 192.1 in./208.3 in. Flareside pickups: Wheelbase: 116.8 in. Overall length: 187.8.2 in. Overall width: 116.8 in. wheelbase. Styleside and Flareside: 69.3 in.; SuperCab: Wheelbase: 155 in. Overall length: 230.3 in. Width: 70.8 in.

CAPACITIES: Fuel Tank: 19.2 gal. Optional: Dual fuel tanks with total capacity of 38.7 to 46.2 gal. except for F-150 with 117 in. wheelbase.

ACCOMMODATIONS: 3 occupants. SuperCab: 6 occupants.

INSTRUMENTATION: Speedometer, odometer, fuel level and engine coolant temperature gauges, warning lights for oil pressure and battery charge.

OPTIONS AND PRICES: With the addition of the new 1981 options previously noted, the option content was essentially carried over from 1980. What follows is a listing of major options and prices. Air conditioning: $499.69. Automatic transmission: $190.03. Glow paint: $54.29. Sports Instrumentation Package: $87.08. 351 V-8: $294.92. Digital clock: $42.62. Tool stowage box: $28.89. Chrome grille: $38.62. Ranger XLT: $516. Ranger Lariat Package: $516.29. Sliding rear window: $83.69. Tilt steering wheel: $68.08. Speed control: $123.03. Leather wrapped steering wheel: $60.24. Handling Package: $77.96. AM/FM stereo radio with cassette tape player: $273. Light Group: $75.60. Engine oil cooler: $39.44. Auxiliary fuel tank: $148.64. SuperCab rear seat: $222.70. Power windows: $121.80. Power door locks: $82.38. Security Lock Group: $43.74. Protection Group: $55.52.

HISTORICAL FOOTNOTES: Total 1981 model year sales of all Ford light-duty trucks were 470,756. Total 1981 model year sales of all Ford four-wheel drive light-duty trucks was 68,200.

1982 PICKUP

The latest F series trucks sported a new front end appearance. The FORD lettering was removed from the hood's leading edge. The classic blue-filled Ford logo was mounted in the grille center. New Trim Packages were introduced for 1982. The base or standard trim content included chrome front bumper, bright grille surround, bright windshield molding, bright door-mounted mirrors, all-vinyl seat trim, full-foam seat over springs, folding seat back access to behind seat storage area, glove box, left side door courtesy light switch, engine coolant temperature gauge, color-keyed windshield pillar, header and cowl side trim panels, color-keyed door trim panels with foam-padded armrests, floor insulation and carpet texture rubber mat, and inside hood release.

The new mid-range XL Package included, in addition to or in place of standard items these features: Bright upper body side moldings, tape stripe (Flareside), bright rear window molding, cigarette lighter, courtesy light switches for both doors, tape letters on tailgate applique, bright surround for door trim panels, color-keyed floor mat, woodtone applique for instrument panel (in place of standard black applique), folding, fully covered seat back, Deluxe seat belts, cloth and vinyl seat trim, aluminum scuff plates, vinyl headlining, and belt line molding.

1982 Ford F-250 with Camper Special Package

The XLT Lariat, which Ford depicted as having the "top-of-the-line" look, featured in addition to or in place of XL items these features: exterior body protection molding with vinyl accents, brushed aluminum tailgate applique, bright with woodtone applique door trim, and Deluxe steering wheel with woodtone insert. The new Sport-oriented XLS option was characterized by black-painted front and rear bumpers, XLS side body stripe, tape treatment for tailgate applique, bright surround for door trim panel, brushed aluminum instrument panel applique, and brushed aluminum trim for the steering wheel.

Seventeen exterior colors were offered for 1983. They consisted of raven black, Wimbledon white, silver metallic, medium grey metallic, candyapple red, midnight blue metallic, medium blue metallic, bright blue, dark spruce metallic, light spruce, dark fawn metallic, fawn, medium caramel metallic, tan, dark brown metallic, maroon, and at extra cost, light spruce glow. Interior were offered in fawn, dark blue, red, black, nutmeg or spruce (not available for SuperCab).

I.D. DATA: The V.I.N. had 17 entries. The first three characters identified the manufacturer, make and type of vehicle. The next entry, a letter designated the GVW rating. The next three characters identified the series and body style. The eighth character identified the engine. A check digit following, then an entry identifying the assembly plant. The final digits represented the sequential production number.

Body Type	Factory Price	GVW	Shipping Weight	Prod. Total
Series F-150, 117 in., 133 in. wheelbase. SuperCab-155 in. wheelbase				
Pickup, 6.75 ft. Flareside	$8573	6050[1]	N.A.	—
Pickup, 6.75 ft. Styleside	$8448	6050	3817	—
Pickup, 8.0 ft. Styleside	$8598	6050	4002	—
SuperCab, Styleside	$9489	6050	3962	—

NOTE 1: 6300 and 6400 lb. GVW optional.

Series F-250, 133 in. wheelbase SuperCab-155 in. wheelbase				
Pickup, 8 ft. Flareside	$N.A.	6700[2]	4024	—
Pickup, 8 ft. Styleside	$N.A.	6700	4039	—
SuperCab, Styleside	$N.A.	6700	4312	—

NOTE 2: 7300 lb., 8100 lb., 8400 lb. GVW optional.

Series F-350, 133 in. wheelbase				
Chassis and Cab	$N.A.	8700[3]	N.A.	—
Pickup, 8 ft. Styleside	$N.A.	8700	4465	—

NOTE 3: 9100 lb. GVW optional.

STANDARD ENGINE: All models except F-350: (not available for California where the 302 V-8 is standard). Engine Type: OHV In-line 6-cylinder. Bore x Stroke: 4.00 in. x 3.98 in. Displacement: 300 cu. in. Induction system: Single venturi downdraft carburetor. Number of main bearings-7. Carburetion: Single 1-barrel downdraft. Compression Ratio: 8.9:1. Horsepower: Net: 122 @ 3000 rpm. Torque: Net: 255 lb.-ft. @ 1400 rpm. Fuel Requirements: Unleaded.

OPTIONAL ENGINE: All models except F-150 and F-250 SuperCab and F-350: Engine type: OHV V-8. Cast-iron block and cylinder heads. Bore x Stroke: 4.00 in. x 3.00 in. Lifters: Hydraulic. Number of main bearings-5. Displacement: 302 cu. in. (5.0 liters). Lifters: Hydraulic. Carburetion: Single 2-barrel. Compression Ratio: 8.4:1. Horsepower: Net: 133 @ 3400 rpm. Torque: Net: 233 lb.-ft. @ 2000 rpm. Fuel Requirements: Unleaded. Optional: All models Standard for F-350. Bore x Stroke: 4.00 in. x 3.50 in. Displacement: 351 cu. in. (5.75 liters). Induction system: 2-barrel Motorcraft carburetor. Compression Ratio: 8.0:1. Number of main bearings-5. Horsepower: Net: 136 @ 3000 rpm. Torque: Net: 262 lb.-ft. @ 1600 rpm. Fuel Requirements: Unleaded. Optional: For F-350 models. Engine Type: OHV V-8. Bore x Stroke: 4.00 in. x 4.00 in. Displacement: 400 cu. in. (6.55 liters). Induction system: 4-barrel carburetor. Compression Ratio: 8.0:1. Number of main bearings-5. Horsepower: Net: 136 @ 2800 rpm. Torque: Net: 310 lb.-ft. @ 1200 rpm. Fuel Requirements: Unleaded.

CHASSIS FEATURES: Separate body and frame. Single channel, 36,000 psi. Section modulus: F-150 regular cab: (117 in. wheelbase): 3.95; F-150 regular cab (133 in. wheelbase): 4.33. F-250 (crew cab): 5.67. F-150 and F-250 (SuperCab): 6.67.

SUSPENSION AND RUNNING GEAR: Front Suspension: F-150 regular cab: Coil springs. F-150 SuperCab and all F-250: Semi-elliptical, tapered, constant rate 2-leaf springs. All springs computer selected for GVW rating. Rear Suspension: All models: Semi-elliptical leaf springs. F-150 regular cab and SuperCab: 5-leaf, 55.5 in. x 3.0 in. Capacity: 3750 lb. at ground. F-250 regular cab, crew cab and SuperCab: 5-leaf, 55.5 in. x 3.0 in. Capacity: 4000 lb. at ground. Optional: F-250: 4500 and 5480 lb. capacity at ground. Auxiliary spring, 34.5 in. x 3.0 in. with 7100 lb. rating. Front Axle Type and Capacity: F-150 regular cab and SuperCab: 3550 lb. capacity, full-floating, Hotchkiss. F-250: 3800 lb. capacity, full-floating, Hotchkiss. Optional: F-250: 4500 lb. capacity. The F-250 front axle was of heavier construction than the F-150. It was of open knuckle design and used pen Cardan-type universal joints of alloy steel. Rear Axle Type and Capacity: F-150: Semi-floating, 3750 lb. capacity. F-250: Full-floating, Hotchkiss. Spicer model 60, 5300 lb. capacity. Transfer Case: Type: 2-speed New Process

208. Ratios: 2.6:1, 1.00:1. Brakes: Type: Hydraulic, single-piston, floating caliper, Ford designed disc front and drums rear, power assisted. Dimensions: Front: F-150: 11.54 in. disc, F-250: 12.5 in. disc on all models. Rear: F-150: 11.03 in. x 2.25 in. F-250: Rear: 12.0 in. x 2.50 in. Wheels: F-150: 5-hole stamped disc, 15 in. x 5.5K, disc. Optional: 6.0JK, 15 in. x 8JJ. F-250: 8-hole, stamped disc, 16 x 6.0, disc. Optional: 6.75, 6.0K. Tires: F-150: L78 x 15B. F-250: 8.00 x 16.5D. Optional: F-150: Tubeless: L78 x 15C, LR78 x 15C, 10 x 15C. Tube-type: 7.0 x 15D. F-250: Tubeless: 8.00 x 16.5E, 8.75 x 16.5E, 8.75 x 16.5E, 8.75R x 16.5E, 9.50 x 16.5D, 9.50 x 16.5E, 7.50 x 16C, 7.50 x 16D, 7.50 x 16E. Tube-type: 7.50 x 16D, 7.50 x 16E. Steering: Standard F-150 regular cab: Gemer #375, Worm and Roller. All others: Power assisted, recirculating ball (optional for F-150 regular cab). Ratio: 17:1. Transmission: 4-speed New Process 435. Ratios: New Process 435: 6.69, 3.34, 1.66, 1.0:1. Reverse: 8.26:1. Clutch: Heavy-duty hydraulic. 11.0 in. dia. and 123.7 sq. in. Optional: Cruise-O-Matic 3-speed automatic for 6.6 liter V-8 only.

VEHICLE DIMENSIONS: Styleside pickups: Wheelbase: 116.8 in./133 in. Overall length: 192.1 in./208.3 in. Flareside pickups: Wheelbase: 116.8 in. Overall length: 187.8.2 in. Overall width: 116.8 in. wheelbase. Styleside and Flareside: 69.3 in.; SuperCab: Wheelbase: 155 in. Overall length: 230.3 in. Width: 70.8 in.

CAPACITIES: Fuel Tank: 19.2 gal. Optional: Dual fuel tanks with total capacity of 38.7 to 46.2 gal. except for F-150 with 117 in. wheelbase.

ACCOMMODATIONS: 3 occupants. SuperCab: 6 occupants.

INSTRUMENTATION: Speedometer, odometer, fuel level and engine coolant temperature gauges, warning lights for oil pressure and battery charge.

OPTIONS AND PRICES: 302 V-8. 351 V-8, 400 V-8. Chrome grille. Chromatic tape stripe. Tri-colored tape stripe. Accent tape stripe. Lower body side molding with black insert. Bright box rails for 8 ft. Styleside pickup. Bright wheel-lip moldings. AM radio. AM/FM monaural radio. AM/FM stereo radio with door-panel mounted speakers. AM/FM stereo radio with cassette tape player. AM/FM stereo with 8-track tape player. Air conditioning: $680. High output heater. Convenience Group. Electronic digital clock. Fingertip speed control. Vinyl headliner. Light Group. Power door locks. Power windows. Tinted sliding rear window. Tinted glass for all windows. Tool storage box mounted hood. Slide-out spare tire carrier. Side-mounted spare tire carrier for Styleside box. Center console (for SuperCabs with Captain's chairs). Electric remote swing-away mirrors. Black low-mount black or bright trim 9 in. x 6 in. Western swing-away mirrors. Recreational 9 in. x 6 in. bright 9 in. x 6 in. low-mount or 9.5 in. x 6.75 in. bright swing-away mirrors. SuperCab seats: Reclining Captain's chairs, forward facing rear seats, center-facing rear seats. Heavy-duty black vinyl seat trim. Knitted vinyl seat trim. Auxiliary fuel tank: $208. Oil pressure and ammeter gauges. Automatic transmission: $252. Engine block heater. Roof clearance lights. Exterior Protection Group. Security Lock Group. Sport instrumentation. Black rear step bumper (for XLS Styleside). Argent step bumper (for Styleside). Chrome channel rear bumper (for Flaresides).

HISTORICAL FOOTNOTES: Total 1982 model year sales of all Ford four-wheel drive light-duty trucks was 82,544.

1983 PICKUP

Although the styling of the F series trucks was continued from 1982, major engine changes occurred that substantially strengthened the competitive position of Ford's four-wheel drive models. A new heavy-duty 250HD model as well as the F-350 models were available with either a 6.9 liter diesel V-8 or a 7.5 liter gas V-8. Both engines were offered with a new 4-speed heavy-duty manual transmission, as well as SelectShift automatic transmission. A new F-350 four-door crew cab Styleside model with room for six passengers was introduced.

The exterior colors for 1983 consisted of raven black, dark red metallic, dark teal metallic, copper, Wimbledon white, desert tan, light charcoal metallic, dark charcoal metallic, walnut metallic, candyapple red, midnight blue metallic, bright blue, and at extra cost, light teal glow and blue glow.

I.D. DATA: The V.I.N. had 17 entries. The first three characters identified the manufacturer, make and type of vehicle. The next entry, a letter designated the GVW rating. The next three characters identified the series and body style. The eighth character identified the engine. A check digit following, then an entry identifying the assembly plant. The final digits represented the sequential production number.

Body Type	Factory Price	GVW	Shipping Weight	Prod. Total
Series F-150, 117 in., 133 in. wheelbase. SuperCab-155 in. wheelbase				
Pickup, 6.75 ft. Flareside	$8627	6050[1]	3807	—
Pickup, 6.75 ft. Styleside	$8498	6050	3817	—
Pickup, 8.0 ft. Styleside	$8648	6050	4002	—
SuperCab, Styleside	$9837	6050	3962	—

NOTE 1: 6300 and 6400 lb. GVW optional.

Body Type	Factory Price	GVW	Shipping Weight	Prod. Total
Series F-250, 133 in. wheelbase SuperCab-155 in. wheelbase				
Pickup, 8 ft. Flareside	$N.A.	6700[2]	4024	—
Pickup, 8 ft. Styleside	$N.A.	6700	4039	—
SuperCab, Styleside	$N.A.	6700	4312	—

NOTE 2: 7300 lb., 8100 lb., 8400 lb. GVW optional.

Body Type	Factory Price	GVW	Shipping Weight	Prod. Total
Series F-350, 133 in. wheelbase				
Chassis and Cab	$N.A.	8700[3]	N.A.	—
Pickup, 8 ft. Styleside	$N.A.	8700	4465	—
Crew Cab, 168.8 in. wb.	—	—	—	—

NOTE 3: 9100 lb. GVW optional.

STANDARD ENGINE: All models except F-350 (not available for California where the 302 V-8 is standard): Engine Type: OHV In-line 6-cylinder. Bore x Stroke: 4.00 in. x 3.98 in. Displacement: 300 cu. in. Induction system: Single venturi downdraft carburetor. Number of main bearings-7. Carburetion: Single 1-barrel downdraft. Compression Ratio: 8.9:1. Horsepower: Net: 122 @ 3000 rpm. Torque: Net: 255 lb.-ft. @ 1400 rpm. Fuel Requirements: Unleaded.

OPTIONAL ENGINE: All models except F-150 and F-250 SuperCab and F-350: Engine type: OHV V-8. Cast-iron block and cylinder heads. Bore x Stroke: 4.00 in. x 3.00 in. Lifters: Hydraulic. Number of main bearings-5. Displacement: 302 cu. in. (5.0 liters). Lifters: Hydraulic. Carburetion: Single 2-barrel. Compression Ratio: 8.4:1. Horsepower: Net: 133 @ 3400 rpm. Torque: Net: 233 lb.-ft. @ 2000 rpm. Fuel Requirements: Unleaded. Optional: All models Standard for F-350. Bore x Stroke: 4.00 in. x 3.50 in. Displacement: 351 cu. in. (5.75 liters). Induction system: 2-barrel Motorcraft carburetor. Compression Ratio: 8.0:1. Number of main bearings-5. Horsepower: Net: 136 @ 3000 rpm. Torque: Net: 262 lb.-ft. @ 1600 rpm. Fuel

Requirements: Unleaded. Optional: For F-350 models. Engine Type: OHV V-8. Bore x Stroke: 4.00 in. x 4.00 in. Displacement: 400 cu. in. (6.55 liters). Induction system: 4-barrel carburetor. Compression Ratio: 8.0:1. Number of main bearings-5. Horsepower: Net: 136 @ 2800 rpm. Torque: Net: 310 lb.-ft. @ 1200 rpm. Fuel Requirements: Unleaded. Optional: For F-250 HD and F-350 models. Engine Type: OHV V-8. Bore x Stroke: 4.36 in. x 3.85 in. Displacement: 460 cu. in. (7.5 liters). Induction system: 4-barrel downdraft carburetor. Compression Ratio: 8.0:1. Number of main bearings-5. Horsepower: Net: 245 @ 4200 rpm. Torque: Net: 380 lb.-ft. @ 2600 rpm. Fuel Requirements: Unleaded. Optional: For F-250 HD and F-350 models. Engine Type: OHV diesel V-8. Bore x Stroke: 4.00 in. x 4.18 in. Displacement: 420 cu. in. (6.9 liters). Induction system: 4-barrel carburetor. Compression Ratio: 21.5:1. Number of main bearings-5. Horsepower: Net: 170 @ 3300 rpm. Torque: Net: 315 lb.-ft. @ 1400 rpm. Fuel Requirements: Diesel.

CHASSIS FEATURES: Separate body and frame. Single channel, 36,000 psi. Section modulus: F-150 regular cab: (117 in. wheelbase): 3.95; F-150 regular cab (133 in. wheelbase): 4.33. F-250 (crew cab): 5.67. F-150 and F-250 (SuperCab): 6.67.

SUSPENSION AND RUNNING GEAR: Front Suspension: F-150 regular cab: Coil springs. F-150 SuperCab and all F-250: Semi-elliptical, tapered, constant rate 2-leaf springs. All springs computer selected for GVW rating. Rear Suspension: All models: Semi-elliptical leaf springs. F-150 regular cab and SuperCab: 5-leaf, 55.5 in. x 3.0 in. Capacity: 3750 lb. at ground. F-250 regular cab, crew cab and SuperCab: 5-leaf, 55.5 in. x 3.0 in. Capacity: 4000 lb. at ground. Optional: F-250: 4500 and 5480 lb. capacity at ground. Auxiliary spring, 34.5 in. x 3.0 in. with 7100 lb. rating. Front Axle Type and Capacity: F-150 regular cab and SuperCab: 3550 lb. capacity, full-floating, Hotchkiss. F-250: 3800 lb. capacity, full-floating, Hotchkiss. Optional: F-250: 4500 lb. capacity. The F-250 front axle was of heavier construction than the F-150. It was of open knuckle design and used open Cardan-type universal joints of alloy steel. Rear Axle Type and Capacity: F-150: Semi-floating, 3750 lb. capacity. F-250: Full-floating, Hotchkiss. Spicer model 60, 5300 lb. capacity. Transfer Case: Type: 2-speed New Process 208. Ratios: 2.6:1, 1.00:1. Brakes: Type: Hydraulic, single-piston, floating caliper, Ford-designed disc front and drums rear, power assisted. Dimensions: Front: F-150: 11.54 in. disc, F-250: 12.5 in. disc on all models. Rear: F-150: 11.03 in. x 2.25 in. F-250: Rear: 12.0 in. x 2.50 in. Wheels: F-150: 5-hole stamped disc, 15 in. x 5.5K, disc. Optional: 6.0JK, 15 in. x 8JJ. F-250: 8-hole, stamped disc, 16 x 6.0, disc. Optional: 6.75, 6.0K. Tires: F-150: L78 x 15B. F-250: 8.00 x 16.5D. Optional: F-150: Tubeless: L78 x 15C, LR78 x 15C, 10 x 15C. Tube-type: 7.0 x 15D. F-250: Tubeless: 8.00 x 16.5E, 8.75 x 16.5E, 8.75 x 16.5E, 8.75R x 16.5E, 9.50 x 16.5D, 9.50 x 16.5E, 7.50 x 16C, 7.50 x 16D, 7.50 x 16E. Tube-type: 7.50 x 16D, 7.50 x 16E. Steering: Standard F-150 regular cab: Gemer #375, Worm and Roller. All others: Power assisted, recirculating ball (optional for F-150 regular cab). Ratio: 17:1. Transmission: 4-speed New Process 435. Ratios: New Process 435: 6.69, 3.34, 1.66, 1.0:1. Reverse: 8.26:1. Clutch: Heavy-duty hydraulic. 11.0 in. dia. and 123.7 sq. in. Optional: Cruise-O-Matic 3-speed automatic for 6.6 liter V-8 only.

VEHICLE DIMENSIONS: Styleside pickups: Wheelbase: 116.8 in./133 in. Overall length: 192.1 in./208.3 in. Flareside pickups: Wheelbase: 116.8 in. Overall length: 187.8.2 in. Overall width: 116.8 in. wheelbase. Styleside and Flareside: 69.3 in.; SuperCab: Wheelbase: 155 in. Overall length: 230.3 in. Width: 70.8 in. Crew cab: Wheelbase: 168.4 in. Overall length: 243.6 in.

CAPACITIES: Fuel Tank: 19.2 gal. Optional: Dual fuel tanks with total capacity of 38.7 to 46.2 gal. except for F-150 with 117 in. wheelbase.

ACCOMMODATIONS: 3 occupants. SuperCab and crew cab: 6 occupants.

INSTRUMENTATION: Speedometer, odometer, fuel level and engine coolant temperature gauges, warning lights for oil pressure and battery charge.

OPTIONS:: 302 V-8. 351 V-8, 400 V-8, 460 V-8, 420 diesel V-8. Chrome grille. Chromatic tape stripe. Tri-colored tape stripe. Accent tape stripe.'Lower body side molding with black insert. Bright box rails for 8 ft. Styleside pickup. Bright wheel-lip moldings. AM radio. AM/FM monaural radio. AM/FM stereo radio with door-panel mounted speakers. AM/FM stereo radio with cassette tape player. AM/FM stereo with 8-track tape player. Air conditioning. High output heater. Convenience Group. Electronic digital clock. Fingertip speed control. Vinyl headliner. Light Group. Power door locks. Power windows. Tinted sliding rear window. Tinted glass for all windows. Tool storage box mounted hood. Slide-out spare tire carrier. Side-mounted spare tire carrier for Styleside box. Center console (for SuperCabs with Captain's chairs). Electric remote swing-away mirrors. lack low-mount black or bright trim 9 in. x 6 in. Western swing-away mirrors. Recreational 9 in. x 6 in. bright 9 in. x 6 in. low-mount or 9.5 in. x 6.75 in. bright swing-away mirrors. SuperCab seats: Reclining Captain's chairs, forward facing rear seats, center-facing rear seats. Heavy-duty black vinyl seat trim. Knitted vinyl seat trim. Auxiliary fuel tank. Oil pressure and ammeter gauges. Automatic transmission. Engine block heater. Roof clearance lights. Exterior Protection Group. Security Lock Group. Sport instrumentation. Black rear step bumper (for XLS Styleside). Argent step bumper (for Styleside). Chrome channel rear bumper (for Flaresides).

HISTORICAL FOOTNOTES: Total 1983 model year sales of all Ford four-wheel drive light-duty trucks was 116,404. Sales of all types of Ford four-wheel drive trucks was 264,528.

1984 PICKUP

The styling of the 1984 F series trucks was unchanged from 1983. A new 5.8 liter HO (High Output) engine was introduced as an option for the F-150 and F-250 models. It was available only with automatic transmission. The standard F series pickup's equipment included chrome front bumper, light argent grille with bright surround, bright windshield molding, bright door-mount mirrors, and rectangular halogen headlights. The standard Styleside pickups also had rope-tie down holes, stake pockets and an easily removable tailgate. The standard interior had these features: All-vinyl seat, AM radio (delete option), pivoting vent window, glove box, engine coolant temperature gauge, color-keyed windshield pillar and cowl-side trim panels, a textured steel-roof, cloth headliner with SuperCab and crew cab, color-keyed door trim panels with foam-padded armrests, floor insulation and carpet-texture rubber mat, day/night rearview mirror, inside hood release, key in-ignition warning buzzer, and parking brake engaged warning light. The XL trim option added a number of appearance and comfort features to the standard trim level. Exterior items included bright wheel-lip moldings and bright insert on rear window weatherstrip. Interior appointments included a color-keyed cloth headliner and vinyl seat trim, passenger and driver's side courtesy door light switches, bright door trim surround moldings, cigarette lighter, woodtone instrument panel applique, color-keyed floor mat and Deluxe color-keyed seat belts.

The XLT had a full-length lower body side molding with a black vinyl insert and a brushed aluminum tailgate applique. Interior appointments included wall-to-wall cut-pile carpeting, a Deluxe steering wheel with a woodtone insert and a full-length storage bin on the lower door panels.

The SuperCab models were offered in standard, XL or XLT trim. The crew cab was available in either standard or XL trim levels.

The exterior colors for 1984 consisted of raven black, polar white, light charcoal metallic, bright canyon red, dark canyon red, light blue, medium blue metallic, midnight blue metallic, desert tan, walnut metallic, light desert tan, medium Ccopper metallic, and dark teal. A bright copper glow was listed as an optional "Glamour" color. The interior colors, keyed to the exterior were charcoal, dark blue, canyon red and tan.

1984 Ford F-150 XLT Styleside pickup

I.D. DATA: The V.I.N. had 17 entries. The first three characters identified the manufacturer, make and type of vehicle. The next entry, a letter designated the GVW rating. The next three characters identified the series and body style. The eighth character identified the engine. A check digit following, then an entry identifying the assembly plant. The final digits represented the sequential production number.

Body Type	Factory Price	GVW	Shipping Weight	Prod. Total
Series F-150, 117 in., 133 in. wheelbase. SuperCab-155 in. wheelbase				
Pickup, 6.5 ft. Flareside	$9409	6050[1]	3807	—
Pickup, 6.75 ft. Styleside	$9247	6050	3817	—
Pickup, 8.0 ft. Styleside	$9404	6050	4002	—
SuperCab, Styleside	$N.A.	6050	3962	—
NOTE 1: 6250 lb. GVW optional for regular pickups; 6450 lb. optional for SuperCab.				
Series F-250, 133 in. wheelbase, SuperCab: 155 in. wheelbase				
Pickup, 8 ft. Styleside	$9472	6700	4039	—
Pickup, 8 ft. Styleside HD	$11,506	—	—	—
SuperCab HD	$12,494	—	—	—
Series F-350, 133 in. wheelbase				
Chassis and Cab	$N.A.	9000[2]	N.A.	—
Pickup, 8 ft. Styleside	$N.A.	9000	4465	—
Crew Cab, 168.8 in. wb.	$N.A.	9300	N.A.	—

NOTE 2: Max. GVW available.

STANDARD ENGINE: All models except F-250 HD and F-350: Engine Type: OHV In-line 6-cylinder. Bore x Stroke: 4.00 in. x 3.98 in. Displacement: 300 cu. in. Induction system: Single venturi downdraft carburetor. Number of main bearings-7. Carburetion: Single 1-barrel downdraft. Compression Ratio: 8.5:1. Horsepower: Net: 120 @ 3000 rpm. Torque: Net: 245 lb.-ft. @ 1800 rpm. Fuel Requirements: Unleaded.

OPTIONAL ENGINE: All models except F-250HD and F-250 SuperCab and F-350: Engine type: OHV V-8. Cast-iron block and cylinder heads. Bore x Stroke: 4.00 in. x 3.00 in. Lifters: Hydraulic. Number of main bearings-5. Displacement: 302 cu. in. (5.0 liters). Lifters: Hydraulic. Carburetion: Single 2-barrel. Compression Ratio: 9.0:1. Horsepower: Net: N.A. Torque: Net: N.A. Fuel Requirements: Unleaded. Optional: All models Standard for F-250HD and F-350. Not available in California for F-250 and F-350. Bore x Stroke: 4.00 in. x 3.50 in. Displacement: 351 cu. in. (5.75 liters). Induction system: 2-barrel Motorcraft carburetor. Compression Ratio: 8.0:1. Number of main bearings-5. Horsepower: Net: 136 @ 3000 rpm. Torque: Net: 262 lb.-ft. @ 1600 rpm. Fuel Requirements: Unleaded. Optional: For F-250 HD and F-350 models. Engine Type: OHV V-8. Bore x Stroke: 4.36 in. x 3.85 in. Displacement: 460 cu. in. (7.5 liters). Induction system: 4-barrel downdraft carburetor. Compression Ratio: 8.0:1. Number of main bearings-5. Horsepower: Net: 245 @ 4200 rpm. Torque: Net: 380 lb.-ft. @ 2600 rpm. Fuel Requirements: Unleaded. Optional: For F-250 HD and F-350 models. Engine Type: OHV diesel V-8. Bore x Stroke: 4.00 in. x 4.18 in. Displacement: 420 cu. in. (6.9 liters). Induction system: Fuel injection. Compression Ratio: 21.5:1. Number of main bearings-5. Horsepower: Net: 170 @ 3300 rpm. Torque: Net: 315 lb.-ft. @ 1400 rpm. Fuel Requirements: Diesel.

CHASSIS FEATURES: Separate body and frame. Single channel, 36,000 psi. Section modulus: F-150 regular cab: (117 in. wheelbase): 3.95; F-150 regular cab (133 in. wheelbase): 4.33. F-250 (crew cab): 5.67. F-150 and F-250 (SuperCab): 6.67.

SUSPENSION AND RUNNING GEAR: Front Suspension: F-150 regular cab: Coil springs. F-150 SuperCab and all F-250: Semi-elliptical, tapered, constant rate 2-leaf springs. All springs computer selected for GVW rating. Rear Suspension: All models: Semi-elliptical leaf springs. F-150 regular cab and SuperCab: 5-leaf, 55.5 in. x 3.0 in. Capacity: 3750 lb. at ground. F-250 regular cab, crew cab and SuperCab: 5-leaf, 55.5 in. x 3.0 in. Capacity: 4000 lb. at ground. Optional: F-250: 4500 and 5480 lb. capacity at ground. Auxiliary spring, 34.5 in. x 3.0 in. with 7100 lb. rating. Front Axle Type and Capacity: F-150 regular cab and SuperCab: 3550 lb. capacity, full-floating, Hotchkiss. F-250: 3800 lb. capacity, full-floating, Hotchkiss. Optional: F-250: 4500 lb. capacity. The F-250 front axle was of heavier construction than the F-150. It was of open knuckle design and used open Cardan-type universal joints of alloy steel. Rear Axle Type and Capacity: F-150: Semi-floating, 3750 lb. capacity. F-250: Full-floating, Hotchkiss. Spicer model 60, 5300 lb. capacity. Transfer Case: Type: 2-speed New Process 208. Ratios: 2.6:1, 1.00:1. Brakes: Type: Hydraulic, single-piston, floating caliper, Ford-designed disc front and drums rear, power assisted. Dimensions: Front: F-150: 11.54 in. disc, F-250: 12.5 in. disc on all models. Rear: F-150: 11.03 in. x 2.25 in. F-250: Rear: 12.0 in. x 2.50 in. Wheels: F-150: 5-hole stamped disc, 15 in. x 5.5K, disc. Optional: 6.0JK, 15 in. x 8JJ. F-250 and F-350: 8-hole, stamped disc, 16 x 6K, disc. Optional: 6.75, 6.0K. Tires: F-150:P235/75R -15L. F-250: LT215/75R-16C, F-350: LT235/75R-16E. Optional: Tubeless tires in sizes to match Payload Package requirements. Steering: Standard Power assisted, recirculating ball. Transmission: 4-speed manual. Clutch: Heavy-duty hydraulic. F-150 and F-250: 10 in. dia. and 95.7 sq. in. F-250HD and F-350: 11.0 in. dia. and 123.7 sq. in. Optional: SelectShift 3-speed automatic. 4-speed manual overdrive for F-150.

VEHICLE DIMENSIONS: Styleside pickups: Wheelbase: 116.8 in./133 in. Overall length: 192.1 in./208.3 in. Flareside pickups: Wheelbase: 116.8 in. Overall length: 187.8 in. Overall width: 116.8 in. wheelbase. Styleside and Flareside: 69.3 in.; SuperCab: Wheelbase: 155 in. Overall length: 230.3 in. Width: 70.8 in. Crew cab: Wheelbase: 168.4 in. Overall length: 243.6 in. Headroom: 40.4 in. (40.0 in. for SuperCab). Front legroom: 41 in. Front hip room: 61.7 in. Front shoulder room: 64.2 in.

CAPACITIES: Fuel Tank: F-150: Short wheelbase: 16.5 gal.; Long wheelbase: 19.0 gal. All others: 19.0 gal. Optional: F-150: Short wheelbase: 35.5 gal. All long wheelbase models: 38.0 gal.

ACCOMMODATIONS: 3 occupants. SuperCab and crew cab: 6 occupants.

INSTRUMENTATION: Speedometer, odometer, fuel level and engine coolant temperature gauges, warning lights for oil pressure and battery charge.

OPTIONS: 302 V-8. 351 V-8. 460 V-8. 420 diesel V-8. Chrome grille. Accent tape stripe. Lower body side molding with black insert. Bright wheel-lip moldings. AM/FM monaural radio. AM/FM stereo radio with door-panel mounted speakers. AM/FM stereo radio with cassette tape player. Radio delete credit. Air conditioning. High output heater. Convenience Group. Electronic digital clock. Fingertip speed control. Deluxe Insulation Package. Light Group. Power door locks. Power windows. Tilt steering wheel. Tinted sliding rear window. Tinted glass for all windows. Tool storage box mounted hood. In box, side-mounted spare tire carrier for Styleside box. Center console (for SuperCabs with Captain's chairs). Bright Western low-mount swing-away 8.0 in. x 5.0 in. mirrors. Black or bright trim 9 in. x 6 in. Recreational 9 in. x 6 in. bright swing-out 95 in. x 6.75 in. SuperCab seats: Reclining Captain's chairs, forward facing rear seats, center-facing rear seats. Cloth and vinyl (for standard trim). Heavy-duty charcoal vinyl seat trim. Knitted vinyl seat trim. Special cloth and vinyl trim (for XLT trim). Auxiliary fuel tank. Auxiliary transmission oil cooler. Handling Package. Heavy-Duty Front Suspension Package (for 133 in. wheelbase F-150). Oil pressure and ammeter gauges. Automatic transmission. 4-speed manual overdrive transmission. Engine oil cooler for 7.5 liter V-8. Heavy-duty air cleaner. Dual electric horns. Engine block heater. Roof clearance lights. Exterior Protection Group. Security Lock Group. Sport instrumentation. Black rear step bumper (for XLS Styleside). Argent step bumper (for Styleside). Chrome channel rear bumper (for Flaresides). Skid plates.

HISTORICAL FOOTNOTES: Total 1984 model year sales of all Ford four-wheel drive light-duty trucks was 148,358. Sales of all types of Ford four-wheel drive trucks was 342,008.

1985 PICKUP

Ford emphasized a commitment to total quality in its 1985 trucks. Donald E. Peterson, the president of Ford Motor Company, told prospective customers that "Total quality begins with the design and engineering of our trucks and continues through the life of the product...I think the full-size F series pickup is an excellent example of the type of quality I'm talking about."

1985 Ford F-250 XL Styleside pickup

For 1985, a new 5.0 liter high-performance, high-technology V-8, the 5.0 EFI V-8 was introduced for the F-150 and F-250 models under 8500 lb. GVW. It produced 31 percent more horsepower than the engine it replaced. Still available was Ford's 4.9 liter 6-cylinder, 5.8 High-Output V-8, the 7.5 liter V-8 and the 6.9 liter V-8 engines. Beginning in February, 1985, a new heavy-duty Monobeam front axle allowing gross axle weight ratings of up to 5,000 lb. was standard for the F-350. The content of the Standard, XL and XL Lariat trim levels were revamped for 1985. Exterior features of the standard pickup included chrome front bumper, light argent grille with bright surround molding, black foldaway door-mounted mirrors, and rectangular halogen headlights. The standard interior had a new all vinyl seat trim, AM radio, pivoting vent window, glove box, engine coolant temperature gauge, lighted ashtray, argent instrument panel appliques, (woodtone with 6.9 liter diesel engine), black control knobs, color-keyed door trim panels with foam-padded armrests, floor insulation and rubber mat, 9.625 in. day/night rearview mirror, inside hood release, dome light and reversible keys.

The XL intermediate trim level added numerous refinements to the standard model. Among the exterior features were bright wheel-lip moldings, 2-color full-length side paint stripes, bright insert for rear window weatherstrip. Interior appointments included color-keyed cloth headliner, new cloth and vinyl seat trim, optional knitted vinyl seat trim, door courtesy light switches for passenger and driver's side doors, bright door trim surround molding, cigarette lighter, new woodtone instrument panel applique and 12 in. day/night rearview mirror. The new XLT Lariat had a full-length black with bright insert body side protection molding bright wheel-lip moldings, XLT and Lariat identification plaques, new-styled brushed aluminum tailgate applique, with a red reflective lower portion and bright tailgate release handle. The interior had a new cloth seat trim and matching cloth inserts on door trim panels. In addition, there were new map pockets, carpeted area on lower door panels, cut-pile carpeting and a new soft-wrapped steering wheel with a woodtone insert. The new cloth-covered sun visors had a band on the driver's side and a slide-out removable vanity mirror on the passenger side

1985 Ford F-150 XL Styleside pickup

The SuperCab was fitted with standard rear jump seats and front bench seat. Front Captain's chairs were optional as was a center console. The SuperCab was available in standard, XL or XLT Lariat trim levels. The crew cab had two full-width full-foam bench seats. It was offered in standard or XL form. Ford also offered four (A, B, C or D) Explorer Packages.

The exterior colors for 1985 consisted of raven black, silver metallic, bright canyon red, midnight blue metallic, light regatta blue, dark canyon red, dark teal metallic, dark charcoal metallic, desert tan metallic, Wimbledon white, light desert tan and bright regatta blue metallic. The interior colors, keyed to the exterior were charcoal, regatta blue, canyon red and tan.

I.D. DATA: The V.I.N. had 17 entries. The first three characters identified the manufacturer, make and type of vehicle. The next entry, a letter designated the GVW rating. The next three characters identified the series and body style. The eighth character identified the engine. A check digit following, then an entry identifying the assembly plant. The final digits represented the sequential production number.

Body Type	Factory Price	GVW	Shipping Weight	Prod. Total
Series F-150, 117 in., 133 in. wheelbase. SuperCab-155 in. wheelbase				
Pickup, 6.5 ft. Flareside	$9957[1]	6050[2]	3807	—
Pickup, 6.5 ft. Styleside	$9794	6050	3817	—
Pickup, 8.0 ft. Styleside	$9960	6050	4002	—
SuperCab, Styleside	$10,934	6050	3962	—

NOTE 1: Prices were subsequently raised to these levels:
NOTE 2: 6250 lb. GVW optional for Regular Pickups; 6450 lb. optional for SuperCab.

Pickup, 6.5 ft. Flareside	$10,094	—	—	—
Pickup, 6.5 ft. Styleside	$9930	—	—	—
Pickup, 8.0 ft. Styleside	$10,096	—	—	—
SuperCab, Styleside	$11,071	—	—	—
Series F-250, 133 in. wheelbase, SuperCab: 155 in. wheelbase				
Pickup, 8 ft. Styleside	$10,072[3]	6700	4039	—
Pickup, 8 ft. Styleside HD	$12,089	—	—	—
SuperCab HD	$13,077	—	—	—

NOTE 3: Prices were subsequently raised to these levels:

Pickup, 8 ft. Styleside	$10,155[3]	—	—	—
Pickup, 8 ft. Styleside HD	$12,189	—	—	—
SuperCab HD	$13,177	—	—	—
Series F-350, 133 in. wheelbase				
Chassis and Cab	$12,061[4]	9000[5]	N.A.	—
Pickup, 8 ft. Styleside	$13,344	9000	4465	—
Crew Cab, 168.8 in. wb.	$14,809	9300	N.A.	—

NOTE 4: Prices were subsequently raised to these levels:

Chassis and Cab	$13,063	9000[5]	N.A.	—
Pickup, 8 ft. Styleside	$13,430	—	—	—
Crew Cab, 168.8 in. wb.	$14,910	—	—	—

NOTE 5: Max. GVW available.

STANDARD ENGINE: All models except F-250 HD and F-350: Engine Type: OHV In-line 6-cylinder. Bore x Stroke: 4.00 in. x 3.98 in. Displacement: 300 cu. in. Induction system: Single venturi downdraft carburetor. Number of main bearings-7. Carburetion: Single 1-barrel downdraft. Compression Ratio: 8.5:1. Horsepower: Net: 120 @ 3000 rpm. Torque: Net: 250 lb.-ft. @ 2000 rpm. Fuel Requirements: Unleaded.

OPTIONAL ENGINE: F-150 and F-250, under 8500 lb. GVW. 5.0 EFI. (This engine became available in November, 1984 and replaced the 5.8 liter 2-barrel V-8). Engine type: OHV V-8. Cast-iron block and cylinder heads. Bore x Stroke: 4.00 in. x 3.00 in. Lifters: Hydraulic. Number of main bearings-5. Displacement: 302 cu. in. (5.0 liters). Lifters: Hydraulic. Carburetion: Multiport fuel injection with eight individual ports. Compression Ratio: 9.0:1. Horsepower: 190 @ 3800 rpm. Torque: Net: 285 lb.-ft. @ 2400 rpm. Fuel Requirements: Unleaded. Optional: F-150 and F-250, standard for F-250HD and F-350. Not available in California for F-250HD and F-350. Not offered for F-150 and F-250 after November, 1984. This engine was cancelled for the F-250HD and F-350 with SelectShift in early December, 1984 when the 5.8 liter HO 4-barrel carburetor V-8 was introduced. Bore x Stroke: 4.00 in. x 3.50 in. Displacement: 351 cu. in. (5.75 liters). Induction system: 2-barrel Motorcraft carburetor. Compression Ratio: 8.0:1. Number of main bearings-5. Horsepower: Net: 136 @ 3000 rpm. Torque: Net: 262 lb.-ft. @ 1600 rpm. Fuel Requirements: Unleaded. Optional: 5.8 HO V-8.For F-150 and F-250. Engine type: OHV V-8. Bore x Stroke: 4.00 in. x 3.50 in. Displacement: 351 cu. in. (5.75 liters). Induction system: 4-barrel carburetor. Number of main bearings-5. Horsepower: 210 @ 4000 rpm. Torque: 305 lb.-ft. @ 2800 rpm. Fuel Requirements: Unleaded. Optional: For F-250 HD and F-350 models. Engine Type: OHV V-8. Bore x Stroke: 4.36 in. x 3.85 in. Displacement: 460 cu. in. (7.5 liters). Induction system: 4-barrel downdraft carburetor. Compression Ratio: 8.0:1. Number of main bearings-5. Horsepower: 225 @ 4000 rpm. Torque: Net: 365 lb.-ft. @ 2800 rpm. Fuel Requirements: Unleaded. Optional: For F-250 HD and F-350 models. Engine Type: OHV diesel V-8. Bore x Stroke: 4.00 in. x 4.18 in. Displacement: 420 cu. in. (6.9 liters). Induction system: Fuel injection. Compression Ratio: 21.5:1. Number of main bearings-5. Horsepower: 170 @ 3300 rpm. (High Altitude: 150 @ 3300 rpm). Torque: Net: 315 lb.-ft. @ 1400 rpm. (High Altitude: 285 lb.-ft. @ 1400 rpm). Fuel Requirements: Diesel.

CHASSIS FEATURES: Separate body and frame. Single channel, 36,000 psi. Section modulus: F-150 regular cab: (117 in. wheelbase): 3.95; F-150 regular cab (133 in. wheelbase): 4.33. F-250 (crew cab): 5.67. F-150 and F-250 (SuperCab): 6.67.

SUSPENSION AND RUNNING GEAR: Front Suspension: F-150 regular cab: Coil springs. F-150 SuperCab and all F-250: Semi-elliptical, tapered, constant rate 2-leaf springs. All springs computer selected for GVW rating. Capacity: F-150: Regular cab: 2525 lb., SuperCab: 3100 lb. F-250: 3305 lb. F-250HD: Regular cab. 3305 lb. SuperCab: 3920 lb. F-350: Regular cab: 3375 lb., crew cab: 3920 lb. Rear Suspension: All models: Semi-elliptical leaf springs. F-150 regular cab: 5-leaf, 55.5 in. x 3.0 in. Capacity: 3775 lb. at ground, SuperCab: 3776 lb. at ground. F-250 regular cab: 5-leaf, 55.5 in. x 3.0 in. Capacity: 3938 lb. at ground. F-250HD regular cab and SuperCab: 5878 lb. F-350 regular cab: 6340 lb., crew cab: 5878 lb. Optional: F-250: 4500 and 5480 lb. capacity at ground. Auxiliary spring, 34.5 in. x 3.0 in. with 710 lb. rating. Front Axle Type and Capacity: F-150 regular cab and SuperCab: 3550 lb. capacity, full-floating, Hotchkiss. F-250: 3850 lb. capacity, full-floating, Hotchkiss. F-250HD: Regular cab: 3850 lb., SuperCab: 4600 lb. F-350: 4600 lb. Optional: F-250: 4500 lb. capacity. The F-250 front axle was of heavier construction than the F-150. It was of open knuckle design and used pen Cardan-type universal joints of alloy steel. Rear Axle Type and Capacity: F-150: Semi-floating, 3750 lb. capacity. F-250: Full-floating, Hotchkiss. Spicer model 60, 5300 lb. capacity. F-250HD: Regular cab and SuperCab: 6250 lb. F-350: 6250 lb. Transfer Case: Type: 2-speed New Process 208. Ratios: 2.6:1, 1.00:1. Brakes: Type: Hydraulic, single-piston, floating caliper, Ford-designed disc front and drums rear, power assisted. Dimensions: Front: F-150: 11.54 in. disc, F-250: 12.5 in. disc on all models. Rear: F-150: 11.03 in. x 2.25 in. F-250: Rear: 12.0 in. x 2.50 in. Wheels: F-150: 5-hole stamped disc, 15 in. x 6JK, disc. Optional: 6.0JK, 15 in. x 8JJ. F-250 and F-350: 8-hole, stamped disc, 16 x 6K, disc. Optional: 6.75, 6.0K. Tires: F-150: P235/75R -15XL. F-250: LT215/75R-16C, F-250HD: LT235/85R-16E. F-350: LT235/85R-16E. Optional: Tubeless tires in sizes to match Payload Package requirements. Steering: Standard power assisted, recirculating ball. Transmission: 4-speed manual. Clutch: Heavy-duty hydraulic. F-150 and F-250: 10 in. dia. and 95.7 sq. in. F-250HD and F-350: 11.0 in. dia. and 123.7 sq. in. Optional: SelectShift 3-speed automatic. 4-speed manual overdrive for F-150.

VEHICLE DIMENSIONS: Styleside pickups: Wheelbase: 116.8 in./133 in. Overall length: 192.1 in./208.3 in. Flareside pickups: Wheelbase: 116.8 in. Overall length: 187.8.2 in. Overall width: 116.8 in. wheelbase. Styleside and Flareside: 69.3 in.; SuperCab: Wheelbase: 155 in. Overall length: 230.3 in. Width: 70.8 in. Crew cab: Wheelbase: 168.4 in. Overall length: 243.6 in. Headroom: 40.4 in. (40.0 in. for SuperCab). Front legroom: 41 in. Front hip room: 61.7 in. Front shoulder room: 64.2 in.

CAPACITIES: Fuel Tank: F-150: Short wheelbase: 16.5 gal.; Long wheelbase: 19.0 gal. All others: 19.0 gal. Optional: F-150: Short wheelbase: 35.5 gal. All long wheelbase models: 38.0 gal.

ACCOMMODATIONS: 3 occupants. SuperCab and crew cab: 6 occupants.

INSTRUMENTATION: Speedometer, odometer, fuel level and engine coolant temperature gauges, warning lights for oil pressure and battery charge.

OPTIONS AND PRICES: All prices listed were effective on January 2, 1985. 5.0 EFI V-8: $426. (later raised to $526). 5.8 liter V-8: $787 (later raised to $857). 4-speed manual overdrive transmission: $80. SelectShift automatic transmission: $558.80. Auxiliary transmission oil cooler: $59. Standard rear axle ratio with Traction-Lok: $238. Optional axle ratio: $42.10. Front Dana limited slip differential: $238. Heavy-duty air cleaner: 20.90. Air conditioning: $743.70. 60 amp alternator: $62. Heavy-duty auxiliary battery: $179. Heavy-duty maintenance-free battery: $53. Argent rear step bumper: $120. Chrome rear step bumper: $189. Chrome rear bumper (F-150 only): $103. Roof clearance lights: $50. Electronic digital clock: $84.50. Console: $119.50. Convenience Group: $85.70-$126.50 depending upon trim level. Engine oil cooler: $120. Extra engine cooling: $53. Super engine cooling: $142. Exterior Sound Package: $12.70. Auxiliary fuel tank: $229.50. Outside-of-frame fuel tank: $177.60. Ammeter and oil pressure gauges: $40. Tinted glass, all-windows: $46-$58.20 depending upon body type. Chrome grille: $56.80. Handling Package (F-150 regular cab): $218.50. Headliner and Insulation Package: $19.50-$73.20 depending upon trim and body type. Engine block heater: $31-$62 depending upon engine. High Output Heater: $31.20. Dual electric horns: $17.90. Automatic locking hubs: $40.20. Sports Instrumentation: $132.60. Light Group: $135. Cigarette lighter: $30. Security Lock Group: $64.60 (with dual fuel tanks), $52.70 (with single fuel tank). Bright low-mount Western swing-away mirrors: $88.80. Bright recreational swing-out mirrors: $96. Body side protection moldings: $144. Wheel-lip moldings: $41.20. Regular two-tone paint: $72. Deluxe two-tone paint: $185.40-$367.20 depending upon trim package and body type. Combination two-tone paint: $215.20-$385.90 depending upon trim package and body type. Victoria two-tone paint: $281-$438.40 depending upon trim level. Power door locks and windows: $292.60. Exterior Protection Group: $64.10. AM/FM stereo radio: $100. AM/FM stereo radio with cassette tape player: $235.40. Electronic AM/FM radio with Search and cassette tape player: $400.40. Delete radio credit: $39. SuperCab rear bench seat: $150.50. Skid plates: $90.20 (with auxiliary fuel tank), $165.10 (with auxiliary fuel tank or crew cab models): $165.10. Speed control: $195. In-box spare tire carrier: $29. Auxiliary rear springs: $76.50. Heavy-duty front springs: $59. Tilt steering wheel: $115. Trailering Towing Package: $185.50. Deluxe argent styled steel wheels: $230. White styled steel wheels: $174. Sliding rear window: $77.70. California emissions system: $235. Standard seat trim options: Knitted vinyl bench seat trim: $55.70. Cloth and vinyl bench seat trim: $95.10. Cloth Captain's chairs: $491.70. XL Seat trim options: Cloth Captain's chairs: $491.70. XLT Lariat seat trim options: Cloth Captain's chairs: $491.70. XL trim level: $280.70-$494.10 depending upon body type. XLT Lariat trim level: $665.10.

HISTORICAL FOOTNOTES: For 1985 Ford depicted its F series trucks as "America's Truck-Built Ford Tough."

1986 PICKUP

The new-for-1986 features for the F series Fords were grouped into three key sections-Technical, Design and Options. Shortly after the model year began the F-150 with the 5.8 HO V-8 engine was offered with the M4 4-speed manual transmission. All models had improved corrosion protection for 1986. Among the improvements in this area was the addition of an internal hem flange sealer on all doors and hood, and the use of a cathodic electrocoat primer. A new pin rail disc brake design was incorporated into the front brakes. Several items previously listed as options were now standard equipment on all models. These consisted of dual electric horns, 60 amp alternator and the Exterior Sound Package. Also making the move from option to standard equipment status were: Ammeter and oil pressure gauges, cigarette lighter, glove box lock, rear bench seat on SuperCab and a 12 in. day/night mirror. A rear jump seat, previously optional, as well as an auxiliary fuel tank and tinted glass were added to the SuperCab. Bright low-mount swing-away mirrors were also made standard on the SuperCab, crew cab and chassis cab models. Many new design features were introduced for 1986. A warning chime replaced the buzzer in the XL and XLT Lariat Trim Packages. A chrome grille was added to the XL Trim Package on Flareside and crew cab models as well as the XLT Lariat trim. A bright tailgate release handle was made standard. Flareside models with XL trim no longer had body side/tailgate surround tape. The dual body side accent paint included with the XL trim on Styleside models was changed from two-color to one color. Secondary front door seals were added to the XL trim on Flareside and crew cab pickup models. Five new exterior and two new interior colors were introduced. The coat hook color was changed from black to color-keyed. A brushed aluminum tailgate applique was added to the XL trim on crew cab pickup models. New "4x4" plaques were added to the front fenders below the series nomenclature on all F series models with standard trim unless the 6.8 liter diesel engine was specified. A chrome rear channel bumper was made standard for Flareside pickups. This feature also had delete option status.

1986 Ford F-150 Styleside pickup

Many changes took place in the F series option availability. The speed control and tilt steering wheel were eliminated as separate options. They were now included in a new speed control/tilt steering wheel option. The Captain's chairs and console were now listed as a single option. The optional heavy-duty battery was upgraded from 63 amp-hr. to 71 amp-hr. The Super Cooling system replaced the Extra Cooling system in the Trailer Towing/Camper Package. This Package also included an auxiliary transmission oil cooler when ordered with automatic transmission. The mid-body side protection molding and wheel-lip moldings were combined into a Single Option Package. Black low-mount swing-away mirrors were combined with an argent front bumper to form a new Fleet Special Option Content. A stationary underhood light replaced the movable light in the Light Group. The Sports instrumentation nomenclature was changed to Tachometer and now included a trip odometer. The bright low-mount Western swing-away mirrors nomenclature was changed to bright low-mount swing-away mirrors. The following items were deleted from the option list for 1986: Auxiliary battery, mid-body side protection molding, extra engine cooling, front limited slip axle, heavy-duty air cleaner, in-box spare tire carrier, outside of frame fuel tank, P215 glass-belted tires, P215 All-Terrain tires, regular two-tone paint, white styled steel wheels, and 550 lb. auxiliary rear springs. The engine oil cooler and auxiliary transmission oil cooler were deleted as separate options but were included with selected equipment.

The exterior colors for 1986 consisted of raven black, bright canyon red, colonial white, light regatta blue, medium silver metallic, dark shadow blue metallic, dark grey metallic, light desert tan, bright canyon red, desert tan metallic, and dark spruce metallic. The interior colors, keyed to the exterior were canyon red, chestnut, regatta blue and medium grey (not available on XLT Lariat, SuperCab and crew cab).

I.D. DATA: The V.I.N. had 17 entries. The first three characters identified the manufacturer, make and type of vehicle. The next entry, a letter designated the GVW rating. The next three characters identified the series and body style. The eighth character identified the engine. A check digit following, then an entry identifying the assembly plant. The final digits represented the sequential production number.

Body Type	Factory Price	GVW	Shipping Weight	Prod. Total
Series F-150, 117 in., 133 in. wheelbase. SuperCab-155 in. wheelbase				
Pickup, 6.5 ft. Flareside	$11,243	6050[1]	3807	—
Pickup, 6.5 ft. Styleside	$10,983	6050	3817	—
Pickup, 8.0 ft. Styleside	$11,165	6050	4002	—
SuperCab, Styleside	$12,755	6050	3962	—

NOTE 1: 6250 lb. GVW optional for regular pickups; 6450 lb. optional for SuperCab.

Body Type	Factory Price	GVW	Shipping Weight	Prod. Total
Series F-250, 133 in. wheelbase, SuperCab: 155 in. wheelbase				
Pickup, 8 ft. Styleside	$11,024	6700	4039	—
Pickup, 8 ft. Styleside HD	$12,817	—	—	—
SuperCab HD	$14,421	—	—	—
Series F-350, 133 in. wheelbase				
Chassis and Cab	$13,676	9000[2]	N.A.	—
Pickup, 8 ft. Styleside	$13,925	9000	4465	—
Crew Cab, 168.8 in. wb.	$15,536	9300	N.A.	—

NOTE 2: Max. GVW available.

STANDARD ENGINE: All models except F-250 HD and F-350: Engine Type: OHV In-line 6-cylinder. Bore x Stroke: 4.00 in. x 3.98 in. Displacement: 300 cu. in. Induction system: Single venturi downdraft carburetor. Number of main bearings-7. Carburetion: Single 1-barrel downdraft. Compression Ratio: 8.5:1. Horsepower: Net: 120 @ 3000 rpm. Torque: Net: 250 lb.-ft. @ 2000 rpm. Fuel Requirements: Unleaded.

OPTIONAL ENGINE: F-150 and F-250, under 8500 lb. GVW. 5.0 EFI: Engine type: OHV V-8. Cast-iron block and cylinder heads. Bore x Stroke: 4.00 in. x 3.00 in. Lifters: Hydraulic. Number of main bearings-5. Displacement: 302 cu. in. (5.0 liters). Lifters: Hydraulic. Carburetion: Multiport fuel injection with eight individual ports. Compression Ratio: 9.0:1. Horsepower: 185 @ 3800 rpm. Torque: Net: 275 lb.-ft. @ 2400 rpm. Fuel Requirements: Unleaded. Optional: 5.8 HO V-8 for F-150 and F-250. Engine type: OHV V-8. Bore x Stroke: 4.00 in. x 3.50 in. Displacement: 351 cu. in. (5.75 liters). Induction system: 4-barrel carburetor. Number of main bearings-5. Horsepower: 210 @ 4000 rpm. Torque: 305 lb.-ft. @ 2800 rpm. Fuel Requirements: Unleaded. Optional: For F-250 HD and F-350 models. Engine Type: OHV V-8. Bore x Stroke: 4.36 in. x 3.85 in. Displacement: 460 cu. in. (7.5 liters). Induction system: 4-barrel downdraft carburetor. Compression Ratio: 8.0:1. Number of main bearings-5. Horsepower: 245 @ 4000 rpm. (240 @ 4200 rpm California rating). Torque: Net: 380 lb.-ft. @ 2600 rpm. (365 lb.-ft. @ 3000 rpm California rating). Fuel Requirements: Unleaded. Optional: For F-250 HD and F-350 models. Engine Type: OHV diesel V-8. Bore x Stroke: 4.00 in. x 4.18 in. Displacement: 420 cu. in. (6.9 liters). Induction system: Fuel injection. Compression Ratio: 21.5:1. Number of main bearings-5. Horsepower: 170 @ 3300 rpm. (High Altitude: 150 @ 3300 rpm). Torque: Net: 315 lb.-ft. @ 1400 rpm. (High Altitude: 285 lb.-ft. @ 1400 rpm). Fuel Requirements: Diesel.

CHASSIS FEATURES: Separate body and frame. F-150 regular pickup: Single-channel, 6 cross members, 36,000 psi. Section modulus: 3.21 cu. in. F-150 SuperCab pickup: Single-channel, 7 cross members, 36,000 psi. Section modulus: 3.79 cu. in. F-250 regular pickup: Single-channel, 7 cross members, 36,000 psi. Section modulus: 4.78 cu. in. F-250HD regular pickup: Single-channel, 6 cross members, 36,000 psi. Section modulus: 4.33 cu. in. F-250HD SuperCab pickup: Single-channel, 7 cross members, 36,000 psi. Section modulus: 4.87 cu. in. F-350 regular pickup: Single-channel, 6 cross members, 36,000 psi. Section modulus: 4.33 cu. in. F-350 crew cab pickup: Single-channel, 8 cross members, 36,000 psi. Section modulus: 4.94 cu. in.

SUSPENSION AND RUNNING GEAR: Front Suspension: F-150: Computer selected coil springs. Capacity: Regular cab: 2525 lb., SuperCab: 3100 lb. F-250: Single stage leaf, constant rate. Capacity: 3305 lb. F-250HD regular cab: Single stage, leaf, constant rate. Capacity: 3305 lb. SuperCab: Single stage, leaf, constant rate Capacity: 3920 lb. F-350: Regular cab: Single stage, leaf, constant rate. Capacity: 3400 lb. Crew Cab: Single stage, leaf, constant rate. Capacity: 4100 lb. Rear Suspension: All models: Leaf, 2-stage, variable rate F-150 regular cab: Capacity: 3802 lb. SuperCab: 3802 lb. F-250 regular cab: Capacity: 4018 lb. F-250HD regular cab and SuperCab: Capacity: 5922 lb. F-350 regular cab: Capacity: 7833 lb., crew cab: Capacity: 7370 lb. Front Axle Type and Capacity: F-150 regular cab and SuperCab: 3550 lb. capacity, full-floating, Hotchkiss. F-250: 3850 lb. capacity, full-floating, Hotchkiss. F-250HD: Twin traction beam. Regular cab: 3850 lb. SuperCab: 4600 lb. capacity. F-350: 5000 lb. capacity. Rear Axle Type and Capacity: F-150: Semi-floating, 3750 lb. capacity. F-250: Semi-floating, Hotchkiss. Spicer model 60, 5300 lb. capacity. F-250HD: Regular Cab and SuperCab: Full-floating. 6250 lb. capacity. F-350: 6250 lb. Transfer Case: F-150 and F-250: 2-speed New Process 208. Ratios: 2.6:1, 1.00:1. F-250HD and F-350: Warner model 1345. Ratios: 2.74, 1.00:1. Brakes: Type: Hydraulic, single-piston, floating caliper, Ford-designed disc front and drums rear, power assisted. Dimensions: Front: F-150: 11.54 in. disc, F-250 and F-350: 12.48 in. disc on all models. Rear: F-150: 11.03 in. x 2.25 in. F-250: Rear: 12.0 in. x 2.50 in. F-250 HD and F-350: 12 in. x 3.0 in. Wheels: F-150: 5-hole stamped disc, 15 in. x 6JK, disc. F-250 and F-350: 8-hole, stamped disc, 16 x 6K, disc. O. Tires: F-150: P235/75R-15XL. F-250: LT215/75R-16C, F-250HD: LT235/85R-16E. F-350: LT235/85R-16E. Optional: Tubeless tires in sizes to match Payload Package requirements. Steering: Standard Power assisted, recirculating ball. Overall Ratio: F-150 regular cab and SuperCab: 17.6:1. F-250 regular cab: 19.7:1. F-250 HD regular cab: 21.9:1. F-250 HD SuperCab: 21.3:1. F-350 crew cab: 20.6:1. F-350 chassis and cab: 20.6:1. Transmission: Warner T-18, 4-speed manual. Ratios: F-150: 6.32, 3.09, 1.69, 1.0:1. Reverse: 7.44:1. The New Process 435 was optional and was also used when shortages of the T-18 occurred. Clutch: Heavy-duty hydraulic. F-150 and F-250: 10 in. dia. and 95.7 sq. in. F-250HD and F-350: 11.0 in. dia. and 123.7 sq. in. Optional: SelectShift 3-speed automatic. 4-speed manual overdrive for F-150.

VEHICLE DIMENSIONS: Styleside pickups: Wheelbase: 116.8 in./133 in. Overall length: 192.1 in./208.3 in. Flareside pickups: Wheelbase: 116.8 in. Overall length: 187.8.2 in. Overall width: 116.8 in. wheelbase. Styleside and Flareside: 69.3 in.; SuperCab: Wheelbase: 155 in. Overall length: 230.3 in. Width: 70.8 in. Crew cab: Wheelbase: 168.4 in. Overall length: 243.6 in. Headroom: 40.4 in. (40.0 in. for SuperCab). Front legroom: 41 in. Front hip room: 61.7 in. Front shoulder room: 64.2 in.

CAPACITIES: Fuel Tank: F-150: Short wheelbase: 16.5 gal.; Long wheelbase: 19.0 gal. All others: 19.0 gal. Optional: F-150: Short wheelbase: 35.5 gal. All long wheelbase models: 38.0 gal.

ACCOMMODATIONS: 3 occupants. SuperCab and and crew cab: 6 occupants.

INSTRUMENTATION: Speedometer, odometer, fuel level and engine coolant temperature gauges, warning lights for oil pressure and battery charge.

OPTIONS AND PRICES: 5.0 EFI V-8: $541. 5.8 HO V-8: $946 (F-150). 7.5 V-8: $139. 6.9 diesel V-8: $2,060. SelectShift automatic transmission: $625. XL Trim Package: $392 (F-150 regular cab). XLT Lariat Trim Package: $789 (regular cab). Air conditioning: $744. Heavy-duty battery: $53. Argent rear step battery: $120. Chrome rear step battery: $212. Roof clearance lights: $92. Rear bumper delete: $61 (credit). Electronic digital clock: $85. Convenience Group: $75-$118 depending upon trim package ordered. Super Engine Cooling: $96. Power door and windows: $293. Auxiliary fuel tank: $230. Tinted glass: $46-$56 depending upon body type. Handling Package: $218 (F-150 regular cab), $110 (F-250 HD SuperCab), $124 (all others). Headliner and Insulation Package: $20-$73 depending upon body type. Engine block heater: $31-$62 depending upon engine. High output heater: $31. Automatic locking front hubs: $40. Light Group: $91. Bright low-mount swing-away mirrors: $89. Bright swing-away recreational mirrors: $96. Mid body side and wheel-lip moldings: $124-$195 depending upon trim package. Combination two-tone paint: $180- $324 depending upon trim package. Deluxe two-tone paint $108-$290 depending upon trim package. Victoria two-tone paint: $293-$438 depending upon trim package. Exterior Protecting Group: $64. Rear jump seats delete option (SuperCab): $150 credit. Skid plates: $90 (without auxiliary fuel tank): $165 (with auxiliary fuel tank and SuperCab and crew cab). Heavy-Duty Suspension Package: $158 (F-150), $778 (F-250 and F-250 HD), $14-$48 (F-350, depending upon wheelbase). AM/FM stereo radio: $100. AM/FM stereo radio with cassette tape player: $135-$235 depending upon trim package. Radio credit option: $38 credit.

HISTORICAL FOOTNOTES: Total Ford F series output for 1986 was 540,126.

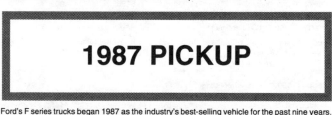

1987 PICKUP

Ford's F series trucks began 1987 as the industry's best-selling vehicle for the past nine years. Changes for 1987 were evolutionary with a focus on improving quality and performance as well as offering new convenience features. Exterior changes included impact-resistent aero headlights, wrap-around parking lights, a new grille, fenders and hood, and a new chrome front bumper with integral spoiler on F-150 models. With the new aero-type headlights, only the halogen bulb had to be replaced — a task that required no tools. Both the headlamp and the parking lamp bulbs were replaced from under the hood. The windshield washer reservoir had an increased capacity of 80 oz. A see-through master cylinder was new for 1987. The interior featured a totally redesigned instrument panel with easier-to-read back-lit gauges. Other highlights were a center-mounted speedometer, a large locking glove box, an electronic AM radio, four climate control outlets and side-window demisters. Access to fuses was through a removable panel below the steering wheel. This process was quicker and easier than in previous years. Five extra replacement fuses were provided. Numerous other service refinements were made in the 1987 F series trucks. A front-wheel caster/camber adjustment provided improved wheel alignment. A new drive belt system was used on the 4.9 liter and 5.0 liter engines. It provided easier access to the alternator, air conditioner compressor, power steering pump, water pump and thermacter pump. It also simplified belt replacement. The new dash arrangement also introduced a number of service improvements. They included the convenient removal of the glove box door for quick access to heater, defroster, ventilation and air conditioning air-flow mechanisms, wiring and antenna cable. The radio, heater and air conditioner controls were reached for servicing by removing a single trim panel. The speedometer/cable, gauges and instrument panel bulbs were accessible for maintenance by removing two screws and two panels.

1987 Ford F-150 XL Styleside pickup

An industry-first for Ford was the use of a standard rear anti-lock brake system. This system utilized an electronic sensor, an on-board computer and special valves to help the driver maintain control during harsh driving maneuvers regardless of the road or load conditions. This system, which operated only when the truck was in the two-wheel drive mode, had its own diagnostic system and did not require adjustment. During braking, the rear anti-lock system, which consisted of an actuation valve, axle sensor and exciter, and computer module, electronically monitored the rear-wheel velocities and adjusted the rear-brake pressure through fast-acting solenoid valves. The driver's ability to brake in a straight line was thus enhanced by limiting rear-wheel lock. All stops, whether normal or in the anti-lock mode, had the same feel to the driver.

Other functional and convenience improvements for 1987 included a new tailgate and latch handle assembly, a new transfer case requiring less shift effort than the previous design, and the addition of a constant-displacement hydraulic pump providing lubrication so that vehicles with manual locking hubs could be towed unlimited distances at speed up to 55 mph without disengaging the drive shaft. New gas-pressurized shock absorbers were also used. All-Season radial tires were installed on F-250 and F-350 models.

The standard 4.9 liter 6-cylinder engine had electronic fuel injection for 1987. This multiple-port system increased horsepower by 20 percent and torque six percent. Numerous changes took place to accommodate the fuel injection system. These included a new air induction system with a tuned cast aluminum plenum and branched intake manifold with individual runners. The optional 5.0 liter V-8 was also refined by the use of new low-friction piston rings and improved control of fuel and spark by a "second generation" EEC-IV electronic engine control system. The 5.0 liter also had a new universal air cleaner and engine oil dip stick. During the model year the 7.5 liter V-8 received electronic fuel injection in place of the 4-barrel carburetor carried over from 1986. A new model introduced during the model year was an F-350 dual rear wheel chassis-cab.

Options from 1986 that were not offered for 1987 included the following: Victoria two-tone paint, electronic digital clock (it was now included with all radios), Deluxe wheelcovers, high-output heater, manual steering, electronic AM/FM stereo Seek-Scan radio with cassette tape player (it was replaced by a new electronic radio) and the Exterior Protection Group. A new option for 1987 was a Roof/Rocker two-tone paint. The exterior colors offered for 1987 were these: Raven black, dark grey metallic, medium silver metallic, bright canyon red, light regatta blue, alpine green metallic, dark canyon red, dark shadow blue metallic, colonial white, desert tan metallic, and light chestnut.

I.D. DATA: The V.I.N. had 17 entries. The first three characters identified the manufacturer, make and type of vehicle. The next entry, a letter designated the GVW rating. The next three characters identified the series and body style. The eighth character identified the engine. A check digit following, then an entry identifying the assembly plant. The final digits represented the sequential production number.

Body Type	Factory Price	GVW	Shipping Weight	Prod. Total
Series F-150, 117 in., 133 in. wheelbase. SuperCab-155 in. wheelbase				
Pickup, 6.5 ft. Flareside	$12,350	6050[1]	3807	—
Pickup, 6.5 ft. Styleside	$12,090	6050	3817	—
Pickup, 8.0 ft. Styleside	$12,272	6050	4002	—
SuperCab, Styleside	$13,862	6050	3962	—

NOTE 1: 6250 lb. GVW optional for regular pickups; 6450 lb. optional for SuperCab.

Body Type	Factory Price	GVW	Shipping Weight	Prod. Total
Series F-250, 133 in. wheelbase, SuperCab: 155 in. wheelbase				
Pickup, 8 ft. Styleside	$11,949	6700	4039	—
Pickup, 8 ft. Styleside HD	$13,742	N.A.	N.A.	—
SuperCab HD	$15,346	N.A.	N.A.	—
Series F-350, 133 in. wheelbase				
Chassis and Cab	$14,489	9000[2]	N.A.	—
Pickup, 8 ft. Styleside	$14,738	9000	4465	—
Crew Cab, 168.8 in. wb.	$16,349	9300	N.A.	—

NOTE 2: Max. GVW available.

STANDARD ENGINE: All models except F-250 HD and F-350: Engine Type: OHV In-line 6-cylinder. Bore x Stroke: 4.00 in. x 3.98 in. Displacement: 300 cu. in. Induction system: Multiple port electronic fuel injection. Number of main bearings-7. Compression Ratio: 8.8:1. Horsepower: Net: 145 @ 3400 rpm (F-150 with 2.73/3.08:1 axle ratios), 150 @ 3400 rpm (all other models under 8500 lb. GVWR). Torque: Net: 265 lb.-ft. @ 2000 rpm. (F-150 with 2.73/3.08:1 axle ratios), 260 @ 2000 rpm (all other models under 8500 lb. GVWR). Fuel Requirements: Unleaded.

OPTIONAL ENGINE: F-150 and F-250, under 8500 lb. GVW. 5.0 EFI: Engine type: OHV V-8. Cast-iron block and cylinder heads. Bore x Stroke: 4.00 in. x 3.00 in. Lifters: Hydraulic. Number of main bearings-5. Displacement: 302 cu. in. (5.0 liters). Lifters: Hydraulic. Carburetion: Multiport fuel injection with eight individual ports. Compression Ratio: 9.0:1. Horsepower: 185 @ 3800 rpm. Torque: Net: 270 lb.-ft. @ 2400 rpm. Fuel Requirements: Unleaded. Optional: 5.8 HO V-8. For F-150 and F-250. Engine type: OHV V-8. Bore x Stroke: 4.00 in. x 3.50 in. Displacement: 351 cu. in. (5.75 liters). Induction system: 4-barrel carburetor. Number of main bearings-5. Horsepower: 190 @ 3800 rpm (models under 8500 lb. GVWR), 180 @ 4000 rpm (manual transmission, models over 8500 lb. GVWR), 190 @ 4000 rpm (automatic transmission, models over 8500 lb. GVWR. Torque: 295 lb.-ft. @ 2600 rpm (models under 8500 lb. GVWR), 270 lb.-ft. @ 2600 rpm (manual transmission, models over 8500 lb. GVWR), 285 lb.-ft. @ 2600 rpm (automatic transmission models over 8500 lb. GVWR). Fuel Requirements: Unleaded. Optional: For F-250 HD and F-350 models. Engine Type: OHV V-8. Bore x Stroke: 4.36 in. x 3.85 in. Displacement: 460 cu. in. (7.5 liters). Induction system: 4-barrel downdraft carburetor. Compression Ratio: 8.0:1 (8.5:1 with EFI). Number of main bearings-5. Horsepower: 245 @ 4000 rpm. (240 @ 4200 rpm California rating). Torque: Net: 380 lb.-ft. @ 2600 rpm. (365 lb.-ft. @ 3000 rpm California rating). Fuel Requirements: Unleaded. Optional: For F-250 HD and F-350 models. Engine Type: OHV diesel V-8. Bore x Stroke: 4.00 in. x 4.18 in. Displacement: 420 cu. in. (6.9 liters). Induction system: Fuel injection. Compression Ratio: 21.5:1. Number of main bearings-5. Horsepower: 170 @ 3300 rpm. (High Altitude: 150 @ 3300 rpm). Torque: Net: 315 lb.-ft. @ 1400 rpm. (High Altitude: 285 lb.-ft. @ 1400 rpm). Fuel Requirements: Diesel.

CHASSIS FEATURES: Separate body and frame. F-150 regular pickup: Single-channel, 6 cross members, 36,000 psi. Section modulus: 3.21 cu. in. F-150 SuperCab pickup: Single-channel, 7 cross members, 36,000 psi. Section modulus: 3.79 cu. in. F-250 regular pickup: Single-channel, 7 cross members, 36,000 psi. Section modulus: 4.78 cu. in. F-250HD regular pickup: Single-channel, 6 cross members, 36,000 psi. Section modulus: 4.33 cu. in. F-250HD SuperCab pickup: Single-channel, 7 cross members, 36,000 psi. Section modulus: 4.87 cu. in. F-350 regular pickup: Single-channel, 6 cross members, 36,000 psi. Section modulus: 4.33 cu. in. F-350 crew cab pickup: Single-channel, 8 cross members, 36,000 psi. Section modulus: 4.94 cu. in.

SUSPENSION AND RUNNING GEAR: Front Suspension: F-150: Computer selected coil springs. Capacity: Regular cab: 2525 lb., SuperCab: 3100 lb. F-250: Single stage leaf, constant rate. Capacity: 3305 lb. F-250HD regular cab: Single stage, leaf, constant rate. Capacity: 3305 lb. SuperCab: Single stage, leaf, constant rate Capacity: 3920 lb. F-350: Regular cab: Single stage, leaf, constant rate. Capacity: 3400 lb. Crew cab: Single stage, leaf, constant rate. Capacity: 4100 lb. Rear Suspension: All models: Leaf, 2-stage, variable rate F-150 regular cab: Capacity: 3802 lb. SuperCab: 3802 lb. F-250 regular cab: Capacity: 4018 lb. F-250HD regular cab and SuperCab: Capacity: 5922 lb. F-350 regular cab: Capacity: 7833 lb., crew cab: Capacity: 7370 lb. Front Axle Type and Capacity: F-150 regular cab and SuperCab: 3550 lb. capacity, full-floating, Hotchkiss. F-250: 3850 lb. capacity, full-floating, Hotchkiss. F-250HD: Twin traction beam. Regular cab: 3850 lb. SuperCab: 4600 lb. capacity. F-350: 5000 lb. capacity. Rear Axle Type and Capacity: F-150: Semi-floating, 3750 lb. capacity. F-250: Semi-floating, Hotchkiss. Spicer model 60, 5300 lb. capacity. F-250HD: Regular cab and SuperCab: Full-floating. 6250 lb. capacity. F-350: 6250 lb. Transfer Case: Warner model 13-56 Ratios: 2.69, 1.00:1. (Some models may be equipped with the older Warner model 135 which was used in case of a shortfall of the model 13-56 units). Brakes: Type: Hydraulic, single-piston, floating caliper, Ford-designed disc front and drums rear, power assisted. Dimensions: Front: F-150: 11.54 in. disc, F-250 and F-350: 12.48 in. disc on all models. Rear: F-150: 11.03 in. x 2.25 in. F-250: Rear: 12.0 in. x 2.50 in. F-250 HD and F-350: 12 in. x 3.0 in. Wheels: F-150: 5-hole stamped disc, 15 in. x 6JK, disc. F-250 and F-350: 8-hole, stamped disc, 16 x 6K, disc. Tires: F-150: P235/75R-15XL. F-250: LT215/75R-16C, F-250HD: LT235/85R-16E. F-350: LT235/85R-16E. Optional: Tubeless tires in sizes to match Payload Package requirements. Steering: Standard Power assisted, recirculating ball. Overall Ratio: F-150 regular cab and SuperCab: 17.6:1. F-250 regular cab: 19.7:1. F-250 HD regular cab: 21.9:1. F-250 HD SuperCab: 21.3:1. F-350 crew cab: 20.6:1. F-350 chassis and cab: 20.6:1. Transmission: F-150/250/350: Warner T-18, 4-speed manual. F-250 HD/F-350: Warner T-19, 4-speed. Ratios: 7.5 V-8: 5.11, 3.03, 1.79, 1.0:1. Reverse: 5.63:1. 6.9 diesel V-8: 4.02, 2.41, 1.41, 1.0:1. Reverse: 4.32:1. During the model year the T-19 was replaced by a 5-speed overdrive with ratios as follows: 7.5 V-8: 5.72, 2.94, 1.61, 1.0. 0.76:1. Reverse: 5.24:1. 6.9 liter diesel: 4.14, 2.37, 1.42, 1.00, 0.77:1. Reverse: 3.79:1. Ratios: F-150/250/350 6.32, 3.09, 1.69, 1.0:1. Reverse: 7.44:1. Clutch: Heavy-duty hydraulic. All engines except 7.5 liter V-8: 11.0 in. dia. and 123.7 sq. in. 7.5 liter V-8: 12 in. dia. and 128.1 sq. in. Optional: 3 and 4-speed automatic transmissions.

VEHICLE DIMENSIONS: Styleside pickups: Wheelbase: 116.8 in./133 in. Overall length: 192.1 in./208.3 in. Flareside pickups: Wheelbase: 116.8 in. Overall length: 187.8 in. Overall width: 116.8 in. wheelbase. Styleside and Flareside: 69.3 in.; SuperCab: Wheelbase: 155 in. Overall length: 230.3 in. Width: 70.8 in. Crew cab: Wheelbase: 168.4 in. Overall length: 243.6 in. Headroom: 40.4 in. (40.0 in. for SuperCab). Front legroom: 41 in. Front hip room: 61.7 in. Front shoulder room: 64.2 in.

CAPACITIES: Fuel Tank: F-150: Short wheelbase: 16.5 gal.; Long wheelbase: 19.0 gal. All others: 19.0 gal. Optional: F-150: Short wheelbase: 35.5 gal. All long wheelbase models: 38.0 gal.

ACCOMMODATIONS: 3 occupants. SuperCab and crew cab: 6 occupants.

INSTRUMENTATION: Speedometer, odometer, fuel level and engine coolant temperature gauges, warning lights for oil pressure and battery charge.

OPTIONS: Air conditioning. Heavy-duty battery. Rear step, argent painted bumper. Chrome rear step bumper. Rear chrome bumper deletion. Convenience Group. Super Cooling Engine Package. California Emission Package. High Altitude Performance Package. Emissions Package. Auxiliary fuel tank. Tinted glass. Chrome grille. Handling Package. Headliner and Insulation Package. Engine block heater. Automatic locking front hubs. Light Group. Clearance lights. Bright low-mount swing-away outside mirrors. Bright recreational swing-out outside mirrors. Lower body side and wheel-lip moldings. Two-tone paint. Deluxe two-tone paint. Roof/Rocker two-tone paint. Power door and window locks. Radio credit option. Electronic AM/FM stereo radio. Electronic AM/FM stereo radio with cassette tape player. Captain's chairs. rear jump seats. Skid plates. Spare tire carrier in-box. Speed control/tilt steering wheel. Heavy-Duty Suspension Package. Tachometer. Various tires. Trailer Towing/Camper Package. Wheelcovers. Sliding rear window.

HISTORICAL FOOTNOTES: In 1987 Ford celebrated its 70th anniversary of truck production.

1988 PICKUP

A new short wheelbase (139 in.) F-150 SuperCab was offered for 1988. Also debuting was a new 161 in. wheelbase dual rear wheel F-350 chassis-cab model. All engines for 1988 were equipped with multi-port electronic fuel injection. Other engine improvements included a self-tensioning serpentine accessory drive system for the 5.8 liter EFI engine, and a two-belt, poly-

V accessory drive system on the 7.5 liter V-8. The cylinder bore of the 6.9 liter diesel V-8 was increased by 0.11 in. for 1988, boosting engine displacement to 7.3 liters. All of last year's four-speed manual transmissions were replaced by five-speed overdrive and heavy-duty five-speed manual overdrive units that were synchronized in all gears, including first and reverse.

1988 Ford F-150 XL Styleside pickup

The interior color selection for 1988 consisted of medium grey and regatta blue, scarlet red and chestnut. The exterior colors offered were raven black, dark grey metallic, medium silver metallic, scarlet red, cabernet red, alpine green metallic, bright regatta blue metallic, deep shadow blue metallic, colonial white, desert tan metallic, light chestnut and dark chestnut metallic.

F-250 XLT Lariat SuperCab 4WD.

1988 Ford F-250 XLT Lariat SuperCab pickup

I.D. DATA: The V.I.N. had 17 entries. The first three characters identified the manufacturer, make and type of vehicle. The next entry, a letter designated the GVW rating. The next three characters identified the series and body style. The eighth character identified the engine. A check digit following, then an entry identifying the assembly plant. The final digits represented the sequential production number.

Body Type	Factory Price	GVW	Shipping Weight	Prod. Total
Series F-150, 117 in., 133 in. wheelbase. SuperCab-155 in. wheelbase				
Pickup, 6.5 ft. Styleside	$12,048	6050	3817	—
Pickup, 8.0 ft. Styleside	$12,243	6050	4002	—
SuperCab, 139 in. wb.	$13,638	6050	3962	—
SuperCab, 155 in. wb.	$13,833	6050	N.A.	—

NOTE 1: 6250 lb. GVW optional for regular pickups; 6450 lb. optional for SuperCab.

Body Type	Factory Price	GVW	Shipping Weight	Prod. Total
Series F-250, 133 in. wheelbase, SuperCab: 155 in. wheelbase				
Pickup, 8 ft. Styleside	$12,358	6700	4039	—
Pickup, 8 ft. Styleside HD	$14,322	6700	N.A.	—
SuperCab HD	$15,825	6700	N.A.	—
Series F-350, 133 in. wheelbase				
Chassis and Cab	$14,495	11,000[2]	N.A.	—
Ch. & Cab, 137 in. wb.	$16,097	11,000	N.A.	—
Pickup, 8 ft. Styleside	$15,873	11,000	4465	—
Crew Cab, 168.8 in. wb.	$18,049	11,000	N.A.	—
Chassis and Cab, 161 in. wb.	$16,082	11,000	N.A.	—

NOTE 2: Max. GVW available.

STANDARD ENGINE: All models except F-250 HD and F-350: Engine Type: OHV In-line 6-cylinder. Bore x Stroke: 4.00 in. x 3.98 in. Displacement: 300 cu. in. Induction system: Multiple port electronic fuel injection. Number of main bearings-7. Compression Ratio: 8.8:1. Horsepower: Net: 145 @ 3400 rpm (F-150 with 2.73/3.08:1 axle ratios), 150 @ 3400 rpm (all other models under 8500 lb. GVWR). Torque: Net: 265 lb.-ft. @ 2000 rpm. (F-150 with 2.73/3.08:1 axle ratios), 260 @ 2000 rpm (all other models under 8500 lb. GVWR). Fuel Requirements: Unleaded.

OPTIONAL ENGINE: F-150 and F-250, under 8500 lb. GVW. 5.0 Fl: Engine type: OHV V-8. Cast-iron block and cylinder heads. Bore x Stroke: 4.00 in. x 3.00 in. Lifters: Hydraulic. Number of main bearings-5. Displacement: 302 cu. in. (5.0 liters). Lifters: Hydraulic. Carburetion: Multiport fuel injection with eight individual ports. Compression Ratio: 9.0:1. Horsepower: 185 @ 3800 rpm. Torque: Net: 270 lb.-ft. @ 2400 rpm. Fuel Requirements: Unleaded. Optional: 5.8 HO V-8. For F-150 and F-250. Engine type: OHV V-8. Bore x Stroke: 4.00 in. x 3.50 in. Displacement: 351 cu. in. (5.75 liters) Induction system: Multiport fuel injection. Number of main bearings-5. Horsepower: 210 @ 3800 rpm. Torque: 315 lb.-ft. @ 2800 rpm. Fuel Requirements: Unleaded. Optional: For F-250 HD and F-350 models. Engine Type: OHV V-8. Bore x Stroke: 4.36 in. x 3.85 in. Displacement: 460 cu. in. (7.5 liters). Compression Ratio: 8.0:1 (8.5:1 with EFI). Number of main bearings-5. Horsepower: 230 @ 3600 rpm. Torque: Net: 390 lb.-ft. @ 2200 rpm. Fuel Requirements: Unleaded. Optional: For F-250 HD and F-350 models. Engine Type: OHV diesel V-8. Bore x Stroke: 4.00 in. x 4.18 in. Displacement: 420 cu. in. (6.9 liters). Induction system: Fuel injection. Compression Ratio: 21.5:1. Number of main bearings-5. Horsepower: Net: 180 @ 3300 rpm. (High Altitude): 150 @ 3300 rpm. Torque: Net: 345 lb.-ft. @ 1400 rpm. (High Altitude: 285 lb.-ft. @ 1400 rpm). Fuel Requirements: Diesel.

CHASSIS FEATURES: Separate body and frame. F-150 regular pickup: Single-channel, 6 cross members, 36,000 psi. Section modulus: 3.21 cu. in. F-150 SuperCab pickup: Single-channel, 7 cross members, 36,000 psi. Section modulus: 3.79 cu. in. F-250 regular pickup: Single-channel, 7 cross members, 36,000 psi. Section modulus: 4.78 cu. in. F-250 regular pickup: Single-channel, 6 cross members, 36,000 psi. Section modulus: 4.33 cu. in. F-250HD SuperCab pickup: Single-channel, 7 cross members, 36,000 psi. Section modulus: 4.87 cu.

in. F-350 regular pickup: Single-channel, 6 cross members, 36,000 psi. Section modulus: 4.33 cu. in. F-350 crew cab pickup: Single-channel, 8 cross members, 36,000 psi. Section modulus: 4.94 cu. in.

SUSPENSION AND RUNNING GEAR: Front Suspension: F-150: Computer selected coil springs. Capacity: Regular cab: 2525 lb., SuperCab: 3100 lb. F-250: Single stage leaf, constant rate. Capacity: 3305 lb. F-250HD regular cab: Single stage, leaf, constant rate. Capacity: 3305 lb. SuperCab: Single stage, leaf, constant rate Capacity: 3920 lb. F-350: regular cab: Single stage, leaf, constant rate. Capacity: 3400 lb. Crew cab: Single stage, leaf, constant rate. Capacity: 4100 lb. Rear Suspension: All models: Leaf, 2-stage, variable rate F-150 regular cab: Capacity: 3802 lb. SuperCab: 3802 lb. F-250 regular cab: Capacity: 4018 lb. F-250HD regular cab and SuperCab: Capacity: 5922 lb. F-350 regular cab: Capacity: 7833 lb., crew cab: Capacity: 7370 lb. Front Axle Type and Capacity: F-150 regular cab and SuperCab: 3550 lb. capacity, full-floating, Hotchkiss. F-250: 3850 lb. capacity, full-floating, Hotchkiss. F-250HD: Twin traction beam. Regular cab: 3850 lb. SuperCab: 4600 lb. capacity. F-350: 5000 lb. capacity. Rear Axle Type and Capacity: F-150: Semi-floating, 3750 lb. capacity. F-250: Semi-floating, Hotchkiss. Spicer model 60, 5300 lb. capacity. F-250HD: regular cab and SuperCab: Full-floating. 6250 lb. capacity. F-350: 6250 lb. Transfer Case: Warner model 13-56 Ratios: 2.69, 1.00:1. Brakes: Type: Hydraulic, single-piston, floating caliper, Ford-designed disc front and drums rear, power assisted. Dimensions: Front: F-150: 11.54 in. disc, F-250 and F-350: 12.48 in. disc on all models. Rear: F-150: 11.03 in. x 2.25 in. F-250: Rear: 12.0 in. x 2.50 in. F-250 HD and F-350: 12 in. x 3.0 in. Wheels: F-150: 5-hole stamped disc, 15 in. x 6JK, disc. F-250 and F-350: 8-hole, stamped disc, 16 x 6K, disc. Tires: F-150: P235/75R-15XL. F-250: LT215/75R-16C, F-250HD: LT235/85R-16E. F-350: LT235/85R-16E. Optional: Tubeless tires in sizes to match Payload Package requirements. Steering: Standard Power assisted, recirculating ball. Overall Ratio: F-150 regular cab and SuperCab: 17.6:1. F-250 regular cab: 19.7:1. F-250 HD regular cab: 21.9:1. F-250 HD SuperCab: 21.3:1. F-350 crew cab: 20.6:1. F-350 chassis and cab: 20.6:1. Transmission: 5-speed manual overdrive. Clutch: Heavy-duty hydraulic. All engines except 7.5 liter V-8: 11.0 in. dia. and 123.7 sq. in. 7.5 liter V-8: 12 in. dia. and 128.1 sq. in. Optional: 3 and 4-speed automatic transmissions.

VEHICLE DIMENSIONS: Styleside pickups: Wheelbase: 116.8 in./133 in. Overall length: 192.1 in./208.3 in. Flareside pickups: Wheelbase: 116.8 in. Overall length: 187.8. in. Overall width: 116.8 in. wheelbase. Styleside and Flareside: 69.3 in. SuperCab: Wheelbase: 155 in. Overall length: 230.3 in. Width: 70.8 in. Crew cab: Wheelbase: 168.4 in. Overall length: 243.6 in. Headroom: 40.4 in. (40.0 in. for SuperCab). Front legroom: 41 in. Front hip room: 61.7 in. Front shoulder room: 64.2 in.

CAPACITIES: Fuel Tank: F-150: Short wheelbase: 16.5 gal.; Long wheelbase: 19.0 gal. All others: 19.0 gal. Optional: F-150: Short wheelbase: 35.5 gal. All long wheelbase models: 38.0 gal.

ACCOMMODATIONS: 3 occupants. SuperCab and crew cab: 6 occupants.

INSTRUMENTATION: Speedometer, odometer, fuel level and engine coolant temperature gauges, warning lights for oil pressure and battery charge.

OPTIONS: Air conditioning. Heavy-duty battery. Rear step, argent painted bumper. Chrome rear step bumper. Rear chrome bumper deletion. Convenience Group. Super Cooling Engine Package. California Emission Package. High Altitude Performance Package. Emissions Package. Auxiliary fuel tank. Tinted glass. Chrome grille. Handling Package. Headliner and Insulation Package. Engine block heater. Automatic locking front hubs. Light Group. Clearance lights. Bright low-mount swing-away outside mirrors. Bright recreational swing-out outside mirrors. Lower body side and wheel-lip moldings. Two-tone paint. Deluxe two-tone paint. Roof/Rocker two-tone paint. Power door and window locks. Radio credit option. Electronic AM/FM stereo radio. Electronic AM/FM stereo radio with cassette tape player. Captain's chairs. Rear jump seats. Skid plates. Spare tire carrier in-box. Speed control/tilt steering wheel. Heavy-Duty Suspension Package. Tachometer. Various tires. Trailer Towing/Camper Package. Wheelcovers. Sliding rear window.

HISTORICAL FOOTNOTES: Ford reported that the F series pickup remained the highest volume unit — car or truck, domestic or import — in the industry.

1989 PICKUP

The exterior of the 1989 Ford F series trucks was highlighted by new grille colors. A light argent /black grille replaced the black grille of 1988 on the base level custom and XL models. A chrome/dark argent grille was used for all other models. A new floor mat in lieu of carpet option was offered for the XLT Lariat. An AM/FM stereo radio with digital clock was made standard with the XLT Lariat. New SuperCab Captain's chairs now included a tip/slide seat mechanism on both the driver and passenger side to improve rear seat ingress/egress. These seats also included a new sew style and folding inboard armrests.

An all-new electronically controlled 4-speed automatic overdrive transmission was offered for F series models with over 8500 lb. GVWR and gasoline engines. Major features of this E4OD transmission included a torque converter clutch and a 0.71:1 overdrive gear.

Five options offered in 1988 were deleted for 1989. They included the Roof/Rocker two-tone feature, the heavy-duty front/rear shock absorbers (these continued to be available as part of the Handling Package and Heavy-Duty Suspension Packages), 7.50R x 16D tires on rear wheel models, IT235/85R x 16D tires on F-250 models and tined glass (made standard on regular cab; already standard on SuperCab/crew cab). No changes were made on the exterior colors selection for the F series trucks. No longer offered as interior color choices were medium grey and regatta blue. In their place were dark charcoal and crystal blue.

1989 Ford XLT Lariat pickup

Standard equipment content of the Custom pickup included these items: Front chrome bumper, tinted glass, aero-style headlights, door-mounted left and right side black fold-away exterior mirrors, bright headlight/parking light bezels, removable tailgate with bright release handle, fully-padded door trim panels, instrument panel-mounted ashtray with ashtray light, carpeted back panel cover, cigarette lighter, right side, color-keyed coat hook, color-keyed cowl side trim panels, color-keyed vinyl door trim panels with molded-in speaker grille, color-keyed rubber floor mat, forced-air heater, inside hood release, dual-note horn, electronic AM radio with digital clock, color-keyed, all-vinyl bench-type seat with folding back, black seat pivot covers, and color-keyed sun visors.

I.D. DATA: The V.I.N. had 17 entries. The first three characters identified the manufacturer, make and type of vehicle. The next entry, a letter designated the GVW rating. The next three characters identified the series and body style. The eighth character identified the engine. A check digit following, then an entry identifying the assembly plant. The final digits represented the sequential production number.

Body Type	Factory Price	GVW	Shipping Weight	Prod. Total
Series F-150, 117 in., 133 in. wheelbase. SuperCab-155 in. wheelbase				
Pickup, 6.5 ft. Styleside	$12,399	6050	3817	—
Pickup, 8.0 ft. Styleside	$12,594	6050	4002	—
SuperCab, 139 in. wb.	$13,989	6050	3962	—
SuperCab, 155 in. wb.	$14,184	6050	N.A.	—

NOTE 1: 6250 lb. GVW optional for regular pickups; 6450 lb. optional for SuperCab.

Body Type	Factory Price	GVW	Shipping Weight	Prod. Total
Series F-250, 133 in. wheelbase, SuperCab: 155 in. wheelbase				
Pickup, 8 ft. Styleside	$12,928	6700	4039	—
Pickup, 8 ft. Styleside HD	$14,892	6700	N.A.	—
SuperCab HD	$16,395	6700	N.A.	—
Series F-350, 133 in. wheelbase				
Chassis & Cab	$14,795	11,000[2]	N.A.	—
Ch & Cab, 137 in.[3]	$16,293	—	—	—
Pickup, 8 ft. Styleside	$16,172	11,000	4465	—
Crew Cab, 168.8 in. wb.	$18,391	11,000	N.A.	—
Ch. & Cab, 161 in. wb.[3]	$16,382	11,000	N.A.	—

NOTE 2: Max. GVW available.
NOTE 3: Dual rear wheels.

STANDARD ENGINE: All models except F-250 HD and F-350: Engine Type: OHV In-line 6-cylinder. Bore x Stroke: 4.00 in. x 3.98 in. Displacement: 300 cu. in. Induction system: Multiple port electronic fuel injection. Number of main bearings-7. Compression Ratio: 8.8:1. Horsepower: Net: 145 @ 3400 rpm (F-150 with 2.73/3.08:1 axle ratios), 150 @ 3400 rpm (all other models under 8500 lb. GVWR). Torque: Net: 265 lb.-ft. @ 2000 rpm. (F-150 with 2.73/3.08:1 axle ratios), 260 @ 2000 rpm (all other models under 8500 lb. GVWR). Fuel Requirements: Unleaded.

OPTIONAL ENGINE: F-150 and F-250, under 8500 lb. GVW. 5.0 EFI: Engine type: OHV V-8. Cast-iron block and cylinder heads. Bore x Stroke: 4.00 in. x 3.00 in. Lifters: Hydraulic. Number of main bearings-5. Displacement: 302 cu. in. (5.0 liters). Lifters: Hydraulic. Carburetion: Multiport fuel injection with eight individual ports. Compression Ratio: 9.0:1. Horsepower: 185 @ 3800 rpm. Torque: Net: 270 lb.-ft. @ 2400 rpm. Fuel Requirements: Unleaded. Optional: 5.8 HO V-8. For F-150 and F-250. Engine type: OHV V-8. Bore x Stroke: 4.00 in. x 3.50 in. Displacement: 351 cu. in. (5.75 liters). Induction system: Multiport fuel injection. Number of main bearings-5. Horsepower: 210 @ 3800 rpm. Torque: 315 lb.-ft. @ 2800 rpm (models under 8500 lb. GVWR), 310 lb.-ft. @ 2800 rpm (models over 8500 lb. GVWR). Fuel Requirements: Unleaded. Optional: For F-250 HD and F-350 models. Engine Type: OHV V-8. Bore x Stroke: 4.36 in. x 3.85 in. Displacement: 460 cu. in. (7.5 liters). Induction system: Multiport fuel injection. Compression Ratio: 8.5:1. Number of main bearings-5. Horsepower: 230 @ 3600 rpm. Torque: Net: 390 lb.-ft. @ 2200 rpm. Fuel Requirements: Unleaded. Optional: For F-250 HD and F-350 models. Engine Type: OHV diesel V-8. Bore x Stroke: 4.00 in. x 4.18 in. Displacement: 420 cu. in. (6.9 liters). Induction system: Fuel injection. Compression Ratio: 21.5:1. Number of main bearings-5. Horsepower: 180 @ 3300 rpm. (High Altitude: 160 @ 3300 rpm). Torque: Net: 345 lb.-ft. @ 1400 rpm (High Altitude: 305 lb.-ft. @ 1400 rpm). Fuel Requirements: Diesel.

CHASSIS FEATURES: Separate body and frame. F-150 regular pickup: Single-channel, 6 cross members, 36,000 psi. Section modulus: 3.21 cu. in. F-150 SuperCab pickup: Single-channel, 7 cross members, 36,000 psi. Section modulus: 3.79 cu. in. F-250 regular pickup: Single-channel, 7 cross members, 36,000 psi. Section modulus: 4.78 cu. in. F-250HD regular pickup: Single-channel, 6 cross members, 36,000 psi. Section modulus: 4.33 cu. in. F-250HD SuperCab pickup: Single-channel, 7 cross members, 36,000 psi. Section modulus: 4.87 cu. in. F-350 regular pickup: Single-channel, 6 cross members, 36,000 psi. Section modulus: 4.33 cu. in. F-350 crew cab pickup: Single-channel, 8 cross members, 36,000 psi. Section modulus: 4.94 cu. in.

SUSPENSION AND RUNNING GEAR: Front Suspension: F-150: Computer selected coil springs. Capacity: Regular cab: 2525 lb., SuperCab: 3100 lb. F-250: Single stage leaf, constant rate. Capacity: 3305 lb. F-250HD regular cab: Single stage, leaf, constant rate. Capacity: 3305 lb. SuperCab: Single stage, leaf, constant rate Capacity: 3920 lb. F-350: Regular cab: Single stage, leaf, constant rate. Capacity: 3400 lb. Crew cab: Single stage, leaf, constant rate. Capacity: 4100 lb. Rear Suspension: All models: Leaf, 2-stage, variable rate F-150 regular cab: Capacity: 3802 lb. SuperCab: 3802 lb. F-250 regular cab: Capacity: 4018 lb. F-250HD regular cab and SuperCab: Capacity: 5922 lb. F-350 regular cab: Capacity: 7833 lb., crew cab: Capacity: 7370 lb. Front Axle Type and Capacity: F-150 regular cab and SuperCab: 3800 lb. capacity, full-floating, Hotchkiss. F-250: 3850 lb. capacity, full-floating, Hotchkiss. F-250HD: Twin traction beam. Regular cab: 3850 lb. SuperCab: 4600 lb. capacity. F-350: 5000 lb. capacity. Rear Axle Type and Capacity: F-150: Semi-floating, 3800 lb. capacity. F-250: Semi-floating, Hotchkiss. Spicer model 60, 5300 lb. capacity. F-250HD: Regular cab and SuperCab: Full-floating. 6250 lb. capacity. F-350: 6250 lb. Transfer Case: Warner model 13-56 Ratios: 2.69, 1.00:1. Brakes: Type: Hydraulic, single-piston, floating caliper, Ford-designed disc front and drums rear, power assisted. Dimensions: Front: F-150: 11.72 in. disc, F-250 and F-350: 12.56 in. disc on all models. Rear: F-150: 11.03 in. x 2.25 in. F-250: Rear: 12.0 in. x 2.50 in. F-250 HD and F-350: 12 in. x 3.0 in. Wheels: F-150: 5-hole stamped disc, 15 in. x 6JK, disc. F-250 and F-350: 8-hole, stamped disc, 16 x 6K, disc. Tires: F-150: P235/75R-15XL. F-250: LT215/85R-16D, F-250HD: LT235/85R-16E. F-350: LT235/85R-16E. Optional: Tubeless tires in sizes to match Payload Package requirements. Steering: Ford XR-50, Power assisted, recirculating ball. Overall Ratio: All models: 17.0:1. Transmission: 5-speed manual overdrive. (Heavy-duty for F-250HD and F-350). Clutch: Heavy-duty hydraulic. F-150: 10.0 in. dia. F-250, F-250HD and F-350: 11.0 in. Optional: 4-speed manual, 3-speed and 4-speed automatics.

VEHICLE DIMENSIONS: Styleside pickups: Wheelbase: 116.8 in./133 in. Overall length: 194.1 in./210.2 in. Flareside pickups: Wheelbase: 116.8 in. Overall length: 194.1 in. Overall width: 116.8 in. wheelbase. Styleside and Flareside: 79.0 in.; SuperCab: Wheelbase: 155 in. Overall length: 232.2 in. Width: 79.0 in. Crew cab: Wheelbase: 168.4 in. Overall length: 245.7 in. Width: 79.0 in. Headroom: 40.4 in. (40.0 in. for SuperCab). Front legroom: 41 in. Front hip room: 61.7 in. Front shoulder room: 64.2 in.

CAPACITIES: Fuel Tank: F-150: Short wheelbase: 18.2 gal.; Long wheelbase: 19.0 gal. Optional: F-150: Short wheelbase: 16.5 gal. auxiliary tank. F-150 long wheelbase: 18.2 gal. auxiliary tank. SuperCab models: 138.8 in. wheelbase: Standard dual tanks with 34.7 gal. capacity. 155.0 in. wheelbase models: 37.2 gal. standard dual tanks. Crew cab models: Standard dual tanks with 37.2 gal. capacity. Chassis & cab models: 19.0 gal. Optional: 133 in. wheelbase: 18.2 gal. auxiliary fuel tank.

ACCOMMODATIONS: 3 occupants. SuperCab and crew cab: 6 occupants.

INSTRUMENTATION: Voltmeter gauge, speedometer, odometer, engine oil pressure gauge, fuel gauge, transfer case indicator light low and high range), anti-lock brake system indicator light, engine coolant temperature gauge, charging system indicator light, check engine warning light, oil pressure/engine temperature indicator light, brake system/parking brake indicator light.

OPTIONS: Air conditioning. Limited slip front axle (F-150 only). Heavy-duty battery. Rear step, argent-painted bumper. Rear step chrome bumper. Convenience Group. Super Cooling Engine Package. California Emissions Package. Special High Altitude Emissions Package. Floor mat in lieu of carpet. Auxiliary fuel tank. Chrome grille. Handling Package. Headliner and Insulation Package. Engine block heater. Automatic locking front hubs. Light Group. Bright low-mount swing-away exterior mirrors. Bright recreational swing-out exterior mirrors. Lower body side and wheel-lip moldings. Deluxe two-tone paint. Power door locks/windows. Electronic AM/FM stereo radio. Electronic AM/FM stereo radio with cassette tape player. Radio credit option. Rear jump seats (for SuperCab). Knitted vinyl bench seat. Cloth and vinyl bench seat. Cloth bench seat (for crew cab). Skid plates. In-box spare tire carrier. Speed control/tilt steering wheel. Heavy-duty Front Suspension Package. Heavy-Duty Rear Suspension Package. tachometer. Spare tire and wheel. Trailer Towing/Camper Package. Sport tire cover. Deluxe argent styled steel wheels. Sliding rear windows. Tires: P235/75R x 15XL white sidewall All Season, P235/75R x 15XL white sidewall All-Terrain, LT215/85R x 16D black sidewall All-Terrain, LT215/85R x 16E black sidewall All-Terrain, LT235/85R x 16E black sidewall, 7.50R x 17D black sidewall highway, 7.50R x 17D black sidewall All-Terrain.

HISTORICAL FOOTNOTES: Ford reported that the light truck market was the hottest growth segment of the U.S. automotive industry. Highlights of this development included a population shift to the West which had a well-defined preference for light trucks and an increase in the allocation of spendable income by new vehicle buyers to the purchase of recreational-type vehicles.

1990 PICKUP

1990 Ford XLT Lariat pickup

The 1990 F series trucks featured chassis and powerplant improvements, including expanded availability of the EOD4 transmission due to increased production capacity. The E4OD transmission replaced the C-6 transmission in trucks with the 4.9 or 5.8 liter engines and a GVWR under 8500 lb. Interior changes were limited to the addition of XLT Lariat trim to the dual rear wheel chassis & cab models. A running change made in 1989 and carried over for 1990 was the use of automatic locking hubs as standard F-150 equipment. Manual locking hubs were optional. Offered after the start of the 1990 model year was a touch drive electric shift on F-150 models with the 5.0 liter/automatic overdrive transmission. A cargo box light was now standard for all models. Improvements to the F series quality and reliability included a EEC-IV module provision on the 4.9 liter and 5.0 liter engines to access engine diagnostic data. The front fuel lines were commonized for serviceability and complexity improvements. The fuel tank pump was revised to a high pressure in-tank design. A new Heavy-Duty Service Package consolidated the heavy-duty battery, super cooling radiator and skid plate options. Another new option, the Light/Convenience Group consolidated the previously separate Light and Convenience Group options. The Trailer/Camper Package was now split into separate options. A new Sport Appearance Package including Sport wheels and tape stripe was now offered. The chrome grille option was deleted for 1990.

Exterior colors for 1990 were as follows: Desert tan metallic, tan, dark chestnut metallic, cabernet red, scarlet red, bright regatta blue metallic, deep shadow blue metallic, alpine green metallic, raven black, medium silver metallic, dark grey metallic and colonial white.

1990 Ford F-250 XLT Lariat SuperCab pickup

I.D. DATA: The V.I.N. had 17 entries. The first three characters identified the manufacturer, make and type of vehicle. The next entry, a letter designated the GVW rating. The next three characters identified the series and body style. The eighth character identified the engine. A check digit following, then an entry identifying the assembly plant. The final digits represented the sequential production number.

Body Type	Factory Price	GVW	Shipping Weight	Prod. Total
Series F-150, 117 in., 133 in. wheelbase. SuperCab: 155 in. wheelbase				
Pickup, 6.5 ft. Styleside	$13,206	6050	3817	—
Pickup, 8.0 ft. Styleside	$13,541	6050	4002	—
SuperCab, 139 in. wb.	$14,591	6050	3962	—
SuperCab, 155 in. wb.	$14,811	6050	N.A.	—

NOTE 1: 6250 lb. GVW optional for regular pickups; 6450 lb. optional for SuperCab.

Body Type	Factory Price	GVW	Shipping Weight	Prod. Total
Series F-250, 133 in. wheelbase, SuperCab: 155 in. wheelbase				
Pickup, 8 ft. Styleside	$13,807	6700	4039	—
Pickup, 8 ft. Styleside HD	$16,137	6700	N.A.	—
SuperCab HD	$17,264	6700	N.A.	—
Series F-350, 133 in. wheelbase				
Ch. & Cab, 133 in. wb.	$15,786	11,000	N.A.	—
Ch. & Cab, 137 in. wb.	$17,178	11,000	N.A.	—
Pickup, 8 ft. Styleside	$17,138	11,000	4465	—
Crew Cab, 168.8 in. wb.	$19,191	11,000	N.A.	—
Ch. & Cab, 161 in. wb.	$16,382	11,000	N.A.	—

STANDARD ENGINE: All models except F-250 HD and F-350: Engine Type: OHV In-line 6-cylinder. Bore x Stroke: 4.00 in. x 3.98 in. Displacement: 300 cu. in. Induction system: Multiple port electronic fuel injection. Number of main bearings-7. Compression Ratio: 8.8:1. Horsepower: Net: 145 @ 3400 rpm (F-150 with 2.73/3.08:1 axle ratios), 150 @ 3400 rpm (all other models under 8500 lb. GVWR). Torque: Net: 265 lb.-ft. @ 2000 rpm. (F-150 with 2.73/3.08:1 axle ratios), 260 @ 2000 rpm (all other models under 8500 lb. GVWR). Fuel Requirements: Unleaded.

OPTIONAL ENGINE: F-150 and F-250, under 8500 lb. GVW. 5.0 EFI: Engine type: OHV V-8. Cast-iron block and cylinder heads. Bore x Stroke: 4.00 in. x 3.00 in. Lifters: Hydraulic. Number of main bearings-5. Displacement: 302 cu. in. (5.0 liters). Lifters: Hydraulic. Carburetion: Multiport fuel injection with eight individual ports. Compression Ratio: 9.0:1. Horsepower: 185 @ 3800 rpm. Torque: Net: 270 lb.-ft. @ 2400 rpm. Fuel Requirements: Unleaded. Optional: 5.8 HO V-8. For F-150 and F-250. Engine type: OHV V-8. Bore x Stroke: 4.00 in. x 3.50 in. Displacement: 351 cu. in. (5.75 liters). Induction system: Multiport fuel injection. Number of main bearings-5. Horsepower: 210 @ 3800 rpm. Torque: 315 lb.-ft. @ 2800 rpm (models under 8500 lb. GVWR), 310 lb.-ft. @ 2800 rpm (models over 8500 lb. GVWR). Fuel Requirements: Unleaded. Optional: For F-250 HD and F-350 models. Engine Type: OHV V-8. Bore x Stroke: 4.36 in. x 3.85 in. Displacement: 460 cu. in. (7.5 liters). Induction system: Multiport fuel injection. Compression Ratio: 8.5:1. Number of main bearings-5. Horsepower: 230 @ 3600 rpm. Torque: Net: 390 lb.-ft. @ 2200 rpm. Fuel Requirements: Unleaded. Optional: For F-250 HD and F-350 models. Engine Type: OHV diesel V-8. Bore x Stroke: 4.00 in. x 4.18 in. Displacement: 420 cu. in. (6.9 liters). Induction system: Fuel injection. Compression Ratio: 21.5:1. Number of main bearings-5. Horsepower: 180 @ 3300 rpm. (High Altitude: 160 @ 3300 rpm). Torque: Net: 345 lb.-ft. @ 1400 rpm. (High Altitude: 305 lb.-ft. @ 1400 rpm). Fuel Requirements: Diesel.

CHASSIS FEATURES: Separate body and frame. F-150 regular pickup: Single-channel, 6 cross members, 36,000 psi. Section modulus: 3.21 cu. in. F-150 SuperCab pickup: Single-channel, 7 cross members, 36,000 psi. Section modulus: 3.79 cu. in. F-250 regular pickup: Single-channel, 7 cross members, 36,000 psi. Section modulus: 4.78 cu. in. F-250HD regular pickup: Single-channel, 6 cross members, 36,000 psi. Section modulus: 4.33 cu. in. F-250HD SuperCab pickup: Single-channel, 7 cross members, 36,000 psi. Section modulus: 4.87 cu. in. F-350 regular pickup: Single-channel, 6 cross members, 36,000 psi. Section modulus: 4.33 cu. in. F-350 crew cab pickup: Single-channel, 8 cross members, 36,000 psi. Section modulus: 4.94 cu. in.

SUSPENSION AND RUNNING GEAR: Front Suspension: F-150: Computer selected coil springs. Capacity: Regular cab: 2525 lb., SuperCab: 3100 lb. F-250: Single stage leaf, constant rate. Capacity: 3305 lb. F-250HD regular cab: Single stage, leaf, constant rate. Capacity: 3305 lb. SuperCab: Single stage, leaf, constant rate Capacity: 3920 lb. F-350: Regular cab: Single stage, leaf, constant rate. Capacity: 3400 lb. Crew cab: Single stage, leaf, constant rate. Capacity: 4100 lb. Rear Suspension: All models: Leaf, 2-stage, variable rate F-150 regular cab: Capacity: 3802 lb. SuperCab: 3802 lb. F-250 regular cab: Capacity: 4018 lb. F-250HD regular cab and SuperCab: Capacity: 5922 lb. F-350 regular cab: Capacity: 7833lb., crew cab: Capacity: 7370lb. Front Axle Type and Capacity: F-150 regular cab and SuperCab: 3800 lb. capacity, full-floating, Hotchkiss. F-250: 3850 lb. capacity, full-floating, Hotchkiss. F-250HD: Twin traction beam. Regular cab: 3850 lb. SuperCab: 4600 lb. capacity. F-350: 5000 lb. capacity. Rear Axle Type and Capacity: F-150: Semi-floating, 3800 lb. capacity. F-250: Semi-floating, Hotchkiss. Spicer model 60, 5300 lb. capacity. F-250HD: Regular cab and SuperCab: Full-floating. 6250 lb. capacity. F-350: 6250 lb. Transfer Case: Warner model 13-56 Ratios: 2.69, 1.00:1. Brakes: Type: Hydraulic, single-piston, floating caliper, Ford-designed disc front and drums rear, power assisted. Dimensions: Front: F-150: 11.72 in. disc, F-250 and F-350: 12.56 in. disc on all models. Rear: F-150: 11.03 in. x 2.25 in. F-250: Rear: 12.0 in. x 2.50 in. F-250 HD and F-350: 12 in. x 3.0 in. Wheels: F-150: 5-hole stamped disc, 15 in. x 6JK, disc. F-250 and F-350: 8-hole, stamped disc, 16 x 6K, disc. Tires: F-150: P235/75R-15XL. F-250: LT215/85R-16D, F-250HD: LT235/85R-16E. F-350: LT235/85R-16E. Optional: Tubeless tires in sizes to match Payload Package requirements. Steering: Ford XR-50, Power assisted, recirculating ball. Overall Ratio: All models: 17.0:1. Transmission: 5-speed manual overdrive. (Heavy-duty for F-250HD and F-350). Clutch: Heavy-duty hydraulic. F-150: 10.0 in. dia. F-250, F-250HD and F-350: 11.0 in. Optional: 4-speed manual, 3-speed and 4-speed automatics.

VEHICLE DIMENSIONS: Styleside pickups: Wheelbase: 116.8 in./133 in. Overall length: 194.1 in./210.2 in. Flareside pickups: Wheelbase: 116.8 in. Overall length: 194.1 in. Overall width: 116.8 in. wheelbase. Styleside and Flareside: 79.0 in.; SuperCab: Wheelbase: 155 in. Overall length: 232.2 in. Width: 79.0 in. Crew cab: Wheelbase: 168.4 in. Overall length: 245.7 in. Width: 79.0 in. Headroom: 40.4 in. (40.0 in. for SuperCab). Front legroom: 41 in. Front hip room: 61.7 in. Front shoulder room: 64.2 in.

CAPACITIES: Fuel Tank: F-150: Short wheelbase: 18.2 gal.; Long wheelbase: 19.0 gal. Optional: F-150: Short wheelbase: 16.5 gal. auxiliary tank. F-150 long wheelbase: 18.2 gal. auxiliary tank. SuperCab models: 138.8 in. wheelbase: Standard dual tanks with 34.7 gal. capacity. 155.0 in. wheelbase models: 37.2 gal. standard dual tanks. Crew cab models: Standard dual tanks with 37.2 gal. capacity. Chassis & cab models: 19.0 gal. Optional: 133 in. wheelbase: 18.2 gal. auxiliary fuel tank.

ACCOMMODATIONS: 3 occupants. SuperCab and Crew cab: 6 occupants.

INSTRUMENTATION: Voltmeter gauge, speedometer, odometer, engine oil pressure gauge, fuel gauge, transfer case indicator light low and high range), anti-lock brake system indicator light, engine coolant temperature gauge, charging system indicator light, check engine warning light, oil pressure/engine temperature indicator light, brake system/parking brake indicator light.

OPTIONS AND PRICES: Air conditioning: $806. Limited slip front axle (F-150 only): $252. Rear step, argent-painted bumper: $130. Rear step chrome bumper: $238 Camper/Trailer Towing Package: $461. Clearance roof lights: $52. Super cooling engine (F-Super-Duty only): $101. Power door locks and windows: $344. Handling Package: $156. Headliner and Insulation Package: $76. Engine block heater: $33 ($66 for diesel engine). Manual locking hubs: $60 credit. Light Convenience Group: $184 with Custom trim; $104 with XL trim. Bright low-mount swing-away mirrors: $91. Bright low-mount swing-out recreational mirrors: $100. Lower body side and wheel-lip moldings: $174 with custom trim. $117 with XL trim. Two-tone paint: $378 with custom trim; $296 with XL trim; $244 with XLT Lariat trim; $166 with Regular Cab Styleside with dual rear wheels. Deluxe tu-tone paint: $350 with custom trim; $267 with XL trim; $215 with XLT Lariat trim; $132 with regular cab Styleside with dual rear wheels. Heavy-Duty Service Package: $101-$332 depending upon engine, fuel tank selection and engine. Speed control/tilt steering wheel: $346. Heavy-duty front suspension: $135 with F-150 regular cab, $790 with F-250 regular cab, $71 with F-250 HD regular cab, $27 with F-350 regular cab. Heavy-duty rear suspension: $130, with F-150, $166, with F-250/F-250HD. Tachometer: $66. Trailer Towing Package: $461. Sport wheelcovers: $83. Deluxe argent styled steel wheels: $205. Forged aluminum deep-dish wheels: $382. Sliding rear window: $113. Electronic AM/FM stereo radio with clock: $96. Electronic AM/FM stereo radio with cassette tape player and clock: $196. Radio credit option: $61.

HISTORICAL FOOTNOTES: The Ford F series trucks were built in Kansas City, Missouri; Wayne, Michigan; Norfolk, Virginia; Twin Cities, Minnesota, and Oakvile, Ontario.

1991 PICKUP

Introduced as a 1990 model year running change and continuing into 1991 was the availability of the 5.0 liter engine with the electronic 4-speed automatic overdrive transmission. Automatic hub locks were added as standard equipment on F-250 and F-350 models (post Job #1, 1991). As a consequence, manual hub locks were revised to optional status on F-250 and F-350 models (post Job #1, 1991). During the 1991 model year improved corrosion protection, including two-sided galvanized steel hood, tailgate, dash panel and doors was implemented. For 1991 a tachometer was made standard for the XLT Trim Package. A new body side two-tone paint option was available for regular cab and SuperCab pickup models. It replaced the combination two-tone paint. A new "Touch Drive" electric shift transfer case was offered (with delayed availability) as an option on F-150 models equipped with the 5.0 liter V-8 and automatic overdrive transmission. Also new for 1991 was a lower accent two-tone on the F-150 XLT Lariat models. When the accent color was Currant Red, the body side moldings and bumper rubstrips were color-keyed to match. An optional Monotone Sport Model was offered (with late availability) for F-150 regular cab XLT Lariat models. Also new for 1991 was a F-150 "Nite" Package for regular cab and SuperCab models with either the 5.0 or 5.9 liter V-8 engines. Its content included XLT Lariat trim, exterior blackout treatment, special body side tape stripe and "NITE" decals, sliding rear window, deep-dish forged aluminum wheels, P235/75R x 15XL OWL All-Season tires, Light/Convenience Group, air conditioning, Handling Package, AM/FM stereo with cassette tape player and clock, and "Nite" floor mats.

The lower body side and wheel-lip moldings were deleted for 1991 as a free-standing option. Also deleted as an option for pickup models was the in-box spare tire carrier. Replacing alpine green in the exterior color selection was Emerald green metallic.

I.D. DATA: The V.I.N. had 17 entries. The first three characters identified the manufacturer, make and type of vehicle. The next entry, a letter designated the GVW rating. The next three characters identified the series and body style. The eighth character identified the engine. A check digit following, then an entry identifying the assembly plant. The final digits represented the sequential production number.

Body Type	Factory Price	GVW	Shipping Weight	Prod. Total
Series F-150, 117 in., 133 in. wheelbase. SuperCab: 155 in. wheelbase				
Pickup, 6.5 ft. Styleside	$14,024	6050	3817	—
Pickup, 8.0 ft. Styleside	$14,365	6050	4002	—
SuperCab, 139 in. wb.	$15,439	6050	3962	—
SuperCab, 155 in. wb.	$15,673	6050	N.A.	—

NOTE 1: 6250 lb. GVW optional for regular pickups; 6450 lb. optional for SuperCab.

Body Type	Factory Price	GVW	Shipping Weight	Prod. Total
Series F-250, 133 in. wheelbase, SuperCab: 155 in. wheelbase				
Pickup, 8 ft. Styleside	$14,867	6700	4039	—
Pickup, 8 ft. Styleside HD	$17,194	6700	N.A.	—
SuperCab HD	$18,362	6700	N.A.	—
Series F-350, 133 in. wheelbase				
Ch. & Cab, 133 in. wb.	$16,849	11,000	N.A.	—
Ch. & Cab, 137 in. wb.	$18,293	11,000	N.A.	—
Pickup, 8 ft. Styleside	$18,196	11,000	4465	—
Crew Cab, 168.8 in. wb.	$20,419	11,000	N.A.	—
Ch. & Cab, 161 in. wb.	$18,422	11,000	N.A.	—

STANDARD ENGINE: All models except F-250 HD and F-350: Engine Type: OHV In-line 6-cylinder. Bore x Stroke: 4.00 in. x 3.98 in. Displacement: 300 cu. in. Induction system: Multiple port electronic fuel injection. Number of main bearings-7. Compression Ratio: 8.8:1. Horsepower: Net: 145 @ 3400 rpm (F-150 with 2.73/3.08:1 axle ratios), 150 @ 3400 rpm (all other models). Torque: Net: 265 lb.-ft. @ 2000 rpm. (F-150 with 2.73/3.08:1 axle ratios), 260 @ 2000 rpm (all other models). Fuel Requirements: Unleaded.

OPTIONAL ENGINE: F-150 and F-250, under 8500 lb. GVW. 5.0 EFI: Engine type: OHV V-8. Cast-iron block and cylinder heads. Bore x Stroke: 4.00 in. x 3.00 in. Lifters: Hydraulic. Number of main bearings-5. Displacement: 302 cu. in. (5.0 liters). Lifters: Hydraulic. Carburetion: Multiport fuel injection with eight individual ports. Compression Ratio: 9.0:1. Horsepower: 185 @ 3800 rpm. Torque: Net: 270 lb.-ft. @ 2400 rpm. Fuel Requirements: Unleaded. Optional: 5.8 HO V-8. For F-150 and F-250. Engine type: OHV V-8. Bore x Stroke: 4.00 in. x 3.50 in. Displacement: 351 cu. in. (5.75 liters). Induction system: Multiport fuel injection. Number of main bearings-5. Horsepower: 210 @ 3800 rpm. Torque: 315 lb.-ft. @ 2800 rpm (models under 8500 lb. GVWR), 310 lb.-ft. @ 2800 rpm (models over 8500 lb. GVWR). Fuel Requirements: Unleaded. Optional: For F-250 HD and F-350 models. Engine Type: OHV V-8. Bore x Stroke: 4.36 in. x 3.85 in. Displacement: 460 cu. in. (7.5 liters). Induction system: Multiport fuel injection. Compression Ratio: 8.5:1. Number of main bearings-5. Horsepower: 230 @ 3600 rpm. Torque: Net: 390 lb.-ft. @ 2200 rpm. Fuel Requirements: Unleaded. Optional: For F-250 HD and F-350 models. Engine Type: OHV diesel V-8. Bore x Stroke: 4.00 in. x 4.18 in. Displacement: 420 cu. in. (6.9 liters). Induction system: Fuel injection. Compression Ratio: 21.5:1. Number of main bearings-5. Horsepower: 180 @ 3300 rpm. (High Altitude: 160 @ 3300 rpm). Torque: Net: 345 lb.-ft. @ 1400 rpm. (High Altitude: 305 lb.-ft. @ 1400 rpm). Fuel Requirements: Diesel.

CHASSIS FEATURES: Separate body and frame. F-150 regular pickup: Single-channel, 6 cross members, 36,000 psi. Section modulus: 3.21 cu. in. F-150 SuperCab pickup: Single-channel, 7 cross members, 36,000 psi. Section modulus: 3.79 cu. in. F-250 Regular Pickup: Single-channel, 7 cross members, 36,000 psi. Section modulus: 4.78 cu. in. F-250HD regular pickup: Single-channel, 6 cross members, 36,000 psi. Section modulus: 4.33 cu. in. F-250HD SuperCab pickup: Single-channel, 7 cross members, 36,000 psi. Section modulus: 4.87 cu. in. F-350 regular pickup: Single-channel, 6 cross members, 36,000 psi. Section modulus: 4.33 cu. in. F-350 crew cab pickup: Single-channel, 8 cross members, 36,000 psi. Section modulus: 4.94 cu. in.

SUSPENSION AND RUNNING GEAR: Front Suspension: F-150: Computer selected coil springs. Capacity: Regular cab: 2525 lb., SuperCab: 3100 lb. F-250: Single stage leaf, constant rate. Capacity: 3305 lb. F-250HD regular cab: Single stage, leaf, constant rate. Capacity: 3305 lb. SuperCab: Single stage, leaf, constant rate Capacity: 3920 lb. F-350: Regular cab: Single stage, leaf, constant rate. Capacity: 3400 lb. Crew cab: Single stage, leaf, constant rate. Capacity: 4100 lb. Rear Suspension: All models: Leaf, 2-stage, variable rate F-150 regular cab: Capacity: 3802 lb. SuperCab: 3802 lb. F-250 regular cab: Capacity: 4018 lb. F-250HD regular cab and SuperCab: Capacity: 5922 lb. F-350 regular cab: Capacity: 7833 lb., crew cab: Capacity: 7370 lb. Front Axle Type and Capacity: F-150 regular cab and SuperCab: 3800 lb. capacity, full-floating, Hotchkiss. F-250: 3850 lb. capacity, full-floating, Hotchkiss. F-250HD: Twin traction beam. Regular cab: 3850 lb. SuperCab: 4600 lb. capacity. F-350: 5000lb. capacity. Rear Axle Type and Capacity: F-150: Semi-floating, 3800 lb. capacity. F-250: Semi-floating, Hotchkiss. Spicer model 60, 5300 lb. capacity. F-250HD: Regular cab and SuperCab: Full-floating. 6250lb. capacity. F-350: 6250lb. Transfer Case: Warner model 13-56 Ratios: 2.69, 1.00:1. Brakes: Type: Hydraulic, single-piston, floating caliper, Ford-designed disc front and drums rear, power assisted. Dimensions: Front: F-150: 11.72 in. disc, F-250 and F-350: 12.56 in. disc on all models. Rear: F-150: 11.03 in. x 2.25 in. F-250: Rear: 12.0 in. x 2.50 in. F-250 HD and F-350: 12 in. x 3.0 in. Wheels: F-150: 5-hole stamped disc, 15 in. x 6JK, disc. F-250 and F-350: 8-hole, stamped disc, 16 x 6K, disc. Tires: F-150: P235/75R-15XL. F-250: LT215/85R-16D, F-250HD: LT235/85R-16E. F-350: LT235/85R-16E. Optional: Tubeless tires in sizes to match Payload Package requirements. Steering: Ford XR-50, Power assisted, recirculating ball. Overall Ratio: All models: 17.0:1. Transmission: 5-speed manual overdrive. (Heavy-duty for F-250HD and F-350). Clutch: Heavy-duty hydraulic. F-150: 10.0 in. dia. F-250, F-250HD and F-350: 11.0 in. Optional: 4-speed manual, 3-speed and 4-speed automatics.

VEHICLE DIMENSIONS: Styleside pickups: Wheelbase: 116.8 in./133 in. Overall length: 194.1 in./210.2 in. Flareside pickups: Wheelbase: 116.8 in. Overall length: 194.1 in. Overall width: 116.8 in. wheelbase. Styleside and Flareside: 79.0 in.; SuperCab: Wheelbase: 155 in. Overall length: 232.2 in. Width: 79.0 in. Crew cab: Wheelbase: 168.4 in. Overall length: 245.7 in. Width: 79.0 in. Headroom: 40.4 in. (40.0 in. for SuperCab). Front legroom: 41 in. Front hip room: 61.7 in. Front shoulder room: 64.2 in.

CAPACITIES: Fuel Tank: F-150: Short wheelbase: 18.2 gal.; Long wheelbase: 19.0 gal. Optional: F-150: Short wheelbase: 16.5 gal. auxiliary tank. F-150 long wheelbase: 18.2 gal. auxiliary tank. SuperCab models: 138.8 in. wheelbase: Standard dual tanks with 34.7 gal. capacity. 155.0 in. wheelbase models: 37.2 gal. standard dual tanks. Crew cab models: Standard dual tanks with 37.2 gal. capacity. Chassis & cab models: 19.0 gal. Optional: 133 in. wheelbase: 18.2 gal. auxiliary fuel tank.

ACCOMMODATIONS: 3 occupants. SuperCab and crew cab: 6 occupants.

INSTRUMENTATION: Voltmeter gauge, speedometer, odometer, engine oil pressure gauge, fuel gauge, transfer case indicator light low and high range), anti-lock brake system indicator light, engine coolant temperature gauge, charging system indicator light, check engine warning light, oil pressure/engine temperature indicator light, brake system/parking brake indicator light.

OPTIONS: Air conditioning. Limited slip front axle (F-150 only). Rear step, argent-painted bumper. Rear step chrome bumper. Camper/Trailer Towing Package. Clearance roof lights. Super cooling engine (F-Super-Duty only). Power door locks and windows. Handling Package. Headliner and Insulation Package. Engine block heater. Manual locking hubs-credit. Light Convenience Group. Bright low-mount swing-away mirrors. Bright low-mount swing-out recreational mirrors. Deluxe tu-tone paint. Heavy-Duty Service Package. Speed control/tilt steering wheel. Heavy-duty front suspension. Heavy-duty rear suspension. Tachometer. Trailer Towing Package. Sport wheelcovers. Deluxe Argent styled steel wheels. Forged aluminum deep-dish wheels. Sliding rear window. Electronic AM/FM stereo radio with clock. Electronic AM/FM stereo radio with cassette tape player and clock. Radio credit option. Body side two-tone paint. Touch Drive electric shift transfer case for F-150. Lower accent two-tone paint for F-150 XLT Lariat.

HISTORICAL FOOTNOTES: At the start of the 1991 model year, the F series Ford trucks had outsold every other vehicle in the U.S. for the past eight years, car or truck, and had been the best-selling pickup in the U.S. for 13 straight years.

1992 PICKUP

The 1992 Ford F series trucks had a freshened exterior appearance due to a new front end design, revised body side moldings, exterior badges, graphics and tailgate. New bright exterior electric aerodynamic mirrors were available for all models except the F-350 regular cab and F-Super-Duty chassis cab. New bright manual aerodynamic mirrors were standard on all models except the 11,000 lb. GVWR F-350 regular chassis cab and F-Super-Duty chassis cab. The 1992 interior featured a new color-keyed instrument panel with black applique, new clusters, larger locking glove box. Heater/air conditioning rotary controls and power point. New door trim panels included a reflector with Custom/XL trim and a light/reflector with XLT Lariat trim. Not offered for 1992 was the F-250 regular cab with an 8500 lb. rating. Also removed from the 1992 model lineup were the F-350 chassis-cab models. A number of new options were available for 1992. A body side accent paint stripe was now optional for the F-150 XL models. It previously had been standard on all XL models. This changes was phased in during the 1992 model run. P265/75R x 15 OWL All-Terrain tires were added (with delayed availability) as an option for all F-150 models. Also offered for all F-150 models were two new wheel options — 15 x 7.5 in. argent styled steel wheels and 15 x 7.5 in. chrome styled steel wheels. A new Custom Upgrade Package which included cloth and vinyl bench seat, Headliner and Insulation Package, bright low-mount swing-out mirrors, and an AM/FM stereo radio with clock was available for F-250/F-350 regular cab and F-Super-Duty models.

1992 Ford F-150 SuperCab pickup

The content of two options were revised for 1992. A removable mini-console which attached to the bench seat was included as part of the Light/Convenience Group on regular cab and crew cab models. The Captain's chairs and cloth flight bench seats now included a power lumbar support. Front bench seats now included adjustable head restraints for outboard seating positions.

New, lower priced special models were added to the F-150 series. Also debuting during the model year were new short wheelbase Flareside F-150 models. Several major technical/functional changes were made for 1992. Automatic hub locks were made standard for all F-250/F-350 models. The manual hub locks were available as an option for all F-250/F-350 models. This development had earlier been instituted as a running change during the 1991 model year. A "Soft Ride" suspension option was now available for all F-250 HD regular cab models over 8500 lb. GVWR.

I.D. DATA: The V.I.N. had 17 entries. The first three characters identified the manufacturer make and type of vehicle. The next entry, a letter designated the GVW rating. The next three characters identified the series and body style. The eighth character identified the engine. A check digit following, then an entry identifying the assembly plant. The final digits represented the sequential production number.

Body Type	Factory Price	GVW	Shipping Weight	Prod. Total
Series F-150, 117 in., 133 in. wheelbase. SuperCab-155 in. wheelbase				
Pickup, 6.5 ft. Styleside S	$13,471	N.A.	N.A.	—
Pickup, 8.0 ft. Styleside S	$13,799	N.A.	N.A.	—
Pickup, 6.5 ft. Styleside Cust.	$15,021	6050	3817	—
Pickup, 8.0 ft. Styleside Cust.	$15,371	6050	4002	—
Pickup Flareside	$16,187	N.A.	N.A.	—
SuperCab, 139 in. wb.	$16,285	6050	3962	—
SuperCab, 155 in. wb.	$16,520	6050	N.A.	—
SuperCab Flareside	$17,296	N.A.	N.A.	—

NOTE 1: 6250 lb. GVW optional for regular pickups; 6450 lb. optional for SuperCab.

Body Type	Factory Price	GVW	Shipping Weight	Prod. Total
Series F-250, 133 in. wheelbase, SuperCab: 155 in. wheelbase				
Pickup, 8 ft. Styleside HD	$18,092	6700	N.A.	—
SuperCab HD	$19,246	6700	N.A.	—
Series F-350, 133 in. wheelbase				
Pickup, 8 ft. Styleside	$18,470	11,000	4465	—
Crew Cab, 168.8 in. wb.	$21,018	11,000	N.A.	—

STANDARD ENGINE: All models except F-250 HD and F-350: Engine Type: OHV In-line 6-cylinder. Bore x Stroke: 4.00 in. x 3.98 in. Displacement: 300 cu. in. Induction system: Multiple port electronic fuel injection. Number of main bearings-7. Compression Ratio: 8.8:1. Horsepower: Net: 145 @ 3400 rpm (F-150 with 2.73/3.08:1 axle ratios), 150 @ 3400 rpm (all other models). Torque: Net: 265 lb.-ft. @ 2000 rpm. (F-150 with 2.73/3.08:1 axle ratios), 260 @ 2000 rpm (all other models). Fuel Requirements: Unleaded.

OPTIONAL ENGINE: F-150 and F-250, under 8500 lb. GVW. 5.0 EFI: Engine type: OHV V-8. Cast-iron block and cylinder heads. Bore x Stroke: 4.00 in. x 3.00 in. Lifters: Hydraulic. Number of main bearings-5. Displacement: 302 cu. in. (5.0 liters). Lifters: Hydraulic. Induction system: Multiport fuel injection with eight individual ports. Compression Ratio: 9.0:1. Horsepower: 185 @ 3800 rpm. Torque: Net: 270 lb.-ft. @ 2400 rpm. Fuel Requirements: Unleaded. Optional: 5.8 HO V-8. For F-150 and F-250. Engine type: OHV V-8. Bore x Stroke: 4.00 in. x 3.50 in. Displacement: 351 cu. in. (5.75 liters). Induction system: Multiport fuel injection. Compression ratio: 8.8:1. Number of main bearings-5. Horsepower: 200 @ 3800 rpm. Torque: 300lb.-ft. @ 2800 rpm. Fuel Requirements: Unleaded. Optional: For F-250 HD and F-350 models. Engine Type: OHV V-8. Bore x Stroke: 4.36 in. x 3.85 in. Displacement: 460 cu. in. (7.5 liters). Induction system: Multiport fuel injection. Compression Ratio: 8.5:1. Number of main bearings-5. Horsepower: 230 @ 3600 rpm. Torque: Net: 390 lb.-ft. @ 2200 rpm. Fuel Requirements: Unleaded. Optional: For F-250 HD and F-350 models. Engine Type: OHV diesel V-8. Bore x Stroke: 4.00 in. x 4.18 in. Displacement: 420 cu. in. (6.9 liters). Induction system: Fuel injection. Compression Ratio: 21.5:1. Number of main bearings-5. Horsepower: 180 @ 3300 rpm. (High Altitude: 160 @ 3300 rpm). Torque: Net: 345 lb.-ft. @ 1400 rpm. (High Altitude: 305 lb.-ft. @ 1400 rpm). Fuel Requirements: Diesel.

CHASSIS FEATURES: Separate body and frame. F-150 regular pickup: Single-channel, 6 cross members, 36,000 psi. Section modulus: 3.21 cu. in. F-150 SuperCab pickup: Single-channel, 7 cross members, 36,000 psi. Section modulus: 3.79 cu. in. F-250 regular pickup: Single-channel, 7 cross members, 36,000 psi. Section modulus: 4.78 cu. in. F-250HD Regular Pickup: Single-channel, 6 cross members, 36,000 psi. Section modulus: 4.33 cu. in. F-250HD SuperCab pickup: Single-channel, 7 cross members, 36,000 psi. Section modulus: 4.87 cu. in. F-350 regular pickup: Single-channel, 6 cross members, 36,000 psi. Section modulus: 4.33 cu. in. F-350 crew cab pickup: Single-channel, 8 cross members, 36,000 psi. Section modulus: 4.94 cu. in.

SUSPENSION AND RUNNING GEAR: Front Suspension: F-150: Computer selected coil springs. Capacity: Regular cab: 2525 lb., SuperCab: 3100 lb. F-250: Single stage leaf, constant rate. Capacity: 3305 lb. F-250HD regular cab: Single stage, leaf, constant rate. Capacity: 3305 lb. SuperCab: Single stage, leaf, constant rate Capacity: 3920 lb. F-350: Regular cab: Single stage, leaf, constant rate. Capacity: 3400 lb. Crew cab: Single stage, leaf, constant rate. Capacity: 4100 lb. Rear Suspension: All models: Leaf, 2-stage, variable rate F-150 regular cab: Capacity: 3802 lb. SuperCab: 3802 lb. F-250 regular cab: Capacity: 4018 lb. F-250HD regular cab and SuperCab: Capacity: 5922 lb. F-350 regular cab: Capacity: 7833 lb., crew cab: Capacity: 7370 lb. Front Axle Type and Capacity: F-150 regular cab and SuperCab: 3800 lb. capacity, full-floating, Hotchkiss. F-250: 3850 lb. capacity, full-floating,

Hotchkiss. F-250HD: Twin traction beam. Regular cab: 3850 lb. SuperCab: 4600 lb. capacity. F-350: 5000 lb. capacity. Rear Axle Type and Capacity: F-150: Semi-floating, 3800 lb. capacity. F-250: Semi-floating, Hotchkiss. Spicer model 60, 5300 lb. capacity. F-250HD: Regular cab and SuperCab: Full-floating. 6250 lb. capacity. F-350: 6250 lb. Transfer Case: Warner model 13-56 Ratios: 2.69, 1.00:1. Brakes: Type: Hydraulic, single-piston, floating caliper, Ford-designed disc front and drums rear, power assisted. Dimensions: Front: F-150: 11.72 in. disc, F-250 and F-350: 12.56 in. disc on all models. Rear: F-150: 11.03 in. x 2.25 in. F-250: Rear: 12.0 in. x 2.50 in. F-250 HD and F-350: 12 in. x 3.0 in. Wheels: F-150: 5-hole stamped disc, 15 in. x 6JK, disc. F-250 and F-350: 8-hole, stamped disc, 16 x 6K, disc. Tires: F-150: P235/75R-15XL. F-250: LT215/85R-16D, F-250HD: LT235/85R-16E. F-350: LT235/85R-16E. Optional: Tubeless tires in sizes to match Payload Package requirements. Steering: Ford XR-50, Power assisted, recirculating ball. Overall Ratio: All models: 17.0:1. Transmission: 5-speed manual overdrive. (Heavy-duty for F-250HD and F-350). Clutch: Heavy-duty hydraulic. F-150: 10.0 in. dia. F-250, F-250HD and F-350: 11.0 in. Optional: 4-speed manual, 3-speed and 4-speed automatics.

VEHICLE DIMENSIONS: Styleside pickups: Wheelbase: 116.8 in./133 in. Overall length: 194.1 in./210.2 in. Flareside pickups: Wheelbase: 116.8 in. Overall length: 194.1 in. Overall width: 116.8 in. wheelbase. Styleside and Flareside: 79.0 in.; SuperCab: Wheelbase: 155 in. Overall length: 232.2 in. Width: 79.0 in. Crew cab: Wheelbase: 168.4 in. Overall length: 245.7 in. Width: 79.0 in. Headroom: 40.4 in. (40.0 in. for SuperCab). Front legroom: 41 in. Front hip room: 61.7 in. Front shoulder room: 64.2 in.

CAPACITIES: Fuel Tank: F-150: Short wheelbase: 18.2 gal.; Long wheelbase: 19.0 gal. Optional: F-150: Short wheelbase: 16.5 gal. auxiliary ιank. F-150 long wheelbase: 18.2 gal. auxiliary tank. SuperCab models: 138.8 in. wheelbase: Standard dual tanks with 34.7 gal. capacity. 155.0 in. wheelbase models: 37.2 gal. standard dual tanks. Crew cab models: Standard dual tanks with 37.2 gal. capacity. Chassis & cab models: 19.0 gal. Optional: 133 in. wheelbase: 18.2 gal. auxiliary fuel tank.

ACCOMMODATIONS: 3 occupants. SuperCab and crew cab: 6 occupants.

INSTRUMENTATION: Voltmeter gauge, speedometer, odometer, engine oil pressure gauge, fuel gauge, transfer case indicator light low and high range), anti-lock brake system indicator light, engine coolant temperature gauge, charging system indicator light, check engine warning light, oil pressure/engine temperature indicator light, brake system/parking brake indicator light.

OPTIONS: Air conditioning. Limited slip front axle (F-150 only). Rear step, argent-painted bumper. Rear step chrome bumper. Camper Towing Package. Clearance roof lights. Captain's chairs (SuperCab). Super cooling engine (F-Super-Duty only). Custom Upgrade Package. 4x4 decal not included. Power door locks and windows. Handling Package. Headliner and Insulation Package. Engine block heater. Manual locking hubs-credit. Light Convenience Group. Bright low-mount swing-away mirrors. Bright electric mirrors. Bright low-mount swing-away mirrors. Bright swing-out recreational mirrors. Body side two-tone paint. Deluxe tu-tone paint. Lower accent two-tone paint. Dual body side paint stripe. Payload Package. Speed control/tilt steering wheel. Heavy-duty front suspension. Heavy-duty rear suspension. Soft Ride suspension. Tachometer. Trailer Towing Package. Sport wheelcovers. Deluxe argent styled steel wheels. Forged aluminum deep-dish wheels. Sliding rear window. Electronic AM/FM stereo radio with clock. Electronic AM/FM stereo radio with cassette tape player and clock. Radio credit option. Touch Drive electric shift transfer case for F-150.

HISTORICAL FOOTNOTES: From its basic plain-Jane work truck origin, the F series Ford truck had, by 1992 evolved into a line of work, personal, and recreational trucks with a bigger choice of models than any single car line. The F series trucks were again the top-selling vehicle in the U.S.

1993 PICKUP

Only minor changes were incorporated into the design of the F series trucks for 1993. The custom name was dropped for 1993. The XL identification replaced custom on the F-150/250/350/ models. Four options were deleted for 1993. These consisted of the dual body side stripe option, the 15 inch Sport wheelcovers, the Sport Appearance Package and the Custom Upgrade Package. Minor option changes involved the use of a new electronic speed control providing faster response, improved speed-holding capacity and a speed tap-up/tap-down feature in 1 mph increments. The SuperCab rear bench seat was redesigned for improved comfort by the raising of its height and the adding of a seat bolster (late availability).

1993 Ford XLT regular cab pickup

I.D. DATA: The V.I.N. had 17 entries. The first three characters identified the manufacturer, make and type of vehicle. The next entry, a letter designated the GVW rating. The next three characters identified the series and body style. The eighth character identified the engine. A check digit following, then an entry identifying the assembly plant. The final digits represented the sequential production number.

Body Type	Factory Price	GVW	Shipping Weight	Prod. Total
Series F-150, 117 in., 133 in. wheelbase. SuperCab-155 in. wheelbase				
Pickup, 6.5 ft. Styleside S	$N.A.	N.A.	N.A.	—
Pickup, 8.0 ft. Styleside S	$N.A.	N.A.	N.A.	—
Pickup, 6.5 ft. Styleside Cust.	$N.A.	6050	3817	—
Pickup, 8.0 ft. Styleside Cust.	$N.A.	6050	4002	—
Pickup Flareside	$N.A.	N.A.	N.A.	—
SuperCab, 139 in. wb.	$N.A.	6050	3962	—
SuperCab, 155 in. wb.	$N.A.	6050	N.A.	—
SuperCab Flareside	$N.A.	N.A.	N.A.	—

NOTE 1: 6250 lb. GVW optional for Regular Pickups; 6450 lb. optional for SuperCab.

Series F-250, 133 in. wheelbase, SuperCab: 155 in. wheelbase				
Pickup, 8 ft. Styleside HD	$N.A.	6700	N.A.	—
SuperCab HD	$N.A.	6700	N.A.	—
Series F-350, 133 in. wheelbase				
Pickup, 8 ft. Styleside	$N.A.	11,000	4465	—
Crew Cab, 168.8 in. wb.	$N.A.	11,000	N.A.	—

STANDARD ENGINE: All models except F-250 HD and F-350: Engine Type: OHV In-line 6-cylinder. Bore x Stroke: 4.00 in. x 3.98 in. Displacement: 300 cu. in. Induction system: Multiple port electronic fuel injection. Number of main bearings-7. Compression Ratio: 8.8:1. Horsepower: Net: 145 @ 3400 rpm (F-150 with 2.73/3.08:1 axle ratios), 150 @ 3400 rpm (all other models). Torque: Net: 265 lb.-ft. @ 2000 rpm. (F-150 with 2.73/3.08:1 axle ratios), 260 @ 2000 rpm (all other models). Fuel Requirements: Unleaded.

OPTIONAL ENGINE: F-150 and F-250, under 8500 lb. GVW. 5.0 EFI: Engine type: OHV V-8. Cast-iron block and cylinder heads. Bore x Stroke: 4.00 in. x 3.00 in. Lifters: Hydraulic. Number of main bearings-5. Displacement: 302 cu. in. (5.0 liters). Lifters: Hydraulic. Induction system: Multiport fuel injection with eight individual ports. Compression Ratio: 9.0:1. Horsepower: 185 @ 3800 rpm. Torque: Net: 270 lb.-ft. @ 2400 rpm. Fuel Requirements: Unleaded. Optional: 5.8 HO V-8. For F-150 and F-250. Engine type: OHV V-8. Bore x Stroke: 4.00 in. x 3.50 in. Displacement: 351 cu. in. (5.75 liters). Induction system: Multiport fuel injection. Compression ratio: 8.8:1. Number of main bearings-5. Horsepower: 200 @ 3800 rpm. Torque: 300 lb.-ft. @ 2800 rpm. Fuel Requirements: Unleaded. Optional: For F-250 HD and F-350 models. Engine Type: OHV V-8. Bore x Stroke: 4.36 in. x 3.85 in. Displacement: 460 cu. in. (7.5 liters). Induction system: Multiport fuel injection. Compression Ratio: 8.5:1. Number of main bearings-5. Horsepower: 230 @ 3600 rpm. Torque: Net: 390 lb.-ft. @ 2200 rpm. Fuel Requirements: Unleaded. Optional: For F-250 HD and F-350 models. Engine Type: OHV diesel V-8. Bore x Stroke: 4.00 in. x 4.18 in. Displacement: 420 cu. in. (6.9 liters). Induction system: Fuel injection. Compression Ratio: 21.5:1. Number of main bearings-5. Horsepower: 180 @ 3300 rpm. (High Altitude: 160 @ 3300 rpm). Torque: Net: 345 lb.-ft. @ 1400 rpm. (High Altitude: 305 lb.-ft. @ 1400 rpm). Fuel Requirements: Diesel.

CHASSIS FEATURES: Separate body and frame. F-150 regular pickup: Single-channel, 6 cross members, 36,000 psi. Section modulus: 3.21 cu. in. F-150 SuperCab pickup: Single-channel, 7 cross members, 36,000 psi. Section modulus: 3.79 cu. in. F-250 regular pickup: Single-channel, 7 cross members, 36,000 psi. Section modulus: 4.78 cu. in. F-250HD regular pickup: Single-channel, 6 cross members, 36,000 psi. Section modulus: 4.33 cu. in. F-250HD SuperCab pickup: Single-channel, 7 cross members, 36,000 psi. Section modulus: 4.87 cu. in. F-350 regular pickup: Single-channel, 6 cross members, 36,000 psi. Section modulus: 4.33 cu. in. F-350 crew cab pickup: Single-channel, 8 cross members, 36,000 psi. Section modulus: 4.94 cu. in.

SUSPENSION AND RUNNING GEAR: Front Suspension: F-150: Computer selected coil springs. Capacity: Regular cab: 2525 lb., SuperCab: 3100 lb. F-250: Single stage leaf, constant rate. Capacity: 3305 lb. F-250HD regular cab: Single stage, leaf, constant rate. Capacity: 3305 lb. SuperCab: Single stage, leaf, constant rate Capacity: 3920 lb. F-350: Regular cab: Single stage, leaf, constant rate. Capacity: 3400 lb. Crew cab: Single stage, leaf, constant rate. Capacity: 4100 lb. Rear Suspension: All models: Leaf, 2-stage, variable rate F-150 regular cab: Capacity: 3802 lb. SuperCab: 3802 lb. F-250 regular cab: Capacity: 4018 lb. F-250HD regular cab and SuperCab: Capacity: 5922 lb. F-350 regular cab: Capacity: 7833 lb., crew cab: Capacity: 7370 lb. Front Axle Type and Capacity: F-150 regular cab and SuperCab: 3800 lb. capacity, full-floating, Hotchkiss. F-250: 3850 lb. capacity, full-floating, Hotchkiss. F-250HD: Twin traction beam. Regular cab: 3850 lb. SuperCab: 4600 lb. capacity. F-350: 5000 lb. capacity. Rear Axle Type and Capacity: F-150: Semi-floating, 3800 lb. capacity. F-250: Semi-floating, Hotchkiss. Spicer model 60, 5300 lb. capacity. F-250HD: Regular cab and SuperCab: Full-floating. 6250 lb. capacity. F-350: 6250 lb. Transfer Case: Warner model 13-56 Ratios: 2.69, 1.00:1. Brakes: Type: Hydraulic, single-piston, floating caliper, Ford-designed disc front and drums rear, power assisted. Dimensions: Front: F-150: 11.72 in. disc, F-250 and F-350: 12.56 in. disc on all models. Rear: F-150: 11.03 in. x 2.25 in. F-250: Rear: 12.0 in. x 2.50 in. F-250 HD and F-350: 12 in. x 3.0 in. Wheels: F-150: 5-hole stamped disc, 15 in. x 6JK, disc. F-250 and F-350: 8-hole, stamped disc, 16 x 6K, disc. Tires: F-150: P235/75R-15XL. F-250: LT215/85R-16D, F-250HD: LT235/85R-16E. F-350: LT235/85R-16E. Optional: Tubeless tires in sizes to match Payload Package requirements. Steering: Ford XR-50, Power assisted, recirculating ball. Overall Ratio: All models: 17.0:1. Transmission: 5-speed manual overdrive. (Heavy-duty for F-250HD and F-350). Clutch: Heavy-duty hydraulic. F-150: 10.0 in. dia. F-250, F-250HD and F-350: 11.0 in. Optional: 4-speed manual, 3-speed and 4-speed automatics.

VEHICLE DIMENSIONS: Styleside pickups: Wheelbase: 116.8 in./133 in. Overall length: 194.1 in./210.2 in. Flareside pickups: Wheelbase: 116.8 in. Overall length: 194.1 in. Overall width: 116.8 in. wheelbase. Styleside and Flareside: 79.0 in. SuperCab: Wheelbase: 155 in. Overall length: 232.2 in. Width: 79.0 in. Crew cab: Wheelbase: 168.4 in. Overall length: 245.7 in. Width: 79.0 in. Headroom: 40.4 in. (40.0 in. for SuperCab). Front legroom: 41 in. Front hip room: 61.7 in. Front shoulder room: 64.2 in.

CAPACITIES: Fuel Tank: F-150: Short wheelbase: 18.2 gal.; Long wheelbase: 19.0 gal. Optional: F-150: Short wheelbase: 16.5 gal. auxiliary tank. F-150 long wheelbase: 18.2 gal. auxiliary tank. SuperCab models: 138.8 in. wheelbase: Standard dual tanks with 34.7 gal. capacity. 155.0 in. wheelbase models: 37.2 gal. standard dual tanks. Crew cab models: Standard dual tanks with 37.2 gal. capacity. Chassis & cab models: 19.0 gal. Optional: 133 in. wheelbase: 18.2 gal. auxiliary fuel tank.

ACCOMMODATIONS: 3 occupants. SuperCab and crew cab: 6 occupants.

INSTRUMENTATION: Voltmeter gauge, speedometer, odometer, engine oil pressure gauge, fuel gauge, transfer case indicator light low and high range), anti-lock brake system indicator light, engine coolant temperature gauge, charging system indicator light, check engine warning light, oil pressure/engine temperature indicator light, brake system/parking brake indicator light.

OPTIONS: Air conditioning. Limited slip front axle (F-150 only). Rear step, argent painted bumper. Rear step chrome bumper. Camper Towing Package. Clearance roof lights. Captain's chairs (SuperCab). Super cooling engine (F-Super-Duty only). 4x4 decal not included. Power door locks and windows. Handling Package. Headliner and Insulation Package. Engine block heater. Manual locking hubs-credit. Light Convenience Group. Bright low-mount swing-away mirrors. Bright electric mirrors. Bright low-mount swing-away mirrors. Bright swing-out recreational mirrors. Body side two-tone paint. Deluxe tu-tone paint. Lower accent two-tone paint. Payload Package. Speed control/tilt steering wheel. Heavy-duty front suspension. Heavy-duty rear suspension. Soft Ride suspension. Tachometer. Trailer Towing Package. Deluxe argent styled steel wheels. Forged aluminum deep-dish wheels. Sliding rear window. Electronic AM/FM stereo radio with clock. Electronic AM/FM stereo radio with cassette tape player and clock. radio credit option. Touch Drive electric shift transfer case for F-150.

HISTORICAL FOOTNOTES: The platform of the 1993 F series trucks had been originally introduced in the fall of 1979 as the 1980 model.

FORD BRONCO
1966-1993

1966 BRONCO

1966 Ford Bronco roadster

Ford introduced the Bronco in August, 1965 as a 1966 model. At the time of the Bronco's introduction some critics questioned Ford's logic in entering as market where only 35,000 units had been sold in 1964. But that number represented a three-fold increase over the level of 1960 and predictions were that by 1970 sales would be approaching the 70,000 level. Ford General Manager Donald N. Frey depicted the Bronco "as neither a car nor a truck, but as a vehicle which combines the best of both worlds. The Bronco can serve as a family sedan, Sports roadster, snowplow, or farm and civil defense vehicle. It has been designed to go nearly anywhere and do nearly anything."

The first Bronco was available in three body styles — a four passenger wagon with a removable full-length roof, a Sports utility (pickup) with a half roof and an open-top, and a two-door Roadster with a choice of two or four passenger seating. If the Bronco was equipped with four passenger seating the spare tire carrier was attached to the tailgate. If the rear seat was not ordered it was positioned on the rear bulkhead. The Roadster lacked both a roof and doors. Neat steel "half-doors" available with or without glass or frame were optional. The other Bronco models had standard roll-up windows. Also offered for the Roadster was a full-length vinyl top. Both the Roadster's and Sports Utility model standard seat was a bench type with room for three people. Both Bronco models could be ordered, at extra cost, with a single driver's side bucket seat or dual bucket seats. If the optional rear bench seat was ordered for the Roadster, either the single or dual front buckets also had to be selected. All seats were upholstered in a smooth-finished vinyl fabric. The roof of both the Wagon and the Sports Utility were removable but the task was not an easy one since the roof was bolted to the body at numerous junctures. However, the Sports Utility top since it weighed only 70 pounds was by far, the easier of the two to remove and install. Once this was accomplished the wagon/Sports Utility windshield could, as was the case with the Roadster's, be folded flat over the hood. The 2 passenger Bronco's rear bed had a 32.1 cu. ft. capacity.

1966 Ford Bronco Sports Utility

Although the Bronco bore a passing resemblance to the International Scout, it possessed its own personality and character. Powering the Bronco was the 170 cu. in. 6-cylinder engine originally developed for the Ford Falcon and also used for the Ford Econoline light-duty trucks. For use in the Bronco a different single-barrel carburetor and a heavier duty fuel pump was used. Coupled to the engine was an all-synchromesh 3-speed transmission with a column-mounted shift lever and a two-speed transfer case. Beginning in mid-March, 1966 Ford's 289 cu. in. V-8 was optional for all models. The Bronco suspension used semi-elliptical rear leaf springs and, for the first time on a stock off-road vehicle, front coil springs.

Standard equipment highlights of the Bronco consisted of a 105 hp. 6-cyl. engine, 3-speed synchromesh manual transmission, four-wheel drive, 2-speed transfer case, Mono-Beam front suspension, full-box-section, all-welded frame, suspended foot pedals, alternator, "Long-Life Sta-Ful" battery, 14.5 gal. fuel tank, 6000 mile oil filter, 2-year coolant-antifreeze, fully aluminized muffler, foam-padded front seat with vinyl upholstery, oil pressure gauge and

ammeter, vinyl-coated rubber floor mat, outside rearview mirror, padded instrument panel, fold-down windshield, front seat belts, liftgate lock (wagon only), windshield washers. Exterior colors offered for the Bronco consisted of holly green, rangoon red, marlin blue, Caribbean turquoise and Springtime yellow. The Bronco interior was offered in grey, chrome yellow, pure white, poppy red, peacock blue and frost turquoise. Ford offered the Bronco with a standard 24,000 mile or 24 month warranty.

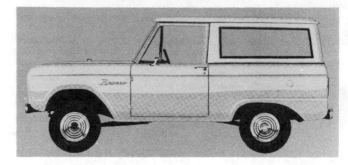

1966 Ford Bronco wagon

I.D. DATA: The Bronco V.I.N. consisted of eleven symbols. The first three (a letter and two digits) represented the series. The fourth digit identified the engine. The fifth letter identified the assembly plant. The last six digits served as the sequential production number.

Body Type	Factory Price	GVW	Shipping Weight	Prod. Total
Bronco U100				
Roadster (U130)	$2404	3900*	2750	4090
Sports Util. (U140)	$2480	3900	2955	6930
Wagon (U150)	$2625	3900	3025	12,756

* An optional 4700 lb. GVW Package was optional. It included a Ford 3300 lb. rear axle, 11 in. x 1.75 in. rear brakes, 1,280 lb. rear springs and 8.15 x 15 8-ply-rated tubeless tires.

STANDARD ENGINE: Engine Type: In-line six. Overhead valve (model prefix-EEW). Bore x Stroke: 3.50 in. x 2.94 in. Lifters: Mechanical. Number of main bearings-7. Displacement: 170 cu. in. Carburetion: Single barrel, Ford 1100-A. Compression Ratio: 9.1:1. Horsepower: Gross: 105 @ 4400 rpm. Net: 89 @ 4400 rpm. Torque: Gross: 158 lb.-ft. @ 2400 rpm. Net: 146 lb.-ft. @ 2400 rpm. Fuel Requirements: Regular.

OPTIONAL ENGINE: (Beginning in March,1966): Engine Type: OHV V-8. Bore x Stroke: 4.00 in. x 2.87 in. Lifters: Hydraulic. Number of main bearings-5. Displacement: 289 cu. in. Carburetion: Single 2-barrel. Compression Ratio: 9.3:1. Horsepower: Gross: 200 @ 4400 rpm. Net: 150 @ 4400 rpm. Torque: Gross: 282 lb.-ft. @ 2400 rpm. Net: 242 lb.-ft. @ 2400 rpm. Fuel Requirements: Regular.

CHASSIS FEATURES: Separate body and frame, box-section welded frame. 2.04 in. section modulus.

SUSPENSION AND RUNNING GEAR: Front Suspension: Coil springs, 760 lb. capacity, 960 lb. for V-8. Rear Suspension: Semi-elliptical leaf springs. Midway through the 1966 model year the Bronco was fitted with progressive-type rear springs. Capacity, 930 lb. Optional: 1280 lb. single-stage. Front Axle Type: Spicer 30. Capacity: 2500 lb. Rear Axle Type and Capacity: 2780 lb. Final Drive Ratio: 4.11:1 Optional: 2780 lb. rear axle: 4.57:1. 3300 lb. rear axle: 4.11, 4.57:1. Ratios for 2780 lb. and 3300 lb. limited slip rear axles: 3.50, 4.11, 4.57:1. Limited slip differential requires front free-running hubs. Transfer Case: Type: Dana 20, constant mesh. Ratios: 1.00:1, 2.46:1. Brakes: Type: Hydraulic, drum, front and rear. Dimensions: Front: 11.0 in. x 2.00 in. Rear: 10.0 in. x 2.50 in. Wheels: 5.5K, 5-hole disc. Optional: 5K, 5-hole disc. Tires: Tubeless, 7.35 x 15, 4-ply passenger car type. Optional: Tube type, 6.50 x 16, 6-ply rating truck type. Steering: Gemmer, worm and lever. Ratio: 24:1. Turning Circle: 33.6 ft. Transmission: Ford-built 3-speed all-synchromesh. Transmission Ratios: 3.41, 1.86, 1.00:1. Clutch: 9.0 in. dia. (6-cyl.), 11.0 in. (V-8). Optional: Heavy-duty 9.375 in. (6-cyl.).

VEHICLE DIMENSIONS: Wheelbase: 92.0 in. Overall Length: 152.1 in. Front/Rear Tread: 57.0 in./57.0 in. Height: 70.4 in., (Sports Utility), 71.4 in., (wagon). Width: 68.8 in. Front/Rear Overhang: 26.9 in./33.2 in. Tailgate: Width and Height: 56 in., 19.3 in. Approach/Departure Degrees: 40.2/30.3. Ground Clearance: 6.6 in. (unsprung components). 11.3 in. (sprung components). Load space: 55.2 in. x 40.0 in. x 38.0 in.

CAPACITIES: Fuel Tank: 14.5 gal. Optional: 11.5 gal. auxiliary tank with skid plate. Engine Coolant: 9 qts.

ACCOMMODATIONS: Seating Capacity: Pickup: 3 passengers, Roadster and Wagon: 3 passengers, 2 passenger rear bench seat optional. Headroom: 37 in. Maximum steering wheel to seat back: 15.6 in. Seat to ground: 36.5 in. Floor to ground: 23 in.

INSTRUMENTATION: Speedometer, odometer, oil pressure gauge, ammeter, engine coolant gauge.

OPTIONS AND PRICES: Limited slip rear axle. Limited slip front axle. Extra-capacity fan. Hand throttle. Extra-capacity battery. Heavy-duty clutch. Clutch skid plate. Vinyl top (Roadster only). Front bucket seats: $80.50. Rear bench seat (Roadster and Wagon only): $70.80. Custom Equipment Package (consists of cigarette lighter, chromed wheelcovers on 15 in. wheels only, chromed front and rear bumpers and taillight bezels, left and right side armrests-available with door models only, chrome horn ring, dual padded sun visors: $29.60. Full-width front floor mat. Oil pressure gauge and ammeter. Horn ring and dual sun visors. Left and right side armrest. Inside rearview mirror. Exterior right side mirror (painted-all models, chromed with doors. Front and rear chrome bumpers. Front bumper guards. Chrome front bumper guards for chrome bumper. Skid plates for fuel tank and transfer case. Inside tailgate-mounted spare tire carrier (included with rear seat option). Bright metal wheelcovers. 9.15 x 15 4-plyrated tubeless high-flotation tires. ICC lamp flashers. Manual AM radio with antenna: $50.20. Padded dash. Fresh Air heater and defroster: $70.20. Electric windshield wipers. Emergency flashers. Luggage rack (wagon only). Convertible top with vinyl doors and plastic windows. Inside handrail. Compass. 2-way radio. Free-running front hubs: $68.00. Limited slip rear axle (with standard axle): $39.70. Front and rear power take-offs. Snowplow. Tow bar. Front tow hooks. Front overload air springs. Trailer hitch. Front-mounted winch. Tachometer. 4700 lb. GVW Package. Fire extinguisher. Locking gas cap. Map light. Tool kit. Auxiliary 12 gal. fuel tank (after May, 1966). The Bronco could also be equipped with such items as a backhoe, boom, fire fighting equipment, grass mower, grille guard, posthole digger, rear step bumper, rotary broom, spray equipment, trencher and wrecker equipment.

HISTORICAL FOOTNOTES: The Bronco body was built by the Budd Company. Total Bronco sales in 1966 were 18,200. The V-8 engine option was introduced in March, 1966.

1967 BRONCO

1967 Ford Bronco wagon

The 1967 Bronco was equipped with numerous new safety-oriented features. These included seat belts, padded instrument panel and sun visors, back-up lights, variable speed electric windshield wipers and a dual hydraulic self-adjusting brake system with dash-mounted warning light. An 11.5 gal auxiliary fuel tank with a skid plate was offered for all Broncos except the Roadster model. The Sports Utility model was now designated a pickup. The design of the Bronco's optional wheelcovers were also changed. A new Sport Option Package was available for both the wagon and pickup. Color choices for 1967 consisted of raven black, Wimbledon white, rangoon red, harbor blue, Springtime yellow, pebble beige, lunar green, holly green, peacock blue, frost turquoise, poppy red and chrome yellow. The Bronco's metal roof as painted Wimbledon white.

1967 Ford Bronco pickup

I.D. DATA: The Bronco V.I.N. consisted of eleven symbols. The first three (a letter and two digits) represented the series. The fourth digit identified the engine. The fifth letter identified the assembly plant. The last six digits served as the sequential production number.

Body Type	Factory Price	GVW	Shipping Weight	Prod. Total
Bronco U100				
Roadster (U130)	$2417	3900	2775	698
Spts. Util. PU (U140)	$2546	3900	2955	2602
Wagon (U150)	$2633	3900	3055	10,930

STANDARD ENGINE: Engine Type: In-line six, Overhead valve (model prefix-EEW). Bore x Stroke: 3.50 in. x 2.94 in. Lifters: Mechanical. Number of main bearings-7. Displacement: 170 cu. in. Carburetion: Single barrel, Ford 1100-A. Compression Ratio: 9.1:1. Horsepower: Gross: 105 @ 4400 rpm. Net: 89 @ 4400 rpm. Torque: Gross: 158 lb.-ft.@ 2400 rpm. Net: 146 lb.-ft. @ 2400 rpm. Fuel Requirements: Regular.

OPTIONAL ENGINE: Engine Type: OHV V-8. Bore x Stroke: 4.00 in. x 2.87 in. Lifters: Hydraulic. Number of main bearings-5. Displacement: 289 cu. in. Carburetion: Single 2-barrel. Compression Ratio: 9.3:1. Horsepower: Gross: 200 @ 4400 rpm. Net: 150 @ 4400 rpm. Torque: Gross: 282 lb.-ft.@ 2400 rpm. Net: 242 lb.-ft. @ 2400 rpm. Fuel Requirements: Regular.

CHASSIS FEATURES: Separate body and frame, box-section welded frame. 2.04 in. section modulus.

SUSPENSION AND RUNNING GEAR: Front Suspension: Coil springs, 760 lb. capacity, 960 lb. for V-8. Rear Suspension: Progressive leaf springs, 930 lb. capacity, 1280 lb. for V-8. Front Axle Type and Capacity: 2500 lb. Rear Axle Type and Capacity: 2780 lb. Final Drive Ratio: 4.11:1 Optional: 3.50:1 and 4.57:1 with optional 3300 lb. axle with or without limited slip differential. Standard 2780 lb. axle also available with limited slip and 3.50, 4.11 and 4.57:1 ratios. Transfer Case: Type: Dana 20, constant mesh. Ratios: 1.00:1, 2.46:1. Brakes: Hydraulic, drum, front and rear. Dimensions: Front: 11.0 in. x 2.00 in. Rear: 10.0 in. x 2.50 in. Wheels: 5.5K, 5-hole disc. Optional: 5K, 5-hole disc. Tires: Tubeless, 7.35 x 15, 4-ply passenger car type. Optional: Tube type, 6.50 x 16, 6-ply rating truck type. Steering: Gemmer, worm and lever. Ratio: 24:1. Turning Circle: 33.6 ft. Transmission: Ford-built 3-speed all-synchromesh. Transmission Ratios: 3.41, 1.86, 1.00:1. Clutch: Type, 9.0 in. dia. (6-cyl.), 11.0 in. (V-8). Optional: Heavy-duty 9.375 in (6-cyl.).

VEHICLE DIMENSIONS: Wheelbase: 92.0 in. Overall Length: 152.1 in. Front/Rear Tread: 57.0 in./57.0 in. Overall Height: 70.4 in., (pickup), 71.4 in., (wagon). Width: 68.8 in. Front/Rear Overhang: 26.9 in./33.2 in. Tailgate: Width and Height: 56 in., 19.3 in. Approach/Departure Degrees: 40.2/30.3. Ground Clearance: 6.6 in. (Unsprung components), 11.3 in. (Sprung components). Load space: 55.2 in. x 40.0 in. x 38.0 in.

CAPACITIES: Fuel Tank: 14.5 gal. Optional: 11.5 gal. auxiliary tank with skid plate. Engine Coolant: 9 qts.

1967 Ford Bronco roadster

ACCOMMODATIONS: Seating Capacity: Pickup: 3 passengers, Roadster and wagon: 3 passengers, 2 passenger rear bench seat optional. Headroom: 37 in. Maximum steering wheel to seat back: 15.6 in. Seat to ground: 36.5 in. Floor to ground: 23 in.

INSTRUMENTATION: Speedometer, odometer, oil pressure gauge, ammeter, engine coolant gauge.

OPTIONS: Sport Bronco Package for wagon and pickup, includes, in addition to or in place of standard features, bright metal instrument panel molding, vinyl-covered door trim panels with bright metal moldings, hardboard headlining with bright metal retainer moldings (wagon only), vinyl floor front mat with bright metal retainers, bright metal seat pivot arm covers, (with optional bucket seats only), left and right armrests, cigar-cigarette lighter, chrome horn ring, bright metal drip rail molding, bright metal windshield and window frames, bright metal grille molding, headlight and taillight bezels, tailgate release handle, front and rear chrome bumpers, chrome front bumper guards, bright metal wheelcovers (available with 15 in. wheels only), "Sport Bronco" emblem. The Bronco was also available with the following factory-installed options: Left and right side armrests. Cigar-cigarette lighter. Horn ring. Right side exterior mirror (painted-all models, chrome with doors), manual radio and antenna. Cab doors (with glass and frames for Roadster). Horn ring. Right side exterior mirror (painted-all models, chrome with doors), manual radio and antenna, bucket seats. Bench-type rear seat (Roadster and Wagon). Fresh-Air heater and defroster. Front and rear chrome bumpers. Front bumper guards (with chrome bumpers only). Skid plates (under standard fuel tank and transfer case). Inside tailgate-mounted spare tire carrier (included with rear seat option). Bright metal wheelcovers (15 in. wheels only). High-flotation tires. Auxiliary 11.5 gal. fuel tank with skid plate. Courtesy lamp, (map) light. Bright body side and tailgate molding (except Roadster). Bright metal rocker panel molding. Extra cooling equipment. Front and rear reflectors, Dana free-running front hubs. Dry element air cleaner. 298 cu. in V-8. 4700 lb. GVW Package. The following items were available as dealer-installed accessories: Convertible top with vinyl doors and plastic windows (Roadster only), chrome inside handrails, power take-off, compass, warn free-running front hubs, 2-way radio, snowplow, front overload air springs, tachometer, front-mounted winch, trailer hitch, fire extinguisher, tool kit and dual tow hooks.

HISTORICAL FOOTNOTES: The 1967 Bronco carried a 5-year/50,000 mile warranty.

1967 Ford Bronco pickup

1968 BRONCO

The Bronco received only a limited number of changes for 1968. A new spare tire carrier was used which was hinged to a mount located on the right rear corner of the body. It was secured to the tailgate by a spring loaded "slam latch." If the Bronco operator wished to carry a load requiring the tailgate to be lowered, the carrier could be swung 270 degrees and secured to the right side panel by a bolt. The Bronco exterior now carried front-fender mounted side-marker lights. Reflectors was positioned on the lower rear quarter panels. The front bumpers now had curved, rather than square ends. Changes in the Bronco interior consisted of the use of new recessed flipper-type door handles, soft window crank knobs, and a reshaped armrest. Mechanical revisions included thermostatically controlled hot and cold air intake systems, standard dry-type, replaceable element air cleaners and thermactor exhaust emission control systems. The free-running front hubs now had improved lubrication sealing and simpler operation. A new kingpin was used with a high density polyurethane-filled bearing cap that automatically compensated for kingpin wear. Ford reported that this provided improved anti-shimmy capability. Added to the Bronco's standard equipment was a heater and defroster. Added to the Sport Package was a frosted horn ring. Additional new options included a steering linkage shock absorber and a 42 amp alternator.

I.D. DATA: The Bronco V.I.N. consisted of eleven symbols. The first three (a letter and two digits) represented the series. The fourth digit identified the engine. The fifth letter identified the assembly plant. The last six digits served as the sequential production number.

Body Type	Factory Price	GVW	Shipping Weight	Prod. Total
Bronco U100				
Roadster (U130)	$2638	3900	2815	—
Pickup (U140)	$2741	3900	2995	—
Wagon (U150)	$2851	3900	3095	—

STANDARD ENGINE: Engine Type: In-line six, Overhead valve (model prefix-EEW). Bore x Stroke: 3.50 in. x 2.94 in. Lifters: Mechanical. Number of main bearings-7. Displacement: 170 cu. in. Carburetion: Single barrel, Ford 1100-A. Compression Ratio: 9.1:1. Horsepower: Gross: 105 @ 4400 rpm. Net: 89 @ 4400 rpm. Torque: Gross: 158 lb.-ft.@ 2400 rpm. Net: 146 lb.-ft. @ 2400 rpm. Fuel Requirements: Regular.

OPTIONAL ENGINE: Engine Type: OHV V-8. Bore x Stroke: 4.00 in. x 2.87 in. Lifters: Hydraulic. Number of main bearings-5. Displacement: 289 cu. in. Carburetion: Single 2-barrel. Compression Ratio: 9.3:1. Horsepower: Gross: 200 @ 4400 rpm. Net: 150 @ 4400 rpm. Torque: Gross: 282 lb.-ft.@ 2400 rpm. Net: 242 lb.-ft. @ 2400 rpm. Fuel Requirements: Regular.

CHASSIS FEATURES: Separate body and frame, box-section welded frame. 2.04 in. section modulus.

SUSPENSION AND RUNNING GEAR: Front Suspension: Coil springs, 760 lb. capacity, 960 lb. for V-8. Rear Suspension: Progressive leaf springs, 930 lb. capacity, 1280 lb. for V-8. Front Axle Type and Capacity: 2500 lb. Rear Axle Type and Capacity: 2780 lb. Final Drive Ratio: 4.11:1 Optional: 3.50:1 and 4.57:1 with optional 3300 lb. axle with or without limited slip differential. Standard 2780 lb. axle also available with limited slip and 3.50, 4.11 and 4.57:1 ratios. Transfer Case: Type: Dana 20, constant mesh. Ratios: 1.00:1, 2.46:1. Brakes: Hydraulic, drum, front and rear. Dimensions: Front: 11.0 in. x 2.00 in. Rear: 10.0 in. x 2.50 in. Wheels: 5.5K, 5-hole disc. Optional: 5K, 5-hole disc. Tires: Tubeless, 7.35 x 15, 4-ply passenger car type. Optional: Tube type, 6.50 x 16, 6-ply rating truck type. Steering: Gemmer, worm and lever. Ratio: 24:1. Turning Circle: 33.6 ft. Transmission: Ford-built 3-speed all-synchromesh. Transmission Ratios: 3.41, 1.86, 1.00:1. Clutch: Type, 9.0 in. dia. (6-cyl.), 11.0 in. (V-8). Optional: Heavy-duty 9.375 in. (6-cyl.).

VEHICLE DIMENSIONS: Wheelbase: 92.0 in. Overall Length: 152.1 in. Front/Rear Tread: 57.0 in./57.0 in. Overall Height: 70.4 in., (pickup), 71.4 in., (wagon). Width: 68.8 in. Front/Rear Overhang: 26.9 in./33.2 in. Tailgate: Width and Height: 56 in., 19.3 in. Approach/Departure Degrees: 40.2/30.3. Ground Clearance: 6.6 in. (Unsprung components), 11.3 in. (Sprung components). Load space: 55.2 in. x 40.0 in. x 38.0 in.

CAPACITIES: Fuel Tank: 14.5 gal. Optional: 11.5 gal. auxiliary tank with skid plate. Engine Coolant: 9 qts.

ACCOMMODATIONS: Seating Capacity: Pickup: 3 passengers, Roadster and Wagon: 3 passengers, 2 passenger rear bench seat optional. Headroom: 37 in. Maximum steering wheel to seat back: 15.6 in. Seat to ground: 36.5 in. Floor to ground: 23 in.

INSTRUMENTATION: Speedometer, odometer, oil pressure gauge, ammeter, engine coolant gauge.

OPTIONS AND PRICES: Sport Bronco Package for wagon and pickup: $189, includes, in addition to or in place of standard features: Bright metal instrument panel molding, vinyl-covered door trim panels with bright metal moldings, hardboard headlining with bright metal retainer moldings (wagon only), vinyl floor front mat with bright metal retainers, bright metal seat pivot arm covers, (with optional bucket seats), left and right armrests, cigar-cigarette lighter, chrome horn ring, bright metal drip rail molding, bright metal windshield and window frames, bright metal grille molding, headlight and taillight bezels, tailgate release handle, front and rear chrome bumpers, front chrome bumper guards, bright metal wheelcovers (available with 15 in. wheels only), "Sport Bronco" emblem. The Bronco was also available with the following factory-installed options: Left and right side armrests, cigar-cigarette lighter, cab doors (with glass and frames for Roadster), horn ring, right side exterior mirror (painted-all models, chrome with doors), manual radio and antenna, bucket seats, bench-type rear seat (Roadster and wagon), fresh air heater and defroster, front and rear chrome bumpers, front bumper guards (with chrome bumpers only), skid plates (under standard fuel tank and transfer case), inside tailgate-mounted spare tire carrier (included with rear seat option), bright metal wheelcovers (15 in. wheels only), high-flotation tires, auxiliary 11.5 gal. fuel tank with skid plate, courtesy lamp, (map) light, bright body side and tailgate molding (except Roadster), bright metal rocker panel molding, extra cooling equipment, front and rear reflectors, Dana free-running front hubs, hand-operated throttle, dry element air cleaner, steering linkage shock absorber, 289 cu. in V-8: $189, 4800 lb. GVW Package. The following items were available as dealer-installed accessories: Convertible top with vinyl doors and plastic windows (Roadster only), chrome inside handrails, power take-off, compass, warn free-running front hubs, 2-way radio, snowplow, front overload air springs, tachometer, front-mounted winch, trailer hitch, fire extinguisher, tool kit and dual tow hooks.

HISTORICAL FOOTNOTES: Semon E. Knudsen became Ford Motor Company president on February 6, 1968.

1969 BRONCO

1969 Ford Sport Bronco wagon

The Bronco Roadster was not available for the 1969 model year. The windshield on the remaining wagon and pickup models was now stationary mounted. The wagon's steel roof was no longer removable. It was also strengthened by the use of reinforcements located in both the roof and body structure. Other areas that were strengthened for 1969 consisted of the side rocker panels, door frames, floor pillar junctions and door hinges. The cowl was redesigned to reduce road noise transfer to the interior. The front fender-mounted side markers were of a lighter amber color. Amber-colored parking light lenses replaced the clear lenses that, along with amber-colored bulbs had been used in 1968. Rear body reflectors were added for 1969. Other revisions and improvements included greater use of insulation, new body sealing to keep out dust and road splash and a black steering wheel grommet. As a running change, two-speed electric windshield wipers were adopted as standard equipment during the model run. Replacing the 289 cu. in. V-8 was a slightly larger 302 cu. in. V-8 as the alternative to the Bronco's standard 170 cu. in. 6-cylinder engine. Broncos with this engine carried "302" identification on their front fenders. Both the previously optional steering linkage shock absorber and the 9.375 inch clutch for the 6-cylinder were now standard. The Sport option was expanded to include aluminum door trim appliques and pleated parchment interior trim. If the rear seat was ordered on a Sport optioned Bronco, a rear floor mat was installed. The 1969 Bronco was available in the following colors: Raven black, Wimbledon white, candy-apple red, royal maroon, reef aqua, sky view blue, pebble beige, lunar green, Norway green, boxwood green, new lime, cordova copper, empire yellow and chrome yellow. The Bronco roof continued to be painted Wimbledon white.

1969 Ford Bronco pickup

I.D. DATA: The Bronco V.I.N. consisted of eleven symbols. The first three (a letter and two digits) represented the series. The fourth digit identified the engine. The fifth letter identified the assembly plant. The last six digits served as the sequential production number.

Body Type	Factory Price	GVW	Shipping Weight	Prod. Total
Bronco U100				
Pickup (U140)	$2834	3900	2990	2317
Wagon (U150)	$2945	3900*	3090	18,639

* 4700 lb. GVW Package available with Ford 3300 lb. capacity rear axle with 11.0 x 1.75 in. rear brakes, 1280 lb. rear springs and 8.15 x 15 load range D 8-ply rating tubeless tires.

STANDARD ENGINE: Engine Type: In-line six, Overhead valve (model prefix-EEW). Bore x Stroke: 3.50 in. x 2.94 in. Lifters: Mechanical. Number of main bearings-7. Displacement: 170 cu. in. Carburetion (type-model ID.): Single barrel, Ford 1100-A. Compression Ratio: 8.7:1. Horsepower: Gross: 100 @ 4000 rpm. Torque: Gross: 156 lb.-ft.@ 2200 rpm. Fuel Requirements: Regular.

OPTIONAL ENGINE: Engine Type: OHV V-8. Bore x Stroke: 4.00 in. x 3.0 in. Lifters: Hydraulic. Number of main bearings-5. Displacement: 302 cu. in. Carburetion: Single 2-barrel. Compression Ratio: 8.6:1. Horsepower: Gross: 205 @ 4600 rpm. Torque: Gross: 300 lb.-ft. @ 2400 rpm. Fuel Requirements: Regular.

CHASSIS FEATURES: Separate body and frame, box-section welded frame. 2.04 in. section modulus.

SUSPENSION AND RUNNING GEAR: Front Suspension: Coil springs, 750 lb. capacity-6 cyl., 800 lb. for V-8. Optional: 850 lb., 1000 lb. Rear Suspension: Progressive leaf springs, 930 lb. capacity-6 cyl. and V-8. Optional: 1280 lb. Front Axle Type and Capacity: 2500 lb. Rear Axle Type and Capacity: 2780 lb. Final Drive Ratio: Front axle: 4.10:1. Rear Axle: 4.11:1. Optional: 2780 lb. with 3.50:1, 3300 lb. with 3.50, 4.11:1 ratios (includes 11 in. x 1.75 in. rear brakes), 2780 and 3300 lb. limited slip available with 3.50 and 4.11:1 ratios. Transfer Case: Dana 20, constant mesh. Ratios: 1.00:1, 2.46:1. Brakes: Type: Hydraulic, drum, front and rear. Dimensions: Front: 11.0 in. x 2.00 in. Rear: 10.0 in. x 2.50 in. Wheels: 5.5K, 5-hole disc. Optional: 5K, 5-hole disc. Tires: Tubeless, 7.35 x 15, load range B, 4-ply passenger car type. Optional: Tube type, 6.50 x 16, 6-ply rating truck type. Steering: Gemmer, worm and lever with linkage shock absorber. Ratio: 24:1. Turning Circle: 33.6 ft. Transmission: Ford-built 3-speed all-synchromesh. Transmission Ratios: 3.41, 1.86, 1.00:1. Clutch: 9.375 in. dia. (6-cyl.), 11.0 in. (V-8). Optional: Heavy-duty 9.375 in (6-cyl.).

VEHICLE DIMENSIONS: Wheelbase: 92.0 in. Overall Length: 152.1 in. Front/Rear Tread: 57.0 in./57.0 in. Overall Height: 68.9 in., (pickup), 71.4 in., (wagon). Width: 68.8 in. Front/Rear Overhang: 26.9 in./33.2 in. Tailgate: Width and Height: 56 in., 19.3 in. Approach/Departure Degrees: 40.2/30.3. Ground Clearance: 6.6 in. (Unsprung components), 11.3 in. (Sprung components). Load space: 55.2 in. x 40.0 in. x 38.0 in.

CAPACITIES: Fuel Tank: 14.5 gal. Optional: 11.5 gal. auxiliary tank with skid plate. Engine Coolant: 9 qts.

ACCOMMODATIONS: Seating Capacity: Pickup: 3 passengers. Wagon: 3 passengers, 2 passenger rear bench seat optional. Headroom: 37 in. Maximum steering wheel to seat back: 15.6 in. Seat to ground: 36.5 in. Floor to ground: 23 in.

INSTRUMENTATION: Speedometer, odometer, oil pressure gauge, ammeter, engine coolant gauge.

OPTIONS AND PRICES: 302 cu. in V-8: $212, Bronco Sport Package: $193. Includes in addition to or in place of standard features: Bright metal "Sport bronco" emblem, pleated parchment vinyl front seat, vinyl door trim panels with bright metal moldings, hardboard headlining with bright metal retaining moldings (wagon only), parchment vinyl simulated-carpet front floor mat with bright metal retainers, rear floor mat (with optional rear seat), cigarette lighter, satin-finish horn ring, bright metal drip rail moldings, bright metal windshield and window frames, bright metal grille molding, headlight and taillight bezels, tailgate release handle, argent-painted grille, chrome front and rear bumpers, chrome front bumper guards, bright metal wheelcovers (15 in. wheels only). Convenience Group Package. Included cigarette lighter, map light, inside day/night mirror and horn ring. One pint oil-bath air cleaner (302 V-8 only). Right-hand chrome rearview mirror. Bucket seats. Rear seat (wagon only with bucket seat option). Chrome bumpers. Skid plate for standard fuel tank and transfer case. Inside tailgate-mounted tire carrier (included with rear seat option). Exterior rear-mounted swing-away tire carrier. Bright metal wheelcovers, (15 in. wheels only). High-flotation tires. Auxiliary 11.5 gal. fuel tank with skid plate. Manual radio and antenna. Bright body side and tailgate molding. Bright metal rocker panel molding. Front and rear reflectors. Dana manual free-running front hubs. Hand-operated throttle. Heavy-duty front axle carrier assembly (on special order). Dealer-installed options consisted of: Chrome inside front handrails, front-mounted power take-off, warn free-running front hubs (manual or automatic), snowplows, snowplow angling kit, front auxiliary air springs, front-mounted winch, trailer hitch, trailer towing mirror, locking gas caps, dual front tow hooks.

HISTORICAL FOOTNOTES: Phil Caldwell served as general manager of the Ford Truck Division.

1970 BRONCO

Although the Sport Package remained an option, Ford marketed pickup and wagon Broncos with this equipment as Sport wagon and pickup models for 1970. Exterior changes for 1970 included flush-mounted front and rear side marker lights. The rear quarter panel reflectors were flush-mounted and positioned higher than in 1969. The height of the wagon was increased by 1.2 in. The pickup was one in. lower. Three new options were introduced for 1970: G78 x 15B highway tread fiberglass tires, Traction-Lok limited slip rear differential and shoulder harnesses. Both the standard and auxiliary fuel tank capacities were reduced if the optional evaporative emissions recovery system was installed. Standard equipment included an all-vinyl 3 passenger front seat with 5 in. travel adjustment, fresh air heater and defroster, lockable glove compartment, padded instrument panel, energy-absorbing sun visors and a vinyl-covered rubber floor mat. Exclusive to the Bronco were two new colors: Acapulco blue and diamond blue. Additional colors consisted of raven black, Wimbledon white, candyapple red, royal maroon, sky view blue, harbor blue, reef aqua, Norway green, boxwood green, Mojave tan, chrome yellow, pinto yellow, caramel bronze metallic, new lime and Yucatan gold.

1970 Ford Sport Bronco wagon

I.D. DATA: The Bronco V.I.N. consisted of eleven symbols. The first three (a letter and two digits) represented the series. The fourth digit identified the engine. The fifth letter identified the assembly plant. The last six digits served as the sequential production number.

Body Type	Factory Price	GVW	Shipping Weight	Prod. Total
Bronco U100				
Pickup (U140)	$3036	3900	2990	1700
Wagon (U150)	$3149	3900*	3090	16,750

* 4700 lb. GVW Package available with Ford 3300 lb. capacity rear axle with 11.0 x 1.75 in. rear brakes, 1280 lb. rear springs and 8.25 x 15 load range D 8-ply rating tubeless tires.

STANDARD ENGINE: Engine Type: In-line six, Overhead valve (model prefix-EEW). Bore x Stroke: 3.50 in. x 2.94 in. Lifters: Mechanical. Number of main bearings-7. Displacement: 170 cu. in. Carburetion (type-model ID.): Single barrel, Ford 1100-A. Compression Ratio: 8.7:1. Horsepower: Gross: 105 @ 4200 rpm. Torque: Gross: 156 lb.-ft.@ 2200 rpm. Fuel Requirements: Regular.

OPTIONAL ENGINE: Engine Type: OHV V-8. Bore x Stroke: 4.00 in. x 3.0 in. Lifters: Hydraulic. Number of main bearings-5. Displacement: 302 cu. in. Carburetion: Single 2-barrel. Compression Ratio: 8.6:1. Horsepower: Gross: 205 @ 4600 rpm. Torque: Gross: 300 lb.-ft. @ 2400 rpm. Fuel Requirements: Regular.

CHASSIS FEATURES: Separate body and frame, box-section welded frame. 2.04 in. section modulus.

SUSPENSION AND RUNNING GEAR: Front Suspension: Coil springs, 750 lb. capacity-6 cyl., 800 lb. for V-8. Optional: 850 lb., 1000 lb. Rear Suspension: Progressive leaf springs, 930 lb. capacity-6 cyl. and V-8. Optional: 1280 lb. Front Axle Type and Capacity: 2500 lb. Rear Axle Type and Capacity: 2780 lb. Final Drive Ratio: Front axle: 4.10:1. Rear Axle: 4.11:1. Optional: 2780 lb. with 3.50:1, 3300 lb. with 3.50, 4.11:1 ratios (includes 11 in. x 1.75 in. rear brakes), 2780 and 3300 lb. limited slip available with 3.50 and 4.11:1 ratios. Transfer Case: Dana 20, constant mesh. Ratios: 1.00:1, 2.46:1. Brakes: Type: Hydraulic, drum, front and rear. Dimensions: Front: 11.0 in. x 2.00 in. Rear: 10.0 in. x 2.50 in. Wheels: 5.5K, 5-hole disc. Optional: 5K, 5-hole disc. Tires: Tubeless, 7.35 x 15, load range B, 4-ply passenger car type. Optional: Tube type, 6.50 x 16, 6-ply rating truck type. Steering: Gemmer, worm and lever with linkage shock absorber. Ratio: 24:1. Turning Circle: 33.6 ft. Transmission: Ford-built 3-speed all-synchromesh. Transmission Ratios: 3.41, 1.86, 1.00:1. Clutch: 9.375 in. dia. (6-cyl.), 11.0 in. (V-8). Optional: Heavy-duty 9.375 in (6-cyl.).

VEHICLE DIMENSIONS: Wheelbase: 92.0 in. Overall Length: 152.1 in. Front/Rear Tread: 57.0 in./57.0 in. Overall Height: 68.9 in., (pickup), 71.4 in., (wagon). Width: 68.8 in. Front/Rear Overhang: 26.9 in./33.2 in. Tailgate: Width and Height: 56 in., 19.3 in. Approach/Departure Degrees: 40.2/30.3. Ground Clearance: 6.6 in. (Unsprung components), 11.3 in. (Sprung components). Load space: 55.2 in. x 40.0 in. x 38.0 in.

CAPACITIES: Fuel Tank: 14.5 gal. (12.7 gal. with optional evaporative control system). Optional: 11.5 gal. auxiliary tank with skid plate (with optional evaporative control system: 10.3 gal). Engine Coolant: 9 qts.

ACCOMMODATIONS: Seating Capacity: Pickup: 3 passengers. Wagon: 3 passengers, 2 passenger rear bench seat optional. Headroom: 37 in. Maximum steering wheel to seat back: 15.6 in. Seat to ground: 36.5 in. Floor to ground: 23 in.

INSTRUMENTATION: Speedometer, odometer, oil pressure gauge, ammeter, engine coolant gauge.

OPTIONS AND PRICES: 302 cu. in V-8: $216. Bronco Sport Package: $197. Includes in addition to or in place of standard features: Bright metal "Sport Bronco" emblem, pleated parchment vinyl front seat, vinyl door trim panels with bright metal moldings, hardboard headlining with bright metal moldings (wagon model only), parchment vinyl simulated-carpet front floor mat with bright metal retainers, rear floor mat (included with optional rear seat (wagon model only), cigarette lighter, satin-finish horn ring, bright metal drip rail moldings, bright metal windshield and window frames, bright metal grille molding and tailgate release handle, argent painted grille with bright FORD letters, chrome front and rear bumpers, chrome front bumper guards, bright metal wheelcovers (15 in. wheels only). Convenience Group Package. Consists of cigarette lighter, map light, inside day/night mirror and horn ring. One pint oil-bath air cleaner (302 V-8 only). Right-hand chrome rearview mirror. Bucket seats. Shoulder harness. Rear seat (wagon only with bucket seat option). Chrome bumpers. Skid plate for standard fuel tank and transfer case. Inside tailgate-mounted tire carrier (included with rear seat option). Exterior rear-mounted swing-away tire carrier. Bright metal wheelcovers, (15 in. wheels only). High-flotation tires. Auxiliary 11.5 gal. fuel tank with skid plate. Manual radio and antenna. Bright body side and tailgate molding. Bright metal rocker panel molding. Dana manual free-running front hubs. Hand-operated throttle. Heavy-duty front axle carrier assembly (on special order). Hand-operated throttle. Heavy-duty front axle carrier (on special order). Dealer-installed options consisted of: Chrome inside front handrails, front-mounted power take-off, warn free-running front hubs (manual or automatic), snowplows, snowplow angling kit, front auxiliary air springs, front-mounted winch, trailer hitch, trailer towing mirror, locking gas caps, dual front tow hooks, tachometer, two-way radio, compass.

HISTORICAL FOOTNOTES: The 1970 Bronco was introduced on September 19, 1969.

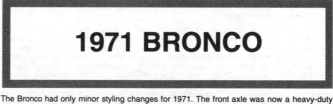

1971 BRONCO

The Bronco had only minor styling changes for 1971. The front axle was now a heavy-duty Spicer 44 unit with a 3100 lb. capacity. The standard tire size was now E78 x 15. Added to the Bronco option list was a driver-side remote control exterior mirror, extra-cooling capacity radiator (for V-8 engines only) and a hardboard headliner for the pickup. During the model year run Ford made front bucket seats and free-running front hubs as standard equipment.

I.D. DATA: The Bronco V.I.N. consisted of eleven symbols. The first three (a letter and two digits) represented the series. For the Bronco this was U-14 (pickup) and U-15 (wagon). The fourth digit identified the engine. For the bronco this was either F (170 cu. in. 6-cyl.) or G (302 cu. in. V-8). The fifth letter identified the assembly plant. The last six digits served as the sequential production number. The starting serial number for all 1971 Ford trucks, except the Econoline was J7000.

Body Type	Factory Price	GVW	Shipping Weight	Prod. Total
Bronco U100				
Pickup (U140)	$3535	3900	3080	1503
Wagon (U150)	$3638	3900*	3185	18,281

* 4700 lb. GVW Package available with Ford 3300 lb. capacity rear axle with 11.0 x 1.75 in. rear brakes, 1280 lb. rear springs and G78 x 15D tubeless tires.

STANDARD ENGINE: Engine Type: In-line six, Overhead valve (model prefix-EEW). Bore x Stroke: 3.50 in. x 2.94 in. Lifters: Mechanical. Number of main bearings-7. Displacement: 170 cu. in. Carburetion (type-model ID.): Single barrel, Ford 1100-A. Compression Ratio: 8.7:1. Horsepower: Gross: 100 @ 4000 rpm. Torque: Gross: 156 lb.-ft.@ 2200 rpm. Fuel Requirements: Regular.

OPTIONAL ENGINE: Engine Type: OHV V-8. Bore x Stroke: 4.00 in. x 3.0 in. Lifters: Hydraulic. Number of main bearings-5. Displacement: 302 cu. in. Carburetion: Single 2-barrel. Compression Ratio: 8.6:1. Horsepower: Gross: 205 @ 4600 rpm. Torque: Gross: 300 lb.-ft. @ 2400 rpm. Fuel Requirements: Regular.

CHASSIS FEATURES: Separate body and frame, box-section welded frame. 2.04 in. section modulus.

SUSPENSION AND RUNNING GEAR: Front Suspension: Coil springs, 750 lb. capacity-6 cyl., 800 lb. for V-8. Optional: 850 lb., 1000 lb. Rear Suspension: Progressive leaf springs, 930 lb. capacity-6 cyl. and V-8. Optional: 1280 lb. Front Axle: Spicer 44. Capacity: 3100 lb. Rear Axle Type and Capacity: 2780 lb. Final Drive Ratio: Front axle: 4.10:1. Rear Axle: 4.11:1. Optional: 2780 lb. with 3.50:1, 3300 lb. with 3.50, 4.11:1 ratios (includes 11 in. x 1.75 in. rear brakes), 2780 and 3300 lb. limited slip available with 3.50 and 4.11:1 ratios. Transfer Case: Dana 20, constant mesh. Ratios: 1.00:1, 2.46:1. Brakes: Type: Hydraulic, drum, front and rear. Dimensions: Front: 11.0 in. x 2.00 in. Rear: 10.0 in. x 2.50 in. Wheels: 5.5K, 5-hole disc. Optional: 5K, 5-hole disc. Tires: Tubeless, 7.35 x 15, load range B, 4-ply passenger car type. Optional: Tube type, 6.50 x 16, 6-ply rating, truck type. Steering: Gemmer, worm and lever with linkage shock absorber. Ratio: 24:1. Turning Circle: 33.6 ft. Transmission: Ford-built 3-speed all-synchromesh. Transmission Ratios: 3.41, 1.86, 1.00:1. Clutch: 9.375 in. dia. (6-cyl.), 11.0 in. (V-8). Optional: Heavy-duty 9.375 in (6-cyl.).

VEHICLE DIMENSIONS: Wheelbase: 92.0 in. Overall Length: 152.1 in. Front/Rear Tread: 57.0 in./57.0 in. Overall Height: 68.9 in., (pickup), 71.4 in., (wagon). Width: 68.8 in. Front/Rear Overhang: 26.9 in./33.2 in. Tailgate: Width and Height: 56 in., 19.3 in. Approach/Departure Degrees: 40.2/30.3. Ground Clearance: 6.6 in. (Unsprung components), 11.3 in. (Sprung components). Load space: 55.2 in. x 40.0 in. x 38.0 in.

CAPACITIES: Fuel Tank: 12.7 gal. Optional: 10.3 gal. auxiliary tank with skid plate. Engine Coolant: 9 qts.

ACCOMMODATIONS: Seating Capacity: Pickup: 3 passengers. Wagon: 3 passengers, 2 passenger rear bench seat optional. Headroom: 37 in. Maximum steering wheel to seat back: 15.6 in. Seat to ground: 36.5 in. Floor to ground: 23 in.

INSTRUMENTATION: 0-100 mph speedometer, 99,999.9 odometer, gauges for fuel level, coolant temperature, ammeter and oil pressure, warning lights for hazard lights operation and brake system malfunction.

OPTIONS: Except for the addition of a driver-side remote control exterior mirror, extra-cooling capacity radiator (for V-8 engines only) and a hardboard headliner for the pickup, the Bronco's options were unchanged for 1971.

HISTORICAL FOOTNOTES: The 1971 Bronco was introduced along with the rest of the Ford truck line on October 30, 1970.

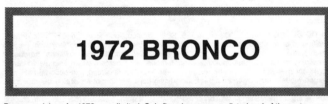

1972 BRONCO

Bronco revisions for 1972 were limited. Only five changes were listed and of those, two were actually running changes made during the 1971 model year. Free-running hubs had been made standard in mid-1971. The other changes incorporated as standard during 1971 were the 1972 Bronco's front bucket seats with pleated all-vinyl upholstery, contoured cushions and seat backs with large bolsters at the front. The 170 cu. in. 6-cylinder engine was not available for use in Broncos sold in California. The standard GVW rating was now 4300 lb. Two optional GVW Packages of 4500 lb. and 4900 lb. were also offered. The fuel tank was slightly reduced in capacity to 12.2 gal. due to the use of new evaporative control equipment. Seven new colors were introduced for 1972. The available colors consisted of Wimbledon white, candyapple red, royal maroon, wind blue, Bahama blue, bay rock blue metallic, seapine green metallic, Swiss aqua, Winter green, chelsa green metallic, mallard green, sequoia brown metallic, hot ginger metallic, prairie yellow, calypso coral, Tampico yellow and chrome yellow. The Bronco top continued to be painted Wimbledon white. In mid-1972 a new Ranger Package were announced for the Bronco. Ranger customers could select from three exterior colors: Ginger, blue or avocado. They were joined by orange-accented striping for the hood and lower body side. Content of the Ranger Package also consisted of an argent-colored grille, front and rear cut-pile carpeting, Deluxe wheelcovers, woodgrain trim for the door panels, a swing-away spare tire carrier with an orange-trimmed white tire cover, bucket seats with cloth seating areas and a fiberglass headliner.

Bill Stroppe & Associates announced a specially modified Bronco, the Baja Bronco, early in 1972. Bill Stroppe had previously developed special Broncos for off-road competition. Among their successes were victories at Riverside, the Mint 400, Stardust 7-11, the Baja 500 and Baja 1000. The Baja Bronco was equipped with a roll bar, dual shock absorbers front and rear, 1280 lb. rear springs, 330 lb. rear axle, Gates 10 x 15 Commando tires mounted on chrome-plated 15 in. wheels, fender flares, Class II (3,50 lb. trailer capacity) rear trailer hitch, fuel tank skid plate, automatic transmission, Saginaw power steering (17:1 ratio), rubberized steering wheel, 302 V-8, Extra Cooling Package, eight gallon auxiliary fuel tank, electric winch, and a special paint treatment. Thus equipped, the Bronco had a GVW of 4,700 lbs. Minimum ground clearance was increased to 11.5 inches The 303 V-8 was available with a 4-barrel carburetor modification that increased its power ratings to 158 hp. @ 5000 rpm and 242 lb.-ft. of torque @ 2000 rpm. Stroppe also added a sliding rear window for the Bronco wagon. The cost of these features added $2,031.67 to the Bronco's price.

I.D. DATA: The Bronco V.I.N. consisted of eleven symbols. The first three, a letter and two digits, indicatedd the series. The fourth entry, a letter, designated the engine. The fifth symbol, a letter, identified the assembly plant. The last six symbols included a letter followed by five sequential production numbers.

Body Type	Factory Price	GVW	Shipping Weight	Prod. Total
Bronco U100				
Pickup (U140)	$3538	4300	3275	—
Wagon (U150)	$3712	4300*	3325	—

* Two GVW Packages, 4500 and 4900 lb. were available. The 4500 lb. Package listed for $49. The 4500 GVW Package consisted of a 2780 lb. rear axle, 1000 lb. rated front springs, 1475 lb. rated rear springs and G78-15B tires. The 4900 lb. Package used the same springs and tires as the 4500 lb. version along with a 330 lb. Traction-Lok rear axle.

STANDARD ENGINE: (Except California where the 302 V-8 was required): EngineType: In-line six, Overhead valve (model prefix-EEW). Bore x Stroke: 3.50 in. x 2.94 in. Lifters: Mechanical. Number of main bearings-7. Displacement: 170 cu. in. Carburetion: Single barrel, Ford 1100-A. Compression Ratio: 8.7:1. Horsepower: Net: 82 @ 4200 rpm. Torque: Net: 131 lb.-ft. @ 2400 rpm. Gross: 156 lb.-ft.@ 2200 rpm. Optional:. Engine Type: OHV V-8. Bore x Stroke: 4.00 in. x 3.0 in. Lifters: Hydraulic. Number of main bearings-5. Displacement: 302 cu. in. Carburetion: Single 2-barrel. Horsepower: Net: 139 @ 4000 rpm. Torque: Net: 237 lb.-ft. @ 2200 rpm. Fuel Requirements: Regular.

CHASSIS FEATURES: Separate body and frame, box-section welded frame. 2.04 in. section modulus.

SUSPENSION AND RUNNING GEAR: Front Suspension: Coil springs, 750 lb. capacity-6 cyl., 800 lb. for V-8. Optional: 850 lb., 1000 lb. Rear Suspension: Progressive leaf springs, 930 lb. capacity-6 cyl. and V-8. Optional: 1280 lb. Front Axle: Spicer 44. Capacity: 3100 lb. Rear Axle Type and Capacity: 2780 lb. Final Drive Ratio: Front axle: 4.10:1. Rear Axle: 4.11:1. Optional: 2780 lb. with 3.50:1, 3300 lb. with 3.50, 4.11:1 ratios (includes 11 in. x 1.75 in. rear brakes), 2780 and 3300 lb. limited slip available with 3.50 and 4.11:1 ratios. Transfer Case: Dana 20, constant mesh. Ratios: 1.00.1, 2.46.1. Brakes: Type: Hydraulic, drum, front and rear. Dimensions: Front: 11.0 in. x 2.00 in. Rear: 10.0 in. x 2.50 in. Wheels: 5.5K, 5-hole disc. Optional: 5K, 5-hole disc. Tires: Tubeless, 7.35 x 15, load range B, 4-ply passenger car type. Optional: Tube type, 6.50 x 16, 6-ply rating, truck type. Steering: Gemmer, worm and lever with linkage shock absorber. Ratio: 24:1. Turning Circle: 33.6 ft. Transmission: Ford-built 3-speed all-synchromesh. Transmission Ratios: 3.41, 1.86, 1.00:1. Clutch: 9.375 in. dia. (6-cyl.), 11.0 in. (V-8). Optional: Heavy-duty 9.375 in (6-cyl.).

VEHICLE DIMENSIONS: Wheelbase: 92.0 in. Overall Length: 152.1 in. Front/Rear Tread: 57.0 in./57.0 in. Overall Height: 68.9 in., (pickup), 71.4 in., (wagon). Width: 68.8 in. Front/Rear Overhang: 26.9 in./33.2 in. Tailgate: Width and Height: 56 in., 19.3 in. Approach/Departure Degrees: 40.2/30.3. Ground Clearance: 6.6 in. (Unsprung components), 11.3 in. (Sprung components). Load space: 55.2 in. x 40.0 in. x 38.0 in.

CAPACITIES: Fuel Tank: 12.2 gal. Optional: 7.5 gal. auxiliary tank with skid plate. Engine Coolant: 9 qts.

ACCOMMODATIONS: Seating Capacity: Pickup: 3 passengers. Wagon: 3 passengers, 2 passenger rear bench seat optional. Headroom: 37 in. Maximum steering wheel to seat back: 15.6 in. Seat to ground: 36.5 in. Floor to ground: 23 in.

INSTRUMENTATION: 0-100 mph speedometer, 99,999.9 odometer, gauges for fuel level, coolant temperature, ammeter and oil pressure, warning lights for hazard lights operation and brake system malfunction.

OPTIONS AND PRICES: 302 cu. in V-8: $128. Auxiliary fuel tank: $38. Limited slip rear axle: $40, Sport group: $213. Rear bench seat (wagon only): $107. AM radio: $60. Extra Cooling Package (302 V-8 only). Left-hand remote control mirror. Hardboard headboard (pickup only). Convenience Group. Includes cigarette lighter, map light and 10 in. inside rearview day/night mirror, horn ring, and right-hand chrome rearview mirror.

HISTORICAL FOOTNOTES: The 1972 Bronco was introduced, along with other Ford trucks on September 24, 1971. Donald E. Peterson was general manager of Truck Operations.

1973 BRONCO

The Bronco pickup model was discontinued for 1973. Two new options introduced were power steering and a 3-speed automatic transmission, SelectShift Cruise-O-Matic, which had been adapted for use with four-wheel drive. It was available only with the 302 V-8. With this transmission, the driver could select either fully automatic or manual control of its three forward speeds. Unlike many other vehicles equipped with automatic transmission, Broncos so-equipped had a brake pedal that was the same size as found on manual transmission Broncos. Included in the price of the automatic transmission was a 55 amp battery and a transmission oil cooler. The power steering option was also limited to installation on V-8 Broncos. The assist mechanism was integral with the steering gear. Giving the Bronco a fresh new appearance as well as an upgraded interior was the new Ranger Package option available in three interior color choices: Ginger, blue and avocado. Primary aspects of the Ranger option included white tape striping with orange accent around the hood power dome and the lower edge of the body side, a white vinyl spare tire cover with orange accents and "Ford Bronco" imprinted in its center, bright window molding, bright front and rear bumpers, bright front bumper guards, cut-pile, color-keyed front and rear carpeting, color-keyed door trim panels with simulated woodgrain upper area, and vinyl lower area, color-keyed front bucket seats with houndstooth cloth inserts, sponge grain-texture fiberboard headliner with bright retainers, a cigarette lighter and a coat hook. The 1973 Bronco interior featured some minor revisions.

1973 Ford Bronco with Ranger Package

The standard Bronco engine was now a 200 cu. in. 6-cylinder. Three new colors were introduced for 1973. The wheel paint color was changed to argent. The controls for the lights, windshield wipers, heater and hazard warning signals had new, lighted identification. Ford also offered, as a new tire choice, passenger car type L78 x 15B wide tread tubeless tires with a 4-ply rating as a replacement for the 9.15 x 15B tires offered in 1972. These were suitable for use with all available GVW Packages, were offered with either highway or Mud and Snow tread and were recommended by Ford for high flotation use. They were also available with black or white sidewalls.

I.D. DATA: The Bronco V.I.N. consisted of eleven symbols. The first three, a letter and two digits, indicatedd the series. The fourth entry, a letter, designated the engine. The fifth symbol, a letter, identified the assembly plant. The last six symbols included a letter followed by five sequential production numbers.

Body Type	Factory Price	GVW	Shipping Weight	Prod. Total
Bronco U100				
Wagon (U150)	$3636	4300*	3090	21,894

* Two GVW Packages, 4450 and 4900 lb. were available. The 4450 lb. Package listed for $49. The 4450 GVW Package, available only on Broncos with the optional rear seat, consisted of a 2780 lb. rear axle, 1000 lb. rated front springs, 1475 lb. rated rear springs and G78-15B tires. The 4900 lb. Package used the same springs and tires as the 4500 lb. version along with a 3300 lb. Traction-Lok rear axle.

STANDARD ENGINE: (Except California where the 302 V-8 was required): EngineType: In-line six, Overhead valve (model prefix-EEW). Bore x Stroke: 3.68 in. x 3.13 in. Lifters: Hydraulic. Number of main bearings-7. Displacement: 200 cu. in. Carburetion: Single barrel. Compression Ratio: 8.3:1. Horsepower: Net: 84 @ 3800 rpm. Torque: Net:131 lb.-ft. @ 2400 rpm. Fuel Requirements: Regular.

OPTIONAL ENGINE: Engine Type: OHV V-8. Bore x Stroke: 4.00 in. x 3.0 in. Lifters: Hydraulic. Number of main bearings-5. Displacement: 302 cu. in. Carburetion: Single 2-barrel. Compression Ratio: 8.6:1. Horsepower: Net: 139 @ 4000 rpm. Torque: Net: 237 lb.-ft. @ 2200 rpm. Fuel Requirements: Regular.

CHASSIS FEATURES: Separate body and frame, box-section welded frame. 2.04 in. section modulus, 36,000 psi.

SUSPENSION AND RUNNING GEAR: Front Suspension: Coil springs, 1025 lb. rated at ground (6-cyl.), 1050 lb. (V-8). Optional: 1075 lb. and 1130 lb. rated at ground. Rear Suspension: Progressive leaf springs, 1237 lb. rated at ground. Optional: 1475 lb. rated at ground. Front Axle: Capacity: 3000 lb. Optional: 3000 lb. Dana with free-running hubs with or without limited slip differential. Rear Axle: Capacity: 2780 lb. Optional: 2780 lb. Ford with or without Traction-Lok, 3300 lb. Ford with Traction-Lok (includes 11 in. x 1.75 in. rear brakes). Final Drive Ratio: Front axle: 4.09:1. Rear Axle: 4.11:1. Optional: 2780 lb. with 3.50:1, 3300 lb. with 3.50, 4.11:1 ratios (includes 11 in. x 1.75 in. rear brakes), 2780 and 3300 lb. limited slip available with 3.50 and 4.11:1 ratios. Transfer Case: Dana 20, constant mesh. Ratios: 1.00:1, 2.46:1. Brakes: Type: Hydraulic, drum, front and rear. Dimensions: Front: 11.0 in. x 2.00 in. Rear: 10.0 in. x 2.50 in. Wheels: 5.5K, 5-hole disc. Optional: 5K, 5-hole disc. Tires: Tubeless, 7.35 x 15, load range B, 4-ply passenger car type. Optional: Tube type, 6.50 x 16, 6-ply rating; 7.00 x 15C truck type, E78 x 15B black sidewall, tubeless, belted, Mud/Snow tread; G78 x 15B black or white sidewall, tubeless, belted, highway or Mud/Snow tread; G78 x 15D black or white sidewall tubeless, belted, highway or Mud/Snow tread; L78 x 15B black or white sidewall, highway or Mud/Snow treads. Steering: Gemmer, worm and lever with linkage shock absorber. Ratio: 24:1. Turning Circle: 33.6 ft. Transmission: Ford-built 3-speed all-synchromesh. Transmission Ratios: 3.41, 1.86, 1.00:1. Clutch: 9.375 in. dia. (6-cyl.), 11.0 in. (V-8). Optional: None.

VEHICLE DIMENSIONS: Wheelbase: 92.0 in. Overall Length: 152.1 in. Front/Rear Tread: 57.0 in./57.0 in. Overall Height: 70.2 in. Width: 68.8 in. Front/Rear Overhang: 26.9 in./33.2 in. Tailgate: Width and Height: 56 in., 19.3 in. Approach/Departure Degrees: 40.2/30.3. Ground Clearance: 6.6 in. (Unsprung components), 11.3 in. (Sprung components). Load space: 55.2 in. x 40.0 in. x 38.0 in.

CAPACITIES: Fuel Tank: 12.2 gal. Optional: 7.5 gal. auxiliary tank with skid plate. Engine Coolant: 9 qts.

ACCOMMODATIONS: Seating Capacity: 3 passengers, 2 passenger rear bench seat optional. Headroom: 37 in. Maximum steering wheel to seat back: 15.6 in. Seat to ground: 36.5 in. Floor to ground: 23 in.

INSTRUMENTATION: 0-100 mph speedometer, 99,999.9 0dometer, gauges for fuel level, coolant temperature, ammeter and oil pressure, warning lights for hazard lights operation and brake system malfunction.

OPTIONS AND PRICES: 302 V8: $124. Ranger Package: $405, Sport Package: $197. Consists of white hardboard headlining with bright retainer, vinyl door trim panel with bright molding, simulated parchment vinyl floor mats with bright metal retainers, (rear mat only with optional wagon rear seat), non-glare horn ring, cigarette lighter, chrome front and rear bumpers with chrome front bumper guards, argent painted grille with bright metal FORD lettering, bright metal bezels for headlights, side marker lights, taillights and rear reflectors, bright metal molding for grille and windshield, bright metal door and vent window frames, rear window frame and wagon side window frames, bright metal tailgate release handle, Bronco wheelcovers and Sport Bronco emblems on front fenders. Dana 44-IF limited slip front axle: $92.38. Traction-Lok rear axle: $39.26. Rear bench seat: $94.39. 4500 lb. GVW Package: $48.48. Skid plates: $50.86. California emissions control: $15.59. Automatic transmission: $236.09. Power steering: $130.78. L78 x 15 belted white sidewall tires: $105.52. Right-hand side exterior chrome mirror: $3.62. Left-hand side exterior remote control mirror: $12.67. AM radio: $58.66. Extra capacity radiator: $25.04. 55 amp alternator: $30.59. 70 amp battery: $7.89. Convenience Package: $11.08. Consists of day/night mirror and map light plus cigarette lighter and non-glare horn ring on Broncos without Sport Package. Auxiliary fuel tank with skid plate: $37.90. Front and rear chrome bumpers with front bumper guards and bright metal bezels on taillights and rear reflectors. Hardboard headlining. Bright metal left door remote control mirror. Bright metal right door rearview mirror. Bright metal body side, rocker panel and tailgate moldings. Radio and antenna. Bronco wheelcovers. Bench-type fixed ear seat with armrests and two seat belts.

HISTORICAL FOOTNOTES: The 1973 Bronco introduction took place in September, 1972.

1974 BRONCO

Many veteran Bronco operators were unhappy to learn that Ford had replaced its single T-handle with a detent control transfer case shifter with a conventional type virtually identical to that used on the Ford four-wheel drive pickups. The shift-lever quadrant for the automatic transmission now was lighted. The Bronco's standard seat trim was available only in a parchment color and had a new embossed pattern intended to suggest the appearance of a knit vinyl. This scheme was also used for the optional rear bench seat when the standard interior was specified. The vinyl floor mat included in the Ranger Package now had a simulated carpet texture. Replacing the map light was a dome light. A total of 17 exterior color choices were offered for the 1974 Bronco. Nine new colors were introduced. Two of these were optional "Glow Metallics" identified as gold glow and ivy glow. The remaining new choices were pastel lime, bright lime, village green, light grabber blue, burnt orange, bold orange and sandpiper yellow. The only engine available for use in California continued to be the 302 V-8. When fitted with California emissions the V-8 was fitted with a solid state ignition. The California 302 V-8 also was equipped with a Thermactor emission system and Monolithic timing.

I.D. DATA: The Bronco V.I.N. consisted of eleven symbols. The first three, a letter and two digits, indicatedd the series. The fourth entry, a letter, designated the engine. The fifth symbol, a letter, identified the assembly plant. The last six symbols included a letter followed by five sequential production numbers.

Body Type	Factory Price	GVW	Shipping Weight	Prod. Total
Bronco U100				
Wagon (U150)	$4182	4300*	3420	18,786

* Two GVW Packages, 4500 and 4900 lb. were available. The 4500 lb. Package listed for $48. The 4900 lb. Package listed for $104. The 4500 GVW Package consisted of a 2780 lb. rear axle, 1000 lb. rated front springs, 1475 lb. rated rear springs and G78-15B tires. The 4900 lb. Package used the same springs and tires as the 4500 lb. version along with a 3300 lb. Traction-Lok rear axle.

STANDARD ENGINE: (Except California where the 302 V-8 was required): EngineType: In-line six, Overhead valve (model prefix-EEW). Bore x Stroke: 3.68 in. x 3.13 in. Lifters: Mechanical. Number of main bearings-7. Displacement: 200 cu. in. Carburetion: Single barrel. Compression Ratio: 8.3:1. Horsepower: Net: 89 @ 3800 rpm. Torque: Net:156 lb.-ft. @ 2200 rpm. Fuel Requirements: 91 octane.

OPTIONAL ENGINE: Engine Type: OHV V-8. Bore x Stroke: 4.00 in. x 3.0 in. Lifters: Hydraulic. Number of main bearings-5. Displacement: 302 cu. in. Carburetion: Single 2-barrel. Compression Ratio: 8.0:1. Horsepower: Net: 137 @ 3800 rpm. Torque: Net: 222 lb.-ft. @ 2600 rpm. Fuel Requirements: 91 octane.

CHASSIS FEATURES: Separate body and frame, box-section welded frame. 2.04 in. section modulus, 36,000 psi.

SUSPENSION AND RUNNING GEAR: Front Suspension: Coil springs, 1025 lb. capacity, rated at ground-6 cyl. 1075 lb. capacity, rated at ground for 302 V-8. Rear Suspension: Progressive leaf springs, 1240 lb. capacity, ground rated. Front Axle Capacity: 3000 lb. with free running hubs. Rear Axle Capacity: 2280 lb. Final Drive Ratio: With 6-cyl.: Front axle: 4.09:1, Rear axle: 4.11:1. With 302 V-8: Front axle: 3.54:1, Rear axle: 3.50:1. Optional ratios: With 6-cyl.: Front axle: 4.55:1, Rear axle: 4.57:1. With V-8: Front axle: 4.09:1, Rear axle: 4.11:1. Transfer Case: Dana 20, constant mesh. Ratios: 1.00:1, 2.46:1. Brakes: Type: Hydraulic, drum, front and rear. Dimensions: Front: 11.0 in. x 2.00 in. Rear: 10.0 in. x 2.50 in. Wheels: 5.5K, 5-hole disc. Optional: None. Tires: E78 x 15B, 4-ply rating, belted tubeless. Optional: G78 x 15B, G78 x 15D, L78 x 15B, 7.00 x 15C. Steering: Ross, worm and lever with linkage shock absorber. Ratio: 24:1. Turning Circle: 33.6 ft. Optional: Power steering: 17:1 ratio. Transmission: Ford-built 3-speed all-synchromesh. Transmission Ratios: 6-cyl.: 3.41, 1.86, 1.00:1. V-8: 2.99:1, 1.75:1, 1.00:1. Optional: 3-speed automatic. Ratios: 2.46:1, 1.46:1, 1.00:1. Clutch: 9.375 in. dia. (6-cyl.), 11.0 in. (V-8). Optional: None.

VEHICLE DIMENSIONS: Wheelbase: 92.0 in. Overall Length: 152.1 in. Front/Rear Tread: 57.0 in./57.0 in. Overall Height: 68.8 in. Width: 68.8 in. Front/Rear Overhang: 27.5 in./33.0 in. Tailgate: Width and Height: 58 in. x 21.5 in. Approach/Departure Degrees: 35/33. Ground Clearance: Front and rear axle: 8.5 in. Oil pan: 17.8 in. Transfer case: 14.5 in. Load space: With rear seat installed: 13 in. x 39 in. x 38 in. With rear seat removed or folded: 49 in. x 39 in. x 38 in.

CAPACITIES: Fuel Tank: 18.5 gal. Optional: 17.5 gal. auxiliary tank with skid plate. Engine Coolant: 6-cyl.: 9 qts.

ACCOMMODATIONS: Seating Capacity: 3 passengers, 2 passenger rear bench seat optional. Headroom: 37 in. Maximum steering wheel to seat back: 15.6 in. Seat to ground: 36.5 in. Floor to ground: 23 in.

INSTRUMENTATION: 0-100 mph speedometer, 99,999.9 0dometer, gauges for fuel level, coolant temperature, ammeter and oil pressure, warning lights for hazard lights operation and brake system malfunction.

OPTIONS AND PRICES: 302 V-8: $124. Automatic transmission: $236. Limited slip differential: $39 (with standard 2780 lb. axle); $55 (with optional 3300 lb. axle). Power steering: $131. Heavy-duty front and rear spring: $11. Ranger Package: $405, consists of argent painted grille, hood and lower body side stripes, fiberboard headliner, vinyl covered seats with fabric inserts, front and rear cut-pile carpeting, full wheelcovers, white spare tire cover with "Bronco Ranger" lettering and Bronco silhouette, Ranger lettering on glove box door and vinyl floor mats. Sport Package: $197, consists of bright metal "Sport Bronco" emblem, pleated parchment vinyl front seat, and vinyl door trim panels. Front and rear chrome bumpers: $32. AM radio: $59. Swing-away spare tire carrier: $32. Rear bench seat: $94.39. Hand throttle: $5. Skid plates: $50.86.

HISTORICAL FOOTNOTES: The 1974 Bronco debuted on September 21, 1973.

1975 BRONCO

1975 Ford Bronco with Ranger Package

The only engine offered for the 1975 Bronco was the 302 cu. in. V-8. The demise of the 200 cu. in. 6-cylinder was due to emissions regulations that made the limited use of the 6-cylinder engine throughout the entire Ford truck line a liability. The V-8 engine as installed in the Bronco was linked to a catalytic converter and required the use of unleaded fuel. Accompanying the use of the catalytic converter were changes in the Bronco's exhaust system and fuel filler. The Bronco continued to be the only vehicle in its class that was available with limited-slip differentials for both the front and rear axles. As in previous years, the shift lever for the optional 3-speed SelectShift Cruise-O-Matic automatic transmission was mounted on the column. Both the Ranger Package and Sport Bronco were fitted with steering wheels from the F series pickup trucks. Bronco's transfer case shifter, which had been severely criticized for its poor operation in 1974 was redesigned for 1975. Some 1974 Broncos were equipped with the new version. Standard equipment for the 1975 Bronco included these items: Fresh-Air heater/defroster, lockable glove compartment, dome light, padded dash panel, two-speed electric windshield wipers, sun visors, vinyl-coated rubber floor mat and painted channel-type steel front and rear bumpers. The standard rear axle capacity was increased to 2900 lb. from 2280 lb. Added to the Bronco's option list was an 800-watt engine block heater, a Reduced Exterior Noise Package and a Northlands Special Cold-Weather Package. The 1975 color choices consisted of Wimbledon white, Viking red, candyapple red, midnight blue metallic, Bahama blue, wind blue, Hatteras green metallic, baytree green, glen green, dark jade metallic, sequoia brown metallic, vineland gold, hot ginger metallic, parrot orange, chrome yellow and raven black. Extra cost Glamour color paints consisted of ginger glow and medium green glow. The Bronco top was painted Wimbledon white. A solid color exterior paint treatment was a special order feature.

1975 Ford Sport Bronco

I.D. DATA: The Bronco V.I.N. consisted of eleven symbols. The first three, a letter and two digits, indicatedd the series. The fourth entry, a letter, designated the engine. The fifth symbol, a letter, identified the assembly plant. The last six symbols included a letter followed by five sequential production numbers.

Body Type	Factory Price	GVW	Shipping Weight	Prod. Total
Bronco U100				
Wagon (U150)	$4979	4300*	3440	11,273

* Three GVW Packages, 4500, 4600 and 4900 lb. were available. Their specifications were as follows:

GVW Package:	—	4500#	4600	4900
Max. Load Rating (lbs.):	—	915	1030	1315
Rear Axle Cap. (lbs.):	—	2900	2900	3300*
Rear Spring Rating (lbs.)	—	1240	1475	1475
Tires:	—	E78-15B	G78-15B	G78-15B

Requires optional rear seat.
* Traction-Lok

STANDARD ENGINE: Engine Type: OHV V-8. Bore x Stroke: 4.00 in. x 3.0 in. Lifters: Hydraulic. Number of main bearings-5. Displacement: 302 cu. in. Carburetion: Single 2-barrel. Compression Ratio: 8.0:1. Horsepower: Net: 125 @ 3600 rpm. (California rating: 121 hp. @ 3400 rpm). Torque: Net: 218 lb.-ft. @ 2200 rpm. (California rating: 216 lb.-ft. @ 1600 rpm). Some sources also quote 135 hp. @ 3600 rpm and 221 lb.-ft. of torque @ 220 rpm-with 3-spd. auto. trans. Fuel Requirements: Unleaded.

CHASSIS FEATURES: Separate body and frame, box-section welded frame. 2.04 in. section modulus, 36,000 psi.

SUSPENSION AND RUNNING GEAR: Front Suspension: Coil springs, 1075 lb. capacity, rated at ground. Optional: 1130 lb. Rear Suspension: Progressive leaf springs, 1240 lb. capacity, ground rated. Optional (for 4300 and 4500 lb. GVW, included in 4600 and 4900 lb. GVW Packages): 1475 lb. Front Axle Type and Capacity: 3000 lb. with free running hubs. Rear Axle Type and Capacity: Semi-floating, hypoid, 2900 lb. Final Drive Ratio: 3.54:1 front/3.50:1 rear. Optional: 4.09:1 front/4.11:1 rear, subsequently revised to 3.50:1 front/4.11:1 rear. Transfer Case: Type: 2-speed Dana 20, constant mesh. Ratios: 1.00:1, 2.46:1. Brakes: Hydraulic, drum, front and rear. Dimensions: Front: 11.0 in. x 2.00 in. Rear: 10.0 in. x 2.50 in. Wheels: 5.5K, 5-hole disc. Optional: None. Tires: E78 x 15B, 4-ply rating, belted tubeless. Optional: G78 x 15B, G78 x 15D, L78 x 15B, 7.00 x 15C. Steering: Gemmer, worm and lever with linkage shock absorber. Ratio: 24:1. Turning Circle: 33.6 ft. Optional: Power steering: 17:1 ratio. Transmission: Type: Ford-built 3-speed all-synchromesh. Ratios: 2.99:1, 1.75:1, 1.00:1. Optional; 3-speed automatic. Ratios: 2.46:1, 1.46:1, 1.00:1. Clutch: Type, 11.0 in. dia. (6-cyl.), 11.0 in. (V-8). Optional: None.

VEHICLE DIMENSIONS: Wheelbase: 92.0 in. Overall Length: 152.1 in. Front/Rear Tread: 57.4 in./57.4 in. Overall Height: 70.6 in. Width: 69.1 in. Front/Rear Overhang: 26.0 in./33.0 in. Tailgate: Width and Height: 58 in. x 21.5 in. Approach/Departure Degrees: 38/29. Ground Clearance: Front and rear axle: 8.2 in. Oil pan: 17.0 in. Transfer case: 14.3 in. Load space: With rear seat installed: 13 in. x 39 in. x 38 in. With rear seat removed or folded: 49 in. x 39 in. x 38 in.

CAPACITIES: Fuel Tank: 12.2 gal. Optional: 7.5 gal. auxiliary tank with skid plate.

ACCOMMODATIONS: Seating Capacity: 3 passengers, 2 passenger rear bench seat optional. Headroom: 37 in. Maximum steering wheel to seat back: 14.8 in. Seat to ground: 33.5 in. Floor to ground: 22.0 in.

INSTRUMENTATION: Speedometer, odometer, fuel gauge, ammeter, oil pressure gauge, coolant temperature gauge, hazard warning light, brake system warning light.

OPTIONS AND PRICES: Rear bench seat: $107.40. Engine Emission Package: $75. Automatic transmission: $288.70. 3300 lb. axle with Traction-Lok: $63.10. 4500 lb. axle with Traction-Lok: $63.10 Limited slip front differential: $106. L78 x 15B Mud and Snow tires: $142. Additional optional tires: G78 x 15B, G78 x 15D, 7.00 x 15C. Heavy-duty front and rear springs: $14. Left-hand chrome remote-control mirror $16. Reduced sound level exhaust system: $7.55. Alternator, 55 amp: $35. Rear seat (includes seat belts and armrests). Chrome bumpers with chrome front guards: $36.10. Skid plates for standard fuel tank and transfer case. Exterior rear-mounted swing-away tire carrier. Bright metal wheelcovers. High-flotation tires. Auxiliary 7.5 gal. fuel tank with skid plate: $43.50. Manual radio. Bright body side and tailgate molding. Bright metal rocker panel molding. Hand-operated throttle. Extra cooling radiator: $30. 70 amp battery: $18.10. Hardboard headliner: $17.90. Reduced External Sound Package. 800 watt dual element engine block heater. Northland Special (includes dual element 800 watt engine block heater, 50%, -35° antifreeze, 70 amp-hr. battery, 55 amp alternator and limited slip differential). Sport Bronco Package: $261, in addition to or in place of standard items includes vinyl door trim panels with bright moldings, hardboard headliner with bright retainers, vinyl parchment simulated carpet front floor mat with bright retainers (matching rear mat with optional rear seat), cigar lighter, steering wheel with woodtone horn ring, bright metal windshield and window frames, bright grille frame molding and tailgate release handle, bright headlight, side marker light and rear reflector bezels, argent painted grille bright bumpers, bright front bumper guards, and bright metal wheelcovers. Ranger Package: $474, includes, in addition to or in place of Sport Bronco features, color-keyed, full carpeting (including tailgate and wheelhousing), color-keyed vinyl door trim panels with burl woodtone accent, color-keyed vinyl trim with insulation on rear quarter panels, cloth and vinyl seat trim in ginger, blue or breen, color-keyed instrument panel paint, hood and lower body side tape stripes (white stripe with orange accent), swing-away spare tire carrier. Spare tire cover (white vinyl with orange accent and Bronco insignia), and coat hook. Convenience Group. (Includes cigarette lighter, inside 10 in. day/night mirror, map light). Dealer installed accessories: Warn free-running front hubs (manual or automatic). Snowplows. Snowplow angling kit. Front auxiliary air springs. Trailer hitch. Locking gas cap. Front tow hooks. Fire extinguisher. Tachometer. Air horns.

HISTORICAL FOOTNOTES: The Bronco represented approximately 2.5 percent of all Ford light-duty truck sales in 1975.

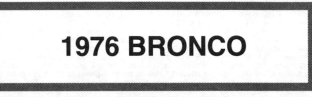

1976 BRONCO

The Bronco was technically updated for 1976. Front disc brakes were standard as were larger 11.0 in. x 2.25 in. rear brakes. Also introduced for 1976 was a variable-ratio parking brake control and a 40 amp alternator. In association with a higher 4400 lb. standard GVW, the Bronco's front axle capacity was increased to 1,090 lb. A number of new handling/capacity options made their debut in 1976 for the Bronco. These included a front stabilizer bar, heavy-duty front and rear shock absorbers and faster-ratio power steering. A new appearance option, the Special Decor Group, was a mid-year addition. Its blacked-out grille treatment accentuated the bold FORD lettering, headlight nacelles and grille perimeter trim all of which retained their chrome finish. Other elements of this package consisted of wide side body tape striping, bright wheelcovers, and bright trim for the windshield and side windows.

I.D. DATA: The Bronco V.I.N. consisted of eleven symbols. The first three, a letter and two digits, indicatedd the series. The fourth entry, a letter, designated the engine. The fifth symbol, a letter, identified the assembly plant. The last six symbols included a letter followed by five sequential production numbers.

Body Type	Factory Price	GVW	Shipping Weight	Prod. Total
Bronco U100				
Wagon (U150)	$5078	4400	3490	13,625

STANDARD ENGINE: Engine Type: OHV V-8. Bore x Stroke: 4.00 in. x 3.0 in. Lifters: Hydraulic. Number of main bearings-5. Displacement: 302 cu. in. Carburetion: Single 2-barrel. Compression Ratio: 8.0:1. Horsepower: Net: 125 @ 3600 rpm. (California rating: 121 hp. @ 3400 rpm). Torque: Net: 218 lb.-ft. @ 2200 rpm. (California rating: 216 lb.-ft. @ 1600 rpm). Fuel Requirements: Unleaded.

CHASSIS FEATURES: Separate body and frame, box-section welded frame. 2.04 in. section modulus, 36,000 psi.

SUSPENSION AND RUNNING GEAR: Front Suspension: Coil springs, 1090 lb. capacity, rated at ground. Optional: 1130 lb. Rear Suspension: Progressive leaf springs, 1240 lb. capacity, ground rated. Optional (for 4300 and 4500 lb. GVW, included in 4600 and 4900 lb. GVW Packages): 1475 lb. Front Axle Type and Capacity: 3000 lb. with free running hubs. Rear Axle Type and Capacity: Semi-floating, hypoid, 2900 lb. Final Drive Ratio: 3.54:1 front/3.50:1 rear. Optional: 4.09:1 front/4.11:1 rear, subsequently revised to 3.50:1 front/4.11:1 rear. Transfer Case: Dana 20, constant mesh. Ratios: 1.00:1, 2.46:1. Brakes: Hydraulic, front: Single piston floating caliper disc. Rear: Drum. Dimensions: Front: 11.0 in. x 2.00 in. Rear: 11.0 in. x 2.20 in. Wheels: 5.5K, 5-hole disc. Optional: None. Tires: E78 x 15B, 4-ply rating, belted tubeless. Optional: G78 x 15B, G78 x 15D, L78 x 15B, 7.00 x 15C. Steering: Gemmer, worm and lever with linkage shock absorber. Ratio: 24:1. Turning Circle: 33.6 ft. Optional: Power steering: 17:1 ratio. Transmission: Ford-built 3-speed all-synchromesh. Transmission Ratios: 2.99:1, 1.75:1, 1.00:1. Optional; 3-speed automatic. Ratios: 2.46:1, 1.46:1, 1.00:1. Clutch: 11.0 in. dia. (6-cyl.), 11.0 in. (V-8). Optional: None.

VEHICLE DIMENSIONS: Wheelbase: 92.0 in. Overall Length: 152.1 in. Front/Rear Tread: 57.4 in./57.4 in. Overall Height: 70.6 in. Width: 69.1 in. Front/Rear Overhang: 26.0 in./33.0 in. Tailgate: Width and Height: 58 in. x 21.5 in. Approach/Departure Degrees: 38/29. Ground Clearance: Front and rear axle: 8.2 in. Oil pan: 17.0 in. Transfer case: 14.3 in. Load space: With rear seat installed: 13 in. x 39 in. x 38 in. With rear seat removed or folded: 49 in. x 39 in. x 38 in.

CAPACITIES: Fuel Tank: 12.2 gal. Optional: 7.5 gal. auxiliary tank with skid plate.

ACCOMMODATIONS: Seating Capacity: 3 passengers, 2 passenger rear bench seat optional. Headroom: 37 in. Maximum steering wheel to seat back: 14.8 in. Seat to ground: 33.5 in. Floor to ground: 22.0 in.

INSTRUMENTATION: Speedometer, odometer, fuel gauge, ammeter, oil pressure gauge, coolant temperature gauge, hazard warning light, brake system warning light.

OPTIONS AND PRICES: Rear bench seat: $107.40. Engine Emission Package: $75. Automatic transmission: $288.70. 4500 lb. axle with Traction-Lok: $63.10. Limited slip front differential: $106. L78 x 15B Mud and Snow tires: $142. Additional optional tires: G78 x 15B,

G78 x 15D, 7.00 x 15C. Heavy-duty front and rear springs: $14. Left-hand chrome remote-control mirror $16. Reduced sound level exhaust system: $7. 55 amp alternator: $35. Rear seat (includes seat belts and armrests). Chrome bumpers with chrome front guards: $36.10. Skid plates for standard fuel tank and transfer case. Exterior rear-mounted swing-away tire carrier. Bright metal wheelcovers. High-flotation tires. Auxiliary 7.5 gal. fuel tank with skid plate: $43.50. Manual radio. Bright body side and tailgate molding. Bright metal rocker panel molding. Hand-operated throttle. Extra cooling radiator: $30. 70 amp battery: $18.10. Hardboard headliner: $17.90. Reduced External Sound Package. 800 watt dual element engine block heater. Northland Special (includes dual element 800 watt engine block heater, 50%, -35° antifreeze, 70 amp-hr. battery, 55 amp alternator and limited slip differential). Sport Bronco Package had in addition to or, in place of standard items the following: Vinyl door trim panels with bright moldings, hardboard headliner with bright retainers, vinyl parchment simulated carpet front floor mat with bright retainers (matching rear mat with optional rear seat, cigar lighter, steering wheel with woodtone horn ring, bright metal windshield and window frames, bright grille frame molding and tailgate release handle, bright headlight, side marker light and rear reflector bezels, argent painted grille, bright bumpers, bright front bumper guards, and bright metal wheelcovers. Ranger Package: $634. Includes, in addition to or, in place of Sport Bronco features: Color-keyed, full carpeting (including tailgate and wheel-housing), color-keyed vinyl door trim panels with burl woodtone accent, color-keyed vinyl trim with insulation on rear quarter panels, cloth and vinyl seat trim in ginger, blue or green; color-keyed instrument panel paint, hood and lower body side tape stripes (white stripe with orange accent), swing-away spare tire carrier, spare tire cover (white vinyl with orange accent and Bronco insignia), and coat hook. Convenience Group. Includes cigarette lighter, inside 10 in. day/night mirror, map light). Dealer installed accessories: Warn free-running front hubs (manual or automatic). Snowplows. Snowplow angling kit. Front auxiliary air springs. Trailer hitch. Locking gas cap. Front tow hooks. Fire extinguisher. Tachometer. Air horns.

HISTORICAL FOOTNOTES: The Bronco represented approximately 2.05 percent of Ford's 1976 light-duty truck sales.

1977 BRONCO

The1977 Bronco as equipped with Ford's new DuraSpark ignition system. The standard 302 V-8 was fitted with a redesigned combustion chamber, and new pistons that raised its compression ratio to 8.4:1. In addition, the Bronco engine had larger cylinder head coolant passages that, said Ford, "would improve spark plug and exhaust valve cooling." The diameter of the intake manifold runner was reduced to increase the velocity of the air/fuel mixture as it entered the combustion chamber. Minor changes also took place in the Bronco's throttle linkage and transmission. A larger 14.4 gallon plastic main fuel tank was introduced for 1977. The optional auxiliary had an 8 gallon capacity and was protected by a skid plate. Absence from the standard equipment of the base model Bronco was the front passenger seat and padded dash. The standard battery was now rated at 41 amp-hr.

I.D. DATA: The Bronco V.I.N. consisted of eleven symbols. The first three, a letter and two digits, indicatedd the series. The fourth entry, a letter, designated the engine. The fifth symbol, a letter, identified the assembly plant. The last six symbols included a letter followed by five sequential production numbers.

Body Type	Factory Price	GVW	Shipping Weight	Prod. Total
Bronco				
Wagon (U150)	$5260	4400*	3490	13,335

STANDARD ENGINE: Engine Type: OHV V-8. Bore x Stroke: 4.00 in. x 3.0 in. Lifters: Hydraulic. Number of main bearings-5. Displacement: 302 cu. in. Carburetion: Single 2-barrel. Compression Ratio: 8.4:1. Horsepower: 133 @ 3600 rpm. Torque: 218 lb.-ft. @ 2200 rpm. Fuel Requirements: Unleaded.

CHASSIS FEATURES: Separate body and frame, box-section welded frame. 2.04 in. section modulus, 36,000 psi.

SUSPENSION AND RUNNING GEAR: Front Suspension: Coil springs, 1090 lb. capacity, rated at ground. Optional: 1130 lb. Rear Suspension: Progressive leaf springs, 1240 lb. capacity, ground rated. Optional (for 4300 and 4500 lb. GVW, included in 4600 and 4900 lb. GVW Packages): 1475 lb. Front Axle Type and Capacity: 3000 lb. with free running hubs. Rear Axle Type and Capacity: Semi-floating, hypoid, 2900 lb. Final Drive Ratio: 3.54:1 front/3.50:1 rear. Optional: 4.09:1 front/4.11:1 rear, subsequently revised to 3.50:1 front/4.11:1 rear. Transfer Case: Dana 20, constant mesh. Ratios: 1.00:1, 2.46:1. Brakes: Hydraulic, front: Single piston floating caliper disc. Rear: Drum. Dimensions: Front: 11.0 in. x 2.00 in. Rear: 11.0 in. x 2.20 in. Wheels: 5.5K, 5-hole disc. Optional: None. Tires: E78 x 15B, 4-ply rating, belted tubeless. Optional: G78 x 15B, G78 x 15D, L78 x 15B, 7.00 x 15C. Steering: Gemmer, worm and lever with linkage shock absorber. Ratio: 24:1. Turning Circle: 33.6 ft. Optional: Power steering: 17:1 ratio. Transmission: Ford-built 3-speed all-synchromesh. Transmission Ratios: 2.99:1, 1.75:1, 1.00:1. Optional; 3-speed automatic. Ratios: 2.46:1, 1.46:1, 1.00:1. Clutch: 11.0 in. dia. (6-cyl.), 11.0 in. (V-8). Optional: None.

VEHICLE DIMENSIONS: Wheelbase: 92.0 in. Overall Length: 152.1 in. Front/Rear Tread: 57.4 in./57.4 in. Overall Height: 70.6 in. Width: 69.1 in. Front/Rear Overhang: 26.0 in./33.0 in. Tailgate: Width and Height: 58 in. x 21.5 in. Approach/Departure Degrees: 38/29. Ground Clearance: Front and rear axle: 8.2 in. Oil pan: 17.0 in. Transfer case: 14.3 in. Load space: With rear seat installed: 13 in. x 39 in. x 38 in. With rear seat removed or folded: 49 in. x 39 in. x 38 in.

CAPACITIES: Fuel Tank: 14.4 gal. plastic main fuel tank. Optional auxiliary with 8 gallon capacity and skid plate.

ACCOMMODATIONS: Seating Capacity: 3 passengers, 2 passenger rear bench seat optional. Headroom: 37 in. Maximum steering wheel to seat back: 14.8 in. Seat to ground: 33.5 in. Floor to ground: 22.0 in.

INSTRUMENTATION: Speedometer, odometer, fuel gauge, ammeter, oil pressure gauge, coolant temperature gauge, hazard warning light, brake system warning light.

OPTIONS: Rear bench seat. Engine Emission Package. Automatic transmission. 4500 lb. axle with Traction-Lok. Limited slip front differential. L78 x 15B Mud and Snow tires. Additional optional tires: G78 x 15B, G78 x 15D, 7.00 x 15C. Heavy-duty front and rear springs. Left-hand chrome remote-control mirror. Reduced sound level exhaust system. 55 amp alternator. Rear seat (includes seat belts and armrests). Chrome bumpers with chrome front guards. Skid plates for standard fuel tank and transfer case. Exterior rear-mounted swing-away tire carrier. Bright metal wheelcovers. High-flotation tires. Auxiliary 8.0 gal. fuel tank with skid plate. Manual radio. Bright body side and tailgate molding. Bright metal rocker panel molding. Hand-operated throttle. Extra cooling radiator 70 amp battery. Hardboard headliner. Reduced External Sound Package. 800 watt dual element engine block heater. Northland Special (includes dual element 800 watt engine block heater, 50%, -35° antifreeze, 70 amp-hr.battery, 55 amp alternator and limited slip differential). Sport Bronco Package. Ranger Package. Convenience Group. Dealer installed accessories: Warn free-running front hubs (manual or automatic). Snowplows. Snowplow angling kit. Front auxiliary air springs. Trailer hitch. Locking gas cap. Front tow hooks. Fire extinguisher. Tachometer. Air horns.

HISTORICAL FOOTNOTES: On July 27, 1977, Ford Motor Company marked the 60th anniversary of the production of its first Model TT one ton truck.

1978 BRONCO

Responding to competitive trends in the four-wheel drive market, the Bronco became a full-sized model with a 104.7 inch wheelbase in 1978. Compared to the original Bronco the new model was ten inches wider, five inches higher and over two feet longer. Its rear hip room was increased by approximately 30 percent. Front hip room was 15 percent greater. Usable space behind the rear seat moved up to 49.3 cu. ft. from 16.6 cu. ft. The rear seat was now designed to fold forward. When positioned in that fashion the Bronco had 81.9 cu. ft. of carrying space. When the seat was removed (by folding the seat forward and removing two pins), this number moved up to 97.4 cu. ft.

With a removable (the top was attached by 13 bolts and required approximately one hour to remove) fiberglass hardtop, it was a more contemporary styled vehicle than its predecessor and had seating for six adults. Its interior was far more "car-like" than previously. Like the Chevrolet Blazer, the new Bronco (which used the F series SuperCab floor pan as well as the steering linkage of the 1978 F-150 four-wheel drive pickup) was essentially a pickup truck from the B-pillar forward. The Bronco interior also borrowed heavily from the F series Ford pickups. The F series instrument panel was used and featured a bright trimmed instrument cluster with a black surround and a full-width padded panel. The standard Bronco model was identified as the custom and among its standard equipment were bright hubcaps, bright left and right side door-mounted mirrors and black painted front and rear bumpers. Other key appearance features included a black cross hatch grillework, black headlight inserts with argent surrounds, and front and rear black bumpers. The Bronco could be ordered without the passenger seat if desired.

1978 Ford Bronco Ranger XLT

Additional standard equipment features included a 5.8 liter (351 cu. in.) V-8 with a 2-barrel carburetor, 4-speed manual transmission (with synchromesh on the top three gears only), part-time four-wheel drive, front bucket seats, padded dash, power front disc brakes, front stabilizer bar, rear passenger footwell and a power tailgate window. The bucket seats of the custom Bronco were vinyl finished. A white sponge-grain hardboard headliner covered the front seat area. The instrument panel and door trim panels were color-keyed with a choice of red, black, green or tan. The steering wheel and horn pad were black. The sun visors were white. The front floor was covered with a black carpet-grain mat. There were also far more features offered as optional equipment. One example was the AM radio which had an LED digital display, controlled by push-button, that displayed either the time or radio frequency. The Bronco suspension consisted of front coil and rear semi-elliptical leaf springs with solid front and rear axles. A front stabilizer bar was standard. Also utilized in the front suspension were two leading arms and a Panhard rod. The Bronco was available with an optional quad front shock absorber option with two front shocks at each front wheel. Another option consisted of four heavy-duty front shock absorbers with two heavy-duty rear shocks and a rear stabilizer bar. It was also possible to order the rear stabilizer bar as a separate option.

The Bronco's front end appearance was that of the Ford pickups with a large egg-crate grille, large FORD lettering on the lower hood surface and recessed headlights. The Bronco profile featured a high-mounted side body protector rub strip into which was incorporated the front and rear side marker lights. Except for the custom model, all 1978 Broncos had a new Zip-Lock windshield weather striping in which the bright molding was inserted instead of applied. The standard large rear side window was fixed. A total of 19 colors were offered: Raven black, Wimbledon white, candyapple red, castillo red, medium copper, silver metallic, midnight blue metallic, light blue, Bahama blue, dark jade metallic, light jade, chrome yellow, tan, cream, dark brown metallic, jade glow, dark cinnamon glow, bright emerald and bright yellow. The last two colors listed were exclusive to the Bronco. The fiberglass Bronco top was available in either black or white. Three "Tu-Tone" color choices were offered as options. The Special Hood and Roof Tu-Tone choice offered those areas in black or white to match either a black or white fiberglass top. The Deluxe Tu-Tone provided an accent color applied within the body side molding and the upper and lower tailgate. It also included a body side molding. The Combination Tu-Tone offered the hood, roof and body side lower panel in black or white to match a black or white roof. It included special hood, roof and Deluxe Tu-Tone with moldings. A Free Wheeling option included tri-color tape stripes for the hood and body sides, black bumpers, L78 x 15C RWL tires mounted on styled steel wheels, black low-mount 6 x 9 in. western mirrors and a Sport steering wheel. A total of five interior color combinations were offered.

1978 Ford Bronco custom

I.D. DATA: The Bronco V.I.N. consisted of eleven symbols. The first three, a letter and two digits, indicatedd the series. The fourth entry, a letter, designated the engine. The fifth symbol, a letter, identified the assembly plant. The last six symbols included a letter followed by five sequential production numbers.

Body Type	Factory Price	GVW	Shipping Weight	Prod. Total
Bronco				
Wagon (U150)	$6543	46010*	4509	70,546

* A 6550 GVW Package was optional.

STANDARD ENGINE: Engine Type: OHV V-8. Cast-iron block and cylinder heads. Bore x Stroke: 4.00 in. x 3.50 in. Lifters: Hydraulic. Number of main bearings-5. Displacement: 351 cu. in. Carburetion: Motorcraft single 2-barrel. Compression Ratio: 8.0:1. Horsepower: Net: 156 @ 4000 rpm. Torque: Net: 262 lb.-ft. @ 2200 rpm. Fuel Requirements: Unleaded.

OPTIONAL ENGINE: OHV V-8. Cast-iron block and cylinder heads. Bore x Stroke: 4.00 in. x 4.00 in. Lifters: Hydraulic. Number of main bearings-5. Displacement: 400 cu. in. Horsepower: Net: 158 @ 3800 rpm. Torque: Net: 276 lb.-ft. @ 2000 rpm. Fuel Requirements: Unleaded.

CHASSIS FEATURES: Separate body and frame, box-section welded frame. 6.7 in. x 2.4 in. side members, 3.95 in. section modulus.

SUSPENSION AND RUNNING GEAR: Front Suspension: Coil springs, computer selected. Rear Suspension: Two-stage, semi-elliptical leaf, computer selected. Front Axle Type and Capacity: 3550 lb. Rear Axle Type and Capacity: 3750 lb. Final Drive Ratio: 3.50:1 front and rear. Transfer Case: 2-speed. Ratios: 1.00:1, 1.96:1. Optional: 2-speed full-time with Cruise-O-Matic. Brakes: Type: Hydraulic power-assisted, vented disc front and cast iron drum rear. Dimensions: Front: 11.5 in. dia. Rear: 11.0 in. x 2.2 in. Wheels: 5.5K, 5-hole disc. Optional: 10-hole aluminum polyurethane-coated, slotted aluminum alloy wheels, 15 x 8 styled steel (available on Broncos built after Nov.1, 1977). Painted white styled 15 x 6 steel wheels. Tires: Fabric cord, bias-belted, tubeless L78 x 15B. Optional: 10.0 x 15C tubeless All-Terrain RWL, tube-type 7.00 x 15D and radials. Steering: Recirculating ball, manual. Turning Circle: 38.0 ft. Optional: Power steering, 4.0, turns Lock-to-Lock. Turning circle: 35.4 ft. Transmission: 4-speed manual, synchromesh on top three gears. Optional: 3-speed automatic. Ratios: 2.46:1, 1.46:1, 1.00:1. Clutch: 11.0 in. dia. Optional: None.

VEHICLE DIMENSIONS: Wheelbase: 104 in. Overall Length: 180.3 in. Front/Rear Tread 64.3 in./64.4 in. Overall Height: 75.5 in. Width: 79.3 in. Approach/Departure Degrees: 37.5/23.4. Ground Clearance: Front axle: 8.1 in. Rear axle: 7.8 in.

CAPACITIES: Fuel Tank: 25.0 gal. Optional: 32 gal. with skid plate.

ACCOMMODATIONS: Seating Capacity: 2 passengers, 3 passenger front bench optional, 3 passenger rear bench seat optional.

OPTIONS AND PRICES: Bright wheel-lip moldings. Inside spare tires cover. Mag style wheel-covers. Narrow body side paint stripe. ComfortVent heater. Console (with front bucket seats only). Tilt steering wheel. Privacy glass. Low mount Western mirrors. Air conditioning. AM digital clock. AM/FM stereo radio. Quad gas-filled shock absorbers. Recreation swing-out mirrors. Sliding side windows. GT roll bar. Sport steering wheel. 5-slot forged aluminum 15 in. wheels. Maintenance-free battery. SelecShift Cruise-O-Matic. Speed control. Swing-away spare tire carrier. CB 40-channel radio. Front tow hooks. Front and rear contour bumpers. Painted white styled 15 x 6 steel wheels, 10-hole, 15 x 6 polyurethane-coated aluminum alloy wheels. Convenience Group. Includes intermittent windshield wipers, gathered map pockets and 12 in. day/night mirror. Heavy-duty scissor-type jack. Insulation Package (included with Ranger XLT and air conditioning). Lighted visor vanity mirror. Rear floor mat (custom). Front bench seat. Rear folding bench seat (includes rear floor mat). Tinted glass all around. Visibility Group. Includes lights in glove box, ashtray and underhood. Also instrument panel courtesy lights and dome light with integral map light. (Not included with front bench seat). Full-time four-wheel drive with automatic transmission. Handling Package. Includes rear stabilizer bar, quad front and heavy-duty rear shock absorbers. Northland Special Package. Includes 68 amp-hr. battery, 60 amp. alternator, dual 600 watt engine block heaters and limited slip rear axle. Rear stabilizer bar. Skid plates for standard fuel tank and transfer case. Towing Packages (light and heavy-duty). 32 gallon fuel tank (in place of standard tank) with skid plate. Inside locking hood release. Protection Group. Includes bright door edge guards, front bumper guards and front bumper rub strip (requires chrome bumper with custom). Security Group. Includes locking gas cap, inside hood release, spare tire lock and locking glove box. Free Wheeling Package: $491. Includes tri-color striping (available in orange/tan/cream or blue/white/green, depending upon body color selected (not available with cream), black bumpers (standard with custom), dual black low-mount mirrors, Sport steering wheel, black glove box applique and five 15 x 6 styled steel wheels with raised white letters (15 x 8 styled wheels available after Nov. 1, 1977). Ranger XLT Package: $669. Includes, in addition to or in place of custom features rectangular headlights, bright front and rear bumpers, bright molding for windshield, rear side windows, wheel-lips and lower tailgate section, body side molding with black vinyl insert and bright taillight bezels.

HISTORICAL FOOTNOTES: The best single year for Bronco retail deliveries was 1978 when they soared to 82,343.

The Ford Bronco was essentially unchanged for 1979.

The Bronco V.I.N. consisted of eleven symbols. The first three, a letter and two digits, indicatedd the series. The fourth entry, a letter, designated the engine. The fifth symbol, a letter, identified the assembly plant. The last six symbols included a letter followed by five sequential production numbers.

Body Type	Factory Price	GVW	Shipping Weight	Prod. Total
Bronco U100 (302 V-8)				
Wagon (U150)	$7733	6100*	4569	75,761

* A 6550 GVW Package was optional.

STANDARD ENGINE: Engine Type: OHV V-8. Cast-iron block and cylinder heads. Bore x Stroke: 4.00 in. x 3.50 in. Lifters: Hydraulic. Number of main bearings-5. Displacement: 351 cu. in. Carburetion: Motorcraft single 2-barrel. Compression Ratio: 8.0:1. Horsepower: Net: 156 @ 4000 rpm. Torque: Net: 262 lb.-ft. @ 2200 rpm. Fuel Requirements: Unleaded.

OPTIONAL ENGINE: OHV V-8. Cast-iron block and cylinder heads. Bore x Stroke: 4.00 in. x 4.00 in. Lifters: Hydraulic. Number of main bearings-5. Displacement: 400 cu. in. Horsepower: Net: 158 @ 3800 rpm. Torque: Net: 276 lb.-ft. @ 2000 rpm. Fuel Requirements: Unleaded.

CHASSIS FEATURES: Separate body and frame, box-section welded frame. 6.7 in. x 2.4 in. side members, 3.95 in. section modulus.

SUSPENSION AND RUNNING GEAR: Front Suspension: Coil springs, computer selected. Rear Suspension: Two-stage, semi-elliptical leaf, computer selected. Front Axle Type and Capacity: 3550 lb. Rear Axle Type and Capacity: 3750 lb. Final Drive Ratio: 3.50:1 front and rear. Transfer Case: 2-speed. Ratios: 1.00:1, 1.96:1. Optional: 2-speed full-time with Cruise-O-Matic. Brakes: Type: Hydraulic power-assisted, vented disc front and cast iron drum rear. Dimensions: Front: 11.5 in. dia. Rear: 11.0 in. x 2.2 in. Wheels: 5.5K, 5-hole disc. Optional: 10-hole aluminum polyurethane-coated, slotted aluminum alloy wheels, 15 x 8 styled steel (available on Broncos built after Nov.1, 1977). Painted white styled 15 x 6 steel wheels. Tires: Fabric cord, bias-belted, tubeless L78 x 15B. Optional: 10.0 x 15C tubeless All-Terrain RWL, tube-type 7.00 x 15D and radials. Steering: Recirculating ball, manual. Turning Circle: 38.0 ft. Optional: Power steering, 4.0, turns Lock-to-Lock. Turning circle: 35.4 ft. Transmission: 4-speed manual, synchromesh on top three gears. Optional: 3-speed automatic. Ratios: 2.46:1, 1.46:1, 1.00:1. Clutch: 11.0 in. dia. Optional: None.

VEHICLE DIMENSIONS: Wheelbase: 104 in. Overall Length: 180.3 in. Front/Rear Tread 64.3 in./64.4 in. Overall Height: 75.5 in. Width: 79.3 in. Approach/Departure Degrees: 37.5/23.4. Ground Clearance: Front axle: 8.1 in. Rear axle: 7.8 in.

CAPACITIES: Fuel Tank: 25.0 gal. Optional: 32 gal. with skid plate.

ACCOMMODATIONS: Seating Capacity: 2 passengers, 3 passenger front bench optional, 3 passenger rear bench seat optional.

OPTIONS AND PRICES: Chrome grille. Accent tape stripe. Tri-color tape stripe on hood and sides in Tri-Tone red, orange/tan/creme, Tri-Tone yellow or Tri-Tone blue (with Free-wheeling options only). Lower body side molding with black vinyl insert (for custom only). Bright wheel-lip molding (for custom only). GT bar, tubular design painted black with black padding. AM radio. AM/FM radio monaural (single speaker). AM/FM stereo (quad speakers). AM/FM stereo with cassette tape player (quad speakers). 40-channel CB radio. Air conditioning. Highout heater. ComfortVent heater. Auxiliary heater. Western low-mount swing-away mirrors. Bright low-mount swing-away recreational mirrors. Simulated leather-wrapped steering wheel (for custom only). Tilt steering wheel. Fingertip speed control with resume feature. Tinted sliding rear quarter windows. Tinted glass for al windows. Privacy glass in fixed quarter windows. Underhood tool storage box. Swing-away outside spare tire carrier with lock and white or black cover. Black spare tire cover for custom with inside carrier. Electronic digital clock. Center console. Captain's chairs (reclining driver and passenger seats), front bench seat. Flip/fold rear bench seat. Cloth seat trim inserts with Ranger XLT Package for front bucket, bench or rear flip/fold bench seats. Automatic locking hubs (with SelectShift transmission only). Select-Shift transmission. Free Wheeling Package: $557. Handling Package. Includes Convenience Group. Includes intermittent windshield wipers, 12 in. day/night mirror, map box in doors, headlamp-on warning buzzer and right hand door courtesy light switch (custom only). Light Group. Includes lights in glove box, ashtray, under instrument panel, dome light with map light (standard dome light only with optional front bucket seat), movable underhood worklight, and headlamp-on warning buzzer

HISTORICAL FOOTNOTES: Broncos with automatic transmission represented 78.8 percent of all Broncos produced.

The third generation Bronco was part of Ford's all-new four-wheel drive line of trucks. It was characterized by a sloping hood and a wraparound front bumper. Aerodynamic drag was reduced by 25 percent over that of the 1979 model. Compared to that model the moderately downsized 1980 Bronco had a shorter front end and a narrower width. Overall length was reduced by 2.7 inches. The Bronco's width was shaved by 1.1 inches. The Bronco's roof was now easier to remove due to bolt locations that were easier to reach. Appearance changes for the 1980 Bronco included a revamped grille and the relocation of the parking lights into a recessed position directly below the headlights. The side body model identification was placed lower on the front fender. The side body rub rail was also positioned lower on the body. At the rear wraparound taillights were used.

1980 Ford Bronco Ranger XLT with FreeWheeling B Package

A new technical development was the use of a Twin Traction beam (Dana 44-IFS) independent front suspension with coil springs. This system reduced unsprung weight and did not use CV joints. As a new option, automatic locking front hubs for Broncos with SelectShift automatic transmission were available. All Broncos used a part-time four-wheel drive New Process 208 transfer case with a 2.61:1 ratio. Compared to the older part-time system the new unit was 55 pounds lighter. The NP 208 also had improved dust and dirt sealing.

The standard Bronco engine was now a 300 cu. in. 6-cylinder. This was the first year a 6-cylinder engine had been offered for the Bronco since 1977. Optional engines consisted of either the 302 or 351 cu. in. V-8s. Interior changes resulted in a one inch increase in front leg room, a functional new two-tier instrument panel with all the warning lights located in a narrow upper level, the relocation of the seat position lever from the side to the front of the seat, an increase of 11% in seat travel and an improved climate control system. Standard Bronco equipment now included a locking steering column, tamper-proof door locks, and an inside hood release with an optional key lock. The Bronco was also equipped with a maintenance free battery and a coolant recovery system. The optional cruise control now had a resume feature. The base model Bronco custom featured black front and rear bumpers, black grille with bright surround, bright hubcaps, bright door-mounted mirrors, swing-down tailgate with power-operated window and bright tailgate letters. The custom interior provided a driver's side bucket seat with increased travel adjustment and tilting back, fixed passenger bucket seat that pivoted forward for entry into the rear, patterned vinyl seat trim, vinyl sun visors, instrument panel with full-width padding, glove box door with horizontal hold position and coin/token holding slots and two cup depressions on the inner side, windshield header and A-pillar moldings, dome light, anti-theft sliding door lock buttons, locking steering column, inside hood release, cowl side trim and textured rubber floor mat for front compartment with insulated backing. The Bronco color choices for 1980 consisted of raven black, Wimbledon white, candyapple red, silver metallic, light sand, maroon, dark chamois metallic, midnight blue metallic, medium blue, light caramel, dark pine metallic, medium grey metallic, dark silver blue metallic, light medium pine, medium copper and bright yellow. Optional "Glamour" colors were: Chamois glow, walnut glow and sand glow. The Bronco's fiberglass roof was available in six colors: Candyapple red, raven black, midnight blue, Wimbledon white, dark chamois and light sand. Three "Tu-Tone" combinations were available. The basic Tu-Tone combined an exterior body color with one of the six roof colors. The Deluxe Tu-Tone consisted of an accent color for the center body panel. The lower molding was brushed aluminum on custom models. The Victoria Tu-Tone provided for an accent color on the roof front, hood, around the door window and the lower body side. An accent tape stripe was available for the Victoria Tu-Tone as well as with any solid color.

1980 Ford Bronco Custom

I.D. DATA: Beginning in 1980 the V.I.N. number was stamped on a metal tag fastened to the instrument panel close to the windshield on the driver's side. The Bronco V.I.N. consisted of eleven symbols. The first three, a letter and two digits, indicatedd the series. The fourth entry, a letter, designated the engine. The fifth symbol, a letter, identified the assembly plant. The last six symbols included a letter followed by five sequential production numbers.

Body Type	Factory Price	GVW	Shipping Weight	Prod. Total
Bronco U100 (302 V-8)				
Wagon (U150)	$8392	5450*	4083	48,837

* 5450, 5700 and 6300 lb. GVW Packages were optional.

STANDARD ENGINE: (All states except California where the 302 V-8 was standard): Engine Type: OHV 6-cyl. Cast-iron block and cylinder heads. Bore x Stroke: 4.0 in. x 3.98 in. Lifters: Hydraulic. Number of main bearings-7. Carburetion: Single 1-barrel downdraft. Compression Ratio: 8.9:1. Displacement: 300 cu. in. (4.9 liters). Horsepower: Net: 119 @ 3200 rpm. Torque: Net: 243 lb.-ft. @ 1200 rpm. Oil capacity: 6 qts. with filter. Fuel Requirements: Unleaded.

OPTIONAL ENGINE: OHV V-8. Cast-iron block and cylinder heads. Bore x Stroke: 4.00 in. x 300 in. Lifters: Hydraulic. Number of main bearings-5. Displacement: 302 cu. in. (5.0 liters). Lifters: Hydraulic. Number of main bearings-5. Carburetion: Single 2-barrel. Compression Ratio: 8.4:1. Horsepower: Net: 137 @ 3400 rpm. Torque: Net: 239 lb.-ft. @ 1800 rpm. Fuel Requirements: Unleaded.

OPTIONAL ENGINE: OHV V-8. Cast-iron block and cylinder heads. Bore x Stroke: 4.00 in. x 3.50 in. Lifters: Hydraulic. Number of main bearings-5. Displacement: 351 cu. in. (5.8 liters). Carburetion: Single 2-barrel. Compression Ratio: 8.0:1. Horsepower: Net: 138 @ 3400 rpm. Torque: Net: 263 lb.-ft. @ 2000 rpm. Fuel Requirements: Unleaded.

CHASSIS FEATURES: Separate body and frame, box-section welded frame. 3.95 in. section modulus.

SUSPENSION AND RUNNING GEAR: Front Suspension: Dana 44 IFS. Coil springs, computer selected. Rear Suspension: Two-stage, semi-elliptical leaf, computer selected. Front Axle: Twin Traction beam. Capacity: 3550 lb. Rear axle beam. Capacity: 3750 lb. Final Drive Ratio: 3.00:1 or 3.50 front and rear. Optional limited slip available only with 3.50:1. Transfer Case: Type: New Process 208, 2-speed. Ratios: 1.00:1, 2.61:1. Brakes: Type: Hydraulic power-assisted, vented disc front and cast iron drum rear. Dimensions: Front: 11.5 in. dia. Rear: 11.0 in. x 2.2 in. Wheels: 15 x 5.5K, 5-hole disc. Optional: Styled steel polished white, 10-hole forged aluminum with clear plastic coating, 5-slot brushed forged aluminum with clear plastic coating. Aluminum, slotted aluminum. Tires: Fabric cord, bias-belted, tubeless L78 x 15B. Optional: L78 x 15C, P235/75R x 15, 10 x 15C, 7,00 x 15D. Steering: Recirculating ball, power assisted. Ratio: 17:1. Turning Circle: 36.7 ft. Optional: Power steering. 4.0, turns Lock-to-Lock. Turning circle: 35.4 ft. Transmission: Warner T-18, 4-speed, synchromesh on top three gears. Transmission Ratios: 6.32, 3.09, 1.69, 1.0:1. Optional (for 302 and 351 engines only); 3-speed automatic. Ratios: 2.46:1, 1.46:1, 1.00:1. Clutch: 11.0 in. dia. Optional: None.

VEHICLE DIMENSIONS: Wheelbase: 104 in. Overall Length: 177.6 in. Front/Rear Tread 64.3 in./64.4 in. Overall Height: 74.4 in. Width: 78.2 in. Front/Rear Overhang: 30.5 in./40.5 in. Tailgate: Width and Height: 58 in. x 36 in. Approach/Departure Degrees: 37.5/23.4. Ground Clearance: Front axle: 8.5 in. Rear axle: 8.5 in. Oil pan: 14.25 in. Transfer case: 11.5 in. Load space: With rear seat installed: 37 in. x 43.5 in. x 43.25 in. With rear seat removed or folded: 54 in. x 43.5 in. x 43.25 in.

CAPACITIES: Fuel Tank: 25.0 gal. Optional: 32 gal. with skid plate.

ACCOMMODATIONS: Seating Capacity: 2 passengers, 3 passenger front bench optional, 3 passenger rear bench seat optional. Headroom: 36 in. Maximum steering wheel to seat back: 18.25 in. Seat to ground: 38.5 in. Floor to ground: 24 in.

INSTRUMENTATION: Speedometer, odometer, temperature and fuel gauges, warning lights for oil pressure, amps, seat belts, turn signals, high beam, brakes, 4x4 operation. Optional: Tachometer, trip odometer, oil pressure gauge and ammeter gauge.

OPTIONS AND PRICES: 302 V-8: $315. 351 V-8: $477. SelectShift automatic transmission: $233. Limited slip rear differential: $197. Chrome grille. Accent tape stripe. Tri-color tape stripe on hood and sides in Tri-Tone red, orange/tan/creme, Tri-Tone yellow or Tri-Tone blue (with Free Wheeling options only). Lower body side molding with black vinyl insert (for custom only). Victoria Tu-Tone paint: $195.00. Bright wheel-lip molding (for custom only). GT bar, tubular design painted black with black padding: $112. AM radio. AM/FM radio monaural (single speaker). AM/FM stereo (quad speakers): $242. AM/FM stereo with cassette tape player (quad speakers). 40-channel CB radio: $361. Air conditioning: $611. High output heater. ComfortVent heater. Auxiliary heater. Western low-mount swing-away mirrors: $78. Bright low-mount swing-away recreational mirrors. GT roll bar: $112.00. Simulated leather-wrapped steering wheel (for custom only). Tilt steering wheel. Fingertip speed control with resume feature. Tinted sliding rear quarter windows. Tinted glass for all windows: $52. Privacy glass in fixed quarter windows. Swing-away outside spare tire carrier with lock and white or black cover. Black spare tire cover for custom with inside carrier. Electronic day/night digital clock: $52. Center console. Captain's chairs (reclining driver and passenger seats), front bench seat. Flip/fold rear bench seat: $339. Cloth seat trim inserts with Ranger XLT Package for front bucket, bench or rear flip/fold bench seats. Automatic locking hubs (with SelectShift transmission only). SelectShift transmission. Quad heavy-duty front and rear shock absorbers. Heavy-duty rear shock absorbers. Heavy-duty air cleaner: $17.00. Sports instrumentation (0-6000 tachometer, ammeter, oil pressure gauge and trip odometer): $107. Gauges for oil pressure and ammeter. Engine block heater (single with 4.2 liter six and 5.0 liter V-8, dual with 5.8 liter V-8). Tool box (includes under hood light and locking inside hood release): $78. Maximum capacity, 32 gal. fuel tank: $101. Tow hooks: $32. Auxiliary transmission oil cooler (with SelectShift automatic transmission). Skid plate: $78. Dual electric horns: $15. Fog lamps (includes plastic covers and bright front bumper guards. Front and/or rear chrome bumpers. Chrome rear step bumper. Argent rear step bumper. Styled steel painted white wheels (4 wheels with steel spare): $642 (with 10 x 15 tires). 10-hole polished forged aluminum with clear plastic coated wheels. (4 wheels with steel spare). Sport wheelcovers (4). 5-slot brushed forged aluminum wheels with clear plastic coating (4 wheels with steel spare). Ranger XLT Package: $814. Includes, in addition to or in place of custom features, brushed aluminum tailgate applique with bright FORD and XLT plaque, chrome bumpers, bright rear side window moldings, bright lower body side molding with black vinyl insert, cloth trim or patterned vinyl, wall-to-wall cut-pile carpeting (includes rear cargo area), bright accents on door trim panels with lower area carpeted, rear quarter trim panels with integral armrests and storage bin, cargo lamp, front vinyl headliner on foam padding, Deluxe seat belts, Ranger XLT dash plaque, black vinyl spare tire cover (not available for 10 x 15 spare), courtesy lighting with passenger and driver's side door switches, simulated leather-wrapped steering wheel, cigar lighter, woodtone accent around steering wheel horn pad, polished woodtone applique on instrument panel with bright molding for instruments, added insulation. Tri-color tape stripe (in lieu of pinstripes on Free Wheeling Packages). Free Wheeling A Package. Includes body side, hood, tailgate and door windows pinstriping, Sport wheelcovers and bright bumpers (standard with Ranger XLT). Free Wheeling B Package. In addition to contents of the A Package includes Sports instrumentation, simulated leather-wrapped steering wheel (standard with Ranger XLT), fog lamps with covers, bumper guards, Handling Package, GT roll bar, white styled wheels (5, in place of Sport wheelcovers). Exterior Protection Group. Includes bright door edge guards and rub strip. Security Lock Group. Includes locking gas cap and locks on inside hood release, glove box and spare tire. Trailer Towing Packages. Super Engine Cooling Package. Extra Engine Cooling Package. Sports Instrumentation Package. Includes 0-6000 rpm tachometer, ammeter, oil pressure gauge and trip odometer. Special Altitude Performance Package. Handling Package. Includes front stabilizer bar and quad heavy-duty hydraulic front and rear shock absorbers. Convenience Group. Includes intermediate windshield wipers, 12 in. day/night mirror, map box in doors, headlamp-on warning buzzer and right hand door courtesy light switch (custom only): $78. Light Group. Includes lights in glove box, ashtray, under instrument panel, dome light with map light (standard dome light only with optional front bucket seat), movable underhood worklight, and headlamp-on warning buzzer.

HISTORICAL FOOTNOTES: The Bronco's new Twin Traction beam front driving axle was the first independent front suspension offered in a full-sized 4x4 truck. *Four Wheeler* magazine recognized the Bronco as its "Four Wheeler of the Year" for 1980.

1981 BRONCO

For 1981 automatic locking front hubs were introduced as an option for all models equipped with the standard front axle. The hubs locked when the transfer case was shifted into four-wheel drive. The hubs disengaged when the transfer case was shifted into two-wheel drive and the Bronco was driven backwards for approximately 10 feet. Also made available as factory options were two new Snowplow Preparation Packages. The Base Package included a heavy-duty alternator, upgraded chassis components and a higher rated front axle. The second package added a heavy-duty battery, Extra Cooling Package, ammeter and oil pressure gauges and roof clearance lights. Also available as new options were a rear window defroster, electric remote mirrors, power door locks and power windows. Cruise control was now available for models with manual transmission. P-metric radial-ply, steel belted radial tires replaced the bias belted tires of 1980 as standard equipment. Available with all Broncos (except in California where it was offered only with the 351 V-8) was Ford's fully synchronized manual transmission with an overdrive fourth gear. The overdrive gearing was 0.71:1 for the 300 and 351 cu. in. engines and 0.72:1 for the 351 V-8. The shift pattern for the overdrive transmission was the same as that for the 4-speed, except that "OD" replaced "4" on the shift pattern. The 1981 Bronco had improved corrosion protection due to increased use of galvanized and pre-coated steel, enhanced-zinc primer paint, aluminum filled wax coating plus vinyl and hot melt sealers. For the front fenders, larger tub-type plastic aprons were used. Highlighting the 1981 Bronco exterior was a new chromatic paint stripe and new trim options. Nine new exterior colors along with two new interior colors were offered.

I.D. DATA: Beginning in 1981 the Bronco V.I.N. consisted of seventeen symbols. The first three characters identified the world manufacturer identifier and type of vehicle. For the Ford Bronco, this was: 1FM (FMC of US, Multipurpose Vehicle). The fourth character (a letter) designated the brake system and GVW range. For the Bronco this was either D (GVW 5001-6000 lb.) or E (6001-7000 lb.). The fifth, sixth and seventh characters identified the line, series, chassis, cab or body style. For the Bronco this was U15. The eighth character identified the engine as follows: 300 6-cyl.-Y, 302 V-8-N, 351 V-8-H. The ninth character was the check digit. The tenth character (a letter) represented the model year. For the years from 1980 through 1992 they were: 1980-A; 1981-B; 1982-C; 1983-D; 1984-E; 1985-F; 1986-G; 1987-H; 1988-J; 1989-K; 1990-L; 1991-M; 1992-N. The eleventh character identified the assembly plant. The remaining digits represented the sequential production number.

Body Type	Factory Price	GVW	Shipping Weight	Prod. Total
Bronco U100				
Wagon (U150)	$9085	5350*	4083	37,396

* A 6300 GVW Package was optional.

STANDARD ENGINE: (All states except California where the 302 V-8 is standard): Engine Type: OHV 6-cyl. Cast-iron block and cylinder heads. Bore x Stroke: 4.0 in. x 3.98 in. Lifters: Hydraulic. Number of main bearings-7. Displacement: 300 cu. in. (4.9 liters). Carburetion: Single 1-barrel. Compression ratio: 8.9:1. Horsepower: 122 @ 3000 rpm. Torque: Net: 255 lb.-ft. @ 1400 rpm. Oil capacity: 6 qts. with filter. Fuel Requirements: Unleaded.

OPTIONAL ENGINE: OHV V-8. Cast-iron block and cylinder heads. Bore x Stroke: 4.00 in. x 300 in. Lifters: Hydraulic. Number of main bearings-5. Displacement: 302 cu. in. (5.0 liters). Lifters: Hydraulic. Number of main bearings-5. Carburetion: Single 2-barrel. Horsepower: 133 @ 3800 rpm. Torque: Net: 222 lb.-ft. @ 2000 rpm. Fuel Requirements: Unleaded.

OPTIONAL ENGINE: OHV V-8. Cast-iron block and cylinder heads. Bore x Stroke: 4.00 in. x 3.50 in. Lifters: Hydraulic. Number of main bearings-5. Displacement: 351 cu. in. (5.8 liters). Carburetion: Single 2-barrel. Horsepower: 136 @ 4000 rpm. Torque: Net: 262 lb.-ft. @ 2200 rpm. Fuel Requirements: Unleaded.

CHASSIS FEATURES: Separate body and frame, box-section welded frame. 3.95 in. section modulus.

SUSPENSION AND RUNNING GEAR: Front Suspension: Coil springs, computer selected. Rear Suspension: Two-stage, semi-elliptical leaf, computer selected. Front Axle: Capacity: 3550 lb. Rear Axle: Capacity: 3750 lb.

Final Drive Ratio

Engine	Trans.	49 states Std./Opt. Ratio	California Std./Opt. Ratio.
300-6 cyl.:	Man.-4 spd.:	3.50/None	Not avail.
	Man.-4 spd. OD:	3.00/3.50	Not avail.
302 V-8:	Man.-4 spd.	3.00/3.50	Not avail.
	Man.-4 spd. OD:	3.00/3.50	Not avail.
	C6 Auto.:	3.00/3.50	3.50 (no opt.)
351 V-8:	Man. 4-spd.:	3.00/3.50	Not avail.
	Man. 4-spd. OD:	3.00/3.50	3.50 (no opt.)
	C6 Auto.:	3.00/3.50	3.50 (no opt.)

Standard transmission for all engines is a wide ratio 4-speed, a close-ratio version is optional. Transfer Case: Type: 2-speed. Ratios: 1.00:1, 2.61:1. Brakes: Type: Hydraulic power-assisted, vented disc front and cast iron drum rear. Dimensions: Front: 11.5 in. dia. Rear: 11.0 in. x 2.2 in. Wheels: 5.5K, 5-hole disc. Optional: 15 x 6, 15 x 7. Tires: L78 x 15B. Optional: L78 x 15C, P235/75R, 10 x 15C, 7.0 x 15D. Steering: Recirculating ball, power assisted. Ratio: 17:1. Turning Circle: 36.75 ft. Optional: None. Transmission: 4-speed manual, synchromesh on top three gears. The 300 6-cyl. engine's standard transmission remained a wide-ratio 4-speed manual. Both a close-ratio version and the manual 4-speed overdrive were optional. Except for California where it was available in California only with the C6 3-spd. automatic. The 302 V-8 was offered with the same transmissions as the 6-cyl. The 351 was available with all transmissions in all states. Optional (for 302 and 351 engines only): 3-speed automatic. Ratios: 2.46:1, 1.46:1, 1.00:1. Clutch: 11. in. dia. Optional: None.

VEHICLE DIMENSIONS: Wheelbase: 104 in. Overall Length: 180.3 in. Front/Rear Tread 64.3 in./64.4 in. Overall Height: 75.5 in. Width: 79.3 in. Front/Rear Overhang: 30.5 in./40.5 in. Tailgate: Width and Height: 58 in. x 36 in. Approach/Departure Degrees: 37.5/23.4. Ground Clearance: Front axle: 8.1 in. Rear axle: 7.8 in. Transfer case: 11.5 in. (at skid plate). Load space: With rear seat installed: 37 in. x 43.5 in. x 43.25 in. With rear seat removed or folded: 54 in. x 43.5 in. x 43.25 in.

CAPACITIES: Fuel Tank: 25.0 gal. Optional: 32 gal. with skid plate.

ACCOMMODATIONS: Seating Capacity: 2 passengers, 3 passenger front bench optional, 3 passenger rear bench seat optional. Headroom: 36 in. Maximum steering wheel to seat back: 18.25 in. Seat to ground: 38.5 in. Floor to ground: 24 in.

INSTRUMENTATION: Speedometer, odometer, temperature and fuel gauges.

OPTIONS AND PRICES: Chrome grille. Accent tape stripe. Tri-color tape stripe on hood and sides in Tri-Tone red, orange/tan/creme, Tri-Tone yellow or Tri-Tone blue (with Free Wheeling options only). Lower body side molding with black vinyl insert (for custom only). Bright wheel-lip molding (for custom only). GT bar, tubular design painted black with black padding. AM radio. AM/FM radio monaural (single speaker). AM/FM stereo (quad speakers). AM/FM stereo with cassette tape player (quad speakers). 40-channel CB radio. Air conditioning: $543.70. High output heater. ComfortVent heater. Auxiliary heater. Western low-mount swing-away mirrors. Bright low-mount swing-away recreational mirrors. Simulated leather-wrapped steering wheel (for custom only). Tilt steering wheel. Fingertip speed control with resume feature. Tinted sliding rear quarter windows. Tinted glass for all windows: $50.70. Privacy glass in fixed quarter windows. Underhood tool storage box. Swing-away outside spare tire carrier with lock and white or black cover: $128.10. Black spare tire cover for custom with inside carrier. Electronic digital clock. Center console. Captain's chairs (reclining driver and passenger seats). Front bench seat. Flip/fold rear bench seat: $270.00. Cloth seat trim inserts with Ranger XLT Package for front bucket, bench or rear flip/fold bench seats. Automatic locking hubs: $94.80. SelectShift transmission. Quad heavy-duty front and rear shock absorbers. Heavy-duty rear shock absorbers. Heavy-duty air cleaner. Heavy-duty battery: $40.00. Gauges for oil pressure and ammeter. Engine block heater (single with 4.2 liter six and 5.0 liter V-8, dual with 5.8 liter V-8). Maximum capacity, 32 gal. fuel tank: $96.10. Auxiliary transmission oil cooler (with SelectShift automatic transmission). Skid plates: $71.00. Dual electric horns. Fog lamps (includes plastic covers and bright front bumper guards. Front and/or rear chrome bumpers. Chrome rear step bumper. Argent rear step bumper. Styled steel painted white wheels (4 wheels with steel spare). 10-hole polished forged aluminum with clear plastic coated wheels. (4 wheels with steel spare). Sport wheelcovers (4). 5-slot brushed forged aluminum wheels with clear plastic coating (4 wheels with steel spare). Ranger XLT Package: $757. Includes, in addition to or in place of custom features, brushed aluminum tailgate applique with bright FORD lettering and XLT plaque, chrome bumpers, bright rear side window moldings, bright lower body side molding with black vinyl insert, cloth trim or patterned vinyl, wall-to-wall cut-pile carpeting (includes rear cargo area), bright accents on door trim panels with lower area carpeted, rear quarter trim panels with integral armrests and storage bin, cargo lamp, front vinyl headliner on foam padding, Deluxe seat belts, Ranger XLT dash plaque, black vinyl spare tire cover (not available for 10 x 15 spare), courtesy lighting with passenger and driver's side door switches, simulated leather-wrapped steering wheel, cigar lighter, woodtone accent around steering wheel horn pad, polished woodtone applique on instrument panel with bright molding for instruments, added insulation. Tri-color tape stripe (in lieu of pinstripes on Free Wheeling Packages). Free Wheeling A Package: $405. Includes body side, hood, tailgate and door windows pinstriping, Sport wheelcovers and bright bumpers (standard with Ranger XLT). Free Wheeling B Package: $1128. In addition to contents of the A Package includes Sports instrumentation, simulated leather-wrapped steering wheel (standard with Ranger XLT), fog lamps with covers, bumper guards, Handling Package, GT bar, white styled wheels (5, in place of Sport wheelcovers). Exterior Protection Group. Includes bright door edge guards and rub strip. Security Lock Group. Includes locking gas cap and locks on inside hood release, glove box and spare tire. Trailer Towing Packages. Super Engine Cooling Package. Extra Engine Cooling Package. Sports Instrumentation Package. Includes 0-6000 rpm tachometer, ammeter, oil pressure gauge and trip odometer. Special Altitude Performance Package. Handling Package. Includes front stabilizer bar and quad heavy-duty hydraulic front and rear shock absorbers. Convenience Group. Includes intermediate windshield wipers, 12 in. day/night mirror, map box in doors, headlamp-on warning buzzer and right hand door courtesy light switch (custom only): $81.90. Light Group. Includes lights in glove box, ashtray, under instrument panel, dome light with map light (standard dome light only with optional front bucket seat), movable underhood worklight, and headlamp-on warning buzzer: $77.60.

HISTORICAL FOOTNOTES: Sales for the 1981 calendar year were 35,700 units.

1982 BRONCO

The latest Bronco was distinguished from the 1980-81 models by its three vertical bar grille and center-mounted Ford oval emblem. This classic Ford identification feature was also found on the tailgate. A new XLT Lariat Package along with a higher level XLS Package was introduced.

I.D. DATA: The Bronco V.I.N. consisted of seventeen symbols. The first three characters identified the manufacturer, make and type of vehicle. The fourth character (a letter) designated the GVW range. The fifth, sixth and seventh characters identified the series and body style. The eighth character identified the engine. The ninth character was the check digit. The tenth character (a letter) represented the model year. The eleventh character identified the assembly plant. The remaining digits represented the sequential production number.

Body Type	Factory Price	GVW	Shipping Weight	Prod. Total
Bronco U100				
Wagon (U150)	$9899	5400*	4079	—

* A 6300 GVW Package was optional.

STANDARD ENGINE: (All states except California where the 302 V-8 is standard): Engine Type: OHV 6-cyl. Cast-iron block and cylinder heads. Bore x Stroke: 4.0 in. x 3.98 in. Lifters: Hydraulic. Number of main bearings-7. Displacement: 300 cu. in. (4.9 liters). Carburetion: Single 1-barrel. Compression ratio: 8.9:1. Horsepower: 122 @ 3000 rpm. Torque: Net: 255 lb.-ft. @ 1400 rpm. Oil capacity: 6 qts. with filter. Fuel Requirements: Unleaded.

OPTIONAL ENGINE: OHV V-8. Cast-iron block and cylinder heads. Bore x Stroke: 4.00 in. x 300 in. Lifters: Hydraulic. Number of main bearings-5. Displacement: 302 cu. in. (5.0 liters). Lifters: Hydraulic. Number of main bearings-5. Carburetion: Single 2-barrel. Horsepower: 133 @ 3800 rpm. Torque: Net: 222 lb.-ft. @ 2000 rpm. Fuel Requirements: Unleaded.

OPTIONAL ENGINE: OHV V-8. Cast-iron block and cylinder heads. Bore x Stroke: 4.00 in. x 3.50 in. Lifters: Hydraulic. Number of main bearings-5. Displacement: 351 cu. in. (5.8 liters). Carburetion: Single 2-barrel. Horsepower: 136 @ 4000 rpm. Torque: Net: 262 lb.-ft. @ 2200 rpm. Fuel Requirements: Unleaded.

CHASSIS FEATURES: Separate body and frame, box-section welded frame. 3.95 in. section modulus.

SUSPENSION AND RUNNING GEAR: Front Suspension: Coil springs, computer selected. Rear Suspension: Two-stage, semi-elliptical leaf, computer selected. Front Axle: Capacity: 3550 lb. Rear Axle: Capacity: 3750 lb.

Final Drive Ratio:

Engine	Trans.	49 states Std./ Opt. Ratio	California Std./Opt. Ratio
300-6 cyl.:	Man.-4 spd.:	3.50/None	Not avail.
	Man.-4 spd. OD:	3.00/3.50	Not avail.
302 V-8:	Man.-4 spd.	3.00/3.50	Not avail.
	Man.-4 spd. OD:	3.00/3.50	Not avail.
	C6 Auto.:	3.00/3.50	3.50 (no opt.)
351 V-8:	Man. 4-spd.:	3.00/3.50	Not avail.
	Man. 4-spd. OD:	3.00/3.50	3.50 (no opt.)
	C6 Auto.:	3.00/3.50	3.50 (no opt.)

Standard transmission for all engines is a wide ratio 4-speed, a close-ratio version is optional. Transfer Case: Type: 2-speed. Ratios: 1.00:1, 2.61:1. Brakes: Type: Hydraulic power-assisted, vented disc front and cast iron drum rear. Dimensions: Front: 11.5 in. dia. Rear: 11.0 in. x 2.2 in. Wheels: 5.5K, 5-hole disc. Optional: 15 x 6, 15 x 7. Tires: L78 x 15B. Optional: L78 x 15C, P235/75R, 10 x 15C, 7.0 x 15D. Steering: Recirculating ball, power assisted. Ratio: 17:1. Turning Circle: 36.75 ft. Optional: None. Transmission: 4-speed manual, synchromesh on top three gears. The 300 6-cyl. engine's standard transmission remained a wide-ratio 4-speed manual. Both a close-ratio version and the manual 4-speed overdrive were optional. Except for California where it was available in California only with the C6 3-spd. automatic. The 302 V-8 was offered with the same transmissions as the 6-cyl. The 351 was available with all transmissions in all states. Optional (for 302 and 351 engines only): 3-speed automatic. Ratios: 2.46:1, 1.46:1, 1.00:1. Clutch: 11. in. dia. Optional: None.

VEHICLE DIMENSIONS: Wheelbase: 104 in. Overall Length: 180.3 in. Front/Rear Tread 64.3 in./64.4 in. Overall Height: 75.5 in. Width: 79.3 in. Front/Rear Overhang: 30.5 in./40.5 in. Tailgate: Width and Height: 58 in. x 36 in. Approach/Departure Degrees: 37.5/23.4. Ground Clearance: Front axle: 8.1 in. Rear axle: 7.8 in. Transfer case: 11.5 in. (at skid plate). Load space: With rear seat installed: 37 in. x 43.5 in. x 43.25 in. With rear seat removed or folded: 54 in. x 43.5 in. x 43.25 in.

CAPACITIES: Fuel Tank: 25.0 gal. Optional: 32 gal. with skid plate.

ACCOMMODATIONS: Seating Capacity: 2 passengers, 3 passenger front bench optional, 3 passenger rear bench seat optional. Headroom: 36 in. Maximum steering wheel to seat back: 18.25 in. Seat to ground: 38.5 in. Floor to ground: 24 in.

INSTRUMENTATION: Speedometer, odometer, temperature and fuel gauges.

OPTIONS AND PRICES: Tri-color tape stripe on hood and sides in Tri-Tone red, orange/tan/creme, Tri-Tone yellow or Tri-Tone blue (with Free Wheeling options only). Lower body side molding with black vinyl insert (for custom only). Bright wheel-lip molding (for custom only). GT bar, tubular design painted black with black padding. AM radio. AM/FM radio monaural (single speaker). AM/FM stereo (quad speakers). AM/FM stereo with cassette tape player (quad speakers). 40-channel CB radio. Air conditioning. Highout heater. ComfortVent heater. Auxiliary heater. Western low-mount swing-away mirrors. Bright low-mount swing-away recreational mirrors. Simulated leather-wrapped steering wheel (for custom only). Tilt steering wheel. Fingertip speed control with resume feature. Tinted sliding rear quarter windows. Tinted glass for all windows. Privacy glass in fixed quarter windows. Underhood tool storage box. Swing-away outside spare tire carrier with lock and white or black cover. Black spare tire cover for custom with inside carrier. Electronic digital clock. Center console. Captain's chairs (reclining driver and passenger seats), front bench seat. Flip/fold rear bench seat. Cloth seat trim inserts with Ranger XLT Package for front bucket, bench or rear flip/fold bench seats. Automatic locking hubs (with SelectShift transmission only). SelectShift transmission. Quad heavy-duty front and rear shock absorbers. Heavy-duty rear shock absorbers. Heavy-duty air cleaner. Gauges for oil pressure and ammeter. Engine block heater (single with 4.2 liter six and 5.0 liter V-8, dual with 5.8 liter V-8). Maximum capacity, 32 gal. fuel tank. Auxiliary transmission oil cooler (with SelectShift automatic transmission). Skid plates. Dual electric horns. Fog lamps (includes plastic covers and bright front bumper guards. Front and/or rear chrome bumpers. Chrome rear step bumper. Argent rear step bumper. Styled steel painted white wheels (4 wheels with steel spare). 10-hole polished forged aluminum with clear plastic coated wheels. (4 wheels with steel spare). Sport wheelcovers (4). 5-slot brushed forged aluminum wheels with clear plastic coating (4 wheels with steel spare). XLT Lariat Package: $908. Includes, in addition to or in place of custom features, brushed aluminum tailgate applique with bright FORD lettering and XLT plaque, chrome bumpers, bright rear side window moldings, bright lower body side molding with black vinyl insert, cloth trim or patterned vinyl, wall-to-wall cut-pile carpeting (includes rear cargo area), bright accents on door trim panels with lower area carpeted, rear quarter trim panels with integral armrests and storage bin, cargo lamp, front vinyl headliner on foam padding, Deluxe seat belts, Ranger XLT dash plaque, black vinyl spare tire cover (not available for 10 x 15 spare), courtesy lighting with passenger and driver's side door switches, simulated leather-wrapped steering wheel, cigar lighter, woodtone accent around steering wheel horn pad, polished woodtone applique on instrument panel with bright molding for instruments, added insulation. Tri-color tape stripe (in lieu of pinstripes on Free Wheeling Packages). XLS Package: $945. Exterior Protection Group. Includes bright door edge guards and rub strip. Security Lock Group. Includes locking gas cap and locks on inside hood release, glove box and spare tire. Trailer Towing Packages. Super Engine Cooling Package. Extra Engine Cooling Package. Sports instrumentation Package. Includes 0-6000 rpm tachometer, ammeter, oil pressure gauge and trip odometer. Special Altitude Performance Package. Handling Package. Includes front stabilizer bar and quad heavy-duty hydraulic front and rear shock absorbers. Convenience Group. Includes intermittent windshield wipers, 12 in. day/night mirror, map box in doors, headlamp-on warning buzzer and right hand door courtesy light switch (custom only). Light Group. Includes lights in glove box, ashtray, under instrument panel, dome light with map light (standard dome light only with optional front bucket seat), movable underhood worklight, and headlamp-on warning buzzer.

HISTORICAL FOOTNOTES: The 1982 Bronco was introduced in the fall of 1981.

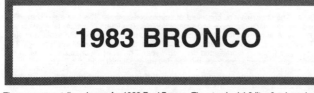

1983 BRONCO

There were no styling change for 1983 Ford Bronco. The standard 4.9 liter 6-cyl. engine was now available with automatic transmission. Joining the Bronco's list of standard equipment features was a rear flip-fold bench seat.

I.D. DATA: The Bronco V.I.N. consisted of seventeen symbols. The first three characters identified the manufacturer, make and type of vehicle. The fourth character (a letter) designated the GVW range. The fifth, sixth and seventh characters identified the series and body style. The eighth character identified the engine. The ninth character was the check digit. The tenth character (a letter) represented the model year. The eleventh character identified the assembly plant. The remaining digits represented the sequential production number.

Body Type	Factory Price	GVW	Shipping Weight	Prod. Total
Bronco U100				
Wagon (U150)	$10,858	5350*	4254	—

* A 6300 GVW Package was optional.

STANDARD ENGINE: (All states except California where the 302 V-8 is standard): Engine Type: OHV 6-cyl. Cast-iron block and cylinder heads. Bore x Stroke: 4.0 in. x 3.98 in. Lifters: Hydraulic. Number of main bearings-7. Displacement: 300 cu. in. (4.9 liters). Carburetion: Single 1-barrel. Compression ratio: 8.9:1. Horsepower: Net: 101 @ 3000 rpm. Torque: Net: 223 lb.-ft. @ 1600 rpm. Oil capacity: 6 qts. with filter. Fuel Requirements: Unleaded.

OPTIONAL ENGINE: OHV V-8. Cast-iron block and cylinder heads. Bore x Stroke: 4.00 in. x 300 in. Lifters: Hydraulic. Number of main bearings-5. Displacement: 302 cu. in. (5.0 liters). Lifters: Hydraulic. Number of main bearings-5. Carburetion: Single 2-barrel. Net: 130 @ 3800 rpm. Torque: Net: 222 lb.-ft. @ 2000 rpm. Fuel Requirements: Unleaded.

OPTIONAL ENGINE: OHV V-8. Cast-iron block and cylinder heads. Bore x Stroke: 4.00 in. x 3.50 in. Lifters: Hydraulic. Number of main bearings-5. Displacement: 351 cu. in. (5.8 liters). Carburetion: Single 2-barrel. Net: 156 @ 4000 rpm. Torque: Net: 262 lb.-ft. @ 2200 rpm. Fuel Requirements: Unleaded.

CHASSIS FEATURES: Separate body and frame, box-section welded frame. 3.95 in. section modulus.

SUSPENSION AND RUNNING GEAR: Front Suspension: Coil springs, computer selected. Rear Suspension: Two-stage, semi-elliptical leaf, computer selected. Front Axle: Capacity: 3550 lb. Rear Axle: Capacity: 3750 lb.

Final Drive Ratio

Engine	Trans.	49 states Std./ Opt. Ratio	California Std./Opt. Ratio
300-6 cyl.:	Man.-4 spd.:	3.50/None	Not avail.
	Man.-4 spd. OD:	3.00/3.50	Not avail.
302 V-8:	Man.-4 spd.	3.00/3.50	Not avail.
	Man.-4 spd. OD:	3.00/3.50	Not avail.
	C6 Auto.:	3.00/3.50	3.50 (no opt.)
351 V-8:	Man. 4-spd.:	3.00/3.50	Not avail.
	Man. 4-spd. OD:	3.00/3.50	3.50 (no opt.)
	C6 Auto.:	3.00/3.50	3.50 (no opt.)

Standard transmission for all engines is a wide ratio 4-speed, a close-ratio version is optional. Transfer Case: Type: 2-speed. Ratios: 1.00:1, 2.61:1. Brakes: Type: Hydraulic power-assisted, vented disc front and cast iron drum rear. Dimensions: Front: 11.5 in. dia. Rear: 11.0 in. x 2.2 in. Wheels: 5.5K, 5-hole disc. Optional: 15 x 6, 15 x 7. Tires: L78 x 15B. Optional: L78 x 15C, P235/75R, 10 x 15C, 7.0 x 15D. Steering: Recirculating ball, power assisted. Ratio: 17:1. Turning Circle: 36.75 ft. Optional: None. Transmission: 4-speed manual, synchromesh on top three gears. The 300 6-cyl. engine's standard transmission remained a wide-ratio 4-speed manual. Both a close-ratio version and the manual 4-speed overdrive were optional. Except for California where it was available in California only with the C6 3-spd. automatic. The 302 V-8 was offered with the same transmissions as the 6-cyl. The 351 was available with all transmissions in all states. Optional (for 302 and 351 engines only): 3-speed automatic. Ratios: 2.46:1, 1.46:1, 1.00:1. Clutch: 11. in. dia. Optional: None.

VEHICLE DIMENSIONS: Wheelbase: 104 in. Overall Length: 180.3 in. Front/Rear Tread 64.3 in./64.4 in. Overall Height: 75.5 in. Width: 79.3 in. Front/Rear Overhang: 30.5 in./40.5 in. Tailgate: Width and Height: 58 in. x 36 in. Approach/Departure Degrees: 37.5/23.4. Ground Clearance: Front axle: 8.1 in. Rear axle: 7.8 in. Transfer case: 11.5 in. (at skid plate). Load space: With rear seat installed: 37 in. x 43.5 in. x 43.25 in. With rear seat removed or folded: 54 in. x 43.5 in. x 43.25 in.

CAPACITIES: Fuel Tank: 25.0 gal. Optional: 32 gal. with skid plate.

ACCOMMODATIONS: Seating Capacity: 2 passengers, 3 passenger front bench optional, 3 passenger rear bench seat optional. Headroom: 36 in. Maximum steering wheel to seat back: 18.25 in. Seat to ground: 38.5 in. Floor to ground: 24 in.

INSTRUMENTATION: Speedometer, odometer, temperature and fuel gauges.

OPTIONS AND PRICES: Chrome grille. Accent tape stripe. Tri-color tape stripe on hood and sides in Tri-Tone red, orange/tan/creme, Tri-Tone yellow or Tri-Tone blue (with Free Wheeling options only). Lower body side molding with black vinyl insert (for custom only). Bright wheel-lip molding (for custom only). GT bar, tubular design painted black with black padding. AM radio. AM/FM radio monaural (single speaker). AM/FM stereo (quad speakers). AM/FM stereo with cassette tape player (quad speakers). 40-channel CB radio. Air conditioning. Highout heater. ComfortVent heater. Auxiliary heater. Western low-mount swing-away mirrors. Bright low-mount swing-away recreational mirrors. Simulated leather-wrapped steering wheel (for custom only). Tilt steering wheel. Fingertip speed control with resume feature. Tinted sliding rear quarter windows. Tinted glass for all windows. Privacy glass in fixed quarter windows. Underhood tool storage box. Swing-away outside spare tire carrier with lock and white or black cover. Black spare tire cover for custom with inside carrier. Electronic digital clock. Center console. Captain's chairs (reclining driver and passenger seats), front bench seat. Flip/fold rear bench seat. Cloth seat trim inserts with Ranger XLT Package for front bucket, bench or rear flip/fold bench seats. Automatic locking hubs (with SelectShift transmission only). SelectShift transmission. Quad heavy-duty front and rear shock absorbers. Heavy-duty rear shock absorbers. Heavy-duty air cleaner. Gauges for oil pressure and ammeter. Engine block heater (single with 4.2 liter six and 5.0 liter V-8, dual with 5.8 liter V-8). Maximum capacity, 32 gal. fuel tank. Auxiliary transmission oil cooler (with SelectShift automatic transmission). Skid plates. Dual electric horns. Fog lamps (includes plastic covers and bright front bumper guards. Front and/or rear chrome bumpers. Chrome rear step bumper. Argent rear step bumper. Styled steel painted white wheels (4 wheels with steel spare). 10-hole polished forged aluminum with clear plastic coated wheels. (4 wheels with steel spare). Sport wheelcovers (4). 5-slot brushed forged aluminum wheels with clear plastic coating (4 wheels with steel spare). XLT Lariat Package: $868 Includes, in addition to or in place of custom features, brushed aluminum tailgate applique with bright FORD lettering and XLT plaque, chrome bumpers, bright rear side window moldings, bright lower body side molding with black vinyl insert, cloth trim or patterned vinyl, wall-to-wall cut-pile carpeting (includes rear cargo area), bright accents on door trim panels with lower area carpeted, rear quarter trim panels with integral armrests and storage bin, cargo lamp, front vinyl headliner on foam padding, Deluxe seat belts, Ranger XLT dash plaque, black vinyl spare tire cover (not available for 10 x 15 spare), courtesy lighting with passenger and driver's side door switches, simulated leather-wrapped steering wheel, cigar lighter, woodtone accent around steering wheel horn pad, polished woodtone applique on instrument panel with bright molding for instruments, added insulation. Tri-color tape stripe (in lieu of pinstripes on Free Wheeling Packages). XLS Package: $899. Exterior Protection Group. Includes bright door edge guards and rub strip. Security Lock Group. Includes locking gas cap and locks on inside hood release, glove box and spare tire. Trailer Towing Packages. Super Engine Cooling Package. Extra Engine Cooling Package. Sports Instrumentation Package. Includes 0-6000 rpm tachometer, ammeter, oil pressure gauge and trip odometer. Special Altitude Performance Package. Handling Package. Includes front stabilizer bar and quad heavy-duty hydraulic front and rear shock absorbers. Convenience Group. Includes intermediate windshield wipers, 12 in. day/night mirror, map box in doors, headlamp-on warning buzzer and right hand door courtesy light switch (custom only). Light Group. Includes lights in glove box, ashtray, under instrument panel, dome light with map light (standard dome light only with optional front bucket seat), movable underhood worklight, and headlamp-on warning buzzer

HISTORICAL FOOTNOTES: The 1983 Bronco was introduced in September, 1982.

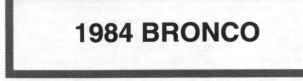

1984 BRONCO

Bronco styling was carried over from 1983 for the 1984 model year. Replacing the 5.8 liter 2-barrel V-8 for automatic transmission applications in all states except California was the 210 horsepower 5.8 liter HO V-8. Broncos with manual transmission now had a hydraulic clutch.

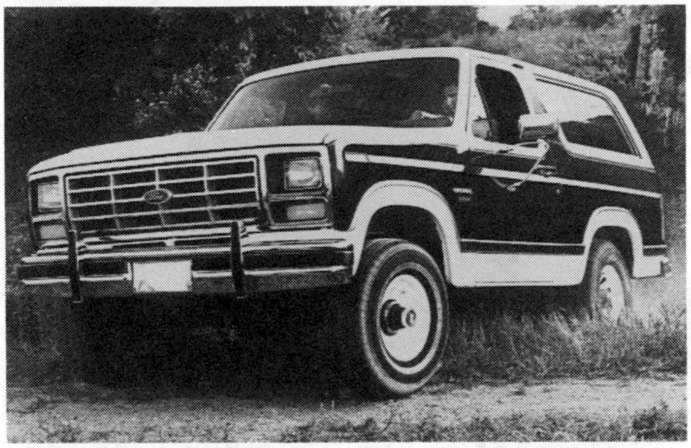

1984 Ford Bronco XLT Ranger

I.D. DATA: The Bronco V.I.N. consisted of seventeen symbols. The first three characters identified the manufacturer, make and type of vehicle. The fourth character (a letter) designated the GVW range. The fifth, sixth and seventh characters identified the series and body style. The eighth character identified the engine. The ninth character was the check digit. The tenth character (a letter) represented the model year. The eleventh character identified the assembly plant. The remaining digits represented the sequential production number.

Body Type	Factory Price	GVW	Shipping Weight	Prod. Total
Bronco U100				
Wagon (U150)	$11,355	5350*	4311	47,589**

* A 6300 GVW Package was optional.
** 1984 calendar year sales.

STANDARD ENGINE: (All states except California where the 302 V-8 is standard): Engine Type: OHV 6-cyl. Cast-iron block and cylinder heads. Bore x Stroke: 4.0 in. x 3.98 in. Lifters: Hydraulic. Number of main bearings-7. Displacement: 300 cu. in. (4.9 liters). Carburetion: Single 1-barrel. Compression ratio: 8.9:1. Horsepower: Net: 101 @ 3000 rpm. Torque: Net: 223 lb.-ft. @ 1600 rpm. Oil capacity: 6 qts. with filter. Fuel Requirements: Unleaded.

OPTIONAL ENGINE: OHV V-8. Cast-iron block and cylinder heads. Bore x Stroke: 4.00 in. x 300 in. Lifters: Hydraulic. Number of main bearings-5. Displacement: 302 cu. in. (5.0 liters). Lifters: Hydraulic. Number of main bearings-5. Carburetion: Single 2-barrel. Net: 130 @ 3800 rpm. Torque: Net: 222 lb.-ft. @ 2000 rpm. Fuel Requirements: Unleaded.

OPTIONAL ENGINE: OHV V-8. Cast-iron block and cylinder heads. Bore x Stroke: 4.00 in. x 3.50 in. Lifters: Hydraulic. Number of main bearings-5. Displacement: 351 cu. in. (5.8 liters). Carburetion: Single 2-barrel. Net: 156 @ 4000 rpm. Torque: Net: 262 lb.-ft. @ 2200 rpm. Fuel Requirements: Unleaded.

OPTIONAL ENGINE: OHV V-8. 351 HO. Cast-iron block and cylinder heads. Bore x Stroke: 4.00 in. x 3.50 in. Lifters: Hydraulic. Number of main bearings-5. Displacement: 351 cu. in. (5.8 liters). Carburetion: Single 4-barrel. Net: 210 @ 4000 rpm. Torque: Net: 305 lb.-ft. @ 2800 rpm. Fuel Requirements: Unleaded.

CHASSIS FEATURES: Separate body and frame, box-section welded frame. 3.95 in. section modulus.

SUSPENSION AND RUNNING GEAR: Front Suspension: Coil springs, computer selected. Rear Suspension: Two-stage, semi-elliptical leaf, computer selected. Front Axle: Capacity: 3550 lb. Rear Axle: Capacity: 3750 lb. Transfer Case: Type: 2-speed. Ratios: 1.00:1, 2.61:1. Brakes: Type: Hydraulic power-assisted, vented disc front and cast iron drum rear. Dimensions: Front: 11.5 in. dia. Rear: 11.0 in. x 2.2 in. Wheels: 5.5K, 5-hole disc. Optional: 15 x 6, 15 x 7. Tires: L78 x 15B. Optional: L78 x 15C, P235/75R, 10 x 15C, 7.0 x 15D. Steering: Recirculating ball, power assisted. Ratio: 17:1. Turning Circle: 36.75 ft. Optional: None. Transmission: 4-speed manual, synchromesh on top three gears. The 300 6-cyl. engine's standard transmission remained a wide-ratio 4-speed manual. Both a close-ratio version and the manual 4-speed overdrive were optional. Replacing the 5.8 liter 2-barrel V-8 for automatic transmission applications in all states except California was the 210 horsepower 5.8 liter HO. Optional (for 302 and 351 engines only): 3-speed automatic. Ratios: 2.46:1, 1.46:1, 1.00:1. Clutch: 11. in. dia. Optional: None.

VEHICLE DIMENSIONS: Wheelbase: 104 in. Overall Length: 180.3 in. Front/Rear Tread 64.3 in./64.4 in. Overall Height: 75.5 in. Width: 79.3 in. Front/Rear Overhang: 30.5 in./40.5 in. Tailgate: Width and Height: 58 in. x 36 in. Approach/Departure Degrees: 37.5/23.4. Ground Clearance: Front axle: 8.1 in. Rear axle: 7.8 in. Transfer case: 11.5 in. (at skid plate). Load space: With rear seat installed: 37 in. x 43.5 in. x 43.25 in. With rear seat removed or folded: 54 in. x 43.5 in. x 43.25 in.

CAPACITIES: Fuel Tank: 25.0 gal. Optional: 32 gal. with skid plate.

ACCOMMODATIONS: Seating Capacity: 2 passengers, 3 passenger front bench optional, 3 passenger rear bench seat optional. Headroom: 36 in. Maximum steering wheel to seat back: 18.25 in. Seat to ground: 38.5 in. Floor to ground: 24 in.

INSTRUMENTATION: Speedometer, odometer, temperature and fuel gauges.

OPTIONS AND PRICES: Chrome grille. Accent tape stripe. Tri-color tape stripe on hood and sides in Tri-Tone red, orange/tan/creme, Tri-Tone yellow or Tri-Tone blue (with Free Wheeling options only). Lower body side molding with black vinyl insert (for custom only). Bright wheel-lip molding (for custom only). GT bar, tubular design painted black with black padding. AM radio. AM/FM radio monaural (single speaker). AM/FM stereo (quad speakers). AM/FM stereo with cassette tape player (quad speakers). 40-channel CB radio. Air conditioning. Highout heater. ComfortVent heater. Auxiliary heater. Western low-mount swing-away mirrors. Bright low-mount swing-away recreational mirrors. Simulated leather-wrapped steering wheel (for custom only). Tilt steering wheel. Fingertip speed control with resume feature. Tinted sliding rear quarter windows. Tinted glass for all windows. Privacy glass in fixed quarter windows. Underhood tool storage box. Swing-away outside spare tire carrier with lock and white or black cover. Black spare tire cover for custom with inside carrier. Electronic digital clock. Center console. Captain's chairs (reclining driver and passenger seats), front bench seat. Flip/fold rear bench seat. Cloth seat trim inserts with Ranger XLT Package for front bucket, bench or rear flip/fold bench seats. Automatic locking hubs (with SelectShift transmission only). SelectShift transmission. Quad heavy-duty front and rear shock absorbers. Heavy-duty rear shock absorbers. Heavy-duty air cleaner. Gauges for oil pressure and ammeter. Engine block heater (single with 4.2 liter six and 5.0 liter V-8, dual with 5.8 liter V-8). Maximum capacity, 32 gal. fuel tank. Auxiliary transmission oil cooler (with SelectShift automatic transmission). Skid plates. Dual electric horns. Fog lamps (includes plastic covers and bright front bumper guards. Front and/or rear chrome bumpers. Chrome rear step bumper. Argent rear step bumper. Styled steel painted white wheels (4 wheels with steel spare). 10-hole polished forged aluminum with clear plastic coated wheels (4 wheels with steel spare). Sport wheelcovers (4). 5-slot brushed forged aluminum wheels with clear plastic coating (4 wheels with steel spare). XLT Lariat Package: $868. Includes, in addition to or in place of custom features, brushed aluminum tailgate applique with bright FORD lettering and XLT plaque, chrome bumpers, bright rear side window moldings, bright lower body side molding with black vinyl insert, cloth trim or patterned vinyl, wall-to-wall cut-pile carpeting (includes rear cargo area), bright accents on door trim panels with lower area carpeted, rear quarter trim panels with integral armrests and storage bin, cargo lamp, front vinyl headliner on foam padding, Deluxe seat belts, Ranger XLT dash plaque, black vinyl spare tire cover (not available for 10 x 15 spare), courtesy lighting with passenger and driver's side door switches, simulated leather-wrapped steering wheel, cigar lighter, woodtone accent around steering wheel horn pad, polished woodtone applique on instrument panel with bright molding for instruments, added insulation. Tri-color tape stripe (in lieu of pinstripes on Free Wheeling Packages). XLS Package: $899. Exterior Protection Group. Includes bright door edge guards and rub strip. Security Lock Group. Includes locking gas cap and locks on inside hood release, glove box and spare tire. Trailer Towing Packages. Super Engine Cooling Package. Extra Engine Cooling Package. Sports Instrumentation Package. Includes 0-6000 rpm tachometer, ammeter, oil pressure gauge and trip odometer. Special Altitude Performance Package. Handling Package. Includes front stabilizer bar and quad heavy-duty hydraulic front and rear shock absorbers. Convenience Group. Includes intermediate windshield wipers, 12 in. day/night mirror, map box in doors, headlamp-on warning buzzer and right hand door courtesy light switch (custom only). Light Group. Includes lights in glove box, ashtray, under instrument panel, dome light with map light (standard dome light only with optional front bucket seat), movable underhood worklight, and headlamp-on warning buzzer

HISTORICAL FOOTNOTES: The full-size Bronco was joined by the Bronco II for 1984.

1985 BRONCO

The major development for 1985 was the introduction of the new Eddie Bauer Package. Also becoming available as an option was an electronic AM/FM stereo radio/cassette player. The 5.0 liter V-8 engine now had multiple port fuel injection. This engine could be ordered with the automatic overdrive transmission. The base custom model's standard exterior equipment consisted of the following: Chrome front and rear bumpers, tinted glass, black grille with bright surround, halogen rectangular headlights, bright, low-mount swing-away western mirrors, bright windshield surround molding, fiberglass roof, wraparound taillights, pivoting vent windows, Sport wheelcovers and interval windshield wipers. Interior features consisted of dual coat hooks, color-keyed plastic cowl side trim, dome light and driver door operated courtesy light, front and rear color-keyed floor mats, color-keyed plastic full panel door trim with fully padded armrest and bright handles, fresh air vents, ammeter and oil pressure gauges, high output heater, inside hood release, dual electric horns, color-keyed instrument panel with full width pad, argent appliques, cluster warning lights, glove box lock and door with cup depressions and coin slots, cigarette lighter, day/night 12 in. mirror, color-keyed A-pillar and windshield header molding, AM radio, black scuff plates, black seat belts, front vinyl bucket seats and rear flip/fold bench seat, black spare tire cover, black steering wheel, color-keyed vinyl sun visors and black rear quarter trim panels with color-keyed molding. The Bronco's exterior colors for 1985 were raven black, silver metallic, bright canyon red, midnight blue metallic, light regatta blue metallic, light desert tan, Wimbledon white, desert tan metallic and dark charcoal metallic. The interior color choices were regatta blue, canyon red and tan. The Bronco's fiberglass roof was offered in black, white, light desert tan and midnight blue.

I.D. DATA: The Bronco V.I.N. consisted of seventeen symbols. The first three characters identified the manufacturer, make and type of vehicle. The fourth character (a letter) designated the GVW range. The fifth, sixth and seventh characters identified the series and body style. The eighth character identified the engine. The ninth character was the check digit. The tenth character (a letter) represented the model year. The eleventh character identified the assembly plant. The remaining digits represented the sequential production number.

Body Type	Factory Price	GVW	Shipping Weight	Prod. Total
Bronco U100				
Wagon (U150)	$11,993[a]	5950*	4373	52,724**

a Subsequently raised to $12,050
* A 6300 GVW Package was optional.
** 1985 calendar year production.

STANDARD ENGINE: (Available in California with 3.55:1 axle ratio): Engine Type: OHV 6-cyl. Cast-iron block and cylinder heads. Bore x Stroke: 4.0 in. x 3.98 in. Lifters: Mechanical. Number of main bearings-7. Carburetion: Single-barrel, downdraft. Compression Ratio: 8.5:1. Displacement: 300 cu. in. (4.9 liters). Horsepower (with 3.08:1 axle ratio): 120 @ 3000 rpm. Not available in California. All others: 125 @ 3200 rpm. Torque (with 3.08:1 axle ratio): 250 lb.-ft. @ 2000 rpm. Not available in California. All others: 245 lb. ft. @ 1800 rpm. Fuel Requirements: Unleaded.

OPTIONAL ENGINE: OHV V-8. Cast-iron block and cylinder heads. (Not available in California with automatic transmission). Bore x Stroke: 4.00 in. x 300 in. Lifters: Hydraulic. Number of main bearings-5. Displacement: 302 cu. in. (5.0 liters). Lifters: Hydraulic. Number of main bearings-7. Fuel induction: Electronic Fuel Injection. Compression Ratio: 9.0:1. Horsepower: 190 @ 3800 rpm. Torque: 285 lb.-ft. @ 2400 rpm. Fuel Requirements: Unleaded.

OPTIONAL ENGINE: OHV V-8. Cast-iron block and cylinder heads. (California only with automatic transmission). Bore x Stroke: 4.00 in. x 3.50 in. Lifters: Hydraulic. Number of main bearings-5. Displacement: 351 cu. in. (5.8 liters). Compression Ratio: 8.3:1. Horsepower: 150 @ 3200 rpm. Torque: 280 lb.-ft. @ 1800 rpm. Fuel Requirements: Unleaded.

OPTIONAL ENGINE: OHV V-8. Cast-iron block and cylinder heads. High Output. (Not available in California). Available only with automatic transmission. Bore x Stroke: 4.00 in. x 3.50 in. Lifters: Hydraulic. Number of main bearings-5. Displacement: 351 cu. in. (5.8 liters). Fuel Induction: Fuel injection. Compression Ratio: 8.3:1. Horsepower: 210 @ 4000 rpm. Torque: 305 lb.-ft. @ 2800 rpm. Fuel Requirements: Unleaded.

CHASSIS FEATURES: Separate body and frame, box-section welded frame. 3.95 in. section modulus.

SUSPENSION AND RUNNING GEAR: Front Suspension: Coil springs, computer selected. Rear Suspension: Two-stage, semi-elliptical leaf, computer selected. Front Axle: Capacity: 3550 lb. Rear Axle: Capacity: 3750 lb. Final Drive Ratio: 3.08:1 front and rear. The 5.9 liter engine with automatic transmission, along with all models equipped with the High Altitude Package have a standard 3.55:1 ratio. All California models have a standard 3.55:1 axle ratio. Transfer Case: NPG 208, 2-speed. Ratios: 2.61, 1.00:1. Brakes: Type: Hydraulic power-assisted, vented disc front and cast iron drum rear. Dimensions: Front: 11.5 in. dia. Rear: 11.0 in. x 2.2 in. Wheels: 6.0JK, 5-hole disc. Tires: P235/75R x 15XL steel belted radial black sidewall All-Season. Optional: P235/75R x 15XL steel belted radial black sidewall All-Terrain, P235/75R x 15XL steel belted radial All-Terrain raised white letters, 31 x 10.50R x 15C All-Terrain raised white letters. Steering: Ford XR-50, power-assisted recirculating ball. Ratio: 17.0:1. Transmission: Type: 4-speed manual. Optional: 4-speed manual overdrive (not available with Heavy-Duty Front Suspension/Snowplow Package or Trailer Tow Package), SelectShift automatic (includes 45 amp battery), automatic overdrive. Clutch: 6-cyl.: 10 in., V-8: 11.0 in. dia.

VEHICLE DIMENSIONS: Wheelbase: 104.7 in. Overall Length: 177.7 in. Front/Rear Tread 65.1 in./64.4 in. Overall Height: 74.0 in. Width: 77.2 in. Front/Rear Overhang: 28.7 in./44.3 in. Approach/Departure Degrees: 34.1/20.6. Ground Clearance: Front axle: 8.1 in. Rear axle: 7.8 in. Transfer case: 9.1 in.

CAPACITIES: Fuel Tank: 32.0 gal. with skid plate.

ACCOMMODATIONS: Seating Capacity: 5 passengers.

INSTRUMENTATION: Speedometer, odometer, gauges for fuel level, ammeter, oil pressure, engine coolant temperature, warning lights for brake system, parking brake engaged.

OPTIONS AND PRICES: The option code follows the option description. 5.0 liter EFI V-8 (99N): $426-subsequently raised to $526. 5.0 liter 2V V-8 (99G) (California only): $672-subsequently raised to $772. 5.8 liter HO V-8 (99G): $757.30 (with Eddie Bauer Package: $331.30). 4-speed manual overdrive (44B): $80.00. SelectShift automatic transmission (44G): $558.80. Automatic overdrive (44T): $694.40. Auxiliary oil cooler: (62H) $59.00. Standard axle ratio with Traction-Lok: $238.00. Optional axle ratios: $42.10. Dana limited slip front axle (Requires 3.50, 3.55 or 4.1:1 Traction-Lok rear axle. Not available with automatic locking hubs or Heavy-Duty Front Suspension/Snowplow Package). (472): $238.00. P235/75R x 15L black sidewall All-Terrain tires (T7/50N): $65.40. P235/75R x 15L raised white letters All-Terrain tires (T7P): $228.30. 31 x 10.50R x 15C raised white letter All-Terrain tires (T1K) $740.30. (With Eddie Bauer Package: $512.00). Air conditioning (572): $743.70. Heavy-duty 63 amp battery: (633) $53. Chrome rear step bumper (768): $109.10. Console (Not available with front bench seat). (604): $119.30. Cooling, super engine (624): $141.50 (without air conditioning or Trailer Towing Package); $88.40 (with air conditioning or Eddie Bauer Package). Rear window defroster (913): $131.10. Privacy glass (924): $144.40. Engine block heater (41H): $31.00 (single element with 4.9 liter or 5.0 liter engines; dual element with 5.8 liter engine: $62.00). Automatic locking front hubs (212) $40.20. Light Group (593): $101.00. Transfer case skid plate (413): $42.20. Swing-away exterior spare tire carrier (51Q): $139.30. Speed ControlTilt steering wheel (554): $279.00. Deluxe argent styled steel wheels: $174.50. White styled steel wheels: $121.00. AM/FM stereo radio (584): $124.90. AM/FM stereo radio with cassette player (587): $255.40 (with standard trim, $130.50 with either Eddie Bauer or XLT trim). Electronic AM/FM stereo search radio with cassette player (586): $295.50. Radio delete option (58Y): $39.00. Cloth and vinyl bucket seat trim (M): $94.80. Cloth and vinyl bench seat (L): $94.80. Cloth and vinyl Captain's chairs (K): $491.70. Deluxe two-tone paint (952): $342.80 (with standard trim, with XLT trim: $160.90). Victoria two-tone (954): $391.80. California emissions system (422): $235.00. High altitude principle use (428): No charge. Trailer Towing Package. Requires SelectShift automatic or automatic overdrive transmission. Includes wiring harness, heavy-duty flashers, Handling Package, heavy-duty battery, heavy-duty alternator, extra engine cooling, auxiliary transmission oil cooler (535): $376.70 (without air conditioning), with air conditioning: $278.90. Heavy-duty Suspension/Snowplow Package (563). The following prices of the heavy-duty option apply to Broncos equipped with XLT Trim Package 682A or Standard Trim Package 680A: $155.10 (with manual trans. and without air conditioning); $93.20 (with manual trans. and air conditioning); $214.10 (with automatic trans. and without air conditioning); $152.20 (with automatic trans. and air conditioning). The following prices apply to Broncos equipped with XLT Trim Package 683A or Eddie Bauer Trim Package 865A: $110.10 (with manual trans. and without air conditioning); $48.20 with manual trans. and air conditioning or Eddie Bauer); $169.10 (with automatic trans. and without air conditioning). Handling Package (553). Includes rear stabilizer bar, quad front and heavy-duty rear shock absorbers; included with Trailer Towing Package): $166.10. Exterior Sound Package: $12.70. Standard Trim Package (681A). Includes heavy-duty maintenance-free battery, Handling Package, transfer case skid plate: $246.10. XLT Trim Package (682A, 683A, 684A). Available in three discount packages ranging in price from $1,237.30 to $2,522.70. The basic XLT Package includes these items: Chrome grille, bright rear quarter window molding, body side protection molding, wheel-lip moldings, brushed aluminum tailgate applique, rear cargo light, color-keyed front and rear carpeting, electronic digital clock, passenger door operated courtesy light, door trim (consisting of bright molding, padded cloth insert, map pocket and carpeted lower panel), color-keyed front vinyl headliner, woodtone instrument panel appliques. Right side visor vanity mirror, AM/FM stereo radio, bright scuff plates, bucket cloth and vinyl seats, Deluxe color-keyed seat belts, soft-wrapped steering wheel with woodtone applique and color-keyed rear quarter trim panel with integral armrest and storage bin. Eddie Bauer Package (686A). Includes air conditioning, heavy-duty battery, console, privacy glass, Light Group, speed ControlTilt steering wheel, Deluxe argent styled steel wheels, AM/FM stereo radio, P235/75R x 15L raised white letter All-Terrain tires, Eddie Bauer two-tone paint, dual body side accent paint stripe, Eddie Bauer gear bag, travel blanket with case and visor organizer (shipped direct to customer from Eddie Bauer), Eddie Bauer nomenclature, "Ford Car" extended service plan. Also included but must be ordered: XLT trim, cloth and vinyl Captain's chairs): $592.60.

HISTORICAL FOOTNOTES: A total of 52,281 Broncos were sold in the 1985 calendar year.

1986 BRONCO

Changes both of a technical and design nature as well as in option availability were found in the 1986 Bronco. The four major technical developments consisted of the use of an internal hem flange on the Bronco's doors, hood and tailgate for improved corrosion protection, inclusion of the Exterior Sound Package into the Bronco's standard equipment, use of a 60 amp alternator, and the upgrading of the heavy-duty battery to 71 amp-hrs. Design developments involved the introduction of three new exterior colors, availability of a new interior color and one new fiberglass roof color, replacement of the buzzer by a warning chime, the addition of a floor console to the XLT and Captain's chairs options and the use of a "4x4" plaque on the front fenders below the "Bronco" nomenclature with standard trim. Restructuring of option availability and content resulted in the replacement of the extra cooling component of the Trailer Towing Package by a Super Engine cooling feature. A stationary underhood light replaced the movable work light in the Light Group. Both the front limited slip axle and the auxiliary transmission cooler were deleted. The Sports instrumentation now included a tachometer.

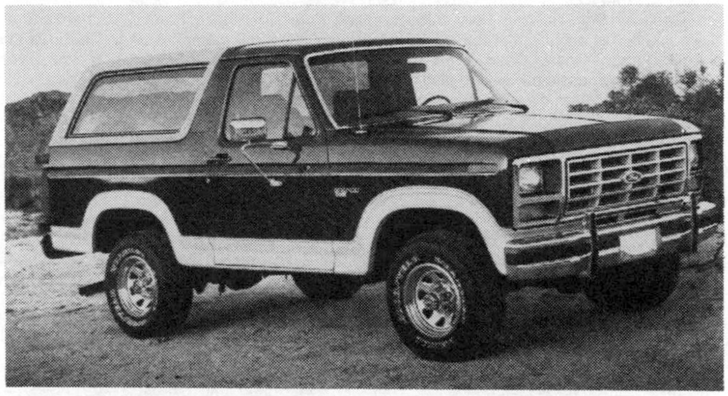

1986 Ford Eddie Bauer Bronco

Standard equipment trim features of the base Bronco included chrome front and rear bumpers, black grille with bright surround, bright windshield molding, Sport wheelcovers, tinted glass, dome light, left hand courtesy light switch, color-keyed rubber floor mat, front floor insulation, inside hood release, color-keyed A-pillar, windshield header moldings and cowl side panels, color-keyed left and right side sun visors, day/night 12 in. rearview mirror, black vinyl spare tire cover (not available with 31 x 10.5R tires), cigarette lighter, interval wipers, warning chime, glove box lock, argent instrument panel appliques. The 1986 Bronco color selection for 1986 consisted of raven black, dark grey metallic, medium silver metallic, bright canyon red, light regatta blue, dark canyon red, dark shadow blue metallic, light desert tan, colonial white and desert tan metallic. Three interior colors were available: Regatta blue, canyon red and chestnut. Four two-tone and paint/tape stripe options were offered. Broncos finished in a monotone color were available with fiberglass roof in white, black, light desert tan or dark shadow blue metallic. The Deluxe Two-Tone option provided an accent color applied to the center body side panel and tailgate between a mid-bodystripe tape stripe below the character depression and lower body side molding. In the Victoria Two-Tone scheme the accent color was applied to the front roof (except for the "basket handle"), hood and the region below the lower body side molding. It also consisted of an upper pinstripe divider tape on the hood and B-pillar and around the fiberglass roof/tailgate and lower body side molding. The accent color of the Eddie Bauer two-tone format was applied below the rocker panel area and two-tone tape stripe at paint break. It also included a two-tone pinstripe below the chamfer.

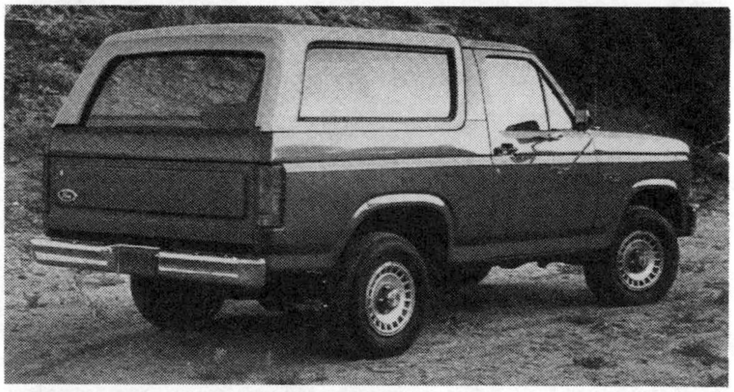

1986 Ford Bronco (standard model)

I.D. DATA: The Bronco V.I.N. consisted of seventeen symbols. The first three functioned as the world manufacturer identifier. The fourth digit identified the brake system and GVWR class. The fifth, sixth and seventh digits identified the line, series, chassis, cab or body type. U15 identified Bronco 4x4. The eighth digit identified the engine type. Y identified the 300 cu. in. 6-cyl.; N identified the 302 V-8 and H identified the 5.8 liter HO engine. The ninth digit was a computer check digit. The tenth digit, G, identified the 1986 model year. The eleventh digit identified the plant of manufacture. L identified the Wayne, Michigan truck plant where the Bronco was built. The twelfth through seventeenth digits were the sequential production numbers for each plant, starting with A00001 through A99999 then B000000, etc.

Body Type	Factory Price	GVW	Shipping Weight	Prod. Total
Bronco U100				
Wagon (U15)	$12,782	6000*	4267	36,102**

* A 6300 GVW Package was optional.
** 1986 calendar year production.

STANDARD ENGINE: Engine Type: OHV 6-cyl. Special high-grade cast-iron block and cylinder heads. Bore x Stroke: 4.0 in. x 3.98 in. Lifters: Hydraulic. Number of main bearings-7. Carburetion: Single venturi downdraft carburetor. Compression Ratio: 8.5:1. Displacement: 300 cu. in. (4.9 liters). Horsepower: 120 @ 3200 rpm (Bronco with manual transmission and 3.08:1 axle ratio). All others: 125 @ 3200 rpm. Torque 250 lb. ft. @ 2000 rpm. (Bronco with manual transmission and 3.08:1 axle ratio). All others: 245 lb.-ft. @ 1800 rpm. Fuel Requirements: Unleaded.

OPTIONAL ENGINE: OHV V-8. Special high-grade cast-iron block and cylinder heads. Bore x Stroke: 4.00 in. x 300 in. Lifters: Hydraulic. Number of main bearings-5. Displacement: 302 cu. in. (5.0 liters). Fuel induction: Eight point synchronous electronic fuel injection. Compression Ratio: 9.0:1. Horsepower: 185 @ 3800 rpm. Torque: 275 lb.-ft. @ 2400 rpm. Fuel Requirements: Unleaded.

OPTIONAL ENGINE: OHV High Output V-8. Special high-grade cast-iron block and cylinder heads. Bore x Stroke: 4.00 in. x 3.50 in. Lifters: Hydraulic. Number of main bearings-5. Displacement: 351 cu. in. (5.8 liters). Carburetion: Four venturi downdraft carburetor. Compression Ratio: 8.3:1. Horsepower: 210 @ 4000 rpm. Torque: 305 lb.-ft. @ 2800 rpm. Fuel Requirements: Unleaded.

CHASSIS FEATURES: Separate body and frame, single channel, 5 cross members, welded frame. 3.66 in. section modulus. Maximum side rail section: 6.95 x 2.12. x 0.170 in.

SUSPENSION AND RUNNING GEAR: Front Suspension: Independent, coil springs, computer selected, 2450 lb. rating. Optional rating of 2600, 2800, 2950 and 3800 lb. available. Rear Suspension: Single-stage, constant rate semi-elliptical 5-leaf, computer selected, 3790 lb. rating. Front Axle Type and Capacity: Twin Traction beam, 3550 lb. rating. Rear Axle Type and Capacity: Semi-floating, Ford, 3750 lb. rating. Final Drive Ratio: Front: 3.07:1 (49 states), 3.5:1 (California and High Altitude). 3.08:1. Rear: 3.08:1 (49 states). 3.50:1 (California and High Altitude). Transfer Case: Type: NPG 208, 2-speed. Ratios: 2.61, 1.0:1. Brakes: Type: Hydraulic power-assisted, vented disc front and cast iron drum rear. Dimensions: Front: 11.61 in. dia. Caliper piston dia.: 2.875 in. Total swept area: 220.76 sq. in. Rear: 11.03 in. x 2.25 in. Total swept area: 155.95 sq. in. Wheels: 6.0JK x 15, 5-hole disc. Optional: 15 x 7JJ Deluxe argent styled steel wheels, 15 x 7JJ white styled steel wheels. Tires: P235/75R x 15SL steel radial. Optional: 31 x 10.50R x 15C. Steering: Power assisted. Ratio: 17.6:1. Turning Circle: 36.5 ft. Optional: None. Transmission: Type: Warner T-18, 4-speed manual, synchromesh on top 3 gears. Transmission Ratios: 6.32, 3.09, 1.69, 1.0:1. Reverse: 7.4:1. Optional: Ford 4-speed manual overdrive (not available with Heavy-Duty Front Suspension/Snowplow Package or Trailer Tow Package. Ratios: 3.25, 1.92, 1.00, 0.71 (overdrive). Reverse: 3.25:1. Optional: Ford C6 automatic. (For use with 4.9 liter 6-cyl. and 5.8 liter HO V-8). Ratios: 2.46, 1.46, 1.0:1. Reverse: 2.18. Converter: 1.80:1. Optional: Ford Automatic Overdrive Drive (AOD). (For use with 5.0 liter EFI V-8). Ratios: 2.40, 1.46, 1.00, 0.667. Reverse: 2.00:1. Converter: 2.28:1. Clutch: Torsion-bend, woven non-asbestos. 10.0 in. dia. (4.9 liter 6-cyl.). Segmented, woven non-asbestos 11.0 in. dia. (5.0 liter EFI V-8). Optional: None.

VEHICLE DIMENSIONS: Wheelbase: 104.7 in. Overall Length: 177.6 in. Front/Rear Tread 65.1 in./64.4 in. Overall Height: 74.0 in. Width: 77.2 in. Front/Rear Overhang: 28.7 in./44.3 in. Tailgate: Width and Height: 63.5 in. x 35.7 in. Approach/Departure Degrees: 35.3/20.9. Ground Clearance: Front axle: 8.1 in. Rear axle: 7.8 in. Transfer case: 9.1 in.

CAPACITIES: Fuel Tank: 32.0 gal. with skid plate.

ACCOMMODATIONS: Seating Capacity: 5 passengers with standard front bucket seats and 3 passenger rear bench seat. 5 passengers with optional dual Captain's chairs and standard rear seat. 6 passengers with optional 3 passenger front bench seat and standard rear seat.

INSTRUMENTATION: Speedometer, odometer, gauges for fuel level, ammeter, oil pressure, engine coolant temperature, warning lights for brake system, parking brake engaged.

OPTIONS AND PRICES: Note: The numbers/letter entry following the option identify its ordering code. Air conditioning (572). Includes Air Conditioning Engine Cooling Package, rear floor mat insulation (standard trim only) and four instrument panel registers: $774. Ford limited slip, 3750 lb. rear axle $238. Optional rear axle ratio: $42. Maintenance-free 71 amp-hr. battery (635): $53. Bright rear step bumper with black rib strip (768): $109. Captain's chairs (886). Includes non-swivel, color-keyed cloth trim seats with armrests and zippered pouch with two external pockets on back. Also includes floor console: $492. Floor console (604). Consists of molded color-keyed plastic construction with lock. Not available with optional front bench seat: $119. Electric rear window defroster (913): $131. California emission system (422). Available only in, and required for California registration: $235. High altitude emission system (428). Required on all vehicles sold in high altitude areas. Not available in California: No charge. Super engine cooling (624): $96.10. 5.0 liter EFI V-8 (99N): $526. 5.8 liter HO V-8 (9H). Available in 49 states only with automatic transmission. $920. With Eddie Bauer: $394. Privacy glass for rear quarter windows (924): $144. Engine block heater (41H): $31. Automatic locking front hubs (212). Not available with Heavy-Duty Front Suspension/Snowplow Package or 4.10:1 axle ratio: $40. Deluxe two-tone paint (952): $379 with standard trim. $235 with XLT trim. Victoria two-tone paint (952): $418. Power door/window locks (903). Includes two switches on driver's door, one on passenger's door for side windows; door lock switches ahead of armrests on both side doors. AM/FM stereo radio (584) Includes quad premium speakers: $125. Electronic AM/FM stereo search radio with cassette tape player (586): $303. Includes quad premium speakers. AM/FM stereo radio with cassette: $255 with standard trim; $130 with XLT or Eddie Bauer. AM radio credit delete option (8Y): $39. Deletes standard AM radio, with standard trim only. Front bench seat (L). Includes cloth and vinyl trim with split back: $95. Seat trim (M). Available with standard trim bucket seats only. Features cloth and vinyl trim: $95. Spare tire carrier (51Q). Consists of outside swing-away unit with spare tire lock, black vinyl tire cover with Bronco horse emblem: $139. Speed ControlTilt steering wheel (554). Includes 15 in., 5-position tilt steering wheel with fingertip speed control: 279. Tachometer (152). Includes trip odometer. Eddie Bauer Package (154.) Includes the following items in addition to or in place of standard equipment and trim items. Exterior: XLT trim components, special two-tone paint treatment, dual body side accent stripe, tan outside spare tire cover when optional swing-away spare tire carrier is ordered (black with 31 x 10.50R tires), choice of three body colors, Deluxe argent styled steel wheels with bright trim rings, "Eddie Bauer" nomenclature, P235/75XL raised white letter All-Terrain tires and light desert tan fiberglass roof. Interior: XLT trim components, dual front cloth-trimmed Captain's chairs, cloth-trimmed rear bench seat, floor console, privacy glass, "Eddie Bauer" nomenclature, chestnut interior trim. Functional: 5.0 liter EFI V-8 (5.8 liter HO V-8 optional), air conditioning, speed ControlTilt steering wheel, Light Group, heavy-duty battery. The Eddie Bauer Package also included an Eddie Bauer garment bag and tote bag, and the "Ford Care" extended service plan: $3705-$4239-depending on package. Handling Package (553). Includes rear stabilizer bar, quad (two gas-pressurized) front shock absorbers and two heavy-duty rear shock absorbers. Not available with Heavy-Duty Front Suspension/Snowplow Package: $166. Heavy-Duty Front Suspension/Snowplow Package (563). Consists of 3800 lb. heavy-duty front axle with 3.50 or 3.54:1 ratio, 3800 lb. heavy-duty front springs with heavy-duty spring tower, heavy-duty rear shock absorbers, heavy-duty 70 amp battery, heavy-duty 71 amp battery and auxiliary oil cooler if automatic transmission is ordered. The following items were not available with this option: Handling Package, Trailer Towing Package, automatic locking front hubs, 4-speed overdrive manual transmission and 31 x 10.50R x 15C tires: $68-$150 depending upon combination with other options. Light Group (593). Consists of glove box light, stationary underhood light, courtesy light (under instrument panel), dome light with integral map light (standard dome light used with optional front bench seat), headlights-on warning chime, and, on standard trim, right side door courtesy light switch: $57. Trailer Towing Package (535). Includes heavy-duty 71 amp-hr. battery, super engine cooling, heavy-duty turn signal flasher, Handling Package and trailer towing harness. Also includes auxiliary transmission air cooler with automatic transmission: $124-$311 depending on combination with other options. XLT Trim Package. Includes these items in addition to or in place of standard trim items. Exterior: Lower body side protection molding, "XLT" emblem below "Bronco" emblem on front fenders, brushed aluminum tailgate applique, chrome grille insert and bright molding on rear quarter windows. Interior: Full-length color-keyed door trim panels with bright surround molding and padded cloth insert with map pocket and carpeting on lower panel; door headliner and quarter panel insulation and floor deadener, bright aluminum scuff plates, cloth and vinyl seat trim and color-keyed Deluxe seat belts, right hand visor vanity mirror, left and right door courtesy light switches, floor console (except with optional front bench seat), color-keyed vinyl front headliner, color-keyed rear quarter panels with armrests, speaker grilles, storage bin (left rear) and left hand panel cargo light. Instrument panel: Woodtone instrument panel cluster appliques, AM/FM stereo radio, electronic digital clock, "XLT" nomenclature and soft-wrapped steering wheel with woodtone insert $492.

HISTORICAL FOOTNOTES: The Bronco's 1986 calendar year sales fell to 49,588. Nonetheless this represented a 38 percent increase from the level of 1981. The general manager of Ford's Truck Operations was Edward E. Hagenlocker. Public relations manager was L.A. Weis. Ford Truck Operations were headquartered at 20000 Rotunda Drive, Dearborn, MI 48121.

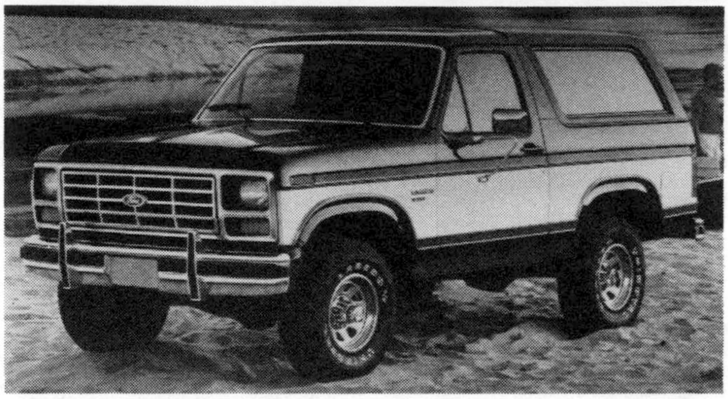

1986 Ford Bronco XLT

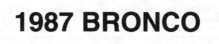

1987 BRONCO

The 1987 Bronco had a new, more aerodynamic front end highlighted by aero-style halogen headlights with impact-resistent plastic lenses and bright surround and wraparound parking/directional lights. The halogen bulb could be removed and replaced using no tools. No realignment of the lenses was necessary when a bulb was replaced. The Bronco grille was similar to last year's but had three, instead of four horizontal segments. A "4x4" identification piece was now installed below the left side headlight. The Bronco front bumper was larger and now had a smooth contour. The front parking/turn signal lights were of a contemporary wraparound design. New taillight lenses were also used. A new wheel-lip opening also helped identify the 1987 Bronco. The paint color of the vanes of the optional Sport wheelcovers were changed from light argent to black. The Deluxe argent styled steel wheels now included a larger 8 inch rim. Numerous trim changes took place in the 1987 Bronco. The standard trim nomenclature was changed to "Custom." New seat trim materials and sew styles along with new door trim panels were also introduced. The XLT Trim Package had a new lower body side molding as well as a black rub strip that was included with the front bumper and chrome rear step bumper. Other trim changes found in the XLT involved cloth sun visors with a band on the left visor and bright headlight/parking light bezels. All models had new black accents on the interior door handles, window regulators, door lock buttons, dome light bezel and door scuff plates.

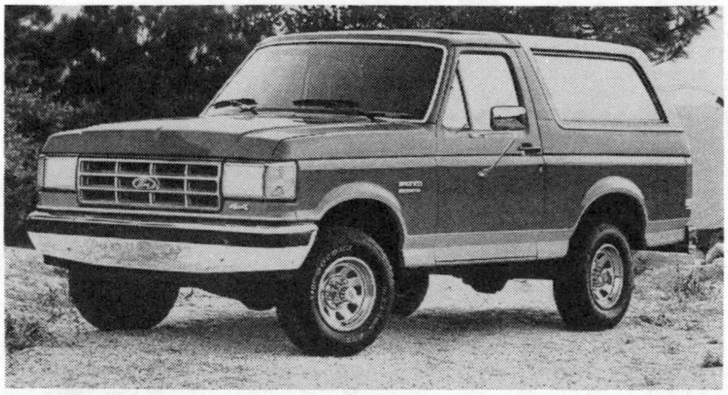

1987 Ford Eddie Bauer Bronco

The 1987 Bronco instrument panel was restyled with a curved shape that centrally positioned the speedometer for an unobstructed driver's view through the steering wheel. Black appliques were applied. Gauges for fuel, oil pressure, engine coolant temperature and battery charge were standard. Redundant indicator lights were provided for the engine coolant

temperature and oil pressure. The panel was backlit and gauge pointers were illuminated. The instrument panel now had four air registers, side window demisters and a larger glove box. Controls for the heater/defroster were located in the center pod. The steering wheel was of a new "A-frame" design and the passenger door courtesy light was now standard equipment. A safety belt comfort regulator feature was made standard with combination color-keyed lap/shoulder belts. A new instrument panel-mounted sensor light was installed for a new standard electronically controlled rear anti-lock brake system. When rear brake lock-up was detected, the computer processes signaled and directed the pressure control valve to modulate rear brake line hydraulic pressure. When the ignition was turned on, a warning light check and a complete computer self-check was made. If the system was experiencing a failure, the warning light notified the driver that the computer had shut the system down and converted the rear brakes to conventional non-anti-lock operation. All radios now included a digital clock. All manual tuning radios were replaced by electronic models.

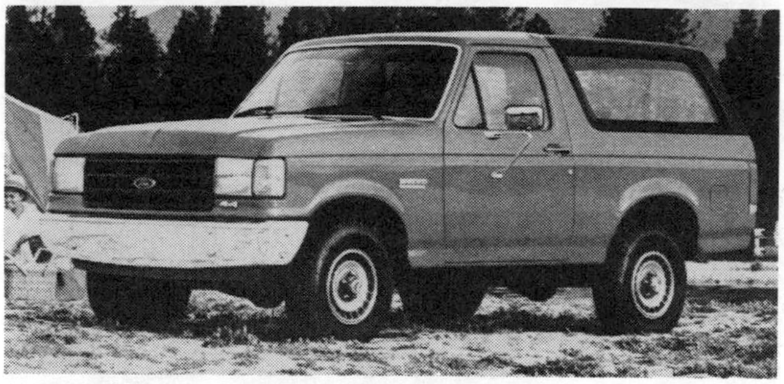

1987 Ford Bronco Custom

Also included among the options updated for 1987 was the Deluxe two-tone feature which had a revised lower paint break and molding. The standard (except for the Eddie Bauer Bronco) 4.9 liter 6-cyl. engine now had multiple port electronic fuel injection and a fast-burn cylinder head design. During the model year the 4.9 liter engine was fitted with hydro-elastic engine mounts. Both the 4.9 liter and 5.0 liter engines were fitted with a serpentine accessory drive. The 2-speed transfer case had interior linkage changes that made the system both quieter and easier shifting. A positive displacement hydraulic oil pump was now used in the transfer case. A new, optional button-operated Touch Drive electric shift transfer case option made it possible to shift on-the-fly from two-wheel drive high to four-wheel drive high and back again at any speed. This option was available with the 5.0 liter EDFI V-8 and automatic overdrive transmission. This feature also provided more interior space since both floor shift levers were eliminated. Both ride and handling were improved by the use of twin tube gas-pressurized shock absorbers and adjustable front caster and camber as standard equipment. Other functional improvements for 1987 included a fuel cap tether, see-through brake master cylinder reservoir and increased capacity windshield washer and radiator overflow reservoirs. The 1987 Bronco also benefited from the additional use of one and two-side galvanized body panels, improved door and vent window sealing and the adoption of an easy access fuse panel. Ford deleted several Bronco options for 1987. These included white styled steel wheels and the Exterior Protection Group. Neither the chrome rear step bumper and the electronic AM/FM stereo Seek-Scan radio with cassette tape player were offered for 1987. But this hardly counted for a loss since a new 4,000 lb. chrome rear step bumper was now standard while the older radio was replaced by an improved model.

Standard exterior features of the custom Bronco consisted of a chrome front bumper, chrome rear step bumper with black rub strip and 4000 lb. towing cap, black grille, fiberglass rear roof, aero headlights with high-impact lenses and replaceable halogen bulbs, wraparound taillights, bright windshield molding, tinted glass in all windows, bright low-mount swing-away mirrors, swing-down tailgate with power window, and "4x4" nomenclature mounted below left headlight. During the model year "Bronco Custom" nomenclature was installed on the front fenders. Standard custom interior appointments were as follows: Dome light, left and right side courtesy light switches, color-keyed rubber floor mat, color-keyed Deluxe seat belts with comfort regulator on shoulder belts, left and right side color-keyed coat hooks, front floor insulation, black scuff plates, inside hood release mounted in cowl trim panel, high output-type heater, two front bucket seats and 3 passenger flip-fold rear bench seat trimmed in vinyl, pivoting vent windows, color-keyed "A"- and "B"-pillar windshield header moldings and cowl side panels, color-keyed left and right side vinyl sun visors, day/night 12 in. rearview mirror and a black vinyl steering wheel. Completing the list of standard custom features was a cigarette lighter, interval windshield wipers, electronic AM radio (may be deleted for credit), glove box lock (the glove box was larger for 1987 and was removable), black instrument panel appliques ammeter, oil pressure and engine coolant temperatures gauges and side window demisters.

The exterior colors offered for the 1987 Bronco consisted of raven black, dark grey metallic, medium silver metallic, bright canyon red, light regatta blue, dark canyon red, dark shadow blue metallic, colonial white, desert tan metallic and light chestnut. Available only for the Eddie Bauer Bronco was alpine green metallic. Bronco roof colors for 1987 were black, dark shadow blue, light chestnut and white. Interior colors for the custom Bronco consisted of regatta blue, canyon red and chestnut. During the model year the XLT was also available in medium grey.

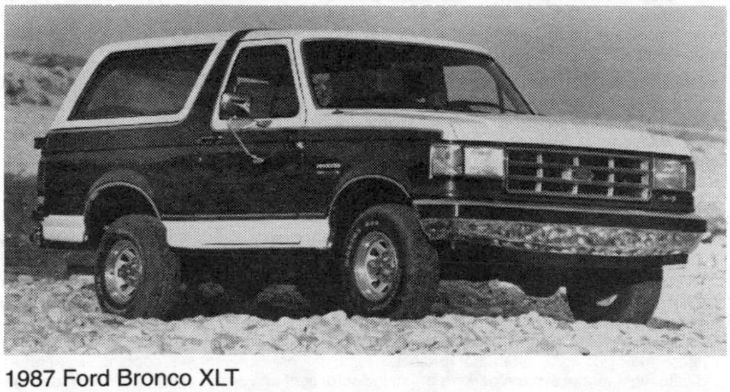

1987 Ford Bronco XLT

I.D. DATA: The Bronco V.I.N. consisted of seventeen symbols. The first three characters identified the manufacturer, make and type of vehicle. The fourth character (a letter) designated the GVW range. The fifth, sixth and seventh characters identified the series and body style. The eighth character identified the engine. The ninth character was the check digit. The tenth character (a letter) represented the model year. The eleventh character identified the assembly plant. The remaining digits represented the sequential production number.

Body Type	Factory Price	GVW	Shipping Weight	Prod. Total
Bronco U100				
Wagon (U15)	$13,924	6000*	4420	57,013

* A 6300 GVW Package was optional.

STANDARD ENGINE: Engine Type: OHV 6-cyl. Special high-grade cast-iron block and cylinder heads. Bore x Stroke: 4.0 in. x 3.98 in. Lifters: Hydraulic. Number of main bearings-7. Fuel induction: Electronic multiple port fuel injection. Compression Ratio: 8.5:1. Displacement: 300 cu. in. (4.9 liters). Horsepower: 145 @ 3400 rpm (Bronco with 2.73 or 3.08:1 axle ratio). All others: 150 @ 3400 rpm. Torque 265 lb. ft. @ 2000 rpm. (Bronco with 2.73 or 3.08:1 axle ratio). All others: 260 lb.-ft. @ 20000 rpm. Fuel Requirements: Unleaded. Oil refill capacity: 4.5 qts. (with filter change), 4.0 qts. (without filter change).

OPTIONAL ENGINE: OHV V-8. Special hlgh-grade cast-iron block and cylinder heads. Bore x Stroke: 4.00 in. x 300 in. Lifters: Hydraulic. Number of main bearings-5. Displacement: 302 cu. in. (5.0 liters). Lifters: Hydraulic. Number of main bearings-7. Fuel induction: Eight point synchronous electronic fuel injection. Compression Ratio: 9.0:1. Horsepower: 185 @ 3800 rpm. Torque: 270 lb.-ft. @ 2400 rpm. Fuel Requirements: Unleaded. Oil Refill Capacity: 6 qts. (with filter change), 5.0 qts. (without filter change).

OPTIONAL ENGINE: OHV High Output V-8. Special high-grade cast-iron block and cylinder heads. Bore x Stroke: 4.00 in. x 3.50 in. Lifters: Hydraulic. Number of main bearings-5. Displacement: 351 cu. in. (5.8 liters). Carburetion: Four venturi downdraft carburetor. Compression Ratio: 8.3:1. Horsepower: 190 @ 3800 rpm. Torque: 295 lb.-ft. @ 2600 rpm. Fuel Requirements: Unleaded. Oil Refill Capacity: 6 qts. (with filter change), 5.0 qts. (without filter change).

CHASSIS FEATURES: Separate body and frame, single channel, 5 cross members, welded frame, 36,000 psi steel. 4.27 in. section modulus. Maximum side rail section: 7.01 x 2.12. x 0.202 in.

SUSPENSION AND RUNNING GEAR: Front Suspension: Independent, coil springs, computer selected, 2450 lb. rating. Optional rating of 2600, 2800, 2950 and 3800 lb. available. Rear Suspension: Single-stage, constant rate semi-elliptical 5-leaf, computer selected, 3770 lb. rating. Front Axle Type and Capacity: Dana 44 Twin Traction beam, 3550 lb. rating. Rear Axle Type and Capacity: Semi-floating, Ford, 3800 lb. rating. Final Drive Ratio: Available Front: 3.07, 3.54, 4.09:1. Available Rear: 3.08, 3.55, 4.10:1. Transfer Case: Type: Borg Warner 1356, 2-speed. Ratios: 1.0:1, 2.69:1. Brakes: Type: Hydraulic power-assisted, vented disc front and cast iron drum rear. Dimensions: Front: 10.90 in. dia. Caliper piston dia.: 2.875 in. Total swept area: 220.76 sq. in. Rear: 11.03 in. x 2.25 in. Total swept area: 155.93 sq. in. Wheels: 6.0JK x 15, 5-hole disc. Optional: 15 x 7JJ Deluxe argent styled steel wheels, 15 x 7JJ white styled steel wheels. Tires: Custom and XLT: P235/75R x 15XL steel radial All-Season black sidewall. Eddie Bauer: P235/75RXL raised white letter All-Terrain. Optional: Custom and XLT: P235/75RXL raised white letter All-Terrain. XLT and Eddie Bauer: 31 x 10.50R x 15C raised white letter All-Terrain. Steering: Power assisted. Ratio: 17.6:1. Turning Circle: 36.5 ft. Optional: None. Transmission: Type: Warner T-18, 4-speed manual, synchromesh on top 3 gears. Transmission Ratios: 6.32, 3.09, 1.69, 1.0:1. Reverse: 7.4:1. Optional: Ford 4-speed manual overdrive (not available with Heavy-Duty Front Suspension/Snowplow Package or Trailer Tow Package Ratios: 3.25, 1.92, 1.00, 0.78 (overdrive). Reverse: 3.25:1. Optional: Ford C6 automatic. (for use with 4.9 liter 6-cyl., 5.0 liter V-8 and 5.8 liter HO V-8). Ratios: 2.46, 1.46, 1.0:1. Reverse: 2.18. Converter: 1.89:1. Optional: Ford Automatic Overdrive Drive (AOD). (For use with 5.0 liter EFI V-8). Ratios: 2.40, 1.46, 1.00, 0.667. Reverse: 2.00:1. Converter: 2.28:1. Clutch: 4.9 liter 6-cyl with overdrive transmission: Torsion-bend, woven non-asbestos. 10.0 in. dia. Belleville pressure plate. Total plate pressure: 1925 lb. Facing thickness for 1987 was changed to 0.137 in. 4.9 liter 6-cyl. and 5.0 liter EFI V-8: Segmented, woven non-asbestos 11.0 in. dia. Total plate pressure: 1796 lb. Belleville pressure plate. Changes for 1987 included an inside diameter of 7.80 in., a facing thickness of 0.130 in. and a facing area of 95.5 sq. in. Optional: None.

VEHICLE DIMENSIONS: Wheelbase: 104.7 in. Overall Length: 180.5 in. Front/Rear Tread 65.1 in./64.4 in. Overall Height: 74.0 in. Width: 79.1 in. Front/Rear Overhang: 30.5 in./45.3 in. Tailgate: Width and Height: 63.4 in. x 35.7 in. Approach/Departure Degrees: 36.3/17.7. Ground Clearance: Front axle: 8.1 in. Rear axle: 7.8 in. Transfer case: 9.1 in. Load space: With rear seat installed: 30.8 in. x 50.8 in. 35.7 in. With rear seat removed or folded: 60.8 in. 50.8 in. x 35.7 in.

CAPACITIES: Fuel Tank: 32.0 gal. with skid plate.

ACCOMMODATIONS: Seating Capacity: 5 passengers with standard front bucket seats and 3 passenger rear bench seat. 5 passengers with optional dual Captain's chairs and standard rear seat. 6 passengers with optional 3 passenger front bench seat and standard rear seat.

INSTRUMENTATION: Speedometer (mph-km/hr.-U.S. kilometers/hr.-Canada), odometer, gauges for fuel level, ammeter, oil pressure and engine coolant temperature; safety belt indicator light, high-beam indicator light, transfer case 4x4 indicator (low and high range), anti-lock brake system indicator light, alternator indicator light, oil pressure/engine coolant temperature indicator light, brake system/parking brake indicator light and emissions system indicator light.

OPTIONS AND PRICES: Note: The numbers/letter entry following the option identify its ordering code. Air conditioning (572). Includes Air Conditioning Engine Cooling Package, rear floor mat insulation (custom trim only) and four instrument panel registers. Ford limited slip, 3800 lb. rear axle. Limited slip 3550 lb. axle with 3.54:1 ratio. Maintenance-free 84 amp-hr. battery (635). Color-keyed cloth trim Captain's chairs (886). Includes inboard armrest and zippered pouch with two external pockets on back. Also includes floor console. Floor Console-(604). Consists of molded color-keyed plastic construction with two cup depressions and lock. Not available with optional front bench seat. Electric rear window defroster (913). California emission system (422). Available only in, and required for, California registration. High altitude emission system (428). Required on all vehicles sold in high altitude areas. Not available in California. 5.0 liter EFI V-8 (99N). 5.8 liter HO V-8 (99H). Available in 49 states only with automatic transmission. Privacy glass for rear quarter windows (924). Automatic locking front hubs (212). Included with Touch Drive electric shift. Not available with Handling Package, Heavy-Duty Front Suspension/Snowplow Package or 4.10:1 axle ratio. Deluxe two-tone paint-(952). Victoria two-tone paint (952). Power door/window locks (903). Includes two switches on driver's door, one on passenger's door for side windows; door lock switches ahead of armrests on both side doors. AM/FM stereo radio (584). Includes quad premium speakers. Electronic AM/FM stereo search radio with cassette tape player (586). Includes quad premium speakers. AM radio credit delete option (58Y). Deletes standard AM radio, with standard trim only. Front bench seat (L). Includes cloth and vinyl color-keyed trim with split back. Seat trim (M). Available with bucket seats only, features cloth and vinyl trim. Spare tire carrier (51Q). Consists of outside swing-away unit with spare tire lock, black vinyl tire cover with Bronco horse emblem. Included with 31 x 10.50R x 15C spare tire. Speed ControlTilt steering wheel (554). Includes 15 in., 5-position tilt steering wheel with fingertip speed control. Tachometer (152). Includes trip odometer. Eddie Bauer Package: $3965 (154). Includes the following items in addition to or in place of custom and XLT equipment and trim items. Exterior: XLT trim components, special two-tone paint treatment, dual body side accent stripe, tan outside spare tire cover when optional swing-away spare tire carrier is ordered (black with 31 x 10.50R tires), wheel-lip moldings, choice of five body colors, Deluxe argent styled steel wheels with bright trim rings, "Eddie Bauer" nomenclature, P235/75XL raised white letter All-Terrain tires and light chestnut fiberglass roof. Interior: XLT trim components, dual front cloth-trimmed Captain's chairs, cloth-trimmed rear bench seat, floor console, privacy glass, "Eddie Bauer" nomenclature, chestnut interior trim. Functional: 5.0 liter EFI V-8 (5.8 liter HO V-8 optional), air conditioning, speed ControlTilt steering wheel, Light Group, heavy-duty battery. The Eddie Bauer Package also included a Eddie Bauer garment bag and tote bag, and the "Ford Care" extended service plan. Handling Package (553). Includes rear stabilizer bar, quad (two gas-pressurized) front shock absorbers and two heavy-duty rear shock absorbers. Not available with Heavy-Duty Front Suspension/Snowplow Package. Heavy-Duty Front Suspension/Snow Plow Package (563). Consists of 3800 lb. heavy-duty front axle with 3.54:1 ratio, 3800 lb. heavy-duty front springs with heavy-duty spring tower, heavy-duty rear shock absorbers, heavy-duty 84 amp battery (late availability), heavy-duty 100 amp alternator and auxiliary oil cooler if automatic transmission is ordered. The following items were not available with this option: Handling Package, Trailer Towing Package, Touch Drive electric shift, automatic locking front hubs, 4-speed overdrive manual transmission and 31 x 10.50R x 15C tires. Light Group (593). Consists of glove box light, stationary underhood light, courtesy light (under instrument panel), dome light with integral map light (standard dome light used with optional front bench seat), headlights-on warning chime, and, on standard trim, right side door courtesy light switch. Trailer Towing Package (535). Includes heavy-duty 84 amp-hr. battery (late availability), super engine cooling, heavy-duty turn signal flasher, Handling Package (includes rear stabilizer bar and quad front and heavy-duty rear shock absorbers) and trailer towing harness. Also includes auxiliary transmission air cooler with automatic transmission. Not available with Heavy-Duty Front Suspension/Snowplow Package. XLT Trim Package. Includes these items in addition to or in place of custom trim items. Exterior: Bright headlight/parking light bezel, lower body side protection and bright wheel-lip moldings, black rub strip included with front and rear bumper, brushed aluminum tailgate applique, chrome grille insert, bright molding on rear quarter windows and "XLT" nomenclature below "Bronco" nomenclature on front fender. Interior: Full-length color-keyed carpeting, door trim panels with cloth insert and map pocket, rear cargo light, floor console (except with bench seat), color-keyed cloth front headliner, woodtone appliques on instrument panel, leather-wrapped steering wheel, electronic AM/FM stereo search radio with digital clock and four speakers, color-keyed rear quarter trim panels, door, headliner and quarter panel insulation and floor deadener, cloth/polyknit seat trim and cloth sun visors with band on left side visor.

HISTORICAL FOOTNOTES: Bronco 1987 calendar year sales totalled 51,782.

1988 BRONCO

All 1988 Broncos were equipped with 5-speed, fully synchronized (including first and reverse) manual overdrive transmissions. A new option was a 5-speed manual overdrive transmission with a creeper 5.72:1 first gear. The respective nomenclature for these two transmissions were M5OD and M5OD-HD. For 1988 the 5.8 liter V-8 was equipped with multiple port fuel injection. This engine's availability was extended to California. All Broncos were now equipped with a standard transfer case skid plate. Other functional changes included increased towing ratings and the addition of a serpentine accessory-drive-belt system to the 5.8 liter engine.

Standard exterior equipment for the base custom model included these items: Chrome front contour bumper, rear bumper with rub strip, tinted glass, chrome grille, aero headlights with bright surround and high-impact lenses with replaceable halogen bulbs, wraparound front turn signal/parking lights/side marker, wraparound taillights/turn signals/stop lights with back-up lights and integral side markers, low-mount, both side doors, swing-away 8 in. x 5 in. bright mirrors (right side mirror surface was convex), bright windshield appliques, bright door handles with black buttons, "Ford" oval in grille center, "Ford" oval emblem, lower left corner of swing-down-type tailgate, "Bronco" nomenclature on front fenders, "4x4" plaque below left headlight, "Custom" emblem below "Bronco" nomenclature, swing-down type tailgate with power window and Sport wheelcovers. Standard custom interior features consisted of front and rear armrests, instrument panel-mounted ashtray at bottom of center pod, rear passenger ashtray located in quarter panel, cigarette lighter, left and right side coat hooks positioned on "B"-pillars, color-keyed rubber front and rear floor mats, high-output type heater and defroster, inside hood release incorporated into cowl side trim panel, dual electric horns and color-keyed instrument panel with black plastic trim panels, full-width pad, upper right side flat storage bin, locking glove box, four air registers and side window demisters. Instrumentation consists of gauges for voltmeter, engine coolant temperature oil pressure, and alert lights. Additional interior standard features include dome light with courtesy light switch at both front doors, windshield-mounted black framed day/night 12 in. mirror, color-keyed windshield pillars, color-keyed rear quarter surround and rear roof header, bright "Custom" on upper right side shelf of instrument panel and above the glove box, electronic AM radio with five push-buttons and digital clock, color-keyed lap/shoulder belts with tension eliminator, black boot stiffeners with bucket seats, black front door scuff plates, bright tailgate, 3 passenger rear flip/fold bench seat, black vinyl spare tire cover (with inside spare tire carrier only), black locking steering column, black vinyl steering wheel, color-keyed cowl side trim panels, color-keyed door trim with speaker grille, black rear quarter trim panels, pivoting vent windows, color-keyed vinyl-covered sun visors, interval windshield wipers.

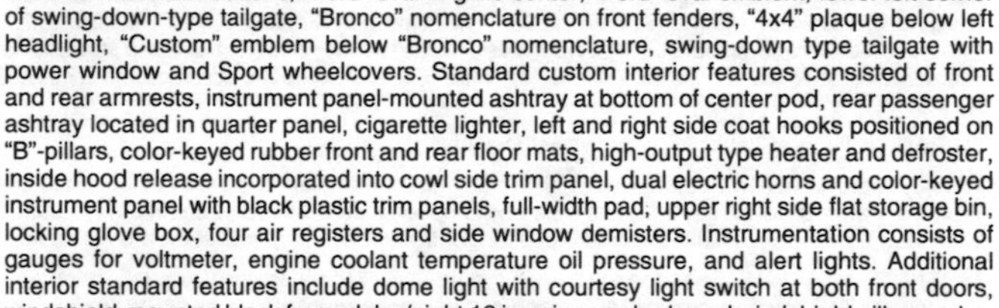

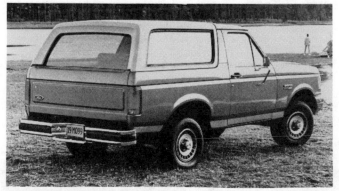

1988 Ford Bronco Custom

The 1988 twelve exterior color selection consisted of raven black, dark grey metallic, medium silver metallic, scarlet red, cabernet red, alpine green (available for Eddie Bauer Bronco only), bright regatta blue metallic, deep shadow blue metallic, colonial white, desert tan metallic, light chestnut and dark chestnut metallic.

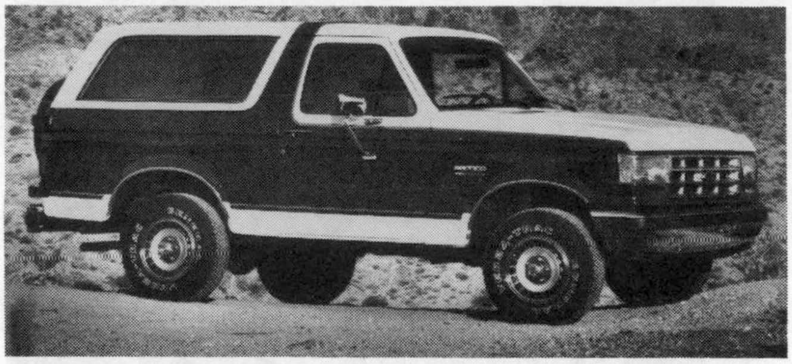

1988 Ford Bronco XLT

I.D. DATA: The Bronco V.I.N. consisted of seventeen symbols. The first three characters identified the manufacturer, make and type of vehicle. The fourth character (a letter) designated the GVW range. The fifth, sixth and seventh characters identified the series and body style. The eighth character identified the engine. The ninth character was the check digit. The tenth character (a letter) represented the model year. The eleventh character identified the assembly plant. The remaining digits represented the sequential production number.

Body Type	Factory Price	GVW	Shipping Weight	Prod. Total
Bronco U100				
Wagon (U15)	$15,397	6050[1]	4532	59,412[2]

NOTE 1: A 6450 GVW Package was optional.
NOTE 2: 1988 calendar year production.

STANDARD ENGINE: Engine Type: OHV 6-cyl. Special high-grade cast-iron block and cylinder heads. Bore x Stroke: 4.0 in. x 3.98 in. Lifters: Hydraulic. Number of main bearings-7. Fuel Induction: Multiple-port electronic fuel injection. Compression Ratio: 8.5:1. Displacement: 300 cu. in. (4.9 liters). Horsepower: 145 @ 3400 rpm. Torque 265 lb. ft. @ 2000 rpm. Fuel Requirements: Unleaded. Oil Refill: 6 qts. with filter change, 5 qts, without filter change.

OPTIONAL ENGINE: OHV V-8. Special high-grade cast-iron block and cylinder heads. Bore x Stroke: 4.00 in. x 300 in. Lifters: Hydraulic. Number of main bearings-5. Displacement: 302 cu. in. (5.0 liters). Lifters: Hydraulic. Number of main bearings-5. Fuel Induction: Multiple-port electronic fuel injection. Compression Ratio: 9.0:1. Horsepower: 185 @ 3800 rpm. Torque: 270 lb.-ft. @ 2400 rpm. Fuel Requirements: Unleaded. Oil Refill: 6 qts. with filter change, 5 qts. without filter change.

OPTIONAL ENGINE: OHV EFI V-8. Special high-grade cast-iron block and cylinder heads. Bore x Stroke: 4.00 in. x 3.50 in. Lifters: Hydraulic. Number of main bearings-5. Displacement: 351 cu. in. (5.8 liters). Fuel Induction: Multiple port electronic fuel injection. Compression Ratio: 8.3:1. Horsepower: 210 @ 3800 rpm. Torque: 315 lb.-ft. @ 2800 rpm. Fuel Requirements: Unleaded. Oil Refill: 6 qts. with filter change, 5 qts. without filter change.

CHASSIS FEATURES: Separate body and frame, single channel, 5 cross members, welded frame, 36,000 psi steel. 4.27 in. section modulus. Maximum side rail section: 7.01 x 2.12. x 0.202 in.

SUSPENSION AND RUNNING GEAR: Front Suspension: Independent, coil springs, computer selected, 2450 lb. rating. Optional rating of 2600, 2800, 2950 and 3800 lb. available. Rear Suspension: Single-stage, constant rate semi-elliptical 5-leaf, computer selected, 3770 lb. rating. Front Axle Type and Capacity: Dana 44 Twin Traction beam, 3550 lb. rating. Rear Axle Type and Capacity: Semi-floating, Ford, 3800 lb. rating. Final Drive Ratio: Available Front: 3.07, 3.54, 4.09:1. Available Rear: 3.08, 3.55, 4.10:1. Transfer Case: Type: Borg Warner 1356, 2-speed. Ratios: 1.0:1, 2.69:1. Brakes: Type: Hydraulic power-assisted, vented disc front and cast iron drum rear. Dimensions: Front: 10.90 in. dia. Caliper piston dia.: 2.875 in. Total swept area: 220.76 sq. in. Rear: 11.03 in. x 2.25 in. Total swept area: 155.93 sq. in. Wheels: 6.0JK x 15, 5-hole disc. Optional: 15 x 7JJ Deluxe argent styled steel wheels, 15 x 7JJ white styled steel wheels. Tires: Custom and XLT: P235/75R x 15XL steel radial All-Season black sidewall. Eddie Bauer: P235/75RXL raised white letter All-Terrain. Optional: Custom and XLT: P235/75RXL raised white letter All-Terrain. XLT and Eddie Bauer: 31 x 10.50R x 15C raised white letter All-Terrain. Steering: Power assisted. Ratio: 17.6:1. Turning Circle: 36.5 ft. Optional: None. Transmission: Standard with 4.9 liter engine (custom and XLT) and 5.0 liter Eddie Bauer: Type: Mazda R2 5-speed overdrive manual, all-synchromesh. (not available with 5.0 liter in California). Transmission Ratios: 3.90, 2.25, 1.49, 1.00, 0.80:1. Reverse: 3.41:1. Optional: 4.9 liter and 5.0 liter engines: Warner T18 4-speed manual. Transmissions ratios: 6.32, 3.09, 1.69, 1.0:1. Reverse: 7.44:1. Optional: Ford C6 automatic. (not available 4.9 liter, 5.0 liter engines in California). Ratios: 2.46, 1.46, 1.0:1. Reverse: 2.18. Converter: 1.80:1. Optional: 5.0 liter engine only: Ford 4-speed Automatic Overdrive Drive Ratios: 2.40, 1.46, 1.00, 0.667. Reverse: 2.00:1. Converter: 2.28:1. Optional: Ford 3-speed automatic (standard for 5.8 liter engine). Ratios: 2.46, 1.46, 1.00:1. Reverse: 2.18. Converter: 1.89. Clutch: 4.9 liter engine with standard 5-speed manual overdrive: Torsion-bend, woven non-asbestos. 10.0 in. dia. Bellevelle pressure plate. Plate pressure: 1925 lb. 5.0 liter engine with 5-speed manual overdrive. Segmented, woven non-asbestos 11.0 in. dia. Belleville pressure plate. Plate pressure: 1796 lb. Optional: None.

VEHICLE DIMENSIONS: Wheelbase: 104.7 in. Overall Length: 180.5 in. Front/Rear Tread 65.1 in./64.4 in. Overall Height: 74.0 in. Width: 79.1 in. Front/Rear Overhang: 30.5 in./45.3 in. Tailgate: Width and Height: 63.4 in. x 35.7 in. Approach/Departure Degrees: 36.3/17.7. Ground Clearance: Front axle: 8.1 in. Rear axle: 7.8 in. Transfer case: 9.1 in. Load space: With rear seat installed: 30.8 in. x 50.8 in. 35.7 in. With rear seat removed or folded: 60.8 in. 50.8 in. x 35.7 in.

CAPACITIES: Fuel Tank: 32.0 gal. with skid plate.

ACCOMMODATIONS: Seating Capacity: 5 passengers with standard front bucket seats and 3 passenger rear bench seat. 5 passengers with optional dual Captain's chairs and standard rear seat. 6 passengers with optional 3 passenger front bench seat and standard rear seat.

INSTRUMENTATION: Speedometer (mph-km/hr.-U.S. km/hr.-Canada), odometer, gauges for fuel level, ammeter, oil pressure and engine coolant temperature; safety belt indicator light, high-beam indicator light, transfer case 4x4 indicator (low and high range), anti-lock brake system indicator light, alternator indicator light, oil pressure/engine coolant temperature indicator light, brake system/parking brake indicator light and emissions system indicator light

OPTIONS: The numbers/letter entry following the option identify its ordering code. Air conditioning (572) Includes Air Conditioning Engine Cooling Package, rear floor mat insulation (custom trim only) and four instrument panel registers. Limited slip front axle (522). requires 3.55:1 limited slip rear axle. Not available with automatic front locking hubs, heavy-duty suspension or Electric Shift. Maintenance-free 84 amp-hr. battery-(632). Molded color-keyed plastic floor console with two cup depressions (414). Super Cooling Engine Package (624). Includes auxiliary transmission cooler on models with automatic transmission. Electric rear window defroster (913), Includes 75 amp alternator with 4.9 liter engine. Power door locks (903). Includes one control panel ahead of door handle for doors and windows, both side doors. Electric Shift (213). Includes 4x2/4x4 shift buttons, HI/LOW 4x4 range shift buttons and automatic locking hubs. Available only with 5.0 liter engine and automatic overdrive transmission and 3.54:1 ratio. Not available with Suspension Package or limited slip front axle. California emissions system (422). Required only in, and required for California registration. Privacy glass (924). Available for rear quarter windows only. Handling Package (553). Includes rear stabilizer bar, quad front shock absorbers and heavy-duty rear shock absorbers. Not available with Heavy-Duty Front Suspension Package. Included with Trailer Towing Package. Engine block heater (41H). Heavy-Duty Front Suspension Package (674). Includes 3.55:1 rear axle ratio, heavy-duty 3800 lb. front springs and heavy-duty rear shock absorbers. Automatic front locking hubs (212). Light Group (593). Includes glove box light, headlights-on audible alert, stationary underhood light, dual-beam dome/map light (dome beam standard with bench seat). Deluxe two-tone paint (952). Victoria two-tone paint (954). Electronic AM/FM stereo radio with quad premium speakers (583). Electronic AM/FM stereo radio search with cassette player and digital clock and quad premium speakers (586). Radio delete credit option (58Y). Cloth and vinyl color-keyed trim, split-back front bench seat (L). Captain's chairs (R). Includes recline feature, color-keyed cloth trim, armrests, zippered pouch with two external pockets on back. Also includes floor console. Cloth and vinyl seat trim (M). Available with bucket seats only. Outside swing-away spare tire carrier (51Q). Includes black vinyl cover with Bronco horse emblem and spare tire lock. Included with 31 x 10.50R x 15C tires. Speed ControlTilt Steering Wheel Package (554). Combines calculator-type buttons, 5-position tilt steering wheel with fingertip speed control. Tachometer (152). Includes trip odometer. P235/75R x 15XL black sidewall All-Terrain tires (T77). P235/75R x 15XL raised white letters All-Terrain (T7P). 31 x 10.50R x 15C raised white letter All-Terrain (T1K). Trailer Towing Package (535). Includes trailer wiring harness, heavy-duty 84 amp battery, super engine cooling, auxiliary transmission cooler with automatic transmission, Heavy-Duty Flasher and Handling Package. Deluxe argent styled wheels (648). Includes trim rings and bright hub covers. XLT Trim Package. Includes in place of or addition to the custom features the following: XLT emblem below "Bronco" nomenclature on front fenders, chrome front bumper with black rub strip, lower body side protection, bright wheel-lips, bright rear quarter window moldings, tailgate applique-bushed aluminum with 3.5 in. red reflective plastic insert on lower portion with "FORD" oval on left side of insert, color-keyed carpeting, floor console (not available with bench seat), front color-keyed cloth headliner, instrument panel with woodtone applique surrounding instrument panel, additional insulation, bright cargo light, "Bronco XLT" bright nomenclature on upper right hand shelf of instrument panel above glove box, electronic AM/FM radio with digital clock, color-keyed door stiffeners with bucket seats/Captain's chairs, color-keyed cloth bucket seats, speed ControlTilt steering wheel, black leather-wrapped steering wheel, color-keyed door trim with bright trim, color-keyed cloth insert and map pocket on lower portion and storage bin below armrest, color-keyed rear quarter trim panels with padded armrests, speaker grilles and storage bin and color-keyed cloth-covered sun visors with band on left side and covered vanity mirror on right side visor. Eddie Bauer Package. Contains in addition to or in place of XLT features, the following: Privacy glass, "Eddie Bauer" emblem below "Bronco" nomenclature on front fenders, dual accent body side paint stripe, two-tone paint on rocker panel, Deluxe argent-styled steel wheels, air conditioning, Light Group, "Eddie Bauer" plaque on upper right hand shelf of instrument panel above glove box, cloth reclining Captain's chairs and 5.0 liter V-8 with 5-speed manual overdrive.

HISTORICAL FOOTNOTES: Sales of Broncos for the 1988 model year were 54,848 units. Sales for the 1988 calendar year were 55,124. Ford reported that the average Bronco buyer was 35 years of age. Eighty-six percent of registered owners of Broncos were male, 76 percent were married and 72 percent had children. Nearly 58 percent had some college education.

1989 BRONCO

![1989 Ford Bronco XLT]

1989 Ford Bronco XLT

Change in the 1989 Bronco were not extensive. New tip/slide front bucket seats were introduced to improve rear seat ingress/egress. This feature was also incorporated into the Captain's chairs. Both the Captain's chairs and bucket seats had a revised sew style. The base model's cooling system was also upgraded. At mid-year automatic front locking hubs were made standard. Standard exterior equipment for the base custom model included these items: Chrome front contour bumper, rear bumper with rub strip, tinted glass, chrome grille, aero headlights with bright surround and high-impact lenses with replaceable halogen bulbs, wraparound front turn signal/parking lights/side marker, wraparound taillights/turn signals/stop lights with back-up lights and integral side markers, low-mount, both side doors, swing-away 8 in. x 5 in. bright mirrors (right side mirror surface was convex), bright windshield appliques, bright door handles with black buttons, "Ford" oval in grille center, "Ford" oval emblem, lower left corner of swing-down-type tailgate, "Bronco" nomenclature on front fenders, "4x4" plaque below left headlight, "Custom" emblem below "Bronco" nomenclature, swing-down type tailgate with power window and Sport wheelcovers. Standard custom interior features consisted of color-keyed vinyl bucket seats with flip-and-slide mechanism, front and rear

armrests, instrument panel-mounted ashtray at bottom of center pod, rear passenger ashtray located in quarter panel, cigarette lighter, left and right side coat hooks positioned on "B"-pillars, color-keyed rubber front and rear floor mats, high-output type heater and defroster, inside hood release incorporated into cowl side trim panel, dual electric horns and color-keyed instrument panel with black plastic trim panels, full-width pad, upper right side flat storage bin, locking glove box, four air registers and side window demisters. Instrumentation consists of gauges for voltmeter, engine coolant temperature oil pressure, and alert lights. Additional interior standard features include dome light with courtesy light switch at both front doors, windshield-mounted black framed day/night 12 in. mirror, color-keyed windshield pillars, color-keyed rear quarter surround and rear roof header, bright "Custom" on upper right side shelf of instrument panel and above the glove box, electronic AM radio with five push-buttons and digital clock, color-keyed lap/shoulder belts with tension eliminator, black boot stiffeners with bucket seats, black front door scuff plates, bright tailgate, 3 passenger rear flip/fold bench seat, black vinyl spare tire cover (with inside spare tire carrier only), black locking steering column, black vinyl steering wheel, color-keyed cowl side trim panels, color-keyed door trim with speaker grille, black rear quarter trim panels, pivoting vent windows, color-keyed vinyl-covered sun visors and interval windshield wipers.

1989 Ford Eddie Bauer Bronco

Exterior colors for 1989 were raven black, dark grey metallic, medium silver metallic, scarlet red, cabernet red, alpine green metallic, bright regatta blue metallic, deep shadow blue metallic, colonial white, desert tan metallic, light chestnut and dark chestnut metallic. The interior trim and fiberglass roof colors for 1989 included two new colors — Dark charcoal and crystal blue. They joined carryover colors scarlet red and chestnut.

1989 Ford Bronco custom

I.D. DATA: The Bronco V.I.N. consisted of seventeen symbols. The first three characters identified the manufacturer, make and type of vehicle. The fourth character (a letter) designated the GVW range. The fifth, sixth and seventh characters identified the series and body style. The eighth character identified the engine. The ninth character was the check digit. The tenth character (a letter) represented the model year. The eleventh character identified the assembly plant. The remaining digits represented the sequential production number.

Body Type	Factory Price	GVW	Shipping Weight	Prod. Total
Bronco U100				
Wagon (U15)	$16,526	6050*	4453	70,156**

* A 6450 GVW Package was optional.
** Calendar year production.

STANDARD ENGINE: Engine Type: OHV 6-cyl. Special high-grade cast-iron block and cylinder heads. Bore x Stroke: 4.0 in. x 3.98 in. Lifters: Hydraulic. Number of main bearings-7. Fuel Induction: Multiple-port electronic fuel injection. Compression Ratio: 8.5:1. Displacement: 300 cu. in. (4.9 liters). Horsepower: 145 @ 3400 rpm. Torque 265 lb. ft. @ 2000 rpm. Fuel Requirements: Unleaded. Oil Refill: 6 qts. with filter change, 5 qts. without filter change.

OPTIONAL ENGINE: OHV V-8. Special high-grade cast-iron block and cylinder heads. Bore x Stroke: 4.00 in. x 300 in. Lifters: Hydraulic. Number of main bearings-5. Displacement: 302 cu. in. (5.0 liters). Lifters: Hydraulic. Number of main bearings-5. Fuel Induction: Multiple-port electronic fuel injection. Compression Ratio: 9.0:1. Horsepower: 185 @ 3800 rpm. Torque: 270 lb.-ft. @ 2400 rpm. Fuel Requirements: Unleaded. Oil Refill: 6 qts. with filter change, 5 qts. without filter change.

OPTIONAL ENGINE: OHV EFI V-8. Special high-grade cast-iron block and cylinder heads. Bore x Stroke: 4.00 in. x 3.50 in. Lifters: Hydraulic. Number of main bearings-5. Displacement: 351 cu. in. (5.8 liters). Fuel Induction: Multiple port electronic fuel injection. Compression Ratio: 8.3:1. Horsepower: 210 @ 3800 rpm. Torque: 315 lb.-ft. @ 2800 rpm. Fuel Requirements: Unleaded. Oil Refill: 6 qts. with filter change, 5 qts. without filter change.

CHASSIS FEATURES: Separate body and frame, single channel, 5 cross members, welded frame, 36,000 psi steel. 4.27 in. section modulus. Maximum side rail section: 7.01 x 2.12. x 0.202 in.

SUSPENSION AND RUNNING GEAR: Front Suspension: Independent, coil springs, computer selected, 2450 lb. rating. Optional rating of 2600, 2800, 2950 and 3800 lb. available. Rear Suspension: Single-stage, constant rate semi-elliptical 5-leaf, computer selected, 3770 lb. rating. Front Axle Type and Capacity: Dana 44 Twin Traction beam, 3550 lb. rating. Rear Axle Type and Capacity: Semi-floating, Ford, 3800 lb. rating. Final Drive Ratio: Available Front: 3.07, 3.54, 4.09:1. Available Rear: 3.08, 3.55, 4.10:1. Transfer Case: Type: Borg Warner 1356, 2-speed. Ratios: 1.0:1, 2.69:1. Brakes: Type: Hydraulic power-assisted, vented disc front and cast iron drum rear. Dimensions: Front: 10.90 in. dia. Caliper piston dia.: 2.875 in. Total swept area: 220.76 sq. in. Rear: 11.03 in. x 2.25 in. Total swept area: 155.93 sq. in. Wheels: 6.0JK x 15, 5-hole disc. Optional: 15 x 7JJ Deluxe argent styled steel wheels, 15 x 7JJ white styled steel wheels. Tires: Custom and XLT: P235/75R x 15XL steel radial All-Season black sidewall. Eddie Bauer: P235/75RXL raised white letter All-Terrain. Optional: Custom and XLT: P235/75RXL raised white letter All-Terrain. XLT and Eddie Bauer: 31 x 10.50R x 15C raised white letter All-Terrain. Steering: Power assisted. Ratio: 17.6:1. Turning Circle: 36.5 ft. Optional: None. Transmission: Standard with 4.9 liter engine (custom and XLT) and 5.0 liter Eddie Bauer: Type: Mazda R2 5-speed overdrive manual, all-synchromesh. (not available with 5.0 liter in California). Transmission Ratios: 3.90, 2.25, 1.49, 1.00, 0.80:1. Reverse: 3.41:1. Optional: 4.9 liter and 5.0 liter engines: Warner T18 4-speed manual. Transmissions ratios: 6.32, 3.09, 1.69, 1.0:1. Reverse: 7.44:1. Optional: Ford C6 automatic. (not available 4.9 liter, 5.0 liter engines in California). Ratios: 2.46, 1.46, 1.0:1. Reverse: 2.18. Converter: 1.80:1. Optional: 5.0 liter engine only: Ford 4-speed Automatic Overdrive Drive Ratios: 2.40, 1.46, 1.00, 0.667. Reverse: 2.00:1. Converter: 2.28:1. Optional: Ford 3-speed automatic (standard for 5.8 liter engine). Ratios: 2.46, 1.46, 1.00:1. Reverse: 2.18. Converter: 1.89. Clutch: 4.9 liter engine with standard 5-speed manual overdrive: Torsion-bend, woven non-asbestos. 10.0 in. dia. Bellevelle pressure plate. Plate pressure: 1925 lb. 5.0 liter engine with 5-speed manual overdrive. Segmented, woven non-asbestos 11.0 in. dia. Belleville pressure plate. Plate pressure: 1796 lb. Optional: None.

VEHICLE DIMENSIONS: Wheelbase: 104.7 in. Overall Length: 180.5 in. Front/Rear Tread 65.1 in./64.4 in. Overall Height: 74.0 in. Width: 79.1 in. Front/Rear Overhang: 30.5 in./45.3 in. Tailgate: Width and Height: 63.4 in. x 35.7 in. Approach/Departure Degrees: 36.3/17.7. Ground Clearance: Front axle: 8.1 in. Rear axle: 7.8 in. Transfer case: 9.1 in. Load space: With rear seat installed: 30.8 in. x 50.8 in. 35.7 in. With rear seat removed or folded: 60.8 in. 50.8 in. x 35.7 in.

CAPACITIES: Fuel Tank: 32.0 gal. with skid plate.

ACCOMMODATIONS: Seating Capacity: 5 passengers with standard front bucket seats and 3 passenger rear bench seat. 5 passengers with optional dual Captain's chairs and standard rear seat. 6 passengers with optional 3 passenger front bench seat and standard rear seat.

INSTRUMENTATION: Speedometer (mph-km/hr.-U.S. kilometers/hr.-Canada), odometer, gauges for fuel level, ammeter, oil pressure and engine coolant temperature; safety belt indicator light, high-beam indicator light, transfer case 4x4 indicator (low and high range), anti-lock brake system indicator light, alternator indicator light, oil pressure/engine coolant temperature indicator light, brake system/parking brake indicator light and emissions system indicator light

OPTIONS: The numbers/letter entry following the option identify its ordering code. Air conditioning (572) Includes Air Conditioning Engine Cooling Package, rear floor mat insulation (custom trim only) and four instrument panel registers. Limited slip front axle (522). requires 3.55:1 limited slip rear axle. Not available with automatic front locking hubs, heavy-duty suspension or Electric Shift. Maintenance-free 84 amp-hr. battery (632). Molded color-keyed plastic floor console with two cup depressions (414). Super Cooling Engine Package (624). Includes auxiliary transmission cooler on models with automatic transmission. Electric rear window defroster (913), Includes 75 amp alternator with 4.9 liter engine. Power door locks (903). Includes one control panel ahead of door handle for doors and windows, both side doors. Electric Shift (213). Includes 4x2/4x4 shift buttons, HI/LOW 4x4 range shift buttons and automatic locking hubs. Available only with 5.0 liter engine and automatic overdrive transmission and 3.54:1 ratio. Not available with Suspension Package or limited slip front axle. California emissions system (422). Required only in, and required for California registration. Privacy glass (924). Available for rear quarter windows only. Handling Package (553). Includes rear stabilizer bar, quad front shock absorbers and heavy-duty rear shock absorbers. Not available with Heavy-Duty Front Suspension Package. Included with Trailer Towing Package. Engine block heater (41H). Heavy-Duty Front Suspension Package (674). Includes 3.55:1 rear axle ratio, heavy-duty 3800 lb. front springs and heavy-duty rear shock absorbers. Automatic front locking hubs (212). Light Group (593). Includes glove box light, headlights-on audible alert, stationary underhood light, dual-beam dome/map light (dome beam standard with bench seat). Deluxe two-tone paint-(952). Victoria two-tone paint (954). Electronic AM/FM stereo radio with digital clock and quad premium speakers (583). Electronic AM/FM stereo radio search with cassette player and digital clock and quad premium speakers (586). Radio delete credit option (58Y). Cloth and vinyl color-keyed trim, split-back front bench seat (L). Captain's chairs (R). Includes recline feature, color-keyed cloth trim, armrests, zippered pouch with two external pockets on back. Also includes floor console. Cloth and vinyl seat trim (M). Available with bucket seats only. Outside swing-away spare tire carrier (51Q). Includes black vinyl cover with Bronco horse emblem and spare tire lock. Included with 31 x 10.50R x 15C tires. Speed ControlTilt Steering Wheel Package (554). Combines calculator-type buttons, 5-position tilt steering wheel with fingertip speed control. Tachometer (152). Includes trip odometer. P235/75R x 15XL black sidewall All-Terrain tires (T77). P235/75R x 15XL raised white letters All-Terrain (T7P). 31 x 10.50R x 15C raised white letter All-Terrain (T1K). Trailer Towing Package (535). Includes trailer wiring harness, heavy-duty 84 amp battery, super engine cooling, auxiliary transmission cooler with automatic transmission, Heavy-Duty Flasher and Handling Package. Deluxe argent styled wheels (648). Includes trim rings and bright hub covers. XLT Trim Package. Includes in place of or addition to the custom features the following: XLT emblem below "Bronco" nomenclature on front fenders, chrome front bumper with black rub strip, lower body side protection, bright wheel-lips, bright rear quarter window moldings, Tailgate applique-bushed aluminum with 3.5 in. Red reflective plastic insert on lower portion with "FORD" oval on left side of insert, color-keyed carpeting, floor console (not available with bench seat), front color-keyed cloth headliner, instrument panel with woodtone applique surrounding instrument panel, additional insulation, rear cargo light, "Bronco XLT" bright nomenclature on upper right hand shelf of instrument panel above glove box, electronic AM/FM radio with digital clock, color-keyed boot stiffeners with bucket seats/ Captain's chairs, color-keyed cloth bucket seats, speed ControlTilt steering wheel, black leather-wrapped steering wheel, color-keyed door trim with bright trim, color-keyed cloth insert and map pocket on lower portion and storage bin below armrest, color-keyed rear quarter trim panels with padded armrests, speaker grilles and storage bin and color-keyed cloth-covered sun visors with band on left side and covered vanity mirror on right side visor. Eddie Bauer Package. Contains in addition to or in place of XLT features, the following: Privacy glass, "Eddie Bauer" emblem below "Bronco" nomenclature on front fenders, dual accent body side paint stripe, two-tone paint on rocker panel, Deluxe argent-styled steel wheels, air conditioning, Light Group, "Eddie Bauer" plaque on upper right hand shelf of instrument panel above glove box, cloth reclining Captain's chairs and 5.0 liter V-8 with 5-speed manual overdrive.

HISTORICAL FOOTNOTES: At the start of the 1989 model year the Bronco was in the admirable position of being the best selling full-size utility truck based on cumulative calendar years for the last ten years. During the 1989 racing season Dave Ashley, driving a Bronco for the Enduro racing team, won seven races in 13 starts. Model year 1989 sales for the Bronco increased to 62,913, up from the 1988 level of 54,848. This marked the third year in which retail deliveries had exceeded 60,000 and the sixth year that Bronco had reached the 50,000-plus sales plateau. Mr. Edward E. Hagenlocker was the general manager of the Ford Truck Division. Responsible for Light Truck Product Development was J.E. Englehart. Public affairs manager was J.J. Emmert.

1990 BRONCO

The physical appearance of the 1990 Bronco was unchanged from 1989. There were, however, a sizable number of changes for the new model year. For use with the 4.9 liter and 5.8 liter engines, an electronically controlled overdrive automatic transmission (E4OD) replaced the older C-6 automatic. Some early 1990 model Broncos continued to use the C-6 transmission until the E4OD became available. The E4OD transmission was an electronically controlled automatic transmission with OVERDRIVE CANCEL switch, mounted on the instrument panel, to prevent upshift to overdrive gears at the operator's discretion. Another running change was the introduction of deep-dish forged aluminum wheels as an option. All 4.9 liter and 5.8 liter engines had a provision on their EEC-IV module to access engine diagnostic data. Added to the Eddie Bauer Package were color-keyed/monogrammed front and rear floor mats. Changes to the Bronco's option program consisted of three developments. The Light Group and console options were combined to form a new Light/Convenience Group. The Handling Package, super cooling and heavy-duty battery options were combined to form a Heavy-Duty Service Package. Reinstated as a Bronco option were P235/75R x 15L black sidewall All-Terrain tires.

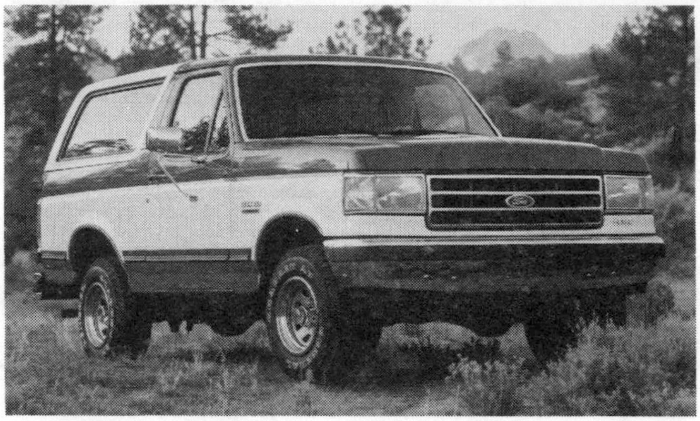

1990 Ford Bronco XLT

Major standard equipment for the base custom model was as follows: Chrome front bumper, chrome rear step bumper with rub strip, rated at 4,000 lbs. for towing, chrome grille, bright headlight surround, bright low-mount swing-away dual mirrors (convex on right side), bright windshield molding, swing-down tailgate with power window, Sport wheelcovers, cigarette lighter, color-keyed dual coat hooks, dome light with courtesy switches, color-keyed rubber floor mat, dual electric horns, color-keyed instrument panel with side window demisters, black appliques and glove box lock, day/night 12 in. mirror, color-keyed windshield pillars, electronic AM/FM stereo radio with digital clock, color-keyed continuous loop lap-shoulder safety belts, front door black scuff plates, front bucket seats with flip/slide mechanism, three passenger rear flip/fold bench seat, black spare tire cover, black vinyl steering wheel, color-keyed, vinyl-covered sun visors, black rear quarter trim panels, pivoting vent windows, and interval windshield wipers. Deleted from the exterior color choices was Light Chestnut. It was replaced by tan. The other exterior colors offered for 1990 were: Desert tan metallic, dark chestnut metallic, cabernet red, scarlet red, bright regatta blue metallic, deep shadow blue metallic, alpine green metallic, raven black, medium blue metallic, dark grey metallic and colonial white. The interior color selection consisted of crystal blue, scarlet red, dark charcoal and chestnut. The fiberglass roof was available in the same choice of colors.

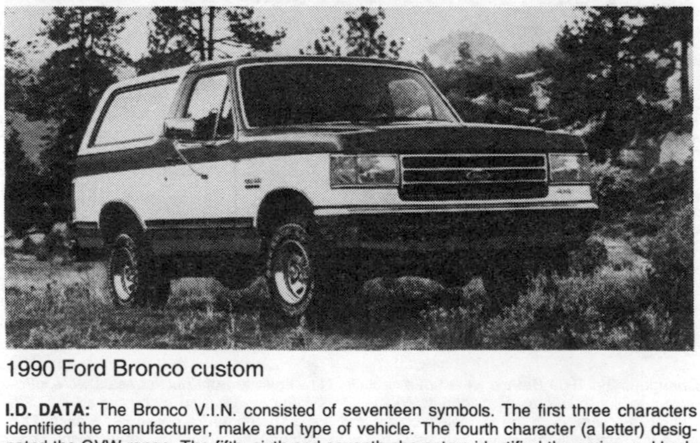

1990 Ford Bronco custom

I.D. DATA: The Bronco V.I.N. consisted of seventeen symbols. The first three characters identified the manufacturer, make and type of vehicle. The fourth character (a letter) designated the GVW range. The fifth, sixth and seventh characters identified the series and body style. The eighth character identified the engine. The ninth character was the check digit. The tenth character (a letter) represented the model year. The eleventh character identified the assembly plant. The remaining digits represented the sequential production number.

Body Type	Factory Price	GVW	Shipping Weight	Prod. Total
Bronco U100				
Wagon (U15)	$16,795	6050*	4453	45,861[a]

a 1990 calendar year production.
* A 6450 GVW Package was optional.

STANDARD ENGINE: Engine Type: OHV 6-cyl. Special high-grade cast-iron block and cylinder heads. Not available with Eddie Bauer Bronco. Bore x Stroke: 4.0 in. x 3.98 in. Lifters: Hydraulic. Number of main bearings-7. Fuel induction: Multiple-port electronic fuel injection. Compression Ratio: 8.8:1. Displacement: 300 cu. in. (4.9 liters).

Power Ratings

Transmission	Horsepower	Torque
5-Spd. Manual Overdrive:	145 @ 3400 rpm	265 lb.-ft. @ 2000 rpm*
4-Spd. Automatic Overdrive:	150 @ 3400 rpm	260 lb.-ft. @ 2000 rpm

* Horsepower and torque ratings are with 3.08:1 rear axle ratio. All other axle ratios use 150 hp. @ 3400 rpm and 260 lb-ft. @ 2000 rpm. Fuel Requirements: Regular Unleaded.

OPTIONAL ENGINE: OHV V-8. Special high-grade cast-iron block and cylinder heads. Standard with Eddie Bauer Bronco. Bore x Stroke: 4.00 in. x 3.00 in. Lifters: Hydraulic. Number of main bearings-5. Displacement: 302 cu. in. (5.0 liters). Fuel Induction: Multiple-port electronic fuel injection. Compression Ratio: 9.0:1. Oil refill: 6 qts. with filter change, 5 qts. without filter change.

Power Ratings

Transmission	Horsepower	Torque
5-Spd. Manual Overdrive[1]:	185 @ 3800 rpm	270 lb.-ft. @ 2400 rpm
3-Spd. Automatic[1]:	185 @ 3800 rpm	270 lb.-ft. @ 2400 rpm
4-Spd. Automatic Overdrive:	185 @ 3800 rpm	270 lb.-ft. @ 2400 rpm

NOTE 1: Not available in California. Fuel Requirements: Regular Unleaded.

OPTIONAL ENGINE: OHV EFI V-8. Special high-grade cast-iron block and cylinder heads. Bore x Stroke: 4.00 in. x 3.50 in. Lifters: Hydraulic. Number of main bearings-5. Displacement: 351 cu. in. (5.8 liters). Fuel Induction: Multiple-port electronic fuel injection. Compression Ratio: 8.8:1. Oil refill: 6 qts. with filter change, 5 qts. without filter change.

Power Ratings

Transmission	Horsepower	Torque
4-Spd. Automatic Overdrive:	210 @ 3800 rpm	315 lb.-ft. @ 2800 rpm.

Fuel Requirements: Regular Unleaded.

CHASSIS FEATURES: Separate body and frame, single channel, 5 cross members, welded frame. 4.27 in. section modulus. Maximum side rail section: 7.01 x 2.12. x 0.202 in. 36,000 psi yield strength. Low carbon steel.

SUSPENSION AND RUNNING GEAR: Front Suspension: Independent, coil springs, computer selected, 2450 lb. rating. Optional rating of 2600, 2800, 2950 and 3800 lb. available. Rear Suspension: Single-stage, constant rate semi-elliptical 5-leaf, computer selected, 3770 lb. rating. Front Axle Type and Capacity: Dana 44 Twin Traction beam, 3800 lb. rating. Rear Axle Type and Capacity: Semi-floating, Ford, 3800 lb. rating. Available Final Drive Ratio: Front: 3.07, 3.54, 4.09:1. Rear: 3.08, 3.55, 4.10:1. Transfer Case: Type: Borg Warner 1356, 2-speed. Ratios: 1.0:1, 2.69:1. Brakes: Type: Hydraulic power-assisted, vented disc front and cast iron drum rear. Dimensions: Front: 11.72 in. dia. Floating Caliper Rear: 11.03 in. x 2.25 in. Total rear swept area: 155.95 sq. in. Wheels: 6.0JK x 15, 5-hole disc. Optional: 15 x 7JJ styled steel wheels, 15 x 8JJ styled steel wheels. Tires: P235/75R x 15SL All-Season steel-belted radial. Optional: P235/75R x 15XL All-Terrain steel-belted radial. 31 x 10.50R x 15C. Steering: Power assisted, recirculating ball. Gear Ratio: 17.0:1, Overall Ratio: 18.1:1. Turning Circle: 36.57 ft. Optional: None. Transmission: Standard for 4.9 and 5.0 liter engines: Type: Mazda R2 5-speed manual overdrive, all-synchromesh. Transmission Ratios: 3.90, 2.25, 1.49, 1.00, 0.80:1. Reverse: 3.41:1. Optional: (For early production Broncos with 4.9 engine, after March, 1990 no longer available): Warner T-18 4-speed manual. Transmission Ratios: 6.32, 3.09, 1.69, 1.00:1. Reverse: 7.44:1. Optional: Ford 3-speed automatic (C-6) Interim for 5.0 liter. Ratios: 2.46, 1.46, 1.0:1. Reverse: 2.18. Optional: For 5.0 liter engines and standard for 5.8 liter engine: 4-speed Electronic Automatic Overdrive (E4OD). Ratios: 2.71, 1.54, 1.00, 0.71. Reverse: 2.18. Clutch: 4.9 liter engine with standard 5-speed manual and optional T18 trans.: Torsion-bend, woven non-asbestos. 10.0 in. dia. Belleville pressure plate. Total plate pressure: 1925 lb. 5.0 liter with standard 5-speed manual and optional T18 trans.: Segmented, woven non-asbestos. 11 in. dia. Belleville pressure plate. Total plate pressure: 1796 lb. Optional: None.

VEHICLE DIMENSIONS: Wheelbase: 104.7 in. Overall Length: 180.5 in. Front/Rear Tread 65.1 in./64.4 in. Overall Height: 74.2 in. Width: 79.1 in. Front/Rear Overhang: 28.7 in./44.3 in. Tailgate: Width and Height: 63.5 in. x 35.7 in. Approach/Departure Degrees: 35.3/20.9. Ground Clearance: Front axle: 8.1 in. Rear axle: 7.8 in. Transfer case: 9.1 in. Load space: With rear seat removed or folded: 60.8 in. x 50.8 in. 43.7 in. Maximum capacity: Without rear seat installed: 101.4 cu. ft. With rear seat folded: 80.2 cu. in. With rear seat up: 50.1 cu. ft.

CAPACITIES: Fuel Tank: 32.0 gal. with skid plate.

ACCOMMODATIONS: Seating Capacity: 5 passengers with standard front bucket seats and 3 passenger rear bench seat. 5 passengers with optional dual Captain's chairs and standard rear seat. 6 passengers with optional 3 passenger front bench seat and standard rear seat. Headroom: Front: 41.1 in. Rear: 39.2 in. Legroom: Front: 41.1 in. Legroom: Rear: 37.7 in. Shoulder room: Front: 65.2 in. Shoulder room: Rear: 64.9 in. Hip room: Front: 61.2 in. Hip room: Rear: 55.3 in.

INSTRUMENTATION: Speedometer, odometer, gauges for fuel level, engine coollant temperature, oil pressure and voltmeter.

OPTIONS AND PRICES: Note: The numbers/letter entry following the option identify its ordering code. Air conditioning (572): $824. Limited slip rear axle (522): $252. Various axle ratios: $44. Captain's chairs (for XLT only-standard on Eddie Bauer): $499. Rear window defroster (913): $139. Power window and door locks (903): $344. California emissions system. (422): $100. Privacy glass (924): $159. 5.0 liter V-8 (99N): $617. 5.8 liter V-8 (99H): $221 (with Eddie Bauer), all others: $838. Engine block heater (41H): $33. Manual locking hubs-deletes standard automatic locking hubs (21M): $60. Two-tone Deluxe paint for custom trim (298): $350. Two-tone paint for XLT (161): $189. Victoria two-tone paint for custom trim (463): $545. Victoria two-tone paint for XLT trim (327): $384. High altitude use (428): No charge. Electronic AM/FM stereo search radio with cassette player and digital clock (586): $112. Radio credit option. (58Y): $130. Cloth and vinyl front bench seat-for custom only. No charge for XLT (M): $100. Cloth and vinyl bucket seats-for custom only (L): $100. Outside swing-away spare tire carrier (51Q): $166. Speed ControlTilt steering wheel (554): $346. Tachometer (152): $66. P235/75R15XL black sidewall All-Terrain tires (T7X): $55. P235/75R15XL OWL All-Terrain tires (T7P): $199. Raised white letter All-Terrain tires. 31 x 10.50R x 15C raised white letter All-Terrain tires. Includes 5 Deluxe argent styled steel wheels and outside spare tire carrier (T1K): $533-$846. Electric Shift Touch Drive (213): $123. Electronic 4-speed automatic transmission (44E): $915. Automatic overdrive (with 5.0 liter engine only) (44T): $860. Deluxe argent styled 15 x 8 in. steel wheels (648): $146. Forged aluminum deep-dish wheels (649): $382. Credit with 31 x 10.5R wheels which include Deluxe argent styled steel wheels: $146. Eddie Bauer Group. Includes 5.0 liter EFI V-8, heavy-duty 84 amp battery, XLT trim (minus XLT nomenclature and exterior moldings), bright wheel-lip molding, specific two-tone paint treatment (tan accent paint in rocker area), tan fiberglass roof, dual body side accent paint stripe, dual cloth Captain's chairs, special cloth seat trim, chestnut interior, Eddie Bauer equipment items, chestnut outside tire cover (black with 31.0 x 10.50R x 15C tires), when outside swing-away spare is ordered, "Ford Care" extended service plan, air conditioning, Light/Convenience group, privacy glass, speed ControlTilt steering wheel, electronic AM/FM stereo radio with cassette player and digital clock, Deluxe argent styled steel wheels, choice of six body colors. Light/Convenience Group. (56L) Includes glove box light, headlights-on audible alert, underhood light, dual beam dome/map light (except with front bench seat), floor console (except with front bench seat): $27 with bench seat; with all other seats: $198. Heavy-Duty Service Package (65D). Includes rear stabilizer bar, quad front and heavy-duty rear shock absorbers, 84 amp-hr. heavy-duty battery, Super engine cooling (includes auxiliary transmission oil cooler with automatic transmission). With Heavy-Duty Front Suspension Package: $157. With Eddie Bauer Package: $242. With all other packages: $298. Heavy-Duty Front Suspension Package (674). Includes 6450 lb. GVW rating, heavy-duty, 3800 lb. rating, front springs, heavy-duty rear shock absorber: $116. Trailer Towing Package (535). Includes seven-wire trailer wiring harness, heavy-duty turn signal flasher, Heavy-Duty Service Package: 332. Credit of $298 with Heavy-Duty Service Package. Credit of $56 with Eddie Bauer Package.

HISTORICAL FOOTNOTES: A total of 46,796 Broncos were sold during the 1990 calendar year.

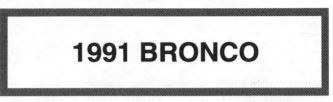

1991 BRONCO

The Ford Bronco celebrated its 25th anniversary in the 1991 model year. Reflecting on 25 years of Broncos, Ford division general manager Thomas J. Wagner noted: "You can look at Bronco as the trunk of the family tree for today's myriad of Sports utility vehicles. It began its long life catering to the personal needs of its owner, without sacrifice to its utility." Recognizing the Bronco's long-standing popularity with four-wheel drive enthusiasts, Mr. Wagner added: "Twenty-five years is a significant milestone, particularly so for the Bronco which achieved sales leadership in its segment of the market in its first year and has been the most popular full-sized utility vehicle in North America for the past 11 years."

During the 1991 model year the Bronco received improved corrosion protection (including two-sided galvanized steel hood, tailgate, dash panel and doors). Added to the Bronco option list were P235/75R x 15XL OWL All-Season tires and a special 25th Anniversary Bronco Option Package. Availability of the Touch Drive Electric Shift was extended to the 5.0 liter/5.8 liter/E4OD powertrains. Standard equipment content of the base custom model was unchanged for 1991.

I.D. DATA: The Bronco V.I.N. consisted of seventeen symbols. The first three characters identified the manufacturer, make and type of vehicle. The fourth character (a letter) designated the GVW range. The fifth, sixth and seventh characters identified the series and body style. The eighth character identified the engine. The ninth character was the check digit. The tenth character (a letter) represented the model year. The eleventh character identified the assembly plant. The remaining digits represented the sequential production number.

Body Type	Factory Price	GVW	Shipping Weight	Prod. Total
Bronco U100				
Wagon (U15)	$17,639	6050*	4453	—
Silver Anniv. Model	$24,866	6050		3000

* A 6450 GVW Package was optional.

STANDARD ENGINE: Engine Type: OHV 6-cyl. Special high-grade cast-iron block and cylinder heads. Not available with Eddie Bauer Bronco. Bore x Stroke: 4.0 in. x 3.98 in. Lifters: Hydraulic. Number of main bearings-7. Fuel induction: Multiple-port electronic fuel injection. Compression Ratio: 8.8:1. Displacement: 300 cu. in. (4.9 liters).

Power Ratings

Transmission	Horsepower	Torque
5-Spd. Manual Overdrive:	145 @ 3400 rpm	265 lb.-ft. @ 2000 rpm*
4-Spd. Automatic Overdrive:	150 @ 3400 rpm	260 lb.-ft. @ 2000 rpm

* Horsepower and torque ratings are with 3.08:1 rear axle ratio. All other applications use 150 hp. @ 3400 rpm and 260 lb-ft. @ 2000 rpm. Fuel Requirements: Regular Unleaded.

OPTIONAL ENGINE: OHV V-8. Special high-grade cast-iron block and cylinder heads. Standard with Eddie Bauer Bronco. Bore x Stroke: 4.00 in. x 3.00 in. Lifters: Hydraulic. Number of main bearings-5. Displacement: 302 cu. in. (5.0 liters). Fuel Induction: Multiple-port electronic fuel injection. Compression Ratio: 9.0:1. Oil refill: 6 qts. with filter change, 5 qts. without filter change.

Power Ratings

Transmission	Horsepower	Torque
5-Spd. Manual Overdrive1:	185 @ 3800 rpm	270 lb.-ft. @ 2400 rpm
3-Spd. Automatic1:	185 @ 3800 rpm	270 lb.-ft. @ 2400 rpm
4-Spd. Automatic Overdrive:	185 @ 3800 rpm	270 lb.-ft. @ 2400 rpm

NOTE 1: Not available in California. Fuel Requirements: Regular Unleaded.

OPTIONAL ENGINE: OHV EFI V-8. Special high-grade cast-iron block and cylinder heads. Bore x Stroke: 4.00 in. x 3.50 in. Lifters: Hydraulic. Number of main bearings-5. Displacement: 351 cu. in. (5.8 liters). Fuel Induction: Multiple-port electronic fuel injection. Compression Ratio: 8.8:1. Oil refill: 6 qts. with filter change, 5 qts. without filter change.

Power Ratings

Transmission	Horsepower	Torque
4-Spd. Automatic Overdrive:	200 @ 3800 rpm	300 lb.-ft. @ 2800 rpm

Fuel Requirements: Regular Unleaded.

CHASSIS FEATURES: Separate body and frame, single channel, 5 cross members, welded frame. 4.27 in. section modulus. Maximum side rail section: 7.01 x 2.12. x 0.202 in. 36,000 psi yield strength. Low carbon steel.

SUSPENSION AND RUNNING GEAR: Front Suspension: Independent, coil springs, computer selected, 2450 lb. rating. Optional rating of 2600, 2800, 2950 and 3800 lb. available. Rear Suspension: Single-stage, constant rate semi-elliptical 5-leaf, computer selected, 3770 lb. rating. Front Axle Type and Capacity: Dana 44 Twin Traction beam, 3800 lb. rating. Rear Axle Type and Capacity: Semi-floating, Ford, 3800 lb. rating. Available Final Drive Ratio: Front: 3.07, 3.54, 4.09:1. Rear: 3.08, 3.55, 4.10:1. Transfer Case: Type: Borg Warner 1356, 2-speed. Ratios: 1.0:1, 2.69:1. Brakes: Type: Hydraulic power-assisted, vented disc front and cast iron drum rear. Dimensions: Front: 11.72 in. dia. Floating Caliper Rear: 11.03 in. x 2.25 in. Total rear swept area: 155.95 sq. in. Wheels: 6.0JK x 15, 5-hole disc. Optional: 15 x 7JJ styled steel wheels, 15 x 8JJ styled steel wheels. Tires: P235/75R x 15SL All-Season steel-belted radial. Optional: P235/75R x 15XL All-Terrain steel-belted radial. 31 x 10.50R x 15C.

Steering: Power assisted, recirculating ball. Gear Ratio: 17.0:1, Overall Ratio: 18.1:1. Turning Circle: 36.57 ft. Optional: None. Transmission: Standard for 4.9 and 5.0 liter engines: Type: Mazda R2 5-speed manual overdrive, all-synchromesh. Transmission Ratios: 3.90, 2.25, 1.49, 1.00, 0.80:1. Reverse: 3.41:1. Optional: Ford 3-speed automatic (C-6). Ratios: 2.46, 1.46, 1.0:1. Reverse: 2.18. Optional: For 5.0 liter engines and standard for 5.8 liter engine: 4-speed Electronic Automatic Overdrive (E4OD). Ratios: 2.71, 1.54, 1.00, 0.71. Reverse: 2.18. Clutch: 4.9 liter engine with standard 5-speed manual and optional T18 trans.: Torsion-bend, woven non-asbestos. 10.0 in. dia. Belleville pressure plate. Total plate pressure: 1925 lb. 5.0 liter with standard 5-speed manual and optional T18 trans.: Segmented, woven non-asbestos. 11 in. dia. Belleville pressure plate. Total plate pressure: 1796 lb. Optional: None.

VEHICLE DIMENSIONS: Wheelbase: 104.7 in. Overall Length: 180.5 in. Front/Rear Tread 65.1 in./64.4 in. Overall Height: 74.2 in. Width: 79.1 in. Front/Rear Overhang: 28.7 in./44.3 in. Tailgate: Width and Height: 63.5 in. x 35.7 in. Approach/Departure Degrees: 35.3/20.9. Ground Clearance: Front axle: 8.1 in. Rear axle: 7.8 in. Transfer case: 9.1 in. Load space: With rear seat removed or folded: 60.8 in. x 50.8 in. 43.7 in. Maximum capacity: Without rear seat installed: 101.4 cu. ft. With rear seat folded: 80.2 cu. in. With rear seat up: 50.1 cu. ft.

CAPACITIES: Fuel Tank: 32.0 gal. with skid plate.

ACCOMMODATIONS: Seating Capacity: 5 passengers with standard front bucket seats and 3 passenger rear bench seat. 5 passengers with optional dual Captain's chairs and standard rear seat. 6 passengers with optional 3 passenger front bench seat and standard rear seat. Headroom: Front: 41.1 in. Rear: 39.2 in. Legroom: Front: 41.1 in. Legroom: Rear: 37.7 in. Shoulder room: Front: 65.2 in. Shoulder room: Rear: 64.9 in. Hip room: Front: 61.2 in. Hip room: Rear: 55.3 in.

INSTRUMENTATION: Speedometer, odometer, gauges for fuel level, engine coolant temperature, oil pressure and voltmeter.

OPTIONS: Air conditioning. Front/rear limited slip axle. Various axle ratios. Captain's chairs. Rear window defroster. Power window and door locks. California emissions system. Privacy glass. 5.0 liter V-8. 5.8 liter V-8. Engine block heater. Automatic locking hubs. Two-tone Deluxe paint. Victoria two-tone paint. High altitude use. Electronic AM/FM stereo search radio with cassette player and digital clock. Radio credit option. Front bench seat. Cloth seat trim. Outside swing-away spare tire carrier. Speed Controltilt steering wheel. Tachometer. P235/75R15XL BSW/OWL All-Terrain tires. 31 x 10.50R x 15C OWL All-Terrain tires. Electric Shift Touch Drive. SelectShift automatic transmission. Automatic overdrive. Deluxe argent styled 15 x 8 in. steel wheels Forged aluminum deep-dished wheels. Front license plate bracket. Eddie Bauer Group. Includes 5.0 liter EFI V-8, heavy-duty 84 amp battery, XLT trim (minus XLT nomenclature and exterior moldings), bright wheel-lip molding, specific two-tone paint treatment (tan accent paint in rocker area), tan fiberglass roof, dual body side accent paint stripe, dual cloth Captain's chairs with floor console, special cloth seat trim, chestnut interior, Eddie Bauer equipment items, chestnut outside tire cover (black with 31.0 x 10.50R x 15C tires), when outside swing-away spare is ordered, "Ford Care" extended service plan, air conditioning, Light/Convenience Group, privacy glass, speed Controltilt steering wheel, electronic AM/FM stereo radio with cassette player and digital clock, Deluxe argent styled steel wheels, tachometer, power door locks/windows, rear window defroster, choice of five body colors. Light/Convenience Group. Includes glove box light, headlights-on audible alert, underhood light, dual beam dome/map light (except with front bench seat), floor console (except with front bench seat). Heavy-Duty Service Package. Includes rear stabilizer bar, quad front and heavy-duty rear shock absorbers, 84 amp-hr. heavy-duty battery (standard on Eddie Bauer Bronco), Super engine cooling (includes auxiliary transmission oil cooler with automatic transmission). Heavy-Duty Front Suspension Package. Includes 6450 lb. GVW rating, heavy-duty, 3800 lb. rating, front springs, heavy-duty rear shock absorber. Trailer Towing Package. Includes seven-wire trailer wiring harness, heavy-duty turn signal flasher, Heavy-Duty Service Package. 25th anniversary Bronco Package. Includes the same items as the Eddie Bauer option, with the following additions and replacements: 5.0 liter EFI engine (upgrade to 5.8 liter if desired), Electronic 4-speed automatic transmission, Touch Drive Electric Shift, deep-dish forged aluminum wheels (set of 4 with conventional steel spare), 31 x 10.50R x 156C OWL All-Terrain tires (set of 5), outside swing-away spare tire carrier, currant red body color (must be ordered), currant red fiberglass roof (must be ordered), 25th anniversary Bronco front fender emblem, currant red bumper rub strips and step pads, currant red body side moldings, special 25th anniversary Bronco B-pillar emblem, dark currant red outside spare tire cover with 25th anniversary logo, dark charcoal interior, leather dual Captain's chairs in dark charcoal with currant red accents (must be ordered), leather rear bench seat in dark charcoal with currant red accents, color-keyed vinyl door trim panel inserts, currant red 22 oz. carpeting, front floor mats with 25th anniversary logo, currant red carpeted map pockets, 25th anniversary Bronco instrument panel emblem, Unique metal key blanks, special Owner's Guide with Silver Anniversary logo, currant red front and rear floor mats with 25th anniversary logo, leather jacket and bag (shipped directly to customer).

HISTORICAL FOOTNOTES: Bronco marked its 25th anniversary in 1991.

1992 BRONCO

The 1992 Ford Bronco revisions included a new grille and more rounded aerodynamic front end appearance. A new instrument panel/steering wheel along with new seat trim was also introduced. The woodgrain instrument panel applique was deleted. New seat trim and styles were introduced. New bright electric aerodynamic mirrors were available for all models except the custom. The custom Bronco had new standard bright manual aerodynamic mirrors. Available as an option for all models were low-mount swing-away mirrors. Also offered as a new option for all models were 15 in. x 7.5 in. chrome styled wheels. Available as options for the Custom and XLT models were new 15 in. x 7.5 in. argent styled steel wheels. Additional changes in the Bronco's option program included the availability (except on early production Broncos) of P265/75R x 15 OWL/BSW All-Terrain tires for all models, leather-trimmed Captain's chairs as an option for the XLT and Eddie Bauer models and a floor console with 2 cupholders, cassette tray and coin holders. Three Bronco series — Custom, XLT and Eddie Bauer were continued into 1992. The XLT and Eddie Bauer models received a full-length headliner. The Captain's chairs now included a new power lumbar support. The XLT and Eddie Bauer models also offered new bright electric aero mirrors. Three engines, all with multi-port fuel injection, were offered: 4.9 liter L-6, 5.0 liter V-8 and 5.8 liter V-8. A 5-speed manual overdrive transmission was standard with all three engines. Optional was an electronic 4-speed automatic that Ford recommended for heavy-duty work such as trailer towing. The optional Touch Drive Electric Shift allowed push-button operation into two or four-wheel drive while moving.

A new NITE option for the Bronco was introduced. It consisted of these items: XLT trim, raven black exterior paint, black fiberglass roof, special body side tape stripe, "NITE" nomenclature (matches tape stripe) located on rear quarter, black front bumper and rear step bumper, black grille, black low-mount outside mirrors, black windshield molding and rear quarter window molding, black body side molding, black appliques and "NITE" nomenclature on instrument panel, special "NITE" color-keyed floor mats, forged aluminum deep-dish wheels, P235/75R OWL All-Season tires, Handling Package, privacy glass and outside swing-away spare tire carrier with black cover with "NITE" logo.

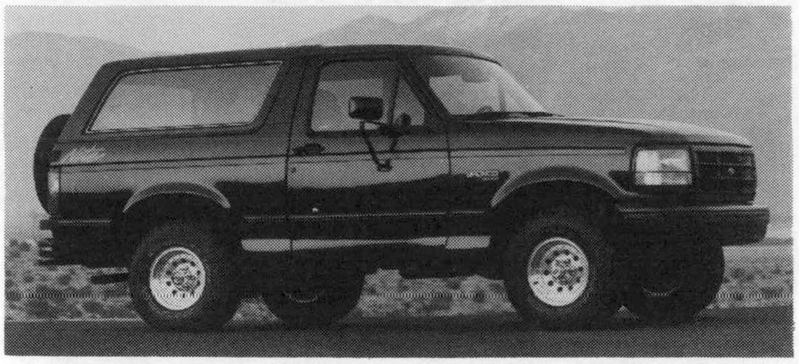

1992 Ford Bronco Nite

Standard equipment for the Bronco custom consisted of these items: Chrome front bumper and rear step bumper, tinted glass, chrome grille, aero halogen headlamps with high impact lenses, bright headlight surround, bright manual mirrors, bright windshield molding, high-mounted stoplight, swing-down tailgate with power window, wraparound taillights with high impact lenses, Sport wheelcovers, cigarette lighter, dual color-keyed coat hooks, dome light with courtesy switches, color-keyed vinyl door trim panels, inside hood release, dual electric horns, color-keyed instrument panel with side window demisters and glove box lock and light, gauges for voltmeter, oil pressure, and temperature plus indicator lights, trip odometer, day/night 12 in. interior mirror, color-keyed windshield pillar moldings, power point, electronic AM/FM stereo radio with digital clock, color-keyed front and rear safety belts, black front door scuff plates, bright tailgate scuff plate, color-keyed vinyl bucket seats with tip/slide mechanism, black spare tire cover, black vinyl steering wheel, color-keyed, vinyl-covered sun visors, black rear quarter trim panels, pivoting vent windows and interval windshield wipers. The XLT had, in addition to or in place of these items, the following: Chrome front bumper with black rub strip, bright rear quarter window molding, lower body protection, bright wheel-lip, rear cargo light, color-keyed carpeting, door trim panels with cloth insert, map pocket and courtesy light, full-length, color-keyed headliner, tachometer, additional insulation, cloth Captain's chairs with tip/slide and power lumbar mechanism, speed ControlTilt steering wheel, black leather-wrapped steering wheel, cloth-covered sun visors with band on left side and covered vanity mirror on right side plus color-keyed trim panels with integral armrests, storage bin, ashtray and cupholder. The Eddie Bauer model had, in addition to or in place of the XLT features, the following: Privacy glass, dual body side accent paint stripes, two-tone paint rocker panels, air conditioning, front and rear carpeted floor mats and the Light Convenience Group.

I.D. DATA: The Bronco V.I.N. consisted of seventeen symbols. The first three characters identified the manufacturer, make and type of vehicle. The fourth character (a letter) designated the GVW range. The fifth, sixth and seventh characters identified the series and body style. The eighth character identified the engine. The ninth character was the check digit. The tenth character (a letter) represented the model year. The eleventh character identified the assembly plant. The remaining digits represented the sequential production number.

Body Type	Factory Price	GVW	Shipping Weight	Prod. Total
Bronco U100				
Wagon Custom (U15)	$18,852	6050*	NA	—
XLT	$20,357	6050	NA	—
XLT Nite	$22,357	6050	NA	—
Eddie Bauer	$23,201	6050	NA	—

* A 6450 GVW Package was optional.

STANDARD ENGINE: Engine Type: OHV 6-cyl. Special high-grade cast-iron block and cylinder heads. Not available with Eddie Bauer Bronco. Bore x Stroke: 4.0 in. x 3.98 in. Lifters: Hydraulic. Number of main bearings-7. Fuel induction: Multiple-port electronic fuel injection. Compression Ratio: 8.8:1. Displacement: 300 cu. in. (4.9 liters).

Power Ratings

Transmission	Horsepower	Torque
5-Spd. Manual Overdrive:	145 @ 3400 rpm	265 lb.-ft. @ 2000 rpm*
4-Spd. Automatic Overdrive:	150 @ 3400 rpm	260 lb.-ft. @ 2000 rpm

* Horsepower and torque ratings are with 3.08:1 rear axle ratio. All other applications use 150 hp. @ 3400 rpm and 260 lb-ft. @ 2000 rpm. Fuel Requirements: Regular Unleaded.

OPTIONAL ENGINE: OHV V-8. Special high-grade cast-iron block and cylinder heads. Standard with Eddie Bauer Bronco. Bore x Stroke: 4.00 in. x 3.00 in. Lifters: Hydraulic. Number of main bearings-5. Displacement: 302 cu. in. (5.0 liters). Fuel Induction: Multiple-port electronic fuel injection. Compression Ratio: 9.0:1. Oil refill: 6 qts. with filter change, 5 qts. without filter change.

Power Ratings

Transmission	Horsepower	Torque
5-Spd. Manual Overdrive[1]:	185 @ 3800 rpm	270 lb.-ft. @ 2400 rpm
3-Spd. Automatic[1]:	185 @ 3800 rpm	270 lb.-ft. @ 2400 rpm
4-Spd. Automatic Overdrive:	185 @ 3800 rpm	270 lb.-ft. @ 2400 rpm

NOTE 1: Not available in California. Fuel Requirements: Regular Unleaded.

OPTIONAL ENGINE: OHV EFI V-8. Special high-grade cast-iron block and cylinder heads. Bore x Stroke: 4.00 in. x 3.50 in. Lifters: Hydraulic. Number of main bearings-5. Displacement: 351 cu. in. (5.8 liters). Fuel Induction: Multiple-port electronic fuel injection. Compression Ratio: 8.8:1. Oil refill: 6 qts. with filter change, 5 qts. without filter change.

Power Ratings

Transmission	Horsepower	Torque
4-Spd. Automatic Overdrive:	200 @ 3800 rpm	300 lb.-ft. @ 2800 rpm

Fuel Requirements: Regular Unleaded.

CHASSIS FEATURES: Separate body and frame, single channel, 5 cross members, welded frame. 4.27 in. section modulus. Maximum side rail section: 7.01 x 2.12. x 0.202 in. 36,000 psi yield strength. Low carbon steel.

SUSPENSION AND RUNNING GEAR: Front Suspension: Independent, coil springs, computer selected, 2450 lb. rating. Optional rating of 2600, 2800, 2950 and 3800 lb. available. Rear Suspension: Single-stage, constant rate semi-elliptical 5-leaf, computer selected, 3770 lb. rating. Front Axle Type and Capacity: Dana 44 Twin Traction beam, 3800 lb. rating. Rear Axle Type and Capacity: Semi-floating, Ford, 3800 lb. rating. Available Final Drive Ratio: Front: 3.07, 3.54, 4.09:1. Rear: 3.08, 3.55, 4.10:1. Transfer Case: Type: Borg Warner 1356,

2-speed. Ratios: 1.0:1, 2.69:1. Brakes: Type: Hydraulic power-assisted, vented disc front and cast iron drum rear. Dimensions: Front: 11.72 in. dia. Floating Caliper Rear: 11.03 in. x 2.25 in. Total rear swept area: 155.95 sq. in. Wheels: 6.0JK x 15, 5-hole disc. Optional: 15 x 7JJ styled steel wheels, 15 x 8JJ styled steel wheels. Tires: P235/75R x 15SL All-Season steel-belted radial. Optional: P235/75R x 15XL All-Terrain steel-belted radial. 31 x 10.50R x 15C. Steering: Power assisted, recirculating ball. Gear Ratio: 17.0:1, Overall Ratio: 18.1:1. Turning Circle: 36.57 ft. Optional: None. Transmission: Standard for 4.9 and 5.0 liter engines: Type: Mazda R2 5-speed manual overdrive, all-synchromesh. Transmission Ratios: 3.90, 2.25, 1.49, 1.00, 0.80:1. Reverse: 3.41:1. Optional: Ford 3-speed automatic (C-6). Ratios: 2.46, 1.46, 1.0:1. Reverse: 2.18. Optional: For 5.0 liter engines and standard for 5.8 liter engine: 4-speed Electronic Automatic Overdrive (E4OD). Ratios: 2.71, 1.54, 1.00, 0.71. Reverse: 2.18. Clutch: 4.9 liter engine with standard 5-speed manual and optional T18 trans.: Torsion-bend, woven non-asbestos. 10.0 in. dia. Belleville pressure plate. Total plate pressure: 1925 lb. 5.0 liter with standard 5-speed manual and optional T18 trans.: Segmented, woven non-asbestos. 11 in. dia. Belleville pressure plate. Total plate pressure: 1796 lb. Optional: None.

VEHICLE DIMENSIONS: Wheelbase: 104.7 in. Overall Length: 180.5 in. Front/Rear Tread 65.1 in./64.4 in. Overall Height: 74.2 in. Width: 79.1 in. Front/Rear Overhang: 28.7 in./44.3 in. Tailgate: Width and Height: 63.5 in. x 35.7 in. Approach/Departure Degrees: 35.3/20.9. Ground Clearance: Front axle: 8.1 in. Rear axle: 7.8 in. Transfer case: 9.1 in. Load space: With rear seat removed or folded: 60.8 in. x 50.8 in. 43.7 in. Maximum capacity: Without rear seat installed: 101.4 cu. ft. With rear seat folded: 80.2 cu. in. With rear seat up: 50.1 cu. ft.

CAPACITIES: Fuel Tank: 32.0 gal. with skid plate.

ACCOMMODATIONS: Seating Capacity: 5 passengers with standard front bucket seats and 3 passenger rear bench seat. 5 passengers with optional dual Captain's chairs and standard rear seat. 6 passengers with optional 3 passenger front bench seat and standard rear seat. Headroom: Front: 41.1 in. Rear: 39.2 in. Legroom: Front: 41.1 in. Legroom: Rear: 37.7 in. Shoulder room: Front: 65.2 in. Shoulder room: Rear: 64.9 in. Hip room: Front: 61.2 in. Hip room: Rear: 55.3 in.

INSTRUMENTATION: Speedometer, odometer, gauges for fuel level, engine coolant temperature, oil pressure and voltmeter.

OPTIONS: Air conditioning. Limited slip front axle. Front license plate bracket. Captain's chairs. Rear window defroster. Power door/window locks. California emissions system. 5.0 liter V-8. 5.8 liter V-8. Privacy glass. Engine block heater. Manual locking front hubs. Bright aero electric mirrors. Bright low-mount swing-away mirrors. Deluxe two-tone paint. Body side two-tone paint. High altitude principal use. Electronic AM/FM stereo radio with digital clock. Electronic AM/FM stereo radio with cassette tape player and digital clock. Radio credit option. Front bench seat. Cloth seat trim. Leather seating surfaces. Outside swing-away spare tire carrier. Speed Controltilt steering wheel. Tachometer. Tires: P235/75R15XL BSW/OWL All-Terrain, P235/75R15XL OWL All-Season, P265/75R15XL OWL All-Terrain (not available for early production run models), 31 x 10, 50R x 15C OWL All-Terrain. Electric Shift Touch Drive. Electronic 4-speed automatic overdrive transmission. Argent styled steel wheels. Chrome styled steel wheels. Forged aluminum deep-dish wheels. Eddie Bauer Package. Includes 5.0 liter V-8 (5.8 liter V-8 is optional), 84 amp-hr. heavy-duty battery, unique two-tone paint treatment (light mocha accent color in rocker area), light mocha fiberglass roof, bright wheel-lip moldings, dual body side accent paint stripe, dual Captain's chairs with floor console, mocha interior, Eddie Bauer equipment items, outside swing-away spare tire carrier, mocha outside spare tire cover (black with P265/75R15XL or 31 x 10.50C tires), "Ford Care" extended service plan, air conditioning, Light/Convenience Group, speed Controltilt steering wheel, privacy glass, electronic AM/FM stereo radio with cassette and digital clock, forged aluminum deep-dish wheels, front and rear carpeted floor mats, rear window defroster, power door/window locks, bright aero electric mirrors, tachometer and choice of six body colors. Light/Convenience Group. Includes headlights-on audible alert, underhood light, dual-beam dome/map light (except with front bench seat) and floor console (except with front bench seat). "NITE" Bronco Package. Heavy-Duty Service Package. Includes rear stabilizer bar (front stabilizer bar standard), quad front and heavy-duty rear shock absorbers, 84 amp-hr. heavy-duty battery, Super engine cooling. Heavy-Duty Front Suspension Package. Includes 6450 lb. GVWR, heavy-duty, 3800 lb. rating front springs, heavy-duty rear shock absorbers and rear stabilizer bar. Trailer Towing Package. Includes 7 wire trailer wiring harness, heavy-duty turn signal flasher, Heavy-Duty Service Package.

HISTORICAL FOOTNOTES: The Bronco continued, as it had since 1978, to dominate the full-size utility vehicle market. At the start of the 1992 model year it had 59 percent of its market segment.

1993 BRONCO

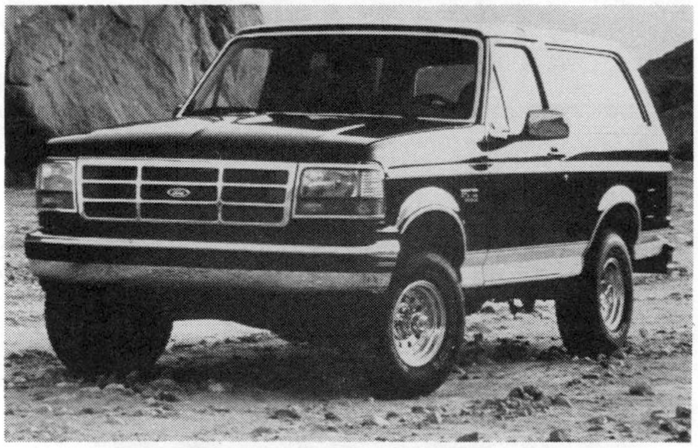

1993 Ford Eddie Bauer Bronco

The Bronco for 1993 was again offered in custom, XLT and Eddie Bauer models. The "Nite" Package was deleted for 1993. A four-wheel anti-lock braking system was added for 1993. The 4.9 liter engine was replaced as the standard Bronco engine by the 5.0 liter V-8 with EFI. Both an automatic transmission and an electric rear window defroster were now standard for the Eddie Bauer Bronco.

Exterior changes were modest in scope for 1993. Bright hubcaps on argent steel wheels were standard for the custom model. The XLT Bronco now had standard argent styled steel wheels. Chrome styled wheels were added to the XLT Preferred Equipment Package. The XLT also had a new monochromatic exterior paint treatment for the cap, body and moldings. The Climate Control, Luxury and Wheel Group options were re-packaged for 1993.

I.D. DATA: The Bronco V.I.N. consisted of seventeen symbols. The first three characters identified the manufacturer, make and type of vehicle. The fourth character (a letter) designated the GVW range. The fifth, sixth and seventh characters identified the series and body style. The eighth character identified the engine. The ninth character was the check digit. The tenth character (a letter) represented the model year. The eleventh character identified the assembly plant. The remaining digits represented the sequential production number.

Body Type	Factory Price	GVW	Shipping Weight	Prod. Total
Bronco U150	—	—	—	—
Custom	—	—	—	—
XLT	—	—	—	—
Eddie Bauer	—	—	—	—

Prices of the 1993 Bronco were not available at press time.

STANDARD ENGINE: Engine type: OHV V-8. Cast-iron block and cylinder heads. Bore x Stroke: 4.00 in. x 3.00 in. Lifters: Hydraulic. Number of main bearings-5. Displacement: 302 cu. in. (5.0 liters). Lifters: Hydraulic. Induction system: Multiport fuel injection with eight individual ports. Compression Ratio: 9.0:1. Horsepower: 185 @ 3800 rpm. Torque: Net: 270 lb.-ft. @ 2400 rpm. Fuel Requirements: Unleaded. Optional: 5.8 V-8. Engine type: OHV V-8. Bore x Stroke: 4.00 in. x 3.50 in. Displacement: 351 cu. in. (5.75 liters). Induction system: Multiport fuel injection. Compression ratio: 8.8:1. Number of main bearings-5. Horsepower: 200 @ 3800 rpm. Torque: 300 lb.-ft. @ 2800 rpm. Fuel Requirements: Unleaded. Note: 1992 Ratings. 1993 ratings not yet available.

CHASSIS FEATURES: Separate body and frame, single channel, 5 cross members, welded frame. 3.66 in. section modulus. Maximum side rail section: 6.95 x 2.12. x 0.170 in. Low carbon steel.

SUSPENSION AND RUNNING GEAR: Front Suspension: Independent, coil springs, computer selected, 2450 lb. rating. Rear Suspension: Single-stage, two-stage constant rate semi-elliptical 5-leaf, computer selected, 3790 lb. rating. Front Axle Type and Capacity: Twin Traction beam, 3800 lb. rating. Rear Axle Type and Capacity: Semi-floating, Ford, 3800 lb. rating. Final Drive Ratio: Front and Rear: 2.73, 3.08:1. Additional ratios optional. Transfer Case: Type: NPG 200, 2-speed. Ratios: 1.0:1, 2.69:1. Brakes: Type: Hydraulic power-assisted, vented disc front and cast iron drum rear. Dimensions: Front: 11.72 in. dia. Floating Caliper Rear: 11.03 in. x 2.25 in. Total rear swept area: 155.95 sq. in. Wheels: 6.0JK x 15, 5-hole disc. Optional: 15 x 7.5 in. argent styled steel wheels, 15 x 7.5 in. chrome styled steel wheels and forged deep-dish aluminum wheels. Tires: P235/75R x 15XL BSW All-Season steel-belted radial. Optional: P235/75R15XL BSW/OWL All-Terrain, P235/75R15XL OWL All-Season, P265/75R15XL OWL All-Terrain (not available for early production run models), 31 x 10, 50R x 15C OWL All-Terrain. Steering: Power assisted, recirculating ball. Ratio: 17.0:1. Turning Circle: 36.6 ft. Optional: None. Transmission: Type: 5-speed manual overdrive, all-synchromesh. 5.8 liter available only with 4-speed E4OD automatic overdrive. Optional: 4-speed Automatic Overdrive Drive 4-speed, Electronic Automatic Overdrive (E4OD). Clutch: Torsion-bend, woven non-asbestos. 10.0 in. dia. Optional: None.

VEHICLE DIMENSIONS: Wheelbase: 104.7 in. Overall Length: 183.6 in. Front/Rear Tread 65.1 in./64.4 in. Overall Height: 74.4 in. Width: 79.1 in. Front/Rear Overhang: 28.7 in./44.3 in. Tailgate: Width and Height: 63.5 in. x 35.7 in. Approach/Departure Degrees: 35.3/20.9. Ground Clearance: Front axle: 8.1 in. Rear axle: 7.8 in. Transfer case: 9.1 in. Load space: With rear seat installed: 63.3 in. x 50.8 in. x 35.8 in. With rear seat removed or folded: 60.8 in. x 50.8 in. x 35.8 in. Maximum capacity: Without rear seat installed: 101.7 cu. ft. With rear seat folded: 78.8 cu. in. With rear seat up: 50.2 cu. ft.

CAPACITIES: Fuel Tank: 32.0 gal.

ACCOMMODATIONS: Seating Capacity: 5 passengers with standard front bucket seats and 3 passenger rear bench seat. 5 passengers with optional dual Captain's chairs and standard rear seat. 6 passengers with optional 3 passenger front bench seat and standard rear seat. Front: Headroom: 41.2 in. Legroom: 41.1 in. Shoulder room: 64.9 in. Hip room: 62.2 in. Rear: Headroom: 39.9 in. Legroom: 37.7 in. Shoulder room: 64.9 in. Hip room: 55.3 in.

INSTRUMENTATION: Speedometer, odometer, gauges for fuel level, engine coolant temperature, oil pressure and voltmeter.

OPTIONS: Optional axle ratio. Front license plate bracket. California emissions system. Climate Control Group. Includes air conditioning and electric rear window defroster. Eddie Bauer Bronco. Includes electronic automatic overdrive transmission, heavy-duty 84 amp battery, bright wheel-lip moldings, two-tone paint treatment with light mocha accent color in rocker area, dual body side accent paint stripe, light mocha fiberglass roof, dual cloth Captain's chairs, mocha interior, Eddie Bauer garment bag and duffel bag, mocha outside spare tire cover (black with P265/75R15XL tires), air conditioning, Light/Convenience Group (headlights-on audible alert, underhood light, dual-beam dome/map light, [except with bench seat], and floor console [except with bench seat]. Privacy glass, speed Controltilt steering wheel, electronic AM/FM stereo radio with digital clock, deep-dish forged aluminum wheels, front and rear carpeted floor mats, electric rear window defroster, bright electric aero mirrors, tachometer, and a choice of five body colors. 5.8 liter V-8. Engine block heater. High altitude principle use. Manual locking hubs. Luxury Group. Includes privacy glass, Light and Convenience Group, power door locks and windows, AM/FM stereo radio with cassette tape player, and bright electric mirrors. Bright low-mount swing-away mirrors. Deluxe two-tone paint (XLT). Electronic AM/FM stereo radio with cassette tape player and digital clock. Radio delete option. Front bench seat. Cloth and vinyl seat trim. Leather seating areas. P235/75R15XL black sidewall OWL All-Terrain tires. P235/75R15XL OWL All-Season tires. P265/75R15XL OQWL All-Terrain tires. Electric Shift Touch Drive. Trailer Towing Package. Includes 7 wire trailer wiring harness, heavy-duty turn signal flasher, rear stabilizer bar, quad front and heavy-duty rear shock absorbers, heavy-duty battery and Super engine cooling (includes auxiliary transmission oil cooler with automatic transmission). Electronic 4-speed overdrive automatic transmission. Wheel Group. Includes outside swing-away tire carrier (includes black cover [mocha with Eddie Bauer] and lock, and argent or chrome styled steel wheels (forged deep-dish aluminum wheels standard on Eddie Bauer). Deep-dish forged aluminum wheels.

HISTORICAL FOOTNOTES: The Bronco was assembled at Ford's Wayne, Michigan facility.

FORD RANGER
1983-1993

1983 RANGER

Ford Motor Company raised the curtain on the first of its 1983 products — the new-size compact Ranger pickup on December 3, 1981. Although production didn't begin until January, 1982, and public announcement wasn't until March, 1982, Harold A Poling, executive vice president, Ford North American Automotive Operations, announced that Ford dealers could begin selling the Ranger immediately. Approximately six months after the March debut of the Ranger a four-wheel drive version was introduced. The Ranger was similar in appearance to the full-size F series Ford trucks. However, its exterior dimensions were closer to those of the imported compact trucks. The interior of the Ranger provided three-across seating with more head, shoulder, leg and hip room than the best-selling imports. The standard 108 in. wheelbase models had six-foot boxes. A seven-foot box was fitted on models with the 114 in. wheelbase. Among the primary features of the Ranger were these: The capability to carry 4x8 foot construction material horizontally in the pickup box with the tailgate down; a quick-removal tailgate, Camper and Light-Duty Towing Packages, double-wall pickup-box and cab-roof construction, weld-on front body structure (this process was intended to provide accurate door and hood-margins and improve the overall quietness of the vehicle), and computer-selected front and rear springs based upon total option weight of each truck. Service features of the Ranger included a virtually lubrication-free chassis, self-adjusting brakes and clutch, computer-set front-end alignment and extensive corrosion protection. The four-wheel drive Ranger was offered in payload capacities of 1,200 and 1,600 pounds. Additional featured included a Twin-Traction independent front suspension similar to the Twin-I-Beam used on the Ranger 4x2, a one inch standard front stabilizer bar, a new variable-ratio steering system, power brakes specifically designed for off-road operation, hot-sealed front and rear driveshafts with extended intervals of 30,000 miles and 15 inch tires that provided ground clearance virtually the same as the F-150 4x4. Initially, the Ranger was offered only with a 2.3 liter 4-cylinder engine. After the introduction of the Bronco II, a European-built 2.8 liter V-6 was offered.

Standard Ranger equipment included a black front bumper, chrome grille and windshield moldings, dual mirrors, argent styled steel wheels with black hub covers, tethered gas cap, vinyl bench seat with folding covered seat back, stalk-mounted controls, instrument panel storage bin and glove box, AM radio, courtesy light switch for driver's door, inside hood release, day/night rearview mirror, color-keyed highlights for instrument panel. The XL trim level added a number of appearance and comfort features to the content of the standard model. These included bright wheel-lip moldings, bright rear window insert molding, Deluxe wheel trim and chrome front bumper, woodtone instrument panel applique, color-keyed cloth headliner, contoured knitted vinyl bench seat, color-keyed seat belts with tension eliminator, color-keyed steering wheel and floor mats, and passenger door courtesy light switch. The XLS Package was the Sporty trim option for the Ranger. It featured blackout trim components, special XLS three-color tape stripe, reclining cloth and vinyl bucket seats, color-keyed steering wheel, and Gauge Package (ammeter, engine coolant temperature, oil pressure gauges and trip odometer). The XLT was the top-of-the line Ranger. This Package included chrome front bumper with black end caps, full-length black lower body side molding with bright accent, dual accent body side paint stripes, Deluxe wheel trim and brushed aluminum tailgate applique, full cloth door trim with color-keyed molding and bright insert, carpeted lower portion and map pockets, cloth seat trim, full color-keyed carpeting, color-keyed deluxe steering wheel, and vent windows. Exterior colors for 1983 consisted of raven black, silver metallic, medium grey metallic, candyapple red, midnight blue metallic, medium blue metallic, bright blue, dark spruce metallic, dark brown metallic, medium yellow, bittersweet glow (extra cost), Wimbledon white, desert tan, and light desert tan. Interior color choices were black, dark blue, red and tan.

I.D. DATA: The Ranger V.I.N. consisted of seventeen symbols. The first three characters identified the manufacturer, make and type of vehicle. The fourth character (a letter) designated the GVW range. The fifth, sixth and seventh characters identified the series and body style. The eighth character identified the engine. The ninth character was the check digit. The tenth character (a letter) represented the model year. The eleventh character identified the assembly plant. The remaining digits represented the sequential production number.

Body Type	Factory Price	GVW	Shipping Weight	Prod. Total
Ranger R10 Styleside				
Pickup, Styleside, 107.9 in. wb.	$7,989	4000[1]	2770	42,300[2]
Pickup, Styleside, 113.9 in. wb.	$8,142	4040[3]	2826	—

NOTE 1: A 4420 GVW Package was optional for the 107.9 in. wheelbase Ranger.
NOTE 2: Total production of all 4x4 Rangers for the 1983 calendar year. An additional 2,798 units were built in 1982.
NOTE 3: A 4480 lb. GVW Package was optional for the 113.9 in. wheelbase Ranger.

STANDARD ENGINE: Engine Type: OHV 4-cyl. Cast-iron block and cylinder heads. Bore x Stroke: 3.78 in. x 3.13 in. Lifters: Hydraulic. Number of main bearings-5. Fuel Induction: Single barrel carburetor. Compression Ratio: 9.0:1. Displacement: 144 cu. in. (2.3 liters). Horsepower: Net: 80 @ 4000 rpm. Torque: Net: 104 lb.-ft. @ 2600 rpm. Fuel Requirements: Unleaded. Oil capacity: 6 qt. with filter change.

OPTIONAL ENGINE: OHV 60 degree V-6. Cast-iron block and cylinder heads. Bore x Stroke: 3.66 in. x 2.70 in. Lifters: Hydraulic. Number of main bearings-4. Displacement: 171 cu. in. (2.8 liters). Fuel Induction: Two-barrel carburetor. Compression Ratio: 8.7:1. Horsepower: Net: 115 @ 4600 rpm. Torque: Net: 150 lb.-ft. @ 2600 rpm. Fuel Requirements: Unleaded. Oil capacity: 5 qt. with filter change.

CHASSIS FEATURES: Frame: Ladder-type, 6 cross members, section modulus: 2.37 cu. in.

SUSPENSION AND RUNNING GEAR: Front Suspension: Coil springs, computer selected. Rear Suspension: Single-stage, semi-elliptical leaf, computer selected. Front Axle Type and Capacity: Twin-Traction beam, Dana 28-IFS, 2750 lb. capacity. Rear Axle Type and Capacity: Ford semi-floating, 2750 lb. capacity. Final Drive Ratio: 3.45:1 front and rear. Transfer Case: Type: Warner 1350, part-time, 2-speed. Ratios: 2.48, 1.00:1. Brakes: Type: Hydraulic, power-assisted, disc front and cast iron drum rear. Dimensions: Front: 10.87 in. dia. Rear: 9.0 in. x 1.75 in. Wheels: 15 x 5.0 in. 5-hole disc. 15 x 5.5 in. with Payload Package and steel belted radial tires. Optional: 15 x 6.0 in. Tires: Glass-belted P195/75R x 15L. Optional: Steel-belted radial tires in sizes to match GVW. Steering: Recirculating ball, manual. Ratio: 23.75:1. Turning Circle: 36.5 ft. Optional: Power steering: 17.1:1 ratio. Transmission: Type: 4-speed, synchromesh on all gears. Transmission Ratios: 3.96, 2.08, 1.39, 1.00:1. Optional: 5-speed manual overdrive. Optional: 3-speed automatic. Ratios: 2.46:1, 1.46:1, 1.00:1. Clutch: 9.0 in. dia. Optional: None.

VEHICLE DIMENSIONS: Wheelbase: 107.8/113.9 in. Overall Length: 175.6 in./187.6 in. (without rear bumper). Front/Rear Tread 56.5 in./55.1 in. Overall Height: 67.1 in. Width: 66.9 in. Front/Rear Overhang: 28.3 in./39.4 in. (107.9 in. wheelbase); 45.4 in. (133.9 in. wheelbase). Tailgate: Width and Height: 51.9 in. x 16.0 in. Approach/Departure Degrees: 107.9 in. wheelbase: 29.2/23.2. 113.9 in. wheelbase: 29.2/25.5. Ground Clearance: Rear axle: 6.9 in. Load space: 107.9 in. wheelbase: 72.2 in. x 54.3 in. x 16.5 in. 133.9 in. wheelbase: 84.2 in. x 54.3 in. x 16.5 in.

CAPACITIES: Fuel Tank: 107.9 in. wheelbase: 15.2 gal. 113.9 in. wheelbase: 17.0 gal. Optional: Auxiliary 10.0 gal. tank.

ACCOMMODATIONS: Seating Capacity: 3 passengers. Headroom: 39.2 in. Maximum Steering wheel to seat back: 23.1 in. Shoulder room: 55.6 in. Hip room: 55.0 in. Legroom: 42.4 in.

INSTRUMENTATION: Speedometer, odometer, warning lights for engine coolant temperature, oil pressure, ammeter, high beam, seat belt, parking brake and turn signals.

OPTIONS AND PRICES: XL Package: $364. XLT Package: $632. XLS Package: $641. Color-Keyed Cloth Headliner Package. Also includes upper door moldings, cowl side trim panels, B-pillar trim panels, rear window moldings and aluminum scuff plates. Sport tri-color tape stripe. 4x4 tape stripe. Regular Tu-Tone paint. Deluxe Tu-Tone paint. Special Tu-Tone paint. AM/FM monaural radio. AM/FM stereo radio. AM/FM stereo radio with cassette tape player. Radio credit option (deletes standard AM radio for credit). Air conditioning. Black rear step bumper. Convenience Group. Includes dual electric horns, interval windshield wipers, passenger's visor vanity mirror, and with standard trim, a driver's sun visor band. Tinted glass. Light Group. Includes ashtray light, cargo box light, passenger door courtesy light switch (standard trim), glove box light and headlights-on warning buzzer. Floor console. Available for bucket seats or XLS trim only. Includes Gauge Package, graphic display module, cassette tape tray, coin holder and storage bin. Overhead console. Requires optional trim or headliner for standard model. Includes pivoting map light and electronic digital clock. Bright low-mounted Western swing-away, 8.0 in. x 5.0 in. Power steering. Tilt steering wheel. Sliding rear window. Cargo tie-down hooks. Pivoting vent windows. Fingertip speed control (includes deluxe steering wheel). Reclining cloth and vinyl bucket seats. Available with XL and XCLT trim. Included with XLS. Includes carpeted back panel and cargo light. Also includes full-length carpeting with XL. Knitted vinyl contoured bench seat. Cloth and vinyl bench seat. Available with standard trim. Payload Packages up to 1,770 lb. Automatic transmission. Heavy-duty air cleaner. Heavy-duty battery. Camper Package. Extra engine cooling. Auxiliary fuel tank. Includes Gauge Package and in-box spare tire carrier with lock. Gauge Package. Standard with XLS. Engine block heater. California emission system. High altitude emission system. Security Lock Group. Includes glove box lock, locking gas cap(s), and under-body spare tire lock. Exterior Protection Group. Includes front chrome bumper, black front bumper guards and end caps, black upper body side moldings with dual red accent stripes (except with Tu-Tones), and bright door edge guards. Chrome front bumper. Cast aluminum wheels. White Sport wheels.

HISTORICAL FOOTNOTES: Ford Motor Company spent approximately $600 million on the Ranger project. A large amount of this expenditure was invested in re-equipping and modernizing Ford's Louisville, Kentucky assembly plant, the sole source of Ranger production.

1984 RANGER

Both the Ranger's Styling and Trim Package content was unchanged for 1984. The exterior color selection for 1984 consisted of raven black, polar white, light charcoal metallic, dark canyon red, light blue, medium blue metallic, midnight blue metallic, medium desert tan, walnut metallic, light desert tan, bright bittersweet, bright copper glow (extra cost). Ranger interiors were available in dark blue, canyon red and tan.

1984 Ford Ranger XLT pickup with Snowplow Special

I.D. DATA: The Ranger V.I.N. consisted of seventeen symbols. The first three characters identified the manufacturer, make and type of vehicle. The fourth character (a letter) designated the GVW range. The fifth, sixth and seventh characters identified the series and body style. The eighth character identified the engine. The ninth character was the check digit. The tenth character (a letter) represented the model year. The eleventh character identified the assembly plant. The remaining digits represented the sequential production number.

Body Type	Factory Price	GVW	Shipping Weight	Prod. Total
Ranger R10 Styleside				
Pickup, Styleside, 107.9 in. wb.	$8,163	4000[1]	2786	48,012
Pickup, Styleside, 113.9 in. wb.	$8,321	4040[2]	2842	—

NOTE 1: A 4420 lb. GVW Package was optional for the 107.9 in. wheelbase Ranger.
NOTE 2: A 4480 lb. GVW Package was optional for the 113.9 in. wheelbase Ranger.

STANDARD ENGINE: Engine Type: OHV 4-cyl. Cast-iron block and cylinder heads. Bore x Stroke: 3.78 in. x 3.13 in. Lifters: Hydraulic. Number of main bearings-5. Fuel Induction: Single barrel carburetor. Compression Ratio: 9.0:1. Displacement: 144 cu. in. (2.3 liters). Horsepower: Net: 80 @ 4000 rpm. Torque: Net: 104 lb.-ft. @ 2600 rpm. Fuel Requirements: Unleaded. Oil capacity: 6 qt. with filter change.

OPTIONAL ENGINE: OHV 60 degree V-6. Cast-iron block and cylinder heads. Bore x Stroke: 3.66 in. x 2.70 in. Lifters: Hydraulic. Number of main bearings-4. Displacement: 171 cu. in. (2.8 liters). Fuel Induction: two-barrel carburetor. Compression Ratio: 8.7:1. Horsepower: Net: 115 @ 4600 rpm. Torque: Net: 150 lb.-ft. @ 2600 rpm. Fuel Requirements: Unleaded. Oil capacity: 5 qt. with filter change.

CHASSIS FEATURES: Frame: Ladder-type, 6 cross members, section modulus: 2.37 cu. in.

SUSPENSION AND RUNNING GEAR: Front Suspension: Coil springs, computer selected. Rear Suspension: Single-stage, semi-elliptical leaf, computer selected. Front Axle Type and Capacity: Twin-Traction beam, Dana 28-IFS, 2750 lb. capacity. Rear Axle Type and Capacity: Ford semi-floating, 2750 lb. capacity. Final Drive Ratio: 3.45:1 front and rear. Transfer Case: Type: Warner 1350, part-time, 2-speed. Ratios: 2.48, 1.00:1. Brakes: Type: Hydraulic, power-assisted, disc front and cast iron drum rear. Dimensions: Front: 10.87 in. dia. Rear: 9.0 in. x 1.75 in. Wheels: 15 x 5.0 in. 5-hole disc. 15 x 5.5 in. with Payload Package and steel belted radial tires. Optional: 15 x 6.0 in. Tires: Glass-belted P195/75R x 15L. Optional: Steel-belted radial tires in sizes to match GVW. Steering: Recirculating ball, manual. Ratio: 23.75:1. Turning Circle: 36.5 ft. Optional: Power steering: 17.1:1 ratio. Transmission: Type: 4-speed, synchromesh on all gears. Transmission Ratios: 3.96, 2.08, 1.39, 1.00:1. Optional: 5-speed manual overdrive. Optional: 3-speed automatic. Ratios: 2.46:1, 1.46:1, 1.00:1. Clutch: 9.0 in. dia. Optional: None.

VEHICLE DIMENSIONS: Wheelbase: 107.8/113.9 in. Overall Length: 175.6 in./187.6 in. (without rear bumper). Front/Rear Tread 56.5 in./55.1 in. Overall Height: 67.1 in. Width: 66.9 in. Front/Rear Overhang: 28.3 in./39.4 in. (107.9 in. wheelbase); 45.4 in. (133.9 in. wheelbase). Tailgate: Width and Height: 51.9 in. x 16.0 in. Approach/Departure Degrees: 107.9 in. wheelbase: 29.2/23./2. 113.9 in. wheelbase: 29.2/25.5. Ground Clearance: Rear axle: 6.9 in. Load space: 107.9 in. wheelbase: 72.2 in. x 54.3 in. x 16.5 in. 133.9 in. wheelbase: 84.2 in. x 54.3 in. x 16.5 in.

CAPACITIES: Fuel Tank: 107.9 in. wheelbase: 15.2 gal. 113.9 in. wheelbase: 17.0 gal. Optional: Auxiliary 10.0 gal. tank.

ACCOMMODATIONS: Seating Capacity: 3 passengers. Headroom: 39.2 in. Maximum Steering wheel to seat back: 23.1 in. Shoulder room: 55.6 in. Hip room: 55.0 in. Legroom: 42.4 in.

INSTRUMENTATION: Speedometer, odometer, warning lights for engine coolant temperature, oil pressure, ammeter, high beam, seat belt, parking brake and turn signals.

OPTIONS AND PRICES: XL Package. XLT Package: $703. XLS Package: $812. Color-Keyed Cloth Headliner Package. Also includes upper door moldings, cowl side trim panels, B-pillar trim panels, rear window moldings and aluminum scuff plates. Sport tri-color tape stripe. 4x4 tape stripe. Regular Tu-Tone paint. Deluxe Tu-Tone paint. Special Tu-Tone paint. AM/FM monaural radio. AM/FM stereo radio. AM/FM stereo radio with cassette tape player. Radio-credit option (deletes standard AM radio for credit). Air conditioning. Black rear step bumper. Convenience Group. Includes dual electric horns, interval windshield wipers, passenger's visor vanity mirror, and with standard trim, a driver's sun visor band. Tinted glass. Light Group. Includes ashtray light, cargo box light, passenger door courtesy light switch (standard trim), glove box light and headlights-on warning buzzer. Floor console. Available for bucket seats or XLS trim only. Includes Gauge Package, graphic display module, cassette tape tray, coin holder and storage bin. Overhead console. Requires optional trim or headliner for standard model. Includes pivoting map light and electronic digital clock. Bright low-mounted Western swing-away, 8.0 in. x 5.0 in. Power steering. Tilt steering wheel. Sliding rear window. Cargo tie-down hooks. Pivoting vent windows. Fingertip speed control (includes deluxe steering wheel). Reclining cloth and vinyl bucket seats. Available with XL and XCLT trim. Included with XLS. Includes carpeted back panel and cargo light. Also includes full-length carpeting with XL. Knitted vinyl contoured bench seat. Cloth and vinyl bench seat. Available with standard trim. Payload Packages up to 1,770 lb. Automatic transmission. Heavy-duty air cleaner. Heavy-duty battery. Camper Package. Extra engine cooling. Auxiliary fuel tank. Includes Gauge Package and in-box spare tire carrier with lock. Gauge Package. Standard with XLS. Engine block heater. California emission system. High altitude emission system. Security Lock Group. Includes glove box lock, locking gas cap(s), and under-body spare tire lock. Exterior Protection Group. Includes front chrome bumper, black front bumper guards and end caps, black upper body side moldings with dual red accent stripes (except with Tu-Tones), and bright door edge guards. Chrome front bumper. Cast aluminum wheels. White Sport wheels.

HISTORICAL FOOTNOTES: Ford reported that on the basis of the most recent (early 1983) data available, customers perceived a 47 percent increase in the quality of Ford light trucks as compared with 1980 models.

1985 RANGER

The 5-speed manual overdrive transmission was now standard equipment for the 1985 Ranger. Standard features of the base model included a black front bumper, chrome grille with chrome surround, rectangular Halogen headlights, dual black fold-away exterior mirrors, bright windshield surround molding, removable tailgate with bright handle, argent styled steel wheels, right side coat hook, dome light with driver door operated courtesy light, color-keyed vinyl panel door trim with fully padded armrest and black handles, black vinyl floor mat with insulation, fresh air vents, Hi-Lo flow-through air ventilation, inside hood release, color-keyed instrument panel with full width pad, brushed pewter-tone cluster finish panel applique, cluster warning lights, black lower instrument panel, day/night rearview mirror, AM radio, black scuff plates, color-keyed steering wheel and color-keyed sun visors. The exterior colors for 1985 were raven black, silver metallic, bright canyon red, midnight blue metallic, light regatta blue, dark spruce metallic, dark canyon red, bright regatta blue metallic, light desert tan, Wimbleton white, dark charcoal metallic and walnut metallic. Interior colors were regatta blue, canyon red and tan.

I.D. DATA: The Ranger V.I.N. consisted of seventeen symbols. The first three characters identified the manufacturer, make and type of vehicle. The fourth character (a letter) designated the GVW range. The fifth, sixth and seventh characters identified the series and body style. The eighth character identified the engine. The ninth character was the check digit. The tenth character (a letter) represented the model year. The eleventh character identified the assembly plant. The remaining digits represented the sequential production number.

Body Type	Factory Price	GVW	Shipping Weight	Prod. Total
Ranger R10 Styleside				
Pickup, Styleside, 107.9 in. wb.	$8,351	4000[1]	2827	—
Pickup, Styleside, 113.9 in. wb.	$8,505	4040[2]	2883	—

NOTE 1: A 4420 lb. GVW Package was optional for the 107.9 in. wheelbase Ranger.
NOTE 2: A 4480 lb. GVW Package was optional for the 113.9 in. wheelbase Ranger.

STANDARD ENGINE: Engine Type: OHV 4-cyl. Cast-iron block and cylinder heads. Bore x Stroke: 3.78 in. x 3.13 in. Lifters: Hydraulic. Number of main bearings-5. Fuel Induction: Single barrel carburetor. Compression Ratio: 9.0:1. Displacement: 144 cu. in. (2.3 liters). Horsepower: Net: 80 @ 4000 rpm. Torque: Net: 104 lb.-ft. @ 2600 rpm. Fuel Requirements: Unleaded. Oil capacity: 6 qt. with filter change. Optional Engine: OHV 60 degree V-6. Cast-iron block and cylinder heads. Bore x Stroke: 3.66 in. x 2.70 in. Lifters: Hydraulic. Number of main bearings-4. Displacement: 171 cu. in. (2.8 liters). Fuel Induction: Two-barrel carburetor. Compression Ratio: 8.7:1. Horsepower: Net: 115 @ 4600 rpm. Torque: Net: 150 lb.-ft. @ 2600 rpm. Fuel Requirements: Unleaded. Oil capacity: 5 qt. with filter change.

CHASSIS FEATURES: Frame: Ladder-type, 6 cross members, section modulus: 2.37 cu. in.

SUSPENSION AND RUNNING GEAR: Front Suspension: Coil springs, computer selected. Rear Suspension: Single-stage, semi-elliptical leaf, computer selected. Front Axle Type and Capacity: Twin-Traction beam, Dana 28-IFS, 2750 lb. capacity. Rear Axle Type and Capacity: Ford semi-floating, 2750 lb. capacity. Final Drive Ratio: 3.45:1 front and rear. Transfer Case: Type: Warner 1350, part-time, 2-speed. Ratios: 2.48, 1.00:1. Brakes: Type: Hydraulic, power-assisted, disc front and cast iron drum rear. Dimensions: Front: 10.87 in. dia. Rear: 9.0 in. x 1.75 in. Wheels: 15 x 5.0 in. 5-hole disc. 15 x 5.5 in. with Payload Package and steel belted radial tires. Optional: 15 x 6.0 in. Tires: Steel-belted P195/75R x 15L. Optional: P205/75R x 15SL, steel-belted radial raised white letter, All-Terrain, P215/75R x 15SL, steel-belted radial raised white letter, All-Terrain. Steering: Recirculating ball, manual. Ratio: 23.75:1. Turning Circle: 36.5 ft. Optional: Power steering: 17.1:1 ratio. Transmission: Type: 5-speed overdrive, synchromesh on all gears. Optional: Automatic overdrive transmission. Clutch: 9.0 in. dia. Optional: None.

VEHICLE DIMENSIONS: Wheelbase: 107.8/113.9 in. Overall Length: 175.6 in./187.6 in. (without rear bumper). Front/Rear Tread 56.5 in./55.1 in. Overall Height: 67.1 in. Width: 66.9 in. Front/Rear Overhang: 28.3 in./39.4 in. (107.9 in. wheelbase); 45.4 in. (133.9 in. wheelbase). Tailgate: Width and Height: 51.9 in. x 16.0 in. Approach/Departure Degrees: 107.9 in. wheelbase: 29.2/23./2. 113.9 in. wheelbase: 29.2/25.5. Ground Clearance: Rear axle: 6.9 in. Load space: 107.9 in. wheelbase: 72.2 in. x 54.3 in. x 16.5 in. 133.9 in. wheelbase: 84.2 in. x 54.3 in. x 16.5 in.

CAPACITIES: Fuel Tank: 107.9 in. wheelbase: 15.2 gal. 113.9 in. wheelbase: 17.0 gal. Optional: Auxiliary 10.0 gal. tank.

ACCOMMODATIONS: Seating Capacity: 3 passengers. Headroom: 39.2 in. Maximum Steering wheel to seat back: 23.1 in. Shoulder room: 55.6 in. Hip room: 55.0 in. Legroom: 42.4 in.

INSTRUMENTATION: Speedometer, odometer, warning lights for engine coolant temperature, oil pressure, ammeter, high beam, seat belt, parking brake and turn signals.

OPTIONS AND PRICES: Heavy-duty air cleaner: $20.70. Air conditioner: $743.70. Heavy-duty battery: $53. Black rear step bumper: $120 (without XLT trim or Protection Group), $134.60, (with XLT trim or Protection Group). Bright front bumper: $46.60. Bright rear step bumper: $170.70. Automatic overdrive transmission: $676.10. Dana limited slip front axle: $238. Traction-Lok rear axle: $238. Optional axle ratio: $42.10. Camper Package: $144.10 (with manual transmission), $203.20 (with automatic transmission). Floor console: $223.50 (with XL or XLT trim), $180 (with XLS trim). Overhead console: $81.70. Convenience group: $104.80 (with standard or XLS trim), $80.70 (all others). Super engine cooling: $53. Auxiliary fuel tank: $228.50, $185 (with XLS trim). Gauge Package: $58. Tinted glass: $46. Handling Package: $72.10 (without heavy-duty suspension or Snowplow Package), $38 (with heavy-duty suspension or Snowplow Package). Headliner: $67.10. Engine block heater: $31. Automatic locking hubs: $40.20. Light Group: $79.10 (with standard trim), $71.10 (with XL or XLT without bucket seats), $37.10 (with XL or XLT with bucket seats), 45.10 (with XLS trim). Security Lock Group: $30.50 (with standard fuel tank), $36.60 (with auxiliary fuel tank). Bright Western low-mount swing-away mirrors: $82.90. Two-tone regular paint: $212.70 (with standard or XL trim), $205 (with XKLT trim). Deluxe two-tone paint: $295.60 (with standard trim), $371.50 (with XL trim), $287.90 (with XKT trim). Special two-tone paint: $349 (with standard trim), $325 (with XL trim), 341.60 (with XLT trim), $185.90 (with XKLS trim). Power Window/Lock Group: $292.60. Exterior Protection Group: $42.20 to $178.30 depending upon trim and paint selection. AM/FM stereo radio: $98.80. AM/FM stereo radio with cassette tape player: $229.30. Electronic AM/FM stereo radio with cassette tape player: $439.10. Premium sound system: $141.20. Radio credit option: $45.10. Tilt-up/Open air roof: $314.60. Heavy-duty shock absorbers: $34. Skid Plates: $116 (with standard fuel tank), $165 (with auxiliary fuel tank). Snowplow Special Package: $345.70. Speed control: $195. Power steering: $263.70. Tilt steering wheel: $115. Heavy-Duty Front Suspension Package: $194 (with manual transmission), $253 (with automatic transmission). Tape stripe 4x4: $68.30 (with standard trim), $60.70 (with XLT trim). Sport tape stripe: $83.20 (with standard trim), $40.70 (with XLT trim). Tie-down hooks: $50.60. Trailer Towing Package: $137 (with manual transmission), $187.10 (with automatic transmission). Deluxe wheel trim: $74.60. Cast aluminum wheels: $281.60 (with standard trim), $222.10 (with optional trim). White Sport wheels: $88.00 (with standard trim), $28.30 (with optional trim). Cast aluminum spare tire wheel: $70.50. Sliding rear window: $77.70. Pivoting vent window: $78.30. Cloth and vinyl bench seat for standard trim: $50.00. Cloth and vinyl bucket seats for XL trim: $219.10. XL Trim Package: $354.80. XLT Trim Package: $737.10. XLS Trim Package: $780.50.

HISTORICAL FOOTNOTES: The general manager of Ford's Truck Operations was Edward E. Hagenlocker.

1986 RANGER

Numerous technical and design changes, as well as major options revisions and additions highlighted the 1986 Ford Ranger. Two new engines were available; a multi-port electronically fuel-injected 2.9 liter V-6, and a 2.3 liter turbo-charged 4-cylinder. The latter engine was limited to installation in regular cab Rangers with standard trim. Joining the model lineup were new SuperCab models. These Rangers had a 125 in. wheelbase, a 6 ft. cargo box and approximately 17 inches of storage space behind the seat. Access to this space was provided by a three passenger 60/40 split bench seat. New options added for the SuperCab were a cargo cover, rear vinyl jump seats and pivoting quarter windows. P215/75R15SL steel-belted All-Season tires were now standard for the Ranger. Power steering was now standard for the regular cab Ranger. Skid plates were now included with the 2.9 liter V-6 engine. They were cancelled as a separate option. Instrument panel gauges as well as interval windshield wipers were now standard on all models. Also added to the standard equipment content were these items: Cigarette lighter, visor band on sun visor, right side door courtesy light switch and a locking glove box.

Option revisions for 1986 began with the replacement of the automatic locking hubs with the electric shift with "Touch Drive" overhead console, and the availability of P215/75R15SL off-road tires for the STX. Also new for 1986 was the inclusion of a bright upper and lower paint break and lower paint break moldings in the deluxe two-tone paint option, and the combination of the speed control and tilt steering wheel into a single option. The following options were either deleted or not offered as separate options for 1986: Trailer Towing Package, heavy-duty air cleaner, Snowplow Special Package, heavy-duty rear springs, XLS trim, Regular and Special two-tone paint, Sport and 4x4 stripes, front limited slip axle, tie-down hooks, floor console, bucket seats, Light Group, Exterior Protection Package, tow hooks, Security Lock Group, black low-mount swing-away mirrors, Premium Sound system, Convenience Group, white Sport steel wheels, and various tires.

1986 Ford Ranger XLT SuperCab pickup

The exterior colors consisted of these choices: Raven black, dark grey metallic, bright canyon red, dark spruce metallic, dark walnut metallic, dark shadow blue metallic, colonial white and desert tan metallic. The following colors were available only for regular cab models: Medium silver metallic, light regatta blue, dark canyon red and light desert tan. Exclusive to the SuperCab were these four colors: Silver clearcoat metallic, medium canyon red clearcoat metallic, light chestnut clearcoat metallic and bright regatta blue clearcoat metallic. The interior colors for 1986 were regatta blue, canyon red and chestnut.

Introduced in 1985 as a regional model for the western states, the Ranger STX Sport truck was available nationwide for 1986. Its features included a Special Handling Suspension Package, P215 15 in. off-road tires, tachometer, dual Captain's chairs and a special two-tone paint treatment. The STX had as its standard engine the 2.9 liter EFI V-6.

The regular cab models were offered in standard, XL or STX trim. The SuperCab was available in standard, XLT or STX trim.

I.D. DATA: The Ranger V.I.N. consisted of seventeen symbols. The first three characters identified the manufacturer, make and type of vehicle. The fourth character (a letter) designated the GVW range. The fifth, sixth and seventh characters identified the series and body style. The eighth character identified the engine. The ninth character was the check digit. The tenth character (a letter) represented the model year. The eleventh character identified the assembly plant. The remaining digits represented the sequential production number.

Body Type	Factory Price	GVW	Shipping Weight	Prod. Total
Ranger R10 Styleside				
Pickup, Styleside, 107.9 in. wb.	$9,467	4040[1]	2833	—
Pickup, Styleside, 113.9 in. wb.	$9,631	4100[2]	2889	—
Ranger R14, SuperCab, 125 in. wheelbase				
Pickup, Styleside	$10,120	4480[3]	3065	—

NOTE 1: A 4480 lb. GVW Package was optional for the 107.9 in. wheelbase Ranger.
NOTE 2: A 4500 lb. GVW Package was optional for the 113.9 in. wheelbase Ranger.
NOTE 3: A 4720 lb. GVW Package was optional for the SuperCab.

STANDARD ENGINE: Engine Type: OHV 4-cyl. Cast-iron block and cylinder heads. Bore x Stroke: 3.78 in. x 3.13 in. Lifters: Hydraulic. Number of main bearings-5. Fuel Induction: Electronic fuel injection. Compression Ratio: 9.5:1. Displacement: 144 cu. in. (2.3 liters). Horsepower: Net: 90 @ 4000 rpm. Torque: Net: 134 lb.-ft. @ 2600 rpm. Fuel Requirements: Unleaded. Oil capacity: 6 qt. with filter change.

OPTIONAL ENGINE: OHV 60 degree V-6. Cast-iron block and cylinder heads. Bore x Stroke: 3.66 in. x 2.83 in. Lifters: Hydraulic. Number of main bearings-4. Displacement: 179 cu. in. (2.9 liters). Fuel Induction: Electronic fuel injection. Compression Ratio: 9.3:1. Horsepower: Net: 140 @ 4600 rpm. Torque: Net: 170 lb.-ft. @ 2600 rpm. Fuel Requirements: Unleaded. Oil capacity: 5 qt. with filter change.

OPTIONAL ENGINE: OHV I-4, turbo diesel. Cast-iron block and cylinder heads. Bore x Stroke: 3.59 in. x 3.54 in. Lifters: Hydraulic. Number of main bearings-5. Displacement: 143 cu. in. (2.3 liters). Fuel Induction: Electronic fuel injection. Compression Ratio: 21:1. Horsepower: Net: 86 @ 4200 rpm. Torque: Net: 134 lb.-ft. @ 2000 rpm. Fuel Requirements: Diesel. Oil capacity: 7 qt. with filter change.

CHASSIS FEATURES: Frame: Ladder-type, 6 cross members, section modulus: 2.37 cu. in.

SUSPENSION AND RUNNING GEAR: Front Suspension: Coil springs, computer selected. Capacity: Regular cab: 1940 lb. SuperCab 2085 lb. Shock absorbers: All models front and rear 1.19 in. dia. 1.125 in. stabilizer bar. Rear Suspension: Single-stage, semi-elliptical 4-leaf, computer selected. Capacity: Regular cab: 2066 lb. SuperCab 2494 lb. Front Axle Type and Capacity: Twin-Traction beam, Dana 28-IFS, 2750 lb. capacity. Rear Axle Type and Capacity: Ford semi-floating, 2750 lb. capacity. Final Drive Ratio: 3.45:1 front and rear. Optional: 3.73, 4.10:1. Transfer Case: Type: Warner 1350, part-time, 2-speed. Ratios: 2.48, 1.00:1. Brakes: Type: Hydraulic, power-assisted, disc front and cast iron drum rear. Dimensions: Front: 10.87 in. dia. Rear: 9.0 in. x 1.75 in. Wheels: 15 x 5.0 in. 5-hole disc. 15 x 5.5 in. with Payload Package and steel belted radial tires. Optional: 15 x 6.0 in. Tires: Steel-belted P195/75R x 15SL. Optional: P205/75R x 15SL, steel-belted radial raised white letter, off-road, P215/75R x 15SL, steel-belted radial raised white letter, off-road. Steering: Recirculating ball, power assisted. Ratio: 17.1:1. Turning Circle: Regular cab: 36.42 ft. SuperCab: 41.34 ft. Transmission: Type: 5-speed overdrive, Mitsubishi or Toyo Kogyo, synchromesh on all gears. Ratios: Mitsubishi: 3.97, 2.14, 1.36, 1.00, 0.86:1. Reverse: 3.58:1. Toyo Kogyo: 3.96, 2.08, 1.39, 1.00, 0.85:1. Reverse: 3.39:1. Optional: Ford A4LD, automatic overdrive transmission. Ratios: 2.47, 1.47, 1.00, 0.75:1. Reverse: 2.10:1. Clutch: 9.0 in. dia. Optional: None.

VEHICLE DIMENSIONS: Wheelbase: Regular cab: 107.8/113.9 in. SuperCab: 125 in. Overall Length: Regular cab:175.6 in./187.6 in. (without rear bumper). SuperCab: 192.7 in. Front/Rear Tread 56.5 in./55.1 in. Overall Height: 107.9 in. wheelbase: 66.9 in., 113.9 in. wheelbase: 66.7 in., SuperCab: 68.1 in. Width: 66.9 in. Front/Rear Overhang: 28.3 in./39.4 in. (107.9 in. wheelbase); 45.4 in. (133.9 in. wheelbase). SuperCab: 28.3 in./39.4 in. Tailgate: Width and Height: 51.9 in. x 16.0 in. Approach/Departure Degrees: 107.9 in. wheelbase: 29.2/23./2. 113.9 in. wheelbase: 29.2/25.5. SuperCab: 29.0/16.1. Ground Clearance: Rear axle: 6.9 in. Load space: 107.9 in. wheelbase: 72.2 in. x 54.3 in. x 16.5 in. 133.9 in. wheelbase: 84.2 in. x 54.3 in. x 16.5 in.

CAPACITIES: Fuel Tank: 107.9 in. wheelbase: 15.2 gal. 113.9 in. wheelbase: 17.0 gal. Optional: Auxiliary 13.0 gal. tank. SuperCab: 14.5 gal. Optional: 13.0 gal.

ACCOMMODATIONS: Seating Capacity: 3 passengers. Headroom: 39.2 in. Maximum Steering wheel to seat back: 23.1 in. Shoulder room: 55.6 in. Hip room: 55.0 in. Legroom: 42.4 in.

INSTRUMENTATION: Speedometer, odometer, gauges for engine coolant temperature, oil pressure, ammeter, fuel level. Warning lights for 4x4 and low range, high beam, seat belt, water in fuel (diesel), parking brake and turn signals.

OPTIONS AND PRICES: Air conditioner: $744. Black rear step bumper: $120. Chrome rear step bumper: $171. Camper Package: $110. Cargo cover: $61. Chrome Package: $244. Overhead console: $82. Super engine cooling: $55. Electric Shift Touch Drive: $168 (regular cab, standard trim), $101 (all other trims on regular cab and SuperCab). Auxiliary fuel tank: $216. Headliner: $67 (with diesel engine). Bright low-mount swing-away mirrors: $83. Power Window/Lock Group: $293. Speed control/tilt steering wheel: $279. Black Sport Appearance Package: $792, $725 (for California SuperCab models). Heavy-duty front suspension: $151. Tachometer: $55. Automatic overdrive transmission: $793. Two-tone Deluxe paint: $342. Two-Tone STX (not included, credit): $68. Cast aluminum wheels: $222. AM/FM stereo radio: $99. AM/FM stereo radio with cassette tape player: $229 (with standard trim), $130 (all other trims). Electronic AM/FM stereo radio with cassette tape player: $269. Radio credit option: $45. Regular Cab XL Trim Package: $80-$1205 depending upon Special Value Package selected. Regular Cab STX Trim Package: 1494-$2286 depending upon Special Value Package selected. 2.9 liter engine: $412. Diesel engine: $896.

HISTORICAL FOOTNOTES: The Ford Ranger was the best-selling domestic compact pickup as the 1986 model year began. The SuperCab model was selected by *4-Wheel and Off-Road* magazine as the 4x4 Truck of the Year for 1986.

1987 RANGER

For 1987 there were significant functional changes in the Ranger, including the introduction of a new High Rider STX regular cab model with increased ride height of nearly 1.5 inches over the 1986 model. High Rider standard equipment included revised suspension geometry, heavy-duty gas shock absorbers, reduced spring rates, 2.9 liter V-6, argent styled steel wheels with bright trim rings and black center caps, off-road tires, unique body side tape treatment, black trim, rear step bumper and STX badge identification. A low engine oil level alert system was now included with the 2.9 liter engine. Improved corrosion protection was provided by the additional use of one and two-sided galvanized body panels. During the model year the use of a single key for ignition and door locks was introduced. What Ford called a "complexity reduction" involved replacing bright finish with black trim for the grille on the STX model along with antenna mast/cap, front/back windshield surround, moldings, door handles/lock cylinders, and window crank handles/door lock buttons. New trim additions for 1987 included a brushed chrome Ranger emblem with black surround. The V6 and tailgate nomenclature was deleted on all models where applicable. The deluxe wheel trim for 1987 included black pockets/hub covers.

1987 Ford Ranger regular cab pickup

The 2.3 liter engine with 5-speed manual overdrive transmission was no longer available for the SuperCab. A number of new options were introduced for 1987. Heading the list was a new pickup box cap and a freshened deluxe wheel trim. The STX paint trim was revised to include three new graduated tape stripes. All electronic radios now had an electronic digital clock. The Deluxe two-tone paint option was revised to resemble the 1986 STX lower two-tone scheme. Clearcoat paint was now available on the regular cab. A carpet delete option was offered for the XLT trim. Both the Sport Appearance Package with STX trim and the custom/XLT trim was available with the 2.3 and 2.9 liter engines and manual transmissions. White Sport wheels were introduced as a new option. P235/75R x 15SL All-Terrain tires were offered (late availability) for the regular cab. Two options — the overhead console and radios without clocks were not offered for 1987.

1987 Ford Ranger STX pickup

The exterior color selection included eight new colors. They were as follows: Raven black, silver clearcoat metallic, bright canyon red, alpine green clearcoat metallic, light chestnut clearcoat metallic, dark canyon red, bright regatta blue clearcoat metallic, colonial white, shadow grey clearcoat metallic, light chestnut and dark walnut clearcoat metallic. The interior color selection consisted of regatta blue, canyon red and chestnut.

1987 Ford Ranger STX High Rider pickup

I.D. DATA: The Ranger V.I.N. consisted of seventeen symbols. The first three characters identified the manufacturer, make and type of vehicle. The fourth character (a letter) designated the GVW range. The fifth, sixth and seventh characters identified the series and body style. The eighth character identified the engine. The ninth character was the check digit. The tenth character (a letter) represented the model year. The eleventh character identified the assembly plant. The remaining digits represented the sequential production number.

Body Type	Factory Price	GVW	Shipping Weight	Prod. Total
Ranger R10				
Ranger R10 Styleside				
Pickup, Styleside, 107.9 in. wb.	$10,317	4040[1]	2833	—
Pickup, Styleside, 113.9 in. wb.	$10,481	4100[2]	2889	—
Ranger R14, SuperCab, 125 in. wheelbase				
Pickup, Styleside	$10,970	4480[3]	3065	—

NOTE 1: A 4480 lb. GVW Package was optional for the 107.9 in. wheelbase Ranger.
NOTE 2: A 4500 lb. GVW Package was optional for the 113.9 in. wheelbase Ranger.
NOTE 3: A 4720 lb. GVW Package was optional for the SuperCab.

STANDARD ENGINE: Engine Type: OHV 4-cyl. Cast-iron block and cylinder heads. Bore x Stroke: 3.78 in. x 3.13 in. Lifters: Hydraulic. Number of main bearings-5. Fuel Induction: Electronic fuel injection. Compression Ratio: 9.5:1. Displacement: 144 cu. in. (2.3 liters). Horsepower: Net: 90 @ 4000 rpm. Torque: Net: 134 lb.-ft. @ 2600 rpm. Fuel Requirements: Unleaded. Oil capacity: 6 qt. with filter change.

OPTIONAL ENGINE: OHV 60 degree V-6. Cast-iron block and cylinder heads. Bore x Stroke: 3.66 in. x 2.83 in. Lifters: Hydraulic. Number of main bearings-4. Displacement: 179 cu. in. (2.9 liters). Fuel Induction: Electronic fuel injection. Compression Ratio: 9.3:1. Horsepower: Net: 140 @ 4600 rpm. Torque: Net: 170 lb.-ft. @ 2600 rpm. Fuel Requirements: Unleaded. Oil capacity: 5 qt. with filter change.

OPTIONAL ENGINE: OHV I-4, turbo diesel. Cast-iron block and cylinder heads. Bore x Stroke: 3.59 in. x 3.54 in. Lifters: Hydraulic. Number of main bearings-5. Displacement: 143 cu. in. (2.3 liters). Fuel Induction: Electronic fuel injection. Compression Ratio: 21:1. Horsepower: Net: 86 @ 4200 rpm. Torque: Net: 134 lb.-ft. @ 2000 rpm. Fuel Requirements: Diesel. Oil capacity: 7 qt. with filter change.

CHASSIS FEATURES: Frame: Ladder-type, 6 cross members, section modulus: 2.37 cu. in.

SUSPENSION AND RUNNING GEAR: Front Suspension: Coil springs, computer selected. Capacity: Regular cab: 1940 lb. SuperCab: 2085 lb. Shock absorbers: All models front and rear 1.19 in. dia. 1.125 in. stabilizer bar. Rear Suspension: Single-stage, semi-elliptical 4-leaf, computer selected. Capacity: Regular cab: 2066 lb. SuperCab 2494 lb. Front Axle Type and Capacity: Twin-Traction beam, Dana 28-IFS, 2750 lb. capacity. Rear Axle Type and Capacity: Ford semi-floating, 2750 lb. capacity. Final Drive Ratio: 3.45:1 front and rear. Optional: 3.73, 4.10:1. Transfer Case: Type: Warner 1350, part-time, 2-speed. Ratios: 2.48, 1.00:1. Brakes: Type: Hydraulic, power-assisted, disc front and cast iron drum rear. Dimensions: Front: 10.87 in. dia. Rear: 9.0 in. x 1.75 in. Wheels: 15 x 5.0 in. 5-hole disc. 15 x 5.5 in. with Payload Package and steel belted radial tires. Optional: 15 x 6.0 in. Tires: Steel-belted P195/75R x 15SL. Optional: P205/75R x 15SL, steel-belted radial raised white letter, off-road, P215/75R x 15SL, steel-belted radial raised white letter, off-road. P235/75R x 15SL All-Terrain tires (regular cab). Steering: Recirculating ball, power assisted. Ratio: 17.1:1. Turning Circle: Regular cab: 36.42 ft. SuperCab: 41.34 ft. Transmission: Type: 5-speed overdrive, Mitsubishi or Toyo Kogyo, synchromesh on all gears. Ratios: Mitsubishi: 3.97, 2.14, 1.36, 1.00, 0.86:1. Reverse: 3.58:1. Toyo Kogyo: 3.96, 2.08, 1.39, 1.00, 0.85:1. Reverse: 3.39:1. Optional: Ford A4LD, automatic overdrive transmission. Ratios: 2.47, 1.47, 1.00, 0.75:1. Reverse: 2.10:1. Clutch: 9.0 in. dia. Optional: None.

VEHICLE DIMENSIONS: Wheelbase: Regular cab: 107.8/113.9 in. SuperCab: 125 in. Overall Length: Regular cab:175.6 in./187.6 in. (without rear bumper). SuperCab: 192.7 in. Front/Rear Tread 56.5 in./55.1 in. Overall Height: 107.9 in. wheelbase: 66.9 in., 113.9 in. wheelbase: 66.7 in., SuperCab: 68.1 in. Width: 66.9 in. Front/Rear Overhang: 28.3 in./39.4 in. (107.9 in. wheelbase); 45.4 in. (133.9 in. wheelbase). SuperCab: 28.3 in./39.4 in. Tailgate: Width and Height: 51.9 in. x 16.0 in. Approach/Departure Degrees: 107.9 in. wheelbase: 29.2/23./2. 113.9 in. wheelbase: 29.2/25.5. SuperCab: 29.0/16.1. Ground Clearance: Rear axle: 6.9 in. Load space: 107.9 in. wheelbase: 72.2 in. x 54.3 in. x 16.5 in. 133.9 in. wheelbase: 84.2 in. x 54.3 in. x 16.5 in.

CAPACITIES: Fuel Tank: 107.9 in. wheelbase: 15.2 gal. 113.9 in. wheelbase: 17.0 gal. Optional: Auxiliary 13.0 gal. tank. SuperCab: 14.5 gal. Optional: 13.0 gal.

ACCOMMODATIONS: Seating Capacity: 3 passengers. Headroom: 39.2 in. Maximum Steering wheel to seat back: 23.1 in. Shoulder room: 55.6 in. Hip room: 55.0 in. Legroom: 42.4 in.

INSTRUMENTATION: Speedometer, odometer, gauges for engine coolant temperature, oil pressure, ammeter, fuel level. Warning lights for 4x4 and low range, high beam, seat belt, water in fuel (diesel), parking brake and turn signals.

OPTIONS AND PRICES: Air conditioner. Black rear step bumper. Chrome rear step bumper. Camper Package. Cargo cover. Chrome Package. Super engine cooling. Electric Shift Touch Drive. Auxiliary fuel tank. Headliner. Bright low-mount swing-away mirrors. Power Window/ Lock Group. Speed control/tilt steering wheel. Black Sport Appearance Package. Heavy-duty front suspension. Tachometer. Automatic overdrive transmission. Two-tone Deluxe paint. Cast aluminum wheels. AM/FM stereo radio. AM/FM stereo radio with cassette tape player. Electronic AM/FM stereo radio with cassette tape player. Radio credit option: $45. Regular Cab XL Trim Package. Regular Cab STX Trim Package. 2.9 liter engine. Diesel engine. Pickup box cap. Regular Cab High Rider STX Trim Package. Carpet delete option for XLT trim. White Sport wheels.

HISTORICAL FOOTNOTES: Robert L. Rewey, Ford Motor Company vice president and Ford Division general manager reported that the "new High Rider model should have the Ford Ranger riding high in the compact truck market in 1987."

1988 RANGER

1988 Ford Ranger STX pickup with Bright Alloy Sport Appearance Package

For 1988, the High Rider Package, standard on STX regular cab models and optional for the 2.9 liter V-6 powered custom and XLT special value models, had new deep-dish cast-aluminum wheels. Other functional improvements for 1988 included optional paddle-type electric remote-control mirrors (late availability), standard tinted glass, interval windshield wipers and improved sound insulation on the custom regular cab. Appearance changes included a standard black rear-step bumper, and a black grille with black surround on STX models. A new five-speed manual overdrive transmission was standard on all models.

The exterior color selection consisted of raven black, scarlet red, cabernet red, colonial white, dark chestnut clearcoat metallic, bright regatta blue clearcoat metallic, deep shadow clearcoat metallic, silver clearcoat metallic, light chestnut, light chestnut clearcoat metallic, shadow grey clearcoat metallic and alpine green clearcoat metallic. The interior color selection consisted of regatta blue, canyon red and chestnut.

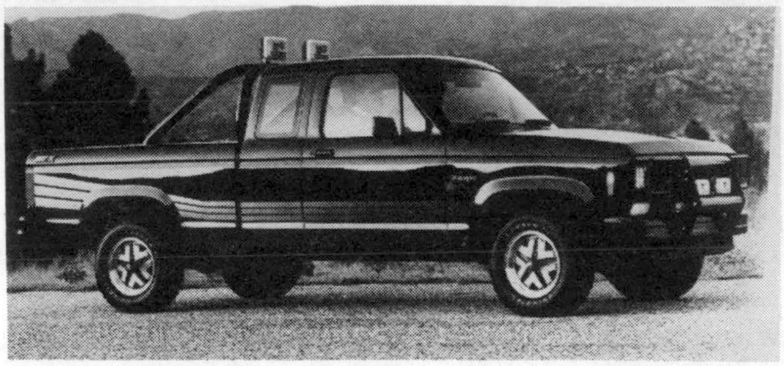

1988 Ford Ranger STX SuperCab pickup with Sport Appearance Package

I.D. DATA: The Ranger V.I.N. consisted of seventeen symbols. The first three characters identified the manufacturer, make and type of vehicle. The fourth character (a letter) designated the GVW range. The fifth, sixth and seventh characters identified the series and body style. The eighth character identified the engine. The ninth character was the check digit. The tenth character (a letter) represented the model year. The eleventh character identified the assembly plant. The remaining digits represented the sequential production number.

Body Type	Factory Price	GVW	Shipping Weight	Prod. Total
Ranger R10 Styleside				
Pickup, Styleside, 107.9 in. wb.	$11,573	4040[1]	2921	—
Pickup, Styleside, 113.9 in. wb.	$11,737	4100[2]	2977	—
Ranger R14, SuperCab, 125 in. wheelbase				
Pickup, Styleside	$12,226	4480[3]	3153	—

NOTE 1: A 4480 lb. GVW Package was optional for the 107.9 in. wheelbase Ranger.
NOTE 2: A 4500 lb. GVW Package was optional for the 113.9 in. wheelbase Ranger.
NOTE 3: A 4720 lb. GVW Package was optional for the SuperCab.

STANDARD ENGINE: Engine Type: OHV 4-cyl. Cast-iron block and cylinder heads. Bore x Stroke: 3.78 in. x 3.13 in. Lifters: Hydraulic. Number of main bearings-5. Fuel Induction: Electronic fuel injection. Compression Ratio: 9.5:1. Displacement: 144 cu. in. (2.3 liters). Horsepower: Net: 90 @ 4000 rpm. Torque: Net: 134 lb.-ft. @ 2600 rpm. Fuel Requirements: Unleaded. Oil capacity: 6 qt. with filter change.

OPTIONAL ENGINE: OHV 60 degree V-6. Cast-iron block and cylinder heads. Bore x Stroke: 3.66 in. x 2.83 in. Lifters: Hydraulic. Number of main bearings-4. Displacement: 179 cu. in. (2.9 liters). Fuel Induction: Electronic fuel injection. Compression Ratio: 9.3:1. Horsepower: Net: 140 @ 4600 rpm. Torque: Net: 170 lb.-ft. @ 2600 rpm. Fuel Requirements: Unleaded. Oil capacity: 5 qt. with filter change.

OPTIONAL ENGINE: OHV I-4, turbo diesel. Cast-iron block and cylinder heads. Bore x Stroke: 3.59 in. x 3.54 in. Lifters: Hydraulic. Number of main bearings-5. Displacement: 143 cu. in. (2.3 liters). Fuel Induction: Electronic fuel injection. Compression Ratio: 21:1. Horsepower: Net: 86 @ 4200 rpm. Torque: Net: 134 lb.-ft. @ 2000 rpm. Fuel Requirements: Diesel. Oil capacity: 7 qt. with filter change.

CHASSIS FEATURES: Frame: Ladder-type, 6 cross members, section modulus: 2.37 cu. in.

SUSPENSION AND RUNNING GEAR: Front Suspension: Coil springs, computer selected. Capacity: Regular cab: 1940 lb. SuperCab: 2085 lb. Shock absorbers: All models front and rear 1.19 in. dia. 1.125 in. stabilizer bar. Rear Suspension: Single-stage, semi-elliptical 4-leaf, computer selected. Capacity: Regular cab: 2066 lb. SuperCab: 2494 lb. Front Axle Type and Capacity: Twin-Traction beam, Dana 28-IFS, 2750 lb. capacity. Rear Axle Type and Capacity: Ford semi-floating, 2750 lb. capacity. Final Drive Ratio: 3.45:1 front and rear. Optional: 3.73, 4.10:1. Transfer Case: Type: Warner 1350, part-time, 2-speed. Ratios: 2.48, 1.00:1. Brakes: Type: Hydraulic, power-assisted, disc front and cast iron drum rear. Dimensions: Front: 10.87 in. dia. Rear: 9.0 in. x 1.75 in. Wheels: 15 x 5.0 in. 5-hole disc. 15 x 5.5 in. with Payload Package and steel belted radial tires. Optional: 15 x 6.0 in. Tires: Steel-belted P195/75R x 15SL. Optional: P205/75R x 15SL, steel-belted radial raised white letter, off-road, P215/75R x 15SL, steel-belted radial raised white letter, off-road. P235/75R x 15SL All-Terrain tires (regular cab). Steering: Recirculating ball, power assisted. Ratio: 17.1:1. Turning Circle: Regular cab: 36.42 ft. SuperCab: 41.34 ft. Transmission: Type: 5-speed overdrive manual, synchromesh on all gears. Optional: Ford A4LD, automatic overdrive transmission. Ratios: 2.47, 1.47, 1.00, 0.75:1. Reverse: 2.10:1. Clutch: 9.0 in. dia. Optional: None.

VEHICLE DIMENSIONS: Wheelbase: Regular cab: 107.8/113.9 in. SuperCab: 125 in. Overall Length: Regular cab:175.6 in./187.6 in. (without rear bumper). SuperCab: 192.7 in. Front/Rear Tread 56.5 in./55.1 in. Overall Height: 107.9 in. wheelbase: 66.9 in., 113.9 in. wheelbase: 66.7 in., SuperCab: 68.1 in. Width: 66.9 in. Front/Rear Overhang: 28.3 in./39.4 in. (107.9 in. wheelbase); 45.4 in. (133.9 in. wheelbase). SuperCab: 28.3 in./39.4 in. Tailgate: Width and Height: 51.9 in. x 16.0 in. Approach/Departure Degrees: 107.9 in. wheelbase: 29.2/23./2. 113.9 in. wheelbase: 29.2/25.5. SuperCab: 29.0/16.1. Ground Clearance: Rear axle: 6.9 in. Load space: 107.9 in. wheelbase: 72.2 in. x 54.3 in. x 16.5 in. 133.9 in. wheelbase: 84.2 in. x 54.3 in. x 16.5 in.

CAPACITIES: Fuel Tank: 107.9 in. wheelbase: 15.2 gal. 113.9 in. wheelbase: 17.0 gal. Optional: Auxiliary 13.0 gal. tank. SuperCab: 14.5 gal. Optional: 13.0 gal.

ACCOMMODATIONS: Seating Capacity: 3 passengers. Headroom: 39.2 in. Maximum Steering wheel to seat back: 23.1 in. Shoulder room: 55.6 in. Hip room: 55.0 in. Legroom: 42.4 in.

INSTRUMENTATION: Speedometer, odometer, gauges for engine coolant temperature, oil pressure, ammeter, fuel level. Warning lights for 4x4 and low range, high beam, seat belt, water in fuel (diesel), parking brake and turn signals.

OPTIONS AND PRICES: Air conditioner. Chrome rear step bumper. Camper Package. Cargo Cover. Chrome Package. Super engine cooling. Electric Shift Touch Drive. Auxiliary fuel tank. Headliner. Bright low-mount swing-away mirrors. Power Window/Lock Group. Speed control/tilt steering wheel. Black Sport Appearance Package. Heavy-duty front suspension. Tachometer. Automatic overdrive transmission. Two-tone Deluxe paint. Cast aluminum wheels. AM/FM stereo radio. AM/FM stereo radio with cassette tape player. Electronic AM/FM stereo radio with cassette tape player. Radio credit option: $45. Regular Cab XL Trim Package. Regular Cab STX Trim Package. 2.9 liter engine. Diesel engine. Pickup box cap. Regular Cab High Rider STX Trim Package. Carpet delete option for XLT trim. White Sport wheels. Paddle-type electric remote-control mirrors.

HISTORICAL FOOTNOTES: The typical 4x4 Ranger buyer was 30.7 years old. Ninety-one percent were married and 58 percent were parents. Only 25 percent of Ranger buyers purchasers bought the base model. Approximately 30 percent bought a SuperCab model. Approximately 30 percent of all Rangers were fitted with automatic transmission and air conditioning.

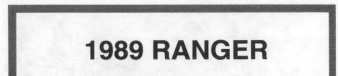

1989 RANGER

The changes found in the 1989 were the most extensive since Ford's compact pickup was introduced in the fall of 1981. New features included a new, more powerful standard engine, a rear anti-lock brake system (ABS), a more aerodynamic front-end look and a restyled instrument panel. The new Ranger engine was a 2.3 liter, four-cylinder "Twin plug" unit developing 100 horsepower, or 10 percent more than the conventional 2.3 liter it replaced. The new engine featured a dual spark plug cylinder head with a redesigned intake manifold, intake ports and combustion chamber and a distributorless ignition.

The Ranger's ABS system used an electronic sensor, an on-board computer and special valves that inhibited rear-wheel lockup under most road conditions. Other functional improvements for 1989 included revised shock absorber valving for improved ride and handling, less noise, vibration and harshness, and a revised tire tread that reduced tire wear.

Changes to the Ranger's front end included aero headlights with integral turn signals and parking lights, wraparound front bumper, front fenders and grille. The XLT models had a bright bumper and grille. The Custom and STX Rangers had a black grille and bumper.

The interior of the 1989 Ranger had a new "foam-in-place" instrument panel with revised mechanical clusters, integral heater/air conditioning ducts, side window demisters and a large glove box. Also new was a column-mounted automatic shift lever that faciliated seating three passengers in the cab, bucket seats and new door trim panels.

New options for 1989 included an expanded capacity "Super Single" 21 gallon fuel tank for long wheelbase regular cab models, and a floor console with an integral armrest and Sport cloth bucket seats with a tip-slide feature on SuperCabs. During the1989 model year this feature was also available for regular cab models.

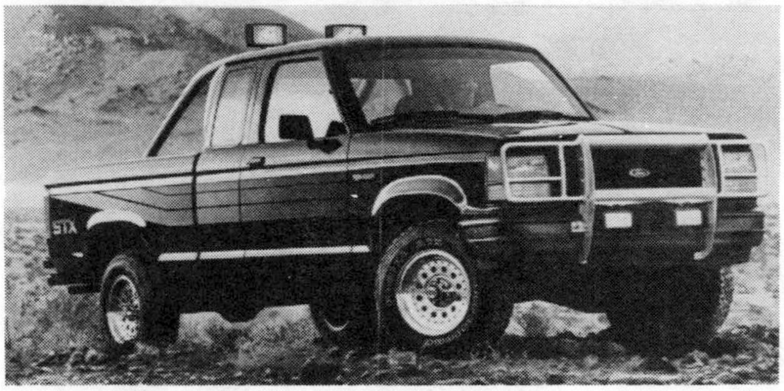

1989 Ford Ranger STX SuperCab pickup

I.D. DATA: The Ranger V.I.N. consisted of seventeen symbols. The first three characters identified the manufacturer, make and type of vehicle. The fourth character (a letter) designated the GVW range. The fifth, sixth and seventh characters identified the series and body style. The eighth character identified the engine. The ninth character was the check digit. The tenth character (a letter) represented the model year. The eleventh character identified the assembly plant. The remaining digits represented the sequential production number.

Body Type	Factory Price	GVW	Shipping Weight	Prod. Total
Ranger R10 Styleside				
Pickup, S, 107.9 in. wb.	$10,837	4040	3020	—
Pickup, Custom, 107.9 in. wb.	$11,641	4040[1]	3058	—
Pickup, Styleside, 113.9 in. wb.	$11,805	4100[2]	3014	—
Ranger R14, SuperCab, 125 in. wheelbase				
Pickup, Styleside	$13,258	4480[3]	3290	—

NOTE 1: A 4480 lb. GVW Package was optional for the 107.9 in. wheelbase Ranger.
NOTE 2: A 4500 lb. GVW Package was optional for the 113.9 in. wheelbase Ranger.
NOTE 3: A 4720 lb. GVW Package was optional for the SuperCab.

STANDARD ENGINE: Engine Type: OHV 4-cyl. Twin plug. Cast-iron block and cylinder heads. Bore x Stroke: 3.78 in. x 3.13 in. Lifters: Hydraulic. Number of main bearings-5. Fuel Induction: Electronic fuel injection. Compression Ratio: 9.5:1. Displacement: 144 cu. in. (2.3 liters). Horsepower: Net: 100 @ 4600 rpm. Torque: Net: 133 lb.-ft. @ 2600 rpm. Fuel Requirements: Unleaded. Oil capacity: 6 qt. with filter change.

OPTIONAL ENGINE: OHV 60 degree V-6. Cast-iron block and cylinder heads. Bore x Stroke: 3.66 in. x 2.83 in. Lifters: Hydraulic. Number of main bearings-4. Displacement: 179 cu. in. (2.9 liters). Fuel Induction: Electronic fuel injection. Compression Ratio: 9.3:1. Horsepower: Net: 140 @ 4600 rpm. Torque: Net: 170 lb.-ft. @ 2600 rpm. Fuel Requirements: Unleaded. Oil capacity: 5 qt. with filter change.

CHASSIS FEATURES: Frame: Ladder-type, low carbon steel, 6 cross members, section modulus: 2.37 cu. in. 36,00 psi.

SUSPENSION AND RUNNING GEAR: Front Suspension: Coil springs, computer selected. Capacity: Regular cab: 1940 lb. SuperCab: 2085 lb. Shock absorbers: All models front and rear 1.19 in. dia. 1.125 in. stabilizer bar. Rear Suspension: Single-stage, semi-elliptical 4-leaf, computer selected. Capacity: Regular cab: 2066 lb. SuperCab: 2494 lb. Front Axle Type and Capacity: Twin-Traction beam, Dana 28-IFS, 2750 lb. capacity. Rear Axle Type and Capacity: Ford semi-floating, 2750 lb. capacity. Final Drive Ratio: 3.45:1 front and rear. Optional: 3.73,

4.10:1. Transfer Case: Type: Warner 1350, part-time, 2-speed. Ratios: 2.48, 1.00:1. Brakes: Type: Hydraulic, power-assisted, disc front and cast iron drum rear. Dimensions: Front: 10.87 in. dia. Rear: 9.0 in. x 1.75 in. Wheels: 15 x 5.0 in. 5-hole disc. 15 x 5.5 in. with Payload Package and steel belted radial tires. Optional: 15 x 6.0 in. Tires: Steel-belted P195/75R x 15SL black sidewall, All-Season radial. Optional: P205/75R x 15SL, steel-belted radial raised white letter, off-road, P215/75R x 15SL, steel-belted radial raised white letter, off-road. P235/75R x 15SL All-Terrain tires (regular cab). Steering: Recirculating ball, power assisted. Ratio: 17.1:1. Turning Circle: Regular cab: 36.42 ft. SuperCab: 41.34 ft. Transmission: 2.3 liter engine: 5-speed overdrive manual, synchromesh on all gears. 2.9 liter engine: 4-speed automatic overdrive. Optional: 2.3 liter: Ford automatic overdrive transmission. Ratios: 2.47, 1.47, 1.00, 0.75:1. Reverse: 2.10:1. Clutch: 9.0 in. dia. Optional: None.

VEHICLE DIMENSIONS: Wheelbase: Regular cab: 107.8/113.9 in. SuperCab: 125 in. Overall Length: Regular cab:175.6 in./187.6 in. (without rear bumper). SuperCab: 192.7 in. Front/Rear Tread 56.5 in./55.1 in. Overall Height: 107.9 in. wheelbase: 66.9 in., 113.9 in. wheelbase: 66.7 in., SuperCab: 68.1 in. Width: 66.9 in. Front/Rear Overhang: 28.3 in./39.4 in. (107.9 in. wheelbase); 45.4 in. (133.9 in. wheelbase). SuperCab: 28.3 in./39.4 in. Tailgate: Width and Height: 51.9 in. x 16.0 in. Approach/Departure Degrees: 107.9 in. wheelbase: 29.2/23./2. 113.9 in. wheelbase: 29.2/25.5. SuperCab: 29.0/16.1. Ground Clearance: Rear axle: 6.9 in. Load space: 107.9 in. wheelbase: 72.2 in. x 54.3 in. x 16.5 in. 133.9 in. wheelbase: 84.2 in. x 54.3 in. x 16.5 in.

CAPACITIES: Fuel Tank: 107.9 in. wheelbase: 15.2 gal. 113.9 in. wheelbase: 17.0 gal. Optional: Auxiliary 13.0 gal. tank. SuperCab: 14.5 gal. Optional: 13.0 gal.

ACCOMMODATIONS: Seating Capacity: 3 passengers. Headroom: 39.2 in. Maximum Steering wheel to seat back: 23.1 in. Shoulder room: 55.6 in. Hip room: 55.0 in. Legroom: 42.4 in.

INSTRUMENTATION: Speedometer, odometer, gauges for engine coolant temperature, oil pressure, ammeter, fuel level. Warning lights for 4x4 and low range, high beam, seat belt, parking brake and turn signals.

OPTIONS AND PRICES: Air conditioner. Chrome rear step bumper. Camper Package. Cargo cover. Chrome Package. Super engine cooling. Electric Shift Touch Drive. Auxiliary fuel tank. Headliner. Bright low-mount swing-away mirrors. Power Window/Lock Group. Speed control/tilt steering wheel. Black Sport Appearance Package. Heavy-duty front suspension. Tachometer. Automatic overdrive transmission. Two-tone Deluxe paint. Cast aluminum wheels. AM/FM stereo radio. AM/FM stereo radio with cassette tape player. Electronic AM/FM stereo radio with cassette tape player. Radio credit option: $45. Regular Cab XL Trim Package. Regular Cab STX Trim Package. 2.9 liter engine. Diesel engine. Pickup box cap. Regular Cab High Rider STX Trim Package. Carpet delete option for XLT trim. White Sport wheels. Paddle-type electric remote-control mirrors. Expanded capacity "Super Single" 21 gallon fuel tank (long wheelbase regular cab models). Floor console with an integral armrest. Sport cloth bucket seats with tip-slide feature.

HISTORICAL FOOTNOTES: Ford reported it expected the Ranger to be built at capacity in 1989 (412,500 units).

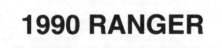

1990 RANGER

Beginning in October, 1989 the custom, XLT and STX Ranger models were available with a 4.0 liter EFI V-6 engine. Exterior changes were limited to the use of a standard black grille for the STX model, a new Rahau windshield molding and revised wheel ornamentation. Interior changes consisted of new color-keyed instrument panel appliques for the XLT and STX, and the mounting of the rear speaker in the B-pillar trim panel (late availability). Functional changes included the replacement of the 17 gallon fuel tank on the regular cab Ranger with a 16.3 gallon unit. A 19.6 gallon unit replaced the 17 gallon tank on the SuperCab. This tank was offered as an option for the regular cab long wheelbase model. The EFI system on 2.9 liter engines for California was improved by the incorporation of a Data Communications Link. This item allowed engine function to be monitored through a computerized diagnostic system. All Canadian Rangers were equipped with running lights. The headlights operated under low voltage (reduced beam) whenever the ignition switch was on. All models had an upgraded tandem brake booster/master cylinder. Routine engine service points were easier to locate through the use of improved callouts and labeling.

In addition to the 4.0 liter V-6, several other new options were offered for 1990. They included a limited production (6 ft.) plastic pickup box for the S Plus model. This component with a RIM exterior and polycarbonate liner provided the advantage of reduced corrosion, less denting and improved durability. A steel pickup box remained a no cost option. An engine compartment light was added to the Light Group. Two other new options were a Rally Bar Package and P235 OWL All-Terrain tires for the regular cab model. The content of the Sport Appearance Package was revised. The black version included these items finished in black: Tubular rear bumper, grille guard, and brush guard. Also included were fog lights and 75 amp alternator. A bright alloy version of the Sport Appearance Package was also available with bright alloy components in place of the black parts. The Rally Bar Package was also offered in either black or bright alloy form. Its elements included tubular rear bumper, rally bar, off-road lights and a 75 amp alternator.

These options were deleted for 1990: Cargo light for SuperCab, Sport Rider Package, and Camper Special. Both the exterior and interior colors were unchanged for 1990. Thus the interior colors were as follows: Exterior: Sandalwood clearcoat metallic, light sandalwood clearcoat metallic, light sandalwood, cabernet red, scarlet red, crystal blue clearcoat metallic, twilight blue clearcoat metallic, hunter green clearcoat metallic, raven black, silver clearcoat metallic, shadow grey clearcoat metallic, and colonial white. The Ranger interiors were offered in crystal blue, scarlet red, medium grey and light sandalwood.

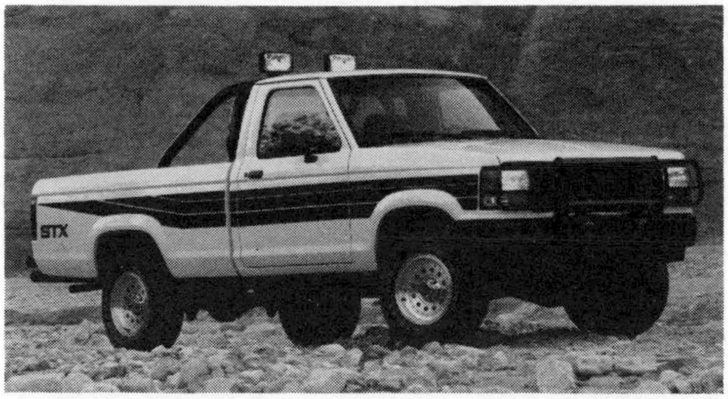

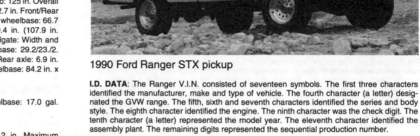

1990 Ford Ranger STX pickup

I.D. DATA: The Ranger V.I.N. consisted of seventeen symbols. The first three characters identified the manufacturer, make and type of vehicle. The fourth character (a letter) designated the GVW range. The fifth, sixth and seventh characters identified the series and body style. The eighth character identified the engine. The ninth character was the check digit. The tenth character (a letter) represented the model year. The eleventh character identified the assembly plant. The remaining digits represented the sequential production number.

Body Type	Factory Price	GVW	Shipping Weight	Prod. Total
Ranger R10 Styleside				
Pickup, S, 107.9 in. wb.	$11,346	4360	3997	—
Pickup, Custom, 107.9 in. wb.	$12,221	4400[1]	3026	—
Pickup, Styleside, 113.9 in. wb.	$12,385	4400[2]	2991	—
Ranger R14, SuperCab, 125 in. wheelbase				
Pickup, Styleside	$13,812	4780	3310	—

NOTE 1: A 4600 lb. GVW Package was optional for the 107.9 in. wheelbase Ranger.
NOTE 2: A 4600 lb. GVW Package was optional for the 113.9 in. wheelbase Ranger.

STANDARD ENGINE: For regular cab only: Engine Type: OHV 4-cyl. Twin plug. Cast-iron block and cylinder heads. Bore x Stroke: 3.78 in. x 3.13 in. Lifters: Hydraulic. Number of main bearings-5. Fuel Induction: Electronic fuel injection. Compression Ratio: 9.2:1. Displacement: 144 cu. in. (2.3 liters). Horsepower: Net: 100 @ 4600 rpm. Torque: Net: 133 lb.-ft. @ 2600 rpm. Fuel Requirements: Unleaded. Oil capacity: 6 qt. with filter change.

OPTIONAL ENGINE: OHV 60 degree V-6. Cast-iron block and cylinder heads. Bore x Stroke: 3.66 in. x 2.83 in. Lifters: Hydraulic. Number of main bearings-4. Displacement: 179 cu. in. (2.9 liters). Fuel Induction: Electronic fuel injection. Compression Ratio: 9.0:1. Horsepower: Net: 140 @ 4600 rpm. Torque: Net: 170 lb.-ft. @ 2600 rpm. Fuel Requirements: Unleaded. Oil capacity: 5 qt. with filter change.

OPTIONAL ENGINE: OHV 60 degree V-6. Cast-iron block and cylinder heads. Bore x Stroke: 3.95 in. x 3.32 in. Lifters: Hydraulic. Number of main bearings-4. Displacement: 245 cu. in. (4.0 liters). Fuel Induction: Electronic fuel injection. Compression Ratio: 9.0:1. Horsepower: Net: 160 @ 4200 rpm. Torque: Net: 225 lb.-ft. @ 2400 rpm. Fuel Requirements: Unleaded. Oil capacity: 6 qt. with filter change.

CHASSIS FEATURES: Frame: Ladder-type, low carbon steel, 6 cross members, section modulus: 2.37 cu. in. 36,00 psi.

SUSPENSION AND RUNNING GEAR: Front Suspension: Coil springs, computer selected. Capacity: Regular cab: 1940 lb. SuperCab: 2085 lb. Shock absorbers: All models front and rear 1.19 in. dia. 1.125 in. stabilizer bar. Rear Suspension: Single-stage, semi-elliptical 4-leaf, computer selected. Capacity: Regular cab: 2066 lb. SuperCab: 2494 lb. Front Axle Type and Capacity: Twin-Traction beam, Dana 28-IFS, 2750 lb. capacity. Rear Axle Type and Capacity: Ford semi-floating, 2750 lb. capacity. Final Drive Ratio: 3.45:1 front and rear. Optional: 3.55, 3.73 (available with limited slip differential), 4.10:1. Transfer Case: Type: Warner 1350, part-time, 2-speed. Ratios: 2.48, 1.00:1. Brakes: Type: Hydraulic, power-assisted, disc front and cast iron drum rear. Dimensions: Front: 10.87 in. dia. Rear: 9.0 in. x 1.75 in. Wheels: 15 x 5.0 in. 5-hole disc. 15 x 5.5 in. with Payload Package and steel belted radial tires. Optional: 15 x 6.0 in. Tires: Steel-belted P195/75R x 15SL black sidewall, All-Season radial. Optional: P205/75R x 15SL, steel-belted radial raised white letter, off-road, P215/75R x 15SL, steel-belted radial raised white letter, off-road. P235/75R x 15SL All-Terrain tires (regular cab). Steering: Recirculating ball, power assisted. Ratio: 17.1:1. Turning Circle: Regular cab: 36.42 ft. SuperCab: 41.34 ft. Transmission: Mitsubishi 5-speed overdrive manual, synchromesh on all gears. Standard transmission for 4.0 liter V-6: Heavy-duty Ford A4LD 4-speed automatic overdrive. Ratios: 5-spd. manual: 3.7, 2.21, 1.52, 1.00, 0.81:1. Reverse: 3.40:1. Optional: Ford A4LD automatic overdrive transmission. Ratios: 2.47, 1.47, 1.00, 0.75:1. Reverse: 2.10:1. Clutch: 9.0 in. dia. Optional: None.

VEHICLE DIMENSIONS: Wheelbase: Regular cab: 107.8/113.9 in. SuperCab: 125 in. Overall Length: Regular cab:175.6 in./187.6 in. (without rear bumper). SuperCab: 192.7 in. Front/Rear Tread 56.5 in./55.1 in. Overall Height: 107.9 in. wheelbase: 66.9 in., 113.9 in. wheelbase: 66.7 in., SuperCab: 68.1 in. Width: 66.9 in. Front/Rear Overhang: 28.3 in./39.4 in. (107.9 in. wheelbase); 45.4 in. (133.9 in. wheelbase). SuperCab: 28.3 in./39.4 in. Tailgate: Width and Height: 51.9 in. x 16.0 in. Approach/Departure Degrees: 107.9 in. wheelbase: 29.2/23./2. 113.9 in. wheelbase: 29.2/25.5. SuperCab: 29.0/16.1. Ground Clearance: Rear axle: 6.9 in. Load space: 107.9 in. wheelbase: 72.2 in. x 54.3 in. x 16.5 in. 133.9 in. wheelbase: 84.2 in. x 54.3 in. x 16.5 in.

CAPACITIES: Fuel Tank: 107.9 in. wheelbase: 15.2 gal. 113.9 in. wheelbase: 17.0 gal. Optional: Auxiliary 13.0 gal. tank. SuperCab: 14.5 gal. Optional: 13.0 gal.

ACCOMMODATIONS: Seating Capacity: 3 passengers. Headroom: 39.2 in. Maximum Steering wheel to seat back: 23.1 in. Shoulder room: 55.6 in. Hip room: 55.0 in. Legroom: 42.4 in.

INSTRUMENTATION: Speedometer, odometer, gauges for engine coolant temperature, oil pressure, ammeter, fuel level. Warning lights for 4x4 and low range, high beam, seat belt, parking brake and turn signals.

OPTIONS AND PRICES: Air conditioner. Chrome rear step bumper. Cargo cover. Chrome Package. Super engine cooling. Electric Shift Touch Drive. Auxiliary fuel tank. Headliner. Bright low-mount swing-away mirrors. Power Window/Lock Group. Speed control/tilt steering wheel. Black Sport Appearance Package. Heavy-duty front suspension. Tachometer. Automatic overdrive transmission. Two-tone Deluxe paint. Cast aluminum wheels. AM/FM stereo radio. AM/FM stereo radio with cassette tape player. Electronic AM/FM stereo radio with cassette tape player. Radio credit option: $45. Regular Cab XL Trim Package. Regular

Cab STX Trim Package. Pickup box cap. Regular Cab High Rider STX Trim Package. Carpet delete option for XLT trim. White Sport wheels. Paddle-type electric remote-control mirrors. Expanded capacity "Super Single" 21 gallon fuel tank (long wheelbase regular cab models). Floor console with an integral armrest. Sport cloth bucket seats with tip-slide feature. Rally Bar Package. P235 OWL All-Terrain tires (for regular cab). Plastic pickup box (S Plus model).

HISTORICAL FOOTNOTES: The Ranger was built in Ford's Louisville, Kentucky and Twin Cities, Minnesota plants.

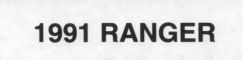

1991 RANGER

Ford's Ranger for 1991 offered a new Sport model, and several exterior appearance updates. The Ranger Sport, available in regular cab form featured a unique tape stripe treatment and deep-dish aluminum wheels. A new two-tone paint treatment was offered for all 1991 Ranger models. The STX was fitted with new tape stripe graphics. Front bumper rubstrips were now standard on the custom model. The rear step bumper for the new Ranger included a step pad. Interior changes were limited to the use of a new 60/40 split bench seat. P235/75R15 All-Terrain tires were now optional for the custom, XLT and STX models. Added to the standard equipment content of the STX and available as an option for the Sport and XLT were fog lamps and bumper guards.

I.D. DATA: The Ranger V.I.N. consisted of seventeen symbols. The first three characters identified the manufacturer, make and type of vehicle. The fourth character (a letter) designated the GVW range. The fifth, sixth and seventh characters identified the series and body style. The eighth character identified the engine. The ninth character was the check digit. The tenth character (a letter) represented the model year. The eleventh character identified the assembly plant. The remaining digits represented the sequential production number.

Body Type	Factory Price	GVW	Shipping Weight	Prod. Total
Ranger R10 Styleside				
Pickup, S, 107.9 in. wb.	$11,935	4400	3097	—
Pickup, Sport, 107.9 in. wb.	$11,935	4400	N.A.	—
Pickup, Sport, 113.9 in. wb.	$12,091	4460	N.A.	—
Pickup, Custom, 107.9 in. wb.	$12,379	4400[1]	3026	—
Pickup, Styleside, 113.9 in. wb.	$12,902	4460[2]	2991	—
Ranger R14, SuperCab, 125 in. wheelbase				
Pickup, Styleside	$14,206	4820	3310	—

NOTE 1: A 4640 lb. GVW Package was optional for the 107.9 in. wheelbase Ranger.
NOTE 2: A 4680 lb. GVW Package was optional for the 113.9 in. wheelbase Ranger.

STANDARD ENGINE: For regular cab only. Engine Type: OHV 4-cyl. Twin plug. Cast-iron block and cylinder heads. Bore x Stroke: 3.78 in. x 3.13 in. Lifters: Hydraulic. Number of main bearings-5. Fuel Induction: Electronic fuel injection. Compression Ratio: 9.2:1. Displacement: 144 cu. in. (2.3 liters). Horsepower: Net: 100 @ 4600 rpm. Torque: Net: 133 lb.-ft. @ 2600 rpm. Fuel Requirements: Unleaded. Oil capacity: 6 qt. with filter change.

OPTIONAL ENGINE: OHV 60 degree V-6. Cast-iron block and cylinder heads. Standard for SuperCab. Bore x Stroke: 3.66 in. x 2.83 in. Lifters: Hydraulic. Number of main bearings-4. Displacement: 179 cu. in. (2.9 liters). Fuel Induction: Electronic fuel injection. Compression Ratio: 9.0:1. Horsepower: Net: 140 @ 4600 rpm. Torque: Net: 170 lb.-ft. @ 2600 rpm. Fuel Requirements: Unleaded. Oil capacity: 5 qt. with filter change.

OPTIONAL ENGINE: OHV 60 degree V-6. Cast-iron block and cylinder heads. Bore x Stroke: 3.95 in. x 3.32 in. Lifters: Hydraulic. Number of main bearings-4. Displacement: 245 cu. in. (4.0 liters). Fuel Induction: Electronic fuel injection. Compression Ratio: 9.0:1. Horsepower: Net: 160 @ 4200 rpm. Torque: Net: 225 lb.-ft. @ 2400 rpm. Fuel Requirements: Unleaded. Oil capacity: 6 qt. with filter change.

CHASSIS FEATURES: Frame: Ladder-type, low carbon steel, 6 cross members, section modulus: 2.37 cu. in. 36,00 psi.

SUSPENSION AND RUNNING GEAR: Front Suspension: Coil springs, computer selected. Capacity: Regular cab: 1940 lb. SuperCab: 2085 lb. Shock absorbers: All models front and rear 1.19 in. dia. 1.125 in. stabilizer bar. Rear Suspension: Single-stage, semi-elliptical 4-leaf, computer selected. Capacity: Regular cab: 2066 lb. SuperCab: 2494 lb. Front Axle Type and Capacity: Twin-Traction beam, Dana 28-IFS, 2750 lb. capacity. Rear Axle Type and Capacity: Ford semi-floating, 2750 lb. capacity. Final Drive Ratio: 3.45:1 front and rear. Optional: 3.55, 3.73 (available with limited slip differential), 4.10:1. Transfer Case: Type: Warner 1350, part-time, 2-speed. Ratios: 2.48, 1.00:1. Brakes: Type: Hydraulic, power-assisted, disc front and cast iron drum rear. Dimensions: Front: 10.87 in. dia. Rear: 9.0 in. x 1.75 in. Wheels: 15 x 5.0 in. 5-hole disc. 15 x 5.5 in. with Payload Package and steel belted radial tires. Optional: 15 x 6.0 in. Tires: Steel-belted P195/75R x 15SL black sidewall, All-Season radial. Optional: P205/75R x 15SL, steel-belted radial raised white letter, off-road, P215/75R x 15SL, steel-belted radial raised white letter, off-road. P235/75R x 15SL All-Terrain tires (regular cab). Steering: Recirculating ball, power assisted. Ratio: 17.1:1. Turning Circle: Regular cab: 36.42 ft. SuperCab: 41.34 ft. Transmission: Mitsubishi 5-speed overdrive manual, synchromesh on all gears. Standard for 4.0 liter V-6: Heavy-duty Ford A4LD automatic overdrive. Ratios: 3.7, 2.21, 1.52, 1.00, 0.81:1. Reverse: 3.40:1. Optional: Ford A4LD automatic overdrive transmission. Ratios: 2.47, 1.47, 1.00, 0.75:1. Reverse: 2.10:1. Clutch: 9.0 in. dia. Optional: None.

VEHICLE DIMENSIONS: Wheelbase: Regular cab: 107.8/113.9 in. SuperCab: 125 in. Overall Length: Regular cab: 175.6 in./187.6 in. (without rear bumper). SuperCab: 192.7 in. Front/Rear Tread 56.5 in./55.1 in. Overall Height: 107.9 in. wheelbase: 66.9 in., 113.9 in. wheelbase: 66.7 in., SuperCab: 68.1 in. Width: 66.9 in. Front/Rear Overhang: 28.3 in./39.4 in. (107.9 in. wheelbase); 45.4 in. (133.9 in. wheelbase). SuperCab: 28.3 in./39.4 in. Tailgate: Width and Height: 51.9 in. x 16.0 in. Approach/Departure Degrees: 107.9 in. wheelbase: 29.2/23./2. 113.9 in. wheelbase: 29.2/25.5. SuperCab: 29.0/16.1. Ground Clearance: Rear axle: 6.9 in. Load space: 107.9 in. wheelbase: 72.2 in. x 54.3 in. x 16.5 in. 133.9 in. wheelbase: 84.2 in. x 54.3 in. x 16.5 in.

CAPACITIES: Fuel Tank: 107.9 in. wheelbase: 15.2 gal. 113.9 in. wheelbase: 17.0 gal. Optional: Auxiliary 13.0 gal. tank. SuperCab: 14.5 gal. Optional: 13.0 gal.

ACCOMMODATIONS: Seating Capacity: 3 passengers. Headroom: 39.2 in. Maximum Steering wheel to seat back: 23.1 in. Shoulder room: 55.6 in. Hip room: 55.0 in. Legroom: 42.4 in.

INSTRUMENTATION: Speedometer, odometer, gauges for engine coolant temperature, oil pressure, ammeter, fuel level. Warning lights for 4x4 and low range, high beam, seat belt, parking brake and turn signals.

OPTIONS AND PRICES: Air conditioner. Chrome rear step bumper. Cargo cover. Chrome Package. Super engine cooling. Electric Shift Touch Drive. Auxiliary fuel tank. Headliner. Bright low-mount swing-away mirrors. Power Window/Lock Group. Speed control/tilt steering wheel. Black Sport Appearance Package. Heavy-duty front suspension. Tachometer. Automatic overdrive transmission. Two-tone Deluxe paint. Cast aluminum wheels. AM/FM stereo radio. AM/FM stereo radio with cassette tape player. Electronic AM/FM stereo radio with cassette tape player. Radio credit option: $45. Regular Cab XL Trim Package. Regular Cab STX Trim Package. Pickup box cap. Regular Cab High Rider STX Trim Package. Carpet delete option for XLT trim. White Sport wheels. Paddle-type electric remote-control mirrors. Expanded capacity "Super Single" 21 gallon fuel tank (long wheelbase regular cab models). Floor console with an integral armrest. Sport cloth bucket seats with tip-slide feature. Rally Bar Package. P235 OWL All-Terrain tires (for regular cab). Plastic pickup box (S Plus model).

HISTORICAL FOOTNOTES: The 1991 Ranger was introduced on September 13, 1990.

1992 RANGER

The 1992 Ranger benefited from improved corrosion protection through the increased use of galvanized steel. Carried over from 1991 when it was introduced as a running change was the addition of an interior cargo cover for the XLT and STX SuperCab models. The Sport Package had new tape stripe graphics for 1992. Fog lights were added to the STX Package (Preferred Equipment Package). Among the interior changes for 1992 was the deletion of the headliner from the S and custom models. It was replaced by a painted interior roof. As a delayed availability revision, a second cupholder was added to the floor console. An improved multifunction wiper switch control was installed on the 1992 Ranger. Rounding out the interior revisions for 1992 was the addition of head restraints to the vinyl bench seats for the outboard seating positions, and the availability of a SuperCab "Comfort Cab" Package on the custom models at no charge.

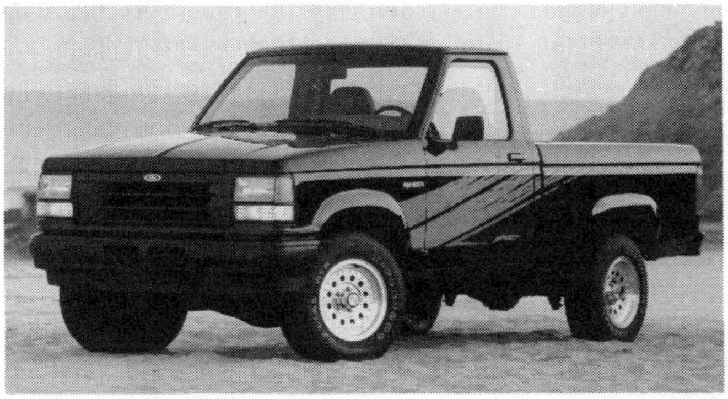

1992 Ford Ranger pickup

I.D. DATA: The Ranger V.I.N. consisted of seventeen symbols. The first three characters identified the manufacturer, make and type of vehicle. The fourth character (a letter) designated the GVW range. The fifth, sixth and seventh characters identified the series and body style. The eighth character identified the engine. The ninth character was the check digit. The tenth character (a letter) represented the model year. The eleventh character identified the assembly plant. The remaining digits represented the sequential production number.

Body Type	Factory Price	GVW	Shipping Weight	Prod. Total
Ranger R10 Styleside				
Pickup, S, 107.9 in. wb.	$12,418	4400	3097	—
Pickup, Sport, 107.9 in. wb.	$12,418	4400	N.A.	—
Pickup, Sport, 113.9 in. wb.	$12,574	4460	N.A.	—
Pickup, Custom, 107.9 in. wb.	$13,345	4400[1]	3026	—
Pickup, Custom, 113.9 in. wb.	$13,556	4460[2]	2991	—
Ranger R14, SuperCab, 125 in. wheelbase				
Pickup, Styleside	$14,840	4820	3310	—

NOTE 1: A 4640 lb. GVW Package was optional for the 107.9 in. wheelbase Ranger.
NOTE 2: A 4680 lb. GVW Package was optional for the 113.9 in. wheelbase Ranger.

STANDARD ENGINE: Engine Type: OHV V-6. Cast-iron block and cylinder heads. Bore x Stroke: 3.66 in. x 2.83 in. Lifters: Hydraulic. Number of main bearings-4. Fuel Induction: Electronic fuel injection. Compression Ratio: 9.0:1. Displacement: 179 cu. in. (2.9 liters). Horsepower: Net: 140 @ 4600 rpm. Torque: Net: 170 lb.-ft. @ 2600 rpm. Fuel Requirements: Unleaded. Oil capacity: 5 qt. with filter change.

OPTIONAL ENGINE: OHV 60 degree V-6. Cast-iron block and cylinder heads. Bore x Stroke: 3.95 in. x 3.32 in. Lifters: Hydraulic. Number of main bearings-4. Displacement: 245 cu. in. (4.0 liters). Fuel Induction: Electronic fuel injection. Compression Ratio: 9.0:1. Horsepower: Net: 160 @ 4200 rpm. Torque: Net: 225 lb.-ft. @ 2400 rpm. Fuel Requirements: Unleaded. Oil capacity: 6 qt. with filter change.

CHASSIS FEATURES: Frame: Ladder-type, low carbon steel, 6 cross members, section modulus: 2.37 cu. in. 36,00 psi.

SUSPENSION AND RUNNING GEAR: Front Suspension: Coil springs, computer selected. Capacity: Regular cab: 1940 lb. SuperCab: 2085 lb. Shock absorbers: All models front and rear 1.19 in. dia. 1.125 in. stabilizer bar. Rear Suspension: Single-stage, semi-elliptical 4-leaf, computer selected. Capacity: Regular cab: 2066 lb. SuperCab: 2494 lb. Front Axle Type and Capacity: Twin-Traction beam, Dana 28-IFS, 2750 lb. capacity. Rear Axle Type and Capacity: Ford semi-floating, 2750 lb. capacity. Final Drive Ratio: 3.45:1 front and rear. Optional: 3.55, 3.73 (available with limited slip differential), 4.10:1. Transfer Case: Type: Warner 1350, part-time, 2-speed. Ratios: 2.48, 1.00:1. Brakes: Type: Hydraulic, power-assisted, disc front and cast iron drum rear. Dimensions: Front: 10.87 in. dia. Rear: 9.0 in. x 1.75 in. Wheels: 15 x 5.0 in. 5-hole disc. 15 x 5.5 in. with Payload Package and steel belted radial tires. Optional: 15 x 6.0 in. Tires: Steel-belted P195/75R x 15SL black sidewall, All-Season radial. Optional: P205/75R x 15SL, steel-belted radial raised white letter, off-road, P215/75R x 15SL, steel-belted radial raised white letter, off-road. P235/75R x 15SL All-Terrain tires (regular cab). Steering:

Recirculating ball, power assisted. Ratio: 17.1:1. Turning Circle: Regular cab: 36.42 ft. SuperCab: 41.34 ft. Transmission: Mitsubishi 5-speed overdrive manual, synchromesh on all gears. Standard for 4.0 liter V-6: Heavy-duty Ford A4LD automatic overdrive. Ratios: 3.7, 2.21, 1.52, 1.00, 0.81:1. Reverse: 3.40:1. Optional: Ford A4LD automatic overdrive transmission. Ratios: 2.47, 1.47, 1.00, 0.75:1. Reverse: 2.10:1. Clutch: 9.0 in. dia. Optional: None.

VEHICLE DIMENSIONS: Wheelbase: Regular cab: 107.8/113.9 in. SuperCab: 125 in. Overall Length: Regular cab: 175.6 in./187.6 in. (without rear bumper). SuperCab: 192.7 in. Front/Rear Tread 56.5 in./55.1 in. Overall Height: 107.9 in. wheelbase: 66.9 in., 113.9 in. wheelbase: 66.7 in., SuperCab: 68.1 in. Width: 66.9 in. Front/Rear Overhang: 28.3 in./39.4 in. (107.9 in. wheelbase); 45.4 in. (133.9 in. wheelbase). SuperCab: 28.3 in./39.4 in. Tailgate: Width and Height: 51.9 in. x 16.0 in. Approach/Departure Degrees: 107.9 in. wheelbase: 29.2/23./2. 113.9 in. wheelbase: 29.2/25.5. SuperCab: 29.0/16.1. Ground Clearance: Rear axle: 6.9 in. Load space: 107.9 in. wheelbase: 72.2 in. x 54.3 in. x 16.5 in. 133.9 in. wheelbase: 84.2 in. x 54.3 in. x 16.5 in.

CAPACITIES: Fuel Tank: 107.9 in. wheelbase: 15.2 gal. 113.9 in. wheelbase: 17.0 gal. Optional: Auxiliary 13.0 gal. tank. SuperCab: 14.5 gal. Optional: 13.0 gal.

ACCOMMODATIONS: Seating Capacity: 3 passengers. Headroom: 39.2 in. Maximum Steering wheel to seat back: 23.1 in. Shoulder room: 55.6 in. Hip room: 55.0 in. Legroom: 42.4 in.

INSTRUMENTATION: Speedometer, odometer, gauges for engine coolant temperature, oil pressure, ammeter, fuel level. Warning lights for 4x4 and low range, high beam, seat belt, parking brake and turn signals.

OPTIONS: Air conditioner. Chrome rear step bumper. Cargo cover. Chrome Package. Super engine cooling. Electric Shift Touch Drive. Auxiliary fuel tank. Headliner. Bright low-mount swing-away mirrors. Power Window/Lock Group. Speed control/tilt steering wheel. Black Sport Appearance Package. Heavy-duty front suspension. Tachometer. Automatic overdrive transmission. Two-tone Deluxe paint. Cast aluminum wheels. AM/FM stereo radio. AM/FM stereo radio with cassette tape player. Electronic AM/FM stereo radio with cassette tape player. Radio credit option. Regular Cab XL Trim Package. Regular Cab STX Trim Package. Pickup box cap. Regular Cab High Rider STX Trim Package. Carpet delete option for XLT trim. White Sport wheels. Paddle-type electric remote-control mirrors. Expanded capacity "Super Single" 21 gallon fuel tank (long wheelbase regular cab models). Floor console with an integral armrest. Sport cloth bucket seats with tip-slide feature. Rally Bar Package. P235 OWL All-Terrain tires (for regular cab). Carpet delete option for Ranger XLT (replaced with black floor mat). SuperCab "Comfort" Package for custom (no charge).

HISTORICAL FOOTNOTES: The 1992 Ranger was introduced on September 17, 1991. In the face of strong competition from the Chevrolet S-10, GMC S-15, Dodge Dakota and Jeep Comanche, the Ranger maintained its position as the top-selling truck in its class.

1993 RANGER

The 1993 Ranger was easily identified by its new exterior, more aerodynamic sheetmetal. Among the highlights of this new look were flusher glass, limo-style doors and a rounded front end appearance. Also new for 1993 were the Ranger's headlights, taillamps and bumpers. Wheel flares were now standard for all models. Added to the distinction of the 4x4 models was the use of an exclusive grille for the 4x4 Rangers. New styled steel and deep-dish cast aluminum wheels were available for 1993. All models were also available with new tape stripe graphics.

Numerous interior changes were apparent in the 1993 Ranger. New door trim panels with ergonomic controls were now used. Also of new design was the steering wheels and seat trim and sew styles on all models. A storage armrest was now included with the 60/40 split bench seat. The optional radios, depicted by Ford as "Next Generation" models were offered with cassette tape player and compact disc options. The instrument panel appliques, cluster graphics and stalk panels were also new for 1993. All models also had new headliners.

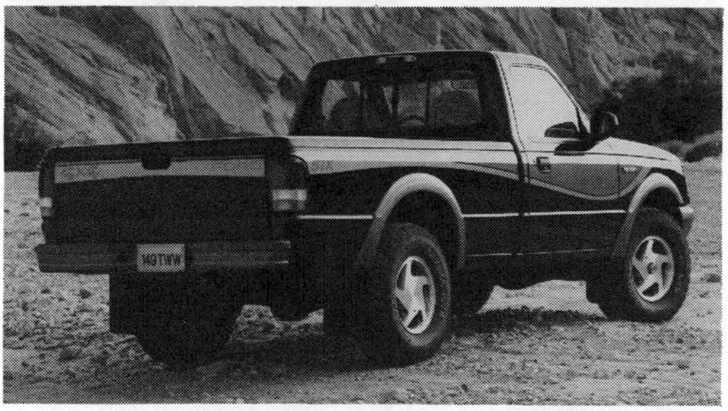

1993 Ford Ranger STX regular cab pickup

The following options were added for 1993: Power mirrors, P235/75R x 15SL All-Terrain OWL tires P265/75R x 15SL All-Terrain OWL tires, round fog lights, electronic premium AM/FM stereo radio with cassette tape player, electronic premium AM/FM stereo radio with CD player, new body side protection moldings, floor consolette with cupholders (bench seat only) and XLT wide tape stripe. Added to the Light Group were map/reading lights.

The list of functional changes for 1993 were headed by the replacement of the 2.9 liter engine with a 3.0 liter V-6. The steering was modified to provide an on-center feel. A center high-mount stop light was adopted as were improvements in the tailgate latch. Single door locks was now used. Regular cab models had increased payload capacity and a new optional Payload Package was available for the SuperCab models. Further upgrades were made in corrosion protection. A 95 amp alternator was now standard. The XL model replaced the custom and S models. The Sport model was replaced by the XL Sport model.

I.D. DATA: The Ranger V.I.N. consisted of seventeen symbols. The first three characters identified the manufacturer, make and type of vehicle. The fourth character (a letter) designated the GVW range. The fifth, sixth and seventh characters identified the series and body style. The eighth character identified the engine. The ninth character was the check digit. The tenth character (a letter) represented the model year. The eleventh character identified the assembly plant. The remaining digits represented the sequential production number.

Body Type	Factory Price	GVW	Shipping Weight	Prod. Total
Ranger R10 Styleside				
Pickup, XL, 107.9 in. wb.	$N.A.	4580[1]	3097	—
Pickup, XL, 113.9 in. wb.	$N.A.	4580[2]	—	—
Pickup XL, Sport, 107.9 in. wb.	$N.A.	4580	N.A.	—
Pickup XL, Sport, 113.9 in. wb.	$N.A.	4580	N.A.	—
Pickup, XLT, 107.9 in. wb.	$N.A.	4580	3026	—
Pickup, XLT, 113.9 in. wb.	$N.A.	4580	2991	—
Pickup, STX, 107.9 in. wb.	—	—	—	—
Pickup, STX, 113.9 in. wb.	—	—	—	—
Ranger SuperCab, 125 in. wheelbase				
Pickup, XL	$N.A.	4840	—	—
Pickup, XLT	$N.A.	4840[3]	3310	—
Pickup, STX	—	—	—	—

NOTE 1: A 4840 lb. GVW Package was optional for the 107.9 in. wheelbase Ranger.
NOTE 2: A 4880 lb. GVW Package was optional for the 113.9 in. wheelbase Ranger.
NOTE 3: A 5040 lb. GVW Package was optional for the SuperCab Ranger.

STANDARD ENGINE: Engine Type: OHV 60 degree V-6. Cast-iron block and cylinder heads. Bore x Stroke: 3.50 in. x 3.14 in. Lifters: Hydraulic. Number of main bearings-4. Fuel Induction: Electronic fuel injection. Compression Ratio: 9.3:1. Displacement: 182 cu. in. (3.0 liters). Horsepower: Net: 145 @ 4800 rpm. Torque: Net: 165 lb.-ft. @ 3000 rpm. Fuel Requirements: Unleaded. Oil capacity: 6 qt. with filter change.

OPTIONAL ENGINE: OHV 60 degree V-6. Cast-iron block and cylinder heads. Bore x Stroke: 3.66 in. x 2.83 in. Lifters: Hydraulic. Number of main bearings-4. Displacement: 179 cu. in. (2.9 liters). Fuel Induction: Electronic fuel injection. Compression Ratio: 9.3:1. Horsepower: Net: 145 @ 4800 rpm. Torque: Net: 165 lb.-ft. @ 3000 rpm. Fuel Requirements: Unleaded. Oil capacity: 5 qt. with filter change.

OPTIONAL ENGINE: OHV 60 degree V-6. Cast-iron block and cylinder heads. Bore x Stroke: 3.95 in. x 3.32 in. Lifters: Hydraulic. Number of main bearings-4. Displacement: 245 cu. in. (4.0 liters). Fuel Induction: Electronic fuel injection. Compression Ratio: 9.0:1. Horsepower: Net: Auto. trans.: 160 @ 4200 rpm. Man. trans.: 145 @ 3800 rpm. Torque: Net: Auto. trans.: 230 lb.-ft. @ 2400 rpm. Fuel Requirements: Unleaded. Oil capacity: 6 qt. with filter change.

CHASSIS FEATURES: Frame: Ladder-type, low carbon steel, 6 cross members, section modulus: 2.37 cu. in. 36,00 psi.

SUSPENSION AND RUNNING GEAR: Front Suspension: Coil springs, computer selected. Capacity: Regular cab: 1940 lb. SuperCab: 2085 lb. Shock absorbers: All models front and rear 1.19 in. dia. 1.125 in. stabilizer bar. Rear Suspension: Single-stage, semi-elliptical 4-leaf, computer selected. Capacity: Regular cab: 2066 lb. SuperCab: 2494 lb. Front Axle Type and Capacity: Twin-Traction beam, Dana 28-IFS, 2750 lb. capacity. Rear Axle Type and Capacity: Ford semi-floating, 2750 lb. capacity. Final Drive Ratio: 3.45:1 front and rear. Optional: 3.55, 3.73 (available with limited slip differential), 4.10:1. Transfer Case: Type: Warner 1350, part-time, 2-speed. Ratios: 2.48, 1.00:1. Brakes: Type: Hydraulic, power-assisted, disc front and cast iron drum rear. Dimensions: Front: 10.87 in. dia. Rear: 9.0 in. x 1.75 in. Wheels: 15 x 5.0 in. 5-hole disc. 15 x 5.5 in. with Payload Package and steel belted radial tires. Optional: 15 x 6.0 in. Tires: Steel-belted P195/75R x 15SL black sidewall, All-Season radial. Optional: P205/75R x 15SL, steel-belted radial raised white letter, off-road, P215/75R x 15SL, steel-belted radial raised white letter, off-road. P235/75R x 15SL All-Terrain tires (regular cab). Steering: Recirculating ball, power assisted. Ratio: 17.1:1. Turning Circle: Regular cab: 36.42 ft. SuperCab: 41.34 ft. Transmission: Mitsubishi 5-speed overdrive manual, synchromesh on all gears. Standard for 4.0 liter V-6: Heavy-duty Ford A4LD automatic overdrive. Ratios: 3.7, 2.21, 1.52, 1.00, 0.81:1. Reverse: 3.40:1. Optional: Ford A4LD automatic overdrive transmission. Ratios: 2.47, 1.47, 1.00, 0.75:1. Reverse: 2.10:1. Clutch: 9.0 in. dia. Optional: None.

VEHICLE DIMENSIONS: Wheelbase: Regular cab: 107.8/113.9 in. SuperCab: 125 in. Overall Length: Regular cab:175.6 in./187.6 in. (without rear bumper). SuperCab: 192.7 in. Front/Rear Tread 56.5 in./55.1 in. Overall Height: 107.9 in. wheelbase: 66.9 in., 113.9 in. wheelbase: 66.7 in., SuperCab: 68.1 in. Width: 66.9 in. Front/Rear Overhang: 28.3 in./39.4 in. (107.9 in. wheelbase); 45.4 in. (133.9 in. wheelbase). SuperCab: 28.3 in./39.4 in. Tailgate: Width and Height: 51.9 in. x 16.0 in. Approach/Departure Degrees: 107.9 in. wheelbase: 29.2/23./2. 113.9 in. wheelbase: 29.2/25.5. SuperCab: 29.0/16.1. Ground Clearance: Rear axle: 6.9 in. Load space: 107.9 in. wheelbase: 72.2 in. x 54.3 in. x 16.5 in. 133.9 in. wheelbase: 84.2 in. x 54.3 in. x 16.5 in.

CAPACITIES: Fuel Tank: 107.9 in. wheelbase: 15.2 gal. 113.9 in. wheelbase: 17.0 gal. Optional: Auxiliary 13.0 gal. tank. SuperCab: 14.5 gal. Optional: 13.0 gal.

ACCOMMODATIONS: Seating Capacity: 3 passengers. Headroom: 39.2 in. Maximum Steering wheel to seat back: 23.1 in. Shoulder room: 55.6 in. Hip room: 55.0 in. Legroom: 42.4 in.

INSTRUMENTATION: Speedometer, odometer, gauges for engine coolant temperature, oil pressure, ammeter, fuel level. Warning lights for 4x4 and low range, high beam, seat belt, parking brake and turn signals.

OPTIONS: Air conditioner. Chrome rear step bumper. Cargo cover. Chrome Package. Super engine cooling. Electric Shift Touch Drive. Auxiliary fuel tank. Headliner. Bright low-mount swing-away mirrors. Power Window/Lock Group. Speed control/tilt steering wheel. Black Sport Appearance Package. Heavy-duty front suspension. Tachometer. Automatic overdrive transmission. Two-tone Deluxe paint. Cast aluminum wheels. AM/FM stereo radio. AM/FM stereo radio with cassette tape player. Electronic AM/FM stereo radio with cassette tape player. Radio credit option. Regular Cab XL Trim Package. Regular Cab STX Trim Package. Pickup box cap. Regular Cab High Rider STX Trim Package. Carpet delete option for XLT trim. White Sport wheels. Paddle-type electric remote-control mirrors. Expanded capacity "Super Single" 21 gallon fuel tank (long wheelbase regular cab models). Floor console with an integral armrest. Sport cloth bucket seats with tip-slide feature. Rally Bar Package. P235 OWL All-Terrain tires (for regular cab). Carpet delete option for Ranger XLT (replaced with black floor mat). SuperCab "Comfort" Package for custom (no charge). Styled steel wheels. Deep-dish cast aluminum wheels. Power mirrors. P235/75R x 15SL All-Terrain OWL tires. P265/75R x 15SL All-Terrain OWL tires. Round fog lights. Electronic premium AM/FM stereo radio with cassette tape player. Electronic premium AM/FM stereo radio with CD player. Body side protection moldings. Floor consolette with cupholders (bench seat only). XLT wide tape stripe.

HISTORICAL FOOTNOTES: The 1993 Ranger was introduced on September 14, 1992. Assembly of the Ranger took place in Louisville, Kentucky, Twin Cities, Minnesota and Edison, New Jersey.

FORD BRONCO II

1984-1990

1984 BRONCO II

1984 Ford Eddie Bauer Bronco II

Ford introduced the Bronco in mid-March 1983 as a 1984 model. Based upon the Ranger pickup, the Bronco II was 19 inches shorter, nine inches narrower and five inches lower than the full-sized Bronco. It also weighed approximately 1000 pounds less than the standard Bronco. Three levels of trim were offered for the Bronco II-Standard, XLT and XLS. Ford subsequently added an Eddie Bauer Package and a 5-speed manual transmission to the Bronco II's option list. Styling of the Bronco II resembled that of the larger Bronco. An egg-crate grille (somewhat shorter and with additional vertical bars as compared to the big Bronco's) with bright trim and encompassing the headlights maintained a close link to Ford truck styling. A unique feature was the Bronco II's rear side windows that curbed upward into the roof segment. The Bronco II top was of all-steel construction and was not removable. The Bronco II's standard engine was a 2.8 liter V-6 manufactured in Germany. No optional engine was offered. Front suspension was a Ford independent Twin I-beam design. Manual locking front hubs were standard as was a 4-speed, manual transmission. The base model's standard exterior features consisted of these items: Bright front and rear bumpers, deep-tinted rear quarter and liftgate glass, black grille with bright surround, halogen rectangular headlights, one-piece, top-hinged liftgate, left and right side black fold-away exterior mirrors, black windshield surround molding, Sport wheelcovers and wrapover rear quarter windows. Interior features consisted of color-keyed carpeting, left and right side coat hooks, color-keyed cowl side trim, dome light with driver and passenger side operation, color-keyed vinyl panel door trim with fully padded armrest, gauge package, Hi-Lo flow-through ventilation, color-keyed cloth headliner, inside hood release, color-keyed instrument panel with black upper panel finish, brushed pewter-tone cluster finish panel applique, cluster warning lights, color-keyed flocked storage bin plus locking glove box, cigarette lighter, day/night rearview mirror, color-keyed "A" pillar and windshield header moldings, AM radio, color-keyed rear quarter and liftgate trim panels, bright scuff plates, black seat belts, knitted vinyl reclining front bucket seats (flip-down front passenger seat) and split fold-down rear bench seat, color-keyed spare tire cover, color-keyed soft vinyl steering wheel and color-keyed sun visors with visor clip.

1984 Ford Bronco II XLT

The exterior colors offered were raven black, polar white, light charcoal metallic, dark canyon red, light blue, medium blue metallic, midnight blue metallic, medium desert tan, walnut metallic, light desert tan, bright bittersweet and bright copper glow. Bronco II interiors were available in dark blue, canyon red and tan.

1984 Standard Ford Bronco II

I.D. DATA: The Bronco II V.I.N. consisted of seventeen symbols. The first three characters identified the manufacturer, make and type of vehicle. The fourth character (a letter) designated the GVW range. The fifth, sixth and seventh characters identified the series and body style. The eighth character identified the engine. The ninth character was the check digit. The tenth character (a letter) represented the model year. The eleventh character identified the assembly plant. The remaining digits represented the sequential production number.

Body Type	Factory Price	GVW	Shipping Weight	Prod. Total
Bronco II				
Wagon (U14)	$9998	4160	3237	*

* Calendar year 1983 sales were 63,178. For the 1984 calendar year they totalled 98,049.

STANDARD ENGINE: Engine Type: OHV, V-6 cast iron head and engine block. Bore x Stroke: 3.66 in. x 2.70 in. Lifters: Hydraulic. Fuel Induction: Single 2-bbl. carburetor. Compression Ratio: 8.7:1. Displacement: 170 cu. in. (2.8 liters). Horsepower: 115 @ 4600 rpm. Torque: 150 lb.-ft. @ 2600 rpm. Fuel Requirements: Regular Unleaded.

CHASSIS FEATURES: Separate body and frame. Full-length frame with rubber-isolated body. Single channel, 5 cross members welded frame. 2.37 in. section modulus. Maximum side rail section: 6.08 in. x 2.26 in. x 0.130 in. Low carbon steel. Yield strength: 36,000 lb. Heavy-duty frame included with Snowplow Package: 2.89 in. section modulus. Maximum side rail section: 6.12 in. x 2.28 in. x 0.150 in. Low carbon steel. Yield strength: 36,000 lb.

1984 Ford Bronco II XLS

SUSPENSION AND RUNNING GEAR: Front Suspension: Independent, coil springs, Twin Traction beam, lateral arms, and leading arms on each side with stabilizer bar. 1970 lb. rating. Rear Suspension: Semi-elliptical leaf springs with stabilizer bar. 4-leaf, 2165 lb. rating. Front Axle Type and Capacity: Twin-Traction, beam, 2750 lb. rating. Rear Axle Type and Capacity: Ford semi-floating 2640 lb. rating. Transfer Case: Type: Warner 1350 2-speed. Ratios: 2.48:1, 1.0:1. Brakes: Type: Hydraulic power-assisted, vented disc front and cast iron drum rear. Dimensions: Front: 10.9 in. dia. x 0.9 in. Floating Caliper. Total front swept area: 188.24 sq. in. Rear: 9.0 in. x 1.8 in. Wheels: 6.0JJ x 15, 5-hole disc. Optional: 6.0 x 15 in. cast aluminum wheels, white Sport wheels. Tires: P195/75R15SL steel radial black sidewall. Optional: P195/75R15SL steel radial All-Terrain black sidewall, P195/75R15SL steel radial All-Terrain raised white letters, P205/75R15SL steel radial All-Terrain raised white letters. Steering: Power assisted, recirculating ball. Ratio: 17:1, overall: 19.8:1, turns Lock-to-Lock: 4.1. Turning Circle: 35.0 ft. Optional: None. Transmission: 4-speed manual. Optional: 5-speed manual overdrive, all-synchromesh. Transmission Ratios: 3.96, 2.08, 1.39, 1.00, 0.84:1. Optional: 3-speed automatic. Clutch: Segmented, woven, non-asbestos lining. Belleville pressure plate, 9 in. dia. Optional: None.

VEHICLE DIMENSIONS: Wheelbase: 94.0 in. Overall Length: 158.4 in. Front/Rear Tread 56.9 in./56.9 in. Overall Height: 68.2 in. Width: 68.0 in. Front/Rear Overhang: 28.2 in./36.0 in. Tailgate: Width and Height: 46.27 in. x 34.3 in. Approach/Departure Degrees: 29.5/24.8. Ground Clearance: Front axle: 6.50 in. Rear axle: 6.90 in. Load space: With rear seat installed: 21 in. x 21.2 in. x 41.9 in. With rear seat removed or folded: 53.2 in. x 21.2 in. x 41.9 in. Maximum capacity: With rear seat folded: 64.9 cu. ft. With rear seat up: 25.6 cu. ft.

CAPACITIES: Fuel Tank: 23.0 gal.

ACCOMMODATIONS: Seating Capacity: 5 passengers. Front headroom: 39.5 in. Rear headroom: 38.5 in. Front legroom: 42.4 in. Rear legroom: 35.2 in. Front shoulder room: 55.5 in. Rear shoulder room: 56.7 in. Front hip room: 54.8 in. Rear hip room: 44.1 in.

INSTRUMENTATION: Speedometer, odometer, fuel level gauge, warning lights for ammeter, oil pressure, engine coolant temperature.

OPTIONS AND PRICES: Chrome grille. Tu-Tone paint: $207. Sport tape stripe. Eddie Bauer Bronco II. AM/FM monaural radio. AM/FM stereo radio with four speakers: $176. AM/FM stereo radio with cassette tape player and four speakers. Dual or Quad Captain's chairs. Includes power lumbar support and zippered map pocket on seat back. Tinted glass. Convenience Group. Includes interval windshield wipers, visor vanity mirror, cigarette lighter, dual electric horns, and driver's sun visor band. Light Group. Includes glove box ashtray and cargo area light, passenger door and liftgate courtesy light switches, and "headlights on" warning buzzer. Fingertip speed control. Tilt steering wheel. Rear window wiper/defroster. Flip-up liftgate window, flip-open removable quarter windows (gray tinted). Pivoting front vent windows. Includes tinted vent and side window glass. Privacy glass. Includes tinted glass. Floor console. Includes Gauge Package, trash bin, coin tray, two cup depressions, and Electronic graphic warning display module: $208. Overhead console. Includes digital clock and pivoting map light. Bright low-mount Western swing-away mirrors. Outside swing-away spare tire carrier. Includes full-size tire, vinyl cover, lock and standard wheel: $206. Roof rack. Rear seat delete. Carpet delete. Includes color-keyed mat. SelectShift automatic transmission. 5-speed manual transmission: $225. Engine block heater. Super engine cooling. Heavy-duty maintenance-free battery. Heavy-duty air cleaner. Gauge Package. Includes ammeter, engine coolant temperature and oil pressure gauges plus resettable trip odometer. Heavy-duty front and rear shock absorbers. Snowplow Special Package. Trailer Towing Package. Two tow hooks. Limited slip front axle. Rear axle Traction-Lok. California emissions system. High altitude emissions system. Exterior Protection Group. Includes bright front and rear bumpers with black end caps, black front bumper guards, black upper body side molding with two red accent stripes. Transfer case skid plate (included with manual transmission). Cast aluminum wheels: $219. White Sport styled steel wheels. Deluxe wheel trim. Includes argent styled steel wheels with bright trim ring, lug nuts and black hub cover.

HISTORICAL FOOTNOTES: The Bronco II was in direct competition with the Chevrolet S-10 Blazer.

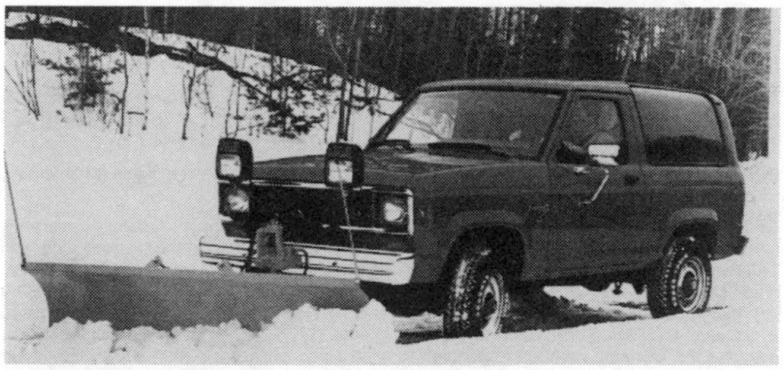

1984 Ford Bronco with Snowplow Package

1985 BRONCO II

No changes were made in the Bronco II's styling for 1985. The previously optional 5-speed overdrive manual transmission was now standard. The base model's standard exterior features consisted of these items: Bright front and rear bumpers, deep-tinted rear quarter and liftgate glass, black grille with bright surround, halogen rectangular headlights, one-piece, top-hinged liftgate, left and right side black fold-away exterior mirrors, black windshield surround molding, Sport wheelcovers and wrapover rear quarter windows. Interior features consisted of color-keyed carpeting, left and right side coat hooks, color-keyed cowl side trim, dome light with driver and passenger side operation, color-keyed vinyl panel door trim with fully padded armrest, gauge package, Hi-Lo flow-through ventilation, color-keyed cloth headliner, inside hood release, color-keyed instrument panel with black upper panel finish, brushed pewter-tone cluster finish panel applique, cluster warning lights, color-keyed flocked storage bin plus locking glove box, cigarette lighter, day/night rearview mirror, color-keyed "A" pillar and windshield header moldings, AM radio, color-keyed rear quarter and liftgate trim panels, bright scuff plates, black seat belts, knitted vinyl reclining front bucket seats (flip-down front passenger seat) and split fold-down rear bench seat, color-keyed spare tire cover, color-keyed soft vinyl steering wheel and color-keyed sun visors with visor clip. Exterior colors for 1985 were raven black, silver metallic, bright canyon red, midnight blue metallic, light regatta blue, dark canyon red, bright regatta blue metallic, light desert tan, Wimbledon white, dark charcoal metallic and walnut metallic. The interior trim colors available were regatta blue, canyon red and tan.

I.D. DATA: The Bronco II V.I.N. consisted of seventeen symbols. The first three functioned as the world manufacturer identifier. The fourth digit identified the brake system and GVWR class. The fifth, sixth and seventh digits identified the line, series, chassis, cab or body type. The eighth digit identified the engine type. The ninth digit was a computer check digit. The tenth entry, a number, E, identified the 1985 model year. The eleventh digit identified the plant of manufacture. The twelvth through seventeenth digits were the sequential production numbers for each plant.

Body Type	Factory Price	GVW	Shipping Weight	Prod. Total
Bronco				
Wagon (U14)	$10,899*	4160	3227	111, 351[a]

* Subsequently increased to $11,102.
a 1985 calendar year production. Included 4x2 models.

STANDARD ENGINE: Engine Type: OHV, V-6 cast iron head and engine block. Bore x Stroke: 3.66 in. x 2.70 in. Lifters: Hydraulic. Number of main bearings-4. Fuel Induction: Single 2-bbl. carburetor. Compression Ratio: 8.7:1. Displacement: 170 cu. in. (2.8 liters). Oil Refill: 5 qt. with filter change. 4 qt. without filter change. Horsepower: 115 @ 4600 rpm. Torque: 150 lb.-ft. @ 2600 rpm. Fuel Requirements: Regular Unleaded.

CHASSIS FEATURES: Separate body and frame. Full-length frame with rubber-isolated body. Single channel, 5 cross members, welded frame. 2.37 in. section modulus. Maximum side rail section: 6.12 in. x 2.28 in. x 0.150 in. Low carbon steel. Yield strength: 36,000 lb.

SUSPENSION AND RUNNING GEAR: Front Suspension: Independent, coil springs, Twin Traction beam, lateral arms, and leading arms on each side with stabilizer bar. 1970 lb. rating. Rear Suspension: Semi-elliptical leaf springs with stabilizer bar, 2165 lb. rating. Front Axle Type and Capacity: Twin-Traction, beam, 2750 lb. rating. Rear Axle Type and Capacity: Ford semi-floating 2640 lb. rating. Final Drive Ratio: Standard for 5-spd. manual trans.: 3.45:1. Standard for auto trans.: 3.73:1. Optional: 3.45, 3.73 and 4.10: 1 with various axle and transmissions. Transfer Case: Type: Warner 1350 2-speed. Ratios: 2.48:1, 1.0:1. Brakes: Type: Hydraulic power-assisted, vented disc front and cast iron drum rear. Dimensions: Front: 10.9 in. dia. x 0.9 in. Floating Caliper. Total front swept area: 18.24 sq. in. Rear: 9.0 in. x 1.8 in. Wheels: 6.0 x 15, 5-hole disc. Optional: 6.0 x 15 in. cast aluminum wheels, white Sport wheels. Tires: P195/75R15SL steel radial black sidewall. Optional: P195/75R15SL steel radial All-Terrain black sidewall, P195/75R15SL steel radial All-Terrain raised white letters, P205/75R15SL steel radial All-Terrain raised white letters. Steering: Power assisted, recirculating ball. Ratio: 17:1:1. Overall ratio: 19.8:1, turns Lock-to-Lock: 4.1. Turning Circle: 35.0 ft. Optional: None. Transmission: Type: 5-speed manual overdrive. Two units were used. Mitsubishi. Transmission Ratios: 3.97, 2.14, 1.36, 1.00, 0.84:1. Reverse: 3.58:1. Toyo Kogyo: Transmission Ratios: 3.96, 2.08, 1.39, 1.00, 0.85:1. Reverse: 3.39:1. Clutch: Segmented, woven, non-asbestos lining. Belleville pressure plate, 9 in. dia. Total plate pressure: 1320 lb. Optional: Type: Ford A4LD automatic overdrive. Ratios: 2.47, 1.47, 1.00, 0.75:1. Clutch: Segmented, woven, non-asbestos lining. Belleville pressure plate, 9 in. dia. Total plate pressure.

VEHICLE DIMENSIONS: Wheelbase: 94.0 in. Overall Length: 158.4 in. Front/Rear Tread 56.9 in./56.9 in. Overall Height: 68.2 in. Width: 68.0 in. Front/Rear Overhang: 28.2 in./36.0 in. Tailgate: Width and Height: 46.27 in. x 34.3 in. Approach/Departure Degrees: 29.3/24.7. Ground Clearance: Front axle: 6.34 in. Rear axle: 6.50 in. Load space: With rear seat installed: 21 in. x 21.2 in. x 41.9 in. With rear seat removed or folded: 52.5 in. x 21.2 in. x 41.9 in. Maximum capacity: With rear seat folded: 64.9 cu. in. With rear seat up: 25.6 cu. ft.

CAPACITIES: Fuel Tank: 23.0 gal.

ACCOMMODATIONS: Seating Capacity: 5 passengers. Front headroom: 39.5 in. Rear headroom: 38.5 in. Front legroom: 42.4 in. Rear legroom: 35.2 in. Front shoulder room: 55.5 in. Rear shoulder room: 56.7 in. Front hip room: 54.8 in. Rear hip room: 44.1 in. Instrumentation: Speedometer, odometer, fuel level gauge, warning lights for ammeter, oil pressure, engine coolant temperature.

OPTIONS AND PRICES: The option code follows the option description. Automatic overdrive transmission (44T): $676.10. Standard rear axle with Traction-Lok: $238. Optional rear axle ratios: $42.10. Dana limited slip front axle (472): $238. P195/75R15SL steel radial All-Terrain black sidewall (T74/50E): $30.10. P195/75R15SL steel radial All-Terrain raised white letters (T7L): $114.10. P205/75R15SL steel radial All-Terrain raised white letters (T7M): $159.40 XLT Trim Package (921B): $201.10. XLT Trim Package (775). Includes bright front and rear bumpers with black end caps, chrome grille, dual electric horns, bright low-mount Western swing-away mirrors, two-color tape stripe, Deluxe wheel trim, color-keyed cloth full door trim with bright surround, map pocket and lower carpet, instrument panel woodtone applique, Light Group, right side visor vanity mirror, molded color-keyed instrument panel with bright surround, color-keyed quarter trim panels with padded armrests and three flocked storage compartments, AM/FM stereo radio, color-keyed Deluxe seat belts with tension eliminator, cloth and vinyl seats, color-keyed Deluxe leather-wrapped steering wheel, color-keyed flocked storage bin, pivoting vent windows and interval wipers: $909.30-$1323.30 (depending on package). XLS Trim Package (776). Includes, in addition to or in place of XLT features: Black front and rear bumpers with black end caps, black grille molding surround, speed control/tilt steering wheel, rocker panel flare molding and XLS tape stripe: $413.20 with cloth and vinyl dual Captain's chairs. $904.90 with quad Captain's chairs. The AM/FM stereo radio is not included in the XLS Package. Eddie Bauer (926B). Includes XLT trim, which must be ordered, speed control/tilt steering wheel, cast aluminum wheels, dual body side accent paint stripe, "Eddie Bauer" gear bag and glove box size map folder (shipped direct to customer from Eddie Bauer). "Eddie Bauer" nomenclature, "Ford Care" extended service plan, AM/FM stereo radio and P205/74R15SL All-Terrain tires: $846. Air conditioning (572): $708.70. Heavy-duty battery (633): $53. Floor console (604): $165.50. Overhead console (606): $81.70. Super cooling engine (624): $53. Floor mat in lieu of carpet (172): $30.20. Privacy glass (924): $135. Engine block heater (41H): $31. Automatic front locking hubs (212): $40.20, Bright low-mount Western swing-away exterior mirrors (547): $82.90. Power window door lock group (962): $292.60. Ski rack (615): $120. Flip-up/Open air roof (566): $314.60. Heavy-duty shock absorbers (664): $34. Skid plate (413): $67. Snowplow Special Package (565). Includes heavy-duty front and rear shock absorbers, heavy-duty alternator, heavy-duty front springs with air bags and auxiliary oil cooler. The front spoiler is deleted: $243.70 (without air conditioning), $191 (with air conditioning). Outside swing-away spare tire carrier (51Q): $179.80-$279 depending on tire size, Speed control/tilt steering wheel (554): $279. Trailer Towing Package (534). $219.10 with manual transmission. $278.20 with automatic transmission. $103 with Snowplow Special Package. Cast aluminum wheels (646): $213.90. White Sport wheels (647): $88 with standard trim, $20.10 with all other trim packages. Flip-out rear window (435): $85.40. Rear window wiper/defroster (913): $238. AM/FM stereo radio (584): $118.80. AM/FM stereo radio with cassette player (587): $439.10 with XLS trim; $320.40 with XLT (except Eddie Bauer Package 926B). Premium Sound system (91A): $96.20. Radio credit potion (58Y): $45. Seat and Trim Options. Standard trim level: Cloth and vinyl bucket seats (A): $94.60. XLT trim level: Cloth and vinyl dual Captain's chairs (B): $413.20. Cloth and vinyl quad Captain's chairs (Y): $904.90. Cloth and vinyl quad Captain's chairs (Eddie Bauer only): $491.70. XLS trim level: Cloth and vinyl quad Captain's chairs: $413.20. Cloth and vinyl quad Captain's chairs: $904.90.Two-tone paint (956): $213.40 with standard trim; $167.10 with XLT trim. Deluxe two-tone paint (952): $250.90 with standard trim; $204.50 with XL trim. California emissions system (422): $99. High altitude principle use (428): No charge.

HISTORICAL FOOTNOTES: Bronco II calendar year sales totalled 104,507 units, including the 4x2 version.

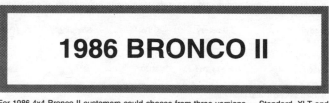

1986 BRONCO II

For 1986 4x4 Bronco II customers could choose from three versions — Standard, XLT and Eddie Bauer. The XLS version was no longer offered. Exterior changes consisted of the addition of bumper rub stripes to the chrome bumpers on the XLT. Six new exterior colors were introduced. The listing of 1986 colors thus contained these colors: Dark grey metallic, raven black, medium silver metallic, bright canyon red, dark canyon red, light regatta blue, dark shadow blue metallic, colonial white, dark walnut metallic, light desert tan and desert tan metallic. Three two-tone paint applications were available. The standard model was available with a Deluxe two-tone paint scheme involving an accent color applied below the side body chamfer to the lower rocker panel area and continued across the liftgate. The colors were separated by upper and lower two-color tape stripes. The XLT exterior in a monotone had a mid-body side tape stripe below the chamfer in two colors with center void. It was available in three different two-color combinations. The Eddie Bauer two-tone paint application consisted of an accent color applied below the rocker area and a two-color tape stripe applied at point break and below the chamfer.

The XLT interior improvements consisted of the use of a tip and slide right side passenger seat and color-keyed seat belts with a tension eliminator added to the base trim. The three interior trim colors for 1986 were regatta blue, canyon red and medium chestnut. The following items were made standard for the base model: Dual note horn, seat belt/headlights-on warning chime, trailer tow bumper, heavy-duty battery and skid plates. Added to the Bronco II's option list were these features: Electric Shift with overhead Touch Drive console, All-Season tires, 60/40 split front bench seat (available on all models except the Eddie Bauer), tachometer with standard trim, P205/75R14 raised white letters off-road tires, electronic AM/FM stereo radio and Electronic AM /FM stereo radio with cassette player. Ford described the Touch Drive option as "a major innovation with strong appeal to suburbanites and first-time off-roaders..." Touch Drive provided the convenience of "on-the-fly" shifting between two-wheel drive and four-wheel drive at the touch of a button located in an overhead console. The console also included a lighted display that indicated the selected operating mode. The options deleted for 1986 consisted of the mechanically tuned AM/FM stereo and AM/FM stereo radio with cassette player, electronic AM/FM stereo radio with cassette player, automatic front locking hubs, limited slip front axle, front mat in lieu of carpet, regular two-tone paint, Trailer Towing Package, quad Captain's chairs, heavy-duty shock absorbers, P205/75 All-Terrain tires and P195/55 All-Terrain tires.

The only engine offered for 1986, a 2.9 liter V-6 was now equipped with electronic fuel injection. It was available with either a 5-spd. manual or automatic overdrive transmission. This engine delivered 12 percent more horsepower than the 1985 2.8 liter 2-barrel carburetor engine it replaced. Among its important features were hydraulic valve lifters, chain-driven camshaft, fast-burn combustion chamber and a 9.3:1 compression ratio. Heavy-duty gas pressurized shock absorbers were now standard. A new tachometer cluster was included in the XLT and Eddie Bauer packages.

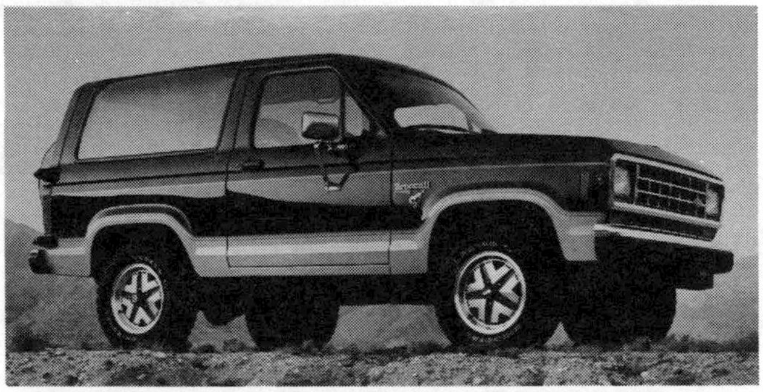

1986 Ford Eddie Bauer Bronco II

Standard exterior trim features were as follows: Chrome front and rear bumpers (the new standard bumper was capable of towing a 2,000 lb. trailer), black grille with bright surround, black windshield molding, black fold-away mirrors, black door handles and locks, wrap over rear quarter windows, deep-tinted rear quarter and liftgate glass, Sport wheelcovers, tinted glass all around, dual-tone horn, "Ford" oval on grille and liftgate, "Bronco II" nomenclature and horse emblem on front fenders and rectangular halogen headlights. The standard interior was fitted with these items: "Bronco II" nomenclature on right side of instrument panel, dome light, driver and passenger door courtesy light switches, color-keyed seat belts with tension eliminator and warning chimes, aluminum left and right side door scuff plates, black plastic with liftgate, bright surround molding on door handle depression, bright window regulator handle with black knob, color-keyed vinyl door trim panels, color-keyed armrests, full-length, color-keyed 16 oz. carpeting with insulation, three color-keyed coat hooks, day/night 9.625 in. mirror, color-keyed vinyl sun visors with visor clip, color-keyed cowl side trim panels, color-keyed garnish moldings, color-keyed rear quarter trim panels with ashtrays and padded armrests, color-keyed liftgate trim panel, color-keyed full-length cloth headliner, knitted vinyl color-keyed seat rim, reclining front bucket seats with color-keyed seat belts, tip-and-slide front passenger bucket seat, split-fold-down rear seats with carpeted seat back and color-keyed seat belts, four color-keyed grab handles, color-keyed spare tire cover, color-keyed "A-frame" steering wheel with center horn blow and color-keyed steering column shroud, liftgate scuff plate and door handles. The standard instrument panel was equipped with gauge package, cigarette lighter, color-keyed instrument panel pad and lower panel, brushed pewter-tone cluster finish pane applique, black instrument panel upper finish panel, color-keyed instrument panel register housings, color-keyed flocked storage bin and locking glove box. AM radio (may be deleted for credit), inside hood release and Hi-Lo flow-through ventilation.

I.D. DATA: The Bronco II V.I.N. consisted of seventeen symbols. The first three functioned as the world manufacturer identifier. The fourth digit identified the brake system and GVWR class. The fifth, sixth and seventh digits identified the line, series, chassis, cab or body type. U14 identified Bronco II 4x4. The eighth digit identified the engine type. T identified the 179 cu. in. V-6 engine. The ninth digit was a computer check digit. The tenth digit, G, identified the 1986 model year. The tenth digit identified the plant of manufacture. U identified the Louisville, Kentucky plant where the Bronco II was built. The twelfth through seventeenth digits were the sequential production numbers for each plant, starting with A00001 through A99999 then B000000, etc.

Body Type	Factory Price	GVW	Shipping Weight	Prod. Total
Bronco				
Wagon (U14)	$11,741	3940*	3219	73,908[a]

* 4160, 4280 and 4500 (Snowplow Package) lb. GVWR packages available.
a 1986 calendar year production.

STANDARD ENGINE: Engine Type: OHV, 60 degree V-6 cast iron head and engine block. Bore x Stroke: 3.66 in. x 2.83 in. Lifters: Hydraulic. Number of main bearings-4. Fuel Induction: Six port-mounted fuel injectors electronically triggered by EEC-IV module. Compression Ratio: 9.3:1. Displacement: 179 cu. in. (2.9 liters). Oil Refill: 5 qt. with filter change. 4 qt. without filter change. Horsepower: 140 @ 4600 rpm. Torque: 170 lb.-ft. @ 2600 rpm. Fuel Requirements: Regular Unleaded.

CHASSIS FEATURES: Separate body and frame. Full-length frame with rubber-isolated body. Single channel, 5 cross members, welded frame. 2.37 in. section modulus. Maximum side rail section: 6.08 in. x 2.26 in. x 0.130 in. Low carbon steel. Yield strength: 36,000 lb. Heavy-duty frame included with Snowplow Package: 2.89 in. section modulus. Maximum side rail section: 6.12 in. x 2.28 in. x 0.150 in. Low carbon steel. Yield strength: 36,000 lb.

SUSPENSION AND RUNNING GEAR: Front Suspension: Independent, coil springs, Twin Traction beam, lateral arms, and leading arms on each side with stabilizer bar. 1970 lb. rating. Optional rating of 2120 and 2240 lb. available. Rear Suspension: Semi-elliptical 4-leaf springs with stabilizer bar, 2177 lb. rating. Optional rating of 2390 lb. available with 5-leaf springs. Front Axle Type and Capacity: Twin-Traction, beam, 2750 lb. rating. Rear Axle Type and Capacity: Ford semi-floating. 2640 lb. rating. Final Drive Ratio: Standard for 5-spd. manual trans.: 3.45:1. Standard for auto trans.: 3.73:1. Standard for High Altitude: 3.73:1 for both transmissions. Standard for Calif. with manual trans.: 3.45:1. Standard for Calif. with auto. trans.: 3.73:1. Optional: Manual trans.: 49 states: 3.73:1 limited slip diff. Calif.: 4.10:1 limited slip diff. High Altitude: manual trans.: 3.73:1 limited slip diff. Auto. trans.: 4.10:1 limited slip. Transfer Case: Type: Warner 1350 2-speed. Ratios: 2.48:1, 1.0:1. Brakes: Type: Hydraulic power-assisted, vented disc front and cast iron drum rear. Dimensions: Front: 10.86 in. dia. x 0.9 in. Floating Caliper. Total front swept area: 188.24 sq. in. Rear: 9.0 in. x 1.75 in. Total rear swept area: 98.96 sq. in. Wheels: 15 x 5.5JJ, 5-hole disc. Optional: 15 x 6.0JJ cast aluminum wheels, 15 x 6.0JJ white Sport wheels. Tires: P195/75R15SL steel radial black sidewall. Optional: P195/75R15SL steel radial All-Terrain black sidewall, P195/75R15SL steel radial All-Terrain raised white letters, P195/75R15SL All-Season black sidewall, P205/75R15SL steel radial All-Terrain raised white letters, P205/75RSL steel radial off-road raised white letters. Steering: Power assisted, recirculating ball. Ratio: 17:1, overall: 19.8:1, turns Lock-to-Lock: 4.1. Turning Circle: 34.42 ft. Optional: None. Transmission: Type: 5-speed manual overdrive. Two units were used. Mitsubishi. Transmission Ratios: 3.97, 2.14, 1.36, 1.00, 0.86:1. Reverse: 3.58:1. Toyo Kogyo: Transmission Ratios: 3.96, 2.08, 1.39, 1.00, 0.85:1. Reverse: 3.39:1. Clutch: Segmented, woven, non-asbestos lining. Belleville pressure plate, 9 in. dia. Total plate pressure: 1320 lb. Optional: Type: Ford A4LD automatic overdrive. Ratios: 2.47, 1.47, 1.00, 0.75:1.

VEHICLE DIMENSIONS: Wheelbase: 94.0 in. Overall Length: 158.2 in. Front/Rear Tread 56.9 in./56.9 in. Overall Height: 68.2 in. Width: 68.0 in. Front/Rear Overhang: 28.2 in./36.0 in. Tailgate: Width and Height: 46.27 in. x 34.3 in. Approach/Departure Degrees: 29.3/24.7. Ground Clearance: Front axle: 6.34 in. Rear axle: 6.50 in. Load space: With rear seat installed: 21.0 in. x 21.2 in. x 41.9 in. With rear seat removed or folded: 53.2 in. x 21.2 in. 41.9 in. Maximum capacity: With rear seat folded: 64.9 cu. in. With rear seat up: 25.6 cu. ft.

CAPACITIES: Fuel Tank: 23.0 gal.

ACCOMMODATIONS: Seating Capacity: 5 passengers. Front headroom: 39.5 in. Rear headroom: 38.5 in. Front legroom: 42.4 in. Rear legroom: 35.2 in. Front shoulder room: 55.5 in. Rear shoulder room: 56.7 in. Front hip room: 54.8 in. Rear hip room: 44.1 in.

INSTRUMENTATION: Speedometer, odometer, fuel level gauge, warning lights for ammeter, oil pressure, engine coolant temperature.

OPTIONS AND PRICES: The option code follows the option description. Automatic overdrive transmission (44T): $701. Electric Shift Touch Drive (213): $101. Standard rear axle with Traction-Lok: $238. Optional rear axle ratios: $42.10. P195/75R15SL steel radial All-Terrain black sidewall (T74/50E): $31. P205/75R15SL off-road raised white letter (T77): $97-$219 depending on additional package ordered. P205/75R15SL steel radial All-Season raised white letters (T7M): $122. Cloth 60/40 bench seat (L): $102. XLT Trim Package (775). Includes the following features in addition to or in place of those in standard trim-exterior: Deluxe wheel trim, chrome grille insert, accent tape stripe on body side and tailgate, low-mount swing-away mirrors and "XLT" nomenclature on front fender. Interior features consist of cloth and vinyl seat trim, additional insulation, additional quarter trim panel features (padded armrests, three storage compartments — one left side, two right side, one lockable), color-keyed cloth full door trim panels with color-keyed molding with bright insert on lower door trim panel, visor mirror, cargo area light, pivoting vent windows, Deluxe leather-wrapped steering wheel, headlights-on warning chime, courtesy lights for ashtray, floor box and engine compartment, electronic AM/FM stereo radio, "XLT" trim nomenclature, interval wipers, color-keyed instrument panel molding with bright surround, color-keyed flocking on glove box interior surface and glove box light, woodtone cluster applique and tachometer: $892-$2062 depending upon package selected. Eddie Bauer (926B). Includes XLT trim, which must be ordered, speed control/tilt steering wheel, cast aluminum wheels, dual body side accent paint stripe, "Eddie Bauer" gear bag and glove box size map folder (shipped direct to customer from Eddie Bauer). "Eddie Bauer" nomenclature, "Ford Care" extended service plan, AM/FM stereo radio and P205/74R15SL All-Terrain tires: $2277-3355 depending upon package selected. Air conditioning (572): $709. Floor console (604): $165. Overhead console (606): $82. Super cooling engine (624): $55. Privacy glass (924): $135. Engine block heater (41H): $31. Bright low-mount Western swing-away exterior mirrors (547): $83. Power window door lock group (962): $293. Luggage rack (615): $120. Flip-up/Open air roof (566): $315. Snowplow Special Package (565). Includes heavy-duty front and rear shock absorbers, heavy-duty alternator, heavy-duty front springs with air bags and auxiliary oil cooler. The front spoiler is deleted: $165 (without air conditioning), $112 (with air conditioning), outside swing-away spare tire carrier (51Q): $271-$326 depending on tire size, Speed control/tilt steering wheel (554): $279. Two-tone Deluxe paint (952): $226 with standard trim. $176 with XLT trim. Cast Aluminum wheels (646): $213. White Sport wheels (647): $88 with standard trim. $19 with all other packages. Flip-open rear window (435): $85. Rear window washer/defroster (913): $238. Electronic AM/FM stereo radio (58F): $147. Electronic AM/FM stereo radio with cassette player and clock (58G): $253 with standard trim. $106 with XLT or Eddie Bauer. Premium sound system (91A): $96. Radio credit option (58Y): $45. California emissions system (422): $9. High altitude principle use (428): No charge.

HISTORICAL FOOTNOTES: Bronco II sales for the 1986 calendar year were 103,020.

1987 BRONCO II

Ford described the 1987 Bronco II as "one of the best all-purpose compact utility vehicles on the market. Today's buyers will appreciate its responsive 2.9 liter EFI V-6 standard engine, rugged chassis and suspension."

For 1987 the standard trim model was redesignated as the XL. Functional changes for 1987 consisted of the inclusion of a rear anti-lock brake system as standard equipment on all models, a new 190mm tandem brake booster, the use of two-sided galvanized body panels in place of the Zincrometal units previously used and replacement of untreated panels by galvanized units. The 1987 Bronco II's standard Sport wheelcover vane paint was changed to black. All electronic radios now had electronic digital clocks. Added to the Bronco II's option list were several clearcoat paints. No longer offered as an option was the overhead console. The standard XL level Bronco II was equipped with these exterior features: Chrome front and rear bumpers with black rub strip, black grille with bright surround, black windshield molding, black fold-away mirrors, wrapover rear quarter windows, deep-tinted rear quarter and tailgate glass, Sport wheelcovers, tinted glass all-around, dual-note horn, Blue "Ford" oval on grille and liftgate, "Bronco II" nomenclature on front fenders and rectangular halogen headlights. The XL interior appointments consisted of bright "Bronco II" nomenclature on right side of instrument panel, dome light, driver and passenger side door courtesy light switches, color-keyed safety belts with tension eliminator and audible alert, aluminum left and right side door scuff plates; black plastic with liftgate, bright surround molding on door handle depressions, black window regulator handle with black knob, color-keyed vinyl door trim panels (starting 3 in. below glass), color-keyed armrests, full-length color-keyed 16 oz. carpeting with insulation, three color-keyed coat hooks, day/night 9.625 in. mirror, color-keyed vinyl sun visors with visor clip, color-keyed cowl side trim panels, color-keyed garnish moldings, color-keyed rear quarter trim panels with ashtrays and padded armrests, color-keyed liftgate trim panel, color-keyed full-length cloth headliner, knitted vinyl color-keyed seat rim, reclining front bucket seats, tip-and-slide front passenger bucket seat, split fold-down rear seats with carpeted seat back and color-keyed seat belts, four color-keyed grab handles, color-keyed spare tire cover, color-keyed "A-frame" steering wheel with center horn blow and color-keyed steering column shroud, liftgate scuff plate and door handles. The standard instrument panel was equipped with Gauge Package, cigarette lighter, color-keyed instrument panel pad and lower panel, brushed pewter-tone cluster finish pane applique, black instrument panel upper finish panel, color-keyed instrument panel register housings, color-keyed flocked storage bin and locking glove box. Electronic AM radio with digital clock (may be deleted for credit), inside hood release and Hi-Lo flow-through ventilation.

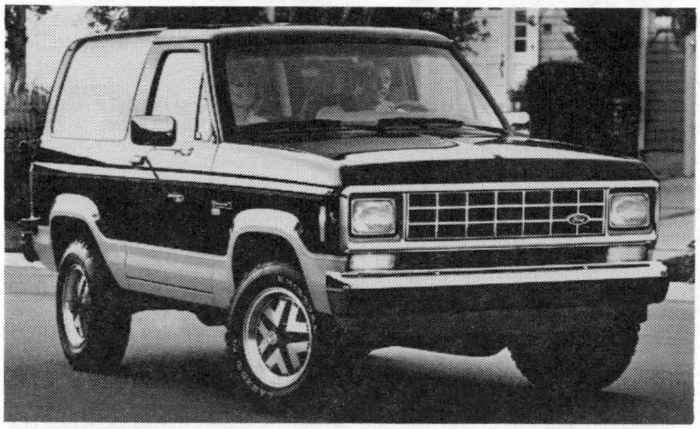

1987 Ford Eddie Bauer Bronco II

The exterior color offered for 1987 included raven black, silver clearcoat metallic, bright canyon red, alpine green clearcoat metallic (Eddie Bauer only), light chestnut clearcoat metallic, dark canyon red, bright regatta, blue clearcoat metallic, dark shadow blue clearcoat metallic, colonial white, shadow grey clearcoat metallic, light chestnut and dark walnut clearcoat metallic. The Bronco interior was available in regatta blue, canyon red and chestnut. The Eddie Bauer interior was available in chestnut only.

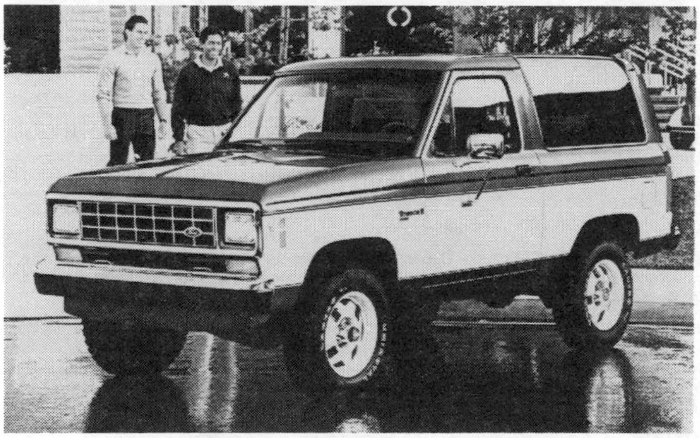

1987 Ford Bronco II XLT

I.D. DATA: The Bronco V.I.N. consisted of seventeen symbols. The first three characters identified the manufacturer, make and type of vehicle. The fourth character (a letter) designated the GVW range. The fifth, sixth and seventh characters identified the series and body style. The eighth character identified the engine. The ninth character was the check digit. The tenth character (a letter) represented the model year. The eleventh character identified the assembly plant. The remaining digits represented the sequential production number.

Body Type	Factory Price	GVW	Shipping Weight	Prod. Total
Bronco				
Wagon (U14)	$12,798	3940[a]	3223	120,905*

a 4160, 4280 and 4500 (Snowplow Package) lb. GVWR packages available.
* 1987 calendar year sales including 4x2 model.

STANDARD ENGINE: Engine Type: OHV, 60 degree V-6 cast iron head and engine block. Bore x Stroke: 3.66 in. x 2.83 in. Lifters: Hydraulic. Number of main bearings-4. Fuel Induction: Six port-mounted fuel injectors electronically triggered by EEC-IV module. Compression Ratio: 9.3:1. Displacement: 179 cu. in. (2.9 liters). Oil Refill: 5 qt. with filter change. 4 qt. without filter change. Horsepower: 140 @ 4600 rpm. Torque: 170 lb.-ft. @ 2600 rpm. Fuel Requirements: Regular Unleaded.

CHASSIS FEATURES: Separate body and frame. Full-length frame with rubber-isolated body. Single channel, 5 cross members, welded frame. 2.37 in. section modulus. Maximum side rail section: 6.08 in. x 2.26 in. x 0.130 in. Low carbon steel. Yield strength: 36,000 lb. Heavy-duty frame included with Snowplow Package: 2.89 in. section modulus. Maximum side rail section: 6.12 in. x 2.28 in. x 0.150 in. Low carbon steel. Yield strength: 36,000 lb.

SUSPENSION AND RUNNING GEAR: Front Suspension: Independent, coil springs, Twin Traction beam, lateral arms, and leading arms on each side with stabilizer bar. 1970 lb. rating. Optional rating of 2120 and 2240 lb. available. Rear Suspension: Semi-elliptical 4-leaf springs with stabilizer bar, 2177 lb. rating. Optional rating of 2390 lb. available with 5-leaf springs. Front Axle Type and Capacity: Twin-Traction, beam, 2750 lb. rating. Rear Axle Type and Capacity: Ford semi-floating. 2640 lb. rating. Final Drive Ratio: Standard for 5-spd. manual trans.: 3.45:1. Standard for auto trans.: 3.73:1. Standard for High Altitude: 3.73:1 for both transmissions. Standard for Calif. with manual trans.: 3.45:1. Standard for Calif. with auto. trans.: 3.73:1. Optional: Manual trans.: 49 states: 3.73:1 limited slip diff. Calif.: 4.10:1 limited slip diff. High Altitude: Manual trans.: 3.73:1 limited slip diff. Auto. trans.: 4.10:1 limited slip. Transfer Case: Type: Warner 1350 2-speed. Ratios: 2.48:1, 1.0:1. Brakes: Type: Hydraulic power-assisted, vented disc front and cast iron drum rear. Dimensions: Front: 10.86 in. dia. x 0.9 in. Floating Caliper. Total front swept area: 188.24 sq. in. Rear: 9.0 in. x 1.75 in. Total rear swept area: 98.96 sq. in. Wheels: 15 x 5.5JJ, 5-hole disc. Optional: 15 x 6.0JJ cast aluminum wheels, 15 x 6.0JJ white Sport wheels. Tires: P195/75R15SL steel radial black sidewall. Optional: P195/75R15SL steel radial All-Terrain black sidewall, P195/75R15SL steel radial All-Terrain raised white letters, P195/75R15SL All-Season black sidewall, P205/75R15SL steel radial All-Terrain raised white letters, P205/75RSL steel radial off-road raised white letters. Steering: Power assisted, recirculating ball. Ratio: 17:1, overall: 19.8:1, turns Lock-to-Lock: 4.1. Turning Circle: 34.42 ft. Optional: None. Transmission: Type: 5-speed manual overdrive. Two units were used. Mitsubishi. Transmission Ratios: 3.97, 2.14, 1.36, 1.00, 0.86:1. Reverse: 3.58:1. Toyo Kogyo: Transmission Ratios: 3.96, 2.08, 1.39, 1.00, 0.85:1. Reverse: 3.39:1. Clutch: Segmented, woven, non-asbestos lining. Belleville pressure plate, 9 in. dia. Total plate pressure: 1320 lb. Optional: Type: Ford A4LD automatic overdrive. Ratios: 2.47, 1.47, 1.00, 0.75:1.

VEHICLE DIMENSIONS: Wheelbase: 94.0 in. Overall Length: 158.2 in. Front/Rear Tread 56.9 in./56.9 in. Overall Height: 68.2 in. Width: 68.0 in. Front/Rear Overhang: 28.2 in./36.0 in. Tailgate: Width and Height: 46.27 in. x 34.3 in. Approach/Departure Degrees: 29.3/24.7. Ground Clearance: Front axle: 6.34 in. Rear axle: 6.50 in. Load space: With rear seat installed: 21.0 in. x 21.2 in. x 41.9 in. With rear seat removed or folded: 53.2 in. x 21.2 in. 41.9 in. Maximum capacity: With rear seat folded: 64.9 cu. in. With rear seat up: 25.6 cu. ft.

CAPACITIES: Fuel Tank: 23.0 gal.

ACCOMMODATIONS: Seating Capacity: 5 passengers. Front headroom: 39.5 in. Rear headroom: 38.5 in. Front legroom: 42.4 in. Rear legroom: 35.2 in. Front shoulder room: 55.5 in. Rear shoulder room: 56.7 in. Front hip room: 54.8 in. Rear hip room: 44.1 in.

INSTRUMENTATION: Speedometer (mph-km/hr.-U.S.; km/hr.-mph.-Canada), Odometer (mile-U.S.; kilometer-Canada), Gauges for engine oil pressure, fuel level, engine coolant temperature, safety belt indicator light, 4x4 indicator light, brake indicator light, low range indicator light, emissions indicator light, check oil level indicator light and battery charge indicator light.

OPTIONS AND PRICES: The option code follows the option description. Automatic overdrive transmission (44T). Electric Shift Touch Drive (213). Standard rear axle with Traction-Lok. Optional rear axle ratios. P195/75R15SL steel radial All-Terrain black sidewall (T74/50E). P205/75R15SL off-road raised white letter (T77). P205/75R15SL steel radial All-Season raised white letters (T7M). Cloth 60/40 bench seat (L). XLT Trim Package (775). Includes the following features in addition to or in place of those in standard trim-exterior: Deluxe wheel trim, chrome grille insert, accent tape stripe on body side and tailgate, low-mount swing-away mirrors and "XLT" nomenclature on front fender. Interior features consist of cloth and vinyl seat trim, additional insulation, additional quarter trim panel features (padded armrests, three storage compartments — one left side, two right side, one lockable), color-keyed cloth full door trim panels with color-keyed molding with bright insert on lower door trim panel, visor mirror, cargo area light, pivoting vent windows, Deluxe leather-wrapped steering wheel, headlights-on warning chime, courtesy lights for ashtray, floor box and engine compartment, electronic AM/FM stereo radio, "XLT" trim nomenclature, interval wipers, color-keyed instrument panel molding with bright surround, color-keyed flocking on glove box interior surface and glove box light, woodtone cluster applique and tachometer. Eddie Bauer (926B). Includes XLT trim, which must be ordered, speed control/tilt steering wheel, cast aluminum wheels, dual body side accent paint stripe, "Eddie Bauer" garment bag and six pocket gear bag (shipped direct to customer from Eddie Bauer). "Eddie Bauer" nomenclature, "Ford Care" extended service plan, AM/FM stereo radio and P205/74R15SL All-Terrain tires. Air conditioning (572). Floor console (604). Super cooling engine (624). Privacy glass (924). Engine block heater (41H). Bright low-mount Western swing-away exterior mirrors (547). Power window door lock group (962). Luggage rack (615). Flip-up/Open air roof (566). Snowplow Special Package (565). Includes heavy-duty front and rear shock absorbers, heavy-duty alternator, heavy-duty front springs with air bags and auxiliary oil cooler. The front spoiler is deleted. Outside swing-away spare tire carrier (51Q). Speed control/tilt steering wheel (554). Two-tone Deluxe paint (952). Cast aluminum wheels (646). White Sport wheels (647). Flip-open rear window (435). Rear window washer/defroster (913). Electronic AM/FM stereo radio (58F) Electronic AM/FM stereo radio with cassette player and clock (58G). Premium sound system (91A). Radio credit option (58Y). California emissions system (422). High altitude principle use (428). Sport Appearance Package. Includes brush/grille guard, fog lamps, contoured tubular rear bumper with matching stone deflector. Available for all trim levels. Mid body side tape stripe. Available for XL only. Tape stripe. Includes horizontal stripes on body side and tailgate. Available later in model year and limited to monotone paint scheme only. Sport tape stripe. Available for body side only, with monotone paint. Includes horizontal stripes at front of body side, rising past "B" pillar. Late model year availability.

HISTORICAL FOOTNOTES: The Bronco II accounted for approximately one out of every five compact utility vehicles sold in 1987. Bronco II owner demographics included these points of interest: The median age of all owners was 33 years, 61 percent were male, 78 percent were married, 64 percent had children, 59 percent had some college education, 67 percent were engaged in white-collar occupations, 59 percent were residents of towns with populations of under 10,000 and 66 percent traded in cars on their Bronco II purchase.

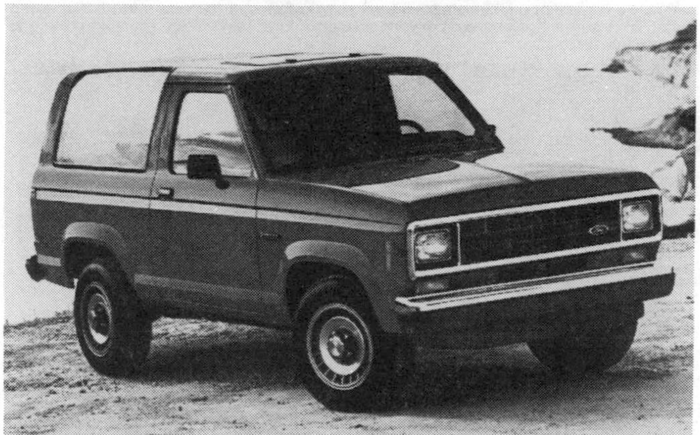

1987 Ford Bronco II XL

1988 BRONCO II

1988 Ford Bronco II XL Sport

Although technically listed as a trim level, Ford added a new XL Sport model to the Bronco II lineup for 1988. The XL Sport model featured raised white-letter tires on deep-dish cast-aluminum wheels, a tachometer and the Sports Appearance Package which included brush/grille guards, fog lamps, black front bumper, black tubular rear bumper and front facia. The Sports Appearance Package was also available for the Bronco II XLT.

A new five-speed overdrive manual transmission that was synchronized in all gears including reverse was standard for all models. New Bronco II options for 1988 included a Sport tape stripe (which had been phased in during the 1987 model year), a Deluxe tape stripe and deep-dish cast-aluminum wheels. Improvements for 1988 included a tip-and-slide driver's seat similar to the passenger seat, use of a standard 60 amp alternator, interval windshield wipers on all models, a limited slip differential on all 4.10:1 rear axles and new shift boots, levers and knobs for the manual transmission and transfer case. Privacy glass was now standard on the Eddie Bauer model.

1988 Ford Eddie Bauer Bronco II

Standard equipment for the XL consisted of the following: Rectangular halogen headlights, black fold-away mirrors, bright front bumper and bright rear trailer-tow bumper, front and rear rub strips, black windshield and quarter panel moldings, one-piece hinged tailgate, tinted windshield and side door windows, black grille with bright surround, Sport wheelcovers, color-keyed front bucket seats and rear split fold seats, knitted vinyl upholstery, color-keyed safety belts with comfort regulators, color-keyed soft vinyl A-frame steering wheel, color-keyed vinyl door trim panel with fully padded armrest, full-length color-keyed cloth headliner, front dome light with courtesy switches for both doors, brushed pewter-tone instrument panel cluster finish applique, locking glove box, inside hood release, dual note horn, gauges for fuel level, and oil pressure; cluster alert lights and trip odometer, interval windshield wipers, full-length color-keyed carpeting, bright aluminum scuff plates, day/night rearview mirror, color-keyed padded sun visors with clipband on driver's side, color-keyed vinyl inside spare tire cover and electronic AM radio.

1988 Ford Bronco II XLT

Interior colors for 1988 consisted of regatta blue, scarlet red and chestnut. The exterior colors choices for 1988 were raven black, scarlet red, caberent red, light chestnut, colonial white, alpine green clearcoat metallic (available only for Eddie Bauer model), silver clearcoat metallic, shadow grey clearcoat metallic, bright regatta blue clearcoat metallic, deep shadow blue clearcoat metallic, light chestnut clearcoat metallic and dark chestnut clearcoat metallic.

I.D. DATA: The Bronco II V.I.N. consisted of seventeen symbols. The first three characters identified the manufacturer, make and type of vehicle. The fourth character (a letter) designated the GVW range. The fifth, sixth and seventh characters identified the series and body style. The eighth character identified the engine. The ninth character was the check digit. The tenth character (a letter) represented the model year. The eleventh character identified the assembly plant. The remaining digits represented the sequential production number.

Body Type	Factory Price	GVW	Shipping Weight	Prod. Total
Bronco II				
Wagon (U14)	$13,316	3940*	3311	—

* 4160, 4280 and 4500 (Snowplow Package) lb. GVWR packages available.

STANDARD ENGINE: Engine Type: OHV, 60 degree V-6 cast iron head and engine block. Bore x Stroke: 3.66 in. x 2.83 in. Lifters: Hydraulic. Number of main bearings-4. Fuel Induction: Six port-mounted fuel injectors electronically triggered by EEC-IV module. Compression Ratio: 9.3:1. Displacement: 179 cu. in. (2.9 liters). Oil Refill: 5 qt. with filter change. 4 qt. without filter change. Horsepower: 140 @ 4600 rpm. Torque: 170 lb.-ft. @ 2600 rpm. Fuel Requirements: Regular Unleaded.

CHASSIS FEATURES: Separate body and frame. Full-length frame with rubber-isolated body. Single channel, 5 cross members, welded frame. 2.37 in. section modulus. Maximum side rail section: 6.08 in. x 2.26 in. x 0.130 in. Low carbon steel. Yield strength: 36,000 lb. Heavy-duty frame included with Snowplow Package: 2.89 in. section modulus. Maximum side rail section: 6.12 in. x 2.28 in. x 0.150 in. Low carbon steel. Yield strength: 36,000 lb.

SUSPENSION AND RUNNING GEAR: Front Suspension: Independent, coil springs, Twin Traction beam, lateral arms, and leading arms on each side with stabilizer bar. 1970 lb. rating. Optional rating of 2120 and 2240 lb. available. Rear Suspension: Semi-elliptical 4-leaf springs with stabilizer bar, 2177 lb. rating. Optional rating of 2390 lb. available with 5-leaf springs. Front Axle Type and Capacity: Twin-Traction, beam, 2750 lb. rating. Rear Axle Type and Capacity: Ford semi-floating. 2640 lb. rating. Final Drive Ratio: Standard for 5-spd. manual trans.: 3.45:1. Standard for auto trans.: 3.73:1. Standard for High Altitude: 3.73:1 for both transmissions. Standard for Calif. with manual trans.: 3.45:1. Standard for Calif. with auto. trans.: 3.73:1. Optional: Calif. 3.73:1 limited slip diff. 49 states: 3.73:1 limited slip diff. High Altitude: Manual trans.: 3.73:1 limited slip diff. Auto. trans.: 4.10:1 limited slip. Transfer Case: Type: Warner 1350 2-speed. Ratios: 2.48:1, 1.0:1. Brakes: Type: Hydraulic power-assisted, vented disc front and cast iron drum rear. Dimensions: Front: 10.86 in. dia. x 0.9 in. Floating Caliper. Total front swept area: 188.24 sq. in. Rear: 9.0 in. x 1.75 in. Total rear swept area: 98.96 sq. in. Wheels: 15 x 5.5JJ, 5-hole disc. Optional: 15 x 6.0JJ cast aluminum wheels, 15 x 6.0JJ white Sport wheels. Tires: P195/75R15SL steel radial black sidewall. Optional: P195/75R15SL steel radial All-Terrain black sidewall, P195/75R15SL steel radial All-Terrain raised white letters, P195/75R15SL All-Season black sidewall, P205/75R15SL steel radial All-Terrain raised white letters, P205/75RSL steel radial off-road raised white letters. Steering: Power assisted, recirculating ball. Ratio: 17:1, overall: 19.8:1, turns Lock-to-Lock: 4.1. Turning Circle: 34.42 ft. Optional: None. Transmission: Type: 5-speed manual overdrive. Two units were used. Mitsubishi: Transmission Ratios: 3.97, 2.14, 1.36, 1.00, 0.86:1. Reverse: 3.58:1. Toyo Kogyo: Transmission Ratios: 3.96, 2.08, 1.39, 1.00, 0.85:1. Reverse: 3.39:1. Clutch: Segmented, woven, non-asbestos lining. Belleville pressure plate, 9 in. dia. Total plate pressure: 1320 lb. Optional: Type: Ford A4LD automatic overdrive. Ratios: 2.47, 1.47, 1.00, 0.75:1.

VEHICLE DIMENSIONS: Wheelbase: 94.0 in. Overall Length: 158.2 in. Front/Rear Tread 56.9 in./56.9 in. Overall Height: 68.2 in. Width: 68.0 in. Front/Rear Overhang: 28.2 in./36.0 in. Tailgate: Width and Height: 46.27 in. x 34.3 in. Approach/Departure Degrees: 29.3/24.7. Ground Clearance: Front axle: 6.34 in. Rear axle: 6.50 in. Load space: With rear seat installed: 21.0 in. x 21.2 in. x 41.9 in. With rear seat removed or folded: 53.2 in. x 21.2 in. 41.9 in. Maximum capacity: With rear seat folded: 64.9 cu. in. With rear seat up: 25.6 cu. ft.

CAPACITIES: Fuel Tank: 23.0 gal.

ACCOMMODATIONS: Seating Capacity: 5 passengers. Front headroom: 39.5 in. Rear headroom: 38.5 in. Front legroom: 42.4 in. Rear legroom: 35.2 in. Front shoulder room: 55.5 in. Rear shoulder room: 56.7 in. Front hip room: 54.8 in. Rear hip room: 44.1 in.

INSTRUMENTATION: Speedometer (mph-km/hr.-U.S.; km/hr.-mph.-Canada), Odometer (mile-U.S.; kilometer-Canada), Gauges for engine oil pressure, fuel level, engine coolant temperature, safety belt indicator light, 4x4 indicator light, brake indicator light, low range indicator light, emissions indicator light, check oil level indicator light and battery charge indicator light.

OPTIONS: The option code follows the option description. Automatic overdrive transmission (44T). Electric Shift Touch Drive (213). Standard rear axle with Traction-Lok. Optional rear axle ratios. P195/75R15SL steel radial All-Terrain black sidewall (T74/50E). P205/75R15SL off-road raised white letter (T77). P205/75R15SL steel radial All-Season raised white letters (T7M). Cloth 60/40 bench seat (L). XLT Trim Package (775). Includes the following features in addition to or in place of those in Standard trim-exterior: Deluxe wheel trim, chrome grille insert, accent tape stripe on body side and tailgate, low-mount swing-away mirrors and "XLT" nomenclature on front fender. Interior features consist of cloth and vinyl seat trim, additional insulation, additional quarter trim panel features (padded armrests, three storage compartments — one left side, two right side, one lockable), color-keyed cloth full door trim panels with color-keyed molding with bright insert on lower door trim panel, visor mirror, cargo area light, pivoting vent windows, Deluxe leather-wrapped steering wheel, headlights-on warning chime, courtesy lights for ashtray, floor box and engine compartment, electronic AM/FM stereo radio, "XLT" trim nomenclature, interval wipers, color-keyed instrument panel molding with bright surround, color-keyed flocking on glove box interior surface and glove box light, woodtone cluster applique and tachometer. Eddie Bauer (926B). Includes XLT trim, which must be ordered, speed control/tilt steering wheel, cast aluminum wheels, dual body side accent paint stripe, "Eddie Bauer" garment bag and six pocket gear bag (shipped direct to customer from Eddie Bauer. "Eddie Bauer" nomenclature, "Ford Care" extended service plan, AM/FM stereo radio and P205/74R15SL All-Terrain tires. Air conditioning (572). Floor console (604. Super cooling engine (624). Privacy glass (924). Engine block heater (41H). Bright low-mount Western swing-away exterior mirrors (547). Power window door lock group (962). Luggage rack (615). Flip-up/Open air roof (566). Snowplow Special Package (565). Includes heavy-duty front and rear shock absorbers, heavy-duty alternator, heavy-duty front springs with air bags and auxiliary oil cooler. The front spoiler is deleted. Outside swing-away spare tire carrier (51Q). Speed control/tilt steering wheel (554). Two-tone Deluxe paint (952). Cast aluminum wheels (646). White Sport wheels (647). Flip-open rear window (435). Rear window washer/defroster (913). Electronic AM/FM stereo radio (58F) Electronic AM/FM stereo radio with cassette player and clock (58G). Premium sound system (91A). Radio credit option (58Y). California emissions system (422). High altitude principle use (428). Sport Appearance Package. Includes brush/grille guard, fog lamps, contoured tubular rear bumper with matching stone deflector. Available for all trim levels. Mid body side tape stripe. Available for XL only. Sport tape stripe. Includes horizontal stripes at front of body side, rising past "B" pillar. Deluxe tape stripe. Deep-dish cast-aluminum wheels.

HISTORICAL FOOTNOTES: The 1988 Bronco II was launched on a strong sales surge illustrated by a 39 percent sales increase from 1981 through 1986.

1989 BRONCO II

A redesigned front-end gave the Bronco II a more aerodynamic and contemporary appearance for 1989. The new front end featured aero headlights with integral turn signals/parking lights, a new wraparound front bumper, a new hood with windsplits, a revised cowl top grille with air intake holes in place of the previously used slots and the use of all-new front end sheetmetal. The vent windows were deleted for the 1989 Bronco II. Two new grille inserts were used. A black format was included on the XL and a bright version was found on the XLT and Eddie Bauer.

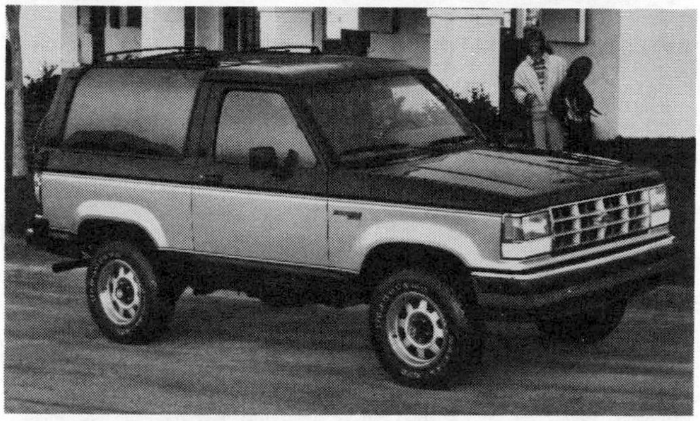

1989 Ford Bronco II XLT

The 1989 Bronco II interior was identified by its new steering column that featured a column shift for models with automatic transmission and a new stalk-mounted turn signal/windshield wiper/washer lever. A repositioned steering wheel located closer to the instrument panel was also used. The steering wheel was also of a new design similar to that used on the Aerostar. The instrument panel was reformated to include revised 1988-type F series mechanical cluster/gauges and improved dash sound absorber. The instrument panel also had a foam-in-place design for additional noise reduction, four new air vents and a new bottom close-out panel. Bronco II seating was redesigned with revised optional high-back Captain's Chair's for improved back support/driver position. New standard high-back bucket seats with a tip-and-slide mechanism were also introduced. The driver's side version of these seats was introduced after the September 7, 1988 debut of the1989 Bronco II. All seats had a new sew style. An AM/FM stereo radio with four speakers was now standard. Other 1989 interior features included: New molder headliner for improved fit/finish and sound insulation, upgraded floor deadener and hood liner on the XL for improved noise reduction, a floor-mounted rear compartment heat vent and new door trim panels. The interior color choices for 1989 were medium grey, crystal blue, scarlet red and light sandlewood. P205/75R15SL black sidewall tires with a new tread design that reduced both tire wear and tire noise were standard. Revised shock absorber valving intended to improve ride and handling was used along with a modified power steering valve to improve handling and steering effort. Added to the Bronco II option list were Sport bucket seats (identical to those available for the Ranger), a new floor console with integral armrest (included with Sport bucket seats and Captain's chairs) and Sport two-tone (available with Sport Appearance Package/XL Sport). This had been introduced in 1988 as a running change. All optional P195 black sidewall tires were deleted. Also no longer available was the Snowplow Special Package and the Power Convenience Group.

Exterior colors for 1989 include five new choices: Light sandlewood clearcoat metallic, light sandlewood, crystal blue clearcoat metallic, twilight blue clearcoat metallic and sandlewood clearcoat metallic. Carried over from 1988 were raven black, scarlet red, cabernet red, shadow grey clearcoat metallic, colonial white and silver clearcoat metallic. The Eddie Bauer Bronco II was offered in any of these colors: Raven black, scarlet red, cabernet red, hunter green clearcoat metallic, twilight blue clearcoat metallic and sandlewood clearcoat metallic.

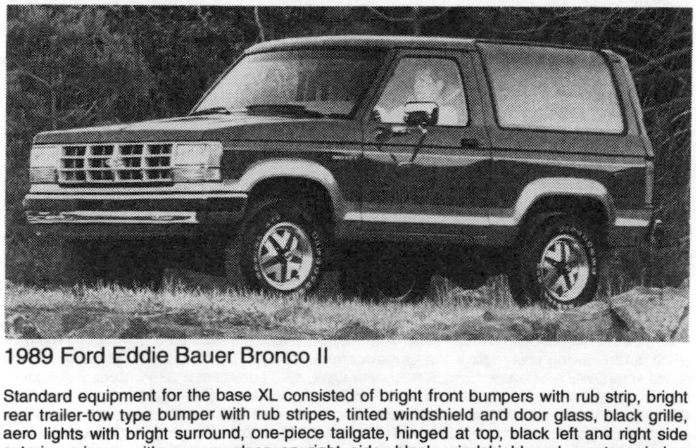

1989 Ford Eddie Bauer Bronco II

Standard equipment for the base XL consisted of bright front bumpers with rub strip, bright rear trailer-tow type bumper with rub stripes, tinted windshield and door glass, black grille, aero lights with bright surround, one-piece tailgate, hinged at top, black left and right side exterior mirrors with convex glass on right side, black windshield and quarter window moldings, blue "Ford" oval in center of grille and lower left hand portion of tailgate, bright "Bronco II" nomenclature on front fenders, black door handles and locks, black liftgate handle, Sport wheelcovers, wrapover rear quarter windows, padded color-keyed (door trim panels) armrests, rear padded color-keyed armrests integral with rear quarter panels with storage compartment, instrument panel and rear quarter trim panel ashtrays, safety belt and "headlights on" audible alert, cigarette lighter, color-keyed coat hooks — one at rear of quarter panel and two integral with rear seat grab handles, front and rear dome lights with left and right door courtesy switches, vinyl color-keyed full length door trim panels, color-keyed 16 oz. cut pile full length carpeting, glove box with lock, color-keyed grab handles at all seating positions except driver's side, color-keyed full length cloth headliner, heater/defroster with Hi/Low flow-through air ventilation, rear seat heat duct, inside hood release, dual-note horn, color-keyed instrument panel with four air registers, black instrument cluster applique, cluster warning lights, trip odometer, gauges for oil pressure, voltmeter, engine coolant temperature and fuel level, color-keyed plastic liftgate, windshield-mounted 9.625 in. day/night rearview mirror, color-keyed windshield pillars, color-keyed cowl side trim panels, color-keyed quarter trim panels with padded armrests and storage compartment on right rear panel, electronic AM/FM radio with digital clock and two speakers in door panels and two speakers in quarter trim panels, color-keyed lap/shoulder belts with tension eliminator, bright aluminum scuff plates on front doors; black plastic on liftgate, color-keyed reclining front bucket seats with tip-and-slide feature, rear split/folding rear seat (rear seat trim matches front seats), knitted-vinyl upholstery, color-keyed vinyl interior spare tire cover, black steering column and shroud, "A-frame" black steering wheel, color-keyed padded left and right side sun visors with clip band on driver's side and right side vanity mirror and interval windshield wipers.

I.D. DATA: The Bronco II V.I.N. consisted of seventeen symbols. The first three characters identified the manufacturer, make and type of vehicle. The fourth character (a letter) designated the GVW range. The fifth, sixth and seventh characters identified the series and body style. The eighth character identified the engine. The ninth character was the check digit. The tenth character (a letter) represented the model year. The eleventh character identified the assembly plant. The remaining digits represented the sequential production number.

Body Type	Factory Price	GVW	Shipping Weight	Prod. Total
Bronco				
Wagon II (U14)	$13,915	4040*	3317	—

* 4280, 4340 and 4400 lb.GVWR packages available.

STANDARD ENGINE: Engine Type: OHV, 60 degree V-6 cast iron head and engine block. Bore x Stroke: 3.66 in. x 2.83 in. Lifters: Hydraulic. Number of main bearings-4. Fuel Induction: Six port-mounted fuel injectors electronically triggered by EEC-IV module. Compression Ratio: 9.3:1. Displacement: 179 cu. in. (2.9 liters). Oil Refill: 5 qt. with filter change. 4 qt. without filter change. Horsepower: 140 @ 4600 rpm. Torque: 170 lb.-ft. @ 2600 rpm. Fuel Requirements: Regular Unleaded.

CHASSIS FEATURES: Separate body and frame. Full-length frame with rubber-isolated body. Single channel, 5 cross members, welded frame. 2.37 in. section modulus. Maximum side rail section: 6.08 in. x 2.26 in. x 0.130 in. Low carbon steel. Yield strength: 36,000 lb. Heavy-duty frame included with Snowplow Package: 2.89 in. section modulus. Maximum side rail section: 6.12 in. x 2.28 in. x 0.150 in. Low carbon steel. Yield strength: 36,000 lb.

SUSPENSION AND RUNNING GEAR: Front Suspension: Independent, coil springs, lateral arms, and leading arms on each side with stabilizer bar. 1970 lb. rating. Optional rating of 2120 and 2240 lb. available. Rear Suspension: Semi-elliptical 4-leaf springs with stabilizer bar, 2172 lb. rating. Optional rating of 2399 lb. available with 5-leaf springs. Front Axle Type and Capacity: Twin-Traction, beam, 2750 lb. rating. Rear Axle Type and Capacity: Ford semi-floating. 2640 lb. rating. Final Drive Ratio: Standard for 5-spd. manual trans.: 3.45:1. Standard for auto trans.: 3.73:1. Standard for High Altitude: Automatic trans.: 3.73:1. Manual trans.: 3.45:1. Standard for Calif. with manual trans.: 3.73:1. Standard for Calif. with auto. trans.: 3.73:1. Optional: Manual trans.: 49 states: 3.73:1 limited slip diff. Calif.: 4.10:1 limited slip diff. High Altitude: Manual trans.: 3.73:1 limited slip diff. Auto. trans.: 4.10:1 limited slip. Transfer Case: Type: Warner 1350 2-speed. Ratios: 2.48:1, 1.0:1. Brakes: Type: Hydraulic power-assisted, vented disc front and cast iron drum rear. Dimensions: Front: 10.86 in. dia. x 0.9 in. Floating Caliper. Total front swept area: 188.24 sq. in. Rear: 9.0 in. x 1.75 in. Total rear swept area: 98.96 sq. in. Wheels: 15 x 5.5JJ, 5-hole disc. Optional: 15 x 6.0JJ cast aluminum wheels, 15 x 6.0JJ White Sport wheels. Tires: P205/75R15SL steel radial All-Season black sidewall. Optional: P205/75R15SL steel radial All-Season raised white letters, P205/75R15SL steel radial All-Terrain. Raised white letters. Steering: Power assisted, recirculating ball. Ratio: 17:1, overall: 19.8:1, turns Lock-to-Lock: 4.1. Turning Circle: 34.42 ft. Optional: None. Transmission: Type: 5-speed manual overdrive. Synchromesh in all gears plus reverse. Mitsubishi. Transmission Ratios: 3.77, 2.21 1.52, 1.00, 0.81:1. Reverse: 3.40:1. Clutch: Segmented, woven, non-asbestos lining. Belleville pressure plate, 9 in. dia. Total plate pressure: 1320 lb. Optional: Type: Ford A4LD automatic overdrive. Ratios: 2.47, 1.47, 1.00, 0.75:1.

VEHICLE DIMENSIONS: Wheelbase: 94.0 in. Overall Length: 158.2 in. Front/Rear Tread 56.9 in./56.9 in. Overall Height: 68.2 in. Width: 68.0 in. Front/Rear Overhang: 28.2 in./36.0 in. Tailgate: Width and Height: 46.27 in. x 34.3 in. Approach/Departure Degrees: 29.3/24.7. Ground Clearance: Front axle: 6.34 in. Rear axle: 6.50 in. Load space: With rear seat installed: 21.0 in. x 21.2 in. x 41.9 in. With rear seat removed or folded: 53.2 in. x 21.2 in. 41.9 in. Maximum capacity: With rear seat folded: 64.9 cu. in. With rear seat up: 25.6 cu. ft.

CAPACITIES: Fuel Tank: 23.0 gal.

ACCOMMODATIONS: Seating Capacity: 5 passengers. Front headroom: 39.5 in. Rear headroom: 38.5 in. Front legroom: 42.4 in. Rear legroom: 35.2 in. Front shoulder room: 55.5 in. Rear shoulder room: 56.7 in. Front hip room: 54.8 in. Rear hip room: 44.1 in.

INSTRUMENTATION: Speedometer (mph-km/hr.-U.S.; km/hr.-mph.-Canada), Odometer (mile-U.S.; kilometer-Canada), Gauges for engine oil pressure, fuel level, engine coolant temperature, safety belt indicator light, 4x4 indicator light, brake indicator light, low range indicator light, emissions indicator light, check oil level indicator light and battery charge indicator light.

OPTIONS AND PRICES: Air conditioning (572). Super cooling engine (624). Privacy glass (924). Engine block heater (41H). Manual locking front hubs credit (21M). Light Group (593). Bright low-mount Western swing-away mirrors (545). Power Window/Lock Group (903). Luggage rack (615). Swing-away spare tire carrier/cargo carrier (51Q). Speed control/tilt steering wheel (554). Black Sport Appearance Package (563). Includes brush/grille guard, fog lights, spats/lower camber moldings, tubular rear bumper, rear stone deflector, all black grille and surround and black bumper without rubstrip. Sport tape stripe (85H). Deluxe two-tone paint (952). Two-tone paint Deluxe deleted. Deep-dish cast aluminum wheels (649). Cast aluminum wheels (646). Deluxe wheel trim (642). Rear window wiper/washer/defroster (913). Electronic AM/FM stereo radio with cassette player and digital clock (586). Electronic premium AM/FM stereo radio with cassette player and digital clock (587). Radio credit option (58Y). Automatic overdrive transmission (44T). Limited slip performance rear axle (XAB). California emissions system (422). Tires: P205/75R15SL steel radial OWL All-Season (T72). P205/75R15SL steel radial OWL All-Terrain (T73). XL Seat and Trim: Cloth Captain's chairs with floor console (8). Cloth Sport bucket seats with power lumbar support and floor console (72). Cloth 60/40 split bench seat (4). XLT seat and trim: Cloth Sport bucket seats with power lumbar support and floor console (7). Cloth 60/40 split bench seat. Preferred Equipment Package Prices: XL Sport (922A). Includes Sport Appearance Package, special two-tone paint treatment, deep-dish aluminum wheels, flip-open rear window, tachometer and headlights-on warning chime. XLT with free air conditioning (923A). Includes, in addition to base XL model features, tachometer, leather-wrapped steering wheel, cloth trimmed reclining front Captain's chairs, 50/50 reclining rear seats, lower section carpeted door trim with map pocket, headlight-on reminder chime, Deluxe wheel trim, bright grille insert and headlight moldings and protective body side moldings. Eddie Bauer with free air conditioning plus (932A). Includes or replaces all XLT equipment plus unique two-tone paint treatment with dual accent stripes, P205 outlined white letter All-Season tires, cast aluminum wheels, privacy glass rear quarter windows, bright low-mount Western swing-away mirrors, outside swing-away spare tire carrier with cover, premium cloth reclining Captain's chairs with power limbar supports, electronic premium AM/FM stereo radio with cassette plater, digital clock and four speakers, speed control and adjustable tilt steering wheel, rear window wiper/washer/defroster and Eddie Bauer two-piece luggage set (shipped directly from Eddie Bauer). Manual transmission Special Value Package (920A). Special Value Package (922A). Special Value Package (923A). Special Value Package (931A).

HISTORICAL FOOTNOTES: The 1989 Bronco II was introduced on September 7, 1988.

1990 BRONCO II

1990 Ford Bronco II XL

There were no Bronco II powertrain or exterior changes for 1990. Interior changes involved the use of color-keyed instrument panel appliques (in place of woodgrain) on XLT and Eddie Bauer models. No changes were made in either the interior or exterior color choices. Several functional changes were noteworthy. A 3.73:1 limited slip axle was made optional for the A4LD transmission (replacing the old optional 4.10:1 limited slip). The EFI system on the 2.9 V-6 for California delivery was improved by the incorporation of a Data Communications Link. This allowed engine functions to be monitored through a computerized diagnostic system (late availability). Canadian vehicles were equipped with running lights. All Bronco II horns had a more throaty sound (late availability). Steering revisions were made for improved tire wear and steering control (late availability). The air conditioning compressor and mounting were redesigned. Also found on the 1990 model were improved callouts and labeling for engine service points.

Except for the splitting of the Sport Appearance Package into a Sport Molding Package and a Sport Appearance Package, there were no option changes for 1990.

1990 Ford Eddie Bauer Bronco II

Standard equipment for the base Bronco II XL consisted of bright front bumpers with rub strip, bright rear trailer-tow type bumper with rub stripes, tinted windshield and door glass, black grille, aero lights with bright surround, one-piece tailgate, hinged at top, black left and right side exterior mirrors with convex glass on right side, black windshield and quarter window moldings, Blue "Ford" oval in center of grille and lower left hand portion of tailgate, bright "Bronco II" nomenclature on front fenders, black door handles and locks, black liftgate handle, Sport wheelcovers, wrapover rear quarter windows, padded color-keyed (door trim panels) armrests, rear padded color-keyed armrests integral with rear quarter panels with storage compartment, instrument panel and rear quarter trim panel ashtrays, safety belt and "headlights-on" audible alert, cigarette lighter, color-keyed coat hooks — one at rear of quarter panel and two integral with rear seat grab handles, front and rear dome lights with left and right door courtesy switches, vinyl color-keyed full length door trim panels, color-keyed 16 oz. cut pile full length carpeting, glove box with lock, color-keyed grab handles at all seating positions except driver's side, color-keyed full length cloth headliner, heater/defroster with Hi/Low flow-through air ventilation, rear seat heat duct, inside hood release, dual-note horn, color-keyed instrument panel with four air registers, black instrument cluster applique, cluster warning lights, trip odometer, gauges for oil pressure, voltmeter, engine coolant temperature and fuel level, color-keyed plastic liftgate, windshield-mounted 9.625 in. day-night rearview mirror, color-keyed windshield pillars, color-keyed cowl side trim panels, color-keyed quarter trim panels with padded armrests and storage compartment on right rear panel, electronic

AM/FM adio with digital clock and two speakers in door panels and two speakers in quarter trim panels, color-keyed lap/shoulder belts with tension eliminator, bright aluminum scuff plates on front doors; black plastic on liftgate, color-keyed reclining front bucket seats with tip-and-slide feature, rear split/folding rear seat (rear seat trim matches front seats), knitted-vinyl upholstery, color-keyed vinyl interior spare tire cover, black steering column and shroud, "A-frame" black steering wheel, color-keyed paded left and right side sun visors with clip band on driver's side and right side vanity mirror and interval windshield wipers.

1990 Ford Bronco II XLT with optional sandlwood Sport tape stripe

I.D. DATA: The Bronco II V.I.N. consisted of seventeen symbols. The first three characters identified the manufacturer, make and type of vehicle. The fourth character (a letter) designated the GVW range. The fifth, sixth and seventh characters identified the series and body style. The eight character identified the engine. The ninth character was the check digit. The tenth character (a letter) represented the model year. The eleventh character identified the assembly plant. The remaining digits represented the sequential production number.

Body Type	Factory Price	GVW	Shipping Weight	Prod. Total
Bronco				
Wagon II (U14)	$13,915	4040*	3317	

* 4280, 4340 and 4400 lb. GVWR packages available.

STANDARD ENGINE: Engine Type: OHV, 60 degree V-6 cast iron head and engine block. Bore x Stroke: 3.66 in. x 2.83 in. Lifters: Hydraulic. Number of main bearings-4. Fuel Induction: Six port-mounted fuel injectors electronically triggered by EEC-IV module. Compression Ratio: 9.3:1. Displacement: 179 cu. in. (2.9 liters). Oil Refill: 5 qt.with filter change. 4 qt. without filter change. Horsepower: 140 @ 4600 rpm. Torque: 170 lb.-ft. @ 2600 rpm. Fuel Requirements: Regular Unleaded.

CHASSIS FEATURES: Separate body and frame. Full-length frame with rubber-isolated body. Single channel, 5 cross members, welded frame. 2.37 in. section modulus. Maximum side rail section: 6.08 in. x 2.26 in. x 0.130 in. Low carbon steel. Yield strength: 36,000 lb. Heavy-duty frame included with Snowplow Package: 2.89 in. section modulus. Maximum side rail section: 6.12 in. x 2.28 in. x 0.150 in. Low carbon steel. Yield strength: 36,000 lb.

SUSPENSION AND RUNNING GEAR: Front Suspension: Independent, coil springs, lateral arms, and leading arms on each side with stabilizer bar. 1970 lb. rating. Optional rating of 2120 and 2240 lb. available. Rear Suspension: Semi-elliptical 4-leaf springs with stabilizer bar, 2172 lb. rating. Optional rating of 2399 lb.available with 5-leaf springs. Front Axle Type and Capacity: Twin-Traction, beam, 2750 lb. rating. Rear Axle Type and Capacity: Ford semi-floating. 2640 lb. rating. Final Drive Ratio: Standard for 5-spd. manual trans.: 3.45:1. Standard for auto trans.: 3.73:1. Standard for High Altitude: Automatic trans.: 3.73:1. Manual trans.: 3.45:1. Standard for Calif. with manual trans.: 3.73:1. Standard for Calif. with auto. trans.: 3.73:1. Optional: Manual trans.: 49 states: 3.73:1 limited slip diff. Calif.: 4.10:1 limited slip diff. High Altitude: Manual trans.: 3.73:1 limited slip diff. Auto. trans.: 3.73:1 limited slip. Transfer Case: Type: Warner 1350 2-speed. Ratios: 2.48:1, 1.0:1. Brakes: Type: Hydraulic power-assisted, vented disc front and cast iron drum rear. Dimensions: Front: 10.86 in. dia. x 0.9 in. Floating Caliper. Total front swept area: 188.24 sq. in. Rear: 9.0 in. x 1.75 in. Total rear swept area: 98.96 sq. in. Wheels: 15 x 5.5JJ, 5-hole disc. Optional: 15 x 6.0JJ cast aluminum wheels, 15 x 6.0JJ white Sport wheels. Tires: P205/75R15SL steel radial All-Season black sidewall. Optional: P205/75R15SL steel radial All-Season. Raised white letters, P205/75R15SL steel radial All-Terrain. Raised white letters. Steering: Power assisted, recirculating ball. Ratio: 17:1, overall: 19.8:1, turns Lock-to-Lock: 4.1. Turning Circle: 34.42 ft. Optional: None. Transmission: Type: 5-speed manual overdrive. Synchromesh in all gears plus reverse. Mitsubishi. Transmission Ratios: 3.77, 2.21, 1.52, 1.00, 0.81:1. Reverse: 3.40:1. Clutch: Segmented, woven, non-asbestos lining. Belleville pressure plate, 9 in. dia. Total plate pressure: 1320 lb. Optional: Type: Ford A4LD automatic overdrive. Ratios: 2.47, 1.47, 1.00, 0.75:1

VEHICLE DIMENSIONS: Wheelbase: 94.0 in. Overall Length: 158.2 in. Front/Rear Tread 56.9 in./56.9 in. Overall Height: 68.2 in. Width: 68.0 in. Front/Rear Overhang: 28.2 in./36.0 in. Tailgate: Width and Height: 46.27 in. x 34.3 in. Approach/Departure Degrees: 29.3/24.7. Ground Clearance: Front axle: 6.34 in. Rear axle: 6.50 in. Load space: With rear seat installed: 21.0 in. x 21.2 in. x 41.9 in. With rear seat removed or folded: 53.2 in. x 21.2 in. 41.9 in. Maximum capacity: With rear seat folded: 64.9 cu. in. With rear seat up: 25.6 cu. ft.

CAPACITIES: Fuel Tank: 23.0 gal.

ACCOMMODATIONS: Seating Capacity: 5 passengers. Front headroom: 39.5 in. Rear headroom: 38.5 in. Front legroom: 42.4 in. Rear legroom: 35.2 in. Front shoulder room: 55.5 in. Rear shoulder room: 56.7 in. Front hip room: 54.8 in. Rear hip room: 44.1 in.

INSTRUMENTATION: Speedometer (mph-km/hr.-U.S.; km/h.r-mph.-Canada), Odometer (mile-U.S.; kilometer-Canada), Gauges for engine oil pressure, fuel level, engine coolant temperature, safety belt indicator light, 4X4 indicator light, brake indicator light, low range indicator light, emissions indicator light, check oil level indicator light and battery charge indicator light.

OPTIONS AND PRICES: Air conditioning (572): $768. Super cooling engine (624): $57. Privacy glass (924): $170. Engine block heater (41H): $33. Manual locking front hubs credit (21M): -$121. Light Group (593): $29. Bright low-mount Western swing-away mirrors (545): $87. Power Window/Lock Group (903): With XL trim: $485; with XLT trim: $344. Luggage rack (615): $126. Swing-away spare tire carrier/cargo carrier (51Q): With BSW All-Season tires: $328; with OWL All-Season tires:$348; with OWL All-Terrain tires: $365. Speed control/tilt steering wheel (554): $312. Black Sport Appearance Package (563): $695; with Sport Trim Package: 389. Bright Alloy Sport Appearance Package (562): $899. Sport Trim Package (564): $824.Sport tape stripe (85H): with XL trim: $159; with XLT trim: $48. Deluxe two-tone paint (952): with XL trim: $241; with XLT trim: $130. Two-tone paint Deluxe deleted: -$68. Deep-dish cast aluminum wheels (649): with Package 920: $326; with Special Value Package or XL trim: $224. Cast aluminum wheels (646): with Package 920: $326; with Package 922:

No charge; with Special Value Package or XLT trim: $224. Deluxe whel trim (642): $110. Rear window wiper/washer/defroster (913): $226. Electronic AM/FM stereo radio with cassette player and digital clock (586): $100. Electronic premium AM/FM stereo radio with cassette player and digital clock (587): with Special Value Package: $121; with all other packages: $221. Radio credit option (58Y): -$61. Automatic overdrive transmission (44T): $957. Limited slip performance rear axle (XAB): $267. California emissions system (422): $100. Tires: P205/75R15SL steel radial OWL All-Season (T72): $96. P205/75R15SL steel radial OWL All-Terrain (T73): $128 (with Special Value Packages and Package 932). All others: $199. XL seat and trim: Cloth Captain's chairs with floor console (8): 274. Cloth Sport bucket seats with power lumbar support and floor console (7): $702. Cloth 60/40 split bench seat (4): $232. XLT seat and trim: Cloth Sport bucket seats with power lumbar support and floor console (7): $450. Cloth 60/40 split bench seat: No charge. Preferred Equipment Package Prices: XL Sport (922A). Includes unique two-tone paint scheme, deep-dish aluminum wheels and Sport Trim Package: $799. XLT with free air conditioning (923A): Includes, in addition to base XL model features, tachometer, leather-wrapped steering wheel, cloth trimmed reclining front Captain's chairs, 50/50 reclining rear seats, lower section carpeted door trim with map pocket, headlight-on reminder chime, Deluxe wheel trim, bright grille insert and headlight moldings and protective body side moldings: $640. Eddie Bauer with free air conditioning plus (932A). Includes or replaces all XLT equipment plus unique two-tone paint treatment with dual accent stripes, P205 outlined white letter All-Season tires, cast aluminum wheels, privacy glass rear quarter windows, bright low-mount Western swing-away mirrors, outside swing-away spare tire carrier with cover, premium cloth reclining Captain's chairs with power limbar supports, electronic premium AM/FM stereo radio with cassette player, digital clock and four speakers, speed control and adjustable tilt steering wheel, rear window wiper/washer/defroster and Eddie Bauer two-piece luggage set (shipped directly from Eddie Bauer): $3,001. Manual Transmission Special Value Package (920A): No charge. Special Value Package (922A): $799. Special Value Package (923A): $641. Special Value Package (931A): $993.

HISTORICAL FOOTNOTES: Job #1 for the 1990 Bronco II was August, 1989. Its introduction took place in October, 1989. In January the last Bronco II moved off the assembly line. The following month the Bronco II was replaced in the Ford truck line by the new Explorer, which was code-named UN-46.

FORD TEMPO

1987-1991

1987 TEMPO

The Ford Tempo was first introduced in May, 1983 as a 1984 model. Mid-way through the 1987 model year a new All-Wheel-Drive model was offered. In the years from its debut until the availability of four-wheel drive, the Tempo experienced numerous evolutionary changes. In the 1985 model year a performance-oriented Tempo Sport GL model was introduced; the 2.3 liter engines offered for the Tempo received EFI and a 5-speed manual transmission was made standard. Significant styling revisions, including the use of aero-design halogen headlights took place for the 1986 model run. Also for 1986, the tires and wheels were upgraded to 14 inches and gas-pressurized struts were made standard for the LX series. For 1987 the All-Wheel -Drive tempo was powered by a 2.3 liter high specific output (HSO) engine with electric fuel injection combined with an automatic transaxle with a fluid link converter. The Tempo All-Wheel-Drive was an On-Demand system. Power was normally supplied to the front wheels only. The All-Wheel-Drive mode was obtained by flipping a rocker switch located in the overhead map light console to the ON position. An indicator light operated when the car was in its All-Wheel-Drive mode. Ford emphasized that the Tempo All-Wheel-Drive was not "designed to take you off-road." The Tempo All-Wheel-Drive was offered in both two-door and four-door form.

I.D. DATA: The Tempo V.I.N. consisted of seventeen symbols. The first three characters identified the manufacturer, make and type of vehicle. The fourth identified the restraint system. The next three entries identified the series and body type. The eighth character identified the engine. The ninth character was the check digit. The tenth (the letter H) identified the model year. The eleventh character identified the assembly plant. The final six digits were the production sequence number.

Body Type	Factory Price	Shipping Weight	Prod. Total
Tempo			
2-door sedan, Model 34	$9984	2667	—
4-door sedan, Model 39	$10,138	2770	—

STANDARD ENGINE: Engine Type: OHV In-line 4-cyl. Cast-iron block and cylinder heads. Bore x Stroke: 3.7 in. x 3.3 in. Lifters: Hydraulic. Fuel induction: Multi-port fuel injection. Compression Ratio: 9.0:1. Displacement: 141 cu. in. (2.3 liters). Horsepower: 94 @ 4000 rpm. Torque 126 lb. ft. @ 3200 rpm. Fuel Requirements: Unleaded.

CHASSIS FEATURES: Unitized body.

SUSPENSION AND RUNNING GEAR: Front Suspension: Independent, MacPherson strut with strut-mounted coil springs, forged lower control arm and cast steering knuckle; hydraulic shock absorbers integral with MacPherson strut. Stabilizer bar diameter: 1.1 in. Rear Suspension: Parallel four-bar, fully independent MacPherson strut with coil spring offset on shock absorber strut, parallel suspension arms and tie bar; hydraulic shock absorbers integral with MacPherson strut. Final Drive Ratio: 3.09:1. Transfer Case: Dana part time power take-off at front driveshaft. 1.00:1 ratio. Brakes: Type: Hydraulic power-assisted, vented disc front and cast iron drum rear. Dimensions: Front: 9.2 in. dia. Rear: 8.0 in. dia. Total brake swept area: 217.2 sq. in. Wheels: Polycast 14 in. x 5.5 in. Tires: P185/70R x 14 black sidewall All-Season steel radial. Optional: P185/75R x 14 white sidewall All-Season steel radial. Steering: Rack and pinion, power assisted. Ratio: 18.3:1, turns Lock-to-Lock: 3.04. Turning Circle: 39.9 ft. Optional: None. Transmission: Three-speed automatic.

VEHICLE DIMENSIONS: Wheelbase: 99.9 in. Overall Length: 176.5 in. Front/Rear Tread 54.9 in./54.9 in. Overall Height: Two-door: 52.7 in.; Four-door: 52.8 in. Width: Two-door: 68.3 in.; Four-door: 66.8 in. Ground Clearance: 5.5 in.

CAPACITIES: Fuel Tank: 15.4 gal.

ACCOMMODATIONS: Seating Capacity: 5 passengers. Headroom: Front: 37.5 in., Rear: 36.8 in. (two-door); 36.9 in. (four-door). Shoulder room: Front: 53.9 in., Rear: 54.0 in. (two-door); 53.3 in. (four-door). Hip room: Front: 48.8 in., Rear: 51.8 in. (two-door); 51.0 in. (four-door). Legroom: Front: 41.5 in., Rear: 36.0 in. (two-door); 36.0 in. (four-door).

INSTRUMENTATION: Speedometer, odometer, fuel level gauge, warning lights for engine coolant temperature, oil pressure and battery charge.

OPTIONS AND PRICES: White sidewall tires. Clearcoat paint. Deck lid luggage rack. Rear window defroster. AM/FM radio with cassette tape player. Tilt steering wheel. Power side windows. Power Lock Group. Air conditioning: $773.

HISTORICAL FOOTNOTES: Ford reported that "Ford engineers took the road handling ability of the front-wheel-drive Tempo one step further for 1987, developing an All-Wheel-Drive model (AWD), to enhance Tempo's traction."

1988 TEMPO

The 1988 Tempo had a new grille and grille opening panel with aero headlights, parking lamps and sidemarkers. The four-door Tempo, the only AWD model offered for 1988, had new fenders, quarter panels, doors, roof and deck lid, as well as new quarter window glass and backlight.

The 1988 Tempo's interior was updated with a new ergonomically-designed instrument panel. New features included backlit cluster lighting, an engine coolant temperature gauge, pod-mounted rotary windshield wiper switch and rotary climate control fan switch. Other interior changes for 1988 included new seat, door and cowl side trim, consolette and standard AM/FM stereo radio with integral clock. Also standard on all 1988 Tempos was a motorized passive restraint system (a two-point motorized shoulder harness with an active seat belt), including knee bolsters. As in 1987, a supplemental driver's side air bag was also available. The standard exterior colors for 1988 were black, light grey, spinmaker blue, sand beige, Oxford white and scarlet red. Available at extra cost were these Cclearcoat metallic colors: Medium red, light sandalwood, twilight blue, dark shadow blue, silver and graphic. The Tempo interior was offered in regatta blue, scarlet red, medium grey and sand beige.

1988 Ford Tempo All-Wheel-Drive

I.D. DATA: The Tempo V.I.N. consisted of seventeen symbols. The first three characters identified the manufacturer, make and type of vehicle. The fourth identified the restraint system. The next three entries identified the series and body type. The eighth character identified the engine. The ninth character was the check digit. The tenth (the letter J) identified the model year. The eleventh character identified the assembly plant. The final six digits were the production sequence number.

Body Type	Factory Price	Shipping Weight	Prod. Total
Tempo			
4-door sedan, Model 39	$10,413	2799	—

STANDARD ENGINE: Engine Type: OHV In-line 4-cyl. Cast-iron block and cylinder heads. Bore x Stroke: 3.7 in. x 3.3 in. Lifters: Hydraulic. Fuel induction: Multi-port fuel injection. Compression Ratio: 9.0:1. Displacement: 141 cu. in. (2.3 liters). Horsepower: 94 @ 4000 rpm. Torque 126 lb. ft. @ 3200 rpm. Fuel Requirements: Unleaded.

CHASSIS FEATURES: Unitized body.

SUSPENSION AND RUNNING GEAR: Front Suspension: Independent, MacPherson strut with strut-mounted coil springs, forged lower control arm and cast steering knuckle; hydraulic shock absorbers integral with MacPherson strut. Stabilizer bar diameter: 1.1 in. Rear Suspension: Parallel four-bar, fully independent MacPherson strut with coil spring offset on shock absorber strut, parallel suspension arms and tie bar; hydraulic shock absorbers integral with MacPherson strut. Final Drive Ratio: 3.09:1. Transfer Case: Dana part time power take-off at front driveshaft. 1.00:1 ratio. Brakes: Type: Hydraulic power-assisted, vented disc front and cast iron drum rear. Dimensions: Front: 9.2 in. dia. Rear: 8.0 in. dia. Total brake swept area: 217.2 sq. in. Wheels: Polycast 14 in. x 5.5 in. Tires: P185/70R x 14 black sidewall All-season steel radial. Optional: P185/75R x 14 white sidewall All-Season steel radial. Steering: Rack and pinion, power assisted. Ratio: 18.3:1, turns Lock-to-Lock: 3.04. Turning Circle: 39.9 ft. Optional: None. Transmission: Type: Three-speed automatic.

VEHICLE DIMENSIONS: Wheelbase: 99.9 in. Overall Length: 176.5 in. Front/Rear Tread 54.9 in./54.9 in. Overall Height: 52.8 in. Width: 66.8 in. Ground Clearance: 5.5 in.

CAPACITIES: Fuel Tank: 15.4 gal.

ACCOMMODATIONS: Seating Capacity: 5 passengers. Headroom: Front: 37.5 in., Rear: 36.9 in. Shoulder room: Front: 53.9 in., Rear: 53.3 in. Hip room: Front: 48.8 in., Rear: 51.0 in. Legroom: Front: 41.5 in., Rear: 36.0 in.

INSTRUMENTATION: Speedometer, odometer, fuel level gauge, warning lights for engine coolant temperature, oil pressure and battery charge.

OPTIONS: White sidewall tires. Clearcoat paint. Deck lid luggage rack. Rear window defroster. AM/FM radio with cassette tape player. Tilt steering wheel. Power side windows: $296. Power Lock Group. Air conditioning

HISTORICAL FOOTNOTES: The Tempo continued to be the only AWD vehicle offered in its class.

1989 TEMPO

New for 1989 was a standard fold-down front-center armrest and a luggage compartment tie-down feature to help keep luggage in place.

I.D. DATA: The Tempo V.I.N. consisted of seventeen symbols. The first three characters identified the manufacturer, make and type of vehicle. The fourth identified the restraint system. The next three entries identified the series and body type. The eighth character identified the engine. The ninth character was the check digit. The tenth (the letter K) identified the model year. The eleventh character identified the assembly plant. The final six digits served as the production sequence number.

Body Type	Factory Price	Shipping Weight	Prod. Total
Tempo			
4-door sedan, Model 39	$10,860	2787	—

STANDARD ENGINE: Engine Type: OHV In-line 4-cyl. Cast-iron block and cylinder heads. Bore x Stroke: 3.7 in. x 3.3 in. Lifters: Hydraulic. Fuel induction: Multi-port fuel injection. Compression Ratio: 9.0:1. Displacement: 141 cu. in. (2.3 liters). Horsepower: 94 @ 4000 rpm. Torque 126 lb. ft. @ 3200 rpm. Fuel Requirements: Unleaded.

CHASSIS FEATURES: Unitized body.

SUSPENSION AND RUNNING GEAR: Front Suspension: Independent, MacPherson strut with strut-mounted coil springs, forged lower control arm and cast steering knuckle; hydraulic shock absorbers integral with MacPherson strut. Stabilizer bar diameter: 1.1 in. Rear Suspension: Parallel four-bar, fully independent MacPherson strut with coil spring offset on shock absorber strut, parallel suspension arms and tie bar; hydraulic shock absorbers integral with MacPherson strut. Final Drive Ratio: 3.09:1. Transfer Case: Dana part time power take-off at front driveshaft. 1.00:1 ratio. Brakes: Type: Hydraulic power-assisted, vented disc front and cast iron drum rear. Dimensions: Front: 9.2 in. dia. Rear: 8.0 in. dia. Total brake swept area: 217.2 sq. in. Wheels: Polycast 14 in. x 5.5 in. Tires: P185/70R x 14 black sidewall All-season steel radial. Optional: P185/75R x 14 white sidewall All-Season steel radial. Steering: Rack and pinion, power assisted. Ratio: 18.3:1, turns Lock-to-Lock: 3.04. Turning Circle: 39.9 ft. Optional: None. Transmission: Type: Three-speed automatic.

VEHICLE DIMENSIONS: Wheelbase: 99.9 in. Overall Length: 176.5 in. Front/Rear Tread 54.9 in./54.9 in. Overall Height: 52.8 in. Width: 66.8 in. Ground Clearance: 5.5 in.

CAPACITIES: Fuel Tank: 15.4 gal.

ACCOMMODATIONS: Seating Capacity: 5 passengers. Headroom: Front: 37.5 in., Rear: 36.9 in. Shoulder room: Front: 53.9 in., Rear: 53.3 in. Hip room: Front: 48.8 in., Rear: 51.0 in. Legroom: Front: 41.5 in., Rear: 36.0 in.

INSTRUMENTATION: Speedometer, odometer, fuel level gauge, warning lights for engine coolant temperature, oil pressure and battery charge.

OPTIONS AND PRICES: White sidewall tires. Clearcoat paint. Deck lid luggage rack. Rear window defroster. AM/FM radio with cassette tape player. Tilt steering wheel. Power side windows. Power Lock Group. Air conditioning: $807

HISTORICAL FOOTNOTES: The 1989 Tempo was introduced on August 24, 1988.

1990 TEMPO

The 1990 Tempo was identified by its revised polycast wheel appearance and AWD decals positioned on the fender sides. Some 1989 models also had the latter feature as it was introduced as a 1989-1/2 update. Interior and functional changes were more extensive. A manual rear lap/shoulder restraint system was added for the outboard seating positions. A single lever emergency passive belt release replaced the dual levers. Front and rear floor mats were added as standard equipment. Also debuting as a new standard feature was footwell illumination and a luggage compartment light.

I.D. DATA: The Tempo V.I.N. consisted of seventeen symbols. The first three characters identified the manufacturer, make and type of vehicle. The fourth identified the restraint system. The next three entries identified the series and body type. The eighth character identified the engine. The ninth character was the check digit. The tenth (the letter L) identified the model year. The eleventh character identified the assembly plant. The final six digits were the production sequence number.

Body Type	Factory Price	Shipping Weight	Prod. Total
Tempo			
4-door sedan, Model 39	$11,331	2808	—

STANDARD ENGINE: Engine Type: OHV In-line 4-cyl. Cast-iron block and cylinder heads. Bore x Stroke: 3.7 in. x 3.3 in. Lifters: Hydraulic. Fuel induction: Multi-port fuel injection. Compression Ratio: 9.0:1. Displacement: 141 cu. in. (2.3 liters). Horsepower: 100 @ 4400 rpm. Torque 130 lb. ft. @ 2600 rpm. Fuel Requirements: Unleaded.

CHASSIS FEATURES: Unitized body.

SUSPENSION AND RUNNING GEAR: Front Suspension: Independent, MacPherson strut with strut-mounted coil springs, forged lower control arm and cast steering knuckle; hydraulic shock absorbers integral with MacPherson strut. Stabilizer bar diameter: 1.1 in. Rear Suspension: Parallel four-bar, fully independent MacPherson strut with coil spring offset on shock absorber strut, parallel suspension arms and tie bar; hydraulic shock absorbers integral with MacPherson strut. Final Drive Ratio: 3.09:1. Transfer Case: Dana part time power take-off at front driveshaft. 1.00:1 ratio. Brakes: Type: Hydraulic power-assisted, vented disc front and cast iron drum rear. Dimensions: Front: 9.2 in. dia. Rear: 8.0 in. dia. Total brake swept area: 217.2 sq. in. Wheels: Polycast 14 in. x 5.5 in. Tires: P185/70R x 14 black sidewall All-season steel radial. Optional: P185/75R x 14 white sidewall All-Season steel radial. Steering: Rack and pinion, power assisted. Ratio: 18.3:1, turns Lock-to-Lock: 3.04. Turning Circle: 39.9 ft. Optional: None. Transmission: Type: Three-speed automatic.

VEHICLE DIMENSIONS: Wheelbase: 99.9 in. Overall Length: 176.5 in. Front/Rear Tread 54.9 in./54.9 in. Overall Height: 52.8 in. Width: 66.8 in. Ground Clearance: 5.5 in.

CAPACITIES: Fuel Tank: 15.4 gal.

ACCOMMODATIONS: Seating Capacity: 5 passengers. Headroom: Front: 37.5 in., Rear: 36.9 in. Shoulder room: Front: 53.9 in., Rear: 53.3 in. Hip room: Front: 48.8 in., Rear: 51.0 in. Legroom: Front: 41.5 in., Rear: 36.0 in.

INSTRUMENTATION: Speedometer, odometer, fuel level gauge, warning lights for engine coolant temperature, oil pressure and battery charge.

OPTIONS AND PRICES: White sidewall tires. Clearcoat paint. Deck lid luggage rack. Rear window defroster. AM/FM radio with cassette tape player. Tilt steering wheel. Power side windows: $306. Power Lock Group. Air conditioning: $807. Power seat: $280.

HISTORICAL FOOTNOTES: The 1990 Tempo was introduced on September 15, 1989.

1991 TEMPO

Changes for 1991 were extremely limited. A four-wheel-drive nomenclature replaced All-Wheel-Drive. Minor improvements were also made in the Tempo's Noise, Vibration and Harshness (NVH).

I.D. DATA: The Tempo V.I.N. consisted of seventeen symbols. The first three characters identified the manufacturer, make and type of vehicle. The fourth identified the restraint system. The next three entries identified the series and body type. The eighth character identified the engine. The ninth character was the check digit. The tenth (the letter M) identified the model year. The eleventh character identified the assembly plant. The final six digits were the production sequence number.

Body Type	Factory Price	Shipping Weight	Prod. Total
Tempo			
4-door sedan, Model 39	$11,436	2808	—

STANDARD ENGINE: Engine Type: OHV In-line 4-cyl. Cast-iron block and cylinder heads. Bore x Stroke: 3.7 in. x 3.3 in. Lifters: Hydraulic. Fuel induction: Multi-port fuel injection. Compression Ratio: 9.0:1. Displacement: 141 cu. in. (2.3 liters). Horsepower: 100 @ 4400 rpm. Torque 130 lb. ft. @ 2600 rpm. Fuel Requirements: Unleaded.

CHASSIS FEATURES: Unitized body.

SUSPENSION AND RUNNING GEAR: Front Suspension: Independent, MacPherson strut with strut-mounted coil springs, forged lower control arm and cast steering knuckle; hydraulic shock absorbers integral with MacPherson strut. Stabilizer bar diameter: 1.1 in. Rear Suspension: Parallel four-bar, fully independent MacPherson strut with coil spring offset on shock absorber strut, parallel suspension arms and tie bar; hydraulic shock absorbers integral with MacPherson strut. Final Drive Ratio: 3.09:1. Transfer Case: Dana part time power take-off at front driveshaft. 1.00:1 ratio. Brakes: Type: Hydraulic power-assisted, vented disc front and cast iron drum rear. Dimensions: Front: 9.2 in. dia. Rear: 8.0 in. dia. Total brake swept area: 217.2 sq. in. Wheels: Polycast 14 in. x 5.5 in. Tires: P185/70R x 14 black sidewall All-season steel radial. Optional: P185/75R x 14 white sidewall All-Season steel radial. Steering: Rack and pinion, power assisted. Ratio: 18.3:1, turns Lock-to-Lock: 3.04. Turning Circle: 39.9 ft. Optional: None. Transmission: Type: Three-speed automatic.

VEHICLE DIMENSIONS: Wheelbase: 99.9 in. Overall Length: 176.5 in. Front/Rear Tread 54.9 in./54.9 in. Overall Height: 52.8 in. Width: 66.8 in. Ground Clearance: 5.5 in.

CAPACITIES: Fuel Tank: 15.4 gal.

ACCOMMODATIONS: Seating Capacity: 5 passengers. Headroom: Front: 37.5 in., Rear: 36.9 in. Shoulder room: Front: 53.9 in., Rear: 53.3 in. Hip room: Front: 48.8 in., Rear: 51.0 in. Legroom: Front: 41.5 in., Rear: 36.0 in.

INSTRUMENTATION: Speedometer, odometer, fuel level gauge, warning lights for engine coolant temperature, oil pressure and battery charge.

OPTIONS AND PRICES: White sidewall tires. Clearcoat paint. Deck lid luggage rack. Rear window defroster. AM/FM radio with cassette tape player. Tilt steering wheel. Power side windows. Power Lock Group. Air conditioning: $817. Power seat.

HISTORICAL FOOTNOTES: This was the final year the four-wheel-drive Tempo was produced.

FORD AEROSTAR
1990-1993

1990 AEROSTAR

The Ford Aerostar, as both cargo and passenger van models, was first introduced on May 31, 1985 as a 1986 model. Between that date and the introduction of the four-wheel drive model for 1990, numerous refinements took place. They included the replacement of the original 2.8 liter V-6 engine with a 3.0 liter multiple-port EFI engine in January, 1986, and the adoption of this engine as standard for the wagon models in 1987. In the 1988 model year the Eddie Bauer model was introduced and the standard wagon model was renamed the XL. Also for 1988, the 5-speed manual transmission was fully synchronized. For the 1989 model year, an extended length model was added and the standard fuel tank capacity was increased to 21 gallons.

For 1990, the electronic four-wheel drive model (with a late availability for the regular length version) debuted. It included a new 4.0 liter V-6 and A4LD-HD transmission, new front suspension, and microprocessor-controlled lock-up and torque split functions. Exterior changes for 1990 included a new deluxe two-tone paint style and five additional new Deluxe two-tone paint combinations.

Interior changes for 1990 consisted of an underseat (right side) locking storage compartment (Nov., 1989 availability) included with Captain's chairs, and the inclusion of carpeted floor mats for front and rear seating positions in the Eddie Bauer trim. Major functional changes consisted of rear anti-lock brakes and a new braking system; the availability of dual rear doors with a 90 degree stop for the van (Nov., 1989 availability) and a Service Diagnostic System with the 4.0 liter V-6 (Nov., 1989 availability). Added to the list of options was a seat/bed combination for the XLT trim (later availability). The exterior colors for 1990 were as follows: Sandalwood clearcoat metallic, light sandalwood clearcoat metallic, light sandalwood, wild strawberry clearcoat metallic, medium red, crystal blue clearcoat metallic, spinmaker blue, twilight blue clearcoat metallic, raven black, silver clearcoat metallic, shadow grey clearcoat metallic, and colonial white. Aerostar interiors were offered in crystal blue, medium grey and light sandalwood.

Major standard equipment for the base XL Aerostar included color-coordinated front and rear bumpers with bright moldings and black paint on center area, tinted glass, dark argent grille with bright surround, black aero-type fold-away exterior mirrors, black flush windshield, body side, and liftgate surrounds, underbody spare tire carrier, front aero black spoiler, full-length color-keyed carpeting, front and rear cigarette lighters, three color-keyed plastic coat hooks, Convenience Group (includes courtesy lamp switches, cargo lamp and instrument panel, vanity panel and locking glove box), color-keyed, vinyl-covered wood fiber door trim panel, carpet-covered engine cover, inside fuel filler release, two-piece full-length color-keyed cloth headliner, four-gauge mechanical instrument cluster, liftgate convenience net, front dome light, stepwell domelight, rearview 10 in. day/night mirror, rear vinyl-covered quarter trim panels, AM electronic radio with digital clock, color-keyed safety belts, color-coordinated plastic scuff plates, dual front bucket seats with fixed back and color-keyed vinyl seat trim, 3 passenger rear bench seat with color-keyed vinyl seat trim and folding seat back, locking, energy-absorbing, color-keyed steering column, color-keyed vinyl A-frame steering wheel with center horn pad, black rubber step well pad, three body side storage bins with fishnet covers, and color-keyed, cloth-covered sun visors with covered vanity mirror, color-keyed, cloth-covered sun visor with sunglasses strap and covered vanity mirror, color-keyed rear body side and upper and lower liftgate trim panels (the lower liftgate trim panel included a pull strap), and two-speed windshield wipers.

1990 Ford Aerostar XL Plus

Primary features of the XL Plus trim level that replaced elements of the XL or were additions to that trim level's content included deluxe three-band stripe on body side, privacy glass (tinted windshield/front door glass), front air conditioning, dual front Captain's chairs with recliners, inboard fold-down armrests, color-keyed cloth seat trim, and right side locking underseat storage compartment; one two-passenger and one three-passenger rear bench seats with color-keyed cloth seat trim, folding seat back and quick release feature, and speed control/tilt steering wheel, two-speed interval windshield wipers and rear wiper/washer.

Primary features of the XLT trim level that replaced elements of the XL Plus or were additions to that trim level's content included color-keyed rear grab handle, dual-note horn, Light Group, electronic AM/FM stereo radio with cassette tape player and digital clock, dual premium Captain's chairs with power lumbar support, recliners, inboard fold-down armrests, seat back

map pockets, and right-side underseat locking storage compartment, and color-keyed luxury cloth seat trim; A-frame color-keyed deluxe leather-wrapped steering wheel with center horn pad, color-keyed, cloth-covered sun visors with covered illuminated vanity mirror, color-coordinated carpet on lower portion of trim panels, and body side panels include contrasting vinyl accent stripe.

Primary features of the XLT Plus trim level that replaced elements of the XLT or were additions to that trim level's content included electric remote exterior mirrors, luggage rack, overhead console with trip odometer and map lights, Electronics Group (includes overhead console, electronic instrument cluster and Super Sound system), electronic instrumentation cluster, electric day/night mirror, and Power Convenience Group (includes power windows, door locks and electric mirrors).

Primary features of the Eddie Bauer trim level that replaced elements of the XLT Plus or were additions to that trim level's content included Eddie Bauer two-tone exterior paint, forged aluminum wheels, high capacity front and rear air conditioning with auxiliary heater, floor console, XLT Plus seats with Eddie Bauer cloth trim, and XLT rear seats with unique Eddie Bauer cloth seat trim.

The Cargo/Window van's standard equipment included shadow grey metallic front and rear bumpers, front and sliding side doors, dual rear doors with glass (could be deleted to obtain rear liftgate with glass), tinted windshield and front door glass, charcoal grey grille, charcoal grey headlight bezels with bright surround, black aero door-mounted fold-away exterior mirrors, black flush windshield and rear window surrounds, black front window/vent surround, black front aero spoiler, single instrument panel-mounted ashtray, front charcoal carpeting, cigarette lighter, one color-keyed coat hook, driver's side courtesy light switch, color-keyed front door trim panels, black engine cover, white grained and painted wood fiber front headliner, heater/defroster, color-keyed instrument panel with black plastic applique, front area dome light, black framed 10 in. day/night mirror, electronic AM radio with digital clock (may be deleted for credit), color-keyed safety belts, black plastic scuff plates, dual front bucket seats with color-keyed vinyl trim, color-keyed A-frame steering wheel with center horn pad, black rubber step well, white vinyl-covered dual sun visors, and interval windshield wipers.

I.D. DATA: The Aerostar V.I.N. consisted of seventeen symbols. The first three characters identified the manufacturer, make and type of vehicle. The fourth character (a letter) designated the GVW range. The fifth, sixth and seventh characters identified the series and body style (A21-Aerostar wagon, A41-Aerostar extended wagon, A24-Aerostar van, A44-Aerostar extended van, A25-Aerostar window van, A45-Aerostar extended window van). The eighth character identified the engine (X-4.0 liter V-6). The ninth character was the check digit. The tenth character (a letter) represented the model year. The eleventh character identified the assembly plant (Z-St. Louis, Missouri). The remaining digits represented the sequential production number.

Body Type	Factory Price	GVW	Shipping Weight	Prod. Total
Wagon, std. length	$14,511	4880[1]	3642	—
Wagon, ext. length	$15,408	4940[2]	3732	—
Van, std. length	$14,065	5200	3470	—
Van, ext. length	$14,832	5240	3550	—
Window Van, std. length	$14,468	5200	N.A.	—
Window Van, ext. length	$15,215	5240	N.A.	—

NOTE 1: 5220 lb. with 7 passenger seating.
NOTE 2: 5180, 5240 and 5300 lb. GVW packages available for 7 passenger version.

STANDARD ENGINE: OHV 60 degree V-6. Cast-iron block and cylinder heads. Bore x Stroke: 3.95 in. x 3.32 in. Lifters: Hydraulic. Number of main bearings: 4. Displacement: 245 cu. in. (4.0 liters). Fuel Induction: Electronic fuel injection. Compression Ratio: 9.0:1. Horsepower: Net: 155 @ 4200 rpm. Torque: Net: 215 lb.-ft. @ 2400 rpm. Fuel Requirements: Unleaded. Oil capacity: 6 qt. with filter change.

CHASSIS FEATURES: Unitized body and frame.

SUSPENSION AND RUNNING GEAR: Front Suspension: Coil springs, computer selected. Capacity: 2650 lb. 1.38 in. dia. stabilizer bar. Shock absorbers: All models front and rear 1.19 in. dia. gas-pressurized. Rear Suspension: Coil springs. Capacity: 2639 lb. Front Axle Type and Capacity: Dana 28 independent. 2750 lb. capacity. Rear Axle Type and Capacity: Ford semi-floating, 2950 lb. capacity. Final Drive Ratio: 3.27:1 front and rear. Optional: 3.55:1. (available with limited slip differential). Brakes: Type: Hydraulic, power-assisted, disc front and cast iron drum rear. Dimensions: Front: 10.28 in. dia. Rear: 10.0 in. x 2.50 in. Wheels: 14 x 5.5 in. JJ.5. Tires: Steel-belted P215/70R x 14SL black sidewall, All-Season radial. Optional: Steel-belted P215/70R x 14SL white sidewall, All-Season radial. Steering: Rack and pinion, power assisted. Ratio: Variable: 19.8-15.0:1. Transmission: Heavy-duty Ford A4LD 4-speed automatic overdrive. Ratios: 5-spd. manual: 3.7, 2.21, 1.52, 1.00, 0.81:1. Reverse: 3.40:1.

VEHICLE DIMENSIONS: Wheelbase: 118.9 in. Overall Length: Regular: 174.9 in.; Extended length: 190.3 in. Front/Rear Tread 61.5 in./60.0 in. Overall Height: Regular: 73.2 in.; Extended length: 73.5 in. Width: 70.1 in. Front/Rear Overhang: 27.1 in./28.9 in. (Extended Length: 44.3 in.). Maximum liftgate width: 55.7 in. Ground Clearance: Axle clearance: 6.1 in. Load space: Regular: 41.3 in. x 46.9 in. x 44.4 in. Extended: 55.7 in. x 46.9 in. x 44.4 in.

CAPACITIES: Fuel Tank: 21.5 gal.

ACCOMMODATIONS: Seating Capacity: 5 or 7 occupants, depending upon package. Headroom: Front: 39.5 in. Legroom: Front: 41.0 in.

INSTRUMENTATION: Speedometer, odometer, gauges for engine coolant temperature, fuel level, battery charge indicator light, brake indicator light, check engine light, voltmeter gauge, oil pressure gauge, check oil light, door ajar indicator light, washer fluid indicator light, rear anti-lock brake indicator light, electronic four-wheel drive indicator light.

OPTIONS: Air conditioner. High capacity air conditioning. Limited slip rear axle. License plate bracket. Bright Package. Floor console. Overhead console. Convenience Group. Power Convenience Group. Heated rear defroster. Electronics Group. California emissions system. Exterior Appearance Group. Privacy glass. Tinted glass. Engine block heater. Light Group. Luggage rack. Swing lock mirrors. Body side protection molding. Deluxe two-tone paint. High Altitude Package. Electronic AM/FM stereo radio with digital clock. Electronic AM/FM stereo radio with cassette tape player and digital clock. Radio credit option. Seat/bed. Dual Captain's chairs. Quad premium Captain's chairs. 7 passenger seating. Super Sound system. Underbody Space Saver spare tire. Speed control/tilt steering wheel. Deluxe tape stripe. Trailer Towing Package. Rear wiper/washer. Forged aluminum wheels. Interval windshield wipers

HISTORICAL FOOTNOTES: The Aerostar was built in Ford's St. Louis, Missouri plant.

1991 AEROSTAR

The 1991 Aerostar was identified by the medium platinum color used on its bumpers, grille and headlamp doors. A graphite color had been used in 1990. XL models with cloth seat trim were available with a new currant red interior color. The right side ashtrays and fishnet-covered storage bins were removed from the rear quarter trim panels of the1991 models. Functional changes were not extensive for 1991 but several were noteworthy. A door ajar light was added for models with dual rear doors. Dual fluidic windshield washers were added to the base equipment content. The trailer towing harness was upgraded to include electric brakes. A memory lock feature was added to the optional sliding door with power locks.

I.D. DATA: The Aerostar V.I.N. consisted of seventeen symbols. The first three characters identified the manufacturer, make and type of vehicle. The fourth character (a letter) designated the GVW range. The fifth, sixth and seventh characters identified the series and body style (A21-Aerostar wagon, A41-Aerostar extended wagon, A24-Aerostar van, A44-Aerostar extended van, A25-Aerostar window van, A45-Aerostar extended window van). The eighth character identified the engine (X-4.0 liter V-6). The ninth character was the check digit. The tenth character (a letter) represented the model year. The eleventh character identified the assembly plant (Z-St. Louis, Missouri). The remaining digits represented the sequential production number.

Body Type	Factory Price	GVW	Shipping Weight	Prod. Total
XL Wagon, std. length	$15,600	4880[1]	3642	—
XL Wagon, ext. length	$16,519	4940[2]	3732	—
XLT Wagon, std. length	$18,132	4880	N.A.	—
XLT Wagon, ext. length	$19,051	4940	N.A.	—
Eddie Bauer, std. length	$21,246	4880	N.A.	—
Eddie Bauer, ext. length	$22,166	4940	N.A.	—
Van, std. length	$15,033	5200	3470	—
Van ext. length	$15,801	5240	3550	—
Window Van, std. length	$15,416	5200	N.A.	—
Window Van, ext. length	$16,185	5240	N.A.	—

NOTE 1: 5220 lb. with 7 passenger seating.
NOTE 2: 5180, 5240 and 5300 lb. GVW packages available for 7 passenger version.

STANDARD ENGINE: OHV 60 degree V-6. Cast-iron block and cylinder heads. Bore x Stroke: 3.95 in. x 3.32 in. Lifters: Hydraulic. Number of main bearings-4. Displacement: 245 cu. in. (4.0 liters). Fuel Induction: Electronic fuel injection. Compression Ratio: 9.0:1. Horsepower: Net: 155 @ 4200 rpm. Torque: Net: 215 lb.-ft. @ 2400 rpm. Fuel Requirements: Unleaded. Oil capacity: 6 qt. with filter change.

CHASSIS FEATURES: Unitized body and frame.

SUSPENSION AND RUNNING GEAR: Front Suspension: Coil springs, computer selected. Capacity: 2650 lb. 1.38 in. dia. stabilizer bar. Shock absorbers: All models front and rear 1.19 in. dia. gas-pressurized. Rear Suspension: Coil springs. Capacity: 2639 lb. Front Axle Type and Capacity: Dana 28 independent. 2750 lb. capacity. Rear Axle Type and Capacity: Ford semi-floating, 2950 lb. capacity. Final Drive Ratio: 3.73:1 front and rear. Brakes: Type: Hydraulic, power-assisted, disc front and cast iron drum rear. Dimensions: Front: 10.28 in. dia. Rear: 10.0 in. x 2.50 in. Wheels: 14 x 5.5 in. JJ. Tires: Steel-belted P215/70R x 14SL black sidewall, All-Season radial. Optional: Steel-belted P215/70R x 14SL white sidewall, All-Season radial. Steering: Rack and pinion, power assisted. Ratio: Variable: 19.8-15.0:1. Transmission: Heavy-duty Ford A4LD 4-speed automatic overdrive. Ratios: 5-spd. manual: 3.7, 2.21, 1.52, 1.00, 0.81:1. Reverse: 3.40:1.

VEHICLE DIMENSIONS: Wheelbase: 118.9 in. Overall Length: Regular: 174.9 in.; Extended length: 190.3 in. Front/Rear Tread 61.5 in./60.0 in. Overall Height: Regular: 73.2 in.; Extended length: 73.5 in. Width: 70.1 in. Front/Rear Overhang: 27.1 in./28.9 in. (extended length: 44.3 in.). Maximum liftgate width: 55.7 in. Ground Clearance: Axle clearance: 6.1 in. Load space: Regular: 41.3 in. x 46.9 in. x 44.4 in. Extended: 55.7 in. x 46.9 in. x 44.4 in.

CAPACITIES: Fuel Tank: 21.5 gal.

ACCOMMODATIONS: Seating Capacity: 5 or 7 occupants, depending upon package. Headroom: Front: 39.5 in. Legroom: Front: 41.0 in.

INSTRUMENTATION: Speedometer, odometer, gauges for engine coolant temperature, fuel level, battery charge indicator light, brake indicator light, check engine light, voltmeter gauge, oil pressure gauge, check oil light, door ajar indicator light, washer fluid indicator light, rear anti-lock brake indicator light, electronic four-wheel drive indicator light.

OPTIONS AND PRICES: Air conditioner. High capacity air conditioning. Limited slip rear axle. License plate bracket. Bright Package. Floor console. Overhead console. Convenience Group. Power Convenience Group. Heated rear defroster. Electronics Group. California emissions system. Exterior Appearance Group. Privacy glass. Tinted glass. Engine block heater. Light Group. Luggage rack. Swing lock mirrors. Body side protection molding. Deluxe two-tone paint. High Altitude Package. Electronic AM/FM stereo radio with digital clock. Electronic AM/FM stereo radio with cassette tape player and digital clock. Radio credit option. Seat/bed. Dual Captain's chairs. Quad premium Captain's chairs. 7 passenger seating. Super Sound system. Underbody Space Saver spare tire. Speed control/tilt steering wheel. Deluxe tape stripe. Trailer Towing Package. Rear wiper/washer. Forged aluminum wheels. Interval windshield wipers.

HISTORICAL FOOTNOTES: The 1991 Aerostar was announced on September 13, 1990.

1992 AEROSTAR

For 1992 the Aerostar had a revised grille and flush aero headlights, an all-new, car-like instrument panel with improved ergonomics, a passenger-side glove box and new instrument panel clusters. Added as standard equipment was a driver's side airbag and rear outboard three-point lap and shoulder belts. A mini-consolette with cup holders was also a new standard feature. Revised front door trim inserts were found on the XLT and Eddie Bauer models. High-back bucket seats were made standard and all second row bed seats (2 passenger) now had a storage bin on the right-hand side. The Eddie Bauer wagons for 1992 were fitted with leather seating areas. A new option offered for all wagons was an autolamp system. The overhead console option was deleted since its features were incorporated into the electronic cluster.

1992 Ford Aerostar Eddie Bauer

I.D. DATA: The Aerostar V.I.N. consisted of seventeen symbols. The first three characters identified the manufacturer, make and type of vehicle. The fourth character (a letter) designated the GVW range. The fifth, sixth and seventh characters identified the series and body style (A21-Aerostar wagon, A41-Aerostar extended wagon, A24-Aerostar van, A44-Aerostar extended van, A25-Aerostar window van, A45-Aerostar extended window van). The eighth character identified the engine (X-4.0 liter V-6). The ninth character was the check digit. The tenth character (a letter) represented the model year. The eleventh character identified the assembly plant (Z-St. Louis, Missouri). The remaining digits represented the sequential production number.

Body Type	Factory Price	GVW	Shipping Weight	Prod. Total
XL Wagon, std length	$16,978	4880[1]	3642	—
XL Wagon, ext. length	$17,966	4940[2]	3732	—
XL Plus Wagon, std length	$18,014	4880	N.A.	—
XL Plus Wagon, ext. length	$19,002	4940	N.A.	—
XLT Wagon, std length	$20,119	4880	N.A.	—
XLT Wagon, ext. length	$21,086	4940	N.A.	—
Eddie Bauer, std. length	$23,414	4880	N.A.	—
Eddie Bauer, ext. length	$24,381	4940	N.A.	—
Van, std. length	$16,182	5200	3470	—
Van, ext. length	$16,951	5240	3550	—
Window Van, std. length	$16,509	5200	N.A.	—
Window Van, ext. length	$17,278	5240	N.A.	—

NOTE 1: 5220 lb. with 7 passenger seating.
NOTE 2: 5180, 5240 and 5300 lb. GVW packages available for 7 passenger version.

STANDARD ENGINE: OHV 60 degree V-6. Cast-iron block and cylinder heads. Bore x Stroke: 3.95 in. x 3.32 in. Lifters: Hydraulic. Number of main bearings-4. Displacement: 245 cu. in. (4.0 liters). Fuel Induction: Electronic fuel injection. Compression Ratio: 9.0:1. Horsepower: Net: 155 @ 4200 rpm. Torque: Net: 215 lb.-ft. @ 2400 rpm. Fuel Requirements: Unleaded. Oil capacity: 6 qt. with filter change.

CHASSIS FEATURES: Unitized body and frame.

SUSPENSION AND RUNNING GEAR: Front Suspension: Coil springs, computer selected. Capacity: 2650 lb. 1.38 in. dia. stabilizer bar. Shock absorbers: All models front and rear 1.19 in. dia. gas-pressurized. Rear Suspension: Coil springs. Capacity: 2639 lb. Front Axle Type and Capacity: Dana 28 independent. 2750 lb. capacity. Rear Axle Type and Capacity: Ford semi-floating, 2950 lb. capacity. Final Drive Ratio: 3.73:1 front and rear. Brakes: Type: Hydraulic, power-assisted, disc front and cast iron drum rear. Dimensions: Front: 10.28 in. dia. Rear: 10.0 in. x 2.50 in. Wheels: 14 x 5.5 in. JJ. Tires: Steel-belted P215/70R x 14SL black sidewall, All-Season radial. Optional: Steel-belted P215/70R x 14SL white sidewall, All-Season radial. Steering: Rack and pinion, power assisted. Ratio: Variable: 19.8-15.0:1. Transmission: Heavy-duty Ford A4LD 4-speed automatic overdrive. Ratios: 5-spd. manual: 3.7, 2.21, 1.52, 1.00, 0.81:1. Reverse: 3.40:1.

VEHICLE DIMENSIONS: Wheelbase: 118.9 in. Overall Length: Regular: 174.9 in.; Extended length: 190.3 in. Front/Rear Tread 61.5 in./60.0 in. Overall Height: Regular: 73.2 in.; Extended length: 73.5 in. Width: 70.1 in. Front/Rear Overhang: 27.1 in./28.9 in. (Extended Length: 44.3 In.). Maximum liftgate width: 55.7 in. Ground Clearance: Axle clearance: 6.1 in. Load space: Regular: 41.3 in. x 46.9 in. x 44.4 in. Extended: 55.7 in. x 46.9 in. x 44.4 in.

CAPACITIES: Fuel Tank: 21.5 gal.

ACCOMMODATIONS: Seating Capacity: 5 or 7 occupants, depending upon package. Headroom: Front: 39.5 in. Legroom: Front: 41.0 in.

INSTRUMENTATION: Speedometer, odometer, gauges for engine coolant temperature, fuel level, battery charge indicator light, brake indicator light, check engine light, voltmeter gauge, oil pressure gauge, check oil light, door ajar indicator light, washer fluid indicator light, rear anti-lock brake indicator light, electronic four-wheel drive indicator light.

OPTIONS: Air conditioner. High capacity air conditioning. Limited slip rear axle. License plate bracket. Bright Package. Floor console. Leather seating areas (Eddie Bauer only). Convenience Group. Power Convenience Group. Heated rear defroster. Electronics Group. California emissions system. Exterior Appearance Group. Privacy glass. Tinted glass. Engine block heater. Light Group. Luggage rack. Swing lock mirrors. Body side protection molding. Deluxe two-tone paint. High Altitude Package. Electronic AM/FM stereo radio with digital clock. Electronic AM/FM stereo radio with cassette tape player and digital clock. Radio credit option. Seat/bed. Dual Captain's chairs. Quad premium Captain's chairs. 7 passenger seating. Super Sound system. Underbody Space Saver spare tire. Speed control/tilt steering wheel. Deluxe tape stripe. Trailer Towing Package. Rear wiper/washer. Forged aluminum wheels. Interval windshield wipers.

HISTORICAL FOOTNOTES: The 1992 Aerostar was announced on September 17, 1991.

1993 AEROSTAR

Significant changes in the Ford Aerostar for 1993 were very limited. A new 90 mph mechanical analog speedometer was adopted. A new Euro-perforation treatment was used for leather interiors and child safety belts were integrated into the second row bench seat.

I.D. DATA: The Aerostar V.I.N. consisted of seventeen symbols. The first three characters identified the manufacturer, make and type of vehicle. The fourth character (a letter) designated the GVW range. The fifth, sixth and seventh characters identified the series and body style (A21-Aerostar wagon, A41-Aerostar extended wagon, A24-Aerostar van, A44-Aerostar extended van, A25-Aerostar window van, A45-Aerostar extended van). The eighth character identified the engine (X-4.0 liter V-6). The ninth character was the check digit. The tenth character (a letter) represented the model year. The eleventh character identified the assembly plant (Z-St. Louis, Missouri). The remaining digits represented the sequential production number.

Prices and shipping weights were not available at press time. A list of available models for 1993 follows.

Aerostar
XL Wagon, std. length.
XL Wagon, ext. length.
XL Plus Wagon, std length.
XL Plus Wagon, ext. length.
XLT Wagon, std. length.
XLT Wagon, ext. length.
Eddie Bauer, std. length.
Eddie Bauer, ext. length.
Van, std. length.
Van, ext. length.
Window Van, std. length.
Window Van, ext. length.

STANDARD ENGINE: OHV 60 degree V-6. Cast-iron block and cylinder heads. Bore x Stroke: 3.95 in. x 3.32 in. Lifters: Hydraulic. Number of main bearings-4. Displacement. 245 cu. in. (4.0 liters). Fuel Induction: Electronic fuel injection. Compression Ratio: 9.0:1. Horsepower: Net: 155 @ 4200 rpm. Torque: Net: 215 lb.-ft. @ 2400 rpm. Fuel Requirements: Unleaded. Oil capacity: 6 qt. with filter change.

CHASSIS FEATURES: Unitized body and frame.

SUSPENSION AND RUNNING GEAR: Front Suspension: Coil springs, computer selected. Capacity: 2650 lb. 1.38 in. dia. stabilizer bar. Shock absorbers: All models front and rear 1.19 in. dia. gas-pressurized. Rear Suspension: Coil springs. Capacity: 2639 lb. Front Axle Type and Capacity: Dana 28 independent. 2750 lb. capacity. Rear Axle Type and Capacity: Ford semi-floating, 2950 lb. capacity. Final Drive Ratio: 3.73:1 front and rear. Brakes: Type: Hydraulic, power-assisted, disc front and cast iron drum rear. Dimensions: Front: 10.28 in. dia. Rear: 10.0 in. x 2.50 in. Wheels: 14 x 5.5 in. JJ. Tires: Steel-belted P215/70R x 14SL black sidewall, All-Season radial. Optional: Steel-belted P215/70R x 14SL white sidewall, All-Season radial. Steering: Rack and pinion, power assisted. Ratio: Variable: 19.8-15.0:1. Transmission: Heavy-duty Ford A4LD 4-speed automatic overdrive. Ratios: 5-spd. manual. 3.7, 2.21, 1.52, 1.00, 0.81:1. Reverse: 3.40:1.

VEHICLE DIMENSIONS: Wheelbase: 118.9 in. Overall Length: Regular: 174.9 in.; Extended length: 190.3 in. Front/Rear Tread 61.5 in./60.0 in. Overall Height: Regular: 73.2 in.; Extended length: 73.5 in. Width: 70.1 in. Front/Rear Overhang: 27.1 in./28.9 in. (extended length: 44.3 in.). Maximum liftgate width: 55.7 in. Ground Clearance: Axle clearance: 6.1 in. Load space: Regular: 41.3 in. x 46.9 in. x 44.4 in. Extended: 55.7 in. x 46.9 in. x 44.4 in.

CAPACITIES: Fuel Tank: 21.5 gal.

ACCOMMODATIONS: Seating Capacity: 5 or 7 occupants, depending upon package. Headroom: Front: 39.5 in. Legroom: Front: 41.0 in.

INSTRUMENTATION: Speedometer, odometer, gauges for engine coolant temperature, fuel level, battery charge indicator light, brake indicator light, check engine light, voltmeter gauge, oil pressure gauge, check oil light, door ajar indicator light, washer fluid indicator light, rear anti-lock brake indicator light, electronic four-wheel drive indicator light.

OPTIONS: Air conditioner. High capacity air conditioning. Limited slip rear axle. License plate bracket. Bright Package. Floor console. Leather seating areas (Eddie Bauer only). Convenience Group. Power Convenience Group. Heated rear defroster. Electronics Group. California emissions system. Exterior Appearance Group. Privacy glass. Tinted glass. Engine block heater. Light Group. Luggage rack. Swing lock mirrors. Body side protection molding. Deluxe two-tone paint. High Altitude Package. Electronic AM/FM stereo radio with digital clock. Electronic AM/FM stereo radio with cassette tape player and digital clock. Radio credit option. Seat/bed. Dual Captain's chairs. Quad premium Captain's chairs. 7 passenger seating. Super Sound system. Underbody Space Saver spare tire. Speed control/tilt steering wheel. Deluxe tape stripe. Trailer Towing Package. Rear wiper/washer. Forged aluminum wheels. Interval windshield wipers.

HISTORICAL FOOTNOTES: The 1993 Aerostar was announced on September 14, 1992. The EPA designated the Aerostar as both a cargo van and a passenger van.

FORD EXPLORER

1991-1993

1991 EXPLORER

The Ford Explorer, which replaced the Bronco II in Ford's utility vehicle lineup, was introduced on March 15, 1990 as a 1991 model. It was available in both two and four-door form. "The Explorer is turning heads in the marketplace," said Ford Division general manager, Thomas J. Wagner. "It is blurring the traditional distinctions between cars and trucks."

"Explorer looks more truck-like than car-like, yet it offers some of the same comforts you would expect to find in cars — right down to the lighted vanity mirrors, the optional disc player and leather seats," noted Wagner. "But when you need a truck," he added, "Explorer is there. It offers such features as a commanding view of the road, part-time four-wheel-drive, trailer towing, plenty of cargo space and built-in ruggedness with heavy-duty frame and suspension for durable performance."

The Explorer was offered in four series: The base XL followed by the Sport, XLT and Eddie Bauer series. The XL and Eddie Bauer were offered in both two-door and four-door body styles. The Sport was offered only as a two-door. The XLT was available only as a four-door.

As compared to the superseded Bronco II, the Explorer had all-new sheetmetal except for its hood and stone shield. Included among its most important styling/external features was aerodynamic styling with a 0.43 cd drag coefficient, a standard rear bumper with a 3500 lb. towing capacity, corrosion protection consisting of 2-sided galvanized steel (excluding the roof) and vinyl lower body side spray, "Limo"-style wrap-over doors, flush-mounted glass, hidden drip system, halogen headlamps with damage resistant headlamp lens and replaceable bulbs, steel liftgate with standard flip-open window and side pivoting windows standard on two-door model. The Explorer's interior was available in four colors: Crystal blue, scarlet red, medium grey and light sandlewood. Primary interior features included a forced-air heater/air conditioner system with 4 registers and front door window demisters, rear floor heat duct and a "user friendly" instrument panel.

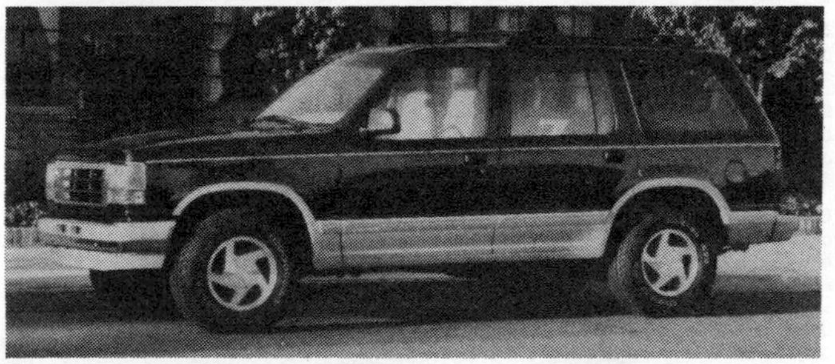

1991 Ford Explorer Eddie Bauer

Standard equipment for the XL Explorer was as follows: 4.0 liter V-6 with electronic fuel injection, 5-speed manual overdrive transmission, part-time 2-speed transfer case, 95 amp, 1425 watt alternator, maintenance-free 72 amp-hr. battery, bucket-type front seats, rear 50/50 split back seat, gauges for fuel level, engine coolant temperature, oil pressure and voltmeter, bright front and rear bumpers with rub strip, tinted windshield and side/rear windows, flip-open "Opera" windows (two-door), bright grille, aero headlights with bright frames, one-piece liftgate, hinged at top with flip-open rear window, black door-mounted exterior mirrors (right side with convex surface), high-mounted stop light, Deluxe wheel trim with trim ring, interval windshield wipers, color-keyed full-length carpeting, cigarette lighter, color-keyed coat hooks, front dome light with left and right door and liftgate courtesy switches, cargo light, plastic color-keyed full length door trim panels with armrest, locking glove box, color-keyed full length headliner, heater/defroster with flow-through air ventilation, rear seat heater duct, inside hood release, dual-tone horn, color-keyed instrument panel with full-width pad and black cluster applique, gauge cluster with trip odometer and tachometer, four load floor tie down hooks, color-keyed "A"-pillar, "B"-pillar, cowlside, rear quarter panel and liftgate, electronic AM/FM stereo with digital clock and two additional speakers in quarter trim panels and two in doors, front and rear color-keyed, continuous loop lap-shoulder safety belts, color-keyed plastic scuff plates at all doors, color-keyed knitted-vinyl front bucket seat and rear split folding seat, black "A" frame steering wheel and color-keyed cloth left and right side sun visors with right side vanity mirror. The four-door version also was equipped with the Light Group and four tie down load floor hooks.

The Explorer's exterior color selection consisted of sandlewood clearcoat metallic, light sandlewood clearcoat metallic, light sandlewood, cabernet red, wild strawberry clearcoat metallic, scarlet red, crystal blue clearcoat metallic, twilight blue clearcoat metallic, hunter green clearcoat metallic, raven black, silver clearcoat metallic, shadow grey clearcoat metallic and colonial white. The Eddie Bauer was available in sandlewood clearcoat metallic, cabernet red, wild strawberry clearcoat metallic, twilight blue clearcoat metallic, hunter green clearcoat metallic and raven black.

I.D. DATA: The Explorer V.I.N. consisted of seventeen symbols. It was stamped on a metal tag fastened to the instrument panel close to the windshield on the driver's side of the vehicle. The first three functioned as the world manufacturer identifier (1FT). The fourth digit identified the brake system and GVWR class. The fifth, sixth and seventh digits identified the line, series, chassis, cab or body type: (U24-Explorer two-door; U34-Explorer four-door). The eighth digit identified the engine type. X identified the 245 cu. in. V-6 engine. The ninth digit was a computer check digit. The tenth digit, M, identified the 1991 model year. The eleventh digit identified the plant of manufacture. U identified the Louisville, Kentucky plant where the Explorer was built. The twelfth through seventeenth digits were the sequential production numbers for each plant, starting with A00001 through A99999 then B000000, etc.

	Body Type	Factory Price
Explorer		
	2-dr. XL	$16,375
	2-dr. Sport	$17,656
	2-dr. Eddie Bauer	$20,534
	4-dr. XL	$17,354
	4-dr. XLT	$19,275
	4-dr. Eddie Bauer	$21,701

STANDARD ENGINE: Engine Type: OHV V-6 Special high-grade cast-iron block and cylinder heads. Bore x Stroke: 3.95 in. x 3.32 in. Lifters: Hydraulic. Fuel Induction: Multiple-port electronic fuel injection. Compression Ratio: 9.3:1. Displacement: 244 cu. in. (4.0 liters). Horsepower: 155 @ 3800 rpm. Torque: 220 lb.-ft. @ 2400 rpm. Oil refill capacity: 6 qt. with filter change. 4.5 qts. without filter change. Fuel Requirements: Regular Unleaded.

OPTIONAL ENGINE: None.

CHASSIS FEATURES: Separate body and frame, Single channel, five cross members, welded frame. 2.89 in. section modulus. Maximum side rail section: 6.08 x 2.28. x 0.150 in. 36,000 psi. Low carbon steel.

SUSPENSION AND RUNNING GEAR: Front Suspension: Computer-selected coil springs, 2260 lb. rating. Optional rating: 2340 lb., 2420 lb., 2540 lb., 2620 lb. Rear Suspension: Variable rate two-stage 5-leaf springs. 2650 lb. rating. Optional Rating: 2750 lb. (for two-door and four-door), 290 lb. (four-door only). Front Axle Type and Capacity: Twin-Traction beam independent with adjustable caster/camber, 2750 lb. capacity. Rear Axle Type and Capacity: Semi-floating, 3200 lb. capacity. Final Drive Ratio: 3.55:1. 3.75:1 limited slip optional with auto. trans. Transfer Case: Warner 1350 part-time, 2-speed. Ratios: 2.48:1, 1.00:1. "Touch Drive" electric shift. Brakes: Type: Hydraulic power-assisted, disc single-piston, self-adjusting front and cast iron drum rear. Dimensions: Front: 10.86 in. dia. Rear: 10.00 in. x 2.25 in. Total swept area: 251.2 sq. in. Wheels: 6.0JK x 15 in., 5-hole styled steel disc. Optional: 7.0JJ x 15 in. Deep dish cast aluminum wheels, 7.0JJ x 15 in. Cast aluminum, 6.0JJ x 15 in. Deluxe steel wheels with trim rings. Tires: P225.70R15SL black sidewall steel-belted, All-Season radial. Optional: P235/75R15SL outline white letters, All-Terrain steel-belted radial. Steering: Power assisted, integral recirculating ball. Ratio: 17.0:1, turns Lock-to-Lock: 3.0.Turning Circle: 37.0 ft. (four-door model); 34.2 ft. (two-door). Optional: None. Transmission: Mazda: 5-speed manual overdrive heavy-duty, all-synchromesh. Transmission Ratios: 3.40, 2.20, 1.50, 1.00, 0.79:1 reverse: 3.42:1. Optional: 4-speed automatic overdrive. Optional: Ford A4LD 4-speed Automatic Overdrive Drive 4-speed. Ratios: 2.47, 1.47, 1.00, 0.75:1. Reverse: 2.10. Converter ratio: 2.80:1. Clutch: Segmented disc, woven non-asbestos lining. Belleville pressure plate. Clutch diameter: 10 in. Total plate pressure: 1515 lb. Optional: None.

VEHICLE DIMENSIONS:

	Two-door	Four-door
Wheelbase:	102.1 in.	111.9 in.
Overall Length:	174.4 in.	184.3 in.
Front/Rear Tread	58.3 in./58.3 in.	same
Overall Height:	67.5 in.	67.3 in.
Width:	70.2 in.	same
Front/Rear Overhang:	29.6 in./42.8 in.	same
Tailgate: Width and Height:	52.4 in./33.7 in.	same
Approach/Departure Degrees:	32.9/22.3	32.6/22.3

Load space: Two-door: With rear seat installed: 29.2 in. x 41.9 in. x 33.7 in. With rear seat removed or folded: 59.5 in. x 41.9 in. x 33.7 in. Four-door: With rear seat installed: 38.1 in. x 41.9 in. x 33.7 in. With rear seat removed or folded: 72.9 in. x 41.9 in. x 33.7 in. Maximum capacity: With rear seat folded: Two-door: 69.4 cu. ft. Four-door: 81.6 cu. ft. Front headroom: 39.9 in. Front leg room: 42.1 in. Front shoulder room: 57.1 in. Front hip room: 51.9 in. Rear headroom: 39.1 in. Rear legroom: 35.6 in. (36.6 in. four-door). Rear shoulder room: 57 in. (51.9 in. four-door). Rear hip room: 43.6 in. (51.9 in. four-door).

CAPACITIES: Fuel Tank: 19.0 gal. with skid plate.

ACCOMMODATIONS: Seating Capacity: Four-door model: 5 passenger. Optional: 6 passenger. Two-door model: 4 passenger.

INSTRUMENTATION: Speedometer, trip odometer, tachometer, gauges for fuel level, engine coolant temperature, oil pressure and volt meter, alert lights for seat belt, 4x4 operation, check engine, battery, brakes, rear anti-lock, low range high beam operation and check oil.

OPTIONS: Option identification follows each option. Air conditioning (572). Limited slip performance axle (XA80). 4-speed electronic automatic overdrive transmission (4T). California emissions system (422). High altitude principle use (428). P235/75R15SL outlined white letter All-terrain steel belted radial tires (T7R). Cloth Captain's chairs (B). Cloth Sport bucket seat with lumbar support (C). Cloth 60/40 split front bench seat (D). Leather Sport bucket seats with power lumbar support (F). Super cooling engine (624). Privacy glass-rear quarter windows only (924). Tilt-up/open air roof. Engine block heater (924). Manual locking hubs (21M). License plate bracket (153). Body side molding (965). Luggage rack (615). Speed control/tilt steering wheel (52N). Deluxe tape stripe (85C). Electronic premium AM/FM stereo with cassette player and digital clock (588). Ford JBL audio system with cassette player (916). Ford JBL audio system with CD player (917). Radio credit option (58Y). Deluxe two-tone paint (952). Deep dish cast aluminum wheels (649). Deluxe steel wheels with trim rings (642). Luxury aluminum wheels (64). Rear window wiper/washer/defroster (17C). Trailer Towing Package (535). Includes wiring harness, heavy-duty flasher and Super engine cooling (required on vehicles over 5000 GVWR). Light group (593). Includes glove box light, ashtray light and engine compartment light. Power Equipment Group (903). Includes power side windows, power door locks and tailgate and dual electric remote-control mirrors. Sport Package (931B). Includes in addition to or in place of XL items the following: Black front and rear bumpers with rub strip, privacy glass (rear quarter windows), black grille, aero headlights with black frames, black with red-orange insert body side molding, black wheel-lips, Sport two-tone black rocker panel paint, deep dish cast aluminum wheels, color-keyed instrument panel applique, Light Group, Deluxe map reading light (deleted with lift-up open air roof), load floor tie down net, black Deluxe leather-wrapped steering wheel, left and right side vanity mirrors and auxiliary visors. Eddie Bauer (932B-two-door; 942B-four-door). Includes in addition to or in place of Sport items the following: Bright front and rear bumpers with rub strip, privacy glass (rear quarter windows on two-door), bright grille, aero headlights with bright frames, electric remote exterior mirrors, light sandlewood with bright insert body side moldings, unique two-tone exterior paint treatment with light sandlewood tape stripes, roof rack, luxury cast aluminum wheels, rear window washer/defroster, cargo area cover, color-keyed soft vinyl door trim appliques with carpeted lower portion with map pocket in front door and courtesy light/reflectors, Eddie Bauer unique items (garment bag and duffle bag, "Ford Care" 24/24 maintenance and warranty program), color-keyed carpeted front and rear floor mats, power window and door locks, premium cloth Captain's chairs and matching split/folding rear seat and floor console, speed control and tilt steering wheel. XLT (941B). Includes in addition to or in place of items found on the four-door XL model the following: Electric remote exterior mirrors, black bright body side moldings, cast aluminum deep dish wheels, color-keyed soft vinyl door trim appliques with carpeted lower portion with map pocket in front door and courtesy light/reflectors, color-keyed instrument panel applique, Deluxe map reading light (deleted with tilt-up open air roof), tie down net for load floor, power windows and door locks, cloth Captain's chairs, rear split/folding seat and floor console, speed control and tilt steering wheel and black Deluxe leather-wrapped steering wheel.

HISTORICAL FOOTNOTES: The Explorer's impact upon sales of Ford utility vehicles was immediate. In July,1990, for example, sales of Ford compact utility vehicles — including the Explorer and the Bronco II, were up 84 percent from the previous year. In March, 1991, the Explorer was the seventh best selling vehicle in the United States with sales exceeding 22,000 units. The Explorer was the first Ford light truck available with the Ford JBL audio system.

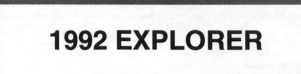

1992 EXPLORER

The Ford Explorer was one of the most important developments in the four-wheel drive field. Just three months after its introduction in April, 1991 it was the best selling vehicle in the compact utility vehicle class. For 1992 the Explorer underwent a number of evolutionary changes. A 3.27:1 axle ratio was now standard on all models except those intended for high altitude use. The air conditioning performance was also improved. Two changes that were phased in during the1991 model year were continued for 1992. These were the availability of privacy glass on four-door models and the addition of the rear window wiper/washer/defroster to the Sport and XLT Packages. The deep dish cast aluminum wheels of the XLT Package were replaced by the luxury cast aluminum wheels. Another running change of 1991 that carried over for 1992 was the addition of a cargo area cover to the Sport two-door model and as a option for the XL. Added to the XLT as an option were front and rear color-keyed floor mats. Rear floor mats were added to the Eddie Bauer. Also new to the Eddie Bauer Explorer were color accented cast aluminum wheels. Phased in during the 1992 model year were new Eddie Bauer cloth Sport bucket seats with 6-way power and the addition of dual front cupholders to the floor console. Several changes took place in the Explorer option content. The tilt-up open air roof was deleted from the Eddie Bauer Preferred Equipment Package. It was still available as a free-standing option. The optional Sport bucket seats now included 6-way power. The power windows now had a one-touch down feature.

The Explorer was again offered in four series: The base XL followed by the Sport, XLT and Eddie Bauer series. The XL and Eddie Bauer were offered in both two-door and four-door body styles. The Sport was offered only as a two-door. The XLT was available only as a four-door.

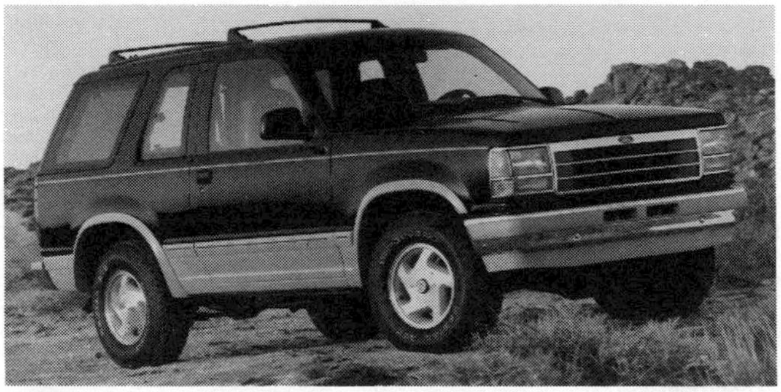

1992 Ford Explorer Eddie Bauer two-door

I. D. DATA: The Explorer V.I.N. consisted of seventeen symbols. It was stamped on a metal tag fastened to the instrument panel close to the windshield on the driver's side of the vehicle. The first three functioned as the world manufacturer identifier (1FT). The fourth digit identified the brake system and GVWR class. The fifth, sixth and seventh digits identified the line, series, chassis, cab or body type: (U24-Explorer two-door; U34-Explorer four-door). The eighth digit identified the engine type. X identified the 245 cu. in. V-6 engine. The ninth digit was a computer check digit. The tenth digit, N identified the 1992 model year. The eleventh digit identified the plant of manufacture. U identified the Louisville, Kentucky plant where the Explorer was built. The twelfth through seventeenth digits were the sequential production numbers for each plant, starting with A00001 through A99999 then B000000 etc.

	Body Type	Factory Price
Explorer		
	2-dr. XL	$17,644
	2-dr. Sport	$18,731
	2-dr. Eddie Bauer	$22,159
	4-dr. XL	$18,505
	4-dr. XLT	$20,401
	4-dr. Eddie Bauer	$23,553

STANDARD ENGINE: Engine Type: OHV V-6 Special high-grade cast-iron block and cylinder heads. Bore x Stroke: 3.95 in. x 3.32 in. Lifters: Hydraulic. Fuel Induction: Multiple-port electronic fuel injection. Compression Ratio: 9.3:1. Displacement: 244 cu. in. (4.0 liters). Horsepower: 155 @ 3800 rpm. Torque: 220 lb.-ft. @ 2400 rpm. Oil refill capacity: 6 qt. with filter change. 4.5 qts. without filter change. Fuel Requirements: Regular Unleaded.

OPTIONAL ENGINE: None.

CHASSIS FEATURES: Separate body and frame, single channel, five cross members, welded frame. 2.89 in. section modulus. Maximum side rail section: 6.08 x 2.28. x 0.150 in. 36,000 psi. Low carbon steel.

SUSPENSION AND RUNNING GEAR: Front Suspension: Computer-selected coil springs, 2260 lb. rating. Optional rating: 2340 lb., 2420 lb., 2540 lb., 2620 lb. Rear Suspension: Variable rate two-stage 5-leaf springs. 2650 lb. rating. Optional Rating: 2750 lb. (for two-door and four-door), 290 lb. (four-door only). Front Axle Type and Capacity: Twin-Traction beam independent with adjustable caster/camber, 2750 lb. capacity. Rear Axle Type and Capacity: Semi-floating, 3200 lb. capacity. Final Drive Ratio: 3.27:1. 3.75:1 limited slip optional with auto. trans. Transfer Case: Warner 1350 part-time, 2-speed. Ratios: 2.48:1, 1.00:1. "Touch Drive" electric shift. Brakes: Type: Hydraulic power-assisted, disc single-piston, self-adjusting front and cast iron drum rear. Dimensions: Front: 10.86 in. dia. Rear: 10.00 in. x 2.25 in. Total swept area: 251.2 sq. in. Wheels: 6.0JK x 15 in., 5-hole styled steel disc. Optional: 7.0JJ x 15 in. Deep dish cast aluminum wheels, 7.0JJ x 15 in. Cast aluminum, 6.0JJ x 15 in. Deluxe steel wheels with trim rings. Tires: P225.70R15SL black sidewall steel-belted, All-Season radial. Optional: P235/75R15SL outline white letters, All-Terrain steel-belted radial. Steering: Power assisted, integral recirculating ball. Ratio: 17.0:1, turns Lock-to-Lock: 3.0.Turning Circle: 37.0 ft. (four-door model); 34.2 ft. (two-door). Optional: None. Transmission: Mazda: 5-speed manual overdrive heavy-duty, all-synchromesh. Transmission Ratios: 3.40, 2.20, 1.50, 1.00, 0.79:1 reverse: 3.42:1. Optional: 4-speed automatic overdrive. Optional: Ford A4LD 4-speed Automatic Overdrive Drive 4-speed. Ratios: 2.47, 1.47, 1.00, 0.75:1. Reverse: 2.10. Converter ratio: 2.80:1. Clutch: Segmented disc, woven non-asbestos lining. Belleville pressure plate. Clutch diameter: 10 in. Total plate pressure: 1515 lb. Optional: None.

VEHICLE DIMENSIONS:

	Two-door	Four-door
Wheelbase:	102.1 in.	111.9 in.
Overall Length:	174.4 in.	184.3 in.
Front/Rear Tread	58.3 in./58.3 in.	same
Overall Height:	67.5 in.	67.3 in.
Width:	70.2 in.	same
Front/Rear Overhang:	29.6 in./42.8 in.	same
Tailgate: Width and Height:	52.4 in./33.7 in.	same
Approach/Departure Degrees:	32.9/22.3	32.6/22.3

Load space: Two-door: With rear seat installed: 29.2 in. x 41.9 in. x 33.7 in. With rear seat removed or folded: 59.5 in. x 41.9 in. x 33.7 in. four-door: With rear seat installed: 38.1 in. x 41.9 in. x 33.7 in. With rear seat removed or folded: 72.9 in. x 41.9 in. x 33.7 in. Maximum capacity: With rear seat folded: Two-door: 69.4 cu. ft. Four-door: 81.6 cu. ft. Front headroom: 39.9 in. Front legroom: 42.1 in. Front shoulder room: 57.1 in. Front hip room: 51.9 in. Rear headroom: 39.1 in. Rear legroom: 35.6 in. (36.6 in. four-door). Rear shoulder room: 57 in. (51.9 in. four-door). Rear hip room: 43.6 in. (51.9 in. four-door).

CAPACITIES: Fuel Tank: 19.0 gal. with skid plate.

ACCOMMODATIONS: Seating Capacity: Four-door model: 5 passenger. Optional: 6 passenger. Two-door model: 4 passenger.

INSTRUMENTATION: Speedometer, trip odometer, tachometer, gauges for fuel level, engine coolant temperature, oil pressure and volt meter, alert lights for seat belt, 4x4 operation, check engine, battery, brakes, rear anti-lock, low range high beam operation and check oil.

OPTIONS: Option identification follows each option. Air conditioning (572). Limited slip performance axle (XA80). 4-speed electronic automatic overdrive transmission (4T). California emissions system (422). High altitude principle use (428). P235/75R15SL outlined white letter All-Terrain steel belted radial tires (T7R). Cloth Captain's chairs (B). Cloth Sport bucket seat with lumbar support (C). Cloth 60/40 split front bench seat (D). Leather Sport bucket seats with power lumbar support (F). Super cooling engine (624). Privacy glass-rear quarter windows only (924). Tilt-up/open air roof. Engine block heater (924). Manual locking hubs (21M). License plate bracket (153). Body side molding (965). Luggage rack (615). Speed control/tilt steering wheel (52N). Deluxe tape stripe (85C). Electronic premium AM/FM stereo with cassette player and digital clock (588). Ford JBL audio system with cassette player (916). Ford JBL audio system with CD player (917). Radio credit option (58Y). Deluxe two-tone paint (952). Deep dish cast aluminum wheels (649). Deluxe steel wheels with trim rings (642). Luxury aluminum wheels (64). Rear window wiper/washer/defroster (17C). Trailer Towing Package (535). Includes wiring harness, heavy-duty flasher and Super engine cooling (required on vehicles over 5000 GVWR). Light group (593). Includes glove box light, ashtray light and engine compartment light. Power Equipment Group (903). Includes power side windows, power door locks and tailgate and dual electric remote-control mirrors. Sport Package (931B). Includes in addition to or in place of XL items the following: Rear window wiper/washer/defroster, black front and rear bumpers with rub strip, privacy glass (rear quarter windows), black grille, aero headlights with black frames, black with red-orange insert body side molding, black wheel-lips, Sport two-tone black rocker panel paint, deep dish cast aluminum wheels, color-keyed instrument panel applique, Light Group, Deluxe map reading light (deleted with lift-up open air roof), load floor tie down net, black Deluxe leather-wrapped steering wheel, left and right side vanity mirrors and auxiliary visors. Eddie Bauer (932B-two-door; 942B-four-door). Includes in addition to or in place of Sport items the following: Rear floor mats, color accented cast aluminum wheels, bright front and rear bumpers with rub strip, privacy glass (rear quarter windows on two-door), bright grille, aero headlights with bright frames, electric remote exterior mirrors, light sandlewood with bright insert body side moldings, unique two-tone exterior paint treatment with light sandlewood tape stripes, roof rack, rear window washer/defroster, cargo area cover, color-keyed soft vinyl door trim appliques with carpeted lower portion with map pocket in front door and courtesy light/reflectors, Eddie Bauer unique items (garment bag and duffle bag, "Ford Care" 24/24 maintenance and warranty program), color-keyed carpeted front and rear floor mats, power window and door locks, premium cloth Captain's chairs and matching split/folding rear seat and floor console, speed control and tilt steering wheel. XLT (941B). Includes in addition to or in place of items found on the four-door XL model the following: Rear window wiper/washer/defroster, electric remote exterior mirrors, black bright body side moldings, luxury cast aluminum wheels, color-keyed soft vinyl door trim appliques with carpeted lower portion with map pocket in front door and courtesy light/reflectors, color-keyed instrument panel applique, Deluxe map reading light (deleted with tilt-up open air roof), tie down net for load floor, power windows and door locks, cloth Captain's chairs, rear split/folding seat and floor console, speed control and tilt steering wheel and black Deluxe leather-wrapped steering wheel. Front and rear color-keyed floor mats (for XLT).

HISTORICAL FOOTNOTES: The 1992 Explorer was introduced on September 21,1992.

1992 Ford Explorer XLT four-door

1993 EXPLORER

The Explorer for 1993 was offered in both two and four-door version in four trim levels: XL, Sport, XLT and Eddie Bauer. All models were equipped with standard equipment four-wheel ABS that functioned in all driving modes. Exterior changes for 1993 consisted of new optional deep dish cast aluminum wheels and styled steel wheels with a spoke design. A new standard lower rocker panel molding was also introduced.

The Explorer's standard knit vinyl seats had a new sew style. Both the cloth premium bucket seats and cloth bucket seats had a cloth and sew style. The 60/40 cloth bench seat also had a cloth and sew style as well as a new storage fold down armrest. Also found in the 1993 Explorer interior was a new steering wheel, instrument panel appliques, instrument cluster graphics and climate control graphics. The two right-hand air conditioning registers and the glove box latch were color-keyed. The 1992 model radios were replaced by "next generation" radios.

The Explorer's options were slightly revised. Floor-mounted consolette cupholders were now available with the 60/40 split bench seat. Scheduled for delayed availability were running boards for the four-door model. The Power Equipment Group option was available for the XL model.

1993 Ford Explorer Eddie Bauer four-door

I.D. DATA: The Explorer V.I.N. consisted of seventeen symbols. It was stamped on a metal tag fastened to the instrument panel close to the windshield on the driver's side of the vehicle. The first three functioned as the world manufacturer identifier (1FT). The fourth digit identified the brake system and GVWR class. The fifth, sixth and seventh digits identified the line, series, chassis, cab or body type: (U24-Explorer two-door; U34-Explorer four-door). The eighth digit identified the engine type. X identified the 245 cu. in. V-6 engine. The ninth digit was a computer check digit. The tenth digit, O identified the 1993 model year. The eleventh digit identified the plant of manufacture. U identified the Louisville, Kentucky plant where the Explorer was built. The twelfth through seventeenth digits were the sequential production numbers for each plant. starting with A00001 through A99999 then B000000, etc.

Prices of the 1993 models were not available at press time.

Model availability:

Explorer XL — two-door, four-door
Explorer Sport — two-door
Explorer XLT — four-door
Explorer Eddie Bauer — two-door, four-door

STANDARD ENGINE: Engine Type: OHV V-6 Special high-grade cast-iron block and cylinder heads. Bore x Stroke: 3.95 in. x 3.32 in. Lifters: Hydraulic. Number of main bearings-4. Fuel Induction: Multiple-port electronic fuel injection. Compression Ratio: 9.0:1. Displacement: 244 cu. in. (4.0 liters). Horsepower: 5-spd. manual: 145 @ 3800 rpm. 4-spd. auto.: 160 @ 4400 rpm. (1992 ratings, 1993 rating not yet available). Torque: 5-spd. manual: 220 lb.-ft. @ 2400 rpm. 4-spd. auto.: 225 lb.-ft. @ 2400 rpm. (1992 ratings, 1993 rating not yet available). Oil refill capacity: 6 qt. with filter change. 4.5 qts. without filter change. Fuel Requirements: Regular Unleaded.

OPTIONAL ENGINE: None.

CHASSIS FEATURES: Separate body and frame, single channel, five cross members, welded frame. 2.89 in. section modulus. Maximum side rail section: 6.08 x 2.28. x 0.150 in. 36,000 psi. Low carbon steel.

SUSPENSION AND RUNNING GEAR: Front Suspension: Computer-selected coil springs, 2260 lb. rating. Optional rating: 2340 lb., 2420 lb., 2540 lb., 2620 lb. Rear Suspension: Variable rate two-stage 5-leaf springs. 2650 lb. rating. Optional Rating: 2750 lb. (for two-door and four-door), 290 lb. (four-door only). Front Axle Type and Capacity: Twin-Traction beam independent with adjustable caster/camber, 2750 lb. capacity. Rear Axle Type and Capacity: Semi-floating, 3200 lb. capacity. Final Drive Ratio: 3.27:1. (3.75:1 limited slip optional with auto. trans. Transfer Case: Warner 1350 Part-time, 2-speed. Ratios: 2.48:1, 1.00:1. "Touch Drive" electric shift. Brakes: Type: Hydraulic power-assisted, disc single-piston, self-adjusting front and cast iron drum rear. Dimensions: Front: 10.86 in. dia. Rear: 10.00 in. x 2.25 in. Total swept area: 251.2 sq. in. Wheels: 6.0JK x 15 in., 5-hole styled steel disc. Optional: Deep dish cast aluminum wheels. Styled steel wheels with spoke design. Tires: P225.70R15SL black sidewall steel-belted, All-Season radial. Optional: P235/75R15SL outline white letters, all-terrain steel-belted radial. Steering: Power assisted, integral recirculating ball. Ratio: 17.0:1, turns Lock-to-Lock: 3.0.Turning Circle: 37.0 ft. (four-door model); 34.2 ft. (two-door). Optional: Transmission: Mazda: 5-speed manual overdrive heavy-duty, all-synchromesh. Transmission Ratios: 3.40, 2.20, 1.50, 1.00, 0.79:1 reverse: 3.42:1. Optional: Ford A4LD 4-speed Automatic Overdrive Drive 4-speed. Ratios: 2.47, 1.47, 1.00, 0.75:1. Reverse: 2.10. Converter ratio: 2.80:1. Clutch: Segmented disc, woven non-asbestos lining. Belleville pressure plate. Clutch diameter: 10 in. Total plate pressure: 1515 lb. Optional: None.

VEHICLE DIMENSIONS:

	Two-door	Four-door
Wheelbase:	102.1 in.	111.9 in.
Overall Length:	174.4 in.	184.3 in.
Front/Rear Tread:	58.3 in./58.3 in.	same
Overall Height:	67.5 in.	67.3 in.
Width:	70.2 in.	same
Front/Rear Overhang:	29.6 in./42.8 in.	same
Tailgate: Width and Height:	52.4 in./33.7 in.	same
Approach/Departure Degrees:	32.9/22.3	32.6/22.3

Load space: Two-door: With rear seat installed: 29.2 in. x 41.9 in. x 33.7 in. With rear seat removed or folded: 59.5 in. x 41.9 in. x 33.7 in. Four-door: With rear seat installed: 38.1 in. x 41.9 in. x 33.7 in. With rear seat removed or folded: 72.9 in. x 41.9 in. x 33.7 in. Maximum capacity: With rear seat folded: Two-door: 69.4 cu. ft. Four-door: 81.6 cu. ft. Front headroom: 39.9 in. Front legroom: 42.1 in. Front shoulder room: 57.1 in. Front hip room: 51.9 in. Rear headroom: 39.1 in. Rear legroom: 35.6 in. (36.6 in. four-door). Rear shoulder room: 57 in. (51.9 in. four-door). Rear hip room: 43.6 in. (51.9 in. four-door).

CAPACITIES: Fuel Tank: 19.0 gal. with skid plate.

ACCOMMODATIONS: Seating Capacity: Four-door model: 5 passenger. Optional: 6 passenger. Two-door model: 4 passenger.

INSTRUMENTATION: Speedometer, trip odometer, tachometer, gauges for fuel level, engine coolant temperature, oil pressure and voltmeter, alert lights for seat belt, 4x4 operation, check engine, battery, brakes, rear anti-lock, low range high beam operation and check oil.

OPTIONS: Air conditioning. Limited slip performance axle (XA80). 4-speed electronic automatic overdrive transmission. California emissions system. High altitude principle use. P235/75R15SL outlined white letter All-Terrain steel belted radial tires. Cloth Captain's chairs. Cloth Sport bucket seat with lumbar support. Cloth 60/40 split front bench seat. Leather Sport bucket seats with power lumbar support. Super cooling engine. Privacy glass for both two- and four-door models. Tilt-up/open air roof. Cargo area cover. Color-keyed front and rear floor mats. Engine block heater. Manual locking hubs. License plate bracket. Body side molding. Luggage rack. Speed control/tilt steering wheel. Deluxe tape stripe. Electronic premium AM/FM stereo with cassette player and digital clock. Electronic AM/FM stereo with cassette player and digital clock. Radio credit option. Deluxe two-tone paint. Deep dish cast aluminum wheels. Deluxe steel wheels. Luxury aluminum wheels. Rear window wiper/washer/defroster. Trailer Towing Package. Includes wiring harness, heavy-duty flasher and ·Super engine cooling (required on vehicles over 5000 GVWR). Light Group. Includes glove box light, ashtray light and engine compartment light. Power Equipment Group. Includes power side windows, power door locks and tailgate and dual electric remote-control mirrors.

HISTORICAL FOOTNOTES: The Ford Explorer was built at Ford's Louisville, Kentucky plant.

GMC PICKUP & SUBURBAN
1956-1993

GMC's origin dates back to 1902 when the American Garment Cleaning Company of Detroit purchased a truck from Max and Morris Grabowsky. This single-cylinder vehicle with chain drive and wooden wheels is regarded by GMC as the "great grandfather" of its modern trucks.

The Grabowsky Motor Vehicle Company was subsequently reorganized and was renamed the Rapid Motor Vehicle Company. By 1909 it was operating the world's largest truck-making facility as well as enjoying the distinction of having built the first truck to successfully climb Pikes Peak.

In 1909 controling interest in the Rapid Motor Vehicle Company was purchased by General Motors. Three years later, in January, 1912, the trade name "GMC Trucks" was first exhibited at the New York auto show and eight months later the GMC trademark (signifying General Motors Company) was registered with the U.S. patent office.

During 1915 GMC began to phase out its use of chain drive in favor of propshaft and universal joints in a series of new gear-driven models. In 1916 a GMC 1-1/2 ton truck made another entry into transportation history by making the first successful transcontinental crossing by a northern route from Seattle, Washington, to New York, New York.

During the First World War, GMC produced approximately 8,500 vehicles for the U.S. Army. These trucks with pneumatic tires, gear-driven axles and fully enclosed cabs functioned as ambulances, troop carriers and cargo haulers. At the end of the war many were purchased for civilian use.

In 1925, GM merged with the Yellow Cab Manufacturing Company of Chicago to form the Yellow Truck and Coach Manufacturing Company. The General Motors Truck Company then became a sales subsidiary of the new venture. Products included yellow coaches, yellow taxicabs and GMC trucks. The property and assets of Yellow Truck and Cab were acquired by GM in 1943 and at that time, the GMC truck & Coach Division of GM was established.

GMC Truck took an active part in military production during World War II. Civilian-truck production ceased in 1942 and GM truck resources were focused upon two products for military use: the DUKW amphibious craft and a 2-1/2 ton 6x6 cargo truck. Both vehicles operated off the same driveline and were powered by the same In-line 6-cylinder gasoline engine. The DUKW-353 became known as the "Duck" and the 6x6 GMC as the "Jimmy." Over 500,000 trucks and 20,000 DUKWs were supplied to the military.

GMC introduced its first Suburban model, based on Chevrolet's commerical panel truck, in 1936. The concept of the Suburban was to provide car-like comfort with the durability and carrying capacity of a truck. Instead of the panel truck's swing rear doors, a horizontally hinged tailgate and a liftgate were fitted to ease the loading of cargo or luggage. The Suburban had three doors; a driver's door and two right-side doors that provided access to the second and third rows of seats which accommodated six passengers (in addition to the driver and one passenger in front). In 1947, the Suburban was redesigned to move it closer to the needs and interests of post-war suburbanites. During the 1950s, swing-out rear doors were added as well as easily removable seats, power steering and power brakes.

The GMC Jimmy full-size Sport utility was introduced in 1970, to combine the ruggedness of a truck with the utility of a fully-enclosed rear seat and cargo area. With a 104 in. wheelbase, the Jimmy 4x4 was well-received by its projected market. Six and eight-cylinder engines were initially offered through V-8s prevailed beginning with the 1983 model year.

The S15 Jimmy-GMC truck's first compact Sport-utility model-was unveiled for the 1983 model uear. Riding on a 100.5 in. wheelbase and "Jimmy Junior" was an instant success. In the 1990 modlel year, a 4.3 lter V-6 becam the standard engine and the S15 prefix was droped form the Jimmy nameplate in 1992. The sensational 280 horsepower turbocharged Typhoon was spun off the Jimmy in 1992.

The Yukon nameplate came with a ground-up overhaul of GMC's full-size Sports utility in 1992. Key ingredients of this make-over included part-time four-wheel drive, a 5.7 liter fuel-injected V-8 and a longer (111.5 in.) wheelbase.

Two energy crises demonstrated the need for more fuel efficiency to many van customers so GMC truck responded with the mid-size Safari for the 1985 model year. The Safari with full time all-wheel drive was introduced in 1990 and a 4.3 liter V-6 became standard in 1991.

The star of the GMC truck fleet is the Sierra. Its four-wheel drive predecessors date back to the 1956 "Blue Chip" models. The future of the four-wheel drive Sierra, along with other GMC four-wheel drive products is closely linked to the fact that 27 percent of General Motors new-car dealers also hold a GMC Truck franchise. These dealers, primarily Buick, Oldsmobile and Pontiac franchises, are involved in a rapidly changing market mix of truck sales to car sales. Within the past decade the ratio of cars to truck sales has changed from seven to eight cars sold per truck sale to a little less than two cars for every truck sold. Industry expects believe that light-duty trucks will continue to win a larger share of the personal-use market. In regard to this trend and the future path of GMC truck design, GMC general manager Lewis B. Campbell has predicted that "in the future, GMC Truck will demonstrate more independence from Chevrolet. Research has shown that the Chevrolet truck brand and the GMC Truck brand each stand for very different things in the buying public's mind, even though the actual products are sometimes very similar. We are now developing a very specific, phased approach to differentiate GMC truck from Chevrolet where there's value in doing so. Eventually, we'll begin to attract a very different buyer from those that are attracted by Chevrolet."

1956 PICKUP & SUBURBAN

After their all-new styling of 1955, the GMC trucks for 1956 were all but unchanged in appearance. But the introduction of four-wheel drive trucks late in the 1956 model year was a major development. The four-wheel drive GMC's were offered in series 100 (1/2 ton-114-123.25 in. wheelbase), series 150 (3/4 ton-123.25 in wheelbase) and series 250 (1 ton, 114-135 in. wheelbase.) trucks. The four-wheel drive system was offered for all chassis-cab, pickup, Panel, Carryall and Stake models in the three series. The four-wheel drive system included a standard 4-speed transmission, or 4-speed Hydra-Matic and a 2-speed transfer case. It was available with either GMC's 6-cylinder or V-8 engine. For the 3100 and 3600 series it also included RPO 254 (heavy-duty 8-leaf rear springs). For the 3800 series RPO 200 (rear shock absorbers) and RPO 254 (a heavy-duty rear spring) were included.

A 6-stud SAE opening at the bottom of the transfer case provided for both front and rear work applications. A rear-opening was available for auxiliary shaft operation. Rzeppa constant-velocity joints were used for the front axle to reduce front wheel vibration and lessen tire wear. They also delivered an even flow of power at all positions of the front wheels, and kept driving forces from being transmitted to the steering wheel. The tie rods were protected from off-road hazards. The transfer case was located in a 4-position rubber mount.

Equally at home on or off highway, 4-wheel drive GMC's deliver the performance and economy . . . have all the s . . . comfort and standout styling features of regular GMC m These new multi-purpose vehicles, with full-size power . . . full-size . . . and full-size bodies are factory built and factory warranted. They

1956 GMC series 150 pickup

I.D. DATA: The serial number was located inside the cab or on the truck firewall. Stamped on this "GMC Service Parts Identification" was the model of the engine, transmission, service brake and axle. The engine number for the 6-cylinder engine was located on the left side of the cylinder block behind the oil filter.

Body Type	Model Number	Factory Price	GVW	Shipping Weight	Prod. Total
Series 100 1/2 ton 6-cyl., 114 in. wheelbase, model 101					
Chassis & Cab	—	$2306	5600	3271	—
Panel	—	$2705	5600	3860	—
Pickup	—	$2409	5600	3615	—
Suburban	—	$3099	5600	4140	—
Series 100 1/2 ton 6-cyl., 123.25 in. wheelbase, model 102					
Chassis & Cab	—	$2328	5600	3395	—
Pickup	—	$2442	5600	3775	—
Stake Rack	—	$N.A.	5600	3990	—
Series 150 3/4 ton 6-cyl., 123.25 in. wheelbase, model 152					
Chassis & Cab	—	$2485	7600	3690	—
Pickup	—	$2599	7600	4070	—
Stake Rack	—	$2690	7600	4285	—
Series 200 1 ton, 114-135 in. wheelbase					
Ch. & Cab, 114 in. wb.	—	$2597	10,000	3895	—
Ch. & Cab, 123.25 in. wb.	—	$2597	10,000	3900	—
Ch. & Cab, 135 in. wb.	—	$2597	10,000	3925	—
Panel, 9 ft.	—	$3050	10,000	4610	—
Panel Dlx., 9 ft.	—	$3142	10,000	4610	—
Pickup, 9 ft.	—	$2732	10,000	4375	—
Stake Rack	—	$2845	10,000	4765	—

STANDARD ENGINE: All models: GMC 270. Engine Type: OHV, In-line 6-cylinder. Cast iron block and cylinder head. Bore x Stroke: 3.78 in. x 4.0 in. Lifters: Hydraulic. Fuel Induction: Single Holley 1-bbl. carburetor, model 1904. Compression Ratio: 7.75:1. Displacement: 269.5 cu. in. (4.42 liters). Horsepower: Gross: 130 @ 3600 rpm. Net: 121 @ 3400 rpm. Torque: Gross: 238 lb.-ft. @ 1200-2000 rpm. Net: 233 lb.-ft. @ 1200 rpm. Fuel Requirements: Regular.

OPTIONAL ENGINE: V-8, OHV. All models. GMC trucks with this engine are designated 100-8, 150-8 or 250-8. Bore x Stroke: 3.937 in. x 3.25 in. Lifters: Hydraulic. Number of main bearings-5. Fuel Induction: Single Rochester 2-bbl. carburetor. Compression Ratio: 7.08:1. Displacement: 316.6 cu. in. (5.19 liters). Horsepower: 180 @ 4400 rpm. Torque: 276 lb.-ft. @ 2200 rpm. Fuel Requirements: Regular.

CHASSIS FEATURES: Separate body and frame with five cross members. 114 in. wheelbase: 6 in. x 2.25 in. x 0.1406 in. Section modulus: 2.53. 123.25 in. wheelbase: 6.09 in. x 2.25 in. x 0.1875 in. Section modulus: 3.36. 135 in. wheelbase: 7.25 in. x 2.75 in. x 0.21875 in. Section modulus: 5.70.

SUSPENSION AND RUNNING GEAR: Front Suspension: 44 in. x 2.0 in. Series 100 and 150: 7-leaf; series 250: 10-leaf semi-elliptical springs, series 100 and 150: 1.0 in. dia. absorbers. Series 100: 1360 lb. rating (at ground). Optional rating: None. Rear Suspension: 52 in. x 2.0 in. Single-stage, series 100: 8-leaf; series 150 and 250: 10-leaf semi-elliptical springs, series

100 and 150: 1.0 in. dia. shock absorbers. Series 100: 1570 lb. rating (at ground). Optional Rating: None. Front Axle Type and Capacity: Semi-floating, series 100: 3000 lb. capacity. Series 150 and 250: 3500 lb. capacity. Optional: None. Rear Axle Type and Capacity: Semi-floating, hypoid. Series 100: 3300 lb. capacity. Series 150: 5000 lb. capacity. Series 250: 7200 lb. capacity. Optional: None. Final Drive Ratio: Series 100: 3.90:1. Series 150: 4.56:1 or 5.14:1. Series 250: 5.14:1. Transfer Case: Single lever, 4-position, 2-speed: 1.86, 1.00:1. Brakes: Type: Hydraulic, front and rear drums. Dimensions: Series 100 and 150: Front: 11.0 in. x 2.0 in. Rear: 11.0 in. x 2.0 in. Series 250: Front: 12.0 in. x 2.0 in. Rear: 140 in. x 2.50 in. Wheels: Ventilated steel disc. Tires: Series 100: 6.70 x 15, 4-ply rating, tubeless. Series 150: 7 x17.5, 6-ply rating, tubeless. Series 250: 8 x 107.5, 6-ply rating, tubeless. Steering: Recirculating ball, nut and sector type, 18 in. steering wheel. Ratio: 21.30:1. Optional: None. Transmission: 4-speed, synchromesh manual. Transmission Ratios: 7.05, 6.69, 3.19, 1.00:1. Reverse: 12.60:1. Optional: 4-speed Hydra-Matic automatic. Clutch: Single disc with damper. Clutch diameter: Series 100, 150 and 250: 10 in. dia. Total lining area: 100.5 sq. in. Series 100-8, 150-8, series 250-8: 11. in. dia. Total lining area: 123.7 sq. in.

VEHICLE DIMENSIONS: 114 in. wheelbase models. Overall Length: Pickup: 185.5 in. Panel: 197.875 in. Overall Height: Pickup: 79.6875 in. Width: 75.75 in. Front/Rear Overhang: 34.875./ 36.625 in. (pickup). Tailgate: Width and Height: 50 in. x 17.56 in. Load space: Pickup box dimensions: 78.125 in. x 50.0. x 17.56 in. 123.25 in. wheelbase models. Overall Length: Pickup: 205.5625 in. Panel: 204.9375 in. Front/Rear Overhang: 30.6875 in./51.625 in. Stake: 30.6875 in. /50.625 in. 135 in. wheelbase models. Overall Length: Pickup and Chassis & Cab: 215.8125 in. Panel: 228.875 in. Stake: 222.5625 in.

CAPACITIES: Fuel Tank: Pickup: 17.5 gal. Panel: 15.5 gal. Series 150 and 250: 18.5 gal. Optional: None.

ACCOMMODATIONS: Seating Capacity: 3 passenger. Optional: None.

INSTRUMENTATION: Speedometer, odometer, gauges for oil pressure, fuel level, engine coolant temperature, battery charge.

OPTIONS AND PRICES: Oil bath air cleaner. Heavy-duty clutch. Oil filter. Low-cut in generator. Governor. Chrome grille, bumper and insignia. Right-hand stop and tail lamp. Directional signals. Rear shock absorbers (series 250 and 250-8). Power steering. Side-mounted spare tire carrier. Wrap-around cab rear window. Electric windshield wipers. Various tire sizes.

HISTORICAL FOOTNOTES: Calendar year registrations for all GMC trucks totalled 82,266 units.

1957 PICKUP & SUBURBAN

The 1957 GMC trucks were identified by their new grille consisting of a center vertical divider and a series of horizontal bars. The optional V-8 now displaced 347 cubic inches and had a corresponding increase in horsepower and torque.

I.D. DATA: Unchanged from 1956.

Body Type	Model Number	Factory Price	GVW	Shipping Weight	Prod. Total
Series 100 1/2 ton 6-cyl., 114 in. wheelbase, model 101					
Chassis & Cab	—	$2420	5600	3271	—
Panel	—	$2819	5600	3860	—
Pickup	—	$2523	5600	3615	—
Suburban	—	$3214	5600	4140	—
Series 100 1/2 ton 6-cyl., 123.25 in. wheelbase, model 102					
Chassis & Cab	—	$2442	5600	3395	—
Pickup	—	$2556	5600	3775	—
Stake Rack	—	$N.A.	5600	3990	—
Series 150 3/4 ton 6-cyl., 123.25 in. wheelbase, model 152					
Chassis & Cab	—	$2605	7600	3690	—
Pickup	—	$2719	7600	4070	—
Stake Rack	—	$2810	7600	4285	—
Series 250 1 ton, 114-135 in. wheelbase					
Ch. & Cab, 114 in. wb.	—	$2733	10,000	3895	—
Ch. & Cab, 123.25 in.	—	$2733	10,000	3900	—
Ch. & Cab, 135 in. wb.	—	$2733	10,000	3925	—
Panel, 9 ft.	—	$3186	10,000	4610	—
Panel Dlx,. 9 ft.	—	$3278	10,000	4610	—
Pickup, 9 ft.	—	$2868	10,000	4375	—
Stake Rack	—	$2981	10,000	4765	—

STANDARD ENGINE: All models: GMC 270. Engine Type: OHV, In-line 6-cylinder. Cast iron block and cylinder head. Bore x Stroke: 3.78 in. x 4.0 in. Lifters: Hydraulic. Fuel Induction: Single Holley 1-bbl. carburetor, model 1904. Compression Ratio: 7.75:1. Displacement: 269.5 cu. in. (4.42 liters). Horsepower: Gross: 130 @ 3600 rpm. Net: 121 @ 3400 rpm. Torque: Gross 238 lb.-ft. @ 1200-2000 rpm. Net: 233 lb.-ft. @ 1200 rpm. Fuel Requirements: Regular.

OPTIONAL ENGINE: V-8, OHV. All models. GMC trucks with this engine are designated 100-8, 150-8 or 250-8. Bore x Stroke: 3.937 in. x 3.56 in. Lifters: Hydraulic. Number of main bearings-5. Fuel Induction: Single Rochester 2-bbl. carburetor. Displacement: 347 cu. in. (5.68 liters). Horsepower: 206 @ 4400 rpm. Torque: 317 lb.-ft. @ 2200 rpm. Oil refill capacity:. Fuel Requirements: Regular.

CHASSIS FEATURES: Separate body and frame with five cross members. 114 in. wheelbase: 6 in. x 2.25 in. x 0.1406 in. Section modulus: 2.53. 123.25 in. wheelbase: 6.09 in. x 2.25 in. x 0.1875 in. Section modulus: 3.36. 135 in. wheelbase: 7.25 in. x 2.75 in. x 0.21875 in. Section modulus: 5.70.

SUSPENSION AND RUNNING GEAR: Front Suspension: 44 in. x 2.0 in. Series 100 and 150: 7-leaf; series 250: 10-leaf semi-elliptical springs, series 100 and 150: 1.0 in. dia. absorbers. Series 100: 1360 lb. rating (at ground). Optional rating: None. Rear Suspension: 52 in. x 2.0 in. Single-stage, series 100: 8-leaf; series 150 and 250: 10-leaf semi-elliptical springs, series 100 and 150: 1.0 in. dia. shock absorbers. Series 100: 1570 lb. rating (at ground). Optional Rating: None. Front Axle Type and Capacity: Semi-floating, series 100: 3000 lb. capacity. Series 150 and 250: 3500 lb. capacity. Optional: None. Rear Axle Type and Capacity: Semi-floating, hypoid. Series 100: 3300 lb. capacity. Series 150: 5000 lb. capacity. Series 250: 7200 lb. capacity. Optional: None. Final Drive Ratio: Series 100: 3.90:1. Series 150: 4.56:1 or 5.14:1. Series 250: 5.14:1. Transfer Case: Single lever, 4-position, 2-speed: 1.86, 1.00:1. Brakes: Type: Hydraulic, front and rear drums. Dimensions: Series 100 and 150: Front: 11.0 in. x 2.0 in. Rear: 11.0 in. x 2.0 in. Series 250: Front: 12.0 in. x 2.0 in. Rear: 140 in. x 2.50 in. Wheels: Ventilated steel disc. Tires: Series 100: 6.70 x 15, 4-ply rating, tubeless. Series 150: 7 x17.5, 6-ply rating, tubeless. Series 250: 8 x 107.5, 6-ply rating, tubeless. Steering: Recirculating ball, nut and sector type, 18 in. steering wheel. Ratio: 21.30:1. Optional: None. Transmission: 4-speed, synchromesh manual. Transmission Ratios: 7.05, 6.69, 3.19, 1.00:1. Reverse: 12.60:1. Optional: 4-speed Hydra-Matic automatic. Clutch: Single disc with damper. Clutch diameter: Series 100, 150 and 250: 10 in. dia. Total lining area: 100.5 sq. in. Series 100-8, 150-8, series 250-8: 11. in. dia. Total lining area: 123.7 sq. in.

VEHICLE DIMENSIONS: 114 in. wheelbase models. Overall Length: Pickup: 185.5 in. Panel: 197.875 in. Overall Height: Panel: 79.6875 in. Width: 75.75 in. Front/Rear Overhang: 34.875./ 36.625 in. (pickup). Tailgate: Width and Height: 50 in. x 17.56 in. Load space: Pickup box dimensions: 78.125 in. x 50.0 in. x 17.56 in. 123.25 in. wheelbase models. Overall Length: Pickup: 205.5625. Stake: 204.9375 in. Front/Rear Overhang: Pickup: 30.6875 in./51.625 in. Stake: 30.6875 in./50.625 in. 135 in. wheelbase models. Overall Length: Pickup and chassis & cab: 215.8125 in. Panel: 228.875 in. Stake: 222.5625 in.

CAPACITIES: Fuel Tank: Pickup: 17.5 gal. Panel: 15.5 gal. Series 150 and 250: 18.5 gal. Optional: None.

ACCOMMODATIONS: Seating Capacity: 3 passenger. Optional: None.

INSTRUMENTATION: Speedometer, odometer, gauges for oil pressure, fuel level, engine coolant temperature, battery charge.

OPTIONS: Oil bath air cleaner. Heavy-duty clutch. Oil filter. Low-cut in generator. Governor. Chrome grille, bumper and insignia. Right-hand stop and tail lamp. Directional signals. Rear shock absorbers (series 250 and 250-8). Power steering. Side-mounted spare tire carrier. Wrap-around cab rear window. Electric windshield wipers. Various tire sizes.

HISTORICAL FOOTNOTES: Calendar year registration of all series of GMC trucks was 62,165.

1958 PICKUP & SUBURBAN

The 1958 GMC trucks were identified by their revamped front body design. The hood featured the familiar GMC nameplate bracketed by panels enclosing thin horizontal bars. The grille was similar to that used in 1956. The latest version had arrow-shaped parking/directional lights and a center horizontal bar carrying the series designation. Also debuting for 1958 was a dual headlight system. The optional V-8 now displaced 336 cubic inches and developed 200 horsepower. A new Wideside body pickup model was available for 1958 in the 100 and 150 series. Among the features of the 1958 GMC trucks were standard or deluxe appointments, fully adjustable seats, sponge rubber seat cushions, two-tone interiors, All-Weather ventilation, safety steering wheel, non-glare instrument panel, concealed running boards, metal-framed door window glass and dual windshield wipers.

1958 GMC series 100 pickup

I.D. DATA: Unchanged from 1957.

Body Type	Model Number	Factory Price	GVW	Shipping Weight	Prod. Total
Series 100 1/2 ton 6-cyl., 114 in. wheelbase, model 101					
Chassis & Cab	—	$2492	5600	3271	—
Panel	—	$2901	5600	3860	—
Pickup	—	$2595	5600	3615	—
Pickup W-S	—	$2616	5600	3675	—
Suburban	—	$3286	5600	4140	—
Series 100 1/2 ton 6-cyl., 123.25 in. wheelbase, model 102					
Chassis & Cab	—	$2514	5600	3395	—
Pickup	—	$2628	5600	3775	—
Pickup W-S	—	$2649	5600	3825	—
Stake Rack	—	$N.A.	5600	3990	—
Series 150 3/4 ton 6-cyl., 123.25 in. wheelbase, model 152					
Chassis & Cab	—	$2677	7600	3690	—
Pickup	—	$2791	7600	4070	—
Pickup W-S	—	$2812	7600	4170	—
Stake Rack	—	$2882	7600	4285	—
Series 250 1 ton 114-135 in. wheelbase					
Ch. & Cab, 114 in. wb.	—	$2805	10,000	3895	—
Ch. & Cab, 123.25 in.	—	$2805	10,000	3900	—
Ch. & Cab, 135 in. wb.	—	$2805	10,000	3925	—
Panel, 9 ft.	—	$3258	10,000	4610	—
Panel Dlx, 9 ft.	—	$3350	10,000	4610	—
Pickup, 9 ft.	—	$2940	10,000	4375	—
Stake Rack	—	$3053	10,000	4765	—

STANDARD ENGINE: All models: GMC 270. Engine Type: OHV, In-line 6-cylinder. Cast iron block and cylinder head. Bore x Stroke: 3.78 in. x 4.0 in. Lifters: Hydraulic. Fuel Induction: Single Holley 1-bbl. carburetor, model 1904. Compression Ratio: 7.75:1. Displacement: 269.5 cu. in. (4.42 liters). Horsepower: Gross: 130 @ 3600 rpm. Net: 121 @ 3400 rpm. Torque: Gross: 238 lb.-ft. @ 1200-2000 rpm. Net: 233 lb.-ft. @ 1200 rpm. Fuel Requirements: Regular.

OPTIONAL ENGINE: V-8, OHV. All models. GMC trucks with this engine are designated 100-8, 150-8 or 250-8. Bore x Stroke: 3.875 in. x 3.5625 in. Lifters: Hydraulic. Number of main bearings-5. Fuel Induction: Single Rochester 2-bbl. carburetor. Displacement: 336.1 cu. in. (5.50 liters). Horsepower: Gross: 200 @ 4400 rpm. Net: 171 @ 3600 rpm. Torque: Gross: 307 lb.-ft. @ 2000-2400 rpm. Net: 286 lb.-ft. @ 2400 rpm. Compression ratio: 7.5:1.

CHASSIS FEATURES: Separate body and frame with five cross members. 114 in. wheelbase: 6 in. x 2.25 in. x 0.1406 in. Section modulus: 2.53. 123.25 in. wheelbase: 6.09 in. x 2.25 in. x 0.1875 in. Section modulus: 3.36. 135 in. wheelbase: 7.25 in. x 2.75 in. x 0.21875 in. Section modulus: 5.70.

SUSPENSION AND RUNNING GEAR: Front Suspension: 44 in. x 2.0 in. Series 100 and 150: 7-leaf; series 250: 10-leaf semi-elliptical springs, series 100 and 150: 1.0 in. dia. absorbers. Series 100: 1360 lb. rating (at ground) Optional rating: None. Rear Suspension: 52 in. x 2.0 in. Single-stage, series 100: 8-leaf; series 150 and 250: 10-leaf semi-elliptical springs, series 100 and 150: 1.0 in. dia. shock absorbers. Series 100: 1570 lb. rating (at ground). Optional Rating: None. Front Axle Type and Capacity: Semi-floating, series 100: 3000 lb. capacity. Series 150 and 250: 3500 lb. capacity. Optional: None. Rear Axle Type and Capacity: Semi-floating, hypoid. Series 100: 3300 lb. capacity. Series 150: 5000 lb. capacity. Series 250: 7200 lb. capacity. Optional: None. Final Drive Ratio: Series 100: 3.90:1. Series 150: 4.56:1 or 5.14:1. Series 250: 5.14:1. Transfer Case: Single lever, 4-position, 2-speed: 1.86, 1.00:1. Brakes: Type: Hydraulic, front and rear drums. Dimensions - Series 100 and 150: Front: 11.0 in. x 2.0 in. Rear: 11.0 in. x 2.0 in. Series 250: Front: 12.0 in. x 2.0 in. Rear: 140 in. x 2.50 in. Wheels: Ventilated steel disc. Tires: Series 100: 6.70 x 17.5, 4-ply rating, tubeless. Series 150: 7 x17.5, 6-ply rating, tubeless. Series 250: 8 x 107.5, 6-ply rating, tubeless. Steering: Recirculating ball, nut and sector type, 18 in. steering wheel. Ratio: 21.30:1. Optional: None. Transmission: 4-speed, synchromesh manual. Transmission Ratios: 7.05, 6.69, 3.19, 1.00:1. Reverse: 12.60:1. Optional: 4-speed Hydra-Matic automatic. Clutch: Single disc with damper. Clutch diameter: Series 100, 150 and 250: 10 in. dia. Total lining area: 100.5 sq. in. Series 100-8, 150-8, series 250-8: 11. in. dia. Total lining area: 123.7 sq. in.

VEHICLE DIMENSIONS: 114 in. wheelbase models. Overall Length: Pickup: 185.5 in. Panel: 197.875 in. Overall Height: Panel: 79.6875 in. Width: 75.75 in. Front/Rear Overhang: 34.875./ 36.625 in. (pickup). Tailgate: Width and Height: 50 in. x 17.56 in. Load space: Pickup box dimensions: 78.125 in. x 50.0 in. x 17.56 in. 123.25 in. wheelbase models. Overall Length: Pickup: 205.5625. Stake: 204.9375 in. Front/Rear Overhang: Pickup: 30.6875 in./51.625 in. Stake: 30.6875 in./50.625 in. 135 in. wheelbase models. Overall Length: Pickup and chassis & cab: 215.8125 in. Panel: 228.875 in. Stake: 222.5625 in.

CAPACITIES: Fuel Tank: Pickup: 17.5 gal. Panel: 15.5 gal. Series 150 and 250: 18.5 gal. Optional: None.

ACCOMMODATIONS: Seating Capacity: 3 passenger. Optional: None.

INSTRUMENTATION: Speedometer, odometer, gauges for oil pressure, fuel level, engine coolant temperature, battery charge.

OPTIONS: Oil bath air cleaner. Heavy-duty clutch. Oil filter. Low-cut in generator. Governor. Chrome grille, bumper and insignia. Right-hand stop and tail lamp. Directional signals. Rear shock absorbers (series 250 and 250-8). Power steering. Side-mounted spare tire carrier. Wrap-around cab rear window. Electric windshield wipers. Various tire sizes.

HISTORICAL FOOTNOTES: Calendar year registration of all series of GMC trucks was 5,950. Model year production of all models was 64,216.

1958 GMC Suburban

1959 PICKUP & SUBURBAN

Change for 1959 was limited to the use of a front bumper sans the dual pods of 1958

I.D. DATA: Unchanged from 1957.

Body Type	Model Number	Factory Price	GVW	Shipping Weight	Prod. Total
Series 100 1/2 ton 6-cyl., 114 in. wheelbase, model 101					
Chassis & Cab	—	$2557	5600	3271	—
Panel	—	$2966	5600	3860	—
Pickup	—	$2660	5600	3615	—
Pickup W-S	—	$2681	5600	3675	—
Suburban	—	$3351	5600	4140	—

Series 100 1/2 ton 6-cyl., 123.25 in. wheelbase, model 102					
Chassis & Cab	—	$2579	5600	3395	—
Pickup	—	$2693	5600	3775	—
Pickup W-S	—	$2714	5600	3825	—
Stake Rack	—	$2784	5600	3990	—
Series 150 3/4 ton 6-cyl., 123.25 in. wheelbase, model 152					
Chassis & Cab	—	$2741	7600	3690	—
Pickup	—	$2855	7600	4070	—
Pickup W-S	—	$2876	7600	4170	—
Stake Rack	—	$2946	7600	4285	—
Series 250 1 ton, 114-135 in. wheelbase					
Ch. & Cab,114 in. wb.	—	$2869	10,000	3895	—
Ch. & Cab, 123.25 in.	—	$2869	10,000	3900	—
Ch. & Cab, 135 in. wb.	—	$2869	10,000	3925	—
Panel, 9 ft.	—	$3322	10,000	4610	—
Panel Dlx., 9 ft.	—	$3414	10,000	4610	—
Pickup, 9 ft.	—	$3004	10,000	4375	—
Stake Rack	—	$3117	10,000	4765	—

STANDARD ENGINE: All models: GMC 270. Engine Type: OHV, In-line 6-cylinder. Cast iron block and cylinder head. Bore x Stroke: 3.78 in. x 4.0 in. Lifters: Hydraulic. Fuel Induction: Single Holley 1-bbl. carburetor, model 1904. Compression Ratio: 7.75:1. Displacement: 269.5 cu. in. (4.42 liters). Horsepower: Gross: 130 @ 3600 rpm. Net: 121 @ 3400 rpm. Torque: Gross: 238 lb.-ft. @ 1200-2000 rpm. Net: 233 lb.-ft. @ 1200 rpm. Fuel Requirements: Regular.

OPTIONAL ENGINE: V-8, OHV. All models. GMC trucks with this engine are designated 100-8, 150-8 or 250-8. Bore x Stroke: 3.875 in. x 3.5625 in. Lifters: Hydraulic. Number of main bearings-5. Fuel Induction: Single Rochester 2-bbl. carburetor. Displacement: 336.1 cu. in. (5.50 liters). Horsepower: Gross: 200 @ 4400 rpm. Net: 171 @ 3600 rpm. Torque: Gross: 307 lb.-ft. @ 2000-2400 rpm. Net: 286 lb.-ft. @ 2400 rpm. Compression ratio: 7.5:1. Fuel Requirements: Regular.

CHASSIS FEATURES: Separate body and frame with five cross members. 114 in. wheelbase: 6 in. x 2.25 in. x 0.1406 in. Section modulus: 2.53. 123.25 in. wheelbase: 6.09 in. x 2.25 in. x 0.1875 in. Section modulus: 3.36. 135 in. wheelbase: 7.25 in. x 2.75 in. x 0.21875 in. Section modulus: 5.70.

SUSPENSION AND RUNNING GEAR: Front Suspension: 44 in. x 2.0 in. Series 100 and 150: 7-leaf; series 250: 10-leaf semi-elliptical springs, series 100 and 150: 1.0 in. dia. absorbers. Series 100: 1360 lb. rating (at ground). Optional rating: None. Rear Suspension: 52 in. x 2.0 in. Single-stage, series 100: 8-leaf; series 150 and 250: 10-leaf semi-elliptical springs, series 100 and 150: 1.0 in. dia. shock absorbers. Series 100: 1570 lb. rating (at ground). Optional Rating: None. Front Axle Type and Capacity: Semi-floating, series 100: 3000 lb. capacity. Series 150 and 250: 3500 lb. capacity. Optional: None. Rear Axle Type and Capacity: Semi-floating, hypoid. Series 100: 3300 lb. capacity. Series 150: 5000 lb. capacity. Series 250: 7200 lb. capacity. Optional: None. Final Drive Ratio: Series 100: 3.90:1. Series 150: 4.56:1 or 5.14:1. Series 250: 5.14:1. Transfer Case: Single lever, 4-position, 2-speed: 1.86, 1.00:1. Brakes: Type: Hydraulic, front and rear drums. Dimensions: Series 100 and 150: Front: 11.0 in. x 2.0 in. Rear: 11.0 in. x 2.0 in. Series 250: Front: 12.0 in. x 2.0 in. Rear: 140 in. x 2.50 in. Wheels: Ventilated steel disc. Tires: Series 100: 6.70 x 15, 4-ply rating, tubeless. Series 150: 7 x17.5, 6-ply rating, tubeless. Series 250: 8 x 107.5, 6-ply rating, tubeless. Steering: Recirculating ball, nut and sector type, 18 in. steering wheel. Ratio: 21.30:1. Optional: None. Transmission: 4-speed, synchromesh manual. Transmission Ratios: 7.05, 6.69, 3.19, 1.00:1. Reverse: 12.60:1. Optional: 4-speed Hydra-Matic automatic. Clutch: Single disc with damper. Clutch diameter: Series 100, 150 and 250: 10 in. dia. Total lining area: 100.5 sq. in. Series 100-8, 150-8, series 250-8: 11. in. dia. Total lining area: 123.7 sq. in.

VEHICLE DIMENSIONS: 114 in. wheelbase models. Overall Length: Pickup: 185.5 in. Panel: 197.875 in. Overall Height: Panel: 79.6875 in. Width: 75.75 in. Front/Rear Overhang: 34.875./36.625 in. (pickup). Tailgate: Width and Height: 50 in. x 17.56 in. Load space: Pickup box dimensions: 78.125 in. x 50.0 in. x 17.56 in. 123.25 in. wheelbase models. Overall Length: Pickup: 205.5625. Stake: 204.9375 in. Front/Rear Overhang: Pickup: 30.6875 in./51.625 in. Stake: 30.6875 in./50.625 in. 135 in. wheelbase models. Overall Length: Pickup and chassis & cab: 215.8125 in. Panel: 228.875 in. Stake: 222.5625 in.

CAPACITIES: Fuel Tank: Pickup: 17.5 gal. Panel: 15.5 gal. Series 150 and 250: 18.5 gal. Optional: None.

ACCOMMODATIONS: Seating Capacity: 3 passenger. Optional: None.

INSTRUMENTATION: Speedometer, odometer, gauges for oil pressure, fuel level, engine coolant temperature, battery charge.

OPTIONS: Oil bath air cleaner. Heavy-duty clutch. Oil filter. Low-cut in generator. Governor. Chrome grille, bumper and insignia. Right-hand stop and tail lamp. Directional signals. Rear shock absorbers (series 250 and 250-8). Power steering. Side-mounted spare tire carrier. Wrap-around cab rear window. Electric windshield wipers. Various tire sizes.

HISTORICAL FOOTNOTES: Calendar year registration of all series of GMC trucks was 69,509. Model year production of all models was 77,473.

1960 PICKUP & SUBURBAN

The 1960 GMC trucks shared their new bodies with the latest Chevrolet trucks. The wraparound windshield format was retained. The front end was boldly conceived with larger horizontal pods for the parking/directional lights positioned above the primary grille section. The headlights were located in a large lower section that included a grille consisting of horizontal bars. GMC lettering was positioned directly below the larger horizontal bars linking the pods containing the GMC's dual headlights. The side body crease of the new models suggested that its creators had ben influenced by the design of the Corvair. Vying with the new styling for the truck customer's attention was GMC's new V-6 engine. This 600 engine was an exclusive truck engine that had the shortest stroke of any 6-cylinder truck engine. Its peak torque was reached at a low rpm level and it had a very high level of cooling (at 3600 rpm 130 gallons of water were pumped through the engine per minute) and lubrication ability (a high output oil pump pumped 14 gallons of oil per minute) and was characterized by a high degree of parts interchangeability. Other features included a high-mounted camshaft, short push rods, a short, rigid crankshaft, large connecting rods and heavy-duty pistons.

I.D. DATA: The serial number was located on the identification plate found on the cowl left side panel inside the cab or on the left door hinge pillar. It provided information about the vehicle's model number, chassis serial number, certified gross vehicle weight and net horsepower. The numbers began with 10,0001 and up. The engine number for 6-cylinder engines was stamped on the left side of the cylinder block behind the oil filler. The V-8 engine number was stamped on the top of engine block ahead of the right-bank cylinder head.

Body Type	Model Number	Factory Price	GVW	Shipping Weight	Prod. Total
Series 1000 1/2 ton V-6. 115 in. wheelbase					
Chassis & Cab	1001	$2641	5600	3980	—
Pickup W.S.	1001	$2776	5600	4520	—
Panel	1001	$3072	5600	4535	—
Panel Cust.	1001	$3169	5600	4550	—
Pickup F.S	1001	$2755	5600	4350	—
Suburban	1001	$3504	5600	4865	—
Series 1000 1/2 ton V-6. 127 in. wheelbase					
Chassis and Cab	1002	$3504	5600	4050	—
Pickup W.S.	1002	$2826	5600	4520	—
Pickup F.S.	1002	$2805	5600	4470	—
Series 1500 3/4 ton V-6. 127 in. wheelbase					
Chassis & Cab	1502	$2852	8100	4285	—
Pickup W.S.	1502	$2987	8100	2842	—
Pickup F.S.	1502	$2966	8100	4705	—
Stake	1502	$3057	8100	4945	—

STANDARD ENGINE: All models: GMC 305D. Engine Type: OHV, V-6. Cast iron block and cylinder head. Bore x Stroke: 4.25 in. x 3.58 in. Fuel Induction: Single barrel model 1904 Holley. Compression Ratio: 7.75:1. Displacement: 304.7 cu. in. (4.99 liters). Number of main bearing: 4. Horsepower: Gross: 165 @ 3800 rpm. Net: 142 @ 3800 rpm. Torque: Gross: 280 lb.-ft. @ 1600 rpm. Net: 260 lb.-ft. @ 1600 rpm. Fuel Requirements: Regular. Oil capacity: 5 qt.

CHASSIS FEATURES: Separate body and frame. Ladder type. drop-center frame. 7.20 in. x 2.75 in. x 0.1875 in.

SUSPENSION AND RUNNING GEAR: Front Suspension: 44 in. x 2.0 in. 5-leaf semi-elliptical springs. Capacity: 1750 lb. at ground. Rear Suspension: K1000: 52 in. x 2.5 in. 6-leaf semi-elliptical springs. Capacity: 1750 lb. K1500: 52 in. x 2.5 in. 7-leaf semi-elliptical springs. Capacity: 2750 lb. Front Axle Type and Capacity: K1000: Hypoid, 3300 lb. capacity. K1500: Hypoid, 3500 lb. capacity. Rear Axle Type and Capacity: K1000: Hypoid, semi-floating, 3500 lb. K1500: Full-floating, hypoid. 5500 lb. capacity. Final Drive Ratio: K1000: Front and rear: 3.54:1. K1500: Front and rear: 4.56:1. Transfer Case: Single lever, 4-position, 2-speed: 1.86, 1.00:1. Brakes: Type: Hydraulic, front and rear drums. Dimensions: K100: Front: 11.0 in. x 2.0 in. Rear: 11.0 in. x 2.0 in. Effective drum area: 276 sq. in. Effective lining area: 167 sq. in. K1500: Front and Rear: 12.125 in. x 2.0 in. Wheels: Ventilated steel disc. Tires: K1000: 6.70 x 15, 6-ply rating, tubeless. K1500: 7 x 17.5 in. 6-ply rating, tubeless. Steering: Recirculating ball type, 17 in. steering wheel. Ratio: 24.0:1. Optional: None. Transmission: 3-speed synchromesh. Optional: 4-speed synchromesh. Clutch: Hydraulic control, coil-spring. Clutch diameter: 11 in. dia. Total lining area: 124.5 sq. in.

VEHICLE DIMENSIONS: 115 in. wheelbase models. Overall Length: Pickup: 186.625 in. Panel: 201 in. FrontTread: 63.125 in. Overall Height: Pickup: 77.125 in., Panel: 80.5 in. Width: 78.75 in. Front/Rear Overhang: Pickup: 31.75./39.875 in. Panel: 31.75 in./54.25 in. Tailgate: Width and Height: 50 in. x 17.50 in. Load space: Pickup box dimensions: 78.125 in. x 50.0 in. x 17.56 in. 127 in. wheelbase models. Overall Length: 206 in. Front Tread: 63.125 in. Overall Height: 78.25 in. Width: 78.75 in. Front/Rear Overhang: 31.75 in./47.25 in.

CAPACITIES: Fuel Tank: Pickup: 17.5 gal. Panel: 17.0 gal.

ACCOMMODATIONS: Seating Capacity: Pickup and Panel: 3 passenger. Suburban: 6 passenger.

INSTRUMENTATION: Speedometer, odometer, gauges for oil pressure, fuel level, engine coolant temperature, battery charge.

OPTIONS: K1000 tires: 6.50 x 15 6-ply rated tires. 7 x 17.5 6-ply rated tires. K1500 tires: 8 x 17.5 6-ply rated. 8 x 17.5 8-ply rated. 8 x 19.5 6-ply rated. 8 x 18.5 8-plyrated. 1 qt. oil bath air cleaner. Heavy-duty 70 amp-hr. battery. Chrome front bumper (except Panel and Suburban). Chrome front and rear bumper (Panel and Suburban only). Custom cab. Includes custom seat and left door lock. Spare wheel carrier. Directional signals. 35 amp generator. 50 amp generator. Deluxe heater and defroster. Recirculating, inside air heater and defroster. Free wheeling manual front hubs. Left door lock. Lock for side wheel carrier. Lock for left door and side wheel carrier. Exterior left 17.5 in. swinging arm mirror (pickup, chassis and cab). Exterior right 17.5 in. swinging arm mirror (pickup, chassis and cab). Exterior right 8.0 in. fixed bracket. Two-tone paint. Heavy-duty radiator. Auxiliary rear seat for Panel. Custom seat (for Deluxe cab only. Full-view rear window. Windshield washers.

HISTORICAL FOOTNOTES: Calendar year registrations of all GMC truck models was 82,546. Model year production of all GMC models was 104,310.

1961 PICKUP & SUBURBAN

The 1961 GMC trucks were unchanged from their 1960 form.

I.D. DATA: The serial number was located on the identification plate found on the cowl left side panel inside the cab or on the left door hinge pillar. It provided information about the vehicle's model number, chassis serial number, certified gross vehicle weight and net horsepower. The numbers began with 10,0001 and up. The engine number for 6-cylinder engines was stamped on the left side of the cylinder block behind the oil filler. The V-8 engine number was stamped on the top of engine block ahead of the right-bank cylinder head.

Body Type	Model Number	Factory Price	GVW	Shipping Weight	Prod. Total
Series 1000 1/2 ton V-6. 115 in. wheelbase					
Chassis & Cab	1001	$2641	5600	3980	—
Pickup W.S.	1001	$2776	5600	4520	—
Panel	1001	$3072	5600	4535	—
Panel Cust.	1001	$3169	5600	4550	—
Pickup F.S	1001	$2755	5600	4350	—
Suburban	1001	$3504	5600	4865	—

Series 1000 1/2 ton V-6. 127 in. wheelbase					
Chassis & Cab	1002	$3504	5600	4050	—
Pickup W.S.	1002	$2826	5600	4590	—
Pickup F.S.	1002	$2805	5600	4540	—
Series 1500 3/4 ton V-6. 127 in. wheelbase					
Chassis & Cab	1502	$2852	8100	4285	—
Pickup W.S.	1502	$2987	8100	4775	—
Pickup F.S.	1502	$2966	8100	4705	—
Stake	1502	$3057	8100	4945	—

STANDARD ENGINE: All models: GMC 305D. Engine Type: OHV, V-6. Cast iron block and cylinder head. Bore x Stroke: 4.25 in. x 3.58 in. Fuel Induction: Single barrel model 1904 Holley. Compression Ratio: 7.75:1. Displacement: 304.7 cu. in. (4.99 liters). Number of main bearing: 4. Horsepower: Gross: 165 @ 3800 rpm. Net: 142 @ 3800 rpm. Torque: Gross: 280 lb.-ft. @ 1600 rpm. Net: 260 lb.-ft. @ 1600 rpm. Fuel Requirements: Regular. Oil capacity: 5 qt.

CHASSIS FEATURES: Separate body and frame. Ladder type. drop-center frame. 7.20 in. x 2.75 in. x 0.1875 in.

SUSPENSION AND RUNNING GEAR: Front Suspension: 44 in. x 2.0 in. 5-leaf semi-elliptical springs. Capacity: 1750 lb. at ground. Rear Suspension: K1000: 52 in. x 2.5 in. 6-leaf semi-elliptical springs. Capacity: 1750 lb. K1500: 52 in. x 2.5 in. 7-leaf semi-elliptical springs. Capacity: 2750 lb. Front Axle Type and Capacity: K1000: Hypoid, 3300 lb. capacity. K1500: Hypoid, 3500 lb. capacity. Rear Axle Type and Capacity: K1000: Hypoid, semi-floating, 3500 lb. K1500: Full-floating, hypoid. 5500 lb. capacity. Final Drive Ratio: K1000: Front and rear: 3.54:1. K1500: Front and rear: 4.56:1. Transfer Case: Single lever, 4-position, 2-speed: 1.86, 1.00:1. Brakes: Type: Hydraulic, front and rear drums. Dimensions: K100: Front: 11.0 in. x 2.0 in. Rear: 11.0 in. x 2.0 in. Effective drum area: 276 sq. in. Effective lining area: 167 sq. in. K1500: Front and Rear: 12.125 in. x 2.0 in. Wheels: Ventilated steel disc. Tires: K1000: 6.70 x 15, 6-ply rating, tubeless. K1500: 7 x 17.5 in. 6-ply rating, tubeless. Steering: Recirculating ball type, 17 in. steering wheel. Ratio: 24.0:1. Optional: None. Transmission: 3-speed synchromesh. Optional: 4-speed synchromesh. Clutch: Hydraulic control, coil-spring. Clutch diameter: 11 in. dia. Total lining area: 124.5 sq. in.

VEHICLE DIMENSIONS: 115 in. wheelbase models. Overall Length: Pickup: 186.625 in. Panel: 201 in. Front/Rear Tread: 63.125 in./. Overall Height: Pickup: 77.125 in., Panel: 80.5 in. Width: 78.75 in. Front/Rear Overhang: Pickup: 31.75./39.875 in. Panel: 31.75 in./54.25 in. Tailgate: Width and Height: 50 in. x 17.50 in. Load space: Pickup box dimensions: 78.125 in. x 50.0 in. x 17.56 in. 127 in. wheelbase models. Overall Length: 206 in. Front/Rear Tread: 63.125 in./. Overall Height: 78.25 in. Width: 78.75 in. Front/Rear Overhang: 31.75 in./47.25 in.

CAPACITIES: Fuel Tank: Pickup: 17.5 gal. Panel: 17.0 gal.

ACCOMMODATIONS: Seating Capacity: Pickup and Panel: 3 passenger. Suburban: 6.

INSTRUMENTATION: Speedometer, odometer, gauges for oil pressure, fuel level, engine coolant temperature, battery charge.

OPTIONS: K1000 tires: 6.50 x 15 6-ply rated tires. 7 x 17.5 6-ply rated tires. K1500 tires: 8 x 17.5 6-ply rated. 8 x 17.5 8-ply rated. 8 x 19.5 6-ply rated. 8 x 18.5 8-plyrated. 1 qt. oil bath air cleaner. Heavy-duty 70 amp-hr. battery. Chrome front bumper (except Panel and Suburban). Chrome front and rear bumper (Panel and Suburban only). Custom cab. Includes custom seat and left door lock. Spare wheel carrier. Directional signals. 35 amp generator. 50 amp generator. Deluxe heater and defroster. Recirculating, inside air heater and defroster. Free wheeling manual front hubs. Left door lock. Lock for side wheel carrier. Lock for left door and side wheel carrier. Exterior left 17.5 in. swinging arm mirror (pickup, chassis and cab). Exterior right 17.5 in. swinging arm mirror (pickup, chassis and cab). Exterior right 8.0 in. fixed bracket. Two-tone pain. Heavy-duty radiator. Auxiliary rear seat for Panel. Custom seat (for Deluxe cab only. Full-view rear window. Windshield washers.

HISTORICAL FOOTNOTES: Calendar year production of all GMC truck models was 74,996 units.

1962 PICKUP & SUBURBAN

The 1962 GMC featured a new front end with a single upper hood air intake bracketed by the parking/directional lights. The nacelles for the dual headlights were also restyled. The GMC's interior featured a two-tone instrument panel in which the lower panel color harmonized with the cab interior. The standard Deluxe cab had silver fawn vinyl upholstery with dark grey trim. Standard appointments included a key-locked glove box, dome lamp operated by the master light switch on the dash, and electric windshield wipers. The extra cost custom cab featured a two-tone nylon upholstery with complementing solid-color vinyl. Four colors were offered: Delta green, terrace blue, varsity blue and silver fewness. Custom cab dash color matched the cab seat trim.

I.D. DATA: The serial number was located on the identification plate found on the cowl left side panel inside the cab or on the left door hinge pillar. It provided information about the vehicle's model number, chassis serial number, certified gross vehicle weight and net horsepower. The numbers began with 10,0001 and up. The engine number for 6-cylinder engines was stamped on the left side of the cylinder block behind the oil filler. The V-8 engine number was stamped on the top of engine block ahead of the right-bank cylinder head.

Body Type	Model Number	Factory Price	GVW	Shipping Weight	Prod. Total
Series 1000 1/2 ton V-6. 115 in. wheelbase					
Chassis & Cab	1001	$2674	5600	3964	—
Pickup W.S.	1001	$2809	5600	4360	—
Pickup F.S	1001	$2788	5600	4390	—
Panel	1001	$3105	5600	4615	—
Panel Cust.	1001	$3202	5600	4625	—
Suburban	1001	$3574	5600	4950	—
Series 1000 1/2 ton V-6. 127 in. wheelbase					
Chassis & Cab	1002	$2725	5600	4034	—
Pickup W.S.	1002	$2860	5600	4430	—
Pickup F.S.	1002	$2839	5600	4460	—
Series 1500 3/4 ton V-6. 127 in. wheelbase					
Chassis & Cab	1502	$2887	8100	4305	—
Pickup W.S.	1502	$3022	8100	4775	—
Pickup F.S.	1502	$3001	8100	4725	—
Stake	1502	$3092	8100	4965	—

STANDARD ENGINE: All models: GMC 305D Engine Type: OHV, V-6. Cast iron block and cylinder head. Bore x Stroke: 4.25 in. x 3.58 in. Fuel Induction: Single barrel model 1904 Holley. Compression Ratio: 7.75:1. Displacement: 304.7 cu. in. (4.99 liters). Number of main bearing: 4. Horsepower: Gross: 165 @ 3800 rpm. Net: 142 @ 3800 rpm. Torque: Gross: 280 lb.-ft. @ 1600 rpm. Net: 260 lb.-ft. @ 1600 rpm. Fuel Requirements: Regular. Oil capacity: 5 qt.

CHASSIS FEATURES: Separate body and frame. Ladder type. drop-center frame. 7.20 in. x 2.75 in. x 0.1875 in.

SUSPENSION AND RUNNING GEAR: Front Suspension: 44 in. x 2.0 in. 5-leaf semi-elliptical springs. Capacity: 1750 lb. at ground. Rear Suspension: K1000: 52 in. x 2.5 in. 6-leaf semi-elliptical springs. Capacity: 1750 lb. K1500: 52 in. x 2.5 in. 7-leaf semi-elliptical springs. Capacity: 2750 lb. Front Axle Type and Capacity: K1000: Hypoid, 3300 lb. capacity. K1500: Hypoid, 3500 lb. capacity. Rear Axle Type and Capacity: K1000: Hypoid, semi-floating, 3500 lb. K1500: Full-floating, hypoid. 5500 lb. capacity. Final Drive Ratio: K1000: Front and rear: 3.54:1. K1500: Front and rear: 4.56:1. Transfer Case: Single lever, 4-position, 2-speed: 1.86, 1.00:1. Brakes: Type: Hydraulic, front and rear drums. Dimensions: K1000: Front: 11.0 in. x 2.0 in. Rear: 11.0 in. x 2.0 in. Effective drum area: 276 sq. in. Effective lining area: 167 sq. in. K1500: Front and Rear: 12.125 in. x 2.0 in. Wheels: Ventilated steel disc. Tires: K1000: 6.70 x 15, 6-ply rating, tubeless. K1500: 7 x 17.5 in. 6-ply rating, tubeless. Steering: Recirculating ball type, 17 in. steering wheel. Ratio: 24.0:1. Optional: None. Transmission: 3-speed synchromesh. Optional: 4-speed synchromesh. Clutch: Hydraulic control, coil-spring. Clutch diameter: 11 in. dia. Total lining area: 124.5 sq. in.

VEHICLE DIMENSIONS: 115 in. wheelbase models. Overall Length: Pickup: 186.625 in. Panel: 201 in. Front Tread: 63.125 in. Overall Height: Pickup: 77.125 in. Panel: 80.5 in. Width: 78.75 in. Front/Rear Overhang: Pickup: 31.75./39.875 in. Panel: 31.75 in./54.25 in. Tailgate: Width and Height: 50 in. x 17.50 in. Load space: Pickup box dimensions: 78.125 in. x 50.0 in. x 17.56 in. 127 in. wheelbase models. Overall Length: 206 in. Front Tread: 63.125 in. Overall Height: 78.25 in. Width: 78.75 in. Front/Rear Overhang: 31.75 in./47.25 in.

CAPACITIES: Fuel Tank: Pickup: 17.5 gal. Panel: 17.0 gal.

ACCOMMODATIONS: Seating Capacity: Pickup and Panel: 3 passenger. Suburban: 6.

INSTRUMENTATION: Speedometer, odometer, gauges for oil pressure, fuel level, engine coolant temperature, battery charge.

OPTIONS: K1000 tires: 6.50 x 15 6-ply rated tires. 7 x 17.5 6-ply rated tires. K1500 tires: 8 x 17.5 6-ply rated. 8 x 17.5 8-ply rated. 8 x 19.5 6-ply rated. 8 x 18.5 8-plyrated. 1 qt. oil bath air cleaner. Heavy-duty 70 amp-hr. battery. Chrome front bumper (except Panel and Suburban). Chrome front and rear bumper (Panel and Suburban only). Custom cab. Includes custom seat and left door lock. Spare wheel carrier. Directional signals. 35 amp generator. 50 amp generator. Deluxe heater and defroster. Recirculating, inside air heater and defroster. Free wheeling manual front hubs. Left door lock. Lock for side wheel carrier. Lock for left door and side wheel carrier. Exterior left 17.5 in. swinging arm mirror (pickup, chassis and cab). Exterior right 17.5 in. swinging arm mirror (pickup, chassis and cab). Exterior right 8.0 in. fixed bracket. Two-tone pain. Heavy-duty radiator. Auxiliary rear seat for Panel. Custom seat (for Deluxe cab only. Full-view rear window. Windshield washers.

HISTORICAL FOOTNOTES: 1962 calendar year production of all GMC trucks was 89,789.

1963 PICKUP & SUBURBAN

GMC's four-wheel drive models were unchanged for the 1963 model year.

I.D. DATA: Unchanged from 1962.

Body Type	Model Number	Factory Price	GVW	Shipping Weight	Prod. Total
Series 1000 1/2 ton V-6. 115 in. wheelbase					
Chassis & Cab	1001	$2672	5600	3964	—
Pickup W.S.	1001	$2807	5600	4360	—
Pickup F.S	1001	$2786	5600	4390	—
Panel	1001	$3103	5600	4615	—
Panel Cust.	1001	$3200	5600	4625	—
Suburban	1001	$3572	5600	4950	—
Series 1000 1/2 ton V-6. 127 in. wheelbase					
Chassis and Cab	1002	$2723	5600	4034	—
Pickup W.S.	1002	$2858	5600	4430	—
Pickup F.S.	1002	$2837	5600	4460	—
Series 1500 3/4 ton V-6. 127 in. wheelbase					
Chassis & Cab	1502	$2885	8100	4305	—
Pickup W.S.	1502	$3020	8100	4775	—
Pickup F.S.	1502	$3099	8100	4725	—
Stake	1502	$3090	8100	4965	—

STANDARD ENGINE: All models: GMC 305D Engine Type: OHV, V-6. Cast iron block and cylinder head. Bore x Stroke: 4.25 in. x 3.58 in. Fuel Induction: Single barrel model 1904 Holley. Compression Ratio: 7.75:1. Displacement: 304.7 cu. in. (4.99 liters). Number of main bearing: 4. Horsepower: Gross: 165 @ 3800 rpm. Net: 142 @ 3800 rpm. Torque: Gross: 280 lb.-ft. @ 1600 rpm. Net: 260 lb.-ft. @ 1600 rpm. Fuel Requirements: Regular. Oil capacity: 5 qt.

CHASSIS FEATURES: Separate body and frame. Ladder type. drop-center frame. 7.20 in. x 2.75 in. x 0.1875 in.

SUSPENSION AND RUNNING GEAR: Front Suspension: 44 in. x 2.0 in. 5-leaf semi-elliptical springs. Capacity: 1750 lb. at ground. Rear Suspension: K1000: 52 in. x 2.5 in. 6-leaf semi-elliptical springs. Capacity: 1750 lb. K1500: 52 in. x 2.5 in. 7-leaf semi-elliptical springs. Capacity: 2750 lb. Front Axle Type and Capacity: K1000: Hypoid, 3300 lb. capacity. K1500: Hypoid, 3500 lb. capacity. Rear Axle Type and Capacity: K1000: Hypoid, semi-floating, 3500 lb. K1500: Full-floating, hypoid. 5500 lb. capacity. Final Drive Ratio: K1000: Front and rear: 3.54:1. K1500: Front and rear: 4.56:1. Transfer Case: Single lever, 4-position, 2-speed: 1.86, 1.00:1. Brakes: Type: Hydraulic, front and rear drums. Dimensions: K100: Front: 11.0 in. x 2.0 in. Rear: 11.0 in. x 2.0 in. Effective drum area: 276 sq. in. Effective lining area: 167 sq. in. K1500: Front and Rear: 12.125 in. x 2.0 in. Wheels: Ventilated steel disc. Tires: K1000: 6.70 x 15, 6-ply rating, tubeless. K1500: 7 x 17.5 in. 6-ply rating, tubeless. Steering: Recirculating ball type, 17 in. steering wheel. Ratio: 24.0:1. Optional: None. Transmission: 3-speed synchromesh. Optional: 4-speed synchromesh. Clutch: Hydraulic control, coil-spring. Clutch diameter: 11 in. dia. Total lining area: 124.5 sq. in.

VEHICLE DIMENSIONS: 115 in. wheelbase models. Overall Length: Pickup: 186.625 in. Panel: 201 in. Front Tread: 63.125 in. Overall Height: Pickup: 77.125 in. Panel: 80.5 in. Width: 78.75 in. Front/Rear Overhang: Pickup: 31.75./39.875 in. Panel: 31.75 in./54.25 in. Tailgate: Width and Height: 50 in. x 17.50 in. Load space: Pickup box dimensions: 78.125 in. x 50.0 in. x 17.56 in. 127 in. wheelbase models. Overall Length: 206 in. Front Tread: 63.125 in. Overall Height: 78.25 in. Width: 78.75 in. Front/Rear Overhang: 31.75 in./47.25 in.

CAPACITIES: Fuel Tank: Pickup: 17.5 gal. Panel: 17.0 gal.

ACCOMMODATIONS: Seating Capacity: Pickup and Panel: 3 passenger. Suburban: 6 passenger.

INSTRUMENTATION: Speedometer, odometer, gauges for oil pressure, fuel level, engine coolant temperature, battery charge.

OPTIONS AND PRICES: K1000 tires: 6.50 x 15 6-ply rated tires. 7 x 17.5 6-ply rated tires. K1500 tires: 8 x 17.5 6-ply rated. 8 x 17.5 8-ply rated. 8 x 19.5 6-ply rated. 8 x 18.5 8-plyrated. 1 qt. oil bath air cleaner. Heavy-duty 70 amp-hr. battery. Chrome front bumper (except Panel and Suburban). Chrome front and rear bumper (Panel and Suburban only). Custom cab. Includes custom seat and left door lock. Spare wheel carrier. Directional signals. 35 amp generator. 50 amp generator. Deluxe heater and defroster. Recirculating, inside air heater and defroster. Free wheeling manual front hubs. Left door lock. Lock for side wheel carrier. Lock for left door and side wheel carrier. Exterior left 17.5 in. swinging arm mirror (pickup, chassis and cab). Exterior right 17.5 in. swinging arm mirror (pickup, chassis and cab). Exterior right 8.0 in. fixed bracket. Two-tone paint. Heavy-duty radiator. Auxiliary rear seat for Panel. Custom seat (for Deluxe cab only. Full-view rear window. Windshield washers.

HISTORICAL FOOTNOTES: 1963 calendar year production of all GMC trucks was 101,234 units. This was the final year for the wraparound windshield which had been introduced on the 1955 models.

1964 PICKUP & SUBURBAN

No design changes were made in the GMC four-wheel drive trucks for 1964.

I.D. DATA: Unchanged from 1963.

Body Type	Model Number	Factory Price	GVW	Shipping Weight	Prod. Total
Series 1000 1/2 ton V-6. 115 in. wheelbase					
Chassis & Cab	1001	$2682	5600	3964	—
Pickup W.S.	1001	$2817	5600	4360	—
Pickup F.S	1001	$2796	5600	4390	—
Panel	1001	$3113	5600	4615	—
Panel Cust.	1001	$3210	5600	4625	—
Suburban	1001	$3582	5600	4950	—
Series 1000 1/2 ton V-6. 127 in. wheelbase					
Chassis & Cab	1002	$2733	5600	4034	—
Pickup W.S.	1002	$2868	5600	4430	—
Pickup F.S.	1002	$2847	5600	4460	—
Series 1500 3/4 ton V-6. 127 in. wheelbase					
Chassis & Cab	1502	$2895	8100	4305	—
Pickup W.S.	1502	$3030	8100	4775	—
Pickup F.S.	1502	$3109	8100	4725	—
Stake	1502	$3100	8100	4965	—

STANDARD ENGINE: All models: GMC 305D Engine Type: OHV, V-6. Cast iron block and cylinder head. Bore x Stroke: 4.25 in. x 3.58 in. Fuel Induction: Single barrel model 1904 Holley. Compression Ratio: 7.75:1. Displacement: 304.7 cu. in. (4.99 liters). Number of main bearing: 4. Horsepower: Gross: 165 @ 3800 rpm. Net: 142 @ 3800 rpm. Torque: Gross: 280 lb.-ft. @ 1600 rpm. Net: 260 lb.-ft. @ 1600 rpm. Fuel Requirements: Regular. Oil capacity: 5 qt.

CHASSIS FEATURES: Separate body and frame. Ladder type. drop-center frame. 7.20 in. x 2.75 in. x 0.1875 in.

SUSPENSION AND RUNNING GEAR: Front Suspension: 44 in. x 2.0 in. 5-leaf semi-elliptical springs. Capacity: 1750 lb. at ground. Rear Suspension: K1000: 52 in. x 2.5 in. 6-leaf semi-elliptical springs. Capacity: 1750 lb. K1500: 52 in. x 2.5 in. 7-leaf semi-elliptical springs. Capacity: 2750 lb. Front Axle Type and Capacity: K1000: Hypoid, 3300 lb. capacity. K1500: Hypoid, 3500 lb. capacity. Rear Axle Type and Capacity: K1000: Hypoid, semi-floating, 3500 lb. K1500: Full-floating, hypoid. 5500 lb. capacity. Final Drive Ratio: K1000: Front and rear: 3.54:1. K1500: Front and rear: 4.56:1. Transfer Case: Single lever, 4-position, 2-speed: 1.86, 1.00:1. Brakes: Type: Hydraulic, front and rear drums. Dimensions: K1000: Front: 11.0 in. x 2.0 in. Rear: 11.0 in. x 2.0 in. Effective drum area: 276 sq. in. Effective lining area: 167 sq. in. K1500: Front and Rear: 12.125 in. x 2.0 in. Wheels: Ventilated steel disc. Tires: K1000: 6.70 x 15, 6-ply rating, tubeless. K1500: 7 x 17.5 in. 6-ply rating, tubeless. Steering: Recirculating ball type, 17 in. steering wheel. Ratio: 24.0:1. Optional: None. Transmission: 3-speed synchromesh. Optional: 4-speed synchromesh. Clutch: Hydraulic control, coil-spring. Clutch diameter: 11 in. dia. Total lining area: 124.5 sq. in.

VEHICLE DIMENSIONS: 115 in. wheelbase models. Overall Length: Pickup: 186.625 in. Panel: 201 in. Front Tread: 63.125 in. Overall Height: Pickup: 77.125 in. Panel: 80.5 in. Width: 78.75 in. Front/Rear Overhang: Pickup: 31.75./39.875 in. Panel: 31.75 in./54.25 in. Tailgate: Width and Height: 50 in. x 17.50 in. Load space: Pickup box dimensions: 78.125 in. x 50.0 in. x 17.56 in. 127 in. wheelbase models. Overall Length: 206 in. Front Tread: 63.125 in. Overall Height: 78.25 in. Width: 78.75 in. Front/Rear Overhang: 31.75 in./47.25 in.

CAPACITIES: Fuel Tank: Pickup: 17.5 gal. Panel: 17.0 gal.

ACCOMMODATIONS: Seating Capacity: Pickup and Panel: 3 passenger. Suburban: 6.

INSTRUMENTATION: Speedometer, odometer, gauges for oil pressure, fuel level, engine coolant temperature, battery charge.

OPTIONS: K1000 tires: 6.50 x 15 6-ply rated tires. 7 x 17.5 6-ply rated tires. K1500 tires: 8 x 17.5 6-ply rated. 8 x 17.5 8-ply rated. 8 x 19.5 6-ply rated. 8 x 18.5 8-plyrated. 1 qt. oil bath air cleaner. Heavy-duty 70 amp-hr. battery. Chrome front bumper (except Panel and Suburban). Chrome front and rear bumper (Panel and Suburban only). Custom cab. Includes custom seat and left door lock. Spare wheel carrier. Directional signals. 35 amp generator. 50 amp generator. Deluxe heater and defroster. Recirculating, inside air heater and defroster. Free wheeling manual front hubs. Left door lock. Lock for side wheel carrier. Lock for left door and side wheel carrier. Exterior left 17.5 in. swinging arm mirror (pickup, chassis and cab). Exterior

right 17.5 in. swinging arm mirror (pickup, chassis and cab). Exterior right 8.0 in. fixed bracket. Two-tone paint. Heavy-duty radiator. Auxiliary rear seat for Panel. Custom seat (for Deluxe cab only. Full-view rear window. Windshield washers.

HISTORICAL FOOTNOTES: 1964 calendar year production of all GMC trucks was 110,521 units.

1965 PICKUP & SUBURBAN

No design changes were made in the GMC four-wheel drive trucks for 1965. The GMC V-6 engine continued to enjoy a reputation as a strong, heavy and extremely durable workhorse. It weighed nearly 1000 pounds, had an extra-heavy block and crankcase, extremely large intake and exhaust valves, cam ground cast aluminum pistons and aluminum rocker arm brackets. GMC also offered an optional heavy-duty version of the V-6 that used Silchrome XB intake valves, Silchrome 10 hard faced exhaust valves and positive rotation on all valves.

I.D. DATA: Unchanged from 1964.

Body Type	Model Number	Factory Price	GVW	Shipping Weight	Prod. Total
Series 1000 1/2 ton V-6. 115 in. wheelbase					
Chassis & Cab	1001	$2682	5600	3964	—
Pickup W.S.	1001	$2817	5600	4360	—
Pickup F.S	1001	$2796	5600	4390	—
Panel	1001	$3113	5600	4615	—
Panel Cust.	1001	$3210	5600	4625	—
Suburban	1001	$3582	5600	4950	—
Series 1000 1/2 ton V-6. 127 in. wheelbase					
Chassis & Cab	1002	$2733	5600	4034	—
Pickup W.S.	1002	$2868	5600	4430	—
Pickup F.S.	1002	$2847	5600	4460	—
Series 1500 3/4 ton V-6. 127 in. wheelbase					
Chassis & Cab	1502	$2895	8100	4305	—
Pickup W.S.	1502	$3030	8100	4775	—
Pickup F.S.	1502	$3109	8100	4725	—
Stake	1502	$3100	8100	4965	—

STANDARD ENGINE: All models: GMC 305D Engine Type: OHV, V-6. Cast iron block and cylinder head. Bore x Stroke: 4.25 in. x 3.58 in. Fuel Induction: Single barrel model 1904 Holley. Compression Ratio: 7.75:1. Displacement: 304.7 cu. in. (4.99 liters). Number of main bearing: 4. Horsepower: Gross: 165 @ 3800 rpm. Net: 142 @ 3800 rpm. Torque: Gross: 280 lb.-ft. @ 1600 rpm. Net: 260 lb.-ft. @ 1600 rpm. Fuel Requirements: Regular. Oil capacity: 5 qt.

CHASSIS FEATURES: Separate body and frame. Ladder type. Drop-center frame. 115 in. wheelbase: 7.09375 in. x 2.718 in. x 0.140 in. 127 in. wheelbase: 7.1875 in. x 2.75 in. x 0.1875 in.

SUSPENSION AND RUNNING GEAR: Front Suspension: 44 in. x 2.0 in. 5-leaf semi-elliptical springs. Capacity: 1750 lb. at ground. Rear Suspension: K1000: 52 in. x 2.5 in. 6-leaf semi-elliptical springs. Capacity: 1750 lb. K1500: 52 in. x 2.5 in. 7-leaf semi-elliptical springs. Capacity: 2750 lb. Front Axle Type and Capacity: K1000: Hypoid, 3300 lb. capacity. K1500: Hypoid, 3500 lb. capacity. Rear Axle Type and Capacity: K1000: Hypoid, semi-floating, 3500 lb. K1500: Full-floating, hypoid. 5500 lb. capacity. Final Drive Ratio: K1000: Front and rear: 3.54:1. K1500: Front and rear: 4.56:1. Transfer Case: Single lever, 4-position, 2-speed: 1.86, 1.00:1. Brakes: Type: Hydraulic, front and rear drums. Dimensions: K1000: Front: 11.0 in. x 2.0 in. Rear: 11.0 in. x 2.0 in. Effective drum area: 276 sq. in. Effective lining area: 167 sq. in. K1500: Front and Rear: 12.125 in. x 2.0 in. Wheels: Ventilated steel disc. Tires: K1000: 6.70 x 15, 6-ply rating, tubeless. K1500: 7 x 17.5 in. 6-ply rating, tubeless. Steering: Recirculating ball type, 17 in. steering wheel. Ratio: 24.0:1. Optional: None. Transmission: 3-speed synchromesh. Optional: 4-speed synchromesh. Clutch: Hydraulic control, coil-spring. Clutch diameter: 11 in. dia. Total lining area: 124.5 sq. in.

VEHICLE DIMENSIONS: 115 in. wheelbase models. Overall Length: Pickup: 186.625 in. Panel: 201 in. Front Tread: 63.125 in. Overall Height: Pickup: 77.125 in. Panel: 80.5 in. Width: 78.75 in. Front/Rear Overhang: Pickup: 31.75./39.875 in. Panel: 31.75 in./54.25 in. Tailgate: Width and Height: 50 in. x 17.50 in. Load space: Pickup box dimensions: 78.125 in. x 50.0 in. x 17.56 in. 127 in. wheelbase models. Overall Length: 206 in. Front Tread: 63.125 in. Overall Height: 78.25 in. Width: 78.75 in. Front/Rear Overhang: 31.75 in./47.25 in.

CAPACITIES: Fuel Tank: Pickup: 17.5 gal. Panel: 17.0 gal.

ACCOMMODATIONS: Seating Capacity: Pickup and Panel: 3 passenger. Suburban: 6.

INSTRUMENTATION: Speedometer, odometer, gauges for oil pressure, fuel level, engine coolant temperature, battery charge.

OPTIONS: K1000 tires: 6.50 x 15 6-ply rated tires. 7 x 17.5 6-ply rated tires. K1500 tires: 8 x 17.5 6-ply rated. 8 x 17.5 8-ply rated. 8 x 19.5 6-ply rated. 8 x 18.5 8-plyrated. 1 qt. oil bath air cleaner. Heavy-duty 70 amp-hr. battery. Chrome front bumper (except Panel and Suburban). Chrome front and rear bumper (Panel and Suburban only). Custom cab. Includes custom seat and left door lock. Spare wheel carrier. Directional signals. 35 amp generator. 50 amp generator. Deluxe heater and defroster. Recirculating, inside air heater and Defroster. Free wheeling manual front hubs. Left door lock. Lock for side wheel carrier. Lock for left door and side wheel carrier. Exterior left 17.5 in. swinging arm mirror (pickup, chassis and cab). Exterior right 17.5 in. swinging arm mirror (pickup, chassis and cab). Exterior right 8.0 in. fixed bracket. Two-tone paint. Heavy-duty radiator. Auxiliary rear seat for Panel. Custom seat (for Deluxe cab only. Full-view rear window. Windshield washers. Auxiliary inside spare tank with 16.5 gals. capacity. Maximum traction rear differential. Four-speed manual transmission. Air conditioning. Radio, heavy-duty Airflow heater and defroster. Braden winch with Spicer driveline and Chelsea power take-off.

HISTORICAL FOOTNOTES: 1965 calendar year production of all GMC trucks was 136,705 units.

1966 PICKUP & SUBURBAN

The GMC four-wheel drive trucks were unchanged for 1966.

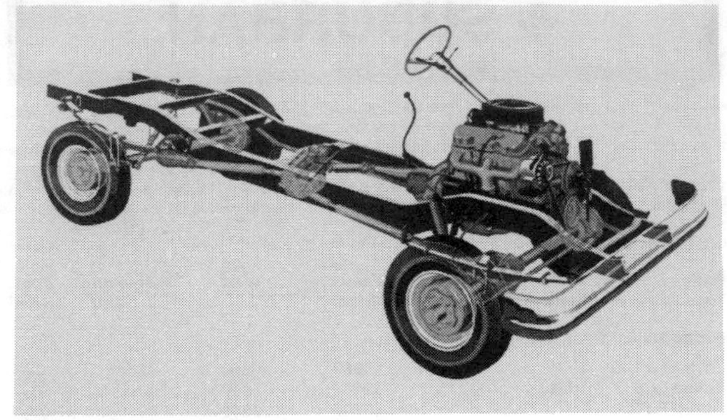

1966 GMC four-wheel drive chassis

I.D. DATA: Unchanged from 1965.

Body Type	Model Number	Factory Price	GVW	Shipping Weight	Prod. Total
Series 1000 1/2 ton V-6. 115 in. wheelbase					
Chassis & Cab	1001	$2719	5600	3964	—
Pickup W.S.	1001	$2864	5600	4360	—
Pickup F.S	1001	$2845	5600	4390	—
Panel	1001	$3153	5600	4615	—
Panel Cust.	1001	$3250	5600	4625	—
Suburban	1001	$3485	5600	4950	—
Series 1000 1/2 ton V-6. 127 in. wheelbase					
Chassis & Cab	1002	$2770	5600	4034	—
Pickup W.S.	1002	$2915	5600	4430	—
Pickup F.S.	1002	$2896	5600	4460	—
Series 1500 3/4 ton V-6. 127 in. wheelbase					
Chassis & Cab	1502	$2933	8100	4305	—
Pickup W.S.	1502	$3078	8100	4775	—
Pickup F.S.	1502	$3056	8100	4725	—
Stake	1502	$3149	8100	4965	—

STANDARD ENGINE: All models: GMC 305D. Engine Type: OHV, V-6. Cast iron block and cylinder head. Bore x Stroke: 4.25 in. x 3.58 in. Fuel Induction: Single barrel model 1904 Holley. Compression Ratio: 7.75:1. Displacement: 304.7 cu. in. (4.99 liters). Number of main bearing-4. Horsepower: Gross: 170 @ 4000 rpm. Net: 157 @ 4000 rpm. Torque: Gross: 277 lb.-ft. @ 1600 rpm. Net: 263 lb.-ft. @ 1600 rpm. Fuel Requirements: Regular. Oil capacity: 5 qt.

CHASSIS FEATURES: Separate body and frame. Ladder type. drop-center frame. 7.20 in. x 2.75 in. x 0.1875 in.

SUSPENSION AND RUNNING GEAR: Front Suspension: 44 in. x 2.0 in. 5-leaf semi-elliptical springs. Capacity: 1750 lb. at ground. Rear Suspension: K1000: 52 in. x 2.5 in. 6-leaf semi-elliptical springs. Capacity: 1750 lb. K1500: 52 in. x 2.5 in. 7-leaf semi-elliptical springs. Capacity: 2750 lb. Front Axle Type and Capacity: K1000: Hypoid, 3300 lb. capacity. K1500: Hypoid, 3500 lb. capacity. Rear Axle Type and Capacity: K1000: Hypoid, semi-floating, 3500 lb. K1500: Full-floating, hypoid. 5500 lb. capacity. Final Drive Ratio: K1000: Front and rear: 3.54:1. K1500: Front and rear: 4.56:1. Transfer Case: Single lever, 4-position, 2-speed: 1.86, 1.00:1. Brakes: Type: Hydraulic, front and rear drums. Dimensions: K1000: Front: 11.0 in. x 2.0 in. Rear: 11.0 in. x 2.0 in. Effective drum area: 276 sq. in. Effective lining area: 167 sq. in. K1500: Front and Rear: 12.125 in. x 2.0 in. Wheels: Ventilated steel disc. Tires: K1000: 6.70 x 15, 6-ply rating, tubeless. K1500: 7 x 17.5 in. 6-ply rating, tubeless. Steering: Recirculating ball type, 17 in. steering wheel. Ratio: 24.0:1. Optional: None. Transmission: 3-speed synchromesh. Optional: 4-speed synchromesh. Clutch: Hydraulic control, coil-spring. Clutch diameter: 11 in. dia. Total lining area: 124.5 sq. in.

VEHICLE DIMENSIONS: 115 in. wheelbase models. Overall Length: Pickup: 186.625 in. Panel: 201 in. Front Tread: 63.125 in. Overall Height: Pickup: 77.125 in. Panel: 80.5 in. Width: 78.75 in. Front/Rear Overhang: Pickup: 31.75./39.875 in. Panel: 31.75 in./54.25 in. Tailgate: Width and Height: 50 in. x 17.50 in. Load space: Pickup box dimensions: 78.125 in. x 50.0 in. x 17.56 in. 127 in. wheelbase models. Overall Length: 206 in. Front Tread: 63.125 in. Overall Height: 78.25 in. Width: 78.75 in. Front/Rear Overhang: 31.75 in./47.25 in.

CAPACITIES: Fuel Tank: Pickup: 17.5 gal. Panel: 17.0 gal.

ACCOMMODATIONS: Seating Capacity: Pickup and Panel: 3 passenger. Suburban: 6.

INSTRUMENTATION: Speedometer, odometer, gauges for oil pressure, fuel level, engine coolant temperature, battery charge.

OPTIONS: K1000 tires: 6.50 x 15 6-ply rated tires. 7 x 17.5 6-ply rated tires. K1500 tires: 8 x 17.5 6-ply rated. 8 x 17.5 8-ply rated. 8 x 19.5 6-ply rated. 8 x 18.5 8-plyrated. 1 qt. oil bath air cleaner. Heavy-duty 70 amp-hr. battery. Chrome front bumper (except Panel and Suburban). Chrome front and rear bumper (Panel and Suburban only). Custom cab. Includes custom seat and left door lock. Spare wheel carrier. Directional signals. 35 amp generator. 50 amp generator. Deluxe heater and defroster. Recirculating, inside air heater and defroster. Free wheeling manual front hubs. Left door lock. Lock for side wheel carrier. Lock for left door and side wheel carrier. Exterior left 17.5 in. swinging arm mirror (pickup, chassis and cab). Exterior right 17.5 in. swinging arm mirror (pickup, chassis and cab). Exterior right 8.0 in. fixed bracket. Two-tone paint. Heavy-duty radiator. Auxiliary rear seat for Panel. Custom seat (for Deluxe cab only). Full-view rear window. Windshield washers. Auxiliary inside spare tank with 16.5 gals. capacity. Maximum traction rear differential. Four-speed manual transmission. Air conditioning. Radio, heavy-duty Airflow heater and defroster. Braden winch with Spicer driveline and Chelsea power take-off.

HISTORICAL FOOTNOTES: 1966 calendar year production of all GMC trucks was 127,294 units.

1967 PICKUP & SUBURBAN

The 1967 GMC four-wheel drive trucks had all-new styling characterized by a lower height, enhanced forward visibility and increased interior space. The windshield glass was of thicker laminate for 1967 as well as being 116 sq. in. greater in area. The cab had a new more rigid roof design that reduced the interior sound level as well as being more sturdy in design. Among its features was a heavily embossed inner roof panel, a stronger roof perimeter and a heavier front header. The side headers were now more closely bound with the front and rear headers. Improved serviceability was achieved the use of embossed door access panels with only four screws and retaining stripes. A new door check built into the upper door hinge permitted the door to be checked in any position. New rotary gear door locks with an outside key lock for both doors were also used.

Interior revisions for 1967 included a deep-dish 3-spoke energy-absorbing steering wheel, a padded instrument panel with recessed switches, flat knobs and non-glare paint. Standard equipment for all models included safety belts, left and right side padded sun visors, 2-speed electric windshield wipers, rubber floor mat, dome light, turn signals with hazard warning switch, back-up lights (except chassis-cabs), and a left-side exterior rearview mirror. Stake and chassis and cab models also had a right side exterior mirror. The redesigned Wideside box had full-depth double-wall side panels and a new quick release tailgate that could be operated with one hand. Improved resistance to corrosion was provided by the use of special bathub-type fender skirts, unitized component construction and wheelhouse undercoating. One-piece outer body side panels were designed with wrap-around ends, thus eliminating coach joints that was often susceptible to corrosion. The Wideside tailgate was of full double-wall construction. The wheelwells of the Wideside models were designed with a flat top to increase pickup box utility. A redesigned powertrain configuration on the four-wheel drive models resulted in a reduction of five inches in their overall height. No reduction was made in the ground clearance of the transfer case which remained at 12.5 in. The transfer case was relocated to a higher position where it was attached directly to the transmission. The four-wheel drive frame continued to be of a heavier gauge than that used on two-wheel drive models. Both the front and rear leaf springs were of a new weight-saving tapered leaf design which also reduced inter-leaf friction and provided a smoother ride.

The standard cab interior had a color-keyed bench seat with vinyl upholstery and foam cushions installed on a steel spring base. The custom cab had a full-depth foam seat with color-keyed woven fabric and vinyl trim, left and right hand armrests, passenger side padded sun visor, cigarette lighter, cowl insulation, underbody coating and embossed vinyl door trim panels with bright retainer. A bucket seat option provided outboard bucket-type seats and a console-type seat for the center passenger. The console seat was a padded cushion which could be raised to reach a storage console. The center passenger's padded backrest could be folded down to provide a center armrest. The bucket seats were covered in textured vinyl. The seat backs were fixed, with the driver's seat adjustable fore and aft.

Available for all pickups and the chassis and cab models was a new Custom Sport Truck option. This included use of bright metal trim for the grille opening, headlights and windshield. A Custom Sport Truck emblem was installed on the doors just below the window sill. The Custom Sport Truck interior featured bucket seats and a center console seat, The floor and fuel tank were carpeted. Additional Custom Sport Truck content included a chrome front bumper, bright metal frames for the clutch, brake and accelerator pedals, chrome-trimmed instrument knobs and horn button, right-hand padded sun visor and underbody coating.

I.D. DATA: The serial number was located on a plate found on the left cab door hinge plate. The engine number for the V-6 engine was stamped on the top of the cylinder block ahead of the right-cylinder head.

Model Number	Body Type	Factory Price	GVW	Shipping Weight	Prod. Total
Series K1500-1/2 ton 6-cyl. 115-127 in. wheelbase					
KS1570V	Chassis and Cab	$2708	4600*	3300	—
KS1570C	6.5 ft. F.S. Pickup	$2833	4600	3645	—
KS1570D	6.5 ft. W.S. Pickup	$2876	4600	3710	—
KS1590C	8 ft. F.S. Pickup	$2883	4600	3725	—
KS1590D	8 ft. W.S. Pickup	$2926	4600	3815	—
KS1590G	Pnl. 127 in. wb.	$3599	4600	4085	—
KS1590K	Sub. 127 in. wb.	$3330	4600	4305	—

* 5600 lb. GVW optional.

Model Number	Body Type	Factory Price	GVW	Shipping Weight	Prod. Total
Series K2500-3/4 ton 6-cyl. 127 in. wheelbase					
KS2590V	Chassis and Cab	$2909	5700*	3645	—
KS2590C	8 ft. F.S. Pickup	$3035	5700	4045	—
KS2590D	8 ft. W.S. Pickup	$3078	5700	4135	—
KS2590F	8 ft. Stake	$3124	5700	4270	—
KS2590G	Panel	$3415	5700	4395	—
KS2590K	Suburban	$3645	5700	4615	—

* 7600 lb. GVW optional.

STANDARD ENGINE: All models: GMC 305D Engine Type: OHV, V-6. Cast iron block and cylinder head. Bore x Stroke: 4.25 in. x 3.58 in. Fuel Induction: Single barrel model 1904 Holley. Compression Ratio: 7.75:1. Displacement: 304.7 cu. in. (4.99 liters). Number of main bearing: 4. Horsepower: Gross: 165 @ 3800 rpm. Net: 142 @ 3800 rpm. Torque: Gross: 280 lb.-ft. @ 1600 rpm. Net: 260 lb.-ft. @ 1600 rpm. Fuel Requirements: Regular. Oil capacity: 5 qt.

CHASSIS FEATURES: Separate body and frame with 2.75 in. channel side rails. Section modulus: K1500: 3.62 in. Optional: 4.85 in. K2500: 4.85 in.

SUSPENSION AND RUNNING GEAR: Front Suspension: Tapered shot-peened springs, shock absorbers. K1500: 1450 lb. rating (at ground). K2500:1510 lb. rating (at ground). Optional rating: None. Rear Suspension: Two or 3-leaf, tapered springs, shock absorbers. K1500: 1800 lb. rating (at ground). K2500: 1900 lb. Optional Rating: K1500 and K2500: 2500 lb. Front Axle Type and Capacity: K1500: Full-floating, 3300 lb. capacity. Optional: None. K2500: Full-floating, 3500 lb. capacity. Rear Axle Type and Capacity: K1500: Semi-floating, 3300 lb. capacity. Optional: None. K2500: Full-floating, 5200 lb. Final Drive Ratio: K1500: Front: 3.73:1. Rear: 3.73:1. K2500: 4.55:1. Rear: 4.75:1. Transfer Case: Single lever, two-speed: 1.94, 1.00:1. Brakes: Type: Hydraulic, front and rear drums. Optional: Power assisted. Wheels: K1500: 15 x 5.5 6-stud disc. Optional: 16 x 5.50 and 16 x 5.0. K2500: 7-17.5 x 5.25. Optional: 8-17.5 x 5.0, 8-17.5 x 5.5, 8-17.5 x 6.0. Tires: K1500: 8.15 x 15. tubeless Optional: Tubeless: 6.50 x 15, 7-17.5. Tube-type: 8.15 x 15, 7.00 x15, 6.50 x 16. K2500: Tubeless: 7-17.5. Optional: Tubeless: 8-17.5, 8-19.5. Tube-type: 7.50 x 16, 7.00 x 17,7.50 x 17.

Steering: Recirculating ball gear. Transmission: 3-speed, synchromesh manual. Optional: 4-speed manual synchromesh and close-ratio 4-speed manual synchromesh. Clutch: Diaphragm, spring. Clutch diameter: 6-cyl.: 10 in. dia. Total lining area: 100.0 sq. in. V-8: 11 in. dia. Total lining area: 124 sq. in. Optional: 6-cyl.: 11 in. dia. Total lining area: 124.0 sq. in. V-8: 12 in. dia. Total lining area: 150 sq. in.

VEHICLE DIMENSIONS: Wheelbase: K1500: 115 in., 127 in. K2500: 127 in. All Suburbans and Panels: 127 in. Overall Length: 115 in. Wideside pickups: 188.75 in. 127 in. Wideside pickups: 208.0 in. 115 in. Fenderside pickups: 188.125 in. 127 in. Fenderside pickups: 208.0 in. Front/Rear Overhang: 115 in. wheelbase pickups: 33.25 in./40.0 in. 127 in. wheelbase. Pickups: 33.25 in./47.75 in.

CAPACITIES: Fuel Tank: Series K1500 and K2500 pickups: 20.0 gal. Optional: None.

ACCOMMODATIONS: Seating Capacity: Pickup and chassis cab models: 3 passenger. Optional: None. Suburban: 3 passenger. Optional: 6 or 9 passenger.

OPTIONS: K1500 tires: 8 x 17.5 6-ply rated. 8 x 17.5 8-ply rated. 8 x 19.5 6-ply rated. 8 x 18.5 8-plyrated. 1 qt. oil bath air cleaner. Heavy-duty 70 amp-hr. battery. Chrome front bumper (except Panel and Suburban). Chrome front and rear bumper (Panel and Suburban only). Custom cab. Includes custom seat and left door lock). Spare wheel carrier. Directional signals. 35 amp generator. 50 amp generator. Deluxe heater and defroster. Recirculating, inside air heater and defroster. Free wheeling manual front hubs. Left door lock. Lock for side wheel carrier. Lock for left door and side wheel carrier. Exterior left 17.5 in. swinging arm mirror (pickup, chassis and cab). Exterior right 17.5 in. swinging arm mirror (pickup, chassis and cab). Exterior right 8.0 in. fixed bracket. Two-tone paint. Heavy-duty radiator. Auxiliary rear seat for Panel. Custom seat (for Deluxe cab only. Full-view rear window. Windshield washers. Auxiliary inside spare tank with 16.5 gals. capacity. Maximum traction rear differential. Four-speed manual transmission. Air conditioning. Radio, heavy-duty Airflow heater and defroster. Braden winch with Spicer driveline and Chelsea power take-off.

HISTORICAL FOOTNOTES: 1967 calendar year production of all GMC trucks was 130,659 units.

1968 PICKUP & SUBURBAN

The 1968 GMC trucks were identified by their safety side marker lamps on the front and rear fenders. Exterior colors for 1968 were the following: Black, dark blue, light blue, medium blue, dark green, orange, red, saddle, silver, vermilion, white, off-white, dark yellow and light yellow. Interior were offered in a choice of white or black. Standard equipment included dual speed electric windshield wipers and washer, directional signals, back-up lights, painted front bumper, Deluxe-Air heater and defroster, exterior left and right side mirrors, driver and passenger seat belts with retractors, and a vinyl trim full-width seat.

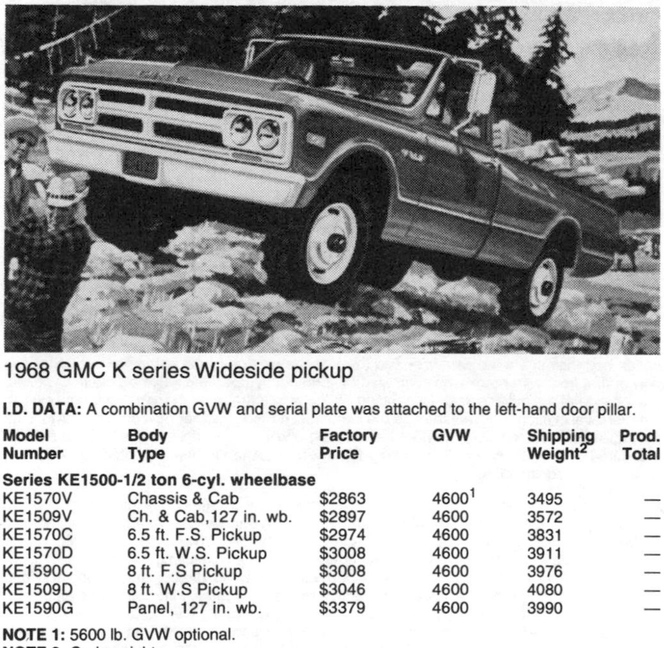

1968 GMC K series Wideside pickup

I.D. DATA: A combination GVW and serial plate was attached to the left-hand door pillar.

Model Number	Body Type	Factory Price	GVW	Shipping Weight[2]	Prod. Total
Series KE1500-1/2 ton 6-cyl. wheelbase					
KE1570V	Chassis & Cab	$2863	4600[1]	3495	—
KE1509V	Ch. & Cab,127 in. wb.	$2897	4600	3572	—
KE1570C	6.5 ft. F.S. Pickup	$2974	4600	3831	—
KE1570D	6.5 ft. W.S. Pickup	$3008	4600	3911	—
KE1590C	8 ft. F.S Pickup	$3008	4600	3976	—
KE1509D	8 ft. W.S Pickup	$3046	4600	4080	—
KE1590G	Panel, 127 in. wb.	$3379	4600	3990	—

NOTE 1: 5600 lb. GVW optional.
NOTE 2: Curb weights.

Series KE2500-3/4 ton 6-cyl. 127 in. wheelbase					
KE20903	Chassis and Cab	$3041	5700*	3610	—
KE20904	8 ft. Fenderside Pickup	$3149	5700	4010	—
KE20934	8 ft. Wideside Pickup	$3187	5700	4100	—
KE20905	Panel	$3521	5700	4445	—

* 7600 lb. GVW optional.

Models with V-6 engine have KM-1500 or KM-2500 identification. An 8100 lb. GVW is optional for these models.

STANDARD ENGINE: KM-1500, KM-2500 Engine Type: OHV, V-6. GMC 305D. Cast iron block and cylinder head. Bore x Stroke: 4.25 in. x 3.58 in. Fuel Induction: Single barrel model 1904 Holley. Compression Ratio: 7.75:1. Displacement: 304.7 cu. in. (4.99 liters). Number of main bearing-4. Horsepower: Gross: 165 @ 3800 rpm. Net: 142 @ 3800 rpm. Torque: Gross: 280 lb.-ft. @ 1600 rpm. Net: 260 lb.-ft. @ 1600 rpm. Fuel Requirements: Regular. Oil capacity: 5 qt.

STANDARD ENGINE: KE models: 307 V-8. Engine Type: OHV, V-8. Cast iron block and cylinder head. Key features include aero-type valve mechanism, and steel-backed babbitt bearings. Bore x Stroke: 3.875 in. x 3.25 in. Lifters: Hydraulic. Number of main bearings-5. Fuel Induction: Single Rochester 2-bbl. carburetor. Compression Ratio: 9.0:1. Displacement: 307 cu. in. (5.03 liters). Horsepower: Gross: 200 @ 4600 rpm. Net: 150 @ 4000 rpm. Torque: Gross: 300 lb.-ft. @ 2400 rpm. Net: 255 lb.-ft. @ 2000 rpm. Oil refill capacity: 5 qt. with filter change. Fuel Requirements: Regular.

OPTIONAL ENGINE: KE models: 327 V-8. Engine Type: OHV, V-8. Cast iron block and alloy iron cylinder head. Key features include chain drive camshaft, molybdenum-filed top piston-rings, premium aluminum main bearings. Bore x Stroke: 4.0 in. x 3.25 in. Lifters: Hydraulic. Number of main bearings-5. Fuel Induction: Single Rochester 4-bbl. carburetor. Model 4G. Compression Ratio: 8.5:1. Displacement: 327 cu. in. (5.35 liters). Horsepower: Gross: 220 @ 4400 rpm. Net: 177 @ 4000 rpm. Torque: Gross: 320 lb.-ft. @ 2800 rpm. Net: 283 lb.-ft. @ 2400 rpm. Oil refill capacity: 5 qt. with filter change. Fuel Requirements: Regular.

CHASSIS FEATURES: Separate body and frame with channel side rails KE1500,115 in. wheelbase: 2.57 in. x 5.98 in. x 0.151 in. Section modulus: 2.70 KE1500,127 in. wheelbase: 2.57 in. x 5.98 in. x 0.186 in. Section modulus: 3.48. KE2500, 2.57 in. x 6.98 in. x 0.186 in. Section modulus: 3.48.

SUSPENSION AND RUNNING GEAR: Front Suspension: KE1500: 2-leaf tapered shot-peened springs. Capacity: 1450 lb. Hydraulic direct action 1.0 in. dia. shock absorbers. KE2500: 2-leaf tapered shot-peened springs. Capacity: 1600 lb. Hydraulic direct action 1.0 in. dia. shock absorbers. Optional rating: KE1500 and KE2500: 3-leaf tapered shot-peened springs. Capacity: 1750 lb. Rear Suspension: KE1500: 5-leaf tapered leaf springs, 52 in. x 2.5 in. Capacity: 1800 lb. at ground. Deflection rate: 280/420 lb./in. shock absorbers. KE2500: 5-leaf tapered leaf springs, 52 in. x 2.5 in. Capacity: 1900 lb. at ground. Deflection rate: 280/420 lb./in. Hydraulic direct action 1.0 in. dia. shock absorbers. Optional Rating: KE1500 and 2500: 2500 lb. capacity, 365/420 lb./in. deflection rate. KE2500:3150 lb. capacity. Front Axle Type and Capacity: KE1500: Spicer 44, semi-floating, 3300 lb. capacity. KE2500: Spicer 44, full-floating, 3500 lb. capacity. Rear Axle Type and Capacity: KE1500: Semi-floating, 3300 lb. capacity. Optional: None. KE2500: Full-floating, 5200 lb. Final Drive Ratio: KE1500: Front: 3.73:1. Rear: 3.73:1. KE2500: 4.55:1. Rear: 4.75:1. Transfer Case: Timken model T-221. Single lever, two-speed: 1.94, 1.00:1. Brakes: Type: Hydraulic, front and rear drums. Dimensions: KE1500: Front: 11.0 in. x 2.0 in. Rear: 11.0 in. x 2.0 in. Total lining area: 167 sq. in. KE2500: Front: 12.0 in. x 2.0 in. Rear: 12.0 in. x 2.0 in. Total lining area: 185.2 sq. in. Optional: Power assisted. Wheels: KE1500: 15 x 5.5, 6-stud disc. KE2500: Optional: 16 x 5.50 and 16 x 5.0. KE2500: 7-17.5 x 5.25. Optional: 8-17.5 x 5.0, 8-17.5 x 5.5, 8-17.5 x 6.0. Tires: KE1500: 8.25 x 15. tubeless Optional: Numerous sizes available. KE2500: Tubeless: 8-16.5. Optional: Numerous sizes available. Steering: Saginaw recirculating ball gear. Ratio: 29.9:1. Optional: None. Transmission: SM330 3-speed, heavy-duty fully-synchromesh manual. Transmission Ratios: 3.03, 1.75, 1.00:1. Reverse: 3.02:1. Optional: SM-465 4-speed manual synchromesh. Ratios: 6.55, 3.58, 1.70, 1.00:1. Reverse: 6.09:1. Clutch: Diaphragm, spring. Clutch diameter: 11.0 in. dia. Total lining area: 124 sq. in.). Total plate pressure: 1875 lb.

VEHICLE DIMENSIONS: Wheelbase: KE1500: 115 in., 127 in. KE2500: 127 in. All Suburbans and Panels: 127 in. Overall Length: 115 in. Wideside pickups: 188.75 in. 127 in. Wideside pickups: 208.0 in. 115 in. Fenderside pickups: 188.125 in. 127 in. Fenderside pickups: 208.0 in. Overall Height: KE1500: 72.5 in. KE2500: 73.25 in. KE1500 Panel: 74.5 in. Width: Pickup: 79 in. Panel: Front/Rear Overhang: 115 in. wheelbase pickups: 33.25 in./40.25 in. 127 in. wheelbase. Pickups: 33.25 in./47.50 in. Tailgate: Width and Height: 50 in. x 19.25 in. Ground Clearance: Lowest point: KE1500 Fenderside: Front axle: 7.25 in. Rear axle: 7.5 in. KE1500 Wideside: Front axle: 7.25 in. Rear axle: 7.0 in. KE2500 Fenderside and Wideside: Front axle: 8.75 in. Rear axle: 7.75 in. Load space: Pickup box dimensions: Stepside115 in. wheelbase: 78 in. x 50 in. x 17.5 in. Wideside 115 in. wheelbase: 78 in. x 60 in. x 17.5 in. Fenderside 127 in. wheelbase: 98 in. x 50 in. x 17.5 in. Wideside 127 in. wheelbase: 98 in. x 66 in. x 17.5 in. Front headroom: 40 in. Front legroom: 40.75 in. Front shoulder room: 58 in.

CAPACITIES: Fuel Tank: Pickups: 21.0 gal. Panels: 23.5 gal. Optional: None.

ACCOMMODATIONS: Seating Capacity: 3 passenger.

INSTRUMENTATION: Speedometer, odometer, fuel gauge. Warning lights for generator, oil pressure, engine coolant temperature, brake system.

OPTIONS AND PRICES: 327 V-8 (KE10 only): $43.05. 4-spd. manual trans.: $96.85. Oil-bath, 1 qt. air cleaner: $10.80. Heavy-duty air cleaner: $53.80. All-Weather air conditioning: $378.25. Heavy-duty front axle (KE2500): $161.40. Driver and passenger armrests: $8.65. Driver's side armrest (Panel only): $4.35. Auxiliary battery: 43.05. Heavy-duty 66 amp-hr. battery: $7.55. Seat belt for third passenger: $6.50. Power brakes: $45.20. Painted rear bumper: $23.70. Rear step painted bumper: $45.20. Chromed front and rear bumpers: $49.50 (pickups), $25.85. (Panel). Front chromed bumper: $12.95. Rear chromed bumper: $36.60. Side-mounted spare wheel carrier: $14 (Wideside), $16.15-21.55 depending on wheelcover and hubcap format. Heavy-duty, 11.0 in. clutch for 250 engine): $5.40. Heavy-duty radiator: $21.55. Heavy-duty radiator and extra-heavy-duty cooling: $46.30. Custom Comfort and Appearance Package: $31.25 (Panels), $86.10, (pickups and cab models). Custom side molding: $26.90 (chassis & cab and Fenderside), $43.05 (Wideside, also includes pickup box moldings), $43.05 (Panels). Custom Sport Truck Package: $161.40. Fuel filter: $7.55. Gauge Package. Includes ammeter, oil pressure and engine coolant temperature: $10.80. Gauge Package. Includes ammeter, oil pressure tachometer and engine coolant temperature: $48.45. 42 amp Delcotron: $21.55. 61 amp Delcotron: $30.15 62 amp Delcotron: $89.35. Soft-Ray glass: $15 (all windows), $14 (windshield only). Governor: $17.25. Door edge guards: $3.25. Camper body wiring: $16.15. Shoulder harness: $26.90. Heater and defroster deletion: $68.35 credit. Two front towing hooks: $16.15. Free wheeling hubs (KE1500 only): $78.55. Marker lamps: $26.90. Side wheel carrier lock: $6.50. Swing arm exterior mirrors: $6.50. West Coast type, 6 in. x 11 in.: $18.30. West Coast type, 7 in. x 16 in.: $31.25. Non-glare interior mirror: $8.65. Two-tone paint: $16.15 (pickups), $26.90 (Panels). Two-tone anniversary gold with off-white secondary color: $49.50 (Wideside), $31.25 (Fenderside). Push-button radio: $58.65. Bucket seats: $113 (with custom Sport truck), $139 (without custom Sport truck). Speed warning indicator: $12.95. Heavy-duty front springs (KE1500): $32.30. Heavy-duty starter motor: $14 (without air conditioning), $29.10 (with air conditioning). Body side paint stripes: $7.55 (Fenderside), $10.80 (Wideside).

HISTORICAL FOOTNOTES: Calendar year production of all models was 148,479.

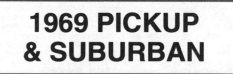

1969 PICKUP & SUBURBAN

The 1969 four-wheel drive GMC trucks had a new hood and front end design with a standard chrome grille. Fifteen solid exterior colors were offered for 1969, five of which were new: Maroon, black, dark blue, light blue, olive green, dark green, light green, orange, red, yellow metallic, silver, saddle metallic, white, turquoise metallic and dark yellow. The interior was offered in six colors: Saddle, blue, green, red, black and turquoise. Both the custom and Super custom interiors had new decorative vinyl door and sidewall trim panels. The 327 V-8 was replaced in the GMC engine line by the 350 cu. in. V-8. Power steering was now optional for four-wheel drive models. The Deluxe cab had as standard equipment dual sun visors and vinyl upholstery. The upholstery of the custom cab was a woven nylon with vinyl trim. The Super custom interior had an all-vinyl upholstery fashioned to resemble tooled leather. It also had bright trim for the foot pedals (except the brake pedal), cowl top insulator and floor insulation under the seat. Bucket seats with a center console were optional for all models.

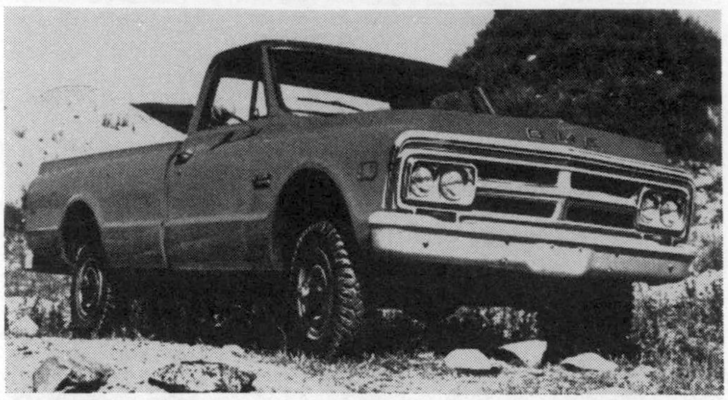

1969 GMC K series Wideside pickup

I.D. DATA: Unchanged from 1968. The final six digits served as the production sequence, beginning with 10,0001. The engine number for the 6-cyl. engine was stamped on the right side of the block next to the distributor. On V-8 engines it was stamped on the forward edge of the block protruding from under the right cylinder head.

Models with the standard 6-cylinder engine had a KS prefix. Those with the standard V-8 engine had a KE prefix.

Model Number	Body Type	Factory Price	GVW	Shipping Weight[2]	Prod. Total
Series KE1500-1/2 ton 6-cyl. wheelbase					
KE1570V	Chassis & Cab	$2913	4600[1]	3510	—
KE1509V	Ch. & Cab,127 in. wb.	$2948	4600	3587	—
KE1570C	6.5 ft. F.S. Pickup	$3025	4600	3846	—
KE1570D	6.5 ft. W.S. Pickup	$3059	4600	3946	—
KE1590C	8 ft. F.S Pickup	$3059	4600	3991	—
KE1509D	8 ft. W.S Pickup	$3097	4600	4095	—
KE1590G	Panel, 127 in. wb.	$3430	4600	4005	—

NOTE 1: 5600 lb. GVW optional.
NOTE 2: Curb weights.

Series KE2500-3/4 ton 6-cyl. 127 in. wheelbase					
KE20903	Chassis and Cab	$3143	5700*	3625	—
KE20904	8 ft. Fenderside Pickup	$3251	5700	4020	—
KE20934	8 ft. Wideside Pickup	$3289	5700	4125	—
KE20905	Panel	$3623	5700	4460	—

* 7600 lb. GVW optional.

Models with V-6 engine have KM-1500 or KM-2500 identification. An 8100 lb. GVW was optional for these models.

STANDARD ENGINE: KM-1500, KM-2500: Engine Type: OHV, V-6. GMC 305D. Cast iron block and cylinder head. Bore x Stroke: 4.25 in. x 3.58 in. Fuel Induction: Single barrel model 1904 Holley. Compression Ratio: 7.75:1. Displacement: 304.7 cu. in. (4.99 liters). Number of main bearing-4. Horsepower: Gross: 165 @ 3800 rpm. Net: 142 @ 3800 rpm. Torque: Gross: 280 lb.-ft. @ 1600 rpm. Net: 260 lb.-ft. @ 1600 rpm. Fuel Requirements: Regular. Oil capacity: 5 qt.

STANDARD ENGINE: KE models: 307 V-8. Engine Type: OHV, V-8. Cast iron block and cylinder head. Key features include aero-type valve mechanism, and steel-backed babbitt bearings. Bore x Stroke: 3.875 in. x 3.25 in. Lifters: Hydraulic. Number of main bearings-5. Fuel Induction: Single Rochester 2-bbl. carburetor. Compression Ratio: 9.0:1. Displacement: 307 cu. in. (5.03 liters). Horsepower: Gross: 200 @ 4600 rpm. Net: 157 @ 4000 rpm. Torque: Gross: 300 lb.-ft. @ 2400 rpm. Net: 260 lb.-ft. @ 2000 rpm. Oil refill capacity: 5 qt. with filter change. Fuel Requirements: Regular.

OPTIONAL ENGINE: KE models: 350 V-8. Engine Type: OHV, V-8. Cast iron block and alloy iron cylinder head. Key features include chain drive camshaft, "Rotocoil" exhaust valve rotators, special coating applied to exhaust valves to reduce deposit formation, molybdenum-filed top piston rings, premium aluminum main bearings. Bore x Stroke: 4.0 in. x 3.50 in. Lifters: Hydraulic. Number of main bearings-5. Fuel Induction: Single Rochester 4-bbl. carburetor. Compression Ratio: 9.0:1. Displacement: 350 cu. in. (5.73 liters). Horsepower: Gross: 255 @ 4600 rpm. Net: 200 @ 4000 rpm. Torque: Gross: 355 lb.-ft. @ 3000 rpm. Net: 315 lb.-ft. @ 2400 rpm. Oil refill capacity: 5 qt. with filter change. Fuel Requirements: Regular.

CHASSIS FEATURES: Separate body and frame with channel side rails KE-1500,115 in. wheelbase: 2.57 in. x 5.98 in. x 0.151 in. Section modulus: 2.70 KE-1500,127 in. wheelbase: 2.57 in. x 5.98 in. x 0.186 in. Section modulus: 3.48. KE-2500, 2.57 in. x 6.98 in. x 0.186 in. Section modulus: 3.48.

SUSPENSION AND RUNNING GEAR: Front Suspension: KE-1500: 2-leaf tapered shot-peened springs. Capacity: 1450 lb. Hydraulic direct action 1.0 in. dia. shock absorbers. KE-2500: 2-leaf tapered shot-peened springs. Capacity: 1600 lb. Hydraulic direct action 1.0 in. dia. shock absorbers. Optional rating: KE-1500 and KE-2500: 3-leaf tapered shot-peened springs. Capacity: 1750 lb. Rear Suspension: KE-1500: 5-leaf tapered leaf springs, 52 in. x 2.5 in. Capacity: 1800 lb. at ground. Deflection rate: 280/420 lb./in. shock absorbers. KE-2500: 5-leaf tapered leaf springs, 52 in. x 2.5 in. Capacity: 1900 lb. at ground. Deflection rate: 280/420 lb./in. Hydraulic direct action 1.0 in. dia. shock absorbers. Optional Rating: KE-2500: 2500 lb. capacity, 365/420 lb./in. deflection rate. Front Axle Type and Capacity: KE-1500: Spicer 44, semi-floating, 3300 lb. capacity. KE-2500: Spicer 44, full-floating, 3500 lb. capacity. Rear Axle Type and Capacity: KE-1500: Semi-floating, 3300 lb. capacity. Optional: None. KE-2500: Full-floating, 5200 lb. Final Drive Ratio: KE-1500: Front: 3.73:1. Rear: 3.73:1. KE-2500: 4.55:1. Rear: 4.75:1. Transfer Case: Timken model T-221. Single lever, two-speed: 1.94, 1.00:1. Brakes: Type: Hydraulic, front and rear drums. Dimensions: KE-1500: Front: 11.0 in. x 2.0 in. Rear: 11.0 in. x 2.0 in. Total lining area: 167 sq. in. KE-2500: Front: 12.0 in. x 2.0 in. Rear: 12.0 in. x 2.0 in. Total lining area: 185.2 sq. in. Optional: Power assisted. Wheels: KE-1500: 15 x 5.5 6-stud disc. Optional: 16 x 5.50 and 16 x 5.0. KE-2500: 17.5 x 5.25 8-stud disc. Optional: 17.5 x 5.0,17.5 x 5.5, 17.5 x 6.0. Tires: KE-1500: 8.25 x 15. tubeless Optional: Tubeless: 7.75 x 15, 6.50 x 16, 8.00 x 16.5. Tube-type: 7.75 x 15, 8.25 x 15, 7.77 x 15, 6.50 x 16. KE-2500: Tubeless: 8.00 x 16.5 Optional: Tubeless: 8.75 x 16.5, 9.50 x 16.5, 10.00 x 16.5 Tube-type: 7.50 x 16. Steering: Saginaw recirculating ball gear. Steering wheel diameter: 17.5 in. Ratio: 29.9:1. Optional: Power-assisted. Transmission: SM-330 3-speed, heavy-duty fully-synchromesh manual. Transmission Ratios: 3.03, 1.75, 1.00:1. Reverse: 3.02:1. Optional: SM465 4-speed manual synchromesh. Ratios: 6.55, 3.58, 1.70, 1.00:1. Reverse: 6.09:1. Clutch: Diaphragm, spring. Clutch diameter: 6-cyl.: 10 in. dia. (11.0 in. with 292 6-cyl.). Total lining area: 100.0 sq. in. (11.0 in.-124 sq. in.). Total plate pressure: 1875 lb. V-8: 12 in. dia. Total lining area: 150 sq. in. Total plate pressure: 1877 lb.

VEHICLE DIMENSIONS: Wheelbase: KE-1500: 115 in. 127 in. KE-2500: 127 in. All Suburbans and Panels: 127 in. Overall Length: 115 in. Wideside pickups: 188.75 in. 127 in. Wideside pickups: 208.0 in. 115 in. Fenderside pickups: 188.125 in. 127 in. Fenderside pickups: 208.0 in. Overall Height: KE-1500: 72.5 in. KE-2500: 73.25 in. KE-1500 Panel: 74.5 in. Width: Pickup: 79 in. Front/Rear Overhang: 115 in. wheelbase pickups: 33.25 in./40.25 in. 127 in. wheelbase. Pickups: 33.25 in./47.50 in. Tailgate: Width and Height: 50 in. x 19.25 in. Ground Clearance: Lowest point: KE-1500 Fenderside: Front axle: 7.25 in. Rear axle: 7.5 in. KE-1500 Wideside: Front axle: 7.25 in. Rear axle: 7.0 in. KE-2500 Fenderside and Wideside: Front axle: 8.75 in. Rear axle: 7.75 in. Load space: Pickup box dimensions: Stepside115 in. wheelbase: 78 in. x 50 in. x 17.5 in. Wideside 115 in. wheelbase: 78 in. x 60 in. x 17.5 in. Fenderside 127 in. wheelbase: 98 in. x 50 in. x 17.5 in. Wideside 127 in. wheelbase: 98 in. x 66 in. x 17.5 in. Capacity: 115 in. wheelbase: 39.7 cu. ft. 127 in. wheelbase: 49.8 cu. ft. Front headroom: 40 in. Front legroom: 40.75 in. Front shoulder room: 58 in. Front hip room: 64.75 in. Steering wheel to seat back (max.): 14.7 in.

CAPACITIES: Fuel Tank: Pickups: 21.0 gal. Panels: 23.5 gal. Optional: None.

ACCOMMODATIONS: Seating Capacity: 3 passenger. Seat Dimensions: 58.75 in.

INSTRUMENTATION: Speedometer, odometer, fuel gauge. Warning lights for generator, oil pressure, engine coolant temperature, brake system.

OPTIONS: With the exception of the addition of power steering, and the replacement of the 327 V-8 cu. in. with the 350 cu. in. V-8, the options offered were unchanged from 1968.

HISTORICAL FOOTNOTES: The 1969 models debuted in the fall of 1968. The 350 cu. in. V-8 was introduced. Total model year production of all GMC trucks established a new record: 150,180.

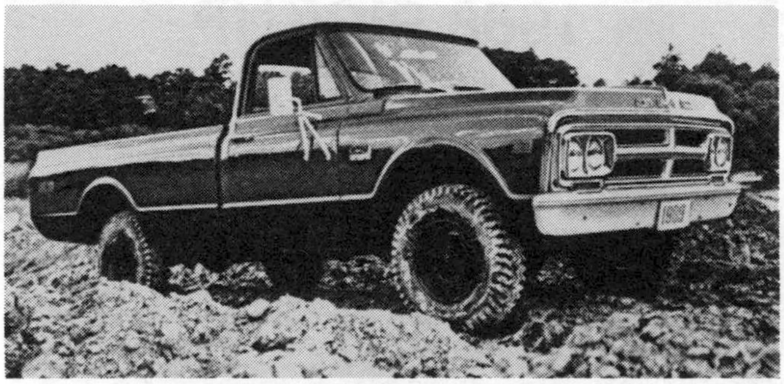

1969 GMC K910 Wideside pickup with optional mirrors

1970 PICKUP & SUBURBAN

The 1970 GMC had a revised grille format with more substantial-appearing crossbars. Half-ton models had new bias-ply, glass-belted tires. The 3/4 ton models were fitted with larger 8.75 x 16.5 highway nylon cord tires. Introduced as an option for the 3/4 ton Wideside pickups was an auxiliary frame-mounted fuel tank positioned just behind the rear axle. Trucks with this option had their spare tire carrier moved towards the rear on frame extension supports. The flow of fuel from either tank was controlled by a manually-operated valve on the floor next to the left side of the driver's seat. Depending on the position of a dash-mounted toggle switch, the fuel level in each tank was read on the same fuel gauge. Another new option for Wideside models was a storage compartment located just ahead of the right rear wheel housing. It measured 7 in. x 28 in. x 127 in. It was fitted with a lockable flush-mounted steel door of double-panel construction

Also added to the option list for 1970 was an adjustable tilting steering column that locked into seven different positions and an AM/FM radio with built in 8-track tape player. For the first time Turbo Hydra-Matic was available for four-wheel drive models. It was used along with a new type transfer case designed to offer quieter operation and easier shifting into four-wheel drive. Four wheel drive models were also equipped with a new 40 degree steer front axle that reduced the turning radius. A maximum traction rear axle was also introduced as an option. Both 1/2 ton and 3/4 ton models had revised standard axle ratios. The 1/2 ton models with the 350 cu. in. V-8 had a 3.07:1 ratio in place of the 3.73:1 used in 1969. The 3/4 ton standard axle with the 350-V-8 now was 4.10:1 instead of 4.57:1. As in 1969 a total of twelve pickup and six chassis-cab models were offered with four-wheel drive. Standard equipment for the pickup models included self-adjusting brakes, dual master cylinder brake system with warning light, back-up lights, directional signals and four-way flasher, side marker and reflectors, left-hand and right-hand exterior rearview mirrors, nonglare interior rearview mirror and heater and defroster. Among the safety related standard equipment found on all models were the following: Energy-absorbing padded instrument panel and sun visors, thick-laminate windshield, non-glare finish on top of dash and instrument panel insert, safety door locks and hinges, low-profile steering wheel, windshield washers and defrosters and 2-speed electric windshield wipers. The standard interior had a 3 passenger bench seat with foam padding, dome light, rubber floor mat and dual armrests. Exterior elements of the Super Comfort option included bright metal around the front and rear windows plus bright ventipane frames and custom nameplates on front fenders. Interior items included color-keyed rubber floor mat, full-depth foam seat with color-keyed fabric and vinyl trim, vinyl trim door panels, cigarette lighter, custom nameplate on glove box door and cowl insulation. The Super Custom option included a chrome front bumper, Super Custom nameplate on front fenders, full-width vinyl seats, bright frames for clutch, brake and accelerator pedals, extra insulation, carpeting and cargo light. The Super Custom option was also available with new two-tone color combinations. All interiors were available in a choice of any one of six colors: Saddle, blue, green, red, black, and turquoise. Among the exterior colors offered were black, white, yellow, medium bronze metallic, medium red, medium olive metallic, dark olive metallic, ochre and red orange.

I.D. DATA: Unchanged from 1969. The serial number was stamped on a plate mounted on the windshield corner post. Models with the standard 6-cylinder engine had a KS prefix. Those with the standard V-8 engine had a KE prefix.

Model Number	Body Type	Factory Price	GVW	Shipping Weight	Prod. Total
Series KS-15001/2 ton 6-cyl. 115 in. wheelbase					
KS15703	Chassis and Cab	$2951	5200*	3320	—
KS15704	6.5 ft. F-S Pickup	$3076	5200	3656	—
KS15734	6.5 ft. W-S Pickup	$3134	5200	3736	—
KS15904	8 ft. Fenderside Pickup	$3134	5200	3740	—
KS15934	8 ft. Wideside Pickup	$3141	5200	3835	—
KS15905	Panel, 127 in. wb.	$3615	5200	3948	—
KS15906	Suburban, 127 in. wb.	$3835	5200	4070	—

* 5600 lb. GVW optional.

Model Number	Body Type	Factory Price	GVW	Shipping Weight	Prod. Total
Series KS-2500-3/4 ton 6-cyl. 127 in. wheelbase					
KS25903	Chassis and Cab	$3378	6400*	3631	—
KS25904	8 ft. Fenderside Pickup	$3478	6400	4031	—
KS25934	8 ft. Wideside Pickup	$3516	6400	4126	—
KS25905	Panel	$3995	6400	4246	—
KS25906	Suburban	$4166	6400	4368	—

* 7500 lb. GVW optional.

STANDARD ENGINE: KS series: 250 Six. Engine Type: OHV, In-line 6-cylinder. Cast iron block and cylinder head. Key features include 12 counterweight crankshaft and torsional damper, and molybdenum-filled top piston rings. Bore x Stroke: 3.875 in. x 3.53 in. Lifters: Hydraulic. Number of main bearings-7. Fuel Induction: Single Rochester 1-bbl. carburetor, model 7028007/7028011. Compression Ratio: 8.5:1. Displacement: 250 cu. in. (4.09 liters). Horsepower: Gross: 155 @ 4000 rpm. Net: 120 @ 3800 rpm. Torque: Gross: 235 lb.-ft. @ 2000 rpm. Net: 210 lb.-ft. @ 2000 rpm. Oil refill capacity: 5 qt. with filter change. Fuel Requirements: Regular.

OPTIONAL ENGINE: KS series: 292 Six. Engine Type: OHV, 6-cyl. Cast iron block and cylinder head. Key features include aluminized intake valves, automatic "Rotocoil" rotors on exhaust valves, special coating applied to exhaust valves to reduce deposit formation, full-chromed top piston rings, and premium aluminum bearings. Bore x Stroke: 3.875 in. x 4.125 in. Lifters: Hydraulic. Number of main bearings-7. Fuel Induction: Single Rochester 1-bbl. carburetor. Model 7028001/7028011. Compression Ratio: 8.5:1. Displacement: 292 cu. in. (4.78 liters). Horsepower: Gross: 170 @ 4000 rpm. Net: 153 @ 3600 rpm. Torque: Gross: 275 lb.-ft. @ 1600 rpm. Net: 240 lb.-ft. @ 1800 rpm. Oil refill capacity: 6 qt. with filter change. Fuel Requirements: Regular.

STANDARD ENGINE: KE models: 307 V-8. Engine Type: OHV, V-8. Cast iron block and cylinder head. Key features include aero-type valve mechanism, and steel-backed babbitt bearings. Bore x Stroke: 3.875 in. x 3.25 in. Lifters: Hydraulic. Number of main bearings-5. Fuel Induction: Single Rochester 2-bbl. carburetor. Compression Ratio: 9.0:1. Displacement: 307 cu. in. (5.03 liters). Horsepower: Gross: 200 @ 4600 rpm. Net: 157 @ 4000 rpm. Torque: Gross: 300 lb.-ft. @ 2400 rpm. Net: 260 lb.-ft. @ 2000 rpm. Oil refill capacity: 5 qt. with filter change. Fuel Requirements: Regular.

OPTIONAL ENGINE: KE models: 350 V-8. Engine Type: OHV, V-8. Cast iron block and alloy iron cylinder head. Key features include chain drive camshaft, "Rotocoil" exhaust valve rotators, special coating applied to exhaust valves to reduce deposit formation, molybdenum-filed top piston rings, premium aluminum main bearings. Bore x Stroke: 4.0 in. x 3.50 in. Lifters: Hydraulic. Number of main bearings-5. Fuel Induction: Single Rochester 4-bbl. carburetor. Compression Ratio: 9.0:1. Displacement: 350 cu. in. (5.73 liters). Horsepower: Gross: 255 @ 4600 rpm. Net: 200 @ 4000 rpm. Torque: Gross: 355 lb.-ft. @ 3000 rpm. Net: 315 lb.-ft. @ 2400 rpm. Oil refill capacity: 5 qt. with filter change. Fuel Requirements: Regular.

CHASSIS FEATURES: Separate body and frame with channel side rails KE-1500,115 in. wheelbase: 2.57 in. x 5.98 in. x 0.151 in. Section modulus: 2.70 KE-1500,127 in. wheelbase: 2.57 in. x 5.98 in. x 0.186 in. Section modulus: 3.48. K20, 2.57 in. x 6.98 in. x 0.186 in. Section modulus: 3.48.

SUSPENSION AND RUNNING GEAR: Front Suspension: K-1500: 2-leaf tapered shot-peened springs. Capacity: 1450 lb. Hydraulic direct action 1.0 in. dia. shock absorbers. K2500: 2-leaf tapered shot-peened springs. Capacity: 1600 lb. Hydraulic direct action 1.0 in. dia. shock absorbers. Optional rating: K-1500 and K-2500: 3-leaf tapered shot-peened springs. Capacity: 1750 lb. Rear Suspension: K-1500: 5-leaf tapered leaf springs, 52 in. x 2.5 in. Capacity: 1800 lb. at ground. Deflection rate: 280/420 lb./in. shock absorbers. K-2500: 5-leaf tapered leaf springs, 52 in. x 2.5 in. Capacity: 1900 lb. at ground. Deflection rate: 280/420 lb./in. Hydraulic direct action 1.0 in. dia. shock absorbers. Optional Rating: K-2500: 2500 lb. capacity, 365/420 lb./in. deflection rate. Front Axle Type and Capacity: K-1500: Spicer 44, semi-floating, 3300 lb. capacity. K-2500: Spicer 44, full-floating, 3500 lb. capacity. Rear Axle Type and Capacity: K-1500: Semi-floating, 3300 lb. capacity. Optional: None. K-2500: Full-floating, 5200 lb. Final Drive Ratio: K-1500: Front: 3.73:1. Rear: 3.73:1. 4.55:1. Rear: 4.75:1. K-1500 with 350 cu. in. V-8: 3.07:1. K-2500 with 350-V-8: 4.10:1. Transfer case: New Process 205. Single lever, 2-speed. Ratios: 1.96, 1.75, 1.0:1. Brakes: Type: Hydraulic, front and rear drums. Dimensions: K-1500: Front: 11.0 in. x 2.0 in. Rear: 11.0 in. x 2.0 in. Total lining area: 167 sq. in. K-2500: Front: 12.0 in. x 2.0 in. Rear: 12.0 in. x 2.0 in. Total lining area: 185.2 sq. in. Optional: Power assisted. Wheels: K-1500: 15 x 5.5 6-stud disc. Optional: 16 x 5.50 and 16 x 5.0. K-2500: 17.5 x 5.25 8-stud disc. Optional: 17.5 5.0,17.5 x 5.5, 17.5 x 6.0. Tires: K-1500: G78 x 15B. tubeless Optional: Tubeless: H78 x 15B. Tube-type: G78 x 15B, 7.00 x 15, 6.50 x 16. K-2500: Tubeless: 8.75 x 16.5 Optional: Tubeless: 10.00 x 16.5, 9.50 x 16.5, Tube-type: 7.50 x 16, 6.50 x 16. Steering: Saginaw recirculating ball gear. Steering wheel diameter: 17.5 in. Ratio: 29.9:1. Optional: Power-assisted. Transmission: SM-330 3-speed, heavy-duty fully-synchromesh manual. Transmission Ratios: 3.03, 1.75, 1.00:1. Reverse: 3.02:1. Optional: SM465 4-speed manual synchromesh. Ratios: 6.55, 3.58, 1.70, 1.00:1. Reverse: 6.09:1. Optional: Hydra-Matic automatic 3-speed automatic. Clutch: Diaphragm, spring. Clutch diameter: 6-cyl.: 10 in. dia. (11.0 in. with 292 6-cyl.) Total lining area: 100.0 sq. in. (11.0 in.-124 sq. in.) Total plate pressure: 1875 lb. V-8: 12 in. dia. Total lining area: 150 sq. in. Total plate pressure: 1877 lb.

VEHICLE DIMENSIONS: Wheelbase: K-1500: 115 in., 127 in. K-2500: 127 in. All Suburbans and Panels: 127 in. Overall Length: 115 in. Wideside pickups: 188.75 in. 127 in. Wideside pickups: 208.0 in. 115 in. Fenderside pickups: 188.125 in. 127 in. Fenderside pickups: 208.0 in. Overall Height: K-1500: 72.5 in. K-2500: 73.25 in. K-1500 Panel: 74.5 in. Width: Pickup: 79 in. Panel: Front/Rear Overhang: 115 in. wheelbase pickups: 33.25 in./40.25 in. 127 in. wheelbase. Pickups: 33.25 in./47.50 in. Tailgate: Width and Height: 50 in. x 19.25 in. Ground Clearance: Lowest point: K-1500 Fenderside: Front axle: 7.25 in. Rear axle: 7.5 in. K-1500 Wideside: Front axle: 7.25 in. Rear axle: 7.0 in. K-2500 Fenderside: Front axle: 8.75 in. Rear axle: 7.75 in. Load space: Pickup box dimensions: Wideside 115 in. wheelbase: 78 in. x 60 in. x 17.5 in. Fenderside 127 in. wheelbase: 98 in. x 50 in. x 17.5 in. Wideside 127

in. wheelbase: 98 in. x 66 in. x 17.5 in. Capacity: 115 in. wheelbase: 39.7 cu. ft., 127 in. wheelbase: 49.8 cu. ft. Front headroom: 40 in. Front legroom: 40.75 in. Front shoulder room: 58 in. Front hip room: 64.75 in. Steering wheel to seat back (max.): 14.7 in.

CAPACITIES: Fuel Tank: Pickups: 21.0 gal. Panels: 23.5 gal. Optional: None.

ACCOMMODATIONS: Seating Capacity: 3 passenger. Seat Dimensions: 58.75 in.

INSTRUMENTATION: Speedometer, odometer, fuel gauge. Warning lights for generator, oil pressure, engine coolant temperature, brake system.

OPTIONS: 292 cu. in. 6-cyl. engine. 350 cu. in. V-8. Power brakes. Power steering. Wooden bed floor for Wideside models. Tachometer. AM radio. Air conditioning. Heavy-duty front and rear shock absorbers. Front stabilizer bar. Chrome below eye-level mirror. Armrests. Engine block heater. Cab clearance lights. Pickup side step. Front bumper guards. Chrome front bumper. Painted rear bumper. Door edge guards. Heavy-duty air cleaner. Heavy-duty battery. Heavy-duty clutch. Heavy-duty cooling. Heavy-duty generator, heavy-duty front and rear springs. Heavy-duty starter. Tinted glass. Two-tone paint. Bucket seats and console. Bright pickup box hand rails. Super Custom Package. Adjustable tilting steering column. AM/FM radio with 8-track tape player.

HISTORICAL FOOTNOTES: Calendar year production of all models was 121,833.

1971 PICKUP & SUBURBAN

1971 GMC Suburban

Exterior changes for 1971 were very limited. Most apparent were the single piece front fender side markers. The standard Deluxe interior/exterior provided dual padded sun visors, and a 3 passenger vinyl covered bench seat with foam padding and available in a choice of black, blue, green, olive or parchment. The custom cab included nylon cloth/vinyl upholstery, vinyl door panels, dual armrests with woodgrain vinyl inserts, dome light and color-keyed vinyl floor mat. The top-ranked Super custom interior added bright trim accents, and deep pile carpeting along with leather upholstery with a leather-like texture. Extra floor and cowl top insulation was also included. Bucket seats finished in soft vinyl along with a center console were optional. Exterior features of the custom option included bright ventipane frames, chrome windshield and rear window reveal moldings, and full underbody protective coating. The Super custom exterior incorporated all custom features plus a chrome front bumper, cowl grille-to-door opening insulators, and cowl-to-fender insulators. Wideside models added special tail and back-up light trim, and special molding with woodgrain vinyl appliques.

1971 GMC K series Wideside pickup with slide-in Camper

Additional standard equipment on all models included a sealed side-terminal battery (54 plate/2350 watts for 250 L-6 and 307 V-8; 66 plate/2900 watts for 292 L-6 and 350 V-8 engines), dual brake system with warning light, high-intensity Power-Beam headlights, back-up lights, directional signals with 4-way flasher, "panoramic" rear window, 2-speed electric windshield wipers, windshield washer, right-hand coat hook and heater/defroster. Front disc brakes were now standard. New rear finned brake drums were standard for the K1500.

A total of 15 exterior colors were offered for 1971: Black, white, yellow, medium bronze metallic, medium red, medium olive metallic, dark olive metallic, ochre, red orange, orange, dark yellow, medium green dark green, medium blue and dark blue. The last six listed were new for 1971.

I.D. DATA: A vehicle identification number was stamped on a combination vehicle identification number and rating plate located on the left door pillar. It contained 12 units. The first, a letter K, identified the truck as a four-wheel drive. The second entry, also a letter identified the engine type. A letter S designated a 6-cyl. engine; an E identified a V-8 engine. Next followed a letter which identified the GVW range. A number 1 represented a 1/2 ton truck; a number 2 represented a 3/4 ton truck. Another number was next in the sequence. It provided information about the type as follows: 3-Cab-chassis; 4-Cab and pickup box. The 1971 model year was next represented by a number 1. A letter or a number, according to this scheme, next identified the assembly plant: A-Lakewood, B-Baltimore, C-Southgate, D-Doraville, F-Flint, G-Framingham, J-Janesville, K-Leeds, L-Van Nuys, N-Norwood, P-GM Truck-Pontiac, R-Arlington, S-St. Louis. T-Tarrytown. U-Lordstown, W-Willow Run, Y-Wilmington, Z-Fremont, 1-Oshawa, 2-Ste. Therese. The final six entries were the unit number. The starting unit number was 600001 or 800001 at each assembly plant regardless of series. The engine number for the 6-cyl. engine was stamped on a boss on the right side of the engine block to the rear of the distributor. On V-8 engines it was stamped on a boss on the right front of the engine block.

Model Number	Body Type	Factory Price	GVW	Shipping Weight	Prod. Total
Series K1500-1/2 ton 6-cyl. 115 in. wheelbase					
KS15704	6.5 ft. Stepside Pickup	$430	5200[1]	3679	—
KS15734	6.5 ft. Fleetside Pickup	$3530	5200	3764	—
KS15904	8 ft. Stepside Pickup	$3469	5200	3772	—
KS15934	8 ft. Fleetside Pickup	$3369	5200	3867	—
KS15906	Suburban Endgate	$4273	5200	4131	—
KS15916	Suburban Pnl.Doors	$4304	5200	4131	—

NOTE 1: 5600 lb. GVW optional.

Models with the standard 6-cylinder engine had a KS prefix. Those with the standard V-8 engine had a KE prefix. The price of an equivalent KE with a 307 V-8 is $124 above that of the respective KS in the K10 series and $124 for the K20 series.

Model Number	Body Type	Factory Price	GVW	Shipping Weight	Prod. Total
Series K2500-3/4 ton 6-cyl. 127 in. wheelbase					
KS25903	Chassis and Cab	$3657	6400*	3599	—
KS25904	8 ft. Stepside Pickup	$3820	6400	4001	—
KS25934	8 ft. Fleetside Pickup	$3820	6400	3094	—
KS25906	Suburban Endgate	$4554	6400	3094	—
KS25916	Suburban Pnl. Doors	$4526	6400	4354	—

* 7500 lb. GVW optional.

STANDARD ENGINE: KS models: 250 Six. Engine Type: OHV, In-line 6-cylinder. Cast iron block and cylinder head. Key features include 12 counterweight crankshaft and torsional damper, and molybdenum-filled top piston rings. Bore x Stroke: 3.875 in. x 3.53 in. Lifters: Hydraulic. Number of main bearings-7. Fuel Induction: Single Rochester 1-bbl. carburetor. Compression Ratio: 8.5:1. Displacement: 250 cu. in. (4.09 liters). Horsepower: Gross: 145 @ 4200 rpm. Net: 110 @ 4000 rpm. Torque: Gross: 230 lb.-ft. @ 1600 rpm. Net: 185 lb.-ft. @ 1600 rpm. Oil refill capacity: 5 qt. with filter change. Fuel Requirements: Regular or reduced lead content fuel.

STANDARD ENGINE: KE models: 307 V-8. Engine Type: OHV, V-8. Cast iron block and cylinder head. Key features include aero-type valve mechanism, and steel-backed babbitt bearings. Bore x Stroke: 3.875 in. x 3.25 in. Lifters: Hydraulic. Number of main bearings-5. Fuel Induction: Single Rochester 2-bbl. carburetor. Compression Ratio: 8.5:1. Displacement: 307 cu. in. (5.03 liters). Horsepower: Series 10: Gross: 200 @ 4600 rpm. Net: 135 @ 4000 rpm. Series 20: Gross: 215 @ 4800 rpm. Net: 135 @ 4000 rpm. Torque: Series 10: Gross: 300 lb.-ft. @ 2400 rpm. Net: 235 lb.-ft. @ 2400 rpm. Series 20: 305 lb.-ft. @ 2800 rpm. Net: 230 lb.-ft. @ 2000 rpm. Oil refill capacity: 5 qt. with filter change. Fuel Requirements: Regular or reduced lead content fuel.

OPTIONAL ENGINE: KS models: 292 Six. Engine Type: OHV, 6-cyl. Cast iron block and cylinder head. Key features include aluminized intake valves, automatic "Rotocoil" rotors on exhaust valves, special coating applied to exhaust valves to reduce deposit formation, full-chromed top piston rings, and premium aluminum bearings. Bore x Stroke: 3.875 in. x 4.125 in. Lifters: Hydraulic. Number of main bearings-7. Fuel Induction: Single Rochester 1-bbl. carburetor. Compression Ratio: 8.0:1. Displacement: 292 cu. in. (4.78 liters). Horsepower: Gross: 165 @ 4000 rpm. Net: 130 @ 4400 rpm. Torque: Gross: 270 lb.-ft. @ 1600 rpm. Net: 225 lb.-ft. @ 1800 rpm. Oil refill capacity: 6 qt. with filter change. Fuel Requirements: Regular or reduced lead content fuel.

OPTIONAL ENGINE: KS models: 350 V-8. Engine Type: OHV, V-8. Cast iron block and alloy iron cylinder head. Key features include chain drive camshaft, "Rotocoil" exhaust valve rotators, special coating applied to exhaust valves to reduce deposit formation, molybdenum-filed top piston rings, premium aluminum main bearings. Bore x Stroke: 4.0 in. x 3.50 in. Lifters: Hydraulic. Number of main bearings-5. Fuel Induction: Single Rochester 4-bbl. carburetor. Compression Ratio: 8.5:1. Displacement: 350 cu. in. (5.73 liters). Horsepower: Gross: 250 @ 4600 rpm. Net: 190 @ 4000 rpm. Torque: Gross: 350 lb.-ft. @ 3000 rpm. Net: 310 lb.-ft. @ 2400 rpm. Oil refill capacity: 5 qt. with filter change. Fuel Requirements: Regular or reduced lead content fuel.

CHASSIS FEATURES: Separate body and frame with channel side rails K1500,115 in. wheelbase: 2.57 in. x 5.98 in. x 0.151 in. Section modulus: 2.70 K1500, 127 in. wheelbase: 2.57 in. x 5.98 in. x 0.186 in. Section modulus: 3.48. K2500, 2.57 in. x 6.98 in. x 0.186 in. Section modulus: 3.48.

SUSPENSION AND RUNNING GEAR: Front Suspension: K1500: 2-leaf tapered shot-peened springs. Capacity: 1450 lb. Hydraulic direct action 1.0 in. dia. shock absorbers. K2500: 2-leaf tapered shot-peened springs. Capacity: 1600 lb. Hydraulic direct action 1.0 in. dia. shock absorbers. Optional rating: K1500 and K2500: 3-leaf tapered shot-peened springs. Capacity: 1750 lb. Rear Suspension: K1500: 5-leaf tapered leaf springs, 52 in. x 2.5 in. Capacity: 1800 lb. at ground. Deflection rate: 280/420 lb./in. shock absorbers. K2500: 5-leaf tapered leaf springs, 52 in. x 2.5 in. Capacity: 1900 lb. at ground. Deflection rate: 280/420 lb./in. Hydraulic direct action 1.0 in. dia. shock absorbers. Optional Rating: K2500: 2500 lb. capacity, 365/420 lb./in. deflection rate. Front Axle Type and Capacity: K1500: Spicer 44, semi-floating, 3300 lb. capacity. K2500: Spicer 44, full-floating, 3500 lb. capacity. Rear Axle Type and Capacity: K1500: Semi-floating, 3300 lb. capacity. Optional: None. K2500: Full-floating, 5200 lb. Final Drive Ratio: K1500: Front and rear: 3.73:1. K2500: Front: 4.55:1, Rear: 4.57:1. Transfer Case: New Process 205. Single lever, two-speed: 1.96, 1.00:1. Brakes: Type: Hydraulic, front disc and rear drums. Dimensions: K1500: Front: 11.86 in. rotor. Rear: 11.0 in. x 2.0 in. Rear brake area: 138.2 sq. in. Lining area: 84.4 sq. in. K2500: Front: 12.50 in. rotor. Rear: 12.0 in. x 2.0 in. Rear brake area: 150.8 sq. in. Lining area: 89.0 sq. in. Optional: Power assisted. Wheels: K1500: 15 x 6.0 6-stud disc. K2500: 16.5 x 5.25 8-stud disc. Tires: K1500: G78 x 15B. tubeless Optional: Tube-type tires: G78 x 15B, 6.50 x 16C. Tubeless: H78 x 15B, G78 x 15B, 10.00 x 16.5C. K2500: Tubeless: 8.75 x 16.5 Optional: Tubeless: 10.00 x 16.5, 9.50 x 16.5, Tube-type: 7.50 x 16, 6.50 x 16, plus numerous other sizes. Steering: Saginaw recirculating ball gear. Steering wheel diameter: 17.5 in. Ratio: 24:1. Optional: Power-assisted. Transmission: SM-330 3-speed, heavy-duty fully-synchromesh manual. Transmission Ratios: 3.03, 1.75, 1.00:1. Reverse: 3.02:1. Optional: SM465 4-speed manual synchromesh. Ratios: 6.55, 3.58, 1.70, 1.00:1. Reverse: 6.09:1. Optional: Turbo Hydra-Matic automatic 3-speed automatic. Clutch: Diaphragm, spring. Clutch diameter: 6-cyl.: 10 in. dia. (11.0 in. with 292 6-cyl.) Total lining area: 100.0 sq. in. (11.0 in.-124 sq. in.) Total plate pressure: 1875 lb. V-8: 12 in. dia. Total lining area: 150 sq. in. Total plate pressure: 1877 lb.

VEHICLE DIMENSIONS: Wheelbase: K1500: 115 in. 127 in. K2500: 127 in. All Suburbans and Panels: 127 in. Overall Length: 115 in. Wideside pickups: 188.75 in. 127 in. Wideside pickups: 208.0 in. 115 in. Fenderside pickups: 188.125 in. 127 in. Fenderside pickups: 208.0 in. Overall Height: K1500: 72.5 in. K2500: 73.25 in. K1500 Suburban Carryall: 75.25 in. Width: Pickup: 79 in. Suburban Carryall: 78.75 in. Front/Rear Overhang: 115 in. wheelbase pickups: 33.25 in./40.25 in. 127 in. wheelbase. Pickups: 33.25 in./47.50 in. Suburban Carryall: 33.25 in./55.25 in. Tailgate: Width and Height: 50 in. x 17.5 in. Ground Clearance: Lowest point: K1500 Fenderside: Front axle: 7.25 in. Rear axle: 7.5 in. K1500 Wideside: Front axle: 7.25 in. Rear axle: 7.0 in. K2500 Fenderside and Wideside: Front axle: 8.75 in. Rear axle: 7.75 in. Suburban Carryall: Front axle: 7.25 in., Rear axle: 7.5 in. Load space: Pickup box dimensions: Wideside 115 in. wheelbase: 78 in. x 60 in. x 17.5 in. Fenderside 127 in. wheelbase: 98 in. x 50 in. x 17.5 in. Wideside 127 in. wheelbase: 98 in. x 66 in. x 17.5 in. Capacity: 115 in. wheelbase: 39.7 cu. ft. 127 in. wheelbase: 49.8 cu. ft. Front headroom: 40 in. Front legroom: 40.75 in. Front shoulder room: 58 in. Front hip room: 64.75 in. Steering wheel to seat back (max.): 14.7 in.

CAPACITIES: Fuel Tank: Pickups: 20.0 gal. Panels and Suburbans: 21.0 gal. Optional: 20.5 gal. auxiliary fuel tank for 3/4 ton Fleetsides.

ACCOMMODATIONS: Seating Capacity: 3 passenger. Seat Dimensions: 58.75 in.

INSTRUMENTATION: Speedometer, odometer, fuel gauge. Warning lights for generator, oil pressure, engine coolant temperature, brake system.

OPTIONS AND PRICES: 292 cu. in. 6-cyl. engine: $95. 307 cu. in. V-8: $124 above price of base 6-cyl. 350 cu. in. V-8: $45 above price of model with 307 V-8. Custom Package. Super Custom Package. Turbo Hydra-Matic: $247.50. 4-speed manual trans.: $113. Optional axle ratios: 12.95. Oil bath air cleaner: $10.80. All-Weather air conditioner (V-8 only): $430.40. Auxiliary battery: $48.45. Heavy-duty 80 amp-hr. battery: $17.25 Seat belts for third passenger: $7.00. Painted rear bumper: $23.70. Rear step bumper: $51.65. Chromed front and rear bumper: $53.80. Chromed front bumper: $16.15. Chromed rear bumper: $37.70. Chromed hubcap (K1500 only): $14. Side-mounted spare wheel carrier: $15.10 (Wideside), $17.25 (Fenderside), additional cost for use with chromed wheels and covers. Heavy-duty cooling: $26.90. Wood pickup box floor for Wideside: $20.45. Gauge Package. Includes ammeter, engine coolant temperature and oil pressure gauges: $12.95. Gauge Package. Includes tachometer, ammeter, engine coolant temperature and oil pressure gauges: $59.20. 42 amp Delcotron generator: $23.70. 61 amp Delcotron generator: $32.30. Soft-Ray tinted glass, all windows: $19.40. Door edge guards: $6.50. Camper body wire harness: $16.15. Two front towing hooks: $19.40. Front free wheeling hubs: $78.55. Cargo area lamp: 20.45. Roof marker lamps: $26.90. Exterior below eye-level painted mirrors: $21. Exterior below eye-level stainless steel mirrors: $37.70. Camper style painted mirrors: $21. Camper style stainless steel mirrors: $52.75. Two-tone paint with white secondary color: $26.90. Custom two-tone paint: $26.90. Deluxe two-tone paint: $123.75, $80.70 (with custom and Super custom). AM radio: $69.95. AM/FM radio: $151.75. Front bucket seats: $148.50, $121.60 (with custom). Full depth foam seat: 30.15. Front and rear heavy-duty shock absorbers: $16.15. Front 1750 lb. springs: $33.40. Rear 2500 lb. springs (K2500): $19.40. Power steering: $150.65. ComforTilt steering wheel: $59.20. Body side paint stripes: $14. Door operated dome lamp switch: $4.35. Manual throttle control: $15.10. Sliding rear window: $53.80.

HISTORICAL FOOTNOTES: GMC introduced its "GMC Sudden Service System" in 1971. This enabled an owner to talk with truck experts at Pontiac, Michigan about truck issues.

1972 PICKUP & SUBURBAN

The 1972 GMC trucks were virtually unchanged externally from the 1971 models. A new Sierra Grande Package was available with features as simulated wood grained inserts for door trim panels, and instrument cluster, Houndstooth checked nylon fabric and coordinated vinyl trim and carpeting, extra floor and top-cowl insulation, interior/exterior bright metal trim and Sierra Grande emblems on pickup box side panels, front fenders and glove box. The standard custom interior offered a color-coordinated, all-vinyl bench seat, door trim panels, and padded sun visors. The Super custom interior included molded interior door trim panels with integral armrests, a tooled Western pattern door trim insert, full-foam bench seat with cloth/vinyl trim, bright trim vent window frames, windshield and rear window moldings, bright instrument panel knob insert, color-keyed vinyl coated rubber floor mats, extra cowl insulation and Super custom emblems on front fenders. Both the 307 and 350 cu. in. V-8 engines now had exhaust valve rotators. The exhaust valves used in the 350 V-8 were now Stellite plated. The 250 cu. in. 6-cylinder engine was fitted with an improved automatic choke as well as higher quality spark plug leads. Replacing the 3300 lb.-rated rear axle on the K1500 models was a 3500 lb.-rated unit. Rear brakes on the 3/4 ton models had revised measurements of 11 in. x 2.75 in. instead of 12 in. x 2.0 in. as used in 1971. This change resulted in a net increase of 25 sq. in. of brake swept area. New dealer-installed items for 1972 included a coolant recovery system and a wrap-around electric blanket for the battery. This item plugged into a 110-volt outlet.

The 1972 Suburban was no longer available with the 292 cu. in. 6-cylinder engine. A new vinyl side body trim was offered for the Suburban models. The Suburban's optional air conditioning system was modified to include a front-mounted condenser and blower in conjunction with corresponding revised rear units. The front system, which also served as the Suburban's heating system, could be ordered separately or with the rear system. If the latter arrangement was chosen, there were individually-controlled front and rear outlets. The rear outlets were integral, unlike the older system in which they were routed to the back along with the full length ceiling duct.

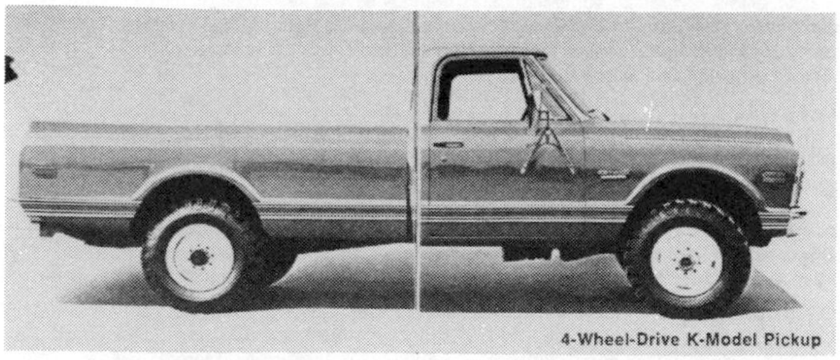

1972 GMC K model pickup

I.D. DATA: Unchanged from 1971.

Model Number	Body Type	Factory Price	GVW	Shipping Weight	Prod. Total
Series K1500-1/2 ton 6-cyl. 115 in. wheelbase					
KS15704	6.5 ft. Fenderside Pickup	$3266	5200*	3766	—
KS15734	6.5 ft. Wideside Pickup	$3266	5200	3836	—
KS15904	8 ft. Fenderside Pickup	$3302	5200	3846	—
KS15934	8 ft. Wideside Pickup	$3302	5200	3926	—
KS15906	Suburban Pnl. Doors	$4288	5200	4206	—
KS15916	Suburban Endgate	$4320	5200	4206	—

* 5600 lb. GVW optional.

Model Number	Body Type	Factory Price	GVW	Shipping Weight	Prod. Total
Series K2500-3/4 ton 6-cyl. 127 in.wheelbase					
KS25903	Chassis and Cab	$3430	6400*	3711	—
KS25904	8 ft. Fenderside Pickup	$3583	6400	4111	—
KS25934	8 ft. Wideside Pickup	$3583	6400	4201	—
KS25906	Suburban Pnl. Doors	$4290	6400	4201	—
KS25916	Suburban Endgate	$4322	6400	4645	—

* 7500 lb. GVW optional.

Models with the standard 6-cylinder engine had a KS prefix. Those with the standard V-8 engine had a KE prefix. The price of an equivalent K1500 model with a 307 V-8 is $120 above that of the 6-cyl. model. The price differential for K2500 is $124.

STANDARD ENGINE: KS models: 250 Six. Engine Type: OHV, In-line 6-cylinder. Cast iron block and cylinder head. Key features include 12 counterweight crankshaft and torsional damper, and molybdenum-filled top piston rings. Bore x Stroke: 3.875 in. x 3.53 in. Lifters: Hydraulic. Number of main bearings-7. Fuel Induction: Single Rochester 1-bbl. carburetor. Compression Ratio: 8.5:1. Displacement: 250 cu. in. (4.09 liters). Horsepower: Gross: 145 @ 4200 rpm. Net: 110 @ 4000 rpm. Torque: Gross: 230 lb.-ft. @ 1600 rpm. Net: 185 lb.-ft. @ 1600 rpm. Oil refill capacity: 5 qt. with filter change. Fuel Requirements: Regular or reduced lead content fuel.

STANDARD ENGINE: KE models: 307 V-8 Engine Type: OHV, V-8. Cast iron block and cylinder head. Key features include aero-type valve mechanism, and steel-backed babbitt bearings. Bore x Stroke: 3.875 in. x 3.25 in. Lifters: Hydraulic. Number of main bearings-5. Fuel Induction: Single Rochester 2-bbl. carburetor. Compression Ratio: 8.5:1. Displacement: 307 cu. in. (5.03 liters). Horsepower: Series 10: Gross: 200 @ 4600 rpm. Net: 135 @ 4000 rpm. Series 20: Gross: 215 @ 4800 rpm. Net: 135 @ 4000 rpm. Torque: Series 10: Gross: 300 lb.-ft. @ 2400 rpm. Net: 235 lb.-ft. @ 2400 rpm. Series 20: 305 lb.-ft. @ 2800 rpm. Net: 230 lb.-ft. @ 2000 rpm. Oil refill capacity: 5 qt. with filter change. Fuel Requirements: Regular or reduced lead content fuel.

OPTIONAL ENGINE: KS models: 292 Six. Engine Type: OHV, 6-cyl. Cast iron block and cylinder head. Key features include aluminized intake valves, automatic "Rotocoil" rotors on exhaust valves, special coating applied to exhaust valves to reduce deposit formation, full-chromed top piston rings, and premium aluminum bearings. Bore x Stroke: 3.875 in. x 4.125 in. Lifters: Hydraulic. Number of main bearings-7. Fuel Induction: Single Rochester 1-bbl. carburetor. Compression Ratio: 8.0:1. Displacement: 292 cu. in. (4.78 liters). Horsepower: Gross: 165 @ 4000 rpm. Net: 130 @ 4400 rpm. Torque: Gross: 270 lb.-ft. @ 1600 rpm. Net: 225 lb.-ft. @ 1800 rpm. Oil refill capacity: 6 qt. with filter change. Fuel Requirements: Regular or reduced lead content fuel.

OPTIONAL ENGINE: KS models: 350 V-8. Engine Type: OHV, V-8. Cast iron block and alloy iron cylinder head. Key features include chain drive camshaft, "Rotocoil" exhaust valve rotators, special coating applied to exhaust valves to reduce deposit formation, molybdenum-filed top piston rings, premium aluminum main bearings. Bore x Stroke: 4.0 in. x 3.50 in. Lifters: Hydraulic. Number of main bearings-5. Fuel Induction: Single Rochester 4-bbl. carburetor. Compression Ratio: 8.5:1. Displacement: 350 cu. in. (5.73 liters). Horsepower: Gross: 250 @ 4600 rpm. Net: 190 @ 4000 rpm. Torque: Gross: 350 lb.-ft. @ 3000 rpm. Net: 310 lb.-ft. @ 2400 rpm. Oil refill capacity: 5 qt. with filter change. Fuel Requirements: Regular or reduced lead content fuel.

CHASSIS FEATURES: Separate body and frame with channel side rails K1500,115 in. wheelbase: 2.57 in. x 5.98 in. x 0.151 in. Section modulus: 2.70 K1500, 127 in. wheelbase: 2.57 in. x 5.98 in. x 0.186 in. Section modulus: 3.48. K2500, 2.57 in. x 6.98 in. x 0.186 in. Section modulus: 3.48.

SUSPENSION AND RUNNING GEAR: Front Suspension: K1500: 2-leaf tapered shot-peened springs. Capacity: 1450 lb. Hydraulic direct action 1.0 in. dia. shock absorbers. K2500: 2-leaf tapered shot-peened springs. Capacity: 1600 lb. Hydraulic direct action 1.0 in. dia. shock absorbers. Optional rating: K1500 and K2500: 3-leaf tapered shot-peened springs. Capacity: 1750 lb. Rear Suspension: K1500: 5-leaf tapered leaf springs, 52 in. x 2.5 in. Capacity: 1800 lb. at ground. Deflection rate: 280/420 lb./in. shock absorbers. K2500: 5-leaf tapered leaf springs, 52 in. x 2.5 in. Capacity: 1900 lb. at ground. Deflection rate: 280/420 lb./in. Hydraulic direct action 1.0 in. dia. shock absorbers. Optional Rating: K2500: 2500 lb. capacity, 365/420 lb./in. deflection rate. Front Axle Type and Capacity: K1500: Spicer 44, semi-floating, 3500 lb. capacity. K2500: Spicer 44, full-floating, 3500 lb. capacity. Rear Axle Type and Capacity: K1500: Semi-floating, 3300 lb. capacity. Optional: None. K2500: Full-floating, 5200 lb. Final Drive Ratio: K1500: Front and rear: 3.73:1. K2500: Front: 4.55:1, Rear: 4.57:1. Transfer Case: Single lever, two-speed: 1.94, 1.00:1. Brakes: Type: Hydraulic, front disc and rear drums. Dimensions: K1500: Front: 11.86 in. rotor. Rear: 11.0 in. x 2.0 in. Rear brake area: 138.2 sq. in. Lining area: 84.4 sq. in. K2500: Front: 12.50 in. rotor. Rear: 11.0 in. x 2.75 in. Rear brake area: 175.8 sq. in. Lining area: 89.0 sq. in. Optional: Power assisted. Wheels: K1500: 15 x 6.0 6-stud disc. K2500: 16.5 x 5.25 8-stud disc. Tires: K1500: G78 x 15B. tubeless Optional: Tube-type tires: G78 x 15B, 6.50 x 16C. Tubeless: H78 x 15B, G78 x 15B, 10.00 x 16.5C. K2500: Tubeless: 8.75 x 16.5 Optional: Tubeless: 10.00 x 16.5, 9.50 x 16.5, Tube-type: 7.50 x 16, 6.50 x 16, plus numerous other sizes. Steering: Saginaw recirculating ball gear. Steering wheel diameter: 17.5 in. Ratio: 24:1. Optional: Power-assisted. Transmission: SM-330 3-speed, heavy-duty fully-synchromesh manual. Transmission Ratios: 3.03, 1.75, 1.00:1. Reverse: 3.02:1. Optional: SM465 4-speed manual synchromesh. Ratios: 6.55, 3.58, 1.70, 1.00:1. Reverse: 6.09:1. Optional: Turbo Hydra-Matic automatic 3-speed automatic. Clutch: Diaphragm, spring. Clutch diameter: 6-cyl.: 10 in. dia. (11.0 in. with 292 6-cyl.) Total lining area: 100.0 sq. in. (11.0 in.-124 sq. in.) Total plate pressure: 1875 lb. V-8: 12 in. dia. Total lining area: 150 sq. in. Total plate pressure: 1877 lb.

VEHICLE DIMENSIONS: Wheelbase: K1500: 115 in. 127 in. K2500: 127 in. All Suburbans and Panels: 127 in. Overall Length: 115 in. Wideside pickups: 188.75 in. 127 in. Wideside pickups: 208.0 in. 115 in. Fenderside pickups: 188.125 in. 127 in. Fenderside pickups: 208.0 in. Overall Height: K1500: 72.5 in. K2500: 73.25 in. K1500 Suburban Carryall: 75.25 in. Width: Pickup: 79 in. Suburban Carryall: 78.75 in. Front/Rear Overhang: 115 in. wheelbase pickups: 33.25 in./40.25 in. 127 in. wheelbase. Pickups: 33.25 in./47.50 in. Suburban Carryall: 33.25 in./55.25 in. Tailgate: Width and Height: 50 in. x 17.5 in. Ground Clearance: Lowest point: K1500 Fenderside: Front axle: 7.25 in. Rear axle: 7.5 in. K1500 Wideside: Front axle: 7.25 in. Rear axle: 7.0 in. K2500 Fenderside and Wideside: Front axle: 8.75 in. Rear axle: 7.75 in. Suburban Carryall: Front axle: 7.25 in. Rear axle: 7.5 in. Load space: Pickup box dimensions: Wideside 115 in. wheelbase: 78 in. x 60 in. x 17.5 in. Fenderside 127 in. wheelbase: 98 in. x 50 in. x 17.5 in. Wideside 127 in. wheelbase: 98 in. x 66 in. x 17.5 in. Capacity: 115 in. wheelbase: 39.7 cu. ft. 127 in. wheelbase: 49.8 cu. ft. Front headroom: 40 in. Front legroom: 40.75 in. Front shoulder room: 58 in. Front hip room: 64.75 in. Steering wheel to seat back (max.): 14.7 in.

CAPACITIES: Fuel Tank: Pickups: 20.0 gal. Panels and Suburbans: 21.0 gal. Optional: 20.5 gal. auxiliary fuel tank for 3/4 ton Fleetsides.

ACCOMMODATIONS: Seating Capacity: 3 passenger. Seat Dimensions: 58.75 in.

INSTRUMENTATION: Speedometer, odometer, fuel gauge. Warning lights for generator, oil pressure, engine coolant temperature, brake system.

OPTIONS AND PRICES: Pickup models: 292 cu. in. 6-cyl. engine: $90. 307 cu. in. V-8: $120 above price of base 6-cyl. model. 350 cu. in. V-8: $49 above price of model with 307 V-8. Power steering: $140. Free-wheeling front hubs: $73. Wooden bed floor for Wideside models: $19. Sliding rear window: $50. Limited slip rear differential. K1500: $67; K2500: $135. Sierra Grande Trim Package: $265. Bucket seats and console $115. Turbo Hydra-Matic: $230. Special instrumentation. Includes ammeter, oil pressure and temperature needle gauges. Available with or without tachometer. Tachometer: $43. AM radio: $65. AM/FM radio. Air conditioning: $400. Heavy-duty front and rear shock absorbers: $15. Heavy-duty front springs (K2500): $6. Heavy-duty rear springs (K2500): $18. Front stabilizer bar. Chrome below eye-level mirror. Armrests. Engine block heater. Cab clearance lights. Cargo compartment light. ComforTilt steering wheel: $55. Auxiliary battery: $45. Heavy-duty battery: $16. Auxiliary fuel tank: $75. Door edge guards: $6. Dual exterior camper-type rearview mirrors: $49. Camper wiring: $15. Two-tone paint: $25. Tinted glass: $18. Pickup side step. Front bumper guards. Chrome front bumper. Painted rear bumper. Rear step bumper: $48. Door edge guards. Heavy-duty air cleaner. Heavy-duty battery. Heavy-duty clutch. Heavy-duty cooling. Heavy-duty generator, heavy-duty front and rear springs. Heavy-duty starter. Bright pickup box hand rails. Tool and storage compartment. 10-16.5 tires and wheels 10-16.5 spare tire and wheel: $137. (K2500): $263. Surburban: 350 V-8: $45 above price of 307-V-8 equipped models. Turbo Hydra-Matic: $242. Air conditioning: $648.Power steering: $147. Free running front hubs: $7. Limited slip rear differential: K1500: $65; K2500: $132.

HISTORICAL FOOTNOTES: Calendar year production of all GMC trucks was 132,243.

1973 PICKUP & SUBURBAN

The GMC four-wheel drive pickups, which once again shared their body shells and technical features with Chevrolet, were handsomely defined, purposeful-appearing vehicles. Single headlamps were positioned on each side of a simple 3-piece grille format. Side body contours created a pleasing format for two-tone color and trim schemes. Additional design features included the use of curved side windows and the elimination of drip moldings. Wheel opening were oblong and flared to accommodate larger tires and wheels. Glass area was increased by 528 sq. in. Total windshield area measured 1447 sq. in. The rear window area was 790 sq. in. The side door window area, including the ventipane, was 546 sq. in. The antenna for the optional radio was imbedded in the windshield. A new one-piece instrument panel, welded in place, reduced shake and vibration. Additional structural changes included a new hood fabricated from two pieces of steel that were welded together to provide improved torsional rigidity. New all-steel, one-piece inner fenders were attached to the inner front fenders for structural integrity. The Wideside pickup box side panel/load floor assembly was redesigned to eliminate exposed flanges and bolt heads. Changes to the exhaust system involved the use of compression-positioned hangers that provided secondary support and lessened the intrusion of exhaust noise into the cab interior. The rear shock absorbers were positioned in a staggered for/aft fashion to reduce axle hop under severe acceleration and deceleration. High capacity 2-speed windshield wipers with 16 inch blades were standard as were new dual-orifice windshield washers. A new energy-absorbing/telescoping steering column provided additional protection for the driver in case of an accident.

The 1973 pickup frames were completely redesigned. Thicker side rails were used as was a new cross member design. The fuel tank was positioned outside the cab on the right frame rail. The front disc brakes were now fitted with a road splash shield. At the rear wheels new finned cast iron-steel brakes were used.

The four-wheel drive models had new wide front springs with lower ride rates and a new front stabilizer bar. The front wheels were moved forward by 2.5 inches. Both the front and rear spring eyes were now rubber bushed. K-2500 models had a new Salisbury type rear axle with a rigid cast differential carrier and steel shaft tubes that were pressed and anchored in the carrier.

The new GMC interior had increased leg, hip, head and shoulder room. A new flow-through power ventilation system provided the interior with a steady supply of outside air. This system used larger inlet valves and a larger plenum chamber. An electric fan directed the air flow through the cab to outlet valves at the bottom of each door. This system also provided for pressure relief when the doors were closed.

The standard custom interior was equipped with a 3 passenger bench seat with ladder-embossed vinyl upholstery with grained vinyl bolsters and foam padding. It was offered in pearl, slate blue, saddle and slate green. Additional standard interior equipment consisted of: Right and left side, individually controlled air vents, right and left side armrests integral with door trim panel, dash-mounted ashtray, right-side mounted coat hook, inside push-button door locks, color-keyed, embossed molded plastic door trim panels, embossed black rubber floor mat, trim rings on gauges and warning lights, white graphic instrumentation identification, soft black knobs for all controls except heater and air conditioner, color-keyed instrument panel with custom nameplate and hardboard top, Deluxe-Air heater and defroster, instrument cluster and courtesy/map lights operated by main switch, 10 in. vinyl edged primatic rearview mirror, three seat belts with push-button release, retractor for driver and rightside passenger, 17 in. dia. steering wheel with black finish and padded two-spoke design, right and left side padded, color-keyed sun visors and door opening scuff plates.

The custom standard model was equipped with bright grille outline molding, headlight bezels, door handles and custom nameplates with series designation located on the upper portion of the front fenders near the door opening. Other standard features included front white-painted bumper, back-up lights (integral with taillights on Wideside models), side markers and reflectors, right and left side exterior mirrors with chrome fixed arms and 5.25 in. x 4.00 in. heads, single electric horn, white GMC lettering on tailgate (painted black on trucks with frost white color), under frame spare tire carrier, mechanical jack, undercoating under wheel-housings and white painted wheels.

The Super custom model option (RPO Z62) included all standard items plus the following additions or substitutions: Super custom nameplates with series designations on front fenders, rear window reveal moldings, windshield reveal moldings, door handles with black plastic insets, additional electric horn with high note, Super custom nameplate on instrument panel, dome light bezel, full length door sill scuff plates, color-keyed molded plastic door trim panels with woodgrain insert and bright trim, color panel insulation, color-keyed rubber floor mat, full-depth foam seat cushion seat with multi-striped nylon cloth/vinyl trim in choice of pearl grey, charcoal, slate blue, saddle or avocado, special all-vinyl trim in choice of pearl grey, charcoal, slate blue, saddle or slate green also available.

The Sierra Grande option (RPO Z84) included all Sierra items plus the following additions or substitutions: Sierra Grande nameplates with series designations on front fenders, GMC nameplate on tailgate panel, chrome front bumper, front side marker lamp moldings, front turn signal lamp moldings, cab back panel molding and applique, hubcaps (except K-1500 with 10.00 x 16.5 tires), upper body side trim moldings (Wideside only), rear lamp molding (Wideside only), tailgate upper and lower moldings with bright finish applique panel insert and nameplate (Wideside only), cab-to-fender seal, hood insulator, Sierra Grande nameplate on instrument panel, chrome transmission and transfer case levers on models with 4-speed transmission, color-keyed carpeting, color-keyed molded plastic door trim panels with storage pockets, teakwood grain inserts with chrome bead and black plastic border, color-keyed plastic headliner with retainer moldings, foam instrument panel pad with color-keyed grained vinyl cover, color-keyed molded plastic trim on windshield pillars, and all-vinyl trim bench seat in choice of pearl grey, slate blue, saddle, charcoal or slate green. A Herringbone striped nylon cloth/vinyl trimmed seat in a choice of pearl grey, charcoal, slate blue, saddle or avocado was also available.

The Sierra Grande option (RPO YE9) included all items in the Cheyenne option plus the following additions or substitutions: Cheyenne Super nameplates with series designation on front fenders, lower body side moldings (on Wideside only), wheel opening lip molding (Wideside only), Cheyenne Super nameplate on instrument panel, color-keyed molded plastic trim on cowl side panels, gauges for battery, engine coolant temperature and oil pressure, bench seat with special Herringbone nylon cloth and vinyl trim in a choice of pearl grey, charcoal, slate blue, saddle or avocado. A special-vinyl trim was offered in a choice of pearl grey, charcoal, slate blue, saddle or slate green.

A total of fifteen exterior colors were offered for 1973. Ten colors were new and five were carried over from 1972. The available colors were: Skyline blue, Glenwood green, Sport silver metallic, Catalina blue metallic, frost white, Hawaiian blue, Spanish gold, crimson red, burnt orange metallic, lime green metallic, sunset gold, desert sand, Mojave tan, moss olive, and Marine turquoise metallic. The fifteen primary colors were available as main body colors in association with white as a secondary color in three different two-tone paint schemes. The conventional two-tone style required RPO BX6 moldings. The Special Two-Tone option was offered for Wideside models with RPO YG1 moldings. A Deluxe version was available for Wideside models with RPO BX6 and RPO YG1.

I.D. DATA: The vehicle identification number was stamped on a plate mounted on the windshield corner post. The first entry, the letter T, represented the GMC division, The second entry, the letter K, identified the chassis type as a four-wheel drive. The third entry, a letter, designated the engine: Q-250-6-cyl., T-292 6-cyl., V-350 V-8, Y-350 4-bbl. V-8. The series identification, by a number, followed: 1-1/2 ton. 2-3/4 ton. The body style was next identified by a number: 3-Cab and Chassis, 4-Cab and pickup box, 6-Suburban. The model year, 1973, was then identified by the number 3. The assembly plant identification, a letter followed. The final six entries, numbers, were the sequential production number.

Model Number	Body Type	Factory Price	GVW	Shipping Weight	Prod. Total
Series K-1500-1/2 ton 350 V-8 117.5 in., 131.5 in. (Suburb.: 129.5 in.) wheelbase					
TK10703	Chassis and Cab	$3324	5200[1]	3663	—
TK10703	6.5 ft. F-S Pickup	$3510	5200	—	—
TK10703	6.5 ft. W-S Pickup	$3510	5200	—	—
TK10903	8 ft. Fenderside Pickup	$3546	5200	4085	—
TK10903	8 ft. Wideside Pickup	$3546	5200	4210	—
TK10906	Suburban [2]	$4338	5200	5034	—

NOTE 1: 5600 lb. and 6000 lb. GVW optional.
NOTE 2: Suburban (both K-1500 and K-2500) available with panel rear doors (ZW9) or endgate (E55).

Model Number	Body Type	Factory Price	GVW	Shipping Weight	Prod. Total
Series K-2500-3/4 ton 307 V-8. (Suburb.: 129.5 in.) 131.5 in. wheelbase					
TK20903	Chassis and Cab	$3562	6800[3]	4119	—
TK20903	8 ft. Fenderside Pickup	$3747	6800	4514	—
TK20903	8 ft. Wideside Pickup	$3747	6800	4640	—
TK20906	Suburban, 129.5 in. wb.	$4668	6800	5136	—

NOTE 3: 7500 lb. and 8200 lb. GVW optional.

A base engine code was added to the model identification for 1973. Models with the standard 6-cylinder engine had an LD4 designation. Those with a standard 350 V-8 (K-2500 models) had a LG8 identification.

STANDARD ENGINE: K-1500, K-2500: 250 Six (LD4 ordering code). Engine Type: OHV, In-line 6-cylinder. Cast iron block and cylinder head. Key features include 12 counterweight crankshaft and torsional damper, and molybdenum-filled top piston rings. Bore x Stroke: 3.875 in. x 3.53 in. Lifters: Hydraulic. Number of main bearings-7. Fuel Induction: Single Rochester 1-bbl. carburetor. Compression Ratio: 8.5:1. Displacement: 250 cu. in. (4.09 liters). Horsepower: Net: 100 @ 4000 rpm. Torque: Net: 175 lb.-ft. @ 1600 rpm. Oil refill capacity: 5 qt. with filter change. Fuel Requirements: Regular.

STANDARD ENGINE: K-2500 V-8 models: 307 V-8 (LG8 Ordering Code). Not available in California. Engine Type: OHV, V-8. Cast iron block and cylinder head. Key features include aero-type valve mechanism, and steel-backed babbitt bearings. Bore x Stroke: 3.875 in. x 3.25 in. Lifters: Hydraulic. Number of main bearings-5. Fuel Induction: Single Rochester 2-bbl carburetor. Compression Ratio: 8.5:1. Displacement: 307 cu. in. (5.03 liters). Horsepower: Net: 130 @ 4000 rpm. Torque: Net: 220 lb.-ft. @ 2200 rpm. Oil refill capacity: 5 qt. with filter change. Fuel Requirements: Regular.

OPTIONAL ENGINE: Available only for 6-cyl. K-2500 pickup models: 292 Six Ordering Code: L25. Engine Type: OHV, 6-cyl. Cast iron block and cylinder head. Key features include aluminized intake valves, automatic "Rotocoil" rotors on exhaust valves, special coating applied to exhaust valves to reduce deposit formation, full-chromed top piston rings, and premium aluminum bearings. Bore x Stroke: 3.875 in. x 4.125 in. Lifters: Hydraulic. Number of main bearings-7. Fuel Induction: Single Rochester 1-bbl. carburetor. Compression Ratio: 8.0:1. Displacement: 292 cu. in. (4.78 liters). Horsepower: Net: 120 @ 3600 rpm. Torque: Net: 215 lb.-ft. @ 2000 rpm. Oil refill capacity: 6 qt. with filter change. Fuel Requirements: Regular.

OPTIONAL ENGINE: K-2500 V-8 models; standard for K-1500 V-8 models: 350 V-8. Ordering Code: LS9: 350 V-8 Engine Type: OHV, V-8. Cast iron block and alloy iron cylinder head. Key features include chain drive camshaft, "Rotocoil" exhaust valve rotators, special coating applied to exhaust valves to reduce deposit formation, molybdenum-filled top piston rings, premium aluminum main bearings. Bore x Stroke: 4.0 in. x 3.50 in. Lifters: Hydraulic. Number of main bearings-5. Fuel Induction: Single Rochester 4-bbl. carburetor. Compression Ratio: 8.5:1. Displacement: 350 cu. in. (5.73 liters). Horsepower: Net: 155 @ 4000 rpm. Torque: Net: 255 lb.-ft. @ 2400 rpm. Oil refill capacity: 5 qt. with filter change. Fuel Requirements: Regular.

CHASSIS FEATURES: Separate body and frame with channel side rails. Carbon-Steel, 39,000 psi. Section modulus: 117.5 in. wheelbase: 3.06. 131.5 in. wheelbase: 3.84. Optional: None.

SUSPENSION AND RUNNING GEAR: Front Suspension: 2-leaf, tapered leaf springs 1.0 in. dia. shock absorbers. K-1500: 1850 lb. rating (at ground). K-2500:1950 lb. rating (at ground). Optional rating: 1900 lb. (both series). Rear Suspension: 52 in. x 2.25 in. Two-stage, 5-leaf. 1.0 in. dia. shock absorbers. K-1500: 1700 lb. rating (at ground). K-2500: 2800 lb. Optional Rating: K-1500: 2000 lb. Front Axle Type and Capacity: K-1500: Spicer 44F Semi-floating. 3400 lb. capacity. Optional: None. K-2500: Full-floating, 3500 lb. capacity. Optional: None. Rear Axle Type and Capacity: K-1500: Chevrolet, semi-floating, 3750 lb. capacity. Optional: None. K-2500: Chevrolet, full-floating, 5700 lb. Final Drive Ratio: K-1500: Front: 6-cyl.:4.11:1; V-8: 3.73:1. (The V-8 ratio was subsequently changed to 3.07:1. Rear: 6-cyl.: 4.11:1. V-8: 3.73:1. K-2500: Front: 6-cyl. and V-8: 4.56:1; V-8. Rear: 6-cyl. and V-8: 4.56:1. Optional K-1500: Rear: 3.73:1, 4.1:1. K-2500: Rear: 4.10:1, 4.56:1. Transfer Case: New Process 205. Single lever, two-speed: 1.94, 1.00:1. Brakes: Type: Hydraulic, power assisted. Dimensions: K-1500: Front: Disc: 11.86 in. dia. Rear: Drums: 11.0 in. x 2.0 in. K-2500: Front: Disc: 12.5 in. dia. Rear: Drums: 11.0 in. x 2.75 in. Optional: None. Wheels: K-1500: 15 x 6.0 6-stud disc. K-2500: 16.5 x 6.0 in. 8-stud disc. Tires: K-1500: G78 x 15B 4-ply rating, tubeless or tube-type. K-2500: 8.75 x 16.5C 6-ply rating, tubeless. Optional: K-1500: G78 x 15B, white stripe; H78 x 15B, tubeless, black sidewall or white stripe; L78 x 15B black sidewall or white stripe, tubeless; 10.00 x 16.5C tubeless; G78 x 15B tube-type; 7.00 x 15C tube-type; 6.50 x 16C tube-type. The following tires were specified for K-1500 models with the 5600 lb. GVW Package which included a front heavy-duty stabilizer bar: H78 x 15B 4-ply rating, tubeless; 6.50 x 16C 6-ply rating, tube-type, truck type. The following tires were specified for K-1500 models with the 6000 lb. GVW Package which included a front heavy-duty stabilizer bar and heavy-duty rear springs: L78 x 15B 4-ply rating, tubeless. Optional K-2500: 8.75 x 16.5D tubeless; 9.50 x 16.5D tubeless; 10.00 x 16.5C tubeless (not available for Fenderside models); 7.50 x 16C 6-ply rating, tube-type; 7.50 x 16D tube-type; 7.50 x 16E tube-type. The following tires were specified for K-2500 models with the 7500 lb. GVW Package which included a front heavy-duty stabilizer bar: 8.75 x 16.5 C 6-ply rating, tubeless; 7.50 x 16C 6-ply rating, tubeless. The following tires were specified for K-2500 models with the 8200 lb. GVW Package which included a front heavy-duty stabilizer bar: 9.50 x 16.5D 8-ply rating, tubeless; 7.50 x 16C 6-ply rating, tube-type. Steering: Recirculating ball gear. Ratio: 20:1, turns Lock-to-Lock: 3.4. Turning Circle: 47 ft. Steering wheel diameter: 17.5 in. Optional: Power-assisted. Ratio: 16.4:1. Transmission: 3-speed, synchromesh manual (ZW4 Ordering Code). Transmission Ratios: 2.85, 1.68, 1.00:1. Optional: Chevrolet CH465. 4-speed manual synchromesh (RPO M20). Ratios: 6.55, 3.58, 1.70, 1.00:1. Optional: 3-speed Turbo Hydra-Matic (RPO M49). Ratios: 2.52, 1.52, 1.00:1. Clutch: Diaphragm, spring. Clutch diameter: K-1500: 6-cyl.: 10 in. dia. Total lining area: 100.0 sq. in. V-8: 12 in. dia. Total lining area: 150 sq. in. K-2500: 10 in. dia. Total lining area: 100.0 sq. in. V-8: 11 in. dia. Total lining area: 124.0 sq. in. K-2500 with 350 V-8: 12 in. dia. Total lining area: 150 sq. in. Optional: K-2500 6-cyl.: 11 in. dia. Total lining area: 124.0 sq. in. 307 V-8: 12 in. dia. Total lining area: 150 sq. in.

VEHICLE DIMENSIONS: Wheelbase: K-1500: 117.5 in. 131.5 in. K-2500: 131.5 in. All Suburbans and Panels: 131.5 in. Overall Length: 117.5 in. Wideside pickups: 191.25 in. 131.5 in. Wideside pickups: 211.25. 117.5 in. Fenderside pickups: 190.5 in. 131.5 in. Fenderside pickups: 210.25. Front/Rear Tread: 67.4 in./65.8 in. Overall Height: K-1500 Pickup and Suburban: 72.25 in., K-2500 Pickup and Suburban: 73.9 in. Width: Pickup: 79.5 in. Front/Rear Overhang: Pickups: 33 in./41 in. Tailgate: Width and Height: 72 in. x 19.25 in. Approach/ Departure Degrees: 30/21. Ground Clearance: Front axle: 7.25 in. Rear axle: 7.0 in. Oil pan: 16.5 in. Transfer case: 12.0 in. Fuel tank: 16.6 in. Load space: Pickup box dimensions: 117.5 in. wheelbase Wideside: 78.25 in. x 50 in. x 19.25 in. 131.5 in. wheelbase Wideside: 98 in. x 50 in. x 19.25 in. Capacity: 117.5 in. wheelbase: 58.4 cu. ft., 131.5 in. wheelbase: 74.3 cu. ft. 117.5 in. wheelbase Fenderside: 78.5 in. x 50 in. x 17.5 in. 131.5 in. wheelbase Fenderside: 96.25 in. x 50 in. x 17.5 in. Front headroom: 38.5 in. (seat to top of cab). Front hip room: 67.25 in. Pedal to seat back (max.): 43.5 in. Steering wheel to seat back (max.): 17.3 in. Seat to ground: 35.0 in. Floor to ground: 23.0 in.

CAPACITIES: Fuel Tank: K-1500: 117.5 in. wheelbase: 160 gal. 131.5 in. wheelbase: 20.0 gal. Optional: 16 gal. auxiliary for 117.5 in. wheelbase; 20 gal. for 131.5 in. wheelbase. K-2500: 20 gal. Optional: 20 gal. auxiliary. Coolant System Capacity: 250 6-cyl.: 14.8 qt. 292 6-cyl.: 13.6 qt. 350 V-8: 17.6 qt. (All figures for vehicles with manual transmission and without air conditioning).

ACCOMMODATIONS: Seating Capacity: Pickup and chassis-cab models: 3 passenger. Optional: None. Suburban: K-1500: 3 passenger. K-2500: 6 passenger. Optional: 6 passenger (K-1500), 9 passenger (K-1500 and K-2500).

INSTRUMENTATION: Speedometer, odometer, fuel level gauge. Warning lights for battery, oil pressure, generator, brake system warning, directional/hazard lights, high beam, and engine coolant temperature.

OPTIONS AND PRICES: Pickup models: 292 cu. in. 6-cyl. engine-RPO L25 (K-2500 only). 307 cu. in. V-8-RPO LG8: $120 above price of base 6-cyl. model. 350 cu. in. V-8-RPO LS9: $161 above price of model with 307 V-8. Turbo Hydra-Matic -RPO M49. Includes extra heavy-duty cooling: $236. 4-speed manual transmission-RPO M20: $108. Positraction rear axle-RPO G80 (available for K-1500 only): $64. NoSPIN rear axle-RPO G86 (available for K-2500 only). Super Custom Package. With cloth bench seat-RPO Z62/YJ4; with custom vinyl bench seat-RPO Z62/YJ5. Sierra Package. With custom cloth bench seat-RPO Z84/YJ6; with custom vinyl bench seat-RPO Z84/YJ5: $213. Sierra Grande Package. With Custom cloth bench seat-RPO YE9/YJ6; with custom vinyl bench seat-RPO YE9/YJ5: $252. Custom Camper Chassis Equipment-Basic Camper Group-RPO Z81. Available with K-2500 V-8 models with 8200 lb. GVW and either 4-spd. manual trans. or Turbo Hydra-Matic. Requires 9.50 x 16.5D tubeless or 7.50 x 16E tube-type rear tires only. Includes heavy-duty front and rear shock absorbers, heavy-duty front springs, heavy-duty front stabilizer, custom camper nameplate and camper body wiring harness. Deluxe Camper Group for cab-over camper bodies-RPO Z83. Available with K-2500 V-8 models with 8200 lb. GVW and either 4-spd. manual trans. or Turbo Hydra-Matic Requires 9.50 x 16.5D tubeless or 7.50 x 16E tube-type rear tires and Wideside body. Not available with wooden floor. Includes Basic Camper Group plus camper body tie-down brackets mounted to pickup box under body, spring loaded turnbuckles shipped loose, horizontal shock absorbers mounted between cab rear panel and pickup box side panels and vertical shock absorber brackets mounted on front fenders. Camper body wiring harness-RPO UY1. Included when custom camper chassis equipment is ordered. Camper-type stainless steel mirrors: RPO DF2. Poly-wrap air cleaner-RPO K43. All-Weather air conditioning-RPO C60. Auxiliary 61 amp battery-RPO TP2. Heavy-duty 80 amp battery-RPO T60. Painted rear bumper-RPO V38. Painted rear step bumper-RPO V43. Chromed front and rear bumper-RPO V37. Front chromed bumper (not available if painted rear bumper is ordered)-RPO V46. Chromed rear bumper (available only when Sierra or Sierra Grande is ordered)-RPO VF1. California assembly line emission test-RPO YF5. Bright metal hubcaps (not available for K-1500 models with 10.00 x 16.5 tires)-RPO PO3. Side-mounted spare tire carrier-RPO P13. Electric clock (available only with Gauge Package, not available if tachometer is ordered)-RPO U35: $18. Heavy-duty clutch (available only for models with 250 engine and 3-spd. manual trans.)-RPO MO1. Exterior tool stowage (available for Wideside only. Not available if auxiliary fuel tank is ordered)-RPO VK4. Coolant recovery system-RPO VQ1. Heavy-duty radiator (requires RPO VQ1)-RPO VO1. Wood 8 ft. Wideside pickup box-RPO E81. Gauge Package-Z53: $12. Tachometer (V-8 models only, not available if electric clock is ordered)-RPO U16: $56. 42 amp Delcotron generator (not available if air conditioning is ordered)-RPO K79.61 amp Delcotron generator (included with air conditioning)-RPO K76. Soft-Ray tinted glass, all windows-RPO V22: $18. Chromed grille-RPO V22. Door edge guards (not available with woodgrained exterior trim)-RPO B93. Free-wheeling front hubs-RP F76. Cargo area lamp-RPO UF2: $19. Dome light-RPO C91. Roof marker lights-RPO U01. Cigarette lighter-RPO U37. Exterior below eye-level 7.5 in. x 10.5 in. painted mirrors-RPO D29. Exterior below eye-level 7.5 in. x 10.5 in. stainless steel mirrors-RPO DG4. Cab back panel applique-RPO BX6. Upper body moldings. For Wideside only. Includes fender, door cab panel, tailgate and pickup box moldings pus bright front turn signal, side marker and taillight trim-RPO B85. Upper and lower body molding (adds lower body side, tailgate and wheel opening moldings to RPO B85)-RPO YG1. Painted roof drip molding-RPO BX5. Soft instrument panel pad-RPO B70. Fuel tank shield-RPO NY1. AM radio-RPO U63: $67. AM/FM radio-RPO U69: $145. Vinyl roof cover-RPO CO8: $36. Bucket seats-RPO A50/YJ5: $135. Full-depth foam bench seat-RPO Z52. Heavy-duty front and rear shock absorbers-RPO F51: $15. Heavy-duty rear shock absorbers-RPO G68. Heavy-duty front springs-RPO F60. Heavy-duty rear springs (K-1500 only)-RPO G50. Heavy-duty front stabilizer-RPO F58. Power steering-RPO N40. ComforTilt steering wheel (not available with 3-spd. manual trans.)-RPO N33: $56. Custom steering wheel (available only with power steering, includes 16 in. steering wheel)-RPO N31. Auxiliary fuel tank (not avail. with K-1500 with 250 engine)-RPO NL2: $77. Manual throttle control (not available with air conditioning)-RPO K31. Front towing hooks-RPO V76. Bright metal wheelcovers (K-1500 only; not avail. with 6.50 x 16 or 10.00 x 16.5 tires)-RPO PO1. Wheel trim rings (not avail. with 10.00 x 16.5 tires on K-1500 or with 7.50 x 16 tires)-RPO PO6. Sliding rear window-RPO A28: $51. Exterior woodgrained trim (avail. only with Wideside models with custom upper and lower moldings or Sierra Grande only. Not avail. with special or Deluxe two-tone paint)-RPO YG2. Surburban: 350 V-8: $45 above price of 307-V-8 equipped models. Turbo Hydra-Matic: $242. Air conditioning: $648. Power steering: $147. Free-running front hubs: $7. Limited slip rear differential: K-1500: $65; K-2500: $132. Super Custom Package (with standard front seat): $186.

HISTORICAL FOOTNOTES: Calendar year production of all GMC models was 166,73 units.

1974 PICKUP & SUBURBAN

At the start of the model year all GMC four-wheel drive models were equipped with the New Process 203 system. During the model year the New Process 205 part-time system returned for use with 6-cylinder models. Due to emissions controls, no 6-cylinder trucks were available for California delivery. The 307 cu. in. V-8 was not available. A brake wearing sensor was a new feature for 1974 as was a new hydraulic booster for higher GVW rated trucks. The K10 models were now available with a 15 in. rally-styled wheel option which in addition to the wheel included a center hub and bright trim ring. Steel-belted, LR78 x 15C white sidewall radial-plytires were introduced for the K-1500 pickup. A telescoping step-type rear bumper was a new option. The 1974 GMC trucks were easy to identify due to the placement of bold GMC letters in the center grille section.

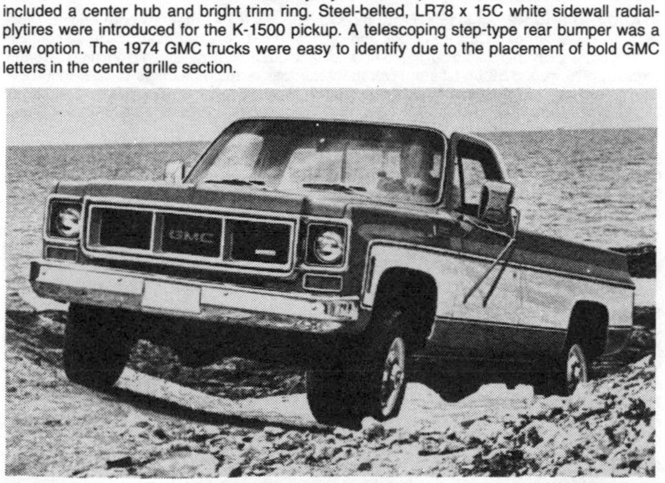

1974 GMC K-1500 Wideside pickup

I.D. DATA: Unchanged from 1973. The 1974 model year, was identified by the number 4.

Model Number	Body Type	Factory Price	GVW	Shipping Weight	Prod. Total
Series K-1500-1/2 ton 350 V-8 117.5 in., 131.5 in. (Suburb.: 129.5 in.) wheelbase					
TK10703	6.5 ft. Stepside Pickup	$3937	5200*	4020	—
TK10703	6.5 ft. Fleetside Pickup	$3937	5200	4124	—
TK10903	8 ft. Stepside Pickup	$3973	5200	4128	—
TK10903	8 ft. Fleetside Pickup	$3973	5200	4238	—
TK10906	Suburban, 129.5 in. wb.	$4846	5200	4578	—

* 5600 lb. and 6000 lb. GVW optional.

Model Number	Body Type	Factory Price	GVW	Shipping Weight	Prod. Total
Series K-2500-3/4 ton 350 V-8. 127 in. wheelbase					
TK20903	Chassis and Cab	$4087	6800*	4183	—
TK20903	8 ft. Stepside Pickup	$4254	6800	4578	—
TK20903	8 ft. Fleetside Pickup	$4254	6800	4688	—
TK20906	Suburban, 129.5 in. wb.	$5753	6800	5415	—

* 7500 lb. and 8200 lb. GVW optional.

STANDARD ENGINE: K-1500, K-2500: 250 Six (LD4 ordering code). Engine Type: OHV, In-line 6-cylinder. Cast iron block and cylinder head. Key features include 12 counterweight crankshaft and torsional damper, and molybdenum-filled top piston rings. Bore x Stroke: 3.875 in. x 3.53 in. Lifters: Hydraulic. Number of main bearings-7. Fuel Induction: Single Rochester 1-bbl. carburetor. Compression Ratio: 8.5:1. Displacement: 250 cu. in. (4.09 liters). Horsepower: Net: 100 @ 4000 rpm. Torque: Net: 175 lb.-ft. @ 1600 rpm. Oil refill capacity: 5 qt. with filter change. Fuel Requirements: 91 octane.

OPTIONAL ENGINE: Available only for 6-cyl. K-2500 pickup models: 292 Six Ordering Code: L25. Engine Type: OHV, 6-cyl. Cast iron block and cylinder head. Key features include aluminized intake valves, automatic "Rotocoil" rotors on exhaust valves, special coating applied to exhaust valves to reduce deposit formation, full-chromed top piston rings, and premium aluminum bearings. Bore x Stroke: 3.875 in. x 4.125 in. Lifters: Hydraulic. Number of main bearings-7. Fuel Induction: Single Rochester 1-bbl. carburetor. Compression Ratio: 8.0:1. Displacement: 292 cu. in. (4.78 liters). Horsepower: Net: 120 @ 3600 rpm. Torque: Net: 215 lb.-ft. @ 2000 rpm. Oil refill capacity: 6 qt. with filter change. Fuel Requirements: 91 octane.

STANDARD ENGINE: K-2500 V-8 models; standard for K-1500 V-8 models: 350 V-8. Ordering Code: LS9: 350 V-8 Engine Type: OHV, V-8. Cast iron block and alloy iron cylinder head. Key features include chain drive camshaft, "Rotocoil" exhaust valve rotators, special coating applied to exhaust valves to reduce deposit formation, molybdenum-filled top piston rings, premium aluminum main bearings. Bore x Stroke: 4.0 in. x 3.50 in. Lifters: Hydraulic. Number of main bearings-5. Fuel Induction: Single Rochester 4-bbl. carburetor. Compression Ratio: 8.5:1. Displacement: 350 cu. in. (5.73 liters). Horsepower: Net: 155 @ 4000 rpm. Torque: Net: 255 lb.-ft. @ 2400 rpm. Oil refill capacity: 5 qt. with filter change. Fuel Requirements: 91 octane.

CHASSIS FEATURES: Separate body and frame with channel side rails. Carbon-Steel, 39,000 psi. Section modulus: 117.5 in. wheelbase: 3.06. 131.5 in. wheelbase: 3.84. Optional: None.

SUSPENSION AND RUNNING GEAR: Front Suspension: 2-leaf, tapered leaf springs 1.0 in. dia. shock absorbers. K-1500: 1850 lb. rating (at ground). K-2500:1950 lb. rating (at ground). Optional rating: 1900 lb. (both series). Rear Suspension: 52 in. x 2.25 in. Two-stage, 5-leaf. 1.0 in. dia. shock absorbers. K-1500: 1700 lb. rating (at ground). K-2500: 2800 lb. Optional Rating: K-1500: 2000 lb. Front Axle Type and Capacity: K-1500: Spicer 44F Semi-floating. 3400 lb. capacity. Optional: None. K-2500: Full-floating, 3500 lb. capacity. Optional: None. Rear Axle Type and Capacity: K-1500: Chevrolet, semi-floating, 3750 lb. capacity. Optional: None. K-2500: Chevrolet, full-floating, 5700 lb. Final Drive Ratio: K-1500: Front: 6-cyl.:4.11:1; V-8: 3.73:1. (The V-8 ratio was subsequently changed to 3.07:1. Rear: 6-cyl.: 4.11:1. V-8: 3.73:1. K-2500: Front: 6-cyl. and V-8: 4.56:1; V-8. Rear: 6-cyl. and V-8: 4.56:1. Optional K-1500: Rear: 3.73:1, 4.1:1. K-2500: Rear: 4.10:1, 4.56:1. Transfer Case: Full Time New Process 203 system for V-8 models only. New Process 205. Single lever, two-speed: 1.94, 1.00:1. Brakes: Type: Hydraulic, power assisted. Dimensions: K-1500: Front: Disc: 11.86 in. dia. Rear: Drums: 11.0 in. x 2.0 in. K-2500: Front: Disc: 12.5 in. dia. Rear: Drums: 11.0 in. x 2.75 in. Optional: None. Wheels: K-1500: 15 x 6.0 6-stud disc. K-2500: 16.5 x 6.0 in. 8-stud disc. Tires: K-1500: G78 x 15B 4-ply rating, tubeless or tube-type. K-2500: 8.75 x 16.5C 6-ply rating, tubeless. Optional: K-1500: G78 x 15B, white stripe; H78 x 15B, tubeless, black sidewall or white stripe; L78 x 15B black sidewall or white stripe, tubeless; 10.00 x 16.5C tubeless; G78 x 15B tube-type; 7.00 x 15C tube-type; 6.50 x 16C tube-type. The following tires were specified for K-1500 models with the 5600 lb. GVW Package which included a front heavy-duty stabilizer bar: H78 x 15B 4-ply rating, tubeless; 6.50 x 16C 6-ply rating, tube-type, truck type. The following tires were specified for K-1500 models with the 6000 lb. GVW Package which included a front heavy-duty stabilizer bar and heavy-duty rear springs: L78 x 15B 4-ply rating, tubeless. Optional K-2500: 8.75 x 16.5D tubeless; 9.50 x 16.5D tubeless; 10.00 x 16.5C tubeless (not available for Fenderside models); 7.50 x 16C 6-ply rating, tube-type; 7.50 x 16D tube-type; 7.50 x 16E tube-type. The following tires were specified for K-2500 models with the 7500 lb. GVW Package which included a front heavy-duty stabilizer bar: 8.75 x 16.5 C 6-ply rating, tubeless; 7.50 x 16C 6-ply rating, tubeless. The following tires were specified for K-2500 models with the 8200 lb. GVW Package which included a front heavy-duty stabilizer bar: 9.50 x 16.5D 8-ply rating, tubeless; 7.50 x 16C 6-ply rating, tube-type. Steering: Recirculating ball gear. Ratio: 20:1, turns Lock-to-Lock: 3.4. Turning Circle: 47 ft. Steering wheel diameter: 17.5 in. Optional: Power-assisted. Ratio: 16.4:1. Transmission: 3-speed, synchromesh manual (ZW4 Ordering Code). Transmission Ratios: 2.85, 1.68, 1.00:1. Optional: CH465. 4-speed manual synchromesh (RPO M20). Ratios: 6.55, 3.58, 1.70, 1.00:1. Optional: 3-speed Turbo Hydra-Matic (RPO M49). Ratios: 2.52, 1.52, 1.00:1. Clutch: Diaphragm, spring. Clutch diameter: K-1500: 6-cyl.: 10 in. dia. Total lining area: 100.0 sq. in. V-8: 12 in. dia. Total lining area: 150 sq. in. K-2500: 10 in. dia. Total lining area: 100.0 sq. in. V-8: 11 in. dia. Total lining area: 124.0 sq. in. K-2500 with 350 V-8: 12 in. dia. Total lining area: 150 sq. in. Optional: K-2500 6-cyl.: 11 in. dia. Total lining area: 124.0 sq. in. 307 V-8: 12 in. dia. Total lining area: 150 sq. in.

VEHICLE DIMENSIONS: Wheelbase: K-1500: 117.5 in., 131.5 in. K-2500: 131.5 in. All Suburbans and Panels: 131.5 in. Overall Length: 117.5 in. Wideside pickups: 191.25 in. 131.5 in. Wideside pickups: 211.25., 117.5 in. Fenderside pickups: 190.5 in. 131.5 in. Fenderside pickups: 210.25. Front/Rear Tread: 67.4 in./65.8 in. Overall Height: K-1500 pickup and Suburban: 72.25 in. K-2500 pickup and Suburban: 73.9 in. Width: Pickup: 79.5 in. Front/Rear Overhang: Pickups: 33 in./41 in. Tailgate: Width and Height: 72 in. x 19.25 in. Approach/Departure Degrees: 30/21. Ground Clearance: Front axle: 7.25 in. Rear axle: 7.0 in. Oil pan: 16.5 in. Transfer case: 12.0 in. Fuel tank: 16.6 in. Load space: Pickup box dimensions: 117.5 in. wheelbase Wideside: 78.25 in. x 50 in. x 19.25 in. 131.5 in. wheelbase Wideside: 98 in. x 50 in. x 19.25 in. Capacity: 117.5 in. wheelbase: 58.4 cu. ft., 131.5 in. wheelbase: 74.3 cu. ft. 117.5 in. wheelbase Fenderside: 78.5 in. x 50 in. x 17.5 in. 131.5 in. wheelbase Fenderside:

96.25 in. x 50 in. x 17.5 in. Front headroom: 38.5 in. (seat to top of cab). Front hip room: 67.25 in. Pedal to seat back (max.): 43.5 in. Steering wheel to seat back (max.): 17.3 in. Seat to ground: 35.0 in. Floor to ground: 23.0 in.

CAPACITIES: Fuel Tank: K-1500: 117.5 in. wheelbase: 160 gal. 131.5 in. wheelbase: 20.0 gal. Optional: 16 gal. auxiliary for 117.5 in. wheelbase; 20 gal. for 131.5 in. wheelbase. K-2500: 20 gal. Optional: 20 gal. auxiliary. Coolant System Capacity: 250 6-cyl.: 14.8 qt. 292 6-cyl.: 13.6 qt. 350 V-8: 17.6 qt. (All figures for vehicles with manual transmission and without air conditioning).

ACCOMMODATIONS: Seating Capacity: Pickup and Chassis Cab models: 3 passenger. Optional: None. Suburban: K-1500: 3 passenger. K-2500: 6 passenger. Optional: 6 passenger (K-1500), 9 passenger (K-1500 and K-2500).

INSTRUMENTATION: Speedometer, odometer, fuel level gauge. Warning lights for battery, oil pressure, generator, brake system warning, directional/hazard lights, high beam, and engine coolant temperature.

OPTIONS AND PRICES: Except as noted above, unchanged from 1973. A sampling of options and their prices follows. Pickup models: Tinted glass: $21. Sliding rear window: $53. Roof drip molding: $16. Air conditioning: $437. Heavy-duty front stabilizer bar: $6. Heavy-duty brakes: $37. Turbo Hydra-Matic: $250. Four-speed manual transmission: $108. Auxiliary fuel tank: 82. Fuel tank skid plate: $101. Bucket seats: $135. Full-depth foam bench seat: $29. Custom steering wheel, 16 in. dia.: $10. Tilt steering wheel: $58. Variable ratio power steering: $152. Tachometer and gauges: $47. Tachometer: $56. Gauge Package (engine coolant temperature, ammeter and oil pressure): $12. AM/FM radio: $145. Chrome rear bumper: $39. 10.00 X 15 tires: $235.44. Sierra Grande Package: $277.

HISTORICAL FOOTNOTES: Sales of GMC light-duty trucks of all types totaled 142,055 in 1974.

1975 PICKUP & SUBURBAN

The 1975 GMC trucks were fitted with a new front grille with a broad center piece with body-color insert and red GMC lettering. The result was an attractive six-portion grille that was distinctive and pleasing to the eye. Clear-lenses parking/directional lights were used. Numbers signifying engine displacement were positioned in the lower right side of the grille. For 1975 they were red in color. New front-fender-mounted model/series identification was used. The Wideside models had a new quick-release tailgate that could be quickly and easily removed or re-installed.

Now offered as an option for V-8 models was a 400 cu. in. V-8. This engine was only available on models with a GVW of 6001 and above. Use of the 250 6-cylinder engine was restricted on K-1500 models to trucks with GVW ratings of 5200 and 5800 lb. The K-1500 models under 6001 GVW along with all other K-1500 and K-2500 with a GVW above 6000 lb. for California sale had a new ducted carburetor air intake system that drew exterior air from outside the engine compartment. The intake was positioned at the side of the radiator. The purpose of this arrangement was to improve both engine performance and fuel economy. Replacing the 250 cu. in. engine as the standard 6-cylinder engine for the K-2500 models was the 292 cu. in. engine. Standard on all engines was a new 35,000 volt transistorized High Energy ignition system. This system provided the GMC trucks with quicker starting, longer mileage between tune-ups and improved performance as a result. The 1975 GMC trucks had new extended maintenance schedules. Pickups rated at 6000 lbs GVW or below had engine oil changes and chassis lubrication mileage intervals of 7500 mile. Previously the recommended mileage had been 6000 miles. The base 250 6-cyl. engine was redesigned to produce more horsepower and torque as well as improved gasoline mileage. Major changes included a new integrally cast intake manifold with more uniform length passages. A new heat sump positioned below the carburetor improved fuel vaporation. All pickups with a GVW below 6001 lb. were equipped with a catalytic converter. All K series trucks used unleaded fuel exclusively and thus were equipped with the new narrow fuel nozzles required for dispensing unleaded fuel. Both V-8 engines had new Mod-Quad 4-barrel carburetors with an integral hot-air choke, a larger primary venturi, larger fuel filter area and additional Teflon coated parts. Also installed on the 1975 models were new fully aluminized mufflers with thicker interior baffles and outer shell.

Standard for all four-wheel drive pickups with a V-8 engine and Turbo Hydra-Matic was a full-time four-wheel drive system. A conventional four-wheel drive system with locking front hubs was found on models with a V-8 engine and manual transmission. All trucks with a 6-cylinder engine and either manual or automatic transmissions also had this system. Initial availability of the conventional four-wheel drive system was restricted to trucks with 6-cylinder engines. During the model year an improved and modified suspension intended to improve the riding quality of these 4x4 trucks became available. Also introduced during the 1975 model year was the All-Weather air conditioning for vehicles equipped with either the 250 or 292 6-cylinder engines. Previously, air conditioning was available only with V-8 engines. Series 10 models with the 250 6-cylinder engine now had a standard 11 in. dia. clutch rather than the 10 in. dia. unit previously used. A new 7-lead, heavy-duty trailer-towing wiring harness was now available both for Suburbans and conventional cab models. Also new-for-1975 was an optional headlights-on warning buzzer.

The base trim level for 1975 was the Sierra Trim Package. It included a full-width foam-padded bench seat upholstered in a plaid pattern vinyl offered in blue, green, saddle or red. The steel roof panel was painted to match the exterior color. Other features included a black rubber floor mat that extended to the firewall, padded armrests and sun visors, courtesy lamp, prismatic rearview mirror, and a foam-padded instrument panel pad. The Sierra exterior also featured bright upper and lower grille outline moldings, bright headlight bezels, silver plastic grille insert, bright outside rearview mirrors, bright door handles, white painted front bumper, hubcaps and wheels and bright Sierra nameplates. Next step up from the base model was the Sierra Grande. Its interior was fitted with a full-depth padded cushion bench seat, door trim panels with simulated woodgrain inserts, ashtray-mounted lighter, door or manually-operated dome and courtesy lights, color-keyed rubber floor mat, full-length bright door sill plates and a high-note horn. The seat upholstery was a grid-patterned nylon cloth with vinyl bolsters and facings. Four color choices were available. The Sierra Grande exterior included all the bright items in the Sierra trim plus chromed front bumper, chromed hubcaps, spear-type upper body side moldings on Wideside models, bright windshield and rear window trim, bright-trimmed parking and side marker lights, bright-trimmed Wideside taillights and Sierra Grande nameplates.

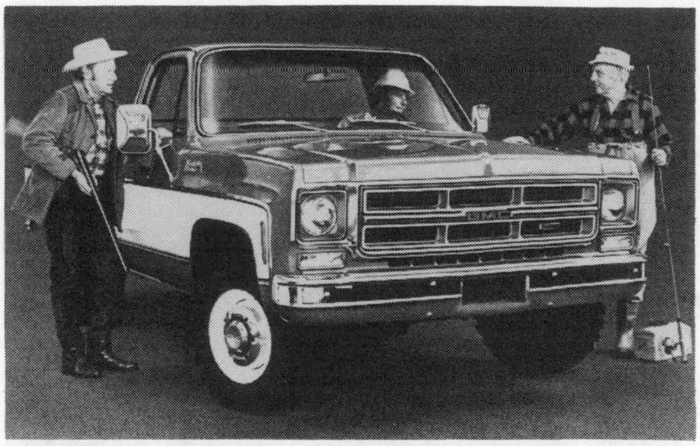
1975 GMC K-2500 Wideside pickup with full-time four-wheel drive

The upscale High Sierra bench seat was fitted with a full-depth foam cushion and was upholstered with either custom-grained vinyl or nylon cloth and vinyl. Vinyl covered bucket seats were optional. Also included in the High Sierra interior were these items: Ashtray-mounted cigarette lighter, simulated woodgrain instrument panel insert, door or manually operated courtesy and dome lights and additional cab insulation. The High Sierra exterior included all bright items found in the Sierra Grande and Sierra options plus these additions or substitutions: Bright metal cab back panel applique and moldings, bright upper body side and tailgate moldings and central tailgate appliques for Fleetsides, and High Sierra nameplates.

The new Sierra Classic had a full-width bench seat had a foam cushion nearly seven inches thick. The Sierra Classic upholstery was a basket weave-patterned nylon cloth with vinyl bolsters and facings. It was available in a choice of five colors. Also offered was a buffalo-hide vinyl in any of six colors. Custom vinyl bucket seats with a center console were also offered. Also included in the Sierra Classic interior was full-gauge instrumentation set in a simulated woodgrain panel with bright trim, simulated woodgrain inserts with bright accent trim and storage pockets on both doors, deep-twist nylon carpeting, insulated headliner and insulation for the floor, cowl, hood and back panel.

The Sierra Classic exterior consisted of all bright items from the High Sierra, Sierra Grande and Sierra models, except that Sierra Classic nameplates were substituted. In addition, the Sierra Classic had bright lower body side and tailgate moldings, wheel-opening moldings and a full tailgate applique on Wideside models.

The color selection for 1975 consisted of these fifteen colors: Skyline blue, Hawaiian blue, Catalina blue, grecian bronze, buckskin, yuba gold, moss gold, willoway green, Spring green, glenwood green, crimson red, rosedale red, Saratoga silver, Santa Fe tan and frost white. The conventional two-tone style required RPO BX6 moldings. The Special two-tone option was offered for Wideside models with RPO YG1 moldings. A Deluxe version was available for Wideside models with RPO BX6 and RPO YG1.

I.D. DATA: Unchanged from 1974 except a number 5 represented the 1975 model year. The letter M indicated the 400 cu. in. V-8. The engine number on 6-cylinders was found on a pad at the right side of the cylinder block at the rear of the distributor. V-8 engine numbers were positioned on a pad at front, right side of cylinder block.

Model Number	Body Type	Factory Price	GVW	Shipping Weight	Prod. Total
Series K-1500-1/2 ton 350 V-8 117.5 in. (Suburban:131.5 in.) wheelbase					
TK10703	Chassis and Cab	$4765	6200[1]	3685	—
TK10703	6.5 ft. F-S Pickup	$4698	6200	4013	—
TK10703	6.5 ft. Fleetside Pickup	$4698	6200	4083	—
TK10903	8 ft. Fenderside Pickup	$4741	6200	4141	—
TK10903	8 ft. Fleetside Pickup	$4741	6200	4211	—
TK10906	Suburban	$5796	6200	4703	—

NOTE 1: 6400 lb. GVW optional.

Model Number	Body Type	Factory Price	GVW	Shipping Weight	Prod. Total
Series K-2500-3/4 ton 350 V-8. 131.5 in. (Suburban-131.5 in.) wheelbase					
TK20903	Chassis and Cab	$4872	6800[2]	4206	—
TK20903	8 ft. Fenderside Pickup	$5039	6800	4606	—
TK20903	8 ft. Fleetside Pickup	$5039	6800	4676	—
TK20906	Suburban	$6054	6800	5133	—

NOTE 2: 8400 lb. GVW optional.

STANDARD ENGINE: All K-1500 6-cyl. models: 250 Six (LD4 ordering code) Engine Type: OHV, In-line 6-cylinder. Cast iron block and cylinder head. Key features include 12 counter-weight crankshaft and torsional damper, and molybdenum-filled top piston rings. Bore x Stroke: 3.875 in. x 3.53 in. Lifters: Hydraulic. Number of main bearings-7. Fuel Induction: Single Rochester 1-bbl. carburetor. Compression Ratio: 8.25:1. Displacement: 250 cu. in. (4.09 liters). Horsepower: Net: 105 @ 3800 rpm. Torque: Net: 185 lb.-ft. @ 1200 rpm. Oil refill capacity: 5 qt. with filter change. Fuel Requirements: Regular.

STANDARD ENGINE: K-2500 6-cyl. models: 292 Six. Ordering Code: L25. Not available in California. Engine Type: OHV, 6-cyl. Cast iron block and cylinder head. Key features include aluminized intake valves, automatic "Rotocoil" rotors on exhaust valves, special coating applied to exhaust valves to reduce deposit formation, full-chromed top piston rings, and premium aluminum bearings. Bore x Stroke: 3.875 in. x 4.125 in. Lifters: Hydraulic. Number of main bearings-7. Fuel Induction: Single Rochester 1-bbl. carburetor. Compression Ratio: 8.0:1. Displacement: 292 cu. in. (4.78 liters). Horsepower: Net: 120 @ 3600 rpm. Torque: Net: 215 lb.-ft. @ 2000 rpm. Oil refill capacity: 6 qt. with filter change. Fuel Requirements: Regular.

STANDARD ENGINE: V-8 models. Ordering Code: LS9: 350 V-8. Engine Type: OHV, V-8. Cast iron block and alloy iron cylinder head. Key features include chain drive camshaft, "Rotocoil" exhaust valve rotators, special coating applied to exhaust valves to reduce deposit formation, molybdenum-filled top piston rings, premium aluminum main bearings. Bore x Stroke: 4.0 in. x 3.50 in. Lifters: Hydraulic. Number of main bearings-5. Fuel Induction: Single Rochester 4-bbl. carburetor. Compression Ratio: 8.5:1. Displacement: 350 cu. in. (5.73 liters). Horsepower: Net: 160 @ 3800 rpm. Torque: Net: 250 lb.-ft. @ 2400 rpm. Oil refill capacity: 5 qt. with filter change. Fuel Requirements: Regular.

OPTIONAL ENGINE: V-8 models. 400 V-8. Available only with heavy-duty emissions for models of 6001 lb. GVW and above. Engine Type: OHV, V-8. Cast iron block and alloy iron cylinder head. Bore x Stroke: 4.125 in. x 4.0 in. Lifters: Hydraulic. Number of main bearings-5.

Fuel Induction: Single Rochester 4-bbl. carburetor. Compression Ratio: 8.5:1. Displacement: 400 cu. in. (6.55 liters). Horsepower: Net: 175 @ 3600 rpm. Torque: Net: 290 lb.-ft. @ 2800 rpm. Oil refill capacity: 5 qt. with filter change. Fuel Requirements: Regular.

CHASSIS FEATURES: Separate body and frame with channel side rails. Carbon-Steel, 39,000 psi. Section modulus: 117.5 in. wheelbase: 3.06. 131.5 in. wheelbase: 3.84. Optional: None.

SUSPENSION AND RUNNING GEAR: Front Suspension: 2-leaf, tapered leaf springs 1.0 in. dia. shock absorbers. K-1500: 1850 lb. rating (at ground). K-2500:1950 lb. rating (at ground). Optional rating: 1900 lb. (both series). Rear Suspension: 52 in. x 2.25 in. Two-stage, 5-leaf. 1.0 in. dia. shock absorbers. K-1500: 1700 lb. rating (at ground). K-2500: 2800 lb. Optional Rating: K-1500: 2000 lb. Front Axle Type and Capacity: K-1500: Spicer 44F Semi-floating. 3400 lb. capacity. Optional: None. K-2500: Full-floating, 3500 lb. capacity. Optional: None. Rear Axle Type and Capacity: K-1500: Chevrolet, semi-floating, 3750 lb. capacity. Optional: None. K-2500: Chevrolet, full-floating, 5700 lb. Final Drive Ratio: K-1500: Front: 6-cyl.:4.11:1; V-8: 3.07:1. Rear: 6-cyl.: 4.11:1. V-8: 3.07:1. K-2500: Front: 6-cyl. 4.56:1; V-8: 4.10:1. Rear: 6-cyl.: 4.56:1; V-8: 4.101. Optional K-1500: 3.07, 3.73:1, 4.1:1. K-2500: None. Transfer Case: 6-cylinder models: New Process 205. Single lever, two-speed: 1.94, 1.00:1. V-8 models: New Process 203. Ratios: 2.0:1, 1.0:1. Tires: K-1500: G78 x 15B 4-ply rating, tubeless or tube-type. K-2500: 8.75 x 16.5C 6-ply rating, tubeless. Optional: K-1500: G78 x 15B, white stripe; H78 x 15B, tubeless, black sidewall or white stripe; L78 x 15B black sidewall or white stripe, tubeless; 10.00 x 16.5C tubeless; G78 x 15B tube-type; 7.00 x 15C tube-type; 6.50 x 16C tube-type and LR78 x 15C white sidewall radial ply. The following tires were specified for K-1500 models with the 5600 lb. GVW Package which included a front heavy-duty stabilizer bar: H78 x 15B 4-ply rating, tubeless; 6.50 x 16C 6-ply rating, tube-type, truck type. The following tires were specified for K-1500 models with the 6000 lb. GVW Package which included a front heavy-duty stabilizer bar and heavy-duty rear springs: L78 x 15B 4-ply rating, tubeless. Optional K-2500: 8.75 x 16.5D tubeless; 9.50 x 16.5D tubeless; 10.00 x 16.5C tubeless (not available for Fenderside models); 7.50 x 16C 6-ply rating, tube-type; 7.50 x 16D tube-type; 7.50 x 16E tube-type. The following tires were specified for K-2500 models with the 7500 lb. GVW Package which included a front heavy-duty stabilizer bar: 8.75 x 16.5 C 6-ply rating, tubeless; 7.50 x 16C 6-ply rating, tubeless. The following tires were specified for K-2500 models with the 8200 lb. GVW Package which included a front heavy-duty stabilizer bar: 9.50 x 16.5D 8-ply rating, tubeless; 7.50 x 16C 6-ply rating, tube-type. Steering: Recirculating ball gear. Ratio: 20:1. Turning Circle: 47 ft. Steering wheel diameter: 17.5 in. Optional: Power-assisted. Ratio: 16.4:1. Transmission: 3-speed, synchromesh manual (ZW4 Ordering Code). Transmission Ratios: 3.03, 1.75, 1.00:1. Optional: Chevrolet CH465. 4-speed manual synchromesh (RPO M20). Ratios: Optional: 3-speed Turbo Hydra-Matic (RPO M49). Ratios: 2.52, 1.52, 1.00:1. Clutch: Diaphragm, spring. Clutch diameter: K-1500: 6-cyl.: 10 in. dia. Total lining area: 100.0 sq. in. V-8: 12 in. dia. Total lining area: 150 sq. in. K-2500: 10 in. dia. Total lining area: 100.0 sq. in. V-8: 11 in. dia. Total lining area: 124.0 sq. in. K-2500 with 350 V-8: 12 in. dia. Total lining area: 150 sq. in. Optional: K-2500 6-cyl.: 11 in. dia. Total lining area: 124.0 sq. in. 307 V-8: 12 in. dia. Total lining area: 150 sq. in.

VEHICLE DIMENSIONS: Wheelbase: K-1500: 117.5 in., 131.5 in. K-2500: 131.5 in. All Suburbans and Panels: 131.5 in. Overall Length: 117.5 in. Fleetside pickups: 191.25 in. 131.5 in. Fleetside pickups: 211.25., 117.5 in. Fenderside pickups: 190.5 in. 131.5 in. Fenderside pickups: 210.25. Front/Rear Tread: 67.4 in./65.8 in. Overall Height: K-1500 pickup and Suburban: 72.25 in., K-2500 pickup and Suburban: 73.9 in. Width: Pickup: 79.5 in. Front/Rear Overhang: Pickups: 33 in./41 in. Tailgate: Width and Height: 72 in. x 19.25 in. Approach/ Departure Degrees: 30/21. Ground Clearance: Front axle: 7.25 in. Rear axle: 7.0 in. Oil pan: 16.5 in. Transfer case: 12.0 in. Fuel tank: 16.6 in. Load space: Pickup box dimensions: 117.5 in. wheelbase Fleetside: 78.25 in. x 50 in. x 19.25 in. 131.5 in. wheelbase Fleetside: 98 in. x 50 in. x 19.25 in. Capacity: 117.5 in. wheelbase: 58.4 cu. ft., 131.5 in. wheelbase: 74.3 cu. ft. 117.5 in. wheelbase Fenderside: 78.5 in. x 50 in. x 17.5 in. 131.5 in. wheelbase Fenderside: 96.25 in. x 50 in. x 17.5 in. Front headroom: 38.5 in. (seat to top of cab). Front hip room: 67.25 in. Pedal to seat back (max.): 43.5 in. Steering wheel to seat back (max.): 17.3 in. Seat to ground: 35.0 in. Floor to ground: 23.0 in.

CAPACITIES: Fuel Tank: K-1500: 117.5 in. wheelbase: 16.0 gal. 131.5 in. wheelbase: 20.0 gal. Optional: 16 gal. auxiliary for 117.5 in. wheelbase; 20 gal. for 131.5 in. wheelbase. K-2500: 20 gal. Optional: 20 gal. auxiliary. Coolant System Capacity: 250 6-cyl.: 14.8 qt. 292 6-cyl.: 13.6 qt. 350 V-8: 17.6 qt. (All figures for vehicles with manual transmission and without air conditioning).

ACCOMMODATIONS: Seating Capacity: Pickup and chassis cab models: 3 passenger. Optional: None. Suburban: K-1500: 3 passenger. K-2500: 6 passenger. Optional: 6 passenger (K-1500), 9 passenger (K-1500 and K-2500).

INSTRUMENTATION: Speedometer, odometer, fuel level gauge. Warning lights for battery, oil pressure, generator, brake system warning, directional/hazard lights, high beam, and engine coolant temperature.

OPTIONS AND PRICES: Positraction rear axle-RPO G80 (available for K-1500 only). NoSPIN rear axle-RPO G86 (available for K-2500 only). Sierra Package. With cloth bench seat-RPO Z62/YJ4; with custom vinyl bench seat-RPO Z62/YJ5. High Sierra Package. With custom cloth bench seat-RPO Z84/YJ6; with custom vinyl bench seat-RPO Z84/YJ5. High Sierra Package. With custom cloth bench seat-RPO YE9/YJ6; with custom vinyl bench seat-RPO YE9/YJ5. Custom camper chassis equipment-Basic Camper Group-RPO Z81. Available with K-2500 V-8 models with 8200 lb. GVW and either 4-spd. manual trans. or Turbo Hydra-Matic. Requires 9.50 x 16.5D tubeless or 7.50 x 16E tube-type rear tires. only. Includes heavy-duty front and rear shock absorbers, heavy-duty front springs, heavy-duty front stabilizer, custom camper nameplate and camper body wiring harness. Deluxe Camper Group for cab-over camper bodies-RPO Z83. Available with K-2500 V-8 models with 8200 lb. GVW and either 4-spd. manual trans. or Turbo Hydra-Matic. Requires 9.50 x 16.5D tubeless or 7.50 x 16E tube-type rear tires and Fleetside body. Not available with wooden floor. Includes Basic Camper Group plus camper body tie-down brackets mounted to pickup box under body, spring loaded turn-buckles shipped loose, horizontal shock absorbers mounted between cab rear panel and pickup box side panels and vertical shock absorber brackets mounted on front fenders. Camper body wiring harness-RPO UY1. Included when custom camper chassis equipment is ordered. Camper-type stainless steel mirrors: RPO DF2. Poly-wrap air cleaner-RPO K43. All-Weather air conditioning-RPO C60. Auxiliary 61 amp battery-RPO TP2. Heavy-duty 80 amp battery-RPO T60. Painted rear bumper-RPO V38. Painted rear step bumper-RPO V43. Chromed front and rear bumper-RPO V37. Front chromed bumper (not available if painted rear bumper is ordered)-RPO V46. Chromed rear bumper (available only with High Sierra or High Sierra Super is ordered)-RPO VF1. California assembly line emission test-RPO YF5. Bright metal hubcaps (not available for K-1500 models with 10.00 x 16.5 tires)-RPO PO3. Side-mounted spare tire carrier-RPO P13. Electric clock (available only with Gauge Package, not available if tachometer is ordered)-RPO U35. Heavy-duty clutch (available only for models with 250 engine and 3-spd. manual trans.)-RPO MO1. Exterior tool stowage (available for Fleetside only. Not available if auxiliary fuel tank is ordered)-RPO VK4. Coolant recovery system-RPO VQ1. Heavy-duty radiator (requires RPO VQ1)-RPO VO1. Wood 8 ft. Fleetside pickup box-RPO E81. Gauge Package-Z53: $12. Tachometer (V-8 models only, not available if electric clock is ordered)-RPO U16: $56. 42 amp Delcotron generator (not available if air conditioning is ordered)-RPO K79. 61 amp Delcotron generator (included with air conditioning)-RPO K76. Soft-Ray tinted glass, all windows-RPO V22: $18. Chromed grille-RPO V22. Door edge guards (not available with woodgrained exterior trim)-RPO B93. Free wheeling front hubs-RP F76. Cargo area lamp-RPO UF2. Dome light-RPO C91. Roof marker lights-RPO U01. Cigarette lighter-RPO U37. Exterior below eye-level 7.5 in. x 10.5 in. painted mirrors-RPO D29. Exterior below eye-level 7.5 in. x 10.5 in. stainless steel mirrors-RPO DG4. Cab back panel applique-RPO BX6. Upper body moldings. For Wideside only. Includes fender, door cab panel, tailgate and pickup box moldings plus bright front turn signal, side marker and taillight trim-RPO B85. Upper and lower body molding (adds lower body side, tailgate and wheel opening moldings to RPO B85)-RPO YG1. Painted roof drip molding-RPO BX5. Soft instrument panel pad-RPO B70. Fuel tank shield-RPO NY1. AM radio-RPO U63. AM/FM radio-RPO U69. Vinyl roof cover-RPO CO8. Bucket seats-RPO A50/YJ5: $135. Full-depth foam bench seat-RPO Z52: $29. Heavy-duty front and rear shock absorbers-RPO F51. Heavy-duty rear shock absorbers-RPO G68. Heavy-duty front springs-RPO F60. Heavy-duty rear springs (K-1500 only)-RPO G50. Heavy-duty front stabilizer-RPO F58. Power steering-RPO N40. ComforTilt steering wheel (not available with 3-spd. manual trans.)-RPO N33. Custom steering wheel (available only with power steering, includes 16 in. steering wheel)-RPO N31. Auxiliary fuel tank (not avail. with K-1500 with 250 engine)-RPO NL2: $77. Manual throttle control (not available with air conditioning)-RPO K31: $410. Front towing hooks-RPO V76. Bright metal wheelcovers (K-1500 only; not avail. with 6.50 x 16 or 10.00 x 16.5 tires)-RPO PO1. Wheel trim rings (not avail. with 10.00 x 16.5 tires on K-1500 or with 7.50 x 16 tires)-RPO PO6. Sliding rear window-RPO A28. Exterior woodgrained trim (avail. only with Wideside models with custom upper and lower moldings or High Sierra only. Not avail. with special or deluxe two-tone paint)-RPO YG2. Suburban: 350 V-8: $45 above price of 307-V-8 equipped models. Turbo Hydra-Matic: $242. Air conditioning: $648. Power steering: $147. Free-running front hubs. Limited slip rear differential: K-1500: $65; K-2500: $132.

HISTORICAL FOOTNOTES: Calendar year sales of all GMC trucks was 140,423.

1976 PICKUP & SUBURBAN

The engine displacement identification was removed from the grillework of the 1976 GMC trucks. A full-time four-wheel drive system was used with all models equipped with Turbo Hydra-Matic transmission. The conventional four-wheel drive system was used with manual transmissions. A heavy-duty stabilizer bar was now standard for the K-1500 and K-2500, previously it had been an option. A new 400 cu. in. V-8 was used for 1976. The optional air conditioning system had a new 7-position control with an "Economy" setting. New options included a new rear chromed step bumper with a skid resistent top surface and a recessed step for Wideside models. It was pre-drilled for a trailer hitch ball and was offered in either 1.875 in. or 2.0 in. sizes. A painted version was available for all pickups. A new two-tone paint scheme employing selected secondary colors in combination with the main body color. A new Trim Package for Fenderside pickups with the 6.5 ft. box included special striping, chromed front and rear bumpers, Rallye wheels, white-lettered tires, and Sierra Grande trim. It was offered in a choice of four exterior colors: Blue, orange, red or black. The Sierra trim level was unchanged. The Sierra Grande level has several changes for 1976. These included the use of simulated wood inserts for the door trim panels and a ribbed velour cloth upholstery with grained vinyl facings or buffalo-hide embossed vinyl. The High Sierra Package was also revised to include the use of ribbed-pattern velour cloth or buffalo-hide vinyl. The seat back folded forward to make the stowage area behind the seat more accessible. Vinyl-upholstered bucket seats with a center console were also available (they were also available for all regular cabs with all trim levels). The door-trim panels and instrument panel had simulated tigerwood inserts. The 1976 Sierra Classic format included new ribbed-pattern velour cloth with grained vinyl facings and bolsters. A buffalo-hide vinyl, with a selection of five colors, was an alternative. The seat back also tilted forward on the Sierra Classic. Simulated tigerwood grain inserts were used for the instrumentation panel and door inserts. A cut-pile floor carpeting was installed. All velour cloth interiors were available in a choice of blue, green, saddle or red. Colors offered for the vinyl interiors were also blue, green, saddle, red or green. The basic standard equipment from the 1975 models and the exterior color selection were carried over into 1976.

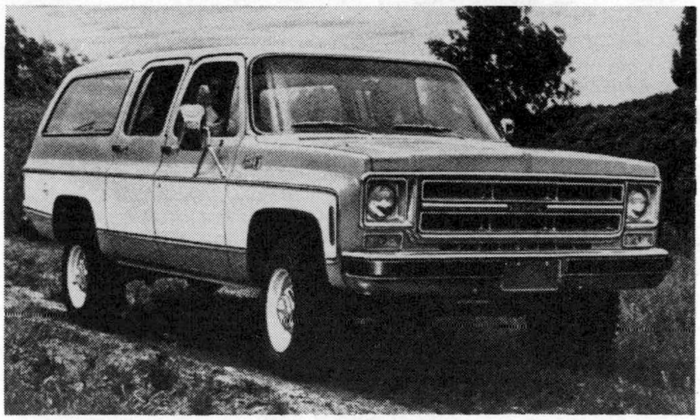

1976 GMC K-1500 Suburban

I.D. DATA: Unchanged from 1975 except the number 6 represented the 1976 model year. The letter U identified trucks with the 400 cu. in. V-8.

Model Number	Body Type	Factory Price	GVW	Shipping Weight	Prod. Total
Series K1500-1/2 ton 350 V-8 117.5 in., 129.5 in. wheelbase					
TK10703	Chassis and Cab	$5104	5200[1]	3816	—
TK10703	6.5 ft. F-S Pickup	$5010	5200	4147	—
TK10703	6.5 ft. W-S Pickup	$5010	5200	4215	—
TK10903	8 ft. Fenderside Pickup	$5055	5200	4244	—
TK10903	8 ft. Wideside Pickup	$5055	5200	4320	—
TK10906	Suburban, 129.5 in. wb.	$6234	5200	4702	—

NOTE 1: 5600 lb. and 6400 lb. GVW optional.

Series K2500-3/4 ton 350 V-8. 131.5 in. (Suburban-129.5 in.) wheelbase

TK20903	Chassis and Cab	$5205	6800[2]	4206	—
TK20903	8 ft. Fenderside Pickup	$5372	6800	4606	—
TK20903	8 ft. Wideside Pickup	$5372	6800	4676	—
TK20906	Suburban	$6441	6800	5133	—

NOTE 2: 7500 lb. and 8200 lb. GVW optional.

STANDARD ENGINE: All K-1500 6-cyl. models: 250 Six (LD4 ordering code) Engine Type: OHV, In-line 6-cylinder. Cast iron block and cylinder head. Key features include 12 counter-weight crankshaft and torsional damper, and molybdenum-filled top piston rings. Bore x Stroke: 3.875 in. x 3.53 in. Lifters: Hydraulic. Number of main bearings-7. Fuel Induction: Single Rochester 1-bbl. carburetor. Compression Ratio: 8.25:1. Displacement: 250 cu. in. (4.09 liters). Horsepower: Net: 105 @ 3800 rpm. Torque: Net: 185 lb.-ft. @ 1200 rpm. Oil refill capacity: 5 qt. with filter change. Fuel Requirements: No-lead, low lead or regular fuel, 91 octane or higher.

STANDARD ENGINE: K-2500 6-cyl. models: 292 Six. Ordering Code: L25. Not available in California. Engine Type: OHV, 6-cyl. Cast iron block and cylinder head. Key features include aluminized intake valves, automatic "Rotocoil" rotors on exhaust valves, special coating applied to exhaust valves to reduce deposit formation, full-chromed top piston rings, and premium aluminum bearings. Bore x Stroke: 3.875 in. x 4.125 in. Lifters: Hydraulic. Number of main bearings-7. Fuel Induction: Single Rochester 1-bbl. carburetor. Compression Ratio: 8.0:1. Displacement: 292 cu. in. (4.78 liters). Horsepower: Net: 120 @ 3600 rpm. Torque: Net: 215 lb.-ft. @ 2000 rpm. Oil refill capacity: 6 qt. with filter change. Fuel Requirements: No-lead, low lead or regular fuel, 91 octane or higher.

STANDARD ENGINE: V-8 models. Ordering Code: LS9: 350 V-8 Engine Type: OHV, V-8. Cast iron block and alloy iron cylinder head. Key features include chain drive camshaft, "Rotocoil" exhaust valve rotators, special coating applied to exhaust valves to reduce deposit formation, molybdenum-filled top piston rings, premium aluminum main bearings. Bore x Stroke: 4.0 in. x 3.50 in. Lifters: Hydraulic. Number of main bearings-5. Fuel Induction: Single Rochester 4-bbl. carburetor. Compression Ratio: 8.5:1. Displacement: 350 cu. in. (5.73 liters). Horsepower: Net: 165 @ 3800 rpm. Torque: Net: 260 lb.-ft. @ 2400 rpm. (255 lb.-ft. @ 2800 rpm for models with heavy-duty emissions and 6001 lb. GVW and above). Oil refill capacity: 5 qt. with filter change. Fuel Requirements: No-lead, low lead or regular fuel, 91 octane or higher.

OPTIONAL ENGINE: V-8 models. 400 V-8. Available only with heavy-duty emissions for models of 6001 lb. GVW and above. Engine Type: OHV, V-8. Cast iron block and alloy iron cylinder head. Bore x Stroke: 4.10 in. x 3.8 in. Lifters: Hydraulic. Number of main bearings-5. Fuel Induction: Single Rochester 4-bbl. carburetor. Compression Ratio: 8.5:1. Displacement: 400 cu. in. (6.55 liters). Horsepower: Net: 175 @ 3600 rpm. Torque: Net: 290 lb.-ft. @ 2800 rpm. Oil refill capacity: 5 qt. with filter change. Fuel Requirements: No-lead, low lead or regular fuel, 91 octane or higher.

CHASSIS FEATURES: Separate body and frame with channel side rails. Carbon-Steel, 39,000 psi. Section modulus: 117.5 in. wheelbase: 3.06 in. 131.5 in. wheelbase: 3.84 in. Optional: None.

SUSPENSION AND RUNNING GEAR: Front Suspension: 2-leaf, tapered. 1.0 in. dia. shock absorbers. K-1500: 1850 lb. rating (at ground). K-2500: 1900 lb. rating (at ground). Optional rating: K-1500: 1900 lb. Rear Suspension: 52 in. x 2.25 in. Two-stage, 5-leaf. 1.0 in. dia. shock absorbers. K-1500: 2000 lb. rating (at ground), K-2500: 2800 lb. Optional Rating: None. Front Axle Type and Capacity: K-1500: Semi-floating. 3600 lb. capacity. Optional: None. K-2500: Full-floating, 3800 lb. capacity. Optional: None. Rear Axle Type and Capacity: K-1500: Chevrolet, semi-floating, 3750 lb. capacity. Optional: None. K-2500: Chevrolet, full-floating, 5700 lb. Final Drive Ratio: K-1500: Front: 6-cyl.: 4.11:1; V-8: 3.07:1. Rear: 6-cyl.: 4.11:1. V-8: 3.07:1. K-2500: Front: 6-cyl. 4.56:1; V-8: 4.10:1. Rear: 6-cyl.: 4.56:1; V-8: 4.101. Optional K-1500: 3.07, 3.73:1, 4.1:1. K-2500: None. Transfer Case: 6-cylinder models: New Process 205. Single lever, two-speed: 1.94, 1.00:1. V-8 models: New Process 203. Ratios: 2.0:1, 1.0:1. Brakes: Type: Hydraulic, power assisted. Dimensions: K-1500: Front: Disc: 11.86 in. dia. Rear: Drums: 11.0 in. x 2.0 in. K-2500: Front: Disc: 12.5 in. dia. Rear: Drums: 11.0 in. x 2.75 in. Optional: K-1500 and K-2500: Heavy-duty. Wheels: K-1500: 15 x 6.0 6-stud disc. K-2500: 16.5 x 6.0 in. 8-stud disc. Tires: K-1500: L78 x 15B. K-2500: 8.75 x 16.5C 6-ply rating, tubeless. Optional: K-1500: G78 x 15B, white stripe; H78 x 15B, tubeless, black sidewall or white stripe; L78 x 15B black sidewall or white stripe, tubeless; 10.00 x 16.5C tubeless; G78 x 15B tube-type; 7.00 x 15C tube-type; 6.50 x 16C tube-type and LR78 x 15C white sidewall radial ply. The following tires were specified for K-1500 models with the 5600 lb. GVW Package which included a front heavy-duty stabilizer bar: H78 x 15B 4-ply rating, tubeless; 6.50 x 16C 6-ply rating, tube-type, truck type. The following tires were specified for K-1500 models with the 6000 lb. GVW Package which included a front heavy-duty stabilizer bar and heavy-duty rear springs: L78 x 15B 4-ply rating, tubeless. Optional K-2500: 8.75 x 16.5D tubeless; 9.50 x 16.5D tubeless; 10.00 x 16.5C tubeless (not available for Fenderside models); 7.50 x 16C 6-ply rating, tube-type; 7.50 x 16D tube-type; 7.50 x 16E tube-type. The following tires were specified for K-2500 models with the 7500 lb. GVW Package which included a front heavy-duty stabilizer bar: 8.75 x 16.5 C 6-ply rating, tubeless; 7.50 x 16C 6-ply rating, tubeless. The following tires were specified for K-2500 models with the 8200 lb. GVW Package which included a front heavy-duty stabilizer bar: 9.50 x 16.5D 8-ply rating, tubeless; 7.50 x 16C 6-ply rating, tube-type. Steering: Recirculating ball gear. Ratio: 20:1. Turning Circle: 47 ft. Steering wheel diameter: 17.5 in. Optional: Power-assisted. Ratio: 16.4:1. In late 1976 as a rolling model change, the power steering gear imput shaft diameter was reduced to provide a common coupling size for all GM vehicles. Transmission: 3-speed, synchromesh manual (ZW4 Ordering Code). Transmission Ratios: 3.03, 1.75, 1.00:1. Optional: CH465. 4-speed manual synchromesh (RPO M20). Ratios: 6.55, 3.58, 1.70, 1.00:1. Optional: 3-speed Turbo Hydra-Matic (RPO M49). Ratios: 2.52, 1.52, 1.00:1. Clutch: Diaphragm, spring. Clutch diameter: K-1500: 6-cyl.: 10 in. dia. Total lining area: 100.0 sq. in. V-8: 12 in. dia. Total lining area: 150 sq. in. K-2500: 10 in. dia. Total lining area: 100.0 sq. in. V-8: 11 in. dia. Total lining area: 124.0 sq. in. K-2500 with 350 V-8: 12 in. dia. Total lining area: 150 sq. in. Optional: K-2500 6-cyl.: 11 in. dia. Total lining area: 124.0 sq. in. 307 V-8: 12 in. dia. Total lining area: 150 sq. in.

VEHICLE DIMENSIONS: Wheelbase: K-1500: 117.5 in., 131.5 in. K-2500: 131.5 in. All Suburbans and Panels: 129.5 in. Overall Length: 117.5 in. Wideside pickups: 191.25 in. 131.5 in. Wideside pickups: 211.25. 117.5 in. Fenderside pickups: 190.5 in. 131.5 in. Fenderside pickups: 210.25. 117.5 in. Front/Rear Tread: 67.4 in./65.8 in. Overall Height: K-1500 pickup: 72.0 in. K-2500 pickup: 74.0 in. K-1500 and K-2500 Suburban: 73.5 in. Width: Pickup: 79.5 in. Front/Rear Overhang: Pickups: 33 in./41 in. Tailgate: Width and Height: 72 in. x 19.25 in. Approach/Departure Degrees: K-1500 117.5 in. Wideside and Fenderside: 33/19. K-1500 131.5 in. Wideside: 33/15. K-1500 131.5 in. wheelbase Fenderside: 33/16. K-2500 131.5 in. wheelbase Wideside: 35/20. K-2500 131.5 in. wheelbase Fenderside: 35/21. Ground Clearance: Front axle: 7.25 in. Rear axle: 7.0 in. Oil pan: 16.5 in. Transfer case: 12.0 in. Fuel tank: 16.6 in. Load space: Pickup box dimensions: 117.5 in. wheelbase Wideside: 78.25 in. x 50 in. x 19.25 in. 131.5 in. wheelbase. Wideside: 98 in. x 50 in. x 19.25 in. Capacity: 117.5 wheelbase: 58.4 cu. ft., 131.5 in. wheelbase: 74.3 cu. ft. 117.5 in. wheelbase. Fenderside: 78.5 in. x 50 in. x 17.5 in. 131.5 in. wheelbase Fenderside: 96.25 in. x 50 in. x 17.5 in. Front headroom: 38.5 in. (seat to top of cab). Front hip room: 67.25 in. Pedal to seat back (max.): 43.5 in. Steering wheel to seat back (max.): 17.3 in. Seat to ground: 35.0 in. Floor to ground: 23.0 in.

CAPACITIES: Fuel Tank: 117.5 in. wheelbase: 16.0 gal. 131.5 in. wheelbase: 20.0 gal. Optional: 17 gal. auxiliary tank. for 117.5 in.; 20 gal. auxiliary for 131.5 in. wheelbase. Coolant System Capacity: 250 6-cyl.: 14.8 qt. 292 6-cyl.: 13.6 qt. 350 V-8: 17.6 qt. (All figures for vehicles with manual transmission and without air conditioning).

ACCOMMODATIONS: Seating Capacity: Pickup and chassis cab models: 3 passenger. Optional: None. Suburban: 3 passenger. Optional: 6 or 9 passenger.

INSTRUMENTATION: Speedometer, odometer, fuel level gauge. Warning lights for battery, oil pressure, generator, brake system warning, directional/hazard lights, high beam, and engine coolant temperature.

OPTIONS: Gauge Package. Includes voltmeter, oil pressure and engine coolant temperature. AM Radio. AM/FM radio. Turbo Hydra-Matic. ComforTilt steering wheel. Tachometer (V-8 only). Delco Freedom battery. Sliding rear window. Air conditioning. Speed and cruise control. Requires V-8 engine and Turbo Hydra-Matic. Cargo area lamp. Below eye-level mirrors. Bucket seats. Two-tone paint. Pickup box side rails. Rear chromed step bumper. Deluxe chrome bumpers (available for front only or front and rear). Chromed front bumper guards with rubber impact stripes. Glide-out spare tire carrier. Stainless steel wheelcovers. Bright hubcaps. Fuel tank skid plate. Transfer case skid plate. Soft-Ray tinted glass. Rallye wheels. Engine oil cooler. Heavy-duty alternator. Weight-equalizing hitch platform. Trailer Special Package. Includes power steering, heavy-duty battery, and trailer special nameplate. Camper Special Package. Includes camper body wiring, heavy-duty front springs, heavy-duty front and rear shock absorbers, added capacity rear springs and camper special nameplate. Available only for K-2500 and requires V-8 engine and either 4-spd. manual or Turbo Hydra-Matic transmission. Deluxe Camper Special Package. Included all camper special equipment plus Camper Tie-Down Package, Elimi-Pitch Package (includes two horizontal shock absorbers mounted between cab rear panel and pickup box, and two vertical shock absorber mounted between camper overhang and front fenders and rear stabilizer (available for cab-over campers on Wideside models only).

HISTORICAL FOOTNOTES: Calendar year production of all GMC 1976 truck classifications was 223,805.

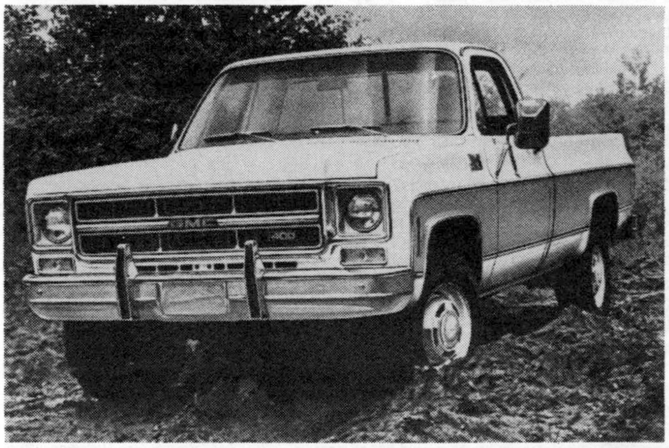

1976 GMC Wideside pickup with 400 cubic inch V-8

1977 PICKUP & SUBURBAN

The GMC front grille was slightly altered for 1977. The center divider was slimmed down as were the vertical dividers. The headlight bezel color was changed from argent to dark grey metallic. The body side moldings for the High Sierra, Sierra Classic and RPO B85 and RPO YG1 Molding Packages had ochre paint in place of the black paint used in 1976. K-1500 models were available with newly styled RPO PO1 black and chrome wheelcovers in a spoked wheel design. Another new option, RPO PA6, white painted wheels, had a spoke-type design.

New K-3500 one-ton four-wheel drive models were available in two-door chassis-cab, two-door Wideside, bonus cab and crew cab Wideside, bonus cab and crew cab chassis-cab. All were equipped with a 4500 lb. Dana-Spicer front axle which utilized a spring loaded kingpin rather than a conventional ball joint. A 7500 lb. rear axle was used. The GVWRs for these trucks ranged from 6600 to 9200 lbs. for single rear-wheel models and 9200 to 10,000 lbs. on dual rear wheel models. All K-3500 pickup boxes were 8 ft. long. Power steering was standard for the K-3500 range. All K series pickups and Suburban models equipped with either the RPO M20 4-speed manual transmission or RPO MC1 3-speed manual transmission and GT4 (3.73:1), HO4 (4.11:1), GT5 or HC4 rear axles had a new two-piece prop shaft. The exhaust systems on the K series trucks incorporated new exhaust hanger assemblies. The exhaust system were also modified to accommodate the new 2-piece propeller shafts on the K pickups and Suburbans. K-1500 and K-2500 models with RPO LS9 350 V-8 engine had a new, quieter muffler. The tail, stop and back-up light assemblies for the Fenderside and chassis-cab models were now combined into a single unit which also included the turn signal function.

1977 GMC series 1500 Sierra Classic Fenderside pickup

Added to the list of K series optional equipment were power windows and power door locks. A new Exterior Package (RPO ZY5) also debuted for 1977. It was available for Wideside pickups and consisted of a choice of six special two-tone paint treatments in which the secondary color was used on the hood, cab roof and between the RPO YG1 body side and rear moldings. This package also included color-coordinated hood stripes (decals) and a bright stand-up hood emblem. Also offered were Sport Packages for both the Wideside and Fenderside pickups. They included special hood and side striping and a choice of new styled or Rallye wheels.

The standard Sierra interior consisted of a full-width foam-padded front bench seat uphol-stered in a new plaid-pattern embossed vinyl offered in a selection of four colors. A matching rear seat was standard for crew cab models. Black rubber floor mats were included as were new larger door trim panels, padded armrests, padded sun visors, courtesy lamp, prismatic inside rearview mirror, foam-padded instrument panel with Sierra nameplate and simulated chestnut woodgrain insert.

The Sierra exterior included bright upper and lower grille outline moldings, bright headlight bezels, silver plastic grille insert, bright outside rearview mirrors, bright door handles, white painted front bumper, hubcaps and wheels, bright drip rails over doors and bright Sierra nameplates.

1977 GMC K-2500 cab & chassis

The Sierra Grande trim level included all Sierra elements plus front bench seat with bright trim for regular cabs, door or manually-operated dome light, full-length bright door sill plates, and high-note horn. The regular cab front seat folded forward for access to the inside stowage area. The upholstery for the regular cabs was a new custom ribbed-pattern velour cloth with grained vinyl facings and bolsters or a custom buffalo-hide embossed vinyl. A striped knit vinyl trim was also available. Standard trim on the crew cabs and bonus cabs was a plaid-pattern vinyl with custom buffalo-hide vinyl also available. The rubber floor mat was color-keyed. On the bonus cab the front mat was color-keyed, the rear was black. The Sierra Grande exterior included all items from the Sierra plus chromed front bumper, bright hubcaps, spear-type side moldings on Widesides, bright windshield and rear window trim, bright-trimmed parking and side-marker lamps, bright-trimmed Wideside taillights and Sierra Grande nameplates. Models with dual-rear wheels had clearance lamps.

The High Sierra option was available for regular cab models only. Its interior included all trim items from the Sierra Grande plus door trim panels with simulated chestnut woodgrain inserts and storage pockets, color-keyed carpeting headliner and garnish moldings, added floor insulation, and High Sierra nameplate on instrument panel. The High Sierra exterior added these items to the Sierra Grande level: Bright cab back panel applique molding, bright upper body side and tailgate moldings on Fleetsides, Wideside tailgate applique and High Sierra nameplates.

The top-of-the-line Sierra Classic Package included all High Sierra items when ordered for a regular cab. When specified for crew cab and bonus cab models it began with these items from the Sierra Grande Package. In addition, these items were included: Full-gauge instrumentation in a simulated chestnut woodgrain panel, full-door trim panels with bright trim and color-keyed carpeting on lower section, full cowl trim panels and Sierra Classic instrument panel nameplate. Crew cabs and bonus cab versions were offered in a choice of custom cloth and vinyl or custom all-vinyl seat trim and cut-pile carpeting. The Sierra Classic exterior incorpo-rated High Sierra items for the regular cabs or the Sierra Grande Package for crew and bonus cabs plus bright upper and lower body side and tailgate moldings, wheel opening moldings, full tailgate applique, bright cab back panel applique molding and Sierra Classic nameplates.

The color selection for 1977 consisted of fifteen choices: Mariner blue, cordova brown, Saratoga silver, light blue, cardinal red, buckskin, holly green, russet metallic, Hawaiian blue, Santa Fe tan, mahogany, red metallic, colonial yellow, frost white and seamist green.

1977 GMC K-3500 crew cab

I.D. DATA: Unchanged from 1976 except the number 7 represented the 1977 model year. The letter U identified trucks with the 400 cu. in. V-8.

Model Number	Body Type	Factory Price	GVW	Shipping Weight	Prod. Total
Series K-1500-1/2 ton 250 6-cyl. 117.5 in., 131.5 in. wheelbase (Suburban: 129.5 in. wheelbase and standard 305 V-8)					
TK10703	Chassis and Cab	$5216	6200	3618[1]	—
TK10703	6.5 ft. F-S Pickup	$5222	6200	3952	—
TK10703	6.5 ft. Wideside Pickup	$5222	6200	4012	—
TK10903	8 ft. Fenderside Pickup	$5272	6200	4539	—
TK10903	8 ft. Wideside Pickup	$5272	6200	4539	—
TK10906	Suburban Panel Drs.	$N.A.	6200	4682	—
TK10906	Suburban Endgate	$6379	6200	—	—

NOTE 1: Weights are for models with V-8 engines.

Model Number	Body Type	Factory Price	GVW	Shipping Weight	Prod. Total
Series K-2500-3/4 ton 350 V-8. 131.5 in. wheelbase. (Suburban-129.5 in. wheelbase), Crew and Bonus Cab: 164.5 in. wheelbase, Suburban weight with standard 305 V-8					
TK20903	Chassis and Cab	$5475	6800*	4131[1]	—
TK20903	8 ft. Fenderside Pickup	$5700	6800	4520	—
TK20903	8 ft. Wideside Pickup	$5700	6800	4611	—
TK20943	Chassis & Bonus Cab	$6122	6800	4633	—
TK20943	Fleetside Bonus Cab	$6347	6800	5740	—
TK20943	Chassis & Crew Cab	$6496	6800	5889	—
TK20943	Fleetside Crew Cab	$6721	6800	5349	—
TK20906	Suburban Panel drs.	$N.A.	6800	5140	—
TK20906	Suburban Endgate	$6851	—	—	—

NOTE 1: Weights are for models with V-8 engines.
* Up to 8400 lb. GVW optional.

Model Number	Body Type	Factory Price	GVW	Shipping Weight	Prod. Total
Series K-3500-1 ton 350 V-8. 131.5 in. wheelbase, Crew and Bonus Cab: 164.5 in. wheelbase					
CK30903	Chassis & Cab	$6657	6600*	3803	—
CK30903	8 ft. Fenderside Pickup	$6882	6600	4192	—
CK30903	8 ft. Wideside Pickup	$6882	6600	4283	—
CK30903	Chassis & Bonus Cab	$7588	6600	4444	—
CK30903	Fleetside Bonus Cab	$7813	6600	4924	—
CK30943	Chassis & Crew Cab	$7698	6600	5475	—
CK30943	Fleetside Crew Cab	$7923	6600	5015	—

* GVW up to 10,000 lb. optional.

STANDARD ENGINE: All K-1500 6-cyl. models: 250 Six (LD4 ordering code) Not available for California where a 350 V-8 is installed. Engine Type: OHV, In-line 6-cylinder. Cast iron block and cylinder head. Key features induction hardened exhaust valve seas, and timing tabs. Bore x Stroke: 3.875 in. x 3.53 in. Lifters: Hydraulic. Number of main bearings-7. Fuel Induction: Single Rochester 1-bbl. carburetor. Compression Ratio: 8.0:1. Displacement: 250 cu. in. (4.09 liters). Horsepower: Net: 100 @ 3600 rpm. Torque: Net: 175 lb.-ft. @ 1800 rpm. Oil refill capacity: 5 qt. with filter change. Fuel Requirements: Regular.

STANDARD ENGINE: K-2500 and K-3500 6-cyl. models: 292 Six. Ordering Code: L25. Engine Type: OHV, 6-cyl. Cast iron block and cylinder head. Key features include cast iron intake manifold, aluminized-face intake valves, Stellite-faced exhaust valves with hardened faces. Bore x Stroke: 3.875 in. x 4.125 in. Lifters: Hydraulic. Number of main bearings-7. Fuel Induction: Single Rochester 1-bbl. carburetor. Compression Ratio: 8.0:1. Displacement: 292 cu. in. (4.78 liters). Horsepower: Net: 120 @ 3600 rpm. Torque: Net: 215 lb.-ft. @ 2000 rpm. Oil refill capacity: 6 qt. with filter change. Fuel Requirements: Regular.

STANDARD ENGINE: K-2500 and K-3500 V-8 models: Ordering Code: LS9: 350 V-8 Engine Type: OHV, V-8. Cast iron block and alloy iron cylinder head. Key features include chain drive camshaft and forged steel connecting rods. Bore x Stroke: 4.0 in. x 3.50 in. Lifters: Hydraulic. Number of main bearings-5. Fuel Induction: Single Rochester 4-bbl. carburetor. Compression Ratio: 8.5:1. Displacement: 350 cu. in. (5.73 liters). Horsepower: Net: 165 @ 3800 rpm. Torque: Net: 255 lb.-ft. @ 2800 rpm. Oil refill capacity: 5 qt. with filter change. Fuel Require-ments: Regular.

OPTIONAL ENGINE: K-2500 and K-3500 V-8 models: Ordering Code: LF4: 400 V-8. Key features include induction-hardened valve seats and cast iron camshaft. Engine Type: OHV, V-8. Cast iron block and alloy iron cylinder head. Bore x Stroke: 4.10 in. x 3.8 in. Lifters: Hydraulic. Number of main bearings-5. Fuel Induction: Single Rochester 4-bbl. carburetor. Compression Ratio: 8.5:1. Displacement: 400 cu. in. (6.55 liters). Horsepower: Net: 175 @ 3600 rpm. Torque: Net: 290 lb.-ft. @ 2800 rpm. Oil refill capacity: 5 qt. with filter change. Fuel Requirements: Regular.

STANDARD ENGINE: K-1500 and K-2500 V-8 Suburban models: Ordering Code: LG9 305 V-8. Not available in California. Engine Type: OHV, V-8. Cast iron block and alloy iron cylinder head. Bore x Stroke: 3.74 in. x 3.48 in. Lifters: Hydraulic. Number of main bearings-5. Fuel Induction: Single Rochester 2-bbl. carburetor. Compression Ratio: 8.5:1. Displacement: 305 cu. in. (4.997 liters). Horsepower: Net: 145 @ 3800 rpm. Torque: Net: 245 lb.-ft. @ 2400 rpm. Oil refill capacity: 5 qt. with filter change. Fuel Requirements: Regular.

CHASSIS FEATURES: Separate body and frame with channel side rails. Carbon-Steel, 39,000 psi. 117.5 in. wheelbase: 2.30 in. x 5.92 in. x 0.156 in. Section modulus: 3.06 in. 129.5 in.: 2.30 in. x 5.92 in. x 0.194. Section modulus: 3.93. 135.5 in. wheelbase: 2.78 in. x 7.74 in.

0.194 in. Section modulus: 6.20. 164.5 in. wheelbase: 2.78 in. x 7.74 in. x 0.224 in. Section modulus: 7.33. 131.5 in. wheelbase: 2.30 in. x 5.92 in. x 0.194 in. Section modulus: 3.84 in. Optional: None.

SUSPENSION AND RUNNING GEAR: Front Suspension: K-1500: Tapered 2-leaf springs. Capacity: 1650 lb. (16), 1850 lb. (03, 06). K15: Tapered 2-leaf springs. Capacity: 1850 lb. K350: Tapered 3-leaf springs. Capacity: 2250 lb. Optional rating: K-1500 and K-2500: 2250 lb. Rear Suspension: K-1500 and K-2500: 52 in. x 2.25 in. Two-stage, 7-leaf. K-3500: 56 in. x 2.50 in. Capacity: K-1500: 2075 lb. K-2500: 2800 lb. K-3500: 3500 lb. 1.0 in. dia. shock absorbers. Optional Rating: K-3500: 3750 lb. Front Axle Type and Capacity: K-1500 and K-2500: GMC or Spicer, K35: Spicer. K-1500: Semi-floating. 3600 lb. capacity. Optional: None. K-2500: Full-floating, 3800 lb. capacity. K-3500: Full-floating, 4500 lb. Optional: None. Rear Axle Type and Capacity: K-1500: Chevrolet, semi-floating, 3750 lb. capacity. K-2500: Chevrolet, full-floating, 5700 lb. K-3500: 7500 lb. Optional: None. Final Drive Ratio: Standard: K-1500: 4.11:1; K-2500 and K-3500: 4.10:1. Optional: K-1500: 2.76, 3.07, 3.73, 4.11:1. Transfer Case: Manual transmission models: New Process 205. Single lever, two-speed: 1.96, 1.00:1. Automatic transmission models: New Process 203. Ratios: 2.01:1, 1.0:1. Brakes: Type: Hydraulic, power assisted. Dimensions: K-1500: Front: Disc: 11.86 in. x 1.28 in. Rear: Drums: 11.15 x 2.75 in. K-2500: Front: Disc: 12.5 in. x 1.28 in. Rear: Drums: 11.15 in. x 2.75 in. Optional: K-2500 (all models including Suburban) (standard with 7500-8400 GVW): Heavy-duty brakes: Front: Disc: 12.50 in. x 1.28 in. Rear: Drums: 13.00 in. x 2.50 in. K-3500: Front: Disc: 121.50 in. x 1.53 in. Rear: Drum: 13.00 in. x 3.50 in. Wheels: K-1500: 15 x 6.0JJ 6-stud disc. Optional: 15 x 8JJ. K-2500: 16.5 x 6.00 in. 8-stud disc. Optional: 16.5 x 6.75. K-3500: 16.5 x 6.75. Tires: K-1500: L78 x 15B. K-2500: 8.75 x 16.5C K-3500: 9.50 x 16.5D. Optional: K-1500: G78 x 15B, white stripe; H78 x 15B, tubeless, black sidewall or white stripe; L78 x 15B black sidewall or white stripe, tubeless; 10.00 x 16.5C tubeless; G78 x 15B tube-type; 7.00 x 15C tube-type; 6.50 x 16C tube-type and LR78 x 15C white sidewall radial ply. The following tires were specified for K-1500 models with the 5600 lb. GVW Package which included a front heavy-duty stabilizer bar: H78 x 15B 4-ply rating, tubeless; 6.50 x 16C 6-ply rating, tube-type, truck type. The following tires were specified for K-1500 models with the 6000 lb. GVW Package which included a front heavy-duty stabilizer bar and heavy-duty rear springs: L78 x 15B 4-ply rating, tubeless. Optional K-2500: 8.75 x 16.5D tubeless; 9.50 x 16.5D tubeless; 10.00 x 16.5C tubeless (not available for Fenderside models); 7.50 x 16C 6-ply rating, tube-type; 7.50 x 16D tube-type; 7.50 x 16E tube-type. The following tires were specified for K-2500 models with the 7500 lb. GVW Package which included a front heavy-duty stabilizer bar: 8.75 x 16.5 C 6-ply rating, tubeless; 7.50 x 16C 6-ply rating, tubeless. The following tires were specified for K-2500 models with the 8200 lb. GVW Package which included a front heavy-duty stabilizer bar: 9.50 x 16.5D 8-ply rating, tubeless; 7.50 x 16C 6-ply rating, tube-type. Steering: Recirculating ball gear. Ratio: 20:1. Turning Circle: 47 ft. Steering wheel diameter: 17.5 in. Optional: Power-assisted. Ratio: 16.4:1. Transmission: K-1500 and K-2500: 3-speed, synchromesh manual (RPO M15). Transmission Ratios: 2.85, 1.68, 1.00:1. Optional: CH465. 4-speed manual synchromesh (RPO M20). Ratios: 6.55, 3.58, 1.70, 1.00:1. Reverse: 6.09:1. The K-2500 crew cab and all K-3500 models had this transmission as standard equipment. Optional: 3-speed Turbo Hydra-Matic 400 (RPO M40). Ratios: 2.1 x 2.48, 1.48, 1.00:1. Reverse: 2.10:1. The 400 cu. in. V-8 was available only with this transmission. Clutch: Diaphragm, spring. Clutch diameter: 6-cyl.: 11 in. dia. Total lining area: 123.5 sq. in. Total plate pressure: 2075 lb. V-8: 12 in. dia. Total lining area: 149.2 sq. in. Total plate pressure: 2060 lb. Optional: K-2500 6-cyl.: 11 in. dia. Total lining area: 124.0 sq. in. 307 V-8: 12 in. dia. Total lining area: 150 sq. in.

VEHICLE DIMENSIONS: Wheelbase: K-1500: 117.5 in., 131.5 in. K-2500: 131.5 in. All Suburbans and Panels: 129.5 in. K-3500: 131.5 in. 164.5 in. Overall Length: 117.5 in. Wideside pickups: 191.30 in. 131.5 in. Wideside pickups: 212.00. 117.5 in. Fenderside pickups: 190.5 in. 131.5 in. Fenderside pickups: 210.25. 117.5 in. Chassis-cab: 186.05 in. K-3500 data: 164.5 in. wheelbase: 244.43 in. Front/Rear Tread: 67.4 in./65.8 in. Overall Height: K-1500 Wideside pickup: 72.0 in. K-2500 Wideside pickup: 74.0 in. K-3500 Wideside pickup: 74.0 in. K-3500 Crew Cab: 75.0 in. K-1500 Suburban: 73.5 in. K-2500 Suburban: 75.5 in. Width: Pickup: 79.5 in. Front/Rear Overhang: Pickups: 33 in./41 in. Tailgate: Width and Height: 72 in. x 19.25 in. Approach/Departure Degrees: K-1500 117.5 in. Wideside and Fenderside: 33/19. K-1500 131.5 in. Wideside: 33/15. K-1500 131.5 in. wheelbase Fenderside: 33/16. K-2500 131.5 in. wheelbase Wideside: 35/20. K-2500 131.5 in. wheelbase Fenderside: 35/21. K-3500 Wideside pickup: 41/19. K-3500 crew cab pickup: 38/18. Ground Clearance: Front axle: 7.25 in. Rear axle: 7.0 in. Oil pan: 16.5 in. Transfer case: 12.0 in. Fuel tank: 16.6 in. Load space: Pickup box dimensions: 117.5 in. wheelbase Wideside: 78.25 in. x 50 in. x 19.25 in. 131.5 in. wheelbase Wideside: 98 in. x 50 in. x 19.25 in. Capacity: 117.5 wheelbase: 58.4 cu. ft. 131.5 in. wheelbase: 74.3 cu. ft. 117.5 in. wheelbase Fenderside: 78.5 in. x 50 in. x 17.5 in. 131.5 in. wheelbase Fenderside: 96.25 in. x 50 in. x 17.5 in. Front headroom: 38.5 in. (seat to top of cab). Front hip room: 67.25 in. Pedal to seat back (max.): 43.5 in. Steering wheel to seat back (max.): 17.3 in. Seat to ground: 35.0 in. Floor to ground: 23.0 in.

CAPACITIES: Fuel Tank: 117.5 in. wheelbase: 16.0 gal. 131.5 in. wheelbase: 20.0 gal. 164.5 in.: 20 gal. Optional: 17 gal. auxiliary tank for 117.5 in. 20 gal. auxiliary for 131.5 in. and 164.5 in. wheelbase. Engine coolant system: 250 6-cyl.: 14.8 qt. 305 V-8: 17.6 qt. 350 V-8: 17.6 qt. 400 V-8: 19.6 qt. (20 qt. on K-2500 and K-3500).

ACCOMMODATIONS: Seating Capacity: Pickup and chassis cab models: 3 passenger. Optional: None. Suburban: 3 passenger. Optional: 6 or 9 passenger.

INSTRUMENTATION: Speedometer, odometer, fuel level gauge. Warning lights for battery, oil pressure, generator, brake system warning, directional/hazard lights, high beam, and engine coolant temperature.

OPTIONS AND PRICES: 350 V-8: $210 above base 250 engine. Variable ratio power steering: $188. Heavy-duty vacuum power brakes (K-2500 only): $53. ComforTilt steering wheel. Turbo Hydra-Matic: $315. Below eye-level mirrors. Gauge Package. Includes voltmeter, oil pressure and engine coolant temperature gauges; available with either tachometer or clock. All-Weather air conditioning: $509. Deluxe chromed bumpers. Chrome front bumper guards with impact stripes. Delco Freedom battery. Heavy-duty battery: $31. Auxiliary battery: $88. Heavy-duty radiator: $34.Stainless steel wheelcovers (K-1500 only). Bright metal hubcaps (K-1500 only). Exterior Decor Package. Cold Climate Package: $120 for K-1500, K-2500 picks with base trim. Prices for vehicles with other trim levels and equipment range from $89 to $129. Speed and cruise control: $80. Sierra Grande Package: $236 (for Fenderside pickups with base equipment). Other prices depend upon model, dual or single rear wheels and installation of bucket seats. Sierra Classic Package: $431. (for Fenderside pickups with base equipment). Other prices depend upon model, dual or single rear wheels and installation of bucket seats. High Sierra Package: $350 (for Fenderside pickups with base equipment). Other prices depend upon model, dual or single rear wheels and installation of bucket seats. Operating Convenience Group: $206. Knit vinyl bench seat: $38. Custom vinyl bench seat bonus cab: $38; crew cab: $76. Fuel tank shield plate. Transfer case shield plate. Extra capacity fuel tank. Soft-Ray tinted glass: Pickups: $27, bonus and crew cab: $34. Special custom cloth bench seat: Bonus cab with Sierra Grande: $38; crew cab with Sierra Grande: $76. Full depth foam seat: $36. Rallye wheels. Electric clock. Two-tone paint. 61 amp alternator. Pickup box side rails. Bucket seats. Glide-out spare tire carrier. Sliding rear window: $62. Cargo area lamp. AM radio: $79. AM/FM radio: $155. Engine oil cooler. Heavy-duty front springs and shock absorbers. Heavy-duty rear springs. Heavy-duty alternator. Weight-equalizing hitch platform. Power door locks. Power windows. Color-keyed front compartment floor mats. Intermittent windshield wipers. Inside hood release. Trailer Special Package, (for K-1500 and K-2500, except for chassis and cab): $219. Includes power steering, heavy-duty battery, trailer wiring harness, rear step bumper, weight-distributing trailer hitch or ball hitch for step bumper. Camper Special Package. Specific equipment content varied with body weight. General content included camper body wiring, heavy-duty front and rear springs, heavy-duty front and rear shock absorbers, and camper special nameplate. Available only for K-2500 and K-3500; requires V-8 engine and either 4-spd. manual or Turbo Hydra-Matic transmission. Deluxe Camper Special Package. Included all camper special equipment plus Camper Tie-Down Package, Elimi-Pitch Package (includes two horizontal shock absorbers mounted between cab rear panel and pickup box, and two vertical shock absorber mounted between camper overhang and front fenders and rear stabilizer (standard on K-3500 with dual rear wheels). Wideside Sport Package. Fenderside Sport Package. Sierra Grande Package. High Sierra Package. Sierra Classic Package.

HISTORICAL FOOTNOTES: Calendar year sales of all GMC trucks for 1977 was 234,992.

1978 PICKUP & SUBURBAN

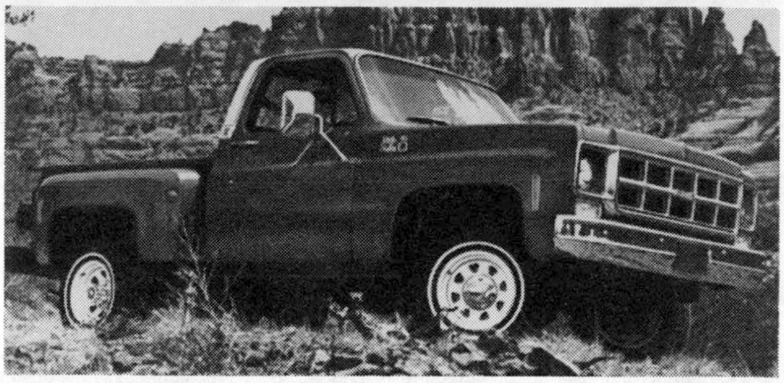

1978 GMC Fenderside with High Sierra trim and optional PA6 wheels

A major effort was applied to refurbishing the interior of the GMC trucks for 1978. Interior changes began with the instrument pad applique. For the Sierra and Sierra Grande models a black diamond-textured applique was used. A silver applique was used for the High Sierra. A bright brush-finished treatment was used for the Sierra Classic. A new brush-finished instrument cluster bezel and instrument panel applique along with a gauge-type instrument cluster comprised the new Deluxe instrument panel option, RPO BC3. It replaced RPO BC2. The windshield wiper/washer system for 1978 had an improved performance wiper motor with an integral washer pump. Because of this motor, the intermittent windshield wiper system, RPO CD4, was all-new.

All front seat safety belts systems now used a single emergency locking retractor for both the lap and shoulder belt. The rear seat lap belt retractors on crew cab models were also changed to this type.

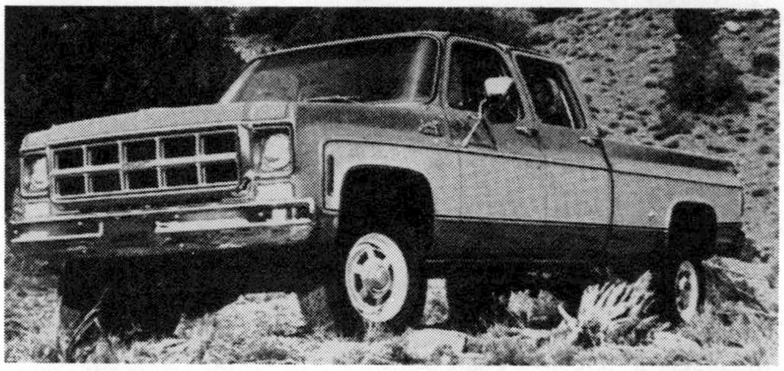

1978 GMC crew cab with Sierra Classic trim

A new hood assembly was used to meet new impact requirements. Replacing the old one-piece hood insulation was a two-piece version. In order to comply with new windshield retention requirements, a new bonded-in urethane rubber strip was used. All models also were equipped with new insulators and deadeners to reduce noise. A new drip gutter over the rear door was added as base equipment for Suburban models. Major improvements in corrosion protection were also found in the GMC trucks for 1978. Galvanized steel was used in such areas as the radiator grille lower panel and all door glass channels. Use of pre-coated steel was extended to the side outer panels and the tailgate of Wideside and Fenderside pickup boxes. The side inner panel extension on those models was redesigned to minimize entry of water and other material between the inner and outer panels. For 1978 front and rear wheel openings were available as separate options. Previously they had been part of other options. The full wheelcovers, RPO PO1, that had been available only for the K-1500 were now offered for the K-2500. The Rallye wheel option had a newly styled chromed plastic center hub. The rear hub of both the Rallye and styled wheels carried four-wheel drive identification. Optional bright metal hubcaps for the K-1500 and K-3500 were revised with the addition of extensions to the front caps which concealed the sides of the axle hub units. Door hardware for all trim levels now featured a bright brushed finish instead of the former pewter finish. The Sierra vinyl bench and bucket seat trims featured a new cover material with an oxen hide grain with a smoother texture than the former buffalo hide grain. The Sierra vinyl trim for bench-type seats also was restyled. The Sierra cloth trim for bench-type seats had new styling and new ribbed velour cloth covers. The color selection and general interior format were unchanged. The vinyl seat trim for the Sierra Grande was restyled. Also, the cover material was changed from knit to porous vinyl. The Sierra Grande color choices were unchanged.

Minor changes were made in the K series frames to accommodate a new catalytic converter exhaust system required in California. The California K series trucks with the 5.7 liter RPO LS9 and 6.6 liter RPO LF4 engines had a single exhaust system with larger diameter pipes and larger muffler, rather than a dual exhaust system. RPO dual exhausts were not available in California. All converter-equipped vehicles had new transmission supports. All two-piece propeller shafts were revised to increase center bearing cushion durability. K-2500 and K-3500 models had new rear spring U-bolts. On all models with V-8 engine and full-time four-wheel drive, struts were added between the engine and transmission, and between the transmission and transfer case to lessen the chance of driveshaft boom. Locking front hubs were not available on the K-3500 series with manual transmission. All steering column assemblies were new to incorporate metric attachments. A newly styled soft vinyl steering wheel and horn button. This wheel had a 16.0 in. diameter and replaced the 17.5 in. diameter unit previously used on K-1500 and K-2500 models. Minor instrument cluster changes involved a lens change for the PRNDL portion on automatic transmission models, and the use of an electric oil pressure gauge for RPO Z53, the Gauge Package option.

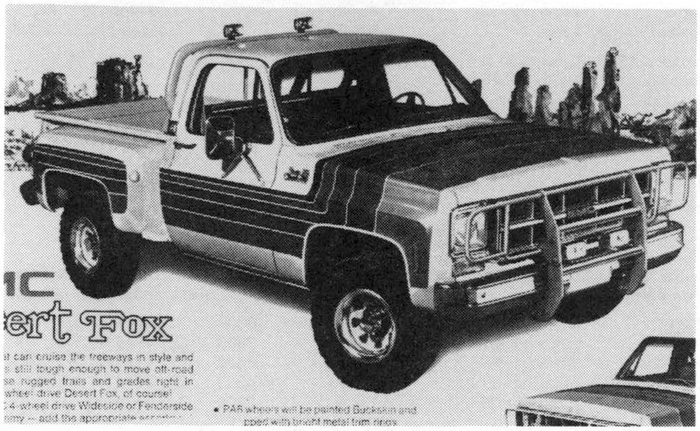

1978 GMC Fenderside with Desert Fox trim

The Wideside and Fenderside Street Coupe Packages were available after January, 1978. They were offered for K-1500 models only. Their content included multi-tone Sport decal striping (either red or gold) down the body sides, hood and tailgate, RPO V22 black painted grille with chrome trim, RPO Z62 Sierra Grande trim (without side moldings), RPO B32 color-keyed floor mats, BC3 Deluxe instrument panel, RPO U35 clock, rear bumper painted body color (Fenderside only), front bumper painted body color with impact strip, rear bumper painted body color with impact strip (Wideside only), bright hood ornament, RPO N67 Rallye wheels, and 10.00 x15B white-lettered on-off highway tires Also available as options were RPO PA6 white-spoked styled wheels, low-profile white-lettered radial LR60-15B tires and RPO PH7 15 x 7 in. aluminum wheels. The Street coupe was offered in midnight black, cardinal red, frost white or colonial yellow. All except the last color had interior trim colors of buckskin and red. The colonial white exterior had a buckskin interior trim. All fifteen exterior color choices were carried over unchanged from 1977.

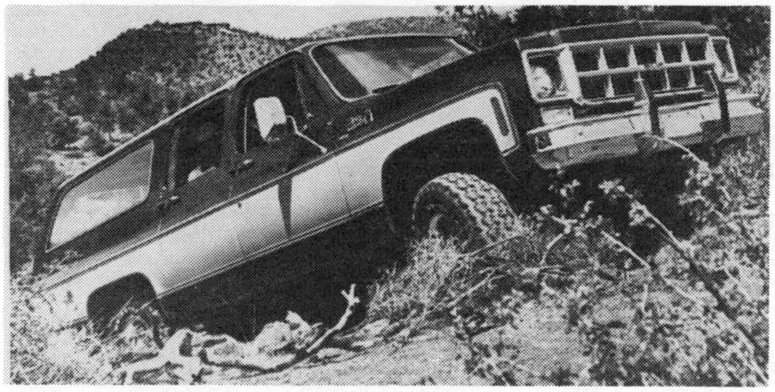

1978 GMC K-2500 Suburban

I.D. DATA: Unchanged from 1976 except the number 8 represented the 1978 model year.

Model Number	Body Type	Factory Price	GVW	Shipping Weight	Prod. Total
Series K-1500-1/2 ton 250 6-cyl. 117.5 in., 131.5 in. wheelbase (Suburban: 129.5 in. wheelbase and standard 305 V-8)					
TK10703	117.5 in. Chassis & Cab	$5006	6200	4143	—
TK10903	131.5 in. Chassis & Cab	—	6200	4250	—
TK10703	6.5 ft. F-S Pickup	$5006	6200	4477	—
TK10703	6.5 ft. Wideside Pickup	$5006	6200	4537	—
TK10903	8 ft. Fenderside Pickup	$5062	6200	4639	—
TK10903	8 ft. Wideside Pickup	$5062	6200	4720	—
TK10906	Suburban Endgate	$6348	6200	5273	—
TK10906	Suburban Pnl. Drs.	—	6200	5235	—
Series K-2500-3/4 ton 292 V-8[1]. 131.5 in. wheelbase. (Suburban-129.5 in. wheelbase), Crew and Bonus Cab: 164.5 in. wheelbase, Suburban weight with standard 305 V-8					
TK20903	Chassis and Cab	$5209	6800*	4485	—
TK20903	8 ft. Fenderside Pickup	$5434	6800	4874	—
TK20903	8 ft. Wideside Pickup	$5434	6800	4955	—
TK20906	Suburban Endgate	$6795	6800	5472	—
TK20906	Suburban Pnl. Drs.	—	6800	5434	—

NOTE 1: Not available in California where the 350 engine is base.
* 7500 and 8400 lb. GVW optional.

Model Number	Body Type	Factory Price	GVW	Shipping Weight	Prod. Total
Series K-3500-1 ton 350 V-8. 131.5 in. wheelbase, Crew and Bonus Cab: 164.5 in. wheelbase					
TK31003	Chassis & Cab[1]	$5589	8400*	4956	—
TK31403	Chassis & Cab[2]	—	8490	5243	—
TK30903	8 ft. Wideside Pickup	$5814	8400	5426	—
TK30943	Chassis & Bonus Cab	$6520	8400	5370	—
TK30943	Fleetside Bonus Cab	$6745	8400	5840	—
TK30943	Chassis & Crew Cab	$6630	8400	5370	—
TK30943	Fleetside Crew Cab	$6855	8400	5840	—

NOTE 1: 135.5 in. wheelbase.
NOTE 2: 159.9 in. wheelbase.
* 9200 and 10,000 lb. GVW optional.

STANDARD ENGINE: All K-1500 6-cyl. models: 250 Six (LD4 ordering code) Not available for California where a 350 V-8 is installed. Engine Type: OHV, In-line 6-cylinder. Cast iron block and cylinder head. Key features induction hardened exhaust valve seas, and timing tabs. Bore x Stroke: 3.875 in. x 3.53 in. Lifters: Hydraulic. Number of main bearings-7. Fuel Induction: Single Rochester 1-bbl. carburetor. Compression Ratio: 8.0:1. Displacement: 250 cu. in. (4.09 liters). Horsepower: Net: 100 @ 3600 rpm. Torque: Net: 175 lb.-ft. @ 1800 rpm. Oil refill capacity: 5 qt. with filter change. Fuel Requirements: Regular.

STANDARD ENGINE: K-2500 and K-3500 6-cyl. models: 292 Six. Ordering Code: L25. Engine Type: OHV, 6-cyl. Cast iron block and cylinder head. Key features include cast iron intake manifold, aluminized-face intake valves, Stellite-faced exhaust valves with hardened faces. Bore x Stroke: 3.875 in. x 4.125 in. Lifters: Hydraulic. Number of main bearings-7. Fuel Induction: Single Rochester 1-bbl. carburetor. Compression Ratio: 8.0:1. Displacement: 292 cu. in. (4.78 liters). Horsepower: Net: 120 @ 3600 rpm. Torque: Net: 215 lb.-ft. @ 2000 rpm. Oil refill capacity: 6 qt. with filter change. Fuel Requirements: Regular.

STANDARD ENGINE: K-2500 and K-3500 V-8 models: Ordering Code: LS9: 350 V-8 Engine Type: OHV, V-8. Cast iron block and alloy iron cylinder head. Key features include chain drive camshaft and forged steel connecting rods. Bore x Stroke: 4.0 in. x 3.50 in. Lifters: Hydraulic. Number of main bearings-5. Fuel Induction: Single Rochester 4-bbl. carburetor. Compression Ratio: 8.5:1. Displacement: 350 cu. in. (5.73 liters). Horsepower: Net: 165 @ 3800 rpm. Torque: Net: 255 lb.-ft. @ 2800 rpm. Oil refill capacity: 5 qt. with filter change. Fuel Requirements: Regular.

OPTIONAL ENGINE: K-2500 and K-3500 V-8 models: Ordering Code: LF4: 400 V-8. Key features include induction-hardened valve seats and cast iron camshaft. Engine Type: OHV, V-8. Cast iron block and alloy iron cylinder head. Bore x Stroke: 4.10 in. x 3.8 in. Lifters: Hydraulic. Number of main bearings-5. Fuel Induction: Single Rochester 4-bbl. carburetor. Compression Ratio: 8.5:1. Displacement: 400 cu. in. (6.55 liters). Horsepower: Net: 175 @ 3600 rpm. Torque: Net: 290 lb.-ft. @ 2800 rpm. Oil refill capacity: 5 qt. with filter change. Fuel Requirements: Regular.

STANDARD ENGINE: K-1500 and K-2500 V-8 Suburban models: Ordering Code: LG9 305 V-8. Not available in California. Engine Type: OHV, V-8. Cast iron block and alloy iron cylinder head. Bore x Stroke: 3.74 in. x 3.48 in. Lifters: Hydraulic. Number of main bearings-5. Fuel Induction: Single Rochester 2-bbl. carburetor. Compression Ratio: 8.5:1. Displacement: 305 cu. in. (4.997 liters). Horsepower: Net: 145 @ 3800 rpm. Torque: Net: 245 lb.-ft. @ 2400 rpm. Oil refill capacity: 5 qt. with filter change. Fuel Requirements: Regular.

CHASSIS FEATURES: Separate body and frame with channel side rails. Carbon-Steel, 39,000 psi. 117.5 in. wheelbase: 2.30 in. x 5.92 in. x 0.156 in. Section modulus: 3.06 in. 129.5 in.: 2.30 in. x 5.92 in. x 0.194. Section modulus: 3.93. 135.5 in. wheelbase: 2.78 in. x 7.74 in. 0.194 in. Section modulus: 6.20. 164.5 in. wheelbase: 2.78 in. x 7.74 in. x 0.224 in. Section modulus: 7.33. 131.5 in. wheelbase: 2.30 in. x 5.92 in. x 0.194 in. Section modulus: 3.84 in. Optional: None.

SUSPENSION AND RUNNING GEAR: Front Suspension: K-1500: Tapered 2-leaf springs. Capacity: 1650 lb. (16), 1850 lb. (03, 06). K2500: Tapered 2-leaf springs. Capacity: 1850 lb. K3500: Tapered 3-leaf springs. Capacity: 2250 lb. Rear Suspension: K-1500 and K-2500: 52 in. x 2.25 in. Two-stage, 7-leaf. K-3500: 56 in. x 2.50 in. Capacity: K-1500: 2075 lb. K-2500: 2800 lb. K-3500: 3500 lb. 1.0 in. dia. shock absorbers. Optional: K-3500: 3750 lb. capacity. Front Axle Type and Capacity: K-1500 and K-2500: GMC or Spicer, K35: Spicer. K-1500: Semi-floating. 3600 lb. capacity. Optional: None. K-2500: Full-floating, 3800 lb. capacity. K-3500: Full-floating, 4500 lb. Optional: None. Rear Axle Type and Capacity: K-1500: Semi-floating, 3750 lb. capacity. K-2500: Full-floating, 5700 lb. K-3500: 7500 lb. Optional: None. Final Drive Ratio: Standard: K-1500: 4.11:1; K-2500 and K-3500: 4.10:1. Optional: K-1500: 2.76, 3.07, 3.73, 4.11:1. Transfer Case: Manual Transmission models: New Process 205. Single lever, two-speed: 1.96, 1.00:1. Automatic transmission models: New Process 203. Ratios: 2.01:1, 1.0:1. Brakes: Type: Hydraulic, power assisted. Dimensions: K-1500: Front: Disc: 11.86 in. x 1.28 in. Rear: Drums: 11.15 x 2.75 in. K-2500: Front: Disc: 12.5 in. x 1.28 in. Rear: Drums: 11.15 in. x 2.75 in. Optional: K-2500 (all models including Suburban) (standard with 7500-8400 GVW): Heavy-duty brakes: Front: Disc: 12.50 in. x 1.28 in. Rear: Drums: 13.00 in. x 2.50 in. K-3500: Front: Disc: 121.50 in. x 1.53 in. Rear: Drum: 13.00 in. x 3.50 in. Wheels: K-1500: 15 x 6.0JJ 6-stud disc. Optional: 15 x 8JJ. K-2500: 16.5 x 6.00 in. 8-stud disc. Optional: 16.5 x 6.75. K-3500: 16.5 x 6.75. Tires: K-1500: L78 x 15B. K-2500: 8.75 x 16.5C K-3500: 9.50 x 16.5D. Optional: K-1500: G78 x 15B, white stripe; H78 x 15B, tubeless, black sidewall or white stripe; L78 x 15B black sidewall or white stripe, tubeless; 10.00 x 16.5C tubeless; G78 x 15B tube-type; 7.00 x 15C tube-type; 6.50 x 16C tube-type and LR78 x 15C white sidewall radial ply. The following tires were specified for K-1500 models with the 5600 lb. GVW Package which included a front heavy-duty stabilizer bar: H78 x 15B 4-ply rating, tubeless; 6.50 x 16C 6-ply rating, tube-type, truck type. The following tires were specified for K-1500 models with the 6000 lb. GVW Package which included a front heavy-duty stabilizer bar and heavy-duty rear springs: L78 x 15B 4-ply rating, tubeless. Optional K-2500: 8.75 x 16.5D tubeless; 9.50 x 16.5D tubeless; 10.00 x 16.5C tubeless (not available for Fenderside models); 7.50 x 16C 6-ply rating, tube-type; 7.50 x 16D tube-type; 7.50 x 16E tube-type. The following tires were specified for K-2500 models with the 7500 lb. GVW Package which included a front heavy-duty stabilizer bar: 8.75 x 16.5 C 6-ply rating, tubeless; 7.50 x 16C 6-ply rating, tubeless. The following tires were specified for K-2500 models with the 8200 lb. GVW Package which included a front heavy-duty stabilizer bar: 9.50 x 16.5D 8-ply rating, tubeless; 7.50 x 16C 6-ply rating, tube-type. Steering: Recirculating ball gear. Ratio: 20:1. Turning Circle: 47 ft. Steering wheel diameter: 17.5 in. Optional: Power-assisted. Ratio: 16.4:1. Transmission: K-1500 and K-2500: 3-speed, synchromesh manual (RPO M15). Transmission Ratios: 2.85, 1.68, 1.00:1. Optional: CH465. 4-speed manual synchromesh (RPO M20). Ratios: 6.55, 3.58, 1.70, 1.00:1. Reverse: 6.09:1. The K-2500 crew cab and all K-3500 models had this transmission as standard equipment. Optional: 3-speed Turbo Hydra-Matic 400 (RPO M40). Ratios: 2.1 x 2.48, 1.48, 1.00:1. Reverse: 2.10:1. The 400 cu. in. V-8 was available only with this transmission. Clutch: Diaphragm, spring. Clutch diameter: 6-cyl.: 11 in. dia. Total lining area: 123.5 sq. in. Total plate pressure: 2075 lb. V-8: 12 in. dia. Total lining area: 149.2 sq. in. Total plate pressure: 2060 lb. Optional: K-2500 6-cyl.: 11 in. dia. Total lining area: 124.0 sq. in. 307 V-8: 12 in. dia. Total lining area: 150 sq. in.

VEHICLE DIMENSIONS: Series K-1500 and K-2500: Wheelbase: K-1500: 117.5 in. 131.5 in. K-2500: 131.5 in. All Suburbans and Panels: 129.5 in. K-3500: 131.5 in. 164.5 in. Overall Length: 117.5 in. Wideside pickups: 191.30 in. 131.5 in. Wideside pickups: 212.00. 117.5 in. Fenderside pickups: 190.5 in. 131.5 in. Fenderside pickups: 210.25. 117.5 in. Chassis-cab: 186.05 in. K-3500 data: 164.5 in. wheelbase: 244.43 in. Front/Rear Tread: 67.4 in./65.8 in. Overall Height: K-1500 Wideside pickup: 72.0 in. K-2500 Wideside pickup: 74.0 in. K-3500 Wideside pickup: 74.0 in. K-3500 crew cab: 75.0 in. K-1500 Suburban: 73.5 in. K-2500 Suburban: 75.5 in. Width: Pickup: 79.5 in. Front/Rear Overhang: Pickups: 33 in./41 in. Tailgate: Width and Height: 72 in. x 19.25 in. Approach/Departure Degrees: K-1500 117.5 in. Wideside and Fenderside: 33/19. K-1500 131.5 in. Wideside: 33/15. K-1500 131.5 in. wheelbase Fenderside: 33/16. K-2500 131.5 in. wheelbase Wideside: 35/20. K-2500 131.5 in. wheelbase Fenderside: 35/21. K-3500 Wideside pickup: 41/19. K-3500 crew cab pickup: 38/18. Ground Clearance: Front axle: 7.25 in. Rear axle: 7.0 in. Oil pan: 16.5 in. Transfer case: 12.0 in. Fuel tank: 16.6 in. Load space: Pickup box dimensions: 117.5 in. wheelbase Wideside: 78.25 in. x 50 in. x 19.25 in. 131.5 in. wheelbase Wideside: 98 in. x 50 in. x 19.25 in. Capacity: 117.5 wheelbase: 58.4 cu. ft. 131.5 in. wheelbase: 74.3 cu. ft. 117.5 in. wheelbase Fenderside: 78.5 in. x 50 in. x 17.5 in. 131.5 in. wheelbase Fenderside: 96.25 in. x 50 in. x 17.5 in. Front headroom: 38.5 in. (seat to top of cab). Front hip room: 67.25 in. Pedal to seat back (max.): 43.5 in. Steering wheel to seat back (max.): 17.3 in. Seat to ground: 35.0 in. Floor to ground: 23.0 in.

CAPACITIES: Fuel Tank: 117.5 in. wheelbase: 16.0 gal. 131.5 in. wheelbase: 20.0 gal. 164.5 in.: 20 gal. Optional: 17 gal. auxiliary tank. for 117.5 in.; 20 gal. auxiliary for 131.5 in. and 164.5 in. wheelbase. Engine coolant system: 250 6-cyl.: 14.8 qt. 305 V-8: 17.6 qt. 350 V-8: 17.6 qt. 400 V-8: 19.6 qt. (20 qt. on K-2500 and K-3500).

ACCOMMODATIONS: Seating Capacity: Pickup and chassis cab models: 3 passenger. Optional: None. Suburban: 3 passenger. Optional: 6 or 9 passenger.

INSTRUMENTATION: Speedometer, odometer, fuel level gauge. Warning lights for battery, oil pressure, generator, brake system warning, directional/hazard lights, high beam, and engine coolant temperature.

OPTIONS AND PRICES: Power steering (K-1500 and K-2500; standard with Trailering Special option. (RPO N41): $187. 350 V-8 (RPO LS9): $300. 400 V-8 (RPO LF4): $465. 4-speed manual synchromesh (RPO MM4): $152.Turbo Hydra-Matic (RPO MX1): $345. Poly-Wrap air cleaner (RPO K43). Air conditioning (RPO C60). Locking rear differential (RPO G80): $175. Auxiliary 3500 watt Delco Freedom battery (RPO TP2). Heavy-duty 4000 watt Delco freedom battery (RPO UA1). Painted rear bumper (RPO V38). Rear step bumper (RPO V43). Front and rear chromed bumpers (RPO V37). Front chrome bumper (RPO V46). Rear chrome bumper (RPO VF1). Rear step bumper-Wideside only (RPO V42). Front and rear deluxe chromed bumpers-Wideside only (RPO VE5). Front deluxe chromed bumper (RPO VG3). Chromed front bumper guards (RPO V31). Glide-out spare wheel carrier (RPO P11). Side-mounted spare wheel carrier (RPO P13). Chevy Sport Package (RPO Z77). Electric clock (RPO U35). Cold Climate Package includes UA1 battery and K76 generator. (RPO Z56). Engine oil cooler. Available for V-8 engines only (RPO KC4). Transmission oil cooler. Available for V-8 engines and auto. trans. only. (RPO VO2). Heavy-duty radiator (RPO VO1). Power door locks (RPO AU3). California emission system (RPO YF5). Dual exhaust system. Requires LS9 (RPO N10). Color-keyed floor mats (RPO B32). Wood pickup box, CK10903 Wideside only (RPO E81). Gauge Package. Includes voltmeter, engine coolant temperature and oil pressure (RPO Z53): $27. Tachometer. Requires V-8 engine. (RPO U16): $87, with Sierra Classic option: $60. 61 amp Delcotron alternator (RPO K76). Soft-Ray tinted glass, all windows (RPO AO1). Chrome grille (RPO V22). Camper body wiring harness (RPO UY1). Headlight warning buzzer (RPO T63). Inside hood lock release (RPO T44). Deluxe instrument panel (RPO BC3). Cargo area lamp (RPO UF2). Dome lamp (RPO C91). Roof marker lights (RPO UO1). Cigarette lighter (RPO U37). Below eye-level painted 7.5 in. x 10.5 in. mirrors (RPO D29). Below eye-level stainless steel 7.5 in. x 10.5 in. mirrors (RPO DG4). Camper-type below eye-level mirrors (RPO DFG4). Body side spear molding, Wideside only (RPO B84). Body upper moldings, Wideside only (RPO B85). Body side upper and lower moldings, Wideside only (RPO YG1). Door edge guard (RPO B93). Wheel opening moldings, Wideside only (RPO B96). Operating Convenience Package. Includes AU3 door locks and A31 windows. (RPO ZQ2). Fuel tank shield (RPO NY1). AM push-button radio (RPO U63). AM/FM push-button radio (RPO U69). Folding seat back (RPO AN1). Full-depth foam seat (RPO Z52). Pickup box side rails (RPO D73). Speed and cruise control (RPO K-3500). Heavy-duty front springs. Includes heavy-duty front and rear shock absorbers. Recommended for snowplow type usage only on K-1500. (RPO F60): $67. ComforTilt steering wheel (RPO N33). Custom steering wheel (RPO N31). Red exterior stripe (RPO 71A). Auxiliary fuel tank (RPO NL2): $150. Two front towing hooks (RPO V76). Weight distributing platform type trailer hitch (RPO VR4). Trailering Special Package. Includes UA1 battery and K76 generator. (RPO Z82). Bright metal hubcaps (RPO PO3). Trim rings (RPO PO6). Wheelcovers (RPO PO1). Special wheelcovers (RPO PA1). Spare dual wheel, K-3500 only (RPO QE2 or QE6 depending upon tire size). Dual rear wheels, K-3500 only (RPO RO5). Single rear wheels, K-3500 only (RPO ZW3). Aluminum wheels, K-1500 only. (RPO PH7). Rallye wheels, K-1500 only. (RPO N67). Styled wheels, K-1500 only. (RPO PA6). Power windows (RPO A31). Sliding rear window (RPO A28). Intermittent windshield wipers (RPO CD4). Heavy-duty vacuum brakes, K-2500 only. (RPO J55). Basic Camper Group, K-2500 and K-3500 only. Includes F60 springs and UY1 harness. (RPO Z81). Deluxe Camper Group, K-2500 and K-3500 only. (RPO Z83). Frame mounted spare wheel carrier, K-3500 only (RPO P10). Senior West Coast type painted mirrors, K-3500 only (RPO DG5). Heavy-duty front and rear shock absorbers (RPO F51). Conventional two-tone paint (RPO ZY2). Special two-tone paint, Wideside only (RPO ZY3). Deluxe two-tone paint, Wideside only (RPO XY4). Exterior Decor Package, Wideside only. Includes YG1 and B96 moldings, hood ornament and hood accent stripes (RPO ZY5).

HISTORICAL FOOTNOTES: Model year sales of all GMC truck series was 283, 540.

1979 PICKUP & SUBURBAN

For 1979 the GMC trucks featured a front-end appearance with new integral head/parking lamp bezels and new lower grille outline molding of bright metal. A new color treatment for the grille was also evident. The hood had a reshaped form resulting in improved aerodynamics. Additional new features included new exterior and interior colors, and a new concealed fuel filler. The 250 6-cylinder engine had a new staged 2-barrel carburetor, new cylinder head with improved porting, and a new dual takedown exhaust system. These changes improved the engine's horsepower output. The 1979 exterior color selection consisted of white, silver metallic, dark bright blue, medium blue, dark blue, medium green metallic, bright green metallic, dark green, yellow, neutral, camel metallic, dark carmine, bright red, russet metallic, dark brown metallic, dark yellow, charcoal and black.

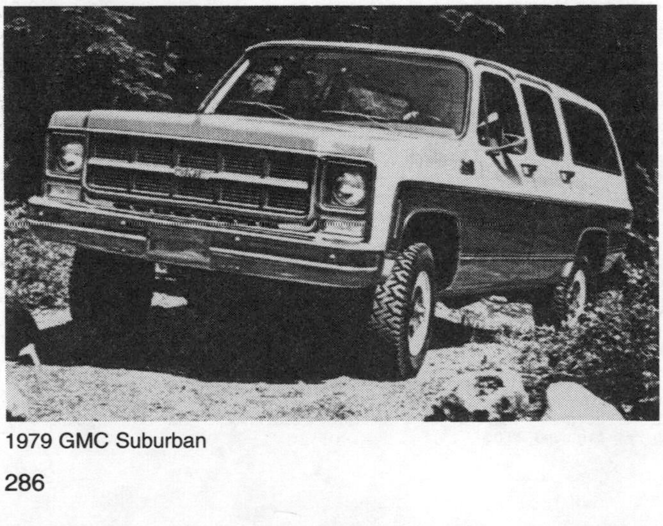

1979 GMC Suburban

I.D. DATA: The vehicle identification number was located on a plate in the lower left side of the windshield. It had 13 units. The first, the letter T, represented the GMC division code. The second entry, the letter K, indicated four-wheel drive. The third letter represented the engine as follows: D-250 6-cyl., L-350 V-8, R-400 V-8, T-292 6-cyl. The fourth entry, a digit, indicated the series: 1-GMC 15,2-GMC 25, 3-GMC 35. The fifth digit identified the body type: 3-Chassis and cab, 4-Pickup, 6-Suburban. The sixth digit, a 9, indicated the 1979 model year. The seventh digit represented the assembly plant. The eighth through thirteenth digit was the assembly sequence number.

Model Number	Body Type	Factory Price	GVW	Shipping Weight	Prod. Total
Series K-1500-1/2 ton 250 6-cyl. 117.5 in., 131.5 in. wheelbase (Suburban: 129.5 in. wheelbase and standard 305 V-8)					
TK10703	117.5 in. Chassis & Cab	$6043	6200	4143	—
TK10903	131.5 in. Chassis & Cab	$6123	6200	4250	—
TK10703	6.5 ft. F-S Pickup	$6191	6200	4477	—
TK10703	6.5 ft. Wideside Pickup	$6191	6200	4537	—
TK10903	8 ft. Fenderside Pickup	$6271	6200	4639	—
TK10903	8 ft. Wideside Pickup	$6271	6200	4720	—
TK10906	Suburban Endgate	$7714	6200	5273	—
TK10906	Suburban Pnl. Drs.	$N.A.	6200	5235	—
Series K-2500-3/4 ton 292 V-8[1]. 131.5 in. wheelbase. (Suburban-129.5 in. wheelbase), Crew and Bonus Cab: 164.5 in. wheelbase, Suburban weight with standard 305 V-8					
TK20903	Chassis and Cab	$6557	6800*	4485	—
TK20903	8 ft. Fenderside Pickup	$6818	6800	4874	—
TK20903	8 ft. Wideside Pickup	$6818	6800	4955	—
TK20906	Suburban Endgate	$8151	6800	5472	—
TK20906	Suburban Pnl. Drs.	$N.A.	6800	5434	—

NOTE 1: Not available in California where the 350 engine is base.
* 7500 and 8400 lb. GVW optional.

Model Number	Body Type	Factory Price	GVW	Shipping Weight	Prod. Total
Series K-3500-1 ton 350 V-8. 131.5 in. wheelbase, Crew and Bonus Cab: 164.5 in. wheelbase					
TK31003	Chassis & Cab[1]	$8059	8400*	4956	—
TK31403	Chassis & Cab[2]	$N.A.	8490	5243	—
TK30903	8 ft. Wideside Pickup	$8355	8400	5426	—
TK30943	Chassis & Bonus Cab	$8858	8400	5370	—
TK30943	Wideside Bonus Cab	$9141	8400	5840	—
TK30943	Chassis & Crew Cab	$9018	8400	5370	—
TK30943	Wideside Crew Cab	$9301	8400	5840	—

NOTE 1: 135.5 in. wheelbase.
NOTE 2: 159.9 in. wheelbase.
* 9200 and 10,000 lb. GVW optional.

STANDARD ENGINE: All K-1500 6-cyl. models: 250 Six (LE3 ordering code) Engine Type: OHV, In-line 6-cylinder. Cast iron block and cylinder head. Key features induction hardened exhaust valve seats, and timing tabs. Not available for California delivery where 350 engine is standard. Bore x Stroke: 3.875 in. x 3.53 in. Lifters: Hydraulic. Number of main bearings-7. Fuel Induction: Single Rochester staged 2-bbl. carburetor. Compression Ratio: 8.3:1. Displacement: 250 cu. in. (4.09 liters). Horsepower: Net: 130 @ 4000 rpm. Torque: Net: 210 lb.-ft. @ 2000 rpm. Oil refill capacity: 5 qt. with filter change. Fuel Requirements: Regular.

STANDARD ENGINE: K-3500 6-cyl. models: 292 Six. Ordering Code: L25. Engine Type: OHV, 6-cyl. Cast iron block and cylinder head. Key features include cast iron intake manifold, aluminized-face intake valves, Stellite-faced exhaust valves with hardened faces. Bore x Stroke: 3.875 in. x 4.125 in. Lifters: Hydraulic. Number of main bearings-7. Fuel Induction: Single Rochester 1-bbl. carburetor. Compression Ratio: 7.8:1. Displacement: 292 cu. in. (4.78 liters). Horsepower: Net: 115 @ 3400 rpm. Torque: Net: 215 lb.-ft. @ 1600 rpm. Oil refill capacity: 6 qt. with filter change. Fuel Requirements: Regular.

STANDARD ENGINE: K-2500 and K-3500 V-8 models: Standard for K-2500 Suburban. Ordering Code: LS9: 350 V-8. Engine Type: OHV, V-8. Cast iron block and alloy iron cylinder head. Key features include chain drive camshaft and forged steel connecting rods. Bore x Stroke: 4.0 in. x 3.50 in. Lifters: Hydraulic. Number of main bearings-5. Fuel Induction: Single Rochester 4-bbl. carburetor. Compression Ratio: 8.2:1. (8500 lb. GVW and below), 8501 lb. and up GVW: 8.3:1. Displacement: 350 cu. in. (5.73 liters). Horsepower: Net: 165 @ 3800 rpm. California and GVW below 8500 lb. GVW: 155 @ 3600 rpm. 8501 lb. and up GVW: 165 @ 3800 rpm. Torque: Net: 8500 lb. and below, except California: 270 lb.-ft. @ 2000 rpm. 8500 lb. and below, for California: 260 lb.-ft.@ 2000 rpm.8501 lb. and up GVW: 255 lb.-ft. @ 2800 rpm. Oil refill capacity: 5 qt. with filter change. Fuel Requirements: Regular.

OPTIONAL ENGINE: K-2500 and K-3500 V-8 models: Ordering Code: LF4: 400 V-8. Key features include induction-hardened valve seats and cast iron camshaft. Engine Type: OHV, V-8. Cast iron block and alloy iron cylinder head. Bore x Stroke: 4.10 in. x 3.8 in. Lifters: Hydraulic. Number of main bearings-5. Fuel Induction: Single Rochester 4-bbl. carburetor. Compression Ratio: 8.5:1. Displacement: 400 cu. in. (6.55 liters). Horsepower: Net: 185 @ 3600 rpm. California and GVW below 8500 lb. GVW: 170 @ 3600 rpm. 8501 lb. and up GVW: 180 @ 3600 rpm. Torque: Net: 8500 lb. and below, except California: 300 lb.-ft. @ 2400 rpm. 8500 lb. and below, for California: 305 lb.-ft.@ 1600 rpm. 8501 lb. and up GVW: 310 lb.-ft. @ 2400 rpm. Oil refill capacity: 5 qt. with filter change. Fuel Requirements: Regular.

STANDARD ENGINE: K-1500 Suburban models: Ordering Code: LG9 305 V-8. Not available in California. Engine Type: OHV, V-8. Cast iron block and alloy iron cylinder head. Bore x Stroke: 3.74 in. x 3.48 in. Lifters: Hydraulic. Number of main bearings-5. Fuel Induction: Single Rochester 2-bbl. carburetor. Compression Ratio: 8.4:1. Displacement: 305 cu. in. (4.997 liters). Horsepower: Net: 140 @ 4000 rpm. Torque: Net: 240 lb.-ft. @ 2000 rpm. Oil refill capacity: 5 qt. with filter change. Fuel Requirements: Regular.

CHASSIS FEATURES: Separate body and frame with channel side rails. Carbon-Steel, 39,000 psi. 117.5 in. wheelbase: 2.30 in. x 5.92 in. x 0.156 in. Section modulus: 3.06 in. 129.5 in.: 2.30 in. x 5.92 in. x 0.194. Section modulus: 3.93. 135.5 in. wheelbase: 2.78 in. x 7.74 in. 0.194 in. Section modulus: 6.20. 164.5 in. wheelbase: 2.78 in. x 7.74 in. x 0.224 in. Section modulus: 7.33. 131.5 in. wheelbase: 2.30 in. x 5.92 in. x 0.194 in. Section modulus: 3.84 in. Optional: None.

SUSPENSION AND RUNNING GEAR: Front Suspension: K-1500: Tapered 2-leaf springs. Capacity: 1650 lb. (16), 1850 lb. (03, 06). K15: Tapered 2-leaf springs. Capacity: 1850 lb. K35: Tapered 3-leaf springs. Capacity: 2250 lb. Rear Suspension: K-1500 and K-2500: 52 in. x 2.25 in. Two-stage, 7-leaf. K-3500: 56 in. x 2.50 in. Capacity: K-1500: 2075 lb. K-2500: 2800 lb. K-3500: 3500 lb. 1.0 in. dia. shock absorbers. Optional: K-3500: 3750 lb. capacity. Front Axle Type and Capacity: K-1500 and K-2500: GMC or Spicer, K35: Spicer. K-1500: Semi-floating. 3600 lb. capacity. Optional: None. K-2500: Full-floating, 3800 lb. capacity. K-3500: Full-floating, 4500 lb. Optional: None. Rear Axle Type and Capacity: K-1500: Semi-floating, 3750 lb. capacity. K-2500: Full-floating, 5700 lb. K-3500: 7500 lb. Optional: None. Final Drive Ratio: Standard: K-1500: 4.11:1; K-2500 and K-3500: 4.10:1. Optional: K-1500: 2.76, 3.07, 3.73, 4.11:1. Transfer Case: Manual Transmission models: New Process 205. Single lever, two-speed: 1.96, 1.00:1. Automatic transmission models: New Process 203. Ratios: 2.01:1, 1.0:1. Brakes: Type: Hydraulic, power assisted. Dimensions: K-1500: Front: Disc: 11.86 in. x 1.28 in. Rear: Drums: 11.15 x 2.75 in. K-2500: Front: Disc: 12.5 in. x 1.28 in. Rear: Drums: 11.15 in. x 2.75 in. Optional: K-2500 (all models including Suburban) (standard with 7500-8400 GVW): Heavy-duty brakes: Front: Disc: 12.50 in. x 1.28 in. Rear: Drums: 13.00 in. x 2.50 in. K-3500: Front: Disc: 121.50 in. x 1.53 in. Rear: Drum: 13.00 in. x 3.50 in. Wheels: K-1500: 15 x 6.0JJ 6-stud disc. Optional: 15 x 8JJ. K-2500: 16.5 x 6.00 in. 8-stud disc. Optional: 16.5 x 6.75. K-3500: 16.5 x 6.75. Tires: K-1500: L78 x 15B. K-2500: 8.75 x 16.5C K-3500: 9.50 x 16.5D. Optional: K-1500: G78 x 15B, white stripe; H78 x 15B, tubeless, black sidewall or white stripe; L78 x 15B black sidewall or white stripe, tubeless; 10.00 x 16.5C tubeless; G78 x 15B tube-type; 7.00 x 15C tube-type; 6.50 x 16C tube-type and LR78 x 15C white sidewall radial ply. The following tires were specified for K-1500 models with the 5600 lb. GVW Package which included a front heavy-duty stabilizer bar: H78 x 15B 4-ply rating, tubeless; 6.50 x 16C 6-ply rating, tube-type, truck type. The following tires were specified for K-1500 models with the 6000 lb. GVW Package which included a front heavy-duty stabilizer bar and heavy-duty rear springs: L78 x 15B 4-ply rating, tubeless. Optional K-2500: 8.75 x 16.5D tubeless; 9.50 x 16.5D tubeless; 10.00 x 16.5C tubeless (not available for Fenderside models); 7.50 x 16C 6-ply rating, tube-type; 7.50 x 16D tube-type; 7.50 x 16E tube-type. The following tires were specified for K-2500 models with the 7500 lb. GVW Package which included a front heavy-duty stabilizer bar: 8.75 x 16.5 C 6-ply rating, tubeless; 7.50 x 16C 6-ply rating, tubeless. The following tires were specified for K-2500 models with the 8200 lb. GVW Package which included a front heavy-duty stabilizer bar: 9.50 x 16.5D 8-ply rating, tubeless; 7.50 x 16C 6-ply rating, tube-type. Steering: Recirculating ball gear. Ratio: 20:1. Turning Circle: 47 ft. Steering wheel diameter: 17.5 in. Optional: Power-assisted. Ratio: 16.4:1. Transmission: K-1500 and K-2500: 3-speed, synchromesh manual (RPO M15). Transmission Ratios: 2.85, 1.68, 1.00:1. Optional: CH465. 4-speed manual synchromesh (RPO M20). Ratios: 6.55, 3.58, 1.70, 1.00:1. Reverse: 6.09:1. The K-2500 crew cab and all K-3500 models had this transmission as standard equipment. Optional: 3-speed Turbo Hydra-Matic 400 (RPO M40). Ratios: 2.1 x 2.48, 1.48, 1.00:1. Reverse: 2.10:1. The 400 cu. in. V-8 was available only with this transmission. Clutch: Diaphragm, spring. Clutch diameter: 6-cyl.: 11 in. dia. Total lining area: 123.5 sq. in. Total plate pressure: 2075 lb. V-8: 12 in. dia. Total lining area: 149.2 sq. in. Total plate pressure: 2060 lb. Optional: K-2500 6-cyl.: 11 in. dia. Total lining area: 124.0 sq. in. 307 V-8: 12 in. dia. Total lining area: 150 sq. in.

VEHICLE DIMENSIONS: Wheelbase: K-1500: 117.5 in. 131.5 in. K-2500: 131.5 in. All Suburbans and Panels: 129.5 in. K-3500: 131.5 in. 164.5 in. Overall Length: 117.5 in. Wideside pickups: 191.30 in. 131.5 in. Wideside pickups: 212.00. 117.5 in. Fenderside pickups: 190.5 in. 131.5 in. Fenderside pickups: 210.25. 117.5 in. Chassis-cab: 186.05 in. K-3500 data: 164.5 in. wheelbase: 244.43 in. Front/Rear Tread: 67.4 in./65.8 in. Overall Height: K-1500 Wideside pickup: 72.0 in. K-2500 Wideside pickup: 74.0 in. K-3500 Wideside pickup: 74.0 in. K-3500 crew cab: 75.0 in. K-1500 Suburban: 73.5 in. K-2500 Suburban: 75.5 in. Width: Pickup: 79.5 in. Front/Rear Overhang: Pickups: 33 in./41 in. Tailgate: Width and Height: 72 in. x 19.25 in. Approach/Departure Degrees: K-1500 117.5 in. Wideside and Fenderside: 33/19. K-1500 131.5 in. Wideside: 33/15. K-1500 131.5 in. wheelbase Fenderside: 33/16. K-2500 131.5 in. wheelbase Wideside: 35/20. K-2500 131.5 in. wheelbase Fenderside: 35/21. K-3500 Wideside pickup: 41/19. K-3500 crew cab pickup: 38/18. Ground Clearance: Front axle: 7.25 in. Rear axle: 7.0 in. Oil pan: 16.5 in. Transfer case: 12.0 in. Fuel tank: 16.6 in. Load space: Pickup box dimensions: 117.5 in. wheelbase Wideside: 78.25 in. x 50 in. x 19.25 in. 131.5 in. wheelbase Wideside: 98 in. x 50 in. x 19.25 in. Capacity: 117.5 wheelbase: 58.4 cu. ft., 131.5 in. wheelbase: 74.3 cu. ft. 117.5 in. wheelbase Fenderside: 78.5 in. x 50 in. x 17.5 in. 131.5 in. wheelbase Fenderside: 96.25 in. x 50 in. x 17.5 in. Front headroom: 38.5 in. (seat to top of cab). Front hip room: 67.25 in. Pedal to seat back (max.): 43.5 in. Steering wheel to seat back (max.): 17.3 in. Seat to ground: 35.0 in. Floor to ground: 23.0 in.

CAPACITIES: Fuel Tank: 117.5 in. wheelbase: 16.0 gal. 131.5 in. wheelbase: 20.0 gal. 164.5 in.: 20 gal. Optional: 17 gal. auxiliary tank. for 117.5 in.; 20 gal. auxiliary for 131.5 in. and 164.5 in. wheelbase. Engine coolant system: 250 6-cyl.: 14.8 qt. 305 V-8: 17.6 qt. 350 V-8: 17.6 qt. 400 V-8: 19.6 qt. (20 qt. on K-2500 and K-3500).

ACCOMMODATIONS: Seating Capacity: Pickup and chassis-cab models: 3 passenger. Optional: None. Suburban: 3 passenger. Optional: 6 or 9 passenger.

INSTRUMENTATION: Speedometer, odometer, fuel level gauge. Warning lights for battery, oil pressure, generator, brake system warning, directional/hazard lights, high beam, and engine coolant temperature.

OPTIONS AND PRICES: Power steering (K-1500 and K-2500; standard with Trailering Special option. (RPO N41): $187. 350 V-8 (RPO LS9): $300. 400 V-8 (RPO LF4): $465. 4-speed manual synchromesh (RPO MM4): $152.Turbo Hydra-Matic (RPO MX1): $345. Poly-Wrap air cleaner (RPO K43). Air conditioning (RPO C60). Locking rear differential (RPO G80): $175. Auxiliary 3500 watt Delco Freedom battery (RPO TP2). Heavy-duty 4000 watt Delco freedom battery (RPO UA1). Painted rear bumper (RPO V38). Rear step bumper (RPO V43). Front and rear chromed bumpers (RPO V37). Front chrome bumper (RPO V46). Rear chrome bumper (RPO VF1). Rear step bumper-Wideside only (RPO V42). Front and rear deluxe chromed bumpers-Wideside only (RPO VE5). Front deluxe chromed bumper (RPO VG3). Chromed front bumper guards (RPO V31). Glide-out spare wheel carrier (RPO P11). Side-mounted spare wheel carrier (RPO P13). Chevy Sport Package (RPO Z77). Electric clock (RPO U35). Cold Climate Package includes UA1 battery and K76 generator. (RPO Z56). Engine oil cooler. Available for V-8 engines only (RPO KC4). Transmission oil cooler. Available for V-8 engines and auto. trans. only. (RPO VO2). Heavy-duty radiator (RPO VO1). Power door locks (RPO AU3). California emission system (RPO YF5). Dual exhaust system. Requires LS9 (RPO N10). Color-keyed floor mats (RPO B32). Wood pickup box, CK10903 Wideside only (RPO E81). Gauge Package. Includes voltmeter, engine coolant temperature and oil pressure (RPO Z53): $27. Tachometer. Requires V-8 engine. (RPO U16): $87, with Sierra Classic option: $60. 61 amp Delcotron alternator (RPO K76). Soft-Ray tinted glass, all windows (RPO AO1). Chrome grille (RPO V22). Camper body wiring harness (RPO UY1). Headlight warning buzzer (RPO T63). Inside hood lock release (RPO T44). Deluxe instrument panel (RPO BC3). Cargo area lamp (RPO UF2). Dome lamp (RPO C91). Roof marker lights (RPO UO1). Cigarette lighter (RPO U37). Below eye-level painted 7.5 in. x 10.5 in. mirrors (RPO D29). Below eye-level stainless steel 7.5 in. x 10.5 in. mirrors (RPO DG4). Camper-type below eye-level mirrors (RPO DFG4). Body side spear molding, Wideside only (RPO B84). Body upper moldings, Wideside only (RPO B85). Body side upper and lower moldings, Wideside only (RPO YG1). Door edge guard (RPO B93). Wheel opening moldings, Wideside only (RPO B96). Operating Convenience Package. Includes AU3 door locks and A31 windows. (RPO ZQ2). Fuel tank shield (RPO NY1). AM push-button radio (RPO U63). AM/FM push-button radio (RPO U69). Folding seat back (RPO AN1). Full-depth foam seat (RPO Z52). Pickup box side rails (RPO D73). Speed and cruise control (RPO K-3500). Heavy-duty front springs. Includes heavy-duty front and rear shock absorbers. Recommended for snowplow type usage only on K-1500. (RPO F60): $67. ComforTilt steering wheel (RPO N33). Custom steering wheel (RPO N31). Red exterior stripe (RPO 71A). Auxiliary fuel tank (RPO NL2): $150. Two front towing hooks (RPO V76). Weight distributing platform type trailer hitch (RPO VR4). Trailering Special Package. Includes UA1 battery and K76 generator. (RPO Z82). Bright metal hubcaps (RPO PO3). Trim rings (RPO PO6). Wheelcovers (RPO PO1). Special wheelcovers (RPO PA1). Spare dual wheel, K-3500 only (RPO QE2 or QE6 depending upon tire size). Dual rear wheels, K-3500 only (RPO RO5). Single rear wheels, K-3500 only (RPO ZW3). Aluminum wheels, K-1500 only. (RPO PH7). Rallye wheels, K-1500 only. (RPO N67). Styled wheels, K-1500 only. (RPO PA6). Power windows (RPO A31). Sliding rear window (RPO A28). Intermittent windshield wipers (RPO CD4). Heavy-duty vacuum brakes, K-2500 only. (RPO J55). Basic Camper Group, K-2500 and K-3500 only. Includes F60 springs and UY1 harness. (RPO Z81). Deluxe Camper Group, K-2500 and K-3500 only. (RPO Z83). Frame mounted spare wheel carrier, K-3500 only (RPO P10). Senior West Coast type painted mirrors, K-3500 only (RPO DG5). Heavy-duty front and rear shock absorbers (RPO F51). Conventional two-tone paint ZY2). Special two-tone paint, Wideside only (RPO ZY3). Deluxe two-tone paint, Wideside only (RPO XY4). Exterior Decor Package, Wideside only. Includes YG1 and B96 moldings, hood ornament and hood accent stripes (RPO ZY5).

HISTORICAL FOOTNOTES: Model sales of all GMC truck series was 283,540.

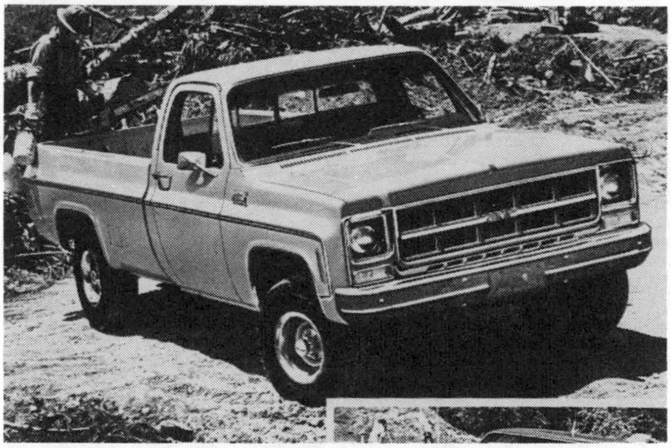

1979 GMC K-1500 Wideside Sierra Grande pickup

1980 PICKUP & SUBURBAN

The 1980 GMC trucks had a standard thermostatically operated fan clutch. A new air dam was added to all K-1500 and K-2500 trucks up to 8500 lb. GVW. A new single-inlet dual-outlet muffler that helped decrease back pressure was used with the 5.7 liter V-8. For 1980 all models regardless of engine or transmission had a New Process 205 2-speed part-time four-wheel drive system. A new painted grille treatment was included in the standard trim level. A new push-button vent window provided improved theft protection. Seven carry-over and eight new exterior colors were available. Two new interior trims colors; dark blue and light green joined camel tan and carmine for 1980. A new Hobnail-pattern custom cloth was optional. The custom vinyl seat trim had a new design. Included in the Sierra Classic Trim Package was a new chrome finish grille treatment with a body-color center bar, new lamp bezels, rectangular headlights and larger parking lamps.

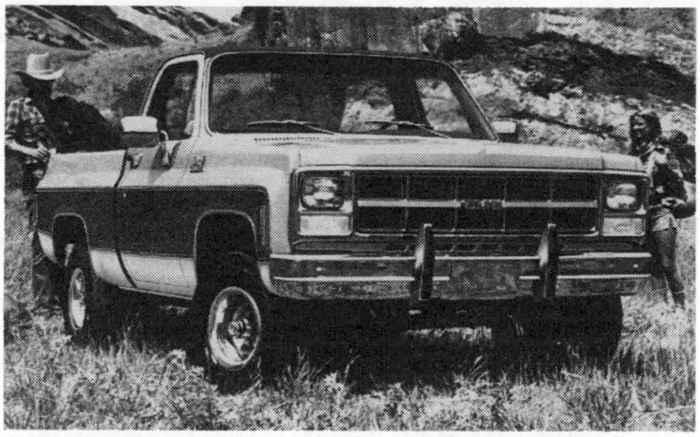

1980 GMC Wideside pickup

I.D. DATA: The vehicle identification number was located on a plate in the lower left side of the windshield. Its content was unchanged except for the sixth entry, the letter A, which indicated the 1980 model year. The eighth through the thirteenth digit was the assembly sequence number.

Model Number	Body Type	Factory Price	GVW	Shipping Weight	Prod. Total
Series K1500-1/2 ton 250 6-cyl. 117.5 in., 131.5 in. wheelbase (Suburban: 129.5 in. wheelbase and standard 305 V-8)					
CK10703	117.5 in. Chassis & Cab	$6965	6200	4143	—
CK10903	131.5 in. Chassis & Cab	$N.A.	6200	4250	—
CK10703	6.5 ft. Fenderside Pickup	$6685	6200	4477	—
CK10703	6.5 ft. Wideside Pickup	$6685	6200	4537	—
CK10903	8 ft. Fenderside Pickup	$6770	6200	4639	—
CK10903	8 ft. Wideside Pickup	$6770	6200	4720	—
CK10906	Suburban Endgate	$8636	6200	5273	—
CK10906	Suburban Pnl. Drs.	$N.A.	6200[1]	5235	—

NOTE 1: Suburban available with optional 6800 and 7300 lb. GVW Packages.

Series K2500-3/4 ton 292 V-8[1]. 131.5 in. wheelbase. (Suburban-129.5 in. wheelbase, Crew and Bonus Cab: 164.5 in. wheelbase, Suburban weight with standard 350 V-8

CK20903	Chassis and Cab	$7404	6800*	4485	—
CK20903	8 ft. Fenderside Pickup	$7514	6800	4874	—
CK20903	8 ft. Wideside Pickup	$7414	6800	4955	—
CK20906	Suburban Endgate	$9111	6800	5472	—
CK20906	Suburban Pnl. Drs.	$N.A.	6800	5434	—

NOTE 1: Not available in California where the 350 engine is base.
* 8600 lb. GVW optional.

Series K3500-1 ton 350 V-8. 131.5 in. wheelbase, Crew and Bonus Cab: 164.5 in. wheelbase

CK31003	Chassis & Cab[1]	$8629	8400*	4956	—
CK31403	Chassis & Cab[2]	$N.A.	8490	5243	—
CK30903	8 ft. Wideside Pickup	$8917	8400	5426	—
CK30903	8 ft. Fenderside Pickup	$8917	8400	5501	—
CK30943	Chassis & Bonus Cab	$9350	8400	5370	—
CK30943	Fleetside Bonus Cab	$9627	8400	5840	—
CK30943	Chassis & Crew Cab	$9604	8400	5370	—
CK30943	Fleetside Crew Cab	$9881	8400	5840	—

NOTE 1: 135.5 in. wheelbase.
NOTE 2: 159.9 in. wheelbase.
* 9200 and 10,000 lb. GVW optional.

STANDARD ENGINE: All K-1500 6-cyl. models: 250 Six (LE3 ordering code) Engine Type: OHV, In-line 6-cylinder. Cast iron block and cylinder head. Key features induction hardened exhaust valve seas, and timing tabs. Not available for California delivery where 350 engine is standard. Bore x Stroke: 3.875 in. x 3.53 in. Lifters: Hydraulic. Number of main bearings-7. Fuel Induction: Single Rochester staged 2-bbl. carburetor. Compression Ratio: 8.3:1. Displacement: 250 cu. in. (4.09 liters). Horsepower: Net: 130 @ 4000 rpm. Torque: Net: 210 lb.-ft. @ 2000 rpm. Oil refill capacity: 5 qt. with filter change. Fuel Requirements: Regular.

STANDARD ENGINE: K-3500 6-cyl. models: 292 Six. Ordering Code: L25. Engine Type: OHV, 6-cyl. Cast iron block and cylinder head. Key features include cast iron intake manifold, aluminized-face intake valves, Stellite-faced exhaust valves with hardened faces. Bore x Stroke: 3.875 in. x 4.125 in. Lifters: Hydraulic. Number of main bearings-7. Fuel Induction: Single Rochester 1-bbl. carburetor. Compression Ratio: 7.8:1. Displacement: 292 cu. in. (4.78 liters). Horsepower: Net: 115 @ 3400 rpm. Torque: Net: 215 lb.-ft. @ 1600 rpm. Oil refill capacity: 6 qt. with filter change. Fuel Requirements: Regular.

STANDARD ENGINE: K-2500 and K-3500 V-8 models. Standard for K-2500 Suburban. Ordering Code: LS9: 350 V-8 Engine Type: OHV, V-8. Cast iron block and alloy iron cylinder head. Key features include chain drive camshaft and forged steel connecting rods. Bore x Stroke: 4.0 in. x 3.50 in. Lifters: Hydraulic. Number of main bearings-5. Fuel Induction: Single Rochester 4-bbl. carburetor. Compression Ratio: 8.2:1. (8500 lb. GVW and below), 8501 lb. and up GVW: 8.3:1. Displacement: 350 cu. in. (5.73 liters). Horsepower: Net: 175 @ 3800 rpm. California and GVW below 8500 lb. GVW: 170 @ 3600 rpm. 8501 lb. and up GVW: 165 @ 3800 rpm. Torque: Net: 8500 lb. and below, except California: 275 lb.-ft. @ 2400 rpm. 8500 lb. and below, for California: 275 lb.-ft.@ 2400 rpm. 8501 lb. and up GVW: 255 lb.-ft. @ 2800 rpm. Oil refill capacity: 5 qt. with filter change. Fuel Requirements: Regular.

OPTIONAL ENGINE: K-2500 and K-3500 V-8 models. Ordering Code: LF4: 400 V-8. Key features include induction-hardened valve seats and cast iron camshaft. Engine Type: OHV, V-8. Cast iron block and alloy iron cylinder head. Bore x Stroke: 4.10 in. x 3.8 in. Lifters: Hydraulic. Number of main bearings-5. Fuel Induction: Single Rochester 4-bbl. carburetor. Compression Ratio: 8.5:1. Displacement: 400 cu. in. (6.55 liters). Horsepower: Net: 185 @ 3600 rpm. California and GVW below 8500 lb. GVW: 170 @ 3600 rpm. 8501 lb. and up GVW: 180 @ 3600 rpm. Torque: Net: 8500 lb. and below, except California: 300 lb.-ft. @ 2400 rpm. 8500 lb. and below, for California: 305 lb.-ft.@ 1600 rpm. 8501 lb. and up GVW: 310 lb.-ft. @ 2400 rpm. Oil refill capacity: 5 qt. with filter change. Fuel Requirements: Regular.

STANDARD ENGINE: K-1500 Suburban models. Ordering Code: LG9 305 V-8. Not available in California. Engine Type: OHV, V-8. Cast iron block and alloy iron cylinder head. Bore x Stroke: 3.74 in. x 3.48 in. Lifters: Hydraulic. Number of main bearings-5. Fuel Induction: Single Rochester 2-bbl. carburetor. Compression Ratio: 8.4:1. Displacement: 305 cu. in. (4.997 liters). Horsepower: Net: 140 @ 4000 rpm. Torque: Net: 240 lb.-ft. @ 2000 rpm. Oil refill capacity: 5 qt. with filter change. Fuel Requirements: Regular.

CHASSIS FEATURES: Separate body and frame with channel side rails. Carbon-Steel, 39,000 psi. 117.5 in. wheelbase: 2.30 in. x 5.92 in. x 0.156 in. Section modulus: 3.06 in. 129.5 in.: 2.30 in. x 5.92 in. x 0.194. Section modulus: 3.93. 135.5 in. wheelbase: 2.78 in. x 7.74 in. 0.194 in. Section modulus: 6.20. 164.5 in. wheelbase: 2.78 in. x 7.74 in. x 0.224 in. Section modulus: 7.33. 131.5 in. wheelbase: 2.30 in. x 5.92 in. x 0.194 in. Section modulus: 3.84 in. Optional: None.

SUSPENSION AND RUNNING GEAR: Front Suspension: K-1500: Tapered 2-leaf springs. Capacity: 1650 lb. (16), 1850 lb. (03, 06). K1500: Tapered 2-leaf springs. Capacity: 1850 lb. K-3500: Tapered 3-leaf springs. Capacity: 2250 lb. Rear Suspension: K-1500 and K-2500: 52 in. x 2.25 in. Two-stage, 7-leaf. K-3500: 56 in. x 2.50 in. Capacity: K-1500: 2075 lb. K-2500: 2800 lb. K-3500: 3500 lb. 1.0 in. dia. shock absorbers. Optional: K-3500: 3750 lb. capacity. Front Axle Type and Capacity: K-1500 and K-2500: GMC or Spicer, K35: Spicer. K-1500: Semi-floating. 3600 lb. capacity. Optional: None. K-2500: Full-floating, 3800 lb. capacity. K-3500: Full-floating, 4500 lb. Optional: None. Rear Axle Type and Capacity: K-1500: Semi-floating, 3750 lb. capacity. K-2500: Full-floating, 5700 lb. K-3500: 7500 lb. Optional: None. Final Drive Ratio: Standard: K-1500: 6-cyl.: 3.42:1; 350 V-8: 2.76:1. K-2500 and K-3500: 292 6-cyl: 4.10:1; 350 and 400 V-8: 4.10:1. K-1500 Suburban: 350 V-8: 3.08:1. Optional: K-1500: 250 6-cyl.: 3.73:1; 350 V-8: 3.08:1. Optional: K-2500 and K-3500: 292 6-cyl.: 4.56:1; 350 V-8: 4.56:1. Transfer Case: New Process 205. Single lever, two-speed: 1.96, 1.00:1. Brakes: Type: Hydraulic, power assisted. Dimensions: K-1500: Front: Disc: 11.86 in. x 1.28 in. Rear: Drums: 11.15 x 2.75 in. K-2500: Front: Disc: 12.5 in. x 1.28 in. Rear: Drums: 11.15 in. x 2.75 in. K-2500 and K-3500: Front: Disc: 12.50 in. x 1.53 in. Rear: Drum: 13.00 in. x 3.50 in. Wheels: K-1500: 15 x 6.0JJ 6-stud disc. Optional: 15 x 8JJ. K-2500: 16.5 x 6.00 in. 8-stud disc. Optional: 16.5 x 6.75. K-3500: 16.5 x 6.75. Tires: K-1500: P215/75R15-P metric radial. K-2500: 8.75 x 16.5C K-3500: 9.50 x 16.5D. Optional: K-1500: G78 x 15B, white stripe; H78 x 15B, tubeless, black sidewall or white stripe; L78 x 15B black sidewall or white stripe, tubeless; 10.00 x 16.5C tubeless; G78 x 15B tube-type; 7.00 x 15C tube-type; 6.50 x 16C tube-type and LR78 x 15C white sidewall radial ply. The following tires were specified for K-1500 models with the 5600 lb. GVW Package which included a front heavy-duty stabilizer bar: H78 x 15B 4-ply rating, tubeless; 6.50 x 16C 6-ply rating, tube-type, truck type. The following tires were specified for K-1500 models with the 6000 lb. GVW Package which included a front heavy-duty stabilizer bar and heavy-duty rear springs: L78 x 15B 4-ply rating, tubeless. Optional K-2500: 9.50 x 16.5E Firestone Town and Country, 8.75 x 16.5D tubeless; 9.50 x 16.5D tubeless; 10.00 x 16.5C tubeless (not available for Fenderside models); 7.50 x 16C 6-ply rating, tube-type; 7.50 x 16D tube-type; 7.50 x 16E tube-type. The following tires were specified for K-2500 models with the 7500 lb. GVW Package which included a front heavy-duty stabilizer bar: 8.75 x 16.5 C 6-ply rating, tubeless; 7.50 x 16C 6-ply rating, tubeless. The following tires were specified for K-2500 models with the 8200 lb. GVW Package which included a front heavy-duty stabilizer bar: 9.50 x 16.5D 8-ply rating, tubeless; 7.50 x 16C 6-ply rating, tube-type. Steering: Recirculating ball gear. Ratio: 20:1. Turning Circle: 47 ft. Steering wheel diameter: 17.5 in. Optional: Power-assisted. Ratio: 16.4:1. Transmission: K-1500 and K-2500: 3-speed, synchromesh manual (RPO M15). Transmission Ratios: 2.85, 1.68, 1.00:1. Optional: CH465. 4-speed manual synchromesh (RPO M20). Ratios: 6.55, 3.58, 1.70, 1.00:1. Reverse: 6.09:1. The K-2500 crew cab and all K-3500 models had this transmission as standard equipment. Optional: 3-speed Turbo Hydra-Matic 400 (RPO M40). Ratios: 2.1 x 2.48, 1.48, 1.00:1. Reverse: 2.10:1. The 400 cu. in. V-8 was available only with this transmission. Clutch: Diaphragm, spring. Clutch diameter: 6-cyl.: 11 in. dia. Total lining area: 123.5 sq. in. Total plate pressure: 2075 lb. V-8: 12 in. dia. Total lining area: 149.2 sq. in. Total plate pressure: 2060 lb. Optional: K-2500 6-cyl.: 11 in. dia. Total lining area: 124.0 sq. in. 307 V-8: 12 in. dia. Total lining area: 150 sq. in.

VEHICLE DIMENSIONS: Wheelbase: K-1500: 117.5 in. 131.5 in. K-2500: 131.5 in. All Suburbans and Panels: 129.5 in. K-3500: 131.5 in. 164.5 in. Overall Length: 117.5 in. Wideside pickups: 191.30 in. 131.5 in. Wideside pickups: 212.00. 117.5 in. Fenderside pickups: 190.5 in. 131.5 in. Fenderside pickups: 210.25. 117.5 in. Chassis-cab: 186.05 in. K-3500 data: 164.5 in. wheelbase: 244.43 in. Front/Rear Tread: 67.4 in./65.8 in. Overall Height: K-1500 Wideside pickup: 72.0 in. K-2500 Wideside pickup: 74.0 in. K-3500 Wideside pickup: 74.0 in. K-3500 crew cab: 75.0 in. K-1500 Suburban: 73.5 in. K-2500 Suburban: 75.5 in. Width: Pickup: 79.5 in. Front/Rear Overhang: Pickups: 33 in./41 in. Tailgate: Width and Height: 72 in. x 19.25 in. Approach/Departure Degrees: K-1500 117.5 in. Wideside and Fenderside: 33/19. K-1500 131.5 in. Wideside: 33/15. K-1500 131.5 in. wheelbase Fenderside: 33/16. K-2500 131.5 in. wheelbase Wideside: 35/20. K-2500 131.5 in. wheelbase Fenderside: 35/21. K-3500 Wideside pickup: 41/19. K-3500 crew cab pickup: 38/18. Ground Clearance: Front axle: 7.25 in. Rear axle: 7.0 in. Oil pan: 16.5 in. Transfer case: 12.0 in. Fuel tank: 16.6 in. Load space: Pickup box dimensions: 117.5 in. wheelbase Wideside: 78.25 in. x 50 in. x 19.25 in. 131.5 in. wheelbase Wideside: 98 in. x 50 in. x 19.25 in. Capacity: 117.5 wheelbase: 58.4 cu. ft. 131.5 in. wheelbase: 74.3 cu. ft. 117.5 in. wheelbase Fenderside: 78.5 in. x 50 in. x 17.5 in. 131.5 in. wheelbase Fenderside: 96.25 in. x 50 in. x 17.5 in. Front headroom: 38.5 in. (seat to top of cab). Front hip room: 67.25 in. Pedal to seat back (max.): 43.5 in. Steering wheel to sea tback (max.): 17.3 in. Seat to ground: 35.0 in. Floor to ground: 23.0 in.

CAPACITIES: Fuel Tank: 117.5 in. wheelbase: 16.0 gal. 131.5 in. wheelbase: 20.0 gal. 164.5 in.: 20 gal. Optional: 17 gal. auxiliary tank. for 117.5 in.; 20 gal. auxiliary for 131.5 in. and 164.5 in. wheelbase. Engine coolant system: 250 6-cyl.: 14.8 qt. 305 V-8: 17.6 qt. 350 V-8: 17.6 qt. 400 V-8: 19.6 qt. (20 qt. on K-2500 and K-3500).

ACCOMMODATIONS: Seating Capacity: Pickup and chassis-cab models: 3 passenger. Optional: None. Suburban: 3 passenger. Optional: 6 or 9 passenger.

INSTRUMENTATION: Speedometer, odometer, fuel level gauge. Warning lights for battery, oil pressure, generator, brake system warning, directional/hazard lights, high beam, and engine coolant temperature.

OPTIONS AND PRICES: Options were essentially unchanged from 1979. This is a representative sampling of options and prices. Tinted glass: $36. Sliding rear window: $90. Power windows: $148. Color-keyed floor mats: $12. Pulse windshield wipers: $35. Air conditioning: $607. Locking rear differential: $197. 400 V-8: $575. Turbo Hydra-Matic: $411. Auxiliary fuel tank: $182. Fuel tank and differential skid plates: $139. Tilt steering wheel: $83. Glide-out spare tire carrier: $34. Tachometer: $62. AM/FM radio: $153. Chrome front bumper: $19. Chrome rear step bumper: $156. Sierra Classic Trim Package: $645. Exterior Decor Package: $236. Vinyl bucket seats: $230. 9.50 x 16.5E tires: $331.46.

HISTORICAL FOOTNOTES: Calendar year sale of all GMC trucks was 141,030, of which 102,130 were pickup models and 4210 were Suburbans.

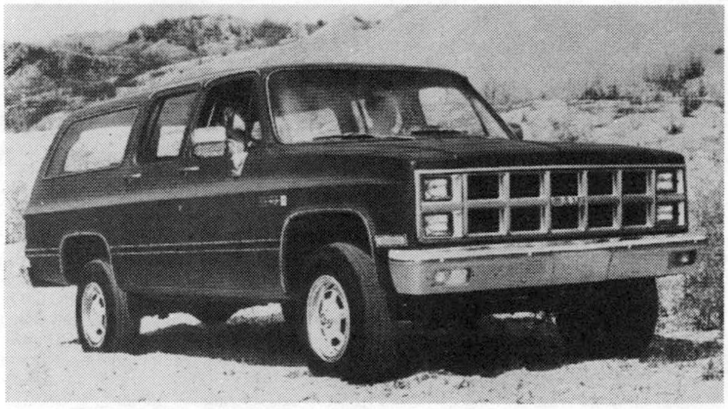

1980 GMC Suburban

1981 PICKUP & SUBURBAN

The 1981 GMC trucks were revised to be more accommodating to the new era of fuel and operating efficiency. The front-end sheet metal was new from the cowl forward. The front fenders were restyled for improved aerodynamics and occupant visibility. Also new were the radiator grille, painted plastic headlight bezels, front bumper, Wideside rear bumper and the parking lights, which were now located in the front bumper. New front bumper braces and an 8-point attachment improved bumper stiffness. The use of HSLA steel for all bumpers except the Fenderside conventional bumper contributed to the vehicle's overall weight reduction. The weight of the K series trucks was reduced from 115 to 309 pounds. New front fender skirts with attached shields helped reduce engine compartment splash. Standard on all K series models with GVW ratings up to 8500 lb. (except for chassis-cab models) was a front air deflector. Single rectangular headlights were now standard. Other changes included a restyled Wideside pickup tailgate and front fender name and series designation plates. All windows had new, thinner glass for weight reduction. Numerous interior changes accompanied these developments. The standard front bench seat was redesigned. The full foam-type seat cushion (previously RPO AQ1) was now standard on both two-door and four-door cabs. The folding seat back (formerly RPO AN1) was now standard for two-door cabs and for the crew cab rear seat. Also restyled for 1981 were the interior side door trim panels, door lock and window control handles. The revised instrument panel now had provision at the top for new stereo radio speakers. The old speaker position had been in the front door trim panels.

Other interior changes included a new instrument panel pad, new instrument panel appliques and name plates, new instrument panel cluster bezels and revised graphics for the windshield wiper-washer switch. A new steering wheel column upper cover matched the new instrument panel bezel. The K-1500 and K-2500 models had a new floor-mounted illuminated transfer case indicator console. The K-3500 retained the shift range graphics on the control lever knob. All K-1500 and K-2500 models under 8500 lb. GVW ratings had drag-free front disc brake calipers with a new quick take-up master cylinder. All K-2500 models had a new standard 6000 lb. capacity, semi-floating rear axle with a 9.5 in. ring gear. Adding incrementally to improved fuel mileage was the deletion of the constant "on" status of the heater blower. A new "off" position was provided.

Revisions to the GMC began with the elimination of RPO LE4, the 6.6 liter, 400 cu. in. V-8 for 1981. A new optional 5.0 liter, 305 V-8 (RPO LE9) with Electronic Spark Control (ESC) was available for K-1500 models. This engine was intended to provide the fuel economy of a 5.0 liter V-8 while delivering performance competitive with a 1980 model year 5.7 liter V-8. This engine's 9.2:1 compression ratio was the highest ever offered in a light-duty GMC truck. This engine was designed to operate on regular unleaded fuel and its ESC system provided protection from audible engine detonation. Other refinements included a camshaft modified to provide less valve overlap a staged 4-barrel carburetor and larger exhaust passages. Internal dimensions were similar to other 5.0 liter GMC V-8 engines except for the combustion chamber volume, which was reduced by approximately 10 percent. This engine was not available in California where a 4-barrel 305 V-8 similar except for the high compression and ESC system was offered. Also refined for 1981 was the LE3, 4.1 liter 6-cylinder which had a carburetor recalibrated to provide smoother operation at cruising speeds. The lift profile of the cam was also modified for improved engine idle operation. The EPA fuel mileage of this engine improved by approximately one mpg over the 1980 level. All engines were cooled by new high-efficiency radiators with more cooling fins in their cores than those used in 1980.

The K-1500 and K-2500 models had a new New Process 208 transfer case which used an aluminum case and included synchronizers for easier shifting. No provision for power take-off was provided in this transfer case. The K-3500 series retained the New Process 205 transfer case which included a power take-off opening. This system was also improved by the inclusion of shifting synchronizers. All four-wheel drive models had automatic locking front hubs. These hubs would freewheel until the vehicle was placed in four-wheel drive and torque was applied to the front wheels. The front hubs were returned to their free-wheeling mode when the transfer case was shifted to two-wheel drive and the vehicle was backed up approximately three feet.

Included among the body and chassis changes for 1981 was the relocation of the standard fuel tank from the right-hand frame rail to the left-hand frame rail. The filler pipe and access door were now located on the driver's side. GMC also announced several significance anti-corrosion features for 1981. The front wheelhousing-to-frame seals were new and the use of corrosion-resistent steel in the pickup boxes was increased. On the Wideside boxes, new urethane stone shields were added ahead of the wheel openings. On the brake and fuel lines of all models, zinc-rich paint was applied over the existing anti-corrosion exterior coating. The Wideside tailgate also had a new hemmed construction for improved anti-corrosion. The standard rear springs on K-1500 and K-2500 models with a GVW rating under 8500 lb. were new and featured greater durability and improved corrosion protection.

Numerous revisions, changes, additions and deletions took place in the K series option list for 1981. The introduction of new exterior colors produced two new exterior two-tone color combinations. The RPO ZY3 Special and RPO ZY4 Deluxe two-tone paint options were limited to single rear wheel Wideside Pickups. Two-tone interiors were discontinued.

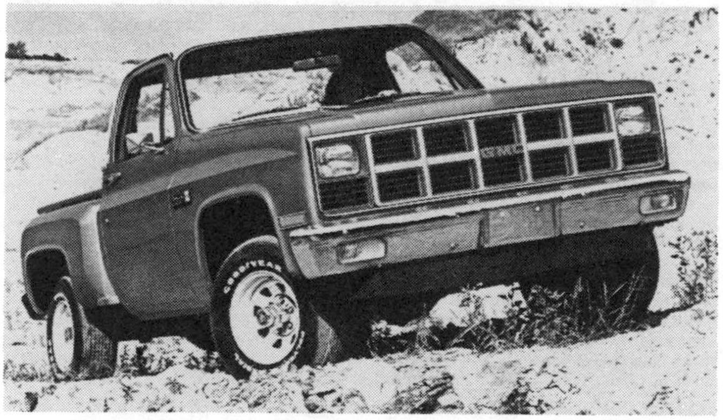

1981 GMC K-1500 Fenderside High Sierra pickup

All body side and rear moldings, except wheel opening moldings, were new for 1981. They continued to be available only for Wideside pickups and Suburbans. Trim moldings were located low on the body and ran between the wheel openings and continued around the side panels and across the rear of the vehicle. RPO B84 moldings were black and trimmed in black plastic. They were included in the Sierra Grande Trim Package and were available for both the Sierra and High Sierra trim levels. The RPO B85 moldings were bright plastic with black paint trim and included bright trimmed front side marker lights and tail lights. They were available for the Sierra, Sierra Grande and High Sierra trim levels. RPO B96 was a carry-over option from 1980. It consisted of bright front and rear opening moldings with black paint trim. These were included in the High Sierra Trim Package and were available for the Sierra and Sierra Grande trim levels.

A new chromed grille option, RPO V22, added a chrome finish on the leading edges of the grille insert. The center bar had a brushed chrome treatment. This finish was also used on the headlight bezels. Also included in this option were dual rectangular head lights. These high-intensity, high-beam halogen lights, listed as RPO TT5 were not available separately. A new RPO K35, automatic speed control, included a resume feature. It was available for 6-cyl. and V-8 models with automatic transmission. New RPO Z75 front quad shock absorbers for K-1500 and K-2500 models included an extra pair of shock absorbers on the front axle, heavy-duty rear shock absorbers, and a front axle pinion nose snubber to limit front axle windup. The electric clock option, RPO U35, had a new solid-state quartz mechanism for improved performance. A new center console in the RPO AV5 bucket seat option was redesigned for a new appearance as well as reduced weight.

The cab back beltline molding was newly styled for 1981 and was available for all pickup and chassis-cab models. It continued to be included in the High Sierra and Sierra Classic Trim Packages and in conventional two-tone and deluxe two-tone paint schemes.

The RPO YG1 Molding Package had new content for 1981. As previously, it was available for Wideside pickups and Suburbans. It consisted of bright trimmed black plastic body side and rear molding, the RPO B84 moldings and the RPO B96 moldings. This package was available for the custom Deluxe, RPO Z62 Sierra Grande or RPO Z84 High Sierra trim levels. It was not available for models with the Sierra Classic trim or with dual rear wheels.

RPO YG3 introduced a new-for-1981 Molding Package for single rear wheel Wideside pickups and Suburbans. It consisted of bright plastic body side and rear moldings with black paint trim, RPO B85 and RPO B96 moldings. It was included with the RPO YE9, Sierra Classic trim and was available for all other trim levels. The RPO ZY5 Exterior Decor Package for both the pickups and Suburban was restyled for 1981. It was offered in a choice of eight colors and included the RPO YG1 and RPO B96 moldings. In addition, it included dual-tone body side and rear tape decal striping keyed to the exterior body color. This striping was applied to the front fenders, side doors and pickup box/body sides and tailgate several inches above the styling crease line. The areas above the striping and below the moldings were painted the primary paint color. The secondary color choice was used between the striping and the molding. A bright, spring-loaded, stand-up type hood emblem was also included.

The RPO Z77 Street Coupe Package, available only for the K-1500 Wideside and Fenderside pickup,s was also modified for 1981. The front bumper in this option was painted the primary body color with resilient black impact stripes. The rear bumper was painted the secondary body color. Impact stripes were fitted on Fleetsides only. Also included was the Deluxe Front End Appearance Package with left- and right-hand dual rectangular head lights. The grille and head light bezels were painted dark grey with a brushed chrome finish applied to the center bar. A chrome stand-up hood ornament was installed. Also included was the new special two-tone paint RPO ZY6 feature, and RPO Z62, the Sierra Grande exterior trim items (except for the body side and rear moldings and chromed front bumper). New Sport striping of this option involved multi-toned decal striping on the front fenders and Fenderside rear fenders, cab and Wideside pickup body sides, and tailgate. The interior contained the Sierra Grande interior trim items and color-keyed carpeting.

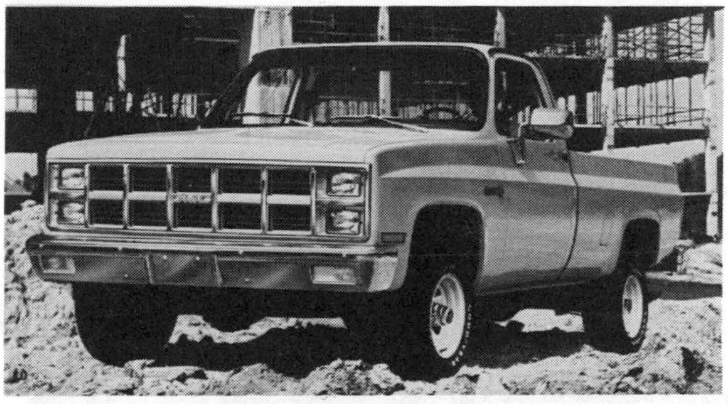

1981 GMC K-1500 Wideside Sierra pickup

Due to the fuel tank location change and low demand in 1980, the RPO P13 side-mounted spare tire carrier for the Fenderside pickups was cancelled for 1981. Also no longer available was RPO E81, the wood floor for the 8 foot Wideside pickup box.

The standard Sierra trim, in addition to the new standard features previously mentioned also included large padded armrests, padded sun shades, cab interior light, prismatic inside rear view mirror, and a nameplate on the new instrument pad panel. Exterior items included bright drip rails over the doors, bright review mirrors, and a white painted front bumper.

Both the Sierra Grande interior and exterior trim included the items from the base trim plus these additions or changes: A choice of either a new custom cloth or custom vinyl seat covering in a selection of five colors with grained vinyl facings; a new black crackle finish insert and bright trim in door panels; color-keyed floor mat, door or manual operated dome light; cigarette lighter and ashtray lamp; and a new Sierra Grande nameplate on the instrument panel. The Sierra Grande exterior for regular pickup cabs began with the Sierra elements and included these major changes or additions: Chromed front bumper, bright-trimmed Wideside tail lamps and dual rear wheel clearance lamps, bright-trimmed black moldings on body sides and tail gate of Wideside pickups, bright windshield/rear window trim, new Sierra Grande front fender-mounted nameplates and dual horns.

Both the High Sierra's interior and exterior trim included all the Sierra Grande items plus numerous additions or changes. The High Sierra interior included a silver instrument cluster bezel, instrument panel pad applique and door trim panels; color-keyed vinyl insert on door trim panels; door storage pockets, perforated, color-keyed headliner; custom steering wheel, extra-thick floor insulation, headliner insulation and new High Sierra nameplate on instrument panel. Additional High Sierra exterior features for regular cab only included bright front/rear wheel opening moldings with black paint trim on the Wideside pickup only; hood and cab-to-fender sound insulators, new bright cab-back panel moldings, bright tailgate panel with GMC lettering on Wideside pickup only, secondary door weather strips and new High Sierra front fender mounted nameplates.

The Sierra Classic interior trim contained all items in the High Sierra Package for regular cabs and all items in the Sierra Grande Package for crew and bonus cabs plus full cowl side trim panels, new door-closing assist strap, new door are carpet trim below door panel, new Sierra Classic nameplate on instrument panel, bright brushed-finish stainless steel instrument cluster frame and matching inset on the instrument panel pad and door trim panels, needle-type and full-gauge instrumentation. The crew cab and bonus cab models were fitted with custom steering wheel, color-keyed carpeting (except for the rear compartment of the bonus cab), and a choice of custom cloth or custom vinyl seats, and extra-thick floor insulation. The Sierra Classic exterior was based on the High Sierra trim and added these additions or changes: New bright-trimmed grille, headlight bezels and dual rectangular headlights, and new Sierra Classic front fender-mounted nameplates.

Four new exterior colors were added for 1981: Light silver metallic, charcoal metallic, colonial yellow and dark chestnut. Also available for 1981 were these colors: Frost white, nordic blue metallic, carmine red, light blue metallic, medium blue, Santa Fe tan, midnight black, cardinal red, dark carmine red, Emerald green and burnt orange metallic. Five interior colors, including three carryovers: Carmine, blue and green was available.

I.D. DATA: The V.I.N. plate was mounted on the lower left side windshield corner. The V.I.N. consisted of 17 elements. The first, the number 1, identified the U.S. as the nation of origin. The letter G followed, for the manufacturer: General Motors. The third entry, the letter T, represented the make as GMC. The GVWR brake system identification followed. Next came the truck line and chassis type; the letter K indicated four-wheel drive. The truck series was identified by a number: 1-1/2 ton; 2-3/4 ton; 3-1 ton. The truck body type identification was next: 3-four-door cab; 4-two-door cab; 6-Suburban. The engine code followed according to this scheme: D-250 6-cyl.; E-350 V-8; T-292 6-cyl.; W-454 V-8. A check digit followed. The model year was identified by the letter B. The assembly plant code followed. The final six digits were the plant sequential production number.

Model Number	Body Type	Factory Price	GVW	Shipping Weight	Prod. Total
Series K-1500-1/2 ton 250 6-cyl. 117.5 in., 131.5 in. wheelbase (Suburban: 129.5 in. wheelbase and standard 305 V-8)					
TK10703	6.5 ft. F-S Pickup	$7762	6200	4442	—
TK10703	6.5 ft. Wideside Pickup	$7762	6200	4485	—
TK10903	8 ft. Fenderside Pickup	$7849	6200	4807	—
TK10903	8 ft. Wideside Pickup	$7849	6200	4686	—
TK10906	Suburban Endgate	$10,267	6200	5273	—
TK10906	Suburban Pnl. Drs.	$N.A.	6200[1]	5250	—

NOTE 1: Suburban available with optional 6800 and 730 lb. GVW Packages.

Model Number	Body Type	Factory Price	GVW	Shipping Weight	Prod. Total
Series K-2500-3/4 ton 292 6-cyl.1. 131.5 in. wheelbase. (Suburban-129.5 in. wheelbase, crew and Bonus cab: 164.5 in. wheelbase, Suburban weight with standard 350 V-8					
TK20903	Chassis and Cab	$7975	6800*	N.A.	—
TK20903	8 ft. Fenderside Pickup	$8479	6800	4807	—
TK20903	8 ft. Wideside Pickup	$8479	6800	4878	—
TK20906	Suburban Endgate	$10,141	6800	5472	—
TK20906	Suburban Pnl. Drs.	$N.A.	6800	5434	—

NOTE 1: Not available in California where the 350 engine is base.

* 8600 lb. GVW optional.

Model Number	Body Type	Factory Price	GVW	Shipping Weight	Prod. Total
Series K-3500-1 ton 350 V-8. 131.5 in. wheelbase, Crew and Bonus Cab: 164.5 in. wheelbase					
TK30903	Chassis & Cab[1]	$9064	8400*	4956	—
TK30903	Chassis & Cab[2]	$N.A.	8400	5243	—
TK30903	8 ft. Wideside Pickup	$9558	8400	5318	—
TK30903	8 ft. Fenderside Pickup	$9558	8400	5330	—
TK30943	Chassis & Bonus Cab	$9969	8400	5370	—
TK30943	Fleetside Bonus Cab	$10,458	8400	5743	—
TK30943	Chassis & Crew Cab	$10,259	8400	5370	—
TK30943	Fleetside Crew Cab	$10,748	8400	5840	—

NOTE 1: 135.5 in. wheelbase.
NOTE 2: 159.9 in. wheelbase.
* 9200 and 10,000 lb. GVW optional.

STANDARD ENGINE: All K-1500 6-cyl. models: 250 Six (LE3 ordering code) Not available for California where a 305 V-8 with 4-bbl. carburetor is installed. Engine Type: OHV, In-line 6-cylinder. Cast iron block and cylinder head. Key features include a staged 2-bbl. carburetor that uses only one barrel for normal operation. The second barrel is used when more power is needed. The emissions control uses engine vacuum pulses instead of an air pump, pulley, and belt. This systems saved about 15 lbs. in weight as compared to the older system. This engine was produced by GM-Chevrolet Motor Division. Bore x Stroke: 3.875 in. x 3.53 in. Lifters: Hydraulic. Number of main bearings-7. Fuel Induction: Single Rochester 2-bbl. carburetor. Compression Ratio: 8.3:1. Displacement: 250 cu. in. (4.1 liters). Horsepower: Net: 115 @ 3600 rpm. Torque: Net: 200 lb.-ft. @ 1800 rpm. Oil refill capacity: 5 qt. with filter change. Fuel Requirements: Regular unleaded.

STANDARD ENGINE: K-2500 with RPO CH6 and K-3500 models: 292 Six. Ordering Code: L25. This engine was produced by GM de Mexico. Engine Type: OHV, 6-cyl. Cast iron block and cylinder head. Key features include cast iron intake manifold, aluminized-face intake valves, Stellite-faced exhaust valves with hardened faces. Bore x Stroke: 3.875 in. x 4.125 in. Lifters: Hydraulic. Number of main bearings-7. Fuel Induction: Single Rochester 1-bbl. carburetor. Compression Ratio: 7.8:1. Displacement: 292 cu. in. (4.8 liters). Horsepower: Net: 115 @ 3400 rpm. Torque: Net: 215 lb.-ft. @ 1600 rpm. Oil refill capacity: 6 qt. with filter change. Fuel Requirements: Regular unleaded.

STANDARD ENGINE: K-2500: Optional for K-2500 with HP6 and all K-3500 models. Ordering Code: LS9: 350 V-8 Engine Type: OHV, V-8. Cast iron block and alloy iron cylinder head. Key features include chain drive camshaft and forged steel connecting rods. This engine was produced by GM-Chevrolet Motor Division. Bore x Stroke: 4.0 in. x 3.50 in. Lifters: Hydraulic. Number of main bearings-5. Fuel Induction: Single Rochester 4-bbl. carburetor. Compression Ratio: 8.2:1. Displacement: 350 cu. in. (5.7 liters). Horsepower: Net: 165 @ 3800 rpm. Torque: Net: 275 lb.-ft. @ 1600 rpm. Oil refill capacity: 5 qt. with filter change. Fuel Requirements: Regular unleaded.

STANDARD ENGINE: K-2500: Optional for K-2500 with HP6 and all K-3500 models with GVW of 8500 lb. and above. Ordering Code: LT9: 350 V-8 Engine Type: OHV, V-8. Cast iron block and alloy iron cylinder head. Key features include chain drive camshaft and forged steel connecting rods. This engine was produced by GM-Chevrolet Motor Division. Bore x Stroke: 4.0 in. x 3.50 in. Lifters: Hydraulic. Number of main bearings-5. Fuel Induction: Single Rochester 4-bbl. carburetor. Compression Ratio: 8.3:1. Displacement: 350 cu. in. (5.7 liters). Horsepower: Net: 160 @ 3800 rpm. (California rating: 155 @ 3600 rpm). Torque: Net: 260 lb.-ft. @ 2800 rpm. (California rating: 240 lb.-ft. @ 2800 rpm). Oil refill capacity: 5 qt. with filter change. Fuel Requirements: Regular unleaded.

OPTIONAL ENGINE: K-1500 models: Ordering Code: LE9: 305 V-8. Key features include Electronic Spark Control, new staged 4-barrel carburetor, camshaft and free-flow exhaust system. Not available for California. This engine was produced by GM-Chevrolet Motor Division and GM of Canada. Engine Type: OHV, V-8. Cast iron block and alloy iron cylinder head. Bore x Stroke: 3.74 in. x 3.48 in. Lifters: Hydraulic. Number of main bearings-5. Fuel Induction: Single Rochester 4-bbl. staged carburetor. Compression Ratio: 9.2:1. Displacement: 305 cu. in. (5.0 liters). Horsepower: 160 @ 4400 rpm. Torque: 235 lb.-ft. @ 2000 rpm. Oil refill capacity: 5 qt. with filter change. Fuel Requirements: Regular unleaded.

OPTIONAL ENGINE: K-1500 models: Ordering Code: LG9: 305 V-8. Key features include 2-barrel carburetor. This engine was produced by GM-Chevrolet Motor Division and GM of Canada. Engine Type: OHV, V-8. Cast iron block and alloy iron cylinder head. Bore x Stroke: 3.74 in. x 3.48 in. Lifters: Hydraulic. Number of main bearings-5. Fuel Induction: Single Rochester 4-bbl. staged carburetor. Compression Ratio: 8.5:1. Displacement: 305 cu. in. (5.0 liters). Horsepower: 130 @ 4000 rpm. Torque: 240 lb.-ft. @ 2000 rpm. Oil refill capacity: 5 qt. with filter change. Fuel Requirements: Regular unleaded.

OPTIONAL ENGINE: K-1500 models for California: Ordering Code: LF3: 305 V-8. Key features include 4-barrel carburetor, camshaft and free-flow exhaust system. This engine was produced by GM-Chevrolet Motor Division and GM of Canada. Engine Type: OHV, V-8. Cast iron block and alloy iron cylinder head. Bore x Stroke: 3.74 in. x 3.48 in. Lifters: Hydraulic. Number of main bearings-5. Fuel Induction: Single Rochester 4-bbl. carburetor. Compression Ratio: 8.6:1. Displacement: 305 cu. in. (5.0 liters). Horsepower: 150 @ 4200 rpm. Torque: 240 lb.-ft. @ 2000 rpm. Oil refill capacity: 5 qt. with filter change. Fuel Requirements: Regular unleaded.

OPTIONAL ENGINE: K-3500 pickup and chassis and cab models. Ordering Code: LE9: 454 V-8. Engine Type: OHV, V-8. Cast iron block and alloy iron cylinder head. Bore x Stroke: 4.25 in. x 4.00 in. Lifters: Hydraulic. Number of main bearings-5. Fuel Induction: Single Rochester 4-bbl. carburetor. Compression Ratio: 7.9:1. Displacement: 454 cu. in. (7.4 liters). Horsepower: 210 @ 3800 rpm. Torque: 340 lb.-ft. @ 2800 rpm. Oil refill capacity: 5 qt. with filter change. Fuel Requirements: Regular unleaded.

CHASSIS FEATURES: Separate body and frame with channel side rails. Carbon-Steel, 39,000 psi. 117.5 in. wheelbase: 2.30 in. x 5.92 in. x 0.156 in. Section modulus: 3.06 in. 129.5 in.: 2.30 in. x 5.92 in. x 0.194. Section modulus: 3.93. 135.5 in. wheelbase: 2.78 in. x 7.74 in. 0.194 in. Section modulus: 6.20. 164.5 in. wheelbase: 2.78 in. x 7.74 in. x 0.224 in. Section modulus: 7.33. 131.5 in. wheelbase: 2.30 in. x 5.92 in. x 0.194 in. Section modulus: 3.84 in. Optional: None.

SUSPENSION AND RUNNING GEAR: Front Suspension: K-1500: Tapered 2-leaf springs. Capacity: 1650 lb. (16), 1850 lb. (03, 06). K-2500: Tapered 2-leaf springs. Capacity: 1850 lb. K-3500: Tapered 3-leaf springs. Capacity: 2250 lb. Rear Suspension: K-1500 and K-2500: 52 in. x 2.25 in. Two-stage, 7-leaf. K-3500: 56 in. x 2.50 in. Capacity: K-1500: 2075 lb. K-2500: 2800 lb. K-3500: 3500 lb. 1.0 in. dia. shock absorbers. Optional Rating: K-2500: 3000 lb. rating at ground. Capacity: 6000 lb., with RPO CP6 K-3500: RPO RO5 (Dual rear wheels): 3750 lb. rating at ground. Capacity: 7500 lb. Front Axle Type and Capacity: K-1500 and K-2500: GMC or Spicer, K35: Spicer. K-1500: Semi-floating. 3600 lb. capacity. Optional: None. K-2500: Full-floating, 3800 lb. capacity. K-3500: Full-floating, 4500 lb. Optional: None. Rear Axle Type and Capacity: K-1500: Chevrolet, semi-floating, 3750 lb. capacity. K-2500: Chevrolet, full-floating, 5700 lb. K-3500: 7500 lb. Optional: None. Final Drive Ratio: Standard: K-1500: 6-cyl. and 3-spd. man. trans. 3.73:1; with 4-spd. man. trans. or 3-spd. auto. trans.: 3.42:1. LE9-305 V-8 and 3-spd. man. trans.: 3.08:1; with 4-spd. man. trans.: 2.73:1; with 3-spd. auto. trans.: 2.56:1. California only: LS9-350 V-8 3-spd. auto. trans.: 2.73:1. Optional K-1500: 6-cyl. with 4-spd. man. trans. or 3-spd. auto. trans.: 3.73:1. LE9-305 V-8 and 4-spd. man. trans.: 3.08:1; with 3-spd. auto. trans.: 2.73:1, 3.73:1 (requires RPO Z82, Trailering Special Package). California only: LS9-350 V-8 3-spd. auto. trans.: 3.08:1. Standard: K-2500 with GVW up to 8500 lb.: LS9 350 V-8 and 3-spd. man. trans.: 3.42:1, with 4-spd. man. trans. or 3-spd. auto. trans.: 3.23:1 (not avail. with locking rear differential). California only: LS9 350 V-8 and 3-spd. auto. trans: 3.23:1; K-2500 with GVW over 8500 lb.: L25 6-cyl.: With 4-spd. man. trans. or 3-spd. auto. trans.: 4.10:1; with LT9 350 V-8: 4-spd. man. trans.: 3.73:1; 3-spd. auto. trans.: 4.10:1. K-2500 with GVW over 8500 lb. L25 292 6-cyl.: 4.10:1 (4-spd. man. and auto. trans.); LT9 350 V-8: 4-spd. man. trans.: 3.73:1; 3-spd. auto. trans.: 4.10:1. Optional: LT9 350 V-8: 4-spd. man. trans.: 4.10:1. Standard K-3500: L25, 6-cyl, 4-spd. man. and auto. trans.: 4.56:1; LT9, 350 V-8, 4-spd. man. and auto. trans. and 9200 lb. GVW: 4.10:1; LT9, 350 V-8, 4-spd. man. and auto. trans. and 10,000 lb. GVW: 4.56:1. Optional K-3500: LT9, 350 V-8, 4-spd. man. and auto. trans. and 9200 lb. GVW: 4.56:1; LT9, 350 V-8, 4-spd. man. and auto. trans. and 10,000 lb. GVW: 4.10:1. Transfer Case: K-1500 and K-2500: New Process 208. Single lever, 2.61, 1.00:1. K-3500: New Process 205, two-speed: 1.96, 1.00:1. Brakes: Type: Hydraulic, power assisted. Dimensions: K-1500: Front: Disc: 11.86 in. x 1.28 in. Rear: Drums: 11.15 x 2.75 in. K-2500: Front: Disc: 12.5 in. x 1.28 in. Rear: Drums: 11.15 in. x 2.75 in. K-2500 and K-3500: Front: Disc: 12.50 in. x 1.53 in. Rear: Drum: 13.00 in. x 3.50 in. Wheels: K-1500: 15 x 6.0JJ 6-stud disc. Optional: 15 x 8JJ. K-2500: 16.5 x 6.00 in. 8-stud disc. Optional: 16.5 x 6.75. K-3500: 16.5 x 6.75. Tires: K-1500: P215/75R15-P metric radial. K-2500: 8.75 x 16.5C K-3500: 9.50 x 16.5D. Optional: K-1500: G78 x 15B, white stripe; H78 x 15B, tubeless, black sidewall or white stripe; L78 x 15B black sidewall or white stripe, tubeless; 10.00 x 16.5C tubeless; G78 x 15B tube-type; 7.00 x 15C tube-type; 6.50 x 16C tube-type and LR78 x 15C white sidewall radial ply. The following tires were specified for K-1500 models with the 5600 lb. GVW Package which included a front heavy-duty stabilizer bar: H78 x 15B 4-ply rating, tubeless; 6.50 x 16C 6-ply rating, tube-type, truck type. The following tires were specified for K-1500 models with the 6000 lb. GVW Package which included a front heavy-duty stabilizer bar and heavy-duty rear springs: L78 x 15B 4-ply rating, tubeless. Optional K-2500: 9.50 x 16.5E Firestone Town and Country, 8.75 x 16.5D tubeless; 9.50 x 16.5D tubeless; 10.00 x 16.5C tubeless (not available for Fenderside models); 7.50 x 16C 6-ply rating, tube-type; 7.50 x 16D tube-type; 7.50 x 16E tube-type. The following tires were specified for K-2500 models with the 7500 lb. GVW Package which included a front heavy-duty stabilizer bar: 8.75 x 16.5 C 6-ply rating, tubeless; 7.50 x 16C 6-ply rating, tubeless. The following tires were specified for K-2500 models with the 8200 lb. GVW Package which included a front heavy-duty stabilizer bar: 9.50 x 16.5D 8-ply rating, tubeless; 7.50 x 16C 6-ply rating, tube-type. Steering: Recirculating ball gear. Ratio: 20:1. Turning Circle: 47 ft. Steering wheel diameter: 17.5 in. Optional: Power-assisted. Ratio: 16.4:1. Transmission: K-1500 and K-2500: 3-speed GMC, synchromesh manual (RPO M15). Transmission Ratios: 5.7 liter V-8: 2.85, 1.68, 1.00:1. Reverse: 2.95:1. 5.0 liter V-8: 3.11, 1.84, 1.0:1 Reverse: 3.22:1. 4.1 liter 6-cyl.: 3.50, 1.89, 1.00:1. Reverse: 3.62:1. Optional: SM465. 4-speed manual synchromesh (RPO M20). Ratios: 6.56, 3.58, 1.70, 1.00:1. Reverse: 6.09:1. The K-2500 crew cab and all K-3500 models had this transmission as standard equipment. Optional: 3-speed Turbo Hydra-Matic 400 (RPO M40). Ratios: 2.1 x 2.48, 1.48, 1.00:1. Reverse: 2.10:1. The 400 cu. in. V-8 was available only with this transmission. Clutch: Diaphragm, spring. Clutch diameter: 6-cyl.: 11 in. dia. Total lining area: 123.5 sq. in. Total plate pressure: 2075 lb. V-8: 12 in. dia. Total lining area: 149.2 sq. in. Total plate pressure: 2060 lb. Optional: K-2500 6-cyl.: 11 in. dia. Total lining area: 124.0 sq. in. 307 V-8: 12 in. dia. Total lining area: 150 sq. in.

VEHICLE DIMENSIONS: Wheelbase: K-1500: 117.5 in. 131.5 in. K-2500: 131.5 in. All Suburbans and Panels: 129.5 in. K-3500: 131.5 in. 164.5 in. Overall Length: 117.5 in. Wideside pickups: 191.30 in. 131.5 in. Wideside pickups: 212.00. 117.5 in. Fenderside pickups: 190.5 in. 131.5 in. Fenderside pickups: 210.25. 117.5 in. Chassis-cab: 186.05 in. K-3500 data: 164.5 in. wheelbase: 244.43 in. Front/Rear Tread: 67.4 in./65.8 in. Overall Height: K-1500 Wideside pickup: 72.0 in. K-2500 Wideside pickup: 74.0 in. K-3500 Wideside pickup: 74.0 in. K-3500 crew cab: 75.0 in. K-1500 Suburban: 73.5 in. K-2500 Suburban: 75.5 in. Width: Pickup: 79.5 in. Front/Rear Overhang: Pickups: 33 in./41 in. Tailgate: Width and Height: 72 in. x 19.25 in. Approach/Departure Degrees: K-1500 117.5 in. Wideside and Fenderside: 33/19. K-1500 131.5 in. Wideside: 33/15. K-1500 131.5 in. wheelbase Fenderside: 33/16. K-2500 131.5 in. wheelbase Wideside: 35/20. K-2500 131.5 in. wheelbase Fenderside: 35/21. K-3500 Wideside pickup: 41/19. K-3500 crew cab pickup: 38/18. Ground Clearance: Front axle: 7.25 in. Rear axle: 7.0 in. Oil pan: 16.5 in. Transfer case: 12.0 in. Fuel tank: 16.6 in. Load space: Pickup box dimensions: 117.5 in. wheelbase Wideside: 78.25 in. x 50 in. x 19.25 in. 131.5 in. wheelbase Wideside: 98 in. x 50 in. x 19.25 in. Capacity: 117.5 wheelbase: 58.4 cu. ft. 131.5 in. wheelbase: 74.3 cu. ft. 117.5 in. wheelbase Fenderside: 78.5 in. x 50 in. x 17.5 in. 131.5 in. wheelbase Fenderside: 96.25 in. x 50 in. x 17.5 in. Front headroom: 38.5 in. (seat to top of cab). Front hip room: 67.25 in. Pedal to seat back (max.): 43.5 in. Steering wheel to seat back (max.): 17.3 in. Seat to ground: 35.0 in. Floor to ground: 23.0 in.

CAPACITIES: Fuel Tank: 117.5 in. wheelbase: 16.0 gal. 131.5 in. wheelbase, 135.5 in. wheelbase and 164.5 in. wheelbase: 20 gal. Optional: 16 gal. auxiliary tank. for 117.5 in.; 20 gal. auxiliary for 131.5 in. 135.5 in. and 164.5 in. wheelbase. Engine coolant system: 250 6-cyl.: 14.8 qt. 305 V-8: 17.6 qt. 350 V-8: 17.6 qt. 400 V-8: 19.6 qt. (20 qt. on K-2500 and K-3500).

ACCOMMODATIONS: Seating Capacity: Pickup and chassis-cab models: 3 passenger. Optional: None. Crew cab: 6 passenger. Suburban: 3 passenger. Optional: 6 or 9 passenger.

INSTRUMENTATION: Speedometer, odometer, fuel level gauge. Warning lights for battery, oil pressure, generator, brake system warning, directional/hazard lights, high beam, and engine coolant temperature.

OPTIONS AND PRICES: 305 V-8 (RPO LE9): $345.00. 305 V-8 (RPO LG9). 350 V-8 (RPO LS9). Air conditioning (RPO C60): $563.00. 2.73:1 axle ratio (RPO GU2): $25.00. Chrome grille (RPO V22). Automatic transmission (RPO MX1): $366.00. Four-speed manual transmission. Chrome front bumper. Chrome front bumper guards. Chrome rear bumper. Chrome rear step bumper. Deluxe front bumper. Deluxe rear bumper. Painted rear step bumper. Cargo area lamp. Cigarette lighter. Color-keyed floor mats (RPO B32): $11.00. ComforTilt steering wheel. Deluxe Front End Appearance Package. Deluxe instrument panel. Dome lamp. Electric clock. Gauge Package. Includes voltmeter, engine coolant temperature and oil pressure gauges. Headlamp warning buzzer. Halogen high-beam headlamps, available with Deluxe Front Appearance Package only (RPO TT5): $25.00. Intermittent windshield wipers (RPO CD4): $32.00. Painted below eye-level mirrors (RPO D44). Stainless steel below eye-level mirrors (RPO D45). Stainless steel camper mirror (RPO DF2). Painted steel below eye-level mirrors (RPO DF1). Visor mirror. Black body moldings. Bright body moldings. Custom Molding Package-black. Deluxe Molding Package-bright. Door edge guards. Wheel opening moldings. Cruise control (RPO K35): 122.00. Power door locks (two-door models only). Power windows. Rear bench seat (K-3500 bonus/crew cab). Painted West Coast mirrors (K-3500 bonus/crew cab only), (RPO DG5). Conventional two-tone paint. Deluxe two-tone paint (RPO ZY4). Exterior Decor Package (RPO ZY5). Special two-tone paint (RPO ZY3). Pickup box side rails. AM radio. AM/FM radio. Operating Convenience Package (RPO ZQ2): $230.00. AM/FM radio with cassette player (RPO UN3): $325.00. AM/FM radio with CB and antenna. Windshield antenna. Roof marker lamps. Sliding rear window (RPO A28): $84.00. Glide-out spare tire carrier (RPO P11): $31.00. Side-mounted spare tire carrier. Tachometer (RPO U16): $86.00. Tinted glass. (RPO AO1): $33.00. Auxiliary fuel tank (RPO NL2): $169.00. Auxiliary battery. Locking rear differential (RPO G80): $182.00. Cold Climate Package. Engine oil cooler (RPO KC4): $90.00. 10R-15B tires white letter, on-off road tires available for K-1500 only (RPO XXN): $170.48. 10R-15B spare tire, available for K-1500 only (RPO ZNX): $85.74. Transmission oil cooler (RPO VO2): $45.00. 55 amp generator. 63 amp generator. Heavy-duty battery. Heavy-duty front and rear shock absorbers. Heavy-duty radiator. Trailering Special. Camper body wiring harness. Dual exhaust system (K-3500 only). Dual rear wheels (K-3500 only). Front tow hooks. Front quad shock absorbers, available for K-1500 and K-2500 only (RPO Z75): $102.00. Fuel tank shield, not available for K-3500 bonus/crew cab (RPO NY1): $129.00. Heavy-duty front springs (K-2500 only.) Extra capacity rear springs (K-2500 and K-3500 bonus/crew cab). Extra capacity rear springs (K-3500 bonus/crew cab only). Main and auxiliary rear springs (K-3500 models only). Special camper chassis equipment-basic (K-2500 HD, and K-3500 models only). Special camper chassis equipment-deluxe (K-2500 HD, and K-3500 models only). Street coupe option (RPO Z77): $868.00. Wheelcovers, available for K-1500 and K-2500 only (RPO PO1). Wheel trim rings (RPO PO6). Aluminum wheels, available for K-1500 only (RPO PA6). Rallye wheels, available for K-1500 only (RPO N67).

HISTORICAL FOOTNOTES: Calendar year sales of GMC trucks of all types totalled 141,335, including 97,599 pickups and 4349 Suburbans.

1982 PICKUP & SUBURBAN

General Motors 379 cu. in. 6.2 liter diesel V-8 was available for all GMC trucks for 1982. Details of this engine are found in the 1982 Chevrolet section. This engine was joined to a new 4-speed manual overdrive transmission. The K-1500 and K-2500 models gasoline models and the K1500 diesel were also available with a new 4-speed overdrive automatic transmission. A standard 3-speed automatic transmission was installed in the K-2500 heavy-duty model (equipped with RPO HD6) and the K-3500 trucks with GVW ratings over 8500 lb. if ordered with the diesel. The K3500 transfer case was now equipped with synchronized gearings, enabling the shifting into four-wheel drive at speeds under 25 mph. To return to two-wheel drive the vehicle was stopped, the transfer case shifted into two-wheel drive at which point the truck was driven in reverse slowly for about 10 feet.

A chrome front bumper was now standard on all models. Improved anti-corrosion methods were also now employed.

The High Sierra level was no longer offered. The standard custom interior provided a full-foam front seat with a new dual-tone leathergrain vinyl trim, an inertia latch seat back that folded forward for access to the cab storage area, color-keyed door trim panels with large padded armrests, padded sunshades, cab interior light, prismatic day/night rearview mirror and a foam-padded instrument panel pad with a Sierra nameplate.

The Sierra Grande trim included these changes or additions to the base level's content: A choice of custom cloth or vinyl seats, black crackle insert and bright trim on door panels, color-keyed floor mat, door or manually operated dome light, extra insulation, cigarette lighter and Sierra Grande nameplate on instrument panel. The Sierra Classic trim included all Sierra Grande items plus the following changes or additions: Full cowl side trim panels, door-closing assist strap, door area carpet trim on lower portion of door panel, nameplate on instrument panel, bright brushed-finish aluminum trim on instrument cluster and door trim panels, needle-type full-gauge instrumentation, right-hand visor mirror, custom steering wheel, color-keyed carpeting, door storage pockets and (except for bonus cab rear compartment), extra-thick floor insulation.

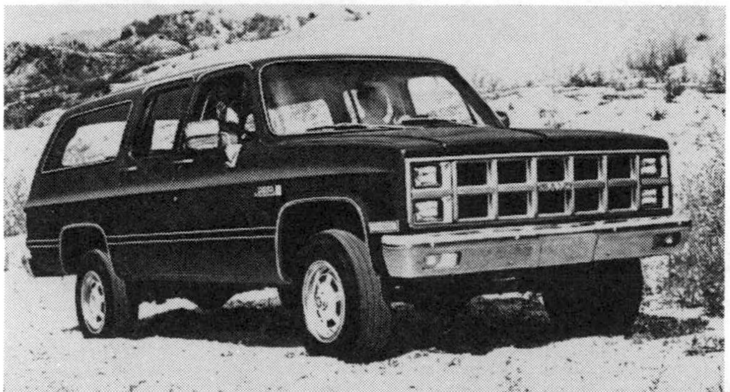

1982 GMC Suburban K-2500

All interior trim offering were available in a choice of two carry over colors: Blue and carmine, or three new colors: Charcoal, mahogany and medium almond. Charcoal and mahogany were limited to application on two-door cab models only.

Four exterior colors were carried over from 1981: Midnight black, frost white, colonial yellow and carmine red. Six new colors debuted for the 1982 models: Silver metallic, light blue metallic, mahogany metallic, almond, midnight blue and light bronze metallic.

I.D. DATA: Unchanged from 1981 except the letter C designated the 1982 model year.

Model Number	Body Type	Factory Price	GVW	Shipping Weight	Prod. Total
Series K-1500-1/2 ton 250 6-cyl. 117.5 in., 131.5 in. wheelbase (Suburban: 129.5 in. wheelbase and standard 305 V-8)					
TK10703	6.5 ft. F-S Pickup	$8874	6200	4442	—
TK10703	6.5 ft. Wideside Pickup	$8749	6200	4485	—
TK10903	8 ft. Wideside Pickup	$8899	6200	4686	—
TK10906	Suburban Endgate	$10,656	6200	5273	—
TK10906	Suburban Pnl. Drs.	$10,622	6200[1]	5250	—

NOTE 1: Surburban available with optional 6800 and 730 lb. GVW Packages.

Model Number	Body Type	Factory Price	GVW	Shipping Weight	Prod. Total
Series K-2500-3/4 ton 292 6-cyl.1. 131.5 in. wheelbase. (Suburban-129.5 in. wheelbase), Crew and Bonus Cab: 164.5 in. wheelbase, Suburban weight with standard 350 V-8					
TK20903	8 ft. Fenderside Pickup	$9815	6800	4807	—
TK20903	8 ft. Wideside Pickup	$9690	6800	4878	—
TK20906	Suburban Endgate	$11,584	6800	5472	—
TK20906	Suburban Pnl. Drs.	$11,550	6800	5434	—

NOTE 1: Not available in California where the 350 engine is base.
* 8600 lb. GVW optional.

Model Number	Body Type	Factory Price	GVW	Shipping Weight	Prod. Total
Series K-3500-1 ton 350 V-8. 131.5 in. wheelbase, Crew and Bonus Cab: 164.5 in. wheelbase					
TK30903	Chassis & Cab[1]	$10,435	8400*	4956	—
TK30903	8 ft. Wideside Pickup	$10,793	8400	5318	—
TK30943	Chassis & Bonus Cab	$11,274	8400	5370	—
TK30943	W-S Bonus Cab	$11,617	8400	5743	—
TK30943	Chassis & Crew Cab	$10,259	8400	5370	—

NOTE 1: 135.5 in. wheelbase.
* 9200 and 10,000 lb. GVW optional.

STANDARD ENGINE: All K-1500 6-cyl. models: 250 Six (LE3 ordering code). Not available for California where a 305 V-8 with 4-bbl. carburetor is installed. Engine Type: OHV, In-line 6-cylinder. Cast iron block and cylinder head. Key features include a staged 2-bbl. carburetor that used only one barrel for normal operation. The second barrel was used when more power was needed. The emissions control used engine vacuum pulses instead of an air pump, pulley, and belt. This systems saved about 15 lbs. in weight as compared to the older system. This engine was produced by GM-Chevrolet Motor Division. Bore x Stroke: 3.875 in. x 3.53 in. Lifters: Hydraulic. Number of main bearings-7. Fuel Induction: Single Rochester 2-bbl. carburetor. Compression Ratio: 8.3:1. Displacement: 250 cu. in. (4.1 liters). Horsepower: Net: 120 @ 3600 rpm. (California: 110 @ 3600 rpm). Torque: Net: 200 lb.-ft. @ 2000 rpm. (California: 195 lb.-ft. @ 2000 rpm). Oil refill capacity: 5 qt. with filter change. Fuel Requirements: Regular unleaded.

STANDARD ENGINE: K-2500 with RPO CH6 and K-3500 models: 292 Six. Ordering Code: L25. This engine was produced by GM de Mexico. Engine Type: OHV, 6-cyl. Cast iron block and cylinder head. Key features include cast iron intake manifold, aluminized-face intake valves, Stellite-faced exhaust valves with hardened faces. Bore x Stroke: 3.875 in. x 4.125 in. Lifters: Hydraulic. Number of main bearings-7. Fuel Induction: Single Rochester 1-bbl. carburetor. Compression Ratio: 7.8:1. Displacement: 292 cu. in. (4.8 liters). Horsepower: Net: 115 @ 3400 rpm. Torque: Net: 215 lb.-ft. @ 1600 rpm. Oil refill capacity: 6 qt. with filter change. Fuel Requirements: Regular unleaded.

STANDARD ENGINE: K-2500: Optional for K-2500 with HP6 and all K-3500 models. Ordering Code: LS9: 350 V-8 Engine Type: OHV, V-8. Cast iron block and alloy iron cylinder head. Key features include chain drive camshaft and forged steel connecting rods. This engine was produced by GM-Chevrolet Motor Division. Bore x Stroke: 4.0 in. x 3.50 in. Lifters: Hydraulic. Number of main bearings-5. Fuel Induction: Single Rochester 4-bbl. carburetor. Compression Ratio: 8.2:1. Displacement: 350 cu. in. (5.7 liters). Horsepower: Net: 165 @ 3800 rpm. Torque: Net: 275 lb.-ft. @ 1600 rpm. Oil refill capacity: 5 qt. with filter change. Fuel Requirements: Regular unleaded.

STANDARD ENGINE: K-2500: Optional for K-2500 with HP6 and all K-3500 models with GVW of 8500 lb. and above. Ordering Code: LT9: 350 V-8 Engine Type: OHV, V-8. Cast iron block and alloy iron cylinder head. Key features include chain drive camshaft and forged steel connecting rods. This engine was produced by GM-Chevrolet Motor Division. Bore x Stroke: 4.0 in. x 3.50 in. Lifters: Hydraulic. Number of main bearings-5. Fuel Induction: Single Rochester 4-bbl. carburetor. Compression Ratio: 8.3:1. Displacement: 350 cu. in. (5.7 liters). Horsepower: Net: 160 @ 3800 rpm. (California rating: 155 @ 3600 rpm). Torque: Net: 260 lb.-ft. @ 2800 rpm. (California rating: 240 lb.-ft. @ 2800 rpm). Oil refill capacity: 5 qt. with filter change. Fuel Requirements: Regular unleaded.

OPTIONAL ENGINE: K-1500 models: Ordering Code: LE9: 305 V-8. Key features include Electronic Spark Control, new staged 4-barrel carburetor, camshaft and free-flow exhaust system. Not available for California. This engine was produced by GM-Chevrolet Motor Division and GM of Canada. Engine Type: OHV, V-8. Cast iron block and alloy iron cylinder head. Bore x Stroke: 3.74 in. x 3.48 in. Lifters: Hydraulic. Number of main bearings-5. Fuel Induction: Single Rochester 4-bbl. staged carburetor. Compression Ratio: 9.2:1. Displacement: 305 cu. in. (5.0 liters). Horsepower: 160 @ 4400 rpm. Torque: 235 lb.-ft. @ 2000 rpm. Oil refill capacity: 5 qt. with filter change. Fuel Requirements: Regular unleaded.

OPTIONAL ENGINE: K-1500 models for California. Ordering Code: LF3: 305 V-8. Key features include 4-barrel carburetor, camshaft and free-flow exhaust system. This engine was produced by GM-Chevrolet Motor Division and GM of Canada. Engine Type: OHV, V-8. Cast iron block and alloy iron cylinder head. Bore x Stroke: 3.74 in. x 3.48 in. Lifters: Hydraulic. Number of main bearings-5. Fuel Induction: Single Rochester 4-bbl. carburetor. Compression Ratio: 8.6:1. Displacement: 305 cu. in. (5.0 liters). Horsepower: 150 @ 4200 rpm. Torque: 240 lb.-ft. @ 2000 rpm. Oil refill capacity: 5 qt. with filter change. Fuel Requirements: Regular unleaded.

OPTIONAL ENGINE: K-3500 pickup and chassis and cab models: Ordering Code: LE9: 454 V-8. Engine Type: OHV, V-8. Cast iron block and alloy iron cylinder head. Bore x Stroke: 4.25 in. x 4.00 in. Lifters: Hydraulic. Number of main bearings-5. Fuel Induction: Single Rochester 4-bbl. carburetor. Compression Ratio: 7.9:1. Displacement: 454 cu. in. (7.4 liters). Horsepower: 210 @ 3800 rpm. Torque: 340 lb.-ft. @ 2800 rpm. Oil refill capacity: 5 qt. with filter change. Fuel Requirements: Regular unleaded.

OPTIONAL ENGINE: All models. Ordering Code: LH4: 379 diesel V-8. Engine Type: OHV, V-8. Cast iron block and alloy iron cylinder head. Bore x Stroke: 3.98 in. x 3.80 in. Lifters: Hydraulic. Number of main bearings-5. Fuel Induction: Fuel injection. Compression Ratio: 21.5:1. Displacement: 379 cu. in. (6.2 liters). Horsepower: 130 @ 3600 rpm. (LL4 for K20 with C6P and K30 has 135 hp. @ 3600 rpm). Torque: 240 lb.-ft. @ 2000 rpm. Oil refill capacity: 7 qt. with filter change. Fuel Requirements: Diesel.

CHASSIS FEATURES: Separate body and frame with channel side rails. Carbon-Steel, 39,000 psi. 117.5 in. wheelbase: 2.30 in. x 5.92 in. x 0.156 in. Section modulus: 3.06 in. 129.5 in.: 2.30 in. x 5.92 in. x 0.194. Section modulus: 3.93. 135.5 in. wheelbase: 2.78 in. x 7.74 in. 0.194 in. Section modulus: 6.20. 164.5 in. wheelbase: 2.78 in. x 7.74 in. x 0.224 in. Section modulus: 7.33. 131.5 in. wheelbase: 2.30 in. x 5.92 in. x 0.194 in. Section modulus: 3.84 in. Optional: None.

SUSPENSION AND RUNNING GEAR: Front Suspension: K-1500: Tapered 2-leaf springs. Capacity: 1650 lb. K-2500: Tapered 2-leaf springs. Capacity: 1850 lb. K-3500: Tapered 3-leaf springs. Capacity: 2250 lb. Rear Suspension: K-1500 and K-2500: 52 in. x 2.25 in. Two-stage, 7-leaf. K-3500: 56 in. x 2.50 in. Capacity: K-1500: 2075 lb. K-2500: 2800 lb. K-3500: 3500 lb. 1.0 in. dia. shock absorbers. Optional Rating: K-2500: 3000 lb. rating at ground. Capacity: 6000 lb., with RPO CP6 K-3500: RPO RO5 (Dual rear wheels): 3750 lb. rating at ground. Capacity: 7500 lb. Front Axle Type and Capacity: K-1500 and K-2500: GMC or Spicer, K35: Spicer. K-1500: Semi-floating. 3600 lb. capacity. Optional: None. K-2500: Full-floating, 3800 lb. capacity. K-3500: Full-floating, 4500 lb. Optional: None. Rear Axle Type and Capacity: K-1500: Chevrolet, semi-floating. K-2500: Chevrolet, full-floating, 5700 lb. K-3500: 7500 lb. Optional: None. Final Drive Ratio: Standard-K-1500: 6-cyl. and 3-spd. man. trans. 3.73:1; with 4-spd. man. trans. or 3-spd. auto. trans.: 3.42:1. LE9-305 V-8 and 3-spd. man. trans.: 3.08:1; with 4-spd. man. trans.: 2.73:1; with 3-spd. auto. trans.: 2.56:1. California only: LS9-350 V-8 3-spd. auto. trans.: 2.73:1. Optional K-1500: 6-cyl. with 4-spd. man. trans. or 3-spd. auto. trans.: 3.73:1. LE9-305 V-8 and 4-spd. man. trans.: 3.08:1; with 3-spd. auto. trans.: 2.73:1, 3.73:1 (requires RPO Z82, Trailering Special Package). California only: LS9-350 V-8 3-spd. auto. trans.: 3.08:1. Standard: K-2500 with GVW up to 8500 lb.: LS9 350 V-8 and 3-spd. man. trans.: 3.42:1, with 4-spd. man. trans. or 3-spd. auto. trans.: 3.23:1 (not avail. with locking rear differential). California only: LS9 350 V-8 3-spd. auto. trans.: 3.23:1; K-2500 with GVW over 8500 lb.: L25 6-cyl.: With 4-spd. man. trans. or 3-spd. auto. trans.: 4.10:1; with LT9 350 V-8: 4-spd. man. trans.: 3.73:1; 3-spd. auto. trans.: 4.10:1. K-2500 with GVW over 8500 lb.: L25 292 6-cyl.: 4.10:1 (4-spd. man. and auto. trans.); LT9 350 V-8: 4-spd. man. trans.: 3.73:1; 3-spd. auto. trans.: 4.10:1. Optional: LT9 350 V-8: 4-spd. man. trans.: 4.10:1. Standard K-3500: L25, 6-cyl. 4-spd. man. and auto. trans.: 4.56:1; LT9, 350 V-8, 4-spd. man. and auto. trans. and 9200 lb. GVW: 4.10:1; LT9, 350 V-8, 4-spd. man. and auto. trans. and 10,000 lb. GVW: 4.56:1. Optional K-3500: LT9, 350 V-8, 4-spd. man. and auto. trans. and 9200 lb. GVW: 4.56:1; LT9, 350 V-8, 4-spd. man. and auto. trans. and 10,000 lb. GVW: 4.10:1. Optional: K-1500 and K-2500: 700R4 4-speed automatic overdrive. Ratios: 3.06, 1.36, 1.00, 0.70. Reverse: 2.29:1. Transfer Case: K-1500 and K-2500: New Process 208. Single lever, 2.61, 1.00:1. K-3500: New Process 205, two-speed: 1.96, 1.00:1. Brakes: Type: Hydraulic, power assisted. Dimensions: K-1500: Front: Disc: 11.86 in. x 1.28 in. Rear: Drums: 11.15 in. x 2.75 in. K-2500: Front: Disc: 12.5 in. x 1.28 in. Rear: Drums: 11.15 in. x 2.75 in. K-2500 and K-3500: Front: Disc: 12.50 in. x 1.53 in. Rear: Drum: 13.00 in. x 3.50 in. Wheels: K-1500: 15 x 6.0JJ 6-stud disc. Optional: 15 x 8JJ. K-2500: 16.5 x 6.00 in. 8-stud disc. Optional: 16.5 x 6.75. K-3500: 16.5 x 6.75. Tires: K-1500: P215/75R15-P metric radial. K-2500: 8.75 x 16.5C K-3500: 9.50 x 16.5D. Optional: K-1500: G78 x 15B, white stripe; H78 x 15B, tubeless, black sidewall or white stripe; L78 x 15B black sidewall or white stripe, tubeless; 10.00 x 16.5C tubeless; G78 x 15B tube-type; 7.00 x 15C tube-type; 6.50 x 16C tube-type and LR78 x 15C white sidewall radial ply. The following tires were specified for K-1500 models with the 5600 lb. GVW Package which included a front heavy-duty stabilizer bar: H78 x 15B 4-ply rating, tubeless; 6.50 x 16C 6-ply rating, tube-type, truck type. The following tires were specified for K-1500 models with the 6000 lb. GVW Package which included a front heavy-duty stabilizer bar and heavy-duty rear springs: L78 x 15B 4-ply rating, tubeless. Optional K-2500: 9.50 x 16.5E Firestone Town and Country, 8.75 x 16.5D tubeless; 9.50 x 16.5D tubeless; 10.00 x 16.5C tubeless (not available for Fenderside models); 7.50 x 16C 6-ply rating, tube-type; 7.50 x 16D tube-type; 7.50 x 16E tube-type. The following tires were specified for K-2500 models with the 7500 lb. GVW Package which included a front heavy-duty stabilizer bar: 8.75 x 16.5 C 6-ply rating, tubeless; 7.50 x 16C 6-ply rating, tubeless. The following tires were specified for K-2500 models with the 8200 lb. GVW Package which included a front heavy-duty stabilizer bar: 9.50 x 16.5D 8-ply rating, tubeless; 7.50 x 16C 6-ply rating, tube-type. Steering: Recirculating ball gear. Ratio: 20:1. Turning Circle: 47 ft. Steering wheel diameter: 17.5 in. Optional: Power-assisted. Ratio: 16.4:1. Transmission: K-1500 and K-2500: 3-speed GMC, synchromesh manual (RPO M15). Transmission Ratios: 5.7 liter V-8: 2.85, 1.68, 1.00:1. Reverse: 2.95:1. 5.0 liter V-8: 3.11, 1.84, 1.0:1 Reverse: 3.22:1. 4.1 liter 6-cyl.: 3.50, 1.89, 1.00:1. Reverse: 3.62:1. Optional: SM465. 4-speed manual synchromesh (RPO M20). Ratios: 6.56, 3.58, 1.70, 1.00:1. Reverse: 6.09:1. The K-2500 crew cab and all K-3500 models had this transmission as standard equipment. Optional: 3-speed Turbo Hydra-Matic 400 (RPO M40). Ratios: 2.1 x 2.48, 1.48, 1.00:1. Reverse: 2.10:1. The 400 cu. in. V-8 was available only with this transmission. Clutch: Diaphragm, spring. Clutch diameter: 6-cyl.: 11 in. dia. Total lining area: 123.5 sq. in. Total plate pressure: 2075 lb. V-8: 12 in. dia. Total lining area: 149.2 sq. in. Total plate pressure: 2060 lb. Optional: K-2500 6-cyl.: 11 in. dia. Total lining area: 124.0 sq. in. 307 V-8: 12 in. dia. Total lining area: 150 sq. in.

VEHICLE DIMENSIONS: Wheelbase: K-1500: 117.5 in. 131.5 in. K-2500: 131.5 in. All Suburbans and Panels: 129.5 in. K-3500: 131.5 in. 164.5 in. Overall Length: 117.5 in. Wideside pickups: 191.30 in. 131.5 in. Wideside pickups: 212.00 in. 117.5 in. Fenderside pickups: 190.5 in. 131.5 in. Fenderside pickups: 210.25. 117.5 in. Chassis-cab: 186.05 in. K-3500 data: 164.5 in. wheelbase: 244.43 in. Front/Rear Tread: 67.4 in./65.8 in. Overall Height: K-1500 Wideside pickup: 72.0 in. K-2500 Wideside pickup: 74.0 in. K-3500 Wideside pickup: 74.0 in. K-1500 crew cab: 75.0 in. K-1500 Suburban: 73.5 in. K-2500 Suburban: 75.5 in. Width: Pickup: 79.5 in. Front/Rear Overhang: Pickups: 33 in./41 in. Tailgate: Width and Height: 72 in. x 19.25 in. Approach/Departure Degrees: K-1500 117.5 in. Wideside and Fenderside: 33/19. K-1500 131.5 in. Wideside: 33/15. K-1500 131.5 in. wheelbase Fenderside: 33/16. K-2500 131.5 in. wheelbase Wideside: 35/20. K-2500 131.5 in. wheelbase Fenderside: 35/21. K-3500 164.5 in. wheelbase Wideside: 41/19. K-3500 crew cab pickup: 38/18. Ground Clearance: Front axle: 7.25 in. Rear axle: 7.0 in. Oil pan: 16.5 in. Transfer case: 12.0 in. Fuel tank: 16.6 in. Load space: Pickup box dimensions: 117.5 in. wheelbase Wideside: 78.25 in. x 50 in. x 19.25 in. 131.5 in. wheelbase Wideside: 98 in. x 50 in. x 19.25 in. Capacity: 117.5 wheelbase: 58.4 cu. ft. 131.5 in. wheelbase: 74.3 cu. ft. 117.5 in. wheelbase Fenderside: 78.5 in. x 50 in. x 17.5 in. 131.5 in. wheelbase Fenderside: 96.25 in. x 50 in. x 17.5 in. Front headroom: 38.5 in. (seat to top of cab). Front hip room: 67.25 in. Pedal to seat back (max.): 43.5 in. Steering wheel to seat back (max.): 17.3 in. Seat to ground: 35.0 in. Floor to ground: 23.0 in.

CAPACITIES: Fuel Tank: 117.5 in. wheelbase: 16.0 gal. 131.5 in. wheelbase: 135.5 in. wheelbase and 164.5 in. wheelbase: 20 gal. Optional: 16 gal. auxiliary tank for 117.5 in. 20 gal. auxiliary for 131.5 in. 135.5 in. and 164.5 in. wheelbase. Engine coolant system: 250 6-cyl.: 14.8 qt. 305 V-8: 17.6 qt. 350 V-8: 17.6 qt. 400 V-8: 19.6 qt. (20 qt. on K-2500 and K-3500).

ACCOMMODATIONS: Seating Capacity: Pickup and chassis-cab models: 3 passenger. Optional: None. Crew cab: 6 passenger. Suburban: 3 passenger. Optional: 6 or 9 passenger.

INSTRUMENTATION: Speedometer, odometer, fuel level gauge. Warning lights for battery, oil pressure, generator, brake system warning, directional/hazard lights, high beam, and engine coolant temperature.

OPTIONS AND PRICES: 5 liter V-8: $170. California emissions: $90. 5.7 liter V-8: $345. 379 cu. in. diesel engine: $1334. 4-speed manual trans.: $198. 4-speed manual with overdrive: $75. 3-speed automatic trans.: $438. 4-speed automatic with overdrive: $637. Optional axle ratios: $35. Rear step painted bumper: $106. Chromed rear bumper: $97. Rear step chromed bumper: $177. Front bumper guards: $39. Glide-out spare tire carrier: $39. Side-mounted spare tire carrier: $27. Quartz analog electric clock: $70, without Sierra Classic, $36 with Sierra Classic. Cold Climate Package: $184, without Trailering Package, $126 with Trailering Package. $172 with High Sierra or Sierra Classic and without Trailering Package, $114 with High Sierra or Sierra Classic and with Trailering Package. Engine oil cooler: $112. Heavy-duty transmission oil cooler: $55. Heavy-duty cooling system: $48. Power door locks: $115. Color-keyed floor mats: $14. Gauges Package. Includes voltmeter, engine coolant temperature and oil pressure: $34. 62 amp Delcotron generator: $58. Tinted glass: $40. Halogen high beam headlights: $15. Halogen high and low beam headlights: $20. Cargo area lamp: $56, with High Sierra or Sierra Classic: $32, without High Sierra or Sierra Classic: $56. Dome light: $24. Cigarette lighter: $28. Below eye-level painted mirrors: $44. Below eye-level stainless steel mirrors: $72. Camper style painted mirrors: $86. Black body side moldings: $105. Bright body side moldings: $131, without High Sierra, $13 with High Sierra. Custom Package: $144 without High Sierra, $26 with High Sierra. Deluxe Package: $157 without High Sierra, $39 with High Sierra. Door edge guard: $13. Pickup box side rails: $88. Operating Convenience Package: $281. AM radio: $92. AM/FM radio: $143. AM/FM stereo radio: $226. AM/FM stereo radio with 8-track tape player: $322. AM/FM stereo radio with cassette tape player: $327. AM/FM stereo radio with CB radio and triband antenna: $559. Windshield antenna: $31. Fuel tank shield: $84, without NL2 tank, $154 with NL tank. Front quad shock absorbers: $117. Speed control: $159 with automatic transmission, $169 with manual trans. Heavy-duty front springs: $84 without quad shocks, $53 with quad shocks. ComforTilt steering wheel: $95. Auxiliary 16 gal. fuel tank: $208. Two front towing hooks: $34. Bright wheelcovers: $38. Aluminum forged wheels: $411. Rallye wheels: $103. Styled wheels: $201. Power windows: $166. Sliding rear window: $100. Intermittent windshield wipers: $45. High Sierra Package: $208, Fenderside, $318, Wideside. Sierra Classic: $614, Fenderside, $780 without Exterior Decor Package, $753 with Exterior Decor Package. Seat trim: $48. Conventional two-tone paint: $69 with Sierra Classic, $42 without Sierra Classic. Special two-tone paint: $291 without High Sierra or Sierra Classic, $173 with High Sierra, $147 with Sierra Classic. Deluxe two-tone paint: $328 without High Sierra Classic or Sierra Classic, $210 with High Sierra, $157 with Sierra Classic. Dual rear wheels for K-3500: $664 to $677. Exterior Decor Package: $503, without High Sierra or Sierra Classic, $385 with High Sierra, $359 with Sierra Classic. Additional Suburban options: Center folding seat: $343. Center and rear folding seats: $640. 31 gal. fuel tank: $39. 40 gal. fuel tank: $91. Heavy-duty trailering Sspecial: $354-$619 depending upon vehicle option content. High Sierra trim: $379. Sierra Classic: $1135. Diesel equipment: $1041. Includes heavy-duty generator, dual batteries, engine oil cooler, engine block heater, sound insulation, water-in-fuel detection and drain system, dual exhaust and in-line fuel heater.

HISTORICAL FOOTNOTES: Calendar year sales of all types of GMC trucks was 200,214, of which 109,762 were full-sized pickups. Suburban sales were 9490.

1983 PICKUP & SUBURBAN

The 1983 GMC trucks had a new front end appearance highlighted by revised grille, lamp bezels and outline moldings. The parking lamps were placed below the standard single headlights. In the Deluxe grille they were positioned behind the lower grille corners. The Sierra Classic and High Sierra had new pewter-toned brushed aluminum finish for the instrument panel cluster bezels. The same trim was used for the High Sierra's instrument panel applique, horn button and door trim panels. A new electronic speed control was introduced. Other new developments included the availability of an air cleaner precleaner and an engine block heater for all gasoline engines; and improved corrosion protection.

1983 GMC Suburban High Sierra K-2500

I.D. DATA: Unchanged from 1982 except the letter D designated the 1983 model year.

Model Number	Body Type	Factory Price	GVW	Shipping Weight	Prod. Total
Series K-1500-1/2 ton 250 6-cyl. 117.5 in., 131.5 in. wheelbase (Suburban: 129.5 in. wheelbase and standard 305 V-8)					
TK10703	6.5 ft. F-S Pickup	$9020	6200	4442	—
TK10703	6.5 ft. Fleetside Pickup	$8895	6200	4485	—
TK10903	8 ft. Fleetside Pickup	$9045	6200	4686	—
TK10906	Suburban Endgate	$10,802	6200	5273	—
TK10906	Suburban Pnl. Drs.	$10,768	6200[1]	5250	—

NOTE 1: Suburban available with optional 6800 and 7300 lb. GVW Packages.

Series K-2500-3/4 ton 292 6-cyl.[1] 131.5 in. wheelbase. (Suburban-129.5 in. wheelbase), Crew and Bonus Cab: 164.5 in. wheelbase, Suburban weight with standard 350 V-8

TK20903	8 ft. Stepside Pickup	$9980	6800	4807	—
TK20903	8 ft. Fleetside Pickup	$9855	6800	4878	—
TK20906	Suburban Endgate	$11,749	6800	5472	—
TK20906	Suburban Pnl. Drs.	$11,715	6800	5434	—

NOTE 1: Not available in California where the 350 engine is base.
* 8600 lb. GVW optional.

Series K-3500-1 ton 350 V-8. 131.5 in. wheelbase, Crew and Bonus Cab: 164.5 in. wheelbase

TK30903	Chassis & Cab[1]	$10,605	8400*	4956	—
TK30903	8 ft. Fleetside Pickup	$10,963	8400	5318	—
TK30943	Chassis & Bonus Cab	$11,444	8400	5370	—
TK30943	W-S Bonus Cab	$11,787	8400	5743	—
TK30943	Chassis & Crew Cab	$10,429	8400	5370	—

NOTE 1: 135.5 in. wheelbase.
* 9200 and 10,000 lb. GVW optional.

STANDARD ENGINE: All K-1500 6-cyl. models: 250 Six (LE3 ordering code) Engine Type: OHV, In-line 6-cylinder. Cast iron block and cylinder head. Bore x Stroke: 3.875 in. x 3.53 in. Lifters: Hydraulic. Number of main bearings-7. Fuel Induction: Single Rochester 2-bbl. carburetor. Compression Ratio: 8.3:1. Displacement: 250 cu. in. (4.1 liters). Horsepower: Net: 115 @ 3600 rpm. (California Rating: 110 @ 3600 rpm). Torque: Net: 200 lb.-ft. @ 2000 rpm. (California Rating: 200 lb.-ft. @ 1600 rpm). Oil refill capacity: 5 qt. with filter change. Fuel Requirements: Regular unleaded.

STANDARD ENGINE: K-2500 with RPO CH6 and K-3500 models: 292 Six. Ordering Code: L25. This engine was produced by GM de Mexico. Not available in California with under 8500 lb. GVW rating. Engine Type: OHV, 6-cyl. Cast iron block and cylinder head. Key features include cast iron intake manifold, aluminized-face intake valves, Stellite-faced exhaust valves with hardened faces. Bore x Stroke: 3.875 in. x 4.125 in. Lifters: Hydraulic. Number of main bearings-7. Fuel Induction: Single Rochester 1-bbl. carburetor. Compression Ratio: 7.8:1. Displacement: 292 cu. in. (4.8 liters). Horsepower: Net: 115 @ 3400 rpm. Torque: Net: 215 lb.-ft. @ 1600 rpm. Oil refill capacity: 6 qt. with filter change. Fuel Requirements: Regular unleaded.

STANDARD ENGINE: K-2500: Optional for K-1500 (California only), K-2500 with HP6 and all K-3500 models. Ordering Code: LS9: 350 V-8 Engine Type: OHV, V-8. Cast iron block and alloy iron cylinder head. Key features include chain drive camshaft and forged steel connecting rods. This engine was produced by GM-Chevrolet Motor Division. Bore x Stroke: 4.0 in. x 3.50 in. Lifters: Hydraulic. Number of main bearings-5. Fuel Induction: Single Rochester 4-bbl. carburetor. Compression Ratio: 8.2:1. Displacement: 350 cu. in. (5.7 liters). Horsepower: Net: 165 @ 3800 rpm. Torque: Net: 275 lb.-ft. @ 1600 rpm. Oil refill capacity: 5 qt. with filter change. Fuel Requirements: Regular unleaded.

OPTIONAL ENGINE: K-2500 with HP6 and all K-3500 models: Ordering Code: LT9: 350 V-8 Engine Type: OHV, V-8. Cast iron block and alloy iron cylinder head. Key features include chain drive camshaft and forged steel connecting rods. This engine was produced by GM-Chevrolet Motor Division. Bore x Stroke: 4.0 in. x 3.50 in. Lifters: Hydraulic. Number of main bearings-5. Fuel Induction: Single Rochester 4-bbl. carburetor. Compression Ratio: 8.3:1. Displacement: 350 cu. in. (5.7 liters). Horsepower: Net: 160 @ 3800 rpm. (California rating: 155 @ 3600 rpm). Torque: Net: 260 lb.-ft. @ 2800 rpm. (California rating: 240 lb.-ft. @ 2800 rpm). Oil refill capacity: 5 qt. with filter change. Fuel Requirements: Regular unleaded.

OPTIONAL ENGINE: K-1500 models: Ordering Code: LE9: 305 V-8. Key features include Electronic Spark Control, new staged 4-barrel carburetor, camshaft and free-flow exhaust system. Not available for California. This engine was produced by GM-Chevrolet Motor Division and GM of Canada. Engine Type: OHV. V-8. Cast iron block and alloy iron cylinder head. Bore x Stroke: 3.74 in. x 3.48 in. Lifters: Hydraulic. Number of main bearings-5. Fuel Induction: Single Rochester 4-bbl. staged carburetor. Compression Ratio: 9.2:1. Displacement: 305 cu. in. (5.0 liters). Horsepower: 160 @ 4400 rpm. Torque: 235 lb.-ft. @ 2000 rpm. Oil refill capacity: 5 qt. with filter change. Fuel Requirements: Regular unleaded.

OPTIONAL ENGINE: K-1500 models for California: Ordering Code: LF3: 305 V-8. Key features include 4-barrel carburetor, camshaft and free-flow exhaust system. This engine was produced by GM-Chevrolet Motor Division and GM of Canada. Engine Type: OHV. V-8. Cast iron block and alloy iron cylinder head. Bore x Stroke: 3.74 in. x 3.48 in. Lifters: Hydraulic. Number of main bearings-5. Fuel Induction: Single Rochester 4-bbl. carburetor. Compression Ratio: 8.6:1. Displacement: 305 cu. in. (5.0 liters). Horsepower: 155 @ 4200 rpm. Torque: 240 lb.-ft. @ 1600 rpm. Oil refill capacity: 5 qt. with filter change. Fuel Requirements: Regular unleaded.

OPTIONAL ENGINE: K-3500 models: Ordering Code: LE8: 454 V-8. This engine was produced by GM-Chevrolet Motor Division. Engine Type: OHV. V-8. Cast iron block and alloy iron cylinder head. Bore x Stroke: 4.3 in. x 4.0 in. Lifters: Hydraulic. Number of main bearings-5. Fuel Induction: Single Rochester 4-bbl. carburetor. Compression Ratio: 7.9:1. Displacement: 454 cu. in. (7.4 liters). Horsepower: 230 @ 3800 rpm. Torque: 360 lb.-ft. @ 2800 rpm. Oil refill capacity: 5 qt. with filter change. Fuel Requirements: Regular unleaded.

OPTIONAL ENGINE: All models. Ordering Code: LH6: 6.2 liter V-8. This engine was produced by GM-Detroit Diesel Allison Division. Engine Type: OHV, diesel V-8. Bore x Stroke: 3.98 in. x 3.80 in. Lifters: Hydraulic. Number of main bearings-5. Fuel Induction: Fuel injection. Compression Ratio: 21.3:1. Displacement: 379.4 cu. in. (6.2 liters). Horsepower: 135 @ 3600 rpm. Torque: 240 lb.-ft. @ 2000 rpm. Oil refill capacity: 7 qt. with filter change. Fuel Requirements: Diesel. An LL4 version of this engine for models with GVW of 8500 lb. and above was also available. Its power ratings were 135 hp. @ 3600 rpm and 240 lb.-ft. of torque at 2000 rpm.

CHASSIS FEATURES: Separate body and frame with channel side rails. Carbon-Steel, 39,000 psi. 117.5 in. wheelbase: 2.30 in. x 5.92 in. x 0.156 in. Section modulus: 3.06 in. 129.5 in. x 5.92 in. x 0.194. Section modulus: 3.93. 135.5 in. wheelbase: 2.78 in. x 7.74 in. 0.194. Section modulus: 6.20. 164.5 in. wheelbase: 2.78 in. x 7.74 in. x 0.224. Section modulus: 7.33. 131.5 in. wheelbase: 2.30 in. x 5.92 in. x 0.194 in. Section modulus: 3.84 in. Optional: None.

SUSPENSION AND RUNNING GEAR: Front Suspension: K-1500: Tapered 2-leaf springs. Capacity: 1650 lb. (16), 1850 lb. (03, 06). K-2500: Tapered 2-leaf springs. Capacity: 1850 lb. K-3500: Tapered 3-leaf springs. Capacity: 2250 lb. Rear Suspension: K-1500 and K-2500: 52 in. x 2.25 in. Two-stage, 7-leaf. K-3500: 56 in. x 2.50 in. Capacity: K-1500: 2075 lb. K-2500: 2800 lb. K-3500: 3500 lb. 1.0 in. dia. shock absorbers. Optional Rating: K-2500: 3000 lb. rating at ground. Capacity: 6000 lb. with RPO CP6 K-3500: RPO RO5 (Dual rear wheels): 3750 lb. rating at ground. Capacity: 7500 lb. Front Axle Type and Capacity: K-1500 and K-2500: GMC or Spicer, K35: Spicer. K-1500: Semi-floating. 3600 lb. capacity. Optional: None. K-2500: Full-floating, 3800 lb. capacity. K-3500: Full-floating, 4500 lb. Optional: None. Rear Axle Type and Capacity: K-1500: Chevrolet, semi-floating, 3750 lb. capacity. K-2500: Chevrolet, full-floating, 5700 lb. K-3500: 7500 lb. Optional: None. Final Drive Ratio: Standard: K-1500: 6-cyl. and 3-spd. man. trans. 3.73:1; with 4-spd. auto. trans. 3.42:1. LE9-305 V-8

and 3-spd. man. trans.: 3.08:1; with 4-spd. man. trans.: 2.73:1; with 3-spd. auto. trans.: 2.56:1. California only: LS9-350 V-8 3-spd. auto. trans.: 2.73:1. Optional K-1500: 6-cyl. with 4-spd. man. trans. or 3-spd. auto. trans.: 3.73:1. LE9-305 V-8 and 4-spd. man. trans.: 3.08:1; with 3-spd. auto. trans.: 2.73:1, 3.73:1 (requires RPO Z82, Trailering Special Package). California only: LS9-350 V-8 3-spd. auto. trans.: 3.08:1. Standard: K-2500 with GVW up to 8500 lb.: LS9 350 V-8 and 3-spd. man. trans.: 3.42:1, with 4-spd. man. trans. or 3-spd. auto. trans.: 3.23:1 (not avail. with locking rear differential). California only: LS9 350 V-8 and 3-spd. auto. trans.: 3.23:1; K-2500 with GVW over 8500 lb. L25 6-cyl.: With 4-spd. man. trans. or 3-spd. auto. trans.: 4.10:1; with LT9 350 V-8: 4-spd. man. trans.: 4.10:1. K-2500 with GVW over 8500 lb. L25 292 6-cyl.: 4.10:1 (4-spd. man. and auto. trans.); LT9 350 V-8: 4-spd. man. trans.: 3.73:1; 3-spd. auto. trans.: 4.10:1. Optional: LT9 350 V-8: 4-spd. man. trans.: 4.10:1. Standard K-3500: L25, 6-cyl. 4-spd. man. and auto. trans.: 4.56:1; LT9, 350 V-8, 4-spd. man. and auto. trans. and 9200 lb. GVW: 4.10:1; LT9, 350 V-8, 4-spd. man. and auto. trans. and 10,000 lb. GVW: 4.56:1; LT9, 350 V-8, 4-spd. man. and auto. trans. and 10,000 lb. GVW: 4.10:1. Optional: K-1500 and K-2500: 700R4 4-speed automatic overdrive. Ratios: 3.06, 1.36, 1.00, 0.70. Reverse: 2.29:1. Transfer Case: K-1500 and K-2500: New Process 208. Single lever, 2.61, 1.00:1. K-3500: New Process 205, two-speed: 1.96, 1.00:1. Brakes: Type: Hydraulic, power assisted. Dimensions: K-1500: Front: Disc: 11.86 in. x 1.28 in. Rear: Drums: 11.15 x 2.75 in. K-2500: Front: Disc: 12.5 in. x 1.28 in. Rear: Drums: 11.15 in. x 2.75 in. K-2500 and K-3500: Front: Disc 12.50 in. x 1.53 in. Rear: Drum: 13.00 in. x 3.50 in. Wheels: K-1500: 15 x 6.0JJ 6-stud disc. Optional: 15 x 8JJ. K-2500: 16.5 x 6.00 in. 8-stud disc. Optional: 16.5 x 6.75. K-3500: 16.5 x 6.75. Tires: K-1500: P215/75R15-P metric radial. K-2500: 8.75 x 16.5C K-3500: 9.50 x 16.5D. Optional: K-1500: G78 x 15B, white stripe; H78 x 15B, tubeless, black sidewall or white stripe; L78 x 15B black sidewall or white stripe, tubeless; 10.00 x 16.5C tubeless; G78 x 15B tube-type; 7.00 x 15C tube-type; 6.50 x 16C tube-type and LR78 x 15C white sidewall radial ply. The following tires were specified for K-1500 models with the 5600 lb. GVW Package which included a front heavy-duty stabilizer bar: H78 x 15B 4-ply rating, tubeless; 6.50 x 16C 6-ply rating, tube-type, truck type. The following tires were specified for K-1500 models with the 6000 lb. GVW Package which included a front heavy-duty rear spring: L78 x 15B 4-ply rating, tubeless. Optional K-2500: 9.50 x 16.5E Firestone Town and Country, 8.75 x 16.5D tubeless; 9.50 x 16.5D tubeless; 10.00 x 16.5C tubeless (not available for Fenderside models); 7.50 x 16C 6-ply rating, tube-type; 7.50 x 16D tube-type; 7.50 x 16E tube-type. The following tires were specified for K-2500 models with the 7500 lb. GVW Package which included a front heavy-duty stabilizer bar: 8.75 x 16.5 C 6-ply rating, tubeless; 7.50 x 16C 6-ply rating, tubeless. The following tires were specified for K-2500 models with the 8200 lb. GVW Package which included a front heavy-duty stabilizer bar: 9.50 x 16.5D 8-ply rating, tubeless; 7.50 x 16C 6-ply rating, tube-type. Steering: Recirculating ball gear. Ratio: 20:1. Turning Circle: 47 ft. Optional: Power-assisted. Ratio: 16.4:1. Transmission: K-1500 and K-2500: 3-speed GMC, synchromesh manual (RPO M15). Transmission Ratios: 5.7 liter V-8: 2.85, 1.68, 1.00:1. Reverse: 2.95:1. 5.0 liter V-8: 3.11, 1.84, 1.0:1 Reverse: 3.22:1. 4.1 liter 6-cyl.: 3.50, 1.89, 1.00:1. Reverse: 3.62:1. Optional: SM465. 4-speed manual synchromesh (RPO M20). Ratios: 6.56, 3.58, 1.70, 1.00:1. Reverse: 6.09:1. The K-2500 crew cab and all K-3500 models had this transmission as standard equipment. Optional: 3-speed Turbo Hydra-Matic 400 (RPO M40). Ratios: 2.1 x 2.48, 1.48, 1.00:1. Reverse: 2.10:1. The 400 cu. in. V-8 was available only with this transmission. Clutch: Diaphragm, spring. Clutch diameter: 6-cyl.: 11 in. dia. Total lining area: 123.5 sq. in. Total plate pressure 2075 lb. V-8: 12 in. dia. Total lining area: 149.2 sq. in. Total plate pressure 2060 lb. Optional: K-2500 6-cyl.: 11 in. dia. Total lining area: 124.0 sq. in. 307 V-8: 12 in. dia. Total lining area: 150 sq. in.

VEHICLE DIMENSIONS: Wheelbase: K-1500: 117.5 in. 131.5 in. K-2500: 131.5 in. All Suburbans and Panels: 129.5 in. K-3500: 131.5 in. 164.5 in. Overall Length: 117.5 in. Wideside pickups: 191.30 in. 131.5 in. Wideside pickups: 212.00. 117.5 in. Fenderside pickups: 190.5 in. 131.5 in. Fenderside pickups: 210.25. 117.5 in. Chassis-cab: 186.05 in. K-3500 data: 164.5 in. wheelbase: 244.43 in. Front/Rear Tread: 67.4 in./65.8 in. Overall Height: K-1500 Wideside pickup: 72.0 in. K-2500 Wideside pickup: 74.0 in. K-3500 Wideside pickup: 74.0 in. K-3500 crew cab: 75.0 in. K-1500 Suburban: 73.5 in. K-2500 Suburban: 75.5 in. Width: Pickup: 79 in. Front/Rear Overhang: 33 in./41 in. Tailgate: Width and Height: 72 in. x 19.25 in. Approach/Departure Degrees: K-1500 117.5 in. Wideside and Fenderside: 33/19. K-1500 131.5 in. Wideside: 33/15. K-1500 131.5 in. wheelbase Fenderside: 33/16. K-2500 131.5 in. wheelbase Wideside: 35/20. K-2500 131.5 in. wheelbase Fenderside: 35/21. K-3500 Wideside pickup: 41/19. K-3500 crew cab pickup: 38/18. Ground Clearance: Front axle: 7.25 in. Rear axle: 7.0 in. Oil pan: 16.5 in. Transfer case: 12.0 in. Fuel tank: 16.6 in. Load space: Pickup box dimensions: 117.5 in. wheelbase Wideside: 78.25 in. x 50 in. x 19.25 in. 131.5 in. wheelbase Wideside: 98 in. x 50 in. x 19.25 in. Capacity: 117.5 wheelbase: 58.4 cu. ft. 131.5 in. wheelbase: 74.3 cu. ft. 117.5 in. wheelbase Fenderside: 78.5 in. x 50 in. x 17.5 in. 131.5 in. wheelbase Fenderside: 96.25 in. x 50 in. x 17.5 in. Front headroom: 38.5 in. (seat to top of cab). Front hip room: 67.25 in. Pedal to seat back (max.): 43.5 in. Steering wheel to seat back (max.): 17.3 in. Seat to ground: 35.0 in. Floor to ground: 23.0 in.

CAPACITIES: Fuel Tank: 117.5 in. wheelbase: 16.0 gal. 131.5 in. wheelbase, 135.5 in. wheelbase and 164.5 in. wheelbase: 20 gal. Optional: 16 gal. auxiliary tank. for 117.5 in.; 20 gal. auxiliary for 131.5 in. 135.5 in. and 164.5 in. wheelbase. Engine coolant system: 250 6-cyl.: 14.8 qt. 305 V-8: 17.6 qt. 350 V-8: 17.6 qt. 400 V-8: 19.6 qt. (20 qt. on K-2500 and K-3500).

ACCOMMODATIONS: Seating Capacity: Pickup and chassis-cab models: 3 passenger. Optional: None. Crew cab: 6 passenger. Suburban: 3 passenger. Optional: 6 or 9 passenger.

INSTRUMENTATION: Speedometer, odometer, fuel level gauge. Warning lights for battery, oil pressure, generator, brake system warning, directional/hazard lights, high beam, and engine coolant temperature.

OPTIONS AND PRICES: 5 liter V-8: $170. California emissions: $90. 5.7 liter V-8: $345. 379 cu. in. diesel: $1334. 4-speed manual trans.: $198. 4-speed manual with overdrive: $75. 3-speed automatic trans.: $438. 4-speed automatic with overdrive: $637. Optional axle ratios: $35. Rear step painted bumper: $106. Chromed rear bumper: $97. Rear step chromed bumper: $177. Front bumper guards: $39. Glide-out spare tire carrier: $39. Side-mounted spare tire carrier: $27. Quartz analog electric clock: $70, without Sierra Classic, $36 with Sierra Classic. Cold Climate Package: $184, without Trailering Package, $126 with Trailering Package. $172 with High Sierra or Sierra Classic and without Trailering Package, $114 with High Sierra or Sierra Classic and with Trailering Package. Engine oil cooler: $112. Heavy-duty transmission oil cooler: $55. Heavy-duty cooling system: $48. Power door locks: $115. Color-keyed floor mats: $14. Gauges Package. Includes voltmeter, engine coolant temperature and oil pressure: $34. 62 amp Delcotron generator: $58. Tinted glass: $40. Halogen high beam headlights: $15. Halogen high and low beam headlights: $20. Cargo area lamp: $56, with High Sierra or Sierra Classic: $32, without High Sierra or Sierra Classic: $56. Dome light: $24. Cigarette lighter: $28. Below eye-level painted mirrors: $44. Below eye-level stainless steel mirrors: $72. Camper style painted mirrors: $86. Black body side moldings: $105. Bright body side moldings: $131, without High Sierra, $13 with High Sierra. Custom Package: $144 without High Sierra, $26 with High Sierra. Deluxe Package: $157 without High Sierra, $39 with High Sierra. Door edge guard: $13. Pickup box side rails: $88. Operating Convenience Package: $281. AM radio: $92. AM/FM radio: $143. AM/FM stereo radio: $226. AM/FM stereo radio with 8-track tape player: $322. AM/FM stereo radio with cassette tape player: $327. AM/FM stereo radio with CB radio and triband antenna: $559. Windshield antenna: $31. Fuel tank shield: $84, without NL2 tank, $154 with NL tank. Front quad shock absorbers: $117. Speed control. $159 with automatic transmission, $169 with manual trans. Heavy-duty front springs: $84 without quad shocks, $53 with quad shocks. ComforTilt steering wheel: $95. Auxiliary 16 gal. fuel tank: $208. Two front towing hooks: $34. Bright wheelcovers: $38. Aluminum forged wheels: $411. Rallye wheels: $103. Styled wheels: $201. Power windows: $166. Sliding rear window: $100. Intermittent windshield wipers: $45. High Sierra Package: $208, Fenderside, $318, Wideside. Sierra Classic: $614, Fenderside, $780 without Exterior Decor Package, $753 with Exterior Decor Package. Seat trim: $48. Conventional two-tone paint: $69 with Sierra Classic, $42 without Sierra Classic. Special two-tone paint: $291 without Sierra Classic or High Sierra, $173 with High Sierra, $147 with Sierra Classic. Deluxe two-tone paint: $328 without High Sierra Classic or Sierra Classic, $210 with High Sierra, $157 with Sierra Classic. Dual rear wheels for K-3500: $664 to $677. Exterior Decor Package: $503, without High Sierra or Sierra Classic, $385 with High Sierra, $359 with Sierra Classic. Additional Suburban options: Center folding seat: $343. Center and rear folding seats: $640. 31 gal. fuel tank: $39. 40 gal. fuel tank: $91. Heavy-duty trailering special: $354-$619 depending upon vehicle option content. High Sierra trim: $379. Sierra Classic: $1135. Diesel equipment: $1041. Includes heavy-duty generator, dual batteries, engine oil cooler, engine block heater, sound insulation, water-in-fuel detection and drain system, dual exhaust and in-line fuel heater.

HISTORICAL FOOTNOTES: Calendar year sales of all types of GMC trucks was 238,411, of which 105,741 were full-sized pickups. Suburban sales were 11,292.

1984 PICKUP & SUBURBAN

The latest GMC trucks were fitted with a buzzer warning for key-left-in-ignition. A new multi-function switch was mounted on the steering column for control of the directionals, windshield washer/wiper, headlight high-beam and optional automatic speed control. The Suburban models were available with the optional diesel engine. Suburban models were also available with new reclining bucket seats. A new anti-chip coating was applied to the lower fender and body sides. The side door panels were now galvanized on both sides. The K-1500 models had new semi-metallic front and rear brake linings. The K-2500 models had a new height-sensing rear brake proportioning valve that provided more balanced braking performance under all load conditions. Other new features included improved parking brake cable corrosion protection and smaller and lighter front locking hubs.

Most K-1500 and K-2500 trucks also had new non-asbestos rear brake linings. All K series pickups and chassis-cabs had new plastic fuel tank stone shields. The standard Sierra interior had a full-foam front seat with a new dual-tone leather-grain vinyl trim. New dual-tone woven Deluxe cloth or custom vinyl were available at extra cost. The seat, as in 1983, folded forward to provide access to the cab storage area. The base interior also included color-keyed door trim panels with padded armrests and a foam-padded instrument panel.

Based on the standard trim, the High Sierra trim offered the customer a choice of either new dual-tone woven Deluxe cloth seats or a new leathergrain vinyl. High Sierra items carried over from 1983 included a pewter-toned brushed aluminum instrument panel, a door-operated dome light, cab back insulation, dual horns, color-keyed vinyl coated floor mats, a cigarette lighter, instrument panel nameplate, plastic door trim panels and fiber optic ashtray illumination. Exterior items consisted of bright rear window and windshield moldings, bright side marker lamp bezels and nameplates on front fenders. Wideside models also had bright taillight trim.

The Sierra Classic trim option included a choice of custom cloth or custom vinyl seats, full cowl side trim panels, a custom steering wheel, door-closing assist straps, color-keyed carpeting for front seat area, plastic door trim panels with storage pockets and bright brushed-finish accents, carpet trim on lower portion of the door panels and needle-type, full-gauge (voltmeter, engine coolant temperature and oil pressure gauges) instrumentation, nameplate on deluxe instrument panel, visor vanity mirror, headliner. Exterior Sierra Classic features consisted of bright side marker lamp bezels, front fender nameplates and Deluxe Front End Appearance Package. Wideside models also had bright taillight trim and cab back panel applique molding, Deluxe Molding Package and tailgate applique.

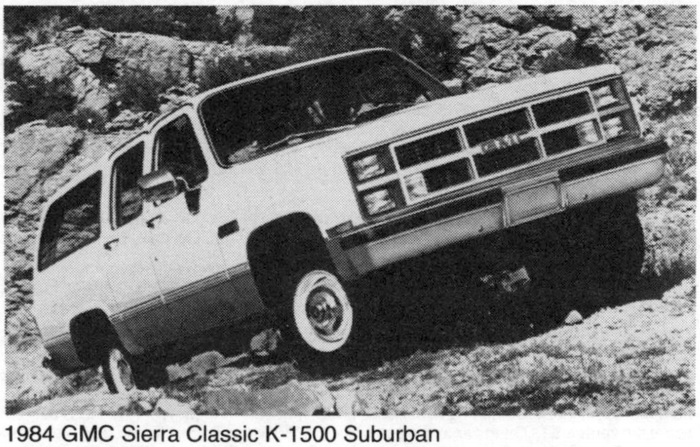

1984 GMC Sierra Classic K-1500 Suburban

Power door locks and power windows were now available for bonus and crew cab models. The electronic speed control now had a feature allowing for the set speed to be increased in one mph increments.

Three exterior paint options for the Wideside pickups with single rear wheels were offered for 1984. The special two-tone version included body side/wheel opening moldings and bright trim for the standard marker and taillights. The secondary body color was installed below the side and rear moldings. The Exterior Decor Package included dual-tone body side/rear tape striping keyed to the body colors and a hood ornament. The secondary color was positioned between the decal stripes and body side moldings. The Deluxe two-tone option included a special two-tone paint option with the secondary color on the roof and cab back panel down to the bright beltline moldings.

Ten exterior colors were offered for 1984: Doeskin tan, desert sand metallic, apple red, frost white, silver metallic, midnight black, light blue metallic, midnight blue and colonial yellow.

I.D. DATA: Unchanged from 1983 except the letter E designated the 1984 model year.

Model Number	Body Type	Factory Price	GVW	Shipping Weight	Prod. Total
Series K-1500-1/2 ton 250 6-cyl. 117.5 in., 131.5 in. wheelbase (Suburban: 129.5 in. wheelbase and standard 350 V-8)					
TK10703	6.5 ft. F-S Pickup	$9527	6100	4453	—
TK10703	6.5 ft. Wideside Pickup	$9392	6100	4500	—
TK10903	8 ft. Wideside Pickup	$9561	6100	4686	—
TK10906	Suburban Endgate	$11,486	6100	5195	—
TK10906	Suburban Pnl. Drs.	$11,449	6100[1]	5161	—

NOTE 1: Suburban available with optional 6600 GVW Package.

Model Number	Body Type	Factory Price	GVW	Shipping Weight	Prod. Total
Series K-2500-3/4 ton 292 V-8. 131.5 in. wheelbase. (Suburban-129.5 in. wheelbase), Crew and Bonus Cab: 164.5 in. wheelbase, Suburban weight with standard 350 V-8. K-2500 Pickup prices include C6P heavy-duty chassis.					
TK20903	8 ft. Fenderside Pickup	$11,977	6600*	4883	—
TK20903	8 ft. Wideside Pickup	$11,843	6600	4945	—
TK20906	Suburban Endgate	$12,998	6600	5579	—
TK20906	Suburban Pnl. Drs.	$13,005	6600	5545	—

* 8600 lb. GVW optional.

Model Number	Body Type	Factory Price	GVW	Shipping Weight	Prod. Total
Series K-3500-1 ton 350 V-8. 131.5 in. wheelbase, Crew and Bonus Cab: 164.5 in. wheelbase					
TK30903	Chassis & Cab[1]	$11,700	9200*	4992	—
TK31003	Chassis & Cab[2]	$11,912	9200	5002	—
TK31403	Chassis & Cab[3]	$12,635	9200	5275	—
TK30903	8 ft. Wideside Pickup	$12,083	9200	5414	—
TK30943	Chassis & Bonus Cab	$12,596	9200	5393	—
TK30943	Fleetside Bonus Cab	$12,962	9200	5816	—
TK30943	Chassis & Crew Cab	$12,935	9200	5905	—
TK30943	Fleetside Crew Cab	$13,300	9200	5816	—

NOTE 1: 131.5 in. wheelbase.
NOTE 2: 135.5 in. wheelbase.
NOTE 3: 159.5 in. wheelbase.
* 10,000 lb. GVW optional.

Diesel engine adds 454 lb. to weights of gasoline-engined models in all series.

STANDARD ENGINE: All K-1500 6-cyl. models: 250 Six (LE3 ordering code) Engine Type: OHV, In-line 6-cylinder. Cast iron block and cylinder head. Bore x Stroke: 3.875 in. x 3.53 in. Lifters: Hydraulic. Number of main bearings-7. Fuel Induction: Single Rochester 2-bbl. carburetor. Compression Ratio: 8.3:1. Displacement: 250 cu. in. (4.1 liters). Horsepower: Net: 115 @ 3600 rpm. (California Rating: 110 @ 3600 rpm). Torque: Net: 200 lb.-ft. @ 2000 rpm. (California Rating: 200 lb.-ft. @ 1600 rpm). Oil refill capacity: 5 qt. with filter change. Fuel Requirements: Regular unleaded.

STANDARD ENGINE: K-2500 with RPO CH6 and K-3500 models: 292 Six. Ordering Code: L25. This engine was produced by GM de Mexico. Not available in California with under 8500 lb. GVW rating. Engine Type: OHV, 6-cyl. Cast iron block and cylinder head. Key features include cast iron intake manifold, aluminized-face intake valves, Stellite-faced exhaust valves with hardened faces. Bore x Stroke: 3.875 in. x 4.125 in. Lifters: Hydraulic. Number of main bearings-7. Fuel Induction: Single Rochester 1-bbl. carburetor. Compression Ratio: 7.8:1. Displacement: 292 cu. in. (4.8 liters). Horsepower: Net: 115 @ 3400 rpm. Torque: Net: 215 lb.-ft. @ 1600 rpm. Oil refill capacity: 6 qt. with filter change. Fuel Requirements: Regular unleaded.

STANDARD ENGINE: K-2500. Optional for K-1500 (California only), K-2500 with HP6 and all K-3500 models. Ordering Code: LS9: 350 V-8 Engine Type: OHV, V-8. Cast iron block and alloy iron cylinder head. Key features include chain drive camshaft and forged steel connecting rods. This engine was produced by GM-Chevrolet Motor Division. Bore x Stroke: 4.0 in. x 3.50 in. Lifters: Hydraulic. Number of main bearings-5. Fuel Induction: Single Rochester 4-bbl. carburetor. Compression Ratio: 8.2:1. Displacement: 350 cu. in. (5.7 liters). Horsepower: Net: 165 @ 3800 rpm. Torque: Net: 275 lb.-ft. @ 1600 rpm. Oil refill capacity: 5 qt. with filter change. Fuel Requirements: Regular unleaded.

OPTIONAL ENGINE: K-2500 with HP6 and all K-3500 models: Ordering Code: LT9: 350 V-8 Engine Type: OHV, V-8. Cast iron block and alloy iron cylinder head. Key features include chain drive camshaft and forged steel connecting rods. This engine was produced by GM-Chevrolet Motor Division. Bore x Stroke: 4.0 in. x 3.50 in. Lifters: Hydraulic. Number of main bearings-5. Fuel Induction: Single Rochester 4-bbl. carburetor. Compression Ratio: 8.3:1. Displacement: 350 cu. in. (5.7 liters). Horsepower: Net: 160 @ 3800 rpm. (California rating: 155 @ 3600 rpm). Torque: Net: 260 lb.-ft. @ 2800 rpm. (California rating: 240 lb.-ft. @ 2800 rpm). Oil refill capacity: 5 qt. with filter change. Fuel Requirements: Regular unleaded.

OPTIONAL ENGINE: K-1500 models: Ordering Code: LE9: 305 V-8. Key features include Electronic Spark Control, new staged 4-barrel carburetor, camshaft and free-flow exhaust system. Not available for California. This engine was produced by GM-Chevrolet Motor Division and GM of Canada. Engine Type: OHV, V-8. Cast iron block and alloy iron cylinder head. Bore x Stroke: 3.74 in. x 3.48 in. Lifters: Hydraulic. Number of main bearings-5. Fuel Induction: Single Rochester 4-bbl. staged carburetor. Compression Ratio: 9.2:1. Displacement: 305 cu. in. (5.0 liters). Horsepower: 160 @ 4400 rpm. Torque: 235 lb.-ft. @ 2000 rpm. Oil refill capacity: 5 qt. with filter change. Fuel Requirements: Regular unleaded.

OPTIONAL ENGINE: K-1500 models for California: Ordering Code: LF3: 305 V-8. Key features include 4-barrel carburetor, camshaft and free-flow exhaust system. This engine was produced by GM-Chevrolet Motor Division and GM of Canada. Engine Type: OHV, V-8. Cast iron block and alloy iron cylinder head. Bore x Stroke: 3.74 in. x 3.48 in. Lifters: Hydraulic. Number of main bearings-5. Fuel Induction: Single Rochester 4-bbl. carburetor. Compression Ratio: 8.6:1. Displacement: 305 cu. in. (5.0 liters). Horsepower: 155 @ 4200 rpm. Torque: 240 lb.-ft. @ 1600 rpm. Oil refill capacity: 5 qt. with filter change. Fuel Requirements: Regular unleaded.

OPTIONAL ENGINE: K-3500 models: Ordering Code: LE8: 454 V-8. This engine was produced by GM-Chevrolet Motor Division. Engine Type: OHV, V-8. Cast iron block and alloy iron cylinder head. Bore x Stroke: 4.3 in. x 4.0 in. Lifters: Hydraulic. Number of main bearings-5. Fuel Induction: Single Rochester 4-bbl. carburetor. Compression Ratio: 7.9:1. Displacement: 454 cu. in. (7.4 liters). Horsepower: 230 @ 3800 rpm. Torque: 360 lb.-ft. @ 2800 rpm. Oil refill capacity: 5 qt. with filter change. Fuel Requirements: Regular unleaded.

OPTIONAL ENGINE: All models: Ordering Code: LH6: 6.2 liter V-8. This engine was produced by GM-Detroit Diesel Allison Division. Engine Type: OHV, diesel V-8. Bore x Stroke: 3.98 in. x 3.80 in. Lifters: Hydraulic. Number of main bearings-5. Fuel Induction: Fuel injection. Compression Ratio: 21.3:1. Displacement: 379.4 cu. in. (6.2 liters). Horsepower: 135 @ 3600 rpm. Torque: 240 lb.-ft. @ 2000 rpm. Oil refill capacity: 7 qt. with filter change. Fuel Requirements: Diesel. An LL4 version of this engine for models with GVW of 8500 lb. and above was also available. Its power ratings were 135 hp. @3600 rpm and 240 lb.-ft. of torque @ 2000 rpm.

CHASSIS FEATURES: Separate body and frame with channel side rails. Carbon-Steel, 39,000 psi. 117.5 in. wheelbase: 2.30 in. x 5.92 in. x 0.156 in. Section modulus: 3.06 in. 129.5 in.: 2.30 in. x 5.92 in. x 0.194. Section modulus: 117.5 in. wheelbase: 3.14 in. 131.5 in. wheelbase: 3.88 in. K-2500 with CP6: 4.53 in. Optional: None.

SUSPENSION AND RUNNING GEAR: Front Suspension: K-1500: Tapered 2-leaf springs. Capacity: 1650 lb. (16), 1850 lb. (03, 06). K-2500: Tapered 2-leaf springs. Capacity: 1850 lb. K-3500: Tapered 3-leaf springs. Capacity: 2250 lb. Rear Suspension: K-1500 and K-2500: 52 in. x 2.25 in. Two-stage, 5-leaf. K-3500: 56 in. x 2.50 in. Rating: K-1500: 2075 lb. K-2500: 2800 lb. K-3500: 3500 lb. K-1500: 22mm. dia. shock absorbers. K-3500: 32mm shock absorbers. Capacity: K-1500: 3750 lb., K-2500: 5700 lb., K-3500: 7000 lb. (7500 lb. for 159.9 in. wheelbase chassis and cab). Optional Rating: K-2500: 3000 lb. rating at ground. Capacity: 6000 lb., with RPO CP6 K-3500: RPO RO5 (Dual rear wheels): 3750 lb. rating at ground. Capacity: 7500 lb. Front Axle Type and Capacity: K-1500: Semi-floating. 3700 lb. capacity. Optional: None. K-2500: Full-floating, 3800 lb. capacity. K-3500: Full-floating, 4500 lb. Optional: None. Rear Axle Type and Capacity: K-1500: Chevrolet, semi-floating, 3750 lb. capacity. K-2500: Semi-floating, 5700 lb. capacity. K-3500: Full-floating, 7500 lb. Optional Rating: K-2500: 3000 lb. rating at ground. Capacity: 6000 lb., with RPO CP6 K-3500: RPO RO5 (Dual rear wheels): 3750 lb. rating at ground. Capacity: 7500 lb. Final Drive Ratio: The following transmission designations were used by GMC: MM3-3-spd. manual; MM4: 4-spd. manual; MM7: 4-spd. manual with overdrive; MXO: 4-spd. auto. with overdrive; MX1: 3-spd. automatic. All ratios are with standard emission equipment. Standard: K-1500: LB1 engine/ MM4, MXO: 3.42:1; LB1/MM7: 3.73:1 (requires engine oil cooler); LS9 /MM7: 3.42:1, LS9/M4: 2.73:1, LS9/MXO: 3.08:1, LH6/MM4, MXO: 3.08:1; LH6/MM7: 3.42:1. Optional: LB1/MM4, MXO: 3.73:1 (requires RPO KC4, engine oil cooler), LE9/MM7: 3.73:1, LE9/MM4: 3.08:1, LH6/ MM4, MXO: 3.42:1. Standard: K-2500: L25/MM4: 4.10:1, LS9/MM4MXO: 3.23:1, LT9/MM4: 3.42:1, LT9/MX1: 4.10:1; LH6/MM4: 3.73:1, LH6/MXO: 3.42:1,LL4/M4:3.73:1, LL4/MX1: 4.10:1. Optional: LS9/MM4: 3.42:1, LS9/MXO: 3.42:1, 3.73:1; LT9/MM4: 3.73:1, 4.10:1; LH6/ MM4: 4.10:1, LH6/MXO: 3.73:1; LL4/MM4: 4.10:1. Standard K-3500: K25/MM4, MX1: 4.56:1; LT9/MM4: 3.73:1; LT9/MX1: 4.10:1; LE8/MM4, MX1: 3.73:1, LL4/MM4, MX1: 4.10:1. Optional: LT9/MM4: 4.10:1, 4.56:1; LT9/MX1: 4.56:1; LE8/MM4, MX1: 4.10:1, 4.56:1; LL4/MM4, MX1: 4.56:1. Transfer Case: K-1500 and K-2500: New Process 208. Single lever, 2.61, 1.00:1. K-3500: New Process 205, two-speed: 1.96, 1.00:1. Brakes: Type: Hydraulic, power assisted. Dimensions: K-1500: Front: Disc: 11.86 in. x 1.28 in. Rear: Drums: 11.15 x 2.75 in. K-2500: Front: Disc: 12.5 in. x 1.28 in. Rear: Drums: 11.15 in. x 2.75 in. K-2500 and K-3500: Front: Disc: 12.50 in. x 1.53 in. Rear: Drum: 13.00 in. x 3.50 in. Wheels: K-1500: 15 x 6.0JJ 6-stud disc. Optional: 15 x 8JJ. K-2500: 16.5 x 6.00 in. 8-stud disc. Optional: 16.5 x 6.75. K-3500: 16.5 x 6.75. Tires: K-1500: P235/75R15 steel belted radial. K-2500: LT215/85R16C, K-2500 with RPO CP6: Front: LT235/85R16D, 8-ply rating; Rear: LT235/85R16E, 10-ply rating. K-3500: Front: LT235/85R16D, 8-ply rating; Rear: LT235/85R16E, 10-ply rating. Optional: K-1500: P235/75R15 white sidewall; P235/75R15R white letters; 31 x 10.50R/15B black wall or white letters (both require RPO N67, N90 or PA6 wheels). Optional K-2500: Tubeless steel belted radials 7.50R/16D, LT215/85R16C, LT215/85R16D, LT235/85R16D, LT235/85R16E. Optional: K-3500: Tube-type, nylon: 7.50-16D. Tubeless steel belted radial: LT215/85R16D, LT235/85R16E. Steering: Recirculating ball gear. Ratio: 20:1. Turning Circle: 47 ft. Steering wheel diameter: 17.5 in. Optional: Power-assisted. Ratio: 16.4:1. Transmission: K-1500, K-2500, K-3500: 4-speed, synchromesh manual. Transmission Ratios: 6.55, 3.58, 1.70, 1.00:1. Optional: K-1500: 4-spd. manual overdrive, 4-spd. automatic overdrive; K-2500: 4-spd. automatic overdrive; K-3500: 3-spd. automatic. Diesel models: K-1500: 4-spd. manual overdrive, 4-spd. automatic overdrive; K-2500: 4-spd. automatic overdrive; K-2500 HD (with RPO C6P) and K-3500: 3-spd. automatic. Clutch: Diaphragm, spring. Clutch diameter: 6-cyl.: 11 in. dia. Total lining area: 123.5 sq. in. Total plate pressure: 2075 lb. V-8: 12 in. dia. Total lining area: 149.2 sq. in. Total plate pressure: 2060 lb. Optional: K-2500 6-cyl.: 11 in. dia. Total lining area: 124.0 sq. in. 307 V-8: 12 in. dia. Total lining area: 150 sq. in.

VEHICLE DIMENSIONS: Wheelbase: K-1500: 117.5 in. 131.5 in. K-2500: 131.5 in. All Suburbans and Panels: 129.5 in. K-3500: 131.5 in. 135.5 in. 164.5 in. Overall Length: 117.5 in. Wideside pickups: 192.60 in. 131.5 in. Wideside pickups: 212.50. 117.5 in. Fenderside pickups: 191.1 in. 131.5 in. Fenderside pickups: 211.00 in. K-3500: 131.5 in. Chassis-cab: 206.20 in.; 135.5 in. wheelbase: 215.6 in.; 159.5 in. wheelbase: 239.7 in.; 164.5 in. wheelbase (bonus/crew cab): 239.3 in. Approach/Departure Degrees: K-1500 117.5 in. Wideside and Fenderside: 33/19. K-1500 131.5 in. Wideside: 33/15. K-1500 131.5 in. wheelbase Fenderside: 33/16. K-2500 131.5 in. wheelbase Wideside: 35/20. K-2500 131.5 in. wheelbase Fenderside: 35/21. K-3500 Wideside pickup: 41/19. K-3500 crew cab pickup: 38/18. Ground Clearance: Wideside models: K-1500 p ickups: Front: 74 in.; rear: 7.1 in., K-2500 pickups: Front: 8.8 in.; rear: 7.2 in. K-3500 pickups: Front: 8.3 in.; rear: 7.8 in. Fenderside models: K-1500 pickups: Front: 7.2 in.; rear: 7.1 in. K-2500 pickups: Front: 8.8 in.; rear: 7.2 in. K-3500 pickups: K-3500 chassis-cab (131.5 in. 135.5 in. and 159.5 in. wheelbase): Front: 8.3 in.; rear: 7.7 in. K-3500 bonus/crew cab: Front: 8.3 in.; rear: 7.7 in. Load space: Pickup box dimensions: 117.5 in. wheelbase Wideside: 78.25 in. x 50 in. x 19.25 in. 131.5 in. wheelbase Wideside: 98 in. x 50 in. x 19.25 in. Capacity: 117.5 wheelbase: 58.4 cu. ft. 131.5 in. wheelbase: 74.3 cu. ft. 117.5 in. wheelbase Fenderside: 78.5 in. x 50 in. x 17.5 in. 131.5 in. wheelbase Fenderside: 96.25 in. x 50 in. x 17.5 in. Front headroom: 38.5 in. (seat to top of cab). Front hip room: 67.25 in. Pedal to seat back (max.): 43.5 in. Steering wheel to seat back (max.): 17.3 in. Seat to ground: 35.0 in. Floor to ground: 23.0 in.

CAPACITIES: Fuel Tank: 117.5 in. wheelbase: 16.0 gal. 131.5 in. wheelbase, 135.5 in. wheelbase and 164.5 in. wheelbase: 20 gal. Optional: 16 gal. auxiliary tank. for 117.5 in.; 20 gal. auxiliary for 131.5 in.135.5 in. and 164.5 in. wheelbase. Engine coolant system: 250 6-cyl.: 14.8 qt. 305 V-8: 17.6 qt. 350 V-8: 17.6 qt. 400 V-8: 19.6 qt. (20 qt. on K-2500 and K-3500).

ACCOMMODATIONS: Seating Capacity: Pickup and chassis-cab models: 3 passenger. Optional: None. Crew cab: 6 passenger. Suburban: 3 passenger. Optional: 6 or 9 passenger.

INSTRUMENTATION: Speedometer, odometer, fuel level gauge. Warning lights for battery, oil pressure, generator, brake system warning, directional/hazard lights, high beam, and engine coolant temperature.

OPTIONS: 292 6-cyl. 305 V-8. 350 V-8. 454 V-8. 379 diesel V-8. Air conditioning. Automatic transmission. Chromed front bumper guards. Chromed rear bumper. Chromed rear step bumper (Wideside only). Painted rear step bumper. Cargo area lamp. Cigarette lighter. Color-keyed floor mats. ComforTilt steering wheel. Deluxe Front End Appearance Package. Dome light. Quartz electric clock. Gauge Package. Includes voltmeter, engine coolant temperature and oil pressure gauges. Halogen headlights. Painted below eye-level mirrors. Stainless steel below eye-level mirrors. Stainless steel camper mirrors. Black body moldings (Wideside only). Bright body moldings (Wideside only). Custom Molding Package-black (Wideside only). Door edge guards. Conventional two-tone paint. Deluxe two-tone paint (Wideside only). Exterior Decor Package (Wideside only). Special two-tone paint (Wideside only). AM radio. AM/FM radio. AM stereo radio. AM/FM stereo radio. AM/FM stereo radio with cassette tape. AM/FM stereo radio with 8-track tape. AM/FM stereo radio with CB. Note: Stereo radios not available for K-3500 bonus/crew cab models. Operating Convenience Package. Pickup box side rails. Power door locks. Power windows. Painted West Coast mirrors. Roof marker lights. Frame-mounted spare tire carrier. Aluminum wheels (for K-1500 only). Rallye wheels (for K-1500 only). Styled wheels (for K-1500 only). Bright metal wheelcovers (not available for K-3500 bonus/crew cab). Bright metal wheel trim rings (available for K-3500 pickup only). Windshield antenna. Sliding rear window. Glide-out spare tire carrier. Side-mounted spare tire carrier (Wideside only). Tinted glass. Pre-cleaner air cleaner (for diesels only). Auxiliary fuel tank. Rear locking differential. Cold Climate Package (Not available for diesels). Cruise control. Engine oil cooler (Not available for diesels). Fuel tank shield. 63 amp generator (standard on (K-3500). Heavy-duty automatic transmission cooler (Not available for diesels). Heavy-duty battery (Not available for diesels). Front and rear heavy-duty shock absorbers (standard on K-2500 with HP6 and all K-3500 models). Heavy-duty radiator (Not available for diesels). Auxiliary battery (Not available for diesels). Camper wiring harness. Dual rear wheels (available for K-3500 only). Front tow hooks. Front quad shocks (K-1500 and K-2500 models only). Heavy-duty front springs (Available for K-1500 and K-2500 only). Main and auxiliary rear springs (available for K-3500 only). Special camper chassis equipment-Basic (available for K-2500 and K-3500 only). Special camper chassis equipment -Deluxe (available for K-2500 and K-3500 only). Heavy-duty trailering special.

HISTORICAL FOOTNOTES: Calendar year sales of all GMC truck models was 280,531 Calendar year full-size pickup sales (all types) were 121,704. Suburban sales totaled 16,132.

1985 PICKUP & SUBURBAN

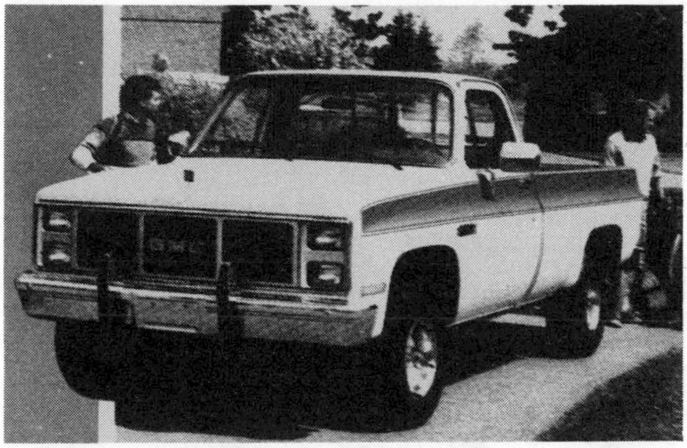

1985 GMC K-1500 Sierra Classic Wideside pickup

The 1985 GMC trucks had a new front end treatment spearheaded by a grille that did not have the center divider as used in 1984. The large GMC letters with red inserts continued to be positioned in the center of what was now a three section grille. Wideside models now were available with a new optional custom two-tone color scheme. New wet-arm-type windshield washers were standard. The custom vinyl and custom cloth fabrics of the Up-Level Trim Packages were also new for 1985. Manual locking hubs were standard for 1985 as were new hydraulic clutch controls and steel-belted radial tires. The seat back angle and seat cushion contour of the pickup truck seat were revised for improved comfort. The K-3500 models now have standard clearance and identification lamps on the roof and tailgate along with a 66 amp generator. The new V-6 Vortex engine was the standard K-1500 gasoline engine. This 90 degree engine had a Quadrajet carburetor. It featured central spark plug location, swirl inlet ports and stainless steel exhaust manifolds. The exterior colors available for 1985 were as follows: Frost white, silver metallic, midnight black, light blue metallic, colonial yellow, doeskin tan, desert sand metallic, Indian bronze metallic and apple red.

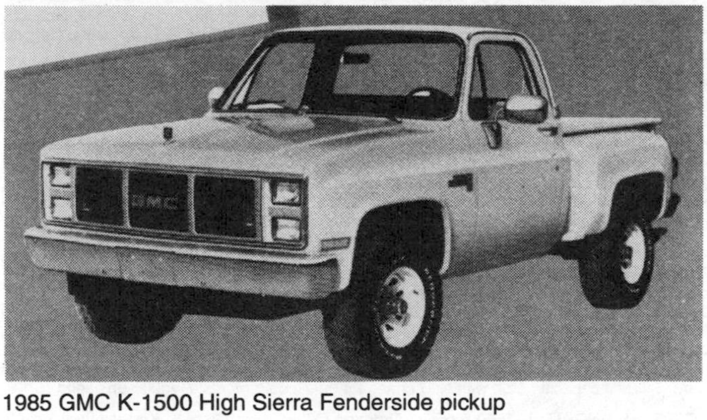

1985 GMC K-1500 High Sierra Fenderside pickup

I.D. DATA: Unchanged from 1983 except the letter F designated the 1985 model year.

Model Number	Body Type	Factory Price	GVW	Shipping Weight	Prod. Total
Series K-1500-1/2 ton 262 V-6. 117.5 in., 131.5 in. wheelbase (Suburban: 129.5 in. wheelbase and standard 350 V-8)					
TK10703	6.5 ft. Fenderside Pickup	$9854	6100	4453	—
TK10703	6.5 ft. Wideside Pickup	$9719	6100	4500	—
TK10903	8 ft. Wideside Pickup	$9888	6100	4686	—
TK10906	Suburban Endgate	$11,813	6100	5195	—
TK10906	Suburban Pnl. Drs.	$11,776	6100[1]	5161	—

NOTE 1: Surburban available with optional 6600 GVW Package.

Series K-2500 3/4 ton 292 V-8. 131.5 in. wheelbase. (Suburban-129.5 in. wheelbase), Crew and Bonus Cab: 164.5 in. wheelbase, Suburban weight with standard 350 V-8. K-2500 Pickup prices include C6P heavy-duty chassis.

TK20903	8 ft. Fenderside Pickup	$11,277	6600*	4883	—
TK20903	8 ft. Wideside Pickup	$11,143	6600	4945	—
TK20906	Suburban Endgate	$13,298	6600	5579	—
TK20906	Suburban Pnl. Drs.	$13,335	6600	5545	—

* 8600 lb. GVW optional.

Series K-3500-1 ton 350 V-8. 131.5 in. wheelbase, Crew and Bonus Cab: 164.5 in. wheelbase

TK30903	Chassis & Cab[1]	$11,900	9200*	4992	—
TK31003	Chassis & Cab[2]	$12,112	9200	5002	—
TK31403	Chassis & Cab[3]	$12,635	9200	5275	—
TK30903	8 ft. Wideside Pickup	$12,283	9200	5414	—
TK30943	Chassis & Bonus Cab	$12,796	9200	5393	—
TK30943	Fleetside Bonus Cab	$13,162	9200	5816	—
TK30943	Chassis & Crew Cab	$13,135	9200	5905	—
TK30943	Fleetside Crew Cab	$13,500	9200	5816	—

NOTE 1: 131.5 in. wheelbase.
NOTE 2: 135.5 in. wheelbase.
NOTE 3: 159.5 in. wheelbase.
* 10,000 lb. GVW optional.

Diesel engine adds 454 lb. to weights of gasoline-engined models in all series.

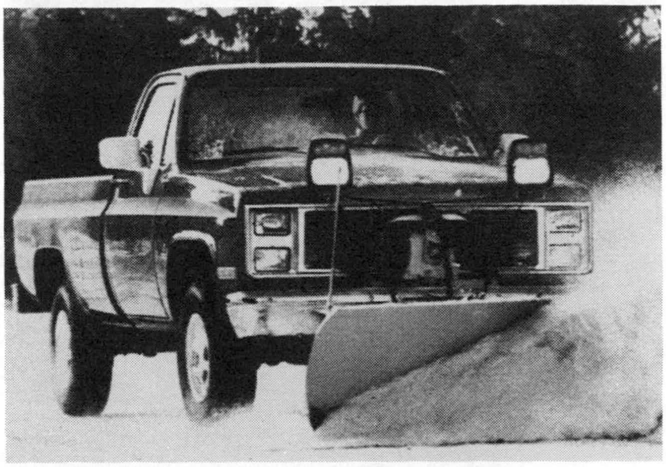

1985 GMC series K-3500 High Sierra Wideside pickup

STANDARD ENGINE: All K-10 6-cyl. models: 262 V-6 (LB1 ordering code) Engine Type: Vortex OHV, V-6-cylinder. Cast iron block. Key features include a 4-bbl. carburetor. Bore x Stroke: 4.0 in. x 3.48 in. Lifters: Hydraulic. Fuel Induction: Single Rochester 4-bbl. carburetor. Compression Ratio: 9.3:1. Displacement: 262 cu. in. (4.3 liters). Horsepower: Net: 155 @ 4000 rpm. Torque: Net: 230 lb.-ft. @ 2400 rpm. Oil refill capacity: 5 qt. with filter change. Fuel Requirements: Regular unleaded.

STANDARD ENGINE: K-2500 with RPO CH6 and K-3500 models: 292 Six. Ordering Code: L25. This engine was produced by GM de Mexico. Not available in California with under 8500 lb. GVW rating. Engine Type: OHV, 6-cyl. Cast iron block and cylinder head. Key features include cast iron intake manifold, aluminized-face intake valves, Stellite-faced exhaust valves with hardened faces. Bore x Stroke: 3.875 in. x 4.125 in. Lifters: Hydraulic. Number of main bearings-7. Fuel Induction: Single Rochester 1-bbl. carburetor. Compression Ratio: 7.8:1. Displacement: 292 cu. in. (4.8 liters). Horsepower: Net: 115 @ 3400 rpm. Torque: Net: 215 lb.-ft. @ 1600 rpm. Oil refill capacity: 6 qt. with filter change. Fuel Requirements: Regular unleaded.

STANDARD ENGINE: K-2500. Optional for K-1500 (California only), K-2500 with HP6 and all K-3500 models: Ordering Code: LS9: 350 V-8 Engine Type: OHV, V-8. Cast iron block and alloy iron cylinder head. Key features include chain drive camshaft and forged steel connecting rods. This engine was produced by GM-Chevrolet Motor Division. Bore x Stroke: 4.0 in. x 3.50 in. Lifters: Hydraulic. Number of main bearings-5. Fuel Induction: Single Rochester 4-bbl. carburetor. Compression Ratio: 8.2:1. Displacement: 350 cu. in. (5.7 liters). Horsepower: Net: 165 @ 3800 rpm. Torque: Net: 275 lb.-ft. @ 1600 rpm. Oil refill capacity: 5 qt. with filter change. Fuel Requirements: Regular unleaded.

OPTIONAL ENGINE: K-2500 with HP6 and all K-3500 models: Ordering Code: LT9: 350 V-8 Engine Type: OHV, V-8. Cast iron block and alloy iron cylinder head. Key features include chain drive camshaft and forged steel connecting rods. This engine was produced by GM-Chevrolet Motor Division. Bore x Stroke: 4.0 in. x 3.50 in. Lifters: Hydraulic. Number of main bearings-5. Fuel Induction: Single Rochester 4-bbl. carburetor. Compression Ratio: 8.3:1. Displacement: 350 cu. in. (5.7 liters). Horsepower: Net: 160 @ 3800 rpm. (California rating: 155 @ 3600 rpm). Torque: Net: 260 lb.-ft. @ 2800 rpm. (California rating: 240 lb.-ft. @ 2800 rpm). Oil refill capacity: 5 qt. with filter change. Fuel Requirements: Regular unleaded.

OPTIONAL ENGINE: K-1500 models: Ordering Code: LE9: 305 V-8. Key features include Electronic Spark Control, new staged 4-barrel carburetor, camshaft and free-flow exhaust system. Not available for California. This engine was produced by GM-Chevrolet Motor Division and GM of Canada. Engine Type: OHV, V-8. Cast iron block and alloy iron cylinder head. Bore x Stroke: 3.74 in. x 3.48 in. Lifters: Hydraulic. Number of main bearings-5. Fuel Induction: Single Rochester 4-bbl. staged carburetor. Compression Ratio: 9.2:1. Displacement: 305 cu. in. (5.0 liters). Horsepower: 160 @ 4400 rpm. Torque: 235 lb.-ft. @ 2000 rpm. Oil refill capacity: 5 qt. with filter change. Fuel Requirements: Regular unleaded.

OPTIONAL ENGINE: K-1500 models for California: Ordering Code: LF3: 305 V-8. Key features include 4-barrel carburetor, camshaft and free-flow exhaust system. This engine was produced by GM-Chevrolet Motor Division and GM of Canada. Engine Type: OHV, V-8. Cast iron block and alloy iron cylinder head. Bore x Stroke: 3.74 in. x 3.48 in. Lifters: Hydraulic. Number of main bearings-5. Fuel Induction: Single Rochester 4-bbl. carburetor. Compression Ratio: 8.6:1. Displacement: 305 cu. in. (5.0 liters). Horsepower: 155 @ 4200 rpm. Torque: 240 lb.-ft. @ 1600 rpm. Oil refill capacity: 5 qt. with filter change. Fuel Requirements: Regular unleaded.

OPTIONAL ENGINE: K-3500 models: Ordering Code: LE8: 454 V-8. This engine was produced by GM-Chevrolet Motor Division. Engine Type: OHV, V-8. Cast iron block and alloy iron cylinder head. Bore x Stroke: 4.3 in. x 4.0 in. Lifters: Hydraulic. Number of main bearings-5. Fuel Induction: Single Rochester 4-bbl. carburetor. Compression Ratio: 7.9:1. Displacement: 454 cu. in. (7.4 liters). Horsepower: 230 @ 3800 rpm. Torque: 360 lb.-ft. @ 2800 rpm. Oil refill capacity: 5 qt. with filter change. Fuel Requirements: Regular unleaded.

OPTIONAL ENGINE: All models: Ordering Code: LH6: 6.2 liter V-8. This engine was produced by GM-Detroit Diesel Allison Division. Engine Type: OHV, diesel V-8. Bore x Stroke: 3.98 in. x 3.80 in. Lifters: Hydraulic. Number of main bearings-5. Fuel Induction: Fuel injection. Compression Ratio: 21.3:1. Displacement: 379.4 cu. in. (6.2 liters). Horsepower: 135 @ 3600 rpm. Torque: 240 lb.-ft. @ 2000 rpm. Oil refill capacity: 7 qt. with filter change. Fuel Requirements: Diesel. An LL4 version of this engine for models with GVW of 8500 lb. and above was also available. Its power ratings were 135 hp. @3600 rpm and 240 lb.-ft. of torque @ 2000 rpm.

CHASSIS FEATURES: Separate body and frame with channel side rails. Carbon-Steel, 39,000 psi. 117.5 in. wheelbase: 2.30 in. x 5.92 in. x 0.156 in. Section modulus: 3.06 in. 129.5 in.: 2.30 in. x 5.92 in. x 0.194. Section modulus: 117.5 in. wheelbase: 3.14 in. 131.5 in. wheelbase: 3.88 in. K-2500 with CP6: 4.53 in. Optional: None.

SUSPENSION AND RUNNING GEAR: Front Suspension: K-1500: Tapered 2-leaf springs. Capacity: 1650 lb. (16), 1850 lb. (03, 06). K-2500: Tapered 2-leaf springs. Capacity: 1850 lb. K-3500: Tapered 3-leaf springs. Capacity: 2250 lb. Rear Suspension: K-1500 and K-2500: 52 in. x 2.25 in. Two-stage, 5-leaf. K-3500: 56 in. x 2.50 in. Rating: K-1500: 2075 lb. K-2500: 2800 lb. K-3500: 3500 lb. K-1500: 22mm. dia. shock absorbers. K-3500: 32mm shock absorbers. Capacity: K-1500: 3750 lb. K-2500: 5700 lb., K-3500: 7000 lb. (7500 lb. for 159.9 in. wheelbase chassis and cab). 000. Optional Rating: K-2500: 3000 lb. rating at ground. Capacity: 6000 lb. with RPO CP6 K-3500: RPO RO5 (Dual rear wheels): 3750 lb. rating at ground. Capacity: 7500 lb. Front Axle Type and Capacity: K-1500: Semi-floating. 3700 lb. capacity. Optional: None. K-2500: Full-floating, 3800 lb. capacity. K-3500: Full-floating, 4500 lb. Optional: None. Rear Axle Type and Capacity: K-1500: Chevrolet, semi-floating, 3750 lb. capacity. K-2500: Semi-floating, 5700 lb. capacity. K-3500: Full-floating, 7500 lb. Optional Rating: K-2500: 3000 lb. rating at ground. Capacity: 6000 lb., with RPO CP6 K-3500: RPO RO5 (Dual rear wheels): 3750 lb. rating at ground. Capacity: 7500 lb. Final Drive Ratio: The following transmission designations were used by Chevrolet: MM3-3-spd. manual; MM4: 4-spd. manual; MM7: 4-spd. manual with overdrive; MXO: 4-spd. auto. with overdrive; MX1: 3-spd. automatic. All ratios are with standard emission equipment. Standard: K-1500: LB1 engine/MM4, MXO: 3.42:1; LB1/MM7: 3.73:1 (requires engine oil cooler); LS9 /MM7: 3.42:1, LS9/M4: 2.73:1, LS9/MXO: 3.08:1, LH6/MM4, MXO: 3.08:1; LH6/MM7: 3.42:1. Optional: LB1/MM4, MXO: 3.73:1 (requires RPO KC4, engine oil cooler), LE9/MM7: 3.73:1, LE9/MM4: 3.08:1, LH6/MM4, MXO: 3.42:1. Standard: K-2500: L25/MM4: 4.10:1, LS9/MM4MXO: 3.23:1, LT9/MM4: 3.42:1, LT9/MX1: 4.10:1; LH6/MM4: 3.73:1, LH6/MXO: 3.42:1,LL4/M4:3.73:1, LL4/MX1: 4.10:1. Optional: LS9/MM4: 3.42:1, LS9/MXO: 3.42:1, 3.73:1; LT9/MM4: 3.73:1, 4.10:1; LH6/MM4: 4.10:1, LH6/MXO: 3.73:1; LL4/MM4: 4.10:1. Standard K-3500: K25/MM4, MX1: 4.56:1; LT9/MM4: 3.73:1; LT9/MX1: 4.10:1; LE8/MM4, MX1: 3.73:1, LL4/MM4, MX1: 4.10:1. Optional: LT9/MM4: 4.10:1, 4.56:1; LT9/MX1: 4.56:1; LE8/MM4, MX1: 4.10:1, 4.56:1; LL4/MM4, MX1: 4.56:1. Transfer Case: K-1500 and K-2500: New Process 208. Single lever, 2.61, 1.00:1. K-3500: New Process 205, two-speed: 1.96, 1.00:1. Brakes: Type: Hydraulic, power assisted. Dimensions: K-1500: Front: Disc: 11.86 in. x 1.28 in. Rear: Drums: 11.15 x 2.75 in. K-2500: Front: Disc: 12.5 in. x 1.28 in. Rear: Drums: 11.15 in. x 2.75 in. K-2500 and K-3500: Front: Disc: 12.50 in. x 1.53 in. Rear: Drum: 13.00 in. x 3.50 in. Wheels: K-1500: 15 x 6.0JJ 6-stud disc. Optional: 15 x 8JJ. K-2500: 16.5 x 6.00 in. 8-stud disc. Optional: 16.5 x 6.75. K-3500: 16.5 x 6.75. Tires: K-1500: P235/75R15 steel belted radial. K-2500: LT215/85R16C, K-2500 with RPO CP6: Front: LT235/85R16D, 8-ply rating; Rear: LT235/85R16E, 10-ply rating. K-3500: Front: LT235/85R16D, 8-ply rating; Rear: LT235/85R16E, 10-ply rating. Optional: K-1500: P235/75R15 white sidewall; P235/75R15R white letters; 31 x 10.50R/15B blackwall or white letters (both require RPO N67, N90 or PA6 wheels). Optional K-2500: Tubeless steel belted radials 7.50R/16D, LT215/85R16C, LT215/85R16D, LT235/85R16D, LT235/85R16E. Optional: K-3500: Tube-type, nylon: 7.50-16D. Tubeless steel belted radial: LT215/85R16D, LT235/85R16E. Steering: Recirculating ball gear. Ratio: 20:1. Turning Circle: 47 ft. Steering wheel diameter: 17.5 in. Optional: Power-assisted. Ratio: 16.4:1. Transmission: K-1500, K-2500, K-3500: 4-speed, synchromesh manual. Transmission Ratios: 6.55, 3.58, 1.70, 1.00:1. Optional: K-1500: 4-spd. manual overdrive, 4-spd. automatic overdrive; K-2500: 4-spd. automatic overdrive; K-3500: 3-spd. automatic. Diesel models: K-1500: 4-spd. manual overdrive, 4-spd. automatic overdrive; K-2500: 4-spd. automatic overdrive; K-2500 HD (with RPO C6P) and K-3500: 3-spd. automatic. Clutch: Diaphragm, spring. Clutch diameter: 6-cyl.: 11 in. dia. Total lining area: 123.5 sq. in. Total plate pressure: 2075 lb. V-8: 12 in. dia. Total lining area: 149.2 sq. in. Total plate pressure: 2060 lb. Optional: K-2500 6-cyl.: 11 in. dia. Total lining area: 124.0 sq. in. 307 V-8: 12 in. dia. Total lining area: 150 sq. in.

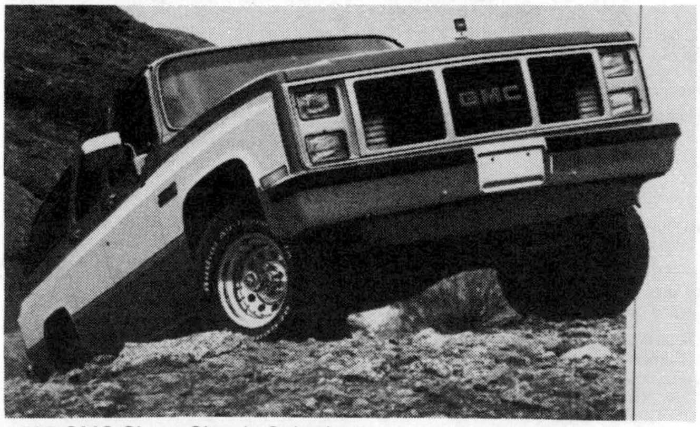

1985 GMC Sierra Classic Suburban

VEHICLE DIMENSIONS: Wheelbase: K-1500: 117.5 in. 131.5 in. K-2500: 131.5 in. All Suburbans and Panels: 129.5 in. K-3500: 131.5 in. 135.5 in. 164.5 in. Overall Length: 117.5 in. Wideside pickups: 192.60 in. 131.5 in. Wideside pickups: 212.50. 117.5 in. Fenderside pickups: 191.1 in. 131.5 in. Fenderside pickups: 211.0 in. K-3500: 131.5 in. Chassis-cab: 206.20 in.; 135.5 in. wheelbase: 215.6 in.; 159.5 in. wheelbase: 239.7 in.; 164.5 in. wheelbase (bonus/crew cab): 239.3 in. Approach/Departure Degrees: K-1500 117.5 in. Wideside and Fenderside: 33/19. K-1500 131.5 in. Wideside: 33/15. K-1500 131.5 in. wheelbase Fenderside: 33/16. K-2500 131.5 in. wheelbase Wideside: 35/20. K-2500 131.5 in. wheelbase Fenderside: 35/21. K-3500 Wideside pickup: 41/19. K-3500 crew cab pickup: 38/18. Ground Clearance: Wideside models: K-1500 pickups: Front: 74 in.; rear: 7.1 in., K-2500 pickups: Front: 8.8 in.; rear: 7.2 in., K-3500 pickups: Front: 8.3 in.; rear: 7.8 in. Fenderside models: K-1500 pickups: Front: 7.2 in.; rear: 7.1 in. K-2500 pickups: Front: 8.8 in.; rear: 7.2 in. K-3500 pickups: K-3500 Chassis-cab (131.5 in. 135.5 in. and 159.5 in. wheelbase): Front: 8.3 in.; rear: 7.7 in. K-3500 bonus/crew cab: Front: 8.3 in.; rear: 7.7 in. Load space: Pickup box dimensions: 117.5 in. wheelbase Wideside: 78.25 in. x 50 in. x 19.25 in. 131.5 in. wheelbase Wideside: 98 in. x 50 in. x 19.25 in. Capacity: 117.5 wheelbase: 58.4 cu. ft. 131.5 in. wheelbase: 74.3 cu. ft. 117.5 in. wheelbase Fenderside: 78.5 in. x 50 in. x 17.5 in. 131.5 in. wheelbase. Fenderside: 96.25 in. x 50 in. x 17.5 in. Front headroom: 38.5 in. (seat to top of cab). Front hip room: 67.25 in. Pedal to seat back (max.): 43.5 in. Steering wheel to seat back (max.): 17.3 in. Seat to ground: 35.0 in. Floor to ground: 23.0 in.

CAPACITIES: Fuel Tank: 117.5 in. wheelbase: 16.0 gal. 131.5 in. wheelbase, 135.5 in. wheelbase and 164.5 in. wheelbase: 20 gal. Optional: 16 gal. auxiliary tank for 117.5 in.; 20 gal. auxiliary for 131.5 in. 135.5 in. and 164.5 in. wheelbase. Engine coolant system: 250 6-cyl.: 14.8 qt. 305 V-8: 17.6 qt. 350 V-8: 17.6 qt. 400 V-8: 19.6 qt. (20 qt. on K-2500 and K-3500).

ACCOMMODATIONS: Seating Capacity: Pickup and chassis-cab models: 3 passenger. Optional: None. Crew cab: 6 passenger. Suburban: 3 passenger. Optional: 6 or 9 passenger.

INSTRUMENTATION: Speedometer, odometer, fuel level gauge. Warning lights for battery, oil pressure, generator, brake system warning, directional/hazard lights, high beam, and engine coolant temperature.

OPTIONS AND PRICES: Sierra Classic Package (RPO YE9): $671-$1016, depending on body and additional packages installed. Deluxe bench seat: $17 with High Sierra Package; $62 without High Sierra Package (RPO Z62). Bonus cab custom bench seat: $50 with RPO Z62. Crew cab bonus seat: $100 with RPO Z62. Regular cab and bonus cab custom vinyl bench seat: $50 without RPO Z62 or RPO YE9. Crew cab custom vinyl bench seat: $100 with RPO YE9. Conventional two-tone paint (RPO ZY2): $43 to $89 depending on body and additional options. Exterior Decor Package (RPO ZY5): $418-$575 depending on body and additional options. Special Big Dooley two-tone paint (RPO ZY9): $444 without RPO Z62; $426 with RPO Z62. California emissions requirement (RPO YF5): $235. 5.0 liter V-8 (RPO LE9 or RPO LF3): $465. 5.7 liter V-8 (RPO LT9): $650. 5.7 liter V-8 (RPO LT9): $620. 7.4 liter V-8 (RPO LE8): $790. 6.2 liter diesel V-8 -3-spd. automatic trans. (RPO MX1): $510. 4-spd. manual overdrive trans.: $80. 4-spd. automatic trans. with overdrive (RPO MXO): $670. Optional axle ratios: $36. Locking rear differential (RPO G80): $238. Heavy-duty power brakes for K-1500 and K-2500 (RPO J55): $103. Heavy-duty front bumper (RPO VF1): $103. Chromed rear step bumper for Wideside only (RPO V42): $189. Painted rear step bumper (RPO V43): $120. Chromed front bumper guards (RPO V31): $41. Camper special chassis equipment (RPO Z81): $108 (for K-2500 with required C6H chassis). $49 for K-3500 with required RPO RO5 dual rear wheels. Glide-Out spare tire carrier (RPO P11): $41. Side-mounted spare tire carrier for Wideside only (RPO P13): $29. Quartz electric clock (RPO U35). Not available when UM6 radio is specified: $79 without RPO YE9. Includes RPO Z53 voltmeter, temperature and oil pressure gauges: $39 with RPO YE9. Cold Climate Package. Not available when RPO C60 air conditioning or RPO B3J diesel equipment is specified. Includes special insulation, RPO K81 66 amp generator, special heater and defroster, RPO KO5 engine block heater, anti-freeze protection to -32 degrees and RPO UA1 heavy-duty battery (RPO V10): $126 to $200 depending upon additional options and series applications. Engine oil cooling system (RPO KC4). Not avail. with RPO L25 engine or RPO B3J: $120. Heavy-duty radiator (RPO VO1): $53. Heavy-duty radiator and transmission oil (RPO VO2). Avail. only with RPO MX1 or RPO MXO transmission are specified. Not avail. with RPO L25 engine or RPO VO1 are specified: $59. Decor Value Package. Includes black-painted radiator grille and headlight bezels, and special body stripe located between body feature lines on front fenders, pickup box and across the tailgate. Not avail. on bonus cab, crew cab and Fenderside models. Not available with the following options: RPO YE9, RO5, V22, PA6, N90, B84 or B85. Requires RPO ZY1 solid paint and blackwall or white lettered tires are specified (RPO YJ6): $256 for K-1500; $141 for K-2500 and K-3500. Power door lock system (RPO AU3): $135 for regular cab; $198 for bonus and crew cab. Color-keyed front floor mats (RPO B32). Requires RPO YE9: $15. Gauge Package. Includes voltmeter, engine coolant temperature and oil pressure (RPO Z53): $40. 66 amp Delcotron generator. Standard on K-3500 except when RPO LE8 engine is ordered (RPO K81): $62. 94 amp Delcotron generator. Included with LE8 engine on K-3500 models (RPO K22): $62. Tinted glass-all windows (RPO AO1): $46 for regular cab; $56 for bonus or crew cab. Halogen high-beam headlamps. Avail. only when RPO V22 or RPO YE9 is specified (RPO TT5): $17. 600 watts engine block heater. Not avail. when RPO BK3 or RPO LF3 engine is specified (RPO KO5): $31. Heavy-duty front heater (RPO C42). Avail. only with RPO B3J is specified. Not avail. with RPO C60 air conditioning: $43. Automatic front locking hubs. Avail. only for K-1500 (RPO X6Z): $30. Cargo lamp (RPO UF2): $40 without RPO Z62 or YE9 (includes RPO C91 dome lamp). Dome lamp (RPO C91): 26. Roof marker lamps. Avail. for K-2500 only. Standard for K-3500 (RPO UO1): $50. Cigarette lighter. Included when RPO Z62 or YE9 is specified (RPO U37): $30. Exterior left and right side below eye-level mirrors: Painted (RPO D44): $50; stainless steel (RPO D45): $83. Camper type stainless steel left and right side exterior mirrors (RPO DF2): $94. Senior West Coast type painted exterior left and right side mirrors (RPO DG5): $65. Black body side molding. Avail. for Wideside only (RPO B84): $115. Bright body side molding. Avail. for Wideside only (RPO B85): $144 without RPO Z62; $15 with RPO Z62. Custom Package (RPO YG1). Avail. for Wideside only. Includes wheel opening moldings, RPO B84, RPO B96 and bright trim for front sidemarker lamps and taillights: $157 without RPO Z62; $29 with RPO Z62. Deluxe Package (RPO YG3). Avail. for Wideside only. Not avail. with RPO YG1 or RPO RO5. Includes bright trim for front side marker lamps and taillights, RPO B85 and RPO B96: $173 without RPO Z62, RPO ZY3, RPO ZY4 or ZY5; $44 with RPO Z62; $16 with RPO ZY3, RPO ZY4 or RPO ZY5. Wheel opening molding (RPO B96). Avail. only with RPO ZY6: $29. Door edge guards (RPO B93): $17 for regular cab; $22 for bonus or crew cab. Operating Convenience Package (RPO ZQ2). Includes RPO AU3 power door locks and RPO A31 power windows: $325 for regular cab; $488 for bonus and crew cab. AM radio (RPO U63): $112. AM/FM radio (RPO U69): 171. AM/FM stereo radio (RPO U58): $198. AM/FM stereo radio with stereo cassette tape player (RPO UN3): $298. Electronically tuned AM/FM stereo radio with Seek-Scan, stereo cassette player and clock (RPO UM6): $419. Windshield antenna (RPO U76): $32. Pickup box side rails (RPO D73): $94. Transfer case shield (RPO NY7): $41. Front quad shock absorbers (RPO Z75): $128 for K-1500 and K-2500 without C6P heavy-duty chassis; $94 for K-2500 with C6P. Electronic speed control (RPO K34). Not avail. for K-1500 with MM7 trans. or K-2500 and K-3500 with LS9, LT9 and LE8 with MM4 trans.: $195. Heavy-duty front springs (RPO F60). Not avail. for K-3500. For K-1500 and K-2500 includes heavy-duty front and rear shock absorbers. Recommended for snowplow use for K-1500: $92 without RPO Z75 front quad shock absorbers; $59 with RPO Z75. Main and auxiliary tank springs (RPO G60): $97. ComforTilt steering wheel (RPO N33). Not avail. when RPO MM3 was specified: $115. Auxiliary fuel tank (RPO NL2): $260-$270 depending on model. Two front towing hooks (RPO V76): $36. Bright metal wheelcovers, for K-1500 only (RPO PO1): $40. Special wheelcovers, for K-2500 only (RPO PA1): $118. Rallye wheels, K-1500 only (RPO N67): $115. Styled wheels (RPO PA6): $174. Aluminum cast wheels (RPO N90): $299. Dual rear wheels for K-3500 only (RPO RO5): $678-740 depending on options and transmission specified. Power windows (RPO A31): $190 for regular cab; $290 for bonus and crew cab. Sliding rear window (RPO A28): $107. Intermittent windshield wiper system (RPO CD4): $55.

HISTORICAL FOOTNOTES: Calendar year production of all GMC truck models was 316,533. Full-size pickup production totalled 105,651. Suburban output was 23,850.

PAYLOA
GVWR

1985 GMC K-3500 cab and chassis

1986 PICKUP & SUBURBAN

The design of the 1986 GMC trucks were little unchanged from 1985. All gasoline engines now had new generator drive belts that increased friction due to their greater area of contact with pulleys. All V-type engines except for the 7.4 liter V-8 had new crankshaft seals and oil pan gaskets. The color selection for 1986 consisted of frost white, steel grey metallic, midnight black, light blue metallic, midnight blue, canyon copper metallic, doeskin tan, Nevada gold metallic, Indian bronze metallic and apple red. All three interior trim levels were available in blue, burgundy, or tan.

1986 GMC Sierra Classic Wideside pickup

I.D. DATA: Unchanged from 1985 except the letter G designated the 1986 model year.

Model Number	Body Type	Factory Price	GVW	Shipping Weight	Prod. Total
Series K-1500-1/2 ton 250 6-cyl. 117.5 in., 131.5 in. wheelbase (Suburban: 129.5 in. wheelbase and standard 350 V-8)					
TK10703	6.5 ft. Stepside Pickup	$10,425	6100	4403	—
TK10703	6.5 ft. Fleetside Pickup	$10,290	6100	4450	—
TK10903	8 ft. Fleetside Pickup	$10,459	6100	4636	—
TK10906	Suburban Endgate	$12,384	6100	5145	—
TK10906	Suburban Pnl. Drs.	$12,347	6100[1]	5111	—

NOTE 1: Surburban available with optional 6600 GVW Package.

Model Number	Body Type	Factory Price	GVW	Shipping Weight	Prod. Total
Series K-2500-3/4 ton 292 V-8. 131.5 in. wheelbase. (Suburban-129.5 in. wheelbase), Crew and Bonus Cab: 164.5 in. wheelbase, Suburban weight with standard 350 V-8.K20 Pickup prices include C6P heavy-duty chassis.					
TK20903	8 ft. Stepside Pickup	$11,947	6600*	4863	—
TK20903	8 ft. Fleetside Pickup	$11,814	6600	4985	—
TK20906	Suburban Endgate	$13,918	6600	5519	—
TK20906	Suburban Pnl. Drs.	$13,996	6600	5585	—

* 8600 lb. GVW optional.

Model Number	Body Type	Factory Price	GVW	Shipping Weight	Prod. Total
Series K-3500-1 ton 350 V-8. 131.5 in. wheelbase, Crew and Bonus Cab: 164.5 in. wheelbase					
TK30903	Chassis & Cab[1]	$13,161	9200*	4512	—
TK31003	Chassis & Cab[2]	$13,373	9200	5022	—
TK31403	Chassis & Cab[3]	$13,896	9200	5295	—
TK30903	8 ft. Fleetside Pickup	$13,547	9200	5434	—
TK30943	Chassis & Bonus Cab	$14,057	9200	5417	—
TK30943	Fleetside Bonus Cab	$14,423	9200	5836	—
TK30943	Chassis & Crew Cab	$14,396	9200	5925	—
TK30943	Fleetside Crew Cab	$14,761	9200	5836	—

297

NOTE 1: 131.5 in. wheelbase.
NOTE 2: 135.5 in. wheelbase.
NOTE 3: 159.5 in. wheelbase.
* 10,000 lb. GVW optional.

Diesel engine adds 454 lb. to weights of gasoline-engined models in all series.

STANDARD ENGINE: All K-10 6-cyl. models: 262 V-6 (LB1 ordering code) Engine Type: Vortex OHV, V-6-cylinder. Cast iron block. Key features include a 4-bbl. carburetor. Bore x Stroke: 4.0 in. x 3.48 in. Lifters: Hydraulic. Fuel Induction: Single Rochester 4-bbl. carburetor. Compression Ratio: 9.3:1. Displacement: 262 cu. in. (4.3 liters). Horsepower: Net: 155 @ 4000 rpm. Torque: Net: 230 lb.-ft. @ 2400 rpm. Oil refill capacity: 5 qt. with filter change. Fuel Requirements: Regular unleaded.

STANDARD ENGINE: K-2500 with RPO CH6 and K-3500 models: 292 Six. Ordering Code: L25. This engine was produced by GM de Mexico. Not available in California with under 8500 lb. GVW rating. Engine Type: OHV, 6-cyl. Cast iron block and cylinder head. Key features include cast iron intake manifold, aluminized-face intake valves, Stellite-faced exhaust valves with hardened faces. Bore x Stroke: 3.875 in. x 4.125 in. Lifters: Hydraulic. Number of main bearings-7. Fuel Induction: Single Rochester 1-bbl. carburetor. Compression Ratio: 7.8:1. Displacement: 292 cu. in. (4.8 liters). Horsepower: Net: 115 @ 3400 rpm. Torque: Net: 215 lb.-ft. @ 1600 rpm. Oil refill capacity: 6 qt. with filter change. Fuel Requirements: Regular unleaded.

STANDARD ENGINE: K-2500: Optional for K-1500 (California only), K-2500 with HP6 and all K-3500 models. Ordering Code: LS9: 350 V-8 Engine Type: OHV, V-8. Cast iron block and alloy iron cylinder head. Key features include chain drive camshaft and forged steel connecting rods. This engine was produced by GM-Chevrolet Motor Division. Bore x Stroke: 4.0 in. x 3.50 in. Lifters: Hydraulic. Number of main bearings-5. Fuel Induction: Single Rochester 4-bbl. carburetor. Compression Ratio: 8.2:1. Displacement: 350 cu. in. (5.7 liters). Horsepower: Net: 165 @ 3800 rpm. Torque: Net: 275 lb.-ft. @ 1600 rpm. Oil refill capacity: 5 qt. with filter change. Fuel Requirements: Regular unleaded.

OPTIONAL ENGINE: K-2500 with HP6 and all K-3500 models: Ordering Code: LT9: 350 V-8. Engine Type: OHV, V-8. Cast iron block and alloy iron cylinder head. Key features include chain drive camshaft and forged steel connecting rods. This engine was produced by GM-Chevrolet Motor Division. Bore x Stroke: 4.0 in. x 3.50 in. Lifters: Hydraulic. Number of main bearings-5. Fuel Induction: Single Rochester 4-bbl. carburetor. Compression Ratio: 8.3:1. Displacement: 350 cu. in. (5.7 liters). Horsepower: Net: 160 @ 3800 rpm. (California rating: 155 @ 3600 rpm). Torque: Net: 260 lb.-ft. @ 2800 rpm. (California rating: 240 lb.-ft. @ 2800 rpm). Oil refill capacity: 5 qt. with filter change. Fuel Requirements: Regular unleaded.

OPTIONAL ENGINE: K-1500 models: 305 V-8. Key features include Electronic Spark Control, new staged 4-barrel carburetor, camshaft and free-flow exhaust system. Not available for California. This engine was produced by GM-Chevrolet Motor Division and GM of Canada. Engine Type: OHV, V-8. Cast iron block and alloy iron cylinder head. Bore x Stroke: 3.74 in. x 3.48 in. Lifters: Hydraulic. Number of main bearings-5. Fuel Induction: Single Rochester 4-bbl. staged carburetor. Compression Ratio: 9.2:1. Displacement: 305 cu. in. (5.0 liters). Horsepower: 160 @ 4400 rpm. Torque: 235 lb.-ft. @ 2000 rpm. Oil refill capacity: 5 qt. with filter change. Fuel Requirements: Regular unleaded.

OPTIONAL ENGINE: K-1500 models for California: Ordering Code: LF3: 305 V-8. Key features include 4-barrel carburetor, camshaft and free-flow exhaust system. This engine was produced by GM-Chevrolet Motor Division and GM of Canada. Engine Type: OHV, V-8. Cast iron block and alloy iron cylinder head. Bore x Stroke: 3.74 in. x 3.48 in. Lifters: Hydraulic. Number of main bearings-5. Fuel Induction: Single Rochester 4-bbl. carburetor. Compression Ratio: 8.6:1. Displacement: 305 cu. in. (5.0 liters). Horsepower: 155 @ 4200 rpm. Torque: 240 lb.-ft. @ 1600 rpm. Oil refill capacity: 5 qt. with filter change. Fuel Requirements: Regular unleaded.

OPTIONAL ENGINE: K-3500 models: Ordering Code: LE8: 454 V-8. This engine was produced by GM-Chevrolet Motor Division. Engine Type: OHV, V-8. Cast iron block and alloy iron cylinder head. Bore x Stroke: 4.3 in. x 4.0 in. Lifters: Hydraulic. Number of main bearings-5. Fuel Induction: Single Rochester 4-bbl. carburetor. Compression Ratio: 7.9:1. Displacement: 454 cu. in. (7.4 liters). Horsepower: 230 @ 3800 rpm. Torque: 360 lb.-ft. @ 2800 rpm. Oil refill capacity: 5 qt. with filter change. Fuel Requirements: Regular unleaded.

OPTIONAL ENGINE: All models: Ordering Code: LH6: 6.2 liter V-8. This engine was produced by GM-Detroit Diesel Allison Division. Engine Type: OHV, diesel V-8. Bore x Stroke: 3.98 in. x 3.80 in. Lifters: Hydraulic. Number of main bearings-5. Fuel Induction: Fuel injection. Compression Ratio: 21.3:1. Displacement: 379.4 cu. in. (6.2 liters). Horsepower: 135 @ 3600 rpm. Torque: 240 lb.-ft. @ 2000 rpm. Oil refill capacity: 7 qt. with filter change. Fuel Requirements: Diesel. An LL4 version of this engine for models with GVW of 8500 lb. and above was also available. Its power ratings were 135 hp. @ 3600 rpm and 240 lb.-ft. of torque @ 2000 rpm.

CHASSIS FEATURES: Separate body and frame with channel side rails. Carbon-Steel, 39,000 psi. 117.5 in. wheelbase: 2.30 in. x 5.92 in. x 0.156 in. Section modulus: 3.06 in. 129.5 in.: 2.30 in. x 5.92 in. x 0.194. Section modulus: 117.5 in. wheelbase: 3.14 in. 131.5 in. wheelbase: 3.88 in. K-2500 with CP6: 4.53 in. Optional: None.

SUSPENSION AND RUNNING GEAR: Front Suspension: K-1500: Tapered 2-leaf springs. Capacity: 1650 lb. (16), 1850 lb. (03, 06). K-2500: Tapered 2-leaf springs. Capacity: 1850 lb. K-3500: Tapered 3-leaf springs. Capacity: 2250 lb. Rear Suspension: K-1500 and K-2500: 52 in. x 2.5 in. Two-stage, 5-leaf. K-3500: 56 in. x 2.50 in. Rating: K-1500: 2075 lb. K-2500: 2800 lb. K-3500: 3500 lb. K-1500: 22mm. dia. shock absorbers. K-3500: 32mm shock absorbers. Capacity: K-1500: 3750 lb., K-2500: 5700 lb., K-3500: 7000 lb. (7500 lb. for 159.9 in. wheelbase chassis and cab). 000. Optional Rating: K-2500: 3000 lb. rating at ground. Capacity: 6000 lb. with RPO CP6 K-3500: RPO RO5 (Dual rear wheels): 3750 lb. rating at ground. Capacity: 7500 lb. Front Axle Type and Capacity: K-1500: Semi-floating, 3700 lb. capacity. Optional: None. K-2500: Full-floating, 3800 lb. capacity. K-3500: Full-floating, 4500 lb. Optional: None. Rear Axle Type and Capacity: K-1500: Chevrolet, semi-floating, 3750 lb. capacity. K-2500: Semi-floating, 5700 lb. capacity. K-3500: Full-floating, 7500 lb. Optional Rating: K-2500: 3000 lb. rating at ground. Capacity: 6000 lb. with RPO CP6 K-3500: RPO RO5 (Dual rear wheels): 3750 lb. rating at ground. Capacity: 7500 lb. Final Drive Ratio: The following transmission designations were used by Chevrolet: MM3-3-spd. manual; MM4: 4-spd. manual; MM7: 4-spd. manual with overdrive; MXO: 4-spd. auto. with overdrive; MX1: 3-spd. automatic. All ratios are with standard emission equipment. Standard: K-1500: LB1 engine/MM4, MXO: 3.73:1 (requires engine oil cooler); LS9 /MM7: 3.42:1, LS9/M4: 2.73:1, LS9/MXO: 3.08:1 LH6/MM4, MXO: 3.08:1; LH6/MM7: 3.42:1 Optional: LB1/ MM4, MXO: 3.73:1 (requires RPO KC4, engine oil cooler), LE9/MM7: 3.73:1, LE9/MM4: 3.08:1, LH6/MM4, MXO: 3.42:1 Standard: K-2500: L25/MM4: 3.42:1, LS9/MM4MXO: 3.23:1, LT9/MM4: 3.42:1, LT9/MX1: 4.10:1; LH6/MM4: 3.73:1, LH6/MXO: 3.42:1,LL4/M4:3.73:1, LL4/ MX1: 4.10:1. Optional: LS9/MM4: 4.10:1, LS9/MXO: 3.42:1, 3.73:1; LT9/MM4: 3.73:1, 4.10:1; LH6/MM4: 4.10:1, LH6/MXO: 3.73:1; LL4/MM4: 4.10:1. Standard K-3500: K25/MM4 4.56:1; LT9/MM4: 3.73:1; LT9/MX1: 4.10:1; LE8/MM4, MX1: 4.10:1, LL4/MM4, MX1: 4.10:1. Optional: LT9/MM4: 4.10:1, 4.56:1; LT9/MX1: 4.56:1; LE8/MM4, MX1: 4.10:1, 4.56:1; LL4/ MM4, MX1: 4.56:1. Transfer Case: K-1500 and K-2500: New Process 208. Single lever, 2.61, 1.00:1. K-3500: New Process 205, two-speed. 1.96, 1.00:1. Brakes: Type: Hydraulic, power assisted. Dimensions: K-1500: Front: Disc. 11.86 in. x 1.28 in. Rear: Drums: 11.15 x 2.75 in. K-2500: Front: Disc 12.5 in. x 1.28 in. Rear: Drums: 11.15 in. x 2.75 in. K-2500 and K-3500:

Front: Disc: 12.50 in. x 1.53 in. Rear: Drum: 13.00 in. x 3.50 in. Wheels: K-1500: 15 x 6.0JJ 6-stud disc. Optional: 15 x 8JJ. K-2500: 16.5 x 6.00 in. 8-stud disc. Optional: 16.5 x 6.75. K-3500: 16.5 x 6.75. Tires: K-1500: P235/75R15 steel belted radial. Optional: K-2500: LT215/85R16C, K-2500 with RPO CP6: Front: LT235/85R16D, 8-ply rating; Rear: LT235/85R16E, 10-ply rating. K-3500: Front: LT235/85R16D, 8-ply rating; Rear: LT235/85R16E, 10-ply rating. Optional: K-1500: P235/75R15 steel belted radial; P235/75R15R white letters; 31 x 10.50R/15B blackwall or white letters (both require RPO N67, N90 or PA6 wheels). Optional K-2500: Tubeless steel belted radials 7.50R/16D, LT215/85R16C, LT215/85R16D, LT235/85R16D, LT235/85R16E. Optional: K-3500: Tube-type, nylon: 7.50-16D. Tubeless steel belted radials: LT215/85R16D, LT235/85R16E. Steering: Recirculating ball gear. Ratio: 20:1. Turning Circle: 47 ft. Steering wheel diameter: 17.5 in. Optional: Power-assisted. Ratio: 16.4:1. Transmission: K-1500, K-2500, K-3500: 4-speed, synchromesh manual. Transmission Ratios: 6.55, 3.58, 1.70, 1.00:1. Optional: K-1500: 4-spd. manual overdrive, 4-spd. automatic overdrive; K-2500: 4-spd. automatic overdrive; K-3500: 3-spd. automatic overdrive; K-2500: 4-spd. automatic overdrive; K-2500: 4-spd. manual overdrive. Diesel models: K-1500: 4-spd. manual overdrive, 4-spd. automatic overdrive; K-2500 HD (with RPO C6P) and K-3500: 3-spd. automatic. Clutch: Diaphragm, spring. Clutch diameter: 6-cyl: 11 in. dia. Total plate pressure: 2075 lb. * 8-cyl: 12 in. dia. Total lining area: 149.2 sq. in. Total plate pressure: 2060 lb. Optional: K-2500 6-cyl.: 11 in. dia. Total lining area: 124.0 sq. in. 307 V-8: 12 in. dia. Total lining area: 150 sq. in.

VEHICLE DIMENSIONS: Wheelbase: K-1500: 117.5 in., 131.5 in. K-2500: 131.5 in. All Suburbans and Panels: 129.5 in. K-3500: 131.5 in. 135.5 in. 164.5 in. Overall Length: 117.5 in. Wideside pickups: 192.60 in. 131.5 in. Wideside pickups: 212.50., 117.5 in. Fenderside pickups: 191.1 in. 131.5 in. Fenderside pickups: 211.00. K-3500: 131.5 in. Chassis-cab: 206.20 in. 135.5 in. wheelbase: 215.6 in.; 159.5 in. wheelbase: 239.7 in.; 164.5 in. wheelbase (bonus/crew cab): 239.3 in. Approach/Departure Degrees: K-1500 117.5 in. Wideside and Fenderside: 33/19. K-1500 131.5 in. Wideside: 33/15. K-1500 131.5 in. Wideside Fenderside: 33/16. K-2500 131.5 in. wheelbase Wideside: 35/20. K-2500 131.5 in. wheelbase Fenderside: 35/21. K-3500 Wideside pickup: 41/19. K-3500 crew cab pickup: 38/18. Ground Clearance: Wideside models: K-1500 pickups: Front: 74 in.; rear: 7.1 in., K-2500 pickups: Front: 8.8 in.; rear: 7.2 in. K-3500 pickups: Front: 8.3 in.; rear: 7.8 in. Fenderside models: K-1500 pickups: Front: 7.2 in.; rear: 7.1 in. K-2500 pickups: Front: 8.8 in.; rear: 7.2 in. K-3500 pickups: K-3500 chassis-cab: Front: 131.5 in. 135.5 in. and 159.5 in. wheelbase): Front: 8.3 in.; rear: 7.7 in. K-3500 bonus/crew cab: Front: 8.3 in.; rear: 7.7 in. Load space: Pickup box dimensions: 117.5 in. wheelbase Wideside: 78.25 in. x 50 in. x 19.25 in. 131.5 in. wheelbase Wideside: 98 in. x 50 in. x 19.25 in. Capacity: 117.5 wheelbase: 58.4 cu. ft. 131.5 in. wheelbase: 74.3 cu. ft. 117.5 in. wheelbase Fenderside: 78.5 in. x 50 in. x 17.5 in. 131.5 in. wheelbase Fenderside: 96.25 in. x 50 in. x 17.5 in. Front headroom: 38.5 in. (seat to top of cab) Front hip room: 67.25 in. Pedal to seat back (max.): 43.5 in. Steering wheel to seat back (max.): 17.3 in. Seat to ground: 35.0 in. Floor to ground: 23.0 in.

CAPACITIES: Fuel Tank: 117.5 in. wheelbase: 16.0 gal. 131.5 in. wheelbase, 135.5 in. wheelbase and 164.5 in. wheelbase: 20 gal. Optional: 16 gal. auxiliary tank. for 117.5 in.; 20 gal. auxiliary for 131.5 in. 135.5 in. and 164.5 in. wheelbase. Engine coolant system: 250 6-cyl.: 14.8 qt. 305 V-8: 17.6 qt. 350 V-8: 17.6 qt. 400 V-8: 19.6 qt. (20 qt. on K-2500 and K-3500).

ACCOMMODATIONS: Seating Capacity: Pickup and chassis-cab models: 3 passenger. Optional: None. Crew cab: 6 passenger. Suburban: 3 passenger. Optional: 6 or 9 passenger.

INSTRUMENTATION: Speedometer, odometer, fuel level gauge. Warning lights for battery, oil pressure, generator, brake system warning, directional/hazard lights, high beam, and engine coolant temperature.

OPTIONS AND PRICES: Sierra Classic Package (RPO YE9): $671-$1016, depending on body and additional packages installed. Deluxe bench seat: $17 with High Sierra Package; $62 without High Sierra Package (RPO Z62). Bonus cab custom bench seat: $50 with RPO Z62. Crew cab bonus seat: $100 with RPO Z62. Regular cab and bonus cab custom vinyl bench seat: $50 without RPO Z62 or RPO YE9. Crew cab custom vinyl bench seat: $100 with RPO YE9. Conventional two-tone paint (RPO ZY2): $43 to $89 depending on body and additional options. Exterior Decor Package (RPO ZY5): $418-$575 depending on body and additional options. Special Big Dooley two-tone paint (RPO ZY9): $444 without RPO Z62; $426 with RPO Z62. California emissions requirement (RPO YF5): $235. 5.0 liter V-8 (RPO LE9 or RPO LF3): $465. 5.7 liter V-8 (RPO LT9): $650. 5.7 liter V-8 (ROP LT9): $620. 7.4 liter V-8 (RPO LE8): $790. 6.2 liter diesel V-8 -3-spd. automatic trans. (RPO MX1): $510. 4-spd. manual overdrive trans.: $80. 4-spd. automatic trans. with overdrive (RPO MXO): $670. Optional axle ratios: $36. Locking rear differential (RPO G80): $238. Heavy-duty power brakes for K-1500 and K-2500 (RPO J55): $104. Chrome rear bumper (RPO VF1): $103. Chromed rear step bumper for Wideside only (RPO V42): $189. Painted rear step bumper (RPO V43): $120. Chromed front bumper guards (RPO V31): $41. Camper special chassis equipment (RPO Z81): $108 (for K-2500 with required C6H chassis) $49 for K-3500 with required RPO RO5 dual rear wheels. Glide-Out spare tire carrier (RPO P11): $41. Side-mounted spare tire carrier for Wideside only (RPO P13): $29. Quartz electric clock (RPO U35): Not available when UM6 radio is specified: $79 without RPO YE9. Includes RPO N53 voltmeter, temperature and oil pressure gauges; $39 with RPO YE9. Cold Climate Package. Not available when RPO C60 air conditioning or RPO B3J equipment is specified. Includes special insulation, RPO K81 66 amp generator, special heater and defroster, RPO KO5 engine block heater, anti-freeze protection to -32 degrees and RPO UA1 heavy-duty battery (RPO V10): $126 to $200 depending upon additional options and series applications. Engine oil cooling system (RPO KC4). Not avail. with RPO L25 engine or RPO B3J: $120. Heavy-duty radiator (RPO VO1): $53. Heavy-duty radiator and transmission oil (RPO VO2). Avail. only with RPO MX1 or RPO MXO transmission are specified. Not avail. with RPO L25 engine or RPO VO1 are specified: $59. Decor Value Package. Includes black-painted radiator grille and headlight bezels, and special body stripe located between body feature lines on front fenders, pickup box and across the tailgate. Not avail. on bonus cab, crew cab and Fenderside models. Not available with the following options: RPO YE9, RO5, V22, PA6, N90, B84 or B85. Requires RPO ZY1 solid paint and blackwall or white lettered tires are specified (RPO YJ6): $256 for K-1500; $141 for K-2500 and K-3500. Power door lock system (RPO AU3): $135 for regular cab; $198 for bonus and crew cab. Color-keyed front floor mats (RPO B32). Requires RPO YE9: $15. Gauge Package. Includes voltmeter, engine coolant temperature and oil pressure (RPO Z53): $40. 66 amp Delcotron generator. Standard on K-3500 except when RPO LE8 engine is ordered (RPO K81): $62. 94 amp Delcotron generator. Included with LE8 engine on K-3500 models (RPO K22): $62. Tinted glass-all windows (RPO AO1): $48 for regular cab; $56 for bonus or crew cab. Halogen high-beam headlamps. Avail. only when RPO V22 or RPO YE9 is specified (RPO TT5): $17. 600 watts engine block heater. Not avail. when RPO BK3 or RPO LF3 engine is specified (RPO KO5): $31. Heavy-duty front heater (RPO C42). Avail. only with RPO B3J is specified. Not avail. with RPO C60 air conditioning: $43. Automatic front locking hubs. Avail. only for K-1500 (RPO X6Z): $40. Cargo lamp (RPO UF2): $60 without RPO Z62 or YE9 (includes RPO C91 dome lamp). Dome lamp (RPO C91): 26. Roof marker lamps. Avail. for K-2500 only. Standard for K-3500 (RPO UO1): $50. Cigarette lighter. Included with RPO Z62 or YE9 and specified (RPO U37): $30. Exterior left and right side below eye-level mirrors: Painted (RPO D44): $50; stainless steel (RPO D45): $83. Camper type stainless steel left and right side exterior mirrors (RPO DF2): $94. Senior West Coast type painted exterior left and right side mirrors (RPO DG5): $65. Black body side molding. Avail. for Wideside only (RPO B84): $115. Bright body side molding. Avail. for Wideside only (RPO B85): $144 without RPO Z62; $15 with RPO Z62. Custom Package (RPO YG1). Avail. for Wideside only. Includes wheel opening moldings, RPO B84, RPO B96 and bright trim for front sidemarker lamps and taillights. $157 without RPO Z62; $29 with RPO Z62. Deluxe Package

(RPO YG3). Avail. for Wideside only. Not avail. with RPO YG1 or RPO RO5. Includes bright trim for front side marker lamps and taillights, RPO B85 and RPO B96: $173 without RPO Z62, RPO ZY3, RPO ZY4 or ZY5; $44 with RPO Z62; $16 with RPO ZY3, RPO ZY4 or RPO ZY5. Wheel opening molding (RPO B96). Avail. only with RPO ZY6: $29. Door edge guards (RPO B93): $17 for regular cab; $22 for bonus or crew cab. Operating Convenience Package (RPO ZQ2). Includes RPO AU3 power door locks and RPO A31 power windows: $325 for regular cab; $488 for bonus and crew cab. AM radio (RPO U63): $112. AM/FM radio (RPO U69): 171. AM/FM stereo radio (RPO U58): $198. AM/FM stereo radio with stereo cassette tape player (RPO UN3): $298. Electronically tuned AM/FM stereo radio with Seek-Scan, stereo cassette player and clock (RPO UM6): $419. Windshield antenna (RPO U76): $32. Pickup box side rails (RPO D73): $94. Transfer case shield (RPO NY7): $41. Front quad shock absorbers (RPO Z75): $128 for K-1500 and K-2500 without C6P heavy-duty chassis; $94 for K-2500 with C6P. Electronic speed control (RPO K34). Not avail. for K-1500 with MM7 trans. or K-2500 and K-3500 with LS9, LT9 and LE8 with MM4 trans.: $195. Heavy-duty front springs (RPO F60). Not avail. for K-3500. For K-1500 and K-2500 series includes heavy-duty front and rear shock absorbers. Recommended for snowplow use for K-1500: $92 without RPO Z75 front quad shock absorbers; $59 with RPO Z75. Main and auxiliary rear springs (RPO G60): $97. ComforTilt steering wheel (RPO N33). Not avail. when RPO MM3 was specified: $115. Auxiliary fuel tank (RPO NL2): $260-$270 depending on model. Two front towing hooks (RPO V76): $36. Bright metal wheelcovers, for K-1500 only (RPO PO1): $40. Special wheelcovers, for K-2500 only (RPO PA1): $118. Rallye wheels, K-1500 only (RPO N67): $115. Styled wheels (RPO PA6): $174. Aluminum cast wheels (RPO N90): $299. Dual rear wheels for K-3500 only (RPO RO5): $678-740 depending on options and transmission specified. Power windows (RPO A31): $190 for regular cab; $290 for bonus and crew cab. Sliding rear window (RPO A28): $107. Intermittent windshield wiper system (RPO CD4): $55.

HISTORICAL FOOTNOTES: The 1986 GMC trucks debuted in Oct., 1985. Model year sales of all GMC truck models was 311,732. Full-size pickup sales were 114,115. Suburban sales were 19,287.

1987 PICKUP & SUBURBAN

GMC reported that its emphasis in 1987 would be on power and performance. All engines had electronic fuel injection. Refinements for 1987 included a serpentine single belt accessory drive for longer belt service life, increased alternator output on selected engines, and the use of lighter-weight Delco Freedom batteries with increased cranking power. GMC offered a special Ducks Unlimited Edition Suburban celebrating the 50th anniversary of Ducks Unlimited, a North American wild fowl and wetlands conservation organization. The four-wheel drive Suburban, customized by Starcraft, was available in exterior camouflage green, Indian bronze or doeskin tan paint treatments.

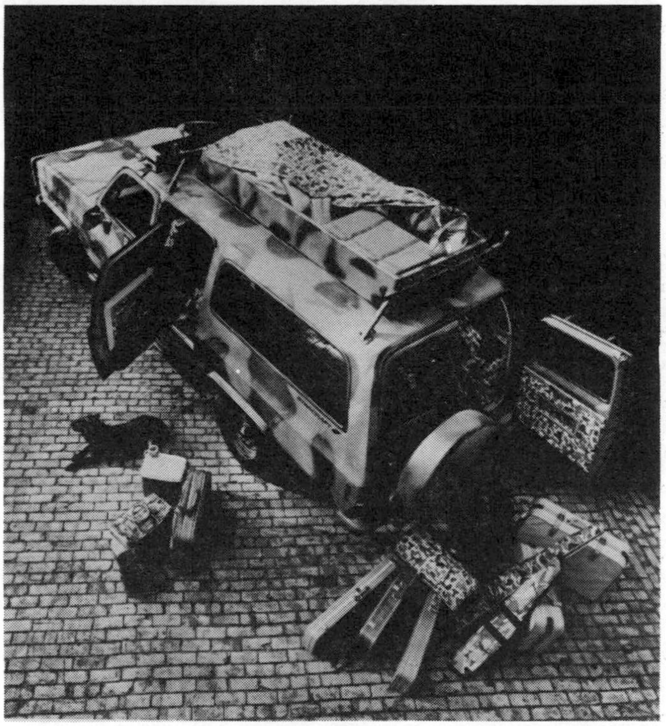

1987 GMC Ducks Unlimited Suburban

I.D. DATA: Unchanged from 1986 except the letter H designated the 1987 model year.

Model Number	Body Type	Factory Price	GVW	Shipping Weight	Prod. Total
Series V-1500-1/2 ton 250 6-cyl. 117.5 in., 131.5 in. wheelbase (Suburban: 129.5 in. wheelbase and standard 350 V-8)					
TV10703	6.5 ft. F-S Pickup	$11,165	6100	4383	—
TV10703	6.5 ft. Wideside Pickup	$11,030	6100	4420	—
TV10903	8 ft. Wideside Pickup	$11,199	6100	4616	—
TV10906	Suburban Endgate	$13,124	6100	5125	—
TV10906	Suburban Pnl. Drs.	$13,087	6100[1]	5179	—

NOTE 1: Surburban available with optional 6600 GVW Package.

Series V-2500-3/4 ton 350 V-8. 131.5 in. wheelbase. (Suburban-129.5 in. wheelbase), Crew and Bonus Cab: 164.5 in. wheelbase, Suburban weight with standard 350 V-8. V-2500 Pickup prices include C6P heavy-duty chassis.

TV20903	8 ft. Fenderside Pickup	$12899	6600*	4848	—
TV20903	8 ft. Wideside Pickup	$12654	6600	4960	—
TV20906	Suburban Endgate	$14819	6600	5496	—
TV20906	Suburban Pnl. Drs.	$14856	6600	5560	—

* 8600 lb. GVW optional.

Series V-3500-1 ton 350 V-8. 131.5 in. wheelbase, Crew and Bonus Cab: 164.5 in. wheelbase

TV30903	Chassis & Cab[1]	$14,461	9200*	4512	—
TV31003	Chassis & Cab[2]	$14,673	9200	5022	—
TV31403	Chassis & Cab[3]	$15,226	9200	5295	—
TV30903	8 ft. Wideside Pickup	$14,874	9200	5434	—
TV30943	Chassis & Bonus Cab	$15,387	9200	5417	—
TV30943	Fleetside Bonus Cab	$15,753	9200	5836	—
TV30943	Chassis & Crew Cab	$15,726	9200	5925	—
TV30943	Fleetside Crew Cab	$16,091	9200	5836	—

NOTE 1: 131.5 in. wheelbase.
NOTE 2: 135.5 in. wheelbase.
NOTE 3: 159.5 in. wheelbase.
* 10,000 lb. GVW optional.
Diesel engine adds 454 lb. to weights of gasoline-engined models in all series.

STANDARD ENGINE: All V-1500 6-cyl. models: 262 V-6 (LB4 ordering code) Engine Type: Vortex OHV, V-6-cylinder. Cast iron block. Bore x Stroke: 4.0 in. x 3.48 in. Lifters: Hydraulic. Fuel Induction: Electronic fuel injection. Compression Ratio: 9.3:1. Displacement: 262 cu. in. (4.3 liters). Horsepower: Net: 155 @ 4000 rpm. Torque: Net: 230 lb.-ft. @ 2400 rpm. Oil refill capacity: 5 qt. with filter change. Fuel Requirements: Regular unleaded. Standard engine: V-2500, V-3500 series, optional for V1500. Ordering Code: LO5. Engine Type: OHV, V-8. 350 V-8. Cast iron block and alloy iron cylinder head. Key features include chain drive camshaft and forged steel connecting rods. This engine was produced by GM-Chevrolet Motor Division. Bore x Stroke: 4.0 in. x 3.50 in. Lifters: Hydraulic. Number of main bearings-5. Fuel Induction: Electronic fuel injection. Compression Ratio: 8.2:1. Displacement: 350 cu. in. (5.7 liters). Horsepower: Net: 210 @ 4000 rpm. Torque: Net: 300 lb.-ft. @ 2800 rpm. Oil refill capacity: 5 qt. with filter change. Fuel Requirements: Regular unleaded.

OPTIONAL ENGINE: V-1500 models: Ordering Code: LO3: 305 V-8. Produced by GM-Chevrolet Motor Division and GM of Canada. Engine Type: OHV, V-8. Cast iron block and alloy iron cylinder head. Bore x Stroke: 3.74 in. x 3.48 in. Lifters: Hydraulic. Number of main bearings-5. Fuel Induction: Electronic fuel injection. Compression Ratio: 9.2:1. Displacement: 305 cu. in. (5.0 liters). Horsepower: 170 @ 4000 rpm. Torque: 260 lb.-ft. @ 2400 rpm. Oil refill capacity: 5 qt. with filter change. Fuel Requirements: Regular unleaded.

OPTIONAL ENGINE: V-3500 models: Ordering Code: L19 454 V-8. This engine was produced by GM-Chevrolet Motor Division. Engine Type: OHV, V-8. Cast iron block and alloy iron cylinder head. Bore x Stroke: 4.3 in. x 4.0 in. Lifters: Hydraulic. Number of main bearings-5. Fuel Induction: Electronic fuel injection. Compression Ratio: 7.9:1. Displacement: 454 cu. in. (7.4 liters). Horsepower: 230 @ 3600 rpm. Torque: 385 lb.-ft. @ 1600 rpm. Oil refill capacity: 5 qt. with filter change. Fuel Requirements: Regular unleaded.

OPTIONAL ENGINE: All V-1500 and V-2500 models: Ordering Code: LH6: 6.2 liter V-8. This engine was produced by GM-Detroit Diesel Allison Division. Engine Type: OHV, diesel V-8. Bore x Stroke: 3.98 in. x 3.80 in. Lifters: Hydraulic. Number of main bearings-5. Fuel Induction: Fuel injection. Compression Ratio: 21.3:1. Displacement: 379.4 cu. in. (6.2 liters). Horsepower: 130 @ 3600 rpm. Torque: 240 lb.-ft. @ 2000 rpm. Oil refill capacity: 5 qt. with filter change. Fuel Requirements: Regular unleaded. An LL4 version of this engine for V-2500 and V-3500 models with GVW of 8600 lb. and above was also available. Use in the V-2500 regular cab required the C6P heavy-duty chassis. Its power ratings were 148 hp. @3600 rpm and 246 lb.-ft. of torque @ 2000 rpm.

CHASSIS FEATURES: Separate body and frame with channel side rails. Carbon-Steel, 39,000 psi. 117.5 in. wheelbase: 2.30 in. x 5.92 in. x 0.156 in. Section modulus: 3.06 in. 129.5 in.: 2.30 in. x 5.92 in. x 0.194. Section modulus: 117.5 in. wheelbase: 3.14 in. 131.5 in. wheelbase: 3.88 in. V2500 with CP6: 4.53 in. Optional: None.

SUSPENSION AND RUNNING GEAR: Front Suspension: V1500: Tapered 2-leaf springs. Capacity: 1650 lb. V2500: Tapered 2-leaf springs. Capacity: 1850 lb. V3500: Tapered 3-leaf springs. Capacity: 2250 lb. Rear Suspension: V1500 and V2500: 52 in. x 2.25 in. Two-stage, 5-leaf. V3500: 56 in. x 2.50 in. Rating: V1500: 2075 lb. V2500: 2800 lb. V3500: 3500 lb. V1500: 22mm. dia. shock absorbers. V3500: 32mm shock absorbers. Capacity: V1500: 3750 lb., V2500: 5700 lb., V3500: 7000 lb. (7500 lb. for 159.9 in. wheelbase chassis and cab). 000. Optional Rating: V2500: 3000 lb. rating at ground. Capacity: 6000 lb., with RPO CP6 V3500: RPO RO5 (Dual rear wheels): 3750 lb. rating at ground. Capacity: 7500 lb. Front Axle Type and Capacity: V1500: Semi-floating. 3700 lb. capacity. Optional: None. V2500: Full-floating, 3800 lb. capacity. V3500: Full-floating, 4500 lb. Optional: None. Rear Axle Type and Capacity: V1500: Semi-floating, 3750 lb. capacity. V2500: Semi-floating, 5700 lb. capacity. V3500: Full-floating, 7500 lb. Optional Rating: V2500: 3000 lb. rating at ground. Capacity: 6000 lb. with RPO CP6 V3500: RPO RO5 (Dual rear wheels): 3750 lb. rating at ground. Capacity: 7500 lb. Final Drive Ratio: The following transmission designations were used by GMC: MM3-3-spd. manual; MM4: 4-spd. manual; MM7: 4-spd. manual with overdrive; MXO: 4-spd. auto. with overdrive; MX1: 3-spd. automatic. All ratios are with standard emission equipment. Standard: V1500: LB1 engine/MM4, MXO: 3.42:1; LB1/MM7: 3.73:1 (requires engine oil cooler); LS9 / MM7: 3.42:1, LS9/M4: 2.73:1, LS9/MXO: 3.08:1, LH6/MM4, MXO: 3.08:1; LH6/MM7: 3.42:1. Optional: LB1/MM4, MXO: 3.73:1 (requires RPO KC4, engine oil cooler), LE9/MM7: 3.73:1, LE9/MM4: 3.08:1, LH6/MM4, MXO: 3.42:1. Standard: V2500: L25/MM4: 4.10:1, LS9/ MM4MXO: 3.23:1, LT9/MM4: 3.42:1, LT9/MX1: 4.10:1; LH6/MM4: 3.73:1, LH6/MXO: 3.42:1,LL4/M4:3.73:1, LL4/MX1: 4.10:1. Optional: LS9/MM4: 3.42:1, LS9/MXO: 3.42:1, 3.73:1; LT9/MM4: 3.73:1, 4.10:1; LH6/MM4: 4.10:1, LH6/MXO: 3.73:1; LL4/MM4: 4.10:1. Standard V3500: K25/MM4, MX1: 4.56:1; LT9/MM4: 3.73:1; LT9/MX1: 4.10:1; LE8/ MM4, MX1: 3.73:1, LL4/MM4, MX1: 4.10:1. Optional: LT9/MM4: 4.10:1, 4.56:1; LT9/MX1: 4.56:1; LE8/MM4, MX1: 4.10:1, 4.56:1; LL4/MM4, MX1: 4.56:1. Transfer Case: V1500 and V2500: New Process 208. Single lever, 2.61, 1.00:1. V3500: New Process 205, two-speed: 1.96, 1.00:1. Brakes: Type: Hydraulic, power assisted. Dimensions: V1500: Front: Disc: 11.86 in. x 1.28 in. Rear: Drums: 11.15 x 2.75 in. V2500: Front: Disc: 12.5 in. x 1.28 in. Rear: Drums: 11.15 in. x 2.75 in. V2500 and V3500: Front: Disc: 12.50 in. x 1.53 in. Rear: Drum: 13.00 in. x 3.50 in. Wheels: V1500: 15 x 6.0JJ 6-stud disc. Optional: 15 x 8JJ. V2500: 16.5 x 6.00 in. 8-stud disc. Optional: 16.5 x 6.75. V30: 16.5 x 6.75. Tires: V1500: P235/75R15 steel belted radial. V2500: LT215/85R16C, V2500 with RPO CP6: Front: LT235/85R16D, 8-ply rating; Rear: LT235/85R16E, 10-ply rating; V3500: Front: LT235/85R16D, 8-ply rating; Rear: LT235/ 85R16E, 10-ply rating. Optional: V1500: P235/75R15 white sidewall; P235/75R15R white letters; 31 x 10.50R/15B blackwall or white letters (both require RPO N67, N90 or PA6 wheels). Optional V2500: Tubeless steel belted radials 7.50R/16D, LT215/85R16C, LT215/ 85R16D, LT235/85R16D, LT235/85R16E. Optional: V3500: Tube-type, nylon: 7.50-16D. Tubeless steel belted radial: LT215/85R16D, LT235/85R16E. Steering: Recirculating ball gear. Ratio: 20:1. Turning Circle: 47 ft. Steering wheel diameter: 17.5 in. Optional: Power-assisted. Ratio: 18.4:1. Transmission: V1500, V2500, V3500: 4-speed, synchromesh manual. Transmission Ratios: 6.55, 3.58, 1.70, 1.00:1. Optional: V1500: 4-spd. manual overdrive, 4-spd. automatic overdrive; V2500: 4-spd. automatic overdrive; V3500: 3-spd. automatic. Diesel models: V1500: 4-spd. manual overdrive, 4-spd. automatic overdrive; V2500: 4-spd. automatic overdrive; V2500 HD (with RPO C6P) and V3500: 3-spd. automatic. Clutch: Diaphragm, spring. Clutch diameter: 6-cyl.: 11 in. dia. Total lining area: 123.5 sq. in. Total plate pressure: 2075 lb. V-8: 12 in. dia. Total lining area: 149.2 sq. in. Total plate pressure: 2060 lb. Optional: V2500 6-cyl.: 11 in. dia. Total lining area: 124.0 sq. in. 307 V-8: 12 in. dia. Total lining area: 150 sq. in.

VEHICLE DIMENSIONS: Wheelbase: V1500: 117.5 in., 131.5 in. V2500: 131.5 in. All Suburbans and Panels: 129.5 in. V3500: 131.5 in., 135.5 in. 164.5 in. Overall Length: 117.5 in. Wideside pickups: 192.60 in. 131.5 in. Wideside pickups: 212.50., 117.5 in. Fenderside pickups: 191.1 in. 131.5 in. Fenderside pickups: 211.00. V3500: 131.5 in. Chassis-cab: 206.20 in. 135.5 in. wheelbase: 215.6 in.; 159.5 in. wheelbase: 239.7 in.; 164.5 in. wheelbase (bonus/crew cab): 239.3 in. Approach/Departure Degrees: V1500 117.5 in. Wideside and Fenderside: 33/19. V1500 131.5 in. Wideside: 33/15. V1500 131.5 in. wheelbase Fenderside: 33/16. V2500 131.5 in. wheelbase Wideside: 35/20. V2500 131.5 in. wheelbase Fenderside: 35/21. V3500 Wideside pickup: 41/19. V3500 crew cab pickup: 38/18. Ground Clearance: Wideside models: V1500 pickups: Front: 74 in.; rear: 7.1 in., V2500 Pickups: Front: 8.8 in.; rear: 7.2 in., V3500 pickups: Front: 8.3 in.; rear: 7.8 in. Fenderside models: V1500 pickups: Front: 7.2 in.; rear: 7.1 in. V2500 pickups: Front: 8.8 in.; rear: 7.2 in. V3500 pickups: V30 Chassis-cab (131.5 in. 135.5 in. and 159.5 in. wheelbase): Front: 8.3 in.; rear: 7.7 in. V3500 bonus/crew cab: Front: 8.3 in.; rear: 7.7 in. Load space: Pickup box dimensions: 117.5 in. wheelbase Wideside: 78.25 in. x 50 in. x 19.25 in. 131.5 in. wheelbase Wideside: 98 in. x 50 in. x 19.25 in. Capacity: 117.5 wheelbase: 58.4 cu. ft., 131.5 in. wheelbase: 74.3 cu. ft. 117.5 in. wheelbase Fenderside: 78.5 in. x 50 in. x 17.5 in. 131.5 in. wheelbase Fenderside: 96.25 in. x 50 in. x 17.5 in. Front headroom: 38.5 in. (seat to top of cab). Front hip room: 67.25 in. Pedal to seat back (max.): 43.5 in. Steering wheel to seat back (max.): 17.3 in. Seat to ground: 35.0 in. Floor to ground: 23.0 in.

CAPACITIES: Fuel Tank: 117.5 in. wheelbase: 16.0 gal. 131.5 in. wheelbase, 135.5 in. wheelbase and 164.5 in. wheelbase: 20 gal. Optional: 16 gal. auxiliary tank. for 117.5 in.; 20 gal. auxiliary for 131.5 in. 135.5 in. and 164.5 in. wheelbase. Engine coolant system: 250 6-cyl.: 14.8 qt. 305 V-8: 17.6 qt. 350 V-8: 17.6 qt. 400 V-8: 19.6 qt. (20 qt. on V20 and V30).

ACCOMMODATIONS: Seating Capacity: Pickup and chassis-cab models: 3 passenger. Optional: None. Crew cab: 6 passenger. Suburban: 3 passenger. Optional: 6 or 9 passenger.

INSTRUMENTATION: Speedometer, odometer, fuel level gauge. Warning lights for battery, oil pressure, generator, brake system warning, directional/hazard lights, high beam, and engine coolant temperature.

OPTIONS AND PRICES: Sierra Classic Package (RPO YE9). Deluxe bench seat. Bonus cab custom bench seat crew cab bonus seats. Regular cab and bonus cab custom vinyl bench seat. Crew cab custom vinyl bench seat. Conventional two-tone paint. Exterior Decor Package (RPO ZY5). Special Big Dooley two-tone paint. California emissions requirement. 5.0 liter V-8 (RPO LE9 or RPO LF3). 5.7 liter V-8 (RPO L05) 7.4 liter V-8 (RPO LE8). 6.2 liter diesel V-8. 3-spd. automatic trans. (RPO MX1). 4-spd. manual overdrive trans. 4-spd. automatic trans. with overdrive (RPO MXO). Optional axle ratios. Locking rear differential (RPO G80). Heavy-duty power brakes for V10 and V20 (RPO J55). Chrome rear bumper (RPO VF1). Chromed rear step bumper for Wideside only (RPO V42). Painted rear step bumper (RPO V43). Chromed front bumper guards (RPO V31). Camper special chassis equipment (RPO Z81). Glide-Out spare tire carrier (RPO P11). Side-mounted spare tire carrier for Wideside only (RPO P13). Quartz electric clock (RPO U35). Not available when UM6 radio is specified. Includes RPO Z53 voltmeter, temperature and oil pressure gauges. Cold Climate Package. Not available when RPO C60 air conditioning or RPO B3J diesel equipment is specified. Includes special insulation, RPO K81 66 amp generator, special heater and defroster, RPO KO5 engine block heater, anti-freeze protection to -32 degrees and RPO UA1 heavy-duty battery (RPO V10). Engine oil cooling system (RPO KC4). Not avail. with RPO L25 engine or RPO B3J. Heavy-duty radiator (RPO VO1). Heavy-duty radiator and transmission oil (RPO VO2). Avail. only with RPO MX1 or RPO MXO transmission are specified. Not avail. with RPO L25 engine or RPO VO1 are specified. Decor Value Package. Includes black painted radiator grille and headlight bezels, and special body stripe located between body feature lines on front fenders, pickup box and across the tailgate. Not avail. on bonus cab, crew cab and Fenderside models. Not available with the following options: RPO YE9, RO5, V22, PA6, N90, B84 or B85. Requires RPO ZY1 solid paint and either blackwall or white lettered tires are specified (RPO YJ6). Power door lock system (RPO AU3). Color-keyed front floor mats (RPO B32). Requires RPO YE9. Gauge Package. Includes voltmeter, engine coolant temperature and oil pressure (RPO Z53). 66 amp Delcotron generator. Standard on V3500 except when RPO LE8 engine is ordered (RPO K81). 94 amp Delcotron generator. Included with LE8 engine on V3500 models (RPO K22). Tinted glass-all windows (RPO AO1). Halogen high-beam headlamps. Avail. only when RPO V22 or RPO YE9 is specified (RPO TT5). 600 watts engine block heater. Not avail. when RPO BK3 or RPO LF3 engine is specified (RPO KO5). Heavy-duty front heater (RPO C42). Avail. only with RPO B3J is specified. Not avail. with RPO C60 air conditioning. Automatic front locking hubs. Avail. only for V1500 (RPO X6Z). Cargo lamp (RPO UF2). Dome lamp (RPO C91). Roof marker lamps. Avail. for V2500 only. Standard for V3500 (RPO UO1). Cigarette lighter. Included when RPO Z62 or YE9 is specified (RPO U37); Exterior left and right side below eye-level mirrors: Painted (RPO D44), stainless steel (RPO D45). Camper type stainless steel left and right side exterior mirrors (RPO DF2). Senior West Coast type painted exterior left and right side mirrors (RPO DG5). Black body side molding. Avail. for Wideside only (RPO B84). Bright body side molding. Avail. for Wideside only (RPO B85). Custom Package (RPO YG1). Avail. for Wideside only. Includes wheel opening moldings, RPO B84, RPO B96 and bright trim for front sidemarker lamps and taillights. Deluxe Package (RPO YG3). Avail. for Wideside only. Not avail. with RPO YG1 or RPO RO5. Includes bright trim for front side marker lamps and taillights. Wheel opening molding (RPO B96). Avail. only with RPO ZY6. Door edge guards (RPO B93). Operating Convenience Package (RPO ZQ2). Includes RPO AU3 power door locks and RPO A31 power windows. AM radio (RPO U63). AM/FM radio (RPO U69). AM/FM stereo radio (RPO U58. AM/FM stereo radio with stereo cassette tape player (RPO UN3). Electronically tuned AM/FM stereo radio with Seek-Scan, stereo cassette player and clock (RPO UM6). Windshield antenna (RPO U76). Pickup box side rails (RPO D73). Transfer case shield (RPO NY7). Front quad shock absorbers (RPO Z75). Electronic speed control (RPO K34). Not avail. for V1500 with MM7 trans. or V2500 and V3500 with LS9, LT9 and LE8 with MM4 trans. Heavy-duty front springs (RPO F60). Not avail. for V3500. For V1500 and V2500 series includes Heavy-duty front and rear shock absorbers. Recommended for snowplow use for V1500. ComforTilt steering wheel (RPO N33). Not avail. when RPO MM3 was specified. Auxiliary fuel tank (RPO NL2). Two front towing hooks (RPO V76). Bright metal wheelcovers, for V1500 only (RPO PO1): $40. Special wheelcovers, for V2500 only (RPO PA1). Rallye wheels, V1500 only (RPO N67). Styled wheels (RPO PA6). Aluminum cast wheels (RPO N90). Dual rear wheels for V3500 only (RPO RO5). Power windows (RPO A31). Sliding rear window (RPO A28): $107. Intermittent windshield wiper system (RPO CD4).

HISTORICAL FOOTNOTES: This was the final year of production for this GMC truck platform which had been originally been introduced in 1973.

1988 PICKUP & SUBURBAN

The new GMC Sierra Pickup, said GMC Truck Operation manager John D. Rock, "rides and handles like a luxury automobile and works like a truck for the best of both worlds." The growth of the full-size pickup truck market, which in 1987 accounted for nearly 25 percent of all trucks purchased in the U.S., saw GM respond with its biggest single truck model investment in history for the GMC Sierra and its Chevrolet counterpart. Highlights of the new model included aerodynamic styling and greater driver and passenger leg and shoulder room. The cargo box was completely welded and robotically assembled for precision fit. Improved corrosion resistance was provided by the use of special steels, primers and coatings. Galvanized steel was used for 73 percent of the Sierra's sheet metal. The frame was fully welded with a boxed front section. The steering-gear system was mounted inside the frame rails for reduced turning diameter and improved maneuverability.

The base Package was the Sierra SL, which was depicted as "a new value standard in full-size work trucks." The mid-range Sierra SLX was described as "a big step up in a sensible blend of function and form." The Sierra SLE was the top-of-the line Trim Package. Standard interior features on all models were the following items: Right and left hand armrests, instrument panel-mounted ashtray, right-side coat hook (also a left-hand unit on extended cabs), painted areas in the same color as the exterior primary color; interior trim identical to seat trim, color-keyed molded plastic door trim panels, left-door jam switch operated dome light, tinted glass in all windows on extended cab models, heater and defroster with side window defoggers, inside-operated hood lock release, speedometer, odometer and fuel gauges, warning lights for generator, oil pressure, engine coolant temperature, safety belt, service/parking brake, direction/hazard signal and high beams; insulation and sound-deadening material installed on firewall, under floor mats and on extended cab rear quarter and cab back panels; storage box located on right side of instrument panel with beverage holder on inside of door, instrument cluster and cab interior lights, shift point indicator light with manual transmission and gasoline engine, 4x4 lighted display, 10 in. inside day/night rearview mirror, foam-padded, full-width bench seat and folding back rear with vinyl trim, safety belts for all seating positions, 15.25 in. soft black plastic 4-spoke steering wheel, energy-absorbing steering column, left and right side padded vinyl sunshades, front chrome bumper, molded plastic argent painted grille, single electric low-tone horn, black plastic hubcaps with 4x4 identification, back-up lights integral with tail lamps, two rectangular headlights, front and rear directional and parking lamps, front side marker lamps, removable tailgate with embossed GMC lettering, mechanical jack and wheel wrench, painted silver wheels and electric two-speed windshield wipers and washers. All models were fitted with new anti-theft door locks in the form of sliding levers integrated into the door trim panels.

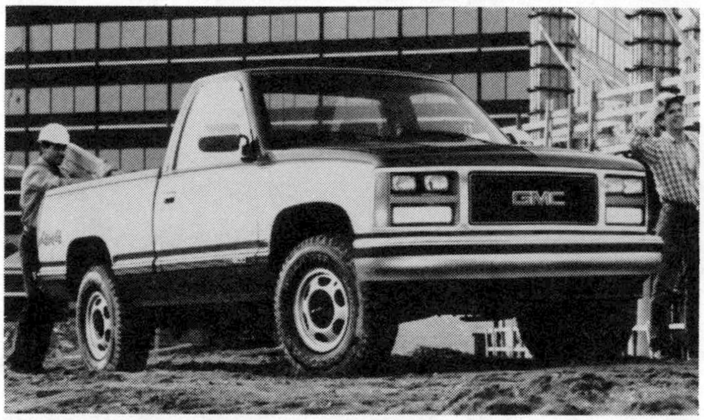

1988 GMC K-2500 Sierra

Contents of the Sierra SL included Sierra SL designation on rear cab side pillars and a choice of five interior colors: Grey, blue, saddle, beige or garnet.

The Sierra SLX Package (RPO Z62) had the following equipment in addition to or replacing that of the Sierra SL level: Dual electric high-note and low-note horn, Sierra SLX nameplates on rear cab side pillars, chrome front bumper with black rub strip, GMC block lettering decal on tailgate, standard bench seat with cloth upholstery and folding backrest in same color selection as Sierra SLX, grained plastic interior door panels with soft-vinyl upper trim, integral armrests, map products and Sierra SLX identification, color-keyed door-sill plates, color-keyed rubber floor mats (front compartment only on bonus cab), full-length mystic-colored insulated cloth headliner with matching retainer moldings, left and right-side coat hooks, and Sierra SLX identification on door trim panels.

The Sierra SLE Package (RPO YE9), included all Sierra SLX features plus the following: Hood and cab-to-fender insulators, Deluxe front end appearance with dark argent grille and quad rectangular halogen headlamps, Deluxe bright-accented front bumper rub strip, bright accent body side moldings, bright accent wheel-opening molding (Wideside single rear wheel models only), Deluxe tailgate trim with GMC lettering over bright aluminum applique, Sierra SLE identification on cab back pillars, custom vinyl seat trim in grey, blue, beige, garnet or saddle (or at no extra cost-custom cloth seat trim), soft-vinyl two-tone door trim panels with integral armrests, map pockets, door closing assist straps and Sierra SLE identification, color-keyed full-length carpeting, carpeted cowl/kick panel with insulator, carpeted cab back panels, color-keyed headliner, cloth-covered sunshades with left-hand storage strap and right-hand vanity mirror, custom four-spoke steering wheel and cigarette lighter in ashtray.

The 4x4 GMCs were fitted with a new independent front suspension utilizing a new wire-form design for the upper control arms that were lighter and stronger than the components previously used. Torsion bar springs and jounce bumpers were connected to the lower control arms. The torsion bars were computer selected to correspond with the truck's GVW rating and balance with the rear springs. The frame used on 4x4 trucks had an additional front cross member located under the transmission case. The 4x4 trucks also had a new "Shift-On-The-Fly Instra-Trac" transfer case system allowing for shifting from two-wheel drive to four-wheel drive high and back without stopping at any speed. The front axle disconnect system locked the front hubs automatically when the single lever operated the four-wheel drive system was pulled backward. This shifter was located in the center of the cab floor and was connected directly to the transfer case rather than using cables. In two-wheel drive the front-axle disconnect allowed the front wheels to turn freely. In four-wheel drive the transfer case split the power and directed it equally to the front and rear wheels. The K1500 was available with an optional Off-Road Chassis Package consisting of a front differential carrier, engine and transfer case shields, front stabilizer bar, Delco/Bilstein high-pressure gas shock absorbers and heavier front and rear jounce bumpers. The standard V-6 engine for the K1500 and K2500 series had a new one-piece rubber oil pan gasket to help prevent oil leakage. As a mid-year treat GMC introduced a new K1500 Sportside model on the 117.5 in. wheelbase chassis with a 6.5 ft. box, fiberglass rear fenders (side panels) flanked by functional steps to aid in loading and unloading. The Sportside was available with any trim level and most appearance, convenience and performance options offered for other 4x4 models. This truck body style identification was E62. Also introduced during the latter part of the 1988 year was a new instrument cluster featuring enhanced cluster graphics that increased clarity of instrument readings at all light levels.

I.D. DATA: Unchanged from 1987. The tenth entry, the letter J, represented the 1988 model year.

Series K1500-1/2 ton 262 V-6-cyl. 117.5 in., 131.5 in. wheelbase. Suburban: 129.5 in. wheelbase and standard 305 V-8.

Model	Body Type	MSRP
TK10703	6.5 ft. Sportside Pickup	$11,957
TK10703	6.5 ft. Fleetside Pickup	$11,827
TK10903	8.0 ft. Fleetside Pickup	$12,091
TK10753	6.5 ft. Extended Pickup	$12,932*
TK10953	8 ft. Extended Pickup	$13,132
TV10906	Suburban Pnl. Drs.	$14,996
TV10906	Suburban Tailgate	$15,046

* Add $2322 for diesel engine and equipment on TK10903.
Add $2518 for diesel equipment on TK10953.
Add $3108 for diesel equipment on Suburbans.

B3J-Diesel equipment

Series K2500-3/4 ton 262 V-6*. 131.5 in. wheelbase. (Suburban-129.5 in. wheelbase), Crew and Bonus Cab: 164.5 in. wheelbase, Suburban weight with standard 350 V-8

TK20903	Chassis and Cab	$13,484
TK20953	Chassis & Ext. Cab	$11,999
TK20903	8 ft. Fleetside Pickup E63	$12,255[1]
TK20753	6.5 ft. Extended Cab	$13,376[2]
TK20953	8.0 ft. Extended Cab	$13,576
TK20906	Suburban Pnl. Drs.	$16,440[3]
TV20906	Suburban Tailgate.	$16,480

NOTE 1: Add $1719.88 to price of E63 for RPO C6P.
Add $1077 to price of chassis & cab for B3J.
Add $1209 to price of E63 with C6P for B3J diesel equipment.
Add $2684 to price of E63 for B3J diesel equipment.
NOTE 2: Add $1450 to price of CK20953 for C6P.
Add $2423 to price of CK20753 and CK20953 for B3J.
Add $1209 to price of CK20953 with C6P for B3J.
NOTE 3: Add $2283 to price of Suburbans for B3J diesel equipment.
* GVW optional.

Series K3500-1 ton 350 V-8. 131.5 in. wheelbase, Crew and Bonus Cab: 164.5 in. wheelbase

Model	Body Type	MSRP
TK30903	Chassis & Cab	$13,584[1]
TK30903	8 ft. Fleetside Pickup	$13,998[1]
TV30943	Chassis & Cab Bonus Cab	$15,651
TV30943	Chassis & Cab Crew	$16,165
TV30943	HD Chassis & Cab Bonus	$16,051
TV30943	HD Chassis & Cab Crew	$16,559

NOTE 1: Add $1811.12 for B3J diesel equipment.

STANDARD ENGINE: All K1500, K2500 models: 262 V-6 (LB4 ordering code) Engine Type: Vortex OHV, V-6-cylinder. Cast iron block. Bore x Stroke: 4.0 in. x 3.48 in. Lifters: Hydraulic. Fuel Induction: Electronic fuel injection. Compression Ratio: 9.3:1. Displacement: 262 cu. in. (4.3 liters). Horsepower: Net: 160 @ 4000 rpm. Torque: Net: 235 lb.-ft. @ 2400 rpm. Oil refill capacity: 5 qt. with filter change. Fuel Requirements: Regular unleaded.

STANDARD ENGINE: K2500 with C6P and V3500 and K3500 models: Optional for K1500 and K2500 models. 350 V-8 (LO5 ordering code). Engine Type: OHV, V-8. Cast iron block and cylinder head. Bore x Stroke: 4.0 in. x 3.48 in. Lifters: Hydraulic. Number of main bearings-5. Fuel Induction: Electronic fuel injection. Compression Ratio: K3500: 8.6:1. K1500 and K2500: 9.3:1. Displacement: 350 cu. in. (5.7 liters). Horsepower: K3500: Net: 185 @ 4000 rpm. K1500 and K2500: 210 @ 4000 rpm. Torque: K3500: Net 295 lb.-ft. @ 2400 rpm. K1500 and K2500: 300 lb.-ft. @ 2800 rpm. Oil refill capacity: 5 qt. with filter change. Fuel Requirements: Regular unleaded. Optional: K1500 and K2500: 305 V-8, Ordering Code: LO3. Engine Type: OHV, V-8. Cast iron block and alloy iron cylinder head. Key features include chain drive camshaft and forged steel connecting rods. This engine was produced in U.S. or Canada. Bore x Stroke: 3.74 in. x 3.48 in. Lifters: Hydraulic. Number of main bearings-5. Fuel Induction: Electronic fuel injection. Compression Ratio: 9.2:1. Displacement: 305 cu. in. (5.0 liters). Horsepower: Net: 175 @ 4000 rpm. Torque: Net: 270 lb.-ft. @ 2400 rpm. Oil refill capacity: 5 qt. with filter change. Fuel Requirements: Regular unleaded.

OPTIONAL ENGINE: K3500 models: Ordering Code: L19: 454 V-8. Engine Type: OHV, V-8. Cast iron block and alloy iron cylinder head. Bore x Stroke: 4.30 in. x 4.0 in. Lifters: Hydraulic. Number of main bearings-5. Fuel Induction: Electronic fuel injection. Compression Ratio: 7.9:1. Displacement: 454 cu. in. (7.4 liters). Horsepower: 230 @ 3600 rpm. Torque: 385 lb.-ft. @ 1600 rpm. Oil refill capacity: 5 qt. with filter change. Fuel Requirements: Regular unleaded.

OPTIONAL ENGINE: K2500: Ordering Code LH6. Not available in California. This engine was produced by GM-Detroit Diesel Allison Division. Engine Type: OHV, diesel V-8. Bore x Stroke: 3.98 in. x 3.80 in. Lifters: Hydraulic. Number of main bearings-5. Fuel Induction: Gear driven mechanical fuel injection. Compression Ratio: 21.3:1. Displacement: 379.4 cu. in. (6.2 liters). Horsepower: 126 @ 3600 rpm. (140 @ 3600 rpm with automatic transmission). Torque: 240 lb.-ft. @ 2000 rpm. (247 lb.-ft. @ 2000 rpm with automatic transmission). Oil refill capacity: 7 qt. with filter change. Fuel Requirements: Diesel.

OPTIONAL ENGINE: K3500 and V3500 models: Ordering Code LL4. This engine was produced by GM-Detroit Diesel Allison Division. Engine Type: OHV, diesel V-8. Bore x Stroke: 3.98 in. x 3.80 in. Lifters: Hydraulic. Number of main bearings-5. Fuel Induction: Fuel injection. Compression Ratio: 21.3:1. Displacement: 379.4 cu. in. (6.2 liters). Horsepower: 143 @ 3600 rpm. Torque: 257 lb.-ft. @ 2000 rpm. Oil refill capacity: 7 qt. with filter change. Fuel Requirements: Diesel.

CHASSIS FEATURES: Semi-perimeter design, all-welded channel beam frame with boxed front end. Dimensions: K1500 and K2500 regular cab: 2.18 x 7.48 x 0.134 in. K1500 extended cab: 2.18 x 7.48 x 0.165 in. K2500 regular cab with C6P: 2.18 x 7.48 x 0.213 in. K2500 extended cab: 2.31 x 7.48 x 0.165 in. K2500 extended cab with C6P: 2.18 x 7.48 x 0.244 in. K3500 regular cab: 2.18 x 7.48 x 0.213 in. K3500 extended cab: 2.18 x 7.48 x 0.244 in. V3500 models: 2.788 x 7.74 x 0.244 in. Section modulus: K1500 regular cab: 3.46; K1500 extended cab: 4.30; K2500: 4.30; K2500 with C6P: 6.48; K3500 regular cab: 5.61; K3500 extended cab: 6.48, V3500: 7.33.

SUSPENSION AND RUNNING GEAR: Front Suspension: Torsion bar springs. K1500 Capacity: 3860 lb. K2500 and K3500 capacity: 3750 lb. V3500: Tapered leaf springs. Capacity: 4500 lb. Shock absorber dia.: K1500; 25mm; K2500, K3500 and V3500: 32mm. 32mm optional for K1500. 1.00 in. stabilizer optional for all series except V3500 which had a standard 1.25 in. bar standard. Optional rating: K1500: RPO F44/F60: 6100 lb. GVW. K2500: 8600 lb. GVW. K3500: 10,000 lb. GVW. Rear Suspension: Semi-elliptical 2-stage, 4-leaf for K1500; 6-leaf for K2500; 6-leaf plus 1-leaf auxiliary for K3500. K1500 capacity: 3750 K2500 capacity: 4800 K3500 capacity: 7500 lb. V3500: Semi-elliptical 2-stage, 9-leaf. Capacity: 7000 lb. Shock absorber dia.: K1500: 25mm; K2500, K3500 and V3500: 32mm. 32mm optional for K1500. Optional Rating: See above for GVW ratings. Front Axle Type and Capacity: Independent, GM or K1500; Spicer on K2500 and K3500. Capacity: K1500 regular cab: 3925; K1500 extended cab: 4800; K2500 and K3500: 4250 V3500: Spicer full-floating. Capacity: 4500, manual hub locks. Optional: K1500: 3925 capacity; K1500 extended cab: 4800 lb. All other K series: 4250 lb. Rear Axle Type: Semi-floating for K1500; full-floating for K2500, K3500 and V3500. GM manufacture for all series. Capacity: K1500: 3750, K2500: 6000; K3500, V3500: 7500 lb. Optional: K2500: Regular cab: 4800 lb.; K250 extended cab: 6000; K3500: 7500. Final Drive Ratio: The following transmission designations were used by GMC: MM4: 4-spd. manual; MM5: 5-spd. manual overdrive; MX1: 3-spd. automatic; MXO: 4-spd. automatic. All ratios are with standard emission equipment. Standard: K1500, K2500: 3.42:1. Optional: 3.73:1. All engine/transmission combinations except K2500 with LL4 diesel engine which had standard 3.73:1 ratio and optional 4.10:1 ratio, and K2500 with 5.7 liter V-8 and C6P which also had an optional 4.56:1 ratio. Standard: K3500: 4.10:1 with 5.7 liter V-8 with 4.56:1 optional; 3.42:1 standard for 7.4 liter V-8 with 3.73 and 4.10:1 optional; 6.2 liter diesel (LL4) had standard 4.10:1 ratio with 4.56:1 optional. Standard for V3500: 3.73:1 with 5.7 liter and manual 4-spd. trans.; 4.10:1 with 3-spd. auto. trans.; 3.73:1 with 7.4 liter V-8; 4.10:1 with LL4 diesel. Optional: 4.10 and 4.56:1 for 5.7 liter V-8 with man. 4-spd.; 4.56:1 for 5.7 liter V-8 with 3-spd. auto. trans.; 4.10 and 4.56:1 for 7.4 liter V-8; 4.56:1 for LL4 diesel. Transfer Case: K1500, K2500, K3500: New Process 241. Single lever. Ratios: 2.72:1, 1.00:1. K3500 with RPO RO5: Borg Warner 1370: Ratios: 2.69:1, 1.00:1. The Borg Warner unit has a right hand side power take-off. Brakes: Type: Hydraulic, power assisted. Dimensions: K1500: Front: Disc: 11.86 in. x 1.00 in. Rear: Drums: 10.0 x 2.25 in. K1500 regular cab with RPO F44/F60 had 11.57 in. x 1.25 in. front disc brakes. K2500 regular cab: Front: Disc: 11.57 in. x 1.20 in. Rear: Drums: 11.15 in. x 2.75 in. K2500 extended cab: Front Disc: 11.57 in. x 1.25 in. Rear: 10.0 in. x 2.25 in. drums. All K2500 with 8600 lb. GVW Package had 12.50 in. x 1.26 in. front disc brakes and 13.0 in. x 2.5 in. rear drum brakes. K3500 All models: Front: Disc: 12.50 in. x 1.26 in. Rear: Drum: 13.00 in. x 2.50 in. V3500 All models: Front Disc: 12.54 in. x 1.54 in. Rear: Drums: 13.0 in. x 3.5 in. Wheels: K1500 and K2500: 16 x 6.5, 6-stud disc. K3500 and V3500: 16.0 x 6.0. Tires: K1500 Sportside and regular cab: LT225/75R-16C steel belted radial. K1500 extended cab: LT245/75R16C. K2500 all models: LT245/75R-16E. K3500: LT225/75RD. V3500 all models: 7.50-16D tubeless nylon. Optional: K1500: LT225/75R16C, blackwall, LT225/75R16C on-off road; blackwall, white stripe or white lettered. Available for K10903 only with the following engines: LB4, LO3 and LH6 and RPO GVT4 axle; and K10703 with LB4 or LO3 engine with RPO GT4 axle: LT265/75R16C blackwall or white letter, on-off road. Optional K2500: LTR225/75R16D steel belted radial blackwall or white stripe, LT245/75R16E highway or on-off road, LT225/75R16D blackwall, on-off road, LT245/75R16E blackwall (K20903 only). Optional: K3500: LT225/75R16D, blackwall, LT245/75R16E blackwall, LT245/75R16E on-off road blackwall, LT245/75R16E blackwall, 7.50 x 16D highway and on-off road. Optional: V3500: V30943 only: 7.50 x 16 D tubeless nylon, dual rear, LT215/85R16D dual rear tubeless steel belted radial; LT235/85R16E. Steering: Integral power. Ratio: K1500 regular cab Sportside and Fleetside: 17.44:1. K1500 extended cab model K10753: 18.8:1, model K10953: 17.44:1. K2500 regular cab: 17.44:1. K2500 extended cab: K20753: 18.88:1; model K20953: 17.44:1. K3500 regular cab: 127.44:1. K3500 extended cab: 17.44:1. V3500: 13.5:1. Turning Diameter (curb-to-curb): K1500 regular cab Sportside: 40.3 ft. K1500 regular cab Fleetside: 44.4 ft. K1500 extended cab Model K10753: 47.9 ft., model K10953: 52.2 ft. K2500 regular cab: 44.4 ft. (with C6P: 45.1 ft.). K2500 extended cab: Model K20753: 47.9 ft., model 52.2 ft. K3500 regular cab: 45.1 ft. K3500 extended cab: 52.2 ft. V3500: 54.5 ft. Transmission: Standard K1500/2500: With gasoline engines: RPO MM5-5-spd. manual with overdrive fully-synchronized. Transmission Ratios: 4.02, 2.32, 1.40, 1.00, 0.73:1; Reverse: 3.74:1. Standard: K3500, V3500 and K2500 with C6P, and K1500 and K2500 with diesel engine: RPO MM4 4-spd. SM465 manual, synchromesh on top three gears (optional: K1500/2500). Transmission ratios: 6.55, 3.58, 1.70, 1.00:1. Reverse: 6.09:1. Optional: All series: RPO MX1-3-spd. 400 automatic. Transmission ratios: 2.48, 1.48, 1.0:1. Reverse: 2.08:1. Optional: K1500/2500, (except K2500 regular cab and extended cab chassis-cab, and all V3500 models): RPO MXO-4-spd. automatic overdrive 700R4: 3.06, 1.63, 1.0, 0.70:1. Reverse: 2.29:1.

VEHICLE DIMENSIONS: Wheelbase: All series regular cab: 117.5 in. 131.5 in. Extended cab: 6.5 ft. box models: 141.5 in.; 8.0 ft. box models: 155.5 in.; V3500 models: 164.5 in. Overall Length (without rear bumper): K1500 Sportside: 194.0 in., K1500 regular cab: 194.1 in. K1500 extended cab: Model K10753 (6.5 ft. box): 223.0 in., K10953 (8.0 ft. box): 237.0 in. K2500 regular cab: 212.6 in. K2500 extended cab: Model K20753: 223.0 in., model K20953: 237.0 in. K3500 Regular cab: 212.6 in. V3500: 246.4 in. Front/Rear Tread: 74 in./74 in. Overall Height: K1500 all models: 73.8 in. K2500 regular cab: 74.3 in. (75.8 in. if equipped with C6P). K2500 extended cab: 74.4 in. (75.8 in. if equipped with C6P). K3500 75.8 in. V3500: 76.3 in. Width: All models except V3500 and those equipped with RO5: 76.8 in. V3500: 79.6 in. V3500 and K3500 with RO5: 107.3 in. Front/Rear Overhang: 117.5 in. wheelbase. Pickups: 34.9 in./41.6 in. 131.5 in. wheelbase Pickups: 34.9 in./46.5 in. Extended cab: 34.9/46.5 in. Chassis-cab models: 34.9/41.8 in. Tailgate: Width and Height: K1500 Sportside: 50.9 x 19.3 in. All others: 62.0 in. x19.3 in. Approach/Departure Degrees: K1500 117.5 in.: 22/28. Ground Clearance (Front/Rear in inches): K1500 Sportside and Fleetside: 8.6/9.0. K1500 extended cab: 9.2/9.6. K2500 regular cab: 8.7/7.7 (with C6P: 7.8/8.1). K2500 extended cab: Model K20753: 9.2/8.2, model K20953: 9.2/8.1. K3500 regular and extended cab: 9.2/8.1 (with RO5 dual rear wheels: 7.2/7.4). V3500: 8.3/7.8. Front headroom, all models: 40.0 in. Front legroom, all models: 41.7 in. Front shoulder room, all models: 66.0 in.

CAPACITIES: Fuel Tank: All K series: 25.0 gal. All V3500 models: 20 gal. Optional: Models K10903, K10753, K10953, K20903, K20953, K30903: 34 gal. V3500 models: 20 gal.

ACCOMMODATIONS: Seating Capacity: Pickup, extended cab and chassis cab models: 3 passenger. Optional: Extended cab: 6 passenger. Suburban: 6 passenger. Optional: 9 passenger.

INSTRUMENTATION: Speedometer, odometer, fuel level gauge. Warning lights for battery, oil pressure, generator, brake system warning, directional/hazard lights, high beam, and engine coolant temperature.

OPTIONS: Pre-cleaner air cleaner (RPO K46). Air conditioning (RPO C60). Deluxe front appearance (RPO V22). Optional axle ratio. Locking rear differential (RPO G80). Heavy-duty Delco Freedom auxiliary battery with 540 cold cranking amps. Not avail. with B3J diesel equipment. (RPO TP2). Heavy-duty Delco Freedom battery with 630 cold cranking amps (RPO UA1). Painted rear step bumper (RPO V43). Chromed front Deluxe bumper with rub strip. Included with RPO Z62 and RPO YE9. (RPO VB3). Rear step bumper with rub strip (RPO VB3). Black front bumper guards. Requires RPO VG3. (RPO V 27). Spare tire and wheel carrier. Not avail. with K10753. (RPO P13): No charge. Heavy-duty chassis. Included with B3J diesel equip. (RPO F44). Cold Climate Package. Not avail. with RPO C60. Includes UA1 battery, KO5 block heater and C42 heater. (RPO V10). Console. Requires bucket seats. (RPO D55). Engine oil cooling system. Not available with B3J diesel equip., with RPO MXO transmission requires VO2 cooling, included with Z82 trailering option. (RPO KC4). Heavy-duty radiator. Not avail. with RPO VO2. (RPO VO1). Heavy-duty radiator and transmission oil cooler. Requires RPO MXO transmission. Included with RPO Z823. (RPO VO2). Sierra SLX Trim Package. (RPO Z62). Sierra SLE Trim Package (RPO YE). Rear window defogger. Requires RPO YE9 or RPO Z62. Not avail. with RPO A28 window or RPO AJ1 glass. (RPO C49). 5.0 liter V-8 (RPO LO3). 5.7 liter V-8 (RPO LO5).Locking fuel filler cap (RPO NO5). Front color-keyed floor mats. Requires RPO YE9 (RPO B32). Rear color-keyed floor mats. Requires RPO AM7 seat and RPO B32. (RPO B33). Gauge Package. Includes voltmeter, engine coolant temperature and oil pressure gauges. Included with RPO YE9. (RPO Z53). Deep tinted glass with light tinted rear window. Not avail. with RPO AJ1. Includes RPO A20 window. (RPO AA3). Deep, tinted glass. Not avail. with RPO C49 defogger. Includes A20 window. (RPO AJ1). Heavy-duty trailering wiring harness. Included with RPO Z82. (RPO UY7). Halogen headlights. Not avail. with RPO V22 or RPO YE9. (RPO TT4). Engine block heater. Included with RPO V10. (RPO KO5). Front heavy-duty heater. Included with V10; not avail. with RPO C60. (RPO C42). Cargo area lamp (RPO UF2). Roof marker lamps. Not avail. with Calif. emissions. (RPO UO1). Dome and reading lamps. Included with RPO TR9. (RPO C95). Cigarette lighter (RPO U37). Auxiliary lighting (RPO TR9). Below eye-level black painted exterior mirrors (RPO D44). Below eye-level stainless steel exterior mirrors (RPO D45). Camper-type exterior mirrors (RPO DF2). Black body side moldings (RPO B84). Bright body side moldings (RPO B85). Black wheel opening moldings (RPO B74). Bright wheel opening moldings (RPO B96). Operating Convenience Package. Includes power door locks and power windows. (RPO ZQ2). Conventional two-tone paint (RPO YZ2). Special two-tone paint (RPO YZ3). Deluxe two-tone paint (RPO 243.00. AM radio (RPO U63). Electronically tuned AM/FM stereo radio with Seek-Scan. Electronically tuned AM/FM stereo radio with Seek-Scan and digital clock (RPO UM7). Electronically tuned AM/FM stereo radio with Seek-Scan and stereo cassette tape player (RPO UK5). Electronically tuned AM/FM stereo radio with Seek-Scan, stereo cassette tape player and digital clock (RPO UM6). Electronically tuned AM/FM stereo radio with Seek-Scan, stereo cassette tape player with Search and Repeat, graphic equalizer and digital clock (RPO UX1). Fixed mast antenna. Included with RPO U63, UK4, UK5, UM6, or UX1 radio. (RPO U73). Rear folding seat. Requires bucket or split front seat. (RPO AM7). Heavy-duty front and rear shock absorbers (RPO F51). Off-road skid plate. Avail. for K1500 only. (RPO NZZ). Electronic speed control (RPO K34). 4x4 Sports Graphic Package (RPO BQ4). Heavy-duty front springs. Not avail. with B3J diesel equip. (RPO F60). Front stabilizer bar (RPO F59). ComforTilt steering wheel (RPO N33). Custom steering wheel (RPO N31). Sport steering wheel (RPO NKJ3). Striping (RPO D85). Fuel tank with approx. 34 gal. total vehicle capacity. Not avail. with K10753. (RPO NJ8). Two front towing hooks (RPO B76). Weight distributing platform trailer hitch (RPO VR4). Heavy-duty trailering special equipment (RPO Z82). 4-speed manual trans. (RPO MM4). 4-spd. auto. with overdrive trans (RPO MXO). Wheelcovers (RPO PO1). Rallye wheels (RPO N67). Swing-out quarter windows (RPO A20). Sliding rear window (RPO A28). Intermittent windshield wipers (RPO CD4).

HISTORICAL FOOTNOTES: Total production of GMC light-duty trucks for 1988 totalled 352,326. Total pickup output were 115,351. Suburban production totalled 31,880.

1989 PICKUP & SUBURBAN

The GMC regular cab and extended cab models had a new optional 4x4 Sport Graphic Package with blackout wheel opening flares, bumpers, mirrors and front air dam with tow hooks.

A new Borg-Warner Model 1370 transfer case with an electronically actuated synchronizer was available for K3500 models with dual rear wheels. This made it possible for RPO RO5 dual rear wheels to be ordered on 1 ton pickups and chassis-cabs which increased the available GVW on the K3500 to 10,000 lbs.

The brake system for the K series trucks was revised. The parking brake cable was given increased protection form rocks and road debris by revised routing and the addition of a shield. To reduce brake noise a new molded, semi-metallic brake lining material was used. A new 28MT starter motor and revised engine dipstick lettering was used on 6.2 liter diesel engine-equipped models.

The following exterior colors were carried over from 1988: Brandywine metallic, sandstone metallic, adobe gold metallic, sable black metallic, quicksilver metallic, summit white, and flame red. Three new colors were available: Smoke blue metallic, caramel brown metallic and midnight blue metallic. Initially, a new dark cognac replaced saddle in the interior color offering. Beginning in January, 1989 saddle rejoined beige, blue, garnet and grey as available interior colors. Beige and grey were not available for the extended cab models. Three optional exterior two-tone schemes were available. The conventional two-tone (RPO ZY2) was available only on single rear wheel Wideside pickup models. The primary color was applied to the areas above the lower side body styling crease line (including the roof) with the secondary color below the crease line. Outlined block "GMC" decal lettering was applied to the tailgate. A bright trim panel with lettering was applied when the SLE option was ordered. The special two-tone (RPO ZY3) also available only on single rear wheel Wideside pickup models, included a multi-stripe decal applied over the paint break at the beltline. One color paint was applied to the areas above the decal (including the roof) with the second color applied to the areas below. The Deluxe two-tone (RPO ZY4) also featured a multi-stripe decal at the upper styling line and the accent color between the decal and the lower feature line. Outlined block "GMC" decal lettering was applied to the tailgate. A bright trim panel with lettering was applied when the SLE option was ordered.

The base SL, mid-range SLX and top-ranked SLE trim levels were carried into 1989 with minor changes. Features of the SL were as follows: Single electric low-note horn, power steering, rear brake drums with anti-lock brake system (operated in two-wheel drive only), front chromed bumper, molded plastic grille painted light argent with dark argent air intake areas, single rectangular headlights, silver painted wheels with black hub ornament, All-Season steel-belted radial tires (steel-belted radials on RPO RO5), winch-type spare tire carrier mounted under frame (K1500 models only), right and left side fixed arm mirrors with adjustable heads and black finish, right and right hand padded armrests integral with door panels with grained molded plastic finish, 3 passenger all-vinyl trim bench seat with folding backrest, right hand coat hook, left hand coat hook on extended cab models, dark grey door sill plate, dome light with switch in left hand door jamb, embossed black rubber floor mats, tinted glass in all windows on extended cab models, padded, color-keyed left and right side sunshades, 4-spoke steering wheel, 10 in. rearview mirror, vinyl headliner (same color as retrainer moldings, extended cab models had cab upper, lower and side trim panels and a molded cloth color-keyed headliner with matching retainer moldings), insulation on dash panel, cowl top and sides and doors, extended cab rear quarter and back panels and on floor covering, extra insulation for models with diesel engines.

The SLX Trim Package (RPO Z62) contained the following equipment in addition to or in place of that of the SL trim level: Front chromed bumper with bumper rub stripes, black plastic body side moldings, black wheel opening lip moldings (except on K2500 C6P models, dual rear wheel models and Sportside models), color-keyed door panels with grained molded plastic finish with soft vinyl trim, map pocket and SLX emblem, left and right hand coat hooks, color-keyed door sill plate, dome light with switches in left and right side door jambs, color-keyed embossed rubber floor mats, full width storage tray behind seat on floor, color-keyed cloth headliner; regular cab and extended cab models had matching retainer moldings, color-keyed door pillar and roof side panels, additional insulation on headliner.

The SLE Trim Package (RPO YE9) had this equipment in addition to or replacing that of the SLX trim level: Additional electric high-note horn, SLE exterior nameplates, dual rectangular halogen headlights, black plastic body side moldings with bright trim, hod and cab-to-fender insulators, door panels with two-toned soft vinyl over plastic trim with map pocket and door closing assist straps and SLE emblem, color-keyed floor carpeting, padded, color-keyed left and right hand sunshades with cloth covering, storage strap on left side unit and visor mirror on right side unit, gauges for voltmeter, engine coolant temperature and oil pressure (replacing warning lights), cigarette lighter in ashtray, color-keyed carpet on cab back panel and insulation on regular cab back panels. The content of the V3500 crew and bonus cab models differed slightly from the other four-wheel drive GMC. The SL Package had white painted wheels, bright metal hubcaps with black trim (on single rear wheel models) exterior below eye-level mirrors, an AM radio, 2-spoke steering wheel and a heavy-duty heater/defogger.

The primary differences in the SLX Package for the V3500 models included a full-width front bench seat in a choice of dual-woven cloth vinyl trim or all-vinyl pigskin trim, door-operated dome lamp with bright trim, color-keyed rubber floor mats (for front compartment only of bonus cab), full-length, mystic-colored insulated headliner with matching retainer moldings and insulation under cowl panel or headliner and on cab back panel. The V3500 SLE Package differed from the content for other 4x4 GMCs in having bright body side and rear moldings with black trim plus bright wheel opening (Wideside single rear wheel models only), under hood reel-type lamp, bright tailgate applique, bright trim for front marker lights and taillights, special color-keyed plastic door panels with cloth inserts, vinyl stowage pockets, plus carpeting and bright trim strips on lower portions, right hand visor mirror, headlamp warning buzzer, 2-spoke steering wheel with bright trim on horn buttons, mystic-colored full-length cloth headliner and extra-thick insulation on floor panels.

I.D. DATA: Unchanged from 1988. The tenth entry, the letter K, represented the 1989 model year.

Series K1500-1/2 ton 262 V-6-cyl. 117.5 in., 131.5 in. wheelbase. (Suburban: 129.5 in. wheelbase and standard 305 V-8)

Model	Body Type	MSRP
TK10703	6.5 ft. Sportside Pickup	$12,636
TK10703	6.5 ft. Wideside Pickup	$12,425
TK10903	8.0 ft. Wideside Pickup	$12,620
TK10753	6.5 ft. Club Coupe Pickup	$13,551*
TK10953	8 ft. Club Coupe Pickup	$13,751
TV10906	Suburban Pnl. Drs.	$15,565
CV10906	Suburban Tailgate	$15,605

* Add $2322 for diesel engine and equipment on TK10753
Add $2518 for diesel equipment on TK10953.
Add $3108 for diesel equipment on Suburbans.

B3J-Diesel equipment

Series K2500-3/4 ton 262 V-61. 131.5 in. wheelbase. (Suburban-129.5 in. wheelbase), Crew and Bonus Cab: 164.5 in. wheelbase, Suburban weight with standard 350 V-8

TK20903	Chassis and Cab	$14,042.88
TK20953	Chassis & Ext. Cab	$12,558.00
TK20903	8 ft. Wideside Pickup E63	$12,814.00[1]
TK20753	6.5 ft. Extended Cab	$13,931.00[2]
TK20953	8.0 ft. Extended Cab	$14,131.00
TK20906	Suburban Pnl. Drs.	$16,998.76[3]
TV20906	Suburban Tailgate.	$17,038.76

NOTE 1: Add $1719.88 to price of E63 for RPO C6P.
Add $1077 to price of chassis & cab for B3J.
Add $1209 to price of E63 with C6P for B3J diesel equipment.
Add $2684 to price of E63 for B3J diesel equipment.
NOTE 2: Add $1450 to price of TK20953 for C6P.
Add $2423 to price of TK20753 and TK20953 for B3J.
Add $1209 to price of TK20953 with C6P for B3J.
NOTE 3: Add $2283 to price of Suburbans for B3J diesel equipment.

1 GVW optional.

Series K3500-1 ton 350 V-8. 131.5 in. wheelbase, Crew and Bonus Cab: 164.5 in. wheelbase

Model	Body Type	MSRP
TK30903	Chassis & Cab	$14,442.88[1]
TK30903	8 ft. Wideside Pickup	$14,442.88[1]
TV30943	Chassis & Cab Bonus Cab	$16,509.76
TV30943	Chassis & Cab Crew	$17,023.76
TV30943	HD Chassis & Cab Bonus	$16,905.00
TV30943	HD Chassis & Cab Crew	$17,418.00

NOTE 1: Add $1811.12 for B3J diesel equipment.

STANDARD ENGINE: All K1500, K2500 models: 262 V-6 (LB4 ordering code) Engine Type: Vortex OHV, V-6-cylinder. Cast iron block. Bore x Stroke: 4.0 in. x 3.48 in. Lifters: Hydraulic. Fuel Induction: Electronic fuel injection. Compression Ratio: 9.3:1. Displacement: 262 cu. in. (4.3 liters). Horsepower: Net: 160 @ 4000 rpm. Torque: Net: 235 lb.-ft. @ 2400 rpm. Oil refill capacity: 5 qt. with filter change. Fuel Requirements: Regular unleaded.

STANDARD ENGINE: K2500 with C6P and V3500 and K3500 models: Optional for K150 and K2500 models. 350 V-8 (LO5 ordering code). Engine Type: OHV, V-8. Cast iron block and cylinder head. Bore x Stroke: 4.0 in. x 3.48 in. Lifters: Hydraulic. Number of main bearings-5. Fuel Induction: Electronic fuel injection. Compression Ratio: K3500: 8.6:1. K1500 and K2500: 9.3:1. Displacement: 350 cu. in. (5.7 liters). Horsepower: K3500: Net: 190 @ 4000 rpm. K1500 and K2500: 210 @ 4000 rpm. Torque: K3500: Net 300 lb.-ft. @ 2400 rpm. K1500 and K2500: 300 lb.-ft. @ 2800 rpm. Oil refill capacity: 5 qt. with filter change. Fuel Requirements: Regular unleaded. Optional: K1500 and K2500: 305 V-8, Ordering Code: LO3. Engine Type: OHV, V-8. Cast iron block and alloy iron cylinder head. Key features include chain drive camshaft and forged steel connecting rods. This engine was produced in U.S. or Canada. Bore x Stroke: 3.74 in. x 3.48 in. Lifters: Hydraulic. Number of main bearings-5. Fuel Induction: Electronic fuel injection. Compression Ratio: 9.2:1. Displacement: 305 cu. in. (5.0 liters). Horsepower: Net: 175 @ 4000 rpm. Torque: Net: 270 lb.-ft. @ 2400 rpm. Oil refill capacity: 5 qt. with filter change. Fuel Requirements: Regular unleaded.

STANDARD ENGINE: K3500 models with dual rear wheels. Optional: Other K3500 models. Ordering Code: L19: 454 V-8. Engine Type: OHV, V-8. Cast iron block and alloy iron cylinder head. Bore x Stroke: 4.30 in. x 4.0 in. Lifters: Hydraulic. Number of main bearings-5. Fuel Induction: Electronic fuel injection. Compression Ratio: 7.9:1. Displacement: 454 cu. in. (7.4 liters). Horsepower: 230 @ 3600 rpm. Torque: 385 lb.-ft. @ 1600 rpm. Oil refill capacity: 5 qt. with filter change. Fuel Requirements: Regular unleaded.

OPTIONAL ENGINE: K1500 and K2500: Ordering Code LH6. Not available in California for K2500. This engine was produced by GM-Detroit Diesel Allison Division. Engine Type: OHV, diesel V-8. Bore x Stroke: 3.98 in. x 3.80 in. Lifters: Hydraulic. Number of main bearings-5. Fuel Induction: Gear driven mechanical fuel injection. Compression Ratio: 21.3:1. Displacement: 379.4 cu. in. (6.2 liters). Horsepower: 126 @ 3600 rpm. (140 @ 3600 rpm with automatic transmission). Torque: 240 lb.-ft. @ 2000 rpm. (247 lb.-ft. @ 2000 rpm with automatic transmission). Oil refill capacity: 7 qt. with filter change. Fuel Requirements: Diesel.

OPTIONAL ENGINE: K3500 and V3500 models. Ordering Code LL4. This engine was produced by GM-Detroit Diesel Allison Division. Engine Type: OHV, diesel V-8. Bore x Stroke: 3.98 in. x 3.80 in. Lifters: Hydraulic. Number of main bearings-5. Fuel Induction: Fuel injection. Compression Ratio: 21.3:1. Displacement: 379.4 cu. in. (6.2 liters). Horsepower: 143 @ 3600 rpm. Torque: 257 lb.-ft. @ 2000 rpm. Oil refill capacity: 7 qt. with filter change. Fuel Requirements: Diesel.

CHASSIS FEATURES: Semi-perimeter design, all-welded channel beam frame with boxed front end. Dimensions: K1500 and K2500 regular cab: 2.18 x 7.48 x 0.134 in. K1500 extended cab: 2.18 x 7.48 x 0.165 in. K2500 regular cab with C6P: 2.18 x 7.48 x 0.213 in. K2500 extended cab: 2.31 x 7.48 x 0.165 in. K2500 extended cab with C6P: 2.18 x 7.48 x 0.244 in. K3500 regular cab: 2.18 x 7.48 x 0.213 in. K3500 extended cab: 2.18 x 7.48 x 0.244 in. V3500 models: 2.788 x 7.74 x 0.244 in. Section modulus: K1500 regular cab: 3.46; K1500 extended cab: 4.30; K2500: 4.30; K2500 with C6P: 6.48; K3500 regular cab: 5.61; K3500 extended cab: 6.48, V3500: 7.33.

SUSPENSION AND RUNNING GEAR: Front Suspension: Torsion bar springs. K1500 Capacity: 3860 lb. K2500 and K3500 capacity: 3750 lb. V3500: Tapered leaf springs. Capacity: 4500 lb. Shock absorber dia.: K1500; 25mm; K2500, K3500 and V3500: 32mm. 32mm optional for K1500. 1.00 in. stabilizer optional for all series except V3500 which had a standard 1.25 in. bar standard. Optional rating: K1500: RPO F44/F60: 6100 lb. GVW. K2500: 8600 lb. GVW. K3500: 10,000 lb. GVW. Rear Suspension: Semi-elliptical 2-stage, 4-leaf for K1500; 6-leaf for K2500; 6-leaf plus 1-leaf auxiliary for K3500. K1500 capacity: 3750 K2500 capacity: 4800 K3500 capacity: 7500 lb. V3500: Semi-elliptical 2-stage, 9-leaf. Capacity: 7000. Shock absorber dia.: K1500: 25mm; K2500, K3500 and V3500: 32mm. 32mm optional for K1500. Optional Rating: See above for GVW ratings. Front Axle Type and Capacity: Independent, GM or K1500; Spicer on K2500 and K3500. Capacity: K1500 regular cab: 3925; K1500 extended cab: 4800; K2500 and K3500: 4250 V3500: Spicer full-floating. Capacity: 4500, manual hub locks. Optional: K1500: 3925 capacity; K1500 extended cab: 4800 lb. All other K series: 4250. Rear Axle Type: Semi-floating for K1500; full-floating for K2500, K3500 and V3500. GM manufacture for all series. Capacity: K1500: 3750, K2500: 6000; K3500, V3500: 7500 lb. Optional: K2500: Regular cab: 4800 lb.; K250 extended cab: 6000; K3500: 7500. Final Drive Ratio: The following transmission designations were used by GMC: MM4: 4-spd. manual; MM5: 5-spd. manual overdrive; MX1: 3-spd. automatic; MXO: 4-spd. automatic. All ratios are with standard emission equipment. Standard: K1500, K2500: 3.42:1. Optional: 3.73:1. All engine/transmission combinations except K2500 with LL4 diesel engine which had standard 3.73:1 ratio and optional 4.10:1 ratio, and K2500 with 5.7 liter V-8 and C6P which also had an optional 4.56:1 ratio. Standard: K3500: 4.10:1 with 5.7 liter V-8 with 4.56:1 optional; 3.42:1 standard for 7.4 liter V-8 with 3.73 and 4.10:1 optional; 6.2 liter diesel (LL4) had standard 4.10:1 ratio with 4.56:1 optional. Standard for V3500: 3.73:1 with 5.7 liter and manual 4-spd. trans.; 4.10:1 with 3-spd. auto. trans.; 3.73:1 with 7.4 liter V-8; 4.10:1 with LL4 diesel. Optional: 4.10 and 4.56:1 for 5.7 liter V-8 with man. 4-spd.; 4.56:1 for 5.7 liter V-8 with 3-spd. auto. trans.; 4.10 and 4.56:1 for 7.4 liter V-8; 4.56:1 for LL4 diesel. Transfer Case: K1500, K2500, K3500: New Process 241. Single lever. Ratios: 2.72:1, 1.00:1. K3500 with RPO RO5: Borg Warner 1370: Ratios: 2.69:1, 1.00:1. The Borg Warner unit has a right hand side power take-off. Brakes: Type: Hydraulic, power assisted. Dimensions: K1500: Front: Disc: 11.86 in. x 1.0 in. Rear: Drums: 10.0 x 2.25 in. K1500 regular cab with RPO F44/F60 had 11.57 in. x 1.25 in. front disc brakes. K2500 regular cab: Front: Disc: 11.57 in. x 1.20 in. Rear: Drums: 11.15 in. x 2.75 in. K2500 extended cab: Front Disc: 11.57 in. x 1.25 in. Rear: 10.0 in. x 2.25 in. drums. All K2500 with 8600 lb. GVW package had 12.50 in. x 1.26 in. front disc brakes and 13.0 in. x 2.5 in. rear drum brakes. K3500 All models: Front: Disc: 12.50 in. x 1.26 in. Rear: Drum: 13.00 in. x 2.50 in. V3500 All models: Front Disc: 12.54 in. x 1.54 in. Rear: Drums: 13.0 in. x 3.5 in. Wheels: K1500 and K2500: 16 x 6.5, 6-stud disc. K3500 and V3500: 16.0 x 6.0. Tires: K1500 Sportside and regular cab: LT225/75R-16C steel belted radial. K1500 extended cab: LT245/75R16C. K2500 all models: LT245/75R-16E. K3500: LT225/75RD. V3500 all models: 7.50-16D tubeless nylon. Optional: K1500: LT225/75R16C, blackwall, LT225/75R16C on-off road; blackwall, white stripe or white lettered. Available for K10903 only with the following engines: LB4, LO3 and LH6 and RPO GVT4 axle; and K10703 with LB4 or LO3 engine with RPO GT4 axle. LT265/75R16C blackwall or white letter, on-off road. Optional K2500: LTR225/75R16D steel belted radial blackwall or white stripe, LT245/75R16E highway or on-off road, LT225/75R16D blackwall, on-off road, LT245/75R16E blackwall (K20903 only). Optional: LT225/75R16D blackwall, LT245/75R16E blackwall, LT245/75R16E on-off road blackwall, LT245/75R16E blackwall, 7.50 x 16D highway and on-off road. Optional: V3500: V30943 only: 7.50 x 16 D tubeless nylon, dual rear, LT215/85R16D dual rear tubeless steel belted radial; LT235/85R16E. Steering: Integral power. Ratio: K1500 regular cab Sportside and Wideside: 17.44:1. K1500 extended cab model K10753: 18.8:1, model K10953: 17.44:1. K2500 regular cab: 17.44:1. K2500 extended cab K20753: 18.88:1; model K20953: 17.44:1. K3500 regular cab: 127.44:1. K3500 extended cab: 17.44:1. V3500: 13.5:1. Turning Diameter (curb-to-curb): K1500 regular cab Sportside: 40.3 ft. K1500 regular cab Wideside: 44.4 ft. K1500 extended cab model K10753: 47.9 ft., model K10953: 52.2 ft. K2500 regular cab: 44.4 ft. (with C6P: 45.1 ft.). K2500 extended cab: Model K20753: 47.9 ft., model 52.2 ft. K3500 regular cab: 45.1 ft. K3500 extended cab: 52.2 ft. V3500: 54.5 ft. Transmission: Standard K1500/2500: With gasoline engines: RPO MM5-5-spd. manual with overdrive fully-synchronized. Transmission Ratios: 4.02, 2.32, 1.40, 1.00, 0.73:1; Reverse: 3.74:1. Standard: K3500, V3500 and K2500 with C6P, and K1500 and K2500 with diesel engine: RPO MM4 4-spd. manual, SM465 manual, synchromesh on last three gears (optional: K1500/2500). Transmission Ratios: 6.55, 3.58, 1.70, 1.00:1. Reverse: 6.09:1. Optional: All series: RPO MX1-3-spd. 400 automatic. Transmission ratios: 2.48, 1.48, 1.0:1. Reverse: 2.08:1. Optional: K1500/2500, (except K2500 regular cab chassis-cab, and all V3500 models): RPO MXO-4-spd. automatic overdrive 700R4: 3.06, 1.63, 1.0, 0.70:1. Reverse: 2.29:1.

VEHICLE DIMENSIONS: Wheelbase: All series regular cab: 117.5 in., 131.5 in. Extended cab: 6.5 ft. box model: 141.5 in.; 8.0 ft. box model: 155.5 in.; V3500 models: 164.5 in. Overall Length (without rear bumper): K1500 Sportside: 194.0 in., K1500 regular cab: 194.1 in. K1500 extended cab: Model K10753 (6.5 ft. box): 223.0 in., K10953 (8.0 ft. box): 237.0 in. K2500 regular cab: 212.6 in. K2500 extended cab: Model K20753: 223.0 in., model K20953: 237.0 in. K3500 regular cab: 212.6 in. V3500: 246.4 in. Front/Rear Tread: 74 in./74 in. Overall Height: K1500 all models: 73.8 in. K2500 regular cab: 74.3 in. (75.8 in. if equipped with C6P).

K2500 extended cab: 74.4 in. (75.8 in. if equipped with C6P). K3500 75.8 in. V3500: 76.3 in. Width: All models except V3500 and those equipped with RO5: 76.8 in. V3500: 79.6 in. V3500 and K3500 with RO5: 107.3 in. Front/Rear Overhang: 117.5 in. wheelbase. Pickups: 34.9 in./ 41.6 in. 131.5 in. wheelbase Pickups: 34.9 in./46.5 in. Extended cab: 34.9/46.5 in. Chassis-cab models: 34.9/41.8 in. Tailgate: Width and Height: K1500 Sportside: 50.9 x 19.3 in. All others: 62.0 in. x19.3 in. Approach/Departure Degrees: K1500 117.5 in.: 22/28. Ground Clearance (Front/Rear in inches): K1500 Sportside and Fleetside: 8.6/9.0. K1500 extended cab: 9.2/9.6. K2500 regular cab: 8.7/7.7 (with C6P: 7.8/8.1). K2500 extended cab: 34.9 in./ 41.6 in. x19.3 in. Ground Clearance (Front/Rear in inches): K1500 Sportside and Fleetside: 8.6/9.0. K1500 extended cab: 9.2/9.6. K2500 regular cab: 8.7/7.7 (with C6P: 7.8/8.1). K2500 extended cab: 9.2/9.6, model K20953: 9.2/8.1. K3500 regular and extended cab: 9.2/8.1 (with RO5 dual rear wheels: 7.2/7.4). V3500: 8.3/7.8. Front headroom, all models: 40.0 in. Front legroom, all models: 41.7 in. Front shoulder room, all models: 66.0 in.

CAPACITIES: Fuel Tank: All K series: 25.0 gal. All V3500 models: 20 gal. Optional: Models K10903, K10753, K10953, K20903, K20953, K30903: 34 gal. V3500 models: 20 gal.

ACCOMMODATIONS: Seating Capacity: Pickup, extended cab and chassis cab models: 3 passenger. Optional: Extended cab: 6 passenger. Suburban: 6 passenger. Optional: 9 passenger.

INSTRUMENTATION: Speedometer, odometer, fuel level gauge. Warning lights for battery, oil pressure, generator, brake system warning, directional/hazard lights, high beam, and engine coolant temperature.

OPTIONS AND PRICES: Pre-cleaner air cleaner (RPO K46): $44.00. Air conditioning (RPO C60): $781.00. Deluxe front appearance (RPO V22): $145.00. Optional axle ratio: $38. Locking rear differential (RPO G80): $252. Heavy-duty Delco Freedom auxiliary battery with 540 cold cranking amps. Not avail. with B3J diesel equipment. (RPO TP2): $134.00. Heavy-duty Delco Freedom battery with 630 cold cranking amps RPO UA1: $56.00 Painted rear step bumper (RPO V43): $130.00. Chromed front Deluxe bumper with rub strip. Included with RPO Z62 and RPO YE9. (RPO VB3): $229.00. Rear step bumper with rub strip (RPO VB3): $229.00. Black front bumper guards. Requires RPO VG3. (RPO V 27): $32.00. Spare tire and wheel carrier. Not avail. with K10753. (RPO P13): No charge. Heavy-duty chassis. Included with B3J diesel equip. (RPO F44): $230.00. Cold Climate Package. Not avail. with RPO C60. Includes UA1 battery, KO5 block heater and C42 heater. (RPO V10): $134.00. Console, requires bucket seats. (RPO D55): $114.00.Engine oil cooling system. Not available with B3J diesel equip., with RPO MXO transmission requires VO2 cooling, included with Z82 trailering option. (RPO KC4): $126.00. Heavy-duty radiator. Not avail. with RPO VO2. (RPO VO1): $56.00. Heavy-duty radiator and transmission oil cooler. Requires RPO MXO transmission. Included with RPO Z823. (RPO VO2): $63.00. Scottsdale Trim Package (RPO Z62): $223. SLE Trim Package (RPO YE9): $665.00. Rear window defogger. Requires RPO YE9 or RPO Z62. Not avail. with RPO A28 window or RPO AJ1 glass. (RPO C49): $1564.00. 5.0 liter V-8 (RPO LO3): $555.00. 5.7 liter V-8 (RPO LO5): $755.00. Locking fuel filler cap (RPO NO5): $18.00. Front color-keyed floor mats. Requires RPO YE9. (RPO B32): $16.00. Rear color-keyed floor mats. Requires RPO AM7 seat and RPO B32. (RPO B33): $12.00. Gauge Package. Includes voltmeter, engine coolant temperature and oil pressure gauges. Included with RPO YE9. (RPO Z53): $42.00. Deep tinted glass with light tinted rear window. Not avail. with RPO AJ1. Includes RPO A20 window. (RPO AA3): $98.00. Deep, tinted glass. Not avail. with RPO C49 defogger. Includes A20 window. (RPO AJ1): $144.00. Heavy-duty trailering wiring harness. Included with RPO Z82. (RPO UY7): $46.00. Halogen headlights. Not avail. with RPO V22 or RPO YE9. (RPO TT4): $24.00. Engine block heater. Included with RPO V10. (RPO KO5): $33.00. Front heavy-duty heater. Included with V10; not avail. with RPO C60. (RPO C42): $45.00. Cargo area lamp (RPO UF2): $36.00. Roog marker lamps. Not avail. with Calif. emissions. (RPO UO1): $52.00. Dome and reading lamps. Included with RPO TR9. (RPO C95): $33.00.Cigarette lighter (RPO U37): $25.00. Auxiliary lighting (RPO TR9): $90.00. Below eye-level black painted exterior mirrors (RPO D44): $52.00. Below eye-level stainless steel exterior mirrors (RPO D45): $87.00. Camper-type exterior mirrors (RPO DF2): $100.00. Black body side moldings (RPO B84): $59.00. Bright body side moldings (RPO B85): $17.0. Black wheel opening moldings (RPO B74): $31.00. Bright wheel opening moldings (RPO B96): No charge. Operating Convenience Package. Includes power door locks and power windows. (RPO ZQ2): $344.00. Conventional two-tone paint (RPO YZ2): $132.00. Special two-tone paint (RPO YZ3): $215.00. Deluxe two-tone paint (RPO 243.00. AM radio (RPO U63): $122.00. Electronically tuned AM/FM stereo radio with Seek-Scan (RPO UK4): $268.00. Electronically tuned AM/FM stereo radio with Seek-Scan and digital clock (RPO UM7): $333.00. Electronically tuned AM/FM stereo radio with Seek-Scan and stereo cassette tape player (RPO UK5): $390.00. Electronically tuned AM/FM stereo radio with Seek/-Scan, stereo cassette tape player and digital clock (RPO UM6): $454.00. Electronically tuned AM/FM stereo radio with Seek-Scan, stereo cassette tape player with Search and Repeat, graphic equalizer and digital clock (RPO UX1): $604.00. Fixed mast antenna. Included with RPO U63, UK4, UK5, UM6, or UX1 radio. (RPO U73): $41.00. Rear folding seat. Requires bucket or split front seat. (RPO AM7): $385.00. Heavy-duty front and rear shock absorbers (RPO F51): $36.00. Off-road skid plate. Avail. for K1500 only. (RPO NZZ): $95.00. Electronic speed control (RPO K34): $205.00. 4x4 Sports Graphic Package (RPO BQ4): $110.00. Heavy-duty front springs. Not avail. with B3J diesel equip. (RPO F60): $63.00. Front stabilizer bar (RPO F59): $40.00. ComfortTilt steering wheel (RPO N33): $121.00. Custom steering wheel (RPO N31): $28.00. Sport steering wheel (RPO NKJ3): $7.0 with RPO YE9; $35.0 with RPO Z62. Striping (RPO D85): $69.00. Fuel tank with approx. 34 gal. total vehicle capacity. Not avail. with K10753. (RPO NJ8): $56.00. Two front towing hooks (RPO B76): $38.00. Weight distributing platform trailer hitch (RPO VR4): $164.00. Heavy-duty trailering special equipment (RPO Z82): $230.00 without B3J diesel equip.; (RPO Z82): $273.00 with B3J. 4-speed manual trans. (RPO MM4): $98.00 without B3J. 4-spd. auto. with overdrive trans (RPO MXO): $795.00. Wheelcovers (RPO PO1): $42.00. Rallye wheels (RPO N67): $75.00. Swing-out quarter windows (RPO A20): $43.00. Sliding rear window (RPO A28): $113.00. Intermittent windshield wipers (RPO CD4): $59.00.

HISTORICAL FOOTNOTES: GMC's truck market share for 1989 was 2.43 percent. Total GMC truck sales for 1989 were 353,788.

1990 PICKUP & SUBURBAN

The GMC trucks along with their Chevrolet counterparts were affected by General Motors efforts to simplify the production, ordering and sales of light-duty trucks. One result was a "deproliferation" of optional equipment. Numerous previously optional items were now either standard equipment on the 1990 models or included in larger Option Packages. Details of these developments are found in the 1990 Chevrolet section.

A heavy-duty version of the 4.3 liter V-6 with electronic fuel injection was standard on K2500 series pickups with C6P. It was also available as a credit option on the K3500 pickups. The primary features of this engine that set it apart from the standard V-6 included a lower 8.6:1 compression ratio and a larger, 3.0 in. low restriction exhaust system for improved performance in heavy-duty applications. The 7.4 liter V-8 now had electronic spark control to control spark knock. The standard and heavy-duty 6.2 liter diesel engines had different horsepower and torque ratings for 1990-actual engine output was not changed, however. Both the RPO LO3, 5.0 liter V-8 and the RPO LO5, 5.7 liter V-8 were upgraded for 1990 by the use of improved oil control rings, a redesigned rear crankshaft seal, a new camshaft sprocket design, the use of a non-asbestos intake manifold gasket and the adoption of heavy-duty intake valves.

1990 GMC Sierra K-1500 SLX regular cab

The content of the base Sierra SL trim were substantially increased for 1990 by the addition of the following items (RPO numbers are included for reference purposes): RPO AO1-tinted glass in all windows, RPO C42-Deluxe heater, RPO F59-1.00 in. dia. front stabilizer bar, RPO NJ8-34 gal. (approx.) fuel tank, standard for all models except K10703 and K10753, RPO TT4-halogen headlights, RPO CCA heavy-duty, 630 cold cranking amps battery, standard for all gasoline engine models, RPO U37-cigarette lighter, RPO U63-AM radio, RPO U73-fixed mast radio antenna, RPO V76-two front towing hooks, RPO Z53-voltmeter, temperature and oil pressure gauges, and RPO CD4-intermittent windshield wiper system.

Equipment added to the content of the Sierra SLX trim level consisted of RPO B84-Black body side moldings, RPO N31-Custom steering wheel, RPO N67-Rallye wheels, standard on all models except those with RPO RO5 (dual rear wheels), RPO V22-Deluxe front appearance containing dark argent grille with bright trim, composite halogen headlights and a dual note horn; and RPO V27-front bumper guards with rub strip.

New standard features of the Sierra SLE Package were as follows: RPO A20-swing-out rear quarter windows on club coupe models, RPO B32-Front removable color-keyed floor mats, RPO B33-Rear removable color-keyed floor mats on club coupe models, RPO NK3-Sport steering wheel and RPO UM7-Electronically-tuned AM/FM stereo radio with Seek-Scan and digital clock.

Also included in the list of 1989 model year options that were part of other options for 1990 were these: RPO N33-ComforTilt steering wheel and RPO K34-Electronic speed control (now included in RPO ZQ3-Convenience Package), RPO D55-Console (now included in RPO A55 low back or RPO A95 bucket seats), RPO KO5-Engine block heater (now included in RPO V10-Cold climate Package), RPO VR4-Weight distributing platform type trailer hitch (now included in RPO Z82-Heavy-duty trailering equipment), and RPO UF2-Cargo area light (now included in RPO TR9-Auxiliary lighting).

1990 GMC Sierra K-2500 SLE club coupe pickup

A new base model, the Wideside Special, was available for 1990. It had a specific level of features and limited option availability. The Wideside Special was offered only in K10903/E63 form and had the Sierra SL trim except for a number of items specific to the Wideside Special. These consisted of a dark charcoal painted front bumper, air deflector and bumper filler, blackout grille and special "W/T1500" body-side decals with integrated GMC Bowtie. This truck was available only in blue, red, silver or white, The only powerteam initially offered was the 4.3 liter Vortex V-6 and a 5-spd. manual transmisson (MM5) with a 3.08:1 axle ratio. Effective December 8, 1989 the Wideside Special was also offered with RPO MX1, the 3-speed automatic transmission. The following items comprised the work truck's standard equipment: Power steering, power brakes, rear-wheel anti-lock brake system (operative in two-wheel drive mode only), power front disc/rear drum brakes, double wall construction in cargo boxsides, tailgate, fenders and doors, All-Season steel-belted radial-plytires, electric speedometer, dome light, glove compartment with latched door and two-side galvanized exterior sheet metal surfaces (except for roof). Options for the Wideside Special were limited to a single Preferred Equipment Group 2 Package consisting of the RPO F4 heavy-duty chassis, RPO F51 heavy-duty shock absorbers and RPO D44 painted below eye-level mirrors and the following individual items in addition to those previously mentioned: Air conditioning, optional axle ratio, locking differential, heavy-duty auxiliary battery, painted rear step bumper, heavy-duty chassis, Cold Climate Package, engine oil cooler, heavy-duty engine and transmission cooler, black painted below eye-level mirrors, AM radio, AM/FM stereo radio with Seek-Scan, stereo cassette tape and digital clock, AM stereo/FM stereo radio and Seek-Scan, stereo cassette tape with Search and Repeat, graphic equalizer and digital clock, heavy-duty front and rear shock absorbers, wheelcovers and sliding rear window.

The content of the trim levels for the V3500 crew and bonus cab models were also revised for 1990. Added to the Sierra SL Trim Package were: RPO C91-Dome light, RPO C91-Pulse windshield wiper system, RPO T63-Headlight warning buzzer, RPO UA1-Heavy-duty batterey with 630 CCA, RPO UT5-AM radio (this item replaced RPO U63), RPO U37-Cigarette lighter and RPO NL2-Auxiliary fuel tank.

Three additonal items were now included in the Sierra SLE Package: RPO TR9-Auxiliary lighting, RPO V22-Deluxe Front Appearance Package and RPO YG3-Deluxe Molding Package. Several options for the V3500 that carried over for 1990 were revised. RPO K34-Electronic speed control and RPO N33-ComforTilt steering wheel was now part of RPO ZQ3, the Convenience Package. RPO B85-Body side molding was incorporated into RPO YG3, the

Deluxe Molding Package which, in turn, was now included in the Sierra SLE Package. The RPO V22, Deluxe Front Appearance Package now required the Sierra SLE Package. Three options were no longer available for the V3500 models: RPO K46-Pre-cleaner air cleaner, RPO B93-Door edge molding guards and RPO UU9-Electronically-tuned AM/FM stereo radio with clock.

The K1500 Sierra ST (Sport Truck) which was introduced during 1989, continued for 1990. It was limited to the short wheelbase Wideside pickup body/chassis. It was available in three two-tone colors: Onyx black metallic, Catalina blue metallic or crimson red metallic upper body colors over a quicksilver metallic lower body. The ST had as standard equiment a deluxe front end with body color surround, quad halogen headlights, silver painted bumpers, striping on front bumper and body sides, Sierra ST decals on tailgate, aluminum wheels and silver painted wheel flares.

1990 GMS Sierra series K-1500 SLE Sportside pickup with Z71 Off-Road Package

Three new exterior colors were offered for 1990. Replacing sable black metallic was black onyx, replacing midnight blue metallic was Catalina blue metallic, and replacing brandywine metallic was crimson red metallic. Carried over from 1989 were blue smoke metallic, caramel brown metallic, adobe gold metallic and quicksilver metallic. A new garnet interior color was available for 1990. Both the Sierra SLX and Sierra SLE interiors had all-new molded seats. The regular cab models were now available with 60/40 seats.

Once again available were the three optional exterior two-tone schemes — Conventional two-tone (RPO ZY2), Special two-tone (RPO ZY3) and the Deluxe two–tone (RPO ZY4). Their format and content were unchanged from those of 1989.

I.D. DATA: Unchanged from 1989. The tenth entry, the letter L, represented the 1990 model year.

Model	Body Type	MSRP
Series K1500-1/2 ton 262 V-6-cyl. 117.5 in., 131.5 in. wheelbase (Suburban: 129.5 in. wheelbase and standard 350 V-8)		
TK10903	8.0 ft. Worktruck	$13,020
TK10703	6.5 ft. Sportside Pickup	$14,300
TK10703	6.5 ft. Wideside Pickup	$13,980
TK10903	8.0 ft. Wideside Pickup	$14,255
TK10753	6.5 ft. Club Coupe Wideside	$14,929
TK10953	8.0 ft. Club Coupe Wideside	$15,204
TV10906	Suburban, Pnl. Drs.	$17,255
TV10906	Suburban, Tailgate	$17,405
TV 10906	Suburban Pnl. Drs.	$15,565
TV10906	Suburban Tailgate	$15,605

The above prices were placed in effect on December 8, 1989. Subsequently these prices were effective with vehicles produced on and after April 2, 1990:

TK10903	8.0 ft. Wideside Special	$12,470
TK10703	6.5 ft. Sportside Pickup	$13,750
TK10703	6.5 ft. Wideside Pickup	$13,430
TK10903	8.0 ft. Wideside Pickup	$13,705
TK10753	6.5 ft. Club Coupe Wideside	$14,379
TK10953	8.0 ft. Club Coupe Wideside	$14,654

Add $2335 for diesel equipment B3J on club coupe TK10953, $2530 on club coupe TK10753. Add $3100 for B3J on Suburban Tailgate and $3105 on Suburban Panel Doors.

K2500-3/4 ton 262 V-61. 131.5 in. wb. (Suburban-129.5 in. wheelbase), Crew and Bonus Cab: 164.5 in. wbheelbase, Suburban weight with standard 350 V-8

TK20903	Chassis & Cab	$15,234
TK20953	Chassis & Club Coupe Cab	$16,264
TK20903	8.0 ft. Wideside Pickup	$14,455
TK20903	8.0 ft. C6P Wideside Pickup	$15,571
TK20753	6.5 ft. Club Coupe Pickup	$15,483
TK20953	8.0 ft. Club Coupe Pickup	$15,763
TK20953	8.0 ft. C6P Club Coupe Pickup	$16,608

Add $1050 for B3J for TK20903 chassis & cab and TK20903 club coupe chassis & cab. Add $1830 for B3J for TK20903 with C6P, add $2710 for B3J on TK20903. Add $1835 for B3J for TK20953 with C6P, add $2435 for B3J for TK20953 Add $2440 for TK20753 with C6P.

The above prices were placed in effect on December 8, 1989. Subseqently these prices were effective with vehicles produced on and after April 2, 1990:

TK20903	8.0 ft. Wideside Pickup	$13,905
TK20903	8.0 ft. C6P Wideside Pickup	$15,029
TK20753	6.5 ft. Club Coupe Pickup	$14,933
TK20953	8.0 ft. Club Coupe Pickup	$15,213
TK20953	8.0 ft. C6P Club Coupe Pickup	$16,059

ZW9-Suburban Panel doors
E55-Suburban Tailgate

Series K3500-1 ton 350 V-8. 131.5 in.wheelbase, Crew and Bonus Cab: 164.5 in. wheelbase

TK30903	8.0 ft. Wideside Pickup	$16,584
TK30953	8.0 ft. Ex. Cab Fleetside Pickup	$17,609
TK30903	Chassis & Cab, 131.5 in. wb	$16,133
TK31003	Chassis & Cab, 135.5 in. wb.	$16,560*
TK31403	Chassis & Cab, 159.9 in. wb	$16,675*
TK30953	Extended Cab Chassis & Cab	$17,167

* Prices for these models were not available on December 8, 1989. These prices are those effective April 2, 1990.

Add $1868 for B3J for TK30953. Add $2281 for B3J for TK30903.
Add $2287 for B3J for TK30953. Add $1871 to TK30903 for B3J.
Add $1621 for B3J to price of TK31003.

TK30903 price was subsequently changed to $16,033 on vehicles produced on or after April,1, 1990. The revised price for TK30953 was $17,059. The revised price for TK30903 was $15584. The revised price for TK30953 was $16,619.

STANDARD ENGINE: All K1500, K2500 models: 262 V-6 (LB4 ordering code). Engine Type: Vortex OHV, V-6-cylinder. Cast iron block. Bore x Stroke: 4.0 in. x 3.48 in. Lifters: Hydraulic. Fuel Induction: Electronic fuel injection. Compression Ratio: For models under 8500 GVWR: 9.3:1. For models over 8500 lb. GVWR: 8.6:1. Displacement: 262 cu. in. (4.3 liters). Horsepower: Net: For models under 8500 lb. GVWR: 160 @ 4000 rpm. For models over 85900 lb. GVWR: 155 @ 4000 rpm. Torque: Net: For models under 8500 lb. GVWR: 235 lb.-ft. @ 2400 rpm. For models over 85900 lb. GVWR: 230 lb.-ft. @ 2400 rpm. Oil refill capacity: 5 qt. with filter change. Fuel Requirements: Regular unleaded.

OPTIONAL ENGINE: K1500, K2500, V3500 and K3500 models: Optional for K150 and K2500 models. 350 V-8 (LO5 ordering code). Engine Type: OHV, V-8. Cast iron block and cylinder head. Bore x Stroke: 4.0 in. x 3.48 in. Lifters: Hydraulic. Number of main bearings-5. Fuel Induction: Electronic fuel injection. Compression Ratio: K3500: 8.6:1. K1500 and K2500: 9.3:1. Displacement: 350 cu. in. (5.7 liters). Horsepower: K3500: Net: 190 @ 4000 rpm. K1500 and K2500: 210 @ 4000 rpm. Torque: K3500: Net 300 lb.-ft. @ 2400 rpm. K1500 and K2500: 300 lb.-ft. @ 2800 rpm. Oil refill capacity: 5 qt. with filter change. Fuel Requirements: Regular unleaded.

OPTIONAL ENGINE: K1500 and K2500: 305 V-8, Ordering Code: LO3. Engine Type: OHV, V-8. Cast iron block and alloy iron cylinder head. Key features include chain drive camshaft and forged steel connecting rods. This engine was produced in U.S. or Canada. Bore x Stroke: 3.74 in. x 3.48 in. Lifters: Hydraulic. Number of main bearings-5. Fuel Induction: Electronic fuel injection. Compression Ratio: 9.2:1. Displacement: 305 cu. in. (5.0 liters). Horsepower: Net: 175 @ 4000 rpm. Torque: Net: 270 lb.-ft. @ 2400 rpm. Oil refill capacity: 5 qt. with filter change. Fuel Requirements: Regular unleaded.

STANDARD ENGINE: K3500 models with rear wheels. Optional: Other K3500 models. Ordering Code: L19: 454 V-8. Engine Type: OHV, V-8. Cast iron block and alloy iron cylinder head. Bore x Stroke: 4.30 in. x 4.0 in. Lifters: Hydraulic. Number of main bearings-5. Fuel Induction: Electronic fuel injection. Compression Ratio: 7.9:1. Displacement: 454 cu. in. (7.4 liters). Horsepower: 230 @ 3600 rpm. Torque: 385 lb.-ft. @ 1600 rpm. Oil refill capacity: 5 qt. with filter change. Fuel Requirements: Regular unleaded.

OPTIONAL ENGINE: K1500 and K2500: Ordering Code LH6. Not available in California for K2500. This engine was produced by GM-Detroit Diesel Allison Division. Engine Type: OHV, diesel V-8. Bore x Stroke: 3.98 in. x 3.80 in. Lifters: Hydraulic. Number of main bearings-5. Fuel Induction: Gear driven mechanical fuel injection. Compression Ratio: 21.3:1. Displacement: 379.4 cu. in. (6.2 liters). Horsepower: 126 @ 3600 rpm. (140 @ 3600 rpm with automatic transmission). Torque: 240 lb.-ft. @ 2000 rpm. (247 lb.-ft. @ 2000 rpm with automatic transmission). Oil refill capacity: 7 qt. with filter change. Fuel Requirements: Diesel.

OPTIONAL ENGINE: K3500 and V3500 models: Ordering Code LL4. This engine was produced by GM-Detroit Diesel Allison Division. Engine Type: OHV, diesel V-8. Bore x Stroke: 3.98 in. x 3.80 in. Lifters: Hydraulic. Number of main bearings-5. Fuel Induction: Fuel injection. Compression Ratio: 21.3:1. Displacement: 379.4 cu. in. (6.2 liters). Horsepower: 143 @ 3600 rpm. Torque: 257 lb.-ft. @ 2000 rpm. Oil refill capacity: 7 qt. with filter change. Fuel Requirements: Diesel.

CHASSIS FEATURES: Semi-perimeter design, all-welded channel beam frame with boxed front end. Dimensions: K1500 and K2500 regular cab: 2.18 x 7.48 x 0.134 in. K1500 club coupe: 2.18 x 7.48 x 0.165 in. K2500 regular cab with C6P: 2.18 x 7.48 x 0.213 in. K2500 club coupe: 2.31 x 7.48 x 0.165 in. K2500 club coupe with C6P: 2.18 x 7.48 x 0.244 in. K3500 regular cab: 2.18 x 7.48 x 0.213 in. K3500 club coupe: 2.18 x 7.48 x 0.244 in. V3500 models: 2.788 x 7.74 x 0.244 in. Section modulus: K1500 regular cab: 3.46; K1500 club coupe: 4.30; K2500: 4.30; K2500 with C6P: 6.48; K3500 regular cab: 5.61; K3500 club coupe: 6.48, V3500: 7.33.

SUSPENSION AND RUNNING GEAR: Front Suspension: Torsion bar springs. K1500 Capacity: 3860 lb. K2500 and K3500 capacity: 3750 lb. V3500: Tapered leaf springs. Capacity: 4500 lb. Shock absorber dia.: K1500; 25mm; K2500, K3500 and V3500: 32mm. 32mm optional for K1500. 1.00 in. stabilizer optional for all series except V3500 which had a standard 1.25 in. bar standard. Optional rating: K1500: RPO F44/F60: 6100 lb. GVW. K2500: 8600 lb. GVW. K3500: 10,000 lb. GVW. Rear Suspension: Semi-elliptical 2-stage, 4-leaf for K1500; 6-leaf for K2500; 6-leaf plus 1-leaf auxiliary for K1500. K2500 capacity: 3750 K2500 capacity; 4800 K2500 capacity: 7500 lb. V3500: Semi-elliptical 2-stage, 9-leaf. Capacity: 7000 lb. Shock absorber dia.: K1500: 25mm; K2500, K3500 and V3500: 32mm. 32mm optional for K1500. Optional Rating: See above for GVW ratings. Front Axle Type and Capacity: Independent, GM or K1500: Spicer on K2500 and K3500. Capacity: K1500 regular cab: 3925; K1500 club coupe: 4800; K2500 and K3500. 4500 V3500: Spicer full-floating. Capacity: 4500, manual hub locks. Optional: K1500: 3925 capacity; K1500 club coupe 4800 lb. All other K series: 4250 Rear Axle Type: Semi-floating for K1500; full-floating for K2500, K3500 and V3500. GM manufacture for all series. Capacity: K1500: 3750, K2500: 6000; K3500, V3500: 7500 lb. Optional: K2500: Regular cab: 4800 lb.; K250 Club Coupe: 6000; K3500: 7500 lb. Final Drive Ratio: The following transmission designations were used by GMC: MM4: 4-spd. manual; MM5: 5-spd. manual overdrive; MX1: 3-spd. automatic; MXO: 4-spd. automatic. All ratios are with standard emission equipment. Standard: K1500, K2500: 3.42:1. Optional: 3.73:1. All engine/transmission combinations except K2500 with LL4 diesel engine which had standard 3.73:1 ratio and optional 4.10:1 ratio, and K2500 with 5.7 liter V-8 and C6P which also had an optional 4.56:1 ratio. Standard: K3500: 4.10:1 with 5.7 liter V-8 and 4.56:1 optional; 3.42:1 standard for 7.4 liter V-8 with 3.73 and 4.10:1 optional; 6.2 liter diesel (LL4) had standard 4.10:1 ratio with 4.56:1 optional. Standard for V3500: 4.10:1 with 5.7 liter V-8 and manual 4-spd. trans.; 4.10:1 with 3-spd. auto. trans. 3.73:1 with 7.4 liter V-8; 4.10:1 with LL4 diesel. Optional: 4.10 and 4.56:1 for 5.7 liter V-8 with man. 4-spd.; 4.56:1 for 5.7 liter V-8 with 3-spd. auto. trans.; 4.10 and 4.56:1 for 7.4 liter V-8; 4.56:1 for LL4 diesel. Transfer Case: K1500, K2500, K3500: New Process 241. Single lever. Ratios: 2.72:1, 1.00:1. K3500 with RPO RO5: Borg Warner 1370. Ratios: 2.69:1, 1.00:1. The Borg Warner unit has a right hand side power take-off. Brakes: Type: Hydraulic, power assisted. Dimensions: K1500: Front: Disc: 11.86 in. x 1.00 in. Rear: Drums: 10.0 x 2.25 in. K1500 regular cab with RPO F44/F60 had 11.57 in. x 1.25 in. front disc brakes. K2500 regular cab: Front: Disc: 11.57 in. x 1.20 in. Rear: Drums: 11.15 in. x 2.75 in. K2500 club coupe: Front Disc: 11.57 in. x 1.25 in. Rear: 10.0 in. x 2.25 in. drums. All K2500 with 8600 lb. GVW Package had 12.50 in. x 1.26 in. front disc

brakes and 13.0 in. x 2.5 in rear drum brakes. K3500 All models: Front: Disc: 12.50 in. x 1.26 in. Rear: Drum: 13.00 in. x 2.50. in. V3500 All models: Front Disc: 12.54 in. x 1.54 in. Rear: Drums: 13.0 in. x 3.5 in. Wheels: K1500 and K2500: 16 x 6.5, 6-stud disc. K3500 and V3500: 16.0 x 6.0. Tires: K1500 Sportside and regular cab: LT225/75R-16C steel belted radial. K1500 club coupe: LT245/75R16C. K2500 all models: LT245/75R-16E. K3500: LT225/75RD. V3500 all models: 7.50-16D tubeless nylon. Optional: K1500: LT225/75R16C, blackwall, LT225/75R16C on-off road; blackwall, white stripe or white lettered. Available for K10903 only with the following engines: LB4, LO3 and LH6 and RPO GVT4 axle; and K10703 with LB4 or LO3 engine with RPO GT4 axle. Optional K2500: LTR225/75R16C blackwall or white letter, on-off road. Optional K2500: LTR225/75R16D steel belted radial blackwall or white stripe, LT245/75R16E highway or on-off road, LT225/75R16D blackwall, on-off road, LT245/75R16E blackwall (K20903 only). Optional: K3500: LT225/75R16D, blackwall, LT245/75R16E blackwall, LT245/75R16E on-off road blackwall, LT245/75R16E blackwall, 7.50 x 16D highway and on-off road. Optional: V3500: V30943 only: 7.50 x 16 D tubeless nylon, dual rear, LT215/85R16D dual rear tubeless steel belted radial, LT235/85R16E. Steering: Integral power. Ratio: K1500 regular cab Sportside and Wideside: 17.44:1. K1500 club coupe model K10753: 18.8:1, model K10953: 17.44:1. K2500 regular cab: 17.44:1. K2500 club coupe: 18.88:1 model K20753: 17.44:1. K3500 regular cab: 127.44:1. K3500 club coupe: 17.44:1. V3500: 13.5:1. Turning Diameter (curb-to-curb): K1500 regular cab Sportside: 40.3 ft. K1500 regular cab Wideside: 44.4 ft. K1500 club coupe model K10753: 52.2 ft. K10953: 44.4 ft. (with C6P: 45.1 ft.). K2500 club coupe: Model K20753: 47.9 ft., model 52.2 ft. K3500 regular cab: 45.1 ft. K3500 club coupe: 52.2 ft. V3500: 54.5 ft. Transmission: Standard K1500/2500: With gasoline engines: RPO MM5-5-spd. manual with overdrive fully-synchronized. Transmission Ratios: 4.02, 2.32, 1.40, 1.00, 0.73:1. Reverse: 3.74:1. Standard: K3500, V3500 and K2500 with C6P, and K1500 and K2500 with diesel engine: RPO MM4 4-spd. SM465 manual, synchromesh on top three gears (optional: K1500/2500). Transmission ratios: 6.55, 3.58, 1.70, 1.00:1. Reverse: 6.09:1. Optional: All series: RPO MX1-3-spd. 400 automatic: Transmission ratios: 2.48, 1.48, 1.0:1. Reverse: 2.08:1. Optional: K1500/2500, (except K2500 regular cab and club coupe chassis-cab, and all V3500 models): RPO MXO-4-spd. automatic overdrive 700R4: 3.06, 1.63, 1.0, 0.70:1. Reverse: 2.29:1.

VEHICLE DIMENSIONS: Wheelbase: All series regular cab: 117.5 in., 131.5 in. Club coupe: 6.5 ft. box models: 141.5 in.; 8.0 ft. box models: 155.5 in.; V3500 models: 164.5 in. Overall Length (without rear bumper): K1500 Sportside: 194.0 in. K1500 regular cab: 194.1 in. K1500 club coupe: Model K10753 (6.5 ft. box) 223.0 in., K10953 (8.0 ft. box): 237.0 in. K2500 regular cab: 212.6 in. K2500 club coupe: Model K20753: 223.0 in., model K20953: 237.0 in. K3500 Regular cab: 212.6 in. V3500: 246.4 in. Front/Rear Tread: 74 in./74 in. Overall Height: K1500 all models: 73.8 in. K2500 regular cab: 74.3 in. (75.8 in. if equipped with C6P). K2500 club coupe: 74.4 in. (75.8 in. if equipped with C6P). K3500 75.8 in. V3500: 76.3 in. Width: All models except V3500 and those equipped with RO5: 76.8 in. V3500: 79.6 in. V3500 and K3500 with RO5: 107.3 in. Front/Rear Overhang: 117.5 in. wheelbase. Pickups: 34.9 in./41.6 in. 131.5 in. wheelbase. Pickups: 34.9 in./46.5 in. Club coupe: 34.9/46.5 in. Chassis-cab models: 34.9/41.8 in. Tailgate: Width and Height: K1500 Sportside: 50.9 x 19.3 in. All others: 62.0 in. x19.3 in. Approach/Departure Degrees: K1500 117.5 in.: 22/28. Ground Clearance (Front/Rear in inches): K1500 Sportside and Fleetside: 8.6/9.0. K1500 club coupe: 9.2/9.6. K2500 regular cab: 8.7/7.7 (with C6P: 7.8/8.1). K2500 club coupe: Model K20753: 9.2/8.2, model K20953: 9.2/8.1. V3500 regular cab and club coupe: 9.2/8.1 (with RO5 dual rear wheels: 7.2/7.4). V3500: 8.3/7.8. Front headroom: all models: 40.0 in. Front legroom: all models: 41.7 in. Front shoulder room, all models: 66.0 in.

CAPACITIES: Fuel Tank: All K series: 25.0 gal. All V3500 models: 20 gal. Optional: Models K10903, K10753, K10953, K20903, K20953, K30903: 34 gal. V3500 models: 20 gal.

ACCOMMODATIONS: Seating Capacity: Pickup, club coupe and chassis cab models: 3 passenger. Optional: Club coupe: 6 passenger. Suburban: 6 passenger. Optional: 9 passenger.

INSTRUMENTATION: Speedometer, odometer, fuel level gauge. Warning lights for battery, oil pressure, generator, brake system warning, directional/hazard lights, high beam, and engine coolant temperature.

OPTIONS AND PRICES: Air conditioning (RPO C60): $780, $820 for V350 without B3J, $758 for V3500 with B3J. Optional axle ratios: $38. Locking differential (RPO G80): $252. Auxiliary heavy-duty battery, not avail. with B3J (RPO TP2): $134. Painted rear step bumper, requires E63 body (RPO V43): $130. Front Deluxe chromed bumper with rub strip, k10703 only (RPO VG3): $26. Chromed rear step bumper with rub strip (RPO VB3): $229. Front black bumper guards (RPO V27): $32. Heavy-duty chassis equipment, K1500 only (RPO F44): $38. Off-Road Package, avail. for K1500 only. Includes skid plate and Bilstein shock absorbers (RPO Z71): $270. Cold Climate Package, not avail. with B3J. Includes engine block heater (RPO V10): $33. Convenience Group. Includes power door locks and windows (RPO ZQ2): $344. Convenience Group. Includes tilt wheel and speed control (RPO ZQ3): $346. Engine oil cooling system (RPO KC4): $135. Heavy-duty radiator (RPO VO1): $56. Heavy-duty radiator and transmission oil cooler (RPO VO2): $63. Rear window defogger (RPO C49): $154. 5.0 liter V-8 (RPO LO3): $555. 5.7 liter V-8 (RPO LO5): $800. 6.2 liter diesel V-8 (RPO LH6). Locking fuel filler cap (RPO NO5): $18. Cargo area lamp (RPO UF2): $36. Dome and reading lamp (RPO C95): $33. Roof marker lamps, not avail. with Calif. emissions (RPO UO1): $52. Auxiliary lighting. Includes dome and reading lamps and ashtray, glovebox and under hood lamps (RPO TR9): $125. Below eye-level type painted mirrors (RPO D44): $52. Below eye-level type stainless steel mirrors (RPO D45): $92. Camper-type stainless steel mirrors (RPO DF2): $100. Black exterior moldings (RPO B84): $90. Exterior bright moldings (RPO B85): $17. Conventional two-tone exterior paint (RPO ZY2): $132. Special two-tone exterior paint (RPO ZY3): $215. Deluxe two-tone exterior paint (RPO ZY4): $243. Electronically tuned AM/FM stereo radio with Seek-Scan and digital clock (RPO UM7): $210. Electronically tuned AM/FM stereo radio with Seek-Scan, stereo cassette tape and digital clock (RPO UM6): $332. Electronically tuned AM/FM stereo radio with Seek-Scan, stereo cassette player with Search and Repeat, graphic equalizer and digital clock (RPO UX1): $482. Radio delete option (RPO UL5): -$77. Sierra SLX Trim Package (RPO Z62): K series pickups: E62: $601 without RPO ZQB, $526 with RPO ZQB. E63: $632 without RPO ZQB, $557 with RPO ZQB, $235 for K1500 Sport pickup. K series chassis & cab: $452 for regular cab with RPO RO5, $527 without RO5, $337 for club coupe with RO5, $412 without RO5. Heavy-duty front and rear shock absorbers (RPO F51): $40. Sierra SLE Trim Package (RPO YE9): K1500 regular cab pickup E62: $1009. E63: $1040 without RPO ZQB, $934 with RPO ZQB. Sierra SLE Trim Package for K1500 club coupe pickup: $1056 without RPO ZQB, $950 with ZQB, $1056 for K2500 club coupe without RPO ZQB, $1025 for K2500 club coupe with C6P, $883 for K2500 regular cab chassis & cab, $1025 for K3500 club coupe pickup, $899 for K2500 club coupe chassis & cab, $942 for V3500 bonus cab pickup, $976 for V3500 crew cab pickup, $734 for V3500 bonus cab pickup with RPO RO5, $768 for V3500 crew cab with RPO RO5. Off-road skid plate, K1500 only (RPO PO1): $95. Heavy-duty front springs K1500 only, requires F44 heavy-duty chassis, not avail. with B3J or RPO Z71 off-road chassis (RPO F60): $63. Body striping (RPO D85): $69. Tow hooks, standard on K1500 (RPO V76): $38. Heavy-duty trailering special equipment (RPO ZQ8): $408 with RPO Z71 or XQ8, $448 without RPO Z71 or ZQ8. Four-speed manual trans. (RPO MM4): $98. Four-speed auto. trans. with overdrive (RPO MXO): $860. Three-speed auto. (RPO MX1): $625. Wheelcovers (RPO PO1): $42. Aluminum wheels, K1500 only (RPO PF4): $295. Sliding rear window (RPO A28): $113. Camper special chassis equipment K2500 and K3500 only (RPO Z81): $280 without B2J, $148 with B3J. Deep tinted glass, (RPO AJ1): $101. Sport Equipment Package (Sport Truck) K10703 only. Includes V43 black bumpers, black wheel flares, deluxe front appearance, black mirrors, GL LT265/75R16 blackwall tires, PF4 aluminum wheels with special hubcaps and 4x4

Sport decal (RPO BPY): $1140.20. Sport steering wheel (RPO NK3): $7.00. Rear-mounted fuel tank, avail for K2500 and K3500 chassis & cab models, approximate capacity of 31 gal. (RPO NK7): $63. Special chassis camper equipment. Includes TP2 auxiliary battery without B3J equipment, camper wiring harness and DF2 mirrors (RPO Z81): $280 for K series pickups, $1436 with B3J, $81 for V3500. Dual rear wheels, available for 3500 models only. Includes plastic rear fender extensions with side marker lamps on front and rear siders and dual rear chasi provisions (RPO RO5): $1038, $1101 with MX1 trans. Includes VO2 heavy-duty radiator and trans. oil cooler, $785 for V3500. The following options and prices applied to the V3500 models: Glide-Out spare tire carrier (RPO P11): $43. Side-mounted spare tire carrier (RPO P13): $31. Door edge guards (RPO B93): $24.

HISTORICAL FOOTNOTES: GMC truck sales for the 1990 calendar year totaled 326,370.

1991 PICKUP & SUBURBAN

Numerous detail changes were evident in the technical design of the 1991 GMC trucks. The 7.4 liter "Mark V" V-8 engine used a new one-piece intake manifold with a relocated throttle body injector in place of the old TYBI mounting adaptors. Other revisions included improved piston-to-cylinder tolerances, improved oil pan gaskets to help eliminate oil leaks, rigid cast iron rocker covers and new engine oil cooler lines with improved bracketing. This engine also was produced via a new manufacturing process and updated tooling that GMC reported was intended to improve the engine's overall reliability. General Motors all-new 4L80-E heavy-duty electronic electronic control 4-speed automatic overdrive transmission (RPO MXO) was available for all models rated at or above 8600 lb. GVWR. The 4L80-E nomenclature had the following significance: 4-4 forward speeds, L-Longitudinal type, 80-transmission gears based on relative torque capacity. This transmisson could handle 885 lbs.-ft of gearbox torque which represented 440 lb.-ft. of imput torque, E-electronic controls. Aside from its 4-speed overdrive configuration this transmission also featured an aluminum case and a Powertrain Control Module (PCM) which combined engine and transmission functions on all gasoline engines and compensated for variations in temperature, altitude and engine performance. A Transmission Control Module (TCM) was used with the diesel V-8. A new dual stator 310mm torque converter was also included for increased low-speed torque.

Powertrain improvements on all K series trucks included a new 220 series throttle body injection system. A new SD 260 starter motor was used for the 4.3 liter V-6 and the 5.0 liter V-8. It was lighter in weight and more durable and reliable than the SD300 motor it replaced. The new TBI system was used on the 4.3 liter V-6, 5.0 liter V-8, 5.7 liter V-8 and the 7.4 liter V-8 engines. It incorporated longer throttle shaft bearings, new throttle return springs and improved fuel mixture distribution. The 4.3 liter V-6 was also improved by the use of a revised air cleaner system and a processing changes in manufacturing spark plugs. Both the 5.0 liter V-8 and 5.7 liter V-8 were upgraded with heavy-duty intake valves, powdered metal camshaft sprockets and improved oil pan baffling on the heavy-duty 5.7 liter engine. Replacing the 12-SI-100 alternator was a lighter weight, more reliable CS130 alternator. A 100 amp alternator was now standard on the V3500 pickup and chassis-cab models.

The Sierra Special continued as the basic four-wheel drive GMC pickup. Revisions for 1991 included a new four spoke steering wheel and larger outside rear view mirrors. A custom urethane 4-spoke steering wheel was standard. Below eye-level type exterior painted mirrors were now standard on the K series pickups and chassis & cab models. These mirrors had adjustable heads in a black finish and measured 9.0 in. x 6.5 in. The standard AM/FM stereo radio in the V series pickups and chassis & cab had improved signal sensitivity and reduced signal interference and signal tracking. The RPO C60 air conditioning option for the K series models included a HVAC climate control incorporating new controls allowing for manual selection of the recirculation air inlet mode. Revised air conditioning display graphics provided improved identification in a dark cab. A software change provided an indication that the system required refrigerant servicing.

New options for 1991 included a bed liner for Wideside and club coupe models, high back reclining front bucket seats and gauge cluster with tachometer. The SL Trim Package had a new impact-resistant metal grille for 991. Two new metallic colors, briliant blue and slate brought the total number of exterior colors to ten. A light grey color was added to the list of available interior colors.

I. D. DATA: Unchanged for 1991. The letter M represented the 1991 model year.

Series K1500-1/2 ton 262 V-6-cyl. 117.5 in., 131.5 in. wheelbase (Suburban: 129.5 in. wheelbase and standard 350 V-8)

Model	Price.
TK10903, 8.0 ft. Sierra Special	$12,665
TK10703, 6.5 ft. Sportside Pickup	$14,959
TK10703, 6.5 ft. Wideside Pickup	$14,629
TK10903, 8.0 ft. Wideside Pickup	$14,909
TK10753, 6.5 ft. Club Coupe Wideside	$15,613
TK10953, 8.0 ft. Club Coupe Wideside	$15,903
TV10906, Suburban, Panel Doors	$18,755
TV10906, Suburban, Tailgate	$18,905

Add $2540 for Wideside TK 10753 with LH6 diesel engine. The diesel engine is not available on TK10703 models.
Add $2740 for TK10753 with diesel engine.
Add $2174 for TK10953 with LH6 diesel engine.
Add $2440 for LH6 diesel on TV10906 models.

K2500-3/4 ton 262 V-61. 131.5 in.wheelbase. (V2500 Suburban-129.5 in. wheelbase), Crew and Bonus Cab: 164.5 in. wheelbase, Suburban with standard 350 V-8

TK20903, Chassis & Cab	$16,428.00
TK20953, Club Coupe Chassis & Cab	$17,508.80
TK20903, 8.0 ft. Wideside Pickup	$15,119.00
TK20903, 8.0 ft. C6P Wideside Pickup	$16,283.00
TK20753, 6.5 ft. Club Coupe Pickup	$16,182.00
TK20953, 8.0 ft. Club Coupe Pickup	$16,482.00
TK20953, 8.0 ft. C6P Club Coupe Pickup	$17,352.00
TV20906 Suburban, Panel Doors	$20,248.00
TV20906 Suburban, Tailgate	$20,403.00

Add $2940 to TK20903 for LH6 diesel engine.
Add $2030 to TK20903 C6P for LL4 diesel engine.
Add $2660 to TK20753 for LH6 diesel engine.
Add $2640 to TK20953 for diesel engine.
Add $2030 to TK20953 with C6P for LL4 diesel engine.
Add $1210 to TK20953 club coupe chassis cab for LL4 diesel engine.
Add $1855 for LH6 diesel on Suburban models.

Series K3500-1 ton 350 V-8. 131.5 in.wheelbase, Club Coupe: 155.5 in. wheelbase, Crew and Bonus Cab: 164.5 in. wheelbase

TK30903, 8.0 ft. Wideside Pickup	$18,350
TK30953, 8.0 ft. Club Coupe W-S Pickup	$19,410
TK30903, Chassis & Cab, 131.5 in. wb	$17,605
TK31003, Chassis & Cab, 135.5 in. wb.	$17,595*
TK31403, Chassis & Cab, 159.9 in. wb.	$17,725*
TK30953, Club Coupe Chassis & Cab	$19,935

Add $1405 for LL4 diesel engine with TK30903.
Add $1415 for LL4 diesel engine with TK30953.
Add $1260 to TK30953, ext. cab chassis & cab for LL4 diesel engine.

Series V3500-1 ton 350 V-8. 164.5 in.wheelbase, Fleetside Crew and Bonus Cab: 164.5 in. wheelbase

TV30943 Bonus Cab	$19,068.08
TV30943 Crew Cab	$19,168.08
TV30943 Bonus Cab Chassis & Cab	$18,598.08
TV30943 Crew Cab Chassis & Cab	$19,148.08
TV30943 HD Bonus Cab Chassis & Cab	$19,025.00
TV30943 HD Crew Cab Chassis & Cab	$19,565.00

Add $1140 for all bonus and crew cab with LL4 diesel engine.
Add $1510 for LL4 diesel engine for HD chassis & cab bonus cab models.
Add $1520 for LL4 diesel engine for HD chassis & cab crew cab models.

STANDARD ENGINE: All K1500, K2500 models: 262 V-6 (LB4 ordering code). Engine Type: Vortex OHV, V-6-cylinder. Cast iron block. Bore x Stroke: 4.0 in. x 3.48 in. Lifters: Hydraulic. Fuel Induction: Electronic fuel injection. Compression Ratio: For models under 8500 GVWR: 9.3:1. For models over 8500 lb. GVWR: 8.6:1. Displacement: 262 cu. in. (4.3 liters). Horsepower: Net: For models under 8500 lb. GVWR: 160 @ 4000 rpm. For models over 85900 lb. GVWR: 155 @ 4000 rpm. Torque: Net: For models under 8500 lb. GVWR: 235 lb.-ft. @ 2400 rpm. For models over 85900 lb. GVWR: 230 lb.-ft. @ 2400 rpm. Oil refill capacity: 5 qt. with filter change. Fuel Requirements: Regular unleaded.

OPTIONAL ENGINE: K1500, K2500, Standard: V3500 and K3500 models. 350 V-8 (LO5 ordering code). Engine Type: OHV, V-8. Cast iron block and cylinder head. Bore x Stroke: 4.0 in. x 3.48 in. Lifters: Hydraulic. Number of main bearings-5. Fuel Induction: Electronic fuel injection. Compression Ratio: K3500: 8.6:1. K1500 and K2500: 9.3:1. Displacement: 350 cu. in. (5.7 liters). Horsepower: K3500: Net: 190 @ 4000 rpm. K1500 and K2500: 210 @ 4000 rpm. Torque: K3500: Net 300 lb.-ft. @ 2400 rpm. K1500 and K2500: 300 lb.-ft. @ 2800 rpm. Oil refill capacity: 5 qt. with filter change. Fuel Requirements: Regular unleaded.

OPTIONAL ENGINE: K1500 and K2500: 305 V-8, Ordering Code: LO3. Engine Type: OHV, V-8. Cast iron block and alloy iron cylinder head. Key features include chain drive camshaft and forged steel connecting rods. This engine was produced in U.S. or Canada. Bore x Stroke: 3.74 in. x 3.48 in. Lifters: Hydraulic. Number of main bearings-5. Fuel Induction: Electronic fuel injection. Compression Ratio: 9.2:1. Displacement: 305 cu. in. (5.0 liters). Horsepower: Net: 175 @ 4000 rpm. Torque: Net: 270 lb.-ft. @ 2400 rpm. Oil refill capacity: 5 qt. with filter change. Fuel Requirements: Regular unleaded.

STANDARD ENGINE: K3500 models with dual rear wheels. Optional: Other K3500 models. Ordering Code: L19: 454 V-8. Engine Type: OHV, V-8. Cast iron block and alloy iron cylinder head. Bore x Stroke: 4.30 in. x 4.0 in. Lifters: Hydraulic. Number of main bearings-5. Fuel Induction: Electronic fuel injection. Compression Ratio: 7.9:1. Displacement: 454 cu. in. (7.4 liters). Horsepower: 230 @ 3600 rpm. Torque: 385 lb.-ft. @ 1600 rpm. Oil refill capacity: 5 qt. with filter change. Fuel Requirements: Regular unleaded.

OPTIONAL ENGINE: K1500 and K2500: Ordering Code LH6. Not available in California for K2500. This engine was produced by GM-Detroit Diesel Allison Division. Engine Type: OHV, diesel V-8. Bore x Stroke: 3.98 in. x 3.80 in. Lifters: Hydraulic. Number of main bearings-5. Fuel Induction: Gear driven mechanical fuel injection. Compression Ratio: 21.3:1. Displacement: 379.4 cu. in. (6.2 liters). Horsepower: 126 @ 3600 rpm. (140 @ 3600 rpm with automatic transmission). Torque: 240 lb.-ft. @ 2000 rpm. (247 lb.-ft. @ 2000 rpm with automatic transmission). Oil refill capacity: 7 qt. with filter change. Fuel Requirements: Diesel.

OPTIONAL ENGINE: K3500 and V3500 models: Ordering Code LL4. This engine was produced by GM-Detroit Diesel Allison Division. Engine Type: OHV, diesel V-8. Bore x Stroke: 3.98 in. x 3.80 in. Lifters: Hydraulic. Number of main bearings-5. Fuel Induction: Fuel injection. Compression Ratio: 21.3:1. Displacement: 379.4 cu. in. (6.2 liters). Horsepower: 143 @ 3600 rpm. Torque: 257 lb.-ft. @ 2000 rpm. Oil refill capacity: 7 qt. with filter change. Fuel Requirements: Diesel.

CHASSIS FEATURES: Semi-perimeter design, all-welded channel beam frame with boxed front end. Dimensions: K1500 and K2500 regular cab: 2.18 x 7.48 x 0.134 in. K1500 club coupe: 2.18 x 7.48 x 0.165 in. K2500 regular cab with C6P: 2.18 x 7.48 x 0.213 in. K2500 club coupe: 2.31 x 7.48 x 0.165 in. K2500 club coupe with C6P: 2.18 x 7.48 x 0.244 in. K3500 regular cab: 2.18 x 7.48 x 0.213 in. K3500 club coupe: 2.18 x 7.48 x 0.244 in. V3500 models: 2.788 x 7.74 x 0.244 in. Section modulus: K1500 regular cab: 3.46; K1500 club coupe: 4.30; K2500: 4.30; K2500 with C6P: 6.48; K3500 regular cab: 5.61; K3500 club coupe: 6.48, V3500: 7.33.

SUSPENSION AND RUNNING GEAR: Front Suspension: Torsion bar springs. K1500 Capacity: 3860 lb. K2500 and K3500 capacity: 3750 lb. V3500: Tapered leaf springs. Capacity: 4500 lb. Shock absorber dia.: K1500; 25mm; K2500, K3500 and V3500: 32mm. 32mm optional for K1500. 1.00 in. stabilizer optional for all series except V3500 which had a standard 1.25 in. bar standard. Optional rating: K1500: RPO F44/F60: 6100 lb. GVW. K2500: 8600 lb. GVW. K3500: 10,000 lb. GVW. Rear Suspension: Semi-elliptical 2-stage, 4-leaf for K1500; 6-leaf for K2500; 6-leaf plus 1-leaf auxiliary for K3500. K1500 capacity: 3750 K2500 capacity: 4800 K3500 capacity: 7500 lb. V3500: Semi-elliptical 2-stage, 9-leaf. Capacity: 7000. Shock absorber dia.: K1500: 25mm; K2500, K3500 and V3500: 32mm. 32mm optional for K1500. Optional Rating: See above for GVW ratings. Front Axle Type and Capacity: Independent, GM or K1500; Spicer on K2500 and K3500. Capacity: K1500 regular cab: 3925; K1500 club coupe: 4800; K2500 and K3500: 4250 V3500: Spicer full-floating. Capacity: 4500, manual hub locks. Optional: K1500: 3925 capacity; K1500 club coupe: 4800 lb. All other K series: 4250. Rear Axle Type: Semi-floating for K1500; full-floating for K2500, K3500 and V3500. GM manufacture for all series. Capacity: K1500: 3750, K2500: 6000; K3500, V3500: 7500 lb. Optional: K2500: Regular cab: 4800 lb.; K250 Club Coupe: 6000; K3500: 7500. Final Drive Ratio: The following transmission designations were used by GMC: MM4: 4-spd. manual; MM5: 5-spd. manual overdrive; MX1: 3-spd. automatic; MXO: 4-spd. automatic. All ratios are with standard emission equipment. Standard: K1500, K2500: 3.42:1. Optional: 3.73:1. All engine/transmission combinations except K2500 with LL4 diesel engine which had standard 3.73:1 ratio and optional 4.10:1 ratio, and K2500 with 5.7 liter V-8 and C6P which also had an optional 4.56:1 ratio. Standard: K3500: 4.10:1 with 5.7 liter V-8 with 4.56:1 optional; 3.42:1 standard for 7.4 liter V-8 with 3.73 and 4.10:1 optional; 6.2 liter diesel (LL4) had standard 4.10:1 ratio with 4.56:1 optional. Standard for V3500: 3.73:1 with 5.7 liter and manual 4-spd. trans.; 4.10:1 with 3-spd. auto. trans.; 3.73:1 with 7.4 liter V-8; 4.10:1 with LL4 diesel. Optional: 4.10 and 4.56:1 for 5.7 liter V-8 with man. 4-spd.; 4.56:1 for 5.7 liter V-8 with 3-spd. auto. trans.; 4.10 and 4.56:1 for 7.4 liter V-8; 4.56:1 for LL4 diesel. Transfer Case: K1500, K2500, K3500: New Process 241. Single lever. Ratios: 2.72:1, 1.00:1. K3500 with RPO RO5: Borg Warner 1370: Ratios: 2.69:1, 1.00:1. The Borg Warner unit has a right hand side power take-off. Brakes: Type: Hydraulic, power assisted. Dimensions: K1500: Front: Disc: 11.86 in. x 1.00 in. Rear: Drums: 10.0 x 2.25 in. K1500 regular cab with RPO F44/F60 had 11.57 in. x 1.25 in. front disc brakes. K2500 regular cab: Front: Disc: 11.57 in. x 1.20 in. Rear: Drums: 11.15 in. x 2.75 in. K2500 club coupe: Front Disc: 11.57 in. x 1.25 in. Rear: 10.0 in. x 2.25 in. drums. All K2500 with 8600 lb. GVW Package had 12.50 in. x 1.26 in. front disc brakes and 13.0 in. x 2.5 in. rear drum brakes. K3500 All models: Front: Disc: 12.50 in. x 1.26 in. Rear: Drum: 13.00 in.x 2.50 in. V3500 All models: Front Disc: 12.54 in. x 1.54 in. Rear: Drums: 13.0 in. x 3.5 in. Wheels: K1500 and K2500: 16 x 6.5, 6-stud disc. K3500 and V3500: 16.0 x 6.0. Tires: K1500 Sportside and regular cab: LT225/75R-16C steel belted radial. K1500 club coupe: LT245/75R16C. K2500 all models: LT245/75R-16E. K3500: LT225/75RD. V3500 all models: 7.50-16D tubeless nylon. Optional: K1500: LT225/75R16C, blackwall, LT225/75R16C on-off road; blackwall, white stripe or white lettered. Available for K10903 only with the following engines: LB4, LO3 and LH6 and RPO GVT4 axle; and K10703 with LB4 or LO3 engine with RPO GT4 axle: LT265/75R16C blackwall or white letter, on-off road. Optional K2500: LTR225/75R16D steel belted radial blackwall or white stripe, LT245/75R16E highway or on-off road, LT225/75R16D blackwall, on-off road, LT245/75R16E blackwall (K20903 only). Optional: K3500: LT225/75R16D, blackwall, LT245/75R16E blackwall, LT245/75R16E on-off road blackwall, LT245/75R16E blackwall, 7.50 x 16D highway and on-off road. Optional: V3500: V30943 only: 7.50 x 16 D tubeless nylon, dual rear, LT215/85R16D dual rear tubeless steel belted radial; LT235/85R16E. Steering: Integral power. Ratio: K1500 regular cab Sportside and Wideside: 17.44:1. K1500 club coupe model K10753: 18.8:1, model K10953: 17.44:1. K2500 regular cab: 17.44:1. K2500 club coupe: K20753: 18.88:1; model K20953: 17.44:1. K3500 regular cab: 127.44:1. K3500 club coupe: 17.44:1. V3500: 13.5:1. Turning Diameter (curb-to-curb): K1500 regular cab Sportside: 40.3 ft. K1500 regular cab Wideside: 44.4 ft. K1500 club coupe model K10753: 47.9 ft., model K10953: 52.2 ft. K2500 regular cab: 44.4 ft. (with C6P: 45.1 ft.). K2500 club coupe: Model K20753: 47.9 ft., model 52.2 ft. K3500 regular cab: 45.1 ft. K3500 club coupe: 52.2 ft. V3500: 54.5 ft. Transmission: Standard K1500/2500: With gasoline engines: RPO MM5-5-spd. manual with overdrive fully-synchronized: Transmission Ratios: 4.02, 2.32, 1.40, 1.00, 0.73:1; Reverse: 3.74:1. Standard: K3500, V3500 and K2500 with C6P, and K1500 and K2500 with diesel engine: RPO MM4 4-spd. SM465 manual, synchromesh on top three gears (optional: K1500/2500). Transmission ratios: 6.55, 3.58, 1.70, 1.00:1. Reverse: 6.09:1. Optional: All series: RPO MX1-3-spd. 400 automatic. Transmission ratios: 2.48, 1.48, 1.0:1. Reverse: 2.08:1. Optional: K1500/2500, (except K2500 regular cab and club coupe chassis-cab, and all V3500 models): RPO MXO-4-spd. automatic overdrive 700R4: 3.06, 1.63, 1.0, 0.70:1. Reverse: 2.29:1

VEHICLE DIMENSIONS: Wheelbase: All series regular cab: 117.5 in., 131.5 in. Club coupe: 6.5 ft. box models: 141.5 in.; 8.0 ft. box models: 155.5 in.; V3500 models: 164.5 in. Overall Length (without rear bumper): K1500 Sportside: 194.0 in., K1500 regular cab: 194.1 in. K1500 club coupe: Model K10753 (6.5 ft. box): 223.0 in., K10953 (8.0 ft. box): 237.0 in. K2500 regular cab: 212.6 in. K2500 club coupe: Model K20753: 223.0 in., model K20953: 237.0 in. K3500 Regular cab: 212.6 in. V3500: 246.4 in. Front/Rear Tread: 74 in./74 in. Overall Height: K1500 all models: 73.8 in. K2500 regular cab: 74.3 in. (75.8 in. if equipped with C6P). K2500 club coupe: 74.4 in. (75.8 in. if equipped with C6P). K3500 75.8 in. V3500: 76.3 in. Width: All models except V3500 and those equipped with RO5: 76.8 in. V3500: 79.6 in. V3500 and K3500 with RO5: 107.3 in. Front/Rear Overhang: 117.5 in. wheelbase pickups: 34.9 in./41.6 in. 131.5 in. wheelbase. Pickups: 34.9 in./46.5 in. Club coupe: 34.9/46.5 in. Chassis-cab models: 34.9/41.8 in. Tailgate: Width and Height: K1500 Sportside: 50.9 x 19.3 in. All others: 62.0 in. x19.3 in. Approach/Departure Degrees: K1500 117.5 in.: 22/28. Ground Clearance (Front/Rear in inches): K1500 Sportside and Fleetside: 8.6/9.0. K1500 club coupe: 9.2/9.6. K2500 regular cab: 8.7/7.7 (with C6P: 7.8/8.1). K2500 club coupe: Model K20753: 9.2/8.2, model K20953: 9.2/8.1. K3500 regular and club coupe: 9.2/8.1 (with RO5 dual rear wheels: 7.2/7.4). V3500: 8.3/7.8. Front headroom, all models: 40.0 in. Front legroom, all models: 41.7 in. Front shoulder room, all models: 66.0 in.

CAPACITIES: Fuel Tank: All K series: 25.0 gal. All V3500 models: 20 gal. Optional: Models K10903, K10753, K10953, K20903, K20953, K30903: 34 gal. V3500 models: 20 gal.

ACCOMMODATIONS: Seating Capacity: Pickup, club coupe and chassis cab models: 3 passenger. Optional: Club coupe: 6 passenger. Suburban: 6 passenger. Optional: 9 passenger.

INSTRUMENTATION: Speedometer, odometer, fuel level gauge. Warning lights for battery, oil pressure, generator, brake system warning, directional/hazard lights, high beam, and engine coolant temperature.

OPTIONS AND PRICES: All K series: Air conditioning (RPO C60): $705, Optional axle ratios: $44. Locking differential (RPO G80): $252. Auxiliary heavy-duty battery, not avail. with B3J (RPO TP2): $134. Painted rear step bumper, requires E63 body (RPO V43): $130. Front Deluxe chromed bumper with rub strip, K10703 only (RPO VG3): $26. Chromed rear step bumper with rub strip (RPO VB3): $229. Front black bumper guards (RPO V27): $32. Heavy-duty chassis equipment, K1500 only (RPO F44): $38. Off-Road Package, avail. for K1500 only. Includes skid plate and Bilstein shock absorbers (RPO Z71: $270. Cold Climate Package, not avail. with B3J. Includes engine block heater (RPO V10): $33. Convenience Group. Includes power door locks and windows (RPO ZQ2): $367. Convenience Group. Includes tilt wheel and speed control (RPO ZQ3): $383. Engine oil cooling system (RPO KC4): $135. Heavy-duty radiator (RPO VO1): $56. Heavy-duty radiator and transmission oil cooler (RPO VO2): $63. Rear window defogger (RPO C49): $154. 5.0 liter V-8 (RPO LO3): $575. 5.7 liter V-8 (RPO LO5): $840. 6.2 liter diesel V-8 (RPO LH6). Locking fuel filler cap (RPO NO5): $18. Cargo area lamp (RPO UF2): $36. Dome and reading lamp (RPO C95): $33. Roof marker lamps, not avail. with Calif. emissions (RPO UO1): $52. Auxiliary lighting. Includes dome and reading lamps and ashtray, glovebox and under hood lamps (RPO TR9): $94. Below eye-level type stainless steel mirrors (RPO D45): $45. Camper-type stainless steel mirrors (RPO DF2): $53. Black exterior moldings (RPO B84): $90. Exterior bright moldings (RPO B85): $17. Conventional two-tone exterior paint (RPO ZY2): $132. Special two-tone exterior paint (RPO ZY3): $215. Deluxe two-tone exterior paint (RPO ZY4): $243. Electronically tuned AM/FM stereo radio with Seek-Scan and digital clock (RPO UM7): $210. Electronically tuned AM/FM stereo radio with Seek-Scan, stereo cassette tape and digital clock (RPO UM6): $332. Electronically tuned AM/FM stereo radio with Seek-Scan, stereo cassette player with Search and Repeat, graphic equalizer and digital clock (RPO UX1): $482. Radio delete option (RPO UL5): -$77. SLX Trim Package (RPO Z62): K series pickups: $573 to $604. Heavy-duty front and rear shock absorbers (RPO F51): $40. SLE Trim Package (RPO YE9): K1500 regular cab pickup: $981 to $1012. Off-road skid plate, K1500 only (RPO NZZ): $95. Heavy-duty front springs K1500 only, requires F44 heavy-duty chassis, not avail. with B3J or RPO Z71 off-road chassis (RPO F60: $63. Body striping (RPO D85): $69. Tow hooks, standard on K1500 (RPO V76): $38. Heavy-duty trailering special equipment (RPO Z82): $408 with RPO Z71 or XQ8, $448 without RPO Z71 or ZQ8. Four-Speed manual trans. (RPO MM4): $98. Four-Speed auto. trans. with overdrive (RPO MXO): $860. Three-speed auto. trans. (RPO MX1): $625. Wheelcovers (RPO PO1): $42. Aluminum wheels, K1500 only (RPO PF4): $295. Sliding rear window (RPO A28): $113. Camper special chassis equipment K2500 and K3500 only (RPO Z81): $280 without B2J, $148 with B3J. Deep tinted glass, (RPO AJ1): $150. Sport Equipment Package (Sport Truck), K10703 only. Includes V43 black bumpers, black wheel flares, deluxe front appearance, black mirrors, GL LT265/75R16 blackwall tires, PF4 aluminum wheels with special hubcaps and 4x4 Sport decal (RPO BPY): $1140.20. Sport steering wheel (RPO NK3): $7.00. Rear-mounted fuel tank, avail for K2500 and K3500 chassis & cab models, approximate capacity of 31 gal. (RPO NK7): $63. Special chassis camper equipment. Includes TP2 auxiliary battery without B3J equipment, camper wiring harness and DF2 mirrors (RPO Z81): $280 for K series pickups, $1436 with B3J, $81 for V3500. Dual rear wheels, available for 3500 models only. Includes plastic rear fender extensions with side marker lamps on front and rear siders and dual rear chassis provisions (RPO RO5): $1038, $1101 with MX1 trans. Includes VO2 heavy-duty radiator and trans. oil cooler, $785 for V3500.

HISTORICAL FOOTNOTES: Total registration of GMC trucks for 1991 was 306,149. Total pickup sales for 1991 were 123,416. Suburban sales were 16,116.

1992 PICKUP & SUBURBAN

The GMC Suburban and four-door crew cab pickup models adopted the styling introduced in 1988 for the full-size GMC pickups. The Suburban's new format provided a lower step-in height and load floor height. Enhancing the Suburban's recreational vehicle appeal were its increased towing capacity, load space, and front and rear leg, shoulder and hip room. Anti-lock brakes were standard for all Suburbans. The Suburban's suspension design closely folowed that of the full-size Pickups The front suspension was independent with upper and lower contorl arms and a stabilizer bar. The rear suspension was of semi-elliptical, two-stage, multi-leaf design. A 5.7 liter fuel injected V-8 was standard. Suburbans with a GVW over 8500 lbs. used a heavy-duty version of the 5.7 liter V-8. The 7.4 liter V-8 was optional for Suburbans with GVW over 8600 lb. Standard Suburban equipment included seats with additional foam support, head restraints for the front outboard seat position (all GMC pickups had new front seats with this feature), a full gauge cluster, All-Season radial tires and an extended-range AM radio. A lift-glass/drop gate was optional.

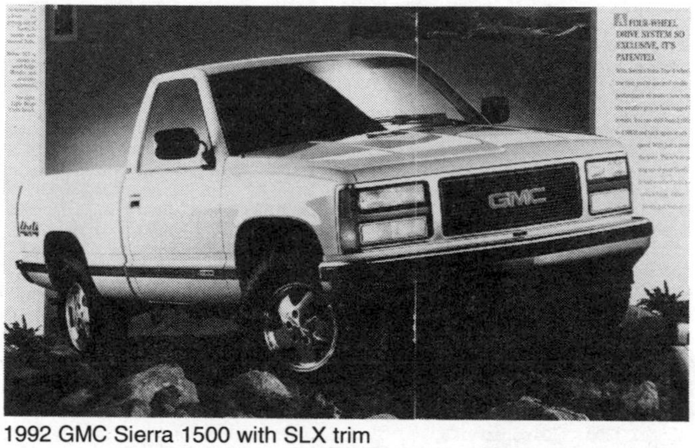

1992 GMC Sierra 1500 with SLX trim

Along with the Blazer and Suburban, the crew cab K3500 pickup had the new generation GMC styling. The crew cab had a 4 inch longer wheelbase, nearly 7 inches more rear seat legroom and increased front leg and shoulder room. The crew cab also had anti-lock brakes. The standard crew cab engine-transmission was a 5.7 liter V-8 with a 5-speed heavy-duty manual transmission with "deep low" and overdrive. Available for all trucks with a GVW rating of 8600 lb. and up was a new 6.5 liter turbo diesel. This engine, built at the General Motors Moraine Engine plant in Dayton, Ohio had a special warranty of five years or 100,00 miles. Among its features were an all-new cylinder case design, and an optimized combustion chamber for totally smokeless performance. Added to the interior color availability for 1992 was beige. New exterior colors were bright red and beige metallic.

I.D. DATA: Unchanged for 1992. The letter N represented the 1992 model year.

Model	Price
Series K1500-1/2 ton 262 V-6-cyl. 117.5 in., 131.5 in. wheelbase (Suburban: 129.5 in. wheelbase and standard 350 V-8)	
TK10903, 8.0 ft. Sierra Special	$13,617
TK10703, 6.5 ft. Sportside Pickup	$15,983
TK10703, 6.5 ft. Fleetside Pickup	$15,583
TK10903, 8.0 ft. Fleetside Pickup	$15,873
TK10753, 6.5 ft. Club Coupe S-S	$16,935
TK10953, 8.0 ft. Club Coupe W-S	$16,535
TV10906, Suburban, Panel Doors	$20,593
TV10906, Suburban, Tailgate	$20,743
K2500-3/4 ton 262 V-6[1], 131.5 in. wheelbase. Suburban with standard 350 V-8	
TK20903, 8.0 ft. W-S Pickup	$16,043
TK20753, 6.5 ft. Club Cpe W-S Pickup	$17,105
TK20953, 8.0 ft. Club Cpe W-S Pickup	$17,405
TV20906 Suburban, Panel Doors	$21,797
TV20906 Suburban, Tailgate	$21,947
Series K3500-1 ton 350 V-8. 131.5 in.wheelbase	
TK30903, 8.0 ft. Club Cpe W-S Pickup	$18,060
TK30953, 8.0 ft. Club Cpe W-S Pickup	$20,579
Series V3500-1 ton 350 V-8.	
TV30943 Bonus Cab	$N.A.
TV30943 Crew Cab	$N.A.
TV30943 Bonus Cab Chassis & Cab	$N.A.
TV30943 Crew Cab Chassis & Cab	$N.A.
TV30943 HD Bonus Cab Chassis & Cab	$N.A.
TV30943 HD Crew Cab Chassis & Cab	$N.A.

STANDARD ENGINE: All K1500, K2500 models: 262 V-6 (LB4 ordering code). Engine Type: Vortex OHV, V-6-cylinder. Cast iron block. Bore x Stroke: 4.0 in. x 3.48 in. Lifters: Hydraulic. Fuel Induction: Electronic fuel injection. Compression Ratio: 9.3:1. Displacement: 262 cu. in. (4.3 liters). Horsepower: Net:160 @ 4000 rpm. Torque: Net 235 lb.-ft. @ 2400 rpm. Oil refill capacity: 5 qt. with filter change. Fuel Requirements: Regular unleaded.

OPTIONAL ENGINE: K1500, K2500, Standard: V3500 and K3500 models. Optional for K150 and K2500 models. 350 V-8 (LO5 ordering code). Engine Type: OHV, V-8. Cast iron block and cylinder head. Bore x Stroke: 4.0 in. x 3.48 in. Lifters: Hydraulic. Number of main bearings-5. Fuel Induction: Electronic fuel injection. Compression Ratio: 8.6:1. K1500 and K2500: 9.3:1. Displacement: 350 cu. in. (5.7 liters). Horsepower: K3500: Net: 190 @ 4000 rpm. K1500 and K2500: 210 @ 4000 rpm. Torque: K3500: Net 300 lb.-ft @ 2400 rpm. K1500 and K2500: 300 lb.-ft. @ 2800 rpm. Oil refill capacity: 5 qt. with filter change. Fuel Requirements: Regular unleaded.

STANDARD ENGINE: K3500 models with dual rear wheels. Optional: Other K3500 models. Ordering Code: L19: 454 V-8. Engine Type: OHV, V-8. Cast iron block and alloy iron cylinder head. Bore x Stroke: 4.30 in. x 4.0 in. Lifters: Hydraulic. Number of main bearings-5. Fuel Induction: Electronic fuel injection. Compression Ratio: 7.9:1. Displacement: 454 cu. in. (7.4 liters). Horsepower: 230 @ 3600 rpm. Torque: 385 lb.-ft. @ 1600 rpm. Oil refill capacity: 5 qt. with filter change. Fuel Requirements: Regular unleaded.

OPTIONAL ENGINE: K1500 and K2500: Ordering Code LH6. Not available in California for K2500. This engine was produced by GM-Detroit Diesel Allison Division. Engine Type: OHV, diesel V-8. Bore x Stroke: 3.98 in. x 3.80 in. Lifters: Hydraulic. Number of main bearings-5. Fuel Induction: Gear driven mechanical fuel injection. Compression Ratio: 21.3:1. Displacement: 379.4 cu. in. (6.2 liters). Horsepower: 126 @ 3600 rpm. (140 @ 3600 rpm with automatic transmission). Torque: 240 lb.-ft. @ 2000 rpm. (247 lb.-ft. @ 2000 rpm with automatic transmission). Oil refill capacity: 7 qt. with filter change. Fuel Requirements: Diesel.

OPTIONAL ENGINE: K3500 and V3500 models: Ordering Code LL4. This engine was produced by GM-Detroit Diesel Allison Division. Engine Type: OHV, diesel V-8. Bore x Stroke: 3.98 in. x 3.80 in. Lifters: Hydraulic. Number of main bearings-5. Fuel Induction: Fuel injection. Compression Ratio: 21.3:1. Displacement: 379.4 cu. in. (6.2 liters). Horsepower: 143 @ 3600 rpm. Torque: 257 lb.-ft. @ 2000 rpm. Oil refill capacity: 7 qt. with filter change. Fuel Requirements: Diesel.

OPTIONAL ENGINE: All 8600 lb. and up GVWR models: Ordering Code L65. This engine was produced by GM-Detroit Diesel Allison Division. Engine Type: OHV, diesel V-8. Bore x Stroke: 4.52 in. x 3.82 in. Lifters: Hydraulic. Number of main bearings-5. Fuel Induction: Fuel injection. Compression Ratio: 21.5:1. Displacement: 396.67 cu. in. (6.5 liters). Horsepower: 190 @ 3400 rpm. Torque: 380 lb.-ft. @ 1700 rpm. Oil refill capacity: 7 qt. with filter change. Fuel Requirements: Diesel.

CHASSIS FEATURES: Semi-perimeter design, all-welded channel beam frame with boxed front end. Dimensions: K1500 and K2500 regular cab: 2.18 x 7.48 x 0.134 in. K1500 club coupe: 2.18 x 7.48 x 0.165 in. K2500 regular cab with C6P: 2.18 x 7.48 x 0.213 in. K2500 club coupe: 2.31 x 7.48 x 0.165 in. K2500 club coupe with C6P: 2.18 x 7.48 x 0.244 in. K3500 regular cab: 2.18 x 7.48 x 0.213 in. K3500 club coupe: 2.18 x 7.48 x 0.244 in. V3500 models: 2.788 x 7.74 x 0.244 in. Section modulus: K1500 regular cab: 3.46; K1500 club coupe: 4.30; K2500: 4.30; K2500 with C6P: 6.48; K3500 regular cab: 5.61; K3500 club coupe: 6.48, V3500: 7.33.

SUSPENSION AND RUNNING GEAR: Front Suspension: Torsion bar springs. K1500 Capacity: 3860 lb. K2500 and K3500 capacity: 3750 lb. V3500: Tapered leaf springs. Capacity: 4500 lb. Shock absorber dia.: K1500: 25mm; K2500, K3500 and V3500: 32mm. 32mm optional for K1500. 1.00 in. stabilizer optional for all series except V3500 which had a standard 1.25 in. bar standard. Optional rating: K1500: RPO F44/F60: 6100 lb. GVW. K2500: 8600 lb. GVW. K3500: 10,000 lb. GVW. Rear Suspension: Semi-elliptical 2-stage, 4-leaf for K1500; 6-leaf for K2500; 6-leaf plus 1-leaf auxiliary for K3500. K1500 capacity: 3750 K2500 capacity: 4800 K3500 capacity: 7500 lb. V3500: Semi-elliptical 2-stage, 9-leaf. Capacity: 7000 lb. Shock absorber dia.: K1500: 25mm; K2500, K3500 and V3500: 32mm. 32mm optional for K1500. Optional Rating: See above for GVW ratings. Front Axle Type and Capacity: Independent, GM or K1500: Spicer on K2500 and K3500. Capacity: K1500 regular cab: 3925; K1500 club coupe: 4800; K2500 and K3500: 4250 V3500: Spicer full-floating. Capacity: 4500, manual hub locks. Optional: K1500: 3925 capacity; K1500 club coupe: 4800 lb. All other K series: 4250 lb. Rear Axle Type: Semi-floating for K1500; full-floating for K2500, K3500 and V3500. GM manufacture for all series. Capacity: K1500: 3750, K2500: 6000; K3500, V3500: 7500 lb. Optional: K2500: Regular cab: 4800 lb.; K250 club coupe: 6000; K3500: 7500. Final Drive Ratio: The following transmission designations were used by GMC: MM4: 4-spd. manual; MM5: 5-spd. manual overdrive; MX1: 3-spd. automatic; MXO: 4-spd. automatic. All ratios are with standard emission equipment. Standard: K1500, K2500: 3.42:1. Optional: 3.73:1. All engine/transmission combinations except K2500 with LL4 diesel engine which had standard 3.73:1 ratio and optional 4.10:1 ratio, and K2500 with 5.7 liter V-8 and C6P which also had an optional 4.56:1 ratio. Standard: K3500: 4.10:1 with 5.7 liter V-8 with 4.56:1 optional; 3.42:1 optional for 7.4 liter V-8 with 3.73 and 4.10:1 optional; 6.2 liter diesel (LL4) had standard 4.10:1 ratio with 4.56:1 optional. Standard for V3500: 3.73:1 with 5.7 liter and manual 4-spd. trans.; 4.10:1 with 3-spd. auto. trans.; 3.73:1 with 7.4 liter V-8; 4.10:1 with LL4 diesel. Optional: 4.10 and 4.56:1 for 5.7 liter V-8 with man. 4-spd.; 4.56:1 for 5.7 liter V-8 with 3-spd. auto. trans.; 4.10 and 4.56:1 for 7.4 liter V-8; 4.56:1 for LL4 diesel. Transfer Case: K1500, K2500, K3500: New Process 241. Single lever. Ratios: 2.72:1, 1.00:1. K3500 with RPO RO5: Borg Warner 1370: Ratios: 2.69:1, 1.00:1. The Borg Warner unit has a right hand side power take-off. Brakes: Type: Hydraulic, power assisted. Dimensions: K1500: Front: Disc: 11.86 in. x 1.00 in. Rear: Drums: 10.0 x 2.25 in. K1500 regular cab with RPO F44/F60 had 11.57 in. x 1.25 in. front disc brakes. K2500 regular cab: Front: Disc: 11.57 in. x 1.20 in. Rear: Drums: 11.15 in. x 2.75 in. K2500 club coupe: Front Disc: 11.57 in. x 1.25 in. Rear: 10.0 in. x 2.25 in. drums. All K2500 with 8600 lb. GVW Package had 12.50 in. x 1.26 in. front disc brakes and 13.0 in. x 2.5 in. rear drum brakes. K3500 All models: Front: Disc: 12.50 in. x 1.26 in. Rear: Drum: 13.00 in. x 2.50 in. V3500 All models: Front Disc: 12.54 in. x 1.54 in. Rear: Drums: 13.0 in. x 3.5 in. Wheels: K1500 and K2500: 16 x 6.5, 6-stud disc. K3500 and V3500: 16.0 x 6.5. Tires: K1500 Sportside and regular cab: LT225/75R-16C steel belted radial. K1500 club coupe: LT245/75R16C. K2500 all models: LT245/75R-16E. K3500: LT225/75RD. V3500 all models: 7.50-16D tubeless nylon. Optional: K1500: LT225/75R16C, blackwall, LT225/75R16C on-off road; blackwall, white stripe or white lettered. Available for K10903 with the following engines: LB4, LO3 and LH6 and RPO GVT4 axle; and K10703 with LB4 or LO3 engine with RPO GT4 axle: LT265/75R16C blackwall or white letter, on-off road. Optional K2500: LTR225/75R16D steel belted radial blackwall or white stripe, LT225/75R16E highway or on-off road, LT225/75R16D blackwall, on-off road, LT245/75R16E blackwall (K20903 only). Optional: K3500: LT225/75R16D, blackwall, LT245/75R16E blackwall, LT245/75R16E on-off road blackwall, LT245/75R16D blackwall or white stripe, 7.50 x 16D highway and on-off road. Optional: V3500: V30943 only: 7.50 x 16 D tubeless nylon, dual rear, LT215/85R16D dual rear tubeless steel belted radial; LT235/85R16E. Steering: Integral power. Ratio: K1500 regular cab Sportside and Wideside: 17.44:1. K1500 regular cab Wideside model K10753: 18.8:1, model K10953: 17.44:1. K2500 regular cab: 17.44:1. K2500 club coupe: K20753: 18.88:1; model K20953: 17.44:1. K3500 regular cab: 127.44:1. K3500 club coupe: 17.44:1. V3500: 13.5:1. Turning Diameter (curb-to-curb): K1500 regular cab Sportside: 40.3 ft. K1500 regular cab Wideside:

44.4 ft. K1500 club coupe model K10753: 47.9 ft., model K10953: 52.2 ft. K2500 regular cab: 44.4 ft. (with C6P: 45.1 ft.). K2500 club coupe. Model K20753: 47.9 ft., model 52.2 ft. K3500 regular cab: 45.1 ft. K3500 club coupe: 52.2 ft. V3500: 54.5 ft. Transmission: Standard K1500/2500: With gasoline engines: RPO MM5-5-spd. manual with overdrive fully-synchronized: Transmission Ratios: 4.02, 2.32, 1.40, 1.00, 0.73:1. Reverse: 3.74:1. Standard: K3500, V3500 and K2500 with C6P, and K1500 and K2500 with diesel engine: RPO MM4 4-spd. SM465 manual, synchromesh on top three gears (optional: K1500/2500). Transmission ratios: 6.55, 3.58, 1.70, 1.00:1. Reverse: 6.09:1. Optional: All series: RPO MX1-3-spd. 400 automatic. Transmission ratios: 2.48, 1.48, 1.0:1. Reverse: 2.08:1. Optional: K1500/2500, (except K2500 regular cab and club coupe chassis-cab, and all V3500 models): RPO MXO-4-spd. automatic overdrive 700R4: 3.06, 1.63, 1.0, 0.70:1. Reverse: 2.29:1

VEHICLE DIMENSIONS: Wheelbase: All series regular cab: 117.5 in., 131.5 in. Club coupe: 6.5 ft. box models: 141.5 in.; 8.0 ft. box models: 155.5 in.; V3500 models: 164.5 in. Overall Length (without rear bumper): K1500 Sportside: 194.0 in., K1500 regular cab: 194.1 in. K1500 club coupe: Model K10753 (6.5 ft. box): 223.0 in., K10953 (8.0 ft. box): 237.0 in. K2500 regular cab: 212.6 in. K2500 club coupe: Model K20753: 223.0 in., model K20953: 237.0 in. K3500 Regular cab: 212.6 in. V3500: 246.4 in. Front/Rear Tread: 74 in./74 in. Overall Height: K1500 all models: 73.8 in. K2500 regular cab: 74.3 in. (75.8 in. if equipped with C6P). K2500 club coupe: 74.4 in. (75.8 in. if equipped with C6P). K3500 75.8 in. V3500: 76.3 in. Width: All models except V3500 and those equipped with RO5: 76.8 in. V3500: 79.6 in. V3500 and K3500 with RO5: 107.3 in. Front/Rear Overhang: 117.5 in. wheelbase. Pickups: 34.9 in./41.6 in. 131.5 in. wheelbase. Pickups: 34.9 in./46.5 in. Club coupe: 34.9/46.5 in. Chassis-cab models: 34.9/41.8 in. Tailgate: Width and Height: K1500 Sportside: 50.9 x 19.3 in. All others: 62.0 in. x19.3 in. Approach/Departure Degrees: K1500 117.5 in.: 22/28. Ground Clearance (Front/Rear in inches): K1500 Sportside and Fleestside: 8.6/9.0. K1500 club coupe: 9.2/9.6. K2500 regular cab: 8.7/7.7 (with C6P: 7.8/8.1). K2500 club coupe: Model K20753: 9.2/8.2, model K20953: 9.2/8.1. K3500 regular and club coupe: 9.2/8.1 (with RO5 dual rear wheels: 7.2/7.4). V3500: 8.3/7.8. Front headroom, all models: 40.0 in. Front legroom, all models: 41.7 in. Front shoulder room, all models: 66.0 in.

CAPACITIES: Fuel Tank: All K series: 25.0 gal. All V3500 models: 20 gal. Optional: Models K10903, K10753, K10953, K20903, K20953, K30903: 34 gal. V3500 models: 20 gal.

ACCOMMODATIONS: Seating Capacity: Pickup, club coupe and chassis cab models: 3 passenger. Optional: Club coupe: 6 passenger. Suburban: 6 passenger. Optional: 9 passenger.

INSTRUMENTATION: Speedometer, odometer, fuel level gauge. Warning lights for battery, oil pressure, generator, brake system warning, directional/hazard lights, high beam, and engine coolant temperature.

OPTIONS AND PRICES: All K series: Air conditioning (RPO C60): $705, Optional Axle ratios: $44. Locking Differential (RPO G80): $252. Auxiliary heavy-duty battery, not avail. with B3J (RPO TP2): $134. Painted rear step bumper, requires E63 body (RPO V43): $130. Front Deluxe chromed bumper with rub strip, K10703 only (RPO VG3): $26. Chromed rear step bumper with rub strip (RPO VB3): $229. Front black bumper guards (RPO V27): $32. Heavy-duty chassis equipment, K1500 only (RPO F44): $38. Off-Road Package, avail. for K1500 only. Includes skid plate and Bilstein shock absorbers (RPO Z71): $270. Cold Climate Package, not avail. with B3J. Includes engine block heater (RPO V10): $33. Convenience Group. Includes power door locks and windows (RPO ZQ2): $367. Convenience Group. Includes tilt wheel and speed control (RPO ZQ3): $383. Engine oil cooling system (RPO KC4): $135. Heavy-duty radiator (RPO VO1): $56. Heavy-duty radiator and transmission oil cooler (RPO VO2): $63. Rear window defogger (RPO C49): $154. 5.0 liter V-8 (RPO LO3): $575. 5.7 liter V-8 (RPO LO5): $840. 6.2 liter diesel V-8 (RPO LH6): $... Locking fuel filler cap (RPO NO5): $18. Cargo area lamp (RPO UF2): $36. Dome and reading lamp (RPO C95): $33. Roof marker lamps, not avail. with Calif. emissions (RPO UO1): $52. Auxiliary lighting. Includes dome and reading lamps and ashtray, glovebox and under hood lamps (RPO TR9): $94. Below eye-level type stainless steel mirrors (RPO D45): $45. Camper-type stainless steel mirrors (RPO DF2): $53. Black exterior moldings (RPO B84): $90. Exterior bright moldings (RPO B85): $17. Conventional two-tone exterior paint (RPO ZY2): $132. Special two-tone exterior paint (RPO ZY3): $215. Deluxe two-tone exterior paint (RPO ZY4): $243. Electronically tuned AM/FM stereo radio with Seek-Scan and digital clock (RPO UM7): $210. Electronically tuned AM/FM stereo radio with Seek-Scan, stereo cassette tape and digital clock (RPO UM6): $332. Electronically tuned AM/FM stereo radio with Seek-Scan, stereo cassette player with Search and Repeat, graphic equalizer and digital clock (RPO UX1): $482. Radio delete option (RPO UL5): -$77. SLX Trim Package (RPO Z62): K series pickups: $573 to $604. Heavy-duty front and rear shock absorbers (RPO F51): $40. SLE Trim Package (RPO YE9): K1500 regular cab pickup: $981 to $1012. Off-road skid plate, K1500 only (RPO NZZ): $95. Heavy-duty front springs K1500 only, requires F44 heavy-duty chassis, not avail. with B3J or RPO Z71 off-road chassis (RPO F60): $63. Body striping (RPO D85): $69. Tow hooks, standard on K1500 (RPO V76): $38. Heavy-duty trailering special equipment (RPO Z82): $408 with RPO Z71 or XQ8, $448 without Z71 or ZQ8. Four-speed manual trans. (RPO MM4): $96. Four-speed auto. trans. with overdrive (RPO MXO): $860. Three-speed auto. trans. (RPO MX1): $625. Wheel-covers (RPO PO1): $42. Aluminum wheels, K1500 only (RPO PF4): $295. Sliding rear window (RPO A28): $113. Camper special chassis equipment K2500 and K3500 only (RPO Z81): $280 without B2J, $148 with B3J. Deep tinted glass, (RPO AJ1): $150. Sport Equipment Package (Sport truck), K10703 only. Includes V43 black bumpers, black wheel flares, deluxe front appearance, black mirrors, GL LT265/75R16 blackwall tires, PF4 aluminum wheels with special hubcaps and 4x4 Sport decal (RPO BPY): $1140.20. Sport steering wheel (RPO NK3): $7.00. Rear-mounted fuel tank, avail for K2500 and K3500 chassis & cab models, approximate capacity of 31 gal. (RPO NK7): $63. Special chassis camper equipment. Includes TP2 auxiliary battery without B3J equipment, camper wiring harness and DF2 mirrors (RPO Z81): $280 for K series pickups, $1436 with B3J, $81 for V3500. Dual rear wheels, available for 3500 models only. Includes plastic rear fender extensions with side marker lamps on front and rear siders and dual rear chassis provisions (RPO RO5): $1038, $1101 with MX1 trans. Includes VO2 heavy-duty radiator and trans. oil cooler, $785 for V3500.

HISTORICAL FOOTNOTES: As of July 1,1992, GMC sales were 162,486, or 22,604 ahead of the same date in 1991.

1993 PICKUP & SUBURBAN

Major mechanical improvements for 1993 included the availability of a new Hydra-Matic 4L60-E 4-speed automatic transmission as optional equipment for the Sierra pickup and standard equipment for the Suburban (on Suburbans with a GVWR over 8500 lb. a higher-capacity 4L80-E was standard). All shifts of this transmission were controlled by four solenoids that received information from the powertrain computer. Several times per second, sensors reported key information-such as engine coolant temperature, engine rpm and intake manifold pressure to the powertrain computer. The 4L60-E was used with gasoline engines with displacements between 4.3 and 5.7 liters and also the 6.2 liter diesel V-8. First gear ratio of the 4L60-E was 3.059:1 for strong take-off power while the fourth gear is 0.696:1 for highway cruising.

A new single-rail shifter for the five-speed manual transmisson reduced shift lever shake and minimized the likelihood of blocked shifts. Sierras and Suburbans with the 7.4 liter V-8 were fitted with a much larger radiator to improve cooling and reduce the likelihood of premature engine wear. The 5.0 liter V-8 had new piston rings with reduced tension for better cylinder-wall conformity, less oil consumption and higher fuel efficiency. The standard 4.3 liter V6 Sierra engine had a new, more reliable thermostat, a revised camshaft for better idle stability, and new intake manifold and cylinder head passages for better breathing. To reduce the possibility of vehicle theft, a new internal steel steering column sleeve helped protect the ignition cylinder lock on the 1993 Sierra and Suburban. Both the Sierra's and Suburban's Heating Ventilation and Air Conditioning (HVAC) was now available with a four-speed (versus three-speed) blower motor for greater passenger comfort. A revised cruise control mechanism for the Sierra and Suburban improved system performance.

A new GT Sport Truck Package featuring a monochromatic look in either fire red or bright teal metallic was available for Sierra series 1500 trucks. It also included aluminum wheels, Sport handling suspension, and Sport appearance with painted body-color grille, wheel flares and bumpers.

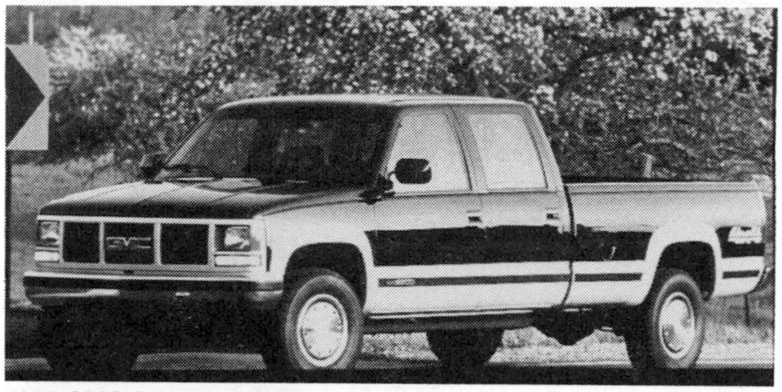

1993 GMC Sierra crew cab

The Sierra's front seats — both the optional high-back buckets and the 40/60 split bench seat had a new seat back recliner on the driver's side for additional comfort. The Suburban's available 40/60 split-bench seat and high-back bucket seats were available with a new passenger-side seat back recliner. An improved fan clutch for all Suburbans provided quieter engine operation on cold startups. All Sierras and Suburbans equipped with cloth upholstery had Scotchgard protection. Sierras and Suburbans with bench or split-bench seats had new instrument panel-mounted cupholders. All Sierra and Suburban sound systems were redesigned with larger, more user-friendly controls for more intuititive use and better overall performance. A new type of glass is standard in all Sierra and Suburban models called "Solar Ray™", it reflected undesirable wave lengths of light to keep the interior cooler on bright summer days while reducing the deteriorating effects of ultraviolet light on interior fabrics and plastics.

The Sierra was available in what even GMC admiited was "an incredibly diverse array of cab, box, trim, powertrain and chassis combinations." Major highlights of this selection included the regular cab, club coupe extended cab and four-door crew cab. The cargo boxes were offered in two interior and exterior choices. The Wideside box used all-steel construction with flush exterior design and a choice between 6.5 and 8.0 ft. bed lengths. The Sportside had composite-construction exterior panels and classic-fender styling and a 6.5 ft. bed length. Both cargo beds carried the standard 4 x 8 ft. plywood sheet between their wheelhouses. A bed delete optoin was also available. Three interior trimlevcles were again offered for the Sierra — SL, SLX and SLE — plus a special Sport model designated Sierra GT. The crew cab was offered in SL or SLE trim.

Basics of the Suburban platform continued to emphasis a variety of building blocks from which customers could select a vehicle to suit their specific needs. Five seating configurations were offered for two, three, five, six or nine passengers. A total of 149.5 cu. ft. of space was available for cargo. Two interior trim levels, SL and SE were once again available. New for 1993 was an indigo blue metallic exterior color. The standard Suburban engine was the 5.7 liter V-8 with the 7.4 liter V-8 available for the 2500 series models with GVWR of over 8500 lb. A four-wheel Anti-lock Braking System(ABS) was standard for all 1993 Suburbans. It operated in both two and four-wheel drive (four-wheel drive High).

I.D. DATA: Unchanged for 1993. The letter O represented the 1993 model year.

Prices for the 1993 models were not available at press time. What follows is a listing of 1993 models, their GVWR and Payload capacities.

Model Series	GVRW*	Payload*
K1500 Sierra Reg. Cab, 117.5 in. wb.	5600	1312/1950
K1500 Sierra Reg. Cab, 131.5 in. wb.	5600/6100	1189/1828
K2500 Sierra Reg. Cab, 131.5 in. wb.	7200/8600	2302/3811
K3500 Sierra Reg. Cab, 131.5 in. wb.	9200/10,000	3839/4670
K1500 Sierra Club Cpe., 141.5 in. wb.	6200/6600	1575/2105
K2500 Sierra Club Cpe., 141.5 in. wb.	7200	2166/2663
K1500 Sierra Club Cpe., 155.5 in. wb.	6200/6600	1323/1854
K2500 Sierra Club Cpe., 155.5 in. wb.	7200/8600	2010/3514
K3500 Sierra Club Cpe., 155.5 in. wb.	9200/10,000	3550/4394
K30943 Sierra Crew Cab, 168.5 in. wb.	9200/10,000	3154/4004
K1500 Suburban, 131.5 in. wb.	7200	2054
K2500 Suburban, 131.5 in. wb.	8600	2944

* Ratings reflect the Minimum/Maximum available.

STANDARD ENGINE: All Sierra K1500 models: 262 V-6 (LB4 ordering code). Engine Type: Vortex OHV, V-6-cylinder. Cast iron block. Bore x Stroke: 4.0 in. x 3.48 in. Lifters: Hydraulic. Fuel Induction: Electronic fuel injection. Compression Ratio: 9.1:1 (under 8500 lb. GVWR), 8.3:1 (over 8500 GVWR. Displacement: 262 cu. in. (4.3 liters). Horsepower: Net:165 @ 4000 rpm. Torque: Net: 235 lb.-ft. @ 2400 rpm. Oil refill capacity: 5 qt. with filter change. Fuel Requirements: Regular unleaded.

OPTIONAL ENGINE: Sierra models. 305 V-8 (LO3 ordering code). Engine Type: OHV, V-8. Cast iron block and cylinder head. Bore x Stroke: 3.74 in. x 3.48 in. Lifters: Hydraulic. Number of main bearings-5. Fuel Induction: Electronic fuel injection. Compression Ratio: 9.1:1. Displacement: 305 cu. in. (5.0 liters). Horsepower: 175 @ 4000 rpm. Torque: Net 270 lb.-ft. @ 2400 rpm. Oil refill capacity: 5 qt. with filter change. Fuel Requirements: Regular unleaded.

STANDARD ENGINE: Suburban, 2500 and 3500 Sierra models. 350 V-8 (LO5 ordering code). Optional other Sierra models. Engine Type: OHV, V-8. Cast iron block and cylinder head. Bore x Stroke: 4.00 in. x 3.48 in. Lifters: Hydraulic. Number of main bearings-5. Fuel Induction: Electronic fuel injection. Compression Ratio: 9.1:1 (under 8500 lb. GVWR), 8.3:1 (over 8500 lb. GVWR). Displacement: 350 cu. in. (5.7 liters). Horsepower: 210 @ 4000 rpm. (190 @ 4000 rpm for models over 8500 lb. GVWR). Torque: 300 lb.-ft. @ 2800 rpm. (300 lb.-ft. @ 2400 rpm for modesl under 8500 lb. GVWR). Oil refill capacity: 5 qt. with filter change. Fuel Requirements: Regular unleaded.

OPTIONAL ENGINE: Suburban and Sierra models. Ordering Code: L19: 454 V-8. Engine Type: OHV, V-8. Cast iron block and alloy iron cylinder head. Bore x Stroke: 4.30 in. x 4.0 in. Lifters: Hydraulic. Number of main bearings-5. Fuel Induction: Electronic fuel injection. Compression Ratio: 7.9:1. Displacement: 454 cu. in. (7.4 liters). Horsepower: 230 @ 3600 rpm. Torque: 385 lb.-ft. @ 1600 rpm. Oil refill capacity: 5 qt. with filter change. Fuel Requirements: Regular unleaded.

OPTIONAL ENGINE: Sierra models: Ordering Code LH6. Engine Type: OHV, diesel V-8. Bore x Stroke: 3.98 in. x 3.80 in. Lifters: Hydraulic. Number of main bearings-5. Fuel Induction: Gear driven mechanical fuel injection. Compression Ratio: 21.3:1. Displacement: 379.4 cu. in. (6.2 liters). Horsepower: 140 @ 3600 rpm. (LL4 heavy-duty version: 150 @ 3500 rpm). Torque: 255 lb.-ft. @ 1900 rpm. (LL4 heavy-duty version: 280 lb.-ft. @ @ 2000 rpm). Oil refill capacity: 7 qt. with filter change. Fuel Requirements: Diesel.

OPTIONAL ENGINE: Sierra pickups, and chassis and cab models over 8500 lb. GVWR and Sierra crew cab: Ordering Code L65. Engine Type: OHV, Turbocharged Diesel V-8. Bore x Stroke: 3.98 in. x 3.80 in. Lifters: Hydraulic. Number of main bearings-5. Fuel Induction: Indirect fuel injection. Compression Ratio: 21.5:1. Displacement: 379.4 cu. in. (6.2 liters). Horsepower: 190 @ 3400 rpm. Torque: 380 lb.-ft. @ 1700 rpm. Oil refill capacity: 7 qt. with filter change. Fuel Requirements: Diesel.

CHASSIS FEATURES: Semi-perimeter design, all-welded channel beam frame with boxed front end. Dimensions: K1500 and K2500 regular cab: 2.18 x 7.48 x 0.134 in. K1500 club coupe: 2.18 x 7.48 x 0.165 in. K2500 regular cab with C6P: 2.18 x 7.48 x 0.213 in. K2500 club coupe: 2.31 x 7.48 x 0.165 in. K2500 club coupe with C6P: 2.18 x 7.48 x 0.244 in. K3500 regular cab: 2.18 x 7.48 x 0.213 in. K3500 club coupe: 2.18 x 7.48 x 0.244 in. V3500 models: 2.788 x 7.74 x 0.244 in. Section modulus: K1500 regular cab: 3.46; K1500 club coupe: 4.30; K2500: 4.30; K2500 with C6P: 6.48; K3500 regular cab: 5.61; K3500 club coupe: 6.48, V3500: 7.33.

SUSPENSION AND RUNNING GEAR: Front Suspension: Torsion bar springs. K1500 Capacity: 3860 lb. K2500 and K3500 capacity: 3750 lb. V3500: Tapered leaf springs. Capacity: 4500 lb. Shock absorber dia.: K1500; 25mm; K2500, K3500 and V3500: 32mm. 32mm optional for K1500. 1.00 in. stabilizer optional for all series except V3500 which had a standard 1.25 in. bar standard. Optional rating: K1500: RPO F44/F60: 6100 lb. GVW. K2500: 8600 lb. GVW. K3500: 10,000 lb. GVW. Rear Suspension: Semi-elliptical 2-stage, 4-leaf for K1500; 6-leaf for K2500; 6-leaf plus 1-leaf auxiliary for K3500. K1500 capacity: 3750 K2500 capacity: 4800 K3500 capacity: 7500 lb. V3500: Semi-elliptical 2-stage, 9-leaf. Capacity: 7000 lb. Shock absorber dia.: K1500: 25mm; K2500, K3500 and V3500: 32mm. 32mm optional for K1500. Optional Rating: See above for GVW ratings. Front Axle Type and Capacity: Independent, GM or K1500; Spicer on K2500 and K3500. Capacity: K1500 regular cab: 3925; K1500 club coupe: 4800; K2500 and K3500: 4250 V3500: Spicer full-floating. Capacity: 4500, manual hub locks. Optional: K1500: 3925 capacity; K1500 club coupe: 4800 lb. All other K series: 4250 lb. Rear Axle Type: Semi-floating for K1500; full-floating for K2500, K3500 and V3500. GM manufacture for all series. Capacity: K1500: 3750, K2500: 6000; K3500, V3500: 7500 lb. Optional: K2500: Regular cab: 4800 lb.; K2500 club coupe: 6000; K3500: 7500. Final Drive Ratio: Standard: Suburban and Sierra: 3.08:1 Sierra crew cab: 4.10:1. Optional: Suburban and Sierra: 3.42 (Suburban, available only with 5.7 liter V-8), 3.43 (Sierra), 3.73, 4.10:1. Sierra crew cab: 4.56:1. Transfer Case: K1500, K2500, K3500: New Process 241. Single lever. Ratios: 2.72:1, 1.00:1. K3500 with RPO RO5: Borg Warner 1370: Ratios: 2.69:1, 1.00:1. The Borg Warner unit has a right hand side power take-off. Brakes: Type: Hydraulic, power assisted. Dimensions: K1500: Front: Disc: 11.86 in. x 1.00 in. Rear: Drums: 10.0 x 2.25 in. K1500 regular cab with RPO F44/F60 had 11.57 in. x 1.25 in. front disc brakes. K2500 regular cab: Front: Disc: 11.57 in. x 1.20 in. Rear: Drums: 11.15 in. x 2.75 in. K2500 club coupe: Front Disc: 11.57 in. x 1.25 in. Rear: 10.0 in. x 2.25 in. drums. All K2500 with 8600 lb. GVW Package had 12.50 in. x 1.26 in. front disc brakes and 13.0 in. x 2.5 in. rear drum brakes. K3500 All models: Front: Disc: 12.50 in. x 1.26 in. Rear: Drum: 13.00 in.x 2.50 in. V3500 All models: Front Disc: 12.54 in. x 1.54 in. Rear: Drums: 13.0 in. x 3.5 in. Wheels: K1500 and K2500: 16 x 6.5, 6-stud disc. K3500 and V3500: 16.0 x 6.0. Tires: K1500 Sportside and regular cab: LT225/75R-16C steel belted radial. K1500 club coupe: LT245/75R16C. K2500 all models: LT245/75R-16E. K3500: LT225/75RD. V3500 all models: 7.50-16D tubeless nylon. Optional: K1500: LT225/75R16C, blackwall, LT225/75R16C on-off road; blackwall, white stripe or white lettered. Available for K10903 only with the following engines: LB4, LO3 and LH6 and RPO GVT4 axle; and K10703 with LB4 or LO3 engine with RPO GT4 axle: LT265/75R16C blackwall or white letter, on-off road. Optional K2500: LTR225/75R16D steel belted radial blackwall or white stripe, LT245/75R16E highway or on-off road, LT225/75R16D blackwall, on-off road, LT245/75R16E blackwall (K20903 only). Optional: K3500: LT225/75R16D, blackwall, LT245/75R16E blackwall, LT245/75R16E on-off road blackwall, LT245/75R16E blackwall, 7.50 x 16D highway and on-off road. Optional: V3500: V30943 only: 7.50 x 16 D tubeless nylon, dual rear, LT215/85R16D dual rear tubeless steel belted radial; LT235/85R16E. Steering: Integral power. Ratio: K1500 regular cab Sportside and Wideside: 17.44:1. K1500 club coupe model K10753: 18.8:1, model K10953: 17.44:1. K2500 regular cab: 17.44:1. K2500 club coupe: K20753: 18.88:1; model K20953: 17.44:1. K3500 regular cab: 127.44:1. K3500 club coupe: 17.44:1. V3500: 13.5:1. Turning Diameter (curb-to-curb): K1500 regular cab Sportside: 40.3 ft. K1500 regular cab Wideside: 44.4 ft. K1500 club coupe model K10753: 47.9 ft., model K10953: 52.2 ft. K2500 regular cab: 44.4 ft. (with C6P: 45.1 ft.). K2500 club coupe: Model K20753: 47.9 ft., model 52.2 ft. K3500 regular cab: 45.1 ft. K3500 club coupe: 52.2 ft. V3500: 54.5 ft. Transmission: Standard K1500/2500: With gasoline engines: RPO MM5-5-spd. manual with overdrive fully-synchronized: Transmission Ratios: 4.02, 2.32, 1.40, 1.00, 0.73:1; Reverse: 3.74:1. Standard: K3500, V3500 and K2500 with C6P, and K1500 and K2500 with diesel engine: RPO MM4 4-spd. SM465 manual, synchromesh on top three gears (optional: K1500/2500). Transmission ratios: 6.55, 3.58, 1.70, 1.00:1. Reverse: 6.09:1. Optional: Sierra: Hydra-Matic 4L60-E. Suburban: Hydra-Matic 4L80-E. Transmission ratios: Hydra-Matic 4L60-E: 3.06, 1.63, 1.00, 0.70:1. Reverse: 2.29:1 Hydra-Matic 4L80-E: 2.48, 1.48, 1.00, 0.75:1. Reverse: 2.08:1.

VEHICLE DIMENSIONS: Wheelbase: Suburban: 131.5 in. Sierra regular cab: 117.5 in., 131.5 in. Club coupe: 6.5 ft. box models: 141.5 in.; 8.0 ft. box models: 155.5 in.; crew cab: 168.5 in. Overall Length Suburban: 219.5 in. Sierra regular cab: Short Box: 194.1 in. Long Box: 212.6 in. Sierra club coupe: Short Box: 218.0 in. Long Box: 237.0 in. Sierra crew cab: 255.4 in. Front/Rear Tread: Suburban: Series 1500: 645.1 in./63.5 in.; series 2500: 68.6 in./53.9 in. Sierra regular cab and club coupe: 64.1 in./63.5 in. Sierra crew cab: 68.6 in./67.1 in. Overall Height: Suburban: 73.6 in. Sierra regular cab and club coupe: 73.8 in. Sierra crew cab: 71.7 in. Width: Suburban: 77.0 in. Sierra regular cab and club coupe: Wideside: 76.8 in.; Sportside: 77.1 in. Sierra crew cab:76.8 in. Ground Clearance Minimum: Suburban and Sierra regular cab: 8.6 in. Sierra club coupe: 9.2 in. Sierra crew cab: 7.7 in. Front headroom: All models 40.0 in. Front legroom, all models: 41.7 in. Front shoulder room, all models: 66.0 in.

CAPACITIES: Fuel Tank: Sierra regular cab and club coupe: 34 gal. Sportside and Short box: 25 gal. Suburban: 42 gal. Sierra crew cab: 34 gal.

ACCOMMODATIONS: Seating Capacity: Pickup, club coupe and chassis cab models: 3 passenger. Optional: Club coupe: 6 passenger. Suburban: 6 passenger. Optional: 9 passenger.

INSTRUMENTATION: Speedometer, odometer, fuel level gauge. Warning lights for battery, oil pressure, generator, brake system warning, directional/hazard lights, high beam, and engine coolant temperature.

OPTIONS AND PRICES: A full listing of GMC options and prices was not available at press time. However, it was expected that most of the items offered for 1992 would be carried into 1993 with modest price increases.

HISTORICAL FOOTNOTES: The truck wagon market, where the GMC Suburban was positioned, represented between 2.0 and 2.5 percent of the total light-duty truck market. In that segment, the GMC Suburban and its Chevrolet counterpart acounted for 90 percent of all sales as the 1993 model year began.

GMC JIMMY
1970-1991

1970 JIMMY

The GMC Jimmy followed Chevrolet's Blazer to the four-wheel drive market by one year. The two vehicles were virtually identical in their technical specifications. The Jimmy had a familiar GMC grille with broad vertical and horizontal divider bars. Large GMC lettering was positioned on the leading edge of the hood. A choice of 15 exterior colors were offered. The Jimmy's optional fiberglass top was available in either a black or white textured paint finish. It was equipped with a lockable lift gate. Standard Jimmy equipment included heater and defroster, two-speed windshield wipers, side marker reflectors, hazard warning switch, directional signals, dual hydraulic brake system, back-up lights, driver's seat belt, padded sun visors, inside mirror, left and right-side exterior mirrors and water-proofed horn button, ignition switch and instrument cluster.

1970 GMC Jimmy

I.D. DATA: The Jimmy's V.I.N. consisted of 12 symbols. The first (a letter) identified the chassis. The second (a letter) identified the engine. The third (a digit) indicated the GVW range. The fourth entry (a digit) identified the model type. The fifth (a digit) identified the model year. The sixth (a letter) identified the assembly plant. The last six elements (all digits) served as the sequential production numbers. The combination V.I.N./GVW number was located on the left door pillar. The engine number indicated the manufacturing plant, day of manufacture and transmission type. It was located on a pad positioned on the right-hand side of the cylinder block at the rear of the distributor on V-8 engines and on a pad located at the front right hand side of the cylinder block of 6-cylinder engines.

Model Number	Body Type & Seating	Factory Price	GVW	Shipping Weight	Prod. Total
Jimmy K1550					
KS11514	Utility	$2947	4600*	3595	—

* 5000 lb. GVW optional.

STANDARD ENGINE: High Torque 250 Six: (KS prefix). Engine Type: OHV, In-line 6-cylinder. Bore x Stroke: 3.875 in. x 3.50 in. Lifters: Hydraulic. Number of main bearings-7. Carburetion: Single barrel Rochester downdraft. Compression Ratio: 8.5:1. Displacement: 250 cu. in. (4.09 liters). Horsepower: Gross: 155 @ 4200 rpm. Net: 125 @ 3800 rpm. Torque: Gross: 235 lb.-ft. @ 1600 rpm. Net: 215 @ 2000 rpm. Oil capacity: 5 qt. with filter change. Fuel Requirements: Regular.

STANDARD ENGINE: V-8 models (KE prefix): Engine Type: OHV, V-8. Bore x Stroke: 3.875 in. x 3.25 in. Lifters: Hydraulic. Number of main bearings-5. Carburetion: 2-barrel Rochester. Compression Ratio: 9.0:1. Displacement: 307 cu. in. (5.03 liters). Horsepower: Gross: 200 @ 4600 rpm. Net: 157 @ 4000 rpm. Torque: Gross: 300 lb.-ft. @ 2400 rpm. Net: 260 @ 2000 rpm. Oil capacity: 5 qt. with filter change. Fuel Requirements: Regular.

OPTIONAL ENGINE: V-8 models: Engine Type: OHV V-8. Bore x Stroke: 4.00 in. x 3.50 in. Lifters: Hydraulic. Number of main bearings-5. Displacement: 350 cu. in. (5.73 liters). Carburetion: Single 4-barrel Rochester. Compression Ratio: 9.0:1. Horsepower: Gross: 255 @ 4600 rpm. Net: 200 @ 4000 rpm. Torque: Gross: 355 lb.-ft. @ 3000 rpm. Net: 310 @ 2400 rpm. Fuel Requirements: Regular.

CHASSIS FEATURES: Ladder-type, heavy-gauge channel side members, alligator-jaw cross members. Section modulus: 2.70 in.

SUSPENSION AND RUNNING GEAR: Front Suspension: Tapered single leaf. Capacity: 2900 lb. Optional: 3500 lb. capacity. Rear Suspension: Two-stage tapered and multi-leaf (four-conventional leaves, one tapered leaf). Capacity: 3600 lb. Optional: None. Front Axle. Type: Hypoid, tubular driving. Capacity: 3300 lb. Rear Axle. Type: Hypoid, semi-floating. Capacity: 3300 lb. Final Drive Ratio: 3.73:1 (3.07:1 with 350 V-8). Optional: 3.07:1. Transfer Case: Type: Manual transmission: Dana 20. Ratios: 2.03:1, 1.00:1. Automatic transmission: New Process 205. Ratios: 1.96:1, 1.00:1. Brakes: Type: Hydraulic, drums. Optional: Power. Dimensions:

Front and rear: 11.0 in. x 2.00 in. Total lining area: 167 sq. in. Wheels: 6-stud, 5.5 in. Optional: 6-stud, 5.0 in. and 6.0 in. Tires: E78 x 15B. Optional: Nine different tires sizes were offered including G78 x 15B, H78 x 15B, 8.75 x 16.5, 10.00 x 16.5, G78 x 15B, 6.50 x 16, 7.00 x 15. Steering: Manual recirculating ball. Ratio: 24.0:1. Optional: Power-assisted. Transmission: Type: Saginaw 3-speed manual, fully synchronized. Steering column-mounted shifter. Transmission Ratios: 2.85, 1.68, 1.0:1. Reverse: 2.95:1. Optional: CH465 4-speed manual floor-mounted shift lever. Optional: Turbo Hydra-Matic 3-speed automatic. Clutch: Six-cylinder: 10.0 in. dia.,100 sq. in. area. V-8: Type: 11.0 in. dia., 124 sq. in. area. Optional: V-8-cylinder: 12.0 in., 150 sq. in.

VEHICLE DIMENSIONS: Wheelbase: 104 in. Overall Length: 177.5 in. Front/Rear Tread 64.0 in./61.0 in. Overall Height: 68.5 in. With optional hardtop: 72.75 in. Width: 79.0 in. Front/Rear Overhang: 33.25 in./40.25 in. Tailgate: Width and Height: 65.0 in. x 19.25 in. Approach/Departure Degrees: 35.2/25.0. Ground Clearance: Front axle: 8.0 in. Rear axle: 8.0 in. Load space: With rear seat removed or folded: 70.0 in. x 65.0 in. x 19.25 in.

CAPACITIES: Fuel Tank: 23.5 gal. Optional: None. Coolant system: 250 6-cyl.: 12.2 qt. 307 V-8: 18.5 qt. 350 V-8: 17.1 qt.

ACCOMMODATIONS: Seating Capacity: Standard: Driver. Optional: Driver and front passenger and/or 3 passenger rear bench seat.

INSTRUMENTATION: Speedometer, odometer, fuel level gauge; warning lights for generator, engine coolant temperature and oil pressure. Brake warning light. Hazard warning switch.

OPTIONS AND PRICES: Fiberglass top. 11 in. clutch for 6-cyl. Front passenger seat. Rear bench seat. 307 cu. in. V-8. 350 cu. in. V-8. various tire sizes. 3.07:1 axle ratio (350 and 307 engines only). Oil bath air cleaner (not available with 350 V-8 and automatic transmission). Engine governor (not available with 350 V-8 and automatic transmission). Power steering. Power brakes. Front bucket seats. Carpeting. Radio. Soft-Ray tinted glass. Air conditioning. Bright exterior trim. Bright wheelcovers. Chrome hubcaps. Chrome front and rear bumpers. Chrome shift lever. Heavy-duty shock absorbers. Heavy-duty clutch. Heavy-duty radiator (standard with 350 V-8). Fuel filter. Heavy-duty shock absorbers. Heavy-duty starter. Shoulder harnesses. Super custom truck option: $358. Includes special exterior trim, front bucket seats, right-hand armrest and color-keyed floor coverings. Towing hooks. Free wheeling front hubs. Courtesy lights. Spare tire lock.

HISTORICAL FOOTNOTES: GMC described the new Jimmy as "the all-new, all-purpose mini-taskmaster...the size surprise of the year."

1971 JIMMY

Except for the positioning of engine identification plaques below the front fender side marker lights, the 1971 Jimmy was unchanged in external appearance. The latest models was fitted with standard front disc brakes and continued to be offered with an optional removable fiberglass top in either black or textured white finish. A choice of 15 external colors were offered. As in 1970, standard equipment included front and rear painted bumpers, front compartment black, embossed floor mat, Deluxe-Air heater and defroster, exterior chrome plated right side mirror, and electric 2-speed windshield wipers and windshield washer.

1971 GMC Jimmy

I.D. DATA: The Jimmy's V.I.N. consisted of 12 symbols. The first (a letter) identified the chassis. The second (a letter) identified the engine. The third (a digit) indicated the GVW range. The fourth entry (a digit) identified the model type. The fifth (a digit) identified the model year. The sixth (a letter) identified the assembly plant. The last six elements (all digits) served as the sequential production numbers. The combination V.I.N./GVW number was located on the left door pillar. The engine number indicated the manufacturing plant, day of manufacture and transmission type. It was located on a pad positioned on the right-hand side of the cylinder block at the rear of the distributor on V-8 engines and on a pad located at the front right hand side of the cylinder block of 6-cylinder engines.

Jimmy K1550

Model Number	Body Type & Seating	Factory Price	GVW	Shipping Weight	Prod. Total
KS15514	Util. (6-cyl.)	$3253	4600*	3595	—
KE15514	Util. (V-8)	$3374	4600	3690	—

* 5000 GVW Package optional.

STANDARD ENGINE: 250 Six: (KS prefix). Engine Type: OHV, In-line 6-cylinder. Bore x Stroke: 3.875 in. x 3.50 in. Lifters: Hydraulic. Number of main bearings-7. Carburetion: Rochester downdraft one-barrel, model M7028007 or M7028011. Compression Ratio: 8.5:1. Displacement: 250 cu. in. (4.09 liters). Horsepower: Gross. 145 @ 4200 rpm. Net: 110 @ 4000 rpm. Torque: Gross: 230 lb.-ft. @ 1600 rpm. Net: 185 @ 1600 rpm. Oil capacity: 5 qt. with filter change. Fuel Requirements: Regular.

STANDARD ENGINE: V-8 models (KE prefix): Engine Type: OHV, V-8. Bore x Stroke: 3.875 in. x 3.25 in. Lifters: Hydraulic. Number of main bearings-5. Carburetion: 2-barrel Rochester. Compression Ratio: 8.5:1. Displacement: 307 cu. in. (5.03 liters). Horsepower: Gross: 200 @ 4600 rpm. Net: 135 @ 4000 rpm. Torque: Gross: 300 lb.-ft. @ 2400 rpm. Net: 235 @ 2000 rpm. Oil capacity: 5 qt. with filter change. Fuel Requirements: Regular.

OPTIONAL ENGINE: V-8 models: Engine Type: OHV V-8. Bore x Stroke: 4.00 in. x 3.50 in. Lifters: Hydraulic. Number of main bearings-5. Displacement: 350 cu. in. (5.73 liters). Carburetion: Single 4-barrel Rochester. Compression Ratio: 8.5:1. Horsepower: Gross: 250 @ 4600 rpm. Net: 170 @ 3600 rpm. Torque: Gross: 350 lb.-ft. @ 3000 rpm. Net: 310 @ 2400 rpm. Fuel Requirements: Regular.

CHASSIS FEATURES: Ladder-type, heavy-gauge channel side members, alligator-jaw cross members. Section modulus: 2.70 in.

SUSPENSION AND RUNNING GEAR: Front Suspension: Tapered single leaf. Capacity: 2900 lb. Optional: 3500 lb. capacity springs and heavy-duty shock absorbers. Rear Suspension: Two-stage tapered and multi-leaf (four-conventional leaves, one tapered leaf). Capacity: 3600 lb. Optional: None. Front Axle. Type: Hypoid, tubular driving. Capacity: 3300 lb. Rear Axle. Type: Hypoid, semi-floating. Capacity: 3300 lb. Final Drive Ratio: 6-cyl.: 3.73:1. 307 V-8: 3.73:1 with 3-speed manual and CH465 4-speed manual; 3.07:1 with Turbo Hydra-Matic. 350 V-8: 3.07:1. Optional: 3.73:1, for 350 V-8 only. Transfer Case: Type: Manual transmission: Dana 20. Ratios: 2.03:1, 1.00:1. Automatic transmission: New Process 205. Ratios: 1.96:1, 1.00:1. Brakes: Type: Hydraulic, Front: Disc. Rear: Drums. Optional: Power. Dimensions: Front disc: 11.86 in. rotor. Rear: 11.0 in. x 2.00 in. Rear brake area: 138.2 sq. in. Wheels: 6-stud,15 x 6.0 in. Tires: E78 x 15B. Optional: Steering: Manual recirculating ball. Ratio: 24.0:1. Optional: Power-assisted. Transmission: Type: SM-326 3-speed manual, fully synchronized. Steering column-mounted shifter. Transmission Ratios: 2.85, 1.68, 1.0:1. Reverse: 2.95:1. Optional: SM-465 4-speed manual floor-mounted shift lever. Optional: Turbo Hydra-Matic 3-speed automatic. 350 V-8 available only with CH465 or Turbo Hydra-Matic. Clutch: Six-cylinder: 10.0 in. dia.,100 sq. in. area. 307 V-8: Type: 11.0 in. dia., 124 sq. in. area. 350 V-8: 12 in. clutch, 150 sq. in. area. Optional: 11.0 in. heavy-duty. available for standard 3-speed only; included when 4-speed manual transmission is ordered.

VEHICLE DIMENSIONS: Wheelbase: 104 in. Overall Length: 177.5 in. Front/Rear Tread 64.0 in./61.0 in. Overall Height: 68.5 in. With optional hardtop; 72.75 in. Width: 79.0 in. Front/Rear Overhang: 33.25 in./40.25 in. Tailgate: Width and Height: 65.0 in. x 19.25 in. Approach/ Departure Degrees: 35.2/25.0. Ground Clearance: Front axle: 8.0 in. Rear axle: 8.0 in. Load space: With rear seat removed or folded: 70.0 in. x 65.0 in. x 19.25 in.

CAPACITIES: Fuel Tank: 21.0 gal. Optional: None. Coolant system: 250 6-cyl.: 12.2 qt. 307 V-8: 18.5 qt. 350 V-8: 17.1 qt.

ACCOMMODATIONS: Seating Capacity: Standard: Driver. Optional: Driver and front passenger and/or 3 passenger rear bench seat.

INSTRUMENTATION: Speedometer, odometer, fuel level gauge; warning lights for generator, engine coolant temperature and oil pressure. Brake warning light. Hazard warning switch.

OPTIONS AND PRICES: Super Custom Truck Package. Includes bucket seats, console, right hand sunshade and armrest, cigarette lighter, nameplates, special insulation, undercoating, chromed bumpers, bright control knob and pedal trim, bright windshield, body side, tailgate, taillight and back-up light molding, bright fuel filler cap, side marker reflectors and bright transfer case shift lever: $364.45 (With auxiliary top). Also includes bright vent window molding, door and body trim panels with bright upper retainers, spare tire cover and front color-keyed carpeting: $301.25. (Without auxiliary top). Also includes front color-keyed vinyl coated rubber floor mat). 350 V-8: Turbo Hydra-Matic: $242.25. 4-speed manual transmission: $110.60. 3.07:1 rear axle: $12.65 with 3-spd. trans.; $19.00 with 4-spd. or Turbo Hydra-Matic. 3.73:1 axle ratio. Available only when 350 engine is ordered with 4-spd. or Turbo Hydra-Matic is ordered with 307 V-8: $12.65. Positraction: $65.30. Oil bath air cleaner. Not available with 350 engine: $10.55. All-Weather air conditioning, V-8 models only: $421.30. Auxiliary battery: $47.40. Heavy-duty 80 amp-hr. battery: $16.90. Rear seat belts: $6.85. Chrome front and rear bumpers: $31.60. Chrome hubcaps: $13.70. Heavy-duty 11 in. clutch. Available only for KS1550 with 3-spd. trans.: $6.85. Heavy-duty radiator: $26.35. Ammeter, engine coolant temperature and oil pressure gauges: $12.65. Tachometer, ammeter, engine coolant temperature and oil pressure gauges: $57.95. 402 amp Delcotron generator: $23.20. 61 amp Delcotron generator: $31.60. Door glass (frameless drop glass windows and framed vent window glass). Included when auxiliary top is ordered: $42.15 without Super custom truck; $52.70 with Super custom truck. Also includes chromed vent window moldings. Soft-Ray glass. Available only when auxiliary top or door glass is ordered: $19.00 with door glass: $30.55 with auxiliary top. Door edge guards: $6.35. Two front towing hooks. Not available when chromed bumpers or Super custom truck are ordered: $19.

HISTORICAL FOOTNOTES: GMC reminded potential customers that "Good things come in small packages. GMC's Jimmy is no exception."

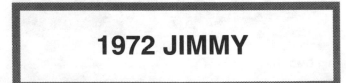

1972 JIMMY

The 1972 Jimmy was essentially unchanged in exterior appearance from its 1971 form. Both the 307 and 350 cu. in. V-8 engines now were fitted with exhaust valve rotators. For 1972 all GMC engines were designed to operate on no-lead or low-lead gasoline. If neither type was available, any leaded regular gasoline with a Research Octane Rating Number of 91 or higher could be used. The Super custom truck option was continued. It included special exterior trim items, twin front bucket seats with simulated tooled western motif, color-keyed floor covering and cigarette lighter.

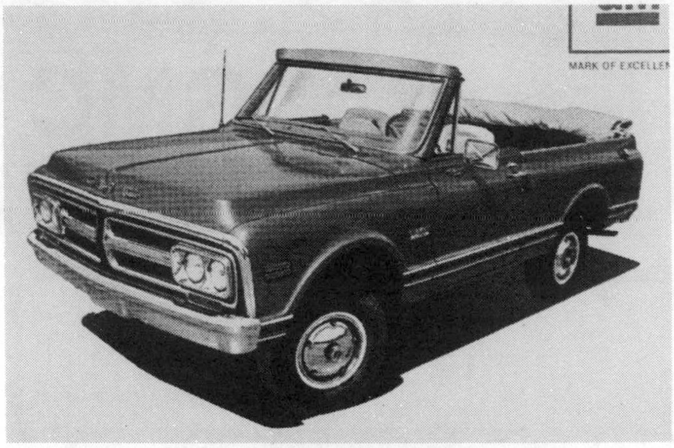

1972 GMC Jimmy with dealer-installed soft top

I.D. DATA: The Jimmy's V.I.N. consisted of 13 symbols. The first symbol (a letter) identified the GMC Division. The second symbol (a letter) indicated vehicle type. The third symbol (a letter) indicated engine type. The fourth symbol (a number) identified the tonnage. The fifth symbol indicatedmodel type. The sixth symbol identified the model year. The seventh symbol (a letter) indicated the assembly plant. The remaining six digits served as the sequential production numbers. The V.I.N. number was located on the left door pillar. The engine number indicated the manufacturing plant, day of manufacture and transmission type. It was located on a pad positioned on the right-hand side of the cylinder block at the rear of the distributor on V-8 engines and on a pad located at the front right hand side of the cylinder block of 6-cylinder engines.

Model Number	Body Type & Seating	Factory Price	GVW	Shipping Weight	Prod. Total
Jimmy K1550. With 307 V-8: Model KE10514. With 6-cyl.: Model KS10514					
KE15514	Utility	$3266	4600*	3830	—

* 5600 GVW Package optional.

STANDARD ENGINE: In-Line 250 Six. (KS prefix). Engine Type: OHV, In-line 6-cylinder. Bore x Stroke: 3.875 in. x 3.50 in. Lifters: Hydraulic. Number of main bearings-7. Carburetion: Rochester downdraft one-barrel, model M7028007 or M7028011. Compression Ratio: 8.5:1. Displacement: 250 cu. in. (4.09 liters). Horsepower: Net: 110 @ 3800 rpm. Torque: Gross: Net: 185 @ 1600 rpm. Oil capacity: 5 qt. with filter change. Fuel Requirements: No-lead or low-lead gasoline.

STANDARD ENGINE: Invader V-8, V-8 models (KE prefix). Not available in California. Engine Type: OHV, V-8. Bore x Stroke: 3.875 in. x 3.25 in. Lifters: Hydraulic. Number of main bearings-5. Carburetion: 2-barrel Rochester. Compression Ratio: 8.5:1. Displacement: 307 cu. in. (5.03 liters). Horsepower: Net: 135 @ 4000 rpm. Torque: Gross: Net: 230 @ 2400 rpm. Oil capacity: 5 qt. with filter change. Fuel Requirements: No-lead or low-lead gasoline.

OPTIONAL ENGINE: Invader V-8: V-8 models: Engine Type: OHV V-8. Bore x Stroke: 4.00 in. x 3.50 in. Lifters: Hydraulic. Number of main bearings-5. Displacement: 350 cu. in. (5.73 liters). Carburetion: Single 4-barrel Rochester. Compression Ratio: 8.5:1. Horsepower: Net: 175 @ 4000 rpm. Torque: Net: 290 @ 2400 rpm. Fuel Requirements: No-lead or low-lead gasoline.

CHASSIS FEATURES: Ladder-type, heavy-gauge channel side members, alligator-jaw cross members. Section modulus: 2.70 in.

SUSPENSION AND RUNNING GEAR: Front Suspension: Tapered single leaf. Capacity: 2900 lb. Optional: 3500 lb. capacity springs and heavy-duty shock absorbers. Rear Suspension: Two-stage tapered and multi-leaf (four-conventional leaves, one tapered leaf). Capacity: 3600 lb. Optional: None. Front Axle. Type: Hypoid, tubular driving. Capacity: 3300 lb. Rear Axle. Type: Hypoid, semi-floating. Capacity: 3300 lb. Final Drive Ratio: 6-cyl.: 3.73:1. 307 V-8: 3.73:1 with 3-speed manual and CH465 4-speed manual; 3.07:1 with Turbo Hydra-Matic. 350 V-8: 3.07:1. Optional: 3.73:1, for 350 V-8 only. Transfer Case: Type: Manual transmission: Dana 20. Ratios: 2.03:1, 1.00:1. Automatic transmission: New Process 205. Ratios: 1.96:1, 1.00:1. Brakes: Type: Hydraulic, Front: Disc. Rear: Drums. Optional: Power. Dimensions: Front disc: 11.86 in. rotor. Rear: 11.0 in. x 2.00 in. Rear brake area: 138.2 sq. in. Wheels: 6-stud,15 x 6.0 in. Tires: E78 x 15B. Optional: Steering: Manual recirculating ball. Ratio: 24.0:1. Optional: Power-assisted. Transmission: Type: SM-326 3-speed manual, fully synchronized. Steering column-mounted shifter. Transmission Ratios: 2.85, 1.68, 1.0:1. Reverse: 2.95:1. Optional: SM-465 4-speed manual.floor-mounted shift lever. Optional: Turbo Hydra-Matic 3-speed automatic. 350 V-8 available only with SM-465 or Turbo Hydra-Matic. Clutch: Six-cylinder: 10.0 in. dia.,100 sq. in. area. 307 V-8: Type: 11.0 in. dia., 124 sq. in. area. 350 V-8: 12 in. clutch, 150 sq. in. area. Optional: 11.0 in. heavy-duty. Available for standard 3-speed only; included when 4-speed manual transmission is ordered.

VEHICLE DIMENSIONS: Wheelbase: 104 in. Overall Length: 177.5 in. Front/Rear Tread 64.0 in./ 61.0 in. Overall Height: 68.5 in. With optional hardtop; 72.75 in. Width: 79.0 in. Front/Rear Overhang: 33.25 in./40.25 in. Tailgate: Width and Height: 65.0 in. x 19.25 in. Approach/ Departure Degrees: 35.2/25.0. Ground Clearance: Front axle: 8.0 in. Rear axle: 8.0 in. Load space: With rear seat removed or folded: 70.0 in. x 65.0 in. x 19.25 in.

CAPACITIES: Fuel Tank: 21.0 gal. Optional: None. Coolant system: 250 6-cyl.: 12.2 qt. 307 V-8: 18.5 qt. 350 V-8: 17.1 qt.

ACCOMMODATIONS: Seating Capacity: Standard: Driver. Optional: Driver and front passenger and/or 3 passenger rear bench seat.

INSTRUMENTATION: Speedometer, odometer, fuel level gauge; warning lights for generator, engine coolant temperature and oil pressure. Brake warning light. Hazard warning switch.

OPTIONS AND PRICES: Fiberglass top. 10 in., 11 in. and 12 in. clutches. Front passenger seat. Rear bench seat. 307 cu. in. V-8. 350 cu. in. V-8. various tire sizes. 3.07:1 axle ratio (350 and 307 engines only). Oil bath air cleaner (not available with 350 V-8 and automatic transmission). Engine governor (not available with 350 V-8 and automatic transmission). Power steering. Power brakes. Auxiliary battery. Front bucket seats. Carpeting. Radio. Soft-Ray tinted glass. Air conditioning. Bright exterior trim. Bright wheelcovers. Chrome hubcaps. Chrome front and rear bumpers. Chrome shift lever. Heavy-duty shock absorbers. Heavy-duty clutch. Heavy-duty radiator (standard with 350 V-8). Fuel filter. Heavy-duty shock absorbers. Heavy-duty starter. Shoulder harnesses. Super custom truck option: $365. Towing hooks. Free wheeling front hubs. Courtesy lights. Spare tire lock.

HISTORICAL FOOTNOTES: GMC referred to the Jimmy as a vehicle with an "Old Name" but of a "New Breed" that "wears its nameplate with pride as it carries on a worldwide tradition for on/off road dependability."

1973 JIMMY

The 1973 Jimmy was easily identified by its all-new exterior. Highlighted by the use of curved glass for the door and rear quarter windows and rectangular-shaped and flared wheel cutouts. Total glass area was also substantially increased. Replacing the liftgate used on the older model was a crank up or down rear window. At the rear functional wraparound taillights were used. A new design fiberglass top with thicker side sections, thinner top and stiffening ribs in the roof for increased rigidity was offered. Models with automatic transmission and V-8 engines, a full-time four-wheel drive system. Details of this system are found in the 1973 Chevrolet Blazer section. The latest Jimmy was slighter larger than the original model. Its wheelbase was increased by 2.5 inches and overall length was extended 4 inches. The 1973 Jimmy, also had a cooling system in which the older tube and center type radiator core was replaced by a multi-louver unit with increased surface area to more efficiently transfer engine heat. A larger water pump was installed with V-8 engines and all units were of a more durable design.

The new GMC Jimmy front suspension now included a standard stabilizer bar. Both the length and width of the front springs were increased. The rear springs were now canted outward. The front spring rates were lowered for 1973 while those at the rear were stiffer. The Jimmy interior was also modernized to incorporate a cockpit-type instrument panel format with the controls and instruments located in a partial oval mounted directly in front of the driver. It included an integral automatic transmission indicator dial, courtesy light, labeled control knobs and, if factory air conditioning was installed, four (three were provided in 1972) air outlets. The air conditioning system was also upgraded for 1973 with an improved condenser and increased air flow. An energy absorbing steering column was introduced for 1973. The Jimmy's front doors were equipped with interior push-button locks that, if depressed while closing the door, locked the doors automatically. The front bucket seats and optional rear bench seat were carried over for 1973 but new vinyl covered door panels were used incorporating elastic topped pockets useful for storage of small items. The 1973 Jimmy's factory installed radio used an antenna embedded in the windshield. The Jimmy was offered in either standard custom or optional Sierra trim. The standard trim included bright grille work, chrome finished left and right hand exterior mirrors, front and rear white painted bumpers and white painted wheels. Except for slightly lower power ratings the same three engines offered in 1972 were available for the 1973 Jimmy. The 1973 exterior color selection consisted of light skyline blue, medium Hawaiian blue, dark Catalina blue, lime green, moss green, dark glenwood green, Spanish gold, sunset gold, burnt orange, crimson red, desert sand, Sport silver, Mojave tan, Marine turquoise and frost white.

I.D. DATA: The Jimmy's V.I.N. consisted of 13 symbols. The first symbol (a letter) identified the GMC Division. The second symbol (a letter) indicated vehicle type. The third symbol (a letter) indicated engine type. The fourth symbol (a number) identified the tonnage. The fifth symbol indicated model type. The sixth symbol identified the model year. The seventh symbol (a letter) indicated the assembly plant. The remaining six digits served as the sequential production numbers. The V.I.N. number was located on the left door pillar. The engine number indicated the manufacturing plant, day of manufacture and transmission type. It was located on a pad positioned on the right-hand side of the cylinder block at the rear of the distributor on V-8 engines and on a pad located at the front right hand side of the cylinder block of 6-cylinder engines. GMC adopted a new light-duty model series identification for 1973. The first symbol (a letter-T) identified the GMC division. The second symbol (a letter-K) indicated vehicle type-four-wheel drive. The third symbol (a number) indicated series 1-series 10. The next two entries (digits) indicated CA dimensions-05. The next two components (digits) identify body style; Jimmy-14. Finally, three entries (a letter followed by two numbers) served as the body code, Jimmy-ZW9.

Model Number	Body Type & Seating	Factory Price	GVW	Shipping Weight	Prod. Total
Jimmy K10. (with 307 V-8)					
TK10514	Utility	$3319	4600*	3757	—

* 4900, 5350, 5800, 6200 lb. GVW Package optional.

STANDARD ENGINE: 250 Six: Ordering Code: LD4. Engine Type: OHV, In-line 6-cylinder. Bore x Stroke: 3.875 in. x 3.50 in. Lifters: Hydraulic. Number of main bearings-7. Carburetion: Rochester downdraft one-barrel, model M7028007 or M7028011. Compression Ratio: 8.5:1. Displacement: 250 cu. in. (4.09 liters). Horsepower: Net: 100 @ 3600 rpm. Torque: Net: 175 lb.-ft. @ 2000 rpm. Oil capacity: 5 qt. with filter change. Fuel Requirements: No-lead or low-lead gasoline.

STANDARD ENGINE: Invader V-8, V-8 models: Ordering Code: LG8. Engine Type: OHV, V-8. Bore x Stroke: 3.875 in. x 3.25 in. Lifters: Hydraulic. Number of main bearings-5. Carburetion: 2-barrel Rochester. Compression Ratio: 8.5:1. Displacement: 307 cu. in. (5.03 liters). Horsepower: Net: 115 @ 3600 rpm. Torque: Gross: Net: 205 lb.-ft. @ 2000 rpm. Oil capacity: 5 qt. with filter change. Fuel Requirements: No-lead or low-lead gasoline.

OPTIONAL ENGINE: Invader V-8, V-8 models: Ordering Code: LS9. Engine Type: OHV V-8. Bore x Stroke: 4.00 in. x 3.50 in. Lifters: Hydraulic. Number of main bearings-5. Displacement: 350 cu. in. (5.73 liters). Carburetion: Single 4-barrel Rochester. Compression Ratio: 8.5:1. Horsepower: Net: 155 @ 4000 rpm. Torque: Net: 225 lb.-ft. @ 2400 rpm. Fuel Requirements: No-lead or low-lead gasoline.

CHASSIS FEATURES: Ladder-type. Carbon steel, 39,000 psi. Heavy-gauge channel side members, alligator-jaw cross members. Section modulus: 3.06 in.

SUSPENSION AND RUNNING GEAR: Front Suspension: Tapered leaf springs. Capacity: 1650 lb. Rating: 340 lb./in. Optional: 1900 lb. Rear Suspension: Two-stage tapered and multi-leaf (four-conventional leaves, one tapered leaf). Capacity: 1700 lb. Rating: 386/632 lb./in. Optional: None. Front Axle. Type: Hypoid, tubular driving. Capacity: 3400 lb. Rear Axle. Type: Hypoid, semi-floating. Capacity: 3750 lb. Final Drive Ratio: 4.11:1 (3.73:1 with 307 V-8). Optional: 3.07, 3.73, 4.11:1. Transfer Case: Type: Manual transmission: Dana 20. Ratios: 2.03:1, 1.00:1. New Process 203 (automatic transmission full-time). Ratios: 1.96:1, 1.00:1. New Process 205 (conventional). Ratios: 2.01, 1.00:1. Brakes: Type: Hydraulic, self-adjusting. Front: Discs. Rear: Drums. Optional: Power. Dimensions: Front: 11.86 in. dia. rotor. Rear: 11.0 in. x 2.0 in.Wheels: 6-stud, 15 x 6.0 in. Optional: 16 x 5.0, 16 x 5.5, 15 x 8.0. Tires: E78 x 15B, 4-ply rating. Optional: G78 x 15B, 6.50 x 16C, 7.00 x 16C, H78 x 15B, L78 x 15C, LR78 x 15C and 10.00 x 15C. Steering: Manual recirculating ball. Ratio: 24.0:1. Turns Lock-to-Lock: 3.4. Optional: Power-assisted. Ratio. Turns Lock-to-Lock. Turning circle: 37.6 ft. Transmission: Type: Saginaw 3-speed manual, fully synchronized. Steering column-mounted shifter. The Muncie 4-speed manual is the only manual transmission available for the 350 cu. in. V-8. Transmission Ratios: 2.85, 1.68, 1.0:1. Optional: Muncie 4-speed manual, synchromesh on to three gears, floor-mounted shift lever. Ratios: 6.55, 3.58, 1.70, 1.00:1. Optional: Turbo Hydra-Matic 3-speed automatic. Ratios: 2.52, 1.52, 1.00:1. Clutch: Six-cylinder: 10.0 in. dia., 100 sq. in. area. 307 V-8: 11.0 in. dia., 124 sq. in. area. 350 V-8: 12.0 in. dia., 150 sq. in. area. Optional: 6-cylinder: 11.0 in.

VEHICLE DIMENSIONS: Wheelbase: 106.5 in. Overall Length: 184.5 in. Front/Rear Tread 65.75 in./ 62.75 in. Overall Height: 69.5 in. With optional hardtop; 71.50 in. Width: 79.5 in. Front/Rear Overhang: 33.5 in./44.5 in. Tailgate: Width and Height: 66.8 in. x 22.0 in. Approach/Departure Degrees: 31/24. Ground Clearance: Front axle: 7.7 in. Rear axle: 8.0 in. Oil pan: 15.5 in. Transfer case: 10.0 in. Fuel tank: 14.3 in. Load space: With rear seat installed: 33 in. x 50 in. x 41.6 in. With rear seat removed or folded: 76.5 in. x 50 in. x 41.6 in.

CAPACITIES: Fuel Tank: 24.0 gal. Coolant system: 250 6-cyl.: 12.2 qt. 307 V-8: 18.5 qt. 350 V-8: 17.1 qt.

ACCOMMODATIONS: Seating Capacity: Standard: Driver. Optional: Driver and front passenger and/or 3 passenger rear bench seat. Headroom: 38.8 in. Maximum steering wheel to seat back: 18.3 in. Seat to ground: 35.0 in. Floor to ground: 20.2 in.

INSTRUMENTATION: 0-100 mph speedometer, 99,999.9 mi. odometer, fuel gauge, warning lights for alternator, oil pressure, engine coolant temperature, brake operating system, hazard warning lights, directional lights.

OPTIONS: Sierra Package. Includes tachometer, temperature, fuel level, and oil pressure instrumentation. Tinted glass. Custom instrument panel. Includes tachometer, temperature, fuel level, and oil pressure instrumentation. Air conditioning. Camper mirrors. Heavy-duty rear spring. Positraction rear axle. Heavy-duty rear springs. 61 amp alternator. 32 gal. fuel tank. Custom steering wheel. Tilt steering wheel. Power steering. Chrome hubcaps. Heavy-duty battery. Tachometer. AM/FM radio. Chrome front and rear bumpers. Dual front tow hooks.

HISTORICAL FOOTNOTES: GMC offered customers a "Sudden Service System" that provided answers to truck service and maintenance questions.

1974 JIMMY

GMC's 1974 Jimmy was easy to identify due to the placement of bold GMC letters in the center grille section. The 1974 Jimmy was available with a factory-installed padded roll bar. Previously it had been available only as a dealer-installed option. Also available for 1974 was a new factory-installed swing-away tire carrier. The limited-slip rear differential could now be ordered with the full-time four-wheel drive system. Jimmy models with optional GVW ratings above the 5600 lb. level were equipped with larger 11.15 in. x 2.75 in. rear drum brakes. The rear drums were finned for improved cooling. New options included steel belted radial tires and a new trailer weight distributing hitch platform. The base level custom interior and exterior included a foam-cushioned driver's side bucket trimmed in vinyl in a choice of four colors, driver's side sun visor, one-piece molded door trim panels, rubber front floor matting, padded sun visors, courtesy lamp, prismatic rearview mirror, 2-speed electric windshield wipers, windshield washers, back-up lights, power brakes, heater/defroster, chrome finished left and right exterior mirrors and white painted front and rear bumpers. A brake lining wear sensor that emitted a warning sound just before the lining rivets contact the front disc brake rotor was new for 1974. The 307 cu. in. V-8 was not offered for the 1974. Six-cylinder engines were not available in California. A dealer installed convertible top was available. The Jimmy's removable top was available in either black or white. Color choices for 1974 consisted of skyline blue, Spanish gold, sunset gold, glenwood green, crimson red, desert sand, grecian bronze, rosedale red, Granada beige, Catalina blue, lime green, moss olive, Hawaiian blue, frost white and Killarney green.

1974 GMC Jimmy

I.D. DATA: The Jimmy's V.I.N. consisted of 13 symbols. The first symbol (a letter T) identified the GMC Motor Division. The second symbol (a letter K) indicated vehicle type. The third symbol (a letter) indicated engine type: Q-250 cu. in. L-6, X-307 cu. in. V-8, Y-350 cu. in. V-8. The fourth symbol (a number) identified the tonnage. The fifth symbol indicated model type. The sixth symbol, a number 4, identified the 1974 model year. The seventh symbol (a letter) indicated the assembly plant. The remaining six digits served as the sequential production numbers beginning with 100083. The V.I.N. number was located on the left door pillar. The engine number indicated the manufacturing plant, day of manufacture and transmission type. It was located on a pad positioned on the right-hand side of the cylinder block at the rear of the distributor on V-8 engines and on a pad located at the front right hand side of the cylinder block of 6-cylinder engines.

Model Number	Body Type & Seating	Factory Price	GVW	Shipping Weight	Prod. Total
Jimmy K10. (with 307 V-8)					
TK10514	Utility	$3798[1]	4600*	3796	—

NOTE 1: Deduct $216.00 for 250 cu. in. 6-cyl. engine.
* 6200 GVW Package optional.

STANDARD ENGINE: 250 Six: Ordering Code: LD4. Engine Type: OHV, In-line 6-cylinder. Bore x Stroke: 3.875 in. x 3.50 in. Lifters: Hydraulic. Number of main bearings-7. Carburetion: Rochester downdraft one-barrel, model M7028007 or M7028011. Compression Ratio: 8.5:1. Displacement: 250 cu. in. (4.09 liters). Horsepower: Net: 100 @ 3600 rpm. Torque: Net: 175 lb.-ft. @ 1600 rpm. Oil capacity: 5 qt. with filter change. Fuel Requirements: Unleaded or low-lead gasoline of at least 91 Research Octane.

STANDARD ENGINE: Invader V-8, V-8 models: Engine Type: Cast iron block. OHV, V-8. Bore x Stroke: 4.0 in. x 3.50 in. Lifters: Hydraulic. Number of main bearings-5. Carburetion: Rochester two-barrel. Compression Ratio: 8.51. Displacement: 350 cu. in. Horsepower: Net: 145 @ 3800 rpm. Torque: Gross: Net: 250 lb.-ft. @ 2200 rpm. Oil capacity: 5 qt. with filter change. Fuel Requirements: Unleaded or low-lead gasoline of at least 91 Research Octane.

OPTIONAL ENGINE: Invader V-8, V-8 models: Engine Type: OHV V-8. Bore x Stroke: 4.00 in. x 3.50 in. Lifters: Hydraulic. Number of main bearings-5. Displacement: 350 cu. in. (5.73 liters). Carburetion: Single 4-barrel Rochester. Compression Ratio: 8.5:1. Horsepower: Net: 160 @ 3800 rpm. Torque: Net: 250 lb.-ft. @ 2400 rpm. Fuel Requirements: No-lead or low-lead gasoline.

CHASSIS FEATURES: Ladder-type. Carbon steel, 39,000 psi. Heavy-gauge channel side members, alligator-jaw cross members. Section modulus: 3.06 in.

SUSPENSION AND RUNNING GEAR: Front Suspension: Tapered leaf springs. Capacity: 1650 lb. Rating: 340 lb./in. Optional: 1900 lb. Front stabilizer bar. Rear Suspension: Two-stage tapered and multi-leaf (four-conventional leaves, one tapered leaf). Capacity: 1700 lb. Rating: 386/632 lb./in. Optional: None. Front Axle. Type: Hypoid, tubular driving. Capacity: 3400 lb. Rear Axle. Type: Hypoid, semi-floating. Capacity: 3750 lb. Final Drive Ratio: 4.11:1 (3.73:1 with 350 V-8). Optional: 3.07, 3.73, 4.11:1. Transfer Case: Type: Manual transmission: Dana 20. Ratios: 2.03:1, 1.00:1. New Process 203 (automatic transmission full-time). Ratios: 1.96:1, 1.00:1. New Process 205 (conventional). Ratios: 2.01, 1.00:1. Brakes: Type: Hydraulic, self-adjusting. Front: Discs. Rear: Drums. Optional: Power. Dimensions: Front: 11.86 in. dia. rotor. Rear: 11.0 in. x 2.0 in.Wheels: 6-stud, 15 x 6.0 in. Optional: 16 x 5.0, 16 x 5.5, 15 x 8.0. Tires: E78 x 15B, 4-ply rating. Optional: G78 x 15B, 6.50 x 16C, 7.00 x 16C, H78 x 15B, L78 x 15C, LR78 x 15C and 10.00 x 15C. Steering: Manual recirculating ball. Ratio: 24.0:1. Turns Lock-to-Lock: 3.4. Optional: Power-assisted. ratio. Turns Lock-to-Lock. Turning circle: 37.6 ft. Transmission: Type: Saginaw 3-speed manual, fully synchronized. Steering column-mounted shifter. Saginaw 3-speed manual, fully synchronized. Steering column-mounted shifter. This transmission is not available for the 2-bbl. 350 cu. in. V-8. The Muncie 4-speed manual is the only manual transmission available for the 350 cu. in. V-8. Transmission Ratios: 2.85, 1.68, 1.0:1. Optional: Muncie 4-speed manual, synchromesh on to three gears, floor-mounted shift lever. Ratios: 6.55, 3.58, 1.70, 1.00:1. Optional: Turbo Hydra-Matic 3-speed automatic. Ratios: 2.52, 1.52, 1.00:1. Clutch: Six-cylinder: 10.0 in. dia., 100 sq. in. area. 307 V-8: 11.0 in. dia., 124 sq. in. area. 350 V-8: 12.0 in. dia., 150 sq. in. area. Optional: 6-cylinder: 11.0 in.

VEHICLE DIMENSIONS: Wheelbase: 106.5 in. Overall Length: 184.5 in. Front/Rear Tread 65.75 in./ 62.75 in. Overall Height: 69.5 in. With optional hardtop; 71.50 in. Width: 79.5 in. Front/Rear Overhang: 33.5 in./44.5 in. Tailgate: Width and Height: 66.8 in. x 22.0 in. Approach/Departure Degrees: 31/24. Ground Clearance: Front axle: 7.7 in. Rear axle: 8.0 in. Oil pan: 15.5 in. Transfer case: 10.0 in. Fuel tank: 14.3 in. Load space: With rear seat installed: 33 in. x 50 in. x 41.6 in. With rear seat removed or folded: 76.5 in. x 50 in. x 41.6 in.

CAPACITIES: Fuel Tank: 24.0 gal. Coolant system: 250 6-cyl.: 12.2 qt. 307 V-8: 18.5 qt. 350 V-8: 17.1 qt.

ACCOMMODATIONS: Seating Capacity: Standard: Driver. Optional: Driver and front passenger and/or 3 passenger rear bench seat. Headroom: 38.8 in. Maximum steering wheel to seat back: 18.3 in. Seat to ground: 35.0 in. Floor to ground: 20.2 in.

INSTRUMENTATION: 0-100 mph speedometer, 99,999.9 mi. odometer, fuel gauge, warning lights for alternator, oil pressure, engine coolant temperature, brake operating system, hazard warning lights, directional lights.

OPTIONS: Sierra Package. Includes tachometer, temperature, fuel level, and oil pressure instrumentation. Tinted glass. Custom instrument panel. Includes tachometer, temperature, fuel level, and oil pressure instrumentation. Air conditioning. Camper mirrors. Heavy-duty rear spring. Positraction rear axle. Heavy-duty rear springs. 61 amp alternator. 32 gal. fuel tank. Custom steering wheel. Tilt steering wheel. Power steering. Chrome hubcaps. Heavy-duty battery. Tachometer. AM/FM radio. Chrome front and rear bumpers. Dual front tow hooks.

HISTORICAL FOOTNOTES: For owners of the 1974 Jimmy, GMC said: "Where you go depends on you."

1975 JIMMY

The 1975 Jimmy had a new front end with a wide center bar within which were positioned GMC letters. A color insert was keyed to the body color. The Jimmy could be ordered with a new extra-cost, "Soft Ride" front suspension with recambered springs, revalved shock absorbers and eight instead of four degrees of caster. This suspension was not recommended by GMC for heavy-duty use such as snowplowing. A 400 cu. in. V-8 was now optional. Standard on all Jimmy engines was a new transistorized high energy ignition system that delivered up to 35,000 volts to the spark plugs. The optional hardtop was now available with optional sliding side glass windows. Open Jimmy models had a restyled tailgate with a quick release feature. The hardtop model had a tailgate and a manually operated drop window. The 1975 Jimmy's front passenger seat was of a new counterbalanced design making for easier exit by rear compartment occupants. The standard single front driver's seat was covered in a plaid patterned vinyl in blue, saddle, red or green. The standard interior appointments also included one-piece molded door trim panels, rubber front floor covering, padded sun visor, and a prismatic rearview mirror. Standard exterior trim included bright grille surround, chrome left and right side exterior mirrors, white painted front and rear bumpers. The optional High Sierra Package included color-keyed front compartment carpeting, Deluxe front bucket seats, console, molded door insert panels with simulated woodgrain inserts and stretch vinyl storage pockets. The High Sierra also included a gauge-type instrument cluster with simulated woodgrain trim. in a new leather grain. Fifteen colors were offered for the 1975 Jimmy: Skyline blue, Hawaiian blue, Catalina blue, grecian bronze, buckskin, yuba gold, moss gold, willoway green, Spring green, glenwood green, crimson red, rocodale red, Saratoga silver, Santa Fe tan and frost white.

1975 GMC Jimmy

I.D. DATA: The Jimmy's V.I.N. consisted of 13 symbols. The first symbol (a letter T) identified the GMC Motor Division. The second symbol (a letter K) indicated vehicle type. The third symbol (a letter) indicated engine type: Q-250 cu. in. L-6, M-4-bbl. 400 cu. in. V-8 Y-4-bbl. 350 cu. in. V-8. The fourth symbol (a number) identified the tonnage. The fifth symbol indicated model type. The sixth symbol identified the model year. The seventh symbol (a letter) indicated the assembly plant. The remaining six digits served as the sequential production numbers. The V.I.N. number was located on the left door pillar. The engine number indicated the manufacturing plant, day of manufacture and transmission type. It was located on a pad positioned on the right-hand side of the cylinder block at the rear of the distributor on V-8 engines and on a pad located at the front right hand side of the cylinder block of 6-cylinder engines.

Model Number	Body Type & Seating	Factory Price	GVW	Shipping Weight	Prod. Total
Jimmy K10. (with 350 V-8)					
TK10514	Util. (no top)	$4569	4900*	4026	—
TK10516	Util. (top)	$4998	4900	4272	—

* 6300 GVW Package optional.

STANDARD ENGINE: 250 Six: Engine Type: OHV, In-line 6-cylinder. Bore x Stroke: 3.875 in. x 3.50 in. Lifters: Hydraulic. Number of main bearings-7. Carburetion: Rochester downdraft one-barrel, model M7028007 or M7028011. Compression Ratio: 8.5:1. Displacement: 250 cu. in. (4.09 liters). Horsepower: Net: 100 @ 3800 rpm. Torque: Net: 175 lb.-ft. @ 1800 rpm. Oil capacity: 5 qt. with filter change. Fuel Requirements: Unleaded or low-lead gasoline of at least 91 Research Octane.

STANDARD ENGINE: V-8 models: Engine Type: Cast iron block. OHV, V-8. Bore x Stroke: 4.0 in. x 3.50 in. Lifters: Hydraulic. Number of main bearings-5. Carburetion: Rochester four-barrel. Compression Ratio: 8.51. Displacement: 350 cu. in. Horsepower: Net: 160 @ 3800 rpm. Torque: Gross: Net: 250 lb.-ft. @ 2400 rpm. Oil capacity: 5 qt. with filter change. Fuel Requirements: Unleaded or low-lead gasoline of at least 91 Research Octane.

OPTIONAL ENGINE: V-8 models: Engine Type: Cast Iron block. OHV V-8. Bore x Stroke: 4.125 in. x 4.75 in. Lifters: Hydraulic. Number of main bearings-5. Displacement: 400 cu. in. (6.55 liters). Carburetion: Single Rochester 4-barrel. Compression Ratio: 8.5:1. Horsepower: Net: 175 @ 3600 rpm. Torque: Net: 290 lb.-ft. @ 2800 rpm. Fuel Requirements: Unleaded or low-lead gasoline of at least 91 Research Octane.

CHASSIS FEATURES: Ladder-type. Carbon steel, 39,000 psi. Heavy-gauge channel side members, alligator-jaw cross members. Section modulus: 3.06 in.

SUSPENSION AND RUNNING GEAR: Front Suspension: Four tapered leaf springs. Capacity: 1650 lb. Rating: Standard: 380 lb./in. Soft Ride: 250 lb./in. Optional Capacity: 1900 lb. Rear Suspension: Two-stage tapered and multi-leaf (four-conventional leaves, one tapered leaf). Capacity: 1700 lb. Rating: Standard: 386/632 lb. in. Soft Ride: 270/510 lb./in. Optional: None. Front Axle. Type: Hypoid, tubular driving. Capacity: 3600 lb. Rear Axle. Type: Hypoid, semi-floating. Capacity: 3750 lb. Final Drive Ratio: 6-cyl.: 4.11:1; V-8: 3.07:1. Optional: 3.07, 3.73, 4.11:1. Transfer Case: Type: Manual transmission: New Process 205. Ratios: 1.96:1, 1.00:1. Automatic transmission: New Process 203. Ratios: 2.00:1, 1.00:1. Brakes: Type: Hydraulic, self-adjusting. Front: Discs. Rear: Drums. Optional: Power. Dimensions: Front: 11.86 in. dia. rotor. Rear: 11.15 in. x 2.75 in. Wheels: 6-stud, 15 x 6JJ. Optional: 15 x 7JJ Rallye, 15 x 8JJ, 15 x 8JJ Rallye, 16 x 5K. Tires: H78 x 15B, 4-ply rating. Optional: L78 x 15B, LR78 x 15B, 6.50 x 16C, 7.00 x 15C, 7.00 x 16C, 10 x 15B. Steering: Manual recirculating ball. Ratio: 24.0:1. Turns Lock-to-Lock: 3.4. Turning circle: 37.6 ft. Optional: Power-assisted. Ratio: 20/16.4:1. Turns Lock-to-Lock. Turning circle: 37.58 ft. Transmission: Type: Saginaw 3-speed manual, fully synchronized. Steering column-mounted shifter. This transmission was not available for the 350 and 400 cu. in. V-8 engine with 4-bbl. carburetor. Transmission Ratios: 2.85, 1.68, 1.0:1. Optional: Muncie 4-speed manual, synchromesh on top three gears, floor-mounted shift lever. Ratios: 6.55, 3.58, 1.70, 1.00:1. Optional: Turbo Hydra-Matic 3-speed automatic. Ratios: 2.52, 1.52, 1.00:1. Clutch: Six-cylinder: 11.0 in. dia., 124 sq. in. area. V-8 engines: 12.0 in. dia., 150 sq. in. area. Optional: None.

VEHICLE DIMENSIONS: Wheelbase: 106.5 in. Overall Length: 184.5 in. Front/Rear Tread 65.75 in./ 62.75 in. Overall Height: 69.0 in. With optional hardtop; 71.0 in. Width: 79.5 in. Tailgate: Width and Height: 66.8 in. x 22.0 in. Approach/Departure Degrees: 34/22. Ground Clearance: Front axle: 8.9 in. Rear axle: 8.5 in. Oil pan: 17.2 in. Transfer case: 11.5 in. Fuel tank: 14.0 in. Load space: With rear seat installed: 38.8 in. x 50 in. x 42.3 in. With rear seat removed or folded: 76.0 in. x 50 in. x 42.3 in.

CAPACITIES: Fuel Tank: 25.0 gal. Optional: Replacement 30 gal. tank. Coolant system: 250 6-cyl.: 12.2 qt.350 V-8: 17.1 qt.

ACCOMMODATIONS: Seating Capacity: Standard: Driver. Optional: Driver and front passenger and/or 3 passenger rear bench seat. Headroom: 38.3 in. Maximum steering wheel to seat back: 18.5 in. Seat to ground: 36.3 in. Floor to ground: 21.9 in.

INSTRUMENTATION: 0-100 mph speedometer, 99,999.9 mi. odometer, fuel gauge, warning lights for alternator, oil pressure, engine coolant temperature, brake operating system, hazard warning lights, directional lights.

OPTIONS AND PRICES: Heavy-duty rear shock absorbers. Instrumentation Package. Includes ammeter, oil pressure gauge, and engine coolant temperature gauges: $17. Clock. Tachometer: $67. High Sierra Package. Includes front and rear chrome bumpers, bright upper and lower body side and rear moldings, bright hubcaps, bright accents, High Sierra nameplate, front bucket seats, front console, gauge instrumentation with simulated woodgrain trim and added insulation. Hardtop version was fitted with color-keyed carpeting, special front door and rear sidewall trim panels with bright accents and simulated woodgrain trim. Map pockets were included in front door trim panels. Special two-tone exterior paint treatment. ComforTilt steering wheel (available with 4-speed manual or Hydra-Matic transmissions only). Air conditioning (an increased capacity engine cooling system plus a 61 amp Delcotron are included). Passenger-side bucket seat (for base Jimmy): $87. Full-width rear bench seat: $153. Skid plates for fuel tank and transfer case. Sliding side glass windows. Below eye-level mirrors. Rear window air deflector, Heavy-duty 80 amp battery. Heavy-duty 42 or 61 amp generator (37 amp is standard). Heavy-duty radiator. Heavy-duty front shock absorbers: $18. Heavy-duty rear shock absorber: $10. Heavy-duty front springs: $36. Replacement 30 gal. fuel tank: $21. Soft-Ray tinted glass. Free wheeling front hubs. Locking differential rear axle: $145. Power steering: $170. Various rare axle ratios. Front tow hooks. Trailer weight-distributing hitch. Woodgrain vinyl exterior trim. Rallye wheels. Special tires. Rooftop luggage carrier. AM radio. AM/FM radio. 400 cu. in. V-8: $144. 4-speed manual transmission: $123. Hydra-Matic transmission: $286.

HISTORICAL FOOTNOTES: The latest Jimmy was touted by GMC as "a hard working truck that is great for fun too!"

1976 JIMMY

The Jimmy's standard interior was identified as the Sierra trim level for 1976. It featured a color-keyed instrument panel pad, dome lights, mats in front and rear areas, and plaid patterned vinyl trim in a choice of four colors. The High Sierra trim included color-keyed front floor covering and dash pad, full gauge instrumentation, bucket seats with center console, and side door panel trim with storage pockets. Exterior trim of the High Sierra models included bright metal garnish on body sides and tailgate, front and rear bumpers; body to fender and hood insulators and special insulation under the cowl panel. The Jimmy's new design includes a new double-walled steel front roof section with standard sound insulation materials. The shorter removable fiberglass reinforced plastic rear roof section was relatively light and easy to handle. New one-piece door frames and full side windows provided a stronger cab area, improved door alignment and sealing.

I.D. DATA: The Blazer's V.I.N. consisted of 13 symbols. The first symbol (a letter C) identified the GMC Motor Division. The second symbol (a letter K) indicated vehicle type. The third symbol (a letter) indicated engine type: Q-250 cu. in. L-6, M-4-bbl. 400 cu. in. V-8, Y-4-bbl. 350 cu. in. V-8. The fourth symbol (a number) identified the tonnage. The fifth symbol indicated model type. The sixth symbol identified the model year. The seventh symbol (a letter) indicated the assembly plant. The remaining six digits served as the sequential production numbers. The V.I.N. number was located on the left door pillar. The engine number indicated the manufacturing plant, day of manufacture and transmission type. It was located on a pad positioned on the right-hand side of the cylinder block at the rear of the distributor on V-8 engines and on a pad located at the front right hand side of the cylinder block of 6-cylinder engines.

Model Number	Body Type & Seating	Factory Price	GVW	Shipping Weight	Prod. Total
Jimmy K10 (with 350 V-8)					
TK10516	Util. (with top)	$5364	6200	4496	—

STANDARD ENGINE: 250 Six: Ordering Code: LD4. Engine Type: OHV, In-line 6-cylinder. Bore x Stroke: 3.875 in. x 3.50 in. Lifters: Hydraulic. Number of main bearings-7. Carburetion: Rochester downdraft one-barrel, model M7028007 or M7028011. Compression Ratio: 8.5:1. Displacement: 250 cu. in. (4.09 liters). Horsepower: Net: 100 @ 3800 rpm. Torque: Net: 175 lb.-ft. @ 1800 rpm. Oil capacity: 5 qt. with filter change. Fuel Requirements: Unleaded or low-lead gasoline of at least 91 Research Octane.

STANDARD ENGINE: V-8 models: Engine Type: Cast iron block. OHV, V-8. Bore x Stroke: 4.0 in. x 3.50 in. Lifters: Hydraulic. Number of main bearings-5. Carburetion: Rochester four-barrel. Compression Ratio: 8.51. Displacement: 350 cu. in. Horsepower: Net: 160 @ 3800 rpm. Torque: Gross: Net: 250 lb.-ft. @ 2400 rpm. Oil capacity: 5 qt. with filter change. Fuel Requirements: Unleaded or low-lead gasoline of at least 91 Research Octane.

OPTIONAL ENGINE: V-8 models: Engine Type: Cast Iron block. OHV V-8. Bore x Stroke: 4.125 in. x 4.75 in. Lifters: Hydraulic. Number of main bearings-5. Displacement: 400 cu. in. (6.55 liters). Carburetion: Single Rochester 4-barrel. Compression Ratio: 8.5:1. Horsepower: Net: 175 @ 3600 rpm. Torque: Net: 290 lb.-ft. @ 2800 rpm. Fuel Requirements: Unleaded or low-lead gasoline of at least 91 Research Octane.

CHASSIS FEATURES: Ladder-type. Carbon steel, 39,000 psi. Heavy-gauge channel side members, alligator-jaw cross members. Section modulus: 3.06 in.

SUSPENSION AND RUNNING GEAR: Front Suspension: Four tapered leaf springs. Capacity: 1650 lb. Optional Capacity: 1900 lb. Rear Suspension: Two-stage tapered and multi-leaf (four-conventional leaves, one tapered leaf). Capacity: 1700 lb. Optional: None. Front Axle. Type: Hypoid, tubular driving. Capacity: 3600 lb. Rear Axle. Type: Hypoid, semi-floating. Capacity: 3750 lb. Final Drive Ratio: 6-cyl.: 4.11:1; V-8: 3.07:1. Optional: 3.07, 3.73, 4.11:1. Transfer Case: Type: Manual transmission: New Process 205. Ratios: 1.96:1, 1.00:1. Automatic transmission: New Process 203. Ratios: 2.00:1, 1.00:1. Brakes: Type: Hydraulic, self-adjusting. Front: Discs. Rear: Drums. Optional: Power. Dimensions: Front: 11.86 in. dia. rotor. Rear: 11.15 in. x 2.75 in. Wheels: 6-stud, 15 x 6JJ. Optional: 15 x 7JJ Rallye, 15 x 8JJ, 15 x 8JJ Rallye, 16 x 5K. Tires: H78 x 15B, 4-ply rating. Optional: L78 x 15B, LR78 x 15B, 6.50 x 16C, 7.00 x 15C, 7.00 x 16C, 10 x 15B. Steering: Manual recirculating ball. Ratio: 24.0:1. Turns Lock-to-Lock: 3.4. Turning circle: 37.6 ft. Optional: Power-assisted. Ratio: 20/16.4:1. Turns Lock-to-Lock. Turning circle: 37.58 ft. Transmission: Type: Saginaw 3-speed manual, fully synchronized. Steering column-mounted shifter. This transmission was not available for the 350 and 400 cu. in. V-8 engine with 4-bbl. carburetor. Transmission Ratios: 2.85, 1.68, 1.0:1. Optional: Muncie 4-speed manual, synchromesh on top three gears, floor-mounted shift lever. Ratios: 6.55, 3.58, 1.70, 1.00:1. Optional: Turbo Hydra-Matic 3-speed automatic. Ratios: 2.52, 1.52, 1.00:1. Clutch: Six-cylinder: 11.0 in. dia., 124 sq. in. area. V-8 engines: 12.0 in. dia., 150 sq. in. area. Optional: None.

VEHICLE DIMENSIONS: Wheelbase: 106.5 in. Overall Length: 184.5 in. Front/Rear Tread 65.75 in./ 62.75 in. Overall Height: 69.0 in. With optional hardtop; 71.0 in. Width: 79.5 in. Tailgate: Width and Height: 66.8 in. x 22.0 in. Approach/Departure Degrees: 34/22. Ground Clearance: Front axle: 8.9 in. Rear axle: 8.5 in. Oil pan: 17.2 in. Transfer case: 11.5 in. Fuel tank: 14.0 in. Load space: With rear seat installed: 38.8 in. x 50 in. x 42.3 in. With rear seat removed or folded: 76.0 in. x 50 in. x 42.3 in.

CAPACITIES: Fuel Tank: 25.0 gal. Optional: Replacement 30 gal. tank. Coolant system: 250 6-cyl.: 12.2 qt.350 V-8: 17.1 qt.

ACCOMMODATIONS: Seating Capacity: Standard: Driver. Optional: Driver and front passenger and/or 3 passenger rear bench seat. Headroom: 38.3 in. Maximum steering wheel to seat back: 18.5 in. Seat to ground: 36.3 in. Floor to ground: 21.9 in.

INSTRUMENTATION: 0-100 mph speedometer, 99,999.9 mi. odometer, fuel gauge, warning lights for alternator, oil pressure, engine coolant temperature, brake operating system, hazard warning lights, directional lights.

OPTIONS AND PRICES: Heavy-duty rear shock absorbers. Instrumentation Package. Includes ammeter, oil pressure gauge, and engine coolant temperature gauges. Clock. Tachometer. High Sierra Package: $626. Includes front and rear chrome bumpers, bright upper and lower body side and rear moldings, bright hubcaps, bright accents, High Sierra nameplate, front bucket seats, front console, gauge instrumentation with simulated woodgrain trim and added insulation. Hardtop version was fitted with color-keyed carpeting, special front door and rear sidewall trim panels with bright accents and simulated woodgrain trim. Map pockets were included in front door trim panels. Special two-tone exterior paint treatment. ComforTilt steering wheel (available with 4-speed manual or Hydra-Matic transmissions only). Air conditioning (an increased capacity engine cooling system plus a 61 amp Delcotron are included). Passenger-side bucket seat (for Jimmy Sierra). Full-width rear bench seat. Skid plates for fuel tank and transfer case. Sliding side glass windows. Below eye-level mirrors. Rear window air deflector, Heavy-duty 80 amp battery. Heavy-duty 42 or 61 amp generator (37 amp is standard). Heavy-duty radiator. Heavy-duty front shock absorbers. Heavy-duty rear shock absorber. Heavy-duty front springs. Replacement 30 gal. fuel tank. Soft-Ray tinted glass. Free wheeling front hubs. Locking differential rear axle. Power steering. Various rear axle ratios. Front tow hooks. Trailer weight-distributing hitch. Woodgrain vinyl exterior trim. Rallye wheels. Special tires. Rooftop luggage carrier. AM radio. AM/FM radio. 400 cu. in. V-8. 4-speed manual transmission. Hydra-Matic transmission. California emission certification: $75.

HISTORICAL FOOTNOTES: The latest GMC Jimmy was introduced in the fall of 1975.

1977 JIMMY

The grille of the 1977 GMC Jimmy grille had four narrow upright dividers along with a center horizontal bar carrying the GMC name. The headlight bezel paint color was changed from argent to dark grey metallic. The High Sierra Option Package had color-keyed front carpeting, dash pad and seats. The full gauge instrument cluster had a new simulated chestnut woodgrained face plate. The front bucket seats were trimmed in custom cloth or vinyl. A large capacity center console was installed as were new side door panels with simulated woodgrained inserts and vinyl storage pockets. A special insulator was installed under the cowl front panel. The rear compartment sidewalls had new full-length vinyl trim panels with simulated woodgrain inserts. A new optional rear speaker was located in the right hand rear panel. Matching carpeting for the rear compartment was included with the optional rear passenger seat. Exterior High Sierra trim consisted of bright metal trim on body sides and tailgate. Chromed front and rear bumpers were installed. Bright wheel opening trim was used along with bright hubcaps and body-to-fender insulators. The standard Sierra interior of plaid-pattern vinyl or optional custom leather-grained vinyl was offered in a choice of four colors. Also included in the Sierra interior were embossed black rubber floor mats, molded plastic door trim panels with integral armrests, dual color-keyed sunshades and a 10 in. prismatic rearview mirror. New options for 1977 included intermittent windshield wipers system, inside hood release latch and color-keyed front floor mats.

1977 GMC Jimmy

Offered as an alternative to Jimmys with the full or partial tops was a factory soft rear top option available in a choice of four colors: White, black, blue or beige. A hardboard-backed foam rubber front compartment headliner with perforated light fawn vinyl skin (RPO BB5) was introduced for 1977. The interior color of the standard hardtop headliner was changed from white to light fawn. New for 1977 was RPO ZY5, an Exterior Decor Package, with distinctive hood stripes and a bright stand-up spring-loaded hood ornament. Six two-tone choices were offered for this package which was not available on Jimmys with black tops. Both the optional styled steel wheels and bright metal wheelcovers were redesigned. Joining the 250 cu. in. L-6 and the 350 and 400 cu. in. V-8 engines in the Jimmy engine line was a new 305 cu. in. V-8. Neither this engine nor the 250 L-6 were available in California. The 250 engine was equipped with a new electric carburetor choke. A new accelerator pedal and rod that were relocated further inboard towards the tunnel hump for improved right foot riding comfort were adopted for 1977.

A new fiberglass Casa Grande camper unit with a steel frame that bolted onto the Jimmy was introduced for 1977. The Casa Grande was available as a Base Package or in three additional packages offering such features as sleeping capacity for four, a refrigerator and an electrical power hook-up. Standard power for the Casa Grande was the 350 V-8 with 4-barrel carburotor. The High Sierra Package was also required. Standard equipment included power steering, front auxiliary seat, deluxe chrome front bumper, rear step bumper, stand-up type spring loaded hood ornament and front-mounted spare tire carrier. The standard tires were L78-15D blackwall. The length of a Jimmy with this package was extended 26 inches beyond the rear tailgate. The Casa Grande Jimmy had a 6700 lb. GVWR (Gross Vehicle Weight Rating). Its equipment included a 350 cu. in. V-8, 3-speed manual transmission, front bucket seats, chromed bumpers, front-mounted spare tire carrier and power steering. GMC offered the following colors for the 1977 Jimmy: Frost white, mariner blue, buckskin, mahogany, Hawaiian blue, Santa Fe tan, red metallic, light blue, colonial yellow, cardinal red, midnight black, Saratoga silver, seamist green, russet metallic and cordova brown.

1977 GMC Jimmy with Casa Grande camper

I.D. DATA: The Jimmy's V.I.N. consisted of 13 symbols. The first symbol (a letter T) identified the GMC Motor Division. The second symbol (a letter K) indicated vehicle type. The third symbol (a letter) indicated engine type: D-250 cu. in. L-6, U-305 V-8, R-4-bbl. 400 cu. in. V-8, L-4-bbl. 350 cu. in. V-8. The fourth symbol (a number) identified the tonnage. The fifth symbol indicated model type. The sixth symbol identified the model year. The seventh symbol (a letter) indicated the assembly plant. The remaining six digits served as the sequential production numbers. The V.I.N. number was located on the left door pillar. The engine number indicated the manufacturing plant, day of manufacture and transmission type. It was located on a pad positioned on the right-hand side of the cylinder block at the rear of the distributor on V-8 engines and on a pad located at the front right hand side of the cylinder block of 6-cylinder engines.

Model Number	Body Type & Seating	Factory Price	GVW	Shipping Weight	Prod. Total
Jimmy K10. (with 305 V-8)					
TK10516	Util. (Hardtop)	$5603	6050	3914	—
TK10516	Util. (folding top)	$5503	6050	3864	—

STANDARD ENGINE: 250 Six: Ordering Code: LD4. Engine Type: OHV, In-line 6-cylinder. Bore x Stroke: 3.875 in. x 3.50 in. Lifters: Hydraulic. Number of main bearings-7. Carburetion: Rochester downdraft one-barrel, model M7028007 or M7028011. Compression Ratio: 8.5:1. Displacement: 250 cu. in. (4.09 liters). Horsepower: Net: 100 @ 3800 rpm. Torque: Net: 175 lb.-ft. @ 1800 rpm. Oil capacity: 5 qt. with filter change. Fuel Requirements: Unleaded or low-lead gasoline of at least 91 Research Octane.

STANDARD ENGINE: V-8 models: Available in all states except California. Engine Type: Cast iron block. OHV, V-8. Bore x Stroke: 3.74 in. x 3.48 in. Lifters: Hydraulic. Number of main bearings-5. Carburetion: Rochester two-barrel. Compression Ratio: 8.5:1. Displacement: 305 cu. in. Horsepower: 140 @ 3800 rpm. Torque: Gross: 235 lb.-ft. @ 2000 rpm. Oil capacity: 5 qt. with filter change. Fuel Requirements: Unleaded or low-lead gasoline of at least 91 Research Octane.

OPTIONAL ENGINE: V-8 models: Engine Type: Cast iron block. OHV, V-8. Bore x Stroke: 4.0 in. x 3.50 in. Lifters: Hydraulic. Number of main bearings-5. Carburetion: Rochester four-barrel. Compression Ratio: 8.51. Displacement: 350 cu. in. Horsepower: Net: 160 @ 3800 rpm. Torque: Gross: Net: 250 lb.-ft. @ 2400 rpm. Oil capacity: 5 qt. with filter change. Fuel Requirements: Unleaded or low-lead gasoline of at least 91 Research Octane.

OPTIONAL ENGINE: V-8 models: Option LF4. Engine Type: Cast Iron block. OHV V-8. Bore x Stroke: 4.125 in. x 4.75 in. Lifters: Hydraulic. Number of main bearings-5. Displacement: 400 cu. in. (6.55 liters). Carburetion: Single Rochester 4-barrel. Compression Ratio: 8.5:1. Horsepower: Net: 175 @ 3600 rpm. Torque: Net: 290 lb.-ft. @ 2800 rpm. Fuel Requirements: Unleaded or low-lead gasoline of at least 91 Research Octane.

CHASSIS FEATURES: Ladder-type. Carbon steel, 39,000 psi. Heavy-gauge channel side members, alligator-jaw cross members. Section modulus: 3.06 in.

SUSPENSION AND RUNNING GEAR: Front Suspension: Two tapered semi-elliptical leaf springs. Capacity: 1650 lb. Rating: 250 lb./in. 1.0 in. shock absorbers, 1.25 in. stabilizer bar. Optional Capacity: 2250 lb. 32mm shock absorbers (available with RPO F60 heavy-duty springs only). Rear Suspension: Two-stage tapered and multi-leaf (six-conventional leaves, one tapered leaf). Capacity: 1700 lb. Rating: 270/510 lb./in. Optional: None. Front Axle. Type: Hypoid, tubular driving. Capacity: 3600 lb. Rear Axle. Type: Hypoid, semi floating. Capacity: 3750 lb. Final Drive Ratio: 6-cyl.: 4.11:1; 305 V-8: 3.73:1; 350 V-8: 3.07:1, 400 V-8: 2.77:1 (initial production), 3.07:1 (interim 1977). Optional: 6-cyl.: 3.73:1; 305 V-8: 2.76, 3.07, 4.11:1; 350 V-8: 2.76, 3.73, 4.11:1, 400 V-8: 3.07, 3.73, 4.11:1. Transfer Case: Type: Manual transmission: New Process 205. Ratios: 1.96:1, 1.00:1. Automatic transmission: New Process 203. Ratios: 2.00:1, 1.00:1. Brakes: Type: Hydraulic, self-adjusting. Front: Discs. Rear: Drums. Optional: Power. Dimensions: Front: 11.86 in. dia. rotor. Rear: 11.15 in. x 2.75 in. Wheels: 6-stud, 15 x 6JJ. Optional: 15 x 7JJ Rallye, 15 x 8JJ, 15 x 8JJ Rallye, 16 x 5K. Tires: H78 x 15B, 4-ply rating. Optional: L78 x 15B, LR78 x 15B, 6.50 x 16C, 7.00 x 15C, 7.00 x 16C, 10 x 15B. Steering: Manual recirculating ball. Ratio: 24.0:1. Turns Lock-to-Lock: 3.4. Turning circle: 37.6 ft. Optional: Power-assisted. Ratio: 20/16.4:1. Turning circle: 37.58 ft. Transmission: Type: Saginaw 3-speed manual, fully synchronized. Steering column-mounted shifter. This transmission was not available for the 350 and 400 cu. in. V-8 engine with 4-bbl. carburetor.

Transmission Ratios: 2.85, 1.68, 1.0:1. Optional: Muncie 4-speed manual, synchromesh on top three gears, floor-mounted shift lever. Ratios: 6.55, 3.58, 1.70, 1.00:1. Optional: Turbo Hydra-Matic 3-speed automatic. Ratios: 2.52, 1.52, 1.00:1. Clutch: Six-cylinder: 11.0 in. dia., 124 sq. in. area. V-8 engines: 12.0 in. dia., 150 sq. in. area. Optional: None.

VEHICLE DIMENSIONS: Wheelbase: 106.5 in. Overall Length: 184.5 in. Front/Rear Tread 65.75 in./ 62.75 in. Overall Height: 69.0 in. With optional hardtop: 71.0 in. Width: 79.5 in. Tailgate: Width and Height: 66.8 in. x 22.0 in. Approach/Departure Degrees: 34/22. Ground Clearance: Front axle: 8.9 in. Rear axle: 8.5 in. Oil pan: 17.2 in. Transfer case: 11.5 in. Fuel tank: 14.0 in. Load space: With rear seat installed: 38.8 in. x 50 in. x 42.3 in. With rear seat removed or folded: 76.0 in. x 50 in. x 42.3 in.

CAPACITIES: Fuel Tank: 25.0 gal. Optional: Replacement 30 gal. tank. Coolant system: 250 6-cyl.: 12.2 qt. 350 V-8: 17.1 qt.

ACCOMMODATIONS: Seating Capacity: Standard: Driver. Optional: Driver and front passenger and/or 3 passenger rear bench seat. Headroom: 38.3 in. Maximum steering wheel to seat back: 18.5 in. Seat to ground: 36.3 in. Floor to ground: 21.9 in.

INSTRUMENTATION: 0-100 mph speedometer, 99,999.9 mi. odometer, fuel gauge, warning lights for alternator, oil pressure, engine coolant temperature, brake operating system, hazard warning lights, directional lights.

OPTIONS AND PRICES: 305 cu. in. V-8 (RPO LG9): $150. 350 cu. in. V-8 (RPO LS9). 400 cu. in. V-8 (RPO LF4): $160. Four-speed manual transmission (RPO MM4): $142. Front passenger bucket seat (RPO A57). Full-width rear bench seat (RPO AM7). Three-speed automatic transmission (RPO MX1): $300. Power steering (RPO N41): $188. Gauge instrumentation (RPO Z53): $21. Tachometer (RPO U16): $76. High Sierra interior (RPO Z84). Includes front bucket seats in leather-grained custom vinyl in a selection of four colors (custom cloth upholstery in buckskin and blue also available), center console, gauge instrumentation, simulated woodgrain trim, additional insulation, color-keyed carpeting (carpeting covers rear floor if rear bench seat is ordered), and rear sidewall trim panels with bright accents and simulated woodgrain trim. Custom Deluxe interior. Includes foam-cushioned driver's bucket seat trimmed in plaid-pattern vinyl in a choice of four colors (matching auxiliary front bucket seat and rear bench seat available), one-piece molded door trim panels, foam-cushioned instrument panel pad, padded sun visors, rubber floor covering and driver combination lap-shoulder belt. Exterior Decor Package (RPO ZY5). Inside hood release. (RPO T44). AM radio (RPO U63): $80. AM/FM radio (RPO U69): $130. Windshield antenna (RPO U76). Auxiliary rear radio speaker (RPO U80). Deluxe front and rear chrome bumpers with impact strips (RPO V37): $75. Deluxe front and rear bumpers (RPO VE5). Stainless steel camper-type exterior mirrors (RPO DF2). Stainless steel below eye-level type exterior mirrors (RPO DG4). Painted below eye-level type exterior mirrors (RPO D29). Soft-Ray tinted glass (RPO AO1). Front stabilizer bar (RPO F59). Engine oil cooler (RPO KC4). Dual exhaust system (RPO N10). Simulated woodgrain exterior trim (RPO YG2). Special two-tone paint (RPO ZY3). Styled steel wheels (PA6). Bright metal wheelcovers (RPO PO1): $35. Rallye wheels (RPO N67). Wheel trim rings (RPO PO6). Speed and cruise control (RPO K30). Intermittent windshield wipers (RPO CD4) . Chromed bumper guards (RPO V31): $50. Luggage carrier. Replacement 31 gal. fuel tank (RPO NK7): $25. Rear window air deflector. 61 amp Delcotron generator (RPO K76). Heavy-duty radiator (RPO VO1). Transmission oil cooler (RPO VO2). Towing device (RPO V76). Special tires. Custom steering wheel (RPO N31). Cigarette lighter (RPO U37): $15. Swing-away spare tire carrier: $100. Locking differential rear axle (RPO G80): $155. Special Trailering Equipment Package (RPO Z82). Includes power steering, heavy-duty battery, trailering special nameplate with GVW rating. Heavy-duty trailer wiring harness (RPO UY7). Auxiliary battery (RPO TP2). Heavy-duty front and rear shock absorbers (F51): $20. Heavy-duty front springs (F60): $36. Weight-distributing hitch platform (RPO VR4). Deadweight trailer hitch (RPO VR2). Fuel tank shield plates (RPO NY1). Convertible top (RPO C1A-White, RPO C1B-Black, C1C-Blue, RPO C1D-Buckskin). ComforTilt steering wheel (RPO N33). Air conditioning (RPO C60). Sliding rear side windows (RPO AD5): $156. Color-keyed front floor mats (RPO B32). Rear roll bar (RPO E50). Spare tire cover (RPO P17).

HISTORICAL FOOTNOTES: The latest Jimmy was called "The Tracker Maker" by GMC.

1978 JIMMY

The Jimmy's optional rear seat for 1978 included outboard armrests color coordinated to match the front seating compartment. Rear passenger legroom was increased by dropping the floor level between the front and rear seats to the same level as the front compartment. The High Sierra trim had new high-back bucket seats in saddle custom cloth and vinyl trim. All vinyl open high-grain trim was also available. Both versions were offered in blue, buckskin and a new (for the cloth and vinyl trim) red color. Mandarin orange was also available for the all-vinyl trim. A new fold-up rear passenger seat was also offered for 1978. It replaced the older rear bench seat (RPO AS3). The new seat could be folded forward by first unlatching the backrest, which then folded forward and down to the cushion. The cushion was then unlatched to allow the entire assembly to swing up and forward against the front seat. The entire assembly could be removed by unbolting four bolts. On some early 1978 models a 3-bolt attachment may be found.

1978 GMC Jimmy High Sierra wtih optional PA6 wheels

The windshield wiper/washer system had an improved performance wiper motor. The intermittent wiper option (RPO CD4) was also of all-new design. The front seat belt system now used one emergency locking retractor for both the lap and shoulder belt. The Jimmy's lap and shoulder belt retractor was now mounted on the door lock pillar instead of the floor as on the 1977 model. This improved rear compartment exit and entry. Jimmy models with a folding rear seat also have new seat belts similar in design to those used in 1977 with the 3 passenger rear seat. The Jimmy windshield was fitted with a new bonded-in urethane rubber strip was used. New insulators and sound deadeners were incorporated into the Jimmy's manufacture. All body side outer panels and, on models with the optional folding seat, the tailgate panel, were now constructed of pre-coated steel. The Jimmy's side inner panel extension was redesigned to minimize entry of water and other matter between the inner and outer panels. The 1978 Jimmy was available with front and rear wheel opening moldings as a separate option (RPO B96). Previously, they had been included with other optional equipment. Bright plastic decorative molding was added to the hood's rear edge. The optional Rallye wheels had a new style center hub of chromed plastic. These hubcaps were also used in conjunction with the optional styled wheels. The rear hubs of both the Rallye and styled wheels carried a new four-wheel drive center insert identification. Replacing the previous woodgrain door trim appliques on High Sierra models were new bright brush-finished appliques. This same change was made to the rear quarter trim panel appliques for High Sierra Jimmy models which also had a new bright molding. Door hardware inserts for all Jimmy trim levels now had a bright brushed finish instead of the former pewter finish. The Custom vinyl bench and bucket seat trims had a new cover material with an oxen hide grain which had a smoother texture than the former buffalo hide grain.

A new latch mechanism facilitated the folding of the auxiliary front seat (RPO A57) out of the way for easier rear seat access. New standard high-back bucket seats were also introduced for the Blazer. The Jimmy was now offered with power front door locks (RPO AU3), power front door windows (RPO A31) and a power tailgate (RPO A33). The power front door locks and power windows were also included in a new Operating Convenience Package (RPO ZQ2). Replacing the 17.5 in. diameter steering wheel used on earlier Jimmys was a smaller 16.0 in. diameter soft vinyl steering wheel with a soft vinyl horn button cap. The custom steering wheel (RPO N31) had a bright trimmed horn button cap. The Jimmy exterior color selection for 1978 consisted of frost white, mariner blue, buckskin, mahogany, Hawaiian blue, Santa Fe tan, red metallic, kite blue, colonial yellow, cardinal red, midnight black, Saratoga silver, seamist green, russet metallic and cordova brown.

1978 GMC Jimmy with Desert Fox equipment

I.D. DATA: The Jimmy's V.I.N. consisted of 13 symbols. The first symbol (a letter T) identified the GMC motor Ddivision. The second symbol (a letter K) indicated vehicle type. The third symbol (a letter) indicated engine type: D-250 cu. in. L-6, U-305 V-8, R-4-bbl. 400 cu. in. V-8, L-4-bbl. 350 cu. in. V-8. The fourth symbol (a number) identified the tonnage. The fifth symbol indicated model type. The sixth symbol identified the model year. The seventh symbol (a letter) indicated the assembly plant. The remaining six digits served as the sequential production numbers. The V.I.N. number was located on the left door pillar. The engine number indicated the manufacturing plant, day of manufacture and transmission type. It was located on a pad positioned on the right-hand side of the cylinder block at the rear of the distributor on V-8 engines and on a pad located at the front right hand side of the cylinder block of 6-cylinder engines.

Model Number	Body Type & Seating	Factory Price	GVW	Shipping Weight	Prod. Total
Jimmy K-1500. (with 250 6-cyl.)					
TK10516	Util. (Hardtop)	$6193.40	6050	4268	—
TK10516	Util. (folding top)	$6093.40	6050*	N.A.	—

* 6200 lb. GVW optional.

Prices listed are for vehicles produced on or after February 6, 1978.

STANDARD ENGINE: 250 Six: Ordering Code: LD4. Engine Type: OHV, In-line 6-cylinder. Bore x Stroke: 3.875 in. x 3.50 in. Lifters: Hydraulic. Number of main bearings-7. Carburetion: Rochester downdraft one-barrel, model M7028007 or M7028011. Compression Ratio: 8.5:1. Displacement: 250 cu. in. (4.09 liters). Horsepower: Net: 100 @ 3800 rpm. Torque: Net: 175 lb.-ft. @ 1800 rpm. Oil capacity: 5 qt. with filter change. Fuel Requirements: Unleaded or low-lead gasoline of at least 91 Research Octane.

STANDARD ENGINE: V-8 models: Available in all states except California. Ordering Code: LG9. Engine Type: Cast iron block. OHV, V-8. Bore x Stroke: 3.74 in. x 3.48 in. Lifters: Hydraulic. Number of main bearings-5. Carburetion: Rochester two-barrel. Compression Ratio: 8.5:1. Displacement: 305 cu. in. Horsepower: 140 @ 3800 rpm. Torque: Gross: 235 lb.-ft. @ 2000 rpm. Oil capacity: 5 qt. with filter change. Fuel Requirements: Unleaded or low-lead gasoline of at least 91 Research Octane.

OPTIONAL ENGINE: V-8 models: Ordering Code: LS9. Engine Type: Cast iron block. OHV, V-8. Bore x Stroke: 4.0 in. x 3.50 in. Lifters: Hydraulic. Number of main bearings-5. Carburetion: Rochester four-barrel. Compression Ratio: 8.5:1. Displacement: 350 cu. in. Horsepower: Net: 160 @ 3800 rpm. Torque: Gross: Net: 250 lb.-ft. @ 2400 rpm. Oil capacity: 5 qt. with filter change. Fuel Requirements: Unleaded or low-lead gasoline of at least 91 Research Octane.

OPTIONAL ENGINE: V-8 models: Option LF4. Engine Type: Cast Iron block. OHV V-8. Bore x Stroke: 4.125 in. x 4.75 in. Lifters: Hydraulic. Number of main bearings-5. Displacement: 400 cu. in. (6.55 liters). Carburetion: Single Rochester 4-barrel. Compression Ratio: 8.5:1. Horsepower: Net: 175 @ 3600 rpm. Torque: Net: 290 lb.-ft. @ 2800 rpm. Fuel Requirements: Unleaded or low-lead gasoline of at least 91 Research Octane.

CHASSIS FEATURES: Ladder-type. Carbon steel, 39,000 psi. Heavy-gauge channel side members, alligator-jaw cross members. Section modulus: 3.06 in.

SUSPENSION AND RUNNING GEAR: Front Suspension: Two tapered semi-elliptical leaf springs. Capacity: 1650 lb. Rating: 250 lb./in. 1.0 in. shock absorbers, 1.25 in. stabilizer bar. Optional Capacity: 2250 lb. 32mm shock absorbers (available with RPO F60 heavy-duty springs only). Rear Suspension: Two-stage tapered and multi-leaf (six-conventional leaves, one tapered leaf). Capacity: 1700 lb. Rating: 270/510 lb./in. Optional: None. Front Axle. Type: Hypoid, tubular driving. Capacity: 3600 lb. Rear Axle. Type: Hypoid, semi-floating. Capacity: 3750 lb. Final Drive Ratio: 6-cyl.: 4.11:1; 305 V-8: 3.40:1; 350 and V-8: 3.07:1. Optional: 6-cyl.: 3.40:1; 305 V-8: 2.76, 3.07, 3.73:1; 350 and 400 V-8: 2.76, 3.40, 3.73:1. Transfer Case: Type: Manual transmission: New Process 205. Ratios: 1.96:1, 1.00:1. Automatic transmission: New Process 203. Ratios: 2.00:1, 1.00:1. Brakes: Type: Hydraulic, self-adjusting. Front: Discs. Rear: Drums. Optional: Power. Dimensions: Front: 11.86 in. dia. rotor. Rear: 11.15 in. x 2.75 in. Wheels: 6-stud, 15 x 6JJ. Optional: 15 x 7JJ Rallye, 15 x 8JJ, 15 x 8JJ Rallye, 16 x 5K. Tires: H78 x 15B, 4-ply rating. Optional: LR78 x 15C (highway steel belted radial white stripe), H78 x 15B (highway), H78 x 15B (highway, white stripe), H78 x 15B (on-off road), L78 x 15B (highway), L78 x15B (on-off road), L78 x 15B (highway, white stripe), 6.50 x 16C (highway), 7.00 x 15C (highway), 10.00 x 15B (polyester), 10.00 x 15B (polyester white lettered). Steering: Manual recirculating ball. Ratio: 24.0:1. Turns Lock-to-Lock: 3.4. Turning circle: 37.6 ft. Optional: Power-assisted. Ratio: 20/16.4:1. Turns Lock-to-Lock. Turning circle: 37.58 ft. Transmission: Type: Saginaw 3-speed manual, fully synchronized. Steering column-mounted shifter. This transmission was not available for the 350 and 400 cu. in. V-8 engine with 4-bbl. carburetor. Transmission Ratios: 2.85, 1.68, 1.0:1. Optional: Muncie 4-speed manual, synchromesh on top three gears, floor-mounted shift lever. Ratios: 6.55, 3.58, 1.70, 1.00:1. Optional: Turbo Hydra-Matic 3-speed automatic. Ratios: 2.52, 1.52, 1.00:1. Clutch: Six-cylinder: 11.0 in. dia., 124 sq. in. area. V-8 engines: 12.0 in. dia., 150 sq. in. area. Optional: None.

VEHICLE DIMENSIONS: Wheelbase: 106.5 in. Overall Length: 184.5 in. Front/Rear Tread 65.75 in./ 62.75 in. Overall Height: 69.0 in. With optional hardtop; 71.0 in. Width: 79.5 in. Tailgate: Width and Height: 66.8 in. x 22.0 in. Approach/Departure Degrees: 34/22. Ground Clearance: Front axle: 8.9 in. Rear axle: 8.5 in. Oil pan: 17.2 in. Transfer case: 11.5 in. Fuel tank: 14.0 in. Load space: With rear seat installed: 38.8 in. x 50 in. x 42.3 in. With rear seat removed or folded: 76.0 in. x 50 in. x 42.3 in.

CAPACITIES: Fuel Tank: 25.0 gal. Optional: Replacement 30 gal. tank. Coolant system: 250 6-cyl.: 12.2 qt. 350 V-8: 17.1 qt. 400 V-8: 20 qt.

ACCOMMODATIONS: Seating Capacity: Standard: Driver. Optional: Driver and front passenger and/or 3 passenger rear bench seat. Headroom: 38.3 in. Maximum steering wheel to seat back: 18.5 in. Seat to ground: 36.3 in. Floor to ground: 21.9 in.

INSTRUMENTATION: 0-100 mph speedometer, 99,999.9 mi. odometer, fuel gauge, warning lights for alternator, oil pressure, engine coolant temperature, brake operating system, hazard warning lights, directional lights.

OPTIONS AND PRICES: Prices shown were in effect on and after February 6, 1978. 305 cu. in. V-8 (RPO LG9): $185. 350 cu. in. V-8 (RPO LS9): $300. 400 cu. in. V-8 (RPO LF4): $485. Automatic transmission (RPO MX1): $345. Four-speed manual transmission (RPO MM4): $152. High Sierra Package (RPO Z84): $758-$781 depending upon tire selection. Poly Wrap air cleaner (RPO K43): $15. All-Weather air conditioning: (RPO C60): $550. Auxiliary batter (RPO TP2): $92. Heavy-duty battery (RPO UA1): $36. Chromed front and rear bumpers (RPO VE5): $84, without High Sierra, $32 with High Sierra. Chromed front bumper guards: $31. California emissions requirements (RPO YF5): $93. Electric clock (RPO YF5): $52 without Cheyenne, $25 with High Sierra. Cold Climate Package (RPO Z56): $97-$133. Engine oil cooler (RPO KC4): $86. Transmission oil cooler (RPO VO2): $42. Heavy-duty radiator (RPO VO1): $39. Spare tire cover (RPO P17): $23. Power door lock system (RPO AU3): $90. Dual exhaust system, K1500 only (RPO N10): $37. Color-keyed front floor mats (RPO B32): $10. Gauge Package. Includes voltmeter, oil pressure and engine coolant temperature (RPO Z53): $27. Tachometer. Available only with V-8 engine (RPO U16) $87. 61 amp Delcotron generator (RPO K76): $45. Sliding side window (RPO AD5): $163. Tinted glass (RPO AO1): $46. Chromed grille (RPO V22): $26. Heavy-duty trailer wiring harness (RPO UY7): $31. Headlight warning buzzer (RPO T63): $7. Full length interior headliner (RPO BB5): $59. Inside hood release (RPO T44): $21. Deluxe instrument panel (RPO BC3): $35. Cigarette lighter (RPO U37): $17. Exterior below eye-level painted mirrors (RPO D29): $28. Exterior below eye-level stainless steel mirrors (RPO DG4): $52. Camper style stainless steel mirrors (RPO DF2): $67. Body spear molding (RPO B84): $59. Body side upper molding (RPO B85): $61. Upper and lower body side moldings (RPO YG1): $150. Door edge guards (RPO B93): $10. Wheel opening moldings (RPO B96): $21. Operating Convenience Group. Includes power door locks and power windows (RPO ZQ2): $221. Special two-tone exterior paint (RPO YZ3): $244, without High Sierra, $94 with High Sierra. Exterior Decor Package (RPO ZY5): $349 without High Sierra, $199 with High Sierra. Fuel tank and transfer case skid plates (RPO NY1): $123. AM radio: $86. AM/FM radio: $167. Rear seat speaker. (RPO U80): $38. Windshield antenna. Included when AM or AM/FM radio is ordered (RPO U76): 24. Rear roll bar (RPOE50): $9. Front passenger seat (RPO A57): $13. Rear 3 passenger seat (RPO AM7): $243, without custom trim, $264 with custom trim. High-back bucket seats $74 to $284 depending on seat trim and seat options. Speed and cruise control, V-8 only (RPO K30): $90. Heavy-duty front springs, K1500 only (RPO F60): $67. Tilt-type steering wheel (N33): $72. Custom steering wheel (RPO N31): $14. 31 gal. fuel tank (RPO N7O): $31. Two front towing hooks (RPO V76): $28. Deadweight towing hitch (RPO VR2): $41. Platform type towing hitch (RPO VR4): $115. Trailering Special Package (RPO Z82): $36-$81. Bright metal hubcaps (RPO PO3): $19. Bright wheel trim rings (RPO PO6): $41. Bright wheelcovers (RPO PO1): $20 with High Sierra, $29 with High Sierra. Rallye wheels (RPO N67): $93. Styled wheels (RPO PA6): $108. Power side door windows (RPO A31): $131. Power tailgate (RPO A33): $62. Intermittent windshield wiper system (RPO 30. Woodgrained exterior trim (RPO YG2): $279 without High Sierra, $129 with High Sierra.

HISTORICAL FOOTNOTES: GMC reported that the 1978 Jimmy "lets you get trackin'."

1979 JIMMY

The 1979 Jimmy had a new front end appearance with new integral headlight/parking light bezels, a lower grille outline molding of bright metal, a new paint treatment for the grille, a more aerodynamic hood contour to improve airflow for better economy, a new concealed fuel filler door and new interior and exterior colors. A wider vent post was used for improved anti-theft protection. In addition, improved anti-corrosion protection was provided by extending the use of zinc-rich precoated metal to the side door hinges and door panels, front fender and hood inner panels, front fender outer panels, standard tailgate, and radiator grille upper panel. The standard Sierra interior had high-back bucket seats (the passenger seat was included in both the custom vinyl trim and High Sierra options) in a choice of blue or camel tan Houndstooth pattern vinyl. Also included was a padded instrument panel with bright-trimmed applique and nameplate. The full floor covering was black embossed rubber. The door trim panels were color-keyed plastic with right-hand and left-hand integral armrests. Hardtop models had two dome lights with door-activated switches. Optional was a custom vinyl seat trim in blue or camel tan. This option also included color-keyed carpeting for the front compartment and color-keyed plastic console between the seats. A matching floor covering was included if the optional rear bench seat was ordered.

The High Sierra interior included all the standard features plus these additions or substitutions: Custom vinyl seat trim in blue, carmine or camel tan or custom cloth seat trim in carmine or camel tan. Also included was bright trim and color-keyed carpeting for the front compartment and color-keyed plastic console. Matching floor covering for the rear compartment was included when the optional rear bench seat was ordered. New for 1979 was the inclusion of a custom steering wheel plus available two-tone interior in a choice of blue, carmine or camel tan in combination with mystic custom vinyl or cloth seat rim or cloth seat trim, door trim panels and sunshades. The High Sierra instrument panel cluster had a bright finish and gauges for engine coolant temperature, voltmeter and oil pressure. Also part of the High Sierra's interior was special front door trim and rear sidewall trim panels with ashtrays.

1979 GMC Jimmy

I.D. DATA: The Jimmy's V.I.N. consisted of 13 symbols. The first symbol (a letter T) identified the GMC Motor Division. The second symbol (a letter K) indicated vehicle type. The third symbol (a letter) indicated engine type: D-250 cu. in. L-6, U-305 V-8, R-4-bbl. 400 cu. in. V-8, L-4-bbl. 350 cu. in. V-8. The fourth symbol (a number) identified the tonnage. The fifth symbol indicated model type. The sixth symbol identified the model year. The seventh symbol (a letter) indicated the assembly plant. The remaining six digits served as the sequential production numbers. The V.I.N. number was located on the left door pillar. The engine number indicated the manufacturing plant, day of manufacture and transmission type. It was located on a pad positioned on the right-hand side of the cylinder block at the rear of the distributor on V-8 engines and on a pad located at the front right hand side of the cylinder block of 6-cylinder engines.

Model Number	Body Type & Seating	Factory Price	GVW	Shipping Weight	Prod. Total
Jimmy K10. (with 305 V-8)					
CK10516	Util. (hardtop)	$7373	6200	4490[1]	11,804[2]
CK10516	Util. (folding top)	$7273	6200	4342[1]	—

NOTE 1: With 6-cyl. engine.
NOTE 2: Includes both two-wheel drive and four-wheel drive Jimmy models.

STANDARD ENGINE: 250 Six: Ordering Code: LD4. Engine Type: OHV, In-line 6-cylinder. Bore x Stroke: 3.875 in. x 3.50 in. Lifters: Hydraulic. Number of main bearings-7. Carburetion: Rochester downdraft one-barrel, model M7028007 or M7028011. Compression Ratio: 8.5:1. Displacement: 250 cu. in. (4.09 liters). Horsepower: Net: 100 @ 3800 rpm. Torque: Net: 175 lb.-ft. @ 1800 rpm. Oil capacity: 5 qt. with filter change. Fuel Requirements: Unleaded or low-lead gasoline of at least 91 Research Octane.

STANDARD ENGINE: V-8 models: Available in all states except California. Ordering Code: LG9. Engine Type: Cast iron block. OHV, V-8. Bore x Stroke: 3.74 in. x 3.48 in. Lifters: Hydraulic. Number of main bearings-5. Carburetion: Rochester two-barrel. Compression Ratio: 8.5:1. Displacement: 305 cu. in. Horsepower: 140 @ 3800 rpm. Torque: Gross: 235 lb.-ft. @ 2000 rpm. Oil capacity: 5 qt. with filter change. Fuel Requirements: Unleaded or low-lead gasoline of at least 91 Research Octane.

OPTIONAL ENGINE: V-8 models: Ordering Code: LS9. Engine Type: Cast iron block. OHV, V-8. Bore x Stroke: 4.0 in. x 3.50 in. Lifters: Hydraulic. Number of main bearings-5. Carburetion: Rochester four-barrel. Compression Ratio: 8.5:1. Displacement: 350 cu. in. Horsepower: Net: 160 @ 3800 rpm. Torque: Gross: Net: 250 lb.-ft. @ 2400 rpm. Oil capacity: 5 qt. with filter change. Fuel Requirements: Unleaded or low-lead gasoline of at least 91 Research Octane.

OPTIONAL ENGINE: V-8 models: Option LF4. Engine Type: Cast Iron block. OHV V-8. Bore x Stroke: 4.125 in. x 4.75 in. Lifters: Hydraulic. Number of main bearings-5. Displacement: 400 cu. in. (6.55 liters). Carburetion: Single Rochester 4-barrel. Compression Ratio: 8.5:1. (California rating: 8.2:1). Horsepower: 175 @ 3600 rpm. (California rating: 170 @ 3600 rpm). Torque: 290 lb.-ft. @ 2800 rpm. Fuel Requirements: Unleaded or low-lead gasoline of at least 91 Research Octane.

CHASSIS FEATURES: Ladder-type. Carbon steel, 39,000 psi. Heavy-gauge channel side members, alligator-jaw cross members. Section modulus: 3.06.

SUSPENSION AND RUNNING GEAR: Front Suspension: Two tapered semi-elliptical leaf springs. Capacity: 1650 lb. Rating: 250 lb./in. 1.0 in. shock absorbers, 1.25 in. stabilizer bar. Optional Capacity: 2250 lb. 32mm shock absorbers (available with RPO F60 heavy-duty springs only). Rear Suspension: Two-stage tapered and multi-leaf (six-conventional leaves, one tapered leaf). Capacity: 1700 lb. Rating: 270/510 lb./in. Optional: None. Front Axle. Type: Hypoid, tubular driving. Capacity: 3600 lb. Rear Axle. Type: Hypoid, semi-floating. Capacity: 3750 lb. Final Drive Ratio: 250 cu. in. 6-cyl.: 3.40:1. 305 V-8: 3.40:1; 350 and 400 cu. in. V-8 engines: 3.07:1. Optional: 250 cu. in. 6-cyl.: 3.40:1; 305, 350 V-8: and 400 cu. in. V-8 engines: 2.76, 3.40, 3.73:1. Transfer Case: Type: Manual transmission: New Process 205. Ratios: 1.96:1, 1.00:1. Automatic transmission: New Process 203. Ratios: 2.00:1, 1.00:1. Brakes: Type: Hydraulic, self-adjusting. Front: Discs. Rear: Drums. Optional: Power. Dimensions: Front: 11.86 in. dia. rotor. Rear: 11.15 in. x 2.75 in. Wheels: 6-stud, 15 x 6JJ. Optional: 15 x 7JJ Rallye, 15 x 8JJ, 15 x 8JJ Rallye, 16 x 5K. Tires: H78 x 15B, 4-ply rating. Optional: LR78 x 15C (highway steel belted radial white stripe), H78 x 15B (highway), H78 x 15B (highway, white stripe), H78 x 15B (on-off road), L78 x 15B (highway), L78 x15B (on-off road), L78 x 15B (highway, white stripe), 6.50 x 16C (highway), 7.00 x 15C (highway), 10.00 x 15B (polyester), 10.00 x 15B (polyester white lettered). Steering: Power assisted. Ratio: 20/16.4:1. Turns Lock-to-Lock. Turning circle: 37.58 ft. Transmission: Type: Saginaw 3-speed manual, fully synchronized. Steering column-mounted shifter. This transmission was not available for the 350 and 400 cu. in. V-8 engine with 4-bbl. carburetor. Transmission Ratios: 2.85, 1.68, 1.0:1. Optional: Muncie 4-speed manual, synchromesh on top three gears, floor-mounted shift lever. Ratios: 6.55, 3.58, 1.70, 1.00:1. Optional: Turbo Hydra-Matic 3-speed automatic. Ratios: 2.52, 1.52, 1.00:1. Clutch: Six-cylinder: 11.0 in. dia., 124 sq. in. area. V-8 engines: 12.0 in. dia., 150 sq. in. area. Optional: None.

VEHICLE DIMENSIONS: Wheelbase: 106.5 in. Overall Length: 184.5 in. Front/Rear Tread 65.75 in./ 62.75 in. Overall Height: 69.0 in. With optional hardtop; 71.0 in. Width: 79.5 in. Tailgate: Width and Height: 66.8 in. x 22.0 in. Approach/Departure Degrees: 34/22. Ground Clearance: Front axle: 8.9 in. Rear axle: 8.5 in. Oil pan: 17.2 in. Transfer case: 11.5 in. Fuel tank: 14.0 in. Load space: With rear seat installed: 38.8 in. x 50 in. x 42.3 in. With rear seat removed or folded: 76.0 in. x 50 in. x 42.3 in.

CAPACITIES: Fuel Tank: 25.0 gal. Optional: Replacement 30 gal. tank. Coolant system: 250 6-cyl.: 12.2 qt. 350 V-8: 17.1 qt.

ACCOMMODATIONS: Seating Capacity: Standard: Driver. Optional: Driver and front passenger and/or 3 passenger rear bench seat. Headroom: 38.3 in. Maximum steering wheel to seat back: 18.5 in. Seat to ground: 36.3 in. Floor to ground: 21.9 in.

INSTRUMENTATION: 0-100 mph speedometer, 99,999.9 mi. odometer, fuel gauge, warning lights for alternator, oil pressure, engine coolant temperature, brake operating system, hazard warning lights, directional lights.

OPTIONS AND PRICES: 305 cu. in. V-8 (RPO LG9). 350 cu. in. V-8 (RPO LS9). 400 cu. in. V-8 (RPO LF4). Automatic transmission (RPO MX1). Four-speed manual transmission (RPO MM4). High Sierra Package (RPO Z84). Poly Wrap air cleaner (RPO K43). All-Weather air conditioning. (RPO C60). Auxiliary Battery (RPO TP2). Heavy-duty battery (RPO UA1). Chromed front and rear bumpers (RPO VE5). Chromed front bumper guards. California emissions requirements (RPO YF5). Electric clock (RPO YF5). Cold Climate Package (RPO Z56). Engine oil cooler (RPO KC4). Transmission oil cooler (RPO VO2). Heavy-duty radiator (RPO VO1). Spare tire cover (RPO P17). Power door lock system (RPO AU3). Dual exhaust system, K1500 only (RPO N10). Color-keyed front floor mats (RPO B32). Gauge Package. Includes voltmeter, oil pressure and engine coolant temperature (RPO Z53). Tachometer. Available only with V-8 engine (RPO U16). 61 amp Delcotron generator (RPO K76). Sliding side window (RPO AD5). Tinted glass (RPO AO1). Chromed grille (RPO V22). Heavy-duty trailer wiring harness (RPO UY7). Headlight warning buzzer (RPO T63). Full length interior headliner (RPO BB5). Inside hood release (RPO T44). Deluxe instrument panel (RPO BC3. Cigarette lighter (RPO U37). Exterior below eye-level painted mirrors (RPO D29). Exterior below eye-level stainless steel mirrors (RPO DG4). Camper style stainless steel mirrors (RPO DF2). Body spear molding (RPO B84). Body side upper molding (RPO B85). Upper and lower body side moldings (RPO YG1). Door edge guards (RPO B93). Wheel opening moldings (RPO B96). Operating Convenience Group. Includes power door locks and power windows (RPO ZQ2). Special two-tone exterior paint (RPO YZ3). Exterior Decor Package (RPO ZY5. Fuel tank and transfer case skid plates (RPO NY1). AM radio. AM/FM radio. Rear seat speaker. (RPO U80). Windshield antenna. Included when AM or AM/FM radio is ordered (RPO U76). Rear roll bar (RPO E50). Front passenger seat (RPO A57). Rear 3 passenger seat (RPO AM7). High-back bucket seats. Speed and cruise control, V-8 only (RPO K30). Heavy-duty front springs, K1500 only (RPO F60). Tilt-type steering wheel (RPO N33). Custom steering wheel (RPO N31) 31 gal. fuel tank (RPO NK7). Two front towing hooks (RPO V76). Deadweight towing hitch (RPO VR2). Platform type towing hitch (RPO VR4). Trailering Special Package (RPO Z82). Bright metal hubcaps (RPO PO3). Bright wheel trim rings (RPO PO6). Bright wheelcovers (RPO PO1). Rallye wheels (RPO N67). Styled wheels (RPO PA6). Power side door windows (RPO A31). Power tailgate (RPO A33). Intermittent windshield wiper system (RPO CD4). Woodgrained exterior trim (RPO YG2).

HISTORICAL FOOTNOTES: For 1979 GMC assured customers that "Jimmy is tough."

1980 JIMMY

New features for the 1980 Jimmy included a new standard front-end paint treatment with argent-silver painted grille insert, eight new exterior colors, new push-button vent window latches, new optional outside mirrors designed to reduce glare, the addition of new international symbols to the instrument cluster gauges, and revised gauge graphics to meet federal standards. The optional RPO V22 grille included with the new Sierra Classic trim now included a chromed grille with rectangular headlights, body-color center bar and larger parking lights. A new one-piece front air dam was standard on all models. New exterior rear quarter panel nameplates and a new visor-mounted mirror were also included in the Sierra Classic. Interior features of the Sierra Classic included new custom cloth or Brahman-grain vinyl seat trim in blue (vinyl only), carmine or camel tan, new visor mirror, new interior nameplates, trimmed cowl side panels, and new front door trim panels with assist straps and carpet trim. The Sierra Classic two-tone interior (seat trim, door trim panels and sunshades) was available with blue, carmine or camel tan in combination with mystic custom vinyl (all colors) or custom cloth in either blue or carmine. The Sierra Classic option also included custom steering wheel, mystic headliner, color-keyed center console and carpeting, bright trim instrument cluster gauges for speedometer, odometer, fuel level, voltmeter, engine coolant temperature and oil pressure. A new part time New Process transfer case was used for 1980. A dash-mounted light operated when the Jimmy was in four-wheel drive. The 350 cu. in. V-8 had a new single inlet, dual outlet exhaust system designed to reduce back pressure. A new engine fan clutch allowed the fan to operate only when it was needed. Both the 305 and 400 cu. in. engines were dropped for 1980. Other changes made for 1980 in order to improve the Jimmy's fuel economy included the use of radial tires. The Jimmy's front seat back angle was increased by 3.0 to 3.5 degrees. A new four speaker system for the Jimmy with the front speakers mounted high in the door panels and the rear speakers positioned in the sidewalls ahead of the wheelhousings was introduced. Also joining the option list were new forged aluminum wheels. The 1980 Jimmy color selection consisted of frost white, medium blue, light blue metallic, nordic blue metallic, Emerald green, Santa Fe tan, carmine red, cardinal red, midnight black and brunt orange metallic.

1980 GMC Jimmy with Sierra Classic trim and V22 grille

I.D. DATA: The Jimmy's V.I.N. consisted of 13 symbols. The first symbol (a letter T) identified the GMC Motor Division. The second symbol (a letter K) indicated vehicle type. The third symbol (a letter) indicated engine type: D-250 cu. in. L-6, L-4-bbl. 350 cu. in. V-8. The fourth symbol (a number) identified the tonnage. The fifth symbol indicated model type. The sixth symbol identified the model year. The seventh symbol (a letter) indicated the assembly plant. The remaining six digits served as the sequential production numbers. The V.I.N. number was located on the left door pillar. The engine number indicated the manufacturing plant, day of manufacture and transmission type. It was located on a pad positioned on the right-hand side of the cylinder block at the rear of the distributor on V-8 engines and on a pad located at the front right hand side of the cylinder block of 6-cylinder engines.

Model Number	Body Type & Seating	Factory Price	GVW	Shipping Weight	Prod. Total
Jimmy K-1500 (with 305 V-8)					
TK10516	Util. (hardtop)	$8078	6200	4418	5606*
TK10516	Util. (folding top)	$7975	6200	N.A.	—

* Includes two-wheel drive and four-wheel drive models of both body styles.

STANDARD ENGINE: All states except California: Order Code LE3. Engine Type: OHV, cast iron block. In-line 6-cylinder. Bore x Stroke: 3.875 in. x 3.50 in. Lifters: Mechanical. Number of main bearings-7. Carburetion: Rochester Staged two-barrel. Compression Ratio: 8.3:1. Displacement: 250 cu. in. (4.09 liters). Horsepower: Net: 130 @ 4000 rpm. Torque: Net: 210 lb.-ft. @ 2000 rpm. Oil capacity: 5 qt. with filter change. Fuel Requirements: Leaded or unleaded.

OPTIONAL ENGINE: 350 V-8: Order Code LG9. Engine Type: Cast iron block. OHV, V-8. Bore x Stroke: 4.0 in. x 3.50 in. Lifters: Hydraulic. Number of main bearings-5. Carburetion: Rochester four-barrel. Compression Ratio: 8.2:1. Displacement: 350 cu. in. Horsepower: 170 @ 4000 rpm. Torque: Gross: 270 lb.-ft. @ 2400 rpm. (California: 275 lb.-ft. @ 2400 rpm. Available in California only with 4-speed manual or automatic transmission. Oil capacity: 5 qt. with filter change. Fuel Requirements: Unleaded.

CHASSIS FEATURES: Ladder-type. Carbon steel, 39,000 psi. Heavy-gauge channel side members, alligator-jaw cross members. Section modulus: 3.06 in.

SUSPENSION AND RUNNING GEAR: Front Suspension: Two tapered semi-elliptical leaf springs. Capacity: 1650 lb. Rating: 250 lb./in. 1.0 in. shock absorbers, 1.25 in. stabilizer bar. Optional Capacity: 2250 lb. 32mm shock absorbers (available with RPO F60 heavy-duty springs only). Rear Suspension: Two-stage tapered and multi-leaf (six-conventional leaves, one tapered leaf). Capacity: 1700 lb. Rating: 270/510 lb./in. Optional: None. Front Axle. Type: Hypoid, tubular driving. Capacity: 3600 lb. Rear Axle. Type: Hypoid, semi-floating. Capacity: 3750 lb. Final Drive Ratio: 6-cyl.: 3.73:1, 350 V-8: 2.76:1. Optional: 6-cyl.: 3.42, V-8: 3.08:1. Transfer Case: Type: 2-speed. Brakes: Type: Hydraulic, self-adjusting. Front: Discs. Rear: Drums. Optional: Power. Dimensions: Front: 11.86 in. dia. rotor. Rear: 11.15 in. x 2.75 in. Wheels: 6-stud, 15 x 6JJ. Optional: 15 x 7JJ Rallye, 15 x 8JJ, 15 x 8JJ Rallye, 16 x 5K. Tires: P215/75R15 steel belted radial. Optional: P215/75R15 steel belted radial whitewall, P235/75R15 steel belted radial, P235/75R15 steel belted whitewall, P235/75R15 white lettered steel belted radial, 10R-15B steel belted radial, 10R-15B white lettered steel belted radial. Steering: Power assisted recirculating ball, variable ratio. Ratio: 17.6/13.1. Turns Lock-to-Lock: 3.4. Turning circle: 37.6 ft. Transmission: Type: Saginaw 3-speed manual, fully synchronized. Steering column-mounted shifter. This transmission was not available for the state of California. Transmission Ratios: 2.85, 1.68, 1.0:1. Optional: Muncie 4-speed manual, synchromesh on top three gears, floor-mounted shift lever. Ratios: 6.55, 3.58, 1.70, 1.00:1. Optional: Turbo Hydra-Matic 3-speed automatic. Ratios: 2.52, 1.52, 1.00:1. Clutch: 11.0 in. dia., 124 sq. in. area. 12 in. clutch included with 350 V-8 engines.

VEHICLE DIMENSIONS: Wheelbase: 106.5 in. Overall Length: 184.4 in. Front/Rear Tread 66.70 in./ 63.70 in. Overall Height: 72.0 in. Width: 79.5 in. Tailgate: Width and Height: 66.8 in. x 22.0 in. Approach/Departure Degrees: 27/23. Ground Clearance: Front axle: 7.4 in. Rear axle: 7.0 in. Oil pan: 17.2 in. Transfer case: 11.5 in. Fuel tank: 14.0 in. Load space: With rear seat installed: 38.8 in. x 50 in. x 42.3 in. With rear seat removed or folded: 76.0 in. x 50 in. x 42.3 in.

CAPACITIES: Fuel Tank: 25.0 gal. Optional: Replacement 31 gal. tank. Coolant system: 250 6-cyl.: 12.2 qt. 350 V-8: 17.1 qt.

ACCOMMODATIONS: Seating Capacity: Standard: Driver and front passenger bucket seats. Optional: 3 passenger rear bench seat. Headroom: 38.3 in. Maximum steering wheel to seat back: 18.5 in. Seat to ground: 36.3 in. Floor to ground: 21 in.

INSTRUMENTATION: 0-100 mph speedometer, 99,999.9 mi. odometer, fuel gauge, warning lights for alternator, oil pressure, engine coolant temperature, brake operating system, hazard warning lights, directional lights, seat belt warning.

OPTIONS AND PRICES: Most options were carried over from 1979; this is a representative sampling. 350 cu. in. V-8: $470. Sliding rear windows: $18. Folding rear seat: $300. Tinted window glass (RPO AO1): $52. Woodgrained trim (RPO YG2): $69. Electric tailgate window: $69. Intermittent windshield wipers: $35. Air conditioning: $607. Rear roll bar: $112. Locking rear differential: $197. 3.07:1 rear axle: $27. Engine oil cooler: $97. 4-speed manual transmission: $175. 31 gal. replacement fuel tank: $35. Fuel tank skid plate: $139. Tilt steering wheel: $83. 3500 watt Delco auxiliary battery: $103. 4000 watt Delco Freedom battery: $41. AM/FM cassette 351. Sierra Classic Package (RPO YE9): $895. Operating Convenience Package: $248. Inside hood lock release: $25. Power windows. Power door locks. Four AM/FM/Tape/CB options were available.

HISTORICAL FOOTNOTES: The 1980 Jimmy was depicted by GMC as "four-wheelin' action."

1981 JIMMY

The GMC Jimmy had new front end sheet metal that was redesigned for reduced weight. The Jimmy's new appearance was more aerodynamic and included standard single rectangular headlights or dual rectangular headlights for the optional Deluxe Front End Appearance Package. Other evident changes included restyled bumpers, and the relocation of the parking lights to the bumper. New optional moldings were installed low on the body side. Other changes included restyled model designation plates.

Other revisions consisted of new front fender skirts with attached shields was used to help reduce engine compartment splash, use of a HSLA-type steel for lighter weight bumpers, and an 8-point front bumper attachment for improved bumper stiffness. Overall weight of K-1500 models were reduced as much as 263 pounds. Also found on the 1981 models were new front door hinge reinforcements and anchor plates and new compression-rebound-type cab body mounts.

Improved anti-corrosion characteristics resulted from the use of two-sided galvanized steel was used for the side inner panels and the rear wheel housings. Urethane stone shields were added forward of the rear wheel openings. A zinc-rich paint was added to the anti-corrosion coating of the brake and fuel lines. Drag-free front disc brakes and a new quick take-up master cylinder also helped improve fuel economy. Four new colors were added for 1981. They were: Light silver metallic, charcoal metallic, colonial yellow and dark chestnut metallic. They joined these colors carried over from 1980: Frost white, medium blue, light blue metallic, nordic blue metallic, Emerald green, Santa Fe tan, carmine red, cardinal red, midnight black and burnt orange metallic. Four interior colors were available for 1981. Continued from 1980 were carmine and blue. New for 1981 were doeskin and slate. All of the Blazer's interior trim panels were new for 1981. In addition, new chromed diecast hardware was used. All models had a color-keyed plastic door trim panel with an integrated armrest. The two-tone interior was discontinued. The driver's seat adjuster was modified for improved stability and greater seat travel. A new bucket seat center console, designed to reduced weight, had a positive-type latch with key lock and a torsion bar hinge which permitted the cover, after being released, to pop up for easy access to the interior. The cover could be lifted to a 110 degree position and was held in place by a check strap. If the check strap was released, the cover could be rotated to a 180 degree position to be used a a tray for rear seat occupants. The console also had two beverage pockets and a loose article storage pocket for the driver and front seat passenger. Helping to lower overall vehicle weight was reduced-thickness glass used in all the Jimmy's windows. In place of the old RPO AO1 option, the Jimmy now had tinted glass in all windows. The Jimmy instrument panel was revised to accommodate a new stereo radio speaker. A new instrument panel pad with new appliques and nameplate was used. New international operating symbols for the windshield wiper-washer control were installed as was a new illuminated transfer case range indicator. Replacing the constant "on" function of the heater blower was a new "off" position. The Jimmy's standard vinyl seats now had a striped design available in either blue or doeskin. The custom vinyl bucket seats had a leather-grained vinyl seat trim material. If the High Sierra Package was ordered the seats were available in any of four colors: blue, carmine, doeskin or slate. Colors for the Sierra interior were blue or doeskin. The custom cloth bucket seats had a carryover houndstooth-patterned cloth cover available in carmine, doeskin or slate.

1981 GMC Jimmy

The Jimmy's 4.1 liter 6-cylinder engine had a recalibrated carburetor as well as a redesigned cam. The 5.7 liter 350 cu. in. V-8 continued to be available only in California. The 5.0 liter 305 cu. in. V-8 was available in all states but California. It was equipped with a staged four-barrel carburetor with a large dual-element air filter and Electronic Spark Control. This system had a sensor that retarded spark advance under engine knock conditions. This allowed the higher compression engine to operate at the highest spark curve possible for increased performance with unleaded fuel. A modified cam that provided less valve overlap was also used as were larger diameter exhaust ports.

The transfer case was a new New Process 208 unit with an aluminum case and synchronizers for smoother shifting. This system also included automatic front locking hubs that freewheeled until the vehicle was placed in four-wheel drive and torque was applied to the front wheels. The hubs returned to their freewheeling mode when the transfer case was shifted back to two-wheel drive and the Jimmy was driven in reverse for approximately three feet. The Jimmy as also equipped with a lighter rear axle with 9.5 in. ring gears. Axle ratios were also changed to improve fuel economy. The standard rear springs had a higher capacity for 1981. They were also of a more durable, lighter weight design and had improved corrosion protection. A new jack with a larger base, more suitable for off-road use was standard Jimmy equipment.

A number of changes took place in the Jimmy's optional equipment content and availability. The bright trimmed black plastic RPO B84 moldings were available for Jimmys with the Sierra Trim Package. The Sierra Jimmy was also available with RPO B85 moldings of bright plastic with black paint trim and bright trimmed front side marker lights and tail lights. Another Molding Package available for the Sierra Jimmy was RPO B96 consisted of bright front and rear front and rear wheel opening moldings with black paint trim. The RPO YG1 Molding Package had new content for 1981. Included in the RPO YE9 High Sierra Package and available for all other trim levels was RPO YG3. This introduced a new Molding Package for the Jimmy consisting of bright plastic body side and rear moldings with black paint trim, RPO B96, plus bright trimmed front side marker lights and tail lights. Included in the High Sierra trim level was a new tailgate trim panel of bright anodized aluminum. Additional aspects of the 1981 High Sierra Package included full foam front bucket seats in either custom vinyl (in any of four colors) or custom cloth, also offered in four colors. The High Sierra instrument panel had brushed stainless steel accents on cluster and pad, and cluster gauges. Other features included a new console, custom steering wheel, visor mirror, color-keyed front carpeting, full door trim panels with brushed stainless steel inserts, a soft vinyl insert in the armrest area, carpet trim below the trim panel, a door-closing assist strap and storage pockets The High Sierra exterior was highlighted by a chrome-trimmed grille with stacked dual rectangular headlights and a bright anodized aluminum tailgate trim panel. The High Sierra grille was also available as RPO V22. It featured a chrome finish on the leading edge of the grille insert. Both its center bar and head light bezels had a brushed chrome finish. It could also be ordered with RPO TT5, high-intensity, high-beam halogen headlights. A new one-way glass, RPO AJ1 option for the side and rear windows back of the driver was introduced for hardtop model Jimmys. A new automatic speed control, RPO K35, included a resume feature and was available on 6-cylinder models. The RPO U35 electric clock now had a solid-state quartz mechanism. The RPO YG2 exterior woodgrain trim was discontinued. A new Front Quad Shock Package, RPO Z75, was introduced which included an extra pair of 25mm shock absorbers on the front axle, heavy-duty 32mm rear shock absorbers and a front axle pinion nose snubber to limit front axle windup to help improve off-road handling.

I.D. DATA: The V.I.N. plate was mounted on the lower left side windshield corner. The V.I.N. consisted of 17 elements. The first, the number 1, identified the U.S. as the nation of origin. The letter G followed, for the manufacturer: General Motors. The third entry, the letter T, represented the make as GMC. The GVWR brake system identification followed. Next came the truck line and chassis type; the letter K indicated four-wheel drive. The truck series was identified by a number: 1-1/2 ton. The truck body yype identification was next: 8-Utility. The engine code was next, followed by a check digit. The model year was identified by the letter B. The assembly plant code followed. The final six digits were the plant sequential production number.

Model Number	Body Type & Seating	Factory Price	GVW	Shipping Weight	Prod. Total
Jimmy K-1500. (with 250 6-cyl.)					
TK10516	Util. (hardtop)	$8856	6100	4087	4689*
TK10516	Util. (folding top)	$8750	6100	N.A.	—

* Includes all two-wheel drive and four-wheel drive Jimmy models.

STANDARD ENGINE: All states except California: Order Code LE3. Engine Type: OHV, cast iron block. In-line 6-cylinder. Bore x Stroke: 3.875 in. x 3.50 in. Lifters: Mechanical. Number of main bearings-7. Carburetion: Rochester Staged two-barrel. Compression Ratio: 8.30:1. Displacement: 250 cu. in. Horsepower: Net: 115 @ 3600 rpm. Torque: Net: 200 lb.-ft. @ 1800 rpm. Oil capacity: 5 qt. with filter change. Fuel Requirements: Unleaded. Optional: Engine Type: OHV, cast iron block. V-8. Order Code LE9 with Electronic Spark Control. Not available for California. Bore x Stroke: 3.74 in. x 3.48 in. Lifters: Hydraulic. Number of main bearings-5. Carburetion: Four-barrel. Compression Ratio: 9.2:1. Displacement: 305 cu. in. Horsepower: Net: 165 @ 4400 rpm. Torque: Net: 240 lb.-ft. @ 2000 rpm. Oil capacity: 5 qt. with filter change. Fuel Requirements: Unleaded. Optional: Engine Type: OHV, cast iron block. V-8. Order Code LS9. Required for California. Bore x Stroke: 4.0 in. x 3.50 in. Lifters: Hydraulic. Number of main bearings-5. Carburetion: Four-barrel. Compression Ratio: 8.2:1. Displacement: 350 cu. in. Horsepower: Net: 150 @ 3600 rpm. Torque: Net: 255 lb.-ft. @ 1600 rpm. Oil capacity: 5 qt. with filter change. Fuel Requirements: Unleaded.

CHASSIS FEATURES: Ladder-type. Carbon steel, 39,000 psi. Heavy-gauge channel side members, alligator-jaw cross members. Section modulus: 3.06 in.

SUSPENSION AND RUNNING GEAR: Front Suspension: Two tapered semi-elliptical leaf springs. Capacity: 1650 lb. Rating: 250 lb./in. 1.0 in. shock absorbers, 1.25 in. stabilizer bar. Optional Capacity: 2250 lb. 32mm shock absorbers (available with RPO F60 heavy-duty springs only). Rear Suspension: Two-stage tapered and multi-leaf (six-conventional leaves, one tapered leaf). Capacity: 1700 lb. Rating: 270/510 lb./in. Optional: None. Front Axle. Type: Hypoid, tubular driving. Capacity: 3600 lb. Rear Axle. Type: Hypoid, semi-floating. Capacity: 3750 lb. Final Drive Ratio: 6-cyl.: 3.73:1, 305 V-8: 2.73:1, 350 V-8: 2.73:1. Optional: 6-cyl.: 3.42; 305 V-8: 2.56, 3.08, 3.73:1; 350 V-8: 3.08:1. Transfer Case: New Process 208. Ratios: 2.61, 1.00:1. Brakes: Type: Hydraulic, self-adjusting. Front: Discs. Rear: Drums. Optional: Power. Dimensions: Front: 11.86 in. dia. rotor. Rear: 11.15 in. x 2.75 in. Wheels: 6-stud, 15 x 6JJ. Optional: 15 x 7JJ Rallye, 15 x 8JJ, 15 x 8JJ Rallye, 16 x 5K. Tires: P215/75R15 steel belted radial. Optional: P215/75R15 steel belted radial whitewall, P235/75R15 steel belted radial, P235/75R15 steel belted radial whitewall, P235/75R15 white lettered steel belted radial, 10R-15B steel belted radial, 10R-15B white lettered steel belted radial. Steering: Power assisted recirculating ball, variable ratio. Ratio: 17.6/13.1. Turns Lock-to-Lock: 3.4. Turning circle: 37.6 ft. Transmission: Type: Saginaw 3-speed manual, fully synchronized. Steering column-mounted shifter. This transmission was not available for the state of California. Transmission Ratios: 2.85, 1.68, 1.0:1. Optional: Muncie 4-speed manual, synchromesh on top three gears, floor-mounted shift lever. Ratios: 6.55, 3.58, 1.70, 1.00:1. Optional: Turbo Hydra-Matic 3-speed automatic. Ratios: 2.52, 1.52, 1.00:1. Clutch: 11.0 in. dia., 124 sq. in. area. 12 in. clutch included with 350 V-8 engines.

VEHICLE DIMENSIONS: Wheelbase: 106.5 in. Overall Length: 184.8 in. Front/Rear Tread 66.10 in./ 63.0 in. Overall Height: 73.40 in. Width: 79.6 in. Tailgate: Width and Height: 66.8 in. x 22.0 in. Approach/Departure Degrees: 34/25. Ground Clearance: Front axle: 7.4 in. Rear axle: 6.7 in. Oil pan: 17.2 in. Transfer case: 11.5 in. Fuel tank: 14.0 in. Load space: With rear seat installed: 38.8 in. x 50 in. x 42.3 in. With rear seat removed or folded: 76.0 in. x 50 in. x 42.3 in.

CAPACITIES: Fuel Tank: 25.0 gal. Optional: Replacement 31 gal. tank. Coolant system: 250 6-cyl.: 12.2 qt. 305 V-8: 17.6 qt. 350 V-8: 17.6 qt.

ACCOMMODATIONS: Seating Capacity: Standard: Driver and front passenger bucket seats. Optional: 3 passenger rear bench seat. Headroom: 38.3 in. Maximum steering wheel to seat back: 18.5 in. Seat to ground: 36.3 in. Floor to ground: 21.0 in.

INSTRUMENTATION: 0-100 mph speedometer, 99,999.9 mi. odometer, fuel gauge, warning lights for alternator, oil pressure, engine coolant temperature, brake operating system, hazard warning lights, directional lights, seat belt warning.

OPTIONS AND PRICES: Air conditioning. Bright metal wheelcovers. Bright metal wheel trim rings. Chromed front and rear bumpers. Chromed front bumper guards. Deluxe front and rear bumpers. Cigarette lighter. Color-keyed floor mats. ComforTilt steering wheel. Custom steering wheel. Chromed grille (RPO V22). Deluxe instrument panel. Electric clock (RPO U35). Folding top (available in either black or white). One-way glass RPO AJ1). Sliding glass rear side windows. Halogen headlights (RPO TT5). Headlight warning buzzer. Intermittent windshield wipers. Painted below eye-level mirrors (RPO D44). Stainless steel below eye-level mirrors (RPO D45). Stainless steel camper mirrors (RPO DF2). Black body side moldings (RPO B84). Bright body side moldings (RPOB85). Black Molding Package. Bright Molding Package. Operating Convenience Package. Power door locks. Power windows. Special two-tone paint. Exterior Decor Package. AM radio. AM/FM radio. AM/FM radio with 8-track tape player. AM/FM radio with cassette tape player. AM/FM stereo radio with cassette tape player. AM/FM radio with CB and antenna. Rear auxiliary speaker. Windshield antenna. Rear roll bar. Spare tire carrier. Folding rear seat. Tachometer. Electric tailgate window. Aluminum wheels (RPO PH7). Rallye wheels (RPO N67). Styled wheels (RPO PA6). High Sierra Trim Package (RPO YE9): $881. Auxiliary battery. Cold Climate Package. Engine oil cooler. Transmission oil cooler. Cruise control. Deadweight trailer hitch. Front quad shock absorbers (RPO Z75). Front tow hooks. 31 gal. fuel tank. Fuel tank shield plate. Gauge Package. Includes voltmeter, engine coolant temperature and oil pressure gauges. 55 amp generator. 61 amp generator. Heavy-duty battery. Heavy-duty front and rear shock absorbers. Heavy-duty front springs. Heavy-duty radiator. Locking rear differential. Trailering special equipment. Trailer wiring harness. Weight-distributing hitch platform.

HISTORICAL FOOTNOTES: For 1981 GMC noted that "trucks are what we are all about."

1982 JIMMY

The 1982 Jimmy was offered only in removable hardtop form. Standard equipment included left and right side padded armrests, ashtray, two coat hooks, two dome lights, color-keyed embossed plastic door trim panels, embossed black molded plastic floor mats, Deluxe-Air heater and defroster, color-keyed padded left and right side sunshades, chromed front and rear bumpers, tinted glass, bright metal hubcaps, left and right side fixed arm adjustable exterior mirrors, white painted wheels and electric 2-speed windshield wipers and washers. General Motors 6.2 liter diesel V-8 engine was introduced as an option. This engine was available only with a new optional 4-speed automatic overdrive transmission. The required diesel equipment option included two heavy-duty Freedom batteries, 63 amp Delcotron generator, hydraulic power brakes, heavy-duty radiator, engine oil cooler, dual exhaust system, heavy-duty front springs, Special Sound Insulation Package, warning lights for glow plugs, water-in-fuel and low coolant, 6.2 LITRE DIESEL hood emblem, and fender and tailgate identification nameplates. The standard Jimmy engine continued to be the 4.1 liter 6-cylinder. For California the 5.7 liter V-8 was specified for the Jimmy. The standard transmission, (except for the LS9 and LH6 engines which both had the 4-speed automatic overdrive transmission as standard) was an all-synchromesh 4-speed manual. Other developments for 1982 included new two-tone paint combinations, new permanent magnet motors for the optional power windows, single rectangular headlights for the Sierra model, automatic speed control for both manual and automatic transmission, and a new AM/FM/CB stereo radio with antenna. Exterior colors for 1982 were white, light slate metallic, black, light blue metallic, dark blue, yellow, light tan, light bronze, dark bronze and carmine.

1982 GMC Jimmy

I.D. DATA: The V.I.N. plate was mounted on the lower left side windshield corner. The V.I.N. consisted of 17 elements. The first, the number 1, identified the U.S. as the nation of origin. The letter G followed, for the manufacturer: General Motors. The third entry, the letter T, represented the make as GMC. The GVWR brake system identification followed. Next came the truck line and chassis type; the letter K indicated four-wheel drive. The truck series was identified by a number: 1-1/2 ton. The truck body type identification was next: 8-Utility. The engine code was next, followed by a check digit. The model year was identified by the letter C. The assembly plant code followed. The final six digits were the plant sequential production number.

Model Number	Body Type & Seating	Factory Price	GVW	Shipping Weight	Prod. Total
Jimmy K1500 (with 250 6-cyl.)					
TK10516	Util. (hardtop)	$9874.20[1]	6100	4294	24,004[2]

NOTE 1: Add $1334 for diesel engine and $1125 for diesel equipment RPO B3J.
NOTE 2: Included both two-wheel drive and four-wheel drive Blazers.

STANDARD ENGINE: All states except California: Order Code LE3. Engine Type: OHV, cast iron block. In-line 6-cylinder. Bore x Stroke: 3.875 in. x 3.50 in. Lifters: Mechanical. Number of main bearings-7. Carburetion: Rochester Staged two-barrel. Compression Ratio: 8.30:1. Displacement: 250 cu. in. Horsepower: Net: 120 @ 3600 rpm. Torque: Net: 200 lb.-ft. @ 1800 rpm. Oil capacity: 5 qt. with filter change. Fuel Requirements: Unleaded. Optional: Engine Type: OHV, cast iron block. V-8. Order Code LE9 with Electronic Spark Control. Not available for California. Bore x Stroke: 3.74 in. x 3.48 in. Lifters: Hydraulic. Number of main bearings-5. Carburetion: Four-barrel. Compression Ratio: 9.2:1. Displacement: 305 cu. in. Horsepower: Net: 165 @ 4400 rpm. Torque: Net: 240 lb.-ft. @ 2000 rpm. Oil capacity: 5 qt. with filter change. Fuel Requirements: Unleaded. Optional: Engine Type: OHV, cast iron block. V-8. Order Code LS9. Required for California. Bore x Stroke: 4.0 in. x 3.50 in. Lifters: Hydraulic. Number of main bearings-5. Carburetion: Four-barrel. Compression Ratio: 8.2:1. Displacement: 350 cu. in. Horsepower: Net: 165 @ 3800 rpm. Torque: Net: 275 lb.-ft. @ 1600 rpm. Oil capacity: 5 qt. with filter change. Fuel Requirements: Unleaded. Optional: Engine Type: OHV, cast iron block. Diesel V-8. Order Code LH6. Bore x Stroke: 3.98 in. x 3.80 in. Lifters: Hydraulic. Number of main bearings-5. Carburetion: Fuel injection. Compression Ratio: 21.5:1. Displacement: 379 cu. in. (6.2 liter). Horsepower: Net: 130 @ 3600 rpm. Torque: Net: 240 lb.-ft. @ 2000 rpm. Oil capacity: 7 qt. with filter change. Fuel Requirements: Diesel.

CHASSIS FEATURES: Ladder-type. Carbon steel, 39,000 psi. Heavy-gauge channel side members, alligator-jaw cross members. Section modulus: 3.06 in.

SUSPENSION AND RUNNING GEAR: Front Suspension: Two tapered semi-elliptical leaf springs. Capacity: 1650 lb. Rating: 250 lb./in. 1.0 in. shock absorbers, 1.25 in. stabilizer bar. Optional Capacity: 2250 lb. 32mm shock absorbers (available with RPO F60 heavy-duty springs only). Front quad shock absorbers. Rear Suspension: Two-stage tapered and multi-leaf (six-conventional leaves, one tapered leaf). Capacity: 1700 lb. Rating: 270/510 lb./in. Optional: None. Front Axle. Type: Hypoid, tubular driving. Capacity: 3600 lb. Rear Axle. Type: Hypoid, semi-floating. Capacity: 3750 lb. Final Drive Ratio: 6-cyl.: 3.42:1; 305 V-8 with ESC: 2.73:1; 350 V-8: 2.73:1; 379 diesel V-8: 3.08:1. Optional: 6-cyl.: 3.73; 305 V-8: 3.08, 3.73:1; 350 V-8: 3.08:1; 379 diesel V-8: 3.42, 3.73:1. Transfer Case: New Process 208. Ratios: 2.61, 1.00:1. Brakes: Type: Hydraulic, self-adjusting. Front: Discs. Rear: Drums. Optional: Power. Dimensions: Front: 11.86 in. dia. rotor. Rear: 11.15 in. x 2.75 in. Wheels: 6-stud, 15 x 6JJ. Optional: 15 x 7JJ Rallye, 15 x 8JJ, 15 x 8JJ Rallye, 16 x 5K. Tires: P215/75R15 steel belted radial. Optional: P215/75R15 steel belted radial whitewall, P235/75R15 steel belted radial, P235/75R15 steel belted radial whitewall, P235/75R15 white lettered steel belted radial, 10R-15B steel belted radial, 10R-15B white lettered steel belted radial. Steering: Power assisted recirculating ball, variable ratio. Ratio: 17.6/13.1. Turns Lock-to-Lock: 3.4. Turning circle: 37.6 ft. Transmission: No standard manual transmissions were available in California. Type: Muncie 4-speed manual, synchromesh on top three gears, floor-mounted shift lever. Ratios: 6.55, 3.58, 1.70, 1.00:1. Optional: 700R4 4-speed automatic with overdrive. Ratios: 3.06, 1.36, 1.00, 0.70:1. R2.29:1. Reverse: Clutch: 11.0 in. dia., 124 sq. in. area. 12 in. clutch included with 350 V-8 engines.

VEHICLE DIMENSIONS: Wheelbase: 106.5 in. Overall Length: 184.8 in. Front/Rear Tread 66.10 in./ 63.0 in. Overall Height: 73.40 in. Width: 79.6 in. Tailgate: Width and Height: 66.8 in. x 22.0 in. Approach/Departure Degrees: 34/25. Ground Clearance: Front axle: 7.4 in. Rear axle: 6.7 in. Oil pan: 17.2 in. Transfer case: 11.5 in. Fuel tank: 14.0 in. Load space: With rear seat installed: 38.8 in. x 50 in. x 42.3 in. With rear seat removed or folded: 76.0 in. x 50 in. x 42.3 in.

CAPACITIES: Fuel Tank: 25.0 gal. Optional: Replacement 31 gal. tank. Coolant system: 250 6-cyl.: 12.2 qt. 305 V-8: 17.6 qt. 350 V-8: 17.6 qt.

ACCOMMODATIONS: Seating Capacity: Standard: Driver and front passenger bucket seats. Optional: 3 passenger rear bench seat. Headroom: 38.3 in. Maximum steering wheel to seat back: 18.5 in. Seat to ground: 36.3 in. Floor to ground: 21 in.

INSTRUMENTATION: 0-100 mph speedometer, 99,999.9 mi. odometer, fuel gauge, warning lights for alternator, oil pressure, engine coolant temperature, brake operating system, hazard warning lights, directional lights, seat belt warning.

OPTIONS AND PRICES: Air conditioning: $677. Deluxe front appearance: $100. Locking rear differential: $217. Heavy-duty battery: $45. Deluxe chromed front and rear bumpers: $44. Front chromed bumper guards: $39. Quartz analog electric clock: $36 without YE9 trim; $70 without YE9 trim. Cold Climate Package: $114-$172. Engine oil cooler: $112. Engine transmission oil cooler: $55. Heavy-duty radiator: $48. Power door locks: $115. Color-keyed front floor mats: $14. Gauges: Voltmeter, engine coolant temperature and oil pressure: $34. 63 amp generator: $58. Deep tinted with tinted rear window: $119. Deep tinted with deep tinted rear window: $168. Sliding side windows with air deflectors: $216. Halogen high-beam headlamps: $15. High and low beam halogen headlamps: $20. Trailer wiring harness: $42. Headlight warning buzzer: $11. Headliner interior: $74. Cigarette lighter: $28. Exterior below eye-level painted mirrors: $44. Exterior below eye-level stainless steel mirrors: $72. Black body side moldings: $105. Bright body side moldings: 131. Custom Package moldings: $144. Deluxe Package moldings: $157. Door edge guards: $15. Operating Convenience Package: $281. AM radio: $92. AM/FM radio: $143. AM/FM stereo radio: $226. AM/FM stereo radio with 8-track stereo tape player: $322. AM/FM stereo radio with cassette stereo tape player: $327. AM/FM stereo radio and CB radio: $559. Rear roll bar: $123. Folding rear seat: $308. Fuel tank and transfer case shield: $84. Front quad shock absorbers: $117. Speed control: $159 with auto. trans., $169 with manual trans. Heavy-duty front shock absorbers: $53. ComforTilt steering wheel: $234. 31 gal. fuel tank: $39. Two front towing hooks: $34. Deadweight trailer hitch: $53. Platform type trailer hitch: $145. Trailering Special Package: $354-$619. Bright metal wheelcovers: $38. Aluminum forged wheels: $411. Rallye wheels: $103. Styled wheels: $201. Power side door windows: $166. Power tailgate: $79. Intermittent windshield wipers: $45. Sierra Classic Package: $931. Special tone-tone paint: $147-$291. Exterior Decor Package: $279-$423.

HISTORICAL FOOTNOTES: GMC reported that the 1982 Jimmy: "...Looks great outside... built for value... feels great inside!"

1983 JIMMY

The 1983 Jimmy, also identified as the K Jimmy to distinguish it from the new S-15 Jimmy, had a new hood inner panel formed of Zincometal for added protection from corrosion. New exhaust fasteners with a spring retention of the exhaust pipe flanges reduced stress to the system. Initially, the standard transmission for the V-8 gasoline engine was the 4-speed automatic overdrive unit. The standard 4-speed manual transmission was available after January, 1983. The standard Jimmy engine was the 5.0 liter, 305 cu. in. V-8. For 1983 the Jimmy had a new front end treatment consisting of new lamp bezels and grille. Those on the standard model were painted light argent and surrounded by new bright outline moldings. The parking lamps were located below the single rectangular headlights. With the optional deluxe front end which was included in the Sierra Classic Package, the lamp bezels and grille were painted light and dark argent. The parking lamps were placed behind the lower corners of the grille. The deluxe front end also included dual rectangular headlights. Standard equipment for the Sierra base level trim included foam-padded high-back front bucket seats in grained vinyl. If the optional custom leather-grained vinyl was ordered, a center console and color-keyed front floor carpeting was included. If the optional rear folding rear seat was ordered, full-length carpeting was installed. Both interior were available in blue or almond. Color-keyed features included the padded instrument panel, plastic door trim panels with integral armrests, and dual padded sun visors. Standard embossed black rubber floor mats were installed except as noted above. Power steering, inside hood-lock and two door-activated dome lights were also part of the Sierra Package. Exterior Sierra features included tinted glass in all windows including tailgate, chromed front and rear bumpers, bright right and left mirrors with adjustable heads, bright hubcaps, single-note electric horn, two-speed windshield wipers, and identifying nameplates. Diesel models had a stand-up hood ornament and "6.2 LITRE DIESEL" lettering. The Sierra Classic had a deluxe instrument panel with new pewter-toned brushed aluminum finish for the instrument cluster bezel and for the appliques on the instrument panel pad, horn button and door trim panels. Gauges replaced the Sierra's warning lights for generator, oil pressure and engine coolant temperature. Also, included was a custom steering wheel, cigarette lighter and fiber optic illuminated ashtray, and visor mirror. The Sierra Classic was offered with custom leather-grained vinyl or a new custom-cut pile velour cloth for the front high-back bucket sears. Both were offered in almond, blue, carmine or grey. A center console with storage space and beverage pockets was also included. Full-length floor carpeting was included if the optional rear folding seat was specified.

1983 GMC Jimmy Sierra Classic

High Sierra doors had full trim panels with padded armrests, map pockets and closing-assist straps.The rear compartment sidewalls were trimmed and carpet was added to the lower portion of doors and sidewalls. The Sierra Classic exterior had bright lower body side and rear moldings, bright wheel openings, and bright windshield and removable top window trim. Also included was a two-tone electric horn, deluxe front end appearance with dual stacked rectangular headlights. Standard exterior colors for 1983 were almond, midnight black, light blue metallic, midnight blue, light bronze metallic, mahogany metallic, carmine red, silver metallic, frost white and colonial white. The removable hardtop was available in black or white, coordinated to the body color selected.

I.D. DATA: The V.I.N. plate was mounted on the lower left side windshield corner. The V.I.N. consisted of 17 elements. The first, the number 1, identified the U.S. as the nation of origin. The letter G followed, for the manufacturer: General Motors. The third entry, the letter T, represented the make as GMC. The GVWR brake system identification followed. Next came the truck line and chassis type; the letter K indicated four-wheel drive. The truck series was identified by a number: 1-1/2 ton. The truck body type identification was next: 8-Utility. The engine code was next, followed by a check digit. The model year was identified by the letter D. The assembly plant code followed. The final six digits were the plant sequential production number.

Model Number	Body Type & Seating	Factory Price	GVW	Shipping Weight	Prod. Total
Jimmy K-1500. (with 305 V-8)					
TK10516	Util. (with top)	$10,287	6100[1]	4426	7361[2]

* 6250 GVW Package available.

NOTE 1: Includes both two-wheel drive and four-wheel drive models.
NOTE 2: Calendar year sales of all models.

STANDARD ENGINE: All states except California: Engine Type: Cast iron block. OHV, V-8 with Electronic Spark Control. Ordering Code: LE9. Produced by GM-Chevrolet Motor Division and GM of Canada. Bore x Stroke: 3.74 in. x 3.48 in. Lifters: Hydraulic. Number of main bearings-5. Carburetion: Rochester 2-barrel. Compression Ratio: 9.2:1. Displacement: 305 cu. in. Horsepower: Net: 160 @ 4000 rpm. Torque: Net: 235 lb.-ft. @ 2000 rpm. Oil capacity: 5 qt. with filter change. Fuel Requirements: Unleaded.

STANDARD ENGINE: California only: Engine Type: Cast iron block. OHV, V-8. Ordering Code: LS9. Produced by GM-Chevrolet Motor Division. Bore x Stroke: 4.0 in. x 3.48 in. Lifters: Hydraulic. Number of main bearings-5. Carburetion: Rochester 4-barrel. Compression Ratio: 8.2:1. Displacement: 350 cu. in. (5.7 liters). Horsepower: Net: 165 @ 3800 rpm. Torque: Net: 275 lb.-ft. @ 1600 rpm. Oil capacity: 5 qt. with filter change. Fuel Requirements: Unleaded.

OPTIONAL ENGINE: 50 states: Engine Type: OHV, cast iron block. Diesel V-8. Order Code LH6. Produced by GM-Detroit Diesel Allison Division. Requires B3J Diesel Equipment Package which consists of dual batteries, hydraulic power-assisted brakes, engine block heater, heavy-duty radiator, K81 alternator, engine oil cooler and additional insulation. Bore x Stroke: 3.98 in. x 3.80 in. Lifters: Hydraulic. Number of main bearings-5. Carburetion: Fuel injection. Compression Ratio: 21.5:1. Displacement: 379 cu. in. (6.2 liter). Horsepower: Net: 130 @ 3600 rpm. Torque: Net: 240 lb.-ft. @ 2000 rpm. Oil capacity: 7 qt. with filter change. Fuel Requirements: Diesel.

CHASSIS FEATURES: Ladder-type. Carbon steel, 36,000-39,000 psi. Heavy-gauge channel side members, alligator-jaw cross members. Section modulus: 3.14 in.

SUSPENSION AND RUNNING GEAR: Front Suspension: Two tapered semi-elliptical leaf springs. Capacity: Gasoline engines: 1650 lb. Optional Capacity: 2250 lb. Diesel engine: 1850 lb. Optional: 2250 lb. Standard 1.25 in. stabilizer bar and 25mm shock absorbers. Optional: 32mm shock absorbers. Rear Suspension: Two-stage tapered and multi-leaf (six-conventional leaves, one tapered leaf). Capacity: 1875 lb. Optional: None. Front Axle. Type: Hypoid, tubular driving. Capacity: 3600 lb. Rear Axle. Type: Hypoid, semi-floating. Capacity: 3750 lb. Final Drive Ratio: Gasoline engines: 2.73:1. Diesel engine: 3.08:1. Optional: Gasoline engines: 3.08:1, 3.73:1 (not available for California). Diesel engine: 3.42, 3.73:1. Transfer Case: Type: New Process 208. Ratios: 2.61, 1.00:1. Brakes: Type: Hydraulic, self-adjusting. Front: Discs. Rear: Drums. Optional: Power. Dimensions: Front: 11.86 in. dia. rotor. Rear: 11.15 in. x 2.75 in. Wheels: 6-stud, 15 x 6JJ. Optional: 15 x 7JJ Rallye, 15 x 8JJ, 15 x 8JJ Rallye, 16 x 5K. Tires: P215/75R15 steel belted radial. Optional: P215/75R15 steel belted radial whitewall, P235/75R15 steel belted radial, P235/75R15 steel belted radial whitewall, P235/75R15 white lettered steel belted radial, 10R-15B steel belted radial, 10R-15B white lettered steel belted radial. Steering: Power assisted recirculating ball, variable ratio. Ratio: 17.6/13.1. Turns Lock-to-Lock: 4.0. Turning circle: 37.6 ft. Optional: None. Transmission: Gasoline engines: Muncie 4-speed manual, synchromesh on top three gears, floor-mounted shift lever. Ratios: 6.55, 3.58, 1.70, 1.00:1 Interim 1983. Not available in California,. Standard: Diesel, optional gasoline engines: 700R4 4-speed automatic with overdrive. Ratios: 3.06, 1.36, 1.00, 0.70:1. Reverse: 2.29:1. Clutch: 11.0 in. dia., 124 sq. in. area. 12 in. clutch included with 350 V-8 engines).

VEHICLE DIMENSIONS: Wheelbase: 106.5 in. Overall Length: 184.8 in. Front/Rear Tread 66.10 in./ 63.00 in. Overall Height: 73.4 in. Width: 79.6 in. Tailgate: Width and Height: 66.8 in. x 22.0 in. Approach/Departure Degrees: 34/25. Ground Clearance: Front axle: 7.4 in. Rear axle: 7.0 in. Oil pan: 17.2 in. Transfer case: 11.5 in. Fuel tank: 14.0 in. Load space: With rear seat installed: 38.8 in. x 50 in. x 42.3 in. With rear seat removed or folded: 76.0 in. x 50 in. x 42.3 in.

CAPACITIES: Fuel Tank: 25.0 gal. Optional: Replacement 31 gal. tank. Coolant system: 305 V-8: 17.6 qt. 350 V-8: 17.6 qt.

ACCOMMODATIONS: Seating Capacity: Standard: Driver and passenger front high-back bucket sets. Optional: 3 passenger rear bench seat. Headroom: 38.3 in. Maximum steering wheel to seat back: 18.5 in. Seat to ground: 36.3 in. Floor to ground: 21.9 in.

INSTRUMENTATION: 0-100 mph speedometer, 99,999.9 mi. odometer, fuel gauge, warning lights for alternator, oil pressure, engine coolant temperature, brake operating system, hazard warning lights, directional lights, seat belt warning.

OPTIONS AND PRICES: Tinted glass: $177. Air conditioning: $725. Bright metal wheelcovers. Bright metal wheel trim rings. Deluxe front and rear bumpers: $47. Chromed front bumper guards. Deluxe front and rear bumpers. Cigarette lighter. Color-keyed floor mats. ComforTilt steering wheel: $105. Custom steering wheel. Chromed grille (RPO V22). Deluxe instrument panel. Electric clock (RPO U35). One-way glass RPO AJ1). Sliding glass rear side windows. Halogen high-beam headlights (RPO TT5): $16. Headlight warning buzzer: $11. Intermittent windshield wipers/washer: $49. Painted below eye-level mirrors (RPO D44). Stainless steel below eye-level mirrors (RPO D45): $76. Stainless steel camper mirrors (RPO DF2). Black body side moldings (RPO B84). Bright body side moldings (RPO B85). Black Molding Package. Bright Molding Package. Operating Convenience Package. Power door locks. Power windows. Special two-tone paint. Exterior Decor Package. AM radio. AM/FM radio. AM/FM radio with 8-track tape player. AM/FM radio with cassette tape player. AM/FM stereo radio with cassette tape player: $298. AM/FM radio with CB and antenna. Rear auxiliary speaker. Windshield antenna. Quartz electric clock: $38. Rear roll bar. Spare tire carrier. Folding rear seat: 353. Tachometer. Electric tailgate window: $85. Aluminum wheels (RPO PH7). Rallye wheels (RPO N67). Styled wheels (RPO PA6): $208. Sierra Classic Package (RPO YE9): $983. Operating Convenience Package: $300. Exterior Decor Package: $294. Auxiliary battery. Cold Climate Package. Engine oil cooler. Transmission oil cooler: $57. Cruise control: $185. Deadweight trailer hitch: $56. Heavy-duty front springs: $57. Front quad shock absorbers: $123. Front tow hooks. 31 gal. fuel tank. Fuel tank shield plate. Gauge Package (includes voltmeter, engine coolant temperature and oil pressure gauges. 55 amp generator. 61 amp generator. Heavy-duty battery. Heavy-duty radiator. Locking rear differential. Trailering special equipment. Trailer wiring harness. Weight-distributing hitch platform. Automatic 4-speed overdrive transmission: $650.10-15LT radial tires: $728.45.

HISTORICAL FOOTNOTES: GMC proclaimed the 1983 Jimmy as "full-size and tough!"

1984 JIMMY

The appearance of the 1984 Jimmy was unchanged from its 1983 version. Many sales literature pieces for 1984 carried the same illustrations used in1983. The standard Sierra interior was now available in a new saddle tan or blue color. New colors for the Sierra Classic included burgundy, saddle tan and slate grey. Blue was a carry over color. The Sierra Classic also had a new neutral-colored cloth-covered headliner. The Jimmy exterior featured a new anti-chip coating on lower fender and body areas. The optional diesel engine had a new integral fuel/water separator. Carried over from 1983 was the optional Exterior Decor Package. It included moldings and lamp trim in a special two-tone scheme, plus dual-tone decal striping on body sides and across the rear of the vehicle. The accent color was applied on the body sides and rear between the striping and molding. Also included was a stand-up hood emblem on gasoline models. A total of ten two-tone color combinations were offered for this package. The 1984 Jimmy color selection consisted of frost white, silver metallic, midnight black, light blue metallic, midnight blue, colonial yellow, doeskin tan, desert sand metallic, Indian bronze metallic and apple red.

1984 K-Jimmy with Sierra Classic trim

I.D. DATA: The V.I.N. plate was mounted on the lower left side windshield corner. The V.I.N. consisted of 17 elements. The first, the number 1, identified the U.S. as the nation of origin. The letter G followed, for the manufacturer: General Motors. The third entry, the letter T, represented the make as GMC. The GVWR brake system identification followed. Next came the truck line and chassis type; the letter K indicated four-wheel drive. The truck series was identified by a number: 1-1/2 ton. The truck body type identification was next: 8-Utility. The engine code was next, followed by a check digit. The model year was identified by the letter E. The assembly plant code followed. The final six digits were the plant sequential production number.

Model Number	Body Type & Seating	Factory Price	GVW	Shipping Weight	Prod. Total
Jimmy K-1500. (with 305 V-8)					
TK10516	Util. (with top)	$10,819	6100[1*]	4409	8488[2]

NOTE 1: 6250 GVW Package available.
NOTE 2: Calendar year sales: All models.

* Includes both two-wheel drive and four-wheel drive models.

STANDARD ENGINE: All states except California: Engine Type: Cast iron block. OHV, V-8 with Electronic Spark Control. Ordering Code: LE9. Produced by GM-Chevrolet Motor Division and GM of Canada. Bore x Stroke: 3.74 in. x 3.48 in. Lifters: Hydraulic. Number of main bearings-5. Carburetion: Rochester 2-barrel. Compression Ratio: 9.2:1. Displacement: 305 cu. in. Horsepower: Net: 160 @ 4000 rpm. Torque: Net: 235 lb.-ft. @ 2000 rpm. Oil capacity: 5 qt. with filter change. Fuel Requirements: Unleaded.

STANDARD ENGINE: California only: Engine Type: Cast iron block. OHV, V-8. Ordering Code: LS9. Produced by GM-Chevrolet Motor Division. Bore x Stroke: 4.0 in. x 3.48 in. Lifters: Hydraulic. Number of main bearings-5. Carburetion: Rochester 4-barrel. Compression Ratio: 8.2:1. Displacement: 350 cu. in. (5.7 liters). Horsepower: Net: 165 @ 3800 rpm. Torque: Net: 275 lb.-ft. @ 1600 rpm. Oil capacity: 5 qt. with filter change. Fuel Requirements: Unleaded.

OPTIONAL ENGINE: 50 states: Engine Type: OHV, cast iron block. Diesel V-8. Order Code LH6. Produced by GM-Detroit Diesel Allison Division. Requires B3J Diesel Equipment Package which consists of dual batteries, hydraulic power-assisted brakes, engine block heater, heavy-duty radiator, K81 alternator, engine oil cooler and additional insulation. Bore x Stroke: 3.98 in. x 3.80 in. Lifters: Hydraulic. Number of main bearings-5. Carburetion: Fuel injection. Compression Ratio: 21.5:1. Displacement: 379 cu. in. (6.2 liter). Horsepower: Net: 130 @ 3600 rpm. Torque: Net: 240 lb.-ft. @ 2000 rpm. Oil capacity: 7 qt. with filter change. Fuel Requirements: Diesel.

CHASSIS FEATURES: Ladder-type. Carbon steel, 36,000-39,000 psi. Heavy-gauge channel side members, alligator-jaw cross members. Section modulus: 3.14 in.

SUSPENSION AND RUNNING GEAR: Front Suspension: Two tapered semi-elliptical leaf springs. Capacity: Gasoline engines: 1650 lb. Optional Capacity: 2250 lb. Diesel engine: 1850 lb. Optional: 2250 lb. Standard 1.25 in. stabilizer bar and 25mm shock absorbers. Optional: 32mm shock absorbers. Rear Suspension: Two-stage tapered and multi-leaf (six-conventional leaves, one tapered leaf). Capacity: 1875 lb. Optional: None. Front Axle. Type: Hypoid, tubular driving. Capacity: 3600 lb. Rear Axle. Type: Hypoid, semi-floating. Capacity: 3750 lb. Final Drive Ratio: Gasoline engines: 2.73:1. Diesel engine: 3.08:1. Optional: Gasoline engines: 3.08:1, 3.73:1 (not available for California). Diesel engine: 3.42, 3.73:1. Transfer Case: Type: New Process 208. Ratios: 2.61, 1.00:1. Brakes: Type: Hydraulic, self-adjusting. Front: Discs. Rear: Drums. Optional: Power. Dimensions: Front: 11.86 in. dia. rotor. Rear: 11.15 in. x 2.75 in. Wheels: 6-stud, 15 x 6JJ. Optional: 15 x 7JJ Rallye, 15 x 8JJ, 15 x 8JJ Rallye, 16 x 5K. Tires: P215/75R15 steel belted radial. Optional: P215/75R15 steel belted radial whitewall, P235/75R15 steel belted radial, P235/75R15 steel belted radial whitewall, P235/75R15 white lettered steel belted radial, 10R-15B steel belted radial, 10R-15B Wwhite lettered steel belted radial. Steering: Power assisted recirculating ball, variable ratio. Ratio: 17.6/13.1. Turns Lock-to-Lock: 4.0. Turning circle: 37.6 ft. Optional: None. Transmission: Gasoline engines: Muncie 4-speed manual, synchromesh on top three gears, floor-mounted shift lever. Ratios: 6.55, 3.58, 1.70, 1.00:1. Not available in California. Standard: Diesel, optional gasoline engines: 700R4 4-speed automatic with overdrive. Ratios: 3.06, 1.36, 1.00, 0.70:1. Reverse: 2.29:1. Clutch: 11.0 in. dia., 124 sq. in. area. 12 in. clutch included with 350 V-8 engines).

VEHICLE DIMENSIONS: Wheelbase: 106.5 in. Overall Length: 184.8 in. Front/Rear Tread 66.10 in./ 63.00 in. Overall Height: 73.4 in. Width: 79.6 in. Tailgate: Width and Height: 66.8 in. x 22.0 in. Approach/Departure Degrees: 34/25. Ground Clearance: Front axle: 7.4 in. Rear axle: 7.0 in. Oil pan: 17.2 in. Transfer case: 11.5 in. Fuel tank: 14.0 in. Load space: With rear seat installed: 38.8 in. x 50 in. x 42.3 in. With rear seat removed or folded: 76.0 In. x 50 in. x 42.3 in.

CAPACITIES: Fuel Tank: 25.0 gal. Optional: Replacement 31 gal. tank. Coolant system: 305 V-8: 17.6 qt. 350 V-8: 17.6 qt.

ACCOMMODATIONS: Seating Capacity: Standard: Driver and passenger front high-back bucket seats. Optional: 3 passenger rear bench seat. Headroom: 38.3 in. Maximum steering wheel to seat back: 18.5 in. Seat to ground: 36.3 in. Floor to ground: 21.9 in.

INSTRUMENTATION: 0-100 mph speedometer, 99,999.9 mi. odometer, fuel gauge, warning lights for alternator, oil pressure, engine coolant temperature, brake operating system, hazard warning lights, directional lights, seat belt warning.

OPTIONS: Tinted glass. Air conditioning. Bright metal wheelcovers. Bright metal wheel trim rings. Deluxe front and rear bumpers. Chromed front bumper guards. Deluxe front and rear bumpers. Cigarette lighter. Color-keyed floor mats. ComforTilt steering wheel. Custom steering wheel. Chromed grille (RPO V22). Deluxe instrument panel. Electric clock (RPO U35). One-way glass (RPO AJ1). Sliding glass rear side windows. Halogen high-beam headlights (RPO TT5). Headlight warning buzzer. Intermittent windshield wipers/washer. Painted below eye-level mirrors (RPO D44). Stainless steel below eye-level mirrors (RPO D45). Stainless steel camper mirrors (RPO DF2). Black body side moldings (RPO B84). Bright body side moldings (RPO B85). Black Molding Package. Bright Molding Package. Operating Convenience Package. Power door locks. Power windows. Special two-tone paint. Exterior Decor Package. AM radio. AM/FM radio. AM/FM radio with 8-track tape player. AM/FM radio with cassette tape player. AM/FM stereo radio with cassette tape player. AM/FM radio with CB and antenna. Rear auxiliary speaker. Windshield antenna. Quartz electric clock. Rear roll bar. Spare tire carrier. Folding rear seat. Tachometer. Electric tailgate window. Aluminum wheels (RPO PH7). Rallye wheels (RPO N67). Styled wheels (RPO PA6). Sierra Classic Package (RPO YE9). Operating Convenience Package. Exterior Decor Package. Auxiliary battery. Cold Climate Package. Engine oil cooler. Transmission oil cooler. Cruise Control. Deadweight trailer hitch. Heavy-duty front springs. Front quad shock absorbers. Front tow hooks. 31 gal. fuel tank. Fuel tank shield plate. Gauge Package (includes voltmeter, engine coolant temperature and oil pressure gauges. 55 amp generator. 61 amp generator. Heavy-duty battery. Heavy-duty radiator. Locking rear differential. Trailering special equipment. Trailer wiring harness. Weight-distributing hitch platform. Automatic 4-speed overdrive transmission. 10-15LT radial tires.

HISTORICAL FOOTNOTES: GMC was the official truck of the XXIIIrd Olympiad held in Los Angeles.

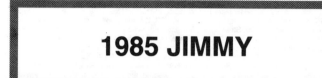

1985 JIMMY

The 1985 GMC K-Jimmy was available with new optional cast aluminum wheels, new standard and optional Front End Packages, a new wet-arm windshield/wiper/washer system, and a new optional custom textured velour seat trim for the Sierra Classic. The base Sierra trim was available in new custom pigskin-grained vinyl. Standard tires were now steel-belted All-Season radial tires. A new fuse box made it easier to replace fuses. The Sierra Classic front end was identified by its dual headlights, bright-trimmed grille, bright moldings for body sides and rear, side quarter windows, front side marker lights and tail lights.

The hardtop, previously available in only black or white was now color-keyed in a choice of midnight black, blue, bronze, silver, tan or frost white. The special two-tone paint treatment included black vinyl body side and rear moldings, with a secondary body color applied below. The Exterior Decor Package included black vinyl body side and rear moldings with side and rear decal striping. The secondary body color was applied between the moldings and the decal striping. The Sierra Classic's interior had a pewter-toned brushed aluminum instrument panel; trim, color-keyed front carpeting and a custom steering wheel. The exterior colors offered for 1985 consisted of frost white, silver metallic, midnight black, light blue metallic, midnight blue, doeskin tan, Indian bronze metallic and apple red.

1985 K-Jimmy Sierra Classic

I.D. DATA: The V.I.N. plate was mounted on the lower left side windshield corner. The V.I.N. consisted of 17 elements. The first, the number 1, identified the U.S. as the nation of origin. The letter G followed, for the manufacturer: General Motors. The third entry, the letter T, represented the make as GMC. The GVWR brake system identification followed. Next came the truck line and chassis type; the letter K indicated four-wheel drive. The truck series was identified by a number: 1-1/2 ton. The truck body type identification was next: 8-Utility. The engine code was next, followed by a check digit. The model year was identified by the letter F. The assembly plant code followed. The final six digits were the plant sequential production number.

Model Number	Body Type & Seating	Factory Price	GVW	Shipping Weight	Prod. Total
Jimmy K-1500 (with 305 V-8)					
TK10516	Util. ZW9	$11,340[1]	6100[2]	4462	—

NOTE 1: $14070 with 379 cu. in. diesel V-8 and B3J Diesel Equipment Package consisting of dual batteries, hydraulic power-assisted brakes, engine block heater, heavy-duty radiator, K81 alternator, engine oil cooler and additional insulation.
NOTE 2: 6250 lb. GVW Package available. Its content, compared to the standard GVW follows:

GVW Rating	GVWR (lbs.) Front Rear	Tire Capacities Front Rear	Chassis Equip.
6100	3166 - 3166	1583 - 1583	None
6250	3550 - 3550	1775 - 1775	Requires B3J

STANDARD ENGINE: All states except California: Engine Type: Cast iron block. OHV, V-8 with Electronic Spark Control. Ordering Code: LE9. Produced by GM-Chevrolet Motor Division and GM of Canada. Bore x Stroke: 3.74 in. x 3.48 in. Lifters: Hydraulic. Number of main bearings-5. Carburetion: Rochester 2-barrel. Compression Ratio: 9.2:1. Displacement: 305 cu. in. Horsepower: Net: 160 @ 4000 rpm. Torque: Net: 235 lb.-ft. @ 2000 rpm. Oil capacity: 5 qt. with filter change. Fuel Requirements: Unleaded.

STANDARD ENGINE: California only: Engine Type: Cast iron block. OHV, V-8. Ordering Code: LS9. Produced by GM-Chevrolet Motor Division. Bore x Stroke: 4.0 in. x 3.48 in. Lifters: Hydraulic. Number of main bearings-5. Carburetion: Rochester 4-barrel. Compression Ratio: 8.2:1. Displacement: 350 cu. in. (5.7 liters). Horsepower: Net: 165 @ 3800 rpm. Torque: Net: 275 lb.-ft. @ 1600 rpm. Oil capacity: 5 qt. with filter change. Fuel Requirements: Unleaded.

OPTIONAL ENGINE: 50 states: Engine Type: OHV, cast iron block. Diesel V-8. Order Code LH6. Produced by GM-Detroit Diesel Allison Division. Requires B3J Diesel Equipment Package which consists of dual batteries, hydraulic power-assisted brakes, engine block heater, heavy-duty radiator, K81 alternator, engine oil cooler and additional insulation. Bore x Stroke: 3.98 in. x 3.80 in. Lifters: Hydraulic. Number of main bearings-5. Carburetion: Fuel injection. Compression Ratio: 21.5:1. Displacement: 379 cu. in. (6.2 liter). Horsepower: Net: 130 @ 3600 rpm. Torque: Net: 240 lb.-ft. @ 2000 rpm. Oil capacity: 7 qt. with filter change. Fuel Requirements: Diesel.

CHASSIS FEATURES: Ladder-type. Carbon steel, 36,000-39,000 psi. Heavy-gauge channel side members, alligator-jaw cross members. Section modulus: 3.14 in.

SUSPENSION AND RUNNING GEAR: Front Suspension: Two tapered semi-elliptical leaf springs. Capacity: Gasoline engines: 1650 lb. Optional Capacity: 2250 lb. Diesel engine: 1850 lb. Optional: 2250 lb. Standard 1.25 in. stabilizer bar and 25mm shock absorbers. Optional: 32mm shock absorbers. Rear Suspension: Two-stage tapered and multi-leaf (six-conventional leaves, one tapered leaf). Capacity: 1875 lb. Optional: None. Front Axle. Type: Hypoid, tubular driving. Capacity: 3600 lb. Rear Axle. Type: Hypoid, semi-floating. Capacity: 3750 lb. Final Drive Ratio: Gasoline engines: 2.73:1. Diesel engine: 3.08:1. Optional: Gasoline engines: 3.08:1, 3.73:1 (not available for California). Diesel engine: 3.42, 3.73:1. Transfer Case: Type: New Process 208. Ratios: 2.61, 1.00:1. Brakes: Type: Hydraulic, self-adjusting. Front: Discs. Rear: Drums. Optional: Power. Dimensions: Front: 11.86 in. dia. rotor. Rear: 11.15 in. x 2.75 in. Wheels: 6-stud, 15 x 6JJ. Optional: 15 x 7JJ Rallye, 15 x 8JJ, 15 x 8JJ Rallye, 16 x 5K. Tires: P215/75R15 steel belted radial. Optional: P215/75R15 steel belted radial whitewall, P235/75R15 steel belted radial, P235/75R15 steel belted radial whitewall, P235/75R15 white lettered steel belted radial, 10R-15B steel belted radial, 10R-15B white lettered steel belted radial. Steering: Power assisted recirculating ball, variable ratio. Ratio: 17.6/13.1. Turns Lock-to-Lock: 4.0. Turning circle: 37.6 ft. Optional: None. Transmission: Gasoline engines: Muncie 4-speed manual, synchromesh on top three gears, floor-mounted shift lever. Ratios: 6.55, 3.58, 1.70, 1.00:1. Not available in California. Standard: Diesel, optional gasoline engines: 700R4 4-speed automatic with overdrive. Ratios: 3.06, 1.36, 1.00, 0.70:1. Reverse: 2.29:1. Clutch: 11.0 in. dia., 124 sq. in. area. 12 in. clutch included with 350 V-8 engines).

VEHICLE DIMENSIONS: Wheelbase: 106.5 in. Overall Length: 184.8 in. Front/Rear Tread 66.10 in./ 63.00 in. Overall Height: 73.4 in. Width: 79.6 in. Tailgate: Width and Height: 66.8 in. x 22.0 in. Approach/Departure Degrees: 34/25. Ground Clearance: Front axle: 7.4 in. Rear axle: 7.0 in. Oil pan: 17.2 in. Transfer case: 11.5 in. Fuel tank: 14.0 in. Load space: With rear seat installed: 38.8 in. x 50 in. x 42.3 in. With rear seat removed or folded: 76.0 in. x 50 in. x 42.3 in.

CAPACITIES: Fuel Tank: 25.0 gal. Optional: Replacement 31 gal. tank. Coolant system: 305 V-8: 17.6 qt. 350 V-8: 17.6 qt.

ACCOMMODATIONS: Seating Capacity: Standard: Driver and passenger front high-back bucket sets. Optional: 3 passenger rear bench seat. Headroom: 38.3 in. Maximum steering wheel to seat back: 18.5 in. Seat to ground: 36.3 in. Floor to ground: 21.9 in.

INSTRUMENTATION: 0-100 mph speedometer, 99,999.9 mi. odometer, fuel gauge, warning lights for alternator, oil pressure, engine coolant temperature, brake operating system, hazard warning lights, directional lights, seat belt warning.

OPTIONS AND PRICES: High Sierra Package (RPO YE9): $1015. Includes either custom cloth or custom vinyl seats, custom steering wheel, Deluxe Molding Package, taillight and rear door or tailgate moldings, bright front turn signal and front side marker lamp bezels, fender nameplates, bright windshield and side rear window moldings, color-keyed carpeting with bright sill plates, plastic door trim panels with storage pockets, and bright brushed finish accents, visor vanity mirror, Deluxe Front Appearance Package, dual horns, nameplate on instrument panel, cigarette lighter, headliner, wheel opening moldings, special insulation, bright body side moldings, pillar trim panels, storage console between front seats, floor and wheelwell carpeting, spare tire cover and voltmeter, engine coolant temperature and oil pressure gauges. Custom vinyl bucket seats (without YE9): $200 (without rear seat), $250 (with rear seat). Custom vinyl seats (with YE9): $50 (with rear seat). No extra charge without rear seat. Special two-tone paint: $327 (without YE9), $170 (with YE9). Includes Custom Molding Package and wheel opening moldings. Exterior decor: $471 (without YE9), $414 (with YE9). Includes hood ornament. California emission systems (RPO YF5): $235. 5.7 liter V-8 (available only with YF5): $290. 4-speed with overdrive automatic transmission (standard on B3J diesel): $670. Optional axle ratio: $36. Locking rear differential (RPO G80): $238. P215/75R15 All-Season steel belted radial blackwall: $70. P215/75R15 highway steel belted radial blackwall: $125. P235/75R15 highway steel belted radial whitewall: $210. P235/75R15 highway steel belted radial white lettered: $240. P235/75R15 All-Season steel belted radial blackwall: $125. P235/75R 15 on-off road steel belted radial blackwall: $175. P235/75R15 All-Season steel belted radial whitewall: $210. P235/75R15 All-Season steel belted radial white lettered: $240. 31 x 10.50R/15LTB on-off road steel belted radial blackwall (available only if N67, N90 or PA6 wheels are specified): $564. 31 x 10.50R/15LTB (available only if N67, N90 or PA6 wheels are specified): $720. Pre-cleaner air cleaner (RPO K46): $42. Air conditioning (not available with Cold Climate Package): $740. Deluxe Front Appearance Package (RPO V22). Includes dark argent grille with bright trim and dual rectangular headlights): $109. Heavy-duty battery: $53. Deluxe chromed front and rear bumpers (RPO VE5): $49. Chromed front bumper guards (RPO V31): $41. Quartz electric clock (RPO U35). Not available with UM6 radio: $79 (without YE9. Includes Z53 Gauge Package). With YE9: $39. Cold Climate Package (RPO V10). Includes special insulation, special heater and defroster, engine block heater, anti-freeze protection to -31 degrees, heavy-duty battery: $188 (without Trailering Special Package. Also includes 66 amp generator). With Trailering Special Package: $126. Engine oil cooling system (RPO KC4): $120. Heavy-duty radiator (RPO VO1): $53. Heavy-duty radiator and transmission oil cooler (RPO VO2): $59. Power door locks (RPO AU3): $135. Color-keyed front floor mats (RPO B32): $15. Gauge Package (RPO Z54). Includes voltmeter, engine coolant temperature and oil pressure gauges: $40. 66 amp generator (RPO K81): $62. Deep tinted glass (RPO AJ1). Includes dark laminated glass on side windows and rear tailgate glass: $194. Deep tinted glass with light tinted rear window (RPO AA3). Includes tinted glass on rear tailgate glass, passenger and driver's side door and dark laminated glass on side windows: $140. Heavy-duty, 7-lead wiring harness (RPO UY7): $44. Halogen light-beam headlights (RPO TT5). Available only with V22 or YE9 was ordered: $17. Headlight warning buzzer (RPO T63): $11. Interior headliner (RPO BB5): $80. 600 watt engine block heater (RPO KO5). Not available for diesel engine: $31. Heavy-duty front heater (RPO C42). Available only with diesel engine: $43. Automatic locking hubs (RPO X6Z): $40. Cigarette lighter (RPO U37): $30. Painted exterior below eye-level mirrors (RPO D44): $50. Stainless steel exterior below eye-level mirrors (RPO D45): $83. Black body side molding (RPO B84). Includes lower side and rear moldings of black plastic with bright trim: $115. Bright body side molding (RPO B85). Includes bright plastic body side and rear lower moldings with black paint trim, plus bright trim for front sidemarker lamps and taillights, fender, door, rear side panel and tailgate moldings: $144. Custom Molding Package (RP0 YG1). Includes B84 black body side moldings, wheel opening moldings and bright trim for front side marker lights and taillight trim. Included with ZY3 or ZY5 Packages: $157. Deluxe Molding Package (RPO YG3). Includes bright trim for front side marker lamps and taillight trim wheel opening molding and B85 bright body side moldings: $173 (without ZY3 or ZY5). With ZY3 or ZY5: $16. Door edge guards (RPO B93): $17. Operating Convenience Package (RPO ZQ2). Includes power door locks and power windows: $325. AM radio (RPO U63): $112. AM/FM radio (RPO U69) $171. AM/FM stereo radio (RPO U58), available only with YE9: $198. AM/FM electronically tuned stereo radio with Seek-Scan, stereo cassette tape player and clock: $419. Windshield antenna (RPO U76), included with radio: $32. Rear seat (RPO AM7). With custom trim: $369. Without Custom trim: $341. Fuel tank shield (RPO NY1): $164. Front quad shock absorbers (RPO Z75). Includes dual left and right hand shock absorbers on front axle, heavy-duty shock absorbers on rear axle and a front axle nose bumper to limit axle windup: $128. Electronic speed control (RPO K34): $195. Front heavy-duty 2250 lb. capacity springs with heavy-duty front and rear shock absorbers. Recommended for snowplow type usage only: $92 (with Z75). Without Z75: $59. ComforTilt steering wheel (RPO N33): $115. 31 gal. replacement fuel tank (RPO NK7): $43. Two front towing hooks (RPO V76): $36. Deadweight type trailer hitch (RPO VR2). Not available with Z82: $58. Weight distributing platform trailer hitch (RPO VR4). Included with Z82: $155. Trailering special equipment (RPO Z82). Available only with 3.24 or 3.73:1 rear axle ratio and MXO automatic transmission were ordered. Not available with 5.7 liter LS9 engine. Includes VR4, UY7 and V02 options: $440. With B3J diesel equipment: $258. With C80 air conditioning: $378. Bright metal wheelcovers (RPO P01): $40. Rallye 15 x 8 wheels (RPO N67). Not available with P215 tires: $115. Styled 15 x 8 wheels (RPO PA6). Not available with P215 tires: $174. Cast aluminum 15 x 7 wheels with special hubcaps. (RPO N90). Not available with P215 tires: $299. Power side door electric windows (RPO A31): $10. Power tailgate electric window (RPO A33): $95. Sliding side quarter windows (RPO AD5): $243. Intermittent windshield wipers (RPO CD4): $55.

HISTORICAL FOOTNOTES: The 1985 Jimmy, when delivered in the United States by a GMC dealer, came with a one year, $10,000 seat belt insurance certificate from MIC General Insurance Corporation at no additional charge. It paid $10,000 to the estate of any occupant who suffered fatal injuries as a result of an accident involving that vehicle while wearing a GM seat belt.

1986 JIMMY

Changes for 1986 were limited. New front bucket seats expanded the Jimmy's rear legroom. Key features of the new seats included folding backrests. The passenger seat slid forward for easier entry and exit from the rear compartment, and, for the Sierra Classic, had built-in recliners. The gasoline engines were fitted with new-design generator drive belts with increased drive friction. New crankshaft seals and oil pan gaskets were also used. Exterior colors for 1986 were frost white, steel grey metallic, midnight black, midnight blue, doeskin tan, Indian bronze metallic, apple red and light blue metallic.

1986 Sierra Classic K-Jimmy with Exterior Decor

I.D. DATA: The V.I.N. plate was mounted on the lower left side windshield corner. The V.I.N. consisted of 17 elements. The first, the number 1, identified the U.S. as the nation of origin. The letter G followed, for the manufacturer: General Motors. The third entry, the letter T, represented the make as GMC. The GVWR brake system identification followed. Next came the truck line and chassis type; the letter K indicated four-wheel drive. The truck series was identified by a number: 1-1/2 ton. The truck body type identification was next: 8-Utility. The engine code was next, followed by a check digit. The model year was identified by the letter G. The assembly plant code followed. The final six digits were the plant sequential production number.

Model Number	Body Type & Seating	Factory Price	GVW	Shipping Weight	Prod. Total
Jimmy K-1500 Body Code: ZW9 (with 305 V-8)					
TK10516	Util.	$12,085	6100[1]	4444	9686[2]

NOTE 1: 6250 GVW Package available. Its content was unchanged from 1985.
NOTE 2: Model year sales of all models.

STANDARD ENGINE: All states except California: Engine Type: Cast iron block. OHV, V-8 with Electronic Spark Control. Ordering Code: LE9. Produced by GM-Chevrolet Motor Division and GM of Canada. Bore x Stroke: 3.74 in. x 3.48 in. Lifters: Hydraulic. Number of main bearings-5. Carburetion: Rochester 2-barrel. Compression Ratio: 9.2:1. Displacement: 305 cu. in. Horsepower: Net: 160 @ 4000 rpm. Torque: Net: 235 lb.-ft. @ 2000 rpm. Oil capacity: 5 qt. with filter change. Fuel Requirements: Unleaded.

STANDARD ENGINE: California only: Engine Type: Cast iron block. OHV, V-8. Ordering Code: LS9. Produced by GM-Chevrolet Motor Division. Bore x Stroke: 4.0 in. x 3.48 in. Lifters: Hydraulic. Number of main bearings-5. Carburetion: Rochester 4-barrel. Compression Ratio: 8.2:1. Displacement: 350 cu. in. (5.7 liters). Horsepower: Net: 165 @ 3800 rpm. Torque: Net: 275 lb.-ft. @ 1600 rpm. Oil capacity: 5 qt. with filter change. Fuel Requirements: Unleaded.

OPTIONAL ENGINE: 50 states: Engine Type: OHV, cast iron block. Diesel V-8. Order Code LH6. Produced by GM-Detroit Diesel Allison Division. Requires B3J Diesel Equipment Package which consists of dual batteries, hydraulic power-assisted brakes, engine block heater, heavy-duty radiator, K81 alternator, engine oil cooler and additional insulation. Bore x Stroke: 3.98 in. x 3.80 in. Lifters: Hydraulic. Number of main bearings-5. Carburetion: Fuel injection. Compression Ratio: 21.5:1. Displacement: 379 cu. in. (6.2 liter). Horsepower: Net: 130 @ 3600 rpm. Torque: Net: 240 lb.-ft. @ 2000 rpm. Oil capacity: 7 qt. with filter change. Fuel Requirements: Diesel.

CHASSIS FEATURES: Ladder-type. Carbon steel, 36,000-39,000 psi. Heavy-gauge channel side members, alligator-jaw cross members. Section modulus: 3.14 in.

SUSPENSION AND RUNNING GEAR: Front Suspension: Two tapered semi-elliptical leaf springs. Capacity: Gasoline engines: 1650 lb. Optional Capacity: 2250 lb. Diesel engine: 1850 lb. Optional: 2250 lb. Standard 1.25 in. stabilizer bar and 25mm shock absorbers. Optional: 32mm shock absorbers. Rear Suspension: Two-stage tapered and multi-leaf (six-conventional leaves, one tapered leaf). Capacity: 1875 lb. Optional: None. Front Axle. Type: Hypoid, tubular driving. Capacity: 3600 lb. Rear Axle. Type: Hypoid, semi-floating. Capacity: 3750 lb. Final Drive Ratio: Gasoline engines: 2.73:1. Diesel engine: 3.08:1. Optional: Gasoline engines: 3.08:1, 3.73:1 (not available for California). Diesel engine: 3.42, 3.73:1. Transfer Case: Type: New Process 208. Ratios: 2.61, 1.00:1. Brakes: Type: Hydraulic, self-adjusting. Front: Discs. Rear: Drums. Optional: Power. Dimensions: Front: 11.86 in. dia. rotor. Rear: 11.15 in. x 2.75 in. Wheels: 6-stud, 15 x 6JJ. Optional: 15 x 7JJ Rallye, 15 x 8JJ, 15 x 8JJ Rallye, 16 x 5K. Tires: P215/75R15 steel belted radial. Optional: P215/75R15 steel belted radial whitewall, P235/75R15 steel belted radial, P235/75R15 steel belted radial whitewall, P235/75R15 white lettered steel belted radial, 10R-15B steel belted radial, 10R-15B white lettered steel belted radial. Steering: Power assisted recirculating ball, variable ratio. Ratio: 17.6/13.1. Turns Lock-to-Lock: 4.0. Turning circle: 37.6 ft. Optional: None. Transmission: Gasoline engines: Muncie 4-speed manual, synchromesh on top three gears, floor-mounted shift lever. Ratios: 6.55, 3.58, 1.70, 1.00:1. Not available in California. Standard: Diesel, optional gasoline engines: 700R4 4-speed automatic with overdrive. Ratios: 3.06, 1.36, 1.00, 0.70:1. Reverse: 2.29:1. Clutch: 11.0 in. dia., 124 sq. in. area. 12 in. clutch included with 350 V-8 engines).

VEHICLE DIMENSIONS: Wheelbase: 106.5 in. Overall Length: 184.8 in. Front/Rear Tread 66.10 in./ 63.00 in. Overall Height: 73.4 in. Width: 79.6 in. Tailgate: Width and Height: 66.8 in. x 22.0 in. Approach/Departure Degrees: 34/25. Ground Clearance: Front axle: 7.4 in. Rear axle: 7.0 in. Oil pan: 17.2 in. Transfer case: 11.5 in. Fuel tank: 14.0 in. Load space: With rear seat installed: 38.8 in. x 50 in. x 42.3 in. With rear seat removed or folded: 76.0 in. x 50 in. x 42.3 in.

CAPACITIES: Fuel Tank: 25.0 gal. Optional: Replacement 31 gal. tank. Coolant system: 305 V-8: 17.6 qt. 350 V-8: 17.6 qt.

ACCOMMODATIONS: Seating Capacity: Standard: Driver and passenger front high-back bucket sets. Optional: 3 passenger rear bench seat. Headroom: 38.3 in. Maximum steering wheel to seat back: 18.5 in. Seat to ground: 36.3 in. Floor to ground: 21.9 in.

INSTRUMENTATION: 0-100 mph speedometer, 99,999.9 mi. odometer, fuel gauge, warning lights for alternator, oil pressure, engine coolant temperature, brake operating system, hazard warning lights, directional lights, seat belt warning.

OPTIONS AND PRICES: Sierra Classic Package (RPO YE9): $1015. Includes either custom cloth or custom vinyl seats, custom steering wheel, Deluxe Molding Package, taillight and rear door or tailgate moldings, bright front turn signal and front side marker lamp bezels, fender nameplates, bright windshield and side rear window moldings, color-keyed carpeting with bright sill plates, plastic door trim panels with storage pockets, and bright brushed finish accents, visor vanity mirror, Deluxe Front Appearance Package, dual horns, nameplate on instrument panel, cigarette lighter, headliner, wheel opening moldings, special insulation, bright body side moldings, pillar trim panels, storage console between front seats, floor and wheelwell carpeting, spare tire cover and voltmeter, engine coolant temperature and oil pressure gauges. Custom vinyl bucket seats (without YE9): $200 (without rear seat), $250 (with rear seat). Custom vinyl seats (with YE9): $50 (with rear seat). No extra charge without rear seat. Special two-tone paint: $327 (without YE9), $170 (with YE9). Includes Custom Molding Package and wheel opening moldings. Exterior Decor: $471 (without YE9), $414 (with YE9). Includes hood ornament. California emission systems (RPO YF5): $235. 5.7 liter V-8 (available only with YF5): $290. 4-speed with overdrive automatic transmission (standard on B3J diesel): $670. Optional axle ratio: $36. Locking rear differential (RPO G80): $238. P215/75R15 All-Season steel belted radial blackwall: $70. P215/75R15 highway steel belted radial blackwall: $125. P235/75R15 highway steel belted radial whitewall: $210. P235/75R15 highway steel belted radial white lettered: $240. P235/75R15 All-Season steel belted radial blackwall: $125. P235/75R 15 on-off road steel belted radial blackwall: $175. P235/75R15 All-Season steel belted radial whitewall: $210. P235/75R15 All-Season steel belted radial white lettered: $240. 31 x 10.50R/15LTB on-off road steel belted radial blackwall (available only if N67, N90 or PA6 wheels are specified): $564. 31 x 10.50R/15LTB (available only if N67, N90 or PA6 wheels are specified): $720. Pre-cleaner air cleaner (RPO K46): $42. Air conditioning (not available with Cold Climate Package): $740. Deluxe Front Appearance (RPO V22). Includes dark argent grille with bright trim and dual rectangular headlights): $109. Heavy-duty battery (RPO UA1): $53. Deluxe chromed front and rear bumpers (RPO VE5): $49. Chromed front bumper guards (RPO V31): $41. Quartz electric clock (RPO U35). Not available with UM6 radio: $79 (without YE9. Includes Z53 Gauge Package). With YE9: $39. Cold Climate Package (RPO V10). Includes special insulation, special heater and defroster, engine block heater, anti-freeze protection to -31 degrees, heavy-duty battery: $188 (without Trailering Special Package. Also includes 66 amp generator). With Trailering Special Package: $126. Engine oil cooling system (RPO KC4): $120. Heavy-duty radiator (RPO VO1): $53. Heavy-duty radiator and transmission oil cooler (RPO VO2): $59. Power door locks (RPO AU3): $135. Color-keyed front floor mats (RPO B32): $15. Gauge Package (RPO Z54). Includes voltmeter, engine coolant temperature and oil pressure gauges: $40. 66 amp generator (RPO K81): $62. Deep tinted glass (RPO AJ1). Includes dark laminated glass on side windows and rear tailgate glass: $194. Deep tinted glass with light tinted rear window (RPO AA3). Includes tinted glass on rear tailgate glass, passenger and driver's side door and dark laminated glass on side windows: $140. Heavy-duty, 7-lead wiring harness (RPO UY7): $44. Halogen light-beam headlights (RPO TT5). Available only with V22 or YE9 was ordered: $17. Headlight warning buzzer (RPO T63): $11. Interior headliner (RPO BB5): $80. 600 watt engine block heater (RPO KO5). Not available for diesel engine: $31. Heavy-duty front heater (RPO C42). Available only with diesel engine: $43. Automatic locking hubs (RPO X6Z): $40. Cigarette lighter (RPO U37): $30. Painted exterior below eye-level mirrors (RPO D44): $50. Stainless steel exterior below eye-level mirrors (RPO D45): $83. Black body side molding (RPO B84). Includes lower side and rear moldings of black plastic with bright trim: $115. Bright body side molding (RPO B85). Includes bright plastic body side and rear lower moldings with black paint trim, plus bright trim for front sidemarker lamps and taillights, fender, door, rear side panel and tailgate moldings: $144. Custom Molding Package (RP0 YG1). Includes B84 black body side moldings, wheel opening moldings and bright trim for front side marker lights and taillight trim. Included with ZY3 or ZY5 Packages: $157. Deluxe Molding Package (RPO YG3). Includes bright trim for front side marker lamps and taillight trim wheel opening molding and B85 bright body side moldings: $173 (without ZY3 or ZY5). With ZY3 or ZY5: $16. Door edge guards (RPO B93): $17. Operating Convenience Package (RPO ZQ2). Includes power door locks and power windows: $325. AM radio (RPO U63): $112. AM/FM radio (RPO U69) $171. AM/FM stereo radio (RPO U58), available only with YE9: $198. AM/FM electronically tuned stereo radio with Seek-Scan, stereo cassette tape player and clock: $419. Windshield antenna (RPO U76), included with radio: $32. Rear seat (RPO AM7). With custom trim: $369. Without custom trim: $341. Fuel tank shield (RPO NY1): $164. Front quad shock absorbers (RPO Z75). Includes dual left and right hand shock absorbers on front axle, heavy-duty shock absorbers on rear axle and a front axle nose bumper to limit axle windup: $128. Electronic speed control (RPO K34): $195. Front heavy-duty 2250 lb. capacity springs with heavy-duty front and rear shock absorbers. Recommended for snowplow type usage only: $92 (with Z75). Without Z75: $59. ComforTilt steering wheel (RPO N33): $115. 31 gal. replacement fuel tank (RPO NK7): $43. Two front towing hooks (RPO V76): $36. Deadweight type trailer hitch (RPO VR2). Not available with Z82: $58. Weight distributing platform trailer hitch (RPO VR4). Included with Z82: $155. Trailering special equipment (RPO Z82). Available only with 3.24 or 3.73:1 rear axle ratio and MXO automatic transmission were ordered. Not available with 5.7 liter LS9 engine. Includes VR4, UY7 and V02 options: $440. With B3J diesel equipment: $258. With C80 air conditioning: $378. Bright metal wheelcovers (RPO P01): $40. Rallye 15 x 8 wheels (RPO N67). Not available with P215 tires: $115. Styled 15 x 8 wheels (RPO PA6). Not available with P215 tires: $174. Cast aluminum 15 x 7 wheels with special hubcaps. (RPO N90). Not available with P215 tires: $299. Power side door electric windows (RPO A31): $10. Power tailgate electric window (RPO A33): $95. Sliding side quarter windows (RPO AD5): $243. Intermittent windshield wipers (RPO CD4): $55.

HISTORICAL FOOTNOTES: The 1986 Jimmy was introduced in Oct, 1985.

1987 JIMMY

Changes for 1987 were primarily of a technical nature, lead by the use electronic fuel injection for all engines. New lighter-weight Delco batteries with increased cranking power were used for the 5.0 and 5.7 liter engine. Jimmys equipped with the 5.7 liter V-8 and those with the 5.0 liter V-8 and automatic transmission had batteries with 525 cold cranking amps. The previous rating had been 405. The previously optional 66 amp alternator was now standard. It replaced a 37 amp unit. The heavy-duty battery option now included an increased performance cranking motor on Jimmys with the 5.7 liter V-8. The exterior colors for 1987 were carry-over 1986 colors: Midnight black, light blue metallic, midnight blue, Indian bronze metallic, steel grey metallic, apple red, doeskin tan, and frost white.

1987 K-Jimmy Sierra Classic

I.D. DATA: The V.I.N. plate was mounted on the lower left side windshield corner. The V.I.N. consisted of 17 elements. The first, the number 1, identified the U.S. as the nation of origin. The letter G followed, for the manufacturer: General Motors. The third entry, the letter T, represented the make as GMC. The GVWR brake system identification followed. Next came the truck line and chassis type; the letter K indicated four-wheel drive. The truck series was identified by a number: 1-1/2 ton. The truck body type identification was next: 8-Utility. The engine code was next, followed by a check digit. The model year was identified by the letter H. The assembly plant code followed. The final six digits were the plant sequential production number.

Model Number	Body Type & Seating	Factory Price	GVW	Shipping Weight	Prod. Total
Jimmy V-1500 Body Code: ZW9 (with 305 V-8)					
TV10516	Util.	$13,117	6100[1]	4379	—

NOTE 1: 6250 GVW Package available. Its content was unchanged from 1986.

STANDARD ENGINE: All states: Engine Type: Cast iron block. OHV, V-8 with Electronic Spark Control. Ordering Code: L03 Produced by GM-Chevrolet Motor Division and GM of Canada. Bore x Stroke: 3.74 in. x 3.48 in. Lifters: Hydraulic. Number of main bearings-5. Carburetion: Electronic fuel injection. Compression Ratio: 9.3:1. Displacement: 305 cu. in. Horsepower: Net: 170 @ 4400 rpm. Torque: Net: 260 lb.-ft. @ 2400 rpm. Oil capacity: 5 qt. with filter change. Fuel Requirements: Unleaded.

OPTIONAL ENGINE: All states: Engine Type: Cast iron block. OHV, V-8. Ordering Code: L05. Produced by GM-Chevrolet Motor Division. Bore x Stroke: 4.0 in. x 3.48 in. Lifters: Hydraulic. Number of main bearings-5. Carburetion: Electronic fuel injection. Compression Ratio: 9.2:1. Displacement: 350 cu. in. (5.7 liters). Horsepower: Net: 210 @ 4000 rpm. Torque: Net: 300 lb.-ft. @ 2800 rpm. Oil capacity: 5 qt. with filter change. Fuel Requirements: Unleaded.

OPTIONAL ENGINE: Not available for California: Engine Type: OHV, cast iron block. Diesel V-8. Order Code LH6. Produced by GM-Detroit Diesel Allison Division. Requires B3J Diesel Equipment Package which consists of dual batteries, hydraulic power-assisted brakes, engine block heater, heavy-duty radiator, K81 alternator, engine oil cooler and additional insulation. Bore x Stroke: 3.98 in. x 3.80 in. Lifters: Hydraulic. Number of main bearings-5. Carburetion: Fuel injection. Compression Ratio: 21.5:1. Displacement: 379 cu. in. (6.2 liter). Horsepower: Net: 130 @ 3600 rpm. Torque: Net: 240 lb.-ft. @ 2000 rpm. Oil capacity: 7 qt. with filter change. Fuel Requirements: Diesel.

CHASSIS FEATURES: Ladder-type. Carbon steel, 36,000-39,000 psi. Heavy-gauge channel side members, alligator-jaw cross members. Section modulus: 3.14 in.

SUSPENSION AND RUNNING GEAR: Front Suspension: Two tapered semi-elliptical leaf springs. Capacity: Gasoline engines: 1650 lb. Optional Capacity: 2250 lb. Diesel engine: 1850 lb. Optional: 2250 lb. Standard 1.25 in. stabilizer bar and 25mm shock absorbers. Optional: 32mm shock absorbers. Rear Suspension: Two-stage tapered and multi-leaf (six-conventional leaves, one tapered leaf). Capacity: 1875 lb. Optional: None. Front Axle. Type: Hypoid, tubular driving. Capacity: 3600 lb. Rear Axle. Type: Hypoid, semi-floating. Capacity: 3750 lb. Final Drive Ratio: 305 V-8: 3.08:1; 350 V-8: 3.42:1; diesel engine: 3.73:1. Optional: Gasoline engines: 3.73:1; diesel engine: 3.42, 3.73:1. Transfer Case: Type: New Process 208. Ratios: 2.61, 1.00:1. Brakes: Type: Hydraulic, self-adjusting. Front: Discs. Rear: Drums. Optional: Power. Dimensions: Front: 11.86 in. dia. rotor. Rear: 11.15 in. x 2.75 in. Wheels: 6-stud, 15 x 6JJ. Optional: 15 x 7JJ Rallye, 15 x 8JJ, 15 x 8JJ Rallye, 16 x 5K. Tires: P215/75R15 steel belted radial. Optional: P215/75R15 steel belted radial whitewall, P235/75R15 steel belted radial, P235/75R15 steel belted radial whitewall, P235/75R15 white lettered steel belted radial, 10R-15B steel belted radial, 10R-15B white lettered steel belted radial. Steering: Power assisted recirculating ball, variable ratio. Ratio: 17.6/13.1. Turns Lock-to-Lock: 4.0. Turning circle: 37.6 ft. Optional: None. Transmission: Gasoline engines: Muncie 4-speed manual, synchromesh on top three gears, floor-mounted shift lever. Ratios: 6.55, 3.58, 1.70, 1.00:1. Standard: Diesel, optional gasoline engines: 700R4 4-speed automatic with overdrive. Ratios: 3.06, 1.36, 1.00, 0.70:1. Reverse: 2.29:1. Clutch: 11.0 in. dia., 124 sq. in. area. 12 in. clutch included with 350 V-8 engines).

VEHICLE DIMENSIONS: Wheelbase: 106.5 in. Overall Length: 184.8 in. Front/Rear Tread 66.10 in./ 63.00 in. Overall Height: 73.4 in. Width: 79.6 in. Tailgate: Width and Height: 66.8 in. x 22.0 in. Approach/Departure Degrees: 34/25. Ground Clearance: Front axle: 7.4 in. Rear axle: 7.0 in. Oil pan: 17.2 in. Transfer case: 11.5 in. Fuel tank: 14.0 in. Load space: With rear seat installed: 38.8 in. x 50 in. x 42.3 in. With rear seat removed or folded: 76.0 in. x 50 in. x 42.3 in.

CAPACITIES: Fuel Tank: 25.0 gal. Optional: Replacement 31 gal. tank. Coolant system: 305 V-8: 17.6 qt. 350 V-8: 17.6 qt.

ACCOMMODATIONS: Seating Capacity: Standard: Driver and passenger front high-back bucket sets. Optional: 3 passenger rear bench seat. Headroom: 38.3 in. Maximum steering wheel to seat back: 18.5 in. Seat to ground: 36.3 in. Floor to ground: 21.9 in.

INSTRUMENTATION: 0-100 mph speedometer, 99,999.9 mi. odometer, fuel gauge, warning lights for alternator, oil pressure, engine coolant temperature, brake operating system, hazard warning lights, directional lights, seat belt warning.

OPTIONS AND PRICES: Sierra Classic Package (RPO YE9): $1073. Includes either custom cloth or custom vinyl seats, custom steering wheel, Deluxe Molding Package, taillight and rear door or tailgate moldings, bright front turn signal and front side marker lamp bezels, fender nameplates, bright windshield and side rear window moldings, color-keyed carpeting with bright sill plates, plastic door trim panels with storage pockets, and bright brushed finish accents, visor vanity mirror, Deluxe Front Appearance Package, dual horns, nameplate on instrument panel, cigarette lighter, headliner, wheel opening moldings, special insulation, bright body side moldings, pillar trim panels, storage console between front seats, floor and wheelwell carpeting, spare tire cover and voltmeter, engine coolant temperature and oil pressure gauges. Custom vinyl bucket seats, custom vinyl seats. Special two-tone paint. Includes Custom Molding Package and wheel opening moldings. Exterior decor. Includes hood ornament. California emission systems (RPO YF5). 5.7 liter V-8. 4-speed with overdrive automatic transmission (standard on B3J diesel). Optional axle ratio. Locking rear differential (RPO G80). P215/75R15 All-Season steel belted radial blackwall. P215/75R15 highway steel belted radial blackwall. P235/75R15 highway steel belted radial whitewall. P235/75R15 highway steel belted radial white lettered. P235/75R15 All-Season steel belted radial blackwall. P235/75R 15 on-off road steel belted radial blackwall. P235/75R15 All-Season steel belted radial whitewall. P235/75R15 All-Season steel belted radial white lettered 31 x 10.50R/15LTB on-off road steel belted radial blackwall. 31 x 10.50R/15LTB (available only if N67, N90 or PA6 wheels are specified). Pre-cleaner air cleaner (RPO K46). Air conditioning (not available with Cold Climate Package). Deluxe Front Appearance Package (RPO V22). Includes dark argent grille with bright trim and dual rectangular headlights). Heavy-duty battery (RPO UA1). Deluxe chromed front and rear bumpers (RPO VE5). Chromed front bumper guards (RPO V31). Quartz electric clock (RPO U35). Not available with UM6 radio. Includes Z53 Gauge Package. Cold Climate Package (RPO V10). Includes special insulation, special heater and defroster, engine block heater, anti-freeze protection to -31 degrees, heavy-duty battery. Engine oil cooling system (RPO KC4). Heavy-duty radiator (RPO VO1). Heavy-duty radiator and transmission oil cooler (RPO VO2). Power door locks (RPO AU3). Color-keyed front floor mats (RPO B32). Gauge Package (RPO Z54). Includes voltmeter, engine coolant temperature and oil pressure gauges. 66 amp generator (RPO K81). Deep tinted glass (RPO AJ1). Includes dark laminated glass on side windows and rear tailgate glass. Deep tinted glass with light tinted rear window (RPO AA3). Includes tinted glass on rear tailgate glass, passenger and driver's side door and dark laminated glass on side windows. Heavy-duty, 7-lead wiring harness (RPO UY7). Halogen light-beam headlights (RPO TT5). Available only with V22 or when YE9 was ordered. Headlight warning buzzer (RPO T63). Interior headliner (RPO BB5). 600 watt engine block heater (RPO KO5). Not available for diesel engine. Heavy-duty front heater (RPO C42). Available only with diesel engine. Automatic locking hubs (RPO X6Z). Cigarette lighter (RPO U37). Painted exterior below eye-level mirrors (RPO D44). Stainless steel exterior below eye-level mirrors (RPO D45). Black body side molding (RPO B84). Includes lower side and rear moldings of black plastic with bright trim. Bright body side molding (RPO B85). Includes bright plastic body side and rear lower moldings with black paint trim, plus bright trim for front side marker lamps and taillights, fender, door, rear side panel and tailgate moldings. Custom Molding Package (RPO YG1). Includes B84 black body side moldings, wheel opening moldings and bright trim for front side marker lights and taillight trim. Included with ZY3 or ZY5 Packages. Deluxe Molding Package (RPO YG3). Includes bright trim for front side marker lamps and taillight trim wheel opening molding and B85 bright body side moldings. Door edge guards (RPO B93). Operating Convenience Package (RPO ZQ2). Includes power door locks and power windows. AM radio (RPO U63). AM/FM radio (RPO U69). AM/FM stereo radio (RPO U58), available only with YE9. AM/FM electronically tuned stereo radio with Seek-Scan, stereo cassette tape player and clock. Windshield antenna (RPO U76), included with radio. Rear seat (RPO AM7). Fuel tank shield (RPO NY1). Front quad shock absorbers (RPO Z75). Includes dual left and right hand shock absorbers on front axle, heavy-duty shock absorbers on rear axle and a front axle nose bumper to limit axle windup. Electronic speed control (RPO K34). Front heavy-duty 2250 lb. capacity springs with heavy-duty front and rear shock absorbers. Recommended for snowplow type usage only.ComforTilt steering wheel (RPO N33). 31 gal. replacement fuel tank (RPO NK7). Two front towing hooks (RPO V76). Deadweight type trailer hitch (RPO VR2). Not available with Z82. Weight distributing platform trailer hitch (RPO VR4). Included with Z82. Trailering special equipment (RPO Z82). Available only with 3.24 or 3.73:1 rear axle ratio and MXO automatic transmission were ordered. Not available with 5.7 liter LS9 engine. Includes VR4, UY7 and V02 options. Bright metal wheelcovers (RPO P01): $40. Rallye 15 x 8 wheels (RPO N67). Not available with P215 tires. Styled 15 x 8 wheels (RPO PA6). Not available with P215 tires. Cast aluminum 15 x 7 wheels with special hubcaps. (RPO N90). Not available with P215 tires. Power side door electric windows (RPO A31). Power tailgate electric window (RPO A33). Sliding side quarter windows (RPO AD5). Intermittent windshield wipers (RPO CD4).

HISTORICAL FOOTNOTES: GMC reported that the full-size Jimmy "features high styling, power and four-wheel drive for rough off-road or smooth highway driving...".

1988 JIMMY

Only two engines were offered for the 1988 Jimmy. Standard was the 5.7 liter electronic fuel injected V-8. The 6.2 liter diesel was optional. Both were equipped with electronic fuel injection. Four new colors were introduced for 1988: Bright blue metallic, forest green metallic, light mesa brown metallic and dark mesa brown metallic. Refinements for 1988 included a fixed mast antenna in place of the old windshield antenna, the inclusion of a trip odometer in the Gauge Package cluster and an improved pulse windshield wiper control. New door handle seals were used to lessen air leaks. New front lining noise insulators reduced brake noise. Improved fuel tank corrosion protection was provided in response to the increased use of methanol fuel.

I.D. DATA: The V.I.N. plate was mounted on the lower left side windshield corner. The V.I.N. consisted of 17 elements. The first, the number 1, identified the U.S. as the nation of origin. The letter G followed, for the manufacturer: General Motors. The third entry, the letter T, represented the make as GMC. The GVWR brake system identification followed. Next came the truck line and chassis type; the letter K indicated four-wheel drive. The truck series was identified by a number: 1-1/2 ton. The truck body type identification was next: 8-Utility. The engine code was next, followed by a check digit. The model year was identified by the letter J. The assembly plant code followed. The final six digits were the plant sequential production number.

Model Number	Body Type & Seating	Factory Price	GVW	Shipping Weight	Prod. Total
Jimmy V-1500 Body Code: ZW9 (with 350 V-8)					
TV10516	Util.	$14,560	6100[1]	4676	9439

NOTE 1: 6250 GVW Package available. Its content was unchanged from 1987.

STANDARD ENGINE: All states: Engine Type: Cast iron block. OHV, V-8. Ordering Code: L05. Produced by GM-Chevrolet Motor Division. Bore x Stroke: 4.0 in. x 3.48 in. Lifters: Hydraulic. Number of main bearings-5. Carburetion: Electronic fuel injection. Compression Ratio: 9.2:1. Displacement: 350 cu. in. (5.7 liters). Horsepower: Net: 210 @ 4000 rpm. Torque: Net: 300 lb.-ft. @ 2800 rpm. Oil capacity: 5 qt. with filter change. Fuel Requirements: Unleaded.

OPTIONAL ENGINE: Engine Type: OHV, cast iron block. Diesel V-8. Order Code LH6. Produced by GM-Detroit Diesel Allison Division. Requires B3J Diesel Equipment Package which consists of dual batteries, hydraulic power-assisted brakes, engine block heater, heavy-duty radiator, K81 alternator, engine oil cooler and additional insulation. Bore x Stroke: 3.98 in. x 3.80 in. Lifters: Hydraulic. Number of main bearings-5. Carburetion: Fuel injection. Compression Ratio: 21.5:1. Displacement: 379 cu. in. (6.2 liter). Horsepower: Net: 130 @ 3600 rpm. Torque: Net: 240 lb.-ft. @ 2000 rpm. Oil capacity: 7 qt. with filter change. Fuel Requirements: Diesel.

CHASSIS FEATURES: Ladder-type. Carbon steel, 36,000-39,000 psi. Heavy-gauge channel side members, alligator-jaw cross members. Section modulus: 3.14 in.

SUSPENSION AND RUNNING GEAR: Front Suspension: Two tapered semi-elliptical leaf springs. Capacity: Gasoline engines: 1650 lb. Optional Capacity: 2250 lb. Diesel engine: 1850 lb. Optional: 2250 lb. Standard 1.25 in. stabilizer bar and 25mm shock absorbers. Optional: 32mm shock absorbers. Rear Suspension: Two-stage tapered and multi-leaf (six-conventional leaves, one tapered leaf). Capacity: 1875 lb. Optional: None. Front Axle. Type: Hypoid, tubular driving. Capacity: 3600 lb. Rear Axle. Type: Hypoid, semi-floating. Capacity: 3750 lb. Final Drive Ratio: 305 V-8: 3.08:1; 350 V-8: 3.42:1; diesel engine: 3.73:1. Optional: Gasoline engines: 3.73:1; diesel engine: 3.42, 3.73:1. Transfer Case: Type: New Process 208. Ratios: 2.61, 1.00:1. Brakes: Type: Hydraulic, self-adjusting. Front: Discs. Rear: Drums. Optional: Power. Dimensions: Front: 11.86 in. dia. rotor. Rear: 11.15 in. x 2.75 in. Wheels: 6-stud, 15 x 6JJ. Optional: 15 x 7JJ Rallye, 15 x 8JJ, 15 x 8JJ Rallye, 16 x 5K. Tires: P215/75R15 steel belted radial. Optional: P215/75R15 steel belted radial whitewall, P235/75R15 steel belted radial, P235/75R15 steel belted radial whitewall, P235/75R15 white lettered steel belted radial, 10R-15B steel belted radial, 10R-15B white lettered steel belted radial. Steering: Power assisted recirculating ball, variable ratio. Ratio: 17.6/13.1. Turns Lock-to-Lock: 4.0. Turning circle: 37.6 ft. Optional: None. Transmission: Gasoline engines: Muncie 4-speed manual, synchromesh on top three gears, floor-mounted shift lever. Ratios: 6.55, 3.58, 1.70, 1.00:1. Not available in California. Standard: Diesel, optional gasoline engines: 700R4 4-speed automatic with overdrive. Ratios: 3.06, 1.36, 1.00, 0.70:1. Reverse: 2.29:1. Clutch: 11.0 in. dia., 124 sq. in. area. 12 in. clutch included with 350 V-8 engines).

VEHICLE DIMENSIONS: Wheelbase: 106.5 in. Overall Length: 184.8 in. Front/Rear Tread 66.10 in./ 63.00 in. Overall Height: 73.4 in. Width: 79.6 in. Tailgate: Width and Height: 66.8 in. x 22.0 in. Approach/Departure Degrees: 34/25. Ground Clearance: Front axle: 7.4 in. Rear axle: 7.0 in. Oil pan: 17.2 in. Transfer case: 11.5 in. Fuel tank: 14.0 in. Load space: With rear seat installed: 38.8 in. x 50 in. x 42.3 in. With rear seat removed or folded: 76.0 in. x 50 in. x 42.3 in.

CAPACITIES: Fuel Tank: 25.0 gal. Optional: Replacement 31 gal. tank. Coolant system: 305 V-8: 17.6 qt. 350 V-8: 17.6 qt.

ACCOMMODATIONS: Seating Capacity: Standard: Driver and passenger front high-back bucket sets. Optional: 3 passenger rear bench seat. Headroom: 38.3 in. Maximum steering wheel to seat back: 18.5 in. Seat to ground: 36.3 in. Floor to ground: 21.9 in.

INSTRUMENTATION: 0-100 mph speedometer, 99,999.9 mi. odometer, fuel gauge, warning lights for alternator, oil pressure, engine coolant temperature, brake operating system, hazard warning lights, directional lights, seat belt warning.

OPTIONS AND PRICES: Sierra Classic Package (RPO YE9): $1249. Includes either custom cloth or custom vinyl seats, custom steering wheel, Deluxe Molding Package, taillight and rear door or tailgate moldings, bright front turn signal and front side marker lamp bezels, fender nameplates, bright windshield and side rear window moldings, color-keyed carpeting with bright sill plates, plastic door trim panels with storage pockets, and bright brushed finish accents, visor vanity mirror, Deluxe Front Appearance Package, dual horns, nameplate on instrument panel, cigarette lighter, headliner, wheel opening moldings, special insulation, bright body side moldings, pillar trim panels, storage console between front seats, floor and wheelwell carpeting, spare tire cover and voltmeter, engine coolant temperature and oil pressure gauges. Custom vinyl bucket seats, custom vinyl seats. Special two-tone paint. Includes Custom Molding Package and wheel opening moldings. Exterior Decor. Includes hood ornament. California emission systems (RPO YF5). 5.7 liter V-8. 4-speed with overdrive automatic transmission (standard on B3J diesel). Optional axle ratio. Locking rear differential (RPO G80). P215/75R15 All-Season steel belted radial blackwall. P215/75R15 highway steel belted radial blackwall. P235/75R15 highway steel belted radial whitewall. P235/75R15 highway steel belted radial white lettered. P235/75R15 All-Season steel belted radial blackwall. P235/75R 15 on-off road steel belted radial blackwall. P235/75R15 All-Season steel belted radial whitewall. P235/75R15 All-Season steel belted radial white lettered 31 x 10.50R/15LTB on-off road steel belted radial blackwall. 31 x 10.50R/15LTB (available only if N67, N90 or PA6 wheels are specified). Pre-cleaner air cleaner (RPO K46). Air conditioning (not available with Cold Climate Package). Deluxe Front Appearance (RPO V22). Includes dark argent grille with bright trim and dual rectangular headlights). Heavy-duty battery (RPO UA1). Deluxe chromed front and rear bumpers (RPO VE5). Chromed front bumper guards (RPO V31). Quartz electric clock (RPO U35). Not available with UM6 radio. Includes Z53 Gauge Package). Cold Climate Package (RPO V10). Includes special insulation, special heater and defroster, engine block heater, anti-freeze protection to -31 degrees, heavy-duty battery. Engine oil cooling system (RPO KC4). Heavy-duty radiator (RPO VO1). Heavy-duty radiator and transmission oil cooler (RPO VO2). Power door locks (RPO AU3). Color-keyed front floor mats (RPO B32). Gauge Package (RPO Z54). Includes voltmeter, engine coolant temperature and oil pressure gauges. 66 amp generator (RPO K81). Deep tinted glass (RPO AJ1). Includes dark laminated glass on side windows and rear tailgate glass. Deep tinted glass with light tinted rear window (RPO AA3). Includes tinted glass on rear tailgate glass, passenger and driver's side door and dark laminated glass on side windows. Heavy-duty, 7-lead wiring harness (RPO UY7). Halogen light-beam headlights (RPO TT5). Available only with V22 or when YE9 was ordered. Headlight warning buzzer (RPO T63). Interior headliner (RPO BB5). 600 watt engine block heater (RPO KO5). Not available for diesel engine. Heavy-duty front heater (RPO C42). Available only with diesel engine. Automatic locking hubs (RPO X6Z). Cigarette lighter (RPO U37). Painted exterior below eye-level mirrors (RPO D44). Stainless steel exterior below eye-level mirrors (RPO D45). Black body side molding (RPO B84). Includes lower side and rear moldings of black plastic with bright trim. Bright body side molding (RPO B85). Includes bright plastic body side and rear lower moldings with black paint trim, plus bright trim for front side marker lamps and taillights, fender, door, rear side panel and tailgate moldings. Custom Molding Package (RP0 YG1). Includes B84 black body side moldings, wheel opening moldings and bright trim for front side marker lights and taillight trim. Included with ZY3 or ZY5 Packages. Deluxe Molding Package (RPO YG3). Includes bright trim for front side marker lamps and taillight trim wheel opening molding and B85 bright body side moldings. Door edge guards (RPO B93). Operating Convenience Package (RPO ZQ2). Includes power door locks and power windows. AM radio (RPO U63). AM/FM radio (RPO U69). AM/FM stereo radio (RPO U58), available only with YE9. AM/FM electronically tuned stereo radio with Seek-Scan, stereo cassette tape player and clock. Windshield antenna (RPO U76), included with radio. Rear seat (RPO AM7). Fuel tank shield (RPO NY1). Front quad shock absorbers (RPO Z75). Includes dual left and right hand shock absorbers on front axle, heavy-duty shock absorbers on rear axle and a front axle nose bumper to limit axle windup. Electronic speed control (RPO K34). Front heavy-duty 2250 lb. capacity springs with heavy-duty front and rear shock absorbers. Recommended for snowplow type usage only.ComforTilt steering wheel (RPO N33). 31 gal. replacement fuel tank (RPO NK7). Two front towing hooks (RPO V76). Deadweight type trailer hitch (RPO VR2). Not available with Z82. Weight distributing platform trailer hitch (RPO VR4). Included with Z82. Trailering special equipment (RPO Z82). Available only with 3.24 or 3.73:1 rear axle ratio and MXO automatic transmission were ordered. Not available with 5.7 liter LS9 engine. Includes VR4, UY7 and V02 options. Bright metal wheelcovers (RPO P01): $40. Rallye 15 x 8 wheels (RPO N67). Not available with P215 tires. Styled 15 x 8 wheels (RPO PA6). Not available with P215 tires. Cast aluminum 15 x 7 wheels with special hubcaps. (RPO N90). Not available with P215 tires. Power side door electric windows (RPO A31). Power tailgate electric window (RPO A33). Sliding side quarter windows (RPO AD5). Intermittent windshield wipers (RPO CD4).

HISTORICAL FOOTNOTES: The GMC Jimmy was built at two locations: Flint, Michigan, and Shreveport, Louisiana.

1989 JIMMY

The 1989 Jimmy had both a new base and up-level grille as well as new headlight bezels. The Jimmy's body nameplate and emblems were identical to those used on the four-wheel drive K series pickups. Also shared with the K models were the Jimmy's new body side moldings and bumper rub strips. The Jimmy exterior had a new "wet-look" shine that was credited to the replacement of the older high solid enamel paint with an all-new base coat/clear coat paint. Ten solid colors were offered: Onyx black, smoke blue metallic, mojave beige, sunset gold metallic, wintergreen metallic, summit white, fire red, grey metallic, quicksilver metallic and midnight blue metallic. In addition, the Jimmy could be ordered in 114 different two-tone combinations with new colors breaks for 1989. The Jimmy's new styling was enhanced by its new body-color side door drip moldings and newly styled full wheelcovers. Other changes for 1989 included new black below eye-level mirrors, standard sun visors on the SLE that were color-keyed and fitted with plastic extenders. The driver's side visor had a map strap and the passenger side had a lighted vanity mirror. Vehicle corrosion protection was upgraded by extending the use of additional body and front end metal components with two-sided galvanized coatings. Ride characteristics of the Jimmy were improved by adding five new spring assemblies and 16 new front and rear shock absorber assemblies. The LO5 5.7 liter V-8 now had serpentine accessory drive belts in place of the older multi-belt accessory drive. New combination lap/shoulder belts were now standard for the Jimmy. The Auxiliary Lighting Package now included a glove box light and an underhood reel lamp. The new series of Delco 2000 electronic tuned radios were offered for the Jimmy. Standard Jimmy trim was SLX. Optional was SLE. Standard equipment for the Jimmy consisted of the following chassis items: Dual electric high-note and low-tone horns, front stabilizer bar, 2-speed transfer case and manual-locking front hubs, and power steering and brakes. Standard exterior features included: Front and rear chromed bumpers, molded plastic grille and front lamp bezels painted light and dark argent, bright metal hubcaps with black trim, argent painted wheels, All-Season steel-belted radial tires, full-size spare and wheel, tool kit (includes mechanical jack and wheel wrench), SLX nameplates, black below eye-level exterior mirrors and roll-down rear tailgate glass window.

The standard SLX interior consisted of right and left side padded armrests, high-back front bucket seats with custom vinyl pigskin-grained trim in any of four colors: Dark blue, burgundy, saddle or slate grey; easy rear entry passenger seat front sliding mechanism, two coat hooks on left side, full-length bright sill plates at front doors and rear of rear compartment floor, map light, two dome lamps with door-operated switches, floor covering of embossed black rubber mats in front and rear, insulation on dash panel, floor panel and between double-wall cab roof, tinted glass on all windows, padded, color-keyed left and right side sunshades, gauges for fuel level, voltmeter, oil pressure and engine pressure, trip odometer, heavy-duty heater and defogger, AM radio with fixed mast antenna, 2-spoke steering wheel and anti-theft locking feature on steering column, 10 in. rearview mirror, color-keyed, molded plastic door trim panels, cigarette lighter with ashtray illumination and spare tire carrier on right hand rear panel.

I.D. DATA: The V.I.N. plate was mounted on the lower left side windshield corner. The V.I.N. consisted of 17 elements. The first, the number 1, identified the U.S. as the nation of origin. The letter G followed, for the manufacturer: General Motors. The third entry, the letter T, represented the make as GMC. The GVWR brake system identification followed. Next came the truck line and chassis type; the letter K indicated four-wheel drive. The truck series was identified by a number: 1-1/2 ton. The truck body type identification was next: 8-Utility. The engine code was next, followed by a check digit. The model year was identified by the letter K. The assembly plant code followed. The final six digits were the plant sequential production number.

Model Number	Body Type & Seating	Factory Price	GVW	Shipping Weight	Prod. Total
Jimmy V-1500 Body Code: ZW9 (with 350 V-8)					
TV10516	Util.	$15,415	6100	4797	—
8339	(with Diesel V-8)	$18,148	6250	N.A.	—

STANDARD ENGINE: All states: Engine Type: Cast iron block. OHV, V-8. Ordering Code: L05. Produced by GM-Chevrolet Motor Division. Bore x Stroke: 4.0 in. x 3.48 in. Lifters: Hydraulic. Number of main bearings-5. Carburetion: Electronic fuel injection. Compression Ratio: 9.2:1. Displacement: 350 cu. in. (5.7 liters). Horsepower: Net: 210 @ 4000 rpm. Torque: Net: 300 lb.-ft. @ 2800 rpm. Oil capacity: 5 qt. with filter change. Fuel Requirements: Unleaded.

OPTIONAL ENGINE: Not available for California: Engine Type: OHV, cast iron block. Diesel V-8. Order Code LH6. Produced by GM-Detroit Diesel Allison Division. Requires B3J Diesel Equipment Package which consists of dual batteries, hydraulic power-assisted brakes, engine block heater, heavy-duty radiator, K81 alternator, engine oil cooler and additional insulation. Bore x Stroke: 3.98 in. x 3.80 in. Lifters: Hydraulic. Number of main bearings-5. Carburetion: Fuel injection. Compression Ratio: 21.5:1. Displacement: 379 cu. in. (6.2 liter). Horsepower: Net: 130 @ 3600 rpm. Torque: Net: 240 lb.-ft. @ 2000 rpm. Oil capacity: 7 qt. with filter change. Fuel Requirements: Diesel.

CHASSIS FEATURES: Ladder-type. Carbon steel, 36,000-39,000 psi. Heavy-gauge channel side members, alligator-jaw cross members. Section modulus: 3.14 in.

SUSPENSION AND RUNNING GEAR: Front Suspension: Two tapered semi-elliptical leaf springs. Capacity: Gasoline engines: 1650 lb. Optional Capacity: 2250 lb. Diesel engine: 1850 lb. Optional: 2250 lb. Standard 1.25 in. stabilizer bar and 25mm shock absorbers. Optional: 32mm shock absorbers. Rear Suspension: Two-stage tapered and multi-leaf (six-conventional leaves, one tapered leaf). Capacity: 1875 lb. Optional: None. Front Axle. Type: Hypoid, tubular driving. Capacity: 3600 lb. Rear Axle. Type: Hypoid, semi-floating. Capacity: 3750 lb. Final Drive Ratio: 350 V-8: 3.42:1; diesel engine: 3.73:1. Optional: Gasoline engines: 3.73:1; diesel engine: 3.42, 3.73:1. Transfer Case: Type: New Process 208. Ratios: 2.61, 1.00:1. Brakes: Type: Hydraulic, self-adjusting. Front: Discs. Rear: Drums. Maximum steering. Optional: Power. Dimensions: Front: 11.86 in. dia. rotor. Rear: 11.15 in. x 2.75 in. Wheels: 6-stud, 15 x 6JJ. Optional: 15 x 7JJ Rallye, 15 x 8JJ, 15 x 8JJ Rallye, 16 x 5K. Tires: P215/75R15 steel belted radial. Optional: P215/75R15 steel belted radial whitewall, P235/75R15 steel belted radial, P235/75R15 steel belted radial whitewall, P235/75R15 white lettered steel belted radial, 10R-15B steel belted radial, 10R-15B white lettered steel belted radial. Steering: Power assisted recirculating ball, variable ratio. Ratio: 17.6/13.1. Turns Lock-to-Lock: 4.0. Turning circle: 37.6 ft. Optional: None. Transmission: Gasoline engines: Muncie 4-speed manual, synchromesh on top three gears, floor-mounted shift lever. Ratios: 6.55, 3.58, 1.70, 1.00:1 Not available in California. Standard: Diesel, optional gasoline engines: 700R4 4-speed automatic with overdrive. Ratios: 3.06, 1.36, 1.00, 0.70:1. Reverse: 2.29:1. Clutch: 11.0 in. dia., 124 sq. in. area. 12 in. clutch included with 350 V-8 engines).

VEHICLE DIMENSIONS: Wheelbase: 106.5 in. Overall Length: 184.8 in. Front/Rear Tread 66.10 in./ 63.00 in. Overall Height: 73.4 in. Width: 79.6 in. Tailgate: Width and Height: 66.8 in. x 22.0 in. Approach/Departure Degrees: 34/25. Ground Clearance: Front axle: 7.4 in. Rear axle: 7.0 in. Oil pan: 17.2 in. Transfer case: 11.5 in. Fuel tank: 14.0 in. Load space: With rear seat installed: 38.8 in. x 50 in. x 42.3 in. With rear seat removed or folded: 76.0 in. x 50 in. x 42.3 in.

CAPACITIES: Fuel Tank: 350 V-8: 31.0 gal. Diesel: 32 gal. Coolant system: 350 V-8: 17.6 qt.

ACCOMMODATIONS: Seating Capacity: Standard: Driver and passenger front high-back bucket sets. Optional: 3 passenger rear bench seat. Headroom: 38.3 in. Maximum steering wheel to seat back: 18.5 in. Seat to ground: 36.3 in. Floor to ground: 21.9 in.

INSTRUMENTATION: 0-100 mph speedometer, 99,999.9 mi. odometer, fuel gauge, warning lights for alternator, oil pressure, engine coolant temperature, brake operating system, hazard warning lights, directional lights, seat belt warning.

OPTIONS AND PRICES: SLE Package (RPO YE9): $1340. Exterior features in addition to or in place of SLX items consisted of front and rear chromed bumpers with black rub stripes (front rub strip has bright trim), SLE nameplates, molded plastic grille and front lamp bezels painted dark argent with chrome trim, rectangular dual halogen headlamps, body side and rear black moldings with bright trim, bright wheel opening moldings, bright metal wheelcovers, cab-to-fender and hood insulators, underhood reel-type lamp and electric power rear tailgate window and bright applique. The SLE interior had, in addition to or in place of the standard items the following: Highback reclining front bucket seats with choice of custom vinyl pigskin-grained trim (available in either dark blue or saddle) or textured velour custom cloth trim (in a choice of dark blue, burgundy, saddle or slate grey), right side front and left and right side rear assist straps, glove box light, floor covering of color-keyed front compartment carpeting (matching rear compartment floor covering including wheelhousings, was also provided with optional rear seat), insulation on dash panel, between double-wall cab roof, on floor panel (extras thick at front, extra-thick at rear when rear seat was ordered), under cowl panel, on headliner and on body side trim panels, extra insulation on diesel engine models, sunshades with flexible outboard ends and sliding extenders at inboard ends, storage strap on left side sunshade, illuminated mirror on right sunshade, brushed pewter-toned instrument panel trim, 4-spoke Sport steering wheel with simulated stitched leather appearance, front compartment foam-backed cloth headliner with matching retainer moldings, special door trim panels, including door closing assist strips, decorative inserts, map pockets and carpet trim, rear sidewall trim panels with ashtrays and carpet trim, cigarette lighter with ashtray illumination, black vinyl spare tire cover, headlight warning buzzer, and color-keyed molded plastic console with storage and beverage pockets. Air cleaner pre-cleaner (RPO K46): $44. Air conditioning (RPO C60) $781 (without B3J); $719 (with B3J). Deluxe front end appearance (RPO V22). Includes dark argent grille with chrome trim and quad halogen headlamps. Included with SLE: $145. Optional rear axle ratios: $38. Locking rear differential (RPO G80): $252. Heavy-duty Delco Freedom Battery with 630 cold cranking amps (RPO UA1), included with V10 Cold Climate Package: $56. Chromed front bumper guards (RPO V31): $43. Cold Climate Package (RPO V10). Includes UA1 battery and KO5 engine block heater: $104. Engine oil cooler (RPO KC4): $126. Heavy-duty radiator (RPO VO1): $56. Heavy-duty radiator and transmission oil cooler (RPO VO2): $63. Front floor mats (RPO B32): $16. Rear floor mats (RPO B33): $22. Deep tinted glass with light tinted rear glass (RPO AA3): $149. Deep tinted glass (RPO AJ1): $205. Wiring harness (RPO UY7): $46. Headlamp warning buzzer (RPO T63): $12. Engine block heater (RPO KO5): $33. Locking front hubs (RPO X6Z): $60. Auxiliary lighting (RPO TR9) Includes glove box and underhood lights: $26. Below eye-level stainless steel exterior mirrors (RPO D45): $35. Deluxe Molding Package (RPO YG3). Includes deluxe front and rear chrome bumpers with rub strips, bright trim for front side marker lights and taillights, bright wheel opening moldings and black body side and rear moldings with bright trim: $234. Operating Convenience Package (RPO ZQ2). Includes power door locks and front door power windows: $344. Conventional two-tone exterior paint (RPO ZY2): $413 (without YE9), $180 (with YE9). Special two-tone exterior paint (RPO ZY3): $464 (without YE9), $450 (with YE9). Deluxe two-tone exterior paint (RPO ZY4): $566 (without YE9), $332 (with YE9). Puncture sealant tires (RPO P42): $230. Electronically tuned AM/FM stereo radio (RPO UU9: $148. Electronically tuned AM/FM stereo radio with Seek-Scan and digital clock (RPO UM7): $208. Electronically tuned AM/FM stereo radio with Seek-Scan, stereo cassette tape player and digital clock (RPO UM6): $329. Electronically tuned AM/FM stereo radio with Seek-Scan, stereo cassette tape player with Search and Repeat, graphic equalizer and digital clock (RPO UX1): $504 . Radio delete (RPO UL5): $77. Fuel tank shield (RPO NY1). Includes protective shield on transfer case: $175. Rear folding 3 passenger seat (AM7): $411. Rear seat not desired (RPO YG4): No charge. Electronic speed control (RPO K34): $205. Heavy-duty 2250 lb. front springs (F60). Includes heavy-duty front and rear shock absorbers, recommended for front-mounted accessory applications only: $62. ComforTilt steering wheel (RPO N33): $121. Two front towing hooks (RPO V76): $38. Deadweight type trailer hitch (RPO VR2): $62. Weight distributing platform type trailer hitch (RPO VR4): $164. Trailering special equipment (RPO Z82). Includes VR4 hitch, UY7 wiring and VO2 trans. oil cooler; without BJ3 includes KC4 engine oil cooler: $398. 4-speed automatic with overdrive (RPO MXO): $795-No charge with B3J equipment. Wheelcovers (RPO PO1): $42. Rallye wheels (RPO N67): $121 (without YE90, $79 (with YE9). Aluminum cast wheels (RPO N90): $318 (without YE9), $278 (with YE9). Power electric tailgate window (RPO A33): $103. Sliding rear quarter windows (AD5): $257. Intermittent windshield wipers (RPO CD4): $59.

HISTORICAL FOOTNOTES: GMC reported that the Jimmy, when properly equipped, had the ability to tow a trailer with a GTW of up to 6000 lbs.

1990 JIMMY

There were no major changes in the Jimmy's external appearance for 1990. All Jimmys now had a standard rear wheel anti-lock braking system. A new electronic speedometer was also introduced for 1990 along with non-asbestos brake linings. The Jimmy body also used two-side galvanized exterior sheet metal. The 5.7 liter V-8 (LO5) engine was improved for 1990 with the addition of the following: Improved oil control rings, redesigned rear crankshaft seal, new camshaft sprocket design, non-asbestos intake manifold gasket and heavy-duty intake valves. The 6.2 liter diesel had new horsepower and torque ratings for 1990 but these were due to changes in the horsepower and torque rating methodology and did not affect actual engine performance.

Many options of 1989 became standard for 1990. Many other items that had proven to be low volume options were eliminated. These consisted of deep tinted glass with light tinted rear window (RPO AA3), pre-cleaner air cleaner (RPO K46), electronically-tuned AM/FM stereo radio with clock (RPO UU9), front bumper guards (RPO V31), puncture proof tires (RPO P42) and the auxiliary battery (RPO TP2). Options that were previously available separately now were combined into packages with other options. Added to the Standard SLX Package was a power-operated tailgate window, pulse windshield wiper system, headlight warning buzzer and front towhooks. A heavy-duty battery with 630 CCA was also standard on the SLX model. An AM radio (RPO UT5) replaced the RPO U63 version. The full range of SLX exterior features consisted of the following: Front and rear chromed bumpers, SLX nameplates, molded plastic grille and front lamp bezels painted light and dark argent, bright metal hubcaps with black trim, argent painted 15 x 6.0 wheels, four All-Season steel-belted radial ply tires, tools including a mechanical jack and wheel wrench, intermittent windshield wipers, left and right side below eye-level 6.5 in. x 9.0 in. black painted exterior bumpers, power-operated tailgate and front tow hooks.

The standard SLX interior consisted of right and left side padded armrests, high-back front bucket seats with custom vinyl pigskin-grained trim in any of four colors: Dark blue, garnet, saddle or slate grey; easy rear entry passenger seat front sliding mechanism, two coat hooks on left side, full-length bright sill plates at front doors and rear of rear compartment floor, map light, two dome lamps with door-operated switches, floor covering of embossed black rubber mats in front and rear, insulation on dash panel, floor panel and between double-wall cab roof, tinted glass on all windows, padded, color-keyed left and right side sunshades, gauges for fuel level, voltmeter, oil pressure and engine pressure, trip odometer, heavy-duty heater and defogger, AM radio with fixed mast antenna, 2-spoke steering wheel and anti-theft locking feature on steering column, 10 in. rearview mirror, color-keyed, molded plastic door trim panels, cigarette lighter with ashtray illumination and spare tire carrier on right hand rear panel. Now included in the SLE option was auxiliary ;ighting (RPO TR9), Deluxe Front Appearance Package (RPO V22) and a Deluxe Molding Package (RPO YG3). The electronic speed control was now included in the Convenience Package (RPO ZQ3). New options for 1990 were: An outside electric mirror (RPO D48), rear seat shoulder belts (RPO AK9) and the Convenience Package (RO ZQ3). The Jimmy's exterior colors were onyx black, smoke blue metallic, mojave beige, sunset gold metallic, wintergreen metallic, summit white, fire red, grey metallic, quicksilver metallic and midnight blue metallic. Garnet replaced burgundy in the Jimmy's interior trim color selection.

1990 SLE V-Jimmy

I.D. DATA: The V.I.N. plate was mounted on the lower left side windshield corner. The V.I.N. consisted of 17 elements. The first, the number 1, identified the U.S. as the nation of origin. The letter G followed, for the manufacturer: General Motors. The third entry, the letter T, represented the make as GMC. The GVWR brake system identification followed. Next came the truck line and chassis type; the letter K indicated four-wheel drive. The truck series was identified by a number: 1-1/2 ton. The truck body type identification was next: 8-Utility. The engine code was next, followed by a check digit. The model year was identified by the letter L. The assembly plant code followed. The final six digits were the plant sequential production number.

Model Number	Body Type & Seating	Factory Price	GVW	Shipping Weight	Prod. Total
Jimmy V10 Body Code: ZW9 (with 350 V-8)					
TV10516	Util.	$16547	6100	4797	—
4,685*	W/Diesel V-8 & B3J	$19,302	6250	N.A.	—

* Production of all models.

STANDARD ENGINE: All states: Engine Type: Cast iron block. OHV, V-8. Ordering Code: L05. Produced by GM-Chevrolet Motor Division. Bore x Stroke: 4.0 in. x 3.48 in. Lifters: Hydraulic. Number of main bearings-5. Carburetion: Electronic fuel injection. Compression Ratio: 9.2:1. Displacement: 350 cu. in. (5.7 liters). Horsepower: Net: 210 @ 4000 rpm. Torque: Net: 300 lb.-ft. @ 2800 rpm. Oil capacity: 5 qt. with filter change. Fuel Requirements: Unleaded.

OPTIONAL ENGINE: Not available for California: Engine Type: OHV, cast iron block. Diesel V-8. Order Code LH6. Produced by GM-Detroit Diesel Allison Division. Requires B3J Diesel Equipment Package which consists of dual batteries, hydraulic power-assisted brakes, engine block heater, heavy-duty radiator, K81 alternator, engine oil cooler and additional insulation. Bore x Stroke: 3.98 in. x 3.80 in. Lifters: Hydraulic. Number of main bearings-5. Carburetion: Fuel injection. Compression Ratio: 21.5:1. Displacement: 379 cu. in. (6.2 liter). Horsepower: Net: 130 @ 3600 rpm. Torque: Net: 240 lb.-ft. @ 2000 rpm. Oil capacity: 7 qt. with filter change. Fuel Requirements: Diesel.

CHASSIS FEATURES: Ladder-type. Carbon steel, 36,000-39,000 psi. Heavy-gauge channel side members, alligator-jaw cross members. Section modulus: 3.14.

SUSPENSION AND RUNNING GEAR: Front Suspension: Two tapered semi-elliptical leaf springs. Capacity: Gasoline engines: 1650 lb. Optional Capacity: 2250 lb. Diesel engine: 1850 lb. Optional: 2250 lb. Standard 1.25 in. stabilizer bar and 25mm shock absorbers. Optional: 32mm shock absorbers. Rear Suspension: Two-stage tapered and multi-leaf (six-conventional leaves, one tapered leaf). Capacity: 1875 lb. Optional: None. Front Axle. Type: Hypoid, tubular driving. Capacity: 3600 lb. Rear Axle. Type: Hypoid, semi-floating. Capacity: 3750 lb. Final Drive Ratio: 5.7 liter V-8 with manual 4-spd. trans.: 3.08:1. Optional: 3.42:1. 5.7 liter V-8 with 4-spd. auto. trans.: 2.73:1. Optional: 3.08, 3.42, 3.731, 2. 1-Requires Z82 Trailering without California emissions. With California emissions requires KC4 engine oil cooler. 2-Requires Z82 trailering special or high altitude emissions. Final Drive Ratio: 6.2 liter diesel V-8: 3.08:1. Optional: 3,42, 3.73:1. 1-Requires Z82 trailering special or high altitude emissions. Transfer Case: Type: New Process 208. Ratios: 2.61, 1.00:1. Brakes: Type: Hydraulic, self-adjusting. Front: Discs. Rear: Drums. Optional: Power. Dimensions: Front: 11.86 in. dia. rotor. Rear: 11.15 in. x 2.75 in. Wheels: 6-stud, 15 x 6.00JJ. Optional: 15 x 7JJ Rallye, 15 x 8JJ, 15 x 8JJ Rallye, 16 x 5K. Tires: P235/75R15 steel belted radial. Optional: P235/75R15 steel belted radial on-off road, P235/75R15 steel belted radial whitewall, P235/75R15 steel belted radial white letters, P235/75R15 steel belted radial whitewall XL (requires N67 or N90 wheels), 31 x 10.50R15B white letters steel belted radial on-off road. Steering: Power assisted recirculating ball, variable ratio. Ratio: 17.6/13.1. Turns Lock-to-Lock: 4.0. Turning circle: 37.6 ft. Optional: None. Transmission: Type: SM465, RPO MM4. 4-speed manual, fully synchronized. Floor-mounted shifter. Standard transmission with diesel V-8: 4-speed automatic overdrive. Optional (gasoline engined models, and models with California emissions): 4-speed automatic overdrive. Transmission Ratios: SM465. Synchromesh on top three gears, floor-mounted shift lever. Ratios: 6.55, 3.58, 1.70, 1.00:1. Reverse: 6.09:1. 700R4 Automatic: 3.06, 1.63, 1.00, 0.70. Reverse: 2.29. Clutch: 12.0 in. dia.

VEHICLE DIMENSIONS: Wheelbase: 106.5 in. Overall Length: 184.8 in. Front/Rear Tread: 66.10 in./ 63.00 in. Overall Height: 73.4 in. Width: 79.6 in. Tailgate: Width and Height: 66.8 in. x 22.0 in. Approach/Departure Degrees: 34/25. Ground Clearance: Front axle: 7.4 in. Rear axle: 7.0 in. Oil pan: 17.2 in. Transfer case: 11.5 in. Fuel tank: 14.0 in. Load space: With rear seat installed: 38.8 in. x 50 in. x 42.3 in. With rear seat removed or folded: 76.0 in. x 50 in. x 42.3 in.

CAPACITIES: Fuel Tank: 350 V-8: 31.0 gal. Diesel: 32 gal. Coolant system: 350 V-8: 17.6 qt.

ACCOMMODATIONS: Seating Capacity: Standard: Driver and passenger front high-back bucket sets. Optional: 3 passenger rear bench seat. Headroom: 38.3 in. Maximum steering wheel to seat back: 18.5 in. Seat to ground: 36.3 in. Floor to ground: 21.9 in.

INSTRUMENTATION: 0-100 mph speedometer, 99,999.9 mi. odometer, fuel gauge, warning lights for alternator, oil pressure, engine coolant temperature, brake operating system, hazard warning lights, directional lights, seat belt warning.

OPTIONS AND PRICES: SLE Package (RPO YE9): $1281. Exterior features in addition to or in place of SLX items consisted of front and rear chromed bumpers with black rub stripes (front rub strip has bright trim), SLE nameplates, molded plastic grille and front lamp bezels painted dark argent with chrome trim, rectangular dual halogen headlamps, body side and rear black moldings with bright trim, bright wheel opening moldings, bright metal wheelcovers, cab-to-fender and hood insulators, underhood reel-type lamp and electric power rear tailgate window and bright applique. The SLE interior had, in addition to or in place of the standard items the following: High-back reclining front bucket seats with choice of custom vinyl pigskin-grained trim (available in either dark blue, garnet, slate grey or saddle) or textured velour custom cloth trim (in a choice of dark blue, garnet, saddle or Slate grey), right side front and left and right side rear assist straps, glove box light, auxiliary lighting, floor covering of color-keyed front compartment carpeting (matching rear compartment floor covering including wheelhousings, was also provided with optional rear seat), insulation on dash panel, between double-wall cab roof, on floor panel (extras thick at front, extra-thick at rear when rear seat was ordered), under cowl panel, on headliner and on body side trim panels, extra insulation on diesel engine models, sunshades with flexible outboard ends and sliding extenders at inboard ends, storage strap on left side sunshade, illuminated mirror on right sunshade, brushed pewter-toned instrument panel trim, 4-spoke Sport steering wheel with simulated stitched leather appearance, front compartment foam-backed cloth headliner with matching retainer moldings, special door trim panels, including door closing assist strips, decorative inserts, map pockets and carpet trim, rear sidewall trim panels with ashtrays and carpet trim, cigarette lighter with ashtray illumination, black vinyl spare tire cover, and color-keyed molded plastic console with storage and beverage pockets. Air conditioning (RPO C60) $820 (without B3J); $758 (with B3J). Optional rear axle ratios: $38. Locking rear differential (RPO G80): $252. Cold Climate Package (RPO V10). Includes special insulation, special heater and defroster, engine block heater, anti-freeze protection to -32 degrees and heavy-duty battery: $48. Engine oil cooler (RPO KC4): $135 Heavy-duty radiator (RPO VO1): $56. Heavy-duty radiator and transmission oil cooler (RPO VO2): $63. Deep tinted glass (RPO AJ1): $215. Locking front hubs (RPO X6Z): $60. Below eye-level stainless steel exterior mirrors (RPO D45): $40. Operating Convenience Package (RPO ZQ2). Includes power door locks and front door power windows: $344. Operating Convenience Package (RPO ZQ3). Includes tilt wheel and speed control: $346. Conventional two-tone exterior paint (RPO ZY2): $413 (without YE9), $180 (with YE9). Special two-tone exterior paint (RPO ZY3): $464 (without YE9), $450 (with YE9). Deluxe two-tone exterior paint (RPO ZY4): $566 (without YE9), $332 (with YE9). Electronically tuned AM/FM stereo radio with Seek-Scan and digital clock (RPO UM7): $131. Electronically tuned AM/FM stereo radio with Seek-Scan, stereo cassette tape player and digital clock (RPO UM6): $253. Electronically tuned AM/FM stereo radio with Seek-Scan, stereo cassette tape player with Searchand Repeat, graphic equalizer and digital clock (RPO UX1): $403 . Radio delete (RPO UL5): $95. Fuel tank shield (RPO NY1). Includes protective shield on transfer case: $175. Rear folding 3 passenger seat (AM7): $411 (without shoulder harness, $461 (with shoulder harness). Rear seat not desired (RPO YG4): No charge. Heavy-duty 2250 lb. front springs (F60). Includes heavy-duty front and rear shock absorbers. recommended for front mounted accessory applications only: $62. Trailering special equipment (RPO Z82). Includes trailer hitch platform and hitch, wiring harness and transmission oil cooler. Requires either 3.42 or 3.73 rear axle, without B3J includes engine oil cooler: $407 (without B3J diesel equipment, $272 (with B3J diesel equipment. 4-speed automatic with overdrive (RPO MXO): $879 (standard with B3J equipment. Wheelcovers (RPO PO1): $42. Rallye wheels (RPO N67): $121 (without YE9), $79 (with YE9). Aluminum cast wheels (RPO N90): $318 (without YE9), $276 (with YE9). Sliding rear quarter windows (RPO AD5): $257. Electric remote exterior mirror (RPO D48): $98. California emission system (RPO YF5): $100. P235/75R15 steel belted radial on-off road blackwall tires: $55. P235/75R15 steel belted All-Season radial whitewall: $90. P235/75R15 steel belted radial All-Season white letters: $125. 31 x 10.50R15B white letters steel belted radial on-off road: $630.40.

HISTORICAL FOOTNOTES: GMC reported that the Jimmy offered the rugged versatility of four wheel-drive with the choice of a gasoline or diesel engine.

1991 JIMMY

Powertrain refinements characterized the 1991 Jimmy. The 200 series throttle body fuel injection system used on the Jimmy's standard 5.7 liter V-8 had longer throttle shaft bearings, new throttle return springs and improved fuel mixture distribution. The 5.7 liter V-8 also had new heavy-duty intake valves and powdered metal camshaft sprockets. Standard on all engines was a lighter and more powerful 100 amp CS130 alternator. This unit replaced an 12-SI-100 alternator. Two new exterior colors — Brilliant blue and slate metallic were offered. The Jimmy top was now available in dark grey. A new light grey joined the four interior colors for 1991. The standard AM radio on the SLX model and the standard AM/FM radio for the SLE model had improved reception. The stereo radios had increased signal sensitivity, reduced signal interference and signal tracking.

I.D. DATA: The V.I.N. plate was mounted on the lower left side windshield corner. The V.I.N. consisted of 17 elements. The first, the number 1, identified the U.S. as the nation of origin. The letter G followed, for the manufacturer: General Motors. The third entry, the letter T, represented the make as GMC. The GVWR brake system identification followed. Next came the truck line and chassis type; the letter K indicated four-wheel drive. The truck series was identified by a number: 1-1/2 ton. The truck body type identification was next: 8-Utility. The engine code was next, followed by a check digit. The model year was identified by the letter M. The assembly plant code followed. The final six digits were the plant sequential production number.

Model Number	Body Type & Seating	Factory Price	GVW	Shipping Weight	Prod. Total
Jimmy V10 Body Code: ZW9 (with 350 V-8)					
TV10516	Util.	$17,674	6100	4797	—
15,352*	W/Diesel V-8 & B3J	$20,664	6250	N.A.	—

* Production of all models.

STANDARD ENGINE: All states: Engine Type: Cast iron block. OHV, V-8. Ordering Code: L05. Produced by GM-Chevrolet Motor Division. Bore x Stroke: 4.0 in. x 3.48 in. Lifters: Hydraulic. Number of main bearings-5. Carburetion: Electronic fuel injection. Compression Ratio: 9.2:1. Displacement: 350 cu. in. (5.7 liters). Horsepower: Net: 210 @ 4000 rpm. Torque: Net: 300 lb.-ft. @ 2800 rpm. Oil capacity: 5 qt. with filter change. Fuel Requirements: Unleaded.

OPTIONAL ENGINE: Not available for Californi: Engine Type: OHV, cast iron block. Diesel V-8. Order Code LH6. Produced by GM-Detroit Diesel Allison Division. Requires B3J Diesel Equipment Package which consists of dual batteries, hydraulic power-assisted brakes, engine block heater, heavy-duty radiator, K81 alternator, engine oil cooler and additional insulation. Bore x Stroke: 3.98 in. x 3.80 in. Lifters: Hydraulic. Number of main bearings-5. Carburetion: Fuel injection. Compression Ratio: 21.5:1. Displacement: 379 cu. in. (6.2 liter). Horsepower: Net: 130 @ 3600 rpm. Torque: Net: 240 lb.-ft. @ 2000 rpm. Oil capacity: 7 qt. with filter change. Fuel Requirements: Diesel.

CHASSIS FEATURES: Ladder-type. Carbon steel, 36,000-39,000 psi. Heavy-gauge channel side members, alligator-jaw cross members. Section modulus: 3.14.

SUSPENSION AND RUNNING GEAR: Front Suspension: Two tapered semi-elliptical leaf springs. Capacity: Gasoline engines: 1650 lb. Optional Capacity: 2250 lb. Diesel engine: 1850 lb. Optional: 2250 lb. Standard 1.25 in. stabilizer bar and 25mm shock absorbers. Optional: 32mm shock absorbers. Rear Suspension: Two-stage tapered and multi-leaf (six-conventional leaves, one tapered leaf). Capacity: 1875 lb. Optional: None. Front Axle. Type: Hypoid, tubular driving. Capacity: 3600 lb. Rear Axle. Type: Hypoid, semi-floating. Capacity: 3750 lb. Final Drive Ratio: 5.7 liter V-8 with manual 4-spd. trans.: 3.08:1. Optional: 3.42:1. 5.7 liter V-8 with 4-spd. auto. trans.: 2.73:1. Optional: 3.08, 3.42, 3.731, 2. 1-Requires Z82 trailering without California emissions. With California emissions requires KC4 engine oil cooler. 2-Requires Z82 trailering special or high altitude emissions. Final Drive Ratio: 6.2 liter diesel V-8: 3.08:1. Optional: 3,42, 3.73:11. 1-Requires Z82 trailering special or high altitude emissions. Transfer Case: Type: New Process 208. Ratios: 2.61, 1.00:1. Brakes: Type: Hydraulic, self-adjusting. Front: Discs. Rear: Drums. Optional: Power. Dimensions: Front: 11.86 in. dia. rotor. Rear: 11.15 in. x 2.75 in. Wheels: 6-stud, 15 x 6.00JJ. Optional: 15 x 7JJ Rallye, 15 x 8JJ, 15 x 8JJ Rallye, 16 x 5K. Tires: P235/75R15 steel belted radial. Optional: P235/75R15 steel belted radial on-off road, P235/75R15 steel belted radial whitewall, P235/75R15 steel belted radial white letters, P235/75R15 steel belted radial whitewall XL (requires N67 or N90 wheels), 31 x 10.50R15B white letters steel belted radial on-off road. Steering: Power assisted recirculating ball, variable ratio. Ratio: 17.6/13.1. Turns Lock-to-Lock: 4.0. Turning circle: 37.6 ft. Optional: None. Transmission: Type: SM465, RPO MM4. 4-speed manual, fully synchronized. Floor-mounted shifter. Standard transmission with diesel V-8: 4-speed automatic overdrive. Optional (gasoline engined models, and models with California emissions): 4-speed automatic overdrive. Transmission Ratios: SM465. Synchromesh on top three gears, floor-mounted shift lever. Ratios: 6.55, 3.58, 1.70, 1.00:1. Reverse: 6.09:1. 700R4 Automatic: 3.06, 1.63, 1.00, 0.70. Reverse: 2.29. Clutch: 12.0 in. dia.

VEHICLE DIMENSIONS: Wheelbase: 106.5 in. Overall Length: 184.8 in. Front/Rear Tread 66.10 in./ 63.00 in. Overall Height: 73.4 in. Width: 79.6 in. Tailgate: Width and Height: 66.8 in. x 22.0 in. Approach/Departure Degrees: 34/25. Ground Clearance: Front axle: 7.4 in. Rear axle: 7.0 in. Oil pan: 17.2 in. Transfer case: 11.5 in. Fuel tank: 14.0 in. Load space: With rear seat installed: 38.8 in. x 50 in. x 42.3 in. With rear seat removed or folded: 76.0 in. x 50 in. x 42.3 in.

CAPACITIES: Fuel Tank: 350 V-8: 31.0 gal. Diesel: 32 gal. Coolant system: 350 V-8: 17.6 qt.

ACCOMMODATIONS: Seating Capacity: Standard: Driver and passenger front high-back bucket sets. Optional: 3 passenger rear bench seat. Headroom: 38.3 in. Maximum steering wheel to seat back: 18.5 in. Seat to ground: 36.3 in. Floor to ground: 21.9 in.

INSTRUMENTATION: 0-100 mph speedometer, 99,999.9 mi. odometer, fuel gauge, warning lights for alternator, oil pressure, engine coolant temperature, brake operating system, hazard warning lights, directional lights, seat belt warning.

OPTIONS AND PRICES: SLE Package (RPO YE9): $1281. Air conditioning (RPO C60) $820 (without B3J); $758 (with B3J). Optional rear axle ratios: $38. Locking rear differential (RPO G80): $252. Cold Climate Package (RPO V10). Includes special insulation, special heater and defroster, engine block heater, anti-freeze protection to -32 degrees and heavy-duty battery $48. Engine oil cooler (RPO KC4): $135 Heavy-duty radiator (RPO VO1): $56. Heavy-duty radiator and transmission oil cooler (RPO VO2): $63. Deep tinted glass (RPO AJ1): $215. Locking front hubs (RPO X6Z): $60. Below eye-level stainless steel exterior mirrors (RPO D45): $45. Below eye-level electric remote painted mirrors: $58-$98 depending upon other options selected. Operating Convenience Package (RPO ZQ2). Includes power door locks and front door power windows: $344. Operating Convenience Package (RPO ZQ3). Includes tilt wheel and speed control: $346. Conventional two-tone exterior paint (RPO ZY2) $413 (without YE9), $180 (with YE9). Special two-tone exterior paint (RPO ZY3): $464 (without YE9), $450 (with YE9). Deluxe two-tone exterior paint (RPO ZY4): $566 (without YE9), $332 (with YE9). Electronically tuned AM/FM stereo radio with Seek-Scan and digital clock (RPO UM7): $131. Electronically tuned AM/FM stereo radio with Seek-Scan, stereo cassette tape player and digital clock (RPO UM6): $253. Electronically tuned AM/FM stereo radio with Seek-Scan, stereo cassette tape player with Search and Repeat, graphic equalizer and digital clock (RPO UX1): $403. Radio delete (RPO UL5): $95. Fuel tank shield (RPO NY1). Includes protective shield on transfer case: $175. Rear folding 3 passenger seat (AM7): $411 (without shoulder harness, $461 (with shoulder harness). Rear seat not desired (RPO YG4): No charge. Heavy-duty 2250 lb. front springs (F60). Includes heavy-duty front and rear shock absorbers. recommended for front mounted accessory applications only: $62. Front quad shock absorbers: $100. Trailering special equipment (RPO Z82). Includes trailer hitch platform and hitch, wiring harness and transmission oil cooler. Requires either 3.42 or 3.73 rear axle, without B3J includes engine oil cooler: $407 (without B3J diesel equipment, $272 (with B3J diesel equipment. 4-speed automatic with overdrive (RPO MXO): $890 (standard with B3J equipment. Wheelcovers (RPO PO1): $42. Rallye wheels (RPO N67): $121 (without YE9), $79 (with YE9). Aluminum cast wheels (RPO N90): $212-$333 (without YE9 and depending upon other options selected.), $291 (with YE9). Sliding rear quarter windows (AD5): $257. P235/75R15 steel belted radial on-off road blackwall tires: $55 P235/75R15 steel belted All-Season radial whitewall: $90. P235/75R15 steel belted radial All-Season white letters: $125. 31 x 10.50 R15B white letters steel belted radial on-off road: $631.10.

HISTORICAL FOOTNOTES: GMC said the Jimmy was "truly built for the great outdoors...." It provided, said GMC: "up-market comfort and convenience features, increased reliability and improved driveability."

GMC S-15 JIMMY
1983-1993

1983 S-15 JIMMY

The new S-15 Jimmy was a compact, high-mileage 4x4 that was based on the S-10 pickup models. Among its features were a 1000 lb. payload capacity, 5 passenger seating with front bucket seats and an optional rear bench seat. Three trim levels were offered-the standard Sierra, the up-scale Sierra Classic and the Gypsy Sport option. All had a full-length steel top, 15 inch wheels, tinted glass and a fold-down tailgate with lift glass. The Sierra trim level included chrome and black grille, headlight and parking lamp bezels with chrome finish and black trim, chromed front and rear bumpers with rub strips, black windshield and rear window moldings, left and right black outside mirrors, radial ply tires and 15 inch argent wheels with hubcaps. The Sierra interior provided front bucket seats, in vinyl trim in a choice of four colors, and color-keyed instrument panel, sun shades, headliner and windshield pillars. Also included were these items: Front and rear passenger assist handles, headlights-on warning buzzer, rubber floor covering, interior light, door/roof sound deadener, and front floor insulation. The optional Sierra Classic Package included a chromed grille, cigarette lighter, right hand sun visor, body side and wheel opening moldings, spare tire cover, and gauges for voltmeter, engine coolant temperature, oil pressure and trip odometer. Other Sierra Classic features included bucket seats in custom vinyl or special custom cloth, side window defoggers, Deluxe color-keyed steering wheel and zippered rear armrest pockets.

The Gypsy Sport Package added to or replaced the Sierra Classic features with the following: Front bucket seat with reclining seat backs trimmed in woven sport cloth with accent stripe, locking center console, and color-keyed sport steering wheel. Available exterior colors for the S-10 Jimmy were midnight blue, silver metallic, midnight black, light blue metallic, frost white, Sunshine yellow, almond, nugget gold metallic, cinnamon red, apple red and, as a secondary color only, satin black.

The S-15 was fitted with the new Insta-Trac four-wheel drive system. Details of its operation may be found in the 1983 Chevrolet S-10 Blazer section.

1983 S-15 Jimmy Sierra Classic

I.D. DATA: The V.I.N. plate was mounted on the lower left side windshield corner. The V.I.N. consisted of 17 elements. The first, the number 1, identified the U.S. as the nation of origin. The letter G followed for the manufacturer: General Motors. The third entry, the letter T, represented the make as GMC. The GVWR brake system identification followed. Next came the truck line and chassis type; the letter K indicated four-wheel drive. The truck series was identified by a number: 1-1/2 ton. The truck body type identification was next: 8-Utility. The engine code was next: Y-2.0 liter, A-1.9 liter, B-2.8 liter V-6, followed by a check digit. The model year was identified by the letter D. The assembly plant code followed. The final six digits were the plant sequential production number.

Model Number	Body Type	Factory Price	GVW	Shipping Weight	Prod. Total
Jimmy S-15 with V-6 engine					
CT10516	Util. (with top)	$9433	4075[1]	3106	—

NOTE 1: 4850 lb. GVW optional.

STANDARD ENGINE: All states except California: Ordering Code LQ2. Produced by GM-Chevrolet Motor Division. Engine Type: Cast iron block. OHV, In-line 4. Bore x Stroke: 3.50 in. x 3.15 in. Lifters: Hydraulic. Carburetion: Two barrel. Compression Ratio: 9.3:1. Displacement: 121 cu. in. (2.0 liter). Horsepower: Net: 83 @ 4600 rpm. Torque: Net: 108 lb.-ft. @ 2400 rpm. Oil capacity: 5 qt. with filter change. Fuel Requirements: Unleaded.

STANDARD ENGINE: California only: Engine Type: Cast iron block. OHV, In-line 4. Ordering Code: LR1. Produced by Isuzu Motors Limited, Japan. Bore x Stroke: 3.42 in. x 3.23 in. Lifters: Hydraulic. Carburetion: Two barrel. Compression Ratio: 8.4:1. Displacement: 119 cu. in. (1.9 liters). Horsepower: Net: 82 @ 4600 rpm. Torque: Net: 101 lb.-ft. @ 3000 rpm. Oil capacity: 5 qt. with filter change. Fuel Requirements: Unleaded.

OPTIONAL ENGINE: 50 states. Engine Type: OHV, cast iron block. V-6. Order Code LR2. Produced by GM-Chevrolet Motor Division. Bore x Stroke: 3.50 in. x 2.99 in. Lifters: Hydraulic. Number of main bearings-5. Carburetion: 2-barrel. Compression Ratio: 8.5. Displacement: 173 cu. in. (2.8 liter). Horsepower: Net: 110 @ 4800 rpm. Torque: Net: 145 lb.-ft. @ 2100 rpm. Oil capacity: 5 qt. with filter change. Fuel Requirements: Unleaded.

CHASSIS FEATURES: Carbon steel, welded front box section and open channel rear section.

SUSPENSION AND RUNNING GEAR: Front Suspension: Independent with torsion bar springs, 25mm dia. shock absorbers. 32mm stabilizer bar. Capacity: 1150 lbs. each at ground. Optional: 32mm shock absorbers. Rear Suspension: Two-stage multi-leaf shot-peened springs. Capacity: 1350 lbs. each at ground. 25mm shock absorbers. Optional: 32mm shock absorbers. Front Axle. Type: Hypoid, tubular driving. Capacity: 2300 lb. Rear Axle. Type: Salisbury, hypoid. Capacity: 2700 lb. Final Drive Ratio: 4-spd. manual transmission and optional 5-spd. manual overdrive: 3.73:1 (3.08:1 for high altitude emission system). Automatic transmission: 3.42:1 (3.73:1 for high altitude emission system). Optional: 4-spd. manual transmission and optional 5-spd. manual overdrive: 4.11:1 (3.73:1 for high altitude emission system). Automatic transmission: 3.73:1. Transfer Case: New Process 207. Brakes: Type: Hydraulic, power assisted self-adjusting. Front: Discs. Rear: Drums. Dimensions: Front: 9.5 in. x 2.0 in. rotor. Rear: 9.5 in. x 2.0 in. Wheels: 15 in. Tires: P195/75R15 glass belted radial black sidewall. Optional: P195/75R15 black sidewall, P205/75R15 black sidewall, P205/75R15 white sidewall, P205/75R15 white letters, P205/75R15 on/off road black sidewall. Steering: Manual. Optional: Power. Transmission: 4-speed manual. Optional: 5-speed manual with overdrive, 4-speed automatic with overdrive (with V-6 engine only). Clutch: 4-cyl. engine: 9.12 in. dia., V-6: 9.76 in. dia.

VEHICLE DIMENSIONS: Wheelbase: 100.5 in. Overall Length: 170.3 in. Front/Rear Tread 55.6 in./ 54.1 in. Overall Height: 64.9 in. Width: 64.7 in. Approach/Departure Degrees: 28° 17'/ 25.5° 30'. Ground Clearance: Front axle: 8.1 in. Rear axle: 6.9 in.

CAPACITIES: Fuel Tank: 13.2 gal. Optional: Replacement 20 gal. tank.

ACCOMMODATIONS: Seating Capacity: Driver and passenger front high-back bucket sets. Optional: 3 passenger rear bench seat.

INSTRUMENTATION: 0-100 mph speedometer, 99,999.9 mi.odometer, fuel gauge, warning lights for alternator, oil pressure, engine coolant temperature, brake operating system, hazard warning lights, directional lights, seat belt warning.

OPTIONS AND PRICES: Sierra Classic Package: $576. Gypsy Sport Package. Air conditioning. Automatic speed control. ComforTilt steering wheel. Power steering. Gauges for oil pressure, engine coolant temperature and voltmeter with trip odometer. Tachometer with gauges. Digital clock (with radio only). Delco radios. Premium rear speakers. Below eye-level mirrors. Styled wheels with special hub ornament and bright trim rings. Operating Convenience Package. Includes power windows and door locks. Dome/reading light. Halogen headlamps. 66 amp Delcotron generator. Heavy-duty Freedom battery. Reclining bucket seat backs. Center console. Color-keyed floor mats. Visor mirror. Door edge guards. Body striping. Spare tire cover. Body side/wheel-opening moldings. Color-keyed front/rear bumpers. Black front bumper guards. Rear air deflector. Front tow hooks. Black or bright wheel-opening moldings. Cast aluminum wheels. Bright wheel trim rings. Full-size spare tire. Heavy-duty radiator. Heavy-duty radiator with transmission or engine cooler with V-6 and automatic transmission. Locking differential rear axle. Heavy-duty front and rear shock absorbers. Off-Road Chassis Package. Stone shield for transfer case and differential carrier. Intermittent windshield wipers. Engine block heater. Deadweight trailer hitch. Trailering Package (either 4,000 or 5,000 lb)

HISTORICAL FOOTNOTES: The new-size Jimmy was introduced on September 14, 1982.

1984 S-15 JIMMY

The S-15 Jimmy for 1984 had a number of revised or new convenience items. Dual sliding sun visors were now standard. The rear passenger assist handles were relocated to the upper side panels for a more convenient grip. These handles were installed only when the optional rear seat was ordered. A new ignition key warning buzzer was standard for 1984. The optional automatic speed control had a new tap-up/tap-down feature for a quicker change of vehicle speed. New optional remote control below eye-line rearview mirrors were available. A new 56 amp Delcotron generator was now standard. A new automatic adjusting hydraulic clutch release mechanism had fewer parts than the former cable-type system. It also offered smoother operation. The optional automatic transmission had a new torque converter.

Models with the V-6 engine had new "2.8 liter V-6" identification below the driver's side headlight. A small V6 emblem mounted on the front fender had been used in 1983. A new Off-Road Package was introduced, with availability beginning in October, 1983, featuring Delco Bilstein gas-pressure shock absorbers, transfer case shield, fuel tank shield, front tow hooks and jounce bumpers. This option requires the optional 1500 lb. Payload Package and P235 steel belted, on/off-road white-lettered ties, including full-size spare. Front and axle clearance with this option was respectively, 7.1 in. and 8.2 in. The 1984 interior color selection consisted of blue, carmine, charcoal or saddle tan. Exterior colors were: Silver metallic, frost white, midnight black, light blue metallic, galaxy blue metallic, doeskin tan, Indian bronze metallic, desert sand metallic, apple red, cinnamon red and, as a secondary color only, satin black.

1984 S-15 Jimmy Sierra Classic

I.D. DATA: The V.I.N. plate was mounted on the lower left side windshield corner. The V.I.N. consisted of 17 elements. The first, the number 1, identified the U.S. as the nation of origin. The letter G followed for the manufacturer: General Motors. The third entry, the letter T, represented the make as GMC. The GVWR brake system identification followed. Next came the truck line and chassis type; the letter K indicated four-wheel drive. The truck series was identified by a number: 1-1/2 ton. The truck body type identification was next: 8-Utility. The engine code was next: Y-2.0 liter, A-1.9 liter, B-2.8 liter V-6, followed by a check digit. The model year was identified by the letter E. The assembly plant code followed. The final six digits were the plant sequential production number.

Model Number	Body Type	Factory Price	GVW	Shipping Weight	Prod. Total
Jimmy S15. with V-6 engine					
CT10516	Util. (with top)	$9685	4075[1]	3146	34,519[2]

NOTE 1: 4850 lb. GVW optional.
NOTE 2: Calendar years for both two-wheel drive and four-wheel drive models.

STANDARD ENGINE: All states except California: Ordering Code LQ2. Produced by GM-Chevrolet Motor Division. Engine Type: Cast iron block. OHV, In-line 4. Bore x Stroke: 3.50 in. x 3.15 in. Lifters: Hydraulic. Carburetion: Two barrel. Compression Ratio: 9.3:1. Displacement: 121 cu. in. (2.0 liter). Horsepower: Net: 83 @ 4600 rpm. Torque: Net: 108 lb.-ft. @ 2400 rpm. Oil capacity: 5 qt. with filter change. Fuel Requirements: Unleaded.

STANDARD ENGINE: California only: Engine Type: Cast iron block. OHV, In-line 4. Ordering Code: LR1. Produced by Isuzu Motors Limited, Japan. Bore x Stroke: 3.42 in. x 3.23 in. Lifters: Hydraulic. Carburetion: Two barrel. Compression Ratio: 8.4:1. Displacement:119 cu. in. (1.9 liters). Horsepower: Net: 82 @ 4600 rpm. Torque: Net: 101 lb.-ft. @ 3000 rpm. Oil capacity: 5 qt. with filter change. Fuel Requirements: Unleaded.

OPTIONAL ENGINE: 50 states. Engine Type: OHV, cast iron block. V-6. Order Code LR2. Produced by GM-Chevrolet Motor Division. Bore x Stroke: 3.50 in. x 2.99 in. Lifters: Hydraulic. Number of main bearings-5. Carburetion: 2-barrel. Compression Ratio: 8.5. Displacement: 173 cu. in. (2.8 liter). Horsepower: Net: 110 @ 4800 rpm. Torque: Net: 145 lb.-ft. @ 2100 rpm. Oil capacity: 5 qt. with filter change. Fuel Requirements: Unleaded.

CHASSIS FEATURES: Carbon steel, welded front box section and open channel rear section.

SUSPENSION AND RUNNING GEAR: Front Suspension: Independent with torsion bar springs, 25mm dia. shock absorbers. 32mm stabilizer bar. Capacity: 1200 lbs. each at ground. Optional: 32mm shock absorbers. Rear Suspension: Two-stage multi-leaf shot-peened springs. Capacity: 1350 lbs. each at ground. 25mm shock absorbers. Optional: 32mm shock absorbers. Front Axle. Type: Hypoid, tubular driving. Capacity: 2400 lb. Rear Axle. Type: Salisbury, hypoid. Capacity: 2700 lb. Final Drive Ratio: Sierra 4-spd. manual transmission and optional 5-spd. manual overdrive: 3.73:1 (3.08:1 for high altitude emission system). Automatic transmission: 3.42:1 (3.73:1 for high altitude emission system). Optional: 4-spd. manual transmission and optional 5-spd. manual overdrive: 4.11:1 (3.73:1 for high altitude emission system). Automatic transmission: 3.73:1. Transfer Case: New Process 207. Brakes: Type: Hydraulic, power assisted self-adjusting. Front: Discs. Rear: Drums. Dimensions: Front: 9.5 in. x 2.0 in. rotor. Rear: 9.5 in. x 2.0 in. Wheels: 15 in. Tires: P195/75R15 glass belted radial black sidewall. Optional: P195/75R15 black sidewall, P205/75R15 black sidewall, P205/75R15 white sidewall, P205/75R15 white letters, P205/75R15 on/off road black sidewall. Steering: Manual. Optional: Power. Transmission: 4-speed manual. Optional: 5-speed manual with overdrive, 4-speed automatic with overdrive (with V-6 engine only). Clutch: 4-cyl. engine: 9.12 in. dia., V-6: 9.76 in. dia.

VEHICLE DIMENSIONS: Wheelbase: 100.5 in. Overall Length: 170.3 in. Front/Rear Tread 55.6 in./ 54.1 in. Overall Height: 64.9 in. Width: 64.7 in. Approach/Departure Degrees: 28° 17'/ 25.5° 30'. Ground Clearance: Front axle: 8.1 in. Rear axle: 6.9 in.

CAPACITIES: Fuel Tank: 13.2 gal. Optional: Replacement 20 gal. tank.

ACCOMMODATIONS: Seating Capacity: Driver and passenger front high back bucket sets. Optional: 3 passenger rear bench seat.

INSTRUMENTATION: 0-100 mph speedometer, 99,999.9 mi.odometer, fuel gauge, warning lights for alternator, oil pressure, engine coolant temperature, brake operating system, hazard warning lights, directional lights, seat belt warning.

OPTIONS AND PRICES: Sierra Classic Package: $576. Gypsy Sport Package. Air conditioning. Automatic speed control. ComforTilt steering wheel. Power steering. Gauges for oil pressure, engine coolant temperature and voltmeter with trip odometer. Tachometer with gauges. Digital clock (with radio only). Delco radios. Premium rear speakers. Below eye-level mirrors. Styled wheels with special hub ornament and bright trim rings. Operating Convenience Package. Includes power windows and door locks. Dome/reading light. Halogen headlamps. 66 amp Delcotron generator. Heavy-duty Freedom battery. Reclining bucket seat backs. Center console. Color-keyed floor mats. Visor mirror. Door edge guards. Body striping. Spare tire cover. Body side/wheel opening moldings. Color-keyed front/rear bumpers. Black front bumper guards. Rear air deflector. Front tow hooks. Black or bright wheel opening moldings. Cast aluminum wheels. Bright wheel trim rings. Full-size spare tire. Heavy-duty radiator. Heavy-duty radiator with transmission or engine cooler with V-6 and automatic transmission. Locking differential rear axle. Heavy-duty front and rear shock absorbers. Off-Road

Chassis Package. Stone shield for transfer case and differential carrier. Intermittent windshield wipers. Engine block heater. Deadweight trailer hitch. Trailering Package (either 4,000 or 5,000 lb).

HISTORICAL FOOTNOTES: GMC reported that the S-15 Jimmy had been wind tunnel tested for air drag.

1985 S-15 JIMMY

All 1985 Jimmy models had a new black chrome finish for the tailgate release handle and lock cylinders plus the antenna if a radio was installed. The controls for the optional intermittent windshield wipers was now fully integral with the multifunction switch mounted on the steering column. A new partitioned fuse panel was used. The Gypsy Sport trim for the latest S-15 Jimmy featured a new black chrome grille and headlamp bezels, door handles, key cylinder covers and taillight trim. A new optional black rooftop luggage rack was also available. A new electronically fuel injected 2.5 liter 4-cylinder engine was now standard. The 2.8 liter V-6 remained an option. Either engine could be ordered with the optional 5-speed manual or 4-speed automatic transmission. New low-pressure gas shock absorbers were standard. They were not available with on/off road tires.

Both the interior and exterior color selections of 1984 were carried over into 1985.

1985 S-15 Jimmy Sierra Classic

I.D. DATA: The V.I.N. plate was mounted on the lower left side windshield corner. The V.I.N. consisted of 17 elements. The first, the number 1, identified the U.S. as the nation of origin. The letter G followed for the manufacturer: General Motors. The third entry, the letter T, represented the make as GMC. The GVWR brake system identification followed. Next came the truck line and chassis type; the letter K indicated four-wheel drive. The truck series was identified by a number: 1-1/2 ton. The truck body type identification was next: 8-Utility. The engine code was next: E-2.5 liter, B-2.8 liter V-6, followed by a check digit. The model year was identified by the letter E. The assembly plant code followed. The final six digits were the plant sequential production number.

Model Number	Body Type	Factory Price	GVW	Shipping Weight	Prod. Total
Jimmy S-15					
CT10516	Util. (with top)	$10,134[1]	4075[2]	3156	150,599[3]

NOTE 1: Price effective with vehicles produced after January 2, 1985. Earlier price sources indicate a price of $9994.
NOTE 2: 4850 lb. GVW optional.
NOTE 3: Calendar year sales, both two-wheel drive and four-wheel drive.

STANDARD ENGINE: Ordering Code LN8: Produced by Pontiac Motor Division. Engine Type: Cast iron block. OHV, In-line 4. Bore x Stroke: 4.0 in. x 3.0 in. Lifters: Hydraulic. Fuel induction: Electronic fuel injection. Compression Ratio: 9.0:1. Displacement: 151 cu. in. (2.5 liter). Horsepower: Net: 92 @ 4400 rpm. Torque: Net: 134 lb.-ft. @ 2800 rpm. Oil capacity: 5 qt. with filter change. Fuel Requirements: Unleaded.

OPTIONAL ENGINE: Engine Type: OHV, cast iron block. V-6. Order Code LR2. Produced by GM-Chevrolet Motor Division. Bore x Stroke: 3.50 in. x 2.99 in. Lifters: Hydraulic. Number of main bearings-5. Carburetion: 2-barrel. Compression Ratio: 8.5. Displacement: 173 cu. in. (2.8 liter). Horsepower: Net: 115 @ 4800 rpm. Torque: Net: 150 lb.-ft. @ 2100 rpm. Oil capacity: 5 qt. with filter change. Fuel Requirements: Unleaded.

CHASSIS FEATURES: Carbon steel, welded front box section and open channel rear section.

SUSPENSION AND RUNNING GEAR: Front Suspension: Independent with torsion bar springs, 25mm dia. shock absorbers. 32mm stabilizer bar. Capacity: 1200 lbs. each at ground. Optional: 32mm shock absorbers. Rear Suspension: Two-stage multi-leaf shot-peened springs. Capacity: 1350 lbs. each at ground. 25mm shock absorbers. Optional: 32mm shock absorbers. Front Axle. Type: Hypoid, tubular driving. Capacity: 2400 lb. Rear Axle. Type: Salisbury, hypoid. Capacity: 2700 lb. Final Drive Ratio: Standard 4-spd. manual transmission and optional 5-spd. manual overdrive: 3.73:1 (3.08:1 for high altitude emission system). Automatic transmission: 3.42:1 (3.73:1 for high altitude emission system). Optional: Standard 4-spd. manual transmission and optional 5-spd. manual overdrive: 4.11:1 (3.73:1 for high altitude emission system). Automatic transmission: 3.73:1. Transfer Case: New Process 207. Brakes: Type: Hydraulic, power assisted self-adjusting. Front: Discs. Rear: Drums. Dimensions: Front: 9.5 in. x 2.0 in. rotor. Rear: 9.5 in. x 2.0 in. Wheels: 15 in. Tires: P195/75R15 glass belted radial black sidewall. Optional: P195/75R15 black sidewall, P205/75R15 black sidewall, P205/75R15 white sidewall, P205/75R15 white letters, P205/75R15 on/off road black sidewall. Steering: Manual. Optional: Power. Transmission: 4-speed manual. Optional: 5-speed manual with overdrive, 4-speed automatic with overdrive. Clutch: 4-cyl. engine: 9.12 in. dia., V-6: 9.76 in. dia.

VEHICLE DIMENSIONS: Wheelbase: 100.5 in. Overall Length: 170.3 in. Front/Rear Tread 55.6 in./ 54.1 in. Overall Height: 64.9 in. Width: 64.7 in. Approach/Departure Degrees: 28° 17'/ 25.5° 30'. Ground Clearance: Front axle: 8.1 in. Rear axle: 6.9 in.

CAPACITIES: Fuel Tank: 13.2 gal. Optional: Replacement 20 gal. tank.

ACCOMMODATIONS: Seating Capacity: Standard: Driver and passenger front high back bucket sets. Optional: 3 passenger rear bench seat.

INSTRUMENTATION: 0-100 mph speedometer, 99,999.9 mi.odometer, fuel gauge, warning lights for alternator, oil pressure, engine coolant temperature, brake operating system, hazard warning lights, directional lights, seat belt warning.

OPTIONS AND PRICES: Sierra Classic Package. $595. Gypsy Sport Package: $940. Sport cloth vinyl high-back bucket seat trim: $24. High Country Sheepskin high-back bucket seats: $295. Custom two-tone paint: $200. Special two-tone paint: $167-$311 depending upon Trim Package. Sport two-tone paint: $162-$227 depending upon Trim Package. California emissions system: $99. 2.6 liter V-6 engine: $225. 4-speed overdrive automatic transmission: $670. Optional axle ratio: $36. Locking rear differential: $238. Pre-cleaner air cleaner: 49. 5-speed manual overdrive transmission: $175. All-Weather air conditioning: 705. Heavy-duty battery: $53. Front black bumper guards: $30. Luggage carrier, black or bright finish: $120. Spare wheel and tire carrier: $118-$150 depending upon Trim Package. Off-Road Package: $602-$658 depending upon Trim Package. Cold Climate Package: $107-$179 depending upon Trim Package. Front compartment console: $108. Engine oil cooling system: $120. Heavy-duty radiator: $53. Heavy-duty radiator and transmission oil cooler: $59 with air conditioning, $112 without air conditioning. Spare tire cover: $32. Air deflector: $41. Rear window defogger: $114 with air conditioning, $145 without air conditioning. Power door locks: $135. Color-keyed floor mats: Front: $15, Rear: $11. Gauge Package. Includes voltmeter, engine coolant temperature, oil pressure: $58. Gauge Package plus tachometer: $55-$113 depending upon Trim Package. 66 amp Delcotron generator: $31. Deep tinted glass: $190. Deep tinted glass with light tinted rear window: $135. Halogen headlights: $22. Engine block heater: $31. Engine compartment light: $15. Exterior left and right side painted mirrors: $50. Exterior left and right side bright mirrors: $83. Body side and wheel opening moldings: $17-$144 depending upon Trim Package. Door edge guards: $17. Bright wheel opening moldings: $28. Black wheel opening moldings: $12-$41 depending upon Trim Package. Operating Convenience Package: $325. AM radio: $112. AM/FM radio: $171. AM/FM radio with clock: $210. AM/FM stereo radio with electronic tuning: $238 AM/FM stereo radio and clock with electronic tuning: 277. AM/FM stereo radio with Seek-Scan, stereo cassette tape, clock and graphic equalizer and electronic tuning and premium rear speakers: $594. Premium rear speakers: $25. Folding rear bench seat: $341. Reclining front seat backs: $70.Transfer case shield: $67. Heavy-duty front and rear shock absorbers: $34. Full size spare tire: $46-90 depending upon size. Electronic speed control: $260. ComforTilt steering wheel: $115. Striping: $65. Heavy-duty suspension equipment: $59. Power release tailgate window: $41. 20 gal. fuel tank: $49. Two front towing hooks: $36. Dead weight trailer hitch: $64. Heavy-duty trailering special: $199. Light-duty trailering special: $103. Wheel trim rings: $56. Rallye wheels: $32-$88 depending upon Trim Package. Styled wheels: $32-$88 depending upon Trim Package. Cast aluminum wheels: $238-$294 depending upon Trim Package. Power side door windows: $190. Intermittent windshield wiper system: $55.

HISTORICAL FOOTNOTES: The 1985 S-15 Jimmy was introduced in October, 1984.

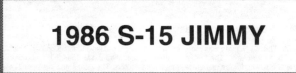

1986 S-15 JIMMY

The latest S-15 Jimmy was characterized by a number of refinements rather than a startling new design. The instrument panel was completely redesigned. The instrument cluster had what GMC called a "high tech look." A tray was installed at the panel bottom. The optional gauge cluster, which was standard for the Sierra Classic and Gypsy Sport models now included tell-tale lights in addition to the voltmeter, oil pressure and engine coolant temperature gauges. Other interior revisions included restyled door trim panels and relocated door panel switches for the optional power windows. All models had a new black molded urethane steering wheel. The Gypsy Sport steering wheel now had a simulated leather look. Also new for the Gypsy Sport was a tweed-pattern cloth seat trim. Exterior changes included two new colors, with resultant new two-tone combinations as well as a new six-stripe Rallye decal available with solid color paint schemes. The standard 2.5 liter engine had lighter-weight high silicon pistons. The 2.8 liter V-6 was equipped with electronic fuel injection. Jimmys with this engine had exterior front body identification reading "2.8 Fuel Injection." Models with the V-6 also had a higher-capacity Delco Freedom III battery. The optional heavy-duty battery offered for both engines had a higher capacity for 1986. All 1986 Jimmys had a lighter-weight radiator with a standard copper-brass core arranged for crossflow coolant movement and plastic side tanks. The exterior color selection for 1986 consisted of midnight black, steel grey metallic, light blue metallic, galaxy blue metallic, doeskin tan, Indian bronze metallic, cinnamon red, apple red, Nevada gold and silver metallic (used as a secondary color only).

1986 S-15 Jimmy Sierra Classic

I.D. DATA: The V.I.N. plate was mounted on the lower left side windshield corner. The V.I.N. consisted of 17 elements. The first, the number 1, identified the U.S. as the nation of origin. The letter G followed for the manufacturer: General Motors. The third entry, the letter T, represented the make as GMC. The GVWR brake system identification followed. Next came the truck line and chassis type; the letter K indicated four-wheel drive. The truck series was identified by a number: 1-1/2 ton. The truck body type identification was next: 8-Utility. The engine code was next: E-2.5 liter, B-2.8 liter V-6, followed by a check digit. The model year was identified by the letter G. The assembly plant code followed. The final six digits were the plant sequential production number.

Model Number	Body Type	Factory Price	GVW	Shipping Weight	Prod. Total
Jimmy S-15					
T18	Util. (with top)	$10,698	4075[1]	3152	43,710[2]

NOTE 1: 4850 lb. GVW optional.
NOTE 2: Model year sales, both two-wheel drive and four-wheel drive.

STANDARD ENGINE: Ordering Code LN8: Produced by Pontiac Motor Division. Engine Type: Cast iron block. OHV, In-line 4. Bore x Stroke: 4.0 in. x 3.0 in. Lifters: Hydraulic. Fuel induction: Electronic fuel injection. Compression Ratio: 9.0:1. Displacement: 151 cu. in. (2.5 liter). Horsepower: Net: 92 @ 4400 rpm. Torque: Net: 134 lb.-ft. @ 2800 rpm. Oil capacity: 5 qt. with filter change. Fuel Requirements: Unleaded.

OPTIONAL ENGINE: Engine Type: OHV, cast iron block. V-6. Order Code LR2. Produced by GM-Chevrolet Motor Division. Bore x Stroke: 3.50 in. x 2.99 in. Lifters: Hydraulic. Number of main bearings-5. Fuel Induction: Electronic fuel injection. Compression Ratio: 8.9:1. Displacement: 173 cu. in. (2.8 liter). Horsepower: Net: 125 @ 4800 rpm. Torque: Net: 150 lb.-ft. @ 2200 rpm. Oil capacity: 5 qt. with filter change. Fuel Requirements: Unleaded.

CHASSIS FEATURES: Carbon steel, welded front box section and open channel rear section.

SUSPENSION AND RUNNING GEAR: Front Suspension: Independent with torsion bar springs, 25mm dia. shock absorbers. 32mm stabilizer bar. Capacity: 1200 lbs. each at ground. Optional: 32mm shock absorbers. Rear Suspension: Two-stage multi-leaf shot-peened springs. Capacity: 1350 lbs. each at ground. 25mm shock absorbers. Optional: 32mm shock absorbers. Front Axle. Type: Hypoid, tubular driving. Capacity: 2400 lb. Rear Axle. Type: Salisbury, hypoid. Capacity: 2700 lb. Final Drive Ratio: Standard 4-spd. manual transmission and optional 5-spd. manual overdrive: 3.73:1 (3.08:1 for high altitude emission system). Automatic transmission: 3.42:1 (3.73:1 for high altitude emission system). Optional: Standard 4-spd. manual transmission and optional 5-spd. manual overdrive: 4.11:1 (3.73:1 for high altitude emission system). Automatic transmission: 3.73:1. Transfer Case: New Process 207. Brakes: Type: Hydraulic, power assisted self-adjusting. Front: Discs. Rear: Drums. Dimensions: Front: 9.5 in. x 2.0 in. rotor. Rear: 9.5 in. x 2.0 in. Wheels: 15 in. Tires: P195/75R15 glass belted radial black sidewall. Optional: P195/75R15 black sidewall, P205/75R15 black sidewall, P205/75R15 white sidewall, P205/75R15 white letters, P205/75R15 on/off road black sidewall. Steering: Manual. Optional: Power. Transmission: 4-speed manual. Optional: 5-speed manual with overdrive, 4-speed automatic with overdrive. Clutch: 4-cyl. engine: 9.12 in. dia., V-6: 9.76 in. dia.

VEHICLE DIMENSIONS: Wheelbase: 100.5 in. Overall Length: 170.3 in. Front/Rear Tread 55.6 in./ 54.1 in. Overall Height: 64.9 in. Width: 64.7 in. Approach/Departure Degrees: 28° 17'/ 25.5° 30'. Ground Clearance: Front axle: 8.1 in. Rear axle: 6.9 in.

CAPACITIES: Fuel Tank: 13.2 gal. Optional: Replacement 20 gal. tank.

ACCOMMODATIONS: Seating Capacity: Standard: Driver and passenger front high back bucket sets. Optional: 3 passenger rear bench seat.

INSTRUMENTATION: 0-100 mph speedometer, 99,999.9 mi.odometer, fuel gauge, warning lights for alternator, oil pressure, engine coolant temperature, brake operating system, hazard warning lights, directional lights, seat belt warning.

OPTIONS AND PRICES: High Sierra Package: $595. Gypsy Sport Package: $940. Sport cloth vinyl high-back bucket seat trim: $24. High Country Sheepskin high-back bucket seats: $295. Custom two-tone paint: $200. Special two-tone paint: $167-$311 depending upon Trim Package. Sport two-tone paint: $162-$227 depending upon Trim Package. California emissions system: $99. 2.6 liter V-6 engine: $225. 4-speed overdrive automatic transmission: $670. Optional axle ratio: $36. Locking rear differential: $238. Pre-cleaner air cleaner: 49. 5-speed manual overdrive transmission: $175. All-Weather air conditioning: 705. Heavy-duty battery: $53. Front black bumper guards: $30. Luggage carrier, black or bright finish: $120. Spare wheel and tire carrier: $118-$150 depending upon Trim Package. Off-Road Package: $602-$658 depending upon Trim Package. Cold Climate Package: $107-$179 depending upon Trim Package. Front compartment console: $108. Engine oil cooling system: $120. Heavy-duty radiator: $53. Heavy-duty radiator and transmission oil cooler: $59 with air conditioning, $112 without air conditioning. Spare tire cover: $32. Air deflector: $41. Rear window defogger: $114 with air conditioning, $145 without air conditioning. Power door locks: $135. Color-keyed floor mats: Front: $15; Rear: $11. Gauge Package. Includes voltmeter, engine coolant temperature, oil pressure: $58. Gauge Package plus tachometer: $55-$113 depending upon Trim Package. 66 amp Delcotron generator: $31. Deep tinted glass: $190. Deep tinted glass with light tinted rear window: $135. Halogen headlights: $22. Engine block heater: $31. Engine compartment light: $15. Exterior left and right side painted mirrors: $50. Exterior left and right side bright mirrors: $83. Body side and wheel opening moldings: $17-$144 depending upon Trim Package. Door edge guards: $17. Bright wheel opening moldings: $28. Black wheel opening moldings: $12-$41 depending upon Trim Package. Operating Convenience Package: $325. AM radio: $112. AM/FM radio: $171. AM/FM radio with clock: $210. AM/FM stereo radio with electronic tuning: $238 AM/FM stereo radio and clock with electronic tuning: 277. AM/FM stereo radio with Seek-Scan, stereo cassette tape, clock and graphic equalizer and electronic tuning and premium rear speakers: $594. Premium rear speakers: $25. Folding rear bench seat: $341. Reclining front seat backs: $70. Transfer case shield: $67. Heavy-duty front and rear shock absorbers: $34. Full-size spare tire: $46-90 depending upon size. Electronic speed control: $260. ComforTilt steering wheel: $115. Striping: $65. Heavy-duty suspension equipment: $59. Power release tailgate window: $41. 20 gal. fuel tank: $49. Two front towing hooks: $36. Deadweight trailer hitch: $64. Heavy-duty trailering special: $199. Light-duty trailering special: $103. Wheel trim rings: $56. Rallye wheels: $32-$88 depending upon Trim Package. Styled wheels: $32-$88 depending upon Trim Package. Cast aluminum wheels: $238-$294 depending upon Trim Package. Power side door windows: $190. Intermittent windshield wiper system: $55.

HISTORICAL FOOTNOTES: The 1986 Jimmy was introduced in October, 1985.

1987 S-15 JIMMY

A new "Timberline" Package was offered for the 1987 S-15 Jimmy. Its features included a gold lower paint color that gradually blended into the black upper body color, special gold color aluminum wheels, gold color key bumpers with rub strips, gold fender name plates, black grille, black exterior mirrors, black body side moldings, and black wheel opening moldings. The standard 2.5 liter engine had a redesigned intake manifold and high flow ports in the cylinder head. A single belt accessory "serpentine" drive replaced the conventional multiple V belts on both the 2.5 and 2.8 liter engines. This system featured automatic belt tensioning that eliminated the need for adjustments throughout the life of the truck. The expected belt life was 100,000 miles. Both the standard Delcotron generator and all batteries had higher capacities for 1987. Replacing the paint previously applied to the two-stage rear springs and rear axle was a special wax-base coating that served as added protection from road salt, water and mud.

The tailgate applique for the High Sierra and Gypsy Sport models was restyled. Not available for 1987 was the cinnamon red exterior color. Joining the colors carried over from 1986 was Emerald metallic. A new-for-1987 Vaquaro upholstery which included genuine leather seat coverings was available with the Sierra Classic, Gypsy Sport or Timberline Packages.

1987 S-15 Jimmy Sierra Classic

I.D. DATA: The V.I.N. plate was mounted on the lower left side windshield corner. The V.I.N. consisted of 17 elements. The first, the number 1, identified the U.S. as the nation of origin. The letter G followed for the manufacturer: General Motors. The third entry, the letter T, represented the make as GMC. The GVWR brake system identification followed. Next came the truck line and chassis type; the letter K indicated four-wheel drive. The truck series was identified by a number: 1-1/2 ton. The truck body type identification was next: 8-Utility. The engine code was next: E-2.5 liter, B-2.8 liter V-6, followed by a check digit. The model year was identified by the letter H. The assembly plant code followed. The final six digits were the plant sequential production number.

Model Number	Body Type	Factory Price	GVW	Shipping Weight	Prod. Total
Jimmy S-15					
T18	Util. (with top)	$11,635	4075[1]	3140	—

NOTE 1: 4850 lb. GVW optional.

STANDARD ENGINE: Ordering Code LN8: Produced by Pontiac Motor Division. Engine Type: Cast iron block. OHV, In-line 4. Bore x Stroke: 4.0 in. x 3.0 in. Lifters: Hydraulic. Fuel induction: Electronic fuel injection. Compression Ratio: 9.0:1. Displacement: 151 cu. in. (2.5 liter). Horsepower: Net: 92 @ 4400 rpm. Torque: Net: 134 lb.-ft. @ 2800 rpm. Oil capacity: 5 qt. with filter change. Fuel Requirements: Unleaded.

OPTIONAL ENGINE: Engine Type: OHV, cast iron block. V-6. Order Code LR2. Produced by GM-Chevrolet Motor Division. Bore x Stroke: 3.50 in. x 2.99 in. Lifters: Hydraulic. Number of main bearings-5. Fuel Induction: Electronic fuel injection. Compression Ratio: 8.9:1. Displacement: 173 cu. in. (2.8 liter). Horsepower: Net: 125 @ 4800 rpm. Torque: Net: 150 lb.-ft. @ 2200 rpm. Oil capacity: 5 qt. with filter change. Fuel Requirements: Unleaded.

CHASSIS FEATURES: Carbon steel, welded front box section and open channel rear section.

SUSPENSION AND RUNNING GEAR: Front Suspension: Independent with torsion bar springs, 25mm dia. shock absorbers. 32mm stabilizer bar. Capacity: 1200 lbs. each at ground. Optional: 32mm shock absorbers. Rear Suspension: Two-stage multi-leaf shot-peened springs. Capacity: 1350 lbs. each at ground. 25mm shock absorbers. Optional: 32mm shock absorbers. Front Axle. Type: Hypoid, tubular driving. Capacity: 2400 lb. Rear Axle. Type: Salisbury, hypoid. Capacity: 2700 lb. Final Drive Ratio: Standard 4-spd. manual transmission and optional 5-spd. manual overdrive: 3.73:1 (3.08:1 for high altitude emission system). Automatic transmission: 3.42:1 (3.73:1 for high altitude emission system). Optional: Standard 4-spd. manual transmission and optional 5-spd. manual overdrive: 4.11:1 (3.73:1 for high altitude emission system). Automatic transmission: 3.73:1. Transfer Case: New Process 207. Brakes: Type: Hydraulic, power assisted self-adjusting. Front: Discs. Rear: Drums. Dimensions: Front: 9.5 in. x 2.0 in. rotor. Rear: 9.5 in. x 2.0 in. Wheels: 15 in. Tires: P195/75R15 glass belted radial black sidewall. Optional: P195/75R15 black sidewall, P205/75R15 black sidewall, P205/75R15 white sidewall, P205/75R15 white letters, P205/75R15 on/off road black sidewall. Steering: Manual. Optional: Power. Transmission: 4-speed manual. Optional: 5-speed manual with overdrive, 4-speed automatic with overdrive. Clutch: 4-cyl. engine: 9.12 in. dia., V-6: 9.76 in. dia.

VEHICLE DIMENSIONS: Wheelbase: 100.5 in. Overall Length: 170.3 in. Front/Rear Tread 55.6 in./ 54.1 in. Overall Height: 64.9 in. Width: 64.7 in. Approach/Departure Degrees: 28° 17'/ 25.5° 30'. Ground Clearance: Front axle: 8.1 in. Rear axle: 6.9 in.

CAPACITIES:: Fuel Tank: 13.2 gal. Optional: Replacement 20 gal. tank.

ACCOMMODATIONS: Seating Capacity: Standard: Driver and passenger front high back bucket sets. Optional: 3-passenger rear bench seat.

INSTRUMENTATION: 0-100 mph speedometer, 99,999.9 mi.odometer, fuel gauge, warning lights for alternator, oil pressure, engine coolant temperature, brake operating system, hazard warning lights, directional lights, seat belt warning.

OPTIONS AND PRICES: Sierra Classic Package. Gypsy Sport Package. Timberline Package. Sport cloth vinyl high-back bucket seat trim. High Country Sheepskin high-back bucket seats. Custom two-tone pain. Special two-tone paint. Sport two-tone paint. California emissions system. 2.6 liter V-6 engine. 4-speed overdrive automatic transmission. Optional axle ratio. Locking rear differential. Pre-cleaner air cleaner. 5-speed manual overdrive transmission. All-Weather air conditioning. Heavy-duty battery. Front black bumper guards. Luggage carrier, black or bright finish. Spare wheel and tire carrier. Off-Road Package. Cold Climate Package. Front compartment console. Engine oil cooling system. Heavy-duty radiator. Heavy-duty radiator and transmission oil cooler. Spare tire cover. Air deflector. Rear window defogger. Power door locks: $135. Color-keyed floor mats. Gauge Package. Includes voltmeter, engine coolant temperature, oil pressure. Gauge Package plus tachometer. 66 amp Delcotron generator. Deep tinted glass. Deep tinted glass with light tinted rear window. Halogen headlights. Engine block heater. Engine compartment light. Exterior left and right side painted mirrors. Exterior left and right side bright mirrors. Body side and wheel opening moldings. Door edge guards. Bright wheel opening moldings. Black wheel opening moldings. Operating Convenience Package. AM radio. AM/FM radio. AM/FM radio with clock. AM/FM stereo radio with electronic tuning. AM/FM stereo radio and clock with electronic tuning. AM/FM stereo radio with Seek-Scan, stereo cassette tape, clock and graphic equalizer and electronic tuning and premium rear speakers. Premium rear speakers. Folding rear bench seat. Reclining front seat backs. Transfer case shield. Heavy-duty front and rear shock absorbers. Full size spare tire. Electronic speed control. ComforTilt steering wheel. Striping. Heavy-duty suspension equipment. Power release tailgate window. 20 gal. fuel tank. Two front towing hooks. Deadweight trailer hitch. Heavy-duty trailering special. Light-duty trailering special. Wheel trim rings. Rallye wheels. Styled wheels. Cast aluminum wheels. Power side door windows. Intermittent windshield wiper system.

HISTORICAL FOOTNOTES: The 1987 S-15 Jimmy was introduced in October, 1986.

1988 S-15 JIMMY

The 2.8 liter V-6 became the Jimmy's standard engine for 1988. In addition, several mid-year changes highlighted the 1988 Jimmy. One development involved the installation of rear seat shoulder belts on models ordered with the optional rear seat. Secondly, beginning in April, 1988, a new 4.3 liter Vortex V-6 became an option for the S-15 Jimmy. Also debuting during the model year for Jimmy's with air conditioning was a new blue illumination for the heating, ventilation, and air-conditioning controls. Other changes for 1988 included the availability of new All-Season tires, the use of "SAS II" brake lining insulators that reduced brake noise on all front brakes. A new option was a factory-installed, manually-operated tinted, non-removable sunroof with five different opening positions. Interior changes included a revised instrument panel with grey trim plate accents. The knobs and switches remained black. L.E.D. displays on stereo radios were replaced by vacuum fluorescent lights. Map lights were added to the inside rearview mirror. Four new exterior colors were added for 1988: Light mesa brown, bright blue metallic, light mesa brown metallic and dark mesa brown metallic. Replacing saddle tan as an interior color was cognac.

I.D. DATA: The V.I.N. plate was mounted on the lower left side windshield corner. The V.I.N. consisted of 17 elements. The first, the number 1, identified the U.S. as the nation of origin. The letter G followed for the manufacturer: General Motors. The third entry, the letter T, represented the make as GMC. The GVWR brake system identification followed. Next came the truck line and chassis type; the letter K indicated four-wheel drive. The truck series was identified by a number: 1-1/2 ton. The truck body type identification was next: 8-Utility. The engine code was next: B-2.8 liter V-6, H-4.3 liter V-6, followed by a check digit. The model year was identified by the letter H. The assembly plant code followed. The final six digits were the plant sequential production number.

Model Number	Body Type	Factory Price	GVW	Shipping Weight	Prod. Total
Jimmy S-15					
T18	Util. (with top)	$12,784	4075[1]	3217	—

NOTE 1: 5013 lb. GVW optional.

STANDARD ENGINE: Engine Type: OHV, cast iron block. V-6. Order Code LL2. Produced by GM-Chevrolet Motor Division in Canada and Mexico. Bore x Stroke: 3.50 in. x 2.99 in. Lifters: Hydraulic. Number of main bearings-5. Fuel Induction: Electronic fuel injection. Compression Ratio: 8.9:1. Displacement: 173 cu. in. (2.8 liter). Horsepower: Net: 125 @ 4800 rpm. Torque: Net: 150 lb.-ft. @ 2200 rpm. Oil capacity: 5 qt. with filter change. Fuel Requirements: Unleaded.

OPTIONAL ENGINE: Engine Type: OHV, cast iron block. V-6. Order Code LB4. Bore x Stroke: 4.00 in. x 3.48 in. Lifters: Hydraulic. Number of main bearings-5. Fuel Induction: Electronic fuel injection. Compression Ratio: 9.3:1. Displacement: 262 cu. in. (4.3 liter). Horsepower: Net: 160 @ 4000 rpm. Torque: Net: 230 lb.-ft. @ 2400 rpm. Oil capacity: 5 qt. with filter change. Fuel Requirements: Unleaded.

CHASSIS FEATURES: Carbon steel, welded front box section and open channel rear section.

SUSPENSION AND RUNNING GEAR: Front Suspension: Independent with torsion bar springs, 25mm dia. shock absorbers. 32mm stabilizer bar. Capacity: 1200 lbs. each at ground. Optional: 32mm shock absorbers. Rear Suspension: Two-stage multi-leaf shot-peened springs. Capacity: 1350 lbs. each at ground. 25mm shock absorbers. Optional: 32mm shock absorbers. Front Axle. Type: Hypoid, tubular driving. Capacity: 2400 lb. Rear Axle. Type: Salisbury, hypoid. Capacity: 2700 lb. Final Drive Ratio: Standard 4-spd. manual transmission and optional 5-spd. manual overdrive: 3.73:1 (3.08:1 for high altitude emission system). Automatic transmission: 3.42:1 (3.73:1 for high altitude emission system). Optional: Standard 4-spd. manual transmission and optional 5-spd. manual overdrive: 4.11:1 (3.73:1 for high altitude emission system). Automatic transmission: 3.73:1. Transfer Case: New Process 207. Brakes: Type: Hydraulic, power assisted self-adjusting. Front: Discs. Rear: Drums. Dimensions: Front: 9.5 in. x 2.0 in. rotor. Rear: 9.5 in. x 2.0 in. Wheels: 15 in. Tires: P195/75R15 glass belted radial black sidewall. Optional: P195/75R15 black sidewall, P205/75R15 black sidewall, P205/75R15 white sidewall, P205/75R15 white letters, P205/75R15 on/off road black sidewall. Steering: Manual. Optional: Power. Transmission: 2.8 liter V-6: 5-speed manual with overdrive. 4.2 liter V-6: 4-speed automatic with overdrive. Optional: 2.8 liter V-6: 4-speed automatic with overdrive. Clutch: 9.76 in. dia.

VEHICLE DIMENSIONS: Wheelbase: 100.5 in. Overall Length: 170.3 in. Front/Rear Tread 54.1 in./ 54.1 in. Overall Height: 64.3 in. Width: 65.4 in. Approach/Departure Degrees: 28° 17'/ 25.5° 30'. Ground Clearance: Front axle: 6.3 in. Rear axle: 7.2 in.

CAPACITIES: Fuel Tank: 20 gal. tank.

ACCOMMODATIONS: Seating Capacity: Standard: Driver and passenger front high back bucket sets. Optional: 3 passenger rear bench seat.

INSTRUMENTATION: 0-100 mph speedometer, 99,999.9 mi.odometer, fuel gauge, warning lights for alternator, oil pressure, engine coolant temperature, brake operating system, hazard warning lights, directional lights, seat belt warning.

OPTIONS AND PRICES: Sierra Classic Package. Gypsy Sport Package. Timberline Package. Sport cloth vinyl high-back bucket seat trim. High Country Sheepskin high-back bucket seats. Custom two-tone pain. Special two-tone paint. Sport two-tone paint. California emissions system. 2.6 liter V-6 engine. 4-speed overdrive automatic transmission. Optional axle ratio. Locking rear differential. Pre-cleaner air cleaner. 5-speed manual overdrive transmission. All-Weather air conditioning. Heavy-duty battery. Front black bumper guards. Luggage carrier, black or bright fihish. Spare wheel and tire carrier. Off-Road Package. Cold Climate Package. Front compartment console. Engine oil cooling system. Heavy-duty radiator. Heavy-duty radiator and transmission oil cooler. Spare tire cover. Air deflector. Rear window defogger. Power door locks: $135. Color-keyed floor mats. Gauge Package. Includes voltmeter, engine coolant temperature, oil pressure. Gauge Package plus tachometer. 66 amp Delcotron generator. Deep tinted glass. Deep tinted glass with light tinted rear window. Halogen headlights. Engine block heater. Engine compartment light. Exterior left and right side painted mirrors. Exterior left and right side bright mirrors. Body side and wheel opening moldings. Door edge guards. Bright wheel opening moldings. Black wheel opening moldings. Operating Convenience Package. AM radio. AM/FM radio. AM/FM radio with clock. AM/FM stereo radio with electronic tuning. AM/FM stereo radio and clock with electronic tuning. AM/FM stereo radio with Seek-Scan, stereo cassette tape, clock and graphic equalizer and electronic tuning and premium rear speakers. Premium rear speakers. Folding rear bench seat. Reclining front seat backs. Transfer case shield. Heavy-duty front and rear shock absorbers. Full-size spare tire. Electronic speed control. ComforTilt steering wheel. Striping. Heavy-duty suspension equipment. Power release tailgate window. 20 gal. fuel tank. Two front towing hooks. Deadweight trailer hitch: $64. Heavy-duty trailering special: $199. Light-duty trailering special. Wheel trim rings. Rallye wheels. Styled wheels. Cast aluminum wheels. Power side door windows. Intermittent windshield wiper system.

HISTORICAL FOOTNOTES: The S-15 Jimmy was produced at three assembly plants — Pontiac, Michigan; Moraine, Ohio, and Shreveport, Louisiana.

1989 S-15 JIMMY

The S-10 Jimmy was fitted with standard rear-wheel anti-lock (RWAL) brakes for 1989. Details of this system are found in the1989 S-10 Blazer section. Now included in the Jimmy's standard equipment was power steering. A new electronic instrument panel cluster including speedometer, tachometer, voltmeter and fuel, oil pressure and engine coolant temperature gauges utilizing high-brightness vacuum fluorescent display tubes was another new option for 1989. Models with the standard 2.8 liter engine had a new transfer case with redesigned gear sets for reduced noise and smoother operation. This new system also involved new controls, a longer shift lever, a new vacuum switch and a relocated vent tube. Also available as a new option was a rear window wiper/washer system attached to the rear window in the upper right corner. This system included a glass-mounted motor, a wet arm nozzle, single-bottle reservoir and two high-pressure pumps-one for the front and one for the rear. The exterior colors for 1989 were frost white, midnight black, Aspen blue metallic, galaxy blue metallic, wheat, woodlands brown metallic, Emerald metallic, Nevada gold metallic, apple red and steel grey metallic. Dark blue replaced medium blue in the choice of interior colors. Premium rear speakers were now included with all optional stereo radios. The base Sierra model included these exterior features: Single electric horn, power brakes, power steering, front and rear chromed bumpers with black rub strips, chrome and black molded plastic grille and headlamp/ side marker lamp bezels, black hubcaps, bright finish door handles/lock cylinders, bright taillight trim, All-Season steel-belted radial tires, and right and left side fixed arm black finish mirrors. Interior features consisted of right and left hand padded armrests integral with door panels, color-keyed plastic door panels with map pockets and grey housing for the door latch release area, high-back bucket seats with folding seat backs and leather-grained custom vinyl, right and left side coat hooks, black plastic door sill plate, color-keyed plastic endgate scuff plate, door-operated courtesy and front and rear dome lights with bright trim, color-keyed rubber mat floor-covering, tinted glass for all windows, convenience tray, front and rear passenger grab handles, deluxe heater with side window defoggers, cigarette lighter with ashtray illumination, padded, color-keyed left and right side sunshades, gages for speedometer, odometer and fuel level, deluxe color-keyed 2-spoke steering wheel, headlamp warning buzzer, 10 in. rearview mirror and full-foam headliner with color-keyed cloth cover.

The Sierra Classic trim level (RPO YC2) had the following items in addition to or replacing the Sierra trim level: Bright wheel opening moldings, black bodyside moldings with bright insert plus rear quarter window moldings, hood insulators and cowl to fender seals, wheel trim rings, body color door handle inserts, and black tailgate applique. Sierra Classic interior features consisted of door panels with custom cloth upper insert, carpeted lower insert with map pocket and coin holder in left hand door, color-keyed floor carpeting, right side sunshade with mirror, trip odometer, gauges for voltmeter, oil pressure and engine coolant temperature (replace warning lamps), dual reading lamps, spare tire cover, color-keyed cowl kick panels and carpeted lower rear quarter and endgate panels.

The Gypsy trim level had the following items in addition to or replacing the Sierra Classic trim level: Bumpers color-keyed to lower accent color with black rub strips, black chrome grille with matching headlamp bezels, black finish for door handles and lock cylinders, two-tone paint (conventional or special), and black chrome taillamp trims. Interior features consisted of reclining bucket seats with folding seat backs and deluxe cloth, floor console, Gypsy steering wheel with simulated leather look and Deluxe cloth trim panel inserts.

I.D. DATA: The V.I.N. plate was mounted on the lower left side windshield corner. The V.I.N. consisted of 17 elements. The first, the number 1, identified the U.S. as the nation of origin. The letter G followed for the manufacturer: General Motors. The third entry, the letter T, represented the make as GMC. The GVWR brake system identification followed. Next came the truck line and chassis type; the letter K indicated four-wheel drive. The truck series was identified by a number: 1-1/2 ton. The truck body type identification was next: 8-Utility. The engine code was next: B-2.8 liter V-6, N-4.3 liter V-6 followed by a check digit. The model year was identified by the letter H. The assembly plant code followed. The final six digits were the plant sequential production number.

Model Number	Body Type	Factory Price	GVW	Shipping Weight	Prod. Total
Jimmy S15					
T18	Util. (with top)	$13,313	4075[1]	3295	—

NOTE 1: 4850 lb. GVW optional.

STANDARD ENGINE: Engine Type: OHV, cast iron block. V-6. Order Code LL2. Produced by GM-Chevrolet Motor Division in Canada and Mexico. Bore x Stroke: 3.50 in. x 2.99 in. Lifters: Hydraulic. Number of main bearings-5. Fuel Induction: Electronic fuel injection. Compression Ratio: 9:13:1. Displacement: 173 cu. in. (2.8 liter). Horsepower: Net: 125 @ 4800 rpm. Torque: Net: 150 lb.-ft. @ 2400 rpm. Oil capacity: 5 qt. with filter change. Fuel Requirements: Unleaded.

OPTIONAL ENGINE: Engine Type: OHV, cast iron block. V-6. Order Code LB4. Bore x Stroke: 4.00 in. x 3.48 in. Lifters: Hydraulic. Number of main bearings-5. Fuel Induction: Electronic fuel injection. Compression Ratio: 9.3:1. Displacement: 262 cu. in. (4.3 liter). Horsepower: Net: 160 @ 4000 rpm. Torque: Net: 230 lb.-ft. @ 2800 rpm. Oil capacity: 5 qt. with filter change. Fuel Requirements: Unleaded.

CHASSIS FEATURES: Carbon steel, welded front box section and open channel rear section. Side rail dimensions: 2.28 in. (width) x 5.00 in. (depth) x 0.118 in. (thickness). Overall length: 162.46 in. Side rail section modulus: 1.78.

SUSPENSION AND RUNNING GEAR: Front Suspension: Independent with torsion bar springs, 25mm dia. shock absorbers. 32mm stabilizer bar. Capacity: 1350 lbs. each at ground. Optional: 32mm shock absorbers. Rear Suspension: Two-stage 4-leaf shot-peened springs. Capacity: 1350 lbs. each at ground. 25mm shock absorbers. Optional: 32mm shock absorbers. Front Axle. Type: Hypoid, tubular driving. Capacity: 2400 lb. Rear Axle. Type: Salisbury, hypoid. Capacity: 2700 lb. Final Drive Ratio: 2.8 V-6 with manual trans.: 3.73:1. 4.3 liter V-6 with 4-speed automatic: 3.08:1. Optional: 2.8 V-6 with manual trans.: 4.11:1. 4.3 liter V-6 with 4-speed automatic: 3.42:1. Transfer Case: New Process 231. Ratios: 2.72,1.00:1. Brakes: Type: Hydraulic, power assisted self-adjusting. Front: Discs. Rear: Drums. Dimensions: Front: 10.5 in. x 1.03 in. rotor. Rear: 9.5 in. x 2.0 in. Wheels: 15 x 6.00 in. Tires: P195/ 75R15 steel belted radial All-Season black sidewall. Optional: P20575R15 black sidewall, All-Season steel-belted radial, P205/75R15 white letter All-Season steel-belted radial, P205/ 75R15 black or white sidewall front highway and rear on-off road All-Season steel-belted radial, P205/75R15 black or white sidewall front/rear on-off road All-Season steel-belted radial, All-Season steel-belted radial, P205/75R15 white letter front/rear on-off road All-Season steel-belted radial, P235/75R15 white letter front/rear on-off road All-Season steel-belted radial. Steering: Power assisted. Ratio: 17.5:1. Turning diameter: 35.4 ft. Transmission: 2.8 liter V-6: 5-speed manual with overdrive. 4.2 liter V-6: 4-speed automatic with overdrive. Ratios: 5-speed manual: 4.02, 2.32, 1.40, 1.00, 0.83:1. Reverse: 3.74:1. 4-speed automatic: 3.06, 1.63, 1.0, 0.70:1. Reverse: 2.29:1.

VEHICLE DIMENSIONS: Wheelbase: 100.5 in. Overall Length: 170.3 in. Front/Rear Tread 54.1 in./ 54.1 in. Overall Height: 64.3 in. Width: 65.4 in. Approach/Departure Degrees: 28° 17'/ 25.5° 30'. Ground Clearance: Front axle: 6.1 in. Rear axle: 7.2 in. Load space: With rear seat installed: 35.5 in. x 53.4 in. x 35.0 in. With rear seat removed or folded: 68.6 in. x 53.4 in. x 35.0 in.

CAPACITIES: Fuel Tank: 20 gal. tank. Coolant system capacity: 2.8 liter V-6: 11.6 qt., 4.2 liter V-6: 12.0 qt.

ACCOMMODATIONS: Seating Capacity: Standard: Driver and passenger front high back bucket sets. Optional: 3 passenger rear bench seat. Front headroom: 39.1 in. Rear headroom: 38.1 in. Front leg room: 42.5 in. Rear leg room: 35.5 in. Front hip room: 50.5 in. Rear hip room: 37.6 in.

INSTRUMENTATION: 0-100 mph speedometer, 99,999.9 mi.odometer, fuel gauge, warning lights for alternator, oil pressure, engine coolant temperature, brake operating system, hazard warning lights, directional lights, seat belt warning.

OPTIONS AND PRICES: Air conditioning: $736 without LL2 engine, $680 with LL2 engine. Optional axle ratio: $38. Locking rear differential: $252. Heavy-duty battery: 56. Luggage carrier: $126. Spare tire and wheel carrier: $159-$192 depending upon trim option. Cold Climate Package: $113-$156 depending upon trim option. Center console: $114. Engine oil cooler: $126. Heavy-duty radiator: $56. Heavy-duty radiator and engine oil cooler: $63, with air conditioning, $118 without air conditioning. Spare tire cover: $33. Gypsy Package: $1038 without Timberline option, $671 with Timberline option. Sierra Classic Package: $683 without Timberline option, $473 with Timberline option. Air deflector: $43. Driver Convenience Package. Includes ComforTilt steering wheel and intermittent wiper system: $180. Rear window Convenience Package. Includes electric tailgate release and rear window defogger: $197. 4.3 liter V-6: $255. Color-keyed front floor mats: $16. Color-keyed rear floor mats: $12. Gauge Package: $62. Deep tinted glass with light tinted rear window: $56-$200 depending on Trim Package. Halogen headlights: $24. Engine block heater: $33. Electronic instrumentation: $296-$358 depending on Trim Package. Engine compartment light: $16. Interior visor mirror: $7. Exterior below eye-level black mirrors: $52. Exterior below eye-level bright mirrors: $87. Interior rearview tilting mirror with dual reading lamps: $26. Body side and wheel opening moldings: $152. Black wheel opening molding: $13-$43 depending upon Trim Package. Bright wheel opening molding: 31. Operating Convenience Package. Includes power door locks and power windows: $344. Custom two-tone paint: $172-$344 depending upon Trim Package. Special two-tone paint: $163-$212 depending upon Trim Package. Deluxe two-tone paint: $177-$329 depending upon Trim Package. Electronically tuned AM/FM stereo radio: $275. Electronically tuned AM/FM stereo radio with Seek-Scan, stereo cassette tape player and digital clock: $454. Electronically tuned AM/FM stereo radio with Seek-Scan, stereo cassette tape player with Search and Repeat, graphic equalizer and digital clock: $604. Rear folding rear seat: $409. Reclining seat backs: $74. Transfer case and front differential skid plates and steering linkage shield: $75. Front and rear heavy-duty shock absorbers: $36. Electronic speed control: $205. Heavy-duty front springs: $63. Body striping: $49. Sunshine striping: $116. Manual sun roof: $250. Suspension Package: $160-$220 depending upon Trim Package. Timberline Package: $925 with Gypsy Package, $1026 with Sierra Classic Package. Two front tow hooks: $38. Deadweight trailer hitch: $68. Light-Duty Trailering Package: $109. Heavy-Duty Trailering Special Package: $211. 4-speed automatic transmission: $795. Wheel trim rings: $60. Cast aluminum wheels: $252-$308 depending upon Trim Package. Sliding rear window: $257. Rear window wiper/washer: $125.

HISTORICAL FOOTNOTES: The 1989 S-10 Jimmy was produced at Pontiac, Michigan and Shreveport, Louisiana.

1990 S-15 JIMMY

The S-15 Jimmy had a more powerful standard engine, increased standard equipment content and a new gross vehicle weight rating system for 1990. A new manual 5-speed transmission was used with the 4.3 liter engine. which was now standard. The 4.3 liter Vortex engine's power ratings were unchanged from 1989. Three trim levels were again offered — Sierra, Sierra Classic and Sport — but their standard equipment content was significantly increased. All three trim levels had the following new-for-1990 items: Full-size spare tire, inside spare tire cover, P205/75R15 All-Season steel-belted radial tires, Deluxe Front Appearance Package, right and left-side exterior black finish mirrors, Halogen headlights, redesigned instrument cluster, voltmeter, engine coolant temperature and oil pressure gauges, electronically tuned AM radio, and front tow hooks. The Gypsy Package now includes cast aluminum wheels. The new Gross Vehicle Weight Rating (GVRW) system for 1990 replaced the older net payload system in which trucks were assigned a net payload rating and were rated to carry that payload regardless of the factory option content or aftermarket accessories. With the new fixed system, ratings were done on an individual, truck-by-truck basis. The net cargo rating was more accurately calculated by subtracting the curb weight and the weight of the options, passengers and any aftermarket equipment. Two new exterior colors were offered for 1990. The total selection of exterior colors were frost white, silver metallic, midnight black, Aspen blue metallic, wheat, woodlands brown metallic, royal blue metallic, garnet, Nevada gold metallic, apple red and steel grey metallic. One new interior color was offered for 1990. The custom vinyl and custom cloth interiors were offered in blue, garnet, charcoal or saddle. The Deluxe cloth and leather upholsteries were offered in either charcoal or saddle. The Timberline Package was cancelled for 1990.

I.D. DATA: The V.I.N. plate was mounted on the lower left side windshield corner. The V.I.N. consisted of 17 elements. The first, the number 1, identified the U.S. as the nation of origin. The letter G followed for the manufacturer: General Motors. The third entry, the letter T, represented the make as Chevrolet. The GVWR brake system identification followed. Next came the truck line and chassis type; the letter K indicated four-wheel drive. The truck series was identified by a number: 1-1/2 ton. The truck body type identification was next: 8-Utility. The engine code was next: N-4.3 liter V-6 followed by a check digit. The model year was identified by the letter L. The assembly plant code followed. The final six digits were the plant sequential production number.

Model Number	Body Type	Factory Price	GVW	Shipping Weight	Prod. Total
Jimmy S-15					
TT10516	Util.	$14,798	4700	3279	—

STANDARD ENGINE: Engine Type: OHV, cast iron block. V-6. Order Code LB4. Bore x Stroke: 4.00 in. x 3.48 in. Lifters: Hydraulic. Number of main bearings-5. Fuel Induction: Electronic fuel injection. Compression Ratio: 9.3:1. Displacement: 262 cu. in. (4.3 liter). Horsepower: Net: 160 @ 4000 rpm. Torque: Net: 230 lb.-ft. @ 2800 rpm. Oil capacity: 5 qt. with filter change. Fuel Requirements: Unleaded.

CHASSIS FEATURES: Carbon steel, welded front box section and open channel rear section. Side rail dimensions: 2.28 in. (width) x 5.00 in. (depth) x 0.118 in. (thickness). Overall length: 162.46 in. Side rail section modulus: 1.78.

SUSPENSION AND RUNNING GEAR: Front Suspension: Independent with torsion bar springs, 25mm dia. shock absorbers. 32mm stabilizer bar. Capacity:1200 lbs. each at ground. Optional: 32mm, 46mm shock absorbers. Rear Suspension: Two-stage 4-leaf shot-peened springs. Capacity: 1350 lbs. each at ground. 25mm shock absorbers. Optional: 32mm, 46mm shock absorbers. Front Axle. Type: Independent GM Hypoid, tubular driving. Capacity: 2400 lb. Rear Axle. Type: Semi-floating GM Hypoid Capacity: 2700 lb. Final Drive Ratio: 3.08:1. Optional: 3.42:1. Transfer Case: New Process 231. Ratios: 2.72,1.00:1. Brakes: Type: Hydraulic, power assisted self-adjusting. Front: Discs. Rear: Drums. Dimensions: Front: 10.5 in. x 1.03 in. rotor. Rear: 9.5 in. x 2.0 in. Wheels: 15 x 6.00 in. Optional: 15 x 7.0 in. Rally wheels, 15 x 7.0 in. Cast aluminum (RPO N90), 15 x 7.0 in. cast aluminum (RPO N60). Tires: P205/75R15 steel belted radial All-Season black sidewall. Optional: P205/75R15 black sidewall, All-Season steel-belted radial, P205/75R15 on-off road steel belted radial, white letters, P205/75R15 All-Season steel belted radial, white letters, P205/75R15 on-off road steel belted radial black sidewall, P205/75R15 steel belted radial. Front: Highway. Rear: On-off road, P235/75R15 on-off road steel belted radial white letters. Steering: Variable ratio, integral power. Ratio: 17.5:1. Turning diameter: 35.4 ft. Transmission: 5-speed manual with overdrive (RPO MM5). Ratios: 4.02, 2.32, 1.40, 1.00, 0.83:1. Reverse: 3.74:1. Optional: 4-speed automatic with overdrive (RPO MXO): 3.06, 1.63, 1.0, 0.70:1. Reverse: 2.29:1.

VEHICLE DIMENSIONS: Wheelbase: 100.5 in. Overall Length: 170.3 in. Front/Rear Tread 54.1 in./54.1 in. Overall Height: 64.3 in. Width: 65.4 in. Front/Rear Overhang: 30.6/39.2 in. Approach/Departure Degrees: 28° 17'/25.5° 30'. Ground Clearance: Front axle: 6.1 in. Rear axle: 7.2 in. Load space: With rear seat installed: 35.5 in. x 53.4 in. x 35.0 in. With rear seat removed or folded: 68.6 in. x 53.4 in. x 35.0 in.

CAPACITIES: Fuel Tank: 20 gal. tank. Coolant system capacity: 12.0 qt.

ACCOMMODATIONS: Seating Capacity: Standard: Driver and passenger front high back bucket sets. Optional: 3-passenger rear bench seat. Front headroom: 39.1 in. Rear headroom: 38.1 in. Front legroom: 42.5 in. Rear legroom: 35.5 in. Front hip room: 50.5 in. Rear hip room: 37.6 in.

INSTRUMENTATION: 0-100 mph speedometer, 99,999.9 mi. odometer, fuel gauge, gauges for voltmeter, oil pressure, engine coolant temperature.Warning lights for brake operating system, hazard warning lights, directional lights, seat belt warning.

OPTIONS AND PRICES: Air conditioning: $755. Optional axle ratio: $38. Locking rear differential: $252. Heavy-duty battery: $56. Luggage carrier: $169. Spare tire and wheel carrier: $159. Cold Climate Package: $146-$189 depending upon trim option. Center console: $135. Heavy-duty radiator: $56. Heavy-duty radiator and engine oil cooler: $63, with air conditioning, $118 without air conditioning. Gypsy Package: $1239. Sierra Classic Package: $809. Driver Convenience Package. Includes ComforTilt steering wheel and intermittent wiper system: $197. Color-keyed front floor mats: $20. Color-keyed rear floor mats: $16. Deep tinted glass with light tinted rear window: $225. Electronic instrumentation: $296. Lighted interior visor mirror: $68-$75 depending upon Trim Package. Body side and wheel opening moldings: $152. Black wheel opening molding: $13-$43 depending upon Trim Package. Bright wheel opening molding: $31. Operating Convenience Package. Includes power door locks and power windows: $344. Custom two-tone paint: $172-$344 depending upon Trim Package. Special two-tone paint: $163-$218 depending upon Trim Package. Deluxe two-tone paint: $177-$329 depending upon Trim Package. Electronically tuned AM/FM stereo radio with Seek-Scan, stereo cassette tape player and digital clock: $122. Electronically tuned AM/FM stereo radio with Seek-Scan, stereo cassette tape player with Search and Repeat, graphic equalizer and digital clock: $272. Delete radio: $226 credit.Rear folding rear seat: $409. Transfer case and front differential skid plates and steering linkage shield: $75. Front and rear heavy-duty shock absorbers: $40. Electronic speed control: $225. Heavy-duty front springs. Includes heavy-duty shock absorbers: $63. Body striping: $49. Sunshine striping: $70 to $125 depending upon Trim Package. Manual sun roof: $250. Off-road suspension equipment: 122-$182 depending upon Trim Package. Light-Duty Trailering Package: $165. Heavy-duty trailering special Package: $211. 4-speed automatic transmission: $860. Wheel trim rings: $60. Cast aluminum wheels: $269-$325 depending upon Trim Package. Grey aluminum wheels: $233-$325 depending upon trim option. Sliding rear window: $257. Rear window wiper/washer: $125.

HISTORICAL FOOTNOTES: GMC noted that the GMC Jimmy was designed to offer compact sport/utility buyers looking for value, comfort and convenience.

1991 S-15 JIMMY

GMC added a four-door model to the Jimmy lineup as a 1991 model early in 1990. The new model's rear doors provided easier access and exit from a standard 3 passenger rear seat. It also had as standard, the SLE level of interior trim, four-wheel anti-lock brake system (ABS) and a 2900 lb. capacity rear axle. The two-door model had a standard rear-wheel anti-lock brake system that operated in two-wheel drive only. New for 1991 were the Jimmy's exterior nameplates, emblems, bumper rub stripes, body side moldings, and body stripes and decals. New wheels and wheel trim designs were also introduced. The new front end styling featured a simple grille of narrow horizontal with three vertical dividers and red-insert GMC lettering. High-back front bucket seats were standard. During the 1991 model year numerous changes were introduced. These included a 220 TBI (Throttle Body Injection) system, use of Hydra-Matic 5LM60 5-speed manual transmission in place of the 290 unit, revised Thermac III air cleaner, use of a revised accessory drive, a new Geolast PCV connector, and new Quantum spark plugs. Additional interim 1991 improvements involved front and rear suspension changes, accelerator pedal effort reduction, revised floor console latch, revised Rallye wheel center insert, use of a lever-type power door lock switch, improved AM/FM radio reception, availability of aluminum wheel colors, inclusion of a heavy-duty battery as standard equipment, improved front axle half-shaft, improved heating/ventilation and the introduction of a front bench seat for maximum 6 passenger capacity. All models were available with new RPO D48 electric OSRV mirrors with control on the instrument cluster. The two-door model had single-rate rear springs with revised rates for an improved ride. The SLE trim had new seat fabric, door panels and rear quarter panels. The standard trim level for the two-door Jimmy was the SL. The front floor console had a revised catch for easy, keyless entry. Exterior colors for 1991 were midnight black, Aspen blue metallic, sky blue, royal blue metallic, garnet red, steel grey metallic, mint green, apple red, wheat, frost white and silver metallic. The two-door models were available in four interior colors: Blue, charcoal, garnet or saddle. Blue and charcoal were initially offered for four-door model interiors. By the fall of 1991 the standard SLE interior for the four-door was also available in blue, charcoal, garnet or saddle.

A new SLX Package was available for the two-door model. It was offered in five exterior colors: Midnight black, apple red, frost white, Aspen blue metallic or seafoam green. Key features included body-colored bumpers, special decals for the doors and tailgate, red decal striping on the lower body and tailgate, bright aluminum wheels, black chrome finish for door handles and taillight trim, bright-trimmed grey rub strips on bumpers, and front bucket seats in Deluxe cloth with red accents in a choice of blue or charcoal.

1991 S-15 Jimmy two and four-door SLE models

I.D. DATA: The V.I.N. plate was mounted on the lower left side windshield corner. The V.I.N. consisted of 17 elements. The first, the number 1, identified the U.S. as the nation of origin. The letter G followed for the manufacturer: General Motors. The third entry, the letter T, represented the make as GMC. The GVWR brake system identification followed. Next came the truck line and chassis type; the letter K indicated four-wheel drive. The truck series was identified by a number: 1-1/2 ton. The truck body type identification was next: 8-Utility. The engine code was next: N-4.3 liter V-6 followed by a check digit. The model year was identified by the letter M. The assembly plant code followed. The final six digits were the plant sequential production number.

Model Number	Body Type	Factory Price	GVW	Shipping Weight	Prod. Total
Jimmy S-15					
TT10506	2-dr. Util.	$15,811	4700	3295	21,641[1]
TT10506	3-dr. Util.	$17,451	5100	—	—

NOTE 1: All models.

STANDARD ENGINE: Engine Type: OHV, cast iron block. V-6. Order Code LB4. Bore x Stroke: 4.00 in. x 3.48 in. Lifters: Hydraulic. Number of main bearings-5. Fuel Induction: Electronic fuel injection. Compression Ratio: 9.3:1. Displacement: 262 cu. in. (4.3 liter). Horsepower: Net: 160 @ 4000 rpm. Torque: Net: 230 lb.-ft. @ 2800 rpm. Oil capacity: 5 qt. with filter change. Fuel Requirements: Unleaded.

CHASSIS FEATURES: Carbon steel, welded front box section and open channel rear section. Dimensions: Two-door: Side rail dimensions: 2.28 in. (width) x 5.00 in. (depth) x 0.118 in. (thickness). Overall length: 162.46 in. Side rail section modulus: 1.78. Dimensions: Four-door: Side rail dimensions: 2.28 in. (width) x 5.00 in. (depth) x 0.118 in. (thickness). Overall length: 168.96 in. Side rail section modulus: 1.78.

SUSPENSION AND RUNNING GEAR: Front Suspension: Independent with torsion bar springs, 25mm dia. shock absorbers. 32mm stabilizer bar. Capacity: 1200 lbs. each at ground. Optional: 32mm, 46mm shock absorbers. Rear Suspension: Two-stage 4-leaf shot-peened springs. Capacity: Two-door: 1350 lbs. each at ground, Four-door: 1450 lb. each at ground. 25mm shock absorbers. Optional: 32mm, 46mm shock absorbers. Front Axle. Type: Independent GM Hypoid, tubular driving. Capacity: 2400 lb. Rear Axle. Type: Semi-floating GM Hypoid Capacity: Two-door: 2700 lb. Four-door: 2900 lb. Final Drive Ratio: 3.08:1. Optional: 3.42:1. Transfer Case: New Process 231. Ratios: 2.72, 1.00:1. Brakes: Type: Hydraulic, power assisted self-adjusting. Front: Discs. Rear: Drums. Dimensions: Front: 10.5 in. x 1.03 in. rotor. Rear: 9.5 in. x 2.0 in. Wheels: 15 x 6.00 in. Optional: 15 x 7.0 in. Rally wheels, 15 x 7.0 in. Cast aluminum (RPO N90), 15 x 7.0 in. cast aluminum (RPO N60). Tires: P205/75R15 steel belted radial All-Season black sidewall. Optional: P205/75R15 black sidewall, All-Season steel-belted radial, P205/75R15 on-off road steel belted radial, white letters, P205/75R15 All-Season steel belted radial, white letters, P205/75R15 on-off road steel belted radial black sidewall, P205/75R15 steel belted radial. Front: Highway. Rear: On-off road, P235/75R15 on-off road steel belted radial white letters. Steering: Variable ratio, integral power. Ratio: 17.5:1. Turning diameter: 35.4 ft. Transmission: 5-speed manual with overdrive (RPO MM5). Ratios: 4.02, 2.32, 1.40, 1.00, 0.83:1. Reverse: 3.74:1. Optional: 4-speed automatic with overdrive (RPO MXO): 3.06, 1.63, 1.0, 0.70:1. Reverse: 2.29:1.

VEHICLE DIMENSIONS: Wheelbase: Two-door/Four-door: 100.5 in./107.0 in. Overall Length: Two-door/Four-door: 170.3 in./176.8. Front/Rear Tread 54.1 in./54.1 in. Overall Height: 62.8 in. Width: 65.4 in. Front/Rear Overhang: 30.6/39.2 in. Approach/Departure Degrees: 28° 17'/25.5° 30'. Ground Clearance: Front axle: 8.5 in. Rear axle: 8.1 in. Load space: Two-door: With rear seat installed: 35.5 in. x 50.0 in. x 35.0 in. With rear seat removed or folded: 68.6 in. x 53.4 in. x 35.0 in. Four-door: With rear seat installed: 38.5 in. x 52.5 in. x 34.5 in. With rear seat removed or folded: 76.1 in. x 52.5 in. x 34.5 in. Maximum cargo space: Two-door: 67.3 cu. ft. Four-door: 74.3 cu. ft.

CAPACITIES: Fuel Tank: 20 gal. tank. Coolant system capacity: 12.0 qt.

ACCOMMODATIONS: Seating Capacity: Standard: Two-door: Driver and passenger front high back bucket sets. Optional: 3-passenger rear bench seat. Four-door: 5 passenger with standard rear bench seat. Front headroom: 39.1 in. Rear headroom: 38.1 in. Front legroom: 42.5 in. Rear legroom: 35.5 in. Front hip room: 50.5 in. Rear hip room: 37.6 in.

INSTRUMENTATION: 0-100 mph speedometer, 99,999.9 mi.odometer, fuel gauge, gauges for voltmeter, oil pressure, engine coolant temperature.Warning lights for brake operating system, hazard warning lights, directional lights, seat belt warning.

OPTIONS AND PRICES: Air conditioning: $724 with engine oil cooler, $780 without engine oil cooler. Air dam with fog lamps: $115. Optional axle ratio: $44. Locking rear differential: $252. Heavy-duty battery: $56. Spare tire and wheel carrier: $159. Cold Climate Package: $146. Heavy-duty radiator: $56. Heavy-duty radiator and engine oil cooler: $63, with air conditioning, $118 without air conditioning. Driver Convenience Package (RPO ZM7). Includes ComforTilt steering wheel and Intermittent wiper system: $204. Driver Convenience Package (RPO ZM8). Includes rear window defroster and tailgate release: $197. California Emissions Package: $100. Color-keyed front floor mats (two-door only): $20. Rear color-keyed floor mats: $16. Deep tinted glass (RPO AJ1): $225. Deep tinted glass with light tinted rear window (RPO AA3): $144. Electronic instrumentation: $195. Black luggage carrier: $169. Exterior electric remote mirrors: $83. Visor mirrors, left and right side: $68. Black wheel opening molding: $13-$43 depending on Trim Package. Operating Convenience Package. Includes power door locks and power windows: $542, four-door, $367, two-door. Special two-tone paint: $218. Deluxe two-tone paint: $177. Electronically tuned AM/FM stereo radio with Seek-Scan, and digital clock: $131. Electronically tuned AM/FM stereo radio with Seek-Scan, stereo cassette tape player: $122-$253 depending upon other options selected. Electronically tuned AM/FM stereo radio with Seek-Scan, stereo cassette tape player with Search and Repeat, graphic equalizer and digital clock: $403. Delete radio: $95 credit. Special custom cloth reclining high-back bucket seats: $345. Deluxe cloth reclining high-back bucket seats: $26 with rear seat. Folding rear bench seat: $409. Leather reclining high-back bucket seats, two-door only: $312 with folding rear bench seat, $412 without folding rear seat. Transfer case and front differential skid plates and steering linkage shield: $75. Front and rear heavy-duty shock absorbers: $40. Electronic speed control: $238. SLS Sport equipment: $699. Body striping: $55. Sun roof, manual, non-removable, two-door only: $250. Heavy-duty front springs: $63. Off-road suspension, two-door only: $122-$182 depending on other options selected. Light-Duty Trailering Package: $165 with oil cooler, $109 without oil cooler. Heavy-Duty Trailering Special Package: $211. 4-speed automatic transmission: $890. Rallye wheels: $92. Cast aluminum wheels: $284-$340 depending upon Trim Package. Grey aluminum wheels: $248-$340 depending upon trim option. Sliding rear side window, two-door only: $257. Rear window wiper/washer: $125.

HISTORICAL FOOTNOTES: The two-door Jimmys were built at GM manufacturing facilities in Pontiac, Michigan and Moraine, Ohio. The four-door Jimmy was built only at the Moraine plant.

1992 S-15 JIMMY

The S-15 Jimmy received minor mechanical and trim revisions for 1992. These included a new optional two-speed electronic shift transfer, new seats with integral head restraints for front bucket seats in four-door models, and high-back bucket seats with optional leather. A new compact disc player was added to the optional list.

I.D. DATA: The V.I.N. plate was mounted on the lower left side windshield corner. The V.I.N. consisted of 17 elements. The first, the number 1, identified the U.S. as the nation of origin. The letter G followed for the manufacturer: General Motors. The third entry, the letter T, represented the make as GMC. The GVWR brake system identification followed. Next came the truck line and chassis type; the letter K indicated four-wheel drive. The truck series was identified by a number: 1-1/2 ton. The truck body type identification was next: 8-Utility. The engine code was next: N-4.3 liter V-6 followed by a check digit. The model year was identified by the letter N. The assembly plant code followed. The final six digits were the plant sequential production number.

Model Number	Body Type	Factory Price	GVW	Shipping Weight	Prod. Total
Jimmy S-15					
TT10506	2-dr. Util.	$16,803	4700	3295	—
TT10506	4-dr. Util.	$18,173	5100	—	—

STANDARD ENGINE: Engine Type: OHV, cast iron block. V-6. Order Code LB4. Bore x Stroke: 4.00 in. x 3.48 in. Lifters: Hydraulic. Number of main bearings-5. Fuel Induction: Electronic fuel injection. Compression Ratio: 9.3:1. Displacement: 262 cu. in. (4.3 liter). Horsepower: Net: 160 @ 4000 rpm. Torque: Net: 230 lb.-ft. @ 2800 rpm. Oil capacity: 5 qt. with filter change. Fuel Requirements: Unleaded.

CHASSIS FEATURES: Carbon steel, welded front box section and open channel rear section. Dimensions: Two-door: Side rail dimensions: 2.28 in. (width) x 5.00 in. (depth) x 0.118 in. (thickness). Overall length: 162.46 in. Side rail section modulus: 1.78. Dimensions: Four-door: Side rail dimensions: 2.28 in. (width) x 5.00 in. (depth) x 0.118 in. (thickness). Overall length: 168.96 in. Side rail section modulus: 1.78.

SUSPENSION AND RUNNING GEAR: Front Suspension: Independent with torsion bar springs, 25mm dia. shock absorbers. 32mm stabilizer bar. Capacity:1200 lbs. each at ground. Optional: 32mm, 46mm shock absorbers. Rear Suspension: Two-stage 4-leaf shot-peened springs. Capacity: Two-door: 1350 lbs. each at ground, four-door: 1450 lb. each at ground. 25mm shock absorbers. Optional: 32mm, 46mm shock absorbers. Front Axle. Type: Independent GM Hypoid, tubular driving. Capacity: 2400 lb. Rear Axle. Type: Semi-floating GM Hypoid Capacity: 2-door: 2700 lb. 4-door: 2900 lb. Final Drive Ratio: 3.08:1. Optional: 3.42:1. Transfer Case: New Process 231. Ratios: 2.72,1.00:1. Brakes: Type: Hydraulic, power assisted self-adjusting. Front: Discs. Rear: Drums. Dimensions: Front: 10.5 in. x 1.03 in. rotor. Rear: 9.5 in. x 2.0 in. Wheels: 15 x 6.00 in. Optional: 15 x 7.0 in. Rally wheels, 15 x 7.0 in. Cast aluminum (RPO N90), 15 x 7.0 in. cast aluminum (RPO N60). Tires: P205/75R15 steel belted radial All-Season black sidewall. Optional: P205/75R15 black sidewall, All-Season steel-belted radial, P205/75R15 on-off road steel belted radial, white letters, P205/75R15 All-Season steel belted radial, white letters, P205/75R15 on-off road steel belted radial black sidewall, P205/75R15 steel belted radial, front: Highway, Rear: On-off road, P235/75R15 on-off road steel belted radial white letters. Steering: Variable ratio, integral power. Ratio: 17.5:1. Turning diameter: 35.4 ft. Transmission: 5-speed manual with overdrive (RPO MM5). Ratios: 4.02, 2.32, 1.40, 1.00, 0.83:1. Reverse: 3.74:1. Optional: 4-speed automatic with overdrive (RPO MXO): 3.06, 1.63, 1.0, 0.70:1. Reverse: 2.29:1.

VEHICLE DIMENSIONS: Wheelbase: Two-door/Four-door: 100.5 in./107.0 in. Overall Length: Two-door/Four-door: 170.3 in./176.8. Front/Rear Tread 54.1 in./54.1 in. Overall Height: 62.8 in. Width: 65.4 in. Front/Rear Overhang: 30.6/39.2 in. Approach/Departure Degrees: 28° 17'/25.5° 30'. Ground Clearance: Front axle: 8.5 in. Rear axle: 8.1 in. Load space: Two-door: With rear seat installed: 35.5 in. x 50.0 in. x 35.0 in. With rear seat removed or folded: 68.6 in. x 53.4 in. x 35.0 in. Four-door: With rear seat installed: 38.5 in. x 52.5 in. x 34.5 in. With rear seat removed or folded: 76.1 in. x 52.5 in. x 34.5 in. Maximum cargo space: Two-door: 67.3 cu. ft. Four-door: 74.3 cu. ft.

CAPACITIES::Fuel Tank: 20 gal. tank. Coolant system capacity: 12.0 qt.

ACCOMMODATIONS: Seating Capacity: Standard: Two-door: Driver and passenger front high back bucket sets. Optional: 3 passenger rear bench seat. Four-door: 5 passenger with standard rear bench seat. Front headroom: 39.1 in. Rear Headroom: 38.1 in. Front legroom: 42.5 in. Rear legroom: 35.5 in. Front hip room: 50.5 in. Rear hip room: 37.6 in.

INSTRUMENTATION: 0-100 mph speedometer, 99,999.9 mi.odometer, fuel gauge, gauges for voltmeter, oil pressure, engine coolant temperature.Warning lights for brake operating system, hazard warning lights, directional lights, seat belt warning.

OPTIONS AND PRICES: Air conditioning: Air dam with fog lamps. Optional axle ratio. Locking rear differential. Heavy-duty battery. Spare tire and wheel carrier. Cold Climate Package. Heavy-duty radiator. Heavy-duty radiator and engine oil cooler. Driver Convenience Package (RPO ZM7). Includes ComforTilt steering wheel and intermittent wiper system. Driver Convenience Package (RPO ZM8). Includes rear window defroster and tailgate release. California Emissions Package. Color-keyed front floor mats (two-door only). Rear color-keyed floor mats. Deep tinted glass (RPO AJ1). Deep tinted glass with light tinted rear window (RPO AA3). Electronic instrumentation. Black luggage carrier. Exterior electric remote mirrors. Visor mirrors, left and right side. Black wheel opening molding. Operating Convenience Package. Includes power door locks and power windows. Special two-tone paint. Deluxe two-tone paint. Electronically tuned AM/FM stereo radio with Seek-Scan and digital clock. Electronically tuned AM/FM stereo radio with Seek-Scan, stereo cassette tape player. Electronically tuned AM/FM stereo radio with Seek-Scan, stereo cassette tape player with Search and Repeat, graphic equalizer and digital clock. Delete radio: $95 credit. Special custom cloth reclining high-back bucket seats. Deluxe cloth reclining high-back bucket seats. Folding rear bench seat. Leather reclining high-back bucket seats, two-door. Transfer case and front differential skid plates and steering linkage shield. Front and rear heavy-duty shock absorbers. Electronic speed control. SLS Sport Equipment. Body striping. Sun roof, manual, non-removable, two-door only. Heavy-duty front springs. Off-road suspension, two-door only. Light-Duty Trailering Package. Heavy-Duty Trailering Special Package. Tahoe Package: Sport Package. 4-speed automatic transmission. Rallye wheels. Cast aluminum wheels. Grey aluminum wheels. Sliding rear side window, two-door only. Rear window wiper/washer.

HISTORICAL FOOTNOTES: Along with GMC vehicles, the 1992 S-15 Jimmy was protected by a 3 year or 36,000 mile bumper to bumper warranty. Body sheet metal rust-through was covered for 6 years or 60,000 miles.

1993 S-15 JIMMY

The 1993 GMC Jimmy was marked by a number of significant changes. The SLT Touring Package was now available for two-door models. Introduced on the four-door models in 1992, this package featured a leather trim interior with power driver's seat, standard overhead console, keyless entry system, luggage rack and all-season highway radial tires. The SLT leather trim was offered in three color choices: Charcoal, grey and garnet. The SLS Trim Package was also overhauled. It included a full chromatic look with a body-color grille, wheel-lip moldings, and painted body-color aluminum wheels. New nameplates and badges (revised on all 1993 GMC trucks) were also included. An all-new "Flexolator" front seat design improved lumbar and thigh support. All cloth manual seats also now included a manual lumbar support. The illuminated entry system that activated the interior lights when the driver's door opened, now had a courtesy delay feature for lights off. The center console provided integral cupholders, storage space, a higher, more comfortable armrest, and an auxiliary 12-volt DC power jack. A new overhead console included adjustable map lights and dedicated storage space for sunglasses and a garage door opener. Dual sun visors with lighted vanity mirrors now included pull-out extensions to help block out glare. A convenience strap was provided on the visors. A new convenience net secured loose parcels in the luggage area. A cargo-area security shade was provided for the luggage area. A remote keyless entry system was now offered. The Jimmy also had a new integral steel sleeve in the steering column to protect the ignition lock cylinder. An available power driver's seat, adjustable in six directions also featured a power lumbar adjustment for the driver and front passenger seats.

Exterior functional improvements included a more aerodynamic and functional luggage rack, a larger tailgate handle, and an easier-to-use spare-tire carrier. The Solar-Ray™ window glass was standard on all Jimmys. Available for all Jimmys was the new Hydra-Matic 4L60-E automatic transmission. Both the standard 4.3 liter (LB4) and the enhanced 4.3 liter (L35) V-6 engines had several improvements. They included a balance shaft, a more reliable thermostat, revised camshaft profiles for better idle stability, and new intake manifolds and cylinder-head passages for better breathing. A single-rail shifter for the five-speed manual transmission reduced lateral movement of the gear lever and minimized the possibility of blocked shifts.

1993 Jimmy two-door

I.D. DATA: The V.I.N. plate was mounted on the lower left side windshield corner. The V.I.N. consisted of 17 elements. The first, the number 1, identified the U.S. as the nation of origin. The letter G followed for the manufacturer: General Motors. The third entry, the letter T, represented the make as GMC. The GVWR brake system identification followed. Next came the truck line and chassis type; the letter K indicated four-wheel drive. The truck series was identified by a number: 1-1/2 ton. The truck body type identification was next: 8-Utility. The engine code was next: N-4.3 liter V-6 followed by a check digit. The model year was identified by the letter N. The assembly plant code followed. The final six digits were the plant sequential production number.

Model Number	Body Type	Factory Price	GVW	Shipping Weight	Prod. Total
Jimmy					
TT10506	2-dr. Util.	$N.A.	4700	3295	—
TT10506	4-dr. Util.	$N.A.	5100	—	—

STANDARD ENGINE: Engine Type: OHV, cast iron block. V-6. Order Code LB4. Bore x Stroke: 4.00 in. x 3.48 in. Lifters: Hydraulic. Number of main bearings-5. Fuel Induction: Electronic fuel injection. Compression Ratio: 9.1:1. Displacement: 262 cu. in. (4.3 liter). Horsepower: Net: 165 @ 4000 rpm. Torque: Net: 235 lb.-ft. @ 2800 rpm. Oil capacity: 5 qt. with filter change. Fuel Requirements: Unleaded.

OPTIONAL ENGINE: Engine Type: OHV, cast iron block. V-6. 4.3 L Enhanced. Order Code L35. Bore x Stroke: 4.00 in. x 3.48 in. Lifters: Hydraulic. Number of main bearings-5. Fuel Induction: Electronic fuel injection. Compression Ratio: 9.1:1. Displacement: 262 cu. in. (4.3 liter). Horsepower: Net: 200 @ 4500 rpm. Torque: Net: 260 lb.-ft. @ 3600 rpm. Oil capacity: 5 qt. with filter change. Fuel Requirements: Unleaded.

CHASSIS FEATURES: Carbon steel, welded front box section and open channel rear section. Dimensions: Two-door: Side rail dimensions: 2.28 in. (width) x 5.00 in. (depth) x 0.118 in. (thickness). Overall length: 162.46 in. Side rail section modulus: 1.78. Dimensions: Four-door: Side rail dimensions: 2.28 in. (width) x 5.00 in. (depth) x 0.118 in. (thickness). Overall length: 168.96 in. Side rail section modulus: 1.78.

SUSPENSION AND RUNNING GEAR: Front Suspension: Independent with torsion bar springs, 25mm dia. shock absorbers. 1.26 in. stabilizer bar. Capacity: 1200 lbs. each at ground. Optional: 32mm, 46mm shock absorbers. Rear Suspension: Two-stage 4-leaf shot-peened springs. Capacity: Two-door: 1350 lbs. each at ground, Four-door: 1450 lb. each at ground. 25mm shock absorbers. Optional: 32mm, 46mm shock absorbers. Front Axle. Type: Independent GM Hypoid, tubular driving. Capacity: 2400 lb. Rear Axle. Type: Semi-floating GM Hypoid Capacity: Two-door: 2700 lb. Four-door: 2900 lb. Final Drive Ratio: 3.08:1. Optional: 3.42:1. Transfer Case: New Process 231. Ratios: 2.72,1.00:1. Brakes: Type: Hydraulic, power assisted self-adjusting. Front: Discs. Rear: Drums. Dimensions: Front: 10.5 in. x 1.03 in. rotor. Rear: 9.5 in. x 2.0 in. Wheels: 15 x 6.00 in. Optional: 15 x 7.0 in. Rally wheels, 15 x 7.0 in. Cast aluminum (RPO N90), 15 x 7.0 in. cast aluminum (RPO N60). Tires: P205/75R15 steel belted radial All-Season black sidewall. Optional: P205/75R15 black sidewall, All-Season steel-belted radial, P205/75R15 on-off road steel belted radial, white letters, P205/75R15 All-Season steel belted radial, white letters, P205/75R15 on-off road steel belted radial black sidewall, P205/75R15 steel belted radial, front: Highway, Rear: On-off road, P235/75R15 on-off road steel belted radial white letters. Steering: Variable ratio, integral power. Ratio: 17.5:1. Turning diameter: 35.4 ft. Transmission: 5-speed manual with overdrive. Ratios: 4.02, 2.32, 1.40, 1.00, 0.83:1. Reverse: 3.74:1. Optional: 4-speed electronic Hydra-Matic 4L60-E (available only with L35). Ratios: 3.06, 1.63, 1.0, 0.70:1. Reverse: 2.29:1.

VEHICLE DIMENSIONS: Wheelbase: Two-door/Four-door: 100.5 in./107.0 in. Overall Length: Two-door/Four-door: 170.3 in./176.8 in. Front/Rear Tread 54.1 in./ 54.1 in. Overall Height: 62.8 in. Width: 65.4 in. Front/Rear Overhang: 30.6/39.2 in. Approach/Departure Degrees: 28° 17'/25.5° 30'. Ground Clearance: Front axle: 8.5 in. Rear axle: 8.1 in. Load space: Two-door: With rear seat installed: 35.5 in. x 50.0 in. x 35.0 in. With rear seat removed or folded: 68.6 in. x 53.4 in. x 35.0 in. Four-door: With rear seat installed: 38.5 in. x 52.5 in. x 34.5 in. With rear seat removed or folded: 76.1 in. x 52.5 in. x 34.5 in. Maximum cargo space: 2-door: 67.3 cu. ft. 4-door: 74.3 cu. ft.

CAPACITIES: Fuel Tank: 20 gal. tank. Coolant system capacity: 12.0 qt.

ACCOMMODATIONS: Seating Capacity: Standard: Two-door: Driver and passenger front high back bucket sets. Optional: 3 passenger rear bench seat. Four-door: 5 passenger with standard rear bench seat. The following dimensions apply to the Jimmy two-door: Front legroom: 42.5 in. Rear legroom: 35.5 in. Front shoulder room: 53.9 in. Rear shoulder room: 56.1 in. Front hip room: 50.5 in. Rear hip room: 37.5 in.

INSTRUMENTATION: 0-100 mph speedometer, 99,999.9 mi.odometer, fuel gauge, gauges for voltmeter, oil pressure, engine coolant temperature.Warning lights for brake operating system, hazard warning lights, directional lights, seat belt warning.

OPTIONS AND PRICES: Air conditioning: Air dam with fog lamps. Optional axle ratio. Locking rear differential. Heavy-duty battery. Spare tire and wheel carrier. Cold Climate Package. Heavy-duty radiator. Heavy-duty radiator and engine oil cooler. Driver Convenience Package (RPO ZM7). Includes ComforTilt steering wheel and intermittent wiper system. Driver Convenience Package (RPO ZM8). Includes rear window defroster and tailgate release. California Emissions Package. Color-keyed front floor mats (two-door only). Rear color-keyed floor mats. Deep tinted glass (RPO AJ1). Deep tinted glass with light tinted rear window (RPO AA3). Electronic instrumentation. Black luggage carrier. Exterior electric remote mirrors. Visor mirrors, left and right side. Black wheel opening molding. Operating Convenience Package. Includes power door locks and power windows. Special two-tone paint. Deluxe two-tone paint. Electronically tuned AM/FM stereo radio with Seek-Scan and digital clock. Electronically tuned AM/FM stereo radio with Seek-Scan, stereo cassette tape player. Electronically tuned AM/FM stereo radio with Seek-Scan, stereo cassette tape player with Search and Repeat, graphic equalizer and digital clock. Delete radio: $95 credit. Special custom cloth reclining high-back bucket seats. Deluxe cloth reclining high-back bucket seats. Folding rear bench seat. Leather reclining high-back bucket seats, two-door. Transfer case and front differential skid plates and steering linkage shield. Front and rear heavy-duty shock absorbers. Electronic speed control. SLS Sport Equipment. Body striping. Sunroof, manual, non-removable, two-door only. Heavy-duty front springs. Off-road suspension, two-door only. Light-Duty Trailering Package. Heavy-Duty Trailering Special Package. Tahoe Package: Sport Package. 4-speed automatic transmission. Rallye wheels. Cast aluminum wheels. Grey aluminum wheels. Sliding rear side window, two-door only. Rear window wiper/washer.

HISTORICAL FOOTNOTES: The 1993 Jimmy was announced on September 1, 1992.

GMC S-15 PICKUPS

1983-1990

1983 S-15 PICKUP

The S-15 GMC trucks were available as four-wheel drive models for 1983. The only S-15 versions not offered as 4x4s were the chassis and Utility cab models. An extended cab model, new for the S-15 line in 1983, was also available in four-wheel drive form. The extension added 14.5 inches to cab length, sufficient for 18.8 cu. ft. of additional cargo room or two side-mounted jump seats. The extended cab model had a 73 in. pickup box and a 122.9 in. wheelbase. The right front seat on extended cab models automatically moved forward on its track when folded. Both short and long wheelbase conventional models were also listed.

The standard Sierra trim level included chrome and black grille, headlight and parking lamp bezels with chrome finish and black trim, chromed front and rear bumpers with rub strips, black windshield and rear window moldings, left and right black outside mirrors, radial-ply tires and 15 in. argent wheels with hubcaps. The Sierra interior provided a front bench seat in vinyl trim in a choice of four colors, and color-keyed instrument panel, sun shades, headliner and windshield pillars. Also included were these items: Front and rear passenger assist handles, headlights-on warning buzzer, rubber floor covering, interior light, door/roof sound deadener, and front floor insulation. The optional High Sierra Classic Package replaced counterpart items or added these new items to the Sierra trim content: Deluxe chrome front end with rub strips, chrome grille, cigarette lighter, cargo area lamp, and bright wheel trim rings. The optional Sierra Classic Package contained these items: Chromed grille, cigarette lighter, right hand sun visor, body side and wheel opening moldings, spare tire cover, and gauges for voltmeter, engine coolant temperature, oil pressure and trip odometer.

The Gypsy Package added to or replaced the Sierra Classic features with the following: Painted color-keyed front bumper and Gypsy two-tone paint. Available exterior colors for the S-15 trucks were midnight blue, silver metallic, midnight black, light blue metallic, frost white, sunshine yellow, almond, nugget gold metallic, cinnamon red, apple red and, as a secondary color only, satin black.

The S-15's Insta-Trac four-wheel drive system was the first 4x4 system to have a lighted action display of the gear position. To shift from rear-wheel drive into four-wheel drive the driver moved the shift lever on the lighted shift console from 2 Wheel to 4 High. When the lever is moved from 2 Wheel to 4 High the transfer case divided the torque. At the same time a locking sleeve in the front axle engaged the central disconnect to provide power to both front axle shafts. Shifting from 4x4 to rear-wheel drive was accomplished by shifting from 4 High to 2 Wheel and the locking sleeve disengaged the central disconnect, allowing the front axle to freewheel. The truck had to be stopped only when shifting into and out of four-wheel drive low.

1983 GMC S-15 Sierra Classic club coupe

I.D. DATA: The V.I.N. plate was mounted on the lower left side windshield corner. The V.I.N. consisted of 17 elements. The first, the number 1, identified the U.S. as the nation of origin. The letter G followed for the manufacturer: General Motors. The third entry, the letter T, represented the make as GMC. The GVWR brake system identification followed. Next came the truck line and chassis type; the letter K indicated four-wheel drive. The truck series was identified by a number: 1-1/2 ton. The truck body type identification was next: 4-Two-door cab. The engine code was next: Y-2.0 liter, A-1.9 liter, B-2.8 liter V-6, followed by a check digit. The model year was identified by the letter D. The assembly plant code followed. The final six digits were the plant sequential production number.

Model Number	Body Type	Factory Price	GVW	Shipping Weight	Prod. Total
S-15					
T10603	108.3 in. wb. Pickup	$7537	3825[1]	2886	40,491[2]
T10803	117.9 in. wb. Pickup	$7690	3825[1]	2966	—
T10653	122.9 in. wb. Ext. Cab	$7919	3825[1]	3024	—

NOTE 1: 4650 lb. GVW optional for 1000 lb. payload, standard GVW for 1500 lb. payload is 4050 lb. with 4750 lb. optional.
NOTE 2: Calendar year sales for both two-wheel drive and four-wheel drive models.

STANDARD ENGINE: All states except California: Ordering Code LQ2. Produced by GM-Chevrolet Motor Division. Engine Type: Cast iron block. OHV, In-line 4. Bore x Stroke: 3.50 in. x 3.15 in. Lifters: Hydraulic. Carburetion: Two barrel. Compression Ratio: 9.3:1. Displacement: 121 cu. in. (2.0 liter). Horsepower: Net: 83 @ 4600 rpm. Torque: Net: 108 lb.-ft. @ 2400 rpm. Oil capacity: 5 qt. with filter change. Fuel Requirements: Unleaded.

STANDARD ENGINE: California only: Engine Type: Cast iron block. OHV, In-line 4. Ordering Code: LR1. Produced by Isuzu Motors Limited, Japan. Bore x Stroke: 3.42 in. x 3.23 in. Lifters: Hydraulic. Carburetion: Two barrel. Compression Ratio: 8.4:1. Displacement: 119 cu. in. (1.9 liters). Horsepower: Net: 82 @ 4600 rpm. Torque: Net: 101 lb.-ft. @ 3000 rpm. Oil capacity: qt. with filter change. Fuel Requirements: Unleaded.

OPTIONAL ENGINE: 50 states: Engine Type: OHV, cast iron block. V-6. Order Code LR2. Produced by GM-Chevrolet Motor Division. Bore x Stroke: 3.50 in. x 2.99 in. Lifters: Hydraulic. Number of main bearings-5. Carburetion: 2-barrel. Compression Ratio: 8.5:1. Displacement: 173 cu. in. (2.8 liter). Horsepower: Net: 110 @ 4800 rpm. Torque: Net: 145 lb.-ft. @ 2100 rpm. Oil capacity: 5 qt. with filter change. Fuel Requirements: Unleaded.

CHASSIS FEATURES: Carbon steel, 39,000 psi., welded front box section and open channel rear section, section modulus: 2.19.

SUSPENSION AND RUNNING GEAR: Front Suspension: Independent with torsion bar springs, 25mm dia. shock absorbers. 32mm stabilizer bar. Capacity: 1250 lbs. each at ground. Optional: 32mm shock absorbers. Rear Suspension: Two-stage multi-leaf shot-peened springs. Capacity: 1150 lbs. each at ground. 25mm shock absorbers. Optional: 32mm shock absorbers. Front Axle. Type: Hypoid, tubular driving. Capacity: 2300 lb. Rear Axle. Type: Salisbury, hypoid. Capacity: 2700 lb. Final Drive Ratio: Standard 4-spd. manual transmission and optional 5-spd. manual overdrive: 3.73:1 (3.08:1 for high altitude emission system). Automatic transmission: 3.42:1 (3.73:1 for high altitude emission system). Optional: Standard 4-spd. manual transmission and optional 5-spd. manual overdrive: 4.11:1 (3.73:1 for high altitude emission system). Automatic transmission: 3.73:1. Transfer Case: New Process 207. Brakes: Type: Hydraulic, power assisted self-adjusting. Front: Discs. Rear: Drums. Dimensions: Front: 10.51 in. x 2.0 in. rotor. Rear: 9.49 in. x 2.0 in. Wheels: 15 in. Tires: P195/75R15 glass belted radial black sidewall. Optional: P195/75R15 black sidewall, P205/75R15 black sidewall, P205/75R15 white sidewall, P205/75R15 white letters, P205/75R15 on/off road black sidewall. Steering: Manual. Optional: Power. Transmission: 4-speed manual. Optional: 5-speed manual with overdrive, 4-speed automatic with overdrive (with V-6 engine only). Clutch: 4-cyl. engine: 9.13 in. dia., V-6: 9.76 in. dia.

VEHICLE DIMENSIONS: Wheelbase: Short wheelbase/Long wheelbase/Extended cab: 108.5 in./117.9 in./122.9 in. Overall Length: Short wheelbase/Long wheelbase/Extended cab: 178.2 in./170.3 in./194.1 in./208.6 in. Front/Rear overhang: Short wheelbase/Long wheelbase/Extended cab: 30.6 in./39.3 in.-30.6 in./45.6 in.-30.6 in./39.3 in. Overall Height: 61.2 in. Width: 64.8 in. Tailgate Height: 16.0 in.

CAPACITIES: Fuel Tank: 13.2 gal. Optional: Replacement 20 gal. tank.

ACCOMMODATIONS: Seating Capacity: Standard: 3. Headroom: 39.5 in. Legroom: 42.4 in.

INSTRUMENTATION: 0-100 mph speedometer, 99,999.9 mi. odometer, fuel gauge, warning lights for alternator, oil pressure, engine coolant temperature, brake operating system, hazard warning lights, directional lights, seat belt warning.

OPTIONS AND PRICES: High Sierra Package. Sierra Classic Package. Gypsy Package. Air conditioning. Automatic speed control. ComforTilt steering wheel. Power steering. Gauges for oil pressure, engine coolant temperature and voltmeter with trip odometer. Tachometer with gauges. Digital clock (with radio only). Delco radios. Below eye-level mirrors. Styled wheels with special hub ornament and bright trim rings. Operating Convenience Package. Includes power windows and door locks. Dome/reading light. Halogen headlamps. 66 amp Delcotron generator. Heavy-duty Freedom battery. Reclining bucket seat backs. Center console. Color-keyed floor mats. Visor mirror. Door edge guards. Body striping. Spare tire cover. Body side/wheel opening moldings. Color-keyed front/rear bumpers. Black front bumper guards. Rear air deflector. Front tow hooks. Black or bright wheel-opening moldings. Cast aluminum wheels. Bright wheel trim rings. Full-size spare tire. Heavy-duty radiator. Heavy-duty radiator with transmission or engine cooler with V-6 and automatic transmission. Locking differential rear axle. Heavy-duty front and rear shock absorbers. Off-Road Chassis Package. Stone shield for transfer case and differential carrier. Intermittent windshield wipers. Engine block heater. Deadweight trailer hitch. Trailering Package (either 4,000 or 5,000 lb).

HISTORICAL FOOTNOTES: GMC reported that its S series high-mileage trucks "revitalized the American trucking scene in 1982 [and] rolled into '83 with more to offer compact-truck enthusiasts...."

1984 S-15 PICKUP

Four new colors were added to the S-15 color selection for 1984. All models with manual transmission had a new automatic-adjusting clutch for smoother operation. The optional automatic transmission was equipped with a new torque converter. The optional automatic speed control had a new one mph tap-up/tap-down feature for easy adjustment of the pre-set speed. A new option was a Heavy-Duty Front Suspension Package recommended for snow-plow equipped four-wheel drive models. The sun visors had a new sliding feature for larger sun-blocking coverage. Trucks with the V-6 engine had "2.8 liter V-6" identification below the driver's side headlight. This replaced the small V-6 emblem mounted on the front fender of 1983 models. A new Off-Road Package was introduced in October, 1983. Among its features were Delco Bilstein gas-pressure shock absorbers, transfer case shield, fuel tank shield, front tow hooks and jounce bumpers. This option required the optional 1500 lb. Payload Package and P235 steel belted on/off-road white-lettered tires, including full-size spare. The 1984 interior color selection consisted of blue, carmine, charcoal or saddle tan. Exterior colors were:

Standard Catalog of American Four-Wheel Drive Vehicles

Silver metallic, frost white, midnight black, light blue metallic, galaxy blue metallic, doeskin tan, Indian bronze metallic, desert sand metallic, apple red, cinnamon red and, as a secondary color only, satin black. The Sport interior was available with optional High Country Sheepskin in saddle tan.

1984 S-15 Sierra Classic pickup with dealer-installed equipment

I.D. DATA: The V.I.N. plate was mounted on the lower left side windshield corner. The V.I.N. consisted of 17 elements. The first, the number 1, identified the U.S. as the nation of origin. The letter G followed for the manufacturer: General Motors. The third entry, the letter T, represented the make as GMC. The GVWR brake system identification followed. Next came the truck line and chassis type; the letter K indicated four-wheel drive. The truck series was identified by a number: 1-1/2 ton. The truck body type identification was next: 4-Two-door cab. The engine code was next: Y-2.0 liter, A-1.9 liter, B-2.8 liter V-6, followed by a check digit. The model year was identified by the letter E. The assembly plant code followed. The final six digits were the plant sequential production number.

Model Number	Body Type	Factory Price	GVW	Shipping Weight	Prod. Total
S-15					
T10603	108.3 in. wb. Pickup	$7592	3825[1]	2923	43,712[2]
T10803	117.9 in. wb. Pickup	$7745	3825[1]	2997	—
T10653	122.9 in. wb. Ext. Cab	$7974	3825[1]	3066	—

NOTE 1: 4650 lb. GVW optional for 1000 lb. payload, standard GVW for 1500 lb. payload is 4050 lb. with 4750 lb. optional.
NOTE 2: Calendar year sales for both two-wheel drive and four-wheel drive models.

STANDARD ENGINE: All states except California: Ordering Code LQ2. Produced by GM-Chevrolet Motor Division. Engine Type: Cast iron block. OHV, In-line 4. Bore x Stroke: 3.50 in. x 3.15 in. Lifters: Hydraulic. Carburetion: Two barrel. Compression Ratio: 9.3:1. Displacement: 121 cu. in. (2.0 liter). Horsepower: Net: 83 @ 4600 rpm. Torque: Net: 108 lb.-ft. @ 2400 rpm. Oil capacity: 5 qt. with filter change. Fuel Requirements: Unleaded.

STANDARD ENGINE: California only: Engine Type: Cast iron block. OHV, In-line 4. Ordering Code: LR1. Produced by Isuzu Motors Limited, Japan. Bore x Stroke: 3.42 in. x 3.23 in. Lifters: Hydraulic. Carburetion: Two barrel. Compression Ratio: 8.4:1. Displacement: 119 cu. in. (1.9 liters). Horsepower: Net: 82 @ 4600 rpm. Torque: Net: 101 lb.-ft. @ 3000 rpm. Oil capacity: 5 qt. with filter change. Fuel Requirements: Unleaded.

OPTIONAL ENGINE: 50 states: Required for 1500 lb. payload option. Engine Type: OHV, cast iron block. V-6. Order Code LR2. Produced by GM-Chevrolet Motor Division. Bore x Stroke: 3.50 in. x 2.99 in. Lifters: Hydraulic. Number of main bearings-5. Carburetion: 2-barrel. Compression Ratio: 8.5:1. Displacement: 173 cu. in. (2.8 liter). Horsepower: Net: 110 @ 4800 rpm. Torque: Net: 145 lb.-ft. @ 2100 rpm. Oil capacity: 5 qt. with filter change. Fuel Requirements: Unleaded.

CHASSIS FEATURES: Carbon steel, 39,000 psi., welded front box section and open channel rear section, section modulus: 2.19.

SUSPENSION AND RUNNING GEAR: Front Suspension: Independent with torsion bar springs, 25mm dia. shock absorbers. 32mm stabilizer bar. Capacity: 1250 lbs. each at ground. Optional: 32mm shock absorbers. Rear Suspension: Two-stage multi-leaf shot-peened springs. Capacity: 1150 lbs. each at ground. 25mm shock absorbers. Optional: 32mm shock absorbers. Front Axle. Type: Hypoid, tubular driving. Capacity: 2300 lb. Rear Axle. Type: Salisbury, hypoid. Capacity: 2700 lb. Final Drive Ratio: Standard 4-spd. manual transmission and optional 5-spd. manual overdrive: 3.73:1 (3.08:1 for high altitude emission system). Automatic transmission: 3.42:1 (3.73:1 for high altitude emission system). Optional: Standard 4-spd. manual transmission and optional 5-spd. manual overdrive: 4.11:1 (3.73:1 for high altitude emission system). Automatic transmission: 3.73:1. Transfer Case: New Process 207. Brakes: Type: Hydraulic, power assisted self-adjusting. Front: Discs. Rear: Drums. Dimensions: Front: 10.51 in. x 2.0 in. rotor. Rear: 9.49 in. x 2.0 in. Wheels: 15 in. Tires: P195/75R15 glass belted radial black sidewall. Optional: P195/75R15 black sidewall, P205/75R15 black sidewall, P205/75R15 white sidewall, P205/75R15 white letters, P205/75R15 on/off road black sidewall. Steering: Manual. Optional: Power. Transmission: 4-speed manual. Optional: 5-speed manual with overdrive, 4-speed automatic with overdrive (with V-6 engine only). Clutch: 4-cyl. engine: 9.13 in. dia., V-6: 9.76 in. dia.

VEHICLE DIMENSIONS: Wheelbase: Short wheelbase/Long wheelbase/Extended cab: 108.5 in./117.9 in./122.9 in. Overall Length: Short wheelbase/Long wheelbase/Extended cab: 178.2 in./170.3 in./194.1 in./208.6 in. Front/Rear overhang: Short wheelbase/Long wheelbase/Extended cab: 30.6 in./39.3 in.-30.6 in./45.6 in.-30.6 in./39.3 in. Overall Height: 61.2 in. Width: 64.8 in. Tailgate Height: 16.0 in.

CAPACITIES: Fuel Tank: 13.2 gal. Optional: Replacement 20 gal. tank.

ACCOMMODATIONS: Seating Capacity: Standard: 3. Headroom: 39.5 in. Legroom: 42.4 in.

INSTRUMENTATION: 0-100 mph speedometer, 99,999.9 mi. odometer, fuel gauge, warning lights for alternator, oil pressure, engine coolant temperature, brake operating system, hazard warning lights, directional lights, seat belt warning.

OPTIONS AND PRICES: High Sierra Package. Sierra Classic Package. Gypsy Package. Air conditioning. Automatic speed control. ComforTilt steering wheel. Power steering. Gauges for oil pressure, engine coolant temperature and voltmeter with trip odometer. Tachometer with gauges. Digital clock (with radio only). Delco radios. Below eye-level mirrors. Styled wheels with special hub ornament and bright trim rings. Operating Convenience Package. Includes power windows and door locks. Dome/reading light. Halogen headlamps. 66 amp Delcotron generator. Heavy-duty Freedom battery. Reclining bucket seat backs. Center console. Color-keyed floor mats. Visor mirror. Door edge guards. Body striping. Spare tire cover. Body side/wheel opening moldings. Color-keyed front/rear bumpers. Black front bumper guards. Rear

air deflector. Front tow hooks. Black or bright wheel opening moldings. Cast aluminum wheels. Bright wheel trim rings. Full-size spare tire. Heavy-duty radiator. Heavy-duty radiator with transmission or engine cooler with V-6 and automatic transmission. Locking differential rear axle. Heavy-duty front and rear shock absorbers. Off-Road Chassis Package. Stone shield for transfer case and differential carrier. Intermittent windshield wipers. Engine block heater. Deadweight trailer hitch. Trailering Package (either 4,000 or 5,000 lb)

HISTORICAL FOOTNOTES: Referring to its S-15 trucks, GMC reported that for '84 "these amazingly popular trucks surpass even themselves!"

1985 S-15 PICKUP

S-15 innovations for 1985 included a new two-tone paint option with new sunshine body striping, restyled fender nameplates and a new paint scheme for the optional styled wheels. The Gypsy Sport grille, headlamp/side marker lamp bezels, key cylinder covers and taillamps had a new black finish. Antennas for the optional radios also had this new black finish. Both the High Sierra and Sierra Classic trim offered a choice of new custom vinyl or extra cost custom cloth upholstery. The custom cloth fabric was also used for the Sierra Classic door trim panel inserts. A new computer-controlled Tech IV, 2.5 liter, 4-cylinder, electronically fuel injected was the standard 4x4 S-15 engine for 1985. It had low friction roller hydraulic lifters, and swirl inlet ports. Its 92 horsepower and 134 lb.-ft. of torque represented 10 percent more horsepower and 22 percent more torque than the previous standard engine. Other developments for 1985 included use of a partitioned fuse panel, 2-side galvanized steel for the hood inner panel and fender skirts; welded-on bumper brackets, new adjust-on-release rear brake adjusters, new valving for shock absorbers, new controls for the optional intermittent windshield wipers, and new variable-ratio manual steering gear. The interior colors for 1985 were blue, carmine, charcoal and saddle tan. Exterior colors were midnight black, galaxy blue metallic, Indian bronze metallic, apple red, cinnamon red, desert sand metallic, silver metallic, doeskin tan, and frost white.

1985 S-15 Sierra Classic pickup

I.D. DATA: The V.I.N. plate was mounted on the lower left side windshield corner. The V.I.N. consisted of 17 elements. The first, the number 1, identified the U.S. as the nation of origin. The letter G followed for the manufacturer: General Motors. The third entry, the letter T, represented the make as GMC. The GVWR brake system identification followed. Next came the truck line and chassis type; the letter K indicated four-wheel drive. The truck series was identified by a number: 1-1/2 ton. The truck body type identification was next: 4-Two-door cab. The engine code was next: E-2.5 liter, B-2.8 liter V-6, followed by a check digit. The model year was identified by the letter F. The assembly plant code followed. The final six digits were the plant sequential production number.

Model Number	Body Type	Factory Price	GVW	Shipping Weight	Prod. Total
S-15 with 2.8 liter V-6					
T10603	108.3 in. wb. Pickup	$7802	3825[1]	2918	—
T10803	117.9 in. wb. Pickup	$7955	3825[1]	3004	—
T10653	122.9 in. wb. Club Coupe	$8420	3825[1]	3072	—

NOTE 1: 4650 lb. GVW optional for 1000 lb. payload, standard GVW for 1500 lb. payload is 4050 lb. with 4750 lb. optional.

STANDARD ENGINE: Ordering Code LN8: Produced by Pontiac Motor Division. Engine Type: Cast iron block. OHV, In-line 4. Bore x Stroke: 4.0 in. x 3.0 in. Lifters: Hydraulic. Fuel induction: Electronic fuel injection. Compression Ratio: 9.0:1. Displacement: 151 cu. in. (2.5 liter). Horsepower: Net: 92 @ 4400 rpm. Torque: Net: 134 lb.-ft. @ 2800 rpm. Oil capacity: 5 qt. with filter change. Fuel Requirements: Unleaded.

OPTIONAL ENGINE: Engine Type: OHV, cast iron block. V-6. Order Code LR2. Produced by GM-Chevrolet Motor Division. Bore x Stroke: 3.50 in. x 2.99 in. Lifters: Hydraulic. Number of main bearings-5. Carburetion: 2-barrel. Compression Ratio: 8.5:1. Displacement: 173 cu. in. (2.8 liter). Horsepower: Net: 115 @ 4800 rpm. Torque: Net: 150 lb.-ft. @ 2100 rpm. Oil capacity: 5 qt. with filter change. Fuel Requirements: Unleaded.

CHASSIS FEATURES: Carbon steel, 39,000 psi., welded front box section and open channel rear section, section modulus: 2.19.

SUSPENSION AND RUNNING GEAR: Front Suspension: Independent with torsion bar springs, 25mm dia. shock absorbers. 32mm stabilizer bar. Capacity: 1250 lbs. each at ground. Optional: 32mm shock absorbers. Rear Suspension: Two-stage multi-leaf shot-peened springs. Capacity: 1150 lbs. each at ground. 25mm shock absorbers. Optional: 32mm shock absorbers. Front Axle. Type: Hypoid, tubular driving. Capacity: 2300 lb. Rear Axle. Type: Salisbury, hypoid. Capacity: 2700 lb. Final Drive Ratio: Standard 4-spd. manual transmission and optional 5-spd. manual overdrive: 3.73:1 (3.08:1 for high altitude emission system). Automatic transmission: 3.42:1 (3.73:1 for high altitude emission system). Optional: Standard 4-spd. manual transmission and optional 5-spd. manual overdrive: 4.11:1 (3.73:1 for high altitude emission system). Automatic transmission: 3.73:1. Transfer Case: New Process 207. Brakes: Type: Hydraulic, power assisted self-adjusting. Front: Discs. Rear: Drums. Dimensions: Front: 10.51 in. x 2.0 in. rotor. Rear: 9.49 in. x 2.0 in. Wheels: 15 in. Tires: P195/75R15 glass belted radial black sidewall. Optional: P195/75R15 black sidewall, P205/75R15 black sidewall, P205/75R15 white sidewall, P205/75R15 white letters, P205/75R15 on/off road black sidewall. Steering: Manual, variable ratio. Optional: Power. Transmission: 4-speed manual. Optional: 5-speed manual with overdrive, 4-speed automatic with overdrive (with V-6 engine only). Clutch: 4-cyl. engine: 9.13 in. dia., V-6: 9.76 in. dia.

VEHICLE DIMENSIONS: Wheelbase: Short wheelbase/Long wheelbase/Extended cab: 108.5 in./117.9 in./122.9 in. Overall Length: Short wheelbase/Long wheelbase/Extended cab: 178.2 in./170.3 in./194.1 in./208.6 in. Overall Height: 61.2 in. Width: 64.8 in. Tailgate Height: 16.0 in.

CAPACITIES: Fuel Tank: 13.2 gal. Optional: Replacement 20 gal. tank.

ACCOMMODATIONS: Seating Capacity: Standard: 3. Headroom: 39.5 in. Legroom: 42.4 in.

INSTRUMENTATION: 0-100 mph speedometer, 99,999.9 mi. odometer, fuel gauge, warning lights for alternator, oil pressure, engine coolant temperature, brake operating system, hazard warning lights, directional lights, seat belt warning.

OPTIONS AND PRICES: High Sierra Package: $339. Sierra Classic Package: $442. Gypsy Package: $940. Custom vinyl bench seat: $50. Custom vinyl high-back bucket seats: $128-$178 depending upon Trim Package. Custom two-tone paint: $200. Special two-tone paint: $167-$311 depending upon Trim Package. Sport two-tone paint: $162-$227 depending upon Trim Package. California emissions system: $99. 2.6 liter V-6 engine: $225. 4-speed overdrive automatic transmission: $670. Optional axle ratio: $36. Locking rear differential: $238. Pre-cleaner air cleaner: 49. 5-speed manual overdrive transmission: $175. All-Weather air conditioning: 705. Heavy-duty battery: $53. Front black bumper guards: $30. Off-Road Package: $602-$658 depending upon Trim Package. Cold Climate Package: $107-$179 depending upon Trim Package. Front compartment console: $108. Engine oil cooling system: $120. Heavy-duty radiator: $53. Heavy-duty radiator and transmission oil cooler: $59 with air conditioning, $112 without air conditioning. Spare tire cover: $32. Air deflector: $41. Rear window defogger: $114 with air conditioning, $145 without air conditioning. Power door locks: $135. Color-keyed floor mats: $15. Gauge Package. Includes voltmeter, engine coolant temperature, oil pressure: $58. Gauge Package plus tachometer: $55-$113 depending upon Trim Package. 66 amp Delcotron generator: $31. Deep tinted back window glass with light tinted windshield and side door glass: $55. Tinted glass, all windows: $46. Halogen headlights: $22. Engine block heater: $31. Engine compartment light: $15. Exterior left and right side painted mirrors: $50. Exterior left and right side bright mirrors: $83. Body side and wheel opening moldings: $17-$144 depending upon Trim Package. Door edge guards: $17. Bright wheel opening moldings: $28. Black wheel opening moldings: $12-$41 depending upon Trim Package. Operating Convenience Package: $325. AM radio: $112. AM/FM radio: $171. AM/FM radio with clock: $210. AM/FM stereo radio with electronic tuning: $238 AM/FM stereo radio and clock with electronic tuning: $277. AM/FM stereo radio with Seek-Scan, stereo cassette tape, clock and graphic equalizer and electronic tuning and premium rear speakers: $594. Premium rear speakers: $25. Transfer case shield: $67. Heavy-duty front and rear shock absorbers: $34. Full-size spare tire: $46-90 depending upon size. Electronic speed control: $260. ComforTilt steering wheel: $115. Striping: $65. Heavy-duty suspension equipment: $59. 20 gal. fuel tank: $49. Two front towing hooks: $36. Deadweight trailer hitch: $64. Heavy-duty trailering special: $199. Light-duty trailering special: $103. Wheel trim rings: $56. Rallye wheels: $32-$88 depending upon Trim Package. Styled wheels: $32-$88 depending upon Trim Package. Cast aluminum wheels: $238-$294 depending upon Trim Package. Power side door windows: $190. Intermittent windshield wiper system: $55.

HISTORICAL FOOTNOTES: GMC said the S-15 models were "big wheels on the compact truck scene."

1986 S-15 PICKUP

Changes found in the 1986 S15 were mainly cosmetic. The instrument panel now included an instrument cluster with tell-tale lights as well as the voltmeter, oil pressure and engine coolant temperature gauges. A panel bottom-mounted tray was a useful addition. Restyled door trim panels were installed. The switches for the optional power windows were repositioned on the door panels. A new black molded urethane steering wheel was used for all models. A simulated leather look highlighted the Sport steering wheel. New tweed-pattern cloth seat trim was used for the Sport Package. Lighter-weight high silicon pistons was used for the standard 2.5 liter engine. The 2.8 liter V-6 was equipped with electronic fuel injection. Exterior front body identification for models with this engine now read "2.8 Fuel Injection." A higher-capacity Delco Freedom III battery was installed on trucks with the V-6 engine. The optional heavy-duty battery offered for both engines had a higher capacity for 1986. Also new for 1986 was a lighter-weight radiator with a standard copper-brass core with crossflow coolant movement and plastic side tanks. The exterior color selection for 1986 consisted of midnight black, steel grey metallic, light blue metallic, galaxy blue metallic, doeskin tan, Indian bronze metallic, cinnamon red, apple red, black gold and silver metallic (used as a secondary color only).

I.D. DATA: The V.I.N. plate was mounted on the lower left side windshield corner. The V.I.N. consisted of 17 elements. The first, the number 1, identified the U.S. as the nation of origin. The letter G followed for the manufacturer: General Motors. The third entry, the letter T, represented the make as GMC. The GVWR brake system identification followed. Next came the truck line and chassis type; the letter K indicated four-wheel drive. The truck series was identified by a number: 1-1/2 ton. The truck body type identification was next: 4-Two-door cab. The engine code was next: E-2.5 liter, B-2.8 liter V-6, followed by a check digit. The model year was identified by the letter G. The assembly plant code followed. The final six digits were the plant sequential production number.

Model Number	Body Type	Factory Price	GVW	Shipping Weight	Prod. Total
S-15 with 2.8 liter V-6					
T10603	108.3 in. wb. Pickup	$8162	3825[1]	2918	49,139[2]
T10803	117.9 in. wb. Pickup	$8397	3825[1]	3004	—
T10653	122.9 in. wb. Ext. Cab	$8849	3825[1]	3072	—

NOTE 1: 4650 lb. GVW optional for 1000 lb. payload, standard GVW for 1500 lb. payload is 4050 lb. with 4750 lb. optional.
NOTE 2: 1986 model year sales, all S-15 models.

STANDARD ENGINE: Ordering Code LN8: Produced by Pontiac Motor Division. Engine Type: Cast iron block. OHV, In-line 4. Bore x Stroke: 4.0 in. x 3.0 in. Lifters: Hydraulic. Number of main bearings-5. Fuel induction: Electronic fuel injection. Compression Ratio: 9.0:1. Displacement: 151 cu. in. (2.5 liter). Horsepower: Net: 92 @ 4400 rpm. Torque: Net: 134 lb.-ft. @ 2800 rpm. Oil capacity: 5 qt. with filter change. Fuel Requirements: Unleaded.

OPTIONAL ENGINE: Engine Type: OHV, cast iron block. V-6. Order Code LR2. Produced by GM-Chevrolet Motor Division. Bore x Stroke: 3.50 in. x 2.99 in. Lifters: Hydraulic. Number of main bearings-5. Fuel Induction: Electronic fuel injection. Compression Ratio: 8.9:1. Displacement: 173 cu. in. (2.8 liter). Horsepower: Net: 125 @ 4800 rpm. Torque: Net: 150 lb.-ft. @ 2200 rpm. Oil capacity: 5 qt. with filter change. Fuel Requirements: Unleaded.

CHASSIS FEATURES: Carbon steel, 39,000 psi., welded front box section and open channel rear section, section modulus: 2.19.

SUSPENSION AND RUNNING GEAR: Front Suspension: Independent with torsion bar springs, 25mm dia. shock absorbers. 32mm stabilizer bar. Capacity: 1250 lbs. each at ground. Optional: 32mm shock absorbers. Rear Suspension: Two-stage multi-leaf shot-peened springs. Capacity: 1150 lbs. each at ground. 25mm shock absorbers. Optional: 32mm shock absorbers. Front Axle. Type: Hypoid, tubular driving. Capacity: 2300 lb. Rear Axle. Type: Salisbury, hypoid. Capacity: 2700 lb. Final Drive Ratio: Standard 4-spd. manual transmission and optional 5-spd. manual overdrive: 3.73:1 (3.08:1 for high altitude emission system). Automatic transmission: 3.42:1 (3.73:1 for high altitude emission system). Optional: Standard 4-spd. manual transmission and optional 5-spd. manual overdrive: 4.11:1 (3.73:1 for high altitude emission system). Automatic transmission: 3.73:1. Transfer Case: New Process 207. Brakes: Type: Hydraulic, power assisted self-adjusting. Front: Discs. Rear: Drums. Dimensions: Front: 10.51 in. x 2.0 in. rotor. Rear: 9.49 in. x 2.0 in. wheels: 15 in. Tires: P195/75R15 glass belted radial black sidewall. Optional: P195/75R15 black sidewall, P205/75R15 black sidewall, P205/75R15 white sidewall, P205/75R15 white letters, P205/75R15 on/off road black sidewall. Steering: Manual, variable ratio. Optional: Power. Transmission: 4-speed manual. Optional: 5-speed manual with overdrive, 4-speed automatic with overdrive (with V-6 engine only). Clutch: 4-cyl. engine: 9.13 in. dia., V-6: 9.76 in. dia.

VEHICLE DIMENSIONS: Wheelbase: Short wheelbase/Long wheelbase/Extended cab: 108.5 in./ 117.9 in./122.9 in. Overall Length: Short wheelbase/Long wheelbase/Extended cab: 178.2 in./170.3 in./194.1 in./208.6 in. Overall Height: 61.2 in. Width: 64.8 in. Tailgate Height: 16.0 in.

CAPACITIES: Fuel Tank: 13.2 gal. Optional: Replacement 20 gal. tank.

ACCOMMODATIONS: Seating Capacity: Standard: 3. Headroom: 39.5 in. Legroom: 42.4 in.

INSTRUMENTATION: 0-100 mph speedometer, 99,999.9 mi. odometer, fuel gauge, warning lights for alternator, oil pressure, engine coolant temperature, brake operating system, hazard warning lights, directional lights, seat belt warning.

OPTIONS AND PRICES: High Sierra Package: $339. Sierra Classic Package: $442. Gypsy Package: $940. Custom vinyl bench seat: $50. Custom vinyl high-back bucket seats: $128-$178 depending upon Trim Package. Custom two-tone paint: $200. Special two-tone paint: $167-$311 depending upon Trim Package. Sport two-tone paint: $162-$227 depending upon Trim Package. California emissions system: $99. 2.6 liter V-6 engine: $225. 4-speed overdrive automatic transmission: $670. Optional axle ratio: $36. Locking rear differential: $238. Pre-cleaner air cleaner: $49. 5-speed manual overdrive transmission: $175. All-Weather air conditioning: 705. Heavy-duty battery: $53. Front black bumper guards: $30. Off-Road Package: $602-$658 depending upon Trim Package. Cold Climate Package: $107-$179 depending upon Trim Package. Front compartment console: $108. Engine oil cooling system: $120. heavy-duty radiator: $53. Heavy-duty radiator and transmission oil cooler: $59 with air conditioning, $112 without air conditioning. Spare tire cover: $32. Air deflector: $41. Rear window defogger: $114 with air conditioning, $145 without air conditioning. Power door locks: $135. Color-keyed floor mats: $15. Gauge Package. Includes voltmeter, engine coolant temperature, oil pressure: $58. Gauge Package plus tachometer: $55-$113 depending upon Trim Package. 66 amp Delcotron generator: $31. Deep tinted back window glass with light tinted windshield and side door glass: $55. Tinted glass, all windows: $46. Halogen headlights: $22. Engine block heater: $31. Engine compartment light: $15. Exterior left and right side painted mirrors: $50. Exterior left and right side bright mirrors: $83. Body side and wheel opening moldings: $17-$144 depending upon Trim Package. Door edge guards: $17. Bright wheel opening moldings: $28. Black wheel opening moldings: $12-$41 depending upon Trim Package. Operating Convenience Package: $325. AM radio: $112. AM/FM radio: $171. AM/FM radio with clock: $210. AM/FM stereo radio with electronic tuning: $238 AM/FM stereo radio and clock with electronic tuning: $277. AM/FM stereo radio with Seek-Scan, stereo cassette tape, clock and graphic equalizer and electronic tuning and premium rear speakers: $594. Premium rear speakers: $25. Transfer case shield: $67. Heavy-duty front and rear shock absorbers: $34. Full-size spare tire: $46-90 depending upon size. Electronic speed control: $260. ComforTilt steering wheel: $115. Striping: $65. Heavy-duty suspension equipment: $59. 20 gal. fuel tank: $49. Two front towing hooks: $36. Deadweight trailer hitch: $64. Heavy-duty trailering special: $199. Light-duty trailering special: $103. Wheel trim rings: $56. Rallye wheels: $32-$88 depending upon Trim Package. Styled wheels: $32-$88 depending upon Trim Package. Cast aluminum wheels: $238-$294 depending upon Trim Package. Power side door windows: $190. Intermittent windshield wiper system: $55.

HISTORICAL FOOTNOTES: The 1986 S-15 models were introduced in Oct.,1985.

1987 S-15 PICKUP

A serpentine single belt accessory drive system replaced the conventional multiple V belts on both the 2.5 and 2.8 liter S-15 engines. The 2.5 liter Tech IV engine also had a new throttle modulation system that provided better control of engine speed with both manual and automatic transmissions. A new lightweight 85 amp generator featured improved performance over the older 78 amp unit. The new belt system featured longer service life and an automatic tensioner helped maintain proper belt adjustment. A special wax base undercoating was applied to the front stabilizer bar, rear axle and rear springs for added chassis protection against corrosion. A new Vaquaro upholstery including leather seat covering for the front bucket seats was offered for club coupe models fitted with either the Gypsy or High Sierra Package. A new color-keyed vinyl floor covering could be specified to replace the Gypsy's carpeting. The Gypsy exterior of a Sport two-tone paint style had black accents and a new-for-1987 black applique with red GMC letters for the tailgate. This applique was also used for the Sierra Classic.

1987 S-15 Jimmy High Sierra

I.D. DATA: The V.I.N. plate was mounted on the lower left side windshield corner. The V.I.N. consisted of 17 elements. The first, the number 1, identified the U.S. as the nation of origin. The letter G followed for the manufacturer: General Motors. The third entry, the letter T, represented the make as GMC. The GVWR brake system identification followed. Next came the truck line and chassis type; the letter K indicated four-wheel drive. The truck series was identified by a number: 1-1/2 ton. The truck body type identification was next: 4-Two-door cab. The engine code was next: E-2.5 liter, B-2.8 liter V-6, followed by a check digit. The model year was identified by the letter H. The assembly plant code followed. The final six digits were the plant sequential production number.

Model Number	Body Type	Factory Price	GVW	Shipping Weight	Prod. Total
S-15 with 2.8 liter V-6					
T10603	108.3 in. wb. Pickup	$9598	3825[1]	2923	—
T10803	117.9 in. wb. Pickup	$9865	3825[1]	3016	—
T10653	122.9 in. wb. Club Coupe	$10,330	3825[1]	3080	—

NOTE 1: 4650 lb. GVW optional for 1000 lb. payload, standard GVW for 1500 lb. payload is 4050 lb. with 4750 lb. optional.

STANDARD ENGINE: Ordering Code LN8: Produced by Pontiac Motor Division. Engine Type: Cast iron block. OHV, In-line 4. Bore x Stroke: 4.0 in. x 3.0 in. Lifters: Hydraulic. Number of main bearings-5. Fuel induction: Electronic fuel injection. Compression Ratio: 9.0:1. Displacement: 151 cu. in. (2.5 liter). Horsepower: Net: 92 @ 4400 rpm. Torque: Net: 134 lb.-ft. @ 2800 rpm. Oil capacity: 5 qt. with filter change. Fuel Requirements: Unleaded.

OPTIONAL ENGINE: Engine Type: OHV, cast iron block. V-6. Order Code LR2. Produced by GM-Chevrolet Motor Division. Bore x Stroke: 3.50 in. x 2.99 in. Lifters: Hydraulic. Number of main bearings-5. Fuel Induction: Electronic fuel injection. Compression Ratio: 8.9:1. Displacement: 173 cu. in. (2.8 liter). Horsepower: Net: 125 @ 4800 rpm. Torque: Net: 150 lb.-ft. @ 2100 rpm. Oil capacity: 5 qt. with filter change. Fuel Requirements: Unleaded.

CHASSIS FEATURES: Carbon steel, 39,000 psi., welded front box section and open channel rear section, section modulus: 2.19.

SUSPENSION AND RUNNING GEAR: Front Suspension: Independent with torsion bar springs, 25mm dia. shock absorbers. 32mm stabilizer bar. Capacity: 1250 lbs. each at ground. Optional: 32mm shock absorbers. Rear Suspension: Two-stage multi-leaf shot-peened springs. Capacity: 1150 lbs. each at ground. 25mm shock absorbers. Optional: 32mm shock absorbers. Front Axle. Type: Hypoid, tubular driving. Capacity: 2300 lb. Rear Axle. Type: Salisbury, hypoid. Capacity: 2700 lb. Final Drive Ratio: Standard 4-spd. manual transmission and optional 5-spd. manual overdrive: 3.73:1 (3.08:1 for high altitude emission system). Automatic transmission: 3.42:1 (3.73:1 for high altitude emission system). Optional: Standard 4-spd. manual transmission and optional 5-spd. manual overdrive: 4.11:1 (3.73:1 for high altitude emission system). Automatic transmission: 3.73:1. Transfer Case: New Process 207. Brakes: Type: Hydraulic, power assisted self-adjusting. Front: Discs. Rear: Drums. Dimensions: Front: 10.51 in. x 2.0 in. rotor. Rear: 9.49 in. x 2.0 in. Wheels: 15 in. Tires: P195/75R15 glass belted radial black sidewall. Optional: P195/75R15 black sidewall, P205/75R15 black sidewall, P205/75R15 white sidewall, P205/75R15 white letters, P205/75R15 on/off road black sidewall. Steering: Manual, variable ratio. Optional: Power. Transmission: 4-speed manual. Optional: 5-speed manual with overdrive, 4-speed automatic with overdrive (with V-6 engine only). Clutch: 4-cyl. engine: 9.13 in. dia., V-6: 9.76 in. dia.

VEHICLE DIMENSIONS: Wheelbase: Short wheelbase/Long wheelbase/Extended cab: 108.5 in./117.9 in./122.9 in. Overall Length: Short wheelbase/Long wheelbase/Extended cab: 178.2 in./170.3 in./194.1 in./208.6 in. Overall Height: 61.2 in. Width: 64.8 in. Tailgate Height: 16.0 in.

CAPACITIES: Fuel Tank: 13.2 gal. Optional: Replacement 20 gal. tank.

ACCOMMODATIONS: Seating Capacity: Standard: 3. Headroom: 39.5 in. Legroom: 42.4 in.

INSTRUMENTATION: 0-100 mph speedometer, 99,999.9 mi. odometer, fuel gauge, warning lights for alternator, oil pressure, engine coolant temperature, brake operating system, hazard warning lights, directional lights, seat belt warning.

OPTIONS AND PRICES: High Sierra Package: $339. Sierra Classic Package: $442. Gypsy Package: $940. Custom vinyl bench seat: $50. Custom vinyl high-back bucket seats: $128-$178 depending upon Trim Package. Custom two-tone paint: $200. Special two-tone paint: $167-$311 depending upon Trim Package. Sport two-tone paint: $162-$227 depending upon Trim Package. California emissions system: $99. 2.6 liter V-6 engine: $225. 4-speed overdrive automatic transmission: $670. Optional axle ratio: $36. Locking rear differential: $238. Pre-cleaner air cleaner: $49. 5-speed manual overdrive transmission: $175. All-Weather air conditioning: 705. Heavy-duty battery: $53. Front black bumper guards: $30. Off-Road Package: $602-$658 depending upon Trim Package. Cold Climate Package: $107-$179 depending upon Trim Package. Front compartment console: $108. Engine oil cooling system: $120. heavy-duty radiator: $53. Heavy-duty radiator and transmission oil cooler: $59 with air conditioning, $112 without air conditioning. Spare tire cover: $32. Air deflector: $41. Rear window defogger: $114 with air conditioning, $145 without air conditioning. Power door locks: $135. Color-keyed floor mats: $15. Gauge Package. Includes voltmeter, engine coolant temperature, oil pressure: $58. Gauge Package plus tachometer: $55-$113 depending upon Trim Package. 66 amp Delcotron generator: $31. Deep tinted back window glass with light tinted windshield and side door glass: $55. Tinted glass, all windows: $46. Halogen headlights: $22. Engine block heater: $31. Engine compartment light: $15. Exterior left and right side painted mirrors: $50. Exterior left and right side bright mirrors: $83. Body side and wheel opening moldings: $17-$144 depending upon Trim Package. Door edge guards: $17. Bright wheel opening moldings: $28. Black wheel opening moldings: $12-$41 depending upon Trim Package. Operating Convenience Package: $325. AM radio: $112. AM/FM radio: $171. AM/FM radio with clock: $210. AM/FM stereo radio with electronic tuning: $238 AM/FM stereo radio and clock with electronic tuning: $277. AM/FM stereo radio with Seek-Scan, stereo cassette tape, clock and graphic equalizer and electronic tuning and premium rear speakers: $594. Premium rear speakers: $25. Transfer case shield: $67. Heavy-duty front and rear shock absorbers: $34. Full-size spare tire: $46-90 depending upon size. Electronic speed control: $260. ComforTilt steering wheel: $115. Striping: $65. Heavy-duty suspension equipment: $59. 20 gal. fuel tank: $49. Two front towing hooks: $36. Deadweight trailer hitch: $64. Heavy-duty trailering special: $199. Light-duty trailering special: $103. Wheel trim rings: $56. Rallye wheels: $32-$88 depending upon Trim Package. Styled wheels: $32-$88 depending upon Trim Package. Cast aluminum wheels: $238-$294 depending upon Trim Package. Power side door windows: $190. Intermittent windshield wiper system: $55.

HISTORICAL FOOTNOTES: The 1987 S-15 models were introduced in Oct.,1986.

1988 S-15 PICKUP

The 1988 S-15 opened the model year with a choice of the 2.5 liter or 2.8 liter engines. Beginning in April, 1988, General Motors new 4.3 liter Vortex V-6 became an option. Redeveloped All-Season tires were available for the 1988 S-15. Front brakes had new noise reducing "SAS II" brake lining insulators. The S-15 instrument panel now had grey trim plate accents. The knobs and switches remained black. L.E.D. displays on stereo radios were replaced by vacuum fluorescent lights. During the 1988 model the optional air conditioning system was fitted with illuminated blue heating, ventilation, and air-conditioning control lighting for improved indication of knob locations. Map lights were added to the inside rearview mirror. For 1988 the S-15 was available with an optional factory-installed tinted sun roof. This non-removable roof had manual operation for its five different opening positions. Four new exterior colors were added for 1988: Light mesa brown, bright blue metallic, light mesa brown metallic and dark mesa brown metallic. Replacing saddle tan as an interior color was cognac. The base Sierra's standard equipment included a 3 passenger vinyl bench seat with folding back rest, padded armrests for both doors, passenger side coat hook, color-keyed molded plastic door trim panels, black rubber floor mat, grab handle over passenger door, sound insulation and sound-deadening material installed in dash, doors and roof, 10 in. interior mirror, soft black plastic 15.25 in. steering wheel, padded color-keyed left and right side sunshades, embossed color-keyed headliner, and AM radio.

The High Sierra enhanced the base interior equipment to include bright High Sierra nameplate on storage box door, choice of custom vinyl or special custom cloth seat trim, color-keyed rubber matting for floor area, deluxe steering wheel, side window defoggers, bright dome lamp trim, cigarette lighter, headlamps-on warning buzzer and deluxe heater and defogger. The High Sierra exterior included bright High Sierra nameplates with series designation on front fenders, bright front bumper with black rub strips, bright trim on black grille, bright taillight trim bright wheel trim rings and reflectorized GMC tailgate lettering. The Sierra Classic Package included all interior High Sierra items plus the following additions or substitutions: Bright Sierra Classic nameplate on stowage box, color-keyed carpeting for floor area and cab back panel, color-keyed cowl kick panels, visor mirror on right side sun visor, special custom cloth inserts in door trim panels, carpeted lower door panel insert with storage pocket, plus coin holder in left side door, full-coverage molded styrene headliner of full foam, with color-keyed cloth (in regular cab) and an instrument panel cluster including voltmeter, oil pressure gauge, engine coolant temperature gauge and trip odometer. The Sierra Classic exterior had these features: Bright Sierra Classic nameplates with series designations on front fenders, black body side moldings with bright trim, bright wheel opening lip moldings, black hub covers, body-color door handle inserts, black applique tailgate trim with GMC lettering, and argent colored wheels.

The Sport Package included all interior Sierra Classic items plus the following additions or substitutions: Bright Sport nameplate on stowage box door, Sport cloth high-back front bucket seats, Sport steering wheel, door trim panels with Sport cloth inserts that matched the seat trim, and a color-keyed console with lockable storage compartment operated by door key. The Sport exterior featured these items: Sport nameplates with series designation on front fenders, Sport two-tone paint, bumper color-keyed to lower accent stripe of two-tone paint with black rib strips, base argent wheels with black ornamental hubs and bright trim rings, black chrome door handles, grille and headlamp bezels, and black wheel opening lip moldings.

I.D. DATA: The V.I.N. plate was mounted on the lower left side windshield corner. The V.I.N. consisted of 17 elements. The first, the number 1, identified the U.S. as the nation of origin. The letter G followed for the manufacturer: General Motors. The third entry, the letter T, represented the make as GMC. The GVWR brake system identification followed. Next came the truck line and chassis type; the letter K indicated four-wheel drive. The truck series was identified by a number: 1-1/2 ton. The truck body type identification was next: 4-Two-door cab. The engine code was next: E-2.5 liter, B-2.8 liter V-6, N-4.3 liter V-6, followed by a check digit. The model year was identified by the letter J. The assembly plant code followed. The final six digits were the plant sequential production number.

Model Number	Body Type	Factory Price	GVW	Shipping Weight	Prod. Total
S-15 with 2.8 liter V-6					
T10603	108.3 in. wb. Pickup	$10,354	3825[1]	2974	68,489[2]
T10803	117.9 in. wb. Pickup	$10,528	3825[1]	3060	—
T10653	122.9 in. wb. Club Coupe	$11,373	3825[1]	3128	—

NOTE 1: 4650 lb. GVW optional for 1000 lb. payload, standard GVW for 1500 lb. payload is 4050 lb. with 4750 lb. optional.
NOTE 2: 1988 calendar year production, both two-wheel drive and four-wheel drive models.

STANDARD ENGINE: Ordering Code LN8: Produced by Pontiac Motor Division. Engine Type: Cast iron block. OHV, In-line 4. Bore x Stroke: 4.0 in. x 3.0 in. Lifters: Hydraulic. Number of main bearings-5. Fuel induction: Electronic fuel injection. Compression Ratio: 9.0:1. Displacement: 151 cu. in. (2.5 liter). Horsepower: Net: 92 @ 4400 rpm. Torque: Net: 134 lb.-ft. @ 2800 rpm. Oil capacity: 5 qt. with filter change. Fuel Requirements: Unleaded.

OPTIONAL ENGINE: Engine Type: OHV, cast iron block. V-6. Order Code LL2. Produced by GM-Chevrolet Motor Division in Canada and Mexico. Bore x Stroke: 3.50 in. x 2.99 in. Lifters: Hydraulic. Number of main bearings-5. Fuel Induction: Electronic fuel injection. Compression

Ratio: 8.9:1. Displacement: 173 cu. in. (2.8 liter). Horsepower: Net: 125 @ 4800 rpm. Torque: Net: 150 lb.-ft. @ 2200 rpm. Oil capacity: 5 qt. with filter change. Fuel Requirements: Unleaded.

OPTIONAL ENGINE: Engine Type: OHV, cast iron block. V-6. Order Code LB4. Bore x Stroke: 4.00 in. x 3.48 in. Lifters: Hydraulic. Number of main bearings-5. Fuel Induction: Electronic fuel injection. Compression Ratio: 9.3:1. Displacement: 262 cu. in. (4.3 liter). Horsepower: Net: 160 @ 4000 rpm. Torque: Net: 230 lb.-ft. @ 2400 rpm. Oil capacity: 5 qt. with filter change. Fuel Requirements: Unleaded.

CHASSIS FEATURES: Carbon steel, 39,000 psi., welded front box section and open channel rear section, section modulus: 2.19.

SUSPENSION AND RUNNING GEAR: Front Suspension: Independent with torsion bar springs, 25mm dia. shock absorbers. 32mm stabilizer bar. Capacity: 1250 lbs. each at ground. Optional: 32mm shock absorbers. Rear Suspension: Two-stage multi-leaf shot-peened springs. Capacity: 1150 lbs. each at ground. 25mm shock absorbers. Optional: 32mm shock absorbers. Front Axle. Type: Hypoid, tubular driving. Capacity: 2300 lb. Rear Axle. Type: Salisbury, hypoid. Capacity: 2700 lb. Final Drive Ratio: Standard 4-spd. manual transmission and optional 5-spd. manual overdrive: 3.73:1 (3.08:1 for high altitude emission system). Automatic transmission: 3.42:1 (3.73:1 for high altitude emission system). Optional: Standard 4-spd. manual transmission and optional 5-spd. manual overdrive: 4.11:1 (3.73:1 for high altitude emission system). Automatic transmission: 3.73:1. Transfer Case: New Process 207. Brakes: Type: Hydraulic, power assisted self-adjusting. Front: Discs. Rear: Drums. Dimensions: Front: 10.51 in. x 2.0 in. rotor. Rear: 9.49 in. x 2.0 in. Wheels: 15 in. Tires: P195/75R15 glass belted radial black sidewall. Optional: P195/75R15 black sidewall, P205/75R15 black sidewall, P205/75R15 white sidewall, P205/75R15 white letters, P205/75R15 on/off road black sidewall. Steering: Manual. Optional: Power. Transmission: 4-speed manual. Optional: 5-speed manual with overdrive, 4-speed automatic with overdrive (with V-6 engine only). Clutch: 4-cyl. engine: 9.13 in. dia., V-6: 9.76 in. dia.

VEHICLE DIMENSIONS: Wheelbase: Short wheelbase/Long wheelbase/Extended cab: 108.5 in./117.9 in./122.9 in. Overall Length: Short wheelbase/Long wheelbase/Extended cab: 178.2 in./170.3 in./194.1 in./208.6 in. Overall Height: 61.2 in. Width: 64.8 in. Tailgate Height:16.0 in.

CAPACITIES: Fuel Tank: 20 gal. tank.

ACCOMMODATIONS: Seating Capacity: Standard: 3. Headroom: 39.5 in. Legroom: 42.4 in.

INSTRUMENTATION: 0-100 mph speedometer, 99,999.9 mi. odometer, fuel gauge, warning lights for alternator, oil pressure, engine coolant temperature, brake operating system, hazard warning lights, directional lights, seat belt warning.

OPTIONS AND PRICES: High Sierra Package. Sierra Classic Package. Sport Package. Custom two-tone paint. Special two-tone paint. Sport two-tone paint. California emissions system. 2.6 liter V-6 engine. 4-speed overdrive automatic transmission. Optional axle ratio. Locking rear differential. Pre-cleaner air cleaner. 5-speed manual overdrive transmission. All-Weather air conditioning. Heavy-duty battery. Front black bumper guards. Luggage carrier, black or bright finish. Off-Road Package. Cold Climate Package. Front console. Engine oil cooling system. Heavy-duty radiator. Heavy-duty radiator and transmission oil cooler. Air deflector. Power door locks. Color-keyed floor mats. Gauge Package. Includes voltmeter, engine coolant temperature, oil pressure. Gauge Package plus tachometer. 66 amp Delcotron generator. Deep tinted glass. Deep tinted glass with light tinted rear window. Halogen headlights. Engine block heater. Engine compartment light. Exterior left and right side painted mirrors. Exterior left and right side bright mirrors. Body side and wheel opening moldings. Door edge guards. Bright wheel opening moldings. Black wheel opening moldings. Operating Convenience Package. AM radio. AM/FM radio. AM/FM radio with clock. AM/FM stereo radio with electronic tuning. AM/FM stereo radio and clock with electronic tuning. AM/FM stereo radio with Seek-Scan, stereo cassette tape, clock and graphic equalizer and electronic tuning and premium rear speakers. Premium rear speakers. Transfer case shield. Heavy-duty front and rear shock absorbers. Full-size spare tire. Electronic speed control. ComforTilt steering wheel. Striping. Heavy-duty suspension equipment. 20 gal. fuel tank. Two front towing hooks. Deadweight trailer hitch: $64. Heavy-duty trailering special: $199. Light-duty trailering special. Wheel trim rings. Rallye wheels. Styled wheels. Cast aluminum wheels. Power side door windows. Intermittent windshield wiper system.

HISTORICAL FOOTNOTES: The top-selling GMC dealer of 1988 was Courtesy Pontiac-GMC of Tampa, Florida which sold 2,057 trucks in 1988.

1989 S-15 PICKUP

The 1989 S-15 pickups had a new standard rear-wheel anti-lock (RWAL) system on all models. Also standard was a new electric speedometer. Added to the option list was an electronic instrument panel cluster with speedometer, tachometer, voltmeter and fuel, oil pressure and engine coolant temperature gauges. The gauges utilized high-brightness vacuum fluorescent tubes for sharper visibility. Models with the standard 2.8 liter V-6 had a new transfer case with redesigned gear sets for reduced noise and smoother operation. The new transfer case also had new controls, longer shift lever, new vacuum switch and relocated vent tube. For 1989 the standard models had an upgraded vinyl interior and a heavy-duty heater. A new exterior color was woodlands brown. Dark blue replaced medium blue as an interior color. The 4.4 liter V-6 was in greater supply for 1989. It was available only with the overdrive automatic transmission. Models with the 4.3 liter were changed in a number of ways to accommodate this larger V-6. The steering column was moved to the left to provide additional clearance for the left exhaust manifold and the frame was changed to gain clearance in several locations on the right side. When the maxi-cab was ordered with the optional jump seats, rear shoulder safety belts were installed.

1989 S-15 Sierra Classic pickup

I.D. DATA: The V.I.N. plate was mounted on the lower left side windshield corner. The V.I.N. consisted of 17 elements. The first, the number 1, identified the U.S. as the nation of origin. The letter G followed for the manufacturer: General Motors. The third entry, the letter T, represented the make as GMC. The GVWR brake system identification followed. Next came the truck line and chassis type; the letter K indicated four-wheel drive. The truck series was identified by a number: 1-1/2 ton. The truck body type identification was next: 4-Two-door cab. The engine code was next: B-2.8 liter V-6, N-4.3 liter V-6, followed by a check digit. The model year was identified by the letter K. The assembly plant code followed. The final six digits were the plant sequential production number.

Model Number	Body Type	Factory Price	GVW	Shipping Weight	Prod. Total
S-15 with 2.8 liter V-6					
T10603	108.3 in. wb. Pickup	$11,511	3570[1]	2998	58,355[2]
T10803	117.9 in. wb. Pickup	$12,141	3825[1]	3084	—
T10653	122.9 in. wb. Club Coupe	$12,321	3825[1]	3152	—

NOTE 1: 4710 lb. optional.
NOTE 2: 1989 calendar year production, both two-wheel drive and four-wheel drive models.

STANDARD ENGINE: Engine Type: OHV, cast iron block. V-6. Order Code LL2. Produced by GM-Chevrolet Motor Division in Canada and Mexico. Bore x Stroke: 3.50 in. x 2.99 in. Lifters: Hydraulic. Number of main bearings-5. Fuel Induction: Electronic fuel injection. Compression Ratio: 8.9:1. Displacement: 173 cu. in. (2.8 liter). Horsepower: Net: 125 @ 4800 rpm. Torque: Net: 150 lb.-ft. @ 2200 rpm. Oil capacity: 5 qt. with filter change. Fuel Requirements: Unleaded.

OPTIONAL ENGINE: Engine Type: OHV, cast iron block. V-6. Order Code LB4. Bore x Stroke: 4.00 in. x 3.48 in. Lifters: Hydraulic. Number of main bearings-5. Fuel Induction: Electronic fuel injection. Compression Ratio: 9.3:1. Displacement: 262 cu. in. (4.3 liter). Horsepower: Net: 160 @ 4000 rpm. Torque: Net: 230 lb.-ft. @ 2400 rpm. Oil capacity: 5 qt. with filter change. Fuel Requirements: Unleaded.

CHASSIS FEATURES: Carbon steel, 39,000 psi., welded front box section and open channel rear section, section modulus: 2.19.

SUSPENSION AND RUNNING GEAR: Front Suspension: Independent with torsion bar springs, 25mm dia. shock absorbers. 32mm stabilizer bar. Capacity: 1350 lbs. each at ground. Optional: 32mm shock absorbers. Rear Suspension: Two-stage multi-leaf shot-peened springs. Capacity: 1150 lbs. each at ground. 25mm shock absorbers. Optional: 32mm shock absorbers. Front Axle. Type: Hypoid, tubular driving. Capacity: 2700 lb. Rear Axle. Type: Salisbury, hypoid. Capacity: 2700 lb. Final Drive Ratio: Standard 5-spd. manual overdrive for 2.8 liter engine: 3.73:1; 4-speed automatic overdrive standard for 4.3 liter V-6: 3.08:1. Optional: Standard 5-spd. manual overdrive for 2.8 liter engine: 4.11:1 4-speed automatic overdrive standard for 4.3 liter V-6: 4.42:1. Transfer Case: New Process 207. Brakes: Type: Hydraulic, power assisted self-adjusting. Front: Discs. Rear: Drums. Dimensions: Front: 10.51 in. x 2.0 in. rotor. Rear: 9.49 in. x 2.0 in. Wheels: 15 in. Tires: P195/75R15 glass belted radial black sidewall. Optional: P195/75R15 black sidewall, P205/75R15 black sidewall, P205/75R15 white sidewall, P205/75R15 white letters, P205/75R15 on/off road black sidewall. Steering: Integral variable ratio power. Ratios: 13-16.0:1. Transmission: Standard 5-spd. manual overdrive for 2.8 liter engine; 4-speed automatic overdrive standard for 4.3 liter V-6. Clutch: 9.13 in. dia.

VEHICLE DIMENSIONS: Wheelbase: Short wheelbase/Long wheelbase/Max. cab: 108.5 in./117.9 in./122.9 in. Overall Length: Short wheelbase/Long wheelbase/Extended cab: 178.2 in./170.3 in./194.1 in./208.6 in. Overall Height: 61.2 in. Width: 64.8 in. Tailgate Height:16.0 in.

CAPACITIES: Fuel Tank: 20 gal. tank.

ACCOMMODATIONS: Seating Capacity: Standard: 3. Headroom: 39.5 in. Legroom: 42.4 in.

INSTRUMENTATION: 0-100 mph speedometer, 99,999.9 mi. odometer, fuel gauge, warning lights for alternator, oil pressure, engine coolant temperature, brake operating system, hazard warning lights, directional lights, seat belt warning.

OPTIONS AND PRICES: High Sierra Package. Sierra Classic Package: Air conditioning: $736 without LL2 engine, $680 with LL2 engine. Optional axle ratio: $38. Locking rear differential: $252. Heavy-duty battery: $56. Cold Climate Package: $113-$156 depending upon trim option. Center console: $114. Engine oil cooler: $126. Heavy-duty radiator: $56. Heavy-duty radiator and engine oil cooler: $63, with air conditioning, $118 without air conditioning. Spare tire cover: $33. Air deflector: $43. Driver Convenience Package. Includes ComforTilt steering wheel and intermittent wiper system: $180. Rear window Convenience Package. Includes electric tailgate release and rear window defogger: $197. 4.3 liter V-6: $255. Color-keyed front floor mats: $16. Color-keyed rear floor mats: $12. Gauge Package: $62. Deep tinted glass with light tinted rear window: $56-$200 depending on Trim Package. Halogen headlights: $24. Engine block heater: $33. Electronic instrumentation: $296-$358 depending on Trim Package. Engine compartment light: $16. Interior visor mirror: $7. Exterior below eye-level black mirrors: $52. Exterior below eye-level bright mirrors: $87. Interior rearview tilting mirror with dual reading lamps: $26. Body side and wheel opening moldings: $152. Black wheel opening molding: $13-$43 depending upon Trim Package. Bright wheel opening molding: 31. Operating Convenience Package. Includes power door locks and power windows: $344. Custom two-tone paint: $172-$344 depending upon Trim Package. Special two-tone paint: $163-$212 depending upon Trim Package. Deluxe two-tone paint: $177-$329 depending upon Trim Package. Electronically tuned AM/FM stereo radio: $275. Electronically tuned AM/FM stereo radio with Seek-Scan, stereo cassette tape player and digital clock: $454. Electronically tuned AM/FM stereo radio with Seek-Scan, stereo cassette tape player with Search and Repeat, graphic equalizer and digital clock: $604. Reclining seat backs: $74. Transfer case and front differential skid plates and steering linkage shield: $75. Front and rear heavy-duty shock absorbers: $36. Electronic speed control: $205. Heavy-duty front springs: $63. Body striping: $49. Sunshine striping: $116. Manual sun roof: $250. Suspension Package: $160-$220 depending upon Trim Package. Two front tow hooks: $38. Deadweight trailer hitch: $68. Light-duty Trailering Package: $109. Heavy-Duty Trailering Special Package: $211. 4-speed automatic transmission: $795. Wheel trim rings: $60. Cast aluminum wheels: $252-$308 depending upon Trim Package. Sliding rear window: $257. Rear window wiper/washer: $125.

HISTORICAL FOOTNOTES: S-15 trucks were assembly in Moraine, Ohio; Pontiac, Michigan and Shreveport, Louisiana.

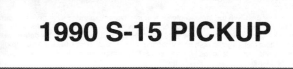

1990 S-15 PICKUP

The S-15 continued to be offered in the base Sierra form and the upscale High Sierra and Sierra Classic Packages. GMC described the Sierra as "designed to offer truck buyers a high level of standard features when purchasing a base-level truck." The High Sierra was, said GMC, "designed to offer truck buyers an increased level of comfort and convenience features compared to the Sierra trim level." Similarly, the Sierra Classic was regarded as offering "truck buyers an increased level of comfort and convenience features compared to the High Sierra trim level."

The 4.3 liter V-6 was now available with a new Getrag-designed, Hydra-Matic-built 5-speed manual transmission with fifth gear overdrive for 1990. Neither the 2.8 liter V-6 and 5-speed manual transmission were available for the 1990 4x4 S-15. A new fixed Gross Vehicle Weight Rating replaced the net payload system. All S-15 models had a redesigned instrument cluster with improved legibility. The panel now included voltmeter, engine coolant temperature and oil pressure gauges. Added to The standard S-15 equipment were enhanced by the inclusion of front tow hooks, P205/75R15 All-Season steel belted tires, reclining seat back on club coupe models and electronically tuned AM radio into the base vehicle's content. New 1990 features of the High Sierra included swing-out quarter windows, right-hand visor mirror, deluxe front chromed bumper and chromed grille. New for the Sierra Classic were right and left-hand black exterior mirrors, color-keyed floor mats and engine compartment lamp. The exterior color selection for 1990 consisted of new royal blue metallic and garnet colors plus midnight black, blue Aspen metallic, woodlands brown metallic, Nevada gold metallic, steel grey metallic, apple red, wheat and frost white. The custom vinyl and custom cloth trims were offered in four colors: Blue, garnet, charcoal and saddle. The leather upholstery was available in either charcoal or saddle.

1990 S-15 Jimmy Sierra Classic

I.D. DATA: The V.I.N. plate was mounted on the lower left side windshield corner. The V.I.N. consisted of 17 elements. The first, the number 1, identified the U.S. as the nation of origin. The letter G followed for the manufacturer: General Motors. The third entry, the letter T, represented the make as GMC. The GVWR brake system identification followed. Next came the truck line and chassis type; the letter K indicated four-wheel drive. The truck series was identified by a number: 1-1/2 ton. The truck body type identification was next: 4-Two-door cab. The engine code was next: N-4.3 liter V-6, followed by a check digit. The model year was identified by the letter L. The assembly plant code followed. The final six digits were the plant sequential production number.

Model Number	Body Type	Factory Price	GVW	Shipping Weight	Prod. Total
S-15 with 4.3 liter V-6					
T10603	108.3 in. wb. Pickup	$12,623	4650[1]	2974	53,330[2]
T10803	117.9 in. wb. Pickup	$12808	4650[1]	3060	—
T10653	122.9 in. wb. Club Coupe	$13,408	4650[1]	3128	—

NOTE 1: 5150 lb. optional.
NOTE 2: 1990 calendar year production, includes 1991 Sonoma models built in 1990 and both two-wheel drive and four-wheel drive models.

STANDARD ENGINE: Engine Type: OHV, cast iron block. V-6. Order Code LB4. Bore x Stroke: 4.00 in. x 3.48 in. Lifters: Hydraulic. Number of main bearings-5. Fuel Induction: Electronic fuel injection. Compression Ratio: 9.3:1. Displacement: 262 cu. in. (4.3 liter). Horsepower: Net: 160 @ 4000 rpm. Torque: Net: 230 lb.-ft. @ 2400 rpm. Oil capacity: 5 qt. with filter change. Fuel Requirements: Unleaded.

CHASSIS FEATURES: Carbon steel, 39,000 psi., welded front box section and open channel rear section, section modulus: 2.19.

SUSPENSION AND RUNNING GEAR: Front Suspension: Independent with torsion bar springs, 25mm dia. shock absorbers. 32mm stabilizer bar. Capacity: 1350 lbs. each at ground. Optional: 32mm shock absorbers. Rear Suspension: Two-stage multi-leaf shot-peened springs. Capacity: 1150 lbs. each at ground. 25mm shock absorbers. Optional: 32mm shock absorbers. Front Axle. Type: Hypoid, tubular driving. Capacity: 2700 lb. Rear Axle. Type: Salisbury, hypoid. Capacity: 2700 lb. Final Drive Ratio: 3.08:1. Optional: 3.42:1. Transfer Case: New Process 231. Ratios: 2.72,1.00:1. Brakes: Type: Hydraulic, power assisted self-adjusting. Front: Discs. Rear: Drums. Dimensions: Front: 10.51 in. x 2.0 in. rotor. Rear: 9.49 in. x 2.0 in. Wheels: 15 in. Tires: P205/75R15 steel belted radial All-Season black sidewall. Optional: P205/75R15 black sidewall, All-Season steel-belted radial, P205/75R15 on-off road steel belted radial, white letters, P205/75R15 All-Season steel belted radial, white letters, P205/75R15 on-off road steel belted radial black sidewall, P205/75R15 steel belted radial, front: Highway, Rear: On-off road, P235/75R15 on-off road steel belted radial white letters. Steering: Variable ratio, integral power. Ratio: 17.5:1. Turning diameter: 35.4 ft. Transmission: 5-speed manual with overdrive (RPO MM5). Ratios: 4.02, 2.32, 1.40, 1.00, 0.83:1. Reverse: 3.74:1. Optional: 4-speed automatic with overdrive (RPO MXO): 3.06, 1.63, 1.0, 0.70:1. Reverse: 2.29:1. Clutch: 9.13 in. dia.

VEHICLE DIMENSIONS: Wheelbase: Short wheelbase/Long wheelbase/Club coupe: 108.5 in./ 117.9 in./122.9 in. Overall Length: Short wheelbase/Long wheelbase/Club coupe: 178.2 in./170.3 in./194.1 in./208.6 in. Overall Height: 61.2 in. Width: 64.8 in. Tailgate Height: 16.0 in.

CAPACITIES: Fuel Tank: 20 gal. tank.

ACCOMMODATIONS: Seating Capacity: Standard: 3. Headroom: 39.5 in. Legroom: 42.4 in.

INSTRUMENTATION: 0-100 mph speedometer, 99,999.9 mi. odometer, fuel gauge, gauges for voltmeter, oil pressure, and engine coolant temperature; warning lights for brake operating system, hazard warning lights, directional lights, seat belt warning.

OPTIONS AND PRICES: (All prices effective with initial shipment of 1990 models) High Sierra Package: $79 to $253 depending on body style and other options ordered. Sierra Classic Package: $359-$709 depending on body style and other options ordered. Air conditioning: $755. Air dam with fog lamps: $115. Optional axle ratio: $38. Locking rear differential: $252. Heavy-duty battery: $56. Spare tire carrier: $100. Cold Climate Package: $140-$243 depending upon trim option. Center console: $135. Heavy-duty radiator: $56. Heavy-duty radiator and engine oil cooler: $63, with air conditioning, $118 without air conditioning. Engine oil cooler: $135. Driver Convenience Package. Includes ComforTilt steering wheel and intermittent wiper system: $180. Color-keyed front floor mats: $20. Full floor carpeting: $40. Deep tinted glass: Extended cab: $101-$140 depending upon ption Package; regular cab: $11. Electronic instrumentation: $296. Lighted interior visor mirror: $68-$75 depending upon Trim Package. Body side and wheel opening moldings: $152. Black wheel opening molding: $13-$43 depending upon Trim Package. Bright wheel opening molding: $31. Endgate net: $110. Operating Convenience Package. Includes power door locks and power windows: $344. Custom two-tone paint: $172-$344 depending upon Trim Package. Special two-tone paint. Includes pin striping: $296. Deluxe two-tone paint: $177. Electronically tuned AM/FM stereo radio with Seek-Scan, stereo cassette tape player and digital clock: $122. Electronically tuned AM/FM stereo radio with Seek-Scan, stereo cassette tape player with Search and Repeat, graphic equalizer and digital clock: $272. Delete radio: $226 credit. Rear jump seats with vinyl trim: $240. Shield Package. Includes transfer case and front differential skid plates and steering linkage shield: $126. Front and rear heavy-duty shock absorbers: $40. Electronic speed control: $225. Heavy-duty rear springs: $64. Heavy duty front suspension with heavy-duty front and rear shock absorbers: $63. Sport Suspension: $415. Body striping: $55. Manual sun roof: $250. Heavy-Duty Trailering Special Package: $211. 4-speed automatic transmission: $860. Wheel trim rings: $60. Cast aluminum wheels: $269-$325 depending upon Trim Package. Aluminum Special wheels: $395 without spare tire carrier, $495 with spare tire carrier. Sliding rear window: $113.

HISTORICAL FOOTNOTES: The S-15 models were replaced by the 1991 Sonoma models in January, 1990.

1990 SAFARI AWD

The 1990 AWD GMC Safari, joined a two-wheel drive version that had been offered since 1985. The AWD Safari had a higher axle ratio (3.34:1 versus the 3.23:1 of the two-wheel drive model) to help compensate for the additional weight of the AWD system. Power in the AWD system was transmitted to the rear through a planetary gear set in the transfer case to the standard open or optional limited-slip rear axle. At the front, the power moved via a random toothed-chain to an open differential front axle. Inside the transfer case was a viscous clutch connecting the front and rear through a series of closely spaced and heavily lubricated plates. When all the plates — alternately splined to the front or rear drive — rotated at the same rate, the viscous clutch was not active. When the front and rear wheel speed varied, the clutch transferred torque in proportion to the speed differential. The torque transfer was immediate, substantial and in direct proportion to need. The AWD Safari used the front suspension, steering and brake system of the 3/4 ton full-size GMC pickup. The body, rear drivetrain and wheels were from the Safari two-wheel drive M-van. The T-15's front axle and drive shafts were also used. Four-wheel anti-lock brakes were standard on the AWD Safari.

New components for the AWD Safari included stub frame, single-speed transfer case, front stabilizer shaft, front prop shaft with constant velocity joints, and specific exhaust manifolds for frame clearance. The AWD Safari exterior was distinguished by its black bumper guards, acrylic emblems with "ALL WHEEL DRIVE" lettering on the rear and side doors that ran the length of both lower sides. The GMC 4.3 liter Vortex V-6 was standard as was a 4-speed automatic overdrive transmission. Initially, the AWD system was offered for the regular length Safari in either cargo or passenger configurations. Available interim 1990 was an extended model that increased cargo capacity by nearly 19 cubic feet by adding 10 inches behind the rear wheels. The extended model was available with an optional platform trailer hitch that fitted flush with the rear bumper. A new-for-1990 high-output (H.O.) version of the 4.3 liter V-6 was available at mid-year. Its horsepower and torque ratings were 170 hp. @ 4800 rpm and 235 lb.-ft. @ 3200 rpm respectively. The added power of the H.O. engine came from a low-restriction intake and exhaust system and a high-lift camshaft. The H.O. engine also featured a high-stall torque converter, performance calibrations for the automatic transmission, and a dual sport exhaust. As compared to the 1989 V-6, the latest Vortex engine had improved durability and reliability due to the use of a closed-bottom charcoal canister, revised exhaust manifold heat stove and improved piston pin.

1990 GMC Safari XT with SLT trim

The Safari AWD was offered in three trim levels — SLX, SLE and SLT. Standard exterior features of the SLX trim level were as follows: Front and rear bumpers painted lower body color, bright Safari nameplates, molded plastic black painted grille, halogen headlights, bright metal hubcaps with black trim, 15 x 6.00 in. steel wheels painted argent, All-Season steel-belted tires, compact spare tire and wheel, intermittent windshield wiper system, right and left side black painted mirrors with pivoting arm and adjustable 4.75 in. x 7.0 in. heads, hot melt wax on underbody, and front license plate bracket. Interior appointments consisted of right and left side armrests, color-keyed vinyl door trim panels with front door map pockets, front high-back adjustable bucket seats with all-vinyl trim plus center removable 3 passenger bench seat, two left and one right side coat hooks, latex foam rubber door seals, black plastic door sill plates, two dome lamps with front door-activated switches, headlight warning chimes, color-keyed carpeting on wheelhousings and floor, left and right side color-keyed sunshades with right side visor mirror, tinted glass in all windows, gauges for speedometer, odometer, fuel level, voltmeter, oil pressure, engine coolant temperature, and trip odometer, remote release for fuel filler door, black vinyl 4-spoke steering wheel with anti-theft device locking features, cigarette lighter and ashtray light, molded color-keyed plastic storage compartment in left side rear quarter area, full-length color-keyed, foam-backed cloth headliner, stowage box including beverage holder in front face of engine cover extension, swing-out glass on sliding side door, electronically-tuned AM radio with fixed mast antenna, and deluxe heater and defogger with side window defogger.

The SLE trim level had the following interior and exterior equipment in addition to or replacing that of the SLX trim: Exterior: Front and rear bumpers with matching color-keyed end caps, rub strips and rear black combination top step surface, grille with argent paint on feature surfaces, black body-side moldings and wheel opening moldings, 15 x 6.5 in. steel Rallye

wheels, and air dam with fog lamps. Interior features were: Expanded vinyl door trim panels with carpet inserts and insulation, choice of custom vinyl trim or custom cloth for seats, rear door and sliding door-actuated dome light switches as well as a door-jamb defeat switch, color-keyed floor mats, lighted right side visor mirror, custom steering wheel, storage box light, swing-out glass for rear door, convenience tray lamp, stepwell lamp, and storage compartment lamp.

The SLT trim had in addition to or replacing equipment of the SLE trim these items: Exterior: special nameplates on front side door B pillars, wide, color-keyed, graduated-tone striping at beltline, and 15 x 6.5 in. Rallye wheels color-keyed to body. Interior features were: Special front bucket seats with reclining backs, folding integral armrests and full-width adjustable headrests, split-back center seat including fold-down center console with convenience tray and cup pockets, right side seat folded forward for access to rear, special velour fabric upholstery, deep tinted glass, special luxury sport-type leather-wrapped steering wheel, and storage pouch with zipper on left side trim panel of storage compartment in rear quarter area. Exterior colors for 1990 were ivory white, sterling silver metallic, onyx black, smoke blue metallic, Catalina blue metallic (available only for Safari SLT), mojave beige, sunset gold metallic, caramel brown metallic (available only for Safari SLT), deep red metallic, burnt red metallic, grey metallic and midnight blue metallic. Four colors were offered for the vinyl, custom vinyl and custom cloth interiors: Blue, garnet, saddle and slate grey. The velour option was offered in blue or saddle.

I.D. DATA: The V.I.N. plate was mounted on the lower left side windshield corner. The V.I.N. consisted of 17 elements. The first, the number 1, identified the U.S. as the nation of origin. The letter G followed for the manufacturer: General Motors. The third entry, the letter T, represented the make as GMC. The GVWR brake system identification followed. Next came the truck line and chassis type; the letter K indicated four-wheel drive. The truck series was identified by a number: 1-1/2 ton. The truck body type identification was next. The engine code was next: N-4.3 liter V-6, followed by a check digit. The model year was identified by the letter L. The assembly plant code followed. The final six digits were the plant sequential production number.

Model Number	Body Type & Seating	Factory Price	GVW	Shipping Weight	Prod. Total
Safari Cargo Van					
TL10905	—	$15,012	5600	N.A.	43,562[1]
TL11005	Extended	$15,672	5850	N.A.	—
Safari Passenger Van					
TL10906	Safari Van-SLX	$15,978	5800	N.A.	—
TL10906	Safari Van-SLE	$17,018	5800	N.A.	—
TL10906	Safari Van-SLT	$18,513	5800	N.A.	—
TL11006	Safari Van-SLX	$16,140	6100	N.A.	—
TL11006	Safari Van-SLE	$17,180	6100	N.A.	—
TL11006	Safari Van-SLT	$18,675	6100	N.A.	—

NOTE 1: 1990 calendar year production, both two-wheel drive and four-wheel drive models.

STANDARD ENGINE: Engine Type: OHV, cast iron block. V-6. Order Code LB4. Bore x Stroke: 4.00 in. x3.48 in. Lifters: Hydraulic. Number of main bearings-5. Fuel Induction: Electronic fuel injection. Compression Ratio: 9.3:1. Displacement: 262 cu. in. (4.3 liter). Horsepower: Net: 150 @ 4000 rpm. Torque: Net: 230 lb.-ft. @ 2400 rpm. Oil capacity: 5 qt. with filter change. Fuel Requirements: Unleaded.

OPTIONAL ENGINE: 4.3 liter V-6 H.O: Order Code LU2. Engine Type: OHV, cast iron block. V-6. Order Code LB4. Bore x Stroke: 4.00 in. x 3.48 in. Lifters: Hydraulic. Number of main bearings-5. Fuel Induction: Electronic fuel injection. Compression Ratio: 9.3:1. Displacement: 262 cu. in. (4.3 liter). Horsepower: Net: 175 @ 4600 rpm. Torque: Net: 235 lb-ft. @ 3200 rpm (early 1990 data quotes 230 lb.-ft. @ 2800 rpm). Oil capacity: 5 qt. with filter change. Fuel Requirements: Unleaded.

CHASSIS FEATURES: Integral body frame design with boxed section front stub frame.

SUSPENSION AND RUNNING GEAR: Front Suspension: Independent with torsion bar springs, 32mm dia. shock absorbers. 1.18 in. stabilizer bar. Capacity: 3050 lb. at ground. Rear Suspension: Composite leaf springs. Capacity: 3150 lb. at ground. 32mm shock absorbers. Front Axle. Type: Independent hypoid GM. Capacity: 3050 lb. Rear Axle. Type: GM, semi-floating, hypoid. Capacity: 3150 lb. Final Drive Ratio: LB4: 3.34:1 LU2: 4.10:1. Optional: 3.73, 4.10:1. Transfer Case: Single speed. Brakes: Type: Hydraulic, power assisted with four-wheel anti-lock system. Front: Discs. Rear: Drums. Dimensions: Front: 11.57 in. x 1.25 in. rotor. Rear: 9.50 in. x 2.0 in. Wheels: 15 x 6.00 in. SLE and SLT: 15 x 6.5 in. Tires: P205/75R15 steel belted radial All-Season black sidewall. Optional: P205/75R15 black sidewall, All-Season steel-belted radial, P205/75R15 on-off road steel belted radial, white sidewall, P205/75R15 All-Season steel belted radial, black sidewall, P215/75R15 All-Season, steel belted radial black sidewall, P215/75R15 All-Season, steel belted radial, P245/60HR15, All-Season, steel belted radial, white outlined letters, GT. Steering: Integral power. Ratio: 16/13:1. Turning diameter: 40.5 ft. Transmission: Automatic 4-speed with overdrive (RPO MXO). Ratios: 3.06, 1.63, 1.00, 0.70:1. Reverse: 2.29:1.

VEHICLE DIMENSIONS: Wheelbase: 111.0 in. Overall Length: 176.8 in.; Extended Passenger/Cargo Van: 186.8 in. 178.2 in./170.3 in./194.1 in./208.6 in. Overall Height: 74.1 in. Width: 77.0 in. Headroom: Front/Middle/Rear: 39.2/37.9/38.3 in. Legroom: Front/Middle/Rear: 41.6/36.5/38.5 in. Shoulder room: Front/Middle/Rear: 64.0/67.8/67.8 in. Hip room: Front/Middle/Rear: 64.9/50.9/50.9 in. Ground Clearance: Front: 6.8 in. Rear: 7.7 in. Extended Passenger/Cargo Van: Front: 7.0 in. Rear: 7.8 in. Load space: 88.9.1 in. x 51.6 in. x 47.5 in. Extended Passenger/Cargo Van: 98.9 in. x 51.6 in. x 47.5 in.

CAPACITIES: Fuel Tank: 27 gal. tank. Coolant system: 13.6 gal.

ACCOMMODATIONS: Seating Capacity: Standard: 5, Optional: 8. Cargo Van: 1. 2.

INSTRUMENTATION: 0-100 mph speedometer, 99,999.9 mi. odometer, fuel gauge, gauges for voltmeter, oil pressure, and engine coolant temperature; warning lights for brake operating system, hazard warning lights, directional lights, seat belt warning.

OPTIONS AND PRICES: Air conditioning: Front: $820, front and rear: $1343. Optional axle ratio: $38. Locking rear differential: $252. Deluxe front and rear chromed bumpers: $76-$128 depending upon Option Packages, black luggage carrier: $126. Engine oil cooler: $135.

Heavy-duty radiator: $56. Heavy-duty radiator and engine oil cooler: $63, with air conditioning, $118 without air conditioning. Power door locks: $211. Driver Convenience Package. Includes ComforTilt steering wheel and intermittent wiper system: $346. Operating Convenience Package. Includes power door locks and power windows: $411. Deep tinted glass: $161-$211 depending on body glass selected. Rear heater: $267. Electronic instrumentation: $88. Auxiliary lighting: $96 with roof console; $129 without roof console. Black below eye-level exterior mirrors: $52. Exterior remote electric mirrors: $150. Special two-tone paint: $172. Deluxe two-tone paint: $172-$334 depending upon other options. Custom two-tone: $187 with SLE, $329 without SLE. Electronically tuned AM/FM stereo radio with Seek-Scan, digital clock, stereo cassette player and premium speakers: $122. Electronically tuned AM/FM stereo radio with Seek-Scan, stereo cassette tape player with Search and Repeat, graphic equalizer, digital clock and premium speakers: $272. Delete radio: $226 credit. Seven passenger seating: $878-$1069 depending upon other options. Eight passenger seating: $344-878 depending upon other options. Seat back recliner and dual armrests: $241. 6-way power seat: $240. Front and rear heavy-duty shock absorbers: $40. Sport Suspension: $417-$509 depending upon other options ordered. Heavy-duty trailering equipment: $507-$564 depending upon other equipment ordered. Light-duty trailering equipment: $109. Aluminum wheels: $233-$325, depending upon other options ordered. Rallye wheels: $92.

HISTORICAL FOOTNOTES: GMC held 7.1 percent of the U.S. light truck market in 1990.

1991 SAFARI AWD

No major changes took place for 1991 in the basic design of the AWD GMC Safari. The sliding side door swing-out glass on all models now had latches with detents for positive locking. The center right side passenger seat incorporated a lap and shoulder belt. Stereo radio reception was improved by increasing signal sensitivity and reducing signal interference and signal tracking. A storage tray positioned under the front passenger seat was available for all models. P245/60R15 white outline tires were a new 1991 option.

An improved version of the 4.3 liter Vortex V-6 was standard as was the 4-speed overdrive automatic transmission. Changes to the engine's 220 throttle body injection included longer throttle shaft bearings, new throttle return springs and improved fuel mixture distribution for better start and idle quality, reliability and performance. A Vortex III air cleaner system and "Quantum" spark plugs were added for improved cold sparks. A SD 260 starter motor replaced the SD300 to reduce overall weight and to increase starter motor reliability and life-span.

Twelve exterior colors were available with the addition of field stone metallic for the SLX and SLE models. Slate metallic red and a two-tone light grey metallic were new for the Astro SLT. The caramel brown and grey metallic colors were discontinued. Four interior colors were offered including a new light grey. Suspension components were carried over from 1990.

I.D. DATA: The V.I.N. plate was mounted on the lower left side windshield corner. The V.I.N. consisted of 17 elements. The first, the number 1, identified the U.S. as the nation of origin. The letter G followed for the manufacturer: General Motors. The third entry, the letter T, represented the make as GMC. The GVWR brake system identification followed. Next came the truck line and chassis type; the letter K indicated four-wheel drive. The truck series was identified by a number: 1-1/2 ton. The truck body type identification was next. The engine code was next: N-4.3 liter V-6, followed by a check digit. The model year was identified by the letter L. The assembly plant code followed. The final six digits were the plant sequential production number.

Model Number	Body Type & Seating	Factory Price	GVW	Shipping Weight	Prod. Total
Safari Cargo Van					
TL10905	—	$15,824	5600	N.A.	41,346[1]
TL11005	Extended	$16,514	5850	N.A.	—
Safari Passenger Van (TL11006 identifies extended models)					
TL10906	Safari Van-SLX	$16,825	5800	N.A.	—
TL10906	Safari Van-SLE	$17,905	5800	N.A.	—
TL10906	Safari Van-SLT	$19,455	5800	N.A.	—
TL11006	Safari Van-SLX	$17,515	6100	N.A.	—
TL11006	Safari Van-SLE	$18,595	6100	N.A.	—
TL11006	Safari Van-SLT	$20,145	6100	N.A.	—

NOTE 1: 1991 calendar year production, both two-wheel drive and four-wheel drive models.

STANDARD ENGINE: Engine Type: OHV, cast iron block. V-6. Order Code LB4. Bore x Stroke: 4.00 in. x 3.48 in. Lifters: Hydraulic. Number of main bearings-5. Fuel Induction: Electronic fuel injection. Compression Ratio: 9.3:1. Displacement: 262 cu. in. (4.3 liter). Horsepower: Net: 150 @ 4000 rpm. Torque: Net: 230 lb.-ft. @ 2400 rpm. Oil capacity: 5 qt. with filter change. Fuel Requirements: Unleaded.

OPTIONAL ENGINE: 4.3 liter V-6 H.O. Order Code LU2. Engine Type: OHV, cast iron block. V-6. Order Code LB4. Bore x Stroke: 4.00 in. x 3.48 in. Lifters: Hydraulic. Number of main bearings-5. Fuel Induction: Electronic fuel injection. Compression Ratio: 9.3:1. Displacement: 262 cu. in. (4.3 liter). Horsepower: Net: 175 @ 4600 rpm. Torque: Net: 235 lb-ft. @ 3200 rpm. Oil capacity: 5 qt. with filter change. Fuel Requirements: Unleaded.

CHASSIS FEATURES: Integral body frame design with boxed section front stub frame.

SUSPENSION AND RUNNING GEAR: Front Suspension: Independent with torsion bar springs, 32mm dia. shock absorbers. 1.18 in. stabilizer bar. Capacity: 3050 lb. at ground. Rear Suspension: Composite leaf springs. Capacity: 3150 lb. at ground. 32mm shock absorbers. Front Axle. Type: Independent hypoid GM. Capacity: 3050 lb. Rear Axle. Type: GM, semi-floating, hypoid. Capacity: 3150 lb. Final Drive Ratio: LB4: 3.34:1 LU2: 4.10:1. Optional: 3.73, 4.10:1. Transfer Case: Single speed. Brakes: Type: Hydraulic, power assisted with four-wheel anti-lock system. Front: Discs. Rear: Drums. Dimensions: Front: 11.57 in. x 1.25 in. rotor. Rear: 9.50 in. x 2.0 in. Wheels: 15 x 6.00 in. SLE and SLT: 15 x 6.5 in. Tires: P205/75R15 steel belted radial All-Season black sidewall. Optional: P205/75R15 black sidewall, All-Season steel-belted radial, P205/75R15 on-off road steel belted radial, white sidewall, P205/75R15 All-Season steel belted radial, black sidewall, P215/75R15 All-Season, steel belted radial black sidewall, P215/75R15 All-Season, steel belted radial, P245/60R15, All-Season, steel belted radial, white outlined letters, GT. Steering: Integral power. Ratio: 16/13:1. Turning diameter: 40.5 ft. Transmission: Automatic 4-speed with overdrive (RPO MXO). Ratios: 3.06, 1.63, 1.00, 0.70:1. Reverse: 2.29:1.

VEHICLE DIMENSIONS: Wheelbase: 111.0 in. Overall Length: 176.8 in.; Extended Passenger/Cargo Van: 186.8 in. 178.2 in./170.3 in./194.1 in./208.6 in. Overall Height: 74.1 in. Width: 77.0 in. Headroom: Front/Middle/Rear: 39.2/37.9/38.3 in. Legroom: Front/Middle/Rear: 41.6/36.5/38.5 in. Shoulder room: Front/Middle/Rear: 64.0/67.8/67.8 in. Hip room: Front/

Middle/Rear: 64.9/50.9/50.9 in. Ground Clearance: Front: 6.8 in. Rear: 7.7 in. Extended Passenger/Cargo Van: Front: 7.0 in. Rear: 7.8 in. Load space: 88.9.1 in. x 51.6 in. x 47.5 in. Extended Passenger/Cargo Van: 98.9 in. x 51.6 in. x 47.5 in.

CAPACITIES: Fuel Tank: 27 gal. tank. Coolant system: 13.6 gal.

ACCOMMODATIONS: Seating Capacity: Standard: 5, Optional: 8. Cargo Van: 1. 2.

INSTRUMENTATION: 0-100 mph speedometer, 99,999.9 mi. odometer, fuel gauge, gauges for voltmeter, oil pressure, and engine coolant temperature; warning lights for brake operating system, hazard warning lights, directional lights, seat belt warning.

OPTIONS AND PRICES: Air conditioning: Front: $820, front and rear: $1343. Optional axle ratio: $38. Locking rear differential: $252. Deluxe front and rear chromed bumpers: $76-$128 depending upon Option Packages, black luggage carrier: $126. Engine oil cooler: $135. Heavy-duty radiator: $56. Heavy-duty radiator and engine oil cooler: $63, with air conditioning, $118 without air conditioning. Power door locks: $211. Driver Convenience Package. Includes ComforTilt steering wheel and Intermittent wiper system: $346. Operating Convenience Package. Includes power door locks and power windows: $411. Deep tinted glass: $161-$211 depending on body glass selected. Rear heater: $267. Electronic instrumentation: $88. Auxiliary lighting: $96 with roof console; $129 without roof console. Black below eye-level exterior mirrors: $52. Exterior remote electric mirrors: $150. Special two-tone paint: $172. Deluxe two-tone paint: $172-$334 depending upon other options. Custom two-tone: $187 with SLE, $329 without SLE. Electronically tuned AM/FM stereo radio with Seek-Scan, digital clock, stereo cassette player and premium speakers: $122. Electronically tuned AM/FM stereo radio with Seek-Scan, stereo cassette tape player with Search and Repeat, graphic equalizer, digital clock and premium speakers: $272. Delete radio: $226 credit. Seven passenger seating: $878-$1069 depending upon other options. Eight passenger seating: $344-878 depending upon other options. Seat back recliner and dual armrests: $241. 6-way power seat: $240. Front and rear heavy-duty shock absorbers: $40. Sport Suspension: $417-$509 depending upon other options ordered. Heavy-duty trailering equipment: $507-$564 depending upon other equipment ordered. Light-duty trailering equipment: $109. Aluminum wheels: $233-$325, depending upon other options ordered. Rallye wheels: $92.

HISTORICAL FOOTNOTES: Safari buyer studies indicated it was purchased for multiple uses.

1992 SAFARI AWD

The standard 1992 AWD Safari V-6 engine had a rating of 200 horsepower. Credit for this substantial increase over the 1991 level was due to the use of central port fuel injection. During the 1992 model run a new option was introduced, a rear "Dutch Door" feature with a one-piece lift-gate with split panel doors below with an electronic release. Among the Safari's new interior features were adjustable bench seats, an optional premium sound system with a compact disc player and a new beige interior color.

I.D. DATA: The V.I.N. plate was mounted on the lower left side windshield corner. The V.I.N. consisted of 17 elements. The first, the number 1, identified the U.S. as the nation of origin. The letter G followed for the manufacturer: General Motors. The third entry, the letter T, represented the make as GMC. The GVWR brake system identification followed. Next came the truck line and chassis type; the letter K indicated four-wheel drive. The truck series was identified by a number: 1-1/2 ton. The truck body type identification was next. The engine code was next: N-4.3 liter V-6, followed by a check digit. The model year was identified by the letter N. The assembly plant code followed. The final six digits were the plant sequential production number.

Model Number	Body Type & Seating	Factory Price	GVW	Shipping Weight	Prod. Total
Safari Cargo Van					
TL10905	—	$16,653	5600	N.A.	—
TL11005	Extended	$17,293	5850	N.A.	—
Safari Passenger Van (TL11006- Extended length models)					
TL10906	Safari Van-CS	$17,573	5800	N.A.	—
TL10906	Safari Van-CL	$18,653	5800	N.A.	—
TL10906	Safari Van-LT	$20,203	5800	N.A.	—
TL11006	Safari Van-CS	$18,213	6100	N.A.	—
TL11006	Safari Van-CL	$19,298	6100	N.A.	—
TL11006	Safari Van-LT	$20,843	6100	N.A.	—

STANDARD ENGINE: Engine Type: OHV, cast iron block. V-6. Order Code L35. Bore x Stroke: 4.00 in. x 3.48 in. Lifters: Hydraulic. Number of main bearings-5. Fuel Induction: Electronic fuel injection. Compression Ratio: 9.3:1. Displacement: 262 cu. in. (4.3 liter). Horsepower: Net: 200 @ 4400 rpm. Torque: Net: 260 lb.-ft. @ 3600 rpm. Oil capacity: 5 qt. with filter change. Fuel Requirements: Unleaded.

CHASSIS FEATURES: Integral body frame design with boxed section front stub frame.

SUSPENSION AND RUNNING GEAR: Front Suspension: Independent with torsion bar springs, 32mm dia. shock absorbers. 1.18 in. stabilizer bar. Capacity: 3050 lb. at ground. Rear Suspension: Composite leaf springs. Capacity: 3150 lb. at ground. 32mm shock absorbers. Front Axle. Type: Independent hypoid GM. Capacity: 3050 lb. Rear Axle. Type: GM, semi-floating, hypoid. Capacity: 3150 lb. Final Drive Ratio: 3.42:1. Optional: 3.73. Transfer Case: Single speed. Brakes: Type: Hydraulic, power assisted with four-wheel anti-lock system. Front: Discs. Rear: Drums. Dimensions: Front: 11.57 in. x 1.25 in. rotor. Rear: 9.50 in. x 2.0 in. Wheels: 15 x 6.00 in. SLE and SLT: 15 x 6.5 in. Tires: Passenger and Cargo Van: P205/75R15 All-Weather steel belted radial. Extended Passenger and Cargo Van: P215/75R15 All-Weather steel belted radial. Optional: P205/75R15 black sidewall, All-Season steel-belted radial, P205/75R15 on-off road steel belted radial, white sidewall, P205/75R15 All-Season steel belted radial, black sidewall, P215/75R15 All-Season, steel belted radial black sidewall, P215/75R15 All-Season, steel belted radial, P245/60HR15, All-Season, steel belted radial, white outlined letters, GT. Steering: Integral power. Ratio: 16/13:1. Turning diameter: 40.5 ft. Transmission: Automatic 4-speed with overdrive (RPO MXO). Ratios: 3.06, 1.63, 1.00, 0.70:1. Reverse: 2.29:1.

VEHICLE DIMENSIONS: Wheelbase: 111.0 in. Overall Length: 176.8 in.; Extended Passenger/Cargo Van: 186.8 in. 178.2 in./170.3 in./194.1 in./208.6 in. Overall Height: 74.1 in. Width: 77.0 in. Headroom: Front/Middle/Rear: 39.2/37.9/38.3 in. Legroom: Front/Middle/Rear: 41.6/36.5/38.5 in. Shoulder room: Front/Middle/Rear: 64.0/67.8/67.8 in. Hip room: Front/Middle/Rear: 64.9/50.9/50.9 in. Ground Clearance: Front: 6.8 in. Rear: 7.7 in. Extended Passenger/Cargo Van: Front: 7.0 in. Rear: 7.8 in. Load space: 88.9.1 in. x 51.6 in. x 47.5 in. Extended Passenger/Cargo Van: 98.9 in. x 51.6 in. x 47.5 in.

CAPACITIES: Fuel Tank: 27 gal. tank. Coolant system: 13.6 qt.

ACCOMMODATIONS: Seating Capacity: Standard: 5, Optional: 8. Cargo Van: 1. 2.

INSTRUMENTATION: 0-100 mph speedometer, 99,999.9 mi. odometer, fuel gauge, gauges for voltmeter, oil pressure, and engine coolant temperature; warning lights for brake operating system, hazard warning lights, directional lights, seat belt warning.

OPTIONS: Air conditioning. Optional axle ratio. Locking rear differential. Deluxe front and rear chromed bumpers. Black luggage carrier. Cold Climate Package. Console Roof. Engine oil cooler. Heavy-duty radiator. Heavy-duty radiator and engine oil cooler. Power door locks. Driver Convenience Package. Includes ComforTilt steering wheel and speed control. Operating Convenience Package. Includes power door locks and power windows. Tinted glass, complete body. Deep tinted glass. Rear heater. Electronic instrumentation. Auxiliary lighting. Black below eye-level exterior mirrors. Exterior remote electric mirrors. Special two-tone paint. Deluxe two-tone paint. Custom two-tone. Electronically tuned AM/FM stereo radio with Seek-Scan, digital clock, stereo cassette player and premium speakers. Electronically tuned AM/FM stereo radio with Seek-Scan, stereo cassette tape player with Search and Repeat, graphic equalizer, digital clock and premium speakers. Electronically tuned AM stereo and FM stereo radio with Seek-Scan, stereo cassette tape player with Search and Repeat, graphic equalizer, digital clock and premium speakers. Premium sound system with CD player. Delete radio. Seven passenger seating. Eight passenger seating. Seat back recliner and dual armrests. 6-way power seat. Front and rear heavy-duty shock absorbers. Heavy-duty trailering equipment. Light-duty trailering equipment. Aluminum wheels. Rallye wheels. Rear "Dutch Doors."

HISTORICAL FOOTNOTES: The AWD Safari represented approximately 12 percent of all Safari sales in 1992.

1993 SAFARI AWD

The 1993 Safari offered a number of improvements intended to improve its performance, comfort level, convenience, safety and overall value. Four-wheel anti-lock brakes (ABS), already standard for the passenger models was now standard for the cargo van models. The Enhanced 4.3 liter V-6, L35 engine now idled more smoothly due to improved electronic spark control and altered camshaft profile. A heavy-duty cooling equipment was now standard on every model. Also standard for all models was the new electronically controlled 4-speed Hydra-Matic transmission. The 4L60-E transmission included a second-gear start-up feature and provided more accurate and smother shifting. Revisions to the air conditioning compressor and radiator-fan clutch significantly reduced engine noise, especially during cold start-ups. New brushed aluminum wheels for 1993, featured a smooth center cap that completely covered the lug nuts. A new analog instrument cluster was easier to read than the 1992 version. A new brake/transmission shift interlock featured required that the brake be applied before the vehicle was shifted out of "Park." The shifting column had a new internal steel sleeve to protect the ignition lock cylinder and reduce the possibility of theft. A new Scotchguard protection was standard for all Safaris with cloth seats. Three new exterior colors and five new decal colors were available for 1993.

The Safari continued to be offered in two body lengths-regular and extended (XT). A choice of three trim levels-standard SLX, mid-level SLE and the top-line SLT were retained for 1993.

1993 GMC Safari XT with SLT trim

I.D. DATA: The V.I.N. plate was mounted on the lower left side windshield corner. The V.I.N. consisted of 17 elements. The first, the number 1, identified the U.S. as the nation of origin. The letter G followed for the manufacturer: General Motors. The third entry, the letter T, represented the make as GMC. The GVWR brake system identification followed. Next came the truck line and chassis type; the letter K indicated four-wheel drive. The truck series was identified by a number: 1-1/2 ton. The truck body type identification was next. The engine code

was next: N-4.3 liter V-6, followed by a check digit. The model year was identified by the letter N. The assembly plant code followed. The final six digits were the plant sequential production number.

Model Number	Body Type & Seating	Factory Price	GVW	Shipping Weight	Prod. Total
Safari Cargo Van					
TL10905	—	$N.A.*	5950	N.A.	—
TL11005	Extended	$N.A.	6100	N.A.	—
Safari Passenger Van (TL11006- Extended length models)					
TL10906	Safari Van-CS	$N.A.	5950	N.A.	—
TL10906	Safari Van-CL	$N.A.	5950	N.A.	—
TL10906	Safari Van-LT	$N.A.	5950	N.A.	—
TL11006	Safari Van-CS	$N.A.	6100	N.A.	—
TL11006	Safari Van-CL	$N.A.	6100	N.A.	—
TL11006	Safari Van-LT	$N.A.	6100	N.A.	—

* 1993 model year prices were not available at press time, but it was expected that they would be only modestly increased over the 1992 level.

STANDARD ENGINE: Engine Type: OHV, cast iron block. V-6. Order Code L35. Bore x Stroke: 4.00 in. x 3.48 in. Lifters: Hydraulic. Number of main bearings-5. Fuel Induction: Electronic central port fuel injection. Compression Ratio: 9.1:1. Displacement: 262 cu. in. (4.3 liter). Horsepower: Net: 200 @ 4500 rpm. Torque: Net: 260 lb.-ft. @ 3600 rpm. Oil capacity: 5 qt. with filter change. Fuel Requirements: Unleaded.

CHASSIS FEATURES: Integral body frame design with boxed section front stub frame.

SUSPENSION AND RUNNING GEAR: Front Suspension: Independent with torsion bar springs, 32mm dia. shock absorbers. 1.18 in. stabilizer bar. Capacity: 3050 lb. at ground. Rear Suspension: Composite leaf springs. Capacity: 3150 lb. at ground. 32mm shock absorbers. Front Axle. Type: Independent hypoid GM. Capacity: 3050 lb. Rear Axle. Type: GM, semi-floating, hypoid. Capacity: 3150 lb. Final Drive Ratio: 3.42:1. Optional: 3.73. Transfer Case: Single speed. Brakes: Type: Hydraulic, power assisted with four-wheel anti-lock system. Front: Discs. Rear: Drums. Dimensions: Front: 11.57 in. x 1.25 in. rotor. Rear: 9.50 in. x 2.0 in. Wheels: 15 x 6.00 in. SLE and SLT: 15 x 6.5 in. Tires: Passenger and Cargo Van: P205/75R15 All-Weather steel belted radial. Extended Passenger and Cargo Van: P215/75R15 All-Weather steel belted radial. Optional: P205/75R15 black sidewall, All-Season steel-belted radial, P205/75R15 on-off road steel belted radial, white sidewall, P205/75R15 All-Season steel belted radial, black sidewall, P215/75R15 All-Season, steel belted radial black sidewall, P215/75R15 All-Season, steel belted radial, P245/60HR15, All-Season, steel belted radial, white outlined letters, GT. Steering: Integral power. Ratio: 16/13:1. Turning diameter: 40.5 ft. Transmission: Automatic 4-speed with overdrive Hydra-Matic 4L60-E. Ratios: 3.06, 1.63, 1.00, 0.70:1. Reverse: 2.29:1.

VEHICLE DIMENSIONS: Wheelbase: 111.0 in. Overall Length: 176.8 in.; Extended Passenger/Cargo Van: 186.8 in. 178.2 in./170.3 in./194.1 in./208.6 in. Overall Height: 74.1 in. Width: 77.0 in. Headroom: Front/Middle/Rear: 39.2/37.9/38.3 in. Legroom: Front/Middle/Rear: 41.6/36.5/38.5 in. Shoulder room: Front/Middle/Rear: 64.0/67.8/67.8 in. Hip room: Front/Middle/Rear: 64.9/50.9/50.9 in. Ground Clearance: Front: 6.8 in. Rear: 7.7 in. Extended Passenger/Cargo Van: Front: 7.0 in. Rear: 7.8 in. Load space: 88.9.1 in. x 51.6 in. x 47.5 in. Extended Passenger/Cargo Van: 98.9 in. x 51.6 in. x 47.5 in.

CAPACITIES: Fuel Tank: 27 gal. tank. Coolant system: 13.6 qt.

ACCOMMODATIONS: Seating Capacity: Standard: 5, Optional: 8. Cargo Van: 1. 2.

INSTRUMENTATION: 0-100 mph speedometer, 99,999.9 mi. odometer, fuel gauge, gauges for voltmeter, oil pressure, and engine coolant temperature; warning lights for brake operating system, hazard warning lights, directional lights, seat belt warning.

OPTIONS: Air conditioning. Optional axle ratio. Locking rear differential. Deluxe front and rear chromed bumpers. Black luggage carrier. Cold Climate Package. Console roof. Engine oil cooler. Heavy-duty radiator. Heavy-duty radiator and engine oil cooler. Power door locks. Driver Convenience Package. Includes ComforTilt steering wheel and speed control. Operating Convenience Package. Includes power door locks and power windows. Tinted glass, complete body. Deep tinted glass. Rear heater. Electronic instrumentation. Auxiliary lighting. Black below eye-level exterior mirrors. Exterior remote electric mirrors. Special two-tone paint. Deluxe two-tone paint. Custom two-tone. Electronically tuned AM/FM stereo radio with Seek-Scan, digital clock, stereo cassette player and premium speakers. Electronically tuned AM/FM stereo radio with Seek-Scan, stereo cassette tape player with Search and Repeat, graphic equalizer, digital clock and premium speakers. Electronically tuned AM stereo and FM stereo radio with Seek-Scan, stereo cassette tape player with Search and Repeat, graphic equalizer, digital clock and premium speakers. Premium sound system with CD player. Delete radio. Seven passenger seating. Eight passenger seating. Seat back recliner and dual armrests. 6-way power seat. Front and rear heavy-duty shock absorbers. Heavy-duty trailering equipment. Light-duty trailering equipment. Aluminum wheels. Rallye wheels. Rear "Dutch Doors."

HISTORICAL FOOTNOTES: GMC reported that the Safari was positioned in the mid-size van category which was the third largest segment of the light-truck market.

GMC SONOMA/SYCLONE

1991-1993

1991 SONOMA

Replacing the 1990 S-15 models were the Sonoma models introduced early in 1990. Their exterior appearance was highlighted, in contrast to the older S-15 models, with a new grille, nameplates, emblems, bumper rub strips and body side moldings. The body striping, decals, wheels and wheel trim were also new as were the optional aluminum wheels. Two new exterior colors — Sky blue and mint green were offered. Woodlands brown metallic and Nevada gold metallic were cancelled.

The 4.3 liter V-6 had an improved 220 series throttle body injection system with longer throttle shaft bearings, new throttle return springs and improved fuel mixture distribution. These changes were designed to improve engine starts, idle and overall engine reliability and durability. A new Thermac III modified air cleaner system and Quantum spark plugs were adopted to improve cold starts and overall engine reliability. A lighter, more durable starting motor was also new for 1991. A "hardened" 72mm distributor replaced the 89mm Hall-Effect distributor to make the ignition more impervious to electromagnetic induction interference from other electrical components. The suspension was improved by the use of new rear springs with revised spring rates for improved ride balance. The rear shock absorber valving was also revised. The front axle half-shaft boots were strengthened for improved durability. Accelerator pedal effort was reduced for easier operation. The three trim levels for 1991 were the Base Special, the SLS Sport equipment and the SLE comfort equipment. Major SLS features included visor mirror, interior courtesy and ashtray lights, headlamp-on warning buzzer, body-color painted front bumper and grille, Sonoma ST decals on doors and tailgate; and red lower body side stripe. The SLE equipment included black exterior mirrors, visor mirror, interior courtesy and ashtray lights, headlamp-on warning buzzer, color-keyed floor mats, bright wheel opening moldings, and Deluxe front bumper painted grey with rub stripes. The optional front compartment floor console for models equipped with bucket seats had a revised thumb operated catch for easier, keyless entry. Replacing the rocker type switch previously used to control the power door locks in the Operating Convenience Package was a more convenient, redesigned lever type switch. Reception for both the AM and FM radios was also improved. The 15-7.0 in. aluminum wheels had black painted vent and lug nut pockets, and a 4x4 logo.

I.D. DATA: The V.I.N. plate was mounted on the lower left side windshield corner. The V.I.N. consisted of 17 elements. The first, the number 1, identified the U.S. as the nation of origin. The letter G followed for the manufacturer: General Motors. The third entry, the letter T, represented the make as GMC. The GVWR brake system identification followed. Next came the truck line and chassis type; the letter K indicated four-wheel drive. The truck series was identified by a number: 1-1/2 ton. The truck body type identification was next: 4-Two-door cab. The engine code was next: N-4.3 liter V-6, followed by a check digit. The model year was identified by the letter M. The assembly plant code followed. The final six digits were the plant sequential production number.

Model Number	Body Type & Seating	Factory Price	GVW	Shipping Weight	Prod. Total
Sonoma with 4.3 liter V-6. (Prices effective October 1, 1990)					
TT10603	108.3 in. wb Pickup	$13,256	4650[1]	2974	57,159[2]
TT10803	117.9 in. wb. Pickup	$13,446	4650[1]	3060	—
TT10653	122.9 in. wb. Club Coupe	$14,066	4650[1]	3128	—

NOTE 1: 5150 lb. optional.
NOTE 2: 1991 calendar year production, S-15 and Sonoma models, and both two-wheel drive and four-wheel drive models.

STANDARD ENGINE: Engine Type: OHV, cast iron block. V-6. Order Code LB4. Bore x Stroke: 4.00 in. x 3.48 in. Lifters: Hydraulic. Number of main bearings-5. Fuel Induction: Electronic fuel injection. Compression Ratio: 9.3:1. Displacement: 262 cu. in. (4.3 liter). Horsepower: Net: 160 @ 4000 rpm. Torque: Net: 230 lb.-ft. @ 2400 rpm. Oil capacity: 5 qt. with filter change. Fuel Requirements: Unleaded.

CHASSIS FEATURES: Carbon steel, 39,000 psi., welded front box section and open channel rear section, section modulus: 2.19. Dimensions: 108.3 in. wheelbase: 2.34 in. x 6.50 in. x 0.118 in. Overall length: 170.31 in. 117.9 in. wheelbase: 2.34 in. x 6.50 in. x 0.134 in. Overall length: 186.26 in. 122.9 in. wheelbase: 2.34 in. x 6.50 in. x 0.134 in. Overall length: 184.46 in.

SUSPENSION AND RUNNING GEAR: Front Suspension: Independent with torsion bar springs, 25mm dia. shock absorbers. 32mm stabilizer bar. Capacity: 1350 lbs. each at ground. Optional: 32mm shock absorbers. Rear Suspension: Two-stage multi-leaf shot-peened springs. Capacity: 1150 lbs. each at ground. 25mm shock absorbers. Optional: 32mm shock absorbers. Front Axle. Type: Hypoid, tubular driving. Capacity: 2700 lb. Rear Axle. Type: Salisbury, hypoid. Capacity: 2700 lb. Final Drive Ratio: 3.08:1. Optional: 3.42:1. Transfer Case: New Process 231. Ratios: 2.72,1.00:1. Brakes: Type: Hydraulic, power assisted self-adjusting. Front: Discs. Rear: Drums. Dimensions: Front: 10.51 in. x 2.0 in. rotor. Rear: 9.49 in. x 2.0 in. Wheels: 15 in. x 6.00 in. Tires: P205/75R15 steel belted radial All-Season black sidewall. Optional: P205/75R15 black sidewall, All-Season steel-belted radial, P205/75R15 on-off road steel belted radial, white letters, P205/75R15 All-Season steel belted radial, white letters, P205/75R15 on-off road steel belted radial black sidewall, P205/75R15 steel belted radial. Front: Highway. Rear: On-off road, P235/75R15 on-off road steel belted radial white letters. Steering: Variable ratio, integral power. Ratio: 17.5:1. Turning diameter: 35.4 ft. Transmission: 5-speed manual with overdrive (RPO MM5). Ratios: 4.02, 2.32, 1.40, 1.00, 0.83:1. Reverse: 3.74:1. Optional: 4-speed automatic with overdrive (RPO MXO): 3.06, 1.63, 1.0, 0.70:1. Reverse: 2.29:1. Clutch: 9.13 in. dia.

VEHICLE DIMENSIONS: Wheelbase: Short wheelbase/Long wheelbase/Club coupe: 108.5 in./ 117.9 in./122.9 in. Overall Length: Short wheelbase/Long wheelbase/Club coupe: 178.2 in./194.2 in./192.8 in. Overall Height: 61.2 in. Width: 64.8 in. Tailgate: Width and Height: 53.6 in. x 16.0 in. Load space: Short wheelbase and extended cab: 73.1 in. x 55.3 in. x 15.9 in. Long wheelbase: 90.1 in. x 55.3 in. x 16.0 in.

CAPACITIES: Fuel Tank: 20 gal. tank. Coolant System: 12 qt.

ACCOMMODATIONS: Seating Capacity: Standard: 3. Headroom: 39.5 in. Legroom: 42.4 in.

INSTRUMENTATION: 0-100 mph speedometer, 99,999.9 mi. odometer, fuel gauge, gauges for voltmeter, oil pressure, and engine coolant temperature; warning lights for brake operating system, hazard warning lights, directional lights, seat belt warning.

OPTIONS AND PRICES: (Prices listed were effective Oct. 1, 1990): SLS Sport Package: $87. SLE Package: $493. Air conditioning: $755. Air dam with fog lamps: $115. Optional axle ratio: $44. Locking rear differential: $252. Heavy-duty battery: $56. Rear step bumper: $130-$229 depending upon paint option. Spare tire carrier: $110. Cold Climate Package: $140-$243 depending upon trim option. Center console: $135. Heavy-duty radiator: $56. Heavy-duty radiator and transmission oil cooler: $63, with air conditioning, $118 without air conditioning. Engine oil cooler: $135. Driver Convenience Package. Includes ComforTilt steering wheel and intermittent wiper system: $204. Full floor carpeting: $40. Deep tinted glass: Club coupe: $101-$140 depending upon Option Package; regular cab: $11. Electronic instrumentation: $195. Auxiliary lighting: $44-$66 depending upon other options ordered. Exterior below eye-level painted mirrors: $52. Lighted interior visor mirror: $68-$75 depending upon Trim Package. Body side and wheel opening moldings: $152. Black wheel opening molding: $13-$43 depending upon Trim Package. Bright wheel opening molding: $31. Endgate net: $110. Operating Convenience Package. Includes power door locks and power windows: $367. Special two-tone paint. Includes pinstriping: $296. Deluxe two-tone paint: $177. Electronically tuned AM/FM stereo radio with digital clock: $201. Electronically tuned AM/FM stereo radio with Seek-Scan, stereo cassette tape player and digital clock: $131. Electronically tuned AM/FM stereo radio with Seek-Scan, stereo cassette tape player with Search and Repeat, and digital clock: $253. Electronically tuned AM/FM stereo radio with Seek-Scan, stereo cassette tape player with Search and Repeat, graphic equalizer and digital clock: $150-$403 depending upon other options ordered. Delete radio: $95 credit. Rear jump seats with vinyl trim: $240. Shield Package. Includes transfer case and front differential skid plates and steering linkage shield: $126. Heavy-duty front springs: $63. Sport suspension: $252. Off-road suspension: $122 with SLE equipment, $182 without SLE equipment. Front and rear heavy-duty shock absorbers: $40. Electronic speed control: $238. Heavy-duty rear springs: $64. Heavy duty front suspension with heavy-duty front and rear shock absorbers: $63. Body striping: $55. Manual sun roof: $250. Heavy-duty Trailering Special Package: $211. 4-speed automatic transmission: $890. Wheel trim rings: $60. Cast aluminum wheels: $284-$340 depending upon Trim Package. Sliding rear window: $113.

HISTORICAL FOOTNOTES: GMC truck sales in 1991 per outlet were 122 units.

1991 SONOMA

New for 1992 was the availability of a four-wheel drive special price leader model. Its base equipment included a 160 hp Vortex V-6 engine, 5-speed manual transmission, power steering, compact spare and wheel and a solid exterior color. The standard SL and upgrade SLE models were offered with an optional new 2-speed electronic-shift transfer case. Revisions for 1992 included seats with integral head restraints for front bench seat positions and high-back buckets with optional leather (club coupe) seating, a standard self-aligning steering wheel, and an optional premium sound system with compact disc player. Exterior colors for 1992 were consisted of midnight black, Aspen blue metallic, royal blue metallic, sky blue, garnet red, steel grey metallic, aquamarine green, forest green metallic, apple red, frost white and as a secondary color only, silver metallic.

I.D. DATA: The V.I.N. plate was mounted on the lower left side windshield corner. The V.I.N. consisted of 17 elements. The first, the number 1, identified the U.S. as the nation of origin. The letter G followed for the manufacturer: General Motors. The third entry, the letter T, represented the make as GMC. The GVWR brake system identification followed. Next came the truck line and chassis type; the letter K indicated four-wheel drive. The truck series was identified by a number: 1-1/2 ton. The truck body type identification was next: 4-Two-door cab. The engine code was next: N-4.3 liter V-6, followed by a check digit. The model year was identified by the letter N. The assembly plant code followed. The final six digits were the plant sequential production number.

Model Number	Body Type & Seating	Factory Price	GVW	Shipping Weight	Prod. Total
Sonoma with 4.3 liter V-6. (Prices effective October 1, 1990)					
TT10603	108.3 in. wb. Spl. Pickup	$12,362	4650[1]	N.A.	—
TT10603	108.3 in. wb. Pickup	$13,644	4650[1]	2974	—
TT10803	117.9 in. wb. Pickup	$13,944	4650[1]	3060	—
TT10653	122.9 in. wb. Club Coupe	$15,144	4650[1]	3128	—

NOTE 1: 5150 lb. optional.

STANDARD ENGINE: Engine Type: OHV, cast iron block. V-6. Order Code LB4. Bore x Stroke: 4.00 in. x 3.48 in. Lifters: Hydraulic. Number of main bearings-5. Fuel Induction: Electronic fuel injection. Compression Ratio: 9.3:1. Displacement: 262 cu. in. (4.3 liter). Horsepower: Net: 160 @ 4000 rpm. Torque: Net: 230 lb.-ft. @ 2400 rpm. Oil capacity: 5 qt. with filter change. Fuel Requirements: Unleaded.

CHASSIS FEATURES: Carbon steel, 39,000 psi., welded front box section and open channel rear section, section modulus: 2.19. Dimensions: 108.3 in. wheelbase: 2.34 in. x 6.50 in. x 0.118 in. Overall length: 170.31 in. 117.9 in. wheelbase: 2.34 in. x 6.50 in. x 0.134 in. Overall length: 186.26 in. 122.9 in. wheelbase: 2.34 in. x 6.50 in. x 0.134 in. Overall length: 184.46 in.

SUSPENSION AND RUNNING GEAR: Front Suspension: Independent with torsion bar springs, 25mm dia. shock absorbers. 32mm stabilizer bar. Capacity:1350 lbs. each at ground. Optional: 32mm shock absorbers. Rear Suspension: Two-stage multi-leaf shot-peened springs. Capacity: 1150 lbs. each at ground. 25mm shock absorbers. Optional: 32mm shock absorbers. Front Axle. Type: Hypoid, tubular driving. Capacity: 2700 lb. Rear Axle. Type: Salisbury, hypoid. Capacity: 2700 lb. Final Drive Ratio: 3.08:1. Optional: 3.42:1. Transfer Case: New Process 231. Ratios: 2.72,1.00:1. Brakes: Type: Hydraulic, power assisted self-adjusting. Front: Discs. Rear: Drums. Dimensions: Front: 10.51 in. x 2.0 in. rotor. Rear: 9.49 in. x 2.0 in. Wheels: 15 in. x 6.00 in. Tires: P205/75R15 steel belted radial All-Season black sidewall. Optional: P205/75R15 black sidewall, All-Season steel-belted radial, P205/75R15 on-off road steel belted radial, White letters, P205/75R15 All-Season steel belted radial, white letters, P205/75R15 Oon-off road steel belted radial black sidewall, P205/75R15 steel belted radial. Front: Highway. Rear: On-off road, P235/75R15 on-off road steel belted radial white letters. Steering: Variable ratio, integral power. Ratio: 17.5:1. Turning diameter: 35.4 ft. Transmission: 5-speed manual with overdrive (RPO MM5). Ratios: 4.02, 2.32, 1.40, 1.00, 0.83:1. Reverse: 3.74:1. Optional: 4-speed automatic with overdrive (RPO MXO): 3.06, 1.63, 1.0, 0.70:1. Reverse: 2.29:1. Clutch: 9.13 in. dia.

VEHICLE DIMENSIONS: Wheelbase: Short wheelbase/Long wheelbase/Club coupe: 108.5 in./ 117.9 in./122.9 in. Overall Length: Short wheelbase/Long wheelbase/Club coupe: 178.2 in./194.2 in./192.8 in. Overall Height: 61.2 in. Width: 64.8 in. Tailgate: Width and Height: 53.6 in. x 16.0 in. Load space: Short wheelbase and extended cab: 73.1 in. x 55.3 in. x 15.9 in. Long wheelbase: 90.1 in. x 55.3 in. x 16.0 in.

CAPACITIES: Fuel Tank: 20 gal. tank. Coolant System: 12 qt.

ACCOMMODATIONS: Seating Capacity: Standard: 3. Headroom: 39.5 in. Legroom: 42.4 in.

INSTRUMENTATION: 0-100 mph speedometer, 99,999.9 mi. odometer, fuel gauge, gauges for voltmeter, oil pressure, and engine coolant temperature; warning lights for brake operating system, hazard warning lights, directional lights, seat belt warning.

OPTIONS: SLE Package. Air conditioning: Air dam with fog lamps. Optional axle ratio. Locking rear differential. Heavy-duty battery. Spare tire and wheel carrier. Cold Climate Package. Heavy-duty radiator. Heavy-duty radiator and engine oil cooler. Driver Convenience Package (RPO ZM7). Includes ComforTilt steering wheel and intermittent wiper system. Driver Convenience Package (RPO ZM8). Includes rear window defroster and tailgate release. California Emissions Package. Color-keyed front floor mats (two-door only). Rear color-keyed floor mats. Deep tinted glass (RPO AJ1). Deep tinted glass with light tinted rear window (RPO AA3). Electronic instrumentation. Exterior electric remote mirrors. Visor mirrors, left and right side. Black wheel opening molding. Operating Convenience Package. Includes power door locks and power windows. Special two-tone paint. Deluxe two-tone paint. Electronically tuned AM/FM stereo radio with Seek-Scan and digital clock. Electronically tuned AM/FM stereo radio with Seek-Scan, stereo cassette tape player. Electronically tuned AM/FM stereo radio with Seek-Scan, stereo cassette tape player with Search and Repeat, graphic equalizer and digital clock. Delete radio. Special custom cloth reclining high-back bucket seats. Deluxe cloth reclining high-back bucket seats. Leather reclining high-back bucket seats. Transfer case and front differential skid plates and steering linkage shield. Front and rear heavy-duty shock absorbers. Electronic speed control. Body striping. Sunroof, manual, non-removable. Heavy-duty front springs. Off-road suspension. Light-Duty Trailering Package. Heavy-Duty Trailering Special Package. 4-speed automatic transmission. Rallye wheels. Cast aluminum wheels. Grey aluminum wheels. Sliding rear side window.

HISTORICAL FOOTNOTES: Observing that its first truck was built in 1912, GMC declared that in 1992 "There's no substitute for 80 years of experience."

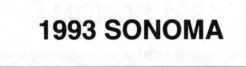

1993 SONOMA

GMC focused upon four major areas — quality, reliability, durability and performance to improve the Sonoma for 1993. The optional enhanced 4.3 liter V-6 engine now had a balance shaft for smoother overall engine performance. It also was equipped with a more reliable thermostat, revised camshaft profile for improved idle performance, new intake manifold and new cylinder-head passages. The all-new, electronically controlled four-speed Hydra-Matic 4L60-E was offered for the Sonoma. The base cooling system for all models was upgraded to include larger radiators. A single rail shifter for the five-speed manual transmission matched to the 4.3 liter V-6 tightened the shift pattern of the gear lever and minimized the possibility of a blocked shift. Revisions to the air conditioning compressor increased the system's reliability and durability. All bucket seats for 1993 offered adjustable seat-back recliners as standard equipment. The cloth bucket seats now had manually adjustable lumbar supports. For club coupe models with the SLS trim, carpeting was added to the back panel of the cab and a convenience net was included with the SLS and SLE trim levels. A more functional center console with integral cup holders, storage space, a higher, more comfortable center armrest, and an auxiliary 12-volt DC power jack was also new for 1993. The instrument panel storage area for smaller items was also improved. Included in the SLS and SLE trim levels were new dual sun visors. In-lines with lighted vanity mirrors, pull-out extensions and a convenience strap. Power outside rearview mirrors were now available. A new internal steel steering column sleeve provided ignition lock cylinder protection and additional vehicle theft prevention. The Sonoma SLS had a monochromatic look with a body-color grille, wheel-lip moldings and available painted body-color aluminum wheels. Solar-Ray & glass was standard in all models.

I.D. DATA: The V.I.N. plate was mounted on the lower left side windshield corner. The V.I.N. consisted of 17 elements. The first, the number 1, identified the U.S. as the nation of origin. The letter G followed for the manufacturer: General Motors. The third entry, the letter T, represented the make as GMC. The GVWR brake system identification followed. Next came the truck line and chassis type; the letter K indicated four-wheel drive. The truck series was identified by a number: 1-1/2 ton. The truck body type identification was next: 4-Two-door cab. The engine code was next: N-4.3 liter V-6, followed by a check digit. The model year was identified by the letter N. The assembly plant code followed. The final six digits were the plant sequential production number.

Sonoma prices for 1993 were not available at press time. What follows is the Sonoma model offerings and their min./max. GVW ratings for 1993.

Model	Body Type	GVWR (min./max.)
T10603	Regular Cab, 108.3 in. wb.	4650/5150
T10803	Regular Cab,117.9 in. wb.	4650/5150
T10653	Club Coupe, 122.9 in. wb.	4650/5150

STANDARD ENGINE: Engine Type: OHV, cast iron block. V-6. Order Code LB4. Bore x Stroke: 4.00 in. x 3.48 in. Lifters: Hydraulic. Number of main bearings-5. Fuel Induction: Electronic throttle-body fuel injection. Compression Ratio: 9.1:1. Displacement: 262 cu. in. (4.3 liter). Horsepower: Net: 165 @ 4000 rpm. Torque: Net: 235 lb.-ft. @ 2400 rpm. Oil capacity: 5 qt. with filter change. Fuel Requirements: Unleaded.

CHASSIS FEATURES: Carbon steel, 39,000 psi., welded front box section and open channel rear section, section modulus: 2.19. Dimensions: 108.3 in. wheelbase: 2.34 in. x 6.50 in. x 0.118 in. Overall length: 170.31 in. 117.9 in. wheelbase: 2.34 in. x 6.50 in. x 0.134 in. Overall length: 186.26 in. 122.9 in. wheelbase: 2.34 in. x 6.50 in. x 0.134 in. Overall length: 184.46 in.

SUSPENSION AND RUNNING GEAR: Front Suspension: Independent with torsion bar springs, 25mm dia. shock absorbers. 1.10 in. stabilizer bar. Capacity: 1350 lbs. each at ground. Optional: 32mm shock absorbers. Rear Suspension: Two-stage multi-leaf shot-peened springs. Capacity: 1150 lbs. each at ground. 25mm shock absorbers. Optional: 32mm shock absorbers. Front Axle. Type: Hypoid, tubular driving. Capacity: 2700 lb. Rear Axle. Type: Salisbury, hypoid. Capacity: 2700 lb. Final Drive Ratio: 3.08:1. Optional: 3.42:1. Transfer Case: New Process 231. Ratios: 2.72,1.00:1. Brakes: Type: Hydraulic, power assisted self-adjusting. Front: Vented discs. Rear: Drums. Dimensions: Front: 10.50 in. x 1.03 in. rotor. Rear: 9.50 in. x 2.0 in. Wheels: 15 in. x 6.00 in. Optional: Aluminum wheels. Tires: P205/75R15 steel belted radial All-Season black sidewall. Optional: P235/75R15 black sidewall, All-Season steel-belted radial. Steering: Variable ratio, integral power. Ratio: 17.5:1. Turning diameter: 35.4 ft. Transmission: New Venture Gear 3500 5-speed manual with overdrive (RPO MY2). Ratios: 4.02, 2.32, 1.40, 1.00, 0.83:1. Reverse: 3.74:1. Optional: Hydra-Matic 4L60-E electronic 4-speed automatic with overdrive (RPO M30): 3.06, 1.63, 1.0, 0.70:1. Reverse: 2.29:1. Clutch: 9.13 in. dia.

VEHICLE DIMENSIONS: Wheelbase: Short wheelbase/Long wheelbase/Club coupe: 108.5 in./ 117.9 in./122.9 in. Overall Length: Short wheelbase/Long wheelbase/Club coupe: 178.2 in./194.2 in./192.8 in. Overall Height: 61.2 in. sun visor. Width: 64.8 in. Tailgate: Width and Height: 53.6 in. x 16.0 in. Load space: Short wheelbase and extended cab: 73.1 in. x 55.3 in. x 15.9 in. Long wheelbase: 90.1 in. x 55.3 in. x 16.0 in.

CAPACITIES: Fuel Tank: 20 gal. tank.

ACCOMMODATIONS: Seating Capacity: Standard: 3. Headroom: 39.5 in. Legroom: 42.4 in.

INSTRUMENTATION: 0-100 mph speedometer, 99,999.9 mi. odometer, fuel gauge, gauges for voltmeter, oil pressure, and engine coolant temperature; warning lights for brake operating system, hazard warning lights, directional lights, seat belt warning.

OPTIONS: SLE Package. Air conditioning: Air dam with fog lamps. Optional axle ratio. Locking rear differential. Heavy-duty battery. Spare tire and wheel carrier. Cold Climate Package. Heavy-duty radiator. Heavy-duty radiator and engine oil cooler. Driver Convenience Package (RPO ZM7). Includes ComforTilt steering wheel and intermittent wiper system. Driver Convenience Package (RPO ZM8). Includes rear window defroster and tailgate release. California Emissions Package. Color-keyed front floor mats (two-door only). Rear color-keyed floor mats. Deep tinted glass (RPO AJ1). Deep tinted glass with light tinted rear window (RPO AA3). Electronic instrumentation. Exterior electric remote mirrors. Visor mirrors, left and right side. Black wheel opening molding. Operating Convenience Package. Includes power door locks and power windows. Special two-tone paint. Deluxe two-tone paint. Electronically tuned AM/FM stereo radio with Seek-Scan and digital clock. Electronically tuned AM/FM stereo radio with Seek-Scan, stereo cassette tape player. Electronically tuned AM/FM stereo radio with Seek-Scan, stereo cassette tape player with Search and Repeat, graphic equalizer and digital clock. Delete radio. Delco CD player. Special custom cloth reclining high-back bucket seats. Deluxe cloth reclining high-back bucket seats. Leather reclining high-back bucket seats. Transfer case and front differential skid plates and steering linkage shield. Front and rear heavy-duty shock absorbers. Electronic speed control. Body striping. Sunroof, manual, non-removable. Heavy-duty front springs. Off-road suspension. Light-Duty Trailering Package. Heavy-Duty Trailering Special Package. 4-speed automatic transmission. Rallye wheels. Cast aluminum wheels. Grey aluminum wheels. Sliding rear side window.

HISTORICAL FOOTNOTES: GMC offered its customers a toll-free 1-800-GMC-Truck phone number for consumer problems and concerns. In one instance it reported a lockout problem was solved in 30 minutes using this service.

1991-1992 SYCLONE

The Syclone, based upon the Sonoma compact pickup, was capable of zero to 60 mph acceleration in less than five seconds and a standing-start 1/4 mile time of 13.4 seconds. It was powered by a turbocharged 4.3 liter V-6 Vortex engine with port fuel injection and an intercooler. Other specific engine equipment included new pistons, new left/right side exhaust manifolds with a special exhaust system, pintle style individual injectors and L88 throttle body. The standard transmission was a Hydra-Matic 4L60 4-speed automatic with unique sport calibration.

The Syclone featured a full-time all-wheel-drive system and the first four-wheel anti-lock braking system available on a pickup truck. Standard equipment included air conditioning, power windows and door locks, AM/FM stereo radio and cassette tape player, tilt wheel, intermittent windshield wipers, analog gauges with tachometer and turbo boost, cruise control and tinted glass. Also standard was a Lexxus TruxCover tonneau cover. The tonneau cover snapped to an aluminum frame that attached to the truck bed without drilled holes.

1991 GMC Syclone

The Syclone's interior contained contoured sport bucket seats with lumbar support, a floor-mounted shifter, center console with two cupholders, storage area, Syclone insignia and leather wrapped steering wheel.

The exterior of the Syclone had a monochromatic black finish with red graphic accents, Body Applique Package, and exclusive badging. High performance Firestone Firehawk tires and turbine aluminum wheels were specifically tailored and produced for the Syclone.

I.D. DATA: The V.I.N. plate was mounted on the lower left side windshield corner. The V.I.N. consisted of 17 elements. The first, the number 1, identified the U.S. as the nation of origin. The letter G followed for the manufacturer: General Motors. The third entry, the letter T, represented the make as GMC. The GVWR brake system identification followed. Next came the truck line and chassis type; the letter K indicated four-wheel drive. The truck series was identified by a number: 1-1/2 ton. The truck body type identification was next: 4-Two-door cab. The engine code was next: N-4.3 liter V-6, followed by a check digit. The model year was identified by the letter M (1991) and N (1992). The assembly plant code followed. The final six digits were the plant sequential production number.

Model	Body Type	Factory Price
Syclone	108.3 in. wb. Pickup	$25,500 ($26,995 for 1992)

STANDARD ENGINE: Engine Type: OHV, cast iron block. V-6. Bore x Stroke: 4.00 in. x 3.48 in. Lifters: Hydraulic. Number of main bearings-5. Fuel Induction: Electronic fuel injection, turbo-charged (max. boost: 14 psi.), intercooled. Compression Ratio: 8.35:1. Displacement: 262 cu. in. (4.3 liter). Horsepower: Net: 280 @ 4400 rpm. Torque: Net: 250 lb.-ft. @ 3600 rpm. Oil capacity: 5 qt. with filter change. Fuel Requirements: Unleaded.

CHASSIS FEATURES: Carbon steel, 39,000 psi., welded front box section and open channel rear section, section modulus: 2.19. Dimensions: 108.3 in. wheelbase: 2.34 in. x 6.50 in. x 0.118 in. Overall length: 170.31 in.

SUSPENSION AND RUNNING GEAR: Front Suspension: Independent with torsion bar springs, 25mm dia. shock absorbers. 32mm stabilizer bar, revised jounce bumpers, lower ride height. Rear Suspension: Reduced rate two-stage multi-leaf shot-peened springs. Front Axle. Type: Hypoid, tubular driving. Capacity: 2700 lb. Rear Axle. Type: Salisbury, hypoid. Capacity: 2700 lb. Final Drive Ratio: 3.42:1, limited slip. Transfer Case: Safari L-van, torque split front/rear: 35%/65%. Brakes: Type: Hydraulic, power assisted self-adjusting. Front: Ventilated discs. Rear: Drums. Dimensions: Front: 10.50 in. x 1.03 in. rotor. Rear: 9.50 in. x 2.0 in. Wheels: Front: 16 in. x 8.00 in., aluminum, 44mm offset. Rear: 16 in. x 8.00 in., aluminum, 20.5mm offset. Tires: 245/50VR-16 Firestone Firehawk. Steering: Power assisted, recirculating ball. Ratio: variable-13/16.0:1. Turning diameter: 37.9 ft. Transmission: Hydra-Matic 4L60 (700R4), 4-speed automatic. Ratios: 3.06, 1.63, 100, 0.701. Reverse: 2.291.

VEHICLE DIMENSIONS: Wheelbase: 108.5 in. Overall Length: 180.5 in. Overall Height: 60.0 in. Width: 64.8 in. Tailgate: Width and Height: 53.6 in. x 16.0 in. Load space: 73.1 in. x 55.3 in. x 15.9 in.

CAPACITIES: Fuel Tank: 20 gal. tank. Coolant system: 12 qt.

ACCOMMODATIONS: Seating Capacity: Standard: 3. Headroom: 39.1 in. Legroom: 42.5 in. Shoulder room: 53.9 in.

INSTRUMENTATION: 0-100 mph speedometer, 99,999.9 mi. odometer, fuel gauge, gauges for voltmeter, oil pressure, tachometer, turbo-boost and engine coolant temperature; warning lights for brake operating system, hazard warning lights, directional lights, seat belt warning.

HISTORICAL FOOTNOTES: *Popular Hot Rodding*, October, 1990 called the Syclone "the performance enthusiast's dream come true."

GMC YUKON
1992-1993

1992 YUKON

Noting that its only business was trucks, and had been for over 80 years, GMC said that its full-size 4x4 utility for 1992 was so improved that a new name — Yukon — was appropriate. With a longer wheelbase than the old Jimmy the Yukon had a 6 passenger capacity, improved on and off-road performance and a towing capability of 7,000 lbs; 1,000 lbs. more than its predecessor. A new front suspension with independent upper and lower control arms and torsion bars provided improved tracking, stability and control. The appearance of the Yukon was similar to GMC full-size pickup models.

New standard features included anti-lock brakes and an Insta-Trac four-wheel drive shift-on-the-fly system. The 5.7 liter Electronic Fuel Injection (EFI) V-8 was standard as was a 5-speed manual transmission with overdrive. The diesel engine was not offered. A 4-speed automatic with locking torque converter and overdrive was optional. New exterior and interior appointments for the Yukon included improved seats with head restraints for the front outboard positions, a standard full gauge cluster and an extended range AM radio. An optional new Sport Appearance Package provided an up-level sport look with two-tone paint, special grille and bumpers and wheel flares. New safety enhancements included a self-aligning steering wheel that aligned parallel to the driver's body to distribute force more equally in the event of a crash. The interior color selection consisted of light beige, blue, garnet and grey. Exterior colors consisted of brilliant blue metallic, smoke blue metallic, dark teal metallic, onyx black, summit white, beige metallic, fire red, dark garnet metallic, quicksilver metallic and slate metallic.

1992 Yukon SLE with Sport Package

Standard equipment for the base SL model included LT225 All-Season steel-belted radial tires, power steering, power brakes, tinted glass, black, below eye-level dual outside rearview mirrors, base-coat/clear coat paint, chrome front and black rear bumpers, high-back front bucket seats with custom vinyl trim and matching rear vinyl seat, inside spare tire carrier on left rear panel, full-coverage, intermittent wet-arm windshield wiper/washer system, electronically tuned AM radio, dual horns, glove box with beverage wells on door back, heavy-duty battery, dual dome lights, headlights-on reminder, voltmeter, oil pressure and engine coolant temperature gauges, trip odometer, lift glass/drop tailgate system with electric tailgate release. The SLE Package added these items: Custom cloth 40/60 split front bench seat and matching rear cloth seat with armrests, chrome front and rear bumpers with rub strips, body-side and wheel-opening moldings, dark argent grille with quad halogen headlights, deluxe bumper guards, Rallye wheel trim, bright, below eye-level dual outside rearview mirrors, electronically-tuned AM/FM stereo radio with Seek-Scan, spare wheel carpet cover, full-length color-keyed cloth headliner, color-keyed carpeting, front and rear color-keyed floormats, interior assist straps, front and rear map lights, illuminated mirror on passenger's side sun visor, vinyl storage pockets and assist straps on doors.

I.D. DATA: The V.I.N. plate was mounted on the lower left side windshield corner. The V.I.N. consisted of 17 elements. The first, the number 1, identified the U.S. as the nation of origin. The letter G followed for the manufacturer: General Motors. The third entry, the letter T, represented the make as GMC. The GVWR brake system identification followed. Next came the truck line and chassis type; the letter K indicated four-wheel drive. The truck series was identified by a number: 1-1/2 ton. The truck body type identification was next: 8-Utility. The engine code was next, followed by a check digit. The model year was identified by the letter N. The assembly plant code followed. The final six digits were the plant sequential production number.

Model Number	Body Type & Seating	Factory Price	GVW	Shipping Weight	Prod. Total
K1500 Yukon					
K10516	Util.	$19,518	6250	N.A.	—

STANDARD ENGINE: All states: Engine Type: Cast iron block. OHV, V-8. Ordering Code: L05. Produced by GM-Chevrolet Motor Division. Bore x Stroke: 4.0 in. x 3.48 in. Lifters: Hydraulic. Number of main bearings-5. Carburetion: Electronic fuel injection. Compression

Ratio: 9.3:1. Displacement: 350 cu. in. (5.7 liters). Horsepower: Net: 210 @ 4000 rpm. Torque: Net: 300 lb.-ft. @ 2800 rpm. Oil capacity: 5 qt. with filter change. Fuel Requirements: 87 octane minimum, unleaded.

CHASSIS FEATURES. Ladder-type. All-welded, ladder-type channel-design with boxed front end.

SUSPENSION AND RUNNING GEAR: Front Suspension: Independent with torsion bars, 1.25 in. anti-roll bar, steel upper and lower control arms. Capacity: 1900 lb. each. Optional: 2500 lb. capacity. 32mm shock absorbers. Rear Suspension: Variable-rate, two-stage, multi-leaf semi-elliptical springs. Capacity: 1875 lb. each. 32mm shock absorbers. Front Axle. Type: Hypoid, tubular driving. Capacity: 3600 lb. Rear Axle. Type: Hypoid, semi-floating. Capacity: 3750 lb. Final Drive Ratio: 3.42:1. Optional: 3.73:1 (manual transmission only). Transfer Case: New Process 241. Part-time, two-speed. Ratios: 2.721, 1.00:1. Brakes: Type: Hydraulic, self-adjusting. Front: Discs. Rear: Drums. Optional: Power. Dimensions: Front: 11.50 in. x 1.25 in. rotor. Rear: 10.0 in. x 2.25 in. Wheels: 16 x 6.50. Tires: LT225/75R16C. Optional: Various sizes available. Steering: Power assisted recirculating ball, variable ratio. Ratio: 13:1. Turning circle: 41.5 ft. Optional: None. Transmission: 5-speed manual with overdrive. Transmission Ratios: 4.02, 2.32, 1.40, 1.00, 0.73:1. Reverse: 3.75:1. Clutch: 12.0 in. dia. Optional: Automatic 4-speed with overdrive.

VEHICLE DIMENSIONS: Wheelbase: 111.5 in. Overall Length: 187.7 in. Front/Rear overhang: 34.9 in./41.2 in. Front/Rear Tread 64.1 in./63.50 in. Overall Height: 71.0 in. Width: 76.4 in. Approach/Departure angle: 13/27. Ground Clearance: Minimum Front: 6.9 in. Minimum Rear axle: 7.1 in. Rear door opening: 61.4 in. width, 53.5 in. height. Load space: With rear seat installed: 38.9 in. x 61.4 in. x 41.7 in. Without rear seat: 74.0 in. x 61.4 in. x 41.7 in.

CAPACITIES: Fuel Tank: 30.0 gal. Coolant system: 15.6 qt.

ACCOMMODATIONS: Seating Capacity: 5. Optional front 40/60 split seat provides room for 6 occupants. Front headroom: 40.2 in. Rear headroom: 38.0 in. Front legroom: 41.7 in. Rear legroom: 37.6 in. Front shoulder room: 66.0 in. Rear shoulder room: 63.2 in. Front hip room: 60.5 in. Rear hip room: 53.1 in.

INSTRUMENTATION: 0-100 mph speedometer, 99,999.9 mi. odometer, gauges for fuel level, voltmeter, oil pressure, and engine coolant temperature; warning lights for brake operating system, hazard warning lights, directional lights, seat belt warning.

OPTIONS: SLE Package. Sport Appearance Package. Air conditioning. Operating Convenience Package. Driver's Convenience Package.

HISTORICAL FOOTNOTES: The 1992 GMC Yukon was offered with a customer satisfaction program called Commitment Plus. Among its features was a complimentary 3000 mile inspection and maintenance service including oil and oil filter change.

1993 YUKON

After debuting as an all-new vehicle in 1992, the 1993 model was improved with technical refinements and revised features keyed towards improved quality and reliability, operational convenience and comfort. The Yukon was available with General Motors new Hydra-Matic 4L60E transmission. The standard 5-speed manual transmission had a new single-rail shifter for improved shift feel and reduced lever shake. This arrangement also minimized blocked shifts. An improved fan clutch and revised air induction system on the standard 5.7 liter V-8 reduced engine noise level, especially during cold start-ups. A new steel sleeve and an improved lock cylinder reduced the likelihood of vehicle theft. The Yukon's HVAC system was now available with a 4-speed blower control and a larger-displacement air compressor. The results included increased reliability, greater passenger comfort and less blower and air rush noise. An improved cruise-control system now featured a soft-pedal release to disengage the system. It also incorporated other modifications for improved system performance. New passenger-side seat back recliners were standard on 60/40 split-bench and high-back bucket seats. Scotchguard protection was applied to all cloth seats. Yukons with full-width bench or split-bench front seats featured new instrument panel-mounted cupholders. All radios were redesigned with larger and rearranged controls. Standard on all Yukons was Solar-Ray™ window glass. A new optional GT sport appearance package with a monochromatic look was offered in either black or dark garnet. It included body-color grille and wheel moldings, and aluminum wheels.

1993 GMC Yukon two-door

The Yukon continued to be available with either 5 or 6 passenger seating. The choice was between bench, 60/40 split-bench or high-back bucket seats for the front. A full-width folding bench rear seat was standard. Roof and floor-mounted consoles were standard when bucket seas were ordered. Two interior trim levels were again offered — SL and the up-scale SLE. A new indigo blue metallic color was offered to provide eleven exterior colors for 1993.

I.D. DATA: The V.I.N. plate was mounted on the lower left side windshield corner. The V.I.N. consisted of 17 elements. The first, the number 1, identified the U.S. as the nation of origin. The letter G followed, for the manufacturer: General Motors. The third entry, the letter T, represented the make as GMC. The GVWR brake system identification followed. Next came the truck line and chassis type; the letter K indicated four-wheel drive. The truck series was identified by a number: 1-1/2 ton. The truck body type identification was next: 8-Utility. The engine code was next, followed by a check digit. The model year was identified by the letter N. The assembly plant code followed. The final six digits were the plant sequential production number.

Model Number	Body Type & Seating	Factory Price	GVW	Shipping Weight	Prod. Total
K1500 Yukon					
K10516	Util.	$19,518	6250	N.A.	—

STANDARD ENGINE: All states: Engine Type: Cast iron block. OHV, V-8. Ordering Code: L05. Produced by GM-Chevrolet Motor Division. Bore x Stroke: 4.0 in. x 3.48 in. Lifters: Hydraulic. Number of main bearings-5. Carburetion: Electronic fuel injection. Compression Ratio: 9.3:1. Displacement: 350 cu. in. (5.7 liters). Horsepower: Net: 210 @ 4000 rpm. Torque: Net: 300 lb.-ft. @ 2800 rpm. Oil capacity: 5 qt. with filter change. Fuel Requirements: 87 octane minimum, unleaded.

CHASSIS FEATURES: Ladder-type. All-welded, ladder-type channel-design with boxed front end.

SUSPENSION AND RUNNING GEAR: Front Suspension: Independent with torsion bars, 1.25 in. anti-roll bar, steel upper and lower control arms. Capacity: 1900 lb. each. Optional: 2500 lb. capacity. 32mm shock absorbers. Rear Suspension: Variable-rate, two-stage, multi-leaf semi-elliptical springs. Capacity: 1875 lb. each. 32mm shock absorbers. Front Axle. Type: Hypoid, tubular driving. Capacity: 3600 lb. Rear Axle. Type: Hypoid, semi-floating. Capacity: 3750 lb. Final Drive Ratio: 3.42:1. Optional: 3.73:1 (manual transmission only). Transfer Case: New Process 241. Part-time, two-speed. Ratios: 2.721, 1.00:1. Brakes: Type: Hydraulic, self-adjusting. Front: Discs. Rear: Drums. Optional: Power. Dimensions: Front: 11.50 in. x 1.25 in. rotor. Rear: 10.0 in. x 2.25 in. Wheels: 16 x 6.50. Tires: LT225/75R16C. Optional: Various sizes available. Steering: Power assisted recirculating ball, variable ratio. Ratio: 13:1. Turning circle: 41.5 ft. Optional: None. Transmission: 5-speed manual with overdrive. Transmission Ratios: 4.02, 2.32, 1.40, 1.00, 0.73:1. Reverse: 3.75:1. Clutch: 12.0 in. dia. Optional: Automatic 4-speed with overdrive.

VEHICLE DIMENSIONS: Wheelbase: 111.5 in. Overall Length: 187.7 in. Front/Rear overhang: 34.9 in./41.2 in. Front/Rear Tread 64.1 in./63.50 in. Overall Height: 71.0 in. Width: 76.4 in. Approach/Departure angle: 13/27. Ground Clearance: Minimum Front: 6.9 in. Minimum Rear axle: 7.1 in. Rear door opening: 61.4 in. width, 53.5 in. height. Load space: With rear seat installed: 38.9 in. x 61.4 in. x 41.7 in. Without rear seat: 74.0 in. x 61.4 in. x 41.7 in.

CAPACITIES: Fuel Tank: 30.0 gal. Coolant system: 15.6 qt.

ACCOMMODATIONS: Seating Capacity: 5. Optional front 40/60 split seat provides room for 6 occupants. Front headroom: 40.2 in. Rear headroom: 38.0 in. Front legroom: 41.7 in. Rear legroom: 37.6 in. Front shoulder room: 66.0 in. Rear shoulder room: 63.2 in. Front hip room: 60.5 in. Rear hip room: 53.1 in.

INSTRUMENTATION: 0-100 mph speedometer, 99,999.9 mi. odometer, gauges for fuel level, voltmeter, oil pressure, and engine coolant temperature; warning lights for brake operating system, hazard warning lights, directional lights, seat belt warning.

OPTIONS: SLE Package. Sport Appearance Package. Air conditioning. Operating Convenience Package. Driver's Convenience Package.

HISTORICAL FOOTNOTES: The 1993 GMC Yukon was offered with a customer satisfaction program called Commitment Plus. Among its features was a complimentary 3000 mile inspection and maintenance service including oil and oil filter change.

GMC TYPHOON
1992-1993

1992 TYPHOON

A super four-wheel drive compact Sport utility truck, the Typhoon, was offered for 1992. It was powered by an intercooled, turbo-charged V-6 Vortex engine with electronic port fuel injection. It developed 280 horsepower @ 4400 rpm and 350 lb.-ft. of torque @ 3600 rpm and required a minimum 93 octane fuel. A recalibrated four-speed automatic transmission was standard. Additional features of the Typhoon included a limited slip rear differential, P245/50VR-16 tires, and electronic load leveling with air-bag assisted shock absorbers. The Typhoon interior had charcoal-colored leather seats, front bucket seats with inflatable lumbar support, and center console. The Typhoon's base price also included air conditioning and cruise control. The standard sound system, specific to the Typhoon could be ordered with an optional CD player. The Typhoon was available in a monochromatic paint scheme in these colors: Black, grey metallic, red, white, Aspen blue or teal. The lower body cladding had a dark gray finish. A front air dam with integral fog lights was included as were aero moldings for the fenders, doors, and rear fascia.

I.D. DATA: The V.I.N. plate was mounted on the lower left side windshield corner. The V.I.N. consisted of 17 elements. The first, the number 1, identified the U.S. as the nation of origin. The letter G followed for the manufacturer: General Motors. The third entry, the letter T, represented the make as GMC. The GVWR brake system identification followed. Next came the truck line and chassis type; the letter K indicated four-wheel drive. The truck series was identified by a number: 1-1/2 ton. The truck body type identification was next: 8-Utility. The engine code was next, followed by a check digit. The model year was identified by the letter N. The assembly plant code followed. The final six digits were the plant sequential production number.

Model Number	Body Type & Seating	Factory Price	GVW	Shipping Weight	Prod. Total
GMC Truck Typhoon					
—	2-dr. Sport Utility	$28,995	4700	N.A.	—

STANDARD ENGINE: All states: Engine Type: Cast iron block. OHV, turbocharged and intercooled V-6. Ordering Code: LB4/ZR9. Bore x Stroke: 4.0 in. x 3.48 in. Lifters: Hydraulic. Number of main bearings-5. Induction system: Electronic port fuel injection. Compression Ratio: 8.35:1. Displacement: 262 cu. in. (4.3 liters). Horsepower: Net: 285 @ 4400 rpm. Torque: Net: 360 lb.-ft. @ 3600 rpm. Oil capacity: 5 qt. with filter change. Fuel Requirements: 93 octane minimum, unleaded.

CHASSIS FEATURES: Ladder-type. All-welded, ladder-type channel-design with boxed front end.

SUSPENSION AND RUNNING GEAR: Front Suspension: Independent with torsion bars, 32mm anti-roll bar, unequal length upper and lower control arms. Rear Suspension: Two-stage, multi-leaf semi-elliptical springs with shock absorbers fitted with integral air bags. Rear Axle: Type: Semi-floating. Final Drive Ratio: 3.42:1. Transfer Case: Borg Warner 4472 with limited slip viscous coupling. Torque split: Front: 35 percent, Rear: 65 percent. Brakes: Type: Hydraulic, self-adjusting. Front: vented discs. Rear: drums with four-wheel ABS. Dimensions: Front: 11.86 in. x 1.29 in. rotor. Rear: 11.15 in. x 2.75 in. Wheels: 16 x 8.0 in. aluminum. Tires: Firestone Firehawk SVX P245/50VR16 speed-rated. Steering: Integral, power assist. Ratio: 17.5:1.Turning Circle: 35.4 ft. Transmission: Hydra-Matic 4L60 4-speed automatic with overdrive. Transmission Ratios: 3.06, 1.63, 1.00, 0.70. Reverse: 2.29:1.

VEHICLE DIMENSIONS: Wheelbase: 100.5 in. Overall Length: 170.3 in. Front/Rear Tread 57.7 in./58.0 in. Overall Height: 60.0 in. Width: 68.2 in. Ground Clearance: Minimum: 7.1 in. Cargo volume, Min./Max. (cu. ft.): 28.1/67.2.

CAPACITIES: Fuel Tank: 20.0 gal.

ACCOMMODATIONS: Seating Capacity: 5. Front headroom: 39.1 in. Rear headroom: 38.7 in. Front legroom: 42.5 in. Rear legroom: 35.5 in. Front shoulder room: 53.9 in. Rear shoulder room: 56.1 in. Front hip room: 50.5 in. Rear hip room: 37.6 in.

INSTRUMENTATION: 0-100 mph speedometer, 99,999.9 mi. odometer, gauges for fuel level, voltmeter, oil pressure, and engine coolant temperature; warning lights for brake operating system, hazard warning lights, directional lights, seat belt warning.

OPTIONS: With a lengthy standard equipment list, the Typhoon's optional equipment was not extensive. Options included a roof-mounted luggage carrier, a compact disc player and exterior paint/cladding combinations.

HISTORICAL FOOTNOTES: The Typhoon was regarded as a technical showcase which helped define GMC's mission as a truck producer.

1993 TYPHOON

After storming onto the performance truck scene in 1992 and becoming an instant legend in the process, the Typhoon featured a number of technical and interior enhancements designed to augment and refine the existing package. The rear suspension was retuned to provide better road feel, reduced harshness and increased maximum lateral acceleration. An overhead console was added that provided two reading lamps plus a convenient storage area for sunglasses and a garage door opener. The standard leather trim driver's seat featured 6-way power adjustments and power lumbar support. The front passenger seat also had a power lumbar support as standard equipment. A door-activated illuminated entry system provided additional nighttime convenience. A cargo area convenience net was added to keep packages and gear secure. A new body-color grille and bolder tailgate graphics were introduced for 1993. Also offered for 1993 was a new monochromatic white-on-white exterior color package.

The Typhoon's basic attributes remained impressive. They included: A 4.3 liter turbocharged and intercooler V-6 engine, a four-speed automatic overdrive transmission (previously fitted to L98-equipped Corvettes), full-time all-wheel drive, leather-trimmed front Sport bucket seats and a front fascia with integral fog lights.

1993 GMC Typhoon

I.D. DATA: The V.I.N. plate was mounted on the lower left side windshield corner. The V.I.N. consisted of 17 elements. The first, the number 1, identified the U.S. as the nation of origin. The letter G followed for the manufacturer: General Motors. The third entry, the letter T, represented the make as GMC. The GVWR brake system identification followed. Next came the truck line and chassis type; the letter K indicated four-wheel drive. The truck series was identified by a number: 1-1/2 ton. The truck body type identification was next: 8-Utility. The engine code was next, followed by a check digit. The model year was identified by the letter N. The assembly plant code followed. The final six digits were the plant sequential production number.

Model Number	Body Type & Seating	Factory Price	GVW	Shipping Weight	Prod. Total
GMC Truck Typhoon					
—	2-dr. Sport Utility	$N.A.	4700	N.A.	—

STANDARD ENGINE: All states: Engine Type: Cast iron block. OHV, turbocharged and intercooled V-6. Ordering Code: LB4/ZR9. Bore x Stroke: 4.0 in. x 3.48 in. Lifters: Hydraulic. Number of main bearings-5. Induction system: Electronic port fuel injection. Compression Ratio: 8.35:1. Displacement: 262 cu. in. (4.3 liters). Horsepower: Net: 285 @ 4400 rpm. Torque: Net: 360 lb.-ft. @ 3600 rpm. Oil capacity: 5 qt. with filter change. Fuel Requirements: 93 octane minimum, unleaded.

CHASSIS FEATURES: Ladder-type. All-welded, ladder-type channel-design with boxed front end.

SUSPENSION AND RUNNING GEAR: Front Suspension: Independent with torsion bars, 32mm anti-roll bar, unequal length upper and lower control arms. Rear Suspension: Two-stage, multi-leaf semi-elliptical springs with shock absorbers fitted with integral air bags. Rear Axle: Type: semi-floating. Final Drive Ratio: 3.42:1. Transfer Case: Borg Warner 4472 with limited slip viscous coupling. Torque split: Front: 35 percent, Rear: 65 percent. Brakes: Type: Hydraulic, self-adjusting. Front: Vented discs. Rear: Drums with four-wheel ABS. Dimensions: Front: 11.86 in. x 1.29 in. rotor. Rear: 11.15 in. x 2.75 in. Wheels: 16 x 8.0 in. aluminum. Tires: Firestone Firehawk SVX P245/50VR16 speed-rated. Steering: Integral, power assist. Ratio: 17.5:1.Turning Circle: 35.4 ft. Transmission: Hydra-Matic 4L60 4-speed automatic with overdrive. Transmission Ratios: 3.06, 1.63, 1.00, 0.70. Reverse: 2.29:1.

VEHICLE DIMENSIONS: Wheelbase: 100.5 in. Overall Length: 170.3 in. Front/Rear Tread 57.7 in./58.0 in. Overall Height: 60.0 in. Width: 68.2 in. Ground Clearance: Minimum: 7.1 in. Cargo volume, Min./Max. (cu. ft.): 28.1/67.2.

CAPACITIES: Fuel Tank: 20.0 gal.

ACCOMMODATIONS: Seating Capacity: 5. Front headroom: 39.1 in. Rear headroom: 38.7 in. Front legroom: 42.5 in. Rear legroom: 35.5 in. Front shoulder room: 53.9 in. Rear shoulder room: 56.1 in. Front hip room: 50.5 in. Rear hip room: 37.6 in.

INSTRUMENTATION: 0-100 mph speedometer, 99,999.9 mi. odometer, gauges for fuel level, voltmeter, oil pressure, and engine coolant temperature; warning lights for brake operating system, hazard warning lights, directional lights, seat belt warning.

OPTIONS: With a lengthy standard equipment list, the Typhoon's optional equipment was not extensive. Options included a roof-mounted luggage carrier, a compact disc player and exterior paint/cladding combinations.

HISTORICAL FOOTNOTES: In regard to the Typhoon, GMC noted: "For 1993, this outrageous sport utility continues to offer the U.S. a limited number of enthusiasts a most brilliant and civil blend of luxury, versatility and awesome performance."

INTERNATIONAL PICKUP & TRAVELALL
1953-1975

International Harvester's early history reflected the dichotomy of the four-wheel drive models it manufactured between 1953 and 1980. With roots reaching into the mid-19th century via Cyrus Hall McCormick's production of numerous farm implements, it was appropriate that its first automotive efforts were tilted towards the perspectives of America's farmers. These vehicles were the International Highwheelers that first appeared in 1907. Even by the admittedly primitive standards for the time, these machines were prime examples of a functional, no-nonsense attitude towards the manufacture of motorized vehicles. The tilt was towards the offering of utilitarian vehicles that offered little in the way of passenger comforts. Instead, International Harvester placed a high priority upon the provision of rugged and reliable mechanical beasts of transportation. The Highwheelers/Auto Wagon/Express International models were, even as late as 1915, characterized by a wagon-like appearance, accentuated by wheels as high as 44 in.. A typical model could be fitted with a rear seat that when conditions required could be removed for additional load space. Mechanically, the Highwheeler's planetary 2-speed transmission, air-cooled 2-cylinder engine and solid rubber tires reflected the thinking of many designers of the era. But the Highwheelers were living on borrowed time and as the teens ended International made the transition towards more contemporary, conventional models. There were exceptions to this course correction, most apparent being the shovel-nose models of the mid-teens that bore a close physical resemblance to the French Renaults of the time. During the 1920s International Harvester catered to both the farm truck market and the rapidly expanding heavy-duty truck industry. A prime example of the former was the S series or "Red Babies" introduced in 1921. These were followed by models with contemporary styling features such as V-eed radiator shells, slanted windshields and flowing fender lines. International Harvester also offered station wagon models during the 1930s that were successful blends of utilitarian reliability and sturdy design with styling, that if not exceptional, was pleasing to the eye. During the 1940 model year, International Harvester introduced a new Model K line with styling that would characterize most International light and heavy-duty trucks until 1950. The use of front fenders incorporating the headlights, a narrow grille with thin horizontal bars and a two-piece windshield of slanted flat glass gave these models a distinctive if conservative appearance. A review of the International's mechanical specifications reinforced the impression that these were trucks, not warmed-over, beefed-up passenger cars. The engine of the K-1-1/2 ton trucks of 1940, the L-head, 6-cylinder "Green Diamond" with a 213 cu. in. displacement produced 82 horsepower.

These models were carried over for the postwar market until replaced by the all-new L series of 1950. Once again, both the styling and design of these Internationals reflected a philosophy of a company committed to a quality product. Over-engineered (International depicted them as "Heavy-Duty Engineered") and possessing a capacity to endure conditions far beyond their paper specifications, the new Internationals became a mainstay of American agriculture. In 1951, International reported that one million of its trucks were still on the road. This number represented more than half of all International trucks built in the past 44 years. In 1953, International announced its first four-wheel drive light R series models. International's position in the four-wheel drive market was strengthened by the availability of the Travelall and Travelette models in four-wheel drive form. But the general public really began to take notice of International as a producer of four-wheel drive models with the arrival of the Scout in 1961. Here was a vehicle that offered the Jeep its first significant domestic competition. As was common International practice, the Scout was built according to true truck design philosophy. Its 4-cylinder engine, for example, was essentially half of International's V-304 V-8 which was used in International trucks capable of transporting a 20,000 lb. gross vehicle weight. The Scout as well as International's other light-duty four-wheel drive models rode the wave of four-wheel drive popularity as the market for such vehicles moved away from its utilitarian/agricultural roots towards what was to become the recreational vehicle market. Soon Scouts were being offered with V-8 engines, power steering, automatic transmission and air conditioning. But just as this market was poised to experience an even more significant burst of popularity, the fuel shortages of the late seventies made a rude but short-lived interruption of what had been a seemingly endless expanse of sales. This event, which other four-wheel drive manufacturers were able to survive, impacted upon International at a time when both its farm implementation and heavy-truck sales were in decline. Eventually these developments brought International Harvester to near collapse, forcing the sale of its farm machinery operations. The loss of its historic farm-oriented business tradition was a heavy price that International paid for its survival. In that content the demise of all International four-wheel drive models after the 1980 model year was predictable. Plans did exist for a new generation Scout; even after the decision was made to focus International's resources on the production of heavy-duty trucks, hopes existed that the Scout division would be acquired by a group of Texas investors. This did not come to pass and in late October, 1980, the last Scout was produced. Its completion ended an illustrious phase of International's grand and glorious history.

1953-56 PICKUP & TRAVELALL

International introduced its first four-wheel drive pickups during 1953. They were R series vehicles. The R series trucks used the basic shell of the L series trucks that were introduced in January, 1950. They featured a one-piece curved windshield, a handsome grille with vertical bars and broad front fenders that in total maintained an appearance continuity with the pre-war derived model K trucks while offering the International truck buyer a vehicle that was up-to-date and contemporary. The basic format of these trucks was continued through the start of the 1955 calendar year.

The 1956 International four-wheel drive models were introduced along with the rest of International's extremely large product offering in mid-1955. Styling revisions made it very easy to identify the new models. The front fender line was raised and the headlights were moved from their former position in the grille to the fenders. The wider hood retained the front air intake feature of the older models but the greater width of the latest version gave the vehicle a more modern and graceful appearance. The trapezoidal-shaped grille encompassed the parking/directional lights. The International's "Comfo-Vision" cabs offered such amenities as a comfort-angled steering wheel, a "Quiet-ride" roof lining and draft-free doors. The optional deluxe cab had a color-keyed interior and chrome trim. A choice of 24 solid and optional two-tone exterior colors were offered. Powering the S-120 and S-140 models was a new overhead valve In-line 6-cylinder engine known as the "240 Black Diamond" engine.

1955 International S-Line

I.D. DATA: The serial number was positioned both on the left-side frame rail behind the front spring hanger, and the vehicle capacity plate attached to the left door pillar. The serial numbers followed the sequence that began in 1953. Engine numbers were stamped on a boss found on the left-hand upper side of the crankcase.

1956:

Body Type	Factory Price	GVW	Shipping Weight	Prod. Total
Series S-120 (S-122)[1], 115 in. wheelbase				
Chassis & Cab	$2027	7000	3880	—
Pickup	$2128	7000	4210	—
Panel	$2355	7000	4485	—
Travelall	$2628	7000	4765	—
Series S-120, 122 in. wheelbase				
Chassis & Cab	$2037	7000	3908	—
Series S-120, 127 in. wheelbase				
Chassis & Cab	$2047	7000	3922	—
Platform	$2185	7000	—	—
Stake	$2238	7000	4527	—
Pickup	$2194	7000	4348	—
Series S-144, 130 in. wheelbase				
Chassis & Cab	$3089	11,000[2]	4725	—
Pickup 9 ft.	$3256	11,000	5135	—
Series S-144, 142 in. wheelbase				
Chassis & Cab	$3116	11,000	4795	—

NOTE 1: International offered a heavy-duty version of its 1/2 and 3/4 ton four-wheel drive pickups. The series in parenthesis refers to those models.
NOTE 2: GVW up to 13,000 lb. optional for S-144 models.

STANDARD ENGINE: S-120, S-140: Engine Type: OHV In-line 6-cylinder. Bore x Stroke: 3.5625 in. x 4.0218 in. Lifters: Solid. Number of main bearings-4. Displacement: 240.3 cu. in. (3.93 liters). Carburetion (type-model id.). Compression Ratio. Horsepower: 131 @ 3800 rpm. Torque: 208.5 lb.-ft. Fuel Requirements: Regular.

CHASSIS FEATURES: Separate body and frame, high-tensile steel channel rails, five cross members.

SUSPENSION AND RUNNING GEAR: Front Suspension: Semi-elliptical leaf springs. Rear Suspension: Semi-elliptical leaf springs.

VEHICLE DIMENSIONS: Series S-120. Wheelbase: 115, 122, 127, 134 in. Series S-140 (S-144): Wheelbase: 130 in., 144 in. Front/Rear Tread: (115, 127 in. wheelbase): 58.281 in./58.8125 in.

OPTIONS AND PRICES: Chrome front bumper, rear bumper, body side spare tire mount, Deluxe cab interior, foam rubber sears, dome light, bumper guards, AM radio, antenna, heater, clock, cigar lighter, seat covers, external sun shade, spotlight, passenger-side sun

visor, door armrests, electric windshield wipers, locking glove compartment, special paint, two-tone paint, wheel trim rings, directional signals, whitewall tires, pickup box side panels, OSRV mirror, deluxe equipment package.

HISTORICAL FOOTNOTES: International was the nation's number three truck producer.

1957 PICKUP & TRAVELALL

International continued its S series four-wheel drive trucks into mid-1957 when they were succeeded by a new A-120 series. The former are usually identified as the 1st 1957 series, the latter as the 2nd 1957 series. The new A models had wraparound windshields, front fenders that flowed into the body sides and headlight nacelles that included the parking/directional lights. The new bodies retained International's familiar front hood scoop in a broader and flatter form. Except for the absence of the parking/directional lights, the A series grille was similar to that of the S series.

I.D. DATA: The serial number was found in two locations: on the left side of the frame rail behind the front spring hanger, and on the capacity plate attached to the left door pillar. The engine number was stamped on a boss on the left-hand upper front side of the crankcase.

Except for a minor price increase averaging $100.00, the first series 1957 models were unchanged from 1956.

Second Series

Body Type	Factory Price	GVW	Shipping Weight	Prod. Total
Series A-120, (A-122), 3/4 ton, 110 in. wheelbase				
Chassis & Cab	$2516	7000	3825	—
Series A-120, (A-122), 3/4 ton, 114 in. wheelbase				
Chassis & Cab	$2516	7000	3825	—
Pickup 7 ft.	$2637	7000	4165	—
Pickup 7 ft. Cust.	$2943	7000	4165	—
Panel 7 ft.	$2912	7000	4440	—
Travelall 7 ft.	$3205	7000	4720	—
Series A-120, (A-122), 3/4 ton, 126 in. wheelbase				
Chassis & Cab	$2543	7000	3855	—
Pickup 8.5 ft.	$2681	7000	4240	—
Series A-140, 129 in. wheelbase				
Chassis & Cab	$3456	11,000	4555	—
Pickup	$3594	11,000	4940	—
Series A-140 141 in. wheelbase				
Chassis & Cab	$3483	11,000	4585	—
Series A-140, 153 in. wheelbase				
Chassis & Cab	$3510	11,000	4645	—

STANDARD ENGINE: A-120, A-122, A-140, A-144: Engine Type: OHV, In-line 6-cylinder "240 Black Diamond." Bore x Stroke: 3.5625 in. x 4.018 in. Lifters: Solid. Number of main bearings-4. Displacement: 240.3 cu. in. Horsepower: 140.8 @ 3800 rpm. Torque: 223.5 lb.-ft. @ 2000 rpm. Fuel Requirements: Regular.

OPTIONAL ENGINE: A-122, A-122: Engine Type: OHV, In-line 6-cylinder "264 Black Diamond." Bore x Stroke: 3.6875 in. x 4.125 in. Displacement: 264.330 cu. in. Lifters: Solid. Number of main bearings-4. Horsepower: 153.5 @ 3800 rpm. Torque: 248 lb.-ft. @ 2400 rpm. Fuel Requirements: Regular.

CHASSIS FEATURES: Separate body and frame, high-tensile steel channel rails, closely spaced cross members.

SUSPENSION AND RUNNING GEAR: Front Suspension: Semi-elliptical leaf springs. Rear Suspension: Semi-elliptical leaf springs. Brakes: Type: Hydraulic front and rear. Tires: A-120: 7. 17.5 in., 6-ply. A-140: 8.00 x 19.5 in., 8-ply.

VEHICLE DIMENSIONS: Wheelbase: S-120, S-122: 110 in. 114 in., 126 in.

OPTIONS: Chrome front bumper, rear bumper, deluxe cab interior, foam rubber seats, dome light, door armrest, bumper guards, AM radio, antenna, fresh air or recirculating type heaters, clock, cigarette lighter, seat covers, custom exterior trim, spotlight, passenger-side sun visor, electric windshield wipers, locking glove box, special paint, two-tone paint, directional signals, white sidewall tires, pickup box panels, wheel trim rings, OSRV mirror, right-side OSRV mirror.

HISTORICAL FOOTNOTES: International Harvester celebrated its fiftieth anniversary as a truck manufacturer in 1957.

1958 PICKUP & TRAVELALL

The 1958 four-wheel drive International models were unchanged in design from the second series models introduced in mid-1957. A slight increase in prices was adopted.

I.D. DATA: The serial number was found in two locations: On the left side of the frame rail behind the front spring hanger, and on the capacity plate attached to the left door pillar. The engine number was stamped on a boss on the left-hand upper front side of the crankcase.

Body Type	Factory Price	GVW	Shipping Weight	Prod. Total
Series A-120, (A-122), 110 in. wheelbase				
Chassis & Cab	$2663	7000	3410	—
Series A-120, (A-122), 114 in. wheelbase				
Chassis & Cab	$2529	7000	3420	—
Pickup 7 ft.	$2650	7000	3750	—
Pickup Cust. 7 ft.	$2956	7000	3750	—
Panel 7 ft.	$2942	7000	4005	—
Travelall	$3261	7000	4305	—
Series A-120, (A-122), 126 in. wheelbase				
Chassis & Cab	$2556	7000	3440	—
Pickup 8.5 ft.	$2694	7000	3825	—
Util. Chassis & Cab	$3648	7000	N.A.	—
Util. Chassis & Cab Cust.	$3756	7000	N.A.	—
Util. Pickup 6 ft.	$3777	7000	N.A.	—
Util. Pickup 6 ft. Cust.	$3939	7000	N.A.	—
Series A-140, 129 in. wheelbase				
Chassis & Cab	$3589	11,000	4555	—
Pickup 8.5 ft.	$3727	11,000	4940	—
Series A-140, 141 in. wheelbase				
Chassis & Cab	$3616	11,000	4585	—
Series A-140, 153 in. wheelbase				
Chassis & Cab	$3643	11,000	4645	—

STANDARD ENGINE: A-120, A-122, A-140, A-144: Engine Type: OHV, In-line 6-cylinder "240 Black Diamond". Bore x Stroke: 3.5625 in. x 4.018 in. Lifters: Solid. Number of main bearings-4. Displacement: 240.3 cu. in. Horsepower: 140.8 @ 3800 rpm. Torque: 223.5 lb.-ft. @ 2000 rpm. Fuel Requirements: Regular.

OPTIONAL ENGINE: A-122, A-122: Engine Type: OHV, In-line 6-cylinder "264 Black Diamond". Bore x Stroke: 3.6875 in. x 4.125 in. Displacement: 264.330 cu. in. Lifters: Solid. Number of main bearings-4. Horsepower: 153.5 @ 3800 rpm. Torque: 248 lb.-ft. @ 2400 rpm. Fuel Requirements: Regular.

CHASSIS FEATURES: Separate body and frame, high-tensile steel channel rails, closely spaced cross members.

SUSPENSION AND RUNNING GEAR: Front Suspension: Semi-elliptical leaf springs. Rear Suspension: Semi-elliptical leaf springs. Brakes: Type: Hydraulic front and rear. Tires: A-120: 7. 17.5 in., 6-ply. A-140: 8.00 x 19.5 in., 8-ply.

VEHICLE DIMENSIONS: Wheelbase: S-120, S-122: 110 in. 114 in., 126 in.

OPTIONS: Chrome front bumper, rear bumper, deluxe cab interior, foam rubber seats, dome light, door armrest, bumper guards, AM radio, antenna, fresh air or recirculating type heaters, clock, cigarette lighter, seat covers, custom exterior trim, spotlight, passenger-side sun visor, electric windshield wipers, locking glove box, special paint, two-tone paint, directional signals, white sidewall tires, pickup box panels, wheel trim rings, OSRV mirror, right-side OSRV mirror.

HISTORICAL FOOTNOTES: The 1958 models, introduced in the fall of 1957, were promoted as the "Golden Anniversary" models.

1959 PICKUP & TRAVELALL

1959 International model B-120 (4x4) with Service Body

International was proud of the "Action Styling" of its new B series 4x4 trucks. "Its external appearance," said International, "starting with the largest, one-piece anodized aluminum meshed grille on any vehicle, flanged by chrome-mounted dual headlights, will convince you that this is truck styling at its best." Specific styling changes for 1959 included a new rectangularly-shaped grille with an egg-crate insert, vertically-mounted dual headlights and bright-rimmed circular parking/directional positioned directly below the headlights. Standard equipment for the B-120 models included an adjustable, full-width, full-depth, padded coil spring front seat and back cushions with two-tone vinyl-coated covering, safety glass "Sweep-Around" windshield, "Silent-Vent" window wings, safety-type door latches, right door lock, inside

overhead rearview mirror, dual electric windshield wipers, left-hand side sun visor, ashtray, map compartment, tool compartment, vinyl-coated insulated headliner, heavy-duty floor mat, front bumper, combination tail and stop light, parking lights, horn and spare wheel. The frame and wheels were painted black. International offered 14 solid exterior color choices.

I.D. DATA: The serial number was found in two locations: on the left side of the frame rail behind the front spring hanger, and on the capacity plate attached to the left door pillar. The engine number was stamped on a boss on the left-hand upper front side of the crankcase.

Body Type	Factory Price	GVW	Shipping Weight	Prod. Total
Series B-120, B-122, 110 in. wheelbase				
Chassis & Cab	$2917	7000	3825	—
Series B-120, B-122, 114 in. wheelbase				
Chassis & Cab	$2917	7000	3835	—
Pickup 7 ft.	$3035	7000	4165	—
Panel 7 ft.	$3313	7000	4440	—
Travelall	$3605	7000	4720	—
Series B-120, B-122, 125 in. wheelbase				
Chassis & Cab	$2944	7000	3855	—
Pickup 8.5 ft.	$3073	7000	4240	—
Series B-120, B-122, 129 in. wheelbase				
Util. Chassis & Cab	$4039	7000	N.A.	—
Util. Pickup 6 ft.	$4166	7000	N.A.	—
Series B-140, 129 in. wheelbase				
Chassis & Cab	$3624	11,000	4555	—
Pickup 8.5 ft.	$3754	11,000	4940	—
Series B-140, 141 in. wheelbase				
Chassis & Cab	$3651	11,000	4585	—
Series B-140, 151 in. wheelbase				
Chassis & Cab	$3678	11,000	4645	—

Model wheelbase identification: Series B-120, B-122: 110, 114, 125, 129 in.; Series B-140: 129, 141, 153 in.

Initially, for 1959, the B-120 and B-140 models had the International Black Diamond 240 engine standard with either the International Black Diamond 264 or the new International V-266 optional. By July, 1959 the V-266 became the standard engine for all models. The B series was continued into 1960 when the V-266 was made standard for the Series 120 and 140.

STANDARD ENGINE: Series B-120, B-140: International Black Diamond. 240 (BD-240). Engine Type: I-block, OHV, 6-cyl. Bore x Stroke: 3.5625 in. x 4.018 in. Lifters: Solid. Number of main bearings-4. Displacement: 240.3 cu. in. Carburetion: Single 1-barrel, downdraft. Compression Ratio: 7.5:1. Horsepower: 140.8 @ 3800 rpm. Torque: 223.5 lb.-ft. @ 2000 rpm. Fuel Requirements: Regular. Oil capacity: 7 qt.

OPTIONAL ENGINE: International Black Diamond 264 (BD-264): Engine Type: I-6 cyl. OHV. Bore x Stroke: 3.5625 in. x 4.125 in. Displacement: 264 cu. in. Carburetion: Single 1-barrel, downdraft. Compression Ratio: 7.5:1. Number of main bearings-4. Horsepower: 153.5 @ 3800 rpm. Torque: 248 lb.-ft. @ 2400 rpm. Fuel Requirements: Regular. Both the BD-240 and BD-264 could be ordered equipped for operation on LP gas. Oil Capacity: 7 qt.

OPTIONAL ENGINE: Standard after July, 1959: International V-266. Engine Type: OHV V-8. Bore x Stroke: 3.625 in. x 3.218 in. Displacement: 266 cu. in. Carburetion: Single 1-barrel, downdraft. Compression Ratio: 8.4:1. Horsepower: 154.8 @ 4400 rpm. Torque: 227,1 lb.-ft. @ 2800 rpm. Fuel Requirements: Regular. Oil Capacity: 7 qt.

CHASSIS FEATURES: Separate body and frame, type (B-120): Pressed steel channel, 7 in. x 3 in. x 0.1875 in.

SUSPENSION AND RUNNING GEAR: (B-120). Front Suspension: 46 in. x 2.5 in. semi-elliptical leaf springs, direct acting shock absorbers. Rear Suspension: 52 in. x 2.5 in. semi-elliptical leaf springs, direct acting shock absorbers. Front Axle Type and Capacity: Single-reduction, hypoid type. Capacity: 2,800 lb. Rear Axle Type and Capacity: Full-floating, single-reduction, Hotchkiss type final drive. Capacity: 4,500 lb. Final Drive Ratio: 4.1 or 4.777:1 (front and rear). Transfer Case: 2-speed. Ratios: 1.98:1, 1.00:1. Brakes: Type: Front and Rear: Hydraulic, internal-expanding, two-shoe, single-anchor type. Lining Area: 172.9 sq. in. Wheels: Disc type, 5.25 in. rims. Optional: None. Tires: Series B-120, B-122: 7 x 17.5, 6-ply. Series B-140: 8 x 19.5 in., 8-ply. Optional: Tubeless or tubed, alternate sizes and special treads. Steering: Type: Semi-reversible dual ratio, cam and roller-mounted twin lever gear. Four-spoke,18 in. safety type steering wheel. Turning circle (B-120): 110 in. wheelbase: 47 ft., 114 in. wheelbase: 48 in., 117 in. wheelbase: 49 ft., 126 in. wheelbase: 53 ft., 129 in. wheelbase: 54 ft. Transmission: Manual, 3-speed. Shift lever mounted on steering column. Ratios: 3.039, 1.641, 1.00:1. Optional: Four-speed, selective sliding gear type manual transmission. Heavy-duty four-speed manual transmission. Clutch: Type, 11.0 in. Optional: 12 in. dia. (V-8 only).

VEHICLE DIMENSIONS:

B-120 Models:

Wheelbase (in.):	110	114	117	126	129
Overall Length (in.):	188.43	188.56	197.56	206.56	209.56
Front Overhang (in.):	36.43	36.43	36.43	36.43	36.43
Rear Overhang (in.):	42	38	44	44	44

Width: 79.375 in. (all models). Ground Clearance (B-120 models): Front axle: 9.125 in. Rear axle: 8.5625 in.

CAPACITIES: Fuel tank: Choice of 18 gal. under cab or 15 gal. underbody fuel tank. Cooling system: Black Diamond. 240 and Black Diamond 264: 15 qt.

ACCOMMODATIONS: Seating Capacity: 3 passenger.

INSTRUMENTATION: 0-100 mph speedometer, odometer reading to 99,999.9 miles, gauges for oil pressure, generator charging rate, engine coolant temperature, fuel level.

OPTIONS: (B-120): Full depth foam rubber or rubber-topped seat and back cushions. Individual foam-rubber topped driver's seat with standard construction passenger's seat. Exterior fixed arm type or chrome cowl-mounted rearview mirrors. Dome light. Armrests. Right-side sun visor. Tinted glass. Cigarette lighter. Grab handles. Left-door lock. Map compartment light. Sliding rear window and screen. Custom cab. Includes: Two sun visors, two armrests, dome light, vinyl-coated padded door panels and padded headliner and foam-rubber-topped seat and back cushions. Special trim for the Custom cab consists of chrome door molding and special matched colors of interior materials. 60 amp battery. 50 amp heavy-duty generator. 20 or 35 amp charge at idle generator. Front axle warning light. Dual stop and taillights. Corner and marker lights. Power steering. Power brakes. Directional signals. Engine governor. Hand-throttle control. Special paint or two-tone combinations. Increased capacity cooling system. Recirculating and fresh-air heaters. Auxiliary rear springs. Four-speed manual transmission. Heavy-duty 4-speed manual transmission. Front-mounted winch.

HISTORICAL FOOTNOTES: International was a major player in the American truck market with a 12.74 percent share of the market.

1960 PICKUP & TRAVELALL

In 1960 the V-266 engine remained standard for the four-wheel drive B-120 and B-140 models. Customers who preferred the older 240 cu. in. 6-cylinder could select that engine as a delete-option. Appearance changes were very limited. The front hood emblem now had a silver background. Trucks with V-8 engines had a "V" identification on the front fenders.

I.D. Data. Unchanged from 1959.

Body Type	Factory Price	GVW	Shipping Weight	Prod. Total
Series B-120, B-122, 110 in. wheelbase				
Chassis & Cab	$3024	7000	3947	—
Series B-120, B-122, 114 in. wheelbase				
Chassis & Cab	$3034	7000	3957	—
Pickup 7 ft.	$3142	7000	4287	—
Panel 7 ft.	$3420	7000	4562	—
Travelall	3784	7000	4842	—
Series B-120, B-122, 126 in. wheelbase				
Chassis & Cab	$3051	7000	3977	—
Pickup 8.5 ft.	$3180	7000	4362	—
Series B-120, B-122, 129 in. wheelbase				
Util. Chassis & Cab	$4142	7000	N.A.	—
Util. Pickup 6 ft.	$4273	7000	N.A.	—
Series B-140, B-142, 129 in. wheelbase				
Chassis & Cab	$3820	11,000-14,000	4677	—
Pickup 8.5 ft.	$3949	11,000-14,000	5062	—
Series B-140, B-142, 141 in. wheelbase				
Chassis & Cab	$3847	11,000-14,000	4707	—
Series B-140, B-142, 153 in. wheelbase				
Chassis & Cab	$3874	11,000-14,000	4767	—

STANDARD ENGINE: B-120, B-122. B-140, B-142: Engine Type: OHV V-8. Bore x Stroke: 3.625 in. x 3.218 in. Displacement: 266 cu. in. Carburetion: Single 1-barrel, downdraft. Compression Ratio: 8.4:1. Horsepower: 154.8 @ 4400 rpm. Torque: 227.1 lb.-ft. @ 2800 rpm. Fuel Requirements: Regular. Oil Capacity: 7 qt.

OPTIONAL ENGINE: (Delete-option). Series B-120, B-140: International Black Diamond 240 (BD-240). Engine Type: I-block, OHV, 6-cyl. Bore x Stroke: 3.5625 in. x 4.018 in. Lifters: Solid. Number of main bearings-4. Displacement: 240.3 cu. in. Carburetion: Single 1-barrel, downdraft. Compression Ratio: 7.5:1. Horsepower: 140.8 @ 3800 rpm. Torque: 223.5 lb.-ft. @ 2000 rpm. Fuel Requirements: Regular. Oil capacity: 7 qt. .

CHASSIS FEATURES: Separate body and frame, type (B-120): Pressed steel channel, 7 in. x 3 in. x 0.1875 in.

SUSPENSION AND RUNNING GEAR: (B-120). Front Suspension: 46 in. x 2.5 in. semi-elliptical leaf springs, direct acting shock absorbers. Rear Suspension: 52 in. x 2.5 in. semi-elliptical leaf springs, direct acting shock absorbers. Front Axle Type and Capacity: Single-reduction, hypoid type. Capacity: 2,800 lb. Rear Axle Type and Capacity: Full-floating, single-reduction, Hotchkiss type final drive. Capacity: 4,500 lb. Final Drive Ratio: 4.1 or 4.777:1 (front and rear). Transfer Case: 2-speed. Ratios: 1.98:1, 1.00:1. Brakes: Type: Front and Rear: Hydraulic, internal-expanding, two-shoe, single-anchor type. Lining Area: 172.9 sq. in. Wheels: Disc type, 5.25 in. rims. Optional: None. Tires: Series B-120, B-122: 7 x 17.5, 6-ply. Series B-140: 8 x 19.5 in., 8-ply. Optional: Tubeless or tubed, alternate sizes and special treads. Steering: Type: Semi-reversible dual ratio, cam and roller-mounted twin lever gear. Four-spoke,18 in. safety type steering wheel. Turning circle (B-120): 110 in. wheelbase: 47 ft., 114 in. wheelbase: 48 ft., 117 in. wheelbase: 49 ft., 126 in. wheelbase: 53 ft., 129 in. wheelbase: 54 ft. Transmission: Manual, 3-speed. Shift lever mounted on steering column. Ratios: 3.039, 1.641, 1.00:1. Optional: Four-speed, selective sliding gear type manual transmission. Heavy-duty four-speed manual transmission. Clutch: Type, 11.0 in. Optional: 12 in. dia. (V-8 only).

VEHICLE DIMENSIONS:

B-120 Models:

Wheelbase (in.):	110	114	117	126	129
Overall Length (in.):	188.43	188.56	197.56	206.56	209.56
Front Overhang (in.):	36.43	36.43	36.43	36.43	36.43
Rear Overhang (in.):	42	38	44	44	44

Width: 79.375 in. (all models). Ground Clearance (B-120 models): Front axle: 9.125 in. Rear axle: 8.5625 in.

CAPACITIES: Fuel tank: Choice of 18 gal. under cab or 15 gal. underbody fuel tank. Cooling system: Black Diamond. 240 and Black Diamond 264: 15 qt.

ACCOMMODATIONS: Seating Capacity: 3 passenger.

INSTRUMENTATION: 0-100 mph speedometer, odometer reading to 99,999.9 miles, gauges for oil pressure, generator charging rate, engine coolant temperature, fuel level.

OPTIONS: (B-120): Full depth foam rubber or rubber-topped seat and back cushions. Individual foam-rubber topped driver's seat with standard construction passenger's seat. Exterior fixed arm type or chrome cowl-mounted rearview mirrors. Dome light. Armrests. Right side sun visor. Tinted glass. Cigarette lighter. Grab handles. Left door lock. Map compartment light. Sliding rear window and screen. Custom cab: Includes: Two sun visors, two armrests, dome light, vinyl-coated padded door panels and padded headliner and foam-rubber-topped

seat and back cushions. Special trim for the Custom cab consists of chrome door molding and special matched colors of interior materials. 60 amp battery. 50 amp heavy-duty generator. 20 or 35 amp charge at idle generator. Front axle warning light. Dual stop and taillights. Corner and marker lights. Power steering. Power brakes. Directional signals. Engine governor. Hand-throttle control. Special paint or two-tone combinations. Increased capacity cooling system. Recirculating and fresh air heaters. Auxiliary rear springs. Four-speed manual transmission. Heavy-duty 4-speed manual transmission. Front-mounted winch.

HISTORICAL FOOTNOTES: The 1960 International trucks were introduced in January, 1960.

1961 PICKUP & TRAVELALL

Although the new Scout attracted the bulk of attention from prospective four-wheel drive vehicle customers, the established line of International pickups and Travelall models were given a face-lift that gave them a more curvaceous, up-to-date appearance. The front end continued to use dual headlights, but they were now mounted horizontally. Use of a lower fender line along with a lowered and wider hood, a concave-curved grille with an anodized aluminum insert with six vertical and horizontal dividers, and oval parking/directional lights served as primary identification features. A long and narrow hood scoop also continued to be part of International's styling format. Overall height was lowered 5 in. while wheelbase was increased 5 in. with no increase in overall length.

1961 International C-120 (4x4) Travelette

The interior was highlighted by a new instrument panel with chrome knobs and a center mounting of the heater controls and the radio. New suspended brake and hydraulic clutch pedals were 2 in. lower. There was increased distance between the clutch and brake pedals. The parking brake was now set by a new floor pedal and released by a separate, hand-controlled lever just below the dash. The upholstery consisted of a foam-rubber topper with Charcoal grey nylon covering and vinyl trim. A vinyl headliner was installed. Mounted on the firewall inside the cab was a nine-circuit fuse panel. Both doors had safety catches and had locks operated by the ignition key. The International frame was redesigned with increased section modulus. A new hydraulic clutch which reduced pressure by as much as 50 percent was also adopted.

1961 International Travelall C-120 (4x4)

The C-120 Travelall had a lower silhouette, four side doors and numerous detail improvements. The Standard Travelall was fitted with a front seat only. The second and third seats were optional. The Custom Travelall was equipped with a standard second seat. It was of a fold-down type and could be easily removed if desired. The optional third seat was attached to the body floor at a slightly higher level than the front seats and was also removable. The Standard Travelall was fitted with two panel type full-length swingout doors. The tailgate and electrically operated roll-down window of the Custom model was optional for the Standard Travelall. Both the Standard and Custom Travelall models had standard door locks, instrument panel-mounted ashtray, chrome-plated knobs, stainless steel-lined adjustable-tension vent wings, front dome light, map compartment, headliner with roof bows and floor mats. The Custom model had higher quality door trim panels, seat covering material, roof insulation, headliner with roof bows, and left side sun visor. Equipment that was standard for the Custom Travelall and optional for the Standard model included a tailgate with electrically operated window, rear dome light, armrests next to all seats, right-side sun visor, back-of-seat ashtray, and plastic spare tire cover. Supplied only with the Custom Travelall were exterior body chrome trim stripes and interior pillar and halo panel Royalite trim.

I.D. DATA: The serial number was placed on both a dash plate and on the left front frame siderail. With the exception of a "1" suffix (indicating the 1961 calendar year), a numerical sequence was continued from 1960. These changes were recognized by a change in International nomenclature as the "B" prefix was replaced by a "C" prefix in the 3/4 ton series identification. The use of longer wheelbases in the C-122 series was accompanied by the introduction of new body styles such as the Travelall pickup with a six-foot box. No longer offered were the Utility versions. The offerings in the medium duty B-140, B-142 series was reduced to just chassis and cab units on three different wheelbase lengths.

4 x 4's

1961 International C-120 (4x4) pickup

Body Type	Factory Price	GVW	Shipping Weight	Prod. Total
Series C-120, (C-122), 115 in. wheelbase				
Ch.& Cab	$2861	7000	3746	—
Series C-120, (C-122), 119 in. wheelbase				
Chassis & Cab	$2861	7000	3750	—
Pickup 7 ft.	$2979	7000	4125	—
Panel 7 ft.	$3293	7000	4305	—
Travelall	$3584	7000	4450	—
Travelall Cust.	$3863	7000	—	—
Series C-120, (C-122), 122 in. wheelbase				
Chassis & Cab	$2877	7000	3756	—
Series C-120, (C-122), 131 in. wheelbase				
Chassis & Cab	$2887	7000	3874	—
Pickup 8 ft.	$3017	7000	4299	—
Series C-120, (C-122), 140 in. wheelbase				
Travelette Ch. &Cab	$3468	7000	4322	—
Travelette Pickup 6 ft. Dlx.	$3612	7000	—	—

The C-120, C-122 models could be ordered with the 240 Black Diamond 6-cylinder engine in lieu of the standard V-266 engine for a credit of $54.00.

Series B-140, (B-142), 129 in. wheelbase				
Chassis & Cab	$3793	11,000-14,000	4677	—
Series B-140, (B-142), 141 in. wheelbase				
Chassis & Cab	$3920	11,000-14,000	4707	—
Series B-140, (B-142), 153 in. wheelbase				
Chassis & Cab	$3947	11,000-14,000	4767	—

STANDARD ENGINE: C-120, C-122. B-140, B-142: Engine Type: OHV V-8. Bore x Stroke: 3.625 in. x 3.218 in. Displacement: 266 cu. in. Carburetion: Single 1-barrel, downdraft. Compression Ratio: 8.4:1. Horsepower: 154.8 @ 4400 rpm. Torque: 227.1 lb.-ft. @ 2800 rpm. Fuel Requirements: Regular. Oil Capacity: 7 qt.

OPTIONAL ENGINE: (Delete-option). Series C-120, B-140: International Black Diamond 240 (BD-240). Engine Type: I-block, OHV, 6-cyl. Bore x Stroke: 3.5625 in. x 4.018 in. Lifters: Solid. Number of main bearings-4. Displacement: 240.3 cu. in. Carburetion: Single 1-barrel, downdraft. Compression Ratio: 7.5:1. Horsepower: 140.8 @ 3800 rpm. Torque: 223.5 lb.-ft. @ 2000 rpm. Fuel Requirements: Regular. Oil capacity: 7 qt.

CHASSIS FEATURES: Separate body and frame, type (C-120): Pressed steel channel, 7 in. x 3 in. x 0.1875 in.

SUSPENSION AND RUNNING GEAR: (C-120). Front Suspension: 46 in. x 2.5 in. semi-elliptical leaf springs, direct acting shock absorbers. Rear Suspension: 52 in. x 2.5 in. semi-elliptical leaf springs, direct acting shock absorbers. Front Axle Type and Capacity: Single-reduction, hypoid type. Capacity: 2,800 lb. Rear Axle Type and Capacity: Full-floating, single-reduction, Hotchkiss type final drive. Capacity: 4,500 lb. Final Drive Ratio: 4.1 or 4.777:1 (front and rear). Transfer Case: 2-speed. Ratios: 1.98:1, 1.00:1. Brakes: Type: Front and Rear: Hydraulic, internal-expanding, two-shoe, single-anchor type. Lining Area: 172.9 sq. in. Wheels: Disc type, 5.25 in. rims. Optional: None. Tires: Series C-120, C-122: 7 x 17.5, 6-ply. Series B-140: 8 x 19.5 in., 8-ply. Optional: Tubeless or tubed, alternate sizes and special treads. Steering: Type: Semi-reversible dual ratio, cam and roller-mounted twin lever gear. Four-spoke,18 in. safety type steering wheel. Turning circle (C-120): 110 in. wheelbase: 47 ft., 114 in. wheelbase: 48 ft., 117 in. wheelbase: 49 ft., 126 in. wheelbase: 53 ft., 129 in. wheelbase: 54 ft. Transmission: Manual, 3-speed. Shift lever mounted on steering column. Ratios: 3.039, 1.641, 1.00:1. Optional: Four-speed, selective sliding gear type manual transmission. Heavy-duty four-speed manual transmission. Clutch: Type, 11.0 in. Optional: 12 in. dia. (V-8 only).

VEHICLE DIMENSIONS:

C-120 Models:

Wheelbase (in.):	114	118	121	130	133
Overall Length (in.):	188.43	188.56	197.56	206.56	209.56
Front Overhang (in.):	36.43	36.43	36.43	36.43	36.43
Rear Overhang (in.):	42	38	44	44	44

Width: 79.375 in. (all models). Ground Clearance (B-120 models): Front axle: 9.125 in. Rear axle: 8.5625 in. Load space: Standard box: 54.5 in. x 17.75 in. x 84 in. or 104 in. Travelall: 49.5 in. x 45 in. x 98 in. (72 in. with second seat).

CAPACITIES: Fuel tank: Choice of 18 gal. under cab or 15 gal. underbody fuel tank. Cooling system: Black Diamond 240 and Black Diamond 264: 15 qt.

ACCOMMODATIONS: Seating Capacity: 3 passenger.

INSTRUMENTATION: 0-100 mph speedometer, odometer reading to 99,999.9 miles, gauges for oil pressure, generator charging rate, engine coolant temperature, fuel level.

OPTIONS: Pickups: Chrome front bumper. Rear bumper. OSRV mirror(s). Undercoating. Trailer hitch. Grille guard. Bumper guards. AM radio. Antenna. Fresh-air or circulating air heater. Clock. Cigarette lighter. Seat covers. Dual sun visors. Spotlight. Electric windshield wipers. Special paint. Two-tone finish. Custom trim package. Deluxe cab package. Front-mounted winch. Directional turn signals. Safety belts. High-side pickup box panels. Clearance marker lights. Armrests. Increased capacity radiator. Heavy-duty battery. Power-Lok differential. Foam seat cushions. Floor mats. 40 amp alternator. Snowplow. Power steering. Power brakes. Travelall: Many of the above options were available for the Travelall. Other Travelall options included: High capacity fresh-air heater/defroster. Instrument panel-mounted semi-transistor, push-button radio with outside antenna. Whitewall tires. Chrome-plated bumpers. Outside cowl-mounted rearview mirror. Tinted glass windshield. Cigarette lighter. Windshield washer. Map compartment lock. Air conditioning.

HISTORICAL FOOTNOTES: The 1961 models were introduced on Nov.1, 1960.

1962 PICKUP & TRAVELALL

Both the technical nature and external appearance of the four-wheel drive International pickups/Travelall models were unchanged from 1961. An important development was the extension of four-wheel drive into the 1 ton C-130 range of vehicles. With a 10,000 lb. GVW rating the C-130 offered in wheelbases of 122 in., 131 in., 143 in. and 140 in. was a robust 4-wheeler. Among its features were steel-bushed front and rear springs, variable ratio steering, heavy-duty 3-speed manual transmission and a solid rectangular section steel front bumper. I-H designed the C-130 to allow the tie rod to be located behind the front axle for added protection. The B-140 four-wheel drive model was not offered for 1962.

I.D. DATA: International's vehicle identification system remained unchanged for 1962. The 1962 models had a "2" suffix after the serial number to indicate 1962.

Body Type	Factory Price	GVW	Shipping Weight	Prod. Total
Series C-120, (C-122), 115 in. wheelbase				
Chassis & Cab	$2865	7400	3746	—
Series C-120, (C-22),119 in. wheelbase				
Pickup	$2983	7400	3125	—
Pickup B.L.	$2844	7400	3930	—
Panel 7 ft.	$3142	7400	4305	—
Travelall	$3433	7400	4265	—
Travelall Cust.	$3868	7400	—	—
Series C-120 (122), 131 in. wheelbase				
Chassis & Cab	$2892	7400	3874	—
Pickup 8.5 ft.	$3021	7400	4299	—
Pickup 8.5 ft. B.L.	$3073	7400	4289	—
Series C-120, (C-122), 140 in. wheelbase				
Travelette Chassis & Cab	$3318	7400	4099	—
Travelette Pickup	$3636	7400	—	—
Series C-130, 122 in wheelbase				
Chassis & Cab	$3459	10,000	3915	—
Series C-130, (C-132) 131 in. wheelbase				
Pickup 8.5 ft.	$3599	10,000	4365	—
Pickup 8.5 ft. B.L.	$3616	10,000	4355	—
Series C-130, (C-132) 134 in. wheelbase				
Chassis & Cab	$3481	10,000	3951	—
Series C-130, (C-132) 140 in. wheelbase				
Travelette Chassis & Cab	$4051	10,000	4399	—

STANDARD ENGINE: C-120, C-122. B-140, B-142: Engine Type: OHV V-8. Bore x Stroke: 3.625 in. x 3.218 in. Displacement: 266 cu. in. Carburetion: Single 1-barrel, downdraft. Compression Ratio: 8.4:1. Horsepower: 154.8 @ 4400 rpm. Torque: 227.1 lb.-ft. @ 2800 rpm. Fuel Requirements: Regular. Oil Capacity: 7 qt.

OPTIONAL ENGINE: (Delete-option). Series C-120, B-140: International Black Diamond. 240 (BD-240). Engine Type: I-block, OHV, 6-cyl. Bore x Stroke: 3.5625 in. x 4.018 in. Lifters: Solid. Number of main bearings-4. Displacement: 240.3 cu. in. Carburetion: Single 1-barrel, downdraft. Compression Ratio: 7.5:1. Horsepower: 140.8 @ 3800 rpm. Torque: 223.5 lb.-ft. @ 2000 rpm. Fuel Requirements: Regular. Oil capacity: 7 qt.

CHASSIS FEATURES: Separate body and frame, type (C-120): Pressed steel channel, 7 in. x 3 in. x 0.1875 in.

SUSPENSION AND RUNNING GEAR: (C-120). Front Suspension: 46 in. x 2.5 in. semi-elliptical leaf springs, direct acting shock absorbers. Rear Suspension: 52 in. x 2.5 in. semi-elliptical leaf springs, direct acting shock absorbers. Front Axle Type and Capacity: Single-reduction, hypoid type. Capacity: 2,800 lb. Rear Axle Type and Capacity: Full-floating, single-reduction, Hotchkiss type final drive. Capacity: 4,500 lb. Final Drive Ratio: 4.1 or 4.777:1 (front and rear). Transfer Case: 2-speed. Ratios: 1.98:1, 1.00:1. Brakes: Type: Front and Rear: Hydraulic, internal-expanding, two-shoe, single-anchor type. Lining Area: 172.9 sq. in. Wheels: Disc type, 5.25 in. rims. Optional: None. Tires: Series C-120, C-122: 7 x 17.5, 6-ply. Series B-140: 8 x 19.5 in., 8-ply. Optional: Tubeless or tubed, alternate sizes and special treads. Steering: Type: Semi-reversible dual ratio, cam and roller-mounted twin lever gear. Four-spoke,18 in. safety type steering wheel. Turning circle (C-120): 110 in. wheelbase: 47 ft., 114 in. wheelbase: 48 ft., 117 in. wheelbase: 49 ft., 126 in. wheelbase: 53 ft., 129 in. wheelbase: 54 ft. Transmission: Manual, 3-speed. Shift lever mounted on steering column.

Ratios: 3.039, 1.641, 1.00:1. Optional: Four-speed, selective sliding gear type manual transmission. Heavy-duty four-speed manual transmission. Clutch: Type, 11.0 in. Optional: 12 in. dia. (V-8 only).

VEHICLE DIMENSIONS:

C-120 Models:

Wheelbase (in.):	114	118	121	130	133
Overall Length (in.):	188.43	188.56	197.56	206.56	209.56
Front Overhang (in.):	36.43	36.43	36.43	36.43	36.43
Rear Overhang (in.):	42	38	44	44	44

Width: 79.375 in. (all models). Ground Clearance (C-120 models): Front axle: 9.125 in. Rear axle: 8.5625 in. Load space: Standard box: 54.5 in. x 17.75 in. x 84 in. or 104 in. Travelall: 49.5 in. x 45 in. x 98 in. (72 in. with second seat).

CAPACITIES: Fuel tank: Choice of 18 gal. under cab or 15 gal. underbody fuel tank. Cooling system: Black Diamond 240 and Black Diamond 264: 15 qt.

ACCOMMODATIONS: Seating Capacity: 3 passenger.

INSTRUMENTATION: 0-100 mph speedometer, odometer reading to 99,999.9 miles, gauges for oil pressure, generator charging rate, engine coolant temperature, fuel level.

OPTIONS: Pickups: Chrome front bumper. Rear bumper. OSRV mirror(s). Undercoating. Trailer hitch. Grille guard. Bumper guards. AM radio. Antenna. Fresh air or circulating air heater. Clock. Cigarette lighter. Seat covers. Dual sun visors. Spotlight. Electric windshield wipers. Special paint. Two-tone finish. Custom Trim Package. Deluxe Cab Package. Front-mounted winch. Directional turn signals. Safety belts. High-side pickup box panels. Clearance marker lights. Armrests. Increased capacity radiator. Heavy-duty battery. Power-Lok differential. Foam seat cushions. Floor mats. 40 amp alternator. Snowplow. Power steering. Power brakes. Travelall: Many of the above options were available for the Travelall. Other Travelall options included: High capacity fresh-air heater/defroster. Instrument panel-mounted semi-transistor, push-button radio with outside antenna. Whitewall tires. Chrome-plated bumpers. Outside cowl-mounted rearview mirror. Tinted glass windshield. Cigarette lighter. Windshield washer. Map compartment lock. Air conditioning.

HISTORICAL FOOTNOTES: The 1962 models debuted on Nov. 1, 1961.

1963 PICKUP & TRAVELALL

International adopted a new model designation system for 1963 that identified its 3/4 ton models as series 1200. The series 1300 consisted of the 1 ton models. Replacing the V-266 V-8 as the base engine for its 3/4 ton and 1 ton four-wheel drive models was the BG-241 6-cylinder engine. This was not a new engine, rather being the old 240 cu. in. "Black Diamond" engine with a new identification. The V-266 remained available as an option. Along with their two-wheel drive counterparts, the latest four-wheel drive models from International reverted to the use of single headlights. The grille now consisted of two horizontal bars and nine vertical dividers. The International name was positioned in the grille center. A simplified International logo sans its 1962-era wings was positioned on the leading edge of the hood. Additional features for 1963 included black painted wheels and front bumper, an anodized aluminum front grille insert and a choice of 13 standard solid exterior body colors. Also included in the International's standard equipment were these items: Dual 2-speed electric windshield wipers, inside overhead rearview mirror, door locks, safety catches and hold-open stops; insulated headliner, heavy-duty floor mat, ashtray and driver's side sun visor. A 37 amp alternator and a 12-volt, 54 plate, 50 amp-hr. battery were also standard.

1963 International Travelall 1200 (4x4)

I.D. DATA: The serial number was stamped both on a dash plate and on the left front frame side rail. The numbers followed in sequence from those used in 1962 with a "3" digit at the end to indicate 1963 production.

Body Type	Factory Price	GVW	Shipping Weight	Prod. Total
Series 1200, 115 in., 131 in. wheelbase				
Chassis & Cab	$2727	7400	3730	—
Series 1200, 119 in., 131 in. wheelbase				
Pickup	$2848	7400	4124	—
Pickup B.L.	$2864	7400	4115	—
Series 1200, 119 in. wheelbase				
Panel 7 ft.	$3160	7400	4305	—
Travelall Cust.	$3497	7400	4450	—
Series 1200, 140 in. wheelbase				
Travelette Chassis & Cab	$3332	7400	4320	—
Travelette Pickup B.L.	$3476	7400	—	—
Series 1300, 120 in., 129 in. wheelbase				
Chassis & Cab	$3337	10,000	3915	—
Series 1300, 132 in. wheelbase				
Pickup 8.5 ft.	$3474	10,000	4365	—
Pickup 8.5 ft. B.L.	$3490	10,000	4365	—

STANDARD ENGINE: Series 1200 and 1300. Engine Type: OHV L-6 ("BG-240"). Bore x Stroke: 3.5625 in. x 4.018 in. Number of main bearings-4. Compression ratio: 7.5:1. Displacement: 240.3 cu. in. Carburetion: Single-barrel, downdraft. Lifters: Solid. Horsepower: 140.8 @ 3800 rpm. Torque: 223.5 lb.-ft. @ 2000 rpm. Fuel Requirements: Regular.

OPTIONAL ENGINE: All models: Engine Type: OHV V-8 ("V-266"). Bore x Stroke: 3.625 in. x 3.21875 in. Displacement: 265.761 cu. in. Carburetion: Single barrel, downdraft. Lifters: Solid. Horsepower: 154.8 @ 4400 rpm. Torque: 227.1 lb.-ft. @ 2800 rpm. Oil capacity: 7 qt. Fuel Requirements: Regular.

OPTIONAL ENGINE: 1300 models. Engine Type: OHV V-8 ("V-304"). Bore x Stroke: 3.875 in. x 3.21875 in. Displacement: 304 cu. in. Carburetion: Single barrel, downdraft. Lifters: Solid. Horsepower: 193 @ 4400 rpm. Torque: 272.5 lb.-ft. @ 2800 rpm. Fuel Requirements: Regular.

CHASSIS FEATURES: All material that follows, except when noted, applies to the 1300 models. Separate body and frame. Frame: Pressed steel channel, 7 in. x 3.0 in. x 0.1875 in. Section modulus: 4.81.

SUSPENSION AND RUNNING GEAR: Front Suspension: Semi-elliptical leaf springs, 42 in. x 2.25 in. Capacity: 2000 lb. Rear Suspension: Semi-elliptical leaf springs, 52 in. x 2.25 in. Capacity: 3000 lb. Front Axle Type and Capacity: Model FA-52, 4000 lb. Rear Axle Type and Capacity: RA-15, 6000 lb. Final Drive Ratio: 4.88:1 or 6.17:1. Transfer Case: Type: TC-141. Ratios: 1.96:1, 1.00:1. Brakes: Type: Hydraulic, front and rear. Dimensions: Front: 12.0 in. x 2.0 in. Rear: 14 in. x 2.125 in. Total effective lining area: 213.6 sq. in. Wheels: Steel rims with 5.25 in. rims. Tires: 1200: 7 x 17.5; 1300: 8 x17.5 truck type, 6-ply tubeless. Optional: Various sizes and treads, dual rear for 1300. Steering: Variable ratio gear, outboard-mounted, 17 in. dia. safety steering wheel. Turning circle: Series 1300: 120 in. wheelbase: 53.16 ft.; 129 in. wheelbase: 56.66 ft.; 132 in. wheelbase: 57.66 ft. Transmission: International T-7, 3-speed, synchromesh. Transmission Ratios: 3.714, 1.871, 1.0:1. Reverse: 4.588:1. Optional: International T-16 4-speed, direct, synchromesh. Clutch: 10.0 in. dia., 9-spring, single plate dry disc with hydraulic action. Optional: 11.0 in. dia., 9-spring (12-spring with V-8 engine), single plate dry disc with hydraulic action.

VEHICLE DIMENSIONS: Wheelbase: Series 1200: Chassis & cab: 115 in.-131 in.; pickup and bonus load pickup: 119 in.-131 in.; Travelette chassis & cab and bonus load pickup: 140 in. Series 1300: Chassis & cab: 120 in., 129 in., 132 in. Overall Length: Series 1300: 120 in. wheelbase: 193.7 in.; 129 in. wheelbase: 202.7 in.; 132 in. wheelbase: 205.7 in. Front/Rear Tread: Series 1300: 63 in./59.9 in. Overall Width: 78 in. Front/Rear Overhang: Series 1300: 29.3 in./44.4 in. Ground Clearance: Series 1300: Front: 8.5 in. Rear: 7.9 in.

CAPACITIES: Fuel tank: 19 gal. right side, under cab or body. Optional: 15 gal fuel tank under cab. Coolant system: 16 qt.

ACCOMMODATIONS: Seating Capacity: 3 passengers.

INSTRUMENTATION: Speedometer, odometer, gauges for fuel level, oil pressure, engine coolant temperature and battery charging.

OPTIONS: Series 1300: Outside, rearview mirrors. Right-side sun visor. Armrests. Tinted glass. Dome light. Heater and defroster. Cigarette lighter. Map compartment lock. Right-hand drive. 52 amp alternator. 60 amp-hr. battery. Dual stop and taillights. Directional signals. Auxiliary oil filter. Increased capacity cooling. Heavy-duty oil-bath air cleaner. Governor, hand throttle control. High temperature thermostat. Magnetic drain plug. Carburetor heater. High altitude equipment. Front axle warning light. Black painted rear bumper. Two front tow hooks. Front or rear chrome bumpers. Power take-off, model AT-640, full torque, mounted on transfer case. Heavy-duty front springs. Heavy-duty main and auxiliary rear springs. Semi-integral power steering. Front-mounted winch with or without cable and hook.

HISTORICAL FOOTNOTES: Introduction date for the 1963 models was Nov. 1, 1962. International Harvester enjoyed a record year in 1963.

1964 PICKUP & TRAVELALL

The 1964 International four-wheel drive pickup and Travelall series were unchanged in appearance for 1964. For the first time the 1100 heavy-duty 1/2 ton series models were available in four-wheel drive form. International made certain that buyers of the 1200 4x4 fully realized the nature of the vehicle they were acquiring. "The Travelall," said International, "is a fleet, agile and well-designed station wagon. Unlike other vehicles of the type which have been so modified by modern stylists and engineers that they are little more than low ground-hugging automobiles with elongated bodies, the Travelall retains the original concept of a station wagon as a dual-purpose passenger and load carrier...The Model 1200 (4x4) Travelall adds not only the ground-gripping traction of power applied to all four wheels, but also nearly doubled torque to the wheels when needed to pull through slippery going or up steep grades...This model makes an altogether superior work wagon with needed extra capacity, traction and power for operation under severe road, load, grade and weather conditions." International also noted that the optional V-304 engine and T-15 4-speed transmission for the Travelall were the same as the standard units in its tractor models approved for 29,000 lb.

gross tractor-trailer combination weights. During 1964 International extended the Travelall 4x4 availability to include the 1/2 ton 1100 model. Joining the 266 cu. in. "V-266" V-8 engine as an option for the 1100, 1200 and 1300 series was International's 304 cu. in. "V-304" V-8. This engine had previously been limited for use in International trucks with ratings over the 1 ton mark.

I.D. DATA: The vehicle serial number was found in three locations: The dash, right-side running board shield and left front frame side rail. The suffix "4" was added to the serial number to indicate the 1964 calendar year.

Body Type	Factory Price	GVW	Shipping Weight	Prod. Total
Series 1100, 115 in. wheelbase				
Chassis & Cab	$2575	5600	3675	—
Series 1100, 119 in. wheelbase				
Pickup	$2696	5600	4085	—
Pickup B.L.	$2707	5600	4075	—
Panel 7 ft.	$2999	5600	4265	—
Series 1100, 131 in. wheelbase				
Chassis & Cab	$2575	5600	370	—
Pickup	$2696	5600	4265	—
Pickup B.L.	$2707	5600	4075	—
Series 1100, 140 in. wheelbase				
Travelette Chassis & Cab	$3203	5600	4135	—
Travelette Pickup 6 ft. B.L.	$3342	5600	N.A.	—
Series 1200, 115 in. wheelbase				
Chassis & Cab	$2736	7400	3760	—
Series 1200, 119 in. wheelbase				
Pickup	$2856	7400	3760	—
Pickup B.L.	$2868	7400	4130	—
Panel 7 ft.	$3160	7400	4320	—
Series 1200, 131 in. wheelbase				
Chassis & Cab	$2736	7400	3885	—
Pickup	$2856	7400	4265	—
Pickup B.L.	$2868	7400	4255	—
Series 1200, 140 in. wheelbase				
Travelette Chassis & Cab	$3364	7400	4460	—
Travelette Pickup B.L. 6 ft.	$3503	7400	N.A.	—
Series 1300, (one ton) 120 in. wheelbase				
Chassis & Cab	$3348	10,000	4375	—
Series 1300, 129 in. wheelbase				
Pickup 8.5 ft.	$3484	10,000	4825	—
Pickup B.L. 8.5 ft.	$3496	10,000	4815	—
Series 1300, 132 in. wheelbase				
Chassis & Cab	$3348	10,000	4375	—
Series 1100, 119 in. wheelbase				
Travelall Cust.	$3426	5600	4240	—
Series C-1200, 119 in. wheelbase				
Travelall Cust.	$3464	7000*	4320	—

* 7400 lb. GVW optional, requires optional heavy-duty front axle.

STANDARD ENGINE: All series: Engine Type: OHV L-6 ("BG-240"). Bore x Stroke: 3.5625 in. x 4.018 in. Number of main bearings-4. Compression ratio: 7.5:1. Displacement: 240.3 cu. in. Carburetion: Single-barrel, downdraft. Lifters: Solid. Horsepower: 140.8 @ 3800 rpm. Torque: 223.5 lb.-ft. @ 2000 rpm. Fuel Requirements: Regular.

OPTIONAL ENGINE: All models: Engine Type: OHV V-8 ("V-266"). Bore x Stroke: 3.625 in. x 3.21875 in. Displacement: 265.761 cu. in. Carburetion: Single barrel, downdraft. Lifters: Solid. Horsepower: 154.8 @ 4400 rpm. Torque: 227.1 lb.-ft. @ 2800 rpm. Oil capacity: 7 qt. Fuel Requirements: Regular.

OPTIONAL ENGINE: All models: Engine Type: OHV V-8 ("V-304"). Bore x Stroke: 3.875 in. x 3.21875 in. Displacement: 304 cu. in. Carburetion: Single barrel, downdraft. Lifters: Solid. Horsepower: 193 @ 4400 rpm. Torque: 272.5 lb.-ft. @ 2800 rpm. Fuel Requirements: Regular.

CHASSIS FEATURES: All material that follows, except when noted, applies to the 1300 models. Separate body and frame. Frame: Pressed steel channel, 7 in. x 3.0 in. x 0.1875 in. Section modulus: 4.81.

SUSPENSION AND RUNNING GEAR: Front Suspension: Semi-elliptical leaf springs, 42 in. x 2.25 in. Capacity: 2000 lb. Rear Suspension: Semi-elliptical leaf springs, 52 in. x 2.25 in. Capacity: 3000 lb. Front Axle Type and Capacity: Model FA-52, 4000 lb. Rear Axle Type and Capacity: RA-15, 6000 lb. Final Drive Ratio: 4.88:1 or 6.17:1. Transfer Case: TC-141. Ratios: 1.96:1, 1.00:1. Brakes: Type: Hydraulic, front and rear. Dimensions: Front: 12.0 in. x 2.0 in. Rear: 14 in. x 2.125 in. Total effective lining area: 213.6 sq. in. Wheels: Steel rims with 5.25 in. rims. Tires: 1200: 7 x 17.5; 1300: 8 x17.5 truck type, 6-ply tubeless. Optional: Various sizes and treads, dual rear for 1300. Steering: Variable ratio gear, outboard-mounted, 17 in. dia. safety steering wheel. Turning circle: Series 1300: 120 in. wheelbase: 53.16 ft.; 129 in. wheelbase: 56.66 ft.; 132 in. wheelbase: 57.66 ft. Transmission: International T-7, 3-speed, synchromesh. Transmission Ratios: 3.714, 1.871, 1.0:1. Reverse: 4.588:1. Optional: International T-16 4-speed, direct, synchromesh. Clutch: 10.0 in. dia., 9-spring, single plate dry disc with hydraulic action. Optional: 11.0 in. dia., 9-spring (12-spring with V-8 engine), single plate dry disc with hydraulic action.

VEHICLE DIMENSIONS: Wheelbase: Series 1200: Chassis & cab: 115 in.-131 in.; pickup and bonus load pickup: 119 in.-131 in.; Travelette chassis & cab and bonus load pickup: 140 in. Series 1300: Chassis & cab: 120 in., 129 in., 132 in. Overall Length: Series 1300: 120 in. wheelbase: 193.7 in.; 129 in. wheelbase: 202.7 in.; 132 in. wheelbase: 205.7 in. Front/Rear Tread: Series 1300: 63 in./59.9 in. Overall Width: 78 in. Front/Rear Overhang: Series 1300: 29.3 in./44.4 in. Ground Clearance: Series 1300: Front: 8.5 in. Rear: 7.9 in.

CAPACITIES: Fuel tank: 19 gal. right side, under cab or body. Optional: 15 gal fuel tank under cab. Coolant system: 16 qt.

ACCOMMODATIONS: Seating Capacity: 3 passengers.

INSTRUMENTATION: Speedometer, odometer, gauges for fuel level, oil pressure, engine coolant temperature and battery charging.

OPTIONS AND PRICES: Series 1300: V-266 engine: $118. V-304 engine: $179. Outside, rearview mirrors. Right-side sun visor. Armrests. Tinted glass. Dome light. Heater and defroster. Cigarette lighter. Map compartment lock. Right-hand drive. 52 amp alternator. 60

amp-hr. battery. Dual stop and taillights. Directional signals. Auxiliary oil filter. Increased capacity cooling. Heavy-duty oil-bath air cleaner. Governor, hand throttle control. High temperature thermostat. Magnetic drain plug. Carburetor heater. High altitude equipment. Front axle warning light. Black painted rear bumper. Two front tow hooks. Front or rear chrome bumpers. Power take-off, model AT-640, full torque, mounted on transfer case. Heavy-duty front springs. Heavy-duty main and auxiliary rear springs. T-16 4-speed transmission: $74. Semi-integral power steering: $174. Front-mounted winch with or without cable and hook.

HISTORICAL FOOTNOTES: The 1964 models debuted in Nov., 1963.

1965 PICKUP & TRAVELALL

The 1965 four-wheel drive pickups and Travelalls had a new grille design consisting of 31 thin vertical bars in the center of which an International nameplate was positioned. As in previous years both flared side pickup bodies or the bonus load version with box side flush with the cab were offered. The International cab was revamped with use of silver amber and antique gold colors in many trim areas. A new 2-spoke steering wheel, in place of the 4-spoke unit previously used, is of a deep-dish safety design. The pads on the pedals had vertical rather than horizontal ribbing to prevent foot slippage. The adjustable full-width seat had a full foam polyurethane pad molded to burlap with a wire flexilator. The standard all-vinyl covering material had an embossed pattern slightly altered in design from the 1964 version. The standard doors had inner panels of textured steel. A heavy-duty jute-backed rubber floor mat and acoustical-type headliner were also standard. The Custom Trim Interior Package included these features: Padded door panels, deluxe seat with nylon inserts, high-quality vinyl-coated rubber floor mat with carpet-like texture, and chrome finish on the rearview mirror. The second seat area for the Travelall and Travelette models with this package had a similar floor mat. Travelalls with the custom trim had a silver amber decking in the cargo area. All models with custom trim also had an exterior custom nameplate and deluxe chrome hubcaps. Standard for the Travelall was an electric-powered roll-down rear window.

1965 International D-1100 (4x4) pickup

I.D. DATA: Serial numbers were found in the same positions as in 1964. A "5" suffix followed the series number to indicate the 1965 calendar year. A new "D" designation was used for the latest International models.

Body Type	Factory Price	GVW	Shipping Weight	Prod. Total
Series D-1100, wheelbase: 119 in. to 140 in.				
Chassis & Cab	$2585	5600	3485	—
Pickup 7 ft.	$2706	5600	3855	—
Pickup 7 ft. B.L.	$2717	5600	N.A.	—
Pickup 8.5 ft.	$2738	5600	3920	—
Pickup 8.5 ft. B.L.	$2750	5600	3935	—
Panel 7 ft.	$3009	5600	4155	—
Travelette Cab	$3221	5600	3930	—
Travelette Pickup 8 ft. B.L.	$3360	5600	N.A.	—
Series D-1200, wheelbase: 119 in.-140 in.				
Chassis & Cab	$2744	7000*	3825	—
Pickup 7 ft.	$2865	7000*	4195	—
Pickup 7 ft. B.L.	$2877	7000*	N.A.	—
Pickup 8.5 ft.	$2897	7000*	4250	—
Pickup 8.5 ft. B.L.	$2909	7000*	4265	—
Panel 7 ft.	$3169	7000*	4495	—
Travelette Cab	$3381	7000*	4260	—
Travelette 6 ft. Pickup B.L.	$3520	7000*	N.A.	—
D-1300, wheelbase: 131 in. to 134 in.				
Chassis & Cab	$3367	10,000	4375	—
Pickup 8.5 ft.	$3494	10,000	4785	—
Pickup 8.5 ft. B.L.	$3506	10,000	4800	—

* GVW range extends to 7400 lb.

Series D-1100 Travelall, 119 in. wheelbase

Body Type	Factory Price	GVW	Shipping Weight	Prod. Total
Travelall Cust.	$3319	5600	3055	

Series D-1200 Travelall 119 in. wheelbase

Body Type	Factory Price	GVW	Shipping Weight	Prod. Total
Travelall Cust.	$3479	7400	N.A.	—

STANDARD ENGINE: All series: Engine Type: OHV L-6 ("BG-240"). Bore x Stroke: 3.5625 in. x 4.018 in. Number of main bearings-4. Compression ratio: 7.5:1. Displacement: 240.3 cu. in. Carburetion: Single-barrel, downdraft. Lifters: Solid. Horsepower: 140.8 @ 3800 rpm. Torque: 223.5 lb.-ft. @ 2000 rpm. Fuel Requirements: Regular.

OPTIONAL ENGINE: All models: Engine Type: OHV V-8 ("V-266"). Bore x Stroke: 3.625 in. x 3.21875 in. Displacement: 265.761 cu. in. Carburetion: Single barrel, downdraft. Lifters: Solid. Horsepower: 154.8 @ 4400 rpm. Torque: 227.1 lb.-ft. @ 2800 rpm. Oil capacity: 7 qt. Fuel Requirements: Regular.

OPTIONAL ENGINE: All models: Engine Type: OHV V-8 ("V-304"). Bore x Stroke: 3.875 in. x 3.21875 in. Displacement: 304 cu. in. Carburetion: Single barrel, downdraft. Lifters: Solid. Horsepower: 193 @ 4400 rpm. Torque: 272.5 lb.-ft. @ 2800 rpm. Fuel Requirements: Regular.

CHASSIS FEATURES: All material that follows, except when noted, applies to the 1300 models. Separate body and frame. Frame: Pressed steel channel, 7 in. x 3.0 in. x 0.1875 in. Section modulus: 4.81.

SUSPENSION AND RUNNING GEAR: Front Suspension: Semi-elliptical leaf springs, 42 in. x 2.25 in. Capacity: 2000 lb. Rear Suspension: Semi-elliptical leaf springs, 52 in. x 2.25 in. Capacity: 3000 lb. Front Axle Type and Capacity: Model FA-52, 4000 lb. Rear Axle Type and Capacity: RA-15, 6000 lb. Final Drive Ratio: 4.88:1 or 6.17:1. Transfer Case: Type: TC-141. Ratios: 1.96:1, 1.00:1. Brakes: Type: Hydraulic, front and rear. Dimensions: Front: 12.0 in. x 2.0 in. Rear: 14 in. x 2.125 in. Total effective lining area: 213.6 sq. in. Wheels: Steel rims with 5.25 in. rims. Tires: 1100: 8.15 x 15 in., 1200: 7 x 17.5; 1300: 8 x17.5 truck type, 6-ply tubeless. Optional: Various sizes and treads, dual rear for 1300. Steering: Variable ratio gear, outboard-mounted, 17 in. dia. safety steering wheel. Turning circle: Series 1300: 120 in. wheelbase: 53.16 ft.; 129 in. wheelbase: 56.66 ft.; 132 in. wheelbase: 57.66 ft. Transmission: International T-7, 3-speed, synchromesh. Transmission Ratios: 3.714, 1.871, 1.0:1. Reverse: 4.588:1. Optional: International T-16 4-speed, direct, synchromesh. Clutch: 10.0 in. dia., 9-spring, single plate dry disc with hydraulic action. Optional: 11.0 in. dia., 9-spring (12-spring with V-8 engine), single plate dry disc with hydraulic action.

VEHICLE DIMENSIONS: Wheelbase: Series 1200: Chassis & cab: 115 in.-131 in.; pickup and bonus load pickup: 119 in.-131 in.; Travelette chassis & cab and bonus load pickup: 140 in. Series 1300: Chassis & cab: 120 in., 129 in., 132 in. Overall Length: Series 1300: 120 in. wheelbase: 193.7 in.; 129 in. wheelbase: 202.7 in.; 132 in. wheelbase: 205.7 in. Front/Rear Tread: Series 1300: 63 in./59.9 in. Overall Width: 78 in. Front/Rear Overhang: Series 1300: 29.3 in./44.4 in. Ground Clearance: Series 1300: Front: 8.5 in. Rear: 7.9 in.

CAPACITIES: Fuel tank: 19 gal. right side, under cab or body. Optional: 15 gal. fuel tank under cab. Coolant system: 16 qt.

ACCOMMODATIONS: Seating Capacity: 3 passengers.

INSTRUMENTATION: Speedometer, odometer, gauges for fuel level, oil pressure, engine coolant temperature and battery charging.

OPTIONS AND PRICES: V-266 engine: $120. V-304 engine: $180. Outside, rearview mirrors. Right-side sun visor. Armrests. Tinted glass. Dome light. Heater and defroster. Cigarette lighter. Map compartment lock. Right-hand drive. 52 amp alternator. 60 amp-hr. battery. Dual stop and taillights. Directional signals. Auxiliary oil filter. Increased capacity cooling. Heavy-duty oil-bath air cleaner. Governor, hand throttle control. High temperature thermostat. Magnetic drain plug. Carburetor heater. High altitude equipment. Front axle warning light. Black painted rear bumper. Two front tow hooks. Front or rear chrome bumpers. Power take-off, model AT-640, full torque, mounted on transfer case. Front wheel locking hubs. Heavy-duty front springs. Heavy-duty main and auxiliary rear springs. T-16 4-speed transmission: $75. Semi-integral power steering: $174. Power brakes: $50.00 (D-1300-$60.00). 8-ft. platform body: $185.00., 8 ft. stake body: $255.00. 9 ft. stake body: $320.00. Front-mounted winch with or without cable and hook.

HISTORICAL FOOTNOTES: The 1965 models were announced in Nov., 1964. International Harvester's sale in all its truck series set a new calendar year record.

1966 PICKUP & TRAVELALL

Aside from new series designations, identification of the 1966 four-wheel drive International models was by their revised grille format featuring a center divider which carried the International name. International offered a new 131 in. wheelbase Campermobile model with a specially-built 8 ft. pickup body suitable for virtually any 8 to 10.5 ft. camper insert. It had as standard equipment such items as an electrical connector that eliminated the need for disorderly spaghetti-wire hookups, increased engine cooling capacity, large exterior mirrors and a heavy-duty electrical system including a 52 amp alternator and a 70 amp-hr. battery. Optional for the Campermobile was a sliding rear window. A special Campermobile emblem was mounted on the side of the hood. The Campermobile was available in either 1100A or 1200A form. The 1200A version was also available in chassis-mounted form with a 140 in. wheelbase.

Standard equipment for the 1966 International pickup and Travelall models included color-keyed champagne, foam-padded seats with embossed vinyl upholstery; full-instrumentation dash, ashtray, suspended step-on parking brake, insulated rubber floor mat, driver's side sun visor (dual on Travelall) and acoustical headliner. Two interior options were offered. The Deluxe Trim Pack included color-coordinated instrument panel with grained walnut insert, chrome integral horn ring and button, steel, color-coordinated door panel covers, vinyl floor mats, steering column boot, painted interior mirror, rear dome light for Travelette and Travelall, door-operated front dome light, cigarette lighter, under-hood insulation, aluminum door steps, driver's side armrest (rear armrests are included on Travelalls with rear seats) and chrome interior mirror. The Custom Trim Pack had these items in addition to or in place of features from the Deluxe Pack: Custom vinyl and nylon upholstery, additional chrome trim, soft padded vinyl door panel covers, dual horns, nylon carpet floor covering, spare tire cover, parking brake pedal bracket cover with red "on" light, and dual front armrests (rear armrests are included on Travelalls with rear seats). An Exterior Dress Pack was offered with these features: Bright-finish windshield molding, chrome front bumper (front and rear on Travelall), chrome hubcaps, chrome body strip (not included on chassis-mounted campers), and chrome rocker panel strip on Travelall wagons. Standard on the Travelall and optional for other models was a new International Safety Pack. It consisted of padded instrument panel, padded sun visors, chrome exterior rearview mirror, switch for front and rear flasher lights, seat belts for all seats ordered and 2-speed electric windshield wipers with windshield washer. The 13 exterior colors for 1966 were as follows: Dark green, turquoise metallic, Bahama blue metallic, Malibu beige, Tahitian yellow, Apache gold, Tam O'Shanter green metallic, Aspen green, schoolbus yellow, alpine white, orange, black and red.

I.D. DATA: Unchanged from 1965 except for use of "6" suffix after serial number to indicate 1966.

Body Type	Factory Price	GVW	Shipping Weight	Prod. Total
Series 1100A, 119-131 in. wheelbase				
Chassis & Cab	$2604	5600	3485	—
Pickup 7 ft.	$2725	5600	3855	—
Pickup 7 ft. B.L.	$2737	5600	N.A.	—
Pickup 8.5 ft.	$2757	5600	3920	—
Pickup 8.5 ft. B.L.	$2769	5600	3935	—
Series 1100A, 119 in. wheelbase				
Panel 7 ft.	$3029	5600	4155	—
Series 1100A, 140 in. wheelbase				
Travelette Cab	$3241	5600	3930	—
Travelette 6 ft. Pickup B.L.	$3380	5600	N.A.	—
Series 1200A, 119 in.-140 in. wheelbase				
Chassis & Cab	$2764	7000[1]	3825	—
Pickup 7 ft.	$2884	7000	4195	—
Pickup 7 ft. B.L.	$2896	7000	N.A.	—
Pickup 8.5 ft.	$2917	7000	4250	—
Series 1200A, 119 in. wheelbase				
Panel 7 ft.	$3188	7000	4495	—
Series 1200A, 140 in. wheelbase				
Travelette Cab	$3400	7000	4260	—
Travelette Pickup 6 ft. B.L.	$3539	7000	N.A.	—
Series 1300A, 131 in. wheelbase				
Chassis & Cab	$3388	10,000	4375	—
Pickup 8.5 ft.	$3514	10,000	4785	—
Pickup 8.5 ft. B.L.	$3526	10,000	4800	—
Series 1300A, 140 in. wheelbase				
Travelette Cab	$3998	10,000	4800	—
Travelette 6 ft. Pickup B.L.	$4140	10,000	N.A.	—
Series 1100A, 119 in. wheelbase				
Station Wagon	$3365	5600	4335	—
Series 1200A,119 in. wheelbase				
Station Wagon	$3522	7000[1]	4670	—

NOTE 1: GVW range for Series 1200A extends to 7400 lbs.

STANDARD ENGINE: All series: Engine Type: OHV L-6 ("BG-240"). Bore x Stroke: 3.5625 in. x 4.018 in. Number of main bearings-4. Compression ratio: 7.5:1. Displacement: 240.3 cu. in. Carburetion: Single-barrel, downdraft. Lifters: Solid. Horsepower: 140.8 @ 3800 rpm. Torque: 223.5 lb.-ft. @ 2000 rpm. Fuel Requirements: Regular.

OPTIONAL ENGINE: All models: Engine Type: OHV I-6 ("BG-265"). Bore x Stroke: 3.343 in. x 4.125 in. Number of main bearings-4. Displacement: 264.33 in. Carburetion: Single barrel, downdraft. Lifters: Solid. Horsepower: 153.5 @ 3800 rpm. Torque: 248 lb.-ft. @ 2400 rpm. Oil capacity: 7 qt. Fuel Requirements: Regular.

OPTIONAL ENGINE: All models: Engine Type: OHV V-8 ("V-266"). Bore x Stroke: 3.625 in. x 3.21875 in. Displacement: 265.761 cu. in. Carburetion: Single barrel, downdraft. Lifters: Solid. Horsepower: 154.8 @ 4400 rpm. Torque: 227.1 lb.-ft. @ 2800 rpm. Oil capacity: 7 qt. Fuel Requirements: Regular.

OPTIONAL ENGINE: All models: Engine Type: OHV V-8 ("V-304"). Bore x Stroke: 3.875 in. x 3.21875 in. Displacement: 304 cu. in. Carburetion: Single barrel, downdraft. Lifters: Solid. Horsepower: 193 @ 4400 rpm. Torque: 272.5 lb.-ft. @ 2800 rpm. Fuel Requirements: Regular.

CHASSIS FEATURES: All material that follows, except when noted, applies to the 1300 models. Separate body and frame. Frame: Pressed steel channel, 7 in. x 3.0 in. x 0.1875 in. Section modulus: 4.81.

SUSPENSION AND RUNNING GEAR: Front Suspension: Semi-elliptical leaf springs, 42 in. x 2.25 in. Capacity: 2000 lb. Rear Suspension: Semi-elliptical leaf springs, 52 in. x 2.25 in. Capacity: 3000 lb. Front Axle Type and Capacity: Model FA-52, 4000 lb. Rear Axle Type and Capacity: RA-15, 6000 lb. Final Drive Ratio: 4.88:1 or 6.17:1. Transfer Case: Type: TC-141. Ratios: 1.96:1, 1.00:1. Brakes: Type: Hydraulic, front and rear. Dimensions: Front: 12.0 in. x 2.0 in. Rear: 14 in. x 2.125 in. Total effective lining area: 213.6 sq. in. Wheels: Steel rims with 5.25 in. rims. Tires: 1100: 8.15 x 15 in., 1200: 7 x 17.5; 1300: 8 x17.5. truck type, 6-ply tubeless. Optional: Various sizes and treads, dual rear for 1300. Steering: Variable ratio gear, outboard-mounted, 17 in. dia. safety steering wheel. Turning circle: Series 1300: 120 in. wheelbase: 53.16 ft.; 129 in. wheelbase: 56.66 ft.; 132 in. wheelbase: 57.66 ft. Transmission: International T-7, 3-speed, synchromesh. Transmission Ratios: 3.714, 1.871, 1.0:1. Reverse: 4.588:1. Optional: International T-16 4-speed, direct, synchromesh. Clutch: 10.0 in. dia., 9-spring, single plate dry disc with hydraulic action. Optional: 11.0 in. dia., 9-spring (12-spring with V-8 engine), single plate dry disc with hydraulic action.

VEHICLE DIMENSIONS: Wheelbase: Series 1200: Chassis & cab: 115 in.-131 in.; pickup and bonus load pickup: 119 in.-131 in.; Travelette chassis & cab and bonus load pickup: 140 in. Series 1300: Chassis & cab: 120 in., 129 in., 132 in. Overall Length: Series 1300: 120 in. wheelbase: 193.7 in.; 129 in. wheelbase: 202.7 in.; 132 in. wheelbase: 205.7 in. Front/Rear Tread: Series 1300: 63 in./59.9 in. Overall Width: 78 in. Front/Rear Overhang: Series 1300: 29.3 in./44.4 in. Ground Clearance: Series 1300: Front: 8.5 in. Rear: 7.9 in.

CAPACITIES: Fuel tank: 19 gal. right side, under cab or body. Optional: 15 gal. fuel tank under cab. Coolant system: 16 qt.

ACCOMMODATIONS: Seating Capacity: 3 passengers.

INSTRUMENTATION: Speedometer, odometer, gauges for fuel level, oil pressure, engine coolant temperature and battery charging.

OPTIONS: Full-width fold-down second seat (Travelall). Removable third seat (Travelall). Tinted glass. Cigarette lighter. Right outside rearview mirror. Armrest, left or right side. Glove compartment lock. Heater-defroster; Fresh air, recirculating or super-capacity. Air conditioning. Power steering. Power brakes. Radio. Increased capacity engine cooling system. 52 amp alternator. 60 or 70 amp-hr. battery. Dual electric horns. High altitude engine equipment. Exhaust emission control. Automatic choke for V-8 engines. Hand throttle. Engine governors. Heavy-duty oil bath air cleaner for 6-cyl. engines. White rear bumper. Panel rear door in place of Travelall standard tailgate. 14 gal. auxiliary fuel tank. Underslung spare tire carrier. Spare tire lock. Extra-heavy-duty axles and springs. Extra-heavy-duty clutches. Specific axle ratios with Power-Lok limited slip differential. Front-mounted winch. Snowplows. Larger tires and rims. Two front tow hooks.

1967 PICKUP & TRAVELALL

Use of a series B designation for 1967 was accompanied by a new grille design for the four-wheel drive Internationals. The latest grille format featured a segmented bright metal surround with a darker insert. A horizontal bar continued to carry the International name. The latest Internationals had a more durable finish benefiting from the use of zinc-coated steel in critical corrosion areas and the application of a zinc-rich primer underneath the body and in specific corrosion-prone areas. Body joints were permanently sealed with a thermo-setting plastic. Standard equipment for 1967 included a color-keyed interior, color-keyed beige foam-padded seats with all-vinyl upholstery, fully-instrumented dash, insulated rubber floor mat, acoustical headliner, dome light, ashtray, step-on parking and two-pint oil bath air cleaner. Standard safety equipment consisted of padded dash and driver's side sun visor, seat belts, shoulder belt anchors, safety door latches, two-speed electric windshield wipers with non-glare arms, windshield washer, four-way emergency light flasher, back-up lights (except for stake/platform bodies), dual operation hydraulic brake system and inside and outside rearview mirrors. The Deluxe interior option consisted of the standard equipment features plus black leather-texture dash inserts, chrome horn ring, dual sun visors, cigarette lighter, door-operated dome light, armrest, vinyl floor mat, aluminum step door plates and underhood insulation. The custom interior option included both the standard and Deluxe equipment plus these items: Custom olive and ivy vinyl-trimmed nylon upholstery, matching padded door panels, retracting seat belts, custom chrome dash trim, nylon carpeting, dual electric horns, dual armrests, chrome inside rearview mirror and parking brake "on" light. The Exterior Dress Pack included bright-finish windshield molding, chrome front bumper and chrome hubcaps. The optional Chrome Body Trim Strip option was available for the bonus load pickup bodies. The color selection for 1967 was as follows: Dark green, turquoise metallic, Bahama blue metallic, Malibu beige, Tahitian yellow, Apache gold, Tam O'Shanter green metallic, dark green, schoolbus yellow, alpine white, orange, black and red.

1967 International 1100B All-Wheel Drive Pickup

I.D. DATA: Vehicle identification data was located on the left door pillar. Thirteen digits were included, the first six indicating the vehicle's serial number. The next entry identified the manufacturing plant. The final six digits were the vehicle's sequential production number. The engine number, located on a machined boss on the block, added an engine identification (BG-241, BG-255, V-266, etc.) to the vehicle's thirteen identification number.

Body Type	Factory Price	GVW	Shipping Weight	Prod. Total
Series 1100B, 115, 131 in. wheelbase				
Chassis & Cab	$2646	5600	3485	—
Pickup 6 ft., 8 in.	$2767	5600	3855	—
Pickup 6 ft., 8 in. B.L.	$2779	5600	N.A.	—
Pickup 8 ft.	$2799	5600	3935	—
Pickup 8 ft. B.L.	$2811	5600	N.A.	—
Panel 7 ft.	$3199	5600	4155	—
Travelette Cab	$3353	5600	3930	—
Travelette Pickup 6 ft. B.L.	$3492	5600	N.A.	—
Series 1200B, 119-166 in. wheelbase				
Chassis & Cab	$2853	7400	3825	—
Pickup 7 ft.	$2974	7400	4195	—
Pickup 7 ft. B.L.	$2986	7400	N.A.	—
Pickup 8.5 ft.	$3006	7400	4265	—
Pickup 8.5 ft. B.L.	$3018	7400	N.A.	—
Panel 7 ft.	$3294	7400	4495	—
Travelette Cab	$3528	7400	4260	—
Travelette 6 ft. Pickup B.L.	$3667	7400	N.A.	—
Series 1300B, 131 in.-156 in. wheelbase				
Chassis & Cab	$3480	10,000	4375	—
Pickup 8.5 ft.	$3606	10,000	4800	—
Travelette Cab	$4127	10,000	4800	—
Travelette 6 ft. Pickup B.L.	$4269	10,000	N.A.	—
Series 1100B, 119 in. wheelbase				
Travelall Custom	$3365	7400	4510	—
Series 1200B, 119 in. wheelbase				
Travelall Custom	$3571	7400	4740	—

STANDARD ENGINE: All series: Engine Type: OHV L-6 ("BG-240"). Bore x Stroke: 3.5625 in. x 4.018 in. Number of main bearings-4. Compression ratio: 7.5:1. Displacement: 240.3 cu. in. Carburetion: Single-barrel, downdraft. Lifters: Solid. Horsepower: 140.8 @ 3800 rpm. Torque: 223.5 lb.-ft. @ 2000 rpm. Fuel Requirements: Regular.

OPTIONAL ENGINE: All models: Engine Type: OHV I-6 ("BG-265"). Bore x Stroke: 3.343 in. x 4.125 in. Number of main bearings-4. Displacement: 264.33 cu. in. Carburetion: Single barrel, downdraft. Lifters: Solid. Horsepower: 153.5 @ 3800 rpm. Torque: 248 lb.-ft. @ 2400 rpm. Oil capacity: 7 qt. Fuel Requirements: Regular.

OPTIONAL ENGINE: All models: Engine Type: OHV V-8 ("V-266"). Bore x Stroke: 3.625 in. x 3.21875 in. Displacement: 265.761 cu. in. Carburetion: Single barrel, downdraft. Lifters: Solid. Horsepower: 154.8 @ 4400 rpm. Torque: 227.1 lb.-ft. @ 2800 rpm. Oil capacity: 7 qt. Fuel Requirements: Regular.

OPTIONAL ENGINE: All models: Engine Type: OHV V-8 ("V-304"). Bore x Stroke: 3.875 in. x 3.21875 in. Displacement: 304 cu. in. Carburetion: Single barrel, downdraft. Lifters: Solid. Horsepower: 193 @ 4400 rpm. Torque: 272.5 lb.-ft. @ 2800 rpm. Fuel Requirements: Regular.

OPTIONAL ENGINE: All models: Engine Type: OHV V-8 ("V-345"). Bore x Stroke: 3.875 in. x 3.656 in. Displacement: 344.96 cu. in. Carburetion: Single barrel, downdraft. Lifters: Solid. Horsepower: 196.7 @ 4000 rpm. Torque: 309 lb.-ft. @ 2200 rpm. Fuel Requirements: Regular.

CHASSIS FEATURES: All material that follows, except when noted, applies to the 1300 models. Separate body and frame. Frame: Pressed steel channel, 7 in. x 3.0 in. x 0.1875 in. Section modulus: 4.81.

SUSPENSION AND RUNNING GEAR: Front Suspension: Semi-elliptical leaf springs, 42 in. x 2.25 in. Capacity: 2000 lb. Rear Suspension: Semi-elliptical leaf springs, 52 in. x 2.25 in. Capacity: 3000 lb. Front Axle Type and Capacity: Model FA-52, 4000 lb. Rear Axle Type and Capacity: RA-15, 6000 lb. Final Drive Ratio: 4.88:1 or 6.17:1. Transfer Case: Type: TC-141. Ratios: 1.96:1, 1.00:1. Brakes: Type: Hydraulic, front and rear. Dimensions: Front: 12.0 in. x 2.0 in. Rear: 14 in. x 2.125 in. Total effective lining area: 213.6 sq. in. Wheels: Steel rims with 5.25 in. rims. Tires: 1100B: 8.15 x 15 in., 1200B: 7 x 17.5 in., 1300B: 8 x 17.5 in. Steering: Variable ratio gear, outboard-mounted, 17 in. dia. safety steering wheel. Turning circle: Series 1300: 120 in. wheelbase: 53.16 ft.; 129 in. wheelbase: 56.66 ft.; 132 in. wheelbase: 57.66 ft. Transmission: International T-7, 3-speed, synchromesh. Transmission Ratios: 3.714, 1.871, 1.0:1. Reverse: 4.588:1. Optional: International T-16 4-speed, direct, synchromesh. Clutch: 10.0 in. dia., 9-spring, single plate dry disc with hydraulic action. Optional: 11.0 in. dia., 9-spring (12-spring with V-8 engine), single plate dry disc with hydraulic action.

VEHICLE DIMENSIONS: Wheelbase: Series 1200: Chassis & cab: 115 in.-131 in.; pickup and bonus load pickup: 119 in.-131 in. Travelette chassis & cab and bonus load pickup: 140 in. Series 1300: Chassis & cab: 120 in., 129 in., 132 in. Overall Length: Series 1300: 120 in. wheelbase: 193.7 in.; 129 in. wheelbase: 202.7 in.; 132 in. wheelbase: 205.7 in. Front/Rear Tread: Series 1300: 63 in./59.9 in. Overall Width: 78 in. Front/Rear Overhang: Series 1300: 29.3 in./44.4 in. Ground Clearance: Series 1300: Front: 8.5 in. Rear: 7.9 in.

CAPACITIES: Fuel tank: 19 gal. right side, under cab or body. Optional: 15 gal fuel tank under cab. Coolant system: 16 qt.

ACCOMMODATIONS: Seating Capacity: 3 passengers.

INSTRUMENTATION: Speedometer, odometer, gauges for fuel level, oil pressure, engine coolant temperature and battery charging.

OPTIONS AND PRICES: V-266 engine: $62.00. White sidewall tires. Rear bumper (painted or chrome). Bumper guards. Transistor radio. Radio antenna. Fresh-air, recirculating or super-capacity heater and defroster. ODSRV mirror(s). Cigarette lighter. "California" towing mirrors. Over-size tires. Foam rubber seat cushions. Pickup box rails. Heavy-duty 4-speed transmission. Heavy-duty 3-speed transmission (for 1100B and 1200B). Power steering: $126.00. Automatic transmission: $210.00. Roof rack (Travelall). Deluxe Interior Package. Custom Interior Package. Clock. Seat covers. Wheel trim rings. Two-tone paint. "California" towing mirrors, oversize tires, vinyl roof (Travelall). Bucket seats (available with any interior). Eight-track stereo tape player. Air conditioning. Tinted glass. Sliding rear window for Camper models. Rear step bumper. Utility hitch. Front tow hooks. Increased capacity engine cooling. Increased capacity alternator. Limited slip rear differential. 14 gal. auxiliary fuel tank.

HISTORICAL FOOTNOTES: International celebrated its 60th anniversary in 1967 as a truck producer. The 1967 models were introduced on Nov. 1, 1966.

1968 PICKUP & TRAVELALL

The "IH" badge was removed from the hood above the grille center for 1968. Custom pickup models and the Travelall were available with a new optional rough-grain, pebble-finish simulated-vinyl black top. The optional power steering was refined to offer an improved road feel. The same color selection as in 1967 was available for 1968. A new oven-baked super-enamel paint was used. Added to the optional transmissions were a 5-speed overdrive manual unit and a 5-speed direct manual unit.

1968 International 1100C Travelall

I.D. DATA: Unchanged from 1967.

Body Type	Factory Price	GVW	Shipping Weight	Prod. Total
Series 1100C, 115 in.-140 in. wheelbase				
Chassis & Cab	$2926	5600	3485	—
Pickup 6 ft., 8 in.	$3047	5600	3845	—
Pickup 6 ft., 8 in. B.L.	$3059	5600	3845	—
Pickup 8.5 ft.	$3079	5600	3935	—
Pickup 8 ft. B.L.	$3091	5600	3920	—
Panel 7 ft.	$3428	5600	4155	—
Travelette Cab	$3633	5600	3930	—
Travelette 6 ft. Pickup B.L.	$3772	5600	4265	—
Series 1200C, 119 in.-166 in. wheelbase				
Chassis & Cab	$3096	7000*	3825	—
Pickup 7 ft.	$3216	7000	4195	—
Pickup 7 ft. B.L.	$3228	7000	4195	—
Pickup 8.5 ft.	$3249	7000	4265	—
Pickup 8 ft. B.L.	$3261	7000	4265	—
Panel 7 ft.	$3565	7000	4495	—
Travelette Cab	$3771	7000	4260	—
Travelette 6 ft. Pickup B.L.	$3909	7000	4595	—
Series 1300C, 131 in.-156 in. wheelbase				
Chassis & Cab	$3695	10,000	4375	—
Pickup 8.5 ft.	$3821	10,000	4800	—
Travelette Cab	$4343	10,000	4800	—
Travelette 6 ft. Pickup B.L.	$4485	10,000	5135	—

* 7400 GVW optional for all series 1200C models.

Body Type	Factory Price	GVW	Shipping Weight	Prod. Total
Series 1100C, 119 in. wheelbase				
Travelall	$3729	7400	4510	—
Series 1200C, 119 in. wheelbase				
Travelall	$3809	7400	4740	—

1968 International 1200

STANDARD ENGINE: All series: Engine Type: OHV L-6 ("BG-240"). Bore x Stroke: 3.5625 in. x 4.018 in. Number of main bearings-4. Compression ratio: 7.5:1. Displacement: 240.3 cu. in. Carburetion: Single-barrel, downdraft. Lifters: Solid. Horsepower: 140.8 @ 3800 rpm. Torque: 223.5 lb.-ft. @ 2000 rpm. Fuel Requirements: Regular.

OPTIONAL ENGINE: All models: Engine Type: OHV I-6 ("BG-265"). Bore x Stroke: 3.343 in. x 4.125 in. Number of main bearings-4. Displacement: 264.33 cu. in. Carburetion: Single barrel, downdraft. Lifters: Solid. Horsepower: 153.5 @ 3800 rpm. Torque: 248 lb.-ft. @ 2400 rpm. Oil capacity: 7 qt. Fuel Requirements: Regular.

OPTIONAL ENGINE: All models: Engine Type: OHV V-8 ("V-266"). Bore x Stroke: 3.625 in. x 3.21875 in. Displacement: 265.761 cu. in. Carburetion: Single barrel, downdraft. Lifters: Solid. Horsepower: 154.8 @ 4400 rpm. Torque: 227.1 lb.-ft. @ 2800 rpm. Oil capacity: 7 qt. Fuel Requirements: Regular.

OPTIONAL ENGINE: All models: Engine Type: OHV V-8 ("V-304"). Bore x Stroke: 3.875 in. x 3.21875 in. Displacement: 304 cu. in. Carburetion: Single barrel, downdraft. Lifters: Solid. Horsepower: 193 @ 4400 rpm. Torque: 272.5 lb.-ft. @ 2800 rpm. Fuel Requirements: Regular.

OPTIONAL ENGINE: All models: Engine Type: OHV V-8 ("V-345"). Bore x Stroke: 3.875 in. x 3.656 in. Displacement: 344.96 cu. in. Carburetion: Single barrel, downdraft. Lifters: Solid. Horsepower: 196.7 @ 4000 rpm. Torque: 309 lb.-ft. @ 2200 rpm. Fuel Requirements: Regular.

CHASSIS FEATURES: All material that follows, except when noted, applies to the 1300 models. Separate body and frame. Frame: Pressed steel channel, 7 in. x 3.0 in. x 0.1875 in. Section modulus: 4.81.

1968 International 1200 C All-Wheel Drive Travelette

SUSPENSION AND RUNNING GEAR: Front Suspension: Semi-elliptical leaf springs, 42 in. x 2.25 in. Capacity: 2000 lb. Rear Suspension: Semi-elliptical leaf springs, 52 in. x 2.26 in. Capacity: 3000 lb. Front Axle Type and Capacity: Model FA-52, 4000 lb. Rear Axle Type and Capacity: RA-15, 6000 lb. Final Drive Ratio: 4.88:1 or 6.17:1. Transfer Case: Type: TC-141. Ratios: 1.96:1, 1.00:1. Brakes: Type: Hydraulic, front and rear. Dimensions: Front: 12.0 in. x 2.0 in. Rear: 14 in. x 2.125 in. Total effective lining area: 213.6 sq. in. Wheels: Steel rims with 5.25 in. rims. Tires: 1100C: 8.15 x 15 in., 1200C: 7 x 17.5 in., 1300C: 8 x 17.5 in. Steering: Variable ratio gear, outboard-mounted, 17 in. dia. safety steering wheel. Turning circle: Series 1300: 120 in. wheelbase: 53.16 ft.; 129 in. wheelbase: 56.66 ft.; 132 in. wheelbase: 57.66 ft. Transmission: International T-7, 3-speed, synchromesh. Transmission Ratios: 3.714, 1.871, 1.0:1. Reverse: 4.588:1. Optional: International T-16 4-speed, direct, synchromesh. Clutch: 10.0 in. dia., 9-spring, single plate dry disc with hydraulic action. Optional: 11.0 in. dia., 9-spring (12-spring with V-8 engine), single plate dry disc with hydraulic action.

VEHICLE DIMENSIONS: Wheelbase: Series 1200C: Chassis & cab: 115 in.-131 in.; pickup and bonus load pickup: 119 in.-131 in.; Travelette chassis & cab and bonus load pickup: 140 in. Series 1300C: Chassis & cab: 120 in., 129 in., 132 in. Overall Length: Series 1300: 120 in. wheelbase: 193.7 in.; 129 in. wheelbase: 202.7 in.; 132 in. wheelbase: 205.7 in. Front/Rear Tread: Series 1300C: 63 in./59.9 in. Overall Width: 78 in. Front/Rear Overhang: Series 1300C: 29.3 in./44.4 in. Ground Clearance: Series 1300C: Front: 8.5 in. Rear: 7.9 in.

CAPACITIES: Fuel tank: 19 gal. right side, under cab or body. Optional: 15 gal. fuel tank under cab. Coolant system: 16 qt.

ACCOMMODATIONS: Seating Capacity: 3 passengers.

INSTRUMENTATION: Speedometer, odometer, gauges for fuel level, oil pressure, engine coolant temperature and battery charging.

OPTIONS AND PRICES: Automatic transmission: $244.00. Five-speed overdrive manual transmission. Five-speed direct manual transmission. Camper Package: $67.00, V-266 engine: $40.00, power steering: $132.00. Simulated-vinyl top. White sidewall tires. Rear bumper (painted or chrome). Bumper guards. Transistor radio. Radio antenna. Fresh-air, recirculating or super-capacity heater and defroster. ODSRV mirror(s). Cigarette lighter. "California" towing mirrors. Over-size tires. Foam rubber seat cushions. Pickup box rails. Heavy-duty 4-speed transmission. Heavy-duty 3-speed transmission (for 1100B and 1200B). Power steering: $126.00. Roof rack (Travelall). Deluxe Interior Package. Custom Interior Package. Exterior trim option. Includes chrome front bumper, chrome hubcaps and aluminum body molding strips. Exterior Trim Package. Includes features of Exterior trim option plus bright-finish windshield molding and aluminum rocker panels under doors. Clock. Seat covers. Wheel trim rings. Two-tone paint. "California" towing mirrors. Oversize tires. Bucket seats (available with any interior). Bucket seats with center console (Travelall). Eight-track stereo tape player. Air conditioning. Tinted glass. Sliding rear window for Camper models. Rear step bumper. Utility hitch. Front tow hooks. Increased capacity engine cooling. Increased capacity alternator. Choice of ten axle ratios from 3.31 to 6.17:1. Limited slip rear differential. 14 gal. auxiliary fuel tank.

HISTORICAL FOOTNOTES: The 1968 models were introduced on Nov.1, 1967. Calendar year production of all International truck models was 145,549.

1968 International 1300 B 4x4

1969 PICKUP & TRAVELALL

Significant styling and engineering changes that were depicted as the most important in International Harvester history characterized its four-wheel drive models for 1969. A total of 82 major changes could be identified including new body shells, updated styling, larger brakes as well as a new engine and transmission. Replacing the somewhat disjointed lines of the older Travelall and pickup models was a much smoother, squared-off styling theme that was influenced by the lines of the Scout. International identified its new styling as the "all-new 'NOW' look." The combination of the new exterior plus new trim, new exterior colors and revised engine lineup was collectively depicted as "Fashion/Action from International." The 1969 models had bigger engines, larger brakes, smoother ride, stronger frames and bodies, longer wheelbases and greater carrying capacities. New body mounts significantly reduced road vibrations. Low friction leaf springs provided a smoother ride, especially when the vehicle was not under load. A new double-jointed steering column absorbed steering vibrations. Stronger bumpers were installed and heavier wheels and tie-rods were specified. A new recirculating ball-type steering was adopted as was a revised exhaust system that was quieter than the old system. Cross-flow radiators with increased capacity was installed along with a more reliable electrical system. The interior was revamped along what International regarded as "car-like" styling. The optional air conditioning was now a built-in unit.

1969 International 1100 4x4 pickup

The new base engine was identified as the Power-Thrift-6. Compared to the older version used in 1968 this engine had seven, instead of five main bearings, revised valve timing, new intake manifold and a redesigned combustion chamber. All models had printed electronic circuits for their instrumentation. Also introduced for 1969 were self-adjusting brakes and, depending on model, brakes with 30 to 50% more lining area. The standard equipment for the pickups was as follows: Foam-padded bench seat with choice of red, blue, green or black all-vinyl upholstery, harmonizing acoustical headliner and trim, full-instrumented padded dash, dual padded sun visors and armrests, fresh air heater and defroster, black rubber floor covering, ashtray, dome light, aluminum doorsill covers, seat belts (front and rear on six passenger Travelette and Travelall models), front seat shoulder harness anchors, two-speed electric windshield wipers with non-glare arms, windshield washer, hazard warning flashing lights, recessed steering wheel, impact-absorbing anti-penetration steering column, breakaway inside mirror, outside mirrors, non-glare interior metal trim, safety door latches, back-up lights, side fender running reflectors, split hydraulic brake system with warning light, safety glass, and outside-mounted fuel tank with built-in filter. The standard exterior trim consisted of a White enameled grille and front bumper. A Deluxe trim was available with a bright finish for the grille, headlight and parking light bezels, windshield trim, drip molding, bonus load body trim, molding rocker panel trim and vent wings. A custom trim option included all the items in the Deluxe Package plus woodgrain side panels with bright trim. This feature was available only on bonus load pickup bodies. The custom interior, in addition to the standard items had a bench seat in red, blue, green or black in custom upholstery with vinyl bolsters and "breathing" nylon inserts, matching padded door panels and vinyl floor covering, brushed aluminum instrument panel trim, padded horn button, cigarette lighter, safety belt retractors, coat hook, underhood insulation and dual electric horns. The 1969 color selection consisted of alpine white, plum metallic, dark bright blue metallic, Tam O'Shanter green metallic, red, schoolbus yellow, orange, copper metallic, lime green metallic, medium blue metallic, black, dark green and gold metallic.

1969 International 1100 4x4 Travelette

I.D. DATA: Vehicle Identification Number was located on left door pillar post.

Body Type	Factory Price	GVW	Shipping Weight	Prod. Total
Series 1100D, 115 in-131 in. wheelbase				
Chassis & Cab	$2988	4800	N.A.	—
Pickup 6.5 ft.	$3108	4800	N.A.	—
Pickup 6.5 ft. B.L.	$4147	4800	N.A.	—
Panel 7 ft.	$3622	4800	N.A.	—
Pickup 8 ft.	$3146	4800	N.A.	—
Pickup 8 ft. B.L.	$3184	4800[1]	N.A.	—

NOTE 1: 5600 lb. GVW optional with heavy-duty front and rear springs.

Series 1200D, 115 in.-164 in. wheelbase				
Chassis & Cab	$3173	6100[2]	N.A.	—
Pickup 6.5 ft.	$3294	6100	N.A.	—
Pickup 6.5 ft. B.L.	$3333	6100	N.A.	—
Panel 7 ft.	$3807	6100	N.A.	—
Pickup 8 ft.	$3331	6100	N.A.	—
Pickup 8 ft. B.L.	$3370	6100	N.A.	—
Travelette Cab	$3835	6100	N.A.	—
Travelette 6.5 ft. Pickup	$4003	6100	N.A.	—
Travelette 8 ft. Pickup B.L.	$4162	6100	N.A.	—

NOTE 2: 7700 lb. GVW with FA-25 front axle and heavy-duty rear springs for 115, 119, 131 in. wheelbase only. 7700 lb. GVW with heavy-duty rear springs for 149, 156 and 164 in. wheelbase.

Series 1300D, 134 in.-156 in. wheelbase				
Chassis & Cab	$3872	7000[3]	N.A.	—
Pickup 9 ft.	$4012	7000	N.A.	—
Travelette Cab	$4507	7000	N.A.	—
Travelette 6.5 ft. Pickup B.L.	$4667	7000	N.A.	—

NOTE 3: 10,000 lb. GVW optional.

Travelall Series 1100D, 119 in. wheelbase				
Station Wagon	$3844	4800	N.A.	—

Travelall Series 1200D, 119 in. wheelbase				
Station Wagon	$4019	6100	N.A.	—

STANDARD ENGINE: 1100D Engine Type: OHV In-line 6-cylinder "Power Thrift-6-232." Bore x Stroke: 3.75 in. x 3.5 in. Displacement: 232 cu. in. Carburetion: Single bbl. Compression Ratio: 8.5:1. Horsepower: 145 @ 4300 rpm. Torque: 215 lb.-ft. @ 1600 rpm. Fuel Requirements: Regular. Standard: 1200D and 1300D. Not available for California where customers selected from V-304, V-345 or V-392. Engine Type: OHV V-8 ("V-266"). Bore x Stroke: 3.625 in. x 3.21875 in. Displacement: 265.761 cu. in. Carburetion: Single barrel, downdraft. Lifters: Solid. Horsepower: 154.8 @ 4400 rpm. Torque: 227.1 lb.-ft. @ 2800 rpm. Oil capacity: 7 qt. Fuel Requirements: Regular.

OPTIONAL ENGINE: All models: Engine Type: OHV V-8 ("V-304"). Bore x Stroke: 3.875 in. x 3.21875 in. Displacement: 304 cu. in. Carburetion: Single barrel, downdraft. Lifters: Solid. Horsepower: 193 @ 4400 rpm. Torque: 272.5 lb.-ft. @ 2800 rpm. Fuel Requirements: Regular.

OPTIONAL ENGINE: All models: Engine Type: OHV V-8 ("V-345"). Bore x Stroke: 3.875 in. x 3.656 in. Displacement: 344.96 cu. in. Carburetion: Holley model 2300G 2-barrel. Lifters: Solid. Horsepower: 196.7 @ 4000 rpm. Torque: 309 lb.-ft. @ 2200 rpm. Fuel Requirements: Regular.

OPTIONAL ENGINE: All models: Engine Type: OHV V-8 ("V-392"). Bore x Stroke: 4.125 in. x 3.656 in. Displacement: 390.89 cu. in. Carburetion: 4-barrel, downdraft. Lifters: Solid. Horsepower: 235 @ 4000 rpm. Torque: 354 lb.-ft. @ 2600 rpm. Fuel Requirements: Regular.

CHASSIS FEATURES: 1100D, 1200D series. Separate body and frame: 1100D: Pressed steel channel main rails, 3.93 in. x 2.968 in. x 0.50 in. Section modulus: 3.98. 1200D: Pressed steel channel main rails, 115-149 in. wheelbase: 7 in. x 3.0 in. x 0.179 in. Section modulus: 4.81. 156-164 in. wheelbase: 7.0625 in. x 3.0312 in. x 0.209 in. Section modulus: 5.65.

SUSPENSION AND RUNNING GEAR: Front Suspension: 1100D: Semi-elliptical leaf springs, 2.5 in. x 42 in. Capacity 2600 lb. 1200D: Semi-elliptical leaf springs, Capacity: 115, 119, 131 in. wheelbase: 2800 lb.; 149, 156, 164 in. wheelbase: 3500 lb. Shock absorbers. Rear Suspension: 1100D: Semi-elliptical leaf springs, 2.5 in. x 52 in. Capacity: 2500 lb. 1200D: Semi-elliptical leaf springs. Capacity 3500 lb. Shock absorbers. Front Axle Type and Capacity: 1100D: FA-16, hypoid, 3500 lb. 1200D: 115, 119, 131 in. wheelbase: FA-15, hypoid, 2800 lb.; 149, 156, 164 in. wheelbase: FA-18, hypoid, 3500 lb. Rear Axle Type and Capacity: 1100D: RA-18, hypoid, 3500 lb. 120D: RA-16, hypoid, 5500 lb. Final Drive Ratio: 1100D: 3.54, 3.73, 4.09:1. 1200D: Front: 4.09:1. Rear: 4.10:1. Transfer Case: Type: TC-141. Ratios: 1.93, 1.00:1. Brakes: Type: Self-adjusting, hydraulic, dual operation, front and rear. Dimensions: 1100D: Front: 11.03 in. x 3.0 in. Rear: 11.03 in. x 2.25 in. Total lining area: 244.8 sq. in. 1200D: Front: 12 in. x 2.5 in. Rear: 12.0 in. x 2.5 in. Total lining area: 245.5 sq. in. Wheels: 1100D: 5-stud wheels with 5.50K rims, 5.5 in. bolt circles. 1200D: 8-stud disc wheels with 6.00 rims, 6.5 in. bolt circles. Optional: Tires: 1100D: 8.25 x 15 2-ply tubeless. 1200D: 8.00 x 16.5 6-ply rated truck type tires. Optional: 1100D: 8.55 x 15, 6.50 x 16, 7.00 x 15 (with tubes). 1200D: 8.75 x 16.5, 9.50 x 16.5, 7.00 x 16 (tubes), 7.50 x 16 (tubes). Steering: Type: S-55 gear, with 17 in. steering wheel. Turning circle: 1100D: 115 in. wheelbase: 46.16 ft., 119 in. wheelbase: 48.5 ft., 131 in. wheelbase: 53.67 ft. 1200D: ranges from 46 ft. to 62.75 ft. depending on wheelbase. Transmission: Type: T-24 3-speed synchromesh manual. Transmission Ratios: 3.06, 1.55, 1.00:1. Optional: See Options and Prices. Clutch: 1100D: 10.5 in. diaphragm type. 1200D: 10.5 in. mechanical control. Optional: 1100D: 11 in. angle link, 11 in. diaphragm type, heavy-duty 11 in. diaphragm type. 1200D: Heavy-duty 11 in. diaphragm type, 11 in. angle link.

VEHICLE DIMENSIONS:

	Wheelbase	Overall Length
1100D:	115 in.	183.7 in.
	119 in.	—
	131 in.	201.7 in.
1200D:	115 in.	183.7 in.
	119 in.	—
	131 in.	201.7 in.
	149 in.	217.2 in.
	156 in.	244.1 in.
	164 in.	235.2 in.

Overall Height: 1100D (with 8.25 x 15 tires): 71.8 in. 1200D: (with 8.00 x 16.5.tires): 72.8 in. 77.6 in. Width: Front Overhang: 1100D: 30.6 in. 1200D: 30.5 in. Rear Overhang: 1100D: 115 in. wheelbase: 37.7 in., 131 in. wheelbase: 40.2 in. 1200D: 115 in. wheelbase: 37.7 in., 131 in. wheelbase: 40.2 in., 149 in. wheelbase: 37.7 in., 156 in. wheelbase: 57.6 in., 164 in. wheelbase: 40.2 in. Ground Clearance: 1100D: Front axle: 7.4 in. Rear axle: 7.3 in. 1200D: Front axle: 8.0 in. Rear axle: 7.4 in.

CAPACITIES: Fuel tank: 16 gal. Travelall: 21 gal. Engine coolant: 12 qt.

ACCOMMODATIONS: Seating Capacity: Pickups: 3 passengers. Travelette: 6 passengers. Travelall: 6/9 passengers.

INSTRUMENTATION: Speedometer, odometer, gauges for fuel level, oil pressure, alternator, engine coolant temperature.

OPTIONS AND PRICES: 304 cu. in. V-8: $100.00. 345 cu. in. V-8: $125.00. 392 cu. in V-8: $125.00. Integral power steering: $100.00. Automatic transmission: $226. Air conditioning: $200.00. Custom Trim Package. Camper Package: (1200D and 1300D) $69.00. OSRV mirror(s). Dual "California" trailer mirrors. Custom Exterior Trim Package. Foam rubber seat cushions. Tinted glass. Solid-state AM or AM/FM push-button radio. Eight-track tape player. Antenna package. High-side pickup box package, pickup box rails. Sliding rear window (camper models). Automatic choke. Super-capacity heater-defroster. Rear bumper. Rear step bumper. White sidewall tires. Power brakes. Auxiliary 16 gal. fuel tank under right side with dash-mounted selector. 15 gal. tank in lieu of standard unit, mounted under cab. T-7 heavy-duty 3-speed manual transmission with floor-mounted control lever. T-34 5-speed overdrive manual transmission. (1100D, 1200D). T-36 5-speed direct manual transmission (1100D,1200D). T-44 4-speed manual transmission (1100D, 1200D). T-419 heavy-duty 4-speed manual transmission (1100D and 1200D). Three-speed automatic transmission with oil cooler. Choice of axle ratios. Larger-size tires and rims. Traction tires. Modulated air control for fast engine warm-up. Undercoating. Front locking hubs with tie rod guard. Power-Lok rear axle: 1100D and 1200D: RA28, 3500 lb. Power-Lok rear axle, 3.54, 3.73, 409:1 ratios. RA-53 rear axle, 3700 lb. capacity, 3.54, 3.73, 4.10:1 ratios. RA-54 Power-Lok rear axle, 3.54, 3.73, 4.10:1 ratios. 52 or 61 amp alternator. Dual electric horns. Two front corner lamps. Front axle warning light. Five front cab clearance and identification lamps. Front or rear marker lamps. Double face, fender-mounted directional signals. Modulated fan. High altitude equipment. Underslung tire carrier, carrier lock. Heavy-duty front springs. Heavy-duty rear shock absorbers. Rear sway bar. Level-Aire ride (1200D).

HISTORICAL FOOTNOTES: This was the last year for the V-266 engine.

1970 PICKUP & TRAVELALL

The only major change made for 1970 was the use of the 145 hp. engine as standard for the 1100D, 1200D and 1300D models. The V-304, V-345 and V-392 were optional for all models.

1970 International 1100D 4x4 pickup

Body Type	Factory Price	GVW	Shipping Weight	Prod. Total
Series 1100D, 115 in.-132 in. wheelbase				
Chassis & Cab	$3351	4800*	N.A.	—
Pickup 6.5 ft.	$3472	4800	N.A.	—
Pickup 6.5 ft. B.L.	$3510	4800	N.A.	—
Panel 7 ft.	$4052	4800	N.A.	—
Pickup 8 ft.	$3509	4800	N.A.	—
Pickup 8 ft. B.L.	$3548	4800	N.A.	—
Series 1200D, 115 in.-164 in. wheelbase				
Chassis & Cab	$3452	6100*	N.A.	—
Pickup 6.5 ft.	$3573	6100	N.A.	—
Pickup 6.5 ft. B.L.	$3611	6100	N.A.	—
Panel 7 ft.	$4153	6100	N.A.	—
Pickup 8 ft.	$3611	6100	N.A.	—
Pickup 8 ft. B.L.	$3649	6100	N.A.	—
Travelette Cab	$4115	6100	N.A.	—
Travelette 6.5 ft. Pickup	$4244	6100	N.A.	—
Travelette 8 ft. Pickup B.L.	$4441	6100	N.A.	—
Series 1300D, 134 in.-156 in. wheelbase				
Chassis & Cab	$4325	7000*	N.A.	—
Pickup 9 ft.	$4456	7000	N.A.	—
Travelette Cab	$4960	7000	N.A.	—
Travelette 8.5 ft. Pickup B.L.	$5119	7000	N.A.	—

* 5600 GVW optional for Series 1100D; 7700 lb. for Series 1200D; 10,000 for Series 1300D.

Travelall Series 1100D, 119 in. wheelbase				
Station Wagon	$4218	4800	N.A.	—
Travelall Series 1200D, 119 in wheelbase				
Station Wagon	$4313	6100	N.A.	—

STANDARD ENGINE: 1100D, 1200D, 1300D Engine Type: OHV In-line 6-cylinder "Power Thrift-6-232". Bore x Stroke: 3.75 in. x 3.5 in. Displacement: 232 cu. in. Carburetion: Single bbl. Compression Ratio: 8.5:1. Horsepower: 145 @ 4300 rpm. Torque: 215 lb.-ft. @ 1600 rpm. Fuel Requirements: Regular.

OPTIONAL ENGINE: All models: Engine Type: OHV V-8 ("V-304"). Bore x Stroke: 3.875 in. x 3.21875 in. Displacement: 304 cu. in. Carburetion: Single barrel, downdraft. Lifters: Solid. Horsepower: 193 @ 4400 rpm. Torque: 272.5 lb.-ft. @ 2800 rpm. Fuel Requirements: Regular.

OPTIONAL ENGINE: All models: Engine Type: OHV V-8 ("V-345"). Bore x Stroke: 3.875 in. x 3.656 in. Displacement: 344.96 cu. in. Carburetion: Holley model 2300G 2-barrel. Lifters: Solid. Horsepower: 196.7 @ 4000 rpm. Torque: 309 lb.-ft. @ 2200 rpm. Fuel Requirements: Regular.

OPTIONAL ENGINE: All models: Engine Type: OHV V-8 ("V-392"). Bore x Stroke: 4.125 in. x 3.656 in. Displacement: 390.89 cu. in. Carburetion: 4-barrel, downdraft. Lifters: Solid. Horsepower: 235 @ 4000 rpm. Torque: 354 lb.-ft. @ 2600 rpm. Fuel Requirements: Regular.

CHASSIS FEATURES: 1100D, 1200D series. Separate body and frame: 1100D: Pressed steel channel main rails, 6.9375 in. x 2.968 in. x 0.50 in. Section modulus: 3.98. 1200D: Pressed steel channel main rails, 115-149 in. wheelbase: 7 in. x 3.0 in. x 0.179 in. Section modulus: 4.81. 156-164 in. wheelbase: 7.0625 in. x 3.0312 in. x 0.209 in. Section modulus: 5.65.

SUSPENSION AND RUNNING GEAR: Front Suspension: 1100D: Semi-elliptical leaf springs, 2.5 in. x 42 in. Capacity: 2600 lb. 1200D: Semi-elliptical leaf springs, Capacity: 115, 119, 131 in. wheelbase: 2800 lb.; 149, 156, 164 in. wheelbase: 3500 lb. Shock absorbers. Rear Suspension: 1100D: Semi-elliptical leaf springs, 2.5 in. x 52 in. Capacity: 2500 lb. 1200D: Semi-elliptical leaf springs. Capacity 3500 lb. Shock absorbers. Front Axle Type and Capacity: 1100D: FA-16, hypoid, 3500 lb. 1200D: 115, 119, 131 in. wheelbase: FA-15, hypoid, 2800 lb.; 149, 156, 164 in. wheelbase: FA-18, hypoid, 3500 lb. Rear Axle Type and Capacity: 1100D: RA-18, hypoid, 3500 lb. 120D: RA-16, hypoid, 5500 lb. Final Drive Ratio: 1100D: 3.54, 3.73, 4.09:1. 1200D: Front: 4.09:1. Rear: 4.10:1. Transfer Case: Type: TC-141. Ratios: 1.93, 1.00:1. Brakes: Type: Self-adjusting, hydraulic, dual operation, front and rear. Dimensions: 1100D: Front: 11.03 in. x 3.0 in. Rear: 11.03 in. x 2.25 in. Total lining area: 244.8 sq. in. 1200D: Front: 12 in. x 2.5 in. Rear: 12.0 in. x 2.5 in. Total lining area: 245.5 sq. in. Wheels: 1100D: 5-stud wheels with 5.50K rims, 5.5 in. bolt circles. 1200D: 8-stud disc wheels with 6.00 rims, 6.5 in. bolt circles. Tires: 1100D: 8.25 x 15 2-ply tubeless. 1200D: 8.00 x 16.5 6-ply rated truck type tires. Optional: 1100D: 8.55 x 15, 6.50 x 16, 7.00 x 15 (with tubes). 1200D: 8.75 x 16.5, 9.50 x 16.5, 7.00 x 16 (tubes), 7.50 x 16 (tubes). Steering: Type: S-55 gear, with 17 in. steering wheel. Turning circle: 1100D: 115 in. wheelbase: 46.16 ft., 119 in. wheelbase: 48.5 ft., 131 in. wheelbase: 53.67 ft. 1200D: ranges from 46 ft. to 62.75 ft. depending on wheelbase. Transmission: Type: T-24 3-speed synchromesh manual. Transmission Ratios: 3.06, 1.55, 1.00:1. Optional: See Options and Prices. Clutch: 1100D: 10.5 in. diaphragm type. 1200D: 10.5 in. mechanical control. Optional: 1100D: 11 in. angle link, 11 in. diaphragm type, heavy-duty 11 in. diaphragm type. 1200D: Heavy-duty 11 in. diaphragm type, 11 in. angle link.

VEHICLE DIMENSIONS:

	Wheelbase	Overall Length
1100D:	115 in.	183.7 in.
	119 in.	—
	131 in.	201.7 in.
1200D:	115 in.	183.7 in.
	119 in.	—
	131 in.	201.7 in.
	149 in.	217.2 in.
	156 in.	244.1 in.
	164 in.	235.2 in.

Overall Height: 1100D (with 8.25 x 15 tires): 71.8 in. 1200D: (with 8.00 x 16.5 tires): 72.8 in. 77.6 in. Width. Front Overhang: 1100D: 30.6 in. 1200D: 30.5 in. Rear Overhang: 1100D: 115 in. wheelbase: 37.7 in., 131 in. wheelbase: 40.2 in. 1200D: 115 in. wheelbase: 37.7 in., 131 in. wheelbase: 40.2 in., 149 in. wheelbase: 37.7 in. 156 in. wheelbase: 57.6 in. 164 in. wheelbase: 40.2 in. Ground Clearance: 1100D: Front axle: 7.4 in. Rear axle: 7.3 in. 1200D: Front axle: 8.0 in. Rear axle: 7.4 in.

CAPACITIES: Fuel tank: 16 gal. Travelall: 21 gal. Engine coolant: 12 qt.

ACCOMMODATIONS: Seating Capacity: Pickups: 3 passengers. Travelette: 6 passengers. Travelall: 6/9 passengers.

INSTRUMENTATION: Speedometer, odometer, gauges for fuel level, oil pressure, alternator, engine coolant temperature.

OPTIONS AND PRICES: Power steering: $125.00. Automatic transmission: $236.00. Factory air conditioning: $385.00. 304 cu. in. V-8. 345 cu. in. V-8. 392 cu. in V-8: Integral Power steering. Custom Trim Package. OSRV mirror(s). Dual "California" trailer mirrors. Custom Exterior Trim Package. Foam rubber seat cushions. Tinted glass. Solid-state AM or AM/FM push-button radio. Eight-track tape player. Antenna Package. High-Side Pickup Box Package, pickup box rails. Sliding rear window (camper models). Automatic choke. Super-capacity heater-defroster. Rear bumper. Rear step bumper. White sidewall tires. Power brakes. Auxiliary 16 gal. fuel tank under right side with dash-mounted selector. 15 gal. tank in lieu of standard unit, mounted under cab. T-7 heavy-duty 3-speed manual transmission with floor-mounted control lever. T-34 5-speed overdrive manual transmission. (1100D,1200D). T-36 5-speed direct manual transmission (1100D,1200D). T-44 4-speed manual transmission (1100D,1200D). T-419 heavy-duty 4-speed manual transmission (1100D and 1200D). Three-speed automatic transmission with oil cooler. Choice of axle ratios. Larger-size tires and rims. Traction tires. Modulated air control for fast engine warm-up. Undercoating. Front locking hubs with tie rod guard. Axles for 1100D and 1200D: RA28, 3500 lb. Power-Lok rear axle, 3.54, 3.73, 409:1 ratios. RA-53 rear axle, 3700 lb. capacity, 3.54, 3.73, 4.10:1 ratios. RA-54 Power-Lok rear axle, 3.54, 3.73, 4.10:1 ratios. Dual electric horns. Two front corner lamps. Front axle warning light. Five front cab clearance and identification lamps. Front or rear marker lamps. Double face, fender-mounted directional signals. Modulated fan. High altitude equipment. Underslung tire carrier, carrier lock. Heavy-duty front springs. Heavy-duty rear springs. Heavy-duty rear shock absorbers. Rear sway bar. Level-Aire ride (1200D). Camper Package (1200D, 1300D): $72.00.

HISTORICAL FOOTNOTES: The 1970 models were announced in Nov., 1969.

1970 International 1100D 4x4 Travelall

1971 PICKUP & TRAVELALL

The 1971 four-wheel drive Internationals had a new grille that closely resembled that of the Scout II. The "IH" logo was found in the left-hand side of the grille insert. Also adopted were new hubcaps that no longer carried the small fins of those used in 1969 and 1970, vertically-positioned rectangular taillights, a revised tailgate design and new rocker panel trim. Model identification badges were located on the front fenders above the side-marker reflectors. Two sets of cowl-mounted air vents were also new for 1971. International also adopted a new series identification nomenclature. Series 1110 was replaced by Series 1110. Replacing the 1210 series was Series 1210. Series 1310 replaced Series 1310. Fourteen acrylic, high-luster exterior colors were offered: Alpine White, Schoolbus Yellow, Omaha Orange, Gold metallic, Red, Flame Red, Medium Blue metallic, Aegean Blue metallic, Medium Green metallic, Frost Green metallic, Lime Green metallic and Sundance Yellow. The standard International interior featured foam padded seats with all-vinyl upholstery available in a choice of black, red, blue or green. The Deluxe Interior Package had a color coded vinyl and nylon seat upholstery, nylon colored coded floor mats (first and second seat areas on Travelall), soft inner color coded door trim panels, brushed aluminum instrument panel with black trim, cigarette lighter, seat belt retractors, coat hook, tinted glass and an intermediate folding seat on Travelall. The Custom Interior Trim Package added these items to the Deluxe Package's content: Padded horn button, rear dome light on Travelall, parking brake warning light, electric rear window with safety switch on Travelall, dual electric horns and a glove compartment lock. The Deluxe Exterior Trim Package contained bright finish hubcaps, rocker panel trim molding, drip rail moldings, windshield molding, headlight and parking light bezels, and vent wing moldings. Also included were chrome front and rear bumpers. The Custom Trim Package included all of the Deluxe Package plus woodgrain side panels and stainless steel wheel covers (hubcaps on 1210). A Special Towing Package provided a heavy-duty front suspension, heavy-duty progressive rear springs, weight equalizer trailer hitch, auxiliary fuel tank, increased engine cooling, power brakes, power steering, 70 amp battery and 61 amp alternator.

1971 International Travelall 1110 4x4

I.D. DATA: Unchanged from 1970.

Body Type	Factory Price	GVW	Shipping Weight	Prod. Total
Series 1110, 115 in.-131 in. wheelbase				
Chassis & Cab	$3325	4800*	N.A.	—
Pickup 6.5 ft.	$3471	4800	N.A.	—
Pickup 6.5 ft. B.L.	$3483	4800	N.A.	—
Panel 7 ft.	$4227	4800	N.A.	—
Pickup 8 ft.	$3600	4800	N.A.	—
Pickup 8 ft. B.L.	$3612	4800	N.A.	—
Series 1210, 115 in.-164 in. wheelbase				
Chassis & Cab	$3632	6100*	N.A.	—
Pickup 6.5 ft.	$3780	6100	N.A.	—
Pickup 6.5 ft. B.L.	$3791	6100	N.A.	—
Panel 7 ft.	$4632	6100	N.A.	—
Pickup 8 ft.	$4005	6100	N.A.	—
Pickup 8 ft. B.L.	$4017	6100	N.A.	—
Travelette Cab 6.5 ft.	$4482	6100	N.A.	—
Travelette Pickup 6.5 ft.	$4638	6100	N.A.	—
Travelette Pickup 8 ft. B.L.	$4809			
Series 1310, 134-156 in. wheelbase				
Chassis & Cab	$4148	7000*	N.A.	—
Pickup 9 ft.	$4307	7000	N.A.	—
Travelette Cab	$4783	7000	N.A.	—
Travelette 6.5 ft. Pickup B.L.	$4943	7000	N.A.	—
Travelall Series 1110, 119 in. wheelbase				
Station Wagon	$4399	4800	N.A.	—
Travelall Series 1210, 119 in. wheelbase				
Station Wagon	$4529	6100	N.A.	—

* Optional GVW range is 5600 lb. for 1110; 7500 lb. for 1210 and 10,000 lb. for 1310.

STANDARD ENGINE: 1110, 1200, 1300: Engine Type: OHV In-line 6-cylinder "Power Thrift-6-232." Bore x Stroke: 3.75 in. x 3.5 in. Displacement: 232 cu. in. Carburetion: Single bbl. Compression Ratio: 8.5:1. Horsepower: 145 @ 4300 rpm. Torque: 215 lb.-ft. @ 1600 rpm. Fuel Requirements: Regular.

OPTIONAL ENGINE: All models: Engine Type: OHV V-8 ("V-304"). Bore x Stroke: 3.875 in. x 3.21875 in. Displacement: 304 cu. in. Carburetion: Single barrel, downdraft. Lifters: Solid. Horsepower: 193 @ 4400 rpm. Torque: 272.5 lb.-ft. @ 2800 rpm. Fuel Requirements: Regular.

OPTIONAL ENGINE: All models: Engine Type: OHV V-8 ("V-345"). Bore x Stroke: 3.875 in. x 3.656 in. Displacement: 344.96 cu. in. Carburetion: Holley model 2300G 2-barrel. Lifters: Solid. Horsepower: 196.7 @ 4000 rpm. Torque: 309 lb.-ft. @ 2200 rpm. Fuel Requirements: Regular.

OPTIONAL ENGINE: All models: Engine Type: OHV V-8 ("V-392"). Bore x Stroke: 4.125 in. x 3.656 in. Displacement: 390.89 cu. in. Carburetion: 4-barrel, downdraft. Lifters: Solid. Horsepower: 235 @ 4000 rpm. Torque: 354 lb.-ft. @ 2600 rpm. Fuel Requirements: Regular.

CHASSIS FEATURES: 1110, 1210 series. Separate body and frame: 1110: Pressed steel channel main rails, 6.9375 in. x 2.968 in. x 0.50 in. Section modulus: 3.98. 1210: Pressed steel channel main rails, 115-149 in. wheelbase: 7 in. x 3.0 in. x 0.179 in. Section modulus: 4.81. 156-164 in. wheelbase: 7.0625 in. x 3.0312 in. x 0.209 in. Section modulus: 5.65.

SUSPENSION AND RUNNING GEAR: Front Suspension: 1110: Semi-elliptical leaf springs, 2.5 in. x 42 in. Capacity: 2600 lb. 1210: Semi-elliptical leaf springs, Capacity: 115, 119, 131 in. wheelbase: 2800 lb.; 149, 156, 164 in. wheelbase: 3500 lb. Shock absorbers. Rear Suspension: 1110: Semi-elliptical leaf springs, 2.5 in. x 52 in. Capacity: 2500 lb. 1210: Semi-elliptical leaf springs. Capacity 3500 lb. Shock absorbers. Front Axle Type and Capacity: 1110: FA-16, hypoid, 3500 lb. 1210: 115, 119, 131 in. wheelbase: FA-15, hypoid, 2800 lb.; 149, 156, 164 in. wheelbase: FA-18, hypoid, 3500 lb. Rear Axle Type and Capacity: 1110: RA-18, hypoid, 3500 lb. 1200D: RA-16, Hhypoid, 5500 lb. Final Drive Ratio: 1110: 3.54, 3.73, 4.09:1. 1210: Front: 4.09:1. Rear: 4.10:1. Transfer Case: Type: TC-141. Ratios: 1.93, 1.00:1. Brakes: Type: Self-adjusting, hydraulic, dual operation, front and rear. Dimensions: 1110: Front: 11.03 in. x 3.0. Rear: 11.03 in. x 2.25 in. Total lining area: 244.8 sq. in. 1210: Front: 12 in. x 2.5 in. Rear: 12.0 in. x 2.5 in. Total lining area: 245.5 sq. in. Wheels: 1110: 5-stud wheels with 5.50K rims, 5.5 in. bolt circles. 1200D: 8-stud wheels with 6.00 rims, 6.5 in. bolt circles. Optional: Tires: 1110: 8.25 x 15 2-ply tubeless. 1210: 8.00 x 16.5 6-ply rated truck type tires. Optional: 1110: 8.55 x 15, 6.50 x 16, 7.00 x 15 (with tubes). 1210: 8.75 x 16.5, 9.50 x 16.5, 7.00 x 16 (tubes), 7.50 x 16 (tubes). Steering: Type: S-55 gear, with 17 in. steering wheel. Turning circle: 1110: 115 in. wheelbase: 46.16 ft., 119 in. wheelbase: 48.5 ft., 131 in. wheelbase: 53.67 ft. 1210: ranges from 46 ft. to 62.75 ft. depending on wheelbase. Transmission: Type: T-24 3-speed synchromesh manual. Transmission Ratios: 3.06, 1.55, 1.00:1. Optional: See Options and Prices. Clutch: 1110: 10.5 in. diaphragm type. 1210: 10.5 in. mechanical control. Optional: 1110: 11 in. angle link, 11 in. diaphragm type, heavy-duty 11 in. diaphragm type. 1210: Heavy-duty 11 in. diaphragm type, 11 in. angle link.

VEHICLE DIMENSIONS:

	Wheelbase	Overall Length
1110:	115 in.	183.7 in.
	119 in.	—
	131 in.	201.7 in.
1210:	115 in.	183.7 in.
	119 in.	—
	131 in.	201.7 in.
	149 in.	217.2 in.
	156 in.	244.1 in.
	164 in.	235.2 in.

Overall Height: 1110 (with 8.25 x 15 tires): 71.8 in. 1210: (with 8.00 x 16.5 tires): 72.8 in. 77.6 in. Width: Front Overhang: 1110: 30.6 in. 1210: 30.5 in. Rear Overhang: 1110: 115 in. wheelbase: 37.7 in., 131 in. wheelbase: 40.2 in. 1210: 115 in. wheelbase: 37.7 in., 131 in. wheelbase: 40.2 in., 149 in. wheelbase: 37.7 in. 156 in. wheelbase: 57.6 in. 164 in. wheelbase: 40.2 in. Ground Clearance: 1110: Front axle: 7.4 in. Rear axle: 7.3 in. 1210: Front axle: 8.0 in. Rear axle: 7.4 in.

CAPACITIES: Fuel tank: 16 gal. Travelall: 21 gal. Engine coolant: 12 qt.

ACCOMMODATIONS: Seating Capacity: Pickups: 3 passengers. Travelette: 6 passengers. Travelall: 6/9 passengers.

INSTRUMENTATION: Speedometer, odometer, gauges for fuel level, oil pressure, alternator, engine coolant temperature.

OPTIONS AND PRICES: Power steering: $126.00; Automatic transmission: $230.00; Factory air conditioning: $411.00. 304 cu. in. V-8. 345 cu. in. V-8. 392 cu. in V-8: Integral Power steering Custom Trim Package. OSRV mirror(s). Dual "California" trailer mirrors. Custom Exterior Trim Package. Foam rubber seat cushions. Tinted glass. Solid-state AM or AM/FM push-button radio. Eight-track tape player. Antenna Package. High-Side Pickup Box Package, pickup box skids. Sliding rear window (camper models). Automatic choke. Super-capacity heater-defroster. Rear bumper. Rear step bumper. White sidewall tires. Power brakes. Auxiliary 16 gal. fuel tank under right side with dash-mounted selector. 15 gal. tank in lieu of standard unit, mounted under cab. T-7 heavy-duty 3-speed manual transmission with floor-mounted control lever. T-34 5-speed overdrive manual transmission. (1100,1200D). T-36 5-speed direct manual transmission (1100,1200D). T-44 4-speed manual transmission (1100,1200D). T-419 heavy-duty 4-speed manual transmission (1110 and 1210). Three-speed automatic transmission with oil cooler. Choice of axle ratios. Larger-size tires and rims. Traction tires. Modulated air control for fast engine warm-up. Undercoating. Front locking hubs with tie rod guard. Axles for 1110 and 1210: RA28, 3500 lb. Power-Lok rear axle, 3.54, 3.73, 409:1 ratios. RA-53 rear axle, 3700 lb. capacity, 3.54, 3.73, 4.10:1 ratios. RA-54 Power-Lok rear axle, 3.54, 3.73, 4.10:1 ratios. 52 or 61 amp alternator. Dual electric horns. Two front corner lamps. Front axle warning light. Five front cab clearance and identification lamps. Front or rear marker lamps. Double face, fender-mounted directional signals. Modulated fan. High altitude equipment. Underslung tire carrier, carrier lock. Heavy-duty front springs. Heavy-duty rear springs. Heavy-duty rear shock absorbers. Rear sway bar. Level-Aire ride (1210). Camper Package (1210, 1310). $72.00.

HISTORICAL FOOTNOTES: The 1971 models were announced in the fall of 1970.

1972 PICKUP & TRAVELALL

The 1972 Internationals were identified by a new grille and dashboard. The new grille had five horizontal bars divided by a center rectangular-shaped centerpiece. The standard engine was now the 258 cu. in. unit. International referred to the four-wheel drive 1100 and 1210 Travelalls

as possessing "all-wheel drive." Standard equipment included seats with foam padding over spring construction, all-vinyl upholstery in a selection of four body color-coordinated colors (Dark Red, Dark Blue, Sage and Jet Black), dual full-size armrests, padded dash, padded sun visors, fresh air heating and defrosting system, hard acoustical headliner with bright metal ribs, front seat shoulder harness anchors, windshield washers, two-speed electric windshield wipers with non-glare arms, impact-absorbing anti-penetration steering column, recessed steering wheel, breakaway interior mirror, dual exterior mirrors, non-glare interior trim, safety door latches, hazard warning lights, and back-up lights. The thirteen exterior colors for 1972 were: Alpine White, Schoolbus Yellow, Yuma Yellow, Omaha Orange, Gold metallic Red, Flame Red, Cosmic Blue metallic, Aegean Blue metallic, Medium Green metallic, Frost Green metallic, Burnished Gold metallic and Sundance Yellow metallic. As in earlier years these designations identified various tonnage ratings. The Series 1100 models were 1/2 ton trucks; the Series 1210 were 3/4 ton trucks and the 1310 Internationals were 1 ton trucks.

I.D. DATA: A thirteen-digit vehicle identification number was located on the left front door pillar post. The first six digits served as the vehicle's serial number. The seventh digit identified the manufacturing plant. The last six digits were the vehicle's sequential production number. The engine number was located on a machined boss on the cylinder block. It consisted of the vehicle's identification number, along with a suffix representing the engine type.

Body Type	Factory Price	GVW	Shipping Weight	Prod. Total
Series 1110, 115 in.-131 in. wheelbase				
Chassis & Cab	$3355	4800*	N.A.	—
Pickup 6.5 ft.	$3495	4800	N.A.	—
Pickup 6.5 ft. B.L.	$3507	4800	N.A.	—
Pickup 8 ft.	$3532	4800	N.A.	—
Pickup 8 ft. B.L.	$3543	4800	N.A.	—
Series 1210, 115 in.-164 in. wheelbase				
Pickup 6.5 ft.	$3440	6100*	N.A.	—
Pickup 6.5 ft. B.L.	$3282	6100	N.A.	—
Pickup 8 ft.	$3619	6100	N.A.	—
Pickup 8 ft. B.L.	$3630	6100	N.A.	—
Travelette Cab	$4079	6100	N.A.	—
Travelette 6.5 ft. Pickup	$4230	6100	N.A.	—
Travelette 6.5 ft. Pickup B.L.	$4241	6100	N.A.	—
Travelette 8 ft. Pickup	$4383	6100	N.A.	—
Travelette 8 ft. Pickup B.L.	$4394	6100	N.A.	—
Series 1310, 131 in.-156 in. wheelbase				
Chassis & Cab	$4154	7000*	N.A.	—
Pickup 8 ft.	$4296	7000	N.A.	—
Pickup 8 ft. B.L.	$4307	7000	N.A.	—
Pickup 9 ft.	4307	7000	N.A.	—
Travelette Cab	$4767	7000	N.A.	—
Travelette 6.5 ft. Pickup B.L.	$4921	7000	N.A.	—
Series 1110, 119 in. wheelbase				
Station Wagon, 119 in. wheelbase	$4295	4800	5475	—
Series 1210, 119 in. wheelbase				
Station Wagon, 119 in. wheelbase	$4515	6100	5990	—

* 5600 lb. GVW optional for series 1100; 7700 lb. for series 1210 and 10,000 lb. for Series1310.

STANDARD ENGINE: Engine Type: OHV, In-line 6-cylinder. Bore x Stroke: 3.75 in. x 3.9 in. Lifters: Hydraulic. Number of main bearings-7. Displacement: 258 cu. in. Carburetion: Model 1904D Holley single barrel. Compression Ratio: 8.0:1. Horsepower: 135 @ 3800 rpm. Torque: 235 lb.-ft. @ 2000 rpm. Fuel Requirements: Regular.

OPTIONAL ENGINE: All models: Engine Type: OHV V-8 ("V-304"). Bore x Stroke: 3.875 in. x 3.21875 in. Displacement: 304 cu. in. Carburetion: Single barrel, downdraft. Lifters: Solid. Horsepower: 193 @ 4400 rpm. Torque: 272.5 lb.-ft. @ 2800 rpm. Fuel Requirements: Regular.

OPTIONAL ENGINE: All models: Engine Type: OHV V-8 ("V-345"). Bore x Stroke: 3.875 in. x 3.656 in. Displacement: 344.96 cu. in. Carburetion: Holley model 2300G 2-barrel. Lifters: Solid. Horsepower: 196.7 @ 4000 rpm. Torque: 309 lb.-ft. @ 2200 rpm. Fuel Requirements: Regular.

OPTIONAL ENGINE: All models: Engine Type: OHV V-8 ("V-392"). Bore x Stroke: 4.125 in. x 3.656 in. Displacement: 390.89 cu. in. Carburetion: 4-barrel, downdraft. Lifters: Solid. Horsepower: 235 @ 4000 rpm. Torque: 354 lb.-ft. @ 2600 rpm. Fuel Requirements: Regular.

CHASSIS FEATURES: 1110, 1210 series. Separate body and frame: 1110: Pressed steel channel main rails, 6.9375 in. x 2.968 in. x 0.50 in. Section modulus: 3.98. 1210: Pressed steel channel main rails, 115-149 in. wheelbase: 7 in. x 3.0 in. x 0.179 in. Section modulus: 4.81. 156-164 in. wheelbase: 7.0625 in. x 3.0312 in. x 0.209 in. Section modulus: 5.65.

SUSPENSION AND RUNNING GEAR: Front Suspension: 1110: Semi-elliptical leaf springs, 2.5 in. x 42 in. Capacity: 2600 lb. 1210: Semi-elliptical leaf springs, Capacity: 115, 119, 131 in. wheelbase: 2800 lb.; 149, 156, 164 in. wheelbase: 3500 lb. Shock absorbers. Rear Suspension: 1110: Semi-elliptical leaf springs, 2.5 in. x 52 in. Capacity: 2500 lb. 1210: Semi-elliptical leaf springs. Capacity 3500 lb. Shock absorbers. Front Axle Type and Capacity: 1110: FA-16, hypoid, 3500 lb. 1210: 115, 119, 131 in. wheelbase: FA-15, hypoid, 2800 lb.; 149, 156, 164 in. wheelbase: FA-18, hypoid, 3500 lb. Rear Axle Type and Capacity: 1110: RA-18, hypoid, 3500 lb. 120D: RA-16, hypoid, 5500 lb. Final Drive Ratio: 1110: 3.54, 3.73, 4.09:1. 1210: Front: 4.09:1. Rear: 4.10:1. Transfer Case: Type: TC-141. Ratios: 1.93, 1.00:1. Brakes: Type: Self-adjusting, hydraulic, dual operation, front and rear. Dimensions: 1110: Front: 11.03 in. x 3.0 in. Rear: 11.03 in. x 2.25 in. Total lining area: 244.8 sq. in. 1210: Front: 12 in. x 2.5 in. Rear: 12.0 in. x 2.5 in. Total lining area: 245.5 sq. in. Wheels: 1110: 5-stud wheels with 5.50K rims, 5.5 in. bolt circles. 1200D: 8-stud disc wheels with 6.00 rims, 6.5 in. bolt circles. Optional: Tires: 1110: 8.25 x 15 2-ply tubeless. 1210: 8.00 x 16.5 6-ply rated truck type tires. Optional: 1110: 8.55 x 15, 6.50 x 16, 7.00 x 15 (with tubes). 1210: 8.75 x 16.5, 9.50 x 16.5, 7.00 x 16 (tubes), 7.50 x 16 (tubes). Steering: Type: S-55 gear, with 17 in. steering wheel. Turning circle: 1110: 115 in. wheelbase: 46.16 ft., 119 in. wheelbase: 48.5 ft., 131 in. wheelbase: 53.67 ft. 1210: ranges from 46 ft. to 62.75 ft. depending on wheelbase. Transmission: Type: T-24 3-speed synchromesh manual. Transmission Ratios: 3.06, 1.55, 1.00:1. Optional: See Options and Prices. Clutch: 1110: 10.5 in. diaphragm type. 1210: 10.5 in. mechanical control. Optional: 1110: 11 in. angle link, 11 in. diaphragm type, heavy-duty 11 in. diaphragm type. 1210: Heavy-duty11 in. diaphragm type, 11 in. angle link.

VEHICLE DIMENSIONS:

	Wheelbase	Overall Length
1110:	115 in.	183.7 in.
	119 in.	—
	131 in.	201.7 in.
1210:	115 in.	183.7 in.
	119 in.	—
	131 in.	201.7 in.
	149 in.	217.2 in.
	156 in.	244.1 in.
	164 in.	235.2 in.

Overall Height: 1110 (with 8.25 x 15 tires): 71.8 in. 1210: (with 8.00 x 16.5.tires): 72.8 in. 77.6 in. Width: Front Overhang: 1110: 30.6 in. 1210: 30.5 in. Rear Overhang: 1110: 115 in. wheelbase: 37.7 in., 131 in. wheelbase: 40.2 in. 1210: 115 in. wheelbase: 37.7 in., 131 in. wheelbase: 40.2 in., 149 in. wheelbase: 37.7 in. 156 in. wheelbase: 57.6 in. 164 in. wheelbase: 40.2 in. Ground Clearance:1110: Front axle: 7.4 in. Rear axle: 7.3 in. 1210: Front axle: 8.0 in. Rear axle: 7.4 in.

CAPACITIES: Fuel tank: 16 gal. Travelall: 21 gal. Engine coolant: 12 qt.

ACCOMMODATIONS: Seating Capacity: Pickups: 3 passengers. Travelette: 6 passengers. Travelall: 6/9 passengers.

INSTRUMENTATION: Speedometer, odometer, gauges for fuel level, oil pressure, alternator, engine coolant temperature.

OPTIONS AND PRICES: Chrome front bumper. Chrome rear bumper. Two-tone paint. Special paint. Bumper guards. Clock. Cigarette lighter. Seat covers. Clearance lights. Dual "California" mirrors. Deluxe hubcaps. White sidewall tires. License plate frame. V-304 engine (series 1110 and 1210): $240; Series 1310: $80.00. 392 cu. in V-8. Heavy-duty rear springs: $14.60. Heavy-duty front shock absorbers: $8.25. Heavy-duty rear shock absorbers: $8.25. Hand throttle control: $4.75. Locking front hubs: $80.00. Eleven in. clutch: $15.00. Power brakes: $45.50. Power steering: $134.00. Dual exhausts: $38.00. Underslung spare tire carrier: $6.00. Tie rod protector: $20.00. Front axle engaged warning light: $8.25. Undercoating: $37.50. Heavy-duty 4-speed manual transmission. Four-speed manual transmission: $91.00. Three-speed automatic transmission. Firestone Transport wide oval tires: $220.00, AM radio and antenna: $65.00. Rear seat speaker: $19.00. Undercoating: $15.00. 16 gallon auxiliary tank (1210, 1300): $106.00. Trac-Lok limited slip rear differential. 15 gallon auxiliary fuel tank (1110). Automatic choke. Larger size rims and tires. Traction tires. Level-Aire ride. Three passages aluminized muffler. Air conditioning: $405.00. Deluxe Exterior Trim Package. Includes standard features in addition to vinyl and nylon color coded seat upholstery, nylon color coded mats (first and second seats for Travelall), soft inner color coded door trim panels, brushed aluminum instrument panel with black trim, cigarette lighter, seat belt retractors, coat hook and intermediate folding seat: $90.00. Custom Interior Trim Package. Includes Deluxe interior features plus: Padded horn button, rear dome light, parking light warning light, electric rear window with safety switch (Travelall), dual electric horns, glove compartment light and tinted glass. Deluxe Exterior Trim Package. Includes bright finish grille, hubcaps, rocker panel trim molding, headlights and parking lamp bezel and vent wing molding. Custom Exterior Trim Package. Includes Deluxe Trim Package features plus: Chrome front and rear bumpers, woodgrain side panels, stainless steel wheel covers (model 1110), and bright finish hubcaps (model 1210). Special Towing Package. Includes heavy-duty front suspension, weight equalizer trailer hitch mount, auxiliary fuel tank, increased engine cooling capacity, power brakes, power steering, 12 volt-70 amp hr. battery. 12 volt-61 amp alternator.

HISTORICAL FOOTNOTES: The 1972 models debuted in the fall of 1971.

1973 PICKUP & TRAVELALL

The International line of four wheel drive trucks continued to consist of 1/2 ton 1110, 3/4 ton 1210 and 1 ton 1310 versions. Along with all 1973 four-wheel drive International Harvester models, the pickups and Travelalls were offered with the "silent drive" transfer case. Details of this innovation are found in the 1973 Scout section. If an International pickup was intended for serious off-road operations, the two-speed transfer case was recommended. New fully synchronized transmissions were now offered.

Both the 1210 and 1310 versions were available with a Camper Package Special Package which included such items as heavy-duty front and rear springs and shock absorbers, a front-mounted stabilizer bar, heavy-duty front axle, dual exhausts and power brakes. A sliding rear window was installed along with a camper wiring harness. The Travelette crew cab pickup continued to be offered with four-wheel drive in the 1210 line. A new hubcap with turbine fins was installed on all four-wheel drive models. A new grip rail for the pickup models was offered. International pickups continued to be available in either Deluxe or custom trim levels. The standard level included a painted front bumper with a rear painted unit optional. The Deluxe option included lower body side molding that extended back from the front fender wheel. This trim was joined by upper body trim that also encompassed both the front and rear fender wells. The area within the custom trim molding could be filled with a contrasting color to the rest of the body. Customers could also purchase chromed front and rear bumpers. Other appearance changes consisted of smaller front fender badges, hubcaps with a more pointed center and trapezoidally-shaped taillights. The cab upholstery was all new for 1973. Four interior colors were offered: Dark blue, sage, jet black and dark red. The Standard interior included a thick foam-padded bench seat with all-vinyl upholstery, dual full-size armrests, padded sun visors, and acoustical headliner. The Deluxe interior added vinyl and nylon upholstery with matching soft padded door panels, vinyl floor mat, cigarette lighter, seat belt retractors, coat hooks and tinted glass. The custom interior provided color-coordinated nylon carpeting, custom steering wheel with padded horn button, locking glove compartment, door operated dome light and dual electric horns. Each interior could be ordered with the standard, Deluxe or custom body trim. The standard exterior colors for 1973 were Ceylon green, red, sunrise yellow, Mayan mist, schoolbus yellow, Omaha orange, Brittany blue, frost green, white, flame red, glacier blue, medium green and burnished gold.

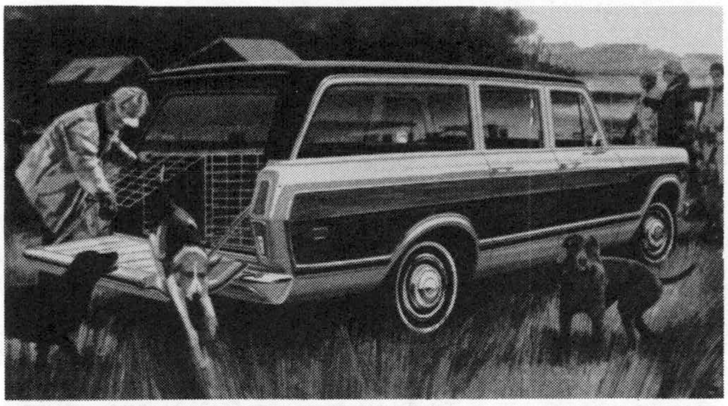

1973 International Model 1100 4x4

I.D. DATA: The vehicle identification number, consisting of 13 digits, was positioned on the left front door pillar post. The first six digits were the vehicle's serial number. The seventh identified the assembly plant and the remaining digits were the vehicle's sequential production number. The engine model identification, located on a machined boss on the block, was a prefix to the V.I.N. number.

Body Type	Factory Price	GVW	Shipping Weight	Prod. Total
Series 1110, 115 in.-134 in. wheelbase				
Chassis & Cab	$3348	4800*	3702	—
Pickup 6.5 ft.	$3494	4800	4062	—
Pickup 6.5 ft. B.L.	$3506	4800	4062	—
Panel 7 ft.	$4158	4800	4392	—
Pickup 8 ft.	$3531	4800	4112	—
Pickup 8 ft. B.L.	$3543	4800	4112	—
Series 1210, 115 in.-164 in. wheelbase				
Chassis & Cab	$3524	6100*	4121	—
Pickup 6.5 ft.	$3366	6100	4491	—
Pickup 6.5 ft. B.L.	$3678	6100	4491	—
Pickup 8 ft.	$3703	6100	4561	—
Pickup 8 ft. B.L.	$3714	6100	4561	—
Travelette Cab	$4163	6100	4166	—
Travelette 6.5 ft. Pickup	$4314	6100	4525	—
Travelette 6.5 ft. Pickup B.L.	$4325	6100	4525	—
Travelette 8 ft. Pickup	$4467	6100	5081	—
Travelette 8 ft. Pickup B.L.	$4478	6100	5081	—
Series 1310, 134 in.-156 in. wheelbase				
Chassis & Cab	$4310	4375	7000*	—
Pickup 8 ft.	$4452	4765	7000	—
Pickup 8 ft. B.L.	$4463	4765	7000	—
Pickup 9 ft.	$4463	4835	7000	—
Travelette Cab	$4923	4975	7000	—
Travelette Cab 6.5 ft. B.L.	$5077	5155	7000	—
Series 1110 Travelall, 119 in. wheelbase				
Station Wagon	$4251	4756	4800	—
Series 1210 Travelall,119 in. wheelbase				
Station Wagon	$4351	5125	6100	—

* 5600 GVW optional for series 1110. 7700 for series 1210, 10,000 for series 1310.

STANDARD ENGINE: Engine Type: OHV, In-line 6-cylinder. Bore x Stroke: 3.75 in. x 3.9 in. Lifters: Hydraulic. Number of main bearings-7. Displacement: 258 cu. in. Carburetion: Model 1904D Holley single barrel. Compression Ratio: 8.0:1. Horsepower: Net: 113 @ 4000. Torque: 191 lb.-ft. @ 2000 rpm. Fuel Requirements: International truck engines for 1973 operated on the new low-lead or non-leaded fuel. International advised its customers that "because consistent use of non-leaded fuels could cause premature valve wear, it is recommended, if non-leaded fuels are used, alternating to a regular grade fuel every fourth tank."

OPTIONAL ENGINE: All models: Engine Type: OHV V-8 ("V-304"). Bore x Stroke: 3.875 in. x 3.21875 in. Displacement: 304 cu. in. Carburetion: Single barrel, downdraft. Lifters: Solid. Horsepower: net: 137 @ 4000 rpm. Torque: 233 lb.-ft. @2400 rpm. Fuel Requirements: See above.

OPTIONAL ENGINE: All models: Engine Type: OHV V-8 ("V-345"). Bore x Stroke: 3.875 in. x 3.656 in. Displacement: 344.96 cu. in. Carburetion: Holley model 2300G 2-barrel. Lifters: Solid. Horsepower: Net: 144 hp. @ 3600 rpm; 156 with dual exhausts. Torque: 263 lb.-ft. @ 2000 rpm, 269 lb.-ft. with dual exhausts. Fuel Requirements: See 258 engine data.

OPTIONAL ENGINE: All models: Engine Type: OHV V-8 ("V-392"). Bore x Stroke: 4.125 in. x 3.656 in. Displacement: 390.89 cu. in. Carburetion: 4-barrel, downdraft. Lifters: Solid. Horsepower: Net: 179 @ 3600 rpm; 193 with dual exhaust. Torque: 297 lb.-ft. @ 2800 rpm. 305 lb.-ft. with dual exhaust. Fuel Requirements: See data for 258 engine.

CHASSIS FEATURES: Separate body and frame: 1110: Pressed steel channel main rails, 6.9375 in. x 2.968 in. x 0.50 in. Section modulus: 3.98. 1210: Pressed steel channel main rails, 115-149 in. wheelbase: 7 in. x 3.0 in. x 0.179 in. Section modulus: 4.81. 156-164 in. wheelbase: 7.0625 in. x 3.0312 in. x 0.209 in. Section modulus: 5.65.

SUSPENSION AND RUNNING GEAR: Front Suspension: 1110: Semi-elliptical leaf springs, 2.5 in. x 42 in. Capacity: 2600 lb. 1210: Semi-elliptical leaf springs, Capacity: 115, 119, 131 in. wheelbase: 2800 lb.; 149, 156, 164 in. wheelbase: 3500 lb. Shock absorbers. Rear Suspension: 1110: Semi-elliptical leaf springs, 2.5 in. x 52 in. Capacity: 2500 lb. 1210: Semi-elliptical leaf springs. Capacity 3500 lb. Shock absorbers. Front Axle Type and Capacity: 1110: FA-16, hypoid, 3000 lb. 1210: 115, 119, 131 in. wheelbase: FA-15, hypoid, 2800 lb.; 149, 156, 164 in. wheelbase: FA-18, hypoid, 3500 lb. Rear Axle Type and Capacity: 1110: RA-18, hypoid, semi-floating. 3500 lb. 1210: RA-16, hypoid, 5500 lb. Final Drive Ratio: 1110: 3.54, 3.73, 4.09:1. 1210: Front: 4.09:1. Rear: 4.10:1. Transfer Case: 1-speed chain drive. Optional: NP-250 2-speed, ratios; Ratios: 1.93, 1.00:1. Brakes: Type: Self-adjusting, hydraulic, dual operation, front and rear. Dimensions: 1110: Front: 11.03 in. x 3.0 in. Rear: 11.03 in. x 2.25 in. Total lining area: 244.8 sq. in. 1210: Front: 12 in. x 2.5 in. Rear: 12.0 in. x 2.5 in. Total lining area: 245.5 sq. in. Wheels: 1110: 5-stud wheels with 5.50K rims, 5.5 in. bolt circles. 1200D: 8-stud disc wheels with 6.00 rims, 6.5 in. bolt circles. Optional: Tires: 1110: 8.25 x 15 2-ply tubeless. 1210: 8.00 x 16.5 6-ply rated truck type tires. Optional: 1110: G78 x 158 (4PR), 8.55 x 15, 6.50 x 16, 7.00 x 15 (with tubes). 1210: 8.75 x 16.5, 9.50 x 16.5, 7.00 x 16 (tubes), 7.50 x 16 (tubes). Steering: Type: S-55 gear, with 17 in. steering wheel. Steering: Recirculating ball. Ratio: 24.0:1. Optional: Power steering with 17.5:1 ratio: Turning circle: 1110: 115 in. wheelbase: 46.16 ft., 119 in. wheelbase: 48.5 ft., 131 in. wheelbase: 53.67 ft. 1210: ranges from 46 ft. to 62.75 ft. depending on wheelbase. Transmission: Type: T-24 3-speed synchromesh manual. Transmission Ratios: 3.06, 1.55, 1.00:1. Optional: T-7, 3-speed manual, floor-mounted shifter. Transmission ratios: 3.17, 1.87,1.00:1. Optional: T-427 heavy-duty all-synchromesh, 4-speed manual. Transmission ratios: 6.32, 3.09, 1.68, 1.00:1. Optional: T-428 Heavy-duty all-synchromesh, 4-speed manual transmission ratios: 4.02, 3.09, 1.68,1.00:1. Optional: T-36 5-speed manual (not available with 258 cu. in. 6-cylinder engine. (first gear not synchromesh). Transmission ratios: 6.21, 3.43, 2.05, 1.11, 1.00:1. Optional: 3-speed automatic with oil cooler. Transmission ratios: 2.40, 1.47,1.00:1. T-34 5-speed overdrive manual transmission. Clutch: 10.5 in. single plate, dry disc, 103.2 sq. in. Optional: 11 in. heavy-duty diaphragm, 11 in. single link, 123.8 sq. in.

VEHICLE DIMENSIONS: 1110 Pickups: Wheelbase: 115, 131 in. Overall length: 183.7 in./ 201.7 in. Front/Rear tread: 61.4 in./61.4 in. Overall height: 68.9 in. Width: 77.6 in. Front/Rear Overhang: 30.6 in./44.0 in. Tailgate: 23.5 in. x 66.5 in. Approach/Departure Angles: 25/21 degree. Ground Clearance: Front and rear axles: 8.5 in. Oil pan: 18.5 in. Transfer case: 17.8 in. Fuel tank: 17.0 in. Exhaust system: 13.0 in. Load space: 79 in. x 49 in. x 19.5 in. Overall Height: 1110 (with 8.25 x 15 tires): 71.8 in. 1210: (with 8.00 x 16.5.tires): 72.8 in. Width: 77.6 in. Front Overhang: 1110: 30.6 in. 1210: 30.5 in. Rear Overhang: 1110: 115 in. wheelbase: 37.7 in., 131 in. wheelbase: 40.2 in. 1210: 115 in. wheelbase: 37.7 in., 131 in. wheelbase: 40.2 in., 149 in. wheelbase: 37.7 in. 156 in. wheelbase: 57.6 in. 164 in. wheelbase: 40.2 in. Ground Clearance:1110: Front axle: 7.4 in. Rear axle: 7.3 in. 1210: Front axle: 8.0 in. Rear axle: 7.4 in. Headroom: 36.0 in. Maximum. Pedal steering wheel to seat back: 24.0 in. Seat to ground: 33.5 in. Floor to ground: 19.5 in. Pedal to seat back: 44.5 in.

CAPACITIES: Fuel tank: Series1110: 15 gal. Series 1220 and 1320: 16 gal. Travelall: 20 gal. Engine coolant: 12 qt.

ACCOMMODATIONS: Seating Capacity: Pickups: 3 passengers. Travelette: 6 passengers. Travelall: 6/9 passengers.

INSTRUMENTATION: 0-120 mph speedometer, 99,999.9 odometer, gauges for oil pressure, temperature, ammeter, fuel level. Warning lights for parking brake, high beams, directionals and hazard flasher.

OPTIONS AND PRICES: Front axle with locking hubs: $73.00. Front axle warning light: $8.25. Rear axle Trac-Lok: $142.00. Heavy-duty front shock absorbers: $8.25. Heavy-duty rear shock absorbers: $8.25. Heavy-duty front springs: $9.00. Heavy-duty rear springs: $14.50. Rear stabilizer bar: $25.50. Level-Ride air shocks: $99.00. Power brakes: $45.50. Power steering: $134.00. 304 cu. in. V-8: $77.00. 345 cu. in. V-8: $113.00. 392 cu. in. V-8: $227.00. Dual exhaust for V-8 engines $38.00. Two-speed transfer case: $50.00. T-407 automatic transmission: $239.00. T-427 4-speed manual transmission: $130.00. T-36 5-speed manual transmission: $312. 11 in. clutch: $15.00. 3800 lb. rear axle: $41.00. 15 gal. auxiliary fuel tank: $106.00. AM solid state radio and antenna: $65.00. AM/FM radio. Air conditioning: $385.00. Tinted glass; $17.00. Bucket seats with console: $129.00. Extra-capacity heater/defroster. Vinyl roof cover. Sliding rear window. 5600 lb. GVW Package. 1100 and 1210 Travelall: Front axle with locking hubs: $80.00. Front axle warning light: $8.25. Rear axle Trac-Lok: $109.00. Tie rod shield: $20.00. Heavy-duty front shock absorbers: $8.25. Heavy-duty rear shock absorbers: $8.25. Heavy-duty rear springs: $14.50. Rear stabilizer bar: $25.50. Power brakes: $45.50. Power steering: $134.00. 345 cu. in. V-8: $60.00. 392 cu. in. V-8: $227.00. Dual exhaust for V-8 engines $38.00. Two-speed transfer case: $50.00. T-407 automatic transmission: $239.00. T-427/T-428 4-speed manual transmission: $91.00. Auxiliary oil cooler for automatic transmission: $43.50. 11 in. clutch: $15.00. 16 gal. auxiliary fuel tank: $106.00. AM solid state radio and antenna: $65.00. Rear speaker: $19.00. Air conditioning: $405.00. Electric tailgate: $37.00. Undercoating: $37.50. Deluxe Exterior Trim Package: $91.00. Door trim guards: $10.25. Underslung spare tire carrier: $6.00.

HISTORICAL FOOTNOTES: The 1974 models were launched in the fall of 1973.

1974 PICKUP & TRAVELALL

International changed its model identification for both the Travelall and pickup models for 1974 from 1210 and 1320 to the 100 and 200 series. A new 401 cu. in V-8 (also identified as a 400 cu. in. in some literature) was introduced. The Travelette was not available with All-Wheel Drive (International used this term for its four-wheel drive vehicles in both 1973 and 1974). Pickups with the 8 foot bonus load box were available with three slide-in camper units of 8, 9-1/2 or 10-1/2 foot length in standard and deluxe form. Both trim levels were available in a special International alpine white finish and were constructed of a fiberglass-reinforced plexiglas. International also offered two caps for its pickups as well as over 250 individual options intended for the camping enthusiast. All models had a new chassis with a 4 inch wider wheel track. Power front disc brakes were also standard for 1974. A heavier frame was used on all models. Also new for 1974 were keyless button-lock doors and a fully-synchronized 3-speed standard manual transmission.

The 1974 pickups and Travelalls had a new rectangular grille with five horizontal bars and more prominent side markers. The rectangular front fender IH badges were positioned closer to the side-markers. The Travelall received new designations for 1974. The old 1010 and 1210 models were superseded by the 100 and 200 Travelalls. Their respective tonnage ratings were 1/2 and 3/4 ton. Unlike previous years when the four-wheel drive Travelall was available with a variety of six-cylinder and V-8 engines, the standard engine offered was the 392 cu. in. V-8 with the 400 cu. in. V-8 optional. The "Silent Drive" one-speed transfer case with its patented International Harvester shift linkage was standard with the 2-speed New Process 250, single lever transfer case continued to be optional. Three trim levels, standard, deluxe and custom were offered. The base level included a padded dash with full instrumentation, an all-vinyl full width bench front seat, a stationary rear seat and a lockable energy-absorbing steering column. The standard exterior mirror on all models had a new and larger 2-piece (instead of 3-piece) rectangular-shaped head that was redesigned for improved visibility. The Travelall's wheelbase was increased 1 in. to 120 in.. The engine was also repositioned further back in the chassis to allow for improved cooling and a reduction in fan noise. The exterior color selection for 1974 consisted of these colors: Ivy metallic, Bimini blue metallic, sunburst yellow, Grenoble green, flame red, alpine white, flame red, glacier blue, burnished gold metallic, Mayan mist, red, Omaha orange and schoolbus yellow. Special colors were available at extra cost.

1974 International Series 100 All-Wheel Drive pickup

I.D. DATA: The vehicle identification number, consisting of 13 digits, was positioned on the left front door pillar post. The first six digits were the vehicle's serial number. The seventh identified the assembly plant and the remaining digits were the vehicle's sequential production number. The engine model identification, located on a machined boss on the block, was a prefix to the V.I.N. number.

Body Type	Factory Price	GVW	Shipping Weight	Prod. Total
Series 100, 115 in.-132 in. wheelbase				
Chassis & Cab, 115 in. wheelbase	$3877	5200*	3571	—
Chassis & Cab, 132 in. wheelbase	$3903	5200	3794	—
Pickup 6.5 ft.	$4031	5200	4143	—
Pickup 6.5 ft. B.L.	$4031	5200	4196	—
Pickup 8 ft.	$4067	5200	4214	—
Pickup 8 ft. B.L.	$4067	5200	4274	—
Series 200, 132 in.				
Chassis & Cab, 132 in. wheelbase	$4016	6800*	N.A.	—
Pickup 8 ft.	$4278	6800	N.A.	—
Pickup 8 ft. B.L.	$4278	6800	N.A.	—
Series 100 Travelall				
Station Wagon	$5320	6500*	4795	—
Series 200 Travelall				
Station Wagon	$5498	6800	4899	—

* 6000 lb. GVW optional for series 100; 7,000, 7700, 8200 and 9,000 lb. GVW optional for series 200. Total 1974 model year production of International pickup trucks was 36, 584.

STANDARD ENGINE: Series 200. Engine Type: OHV, In-line 6-cylinder. Bore x Stroke: 3.75 in. x 3.9 in. Lifters: Hydraulic. Number of main bearings-7. Displacement: 258 cu. in. Carburetion: Model 1904D Holley single barrel. Compression Ratio: 8.0:1. Horsepower: Net 113 @ 4000 rpm. Torque: 191 lb.-ft. @ 2000 rpm. Fuel Requirements: 91 octane.

STANDARD ENGINE: Series 100. Optional for Series 200. Engine Type: OHV V-8 ("V-304"). Bore x Stroke: 3.875 in. x 3.21875 in. Displacement: 304 cu. in. Carburetion: Single barrel, downdraft. Compression ratio: 8.19:1. Lifters: Solid. Horsepower: net 137 @ 4000 rpm. Torque: 233 lb.-ft. @ 2400 rpm. Fuel Requirements: 91 octane.

OPTIONAL ENGINE: All models: Engine Type: OHV V-8 ("V-345"). Bore x Stroke: 3.875 in. x 3.656 in. Displacement: 344.96 cu. in. Carburetion: Holley model 2300G 2-barrel. Compression Ratio: 8.05:1. Lifters: Solid. Horsepower: Net: 144 hp. @ 3600 rpm; 156 with dual exhausts. Torque: 263 lb.-ft. @ 2000 rpm, 269 lb.-ft. with dual exhausts. Fuel Requirements: 91 octane.

STANDARD ENGINE: Travelall Series 100 and 200. Optional for all other models. Engine Type: OHV V-8 ("V-392"). Bore x Stroke: 4.125 in. x 3.656 in. Displacement: 390.89 cu. in. Carburetion: 4-barrel, downdraft. Compression Ratio: 8.02:1. Lifters: Solid. Horsepower: Net: 179 @ 3600 rpm; 193 with dual exhaust. Torque: 297 lb.-ft. @ 2800 rpm. 305 lb.-ft. with dual exhaust. Fuel Requirements: 91 octane.

OPTIONAL ENGINE: All series, not available in California. Engine Type: OHV V-8. Bore x Stroke: 4.165 in. x 3.68 in. Displacement: 400 cu. in. Carburetion Single 4-barrel. Compression Ratio: 8.35:1. Horsepower: 210 @ 4400 rpm, with dual exhaust. Torque: 320 lb.-ft. @ 2800 rpm. Fuel Requirements: 91 octane.

CHASSIS FEATURES: Separate body and frame. Pressed steel channel main rails.

SUSPENSION AND RUNNING GEAR: Front Suspension: Series 100: Semi-elliptical leaf springs, 2.5 in. x 42 in. Capacity: 3400 lb. Series 200: Semi-elliptical leaf springs, Capacity: 3500 lb. Shock absorbers. Rear Suspension: Series 100: and 200: Semi-elliptical leaf springs. Shock absorbers. Front Axle Type and Capacity: Series 100: Hypoid, 3400 lb. Rear Axle Type and Capacity: Series 100: Hypoid, semi-floating. 3600 lb. Final Drive Ratio: Series 100: 3.54:1. Series 200: 3.73:1. Optional: Series 100: 3.73, 4.09:1. Series 200: 4.10:1. Transfer Case: 1-speed chain drive. Optional: NP-250 2-speed, ratios: 1.93, 1.00:1. Brakes: Type: Self-adjusting, hydraulic, dual operation power assisted. Front disc, and rear. Dimensions: 100: Front: 11.75 in. dia. disc. Rear: 11.0 in. x 2.25 in. Total swept area: 328.7 sq. in. Series 200: Front: Disc. in. Rear: 12.0 in. x 2.5 in. Total lining area: 373.7 sq. in. Wheels: Series 100: 15 x 6.00K, 5.5 in. bolt circles. Series 200: 16.5 x 6.00JK, 8-stud disc wheels. Tires: Series 100: L78 x 15B. Optional: H78 x 15C, H78 x 15D, 7.00 x 15C series 200: 8.00 x 16.5 LRC. Steering: Type: Recirculating ball. Ratio: 24:1, turns-3.5 Lock-to-Lock. Turning circle: 40.6 ft. Optional: Power steering, 17.5:1 ratio. Transmission: Type: 3-speed all-synchromesh manual with column shift. Transmission Ratios: 3.06, 1.50, 1.0:01. Optional: T-427 4-speed, all-synchromesh manual transmission, ratios: 6.32, 3.09, 1.68, 1.00:1; 3-spd automatic, ratios: 2.45, 1.45, 1.00:1. Optional: T-427 heavy-duty all-synchromesh, 4-speed manual. Transmission ratios: 6.32, 3.09, 1.68, 1.00:1. Optional: T-36 5-speed manual (not available with 258 cu. in. 6-cylinder engine. (First gear not synchromesh). Transmission ratios: 6.21, 3.43, 2.05, 1.11, 1.00:1. Optional: 3-speed automatic with oil cooler. Transmission ratios: 2.40, 1.47,1.00:1. T-34 5-speed overdrive manual transmission. Clutch: 10.5 in. disc, single dry plate. Optional: 11.0 in. heavy-duty diaphragm type or 11 in. angle link.

VEHICLE DIMENSIONS: Wheelbase: Series 100: 115 in./132 in. Overall Length: Series 100: 183.7 in./202.8 in. Front/Rear Tread: 65.1 in./65.5 in. Overall Height: Series 100: 68.9 in. Series 200: 73.8 in. Width: 77.6 in. Front/Rear Overhang: 29 in./44 in. Tailgate: Width and Height: in. 66.5 in. x 19.2 in. Approach/Departure Degrees: 24/22 degrees. Ground Clearance: Series 200: Front differential: 8.0 in. rear differential: 7.3 in. Series 100: Front axle: 7.8 in. Rear

axle: 6.6 in. Oil pan: 15.5 in. Transfer case: 11.0 in. Fuel tank: 14.5 in. Load space: (8 ft. box) 97.2 in. x 49.5 in. x 19.2 in. Headroom: 36.0 in. Maximum steering wheel to seat back: 24.0 in. Seat to ground: 33.5 in. Floor to ground: 19.5 in. Pedal to seat back: 44.5 in.

CAPACITIES: Fuel tank: Series100: 20 gal. Series 200: 16 gal. Travelall: 20 gal. Optional for all Series: 16 gal. auxiliary fuel tank. Engine coolant: 12 qt.

ACCOMMODATIONS: Seating Capacity: Pickups: 3 passengers. Travelall: 6/9 passengers.

INSTRUMENTATION: 0-120 mph speedometer, 99,999.9 odometer, gauges for oil pressure, temperature, ammeter, fuel level. Warning lights for parking brake, high beams, directionals and hazard flasher.

OPTIONS AND PRICES: 304 cu. in. V-8: $98.00. 345 cu. in. V-8: $135.00. 392 cu. in. V-8: $255.00. 400 cu. in. V-8: $309. Power steering: $152.00. Locking front hubs: $81.00. Front axle warning light: $8.75. 2-speed transfer case: $54.00. Spicer rear axle with Track-Lok: $150.00. 7700 lb. GVW package (series 200): $67.00. Extra transmission oil cooler: $53.00. Rear step bumper with trailer hitch: $71.00. Tilt steering wheel: $59.00. AM radio: $72.00. Custom Interior Trim Package: $186.00. Exterior Custom Trim Package: $278.00. Camper Package with air conditioner: $740.00. Door guards: $6.25. Air conditioning: $500. "California" exterior mirrors. Oversize tires. Tinted glass. Two-tone paint. AM radio: $70.00. Deluxe Exterior Trim Package: $120.00. Custom Exterior Trim Package: $275.00. Camper Special Package for series 200: $275.00. T-427 4-speed man. trans.: $130.00. 3-speed automatic trans.: $250.00. Free-running front hubs: $81.00. Limited slip rear differential: $116.00. 2-speed transfer case: $54.00. Power steering: $134.00. Heavy-duty front and rear shock absorbers: $17.00. Rear stabilizer bar: $28.00. High-back front bucket seats with folding armrests: $191.00. Folding intermediate rear bench seat (Travelall): $36.00. 2/3 stationary rear seat with snap-out full-width third bench seat (Travelall): $124.00. Tinted windshield glass: $17.00. Air conditioning: $405.00. Auxiliary fuel tank: $69.00. Trailer Tow Package (includes electric trailer brake control, trailer wiring, Class IV equalizing trailer hitch receiver. Heavy-duty 70 amp-hr. battery and 61 amp alternator, front stabilizer bar, power steering and added capacity cooling system): $464.00

HISTORICAL FOOTNOTES: The 1974 models were introduced in the fall of 1973.

1975 PICKUP & TRAVELALL

This was the final year for International's line of full-size four-wheel drive pickup and Travelall models. For 1975 a new series 150 designation replaced the previously used 150 series. The 200 series continued. A total of 17 (eight of which were new) exterior colors were available. Interior color choices included sage, blue, red or black. A new Optional Lighting Package was introduced for 1975 that included underhood, map, rear cargo area and glove box lights. Both the ashtrays and control knobs were also lighted. Along with the Scout and Travelall models the four-wheel drive pickup engines had a new electronic ignition system consisting of a distributor with no points, a coil and a special control module. Replacing the 258 cu. in. 6-cylinder as the four-wheel drive pickup's base engine was the "V304 A Comanche" 304 cu. in. V-8. Both the 345 and 392 cu. in. V-8 engines were optional. All the four-wheel drive pickups and Travelette models had the flush-fender "bonus load" box design.

1975 International Travelall 150 4x4

I.D. DATA: Unchanged from 1974.

Body Type	Factory Price	GVW	Shipping Weight	Prod. Total
Series 150, 115 in.-132 in. wheelbase				
Chassis & Cab (115 in. wb.)	$4575	6200	3872	—
Chassis & Cab (132 in. wb.)	$4601	6200	3938	—
Pickup 6.5 ft. B.L.	$4729	6200	4283	—
Pickup 8 ft. B.L.	$4765	6200	4394	—
Series 200, 132 in. wheelbase				
Chassis & Cab	$5009	6900	4136	—
Pickup 8 ft. B.L.	$5173	6900	4592	—
Series 150, Travelall, 120 in. wheelbase				
Station Wagon	$5836	6200	4803	—
Series 200,Travelall, 120 in. wheelbase				
Station Wagon	$6024	6900	5051	—

Total pickup (both two-wheel drive and four-wheel drive) production for 1975 was 6329 units.

STANDARD ENGINE: Engine Type: OHV V-8 ("V-304"). Bore x Stroke: 3.875 in. x 3.21875 in. Displacement: 304 cu. in. Carburetion: Single barrel, downdraft. Compression ratio: 8.19:1. Lifters: Solid. Horsepower: net 141 @ 4000 rpm. Torque: 243 lb. @ 2400 rpm. Fuel Requirements: Leaded or Unleaded.

OPTIONAL ENGINE: All models: Engine Type: OHV V-8 ("V-345"). Bore x Stroke: 3.875 in. x 3.656 in. Displacement: 344.96 cu. in. Carburetion: Holley model 2210G 2-barrel. Compression Ratio: 8.05:1. Lifters: Solid. Horsepower: 158 @ 3600 rpm. Torque: Torque: 288 lb.-ft. @ 2000 rpm. Fuel Requirements: Leaded or Unleaded.

STANDARD ENGINE: Travelall Series 150 and 200. Optional for all other models. Engine Type: OHV V-8 ("V-392"). Bore x Stroke: 4.125 in. x 3.656 in. Displacement: 390.89 cu. in. Carburetion: Model 4510 Holley four-barrel. Compression Ratio: 8.02:1. Lifters: Solid. Horsepower: 187 @ 3600 rpm. Torque: 307 lb.-ft. @ 2400 rpm. Fuel Requirements: Leaded or Unleaded.

OPTIONAL ENGINE: All series, not available in California. Engine Type: OHV V-8. Bore x Stroke: 4.165 in. x 3.68 in. Displacement: 400 cu. in. Carburetion Single 4-barrel. Compression Ratio: 8.35:1. Horsepower: 210 @ 4400 rpm, with dual exhaust. Torque: 320 lb.-ft. @ 2800 rpm. Fuel Requirements: Leaded or Unleaded.

CHASSIS FEATURES: Separate body and frame. Pressed steel channel main rails.

SUSPENSION AND RUNNING GEAR: Front Suspension: Series 150: Semi-elliptical leaf springs, 2.5 in. x 42 in. Capacity: 3400 lb. Series 200: Semi-elliptical leaf springs, Capacity: 3500 lb. Shock absorbers. Rear Suspension: Series 150: and 200: Semi-elliptical leaf springs. Shock absorbers. Front Axle Type and Capacity: Series 150: Hypoid, 3400 lb. Rear Axle Type and Capacity: Series 150: Hypoid, semi-floating. 3600 lb. Final Drive Ratio: Series 150: 3.54:1. Series 200: 3.73:1. Optional: Series 150: 3.73, 4.09:1. Series 200: 4.10:1. Transfer Case: 1-speed chain drive. Optional: NP-250 2-speed, ratios; Ratios: 1.93, 1.00:1. Brakes: Type: Self-adjusting, hydraulic, dual operation power assisted. Front disc, and rear. Dimensions: 150: Front: 11.75 in. dia. disc. Rear: 11.0 in. x 2.25 in. Total swept area: 328.7 sq. in. Series 200: Front: Disc. in. Rear: 12.0 in. x 2.5 in. Total lining area: 373.7 sq. in. Wheels: Series100: 15 x 6.00K, 5.5 in. bolt circles. Series 200: 16.5 x 6.00JK, 8-stud disc wheels. Tires: Series 150: L78 x 15B. Optional: H78 x 15C, H78 x 15D, 7.00 x 15C series 200: 8.00 x 16.5 LRC. Steering: Type: Recirculating ball. Ratio: 24:1, turns-3.5 Lock-to-Lock. Turning circle: 40.6 ft. Optional: Power steering, 17.5:1 ratio. Transmission: Type: 3-speed all-synchromesh manual with column shift. Transmission Ratios: 3.06, 1.50, 1.0:01. Optional: T-427 4-speed, all-synchromesh manual transmission, ratios: 6.32, 3.09, 1.68, 1.00:1; 3-speed automatic, ratios: 2.45, 1.45, 1.00:1. Optional: T-427 heavy-duty all-synchromesh, 4-speed manual. Transmission ratios: 6.32, 3.09, 1.68, 1.00:1. Optional: T-36 5-speed manual (not available with 258 cu. in. 6-cylinder engine. (first gear not synchromesh). Transmission ratios: 6.21, 3.43, 2.05, 1.11, 1.00:1. Optional: 3-speed automatic with oil cooler. Transmission ratios: 2.40, 1.47,1.00:1. T-34 5-speed overdrive manual transmission. Clutch: 10.5 in. disc, single dry plate. Optional: 11.0 in. heavy-duty diaphragm type or 11 in. angle link.

VEHICLE DIMENSIONS: Wheelbase: Series 150: 115 in./132 in. Overall Length: Series 150: 183.7 in./202.8 in. Front/Rear Tread: 65.1 in./65.5 in. Overall Height: Series 150: 68.9 in. Series 200: 73.8 in. Width: 77.6 in. Front/Rear Overhang: 29 in./44 in. Tailgate: Width and Height: in. 66.5 in. x 19.2 in. Approach/Departure Degrees: 24/22 degrees. Ground Clearance: Series 200: Front differential: 8.0 in. Rear differential: 7.3 in. Series 150: Front axle: 7.8 in. Rear axle: 6.6 in. Oil pan: 15.5 in. Transfer case: 11.0 in. Fuel tank: 14.5 in. Load space: (8 ft. box) 97.2 in. x 49.5 in. x 19.2 in. Headroom: 36.0 in. Maximum steering wheel to seat back: 24.0 in. Seat to ground: 33.5 in. Floor to ground: 19.5 in. Pedal to seat back: 44.5 in.

CAPACITIES: Fuel tank: Series100: 20 gal. Series 200: 16 gal. Travelall: 20 gal. Optional for all Series: 16 gal. auxiliary fuel tank. Engine coolant: 12 qt.

ACCOMMODATIONS: Seating Capacity: Pickups: 3 passengers. Travelall: 6/9 passengers.

INSTRUMENTATION: 0-120 mph speedometer, 99,999.9 odometer, gauges for oil pressure, temperature, ammeter, fuel level. Warning lights for parking brake, high beams, directionals and hazard flasher.

OPTIONS AND PRICES: Chrome front bumper. Rear bumper. Chrome rear bumper. Rear step bumper. Air conditioning: $540.00. Automatic transmission: $287.00. Power steering: $154.00. Power brakes. Bumper guards. AM radio: $70.00. Radio antenna. AM/FM radio. Seat covers. Heater. Clock. Cigarette lighter. Trailer Towing Package: $451.00. Deluxe Exterior Trim Package: $144.00. Custom Exterior Trim Package: $299.00. Camper Special Package (series 200): $302.00. Tinted glass. 345 cu. in. V-8: $40,00. 392 cu. in. V-8: $167.00. Wheel trim rings. Clearance lights (series 200). Dual OSRV exterior mirrors. "California" exterior mirrors. Spare tire and carrier.

HISTORICAL FOOTNOTES: Production of the full-size International trucks was ended after the 1975 model year.

INTERNATIONAL SCOUT
1961-1980

1961 SCOUT

The Scout was International Harvester's entry into the four-wheel drive sports utility market. The inevitable comparison with the CJ Jeep was a common denominator in most early evaluations of the Scout. Critics were quick to learn that the Scout was not a simple clone of the Jeep. Offered in a two-wheel drive version as well as four-wheel drive, the Scout reflected both International Harvester's deservedly excellent reputation as a quality truck manufacturer as well the years spent by I-H engineers in developing the Scout. The Scout was not a substitute for a passenger car but with a 100 in. wheelbase its ride quality was tolerable and it proved capable of 65 mph highway travel without an inordinate amount of strain upon either machine or driver. Styling was typically International Harvester; simple and straightforward. Moreover, both the Scout's standard top as well as the various optional steel tops could be easily converted back and forth respectively from pickup body style to a panel truck/station wagon. Regardless of top installed they had a well-deserved reputation for leaks. It was also possible to transform the Scout into an ultra-open air model without top, windshield or doors. In true utility vehicle fashion the windshield also folded down. The exterior body color selection consisted red and metallic green with the steel top painted white or yellow, metallic blue, tan or white bodies with the steel top painted in the same color as the body.

The Scout's 152 cubic inch, 4-cylinder engine was derived from International Harvester's existing V-8 engine. As essentially half of an outstanding V-304 truck engine it proved a durable and reliable performer.

1961 Scout

I.D. DATA: The serial number was located on a dash-mounted plate as well as on the left front frame side rail. A number "1" suffix indicating 1961 followed the serial number. The engine number was found on the right side of the crankcase at the upper front.

Body Type	Factory Price	GVW	Shipping Weight	Prod. Total
Scout 80, 1/4 ton 100 in. wheelbase				
Utility Pickup	$2149	3000	3000	*

* Total production of all Scouts, including the two-wheel drive version exceeded 28,000.

STANDARD ENGINE: Engine Type: OHV I-4. Bore x Stroke: 3.88 in. x 3.219 in. Lifters: Mechanical. Number of main bearings-5. Displacement: 152 cu. in. (2.49 liters). Carburetion: Single down-draft carburetor. Compression Ratio: 8.19:1. Horsepower: 93.4 @ 4000 rpm. Torque: 135 lb.-ft. @ 2400 rpm. Fuel Requirements: Regular.

SUSPENSION AND RUNNING GEAR: Front Suspension: Semi-elliptical leaf springs, 1.75 in. x 40 in. Capacity: 1820 lb. direct-action shock absorbers. Rear Suspension: Semi-elliptical leaf springs, 1.75 in. x 46 in. Capacity: 2080 lb. direct-action shock absorbers. Front Axle Type and Capacity: Hypoid, 2000 lbs. Rear Axle Type and Capacity: Semi-floating 2300 lb. capacity. Final Drive Ratio: 4.27:1. Transfer Case: Two-speed: 2.46, 1.00:1. Brakes: Type: Hydraulic drums both front and rear. Lining area: 139 sq. in. Wheels: Steel disc. Tires: 6.50 x 15. Steering: Cam and lever, 17 in. dia. steering wheel. Turns Lock-to-Lock: 4.6. Turning circle: 38.0 ft. Transmission: Type: 3-speed manual, synchromesh on top two gears. Transmission Ratios: 3.33:1, 1.85:1, 1.00:1. Clutch: Girling Hydraulic, 10 dia., 6-spring, single plate.

VEHICLE DIMENSIONS: Wheelbase: 100 in. Overall Length: 154 in. Front/Rear Tread: 55.1 in./55.1 in. Overall Height: 67.0 in. Width: 68.6 in. Front/Rear Overhang: 24 in./30 in. Tailgate: Width and Height: 20.5 in. x 38 in. Approach/Departure Degrees: 47/35. Ground Clearance: Front axle: 9.25 in. Rear axle: 9.125 in. Load space: 60 in. x 41 in. x 20.5 in.

CAPACITIES: Fuel Tank: 9 gal. Coolant system: 10.5 qt.

ACCOMMODATIONS: Seating Capacity: 2 passenger with standard bench front seat; 2 passenger with optional front bucket seats; 4 passenger with optional rear bench seat; 6 passenger with optional side wheelhouse cushions. Front hip room: 59.0 in. Pedal to seat back: 39.0 in. Floor to ground: 15.0 in.

INSTRUMENTATION: Speedometer, odometer, gauges for ammeter, oil pressure, fuel level and engine coolant temperature.

OPTIONS: Front locking hubs. Traveltop. Sporttop. Paneltop. Sliding rear windows. Convertible Sporttop. Right hand drive. Front and rear power take off. Winch. Snowplow. 3-point hitch. Trailer hitch. Pusher bumper. Front bucket seats. 2 passenger rear seat. Rear wheelhousing seat cushions. Front tailgate spare tire carrier. Rear tailgate spare tire carrier. Radio. Dual 10 gal. fuel tanks.

HISTORICAL FOOTNOTES: The introduction of the Scout illustrated the growing popularity of four-wheel drive vehicles in the United States.

1962 SCOUT

The 1962 Scout was virtually unchanged from its 1961 form.

I.D. DATA: Same location and format as 1961 except the suffix following the serial number was now a "2" signifying 1962.

Body Type	Factory Price	GVW	Shipping Weight	Prod. Total
Scout 80, 1-4 ton 100 in. wheelbase				
Pickup 5 ft.	$2132	3900	3000	—

STANDARD ENGINE: Engine Type: OHV I-4. Bore x Stroke: 3.88 in. x 3.219 in. Lifters: Mechanical. Number of main bearings-5. Displacement: 152 cu. in. (2.49 liters). Carburetion: Single down-draft carburetor. Compression Ratio: 8.19:1. Horsepower: 93.4 @ 4000 rpm. Torque: 135 lb.-ft. @ 2400 rpm. Fuel Requirements: Regular.

SUSPENSION AND RUNNING GEAR: Front Suspension: Semi-elliptical leaf springs, 1.75 in. x 40 in. Capacity: 1820 lb. direct-action shock absorbers. Rear Suspension: Semi-elliptical leaf springs, 1.75 in. x 46 in. Capacity: 2080 lb. direct-action shock absorbers. Front Axle Type and Capacity: Hypoid, 2000 lbs. Rear Axle Type and Capacity: Semi-floating 2300 lb. capacity. Final Drive Ratio: 4.27:1. Transfer Case: Two-speed: 2.46, 1.00:1. Brakes: Type: Hydraulic drums both front and rear. Lining area: 139 sq. in. Wheels: Steel disc. Tires: 6.50 x 15. Steering: Cam and lever, 17 in. dia. steering wheel. Turns Lock-to-Lock: 4.6. Turning circle: 38.0 ft. Transmission: Type: 3-speed manual, synchromesh on top two gears. Transmission Ratios: 3.33:1, 1.85:1, 1.00:1. Clutch: Girling Hydraulic, 10 dia., 6-spring, single plate.

VEHICLE DIMENSIONS: Wheelbase: 100 in. Overall Length: 154 in. Front/Rear Tread: 55.1 in./55.1 in. Overall Height: 67.0 in. Width: 68.6 in. Front/Rear Overhang: 24 in./30 in. Tailgate: Width and Height: 20.5 in. x 38 in. Approach/Departure Degrees: 47/35. Ground Clearance: Front axle: 9.25 in. Rear axle: 9.125 in. Load space: 60 in. x 41 in. x 20.5 in.

CAPACITIES: Fuel Tank: 9 gal. Coolant system: 10.5 qt.

ACCOMMODATIONS: Seating Capacity: 2 passenger with standard bench front seat; 2 passenger with optional front bucket seats; 4 passenger with optional rear bench seat; 6 passenger with optional side wheelhouse cushions. Front hip room: 59.0 in. Pedal to seat back: 39.0 in. Floor to ground: 15.0 in.

INSTRUMENTATION: Speedometer, odometer, gauges for ammeter, oil pressure, fuel level and engine coolant temperature.

OPTIONS: Front locking hubs. Traveltop. Sporttop. Paneltop. Sliding rear windows. Convertible Sporttop. Right hand drive. Front and rear power take off. Winch. Snowplow. 3-point hitch. Trailer hitch. Pusher bumper. Front bucket seats. 2 passenger rear seat. Rear wheelhousing seat cushions. Front tailgate spare tire carrier. Rear tailgate spare tire carrier. Radio. Dual 10 gal. fuel tanks.

HISTORICAL FOOTNOTES: The latest Scout debuted on Nov. 1, 1961.

1963 SCOUT

The 1963 Scout was offered with optional roll-down front windows as an alternative to the standard two-section, horizontal sliding units.

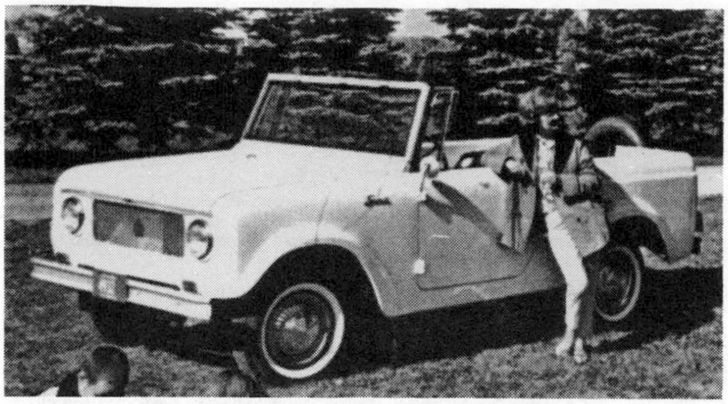

1963 Scout

I.D. DATA: Same location and format as 1962 except the suffix following the serial number was now a "3" signifying 1963.

Body Type	Factory Price	GVW	Shipping Weight	Prod. Total
Scout 80, 1-4 ton 100 in. wheelbase				
Pickup 5 ft.	$2188	3900	3000	—

STANDARD ENGINE: Engine Type: OHV I-4. Bore x Stroke: 3.88 in. x 3.219 in. Lifters: Mechanical. Number of main bearings-5. Displacement: 152 cu. in. (2.49 liters). Carburetion: Single down-draft carburetor. Compression Ratio: 8.19:1. Horsepower: 93.4 @ 4000 rpm. Torque: 135 lb.-ft. @ 2400 rpm. Fuel Requirements: Regular.

SUSPENSION AND RUNNING GEAR: Front Suspension: Semi-elliptical leaf springs, 1.75 in. x 40 in. Capacity: 1820 lb. direct-action shock absorbers. Rear Suspension: Semi-elliptical leaf springs, 1.75 in. x 46 in. Capacity: 2080 lb. direct-action shock absorbers. Front Axle Type and Capacity: Hypoid, 2000 lbs. Rear Axle Type and Capacity: Semi-floating 2300 lb. capacity. Final Drive Ratio: 4.27:1. Transfer Case: Two-speed: 2.46, 1.00:1. Brakes: Type: Hydraulic drums both front and rear. Lining area: 139 sq. in. Wheels: Steel disc. Tires: 6.50 x 15. Steering: Cam and lever, 17 in. dia. steering wheel. Turns Lock-to-Lock: 4.6. Turning circle: 38.0 ft. Transmission: Type: 3-speed manual, synchromesh on top two gears. Transmission Ratios: 3.33:1, 1.85:1, 1.00:1. Clutch: Girling Hydraulic, 10 dia., 6-spring, single plate.

VEHICLE DIMENSIONS: Wheelbase: 100 in. Overall Length: 154 in. Front/Rear Tread: 55.1 in./55.1 in. Overall Height: 67.0 in. Width: 68.6 in. Front/Rear Overhang: 24 in./30 in. Tailgate: Width and Height: 20.5 in. x 38 in. Approach/Departure Degrees: 47/35. Ground Clearance: Front axle: 9.25 in. Rear axle: 9.125 in. Load space: 60 in. x 41 in. x 20.5 in.

CAPACITIES: Fuel Tank: 9 gal. Coolant system: 10.5 qt.

ACCOMMODATIONS: Seating Capacity: 2 passenger with standard bench front seat; 2 passenger with optional front bucket seats; 4 passenger with optional rear bench seat; 6 passenger with optional side wheelhouse cushions. Front hip room: 59.0 in. Pedal to seat back: 39.0 in. Floor to ground: 15.0 in.

INSTRUMENTATION: Speedometer, odometer, gauges for ammeter, oil pressure, fuel level and engine coolant temperature.

OPTIONS: Front locking hubs. Traveltop. Sporttop. Paneltop. Sliding rear windows. Convertible Sporttop. Right hand drive. Front and rear power take off. Winch. Snowplow. 3-point hitch. Trailer hitch. Pusher bumper. Front bucket seats. 2 passenger rear seat. Rear wheelhousing seat cushions. Front tailgate spare tire carrier. Rear tailgate spare tire carrier. Radio. Dual 10 gal. fuel tanks.

HISTORICAL FOOTNOTES: The 1963 Scout was introduced on Nov. 1, 1962.

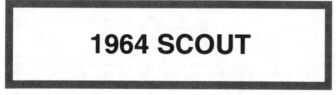

1964 SCOUT

The Scout was unchanged for 1964.

I.D. DATA: Serial number located on dash plaque, right-hand floor board inside cab, left front frame side rail and front right-side running board shield. A "4" suffix after the serial number indicated 1964 calendar year.

Body Type Total	Factory Price	GVW	Shipping Weight	Prod. Total
Scout 80, 1-4 ton 100 in. wheelbase.				
Pickup 5 ft.	$2210	3900	3000	—

STANDARD ENGINE: Engine Type: OHV I-4. Bore x Stroke: 3.88 in. x 3.219 in. Lifters: Mechanical. Number of main bearings-5. Displacement: 152 cu. in. (2.49 liters). Carburetion: Single down-draft carburetor. Compression Ratio: 8.19:1. Horsepower: 93.4 @ 4000 rpm. Torque: 135 lb.-ft. @ 2400 rpm. Fuel Requirements: Regular.

SUSPENSION AND RUNNING GEAR: Front Suspension: Semi-elliptical leaf springs, 1.75 in. x 40 in. Capacity: 1820 lb. direct-action shock absorbers. Rear Suspension: Semi-elliptical leaf springs, 1.75 in. x 46 in. Capacity: 2080 lb. direct-action shock absorbers. Front Axle Type and Capacity: Hypoid, 2000 lbs. Rear Axle Type and Capacity: Semi-floating 2300 lb. capacity. Final Drive Ratio: 4.27:1. Transfer Case: Two-speed: 2.46, 1.00:1. Brakes: Type: Hydraulic drums both front and rear. Lining area: 139 sq. in. Wheels: Steel disc. Tires: 6.50 x 15. Steering: Cam and lever, 17 in. dia. steering wheel. Turns Lock-to-Lock: 4.6. Turning circle: 38.0 ft. Transmission: Type: 3-speed manual, synchromesh on top two gears. Transmission Ratios: 3.33:1, 1.85:1, 1.00:1. Clutch: Girling Hydraulic, 10 dia., 6-spring, single plate.

VEHICLE DIMENSIONS: Wheelbase: 100 in. Overall Length: 154 in. Front/Rear Tread: 55.1 in./55.1 in. Overall Height: 67.0 in. Width: 68.6 in. Front/Rear Overhang: 24 in./30 in. Tailgate: Width and Height: 20.5 in. x 38 in. Approach/Departure Degrees: 47/35. Ground Clearance: Front axle: 9.25 in. Rear axle: 9.125 in. Load space: 60 in. x 41 in. x 20.5 in.

CAPACITIES: Fuel Tank: 9 gal. Coolant system: 10.5 qt.

ACCOMMODATIONS: Seating Capacity: 2 passenger with standard bench front seat; 2 passenger with optional front bucket seats; 4 passenger with optional rear bench seat; 6 passenger with optional side wheelhouse cushions. Front hip room: 59.0 in. Pedal to seat back: 39.0 in. Floor to ground: 15.0 in.

INSTRUMENTATION: Speedometer, odometer, gauges for ammeter, oil pressure, fuel level and engine coolant temperature.

OPTIONS AND PRICES: Front locking hubs. Traveltop. Sporttop. Paneltop: $139. Sliding rear windows. Convertible Sporttop. Right hand drive. Front and rear power take off. Winch. Snowplow. 3-point hitch. Trailer hitch. Pusher bumper. Front bucket seats. 2 passenger rear seat. Rear wheelhousing seat cushions. Front tailgate spare tire carrier. Rear tailgate spare tire carrier. Radio. Dual 10 gal. fuel tanks. R-14 Powr-Lok limited slip differential: $38.00. R-23 Powr-Lok limited slip differential: $92.00.

HISTORICAL FOOTNOTES: International's overall sales increased for the fourth year in succession.

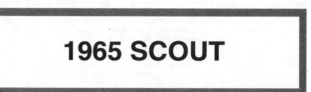

1965 SCOUT

The Scout underwent its first significant engineering and styling changes in 1965. A new 800 series identification was also adopted. The latest Scout had an revamped anodized aluminum grille with horizontal "International" lettering in its center. The hood was fitted an "I-H" emblem. The Scout's older removable windshield was replaced with a permanent unit that offered the advantages of being leak-proof and more substantial. The windshield wipers were mounted at the windshield base instead of the top cross-bar as on the previous models. The Scout now had as standard equipment a safety-styled steering wheel, roll-down windows, tension-adjustable side window vents, rotary door locks that could be activated from the vehicle's interior or exterior, push-button door handles with separate key locks and suspended pedals. The Traveltop had a "Vibradamp" acoustical headliner and sound-deadening outer door panel liners. A new "Easy-View" instrument panel was adopted. Exterior changes included revised drip moldings intended to carry the water below the windows and a new tailgate release lever that was operable by one-hand. On Scouts with their spare tire mounted on the tailgate, two-stage support straps were provided to prevent full drop from the weight of the tire. The standard models had full-width rubber-padded seats, all-vinyl champagne upholstery, ashtray and a silver grey finish front bumper. Additional standard equipment included dual stop and taillights, single electrical horn, directional signals, back-up lights, variable speed vacuum windshield wipers with booster, hand choke, outside left rearview mirror. The custom versions with the full-length Traveltop had deep contoured bucket seats. All custom Scouts had all-vinyl champagne upholstery, harmonizing vinyl-covered door panels, dual sun visors and armrests, front floor mat, cigar lighter, chrome OSRV mirror, chrome wheel discs and chrome front bumper. For the first time an optional engine was offered for the Scout. Specifically, this was a turbo-charged version of the familiar overhead valve, 152 cu. in. 4-cylinder engine known as the Turbo-III. Paint options for 1965 included champagne metallic, Aspen green, Apache gold, white, red, light yellow and moonstone blue.

I.D. DATA: Positions of both vehicle and engine serial numbers were unchanged from 1964. A "5" suffix was added to the vehicle serial number to indicate the 1965 calendar year.

Body Type Total	Factory Price	GVW	Shipping Weight	Prod. Total
Scout 800, 1/4 ton 100 in. wheelbase				
Pickup 5 ft.	$2244	3900*	3000	—

* 4700 lb. with heavy-duty rear springs.

STANDARD ENGINE: Engine Type: OHV I-4. Bore x Stroke: 3.88 in. x 3.219 in. Lifters: Mechanical. Number of main bearings-5. Displacement: 152 cu. in. (2.49 liters). Carburetion: Single down-draft carburetor. Compression Ratio: 8.19:1. Horsepower: 93.4 @ 4000 rpm. Torque: 135 lb.-ft. @ 2400 rpm. Fuel Requirements: Regular.

OPTIONAL ENGINE: Engine Type: OHV, 4-cyl., turbocharged. Bore x Stroke: 3.875 in. x 3.21875 in. Displacement: 151.84 cu. in. Number of main bearings-5. Horsepower: 111.3 @ 4000 rpm. Torque: 166.5 lb.-ft.@ 3200 rpm. Fuel Requirements: Regular.

CHASSIS FEATURES: Separate body and frame, 3 in. x 4 in. x 0.135 in. steel box-section side rails with center drop section. Section modulus: 2.75. Two box section and two channel steel cross members.

SUSPENSION AND RUNNING GEAR: Front Suspension: Semi-elliptical leaf springs, 1.75 in. x 40 in. Capacity: 1820 lb. direct-action shock absorbers. Rear Suspension: Semi-elliptical leaf springs, 1.75 in. x 46 in. Capacity: 2080 lb. direct-action shock absorbers. Front Axle Type and Capacity: Hypoid, 2000 lbs. Rear Axle Type and Capacity: Semi-floating 2300 lb. capacity. Final Drive Ratio: 4.27:1. Transfer Case: Two-speed: 2.46, 1.00:1. Brakes: Type: Hydraulic drums both front and rear. Lining area: 139 sq. in. Wheels: Steel disc. Tires: 6.50 x 15. Steering: Cam and lever, 17 in. dia. steering wheel. Turns Lock-to-Lock: 4.6. Turning circle: 38.0 ft. Transmission: Type: 3-speed manual, synchromesh on top two gears. Transmission Ratios: 3.33:1, 1.85:1, 1.00:1. Reverse: 4.53:1. Clutch: Girling Hydraulic, 10 dia., 6-spring, single plate.

VEHICLE DIMENSIONS: Wheelbase: 100 in. Overall Length: 154 in. Front/Rear Tread: 55.1 in./55.1 in. Overall Height: 67.0 in. Width: 68.6 in. Front/Rear Overhang: 24 in./30 in. Tailgate: Width and Height: 20.5 in. x 38 in. Approach/Departure Degrees: 34/34. Ground Clearance: Front axle: 9.25 in. Rear axle: 9.125 in. Load space: 60 in. x 41 in. x 20.5 in.

CAPACITIES: Fuel Tank: 9 gal. Coolant system: 10.5 qt.

ACCOMMODATIONS: Seating Capacity: 2 passenger with standard bench front seat; 2 passenger with optional front bucket seats; 4 passenger with optional rear bench seat; 6 passenger with optional side wheelhouse cushions. Front hip room: 59.0 in. Pedal to seat back: 39.0 in. Floor to ground: 15.0 in.

INSTRUMENTATION: Speedometer, odometer, gauges for ammeter, oil pressure, fuel level and engine coolant temperature.

OPTIONS AND PRICES: Steel Cabtop. Soft Cabtop. Steel Traveltop. Soft Traveltop. Heavy-duty rear axle. Oversized tires. Undercoating. Ten gallon auxiliary fuel tank. Windshield washers. Full-width upholstered rear seat. Transistorized push-button radio. Fresh air heater/ defroster. 4-speed synchromesh manual transmission. Power take-off. Paneltop in lieu of Cabtop: $140.00. R-14 Powr-Lok differential: $40.00. R-23 Powr-Lok differential: $90.00. Custom Traveltop Rear Seating Package. Included custom-width full-width seat with armrests and floor mat, cushions, rear wheel housing bench cushions, single (driver-side) or dual front armrests for standard model, chrome rear bumper (custom model only).

1966 SCOUT

International expanded the Scout's market potential by introducing two new upscale Sportop models with front bucket seats with matching rear seats, rear wheel housing trim panels, trimmed transmission console and a champagne-colored interior. Both versions of the Sportop Scout (hard or soft top) had a sporty slantback design. The last expensive Utility models had silver grey painted front bumpers and bench seats. Mid-range custom versions featured vinyl-covered door panels, dual sun visors, armrests, front floor mats, cigar lighter, chrome OSRV mirror, chrome wheel discs and a chrome front bumper. If a custom model was fitted with either a soft or all-steel Traveltop, front bucket seats were installed. The Sportop Scouts had roll-down front windows with chrome moldings, swing-out rear windows, dual variable-speed windshield wipers, front bucket seats, deluxe front and rear floor mats, chrome interior and exterior mirrors, chrome front bumper, chrome rear bumperettes, chrome wheel discs and other luxury appointments. Sportop medallions were positioned on the lower rear portion of the hardtop and soft top. During the calendar year International introduced both a larger version of the Scout's 4-cylinder engine and the V-266 V-8 as options. The new Comanche 4-196 engine was available for all 1966 Model 800 Scouts. With 196 cu. in. it was 44 cu. in. larger than the standard Comanche 4-152. Its power ratings were 110.8 horsepower and 180 lb.-ft. of torque. This engine was essentially half of the 392 cu. in. International Harvester V-8 and provided the Scout with much improved acceleration. The factory reported a Scout with the 4-196 engine accelerated from 10 to 60 mph in 26 seconds. Moving from 40 to 60 mph required 12 seconds. Exterior colors for 1966 were Apache gold, red, Bahama blue metallic, Alpine white, Malibu beige, Tahitian yellow and Aspen green.

1966 Scout 800

I.D. DATA: Serial number and engine number locations unchanged from 1965 except for "6" suffix after serial number to indicate 1966 calendar year.

Body Type	Factory Price	GVW	Shipping Wt. Weight	Prod. Total
Scout 800, 1-4 ton 100 in. wheelbase.				
Roadster Utility	$2284	3900*	2800	—
Traveltop Utility	$2458	3900	2900	—
Roadster Custom	$2407	3900	2800	—
Traveltop Custom	$2672	3900	2900	—
Soft Top Sportop	$2995	3900	2800	—
Hardtop Sportop	$2962	3900	2900	—
Pickup Utility	$2368	3900	2800	—
Pickup Custom	$2500	3900	2900	—

* All models available with optional 4700 GVW lb. rating.

STANDARD ENGINE: Engine Type: OHV I-4. Bore x Stroke: 3.88 in. x 3.219 in. Lifters: Hydraulic. Number of main bearings-5. Displacement: 151.84 cu. in. (2.49 liters). Carburetion: Single down-draft carburetor. Compression Ratio: 8.19:1. Horsepower: 93.4 @ 4000 rpm. Torque: 135 lb.-ft. @ 2400 rpm. Fuel Requirements: Regular.

OPTIONAL ENGINE: Engine Type: OHV, 4-cyl., turbocharged. Bore x Stroke: 3.875 in. x 3.21875 in. Lifters: Hydraulic. Displacement: 151.84 cu. in. (2.49 liters). Number of main bearings-5. Horsepower: 111.3 @ 4000 rpm. Torque: 166.5 lb.-ft. @ 3200 rpm. Fuel Requirements: Regular.

OPTIONAL ENGINE: Engine Type: OHV, V-8, "V-266." Bore x Stroke: 3.625 in. x 3.21875 in. Displacement: 266.76 cu. in. Number of main bearings-5. Carburetion: Holley model 2300, 2-barrel carburetor. Compression Ratio: 8.4:1. Horsepower: 154.8 @ 4400 rpm. Torque: 227.1 lb.-ft. @ 2800 rpm. Fuel Requirements: Regular.

OPTIONAL ENGINE: Engine Type: OHV, In-line 4-cylinder "4-196." Bore x Stroke: 4.125 in. x 3.65625 in. Displacement: 195.44 cu. in. (3.20 liters). Lifters: Hydraulic. Carburetion: Single Holley model 1904 downdraft single throat carburetor. Compression Ratio: 8.1:1. Number of main bearings-5. Horsepower: 110.8 @ 4000 rpm. Torque: 180.2 lb.-ft. @ 2800 rpm. Fuel Requirements: Regular.

CHASSIS FEATURES: Separate body and frame, 3 in. x 4 in. x 0.135 in. steel box-section side rails with center drop section. Section modulus: 2.75. Two box section and two channel steel cross members.

SUSPENSION AND RUNNING GEAR: Front Suspension: Semi-elliptical leaf springs, 1.75 in. x 40 in. Capacity: 1820 lb. direct-action shock absorbers. Rear Suspension: Semi-elliptical leaf springs, 1.75 in. x 46 in. Capacity: 2080 lb. direct-action shock absorbers. Front Axle Type and Capacity: Hypoid, 2000 lbs. Rear Axle Type and Capacity: Semi-floating 2300 lb. capacity. Final Drive Ratio: 4.27:1. Transfer Case: Two-speed: 2.46, 1.00:1. Brakes: Type: Hydraulic drums both front and rear. Lining area: 139 sq. in. Wheels: Steel disc. Tires: 6.50 x 15. Steering: Cam and lever, 17 in. dia. steering wheel. Turns Lock-to-Lock: 4.6. Turning circle:

38.0 ft. Transmission: Type: 3-speed manual, synchromesh on top two gears. Transmission Ratios: 3.33:1, 1.85:1, 1.00:1. Reverse: 4.53:1. Clutch: Girling Hydraulic, 10 dia., 6-spring, single plate.

VEHICLE DIMENSIONS: Wheelbase: 100 in. Overall Length: 154 in. Front/Rear Tread: 55.1 in./55.1 in. Overall Height: 67.0 in. Width: 68.6 in. Front/Rear Overhang: 24 in./30 in. Tailgate: Width and Height: 20.5 in. x 38 in. Approach/Departure Degrees: 34/34. Ground Clearance: Front axle: 9.25 in. Rear axle: 9.125 in. Load space: 60 in. x 41 in. x 20.5 in.

CAPACITIES: Fuel Tank: 9 gal. Coolant system: 10.5 qt.

ACCOMMODATIONS: Seating Capacity: 2 passenger with standard bench front seat; 2 passenger with optional front bucket seats; 4 passenger with optional rear bench seat; 6 passenger with optional side wheelhouse cushions. Front hip room: 59.0 in. Pedal to seat back: 39.0 in. Floor to ground: 15.0 in.

INSTRUMENTATION: Speedometer, odometer, gauges for ammeter, oil pressure, fuel level and engine coolant temperature.

OPTIONS AND PRICES: Turbo-charged engine: $262.00, 196 cu. in. 4-cylinder: $81.00. Steel Cabtop. Soft Cabtop. Steel Traveltop. Soft Traveltop. Heavy-duty rear axle. Oversized tires. Undercoating. Ten gallon auxiliary fuel tank. Windshield washers. Full-width upholstered rear seat. Transistorized push-button radio. Fresh air heater/defroster. 4-speed synchromesh manual transmission. Power take-off. Paneltop in lieu of Cabtop: $140.00. R-14 Powr-Lok differential: $40.00. R-23 Powr-Lok differential: $90.00. Custom Traveltop Rear Seating Package. Included custom-width full-width seat with armrests and floor mat, cushions, rear wheel housing bench cushions, single (driver-side) or dual front armrests for standard model, chrome rear bumper (custom model only).

HISTORICAL FOOTNOTES: The new Sportop models gave the Scout additional strength in the four-wheel drive market.

1966 Scout 800 Sportop

1967 SCOUT

Whereas earlier Scouts had the optional ten gallon fuel tanks connected, the 1967 model had them function independently. A floor-mounted switch-over valve was now located at the driver's left side. Depending on the position of this switch, the fuel gauge read the fuel level in either the left or right tank. The Scout continued to be offered in Utility, custom or Sportop versions. All examples had approximately fifty pounds of safety equipment added to meet new government regulations. Color choices for 1968 consisted of Apache gold, red, Bahama blue, alpine white, Malibu beige, Tahitian yellow and Aspen green. Basic standard equipment included silver grey painted front bumper, dual stop and taillights, single electric horn, directional signals, back-up lights, traffic hazard lights, full-width seat with foam rubber padded cushion, two-tone grey vinyl upholstery, seat belts, variable speed vacuum windshield wipers with boosters, electric windshield washer, ashtray, hand choke, outside left side rearview mirror, inside rearview mirror, dual padded sun visors and padded instrument panel.

I.D. DATA: The vehicle number, consisting of 13 digits, was located on the left door pillar. The first six digits of the serial number served as the vehicle's serial number. The seventh identified the manufacturing plant. The remaining digits were the sequential production number. The engine number utilized the vehicle number to which was added a prefix. These would be 4-155, 4-196, or V-266.

Body Type	Factory Price	GVW	Shipping Weight	Prod. Total
Scout 800, 1-4 ton 100 in. wheelbase.				
Utility Roadster	$2407	3900*	2850	—
Utility Traveltop	$2580	3900	2950	—
Custom Roadster	$2529	3900	2850	—
Custom Traveltop	$2795	3900	2950	—
Soft Top Sportop	$3129	3900	2850	—
Hardtop Sportop	$3095	8900	2950	—
Utility Pickup	$2494	3900	2850	—
Custom Pickup	$2626	3900	2950	—

STANDARD ENGINE: Engine Type: OHV I-4. Bore x Stroke: 3.88 in. x 3.219 in. Lifters: Hydraulic. Number of main bearings-5. Displacement: 151.84 cu. in. (2.49 liters). Carburetion: Single down-draft Holley 1904 carburetor. Compression Ratio: 8.19:1. Horsepower: 93.4 @ 4000 rpm. Torque: 143 lb.-ft. of torque @ 2400 rpm. Fuel Requirements: Regular.

OPTIONAL ENGINE: Engine Type: OHV, 4-cyl., turbocharged. Bore x Stroke: 3.875 in. x 3.21875 in. Lifters: Hydraulic. Displacement: 151.84 cu. in. (2.49 liters). Number of main bearings-5. Horsepower: 111.3 @ 4000 rpm. Torque: 166.5 lb.-ft. @ 3200 rpm. Fuel Requirements: Regular.

OPTIONAL ENGINE: Engine Type: OHV, V-8, "V-266." Bore x Stroke: 3.625 in. x 3.21875 in. Displacement: 266.76 cu. in. Number of main bearings-5. Lifters: Hydraulic. Carburetion: Holley model 2300, 2-barrel carburetor. Compression Ratio: 8.4:1. Horsepower: 154.8 @ 4400 rpm. Torque: 227.1 lb.-ft. @ 2800 rpm. Fuel Requirements: Regular.

OPTIONAL ENGINE: Engine Type: OHV, In-line 4-cylinder "4-196." Bore x Stroke: 4.125 in. x 3.65625 in. Displacement: 195.44 cu. in. (3.20 liters). Lifters: Hydraulic. Carburetion: Single Holley model 1904 downdraft single throat carburetor. Compression Ratio: 8.1:1. Number of main bearings-5. Horsepower: 110.8 @ 4000 rpm. Torque: 180.2 lb.-ft. @ 2800 rpm. Fuel Requirements: Regular.

CHASSIS FEATURES: Separate body and frame, 3 in. x 4 in. x 0.135 in. steel box-section side rails with center drop section. Section modulus: 2.75. Two box section and two channel steel cross members.

SUSPENSION AND RUNNING GEAR: Front Suspension: Semi-elliptical leaf springs, 1.75 in. x 40 in. Capacity: 1820 lb. direct-action shock absorbers. Rear Suspension: Semi-elliptical leaf springs, 1.75 in. x 46 in. Capacity: 2080 lb. direct-action shock absorbers. Front Axle Type and Capacity: FA-14, hypoid, 2100 lb. capacity. Rear Axle Type and Capacity: RA-9, hypoid, semi-floating 3500 lb. capacity. Final Drive Ratio: 3.73, 4.27 or 4.88:1. Transfer Case: TC-145, two-speed: 2.03, 1.00:1. Brakes: Type: Dual operation hydraulic, self-adjusting front and rear drums with warning light. Dimensions: Front: 10 in. x 2.0 in., Rear: 11.0 in. x 1.85 in. Total lining area: 169.2 sq. in. Wheels: 5-stud disc with 5.5 in. bolt circles and 5.50K rims. Tires: 7.35 x 15. Optional: Tubeless: 7.75 x 15, 8.15 x 15, 8.45 x 15. Tires and tubes: 6.00 x 16, 8.45 x 15 (available in either black or white sidewalls), 9.00 x 13. Steering: S-12 cam and lever, 17 in. dia. steering wheel. Turns Lock-to-Lock: 4.6. Turning circle: 38.0 ft. Transmission: Type: T-14 3-speed manual, synchromesh on top two gears. Transmission Ratios: 3.34:1, 1.85:1, 1.00:1. Reverse: 4.53:1. Clutch: Girling Hydraulic, 10 dia., 6-spring, single plate.

VEHICLE DIMENSIONS: Wheelbase: 100 in. Overall Length: 154 in. Front/Rear Tread: 55.1 in./55.1 in. Overall Height: 66.5 in. (Cabtop), 67.7 in. (Traveltop). Width: 68.6 in. Front/Rear Overhang: 24 in./30 in. Tailgate: Width and Height: 20.5 in. x 38 in. Approach/Departure Degrees: 44/32. Ground Clearance: Front axle: 7.7 in. Rear axle: 6.8 in. Load space: 60 in. x 41 in. x 20.5 in.

CAPACITIES: Fuel Tank: 10 gal. Coolant system: 10.5 qt.

ACCOMMODATIONS: Seating Capacity: 2 passenger with standard bench front seat; 2 passenger with optional front bucket seats; 4 passenger with optional rear bench seat; 6 passenger with optional side wheelhouse cushions. Front hip room: 59.0 in. Pedal to seat back: 39.0 in. Floor to ground: 15.0 in.

INSTRUMENTATION: Speedometer, odometer, gauges for ammeter, oil pressure, fuel level and engine coolant temperature.

OPTIONS AND PRICES: FA-24 2500 lb. capacity front axle with Powr-Lok limited slip differential with ratios of 3.73, 4.27 or 4.88:1: $40. Front wheel locking hubs. RA-23, 3500 lb. capacity rear Powr-Lok limited slip differential with ratios of 3.73, 4.27 or 4.88:1: $90. Fresh-air heater and defroster. Driver and passenger bucket seats and seat belts with or without bulkhead. Armrests. Floor mats. Full width rear seat (seat belts included with Traveltop). Sliding door glass. Right-hand drive. Chrome door-mounted outside rearview mirror. Heavy-duty clutch. Increased capacity cooling system. 52 amp alternator. 60 amp-hr. battery. Cigarette lighter. Dual electric horns. Courtesy lamp on dash. Push-button radio and antenna. Engine governor, hand throttle. Exhaust emission control. Undercoating. Two front tow hooks. Silver grey rear bumper. Chrome front bumper. Chrome rear bumper. Skid plate. Inside spare tire carrier or outside of tailgate carrier. Snowplows. Dual 10 gal. fuel tanks with selector valve and two-position gauge switch. T-45 4-speed heavy-duty manual transmission. Front-mounted winch. Heavy-duty front springs. Heavy-duty rear springs. Chrome wheel discs. Turbo-charged engine: $262.00. 196 cu. in. 4-cylinder: $81.00. Paneltop in lieu of Cabtop: $140.00. Custom Traveltop Rear Seating Package. Includes custom-width full-width seat with armrests and floor mat, cushions, rear wheel housing bench cushions, single (driver-side) or dual front armrests for standard model, chrome rear bumper (custom model only).

HISTORICAL FOOTNOTES: The latest Scouts debuted on Nov. 1,1966.

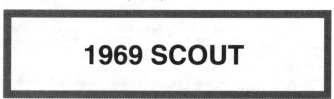

1968 SCOUT

The turbocharged engine was not offered for 1968. Numerous technical refinements and revisions to the Scout's specifications took place in 1968. Among the most apparent was the use of the 196 engine as its standard engine.

I.D. DATA: Location and configuration unchanged from 1967.

Body Type	Factory Price	GVW	Shipping Weight	Prod. Total
Scout Series 800, 100 in. wheelbase				
Utility Roadster	$2659	4000*	3465#	—
Utility Traveltop	$2833	4000	3150	—
Custom Traveltop	$3047	4000	3615#	—
Soft Top Sportop	$3276	4000	3515#	—
Utility Pickup	$2752	4000	N.A.	—
Custom Pickup	$2966	4000	N.A.	—

* 4700 lb. GVW optional
#-weight with V-8 eng.

STANDARD ENGINE: Engine Type: OHV, In-line 4-cylinder "4-196." Bore x Stroke: 4.125 in. x 3.65625 in. Displacement: 195.44 cu. in. (3.20 liters). Lifters: Hydraulic. Carburetion: Single Holley model 1904 downdraft single throat carburetor. Compression Ratio: 8.1:1. Number of main bearings-5. Horsepower: 110.8 @ 4000 rpm. Torque: 180.2 lb.-ft. @ 2800 rpm. Fuel Requirements: Regular.

OPTIONAL ENGINE: Engine Type: OHV, V-8, "V-266." Bore x Stroke: 3.625 in. x 3.21875 in. Displacement: 266.76 cu. in. Number of main bearings-5. Lifters: Hydraulic. Carburetion: Holley model 2300, 2-barrel carburetor. Compression Ratio: 8.4:1. Horsepower: 154.8 @ 4400 rpm. Torque: 227.1 lb.-ft. @ 2800 rpm. Fuel Requirements: Regular.

CHASSIS FEATURES: Separate body and frame, 3 in. x 4 in. x 0.135 in. steel box-section side rails with center drop section. Section modulus: 2.75. Two box section and two channel steel cross members.

SUSPENSION AND RUNNING GEAR: Front Suspension: Semi-elliptical leaf springs, 1.75 in. x 40 in. Capacity: 2060 lb. direct-action shock absorbers. Rear Suspension: Semi-elliptical leaf springs, 1.75 in. x 46 in. Capacity: 2540 lb. direct-action shock absorbers. Front Axle Type and Capacity: FA-14, hypoid, 2000 lb. capacity. Rear Axle Type and Capacity: RA-9, hypoid, semi-floating 3500 lb. capacity. Final Drive Ratio: 4.27 or 4.88:1. Transfer Case: TC-145, two-speed: 2.03, 1.00:1. Brakes: Type: Dual operation hydraulic, self-adjusting front and rear drums with warning light. Dimensions: Front: 10 in. x 2.0 in., Rear: 11.0 in. x 1.75 in. Total lining area: 161.5 sq. in. Wheels: 5-stud disc with 5.5 in. bolt circles and 4.50E rims. Tires: 6.00 x 16, 4-ply rated. Optional: Tires and tubes: 8.45 x 15. Steering: S-9 cam and lever, 17 in. dia. steering wheel. Turns Lock-to-Lock: 4.6. Turning circle: 38.0 ft. Transmission: Type: T-14 3-speed manual, synchromesh on top two gears. Transmission Ratios: 3.34:1, 1.85:1, 1.00:1. Reverse: 4.53:1. Clutch: Girling Hydraulic, 10 dia., 9-spring, single plate, mechanical control, vibration dampener.

VEHICLE DIMENSIONS: Wheelbase: 100 in. Overall Length: 154 in. Front Tread: 53.875 in. Overall Height: 68.0 in. (Cabtop), 69.5 in. (Traveltop). Width: 68.25 in. Front/Rear Overhang: 24 in./30 in. Tailgate: Width and Height: 20.5 in. x 38 in. Approach/Departure Degrees: 47/35. Ground Clearance: Front axle: 9.25 in. Rear axle: 9.125 in. Load space: 60 in. x 41 in. x 20.5 in.

CAPACITIES: Fuel Tank: 9 gal. Coolant system: 10.5 qt.

ACCOMMODATIONS: Seating Capacity: 2 passenger with standard bench front seat; 2 passenger with optional front bucket seats; 4 passenger with optional rear bench seat; 6 passenger with optional side wheelhouse cushions. Front hip room: 59.0 in. Pedal to seat back: 39.0 in. Floor to ground: 15.0 in.

INSTRUMENTATION: Speedometer, odometer, gauges for ammeter, oil pressure, fuel level and engine coolant temperature.

OPTIONS: FA-24 2500 lb. capacity front axle with Powr-Lok limited slip differential with ratios of 4.27 or 4.88:1. Front wheel locking hubs. RA-23, 3500 lb. capacity rear Powr-Lok limited slip differential with ratios of 4.27 or 4.88:1. Fresh-air heater and defroster. Driver and passenger bucket seats and seat belts with or without bulkhead. Armrests. Floor mats. Omit Cabtop. Full width rear seat (seat belts included with Traveltop). Sliding door glass. Right-hand drive. Chrome door-mounted outside rearview mirror. Heavy-duty clutch. Increased capacity cooling system. 52 amp alternator. 60 amp-hr. battery. Cigarette lighter. Dual electric horns. Courtesy lamp on dash. Push-button radio and antenna. Engine governor, hand throttle. Exhaust emission control. Undercoating. Two front tow hooks. Silver grey rear bumper. Chrome front bumper. Chrome rear bumper. Skid plate. Inside spare tire carrier or outside of tailgate carrier. Snowplows. Dual 9 gal. fuel tanks with selector valve and two-position gauge switch. T-45 4-speed heavy-duty manual transmission. Ramsey model 200 Front-mounted winch with 150 ft. 0.3125 in. cable and hook (requires power take off). Power take off for Ramsey winch-transfer case mounted. Heavy-duty front springs. Heavy-duty rear springs. Chrome wheel discs.

HISTORICAL FOOTNOTES: During the 1968 calendar year the 200,000th Scout was produced at International's Fort Wayne facility.

1969 SCOUT

In the spring of 1969 International Harvester introduced the revamped 800A version of the Scout. Among the improvements offered by the 800A was a single lever transfer case and for those Scouts powered by the International V-304 V-8 engine, a new T-39 3-speed automatic transmission. This transmission, which had been previously installed in excess of 20,000 post office trucks, was built by International Harvester. For use in the Scout it was moderately redesigned for smoother shifts, increased torque capacity and quieter operation. It was controlled by a floor-mounted shifter with a "PRND12" range. The transmission could be shifted through its three gears manually, or when the lever was placed in D, would shift automatically.

The transfer case, which had a 2.03:1 low range, had four positions: Two-wheel drive high, four-wheel drive high, four-wheel drive low and neutral. Shifting could be done while the Scout was in motion. The rear spring rate was altered to provide an improved ride and a redesigned flange-type front axle of increased capacity (2100 lbs. for 4-cyl. models and 2500 lbs. on V-8 Scouts) was adopted. The rear axle continued to have a 3500 lb. rating. Replacing the 266 cu. in. V-8 available in 1968, and first used in 1967, was a larger, 304 cu. in. unit identified as the V-304. With 38 more horsepower and 45 more lb.-ft. of torque it was significantly more powerful than the older 266 cu. in. V-8. Also introduced during the 1969 model year was an optional 6-cylinder, 232 cu. in. engine. The latest Scout used an aluminized muffler and a stronger accelerator linkage. All joints now had nylon inserts for smoother operation. Other improvements included a new more durable front engine mount with a large rubber compression pad in place of the older rubber shear load type. This arrangement also reduced the transmitting of vibration into the Scout's interior. The 800A was also moderately restyled with a new grille format consisting of an anodized insert with an bright aluminum outer molding. The headlights were located within aluminum bezels with black inserts. Replacing the center-grille mounted International lettering was a new International nameplate located in the grille's lower left corner. Some early publicity shots of the 800-A show this plate positioned in the opposite corner. The parking/directional lights were now integrated into the lower edge of the bumper splash panel. At the rear the tailgate latch was now located next to the spare tire. The full-length steel top was redesigned to provide an additional 84 sq. in. of window area.

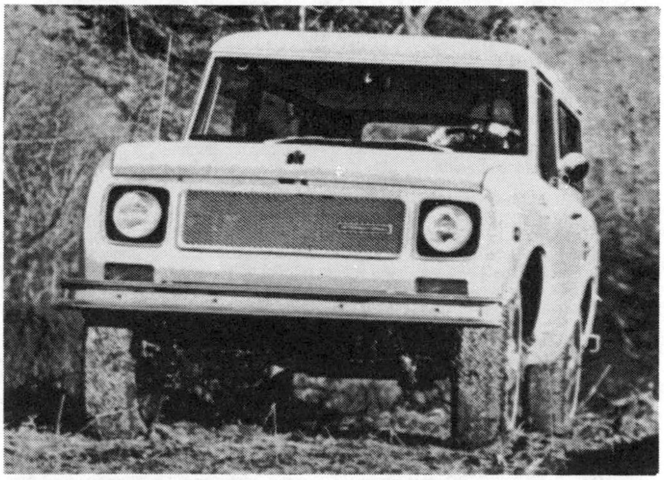

1969 Scout

In addition to the red and white color choices of previous years, the new Scout was also available in five new metallic colors: Gold, copper, lime green, medium blue and plum. A new "Safari" convertible top option was also offered. This feature, constructed of a vinyl-coated, pre-shrunk fabric was of full length style and thanks to its roll-up side and rear windows provided the Scout owner with open air motoring in conjunction with reasonable weather protection. The 1969 models were fitted with amber front and red rear side reflectors. Additional standard equipment included roll down window glass with adjustable vent wings, door locks on both sides, full-width seat with foam rubber padded seat cushion, black upholstery and seat belts, ashtray, hand choke, left and right rearview mirrors, inside rearview mirror, dual padded sun visors, padded instrument panel and fresh air heater and defroster.

Closely following the introduction of the 800A version of the Scout was the announcement of a limited edition "Aristocrat" version of the Scout for 1969. Production was limited to 2500 units (which meant that some of International Harvester's 3500 dealers would not be able to sell even one Aristocrat). All were offered in identical color schemes of a metal blue, full-length Traveltop and a silver lower body finish. The Aristocrat also was fitted with a chrome luggage rack that extended down the roof back. Interior appointments included a blue color decor, all vinyl front bucket and rear bench seats, padded door panels, rear wheel and side pads, blue floor carpeting with bright finish retaining strips and a padded and silver trimmed dash. The Aristocrat was equipped with many items that were optional for the standard Scout. These include chrome dual exterior mirrors, dashboard-mounted interior courtesy light, cigarette lighter, radio and vibration-absorbing antenna. Also included in the Aristocrat's list of features was a limited slip differential, dual fuel tanks, 7 in. wide wheels, glass-belted 2-ply H70-15 low profile tires, and undercoating. The Aristocrat was available only as a four-wheel drive model. Its front suspension used stronger springs than the 800A. In addition, heavy-duty front and rear shocks were installed. The Aristocrat was also the first Scout offered with the 6-cylinder engine.

I.D. DATA: Location and configuration unchanged from 1967

Body Type	Factory Price	GVW	Shipping Weight	Prod. Total
Scout Series 800A				
Roadster	$2798	3900*	3000	—
Pickup	$2920	3900	3050	—
Traveltop	$3000	3900	3150	—

* 4700 lb. GVW optional

STANDARD ENGINE: Engine Type: OHV, In-line 4-cylinder "4-196." Bore x Stroke: 4.125 in. x 3.65625 in. Displacement: 195.44 cu. in. (3.20 liters). Lifters: Hydraulic. Carburetion: Single Holley model 1904 downdraft single throat carburetor. Compression Ratio: 8.1:1. Number of main bearings-5. Horsepower: 110.8 @ 4000 rpm. Torque: 180.2 lb.-ft. @ 2800 rpm. Fuel Requirements: Regular.

OPTIONAL ENGINE: Engine Type: OHV In-line 6-cylinder "Power Thrift"-6-2320Bore x Stroke: 3.75 in. x 3.5 in. Displacement: 232 cu. in. Carburetion: Single bbl. Compression Ratio: 8.5:1. Horsepower: 145 @ 4300 rpm. Torque: 215 lb.-ft. @ 1600 rpm. Fuel Requirements: Regular.

OPTIONAL ENGINE: Engine Type: OHV V-8. Bore x Stroke: 3.875 in. x 4.21875 in. Displacement: 304 cu. in. (4.98 liters). Lifters: Hydraulic. Carburetion: Model 2300G Holley. Compression Ratio: 8.19:1. Number of main bearings-7. Horsepower: 193 @ 4400 rpm. Torque: 272 @ 2800 rpm. Fuel Requirements: Regular.

CHASSIS FEATURES: Separate body and frame, 3 in. x 4 in. x 0.135 in. steel box-section side rails with center drop section. Section modulus: 2.75. Two box section and two channel steel cross members.

SUSPENSION AND RUNNING GEAR: All data applies to models with standard 4-cylinder engine. Front Suspension: Semi-elliptical leaf springs, 1.75 in. x 40 in. Capacity: 2010 lb. direct-action shock absorbers. Rear Suspension: Semi-elliptical leaf springs, 1.75 in. x 46 in. Capacity: 2120 lb. direct-action shock absorbers. Front Axle Type and Capacity: FA-14, hypoid, 2100 lb. capacity. Rear Axle Type and Capacity: RA-18, hypoid, semi-floating 3500 lb. capacity. Final Drive Ratio: 3.31, 3.73 or 4.27:1. Transfer Case: TC-145, two-speed: 2.03, 1.00:1. Brakes: Type: Dual operation hydraulic, self-adjusting front and rear drums with warning light. Dimensions: Front: 10 in. x 2.0 in., Rear: 11.0 in. x 1.75 in. Total lining area: 161.5 sq. in. Wheels: 5-stud disc with 5.5 in. bolt circles and 5.50K rims. Tires: 7.35 x 15, 2-ply tubeless. Optional: Tubeless: 7.35 x 15 white sidewall, 7.75 x 15, 8.25 x 15, 8.55 x 15. Tires and tubes: 6.00 x 16, 8.55 x 15 (black or white sidewall). Steering: S-8 cam and lever, 17 in. dia. steering wheel. Turns Lock-to-Lock: 4.6. Turning circle: 38.0 ft. Transmission: Type: T-14 3-speed manual, synchromesh on top two gears. Transmission Ratios: 3.34:1, 1.85:1, 1.00:1. Reverse: 4.53:1. Clutch: Girling Hydraulic, 10 dia., 9-spring, single plate, mechanical control, vibration dampener.

VEHICLE DIMENSIONS: Wheelbase: 100 in. Overall Length: 154 in. Front Tread: 54.5 in. Overall Height: 66.5 in. (Cabtop), 67.7 in. (Traveltop). Width: 68.6 in. Front/Rear Overhang: 24 in./30 in. Tailgate: Width and Height: 20.5 in. x 38 in. Approach/Departure Degrees: 43/32. Ground Clearance: Front axle: 7.7 in. Rear axle: 6.8 in. Load space: 60 in. x 41 in. x 20.5 in.

CAPACITIES: Fuel Tank: 10 gal. Coolant system: 11.6 qt.

ACCOMMODATIONS: Seating Capacity: 2 passenger with standard bench front seat; 2 passenger with optional front bucket seats; 4 passenger with optional rear bench seat; 6 passenger with optional side wheelhouse cushions. Front hip room: 59.0 in. Pedal to seat back: 39.0 in. Floor to ground: 15.0 in.

INSTRUMENTATION: Speedometer, odometer, gauges for ammeter, oil pressure, fuel level and engine coolant temperature.

OPTIONS: Front wheel locking hubs. RA-28 rear axle with Powr-Lok limited slip differential, available with 3.31, 3.73 or 4.27:1 ratios. Custom Interior Trim Package (Traveltop only). Includes body color interior, black vinyl bucket seats, matching-padded door panels, dual armrests, textured vinyl front floormat, cigar lighter, Traveltop headliner. Individual driver and passenger bucket seats and seat belts with or without bulkhead. Armrests. Floor mats. Full width rear seat (seat belts with Traveltop), Sliding door glass. Right-hand drive. Chrome door-mounted outside rearview mirrors. Increased cooling system capacity. 52 amp alternator. 60 amp-hr. battery. Cigarette lighter. Dual electric horns. Courtesy light on dash. Push-button radio and antenna. 4-way trailer connector. Hand throttle. Undercoating. Two front tow hooks. Rear tow loop. Silver grey rear bumper. Chrome front bumper. Chrome rear bumper. Skid plate. Tire carrier outside of tailgate. Snowplows. Heavy-duty step bumper with trailer hitch. Dual 10 gal. fuel tanks with selector valve and two-position gauge switch. T-45 4-speed heavy-duty manual transmission. Transfer case-mounted power take off. Front-mounted winch. Heavy-duty front springs. Heavy-duty rear springs. Chrome wheelcovers. Aristrocrat Trim Package.

HISTORICAL FOOTNOTES: International Harvester introduced the Aristocrat model at a Playboy resort in Geneva, Wisconsin.

1970 SCOUT

Another new model, the SR-2, highlighted the 1970 Scout line. The SR-2, like the older Aristocrat, was a limited production model with output pegged at approximately 2500 units. The SR-2 was easy to identify. Early versions had a flame red paint finish, two white hood stripes, upper and lower body striping, and chrome wheels fitted with Polyglas tires. Other chromed items included the front bumper, external mirrors, antenna and gas caps. Later versions of the SR-2 (production of the1970 Scouts continued into the spring of 1971 when the all new Scout II was introduced) were offered in a variety of colors including white and bronze. Free wheeling hubs were also standard. The interior was finished in black vinyl with full carpeting, woodgrain applique trim, chrome inserts for the dash gauges and a sound-absorbing headliner.

I.D. DATA: The vehicle identification number was located on the left door pillar post.

Body Type	Factory Price	GVW	Shipping Weight	Prod. Total
Scout Series 800A				
Roadster	$2993	3900*	3000	—
Traveltop	$3195	3900	3150	—
Pickup	$3120	3900	3050	—

* 4700 lb. GVW optional

STANDARD ENGINE: Engine Type: OHV, In-line 4-cylinder "4-196." Bore x Stroke: 4.125 in. x 3.65625 in. Displacement: 195.44 cu. in. (3.20 liters). Lifters: Hydraulic. Carburetion: Single Holley model 1904 downdraft single throat carburetor. Compression Ratio: 8.1:1. Number of main bearings-5. Horsepower: 110.8 @ 4000 rpm. Torque: 180.2 lb.-ft. @ 2800 rpm. Fuel Requirements: Regular.

OPTIONAL ENGINE: Engine Type: OHV In-line 6-cylinder "Power Thrift"-6-2320Bore x Stroke: 3.75 in. x 3.5 in. Displacement: 232 cu. in. Carburetion: Single bbl. Compression Ratio: 8.5:1. Horsepower: 145 @ 4300 rpm. Torque: 215 lb.-ft. @ 1600 rpm. Fuel Requirements: Regular.

OPTIONAL ENGINE: Engine Type: OHV V-8. Bore x Stroke: 3.875 in. x 4.21875 in. Displacement: 304 cu. in. (4.98 liters). Lifters: Hydraulic. Carburetion: Model 2300G Holley. Compression Ratio: 8.19:1. Number of main bearings-7. Horsepower: 193 @ 4400 rpm. Torque: 272 @ 2800 rpm. Fuel Requirements: Regular.

CHASSIS FEATURES: Separate body and frame, 3 in. x 4 in. x 0.135 in. steel box-section side rails with center drop section. Section modulus: 2.75. Two box section and two channel steel cross members.

SUSPENSION AND RUNNING GEAR: All data applies to models with standard 4-cylinder engine. Front Suspension: Semi-elliptical leaf springs, 1.75 in. x 40 in. Capacity: 2010 lb. direct-action shock absorbers. Rear Suspension: Semi-elliptical leaf springs, 1.75 in. x 46 in. Capacity: 2120 lb. direct-action shock absorbers. Front Axle Type and Capacity: FA-14, hypoid, 2100 lb. capacity. Rear Axle Type and Capacity: RA-18, hypoid, semi-floating 3500 lb. capacity. Final Drive Ratio: 3.31, 3.73 or 4.27:1. Transfer Case: TC-145, two-speed: 2.03, 1.00:1. Brakes: Type: Dual operation hydraulic, self-adjusting front and rear drums with warning light. Dimensions: Front: 10 in. x 2.0 in., Rear: 11.0 in. x 1.75 in. Total lining area: 161.5 sq. in. Wheels: 5-stud disc with 5.5 in. bolt circles and 5.50K rims. Tires: 7.35 x 15, 2-ply tubeless. Optional: Tubeless: 7.35 x 15 white sidewall, 7.75 x 15, 8.25 x 15, 8.55 x 15. Tires and tubes: 6.00 x 16, 8.55 x 15 (black or white sidewall). Steering: S-8 cam and lever, 17 in. dia. steering wheel. Turns Lock-to-Lock: 4.6. Turning circle: 38.0 ft. Transmission: Type: T-14 3-speed manual, synchromesh on top two gears. Transmission Ratios: 3.34:1, 1.85:1, 1.00:1. Reverse: 4.53:1. Clutch: Girling Hydraulic, 10 dia., 9-spring, single plate, mechanical control, vibration dampener.

VEHICLE DIMENSIONS: Wheelbase: 100 in. Overall Length: 154 in. Front Tread: 54.5 in. Overall Height: 66.5 in. (Cabtop), 67.7 in. (Traveltop). Width: 68.6 in. Front/Rear Overhang: 24 in./30 in. Tailgate: Width and Height: 20.5 in. x 38 in. Approach/Departure Degrees: 43/32. Ground Clearance: Front axle: 7.7 in. Rear axle: 6.8 in. Load space: 60 in. x 41 in. x 20.5 in.

CAPACITIES: Fuel Tank: 10 gal. Coolant system: 11.6 qt.

ACCOMMODATIONS: Seating Capacity: 2 passenger with standard bench front seat; 2 passenger with optional front bucket seats; 4 passenger with optional rear bench seat; 6 passenger with optional side wheelhouse cushions. Front hip room: 59.0 in. Pedal to seat back: 39.0 in. Floor to ground: 15.0 in.

INSTRUMENTATION: Speedometer, odometer, gauges for ammeter, oil pressure, fuel level and engine coolant temperature.

OPTIONS: Front wheel locking hubs. RA-28 rear axle with Powr-Lok limited slip differential, available with 3.31, 3.73 or 4.27:1 ratios. Custom Interior Trim Package (Traveltop only). Includes body color interior, black vinyl bucket seats, matching-padded door panels, dual armrests, textured vinyl front floormat, cigar lighter, Traveltop headliner. Individual driver and passenger bucket seats and seat belts with or without bulkhead. armrests. Floor mats. Full width rear seat (seat belts with Traveltop), Sliding door glass. Right-hand drive. Chrome door-mounted outside rearview mirrors. Increased cooling system capacity. 52 amp alternator. 60 amp-hr. battery. Cigarette lighter. Dual electric horns. Courtesy light on dash. Push-button radio and antenna. 4-way trailer connector. Hand throttle. Undercoating. Two front tow hooks. Rear tow loop. Silver Gray rear bumper. Chrome front bumper. Chrome rear bumper. Skid plate. Tire carrier outside of tailgate. Snowplows. Heavy-duty step bumper with trailer hitch. Dual 10 gal. fuel tanks with selector valve and two-position gauge switch. T-45 4-speed heavy-duty manual transmission. Transfer case-mounted power take off. Front-mounted winch. Heavy-duty front springs. Heavy-duty rear springs. Chrome wheelcovers.

HISTORICAL FOOTNOTES: In recognition of the numerous options and powertrain combinations available, International promoted the latest Scout as "the do-it-yourself Scout."

1971 SCOUT

In January, 1971 the International Harvester plant assembling the Scout 800 was struck by the union representing its hourly work force. During the interim between the start of the strike and its settlement, the plant was retooled to prepare for production of the model 800C Scout which was far better known as the Scout II. Production of this new model began in the Spring of 1971. The series 800B model of early 1971 was set apart from the preceding 800A by the repositioning of the "IH" badge from the hood to the left side of the grille.

The second generation Scout retained the 100 inch wheelbase of the older model as well as a good deal of its styling format. In other words, there was no difficulty in recognizing the latest Bobcat from International Harvester as a Scout. But the new model's rounded body sections, revamped rear side window profile, and larger overall dimensions also gave it a fresh and pleasing appearance. Relative to the model 800 Scout, the height of the new Scout was unchanged at 66.4 inches. The Scout II was, at 165.7 inches, nearly eleven inches longer. Virtually all of the added length was at the rear which resulted in a change in the Scout's angle of departure. It was now 26 degrees instead of 32 degrees. Overall width was increased to 70.0 in. from 68.6 in. The front and rear track was also increased to 57.1 inches from 55.7 inches. There was no decrease in ground clearance. The Scout's larger size was put to good advantage, providing the occupants with six additional inches of interior, front-to-rear space, and nearly five cubic feet additional cargo space. Also praiseworthy was the revised rear seat which now was of full-width design and positioned ahead of the rear axle and of the same height as the front seat. A flatter door sill, a wider 45.1 inch door and a lower, to 15.2 inches, floor height made for easier entry and exit. The steering column, purchased from General Motors, was of a lockable and energy-absorbing design. All instruments had printed circuits. Standard equipment for the Scout II included painted front bumper, heater and defroster, padded sun visors, armrests black all-vinyl front bench seat and 4-ply E78-15 tires. The interior colors selection consisted of dark blue, sage, jet black and dark red. Seven exterior colors were offered: Flame red, Ceylon green metallic, sunrise yellow, glacier blue, Mayan mist metallic, alpine white, and burnished gold metallic.

The upscale models was fitted with numerous semi-luxury items that included vinyl-covered bucket seats, pile carpeting in blue, gold, black or red, padded dash, quilted side door panels, and a color-coordinated steering wheel.

Numerous technical developments accompanies these design and convenience changes. Both the Scout's ride quality and off-road capability were improved by the use of three inch longer and wider front springs that now measured 40 inches x 2 inches. The rear springs were, at 56 inches, 10 inches longer than those used on the model 800. Their width was also 2 inches. Both sets of springs were moved outward from their former positions to provide improved handling and stability. Joining a new worm-and lever steering system was a new front axle with open Cardon joints. The front suspension now used ball-joint kingpins and the maximum turning angle was now 38 degrees. The Scout's turning circle was reduced from 42 feet to 37 feet. Power steering, with a faster ratio than the manual unit, was now offered as an option. The optional "Track-Loc" limited slip differential was completely redesigned for the new Scout II. No change was made in the Scout's rear drum brakes which measured 11 inches x 1.75 inches. The front brakes were redesigned and were increased in size to 11 inches x 2.0 inches. A power assist was also available.

The Scout II's cooling system capacity was increased and a reservoir was fitted to the cross-flow radiator. Replacing the dual, 10 gallon, side-mounted fuel tanks was a single unit, 19 gallon capacity, fuel tank located amidships between the rear frame rails.

The familiar 4-cylinder, 196 cu. in. engine remained as the Scout's standard powerplant except in California where the 232 cu. in. In-line six was standard. Added to the list of available optional engines was International's 345 cu. in. V-8. The Scout II was available in Cabtop pickup, Traveltop station wagon, or open roadster form.

I.D. DATA: The V.I.N. consisted of 13 symbols. The first six served as the serial number. The seventh identified the manufacturing plant. The final six digits were the sequential production number. The V.I.N. was stamped on a plate located on the right door hinge pillar. The Engine serial number was stamped on the crankcase of 6-cylinder engines, right side near distributor and on the right bank, upper front of V-8 engines. The chassis serial number was stamped on the frame left side rail, front.

Body Type	Factory Price	GVW	Shipping Weight	Prod. Total
Scout Series 800B				
Roadster	$3376	3900*	N.A.	—
Traveltop	$3564	3900	3480	—
Pickup	$3483	3900	3380	—
Scout Series 800C (Scout II)				
Roadster	N.A.	3900	N.A.	—
Traveltop	$3608	3900	3794	—
Pickup	$3528	3900	3694	—

* Prices and weights listed are for vehicles with 304 cu. in. V-8. 4700 lb. GVW optional 3. Standard and optional engines for Scout II (800B engines unchanged from 800A).

STANDARD ENGINE: (except for delivery in California) Engine Type: OHV, In-line 4-cylinder "4-196." Bore x Stroke: 4.125 in. x 3.65625 in. Displacement: 195.44 cu. in. (3.20 liters). Lifters: Hydraulic. Carburetion: Single Holley model 1904 downdraft single throat carburetor. Compression Ratio: 8.1:1. Number of main bearings-5. Horsepower: 110.8 @ 4000 rpm. Torque: 180.2 lb.-ft. @ 2800 rpm. Fuel Requirements: Regular.

OPTIONAL ENGINE: (Standard for Scouts for California delivery): Engine Type: OHV In-line 6-cylinder "Power Thrift"-6-2320Bore x Stroke: 3.75 in. x 3.5 in. Displacement: 232 cu. in. Carburetion: Single bbl. Compression Ratio: 8.5:1. Number of main bearings-7. Horsepower: 145 @ 4300 rpm (also listed at 140 and 150 hp with emission controls.). Torque: 215 lb.-ft. @ 1600 rpm. Fuel Requirements: Regular.

OPTIONAL ENGINE: Engine Type: OHV V-8. Bore x Stroke: 3.875 in. x 4.21875 in. Displacement: 304 cu. in. (4.98 liters). Lifters: Hydraulic. Carburetion: Model 2300G Holley. Compression Ratio: 8.19:1. Number of main bearings-5. Horsepower: 193 @ 4400 rpm. Torque: 272 @ 2800 rpm. Fuel Requirements: Regular.

OPTIONAL ENGINE: Engine Type: OHV V-8. Bore x Stroke: 3.88 in. x 3.66 in. Displacement: 345 cu. in. (5.65 liters). Carburetion: 2-barrel Holley model 2300 G. Compression Ratio: 8.1:1. Number of main bearings-5. Horsepower: 196.7 @ 4000 rpm. Torque: 309 lb.-ft. @ 2200 rpm. Fuel Requirements: Regular. The material that follows relates to the Scout II. The specifications of the Scout 800B were unchanged from those of the 800A.

CHASSIS FEATURES: Separate body and frame, ladder type frame.

SUSPENSION AND RUNNING GEAR: Front Suspension: Semi-elliptical leaf springs, 2.0 in. x 40.0 in. Capacity: 2200 lb. Tubular shock absorbers. Optional: Heavy-duty springs with 2400 lb. capacity. Rear Suspension: Semi-elliptical leaf springs, 2.0 in. x 56.0 in. Capacity: 2000 lb. Tubular shock absorbers. Optional: Heavy-duty springs with 2000 lb. capacity. Heavy-duty progressive springs with 2500 lb. capacity. Front Axle: FA-13, open Cardon. Capacity: 2500 lb. Rear Axle: Semi-floating, hypoid. Capacity: 3500 lb. Final Drive Ratio: 3.31:1, 3.73:1 or 4.27:1. Transfer Case: Type: Two-speed Dana 20. Ratios: 1.00:1, 2.03:1. Brakes: Type: Hydraulic drums front and rear. Dimensions: Front: 11 in. x 2.00 in. Rear: 11 in. x 1.75 in. Swept Area: 259 sq. in. Optional: Power assisted. Not available with 4-cylinder engine. Wheels: Pressed steel,15 in. x 5.5K, Optional: None. Tires: E78 x 15 4-ply. Optional: F78 x 15, G78 x 15, H78 x 15, available in traction tread and white sidewalls. Steering: Type: Worm and Lever. Ratio: 24:1, 4.24. Turns Lock-to-Lock. Turning circle: 36.8 ft. Optional: Power steering with 17.5:1 ratio. Not available with 4-cylinder engine. Transmission: Type: 3-speed fully synchromesh manual. Transmission Ratios: 3.17:1, 1.87:1, 1.0:1. Optional: T-45, 4-speed heavy-duty manual transmission, ratios: 4.02, 2.41, 1.41 and 1.00:1; T-39 3-speed automatic, ratios: 2.40:1, 1.47:1, 1.00:1. T-49 3-speed automatic for 345 engine only. Clutch: 4-cyl.: 10.0 in. dia., 6-spring. 6-cyl.: 10.5 in., 1570 lb. plate pressure. Optional: 11.0 in. angle link with 1800 lb. or 2000 lb. pressure.

VEHICLE DIMENSIONS: Scout II Wheelbase: 100 in. Overall Length: 165.8 in. Front/Rear Tread: 57.1 in./57.1 in. Overall Height: 66.4 in. Width: 70.0 in. Front/Rear Overhang: 24.0 in./ 41.7 in. Tailgate: Width and Height: 53 in. x 23 in. Approach/Departure Degrees: 46/26 degrees. Ground Clearance: Front differential: 8.75 in., Rear differential: 8.5in. Oil pan: 14.3 in. Transfer case: 11.4 in. Fuel tank: 14.8 in. Load space: 40 in. x 33 in. x 36.5 in. (Traveltop with seats in place), 40 in. x 59 in. x 36.5 in. with rear seat folded.

CAPACITIES: Fuel Tank: 19 gal. Engine coolant capacity: 4-cyl.: 10.5 qt., 6-cyl.: 12 qt., V-304: 19 qt., V-345: 20 qt.

ACCOMMODATIONS: Seating Capacity: Traveltop: 5, Cabtop: 2. Headroom: 36.0 in. Maximum Steering wheel to seat back: 22.5 in. Seat to ground: 32.0 in. Floor to ground: 17.2 in.

INSTRUMENTATION: 120 mph speedometer, odometer (reading to 99,999.9 mi.), gauges for fuel level, oil pressure, ammeter and engine coolant.

OPTIONS AND PRICES: Modulated fan (V-8 models only). Track-Lok limited slip rear differential: $61. Free running manual front hubs: $74. Free running automatic front hubs: $108. Heavy-duty manual 4-speed transmission: $102. Three-speed automatic transmission: $239. Power brakes: $44. Heavy-duty front and rear springs: $12. Heavy-duty front and heavy-duty progressive rear springs: $20. Front spring air attachment: $43. Black vinyl front bucket seats: $89. Front vinyl bucket seats in body color coordinated color: $103. Black front 1/3-2/3 seat: $27. Front 1/3-2/3 seat in body color coordinated color: $31. Black rear bench seat: $102. Back rear bench seat in body color coordinated color: $117. Air conditioning. Tow hooks: $17. Chrome front bumper; $16. Painted rear bumper: $13. Chrome rear bumper: $29. Skid plate kit (customer installed): $564. Rear step bumper with trailer hitch: $52. 61 amp alternator: $31. Cigarette lighter: $5. Trailer wiring (without connector): $9. 258 cu. in. 6-cyl.: $85. 304 cu. in. V-8: $164. 345 cu. in. V-8: $192. Deluxe Trim Package: $163. Includes color-keyed interior, vinyl door trim panels, vinyl color keyed floor mats with insulation, cigarette lighter, headliner and rear side panels with insulation (Traveltop), rear dome light (Traveltop), coat hook (Traveltop), courtesy light, parking brake with warning light, 1/3-2/3 vinyl-nylon color coded seat, spare tire cover (Traveltop), and undercoating. Custom Trim Package: $249. Includes Deluxe items plus carpeting in lieu of vinyl floor mats, tinted glass, dual electric horns and cargo area mat with insulation (Traveltop). Deluxe Exterior Trim Package: $118. Includes bright grille molding, bright tail lamp bezels, bright parking light bezels, bright door glass vent window frame, bright windshield trim molding, bright side trim molding, bright liftgate glass molding (Traveltop), bright rear quarter window molding (Traveltop), dual chrome outside rearview mirrors, chrome front and rear bumpers (front only with Cabtop), and stainless steel full wheelcovers.

HISTORICAL FOOTNOTES: The new Scout II was depicted as the "Weekday/Weekend WOW Wagon!."

1972 SCOUT

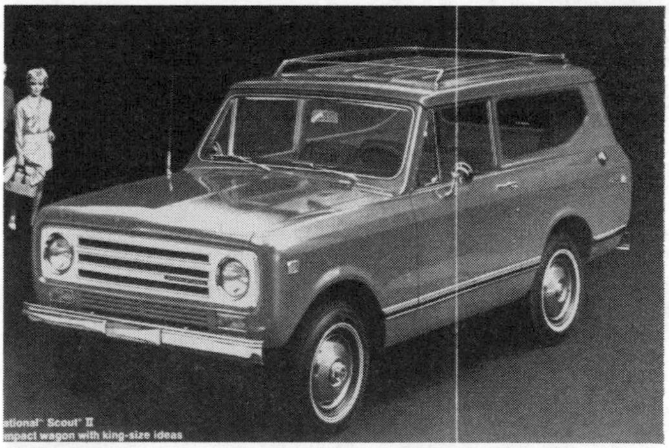

1972 Scout II

Whereas the 1971 Scout II had a grille panel painted to match the body color, the 1972 model used a silver/grey insert. Replacing the 232 cu. in. 6-cyl. engine as an option, except in California where the 4-cyl. engine was not available, was a larger, 258 cu. in. 6-cyl. The Scout Roadster model was not offered for 1972. It was still possible to order a Scout from the factory without a metal top and then obtain a folding soft top as a dealer option. The pickup model was depicted by International as the "Cabtop." The standard Scout transmission was a 3-speed, all-synchromesh unit. A heavy-duty 4-speed manual with a non-synchromesh first gear was available as an option. A new 3200 lb. front axle was also optional. It was a required option for Scouts equipped with snowplowing equipment. Standard Scout II equipment included a painted front bumper, heater and defroster.

I.D. DATA: Unchanged from 1971.

Body Type	Factory Price	GVW	Shipping Weight	Prod. Total
Scout II, 110 in. wheelbase				
Traveltop	$3340	4600*	3050	—
Pickup	$3185	4600	3150	—

* 5200 lb. GVW optional

STANDARD ENGINE: All models except those for California delivery: Engine Type: OHV, In-line 4-cylinder "4-196." Bore x Stroke: 4.125 in. x 3.65625 in. Displacement: 195.44 cu. in. (3.20 liters). Lifters: Hydraulic. Carburetion: Single Holley model 1904 downdraft single throat carburetor. Compression Ratio: 8.1:1. Number of main bearings-5. Horsepower: Net:102 @ 4000 rpm. Torque: Net: 176 lb.-ft. @ 2000 rpm. Fuel Requirements: Regular.

OPTIONAL ENGINE: (Standard for Scouts for California delivery): Engine Type: OHV 6-cyl. Bore x Stroke: 3.75 in. x 3.89 in. Displacement: 258 cu. in. Carburetion: Holley model 1940C. Compression Ratio: 8.0:1. Number of main bearings-7. Horsepower: Net: 113 @ 4000 rpm. Torque: Net: 191 lb.-ft. @ 2000 rpm. Fuel Requirements: Regular.

OPTIONAL ENGINE: Engine Type: OHV V-8. Bore x Stroke: 3.875 in. x 4.21875 in. Displacement: 304 cu. in. (4.98 liters). Lifters: Hydraulic. Carburetion: Model 2300G Holley. Compression Ratio: 8.02:1. Number of main bearings-5. Horsepower: Net: 140 @ 4000 rpm. Torque: Net: 236 lb.-ft. @ 2400 rpm. Fuel Requirements: Regular.

OPTIONAL ENGINE: Engine Type: OHV V-8. Bore x Stroke: 3.88 in. x 3.66 in. Displacement: 345 cu. in. (5.65 liters). Carburetion: 2-barrel Holley model 2300 G. Compression Ratio: 8.1:1. Number of main bearings-5. Horsepower: Net: 144 @ 3600 rpm. Torque: Net: 263 lb.-ft. @ 2000 rpm. Fuel Requirements: Regular.

CHASSIS FEATURES: Separate body and frame, ladder type frame.

SUSPENSION AND RUNNING GEAR: Front Suspension: Semi-elliptical leaf springs, 2.0 in. x 40.0 in. Capacity: 2200 lb. Tubular shock absorbers. Optional: Heavy-duty springs with 2400 lb. capacity. Rear Suspension: Semi-elliptical leaf springs, 2.0 in. x 56.0 in. Capacity: 2000 lb. Tubular shock absorbers. Optional: Heavy-duty springs with 2000 lb. capacity. Heavy-duty progressive springs with 2500 lb. capacity. Front Axle: FA-13, open Cardon. Capacity: 2500 lb. Rear Axle: Semi-floating, hypoid. Capacity: 3500 lb. Final Drive Ratio: 3.31:1, 3.73:1 or 4.27:1. Transfer Case: Type: Two-speed Dana 20. Ratios: 1.00:1, 2.03:1. Brakes: Type: Hydraulic drums front and rear. Dimensions: Front: 11 in. x 2.00 in. Rear: 11 in. x 1.75 in. Swept Area: 259 sq. in. Optional: Power assisted. Not available with 4-cylinder engine. Wheels: Pressed steel,15 in. x 5.5K, Optional: None. Tires: E78 x 15 4-ply. Optional: F78 x 15, G78 x 15, H78 x 15, available in traction tread and white sidewalls. Steering: Type: Worm and Lever. Ratio: 24:1, 4.24. Turns Lock-to-Lock. Turning circle: 36.8 ft. Optional: Power steering with 17.5:1 ratio. Not available with 4-cylinder engine. Transmission: Type: 3-speed fully synchromesh manual. Transmission Ratios: 3.17:1, 1.87:1, 1.0:1. Optional: T-45, 4-speed heavy-duty manual transmission, ratios: 4.02, 2.41, 1.41 and 1.00:1; T-39 3-speed automatic, ratios: 2.40:1, 1.47:1, 1.00:1. T-49 3-speed automatic for 345 engine only. Clutch: 4-cyl.: 10.0 in. dia., 6-spring. 6-cyl.: 10.5 in., 1570 lb. plate pressure. Optional: 11.0 in. angle link with 1800 lb. or 2000 lb. pressure.

VEHICLE DIMENSIONS: Scout II Wheelbase: 100 in. Overall Length: 165.8 in. Front/Rear Tread: 57.1 in./57.1 in. Overall Height: 66.4 in. Width: 70.0 in. Front/Rear Overhang: 24.0 in./ 41.7 in. Tailgate: Width and Height: 53 in. x 23 in. Approach/Departure Degrees: 46/26 degrees. Ground Clearance: Front differential: 8.75 in., Rear differential: 8.5in. Oil pan: 14.3 in. Transfer case: 11.4 in. Fuel tank: 14.8 in. Load space: 40 in. x 33 in. x 36.5 in. (Traveltop with seats in place), 40 in. x 59 in. x 36.5 in. with rear seat folded.

CAPACITIES: Fuel Tank: 19 gal. Engine coolant capacity: 4-cyl.: 10.5 qt., 6-cyl.: 12 qt., V-304: 19 qt., V-345: 20 qt.

ACCOMMODATIONS: Seating Capacity: Traveltop: 5, Cabtop: 2. Headroom: 36.0 in. Maximum Steering wheel to seat back: 22.5 in. Seat to ground: 32.0 in. Floor to ground: 17.2 in.

INSTRUMENTATION: 120 mph speedometer, odometer (reading to 99,999.9 mi.), gauges for fuel level, oil pressure, ammeter and engine coolant.

OPTIONS AND PRICES: 258 cu. in. 6-cyl. engine: $85. 304 cu. in. V-8: $164. 345 cu. in. V-8: $192. Free running manual front hubs: $74. Automatic free running front hubs: $108. Rear limited slip axle: $61. Heavy-duty 4-speed manual transmission: $102. Automatic 3-speed transmission: $239. Power brakes: $44. Power steering: $130. Heavy-duty front and rear springs: $12. Heavy-duty front and heavy-duty rear progressive springs: $20. Front air springs: $43. AM radio: $63. Black front bucket seats: $89. Color-keyed front bucket seats: $103. Black 1/3-2/3 front seat: $27. Color-keyed 1/3-2/3 front seat: $31. Black rear seat: $102. Color-keyed rear seat: $117. Air conditioning (includes 61 amp alternator, 70 amp-hr. battery, increased engine cooling capacity): $409. Tow hooks: $17. Chrome front bumper: $16. Painted rear bumper: $13. Chrome rear bumper: $29. Skid plate kit (not installed): $54. Rear step bumper with trailer hitch: $52. 61 amp alternator: 31. Cigarette lighter: $5. Trailer wiring (does not include connector); $9. Deluxe Trim Package. Includes vinyl door panels, headliner, rear side panels, cigarette lighter, coat hook, courtesy light, spare tire carrier and undercoating: $163. Custom Trim Package. Includes all items from Deluxe Package plus carpeting, tinted glass, dual horns and cargo area mat: $249. Deluxe Exterior Package. Includes bright trim molding, dual chrome mirrors, chrome front and rear bumpers, chrome wheelcovers: $118.

HISTORICAL FOOTNOTES: International referred to the new Scout II as "What you can't get from Germany, Japan, France, England, Italy, Sweden, or even Detroit."

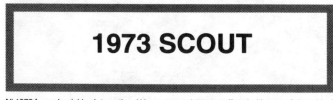

1973 SCOUT

All 1973 four-wheel drive International Harvester models were offered with a new "silent drive" transfer case which consisted of a single speed, chain-driven transfer case which locked into the front driveshaft. This system was extremely simple to operate. A dash-mounted control switch was pulled out to engage four-wheel drive. To return to two-wheel operation the switch was pushed in. This system eliminated the floor-mounted lever and also offered a savings in weight since it was constructed of hardened aluminum. However, this was not a unit intended for rugged off-road operations. For that purpose, International Harvester still offered the two-speed, chain-driven transfer case as an option.

For the first time since its mid-1971 introduction the mechanical nature of the Scout II was revised. The four-cylinder engine that had been standard for the Scout since its introduction in 1961 was replaced by the previously optional 258 cu. in. In-line 6-cylinder engine. Four-wheel drive enthusiasts who preferred the simple, straight-forward philosophy represented by the four-cylinder engine would suffer its loss for only a few years. In 1975 the need for improved fuel efficiency would prompt International Harvester to bring this engine out of hibernation. Visual identification of the latest Scout was ascertained by its new vertically-divided grille. Exterior colors for 1973 were Ceylon green metallic, sunrise yellow, flame red, glacier blue, Mayan mist metallic, alpine white and burbished gold metallic. The interior colors continued to be dark blue, sage, jet black and dark red. The standard interior offered a black all-vinyl front bench seat, 1/2-2/3 split-back front seat or bucket seats. The Deluxe interior had a vinyl and nylon 1/3-2/3 split-back front seat or bucket seats, vinyl padded door panels, Traveltop headliner and color-keyed vinyl floor covering. The custom interior added color-keyed nylon carpeting in passenger areas and a matching cargo area mat in black plus tinted glass and dual electric horns.

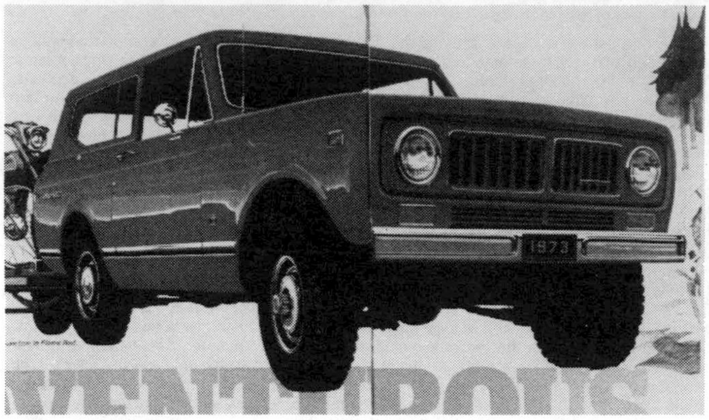

1973 Scout

I.D. DATA: The vehicle identification number, consisting of 13 digits, was positioned on the left front door pillar post. The first six digits were the vehicle's serial number. The seventh identified the assembly plant and the remaining digits were the vehicle's sequential production number. The engine model identification, located on a machined boss on the block, was a prefix to the V.I.N. number. For example: a Scout with the 4-cylinder, 196 cu. in. engine would read: I-196 plus the V.I.N.

Body Type	Factory Price	GVW	Shipping Weight	Prod. Total
Scout II				
Traveltop	$3425	5200*	3744	—
Pickup	$3482	5200	3644	—

* 6700 lb. GVW available with optional suspension options

STANDARD ENGINE: Engine Type: OHV 6-cyl. "Power-Thrift-6." Bore x Stroke: 3.75 in. x 3.89 in. Displacement: 258 cu. in. Carburetion: Holley model 1940C. Compression Ratio: 8.0:1. Number of main bearings-7. Horsepower: Net: 113 @ 4000 rpm. Torque: Net: 191 lb.-ft. @ 2000 rpm. Fuel Requirements: Regular.

OPTIONAL ENGINE: Engine Type: OHV V-8. Bore x Stroke: 3.875 in. x 4.21875 in. Displacement: 304 cu. in. (4.98 liters). Lifters: Hydraulic. Carburetion: Model 2300G Holley. Compression Ratio: 8.02:1. Number of main bearings-5. Horsepower: Net: 137 @ 4000 rpm. Torque: Net: 236 lb.-ft. @ 2400 rpm. Fuel Requirements: Regular.

OPTIONAL ENGINE: Engine Type: OHV V-8. Bore x Stroke: 3.88 in. x 3.66 in. Displacement: 345 cu. in. (5.65 liters). Carburetion: 2-barrel Holley model 2300 G. Compression Ratio: 8.1:1. Number of main bearings-5. Horsepower: Net: 144 @ 3600 rpm. Torque: Net: 263 lb.-ft. @ 2000 rpm. Fuel Requirements: Regular.

CHASSIS FEATURES: Separate body and frame, ladder type frame.

SUSPENSION AND RUNNING GEAR: Front Suspension: Semi-elliptical leaf springs, 2.0 in. x 40.0 in. Capacity: 2200 lb. Tubular shock absorbers. Optional: Heavy-duty springs with 2400 lb. capacity. Rear Suspension: Semi-elliptical leaf springs, 2.0 in. x 56.0 in. Capacity: 2000 lb. Tubular shock absorbers. Optional: Heavy-duty springs with 2000 lb. capacity. Heavy-duty progressive springs with 2500 lb. capacity. Front Axle: FA-13, open Cardon. Capacity: 2500 lb. Optional: 3200 lb. capacity. Rear Axle: Semi-floating, hypoid. Capacity: 3500 lb. Final Drive Ratio: 3.31:1, 3.73:1 or 4.27:1. Transfer Case: TC-143 chain drive, single speed with dash mounted push-pull control. Optional: TC-145 2-speed, floor-mounted control. Brakes: Type: Hydraulic drums front and rear. Dimensions: Front: 11 in. x 2.00 in. Rear: 11 in. x 1.75 in. Swept Area: 259 sq. in. Optional: Power assisted. Wheels: 5-stud, disc wheels with 5.5K rims and 5.5 in. bolt circles. Tires: E78 x 15 4-ply. Optional: F78 x 15, G78 x 15, H78 x 15, available in traction tread and white sidewalls. Steering: Type: Worm and Lever. Ratio: 24:1, 4.24. Turns Lock-to-Lock. Turning circle: 36.8 ft. Optional: Power steering with 17.5:1 ratio. Transmission: Type: 3-speed fully synchromesh manual. Ratios: 3.17, 1.87, 1.00:1. Optional: 4-speed heavy-duty manual. Ratios: 6.32, 3.09, 1.68, 1.00:1. Optional: 3-speed automatic (with oil cooler). Ratios: 2.40, 1.47, 1.00:1. Clutch: 10.5 in. dia. Optional: 11.0 in. angle link with 1800 lb. or 2000 lb. pressure.

VEHICLE DIMENSIONS: Wheelbase: 100 in. Overall Length: 165.8 in. Front/Rear Tread: 57.1 in./57.1 in. Overall Height: 65.2in. Width: 70.0 in. Front/Rear Overhang: 24.0 in./41.8 in. Tailgate: Width and Height: 53 in. x 23 in. Approach/Departure Degrees: 46/26 degrees. Ground Clearance: Front differential: 9.2 in. Rear differential: 8.5 in. Oil pan: 14.0 in. Transfer case: 11.8 in. Fuel tank: 16.5 in. Load space: 40 in. x 33 in. x 36.5 in. (Traveltop with seats in place), 40 in. x 59 in. x 36.5 in. with rear seat folded.

CAPACITIES: Fuel Tank: 19 gal. Engine coolant capacity: 6-cyl.: 12 qt., V-304: 19 qt., V-345: 20 qt.

ACCOMMODATIONS: Seating Capacity: Traveltop: 5, Cabtop: 2. Headroom: 36.0 in. Maximum Steering wheel to seat back: 22.5 in. Seat to ground: 32.0 in. Floor to ground: 17.2 in.

INSTRUMENTATION: 120 mph speedometer, odometer (reading to 99,999.9 mi.), gauges for fuel level, oil pressure, ammeter and engine coolant.

OPTIONS AND PRICES: Dual exhaust system: $37.00. Free running front hubs: $73.00. Manual locking hubs. Automatic locking hubs. Tow hooks: $17.00. Front and rear skid plates. Front power take-off. Auxiliary front level ride air springs: $43.00. Bumper mounted winch.

61-amp alternator: $31.00. 70 amp battery: $14.00. Combined heavy-duty rear step bumper and trailer hitch: $51.00. 11 in. clutch: $20.00. Heavy-duty cooling system: $17.00. Undercoating: $25.00. Power steering: $128.00. Power brakes: $43.00. Heavy-duty 4-speed manual transmission: $100.00. 3-speed automatic transmission: $235.00. 304 cu. in. V-8: $84.00. 345 cu. in. V-8: $118.00. Air conditioning: $402.00. Exterior Trim Package. 3500 lb. Trac-Lok rear axle: $60.00. 3200 lb. capacity front axle: $49.00. Heavy-duty front and rear springs: $12.00. Heavy-duty progressive springs: $19.00. Front bucket seats: $102.00. Split front seat: $31.00. AM radio: $62.00. Electric clock: $17.00. Console (requires bucket option): $36.00. Traveltop model available with front and rear chrome bumpers, metal liftgate molding and metal door edge guards, folding rear seat with cargo bulkhead and solid side panels: $115.00. Deluxe Trim Package.

HISTORICAL FOOTNOTES: The new Scouts were announced in the fall of 1972.

1974 SCOUT

Significant engineering changes and improvements characterized the 1974 Scout II. As in earlier years two body styles were offered; the Traveltop, station wagon version and the Cabtop pickup model. The Traveltop top could be removed but it was a tedious, time-consuming operation. A new chrome grille treatment along with an optional 2-tone vinyl applique for the Scout's side body panels provided a sporty and distinctive appearance. The vinyl trim was offered in four different formats including all-white and woodgrain. Seven paint finishes were offered for the 1974 Scout II: Sunburst yellow, glacier blue, flame red, Ceylon green metallic, alpine white, Mayan mist and burnished gold metallic. International Harvester light-uty truck Marketing Manager, Richard Bakkom noted at the Scout II's press introduction that "The Scout was designed as an all-wheel drive vehicle from the first bolt. It's built to go anywhere...." Emphasizing this design philosophy were the numerous design changes made for 1974. Power front disc brakes were now standard as were heavier front and rear suspensions and increased towing capacities. Specific refinements included a standard front stabilizer bar, F-78 x 15 PCLRB tires and 6.00 JK rims. Scouts with V-8 engines had a standard 3200 lb. capacity front axle. In 1973 this axle had been offered as an option. It remained available at extra cost for 6-cylinder Scouts.

I.D. DATA: Unchanged from 1973.

Body Type	Factory Price	GVW	Shipping Weight	Prod. Total
Scout II				
Traveltop	$3963	4600*	3717	—
Cabtop	$3808	4600	3571	—

* 5200 lb. GVW optional

STANDARD ENGINE: Engine Type: OHV 6-cyl. "Power-Thrift-6." Bore x Stroke: 3.75 in. x 3.89 in. Displacement: 258 cu. in. Carburetion: Holley model 1940C. Compression Ratio: 8.0:1. Number of main bearings-7. Compression Ratio: 8.0:1. Horsepower: 113 @ 4000 rpm. Torque: 191 lb.-ft. @ 2000 rpm. Fuel Requirements: 91 octane.

OPTIONAL ENGINE: Engine Type: OHV V-8. Bore x Stroke: 3.875 in. x 4.21875 in. Displacement: 304 cu. in. (4.98 liters). Lifters: Hydraulic. Carburetion: Model 2300G Holley. Compression Ratio: 8.19:1. Number of main bearings-5. Horsepower: 137 @ 4000 rpm. Torque: 233 lb.-ft. @ 2400 rpm. Fuel Requirements: 91 octane.

OPTIONAL ENGINE: Engine Type: OHV V-8. Bore x Stroke: 3.88 in. x 3.66 in. Displacement: 345 cu. in. (5.65 liters). Carburetion: 2-barrel Holley model 2300 G. Compression Ratio: 8.05:1. Number of main bearings-5. Horsepower: 144 @ 3600 rpm (156 with dual exhaust). Torque: 263 lb.-ft. @ rpm (269 with dual exhaust). Fuel Requirements: 91 octane.

CHASSIS FEATURES: Separate body and frame, ladder type frame.

SUSPENSION AND RUNNING GEAR: Front Suspension: Semi-elliptical leaf springs, 2.0 in. x 40.0 in. Capacity: 2200 lb. Tubular shock absorbers. 1.0 in. stabilizer bar. Optional: Heavy-duty springs with 2400 lb. capacity. Rear Suspension: Semi-elliptical leaf springs, 2.0 in. x 56.0 in. Capacity: 2000 lb. Tubular shock absorbers. Optional: Heavy-duty springs with 2000 lb. capacity. Heavy-duty progressive springs with 2500 lb. capacity. Front Axle: FA-13, open Cardon. Capacity: 2500 lb., 3200 lb. with V-8 engines. Optional: 3200 lb. capacity. Rear Axle: Semi-floating, hypoid. Capacity: 3500 lb. Final Drive Ratio: 3.31:1, 3.73:1 or 4.27:1. Transfer Case: TC-143 chain drive, single speed with dash mounted push-pull control. Optional: TC-145 2-speed, floor-mounted control. Brakes: Type: Power, Front 11.75 in. discs: 11.75 in. Rear 11 in. x 2.5 in. drums. Dimensions: Swept Area: 417 sq. in. Wheels: 15 in. x 6.0JK. Optional: 15 in. x 7.0JJ. Tires: F78 x 15LRB, Optional: G78 x 15LBR, H78 x 15 LRB, HR78 x 15B. Steering: Type: Worm and Lever. Ratio: 24:1, 4.24. Turns Lock-to-Lock. Turning circle: 34 ft. Optional: Power steering with 17.5:1 ratio. Transmission: Type: 3-speed manual (synchromesh on top two gears). Ratios: 2.80, 1.85, 1.00:1. Optional: 4-speed manual transmission. Ratios: 4.02, 2.41, 1.41, 1.00:1. Optional: 3-speed automatic. Ratios: 2.45, 1.45, 1.00:1. Clutch: 10.5 in. dia. Optional: 11.0 in. angle link with 1800 lb. or 2000 lb. pressure.

VEHICLE DIMENSIONS: Wheelbase: 100 in. Overall Length: 165.8 in. Front/Rear Tread: 57.1 in./57.1 in. Overall Height: 65.2 in. Width: 70.0 in. Front/Rear Overhang: 27 in./39.5 in. Tailgate: Width and Height: 53 in. x 23 in. Approach/Departure Degrees: 38/23 degrees. Ground Clearance: Front axle: 9.1 in. Rear axle: 8.2 in. Oil pan: 15.5 in. Transfer case: 12.8 in. Fuel tank: 14.0 in. Exhaust system: 11.7 in. Load space: (with seats in place) 41 in. x 42 in. x 41.5 in.: (with rear seat folded): 59 in. x 42 in. x 41.5 in.

CAPACITIES: Fuel Tank: 19 gal. Engine coolant capacity: 6-cyl.: 12 qt., V-304: 19 qt., V-345: 20 qt.

ACCOMMODATIONS: Seating Capacity: Traveltop: 5, Cabtop: 2. Headroom: 36.0 in. Maximum Steering wheel to seat back: 22.5 in. Seat to ground: 32.0 in. Floor to ground: 17.2 in.

INSTRUMENTATION: 120 mph speedometer, odometer (reading to 99,999.9 mi.), gauges for fuel level, oil pressure, ammeter and engine coolant. Front axle engaged signal light.

OPTIONS AND PRICES: 304 cu. in. V-8: $118.00. 345 cu. in. V-8: $153.00 (when installed on Scouts for California delivery this engine has a 4-bbl. carburetor and electronic ignition. Cost rose to $258.00). 4-spd. manual transmission: $107.00. 3-spd. automatic transmission: $249.00. Free running front hubs: manual: $77.00; automatic: $113.00. Limited slip differential: $64.00. Heavy-Duty Spring and Shock Absorber Package: $22.00. Air-type level ride front springs: $45.00. 1/2-2/3 split back front seat: $33.00. Folding full width rear bench seat: $108.00. Front bucket seats: $92.00. Power steering: $136.00. Tinted glass: Cabtop: $18; Travelall: $30.00. Air conditioning: $427.00. Various GVW Packages including 5200 lb. for Cabtop and 5600 lb. for both models.

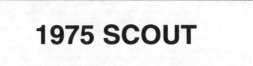

HISTORICAL FOOTNOTES: Nearly 60 percent (58.2 percent) of all Scouts were equipped with automatic transmission in 1974.

1975 SCOUT

The 1975 Scout, now with a new "XLC" designation, returned to use of International's 4-cylinder, 196 cu. in. engine as its standard powerplant. This move, prompted by the need to improve fuel economy was joined by numerous improvements and updates in the Scout's basic design. An electronic ignition was now standard as was a stronger suspension with a higher load carrying capacity. The Scout's standard GVW was now 6200 lbs. thanks in part to its H78 x 15 tires and increased capacity springs. The "silent drive" transfer case was continued as was the optional 2-speed single lever transfer case. Power front disc brakes, a 3-speed manual transmission and a 3200 lb. front axle continued to be standard on the Scout. Both the 304 and 345 cu. in. V-8 engines continued to be Scout options. The 258 cu. in. 6-cylinder engine was no longer available. An electronic ignition was used on all 1975 model year engines. A total of nine exterior colors were offered for the Scout including seven new colors: Glacier blue, winter white, sunburst yellow, pewter metallic, Grenoble green, dark brown metallic, buckskin, fire orange and terra cota. The Scout was available in two-tone color schemes as well as with special vinyl woodgrain or white side panel appliques. Customers could have their Scout fitted at the factory with white striping or could have their dealer install permanent bond self-adhesive vinyl striping if they so preferred. Five interior trim colors were available: Saddle (available with bucket seats only), tanbark, parchment, wedgewood blue and ivy green. The standard Scout interior provided a deep-cushioned bench seat upholstered in tanbark vinyl. Standard appointments included padded swingaway sun visors, armrests, and breakaway mirror. The Deluxe interior had a front split bench seat with nylon trim and vinyl finish, woodgrain instrument panel insert, color-keyed vinyl padded floor covering, vinyl padded door panels with woodgrain inserts, insulated headliner, rear side panels, rear dome lights, parking brake warning light, courtesy lamps, cigarette lighter and a color-keyed spare tire cover. The Custom Interior Trim Package included all features of the Deluxe interior plus nylon carpeting in the passenger area, color-keyed carpet on kick panels, padded vinyl trim for the rear quarter panels, dual electric horns and tinted glass. If automatic transmission was ordered the custom interior also had a color-keyed shift tower and automatic cover with woodgrain insert for the shift console. The bucket seat option could be ordered with a factory dealer installed console between the seats. The console included a convenience tray, lockable storage compartment and an ashtray for rear seat passengers. Scouts for California delivery were fitted with an evaporation loss system. The 1975 Scout also had rust-proof rocker panels and steel-framed side glass.

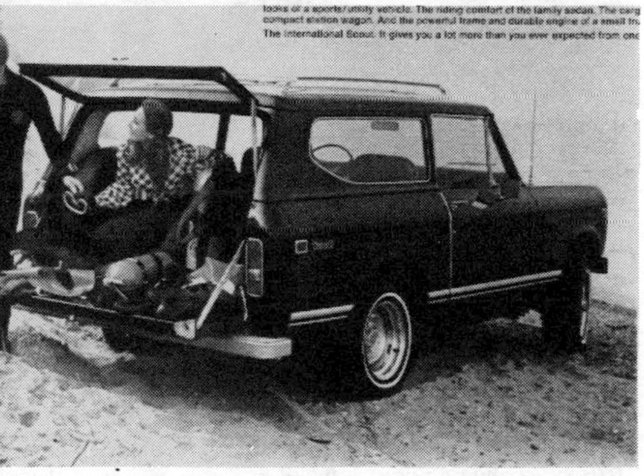

1975 Scout Traveltop

I.D. DATA: Vehicle model stamped on plate on right front door hinge pillar. Engine serial number stamped on engine crankcase; 4-cylinder engines: left side, upper front; V-8 engines: upper front. Chassis serial number stamped on frame left side rail, front. The transfer case number, transmission number, front and rear axle numbers were found on the Scout's specification card.

Body Type	Factory Price	GVW	Shipping Weight	Prod. Total
Scout II XLC				
Traveltop	$4712	6200	3551	25,904
* Cabtop	$4489	6200	3549	—

*Total calendar year production, both two-wheel drive and four-wheel drive models.

STANDARD ENGINE: Engine Type: OHV, In-line 4-cylinder, "Comanche H-196." Bore x Stroke: 4.125 in. x 3.656 in. Lifters: Hydraulic. Number of main bearings-5. Displacement: 196 cu. in. Carburetion: Model 1920 Holley. Compression Ratio: 8.02:1. Horsepower: 92 @ 3600 rpm. Torque: 164 lb.-ft. @ 2000 rpm. Fuel Requirements: low lead, unleaded or regular.

OPTIONAL ENGINE: Engine Type: OHV V-8, "Comanche V-304." Bore x Stroke: 3.875 in. x 3.218 in. Displacement: 304 cu. in. Carburetion: Model 2210C Holley. Compression Ratio: 8.19:1. Number of main bearings-5. Horsepower: 141 @ 4000 rpm. Torque: 243 lb.-ft. @ 2400 rpm. Fuel Requirements: low lead, unleaded or regular.

OPTIONAL ENGINE: Engine Type: OHV V-8, "V-345." Bore x Stroke: 3.875 in. x 3.656 in. Displacement: 345 cu. in. Carburetion: Model 2210 Holley, 2-barrel. Compression Ratio: 8.05:1. Number of main bearings-5. Horsepower: 158 @ 3600 rpm. Torque: 288 lb.-ft. @ 2000 rpm. Fuel Requirements: low lead, unleaded or regular.

CHASSIS FEATURES: Separate body and frame, ladder type frame.

SUSPENSION AND RUNNING GEAR: Front Suspension: Semi-elliptical 6-leaf springs, 2.0 in. x 40.0 in. Capacity: 3100 lb. Tubular shock absorbers. 1.0 in. stabilizer bar. Optional: Heavy-duty springs with 3200 lb. capacity, 1.1875 in. heavy-duty stabilizer bar. Rear Suspension: Semi-elliptical 4-leaf springs, 2.0 in. x 56.0 in. Capacity: 3100 lb. Tubular shock absorbers. Front Axle: FA-44, open Cardon. Capacity: 3200 lb. Rear Axle: Semi-floating, hypoid. Capacity: 3500 lb. Final Drive Ratio: 4.09:1. Optional: 3.07, 3.54:1. Transfer Case: TC-143 chain drive, single speed with dash mounted push-pull control. Optional: TC-145 2-

speed, floor-mounted control. Ratios: 2.03, 1.00:1. Brakes: Type: Power hydraulic, Front 11.75 in. discs: 11.75 in. Rear 11 in. x 2.5 in. drums. Dimensions: Swept Area: 417 sq. in. Wheels: 15 x 6.0JK, Optional: 15 x 7.0JJ. Tires: H78 x 15 PC. Optional: HR78 x 15 Mud and Snow and HR78 steel belted radials. Steering: Type: Worm and Lever. Ratio: 24:1, 4.24. Turns Lock-to-Lock. Turning circle: 34 ft. Optional: Power steering with 17.5:1 ratio. Transmission: Type: 3-speed manual (synchromesh on top two gears). Ratios: 2.80, 1.85, 1.00:1. Optional: 4-speed manual transmission. Ratios: 4.02, 2.41, 1.41, 1.00:1. Optional: 3-speed automatic. Ratios: 2.45, 1.45, 1.00:1. Clutch: 11 in. dia. Optional: 11.0 in. angle link with 1800 lb. or 2000 lb. pressure.

VEHICLE DIMENSIONS: Wheelbase: 100 in. Overall Length: 165.8 in. Front/Rear Tread: 57.1 in./57.1 in. Overall Height: 65.2 in. Width: 70.0 in. Front/Rear Overhang: 27 in./39.5 in. Tailgate: Width and Height: 54.8 in. x 23 in. Approach/Departure Degrees: 42/21 degrees. Ground Clearance: Front axle: 8.2 in. Rear axle: 8.2 in. Oil pan: 13.7 in. Transfer case: 11.9 in. Fuel tank: 13.3 in. Exhaust system: 11.3 in. Load space: (with seats in place) 41 in. x 42 in. x 41.5 in.: (with rear seat folded): 59 in. x 42 in. x 41.5 in.

CAPACITIES: Fuel Tank: 19 gal. Engine coolant capacity: 4-cyl.: 10.50 qt., V-304: 19 qt., V-345: 20 qt.

ACCOMMODATIONS: Seating Capacity: Traveltop: 5, Cabtop: 2. Headroom: 36.0 in. Maximum Steering wheel to seat back: 22.5 in. Seat to ground: 32.0 in. Floor to ground: 17.2 in.

INSTRUMENTATION: 120 mph speedometer, odometer (reading to 99,999.9 mi.), gauges for fuel level, oil pressure, ammeter and engine coolant. Front axle engaged signal light.

OPTIONS AND PRICES: 304 cu. in. V-8: $99.00, 345 cu. in. V-8: $135.00. 4-spd. manual trans.: $125.00. 3-spd. automatic trans.: $269.00. Free running front hubs: Manual: $82.00, automatic: $120.00. Limited slip differential: $68.00. Power steering: $159.00. Heavy-duty front springs and shock absorbers: $10.00. Heavy-duty rear springs: $18.00. Heavy-duty rear step bumper with ball hitch (2000 lb. towing rating). Dealer-installed equalizer hitch receiver with 5,000 lb. towing capacity. 1/3-2/3 split back front bench seat: $40.00. Folding full-width rear bench seat: $136.00. Front bucket seats: $121.00. Custom Trim Package. Air conditioning. AM/FM radio. Roof rack. Tinted glass. Electric clock. Full instrumentation. Front and rear skid plates. Rear bumper. Steel belted radial tires. Mini-shelter.

HISTORICAL FOOTNOTES: The 1975 models debuted in the fall of 1984.

1976 SCOUT

1976 International Scout Traveler

The void left by International Harvester's decision to drop its full-sized pickup, Travelette and Travelall models was at least partially filled by the introduction of two important new four-wheel drive models, the Scout Terra pickup and the Scout Traveler. Keith P. Mazurek, president of International Harvester's Motor Truck Division explained the rationale behind these new models: "We have developed the vehicles for these times. Lower weight and economical engines will reduce the cost of owning the vehicles. Intermediate size will make them easy to operate. Yet, we have not taken out the truck-type durability and we are not offering vehicles which are austere.

"It is our goal to offer the customer a choice, something different, which is in line with present changes in what he wants in a vehicle. A large majority of our light trucks are purchased for personal transportation, not commercial use.

"Our successes with the Scout II models have convinced us of the importance of four-wheel drive in the personal use market. You can bet that four-wheel drive will be emphasized throughout our light-duty line from now on." As far as the recession of 1975-76 was concerned, Mr. Mazurek noted: "We can consider such a period as an opportunity to reassess our position and get our house in order."

1976 International Scout Terra

The new Terra and Traveler models were easily identified as Scout derivatives. Their status as intermediate-sized vehicles was achieved by adding 18 inches to the 100 in. wheelbase of the Scout. Both their width and height were identical to those of the Scout II. The Terra was fitted with a 6 foot pickup box. It also had 11 cu. ft. of storage space behind the split-back seat. The Traveler's station wagon-like body featured a large rear side window with sliding sections as well as a rear hatchback. The Traveler's top, constructed of steel reinforced fiberglass was removable. The hatchback Traveler had a load capacity of 2400 lbs. and was available with Class III trailer towing capability. The Terra's pickup box was of double-walled design. Like the Traveler the Terra had a load capacity of 2400 lbs. It had a GVW rating of 6200 lbs. An interesting engine option for both new Internationals as well as the Scout II was a 198 cu. in. 6-cylinder Nissan CN6-33 diesel engine. This engine had been used extensively in taxi cabs as well as an industrial stationary engine. All 1976 versions had a new grille design with three distinct sections each with five horizontal bars. Numerous side body appliques including white panels, woodgrain with cork finish, a fanciful "red feather" design as well as Rallye "racing stripes" that ran from the sides to the hood were offered. The Rallye Package for the Scout II included special exterior appliques, chrome wheels, AR78 steel belted white sidewall tires, heavy-duty shock absorbers and power steering. Standard equipment for the new Internationals included power front disc brakes, chrome front and rear bumpers, dual chrome door-mounted mirrors, manual locking hubs, increased engine cooling capacity and undercoating. The Scout II models were offered in any of nine exterior colors: Winter white, terra cotta, fire orange, dark brown metallic, solar yellow, pewter metallic, Grenoble green, buckskin and glacier blue. Interior appointments were available in ivy green, wedgewood blue, parchment, tanbark and custom saddle.

I.D. DATA: Unchanged from 1975 except diesel engine serial number located on left rear corner of cylinder head cover.

Body Type	Factory Price	GVW	Shipping Weight	Prod. Total
Scout II XLC				
Traveltop	$5594	6200	3843	—
Scout II XLC Diesel				
Traveltop	$8394	6200	4083	—
Terra XLC				
Terra Pickup	$5550	6200	3831	—
Terra XLC Diesel				
Terra Pickup	$8285	6200	4126	—
Traveler XLC				
Station Wagon	$5844	6200	4201	—
Traveler XLC Diesel				
Station Wagon	$8770	6200	4202	—

STANDARD ENGINE: Engine Type: OHV, In-line 4-cylinder, "Comanche H-196." Bore x Stroke: 4.125 in. x 3.656 in. Lifters: Hydraulic. Number of main bearings-5. Displacement: 196 cu. in. Carburetion: Model 1920 Holley. Compression Ratio: 8.02:1. Horsepower: 86 @ 3800 rpm. Torque: 157 lb.-ft. @ 2200 rpm. Fuel Requirements: low lead, unleaded or regular.

OPTIONAL ENGINE: Engine Type: OHV V-8, "Comanche V-304." Bore x Stroke: 3.875 in. x 3.218 in. Displacement: 304 cu. in. Carburetion: Model 2210C Holley. Compression Ratio: 8.19:1. Number of main bearings-5. Horsepower: 141 @ 4000 rpm. Torque: 243 lb.-ft. @ 2400 rpm. Fuel Requirements: low lead, unleaded or regular.

OPTIONAL ENGINE: Engine Type: OHV V-8, "V-345." Bore x Stroke: 3.875 in. x 3.656 in. Displacement: 345 cu. in. Carburetion: Model 2210 Holley, 2-barrel. Compression Ratio: 8.05:1. Number of main bearings-5. Horsepower: 140 @ 3800 rpm. Torque: 243 lb.-ft. @ 2400 rpm. Fuel Requirements: low lead, unleaded or regular.

OPTIONAL ENGINE: (International marketed the diesel-powered Scout, Terra and Traveler models as a separate model-option). Engine Type: OHV, In-line, 6-cylinder, Nissan CN6-33 Diesel. Bore x Stroke: 3.27 in. x 3.94 in. Displacement: 198 cu. in. Carburetion: Diesel Kiki mechanical fuel injection. Compression Ratio: 21:1. Valve lifters: Mechanical. Horsepower: 92 @ 4000 rpm. Torque: 137.5 lb.-ft. @ 2000 rpm. Fuel Requirements: Diesel. Engine weights: Diesel: (with standard accessories) 662 lbs.; 4-196: 476.5 lbs. (dry, less accessories); V-304: 617.6 lbs. (dry, less accessories); V-345: 640.6 lbs. (dry, less accessories).

CHASSIS FEATURES: Separate body and frame, ladder type frame.

SUSPENSION AND RUNNING GEAR: Front Suspension: Semi-elliptical 6-leaf springs, 2.0 in. x 40.0 in. Capacity: 3100 lb. Tubular shock absorbers. 1.0 in. stabilizer bar. Optional: Heavy-duty springs with 3200 lb. capacity, 1.1875 in. stabilizer bar. Rear Suspension: Semi-elliptical 4-leaf springs, 2.0 in. x 56.0 in. Capacity: 3100 lb. Tubular shock absorbers. Front Axle: FA-44, open Cardon. Capacity: 3200 lb. Rear Axle: Semi-floating, hypoid. Capacity: 3500 lb. Final Drive Ratio: 4.09:1. Optional: 3.07, 3.54:1. Transfer Case: TC-143 chain drive, single speed with dash mounted push-pull control. Optional: TC-145 2-speed, floor-mounted control. Ratios: 2.03, 1.00:1. Brakes: Type: Power hydraulic, Front 11.75 in. discs: 11.75 in. Rear 11 in. x 2.5 in. drums. Dimensions: Swept Area: 417 sq. in. Wheels: 15 x 6.0JK, Optional: 15 x 7.0JJ. Tires: H78 x 15 PC. Optional: HR78 x 15 Mud and Snow and HR78 steel belted radials. Steering: Type: Worm and Lever. Ratio: 24:1, 4.24. Turns Lock-to-Lock. Turning circle: 34 ft. Optional: Power steering with 17.5:1 ratio. Transmission: Type: 3-speed manual (synchromesh on top two gears). Ratios: 2.80, 1.85, 1.00:1. Optional: T-427, wide-ratio, 4-speed, all-synchromesh manual transmission. Ratios: 6.32, 3.09, 1.68, 1.00:1. Optional: T-428, close-ratio, all-synchromesh manual transmission. Ratios: 4.02, 2.41, 1.41, 1.00:1. Optional: 3-speed automatic. Ratios: 2.45, 1.45, 1.00:1. Clutch: 11 in. dia. Optional: 11.0 in. angle link with 1800 lb. or 2000 lb. pressure.

VEHICLE DIMENSIONS: Scout: Wheelbase: 100 in. Overall Length: 165.8 in. Front/Rear Tread: 57.1 in./57.1 in. Overall Height: 65.2 in. Width: 70.0 in. Front/Rear Overhang: 27 in./39.5 in. Tailgate: Width and Height: 54.8 in. x 23 in. Approach/Departure Degrees: 42/21 degrees. Ground Clearance: Front axle: 8.2 in. Rear axle: 8.2 in. Oil pan: 13.7 in. Transfer case: 11.9 in. Fuel tank: 13.3 in. Exhaust system: 11.3 in. Load space: (with seats in place) 41 in. x 42 in. x 41.5 in.: (with rear seat folded): 59 in. x 42 in. x 41.5 in.

VEHICLE DIMENSIONS: Traveler and Terra: Wheelbase: 118 in. Overall Length: 183.8 in. Front/Rear Tread: 57.1 in./57.1 in. Overall Height: 66.2 in. Width: 70.0 in. Front/Rear Overhang: 23.0 in./43.0 in. Tailgate: Width and Height: 54.8 in. x 21.3 in. Approach/Departure Degrees: 49/22 degrees. Ground Clearance: Front and rear axles: 8.2 in., 8.2 in. Oil pan: 13.7 in. Transfer case: 11.9 in. Fuel tank: 13.3 in. Exhaust system: 11.3 in. Load space: Terra: 72 in. x 54.8 in. x 19 in. Traveler: 78.8 in. x 25.2 in. x 54.8 in.

CAPACITIES: Fuel Tank: 19 gal. Engine coolant capacity: 4-cyl.: 10.50 qt. V-304: 19 qt., V-345: 20 qt.

ACCOMMODATIONS: Seating Capacity: Scout II, Traveler: 5, Terra: 2. Headroom: 36.0 in. Maximum Steering wheel to seat back: 22.5 in. Seat to ground: 32.0 in. Floor to ground: 17.2 in.

INSTRUMENTATION: 120 mph speedometer, odometer (reading to 99,999.9 mi.), gauges for fuel level, oil pressure, ammeter and engine coolant. Front axle engaged signal light.

Standard Catalog of American Four-Wheel Drive Vehicles

OPTIONS AND PRICES: Rallye Package: Scout II and Terra: $611.00, Traveler: 595.00. Power steering: $162.00. Automatic transmission (V-8 only): $279.00. 4-speed manual transmission: $155.00. Air conditioning: $462.00. Trailer Towing Package: $595.00. 304 cu. in. V-8: $156.00. 345 cu. in. V-8: $198.00. Diesel engine: $2648. Deluxe exterior trim: $234.00. Custom exterior trim: $357.00. 2-speed transfer case (standard with diesel): $67. Right-hand drive: $144. Custom Interior Package: Traveler: $221, Terra: $198, Traveler: $261. Radial Tire and Chrome Wheel Trim Package: $366. Deluxe Interior Trim Package: $134. California Emissions Package $80 with air pump, $39 without air pump. AM radio: $83. AM/FM radio: $185. Cruise control: $80. Console (available with bucket seat option only): $48. Electric clock: $24, Tilt steering wheel (standard on diesel models): $73. Door edge guards: $8. Bumper step with hitch ball: $37. Body side moldings; $31. Skid plate: $39. Automatic front locking hubs: $72. Dual exterior mirrors: $48. Luggage rack (not available for Terra): $92. Chrome tie down rails (Terra only): $71. 61 amp alternator: $42. Trac-Lok axle: $82. Optional axle ratios: $17. 72 amp battery: $19. Heavy-duty shock absorbers: $13. Heavy-duty front springs and shock absorbers: Traveltop: $17, Terra: $19. Heavy-duty rear springs and shock absorbers: Traveltop: $29. Heavy-duty front and rear springs and shock absorbers: Traveler: $38. Modulated fan: $41. Two tone paint: $115. Tan vinyl bucket seats: $79, other colors: $101. Rear folding seat (not available for Terra): $160. Cargo area mat (not available for Terra): $32. Sliding rear quarter window: Scout II: $51, Traveler: $56.

HISTORICAL FOOTNOTES: A total of 750 diesel-powered Scouts were sold in the 1976 model year.

1976 International Scout Diesel

1977 SCOUT

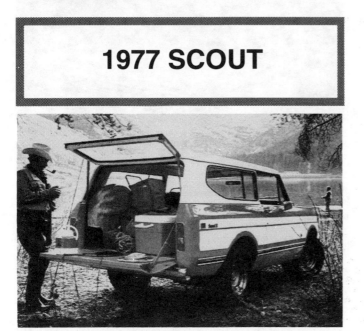
1977 International Scout II

International's carryover Scout Traveltop, Terra and Traveler models were given new grilles for 1977 with squared-off headlight nacelles and an insert with two vertically stacked narrow rectangular inserts. Of much greater interest was the addition of a new Scout SS II model. Based upon the discontinued 100 inch wheelbase Scout pickup the SS II had a unique black plastic grille insert with five vertical dividers. Both the front and rear bumpers were also painted black. No side doors or top were included in the base SS II model. A molded plastic insert covered the door jambs with optional fabric covered doors with metal frames fitted with snaps at the front end to minimize drafts was also offered. Another extra cost item was a Whitco vinyl top that could be completely removed or rolled up on the sides and rear. A sunroof was also available for this top. Included in the SS II's standard equipment was a 2-speed transfer case, 11.0 in. clutch, front stabilizer bar, padded dash, roll bar and a fuel tank skid plate. A special gold and black applique was offered as a special SS II option. All Scout models were offered in nine exterior colors for 1977: Siam yellow, fire orange, buckskin, winter white, Grenoble green, dark brown metallic, terra cotta, elk, and glacier blue. The interior trim color selection consisted of standard tanbark vinyl, saddle vinyl, parchment vinyl, tanbark vinyl/nylon and wedgewood lieu vinyl/nylon. The standard Scout II, Traveler and Terra interior included padded sun visors, tinted glass, 1/3/2/3 front seat, vinyl floor mats, and courtesy lights. It was available only in tanbark vinyl upholstery. The Deluxe interior added interior door trim panels, vinyl cargo and floor mats and vinyl spare tire cover. The custom interior added these items to the content of the Deluxe interior: cut pile carpeting, woodgrain instrument panel and door panel trim, padded steering wheel, custom steering wheel, and vinyl transmission cover pad. A creative dealer-installed option for the Terra pickup, the $250 Suntanner feature, replaced the fiberglass top with a convertible top. Extending over the pickup bed, this top gave the Terra a fastback profile.

I.D. DATA: Unchanged from 1976.

Body Type	Factory Price	GVW	Shipping Weight	Prod. Total
Scout II				
Traveltop	$5751	6200	3846	27,074[1]
Terra Pickup	$5637	6200	3861	2688[2]
Traveler	$6122	6200	4201	9620[3]
SS II	$5251	6200	N.A.	—
Scout II Diesel				
Traveltop	$8394	6200	4083	—
Terra Pickup	$8285	6200	4126	—
Traveler	$8770	6200	4466	—

NOTE 1: Total Scout II Traveltop and SS II production.
NOTE 2: Total Terra production.
NOTE 3: Total Traveler production.

STANDARD ENGINE: Engine Type: OHV, In-line 4-cylinder, "Comanche H-196." Bore x Stroke: 4.125 in. x 3.656 in. Lifters: Hydraulic. Number of main bearings-5. Displacement: 196 cu. in. Carburetion: Model 1920 Holley. Compression Ratio: 8.02:1. Horsepower: 86 @ 3800 rpm (California rating: 79 @ 3600 rpm). Torque: 157 lb.-ft. @ 2200 rpm (California rating: 155 lb.-ft. @ 2000 rpm). Fuel Requirements: leaded or unleaded.

OPTIONAL ENGINE: All Scout II models, except those for California delivery: Engine Type: OHV V-8, "Comanche V-304." Bore x Stroke: 3.875 in. x 3.218 in. Displacement: 304 cu. in. Carburetion: Model 2210C Holley. Compression Ratio: 8.19:1. Number of main bearings-5. Horsepower: 144 @ 3600 rpm. Torque: 247 lb.-ft. @ 2400 rpm. Fuel Requirements: leaded or unleaded.

OPTIONAL ENGINE: Engine Type: OHV V-8, "V-345." Bore x Stroke: 3.875 in. x 3.656 in. Displacement: 345 cu. in. Carburetion: Model 2210 Holley, 2-barrel. Compression Ratio: 8.05:1. Number of main bearings-5. Horsepower: 163 @ 3600 rpm (California rating: 146 @ 3600 rpm). Torque: 275 lb.-ft. @ 2000 rpm. Fuel Requirements: leaded or unleaded.

OPTIONAL ENGINE: All Scout II models except SS II: Engine Type: OHV, In-line, 6-cylinder, Nissan CN6-33 Diesel. Bore x Stroke: 3.27 in. x 3.94 in. Displacement: 198 cu. in. Carburetion: Diesel Kiki mechanical fuel injection. Compression Ratio: 21:1. Valve lifters: Mechanical. Horsepower: 92 @ 4000 rpm. Torque: 137.5 lb.-ft. @ 2000 rpm. Fuel Requirements: Diesel. Engine weights: Diesel: (with standard accessories) 662 lbs.; 4-196: 476.5 lbs. (dry, less accessories); V-304: 617.6 lbs. (dry, less accessories); V-345: 640.6 lbs. (dry, less accessories).

CHASSIS FEATURES: Separate body and frame, ladder type frame.

SUSPENSION AND RUNNING GEAR: Front Suspension: Semi-elliptical 6-leaf springs, 2.0 in. x 40.0 in. Capacity: 3100 lb. Tubular shock absorbers. 1.0 in. stabilizer bar. Optional: Heavy-duty springs with 3200 lb. capacity, 1.1875 in. stabilizer bar. Rear Suspension: Semi-elliptical 4-leaf springs, 2.0 in. x 56.0 in. Capacity: 3100 lb. Tubular shock absorbers. Optional: 3500 lb. with Trac-Lok. Front Axle: FA-44, open Cardon. Capacity: 3200 lb. Rear Axle: Semi-floating, hypoid. Capacity: 3500 lb. Final Drive Ratio: 4.09:1. Optional: 3.07, 3.54:1. Transfer Case: TC-143 chain drive, single speed with dash mounted push-pull control. Optional: TC-145 2-speed, floor-mounted control. Ratios: 2.03, 1.00:1. Brakes: Type: Power hydraulic, Front: 11.75 in. discs, Rear: 11.03 in. x 2.25 in. drums. Swept Area: 381 sq. in. Wheels: 15 x 6.0JK, Optional: 15 x 7.0JJ, 15 x 8.0JJ. Tires: H78 x 15B, Optional: HR78 x 15B, 7.00 x 15C, 10 x 15B. Ratio: 24:1, 4.24. Turns Lock-to-Lock. Turning circle: 33.8 ft. Optional: Power steering, 17.5:1 ratio. Transmission: Type: 3-speed, all-synchromesh manual. Transmission Ratios: 2.99, 1.55, 1.00:1. Clutch: 11.0 in. dia. Optional: 11 in. dia. heavy-duty angle link. Optional: T-427, wide-ratio, 4-speed, all-synchromesh manual transmission. Ratios: 6.32, 3.09, 1.68, 1.00:1. Optional: T-428, close-ratio, all-synchromesh manual transmission. Ratios: 4.02, 2.41, 1.41, 1.00:1. Optional: 3-speed automatic. Ratios: 2.45, 1.45, 1.00:1. Clutch: 11.0 in. dia. Optional: 11.0 in. heavy-duty angle link.

VEHICLE DIMENSIONS: Scout: Overall Length: 166.2 in. Front/Rear Tread: 57.1 in./67.1 in. Overall Height: 65.7 in. Width: 70.0 in. Front/Rear Overhang: 24 in./42.2 in. Tailgate: Width and Height: 54.8 in. x 21.1 in. Approach/Departure Degrees: 49/22. Ground Clearance: Front and rear axles: 8.4 in., 8.2 in. Oil pan: 14.1 in. Transfer case: 13.0 in. Fuel tank: 15.8 in. Exhaust system: 13.3 in. Load space: with seats in place: 40.5 in. x 42.1 in. x 43.7 in.; with rear seat folded or removed: 60.8 in. x 42.0 in. x 43.7 in.

VEHICLE DIMENSIONS: Traveler and Terra: Wheelbase: 118 in. Overall Length: 184.2 in. Front/Rear Tread: 57.1 in./57.1 in. Overall Height: 66.2 in. Width: 70.0 in. Front/Rear Overhang: 23.0 in./43.0 in. Tailgate: Width and Height: 54.8 in. x 21.3 in. Approach/Departure Degrees: 49/20 degrees. Ground Clearance: Front and rear axles: 8.2 in., 8.2 in. Oil pan: 13.7 in. Transfer case: 11.9 in. Fuel tank: 13.3 in. Exhaust system: 11.3 in. Load space: Terra: 72 in. x 54.8 in. x 19 in. Traveler: 78.8 in. x 25.2 in. x 54.8 in.

CAPACITIES: Fuel Tank: 19 gal. Engine coolant capacity: 4-cyl.: 10.50 qt. V-304: 19 qt., V-345: 20 qt.

ACCOMMODATIONS: Seating Capacity: Scout II, Traveler: 5, Terra: 2. Headroom: 36.0 in. Maximum Steering wheel to seat back: 22.5 in. Seat to ground: 32.0 in. Floor to ground: 17.2 in.

INSTRUMENTATION: 120 mph speedometer, odometer (reading to 99,999.9 mi.), gauges for fuel level, oil pressure, ammeter and engine coolant. Front axle engaged signal light.

OPTIONS AND PRICES: 304 cu. in. V-8: $166 (not available in California). 345 cu. in. V-8: $220. 4-speed manual transmission: $165. Automatic transmission: $306, (with diesel engine): $141. 2-speed transfer case (std. on SS II and diesel models): $67. Right hand drive: $144. Power steering: $206. Air conditioning: $497. Trailering Package: $183. Rallye Package: $648. Custom interior trim: Traveler: $261, Traveltop: $221, Terra: $198. Deluxe Interior Package: $134. Deluxe Exterior Trim Package: $60. Passenger front bucket seat (SS II): $95. Folding full-width rear bench seat (SS II): $170. Radial Tire/Chrome Wheel Package: $366. California Emission Package: with air pump $80, without air pump $39, AM radio: $80. AM/FM radio: $184. Cruise control: $80. Console (requires bucket seat option): $48. Electric clock: $24. Tilt steering wheel: (standard on diesel engine): $73. Door edge guards: $8. Rear bumper with hitch ball: $37. Body side molding: $31. Skid plate protector: $39. Manual free running front hubs: $104. Automatic front locking hubs: $72. "Trac-Lok" limited slip differential: $82. Dual exterior mirrors: $48. Luggage rack (not available for Terra and SS II): $92. Chrome pickup box tie-downs (Terra only): $70. Optional axle ratios: $17. Heavy-duty front and rear shock absorbers: SS II: $25. Heavy-duty front springs and shock absorbers: Traveltop: $17. Heavy-duty rear springs and shock absorbers: Traveltop: $29. Heavy-duty front and rear springs and shock absorbers: Traveler: $38. Modulated fan: $41. Two-tone paint: $115. Tan vinyl bucket seats: $79, other colors: $101. Cargo area mat: $32 (not available for Terra). Sliding rear quarter window: Traveltop: $51, Traveler: $66.

1977 International Scout Traveler

1978 SCOUT

1978 International Scout Terra

The grille found on all Scouts except for the SS II model was slightly revised for 1978. The small vertical bars used in 1977 were removed while the bright metal surround was of increased thickness. The twin internal grille loops were continued from 1977. Rather than classifying the diesel-engined Scouts as separate models, International Harvester simply listed the Nissan-built diesel as an extra cost option in 1978. The tape stripe options were slightly revised for 1978. The stripes included in the Rallye Package now included two narrow white stripes extending the full length of the body. Nine colors, including four new tones were offered for 1978: Winter white, Siam yellow, elk, woodbine green, embassy grey, Concord blue, dark brown metallic and rallye gold.

1978 International Scout Traveler

I.D. DATA: The vehicle model was stamped on a plate located on the right door hinge pillar. The engine serial number was stamped on the left side, upper front of the crankcase on 4-cylinder engines and on the right bank, upper right on V-8 engines. The chassis serial number was located on the front of the frame's left side rail. The transmission number, front axle number and rear axle number were found on the vehicle specification card.

Body Type	Factory Price	GVW	Shipping Weight	Prod. Total
Scout XLC Series				
Traveler	$6546	6200	4059	—
Traveltop	$6153	6200	3705	—
Terra Pickup	$6068	6200	3720	—
SS II	$5387	6200	3314	—

Total Scout sales for 1978 were 23,610 of which 21,192 were powered by V-8 engines.

STANDARD ENGINE: Engine Type: OHV, In-line 4-cylinder, "Comanche H-196." Bore x Stroke: 4.125 in. x 3.656 in. Lifters: Hydraulic. Number of main bearings-5. Displacement: 196 cu. in. Carburetion: Model 1920 Holley. Compression Ratio: 8.02:1. Horsepower: 86 @ 3800 rpm (California rating: 79 @ 3600 rpm). Torque: 157 lb.-ft. @ 2200 rpm (California rating: 155 lb.-ft. @ 2000 rpm). Fuel Requirements: leaded or unleaded.

OPTIONAL ENGINE: All Scout II models, except those for California delivery: Engine Type: OHV V-8, "Comanche V-304." Bore x Stroke: 3.875 in. x 3.218 in. Displacement: 304 cu. in. Carburetion: Model 2210C Holley. Compression Ratio: 8.19:1. Number of main bearings-5. Horsepower: 144 @ 3600 rpm. Torque: 247 lb.-ft. @ 2400 rpm. Fuel Requirements: leaded or unleaded.

OPTIONAL ENGINE: Engine Type: OHV V-8, "V-345." Bore x Stroke: 3.875 in. x 3.656 in. Displacement: 345 cu. in. Carburetion: Model 2210 Holley, 2-barrel. Compression Ratio: 8.05:1. Number of main bearings-5. Horsepower: 163 @ 3600 rpm (California rating: 146 @ 3600 rpm). Torque: 275 lb.-ft. @ 2000 rpm. Fuel Requirements: leaded or unleaded.

OPTIONAL ENGINE: All Scout II models except SS II: Engine Type: OHV, In-line, 6-cylinder, Nissan CN6-33 Diesel. Bore x Stroke: 3.27 in. x 3.94 in. Displacement: 198 cu. in. Carburetion: Diesel Kiki mechanical fuel injection. Compression Ratio: 21:1. Valve lifters: Mechanical. Horsepower: 92 @ 4000 rpm. Torque: 137.5 lb.-ft. @ 2000 rpm. Fuel Requirements: Diesel. Engine weights: Diesel: (with standard accessories) 662 lbs.; 4-196: 476.5 lbs. (dry, less accessories); V-304: 617.6 lbs. (dry, less accessories); V-345: 640.6 lbs. (dry, less accessories).

1978 International Scout SSII

CHASSIS FEATURES: Separate body and frame, ladder type frame.

SUSPENSION AND RUNNING GEAR: Front Suspension: Semi-elliptical 6-leaf springs, 2.0 in. x 40.0 in. Capacity: 3100 lb. Tubular shock absorbers. 1.0 in. stabilizer bar. Optional: Heavy-duty springs with 3200 lb. capacity, 1.1875 in. stabilizer bar. Rear Suspension: Semi-elliptical 4-leaf springs, 2.0 in. x 56.0 in. Capacity: 3100 lb. Tubular shock absorbers. Optional: Heavy-duty progressive springs with 3100 lb. capacity, 3500 lb. with Trac-Lok. Front Axle: FA-44, open Cardon. Capacity: 3200 lb. Rear Axle: Semi-floating, hypoid. Capacity: 3500 lb. Final Drive Ratio: 4-cyl. engine with 3-spd. and 4-spd. wide ratio manual transmission: 4.09:1, 4-cyl. with close ratio 4-spd. manual trans.: 3.54:1. 304 and 345 V-8 with 3-spd. and 4-spd. wide ratio manual trans.: 3.54:1; with 4-spd. close ratio manual trans. and 3-spd. auto. trans.: 3.07:1. Diesel engine with 4-spd. wide ratio manual trans.: 4.09:1, with 4-spd. close ratio 4-spd. manual trans.: 3.73:1. Optional: 4-cyl. with 4-spd. wide ratio manual trans.: 3.54, 3.73:1. 4-cyl. with 4-spd. close ratio manual trans.: 3.73, 4.09:1. 304 and 345 V-8 with 3-spd. manual and 4-spd. wide ratio manual trans.: 3.73, 4.09:1 (304 V-8 only), 304 an 345 V-8 with 4-spd. close ratio manual trans. and 3-spd. auto trans.: 3.54, 3.73, 4.09:1 (304 V-8 only). Diesel engine with 4-spd. wide ratio manual trans.: 3.73:1, with 4-spd. close ratio 4-spd. manual trans.: 4.09:1. Transfer Case: TC-143 chain drive, single speed with dash mounted push-pull control. Optional: TC-145 2-speed, floor-mounted control. Ratios: 2.03, 1.00:1. Brakes: Type: Power hydraulic, Front: 11.75 in. discs, Rear: 11.03 in. x 2.25 in. drums. Dimensions: Swept Area: 381 sq. in. Wheels: 15 x 6.0JK, Optional: 15 x 7.0JJ, 15 x 8.0JJ. Tires: H78 x 15B, Optional: HR78 x 15B, 7.00 x 15C, 10 x 15B. Ratio: 24:1, 4.24. Turns Lock-to-Lock. Turning circle: 33.8 ft. Optional: Power steering, 17.5:1 ratio. Transmission: Type: 3-speed, all-synchromesh manual. Transmission Ratios: 2.99, 1.55, 1.00:1. Clutch: 11.0 in. dia. Optional: 11 in. dia. heavy-duty angle link. Optional: T-427, wide-ratio, 4-speed, all-synchromesh manual transmission. Ratios: 6.32, 3.09, 1.68, 1.00:1. Optional: T-428, close-ratio, all-synchromesh manual transmission. Ratios: 4.02, 2.41, 1.41, 1.00:1. Optional: 3-speed automatic. Ratios: 2.45, 1.45, 1.00:1. Clutch: 11.0 in. dia. Optional: 11.0 in. heavy-duty angle link.

VEHICLE DIMENSIONS: Scout: Overall Length: 166.2 in. Front/Rear Tread: 57.1 in./67.1 in. Overall Height: 65.7 in. Width: 70.0 in. Front/Rear Overhang: 24 in./42.2 in. Tailgate: Width and Height: 54.8 in. x 21.1 in. Approach/Departure Degrees: 49/22. Ground Clearance: Front and rear axles: 8.4 in., 8.2 in. Oil pan: 14.1 in. Transfer case: 13.0 in. Fuel tank: 15.8 in. Exhaust system: 13.3 in. Load space: with seats in place: 40.5 in. x 42.1 in. x 43.7 in.; with rear seat folded or removed: 60.8 in. x 42.0 in. x 43.7 in.

VEHICLE DIMENSIONS: Traveler and Terra: Wheelbase: 118 in. Overall Length: 184.2 in. Front/Rear Tread: 57.1 in./57.1 in. Overall Height: 66.2 in. Width: 70.0 in. Front/Rear Overhang: 23.0 in./43.0 in. Tailgate: Width and Height: 54.8 in. x 21.3 in. Approach/Departure Degrees: 49/20 degrees. Ground Clearance: Front and rear axles: 8.2 in., 8.2 in. Oil pan: 13.7 in. Transfer case: 11.9 in. Fuel tank: 13.3 in. Exhaust system: 11.3 in. Load space: Terra: 72 in. x 54.8 in. x 19 in. Traveler: 78.8 in. x 25.2 in. x 54.8 in.

CAPACITIES: Fuel Tank: 19 gal. Engine coolant capacity: 4-cyl.: 10.50 qt. V-304: 19 qt., V-345: 20 qt.

ACCOMMODATIONS: Seating Capacity: Scout II, Traveler: 5, Terra: 2. Headroom: 36.0 in. Maximum Steering wheel to seat back: 22.5 in. Seat to ground: 32.0 in. Floor to ground: 17.2 in.

INSTRUMENTATION: 120 mph speedometer, odometer (reading to 99,999.9 mi.), gauges for fuel level, oil pressure, ammeter and engine coolant. Front axle engaged signal light.

OPTIONS AND PRICES: Most options were unchanged from 1977. Front passenger bucket seat (SS II): $95. Folding rear full-width rear bench seat (SS II, Traveler and Traveltop): $170. 304 cu. in. V-8: $176. 345 cu. in. V-8: $234. Diesel engine: $2581. T-427 4-speed manual transmission: $152. T-428 4-speed manual transmission: $165. Automatic transmission: $324. Free running front hubs: $104. Limited slip differential: $87. Power steering: $206. Heavy-duty front and rear shock absorbers: $25. Heavy-duty front springs and shock absorbers: $37. Heavy-duty rear springs and shocks: $50. Air conditioning: $544. Rallye Package: Traveler: $687.

HISTORICAL FOOTNOTES: The 1978 models were announced in the fall of 1977.

1979 SCOUT

1979 International Scout Terra

No significant design changes took place in the Scout models for 1979. The 1979 Scout Traveler was not offered with the Comanche 4-cylinder engine. The exterior color selection for 1979 consisted of winter white, sunburst yellow, persimmon, embassy grey, Lexington blue, mint green, dark brown metallic, rallye gold and Tahitian red metallic. A new Sport dash option was available either with the Custom or Deluxe Interior Trim Packages. New inner door trim panels with carpeting and map pockets was now part of the Custom Interior Trim Package. The interior colors for 1979 were black, tan, russet and highland blue. The standard vinyl interior was offered in black only.

I.D. DATA: The vehicle model was stamped on a plate located on the right door hinge pillar. The engine serial number was stamped on the left side, upper front of the crankcase on 4-cylinder engines and on the right bank, upper right on V-8 engines. The chassis serial number was located on the front of the frame's left side rail. The transmission number, front axle number and rear axle number were found on the vehicle specification card.

1979 International Scout II

Body Type	Factory Price	GVW	Shipping Weight	Prod. Total
Scout II with 304 V-8				
Traveler	$7657	6200	4200	—
Traveltop	$7212	6200	3846	—
Terra Pickup	$7263	6200	3861	—
SS II	$6406	6200	3314	—

STANDARD ENGINE: All models except Traveler: Engine Type: OHV, In-line 4-cylinder, "Comanche 4-196." Bore x Stroke: 4.125 in. x 3.656 in. Lifters: Hydraulic. Number of main bearings-5. Displacement: 196 cu. in. Carburetion: Model 1920 Holley. Compression Ratio: 8.02:1. Horsepower: 76.5 @ 3600 rpm. Torque: 153.3 lb.-ft. @ 2000 rpm. Fuel Requirements: Unleaded.

OPTIONAL ENGINE: All Scout II models, except those for California delivery: Standard for Traveler, except for those for California delivery. Engine Type: OHV V-8, "Comanche V-8 304A." Bore x Stroke: 3.875 in. x 3.218 in. Displacement: 304 cu. in. Carburetion: Model 2210C Holley. Compression Ratio: 8.19:1. Number of main bearings-5. Horsepower: 122.3 @ 3400 rpm. Torque: 226.3 lb.-ft. @ 2000 rpm. Fuel Requirements: Unleaded.

OPTIONAL ENGINE: Engine Type: OHV V-8, "V-8 345A." Bore x Stroke: 3.875 in. x 3.656 in. Displacement: 345 cu. in. Carburetion: Model 2210 Holley, 2-barrel. Compression Ratio: 8.05:1. Number of main bearings-5. Horsepower: 148 @ 3600 rpm. Torque: 265 lb.-ft. @ 2000 rpm. Fuel Requirements: Unleaded.

OPTIONAL ENGINE: All Scout II models except SS II: Engine Type: OHV, In-line, 6-cylinder, Nissan CN6-33 Diesel. Bore x Stroke: 3.27 in. x 3.94 in. Displacement: 198 cu. in. Carburetion: Diesel Kiki mechanical fuel injection. Compression Ratio: 22:1. Valve lifters: Mechanical. Horsepower: 81 @ 3800 rpm. Torque: 138 lb.-ft. @ 1200-1600 rpm. Fuel Requirements: Diesel. Engine weights: Diesel: (with standard accessories) 662 lbs.; 4-196: 476.5 lbs. (dry, less accessories); V-304: 617.6 lbs. (dry, less accessories); V-345: 640.6 lbs. (dry, less accessories).

1979 International Scout SSII

CHASSIS FEATURES: Separate body and frame, ladder type frame.

SUSPENSION AND RUNNING GEAR: Front Suspension: Semi-elliptical 6-leaf springs, 2.0 in. x 40.0 in. Capacity: 3100 lb. Tubular shock absorbers. 1.0 in. stabilizer bar. Optional: Heavy-duty springs with 3200 lb. capacity, 1.1875 in. stabilizer bar. Rear Suspension: Semi-elliptical 4-leaf springs, 2.0 in. x 56.0 in. Capacity: 3100 lb. Tubular shock absorbers. Optional: Heavy-duty progressive springs with 3100 lb. capacity, 3500 lb. with Trac-Lok. Front Axle: FA-44, open Cardon. Capacity: 3200 lb. Rear Axle: Semi-floating, hypoid. Capacity: 3500 lb. Final Drive Ratio: 4-cyl. engine with 3-spd. and 4-spd. wide ratio manual transmission: 4.09:1, 4-cyl. with close ratio 4-spd. manual trans.: 3.54:1. 304 and 345 V-8 with 3-spd. and 4-spd. wide ratio manual trans.: 3.54:1; with 4-spd. close ratio manual trans. and 3-spd. auto. trans.: 3.07:1. Diesel engine with 4-spd. wide ratio manual trans.: 4.09:1, with 4-spd. close ratio 4-spd. manual trans.: 3.73:1. Optional: 4-cyl. with 4-spd. wide ratio manual trans.: 3.54, 3.73:1. 4-cyl. with 4-spd. close ratio manual trans.: 3.73, 4.09:1. 304 and 345 V-8 with 3-spd. manual and 4-spd. wide ratio manual trans.: 3.73, 4.09:1 (304 V-8 only), 304 an 345 V-8 with 4-spd. close ratio manual trans. and 3-spd.: auto trans.: 3.54, 3.73, 4.09:1 (304 V-8 only). Diesel engine with 4-spd. wide ratio manual trans.: 3.73:1, with 4-spd. close ratio 4-spd. manual trans.: 4.09:1. Transfer Case: TC-143 chain drive, single speed with dash mounted push-pull control. Optional: TC-145 2-speed, floor-mounted control. Ratios: 2.03, 1.00:1. Brakes: Type: Power hydraulic, Front: 11.75 in. discs, Rear: 11.03 in. x 2.25 in. drums. Dimensions: Swept Area: 381 sq. in. Wheels: 15 x 6.0JK, Optional: 15 x 7.0JJ, 15 x 8.0JJ. Tires: H78 x 15B, Optional: HR78 x 15B, 7.00 x 15C, 10 x 15B. Ratio: 24:1, 4.24. Turns Lock-to-Lock. Turning circle: 33.8 ft. Optional: Power steering, 17.5:1 ratio. Transmission: Type: 3-speed, all-synchromesh manual. Transmission Ratios: 2.99, 1.55, 1.00:1. Clutch: 11.0 in. dia. Optional: 11 in. dia. heavy-duty angle link. Optional: T-427, wide-ratio, 4-speed, all-synchromesh manual transmission. Ratios: 6.32, 3.09, 1.68, 1.00:1. Optional: T-428, close-ratio, all-synchromesh manual transmission. Ratios: 4.02, 2.41, 1.41, 1.00:1. Optional: 3-speed automatic. Ratios: 2.45, 1.45, 1.00:1. Clutch: 11.0 in. dia. Optional: 11.0 in. heavy-duty angle link.

VEHICLE DIMENSIONS: Scout: Overall Length: 166.2 in. Front/Rear Tread: 57.1 in./67.1 in. Overall Height: 65.7 in. Width: 70.0 in. Front/Rear Overhang: 24 in./42.2 in. Tailgate: Width and Height: 54.8 in. x 21.1 in. Approach/Departure Degrees: 49/22. Ground Clearance: Front and rear axles: 8.4 in., 8.2 in. Oil pan: 14.1 in. Transfer case: 13.0 in. Fuel tank: 15.8 in. Exhaust system: 13.3 in. Load space: with seats in place: 40.5 in. x 42.1 in. x 43.7 in.; with rear seat folded or removed: 60.8 in. x 42.0 in. x 43.7 in.

VEHICLE DIMENSIONS: Traveler and Terra: Wheelbase: 118 in. Overall Length: 184.2 in. Front/Rear Tread: 57.1 in./57.1 in. Overall Height: 66.2 in. Width: 70.0 in. Front/Rear Overhang: 23.0 in./43.0 in. Tailgate: Width and Height: 54.8 in. x 21.3 in. Approach/Departure Degrees: 49/20 degrees. Ground Clearance: Front and rear axles: 8.2 in., 8.2 in. Oil pan: 13.7 in. Transfer case: 11.9 in. Fuel tank: 13.3 in. Exhaust system: 11.3 in. Load space: Terra: 72 in. x 54.8 in. x 19 in. Traveler: 78.8 in. x 25.2 in. x 54.8 in.

CAPACITIES: Fuel Tank: 19 gal. Engine coolant capacity: 4-cyl.: 10.50 qt. V-304: 19 qt., V-345: 20 qt.

ACCOMMODATIONS: Seating Capacity: Scout II, Traveler: 5, Terra: 2. Headroom: 36.0 in. Maximum Steering wheel to seat back: 22.5 in. Seat to ground: 32.0 in. Floor to ground: 17.2 in.

INSTRUMENTATION: 120 mph speedometer, odometer (reading to 99,999.9 mi.), gauges for fuel level, oil pressure, ammeter and engine coolant. Front axle engaged signal light.

OPTIONS AND PRICES: Except for a new Sport steering wheel and an AM/FM stereo radio with 8-track tape player, Scout options were unchanged from 1978.

HISTORICAL FOOTNOTES: The 1979 models were announced in the fall of 1977.

1979 International Scout Traveler

1980 SCOUT

The final year of Scout production, a condition prompted more by International's severe financial difficulties rather than the Scout's relative lack of popularity, was highlighted by significant technical developments as well as mild appearance refinements. The latter development consisted of a new black outlined grille, a black bumper, rectangular headlights, new side body appliques and six new exterior colors. The side body trim options included "Spear", "See-Thru Flare" and "Rallye." The Traveler was offered with a woodgrain trim pattern. The six new body colors included black canyon, copper, dark brown, saffron yellow, green metallic and Concord blue. International also expended a fair amount of attention to the Scout's interior in an effort to update its appearance and functional value. A 15 inch styled steering wheel replaced the older 17 inch unit (a 15 inch padded version was also offered as an option). Replacing the previously used simulated wood plastic dash cover was a satin finish metal facia. Also apparent were new speedometer mph designations reading from 0 to 85 mph/140 kph. The controls and ducts of the optional air conditioning system (which was also redesigned for quieter operation) were also revised. All Scout models now had power steering as standard equipment. The 3-speed automatic transmission that was optional for gasoline powered Scouts was standard on the Traveler with either its standard 304 cu. in. V-8 or optional 345 cu. in. V-8. No longer offered was the SS II model. The front and rear tread of the Scout models was now 58.5 in. and 57.62 in.

Significant improvements were made in the Scout's corrosion protection. A zinc rich primer was installed on the hood, front fender and tailgate seams, windshield frame and drip molding joints. Galvanized steel was used for the lower grille, rear inner quarter panels, quarter panel end caps, fillers and splash shields. A Zincrometal treatment was applied to the outer doors, inner and outer tailgate, outer windshield frame sides and outer rear quarter panels. The tailgate, quarter panels and caps, and doors were given a hot wax covering. Replacing the previously used Dana 20 transfer case was a new Dana 300 unit. It had a lower low range ratio of 2.62: 1 instead of 2.02:1. With a weight of 70 pounds it was also somewhat lighter than the older model. International also revised the axle ratio availability for the Scout. Those with V-8 engines were offered with either 2.72:1 or 3.31:1. The 3.54:1 axle from 1979 was an extra cost

item for both the 304 and 345 cu. in. V-8 engines with the 3.73:1 gears listed only in conjunction with the 345 cu. in. V-8 and the extra cost Trailer Towing Package. The rating of the International gasoline engines was unchanged from 1979 except for the horsepower output of the 345 cu. in. V-8 which was now cited as 150 @ 3600 rpm. The standard engine for the Traveltop and Terra was the 196 cu. in. 4-cylinder. The Traveler's standard engine was the 304 cu. in. V-8.

Along with the familiar V-8 and 4-cylinder engine choices for the Scout International continued to offer its customers a diesel engine option. But for 1980 this engine took on a new character by virtue of its turbocharger. To cope with the additional stress resulting from the turbocharger's 6.5 pounds of manifold pressure the diesel, now identified as the 6-33T, differed in many ways from its predecessor, the 6-33, which was no longer offered as a Scout option. During each engine cycle a jet of oil was sprayed over the top of each piston for cooling purposes. To meet the requirements of this process and to also properly lubricate the turbocharger the diesel's oil capacity was increased to 9.2 qts. from the previous 8 qt. level. A new higher capacity oil pump provided an oil flow of 12.7 gallons per minute as compared to the older pump's rate of 11.1 gallons per minute. The oil pump drive spindle was also strengthened. Other revisions included use of larger camshaft journals, redesigned crankshaft arms, larger cylinder head ports, an oil cooler with five instead of three cores and a larger air cleaner element. The turbocharged diesel with ratings of 101 horsepower @ 3800 rpm and 178 lb.-ft. of torque @ 2200 rpm was approximately 20 percent more powerful than the older diesel. International's confidence both about the durability of the 6-33T diesel and the effectiveness of its anti-corrosion program was manifested by its five year or 100,000 mile limited engine durability and anti-corrosion warranty. The turbocharged diesel was optional in all four Scout models and its list price of $2496 included a large capacity battery, tilt wheel and either the close or wide-ratio 4-speed manual transmission. Standard axle ratio for the diesel was 3.73:1 with 3.54:1 optional. Diesel Scouts were not available with an automatic transmission.

1980 Scout II

I.D. DATA: Unchanged from 1979.

Body Type	Factory Price	GVW	Shipping Weight	Prod. Total
Scout				
Traveler	$8783	6200	4201	—
Traveltop	$7748	6200	3699	—
Terra Pickup	7649	6200	3723	—

OPTIONS AND PRICES: Diesel engine (includes large battery, tilt wheel, close-ratio 4-spd. manual transmission and power steering): $2496; for Traveler: $1773. 304 cu. in. V-8: $368. 345 cu. in. V-8: $499. 4-spd. close-ratio manual transmission (this transmission could be ordered for the diesel-powered Scout at no extra cost): $216. 4-spd. wide-ratio manual transmission: $172. 3-spd. automatic transmission: $392. Limited slip differential: $199. Front axle Lock-O-Matic hubs: $97. Heavy-duty front springs: $42. Heavy-duty rear springs: $58. AM/FM radio: $167, AM/FM radio with tape player: $358. Spare tire lock: $8.75. Spear applique (Traveler): $125. Woodgrain applique (Traveler): $199. Off-Road Trim and Rim Package: $505. Clutch with continuous 11 inch angle: $16.50. California smoke exhaust certification diesel: $222. Custom interior trim (Traveler): $325. Deluxe Exterior Trim Package (Traveler): $161. Sliding rear quarter windows (Traveler): $104. Luggage rack (Traveler): $116. Fold down rear bench seat (Traveler): $266. Air conditioning: $607. Dual exterior low profile mirrors: $59.

HISTORICAL FOOTNOTES: Scout production ceased on October 31, 1980 after a production run of 523,674 units. A group of investors lead by Mr. Ed Russell had unsuccessfully attempted to raise sufficient capital to purchase the Scout's tooling and possibly relocate the Scout production line in South Bend, Indiana. In mid-1978 International had shown what it depicted as a replacement for the Scout, scheduled to begin production in 1981. It would have used the existing Scout drivetrain but its lightweight non-steel body would have dramatically reduced overall weight.

JEEP

It's impossible for any discussion of four-wheel drive vehicles to take place without Jeep being a focus of the conversation. Debuting in 1945 in civilian form, the first CJ Jeeps seemed out of step with the predictions offered by critics during the war of a new era of automotive sophistication. The postwar cars, we were told, would be streamlined things devoid of familiar automotive forms, bedecked with fins possessing huge expanses of glass and powered by some form of technical exotica that would propel machine and occupants at previously unimagined speeds.

What visitors to Willys-Overland dealers saw in the summer of 1945 was a machine that was arguably the ultimate expression of form following function. Time has honored those CJ Jeeps as worthy of being regarded as Classics. This perspective gains full credence if we accept the view that such an item is of lasting significance and a model of its kind. As early as 1951, the Jeep's special status in automotive history was recognized by the Museum of Modern Art. In that year the museum held a special exhibit of vehicles it deemed as the most significant prewar examples of styling. In such an atmosphere of high-powered marques as Lincoln and Mercedes-Benz was a Jeep.

Foremost a utilitarian vehicle, the Jeep, in its initial civilian form, didn't displace the tractor or farm truck from American agriculture. But it did fill a long-empty niche for a vehicle that was versatile, reliable, tough and at home on or off the road.

The producer of the Jeep, Willys-Overland, had at one time been America's second largest automotive producer, but that had been many years earlier, in 1912. Several years prior to that time, in 1909, John North Willys had gained control of the Overland Company which itself dated back to 1903. Willys-Overland, under Mr. Willys exhibited considerable alacrity during the Boom and Rush years of the 1920s. Products such as the sleeve-valve Willys-Knight cars and the four and six-cylinder Whippets maintained Willys' competitive edge as manifested by its third place in production, with an output of 320,000 vehicles, behind Ford and Chevrolet in 1928.

John North Willys, served as American Ambassador to Poland in 1929. Within three years he returned to a position of active control of Willys-Overland. The company he rejoined had been ravaged by the Depression to the point of near-annihilation. Willys, sometimes characterized as susceptible to grandiose schemes and excessive displays of industrial opulence, counterattacked with a sensible, low-cost vehicle. This common sense approach to the depression was not original with Willys. Nearly every automotive manufacturer realigned its product line in a search for the increasingly elusive new car buyer. But Willys' effort resulted in an excellent automobile, the Willys 77. Competitive, pricewise, with the neo-midget American Austin, the Willys 77 quickly demonstrated that its performance was full-size by averaging 65.6 mph for 24 hours at the Muroc dry lakes in California.

John North Willys' death in 1935 marked the start of another segment of his company's life. Following a time of financial restructuring, Willys-Overland, now under the control of Ward Canaday and George Ritter, had as its chief engineer, Delmar Roos. Possessed of extraordinary talent and a huge reservoir of engineering experience, Roos' skills was linked to the market acumen of Joseph W. Frazer who became Willys-Overland president in 1939. In 1941 the model 441 Willys-Overland, touted as the "lowest-priced full-sized car in the world" was introduced. But few, except for Willys-Overland devotees, recall much about that vehicle. What was about to unfold as the result of the military's quest for a new multi-purpose four-wheel drive transport, was the quintessential Willys product.

The relative merits of the prototypes offered by Ford, Bantam and Willys to the military for evaluation, not to mention the true design origin of what became the Jeep, has long been debated by Historians. Setting this point of disputation aside, the result of the competition, a major contract for Willys-Overland, changed the course not only of military history, but also of American automotive history. The MA and MB military Jeeps established a world-wide reputation for toughness, versatility and dependability. They were recognized as one of the most significant weapons of the war, and at war's end Willys-Overland, a company that had seemed to have little chance of surviving the depression, was poised to offer the American public the world's first low-cost, mass-produced four-wheel drive vehicle.

In the free-wheeling and at times frantic automotive market of the early postwar years, Willys-Overland made the most of the Jeep's solid gold reputation. The CJ Jeep was soon followed by the Willys station wagon and truck models. With their physical and technical kinship to the Jeep readily apparent, their down-to earth format was a refreshing alternative to the conventional products offered by other American manufacturers.

But this did not make Willys-Overland immune to the highly competitive market forces buffeting the industry as the postwar seller's market dried up. At least in part, influenced by this situation, was the 1953 purchase of Willys-Overland by Kaiser-Frazer. The short-lived Aero Willys was soon dropped but the stalwart of Willys, its Jeep vehicles, went from strength to strength. To cite just one example: In 1953 Willys was the third largest exporter of commercial vehicles from the United States. As the Fifties fade into the Sixties the market for what would soon be called recreational vehicles emerged. While some purists bewailed the loss of the CJ Jeep's absolute and uncompromising commitment to farm and country, the appeal of the CJ, to a much larger buyer pool as it evolved into various forms and formats, was of greater consequence. In retrospect, it is apparent that was precisely this type of evolution that was essential to the survival of the marque. A similar, and equally important metamorphic transformation of sorts took place with the Wagoneer. Introduced in 1963 it assumed a life (that seemed for a time to have no bounds) of its own, growing and maturing into a vehicle that opened the vistas of four-wheel drive to owners who had at that time viewed the combination of an automatic transmission, luxurious appointments and full-time four-wheel drive operation, as an irreconcilable contradiction.

There were a few exclusions on four-wheel drive sideroads that were of short duration, the revived Jeepster model, for example. But the mainstream of Jeep product design was highly focused and extremely successful. The Cherokee was a stroke of pure genius, the replacement of the CJ by the Wrangler, if tainted by sentiment and emotionalism over the loss of an old and faithful friend, was appropriate. And as the last decade of the Twentieth Century gained a full head of steam, the Jeep marque, now under the Chrysler pentastar made ready a new generation of Grand Cherokee and Grand Wagoneer models. Introduced as a 1993 model, the new Grand Cherokee and its running mate, the new generation Grand Wagoneer with their available 5.2 liter, 220 horsepower V-8s, will likely bring more honor to this uniquely American marque.

JEEP CJ/WRANGLER SERIES
1945-1993

1945 CJ

The first civilian Jeep, the CJ-2A, differed in many ways from its military predecessors. Not the least of these differences were its power take-off, revised transmission, transfer case and axle gear ratios, and shorter overall length, from front bumper to spare tire, of 130.125 in. due to the relocation of the spare tire mount to the driver's side.

The CJ transmission, a Warner Gear model T090A, was of a larger size than that used for the MB. It had a special rear mainshaft and side-mounted shifting levers to allow for a column-mounted shift lever.

Additional specifications included a 6-volt electrical system and an 11 quart cooling capacity. A radiator shroud was also installed to improve engine cooling at low speeds. During the production life of the CJ-2A numerous changes were introduced. Up to serial number 27926 and serial number 48658 through 48707 the shock absorbers could be disassembled for refilling. After serial number 27926 and in the interval noted they were sealed. The CJ-2A engine's 4-bearing camshaft was driven by a silent type timing chain up to serial number 44417. After that point all CJ-2A engines were equipped with gear driven camshafts. CJ-2A engines with timing gears had a J prefix added to their engine numbers. Beginning with CJ-2A engine number 62054 a double baffle was added to the timing cover case, the oil seal was changed from braided asbestos to a spring loaded leather seal. The fan pulley was also changed to provide a polished surface at the seal contact. This change was made to more effectively prevent dirt and grit from entering the engine. Up to CJ-2A engine number 55137 the drop forged steel crankshaft was built with its four counterweights forged as an integral part of the shaft. After that point the counterweights were independently forged and attached to the shaft with a dowel and cap screw. Initially an AC model 153886 fuel pump was used on CJ-2A's up to serial number 16985. Subsequently a combined fuel and vacuum pump, AC model 1537409 was used. Effective with serial number 24196 oil circulation was provided between the transmission and transfer case by the addition of drilled passages between the two units.

The CJ-2A was available in four exterior body colors: Grey, tan, blue and brown. Standard equipment for the CJ-2A included front bumper, high-frequency horn, driver side vacuum-powered windshield wiper, passenger-side manual windshield wiper, two padded seats, external driver's side rearview mirror, combination stop and taillight, high and low beam corcoran-brown 7 in. sealed beam headlights, parking lights, spare wheel and mount, oil bath type air cleaner, oil filter, tool kit, jack, and safety windshield glass. The gas filler was positioned on the outside of the body just behind the driver's seat. A pressure type fuel tank filler cap was used in order to prevent fuel leakage when the Jeep was positioned on a side slope.

Also used on the CJ-2A was a re-routed exhaust system which exited behind the right rear wheel and used a transversely-mounted muffler. The side hood panel carried Willys lettering. At the rear a chain-supported tailgate was used.

I.D. DATA: The serial number was located on the left front of the frame and the back of the bumper. The engine number was located on the boss for the water pump at the front of the cylinder block. Serial number range: 10,000 to 11,824.

Model Number	Body Type	Factory Price	GVW	Shipping Weight	Prod. Total
Jeep CJ-2A	Utility	$1241	3500	2120	1823

STANDARD ENGINE: Engine Type: Side valve, In-line-4. Cast iron block and cylinder head. Bore x Stroke: 3.125 in. x 4.375 in. Lifters: Mechanical. Number of main bearings-3. Fuel Induction: Single one in. Carter model WO-596S downdraft unit (some CJ-2A's were fitted with the MB military carburetor). Compression Ratio: 6.48:1. Displacement: 134.2 cu. in. (2.199 liters). Horsepower: 60 @ 4000 rpm. Torque: 105 lb.-ft. @ 2000 rpm. Oil refill capacity: 4 qt. with filter change. Fuel Requirements: Regular.

CHASSIS FEATURES: Separate body and channel steel frame construction, 4.125 in. depth x 1.937 in. width, five cross members. Overall frame length: 122.656 in. Section modulus: 1.493 in. cu.

SUSPENSION AND RUNNING GEAR: Front Suspension: 10-leaf semi-elliptical springs, 36.25 in. x by 1.75 in. Spring rate: 260 lb./in. Monroe, 10.75 in. dia. double-acting shock absorbers. Normal load: 650 lbs. Optional: 10-leaf heavy-duty front springs. Rear Suspension: 9-leaf semi-elliptical springs, 42 in. x 1.75 in. Spring rate: 190 lb./in. Monroe 10.75 in. dia. double-acting shock absorbers. Optional: Heavy-duty rear springs option with eleven thicker (2.407 in. to 1.973 in.). Spring rate: 225 lb./in. Front Axle Type and Capacity: Full-floating Spicer model 25, hypoid. Rear Axle Type and Capacity: Full-floating Spicer 23-2, Hypoid. Axle Ratio: 5.38:1. Transfer Case: Spicer model 18. Ratios: 2.46:1, 1.00:1. Brakes: Type: Hydraulic, front and rear. Dimensions: Front and rear: 9.00 in. x 1.75 in. Total braking area: 117.75 sq. in. Wheels: Kelsey-Hayes 16 x 4.50 in., 5-bolt steel disc. Tires: 6.00 x 16 in. 4-ply. Optional: 7.00 x 15 in. 4-ply. Steering: Ross model T-12 cam and lever. Ratio: 14-12:1. Turning Circle: 36 ft. Standard Transmission: Warner-Gear model T090A, 3-speed manual, column shift. Transmission ratios: 2.798:1, 1.551:1, 1.00:1. Reverse: 3.798:1. Clutch: 7.875 in. Borg & Beck single dry plate. Total lining area: 72 sq. in.

VEHICLE DIMENSIONS: Wheelbase: 80.166 in. Overall Length: 130.125 in. Front/Rear Tread: 48.25 in./48.25 in. Overall Height: 69.0 in. Width: 59.0 in. Front/Rear Overhang: 20.75 in./22.31 in. Tailgate: Width and Height: 36 in. x 19.25 in. Ground Clearance: 8.75 in. Load space: 32 in. x 36 in. Steering wheel to seat back (max.): 14 in.

CAPACITIES: Fuel Tank: 10.5 gal. Located under driver's seat. Cooling system: 11 qt.

ACCOMMODATIONS: Seating Capacity: 2/5.

INSTRUMENTATION: Speedometer, odometer, gauges for oil pressure, battery and engine coolant temperature.

OPTIONS AND PRICES: Willys offered a selection of both basic farm implements and industrial tools for use with the CJ-2A "Universal" Jeep. Agricultural options: Power take-off: $96.25. Drawbar. Single 16 in. or double 12 in. mould board plow. Two-disc, 26 in. plow. Brush and bog harrow. Tandem disc harrow. 8.5 in. spring tooth harrow. Six foot field and pasture cultivator. Six foot farm mower. Terracing blade. Industrial equipment options: 60 or 105 C.F.M. compressors. 12.5 K.V.A. generator. 300 amp D.C. arc welder. Hydro-Grader and Terracer. Lift-type overland scraper. Pulley for center power take-off: $57.40. Monroe hydraulic implement lift controlled from the driver's seat. Power take-off and tow bar hitch. Centrifugal-type King-Seeley governor: $28.65. Front brush guards for the front and rear propeller shafts. Baffle plate for the transfer case. Special wheels and 7 in. tires: $4.00. Front 10 oz. soldenized mildew-resistant duck top with double-sewn seams. top, kit no. 667888: $57.50. Rear top, kit no. 667826 (must be ordered with kit no. 667888). Hydraulic lift: $225.00.

HISTORICAL FOOTNOTES: On July 17, 1945, the first CJ-2A Jeep was produced. Willys-Overland ended its fiscal year in September 30, 1945 with a net profit of $2,711,332.

1946 CJ

There were no significant changes made in the CJ-2A for 1946. CJ-2A's built after serial number 38221, in early 1946, reverted to a floor mounted shifter. Other changes introduced at this time included pressure lubrication of the mainshaft pilot bearing, a more durable rear bearing oil seal and needle bearings for the countershaft. Accompanying this development was use of a larger, 8.5 in. clutch with a torque capacity of 144 lb.-ft.

1946 Jeep CJ-2A

I.D. DATA: The serial number was located on the left front of the frame and the back of the bumper. The engine number was located on the boss for the water pump at the front of the cylinder block. Serial number range: 11825 to 83379.

Model Number	Body Type	Factory Price	GVW	Shipping Weight	Prod. Total
Jeep CJ-2A	Utility	$1241	3500	2120	71,554

STANDARD ENGINE: Engine Type: Side valve, In-line-4. Cast iron block and cylinder head. Bore x Stroke: 3.125 in. x 4.375 in. Lifters: Mechanical. Number of main bearings-3. Fuel Induction: Single one in. Carter model WO-596S downdraft unit. Compression Ratio: 6.48:1. Displacement: 134.2 cu. in. (2.199 liters). Horsepower: 60 @ 4000 rpm. Torque: 105 lb.-ft. @ 2000 rpm. Oil refill capacity: 4 qt. with filter change. Fuel Requirements: Regular.

CHASSIS FEATURES: Separate body and channel steel frame construction, 4.125 in. depth x 1.937 in. width, five cross members. Overall frame length: 122.656 in. Section modulus: 1.493 in. cu.

SUSPENSION AND RUNNING GEAR: Front Suspension: 10-leaf semi-elliptical springs, 36.25 in. x by 1.75 in. Spring rate: 260 lb./in. Monroe 10.75 in. dia. double-acting shock absorbers. Normal load: 650 lbs. Optional: 10-leaf heavy-duty front springs. Rear Suspension: 9-leaf semi-elliptical springs, 42 in. x 1.75 in. Spring rate: 190 lb./in. Monroe 10.75 in. dia. double-acting shock absorbers. Optional: Heavy-duty rear springs option with eleven thicker (2.407 in. to 1.973 in.). Spring rate: 225 lb./in. Front Axle Type and Capacity: Full-floating Spicer, hypoid. Rear Axle Type and Capacity: After serial Number 13453: Semi-floating Spicer 41-2, Hypoid. Prior to that number: Full-floating Spicer 23-2. Axle Ratios: 5.38:1. Transfer Case: Spicer model 18. Ratios: 2.46:1, 1.00:1. Brakes: Type: Hydraulic, front and rear. Dimensions: Front and rear: 9.00 in. x 1.75 in. Total braking area: 117.75 sq. in. Wheels: Kelsey-Hayes 16 x 4.50 in., 5-bolt steel disc. Optional: None. Tires: 6.00 x 16 in. 4-ply. Optional: 7.00 x 15 in. 4-ply. Steering: Ross model T-12 cam and lever. Ratio: 14-12:1. Turning Circle: 36 ft. Standard Transmission: Warner-Gear model T090A, 3-speed manual, column shift; after serial number 38221-floor-mounted shift. Transmission ratios: 2.798:1, 1.551:1, 1.00:1. Reverse: 3.798:1. Clutch: 8.5 in. Auburn single dry plate. Total lining area: sq. in.

VEHICLE DIMENSIONS: Wheelbase: 80.166 in. Overall Length: 130.125 in. Front/Rear Tread: 48.25 in./48.25 in. Overall Height: 69.0 in. Width: 59.0 in. Front/Rear Overhang: 20.75 in./22.31 in. Tailgate: Width and Height: 36 in. x 19.25 in. Ground Clearance: Front axle: Full-floating front axle models: 8.625 in.; Semi-floating front axle models: 8.750 in. Load space: 32 in x 36 in. Steering wheel to seat back (max.): 14 in.

CAPACITIES: Fuel Tank: 10.5 gal. Located under driver's seat. Cooling System: 11 qt.

ACCOMMODATIONS: Seating Capacity: 2/5.

INSTRUMENTATION: Speedometer, odometer, gauges for oil pressure, battery and engine coolant temperature.

OPTIONS AND PRICES: Unchanged from 1945.

HISTORICAL FOOTNOTES: In October, 1946, Willys-Overland held its first "Institutional Day" at its Toledo facility. The latest models were on display.

1947 CJ

The CJ-2A was carried over into 1947 in the same basic form as the 1946 model.

1947 Jeep CJ-2A

I.D. DATA: The serial number was located on the left front of the frame and the back of the bumper. The engine number was located on the boss for the water pump at the front of the cylinder block. Serial number range: 83380 and up.

Model Number	Body Type	Factory Price	GVW	Shipping Weight	Prod. Total
Jeep CJ-2A	Utility	$1213	3500	2074	—

STANDARD ENGINE: Engine Type: Side valve, In-line-4. Cast iron block and cylinder head. Bore x Stroke: 3.125 in. x 4.375 in. Lifters: Mechanical. Number of main bearings-3. Fuel Induction: Single one in. Carter model WO-596S downdraft unit. Compression Ratio: 6.48:1. Displacement: 134.2 cu. in. (2.199 liters). Horsepower: 60 @ 4000 rpm. Torque: 105 lb.-ft. @ 2000 rpm. Oil refill capacity: 4 qt. with filter change. Fuel Requirements: Regular.

CHASSIS FEATURES: Separate body and channel steel frame construction, 4.125 in. depth x 1.937 in. width, five cross members. Overall frame length: 122.656 in. Section modulus: 1.493 in. cu.

SUSPENSION AND RUNNING GEAR: Front Suspension: 10-leaf semi-elliptical springs, 36.25 in. x by 1.75 in. Spring rate: 260 lb./in. Monroe 10.75 in. dia. double-acting shock absorbers. Normal load: 650 lbs. Optional: 10-leaf heavy-duty front springs. Rear Suspension: 9-leaf semi-elliptical springs, 42 in. x 1.75 in. Spring rate: 190 lb./in. Monroe 10.75 in. dia. double-acting shock absorbers. Optional: Heavy-duty rear springs option with eleven thicker (2.407 in. to 1.973 in.). Spring rate: 225 lb./in. Front Axle Type and Capacity: Full-floating Spicer, hypoid. Rear Axle Type and Capacity: Semi-floating Spicer 41-2, Hypoid. Axle Ratios: 5.38:1. Transfer Case: Spicer model 18. Ratios: 2.46:1, 1.00:1. Brakes: Type: Hydraulic, front and rear. Dimensions: Front and rear: 9.00 in. x 1.75 in. Total braking area: 117.75 sq. in. Wheels: Kelsey-Hayes 16 x 4.50 in., 5-bolt steel disc. Tires: 6.00 x 16 in. 4-ply. Optional: 7.00 x 15 in. 4-ply. Steering: Ross model T-12 cam and lever. Ratio: 14-12:1. Turning Circle: 36 ft. Standard Transmission: Warner-Gear model T090A, 3-speed manual, floor-mounted shift. Transmission ratios: 2.798:1, 1.551:1, 1.00:1. Reverse: 3.798:1. Clutch: 8.5 in. Auburn single dry plate. Total lining area: 72 sq. in.

VEHICLE DIMENSIONS: Wheelbase: 80.166 in. Overall Length: 130.125 in. Front/Rear Tread: 48.25 in./48.25 in. Overall Height: 69.0 in. Width: 59.0 in. Front/Rear Overhang: 20.75 in./22.31 in. Tailgate: Width and Height: 36 in. x 19.25 in. Ground Clearance: Rear axle: 8.750 in. Load space: 32 in. x 36 in. Steering wheel to seat back (max.): 14 in.

CAPACITIES: Fuel Tank: 10.5 gal. Located under driver's seat. Cooling System: 11 qt.

ACCOMMODATIONS: Seating Capacity: 2/5.

INSTRUMENTATION: Speedometer, odometer, gauges for oil pressure, battery and engine coolant temperature.

OPTIONS AND PRICES: Unchanged from 1946.

HISTORICAL FOOTNOTES: The 1947 Jeeps were introduced in January, 1947.

1948 CJ

The CJ-2A was essentially unchanged for 1948.

I.D. DATA: The serial number was located on the left front of the frame and the back of the bumper. The engine number was located on the boss for the water pump at the front of the cylinder block. Serial number range: 148459 to 219588.

Model Number	Body Type	Factory Price	GVW	Shipping Weight	Prod. Total
Jeep CJ-2A	Utility	$1262	3500	2037	63,170*

* Calendar year production.

STANDARD ENGINE: Engine Type: Side valve, In-line-4. Cast iron block and cylinder head. Bore x Stroke: 3.125 in. x 4.375 in. Lifters: Mechanical. Number of main bearings-3. Fuel Induction: Single one in. Carter model WO-596S downdraft unit. Compression Ratio: 6.48:1. Displacement: 134.2 cu. in. (2.199 liters). Horsepower: 60 @ 4000 rpm. Torque: 105 lb.-ft. @ 2000 rpm. Oil refill capacity: 4 qt. with filter change. Fuel Requirements: Regular.

CHASSIS FEATURES: Separate body and channel steel frame construction, 4.125 in. depth x 1.937 in. width, five cross members. Overall frame length: 122.656 in. Section modulus: 1.493 in. cu.

SUSPENSION AND RUNNING GEAR: Front Suspension: 10-leaf semi-elliptical springs, 36.25 in. x by 1.75 in. Spring rate: 260 lb./in. Monroe 10.75 in. dia. double-acting shock absorbers. Normal load: 650 lbs. Optional: 10-leaf heavy-duty front springs. Rear Suspension: 9-leaf semi-elliptical springs, 42 in. x 1.75 in. Spring rate: 190 lb./in. Monroe 10.75 in. dia. double-acting shock absorbers. Optional: Heavy-duty rear springs option with eleven thicker (2.407 in. to 1.973 in.). Spring rate: 225 lb./in. Front Axle Type and Capacity: Full-floating Spicer, hypoid. Rear Axle Type and Capacity: Semi-floating Spicer 41-2, Hypoid. Axle Ratios: 5.38:1. Transfer Case: Spicer model 18. Ratios: 2.46:1, 1.00:1. Brakes: Type: Hydraulic, front and rear. Dimensions: Front and rear: 9.00 in. x 1.75 in. Total braking area: 117.75 sq. in. Wheels: Kelsey-Hayes 16 x 4.50 in., 5-bolt steel disc. Tires: 6.00 x 16 in. 4-ply. Optional: 7.00 x 15 in. 4-ply. Steering: Ross model T-12 cam and lever. Ratio: 14-12:1. Turning Circle: 36 ft. Standard Transmission: Warner-Gear model T090A, 3-speed manual, column shift; after serial number 38221-floor-mounted shift. Transmission ratios: 2.798:1, 1.551:1, 1.00:1. Reverse: 3.798:1. Optional: None. Clutch: 8.5 in. Auburn single dry plate. Total lining area: 72 sq. in. Optional: None.

VEHICLE DIMENSIONS: Wheelbase: 80.166 in. Overall Length: 130.125 in. Front/Rear Tread: 48.25 in./48.25 in. Overall Height: 69.0 in. Width: 59.0 in. Front/Rear Overhang: 20.75 in./22.31 in. Tailgate: Width and Height: 36 in. x 19.25 in. Ground Clearance: Rear axle: 8.750 in. Load space: 32 in. x 36 in. Steering wheel to seat back (max.): 14 in.

CAPACITIES: Fuel Tank: 10.5 gal. Located under driver's seat. Cooling system: 11 qt.

ACCOMMODATIONS: Seating Capacity: 2/5.

INSTRUMENTATION: Speedometer, odometer, gauges for oil pressure, battery and engine coolant temperature.

OPTIONS AND PRICES: Unchanged from 1947.

HISTORICAL FOOTNOTES: The 1948 models were introduced in November, 1947.

1949 CJ

Production of the CJ-2A, which ended in 1949 overlapped that of its successor, the CJ-3A which was introduced in late 1948. Except for the production and serial number data, the information in this section refers to the CJ-3A. The CJ-3A and its predecessor differed in many ways, including their physical dimensions. The domestic version of the CJ-3A had a one-piece windshield (a two-piece windshield was available for export), dual windshield wipers located on the windshield base and a front end air intake set in a panel with three indented sections.

In place of the CJ-2A's Jamestown J-161 radiator, the CJ-3A used a Harrison unit. The cooling system capacity remained 11 quarts without heater and 12 quarts with heater. The thermostat on early CJ-3A Jeeps was also unchanged from that used on the CJ-2A. It started to open at 150 degrees F and was fully open at 180 degrees F. Later models that used a thermostat had respective levels of 180 degrees F and 202 degrees F. The fan-to-crankshaft ratio of the early CJ-3A was 1.83:1. It was subsequently changed back to the 1.19:1 ratio used on the CJ-2A. The length of the engine drive belt used on the CJ-3A was 44 in. as compared to the 42.34 in. length belt installed on the CJ-2A. The angle of the belt "V" also was different on the two CJ models. The CJ-2A's had a 42 degree angle; the CJ-3A's had a 45 degree angle. Engine changes were of a minor nature. A piston clearance of 0.003 in. was used for the CJ-3A engine. That of the CJ-2A had been 0.004 in. Similarly, a valve tappet clearance of 0.016 in. instead of 0.014 in. was specified for the CJ-3A. The CJ-3A also used a different flywheel.

1949 Jeep CJ-3A

I.D. DATA: The serial number was located on the left front of the frame and the back of the bumper. The engine number was located on the boss for the water pump at the front of the cylinder block. Serial number range: CJ-2A: 219589 to 224762. CJ-3A: 10001 to 35688.

Model Number	Body Type	Factory Price	GVW	Shipping Weight	Prod. Total
Jeep CJ-2A	Utility	$1270	3500	2037	5164
CJ-3A	Utility	$1270	3500	2110	25,687

STANDARD ENGINE: Engine Type: Side valve, In-line-4. Cast iron block and cylinder head. Bore x Stroke: 3.125 in. x 4.375 in. Lifters: Mechanical. Number of main bearings-3. Fuel Induction: Single one in. Carter model 636SA downdraft unit. Compression Ratio: 6.48:1. Displacement: 134.2 cu. in. (2.199 liters). Horsepower: 60 @ 4000 rpm. Torque: 105 lb.-ft. @ 2000 rpm. Oil refill capacity: 4 qt. with filter change. Fuel Requirements: Regular.

CHASSIS FEATURES: Separate body and channel steel frame construction, 4.125 in. depth x 1.937 in. width, five cross members. Overall frame length: 122.656 in. Section modulus: 1.493 in. cu.

SUSPENSION AND RUNNING GEAR: Front Suspension: 10-leaf semi-elliptical springs, 36.25 in. x by 1.75 in. Spring rate: 260 lb./in. Monroe 10.75 in. dia. double-acting shock absorbers. Normal load: 650 lbs. Optional: 10-leaf heavy-duty front springs. Rear Suspension: 9-leaf semi-elliptical springs, 42 in. x 1.75 in. Spring rate: 190 lb./in. Monroe 10.75 in. dia. double-acting shock absorbers. Optional: Heavy-duty rear springs option with eleven thicker (2.407 in. to 1.973 in.). Spring rate: 225 lb./in. Front Axle Type and Capacity: Full-floating Spicer, hypoid. Rear Axle Type and Capacity: Semi-floating Spicer model 44-2. Hypoid. Axle Ratios: 5.38:1. Transfer Case: Spicer model 18. Ratios: 2.46:1, 1.00:1. Brakes: Type: Hydraulic, front and rear. Dimensions: Front and rear: 9.00 in. x 1.75 in. Total braking area: 117.75 sq. in. Wheels: Kelsey-Hayes 16 x 4.50 in., 5-bolt steel disc. Optional: None. Tires: 6.00 x 16 in. 4-ply. Optional: 7.00 x 15 in. 4-ply. Steering: Ross model T-12 cam and lever. Ratio: 14-12:1. Turning Circle: 36 ft. Optional: None. Standard Transmission: Warner-Gear model T090A, 3-speed manual floor-mounted shift. Transmission ratios: 2.798:1, 1.551:1, 1.00:1. Reverse: 3.798:1. Optional: None. Clutch: 8.5 in. Auburn or Rockford single dry plate. Total lining area: 72 sq. in. Optional: Auburn single dry plate, 9.25 in dia. plate.

VEHICLE DIMENSIONS: Wheelbase: 80.166 in. Overall Length: 129.75 in. Front/Rear Tread: 48.25 in./48.25 in. Overall Height: 66.75 in. Width: 68.721 in. Front/Rear Overhang: 20.59 in./22.31 in. Tailgate: Width and Height: 36 in. x 14.125 in. Ground Clearance: 8.750 in. Load space: 32 in. x 52.315 in. x 14.125 in. Steering wheel to seat back (max.): 15.12 in.

CAPACITIES: Fuel Tank: 10.5 gal. Located under driver's seat. Cooling System: 11 qt.

ACCOMMODATIONS: Seating Capacity: 2/5.

INSTRUMENTATION: Instrument panel light, ammeter, heat indicator gauge, speedometer oil pressure gauge, fuel level gauge.

OPTIONS AND PRICES: Unchanged from 1948.

HISTORICAL FOOTNOTES: Tom McCahill called the CJ-3B "one of the greatest vehicles ever conceived by man."

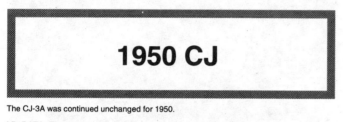

1950 CJ

The CJ-3A was continued unchanged for 1950.

I.D. DATA: The serial number was located on the left front of the frame and the back of the bumper. It was also found on the engine number was located on the boss for the water pump at the front of the cylinder block. Serial number range: CJ-3A: 35689 to 63784.

Model Number	Body Type	Factory Price	GVW	Shipping Weight	Prod. Total
Jeep					
CJ-2A	Utility	$1270	3500	2037	5164
CJ-3A	Utility	$1270	3500	2110	25,687

STANDARD ENGINE: Engine Type: Side valve, In-line-4. Cast iron block and cylinder head. Bore x Stroke: 3.125 in. x 4.375 in. Lifters: Mechanical. Number of main bearings-3. Fuel Induction: Single one in. Carter model 636SA downdraft unit. Compression Ratio: 6.48:1. Displacement: 134.2 cu. in. (2.199 liters). Horsepower: 60 @ 4000 rpm. Torque: 105 lb.-ft. @ 2000 rpm. Oil refill capacity: 4 qt. with filter change. Fuel Requirements: Regular.

CHASSIS FEATURES: Separate body and channel steel frame construction, 4.125 in. depth x 1.937 in. width, five cross members. Overall frame length: 122.656 in. Section modulus: 1.493 in. cu.

SUSPENSION AND RUNNING GEAR: Front Suspension: 10-leaf semi-elliptical springs, 36.25 in. x by 1.75 in. Spring rate: 260 lb./in. Monroe 10.75 in. dia. double-acting shock absorbers. Normal load: 650 lbs. Optional: 10-leaf heavy-duty front springs. Rear Suspension: 9-leaf semi-elliptical springs, 42 in. x 1.75 in. Spring rate: 190 lb./in. Monroe 10.75 in. dia. double-acting shock absorbers. Optional: Heavy-duty rear springs option with eleven thicker (2.407 in. to 1.973 in.). Spring rate: 225 lb./in. Front Axle Type and Capacity: Full-floating Spicer, hypoid. Rear Axle Type and Capacity: Semi-floating Spicer model 44-2. Hypoid. Axle Ratios: 5.38:1. Transfer Case: Spicer model 18. Ratios: 2.46:1, 1.00:1. Brakes: Type: Hydraulic, front and rear. Dimensions: Front and rear: 9.00 in. x 1.75 in. Total braking area: 117.75 sq. in. Wheels: Kelsey-Hayes 16 x 4.50 in., 5-bolt steel disc. Optional: None. Tires: 6.00 x 16 in. 4-ply. Optional: 7.00 x 15 in. 4-ply. Steering: Ross model T-12 cam and lever. Ratio: 14-12:1. Turning Circle: 36 ft. Standard Transmission: Warner-Gear model T090A, 3-speed manual floor-mounted shift. Transmission ratios: 2.798:1, 1.551:1, 1.00:1. Reverse: 3.798:1. Optional: None. Clutch: 8.5 in. Auburn or Rockford single dry plate. Total lining area: 72 sq. in. Optional: Auburn single dry plate, 9.25 in. dia. plate.

VEHICLE DIMENSIONS: Wheelbase: 80.166 in. Overall Length: 129.75 in. Front/Rear Tread: 48.25 in./48.25 in. Overall Height: 66.75 in. Width: 68.721 in. Front/Rear Overhang: 20.59 in. 22.31/ in. Tailgate: Width and Height: 36 in. x 14.125 in. Ground Clearance: 8.750 in. Load space: 32 in. x 52.315 in. x 14.125 in. Steering wheel to seat back (max.): 15.12 in.

CAPACITIES: Fuel Tank: 10.5 gal. Located under driver's seat. Cooling System: 11 qt.

ACCOMMODATIONS: Seating Capacity: 2/5.

INSTRUMENTATION: Instrument panel light, ammeter, heat indicator gauge, speedometer oil pressure gauge, fuel level gauge.

OPTIONS AND PRICES: Unchanged from 1949.

HISTORICAL FOOTNOTES: The CJ Jeep was introduced in November, 1949.

1951 CJ

The CJ-3A was continued unchanged for 1951. Willys promoted the "Universal" Jeep as a vehicle that thrived on tough jobs in al types of climates and seasons. It was a vehicle that its manufacturer claimed could climb a 70 percent grade, carry up to 1200 pounds and handle a drawbar pull of 2,650 pounds. A stripped chassis version as well as a "Farm Jeep" with a standard power take-off were offered for 1951.

I.D. DATA: The serial number was located on the left front of the frame and the back of the bumper. It was also found on the engine. The number was located on the boss for the water pump at the front of the cylinder block. Added to the CJ serial number was a six character prefix. Serial number range: Stripped chassis: 451-GA1-10001 to 10003; CJ3-A: 451-GA1-10001 to 451-GA1-54158.

Model Number	Body Type	Factory Price	GVW	Shipping Weight	Prod. Total
Jeep					
Chassis	—	$1055	3500	1692	3
CJ-3A	Utility	$1290	3500	2108	44,157*

* Includes 62 Farm Jeeps. Calendar year production was 76,571 including military versions.

STANDARD ENGINE: Engine Type: Side valve, In-line-4. Cast iron block and cylinder head. Bore x Stroke: 3.125 in. x 4.375 in. Lifters: Mechanical. Number of main bearings-3. Fuel Induction: Single one in. Carter model 636SA downdraft unit. Compression Ratio: 6.48:1. Displacement: 134.2 cu. in. (2.199 liters). Horsepower: 60 @ 4000 rpm. Torque: 105 lb.-ft. @ 2000 rpm. Oil refill capacity: 4 qt. with filter change. Fuel Requirements: Regular.

CHASSIS FEATURES: Separate body and channel steel frame construction, 4.125 in. depth x 1.937 in. width, five cross members. Overall frame length: 122.656 in. Section modulus: 1.493 in. cu.

SUSPENSION AND RUNNING GEAR: Front Suspension: 10-leaf semi-elliptical springs, 36.25 in. x by 1.75 in. Spring rate: 260 lb./in. Monroe 10.75 in. dia. double-acting shock absorbers. Normal load: 650 lbs. Optional: 10-leaf heavy-duty front springs. Rear Suspension: 9-leaf semi-elliptical springs, 42 in. x 1.75 in. Spring rate: 190 lb./in. Monroe 10.75 in. dia. double-acting shock absorbers. Optional: Heavy-duty rear springs option with eleven thicker (2.407 in. to 1.973 in.). Spring rate: 225 lb./in. Front Axle Type and Capacity: Full-floating Spicer, hypoid. Rear Axle Type and Capacity: Semi-floating Spicer model 44-2. Hypoid. Axle Ratios: 5.38:1. Transfer Case: Spicer model 18. Ratios: 2.46:1, 1.00:1. Brakes: Type: Hydraulic, front and rear. Dimensions: Front and rear: 9.00 in. x 1.75 in. Total braking area: 117.75 sq. in. Wheels: Kelsey-Hayes 16 x 4.50 in., 5-bolt steel disc. Optional: None. Tires: 6.00 x 16 in. 4-ply. Optional: 7.00 x 15 in. 4-ply. Steering: Ross model T-12 cam and lever. Ratio: 14-12:1. Turning Circle: 36 ft. Optional: None. Standard Transmission: Warner-Gear model T090A, 3-speed manual floor-mounted shift. Transmission ratios: 2.798:1, 1.551:1, 1.00:1. Reverse: 3.798:1. Optional: None. Clutch: 8.5 in. Auburn or Rockford single dry plate. Total lining area: 72 sq. in. Optional: Auburn single dry plate, 9.25 in dia. plate.

VEHICLE DIMENSIONS: Wheelbase: 80.166 in. Overall Length: 129.75 in. Front/Rear Tread: 48.25 in./48.25 in. Overall Height: 66.75 in. Width: 68.721 in. Front/Rear Overhang: 20.59 in. 22.31/ in. Tailgate: Width and Height: 36 in. x 14.125 in. Ground Clearance: 8.750 in. Load space: 32 in. x 52.315 in. x 14.125 in. Steering wheel to seat back (max.): 15.12 in.

CAPACITIES: Fuel Tank: 10.5 gal. Located under driver's seat. Coolant System: 11 qt.

ACCOMMODATIONS: Seating Capacity: 2/5.

INSTRUMENTATION: Instrument panel light, ammeter, heat indicator gauge, speedometer oil pressure gauge, fuel level gauge.

OPTIONS AND PRICES: Unchanged from 1950. Power take-off: $96.25. Pulley drive: $57.40. Engine governor: $28.65. Front canvas top: $57.80. High temperature thermostat.

HISTORICAL FOOTNOTES: The Farm Jeep was introduced in July, 1951.

1952 CJ

The CJ-3A was continued unchanged for 1952.

I.D. DATA: The serial number was located on the left front of the frame and the back of the bumper. It was also found on the engine. The number was located on the boss for the water pump at the front of the cylinder block. Added to the CJ serial number was a six character prefix. Serial number range: Stripped chassis: 452-GA1-10001 to 10013. CJ3-A: 452-GA1-10001 to 452-GA1-39652.

Model Number	Body Type	Factory Price	GVW	Shipping Weight	Prod. Total
Jeep					
Chassis	—	$1224	3500	1692	13
CJ-3A	Utility	$1462	3500	2108	29,651

STANDARD ENGINE: Engine Type: Side valve, In-line-4. Cast iron block and cylinder head. Bore x Stroke: 3.125 in. x 4.375 in. Lifters: Mechanical. Number of main bearings-3. Fuel Induction: Single one in. Carter model 636SA downdraft unit. Compression Ratio: 6.48:1. Displacement: 134.2 cu. in. (2.199 liters). Horsepower: 60 @ 4000 rpm. Torque: 105 lb.-ft. @ 2000 rpm. Oil refill capacity: 4 qt. with filter change. Fuel Requirements: Regular.

CHASSIS FEATURES: Separate body and channel steel frame construction, 4.125 in. depth x 1.937 in. width, five cross members. Overall frame length: 122.656 in. Section modulus: 1.493 in. cu.

SUSPENSION AND RUNNING GEAR: Front Suspension: 10-leaf semi-elliptical springs, 36.25 in. x by 1.75 in. Spring rate: 260 lb./in. Monroe 10.75 in. dia. double-acting shock absorbers. Normal load: 650 lbs. Optional: 10-leaf heavy-duty front springs. Rear Suspension: 9-leaf semi-elliptical springs, 42 in. x 1.75 in. Spring rate: 190 lb./in. Monroe 10.75 in. dia. double-acting shock absorbers. Optional: Heavy-duty rear springs option with eleven thicker

(2.407 in. to 1.973 in.). Spring rate: 225 lb./in. Front Axle Type and Capacity: Full-floating Spicer, hypoid. Rear Axle Type and Capacity: Semi-floating Spicer model 44-2. Hypoid. Axle Ratios: 5.38:1. Transfer Case: Spicer model 18. Ratios: 2.46:1, 1.00:1. Brakes: Type: Hydraulic, front and rear. Dimensions: Front and rear: 9.00 in. x 1.75 in. Total braking area: 117.75 sq. in. Wheels: Kelsey-Hayes 16 x 4.50 in., 5-bolt steel disc. Optional: None. Tires: 6.00 x 16 in. 4-ply. Optional: 7.00 x 15 in. 4-ply. Steering: Ross model T-12 cam and lever. Ratio: 14-12:1. Turning Circle: 36 ft. Optional: None. Standard Transmission: Warner-Gear model T090A, 3-speed manual floor-mounted shift. Transmission ratios: 2.798:1, 1.551:1, 1.00:1. Reverse: 3.798:1. Optional: None. Clutch: 8.5 in. Auburn or Rockford single dry plate. Total lining area: 72 sq. in. Optional: Auburn single dry plate, 9.25 in dia. plate.

VEHICLE DIMENSIONS: Wheelbase: 80.166 in. Overall Length: 129.75 in. Front/Rear Tread: 48.25 in./48.25 in. Overall Height: 66.75 in. Width: 68.721 in. Front/Rear Overhang: 20.59 in. 22.31/ in. Tailgate: Width and Height: 36 in. x 14.125 in. Ground Clearance: 8.750 in. Load space: 32 in. x 52.315 in. x 14.125 in. Steering wheel to seat back (max.): 15.12 in.

CAPACITIES: Fuel Tank: 10.5 gal. Located under driver's seat. Coolant System: 11 qt.

ACCOMMODATIONS: Seating Capacity: 2/5.

INSTRUMENTATION: Instrument panel light, ammeter, heat indicator gauge, speedometer oil pressure gauge, fuel level gauge.

OPTIONS AND PRICES: Unchanged from 1950. Power take-off: $96.25. Pulley drive: $57.40. Engine governor: $28.65. Front canvas top: $57.80. High temperature thermostat.

HISTORICAL FOOTNOTES: The one-millionth Jeep was built on March 19, 1952. Calendar output of Jeep models (civilian and military) totaled 88,098.

1953 CJ

On January 28, 1953 the CJ-3B Universal Jeep was made available with the F-head engine already in production for Jeep station wagons and trucks. The CJ-3A was continued for the remainder of the model year.

The hood of the new CJ-3B was much higher than the CJ-3A's, due to the greater height of the F-head engine. Filling the extra space resulting from this revision at the front was large "WILLYS" lettering. The CJ-3A one-piece windshield was retained but the newest Jeep lacked the high-mounted air ventilator of the CJ-3A. The dash arrangement of the CJ-3B was revised to carry a single circular instrument cluster rather the separate gauges as found on the CJ-3A. A somewhat larger exterior rearview mirror was also used for the CJ-3B.

1953 Jeep CJ-3B

I.D. DATA: The serial number was located on the left front of the frame and the back of the bumper. It was also found on the right side of the dash under the hood. The engine number was located on the boss for the water pump at the front of the cylinder block. Serial number range: CJ-3A: 453-GB1-10001 and up. CJ-3B: 453-GB2-10001 to 37550; CJ-3B Farm: 453-GC2-10001 and up.

Model Number	Body Type	Factory Price	GVW	Shipping Weight	Prod. Total
Jeep					
CJ-3A	Utility	$1352	3500	2108	—
CJ-3B	Utility	$1377	3500	2098	—
CJ-3B	Farm	$1439	3500	2098	—

STANDARD ENGINE: Engine Type: F-head, In-line-4. Cast iron block and cylinder head. Bore x Stroke: 3.125 in. x 4.375 in. Lifters: Mechanical. Number of main bearings-3. Fuel Induction: Single Carter model YF-938-SD. Compression Ratio: 6.9:1. Optional High Altitude 7.4:1. Displacement: 134.2 cu. in. (2.199 liters). Horsepower: 72 @ 4000 rpm. Torque: 114 lb.-ft. @ 2000 rpm. Oil refill capacity: 4 qt. with filter change. Fuel Requirements: Regular.

CHASSIS FEATURES: Separate body and channel steel frame construction, 4.125 in. depth x 1.937 in. width, five cross members. Overall frame length: 122.656 in. Section modulus: 1.493 in. cu.

SUSPENSION AND RUNNING GEAR: Front Suspension: 10-leaf semi-elliptical springs, 36.25 in. x 1.75 in. Spring rate: 260 lb./in. Monroe 10.75 in. dia. double-acting shock absorbers. Normal load: 650 lbs. Optional: 10-leaf heavy-duty front springs. Rear Suspension: 9-leaf semi-elliptical springs, 42 in. x 1.75 in. Spring rate: 190 lb./in. Monroe 10.75 in. dia. double-acting shock absorbers. Optional: Heavy-duty rear springs option with eleven thicker (2.407 in. to 1.973 in.). Spring rate: 225 lb./in. Front Axle Type and Capacity: Full-floating Spicer, hypoid. Rear Axle Type and Capacity: Semi-floating Spicer model 44-2. Hypoid. Axle Ratios: 5.38:1. Transfer Case: Spicer model 18. Ratios: 2.46:1, 1.00:1. Brakes: Type: Hydraulic, front and rear. Dimensions: Front and rear: 9.00 in. x 1.75 in. Total braking area: 117.75 sq. in. Wheels: Kelsey-Hayes 16 x 4.50 in., 5-bolt steel disc. Optional: None. Tires: 6.00 x 16 in. 4-ply. Optional: 7.00 x 15 in. 4-ply. Steering: Ross model T-12 cam and lever.

Ratio: 14-12:1. Turning Circle: 36 ft. Optional: None. Standard Transmission: Warner-Gear model T090A, 3-speed manual floor-mounted shift. Transmission ratios: 2.798:1, 1.551:1, 1.00:1. Reverse: 3.798:1. Optional: None. Clutch: 8.5 in. Auburn or Rockford single dry plate. Total lining area: 72 sq. in. Optional: Auburn single dry plate, 9.25 in dia. plate.

VEHICLE DIMENSIONS: Wheelbase: 80.166 in. Overall Length: 129.75 in. Front/Rear Tread: 48.25 in./48.25 in. Overall Height: 66.75 in. Width: 68.721 in. Front/Rear Overhang: 20.59 in./ .22.31 in. Tailgate: Width and Height: 36 in. x 14.125 in. Ground Clearance: 8.750 in. Load space: 32 in. x 52.315 in. x 14.125 in. Steering wheel to seat back (max.): 15.12 in.

CAPACITIES: Fuel Tank: 10.5 gal. Located under driver's seat. Coolant System: 11 qt.

ACCOMMODATIONS: Seating Capacity: 2/5.

INSTRUMENTATION: Instrument panel light, ammeter, heat indicator gauge, speedometer oil pressure gauge, fuel level gauge.

OPTIONS AND PRICES: Power take-off: $96.25. Pulley drive: $57.40. Engine governor: $28.65. Half and full canvas and metal tops. High altitude cylinder head. High temperature thermostat.

HISTORICAL FOOTNOTES: Willys-Overland celebrated its 50th anniversary in 1953. The CJ-3B was introduced on January 28, 1953. Kaiser Manufacturing purchasing Willys-Overland for $62,382,175.

1954 CJ

No changes were made in the CJ-3B for 1954.

1954 Jeep CJ-5

I.D. DATA: The serial number was located on the left front of the frame and the back of the bumper. It was also found on the right side of the dash under the hood. The engine number was located on the boss for the water pump at the front of the cylinder block. Serial number range: CJ-3B: 453-GB2-10001 to 37550; CJ-3B Farm: 453-GC2-10001 and up.

Model Number	Body Type	Factory Price	GVW	Shipping Weight	Prod. Total
Jeep					
CJ-3B	Utility	$1377	3500	2098	—
CJ-3B	Farm	$1439	3500	2098	—

STANDARD ENGINE: Engine Type: F-head, In-line-4. Cast iron block and cylinder head. Bore x Stroke: 3.125 in. x 4.375 in. Lifters: Mechanical. Number of main bearings-3. Fuel Induction: Single Carter model YF-938-SD. Compression Ratio: 6.9:1. Optional High Altitude 7.4:1. Displacement: 134.2 cu. in. (2.199 liters). Horsepower: 72 @ 4000 rpm. Torque: 114 lb.-ft. @ 2000 rpm. Oil refill capacity: 4 qt. with filter change. Fuel Requirements: Regular.

CHASSIS FEATURES: Separate body and channel steel frame construction, 4.125 in. depth x 1.937 in. width, five cross members. Overall frame length: 122.656 in. Section modulus: 1.493 in. cu.

SUSPENSION AND RUNNING GEAR: Front Suspension: 10-leaf semi-elliptical springs, 36.25 in. x 1.75 in. Spring rate: 260 lb./in. Monroe 10.75 in. dia. double-acting shock absorbers. Normal load: 650 lbs. Optional: 10-leaf heavy-duty front springs. Rear Suspension: 9-leaf semi-elliptical springs, 42 in. x 1.75 in. Spring rate: 190 lb./in. Monroe 10.75 in. dia. double-acting shock absorbers. Optional: Heavy-duty rear springs option with eleven thicker (2.407 in. to 1.973 in.). Spring rate: 225 lb./in. Front Axle Type and Capacity: Full-floating Spicer, hypoid. Rear Axle Type and Capacity: Semi-floating Spicer model 44-2. Hypoid. Axle Ratios: 5.38:1. Transfer Case: Spicer model 18. Ratios: 2.46:1, 1.00:1. Brakes: Type: Hydraulic, front and rear. Dimensions: Front and rear: 9.00 in. x 1.75 in. Total braking area: 117.75 sq. in. Wheels: Kelsey-Hayes 16 x 4.50 in., 5-bolt steel disc. Optional: None. Tires: 6.00 x 16 in. 4-ply. Optional: 7.00 x 15 in. 4-ply. Steering: Ross model T-12 cam and lever. Ratio: 14-12:1. Turning Circle: 36 ft. Optional: None. Standard Transmission: Warner-Gear model T090A, 3-speed manual floor-mounted shift. Transmission ratios: 2.798:1, 1.551:1, 1.00:1. Reverse: 3.798:1. Optional: None. Clutch: 8.5 in. Auburn or Rockford single dry plate. Total lining area: 72 sq. in. Optional: Auburn single dry plate, 9.25 in. dia. plate.

VEHICLE DIMENSIONS: Wheelbase: 80.166 in. Overall Length: 129.75 in. Front/Rear Tread: 48.25 in./48.25 in. Overall Height: 66.75 in. Width: 68.721 in. Front/Rear Overhang: 20.59 in./ .22.31 in. Tailgate: Width and Height: 36 in. x 14.125 in. Ground Clearance: 8.750 in. Load space: 32 in. x 52.315 in. x 14.125 in. Steering wheel to seat back (max.): 15.12 in.

CAPACITIES: Fuel Tank: 10.5 gal. Located under driver's seat. Coolant System: 11 qt.

ACCOMMODATIONS: Seating Capacity: 2/5.

INSTRUMENTATION: Instrument panel light, ammeter, heat indicator gauge, speedometer oil pressure gauge, fuel level gauge.

OPTIONS AND PRICES: Power take-off: $96.25. Pulley drive: $57.40. Engine governor: $28.65. Half and full canvas and metal tops. High altitude cylinder head. High temperature thermostat.

HISTORICAL FOOTNOTES: The 1954 CJ Jeeps were introduced on December 1, 1953. On February 23, 1954 the 500,000th postwar Jeep was built.

1955 CJ

A new CJ-5 Universal Jeep was announced on October 11, 1954. It was based on the MD-MB38A1 military Jeep. The CJ-5 had an 81 in. wheelbase (one in. longer than that of the CJ-3B) and an overall length of 135.5 in. (5.75 in. greater than that of the CJ-3B). The overall width of the new CJ-5 was 71.75 as compared to the CJ-3B's 68.75 in. "Jeep" lettering was positioned just ahead of the door cutout on the CJ-5. Respective shipping weights for the CJ-5 and CJ-3B were 2164 and 2134 pounds.

Comparison of the CJ-5 to its MD-MB38A1 military counterpart revealed some noteworthy variations. The CJ-5's headlights extended forward slightly from their openings and carried chrome dress-up rings. As expected, the military model's blacked-out parking lights were replaced by units of conventional design on the CJ-5. A 6-volt electrical system replaced the military's 24-volt system.

Military models used both windshield base and cowl-mounted driver side mirrors. The CJ-5's mirror was positioned on the windshield support base. CJ-5 Jeeps for the domestic market had a one-piece windshield standard with a divided opening type optional. The MB38A1 had a two-piece windshield. All export CJ-5 Jeeps had a standard divided opening windshield.

The CJ-5's reshaped body with its curved hood and fenders made it easy to distinguish from the CJ-3B. The CJ-5's body sheet metal was flanged and overlapped for increased strength. A fully boxed front cross member increased the frame's carrying strength and rigidity and endurance of the new Jeep's frame. The CJ-5's front suspension used lower-rate springs. Those at the rear were slightly stiffer.

1955 Jeep CJ-5

The CJ-5 windshield in comparison with that of the CJ-3B had nearly 100 more square in. of glass area and folded flat on stronger hinges. While the front seat occupant probably welcomed the availability of the added space, the driver was treated to a new dash panel with a back-lighted instrument cluster. Also debuting on the CJ-5 was a passenger-car type handbrake, a glove compartment that could be equipped with a cover and improved seating. The front seats were now softer due to their new coil springs. The driver's seat had three fore and aft adjustments. At the rear a new optional seat allowed four passengers to be carried.

An improved "All-Weather" top with closer tolerance fittings was an extra cost feature. A new passenger safety rail and an optional rear seat making it possible to carry four passengers were added to the CJ's optional equipment list. No changes were made in the CJ-3B for 1954.

I.D. DATA: The serial number was located on the left front of the frame and the back of the bumper. It was also found on the right side of the dash under the hood. The engine number was located on the boss for the water pump at the front of the cylinder block. Serial number range: CJ-3B: 57548-10001 and up. CJ-5: 57548-10001 and up.

Model Number	Body Type	Factory Price	GVW	Shipping Weight	Prod Total
Jeep					
CJ-3B	Utility	$1411	3500	2134	47,432*
CJ-5	Utility	$1476	3500	2164	—

* Calendar production for all Jeep models.

All specifications for the CJ-3B were unchanged for 1954. The information that follows relates to the CJ-5.

STANDARD ENGINE: Engine Type: F-head, In-line-4. Cast iron block and cylinder head. Bore x Stroke: 3.125 in. x 4.375 in. Lifters: Mechanical. Number of main bearings-3. Fuel Induction: Single Carter model YF-938-SD. Compression Ratio: 6.9:1. Optional High Altitude 7.4:1. Displacement: 134.2 cu. in. (2.199 liters). Horsepower: 72 @ 4000 rpm. Torque: 114 lb.-ft. @ 2000 rpm. Oil refill capacity: 4 qt. with filter change. Fuel Requirements: Regular.

CHASSIS FEATURES: Separate body and channel steel frame construction, 4.125 in. depth x 1.937 in. width, five cross members. Overall frame length: 128.4375 in. Section modulus: 1.493 in. cu.

SUSPENSION AND RUNNING GEAR: Front Suspension: 7-leaf semi-elliptical springs, 39.625 in. x by 1.75 in. Spring rate: 240 lb./in. Monroe, 11.4375 in. dia. double-acting shock absorbers. Load capacity: 550 lbs. Optional: 10-leaf heavy-duty front springs. Rear Suspension: 9-leaf semi-elliptical springs, 46 in. x 1.75 in. Spring rate: 200 lb./in. Monroe, 11.9375 in. dia. double-acting shock absorbers. Normal load capacity: 940 lbs. Optional: Heavy-duty rear springs option with eleven thicker (2.407 in. to 1.973 in.). Spring rate: 225 lb./

in. Front Axle Type and Capacity: Full-floating Spicer, hypoid. Rear Axle Type and Capacity: Semi-floating Spicer model 44-2. Hypoid. Axle Ratios: 5.38:1. Transfer Case: Spicer model 18. Ratios: 2.46:1, 1.00:1. Brakes: Type: Hydraulic, front and rear. Dimensions: Front and rear: 9.00 in. x 1.75 in. Total braking area: 117.75 sq. in. Wheels: Kelsey-Hayes 16 x 4.50 in., 5-bolt steel disc. Optional: None. Tires: 6.00 x 16 in. 4-ply. Optional: 7.00 x 15 in. 4-ply. Steering: Ross model T-12 cam and lever. Ratio: 14-12:1. Turning Circle: 36 ft. Optional: None. Standard Transmission: Warner-Gear model T090A, 3-speed manual floor-mounted shift. Transmission ratios: 2.798:1, 1.551:1, 1.00:1. Reverse: 3.798:1. Optional: None. Clutch: 8.5 in. Auburn or Rockford single dry plate. Total lining area: 72 sq. in. Optional: Auburn single dry plate, 9.25 in. dia. plate.

VEHICLE DIMENSIONS: Wheelbase: 80.166 in. Overall Length: 129.75 in. Front/Rear Tread: 48.25 in./48.25 in. Overall Height: 66.75 in. Width: 68.721 in. Front/Rear Overhang: 20.59 in. 22.31/ in. Tailgate: Width and Height: 36 in. x 14.125 in. Ground Clearance: 8.750 in. Load space: CJ-5: 36 in. x 39 in. with tailgate closed, 36 in. by 49 in. with open tailgate. Steering wheel to seat back (max.): 15.12 in.

CAPACITIES: Fuel Tank: 10.5 gal. Located under driver's seat. Coolant System: 11 qt.

ACCOMMODATIONS: Seating Capacity: 2/6.

INSTRUMENTATION: Instrument panel light, ammeter, heat indicator gauge, speedometer oil pressure gauge, fuel level gauge.

OPTIONS AND PRICES: Power take-off: $96.25. Pulley drive: $57.40. Engine governor: $28.65. Half and full canvas and metal tops. High altitude cylinder head. High temperature thermostat. Passenger safety rail. Rear passenger seat.

HISTORICAL FOOTNOTES: The CJ-3B was introduced on October 11, 1954. The CJ-5 debuted on November 12, 1954.

1956 CJ

A longer wheelbase Jeep, the CJ-6 was introduced for 1956. Based on the CJ-5, it had a 20 in. longer wheelbase and additional cargo and passenger space. Except for its longer wheelbase, the CJ-6 was identical to the CJ-5, which along with the CJ-3B was carried over unchanged into 1956.

I.D. DATA: The serial number was located on the left front of the frame and the back of the bumper. It was also found on the right side of the dash under the hood. The engine number was located on the boss for the water pump at the right front of the cylinder block. Serial number range: CJ-3B: 57548-21158 and up. CJ-5: 57548-23233 and up. CJ-6: 57748-10001 and up. Engine and serial numbers were the same in most models.

Model Number	Body Type	Factory Price	GVW	Shipping Weight	Prod. Total
Jeep					
CJ-3B	Utility	$1503	3500	2134	—
CJ-5	Utility	$1577	3750	2164	—
CJ-6	Utility	$1731	3900	2305	—

All specifications for the CJ-3B were unchanged for 1956. The information that follows relates to the CJ-5 and CJ-6.

STANDARD ENGINE: Engine Type: F-head, In-line-4. Cast iron block and cylinder head. Bore x Stroke: 3.125 in. x 4.375 in. Lifters: Mechanical. Number of main bearings-3. Fuel Induction: Single Carter model YF-938-SD. Compression Ratio: 6.9:1. Optional High Altitude 7.4:1. Displacement: 134.2 cu. in. (2.199 liters). Horsepower: 72 @ 4000 rpm. Torque: 114 lb.-ft. @ 2000 rpm. Oil refill capacity: 4 qt. with filter change. Fuel Requirements: Regular.

CHASSIS FEATURES: Separate body and channel steel frame construction, 4.125 in. depth x 1.937 in. width, five cross members. Overall frame length: CJ-5: 128.4375 in. CJ-6: 148.4375 in. Section modulus: 1.493 in. cu.

SUSPENSION AND RUNNING GEAR: Front Suspension: 7-leaf semi-elliptical springs, 39.625 in. x by 1.75 in. Spring rate: 240 lb./in. Monroe, 11.4375 in. dia. double-acting shock absorbers. Load capacity: 550 lbs. Optional: 10-leaf heavy-duty front springs-3. Rear Suspension: 9-leaf semi-elliptical springs, 46 in. x 1.75 in. Spring rate: 200 lb./in. CJ-6: 270 lb./in. Monroe 11.9375 in. dia. double-acting shock absorbers. Normal load capacity: 940 lbs. CJ-6: 845 lbs. Optional: Heavy-duty rear springs option with eleven thicker (2.407 in. to 1.973 in.). Spring rate: 225 lb./in. Front Axle Type and Capacity: Full-floating Spicer model 25, hypoid. Rear Axle Type and Capacity: Semi-floating Spicer model 44-2. Hypoid. Axle Ratios: 5.38:1. Transfer Case: Spicer model 18. Ratios: 2.46:1, 1.00:1. Brakes: Type: Hydraulic, front and rear. Dimensions: Front and rear: 9.00 in. x 1.75 in. Total braking area: 117.75 sq. in. Wheels: Kelsey-Hayes 16 x 4.50 in., 5-bolt steel disc. Optional: None. Tires: 6.00 x 16 in. 4-ply. Optional: 7.00 x 15 in. 4-ply. Steering: Ross model T-12 cam and lever. Ratio: 14-12. Turning Circle: 39 ft. Standard Transmission: Warner-Gear model T090A, 3-speed manual floor-mounted shift. Transmission ratios: 2.798:1, 1.551:1, 1.00:1. Reverse: 3.798:1. Optional: None. Clutch: 8.5 in. Auburn or Rockford single dry plate. Total lining area: 72 sq. in. Optional: Auburn single dry plate, 9.25 in. dia. plate.

VEHICLE DIMENSIONS: Wheelbase: CJ-3B: 80.0625 in. CJ-5: 81.0 in. CJ-6: 101 in. Overall Length: CJ-3B: 129.875 in. CJ-5: 135.50 in. CJ-6: 155.50 in. Front/Rear Tread: 48.4375 in./48.4375 in. Overall Height: CJ-3B: 67.75 in. CJ-5: 69.5 in. CJ-6: 68.25 in. Width: CJ-5, CJ-6: 71.75 in. Front/Rear Overhang: 20.59 in./22.31 in. Tailgate: Width and Height: 36 in. x 14.125 in. Ground Clearance: 8.0 in. Load space: 36 in. x 39 in. (with tailgate closed), 36 in. by 49 in. (tailgate closed). Steering wheel to seat back (max.): 15.12 in.

CAPACITIES: Fuel Tank: 10.5 gal. Located under driver's seat. Coolant System: 11 qt.

ACCOMMODATIONS: Seating Capacity: 2/6.

INSTRUMENTATION: Instrument panel light, ammeter, heat indicator gauge, speedometer oil pressure gauge, fuel level gauge.

OPTIONS AND PRICES: Power take-off: $96.25. Pulley drive: $57.40. Engine governor: $28.65. Half and full canvas and metal tops. High altitude cylinder head. High temperature thermostat. Passenger safety rail. Rear passenger seat.

HISTORICAL FOOTNOTES: The CJ models were introduced on August 17, 1955.

1957 CJ

No changes took place in the design of the CJ Jeeps for 1957.

The exterior colors for 1957 were raven black, president red, metallic steel glow, transport yellow, metallic royal blue, metallic glenwood green and Aztec orange.

I.D. DATA: The serial number was located on the left front of the frame and the back of the bumper. It was also found on the right side of the dash under the hood. The engine number was located on the boss for the water pump at the right front of the cylinder block. Serial number range: CJ-3B: 57548-21158 and up. CJ-5: 57548-23233 and up. CJ-6: 57748-10001 and up. Engine and serial numbers were the same in most models.

Model Number	Body Type	Factory Price	GVW	Shipping Weight	Prod. Total
Jeep					
CJ-3B	Utility	$1799.26	3500	2132	—
CJ-5	Utility	$1885.98	3750	2163	—
CJ-6	Utility	$2068.47	3900	2225	—

All specifications for the CJ models was unchanged for 1957.

STANDARD ENGINE: Engine Type: F-head, In-line-4. Cast iron block and cylinder head. Bore x Stroke: 3.125 in. x 4.375 in. Lifters: Mechanical. Number of main bearings-3. Fuel Induction: Single Carter model YF-938-SD. Compression Ratio: 6.9:1. Optional High Altitude 7.4:1. Displacement: 134.2 cu. in. (2.199 liters). Horsepower: 72 @ 4000 rpm. Torque: 114 lb.-ft. @ 2000 rpm. Oil refill capacity: 4 qt. with filter change. Fuel Requirements: Regular.

CHASSIS FEATURES: Separate body and channel steel frame construction, 4.125 in. depth x 1.937 in. width, five cross members. Overall frame length: CJ-5: 128.4375 in. CJ-6: 148.4375 in. Section modulus: 1.493 in. cu.

SUSPENSION AND RUNNING GEAR: Front Suspension: 7-leaf semi-elliptical springs, 39.625 in. x by 1.75 in. Spring rate: 240 lb./in. Monroe, 11.4375 in. dia. double-acting shock absorbers. Load capacity: 550 lbs. Optional: 10-leaf heavy-duty front springs. Rear Suspension: 9-leaf semi-elliptical springs, 46 in. x 1.75 in. Spring rate: 200 lb./in. CJ-6: 270 lb./in. Monroe 11.9375 in. dia. double-acting shock absorbers. Normal load capacity: 940 lbs. CJ-6: 845 lb. Optional: Heavy-duty rear springs option with eleven thicker (2.407 in. to 1.973 in.). Spring rate: 225 lb./in. Front Axle Type and Capacity: Full-floating Spicer model 25, hypoid. Rear Axle Type and Capacity: Semi-floating Spicer model 44-2. Hypoid. Axle Ratios: 5.38:1. Transfer Case: Spicer model 18. Ratios: 2.46:1, 1.00:1. Brakes: Type: Hydraulic, front and rear. Dimensions: Front and rear: 9.00 in. x 1.75 in. Total braking area: 117.75 sq. in. Wheels: Kelsey-Hayes 16 x 4.50 in., 5-bolt steel disc. Optional: None. Tires: 6.00 x 16 in. 4-ply. Optional: 7.00 x 15 in. 4-ply. Steering: Ross model T-12 cam and lever. Ratio: 14-12. Turning Circle: 39 ft. Standard Transmission: Warner-Gear model T090A, 3-speed manual floor-mounted shift. Transmission ratios: 2.798:1, 1.551:1, 1.00:1. Reverse: 3.798:1. Clutch: 8.5 in. Auburn or Rockford single dry plate. Total lining area: 72 sq. in. Optional: Auburn single dry plate, 9.25 in. dia. plate.

VEHICLE DIMENSIONS: Wheelbase: CJ-3B: 80.0625 in. CJ-5: 81.0 in. CJ-6: 101 in. Overall Length: CJ-3B: 129.875 in. CJ-5: 135.50 in. CJ-6:. Front/Rear Tread: 48.4375 in./48.4375 in. Overall Height: CJ-3B: 67.75 in. CJ-5: 69.5 in. CJ-6: 68.25 in. Width: CJ-3B: 68.875 in. CJ-5, CJ-6: 71.75 in. Front/Rear Overhang: 20.59 in./22.31 in. Tailgate: Width and Height: 36 in. x 14.125 in. Ground Clearance: 8.0 in. Load space: 36 in. x 39 in. (with tailgate closed), 36 in. by 49 in. (tailgate closed). Steering wheel to seat back (max.): 15.12 in.

CAPACITIES: Fuel Tank: 10.5 gal. Located under driver's seat. Coolant System: 11 qt.

ACCOMMODATIONS: Seating Capacity: 2/6.

INSTRUMENTATION: Instrument panel light, ammeter, heat indicator gauge, speedometer oil pressure gauge, fuel level gauge.

OPTIONS AND PRICES: Group #932. Includes drawbar, oil bath air cleaner, oil filter and directional signals: $71.10. Full canvas top (CJ-3B): $135.68. Full canvas top (CJ-5): $157.77. Full canvas top (CJ-6): $172.94. Front canvas top (CJ-3B): $95.71. Front canvas top (CJ-5 and CJ-6): $114.43. CJ-5 full cab with hinged doors: $402.36. CJ-5 full cab with sliding doors: $402.36. Heater: $36.90. Fresh-air heater and defroster (CJ-5 and CJ-6): $79.93. Ventilating windshield (CJ-5 and CJ-6): $21.51. Center power take-off: $51.68. Pulley and pulley drive for power take-off: $95.87. Center and rear power take-off: $169.97. Belt driven governor: $43.34. Monroe hydraulic lift: $308.30. Quick disconnect fittings: $20.50. Front passenger seat (CJ-3B): $32.48. Front passenger seat (1/3 right, CJ-5 and CJ-6): $41.68. Front passenger seat (bucket, CJ-5 and CJ-6): $44.35. Rear seat: $48.31. Front passenger seat (2/3 driver, CJ-5 and CJ-6 with 3-speed transmission): $20.44. Front passenger seat (2/3 driver, CJ-5 and CJ-6 with 4-speed transmission): $20.44. 7.00 x 15 4-ply All-Service tread: $61.89. 7.00 x 15 6-ply All-Service tread: $87.48. 7.00 x 16 6-ply All-Service tread: $148.63. 6.50 x 15 6-ply Deluxe Rib tread: $49.29. 7.60 x 15 4-ply Suburbanite: $26.49. 6.00 x 16 4-ply Deluxe Rib: No extra charge. 6.00 x 16 6-ply All-Service: $38.29. 9.00 x 13 4-ply Rib Sand-Service: $283.70. Front bumper weight: $47.83. 4-speed transmission (CJ-5 and CJ-6): $161.52. Locking differential: $42.96.

HISTORICAL FOOTNOTES: The CJ models were introduced on August 16 and 17,1956.

1958 CJ

No changes took place in the design of the CJ Jeeps for 1958.

I.D. DATA: The serial number was located on the left front of the frame and the back of the bumper. It was also found on the right side of the dash under the hood. The engine number was located on the boss for the water pump at the right front of the cylinder block. Serial number range: CJ-3B: 57548-25017 and up. CJ-5: 57548-25675 and up. CJ-6: 57748-10016 and up. Engine and serial numbers were the same in most models.

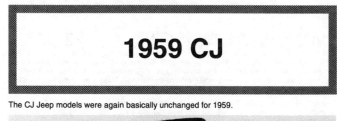

Model Number	Body Type	Factory Price	GVW	Shipping Weight	Prod. Total
Jeep					
CJ-3B	Utility	$1654	3500	2132	—
CJ-5	Utility	$1734	3750	2163	—
CJ-6	Utility	$1904	3900	2225	—

All specifications for the CJ models was unchanged for 1958.

STANDARD ENGINE: Engine Type: F-head, In-line-4. Cast iron block and cylinder head. Bore x Stroke: 3.125 in. x 4.375 in. Lifters: Mechanical. Number of main bearings-3. Fuel Induction: Single Carter model YF-938-SD. Compression Ratio: 6.9:1. Optional High Altitude 7.4:1. Displacement: 134.2 cu. in. (2.199 liters). Horsepower: 72 @ 4000 rpm. Torque: 114 lb.-ft. @ 2000 rpm. Oil refill capacity: 4 qt. with filter change. Fuel Requirements: Regular.

CHASSIS FEATURES: Separate body and channel steel frame construction, 4.125 in. depth x 1.937 in. width, five cross members. Overall frame length: CJ-5: 128.4375 in. CJ-6: 148.4375 in. Section modulus: 1.493 in. cu.

SUSPENSION AND RUNNING GEAR: Front Suspension: 7-leaf semi-elliptical springs, 39.625 in. x by 1.75 in. Spring rate: 240 lb./in. Monroe, 11.4375 in. dia. double-acting shock absorbers. Load capacity: 550 lbs. Optional: 10-leaf heavy-duty front springs. Rear Suspension: 9-leaf semi-elliptical springs, 46 in. x 1.75 in. Spring rate: 200 lb./in. CJ-6: 270 lb./in. Monroe 11.9375 in. dia. double-acting shock absorbers. Normal load capacity: 940 lbs. CJ-6: 845 lb. Optional: Heavy-duty rear springs option with eleven thicker (2.407 in. to 1.973 in.). Spring rate: 225 lb./in. Front Axle Type and Capacity: Full-floating Spicer model 25, hypoid. Rear Axle Type and Capacity: Semi-floating Spicer model 44-2. Hypoid. Axle Ratios: 5.38:1. Transfer Case: Spicer model 18. Ratios: 2.46:1, 1.00:1. Brakes: Type: Hydraulic, front and rear. Dimensions: Front and rear: 9.00 in. x 1.75 in. Total braking area: 117.75 sq. in. Wheels: Kelsey-Hayes 16 x 4.50 in., 5-bolt steel disc. Optional: None. Tires: 6.00 x 16 in. 4-ply. Optional: 7.00 x 15 in. 4-ply. Steering: Ross model T-12 cam and lever. Ratio: 14-12. Turning Circle: 39 ft. Standard Transmission: Warner-Gear model T090A, 3-speed manual floor-mounted shift. Transmission ratios: 2.798:1, 1.551:1, 1.00:1. Reverse: 3.798:1. Clutch: 8.5 in. Auburn or Rockford single dry plate. Total lining area: 72 sq. in. Optional: Auburn single dry plate, 9.25 in. dia. plate.

VEHICLE DIMENSIONS: Wheelbase: CJ-3B: 80.0625 in. CJ-5: 81.0 in. CJ-6: 101 in. Overall Length: CJ-3B: 129.875 in. CJ-5: 135.50 in. CJ-6:. Front/Rear Tread: 48.4375 in./48.4375 in. Overall Height: CJ-3B: 67.75 in. CJ-5: 69.5 in. CJ-6: 68.25 in. Width: CJ-3B: 68.875 in. CJ-5, CJ-6: 71.75 in. Front/Rear Overhang: 20.59 in./22.31 in. Tailgate: Width and Height: 36 in. x 14.125 in. Ground Clearance: 8.0 in. Load space: 36 in. x 39 in. (with tailgate closed), 36 in. by 49 in. (tailgate closed). Steering wheel to seat back (max.): 15.12 in.

CAPACITIES: Fuel Tank: 10.5 gal. Located under driver's seat. Coolant System: 11 qt.

ACCOMMODATIONS: Seating Capacity: 2/6.

INSTRUMENTATION: Instrument panel light, ammeter, heat indicator gauge, speedometer oil pressure gauge, fuel level gauge.

OPTIONS: Group #932. Includes drawbar, oil bath air cleaner, oil filter and directional signals. Full canvas top (CJ-3B). Full canvas top (CJ-5). Full canvas top (CJ-6). Front canvas top (CJ-3B). Front canvas top (CJ-6 and CJ-6). CJ-5 full cab with hinged doors. CJ-5 full cab with sliding doors. Heater. Fresh-air heater and defroster (CJ-5 and CJ-6). Ventilating windshield (CJ-5 and CJ-6). Center power take-off. Pulley and pulley drive for power take-off. Center and rear power take-off. Belt driven governor. Monroe hydraulic lift. Quick disconnect fittings. Front passenger seat (CJ-3B). Front passenger seat (1/3 right, CJ-5 and CJ-6). Front passenger seat (bucket, CJ-5 and CJ-6). Rear seat. Front passenger seat (2/3 driver, CJ-5 and CJ-6 with 3-speed transmission). Front passenger seat (2/3 driver, CJ-5 and CJ-6 with 4-speed transmission). 7.00 x 15 4-ply All-Service tread. 7.00 x 15 6-ply All-Service tread. 7.00 x 16 6-ply All-Service tread. 6.50 x 15 6-ply Deluxe Rib tread. 7.60 x 15 4-ply Suburbanite. 6.00 x 16 4-ply Deluxe Rib: No extra charge. 6.00 x 16 6-ply All-Service. 9.00 x 13 4-ply Rib Sand-Service. Front bumper weight. 4-speed transmission (CJ-5 and CJ-6). Locking differential.

HISTORICAL FOOTNOTES: The CJ models were introduced on August 15, 1957.

1959 CJ

The CJ Jeep models were again basically unchanged for 1959.

1959 Jeep CJ-3B

I.D. DATA: The serial number was located on the left front of the frame and the back of the bumper. It was also found on the right side of the dash under the hood. The engine number was located on the boss for the water pump at the right front of the cylinder block. Serial number range: CJ-3B: 57348-38152 and up. CJ-5: 57548-31799 and up. CJ-6: 57748-10608 and up. Engine and serial numbers were the same in most models.

Model Number	Body Type	Factory Price	GVW	Shipping Weight	Prod. Total
Jeep					
CJ-3B	Utility	$1736	3500	2132	—
CJ-5	Utility	$1821	3750	2163	—
CJ-6	Utility	$1999	3900	2225	—

All specifications for the CJ models was unchanged for 1958.

STANDARD ENGINE: Engine Type: F-head, In-line-4. Cast iron block and cylinder head. Bore x Stroke: 3.125 in. x 4.375 in. Lifters: Mechanical. Number of main bearings-3. Fuel Induction: Single Carter model YF-938-SD. Compression Ratio: 6.9:1. Optional High Altitude 7.4:1. Displacement: 134.2 cu. in. (2.199 liters). Horsepower: 72 @ 4000 rpm. Torque: 114 lb.-ft. @ 2000 rpm. Oil refill capacity: 4 qt. with filter change. Fuel Requirements: Regular.

CHASSIS FEATURES: Separate body and channel steel frame construction, 4.125 in. depth x 1.937 in. width, five cross members. Overall frame length: CJ-5: 128.4375 in. CJ-6: 148.4375 in. Section modulus: 1.493 in. cu.

SUSPENSION AND RUNNING GEAR: Front Suspension: 7-leaf semi-elliptical springs, 39.625 in. x by 1.75 in. Spring rate: 240 lb./in. Monroe, 11.4375 in. dia. double-acting shock absorbers. Load capacity: 550 lbs. Optional: 10-leaf heavy-duty front springs. Rear Suspension: 9-leaf semi-elliptical springs, 46 in. x 1.75 in. Spring rate: 200 lb./in. CJ-6: 270 lb./in. Monroe 11.9375 in. dia. double-acting shock absorbers. Normal load capacity: 940 lbs. CJ-6: 845 lb. Optional: Heavy-duty rear springs option with eleven thicker (2.407 in. to 1.973 in.). Spring rate: 225 lb./in. Front Axle Type and Capacity: Full-floating Spicer model 25, hypoid. Rear Axle Type and Capacity: Semi-floating Spicer model 44-2. Hypoid. Axle Ratios: 5.38:1. Transfer Case: Spicer model 18. Ratios: 2.46:1, 1.00:1. Brakes: Type: Hydraulic, front and rear. Dimensions: Front and rear: 9.00 in. x 1.75 in. Total braking area: 117.75 sq. in. Wheels: Kelsey-Hayes 16 x 4.50 in., 5-bolt steel disc. Optional: None. Tires: 6.00 x 16 in. 4-ply. Optional: 7.00 x 15 in. 4-ply. Steering: Ross model T-12 cam and lever. Ratio: 14-12. Turning Circle: 39 ft. Standard Transmission: Warner-Gear model T090A, 3-speed manual floor-mounted shift. Transmission ratios: 2.798:1, 1.551:1, 1.00:1. Reverse: 3.798:1. Clutch: 8.5 in. Auburn or Rockford single dry plate. Total lining area: 72 sq. in. Optional: Auburn single dry plate, 9.25 in. dia. plate.

VEHICLE DIMENSIONS: Wheelbase: CJ-3B: 80.0625 in. CJ-5: 81.0 in. CJ-6: 101 in. Overall Length: CJ-3B: 129.875 in. CJ-5: 135.50 in. CJ-6:. Front/Rear Tread: 48.4375 in./48.4375 in. Overall Height: CJ-3B: 67.75 in. CJ-5: 69.5 in. CJ-6: 68.25 in. Width: CJ-3B: 68.875 in. CJ-5, CJ-6: 71.75 in. Front/Rear Overhang: 20.59 in./22.31 in. Tailgate: Width and Height: 36 in. x 14.125 in. Ground Clearance: 8.0 in. Load space: 36 in. x 39 in. (with tailgate closed), 36 in. by 49 in. (tailgate closed). Steering wheel to seat back (max.): 15.12 in.

CAPACITIES: Fuel Tank: 10.5 gal. Located under driver's seat. Coolant System: 11 qt.

ACCOMMODATIONS: Seating Capacity: 2/6.

INSTRUMENTATION: Instrument panel light, ammeter, heat indicator gauge, speedometer oil pressure gauge, fuel level gauge.

OPTIONS: Group #932. Includes drawbar, oil bath air cleaner, oil filter and directional signals. Full canvas top (CJ-3B). Full canvas top (CJ-5). Full canvas top (CJ-6). Front canvas top (CJ-3B). Front canvas top (CJ-5 and CJ-6). CJ-5 full cab with hinged doors. CJ-5 full cab with sliding doors. Heater. Fresh-air heater and defroster (CJ-5 and CJ-6). Ventilating windshield (CJ-5 and CJ-6). Center power take-off. Pulley and pulley drive for power take-off. Center and rear power take-off. Belt driven governor. Monroe hydraulic lift. Quick disconnect fittings. Front passenger seat (CJ-3B). Front passenger seat (1/3 right, CJ-5 and CJ-6). Front passenger seat (bucket, CJ-5 and CJ-6). Rear seat. Front passenger seat (2/3 driver, CJ-5 and CJ-6 with 3-speed transmission). Front passenger seat (2/3 driver, CJ-5 and CJ-6 with 4-speed transmission). 7.00 x 15 4-ply All-Service tread. 7.00 x 15 6-ply All-Service tread. 7.00 x 16 6-ply All-Service tread. 6.50 x 15 6-ply Deluxe Rib tread. 7.60 x 15 4-ply Suburbanite. 6.00 x 16 4-ply Deluxe Rib: No extra charge. 6.00 x 16 6-ply All-Service. 9.00 x 13 4-ply Rib Sand-Service. Front bumper weight. 4-speed transmission (CJ-5 and CJ-6). Locking differential. High temperature thermostat. Passenger safety rail. Rear passenger seat.

HISTORICAL FOOTNOTES: A total of 10,576 Jeeps were registered during the 1959 calendar year.

1959 Jeep CJ-5

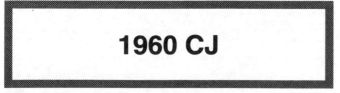
1960 CJ

The CJ Jeep models were again basically unchanged for 1960.

I.D. DATA: The serial number was located on the left front of the frame and the back of the bumper. It was also found on the right side of the dash under the hood. The engine number was located on the boss for the water pump at the right front of the cylinder block. Serial number range: CJ-3B: 57348-41475 and up. CJ-5: 57548-33889 and up. CJ-6: 57748-13886 and up. Engine and serial numbers were the same in most models.

Model Number	Body Type	Factory Price	GVW	Shipping Weight	Prod. Total
Jeep					
CJ-3B	Utility	$1888	3500	2132	—
CJ-5	Utility	$1979	3750	2163	—
CJ-6	Utility	$2171	3900	2225	—

All specifications for the CJ models was unchanged for 1958.

1960 Jeep CJ-6

STANDARD ENGINE: Engine Type: F-head, In-line-4. Cast iron block and cylinder head. Bore x Stroke: 3.125 in. x 4.375 in. Lifters: Mechanical. Number of main bearings-3. Fuel Induction: Single Carter model YF-938-SD. Compression Ratio: 6.9:1. Optional High Altitude 7.4:1. Displacement: 134.2 cu. in. (2.199 liters). Horsepower: 72 @ 4000 rpm. Torque: 114 lb.-ft. @ 2000 rpm. Oil refill capacity: 4 qt. with filter change. Fuel Requirements: Regular.

CHASSIS FEATURES: Separate body and channel steel frame construction, 4.125 in. depth x 1.937 in. width, five cross members. Overall frame length: CJ-5: 128.4375 in. CJ-6: 148.4375 in. Section modulus: 1.493 in. cu.

SUSPENSION AND RUNNING GEAR: Front Suspension: 7-leaf semi-elliptical springs, 39.625 in. x by 1.75 in. Spring rate: 240 lb./in. Monroe, 11.4375 in. dia. double-acting shock absorbers. Load capacity: 550 lbs. Optional: 10-leaf heavy-duty front springs. Rear Suspension: 9-leaf semi-elliptical springs, 46 in. x 1.75 in. Spring rate: 200 lb./in. CJ-6: 270 lb./in. Monroe 11.9375 in. dia. double-acting shock absorbers. Normal load capacity: 940 lbs. CJ-6: 845 lb. Optional: Heavy-duty rear springs option with eleven thicker (2.407 in. to 1.973 in.). Spring rate: 225 lb./in. Front Axle Type and Capacity: Full-floating Spicer model 25, hypoid. Rear Axle Type and Capacity: Semi-floating Spicer model 44-2. Hypoid. Axle Ratios: 5.38:1. Transfer Case: Spicer model 18. Ratios: 2.46:1, 1.00:1. Brakes: Type: Hydraulic, front and rear. Dimensions: Front and rear: 9.00 in. x 1.75 in. Total braking area: 117.75 sq. in. Wheels: Kelsey-Hayes 16 x 4.50 in., 5-bolt steel disc. Optional: None. Tires: 6.00 x 16 in. 4-ply. Optional: 7.00 x 15 in. 4-ply. Steering: Ross model T-12 cam and lever. Ratio: 14-12. Turning Circle: 39 ft. Standard Transmission: Warner-Gear model T090A, 3-speed manual floor-mounted shift. Transmission ratios: 2.798:1, 1.551:1, 1.00:1. Reverse: 3.798:1. Clutch: 8.5 in. Auburn or Rockford single dry plate. Total lining area: 72 sq. in. Optional: Auburn single dry plate, 9.25 in. dia. plate.

VEHICLE DIMENSIONS: Wheelbase: CJ-3B: 80.0625 in. CJ-5: 81.0 in. CJ-6: 101 in. Overall Length: CJ-3B: 129.875 in. CJ-5: 135.50 in. CJ-6:. Front/Rear Tread: 48.4375 in./48.4375 in. Overall Height: CJ-3B: 67.75 in. CJ-5: 69.5 in. CJ-6: 68.25 in. Width: CJ-3B: 68.875 in. CJ-5, CJ-6: 71.75 in. Front/Rear Overhang: 20.59 in./22.31 in. Tailgate: Width and Height: 36 in. x 14.125 in. Ground Clearance: 8.0 in. Load space: 36 in. x 39 in. (with tailgate closed), 36 in. by 49 in. (tailgate closed). Steering wheel to seat back (max.): 15.12 in.

CAPACITIES: Fuel Tank: 10.5 gal. Located under driver's seat. Coolant System: 11 qt.

1960 Jeep CJ-5

ACCOMMODATIONS: Seating Capacity: 2/6.

INSTRUMENTATION: Instrument panel light, ammeter, heat indicator gauge, speedometer oil pressure gauge, fuel level gauge.

OPTIONS: Group #932. Includes drawbar, oil bath air cleaner, oil filter and directional signals. Full canvas top (CJ-3B). Full canvas top (CJ-5). Full canvas top (CJ-6). Front canvas top (CJ-3B). Front canvas top (CJ-5 and CJ-6). CJ-5 full cab with hinged doors. CJ-5 full cab with sliding doors. Heater. Fresh-air heater and defroster (CJ-5 and CJ-6). Ventilating windshield (CJ-5 and CJ-6). Center power take-off. Pulley and pulley drive for power take-off. Center and rear power take-off. Belt driven governor. Monroe hydraulic lift. Quick disconnect fittings. Front passenger seat (CJ-3B). Front passenger seat (1/3 right, CJ-5 and CJ-6). Front passenger seat (bucket, CJ-5 and CJ-6). Rear seat. Front passenger seat (2/3 driver, CJ-5 and CJ-6 with 3-speed transmission). Front passenger seat (2/3 driver, CJ-5 and CJ-6 with 4-speed transmission). 7.00 x 15 4-ply All-Service tread. 7.00 x 15 6-ply All-Service tread. 7.00 x 16 6-ply

All-Service tread. 6.50 x 15 6-ply Deluxe Rib tread. 7.60 x 15 4-ply Suburbanite. 6.00 x 16 4-ply Deluxe Rib: No extra charge. 6.00 x 16 6-ply All-Service. 9.00 x 13 4-ply Rib Sand-Service. Front bumper weight.4-speed transmission (CJ-5 and CJ-6). Locking differential.

HISTORICAL FOOTNOTES: Barney Roos, one of the most prolific of America's automotive engineers and the man who was the engineering driving force behind the original military Jeep, died in 1960.

1960 Jeep CJ-3B

1961 CJ

A near-luxury version of the CJ-5, the Tuxedo Park, was introduced for 1961. It was essentially the CJ-5 with dress-up items such as chromed hood hinges, exterior mirror supports and bumpers; turbine wheels, whitewall tires, spare tire cover and new color combinations. The CJ-5 was available in any of ten exterior colors. The optional CJ-5 convertible top was offered in black or white. Available for the CJ-5 and CJ-6 was the British Perkins 4-cylinder diesel engine.

I.D. DATA: The serial number was located on the left front of the frame and the back of the bumper. It was also found on the right side of the dash under the hood. The engine number was located on the boss for the water pump at the right front of the cylinder block. Serial number range: CJ-3B: 57348-49029 and up. CJ-5: 57548-83109 and up. CJ-6: 57748-15196 and up. Engine and serial numbers were the same in most models.

Model Number	Body Type	Factory Price	GVW	Shipping Weight	Prod. Total
Jeep					
CJ-3B	Utility	$1960	3500	2132	—
CJ-5	Utility	$2054	3750	2163	—
CJ-6	Utility	$2253	3900	2225	—

STANDARD ENGINE: Engine Type: F-head, In-line-4. Cast iron block and cylinder head. Bore x Stroke: 3.125 in. x 4.375 in. Lifters: Mechanical. Number of main bearings-3. Fuel Induction: Single Carter model YF-938-SD. Compression Ratio: 7.4:1. Optional 6.9:1. Displacement: 134.2 cu. in. (2.199 liters). Horsepower: 75 @ 4000 rpm. Torque: 114 lb.-ft. @ 2000 rpm. Oil refill capacity: 4 qt. with filter change. Fuel Requirements: Regular.

OPTIONAL ENGINE: (CJ-5 and CJ-6): Engine Type: OHV In-line-4. Cast iron block and cylinder head. Bore x Stroke: 3.5 in. x 5.0 in. Compression Ratio: 16.5:1 Displacement: 192.2 cu. in. (3.15 liters). Horsepower: 62 @ 3000 rpm. Torque: 143 lb.-ft. @ 1350 rpm. Fuel Requirements: Diesel.

CHASSIS FEATURES: Separate body and channel steel frame construction, 4.125 in. depth x 1.937 in. width, six cross members. Overall frame length: CJ-5: 128.4375 in. CJ-6: 148.4375 in. Section modulus: 1.493 in. cu.

SUSPENSION AND RUNNING GEAR: Front Suspension: CJ-3B: 10-leaf semi-elliptical springs, 36.25 in. x 1.75 in. Spring rate: 260 lb./in. CJ-5 and CJ-6: 7-leaf semi-elliptical springs, 39.625 in. x 1.75 in. Spring rate: 240 lb./in. Monroe, 11.4375 in. dia. double-acting shock absorbers. Load capacity: 550 lbs. Optional: 10-leaf heavy-duty front springs. Rear Suspension: CJ-3B: 9-leaf semi-elliptical springs, 42 in. x 1.75 in. Spring rate: 190 lb/in. Capacity: 800 lb. CJ-5 and CJ-6: 9-leaf semi-elliptical springs, 46 in. x 1.75 in. Spring rate: CJ-5: 200 lb./in. CJ-6: 270 lb./in. Monroe, 11.9375 in. dia. double-acting shock absorbers. Normal load capacity: CJ-5: 940 lb., Optional: Heavy-duty rear springs option with eleven thicker (2.407 in. to 1.973 in.). Spring rate: 225 lb./in. Front Axle Type and Capacity: Full-floating Spicer model 25, hypoid. Capacity: 2000 lb. Rear Axle Type and Capacity: Semi-floating Spicer model 44-2. Hypoid. Capacity: 2500 lb. Axle Ratios: CJ-3B and CJ-6: 5.38:1. CJ-5: 4.27:1. Transfer Case: Spicer model 18. Ratios: 2.46:1, 1.00:1. Brakes: Type: Hydraulic, front and rear. Dimensions: Front and rear: 9.00 in. x 1.75 in. Total braking area: 117.75 sq. in. Wheels: Kelsey-Hayes 16 x 4.50 in., 5-bolt steel disc. Tires: 6.00 x 16 in. 4-ply. Optional: Other sizes including 7.00 x 15 in. 4-ply. Steering: Cam and lever. Ratio: 17.9:1. Turning Circle: CJ-5: 39 ft. Standard Transmission: Warner-Gear model T090A, 3-speed manual floor-mounted shift. Transmission ratios: 2.798:1, 1.551:1, 1.00:1. Reverse: 3.798:1. Clutch: 8.5 in. Auburn or Rockford single dry plate. Total lining area: 72sq. in. Optional: Auburn single dry plate, 9.25 in. dia. plate.

VEHICLE DIMENSIONS: Wheelbase: CJ-3B: 80.0625 in. CJ-5: 81.0 in. CJ-6: 101 in. Overall Length: CJ-3B: 129.875 in. CJ-5: 135.50 in. CJ-6:. Front/Rear Tread: 48.4375 in./48.4375 in. Overall Height: CJ-3B: 67.75 in. CJ-5: 69.5 in. CJ-6: 68.25 in. Width: CJ-3B: 68.875 in. CJ-5, CJ-6: 71.75 in. Front/Rear Overhang: 20.59 in./22.31 in. Tailgate: Width and Height: 36 in. x 14.125 in. Ground Clearance: 8.0 in. Load space: CJ-3B and CJ-5: 36 in. x 39 in. (with tailgate closed), 36 in. by 49 in. (tailgate closed). CJ-6: 36 in. x 64.625 in. (with tailgate closed). Steering wheel to seat back (max.): 15.12 in.

CAPACITIES: Fuel Tank: 10.5 gal. Located under driver's seat. Coolant system: 11 qt. 12 qt. with heater.

ACCOMMODATIONS: Seating Capacity: 2/6.

INSTRUMENTATION: Instrument panel light, ammeter, heat indicator gauge, speedometer oil pressure gauge, fuel level gauge.

OPTIONS: Tuxedo Park Package. Power take-off. Pulley drive. Engine governor. Half and full canvas and metal tops. High altitude cylinder head. High temperature thermostat. Passenger safety rail. Rear passenger seat.

HISTORICAL FOOTNOTES: Introduced Fall, 1960.

1962 CJ

Willys offered a "Parade Blue Convertible Top and Accessory Kit" for the Tuxedo Park Mark II in March, 1962. Parade blue was a new color for the Jeep and it was used for the kit's convertible top, boot and spare tire cover. All of these items were also treated with a "Scotchgard" process for color-fastness and stain resistance. This kit, which retailed for $130.20, was also available for other CJ-5 Jeeps. No other major changes took place in the CJ lineup for 1962.

1962 Jeep CJ-6

I.D. DATA: The serial number was located on the left front of the frame and the back of the bumper. It was also found on the right side of the dash under the hood. The engine number was located on the boss for the water pump at the right front of the cylinder block. Serial number range: CJ-3B: 57348-55345 and up. CJ-5: 57548-86195 and up. CJ-6: 57748-17087 and up. Engine and serial numbers were the same in most models.

Model Number	Body Type	Factory Price	GVW	Shipping Weight	Prod. Total
Jeep					
CJ-3B	Utility	$1960	3500	2132	—
CJ-5	Utility	$2054	3750	2163	—
CJ-6	Utility	$2149	3900	2225	—

STANDARD ENGINE: Engine Type: F-head, In-line-4. Cast iron block and cylinder head. Bore x Stroke: 3.125 in. x 4.375 in. Lifters: Mechanical. Number of main bearings-3. Fuel Induction: Single Carter model YF-938-SD. Compression Ratio: 7.4:1. Optional 6.9:1. Displacement: 134.2 cu. in. (2.199 liters). Horsepower: 75 @ 4000 rpm. Torque: 114 lb.-ft. @ 2000 rpm. Oil refill capacity: 4 qt. with filter change. Fuel Requirements: Regular.

OPTIONAL ENGINE: (CJ-5 and CJ-6): Engine Type: OHV In-line-4. Cast iron block and cylinder head. Bore x Stroke: 3.5 in. x 5.0 in. Compression Ratio: 16.5:1. Displacement: 192.2 cu. in. (3.15 liters). Horsepower: 62 @ 3000 rpm. Torque: 143 lb.-ft. @ 1350 rpm. Fuel Requirements: Diesel.

CHASSIS FEATURES: Separate body and channel steel frame construction, 4.125 in. depth x 1.937 in. width, six cross members. Overall frame length: CJ-5: 128.4375 in. CJ-6: 148.4375 in. Section modulus: 1.493 in. cu.

SUSPENSION AND RUNNING GEAR: Front Suspension: CJ-3B: 10-leaf semi-elliptical springs, 36.25 in. x 1.75 in. Spring rate: 260 lb./in. CJ-5 and CJ-6: 7-leaf semi-elliptical springs, 39.625 in. x 1.75 in. Spring rate: 240 lb./in. Monroe, 11.4375 in. dia. double-acting shock absorbers. Load capacity: 550 lbs. Optional: 10-leaf heavy-duty front springs. Rear Suspension: CJ-3B: 9-leaf semi-elliptical springs, 42 in. x 1.75 in. Spring rate: 190 lb/in. Capacity: 800 lb. CJ-5 and CJ-6: 9-leaf semi-elliptical springs, 46 in. x 1.75 in. Spring rate: CJ-5: 200 lb./in. CJ-6: 270 lb./in. Monroe, 11.9375 in. dia., double-acting shock absorbers. Normal load capacity: CJ-5: 940 lb., CJ-6: 845 lb. Optional: Heavy-duty rear springs option with eleven thicker (2.407 in. to 1.973 in.). Spring rate: 225 lb./in. Front Axle Type and Capacity: Full-floating Spicer model 25, hypoid. Capacity: 2000 lb. Rear Axle Type and Capacity: Semi-floating Spicer model 44-2. Hypoid. Capacity: 2500 lb. Axle Ratios: 4.27:1. 5.38:1 optional. Transfer Case: Spicer model 18. Ratios: 2.46:1, 1.00:1. Brakes: Type: Hydraulic, front and rear. Dimensions: Front and rear: 9.00 in. x 1.75 in. Total braking area: 117.75 sq. in. Wheels: Kelsey-Hayes 16 x 4.50 in., 5-bolt steel disc. Tires: 6.00 x 16 in. 4-ply. Optional: Other sizes including 7.00 x 15 in. 4-ply. Steering: Cam and lever. Ratio: 17.9:1. Turning Circle: CJ-5: 39 ft. Standard Transmission: Warner-Gear model T090A, 3-speed manual floor-mounted shift. Transmission ratios: 2.798:1, 1.551:1, 1.00:1. Reverse: 3.798:1. Clutch: 8.5 in. Auburn or Rockford single dry plate. Total lining area: 72 sq. in. Optional: Auburn single dry plate, 9.25 in. dia. plate.

VEHICLE DIMENSIONS: Wheelbase: CJ-3B: 80.0625 in. CJ-5: 81.0 in. CJ-6: 101 in. Overall Length: CJ-3B: 129.875 in. CJ-5: 135.50 in. CJ-6:. Front/Rear Tread: 48.4375 in./48.4375 in. Overall Height: CJ-3B: 67.75 in. CJ-5: 69.5 in. CJ-6: 68.25 in. Width: CJ-3B: 68.875 in. CJ-5, CJ-6: 71.75 in. Front/Rear Overhang: 20.59 in./22.31 in. Tailgate: Width and Height: 36 in. x 14.125 in. Ground Clearance: 8.0 in. Load space: CJ-3B and CJ-5: 36 in. x 39 in. (with tailgate closed), 36 in. by 49 in. (tailgate closed). CJ-6: 36 in. x 64.625 in. (with tailgate closed). Steering wheel to seat back (max.): 15.12 in.

392

CAPACITIES: Fuel Tank: 10.5 gal. Located under driver's seat. Coolant system: 11 qt. 12 qt. with heater.

ACCOMMODATIONS: Seating Capacity: 2/6.

INSTRUMENTATION: Instrument panel light, ammeter, heat indicator gauge, speedometer oil pressure gauge, fuel level gauge.

OPTIONS: Tuxedo Park Package. Power take-off. Pulley drive. Engine governor. Half and full canvas and metal tops. High altitude cylinder head. High temperature thermostat. Passenger safety rail. Rear passenger seat. Ramsey win., Koenig win., Meyer angle-dozer plows, and Jeep-A-Trench trench diggers.

HISTORICAL FOOTNOTES: The 1962 CJ models were introduced in the fall of 1961.

1962 Jeep CJ-3B

1963 CJ

There were no significant changes in the CJ line for 1963.

I.D. DATA: The serial number was located on the left front of the frame and the back of the bumper. It was also found on the right side of the dash under the hood. The engine number was located on the boss for the water pump at the right front of the cylinder block. Serial number range: CJ-3B: 57348-59127 and up. CJ-5: 57548-90027 and up. CJ-6: 57748-18221 and up. Engine and serial numbers were the same in most models.

Model Number	Body Type	Factory Price	GVW	Shipping Weight	Prod. Total
Jeep					
CJ-3B	Utility	$2015	3500	2132	14,544
CJ-5	Utility	$2109	3750	2163	11,304
CJ-6	Utility	$2204	3900	2225	2,108*

* All CJ production numbers are based on serial number runs of 1962 and 1963.

STANDARD ENGINE: Engine Type: F-head, In-line-4. Cast iron block and cylinder head. Bore x Stroke: 3.125 in. x 4.375 in. Lifters: Mechanical. Number of main bearings-3. Fuel Induction: Single Carter model YF-938-SD. Compression Ratio: 7.4:1. Optional 6.9:1. Displacement: 134.2 cu. in. (2.199 liters). Horsepower: 75 @ 4000 rpm. Torque: 114 lb.-ft. @ 2000 rpm. Oil refill capacity: 4 qt. with filter change. Fuel Requirements: Regular. Optional Engine (CJ-5 and CJ-6). Engine Type: OHV In-line-4. Cast iron block and cylinder head. Bore x Stroke: 3.5 in. x 5.0 in. Compression Ratio: 16.5:1. Displacement: 192.2 cu. in. (3.15 liters). Horsepower: 62 @ 3000 rpm. Torque: 143 lb.-ft. @ 1350 rpm. Fuel Requirements: Diesel.

CHASSIS FEATURES: Separate body and channel steel frame construction, 4.125 in. depth x 1.937 in. width, six cross members. Overall frame length: CJ-5: 128.4375 in. CJ-6: 148.4375 in. Section modulus: 1.493 in. cu.

SUSPENSION AND RUNNING GEAR: Front Suspension: CJ-3B: 10-leaf semi-elliptical springs, 36.25 in. x 1.75 in. Spring rate: 260 lb./in. CJ-5 and CJ-6: 7-leaf semi-elliptical springs, 39.625 in. x 1.75 in. Spring rate: 240 lb./in. Monroe, 11.4375 in. dia. double-acting shock absorbers. Load capacity: 550 lbs. Optional: 10-leaf heavy-duty front springs. Rear Suspension: CJ-3B: 9-leaf semi-elliptical springs, 42 in. x 1.75 in. Spring rate: 190 lb/in. Capacity: 800 lb. CJ-5 and CJ-6: 9-leaf semi-elliptical springs, 46 in. x 1.75 in. Spring rate: CJ-5: 200 lb./in. CJ-6: 270 lb./in. Monroe, 11.9375 in. dia., double-acting shock absorbers. Normal load capacity: CJ-5: 940 lb., CJ-6: 845 lb. Optional: Heavy-duty rear springs option with eleven thicker (2.407 in. to 1.973 in.). Spring rate: 225 lb./in. Front Axle Type and Capacity: Full-floating Spicer model 25, hypoid. Capacity: 2000 lb. Rear Axle Type and Capacity: Semi-floating Spicer model 44-2. Hypoid. Capacity: 2500 lb. Axle Ratios: 4.27:1. 5.38:1 optional. Transfer Case: Spicer model 18. Ratios: 2.46:1, 1.00:1. Brakes: Type: Hydraulic, front and rear. Dimensions: Front and rear: 9.00 in. x 1.75 in. Total braking area: 117.75 sq. in. Wheels: Kelsey-Hayes 16 x 4.50 in., 5-bolt steel disc. Tires: 6.00 x 16 in. 4-ply. Optional: Other sizes including 7.00 x 15 in. 4-ply. Steering: Cam and lever. Ratio: 17.9:1. Turning Circle: CJ-5: 39 ft. Standard Transmission: Warner-Gear model T090A, 3-speed manual floor-mounted shift. Transmission ratios: 2.798:1, 1.551:1, 1.00:1. Reverse: 3.798:1. Optional: For CJ-5 and CJ-6: Warner T98A 4-speed manual transmission. Transmission ratios: 6.398, 3.092, 1.686, 1.0:1. Reverse: 7.820:1. Brakes: Type: Hydraulic, front and rear. Dimensions: Front and rear: 9.00 in. x 1.75 in. Total braking area: 117.75 sq. in. Wheels: Kelsey-Hayes 16 x 4.50 in., 5-bolt steel disc. Tires: 6.00 x 16 in. 4-ply. Optional: Other sizes including 7.00 x 15 in. 4-ply. Steering: Cam and lever. Ratio: 17.9:1. Turning Circle: CJ-5: 39 ft. Standard Transmission: Warner-Gear model T090A, 3-speed manual floor-mounted shift. Transmission ratios: 2.798:1, 1.551:1, 1.00:1. Reverse: 3.798:1. Clutch: 8.5 in. Auburn or Rockford single dry plate. Total lining area: 72sq. in. Optional: Auburn single dry plate, 9.25 in. dia. plate.

VEHICLE DIMENSIONS: Wheelbase: CJ-3B: 80.0625 in. CJ-5: 81.0 in. CJ-6: 101 in. Overall Length: CJ-3B: 129.875 in. CJ-5: 135.50 in. CJ-6:. Front/Rear Tread: 48.4375 in./48.4375 in. Overall Height: CJ-3B: 67.75 in. CJ-5: 69.5 in. CJ-6: 68.25 in. Width: CJ-3B: 68.875 in. CJ-5, CJ-6: 71.75 in. Front/Rear Overhang: 20.59 in./22.31 in. Tailgate: Width and Height: 36 in. x 14.125 in. Ground Clearance: 8.0 in. Load space: CJ-3B and CJ-5: 36 in. x 39 in. (with tailgate closed), 36 in. by 49 in. (tailgate closed). CJ-6: 36 in. x 64.625 in. (with tailgate closed). Steering wheel to seat back (max.): 15.12 in.

CAPACITIES: Fuel Tank: 10.5 gal. Located under driver's seat. Coolant system: 11 qt. 12 qt. with heater.

ACCOMMODATIONS: Seating Capacity: 2/6.

INSTRUMENTATION: Instrument panel light, ammeter, heat indicator gauge, speedometer oil pressure gauge, fuel level gauge.

OPTIONS AND PRICES: Four speed manual transmission: $194. Radio. Warn or Cutlass locking front hubs. Canfield wrecker body. Front bumper guards. Directional signals. Tuxedo Park Package. Power take-off. Pulley drive. Engine governor. Half and full canvas and metal tops. High altitude cylinder head. High temperature thermostat. Passenger safety rail. Rear passenger seat. Ramsey win., Koenig win., Meyer angle-dozer plows, and Jeep-A-Trench trench diggers.

HISTORICAL FOOTNOTES: Calendar year production of the Jeep Universal models totalled 12,615 units. They were introduced in the fall of 1962.

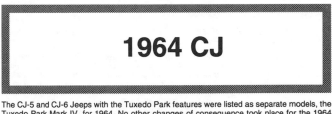

1964 CJ

The CJ-5 and CJ-6 Jeeps with the Tuxedo Park features were listed as separate models, the Tuxedo Park Mark IV, for 1964. No other changes of consequence took place for the 1964 model year. Depicted by Kaiser Jeep as a "new idea in sports cars" the Tuxedo Park Mark IV featured chrome trim for its bumpers, hood latches, gas cap, mirror and tail lamps. The Tuxedo Park's driver's seat was fully adjustable and was cushioned with foam padding. The standard shift lever on the Tuxedo Park was column-mounted. If the optional 4-speed manual transmission was installed a floor-mounted lever was used.

1964 Jeep CJ-5

I.D. DATA: The serial number was located on the left front of the frame and the back of the bumper. It was also found on the right side of the dash under the hood. The engine number was located on the boss for the water pump at the right front of the cylinder block. Serial number range: CJ-3B: 57348 or 8105-73671-59127 and up. CJ-5: 57548 or 8305-101331 and up. CJ-6: 57748 or 8405-20329 and up. CJ-5A: 8322-10001 and up. CJ-6A: 8422-10001 and up. Engine and serial numbers were the same in most models.

Model Number	Body Type	Factory Price	GVW	Shipping Weight	Prod. Total
Jeep					
CJ-3B	Utility	$2117	3500	2132	—
CJ-5	Utility	$2211	3750	2163	—
CJ-6	Utility	$2306	3900	2225	—
CJ-5A	Tuxedo Park	$2306	3750	2163	—
CJ-6A	Tuxedo Park	$2401	3900	2225	—

STANDARD ENGINE: Engine Type: F-head, In-line-4. Cast iron block and cylinder head. Bore x Stroke: 3.125 in. x 4.375 in. Lifters: Mechanical. Number of main bearings-3. Fuel Induction: Single Carter model YF-938-SD. Compression Ratio: 7.4:1. Optional 6.9:1. Displacement: 134.2 cu. in. (2.199 liters). Horsepower: 75 @ 4000 rpm. Torque: 114 lb.-ft. @ 2000 rpm. Oil refill capacity: 5 qt. with filter change. Fuel Requirements: Regular.

OPTIONAL ENGINE: (CJ-5 and CJ-6): Engine Type: OHV In-line-4. Cast iron block and cylinder head. Bore x Stroke: 3.5 in. x 5.0 in. Compression Ratio: 16.5:1. Displacement: 192.2 cu. in. (3.15 liters). Horsepower: 62 @ 3000 rpm. Torque: 143 lb.-ft. @ 1350 rpm. Fuel Requirements: Diesel.

CHASSIS FEATURES: Separate body and channel steel frame construction, 4.125 in. depth x 1.937 in. width, six cross members. Overall frame length: CJ-5: 128.4375 in. CJ-6: 148.4375 in. Section modulus: 1.493 in. cu.

SUSPENSION AND RUNNING GEAR: Front Suspension: CJ-3B: 10-leaf semi-elliptical springs, 36.25 in. x 1.75 in. Spring rate: 260 lb./in. CJ-5 and CJ-6: 7-leaf semi-elliptical springs, 39.625 in. x 1.75 in. Spring rate: 240 lb./in. Monroe, 11.4375 in. dia. double-acting shock absorbers. Load capacity: 550 lbs. Tuxedo Park: 2-stage, variable rate semi-elliptical springs.

Optional: 10-leaf heavy-duty front springs. Rear Suspension: CJ-3B: 9-leaf semi-elliptical springs, 42 in. x 1.75 in. Spring rate: 190 lb/in. Capacity: 800 lb. CJ-5 and CJ-6: 9-leaf semi-elliptical springs, 46 in. x 1.75 in. Spring rate: CJ-5: 200 lb./in. CJ-6: 270 lb./in. Monroe, 11.9375 in. dia., double-acting shock absorbers. Normal load capacity: CJ-5: 940 lb., CJ-6: 845 lb. Tuxedo Park: 2-stage, variable rate semi-elliptical springs. Optional: Heavy-duty rear springs option with eleven thicker (2.407 in. to 1.973 in.). Spring rate: 225 lb./in. Front Axle Type and Capacity: Full-floating Spicer model 25, hypoid. Capacity: 2000 lb. Rear Axle Type and Capacity: Semi-floating Spicer model 44-2. Hypoid. Capacity: 2500 lb. Axle Ratios: 4.27:1. 5.38:1 optional. Transfer Case: Spicer model 18. Ratios: 2.46:1, 1.00:1. Brakes: Type: Hydraulic, front and rear. Dimensions: Front and rear: 9.00 in. drums. Effective lining area: 102.65 sq. in. Tuxedo Park: 10.0 in. drums. Effective lining area: 174 sq. in. Wheels: Kelsey-Hayes 16 x 4.50 in., 5-bolt steel disc. Tires: 6.00 x 16 in. 4-ply non-directional tread. Tuxedo Park: 7.35 x 15 4-ply Highway-Service tread. Optional: Other sizes including 7.00 x 15 in. 4-ply and white sidewalls. Steering: Cam and lever. Ratio: 17.9:1. Turning Circle: CJ-5: 39 ft. Standard Transmission: Warner-Gear model T090A, 3-speed manual floor-mounted shift. Transmission ratios: 2.798:1, 1.551:1, 1.00:1. Reverse: 3.798:1. Optional: For CJ-5 and CJ-6: Warner T98A 4-speed manual transmission. Transmission ratios: 6.398, 3.092, 1.686, 1.0:1. Reverse: 7.820:1.

VEHICLE DIMENSIONS: Wheelbase: CJ-3B: 80.0625 in. CJ-5: 81.0 in. CJ-6: 101 in. Overall Length: CJ-3B: 129.875 in. CJ-5: 135.50 in. CJ-6:. Front/Rear Tread: 48.4375 in./48.4375 in. Overall Height: CJ-3B: 67.75 in. CJ-5: 69.5 in. CJ-6: 68.875 in. Width: CJ-3B: 68.875 in. CJ-5, CJ-6: 71.75 in. Front/Rear Overhang: 20.59 in./22.31 in. Tailgate: Width and Height: 36 in. x 14.125 in. Ground Clearance: 8.0 in. Load space: CJ-3B and CJ-5: 36 in. x 39 in. (with tailgate closed), 36 in. by 49 in. (tailgate closed). CJ-6: 36 in. x 64.625 in. (with tailgate closed). Steering wheel to seat back (max.): 15.12 in.

CAPACITIES: Fuel Tank: 10.5 gal. Located under driver's seat. Coolant system: 11 qt. 12 qt. with heater.

ACCOMMODATIONS: Seating Capacity: 2/6.

INSTRUMENTATION: Instrument panel light, ammeter, heat indicator gauge, speedometer oil pressure gauge, fuel level gauge.

OPTIONS AND PRICES: Fresh-air heater and defroster. Ventilating windshield, One-third front passenger seat. Longitudinal seats. Wheelhouse cushions (CJ-5 only). Rear passenger seat. Full canvas top. Windshield washer. Rear bumperettes. Outside rearview mirror. Locking gas cap. Wheelcovers. Spare tire cover. Overdrive. 50, 60 and 70 amp batteries. 9.25 in. clutch. 40, 60 amp generators. Four-speed transmission: $109. Heavy-duty springs and shock absorbers. Radiator chaff screen. Magnetic drain plug. 2/3 driver's seat. Wrecker equipment. Directional signals with 4-way flasher. Tailgate mounting for spare tire. Pintle hook. Diesel engine. Angledozer. Compressor. Selective drive hubs. Implement lift. Radio. Power take-off. Pulley drive. Engine governor. Half metal cab. Full metal cabs (choice of two styles). Full fabric cab. Half fabric cab. Full fabric cab. Convertible top. High altitude cylinder head. High temperature Thermostat.

HISTORICAL FOOTNOTES: In 1964 Jeep registrations totalled 44,385 which was virtually unchanged from the 44,339 level of 1963.

with a lively new appea

1964 Jeep Tuxedo Park

1965 CJ

The CJ Jeeps were essentially unchanged for 1965. Kaiser Jeep identification was added to the CJ's exterior.

I.D. DATA: The serial number was located on the left front of the frame and the back of the bumper. It was also found on the right side of the dash under the hood. The engine number was located on the boss for the water pump at the right front of the cylinder block. Serial number range: CJ-3B: 57348 or 8105-106405 and up. CJ-5: 57548 or 8305-156383 and up. CJ-6: 57748 or 8405-24391 and up. CJ-5A: 8322-10001 and up. CJ-6A: 8422-10001 and up. Engine and serial numbers were the same in most models.

Model Number	Body Type	Factory Price	GVW	Shipping Weight	Prod. Total
Jeep					
CJ-3B	Utility	$2117	3500	2132	—
CJ-5	Utility	$2211	3750	2163	—
CJ-6	Utility	$2306	3900	2225	—

STANDARD ENGINE: Engine Type: F-head, In-line-4. Cast iron block and cylinder head. Bore x Stroke: 3.125 in. x 4.375 in. Lifters: Mechanical. Number of main bearings-3. Fuel Induction: Single Carter model YF-938-SD. Compression Ratio: 7.4:1. Optional 6.9:1. Displacement: 134.2 cu. in. (2.199 liters). Horsepower: 75 @ 4000 rpm. Torque: 114 lb.-ft. @ 2000 rpm. Oil refill capacity: 5 qt. with filter change. Fuel Requirements: Regular.

OPTIONAL ENGINE: (CJ-5 and CJ-6): Engine Type: OHV In-line-4. Cast iron block and cylinder head. Bore x Stroke: 3.5 in. x 5.0 in. Compression Ratio: 16.5:1. Displacement: 192.2 cu. in. (3.15 liters). Horsepower: 62 @ 3000 rpm. Torque: 143 lb.-ft. @ 1350 rpm. Fuel Requirements: Diesel.

1965 Jeep CJ-5

CHASSIS FEATURES: Separate body and channel steel frame construction, 4.125 in. depth x 1.937 in. width, six cross members. Overall frame length: CJ-5: 128.4375 in. CJ-6: 148.4375 in. Section modulus: 1.493 in. cu.

SUSPENSION AND RUNNING GEAR: Front Suspension: CJ-3B: 10-leaf semi-elliptical springs, 36.25 in. x 1.75 in. Spring rate: 260 lb./in. CJ-5 and CJ-6: 7-leaf semi-elliptical springs, 39.625 in. x 1.75 in. Spring rate: 240 lb./in. Monroe, 11.4375 in. dia. double-acting shock absorbers. Load capacity: 550 lbs. Tuxedo Park: 2-stage, variable rate semi-elliptical springs. Optional: 10-leaf heavy-duty front springs. Rear Suspension: CJ-3B: 9-leaf semi-elliptical springs, 42 in. x 1.75 in. Spring rate: 190 lb/in. Capacity: 800 lb. CJ-5 and CJ-6: 9-leaf semi-elliptical springs, 46 in. x 1.75 in. Spring rate: CJ-5: 200 lb./in. CJ-6: 270 lb./in. Monroe, 11.9375 in. dia., double-acting shock absorbers. Normal load capacity: CJ-5: 940 lb., CJ-6: 845 lb. Tuxedo Park: 2-stage, variable rate semi-elliptical springs. Optional: Heavy-duty rear springs option with eleven thicker (2.407 in. to 1.973 in.). Spring rate: 225 lb./in. Front Axle Type and Capacity: Full-floating Spicer model 25, hypoid. Capacity: 2000 lb. Rear Axle Type and Capacity: Semi-floating Spicer model 44-2. Hypoid. Capacity: 2500 lb. Axle Ratios: 4.27:1. 5.38:1 optional. Transfer Case: Spicer model 18. Ratios: 2.46:1, 1.00:1. Brakes: Type: Hydraulic, front and rear. Dimensions: Front and rear: 9.00 in. drums. Effective lining area: 102.65 sq. in. Tuxedo Park: 10.0 in. drums. Effective lining area: 174 sq. in. Wheels: Kelsey-Hayes 16 x 4.50 in., 5-bolt steel disc. Tires: 6.00 x 16 in. 4-ply non-directional tread. Tuxedo Park: 7.35 x 15 4-ply Highway-Service tread. Optional: Other sizes including 7.00 x 15 in. 4-ply and white sidewalls. Steering: Cam and lever. Ratio: 17.9:1. Turning Circle: CJ-5: 39 ft. Standard Transmission: Warner-Gear model T090A, 3-speed manual floor-mounted shift. Transmission ratios: 2.798:1, 1.551:1, 1.00:1. Reverse: 3.798:1. Optional: For CJ-5 and CJ-6: Warner T98A 4-speed manual transmission. Transmission ratios: 6.398, 3.092, 1.686, 1.0:1. Reverse: 7.820:1.

VEHICLE DIMENSIONS: Wheelbase: CJ-3B: 80.0625 in. CJ-5: 81.0 in. CJ-6: 101 in. Overall Length: CJ-3B: 129.875 in. CJ-5: 135.50 in. CJ-6:. Front/Rear Tread: 48.4375 in./48.4375 in. Overall Height: CJ-3B: 67.75 in. CJ-5: 69.5 in. CJ-6: 68.25 in. Width: CJ-3B: 68.875 in. CJ-5, CJ-6: 71.75 in. Front/Rear Overhang: 20.59 in./22.31 in. Tailgate: Width and Height: 36 in. x 14.125 in. Ground Clearance: 8.0 in. Load space: CJ-3B and CJ-5: 36 in. x 39 in. (with tailgate closed), 36 in. by 49 in. (tailgate closed). CJ-6: 36 in. x 64.625 in. (with tailgate closed). Steering wheel to seat back (max.): 15.12 in.

CAPACITIES: Fuel Tank: 10.5 gal. Located under driver's seat. Coolant system: 11 qt. 12 qt. with heater.

ACCOMMODATIONS: Seating Capacity: 2/6.

INSTRUMENTATION: Instrument panel light, ammeter, heat indicator gauge, speedometer oil pressure gauge, fuel level gauge.

OPTIONS AND PRICES: Fresh-air heater and defroster. Ventilating windshield, One-third front passenger seat. Longitudinal seats. Wheelhouse cushions (CJ-5 only). Rear passenger seat. Full canvas top. Windshield washer. Rear bumperettes. Outside rearview mirror. Locking gas cap. Wheelcovers. Spare tire cover. Overdrive. 50, 60 and 70 amp batteries. 9.25 in. clutch. 40, 60 amp generators. Four-speed transmission: $109. Heavy-duty springs and shock absorbers. Radiator chaff screen. Magnetic drain plug. 2/3 driver's seat. Wrecker equipment. Directional signals with 4-way flasher. Tailgate mounting for spare tire. Pintle hook. Diesel engine. Angledozer. Compressor. Selective drive hubs. Implement lift. Radio. Power take-off. Pulley drive. Engine governor. Half metal cab. Full metal cabs (choice of two styles). Full fabric cab. Half fabric cab. Full fabric cab. Convertible top. High altitude cylinder head. High temperature thermostat.

HISTORICAL FOOTNOTES: This was the final year of production for the CJ-3B.

1966 CJ

For 1966 the CJ-5 and CJ-6 were available with the "Dauntless" V-6. This cast iron block engine's origin was traced back to the 1961 aluminum V-8 offered by General Motors for its then-new Buick, Oldsmobile and Pontiac compacts. By 1965 the V-6, with a 3.75 in. bore and 3.40 in. stroke, displaced 225 in. and had ratings of 155 horsepower at 4400 rpm and 225 lb.-ft. of torque at 2400 rpm.

As in earlier years, the CJ Jeeps, regardless of their engine, were available with optional heavy-duty springs and shock absorbers.

Coinciding with the introduction of the V-6 option were several alterations in the Jeep's specifications. These included use of the single lever, dual range transfer case already installed on Jeep station wagons and trucks in place of the older unit with its front driving control lever. The ratios were unchanged and a power take-off was still available. New Servo brakes with a total effective area of 174 sq. in. were also adopted.

The CJ's with V-6 engines had small identification shields placed below the Jeep lettering located on the lower body panel. Rounding out the features of the latest CJ were several new chromed appearance options and an expanded list of available body colors. A new, more comfortable front driver's vinyl-covered bucket-type seat made by the Bostrom Corporation of Milwaukee, Wisconsin was also introduced for 1966. A matching front passenger's seat as well as a rear seat were optional. The Tuxedo Park model was offered only in CJ-5 form.

1966 Jeep CJ-5

I.D. DATA: The serial number was located on the left front of the frame and the back of the bumper. It was also found on the right side of the dash under the hood. A new serial number code was introduced for 1966. The first character was a J for the manufacturer (Jeep). Next came a digit (6) for the 1966 model year. Then came a letter identifying the type of transmission: E-speed manual, M-4-speed floor shifter or S-3-speed manual. The next entry identified the body/model/group: 83-CJ-5, 84-CJ-6. The engine identification was next, followed by the sequential production numbers. The engine number of 4-cylinder engine was located on the boss for the water pump at the right front of the cylinder block. The V-6 number was located on the right block deck. Serial number range: CJ-5: 8305-166803 and up. CJ-6: 8405-25532 and up. CJ-5A: 8322-10463 and up. The designation "-A" was added to the serial number's first four letters on models with the V-6 engine. Engine and serial numbers were the same in most models.

Model Number	Body Type	Factory Price	GVW	Shipping Weight	Prod. Total
Jeep					
CJ-5	Utility	$2284	3750	2163	—
CJ-5A	Tuxedo Park	$2379	3750	2163	—
CJ-6	Utility	$2379	3900	2225	—
CJ-6A	Tuxedo Park	$2475	3750	2225	—

STANDARD ENGINE: Engine Type: F-head, In-line-4. Cast iron block and cylinder head. Bore x Stroke: 3.125 in. x 4.375 in. Lifters: Mechanical. Number of main bearings-3. Fuel Induction: Single Carter model YF-938-SD. Compression Ratio: 7.4:1. Optional 6.9:1. Displacement: 134.2 cu. in. (2.199 liters). Horsepower: 75 @ 4000 rpm. Torque: 114 lb.-ft. @ 2000 rpm. Oil refill capacity: 5 qt. with filter change. Fuel Requirements: Regular.

OPTIONAL ENGINE: Engine Type: OHV V-6. Cast iron block and cylinder heads. Bore x Stroke: 3.75 in. x 3.40 in. Lifters: Mechanical. Number of main bearings-3. Fuel Induction: 2-barrel carburetor. Compression Ratio: 9.0:1. Displacement: 225 cu. in. (3.68 liters). Horsepower: 160 @ 4200 rpm. (initially 155 @ 4400 rpm). Torque: 235 lb.-ft. @ 2400 rpm. (initially 225 lb.-ft. @ 2400 rpm). Oil refill capacity: 4 qt. with filter change. Fuel Requirements: Regular.

OPTIONAL ENGINE: Engine Type: Perkins "Four 192" diesel In-line-4. Cast iron block and cylinder head. Bore x Stroke: 3.5 in. x 5.0 in. Lifters: Mechanical. Compression Ratio: 16.5:1. Displacement: 192 cu. in. (3.15 liters). Horsepower: 62 @ 3000 rpm. Torque: 143 lb.-ft. @ 1350 rpm. Fuel Requirements: Diesel.

CHASSIS FEATURES: Separate body and channel steel frame construction, 4.125 in. depth x 1.937 in. width, five cross members. Overall frame length: CJ-5: 128.4375 in. CJ-6: 148.4375 in. Section modulus: 1.493 in. cu.

SUSPENSION AND RUNNING GEAR: Front Suspension: 4-cyl.: 5-leaf semi-elliptical springs, Spring rate: 240 lb./in. Monroe, 11.4375 in. dia. double-acting shock absorbers. Load capacity: 550 lbs. V-6: 10-leaf semi-elliptical springs. Spring rate: 176 lb./in. Optional: 10-leaf heavy-duty front springs. Rear Suspension: 5-leaf, two-stage semi-elliptical springs. Spring rate: 4-cyl.: 200 lb./in., V-6: 240.1 lb./in. Monroe, 11.9375 in. dia. double-acting shock absorbers. Normal load capacity: 940 lbs. Optional: Heavy-duty rear springs option with eleven thicker (2.407 in. to 1.973 in.). Spring rate: 225 lb./in. Front Axle Type and Capacity: Full-floating Spicer model 25, hypoid. Capacity: 2500 lb. Early 1966 models: 2000 lb. capacity. Rear Axle Type and Capacity: Semi-floating Spicer model 44-2. Hypoid. Capacity: 2500 lb. Axle Ratios: Three speed models: 4-cyl.: 4.27:1, V-6: 3.73:1. Optional: (at no extra cost): 4-cyl.: 5.38:1, V-6: 4.8:1. Four-speed models: (not available with V-6 engine): 4-cyl.: 4.27:1. Optional: (at no extra cost) 5.38:1. Overdrive: V-6: 4.88:1, 4-cyl.: 5.38:1. Transfer Case: Spicer model 18. Ratios: 2.46:1, 1.00:1. Brakes: Type: Hydraulic, front and rear. Dimensions: Front and rear: 10.00 in. x 1.75 in. Total braking area: 174 sq. in. Wheels: Kelsey-Hayes 16 x 4.50 in., 5-bolt steel disc. Optional: None. Tires: 4-cyl.: 6.00 x 16 in. 4-ply rating. V-6: 7.35 x 15 4-ply rating. Optional: Numerous sizes and tread designs were offered. Steering: Ross model T-12 cam and lever. Ratio: 4-cyl.: 17.9:1, V-6: 24.3:1. Optional: None. Standard Transmission: 3-speed manual floor-mounted shift. (column-mounted on Tuxedo Park). Transmission ratios: 2.798:1, 1.69:1, 1.00:1. Reverse: 3.798:1. Optional: Warner T98A 4-speed manual transmission. Transmission ratios: 6.398, 3.092, 1.686, 1.0:1. Reverse: 7.820:1. Clutch: 4-cyl. 9.25 in., V-6: 10.4 in. Single dry plate. Total lining area: 4-cyl.: 78 sq. in., V-6: 103.4 sq. in.

VEHICLE DIMENSIONS: (CJ-5/CJ-6) Wheelbase: 81.0 in./101.0 in. Overall Length: 136.18 in./156.18 in. Front/Rear Tread: 48.4375 in./48.4375 in. Overall Height: 67.0 in. Width: 71.75 in. Front/Rear Overhang: 20.59 in. 22.31/ in. Tailgate: Width and Height: 36 in. x 14.125 in. Ground Clearance: 8.0 in. Load space: 36 in. x 39 in. (with tailgate closed), 36 in. by 49 in. (tailgate closed).

CAPACITIES: Fuel Tank: 10.5 gal. Located under driver's seat.

ACCOMMODATIONS: Seating Capacity: 2/6.

INSTRUMENTATION: Instrument panel light, ammeter, heat indicator gauge, speedometer oil pressure gauge, fuel level gauge.

OPTIONS: V-6 engine. Perkins diesel engine (not available for Tuxedo Park). Heavy-duty alternator. Compressor. Heavy-duty battery. Power brakes. Rotary broom. Locking gas cap. Heavy-duty clutch (for Hurricane 4-cyl. engine only). 6-volt electrical system. 4-way flasher lights. Governor. Fresh-air heater and defroster. Heavy-duty front and rear shock absorbers. Pintle hook. Selective drive hubs. Cigarette lighter. Spare tire lock. Outside right-side mirror. Inside rearview mirror. Fuel tank skid plate. Power take-offs. Radio. Passenger safety rail. Radiator chaff screen. Snowplow. Push plate. Passenger's side front bucket seat. Driver's 2/3 seat. Passenger's front 1/3 seat. Rear bench seat. Longitudinal rear seats. Wheelhouse cushion pads (CJ-5 only). Trencher. Full or half metal cab. Full or half fabric top. Convertible top. "Bikini" top with half doors. 4-speed manual transmission (available with Hurricane or Perkins engines only). Overdrive. Wheelcovers. Win. Wreckers. Windshield washer. Ventilating windshield. Rear Powr-Lok differential. Front Powr-Lok differential (available with Hurricane engine only). Step rear bumper. Welder. Chrome front and rear bumpers. Options for the Tuxedo Park were as follows: V-6 engine. Heavy-duty battery, Locking gas cap. Heavy-duty clutch (for Hurricane 4-cyl. engine only). 4-way flasher lights. Fresh-air heater and defroster. Heavy-duty front and rear shock absorbers. Front floor mat. Selective drive hubs. Outside right-side mirror. Chrome passenger safety rail. Snowplow. Passenger side front bucket seat. Driver's 2/3 seat. Passenger's front 1/3 seat. Rear bench seat. Longitudinal rear seats. Wheelhouse cushion pads (CJ-5 only). Full or half metal cab. Full or half fabric top. Convertible top. "Bikini" top with half doors. 4-speed manual transmission (available with Hurricane engine only). Wheelcovers. Win. Windshield washer. Ventilating windshield. Rear Powr-Lok differential. Front Powr-Lok differential (available with Hurricane engine only).

HISTORICAL FOOTNOTES: The CJ models were introduced in the fall of 1965.

1967 CJ

No major changes occurred in the CJ models for 1967.

I.D. DATA: The serial number was located on the left front of the frame and the back of the bumper. It was also found on the right side of the dash under the hood. The engine number on 4-cylinder models was located on the boss for the water pump at the right front of the cylinder block. The V-6 number was located right block deck. The same serial number code as used in 1966 was continued for 1967 The second digit was a 7 for the 1967 model year. Serial number range: CJ-5: 8305 (8305C)-14185971 and up. CJ-5A: 8322-14193 and up. CJ-6A: 8422-10164 and up. The designation "-A" was added to the serial number's first four letters on models with the V-6 engine. Engine and serial numbers were the same in most models.

Model Number	Body Type	Factory Price	GVW	Shipping Weight	Prod. Total
Jeep					
CJ-5	Utility	$2361	3750	2163	—
CJ-5A	Tuxedo Park	$2458	3750	2163	—
CJ-6	Utility	$2457	3900	2225	—
CJ-6A	Tuxedo Park	$2553	3750	2217	—

STANDARD ENGINE: Engine Type: F-head, In-line-4. Cast iron block and cylinder head. Bore x Stroke: 3.125 in. x 4.375 in. Lifters: Mechanical. Number of main bearings-3. Fuel Induction: Single Carter model YF-938-SD. Compression Ratio: 7.4:1. Optional 6.9:1. Displacement: 134.2 cu. in. (2.199 liters). Horsepower: 75 @ 4000 rpm. Torque: 114 lb.-ft. @ 2000 rpm. Oil refill capacity: 5 qt. with filter change. Fuel Requirements: Regular

OPTIONAL ENGINE: Engine Type: OHV V-6. Cast iron block and cylinder head. Bore x Stroke: 3.75 in. x 3.40 in. Lifters: Mechanical. Number of main bearings-3. Fuel Induction: 2-barrel carburetor. Compression Ratio: 9.0:1. Displacement: 225 cu. in. (3.68 liters). Horsepower: 160 @ 4200 rpm. (initially 155 @ 4400 rpm) Torque: 235 lb.-ft. @ 2400 rpm. (initially 225 lb.-ft. @ 2400 rpm). Oil refill capacity: 4 qt. with filter change. Fuel Requirements: Regular.

OPTIONAL ENGINE: Engine Type: Perkins "Four 192" diesel In-line-4. Cast iron block and cylinder head. Bore x Stroke: 3.5 in. x 5.0 in. Lifters: Mechanical. Compression Ratio: 16.5:1. Displacement: 192 cu. in. (3.15 liters). Horsepower: 62 @ 3000 rpm. Torque: 143 lb.-ft. @ 1350 rpm. Fuel Requirements: Diesel.

CHASSIS FEATURES: Separate body and channel steel frame construction, 4.125 in. depth x 1.937 in. width, five cross members. Overall frame length: CJ-5: 128.4375 in. CJ-6: 148.4375 in. Section modulus: 1.493 in. cu.

SUSPENSION AND RUNNING GEAR: Front Suspension: 4-cyl.: 5-leaf semi-elliptical springs, Spring rate: 240 lb./in. Monroe, 11.4375 in. dia. double-acting shock absorbers. Load capacity: 550 lbs. V-6: 10-leaf semi-elliptical springs. Spring rate: 176 lb./in. Optional: 10-leaf heavy-duty front springs. Rear Suspension: 5-leaf, two-stage semi-elliptical springs. Spring rate: 4-cyl.: 200 lb./in., V-6: 240.1 lb./in. Monroe, 11.9375 in. dia. double-acting shock absorbers. Normal load capacity: 940 lbs. Optional: Heavy-duty rear springs option with eleven thicker (2.407 in. to 1.973 in.). Spring rate: 225 lb./in. Front Axle Type and Capacity: Full-floating Spicer model 25, hypoid. Capacity: 2500 lb. Early 1966 models: 2000 lb. capacity. Rear Axle Type and Capacity: Semi-floating Spicer model 44-2. Hypoid. Capacity: 2500 lb. Axle Ratios: Three speed models: 4-cyl.: 4.27:1, V-6: 3.73:1. Optional: (at no extra cost): 4-cyl.: 5.38:1, V-6: 4.8:1. Four-speed models: (not available with V-6 engine): 4-cyl.: 4.27:1. Optional: (at no extra cost) 5.38:1. Overdrive: V-6: 4.88:1, 4-cyl.: 5.38:1. Transfer Case: Spicer model 18. Ratios: 2.46:1, 1.00:1. Brakes: Type: Hydraulic, front and rear. Dimensions: Front and rear: 10.00 in. x 1.75 in. Total braking area: 174 sq. in. Wheels: Kelsey-Hayes 16 x 4.50 in., 5-bolt steel disc. Optional: None. Tires: 4-cyl.: 6.00 x 16 in. 4-ply rating. V-6: 7.35 x 15 4-ply rating. Optional: Numerous sizes and tread designs were offered. Steering: Ross model T-12 cam and lever. Ratio: 4-cyl.: 17.9:1, V-6: 24.3:1. Optional: None. Standard Transmission: 3-speed manual floor-mounted shift. (column-mounted on Tuxedo Park). Transmission ratios: 2.798:1, 1.69:1, 1.00:1. Reverse: 3.798:1. Optional: Warner T98A 4-speed manual transmission. Transmission ratios: 6.398, 3.092, 1.686, 1.0:1. Reverse: 7.820:1. Clutch: 4-cyl. 9.25 in., V-6: 10.4 in. Single dry plate. Total lining area: 4-cyl.: 78 sq. in., V-6: 103.4 sq. in.

VEHICLE DIMENSIONS: (CJ-5/CJ-6) Wheelbase: 81.0 in./101.0 in. Overall Length: 136.18 in./156.18 in. Front/Rear Tread: 48.4375 in./48.4375 in. Overall Height: 67.0 in. Width: 71.75 in. Front/Rear Overhang: 20.59 in. 22.31/ in. Tailgate: Width and Height: 36 in. x 14.125 in. Ground Clearance: 8.0 in. Load space: 36 in. x 39 in. (with tailgate closed), 36 in. by 49 in. (tailgate closed).

CAPACITIES: Fuel Tank: 10.5 gal. Located under driver's seat.

ACCOMMODATIONS: Seating Capacity: 2/6.

INSTRUMENTATION: Instrument panel light, ammeter, heat indicator gauge, speedometer oil pressure gauge, fuel level gauge.

OPTIONS: V-6 engine. Perkins diesel engine (not available for Tuxedo Park). Heavy-duty alternator. Compressor. Heavy-duty battery. Power brakes. Rotary broom. Locking gas cap. Heavy-duty clutch (for Hurricane 4-cyl. engine only). 6-volt electrical system. 4-way flasher lights. Governor. Fresh-air heater and defroster. Heavy-duty front and rear shock absorbers. Pintle hook. Selective drive hubs. Cigarette lighter. Spare tire lock. Outside right-side mirror. Inside rearview mirror. Fuel tank skid plate. Power take-offs. Radio. Passenger safety rail. Radiator chaff screen. Snowplow. Push plate. Passenger's side front bucket seat. Driver's 2/3 seat. Passenger's front 1/3 seat. Rear bench seat. Longitudinal rear seats. Wheelhouse cushion pads (CJ-5 only). Trencher. Full or half metal cab. Full or half fabric top. Convertible top. "Bikini" top with half doors. 4-speed manual transmission (available with Hurricane or Perkins engines only). Overdrive. Wheelcovers. Win. Wreckers. Windshield washer. Ventilating windshield. Rear Powr-Lok differential. Front Powr-Lok differential (available with Hurricane engine only). Step rear bumper. Welder. Chrome front and rear bumpers. Options for the Tuxedo Park were as follows: V-6 engine. Heavy-duty battery, Locking gas cap. Heavy-duty clutch (for Hurricane 4-cyl. engine only). 4-way flasher lights. Fresh-air heater and defroster. Heavy-duty front and rear shock absorbers Front floor mat. Selective drive hubs. Outside right-side mirror. Chrome passenger safety rail. Snowplow. Passenger's side front bucket seat. Driver's 2/3 seat. Passenger's front 1/3 seat. Rear bench seat. Longitudinal rear seats. Wheelhouse cushion pads (CJ-5 only). Full or half metal cab. Full or half fabric top. Convertible top. "Bikini" top with half doors. 4-speed manual transmission (available with Hurricane engine only). Wheelcovers. Win. Windshield washer. Ventilating windshield. Rear Powr-Lok differential. Front Powr-Lok differential (available with Hurricane engine only).

HISTORICAL FOOTNOTES: The CJ models debuted in the fall of 1966.

1968 CJ

With the exception of changes mandated by federal government emissions regulations, no major changes occurred in the CJ models for 1968.

I.D. DATA: The serial number was positioned on the left front door hinge pillar post and left firewall. The serial number consisted of from nine to eleven entries. The first four identified the series and bodystyle. The last five or six digits were the sequential production numbers. Serial number range: CJ-5: 8305015 or 8305S or 8305C15-228800 and up. CJ-6: 8405015 or 8405S-33935 and up. CJ-5A: 8322S-17423 and up. CJ-6A: 8422S-10462 and up.

1968 Jeep CJ-5 with Camper option

Model Number	Body Type	Factory Price	GVW	Shipping Weight	Prod. Total
Jeep					
CJ-5	Utility	$2683	3750	2212	—
CJ-5A	Tuxedo Park	$2778	3750	2212	—
CJ-6	Utility	$2778	3900	2274	—
CJ-6A	Tuxedo Park	$2875	3750	2274	—

STANDARD ENGINE: Engine Type: F-head, In-line-4. Cast iron block and cylinder head. Bore x Stroke: 3.125 in. x 4.375 in. Lifters: Mechanical. Number of main bearings-3. Fuel Induction: Single Carter model YF-938-SD. Compression Ratio: 7.4:1. Optional 6.9:1. Displacement: 134.2 cu. in. (2.199 liters). Horsepower: 75 @ 4000 rpm. Torque: 114 lb.-ft. @ 2000 rpm. Oil refill capacity: 5 qt. with filter change. Fuel Requirements: Regular.

OPTIONAL ENGINE: Engine Type: OHV V-6. Cast iron block and cylinder head. Bore x Stroke: 3.75 in. x 3.40 in. Lifters: Mechanical. Number of main bearings-3. Fuel Induction: 2-barrel carburetor. Compression Ratio: 9.0:1. Displacement: 225 cu. in. (3.68 liters). Horsepower: 160 @ 4200 rpm. Torque: 235 lb.-ft. @ 2400 rpm. Oil refill capacity: 4 qt. with filter change. Fuel Requirements: Regular.

OPTIONAL ENGINE: Engine Type: Perkins "Four 192" diesel In-line-4. Cast iron block and cylinder head. Bore x Stroke: 3.5 in. x 5.0 in. Lifters: Mechanical. Compression Ratio: 16.5:1. Displacement: 192 cu. in. (3.15 liters). Horsepower: 62 @ 3000 rpm. Torque: 143 lb.-ft. @ 1350 rpm. Fuel Requirements: Diesel.

CHASSIS FEATURES: Separate body and channel steel frame construction, 4.125 in. depth x 1.937 in. width, five cross members. Overall frame length: CJ-5: 128.4375 in. CJ-6: 148.4375 in. Section modulus: 1.493 in. cu.

SUSPENSION AND RUNNING GEAR: Front Suspension: 4-cyl.: 5-leaf semi-elliptical springs, Spring rate: 240 lb./in. Monroe, 11.4375 in. dia. double-acting shock absorbers. Load capacity: 550 lbs. V-6: 10-leaf semi-elliptical springs. Spring rate: 176 lb./in. Optional: 10-leaf heavy-duty front springs. Rear Suspension: 5-leaf, two-stage semi-elliptical springs. Spring rate: 4-cyl.: 200 lb./in., V-6: 240.1 lb./in. Monroe, 11.9375 in. dia. double-acting shock absorbers. Normal load capacity: 940 lbs. Optional: Heavy-duty rear springs option with eleven thicker (2.407 in. to 1.973 in.). Spring rate: 225 lb./in. Front Axle Type and Capacity: Full-floating Spicer model 25, hypoid. Capacity: 2500 lb. Early 1966 models: 2000 lb. capacity. Rear Axle Type and Capacity: Semi-floating Spicer model 44-2. Hypoid. Capacity: 2500 lb. Axle Ratios: Three speed models: 4-cyl.: 4.27:1, V-6: 3.73:1. Optional: (at no extra cost): 4-cyl.: 5.38:1, V-6: 4.8:1. Four-speed models: (not available with V-6 engine): 4-cyl.: 4.27:1. Optional: (at no extra cost) 5.38:1. Overdrive: V-6: 4.88:1, 4-cyl.: 5.38:1. Transfer Case: Spicer model 18. Ratios: 2.46:1, 1.00:1. Brakes: Type: Hydraulic, front and rear. Dimensions: Front and rear: 10.00 in. x 1.75 in. Total braking area: 174 sq. in. Wheels: Kelsey-Hayes 16 x 4.50 in., 5-bolt steel disc. Optional: None. Tires: 4-cyl.: 6.00 x 16 in. 4-ply rating. V-6: 7.35 x 15 4-ply rating. Optional: Numerous sizes and tread designs were offered. Steering: Ross model T-12 cam and lever. Ratio: 4-cyl.: 17.9:1, V-6: 24.3:1. Optional: None. Standard Transmission: 3-speed manual floor-mounted shift. (column-mounted on Tuxedo Park). Transmission ratios: 2.798:1, 1.69:1, 1.00:1. Reverse: 3.798:1. Optional: Warner T98A 4-speed manual transmission. Transmission ratios: 6.398, 3.092, 1.686, 1.0:1. Reverse: 7.820:1. Clutch: 4-cyl. 9.25 in., V-6: 10.4 in. Single dry plate. Total lining area: 4-cyl.: 78 sq. in., V-6: 103.4 sq. in.

VEHICLE DIMENSIONS: (CJ-5/CJ-6) Wheelbase: 81.0 in./101.0 in. Overall Length: 136.18 in./156.18 in. Front/Rear Tread: 48.4375 in./48.4375 in. Overall Height: 67.0 in. Width: 71.75 in. Front/Rear Overhang: 20.59 in. 22.31/ in. Tailgate: Width and Height: 36 in. x 14.125 in. Ground Clearance: 8.0 in. Load space: 36 in. x 39 in. (with tailgate closed), 36 in. by 49 in. (tailgate closed).

CAPACITIES: Fuel Tank: 10.5 gal. Located under driver's seat.

ACCOMMODATIONS: Seating Capacity: 2/6.

INSTRUMENTATION: Instrument panel light, ammeter, heat indicator gauge, speedometer oil pressure gauge, fuel level gauge.

OPTIONS: V-6 engine. Perkins diesel engine (not available for Tuxedo Park). Heavy-duty alternator. Compressor. Heavy-duty battery. Power brakes. Rotary broom. Locking gas cap. Heavy-duty clutch (for Hurricane 4-cyl. engine only). 6-volt electrical system. 4-way flasher lights. Governor. Fresh-air heater and defroster. Heavy-duty front and rear shock absorbers. Pintle hook. Selective drive hubs. Cigarette lighter. Spare tire lock. Outside right-side mirror. Inside rearview mirror. Fuel tank skid plate. Power take-offs. Radio. Passenger safety rail. Radiator chaff screen. Snowplow. Push plate. Passenger's side front bucket seat. Driver's 2/3 seat. Passenger's front 1/3 seat. Rear bench seat. Longitudinal rear seats. Wheelhouse cushion pads (CJ-5 only). Trencher. Full or half metal cab. Full or half fabric top. Convertible top. "Bikini" top with half doors. 4-speed manual transmission (available with Hurricane or Perkins engines only). Overdrive. Wheelcovers. Win. Wreckers. Windshield washer. Ventilating windshield. Rear Powr-Lok differential. Front Powr-Lok differential (available with Hurricane engine only). Step rear bumper. Welder. Chrome front and rear bumpers. Options for the Tuxedo Park were as follows: V-6 engine. Heavy-duty battery, Locking gas cap. Heavy-duty clutch (for Hurricane 4-cyl. engine only). 4-way flasher lights. Fresh-air heater and defroster. Heavy-duty front and rear shock absorbers. Front floor mat. Selective drive hubs. Outside right-side mirror. Chrome passenger safety rail. Snowplow. Passenger side front bucket seat. Driver's 2/3 seat. Passenger's front 1/3 seat. Rear bench seat. Longitudinal rear seats. Wheelhouse cushion pads (CJ-5 only). Full or half metal cab. Full or half fabric top. Convertible top. "Bikini" top with half doors. 4-speed manual transmission (available with Hurricane engine only). Wheelcovers. Win. Windshield washer. Ventilating windshield. Rear Powr-Lok differential. Front Powr-Lok differential (available with Hurricane engine only).

HISTORICAL FOOTNOTES: Buick sold the manufacturing line for the V-6 to Kaiser after production of Buick's 1967 models ended. By 1968 over 75 percent of all Jeeps were being ordered with the "Dauntless" V-6.

1969 CJ

A new Jeep camper option debuted in 1969. Recommended for CJ-5 Jeeps with the V-6 engine and the 4.88:1 axle ratio, it could be installed on any CJ-5 model. The camper was attached to the Jeep by a hook-up that slipped into the CJ's rear body section. The camper had a two-tone exterior and accommodated four occupants. Its standard features included a kitchen with running water, built-in cabinets, stove and oven. Available options included a 10,000 BTU heater, toilet, gas/electric refrigerator and a second roof vent in addition to the single standard unit.

1969 Jeep CJ-5 with Camper option

Also offered for 1969 was a limited production "462" version of the CJ-5. Its standard features included a roll bar, swing-out spare tire carrier, Polyglas tubeless tires, skid plate, an electric ammeter and oil gauge. The Tuxedo Park models were not offered for 1969.

I.D. DATA: The serial number was positioned on the left front door hinge pillar post and left firewall. The serial number consisted of from nine to eleven entries. The first four identified the series and bodystyle. The last five or six digits were the sequential production numbers. Serial number range: CJ-5: 8305015 or 8305C15-244728 and up. CJ-6: 8405015-35264

Model Number	Body Type	Factory Price	GVW	Shipping Weight	Prod. Total
Jeep					
CJ-5	Utility	$2823	3750	2212	—
CJ-6	Utility	$2918	3900	2274	—

STANDARD ENGINE: Engine Type: F-head, In-line-4. Cast iron block and cylinder head. Bore x Stroke: 3.125 in. x 4.375 in. Lifters: Mechanical. Number of main bearings-3. Fuel Induction: Single Carter model YF-938-SD. Compression Ratio: 7.4:1. Optional 6.9:1. Displacement: 134.2 cu. in. (2.199 liters). Horsepower: 75 @ 4000 rpm. Torque: 114 lb.-ft. @ 2000 rpm. Oil refill capacity: 5 qt. with filter change. Fuel Requirements: Regular.

OPTIONAL ENGINE: Engine Type: OHV V-6. Cast iron block and cylinder head. Bore x Stroke: 3.75 in. x 3.40 in. Lifters: Mechanical. Number of main bearings-3. Fuel Induction: 2-barrel carburetor. Compression Ratio: 9.0:1. Displacement: 225 cu. in. (3.68 liters). Horsepower: 160 @ 4200 rpm. Torque: 235 lb.-ft. @ 2400 rpm. Oil refill capacity: 4 qt. with filter change. Fuel Requirements: Regular.

OPTIONAL ENGINE: Engine Type: Perkins "Four 192" diesel In-line-4. Cast iron block and cylinder head. Bore x Stroke: 3.5 in. x 5.0 in. Lifters: Mechanical. Compression Ratio: 16.5:1. Displacement: 192 cu. in. (3.15 liters). Horsepower: 62 @ 3000 rpm. Torque: 143 lb.-ft. @ 1350 rpm. Fuel Requirements: Diesel.

CHASSIS FEATURES: Separate body and channel steel frame construction, 4.125 in. depth x 1.937 in. width, five cross members. Overall frame length: CJ-5: 128.4375 in. CJ-6: 148.4375 in. Section modulus: 1.493 in. cu.

SUSPENSION AND RUNNING GEAR: Front Suspension: 4-cyl.: 5-leaf semi-elliptical springs, Spring rate: 240 lb./in. Monroe, 11.4375 in. dia. double-acting shock absorbers. Load capacity: 550 lbs. V-6: 10-leaf semi-elliptical springs. Spring rate: 176 lb./in. Optional: 10-leaf heavy-duty front springs. Rear Suspension: 5-leaf, two-stage semi-elliptical springs. Spring rate: 4-cyl.: 200 lb./in., V-6: 240.1 lb./in. Monroe, 11.9375 in. dia. double-acting shock absorbers. Normal load capacity: 940 lbs. Optional: Heavy-duty rear springs option with eleven thicker (2.407 in. to 1.973 in.). Spring rate: 225 lb./in. Front Axle Type and Capacity: Full-floating Spicer model 25, hypoid. Capacity: 2500 lb. Early 1966 models: 2000 lb. capacity. Rear Axle Type and Capacity: Semi-floating Spicer model 44-2. Hypoid. Capacity: 2500 lb. Axle Ratios: Three speed models: 4-cyl.: 4.27:1, V-6: 3.73:1. Optional: (at no extra cost): 4-cyl.: 5.38:1, V-6: 4.8:1. Four-speed models: (not available with V-6 engine): 4-cyl.: 4.27:1. Optional: (at no extra cost) 5.38:1. Overdrive: V-6: 4.88:1, 4-cyl.: 5.38:1. Transfer Case: Spicer model 18. Ratios: 2.46:1, 1.00:1. Brakes: Type: Hydraulic, front and rear. Dimensions: Front and rear: 10.00 in. x 1.75 in. Total braking area: 174 sq. in. Wheels: Kelsey-Hayes 16 x 4.50 in., 5-bolt steel disc. Optional: None. Tires: 4-cyl.: 6.00 x 16 in. 4-ply rating. V-6: 7.35 x 15 4-ply rating. Optional: Numerous sizes and tread designs were offered. Steering: Ross model T-12 cam and lever. Ratio: 4-cyl.: 17.9:1, V-6: 24.3:1. Optional: None. Standard Transmission: 3-speed manual floor-mounted shift. (column-mounted on Tuxedo Park). Transmission ratios: 2.798:1, 1.69:1, 1.00:1. Reverse: 3.798:1. Optional: Warner T98A 4-speed manual transmission. Transmission ratios: 6.398, 3.092, 1.686, 1.0:1. Reverse: 7.820:1. Clutch: 4-cyl. 9.25 in., V-6: 10.4 in. Single dry plate. Total lining area: 4-cyl.: 78 sq. in., V-6: 103.4 sq. in.

VEHICLE DIMENSIONS: (CJ-5/CJ-6) Wheelbase: 81.0 in./101.0 in. Overall Length: 136.18 in./156.18 in. Front/Rear Tread: 48.4375 in./48.4375 in. Overall Height: 67.0 in. Width: 71.75 in. Front/Rear Overhang: 20.59 in. 22.31/ in. Tailgate: Width and Height: 36 in. x 14.125 in. Ground Clearance: 8.0 in. Load space: 36 in. x 39 in. (with tailgate closed), 36 in. by 49 in. (tailgate closed).

CAPACITIES: Fuel Tank: 10.5 gal. Located under driver's seat.

ACCOMMODATIONS: Seating Capacity: 2/6.

INSTRUMENTATION: Instrument panel light, ammeter, heat indicator gauge, speedometer oil pressure gauge, fuel level gauge.

OPTIONS: V-6 engine. Perkins diesel engine (not available for Tuxedo Park). Heavy-duty alternator. Compressor. Heavy-duty battery. Power brakes. Rotary broom. Locking gas cap. Heavy-duty clutch (for Hurricane 4-cyl. engine only). 6-volt electrical system. 4-way flasher lights. Governor. Fresh-air heater and defroster. Heavy-duty front and rear shock absorbers. Pintle hook. Selective drive hubs. Cigarette lighter. Spare tire lock. Outside right-side mirror. Inside rearview mirror. Fuel tank skid plate. Power take-offs. Radio. Passenger safety rail. Radiator chaff screen. Snowplow. Push plate. Passenger's side front bucket seat. Driver's 2/3 seat. Passenger's front 1/3 seat. Rear bench seat. Longitudinal rear seats. Wheelhouse cushion pads (CJ-5 only). Trencher. Full or half metal cab. Full or half fabric top. Convertible top. "Bikini" top with half doors. 4-speed manual transmission (available with Hurricane or Perkins engines only). Overdrive. Wheelcovers. Win. Wreckers. Windshield washer. Ventilating windshield. Rear Powr-Lok differential. Front Powr-Lok differential (available with Hurricane engine only). Step rear bumper. Welder. Chrome front and rear bumpers.

HISTORICAL FOOTNOTES: This was the final year for Kaiser ownership of the Jeep name.

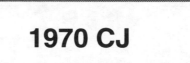

1970 CJ

The CJ Jeeps were unchanged for 1970. Standard equipment for the CJ models included these items: Oil bath air cleaner, 50 amp battery.

I.D. DATA: The serial number was positioned on the left front door hinge pillar post and left firewall. The serial number consisted of from nine to eleven entries. The first four identified the series and bodystyle. The last five or six digits were the sequential production numbers. Serial number range: CJ-5: 8305015 or 8305C15-259487 and up. CJ-6: 8405015-37549.

Model Number	Body Type	Factory Price	GVW	Shipping Weight	Prod. Total
Jeep					
CJ-5	Utility	$2930	3750	2212	—
CJ-6	Utility	$3026	3900	2274	—

STANDARD ENGINE: Engine Type: F-head, In-line-4. Cast iron block and cylinder head. Bore x Stroke: 3.125 in. x 4.375 in. Lifters: Mechanical. Number of main bearings-3. Fuel Induction: Single Carter model YF-938-SD. Compression Ratio: 7.4:1. Optional 6.9:1. Displacement: 134.2 cu. in. (2.199 liters). Horsepower: 75 @ 4000 rpm. Torque: 114 lb.-ft. @ 2000 rpm. Oil refill capacity: 5 qt. with filter change. Fuel Requirements: Regular.

OPTIONAL ENGINE: Engine Type: OHV V-6. Cast iron block and cylinder head. Bore x Stroke: 3.75 in. x 3.40 in. Lifters: Mechanical. Number of main bearings-3. Fuel Induction: 2-barrel carburetor. Compression Ratio: 9.0:1. Displacement: 225 cu. in. (3.68 liters). Horsepower: 160 @ 4200 rpm. Torque: 235 lb.-ft. @ 2400 rpm. Oil refill capacity: 4 qt. with filter change. Fuel Requirements: Regular.

CHASSIS FEATURES: Separate body and channel steel frame construction, 4.125 in. depth x 1.937 in. width, five cross members. Overall frame length: CJ-5: 128.4375 in. CJ-6: 148.4375 in. Section modulus: 1.493 in. cu.

SUSPENSION AND RUNNING GEAR: Front Suspension: 4-cyl.: 5-leaf semi-elliptical springs, 39.63 in. x by 1.75 in. Spring rate: 188 lb./in. Monroe, 11.4375 in. dia. double-acting shock absorbers. Load capacity (at pad): 875 lbs. V-6: 10-leaf semi-elliptical springs, 39.63 in. x 1.75 in. Spring rate: 176 lb./in. Load capacity (at pad): 865 lb. Optional: 12-leaf heavy-duty front springs, 39.50 in. x 1.75 in. Capacity (at pad): 1240 lb. Rear Suspension: 5-leaf, two-stage semi-elliptical springs, 46.0 in. x 1.75 in. Spring rate: 4-cyl. and V-6: 155-230 lb./in. V-6: 240.1 lb./in. Monroe, 11.9375 in. dia. double-acting shock absorbers. Capacity (at pad): 1240 lb. Capacity at ground: 4-cyl.: 1370 lb., V-6: 1405 lb. Optional: Heavy-duty 12-leaf semi-elliptical rear springs, 46 in. x 1.75 in. Spring rate: 410 lb./in. Capacity (at pad): 1850 lb. Mandatory with 12-leaf front spring option: 13-leaf semi-elliptical springs, 46 in. x 1.75 in. Spring rate: 220 lb./in. Capacity (at pad): 1260 lb. Front Axle Type and Capacity: Full-floating Spicer 27-AF, hypoid. Capacity: 2000 lb. Rear Axle Type and Capacity: Semi-floating Spicer model 44. Hypoid. Capacity: 2500 lb. Axle Ratios: Three speed models: 4-cyl.: 4.27:1, V-6: 3.73:1. Optional: (at no extra cost): 4-cyl.: 5.38:1, V-6: 4.8:1. Four-speed models: (not available with V-6 engine): 4-cyl.: 4.27:1. Optional: (at no extra cost) 5.38:1. Overdrive: V-6: 4.88:1, 4-cyl.: 5.38:1. Transfer Case: Spicer model 18. Ratios: 2.46:1, 1.00:1. Brakes: Type: Hydraulic, front and rear. Dimensions: Front and rear: 10.00 in. x 2.00 in. Effective braking area: 156 sq. in. Wheels: Kelsey-Hayes 16 x 4.50 in. E, 5-bolt steel disc. V-6: Kelsey-Hayes 15 x 6K. Optional: None. Tires: 4-cyl.: 6.00 x 16 in. 4-ply rating. V-6: 7.35 x 15 in. 4-ply rating Power-Cushion tubeless. Optional: 8.55 x 15 in. 4-ply, black or white sidewall Suburbanite, 6.00 x 16 in. 6-ply, black sidewall All-Service, 7.00 x 15 in. 6-ply, black sidewall All-Service, 7.00 x 16 in. 6-ply black sidewall All-Service, G-70 x 15 in. white sidewall Polyglas, H-78 x 15 Power Cushion Polyglas white sidewall, H-78 x 15 in. Suburbanite black sidewall. Steering: Ross model T-12 cam and lever. Ratio: 14:1. Turning Circle: CJ-5: 35.0 ft. CJ-6: 42.3 ft. Optional: None. Standard Transmission: 4-cylinder: Warner T90L 3-speed manual floor-mounted shift. V-6: Warner T14A 3-speed manual. Fully synchromesh with V-6, synchromesh on top two gears for 4-cyl. Transmission ratios: 4-cyl.: 3.339, 1,551, 1.00:1 Reverse: 3.798:1. V-6: 3.1, 1.612, 1.00:1. Reverse: 3.1:1. Optional: 4-cyl.: Warner T98A 4-speed manual transmission. V-6: Warner T18. Not available for CJ-6 with V-6. Transmission ratios: 4-cyl.: 6.398, 3.092, 1.686, 1.0:1. Reverse: 7.820:1. V-6: 4.020, 34.092, 1.686, 1.00:1. Reverse: 7.439:1. Clutch: 4-cyl. 9.25 in., V-6: 10.4 in. Single dry plate. Total lining area: 4-cyl.: 78 sq. in., V-6: 103.4 sq. in.

VEHICLE DIMENSIONS: (CJ-5/CJ-6) Wheelbase: 81.0 in./101.0 in. Overall Length: 136.18 in./156.18 in. Front/Rear Tread: 48.4375 in./48.4375 in. Overall Height: 67.0 in. Width: 71.75 in. Front/Rear Overhang: 20.59 in. 22.31/ in. Tailgate: Width and Height: 36 in. x 14.125 in. Ground Clearance: 8.0 in. Load space: 36 in. x 39 in. (with tailgate closed), 36 in. by 49 in. (tailgate closed).

CAPACITIES: Fuel Tank: 15.5 gal. Engine coolant system:. 4-cyl.: 12 qt. V-6: 10 qt.

ACCOMMODATIONS: Seating Capacity: 2/6.

INSTRUMENTATION: Instrument panel light, ammeter, heat indicator gauge, speedometer, oil pressure gauge, fuel level gauge.

HISTORICAL FOOTNOTES: American Motors acquired Jeep in February, 1970.

1970 Jeep CJ-5 Renegade I

1971 CJ

Although the CJ Jeeps were essentially unchanged for 1971 there was a harbinger of things soon to come in the form of the limited edition Jeep Renegade II. The Renegade II was depicted by AMC as a "limited-edition model based on the famed four-wheel drive "Jeep Universal CJ-5." First shown at the 1971 Detroit Auto Show, the Renegade II had such features as body striping, roll bar and tachometer. Jeep's sales manager, Jeffrey C. Williams, noted that the Renegade II was "designed to meet the most exacting tastes of the four-wheel drive enthusiast. It incorporates custom touches that permit Jeep owners to express their individuality in off-road events." The Renegade II was offered only in a "big bad orange" body color with charcoal striping. Standard colors for the CJ line for 1971 were sprucetip green metallic, president red, avocado mist metallic, champagne white, spring green, vintage gold metallic, burnished bronze metallic, island blue metallic and candlelight yellow. The three interior colors offered were buckskin, marlin blue and charcoal. Standard CJ equipment included these items: Oil bath air cleaner, 50 amp battery, 35 amp generator, heater and defroster, single horn, outside driver-side mirror, interior mirror, oil filter, driver's bucket seat with seat belt, and windshield washers and 2-speed electric windshield wipers.

I.D. DATA: The serial number was positioned on the left front door hinge pillar post and left firewall. The serial number consisted of from nine to eleven entries. The first four identified the series and bodystyle. The last five or six digits were the sequential production numbers. Serial number range: CJ-5: 8305015-273245 and up. CJ-6: 8405015-39612 and up.

Model Number	Body Type	Factory Price	GVW	Shipping Weight	Prod. Total
Jeep					
CJ-5	Utility	$2886	3750	2212	—
CJ-6	Utility	$2979	3900*	2274	—

* 4500 GVW available for both CJ-5 and CJ-6.

STANDARD ENGINE: Engine Type: F-head, In-line-4. Cast iron block and cylinder head. Bore x Stroke: 3.125 in. x 4.375 in. Lifters: Mechanical. Number of main bearings-3. Fuel Induction: Single Carter model YF-938-SD. Compression Ratio: 6.7:1. (7.4:1 for California). Displacement: 134.2 cu. in. (2.199 liters). Horsepower: 75 @ 4000 rpm. Torque: 114 lb.-ft. @ 2000 rpm. Oil refill capacity: 5 qt. with filter change. Fuel Requirements: Regular.

OPTIONAL ENGINE: Engine Type: OHV V-6. Cast iron block and cylinder head. Bore x Stroke: 3.75 in. x 3.40 in. Lifters: Mechanical. Number of main bearings-3. Fuel Induction: 2-barrel carburetor. Compression Ratio: 9.0:1 (7.4:1 for California). Displacement: 225 cu. in. (3.68 liters). Horsepower: 160 @ 4200 rpm. Torque: 235 lb.-ft. @ 2400 rpm. Oil refill capacity: 4 qt. with filter change. Fuel Requirements: Regular.

CHASSIS FEATURES: Separate body and channel steel frame construction, 4.125 in. depth x 1.937 in. width, five cross members. Overall frame length: CJ-5: 128.4375 in. CJ-6: 148.4375 in. Section modulus: 1.493 in. cu.

SUSPENSION AND RUNNING GEAR: Front Suspension: 4-cyl.: 5-leaf semi-elliptical springs, 39.63 in. x by 1.75 in. Spring rate: 188 lb./in. Monroe, 11.4375 in. dia. double-acting shock absorbers. Load capacity (at pad): 875 lbs. V-6: 10-leaf semi-elliptical springs, 39.63 in. x 1.75 in. Spring rate: 176 lb./in. Load capacity (at pad): 865 lb. Optional: 12-leaf heavy-duty front springs, 39.50 in. x 1.75 in. Capacity (at pad): 1240 lb. Rear Suspension: 5-leaf, two-stage semi-elliptical springs, 46.0 in. x 1.75 in. Spring rate: 4-cyl. and 6-l.: 155-230 lb./in. V-6: 240.1 lb./in. Monroe, 11.9375 in. dia. double-acting shock absorbers. Capacity (at pad): 1240 lb. Capacity at ground: 4-cyl.: 1370 lb., V-6: 1405 lb. Optional: Heavy-duty 12-leaf semi-elliptical rear springs, 46 in. x 1.75 in. Spring rate: 410 lb./in. Capacity (at pad): 1850 lb. Mandatory with 12-leaf front spring option: 13-leaf semi-elliptical springs, 46 in. x 1.75 in. Spring rate: 220 lb./in. Capacity (at pad): 1260 lb. Front Axle Type and Capacity: Full-floating Spicer 27-AF, hypoid. Capacity: 2000 lb. Rear Axle Type and Capacity: Semi-floating Spicer model 44. Hypoid. Capacity: 2500 lb. Axle Ratios: Three speed models: 4-cyl.: 4.27:1, V-6: 3.73:1. Optional: (at no extra cost): 4-cyl.: 5.38:1, V-6: 4.8:1. Four-speed models: (not available with V-6 engine): 4-cyl.: 4.27:1. Optional: (at no extra cost) 5.38:1. Overdrive: V-6: 4.88:1, 4-cyl.: 5.38:1. Transfer Case: Spicer model 18. Ratios: 2.46:1, 1.00:1. Brakes: Type: Hydraulic, front and rear. Dimensions: Front and rear: 10.00 in. x 2.00 in. Effective braking area: 156 sq. in. Wheels: Kelsey-Hayes 16 x 4.50 in. E, 5-bolt steel disc. V-6: Kelsey-Hayes 15 x 6K. Optional: None. Tires: 4-cyl.: 6.00 x 16 in. 4-ply rating. V-6: 7.35 x 15 in. 4-ply rating Power-Cushion tubeless. Optional: 8.55 x 15 in. 4-ply, black or white sidewall Suburbanite, 6.00 x 16 in. 6-ply,

black sidewall All-Service, 7.00 x 15 in. 6-ply, black sidewall All-Service, 7.00 x 16 in. 6-ply black sidewall All-Service, G-70 x 15 in. white sidewall Polyglas, H-78 x 15 Power Cushion Polyglas white sidewall, H-78 x 15 in. Suburbanite black sidewall. Steering: Ross model T-12 cam and lever. Ratio: 14:1. Turning Circle: CJ-5: 35.0 ft. CJ-6: 42.3 ft. Optional: None. Standard Transmission: 4-cylinder: Warner T90L 3-speed manual floor-mounted shift. V-6: Warner T14A 3-speed manual. Fully synchromesh with V-6, synchromesh on top two gears for 4-cyl. Transmission ratios: 4-cyl.: 3.339, 1.551, 1.00:1 Reverse: 3.798:1. V-6: 3.1, 1.612, 1.00:1. Reverse: 3.1:1. Optional: 4-cyl.: Warner T98A 4-speed manual transmission. V-6: Warner T18. Not available for CJ-6 with V-6. Transmission ratios: 4-cyl.: 6.398, 3.092, 1.686, 1.0:1. Reverse: 7.820:1. V-6: 4.020, 34.092, 1.686, 1.00:1. Reverse: 7.439:1. Clutch: 4-cyl.: 9.25 in., V-6: 10.4 in. Single dry plate. Total lining area: 4-cyl.: 78 sq. in., V-6: 103.4 sq. in.

VEHICLE DIMENSIONS: Wheelbase: 81.0 in./101.0 in. Overall Length: 135.6 in./155.6 in. Front/Rear Tread: 48.4375 in./48.4375 in. Overall Height: CJ-5: 69.5 in. CJ-6: 68.3 in. Width: 59.1 in. (less steps). Front/Rear Overhang: 22.6 in./32.0 in. Tailgate: Width and Height: 36 in. x 14.125 in. Ground Clearance: Front axle: 8.4 in. Rear axle: 8.0 in. Load space: 36 in. x 39 in. (with tailgate closed), 36 in. by 49 in. (tailgate closed).

CAPACITIES: Fuel Tank: 16.5 gal. Coolant System: 4-cyl.: 12 qt., V-6: 10 qt.

ACCOMMODATIONS: Seating Capacity: 2/6.

INSTRUMENTATION: Instrument panel light, ammeter, heat indicator gauge, speedometer oil pressure gauge, fuel level gauge.

OPTIONS AND PRICES: V-6 engine: $100.00. Full Meyer metal cab: $399. 4-speed manual transmission: $174.65. Optional axle ratios: $12.65. Rear Trac-Lok differential: $61.35. Cigarette lighter: $6.50. Dual sun visors: $13.95. Padded instrument panel: $37.95. Heavy-duty battery: $11.70. 55 amp alternator: $27.60. Heavy-duty cooling system. Includes 6 blade fan: $9.75 (4-cyl.), $23.35 (V-6). Heavy-duty frame: $19.50. Front and rear military wrap shock absorbers and springs: $38.85. Heavy-duty 12-leaf rear springs. (Available for V-6 only): $20.15. 8.55 x 15 black Suburbanite tires: $55.15. 8.55 x 15 white Suburbanite tires: $87.05. H78 x 15 black Polyglas Suburbanite tires: $81.05. H78 x 15 white Polyglas Power Cushion tires: $113.40. Drawbar: $27.65. Fuel tank skid plate: $19.95. Spare tire tailgate mount: $9.95. Nitrox emission (V-6 only): $37.00. Warn semi-automatic front hubs: $64.75. Front passenger bucket seat: $74.30. Full bench front seat (2/3-1/3 type): $89.45. Rear seat with dual seat belts: $92.10.

HISTORICAL FOOTNOTES: American Motors reported that the Jeep Universal had won more off-road racing and endurance events than any other four-wheel drive vehicle. Among the events in which the Jeep had been victorious were the Baja 500, the Mint 400 and the Riverside Grand Prix.

1972 CJ

The changes made in the CJ models (the old "Universal" identification gave way to just CJ) for 1972 were the most dramatic sweeping changes made in that series since the CJ-5 debuted in 1955. Both the V-6 engine and the F-head 4-cylinder were no longer available. The F-head was still available for export. Standard for the U.S. market was American Motors' 232 cu. in. 6-cylinder engine.

Both the larger AMC 258 cu. in. 6-cylinder engine and its 305 cu. in. V-8 were CJ options. The 305 engine was the first V-8 ever installed at the factory in a CJ.

A new fixed tailgate option was offered as an alternative to the standard drop-down version. Also new for 1972 were optional gauges for the oil pressure and ammeter, wheelcovers for 15 in. wheels, an improved Whitco vinyl top and a more efficient heater. Other changes for 1972 included a longer handle for the transfer case, cowl-suspended pedals and a foot-operated parking brake.

The CJ-5 was available with the Renegade Package. Its content included American Racing cast aluminum wheels, H78 x 15 white sidewall tires, roll bar, dual exterior mirrors, fender-lips, striped seat upholstery, and a Renegade hood stripe. The Renegade was offered in a choice of three colors: Yellow, orange and plum. A list of mandatory options were also listed for the Renegade Package: Trac-Lok rear differential, 304 V-8, dual sun visors, heavy-duty cooling system, rear seat, fuel tank skid plate, passenger safety rail, ammeter and oil pressure gauges, solid back tail panel with spare tire mount.

1972 Jeep CJ-5 Renegade

I.D. DATA: The serial number was positioned on the left front door hinge pillar post and left firewall. The serial number consisted of from nine to eleven entries. The first four identified the series and bodystyle. The last five or six digits were the sequential production numbers. Model identification: CJ-5: 83050; CJ-6: 84050.

Model Number	Body Type	Factory Price	GVW	Shipping Weight	Prod. Total
Jeep					
CJ-5	Utility	$2955	3750	2437	—
CJ-6	Utility	$3045	3900	2499	—

STANDARD ENGINE: Engine Type: OHV, In-line-6. Cast iron block and cylinder head. Bore x Stroke: 3.75 in. x 3.50 in. Lifters: Hydraulic. Number of main bearings-7. Fuel Induction: 1-bbl. Carter Type RTBS or Holley model 1931C-3705. Compression Ratio: 8.0:1. Displacement: 232 cu. in. (3.8 liters). Horsepower: Net 100 @ 3600 rpm. Torque: Net 185 lb.-ft. @ 1800 rpm. Oil refill capacity: 5 qt. with filter change. Fuel Requirements: Regular.

OPTIONAL ENGINE: Engine Type: OHV, In-line-6. Cast iron block and cylinder head. Bore x Stroke: 3.75 in. x 3.90 in. Lifters: Hydraulic. Number of main bearings-7. Fuel Induction: 1-bbl. Carter Type RTBS or Holley model 1931C-3705. Compression Ratio: 8.0:1. Displacement: 258 cu. in. (4.2 liters). Horsepower: Net 110 @ 3500 rpm. Torque: Net 195 lb.-ft. @ 2000 rpm. Oil refill capacity: 5 qt. with filter change. Fuel Requirements: Regular.

OPTIONAL ENGINE: Engine Type: OHV, V-8. Cast iron block and cylinder head. Bore x Stroke: 3.75 in. x 3.44 in. Lifters: Hydraulic. Number of main bearings-5. Fuel Induction: 2-bbl. carburetor. Compression Ratio: 8.4:1. Displacement: 304 cu. in. (4.98 liters). Horsepower: Net: 150 @ 4200 rpm. Torque: Net: 245 lb.-ft. @ 2500 rpm. Oil refill capacity: 5 qt. with filter change. Fuel Requirements: Regular.

CHASSIS FEATURES: Separate body and ladder steel frame construction, Length: 131.38 in., Width: 29.25 in. six cross members. Section modulus: 1.493 in. cu.

SUSPENSION AND RUNNING GEAR: Front Suspension: CJ-5: 7-leaf semi-elliptical springs, 39.75 in. x by 1.75 in. Spring rate: 190 lb./in. Capacity: 855 lb. (at pad). 1015 lb. (at ground). Hydraulic direct double-action shock absorbers with 1.1875 in. piston diameter. CJ-6: 9-leaf semi-elliptical springs, 39.75 in. x 1.75 in. Spring rate: 210 lb./in. Capacity: 1040 lb. (at pad), 1200 lb. (at ground). Hydraulic direct double-action shock absorbers with 1.1875 in. piston diameter. Optional: 10-leaf semi-elliptical springs, 39.75 in. x 1.75 in. Spring rate: 270 lb./in. Capacity: 1300 lb. (at pad), 1460 lb. (at ground). Rear Suspension: 5-leaf semi-elliptical springs, 46 in. x 1.75 in. Spring rate: 230 lb./in. Capacity: 1240 lb. (at pad), 1405 lb. (at ground). Hydraulic direct double-action shock absorbers with 1.1875 in. piston diameter. Optional: 10-leaf semi-elliptical springs, 46 in. x 1.75 in. Spring rate: 270 lb./in. Capacity 1260 lb. (at pad), 1425 lb. (at ground). Front Axle Type and Capacity: Full-floating Dana 30 front axle, hypoid. Capacity: 2300 lb. Rear Axle Type and Capacity: Semi-floating Dana 44 Hypoid. Capacity: 3000 lb. Axle Ratios: 3.73:1. Optional: 4.27:1. Transfer Case: Dana model 20. Ratios: 2.03:1, 1.00:1. Brakes: Type: Hydraulic, front and rear. Dimensions: Front and rear: 11.00 in. x 2.0 in. Effective lining area: 180.8 sq. in. Wheels: Kelsey-Hayes 15 x 6L in., 5-bolt on 5.5 in. circle steel disc. Optional: 16 x 4.5E with 4500 lb. (CJ-5) or 4750 lb. GVW options. Tires: E78 x 15B Suburbanite Polyglas black sidewall. Optional: F-78 x 15B Power Cushion black sidewall, H-78 x 15B black sidewall, H-78 x 15 white sidewall, 7.35 x 15B Suburbanite XG black sidewall, H-78 x 15B black sidewall, H-78 x 15B white sidewall, 6.00 x 16C All-Service black sidewall, 6.00 x 16C Custom X-Grip black sidewall, H-78 x 15 Power Cushion Polyglas white sidewall, H-78 x 15B Suburbanite Polyglas black sidewall, H-78 x 15D Suburbanite Polyglas black sidewall. Steering: Recirculating ball system. Ratio: 24.1:1t. Turning Circle: CJ-5: 32.75 ft. CJ-6: 37.5 ft. Optional: Saginaw power steering. Ratio: 17.5:1. Standard Transmission: All-synchromesh 3-speed Warner T-14A transmission. Transmission ratios: 3.1, 1.612, 1.00:1. Reverse: 3.1:1. Optional: Warner T-18 4-speed gearbox with a non-synchromesh first gear. Transmission ratios: 4.02, 2.41, 1.431, 1.00:1. Reverse: 4.73:1. Clutch: 10.5 in. Single dry plate. Total lining area: 106.75 sq. in. Total plate pressure: 1640 lb. Optional: None.

VEHICLE DIMENSIONS: CJ-5/CJ-6 Wheelbase: 84 in./104 in. Overall Length: 138.75 in./ 158.75 in. Front/Rear Tread: 51.5 in./50.0 in. Overall Height: 67.0 in. Width: 71.75 in. Front/ Rear Overhang: 22.6 in./32.0 in. Tailgate: Width and Height: 36 in. x 14.125 in. Approach/ Departure Degrees: 45/30. Ground Clearance: Front axle: 8.6 in. Rear axle: 8.0 in. Load space: CJ-5: 36 in. x 39.75 in. (with tailgate closed), 36 in. by 54.5 in. (tailgate closed). CJ-6: 36 in. x 59.75 in. (with tailgate closed), 36 in. x 74.5 in. Cargo area: CJ-5: 10.0 sq. ft., CJ-6: 15.0 sq. ft. Front legroom: 41 in. Front hip room: 55.40 in.

CAPACITIES: Fuel Tank: 16.5 gal. Cooling system: 10.5 qt.

ACCOMMODATIONS: Seating Capacity: 2/6.

INSTRUMENTATION: 0-90 mph speedometer, odometer, gauges for engine coolant temperature, fuel level, and oil pressure and battery warning lights

OPTIONS AND PRICES: Renegade Package: $299.00. Spare tire lock: $4.05. Free-wheeling hubs: $98. Power steering: $148. Power brakes: $46. Trac-Lok rear differential: $62. Oil and ammeter gauges: $17. Heavy-duty frame: $20. Heavy-duty springs and shock absorbers: $39. Front passenger bucket seat: $74. Full width split front bench seat: $89. Rear bench seat: $92. 55-amp alternator: $28. 70-amp. battery: $12. Cigarette lighter: $7. Drawbar: $28. Padded instrument panel: $38. Fuel tank skid panel: $10. Sun visors: $14. 258 cid engine: $56. 304 cid engine: $130 4-speed manual transmission. Full metal top. Full fabric top. Metal half top. Fabric half top. Safari top. Cigarette lighter. Wheelcovers. Chrome bumpers. Swing-out spare tire carrier. Roll bar. Semi-automatic front hubs. Heavy-duty cooling system. Winch. Snowplow.

HISTORICAL FOOTNOTES: AMC no longer used the "Universal" identification for the CJ Jeeps.

1973 CJ

Standard for the CJ-5 and CJ-6 was a fuel skid plate. The U-joints for the front axle and drive shaft were strengthened for an extended service life. AMC also installed upgraded F78-15, four-ply tires standard tires on the 1973 CJ-5 and CJ-6 and an all-new standard two-speed windshield wiper system with an integrated washer system.

The 6-cylinder engines (which for 1973 was designed to operate on regular, low-lead gasoline of 91 octane or higher), had induction-hardened exhaust valve seats. A new mechanical linkage replaced the old cable clutch linkage design.

All dash panel control knobs were of a "Soft-Feel" design with international-code symbols. The gauges had improved green lighting as well as flame orange, instead of white colored, needles. The instrument cluster as well as the optional oil and ammeter gauges (which were now located on each side of the primary instrument dial) were surrounded by bright ring moldings. The parking brake handle was moved from behind the steering wheel to the left side of the dashboard. The heater controls now had a separate fan toggle switch and black and white "standout" knobs. For the first time a factory installed roll bar was offered. New paint was used to highlight the Jeep letters on the cowl side. Simplified model numbers were introduced for 1973: 83 for CJ-5 (was 83050) and 84 for CJ-6 (was 84050).

1973 Jeep CJ-6

The latest Jeep Renegade became available in January, 1973. Its standard features included the 304 cu. in. V-8, roll bar, specially styled wheels, H78-15 whitewall tires, blackout hood, side body racing stripe with Renegade lettering, fender extensions, transmission skid plate, oil and ammeter gauges, dual exterior mirrors, dual visors, custom vinyl interior and a rear-mounted spare.

The Renegade was later joined by another limited-production model CJ-5, the Super Jeep. It had star-studded curving red, white and blue striping on its hood, lower body and rear deck. A similar trim theme was placed on the front fenders.

The Super Jeep's standard equipment included vertically striped front and rear seats, 258 cu. in. 6-cylinder engine, rubber lip extensions on the fenders, chrome front bumper and a passenger safety rail.

The exterior color selection for the CJ models consisted of champagne white, fawn beige, jetset blue metallic, fairway green metallic, avocado mist metallic, copper tan metallic, butterscotch gold, daisy yellow, and Trans-Am red. A Wellington vinyl interior trim was standard.

1973 Jeep CJ-5

I.D. DATA: The serial number was positioned on the left front door hinge pillar post and left firewall. The serial number consisted of 13 entries. The first identified the Jeep Corporation. The second indicated the year of production. The third identified the transmission, drivetrain and assembly plant. The next two numbers identified the vehicle series or model. The sixth symbol (a letter) identified the body style. The next letter identified the type and GVW. A letter then designated the engine. The final five numbers were the sequential production number. Model identification: CJ-5: 83; CJ-6: 84.

Model Number	Body Type	Factory Price	GVW	Shipping Weight	Prod. Total
Jeep					
CJ-5	Utility	$3086	3750	2450	—
CJ-6	Utility	$3176	3900	2510	—

STANDARD ENGINE: Engine Type: OHV, In-line-6. Cast iron block and cylinder head. Bore x Stroke: 3.75 in. x 3.50 in. Lifters: Hydraulic. Number of main bearings-7. Fuel Induction: 1-bbl. Carter Type RTBS or Holley model 1931C-3705. Compression Ratio: 8.0:1. Displacement: 232 cu. in. (3.8 liters). Horsepower: Net 100 @ 3600 rpm. Torque: Net 185 lb.-ft. @ 1800 rpm. Oil refill capacity: 5 qt. with filter change. Fuel Requirements: Regular, low-lead gasoline of 91 octane or higher.

OPTIONAL ENGINE: Engine Type: OHV, In-line-6. Cast iron block and cylinder head. Bore x Stroke: 3.75 in. x 3.90 in. Lifters: Hydraulic. Number of main bearings-7. Fuel Induction: 1-bbl. Carter Type RTBS or Holley model 1931C-3705. Compression Ratio: 8.0:1. Displacement: 258 cu. in. (4.2 liters). Horsepower: Net 110 @ 3500 rpm. Torque: Net 195 lb.-ft. @ 2000 rpm. Oil refill capacity: 5 qt. with filter change. Fuel Requirements: Regular, low-lead gasoline of 91 octane or higher.

OPTIONAL ENGINE: Engine Type: OHV, V-8. Cast iron block and cylinder head. Bore x Stroke: 3.75 in. x 3.44 in. Lifters: Hydraulic. Number of main bearings-5. Fuel Induction: 2-bbl. carburetor. Compression Ratio: 8.4:1. Displacement: 304 cu. in. (4.98 liters). Horsepower: Net: 150 @ 4200 rpm. Torque: Net: 245 lb.-ft. @ 2500 rpm. Oil refill capacity: 5 qt. with filter change. Fuel Requirements: Regular, low-lead gasoline of 91 octane or higher.

CHASSIS FEATURES: Separate body and ladder steel frame construction, Length: 131.38 in., Width: 29.25 in. six cross members. Section modulus: 1.493 in. cu.

SUSPENSION AND RUNNING GEAR: Front Suspension: CJ-5: 7-leaf semi-elliptical springs, 39.75 in. x by 1.75 in. Spring rate: 190 lb./in. Capacity: 855 lb. (at pad). 1015 lb. (at ground). Hydraulic direct double-action shock absorbers with 1.1875 in. piston diameter. CJ-6: 9-leaf semi-elliptical springs, 39.75 in. x 1.75 in. Spring rate: 210 lb./in. Capacity: 1040 lb. (at pad), 1200 lb. (at ground). Hydraulic direct double-action shock absorbers with 1.1875 in. piston diameter. Optional: 10-leaf semi-elliptical springs, 39.75 in. x 1.75 in. Spring rate: 270 lb./in. Capacity: 1300 lb. (at pad), 1460 lb. (at ground). Rear Suspension: 5-leaf semi-elliptical springs, 46 in. x 1.75 in. Spring rate: 230 lb./in. Capacity: 1240 lb. (at pad), 1405 lb. (at ground). Hydraulic direct double-action shock absorbers with 1.1875 in. piston diameter. Optional: 10-leaf semi-elliptical springs, 46 in. x 1.75 in. Spring rate: 270 lb./in. Capacity 1260 lb. (at pad), 1425 lb. (at ground). Front Axle Type and Capacity: Full-floating Dana 30 front axle, hypoid. Capacity: 2300 lb. Rear Axle Type and Capacity: Semi-floating Dana 44 Hypoid. Capacity: 3000 lb. Axle Ratios: 4.27:1. Optional: 3.73:1. Transfer Case: Dana model 20. Ratios: 2.03:1, 1.00:1. Brakes: Type: Hydraulic, front and rear. Dimensions: Front and rear: 11.00 in. x 2.0 in. Effective lining area: 180.8 sq. in. Wheels: Kelsey-Hayes 15 x 6L in., 5-bolt on 5.5 in. circle steel disc. Optional: 16 x 4.5E with 4500 lb. (CJ-5) or 4750 lb. GVW options. Tires: E78 x 15B Suburbanite Polyglas black sidewall. Optional: F-78 x 15B Power Cushion black sidewall, H-78 x 15B black sidewall, H-78 x 15 white sidewall, 7.35 x 15B Suburbanite XG black sidewall, H-78 x 15B black sidewall, H-78 x 15B white sidewall, 6.00 x 16C All-Service black sidewall, 6.00 x 16C Custom X-Grip black sidewall, H-78 x 15 Power Cushion Polyglas white sidewall, H-78 x 15B Suburbanite Polyglas black sidewall, H-78 x 15D Suburbanite Polyglas black sidewall. Steering: Recirculating ball system. Ratio: 24.1:1t. Turning Circle: CJ-5: 32.75 ft. CJ-6: 37.5 ft. Optional: Saginaw power steering. Ratio: 17.5:1. Standard Transmission: All-synchromesh 3-speed Warner T-14A transmission. Transmission ratios: 3.1, 1.612, 1.00:1. Reverse: 3.1:1. Optional: Warner T-18 4-speed gearbox with a non-synchromesh first gear. Transmission ratios: 4.02, 2.41, 1.431, 1.00:1. Reverse: 4.73:1. Clutch: 10.5 in. Single dry plate. Total lining area: 106.75 sq. in. Total plate pressure: 1640 lb. Optional: None.

VEHICLE DIMENSIONS: CJ-5/CJ-6 Wheelbase: 84 in./104 in. Overall Length: 138.75 in./158.75 in. Front/Rear Tread: 51.5 in./50.0 in. Overall Height: 67.0 in. Width: 71.75 in. Front/Rear Overhang: 22.6 in./32.0 in. Tailgate: Width and Height: 36 in. x 14.125 in. Approach/Departure Degrees: 45/30. Ground Clearance: Front axle: 8.6 in. Rear axle: 8.0 in. Load space: CJ-5: 36 in. x 39.75 in. (with tailgate closed), 36 in. by 54.5 in. (tailgate closed). CJ-6: 36 in. x 59.75 in. (with tailgate closed), 36 in. x 74.5 in. Cargo area: CJ-5: 10.0 sq. ft., CJ-6: 15.0 sq. ft. Front legroom: 41 in. Front hip room: 55.40 in.

CAPACITIES: Fuel Tank: 16.5 gal. Cooling system: 10.5 qt.

ACCOMMODATIONS: Seating Capacity: 2/6.

INSTRUMENTATION: 0-90 mph speedometer, odometer, gauges for engine coolant temperature, fuel level, and oil pressure and battery warning lights

OPTIONS AND PRICES: Heavy-duty cooling system: $25.60. Drawbar: $26.80. Power steering: $143.25. Semi-automatic front hubs: $59.80. Heavy-duty frame: $18.90. Heavy-duty 51 amp alternator: $26.75. Trac-Lok 3.73:1 rear differential: $59.40. 4-speed manual transmission: $107.30. H78-15 Polyglas Suburban tires: $81.10. 258 cid engine: $53.85. 304 V-8. Heavy-duty springs and shock absorbers: $37.60. Oil and ammeter gauges: $16.65. Cigarette lighter: $8.65. Dual sun visors: $13.55. Front passenger seat: $72.10. Rear bucket seats: $89.35. Front passenger safety bar: $6.85. Padded instrument panel: $31.90. Roll bar: $54.65. Full metal top. Full fabric top. Half-cab metal top. Half cab fabric top. Safari Top. Heavy-duty snowplow. Electric winches. Power take-off winches. Trailer hitch. Push plate. Power take-off.

HISTORICAL FOOTNOTES: American Motors installed both new and improved factory inspection facilities and equipment for quality control at the Toledo plant for the 1973 model year.

1974 CJ

In appearance, the CJ-5 and CJ-6 were unchanged from their 1973 form. Technical revisions included the use of induction-hardened exhaust valve seats on the 304 cu. in. V-8. All engines met the new evaporative and exhaust emission standards for utility vehicles. All CJ Jeeps had stronger body-to-chassis mounts, a higher output heater and optional bumpers that met the government's 5 mph standard. Providing an improved braking performance was a system with new linings, master cylinders and, for the first time on the CJ's, proportioning valves.

The Renegade Package for the CJ-5 included special paint treatment, hood and cowl decals, 304 V-8 engine, oil and ammeter gauges, spare-tire lock, rear-mounted spare tire, padded instrument panel, passenger safety rail, H78x 15 white sidewall Polyglas tires, forged aluminum-styled wheels, dual sun visors, roll bar, heavy-duty cooling system and wheel well extensions. The exterior color selection for the CJ models consisted of champagne white, fawn beige, mellow yellow, Trans-Am red, golden tan metallic, copper metallic, silver green metallic, fairway green metallic and jetset blue metallic. Any of these colors were also available for the CJ-5 Renegade Special. Renegade colors were Renegade yellow and Renegade plum.

I.D. DATA: The serial number was positioned on the left front door hinge pillar post and left firewall. The serial number consisted of 13 entries. The first identified the Jeep Corporation. The second indicated the year of production. The third identified the transmission, drivetrain and assembly plant. The next two numbers identified the vehicle series or model. The sixth symbol (a letter) identified the body style. The next letter identified the type and GVW. A letter then designated the engine. The final five numbers were the sequential production number. Model identification: CJ-5: 83; CJ-6: 84.

Model Number	Body Type	Factory Price	GVW	Shipping Weight	Prod. Total
Jeep					
CJ-5	Utility	$3574	3750	2450	—
CJ-6	Utility	$3670	3900	2600	—

STANDARD ENGINE: Engine Type: OHV, In-line-6. Cast iron block and cylinder head. Bore x Stroke: 3.75 in. x 3.50 in. Lifters: Hydraulic. Number of main bearings-7. Fuel Induction: 1-bbl. Carter Type RTBS or Holley model 1931C-3705. Compression Ratio: 8.0:1. Displacement: 232 cu. in. (3.8 liters). Horsepower: Net 100 @ 3600 rpm. Torque: Net 185 lb.-ft. @ 1800 rpm. Oil refill capacity: 5 qt. with filter change. Fuel Requirements: Regular, low-lead gasoline of 91 octane or higher.

OPTIONAL ENGINE: Engine Type: OHV, In-line-6. Cast iron block and cylinder head. Bore x Stroke: 3.75 in. x 3.90 in. Lifters: Hydraulic. Number of main bearings-7. Fuel Induction: 1-bbl. Carter Type RTBS or Holley model 1931C-3705. Compression Ratio: 8.0:1. Displacement: 258 cu. in. (4.2 liters). Horsepower: Net 110 @ 3500 rpm. Torque: Net 195 lb.-ft. @ 2000 rpm. Oil refill capacity: 5 qt. with filter change. Fuel Requirements: Regular, low-lead gasoline of 91 octane or higher.

OPTIONAL ENGINE: Engine Type: OHV, V-8. Cast iron block and cylinder head. Bore x Stroke: 3.75 in. x 3.44 in. Lifters: Hydraulic. Number of main bearings-5. Fuel Induction: 2-bbl. carburetor. Compression Ratio: 8.4:1. Displacement: 304 cu. in. (4.98 liters). Horsepower: Net 150 @ 4200 rpm. Torque: Net 245 lb.-ft. @ 2500 rpm. Oil refill capacity: 5 qt. with filter change. Fuel Requirements: Regular, low-lead gasoline of 91 octane or higher.

CHASSIS FEATURES: Separate body and ladder steel frame construction, Length: 131.38 in., Width: 29.25 in. six cross members. Section modulus: 1.493 in. cu.

SUSPENSION AND RUNNING GEAR: Front Suspension: CJ-5: 7-leaf semi-elliptical springs, 39.75 in. x by 1.75 in. Spring rate: 190 lb./in. Capacity: 855 lb. (at pad). 1015 lb. (at ground). Hydraulic direct double-action shock absorbers with 1.1875 in. piston diameter. CJ-6: 9-leaf semi-elliptical springs, 39.75 in. x 1.75 in. Spring rate: 210 lb./in. Capacity: 1040 lb. (at pad), 1200 lb. (at ground). Hydraulic direct double-action shock absorbers with 1.1875 in. piston diameter. Optional: 10-leaf semi-elliptical springs, 39.75 in. x 1.75 in. Spring rate: 270 lb./in. Capacity: 1300 lb. (at pad), 1460 lb. (at ground). Rear Suspension: 5-leaf semi-elliptical springs, 46 in. x 1.75 in. Spring rate: 230 lb./in. Capacity: 1240 lb. (at pad), 1405 lb. (at ground). Hydraulic direct double-action shock absorbers with 1.1875 in. piston diameter. Optional: 10-leaf semi-elliptical springs, 46 in. x 1.75 in. Spring rate: 270 lb./in. Capacity 1260 lb. (at pad), 1425 lb. (at ground). Front Axle Type and Capacity: Full-floating Dana 30 front axle, hypoid. Capacity: 2300 lb. Rear Axle Type and Capacity: Semi-floating Dana 44 Hypoid. Capacity: 3000 lb. Axle Ratios: 4.27:1. Optional: 3.73:1. Transfer Case: Dana model 20. Ratios: 2.03:1, 1.00:1. Brakes: Type: Hydraulic, front and rear. Dimensions: Front and rear: 11.00 in. x 2.0 in. Effective lining area: 180.8 sq. in. Wheels: Kelsey-Hayes 15 x 6L in., 5-bolt on 5.5 in. circle steel disc. Optional: 16 x 4.5E with 4500 lb. (CJ-5) or 4750 lb. GVW options. Tires: E78 x 15B Suburbanite Polyglas black sidewall. Optional: F-78 x 15B Power Cushion black sidewall, H-78 x 15B black sidewall, H-78 x 15 white sidewall, 7.35 x 15B Suburbanite XG black sidewall, H-78 x 15B black sidewall, H-78 x 15B white sidewall, 6.00 x 16C All-Service black sidewall, 6.00 x 16C Custom X-Grip black sidewall, H-78 x 15 Power Cushion Polyglas white sidewall, H-78 x 15B Suburbanite Polyglas black sidewall, H-78 x 15D Suburbanite Polyglas black sidewall. Steering: Recirculating ball system. Ratio: 24.1:1t. Turning Circle: CJ-5: 32.75 ft. CJ-6: 37.5 ft. Optional: Saginaw power steering. Ratio: 17.5:1. Standard Transmission: All-synchromesh 3-speed Warner T-14A transmission. Transmission ratios: 3.1, 1.612, 1.00:1. Reverse: 3.1:1. Optional: Warner T-18 4-speed gearbox with a non-synchromesh first gear. Transmission ratios: 4.02, 2.41, 1.431, 1.00:1. Reverse: 4.73:1. Clutch: 10.5 in. Single dry plate. Total lining area: 106.75 sq. in. Total plate pressure: 1640 lb. Optional: None.

VEHICLE DIMENSIONS: CJ-5/CJ-6 Wheelbase: 84 in./104 in. Overall Length: 138.75 in./158.75 in. Front/Rear Tread: 51.5 in./50.0 in. Overall Height: 67.0 in. Width: 71.75 in. Front/Rear Overhang: 22.6 in./32.0 in. Tailgate: Width and Height: 36 in. x 14.125 in. Approach/Departure Degrees: 45/30. Ground Clearance: Front axle: 8.6 in. Rear axle: 8.0 in. Load space: CJ-5: 36 in. x 39.75 in. (with tailgate closed), 36 in. by 54.5 in. (tailgate closed). CJ-6: 36 in. x 59.75 in. (with tailgate closed), 36 in. x 74.5 in. Cargo area: CJ-5: 10.0 sq. ft., CJ-6: 15.0 sq. ft. Front legroom: 41 in. Front hip room: 55.40 in.

CAPACITIES: Fuel Tank: 16.5 gal. Cooling system: 10.5 qt.

ACCOMMODATIONS: Seating Capacity: 2/6.

INSTRUMENTATION: 0-90 mph speedometer, odometer, gauges for engine coolant temperature, fuel level, and oil pressure and battery warning lights.

OPTIONS AND PRICES: Heavy-duty cooling system: Drawbar. Power steering. Semi-automatic front hubs. Heavy-duty frame. Heavy-duty 51 amp alternator: $26.75. Trac-Lok 3.73:1 rear differential. 4-speed manual transmission. H78-15 Polyglas Suburban tires. 258 cid engine: $53.85. 304 V-8: $126. Heavy-duty springs and shock absorbers. Oil and ammeter gauges. Cigarette lighter. Dual sun visors. Front passenger seat. Rear bucket seats. Front passenger safety bar. Padded instrument panel. Roll bar. Full metal top. Full fabric top. Half-cab metal top. Half cab fabric top. Safari Top. Heavy-duty snowplow. Electric winches. Power take-off winches. Trailer hitch. Push plate. Power take-off.

HISTORICAL FOOTNOTES: The CJ models were introduced in the fall of 1974. The Jeep Renegade was now a regular production model.

1975 CJ

There were many changes for 1975 and for the most part they made the CJ-5 more of a Jeep than ever while providing a few new niceties. The CJ-5 and CJ-6 models had stronger frames with increased gauge steel in the side rails. A new Levi's weather-resistant vinyl interior seat trim option was available for the base CJ-5 model. It was also installed on the 1975 Renegade. With classic Levi's stitching it was available in either blue or tan and covered the front and rear seats, instrument panel pad and padded sun visors. All CJ models had new Jeep lettering on the cowl side. Models with the Levi's option had a Levi's decal positioned above the Jeep name. A CJ-5/6 designation was located at a point just below the passenger side front directional signal on CJ's with the Levi's Package. For the first time a new black or white Whitco top was a factory option. It remained, as in previous years, a dealer-installed option. It was available in blue or tan when ordered with the Levi's Package.

1975 Jeep CJ-5

Another first for the CJ was a factory-installed AM radio. It was mounted below the instrument panel and had a plastic weatherproof case and was connected to a fixed-length whip-type antenna. For the first time a passenger-side sun visor and bucket seat were standard for the CJ Jeep. The CJ Renegade had a new broad two-color hood tape stripe as well as two new exterior colors, Renegade blue and orange. The Renegade Package included 304 V-8 engine, roll bar, forged aluminum styled wheels, H78 x 15 white sidewall Polyglas Suburbanite tires, padded instrument panel, color-keyed Levi's seat material, heavy-duty cooling system, solid back panel with rear-mounted spare tire, wheel-lip extensions, passenger safety rail, spare tire lock, ashtray and cigarette lighter and rear bench seat. With the exception of green apple and reef green, all 1975 Jeep colors were also available for the Renegade. Exclusive to the Renegade were two colors: Renegade blue and Renegade orange.

No changes were made in the CJ engine lineup but they were the only Jeep engines in 1975 to be fitted with catalytic converters. They were required to use unleaded gasoline. Warning labels to this effect were placed on the instrument panel and near the fuel filler. The CJ engines had new electronic ignition systems with a more reliable wiring harness with a dash connect plug permitting easier diagnosis and servicing. Also installed on the 1975 CJ's was an improved exhaust system with quieter mufflers. Six-cylinder engines had a modified intake manifold which enabled operation with a leaner air/fuel mixture. This resulted in improved fuel economy and better throttle response. Both the six-cylinder and V-8 engines had improved insulation which reduced heat input from the engine to the carburetor. A voltmeter and oil pressure gauge were standard for all 1975 CJ models in 1975.

New options included a Cold Climate Group consisting of an engine block heater, 70 amp battery and a 62 amp alternator; a column-mounted tachometer and HR78-15 whitewall radial tires.

Standard CJ equipment included 3-speed fully-synchromesh manual transmission with floor shift, full foam front bucket seats, oil gauge and voltmeter, F78 x 15 tires, electric windshield wipers and washers, 54 plate, 50 amp battery, folding windshield with tie-downs, seat belts, and rear tailgate. The standard interior was finished in a Wellington vinyl in either buff or black.

The exterior color selection for the CJ models consisted of alpine white, medium blue metallic, reef green metallic, green apple, pewter grey metallic, raven black, fawn beige, Trans-Am red, copper metallic and mellow yellow.

1975 Jeep CJ-5 Renegade

I.D. DATA: The serial number was positioned on the left front door hinge pillar post and left firewall. The serial number consisted of 13 entries. The first identified the Jeep Corporation. The second indicated the year of production. The third identified the transmission, drivetrain and assembly plant. The next two numbers identified the vehicle series or model. The sixth symbol (a letter) identified the code model and GVW. The next letter identified the engine. The final six numbers were the sequential production number. Model identification: CJ-5: 83; CJ-6: 84.

Model Number	Body Type	Factory Price	GVW	Shipping Weight	Prod. Total
Jeep					
CJ-5	Utility	$4099	3750	2648	—
CJ-6	Utility	$4195	3900	2714	—

STANDARD ENGINE: Engine Type: OHV, In-line-6. Cast iron block and cylinder head. Bore x Stroke: 3.75 in. x 3.50 in. Lifters: Hydraulic. Number of main bearings-7. Fuel Induction: 1-bbl. Carter Type RTBS or Holley model 1931C-3705. Compression Ratio: 8.0:1. Displacement: 232 cu. in. (3.8 liters). Horsepower: Net 100 @ 3600 rpm. Torque: Net 185 lb.-ft. @ 1800 rpm. Oil refill capacity: 5 qt. with filter change. Fuel Requirements: Regular, low-lead gasoline of 91 octane or higher.

OPTIONAL ENGINE: Engine Type: OHV, In-line-6. Cast iron block and cylinder head. Bore x Stroke: 3.75 in. x 3.90 in. Lifters: Hydraulic. Number of main bearings-7. Fuel Induction: 1-bbl. Carter Type RTBS or Holley model 1931C-3705. Compression Ratio: 8.0:1. Displacement: 258 cu. in. (4.2 liters). Horsepower: Net 110 @ 3500 rpm. Torque: Net 195 lb.-ft. @ 2000 rpm. Oil refill capacity: 5 qt. with filter change. Fuel Requirements: Regular, low-lead gasoline of 91 octane or higher.

OPTIONAL ENGINE: Engine Type: OHV, V-8. Cast iron block and cylinder head. Bore x Stroke: 3.75 in. x 3.44 in. Lifters: Hydraulic. Number of main bearings-5. Fuel Induction: 2-bbl. carburetor. Compression Ratio: 8.4:1. Displacement: 304 cu. in. (4.98 liters). Horsepower: Net: 150 @ 4200 rpm. Torque: Net: 245 lb.-ft. @ 2500 rpm. Oil refill capacity: 5 qt. with filter change. Fuel Requirements: Regular, low-lead gasoline of 91 octane or higher.

CHASSIS FEATURES: Separate body and ladder steel frame construction. Length: 131.38 in. Width: 29.25 in. six cross members. Section modulus: 1.493 in. cu.

SUSPENSION AND RUNNING GEAR: Front Suspension: CJ-5: 7-leaf semi-elliptical springs, 39.75 in. x by 1.75 in. Spring rate: 190 lb./in. Capacity: 855 lb. (at pad). 1015 lb. (at ground). Hydraulic direct double-action shock absorbers with 1.1875 in. piston diameter. CJ-6: 9-leaf semi-elliptical springs, 39.75 in. x 1.75 in. Spring rate: 210 lb./in. Capacity: 1040 lb. (at pad), 1200 lb. (at ground). Hydraulic direct double-action shock absorbers with 1.1875 in. piston diameter. Optional: 10-leaf semi-elliptical springs, 39.75 in. x 1.75 in. Spring rate: 270 lb./in. Capacity: 1300 lb. (at pad), 1460 lb. (at ground). Rear Suspension: 5-leaf semi-elliptical springs, 46 in. x 1.75 in. Spring rate: 230 lb./in. Capacity: 1240 lb. (at pad), 1405 lb. (at ground). Hydraulic direct double-action shock absorbers with 1.1875 in. piston diameter. Optional: 10-leaf semi-elliptical springs, 46 in. x 1.75 in. Spring rate: 270 lb./in. Capacity 1260 lb. (at pad), 1425 lb. (at ground). Front Axle Type and Capacity: Full-floating Dana 30 front axle, hypoid. Capacity: 2300 lb. Rear Axle Type and Capacity: Semi-floating Dana 44 Hypoid. Capacity: 3000 lb. Axle Ratios: 4.27:1. Optional: 3.73:1. Transfer Case: Dana model 20. Ratios: 2.03:1, 1.00:1. Brakes: Type: Hydraulic, front and rear. Dimensions: Front and rear: 11.00 in. x 2.0 in. Effective lining area: 180.8 sq. in. Wheels: Kelsey-Hayes 15 x 6L in., 5-bolt on 5.5 in. circle steel disc. Optional: 16 x 4.5E with 4500 lb. (CJ-5) or 4750 lb. GVW options. Tires: E78 x 15B Suburbanite Polyglas black sidewall. Optional: F-78 x 15B Power Cushion black sidewall, H-78 x 15B black sidewall, H-78 x 15 white sidewall, 7.35 x 15B Suburbanite XG black sidewall, H-78 x 15B black sidewall, H-78 x 15B white sidewall, 6.00 x 16C All-Service black sidewall, 6.00 x 16C Custom X-Grip black sidewall, H-78 x 15 Power Cushion Polyglas white sidewall, H-78 x 15B Suburbanite Polyglas black sidewall, H-78 x 15D Suburbanite Polyglas black sidewall. Steering: Recirculating ball system. Ratio: 24.1:1. Turning Circle: CJ-5: 32.75 ft. CJ-6: 37.5 ft. Optional: Saginaw power steering. Ratio: 17.5:1. Standard Transmission: All-synchromesh 3-speed Warner T-14A transmission. Transmission ratios: 3.1, 1.612, 1.00:1. Reverse: 3.1:1. Optional: Warner T-18 4-speed gearbox with a non-synchromesh first gear. Transmission ratios: 4.02, 2.41, 1.431, 1.00:1. Reverse: 4.73:1. Clutch: 10.5 in. Single dry plate. Total lining area: 106.75 sq. in. Total plate pressure: 1640 lb. Optional: None.

VEHICLE DIMENSIONS: CJ-5/CJ-6 Wheelbase: 84 in./104 in. Overall Length: 138.75 in./ 158.75 in. Front/Rear Tread: 51.5 in./50.0 in. Overall Height: 67.0 in. Width: 71.75 in. Front/ Rear Overhang: 22.6 in./32.0 in. Tailgate: Width and Height: 36 in. x 14.125 in. Approach/ Departure Degrees: 45/30. Ground Clearance: Front axle: 8.6 in. Rear axle: 8.0 in. Load space: CJ-5: 36 in. x 39.75 in. (with tailgate closed), 36 in. by 54.5 in. (tailgate closed). CJ-6: 36 in. x 59.75 in. (with tailgate closed), 36 in. x 74.5 in. Cargo area: CJ-5: 10.0 sq. ft., CJ-6: 15.0 sq. ft. Front legroom: 41 in. Front hip room: 55.40 in.

CAPACITIES: Fuel Tank: 16.5 gal. Cooling system: 10.5 qt.

ACCOMMODATIONS: Seating Capacity: 2/6.

INSTRUMENTATION: 0-90 mph speedometer, odometer, gauges for engine coolant temperature, fuel level, and oil pressure and battery warning lights

OPTIONS AND PRICES: AM radio: $69.00. Heavy-duty cooling system. Drawbar. Power steering. Semi-automatic front hubs. Heavy-duty frame. Heavy-duty 51 amp alternator: $26.75. Heavy-duty 70 amp battery: $18. Exterior passenger side mirror: $8. Trac-Lok 3.73:1 rear differential: $69.40. Rear spare tire mount: $9.60. 4-speed manual transmission. H78-15 Polyglas Suburban tires: $84.75. 258 cid engine: $53.85. 304 V-8: $126. Heavy-duty springs and shock absorbers: $39.65. Oil and ammeter gauges. Cigarette lighter and ashtray: $9.95. Dual sun visors. Front passenger seat. Rear bench seat with seat belts: $89.35. Rear bucket seats. Front passenger safety bar: $7.95. Padded instrument panel: $34.90. Roll bar. Full metal top: $399 (CJ-5). Full fabric top. Half-cab metal top. Half cab fabric top. Safari Top. Heavy-duty snowplow. Electric winches. Power take-off winches. Trailer hitch. Push plate. Power take-off.

HISTORICAL FOOTNOTES: Domestic wholesale sales of 69,300 Jeeps in 1975 was just below the 1974 record level of 69,800. Jeep sales in Canada increased 11 percent over those of 1974. In 1975, AMC and Jeep dealers had their third-best sales year in history. In April, 1975 the 400,000th Jeep vehicle built since American Motors' acquisition of Jeep in 1970 came off the assembly line.

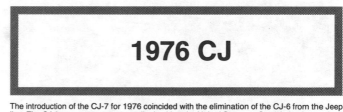

1976 CJ

The introduction of the CJ-7 for 1976 coincided with the elimination of the CJ-6 from the Jeep line. The CJ-6 was never a strong seller in either the United States or Canada but it remained available in 1976 for export. Compared to the CJ-6, the longer wheelbase of the CJ-7 provided more front and rear leg as well as wider, 33.8 inch, door openings. Both the CJ-5 and CJ-7 had new body hold-down mounts, a new frame of splayed side rail design which widened from front to rear, new shock absorbers and suspensions of 4-leaf front and rear springs. The new frame was also noteworthy for its greatly increased bending strength and significantly greater torsional rigidity, side rails with increased depth and full box-section construction from the front to the fuel tank cross member. Integral with the frame were stronger cross members and a combination cross member skid plate for the engine, transmission and transfer case extending the full length of the vehicle. The rear springs on all CJ's were wider spaced than in 1975. Exclusive for the CJ-7 was an optional one-piece injection-molded structural polycarbonate removal hardtop with metal lockable doors, vinyl door trim panels and roll-down windows. Color selections for this top were limited to black or white. CJ-7's with this hardtop had 5-leaf front and rear springs and higher gross weight ratings of 4,150 pounds instead of the standard CJ-7's 3,750 pound rating. The fuel tank skid plate was continued as standard CJ equipment. The CJ-7 was the first CJ available with both Turbo Hydra-Matic and the full-time Quadra-Trac four-wheel drive system. The CJ-7 had a standard tailgate which was flush-mounted with a double-wall, dual-latch construction. A rear-mounted swing-away spare-tire carrier was optional. The Whitco full soft top for both the CJ-5 and CJ-7 was of a new design with improved visibility and larger door openings. Available on all CJ's was a new extra-duty suspension consisting of 7-leaf, two-stage front and rear springs plus heavy-duty shock absorbers and a front frame tie bar. These components increased gross vehicle weight from 3,750 pounds to 4,150 pounds on both open or soft top models. For 1976 the standard CJ all-synchromesh 3-speed transmission was of a new design with heavier gears, shafts and synchronizers and a higher torque capacity.

The CJ 6-cylinder engines used an electric-assist choke and exhaust gas circulation system, and a new fuel return line.

1976 Jeep CJ-5 Renegade

The 1976 CJ Jeeps had new folding windshields with screw-type hold-downs and inside-mounted windshield wiper motor. They had larger taillights that were rectangular rather than circular, as 1975 had integral backup lights. They were mounted higher on the body.

A steering wheel with two instead of three spokes was installed on an energy absorbing steering column with an anti-theft ignition and steering lock. A redesigned dash panel enabled the optional radio and speaker to be located within the panel instead of the under the dash installation used in 1975. The optional tachometer and "Rallye" clock were positioned on each side of the steering column. The gauges for the engine temperature and ammeter were moved from their old locations just below the speedometer to its right side.

New floor and dash panels increased legroom on the CJ-5. Redesigned defroster outlets improved interior air circulation. In place of the old "fold-and-tumble" seat was a four-bar arrangement for the front passenger seat allowing the entire seat to move forward for easier entry to the rear of the vehicle.

Among the new options offered for the CJ-5 and CJ-7 was the Convenience Group Package consisting of courtesy lights, passenger side mirror, passenger assist handle, cigarette lighter, ashtray and eight in. day/night mirror. A new Decor Group contained rocker panel protection molding, instrument panel pad and overlay, and a Sport steering wheel. Additional new options included a full-foam 2/3-1/3 seat, indoor/outdoor carpeting, Sport or leather-wrapped steering wheel and a front stabilizer bar.

Both the CJ-5 and CJ-7 were available with the Renegade Package. When installed on a CJ-7 it included a rear swing-away spare tire carrier. A rear-mounted spare with a solid back panel was used for the CJ-5 Renegade. Added to the Renegade Package were the following items: under dash courtesy lights, eight in. day/night mirror, Sport steering wheel, instrument panel overlay and bright rocker panel protection molding between the front and rear wells. The Levi's seat trim in blue or tan with matching instrument panel and sun visors was again included in the Renegade Package. It remained available as a separate option on models without the Renegade Package. Two hood tape stripe combinations continued to be offered with the Renegade Package — blue with orange and white accents or gold with brown and white accents.

The standard CJ interior provided front bucket seats in a Wellington vinyl. The color selection was either black or buff. Standard equipment included side-mounted spare tire, electric 2-speed windshield wipers and washers, seat belts, rear tailgate, and dual padded sun visors.

The 1976 exterior color selection for the CJ models consisted of alpine white, classic black, dark cocoa metallic, sunshine yellow, sand tan, Renegade orange, firecracker red, pewter grey, reef green metallic (not available for Renegade), medium blue, brilliant blue and nautical blue.

1976 Jeep CJ-7

I.D. DATA: The serial number was positioned on the left front door hinge pillar post and left firewall. The serial number consisted of 13 entries. The first identified the Jeep Corporation. The second indicated the year of production. The third identified the transmission, drivetrain and assembly plant. The next two numbers identified the vehicle series or model. The sixth symbol (a letter) identified the code model and GVW. The next letter identified the engine. The final six numbers were the sequential production number. Model identification: CJ-5: 83; CJ-7: 93.

Model Number	Body Type	Factory Price	GVW	Shipping Weight	Prod. Total
Jeep					
CJ-5	Utility	$4199	3750	2641	—
CJ-7	Utility	$4299	3750	2683	—

STANDARD ENGINE: Engine Type: OHV, In-line-6. Cast iron block and cylinder head. Bore x Stroke: 3.75 in. x 3.50 in. Lifters: Hydraulic. Number of main bearings-7. Fuel Induction: 1-bbl. Carter Type RTBS or Holley model 1931C-3705. Compression Ratio: 8.0:1. Displacement: 232 cu. in. (3.8 liters). Horsepower: Net 100 @ 3600 rpm. Torque: Net 185 lb.-ft. @ 1800 rpm. Oil refill capacity: 5 qt. with filter change. Fuel Requirements: Regular, low-lead gasoline of 91 octane or higher.

OPTIONAL ENGINE: Engine Type: OHV, In-line-6. Cast iron block and cylinder head. Bore x Stroke: 3.75 in. x 3.90 in. Lifters: Hydraulic. Number of main bearings-7. Fuel Induction: 1-bbl. Carter Type RTBS or Holley model 1931C-3705. Compression Ratio: 8.0:1. Displacement: 258 cu. in. (4.2 liters). Horsepower: Net 110 @ 3500 rpm. Torque: Net 195 lb.-ft. @ 2000 rpm. Oil refill capacity: 5 qt. with filter change. Fuel Requirements: Regular, low-lead gasoline of 91 octane or higher.

OPTIONAL ENGINE: Engine Type: OHV, V-8. Cast iron block and cylinder head. Bore x Stroke: 3.75 in. x 3.44 in. Lifters: Hydraulic. Number of main bearings-5. Fuel Induction: 2-bbl. carburetor. Compression Ratio: 8.4:1. Displacement: 304 cu. in. (4.98 liters). Horsepower: Net 150 @ 4200 rpm. Torque: Net 245 lb.-ft. @ 2500 rpm. Oil refill capacity: 5 qt. with filter change. Fuel Requirements: Regular, low-lead gasoline of 91 octane or higher.

CHASSIS FEATURES: Separate body and partial box-section steel frame construction, six cross members.

SUSPENSION AND RUNNING GEAR: Front Suspension: 4-leaf semi-elliptical springs, Spring rate: 170 lb./in. Double-acting shock absorbers. Optional: 7-leaf semi-elliptical two-stage springs. Spring rate: 170/ 230 lb./in. Rear Suspension: 4-leaf semi-elliptical springs, Spring rate: 185 lb./in. Double-acting shock absorbers. Optional: 7-leaf two-stage semi-elliptical springs. Spring rate: 185/250 lb./in. Front Axle Type and Capacity: Full-floating, open end. Capacity: 2200 lb. Rear Axle Type and Capacity: Semi-floating. Capacity: 2700 lb. Axle Ratios: 3.54:1. Optional: 4.09:1. Transfer Case: Dana model 20. Ratios: 2.03:1, 1.00:1. Brakes: Type: Hydraulic, front and rear. Dimensions: Front and rear: 11.00 in. x 2.0 in. Effective lining area: 180.8 sq. in. Optional: Power brakes with 276 sq. in. swept area. Available with V-8 engine only. Wheels: 15 x 6 in. 5-bolt steel disc. Optional: 15 x 8 in. Tires: F78 x 15B. Optional: H78 x 15B White sidewall, steel belted radials. HR78 x 15B Cushion Power Polyglas (white sidewall), and Power Cushion 78 (black sidewall). HR78 x 15 white sidewall steel belted radial, Mud and Snow. HR78 x 15 2/4-ply Suburbanite Polyglas and Suburbanite XG Polyglas blackwall (white sidewall on Renegade). Steering: Recirculating ball system. Ratio: 24.1:1. Turning Circle: CJ-5: 33.416 ft. CJ-7: 35.75 ft. Optional: Saginaw power steering. Ratio: 17.5:1. Standard Transmission: All-synchromesh 3-speed Warner T-14A transmission. Transmission ratios: 3.00, 1.83. 1.00:1. Reverse: 1:1. Optional: Warner T-18 4-speed gearbox with a non-synchromesh first gear. Available with 258 engine only. Transmission ratios: 4.02, 2.41, 1.41, 1.00:1. Reverse: 4.73:1. Clutch: 6-cyl.: 10.5 in., V-8: 11.0 in. Single dry plate. Optional: Turbo Hydra-Matic 3-speed automatic transmission. Transmission ratios: 2.48, 1.415, 1.0:1.

VEHICLE DIMENSIONS: Wheelbase: CJ-5: 83.416 in. CJ-7: 93.416 in. Overall Length: CJ-5: 138.3 in. CJ-7: 147.75 in. Front/Rear Tread: 51.5 in./50.0 in. Overall Height: 67.5 in. Width: 68.5 in. (with side-mounted spare tire). Front/Rear Overhang: CJ-5: 23.416 in./31.3 in. CJ-7: 23.416 in./30.75 in. Tailgate: Width and Height: CJ-5: 35.8 in. x 14.125 in. CJ-7: 34.5 in. x 14.125 in. Approach/Departure Degrees: 45/30. Ground Clearance: 6.75 in. Load space: CJ-5: 36 in. x 39 in. (with tailgate closed), 36 in. by 49 in. (tailgate closed). Maximum capacity (Volume Index): CJ-5: 10.2 cu. ft., CJ-7: 13.6 cu. ft. Front headroom: CJ-5-Soft top/Hardtop: 39.66 in./40.66 in. CJ-7-Soft top/Hardtop 40.5 in./39.75 in. Front legroom: CJ-5: 37.75 in. CJ-7: 39.08 in. Front hip room: CJ-5: 55.33 in. CJ-7: 53.66 in. Floor to ground: CJ-5: 27.0 in. CJ-7: 26.1 in.

CAPACITIES: Fuel Tank: 15.5 gal. Coolant system: 10.2 qt.

ACCOMMODATIONS: Seating Capacity: 2/4.

INSTRUMENTATION: 0-90 mph speedometer, odometer, engine coolant temperature, fuel level gauge, gauges for oil pressure and voltmeter.

OPTIONS: Full and half cab metal top (CJ-5). Steel push bumper. Sport steering wheel. Leather-wrapped steering wheel. Rear step bumper. Forged aluminum styled wheels. Rear seat. Automatic transmission and Quadra-Trac (CJ-7). Passenger grab rail. Swing-out spare tires carrier. Dash-mounted tachometer and Rallye clock. Padded instrument panel. Citizen's Band radio. Removable top (CJ-7). Outside passenger mirror. Roll bar. Full soft top. Locking front hubs. 304 V-8. 258 6-cyl. engine. Mechanical winch. Electric winch. Steel belted radial tires. Carpeting. 4-speed manual transmission (available with 258 engine only). Extra-duty suspension. Front stabilizer bar. Power drum brakes. Low range for Quadra-Trac (CJ-7 only). Convenience Group. Decor Group. Heavy-duty cooling system. Rear Trac-Lok differential. Cold Climate Group. Includes engine block heater, 70 amp battery and heavy-duty alternator.

HISTORICAL FOOTNOTES: The CJ models were introduced in the fall of 1975.

1977 CJ

For the first time the CJ Jeeps were available with air conditioning and front disc brakes with or without power assistance. The designing of air conditioning into the CJ body plus the inclusion of air ducts in the CJ dash resulted in the relocation of the ashtray to the upper dash section. Technical revisions included stronger front axle and wheel spindles and a full boxed frame. New wider wheels and tires were optional. The rear body panels were also strengthened for 1977. The fuel tank was now enclosed in a protective material. The CJ's optional 4-speed (for the 258 cu. in. six only) had a new internal gearset which changed its low gear ratio from 4.02:1 to 6.32:1.

1977 Jeep CJ-7

Production began in January, 1977 of the new Golden Eagle Package for CJ. The Golden Eagle option was priced less than $200 more than a comparably equipped Jeep Renegade and was available for soft top CJ-5 and CJ-7 models. All regular production options were available for the Golden Eagle CJ. The Golden Eagle Package consisted of the following items: A single unique exterior color — Thrush brown, gold, black and white eagle decal on hood, Golden Eagle name on hood side in black lettering edged in gold, "Limited Edition" decal on grille panel, gold stripe on grille panel and 15 x 8 styled wheels, painted gold with a black accent stripe. Regular options included in the Golden Eagle Package consisted of 9-15 Tracker RWL tires, rear mounted spare tire, Levi's tan mounted vinyl soft top, Levi's tan interior, roll bar, Levi's tan instrument panel pad, wheel-lip extensions, spare tire lock, Convenience Group, Decor Group, black anodized rocker molding, tachometer and clock, and full, brown colored carpeting. By late April 2000 had been built and a second batch of 2000 were nearly completed. Of the plant's 560 vehicle daily output, 300 were CJ Jeeps. Added to the Renegade Package in1977 were 9.00 x 15 raised white letter Tracker All-Terrain tires mounted on white-painted, styled steel spoke wheels highlighted by narrow red striping.

The 1977 exterior color selection for the CJ models consisted of five new colors: Autumn red metallic, loden green metallic, midnight blue metallic, mocha brown metallic and tawny orange. Other colors included: Alpine white, classic black, firecracker red, pewter grey metallic, sunshine yellow, sand tan, and brilliant blue.

I.D. DATA: The serial number was positioned on the left front door hinge pillar post and left firewall. The serial number consisted of 13 entries. The first identified the Jeep Corporation. The second indicated the year of production. The third identified the transmission, drivetrain and assembly plant The next two numbers identified the vehicle series or model. The sixth symbol (a letter) identified the code model and GVW. The next letter identified the engine. The final six numbers were the sequential production number. Model identification: CJ-5: 83; CJ-7: 93.

Model Type	Body Type	Factory Price	GVW	Shipping Weight	Prod. Total
Jeep					
CJ-5	Utility	$4399	3750	2659	—
CJ-7	Utility	$4499	3750*	2701	—

* A 4150 lb. GVW was standard with CJ-5 and CJ-7 models with hardtop. It was optional for the open body or soft top models.

STANDARD ENGINE: Engine Type: OHV, In-line-6. Cast iron block and cylinder head. (California models have the 258 engine as standard equipment). Bore x Stroke: 3.75 in. x 3.50 in. Lifters: Hydraulic. Number of main bearings-7. Fuel Induction: 1-bbl. Carter Type RTBS or Holley model 1931C-3705. Compression Ratio: 8.0:1. Displacement: 232 cu. in. (3.8 liters). Horsepower: Net 100 @ 3600 rpm. Torque: Net 185 lb.-ft. @ 1800 rpm. Oil refill capacity: 5 qt. with filter change. Fuel Requirements: Regular, low-lead gasoline of 91 octane or higher.

OPTIONAL ENGINE: Engine Type: OHV, In-line-6. Cast iron block and cylinder head. Bore x Stroke: 3.75 in. x 3.90 in. Lifters: Hydraulic. Number of main bearings-7. Fuel Induction: 1-bbl. Carter Type RTBS or Holley model 1931C-3705. Compression Ratio: 8.0:1. Displacement: 258 cu. in. (4.2 liters). Horsepower: Net 110 @ 3500 rpm. Torque: Net 195 lb.-ft. @ 2000 rpm. Oil refill capacity: 5 qt. with filter change. Fuel Requirements: Regular, low-lead gasoline of 91 octane or higher.

OPTIONAL ENGINE: Engine Type: OHV, V-8. Cast iron block and cylinder head. Bore x Stroke: 3.75 in. x 3.44 in. Lifters: Hydraulic. Number of main bearings-5. Fuel Induction: 2-bbl. carburetor. Compression Ratio: 8.4:1. Displacement: 304 cu. in. (4.98 liters). Horsepower: Net: 150 @ 4200 rpm. Torque: Net: 245 lb.-ft. @ 2500 rpm. Oil refill capacity: 5 qt. with filter change. Fuel Requirements: Regular, low-lead gasoline of 91 octane or higher.

CHASSIS FEATURES: Separate body and partial box-section steel frame construction, six cross members.

SUSPENSION AND RUNNING GEAR: Front Suspension: 4-leaf semi-elliptical springs, Spring rate: 170 lb./in. Double-acting shock absorbers. Optional: 7-leaf semi-elliptical two-stage springs. Spring rate: 170/ 230 lb./in. Rear Suspension: 4-leaf semi-elliptical springs, Spring rate: 185 lb./in. Double-acting shock absorbers. Optional: 7-leaf two-stage semi-elliptical springs. Spring rate: 185/250 lb./in. Front Axle Type and Capacity: Full-floating, open end. Capacity: 2200 lb. Rear Axle Type and Capacity: Semi-floating. Capacity: 2700 lb. Axle Ratios: 3.54:1. Optional: 4.09:1. Transfer Case: Dana model 20. Ratios: 2.03:1, 1.00:1. Brakes: Type: Hydraulic, front and rear. Dimensions: Front and rear: 11.00 in. x 2.0 in. Effective lining area: 180.8 sq. in. a:. Optional: Front 12.0 in. disc brakes (the front disc/rear drum system was available with or without power assist). Wheels: 15 x 6 in. 5-bolt steel disc. Optional: 15 x 8 in. Tires: F78 x 15B. Optional: H78 x 15B, HR78 x 15B, 9.00 x 15B. Steering: Recirculating ball system. Ratio: 24.1:1. Turning Circle: CJ-5: 34.1 ft. CJ-7: 38.0 ft. Optional: Saginaw power steering. Ratio: 17.5:1. Standard Transmission: All-synchromesh 3-speed Warner T-14A transmission. Transmission ratios: 3.00, 1.83. 1.00:1. Reverse: 1.0. Optional: Warner T-18 4-speed gearbox with a non-synchromesh first gear. Available with 258 engine only. Transmission ratios: 6.32, 3.00, 1.69, 1.00:1. Clutch: 6-cyl.: 10.5 in., V-8: 11.0 in. Single dry plate. Total lining area: 6-cyl.: 106.75 sq. in. Optional: Turbo Hydra-Matic 3-speed automatic transmission. Transmission ratios: 2.48, 1.415, 1.0:1.

VEHICLE DIMENSIONS: Wheelbase: CJ-5: 83.5 in. CJ-7: 93.5 in. Overall Length: CJ-5: 138.4 in. CJ-7: 147.9 in. Front/Rear Tread: With standard wheels: 51.5 in./50.0 in. With styled wheels: 53.8 in./52.3 in. Overall Height: 67.6 in. Width: 68.6 in. (with side-mounted spare tire). Front/Rear Overhang: CJ-5: 23.5 in./31.4 in. CJ-7: 23.5 in./30.9 in. Tailgate: Width and Height: CJ-5: 35.8 in. x 14.125 in. CJ-7: 34.5 in. x 14.125 in. Approach/Departure Degrees: CJ-5: 45/30. Ground Clearance: 6.9 in. Load space: CJ-5: 36 in. x 39 in. (with tailgate closed), 36 in. by 49 in. (tailgate closed). Maximum capacity: CJ-5: 10.2 cu. ft. CJ-7: 13.6 cu. ft. Front headroom: CJ-5 Soft top/Hardtop: 39.66 in./40.8 in. CJ-7 Soft top/Hardtop: 40.5 in./39.9 in. Front legroom: CJ-5: 37.9 in. CJ-7: 39.1 in. Front shoulder room: CJ-5: 55.4 in. CJ-7: 53.8 in. Rear shoulder room: CJ-5: 55.4 in. CJ-7: 56.3 in. Front hip room: CJ-5: 55.33 in. CJ-7: 53.66 in. Floor to ground: CJ-5: 27.0 in. CJ-7: 26.1 in.

CAPACITIES: Fuel Tank: 15.5 gal. Coolant system: 10.2 qt.

ACCOMMODATIONS: Seating Capacity: 2/4.

INSTRUMENTATION: 0-90 mph speedometer, odometer, engine coolant temperature, fuel level gauge, gauges for oil pressure and voltmeter.

OPTIONS AND PRICES: Air conditioning: $499. Power assisted disc brakes: $73. 304 V-8 engine: $140. 258 6-cyl. engine: $73. Free-wheeling front hubs: $95. Power steering: $166. Center console: $62. AM radio: $73. Tachometer and Rallye clock: $73. Roll bar: $66. Body side step: $19. Bumperettes: $22. Wheelcovers: $327. Vinyl bucket seats with Levi's trim: $69. Vinyl bench seat: $33. Rear seat: $100. Indoor/outdoor carpeting: $63. Whitco top: $275. Front stabilizer bar: $27. Steering damper: $10. 4-spd. manual trans.: $144. Turbo-Hydra-Matic with Quadra-Trac: $345. Turbo-Hydramatic with Quadra-Trac low range: $482. Extra Duty Suspension Package: $63. Convenience Package: $41. Decor group: $99. High Altitude Package: $50. Soft top (black or white): $239. Soft top in Levi's blue. Requires Levi's interior: $275. CJ-7 hardtop: $525. Heavy-duty cooling system: $34. Heavy-duty battery: $31. Heavy-duty alternator: $40. Swing away spare tie carrier: $52. Renegade Package: $839.

HISTORICAL FOOTNOTES: American Motors observed its 75th anniversary in 1977. Jeep sales reached a record 95,718 units in 1977, up from 67,771 in 1975. Twenty-five percent of CJ-5 and CJ-7 Jeeps built in 1977 had the Renegade Package. Of the total U.S. four-wheel drive market, Jeep controlled 16 percent.

1977 Jeep CJ-5

1978 CJ

All CJ models for 1978 had a redesigned heater with improved heat distribution, especially to the rear seat region; higher defroster temperature and air-flow rate and improved outside fresh-air ventilation. A number of features moved from the optional equipment to the standard equipment list. They included: Manual front disc brakes, ashtray and cigarette lighter, passenger-side exterior mirror and H78 Suburbanite XG fiberglass-belted tires. The Convenience Group now contained an underhood light and the seat and door panels were now flax, rather than buff-colored.

The CJ engines were equipped with a new ambient air intake system which improved overall engine efficiency.

1978 Jeep CJ-5

Available for all Jeep vehicles were 14 body colors including three new colors: Sun orange, golden ginger metallic, and captain blue metallic. Other colors included alpine white, loden green metallic, mocha brown metallic, autumn red metallic, oakleaf brown, brilliant blue, classic black, firecracker red, pewter grey metallic, sand tan and sunshine yellow.

The Golden Eagle Package was again offered for the CJ in 1978. It was priced at $1,249 and was highlighted by a large white, gold and black eagle decal on the hood. On each side of the hood was larger "Golden Eagle" black lettering outlined in gold. The Golden Eagle Package also included special grille and body striping, black fender flares, gold anodized 15 x 8 steel spoke wheels and 9.00-15 LT Goodyear Tracker tires with raised white lettering. In addition to these features the Golden Eagle option included most of the items of the Renegade Package.

The following body colors were available for Golden Eagle equipped CJ's: Loden green metallic, mocha brown metallic, oakleaf brown, alpine white, sand tan, classic black and golden ginger metallic.

1978 Jeep CJ-7 Golden Eagle

I.D. DATA: The serial number was positioned on the left front door hinge pillar post and left firewall. The serial number consisted of 13 entries. The first identified the Jeep Corporation. The second indicated the year of production. The third identified the transmission, drivetrain and assembly plant. The next two numbers identified the vehicle series or model. The sixth symbol (a letter) identified the code model and GVW. The next letter identified the engine. The final six numbers were the sequential production number. Model identification: CJ-5: 83; CJ-7: 93.

Model Number	Body Type	Factory Price	GVW	Shipping Weight	Prod. Total
Jeep					
CJ-5	Utility	$5095	3750	2738	—
CJ-7	Utility	$5195	3750*	2782	—

* A 4150 lb. GVW was standard with CJ-5 and CJ-7 models with hardtop. It was optional for the open body or soft top models.

STANDARD ENGINE: Engine Type: OHV, In-line-6. Cast iron block and cylinder head. (California models have the 258 engine as standard equipment). Bore x Stroke: 3.75 in. x 3.50 in. Lifters: Hydraulic. Number of main bearings-7. Fuel Induction: 1-bbl. Carter Type RTBS or Holley model 1931C-3705. Compression Ratio: 8.0:1. Displacement: 232 cu. in. (3.8 liters). Horsepower: Net 100 @ 3600 rpm. Torque: Net 185 lb.-ft. @ 1800 rpm. Oil refill capacity: 5 qt. with filter change. Fuel Requirements: Regular, low-lead gasoline of 91 octane or higher.

OPTIONAL ENGINE: Engine Type: OHV, In-line-6. Cast iron block and cylinder head. Bore x Stroke: 3.75 in. x 3.90 in. Lifters: Hydraulic. Number of main bearings-7. Fuel Induction: 1-bbl. Carter Type RTBS or Holley model 1931C-3705. Compression Ratio: 8.0:1. Displacement: 258 cu. in. (4.2 liters). Horsepower: Net 110 @ 3500 rpm. Torque: Net 195 lb.-ft. @ 2000 rpm. Oil refill capacity: 5 qt. with filter change. Fuel Requirements: Regular, low-lead gasoline of 91 octane or higher.

OPTIONAL ENGINE: Engine Type: OHV, V-8. Cast iron block and cylinder head. Bore x Stroke: 3.75 in. x 3.44 in. Lifters: Hydraulic. Number of main bearings-5. Fuel Induction: 2-bbl. carburetor. Compression Ratio: 8.4:1. Displacement: 304 cu. in. (4.98 liters). Horsepower: Net: 150 @ 4200 rpm. Torque: Net: 245 lb.-ft. @ 2500 rpm. Oil refill capacity: 5 qt. with filter change. Fuel Requirements: Regular, low-lead gasoline of 91 octane or higher.

CHASSIS FEATURES: Separate body and partial box-section steel frame construction, six cross members.

SUSPENSION AND RUNNING GEAR: Front Suspension: 4-leaf semi-elliptical springs, Spring rate: 170 lb./in. Double-acting shock absorbers. Optional: 7-leaf semi-elliptical two-stage springs. Spring rate: 170/ 230 lb./in. Rear Suspension: 4-leaf semi-elliptical springs, Spring rate: 185 lb./in. Double-acting shock absorbers. Optional: 7-leaf two-stage semi-elliptical springs. Spring rate: 185/250 lb./in. Front Axle Type and Capacity: Full-floating, open end. Capacity: 2200 lb. Rear Axle Type and Capacity: Semi-floating. Capacity: 2700 lb. Axle Ratios: 3.54:1. Optional: 4.09:1. Transfer Case: Dana model 20. Ratios: 2.03:1, 1.00:1. Brakes: Type: Hydraulic, front and rear. Dimensions: Front and rear: 11.00 in. x 2.0 in. Effective lining area: 180.8 sq. in. a.: Optional: Front 12.0 in. disc brakes (the front disc/rear drum system was available with or without power assist). Wheels: 15 x 6 in. 5-bolt steel disc. Optional: 15 x 8 in. Tires: F78 x 15B. Optional: H78 x 15B, HR78 x 15B, 9.00 x 15B. Steering: Recirculating ball system. Ratio: 24.1:1. Turning Circle: CJ-5: 34.1 ft. CJ-7: 38.0 ft. Optional: Saginaw power steering. Ratio: 17.5:1. Standard Transmission: All-synchromesh 3-speed Warner T-14A transmission. Transmission ratios: 3.00, 1.83. 1.00:1. Reverse: 1. Optional: Warner T-18 4-speed gearbox with a non-synchromesh first gear. Available with 258 engine only. Transmission ratios: 6.32, 3.00, 1.69, 1.00:1. Clutch: 6-cyl.: 10.5 in., V-8: 11.0 in. Single dry plate. Total lining area: 6-cyl.: 106.75 sq. in. Optional: Turbo Hydra-Matic 3-speed automatic transmission. Transmission ratios: 2.48, 1.415, 1.0:1.

VEHICLE DIMENSIONS: Wheelbase: CJ-5: 83.5 in. CJ-7: 93.5 in. Overall Length: CJ-5: 138.4 in. CJ-7: 147.9 in. Front/Rear Tread: With standard wheels: 51.5 in./50.0 in. With styled wheels: 53.8 in./52.3 in. Overall Height: 67.6 in. Width: 68.6 in. (with side-mounted spare tire). Front/Rear Overhang: CJ-5: 23.5 in./31.4 in. CJ-7: 23.5 in./30.9 in. Tailgate: Width and Height: CJ-5: 35.8 in. x 14.125 in. CJ-7: 34.5 in. x 14.125 in. Approach/Departure Degrees: CJ-5: 45/30. Ground Clearance: 6.9 in. Load space: CJ-5: 36 in. x 39 in. (with tailgate closed), 36 in. by 49 in. (tailgate closed). Maximum capacity: CJ-5: 10.2 cu. ft., CJ-7: 13.6 cu. ft. Heater headroom: CJ-5-Soft top/Hardtop: 39.66 in./40.8 in. CJ-7-Soft top/Hardtop: 40.5 in./39.9 in. Front legroom: CJ-5: 37.9 in. CJ-7: 39.1 in. Front shoulder room: CJ-5: 55.4 in. CJ-7: 53.8 in. Rear shoulder room: CJ-5: 55.4 in. CJ-7: 56.3 in. Front hip room: CJ-5: 55.33 in. CJ-7: 53.66 in. Floor to ground: CJ-5: 27.0 in. CJ-7: 26.1 in.

CAPACITIES: Fuel Tank: 15.5 gal. Coolant system: 10.2 qt.

ACCOMMODATIONS: Seating Capacity: 2/4.

INSTRUMENTATION: 0-90 mph speedometer, odometer, engine coolant temperature, fuel level gauge, gauges for oil pressure and voltmeter.

OPTIONS AND PRICES: During the year AMC raised the price of all Jeeps by $100 as well as the prices of selected options by an average of $29 per vehicle. Therefore, the following prices may vary slightly from those actually paid by customers during 1978: Golden Eagle

Package: $1,248. Renegade Package: $799. Hardtop: $610. Tachometer and clock: $77. Rear bench seat: $106. 258 cu. in. engine (std. in CA): $77. 304 cu. in. V-8 engine: $186. Four-Speed manual trans. (258 engine): $153. Three-speed Turbo Hydra-Matic with Quadra-Trac: $366. Low range for Quadra-Trac: $145. Free-wheeling front hubs: $101. Limited slip differential (N.A. with Quadra-Trac): $82. Power steering: $176. Power brakes: $73. Extra-duty suspension: $85. Front stabilizer bar: $29.

HISTORICAL FOOTNOTES: In early March, 1978, AMC announced plans to convert its Brampton, Ontario plant over to the production of CJ Jeeps. This operation, which cost $4.8 million, was completed by September, 1978. It added another 50,000 units to AMC's CJ production capacity. Production of Jeep vehicles at Toledo was increased through overtime work beginning in July. Plans were also made to expand capacity at Toledo. On June 27, 1978, the 150,000th Jeep assembled in the 1978 model year, a CJ-7 Renegade, was driven off the assembly line by Ohio governor James A. Rhodes. For the calendar year production totalled 153,000 units while sales increased to 161,912. At the end of 1978 there were 1999 Jeep dealers in the U.S. and Canada along with 1517 dealers selling both passenger cars and Jeeps.

1979 CJ

In order to conform with more stringent federal emissions standards all 1979 CJ Jeeps, had catalytic converters, and used no-lead fuel. The use of several lighter body and chassis components reduced overall weight by approximately eighty pounds.

1979 Jeep CJ-7 Golden Eagle

The standard engine for the CJ now was the 258 cu. in. 6-cylinder fitted with a 2-barrel carburetor. The optional 4-speed manual transmission had an upgraded shift tower and new shift pattern. No change was made in the standard CJ axle ratio which remained at 3.54:1. This did not mean that overall performance was unaltered from 1978 levels since both CJ engines were less powerful then the year-earlier versions. The 304 cu. in. V-8, for example, was rated at 130 horsepower, down 20 horsepower in just one year.

Both the Renegade and Golden Eagle Packages were revised for 1979. The Renegade Package incorporated a new exterior strip design with varying widths in three graduated shades of either blue or orange with gold borders. New painted spoke steel wheels and L78-15 white letter tires were also available. Exclusive to the Golden Eagle was an optional tan injection-molded hardtop with bronze-tone tinted glass in the rear quarter and tailgate windows. A sunroof was also available for the hardtop. All CJ's had a new vinyl convertible top with cotton-polyester fabric backing that was available in blue, black, white or tan.

A limited edition Silver Anniversary CJ-5 recognizing the 25th birthday of the CJ-5 was available for 1979. Its features included a quick silver metallic finish, silver-toned Renegade accent striping, black soft top, black bucket seats with silver accents and a commemorative dash plaque.

Standard equipment content for the CV-5 and CV-7 consisted of these items: Front ashtray, cigarette lighter, gauges for oil pressure, voltmeter and engine coolant temperature, heater and defroster, 8.0 in. inside rearview mirror, padded sun visors, passenger safety rail, front bucket seats with safety belts, energy-absorbing steering column with anti-theft ignition, front painted bumpers, outside left and right-side mirrors, movable tailgate (CJ-7), solid back panel (CJ-5), 37 amp alternator, 45 amp battery, single horn, rear spare tire mount (CJ-5), inside spare tire mount (CJ-7), and electric 2-speed windshield wipers and washers.

Fourteen body colors were available for the 1979 CJ models: Olympic white, classic black, alpaca brown metallic, Cumberland green metallic, wedgewood Blue (not avail. for Golden Eagle), mandarin orange (not avail. for Golden Eagle), russet metallic, arrowhead silver metallic (not avail. for Golden Eagle), Morocco buff, sable brown metallic, Saxon yellow (not avail. for Golden Eagle), ensign blue (not avail. for Golden Eagle), firecracker red (not avail. for Golden Eagle), bordeaux metallic.

1979 Jeep CJ-7 Renegade

I.D. DATA: The serial number was positioned on the left front door hinge pillar post and left firewall. The serial number consisted of 13 entries. The first identified the Jeep Corporation. The second indicated the year of production. The third identified the transmission, drivetrain and assembly plant. The next two numbers identified the vehicle series or model. The sixth symbol (a letter) identified the code model and GVW. The next letter identified the engine. The final six numbers were the sequential production number. Model identification: CJ-5: 83; CJ-7: 93.

Model Number	Body Type	Factory Price	GVW	Shipping Weight	Prod. Total
Jeep					
CJ-5	Utility	$5588	3750	2623	74,878[2]
CJ-7	Utility	$5732	3750[1]	2666	—

NOTE 1: A 4150 lb. GVW was standard with CJ-5 and CJ-7 models with hardtop. It was optional for the open body or soft top models.
NOTE 2: 1979 calendar year sales.

STANDARD ENGINE: Engine Type: OHV, In-line-6. Cast iron block and cylinder head. Bore x Stroke: 3.75 in. x 3.90 in. Lifters: Hydraulic. Number of main bearings-7. Fuel Induction: 1-bbl. Carter model YF. Compression Ratio: 8.3:1. (some factory data specifies an 8.0:1 compression ratio). Displacement: 258 cu. in. (4.2 liters). Horsepower: Net 110 @ 3500 rpm. Torque: Net 195 lb.-ft. @ 2000 rpm. Oil refill capacity: 5 qt. with filter change. Fuel Requirements: Unleaded. Optional Engine. Type: OHV, V-8. Cast iron block and cylinder head. Bore x Stroke: 3.75 in. x 3.44 in. Lifters: Hydraulic. Number of main bearings-5. Fuel Induction: 2-bbl. carburetor. Compression Ratio: 8.4:1. Displacement: 304 cu. in. (4.98 liters). Horsepower: Net: 130 @ 4200 rpm. Torque: Net 245 lb.-ft. @ 2500 rpm. Oil refill capacity: 5 qt. with filter change. Fuel Requirements: Unleaded.

CHASSIS FEATURES: Separate body and partial box-section steel frame construction, six cross members.

SUSPENSION AND RUNNING GEAR: Front Suspension: 4-leaf semi-elliptical springs, Spring rate: 170 lb./in. Double-acting shock absorbers. Optional: 7-leaf semi-elliptical two-stage springs. Spring rate: 170/ 230 lb./in. Rear Suspension: 4-leaf semi-elliptical springs, Spring rate: 185 lb./in. Double-acting shock absorbers. Optional: 7-leaf two-stage semi-elliptical springs. Spring rate: 185/250 lb./in. Front Axle Type and Capacity: Full-floating, open end. Capacity: 2200 lb. Rear Axle Type and Capacity: Semi-floating. Capacity: 2700 lb. Axle Ratios: 3.54:1. Optional: 4.09:1. Transfer Case: Dana model 20. Ratios: 2.03:1, 1.00:1. Brakes: Type: Hydraulic, front and rear. Dimensions: Front and rear: 11.00 in. x 2.0 in. Effective lining area: 180.8 sq. in. Optional: Front 12.0 in. disc brakes (the front disc/rear drum system was available with or without power assist). Wheels: 15 x 6 in. 5-bolt steel disc. Optional: 15 x 8 in. Tires: F78 x 15B. Optional: H78 x 15B, HR78 x 15B, 9.00 x 15B. Steering: Recirculating ball system. Ratio: 24.1:1. Turning Circle: CJ-5: 34.1 ft. CJ-7: 38.0 ft. Optional: Saginaw power steering. Ratio: 17.5:1. Standard Transmission: All-synchromesh 3-speed Warner T-14A transmission. Transmission ratios: 3.00, 1.83, 1.00:1. Reverse: 1. Optional: Warner T-18 4-speed gearbox with a non-synchromesh first gear. Available with 258 engine only. Transmission ratios: 6.32, 3.00, 1.69, 1.00:1. Clutch: 6-cyl.: 10.5 in., V-8: 11.0 in. Single dry plate. Total lining area: 6-cyl.: 106.75 sq. in. Optional: Turbo Hydra-Matic 3-speed automatic transmission. Transmission ratios: 2.48, 1.415, 1.0:1.

VEHICLE DIMENSIONS: Wheelbase: CJ-5: 83.5 in. CJ-7: 93.5 in. Overall Length: CJ-5: 138.4 in. CJ-7: 147.9 in. Front/Rear Tread: With standard wheels: 51.5 in./50.0 in. With styled wheels: 53.8 in./52.3 in. Overall Height: 67.6 in. Width: 68.6 in. (with side-mounted spare tire). Front/Rear Overhang: CJ-5: 23.5 in./31.4 in. CJ-7: 23.5 in./30.9 in. Tailgate: Width and Height: CJ-5: 35.8 in. x 14.125 in. CJ-7: 34.5 in. x 14.125 in. Approach/Departure Degrees: CJ-5: 45/30. Ground Clearance: 6.9 in. Load space: CJ-5: 36 in. x 39 in. (with tailgate closed), 36 in. by 49 in. (tailgate closed). Maximum capacity: CJ-5: 10.2 cu. ft., CJ-7: 13.6 cu. ft. Front headroom: CJ-5-Soft top/Hardtop: 39.66 in./40.8 in. CJ-7-Soft top/Hardtop: 40.5 in./39.9 in. Front legroom: CJ-5: 37.9 in. CJ-7: 39.1 in. Front shoulder room: CJ-5: 55.4 in. CJ-7: 53.8 in. Rear shoulder room: CJ-5: 55.4 in. CJ-7: 56.3 in. Front hip room: CJ-5: 55.33 in. CJ-7: 53.66 in. Floor to ground: CJ-5: 27.0 in. CJ-7: 26.1 in.

CAPACITIES: Fuel Tank: 15.5 gal. Coolant system: 10.2 qt.

ACCOMMODATIONS: Seating Capacity: 2/4.

INSTRUMENTATION: 0-90 mph speedometer, odometer, engine coolant temperature, fuel level gauge, gauges for oil pressure and voltmeter.

OPTIONS AND PRICES: Renegade Package: $849. Convenience Group. Decor Group. Golden Eagle Package: $1210 with black or white top; $1246 with tan top with bronze windows.15 in. wheelcovers. Black Soft-Feel steering wheel. Padded instrument panel. Air conditioning. Tilt steering wheel. Tachometer and Rallye clock. Power steering: $188. Power front disc brakes: $70. AM push-button radio: $91. Body side step. Moonroof (with hardtop only). Side-mounted spare and tailgate (CJ-5). Swing-away spare tire carrier (CJ-7). 304 V-8. Four-speed manual trans.: $161. Turbo-Hydramatic with Quadra-Trac (CJ-7). Rear Trac-Lok differential. Free-wheeling front hubs: $107. Heavy-duty cooling system: $41. Extra-duty Suspension Package. Drawbar: $37. Steering damper: $12. Front stabilizer bar: $31. Heavy-duty 70 amp battery. Heavy-duty 63 amp alternator. Heavy-duty Cold Climate Group. Injection molded hardtop with doors (CJ-7): $656. Full metal cab (CJ-5). Vinyl soft top: $307. Removable carpet: $77. Spare tire lock. Rear bumperettes. Roll bar: $31. Snowplow Package. 9 x 15 Tracker tires: $50.

HISTORICAL FOOTNOTES: Jeep sales for AMC's 1979 fiscal year were a record 207,642 units compared to 180,667 the previous year.

1980 CJ

For 1980 the CJ Jeep's standard powerplant was a 4-cylinder "Hurricane" engine; in reality, the Pontiac "Iron Duke" engine. Its assembled weight was 319 pounds. On all CJ's except those intended for sale in California, the engine was fitted with a PULSAIR Injection Reaction system instead of an air pump which remained part of the Fuel Feedback (FFB) system found on California CJ's. The PULSAIR arrangement used the pulses of the engine's exhaust to draw air into the exhaust ports. CJ's for California had a 3-way catalytic converter; all others had a 2-way unit.

Standard on all CJ models were manually operated free-wheeling front hubs and a new manual all-synchromesh 4-speed SR-4 Borg-Warner transmission with aluminum case, top cover and adapter housing. For CJ's with either the 258 cu. in. 6-cylinder engine or the 304 cu. in. V-8 another new 4-speed, all-synchromesh transmission, a Tremac model T-176.

The top level CJ Trim Package was the new Laredo Package. Offered for both the CJ-5 and CJ-7 in either soft or hardtop form, it contained 15-8 styled steel chrome plated wheels with a center hub cover, new Goodyear Wrangler 9R on-or off-road radial tires, chrome front and rear bumperettes, swing-away spare tire carrier with chrome latch and stop, chrome mirror heads and arms, black rocker moldings, hood insulation, body striping in either silver or blue tones, indoor/outdoor carpeting, leather-wrapped steering wheel and passenger assist bar, chrome grille panel with pin-striped instrument panel, covered console with special trim pad, special door trim panels and a Laredo nameplate on the instrument panel.

1980 Jeep CJ-5 Renegade

CJ-7's with the Laredo option had hardtops with tinted glass in the side quarter windows. Offered for the first time on a Jeep, and standard on the Laredo, were high-back bucket seats available in black and silver or beige and brown. They were joined by matching rear seats on the Laredo. The bucket seats were also included in the Renegade and Golden Eagle Packages.

The Renegade Package was altered for 1980 to include a Soft-Feel Sport steering wheel. The color scheme for its body striping color was now either orange with gold or blue with gold.

Replacing the optional Turbo Hydra-Matic transmission of 1979 was Chrysler's TorqueFlite automatic. CJ-7's with automatic transmission were available only with part-time 4-wheel drive.

With the exception of classic black, all Jeep exterior colors were new for 1980. The 13 new colors were olympic white, cameo tan, medium teal blue, dark green metallic, dark brown metallic, bordeaux metallic, and Saxon yellow. Not offered for the Laredo and Golden Eagle were medium teal blue, smoke grey metallic and cardinal red. Available for the Golden Eagle but not the Laredo were dark green metallic, russet metallic and caramel. Not available for the Golden Eagle was navy blue.

For the first time the CJ-7 soft top was available with steel doors and roll-up windows. Standard on all CJ-7's was a swing-away spare tire mount.

I.D. DATA: The serial number was positioned on the left front door hinge pillar post and left firewall. The serial number consisted of 13 entries. The first identified the Jeep Corporation. The second indicated the year of production. The third identified the transmission, drivetrain and assembly plant. The next two numbers identified the vehicle series or model. The sixth symbol (a letter) identified the code model and GVW. The next letter identified the engine. The final six numbers were the sequential production number. Model identification: CJ-5: 83; CJ-7: 93.

Model Number	Body Type	Factory Price	GVW	Shipping Weight	Prod. Total
Jeep					
CJ-5	Utility	$6195	3750	2439	47,304[2]
CJ-7	Utility	$6445	3750[1]	2464	—

NOTE 1: A 4150 lb. GVW was standard with CJ-5 and CJ-7 models with hardtop. It was optional for the open body or soft top models.
NOTE 2: 1980 calendar year sales.

STANDARD ENGINE: Engine Type: OHV, In-line-4. Cast iron block and cylinder head. Bore x Stroke: 4.00 in. x 3.00 in. Lifters: Hydraulic. Number of main bearings-5. Fuel Induction: Rochester 2SE staged 2-barrel carburetor. Compression Ratio: 8.2:1. Displacement: 151 cu. in. (2.4 liters). Horsepower: Net 82 @ 4000 rpm. Torque: Net 125 lb.-ft. @ 2600 rpm. Oil refill capacity: 5 qt. with filter change. Fuel Requirements: Unleaded.

OPTIONAL ENGINE: Engine Type: OHV, In-line-6. Cast iron block and cylinder head. Bore x Stroke: 3.75 in. x 3.90 in. Lifters: Hydraulic. Number of main bearings-7. Fuel Induction: 1-bbl. Carter model YF. Compression Ratio: 8.3:1. Displacement: 258 cu. in. (4.2 liters). Horsepower: Net 110 @ 3500 rpm. Torque: Net 195 lb.-ft. @ 2000 rpm. Oil refill capacity: 5 qt. with filter change. Fuel Requirements: Unleaded. Optional Engine. Type: OHV, V-8. Cast iron block and cylinder head. Bore x Stroke: 3.75 in. x 3.44 in. Lifters: Hydraulic. Number of main bearings-5. Fuel Induction: 2-bbl. carburetor. Compression Ratio: 8.4:1. Displacement: 304 cu. in. (4.98 liters). Horsepower: Net: 125 @ 3200 rpm. Torque: Net: 220 lb.-ft. @ 2400 rpm. Oil refill capacity: 5 qt. with filter change. Fuel Requirements: Unleaded.

CHASSIS FEATURES: Separate body and partial box-section steel frame construction, six cross members.

SUSPENSION AND RUNNING GEAR: Front Suspension: 4-leaf semi-elliptical springs, Spring rate: 170 lb./in. Double-acting shock absorbers. Optional: 7-leaf semi-elliptical two-stage springs. Spring rate: 170/ 230 lb./in. Rear Suspension: 4-leaf semi-elliptical springs, Spring rate: 185 lb./in. Double-acting shock absorbers. Optional: 7-leaf two-stage semi-elliptical springs. Spring rate: 185/250 lb./in. Front Axle Type and Capacity: Full-floating, open end. Capacity: 2200 lb. Rear Axle Type and Capacity: Semi-floating. Capacity: 2700 lb. Axle Ratios: 4-cyl. models: 3.54:1. 258 or 304 engines: 3.07:1. Optional: 4-cyl. models: 4.09:1, 258 or 304 engines: 3.54:1. Transfer Case: Dana 300 model, Ratios: 2.62:1, 1.00:1. Brakes: Type: Hydraulic, front and rear. Dimensions: Front and rear: 11.00 in. x 2.0 in. Effective lining area: 180.8 sq. in. Optional: Front 12.0 in. disc brakes (the front disc/rear drum system was available with or without power assist). Wheels: 15 x 6 in. 5-bolt steel disc. Optional: 15 x 8 in. Tires: H78 x 15B. Optional: H78 x 15B white or blackwall sidewall Town & Country, L78 x 15 black sidewall Town & Country, L78 x 15 OWL Tracker PG (Included with Renegade), 9 x 15 OWL Tracker All-Terrain (included with Golden Eagle). Steering: Recirculating ball system. Ratio: 24.1:1. Turning Circle: CJ-5: 34.1 ft. CJ-7: 38.0 ft. Optional: Saginaw power steering. Ratio: 17.5:1. Standard Transmission: 4-cyl. models: Four-speed all-synchromesh manual SR-4 Borg-Warner transmission. Transmission ratios: 4.07, 2.39, 1.49, 1.00:1. Standard Transmission: 258 and 304 engines: Four-speed, all-synchromesh manual Tremac model T-176. Transmission ratios: 3.52, 2.27, 1.46, 1.0:1. Clutch: 4-cyl.: 9.12 in. Single dry plate. Total lining area: 71.78 sq. in. 6-cyl. and V-8: 10.5 in. Single dry plate. Total lining area: 106.75 sq. in. Optional: TorqueFlite 3-speed automatic transmission. Transmission ratios: 2.74, 1.55, 1.00:1. Reverse: 2.20:1.

VEHICLE DIMENSIONS: Wheelbase: CJ-5: 83.5 in. CJ-7: 93.5 in. Overall Length: CJ-5: 138.4 in. CJ-7: 147.9 in. Front/Rear Tread: With standard wheels: 51.5 in./50.0 in. With styled wheels: 53.8 in./52.3 in. Overall Height: 67.6 in. Width: 68.6 in. (with side-mounted spare tire). Front/Rear Overhang: CJ-5: 23.5 in./31.4 in. CJ-7: 23.5 in./30.9 in. Tailgate: Width and Height: CJ-5: 35.8 in. x 14.125 in. CJ-7: 34.5 in. x 14.125 in. Approach/Departure Degrees: CJ-5: 45/30. Ground Clearance: 6.9 in. Load space: CJ-5: 36 in. x 39 in. (with tailgate closed), 36 in. by 49 in. (tailgate closed). Maximum capacity: CJ-5: 10.2 cu. ft. CJ-7: 13.6 cu. ft. Front headroom: CJ-5-Soft top/Hardtop: 39.66 in./40.8 in. CJ-7-Soft top/Hardtop: 40.5 in./39.9 in. Front legroom: CJ-5: 37.9 in. CJ-7: 39.1 in. Front shoulder room: CJ-5: 55.4 in. CJ-7: 53.8 in. Rear shoulder room: CJ-5: 55.4 in. CJ-7: 56.3 in. Front hip room: CJ-5: 55.33 in. CJ-7: 53.66 in. Floor to ground: CJ-5: 27.0 in. CJ-7: 26.1 in.

CAPACITIES: Fuel Tank: 15.5 gal. Coolant system: 10.2 qt.

ACCOMMODATIONS: Seating Capacity: 2/4.

INSTRUMENTATION: 0-90 mph speedometer, odometer, engine coolant temperature, fuel level gauge, gauges for oil pressure and voltmeter.

OPTIONS AND PRICES: Renegade Package: $899. Golden Eagle Package: $1,450. Laredo Package: $1,950. Tachometer and Rallye clock: $84. Limited slip differential: $90. Power brakes: $73. Power steering: $194. AM radio: $96. Front anti-roll bar: $41. Steering damper: $21. Stabilizer bar: $41. Tilt steering wheel: $79. Extra-duty suspension: $93. Heavy-duty shock absorbers: $28. 258 cu. in. engine: $129. 304 cu. in. engine: $383. Automatic transmission: $333. Hardtop (CJ-7): $676.

HISTORICAL FOOTNOTES: With its 4-cylinder engine the CJ Jeep became the first conventional four-wheel drive vehicle to break the 20 mpg barrier with an EPA estimated 21 mpg and 25 mpg in highway ratings.

1981 CJ

AMC's redesigned and lighter weight 258 cu. in. 6-cylinder engine was available for the 1981 CJ Jeeps. Also helping improve the CJ's fuel economy was the incorporation of a locking torque convertor in the Chrysler TorqueFlite transmission used in conjunction with the 6-cylinder engine. The 4-cylinder engine was now available for the CJ-7 with a wide ratio automatic transmission.

Several other minor changes took place for 1981. They included a longer optional sidestep, revised body graphics for the Renegade Package and the addition of a vent window to the soft top/metal door option for the CJ-7.

1981 Jeep CJ-5 Renegade

Standard equipment features consisted of free-wheeling front hubs, 42 amp alternator, 55 amp battery, ashtray with cigarette lighter, front stabilizer bar and steering damper, glove box, gauges for oil pressure, ammeter engine coolant temperature and fuel level, single note horn, heater and defroster, inside 8 in. rearview mirror, left and right side exterior mirrors, dual padded sun visors, passenger safety rail, fixed rear spare tire mount (CJ-5), swing-away spare tire mount (CJ-7), roll bar, lap seat belts, two front bucket seats, skid plate for fuel tank and transfer case, three-spoke black molded polypropylene steering wheel, moveable tailgate (CJ-7), two-speed electric windshield wipers and washers, and fold down windshield.

The 1981 color selection consisted of cameo tan, vintage red metallic, classic black, autumn gold, moonlight blue, steel grey metallic, dark brown metallic, deep maroon metallic, olympic white, copper brown metallic, oriental red, montana blue, sherwood green metallic and chestnut brown metallic.

I.D. DATA: The V.I.N. consisted of 17 entries. The first three characters identified country, manufacturer and type of vehicle. The fourth (a letter) identified the engine as follows: B-151 cid, 4-cyl.; C-258 cid 6-cyl.; H-304 cid V-8. The fifth character (a letter) identified the transmission. The sixth and seventh characters identified the series and body style. The eighth character identified the GVW rating. Next followed a check digit. The tenth character (a letter) identified the model year. The eleventh character identified the assembly plant. The last six digits were the sequential production numbers. Model identification: CJ-5: 85; CJ-7: 87.

Model Number	Body Type	Factory Price	GVW	Shipping Weight	Prod. Total
Jeep					
CJ-5	Utility	$7240	3750	2495	30,564[3]
CJ-7	Utility	$7490	3750[1]	2520[2]	—

NOTE 1: A 4150 lb. GVW was standard with CJ-5 and CJ-7 models with hardtop. It was optional for the open body or soft top models.
NOTE 2: Shipping weights are for vehicles with 4-speed trans. and power steering.
NOTE 3: 1981 calendar year sales.

STANDARD ENGINE: Engine Type: OHV, In-line-4. Cast iron block and cylinder head. Bore x Stroke: 4.00 in. x 3.00 in. Lifters: Hydraulic. Number of main bearings-5. Fuel Induction: Rochester 2SE staged 2-barrel carburetor. Compression Ratio: 8.2:1. Displacement: 151 cu. in. (2.4 liters). Horsepower: Net 82 @ 4000 rpm. Torque: Net 125 lb.-ft. @ 2600 rpm. Oil refill capacity: 5 qt. with filter change. Fuel Requirements: Unleaded.

OPTIONAL ENGINE: Engine Type: OHV, In-line-6. Cast iron block and cylinder head. Bore x Stroke: 3.75 in. x 3.90 in. Lifters: Hydraulic. Number of main bearings-7. Fuel Induction: 1-bbl. Carter model YF. Compression Ratio: 8.3:1. Displacement: 258 cu. in. (4.2 liters). Horsepower: Net 110 @ 3500 rpm. Torque: Net 195 lb.-ft. @ 2000 rpm. Oil refill capacity: 5 qt. with filter change. Fuel Requirements: Unleaded.

OPTIONAL ENGINE: Engine Type: OHV, V-8. Cast iron block and cylinder head. Bore x Stroke: 3.75 in. x 3.44 in. Lifters: Hydraulic. Number of main bearings-5. Fuel Induction: 2-bbl. carburetor. Compression Ratio: 8.4:1. Displacement: 304 cu. in. (4.98 liters). Horsepower: Net: 125 @ 3200 rpm. Torque: Net: 220 lb.-ft. @ 2400 rpm. Oil refill capacity: 5 qt. with filter change. Fuel Requirements: Unleaded.

CHASSIS FEATURES: Separate body and partial box-section steel frame construction, six cross members.

SUSPENSION AND RUNNING GEAR: Front Suspension: 4-leaf semi-elliptical springs, Spring rate: 170 lb./in. Double-acting shock absorbers. Optional: 7-leaf semi-elliptical two-stage springs. Spring rate: 170/ 230 lb./in. Rear Suspension: 4-leaf semi-elliptical springs, Spring rate: 185 lb./in. Double-acting shock absorbers. Optional: 7-leaf two-stage semi-elliptical springs. Spring rate: 185/250 lb./in. Front Axle Type and Capacity: Full-floating, open end. Capacity: 2200 lb. Rear Axle Type and Capacity: Semi-floating. Capacity: 2700 lb. Axle Ratios: 4-cyl. models: 3.54:1. 258 or 304 engines: 3.07:1. Optional: 4-cyl. models: 4.09:1, 258 or 304 engines: 3.54:1. Transfer Case: Dana 300 model, Ratios: 2.62:1, 1.00:1. Brakes: Type: Hydraulic, front and rear. Dimensions: Front and rear: 11.00 in. x 2.0 in. Effective lining area: 180.8 sq. in. Optional: Front 12.0 in. disc brakes (the front disc/rear drum system was available with or without power assist). Wheels: 15 x 5.5 in. 5-bolt steel disc. Optional: 15 x 8 in. Tires: H78 x 15B black or white sidewall Cruiser polyester cord diagonal ply. Optional: H78 x 15 black or white sidewall Suburbanite, L78 x 15 black or white sidewall Suburbanite, 9R-15 OWL Wrangler steel radial, L78 x 15 OWL Tracker PG Polyglas belted, 9 x 15 OWL Tracker All-Terrain, All-Weather. Steering: Recirculating ball system. Ratio: 24.1:1. Turning Circle: CJ-5: 34.1 ft. CJ-7: 38.0 ft. Optional: Saginaw power steering. Ratio: 17.51:1. Standard Transmission: 4-cyl. models: Four-speed all-synchromesh manual SR-4 Borg-Warner transmission. Transmission ratios: 4.07, 2.39, 1.49, 1.00:1. Standard Transmission: 258 and 304 engines: Four-speed, all-synchromesh manual Tremac model T-176. Transmission ratios: 3.82, 2.27, 1.46, 1.0:1. Clutch: 4-cyl.: 9.12 in. Single dry plate. Total lining area: 71.78 sq. in. 6-cyl. and V-8: 10.5 in. Single dry plate. Total lining area: 106.75 sq. in. Optional: Chrysler TorqueFlite 3-speed automatic transmission. Transmission ratios: 2.74, 1.55, 1.00:1. Reverse: 2.20:1.

VEHICLE DIMENSIONS: Wheelbase: CJ-5: 83.5 in. CJ-7: 93.5 in. Overall Length: CJ-5: 138.4 in. CJ-7: 147.9 in. Front/Rear Tread: With standard wheels: 51.5 in./50.0 in. With styled wheels: 53.8 in./52.3 in. Overall Height: 67.6 in. Width: 68.6 in. (with side-mounted spare tire). Front/Rear Overhang: CJ-5: 23.5 in./31.4 in. CJ-7: 23.5 in./30.9 in. Tailgate: Width and Height: CJ-5: 35.8 in. x 14.125 in. CJ-7: 34.5 in. x 14.125 in. Approach/Departure Degrees: CJ-5: 45/30. Ground Clearance: 6.9 in. Load space: CJ-5: 36 in. x 39 in. (with tailgate closed), 36 in. by 49 in. (tailgate closed). Maximum capacity: CJ-5: 10.2 cu. ft., CJ-7: 13.6 cu. ft. Front headroom: CJ-5-Soft top/Hardtop: 39.66 in./40.8 in. CJ-7-Soft top/Hardtop: 40.5 in./39.9 in. Front legroom: CJ-5: 37.9 in. CJ-7: 39.1 in. Front shoulder room: CJ-5: 55.4 in. CJ-7: 53.8 in. Rear shoulder room: CJ-5: 55.4 in. CJ-7: 56.3 in. Front hip room: CJ-5: 55.33 in. CJ-7: 53.66 in. Floor to ground: CJ-5: 27.0 in. CJ-7: 26.1 in.

CAPACITIES: Fuel Tank: 15.5 gal. Coolant system: 10.2 qt.

ACCOMMODATIONS: Seating Capacity: 2/4.

INSTRUMENTATION: 0-90 mph speedometer, odometer, engine coolant temperature, fuel level gauge, gauges for oil pressure and voltmeter.

OPTIONS AND PRICES: Renegade Package: $1316. Laredo Package: $2049. Automatic transmission (CJ-7). Air conditioning (not avail. for 4-cyl.). Heavy-duty alternator. Body side step: $22. Bumperettes. Front and rear carpeting. Center console. Convenience Group. Decor Group. Drawbar. 258 engine: $136. 304 V-8: $345. Heavy-duty cooling. Instrument panel pad. Fog lights with clear lens: $79. Quartz halogen headlamps: $45. Sun roof (CJ-7 with hardtop). Front power disc brakes. Power steering: $194. AM radio. AM/FM stereo radio. Lockable rear storage box. Soft-Feel steering wheel. Tilt steering wheel: $83. Leather-wrapped steering wheel. Extra duty suspension. Movable tailgate (CJ-5). Soft top. Soft top with steel doors (CJ-7). Molded hardtop (CJ-7). Full wheelcovers. Styled steel wheels. Painted, styled steel wheels. Chrome wheels. Electric winch. Sun bonnet top. Snowplow. Roll bar padding with saddle bags. Radiator screen. Brush guard.

HISTORICAL FOOTNOTES: In spite of a sales decline to 63,275 from 77,852 in 1980, Jeep's share of its market for 1981 moved up to 21.2 percent.

1981 Jeep CJ-7 Laredo

1982 CJ

A new Jeep CJ Option Package, the Limited, was introduced for 1982. The list of features included in the Limited Package began with the basic CJ equipment. In addition, it included power steering and brakes, Arriva P225/75R15 white sidewall tires AM/FM radio with two speakers, a monochromatic paint theme with color-keyed hardtop and wheel-lip extensions, special dual-color body side striping, special grille panel strips, exterior "Limited" nameplates, chrome front bumpers and rear bumperettes, body side steps, black painted windshield and window frames, special dual exterior mirrors, 15 x 7 steel spoke wheels with bright trim rings, Decor and Convenience Groups, high-back front bucket seats with rear bench seat in slate blue or nutmeg Western Weave (nutmeg leather seats were optional), special sound/heat insulated carpeted floor, trim panels for the wheel housing, tailgate, innerbody and cowl sides, carpeted protective front floor mats, low gloss finish for the Sport console, steering column and bezel and air conditioning housing, color-keyed padded roll bar, special door trim and headlining, door activated dome and courtesy lights, leather-wrapped steering wheel and passenger assist handle, and rear quarter beltline trim molding. The limited CJ-7 was available in five exterior/interior color combinations: Mist silver metallic, slate blue metallic and olympic white exteriors with a slate blue interior or copper brown metallic or olympic white exteriors with nutmeg cloth or optional leather interior.

To honor the 30th anniversary of the Jeepers Jamboree, AMC offered the Commemorative Edition Jeep CJ-7 Jamboree model. Only 2500 were available and each had a numbered instrument panel plaque indicating its chronological placement in the total build. Each owner received a signed, frameable certificate of authenticity. The exterior features of the CJ-7 Jamboree consisted of a Jamboree hood lettering decals, black vinyl spare tire cover with Jamboree logo, special topaz gold metallic paint or olympic white paint, chrome styled wheels, chrome front bumper, chrome rear bumperettes, black vinyl soft top, and Decor Group. The Jamboree interior was fitted with high-back black vinyl bucket seats and rear bench seat with special gold accents, center console, black floor and wheelhouse carpeting, black padded roll bar and saddle bags, and instrument panel mounted numbered identification plaque. Required options that were not part of the Jamboree Package were: 258 engine, 5-speed manual transmission, power steering, power brakes, Wrangler radial tires, 20 gal. fuel tank, tachometer and Rallye clock, halogen fog lamps, tilt steering wheel, heavy-duty battery, heavy-duty alternator, heavy-duty cooling system, heavy-duty suspension. A package of factory approved dealer installed special equipment was also listed for the Jamboree. They were as follows: Ramsey electric win. with mounting kit, AM/FM radio, off-road driving lamps and over windshield light mounting bar, fire extinguisher, grille guard and brush guard. Any or all of these items could be deleted by the dealer.

1982 Jeep CJ-7 Limited

All 1982 CJ Jeeps had a wider front/rear tread and were available with an Improved Ride Package containing softer front and rear springs and shock absorbers. Now low-drag front disc brakes were standard. A new drivetrain option was a five-speed manual transmission. Also available was an optional 20 gal. fuel tank. The 1982 exterior color consisted of olympic white, classic black, Jamaica beige, copper brown metallic, deep night blue, vintage red metallic, mist silver metallic, sherwood green metallic, slate blue metallic, oriental red, sun yellow and chestnut brown metallic. The 304 V-8 engine was not available for 1982.

1982 Commemorative Edition Jeep CJ-7 Jamboree

I.D. DATA: The V.I.N. consisted of 17 entries. The first three characters identified country, manufacturer and type of vehicle. The fourth (a letter) identified the engine as follows: B-151 cid, 4-cyl.; C-258 cid 6-cyl. The fifth character (a letter) identified the transmission. The sixth and seventh characters identified the series and body style. The eighth character identified the GVW rating. Next followed a check digit. The tenth character (a letter) identified the model year. The eleventh character identified the assembly plant. The last six digits were the sequential production numbers. Model identification: CJ-5: 85; CJ-7: 87. Serial number range:

Model Number	Body Type	Factory Price	GVW	Shipping Weight	Prod. Total
Jeep					
CJ-5	Utility	$7515	3750	2489	—
CJ-7	Utility	$7765	3750[1]	2555[2]	—

NOTE 1: A 4150 lb. GVW was standard with CJ-5 and CJ-7 models with hardtop. It was optional for the open and soft top models.
NOTE 2: Shipping weights are for vehicles with 4-speed trans. and power steering.

STANDARD ENGINE: Engine Type: OHV, In-line-4. Cast iron block and cylinder head. Bore x Stroke: 4.00 in. x 3.00 in. Lifters: Hydraulic. Number of main bearings-5. Fuel Induction: Rochester staged 2-barrel carburetor. Compression Ratio: 8.2:1. Displacement: 151 cu. in. (2.45 liters). Horsepower: Net 82 @ 4000 rpm. Torque: Net 125 lb.-ft. @ 2600 rpm. Oil refill capacity: 5 qt. with filter change. Fuel Requirements: Unleaded.

OPTIONAL ENGINE: Engine Type: OHV, In-line-6. Cast iron block and cylinder head. Bore x Stroke: 3.75 in. x 3.90 in. Lifters: Hydraulic. Number of main bearings-7. Fuel Induction: 1-bbl. Carter model YF. Compression Ratio: 8.3:1. Displacement: 258 cu. in. (4.2 liters). Horsepower: Net 115 @ 3200 rpm. Torque: Net 210 lb.-ft. @ 1800 rpm. Oil refill capacity: 5 qt. with filter change. Fuel Requirements: Unleaded.

SUSPENSION AND RUNNING GEAR: Front Suspension: 4-leaf semi-elliptical springs, Spring rate: 170 lb./in. Double-acting shock absorbers. Optional: 7-leaf semi-elliptical two-stage springs. Spring rate: 170/ 230 lb./in. Rear Suspension: 4-leaf semi-elliptical springs, Spring rate: 185 lb./in. Double-acting shock absorbers. Optional: 7-leaf two-stage semi-elliptical springs. Spring rate: 185/250 lb./in. Front Axle Type and Capacity: Full-floating, open end. Capacity: 2200 lb. Rear Axle Type and Capacity: Semi-floating. Capacity: 2700 lb. Axle Ratios: 4-cyl. engine: 6-cyl. engine: 2.73:1. Optional: 6-cyl. engine: 3.73:1. Transfer Case: Dana 300 model, Ratios: 2.62:1, 1.00:1. Brakes: Type: Hydraulic, front and rear. Dimensions: Front and rear: 11.00 in. x 2.0 in. Effective lining area: 180.8 sq. in. Optional: Front 12.0 in. disc brakes (the front disc/rear drum system was available with or without power assist). Wheels: 15 x 5.5 in. 5-bolt steel disc. Optional: 15 x 8 in. Tires: G78 x 15 Black sidewall Suburbanite XG fiberglass belted Town and Country. Optional: 10R-15 OWL Wrangler radial, L78 x 15 OWL Tracker PG Polyglas belted. Steering: Recirculating ball system. Ratio: 24.1:1. Turning Circle: CJ-5: 33.5 ft. CJ-7: 35.9 ft. Optional: Saginaw power steering. Ratio: 17.51:1. Standard Transmission: 4-cyl. models: Four-speed all-synchromesh manual SR-4 Borg-Warner transmission. Transmission ratios: 4.07, 2.39, 1.49, 1.00:1. Reverse: 1. Standard Transmission: 258 engine: Four-speed, all-synchromesh manual Tremac model T-176. Transmission ratios: 3.82, 2.27, 1.46, 1.0:1. Clutch: 4-cyl.: 9.12 in. Single dry plate. Total lining area: 71.78 sq. in. 6-cyl.: 10.5 in. Single dry plate. Total lining area: 106.75 sq. in. Total plate pressure:. Optional: TorqueFlite 3-speed automatic transmission. Transmission ratios: 2.74, 1.55, 1.00:1. Reverse: 2.20:1. Optional: Warner Gear T-5 5-speed manual transmission. Not available for CJ-5 with 6-cyl. engine. Transmission ratios: 4.03, 2.37, 1.50, 1.00, 0.76 or 0.86:1 (depending on engine and axle ratio).

VEHICLE DIMENSIONS: Wheelbase: CJ-5: 83.5 in. CJ-7: 93.5 in. Overall Length: CJ-5: 138.4 in. CJ-7: 147.9 in. Front/Rear Tread: With standard wheels: 51.5 in./50.0 in. With styled wheels: 53.8 in./52.3 in. Overall Height: 67.6 in. Width: 68.6 in. (with side-mounted spare tire). Front/Rear Overhang: CJ-5: 23.5 in./31.4 in. CJ-7: 23.5 in./30.9 in. Tailgate: Width and Height: CJ-5: 35.8 in. x 14.125 in. CJ-7: 34.5 in. x 14.125 in. Approach/Departure Degrees: CJ-5: 45/30. Ground Clearance: 6.9 in. Load space: CJ-5: 36 in. x 39 in. (with tailgate closed), 36 in. by 49 in. (tailgate closed). Maximum capacity: CJ-5: 10.2 cu. ft., CJ-7: 13.6 cu. ft. Front headroom: CJ-5-Soft top/Hardtop: 39.66 in./40.8 in. CJ-7-Soft top/Hardtop: 40.5 in./39.9 in. Front legroom: CJ-5: 37.9 in. CJ-7: 39.1 in. Front shoulder room: CJ-5: 55.4 in. CJ-7: 53.8 in. Rear shoulder room: CJ-5: 55.4 in. CJ-7: 56.3 in. Front hip room: CJ-5: 55.33 in. CJ-7: 53.66 in. Floor to ground: CJ-5: 27.0 in. CJ-7: 26.1 in.

CAPACITIES: Fuel Tank: 15.0 gal. with standard skid plate. 20.0 gal. optional. Coolant system: 10.2 qt.

ACCOMMODATIONS: Seating Capacity: 2/4.

INSTRUMENTATION: 0-90 mph speedometer, odometer, engine coolant temperature, fuel level gauge, gauges for oil pressure and voltmeter.

OPTIONS AND PRICES: The CJ option list was essentially unchanged from 1981. A listing of selected options and prices follows: 258 cu. in. engine: $145. 5-speed manual transmission: $199. Automatic transmission: $409. 3.31:1 axle ratio: $33. Extra duty suspension: $103. Power steering: $229. Power disc brakes: $499. Heavy-duty battery: $45. Cold Climate Group: $115. Renegade Package: $979. Laredo Package: $2149. Limited Package: $2895. Metal cab: $610.

HISTORICAL FOOTNOTES: Jeep Corporation promoted off-roading as a safe positive form of recreation by encouraging its customers to respect the land and help protect the environment for future generations.

1983 CJ

Changes for 1983 were not extensive. The 258 cu. in. engine now had a higher, 9.2:1, compression ratio as well as a fuel feedback system and knock sensor. Unlike 1982 when the four-cylinder was standard in all CJ models, the 1983 CJ-5's base engine was the 258 cu. in. engine. The CJ-7 retained the 4-cyl. engine as standard.

The CJ's were offered with the same Appearance/Equipment Packages as in 1982. The Renegade had revised graphics highlighted by added elements just behind the front fenders.

1983 Jeep CJ-7 Renegade

I.D. DATA: The V.I.N. consisted of 17 entries. The first three characters identified country, manufacturer and type of vehicle. The fourth (a letter) identified the engine as follows: B-151 cid, 4-cyl.; C-258 cid 6-cyl. The fifth character (a letter) identified the transmission. The sixth and seventh characters identified the series and body style. The eighth character identified the GVW rating. Next followed a check digit. The tenth character (a letter) identified the model year. The eleventh character identified the assembly plant. The last six digits were the sequential production numbers. Model identification: CJ-5: 85; CJ-7: 87.

Model Number	Body Type	Factory Price	GVW	Shipping Weight	Prod. Total
Jeep					
CJ-5	Utility	$7515	3750	2699	36,308[3]
CJ-7	Utility	$6995	3750[1]	2595[2]	—

NOTE 1: A 4150 lb. GVW was standard with CJ-5 and CJ-7 models with hardtop. It was optional for the open body or soft top models.
NOTE 2: Shipping weights are for vehicles with 4-speed trans. and power steering.
NOTE 3: 1983 calendar year sales.

STANDARD ENGINE: For CJ-7, optional for CJ-5: Engine Type: OHV, In-line-4. Cast iron block and cylinder head. b. Bore x Stroke: 4.00 in. x 3.00 in. Lifters: Hydraulic. Number of main bearings-5. Fuel Induction: Rochester staged 2-barrel carburetor. Compression Ratio: 8.2:1. Displacement: 151 cu. in. (2.45 liters). Horsepower: Net 82 @ 4000 rpm. Torque: Net 125 lb.-ft. @ 2600 rpm. Oil refill capacity: 5 qt. with filter change. Fuel Requirements: Unleaded.

OPTIONAL ENGINE: For CJ-7, optional for CJ-5: Engine Type: OHV, In-line-6. Cast iron block and cylinder head. Bore x Stroke: 3.75 in. x 3.90 in. Lifters: Hydraulic. Number of main bearings-7. Fuel Induction: 1-bbl. Carter model YF. Compression Ratio: 9.2:1. Displacement: 258 cu. in. (4.2 liters). Horsepower: Net 115 @ 3200 rpm. Torque: Net 210 lb.-ft. @ 1800 rpm. Oil refill capacity: 5 qt. with filter change. Fuel Requirements: Unleaded.

SUSPENSION AND RUNNING GEAR: Front Suspension: 4-leaf semi-elliptical springs, Spring rate: 170 lb./in. Double-acting shock absorbers. Optional: 7-leaf semi-elliptical two-stage springs. Spring rate: 170/ 230 lb./in. Rear Suspension: 4-leaf semi-elliptical springs, Spring rate: 185 lb./in. Double-acting shock absorbers. Optional: 7-leaf two-stage semi-elliptical springs. Spring rate: 185/250 lb./in. Front Axle Type and Capacity: Full-floating, open end. Capacity: 2200 lb. Rear Axle Type and Capacity: Semi-floating. Capacity: 2700 lb. Axle Ratios: 4-cyl. engine: 6-cyl. engine: 2.73:1. Optional: 6-cyl. engine: 3.73:1. Transfer Case: Dana 300 model, Ratios: 2.62:1, 1.00:1. Brakes: Type: Hydraulic, front and rear. Dimensions: Front and rear: 11.00 in. x 2.0 in. Effective lining area: 180.8 sq. in. Optional: Front 12.0 in. disc brakes (the front disc/rear drum system was available with or without power assist). Wheels: 15 x 5.5 in. 5-bolt steel disc. Optional: 15 x 8 in. Tires: G78 x 15 black sidewall Suburbanite XG fiberglass belted Town and Country. Optional: 10R-15 OWL Wrangler radial, L78 x 15 OWL Tracker PG Polyglas belted. Steering: Recirculating ball system. Ratio: 24.1:1. Turning Circle: CJ-5: 33.5 ft. CJ-7: 35.9 ft. Optional: Saginaw power steering. Ratio: 17.51:1. Standard Transmission: 4-cyl. models: Four-speed all-synchromesh manual SR-4 Borg-Warner transmission. Transmission ratios: 4.07, 2.39, 1.49, 1.00:1. Reverse: 1. Standard Transmission: 258 engine: Four-speed, all-synchromesh manual Tremac model T-176. Transmission ratios: 3.82, 2.27, 1.46, 1.0:1. Clutch: 4-cyl.: 9.12 in. Single dry plate. Total lining area: 71.78 sq. in. 6-cyl.: 10.5 in. Single dry plate. Total lining area: 106.75 sq. in. Total plate pressure:. Optional: TorqueFlite 3-speed automatic transmission. Transmission ratios: 2.74, 1.55, 1.00:1. Reverse: 2.20:1. Optional: Warner Gear T-5 5-speed manual transmission. Not available for CJ-5 with 6-cyl. engine. Transmission ratios: 4.03, 2.37, 1.50, 1.00, 0.76 or 0.86:1 (depending on engine and axle ratio).

VEHICLE DIMENSIONS: Wheelbase: CJ-5: 83.5 in. CJ-7: 93.5 in. Overall Length: CJ-5: 138.4 in. CJ-7: 147.9 in. Front/Rear Tread: With standard wheels: 51.5 in./50.0 in. With styled wheels: 53.8 in./52.3 in. Overall Height: 67.6 in. Width: 68.6 in. (with side-mounted spare tire). Front/Rear Overhang: CJ-5: 23.5 in./31.4 in. CJ-7: 23.5 in./30.9 in. Tailgate: Width and Height: CJ-5: 35.8 in. x 14.125 in. CJ-7: 34.5 in. x 14.125 in. Approach/Departure Degrees:

CJ-5: 45/30. Ground Clearance: 6.9 in. Load space: CJ-5: 36 in. x 39 in. (with tailgate closed), 36 in. by 49 in. (tailgate closed). Maximum capacity: CJ-5: 10.2 cu. ft., CJ-7: 13.6 cu. ft. Front headroom: CJ-5-Soft top/Hardtop: 39.66 in./40.8 in. CJ-7-Soft top/Hardtop: 40.5 in./39.9 in. Front legroom: CJ-5: 37.9 in. CJ-7: 39.1 in. Front shoulder room: CJ-5: 55.4 in. CJ-7: 53.8 in. Rear shoulder room: CJ-5: 55.4 in. CJ-7: 56.3 in. Front hip room: CJ-5: 55.33 in. CJ-7: 53.66 in. Floor to ground: CJ-5: 27.0 in. CJ-7: 26.1 in.

CAPACITIES: Fuel Tank: 15.0 gal. with standard skid plate. 20.0 gal. optional. Coolant system: 10.2 qt.

ACCOMMODATIONS: Seating Capacity: 2/4.

INSTRUMENTATION: 0-90 mph speedometer, odometer, engine coolant temperature, fuel level gauge, gauges for oil pressure and voltmeter.

OPTIONS AND PRICES: The CJ option list was essentially unchanged from 1982. Selected options prices were as follows: Renegade Package: $1011. Laredo Package: $2220. Limited Package: $3595.

HISTORICAL FOOTNOTES: After losing money for 14 consecutive years, American Motors reported a 1983 fourth quarter profit of $7.4 million.

1984 CJ

For the 1984 model year the CJ-5 was dropped. Also dropped from the CJ's optional equipment list was the Limited Package. Still available were the Renegade and Laredo Trim Packages.

AMC's newly designed 2.5 liter, 150 cu. in. 4-cylinder engine was the standard CJ-7 engine. The older 4.2 liter, 258 cu. in. 6-cylinder continued to be optional. Transmission choices included the standard 4-speed manual and an optional 5-speed manual. The 3-speed automatic was optionally available for the 6-cylinder engine only.

1984 Jeep CJ-7 Laredo

I.D. DATA: The V.I.N. consisted of 17 entries. The first three characters identified country, manufacturer and type of vehicle. The fourth (a letter) identified the engine as follows: B-151 cid, 4-cyl.; C-258 cid 6-cyl.; H-304 cid V-8. The fifth character (a letter) identified the transmission. The sixth and seventh characters identified the series and body style. The eighth character identified the GVW rating. Next followed a check digit. The tenth character (a letter) identified the model year. The eleventh character identified the assembly plant. The last six digits were the sequential production numbers. Model identification: CJ-7: 87.

Model Number	Body Type	Factory Price	GVW	Shipping Weight	Prod. Total
Jeep					
CJ-7	Utility	$7282	3750[1]	2601[2]	—

NOTE 1: A 4150 lb. GVW was standard with CJ-7 models with hardtop. It was optional for the open body or soft top models.
NOTE 2: Shipping weights are for vehicles with 4-speed trans. and power steering.

STANDARD ENGINE: Engine Type: OHV, In-line-4. Cast iron block and cylinder head. Bore x Stroke: 3.88 in. x 3.19 in. Lifters: Hydraulic. Number of main bearings-5. Fuel Induction: 1-bbl. carburetor. Compression Ratio: 9.2:1. Displacement: 150.45 cu. in. (2.4 liters). Horsepower: Net 105 @ 5000 rpm. Torque: Net 132 lb.-ft. @ 2800 rpm. Oil refill capacity: 5 qt. with filter change. Fuel Requirements: Unleaded. Optional Engine. Engine Type: OHV, In-line-6. Cast iron block and cylinder head. Bore x Stroke: 3.75 in. x 3.90 in. Lifters: Hydraulic. Number of main bearings-7. Fuel Induction: 1-bbl. Carter model YF. Compression Ratio: 9.2:1. Displacement: 258 cu. in. (4.2 liters). Horsepower: Net 115 @ 3200 rpm. Torque: Net 210 lb.-ft. @ 1800 rpm. Oil refill capacity: 5 qt. with filter change. Fuel Requirements: Unleaded.

SUSPENSION AND RUNNING GEAR: Front Suspension: 4-leaf semi-elliptical springs. Spring rate: 170 lb./in. Double-acting shock absorbers. Optional: 7-leaf semi-elliptical two-stage springs. Spring rate: 170/ 230 lb./in. Rear Suspension: 4-leaf semi-elliptical springs, Spring rate: 185 lb./in. Double-acting shock absorbers. Optional: 7-leaf two-stage semi-elliptical springs. Spring rate: 185/250 lb./in. Front Axle Type and Capacity: Full-floating, open end. Capacity: 2200 lb. Rear Axle Type and Capacity: Semi-floating. Capacity: 2700 lb. Axle Ratios: 4-cyl. engine: 6-cyl. engine: 2.73:1. Optional: 6-cyl. engine: 3.73:1. Transfer Case: Dana 300 model, Ratios: 2.62:1, 1.00:1. Brakes: Type: Hydraulic, front and rear. Dimensions: Front and rear: 11.00 in. x 2.0 in. Effective lining area: 180.8 sq. in. Optional: Front 12.0 in. disc brakes (the front disc/rear drum system was available with or without power assist). Wheels: 15 x 6.0 in. L rim, 5-bolt steel disc. Optional: 15 x 7 in. chrome styled steel wheel (standard for Laredo, optional for Base and Renegade Package). 15 x 7 in. White painted style steel wheels (standard on Renegade Package, optional for Base model). Tires: Base: P205/75R15 black Arriva steel belted. Renegade: P235/75R15RB Wrangler steel belted radial. Laredo: P235/75R15 Wrangler OWL radial. Optional: P215/75R15B black sidewall Wrangler steel radial Mud and Snow (optional for Base only), P235/75R15RB Wrangler steel belted radial (optional for Base only), P235/75R15 Wrangler OWL radial (optional for Base and Renegade). Steering: Recirculating ball system. Ratio: 24.1:1. Turning Circle: CJ-5: 33.5 ft. CJ-7: 35.9 ft. Optional: Saginaw power steering. Ratio: 17.51:1. Standard Transmission: 4-cyl. models: Four-speed all-synchromesh manual SR-4 Borg-Warner transmission. Transmission ratios: 4.07, 2.39, 1.49, 1.00:1. Standard Transmission: 258 engine: Four-speed, all-synchromesh manual Tremac model T-176. Transmission ratios: 3.82, 2.27, 1.46, 1.0:1. Clutch: 4-cyl.: 9.12 in. Single dry plate. Total lining area: 71.78 sq. in. 6-cyl.: 10.5 in. Single dry plate. Total lining area: 106.75 sq. in. Optional: 6-cyl.: TorqueFlite 3-speed automatic transmission. Transmission ratios: 2.74, 1.55, 1.00:1. Reverse: 2.20:1. Optional: Warner Gear T-5 5-speed manual transmission. Not available with 6-cyl. engine. Transmission ratios: 3.93, 2.33, 1.45, 1.00, 0.85:1.

VEHICLE DIMENSIONS: Wheelbase: 93.4 in. Overall Length: 153.2 in. Front/Rear Tread: 55.8 in./55.1 in. Overall Height: 69.1 in., 71.0 in. with hardtop. Width: 65.3 in. Front/Rear Overhang: 23.5 in./36.3 in. Tailgate: Width and Height: 34.5 in. x. Maximum capacity (Volume Index): 13.6 cu. ft. Front headroom: Soft top/Hardtop: 40.6 in./39.9 in. Front legroom: 39.1 in. Front shoulder room: 53.8 in. Rear shoulder room: 56.3 in. Front hip room: 53.66 in. Floor to ground: 26.1 in.

CAPACITIES: Fuel Tank: 15.0 gal. with standard skid plate. 20.0 gal. optional. Coolant capacity: 10.2 qt.

ACCOMMODATIONS: Seating Capacity: 2/4.

INSTRUMENTATION: Speedometer calibrated in mph/km/hr., odometer, engine coolant temperature, fuel level gauge, gauges for oil pressure and voltmeter.

OPTIONS: Front and rear carpeting. Center console. Convenience Group. Includes courtesy lights, engine compartment light, 8 in. day/night rearview mirror, intermittent windshield wipers, lockable glove box. Decor group. Includes rocker panel protection moldings, instrument panel overlay, Soft-Feel Sport steering wheel and front frame overlay. AM radio. AM/FM stereo radio with two speakers. AM/FM stereo radio with cassette tape player and two speakers. Requires factory hard or soft top. Roll Bar Accessory Package. Includes padded roll bar and roll bar saddle bags. High-back vinyl bucket seats with denim trim (not available for Laredo). Soft-Feel Sport steering wheel. Leather-wrapped 3-spoke steering wheel. Rear lockable storage box. Tachometer and Rallye clock. Tilt steering wheel. Bumper Accessory Group. Includes two tow hooks, front bumper extensions, rear bumperettes (not available with Laredo). Metal doors. Available with optional soft top. Doors painted same color as body, available with black and honey tops only. Steel doors. Available with fiberglass hardtop (black, white, honey). Full soft top with hard doors. Vinyl soft tops. Available in black or white, honey, denim or garnet denim with denim interior only. Hardtops. Available in black, white or honey with doors. Air conditioning. Includes heavy-duty cooling. Requires power steering and carpeting (not available with 4-cyl. engine). Heavy-duty 63 amp alternator. Heavy-duty 56-450 cold crank battery. Power front disc brakes. Cold Climate Group. Includes heavy-duty battery, heavy-duty alternator and engine block heater. Heavy-duty cooling system. Includes extra capacity radiator, 7-blade fan (6-cyl.), Tempatrol viscous fan drive, fan shroud (6-cyl.) and coolant recovery. Coolant recovery system. Cruise control. Drawbar. Five speed manual overdrive transmission with floor shift. Automatic transmission (not available for 4-cyl.). Rear Trac-Lok differential. California emissions system. High altitude system. 4.2 liter engine. Fog lamps with clear lens. 20 gal. fuel tank. Halogen headlamps. Extra-quiet insulation (hardtop only). Heavy-duty front and rear shock absorbers. Spare wheel lock, included with 7 in. wheels. Power steering. Requires power steering. Extra-Duty Suspension Package. Soft-Ride suspension. Not available for base model.

HISTORICAL FOOTNOTES: In 1984 the CJ-5 model ended a production run that began on October 11, 1954.

1985 CJ

The 1985 CJ-7 had new fold and tumble rear seats in place of the fixed type of 1984. Up front were standard. High-back bucket seats were standard. Both the Renegade and Laredo Packages featured new interior and exterior decors. Common to both were revised tape stripe patterns, three new exterior colors and one new interior color, honey, which replaced nutmeg. The available exterior colors for the 1985 CJ consisted of four standard choices: Olympic white, classic black, almond beige and sebring red. The extra cost metallic colors were sterling, ice blue, charcoal, dark honey, dark brown and garnet. All extra cost colors had a clearcoat finish.

Standard equipment for the CJ-7 consisted of front ashtray, mini carpet mat, cigarette lighter, gauges for oil pressure, voltmeter, engine coolant temperature and fuel level, heater and defroster, 8 in. inside rearview mirror, passenger safety rail, high-back bucket seats in linen grain vinyl, padded sun visors, front painted bumper, outside left-side mirror, movable tailgate, wheel-lip extensions, 42 amp alternator, 55-421 cold crank battery, fuel tank skid plate, single horn, hood insulation, swing-away spare tire mount, and electric 2-speed windshield wipers.

The Renegade Package had these features in place of or in addition to the content of the base model: Courtesy lights, instrument panel overlay, 8 in. day/night rearview mirror, high-back denim vinyl front bucket seats in three color choices: Garnet, black or honey, matching fold and tumble denim-look vinyl rear seat, Soft-Feel Sport steering wheel, front frame cover, hood decal, bright rocker panel moldings, front frame overlay, exterior Renegade graphics in three color choices: Yellow, blue and red, engine compartment light, die cast chrome plated hub covers, and spare tire lock. The Laredo Package had these features in place of or in addition to the content of the Renegade model: Full indoor/outdoor carpeting in either black or honey, console, special door trim panels (hardtop only), pin-striped instrument panel overlay with Laredo nameplate, leather-wrapped passenger assist bar in either black or honey, Celtic Grain vinyl high-back bucket seats with matching fold and tumble rear seat in Celtic Grain vinyl, door vent window (hardtop models only), chrome front bumper and rear bumperettes, chrome grille panel with pinstripe, chrome mirror heads and arms, chrome footman loops, Laredo graphic exterior treatment in two color choices: Silver and grey and brown and gold, black rocker panel moldings, door inserts overlays (textured to match roof, hardtop only), optional hardtop liftgate glass and quarter window tinted in grey tone with black top or bronze-tone with honey top, hood insulation, tachometer and Rallye clock.

1985 Jeep CJ-7

I.D. DATA: The V.I.N. consisted of 17 entries. The first three characters identified country, manufacturer and type of vehicle. The fourth (a letter) identified the engine as follows: B-151 cid, 4-cyl.; C-258 cid 6-cyl.; H-304 cid V-8. The fifth character (a letter) identified the transmission. The sixth and seventh characters identified the series and body style. The eighth character identified the GVW rating. Next followed a check digit. The tenth character (a letter) identified the model year. The eleventh character identified the assembly plant. The last six digits were the sequential production numbers. Model identification: CJ-7: 87.

Model Number	Body Type	Factory Price	GVW	Shipping Weight	Prod. Total
Jeep					
CJ-7	Utility	$7282	3750[1]	2601[2]	46,553[3]

NOTE 1: A 4150 lb. GVW was standard with CJ-7 models with hardtop. It was optional for the open body or soft top models.
NOTE 2: Shipping weights are for vehicles with 4-speed trans. and power steering.
3-Calendar year production.

STANDARD ENGINE: Engine Type: OHV, In-line-4. Cast iron block and cylinder head. Bore x Stroke: 3.88 in. x 3.19 in. Lifters: Hydraulic. Number of main bearings-5. Fuel Induction: 1-bbl. carburetor. Compression Ratio: 9.2:1. Displacement: 150.45 cu. in. (2.4 liters). Horsepower: Net: 105 @ 5000 rpm. Torque: Net: 132 lb.-ft. @ 2800 rpm. Oil refill capacity: 5 qt. with filter change. Fuel Requirements: Unleaded.

OPTIONAL ENGINE: Engine Type: OHV, In-line-6. Cast iron block and cylinder head. Bore x Stroke: 3.75 in. x 3.90 in. Lifters: Hydraulic. Number of main bearings-7. Fuel Induction: 1-bbl. Carter model YF. Compression Ratio: 9.2:1. Displacement: 258 cu. in. (4.2 liters). Horsepower: Net 115 @ 3200 rpm. Torque: Net 210 lb.-ft. @ 1800 rpm. Oil refill capacity: 5 qt. with filter change. Fuel Requirements: Unleaded.

SUSPENSION AND RUNNING GEAR: Front Suspension: 4-leaf semi-elliptical springs. Spring rate: 170 lb./in. Double-acting shock absorbers. Optional: 7-leaf semi-elliptical two-stage springs. Spring rate: 170/ 230 lb./in. Rear Suspension: 4-leaf semi-elliptical springs, Spring rate: 185 lb./in. Double-acting shock absorbers. Optional: 7-leaf two-stage semi-elliptical springs. Spring rate: 185/250 lb./in. Front Axle Type and Capacity: Full-floating, open end. Capacity: 2200 lb. Rear Axle Type and Capacity: Semi-floating. Capacity: 2700 lb. Axle Ratios: 4-cyl. engine: 6-cyl. engine: 2.73:1. Optional: 6-cyl. engine: 3.73:1. Transfer Case: Dana 300 model, Ratios: 2.62:1, 1.00:1. Brakes: Type: Hydraulic, front and rear. Dimensions: Front and rear: 11.00 in. x 2.0 in. Effective lining area: 180.8 sq. in. Optional: Front 12.0 in. disc brakes (the front disc/rear drum system was available with or without power assist). Wheels: 15 x 6.0 in. L rim, 5-bolt steel disc. Optional: 15 x 7 in. chrome styled steel wheel (standard for Laredo, optional for base and Renegade Package). 15 x 7 in. White painted style steel wheels (standard on Renegade Package, optional for base model). Tires: Base: P205/75R15 Black Arriva steel belted. Renegade: P235/75R15RB Wrangler steel belted radial. Laredo: P235/75R15 Wrangler OWL radial. Optional: P215/75R15B Black sidewall Wrangler steel radial Mud and Snow (optional for base only), P235/75R15RB Wrangler steel belted radial (optional for base only), P235/75R15 Wrangler OWL radial (optional for base and Renegade). Steering: Recirculating ball system. Ratio: 24.1:1. Turning Circle: 35.9 ft. Optional: Saginaw power steering. Ratio: 17.51:1.Standard Transmission: 4-cyl. models: Four-speed all-synchromesh manual SR-4 Borg-Warner transmission. Transmission ratios: 4.07, 2.39, 1.49, 1.00:1. Standard Transmission: 258 engine: Four-speed, all-synchromesh manual Tremac model T-176. Transmission ratios: 3.82, 2.27, 1.46, 1.0:1. Clutch: 4-cyl.: 9.12 in. Single dry plate. Total lining area: 71.78 sq. in. 6-cyl.: 10.5 in. Single dry plate. Total lining area: 106.75 sq. in. Optional: 6-cyl.: TorqueFlite 3-speed automatic transmission. Transmission ratios: 2.74, 1.55, 1.00:1. Reverse: 2.20:1. Optional: Warner Gear T-5 5-speed manual transmission. Not available with 6-cyl. engine. Transmission ratios: 3.93, 2.33, 1.45, 1.00, 0.85:1.

VEHICLE DIMENSIONS: Wheelbase: 93.4 in. Overall Length: 153.2 in. Front/Rear Tread: 55.8 in./55.1 in. Overall Height: 69.1 in., 71.0 in. with hardtop. Width: 65.3 in. Front/Rear Overhang: 23.5 in./36.3 in. Tailgate: Width and Height: 34.5 in. x. Maximum capacity (Volume Index): 13.6 cu. ft. Front headroom: Soft top/Hardtop: 40.6 in./39.9 in. Front legroom: 39.1 in. Front shoulder room: 53.8 in. Rear shoulder room: 56.3 in. Front hip room: 53.66 in. Floor to ground: 26.1 in.

CAPACITIES: Fuel Tank: 15.0 gal. with standard skid plate. 20.0 gal. optional. Coolant capacity: 10.2 qt.

ACCOMMODATIONS: Seating Capacity: 2/4.

INSTRUMENTATION: Speedometer calibrated in mph/km/hr., odometer, engine coolant temperature, fuel level gauge, gauges for oil pressure and voltmeter.

OPTIONS: Except for the addition of the fold and tumble rear seat, the option availability of the CJ-7 was unchanged from 1984.

HISTORICAL FOOTNOTES: The CJ Jeep was introduced in the fall of 1984.

1986 CJ

On November 27, 1985 Joseph Cappy, executive vice-president-operations announced that production of the CJ Jeep would end early in 1986. Thus, it isn't surprising that virtually no change took place in the CJ-7 for 1986. All exterior paints now had a clearcoat finish. Like all 1986 Jeeps the CJ-7 was covered by the same warranty as offered in 1985. The basic features of this plan included 12 month/12,000 mile coverage for the entire vehicle (except tires) plus three year corrosion protection. In addition, major engine, transmission and power-train components were covered for 24 months/24,000 miles.

1986 Jeep CJ-7

I.D. DATA: The V.I.N. consisted of 17 entries. The first three characters identified country, manufacturer and type of vehicle. The fourth (a letter) identified the engine as follows: B-151 cid, 4-cyl.; C-258 cid 6-cyl.; H-304 cid V-8. The fifth character (a letter) identified the transmission. The sixth and seventh characters identified the series and body style. The eighth character identified the GVW rating. Next followed a check digit. The tenth character (a letter) identified the model year. The eleventh character identified the assembly plant. The last six digits were the sequential production numbers. Model identification: CJ-7: 87.

Model Number	Body Type	Factory Price	GVW	Shipping Weight	Prod. Total
Jeep					
CJ-7	Utility	$7500	3750[1]	2596[2]	—

NOTE 1: A 4150 lb. GVW was standard with CJ-7 models with hardtop. It was optional for the open body or soft top models.
NOTE 2: Shipping weights are for vehicles with 4-speed trans. and power steering.

STANDARD ENGINE: Engine Type: OHV, In-line-4. Cast iron block and cylinder head. Bore x Stroke: 3.88 in. x 3.19 in. Lifters: Hydraulic. Number of main bearings-5. Fuel Induction: 1-bbl. carburetor. Compression Ratio: 9.2:1. Displacement: 150.45 cu. in. (2.4 liters). Horsepower: Net: 105 @ 5000 rpm. Torque: Net: 132 lb.-ft. @ 2800 rpm. Oil refill capacity: 5 qt. with filter change. Fuel Requirements: Unleaded. Optional Engine. Engine Type: OHV, In-line-6. Cast iron block and cylinder head. Bore x Stroke: 3.75 in. x 3.90 in. Lifters: Hydraulic. Number of main bearings-7. Fuel Induction: 1-bbl. Carter model YF. Compression Ratio: 9.2:1. Displacement: 258 cu. in. (4.2 liters). Horsepower: Net 115 @ 3200 rpm. Torque: Net 210 lb.-ft. @ 1800 rpm. Oil refill capacity: 5 qt. with filter change. Fuel Requirements: Unleaded.

SUSPENSION AND RUNNING GEAR: Front Suspension: 4-leaf semi-elliptical springs. Spring rate: 170 lb./in. Double-acting shock absorbers. Optional: 7-leaf semi-elliptical two-stage springs. Spring rate: 170/ 230 lb./in. Rear Suspension: 4-leaf semi-elliptical springs, Spring rate: 185 lb./in. Double-acting shock absorbers. Optional: 7-leaf two-stage semi-elliptical springs. Spring rate: 185/250 lb./in. Front Axle Type and Capacity: Full-floating, open end. Capacity: 2200 lb. Rear Axle Type and Capacity: Semi-floating. Capacity: 2700 lb. Axle Ratios: 4-cyl. engine: 6-cyl. engine: 2.73:1. Optional: 6-cyl. engine: 3.73:1. Transfer Case: Dana 300 model, Ratios: 2.62:1, 1.00:1. Brakes: Type: Hydraulic, front and rear. Dimensions: Front and rear: 11.00 in. x 2.0 in. Effective lining area: 180.8 sq. in. Optional: Front 12.0 in. disc brakes (the front disc/rear drum system was available with or without power assist). Wheels: 15 x 6.0 in. L rim, 5-bolt steel disc. Optional: 15 x 7 in. chrome styled steel wheel (standard for Laredo, optional for base and Renegade Package). 15 x 7 in. white painted style steel wheels (standard on Renegade Package, optional for base model). Tires: Base: P205/75R15 black Arriva steel belted. Renegade: P235/75R15RB Wrangler steel belted radial. Optional: P235/75R15 Wrangler OWL radial. Optional: P215/75R15B black sidewall Wrangler steel radial Mud and Snow (optional for base only), P235/75R15RB Wrangler steel belted radial (optional for base only), P235/75R15 Wrangler OWL radial (optional for base and Renegade). Steering: Recirculating ball system. Ratio: 24.1:1. Turning Circle: 35.9 ft. Optional: Saginaw power steering. Ratio: 17.51:1.Standard Transmission: 4-cyl. models: Four-speed all-synchromesh manual SR-4 Borg-Warner transmission. Transmission ratios: 4.07, 2.39, 1.49, 1.00:1. Standard Transmission: 258 engine: Four-speed, all-synchromesh manual Tremac model T-176. Transmission ratios: 3.82, 2.27, 1.46, 1.0:1. Clutch: 4-cyl.: 9.12 in. Single dry plate. Total lining area: 71.78 sq. in. 6-cyl.: 10.5 in. Single dry plate. Total lining area: 106.75 sq. in. Optional: 6-cyl.: TorqueFlite 3-speed automatic transmission. Transmission ratios: 2.74, 1.55, 1.00:1. Reverse: 2.20:1. Optional: Warner Gear T-5 5-speed manual transmission. Not available with 6-cyl. engine. Transmission ratios: 3.93, 2.33, 1.45, 1.00, 0.85:1.

VEHICLE DIMENSIONS: Wheelbase: 93.4 in. Overall Length: 153.2 in. Front/Rear Tread: 55.8 in./55.1 in. Overall Height: 69.1 in., 71.0 in. with hardtop. Width: 65.3 in. Front/Rear Overhang: 23.5 in./36.3 in. Tailgate: Width and Height: 34.5 in. x. Maximum capacity (Volume Index): 13.6 cu. ft. Front headroom: Soft top/Hardtop: 40.6 in./39.9 in. Front legroom: 39.1 in. Front shoulder room: 53.8 in. Rear shoulder room: 56.3 in. Front hip room: 53.66 in. Floor to ground: 26.1 in.

CAPACITIES: Fuel Tank: 15.0 gal. with standard skid plate. 20.0 gal. optional. Coolant capacity: 10.2 qt.

ACCOMMODATIONS: Seating Capacity: 2/4.

INSTRUMENTATION: Speedometer calibrated in mph/km/hr., odometer, engine coolant temperature, fuel level gauge, gauges for oil pressure and voltmeter.

OPTIONS AND PRICES: Clearcoat metallic paint: $161. Vinyl denim bucket seats: $123. P215/75R15 black tires: $108. P235/75R15 RBL tires: $346. P235/75R15OWL ties: $389. 4.2 liter engine: $361. 5-spd. man. trans.: $250. Auto. trans.: $585. Rear Trac-Lok differential: $255. California emissions system: $116. Renegade Package: $1253. Laredo Package: $2787 (soft top), $3304 (hardtop). Air conditioning: $804. Heavy-duty alternator: $68. Heavy-duty battery: $55. Rear bumperettes: $35. Bumper Access Package: $130. Front and rear floor carpets: $125. Center console: $74. Cold Climate Group: $132. Convenience Group: $96. Heavy-duty cooling system: $57. Cruise control: $204. Decor Group: $99. Deep tinted glass: $138. Drawbar: $50. Extra capacity fuel tank: $57. Extra-Quiet Insulation Group: $199. Halogen fog lamps: $103. Halogen headlamps: $26. Metal doors: $263. Outside passenger side mirror: $18. Power disc brakes: $125. Power steering: $274. AM radio: $123. AM/FM stereo: $204. AM/FM stereo radio with cassette tape player: $348. Rear seat: $275. Roll Bar Accessory Package: $130. Heavy-duty shock absorbers: $40. Spare tire lock: $14. Soft-Feel steering wheel: $59. Body side step: $30.

Heavy-Duty Suspension Package: $118. Soft-Ride Suspension: $56. Tachometer and Rallye clock: $109. Tilt steering wheel: $118. Vinyl soft top: $378. Denim soft top: $402. Hardtop with doors: $889. White styled wheels: $161. Chrome styled wheels: $321.

HISTORICAL FOOTNOTES: AMC executive vice-president Joseph Cappy, acknowledged the greatness of the CJ Jeep by noting, "Completion of CJ production will signal an end of a very important era in Jeep history."

1986 Jeep CJ-7 Laredo

1987 WRANGLER

On May 13, 1986 the new Jeep Wrangler made its debut as a 1987 model. With the exception of its doors and endgate the Wrangler, from the firewall back, used the old CJ body work. All front-end sheet metal ahead of the cowl was new, including hood, fenders, splash apron and the radiator grille guard. The hood had a beveled edge with rounded outer edges. Standard were flexible wheel flares. Incorporated into the Wrangler's exterior body sides were splash shields extending approximately 10 in. back from the front fenders. Five-spoke cast aluminum wheels carrying the Jeep nameplate were used. All Wrangler exterior body panels were constructed of galvanized steel. Standard metal half doors were installed on the soft top Wrangler model. Both the Wrangler's soft top and its optional hardtop were of entirely new design. The soft top incorporated adjustable snaps for a tight fit around the side rails and half-doors. Velcro fasteners were used. The soft top was factory installed and included a bow structure design that made folding of the top up or down relatively simple. The doors also had easily detached soft upper halves and a "bikini-top" effect could be created by the removal of the side and rear windows. Side curtains were used on the soft top with the hardtop having roll-down flush glass side windows and rear tailgate glass. The hardtop also had air extractors to improve performance of the heater and standard air vents. Both versions had standard tinted glass for the windshield. The spare tire was attached to a swing-away tailgate for convenient access to the Wrangler's rear compartment.

The Wrangler's gauges and instrumentation were arranged in a modern ergonomical fashion. If the optional automatic transmission was installed the gear selection panel was positioned directly in front of the steering column. To the column's left was a circular tachometer balanced by the speedometer (which included a trip odometer) to the right side of the column. Extending across the panel were smaller circular gauges for the temperature, fuel level, clock, oil pressure and voltmeter. Controls for the windshield washer/wiper, high beam lights, and optional cruise control, were mounted on the steering column. Integrated into the padded dash were the passenger assist panel, glove box and defroster ducts. The controls for the heating and ventilation systems were lever-activated.

The Base Wrangler was available with a Sport Decor Group option that included an AM/FM monaural radio, Special "Wrangler" hood decals and striping on the lower body side in either silver or tan, Goodyear "All-Terrain" P215/75R15 OWL steel belted radial tires, conventional tire with lock and Convenience Group. The Convenience Group contained courtesy lights with door switches, engine compartment light, intermittent wipers and glove box lock.

1987 Jeep Wrangler

The interior appointments of the Laredo hardtop featured Buffalo grain vinyl seat trim, front and rear carpeting, center console, extra-quiet insulation, leather-wrapped Sport steering wheel and door panels with a carpeted lower third section and a map pocket.

Laredo exterior trim featured a chrome front bumper, rear bumperettes, grille panel headlight bezels, front bumper extensions and tow hooks. Also included were color-keyed wheel flares and full-length mud guards with integrated body sidesteps, deep tinted glass, door-mounted left and right side mirrors, special stripes in silver or brown for the hood and body side with "Laredo" cutouts in the lower body side stripes, P215/75R15 Goodyear Wrangler OWL radial tires and 15 x 7 in., 5-bolt sport aluminum wheels.

Two standard colors were available for the Laredo: Olympic white and classic black. Three extra cost metallic colors were available: Mist silver, mocha brown and garnet. The standard Wrangler was available in those colors plus beige, Colorado red, sun yellow, medium blue metallic and autumn brown metallic. The available soft and hardtop colors were black, white and honey.

On May 8, 1987 a new version of the Wrangler — the entry level S model was introduced. With a base price of $8795, the Wrangler S was equipped with the 2.5 liter engine, 5-speed transmission, soft top, P205/75R15 Wrangler tires and argent steel wheels. Two exterior colors were available for the Wrangler S: Olympic white and classic black. Only four options were offered: Rear seat, full carpeting, power steering and a radio.

1987 Jeep Wrangler S

The upscale Sahara model Wrangler had its first public showing at the March, 1987 Geneva Auto Show in Switzerland. The Sahara was available in two unique exterior colors — Khaki metallic or coffee. It also featured unique tape stripes, "Sahara" logos on the body side and spare tire cover, khaki-colored spoke wheels, khaki soft top (a tan hardtop was optional), as well as khaki-colored interior trim appointments. Other exterior standard equipment features of the Sahara included special fender-mounted fog lights, color-keyed wheel flares and integrated body sidesteps.

The interior had a Trailcloth seat fabric in khaki with tan accents, khaki-color 20-ounce carpeting, map pocket pouches on both door sides, a leather-wrapped steering wheel, center console with padded cover plus an AM/FM electronically-tuned stereo radio. The unique dealer-installed options for the Sahara included a brush-grille guard and a bug screen kit.

I.D. DATA: The V.I.N. consisted of 17 entries. The first three characters identified country, manufacturer and type of vehicle. The fourth (a letter) identified the engine as follows: B-151 cid, 4-cyl.; C-258 cid 6-cyl.; H-304 cid V-8. The fifth character (a letter) identified the transmission. The sixth and seventh characters identified the series and body style. The eighth character identified the GVW rating. Next followed a check digit. The tenth character (a letter) identified the model year. The eleventh character identified the assembly plant. The last six digits were the sequential production numbers. Model identification: Wrangler: 81.

Model Type	Body Type	Factory Price	GVW	Shipping Weight	Prod. Total
Jeep					
Wrangler	Utility	$9899	3000[1]	3022[2]	30,663[3]
Wrangler S	Utility	$8396	3000	2869	—

NOTE 1: 3500 lb. with 6-cyl. engine. A 4500 lb. GVW was optional.
NOTE 2: Shipping weights are for vehicles with 258 engine.
NOTE 3: Calendar year sales, all models.

STANDARD ENGINE: Engine Type: OHV, In-line-4. Cast iron block and cylinder head. Bore x Stroke: 3.88 in. x 3.19 in. Lifters: Hydraulic. Number of main bearings-5. Fuel Induction: electronic fuel injection. Compression Ratio: 9.2:1. Displacement: 150.45 cu. in. (2.5 liters). Horsepower: Net: 117 horsepower at 5000 rpm. Torque: Net: 135 lb.-ft. of torque at 3500 rpm. Oil refill capacity: 5 qt. with filter change. Fuel Requirements: Unleaded.

OPTIONAL ENGINE: Engine Type: OHV, In-line-6. Cast iron block and cylinder head. Bore x Stroke: 3.75 in. x 3.90 in. Lifters: Hydraulic. Number of main bearings-7. Fuel Induction: 1-bbl. Carter model YF. Compression Ratio: 9.2:1. Displacement: 258 cu. in. (4.2 liters). Horsepower: Net 112 @ 3200 rpm. Torque: Net 210 lb.-ft. @ 2000 rpm. Oil refill capacity: 5 qt. with filter change. Fuel Requirements: Unleaded.

CHASSIS FEATURES: Separate body/chassis, tubular, rectangular-shaped frame side-rails, uniform section modulus throughout the side rails.

SUSPENSION AND RUNNING GEAR: Front Suspension: Hotchkiss multi-leaf longitudinal leaf springs. Spring rate: 113 lb./in. 1.375 in. shock absorbers. Stabilizer bar. Optional: Off-Road Package. Includes high-pressure gas charged Fichtel and Sachs shock absorbers and P225/75 R15 Goodyear Wrangler tires. Rear Suspension: Hotchkiss multi-leaf longitudinal leaf springs. Spring rate: 170 lb./in., 1.375 in. shock absorbers. Spring rate: 170 lb./in. Front Axle Type and Capacity: Dana model 30 semi-floating, open end. Capacity: 2200 lb. Rear Axle Type and Capacity: Dana model 35C semi-floating. Capacity: 2700 lb. Axle Ratios: 4-cyl. engine: 4.11:1. 6-cyl. engine: 3.08:1. Optional: 4-cyl.: None. 6-cyl. engine: 3.55:1. Transfer Case: New Process 207 Command-Trac. Ratios: 2.60:1, 1.00:1. Brakes: Type: Hydraulic, front and rear. Dimensions: Front disc, vented cast iron rotor, 11.02 in. dia. Rear: Drum. Lining dimensions: 9.84 in. x 1.77 in. Wheels: 15 x 7.0 JJ. Tires: Base: P215/75R15 RBL Wrangler steel belted tires. Optional: P225/75R15 steel belted radial. Steering: Saginaw recirculating ball system. Ratio: 24.1:1. Turns lock-to-lock: 5.25. Optional: Saginaw power steering. Ratio: 14:1. Turns lock-to-lock: 4.0. Standard Transmission: 4-cyl. models: Aisin 5-speed overdrive

manual. Transmission ratios: 3.93, 2.33, 1.45, 1.00, 0.84:1. Reverse: 3.76:1. Standard Transmission: 4.2 liter engine: Peugeot 5-speed overdrive manual. Transmission ratios: 4.03, 2.39, 1.52, 1.00, 0.72:1. Reverse: 3.76:1. Clutch: Single dry plate. Optional: 6-cyl.: Chrysler No. 999 3-speed automatic transmission. Transmission ratios: 2.74, 1.55, 1.00:1. Reverse: 2.20:1.

VEHICLE DIMENSIONS: Wheelbase: 93.4 in. Overall Length: 152.0 in. (with P215 spare tire), 153.1 in. (with P225 spare tire). Front/Rear Tread: 58.0 in./58.0 in. Overall Height: Open body: 68.6 in. Soft top: 72.0 in. Width: 66.0 in. Front Overhang: 23.9 in. Rear Overhang: To 215 spare: 34.7 in.; to 225 spare: 35.7 in. Approach/Departure Degrees: 30.77/31.50. Ground Clearance: Rear axle: 8.14 in. (running clearance). Skid plate: 9.65 in. (minimum clearance). Maximum capacity (Volume Index): Rear seat removed: 53.4 cu. ft. Rear cargo volume: 12.5 cu. ft. Rear cargo volume with seat folded: 43.2 cu. ft. Front headroom: Soft top/Hardtop: Driver: 41.4 in./40.2 in. Passenger: 41.0 in./40.0 in. Rear headroom: Soft top/Hardtop: 40.3 in./40.541.0 in./40.0 in. Front legroom: Driver: 39.5 in. Passenger: 39.6 in. Front shoulder room: 53.1 in. Rear shoulder room: 56.3 in. Front hip room: 53.1 in. Rear hip room: 36.0 in.

CAPACITIES: Fuel Tank: 15.0 gal. with standard skid plate. 20.0 gal. optional.

ACCOMMODATIONS: Seating Capacity: 2/4.

INSTRUMENTATION: Speedometer calibrated in mph/km/hr., odometer, engine coolant temperature, fuel level gauge, gauges for oil pressure and voltmeter.

OPTIONS: Full length splash shield with built-in body side step. Hardtop (for the base model). Tilt steering wheel. Rear Trac-Loc differential. Air conditioning. Removable front and rear carpeting. Center console. Convenience Group. Floor mats. Leather-wrapped steering wheel. Deep tinted glass (hardtop only). Hardtop. Sport Decor Group. 15 x 7 in. Sport aluminum wheels. Bumper Accessory Package. Cold Climate Group. Cruise control. Drawbar. Halogen fog lights. Power steering. Electric rear window defogger (hardtop only). Heavy-duty cooling (for 6-cyl. engine only). Halogen fog lamps. Heavy-duty alternator. Heavy-duty battery. Automatic transmission. 20 gal. fuel tank. Outside passenger mirror. AM/FM monaural radio. AM/FM electronically tuned stereo. AM/FM ETR cassette stereo with Dolby. All radios were paired with dual speakers.

HISTORICAL FOOTNOTES: AMC executive vice-president Joseph Cappy, acknowledged the greatness of the CJ Jeep by noting, "Completion of CJ production will signal an end of a very important era in Jeep history."

1988 WRANGLER

A number of appearance and convenience features was made standard for the 1988 Wrangler. These included seven new exterior paint choices; two new soft top and hardtop colors (charcoal and tan); two new interior trim colors (charcoal and tan); a new Trailcloth water resistant seat fabric on the Sahara and Laredo models; new-styled, white spoke wheels; net map pockets; and a new fore/aft adjustment capability for the front passenger seat.

1988 Jeep Wrangler Sahara

I.D. DATA: The V.I.N. consisted of 17 entries. The first three characters identified country, manufacturer and type of vehicle. The fourth (a letter) identified the engine as follows: B-151 cid, 4-cyl.; C-258 cid 6-cyl. The fifth character (a letter) identified the transmission. The sixth and seventh characters identified the series and body style. The eighth character identified the GVW rating. Next followed a check digit. The tenth character (a letter) identified the model year. The eleventh character identified the assembly plant. The last six digits were the sequential production numbers. Model identification: Wrangler: 81.

Model Type	Body Type	Factory Price	GVW	Shipping Weight	Prod. Total
Jeep					
Wrangler	Utility	$10,595	3000[1]	3022[2]	39,962[3]
Wrangler S	Utility	$8995	3000	2914	—

NOTE 1: 3500 lb. with 6-cyl. engine. A 4500 lb. GVW was optional.
NOTE 2: Shipping weights are for vehicles with 258 engine.
NOTE 3: Model year sales, all models.

STANDARD ENGINE: Engine Type: OHV, In-line-4. Cast iron block and cylinder head. Bore x Stroke: 3.88 in. x 3.19 in. Lifters: Hydraulic. Number of main bearings-5. Fuel Induction: electronic fuel injection. Compression Ratio: 9.2:1. Displacement: 150.45 cu. in. (2.5 liters). Horsepower: Net: 117 horsepower at 5000 rpm. Torque: Net: 135 lb.-ft. of torque at 3500 rpm. Oil refill capacity: 5 qt. with filter change. Fuel Requirements: Unleaded. Optional Engine. Engine Type: OHV, In-line-6. Cast iron block and cylinder head. Bore x Stroke: 3.75 in. x 3.90 in. Lifters: Hydraulic. Number of main bearings-7. Fuel Induction: 1-bbl. Carter model YF. Compression Ratio: 9.2:1. Displacement: 150.45 cu. in. (4.2 liters). Horsepower: Net 112 @ 3200 rpm. Torque: Net 210 lb.-ft. @ 2000 rpm. Oil refill capacity: 5 qt. with filter change. Fuel Requirements: Unleaded.

CHASSIS FEATURES: Separate body/chassis, tubular, rectangular-shaped frame side-rails, uniform section modulus throughout the side rails.

SUSPENSION AND RUNNING GEAR: Front Suspension: Hotchkiss multi-leaf longitudinal leaf springs. Spring rate: 113 lb./in. 1.375 in. shock absorbers. Stabilizer bar. Optional: Off-Road Package. Includes high-pressure gas charged Fichtel and Sachs shock absorbers and P225/75 R15 Goodyear Wrangler tires. Rear Suspension: Hotchkiss multi-leaf longitudinal leaf springs. Spring rate: 170 lb./in., 1.375 in. shock absorbers. Spring rate: 170 lb./in. Front Axle Type and Capacity: Dana model 30 semi-floating, open end. Capacity: 2200 lb. Rear Axle Type and Capacity: Dana model 35C semi-floating. Capacity: 2700 lb. Axle Ratios: 4-cyl. engine: 4.11:1. 6-cyl. engine: 3.08:1. Optional: 4-cyl.: None. 6-cyl. engine: 3.55:1. Transfer Case: New Process 207 Command-Trac. Ratios: 2.60:1, 1.00:1. Brakes: Type: Hydraulic, front and rear. Dimensions: Front disc, vented cast iron rotor, 11.02 in. dia. Rear: Drum. Lining dimensions: 9.84 in. x 1.77 in. Wheels: 15 x 7.0 JJ. Tires: Base: P215/75R15 RBL Wrangler steel belted tires. Optional: P225/75R15 steel belted radial. Steering: Saginaw Recirculating ball system. Ratio: 24.1:1. Turns lock-to-lock: 5.25. Optional: Saginaw power steering. Ratio: 14:1. Turns lock-to-lock: 4.0. Standard Transmission: 4-cyl. models: Aisin 5-speed overdrive manual. Transmission ratios: 3.93, 2.33, 1.45, 1.00, 0.84:1. Reverse: 3.76:1. Standard Transmission: 4.2 liter engine: Peugeot 5-speed overdrive manual. Transmission ratios: 4.03, 2.39, 1.52, 1.00, 0.72:1. Reverse: 3.76:1. Clutch: Single dry plate. Optional: 6-cyl.: Chrysler No. 999 3-speed automatic transmission. Transmission ratios: 2.74, 1.55, 1.00:1. Reverse: 2.20:1.

VEHICLE DIMENSIONS: Wheelbase: 93.4 in. Overall Length: 152.0 in. (with P215 spare tire), 153.1 in. (with P225 spare tire). Front/Rear Tread: 58.0 in./58.0 in. Overall Height: Open body: 68.6 in., Soft top: 72.0 in. Width: 66.0 in. Front Overhang: 23.9 in. Rear Overhang: To 215 spare: 34.7 in.; to 225 spare: 35.7 in. Approach/Departure Degrees: 30.77/31.50. Ground Clearance: Rear axle: 8.14 in. (running clearance). Skid plate: 9.65 in. (minimum clearance). Maximum capacity (Volume Index): Rear seat removed: 53.4 cu. ft. Rear cargo volume: 12.5 cu. ft. Rear cargo volume with seat folded: 43.2 cu. ft. Front headroom: Soft top/Hardtop: Driver: 41.4 in./40.2 in. Passenger: 41.0 in./40.0 in. Rear headroom: Soft top/Hardtop: 40.3 in./40.541.0 in./40.0 in. Front legroom: Driver: 39.5 in. Passenger: 39.6 in. Front shoulder room: 53.1 in. Rear shoulder room: 56.3 in. Front hip room: 53.1 in. Rear hip room: 36.0 in.

CAPACITIES: Fuel Tank: 15.0 gal. with standard skid plate. 20.0 gal. optional.

ACCOMMODATIONS: Seating Capacity: 2/4.

INSTRUMENTATION: Speedometer calibrated in mph/km/hr., odometer, engine coolant temperature, fuel level gauge, gauges for oil pressure and voltmeter.

OPTIONS AND PRICES: Unchanged from 1987 with exception of new white spoke wheels. Sport Decor Group: $457. Hardtop: $525.

HISTORICAL FOOTNOTES: All Wranglers were covered by a Jeep New Vehicle Limited Warranty providing 12 month/12,000 mile coverage on vehicle components as well as a three-year corrosion protection. In addition, major engine and powertrain components were covered for 36 months/36,000 miles.

1988 Jeep Wrangler Laredo

1989 WRANGLER

For 1989, the Wrangler was available in a new Islander form. The base, S, Laredo, and Sahara were continued. The Islander's highlights included hood, doors and spare tire cover sunset orange graphics. Special Islander body colors included malibu yellow, red, pearl white and Pacific blue. The Islander was fitted with a soft top, full carpeting, door map pockets, P215/75R15 tires, and six-spoke silver painted wheels. Standard equipment for the S model included 2.4 liter engine, 5-speed manual transmission, power brakes, vinyl front bucket seats, tachometer, engine coolant temperature and oil pressure gauges, voltmeter, trip odometer, padded roll bar, soft top, tinted windshield, fuel tank skid plate, and vinyl spare tire cover. The base model had these additional items: Folding rear seat, AM radio, and right outside rearview mirror. The Islander Package included the features of the S and base models plus charcoal colored carpeting, upholstery, soft top, and spare tire cover; door pockets, and charcoal-colored fender flares. The Laredo added the following to the previous items: 4.2 liter engine, power steering, AM/FM stereo radio, carpeted lower door panels with pockets, front bumper extensions with two hooks, chrome front bumper, chrome rear bumperettes, mud guards, side steps, deep-tinted glass, hardtop with full metal doors, courtesy lights, intermittent windshield wipers, center console, tilt steering wheel, halogen fog lights, spare tire lock, off-road gas-charged shock absorbers, and aluminum wheels.

I.D. DATA: The V.I.N. consisted of 17 entries. The first three characters identified country, manufacturer and type of vehicle. The fourth (a letter) identified the engine as follows: B-151 cid, 4-cyl.; C-258 cid 6-cyl. The fifth character (a letter) identified the transmission. The sixth and seventh characters identified the series and body style. The eighth character identified the GVW rating. Next followed a check digit The tenth character (a letter) identified the model year. The eleventh character identified the assembly plant. The last six digits were the sequential production numbers. Model identification: Wrangler: 81.

Model Type	Body Type	Factory Price	GVW	Shipping Weight	Prod. Total
Jeep					
Wrangler Base	Utility	$11,022	3000[1]	3036[2]	51,788[3]
Wrangler S	Utility	$8995	3000	2914	—
Wrangler Islander	Utility	$11,721	3000	—	—
Wrangler Sahara	Utility	$12,853	3000	—	—
Wrangler Laredo	Utility	$14,367	3000	—	—

NOTE 1: 3500 lb. with 6-cyl. engine. A 4500 lb. GVW was optional.
NOTE 2: Shipping weights are for vehicles with 258 engine.
NOTE 3: Model year sales, all models.

STANDARD ENGINE: Engine Type: OHV, In-line-4. Cast iron block and cylinder head. Bore x Stroke: 3.88 in. x 3.19 in. Lifters: Hydraulic. Number of main bearings-5. Fuel Induction: electronic fuel injection. Compression Ratio: 9.2:1. Displacement: 150.45 cu. in. (2.5 liters). Horsepower: Net: 117 horsepower at 5000 rpm. Torque: Net: 135 lb.-ft. of torque at 3500 rpm. Oil refill capacity: 5 qt. with filter change. Fuel Requirements: Unleaded.

OPTIONAL ENGINE: Engine Type: OHV, In-line-6. Cast iron block and cylinder head. Bore x Stroke: 3.75 in. x 3.90 in. Lifters: Hydraulic. Number of main bearings-7. Fuel Induction: 1-bbl. Carter model YF. Compression Ratio: 9.2:1. Displacement: 258 cu. in. (4.2 liters). Horsepower: Net 112 @ 3200 rpm. Torque: Net 210 lb.-ft. @ 2000 rpm. Oil refill capacity: 5 qt. with filter change. Fuel Requirements: Unleaded.

CHASSIS FEATURES: Separate body/chassis, tubular, rectangular-shaped frame side-rails, uniform section modulus throughout the side rails.

SUSPENSION AND RUNNING GEAR: Front Suspension: Hotchkiss multi-leaf longitudinal leaf springs. Spring rate: 113 lb./in. 1.375 in. shock absorbers. Stabilizer bar. Optional: Off-Road Package. Includes high-pressure gas charged Fichtel and Sachs shock absorbers and P225/75 R15 Goodyear Wrangler tires. Rear Suspension: Hotchkiss multi-leaf longitudinal leaf springs. Spring rate: 170 lb./in., 1.375 in. shock absorbers. Spring rate: 170 lb./in. Front Axle Type and Capacity: Dana model 30 semi-floating, open end. Capacity: 2200 lb. Rear Axle Type and Capacity: Dana model 35C semi-floating. Capacity: 2700 lb. Axle Ratios: 4-cyl. engine: 4.11:1. 6-cyl. engine: 3.08:1. Optional: 4-cyl.: None. 6-cyl. engine: 3.55:1. Transfer Case: New Process 207 Command-Trac. Ratios: 2.60:1, 1.00:1. Brakes: Type: Hydraulic, front and rear. Dimensions: Front disc, vented cast iron rotor, 11.02 in. dia. Rear: Drum. Lining dimensions: 9.84 in. x 1.77 in. Wheels: 15 x 7.0 JJ. Tires: Base: P215/75R15 RBL Wrangler steel belted tires. Optional: P225/75R15 steel belted radial. Steering: Saginaw recirculating ball system. Ratio: 24.1:1. Turns Lock-to-Lock: 5.25. Optional: Saginaw power steering. Ratio: 14:1. Turns lock-to-lock: 4.0. Standard Transmission: 4-cyl. models: Aisin 5-speed overdrive manual. Transmission ratios: 3.93, 2.33, 1.45, 1.00, 0.84:1. Reverse: 3.76:1. Standard Transmission: 4.2 liter engine: Peugeot 5-speed overdrive manual. Transmission ratios: 4.03, 2.39, 1.52, 1.00, 0.72:1. Reverse: 3.76:1. Clutch: Single dry plate. Optional: 6-cyl.: Chrysler No. 999 3-speed automatic transmission. Transmission ratios: 2.74, 1.55, 1.00:1. Reverse: 2.20:1.

VEHICLE DIMENSIONS: Wheelbase: 93.4 in. Overall Length: 152.0 in. (with P215 spare tire), 153.1 in. (with P225 spare tire). Front/Rear Tread: 58.0 in./58.0 in. Overall Height: Open body: 68.6 in., Soft top: 72.0 in. Width: 66.0 in. Front Overhang: 23.9 in. Rear Overhang: To 215 spare: 34.7 in.; to 225 spare: 35.7 in. Approach/Departure Degrees: 30.77/31.50. Ground Clearance: Rear axle: 8.14 in. (running clearance). Skid plate: 9.65 in. (minimum clearance). Maximum capacity (Volume Index): Rear seat removed: 53.4 cu. ft. Rear cargo volume: 12.5 cu. ft. Rear cargo volume with seat folded: 43.2 cu. ft. Front headroom: Soft top/Hardtop: Driver: 41.4 in./40.2 in. Passenger: 41.0 in./40.0 in. Rear headroom: Soft top/Hardtop: 40.3 in./40.541.0 in./40.0 in. Front legroom: Driver: 39.5 in. Passenger: 39.6 in. Front shoulder room: 53.1 in. Rear shoulder room: 56.3 in. Front hip room: 53.1 in. Rear hip room: 36.0 in.

CAPACITIES: Fuel Tank: 15.0 gal. with standard skid plate. 20.0 gal. optional.

ACCOMMODATIONS: Seating Capacity: 2/4.

INSTRUMENTATION: Speedometer calibrated in mph/km/hr., odometer, engine coolant temperature, fuel level gauge, gauges for oil pressure and voltmeter.

OPTIONS AND PRICES: 4.2 liter engine: $417. 3-spd. auto. trans.: $497. Power steering: $294. Air conditioning: $861. Rear Trac-Lok differential (not avail. for S model): $273. Trail-cloth fabric seats (Islander): $105. Hardtop (S and base): $596. Hardtop with deep-tinted glass (Islander and Sahara): $748. California Emissions Package: $125. metallic paint (base, Islander and Laredo): $170. Carpeting (S and base): $134. Convenience Group: $182. Cruise control. Requires 4.2 liter engine, auto. trans. and tilt steering wheel: $218.Rear defogger for hardtop: $161. 20 gal. fuel tank. Not avail. for S model: $161. Heavy-duty Alternator and Battery Group. Not avail. for S model: $132. Floormats. Requires carpeting: $32. Off-Road Package: $299 (for base and Islander with 215 black tires), $190 (for base and Islander with 215 or 225 OWL tires), $316 (for Islander with 215 OWL tires). AM radio (S model): $98. AM/FM stereo, extended range radio: $265 (base and Islander), $167 (Sahara and Laredo). Folding rear seat (S model): $446. Tilt steering wheel: $184 (base and Islander), $122 (Sahara and Islander). 215/75R15 OWL tires: $224 (base and Sahara). 225/75R15 OLW tires: $411 (base and Sahara), $313 (Islander), $187 (Laredo). Aluminum wheels: $441 (for Islander with 215 black spare tire), $424 (for Islander with 205 OWL spare, and Islander with 205 OWL spare). 215 OWL conventional spare tire: $126 (Islander). 215 black conventional spare tire: $109 (base and Sahara). 205 OWL spare tire: 109 (base, Islander and Sahara).

HISTORICAL FOOTNOTES: The top Jeep-Eagle dealer in the United States in 1989 was Don-A-Vee Jeep-Eagle of Bellflower, CA which sold 2453 Jeeps in 1989.

1990 WRANGLER

New for 1990 was a standard rear window wiper/washer system for hardtop models. The model lineup for 1990 consisted of Wrangler, Wrangler base, Wrangler Islander, Wrangler Sahara and Wrangler Laredo models. The exterior body color selection consisted of these colors: Bright white, black, graphic red, sand, Pacific blue, Malibu yellow, charcoal grey metallic, navy blue metallic, and khaki metallic. The interior trim for the Wrangler and Wrangler base models included Jeep denim vinyl seats. The Islander had standard charcoal Islander vinyl seats with optional Trailcoat fabric seats available. The Sahara and Laredo Wranglers had Trailcloth fabric seats offered in charcoal, khaki (Sahara only) and sand. Stripe colors for the Islander were available in midnight blue with yellow-orange and bright orange-red accent colors. The Sahara's stripe color was yellow/red. The Laredo stripe colors were light medium silver/dark silver and light sand/dark sand.

I.D. DATA: The V.I.N. consisted of 17 entries. The first three characters identified country, manufacturer and type of vehicle. The fourth (a letter) identified the engine as follows: B-151 cid, 4-cyl.; C-258 cid 6-cyl. The fifth character (a letter) identified the transmission. The sixth and seventh characters identified the series and body style. The eighth character identified the GVW rating. Next followed a check digit. The tenth character (a letter) identified the model year. The eleventh character identified the assembly plant. The last six digits were the sequential production numbers. Model identification: Wrangler base: Y29, Wrangler: Y19.

Model Type	Body Type	Factory Price	GVW	Shipping Weight	Prod. Total
Jeep					
Wrangler Base	Utility	$11,599	3000[1]	3062[2]	58,184[3]
Wrangler	Utility	$9393	3000	9393	—
Wrangler Islander	Utility	—	3000	—	—
Wrangler Sahara	Utility	—	3000	—	—
Wrangler Laredo	Utility	—	3000	—	—

NOTE 1: 3500 lb. with 6-cyl. engine. A 4500 lb. GVW was optional.
NOTE 2: Shipping weights are for vehicles with 258 engine.
NOTE 3: 1990 calendar year production, all models.

STANDARD ENGINE: Engine Type: OHV, In-line-4. Cast iron block and cylinder head. Bore x Stroke: 3.88 in. x 3.19 in. Lifters: Hydraulic. Number of main bearings-5. Fuel Induction: electronic fuel injection. Compression Ratio: 9.2:1. Displacement: 150.45 cu. in. (2.5 liters). Horsepower: Net: 117 horsepower at 5000 rpm. Torque: Net: 135 lb.-ft. of torque at 3500 rpm. Oil refill capacity: 5 qt. with filter change. Fuel Requirements: Unleaded.

OPTIONAL ENGINE: Engine Type: OHV, In-line-6. Cast iron block and cylinder head. Bore x Stroke: 3.75 in. x 3.90 in. Lifters: Hydraulic. Number of main bearings-7. Fuel Induction: 1-bbl. Carter model YF. Compression Ratio: 9.2:1. Displacement: 258 cu. in. (4.2 liters). Horsepower: Net 112 @ 3200 rpm. Torque: Net 210 lb.-ft. @ 2000 rpm. Oil refill capacity: 5 qt. with filter change. Fuel Requirements: Unleaded.

CHASSIS FEATURES: Separate body/chassis, tubular, rectangular-shaped frame side-rails, uniform section modulus throughout the side rails.

SUSPENSION AND RUNNING GEAR: Front Suspension: Hotchkiss multi-leaf longitudinal leaf springs. Spring rate: 113 lb./in. 1.375 in. shock absorbers. Stabilizer bar. Optional: Off-Road Package. Includes high-pressure gas charged Fichtel and Sachs shock absorbers and P225/75 R15 Goodyear Wrangler tires. Rear Suspension: Hotchkiss multi-leaf longitudinal leaf springs. Spring rate: 170 lb./in., 1.375 in. shock absorbers. Spring rate: 170 lb./in. Front Axle Type and Capacity: Dana model 30 semi-floating, open end. Capacity: 2200 lb. Rear Axle Type and Capacity: Dana model 35C semi-floating. Capacity: 2700 lb. Axle Ratios: 4-cyl. engine: 4.11:1. 6-cyl. engine: 3.08:1. Optional: 4-cyl.: None. 6-cyl. engine: 3.55:1. Transfer Case: New Process 207 Command-Trac. Ratios: 2.60:1, 1.00:1. Brakes: Type: Hydraulic, front and rear. Dimensions: Front disc, vented cast iron rotor, 11.02 in. dia. Rear: Drum. Lining dimensions: 9.84 in. x 1.77 in. Wheels: 15 x 7.0 JJ. Tires: Base: P215/75R15 RBL Wrangler steel belted tires. Optional: P225/75R15 steel belted radial. Steering: Saginaw recirculating ball system. Ratio: 24.1:1. Turns lock-to-lock: 5.25. Optional: Saginaw power steering. Ratio: 14:1. Turns lock-to-lock: 4.0. Standard Transmission: 4-cyl. models: Aisin 5-speed overdrive manual. Transmission ratios: 3.93, 2.33, 1.45, 1.00, 0.84:1. Reverse: 3.76:1. Standard Transmission: 4.2 liter engine: Peugeot 5-speed overdrive manual. Transmission ratios: 4.03, 2.39, 1.52, 1.00, 0.72:1. Reverse: 3.76:1. Clutch: Single dry plate. Optional: 6-cyl.: Chrysler No. 999 3-speed automatic transmission. Transmission ratios: 2.74, 1.55, 1.00:1. Reverse: 2.20:1.

VEHICLE DIMENSIONS: Wheelbase: 93.4 in. Overall Length: 152.0 in. (with P215 spare tire), 153.1 in. (with P225 spare tire). Front/Rear Tread: 58.0 in./58.0 in. Overall Height: Open body: 68.6 in., Soft top: 72.0 in. Width: 66.0 in. Front Overhang: 23.9 in. Rear Overhang: To 215 spare: 34.7 in.; to 225 spare: 35.7 in. Approach/Departure Degrees: 30.77/31.50. Ground Clearance: Rear axle: 8.14 in. (running clearance). Skid plate: 9.65 in. (minimum clearance). Maximum capacity (Volume Index): Rear seat removed: 53.4 cu. ft. Rear cargo volume: 12.5 cu. ft. Rear cargo volume with seat folded: 43.2 cu. ft. Front headroom: Soft top/Hardtop: Driver: 41.4 in./40.2 in. Passenger: 41.0 in./40.0 in. Rear headroom: Soft top/Hardtop: 40.3 in./40.541.0 in./40.0 in. Front legroom: Driver: 39.5 in. Passenger: 39.6 in. Front shoulder room: 53.1 in. Rear shoulder room: 56.3 in. Front hip room: 53.1 in. Rear hip room: 36.0 in.

CAPACITIES: Fuel Tank: 15.0 gal. with standard skid plate. 20.0 gal. optional.

ACCOMMODATIONS: Seating Capacity: 2/4.

INSTRUMENTATION: Speedometer calibrated in mph/km/hr., odometer, engine coolant temperature, fuel level gauge, gauges for oil pressure and voltmeter.

OPTIONS AND PRICES: Unchanged from 1989.

HISTORICAL FOOTNOTES: The top Jeep-Eagle dealer for 1990, based upon new unit sales was Don-A-Vee Jeep-Eagle in Bellflower, CA which sold 2,043 units in 1990.

1991 WRANGLER

Changes for 1991 were lead by the replacement of the 4.2 liter engine by the 180 horsepower 4.0 liter engine. This engine was optional on all models except the Renegade version for which it was standard. The 2.5 liter 4-cylinder engine now had sequential multipoint fuel-injection. The rear window wiper on the hardtop model was redesigned. Now monitoring the engine functions on all models was a single board engine control computer. New underhood identification labels highlighted maintenance points. A new optional sound board included two rear Jensen speakers mounted on the Sport bar. This feature was not available for the S model (the S designation returned for 1991). The Wrangler's front seats were new for 1991. They now incorporated driver and passenger backseat recliners (except for Wrangler S) and had wider cushion and backrest pads for increased comfort. A white color replaced charcoal colored soft and hardtops. "Check Engine" and "Maintenance Required" lights were added to the instrument cluster. A number of new exterior colors were offered for the Wrangler. They were: Radiant fire red, steel blue low gloss metallic, dark silver metallic, Navajo turquoise metallic and canyon blue metallic. Additional colors were: Bright white, Malibu yellow, navy blue metallic, and khaki metallic. During the model year sage green low luster was available. The Sahara was available only in khaki metallic. Color selection restrictions also applied to other Wrangler models.

The Islander Decor Group contained floor carpeting, door map net pocket, denim vinyl high-back front bucket seats, color-keyed fender flares and full mud guard with integrated body side step, spare tire cover with Jeep logo, exterior graphics: Hood stripe, lower body stripes, Jeep decal/logo, and Wrangler decal.

The Sahara Decor group contained khaki floor carpeting, door map pouches, sand with khaki accent Trailcloth fabric high-back front bucket seats, leather wrapped steering wheel, khaki vinyl soft top, spare tire cover with special logo, special tape stripes/decal, color-keyed fender flares and full mud guard with integrated body side steps, front black bumper extensions and tow hooks, Convenience Group, fog lamps, power steering, extra-capacity fuel tank, front floor mats, and off-road gas shock absorbers.

The new top-of-the-line Renegade model featured Trailcloth fabric high-back front bucket seats, floor carpeting, front floor mats, leather-wrapped steering wheel, color-keyed fender flares and full mud guard with integrated body steps, body color: Front bumper, rear bumperettes, grille panel, and headlamp bezels; vinyl soft top with half doors, left and right-side door mounted mirrors, special stripes with Renegade decal, Convenience Group, extra-capacity fuel tank, fog lamps, power steering, and off-road gas shock absorbers. The Renegade's standard tires were specially developed Goodyear Wranglers that measured 29 in. tall by 9.5 in. Exterior monochromatic colors for the Renegade were radiant fire red, bright white and black. The Laredo model was cancelled for 1991. Other items or features cancelled for 1991 were the following: Cruise control, bronze-tone deep tinted glass and P205/75R15 OWL tires. Exterior colors cancelled for 1991 were: Sand, graphic red, Pacific blue and charcoal grey. Standard for all models were double-bited keys. Additional standard features included 75 amp alternator, front ashtray, 58-430 cold crank battery, front mini floor mat, cigarette lighter, front frame overlay, fuel tank skid plate, tinted windshield glass, heater and defroster, halogen headlights, single horn, inside 8.5 in. day/night mirror, left outside mirror, padded sun visors, padded instrument panel, rear swing away tailgate spare tire mount, Sport bar with side bars and padding (padding not included on Wrangler S), three-spoke Soft-Feel steering wheel, and two-speed electric windshield wipers and washers.

I.D. DATA: The V.I.N. consisted of 17 entries. The first entry, a number, identified the country of manufacture (1-U.S., 2-Canada). The next character, a number, identified the vehicle type (4-MPV). The next item, a letter, was the GVW designation. (E-3001-4000, F-4001-5000). The next character, a letter identified the model line (Y-Wrangler). A number followed that identified the series (1-S, 2-Base, 3-Islander, 4-Sahara, 5-Laredo). The body identification in the form of a letter was next (9-2-door open body). The engine identification was next in the form of a letter (P-2.5 liter, S-4.0 liter). A check digit followed. The letter M indicating the 1991 model year was next. The plant location was identified by a letter (J-Brampton). The sequential serial number followed. Body type identification: Wrangler-YJJL77. Decor Trim identification: Wrangler S-ARK, Wrangler Base-ALA, Wrangler Islander-ARR, Wrangler Sahara-ARS, Wrangler Renegade-ARJ.

Model Type	Body Type	Factory Price	GVW	Shipping Weight	Prod. Total
Jeep					
Wrangler S	Utility	$9910	4300	—	—
Wrangler Base	Utility	$12,356	4300	2934[1]	—

NOTE 1: Curb weight with 2.5 liter engine, with 4.0 liter engine-3083 lb.

STANDARD ENGINE: Engine Type: OHV, In-line-4. Cast iron block and cylinder head. Bore x Stroke: 3.88 in. x 3.19 in. Lifters: Hydraulic. Number of main bearings-5. Fuel Induction: multi-point electronic fuel injection. Compression Ratio: 9.2:1. Displacement: 150.45 cu. in. (2.5 liters). Horsepower: Net: 123 horsepower at 5250 rpm. Torque: Net: 139 lb.-ft. of torque at 3250 rpm. Oil refill capacity: 5 qt. with filter change. Fuel Requirements: Unleaded.

OPTIONAL ENGINE: Engine Type: OHV, In-line-6. Cast iron block and cylinder head. Bore x Stroke: 3.88 in. x 3.41 in. Lifters: Hydraulic. Number of main bearings-7. Fuel Induction: multi-point electronic fuel injection. Compression Ratio: 9.2:1. Displacement: 242 cu. in. (4.2 liters). Horsepower: Net 180 @ 4750 rpm. Torque: Net 220 lb.-ft. @ 4000 rpm. Oil refill capacity: 5 qt. with filter change. Fuel Requirements: Unleaded.

CHASSIS FEATURES: Separate body/chassis, tubular, rectangular-shaped frame side-rails, uniform section modulus throughout the side rails.

SUSPENSION AND RUNNING GEAR: Front Suspension: Hotchkiss multi-leaf longitudinal leaf springs. Spring rate: 113 lb./in. 1.375 in. shock absorbers. Optional: Off-Road Package. Includes high-pressure gas charged Fichtel and Sachs shock absorbers and P225/75 R15 Goodyear Wrangler tires. Rear Suspension: Hotchkiss multi-leaf longitudinal leaf springs. Spring rate: 170 lb./in., 1.375 in. shock absorbers. Spring rate: 170 lb./in. Front Axle Type and Capacity: Dana model 30 semi-floating, open end. Capacity: 2200 lb. Rear Axle Type and Capacity: Dana model 35C semi-floating. Capacity: 2700 lb. Axle Ratios: 4-cyl. engine: 4.11:1. 6-cyl. engine: 3.08:1 (with manual trans.), 3.55:1 (with auto. trans.). Optional: None. Transfer Case: New Process 231 Command-Trac. Ratios: 2.721, 1.00:1. Brakes: Type: Hydraulic, front and rear. Dimensions: Front disc, vented cast iron rotor, 11.02 in. dia. Rear: Drum. Lining dimensions: 9.84 in. x 1.77 in. Wheels: Wrangler S: Styled steel argent 15 x 6 with black hubs. Wrangler base and Islander: Styled steel silver six-spoke 15 x 7 in. with black hubs. Wrangler Sahara: Styled steel khaki six spoke 15 x 7 in., black hubs. Wrangler Renegade: Aluminum five hole 15 x 8 in. Optional: Five-spoke aluminum 15 x 7 in. wheels. Tires: Wrangler S: P205/75R15 black sidewall Wrangler steel belted tires. Wrangler base and Sahara: P215/75R15 black sidewall All-Terrain. Wrangler Islander: P215/75R OWL All-Terrain. Wrangler Renegade: 29 x 9.6R15LT OWL All-Terrain. Optional: P215/75R15 OWL Wrangler All-Terrain. (available for Base model only). P225/75R1,OWL Wrangler All-Terrain. (available for S, base and Islander). Steering: Wrangler S, base and Islander: Saginaw Recirculating ball system. Ratio: 24.1:1. Wrangler Sahara and Renegade: Saginaw variable ratio power steering. Ratio: 16:13:1. Optional: For Wrangler S, base and Islander: Saginaw variable ratio power steering. Standard Transmission: 4-cyl. models: Aisin 5-speed overdrive manual. Transmission ratios: 3.93, 2.33, 1.45, 1.00, 0.84:1. Reverse: 3.76:1. Standard Transmission: 4.2 liter engine: Peugeot 5-speed overdrive manual. Transmission ratios: 4.03, 2.39, 1.52, 1.00, 0.72:1. Reverse: 3.76:1. Clutch: 2.5 liter engine: 9.1 in. dia., 4.0 liter engine: 10.5 in. dia. Single dry plate. Optional: 6-cyl.: Chrysler No. 999 3-speed automatic transmission. Transmission ratios: 2.74, 1.55, 1.00:1. Reverse: 2.20:1.

VEHICLE DIMENSIONS: Wheelbase: 93.4 in. Overall Length: 152.6 in. (with P215 spare tire). Front/Rear Tread: 58.0 in./58.0 in. Overall Height: Open body: 68.6 in., Soft top: 72.0 in., Hardtop: 69.5 in. Width: (except Renegade) 66.0 in. Front Overhang: 23.9 in. Rear overhang: To 215 spare: 34.7 in.; to 225 spare: 35.7 in. Approach/Departure Degrees: 32.4/36.1. Ground Clearance: Front axle: 8.1 in. Rear axle: 8.1 in. Minimum running clearance: 9.7 in. Maximum capacity (Volume Index): Rear seat removed: 53.4 cu. ft. Rear cargo volume: 12.5 cu. ft. Rear cargo volume with seat folded: 43.2 cu. ft. Front headroom: Soft top/Hardtop: Driver: 41.4 in./40.2 in. Passenger: 41.0 in./40.0 in. Rear headroom: Soft top/Hardtop: 40.3 in./40.5. Front legroom: Driver: 39.4 in. Passenger: 39.0 in. Front shoulder room: 53.1 in. Rear shoulder room: 56.3 in. Front hip room: 53.1 in. Rear hip room: 36.0 in.

CAPACITIES: Fuel Tank: Wrangler DS, Base and Islander: 15.0 gal. with standard skid plate. 20.0 gal. optional. 20.0 gal. tank standard for Sahara and Renegade.

ACCOMMODATIONS: Seating Capacity: 2/4.

INSTRUMENTATION: Speedometer calibrated in mph/km/hr., odometer, engine coolant temperature, fuel level gauge, gauges for oil pressure and voltmeter.

OPTIONS AND PRICES: Metallic paint: $173. Carpeting and rear seat for Wrangler S: $75. Reclining bucket seats with Trailcloth trim: $107. Black, white, dark sand or red hardtop with full doors, wiper/washer: $755 (with tinted glass); $923 (with grey-tone deep tinted glass). 4.0 liter engine: $612. Auto. trans.: $573. Rear Trac-Lok differential: $278. California emission system: $128. Islander Decor Group: $738. Sahara Decor Group: $1886. Renegade Decor Group: $4266. Air conditioning: $878. Body side steps: $73. Rear black bumperettes: $36. Floor carpeting: $137. Convenience Group: $233. Center console: $170. Rear window defroster: $164. Extra-capacity fuel tank: $62. Heavy-Duty Alternator/Battery Group: $135. Right outside mirror: $27. Off-Road Package: $549. Power steering: $300. AM/FM extended range stereo radio with two speakers: $270. AM/FM extended range stereo radio with cassette tape player and two speakers: $534. Sound bar: $204. Fold and tumble rear seat: $455. Tilt steering column: $193. Five hole aluminum wheels: $399.

HISTORICAL FOOTNOTES: Jeep reported that the typical Wrangler buyer had these characteristics: Average age: 29; average income: $34,000. They were most often single and were usually male.

1992 WRANGLER

For 1992 the Sahara Decor Group was freshened by the availability of new low gloss sand and sage green exterior paints. A new interior color — Dark green was introduced for the Sahara as was a unique 15 x 7 in. full-face steel wheel painted low gloss sand with sand color hub cover. The Sahara also had new exterior graphics.

Additional changes for 1992 included the use of a new radio with a clock function, a Gauge Package with four-wheel drive indicator graphic, three new exterior colors — Bright copper, low gloss sage green and low gloss sand, and three-point rear sear belts.

1992 Jeep Wrangler Sahara

I.D. DATA: The V.I.N. consisted of 17 entries. The first entry a number identified the country of manufacture (1-U.S., 2-Canada). The next character, a number, identified the vehicle type (4-MPV). The next item, a letter, was the GVW designation. (E-3001-4000, F-4001-5000). The next character, a letter identified the model line (Y-Wrangler). A number followed that identified the series (1-S, 2-Base, 3-Islander, 4-Sahara, 5-Laredo). The body identification in the form of a letter was next (9-Two-door open body). The engine identification was next in the form of a letter (P-2.5 liter, S-4.0 liter). A check digit followed. The letter M indicating the 1991 model year was next. The plant location was identified by a letter (J-Brampton). The sequential serial number followed. Body type identification: Wrangler-YJJL77, add the following Decor trim identification: Wrangler S-ARK, Wrangler Base-ALA, Wrangler Islander-ARR, Wrangler Sahara-ARS, Wrangler Renegade-ARJ.

Model Type	Body Type	Factory Price	GVW	Shipping Weight	Prod. Total
Jeep					
Wrangler S	Utility	$9910	4300	—	—
Wrangler Base	Utility	$12,356	4300	2934[1]	—

NOTE 1: Curb weight with 2.5 liter engine, with 4.0 liter engine-3083 lb.

STANDARD ENGINE: Engine Type: OHV, In-line-4. Cast iron block and cylinder head. Bore x Stroke: 3.88 in. x 3.19 in. Lifters: Hydraulic. Number of main bearings-5. Fuel Induction: multi-point electronic fuel injection. Compression Ratio: 9.2:1. Displacement: 150.45 cu. in. (2.5 liters). Horsepower: Net: 123 horsepower at 5250 rpm. Torque: Net: 139 lb.-ft. of torque at 3250 rpm. Oil refill capacity: 5 qt. with filter change. Fuel Requirements: Unleaded.

OPTIONAL ENGINE: Engine Type: OHV, In-line-6. Cast iron block and cylinder head. Bore x Stroke: 3.88 in. x 3.41 in. Lifters: Hydraulic. Number of main bearings-7. Fuel Induction: Multi-point electronic fuel injection. Compression Ratio: 9.2:1. Displacement: 242 cu. in. (4.2 liters). Horsepower: Net 180 @ 4750 rpm. Torque: Net 220 lb.-ft. @ 4000 rpm. Oil refill capacity: 5 qt. with filter change. Fuel Requirements: Unleaded.

CHASSIS FEATURES: Separate body/chassis, tubular, rectangular-shaped frame side-rails, uniform section modulus throughout the side rails.

SUSPENSION AND RUNNING GEAR: Front Suspension: Hotchkiss multi-leaf longitudinal leaf springs. Spring rate: 113 lb./in. 1.375 in. shock absorbers. Optional: Off-Road Package. Includes high-pressure gas charged Fichtel and Sachs shock absorbers and P225/75 R15 Goodyear Wrangler tires. Rear Suspension: Hotchkiss multi-leaf longitudinal leaf springs. Spring rate: 170 lb./in., 1.375 in. shock absorbers. Spring rate: 170 lb./in. Front Axle Type and Capacity: Dana model semi-floating, open end. Capacity: 2200 lb. Rear Axle Type and Capacity: Dana model 35C semi-floating. Capacity: 2700 lb. Axle Ratios: 4-cyl. engine: 4.11:1. 6-cyl. engine: 3.08:1 (with manual trans.), 3.55:1 (with auto. trans.). Optional: None. Transfer Case: New Process 231 Command-Trac. Ratios: 2.721, 1.00:1. Brakes: Type: Hydraulic, front and rear. Dimensions: Front disc, vented cast iron rotor, 11.02 in. dia. Rear: Drum. Lining dimensions: 9.84 in. x 1.77 in. Wheels: Wrangler S: Styled steel argent 15 x 6 with black hubs. Wrangler Base and Islander: Styled steel silver six-spoke 15 x 7 in. with black hubs. Wrangler Sahara: Styled steel khaki six spoke 15 x 7 in., black hubs. Wrangler Renegade: Aluminum five hole 15 x 8 in. Optional: Five-spoke aluminum 15 x 7 in. wheels. Tires: Wrangler S: P205/75R15 black sidewall Wrangler steel belted tires. Wrangler base and Sahara: P215/75R15 black sidewall All-Terrain. Wrangler Islander: P215/75R OWL All-Terrain. Wrangler Renegade: 29 x 9.6R15LT OWL All-Terrain. Optional: P215/75R15 OWL Wrangler All-Terrain. (available for base model only). P225/75R1,OWL Wrangler All-Terrain. (available for S, base and Islander). Steering: Wrangler S, base and Islander: Saginaw recirculating ball system. Ratio: 24.1:1. Wrangler Sahara and Renegade: Saginaw variable ratio power steering. Ratio: 16:13:1. Optional: For Wrangler S, base and Islander: Saginaw variable ratio power steering. Standard Transmission: 4-cyl. models: Aisin 5-speed overdrive manual. Transmission ratios: 3.93, 2.33, 1.45, 1.00, 0.84:1. Reverse: 3.76:1. Standard Transmission: 4.2 liter engine: Peugeot 5-speed overdrive manual. Transmission ratios: 4.03, 2.39, 1.52, 1.00, 0.72:1. Reverse: 3.76:1. Clutch: 2.5 liter engine: 9.1 in. dia., 4.0 liter engine: 10.5 in. dia. Single dry plate. Optional: 6-cyl.: Chrysler No. 999 3-speed automatic transmission. Transmission ratios: 2.74, 1.55, 1.00:1. Reverse: 2.20:1.

VEHICLE DIMENSIONS: Wheelbase: 93.4 in. Overall Length: 152.6 in. (with P215 spare tire). Front/Rear Tread: 58.0 in./58.0 in. Overall Height: Open body: 68.6 in., Soft top: 72.0 in. Hardtop: 69.5 in. Width: (except Renegade) 66.0 in. Front Overhang: 23.9 in. Rear overhang: To 215 spare: 34.7 in.; to 225 spare: 35.7 in. Approach/Departure Degrees: 32.4/36.1. Ground

Clearance: Front axle: 8.1 in. Rear axle: 8.1 in. Minimum running clearance: 9.7 in. Maximum capacity (Volume Index): Rear seat removed: 53.4 cu. ft. Rear cargo volume: 12.5 cu. ft. Rear cargo volume with seat folded: 43.2 cu. ft. Front headroom: Soft top/Hardtop: Driver: 41.4 in./40.2 in. Passenger: 41.0 in./40.0 in. Rear headroom: Soft top/Hardtop: 40.3 in./40.5. Front legroom: Driver: 39.4 in. Passenger: 39.0 in. Front shoulder room: 53.1 in. Rear shoulder room: 56.3 in. Front hip room: 53.1 in. Rear hip room: 36.0 in.

CAPACITIES: Fuel Tank: Wrangler DS, base and Islander: 15.0 gal. with standard skid plate. 20.0 gal. optional. 20.0 gal. tank standard for Sahara and Renegade.

ACCOMMODATIONS: Seating Capacity: 2/4.

INSTRUMENTATION: Speedometer calibrated in mph/km/hr., odometer, engine coolant temperature, fuel level gauge, gauges for oil pressure and voltmeter.

OPTIONS: New options for 1992 included rear bumperettes for the S model, a Bright Package and cloth seat for the base model and a leather-wrapped steering wheel for the base and Islander models.

HISTORICAL FOOTNOTES: Jeep was a charter member of the "Tread Lightly" program, and also supported educational programs designed to promote an off-roader's code of ethics.

1992 Jeep Wrangler

1993 WRANGLER

Changes for 1993 consisted of a stainless steel exhaust system, the availability of a four-wheel anti-lock brake system with the 4.0 liter engine, a tamper resistant odometer, four new exterior colors: Flame red, grey mist, light champagne and deep blue, and blue/grey tinted quarter and rear windows for the soft top.

1993 Jeep Wrangler Sport

I.D. DATA: The V.I.N. consisted of 17 entries.

Total Prices of the Jeep Wrangler models (Wrangler S, base, Sahara and Renegade) were not available at press time.

STANDARD ENGINE: Engine Type: OHV, In-line-4. Cast iron block and cylinder head. Bore x Stroke: 3.88 in. x 3.19 in. Lifters: Hydraulic. Number of main bearings: 5. Fuel Induction: Multi-point electronic fuel injection. Compression Ratio: 9.1:1. Displacement: 150.45 cu. in. (2.5 liters). Horsepower: Net: 123 horsepower at 5250 rpm. Torque: Net: 139 lb.-ft. of torque at 3250 rpm. Oil refill capacity: 5 qt. with filter change. Fuel Requirements: Unleaded.

OPTIONAL ENGINE: Engine Type: OHV, In-line-6. Cast iron block and cylinder head. Bore x Stroke: 3.88 in. x 3.41 in. Lifters: Hydraulic. Number of main bearings: 7. Fuel Induction: Multi-point electronic fuel injection. Compression Ratio: 8.8:1. Displacement: 242 cu. in. (4.2 liters). Horsepower: Net 180 @ 4750 rpm. Torque: Net 220 lb.-ft. @ 4000 rpm. Oil refill capacity: 5 qt. with filter change. Fuel Requirements: Unleaded.

CHASSIS FEATURES: Separate body/chassis, tubular, rectangular-shaped frame side-rails, uniform section modulus throughout the side rails.

SUSPENSION AND RUNNING GEAR: Front Suspension: Hotchkiss multi-leaf longitudinal leaf springs, Spring rate: 113 lb./in. 1.375 in. shock absorbers. Optional: Off-Road Package. Rear Suspension: Hotchkiss multi-leaf longitudinal leaf springs. Spring rate: 170 lb./in., 1.375 in. shock absorbers. Front Axle Type and Capacity: Dana model 30 Semi-floating, open end. Rear Axle Type and Capacity: Dana model 35C semi-floating. Axle Ratios: 4-cyl. engine: 4.11:1. 6-cyl. engine: 3.07:1. Optional: 3.55:1 Non-Trac-Lok for High Altitude Emissions

Package; 3.55:1 Trac-Lok optional for 4.0 liter engine. Transfer Case: New Process 231 Command-Trac. Ratios: 2.721, 1.00:1. Brakes: Type: Hydraulic, front and rear. Dimensions: Front disc, vented cast iron rotor, 11.2 in. dia. Rear: Drum. Lining dimensions: 9.00 in. dia. Optional: ABS power front disc and rear drum. Wheels: Wrangler S: steel 15 x 6. Wrangler Base: Styled steel 15 x 7 in. Wrangler Sahara: Full face steel 15 x 7 in. Wrangler Renegade: Aluminum 15 x 7 in. Tires: Wrangler S: P205/75R15 black sidewall Wrangler steel belted tires. Wrangler Base and Sahara: P215/75R15 black sidewall Wrangler All-Terrain. Wrangler Renegade: 29 x 9.6R15LT OWL All-Terrain. Optional: S, Base and Sahara: P215/75R15 OWL All-Terrain Wrangler, P225/75R15 OWL Traction tread off-road. Steering: Wrangler S, base: Saginaw recirculating ball system. Ratio: 24.1:1. Wrangler Sahara and Renegade: Saginaw variable ratio power steering. Ratio: 16:13:1. Optional: For Wrangler S and base: Saginaw variable ratio power steering. Standard Transmission: 4-cyl. models: Aisin 5-speed overdrive manual. Transmission ratios: 3.93, 2.33, 1.45, 1.00, 0.84:1. Reverse: 3.76:1. Standard Transmission: 4.2 liter engine: Peugeot 5-speed overdrive manual. Transmission ratios: 4.03, 2.39, 1.52, 1.00, 0.72:1. Reverse: 3.76:1. Clutch: 2.5 liter engine: 9.1 in. dia., 4.0 liter engine: 10.5 in. dia. Single dry plate. Optional: 6-cyl.: Chrysler No. 999 3-speed automatic transmission. Transmission ratios: 2.74, 1.55, 1.00:1. Reverse: 2.20:1.

VEHICLE DIMENSIONS: Wheelbase: 93.4 in. Overall Length: 152.6 in. (with P215 spare tire). Front/Rear Tread: 58.0 in./58.0 in. Overall Height: Open body: 68.6 in. Soft top: 72.0 in. Hardtop: 69.5 in. Width: (except Renegade) 66.0 in. Front Overhang: 23.9 in. Rear overhang: To 215 spare: 34.7 in.; to 225 spare: 35.7 in. Approach/Departure Degrees: 32.4/36.1. Ground Clearance: Front axle: 8.1 in. Rear axle: 8.1 in. Minimum running clearance: 9.7 in. Maximum capacity (Volume Index): Rear seat removed: 53.4 cu. ft. Rear cargo volume: 12.5 cu. ft. Rear cargo volume with seat folded: 43.2 cu. ft. Front headroom: Soft top/Hard top: Driver: 41.4 in./40.2 in. Passenger: 41.0 in./40.0 in. Rear headroom: Soft top/Hard top: 40.3 in./40.5 in. Front legroom: Driver: 39.4 in. Passenger: 39.0 in. Front shoulder room: 53.1 in. Rear shoulder room: 56.3 in. Front hip room: 53.1 in. Rear hip room: 36.0 in.

CAPACITIES: Fuel Tank: 15.0 gal. with standard skid plate; 20.0 gal. tank standard for Sahara and Renegade and optional for all others.

ACCOMMODATIONS: Seating Capacity: 2/4.

INSTRUMENTATION: Speedometer calibrated in mph/km/hr., tamper resistant odometer, engine coolant temperature, fuel level gauge, gauges for oil pressure and voltmeter.

OPTIONS: Metallic paint. Carpeting and rear seat for Wrangler S. Reclining bucket seats with Trailcloth trim. Hardtop with full doors. 4.0 liter engine. Auto. trans. Rear Trac-Lok differential. California emission system. Air conditioning. Body side steps. Rear black bumperettes. Floor carpeting. Convenience Group. Center console. Rear window defroster. Extra-capacity fuel tank. Heavy-Duty Alternator/Battery Group. Right outside mirror. Off-Road Package. Power steering. AM/FM extended range stereo radio with two speakers. AM/FM extended range stereo radio with cassette tape player and two speakers. Sound bar. Fold and tumble rear seat. Tilt steering column.

HISTORICAL FOOTNOTES: Chrysler Corporation reported that the "Jeep Wrangler is an icon-synonymous with four-wheel drive... the ultimate, affordable, no-compromise fun and freedom machine."

1993 Jeep Wrangler

JEEP PICKUP TRUCKS
1947-1965

1947 PICKUP TRUCKS

In May, 1947 Willys-Overland introduced a new line of two and four-wheel drive trucks. From 1937 through 1942 Willys-Overland had marketed a pickup truck with a front end virtually identical to its passenger car's and with either a stake-platform or pickup bed. The postwar trucks also had a front end appearance and general styling theme that linked them to the Willys-Overland station wagon models. The straight-forward appearance of the trucks supported Willys' promise to avoid annual model changes merely for the sake of change while making continuing refinements and improvements. Initial model designations for the postwar four-wheel drive truck was 4T. The very early trucks (up to serial number 10342-four-wheel drive were fitted with doors having stationary vent windows. Beyond that point they were movable.

External identification of the earliest models as Willys-Overland products was limited to a W-O logo on the tailgate. This was soon supplanted by a "Jeep Truck" plate mounted on the hood. A 2-spoke steering wheel was used with a large "W-O" logo mounted on the center horn button.

The four-wheel drive models, with a 1 ton rating, had shipping weights of 3,205 pounds (pickup) and 3,431 pounds (platform). Willys also offered 12 other body and chassis forms including canopy tops and demountable steel van versions. The trucks could be equipped with either front or rear power take-off kits.

A divided front seat was standard. A centrally-located instrument cluster assembly was also standard It included a large square speedometer reading from 0 to 80 mph. An odometer was also installed. To the left of the cluster were the fuel and ammeter gauges, balanced on the right by oil pressure and temperature gauges. The windshield wiper control knob was mounted just below the windshield division. Beneath the instrument cluster, from left to right, were the ignition, main light switch, receptacle for the optional cigarette lighter and the choke control. On either side of the main instrument panel cluster were recessed panels with the right side serving as the glove box. The instrument cluster had an engine-turned aluminum finish A burnt coffee color was used for wiper control, cowl ventilator knobs, window regulators and door lock knobs. The ashtray cover was painted. A small garnish molding for the center windshield divider was used. A revised door garnish molding was adopted after serial number 10342-four-wheel drive which fully encircled the window frame instead of just covering the lower portion. Coral grey colored armrests were standard. Either brown or black floor mats in conjunction with either a basket weave were used a gray headliner.

Willys included a tool-kit containing an adjustable nine-inch wrench and handle, hammer, pliers, screwdriver and sparkplug wrench as standard truck equipment.

Willys offered its trucks in a any of a dozen colors choices including Emerald green, Harvard red, jungle green, Luzon red, Manila blue, Michigan yellow, Potomac grey, Princeton black, Tarawa green, tropical silver, universal beige and wake ivory.

1947 Jeep pickup truck

I.D. DATA: The serial number was located on a plate found on the outside of the left frame side rail at the front and also on the left of the driver's seat on the floor riser. The engine number was stamped on top of the cylinder block water pump boss. Serial number range: 10001 to 12346.

Body Type	Factory Price	GVW	Shipping Weight	Prod. Total
Model four-wheel drive (1 ton, four-wheel drive, 118 in. wheelbase)				
Chassis	$1,175	5300	1974	4114*
Chassis and Cab	$1,529	5300	2809	—
Pickup	$1,620	5300	3129	—
Stake	$1,685	5300	3431	—

* Output of all four-wheel drive trucks for 1947.

STANDARD ENGINE: Engine Type: L-head (side valve) In-line-4. Cast iron block and cylinder head. Bore x Stroke: 3.125 in. x 4.375 in. Lifters: Solid. Number of main bearings-3. Fuel Induction: Carter single barrel carburetor, model 626. Compression Ratio: 6.47:1.

Optional: High altitude cylinder head with a 7.0:1 compression ratio. Displacement: 134.2 cu. in. (2.19 liters). Horsepower: 60 @ 4000 rpm. Torque: 106 lb.-ft. @ 2000 rpm. Oil refill capacity: 4 qt. Fuel Requirements: Regular.

CHASSIS FEATURES: Separate body and chassis. Channel steel frame side rails. Six cross members. Dimensions: 5.5 in. x 2.0 in. x 0.179 in. Section modulus: 2.581 cu. in.

SUSPENSION AND RUNNING GEAR: Front Suspension: Nine leaf semi-elliptical springs, 36.25 in. x by 1.75 in. Compression rate: 303 lb./in. Double acting shock absorbers. Rear Suspension: Eleven leaf semi-elliptical springs, 50 in. x 2.0 inches. Spring rate: 370/410 lb./ in. Double acting shock absorbers. Front Axle Type: Spicer model 25 full-floating. Axle ratio: 5.38:1. Rear Axle Type: Semi-floating Timken model 51540. Axle Ratio: 5.38:1. Optional: 6.17, 4.88:1. Transfer Case: Ratios: Spicer model 18. Ratios: 2.43, 1.0:1. Brakes: Type: Hydraulic, front and rear. Dimensions: Front and rear: 11.00 in. x 2.0 in. Wheels: 16 x 5.00. Tires: 7.00 x 16 in. 6-ply. Steering: Cam and twin pin lever, variable ratio. Ratio: 15.4-13.5-10.54:1. Turning circle: 50 ft. Optional None. Standard Transmission: Warner ASI-T909E 3-speed manual transmission. Transmission ratios: 3.44, 1.85 and 1.1:1. Optional: None. Clutch: 8.5 in. dia. Auburn single dry plate clutch with a 120 lb.-ft. of torque capacity. Single dry plate. Total plate pressure: 183-203 lb. Optional: None.

VEHICLE DIMENSIONS: Wheelbase: 118 in. Overall Length: 183.75 in. Front/Rear Tread: 56 in./63.5 in. Overall Height: 74.5 in. Width: Pickup models: 66.625 in. Stake platform: 73.156 in. Front/Rear Overhang: 25.75 in./40 in. Tailgate: Width and Height: 48.50 in. x 15.75 in. Approach/Departure Degrees: 48/50. Ground Clearance: 8.125 in. Load space: Pickup: 80 in. x 48.5 in. Platform body: 81.5 in. x 73 in.

CAPACITIES: Fuel Tank: 15.0 gal. Optional: None. Coolant system: 11 qt.

ACCOMMODATIONS: Seating Capacity: Three.

INSTRUMENTATION: 0-80 mph speedometer, odometer, fuel, ammeter, oil pressure and temperature gauges.

OPTIONS: Zenith, Detroit and Philco radios with speakers mounted in the instrument panel or cowl trim pad. Heater-defroster. Cigarette lighter. Sun visors. Interior and exterior rearview mirrors. License plate frame. Dual horns. Lockable gas cap. Tire pump. Spare tire lock. Dual taillights. Foglights or combination fog-driving lights. Gasoline filter. Starter crank. Spotlight. Underhood light and a deluxe tool kit. Fire extinguisher. Tire inflator. Directional signals. Summer insect bug screen. Winter grille front. Right-hand drive. Front-mounted drum type winch. Power take-off.

HISTORICAL FOOTNOTES: In the first nine months of 1947 Willys-Overland earned a profit of $2,329,900

1948 PICKUP TRUCKS

1948 Jeep model 4T Canopy truck

Willys announced the adoption of a new "four-wheel drive" model identification for its four-wheel drive trucks on March 5, 1948. The first truck with this new designation, serial number 15251-four-wheel drive was built on February 10, 1948.

Until serial number 26719-four-wheel drive the instrument cluster had an engine-turned aluminum finish which at that point was replaced by an aluminum painted mask with black decorative lines. Those built after serial number 23710-four-wheel drive had Ivory-colored controls for the wiper control, cowl ventilator knobs, window regulators and door lock knobs The armrests on trucks produced after 23710-four-wheel drive were Ivory-colored.

I.D. DATA: The serial number was located on a plate found on the outside of the left frame side rail at the front and also on the left of the driver's seat on the floor riser. The engine number was stamped on top of the cylinder block water pump boss. Serial number range: 12347 to 30575.

Body Type	Factory Price	GVW	Shipping Weight	Prod. Total
Model four-wheel drive (1 ton, four-wheel drive, 118 in. wheelbase)				
Chassis and Cab	$1,652	5300	2809	41,462*
Pickup	$1,743	5300	3129	—
Stake	$1,807	5300	3431	—

* Includes both two- and four-wheel drive trucks.

STANDARD ENGINE: Engine Type: L-head (side valve) In-line-4. Cast iron block and cylinder head. Bore x Stroke: 3.125 in. x 4.375 in. Lifters: Solid. Number of main bearings-3. Fuel Induction: Carter single barrel carburetor, model 626. Compression Ratio: 6.47:1. Optional: High altitude cylinder head with a 7.0:1 compression ratio. Displacement: 134.2 cu. in. (2.19 liters). Horsepower: 60 @ 4000 rpm. Torque: 106 lb.-ft. @ 2000 rpm. Oil refill capacity: 4 qt. Fuel Requirements: Regular.

CHASSIS FEATURES: Separate body and chassis. Channel steel frame side rails. Six cross members. Dimensions: 5.5 in. x 2.0 in. x 0.179 in. Section modulus: 2.581 cu. in.

SUSPENSION AND RUNNING GEAR: Front Suspension: Nine leaf semi-elliptical springs, 36.25 in. x by 1.75 in. Compression rate: 303 lb./in. Double acting shock absorbers. Rear Suspension. Eleven leaf semi-elliptical springs, 50 in. x 2.0 inches. Spring rate: 370/410 lb./in. Double acting shock absorbers. Front Axle Type: Spicer model 25 full-floating. Axle ratio: 5.38:1. Rear Axle Type: Semi-floating Timken model 51540. Axle Ratio: 5.38:1. Optional: 6.17, 4.88:1. Transfer Case: Ratios: Spicer model 18. Ratios: 2.43, 1.0:1. Brakes: Type: Hydraulic, front and rear. Dimensions: Front and rear: 11.00 in. x 2.0 in. Wheels: 16 x 5.00. Tires: 7.00 x 16 in. 6-ply. Steering: Cam and twin pin lever, variable ratio. Ratio: 15.4-13.5-10.54:1. Turning circle: 50 ft. Standard Transmission: Warner ASI-T909E 3-speed manual transmission. Transmission ratios: 3.44, 1.85 and 1.1:1. Optional: None. Clutch: 8.5 in. dia. Auburn single dry plate clutch with a 120 lb.-ft. of torque capacity. Single dry plate. Total plate pressure: 183-203 lb. Optional: None.

VEHICLE DIMENSIONS: Wheelbase: 118 in. Overall Length: 183.75 in. Front/Rear Tread: 56 in./63.5 in. Overall Height: 74.5 in. Width: Pickup models: 66.625 in. Stake platform: 73.156 in. Front/Rear Overhang: 25.75 in./40 in. Tailgate: Width and Height: 48.50 in. x 15.75 in. Approach/Departure Degrees: 48/50. Ground Clearance: 8.125 in. Load space: Pickup: 80 in. x 48.5 in. Platform body: 81.5 in. x 73 in.

CAPACITIES: Fuel Tank: 15.0 gal. Optional: None. Coolant system: 11 qt.

ACCOMMODATIONS: Seating Capacity: Three.

INSTRUMENTATION: 0-80 mph speedometer, odometer, fuel, ammeter, oil pressure and temperature gauges.

OPTIONS: Zenith, Detroit and Philco radios with speakers mounted in the instrument panel or cowl trim pad. Heater-defroster. Cigarette lighter. Sun visors. Interior and exterior rearview mirrors. License plate frame. Dual horns. Lockable gas cap. Tire pump. Spare tire lock. Dual taillights. Foglights or combination fog-driving lights. Gasoline filter. Starter crank. Spotlight. Underhood light and a deluxe tool kit. Fire extinguisher. Tire inflator. Directional signals. Summer insect bug screen. Winter grille front. Right hand drive. Front-mounted drum type winch. Power take-off.

HISTORICAL FOOTNOTES: The Jeep trucks for 1948 were introduced in Nov., 1947.

1949 PICKUP TRUCKS

There were numerous examples, in 1949 of Willys-Overland's policy of making revisions to its models on a regular basis during a calendar year. Beginning with 42136-four-wheel drive, a "Four-Wheel Drive" plate was mounted on the hood. After 34679-four-wheel drive a full-length seat cushion replaced the divided front seat. Trucks produced after serial number 33386-four-wheel drive had a shift plate installed on the dash panel. A shift from a remote-control column shift mechanism to a floor-mounted shift lever. was made after serial number 34787-four-wheel drive. It was accompanied by a major interior revision that included the switching of the locations for the windshield wiper control and the ashtray. A floor mat with provision for access to the transmission was also installed.

After serial number 37628-four-wheel drive the ashtray cover was chrome plated. After serial number 30780-four-wheel drive a garnish molding extending the full length of the windshield divider bar entered production. After 34027-four-wheel drive an embossed leather grain, Taupe color, insert was used for the interior door panel.

I.D. DATA: The serial number was located on a plate found on the outside of the left frame side rail at the front and also on the left of the driver's seat on the floor riser. The engine number was stamped on top of the cylinder block water pump boss. The serial number range was 30576 to 43586.

Body Type	Factory Price	GVW	Shipping Weight	Prod. Total
Model four-wheel drive (1 ton, four-wheel drive, 118 in. wheelbase)				
Chassis and Cab	$1700	5300	2809	18,342*
Pickup	$1792	5300	3129	—
Stake	$1856	5300	3431	—

*-Includes both two- and four-wheel drive models.

STANDARD ENGINE: Engine Type: L-head (side valve) In-line-4. Cast iron block and cylinder head. Bore x Stroke: 3.125 in. x 4.375 in. Lifters: Solid. Number of main bearings-3. Fuel Induction: Carter single barrel carburetor, model 626. Compression Ratio: 6.47:1.

Optional: High altitude cylinder head with a 7.0:1 compression ratio. Displacement: 134.2 cu. in. (2.19 liters). Horsepower: 60 @ 4000 rpm. Torque: 106 lb.-ft. @ 2000 rpm. Oil refill capacity: 4 qt. Fuel Requirements: Regular.

CHASSIS FEATURES: Separate body and chassis. Channel steel frame side rails. Six cross members. Dimensions: 5.5 in. x 2.0 in. x 0.179 in. Section modulus: 2.581 cu. in.

SUSPENSION AND RUNNING GEAR: Front Suspension: Nine leaf semi-elliptical springs, 36.25 in. x by 1.75 in. Compression rate: 303 lb./in. Double acting shock absorbers. Rear Suspension: Eleven leaf semi-elliptical springs, 50 in. x 2.0 inches. Spring rate: 370/410 lb./in. Double acting shock absorbers. Front Axle Type: Spicer model 25 full-floating. Axle ratio: 5.38:1. Rear Axle Type: Semi-floating Timken model 51540. Axle Ratio: 5.38:1. Optional: 6.17, 4.88:1. Transfer Case: Ratios: Spicer model 18. Ratios: 2.43, 1.0:1. Brakes: Type: Hydraulic, front and rear. Dimensions: Front and rear: 11.00 in. x 2.0 in. Wheels: 16 x 5.00. Tires: 7.00 x 16 in. 6-ply. Steering: Cam and twin pin lever, variable ratio. Ratio: 15.4-13.5-10.54:1. Turning circle: 50 ft. Optional None. Standard Transmission: Warner ASI-T909E 3-speed manual transmission. Transmission ratios: 3.44, 1.85 and 1.1:1. Optional: None. Clutch: 8.5 in. dia. Auburn single dry plate clutch with a 120 lb.-ft. of torque capacity. Single dry plate. Total plate pressure: 183-203 lb. Optional: None.

VEHICLE DIMENSIONS: Wheelbase: 118 in. Overall Length: 183.75 in. Front/Rear Tread: 56 in./63.5 in. Overall Height: 74.5 in. Width: Pickup models: 66.625 in. Stake platform: 73.156 in. Front/Rear Overhang: 25.75 in./40 in. Tailgate: Width and Height: 48.50 in. x 15.75 in. Approach/Departure Degrees: 48/50. Ground Clearance: 8.125 in. Load space: Pickup: 80 in. x 48.5 in. Platform body: 81.5 in. x 73 in.

CAPACITIES: Fuel Tank: 15.0 gal. Optional: None. Coolant system: 11 qt.

ACCOMMODATIONS: Seating Capacity: Three.

INSTRUMENTATION: 0-80 mph speedometer, odometer, fuel, ammeter, oil pressure and temperature gauges.

OPTIONS: Zenith, Detroit and Philco radios with speakers mounted in the instrument panel or cowl trim pad. Heater-defroster. Cigarette lighter. Sun visors. Interior and exterior rearview mirrors. License plate frame. Dual horns. Lockable gas cap. Tire pump. Spare tire lock. Dual taillights. Foglights or combination fog-driving lights. Gasoline filter. Starter crank. Spotlight. Underhood light and a deluxe tool kit. Fire extinguisher. Tire inflator. Directional signals. Summer insect bug screen. Winter grille front. Right-hand drive. Front-mounted drum type winch. Power take-off.

HISTORICAL FOOTNOTES: The Jeep trucks were introduced in Nov.,1948.

1950 PICKUP TRUCKS

Starting in October, 1949, the 1949 models were carried over as 1950 models. On March 30, 1950 a second series of 1950 model trucks were introduced. These trucks received a major styling change in the form of the same new front end appearance as used on the latest Willys station wagons. Removed was the full length hood ornament that on earlier models had been either painted body color or chromed. The result was a smoother hood line that blended into a new V-shaped front hood with a winged Willys-Overland emblem, five horizontal and nine vertical grille bars. The front edge of the hood was rolled under for added strength and rigidity. The front fenders had deeper, head-on cutouts and crease lines matching the one found on the hood.

At the same time Willys introduced an across-the-board price cut. it introduced a new 4-cylinder F-head engine with its overhead intake and side exhaust valve arrangement. No changes were made in its bore and stroke but the new cylinder head provided for a compression ratio boost to 6.9:1. The high altitude head had a 7.4:1 compression ratio. The repositioned intake valves had a larger, 2.0 inch instead of the 1.53 inch head diameter used on the older engines. Use of the new engine, known as the 473, brought with it new model identifications. Standard equipment included ashtray, sun visor, rearview mirror, glove box, dual windshield wipers, and adjustable seat.

I.D. DATA: The serial number was located on a plate found on the outside of the left frame side rail at the front and also on the left of the driver's seat on the floor riser. The engine number was stamped on top of the cylinder block water pump boss. The serial number range was 43587 to 47708.

Body Type	Factory Price	GVW	Shipping Weight	Prod. Total
First Series 1950 Models				
Model four-wheel drive (1 ton, four-wheel drive, 118 in. wheelbase)				
Chassis and Cab	$1700	5300	2809	—
Pickup	$1792	5300	3129	—
Stake	$1856	5300	3431	—
Second Series 1950 Models				
Model 473-four-wheel drive (1 ton, four-wheel drive, 118 in. wheelbase)				
Chassis and Cab	$1,604	5300	2924	—
Pickup	$1,690	5300	3240	—
Stake	$1,750	5300	3481	—

STANDARD ENGINE: (Second series): Engine Type: F-head (overhead intake valve, side exhaust valve). In-line-4. Cast iron block and cylinder head. Bore x Stroke: 3.125 in. x 4.375 in. Lifters: Solid. Number of main bearings-3. Fuel Induction: Carter single barrel carburetor, model 626. Compression Ratio: 6.9:1. Optional: High altitude cylinder head with a 7.4:1 compression ratio. Displacement: 134.2 cu. in. (2.19 liters). Horsepower: 72 @ 4000 rpm. Torque: 114 lb.-ft. @ 2000 rpm. Oil refill capacity: 4 qt. Fuel Requirements: Regular.

CHASSIS FEATURES: Separate body and chassis. Channel steel frame side rails. Six cross members. Dimensions: 5.5 in. x 2.0 in. x 0.179 in. Section modulus: 2.581 cu. in.

SUSPENSION AND RUNNING GEAR: Front Suspension: Nine leaf semi-elliptical springs, 36.25 in. x by 1.75 in. Compression rate: 303 lb./in. Double acting shock absorbers. Rear Suspension: Eleven leaf semi-elliptical springs, 50 in. x 2.0 inches. Spring rate: 370/410 lb./in. Double acting shock absorbers. Front Axle Type: Spicer model 25 full-floating. Axle Ratio: 5.38:1. Rear Axle Type: Semi-floating Timken model 51540. Axle Ratio: 5.38:1. Optional: 6.17, 4.88:1. Transfer Case: Ratios: Spicer model 18. Ratios: 2.43, 1.0:1. Brakes: Type: Hydraulic, front and rear. Dimensions: Front and rear: 11.00 in. x 2.0 in. Wheels: 16 x 5.00. Tires: 7.00 x 16 in. 6-ply. Steering: Cam and twin pin lever, variable ratio. Ratio: 15.4-13.5-10.54:1. Turning circle: 50 ft. Optional None. Standard Transmission: Warner

ASI-T909E 3-speed manual transmission. Transmission ratios. 3.44, 1.85 and 1.1:1. Optional: None. Clutch: 8.5 in. dia. Auburn single dry plate clutch with a 120 lb.-ft. of torque capacity. Single dry plate. Total plate pressure: 183-203 lb. Optional: None.

VEHICLE DIMENSIONS: Wheelbase: 118 in. Overall Length: 183.75 in. Front/Rear Tread: 56 in./63.5 in. Overall Height: 74.5 in. Width: Pickup models: 66.625 in. Stake platform: 73.156 in. Front/Rear Overhang: 25.75 in./40 in. Tailgate: Width and Height: 48.50 in. x 15.75 in. Approach/Departure Degrees: 48/50. Ground Clearance: 8.125 in. Load space: Pickup: 80 in. x 48.5 in. Platform body: 81.5 in. x 73 in.

CAPACITIES: Fuel Tank: 15.0 gal. Optional: None. Coolant system: 11 qt.

ACCOMMODATIONS: Seating Capacity: Three.

INSTRUMENTATION: 0-80 mph speedometer, odometer, fuel, ammeter, oil pressure and temperature gauges.

OPTIONS AND PRICES: Zenith, Detroit and Philco radios with speakers mounted in the instrument panel or cowl trim pad. Heater-defroster. Cigarette lighter. Sun visors. Interior and exterior rearview mirrors. License plate frame. Dual horns. Lockable gas cap. Tire pump. Spare tire lock. Dual taillights. Foglights or combination fog-driving lights. Gasoline filter. Starter crank. Spotlight. Underhood light and a deluxe tool kit. Fire extinguisher. Tire inflator. Directional signals. Summer insect bug screen. Winter grille front. Right hand drive. Front-mounted drum type winch. Power take-off.

HISTORICAL FOOTNOTES: Willys claimed that the new F-head engined trucks had the "highest-compression engine in any farm truck."

1951 PICKUP TRUCKS

The second series trucks of 1950 became the 1951 models without change.

1951 Willys truck

I.D. DATA: The serial number was located on a plate found on the outside of the left frame side rail at the front and also on the left of the driver's seat on the floor riser. The engine number was stamped on top of the cylinder block water pump boss. The serial number range was as follows: Chassis: 451-EA1-10001 and up. Chassis and cab: 451-EB1-10001 to 11894. Pickup: 451-EC1-10001 to 26029. Platform Stake: 451-ED1-10001 to 10420. The first number of this new system represented the number of cylinders. The next two digits indicated the model year. The first letter identified the basic chassis and body type. The second letter identified the model. The final entry indicated the series.

Body Type	Factory Price	GVW	Shipping Weight	Prod. Total
Model 473-four-wheel drive (1 ton, four-wheel drive, 118 in. wheelbase)				
Chassis	$1205	5300	2109	20,244*
Chassis and Cab	$1595	5300	2799	—
Pickup	$1678	5300	3115	—
Stake	$1736	5300	3356	—

* Calendar year production of both two- and four-wheel drive trucks.

STANDARD ENGINE: Engine Type: F-head (overhead intake valve, side exhaust valve). In-line-4. Cast iron block and cylinder head. Bore x Stroke: 3.125 in. x 4.375 in. Lifters: Solid. Number of main bearings-3. Fuel Induction: Carter single barrel carburetor, model 626. Compression Ratio: 6.9:1. Optional: High altitude cylinder head with a 7.4:1 compression ratio. Displacement: 134.2 cu. in. (2.19 liters). Horsepower: 72 @ 4000 rpm. Torque: 114 lb.-ft. @ 2000 rpm. Oil refill capacity: 4 qt. Fuel Requirements: Regular.

CHASSIS FEATURES: Separate body and chassis. Channel steel frame side rails. Six cross members. Dimensions: 5.5 in. x 2.0 in. x 0.179 in. Section modulus: 2.581 cu. in.

SUSPENSION AND RUNNING GEAR: Front Suspension: Nine leaf semi-elliptical springs, 36.25 in. x by 1.75 in. Compression rate: 303 lb./in. Double acting shock absorbers. Rear Suspension: Eleven leaf semi-elliptical springs, 50 in. x 2.0 inches. Spring rate: 370/410 lb./in. Double acting shock absorbers. Front Axle Type: Spicer model 25 full-floating. Axle ratio: 5.38:1. Rear Axle Type: Semi-floating Timken model 51540. Axle Ratio: 5.38:1. Optional: 6.17, 4.88:1. Transfer Case: Ratios: Spicer model 18. Ratios: 2.43, 1.0:1. Brakes: Type: Hydraulic, front and rear. Dimensions: Front and rear: 11.00 in. x 2.0 in. Wheels: 16 x 5.00. Tires: 7.00 x 16 in. 6-ply. Steering: Cam and twin pin lever, variable ratio. Ratio: 15.4-13.5-10.54:1. Turning circle: 50 ft. Optional None. Standard Transmission: Warner ASI-T909E 3-speed manual transmission. Transmission ratios: 3.44, 1.85 and 1.1:1. Optional: None. Clutch: 8.5 in. dia. Auburn single dry plate clutch with a 120 lb.-ft. of torque capacity. Single dry plate. Total plate pressure: 183-203 lb. Optional: None.

VEHICLE DIMENSIONS: Wheelbase: 118 in. Overall Length: 183.75 in. Front/Rear Tread: 56 in./63.5 in. Overall Height: 74.5 in. Width: Pickup models: 66.625 in. Stake platform: 73.156 in. Front/Rear Overhang: 25.75 in./40. Tailgate: Width and Height: 48.50 in. x 15.75 in. Approach/Departure Degrees: 48/50. Ground Clearance: 8.125 in. Load space: Pickup: 80 in. x 48.5 in. Platform body: 81.5 in. x 73 in.

CAPACITIES: Fuel Tank: 15.0 gal. Optional: None. Coolant system: 11 qt.

ACCOMMODATIONS: Seating Capacity: Three.

INSTRUMENTATION: 0-80 mph speedometer, odometer, fuel, ammeter, oil pressure and temperature gauges.

OPTIONS: Zenith, Detroit and Philco radios with speakers mounted in the instrument panel or cowl trim pad. Heater-defroster. Cigarette lighter. Sun visors. Interior and exterior rearview mirrors. License plate frame. Dual horns. Lockable gas cap. Tire pump. Spare tire lock. Dual taillights. Foglights or combination fog-driving lights. Gasoline filter. Starter crank. Spotlight. Underhood light and a deluxe tool kit. Fire extinguisher. Tire inflator. Directional signals. Summer insect bug screen. Winter grille front. Right hand drive. Front-mounted drum type winch. Power take-off.

HISTORICAL FOOTNOTES: Introduction of the Jeep trucks took place in Nov., 1950.

1952 PICKUP TRUCKS

Beginning in October, 1952 the F-head engine was fitted with a larger 4.5 inch starter motor as well as a 129 tooth ring gear in place of the older 124 tooth unit. The changes required use of a different bellhousing, engine plate and flywheel ring gear. This version of the F-head was identified as the 475 engine. No other changes of significant took place for 1952.

I.D. DATA: The serial number was located on a plate found on the outside of the left frame side rail at the front and also on the left of the driver's seat on the floor riser. The engine number was stamped on top of the cylinder block water pump boss. The serial number range was as follows: Chassis: 452-FA1-10001 and up. Chassis and cab: 452-EB1-10001 and up. Pickup: 452-EC1-10001 and up. Platform Stake: 452-ED1-10001 and up. The first number of this system represented the number of cylinders. The next two digits indicated the model year. The first letter identified the basic chassis and body type. The second letter identified the model. The final entry indicated the series.

Body Type	Factory Price	GVW	Shipping Weight	Prod. Total
Model 473-four-wheel drive (1 ton, four-wheel drive, 118 in. wheelbase(				
Chassis	$1296	5300	2109	31,273*
Chassis and Cab	$1844	5300	2799	—
Pickup	$1943	5300	3115	—
Stake	$2012	5300	335	—

* Includes both two- and four-wheel drive models.

STANDARD ENGINE: Engine Type: F-head (overhead intake valve, side exhaust valve). In-line-4. Cast iron block and cylinder head. Bore x Stroke: 3.125 in. x 4.375 in. Lifters: Solid. Number of main bearings-3. Fuel Induction: Carter single barrel carburetor, model 626. Compression Ratio: 6.9:1. Optional: High altitude cylinder head with a 7.4:1 compression ratio. Displacement: 134.2 cu. in. (2.19 liters). Horsepower: 72 @ 4000 rpm. Torque: 114 lb.-ft. @ 2000 rpm. Oil refill capacity: 4 qt. Fuel Requirements: Regular.

CHASSIS FEATURES: Separate body and chassis. Channel steel frame side rails. Six cross members. Dimensions: 5.5 in. x 2.0 in. x 0.179 in. Section modulus: 2.581 cu. in.

SUSPENSION AND RUNNING GEAR: Front Suspension: Nine leaf semi-elliptical springs, 36.25 in. x by 1.75 in. Compression rate: 303 lb./in. Double acting shock absorbers. Rear Suspension: Eleven leaf semi-elliptical springs, 50 in. x 2.0 inches. Spring rate: 370/410 lb./in. Double acting shock absorbers. Front Axle Type: Spicer model 25 full-floating. Axle ratio: 5.38:1. Rear Axle Type: Semi-floating Timken model 51540. Axle Ratio: 5.38:1. Optional: 6.17, 4.88:1. Transfer Case: Ratios: Spicer model 18. Ratios: 2.43, 1.0:1. Brakes: Type: Hydraulic, front and rear. Dimensions: Front and rear: 11.00 in. x 2.0 in. Wheels: 16 x 5.00. Tires: 7.00 x 16 in. 6-ply. Steering: Cam and twin pin lever, variable ratio. Ratio: 15.4-13.5-10.54:1. Turning circle: 50 ft. Optional None. Standard Transmission: Warner ASI-T909E 3-speed manual transmission. Transmission ratios: 3.44, 1.85 and 1.1:1. Optional: None. Clutch: 8.5 in. dia. Auburn single dry plate clutch with a 120 lb.-ft. of torque capacity. Single dry plate. Total plate pressure: 183-203 lb. Optional: None.

VEHICLE DIMENSIONS: Wheelbase: 118 in. Overall Length: 183.75 in. Front/Rear Tread: 56 in./63.5 in. Overall Height: 74.5 in. Width: Pickup models: 66.625 in. Stake platform: 73.156 in. Front/Rear Overhang: 25.75 in./40 in. Tailgate: Width and Height: 48.50 in. x 15.75 in. Approach/Departure Degrees: 48/50. Ground Clearance: 8.125 in. Load space: Pickup: 80 in. x 48.5 in. Platform body: 81.5 in. x 73 in.

CAPACITIES: Fuel Tank: 15.0 gal. Optional: None. Coolant system: 11 qt.

ACCOMMODATIONS: Seating Capacity: Three.

INSTRUMENTATION: 0-80 mph speedometer, odometer, fuel, ammeter, oil pressure and temperature gauges.

OPTIONS: Zenith, Detroit and Philco radios with speakers mounted in the instrument panel or cowl trim pad, heater-defroster, cigarette lighter, sun visors, interior and exterior rearview mirrors, license plate frame, dual horns, lockable gas cap, tire pump, spare tire lock, dual taillights, foglights or combination fog-driving lights, gasoline filter, starter crank, spotlight, underhood light and a deluxe tool kit. Fire extinguisher. Tire inflator. Directional signals. Summer insect bug screen. Winter grille front. Radios with speakers. Heater-defroster. Cigarette lighter. Sun visors. Interior and exterior rearview mirrors. License plate frame. Dual horns. Lockable gas cap. Tire pump. Spare tire lock. Dual taillights. Foglights or combination fog-driving lights. Gasoline filter. Starter crank. Spotlight. Underhood light and a deluxe tool kit. Fire extinguisher. Tire inflator. Directional signals. Summer insect bug screen. Winter grille front. Right-hand drive. Front-mounted drum type winch. Power take-off.

HISTORICAL FOOTNOTES: The 1952 trucks were introduced on Dec. 10, 1951. The one-millionth Jeep vehicle was built on March 19, 1952.

1953 PICKUP TRUCKS

The Jeep trucks were unchanged for 1953.

I.D. DATA: The serial number was located on a plate found on the outside of the left frame side rail at the front and also on the left of the driver's seat on the floor riser. The engine number was stamped on top of the cylinder block water pump boss. The serial number range was as follows: Chassis: 453-FA1-10001 and up. Chassis and cab: 453-EB1-10001 and up. Pickup: 453-EC1-10001 and up. Platform Stake: 453-ED1-10001 and up.

Body Type	Factory Price	GVW	Shipping Weight	Prod. Total
Model 473-four-wheel drive (1 ton, four-wheel drive, 118 in. wheelbase)				
Chassis and Cab	$1712	5300	2799	—
Pickup	$1805	5300	3115	—
Stake	$1870	5300	3356	—

STANDARD ENGINE: Engine Type: F-head (overhead intake valve, side exhaust valve). In-line-4. Cast iron block and cylinder head. Bore x Stroke: 3.125 in. x 4.375 in. Lifters: Solid. Number of main bearings-3. Fuel Induction: Carter single barrel carburetor, model 626. Compression Ratio: 6.9:1. Optional: High altitude cylinder head with a 7.4:1 compression ratio. Displacement: 134.2 cu. in. (2.19 liters). Horsepower: 72 @ 4000 rpm. Torque: 114 lb.-ft. @ 2000 rpm. Oil refill capacity: 4 qt. Fuel Requirements: Regular.

CHASSIS FEATURES: Separate body and chassis. Channel steel frame side rails. Six cross members. Dimensions: 5.5 in. x 2.0 in. x 0.179 in. Section modulus: 2.581 cu. in.

SUSPENSION AND RUNNING GEAR: Front Suspension: Nine leaf semi-elliptical springs, 36.25 in. x by 1.75 in. Compression rate: 303 lb./in. Double acting shock absorbers. Rear Suspension: Eleven leaf semi-elliptical springs, 50 in. x 2.0 inches. Spring rate: 370/410 lb./in. Double acting shock absorbers. Front Axle Type: Spicer model 25 full-floating. Axle ratio: 5.38:1. Rear Axle Type: Semi-floating Timken model 51540. Axle Ratio: 5.38:1. Optional: 6.17, 4.88:1. Transfer Case: Ratios: Spicer model 18. Ratios: 2.43, 1.0:1. Brakes: Type: Hydraulic, front and rear. Dimensions: Front and rear: 11.00 in. x 2.0 in. Wheels: 16 x 5.00. Tires: 7.00 x 16 in. 6-ply. Steering: Cam and twin pin lever, variable ratio. Ratio: 15.4-13.5-10.54:1. Turning circle: 50 ft. Optional None. Standard Transmission: Warner ASI-T909E 3-speed manual transmission. Transmission ratios: 3.44, 1.85 and 1.1:1. Optional: None. Clutch: 8.5 in. dia. Auburn single dry plate clutch with a 120 lb.-ft. of torque capacity. Single dry plate. Total plate pressure: 183-203 lb. Optional: None.

VEHICLE DIMENSIONS: Wheelbase: 118 in. Overall Length: 183.75 in. Front/Rear Tread: 56 in./63.5 in. Overall Height: 74.5 in. Width: Pickup models: 66.625 in. Stake platform: 73.156 in. Front/Rear Overhang: 25.75 in./40 in. Tailgate: Width and Height: 48.50 in. x 15.75 in. Approach/Departure Degrees: 48/50. Ground Clearance: 8.125 in. Load space: Pickup: 80 in. x 48.5 in. Platform body: 81.5 in. x 73 in.

CAPACITIES: Fuel Tank: 15.0 gal. Optional: None. Coolant system: 11 qt.

ACCOMMODATIONS: Seating Capacity: Three.

INSTRUMENTATION: 0-80 mph speedometer, odometer, fuel, ammeter, oil pressure and temperature gauges.

OPTIONS: Radios with speakers. Heater-defroster. Cigarette lighter. Sun visors. Interior and exterior rearview mirrors. License plate frame. Dual horns. Lockable gas cap. Tire pump. Spare tire lock. Dual taillights. Foglights or combination fog-driving lights. Gasoline filter. Starter crank. Spotlight. Underhood light and a deluxe tool kit. Fire extinguisher. Tire inflator. Directional signals. Summer insect bug screen. Winter grille front. Right hand drive. Front-mounted drum type winch. Power take-off.

HISTORICAL FOOTNOTES: The 1953 Jeep trucks were introduced on Oct. 20, 1952.

1954 PICKUP TRUCKS

For 1954 the Jeep truck's grille had three instead of five horizontal bars The four-wheel drive series could be ordered with the "Super Hurricane" L-head 6-cylinder engine. This engine was essentially the same engine that had been used by Kaiser-Frazer for its line of full-size postwar automobiles. This engine had originated as a Continental design.

1954 Jeep truck

I.D. DATA: The serial number was located on a plate found on the outside of the left frame side rail at the front and also on the left of the driver's seat on the floor riser. The engine number was stamped on top of the cylinder block water pump boss. The serial number range was as follows: Chassis and cab: 454-EB2- 10001 to 10,681; 654-EB2-100001 to 10,439. Pickup: 454-EC2-10001 to 14,927. 654-EC2-10001 to 14,927. Platform Stake: 454-ED2-10001 to 10,185, 654-ED2-10001 and up. The first number of this new system represented the number of cylinders. The next two digits indicated the model year. The first letter identified the basic chassis and body type. The second letter identified the model. The final entry indicated the series.

Body Type	Factory Price	GVW	Shipping Weight	Prod. Total
Model 454-four-wheel drive (1 ton, four-wheel drive, 118 in. wheelbase)				
Chassis and Cab	$1712	5300	2799	9,925*
Pickup	$1805	5300	3115	—
Stake	$1870	5300	3356	—
Model 6-226-four-wheel drive (1 ton, four-wheel drive, 118 in. wheelbase)				
Chassis and Cab	$1802	5300	2850	—
Pickup	$1895	5300	3141	—
Stake	$1960	5300	3362	—

* Calendar year 1954 registrations for both two- and four-wheel drive trucks.

STANDARD ENGINE: 454 series: Engine Type: F-head (overhead intake valve, side exhaust valve) In-line-4. Cast iron block and cylinder head. Bore x Stroke: 3.125 in. x 4.375 in. Lifters: Hydraulic. Number of main bearings-3. Fuel Induction: Carter single barrel carburetor, model 626. Compression Ratio: 6.9:1. Optional: High altitude cylinder head with a 7.4:1 compression ratio. Displacement: 134.2 cu. in. (2.19 liters). Horsepower: 72 @ 4000 rpm. Torque: 114 lb.-ft. @ 2000 rpm. Oil refill capacity: 4 qt. Fuel Requirements: Regular.

STANDARD ENGINE: 6-226 series: Engine Type: L-head In-line-6-cyl. "Super-Hurricane", cast iron block and cylinder head. Bore x Stroke: 3.9375 in. x 4.375 in. Lifters: Solid. Number of main bearings-4. Fuel Induction: Single barrel Carter YF carburetor, model 2052S or 2052A. Compression Ratio: 6.861. Optional: 7.3:1. Displacement: 226.2 cu. in. (3.7 liters). Horsepower: 115 @ 3800 rpm. Torque: 190 lb.-ft. @ 1800 rpm. Oil refill capacity: 5 qt. Fuel Requirements: Regular.

CHASSIS FEATURES: Separate body and chassis. Channel steel frame side rails. Six cross members. Dimensions: 5.5 in. x 2.0 in. x 0.179 in. Section modulus: 2.581 cu. in.

SUSPENSION AND RUNNING GEAR: Front Suspension: Nine leaf semi-elliptical springs, 36.25 in. x by 1.75 in. Compression rate: 303 lb./in. Double acting shock absorbers. Rear Suspension: Eleven leaf semi-elliptical springs, 50 in. x 2.0 inches. Spring rate: 370/410 lb./in. Double acting shock absorbers. Front Axle Type and Capacity: Spicer model 25 full-floating. Axle ratio: 4-cyl.: 5.38:1, 6-cyl.: 4.88:1. Optional: 4-cyl.: 6.17, 4.88:1. 6-cyl.: 5.38:1. Rear Axle Type and Capacity: Semi-floating Timken model 51540. Transfer Case: Spicer model 18. Ratios: 2.43, 1.0:1. Brakes: Type: Hydraulic, front and rear. Dimensions: Front and rear: 11.00 in. x 2.0 in. Wheels: 16 x 5.00. Tires: 7.00 x 16 in. 6-ply. Steering: Cam and twin pin lever, variable ratio. Ratio: 15.4-13.5-10.5:1. Turning circle: 50 ft. Standard Transmission: Warner ASI-T909E 3-speed manual transmission. Transmission ratios: 3.44, 1.85 and 1.0:1. Optional: None. Clutch: Four cyl.: 8.5 in. dia., 6-cyl.: 10.0 in. dia. Optional: None.

VEHICLE DIMENSIONS: Wheelbase: 118 in. Overall Length: 183.75 in. Front/Rear Tread: 56 in./63.5 in. Overall Height: 74.5 in. Width: Pickup models: 66.625 in. Stake platform: 73.156 in. Front/Rear Overhang: 25.75 in./40 in. Tailgate: Width and Height: 48.50 in. x 15.75 in. Approach/Departure Degrees: 48/50. Ground Clearance: 8.125 in. Load space: Pickup: 80 in. x 48.5 in. Platform body: 81.5 in. x 73 in.

CAPACITIES: Fuel Tank: 15.0 gal. Optional: None. Coolant system: 4-cyl.: 11 qt., 6-cyl.: 9 qt.

ACCOMMODATIONS: Seating Capacity: Three.

INSTRUMENTATION: 0-80 mph speedometer, odometer, fuel, ammeter, oil pressure and engine coolant temperature gauges.

OPTIONS AND PRICES: Radios with speakers. Heater-defroster. Cigarette lighter. Sun visors. Interior and exterior rearview mirrors. License plate frame. Dual horns. Lockable gas cap. Tire pump. Spare tire lock. Dual taillights. Foglights or combination fog-driving lights. Gasoline filter. Starter crank. Spotlight. Underhood light and a deluxe tool kit. Fire extinguisher. Tire inflator. Directional signals. Summer insect bug screen. Winter grille front. Right hand drive. Front-mounted drum type winch. Power take-off: $96.25. Pulley drive: $57.40. Special wheels and 7.00 tires: $28.65.

HISTORICAL FOOTNOTES: None.

1955 PICKUP TRUCKS

All four-wheel drive Jeep trucks for 1955 were powered by the 226 cu. in. 6-cylinder engine. The 4-cylinder engine was optional.

1955 Jeep pickup

I.D. DATA: The serial number was located on a plate found on the outside of the left frame side rail at the front and also on the left of the driver's seat on the floor riser. The engine number was stamped on top of the cylinder block water pump boss.

Body Type	Factory Price	GVW	Shipping Weight	Prod. Total
Model 6-226-four-wheel drive (1 ton, four-wheel drive, 118 in. wheelbase)				
Chassis and Cab	$1833	5300	2782	16,811*
Pickup	$1927	5300	3141	—
Stake	$1992	5300	3355	—

* Calendar year 1955 registration for both two- and four-wheel drive trucks.

STANDARD ENGINE: 6-226 series: Engine Type: L-head In-line-6-cyl. "Super-Hurricane", cast iron block and cylinder head. Bore x Stroke: 3.9375 in. x 4.375 in. Lifters: Solid. Number of main bearings-4. Fuel Induction: Single barrel Carter YF carburetor, model 2052S or 2052A. Compression Ratio: 6.861. Optional: 7.3:1. Displacement: 226.2 cu. in. (3.7 liters). Horsepower: 115 @ 3800 rpm. Torque: 190 lb.-ft. @ 1800 rpm. Oil refill capacity: 5 qt. Fuel Requirements: Regular.

OPTIONAL ENGINE: Engine Type: F-head (overhead intake valve, side exhaust valve) In-line-4. Cast iron block and cylinder head. Bore x Stroke: 3.125 in. x 4.375 in. Lifters: Hydraulic. Number of main bearings-3. Fuel Induction: Carter single barrel carburetor, model 626. Compression Ratio: 6.9:1. Optional: High altitude cylinder head with a 7.4:1 compression ratio. Displacement: 134.2 cu. in. (2.19 liters). Horsepower: 72 @ 4000 rpm. Torque: 114 lb.-ft. @ 2000 rpm. Oil refill capacity: 4 qt. Fuel Requirements: Regular.

CHASSIS FEATURES: Separate body and chassis. Channel steel frame side rails. Six cross members. Dimensions: 5.5 in. x 2.0 in. x 0.179 in. Section modulus: 2.581 cu. in.

SUSPENSION AND RUNNING GEAR: Front Suspension: Nine leaf semi-elliptical springs, 36.25 in. x by 1.75 in. Compression rate: 303 lb./in. Double acting shock absorbers. Rear Suspension: Eleven leaf semi-elliptical springs, 50 in. x 2.0 inches. Spring rate: 370/410 lb./in. Double acting shock absorbers. Front Axle Type and Capacity: Spicer model 25 full-floating. Axle ratio: 4-cyl.: 5.38:1, 6-cyl.: 4.88:1. Optional: 4-cyl.: 6.17, 4.88:1. 6-cyl.: 5.38:1. Rear Axle Type and Capacity: Semi-floating Timken model 51540. Transfer Case: Spicer model 18. Ratios: 2.43, 1.0:1. Brakes: Type: Hydraulic, front and rear. Dimensions: Front and rear: 11.00 in. x 2.0 in. Wheels: 16 x 5.00. Tires: 7.00 x 16 in. 6-ply. Steering: Cam and twin pin lever, variable ratio. Ratio: 15.4-13.5-10.5:1. Turning circle: 50 ft. Standard Transmission: Warner ASI-T909E 3-speed manual transmission. Transmission ratios: 3.44, 1.85 and 1.0:1. Optional: None. Clutch: Four cyl.: 8.5 in. dia., 6-cyl.: 10.0 in. dia. Optional: None.

VEHICLE DIMENSIONS: Wheelbase: 118 in. Overall Length: 183.75 in. Front/Rear Tread: 56 in./63.5 in. Overall Height: 74.5 in. Width: Pickup models: 66.625 in. Stake platform: 73.156 in. Front/Rear Overhang: 25.75 in./40 in. Tailgate: Width and Height: 48.50 in. x 15.75 in. Approach/Departure Degrees: 48/50. Ground Clearance: 8.125 in. Load space: Pickup: 80 in. x 48.5 in. Platform body: 81.5 in. x 73 in.

CAPACITIES: Fuel Tank: 15.0 gal. Optional: None. Coolant system: 4-cyl.: 11 qt., 6-cyl.: 9 qt.

ACCOMMODATIONS: Seating Capacity: Three.

INSTRUMENTATION: 0-80 mph speedometer, odometer, fuel, ammeter, oil pressure and engine coolant temperature gauges.

OPTIONS: Radios with speakers. Heater-defroster. Cigarette lighter. Sun visors. Interior and exterior rearview mirrors. License plate frame. Dual horns. Lockable gas cap. Tire pump. Spare tire lock. Dual taillights. Foglights or combination fog-driving lights. Gasoline filter. Starter crank. Spotlight. Underhood light and a deluxe tool kit. Fire extinguisher. Tire inflator. Directional signals. Summer insect bug screen. Winter grille front. Right hand drive. Front-mounted drum type winch. Power take-off.

HISTORICAL FOOTNOTES: The Jeep trucks were introduced on Oct. 11, 1954.

1956 PICKUP TRUCKS

Except for the availability of standard 4-cylinder models, no changes were made in the Jeep trucks for 1956.

I.D. DATA: The serial number was located on a plate found on the outside of the left frame side rail at the front and also on the left of the driver's seat on the floor riser. The engine number was stamped on top of the cylinder block water pump boss. Series number range: 475 Pickup: 55248-010826 and up; 6-226 Chassis and cab: 55168-11022 and up; 6-226 pickup: 55268-20003 and up; 6-226 Stake Platform: 55368-10595 and up.

Body Type	Factory Price	GVW	Shipping Weight	Prod. Total
Model 475-four-wheel drive (1 ton, four-wheel drive, 118 in. wheelbase)				
Pickup	$1946	6000	2786	—
Model 6-226-four-wheel drive (1 ton, four-wheel drive, 118 in. wheelbase)				
Chassis and Cab	$1943	6000	2782	—
Pickup	$2046	6000	3141	—
Stake	$2118	6000	3355	—

STANDARD ENGINE: 6-226 series: Engine Type: L-head In-line-6-cyl. "Super-Hurricane", cast iron block and cylinder head. Bore x Stroke: 3.9375 in. x 4.375 in. Lifters: Solid. Number of main bearings-4. Fuel Induction: Single barrel Carter YF carburetor, model 2052S or 2052A. Compression Ratio: 6.861. Optional: 7.3:1 compression ratio. Displacement: 226.2 cu. in. (3.7 liters). Horsepower: 115 @ 3800 rpm. Torque: 190 lb.-ft. @ 1800 rpm. Oil refill capacity: 5 qt. Fuel Requirements: Regular.

STANDARD ENGINE: 475 series: Engine Type: F-head (overhead intake valve, side exhaust valve) In-line-4. Cast iron block and cylinder head. Bore x Stroke: 3.125 in. x 4.375 in. Lifters: Hydraulic. Number of main bearings-3. Fuel Induction: Carter single barrel carburetor, model 626. Compression Ratio: 6.9:1. Optional: High altitude cylinder head with a 7.4:1 compression ratio. Displacement: 134.2 cu. in. (2.19 liters). Horsepower: 72 @ 4000 rpm. Torque: 114 lb.-ft. @ 2000 rpm. Oil refill capacity: 4 qt. Fuel Requirements: Regular.

CHASSIS FEATURES: Separate body and chassis. Channel steel frame side rails. Six cross members. Dimensions: 5.5 in. x 2.0 in. x 0.179 in. Section modulus: 2.581 cu. in.

SUSPENSION AND RUNNING GEAR: Front Suspension: Nine leaf semi-elliptical springs, 36.25 in. x by 1.75 in. Compression rate: 303 lb./in. Double acting shock absorbers. Rear Suspension: Eleven leaf semi-elliptical springs, 50 in. x 2.0 inches. Spring rate: 370/410 lb./in. Double acting shock absorbers. Front Axle Type and Capacity: Spicer model 25 full-floating. Axle ratio: 4-cyl.: 5.38:1, 6-cyl.: 4.88:1. Optional: 4-cyl.: 6.17, 4.88:1. 6-cyl.: 5.38:1. Rear Axle Type and Capacity: Semi-floating Timken model 51540. Transfer Case: Spicer model 18. Ratios: 2.43, 1.0:1. Brakes: Type: Hydraulic, front and rear. Dimensions: Front and rear: 11.00 in. x 2.0 in. Wheels: 16 x 5.00. Tires: 7.00 x 16 in. 6-ply. Steering: Cam and twin pin lever, variable ratio. Ratio: 15.4-13.5-10.5:1. Turning circle: 50 ft. Standard Transmission: Warner ASI-T909E 3-speed manual transmission. Transmission ratios: 3.44, 1.85 and 1.0:1. Optional: None. Clutch: Four cyl.: 8.5 in. dia., 6-cyl.: 10.0 in. dia. Optional: None.

VEHICLE DIMENSIONS: Wheelbase: 118 in. Overall Length: 183.75 in. Front/Rear Tread: 56 in./63.5 in. Overall Height: 74.5 in. Width: Pickup models: 66.625 in. Stake platform: 73.156 in. Front/Rear Overhang: 25.75 in./40 in. Tailgate: Width and Height: 48.50 in. x 15.75 in. Approach/Departure Degrees: 48/50. Ground Clearance: 8.125 in. Load space: Pickup: 80 in. x 48.5 in. Platform body: 81.5 in. x 73 in.

CAPACITIES: Fuel Tank: 15.0 gal. Optional: None. Coolant system: 4-cyl.: 11 qt., 6-cyl.: 9 qt.

ACCOMMODATIONS: Seating Capacity: Three.

INSTRUMENTATION: 0-80 mph speedometer, odometer, fuel, ammeter, oil pressure and engine coolant temperature gauges.

OPTIONS: Radios with speakers mounted in the instrument panel or cowl trim pad, heater-defroster, cigarette lighter, sun visors, interior and exterior rearview mirrors, license plate frame, dual horns, lockable gas cap, tire pump, spare tire lock, dual taillights, foglights or combination fog-driving lights, gasoline filter, starter crank, spotlight, underhood light and a deluxe tool kit. Fire extinguisher. Tire inflator. Directional signals. Summer insect bug screen. Winter grille front. Right-hand drive. Front-mounted drum type winch.

HISTORICAL FOOTNOTES: The 1956 model Jeep trucks were introduced on Aug. 17, 1955.

1957 PICKUP TRUCKS

The exterior colors for 1957 were raven black, president red, steel glow metallic, transport yellow, royal blue metallic, glenwood green metallic and Aztec orange. Two-tone color scheme base on these colors were also available. Jeep trucks of this era were available with numerous special bodies and highly specialized equipment. Some examples of the type of bodies offered included a service body, a "Dump-O-Matic" hydraulic hoist that converted the pickup into a mini-dump truck, and a hydraulic tailgate. The 6-226-four-wheel drive could also be ordered in two ambulance variations and as an open top Cargo-Personnel Carrier with room for 12 occupants. Another open top version was the Commando fire truck.

I.D. DATA: The serial number was located on a plate found on the outside of the left frame side rail at the front and also on the left of the driver's seat on the floor riser. The engine number was stamped on top of the cylinder block water pump boss. Series number range: 6-226 Chassis and cab: 55168-11022 and up; 6-226 pickup: 55268-20003 and up; 6-226 Stake Platform: 55368-10595 and up.

Body Type	Factory Price	GVW	Shipping Weight	Prod. Total
Model 6-226-four-wheel drive (1 ton, four-wheel drive, 118 in. wheelbase)				
Chassis and Cab	$2251.43	6000	2817	—
Pickup	$2370.22	6000	3176	—
Stake	$2453.29	6000	3341	—

STANDARD ENGINE: 6-226 series: Engine Type: L-head In-line-6-cyl. "Super-Hurricane", cast iron block and cylinder head. Bore x Stroke: 3.9375 in. x 4.375 in. Lifters: Solid. Number of main bearings-4. Fuel Induction: Single barrel Carter YF carburetor, model 2052S or 2052A. Compression Ratio: 6.861. Optional: 7.3:1 compression ratio. Displacement: 226.2 cu. in. (3.7 liters). Horsepower: 115 @ 3800 rpm. Torque: 190 lb.-ft. @ 1800 rpm. Oil refill capacity: 5 qt. Fuel Requirements: Regular.

CHASSIS FEATURES: Separate body and chassis. Channel steel frame side rails. Six cross members. Dimensions: 5.5 in. x 2.0 in. x 0.179 in. Section modulus: 2.581 cu. in.

SUSPENSION AND RUNNING GEAR: Front Suspension: Nine leaf semi-elliptical springs, 36.25 in. x by 1.75 in. Compression rate: 303 lb./in. Double acting shock absorbers. Rear Suspension: Eleven leaf semi-elliptical springs, 50 in. x 2.0 inches. Spring rate: 370/410 lb./in. Double acting shock absorbers. Front Axle Type: Spicer model 25 full-floating. Axle ratio: 4.88:1. Optional: 4.27:1 with locking rear differential. Rear Axle Type: Semi-floating Timken model 51540. Transfer Case: Ratios: Spicer model 18. Ratios: 2.43, 1.0:1. Brakes: Type: Hydraulic, front and rear. Dimensions: Front and rear: 11.00 in. x 2.0 in. Wheels: 16 x 5.00. Tires: 7.00 x 16 in. 6-ply. Steering: Cam and twin pin lever, variable ratio. Ratio: 15.4-13.5-10.54:1. Turning circle: 50 ft. Optional None. Standard Transmission: Warner ASI-T909E 3-speed manual transmission. Transmission ratios: 3.44, 1.85 and 1.0:1. Clutch: 10.0 in. dia.

VEHICLE DIMENSIONS: Wheelbase: 118 in. Overall Length: Pickup:183.75 in. Cab and chassis: 182.5 in. Stake: 183.88 in. Front/Rear Tread: 56 in./63.5 in. Overall Height: 74.38 in. Width: Pickup models: 66.625 in. Stake platform: 73.156 in. Front/Rear Overhang: 25.75 in./40 in. Tailgate: Width and Height: 48.50 in. x 15.75 in. Approach/Departure Degrees: 48/50. Ground Clearance: 8.125 in. Load space: Pickup: 80 in. x 48.5 in. Platform body 81.5 in. x 73 in.

CAPACITIES: Fuel Tank: 15.0 gal. Coolant system capacity: 9 qt.

ACCOMMODATIONS: Seating Capacity: Three.

INSTRUMENTATION: 0-80 mph speedometer, fuel, ammeter, oil pressure and temperature gauges.

OPTIONS AND PRICES: Hydrovac Power brake booster: $53.34. Transmission hand brake: $19.21. Fresh-Air heater and defroster: $79.93. Locking rear differential with 4.88:1 or 4.27:1 ratio: $42.96. Radio and antenna: $101.74. 9.00 x 13 4-ply rib Sand tires: $164.97. 7.00 x 16 6-ply Traction Himiler tires: No charge. 7.00 x 16 6-ply Grip Tread tires: $8.35. High altitude cylinder head: No charge. Front bumper rail and guard: $16.69. Hot climate heater: $10.38. Two-tone paint: $18.67. Heavy-duty rear end modification: $216.09.

HISTORICAL FOOTNOTES: The 1957 trucks were introduced in mid-August, 1956.

1958 PICKUP TRUCKS

No changes were made in the Jeep truck design format for 1958.

I.D. DATA: The serial number was located on a plate found on the outside of the left frame side rail at the front and also on the left of the driver's seat on the floor riser. The engine number was stamped on top of the cylinder block water pump boss. Series number range: 6-226 Chassis and cab: 55168-11189 and up; 6-226 pickup: 55268-22248 and up; 6-226 Stake Platform: 55368-10761 and up.

Body Type	Factory Price	GVW	Shipping Weight	Prod. Total
Model 6-226-four-wheel drive (1 ton, four-wheel drive, 118 in. wheelbase)				
Chassis and Cab	$2279	6000	2817	—
Pickup	$2190	6000	3176	—
Stake	$2267	6000	3341	—

STANDARD ENGINE: 6-226 Series. Engine Type: L-head In-line-6-cyl. "Super-Hurricane", cast iron block and cylinder head. Bore x Stroke: 3.9375 in. x 4.375 in. Lifters: Solid. Number of main bearings-4. Fuel Induction: Single barrel Carter YF carburetor, model 2052S or 2052A. Compression Ratio: 6.861. Optional: 7.3:1 compression ratio. Displacement: 226.2 cu. in. (3.7 liters). Horsepower: 115 @ 3800 rpm. Torque: 190 lb.-ft. @ 1800 rpm. Oil refill capacity: 5 qt. Fuel Requirements: Regular.

CHASSIS FEATURES: Separate body and chassis. Channel steel frame side rails. Six cross members. Dimensions: 5.5 in. x 2.0 in. x 0.179 in. Section modulus: 2.581 cu. in.

SUSPENSION AND RUNNING GEAR: Front Suspension: Nine leaf semi-elliptical springs, 36.25 in. x by 1.75 in. Compression rate: 303 lb./in. Double acting shock absorbers. Rear Suspension: Eleven leaf semi-elliptical springs, 50 in. x 2.0 inches. Spring rate: 370/410 lb./in. Double acting shock absorbers. Front Axle Type: Spicer model 25 full-floating. Axle ratio: 4.88:1. Optional: 4.27:1 with locking rear differential. Rear Axle Type: Semi-floating Timken model 51540. Transfer Case: Ratios: Spicer model 18. Ratios: 2.43, 1.0:1. Brakes: Type: Hydraulic, front and rear. Dimensions: Front and rear: 11.00 in. x 2.0 in. Wheels: 16 x 5.00. Tires: 7.00 x 16. 6-ply. Steering: Cam and twin pin lever, variable ratio. Ratio: 15.4-13.5-10.54:1. Turning circle: 50 ft. Optional None. Standard Transmission: Warner ASI-T909E 3-speed manual transmission. Transmission ratios: 3.44, 1.85 and 1.0:1. Clutch: 10.0 in. dia.

VEHICLE DIMENSIONS: Wheelbase: 118 in. Overall Length: Pickup:183.75 in. Cab and chassis: 182.5 in. Stake: 183.88 in. Front/Rear Tread: 56 in./63.5 in. Overall Height: 74.38 in. Width: Pickup models: 66.625 in. Stake platform: 73.156 in. Front/Rear Overhang: 25.75 in./40 in. Tailgate: Width and Height: 48.50 in. x 15.75 in. Approach/Departure Degrees: 48/50. Ground Clearance: 8.125 in. Load space: Pickup: 80 in. x 48.5 in. Platform body 81.5 in. x 73 in.

CAPACITIES: Fuel Tank: 15.0 gal. Coolant system capacity: 9 qt.

ACCOMMODATIONS: Seating Capacity: Three.

INSTRUMENTATION: 0-80 mph speedometer, fuel, ammeter, oil pressure and temperature gauges.

OPTIONS AND PRICES: Hydrovac power brake booster: $53.34. Transmission hand brake: $19.21. Fresh-Air heater and defroster: $79.93. Locking rear differential with 4.88:1 or 4.27:1 ratio: $42.96. Radio and antenna: $101.74. 9.00 x 13 4-ply rib Sand tires: $164.97. 7.00 x 16 6-ply Traction Himiler tires: No charge. 7.00 x 16 6-ply Grip Tread tires: $8.35. High altitude cylinder head: No charge. Front bumper rail and guard: $16.69. Hot climate heater: $10.38. Two-tone paint: $18.67. Heavy-duty rear end modification: $216.09.

HISTORICAL FOOTNOTES: The Jeep trucks were introduced on Aug. 15,1957.

1959 PICKUP TRUCKS

Although no changes were made for 1959, except for revised horsepower and torque rating for the 226 engine, and the availability of the 4-cylinder engine, the apparently ageless Jeep truck design still compared favorably to many of its competitors. Jeep trucks scored high in comparisons based upon initial cost, variety of special bodies offered, payload length, GVW ratings, standard tire capacity and resale value.

I.D. DATA: The serial number was located on a plate found on the outside of the left frame side rail at the front and also on the left of the driver's seat on the floor riser. The engine number was stamped on top of the cylinder block water pump boss. Series number range: 6-226 Chassis and cab: 55168-11597 and up; 6-226 pickup: 55268-27675 and up; 6-226 Stake Platform: 55368-11229 and up.

Body Type	Factory Price	GVW	Shipping Weight	Prod. Total
Model 6-226-four-wheel drive (1 ton, four-wheel drive, 118 in. wheelbase)				
Chassis and Cab	$2363*	6000	2817	—
Pickup	$2248	6000	3176	—
Stake	$2575	6000	3341	—

Prices of these models with the optional 4-cylinder engine were: Chassis and Cab: $2243, Pickup: $2368, Stake: $2455.

STANDARD ENGINE: 6-226 series: Engine Type: L-head In-line-6-cyl. "Super-Hurricane", cast iron block and cylinder head. Bore x Stroke: 3.9375 in. x 4.375 in. Lifters: Solid. Number of main bearings-4. Fuel Induction: Single barrel Carter YF carburetor, model 2052S or 2052A. Compression Ratio: 6.861. Optional: 7.3:1 compression ratio. Displacement: 226.2 cu. in. (3.7 liters). Horsepower: 105 @ 3600 rpm. Torque: 190 lb.-ft. @ 1400 rpm. Oil refill capacity: 5 qt. Fuel Requirements: Regular.

OPTIONAL ENGINE: Engine Type: F-head (overhead intake valve, side exhaust valve) In-line-4. Cast iron block and cylinder head. Bore x Stroke: 3.125 in. x 4.375 in. Lifters: Hydraulic. Number of main bearings-3. Fuel Induction: Carter single barrel carburetor, model 626.

Compression Ratio: 6.91. Optional: High altitude cylinder head with a 7.4:1 compression ratio. Displacement: 134.2 cu. in. (2.19 liters). Horsepower: 72 @ 4000 rpm. Torque: 114 lb.-ft. @ 2000 rpm. Oil refill capacity: 4 qt. Fuel Requirements: Regular.

CHASSIS FEATURES: Separate body and chassis. Channel steel frame side rails. Six cross members. Dimensions: 5.5 in. x 2.0 in. x 0.179 in. Section modulus: 2.581 cu. in.

SUSPENSION AND RUNNING GEAR: Front Suspension: Nine leaf semi-elliptical springs, 36.25 in. x by 1.75 in. Compression rate: 303 lb./in. Double acting shock absorbers. Rear Suspension: Eleven leaf semi-elliptical springs, 50 in. x 2.0 inches. Spring rate: 370/410 lb./in. Double acting shock absorbers. Front Axle Type: Spicer model 25 full-floating. Axle ratio: 4-cyl.: 5.38:1, 6-cyl.: 4.88:1. Optional: 4-cyl.: 6.17, 4.88:1. 6-cyl.: 5.38:1. Rear Axle Type: Semi-floating Timken model 51540. Transfer Case: Ratios: Spicer model 18. Ratios: 2.43, 1.0:1. Brakes: Type: Hydraulic, front and rear. Dimensions: Front and rear: 11.00 in. x 2.0 in. Wheels: 16 x 5.00. Tires: 7.00 x 16. 6-ply. Steering: Cam and twin pin lever, variable ratio. Ratio: 15.4-13.5-10.54:1. Turning circle: 50 ft. Optional None. Standard Transmission: Warner ASI-T909E 3-speed manual transmission. Transmission ratios: 3.44, 1.85 and 1.0:1. Clutch: 10.0 in. dia.

VEHICLE DIMENSIONS: Wheelbase: 118 in. Overall Length: Pickup:183.75 in. Cab and chassis: 182.5 in. Stake: 183.88 in. Front/Rear Tread: 56 in./63.5 in. Overall Height: 74.38 in. Width: Pickup models: 66.625 in. Stake platform: 73.156 in. Front/Rear Overhang: 25.75 in./40 in. Tailgate: Width and Height: 48.50 in. x 15.75 in. Approach/Departure Degrees: 48/50. Ground Clearance: 8.125 in. Load space: Pickup: 80 in. x 48.5 in. Platform body 81.5 in. x 73 in.

CAPACITIES: Fuel Tank: 15.0 gal. Coolant system capacity: 4-cyl.: 11 qt. 6-cyl.: 9 qt.

ACCOMMODATIONS: Seating Capacity: Three.

INSTRUMENTATION: 0-80 mph speedometer, fuel, ammeter, oil pressure and temperature gauges.

OPTIONS AND PRICES: Hydrovac Power brake booster. Transmission hand brake. Fresh-Air heater and defroster. Locking rear differential with 4.88:1 or 4.27:1 ratio. Radio and antenna. 9.00 x 13 4-ply rib Sand tires. 7.00 x 16 6-ply Traction Himiler tires. 7.00 x 16 6-ply Grip Tread tires. High altitude cylinder head: No charge. Front bumper rail and guard. Hot climate heater. Two-tone paint. Heavy-duty rear end modification.

HISTORICAL FOOTNOTES: The 1959 Jeep trucks were introduced in the fall of 1958. Jeep reported that the prices of its trucks were the lowest in their field.

1960 PICKUP TRUCKS

The latest Jeep trucks were easily identified by their new exterior appearance highlighted by a one-piece windshield, and a new side body trim molding that made possible a rather attractive new two-tone paint scheme. A moderate updating of the interior appointments also took place at this time. Occupants appreciated the use of new Torflex seat springs that provided a better ride and more comfort.

1960 Jeep pickup truck

I.D. DATA: The serial number was located on a plate found on the outside of the left frame side rail at the front and also on the left of the driver's seat on the floor riser. The engine number was stamped on top of the cylinder block water pump boss. Series number range: 6-226 Chassis and cab: 55168-16965 and up; 6-226 pickup: 55268-34561 and up; 6-226 Stake Platform: 55368-12077 and up.

Body Type	Factory Price	GVW	Shipping Weight	Prod. Total
Model 6-226-four-wheel drive (1 ton, four-wheel drive, 118 in. wheelbase)				
Chassis and Cab	$2363	6000	2817	—
Pickup	$2448	6000	3176	—
Stake	$2575	6000	3341	—

STANDARD ENGINE: 6-226 series: Engine Type: L-head In-line-6-cyl. "Super-Hurricane", cast iron block and cylinder head. Bore x Stroke: 3.9375 in. x 4.375 in. Lifters: Solid. Number of main bearings-4. Fuel Induction: Single barrel Carter YF carburetor, model 2052S or 2052A. Compression Ratio: 6.861. Optional: 7.3:1 compression ratio. Displacement: 226.2 cu. in. (3.7 liters). Horsepower: 105 @ 3600 rpm. Torque: 190 lb.-ft. @ 1400 rpm. Oil refill capacity: 5 qt. Fuel Requirements: Regular.

OPTIONAL ENGINE: Engine Type: F-head (overhead intake valve, side exhaust valve) In-line-4. Cast iron block and cylinder head. Bore x Stroke: 3.125 in. x 4.375 in. Lifters: Hydraulic. Number of main bearings-3. Fuel Induction: Carter single barrel carburetor, model 626. Compression Ratio: 7.4:1. Optional: High altitude cylinder head with a 7.8:1 compression ratio. Displacement: 134.2 cu. in. (2.19 liters). Horsepower: 75 @ 4000 rpm. Torque: 114 lb.-ft. @ 2000 rpm. Oil refill capacity: 4 qt. Fuel Requirements: Regular.

CHASSIS FEATURES: Separate body and chassis. Channel steel frame side rails. Six cross members. Dimensions: 5.5 in. x 2.0 in. x 0.179 in. Section modulus: 2.581 cu. in.

SUSPENSION AND RUNNING GEAR: Front Suspension: Nine leaf semi-elliptical springs, 36.25 in. x by 1.75 in. Compression rate: 303 lb./in. Double acting shock absorbers. Rear Suspension: Eleven leaf semi-elliptical springs, 50 in. x 2.0 inches. Spring rate: 370/410 lb./in. Double acting shock absorbers. Front Axle Type: Spicer model 25 full-floating. Axle ratio: 4-cyl.: 5.38:1, 6-cyl.: 4.88:1. Optional: 4-cyl.: 6.17, 4.88:1. 6-cyl.: 5.38:1. Rear Axle Type: Semi-floating Timken model 51540. Transfer Case: Ratios: Spicer model 18. Ratios: 2.43, 1.0:1. Brakes: Type: Hydraulic, front and rear. Dimensions: Front and rear: 11.00 in. x 2.0 in. Wheels: 16 x 5.00. Tires: 7.00 x 16 in. 6-ply. Steering: Cam and twin pin lever, variable ratio. Ratio: 15.4-13.5-10.54:1. Turning circle: 47.25 ft. Optional None. Standard Transmission: Warner ASI-T909E 3-speed manual transmission. Transmission ratios: 3.44, 1.85 and 1.0:1. Clutch: 10.0 in. dia.

VEHICLE DIMENSIONS: Wheelbase: 118 in. Overall Length: Pickup:183.75 in. Cab and chassis: 182.5 in. Stake: 183.88 in. Front/Rear Tread: 56 in./63.5 in. Overall Height: 74.38 in. Width: Pickup models: 66.625 in. Stake platform: 73.156 in. Front/Rear Overhang: 25.75 in./40 in. Tailgate: Width and Height: 48.50 in. x 15.75 in. Approach/Departure Degrees: 48/50. Ground Clearance: 8.125 in. Load space: Pickup: 80 in. x 48.5 in. Platform body 81.5 in. x 73 in.

CAPACITIES: Fuel Tank: 15.0 gal. Coolant system capacity: 4-cyl.: 11 qt. 6-cyl.: 9 qt.

ACCOMMODATIONS: Seating Capacity: Three.

INSTRUMENTATION: 0-80 mph speedometer, fuel, ammeter, oil pressure and temperature gauges.

OPTIONS: Hydrovac Power brake booster. Transmission hand brake. Fresh-Air heater and defroster. Locking rear differential with 4.88:1 or 4.27:1 ratio. Radio and antenna. 9.00 x 13 4-ply rib Sand tires. 7.00 x 16 6-ply Traction Himiler tires. 7.00 x 16 6-ply Grip Tread tires. High altitude cylinder head: No charge. Front bumper rail and guard. Hot climate heater. Two-tone paint. Heavy-duty rear end modification.

HISTORICAL FOOTNOTES: The death of Barney Roos, one of the greatest automotive designers of the age and the "Father of the Jeep" brought an era of Jeep history to a close.

The Platform Stake model was not available with the 4-cylinder Hurricane engine for 1961.

1961 Jeep model 6-226

I.D. DATA: The serial number was located on a plate found on the outside of the left frame side rail at the front and also on the left of the driver's seat on the floor riser. The engine number was stamped on top of the cylinder block water pump boss. Series number range: 6-226 Chassis and cab: 55168-19578 and up; 6-226 pickup: 55268-46569 and up; 6-226 Stake Platform: 55368-12201 and up.

Body Type	Factory Price	GVW	Shipping Weight	Prod. Total
Model 6-226-four-wheel drive (1 ton, four-wheel drive, 118 in. wheelbase)				
Chassis and Cab	$2365	6000	2817	—
Pickup	$2490	6000	3176	—
Stake	$2577	6000	3341	—

STANDARD ENGINE: 6-226 series: Engine Type: L-head In-line-6-cyl. "Super-Hurricane", cast iron block and cylinder head. Bore x Stroke: 3.9375 in. x 4.375 in. Lifters: Solid. Number of main bearings-4. Fuel Induction: Single barrel Carter YF carburetor, model 2052S or 2052A. Compression Ratio: 6.861. Optional: 7.3:1 compression ratio. Displacement: 226.2 cu. in. (3.7 liters). Horsepower: 105 @ 3600 rpm. Torque: 190 lb.-ft. @ 1400 rpm. Oil refill capacity: 5 qt. Fuel Requirements: Regular.

OPTIONAL ENGINE: Engine Type: F-head (overhead intake valve, side exhaust valve) In-line-4. Cast iron block and cylinder head. Bore x Stroke: 3.125 in. x 4.375 in. Lifters: Hydraulic. Number of main bearings-3. Fuel Induction: Carter single barrel carburetor, model 626. Compression Ratio: 7.4:1. Optional: High altitude cylinder head with a 7.8:1 compression ratio. Displacement: 134.2 cu. in. (2.19 liters). Horsepower: 75 @ 4000 rpm. Torque: 114 lb.-ft. @ 2000 rpm. Oil refill capacity: 4 qt. Fuel Requirements: Regular.

CHASSIS FEATURES: Separate body and chassis. Channel steel frame side rails. Six cross members. Dimensions: 5.5 in. x 2.0 in. x 0.179 in. Section modulus: 2.581 cu. in.

SUSPENSION AND RUNNING GEAR: Front Suspension: Nine leaf semi-elliptical springs, 36.25 in. x by 1.75 in. Compression rate: 303 lb./in. Double acting shock absorbers. Rear Suspension: Eleven leaf semi-elliptical springs, 50 in. x 2.0 inches. Spring rate: 370/410 lb./in. Double acting shock absorbers. Front Axle Type: Spicer model 25 full-floating. Axle ratio: 4-cyl.: 5.38:1, 6-cyl.: 4.88:1. Optional: 4-cyl.: 6.17, 4.88:1. 6-cyl.: 5.38:1. Rear Axle Type: Semi-floating Timken model 51540. Transfer Case: Ratios: Spicer model 18. Ratios: 2.43, 1.0:1. Brakes: Type: Hydraulic, front and rear. Dimensions: Front and rear: 11.00 in. x 2.0 in. Wheels: 16 x 5.00. Tires: 7.00 x 16 in. 6-ply. Steering: Cam and twin pin lever, variable ratio.

Ratio: 15.4-13.5-10.54:1. Turning circle: 47.25 ft. Optional None. Standard Transmission: Warner ASI-T909E 3-speed manual transmission. Transmission ratios: 3.44, 1.85 and 1.0:1. Clutch: 10.0 in. dia.

VEHICLE DIMENSIONS: Wheelbase: 118 in. Overall Length: Pickup:183.75 in. Cab and chassis: 182.5 in. Stake: 183.88 in. Front/Rear Tread: 56 in./63.5 in. Overall Height: 74.38 in. Width: Pickup models: 66.625 in. Stake platform: 73.156 in. Front/Rear Overhang: 25.75 in./40 in. Tailgate: Width and Height: 48.50 in. x 15.75 in. Approach/Departure Degrees: 48/50. Ground Clearance: 8.125 in. Load space: Pickup: 80 in. x 48.5 in. Platform body 81.5 in. x 73 in.

CAPACITIES: Fuel Tank: 15.0 gal. Coolant system capacity: 4-cyl.: 11 qt. 6-cyl.: 9 qt.

ACCOMMODATIONS: Seating Capacity: Three.

INSTRUMENTATION: 0-80 mph speedometer, fuel, ammeter, oil pressure and temperature gauges.

OPTIONS: Hydrovac Power brake booster. Transmission hand brake. Fresh-Air heater and defroster. Locking rear differential with 4.88:1 or 4.27:1 ratio. Radio and antenna. 9.00 x 13 4-ply rib Sand tires. 7.00 x 16 6-ply Traction Himiler tires. 7.00 x 16 6-ply Grip Tread tires. High altitude cylinder head: No charge. Front bumper rail and guard. Hot climate heater. Two-tone paint. Heavy-duty rear end modification.

HISTORICAL FOOTNOTES: The 1961 Jeep trucks debuted in the fall of 1960.

No changes were made for 1962 in the Jeep trucks.

I.D. DATA: The serial number was located on a plate found on the outside of the left frame side rail at the front and also on the left of the driver's seat on the floor riser. The engine number was stamped on top of the cylinder block water pump boss. Series number range: 6-226 Chassis and cab: 55168-22058 and up; 6-226 pickup: 55268-49190 and up; 6-226 Stake Platform: 55368-12394 and up.

Body Type	Factory Price	GVW	Shipping Weight	Prod. Total
Model 6-226-four-wheel drive (1 ton, four-wheel drive, 118 in. wheelbase.)				
Chassis and Cab	$2365	6000	2817	—
Pickup	$2490	6000	3176	—
Stake	$2577	6000	3341	—

STANDARD ENGINE: 6-226 series: Engine Type: L-head In-line-6-cyl. "Super-Hurricane", cast iron block and cylinder head. Bore x Stroke: 3.9375 in. x 4.375 in. Lifters: Solid. Number of main bearings-4. Fuel Induction: Single barrel Carter YF carburetor, model 2052S or 2052A. Compression Ratio: 6.861. Optional: 7.3:1 compression ratio. Displacement: 226.2 cu. in. (3.7 liters). Horsepower: 105 @ 3600 rpm. Torque: 190 lb.-ft. @ 1400 rpm. Oil refill capacity: 5 qt. Fuel Requirements: Regular.

OPTIONAL ENGINE: Engine Type: F-head (overhead intake valve, side exhaust valve) In-line-4. Cast iron block and cylinder head. Bore x Stroke: 3.125 in. x 4.375 in. Lifters: Hydraulic. Number of main bearings-3. Fuel Induction: Carter single barrel carburetor, model 626. Compression Ratio: 7.4:1. Optional: High altitude cylinder head with a 7.8:1 compression ratio. Displacement: 134.2 cu. in. (2.19 liters). Horsepower: 75 @ 4000 rpm. Torque: 114 lb.-ft. @ 2000 rpm. Oil refill capacity: 4 qt. Fuel Requirements: Regular.

CHASSIS FEATURES: Separate body and chassis. Channel steel frame side rails. Six cross members. Dimensions: 5.5 in. x 2.0 in. x 0.179 in. Section modulus: 2.581 cu. in.

SUSPENSION AND RUNNING GEAR: Front Suspension: Nine leaf semi-elliptical springs, 36.25 in. x by 1.75 in. Compression rate: 303 lb./in. Double acting shock absorbers. Rear Suspension: Eleven leaf semi-elliptical springs, 50 in. x 2.0 inches. Spring rate: 370/410 lb./in. Double acting shock absorbers. Front Axle Type: Spicer model 25 full-floating. Axle ratio: 4-cyl.: 5.38:1, 6-cyl.: 4.88:1. Optional: 4-cyl.: 6.17, 4.88:1. 6-cyl.: 5.38:1. Rear Axle Type: Semi-floating Timken model 51540. Transfer Case: Ratios: Spicer model 18. Ratios: 2.43, 1.0:1. Brakes: Type: Hydraulic, front and rear. Dimensions: Front and rear: 11.00 in. x 2.0 in. Wheels: 16 x 5.00. Tires: 7.00 x 16 in. 6-ply. Steering: Cam and twin pin lever, variable ratio. Ratio: 15.4-13.5-10.54:1. Turning circle: 47.25 ft. Optional None. Standard Transmission: Warner ASI-T909E 3-speed manual transmission. Transmission ratios: 3.44, 1.85 and 1.0:1. Clutch: 10.0 in. dia.

VEHICLE DIMENSIONS: Wheelbase: 118 in. Overall Length: Pickup:183.75 in. Cab and chassis: 182.5 in. Stake: 183.88 in. Front/Rear Tread: 56 in./63.5 in. Overall Height: 74.38 in. Width: Pickup models: 66.625 in. Stake platform: 73.156 in. Front/Rear Overhang: 25.75 in./40 in. Tailgate: Width and Height: 48.50 in. x 15.75 in. Approach/Departure Degrees: 48/50. Ground Clearance: 8.125 in. Load space: Pickup: 80 in. x 48.5 in. Platform body 81.5 in. x 73 in.

CAPACITIES: Fuel Tank: 15.0 gal. Coolant system capacity: 4-cyl.: 11 qt. 6-cyl.: 9 qt.

ACCOMMODATIONS: Seating Capacity: Three.

INSTRUMENTATION: 0-80 mph speedometer, fuel, ammeter, oil pressure and temperature gauges.

OPTIONS: Hydrovac Power brake booster. Transmission hand brake. Fresh-Air heater and defroster. Locking rear differential with 4.88:1 or 4.27:1 ratio. Radio and antenna. 9.00 x 13 4-ply rib Sand tires. 7.00 x 16 6-ply Traction Himiler tires. 7.00 x 16 6-ply Grip Tread tires. High altitude cylinder head: No charge. Front bumper rail and guard. Hot climate heater. Two-tone paint. Heavy-duty rear end modification.

HISTORICAL FOOTNOTES: The Jeep trucks were introduced in the fall of 1961.

In addition to the familiar 226 engine, the Jeep trucks were available with the 230 cu. in single overhead cam 6-cylinder engine. Models with this engine had a new 6-230 designation. The trucks were not available as 4-cylinder models.

I.D. DATA: The serial number was located on a plate found on the outside of the left frame side rail at the front and also on the left of the driver's seat on the floor riser. The engine number was stamped on top of the cylinder block water pump boss. Series number range: 6-226 Chassis and cab: 55168-24694 and up; 6-226 pickup: 55268-54147 and up; 6-226 Stake Platform: 55368-12752 and up. 6-230 Chassis and cab: 55178-10006 and up, 6-230 Pickup: 5278-10003 and up, 6-230 Platform Stake: 5378-10004 and up.

Body Type	Factory Price	GVW	Shipping Weight	Prod. Total
Model 6-226-four-wheel drive (1 ton, four-wheel drive, 118 in. wheelbase)				
Chassis and Cab	$2365	6000	2817	—
Pickup	$2490	6000	3176	—
Stake	$2577	6000	3341	—
Model 6-230-four-wheel drive (1 ton, four-wheel drive, 118 in. wheelbase)				
Chassis and Cab	$2472	6000	2872	—
Pickup	$2597	6000	3238	—
Stake	$2684	6000	3373	—

STANDARD ENGINE: 6-226 series: Engine Type: L-head In-line-6-cyl. "Super-Hurricane", cast iron block and cylinder head. Bore x Stroke: 3.9375 in. x 4.375 in. Lifters: Solid. Number of main bearings-4. Fuel Induction: Single barrel Carter YF carburetor, model 2052S or 2052A. Compression Ratio: 6.861. Optional: 7.3:1 compression ratio. Displacement: 226.2 cu. in. (3.7 liters). Horsepower: 105 @ 3600 rpm. Torque: 190 lb.-ft. @ 1400 rpm. Oil refill capacity: 5 qt. Fuel Requirements: Regular.

STANDARD ENGINE: 6-230 models: Engine Type: Tornado-230, 6-cyl., OHC, OHV, cast iron block and cylinder head. Bore x Stroke: 3.34 in. x 4.38 in. Lifters: Solid. Number of main bearings-4. Fuel Induction: Carter two barrel carburetor. Compression Ratio: 8.5:1. Displacement: 230 cu. in. (3.77 liters). Horsepower: Net 140 @ 4000 rpm. Torque: Net 210 lb.-ft. @ 1750 rpm. Oil refill capacity: 5 qt. Fuel Requirements: Regular.

CHASSIS FEATURES: Separate body and chassis. Channel steel frame side rails. Six cross members. Dimensions: 5.5 in. x 2.0 in. x 0.179 in. Section modulus: 2.581 cu. in.

SUSPENSION AND RUNNING GEAR: Front Suspension: Nine leaf semi-elliptical springs, 36.25 in. x by 1.75 in. Compression rate: 303 lb./in. Double acting shock absorbers. Rear Suspension: Eleven leaf semi-elliptical springs, 50 in. x 2.0 inches. Spring rate: 370/410 lb./in. Double acting shock absorbers. Front Axle Type: Spicer model 25 full-floating. Axle ratio: 4.88:1. Optional: 5.38:1. Rear Axle Type: Semi-floating Timken model 51540. Transfer Case: Ratios: Spicer model 18. Ratios: 2.43, 1.0:1. Brakes: Type: Hydraulic, front and rear. Dimensions: Front and rear: 11.00 in. x 2.0 in. Wheels: 16 x 5.00. Tires: 7.00 x 16 in. 6-ply. Steering: Cam and twin pin lever, variable ratio. Ratio: 15.4-13.5-10.54:1. Turning circle: 47.25 ft. Optional None. Standard Transmission: Warner ASI-T909E 3-speed manual transmission. Transmission ratios: 3.44, 1.85 and 1.0:1. Clutch: 10.0 in. dia.

VEHICLE DIMENSIONS: Wheelbase: 118 in. Overall Length: Pickup:183.75 in. Cab and chassis: 182.5 in. Stake: 183.88 in. Front/Rear Tread: 56 in./63.5 in. Overall Height: 74.38 in. Width: Pickup models: 66.625 in. Stake platform: 73.156 in. Front/Rear Overhang: 25.75 in./40 in. Tailgate: Width and Height: 48.50 in. x 15.75 in. Approach/Departure Degrees: 48/50. Ground Clearance: 8.125 in. Load space: Pickup: 80 in. x 48.5 in. Platform body 81.5 in. x 73 in.

CAPACITIES: Fuel Tank: 15.0 gal. Coolant system capacity: L-226: 9 qt. 6-230: 11 qt. (12 qt. with heater).

ACCOMMODATIONS: Seating Capacity: Three.

INSTRUMENTATION: 0-80 mph speedometer, fuel, ammeter, oil pressure and temperature gauges.

OPTIONS: Hydrovac Power brake booster. Transmission hand brake. Fresh-Air heater and defroster. Locking rear differential with 4.88:1 or 4.27:1 ratio. Radio and antenna. 9.00 x 13 4-ply rib Sand tires. 7.00 x 16 6-ply Traction Himiler tires. 7.00 x 16 6-ply Grip Tread tires. High altitude cylinder head: No charge. Front bumper rail and guard. Hot climate heater. Two-tone paint. Heavy-duty rear end modification.

HISTORICAL FOOTNOTES: The Jeep trucks were introduced in the fall of 1962.

1964 PICKUP TRUCKS

The L-226 truck was available only in pickup form for 1964. The 6-230 line was unchanged. A lower horsepower version of the OHC engine was available.

I.D. DATA: The serial number was located on a plate found on the outside of the left frame side rail at the front and also on the left of the driver's seat on the floor riser. The engine number was stamped on top of the cylinder block water pump boss. Series number range: 6-226 pickup: 55268-55482 and up; 6-226 Stake Platform: 55368-12752 and up. 6-230 Chassis and cab: 55178 or 6606-11048 and up, 6-230 pickup: 5278 6607-10034 and up, 6-230 Platform Stake: 5378 or 6608-10049 and up.

Body Type	Factory Price	GVW	Shipping Weight	Prod. Total
Model 6-226-four-wheel drive (1 ton, four-wheel drive, 118 in. wheelbase)				
Pickup	$2514	6000	3176	—
Model 6-230-four-wheel drive (1 ton, four-wheel drive, 118 in. wheelbase)				
Chassis and Cab	$2619	6000	2872	—
Pickup	$2744	6000	3238	—
Stake	$2831	6000	3373	—

STANDARD ENGINE: 6-226 series: Engine Type: L-head In-line-6-cyl. "Super-Hurricane", cast iron block and cylinder head. Bore x Stroke: 3.9375 in. x 4.375 in. Lifters: Solid. Number of main bearings-4. Fuel Induction: Single barrel Carter YF carburetor, model 2052S or 2052A. Compression Ratio: 6.861. Optional: 7.3:1 compression ratio. Displacement: 226.2 cu. in. (3.70 liters). Horsepower: 105 @ 3600 rpm. Torque: 190 lb.-ft. @ 1400 rpm. Oil refill capacity: 5 qt. Fuel Requirements: Regular.

STANDARD ENGINE: 6-230 models: Engine Type: Tornado-230, 6-cyl., OHC,OHV, cast iron block and cylinder head. Bore x Stroke: 3.34 in. x 4.38 in. Lifters: Solid. Number of main bearings-4. Fuel Induction: Carter two barrel carburetor. Compression Ratio: 8.5:1. (7.5:1 optional). Displacement: 230 cu. in. (3.77 liters). Horsepower: Net 140 @ 4000 rpm. 133 @ 4000 rpm with 7.5:1 compression ratio. Torque: Net 210 lb.-ft. @ 1750 rpm. 199 @ 2400 rpm with 7.5:1 compression ratio. Oil refill capacity: 5 qt. Fuel Requirements: Regular.

CHASSIS FEATURES: Separate body and chassis. Channel steel frame side rails. Six cross members. Dimensions: 5.5 in. x 2.0 in. x 0.179 in. Section modulus: 2.581 cu. in.

SUSPENSION AND RUNNING GEAR: Front Suspension: Nine leaf semi-elliptical springs, 36.25 in. x by 1.75 in. Compression rate: 303 lb./in. Double acting shock absorbers. Rear Suspension: Eleven leaf semi-elliptical springs, 50 in. x 2.0 inches. Spring rate: 370/410 lb./in. Double acting shock absorbers. Front Axle Type: Spicer model 25 full-floating. Axle ratio: 4.88:1. Optional: 5.38:1. Rear Axle Type: Semi-floating Timken model 51540. Transfer Case: Ratios: Spicer model 18. Ratios: 2.43, 1.0:1. Brakes: Type: Hydraulic, front and rear. Dimensions: Front and rear: 11.00 in. x 2.0 in. Wheels: 16 x 5.00. Tires: 7.00 x 16 in. 6-ply. Steering: Cam and twin pin lever, variable ratio. Ratio: 15.4-13.5-10.54:1. Turning circle: 47.25 ft. Optional None. Standard Transmission: Warner ASI-T909E 3-speed manual transmission. Transmission ratios: 3.44, 1.85 and 1.0:1. Clutch: 10.0 in. dia.

VEHICLE DIMENSIONS: Wheelbase: 118 in. Overall Length: Pickup: 183.75 in. Cab and chassis: 182.5 in. Stake: 183.88 in. Front/Rear Tread: 56 in./63.5 in. Overall Height: 74.38 in. Width: Pickup models: 66.625 in. Stake platform: 73.156 in. Front/Rear Overhang: 25.75 in./40 in. Tailgate: Width and Height: 48.50 in. x 15.75 in. Approach/Departure Degrees: 48/50. Ground Clearance: 8.125 in. Load space: Pickup: 80 in. x 48.5 in. Platform body 81.5 in. x 73 in.

CAPACITIES: Fuel Tank: 15.0 gal. Coolant system capacity: L-226: 9 qt. 6-230: 11 qt. (12 qt. with heater).

ACCOMMODATIONS: Seating Capacity: Three.

INSTRUMENTATION: 0-80 mph speedometer, fuel, ammeter, oil pressure and temperature gauges.

OPTIONS: Hydrovac Power brake booster. Transmission hand brake. Fresh-Air heater and defroster. Locking rear differential with 4.88:1 or 4.27:1 ratio. Radio and antenna. 9.00 x 13 4-ply rib Sand tires. 7.00 x 16 6-ply Traction Himiler tires. 7.00 x 16 6-ply Grip Tread tires. High altitude cylinder head: No charge. Front bumper rail and guard. Hot climate heater. Two-tone paint. Heavy-duty rear end modification.

HISTORICAL FOOTNOTES: The 1964 Jeep trucks were introduced in the fall of 1963.

1965 PICKUP TRUCKS

This was the final year for the classic Jeep truck design. The L-226 version was not available. The 6-230 line was unchanged.

I.D. DATA: The serial number was located on a plate found on the outside of the left frame side rail at the front and also on the left of the driver's seat on the floor riser. The engine number was stamped on top of the cylinder block water pump boss. Series number range: 6-230 Chassis and cab: 6606-12315 and up, 6-230 pickup: 6607-15116 and up, 6-230 Platform Stake:6608-10513 and up.

Body Type	Factory Price	GVW	Shipping Weight	Prod. Total
Model 6-230-four-wheel drive (1 ton, four-wheel drive,118 in. wheelbase)				
Chassis and Cab	$2619	6000	2872	—
Pickup	$2744	6000	3238	—
Stake	$2831	6000	3373	—

STANDARD ENGINE: Engine Type: Tornado-230, 6-cyl., OHC, OHV, cast iron block and cylinder head. Bore x Stroke: 3.34 in. x 4.38 in. Lifters: Solid. Number of main bearings-4. Fuel Induction: Carter two barrel carburetor. Compression Ratio: 8.5:1 (7.5:1 optional). Displacement: 230 cu. in. (3.77 liters). Horsepower: Net 140 @ 4000 rpm. 133 @ 4000 rpm with 7.5:1 compression ratio. Torque: Net 210 lb.-ft. @ 1750 rpm. 199 @ 2400 rpm with 7.5:1 compression ratio. Oil refill capacity: 5 qt. Fuel Requirements: Regular.

CHASSIS FEATURES: Separate body and chassis. Channel steel frame side rails. Six cross members. Dimensions: 5.5 in. x 2.0 in. x 0.179 in. Section modulus: 2.581 cu. in.

SUSPENSION AND RUNNING GEAR: Front Suspension: Nine leaf semi-elliptical springs, 36.25 in. x by 1.75 in. Compression rate: 303 lb./in. Double acting shock absorbers. Rear Suspension: Eleven leaf semi-elliptical springs, 50 in. x 2.0 inches. Spring rate: 370/410 lb./in. Double acting shock absorbers. Front Axle Type: Spicer model 25 full-floating. Axle ratio: 4.88:1. Optional: 5.38:1. Rear Axle Type: Semi-floating Timken model 51540. Transfer Case: Ratios: Spicer model 18. Ratios: 2.43, 1.0:1. Brakes: Type: Hydraulic, front and rear. Dimensions: Front and rear: 11.00 in. x 2.0 in. Wheels: 16 x 5.00. Tires: 7.00 x 16 in. 6-ply. Steering: Cam and twin pin lever, variable ratio. Ratio: 15.4-13.5-10.54:1. Turning circle: 47.25 ft. Optional None. Standard Transmission: Warner ASI-T909E 3-speed manual transmission. Transmission ratios: 3.44, 1.85 and 1.0:1. Clutch: 10.0 in. dia.

VEHICLE DIMENSIONS: Wheelbase: 118 in. Overall Length: Pickup: 183.75 in. Cab and chassis: 182.5 in. Stake: 183.88 in. Front/Rear Tread: 56 in./63.5 in. Overall Height: 74.38 in. Width: Pickup models: 66.625 in. Stake platform: 73.156 in. Front/Rear Overhang: 25.75 in./40 in. Tailgate: Width and Height: 48.50 in. x 15.75 in. Approach/Departure Degrees: 48/50. Ground Clearance: 8.125 in. Load space: Pickup: 80 in. x 48.5 in. Platform body 81.5 in. x 73 in.

CAPACITIES: Fuel Tank: 15.0 gal. Coolant system capacity: L-226: 9 qt. 6-230: 11 qt. (12 qt. with heater).

ACCOMMODATIONS: Seating Capacity: Three.

INSTRUMENTATION: 0-80 mph speedometer, fuel, ammeter, oil pressure and temperature gauges.

OPTIONS: Hydrovac Power brake booster. Transmission hand brake. Fresh-Air heater and defroster. Locking rear differential with 4.88:1 or 4.27:1 ratio. Radio and antenna. 9.00 x 13 4-ply rib Sand tires. 7.00 x 16 6-ply Traction Himiler tires. 7.00 x 16 6-ply Grip Tread tires. High altitude cylinder head: No charge. Front bumper rail and guard. Hot climate heater. Two-tone paint. Heavy-duty rear end modification.

HISTORICAL FOOTNOTES: Although no longer in production the first series of postwar Jeep trucks were destined to be common sights in rural America for many years.

JEEP WAGONS
1949-1965

1949 463 STATION WAGON

Willys introduced its new 463 four-wheel drive station wagon in 1949. Except for "Four-Wheel Drive" identification instead of "Jeep station wagon" on the hood sides, the new model had the same body appearance as the two-wheel drive model 463 Jeep station wagon which had entered production in July, 1946. The headlights were set inward from the fenders next to an attractive grille of simple vertical bars. The body had a ribbed, brown and cream color scheme suggestive of the mahogany and birch colors of wooden station wagon bodies. The only body color offered was dark burgundy. The arrangement of angular front fenders, a grille with narrow vertical opening enclosing seven-inch sealed beamed headlights and circular parking/directional lights plus a simple squared-off passenger/load area were key elements of the 463's functional look.

A two-piece windshield of flat glass was used. The upper portion of the rear section, housing a 2-section glass panel, was controlled by a simple T-handle. When opened it was supported by two hinges. The tailgate lowered to form a flat surface with the interior floor. Both the taillight and license plate holder swiveled 90 degrees so that they were visible when the tailgate was dropped. The front and rear seats were of the 60/40 design with simulated leather upholstery. They were mounted on a tubular steel frame. The headliner was finished in a patterned red washable plastic-coated fabric which contrasted with the body and door panel's aspen-grain finish. The armrest were upholstered to match the seats. A simple dash panel was used with a painted metal surface surrounding a centrally-positioned square-shaped instrument cluster. A glove box was located to the right of these items with the ignition key receptacle, choke and starter controls directly below them. A standard "Deluxe" steering wheel with a horn button rim was fitted as were front and rear dome lights. Other items included in the Willys' base equipment were a storage compartment under the front seat complete with a door, three ashtrays; one dash-mounted, the others located on the rear side panels, dual sun visors, front and rear armrests, combination fuel and vacuum pump, dual horns, rear bumper extensions, and key locks on both front doors. The spare tire was mounted in the Jeep's interior on the right side of the rear load area.

1949 Willys 463 station wagon

I.D. DATA: The serial number was located on a plate on the right side of the dash under the hood. The engine number was found on the right side of the cylinder block; stamped on the water pump boss. Serial number range: 10101-13185.

Model Number	Body Type	Factory Price	GVW	Shipping Weight	Prod. Total
4 x 463	St. Wagon	$1895	4000	3136	—

STANDARD ENGINE: Engine Type: 4-cyl., L-head, cast iron block and cylinder head. Bore x Stroke: 3.125 in. x 4.375 in. Lifters: Solid. Number of main bearings-3. Fuel Induction: Single barrel Carter model WA-1 carburetor. Compression Ratio: 6.5:1. "High Altitude" 7.0:1 cylinder optional. Displacement: 134.2 cu. in. (2.19 liters). Horsepower: 60 @ 4000 rpm. Torque: Net 106 lb.-ft. @ 2000 rpm. Oil refill capacity: 5 qt. Fuel Requirements: Regular.

CHASSIS FEATURES: Separate body and chassis. Heavy side members with 1-piece pressed steel channels. Six cross members of flanged U and channel section.

SUSPENSION AND RUNNING GEAR: Front Suspension: Semi-elliptical 10-leaf springs. 36.25 in. x 1.75 in. Spring rate: 260 lb./in. Capacity: 650 lb. direct acting hydraulic shock absorbers. Optional: None. Rear Suspension: Semi-elliptical 8-leaf springs, 50 in. x 1.75 in. Spring rate: 150 lb./in. Capacity: 900 lb. direct acting hydraulic shock absorbers. Front Axle Type: Spicer full-floating. Axle ratio: 5.38:1. Optional: None. Rear Axle Type: Semi-floating Spicer. Transfer Case: Spicer model 18. Ratios: 2.42:1, 1.00:1. Brakes: Type: Hydraulic, front and rear cast iron drums, dual master cylinder, double hydraulic circuit. Dimensions: Front and rear: 11.00 in. x 2.0 in. Total effective lining area: 176.2 sq. in. Optional: None. Wheels: 15 x 6K. Tires: 6.50 x 15 black sidewall. Steering: Cam and lever. Ratio: 26.0:1. Turning Circle: 37.8 ft. Standard Transmission: 3-speed manual. Transmission ratios: 2.798, 1.551, 1.0:1 Reverse: 3.798:1. Optional: None. Clutch: Single dry plate with torsional damping, 72 sq. in. Optional: None.

VEHICLE DIMENSIONS: Wheelbase: 104.5 in. Overall Length: 176.25 in. Front/Rear Tread: 57 in./57 in. Overall Height: 73.5625 in. Width: 71.75 in. Front/Rear Overhang: 25.75 in./46 in. Tailgate: Width and Height: 49.75 in. x 39.5 in. Approach/Departure Degrees: 38/19. Ground Clearance: Front axle: 9.5 in. Rear axle: 8.3125 in. Load space: 71.0 inches x 43.75 inch x 41.0 in. Maximum capacity (Volume Index): 112 cu. ft. Front headroom: 38.5 in.

CAPACITIES: Fuel Tank: 15.0 gallon capacity. Optional: None. Coolant System: 11 qt., 12 qt. with heater.

ACCOMMODATIONS: Seating Capacity: 4. Seat Dimensions: Front-Driver's: 31.875 in. Passenger's: 15 in. Rear: Divided: 15 in./26.375 in.

INSTRUMENTATION: 0-80 mph speedometer, gauges for fuel level, engine coolant temperature, oil pressure, ammeter.

OPTIONS: Dual horns. Oil bath air cleaner. Vacuum booster pump. One-piece longitudinally-positioned rear seat. Radio. Front bumper guard. Power take-off. Winches. Snowplows.

HISTORICAL FOOTNOTES: The introduction of the 4x4 station wagon marked the start of a new era of expanded market opportunities for Willys.

1950 463 STATION WAGON

Two series of 1950 models were produced. The first were unchanged from 1949 and were available through the spring of 1950. The second series went on sale April 16, 1950. The grille on the new models was slightly V'ed and had five chrome horizontal bars dividing the vertical units which continued to be painted the body's color. The front edge of the hood was now rolled under for added strength and rigidity. Added to the hood's leading edge was an ornament with a circular red Willys emblem. The lower valance found on the front fenders of the older models was removed and the fender's front section now had a slight V-shape and a modest crease line which faded back into the fender's top surface. A new F-head engine with the same bore and stroke replaced the old L-head engine.

I.D. DATA: The serial number was located to the left of the driver's seat on the floor riser. The engine number was found on a boss on top of the cylinder head directly behind the water pump. Serial number range: First series: 13186 and up. Second series: 1001 to 12450.

Model Number	Body Type	Factory Price	GVW	Shipping Weight	Prod. Total
First Series					
4 x 463	St. Wagon	$2010	—	3136	32,218*
Second Series					
4 x 473	St. Wagon	$1990	—	3136	—

* Calendar year production, both two- and four-wheel drive models.

STANDARD ENGINE: First series: Engine Type: 4-cyl., L-head, cast iron block and cylinder head. Bore x Stroke: 3.125 in. x 4.375 in. Lifters: Solid. Number of main bearings-3. Fuel Induction: Single barrel Carter model WA-1carburetor. Compression Ratio: 6.5:1. "High Altitude" 7.0:1 cylinder head optional. Displacement: 134.2 cu. in. (2.19 liters). Horsepower: 60 @ 4000 rpm. Torque: Net 106 lb.-ft. @ 2000 rpm. Oil refill capacity: 5 qt. Fuel Requirements: Regular.

STANDARD ENGINE: Second series: Engine Type: 4-cyl., F-head, cast iron block and cylinder head. Bore x Stroke: 3.125 in. x 4.375 in. Lifters: Solid. Number of main bearings-3. Fuel Induction: Single barrel Carter model WA-1 carburetor. Compression Ratio: 6.91. "High Altitude" 7.4:1 cylinder head optional. Displacement: 134.2 cu. in. (2.19 liters). Horsepower: 72 @ 4000 rpm. Torque: Net 114 lb.-ft. @ 2000 rpm. Oil refill capacity: 5 qt. Fuel Requirements: Regular. No other changes took place for 1950.

CHASSIS FEATURES: Separate body and chassis. Heavy side members with 1-piece pressed steel channels. Six cross members of flanged U and channel section.

SUSPENSION AND RUNNING GEAR: Front Suspension: Semi-elliptical 10-leaf springs. 36.25 in. x 1.75 in. Spring rate: 260 lb. /in. Capacity: 650 lb. direct acting hydraulic shock absorbers. Optional: None. Rear Suspension: Semi-elliptical 8-leaf springs, 50 in. x 1.75 in. Spring rate: 150 lb./in. Capacity: 900 lb. direct acting hydraulic shock absorbers. Front Axle Type: Spicer full-floating. Axle ratio: 5.38:1. Optional: None. Rear Axle Type: Semi-floating Spicer. Transfer Case: Spicer model 18. Ratios: 2.42:1, 1.00:1. Brakes: Type: Hydraulic, front and rear cast iron drums, dual master cylinder, double hydraulic circuit. Dimensions: Front and rear: 11.00 in. x 2.0 in. Total effective lining area: 176.2 sq. in. Optional: None. Wheels: 15 x 6K. Tires: 6.50 x 15 black sidewall. Steering: Cam and lever. Ratio: 26.0:1. Turning Circle: 37.8 ft. Standard Transmission: 3-speed manual. Transmission ratios: 2.798, 1.551, 1.0:1 Reverse: 3.798:1. Optional: None. Clutch: Single dry plate with torsional damping, 72 sq. in. Optional: None.

VEHICLE DIMENSIONS: Wheelbase: 104.5 in. Overall Length: 176.25 in. Front/Rear Tread: 57 in./57 in. Overall Height: 73.5625 in. Width: 71.75 in. Front/Rear Overhang: 25.75 in./46 in. Tailgate: Width and Height: 49.75 in. x 39.5 in. Approach/Departure Degrees: 38/19. Ground Clearance: Front axle: 9.5 in. Rear axle: 8.3125 in. Load space: 71.0 in. x 43.75 in. x 41.0 in. Maximum capacity (Volume Index): 112 cu. ft. Front headroom: 38.5 in.

CAPACITIES: Fuel Tank: 15.0 gallon capacity. Optional: None. Coolant System: 11 qt., 12 qt. with heater.

ACCOMMODATIONS: Seating Capacity: 4. Seat Dimensions: Front-Driver's: 31.875 in. Passenger's: 15 in. Rear: Divided: 15 in./26.375 in.

INSTRUMENTATION: 0-80 mph speedometer, gauges for fuel level, engine coolant temperature, oil pressure, ammeter.

OPTIONS: Dual horns. Oil bath air cleaner. Vacuum booster pump. One-piece longitudinally-positioned rear seat. Radio. Front bumper guard. Power take-off. Winches. Snowplows.

HISTORICAL FOOTNOTES: The first series station wagons were introduced in Nov., 1949, followed by the second series on April 16, 1950.

1951 463
STATION WAGON

No significant changes were made in the station wagon for 1951.

I.D. DATA: A new serial number system was introduced for 1951. The first number indicated the number of cylinders, the next two numbers identified the model year. The next entry, a letter, served to identify the basic chassis and body type. The next letter indicated the model. The next character, a number, indicated the series in a particular model year. Serial number range: 451-FA1-10001 to 21854.

Model Number	Body Type	Factory Price	GVW	Shipping Weight	Prod. Total
4 x 473	St. Wagon	$2204	—	3174	

STANDARD ENGINE: Engine Type: 4-cyl., F-head, cast iron block and cylinder head. Bore x Stroke: 3.125 in. x 4.375 in. Lifters: Solid. Number of main bearings-3. Fuel Induction: Single barrel Carter model WA-1 carburetor. Compression Ratio: 6.91. "High Altitude" 7.4:1 cylinder head optional. Displacement: 134.2 cu. in. (2.19 liters). Horsepower: 72 @ 4000 rpm. Torque: Net 114 lb.-ft. @ 2000 rpm. Oil refill capacity: 5 qt. Fuel Requirements: Regular.

CHASSIS FEATURES: Separate body and chassis. Heavy side members with 1-piece pressed steel channels. Six cross members of flanged U and channel section.

SUSPENSION AND RUNNING GEAR: Front Suspension: Semi-elliptical 10-leaf springs. 36.25 in. x 1.75 in. Spring rate: 260 lb./in. Capacity: 650 lb. direct acting hydraulic shock absorbers. Optional: None. Rear Suspension: Semi-elliptical 8-leaf springs, 50 in. x 1.75 in. Spring rate: 150 lb./in. Capacity: 900 lb. direct acting hydraulic shock absorbers. Front Axle Type: Spicer full-floating. Axle ratio: 5.38:1. Optional: None. Rear Axle Type: Semi-floating Spicer. Transfer Case: Spicer model 18. Ratios: 2.42:1, 1.00:1. Brakes: Type: Hydraulic, front and rear cast iron drums, dual master cylinder, double hydraulic circuit. Dimensions: Front and rear: 11.00 in. x 2.0 in. Total effective lining area: 176.2 sq. in. Optional: None. Wheels: 15 x 6K. Tires: 6.50 x 15 black sidewall. Steering: Cam and lever. Ratio: 26.0:1. Turning Circle: 37.8 ft. Standard Transmission: 3-speed manual. Transmission ratios: 2.798, 1.551, 1.0:1 Reverse: 3.798:1. Optional: None. Clutch: Single dry plate with torsional damping, 72 sq. in. Optional: None.

VEHICLE DIMENSIONS: Wheelbase: 104.5 in. Overall Length: 176.25 in. Front/Rear Tread: 57 in./57 in. Overall Height: 73.5625 in. Width: 71.75 in. Front/Rear Overhang: 25.75 in./46 in. Tailgate: Width and Height: 49.75 in. x 39.5 in. Approach/Departure Degrees: 38/19. Ground Clearance: Front axle: 9.5 in. Rear axle: 8.3125 in. Load space: 71.0 in. x 43.75 in. x 41.0 in. Maximum capacity (Volume Index): 112 cu. ft. Front headroom: 38.5 in.

CAPACITIES: Fuel Tank: 15.0 gallon capacity. Optional: None. Coolant System: 11 qt., 12 qt. with heater.

ACCOMMODATIONS: Seating Capacity: 4. Seat Dimensions: Front-Driver's: 31.875 in. Passenger's: 15 in. Rear: Divided: 15 in./26.375 in.

INSTRUMENTATION: 0-80 mph speedometer, gauges for fuel level, engine coolant temperature, oil pressure, ammeter.

OPTIONS: Dual horns. Oil bath air cleaner. Vacuum booster pump. One-piece longitudinally-positioned rear seat. Radio. Front bumper guard. Power take-off. Winches. Snowplows.

HISTORICAL FOOTNOTES: Willys promoted the four-wheel drive station wagon as a "combination passenger and utility vehicle that provides dependable year-around transportation under conditions that would stop others cold."

1952 463
STATION WAGON

A number of small changes were made in the exterior of the 1952 station wagon. At the rear new flush-mounted, vertically-positioned taillights were installed midway up on the body's side corners. The license plate bracket and light assembly had a new center location on the tailgate. As before, it was adjustable to the position of the tailgate. With the tailgate open or closed the license plate could be brought into full view. A new Deluxe station wagon four-wheel drive model was introduced for 1952. It was identified by its new hood ornament and new side panels with woven inserts. Standard on this model was an all vinyl plastic interior with vertically pleated seat backs and seating areas with contrasting solid bolsters and facing. The seats were also of a new design. The headliner was covered with the same vinyl as the seats. Other changes incorporated into the new wagon included ignition starting, called "Startakey" by Willys, a revised braking system requiring less pedal pressure and improved "live-rubber" engine mounts that were calibrated and positioned to absorb more vibrations.

I.D. DATA: The same nomenclature as introduced in 1951 was used in 1952. Serial number range: 4 x 473 station wagon: 452-FA1-10001 and up. 4 x 475 Deluxe station wagon: 452-FA2-10001 and up.

Model Number	Body Type	Factory Price	GVW	Shipping Weight	Prod. Total
4 x 473	St. Wagon	$2235	4500	3174	9713*
4 x 475	Deluxe St. Wagon	$2304	4500	3174	—

* Calendar year production of all four-wheel drive station wagons.

STANDARD ENGINE: Engine Type: 4-cyl., F-head, cast iron block and cylinder head. Bore x Stroke: 3.125 in. x 4.375 in. Lifters: Solid. Number of main bearings-3. Fuel Induction: Single barrel Carter model WA-1 carburetor. Compression Ratio: 6.91. "High Altitude" 7.4:1 cylinder head optional. Displacement: 134.2 cu. in. (2.19 liters). Horsepower: 72 @ 4000 rpm. Torque: Net 114 lb.-ft. @ 2000 rpm. Oil refill capacity: 5 qt. Fuel Requirements: Regular.

CHASSIS FEATURES: Separate body and chassis. Heavy side members with 1-piece pressed steel channels. Six cross members of flanged U and channel section.

SUSPENSION AND RUNNING GEAR: Front Suspension: Semi-elliptical 10-leaf springs. 36.25 in. x 1.75 in. Spring rate: 260 lb./in. Capacity: 650 lb. direct acting hydraulic shock absorbers. Optional: None. Rear Suspension: Semi-elliptical 8-leaf springs, 50 in. x 1.75 in. Spring rate: 150 lb./in. Capacity: 900 lb. direct acting hydraulic shock absorbers. Front Axle Type: Spicer full-floating. Axle ratio: 5.38:1. Optional: None. Rear Axle Type: Semi-floating Spicer. Transfer Case: Spicer model 18. Ratios: 2.42:1, 1.00:1. Brakes: Type: Hydraulic, front and rear cast iron drums, dual master cylinder, double hydraulic circuit. Dimensions: Front and rear: 11.00 in. x 2.0 in. Total effective lining area: 176.2 sq. in. Optional: None. Wheels: 15 x 6K. Tires: 6.50 x 15 black sidewall. Steering: Cam and lever. Ratio: 26.0:1. Turning Circle: 37.8 ft. Standard Transmission: 3-speed manual. Transmission ratios: 2.798, 1.551, 1.0:1 Reverse: 3.798:1. Optional: None. Clutch: Single dry plate with torsional damping, 72 sq. in. Optional: None.

VEHICLE DIMENSIONS: Wheelbase: 104.5 in. Overall Length: 176.25 in. Front/Rear Tread: 57 in./57 in. Overall Height: 73.5625 in. Width: 71.75 in. Front/Rear Overhang: 25.75 in./46 in. Tailgate: Width and Height: 49.75 in. x 39.5 in. Approach/Departure Degrees: 38/19. Ground Clearance: Front axle: 9.5 in. Rear axle: 8.3125 in. Load space: 71.0 in. x 43.75 in. x 41.0 in. Maximum capacity (Volume Index): 112 cu. ft. Front headroom: 38.5 in.

CAPACITIES: Fuel Tank: 15.0 gallon capacity. Optional: None. Coolant System: 11 qt., 12 qt. with hea.er.

ACCOMMODATIONS: Seating Capacity: 4. Seat Dimensions: Front-Driver's: 31.875 in. Passenger's: 15 in. Rear: Divided: 15 in./26.375 in.

INSTRUMENTATION: 0-80 mph speedometer, gauges for fuel level, engine coolant temperature, oil pressure, ammeter.

OPTIONS: Dual horns. Oil bath air cleaner. Vacuum booster pump. One-piece longitudinally-positioned rear seat. Radio. Front bumper guard. Power take-off. Winches. Snowplows.

HISTORICAL FOOTNOTES: The 1952 models were introduced on Dec. 10, 1951.

1953 463
STATION WAGON

Joining the four-wheel drive station wagon models was a four-wheel drive version of the sedan delivery model which had been offered in two-wheel drive form since 1947. This Willys model had solid side panels and dual rear doors. The 4 x 473 model was not offered for 1953.

1953 four-wheel drive Willys station wagon

I.D. DATA: The same system as introduced in 1951 was used in 1953. Serial number range: 4 x 475 Deluxe station wagon: 453-FA2-10001 and up. 4 x 475 sedan delivery: 453-RA2-10001 to 10,992.

Model Number	Body Type	Factory Price	GVW	Shipping Weight	Prod. Total
4 x 475	Deluxe St. Wagon	$2134	4500	3174	5417*
4 x 475	Sedan Del.	$1920	4500	2976	—

* Calendar year production of two- and four-wheel drive station wagons.

STANDARD ENGINE: Engine Type: 4-cyl., F-head, cast iron block and cylinder head. Bore x Stroke: 3.125 in. x 4.375 in. Lifters: Solid. Number of main bearings-3. Fuel Induction: Single barrel Carter model WA-1 carburetor. Compression Ratio: 6.91. "High Altitude" 7.4:1 cylinder head optional. Displacement: 134.2 cu. in. (2.19 liters). Horsepower: 72 @ 4000 rpm. Torque: Net 114 lb.-ft. @ 2000 rpm. Oil refill capacity: 5 qt. Fuel Requirements: Regular.

CHASSIS FEATURES: Separate body and chassis. Heavy side members with 1-piece pressed steel channels. Six cross members of flanged U and channel section.

SUSPENSION AND RUNNING GEAR: Front Suspension: Semi-elliptical 10-leaf springs. 36.25 in. x 1.75 in. Spring rate: 260 lb./in. Capacity: 650 lb. direct acting hydraulic shock absorbers. Optional: None. Rear Suspension: Semi-elliptical 8-leaf springs, 50 in. x 1.75 in. Spring rate: 150 lb./in. Capacity: 900 lb. direct acting hydraulic shock absorbers. Front Axle Type: Spicer full-floating. Axle ratio: 5.38:1. Optional: None. Rear Axle Type: Semi-floating Spicer. Transfer Case: Spicer model 18. Ratios: 2.42:1, 1.00:1. Brakes: Type: Hydraulic, front and rear cast iron drums, dual master cylinder, double hydraulic circuit. Dimensions: Front and rear: 11.00 in. x 2.0 in. Total effective lining area: 176.2 sq. in. Optional: None. Wheels: 15 x 6K. Tires: 6.50 x 15 black sidewall. Steering: Cam and lever. Ratio: 26.0:1. Turning Circle: 37.8 ft. Standard Transmission: 3-speed manual. Transmission ratios: 2.798, 1.551, 1.0:1 Reverse: 3.798:1. Optional: None. Clutch: Single dry plate with torsional damping, 72 sq. in. Optional: None.

VEHICLE DIMENSIONS: Wheelbase: 104.5 in. Overall Length: 176.25 in. Front/Rear Tread: 57 in./57 in. Overall Height: 73.5625 in. Width: 71.75 in. Front/Rear Overhang: 25.75 in./46 in. Tailgate: Width and Height: 49.75 in. x 39.5 in. Approach/Departure Degrees: 38/19. Ground Clearance: Front axle: 9.5 in. Rear axle: 8.3125 in. Load space: 71.0 in. x 43.75 in. x 41.0 in. Maximum capacity (Volume Index): 112 cu. ft. Front headroom: 38.5 in.

CAPACITIES: Fuel Tank: 15.0 gallon capacity. Optional: None. Coolant System: 11 qt., 12 qt. with heater.

ACCOMMODATIONS: Seating Capacity: 4. Seat Dimensions: Front-Driver's: 31.875 in. Passenger's: 15 in. Rear: Divided: 15 in./26.375 in.

INSTRUMENTATION: 0-80 mph speedometer, gauges for fuel level, engine coolant temperature, oil pressure, ammeter.

OPTIONS: Dual horns. Oil bath air cleaner. Vacuum booster pump. One-piece longitudinally-positioned rear seat. Radio. Front bumper guard. Power take-off. Winches. Snowplows.

HISTORICAL FOOTNOTES: The 1953 models were announced on Oct. 20, 1952.

1954 654
STATION WAGON

Early in 1954, both the station wagon and sedan delivery were made available with the 226 cu. in. 6-cylinder L-head Super-Hurricane engine for 1954. External identification of the latest models was not difficult due to their new grille format of three chrome horizontal bars and nine vertical bars that were painted the body color.

1954 Willys Jeep four-wheel drive sedan delivery

I.D. DATA: The same system as introduced in 1951 was used in 1954. Serial number range: Deluxe station wagon: 654-FA2-10001 to 13528. Sedan delivery: 654-RA2-10001 to 10243.

Model Number	Body Type	Factory Price	GVW	Shipping Weight	Prod. Total
654-FA2	Deluxe St. Wagon	$2134	4500	3174	—
654-RA2	Sedan Del.	$2009	4500	3055	—

STANDARD ENGINE: 654 models: Engine Type: 6-cyl., L-head, cast iron block and cylinder head. Bore x Stroke: 3.9375 in. x 4.375 in. Lifters: Solid. Number of main bearings-4. Fuel Induction: Carter model WDG 1-barrel carburetor. Model 2052S or 2052SA. Compression Ratio: 7.3:1. Displacement: 226.2 cu. in. (3.7 liters). Horsepower: 115 @ 3800 rpm. Torque: 190 lb.-ft. @ 1800 rpm. Oil refill capacity: 5 qt. Fuel Requirements: Regular.

CHASSIS FEATURES: Separate body and chassis. Heavy side members with 1-piece pressed steel channels. Six cross members of flanged U and channel section.

SUSPENSION AND RUNNING GEAR: Front Suspension: Semi-elliptical 10-leaf springs. 36.25 in. x 1.75 in. Spring rate: 260 lb./in. Capacity: 650 lb. direct acting hydraulic shock absorbers. Optional: None. Rear Suspension: Semi-elliptical 8-leaf springs, 50 in. x 1.75 in. Spring rate: 150 lb./in. Capacity: 900 lb. direct acting hydraulic shock absorbers. Front Axle Type and Capacity: Spicer full-floating. 2000 lb. Axle ratio: 4.88:1. Optional: 5.38:1. Optional: None. Rear Axle Type and Capacity: Semi-floating Spicer. 3700 lb. Transfer Case: Spicer model 18. Ratios: 2.42:1, 1.00:1. Brakes: Type: Hydraulic, front and rear cast iron drums, dual master cylinder, double hydraulic circuit. Dimensions: Front and rear: 11.00 in. x 2.0 in. Total effective lining area: 176.2 sq. in. Optional: None. Wheels: 15 x 6K. Tires: 6.50 x 15 black sidewall. Steering: Cam and lever. Ratio: 26.0:1. Turning Circle: 37.8 ft. Optional: None. Standard Transmission: 3-speed manual. Transmission ratios: 2.798, 1.551, 1.0:1 Reverse: 3.798:1. Optional: None. Clutch: 10 in. dia. Single dry plate with torsional damping, 100.5 sq. in. Optional: None.

VEHICLE DIMENSIONS: Wheelbase: 104.5 in. Overall Length: 176.25 in. Front/Rear Tread: 57 in./57 in. Overall Height: 73.5625 in. Width: 71.75 in. Front/Rear Overhang: 25.75 in./46 in. Tailgate: Width and Height: 49.75 in. x 39.5 in. Approach/Departure Degrees: 38/19. Ground Clearance: Front axle: 9.5 in. Rear axle: 8.3125 in. Load space: 71.0 in. x 43.75 in. x 41.0 in. Maximum capacity (Volume Index): 112 cu. ft. Front headroom: 38.5 in.

CAPACITIES: Fuel Tank: 15.0 gallon capacity. Optional: None. Coolant System: 12 qt., 13 qt. with heater.

ACCOMMODATIONS: Seating Capacity: Station wagon: 4. Sedan delivery: 2. Seat Dimensions: Front-Driver's: 31.875 in. Passenger's: 15 in. Station wagon: Rear: Divided: 15 in./26.375 in.

INSTRUMENTATION: 0-80 mph speedometer, gauges for fuel level, engine coolant temperature, oil pressure, ammeter.

OPTIONS: Dual horns. Oil bath air cleaner. Vacuum booster pump. One-piece longitudinally-positioned rear seat (station wagon). Radio. Front bumper guard. Power take-off. Winches. Snowplows.

HISTORICAL FOOTNOTES: Willys reported that the new "Super Hurricane" engine provided the station wagon and sedan delivery with 53 percent more power."

1955 6-226
STATION WAGON

Identifying the latest version was a new optional two-tone paint combination in which the color of the roof and the lower body section contrasted with that of the wagon's mid-section. Beginning in 1955 Willys offered a less expensive utility wagon model as an alternative to the station wagon.

1955 Willys four-wheel drive station wagon

I.D. DATA: The serial number was located on the right side of the dash under hood, on the front frame cross member and on the left floor riser in the back of the driver's seat. The serial numbers began with 55 for 1955, followed by three digits identifying the model. Next was a hyphen and then four or five numbers for the sequential production number.

Model Number	Body Type	Factory Price	GVW	Shipping Weight	Prod. Total
475	Sedan Del.	$2026	4500	2951	—
475	Station Wagon	$2126	4500	3174	—
6-226	Deluxe St. Wagon	$2420	4500	N.A.	—
6-226	Sedan Del.	$2036	4500	3055	—
6-226	Utility Wagon	$2375	4500	3382	—

STANDARD ENGINE: 475 models: Engine Type: 4-cyl., F-head, cast iron block and cylinder head. Bore x Stroke: 3.125 in. x 4.375 in. Lifters: Solid. Number of main bearings-3. Fuel Induction: Single barrel Carter model WA-1 carburetor. Compression Ratio: 6.91. "High Altitude" 7.4:1 cylinder head optional. Displacement: 134.2 cu. in. (2.19 liters). Horsepower: 72 @ 4000 rpm. Torque: Net 114 lb.-ft. @ 2000 rpm. Oil refill capacity: 5 qt. Fuel Requirements: Regular.

STANDARD ENGINE: 6-226 models: Engine Type: 6-cyl., L-head, cast iron block and cylinder head. Bore x Stroke: 3.9375 in. x 4.375 in. Lifters: Solid. Number of main bearings-4. Fuel Induction: Carter model 1-barrel carburetor. Model 2052S or 2052SA. Compression Ratio: 6.86:1 "High Altitude" 7.3:1 cylinder head optional. Displacement: 226.2 cu. in. (3.17 liters). Horsepower: 115 @ 3800 rpm. Torque: 190 lb.-ft. @ 1800 rpm. Oil refill capacity: 5 qt. Fuel Requirements: Regular.

CHASSIS FEATURES: Separate body and chassis. Heavy side members with 1-piece pressed steel channels. Six cross members of flanged U and channel section.

SUSPENSION AND RUNNING GEAR: Front Suspension: Semi-elliptical 10-leaf springs. 36.25 in. x 1.75 in. Spring rate: 260 lb./in. Capacity: 650 lb. direct acting hydraulic shock absorbers. Rear Suspension: Semi-elliptical 8-leaf springs, 50 in. x 1.75 in. Spring rate: 150 lb./in. Capacity: 900 lb. direct acting hydraulic shock absorbers. Front Axle Type and Capacity: Spicer full-floating. Capacity: 2000 lb. Axle ratio: 4.89:1. Optional: 5.38:1. Rear Axle Type and Capacity: Semi-floating Spicer. Capacity: 3700 lb. Transfer Case: Spicer model 18. Ratios: 2.42:1, 1.00:1. Brakes: Type: Hydraulic, front and rear cast iron drums, dual master cylinder, double hydraulic circuit. Dimensions: Front and rear: 11.00 in. x 2.0 in. Total effective lining area: 176.2 sq. in. Optional: None. Wheels: 15 x 6K. Tires: 6.50 x 15 black sidewall. Steering: Cam and lever. Ratio: 26.0:1. Turning Circle: 37.8 ft. Optional: None. Standard Transmission: 3-speed manual. Transmission ratios: 2.798, 1.551, 1.0:1 Reverse: 3.798:1. Optional: None. Clutch: 10 in. dia. Single dry plate with torsional damping, 100.5 sq. in. 6-cyl., data. Optional: None.

VEHICLE DIMENSIONS: Wheelbase: 104.5 in. Overall Length: 176.25 in. Front/Rear Tread: 57 in./57 in. Overall Height: 73.5625 in. Width: 71.75 in. Front/Rear Overhang: 25.75 in./46 in. Tailgate: Width and Height: 49.75 in. x 39.5 in. Approach/Departure Degrees: 38/19. Ground Clearance: Front axle: 9.5 in. Rear axle: 8.3125 in. Load space: 71.0 in. x 43.75 in. x 41.0 in. Maximum capacity (Volume Index): 112 cu. ft. Front headroom: 38.5 in.

CAPACITIES: Fuel Tank: 15.0 gallon capacity. Optional: None. Coolant System: 4-cyl.: 11 qt., 12 qt. with heater. 6-cyl.: 12 qt., 13 qt. with heater.

ACCOMMODATIONS: Seating Capacity: Station wagon: 4. Sedan del.: 1. Seat Dimensions: Front-Station wagon: Driver's: 31.875 in. Passenger's: 15 in. Rear: Station wagon: Divided: 15 in./26.375 in.

INSTRUMENTATION: 0-80 mph speedometer, gauges for fuel level, engine coolant temperature, oil pressure, ammeter.

OPTIONS: Front bumper rail and guards. Two-tone paint. Oil bath air cleaner. High altitude cylinder head. Directional signals. Fresh-air heater and defroster. Back-up light. Oil filter. Radio. Governor. Heavy-duty springs. Power take-off (front and center). Fuel tank skid plate. Selective drive hubs. Trailer hitch. Extra-duty generators. Winches. Snowplows.

HISTORICAL FOOTNOTES: The 1955 models were introduced on May 25, 1955.

1956 6-226 & 475 WAGONS & SEDAN DELIVERY

No changes of substance were made in the Jeep station wagon, utility wagon models and sedan delivery for 1956.

I.D. DATA: The serial number was located on the right side of the dash under the hood, on the front frame cross member and on the left floor riser in the back of the driver's seat. Serial number ranges: 6-226 sedan delivery: 54268-10762 and up. Model 475 sedan delivery: 54128-10140. Model 475 station wagon: 54148-10941 and up. 6-226 station wagon: 54168016514 and up.

Model Number	Body Type	Factory Price	GVW	Shipping Weight	Prod. Total
6-226	Station Wagon	$2250	4500	3278	—
6-226	Sedan Del.	$2160	4500	3055	—
475	Station Wagon	$2152	4500	3174	—
475	Sedan Del.	$2062	4500	2951	—

STANDARD ENGINE: 475 models: Engine Type: 4-cyl., F-head, cast iron block and cylinder head. Bore x Stroke: 3.125 in. x 4.375 in. Lifters: Solid. Number of main bearings-3. Fuel Induction: Single barrel Carter model WA-1 carburetor. Compression Ratio: 6.91. "High Altitude" 7.4:1 cylinder head optional. Displacement: 134.2 cu. in. (2.19 liters). Horsepower: 72 @ 4000 rpm. Torque: Net 114 lb.-ft. @ 2000 rpm. Oil refill capacity: 5 qt. Fuel Requirements: Regular.

STANDARD ENGINE: 6-226 models: Engine Type: 6-cyl., L-head, cast iron block and cylinder head. Bore x Stroke: 3.9375 in. x 4.375 in. Lifters: Solid. Number of main bearings-4. Fuel Induction: Carter model WDG 1-barrel carburetor. Model 2052S or 2052SA. Compression Ratio: 6.86:1 "High Altitude" 7.3:1 cylinder head optional. Displacement: 226.2 cu. in. (3.17 liters). Horsepower: 115 @ 3800 rpm. Torque: 190 lb.-ft. @ 1800 rpm. Oil refill capacity: 5 qt. Fuel Requirements: Regular.

CHASSIS FEATURES: Separate body and chassis. Heavy side members with 1-piece pressed steel channels. Six cross members of flanged U and channel section.

SUSPENSION AND RUNNING GEAR: Front Suspension: Semi-elliptical 10-leaf springs. 36.25 in. x 1.75 in. Spring rate: 260 lb./in. Capacity: 650 lb. direct acting hydraulic shock absorbers. Rear Suspension: Semi-elliptical 8-leaf springs, 50 in. x 1.75 in. Spring rate: 150 lb./in. Capacity: 900 lb. direct acting hydraulic shock absorbers. Front Axle Type and Capacity: Spicer full-floating. Capacity: 2000 lb. Axle ratio: 4.89:1. Optional: 5.38:1. Rear Axle Type and Capacity: Semi-floating Spicer. Capacity: 3700 lb. Transfer Case: Spicer model 18. Ratios: 2.42:1, 1.00:1. Brakes: Type: Hydraulic, front and rear cast iron drums, dual master cylinder, double hydraulic circuit. Dimensions: Front and rear: 11.00 in. x 2.0 in. Total effective lining area: 176.2 sq. in. Optional: None. Wheels: 15 x 6K. Tires: 6.50 x 15 black sidewall. Steering: Cam and lever. Ratio: 26.0:1. Turning Circle: 37.8 ft. Optional: None. Standard Transmission: 3-speed manual. Transmission ratios: 2.798, 1.551, 1.0:1 Reverse: 3.798:1. Optional: None. Clutch: 10 in. dia. Single dry plate with torsional damping, 100.5 sq. in. 6-cyl., data. Optional: None.

VEHICLE DIMENSIONS: Wheelbase: 104.5 in. Overall Length: 176.25 in. Front/Rear Tread: 57 in./57 in. Overall Height: 73.5625 in. Width: 71.75 in. Front/Rear Overhang: 25.75 in./46 in. Tailgate: Width and Height: 49.75 in. x 39.5 in. Approach/Departure Degrees: 38/19. Ground Clearance: Front axle: 9.5 in. Rear axle: 8.3125 in. Load space: 71.0 in. x 43.75 in. x 41.0 in. Maximum capacity (Volume Index): 112 cu. ft. Front headroom: 38.5 in.

CAPACITIES: Fuel Tank: 15.0 gallon capacity. Optional: None. Coolant System: 4-cyl.: 11 qt., 12 qt. with heater. 6-cyl.: 12 qt., 13 qt. with heater.

ACCOMMODATIONS: Seating Capacity: Station wagon: 4. Sedan del.: 1. Seat Dimensions: Front-Station wagon: Driver's: 31.875 in. Passenger's: 15 in. Rear: Station wagon: Divided: 15 in./26.375 in.

INSTRUMENTATION: 0-80 mph speedometer, gauges for fuel level, engine coolant temperature, oil pressure, ammeter.

OPTIONS: Front bumper rail and guards. Two-tone paint. Oil bath air cleaner. High altitude cylinder head. Directional signals. Fresh-air heater and defroster. Back-up light. Oil filter. Radio. Governor. Heavy-duty springs. Power take-off (front and center). Fuel tank skid plate. Selective drive hubs. Trailer hitch. Extra-duty generators. Winches. Snowplows.

HISTORICAL FOOTNOTES: This was the last year Jeep used the station wagon title for its 6-226 and 475 models.

1957 6-226 & F4-134 UTILITY WAGONS

The utility wagon models were only offered in 6-cylinder form for 1957. Although some sources indicate that Willys offered its four-wheel drive utility delivery and wagon models in 4-cyl. form, a January 1, 1957 Willys Motors *Retail Prices and Specifications; 1957 Jeep Commercial Vehicles* publication does not list those models. The two-wheel drive versions were available with the 4-cyl. engine.

The exterior color selection for 1957 consisted of raven black, president red, steel glow metallic, transport yellow, royal blue metallic, glenwood green metallic and Aztec orange. The Utility Wagon was also offered in a wide variety of two-tone color combinations.

I.D. DATA: The serial number was located on the right side of the dash under the hood, on the front frame cross member and on the left floor riser in the back of the driver's seat. Serial number ranges: L6-226 utility wagon: 54167-10451 and up. L6-226 utility delivery: 54267-10134 and up.

Model Number	Body Type	Factory Price	GVW	Shipping Weight	Prod. Total
L6-226	Utility Wagon	$2552.35	4500	3206	—
L6-226	Utility Del.	$2311.70	4500	3008	—

STANDARD ENGINE: 475 models: Engine Type: 4-cyl., F-head, cast iron block and cylinder head. Bore x Stroke: 3.125 in. x 4.375 in. Lifters: Solid. Number of main bearings-3. Fuel Induction: Single barrel Carter model WA-1 carburetor. Compression Ratio: 6.91. "High Altitude" 7.4:1 cylinder head optional. Displacement: 134.2 cu. in. (2.19 liters). Horsepower: 72 @ 4000 rpm. Torque: Net 114 lb.-ft. @ 2000 rpm. Oil refill capacity: 5 qt. Fuel Requirements: Regular.

STANDARD ENGINE: 6-226 models: Engine Type: 6-cyl., L-head, cast iron block and cylinder head. Bore x Stroke: 3.9375 in. x 4.375 in. Lifters: Solid. Number of main bearings-4. Fuel Induction: Carter model WDG 1-barrel carburetor. Model 2052S or 2052SA. Compression Ratio: 6.86:1 "High Altitude" 7.3:1 cylinder head optional. Displacement: 226.2 cu. in. (3.17 liters). Horsepower: 115 @ 3800 rpm. Torque: 190 lb.-ft. @ 1800 rpm. Oil refill capacity: 5 qt. Fuel Requirements: Regular.

CHASSIS FEATURES: Separate body and chassis. Heavy side members with 1-piece pressed steel channels. Six cross members of flanged U and channel section.

SUSPENSION AND RUNNING GEAR: Front Suspension: Semi-elliptical 10-leaf springs. 36.25 in. x 1.75 in. Spring rate: 260 lb./in. Capacity: 650 lb. direct acting hydraulic shock absorbers. Rear Suspension: Semi-elliptical 8-leaf springs, 50 in. x 1.75 in. Spring rate: 150 lb./in. Capacity: 900 lb. direct acting hydraulic shock absorbers. Front Axle Type and Capacity: Spicer full-floating. Capacity: 2000 lb. Axle ratio: 4.89:1. Optional: 5.38:1. Rear Axle Type and Capacity: Semi-floating Spicer. Capacity: 3700 lb. Transfer Case: Spicer model 18. Ratios: 2.42:1, 1.00:1. Brakes: Type: Hydraulic, front and rear cast iron drums, dual master cylinder, double hydraulic circuit. Dimensions: Front and rear: 11.00 in. x 2.0 in. Total effective lining area: 176.2 sq. in. Optional: None. Wheels: 15 x 6K. Tires: 6.50 x 15 black sidewall. Steering: Cam and lever. Ratio: 26.0:1. Turning Circle: 37.8 ft. Optional: None. Standard Transmission: 3-speed manual. Transmission ratios: 2.798, 1.551, 1.0:1 Reverse: 3.798:1. Optional: None. Clutch: 10 in. dia. Single dry plate with torsional damping, 100.5 sq. in. 6-cyl., data. Optional: None.

VEHICLE DIMENSIONS: Wheelbase: 104.5 in. Overall Length: 176.25 in. Front/Rear Tread: 57 in./57 in. Overall Height: 73.5625 in. Width: Utility wagon: 71.75 in. Utility delivery: 68.125 in. Front/Rear Overhang: 25.75 in./46 in. Tailgate: Width and Height: 49.75 in. x 39.5 in. Approach/Departure Degrees: 38/19. Ground Clearance: Front axle: 9.5 in. Rear axle: 8.3125 in. Load space: 71.0 in. x 43.75 in. x 41.0 in. Maximum capacity (Volume Index): 112 cu. ft. Front headroom: 38.5 in.

CAPACITIES: Fuel Tank: 15.0 gallon capacity. Optional: None. Coolant System: 4-cyl.: 11 qt., 12 qt. with heater. 6-cyl.: 12 qt., 13 qt. with heater.

ACCOMMODATIONS: Seating Capacity: Utility wagon: 4. Sedan del.: 1. Seat Dimensions: Front-Utility wagon: Driver's: 31.875 in. Passenger's: 15 in. Rear: Utility wagon: Divided: 15 in./26.375 in.

INSTRUMENTATION: 0-80 mph speedometer, gauges for fuel level, engine coolant temperature, oil pressure, ammeter.

OPTIONS AND PRICES: Group 942 (utility delivery), 943 (utility wagon). Includes oil bath air cleaner, oil filter and directional signals: $55.21. Hydrovac power brake booster: $49.85. Transmission hand brake: $17.95. Front bumper rail and guard: $15.60. Rear bumper bar extension (utility deliveries only): $21.60. Fresh-air heater and defroster: $74.70. Radio and antenna: $98.30. Front passenger seat: $40.65. 7.00 x 15 6-ply All-Service tread: $24.85. 6.50 x 15 6-ply Deluxe Rib tread: No extra charge. 7.60 x 15 4-ply Suburbanite tread: No extra charge. Hot Climate radiator: $9.70. Two-tone paint: $17.45. Locking rear differential: $40.15.

HISTORICAL FOOTNOTES: Willys described itself as "The Company On The Move" in 1957. The 1957 models were introduced in mid-1956.

1958 6-226 & F4-134 UTILITY WAGONS

Both the utility wagon and utility delivery were offered in 4 and 6-cylinder form for 1958. Except for a new 105 horsepower at 3,600 rpm rating for the L-head 6-cylinder engine, there were no changes for 1958.

1958 Willys Jeep four-wheel drive utility wagon

I.D. DATA: The serial number was located on the right side of the dash under the hood, on the front frame cross member and on the left floor riser in the back of the driver's seat. Serial number ranges: F4-134 utility delivery: 54248-10510 and up. F4-134 utility wagon: 54148-13907 and up. L6-226 utility wagon: 54168-18094 and up. L6-226 utility delivery: 54268-10762 and up.

Model Number	Body Type	Factory Price	GVW	Shipping Weight	Prod. Total
L6-226	Utility Wagon	$2764	4500	3206	—
L6-226	Utility Del.	$2312	4500	3008	—
F4-134	Utility Wagon	$2654	4500	2944	—
F4-134	Utility Del.	$2206	4500	2895	—

STANDARD ENGINE: F4-134 models: Engine Type: 4-cyl., F-head, cast iron block and cylinder head. Bore x Stroke: 3.125 in. x 4.375 in. Lifters: Solid. Number of main bearings-3. Fuel Induction: Single barrel Carter model WA-1 carburetor. Compression Ratio: 6.81. "High Altitude" 7.4:1 cylinder available at no extra cost. Displacement: 134.2 cu. in. (2.19 liters). Horsepower: 72 @ 4000 rpm. Torque: Net 114 lb.-ft. @ 2000 rpm. Oil refill capacity: 5 qt. Fuel Requirements: Regular.

STANDARD ENGINE: L6-226 models: Engine Type: 6-cyl., L-head, cast iron block and cylinder head. Bore x Stroke: 3.9375 in. x 4.375 in. Lifters: Solid. Number of main bearings-4. Fuel Induction: Carter model WDG 1-barrel carburetor. Model 2052S or 2052SA. Compression Ratio: 6.86:1 "High Altitude" 7.3:1 cylinder head optional. Displacement: 226.2 cu. in. (3.7 liters). Horsepower: 105 @ 3600 rpm. Torque: 190 lbs.-ft. @ 1400 rpm. Oil refill capacity: 5 qt. Fuel Requirements: Regular.

CHASSIS FEATURES: Separate body and chassis. Heavy side members with 1-piece pressed steel channels. Six cross members of flanged U and channel section.

SUSPENSION AND RUNNING GEAR: Front Suspension: Semi-elliptical 10-leaf springs. 36.25 in. x 1.75 in. Spring rate: 260 lb./in. Capacity: 650 lb. direct acting hydraulic shock absorbers. Rear Suspension: Semi-elliptical 8-leaf springs, 50 in. x 1.75 in. Spring rate: 150 lb./in. Capacity: 900 lb. direct acting hydraulic shock absorbers. Front Axle Type and Capacity: Spicer full-floating. Capacity: 2000 lb. Axle ratio: 4.89:1. Optional: 5.38:1. Rear Axle Type and Capacity: Semi-floating Spicer. Capacity: 3700 lb. Transfer Case: Spicer model 18. Ratios: 2.42:1, 1.00:1. Brakes: Type: Hydraulic, front and rear cast iron drums, dual master cylinder, double hydraulic circuit. Dimensions: Front and rear: 11.00 in. x 2.0 in. Total effective lining area: 176.2 sq. in. Optional: None. Wheels: 15 x 6K. Tires: 6.50 x 15 black sidewall. Steering: Cam and lever. Ratio: 26.0:1. Turning Circle: 37.8 ft. Optional None. Standard Transmission: 3-speed manual. Transmission ratios: 2.798, 1.551, 1.0:1 Reverse: 3.798:1. Optional: None. Clutch: 10 in. dia. Single dry plate with torsional damping, 100.5 sq. in. 6-cyl., data. Optional: None.

VEHICLE DIMENSIONS: Wheelbase: 104.5 in. Overall Length: 176.25 in. Front/Rear Tread: 57 in./57 in. Overall Height: 73.5625 in. Width: Utility wagon: 71.75 in. Utility delivery: 68.125 in. Front/Rear Overhang: 25.75 in./46 in. Tailgate: Width and Height: 49.75 in. x 39.5 in. Approach/Departure Degrees: 38/19. Ground Clearance: Front axle: 9.5 in. Rear axle: 8.3125 in. Load space: 71.0 in. x 43.75 in. x 41.0 in. Maximum capacity (Volume Index): 112 cu. ft. Front headroom: 38.5 in.

CAPACITIES: Fuel Tank: 15.0 gallon capacity. Optional: None. Coolant System: 4-cyl.: 11 qt., 12 qt. with heater. 6-cyl.: 12 qt., 13 qt. with heater.

ACCOMMODATIONS: Seating Capacity: Utility wagon: 4. Sedan del.: 1. Seat Dimensions: Front-Utility wagon: Driver's: 31.875 in. Passenger's: 15 in. Rear: Utility wagon: Divided: 15 in./26.375 in.

INSTRUMENTATION: 0-80 mph speedometer, gauges for fuel level, engine coolant temperature, oil pressure, ammeter.

OPTIONS AND PRICES: Front bumper rail and guards. Two-tone paint. Oil bath air cleaner. High altitude cylinder head. Directional signals. Fresh-air heater and defroster. Back-up light. Oil filter. Radio. Governor. Heavy-duty springs. Power take-off (front and center). Fuel tank skid plate. Selective drive hubs. Trailer hitch. Extra-duty generators. Winches. Snowplows.

HISTORICAL FOOTNOTES: The introduction date for the 1958 models was Aug. 15, 1957.

1959 6-226 & F4-134 UTILITY WAGONS

No changes were made in the four-wheel drive utility wagon and utility delivery models for 1959.

I.D. DATA: The serial number was located on the right side of the dash under hood, on the front frame cross member and on the left floor riser in the back of the driver's seat. Serial number ranges: New-F4-134 utility delivery: 54248-10925 and up. New-F4-134 utility wagon: 54148-114247 and up. New-L6-226 utility wagon: 54168-24102 and up. L6-226 utility delivery: 54268-11022 and up.

Model Number	Body Type	Factory Price	GVW	Shipping Weight	Prod. Total
L6-226	Utility Wagon	$2901	4500	3206	—
L6-226	Utility Del.	$2427	4500	3008	—
F4-134	Utility Wagon	$2654	4500	2944	—
F4-134	Utility Del.	$2317	4500	2895	—

STANDARD ENGINE: F4-134 models: Engine Type: 4-cyl., F-head, cast iron block and cylinder head. Bore x Stroke: 3.125 in. x 4.375 in. Lifters: Solid. Number of main bearings-3. Fuel Induction: Single barrel Carter model WA-1 carburetor. Compression Ratio: 6.81. "High Altitude" 7.4:1 cylinder available at no extra cost. Displacement: 134.2 cu. in. (2.19 liters). Horsepower: 72 @ 4000 rpm. Torque: Net 114 lb.-ft. @ 2000 rpm. Oil refill capacity: 5 qt. Fuel Requirements: Regular.

STANDARD ENGINE: L6-226 models: Engine Type: 6-cyl., L-head, cast iron block and cylinder head. Bore x Stroke: 3.9375 in. x 4.375 in. Lifters: Solid. Number of main bearings-4. Fuel Induction: Carter model WDG 1-barrel carburetor. Model 2052S or 2052SA. Compression Ratio: 6.86:1 "High Altitude" 7.3:1 cylinder head optional. Displacement: 226.2 cu. in. (3.7 liters). Horsepower: 105 @ 3600 rpm. Torque: 190 lb.-ft. @ 1400 rpm. Oil refill capacity: 5 qt. Fuel Requirements: Regular.

CHASSIS FEATURES: Separate body and chassis. Heavy side members with 1-piece pressed steel channels. Six cross members of flanged U and channel section.

SUSPENSION AND RUNNING GEAR: Front Suspension: Semi-elliptical 10-leaf springs. 36.25 in. x 1.75 in. Spring rate: 260 lb./in. Capacity: 650 lb. direct acting hydraulic shock absorbers. Rear Suspension: Semi-elliptical 8-leaf springs, 50 in. x 1.75 in. Spring rate: 150 lb./in. Capacity: 900 lb. direct acting hydraulic shock absorbers. Front Axle Type and Capacity: Spicer full-floating. Capacity: 2000 lb. Axle ratio: 4.89:1. Optional: 5.38:1. Rear Axle Type and Capacity: Semi-floating Spicer. Capacity: 3700 lb. Transfer Case: Spicer model 18. Ratios: 2.42:1, 1.00:1. Brakes: Type: Hydraulic, front and rear cast iron drums, dual master cylinder,

---

double hydraulic circuit. Dimensions: Front and rear: 11.00 in. x 2.0 in. Total effective lining area: 176.2 sq. in. Optional: None. Wheels: 15 x 6K. Tires: 6.50 x 15 black sidewall. Steering: Cam and lever. Ratio: 26.0:1. Turning Circle: 37.8 ft. Optional: None. Standard Transmission: 3-speed manual. Transmission ratios: 2.798, 1.551, 1.0:1 Reverse: 3.798:1. Optional: None. Clutch: 10 in. dia. Single dry plate with torsional damping, 100.5 sq. in. 6-cyl., data. Optional: None.

VEHICLE DIMENSIONS: Wheelbase: 104.5 in. Overall Length: 176.25 in. Front/Rear Tread: 57 in./57 in. Overall Height: 73.5625 in. Width: Utility wagon: 71.75 in. Utility delivery: 68.125 in. Front/Rear Overhang: 25.75 in./46 in. Tailgate: Width and Height: 49.75 in. x 39.5 in. Approach/Departure Degrees: 38/19. Ground Clearance: Front axle: 9.5 in. Rear axle: 8.3125 in. Load space: 71.0 in. x 43.75 in. x 41.0 in. Maximum capacity (Volume Index): 112 cu. ft. Front headroom: 38.5 in.

CAPACITIES: Fuel Tank: 15.0 gallon capacity. Optional: None. Coolant System: 4-cyl.: 11 qt., 12 qt. with heater. 6-cyl.: 12 qt., 13 qt. with heater.

ACCOMMODATIONS: Seating Capacity: Utility wagon: 4. Sedan del.: 1. Seat Dimensions: Front-Utility wagon: Driver's: 31.875 in. Passenger's: 15 in. Rear: Utility wagon: Divided: 15 in./26.375 in.

INSTRUMENTATION: 0-80 mph speedometer, gauges for fuel level, engine coolant temperature, oil pressure, ammeter.

OPTIONS: Front bumper rail and guards. Two-tone paint. Oil bath air cleaner. High altitude cylinder head. Directional signals. Fresh-air heater and defroster. Back-up light. Oil filter. Radio. Governor. Heavy-duty springs. Power take-off (front and center). Fuel tank skid plate. Selective drive hubs. Trailer hitch. Extra-duty generators. Winches. Snowplows.

HISTORICAL FOOTNOTES: The 1959 models were introduced in the fall of 1958.

1960 6-226 & F4-134 UTILITY WAGONS

A new side body trim piece with its forward edge paralleling the form of the front fender's trailing edge allowed a new two-tone color format to be offered. Also new for 1960 was a one-piece windshield, one-piece tailgate glass, new seat fabrics and interiors, and an expanded color selection.

1960 Willys Jeep four-wheel drive utility wagon

I.D. DATA: The serial number was located on the right side of the dash under the hood, on the front frame cross member and on the left floor riser in the back of the driver's seat. Serial number ranges: F4-134 utility delivery: 54248-111721 and up. F4-148 utility wagon: 54148-16096 and up. L6-226 utility wagon: 54168-39730 and up. L6-226 utility delivery: 54268-12900 and up.

Model Number	Body Type	Factory Price	GVW	Shipping Weight	Prod. Total
L6-226	Utility Wagon	$3010	4500	3206	—
L6-226	Utility Del.	$2630	4500	3008	—
F4-134	Utility Wagon	$2887	4500	3093	—
F4-134	Utility Del.	$2510	4500	2893	—

STANDARD ENGINE: F4-134 models: Engine Type: 4-cyl., F-head, cast iron block and cylinder head. Bore x Stroke: 3.125 in. x 4.375 in. Lifters: Solid. Number of main bearings-3. Fuel Induction: Single barrel Carter model WA-1 carburetor. Compression Ratio: 6.81. "High Altitude" 7.4:1 cylinder available at no extra cost. Displacement: 134.2 cu. in. (2.19 liters). Horsepower: 72 @ 4000 rpm. Torque: Net 114 lb.-ft. @ 2000 rpm. Oil refill capacity: 5 qt. Fuel Requirements: Regular.

STANDARD ENGINE: 6-226 models: Engine Type: 6-cyl., L-head, cast iron block and cylinder head. Bore x Stroke: 3.9375 in. x 4.375 in. Lifters: Solid. Number of main bearings-4. Fuel Induction: Carter model WDG 1-barrel carburetor. Model 2052S or 2052SA. Compression Ratio: 6.86:1 "High Altitude" 7.3:1 cylinder head optional. Displacement: 226.2 cu. in. (3.7 liters). Horsepower: 105 @ 3600 rpm. Torque: 190 lbs.-ft. @ 1400 rpm. Oil refill capacity: 5 qt. Fuel Requirements: Regular.

CHASSIS FEATURES: Separate body and chassis. Heavy side members with 1-piece pressed steel channels. Six cross members of flanged U and channel section.

SUSPENSION AND RUNNING GEAR: Front Suspension: Semi-elliptical 10-leaf springs. 36.25 in. x 1.75 in. Spring rate: 260 lb./in. Capacity: 650 lb. direct acting hydraulic shock absorbers. Rear Suspension: Semi-elliptical 8-leaf springs, 50 in. x 1.75 in. Spring rate: 150 lb./in. Capacity: 900 lb. direct acting hydraulic shock absorbers. Front Axle Type and Capacity: Spicer full-floating. Capacity: 2000 lb. Axle ratio: 4.89:1. Optional: 5.38:1. Rear Axle Type and Capacity: Semi-floating Spicer. Capacity: 3700 lb. Transfer Case: Spicer model 18. Ratios: 2.42:1, 1.00:1. Brakes: Type: Hydraulic, front and rear cast iron drums, dual master cylinder, double hydraulic circuit. Dimensions: Front and rear: 11.00 in. x 2.0 in. Total effective lining area: 176.2 sq. in. Optional: None. Wheels: 15 x 6K. Tires: 6.50 x 15 black sidewall. Steering: Cam and lever. Ratio: 26.0:1. Turning Circle: 37.8 ft. Optional: None. Standard Transmission: 3-speed manual. Transmission ratios: 2.798, 1.551, 1.0:1 Reverse: 3.798:1. Optional: None. Clutch: 10 in. dia. Single dry plate with torsional damping, 100.5 sq. in. 6-cyl., data. Optional: None.

VEHICLE DIMENSIONS: Wheelbase: 104.5 in. Overall Length: 176.25 in. Front/Rear Tread: 57 in./57 in. Overall Height: 73.5625 in. Width: Utility wagon: 71.75 in. Utility delivery: 68.125 in. Front/Rear Overhang: 25.75 in./46 in. Tailgate: Width and Height: 49.75 in. x 39.5 in. Approach/Departure Degrees: 38/19. Ground Clearance: Front axle: 9.5 in. Rear axle: 8.3125 in. Load space: 71.0 in. x 43.75 in. x 41.0 in. Maximum capacity (Volume Index): 112 cu. ft. Front headroom: 38.5 in.

CAPACITIES: Fuel Tank: 15.0 gallon capacity. Optional: None. Coolant System: 4-cyl.: 11 qt., 12 qt. with heater. 6-cyl.: 12 qt., 13 qt. with heater.

ACCOMMODATIONS: Seating Capacity: Utility wagon: 4. Sedan del.: 1. Seat Dimensions: Front-Utility wagon: Driver's: 31.875 in. Passenger's: 15 in. Rear: Utility wagon: Divided: 15 in./26.375 in.

INSTRUMENTATION: 0-80 mph speedometer, gauges for fuel level, engine coolant temperature, oil pressure, ammeter.

OPTIONS: Front bumper rail and guards. Two-tone paint. Oil bath air cleaner. High altitude cylinder head. Directional signals. Fresh-air heater and defroster. Back-up light. Oil filter. Radio. Governor. Heavy-duty springs. Power take-off (front and center). Fuel tank skid plate. Selective drive hubs. Trailer hitch. Extra-duty generators. Winches. Snowplows.

HISTORICAL FOOTNOTES: The 1960 models were introduced in the fall of 1959.

1961 6-226 & F4-134 UTILITY WAGONS

Except for a new horsepower rating for the F-head engine, no changes took place in the utility delivery and utility wagons for 1961.

1961 Willys 6-226 four-wheel drive utility wagon

I.D. DATA: The serial number was located on the right side of the dash under the hood, on the front frame cross member and on the left floor riser in the back of the driver's seat. Serial number ranges: F4-134 utility delivery: 54248-11219 and up. F4-134 utility wagon: 54148-18111 and up. L6-226 utility wagon: 54168-42839 and up. L6-226 utility delivery: 54268-14157 and up. 6-230 utility wagon: 54178-10001 and up. 6-230 utility delivery: 54278-10001 and up.

Model Number	Body Type	Factory Price	GVW	Shipping Weight	Prod. Total
L6-226	Utility Wagon	$3010	4500	3206	—
L6-226	Utility Del.	$2728	4500	3008	—
F4-134	Utility Wagon	$2887	4500	3093	—
F4-134	Utility Del.	$2605	4500	2893	—

STANDARD ENGINE: F4-134 models: Engine Type: 4-cyl., F-head, cast iron block and cylinder head. Bore x Stroke: 3.125 in. x 4.375 in. Lifters: Solid. Number of main bearings-3. Fuel Induction: Single barrel Carter model WA-1 carburetor. Compression Ratio: 7.4:1 (6.9 and 7.4:1 optional at no extra cost). Displacement: 134.2 cu. in. (2.19 liters). Horsepower: 75 @ 4000 rpm. Torque: Net 114 lb.-ft. @ 2000 rpm. Oil refill capacity: 5 qt. Fuel Requirements: Regular.

STANDARD ENGINE: 6-226 models: Engine Type: 6-cyl., L-head, cast iron block and cylinder head. Bore x Stroke: 3.9375 in. x 4.375 in. Lifters: Solid. Number of main bearings-4. Fuel Induction: Carter model WDG 1-barrel carburetor. Model 2052S or 2052SA. Compression Ratio: 6.86:1 "High Altitude" 7.3:1 cylinder head optional. Displacement: 226.2 cu. in. (3.7 liters). Horsepower: 105 @ 3600 rpm. Torque: 190 lb.-ft. @ 1400 rpm. Oil refill capacity: 5 qt. Fuel Requirements: Regular.

CHASSIS FEATURES: Separate body and chassis. Heavy side members with 1-piece pressed steel channels. Six cross members of flanged U and channel section.

SUSPENSION AND RUNNING GEAR: Front Suspension: Semi-elliptical 10-leaf springs. 36.25 in. x 1.75 in. Spring rate: 260 lb./in. Capacity: 650 lb. direct acting hydraulic shock absorbers. Rear Suspension: Semi-elliptical 8-leaf springs, 50 in. x 1.75 in. Spring rate: 150 lb./in. Capacity: 900 lb. direct acting hydraulic shock absorbers. Front Axle Type and Capacity: Spicer full-floating. Capacity: 2000 lb. Axle ratio: 4.89:1. Optional: 5.38:1. Rear Axle Type and Capacity: Semi-floating Spicer. Capacity: 3700 lb. Transfer Case: Spicer model 18. Ratios: 2.42:1, 1.00:1. Brakes: Type: Hydraulic, front and rear cast iron drums, dual master cylinder, double hydraulic circuit. Dimensions: Front axle: 11.00 in. x 2.0 in. Total effective lining area: 176.2 sq. in. Optional: None. Wheels: 15 x 6K. Tires: 6.50 x 15 black sidewall. Steering: Cam and lever. Ratio: 26.0:1. Turning Circle: 37.8 ft. Optional: None. Standard Transmission:

3-speed manual. Transmission ratios: 2.798, 1.551, 1.0:1 Reverse: 3.798:1. Optional: None. Clutch: 10 in. dia. Single dry plate with torsional damping, 100.5 sq. in. 6-cyl., data. Optional: None.

VEHICLE DIMENSIONS: Wheelbase: 104.5 in. Overall Length: 176.25 in. Front/Rear Tread: 57 in./57 in. Overall Height: 73.5625 in. Width: Utility wagon: 71.75 in. Utility delivery: 68.125 in. Front/Rear Overhang: 25.75 in./46 in. Tailgate: Width and Height: 49.75 in. x 39.5 in. Approach/Departure Degrees: 38/19. Ground Clearance: Front axle: 9.5 in. Rear axle: 8.3125 in. Load space: 71.0 in. x 43.75 in. x 41.0 in. Maximum capacity (Volume Index): 112 cu. ft. Front headroom: 38.5 in.

CAPACITIES: Fuel Tank: 15.0 gallon capacity. Optional: None. Coolant System: 4-cyl.: 11 qt., 12 qt. with heater. 6-cyl.: 12 qt., 13 qt. with heater.

ACCOMMODATIONS: Seating Capacity: Utility wagon: 4. Utility del.: 1. Seat Dimensions: Front-Utility wagon: Driver's: 31.875 in. Passenger's: 15 in. Rear: Utility wagon: Divided: 15 in./26.375 in.

INSTRUMENTATION: 0-80 mph speedometer, gauges for fuel level, engine coolant temperature, oil pressure, ammeter.

OPTIONS: Front bumper rail and guards. Two-tone paint. Oil bath air cleaner. High altitude cylinder head. Directional signals. Fresh-air heater and defroster. Back-up light. Oil filter. Radio. Governor. Heavy-duty springs. Power take-off (front and center). Fuel tank skid plate. Selective drive hubs. Trailer hitch. Extra-duty generators. Winches. Snowplows.

HISTORICAL FOOTNOTES: The 1961 Utility models were introduced in the fall of 1960.

1962 6-226 & F4-134 UTILITY WAGONS

In May, 1962, Willys replaced the L-head 6-cylinder engine with the new Tornado OHC 6-cylinder engine. No other changes took place for 1962.

1962 Willys Jeep four-wheel drive utility wagon

I.D. DATA: The serial number was located on the right side of the dash under the hood, on the front frame cross member and on the left floor riser in the back of the driver's seat. Serial number ranges: F4-134 utility delivery: 54248-11219 and up. F4-134 utility wagon: 54148-18111 and up. L6-226 utility wagon: 54168-11309 and up. L6-226 utility delivery: 54268-14157 and up. 6-230 utility wagon: 54178-10001 and up. 6-230 utility delivery: 54278-10001 and up.

Model Number	Body Type	Factory Price	GVW	Shipping Weight	Prod. Total
L6-226	Utility Wagon	$3010	4500	3206	—
L6-226	Utility Del.	$2728	4500	3008	—
F4-134	Utility Wagon	$2887	4500	3093	—
F4-134	Utility Del.	$2605	4500	2893	—
6-230	Utility Del.	$2835	4500	3028	—
6-230	Utility Wagon	$3117	4500	3307	—

STANDARD ENGINE: F4-134 models: Engine Type: 4-cyl., F-head, cast iron block and cylinder head. Bore x Stroke: 3.125 in. x 4.375 in. Lifters: Solid. Number of main bearings-3. Fuel Induction: Single barrel Carter model WA-1 carburetor. Compression Ratio: 7.4:1. (6.9 and 7.4:1 optional, available at no extra cost). Displacement: 134.2 cu. in. (2.19 liters). Horsepower: 75 @ 4000 rpm. Torque: Net 114 lb.-ft. @ 2000 rpm. Oil refill capacity: 5 qt. Fuel Requirements: Regular.

STANDARD ENGINE: L6-226 models: Engine Type: 6-cyl., L-head, cast iron block and cylinder head. Bore x Stroke: 3.9375 in. x 4.375 in. Lifters: Solid. Number of main bearings-4. Fuel Induction: Carter model WDG 1-barrel carburetor. Model 2052S or 2052SA. Compression Ratio: 6.86:1. "High Altitude" 7.3:1 cylinder head optional. Displacement: 226.2 cu. in. (3.7 liters). Horsepower: 105 @ 3600 rpm. Torque: 190 lb.-ft. @ 1400 rpm. Oil refill capacity: 5 qt. Fuel Requirements: Regular.

STANDARD ENGINE: 6-230 models: Engine Type: 6-cyl., OHV, OHC, cast iron block and cylinder head. Bore x Stroke: 3.34 in. x 4.38 in. Lifters: Solid. Number of main bearings-4. Fuel Induction: 2-barrel downdraft carburetor. Compression Ratio: 8.50:1. Displacement: 230 cu. in. (3.77 liters). Horsepower: 140 @ 4000 rpm. Torque: 210 lb.-ft. @ 1750 rpm. Oil refill capacity: 5 qt. Fuel Requirements: Regular.

CHASSIS FEATURES: Separate body and chassis. Heavy side members with 1-piece pressed steel channels. Six cross members of flanged U and channel section.

SUSPENSION AND RUNNING GEAR: Front Suspension: Semi-elliptical 10-leaf springs. 36.25 in. x 1.75 in. Spring rate: 260 lb./in. Capacity: 650 lb. direct acting hydraulic shock absorbers. Rear Suspension: Semi-elliptical 8-leaf springs, 50 in. x 1.75 in. Spring rate: 150 lb./in. Capacity: 900 lb. direct acting hydraulic shock absorbers. Front Axle Type and Capacity: Spicer full-floating. Capacity: 2000 lb. Axle ratio: 4.89:1. Optional: 5.38:1. Rear Axle Type and Capacity: Semi-floating Spicer. Capacity: 3700 lb. Transfer Case: Spicer model 18. Ratios:

2.42:1, 1.00:1. Brakes: Type: Hydraulic, front and rear cast iron drums, dual master cylinder, double hydraulic circuit. Dimensions: Front and rear: 11.00 in. x 2.0 in. Total effective lining area: 176.2 sq. in. Optional: None. Wheels: 15 x 6K. Tires: 6.50 x 15 black sidewall. Steering: Cam and lever. Ratio: 26.0:1. Turning Circle: 37.8 ft. Optional: None. Standard Transmission: 3-speed manual. Transmission ratios: 2.798, 1.551, 1.0:1 Reverse: 3.798:1. Optional: None. Clutch: 10 in. dia. Single dry plate with torsional damping, 100.5 sq. in. 6-cyl., data. Optional: None.

VEHICLE DIMENSIONS: Wheelbase: 104.5 in. Overall Length: 176.25 in. Front/Rear Tread: 57 in./57 in. Overall Height: 73.5625 in. Width: Utility wagon: 71.75 in. Utility delivery: 68.125 in. Front/Rear Overhang: 25.75 in./46 in. Tailgate: Width and Height: 49.75 in. x 39.5 in. Approach/Departure Degrees: 38/19. Ground Clearance: Front axle: 9.5 in. Rear axle: 8.3125 in. Load space: 71.0 in. x 43.75 in. x 41.0 in. Maximum capacity (Volume Index): 112 cu. ft. Front headroom: 38.5 in.

CAPACITIES: Fuel Tank: 15.0 gallon capacity. Optional: None. Coolant System: 4-cyl.: 11 qt., 12 qt. with heater. 6-cyl.: 12 qt., 13 qt. with heater.

ACCOMMODATIONS: Seating Capacity: Utility wagon: 4. Utility del.: 1. Seat Dimensions: Front-Utility wagon: Driver's: 31.875 in. Passenger's: 15 in. Rear: Utility wagon: Divided: 15 in./26.375 in.

INSTRUMENTATION: 0-80 mph speedometer, gauges for fuel level, engine coolant temperature, oil pressure, ammeter.

OPTIONS: Front bumper rail and guards. Two-tone paint. Oil bath air cleaner. High altitude cylinder head. Directional signals. Fresh-air heater and defroster. Back-up light. Oil filter. Radio. Governor. Heavy-duty springs. Power take-off (front and center). Fuel tank skid plate. Selective drive hubs. Trailer hitch. Extra-duty generators. Winches. Snowplows.

HISTORICAL FOOTNOTES: The availability of the utility wagon and delivery with three distinct engines, originating in different design eras, was another example of the longevity of the basic design of these highly versatile Jeep vehicles.

1963 6-226 & F4-134 UTILITY WAGONS

No changes took place in the design of the Jeep utility vehicles for 1963.

I.D. DATA: The serial number was located on the right side of the dash under the hood, on the front frame cross member and on the left floor riser in the back of the driver's seat. Serial number ranges: F4-134 utility delivery: 54248-11219 and up. F4-134 utility wagon: 54148-18111 and up. F4-134 station wagon Traveler: 54348-1001 and up. L6-226 station wagon Traveler: 54368-10001 and up. L6-226 utility wagon: 54168-42839 and up. L6-226 utility delivery: 54268-15311 and up. 6-230 utility wagon: 54178-10004 and up. 6-230 utility delivery: 54278-10001 and up.

Model Number	Body Type	Factory Price	GVW	Shipping Weight	Prod. Total
L6-226	Utility Wagon	$3010	4500	3206	—
L6-226	Utility Del.	$2728	4500	3008	—
F4-134	Utility Wagon	$2887	4500	3093	—
F4-134	Utility Del.	$2605	4500	2893	—
6-230	Utility Del.	$2835	4500	3028	—
6-230	Utility Wagon	$3117	4500	3307	—

STANDARD ENGINE: F4-134 models: Engine Type: 4-cyl., F-head, cast iron block and cylinder head. Bore x Stroke: 3.125 in. x 4.375 in. Lifters: Solid. Number of main bearings-3. Fuel Induction: Single barrel Carter model WA-1 carburetor. Compression Ratio: 7.4:1. (6.9 and 7.4:1 optional, available at no extra cost). Displacement: 134.2 cu. in. (2.19 liters). Horsepower: 75 @ 4000 rpm. Torque: Net 114 lb.-ft. @ 2000 rpm. Oil refill capacity: 5 qt. Fuel Requirements: Regular.

STANDARD ENGINE: L6-226 models: Engine Type: 6-cyl., L-head, cast iron block and cylinder head. Bore x Stroke: 3.9375 in. x 4.375 in. Lifters: Solid. Number of main bearings-4. Fuel Induction: Carter model WDG 1-barrel carburetor. Model 2052S or 2052SA. Compression Ratio: 6.86:1. "High Altitude" 7.3:1 cylinder head optional. Displacement: 226.2 cu. in. (3.7 liters). Horsepower: 105 @ 3600 rpm. Torque: 190 lb.-ft. @ 1400 rpm. Oil refill capacity: 5 qt. Fuel Requirements: Regular.

STANDARD ENGINE: 6-230 models: Engine Type: 6-cyl., OHV, OHC, cast iron block and cylinder head. Bore x Stroke: 3.34 in. x 4.38 in. Lifters: Solid. Number of main bearings-4. Fuel Induction: 2-barrel downdraft carburetor. Compression Ratio: 8.50:1. Displacement: 230 cu. in. (3.77 liters). Horsepower: 140 @ 4000 rpm. Torque: 210 lb.-ft. @ 1750 rpm. Oil refill capacity: 5 qt. Fuel Requirements: Regular.

CHASSIS FEATURES: Separate body and chassis. Heavy side members with 1-piece pressed steel channels. Six cross members of flanged U and channel section.

SUSPENSION AND RUNNING GEAR: Front Suspension: Semi-elliptical 10-leaf springs. 36.25 in. x 1.75 in. Spring rate: 260 lb./in. Capacity: 650 lb. direct acting hydraulic shock absorbers. Rear Suspension: Semi-elliptical 8-leaf springs, 50 in. x 1.75 in. Spring rate: 150 lb./in. Capacity: 900 lb. direct acting hydraulic shock absorbers. Front Axle Type and Capacity: Spicer full-floating. Capacity: 2000 lb. Axle ratio: 4.89:1. Optional: 5.38:1. Rear Axle Type and Capacity: Semi-floating Spicer. Capacity: 3700 lb. Transfer Case: Spicer model 18. Ratios: 2.42:1, 1.00:1. Brakes: Type: Hydraulic, front and rear cast iron drums, dual master cylinder, double hydraulic circuit. Dimensions: Front and rear: 11.00 in. x 2.0 in. Total effective lining area: 176.2 sq. in. Optional: None. Wheels: 15 x 6K. Tires: 6.50 x 15 black sidewall. Steering: Cam and lever. Ratio: 26.0:1. Turning Circle: 37.8 ft. Optional: None. Standard Transmission: 3-speed manual. Transmission ratios: 2.798, 1.551, 1.0:1 Reverse: 3.798:1. Optional: None. Clutch: 10 in. dia. Single dry plate with torsional damping, 100.5 sq. in. 6-cyl., data. Optional: None.

VEHICLE DIMENSIONS: Wheelbase: 104.5 in. Overall Length: 176.25 in. Front/Rear Tread: 57 in./57 in. Overall Height: 73.5625 in. Width: Utility wagon: 71.75 in. Utility delivery: 68.125 in. Front/Rear Overhang: 25.75 in./46 in. Tailgate: Width and Height: 49.75 in. x 39.5 in. Approach/Departure Degrees: 38/19. Ground Clearance: Front axle: 9.5 in. Rear axle: 8.3125 in. Load space: 71.0 in. x 43.75 in. x 41.0 in. Maximum capacity (Volume Index): 112 cu. ft. Front headroom: 38.5 in.

CAPACITIES: Fuel Tank: 15.0 gallon capacity. Optional: None. Coolant System: 4-cyl.: 11 qt., 12 qt. with heater. 6-cyl.: 12 qt., 13 qt. with heater.

ACCOMMODATIONS: Seating Capacity: Utility wagon: 4. Utility del.: 1. Seat Dimensions: Front-Utility wagon: Driver's: 31.875 in. Passenger's: 15 in. Rear: Utility wagon: Divided: 15 in./26.375 in.

INSTRUMENTATION: 0-80 mph speedometer, gauges for fuel level, engine coolant temperature, oil pressure, ammeter.

OPTIONS: Front bumper rail and guards. Two-tone paint. Oil bath air cleaner. High altitude cylinder head. Directional signals. Fresh-air heater and defroster. Back-up light. Oil filter. Radio. Governor. Heavy-duty springs. Power take-off (front and center). Fuel tank skid plate. Selective drive hubs. Trailer hitch. Extra-duty generators. Winches. Snowplows.

HISTORICAL FOOTNOTES: The 1963 models were introduced in the fall of 1962.

1964 6-226 & F4-134 UTILITY WAGONS

No changes took place in the design of the Jeep utility vehicles for 1964. The L6-226 utility delivery model was not offered for 1964.

I.D. DATA: The serial number was located on the right side of the dash under the hood, on the front frame cross member and on the left floor riser in the back of the driver's seat. Serial number ranges: F4-134 utility delivery: 54248 or 4213-11825 and up. F4-134 utility wagon: 54148 or 4212-18559 and up. L6-226 utility wagon: 54168-50112 and up. 6-230 utility wagon: 54178 or 6512-10039 and up. 6-230 utility delivery: 54278 or 6513-10582 and up.

Model Number	Body Type	Factory Price	GVW	Shipping Weight	Prod. Total
L6-226	Utility Wagon	$3010	4500	3206	—
F4-134	Utility Wagon	$3030	4500	3093	—
F4-134	S.W. Traveler	$3158	4500	2826	—
F4-134	Utility Del.	$2741	4500	2893	—
6-230	Utility Del.	$2973	4500	3028	—
6-230	Utility Wagon	$3263	4500	3307	—
6-230	S.W. Traveler	$3534	4500	3410	—

STANDARD ENGINE: F4-134 models: Engine Type: 4-cyl., F-head, cast iron block and cylinder head. Bore x Stroke: 3.125 in. x 4.375 in. Lifters: Solid. Number of main bearings-3. Fuel Induction: Single barrel Carter model WA-1 carburetor. Compression Ratio: 7.4:1. (6.9 and 7.4:1 optional, available at no extra cost). Displacement: 134.2 cu. in. (2.19 liters). Horsepower: 75 @ 4000 rpm. Torque: Net 114 lb.-ft. @ 2000 rpm. Oil refill capacity: 5 qt. Fuel Requirements: Regular.

STANDARD ENGINE: L6-226 models: Engine Type: 6-cyl., L-head, cast iron block and cylinder head. Bore x Stroke: 3.9375 in. x 4.375 in. Lifters: Solid. Number of main bearings-4. Fuel Induction: Carter model WDG 1-barrel carburetor. Model 2052S or 2052SA. Compression Ratio: 6.86:1. "High Altitude" 7.3:1 cylinder head optional. Displacement: 226.2 cu. in. (3.7 liters). Horsepower: 105 @ 3600 rpm. Torque: 190 lb.-ft. @ 1400 rpm. Oil refill capacity: 5 qt. Fuel Requirements: Regular.

STANDARD ENGINE: 6-230 models: Engine Type: 6-cyl., OHV, OHC, cast iron block and cylinder head. Bore x Stroke: 3.34 in. x 4.38 in. Lifters: Solid. Number of main bearings-4. Fuel Induction: 2-barrel downdraft carburetor. Compression Ratio: 8.50:1. (7.5:1 optional). Displacement: 230 cu. in. (3.77 liters). Horsepower: Net 140 @ 4000 rpm. (133 @ 4000 rpm optional with 7.5:1 compression ratio). Torque: 210 lb.-ft. @ 1750 rpm. (199 lb.-ft. @ 2400 optional with 7.5:1 compression ratio). Oil refill capacity: 5 qt. Fuel Requirements: Regular.

CHASSIS FEATURES: Separate body and chassis. Heavy side members with 1-piece pressed steel channels. Six cross members of flanged U and channel section.

SUSPENSION AND RUNNING GEAR: Front Suspension: Semi-elliptical 10-leaf springs. 36.25 in. x 1.75 in. Spring rate: 260 lb./in. Capacity: 650 lb. direct acting hydraulic shock absorbers. Rear Suspension: Semi-elliptical 8-leaf springs, 50 in. x 1.75 in. Spring rate: 150 lb./in. Capacity: 900 lb. direct acting hydraulic shock absorbers. Front Axle Type and Capacity: Spicer full-floating. Capacity: 2000 lb. Axle ratio: 4.89:1. Optional: 5.38:1. Rear Axle Type and Capacity: Semi-floating Spicer. Capacity: 3700 lb. Transfer Case: Spicer model 18. Ratios: 2.42:1, 1.00:1. Brakes: Type: Hydraulic, front and rear cast iron drums, dual master cylinder, double hydraulic circuit. Dimensions: Front and rear: 11.00 in. x 2.0 in. Total effective lining area: 176.2 sq. in. Optional: None. Wheels: 15 x 6K. Tires: 6.50 x 15 black sidewall. Steering: Cam and lever. Ratio: 26.0:1. Turning Circle: 37.8 ft. Optional: None. Standard Transmission: 3-speed manual. Transmission ratios: 2.798, 1.551, 1.0:1 Reverse: 3.798:1. Optional: None. Clutch: 10 in. dia. Single dry plate with torsional damping, 100.5 sq. in. 6-cyl., data. Optional: None.

VEHICLE DIMENSIONS: Wheelbase: 104.5 in. Overall Length: 176.25 in. Front/Rear Tread: 57 in./57 in. Overall Height: 73.5625 in. Width: Utility Wagon: 71.75 in., Utility Delivery: 68.125 in. Front/Rear Overhang: 25.75 in./46 in. Tailgate: Width and Height: 49.75 in. x 39.5 in. Approach/Departure Degrees: 38/19. Ground Clearance: Front axle: 9.5 in. Rear axle: 8.3125 in. Load space: 71.0 in. x 43.75 in. x 41.0 in. Maximum capacity (Volume Index): 112 cu. ft. Front headroom: 38.5 in.

CAPACITIES: Fuel Tank: 15.0 gallon capacity. Optional: None. Coolant System: 4-cyl.: 11 qt., 12 qt. with heater. 6-cyl.: 12 qt., 13 qt. with heater.

ACCOMMODATIONS: Seating Capacity: Utility wagon: 4. Utility del.: 1. Seat Dimensions: Front-Utility wagon: Driver's: 31.875 in. Passenger's: 15 in. Rear: Utility wagon: Divided: 15 in./26.375 in.

INSTRUMENTATION: 0-80 mph speedometer, gauges for fuel level, engine coolant temperature, oil pressure, ammeter.

OPTIONS: Front bumper rail and guards. Two-tone paint. Oil bath air cleaner. High altitude cylinder head. Directional signals. Fresh-air heater and defroster. Back-up light. Oil filter. Radio. Governor. Heavy-duty springs. Power take-off (front and center). Fuel tank skid plate. Selective drive hubs. Trailer hitch. Extra-duty generators. Winches. Snowplows.

HISTORICAL FOOTNOTES: The 1964 models debuted in the fall of 1963.

1965 6-230 & F4-134 UTILITY WAGONS

This was the final year for these classic Jeep models. No changes took place in their design. The L-6 engine was not offered.

I.D. DATA: The serial number was located on the right side of the dash under the hood, on the front frame cross member and on the left floor riser in the back of the driver's seat. Serial number ranges: F4-134 utility delivery: 4213-12066 and up. F4-134 utility wagon: 4212-18559 and up. 6-230 utility wagon: 6512-15776 and up. 6-230 utility delivery: 6513-10717 and up.

Model Number	Body Type	Factory Price	GVW	Shipping Weight	Prod. Total
F4-134	Utility Wagon	$3030	4500	3093	—
F4-134	S.W. Traveler	$3302	4500	3077	—
F4-134	Utility Del.	$2741	4500	2893	—
6-230	Utility Del.	$2973	4500	3028	—
6-230	Utility Wagon	$3263	4500	3307	—

STANDARD ENGINE: F4-134 models: Engine Type: 4-cyl., F-head, cast iron block and cylinder head. Bore x Stroke: 3.125 in. x 4.375 in. Lifters: Solid. Number of main bearings-3. Fuel Induction: Single barrel Carter model WA-1 carburetor. Compression Ratio: 7.4:1. (6.9 and 7.4:1 optional, available at no extra cost). Displacement: 134.2 cu. in. (2.19 liters). Horsepower: 75 @ 4000 rpm. Torque: Net 114 lb.-ft. @ 2000 rpm. Oil refill capacity: 5 qt. Fuel Requirements: Regular.

STANDARD ENGINE: 6-230 models: Engine Type: 6-cyl., OHV, OHC, cast iron block and cylinder head. Bore x Stroke: 3.34 in. x 4.38 in. Lifters: Solid. Number of main bearings-4. Fuel Induction: 2-barrel downdraft carburetor. Compression Ratio: 8.50:1. (7.5:1 optional). Displacement: 230 cu. in. (3.77 liters). Horsepower: Net 140 @ 4000 rpm. (133 @ 4000 rpm optional with 7.5:1 compression ratio). Torque: 210 lb.-ft. @ 1750 rpm. (199 lb.-ft. @ 2400 optional with 7.5:1 compression ratio). Oil refill capacity: 5 qt. Fuel Requirements: Regular.

CHASSIS FEATURES: Separate body and chassis. Heavy side members with 1-piece pressed steel channels. Six cross members of flanged U and channel section.

SUSPENSION AND RUNNING GEAR: Front Suspension: Semi-elliptical 10-leaf springs. 36.25 in. x 1.75 in. Spring rate: 260 lb./in. Capacity: 650 lb. direct acting hydraulic shock absorbers. Rear Suspension: Semi-elliptical 8-leaf springs, 50 in. x 1.75 in. Spring rate: 150 lb./in. Capacity: 900 lb. direct acting hydraulic shock absorbers. Front Axle Type and Capacity: Spicer full-floating. Capacity: 2000 lb. Axle ratio: 4.89:1. Optional: 5.38:1. Rear Axle Type and Capacity: Semi-floating Spicer. Capacity: 3700 lb. Transfer Case: Spicer model 18. Ratios: 2.42:1, 1.00:1. Brakes: Type: Hydraulic, front and rear cast iron drums, dual master cylinder, double hydraulic circuit. Dimensions: Front and rear: 11.00 in. x 2.0 in. Total effective lining area: 176.2 sq. in. Optional: None. Wheels: 15 x 6K. Tires: 6.50 x 15 black sidewall. Steering: Cam and lever. Ratio: 26.0:1. Turning Circle: 37.8 ft. Optional: None. Standard Transmission: 3-speed manual. Transmission ratios: 2.798, 1.551, 1.0:1 Reverse: 3.798:1. Optional: None. Clutch: 10 in. dia. Single dry plate with torsional damping, 100.5 sq. in. 6-cyl., data. Optional: None.

VEHICLE DIMENSIONS: Wheelbase: 104.5 in. Overall Length: 176.25 in. Front/Rear Tread: 57 in./57 in. Overall Height: 73.5625 in. Width: Utility wagon: 71.75 in. Utility delivery: 68.125 in. Front/Rear Overhang: 25.75 in./46 in. Tailgate: Width and Height: 49.75 in. x 39.5 in. Approach/Departure Degrees: 38/19. Ground Clearance: Front axle: 9.5 in. Rear axle: 8.3125 in. Load space: 71.0 in. x 43.75 in. x 41.0 in. Maximum capacity (Volume Index): 112 cu. ft. Front headroom: 38.5 in.

CAPACITIES: Fuel Tank: 15.0 gallon capacity. Optional: None. Coolant System: 4-cyl.: 11 qt., 12 qt. with heater. 6-cyl.: 12 qt., 13 qt. with heater.

ACCOMMODATIONS: Seating Capacity: Utility wagon: 4. Utility del.: 1. Seat Dimensions: Front-Utility wagon: Driver's: 31.875 in. Passenger's: 15 in. Rear: Utility wagon: Divided: 15 in./26.375 in.

INSTRUMENTATION: 0-80 mph speedometer, gauges for fuel level, engine coolant temperature, oil pressure, ammeter.

OPTIONS: Front bumper rail and guards. Two-tone paint. Oil bath air cleaner. High altitude cylinder head. Directional signals. Fresh-air heater and defroster. Back-up light. Oil filter. Radio. Governor. Heavy-duty springs. Power take-off (front and center). Fuel tank skid plate. Selective drive hubs. Trailer hitch. Extra-duty generators. Winches. Snowplows.

HISTORICAL FOOTNOTES: The demise of these classic and long-lived Jeep models was seen only in retrospect as a major milestone of postwar American automotive history.

JEEP FC-150 & FC-170 TRUCKS

1957-1965

The FC-150 truck was introduced on November 27, 1956. The FC-170 was introduced shortly thereafter on May 20, 1957. Although the Forward Control models used a cab-over-engine design, they were still identifiable as a Jeep product due to a grille arrangement that included seven vertical cutouts plus the head and parking lights within a perimeter shaped to suggest that of the CJ models.

1957 Jeep FC-150

The FC "Safety View" cab had an exceptional amount of glass area. The wrap-around windshield had a surface of nearly 1200 sq. in. while the rear window measured 628 sq. in. In addition there were large side door windows and, on Deluxe cab models, stationary windows in the rear side pillars. The Deluxe FC Jeep's glass area totalled 2747 sq. in.

The angular rear fenders of the FC were almost identical to those used on the conventional Jeep trucks. The FC front fenders were in the form of a simple raised panel of rubber construction extending along the wheel wells. When opened, the wide door revealed a concealed "safety step" area. The cab interior was color-coded to the truck's exterior. A console-type instrument panel grouped the instruments and gauges in a cluster directly in front of the driver. An ignition key-operated starter was used and both the clutch and brake pedals were of suspended design. A useful feature was the placement of the brake fluid access tank cover on the dash panel. Access to the engine was through an easily removed cover. The use of heavy fiberglass insulation limited the amount of engine noise and heat that entered the cab.

Standard FC equipment included a front bumper, two front seats with adjustable driver's seat, single horn, tool kit, driver's side sun visor, dual vacuum windshield wipers, partial roof trim, dome light, ashtray, floor mats, inside mirror, vent windows, spare wheel and mounting bracket, door locks, weed and brush guard, quarter trim panel, rear floor trim panels and glove box.

The FC color selection consisted of these colors: Raven black, president red, steel glow metallic, transport yellow, royal blue metallic, glenwood green metallic and Aztec orange.

1957 Jeep FC-170

I.D. DATA: The serial number was located on the right side of the dash under hood, on the front frame cross member and on the left floor riser in the back of the driver's seat. Serial number ranges: FC-150: 65548-10001 and up. FC-170: 61568-10001 and up.

Model Number	Body Type	Factory Price	GVW	Shipping Weight	Prod. Total
FC-150	Chassis & Cab	$2044.10	5000	2764	—
FC-150	Pickup	$2140.15	5000	3020	—
FC-150	Stake	$2223.00	5000	3187	—
FC-170	Chassis & Cab	$2396.00	7000	2901	—
FC-170	Pickup	$2508.00	7000	3331	—
FC-170	Stake	$2678.00	7000	3564	—

STANDARD ENGINE: FC-150 models: Engine Type: 4-cyl., F-head, cast iron block and cylinder head. Bore x Stroke: 3.125 in. x 4.375 in. Lifters: Solid. Number of main bearings-3. Fuel Induction: Single barrel Carter model WA-1 carburetor. Compression Ratio: 6.9:1. "High Altitude" 7.4:1 cylinder available at no extra cost. Displacement: 134.2 cu. in. (2.19 liters). Horsepower: 75 @ 4000 rpm. Torque: Net 115 lb.-ft. @ 2000 rpm. Oil refill capacity: 5 qt. Fuel Requirements: Regular.

STANDARD ENGINE: FC-170 models: Engine Type: 6-cyl., L-head, cast iron block and cylinder head. Bore x Stroke: 3.9375 in. x 4.375 in. Lifters: Solid. Number of main bearings-4. Fuel Induction: Carter WDG 1-barrel carburetor. Model 2052S or 2052SA. Compression Ratio: 6.86:1 "High Altitude" 7.3:1 cylinder head optional. Displacement: 226.2 cu. in. (3.7 liters). Horsepower: 105 @ 3600 rpm. Torque: 190 lb.-ft. @ 1400 rpm. Oil refill capacity: 5 qt. Fuel Requirements: Regular.

CHASSIS FEATURES: Separate body and chassis. FC-150: Pressed steel channel 1.94 in. x 4.12 in. x 0.149 in., 7 cross members. FC-170: Pressed steel channel, section modulus: 2.581, 6 cross members.

SUSPENSION AND RUNNING GEAR: Front Suspension: FC-150: Semi-elliptical 7-leaf springs. 39.625 in. x 1.75 in. Direct acting shock absorbers. FC-170: Semi-elliptical 6-leaf springs. 46 in. x 2.50 in. Direct acting shock absorbers. Optional: Heavy-duty springs. Rear Suspension: FC-150: Semi-elliptical 9-leaf springs. 52 in. x 2.50 in. Direct acting shock absorbers. FC-170: Semi-elliptical 6-leaf springs. 52 in. x 2.50 in. Direct acting shock absorbers. Front Axle Type and Capacity: FC-150: Full-floating. Capacity: 2300 lbs. FC-170: Full-floating. Capacity: 3700 lbs. Axle ratio: FC-150: 5.38:1. FC-170: 4.88:1. Rear Axle Type and Capacity: FC-150: Semi-floating. Capacity: 3000 lbs. FC-170: Semi-floating. Capacity: 4500 lbs. Axle ratio: FC-150: 5.38:1. FC-170: 4.88:1. Transfer Case: 2-speed. Ratios: 2.46:1, 1.00:1. Brakes: Type: Hydraulic, front and rear cast iron drums, dual master cylinder, double hydraulic circuit. Dimensions: Front and rear: 11.00 in. x 2.0 in. Total effective lining area: 176.2 sq. in. Optional: None. Wheels: 15 x 6K. Tires: 7.00 x 15 4-ply black sidewall. Steering: Cam and lever. Ratio (overall): 32.0:1. Turning Circle: FC-150: 36 ft. FC-170: 43.83 ft. Optional: None. Standard Transmission: 3-speed manual. Transmission Ratios: 2.798, 1.441, 1.0:1. Reverse: 3.798:1. Optional: 4-speed manual transmission. Transmission Ratios: 6.398, 3.092, 1.686, 1.00:1. Reverse: 7.820:1. Clutch: Single dry plate with torsional dampening 10 in. dia. Single dry plate with torsional damping, FC-150: 72 sq. in. FC-170: 100.5 sq. in. Optional: None.

VEHICLE DIMENSIONS: Wheelbase: FC-150: 81.0 in. FC-170: 103.5 in. Overall Length: FC-150: 147.4 in. FC-170: 180.5 in. Front/Rear Tread: FC-150: 48.375 in. FC-170: 63.5 in. Overall Height: FC-150: 77.375 in. FC-170: 79.375 in. Width: FC-150: 71.375 in. FC-170: 76.5 in. Front/Rear Overhang: FC-150: 38.25 in./27.25 in. FC-170: 38.50 in./38.50 in. Tailgate: Width and Height: FC-150: 58.25 in. x 20.0 in. FC-170: 48.25 in. x 13.71 in. Approach/Departure Degrees: FC-150: 36/36. FC-170: 40/30. Ground Clearance: FC-150: Rear axle: .8.0 in. FC-170: 8.25 in. Load space: FC-150: 74.25 in. x 36.0 in. x 20.0 in. FC-170: 109.80 in. x 48.46 in. x 13.71 in. Floor to ground: FC-150: 16.25 in. FC-170: 18.25 in.

CAPACITIES: Fuel Tank: FC-150: 16 gal. FC-170: 22 gal. capacity. Optional: None. Coolant system: FC-150: 11 qt., 12 qt. with heater. FC-170: 12 qt., 13 qt. with heater.

ACCOMMODATIONS: Seating Capacity: Two.

INSTRUMENTATION: Speedometer, odometer, gauges for engine coolant temperature, oil pressure, battery and fuel level.

OPTIONS AND PRICES: Note: The prices quoted refer to options for the FC-150. In most cases the prices were unchanged for the FC-170. Group 901. Includes oil bath air cleaner, oil filter and directional signals: $55.32. Deluxe cab. Includes cigarette lighter, quarter windows, door trim panel, armrests, full roof trim, foam rubber seat pads, front trim panel, passenger side sun visor, vinyl windshield trim with defroster, bezels and chrome safety rail: $45. Heavy-duty rear axle: $33.60. Locking rear differential: $40.15. Locking differential and heavy-duty rear axle: $59.50. Transmission hand brake: $17.95. Pickup box: $6.05. Platform stake: $178.90. Fresh-air heater and defroster: $74.70. Front panel air vent: $8.85. Center power take-off: $60.00. Pulley and pulley drive for power take-off: $108.60. Center and rear power take-off: $203.15. Velocity governor: $24.20. Radio and antenna: $98.30. Passenger 2/3 type seat: $10.00. 7.00 x 15 6-ply All-Service tires: $24.85. 6.50 x 15 6-ply Deluxe Rib tires: No extra charge. 7.60 x 15 4-ply Suburbanite tires: No extra charge. High altitude, 7.8:1, cylinder head: No extra charge. Front bumper guards: $2.65. Drawbar: $24.15. Heavy-duty springs and shock absorbers: $14.95. Windshield washers: $14.85. Two-tone paint: $17.45. E-Z Eye glass: $11.65. Front stabilizer bar: $16.65. 4-speed manual transmission. Dealer installed options included selective drive hubs, winches, snowplows, dozing blades and wrecker equipment.

HISTORICAL FOOTNOTES: Willys depicted the new FC as "a great new Jeep, newest addition to the time-tested ... performance proved Jeep line of four-wheel drive vehicles."

1958 FC-150 & FC-170 TRUCKS

No changes were made in the FC models for 1958.

I.D. DATA: The serial number was located on the right side of the dash under hood, on the front frame cross member and on the left floor riser in the back of the driver's seat. Serial number ranges: FC-150: 65548-10001 and up. FC-170: 61568-10001 and up.

Model Number	Body Type	Factory Price	GVW	Shipping Weight	Prod. Total
FC-150	Chassis & Cab	$2044.10	5000	2764	—
FC-150	Pickup	$2140.15	5000	3020	—
FC-150	Stake	$2223.00	5000	3187	—
FC-170	Chassis & Cab	$2396.00	7000	2901	—
FC-170	Pickup	$2508.00	7000	3331	—
FC-170	Stake	$2678.00	7000	3564	—

STANDARD ENGINE: FC-150 models: Engine Type: 4-cyl., F-head, cast iron block and cylinder head. Bore x Stroke: 3.125 in. x 4.375 in. Lifters: Solid. Number of main bearings-3. Fuel Induction: Single barrel Carter model WA-1 carburetor. Compression Ratio: 6.9:1. "High Altitude" 7.4:1 cylinder available at no extra cost. Displacement: 134.2 cu. in. (2.19 liters). Horsepower: 75 @ 4000 rpm. Torque: Net 115 lb.-ft. @ 2000 rpm. Oil refill capacity: 5 qt. Fuel Requirements: Regular.

STANDARD ENGINE: FC-170 models: Engine Type: 6-cyl., L-head, cast iron block and cylinder head. Bore x Stroke: 3.9375 in. x 4.375 in. Lifters: Solid. Number of main bearings-4. Fuel Induction: Carter model WDG 1-barrel carburetor. Model 2052S or 2052SA. Compression Ratio: 6.86:1 "High Altitude" 7.3:1 cylinder head optional. Displacement: 226.2 cu. in. (3.7 liters). Horsepower: 105 @ 3600 rpm. Torque: 190 lb.-ft. @ 1400 rpm. Oil refill capacity: 5 qt. Fuel Requirements: Regular.

CHASSIS FEATURES: Separate body and chassis. FC-150: Pressed steel channel 1.94 in. x 4.12 in. x 0.149 in., seven cross members. FC-170: Pressed steel channel, section modulus: 2.581, six cross members.

SUSPENSION AND RUNNING GEAR: Front Suspension: FC-150: Semi-elliptical 7-leaf springs. 39.625 in. x 1.75 in. Direct acting shock absorbers. FC-170: Semi-elliptical 6-leaf springs. 46 in. x 2.50 in. Direct acting shock absorbers. Optional: Heavy-duty springs. Rear Suspension: FC-150: Semi-elliptical 9-leaf springs. 52 in. x 2.50 in. Direct acting shock absorbers. FC-170: Semi-elliptical 6-leaf springs. 52 in. x 2.50 in. Direct acting shock absorbers. Front Axle Type and Capacity: FC-150: Full-floating. Capacity: 2300 lbs. FC-170: Full-floating. Capacity: 3700 lbs. Axle ratio: FC-150: 5.38:1. FC-170: 4.88:1. Rear Axle Type and Capacity: FC-150: Semi-floating. Capacity: 3000 lbs. FC-170: Semi-floating. Capacity: 4500 lbs. Axle ratio: FC-150: 5.38:1. FC-170: 4.88:1. Transfer Case: 2-speed. Ratios: 2.46:1, 1.00:1. Brakes: Type: Hydraulic, front and rear cast iron drums, dual master cylinder, double hydraulic circuit. Dimensions: Front and rear: 11.00 in. x 2.0 in. Total effective lining area: 176.2 sq. in. Optional: None. Wheels: 15 x 6K. Tires: 7.00 x 15 4-ply black sidewall. Steering: Cam and lever. Ratio (overall): 32.0:1. Turning Circle: FC-150: 36 ft. FC-170: 43.83-ft. Optional: None. Standard Transmission: 3-speed manual. Transmission Ratios: 2.798, 1.441, 1.0:1. Reverse: 3.798:1. Optional: 4-speed manual transmission. Transmission Ratios: 6.398, 3.092, 1.686, 1.00:1. Reverse: 7.820:1. Clutch: Single dry plate with torsional dampening, 10 in. dia. Single dry plate with torsional damping, FC-150: 72 sq. in. FC-170: 100.5 sq. in. Optional: None.

VEHICLE DIMENSIONS: Wheelbase: FC-150: 81.0 in. FC-170: 103.5 in. Overall Length: FC-150: 147.4 in. FC-170: 180.5 in. Front/Rear Tread: FC-150: 48.375 in. FC-170: 63.5 in. Overall Height: FC-150: 77.375 in. FC-170: 79.375 in. Width: FC-150: 71.375 in. FC-170: 76.5 in. Front/Rear Overhang: FC-150: 38.25 in./27.25 in. FC-170: 38.50 in./38.50 in. Tailgate: Width and Height: FC-150: 58.25 in. x 20.0 in. FC-170: 48.25 in. x 13.71 in. Approach/Departure Degrees: FC-150: 36/36. FC-170: 40/30. Ground Clearance: FC-150: Rear axle: .8.0 in. FC-170: 8.25 in. Load space: FC-150: 74.25 in. x 36.0 in. x 20.0 in. FC-170: 109.80 in. x 48.46 in. x 13.71 in. Floor to ground: FC-150: 16.25 in. FC-170: 18.25 in.

CAPACITIES: Fuel Tank: FC-150: 16 gal. FC-170: 22 gal. capacity. Optional: None. Coolant system: FC-150: 11 qt., 12 qt. with heater. FC-170: 12 qt., 13 qt. with heater.

ACCOMMODATIONS: Seating Capacity: Two.

INSTRUMENTATION: Speedometer, odometer, gauges for engine coolant temperature, oil pressure, battery and fuel level.

OPTIONS AND PRICES: Note: The prices quoted refer to options for the FC-150. In most cases the prices were unchanged for the FC-170. Group 901. Includes oil bath air cleaner, oil filter and directional signals: $55.32. Deluxe cab. Includes cigarette lighter, quarter windows, door trim panel, armrests, full roof trim, foam rubber seat pads, front trim panel, passenger side sun visor, vinyl windshield trim with defroster, bezels and chrome safety rail: $45. Heavy-duty rear axle: $33.60. Locking rear differential: $40.15. Locking differential and heavy-duty rear axle: $59.50. Transmission hand brake: $17.95. Pickup box: $6.05. Platform stake: $178.90. Fresh-air heater and defroster: $74.70. Front panel air vent: $8.85. Center power take-off: $60.00. Pulley and pulley drive for power take-off: $108.60. Center and rear power take-off: $203.15. Velocity governor: $24.20. Radio and antenna: $98.30. Passenger 2/3 type seat: $10.00. 7.00 x 15 6-ply All-Service tires: $24.85.6.50 x 15 6-ply Deluxe Rib tires: No extra charge. 7.60 x 15 4-ply Suburbanite tires: No extra charge. High altitude, 7.8:1, cylinder head: No extra charge. Front bumper guards: $2.65. Drawbar: $24.15. Heavy-duty springs and shock absorbers: $14.95. Windshield washers: $14.85. Two-tone paint: $17.45. E-Z Eye glass: $11.65. Front stabilizer bar: $16.65. 4-speed manual transmission. Dealer installed options included selective drive hubs, winches, snowplows, dozing blades and wrecker equipment.

HISTORICAL FOOTNOTES: The 1958 FC Jeeps were introduced on Aug. 15, 1957.

1959 FC-150 & FC-170 TRUCKS

The latest FC models were available with new color styling, new interior trims and fabrics. Both the FC-150 and FC-170 had numerous revised technical specifications. The FC-170 was offered in a newly modified model with an optional heavy-duty rear end including a stronger rear axle, heavy-duty springs and shock absorbers, increased brake capacity and rear wheels. This heavy-duty FC-170 was available in chassis and cab, pickup and Platform Stake styles with dual rear wheels. The Platform Stake was also offered with dual rear wheels and 4-speed manual transmission. In this form it had a 9000 lb. GVW rating.

1959 Jeep FC-170 Forward Control truck

I.D. DATA: The serial number was located on the right side of the dash under hood, on the front frame cross member and on the left floor riser in the back of the driver's seat. Serial number ranges: FC-150: Chassis and Cab: 65548-10062 and up. Pickup: 65548-10098 and up, Platform Stake: 65548-12150 and up. FC-170: Chassis and cab: 61568-10015 and up. Pickup: 61568-10007 and up. Platform Stake: 61568-11551 and up, heavy-duty: 61568-10015 and up.

Model Number	Body Type	Factory Price	GVW	Shipping Weight	Prod. Total
FC-150	Chassis & Cab	$2229	5000	2764	—
FC-150	Pickup	$2338	5000	3020	—
FC-150	Stake	$2433	5000	3187	—
FC-170	Chassis & Cab	$2516	7000	2901	—
FC-170	Pickup	$2643	7000	3331	—
FC-170	Stake	$2837	7000	3564	—
FC-170 HD	Chassis	$2449	8000	2819	—
FC-170 HD	Chassis & Cab	$2961	8000	3552	—
FC-170 HD	Platform Stake	$3369	8000*	4586	—

* 9000 lb. GVW available for Platform Stake.

STANDARD ENGINE: FC-150 models: Engine Type: 4-cyl., F-head, cast iron block and cylinder head. Bore x Stroke: 3.125 in. x 4.375 in. Lifters: Solid. Number of main bearings-3. Fuel Induction: Single barrel Carter model WA-1 carburetor. Compression Ratio: 6.9:1. "High Altitude" 7.4:1 cylinder available at no extra cost. Displacement: 134.2 cu. in. (2.19 liters). Horsepower: 75 @ 4000 rpm. Torque: Net 115 lb.-ft. @ 2000 rpm. Oil refill capacity: 5 qt. Fuel Requirements: Regular.

STANDARD ENGINE: FC-170 models: Engine Type: 6-cyl., L-head, cast iron block and cylinder head. Bore x Stroke: 3.9375 in. x 4.375 in. Lifters: Solid. Number of main bearings-4. Fuel Induction: Carter model WDG 1-barrel carburetor. Model 2052S or 2052SA. Compression Ratio: 6.86:1 "High Altitude" 7.3:1 cylinder head optional. Displacement: 226.2 cu. in. (3.7 liters). Horsepower: 105 @ 3600 rpm. Torque: 190 lb.-ft. @ 1400 rpm. Oil refill capacity: 5 qt. Fuel Requirements: Regular.

CHASSIS FEATURES: Separate body and chassis. FC-150: Pressed steel channel 1.94 in. x 4.12 in. x 0.149 in., seven cross members. FC-170: Pressed steel channel, section modulus: 2.581, six cross members.

SUSPENSION AND RUNNING GEAR: Front Suspension: FC-150: Semi-elliptical 6-leaf springs 46 in. x 2.50 in. Spring rate: 270 lb./in. Capacity: 1030 lb. Direct acting shock absorbers. FC-170: Semi-elliptical 6-leaf spring. 46 in. x 2.50 in. Spring rate: 260 lb./in. Capacity: 1250 lb. Direct acting shock absorbers. Optional: Heavy-duty springs. Rear Suspension: FC-150: Semi-elliptical 7-leaf spring. 46 in. x 2.50 in. Spring rate: 280 lb./in. Capacity: 1135 lb. shock absorbers. FC-170: Semi-elliptical 6-leaf spring. 52 in. x 2.50 in. Spring rate: 285 lb./in. Capacity: 1450 lbs. FC-170 HD: Semi-elliptical 9-leaf springs. Spring rate: 672 lb./in. Capacity: 2790 lb. Front Axle Type and Capacity: FC-150: Full-floating. Capacity: 3000 lb. FC-170: Full-floating. Capacity: 3000 lbs. Axle ratio: FC-150: 5.38:1. FC-170: 4.88:1. Optional: None. Rear Axle Type and Capacity: FC-150: Semi-floating. Capacity: 3500 lbs. FC-170: Semi-floating. Capacity: 4500 lbs. Axle ratio: FC-150: 5.38:1. FC-170: 4.88:1. Transfer Case: 2-speed. Ratios: 2.46:1, 1.00:1. Brakes: Type: Hydraulic, front and rear cast iron drums, dual master cylinder, double hydraulic circuit. Dimensions: FC-150 and FC-170: Front and rear: 11.00 in. x 2.0 in. Total effective lining area: 176.2 sq. in. FC-170 HD: Front: 12 in. x 2.00 in. rear: 13 in. x 2.5 in. Total effective area: 230.6 sq. in. Optional: None. Wheels: FC-150: 15 x 4.5. FC-170: 16 x 5.00. FC-170 HD: Dual rear 16 x 5.50 wheels. Tires: FC-150: 7.00 x 15 4-ply black sidewall. FC-170: 7.00 x 16.6-ply black sidewall. Other sizes optional. Steering: Cam and lever. Ratio (overall): 32.0:1. Turning Circle: FC-150: 36 ft. FC-170: 43.83-ft. Standard Transmission: 3-speed manual. Transmission ratios: 2.798, 1.441, 1.0:1. Reverse: 3.798:1. Optional: 4-speed manual transmission (standard for FC-170 HD with 9000 lb. GVW). Transmission Ratios: 6.398, 3.092, 1.686, 1.00:1. Reverse: 7.820:1. Clutch: Single dry plate with torsional dampening, 10 in. dia. Single dry plate with torsional damping, FC-150: 72 sq. in. FC-170: 100.5 sq. in. Optional: None.

VEHICLE DIMENSIONS: Wheelbase: FC-150: 81.0 in. FC-170: 103.5 in. Overall Length: FC-150: 147.4 in. FC-170: 180.5 in. FC-170 HD Stake: 203 in. Front/Rear Tread: FC-150: 48.375 in. FC-170: 63.5 in. FC-170 HD: Rear tread: 72.5 in. Overall Height: FC-150: 77.375

in. FC-170: 79.98 in. FC-170 HD: 79.10 in. Width: FC-150: 71.375 in. FC-170: 76.5 in. FC-170 HD Stake: 92.12 in. Front/Rear Overhang: FC-150: 38.25 in./27.25 in. FC-170: 38.50 in./38.50 in. Tailgate: Width and Height: FC-150: 58.25 in. x 20.0 in. FC-170: 48.25 in. x 13.71 in. Approach/Departure Degrees: FC-150: 36/36. FC-170: 40/30. Ground Clearance: Rear axle: FC-150: 8.0 in. FC-170: 8.87 in. FC-170 HD: 7.90 in. Load space: FC-150: 74.25 in. x 36.0 in. x 20.0 in. FC-170: 109.80 in. x 48.46 in. x 13.71 in. FC-170 HD Platform: 132.60 in. x 92.12 in. Floor to ground: FC-150: 16.25 in. FC-170: 18.25 in.

CAPACITIES: Fuel Tank: FC-150: 16 gal. FC-170: 22 gal. capacity. Optional: None. Coolant system: FC-150: 11 qt., 12 qt. with heater. FC-170: 12 qt., 13 qt. with heater.

ACCOMMODATIONS: Seating Capacity: Two.

INSTRUMENTATION: Speedometer, odometer, gauges for engine coolant temperature, oil pressure, battery and fuel level.

OPTIONS: Group 901. Includes oil bath air cleaner, oil filter and directional signals. Deluxe cab. Includes cigarette lighter, quarter windows, door trim panel, armrests, full roof trim, foam rubber seat pads, front trim panel, passenger side sun visor, vinyl windshield trim with defroster, bezels and chrome safety rail. Heavy-duty rear axle. Locking rear differential. Locking differential and heavy-duty rear axle. Transmission hand brake. Pickup box. Platform stake. Fresh-air heater and defroster. Front panel air vent. Center power take-off. Pulley and pulley drive for power take-off. Center and rear power take-off. Velocity governor. Radio and antenna. Passenger 2/3 type seat. 7.00 x 15 6-ply All-Service tires. 6.50 x 15 6-ply Deluxe Rib tires. 7.60 x 15 4-ply. High altitude, 7.8:1, cylinder head: No extra charge. Front bumper guards. Drawbar. Heavy-duty springs and shock absorbers. Windshield washers. Two-tone paint. E-Z Eye glass. Front stabilizer bar. 4-speed manual transmission. Dealer installed options included selective drive hubs, winches, snowplows, dozing blades and wrecker equipment.

HISTORICAL FOOTNOTES: The 1959 FC models were introduced in the fall of 1958.

1960 FC-150 & FC-170 TRUCKS

No changes took place in the FC models for 1960.

1960 Jeep FC-150 Forward Control truck

I.D. DATA: The serial number was located on the right side of the dash under hood, on the front frame cross member and on the left floor riser in the back of the driver's seat. Serial number ranges: FC-150: Chassis and cab: 65548-10403 and up. Pickup: 65548-10101 and up. Platform Stake: 65548-12820 and up. FC-170: Chassis and cab: 61568-11480 and up, Pickup: 61568-10015 and up, Platform Stake: 61568-11692 and up, FC-170 heavy-duty: Chassis and cab: 61568-13-10015 and up. Chassis W. S: 61368-13-10015 and up.

Model Number	Body Type	Factory Price	GVW	Shipping Weight	Prod. Total
FC-150	Chassis & Cab	$2416	5000	2764	—
FC-150	Pickup	$2533	5000	3020	—
FC-150	Stake	$2634	5000	3187	—
FC-170	Chassis & Cab	$2722	7000	2901	—
FC-170	Pickup	$2858	7000	3331	—
FC-170	Stake	$3065	7000	3564	—
FC-170 HD	Chassis W. S.	$3032	8000*	3028	—
FC-170 HD	Chassis & Cab	$3197	8000	3561	—

* 9000 lb. GVW available for Platform Stake.

STANDARD ENGINE: FC-150 models: Engine Type: 4-cyl., F-head, cast iron block and cylinder head. Bore x Stroke: 3.125 in. x 4.375 in. Lifters: Solid. Number of main bearings-3. Fuel Induction: Single barrel Carter model WA-1 carburetor. Compression Ratio: 6.9:1. "High Altitude" 7.4:1 cylinder available at no extra cost. Displacement: 134.2 cu. in. (2.19 liters). Horsepower: 75 @ 4000 rpm. Torque: Net 115 lb.-ft. @ 2000 rpm. Oil refill capacity: 5 qt. Fuel Requirements: Regular.

STANDARD ENGINE: FC-170 models: Engine Type: 6-cyl., L-head, cast iron block and cylinder head. Bore x Stroke: 3.9375 in. x 4.375 in. Lifters: Solid. Number of main bearings-4. Fuel Induction: Carter model WDG 1-barrel carburetor. Model 2052S or 2052SA. Compression Ratio: 6.86:1 "High Altitude" 7.3:1 cylinder head optional. Displacement: 226.2 cu. in. (3.7 liters). Horsepower: 105 @ 3600 rpm. Torque: 190 lb.-ft. @ 1400 rpm. Oil refill capacity: 5 qt. Fuel Requirements: Regular.

CHASSIS FEATURES: Separate body and chassis. FC-150: Pressed steel channel 1.94 in. x 4.12 in. x 0.149 in., seven cross members. FC-170: Pressed steel channel, section modulus: 2.581, six cross members.

SUSPENSION AND RUNNING GEAR: Front Suspension: FC-150: Semi-elliptical 6-leaf springs. 46 in. x 2.50 in. Spring rate: 270 lb./in. Capacity: 1030 lb. Direct acting shock absorbers. FC-170: Semi-elliptical 6-leaf springs. 46 in. x 2.50 in. Spring rate: 260 lb./in. Capacity: 1250 lb. Direct acting shock absorbers. Optional: Heavy-duty springs. Rear Suspension: FC-150: Semi-elliptical 7-leaf springs. 46 in. x 2.50 in. Spring rate: 280 lb./in. Capacity: 1135 lb. shock absorbers. FC-170: Semi-elliptical 6-leaf spring. 52 in. x 2.50 in. Spring rate: 285 lb./in. Capacity: 1450 lbs. FC-170 HD: Semi-elliptical 9-leaf springs. Spring rate: 672 lb./in. Capacity: 2790 lb. Front Axle Type and Capacity: FC-150: Full-floating. Capacity: 3000 lbs. FC-170: Full-floating. Capacity: 3000 lbs. Axle ratio: FC-150: 5.38:1. FC-170: 4.88:1. Optional: None. Rear Axle Type and Capacity: FC-150: Semi-floating. Capacity: 3500 lbs. FC-170: Semi-floating. Capacity: 4500 lbs. Axle ratio: FC-150: 5.38:1. FC-170: 4.88:1. Transfer Case: 2-speed. Ratios: 2.46:1, 1.00:1. Brakes: Type: Hydraulic, front and rear cast iron drums, dual master cylinder, double hydraulic circuit. Dimensions: FC-150 and FC-170: Front and rear: 11.00 in. x 2.0 in. Total effective lining area: 176.2 sq. in. FC-170 HD: Front: 12 in. x 2.00 in. rear: 13 in. x 2.5 in. Total effective area: 230.6 sq. in. Optional: None. Wheels: FC-150: 15 x 4.5. FC-170: 16 x 5.00. FC-170 HD: Dual rear 16 x 5.50 wheels. Tires: FC-150: 7.00 x 15 4-ply black sidewall. FC-170: 7.00 x 16.6-ply black sidewall. Other sizes optional. Steering: Cam and lever. Ratio (overall): 32.0:1. Turning Circle: FC-150: 36 ft. FC-170: 43.83-ft. Standard Transmission: 3-speed manual. Transmission ratios: 2.798, 1.441, 1.0:1. Reverse: 3.798:1. Optional: 4-speed manual transmission (standard for FC-170 HD with 9000 lb. GVW). Transmission Ratios: 6.398, 3.092, 1.686, 1.00:1. Reverse: 7.820:1. Clutch: Single dry plate with torsional dampening, 10 in. dia. Single dry plate with torsional damping, FC-150: 72 sq. in. FC-170: 100.5 sq. in. Optional: None.

VEHICLE DIMENSIONS: Wheelbase: FC-150: 81.0 in. FC-170: 103.5 in. Overall Length: FC-150: 147.4 in. FC-170: 180.5 in. FC-170 HD Stake: 203 in. Front/Rear Tread: FC-150: 48.375 in. FC-170: 63.5 in. FC-170 HD: Rear tread: 72.5 in. Overall Height: FC-150: 77.375 in. FC-170: 79.98 in. FC-170 HD: 79.10 in. Width: FC-150: 71.375 in. FC-170: 76.5 in. FC-170 HD Stake: 92.12 in. Front/Rear Overhang: FC-150: 38.25 in./27.25 in. FC-170: 38.50 in./38.50 in. Tailgate: Width and Height: FC-150: 58.25 in. x 20.0 in. FC-170: 48.25 in. x 13.71 in. Approach/Departure Degrees: FC-150: 36/36. FC-170: 40/30. Ground Clearance: Rear axle: FC-150: 8.0 in. FC-170: 8.87 in. FC-170 HD: 7.90 in. Load space: FC-150: 74.25 in. x 36.0 in. x 20.0 in. FC-170: 109.80 in. x 48.46 in. x 13.71 in. FC-170 HD Platform: 132.60 in. x 92.12 in. Floor to ground: FC-150: 16.25 in. FC-170: 18.25 in.

CAPACITIES: Fuel Tank: FC-150: 16 gal. FC-170: 22 gal. capacity. Optional: None. Coolant system: FC-150: 11 qt., 12 qt. with heater. FC-170: 12 qt., 13 qt. with heater.

ACCOMMODATIONS: Seating Capacity: 2.

INSTRUMENTATION: Speedometer, odometer, gauges for engine coolant temperature, oil pressure, battery and fuel level.

OPTIONS: Group 901. Includes oil bath air cleaner, oil filter and directional signals. Deluxe cab. Includes cigarette lighter, quarter windows, door trim panel, armrests, full roof trim, foam rubber seat pads, front trim panel, passenger side sun visor, vinyl windshield trim with defroster, bezels and chrome safety rail. Heavy-duty rear axle. Locking rear differential. Locking differential and heavy-duty rear axle. Transmission hand brake. Pickup box. Platform stake. Fresh-air heater and defroster. Front panel air vent. Center power take-off. Pulley and pulley drive for power take-off. Center and rear power take-off. Velocity governor. Radio and antenna. Passenger 2/3 type seat. 7.00 x 15 6-ply All-Service tires. 6.50 x 15 6-ply Deluxe Rib tires. 7.60 x 15 4-ply. High altitude, 7.8:1, cylinder head: No extra charge. Front bumper guards. Drawbar. Heavy-duty springs and shock absorbers. Windshield washers. Two-tone paint. E-Z Eye glass. Front stabilizer bar. 4-speed manual transmission. Dealer installed options included selective drive hubs, winches, snowplows, dozing blades and wrecker equipment.

HISTORICAL FOOTNOTES: The 1960 FC trucks were introduced in the fall of 1959.

1961 FC-150 & FC-170 TRUCKS

No changes took place in the FC models for 1961.

I.D. DATA: The serial number was located on the right side of the dash under hood, on the front frame cross member and on the left floor riser in the back of the driver's seat. Serial number ranges: FC-150: Chassis and cab: 65548-18697 and up. FC-170: Chassis and cab: 61568-14610. FC-170 heavy-duty: Ch. and cab: 61568-13-10047 and up. Chassis W. S: 61368-13-10047 and up.

Model Number	Body Type	Factory Price	GVW	Shipping Weight	Prod. Total
FC-150	Chassis & Cab	$2507	5000	2764	—
FC-150	Pickup	$2624	5000	3020	—
FC-150	Stake	$2725	5000	3187	—
FC-170	Chassis & Cab	$2824	7000	2901	—
FC-170	Pickup	$2960	7000	3331	—
FC-170	Stake	$3167	7000	3564	—
FC-170 HD	Chassis W. S.	$3144	8000*	3028	—
FC-170 HD	Chassis & Cab	$3315	8000	3561	—

* 9000 lb. GVW available for Platform Stake.

STANDARD ENGINE: FC-150 models: Engine Type: 4-cyl., F-head, cast iron block and cylinder head. Bore x Stroke: 3.125 in. x 4.375 in. Lifters: Solid. Number of main bearings-3. Fuel Induction: Single barrel Carter model WA-1 carburetor. Compression Ratio: 6.9:1. "High Altitude" 7.4:1 cylinder available at no extra cost. Displacement: 134.2 cu. in. (2.19 liters). Horsepower: 75 @ 4000 rpm. Torque: Net 115 lb.-ft. @ 2000 rpm. Oil refill capacity: 5 qt. Fuel Requirements: Regular.

STANDARD ENGINE: FC-170 models: Engine Type: 6-cyl., L-head, cast iron block and cylinder head. Bore x Stroke: 3.9375 in. x 4.375 in. Lifters: Solid. Number of main bearings-4. Fuel Induction: Carter model WDG 1-barrel carburetor. Model 2052S or 2052SA. Compression Ratio: 6.86:1 "High Altitude" 7.3:1 cylinder head optional. Displacement: 226.2 cu. in. (3.7 liters). Horsepower: 105 @ 3600 rpm. Torque: 190 lb.-ft. @ 1400 rpm. Oil refill capacity: 5 qt. Fuel Requirements: Regular.

CHASSIS FEATURES: Separate body and chassis. FC-150: Pressed steel channel 1.94 in. x 4.12 in. x 0.149 in., seven cross members. FC-170: Pressed steel channel, section modulus: 2.581, six cross members.

SUSPENSION AND RUNNING GEAR: Front Suspension: FC-150: Semi-elliptical 6-leaf spring. 46 in. x 2.50 in. Spring rate: 270 lb./in. Capacity: 1030 lb. Direct acting shock absorbers. FC-170: Semi-elliptical 6-leaf spring. 46 in. x 2.50 in. Spring rate: 260 lb./in. Capacity: 1250 lb. Direct acting shock absorbers. Optional: Heavy-duty springs. Rear Suspension: FC-150: Semi-elliptical 7-leaf spring. 46 in. x 2.50 in. Spring rate: 280 lb./in. Capacity: 1135 lb. shock absorbers. FC-170: Semi-elliptical 6-leaf spring. 52 in. x 2.50 in. Spring rate: 285 lb./in. Capacity: 1450 lbs. FC-170 HD: Semi-elliptical 9-leaf springs. Spring rate: 672 lb./in. Capacity: 2790 lb. Front Axle Type and Capacity: FC-150: Full-floating.

Capacity: 3000 lbs. FC-170: Full-floating. Capacity: 3000 lbs. Axle ratio: FC-150: 5.38:1. FC-170: 4.88:1. Optional: None. Rear Axle Type and Capacity: FC-150: Semi-floating. Capacity: 3500 lbs. FC-170: Semi-floating. Capacity: 4500 lbs. Axle ratio: FC-150: 5.38:1. FC-170: 4.88:1. Transfer Case: 2-speed. Ratios: 2.46:1, 1.00:1. Brakes: Type: Hydraulic, front and rear cast iron drums, dual master cylinder, double hydraulic circuit. Dimensions: FC-150 and FC-170: Front and rear: 11.00 in. x 2.0 in. Total effective lining area: 176.2 sq. in. FC-170 HD: Front: 12 in. x 2.00 in. rear: 13 in. x 2.5 in. Total effective area: 230.6 sq. in. Optional: None. Wheels: FC-150: 15 x 4.5. FC-170: 16 x 5.00. FC-170 HD: Dual rear 16 x 5.50 wheels. Tires: FC-150: 7.00 x 15 4-ply black sidewall. FC-170: 7.00 x 16.6-ply black sidewall. Other sizes optional. Steering: Cam and lever. Ratio (overall): 32.0:1. Turning Circle: FC-150: 36 ft. FC-170: 43.83-ft. Standard Transmission: 3-speed manual. Transmission ratios: 2.798, 1.441, 1.0:1. Reverse: 3.798:1. Optional: 4-speed manual transmission (standard for FC-170 HD with 9000 lb. GVW). Transmission Ratios: 6.398, 3.092, 1.686, 1.00:1. Reverse: 7.820:1. Clutch: Single dry plate with torsional dampening, 10 in. dia. Single dry plate with torsional damping, FC-150: 72 sq. in. FC-170: 100.5 sq. in. Optional: None.

VEHICLE DIMENSIONS: Wheelbase: FC-150: 81.0 in. FC-170: 103.5 in. Overall Length: FC-150: 147.4 in. FC-170: 180.5 in. FC-170 HD Stake: 203 in. Front/Rear Tread: 48.375 in. FC-170: 63.5 in. FC-170 HD: Rear tread: 72.5 in. Overall Height: FC-150: 77.375 in. FC-170: 79.98 in. FC-170 HD: 79.10 in. Width: FC-150: 71.375 in. FC-170: 76.5 in. FC-170 HD Stake: 92.12 in. Front/Rear Overhang: FC-150: 38.25 in./27.25 in. FC-170: 38.50 in./38.50 in. Tailgate: Width and Height: FC-150: 58.25 in. x 20.0 in. FC-170: 48.25 in. x 13.71 in. Approach/Departure Degrees: FC-150: 36/36. FC-170: 40/30. Ground Clearance: Rear axle: FC-150: 8.0 in. FC-170: 8.87 in. FC-170 HD: 7.90 in. Load space: FC-150: 74.25 in. x 36.0 in. x 20.0 in. FC-170: 109.80 in. x 48.46 in. x 13.71 in. FC-170 HD Platform: 132.60 in. x 92.12 in. Floor to ground: FC-150: 16.25 in. FC-170: 18.25 in.

CAPACITIES: Fuel Tank: FC-150: 16 gal. FC-170: 22 gal. capacity. Optional: None. Coolant system: FC-150: 11 qt., 12 qt. with heater. FC-170: 12 qt., 13 qt. with heater.

ACCOMMODATIONS: Seating Capacity: Two.

INSTRUMENTATION: Speedometer, odometer, gauges for engine coolant temperature, oil pressure, battery and fuel level.

OPTION: Group 901. Includes oil bath air cleaner, oil filter and directional signals. Deluxe cab. Includes cigarette lighter, quarter windows, door trim panel, armrests, full roof trim, foam rubber seat pads, front trim panel, passenger side sun visor, vinyl windshield trim with defroster, bezels and chrome safety rail. Heavy-duty rear axle. Locking rear differential. Locking differential and heavy-duty rear axle. Transmission hand brake. Pickup box. Platform stake. Fresh-air heater and defroster. Front panel air vent. Center power take-off. Pulley and pulley drive for power take-off. Center and rear power take-off. Velocity governor. Radio and antenna. Passenger 2/3 type seat. 7.00 x 15 6-ply All-Service tires. 6.50 x 15 6-ply Deluxe Rib tires. 7.60 x 15 4-ply. High altitude, 7.8:1, cylinder head: No extra charge. Front bumper guards. Drawbar. Heavy-duty springs and shock absorbers. Windshield washers. Two-tone paint. E-Z Eye glass. Front stabilizer bar. 4-speed manual transmission. Dealer installed options included selective drive hubs, winches, snowplows, dozing blades and wrecker equipment.

HISTORICAL FOOTNOTES: The 1961 FC trucks debuted in the fall of 1960.

1962 FC-150 & FC-170 TRUCKS

No changes took place in the FC models for 1962.

I.D. DATA: The serial number was located on the right side of the dash under hood, on the front frame cross member and on the left floor riser in the back of the driver's seat. Serial number ranges: FC-150: 65548-20010 and up. FC-170: 61568-15245. FC-170 heavy-duty: Ch. and Cab: 61568-13-10160 and up.

Model Number	Body Type	Factory Price	GVW	Shipping Weight	Prod. Total
FC-150	Chassis & Cab	$2507	5000	2764	—
FC-150	Pickup	$2624	5000	3020	—
FC-150	Stake	$2725	5000	3187	—
FC-170	Chassis & Cab	$2824	7000	2901	—
FC-170	Pickup	$2960	7000	3331	—
FC-170	Stake	$3167	7000	3564	—
FC-170 HD	Chassis & Cab	$3315	8000*	3561	—

* 9000 lb. GVW available.

STANDARD ENGINE: FC-150 models. Engine Type: 4-cyl., F-head, cast iron block and cylinder head. Bore x Stroke: 3.125 in. x 4.375 in. Lifters: Solid. Number of main bearings-3. Fuel Induction: Single barrel Carter model WA-1 carburetor. Compression Ratio: 6.9:1. "High Altitude" 7.4:1 cylinder available at no extra cost. Displacement: 134.2 cu. in. Horsepower: 75 @ 4000 rpm. Torque: Net 115 lb.-ft. @ 2000 rpm. Tach redline: NA. Oil refill capacity: 4 qt. Fuel Requirements: Regular.

STANDARD ENGINE: FC-170 models. Engine Type: 6-cyl., L-head, cast iron block and cylinder head. Bore x Stroke: 3.9375 in. x 4.375 in. Lifters: Solid. Number of main bearings-4. Fuel Induction: Carter model WDG 1-barrel carburetor. Model 2052S or 2052SA. Compression Ratio: 6.86:1 "High Altitude" 7.3:1 cylinder available at no extra cost. Displacement: 226.2 cu. in. Horsepower: 105 @ 3600 rpm. Torque: 190 lb.-ft. @ 1400 rpm. Tach redline: NA. Oil refill capacity: 5 qt. Fuel Requirements: Regular.

OPTIONAL ENGINE: None.

CHASSIS FEATURES: Separate body and chassis. FC-150: Pressed steel channel 1.94 in. x 4.12 in. x 0.149 in., seven cross members. FC-170: Pressed steel channel, section modulus: 2.581, six cross members.

SUSPENSION AND RUNNING GEAR: Front Suspension: FC-150: Semi-elliptical 6-leaf springs. 46 in. x 2.50 in. Spring rate: 270 lb./in. Capacity: 1030 lb. Direct acting shock absorbers. FC-170: Semi-elliptical 6-leaf spring. 46 in. x 2.50 in. Spring rate: 260 lb./in. Capacity: 1250 lb. Direct acting shock absorbers. Optional: Heavy-duty springs. b. Rear Suspension: FC-150: Semi-elliptical 7-leaf spring. 46 in. x 2.50 in. Spring rate: 280 lb./in. Capacity: 1135 lb. shock absorbers. FC-170: Semi-elliptical 6-leaf springs. 52 in. x 2.50 in. Spring rate: 285 lb./in. Capacity: 1450 lbs. FC-170 HD: Semi-elliptical 9-leaf springs. Spring rate: 672 lb./in. Capacity: 2790 lb. Front Axle Type and Capacity: FC-150: Full-floating. Capacity: 3000 lbs. FC-170: Full-floating. Capacity: 3000 lbs. Axle ratio: FC-150: 5.38:1. FC-170: 4.88:1. Optional: None. Rear Axle Type and Capacity: FC-150: Semi-floating. Capacity: 3500 lbs. FC-170: Semi-floating. Capacity: 4500 lbs. Axle ratio: FC-150: 5.38:1. FC-170: 4.88:1. Transfer Case: 2-speed. Ratios: 2.46:1, 1.00:1. Brakes: Type: Hydraulic, front

and rear cast iron drums, dual master cylinder, double hydraulic circuit. Dimensions: FC-150 and FC-170: Front and rear: 11.00 in. x 2.0 in. Total effective lining area: 176.2 sq. in. FC-170 HD: Front: 12 in. x 2.00 in. rear: 13 in. x 2.5 in. Total effective area: 230.6 sq. in. Optional: None. Wheels: FC-150: 15 x 4.5. FC-170" 16 x 5.00. FC-170 HD: Dual rear 16 x 5.50 wheels. Optional: Black. Tires: FC-150: 7.00 x 15 4-ply black sidewall. FC-170: 7.00 x 16.6-ply black sidewall. Other sizes optional. Steering: Cam and lever. Ratio (overall): 32.0:1 Turns Lock-to-Lock. Turning Circle: FC-150: 36 ft. FC-170: 43.83 ft. Optional: None. Standard Transmission: 3-speed manual transmission. Transmission ratios: 2.798, 1.441, 1.0:1. Reverse: 3.798:1. Optional: 4-speed manual transmission (standard for FC-170 HD with 9000 lb. GVW). Transmission Ratios: 6.398, 3.092, 1.686, 1.00:1. Reverse: 7.820:1. Clutch: Single dry plate with torsional damping, 10 in. dia. Single dry plate with torsional damping, FC-150: 72 sq. in. FC-170: 100.5 sq. in. Optional: None.

VEHICLE DIMENSIONS: Wheelbase: FC-150: 81.0 in. FC-170: 103.5 in. Overall Length: FC-150: 147.4 in. FC-170: 180.5 in. FC-170 HD Stake: 203 in. Front/Rear Tread: 48.375 in. FC-170: 63.5 in. FC-170 HD: Rear tread: 72.5 in. Overall Height: FC-150: 77.375 in. FC-170: 79.98 in. FC-170 HD: 79.10 in. Width: FC-150: 71.375 in. FC-170: 76.5 in. FC-170 HD Stake: 92.12 in. Front/Rear Overhang: FC-150: 38.25 in./27.25 in. FC-170: 38.50 in./38.50 in. Tailgate: Width and Height: FC-150: 58.25 in. x 20.0 in. FC-170: 48.25 in. x 13.71 in. Approach/Departure Degrees: FC-150: 36/36. FC-170: 40/30. Ground Clearance: FC-150: Rear axle: .8.0 in. FC-170: 8.87 in. FC-170 HD: 7.90 in. Load space: FC-150: 74.25 in. x 36.0 in. x 20.0 in. FC-170: 109.80 in. x 48.46 in. x 13.71 in. FC-170 HD Platform: 132.60 in. x 92.12 in. Maximum capacity (Volume Index). Floor to ground: FC-150: 16.25 in. FC-170: 18.25 in.

CAPACITIES: Fuel Tank: FC-150: 16 gal. FC-170: 22 gal. capacity. Optional: None.

ACCOMMODATIONS: Seating Capacity: Two. Seat Dimensions: Front-Driver's: ?

INSTRUMENTATION: Speedometer, odometer. gauges for engine coolant temperature, oil pressure, battery and fuel level.

OPTIONS: Group 901. Includes oil bath air cleaner, oil filter and directional signals. Deluxe cab. Includes cigarette lighter, quarter windows, door trim panel, armrests, full roof trim, foam rubber seat pads, front trim panel, passenger side sun visor, vinyl windshield trim with defroster, bezels and chrome safety rail. Heavy-duty rear axle. Locking rear differential. Locking differential and heavy-duty rear axle. Transmission hand brake. Pickup box. Platform stake. Fresh-air heater and defroster. Front panel air vent. Center power take-off. Pulley and pulley drive for power take-off. Center and rear power take-off. Velocity governor. Radio and antenna. Passenger 2/3 type seat. 7.00 x 15 6-ply All-Service tires. 6.50 x 15 6-ply Deluxe Rib tires. 7.60 x 15 4-ply. High altitude, 7.8:1, cylinder head: No extra charge. Front bumper guards. Drawbar. Heavy-duty springs and shock absorbers. Windshield washers. Two-tone paint. E-Z Eye glass. Front stabilizer bar. 4-speed manual transmission. Dealer installed options included selective drive hubs, winches, snowplows, dozing blades and wrecker equipment.

HISTORICAL FOOTNOTES: The 1962 FC trucks were announced in the fall of 1961.

1963 FC-150 & FC-170 TRUCKS

No changes took place in the FC models for 1963.

1963 Jeep FC-170 Forward Control truck

I.D. DATA: The serial number was located on the right side of the dash under hood, on the front frame cross member and on the left floor riser in the back of the driver's seat. Serial number ranges: FC-150: 65548-20683 and up. FC-170: 61568-15897. FC-170 heavy-duty: Ch. and cab: 61568-13-10479 and up.

Model Number	Body Type	Factory Price	GVW	Shipping Weight	Prod. Total
FC-150	Chassis & Cab	$2507	5000	2764	—
FC-150	Pickup	$2624	5000	3020	—
FC-150	Stake	$2725	5000	3187	—
FC-170	Chassis & Cab	$2824	7000	2901	—
FC-170	Pickup	$2960	7000	3331	—
FC-170	Stake	$3167	7000	3564	—
FC-170 HD	Chassis & Cab	$3315	8000*	3561	—

* 9000 lb. GVW available.

STANDARD ENGINE: FC-150 models: Engine Type: 4-cyl., F-head, cast iron block and cylinder head. Bore x Stroke: 3.125 in. x 4.375 in. Lifters: Solid. Number of main bearings-3. Fuel Induction: Single barrel Carter model WA-1 carburetor. Compression Ratio: 6.9:1. "High Altitude" 7.4:1 cylinder available at no extra cost. Displacement: 134.2 cu. in. (2.19 liters). Horsepower: 75 @ 4000 rpm. Torque: Net 115 lb.-ft. @ 2000 rpm. Oil refill capacity: 5 qt. Fuel Requirements: Regular.

STANDARD ENGINE: FC-170 models: Engine Type: 6-cyl., L-head, cast iron block and cylinder head. Bore x Stroke: 3.9375 in. x 4.375 in. Lifters: Solid. Number of main bearings-4. Fuel Induction: Carter model WDG 1-barrel carburetor. Model 2052S or 2052SA. Compression Ratio: 6.86:1 "High Altitude" 7.3:1 cylinder head optional. Displacement: 226.2 cu. in. (3.7 liters). Horsepower: 105 @ 3600 rpm. Torque: 190 lb.-ft. @ 1400 rpm. Oil refill capacity: 5 qt. Fuel Requirements: Regular.

CHASSIS FEATURES: Separate body and chassis. FC-150: Pressed steel channel 1.94 in. x 4.12 in. x 0.149 in., seven cross members. FC-170: Pressed steel channel, section modulus: 2.581, six cross members.

SUSPENSION AND RUNNING GEAR: Front Suspension: FC-150: Semi-elliptical 6-leaf springs. 46 in. x 2.50 in. Spring rate: 270 lb./in. Capacity: 1030 lb. Direct acting shock absorbers. FC-170: Semi-elliptical 6-leaf springs. 46 in. x 2.50 in. Spring rate: 260 lb./in. Capacity: 1250 lb. Direct acting shock absorbers. Optional: Heavy-duty springs. Rear Suspension: FC-150: Semi-elliptical 7-leaf springs. 46 in. x 2.50 in. Spring rate: 280 lb./in. Capacity: 1135 lb. shock absorbers. FC-170: Semi-elliptical 6-leaf springs. 52 in. x 2.50 in. Spring rate: 285 lb./in. Capacity: 1450 lbs. FC-170 HD: Semi-elliptical 9-leaf springs. Spring rate: 672 lb./in. Capacity: 2790 lb. Front Axle Type and Capacity: FC-150: Full-floating. Capacity: 3000 lbs. FC-170: Full-floating. Capacity: 3000 lbs. Axle ratio: FC-150: 5.38:1. FC-170: 4.88:1. Optional: None. Rear Axle Type and Capacity: FC-150: Semi-floating. Capacity: 3500 lbs. FC-170: Semi-floating. Capacity: 4500 lbs. Axle ratio: FC-150: 5.38:1. FC-170: 4.88:1. Transfer Case: 2-speed. Ratios: 2.46:1, 1.00:1. Brakes: Type: Hydraulic, front and rear cast iron drums, dual master cylinder, double hydraulic circuit. Dimensions: FC-150 and FC-170: Front and rear: 11.00 in. x 2.0 in. Total effective lining area: 176.2 sq. in. FC-170 HD: Front: 12 in. x 2.00 in. rear: 13 in. x 2.5 in. Total effective area: 230.6 sq. in. Optional: None. Wheels: FC-150: 15 x 4.5. FC-170: 16 x 5.00. FC-170 HD: Dual rear 16 x 5.50 wheels. Tires: FC-150: 7.00 x 15 4-ply black sidewall. FC-170: 7.00 x 16.6-ply black sidewall. Other sizes optional. Steering: Cam and lever. Ratio (overall): 32.0:1. Turning Circle: FC-150: 36 ft. FC-170: 43.83-ft. Standard Transmission: 3-speed manual. Transmission ratios: 2.798, 1.441, 1.0:1. Reverse: 3.798:1. Optional: 4-speed manual transmission (standard for FC-170 HD with 9000 lb. GVW). Transmission Ratios: 6.398, 3.092, 1.686, 1.00:1. Reverse: 7.820:1. Clutch: Single dry plate with torsional dampening, 10 in. dia. Single dry plate with torsional damping, FC-150: 72 sq. in. FC-170: 100.5 sq. in. Optional: None.

VEHICLE DIMENSIONS: Wheelbase: FC-150: 81.0 in. FC-170: 103.5 in. Overall Length: FC-150: 147.4 in. FC-170: 180.5 in. FC-170 HD Stake: 203 in. Front/Rear Tread: FC-150: 48.375 in. FC-170: 63.5 in. FC-170 HD: Rear tread: 72.5 in. Overall Height: FC-150: 77.375 in. FC-170: 79.98 in. FC-170 HD: 79.10 in. Width: FC-150: 71.375 in. FC-170: 76.5 in. FC-170 HD Stake: 92.12 in. Front/Rear Overhang: FC-150: 38.25 in./27.25 in. FC-170: 38.50 in./38.50 in. Tailgate: Width and Height: FC-150: 58.25 in. x 20.0 in. FC-170: 48.25 in. x 13.71 in. Approach/Departure Degrees: FC-150: 36/36. FC-170: 40/30. Ground Clearance: Rear axle: FC-150: 8.0 in. FC-170: 8.87 in. FC-170 HD: 7.90 in. Load space: FC-150: 74.25 in. x 36.0 in. x 20.0 in. FC-170: 109.80 in. x 48.46 in. x 13.71 in. FC-170 HD Platform: 132.60 in. x 92.12 in. Floor to ground: FC-150: 16.25 in. FC-170: 18.25 in.

CAPACITIES: Fuel Tank: FC-150: 16 gal. FC-170: 22 gal. capacity. Optional: None. Coolant system: FC-150: 11 qt., 12 qt. with heater. FC-170: 12 qt., 13 qt. with heater.

ACCOMMODATIONS: Seating Capacity: Two.

INSTRUMENTATION: Speedometer, odometer, gauges for engine coolant temperature, oil pressure, battery and fuel level.

OPTIONS: Group 901. Includes oil bath air cleaner, oil filter and directional signals. Deluxe cab. Includes cigarette lighter, quarter windows, door trim panel, armrests, full roof trim, foam rubber seat pads, front trim panel, passenger side sun visor, vinyl windshield trim with defroster, bezels and chrome safety rail. Heavy-duty rear axle. Locking rear differential. Locking differential and heavy-duty rear axle. Transmission hand brake. Pickup box. Platform stake. Fresh-air heater and defroster. Front panel air vent. Center power take-off. Pulley and pulley drive for power take-off. Center and rear power take-off. Velocity governor. Radio and antenna. Passenger 2/3 type seat. 7.00 x 15 6-ply All-Service tires. 6.50 x 15 6-ply Deluxe Rib tires. 7.60 x 15 4-ply. High altitude, 7.8:1, cylinder head: No extra charge. Front bumper guards. Draw bar. Heavy-duty springs and shock absorbers. Windshield washers. Two-tone paint. E-Z Eye glass. Front stabilizer bar. 4-speed manual transmission. Dealer installed options included selective drive hubs, winches, snowplows, dozing blades and wrecker equipment.

HISTORICAL FOOTNOTES: The 1963 FC models were introduced in the fall of 1962.

1964 FC-150 & FC-170 TRUCKS

No changes took place in the FC models for 1964.

I.D. DATA: The serial number was located on the right side of the dash under hood, on the front frame cross member and on the left floor riser in the back of the driver's seat. Serial number ranges: FC-150: 65548-or 9209-21774 and up. FC-170: 61568 or 9309-17928 and up. FC-170 heavy-duty: 61568-13 or 9325-10653 and up.

Model Number	Body Type	Factory Price	GVW	Shipping Weight	Prod. Total
FC-150	Chassis & Cab	$2735	5000	2764	—
FC-150	Pickup	$2853	5000	3020	—
FC-150	Stake	$2954	5000	3187	—
FC-170	Chassis & Cab	$3056	7000	2901	—
FC-170	Pickup	$3192	7000	3331	—
FC-170	Stake	$3399	7000	3564	—
FC-170 HD	Chassis & Cab	$3547	8000*	3561	—

* 9000 lb. GVW available.

STANDARD ENGINE: FC-150 models: Engine Type: 4-cyl., F-head, cast iron block and cylinder head. Bore x Stroke: 3.125 in. x 4.375 in. Lifters: Solid. Number of main bearings-3. Fuel Induction: Single barrel Carter model WA-1 carburetor. Compression Ratio: 6.9:1. "High Altitude" 7.4:1 cylinder available at no extra cost. Displacement: 134.2 cu. in. (2.19 liters). Horsepower: 75 @ 4000 rpm. Torque: Net 115 lb.-ft. @ 2000 rpm. Oil refill capacity: 5 qt. Fuel Requirements: Regular.

STANDARD ENGINE: FC-170 models: Engine Type: 6-cyl., L-head, cast iron block and cylinder head. Bore x Stroke: 3.9375 in. x 4.375 in. Lifters: Solid. Number of main bearings-4. Fuel Induction: Carter model WDG 1-barrel carburetor. Model 2052S or 2052SA. Compression Ratio: 6.86:1 "High Altitude" 7.3:1 cylinder head optional. Displacement: 226.2 cu. in. (3.7 liters). Horsepower: 105 @ 3600 rpm. Torque: 190 lb.-ft. @ 1400 rpm. Oil refill capacity: 5 qt. Fuel Requirements: Regular.

CHASSIS FEATURES: Separate body and chassis. FC-150: Pressed steel channel 1.94 in. x 4.12 in. x 0.149 in., seven cross members. FC-170: Pressed steel channel, section modulus: 2.581, six cross members.

SUSPENSION AND RUNNING GEAR: Front Suspension: FC-150: Semi-elliptical 6-leaf springs. 46 in. x 2.50 in. Spring rate: 270 lb./in. Capacity: 1030 lb. Direct acting shock absorbers. FC-170: Semi-elliptical 6-leaf springs. 46 in. x 2.50 in. Spring rate: 260 lb./in. Capacity: 1250 lb. Direct acting shock absorbers. Optional: Heavy-duty springs. Rear Suspension: FC-150: Semi-elliptical 7-leaf springs. 46 in. x 2.50 in. Spring rate: 280 lb./in. Capacity: 1135 lb. shock absorbers. FC-170: Semi-elliptical 6-leaf spring. 52 in. x 2.50 in. Spring rate: 285 lb./in. Capacity: 1450 lbs. FC-170 HD: Semi-elliptical 9-leaf springs. Spring rate: 672 lb./in. Capacity: 2790 lb. Front Axle Type and Capacity: FC-150: Full-floating. Capacity: 3000 lbs. FC-170: Full-floating. Capacity: 3000 lbs. Axle ratio: FC-150: 5.38:1. FC-170: 4.88:1. Optional: None. Rear Axle Type and Capacity: FC-150: Semi-floating. Capacity: 3500 lbs. FC-170: Semi-floating. Capacity: 4500 lbs. Axle ratio: FC-150: 5.38:1. FC-170: 4.88:1. Transfer Case: 2-speed. Ratios: 2.46:1, 1.00:1. Brakes: Type: Hydraulic, front and rear cast iron drums, dual master cylinder, double hydraulic circuit. Dimensions: FC-150 and FC-170: Front and rear: 11.00 in. x 2.0 in. Total effective lining area: 176.2 sq. in. FC-170 HD: Front: 12 in. x 2.00 in. rear: 13 in. x 2.5 in. Total effective area: 230.6 sq. in. Optional: None. Wheels: FC-150: 15 x 4.5. FC-170: 16 x 5.00. FC-170 HD: Dual rear 16 x 5.50 wheels. Tires: FC-150: 7.00 x 15 4-ply black sidewall. FC-170: 7.00 x 16.6-ply black sidewall. Other sizes optional. Steering: Cam and lever. Ratio (overall): 32.0:1. Turning Circle: FC-150: 36 ft. FC-170: 43.83-ft. Standard Transmission: 3-speed manual. Transmission ratios: 2.798, 1.441, 1.0:1. Reverse: 3.798:1. Optional: 4-speed manual transmission (standard for FC-170 HD with 9000 lb. GVW). Transmission Ratios: 6.398, 3.092, 1.686, 1.00:1. Reverse: 7.820:1. Clutch: Single dry plate with torsional dampening, 10 in. dia. Single dry plate with torsional damping, FC-150: 72 sq. in. FC-170: 100.5 sq. in. Optional: None.

VEHICLE DIMENSIONS: Wheelbase: FC-150: 81.0 in. FC-170: 103.5 in. Overall Length: FC-150: 147.4 in. FC-170: 180.5 in. FC-170 HD Stake: 203 in. Front/Rear Tread: FC-150: 48.375 in. FC-170: 63.5 in. FC-170 HD: Rear tread: 72.5 in. Overall Height: FC-150: 77.375 in. FC-170: 79.98 in. FC-170 HD: 79.10 in. Width: FC-150: 71.375 in. FC-170: 76.5 in. FC-170 HD Stake: 92.12 in. Front/Rear Overhang: FC-150: 38.25 in./27.25 in. FC-170: 38.50 in./38.50 in. Tailgate: Width and Height: FC-150: 58.25 in. x 20.0 in. FC-170: 48.25 in. x 13.71 in. Approach/Departure Degrees: FC-150: 36/36. FC-170: 40/30. Ground Clearance: Rear axle: FC-150: 8.0 in. FC-170: 8.87 in. FC-170 HD: 7.90 in. Load space: FC-150: 74.25 in. x 36.0 in. x 20.0 in. FC-170: 109.80 in. x 48.46 in. x 13.71 in. FC-170 HD Platform: 132.60 in. x 92.12 in. Floor to ground: FC-150: 16.25 in. FC-170: 18.25 in.

CAPACITIES: Fuel Tank: FC-150: 16 gal. FC-170: 22 gal. capacity. Optional: None. Coolant system: FC-150: 11 qt., 12 qt. with heater. FC-170: 12 qt., 13 qt. with heater.

ACCOMMODATIONS: Seating Capacity: Two.

INSTRUMENTATION: Speedometer, odometer, gauges for engine coolant temperature, oil pressure, battery and fuel level.

OPTIONS: Group 901. Includes oil bath air cleaner, oil filter and directional signals. Deluxe cab. Includes cigarette lighter, quarter windows, door trim panel, armrests, full roof trim, foam rubber seat pads, front trim panel, passenger side sun visor, vinyl windshield trim with defroster, bezels and chrome safety rail. Heavy-duty rear axle. Locking rear differential. Locking differential and heavy-duty rear axle. Transmission hand brake. Pickup box. Platform stake. Fresh-air heater and defroster. Front panel air vent. Center power take-off. Pulley and pulley drive for power take-off. Center and rear power take-off. Velocity governor. Radio and antenna. Passenger 2/3 type seat. 7.00 x 15 6-ply All-Service tires. 6.50 x 15 6-ply Deluxe Rib tires. 7.60 x 15 4-ply. High altitude, 7.8:1, cylinder head: No extra charge. Front bumper guards. Drawbar. Heavy-duty springs and shock absorbers. Windshield washers. Two-tone paint. E-Z Eye glass. Front stabilizer bar. 4-speed manual transmission. Dealer installed options included selective drive hubs, winches, snowplows, dozing blades and wrecker equipment.

HISTORICAL FOOTNOTES: The 1964 FC trucks were announced in the fall of 1963.

1965 FC-150 & FC-170 TRUCKS

No changes took place in the FC models for 1965. This was the final year of production of the FC models.

I.D. DATA: The serial number was located on the right side of the dash under hood, on the front frame cross member and on the left floor riser in the back of the driver's seat. Serial number ranges: FC-150: 65548-or 9209-25861 and up. FC-170: 61568 or 9309-23617 and up. FC-170 heavy-duty: 61568-13 or 9325-10901 and up.

Model Number	Body Type	Factory Price	GVW	Shipping Weight	Prod. Total
FC-150	Chassis & Cab	$2735	5000	2764	—
FC-150	Pickup	$2853	5000	3020	—
FC-150	Stake	$2954	5000	3187	—
FC-170	Chassis & Cab	$3056	7000	2901	—
FC-170	Pickup	$3192	7000	3331	—
FC-170	Stake	$3399	7000	3564	—
FC-170 HD	Chassis & Cab	$3547	8000*	3561	—

* 9000 lb. GVW available.

STANDARD ENGINE: FC-150 models: Engine Type: 4-cyl., F-head, cast iron block and cylinder head. Bore x Stroke: 3.125 in. x 4.375 in. Lifters: Solid. Number of main bearings-3. Fuel Induction: Single barrel Carter model WA-1 carburetor. Compression Ratio: 6.9:1. "High Altitude" 7.4:1 cylinder available at no extra cost. Displacement: 134.2 cu. in. (2.19 liters). Horsepower: 75 @ 4000 rpm. Torque: Net 115 lb.-ft. @ 2000 rpm. Oil refill capacity: 5 qt. Fuel Requirements: Regular.

STANDARD ENGINE: FC-170 models: Engine Type: 6-cyl., L-head, cast iron block and cylinder head. Bore x Stroke: 3.9375 in. x 4.375 in. Lifters: Solid. Number of main bearings-4. Fuel Induction: Carter model WDG 1-barrel carburetor. Model 2052S or 2052SA. Compression Ratio: 6.86:1 "High Altitude" 7.3:1 cylinder head optional. Displacement: 226.2 cu. in. (3.7 liters). Horsepower: 105 @ 3600 rpm. Torque: 190 lb.-ft. @ 1400 rpm. Oil refill capacity: 5 qt. Fuel Requirements: Regular.

CHASSIS FEATURES: Separate body and chassis. FC-150: Pressed steel channel 1.94 in. x 4.12 in. x 0.149 in., seven cross members. FC-170: Pressed steel channel, section modulus: 2.581, six cross members.

SUSPENSION AND RUNNING GEAR: Front Suspension: FC-150: Semi-elliptical 6-leaf springs. 46 in. x 2.50 in. Spring rate: 270 lb./in. Capacity: 1030 lb. Direct acting shock absorbers. FC-170: Semi-elliptical 6-leaf springs. 46 in. x 2.50 in. Spring rate: 260 lb./in. Capacity: 1250 lb. Direct acting shock absorbers. Optional: Heavy-duty springs. Rear Suspension: FC-150: Semi-elliptical 7-leaf springs. 46 in. x 2.50 in. Spring rate: 280 lb./in. Capacity: 1135 lb. shock absorbers. FC-170: Semi-elliptical 6-leaf springs. 52 in. x 2.50 in. Spring rate: 285 lb./in. Capacity: 1450 lbs. FC-170 HD: Semi-elliptical 9-leaf springs. Spring rate: 672 lb./in. Capacity: 2790 lb. Front Axle Type and Capacity: FC-150: Full-floating. Capacity: 3000 lbs. FC-170: Full-floating. Capacity: 3000 lbs. Axle ratio: FC-150: 5.38:1. FC-170: 4.88:1. Optional: None. Rear Axle Type and Capacity: FC-150: Semi-floating. Capacity: 3500 lbs. FC-170: Semi-floating. Capacity: 4500 lbs. Axle ratio: FC-150: 5.38:1. FC-170: 4.88:1. Transfer Case: 2-speed. Ratios: 2.46:1, 1.00:1. Brakes: Type: Hydraulic, front and rear cast iron drums, dual master cylinder, double hydraulic circuit. Dimensions: FC-150 and FC-170: Front and rear: 11.00 in. x 2.0 in. Total effective lining area: 176.2 sq. in. FC-170 HD: Front: 12 in. x 2.00 in. rear: 13 in. x 2.5 in. Total effective area: 230.6 sq. in. Optional: None. Wheels: FC-150: 15 x 4.5. FC-170: 16 x 5.00. FC-170 HD: Dual rear 16 x 5.50 wheels. Tires: FC-150: 7.00 x 15 4-ply black sidewall. FC-170: 7.00 x 16.6-ply black sidewall. Other sizes optional. Steering: Cam and lever. Ratio (overall): 32.0:1. Turning Circle: FC-150: 36 ft. FC-170: 43.83 ft. Standard Transmission: 3-speed manual. Transmission ratios: 2.798, 1.441, 1.0:1. Reverse: 3.798:1. Optional: 4-speed manual transmission (standard for FC-170 HD with 9000 lb. GVW). Transmission Ratios: 6.398, 3.092, 1.686, 1.00:1. Reverse: 7.820:1. Clutch: Single dry plate with torsional dampening, 10 in. dia. Single dry plate with torsional damping, FC-150: 72 sq. in. FC-170: 100.5 sq. in. Optional: None.

VEHICLE DIMENSIONS: Wheelbase: FC-150: 81.0 in. FC-170: 103.5 in. Overall Length: FC-150: 147.4 in. FC-170: 180.5 in. FC-170 HD Stake: 203 in. Front/Rear Tread: FC-150: 48.375 in. FC-170: 63.5 in. FC-170 HD: Rear tread: 72.5 in. Overall Height: FC-150: 77.375 in. FC-170: 79.98 in. FC-170 HD: 79.10 in. Width: FC-150: 71.375 in. FC-170: 76.5 in. FC-170 HD Stake: 92.12 in. Front/Rear Overhang: FC-150: 38.25 in./27.25 in. FC-170: 38.50 in./38.50 in. Tailgate: Width and Height: FC-150: 58.25 in. x 20.0 in. FC-170:48.25 in. x 13.71 in. Approach/Departure Degrees: FC-150: 36/36. FC-170: 40/30. Ground Clearance: Rear axle: FC-150: 8.0 in. FC-170: 8.87 in. FC-170 HD: 7.90 in. Load space: FC-150: 74.25 in. x 36.0 in. x 20.0 in. FC-170: 109.80 in. x 48.46 in. x 13.71 in. FC-170 HD Platform: 132.60 in. x 92.12 in. Floor to ground: FC-150: 16.25 in. FC-170: 18.25 in.

CAPACITIES: Fuel Tank: FC-150: 16 gal. FC-170: 22 gal. capacity. Optional: None. Coolant system: FC-150: 11 qt., 12 qt. with heater. FC-170: 12 qt., 13 qt. with heater.

ACCOMMODATIONS: Seating Capacity: Two.

INSTRUMENTATION: Speedometer, odometer, gauges for engine coolant temperature, oil pressure, battery and fuel level.

OPTIONS: Group 901. Includes oil bath air cleaner, oil filter and directional signals. Deluxe cab. Includes cigarette lighter, quarter windows, door trim panel, armrests, full roof trim, foam rubber seat pads, front trim panel, passenger side sun visor, vinyl windshield trim with defroster, bezels and chrome safety rail. Heavy-duty rear axle. Locking rear differential. Locking differential and heavy-duty rear axle. Transmission hand brake. Pickup box. Platform stake. Fresh-air heater and defroster. Front panel air vent. Center power take-off. Pulley and pulley drive for power take-off. Center and rear power take-off. Velocity governor. Radio and antenna. Passenger 2/3 type seat. 7.00 x 15 6-ply All-Service tires. 6.50 x 15 6-ply Deluxe Rib tires. 7.60 x 15 4-ply. High altitude, 7.8:1, cylinder head: No extra charge. Front bumper guards. Drawbar. Heavy-duty springs and shock absorbers. Windshield washers. Two-tone paint. E-Z Eye glass. Front stabilizer bar. 4-speed manual transmission. Dealer installed options included selective drive hubs, winches, snowplows, dozing blades and wrecker equipment.

HISTORICAL FOOTNOTES: Both the close-coupled design of the FC trucks which provided them with remarkable maneuverability and their ingenious yet simple design made the FC trucks desirable and versatile vehicles.

JEEP GLADIATOR TRUCKS

1963-1987

1963 GLADIATOR

Coinciding with the introduction of the new Wagoneer station wagons came a new line of Jeep pickups with an imposing Gladiator title. These trucks, available with either pickup or stake platform bodies, shared much of the Wagoneer's styling and general engineering features. The truck models were also offered in two wheelbases — 120 in. (7 ft. box) or 126 in. (8 ft. box) as well as a variety of GVW ratings. The 120 in. wheelbase models were classified as the J-200 series; the 126 in. wheelbase models were identified as the J-300 series. The J-300 stake platforms had either single or dual rear wheels. All J-200 and J-300 models had a full-width seat and were available in either standard or custom interior trim. The base model had a rear header trim panel with a vinyl welt covering the exposed edges of the roof header. The Custom Equipment Package added such features as roof trim, front header panels and arm rests.

Variations on these two basic truck lines, based on different GVW ratings were also available. The J-200 models, in addition to being available with 6.70 x 15 tires were offered as the J-210 models with larger 7.60 x 15 tires. Both were rated as 1/2 ton models.

If a customer wanted a 120 in. wheelbase J series truck with a 3/4 ton rating the J-220 line was offered. The 230 line combined the 120 in. wheelbase with a 1 ton rating and 7.00 x 16 tires. The J-310 trucks had a 126 in. wheelbase and a 3/4 ton rating.

1963 Jeep Gladiator J-300 Townside

Rounding up this diverse offering were the J-320 with a 3/4 ton rating,126 in. wheelbase and 7.50 x 16 tires Both the J-320 and J-230 were available only in chassis and cab or stake platform versions.

Standard equipment for the base models included all vinyl plastic interior trim with rubberized floor mats, dual sun visors, electric windshield wipers, cigarette lighter and compass. Custom models (initially they were referred to as Deluxe models) were identified by their chrome grille, stainless steel door frame trim and windshield molding and wheel rings. Interior custom features included front and rear carpeting, covered cargo floor area, fabric seat inserts, higher grade headliner and door trim panels, interior wheelhouse covers, front and rear chrome-trimmed armrests and rearview mirror, chrome control knobs, rear seat chrome ashtray, courtesy lights, chrome molding for instrument panel and radio speaker, chrome cigarette lighter, foam seat cushions and deluxe horn ring.

Ten exterior colors were offered for the Gladiators: White cap, spruce tip green, parkway green, president red, nordic blue, Sierra tan, parade blue, jet line grey, tree bark brown and amber metallic interior finishes were available in three low gloss paints: Sylvan green for trucks with exterior green paint, nordic blue for those with exterior blues and amber metallic for all others.

I.D. DATA: The serial number was located on the left-hand hinge pillar. The first four digits indicated the model as follows: The fifth symbol was a letter. The sequential production number followed. The starting number for each series was 10001. The engine number was located on the right-hand corner of the block. The engine codes were ND60C and TD60C.

Model Number	Body Type	Factory Price	GVW	Shipping Weight	Prod. Total
Series J-200 1/2, 3/4 and 1 ton					
J-200	Chassis/Cab	$2596	4000	3061	—
J-200	Pickup Thriftside	$2696	4000	3361	—
J-200	Pickup Townside	$2722	4000	3461	—
J-210	Chassis/Cab	$2653	5600	3096	—
J-210	Pickup Thriftside	$2734	5600	3396	—
J-210	Pickup Townside	$2781	5600	3496	—
J-220	Chassis/Cab	$2753	6600	3214	—
J-220	Pickup Thriftside	$2854	6600	3514	—
J-220	Pickup Townside	$2811	6600	3614	—
J-220	Stake Platform	$3060	6600	3894	—
J-230	Chassis/Cab	$3578	7600	3874	—
J-230	Stake Platform	$3870	7600	4714	—

Series J-300 3/4, 1 ton					
J-300	Chassis/Cab	$2654	5000	3091	—
J-300	Pickup Thriftside	$2769	5000	3441	—
J-300	Pickup Townside	$2796	5000	3541	—
J-310	Chassis/Cab	$2771	6600	3239	—
J-310	Pickup Thriftside	$2886	6600	3589	—
J-310	Pickup Townside	$2913	6600	3689	—
J-310	Stake Platform	$3111	6600	4679	—
J-320	Chassis/Cab	$2931	7600	3377	—
J-320	Pickup Thriftside	$3046	7600	3727	—
J-320	Pickup Townside	$3073	7600	3827	—
J-320	Stake Platform	$3271	7600	4117	—
J-330	Chassis/Cab	$3597	8600	3899	—
J-330	Stake Platform	$4011	8600	4799	—

STANDARD ENGINE: Engine Type: OHV, OHC In-line-6. Cast iron block and cylinder head. Bore x Stroke: 3.4375 in. x 4.375 in. Lifters: Hydraulic. Number of main bearings-4. Fuel Induction: 1 bbl. Holley model 1920 (manual trans. models); 2 bbl. Holley model 2415 (auto. trans.). Compression Ratio: 8.5:1. Displacement: 230 cu. in. (3.76 liters). Horsepower: Net:140 @ 4000 rpm. Torque: Net: 210 lb.-ft. @ 1750 rpm. Oil refill capacity: 6 qt. with filter change. Fuel Requirements: Regular.

OPTIONAL ENGINE: None.

CHASSIS FEATURES: Separate body and frame. Deep web frame, wide flange, lightweight pressed steel with five cross members.

SUSPENSION AND RUNNING GEAR: Front Suspension: Multi-Leaf semi-elliptical springs, size varies with GVW rating. Hydraulic double-action shock absorbers: 13.0 in. on solid front axle, 12.375 in. dia. for torsion bar suspension. Optional Torsion bar. Rear Suspension: Semi-elliptical multi-leaf springs with anti-windup top half spring, hydraulic double-action shock absorbers. Optional: 6-leaf semi-elliptical springs. Front Axle Type and Capacity: Dana model 44F, 3000 lb. capacity. Rear Axle Type and Capacity: Dana model 44 semi-floating. Optional: Dana model 70 full-floating. Optional: Powr-Lok differential.

Final Drive Ratio:

J-200 and J-300:	Transmission		
	3-spd.	4-spd.	Auto.
4000 lb. GVW:	4.09:1	—	4.09:1
5000 lb. GVW:	4.09:1	—	4.09:1
5600 lb. GVW:	4.09:1	—	4.09:1
6600 lb. GVW:	4.27:1	4.27:1	4.27:1
7600 lb. GVW:	4.88:1	4.88:1	4.27:1
8800 lb. GVW:	4.88:1	4.88:1	—

Transfer Case: Man. trans. models: 2-speed Spicer model 20, 2.03:1, 1.0:1. Auto. Trans. models: Spicer model 21, single speed (1.00:1). Brakes: Type: Hydraulic, front and rear drums. Optional: Power brakes. Models with auto. trans. had a Bendix system with a wide and low-positioned pedal. Models with manual trans. have a Midland system with a narrower and lower positioned pedal. Wheels: 15 x 5.5 K: Trucks with GVW below 6600 lb., trucks with 6600 lb. GVW: 16 x 5.00K, trucks with 7600 lb. GVW rating: 16 6L, dual 6 x 6.00L rear wheels on J-300 with 8600 GVW lb. rating. Tires: J-200 and J-300:. 4000 lb. GVW: 6.70 x 15. 5000 lb. GVW: 7.10 x 15. 5600 lb. GVW: 7.60 x 15. 6600 lb. GVW: 7.00 x 15. 7600 lb. GVW: 7.50 x 15. 8800 lb. GVW: 7.00 x 15. Steering: Ross cam lever. Ratio: 24:1. Turns Lock-to-Lock: 5.6. Turning Circle: J-200 with independent front suspension: 44 ft. J-300 with independent front suspension: 49.67 ft.; with solid front axle: 57.67 ft. Optional: Thompson power steering. Ratios: 20:1 (later revised to 24:1). Standard: Transmission: Vehicles with GVW of 4000, 5000 and 5600 lb.: GVW: Warner Gear T-90, 3-speed synchromesh manual. Transmission ratios: 2.798:1, 1.551:1, 1.00:1, Reverse: 3.798:1. Vehicles with GVW of 6600, 7600 and 8600 lb. GVW: Warner Gear T-89, heavy-duty 3-spd. manual. ratios: 3.17:1, 1.92:1, 1.00:1. reverse: 4.12:1. Optional: Borg-Warner model AS-8F, three speed torque converter automatic transmission: Ratios: 2.4:1, 1.467:1, 1.00:1, reverse: 2.01:1. Optional: Borg-Warner model T-98A 4-speed trans. Ratios: 6.398:1, 3.092:1, 1.686:1, 1.00:1. See Final Drive Ratio section for specific applications. Clutch: Borg & Beck single dry plate. Clutch diameter: 10.00 in. dia. A 10.5 in. Auburn clutch was used with the T-98A trans. Optional: Borg & Beck or Auburn single dry plate. Clutch Diameter: 10.5 in.

VEHICLE DIMENSIONS: Wheelbase: J-200: 120 in.; J-300: 126 in. Overall Length: J-200: 183.75 in.; J-300: 195.75 in. Front/Rear Tread: J-200: 63.5/63.5 in.; J-300: 63.75/63.75 in. Overall Height: 71.0 in. Width: 75.93 in. Tailgate: Width and Height: Townside: 55.75 in. x 20.20 in. Thriftside: 48.60 in. x 13.75 in. Ground Clearance: Lowest point: 8.75 in. Load space: Townside: J-200-Townside: 84.34 in. x 71.00 in. x 20.20 in. Thriftside: 84.34 in. x 55 in. x 13.75 in. J-300-Townside: 96.34 in. x 71.00 in. x 20.20 in. Front legroom: 45.25 in. Rear legroom: 38.25 in.

CAPACITIES: Fuel Tank: 20.0 gal. Coolant System: 12 qt., 13 qt. with heater.

ACCOMMODATIONS: Seating Capacity: Three.

INSTRUMENTATION: Speedometer, odometer, gauges for fuel level, engine coolant temperature, battery charge and oil pressure, and transfer case indicator lights.

OPTIONS: 40-60 amp alternator, power steering, power brakes, drive line brake, Powr-Lok differential (rear axle only), oil bath air cleaner, front-mounted winch, power take-off (rear-mounted), Warn free-wheeling front hubs and governors, locking gas cap, magnetic drain plug, a speedometer reading in kilometers, dual-speed wipers, windshield washers, fresh air heater and defroster, electric clock, back-up lights, push-button AM radio, parking light indicator, compass, transfer case indicator lights, chrome exterior mirror, padded dash panel, seat belts, E-Z Eye windshield glass and a glove box light.

HISTORICAL FOOTNOTES: Jeep regarded the new Gladiator as "the world's most advanced, most useful four-wheel drive truck."

1964 GLADIATOR

The 1964 Gladiators were essentially unchanged for 1964. Air conditioning was added to its optional equipment list and a lower compression version of the OHC 6-cylinder engine was now available.

I.D. DATA: The serial number was located on the left-hand hinge pillar. The first four digits indicated the model as follows: The fifth symbol was a letter. The sequential production number followed. The starting number for each series was 10001. The engine number was located on the right-hand corner of the block. The engine codes were ND60C and TD60C.

Model Number	Body Type	Factory Price	GVW	Shipping Weight	Prod. Total
Series J-200 1/2, 3/4 and 1 ton					
J-200	Chassis/Cab	$2679	4000	3061	—
J-200	Pickup Thriftside	$2779	4000	3361	—
J-200	Pickup Townside	$2806	4000	3461	—
J-210	Chassis/Cab	$2738	5600	3096	—
J-210	Pickup Thriftside	$2839	5600	3396	—
J-210	Pickup Townside	$2866	5600	3496	—
J-220	Chassis/Cab	$2841	6600	3214	—
J-220	Pickup Thriftside	$2942	6600	3514	—
J-220	Pickup Townside	$2969	6600	3614	—
J-220	Stake Platform	$3148	6600	3894	—
J-230	Chassis/Cab	$3687	8600	3874	—
J-230	Stake Platform	$4079	8600	4714	—
Series J-300 3/4, 1 ton					
J-300	Chassis/Cab	$2739	5000	3091	—
J-300	Pickup Thriftside	$2854	5000	3441	—
J-300	Pickup Townside	$2881	5000	3541	—
J-310	Chassis/Cab	$2860	6600	3239	—
J-310	Pickup Thriftside	$2975	6600	3589	—
J-310	Pickup Townside	$3002	6600	3689	—
J-310	Stake Platform	$3200	6600	4679	—
J-320	Chassis/Cab	$3024	7600	3377	—
J-320	Pickup Thriftside	$3139	7600	3727	—
J-320	Pickup Townside	$3166	7600	3827	—
J-320	Stake Platform	$3364	7600	4117	—
J-330	Chassis/Cab	$3706	8600	3899	—
J-330	Stake Platform	$4120	8600	4799	—

STANDARD ENGINE: Engine Type: OHV, OHC In-line-6. Cast iron block and cylinder head. Bore x Stroke: 3.4375 in. x 4.375 in. Lifters: Hydraulic. Number of main bearings-4. Fuel Induction: 1 bbl. Holley model 1920 (manual trans. models); 2 bbl. Holley model 2415 (auto. trans.). Compression Ratio: 8.5:1. Displacement: 230 cu. in. (3.76 liters). Horsepower: Net:140 @ 4000 rpm. Torque: Net: 210 lb.-ft. @ 1750 rpm. Oil refill capacity: 6 qt. with filter change. Fuel Requirements: Regular.

OPTIONAL ENGINE: Engine Type: OHV, V-6. Cast iron block and cylinder head. Bore x Stroke: 3.4375 in. x 4.375 in. Lifters: Hydraulic. Number of main bearings-4. Fuel Induction: 1-bbl. Holley model 1920 (manual trans. models); 2 bbl. Holley model 2415 (auto. trans.). Compression Ratio: 7.5:1. Displacement: 230 cu. in. (3.76 liters). Horsepower: Net: 133 @ 4000 rpm. Torque: Net: 199 lb.-ft. @ 2400 rpm. Oil refill capacity: 6 qt. with filter change.

CHASSIS FEATURES: Separate body and frame. Deep web frame, wide flange, lightweight pressed steel with five cross members.

SUSPENSION AND RUNNING GEAR: Front Suspension: Multi-Leaf semi-elliptical springs, size varies with GVW rating. Hydraulic double-action shock absorbers: 13.0 in. on solid front axle, 12.375 in. dia. for torsion bar suspension. Optional torsion bar. Rear Suspension: Semi-elliptical multi-leaf springs with anti-windup top half spring, hydraulic double-action shock absorbers. Optional: 6-leaf semi-elliptical springs. Front Axle Type and Capacity: Dana model 44F, 3000 lb. capacity. Rear Axle Type and Capacity: Dana model 44 semi-floating. Optional: Dana model 70 full-floating. Optional: Powr-Lok differential.

Final Drive Ratio:

J-200 and J-300:

	Transmission		
	3-spd.	4-spd.	Auto.
4000 lb. GVW:	4.09:1	—	4.09:1
5000 lb. GVW:	4.09:1	—	4.09:1
5600 lb. GVW:	4.09:1	—	4.09:1
6600 lb. GVW:	4.27:1	4.27:1	4.27:1
7600 lb. GVW:	4.88:1	4.88:1	4.27:1
8800 lb. GVW:	4.88:1	4.88:1	—

Transfer Case: Man. trans. models: 2-speed Spicer model 20, 2.03:1, 1.0:1. Auto. Trans. models: Spicer model 21, single speed (1.00:1). Brakes: Type: Hydraulic, front and rear drums. Optional: Power brakes. Models with auto. trans. had a Bendix system with a wide and low-positioned pedal. Models with manual trans. have a Midland system with a narrower and lower positioned pedal. Wheels: 15 x 5.5 K: Trucks with GVW below 6600 lb., trucks with 6600 lb. GVW: 16 x 5.00K, trucks with 7600 lb. GVW rating: 16 6L, dual 6 x 6.00L rear wheels on J-300 with 8600 GVW lb. rating. Tires: J-200 and J-300. 4000 lb. GVW: 6.70 x 15. 5000 lb. GVW: 7.10 x 15. 5600 lb. GVW: 7.60 X 15. 6600 lb. GVW: 7.00 x 15. 7600 lb. GVW: 7.00 x 15. 8800 lb. GVW: 7.00 x 15. Steering: Ross cam lever. Ratio: 24:1. Turns Lock-to-Lock: 5.6. Turning Circle: J-200 with independent front suspension: 44 ft. J-300 with independent front suspension: 49.67 ft.; with solid front axle: 57.67 ft. Optional: Thompson power steering. Ratios: 20:1 (later revised to 24:1). Standard: Transmission: Vehicles with GVW of 4000, 5000 and 5600 lb.: GVW: Warner Gear T-90, 3-speed synchromesh manual. Transmission ratios: 2.798:1, 1.551:1, 1.00:1, Reverse: 3.798:1. Vehicles with GVW of 6600, 7600 and 8600 lb. GVW: Warner Gear T-89, heavy-duty 3-spd. manual. ratios: 3.17:1, 1.92:1, 1.00:1. reverse: 4.12:1. Optional: Borg-Warner model AS-8F, three speed torque converter automatic transmission: Ratios: 2.4:1, 1.467:1, 1.00:1, reverse: 2.01:1. Optional: Borg-Warner model T-98A 4-speed trans. Ratios: 6.398:1, 3.092:1, 1.686:1, 1.00:1. See Final Drive Ratio section for specific applications. Clutch: Borg & Beck single dry plate. Clutch diameter: 10.00 in. dia. A 10.5 in. auburn clutch was used with the T-98A trans. Optional: Borg & Beck or auburn single dry plate. Clutch Diameter: 10.5 in.

VEHICLE DIMENSIONS: Wheelbase: J-200: 120 in.; J-300: 126 in. Overall Length: J-200: 183.75 in.; J-300: 195.75 in. Front/Rear Tread: J-200: 63.5/63.5 in.; J-300: 63.75/63.75 in. Overall Height: 71.0 in. Width: 75.93 in. Tailgate: Width and Height: Townside: 55.75 in. x 20.20 in. Thriftside: 48.60 in. x 13.75 in. Ground Clearance: Lowest point: 8.75 in. Load space: Townside: J-200-Townside: 84.34 in. x 71.00 in. x 20.20 in. Thriftside: 84.34 in. x 55 in. x 13.75 in. J-300-Townside: 96.34 in. x 71.00 in. x 20.20 in. Front legroom: 45.25 in. Rear legroom: 38.25 in.

CAPACITIES: Fuel Tank: 20.0 gal. Coolant System: 12 qt., 13 qt. with heater.

ACCOMMODATIONS: Seating Capacity: Three.

INSTRUMENTATION: Speedometer, odometer, gauges for fuel level, engine coolant temperature, battery charge and oil pressure, and transfer case indicator lights.

OPTIONS: 40-60 amp alternator, power steering, power brakes, drive line brake, Powr-Lok differential (rear axle only), oil bath air cleaner, front-mounted winch, power take-off (rear-mounted), Warn free-wheeling front hubs and governors, locking gas cap, magnetic drain plug, a speedometer reading in kilometers, dual-speed wipers, windshield washers, fresh air heater and defroster, electric clock, back-up lights, push button AM radio, parking light indicator, compass, transfer case indicator lights, chrome exterior mirror, padded dash panel, seat belts, E-Z Eye windshield glass and a glove box light.

HISTORICAL FOOTNOTES: Introduction of the Gladiator trucks took place in the fall of 1963.

1965 GLADIATOR

Jeep began the 1965 model year with carry-over Gladiator models from 1964. During the model year a revised line of Gladiator trucks with new J-2000 (120 in. wheelbase) and J-3000 (126 in. wheelbase) identifications. The new models were available with the same Hi-Torque Six and Vigilante V-8 engines as the Wagoneer. As standard equipment the new Gladiators had a Safety Package consisting of padded sun visor, padded dash, seat belts, dual sped windshield wipers and washer, outside rearview mirror, 4-way warning flashers, high-impact windshield, dual brake system and self-adjusting brakes.

1965 Jeep Gladiator J-3000 Townside

I.D. DATA: The serial number was located on the left-hand hinge pillar. The first four digits indicated the model as follows: The fifth symbol was a letter. The sequential production number followed. The starting number for each series was 10001. The engine number was located on the right-hand corner of the block. The engine codes were ND60C and TD60C.

Model Number	Body Type	Factory Price	GVW	Shipping Weight	Prod. Total
First Series: Series J-200 1/2, 3/4 and 1 ton					
J-200	Chassis/Cab	$2679	4000	3061	—
J-200	Pickup Thriftside	$2779	4000	3361	—
J-200	Pickup Townside	$2806	4000	3461	—
J-210	Chassis/Cab	$2738	5600	3096	—
J-210	Pickup Thriftside	$2839	5600	3396	—
J-210	Pickup Townside	$2866	5600	3496	—
J-220	Chassis/Cab	$2841	6600	3214	—
J-220	Pickup Thriftside	$2942	6600	3514	—
J-220	Pickup Townside	$2969	6600	3614	—
J-220	Stake Platform	$3148	6600	3894	—
J-230	Chassis/Cab	$3687	8600	3874	—
J-230	Stake Platform	$4079	8600	4714	—
Series J-300 3/4 and 1 ton					
J-300	Chassis/Cab	$2739	5000	3091	—
J-300	Pickup Thriftside	$2854	5000	3441	—
J-300	Pickup Townside	$2881	5000	3541	—
J-310	Chassis/Cab	$2860	6600	3239	—
J-310	Pickup Thriftside	$2975	6600	3589	—
J-310	Pickup Townside	$3002	6600	3689	—
J-310	Stake Platform	$3200	6600	4679	—
J-320	Chassis/Cab	$3024	7600	3377	—
J-320	Pickup Thriftside	$3139	7600	3727	—
J-320	Pickup Townside	$3166	7600	3827	—
J-320	Stake Platform	$3364	7600	4117	—
J-330	Chassis/Cab	$3706	8600	3899	—
J-330	Stake Platform	$4120	8600	4799	—

Second Series 120 in. wheelbase. (J2500 & J2600: 1/2 ton; J-2700: 3/4 ton Series J2800 1 ton)

J-2500	Chassis/Cab	$2802	5000	3128	—
J-2500	Pickup Thriftside	$2903	5000	3423	—
J-2500	Pickup Townside	$2930	5000	3531	—
J-2600	Chassis/Cab	$2923	6000	3269	—
J-2600	Pickup Thriftside	$3024	6000	3564	—
J-2600	Pickup Townside	$3050	6000	3672	—
J-2600	Stake Platform	$3229	6000	3925	—
J-2700	Chassis/Cab	$3087	7000	3356	—
J-2700	Pickup Thriftside	$3188	7000	3651	—
J-2700	Pickup Townside	$3215	7000	3759	—
J-2700	Stake Platform	$3393	7000	4012	—
J-2800	Chassis/Cab	$3770	8600	3789	—
J-2800	Stake Platform	$4163	8600	4534	—

Second Series, 126 in. wheelbase. (J-3500 & J-3600: 1/2 ton; J-3700: 3/4 ton Series J-3800 1 ton)

J-3500	Chassis/Cab	$2821	5000	3152	—
J-3500	Pickup Thriftside	$2935	5000	3472	—
J-3500	Pickup Townside	$2962	5000	3580	—
J-3600	Chassis/Cab	$2942	6000	3290	—
J-3600	Pickup Thriftside	$3056	6000	3610	—
J-3600	Pickup Townside	$3083	6000	3718	—
J-3600	Stake Platform	$3280	6000	3994	—
J-3700	Chassis/Cab	$3106	7000	3377	—
J-3700	Pickup Thriftside	$3220	7000	3697	—
J-3700	Pickup Townside	$3247	7000	3805	—
J-3700	Stake Platform	$3444	7000	4081	—
J-3800	Chassis/Cab	$3788	8600	3822	—
J-3800	Stake Platform	$4203	8600	4620	—

First series had same engines as in 1964.

STANDARD ENGINE: Second series: Engine Type: OHV, L-6. Cast iron block and cylinder head. Bore x Stroke: 3.75 in. x 3.50 in. Lifters: Hydraulic. Number of main bearings-7. Fuel Induction: 1 bbl. Carter Type RTBS or Holley model 1931C-3705. Compression Ratio: 8.5:1. Displacement: 232 cu. in. (3.80 liters). Horsepower: 145 @ 4300 rpm. Torque: 215 lb.-ft. @ 1600 rpm. Oil refill capacity: 5 qt. with filter change. Fuel Requirements: Regular.

OPTIONAL ENGINE: Engine Type: OHV, "Vigilante" V-8. Cast iron block and cylinder head. Bore x Stroke: 4.00 in. x 3.25 in. Lifters: Hydraulic. Number of main bearings-4. Fuel Induction: 2 bbl. downdraft carburetor. Compression Ratio: 8.7:1. Displacement: 327 cu. in. (5.35 liters). Horsepower: 250 @ 4700 rpm. Torque: Net: 340 lb.-ft. @ 2600 rpm. Oil refill capacity: 5 qt. with filter change. Fuel Requirements: Regular.

CHASSIS FEATURES: Separate body and frame. Deep web frame, wide flange, lightweight pressed steel with five cross members.

SUSPENSION AND RUNNING GEAR: Front Suspension: Multi-Leaf semi-elliptical springs, size varies with GVW rating. Hydraulic double-action shock absorbers: 13.0 in. on solid front axle, 12.375 in. dia. for torsion bar suspension. Rear Suspension: Semi-elliptical multi-leaf springs with anti-windup top half spring, Hydraulic double-action shock absorbers. Optional: 6-leaf semi-elliptical springs. Front Axle Type and Capacity: Dana model 44F, 3000 lb. capacity. Rear Axle Type and Capacity: Dana model 44 semi-floating. Optional: Dana model 70 full-floating. Optional: Powr-Lok differential.

Final Drive Ratio:

J-2000 and J-3000		Transmission	
Vigilante V-8	3-spd.	4-spd.	Auto.
5000 lb. GVW:	3.92:1	3.92:1	3.54:1
	4.27:1*	4.27:1*	3.92:1
6000 lb. GVW:	4.09:1	4.09:1	4.09:1
	4.27:1*	4.27:1*	—
7000 lb. GVW:	4.09:1	4.09:1	4.09:1
	4.27:1*	4.27:1	—
8600 lb. GVW:	N.A.	4.88:1	N.A.

* Optional at no extra cost.

J-2000 and J-3000:		Transmission	
High-Torque L-6	3-spd.	4-spd.	Auto.
5000 lb. GVW:	4.27:1	4.27:1	4.27:1
4.88:1*	4.88:1*	4.88:1*	—
6000 lb. GVW:	4.27:1	4.27:1	4.27:1
4.88:1*	4.88:1*	4.88:1*	—
7000 lb. GVW:	4.88:1	4.88:1	4.27:1
8600 lb. GVW:	N.A.	4.88:1	N.A.

* Optional at no extra cost.

Transfer Case: All models: 2-speed Spicer model 20, 2.03:1, 1.0:1. Brakes: Type: Hydraulic, front and rear drums. Dimensions: Front: 11.0 in. x 2.00 in. front and rear. Total effective area: 161.16 sq. in. Optional: Power brakes. Models with auto. trans. had a Bendix system with a wide and low-positioned pedal. Models with manual trans. have a Midland system with a narrower and lower positioned pedal. Wheels: 15 x 5.5 K: Trucks with GVW below 6600 lb., trucks with 6600 lb. GVW: 16 x 5.00K, trucks with 7600 lb. GVW rating: 16 6L, dual 6 x 6.00L rear wheels on J-3800 with 8600 GVW lb. rating. Tires: J-2500: 8.15 x 15, J-2600: 7.00 x16, J-3500: 8.15 x 15, J-3600: 7.00 x 16, J-2700: 7.50 x 16, J-3700: 7.50 x 16, J-2800: 7.00 x16, J-3800: 7.00 x 16. Steering: Ross cam lever. Ratio: 24:1. Turns Lock-to-Lock: 5.6. Turning Circle: J-2600: 49.5 ft., J-3600: 52.5 ft. Optional: Saginaw power steering. Ratios: 24:1. Standard: Transmission: 3-spd. man. trans. except for vehicles with 8600 lb. GVW which have 4-spd. manual standard. Optional: Turbo Hydra-Matic. Not avail. for 8600 lb. GVW vehicles. Optional: 4-spd. Borg-Warner model T-98A 4-speed trans. Ratios: 6.398:1, 3.092:1, 1.686:1, 1.00:1. Clutch: Borg & Beck single dry plate.

VEHICLE DIMENSIONS: Wheelbase: J-2000: 120 in.; J-3000: 126 in. Overall Length: J-2000: 183.75 in.; J-3000: 195.75 in. Front/Rear Tread: J-2000: 63.5/63.5 in.; J-3000: 63.75/63.75 in. Overall Height: 71.0 in. Width: 75.93 in. Tailgate: Width and Height: Townside: 55.75 in. x 20.20 in. Thriftside: 48.60 in. x 13.75 in. Ground Clearance: Lowest point: 8.75 in. Load space: Townside: J-2000-Townside: 84.34 in. x 71.00 in. x 20.20 in. Thriftside: 84.34 in. x 55 in. x 13.75 in. J-3000-Townside: 96.34 in. x 71.00 in. x 20.20 in. Front legroom: 45.25 in.

CAPACITIES: Fuel Tank: 18.0 gal.

ACCOMMODATIONS: Seating Capacity: Three.

INSTRUMENTATION: Speedometer, odometer, gauges for oil pressure, engine coolant temperature, transfer case indicator lights.

OPTIONS: Heavy-duty alternator. Pintle hook. Heavy-duty battery. Power brakes. Transmission brake (standard with 8600 lb. GVW). Step bumper. Front chrome bumper. Rear painted or chrome bumper. Full wheelcovers. Locking gas cap. Electric clock. Heavy-duty clutch. Air conditioning. Fabric box enclosure. Dump body. Vigilante V-8. E-Z Eye glass. Chrome grille. Fresh air heater and defroster. Selective drive hubs. Cigarette lighter. Courtesy lights. Parking brake warning light. Glove box light. Spare tire lock. Right outside rearview mirror. Power take-offs. Push-button transistor radio. Snowplow. Push plate. Power steering. Turbo Hydra-Matic. 4-speed manual trans. (standard with 8600 lb. GVW). Tonneau cover. Winches. Deluxe rear window. Wrecker. Custom cab. Rear Powr-Lok differential. Fuel tank skid plate. Mud flaps. Bucket seats and console (avail. with Custom Cab only), and Camper Package.

HISTORICAL FOOTNOTES: The new models with the available V-8 engine were introduced in the fall of 1964.

1966 GLADIATOR

No changes of consequence took place in the Gladiator trucks for 1966.

1966 Jeep Gladiator pickup

I.D. DATA: The serial number was located on the left-hand hinge pillar. The first four digits indicated the model as follows. The fifth symbol was a letter. The sequential production number followed. The starting number for each series was 10001. The engine number was located on the right-hand corner of the block. The engine codes were ND60C and TD60C. Serial number data: Model J-2500: 6-cyl.: 1406W-10100 and up, (V-8 models: 5001 and up); model J-2600: 2406X-10075 and up, (V-8 models: 5001 and up); J-3500: 3406W-10100 and up (V-8: 5001 and up); J-3800: 3406X-10075 and up, (V-8: 5001 and up); J-2700: 2406Y-10025 and up, (V-8: 5001 and up); J-3700: 3406Y-10025 and up, (V-8: 5001 and up); J-2800: 2406Z-10010 and up, (V-8: 5001 and up), J-3800: 3406Z-10010 and up, (V-8: 5001 and up).

Model Number	Body Type	Factory Price	GVW	Shipping Weight	Prod. Total

J-2000, 120 in. wheelbase. (J2500 & J2600: 1/2 ton; J-2700: 3/4 ton; Series J2800 1 ton)

J-2500	Chassis/Cab	$2861	5000	3128	—
J-2500	Pickup Thriftside	$2961	5000	3423	—
J-2500	Pickup Townside	$2988	5000	3531	—
J-2600	Chassis/Cab	$2981	6000	3269	—
J-2600	Pickup Thriftside	$3082	6000	3564	—
J-2600	Pickup Townside	$3109	6000	3672	—
J-2600	Stake Platform	$3287	6000	3925	—
J-2700	Chassis/Cab	$3146	7000	3356	—
J-2700	Pickup Thriftside	$3246	7000	3651	—
J-2700	Pickup Townside	$3273	7000	3759	—
J-2700	Stake Platform	$3451	7000	4012	—
J-2800	Chassis/Cab	$3831	8600	3789	—
J-2800	Stake Platform	$4233	8600	4534	—

J-3000, 126 in. wheelbase. (J-3500 & J-3600: 1/2 ton; J-3700: 3/4 ton; Series J-3800 1 ton)

J-3500	Chassis/Cab	$2879	5000	3152	—
J-3500	Pickup Thriftside	$2994	5000	3472	—
J-3500	Pickup Townside	$3021	5000	3580	—
J-3600	Chassis/Cab	$3000	6000	3290	—
J-3600	Pickup Thriftside	$3114	6000	3610	—
J-3600	Pickup Townside	$3141	6000	3718	—
J-3600	Stake Platform	$3338	6000	3994	—
J-3700	Chassis/Cab	$3164	7000	3377	—
J-3700	Pickup Thriftside	$3279	7000	3697	—
J-3700	Pickup Townside	$3305	7000	3805	—
J-3700	Stake Platform	$3502	7000	4081	—
J-3800	Chassis/Cab	$3849	8600	3822	—
J-3800	Stake Platform	$4264	8600	4620	—

STANDARD ENGINE: Engine Type: OHV, L-6. Cast iron block and cylinder head. Bore x Stroke: 3.75 in. x 3.50 in. Lifters: Hydraulic. Number of main bearings-7. Fuel Induction: 1 bbl. Carter Type RTBS or Holley model 1931C-3705. Compression Ratio: 8.5:1. Displacement: 232 cu. in. (3.80 liters). Horsepower: 145 @ 4300 rpm. Torque: 215 lb.-ft. @ 1600 rpm. Oil refill capacity: 5 qt. with filter change. Fuel Requirements: Regular.

Standard Catalog of American Four-Wheel Drive Vehicles

OPTIONAL ENGINE: Engine Type: OHV, "Vigilante" V-8. Cast iron block and cylinder head. Bore x Stroke: 4.00 in. x 3.25 in. Lifters: Hydraulic. Number of main bearings-4. Fuel Induction: 2 bbl. downdraft carburetor. Compression Ratio: 8.7:1. Displacement: 327 cu. in. (5.35 liters). Horsepower: 250 @ 4700 rpm. Torque: Net: 340 lb.-ft. @ 2600 rpm. Oil refill capacity: 5 qt. with filter change. Fuel Requirements: Regular.

CHASSIS FEATURES: Separate body and frame. Deep web frame, wide flange, lightweight pressed steel with five cross members.

SUSPENSION AND RUNNING GEAR: Front Suspension: Multi-Leaf semi-elliptical springs, size varies with GVW rating. Hydraulic double-action shock absorbers: 13.0 in. on solid front axle, 12.375 in. dia. for torsion bar suspension. Rear Suspension: Semi-elliptical multi-leaf springs with anti-windup top half spring, hydraulic double-action shock absorbers. Optional: 6-leaf semi-elliptical springs. Front Axle Type and Capacity: Dana model 44F, 3000 lb. capacity. Rear Axle Type and Capacity: Dana model 44 semi-floating. Optional: Dana model 70 full-floating. Optional: Powr-Lok differential.

Final Drive Ratio:

J-2000 and J-3000:		Transmission	
Vigilante V-8	3-spd.	4-spd.	Auto
5000 lb. GVW:	3.92:1	3.92:1	3.54:1
	4.27:1*	4.27:1*	3.92:1
6000 lb. GVW:	4.09:1	4.09:1	4.09:1
	4.27:1*	4.27:1*	—
7000 lb. GVW:	4.09:1	4.09:1	4.09:1
	4.27:1*	4.27:1	—
8600 lb. GVW:	N.A.	4.88:1	NA.

* Optional at no extra cost.

J-2000 and J-3000:		Transmission	
High-Torque L-6	3-spd.	4-spd.	Auto
5000 lb. GVW:	4.27:1	4.27:1	4.27:1
	4.88:1*	4.88:1*	4.88:1*
6000 lb. GVW:	4.27:1	4.27:1	4.27:1
	4.88:1*	4.88:1*	4.88:1*
7000 lb. GVW:	4.88:1	4.88:1	4.27:1
8600 lb. GVW:	N.A.	4.88:1	N.A.

* Optional at no extra cost.

Transfer Case: All models: 2-speed Spicer model 20, 2.03:1, 1.0:1. Brakes: Type: Hydraulic, front and rear drums. Dimensions: Front: 11.0 in. x 2.00 in. front and rear. Total effective area: 161.16 sq. in. Optional: Power brakes. Models with auto. trans. had a Bendix system with a wide and low-positioned pedal. Models with manual trans. have a Midland system with a narrower and lower positioned pedal. Wheels: 15 x 5.5 K: Trucks with GVW below 6600 lb., trucks with 6600 lb. GVW: 16 x 5.00K, trucks with 7600 lb. GVW rating: 16 6L, dual 6 x 6.00L rear wheels on J-3800 with 8600 GVW lb. rating. Tires: J-2500: 8.15 x 15, J-2600: 7.00 x16, J-3500: 8.15 x 15, J-3600: 7.00 x 16, J-2700: 7.50 x 16, J-3700: 7.50 x 16, J-2800: 7.00 x16, J-3800: 7.00 x 16. Steering: Ross Cam lever. Ratio: 24:1. Turns Lock-to-Lock: 5.6. Turning Circle: J-2600: 49.5 ft., J-3600: 52.5 ft. Optional: Saginaw Power steering. Ratios: 24:1. Standard: Transmission: 3-spd. man. trans. except for vehicles with 8600 lb. GVW which have 4-spd. manual standard. Optional: 3-spd. Turbo Hydra-Matic. Not avail. for 8600 lb. GVW vehicles. Optional: 4-spd. Borg-Warner model T-98A 4-speed trans. Ratios: 6.398:1, 3.092:1, 1.686:1, 1.00:1. Clutch: Borg & Beck single dry plate.

VEHICLE DIMENSIONS: Wheelbase: J-2000: 120 in.; J-3000: 126 in. Overall Length: J-2000: 183.75 in.; J-3000: 195.75 in. Front/Rear Tread: J-2000: 63.5/63.5 in.; J-3000: 63.75/63.75 in. Overall Height: 71.0 in. Width: 75.93 in. Tailgate: Width and Height: Townside: 55.75 in. x 20.20 in. Thriftside: 48.60 in. x 13.75 in. Ground Clearance: Lowest point: 8.75 in. Load space: Townside: J-2000-Townside: 84.34 in. x 71.00 in. x 20.20 in. Thriftside: 84.34 in. x 55 in. x 13.75 in. J-3000-Townside: 96.34 in. x 71.00 in. x 20.20 in. Front legroom: 45.25 in.

CAPACITIES: Fuel Tank: 18.0 gal.

ACCOMMODATIONS: Seating Capacity: Three.

INSTRUMENTATION: Transfer case indicator lights.

OPTIONS: Heavy-duty alternator. Pintle hook. Heavy-duty battery. Power brakes. Transmission brake (standard with 8600 lb. GVW). Step bumper. Front chrome bumper. Rear painted or chrome bumper. Full wheelcovers. Locking gas cap. Electric clock. Heavy-duty clutch. Air conditioning. Fabric box enclosure. Dump body. Vigilante V-8. E-Z Eye glass. Chrome grille. Fresh air heater and defroster. Selective drive hubs. Cigarette lighter. Courtesy lights. Parking brake warning light. Glove box light. Spare tire lock. Glove box light. Courtesy lights. Parking brake warning light. Glove box light. Spare tire lock. Glove box light. Outside rearview mirror. Power take-offs. Push-button transistor radio. Snowplow. Push plate. Power steering. Turbo Hydra-Matic. 4-speed manual trans. (standard with 8600 lb. GVW). Tonneau cover. Winches. Deluxe rear window. Wrecker. Custom cab. Rear Powr-Lok differential. Fuel tank skid plate. Mud flaps. Bucket seats and console (avail. with Custom Cab only), and Camper Package.

HISTORICAL FOOTNOTES: The 1966 Jeep trucks were announced in the fall of 1965.

1967 GLADIATOR

Except for minor revisions such as axle ratios and tire availability, no major developments took place for 1967.

I.D. DATA: The serial number was located on the left-hand hinge pillar. The first four digits indicated the model as follows: J-2500: 2406W; J-2600: 2406X; J-2700: 2406Y; J-2800: 2406Z; J-3500: 3406W; J-3600: 3406X; J-3700: 3406Y; J-3800: 3406Z. The sequential production number followed. The starting number for each series was 200001.

Model Number	Body Type	Factory Price	GVW	Shipping Weight	Prod. Total
J-2000, 120 in. wheelbase. (J-2500 & J-2600: 1/2 ton; J-2700: 3/4 ton; Series J-2800 1 ton)					
J-2500	Chassis/Cab	$2957	5000	3096	—
J-2500	Pickup Thriftside	$3058	5000	3391	—
J-2500	Pickup Townside	$3085	5000	3499	—
J-2600	Chassis/Cab	$3078	6000	3237	—
J-2600	Pickup Thriftside	$3178	6000	3532	—
J-2600	Pickup Townside	$3205	6000	3640	—
J-2600	Stake Platform	$3383	6000	3893	—
J-2700	Chassis/Cab	$3242	7000	3324	—
J-2700	Pickup Thriftside	$3343	7000	3619	—
J-2700	Pickup Townside	$3369	7000	3727	—
J-2700	Stake Platform	$3548	7000	3980	—
J-2800	Chassis/Cab	$3920	8600	3757	—
J-2800	Stake Platform	$4312	8600	4502	—
J-3000, 126 in. wheelbase. (J-3500 & J-3600: 1/2 ton; J-3700: 3/4 ton; Series J-3800 1 ton)					
J-3500	Chassis/Cab	$2976	5000	3120	—
J-3500	Pickup Thriftside	$3091	5000	3440	—
J-3500	Pickup Townside	$3117	5000	3548	—
J-3600	Chassis/Cab	$3096	6000	3258	—
J-3600	Pickup Thriftside	$3211	6000	3578	—
J-3600	Pickup Townside	$3238	6000	3686	—
J-3600	Stake Platform	$3435	6000	3962	—
J-3700	Chassis/Cab	$3261	7000	3345	—
J-3700	Pickup Thriftside	$3375	7000	3665	—
J-3700	Pickup Townside	$3402	7000	3773	—
J-3700	Stake Platform	$3599	7000	4049	—
J-3800	Chassis/Cab	$3938	8600	3790	—
J-3800	Stake Platform	$4353	8600	4588	—

STANDARD ENGINE: Engine Type: OHV, L-6. Cast iron block and cylinder head. Bore x Stroke: 3.75 in. x 3.50 in. Lifters: Hydraulic. Number of main bearings-7. Fuel Induction: 1 bbl. Carter Type RTBS or Holley model 1931C-3705. Compression Ratio: 8.5:1. Displacement: 232 cu. in. (3.80 liters). Horsepower: 145 @ 4300 rpm. Torque: 215 lb.-ft. @ 1600 rpm. Oil refill capacity: 5 qt. with filter change. Fuel Requirements: Regular.

OPTIONAL ENGINE: Engine Type: OHV, "Vigilante" V-8. Cast iron block and cylinder head. Bore x Stroke: 4.00 in. x 3.25 in. Lifters: Hydraulic. Number of main bearings-4. Fuel Induction: 2 bbl. downdraft carburetor. Compression Ratio: 8.7:1. Displacement: 327 cu. in. (5.35 liters). Horsepower: 250 @ 4700 rpm. Torque: Net: 340 lb.-ft. @ 2600 rpm. Oil refill capacity: 5 qt. with filter change. Fuel Requirements: Regular.

CHASSIS FEATURES: Separate body and frame. Deep web frame, wide flange, lightweight pressed steel with five cross members.

SUSPENSION AND RUNNING GEAR: Front Suspension: Multi-Leaf semi-elliptical springs, size varies with GVW rating. Hydraulic double-action shock absorbers: 13.0 in. on solid front axle, 12.375 in. dia. for torsion bar suspension. Rear Suspension: Semi-elliptical multi-leaf springs with anti-windup top half spring, Hydraulic double-action shock absorbers. Optional: 6-leaf semi-elliptical springs. Front Axle Type and Capacity: Dana model 44F, 3000 lb. capacity. Rear Axle Type and Capacity: Dana model 44 semi-floating. Optional: Dana model 70 full-floating. Optional: Powr-Lok differential.

Final Drive Ratio:

J-2000 and J-3000:		Transmission	
Vigilante V-8	3-spd.	4-spd.	Auto.
5000 lb. GVW:	3.92:1	3.92:1	3.54:1
	4.27:1*	4.27:1*	3.92:1
6000 lb. GVW:	4.09:1	4.09:1	4.09:1
	4.27:1*	4.27:1*	4.27:1*
7000 lb. GVW:	4.09:1	4.09:1	4.09:1
	4.27:1*	4.27:1*	
8600 lb. GVW:	N.A.	4.88:1	N.A.

* Optional at no extra cost.

J-2000 and J-3000:		Transmission	
High-Torque L-6	3-spd.	4-spd.	Auto
5000 lb. GVW:	4.27:1	4.27:1	4.27:1
	4.88:1*	4.88:1*	4.88:1*
6000 lb. GVW:	4.27:1	4.27:1	4.27:1
	4.88:1*	4.88:1*	4.88:1*
7000 lb. GVW:	4.88:1	4.88:1	4.27:1
8600 lb. GVW:	N.A.	4.88:1	N.A.

* Optional at no extra cost.

Transfer Case: All models: 2-speed Spicer model 20, 2.03:1, 1.0:1. Brakes: Type: Hydraulic, front and rear drums. Dimensions: Front: 11.0 in. x 2.00 in. front and rear. Total effective area: 161.16 sq. in. Optional: Power brakes. Models with auto. trans. had a Bendix system with a wide and low-positioned pedal. Models with manual trans. have a Midland system with a narrower and lower positioned pedal. Wheels: 15 x 5.5 K: Trucks with GVW below 6600 lb., trucks with 6600 lb. GVW: 16 x 5.00K, trucks with 7600 lb. GVW rating: 16 6L, dual 6 x 6.00L rear wheels on J-3800 with 8600 GVW lb. rating. Tires: J-2500: 8.15 x 15, J-2600: 7.00 x16, J-3500: 8.15 x 15, J-3600: 7.00 x 16, J-2700: 7.50 x 16, J-3700: 7.50 x 16, J-2800: 7.00 x16, J-3800: 7.00 x 16. Steering: Ross cam lever. Ratio: 24:1. Turns Lock-to-Lock: 5.6. Turning Circle: J-2600: 49.5 ft., J-3600: 52.5 ft. Optional: Saginaw power steering. Ratios: 24:1. Standard: Transmission: 3-spd. man. trans. except for vehicles with 8600 lb. GVW which have 4-spd. manual standard. Optional: 3-spd. Turbo Hydra-Matic. Not avail. for 8600 lb. GVW vehicles. Optional: 4-spd. Borg-Warner model T-98A 4-speed trans. Ratios: 6.398:1, 3.092:1, 1.686:1, 1.00:1. Clutch: Borg & Beck single dry plate.

VEHICLE DIMENSIONS: Wheelbase: J-2000: 120 in.; J-3000: 126 in. Overall Length: J-2000: 183.75 in.; J-3000: 195.75 in. Front/Rear Tread: J-2000: 63.5/63.5 in.; J-3000: 63.75/63.75 in. Overall Height: 71.0 in. Width: 75.93 in. Tailgate: Width and Height: Townside: 55.75 in. x 20.20 in. Thriftside: 48.60 in. x 13.75 in. Ground Clearance: Lowest point: 8.75 in. Load space: Townside: J-2000-Townside: 84.34 in. x 71.00 in. x 20.20 in. Thriftside: 84.34 in. x 55 in. x 13.75 in. J-3000-Townside: 96.34 in. x 71.00 in. x 20.20 in. Front legroom: 45.25 in.

CAPACITIES: Fuel Tank: 18.0 gal.

ACCOMMODATIONS: Seating Capacity: Three.

INSTRUMENTATION: Transfer case indicator lights.

OPTIONS: Heavy-duty alternator. Pintle hook. Heavy-duty battery. Power brakes. Transmission brake (standard with 8600 lb. GVW). Step bumper. Front chrome bumper. Rear painted or chrome bumper. Full wheelcovers. Locking gas cap. Electric clock. Heavy-duty clutch. Air conditioning. Fabric box enclosure. Dump body. Vigilante V-8. E-Z Eye glass. Chrome grille. Fresh air heater and defroster. Selective drive hubs. Cigarette lighter. Courtesy lights. Parking brake warning light. Glove box light. Spare tire lock. Right outside rearview mirror. Power take-offs. Push-button transistor radio. Snowplow. Push plate. Power steering. Turbo Hydra-Matic. 4-speed manual trans. (standard with 8600 lb. GVW). Tonneau cover. Winches. Deluxe rear window. Wrecker. Custom cab. Rear Powr-Lok differential. Fuel tank skid plate. Mud flaps. Bucket seats and console (avail. with Custom Cab only), and Camper Package.

HISTORICAL FOOTNOTES: The 1967 Gladiator trucks were introduced in the fall of 1967.

1967 Jeep Gladiator J-3000 Townside

1968 GLADIATOR

The Thriftside models were dropped from the J-3500, J-3600 and J-3700 series.

I.D. DATA: The serial number was located on the left-hand hinge pillar. The first four digits indicated the model as follows: J-2500: 2406W17 or 2406WS-202456 and up; J-2600: 2406X17 or 2406XS-20257 and up; J-2700: 2406Y17 or 2406Y or 2406YS-201297 and up; J-2800: 2406Z17 or 2406Z or 2406ZS-20020 and up; J-3500: 3406W17 or 3406WS-201022; J-3600: 3406X17 or 3406XS-200669; J-3700: 3406Y17 or 3406Y or 3406YS-200725; J-3800: 3406Z17 or 3406Z or 3406ZS-200150 and up.

Model Number	Body Type	Factory Price	GVW	Shipping Weight	Prod. Total
J-2000, 120 in. wheelbase. (J-2500 & J-2600: 1/2 ton; J-2700: 3/4 ton; Series J2800 1 ton)					
J-2500	Chassis/Cab	$3119	5000	3152	—
J-2500	Pickup Thriftside	$3225	5000	3447	—
J-2500	Pickup Townside	$3253	5000	3555	—
J-2600	Chassis/Cab	$3240	6000	3293	—
J-2600	Pickup Thriftside	$3345	6000	3588	—
J-2600	Pickup Townside	$3373	6000	3696	—
J-2600	Stake Platform	$3560	6000	3949	—
J-2700	Chassis/Cab	$3404	7000	3380	—
J-2700	Pickup Thriftside	$3510	7000	3675	—
J-2700	Pickup Townside	$3538	7000	3785	—
J-2700	Stake Platform	$3725	7000	4036	—
J-2800	Chassis/Cab	$3996	8600	3813	—
J-2800	Stake Platform	$4411	8600	4558	—
J-3000, 126 in. wheelbase. (J-3500 & J-3600: 1/2 ton; J-3700: 3/4 ton; Series J-3800 1 ton)					
J-3500	Chassis/Cab	$3138	5000	3176	—
J-3500	Pickup Townside	$3286	5000	3604	—
J-3600	Chassis/Cab	$3258	6000	3314	—
J-3600	Pickup Townside	$3407	6000	3742	—
J-3600	Stake Platform	$3614	6000	4018	—
J-3700	Chassis/Cab	$3423	7000	3401	—
J-3700	Pickup Townside	$3571	7000	3829	—
J-3700	Stake Platform	$3778	7000	4105	—
J-3800	Chassis/Cab	$3938	8600	3790	—
J-3800	Stake Platform	$4353	8600	4588	—

STANDARD ENGINE: Engine Type: OHV, L-6. Cast iron block and cylinder head. Bore x Stroke: 3.75 in. x 3.50 in. Lifters: Hydraulic. Number of main bearings-7. Fuel Induction: 1 bbl. Carter Type RTBS or Holley model 1931C-3705. Compression Ratio: 8.5:1. Displacement: 232 cu. in. (3.80 liters). Horsepower: 145 @ 4300 rpm. Torque: 215 lb.-ft. @ 1600 rpm. Oil refill capacity: 5 qt. with filter change. Fuel Requirements: Regular.

OPTIONAL ENGINE: Engine Type: OHV, "Vigilante" V-8. Cast iron block and cylinder head. Bore x Stroke: 4.00 in. x 3.25 in. Lifters: Hydraulic. Number of main bearings-4. Fuel Induction: 2 bbl. downdraft carburetor. Compression Ratio: 8.7:1. Displacement: 327 cu. in. (5.35 liters). Horsepower: 250 @ 4700 rpm. Torque: Net: 340 lb.-ft. @ 2600 rpm. Oil refill capacity: 5 qt. with filter change. Fuel Requirements: Regular.

CHASSIS FEATURES: Separate body and frame. Deep web frame, wide flange, lightweight pressed steel with five cross members.

SUSPENSION AND RUNNING GEAR: Front Suspension: Multi-Leaf semi-elliptical springs, size varies with GVW rating. Hydraulic double-action shock absorbers: 13.0 in. on solid front axle, 12.375 in. dia. for torsion bar suspension. Rear Suspension: Semi-elliptical multi-leaf springs with anti-windup top half spring, hydraulic double-action shock absorbers. Optional:

6 leaf semi-elliptical springs. Front Axle Type and Capacity: Dana model 44F, 3000 lb. capacity. Rear Axle Type and Capacity: Dana model 44 semi-floating. Optional: Dana model 70 full-floating. Optional: Powr-Lok differential.

Final Drive Ratio:

J-2000 and J-3000:		Transmission	
Vigilante V-8	3-spd.	4-spd.	Auto
5000 lb. GVW:	3.92:1	3.92:1	3.54:1
	4.27:1*	4.27:1*	3.92:1
6000 lb. GVW:	4.091	4.09:1	4.09:1
	4.27:1*	4.27:1*	4.27:1*
7000 lb. GVW:	4.09:1	4.09:1	4.09:1
	4.27:1*	4.27:1*	
8600 lb. GVW:	N.A.	4.88:1	N.A.

* Optional at no extra cost.

J-2000 and J-3000:		Transmission	
High-Torque L-6	3-spd.	4-spd.	Auto
5000 lb. GVW:	4.27:1	4.27:1	4.27:1
	4.88:1*	4.88:1*	4.88:1*
6000 lb. GVW:	4.27:1	4.27:1	4.27:1
	4.88:1*	4.88:1*	4.88:1*
7000 lb. GVW:	4.88:1	4.88:1	4.27:1
8600 lb. GVW:	N.A.	4.88:1	N.A.

* Optional at no extra cost.

Transfer Case: All models: 2-speed Spicer model 20, 2.03:1, 1.0:1. Brakes: Type: Hydraulic, front and rear drums. Dimensions: Front: 11.0 in. x 2.00 in. front and rear. Total effective area: 161.16 sq. in. Optional: Power brakes. Models with auto. trans. had a Bendix system with a wide and low-positioned pedal. Models with manual trans. have a Midland system with a narrower and lower positioned pedal. Wheels: 15 x 5.5 K: Trucks with GVW below 6600 lb., trucks with 6600 lb. GVW: 16 x 5.00K, trucks with 7600 lb. GVW rating: 16 6L, dual 6 x 6.00L rear wheels on J-3800 with 8600 GVW lb. rating. Tires: J-2500: 8.15 x 15, J-2600: 7.00 x16, J-3500: 8.15 x 15, J-3600: 7.00 x 16, J-2700: 7.50 x 16, J-3700: 7.50 x 16, J-2800: 7.00 x16, J-3800: 7.00 x 16. Steering: Ross cam lever. Ratio: 24:1. Turns Lock-to-Lock: 5.6. Turning Circle: J-2600: 49.5 ft., J-3600: 52.5 ft. Optional: Saginaw power steering. Ratios: 24:1. Standard: Transmission: 3-spd. man. trans. except for vehicles with 8600 lb. GVW which have 4-spd. manual standard. Optional: 3-spd. Turbo Hydra-Matic. Not avail. for 8600 lb. GVW vehicles. Optional: 4-spd. Borg-Warner model T-98A 4-speed trans. Ratios: 6.398:1, 3.092:1, 1.686:1, 1.00:1. Clutch: Borg & Beck single dry plate.

VEHICLE DIMENSIONS: Wheelbase: J-2000: 120 in.; J-3000: 126 in. Overall Length: J-2000: 183.75 in.; J-3000: 195.75 in. Front/Rear Tread: J-2000: 63.5/63.5 in.; J-3000: 63.75/63.75 in. Overall Height: 71.0 in. Width: 75.93 in. Tailgate: Width and Height: Townside: 55.75 in. x 20.20 in. Thriftside: 48.60 in. x 13.75 in. Ground Clearance: Lowest point: 8.75 in. Load space: Townside: J-2000-Townside: 84.34 in. x 71.00 in. x 20.20 in. Thriftside: 84.34 in. x 55 in. x 13.75 in. J-3000-Townside: 96.34 in. x 71.00 in. x 20.20 in. Front legroom: 45.25 in.

CAPACITIES: Fuel Tank: 18.0 gal.

ACCOMMODATIONS: Seating Capacity: Three.

INSTRUMENTATION: Speedometer, odometer, gauges for oil pressure, engine coolant temperature and battery charge, transfer case indicator lights.

OPTIONS: Heavy-duty alternator. Pintle hook. Heavy-duty battery. Power brakes. Transmission brake (standard with 8600 lb. GVW). Step bumper. Front chrome bumper. Rear painted or chrome bumper. Full wheelcovers. Locking gas cap. Electric clock. Heavy-duty clutch. Air conditioning. Fabric box enclosure. Dump body. Vigilante V-8. E-Z Eye glass. Chrome grille. Fresh air heater and defroster. Selective drive hubs. Cigarette lighter. Courtesy lights. Parking brake warning light. Glove box light. Spare tire lock. Right outside rearview mirror. Power take-offs. Push-button transistor radio. Snowplow. Push plate. Power steering. Turbo Hydra-Matic. 4-speed manual trans. (standard with 8600 lb. GVW). Tonneau cover. Winches. Deluxe rear window. Wrecker. Custom cab. Rear Powr-Lok differential. Fuel tank skid plate. Mud flaps. Bucket seats and console (avail. with custom cab only), and Camper Package.

HISTORICAL FOOTNOTES: The 1968 Gladiator trucks were introduced in the fall of 1967.

1969 GLADIATOR

The latest Gladiators, like the Wagoneer models were offered with the 350 cu. in. Dauntless V-8 as well as a standard 3-speed all-synchromesh manual transmission for 1969. The standard interior was of all-vinyl trim in a rawhide color. The interior components of the custom cab option consisted of deluxe trim, color-keyed instrument panel, cigarette lighter, dual padded sun visors and harmonizing door panels. Comprising the exterior features were: stainless steel rear cab and windshield moldings, chrome front bumper, and chrome hubcaps (available on 5,000 GVW models only). The custom cab interior was available in rawhide, charcoal or marlin blue. A vinyl bucket seat option for the custom cab was offered in charcoal. It included a center seat back that could be folded down to function as a console. A map case was located beneath the center seat. Not offered for 1969 were the J-2800 models. Late in the model year the J-3800 models converted to a 132 in. wheelbase.

I.D. DATA: The serial number was located on the left-hand hinge pillar. The V.I.N. indicated the model as follows: J-2500: 2406W17-202937 and up; J-2600: 2406X17-202823 and up; J-2700: 2406Y17-203184 and up; J-3500: 3406W17-201152 and up; J-3600: 3406X17-200866 and up; J-3700: 3406Y17-200848 and up. The Vehicle Code for the J-2000 line consisted of the 2406W model with a 5000 lb. GVW. The Vehicle Code for this J-3000 line consisted of the 3508W with a 5000 lb. GVW, the 3408X with a 6000 lb. GVW, the 3408Y with a 7000 lb. GVW and the 3407Z with a 8000 lb. GVW. All model were available with either a 6-cyl. or V-8 engine.

Model Number	Body Type	Factory Price	GVW	Shipping Weight	Prod. Total
J-2000, 120 in. wheelbase. (J-2500 & J-2600: 1/2 ton; J-2700: 3/4 ton; Series J2800 1 ton)					
J-2500	Chassis/Cab	$3243	5000	3152	—
J-2500	Pickup Thriftside	$3348	5000	3447	—
J-2500	Pickup Townside	$3376	5000	3555	—
J-2600	Chassis/Cab	$3363	6000	3293	—
J-2600	Pickup Thriftside	$3469	6000	3588	—
J-2600	Pickup Townside	$3497	6000	3696	—
J-2600	Stake Platform	$3684	6000	3949	—
J-2700	Chassis/Cab	$3528	7000	3380	—
J-2700	Pickup Thriftside	$3633	7000	3675	—
J-2700	Pickup Townside	$3661	7000	3785	—
J-2700	Stake Platform	$3849	7000	4036	—
J-3000, 126 in. wheelbase except for J-3800 which had a 132 in. wheelbase. (J-3500 & J-3600: 1/2 ton; J-3700: 3/4 ton; Series J-3800 1 ton)					
J-3500	Chassis/Cab	$3261	5000	3176	—
J-3500	Pickup Townside	$3410	5000	3604	—
J-3600	Chassis/Cab	$3382	6000	3314	—
J-3600	Pickup Townside	$3530	6000	3742	—
J-3600	Stake Platform	$3737	6000	4018	—
J-3700	Chassis/Cab	$3546	7000	3401	—
J-3700	Pickup Townside	$3695	7000	3829	—
J-3700	Stake Platform	$3902	7000	4105	—
J-3800	Chassis/Cab	$4148	8000	3792	—

STANDARD ENGINE: Engine Type: OHV, In-line-6. Cast iron block and cylinder head. Bore x Stroke: 3.75 in. x 3.50 in. Lifters: Hydraulic. Number of main bearings-7. Fuel Induction: 1-bbl. Carter Type RTBS or Holley model 1931C-3705. Compression Ratio: 8.5:1. Displacement: 232 cu. in. (3.8 liters). Horsepower: 145 @ 4300 rpm. Torque: 215 lb.-ft. @ 1600 rpm. Oil refill capacity: 5 qt. with filter change. Fuel Requirements: Regular.

OPTIONAL ENGINE: Engine Type: OHV, "Dauntless" V-8. Cast iron block and cylinder head. Bore x Stroke: 3.80 in. x 3.85 in. Lifters: Hydraulic. Number of main bearings-5. Fuel Induction: 2-bbl. carburetor, barrel sizes: 1.437 in. Compression Ratio: 9.0:1. Displacement: 350 cu. in. (5.73 liters). Horsepower: 230 @ 4400 rpm. Torque: Net: 350 lb.-ft. @ 2400 rpm. Oil refill capacity: 5 qt. with filter change. Fuel Requirements: Regular.

CHASSIS FEATURES: Separate body and frame. Deep web frame, wide flange, lightweight pressed steel with five cross members.

SUSPENSION AND RUNNING GEAR: Front Suspension: 2406W, 3408W with 6-cyl. engine: 6-leaf, semi-elliptical springs, 44 in. x 2.00 in. Spring rate: 216 lb./in. Capacity at Pad: 1275 lb. Capacity at ground: 1470 lb. 2406W, 3408W with V-8: 5000 lb. GVW: 6-leaf, semi-elliptical springs, 44 in. x 2.00 in. Spring rate: 216 lb./in. Capacity at Pad: 1390 lb. Capacity at ground: 1585 lb. 3408X, 3408Y, 3407Z with 6-cyl. engine: 8-leaf, semi-elliptical springs, 44 in. x 2.00 in. Spring rate: 240 lb./in. Capacity at pad: 1330 lb. Capacity at ground: 1575 lb. 3408X, 3408Y with V-8 engine: 8-leaf, semi-elliptical springs, 44 in. x 2.00 in. Spring rate: 240 lb./in. Capacity at pad: 1561 lb. Capacity at ground: 1826 lb. Optional: 2406W, 3408W, 3408X: 6-leaf, semi-elliptical springs, 44 in. x 2.00 in. Spring rate: 271 lb./in. Capacity at pad: 1380 lb. Capacity at ground: 1575 lb. Rear Suspension: 2406W: 8 semi-elliptical leaf springs, 52 in. x 2.50 in. Spring rate: 160-295 lb./in. Capacity at pad: 1500 lb. Capacity at ground: 1680 lb. 3408W: 6 semi-elliptical leaf springs, 57 in. x 2.50 in. Spring rate: 185-375 lb./in. Capacity at pad: 1720 lb. Capacity at ground: 1900 lb. 3408X: 6-semi-elliptical leaf springs, 52 in. x 2.50 in. Spring rate: 185-375 lb./in. Capacity at pad: 2060 lb. Capacity at ground: 2285 lb. 3408Y: 7 semi-elliptical leaf springs, 52 in. x 2.60 in. Spring rate: 375 lb./in. Capacity at pad: 2450 lb. Capacity at ground: 2700 lb. Optional: 2406W: 10 semi-elliptical leaf springs, 52 in. x 2.50 in. Spring rate: 238-400 lb./in. Capacity at pad: 2620 lb. Capacity at ground: 2800 lb. 3408W: 7 semi-elliptical leaf springs, 57 in. x 2.50 in. Spring rate: 270-450 lb./in. Capacity at pad: 2735 lb. Capacity at ground: 2965 lb. 3408X: 7 semi-elliptical leaf springs, 52 in. x 2.50 in. Spring rate: 240-432 lb./in. Capacity at pad: 2735 lb. Capacity at ground: 2965 lb. 3408Y: 7 semi-elliptical leaf springs, 52 in. x 2.50 in. Spring rate: 270-450 lb./in. Capacity at pad: 2735 lb. Capacity at ground: 2975 lb. Front Axle Type and Capacity: Spicer 44-1F, 3000 lb. capacity. Rear Axle Type and Capacity: 2406W, 3408W: Spicer model 44. Capacity: 3500 lb. 3408X, 3408Y: Spicer model 60-2. Capacity: 5000 lb. Optional: Powr-Lok differential.

Final Drive Ratio:

Hi-Torque 6 cyl.		Transmission	
	3-spd.	4-spd.	Auto
2406W	4.09:1	3.92:1	3.54:1
	4.88:1*	4.88:1*	4.88:1
3408W	4.09:1	4.09:1	4.09:1
	4.89:1*	4.89:1*	4.89:1*
3408X, 3408Y	4.10:1	4.10:1	4.10:1
	4.89:1*	4.89:1*	4.89:1*

* Optional at no extra cost.

Dauntless V-8		Transmission	
	3-spd.	4-spd.	Auto
2406W	4.09:1	3.92:1	3.54:1
	4.27:1*	4.27:1*	3.92:1*
3408W	4.09:1	4.09:1	4.09:1
	4.89:1*	4.89:1*	N.A.
3408X, 3408Y	4.10:1	4.10:1	4.10:1
	4.89:1*	4.89:1*	N.A.

* Optional at no extra cost.

Transfer Case: All models: 2-speed Dana model 20, 2.03:1, 1.0:1. Brakes: Type: Hydraulic, front and rear drums. Dimensions: Front: 11.0 in. x 2.00 in. front and rear. Total effective area: 161.16 sq. in. Vehicles with 7000 GVW: 12 in. x 2.00 in. front and rear, total effective lining: 176.0 sq. in. Optional: Power brakes. Wheels: Full drop center. Vehicles with 5000 lb. GVW: 15 x 5.5K; vehicles with 6000 lb. GVW: 16 x 6L; vehicles with 7000 lb. GVW: 16 x 6L. Tires: Vehicles with 5000 lb.GVW: 8.15 x 15, 4-ply; vehicles with 6000 lb. GVW: 7.00 x 16, 8-ply; vehicles with 7000 lb. GVW: 7.50 x 16, 8-ply. Optional: Other sizes available. Steering: Recirculating ball type. Ratio: 24:1. Turns Lock-to-Lock: 5.6. Turning Circle: J-2000: 49.5 ft., J-4000: 52.0 ft. Optional: Saginaw power steering. Ratios: 22.8:1. Standard: Transmission: 3408W, 3408X, 3408Y with 6-cyl. engine, and all models with V-8 engine: Warner T15A 3-speed manual. ratios: 2.997, 1.8332, 1.0:1. Reverse: 2.997:1. Optional: 4-speed Warner T18 4-speed manual. Ratios: 4.020, 3.092, 1.686, 1.00:1. Reverse: 7.439:1. Optional: 3-spd. Turbo Hydra-Matic 400 automatic transmission. Ratios: 2.4815, 1.4815, 1.0:1. Reverse: 2.0769:1. Clutch: V-8 models: 11 in. Single dry plate. Total lining area: 123.7 sq. in. 6-cyl. models: 10.0 in single dry plate. Total lining area: 106.8 sq. in. Optional: Heavy-duty clutch.

VEHICLE DIMENSIONS: Wheelbase: J-2000: 120 in.; J-3000: 126 in. J-3800 132 in. wheelbase. Overall Length: J-2000: 183.75 in.; J-3000: 195.75 in. J-3800: 205.64 in. Front/Rear Tread: J-2000: 63.5/63.5 in.; J-3000: 63.75 in. /63.75 in. Overall Height: 71.0 in. Width: 75.93 in. Front/Rear Overhang: J-2000 Townside: in./54.08 in. J-3000 Townside: in./51.08 in. J-2000 Thriftside: in./44.80 in. J-3000 Thriftside: in./50.86 in. Tailgate: Width and Height: Townside: 55.75 in. x 20.20 in. Thriftside: 48.60 in. x 13.75 in. Approach/Departure Degrees: 45/26 (27 for 4000).Ground Clearance: Lowest point: 8.75 in. Load space: Townside 7 ft.: 84.34 in. x 71 in. x 20.20 in. Thriftside 7 ft.: 84.34 in. x 48.60 in. x 15.60 in. Townside 8 ft.: 96.34 in. x 71.0 in. x 20.20 in. Front legroom: 45.25 in.

CAPACITIES: Fuel Tank: 18.0 gal. Coolant System: 6-cyl.: 9.5 qt., V-8: 15 qt.

ACCOMMODATIONS: Seating Capacity: Three.

INSTRUMENTATION: Speedometer, odometer, gauges for fuel level and engine coolant temperature, indicator lights for alternator charging and oil pressure, transfer case indicator lights.

OPTIONS: Dauntless V-8. 40 amp alternator. Drive line brake. Powr-Lok rear differential. Rear or bed mounted winch. Front mounted winch. Power take-off. Parking brake light indicator. E-Z Eye glass. 4-speed transmission. Chrome front bumper. Air conditioning. Spare tire lock. Dual horns. Heavy-duty clutch. Deluxe horn ring. Front mounted steel push plate. Rotary brooms. Spreaders. Utility service bodies. Trailer hitches. Helper springs. Step rear bumper. Tonneau cover (available only for Townside models). Convertible Pick-up Top (available only for Townside models). Turbo Hydra-Matic. Dump body (not available for 5000 or 6000 lb. GVW models). Power brakes. Power steering. Push button radio. Wrecker Package. Selective drive front hubs. Snowplows.

HISTORICAL FOOTNOTES: The 1969 Gladiators were introduced in the fall of 1968.

1970 GLADIATOR

The Gladiators were given their first significant styling change in 1970 when they adopted the vertical grille style found on Wagoneer models since 1966. New two-tone body color options were available on all Gladiators with the custom cab option. This format consisted of an upper body section painted champagne white, while the lower section could be finished in any of the other eight available color choices. The interior of the Custom Accessory Group was available in buckskin, charcoal or marlin blue. The interior features of the Custom Accessory Group option consisted of deluxe trim, color-keyed instrument panel, cigarette lighter, dual padded sun visors and woodgrained door panels. The Custom Accessory Group's exterior was identified by its stainless steel rear cab, door window frames and windshield molding, chrome front bumper and, on 5000 lb. GVW models only, chrome hubcaps.

Available in J-3800, J-4500 and J-4700 form was a longer, 132 in. wheelbase that had been phased in for the J-3800 in late 1969 and, for the J-3800, an 8000 pound GVW rating. The 8000 lb. GVW J-3800 was available as the first four-wheel drive truck specially built for Campers. It was capable of carrying a slide-in Camper weighing up to 2500 lbs. The 4-speed manual transmission was standard for the Camper Special. Standard equipment for the Gladiator trucks included these items: Oil filter, directional signals, seat belts with retractor boots, padded sun visors, padded instrument panel, outside left rearview mirror, 2-speed electric windshield wipers and washers, 4-way flasher, chrome grille, dual arm rests, heater and defroster and back-up lights. The exterior color selection consisted of sprucetip green metallic, president red, avocado mist metallic, champagne white, spring green, vintage gold metallic, burnished bronze metallic, island blue metallic and candlelight yellow. The two-tone scheme consisted of an upper body section painted champagne white with the lower selection available in any of the remaining standard colors.

Cab and Chassis

Townside
• **Classically Styled pick-up box** • **High capacity load area up to 44 sq. ft.** •
Small wheelhousings increase cargo space

1970 Jeep Gladiator cab and chassis

I.D. DATA: The serial number was located on the left-hand hinge pillar. The V.I.N. indicated the model as follows: J-2500: 2406W17-203892 and up; J-2600: 2406X17-204863 and up; J-2700: 2406Y17-203592 and up; J-3500: 3406W17-203526 and up; J-3600: 3406X17-201326 and up; J-3700: 3406Y17-2201172 and up; J-3800: 3407Z19-300005 and up. J-4500: 3408W17-201374 and up; J-4600: 3408X17-201190; J-4700: 3408Y17-201421.

Model Number	Body Type	Factory Price	GVW	Shipping Weight	Prod. Total
J-2000, 120 in. wheelbase. (J-2500 & J-2600: 1/2 ton; J-2700: 3/4 ton; Series J2800 1 ton)					
J-2500	Chassis/Cab	$3361	5000	3152	—
J-2500	Pickup Thriftside	$3488	5000	3447	—
J-2500	Pickup Townside	$3516	5000	3555	—
J-2600	Chassis/Cab	$3483	6000	3293	—
J-2600	Pickup Thriftside	$3610	6000	3588	—
J-2600	Pickup Townside	$3638	6000	3696	—
J-2600	Stake Platform	$3804	6000	3949	—
J-2700	Chassis/Cab	$3649	7000	3380	—
J-2700	Pickup Thriftside	$3776	7000	3675	—
J-2700	Pickup Townside	$3804	7000	3783	—
J-2700	Stake Platform	$3970	7000	4036	—
J-3000, 126 in. wheelbase except for J-3800 which had a 132 in. wheelbase. (J-3500 & J-3600, 1/2 ton; J-3700: 3/4 ton, J-3800 -1 ton)					
J-3500	Chassis/Cab	$3381	5000	3176	—
J-3500	Pickup Townside	$3544	5000	3604	—
J-3600	Chassis/Cab	$3505	6000	3314	—
J-3600	Pickup Townside	$3667	6000	3742	—
J-3600	Stake Platform	$3860	6000	4018	—
J-3700	Chassis/Cab	$3668	7000	3401	—
J-3700	Pickup Townside	$3831	7000	3829	—
J-3700	Stake Platform	$4024	7000	4105	—
J-3800	Chassis/Cab	$4320*	8000	3792	—
J-4000, 132 in. wheelbase (J-4500 & J-4600: 1/2 ton; J-4700: 3/4 ton)					
J-4500	Chassis & Cab	$3381	5000	3130	—
J-4500	Pickup Townside	$3544	5000	3558	—
J-4600	Chassis & Cab	$3505	6000	3268	—
J-4600	Pickup Townside	$3668	6000	3696	—
J-4700	Chassis & Cab	$3831	7000	3355	—
J-4700	Pickup Townside	$3831	7000	3783	—
J-4800	Chassis & Cab	$4319	8000	—	—
J-4800	Pickup Townside	$4482	8000	3939	—
J-4800	Camper Pickup	$4482	8000	4367	—

STANDARD ENGINE: All models except J-4800: Engine Type: OHV, In-line-6. Cast iron block and cylinder head. Bore x Stroke: 3.75 in. x 3.50 in. Lifters: Hydraulic. Number of main bearings-7. Fuel Induction: 1 bbl. Carter Type RTBS or Holley model 1931C-3705. Barrel size: 1.562 in. Compression Ratio: 8.5:1. Displacement: 232 cu. in. (3.8 liters). Horsepower: 145 @ 4300 rpm. Torque: 215 lb.-ft. @ 1600 rpm. Oil refill capacity: 5 qt. with filter change. Fuel Requirements: Regular.

OPTIONAL ENGINE: (Standard J-4800): Engine Type: OHV, "Dauntless" V-8. Cast iron block and cylinder head. Bore x Stroke: 3.80 in. x 3.85 in. Lifters: Hydraulic. Number of main bearings-5. Fuel Induction: 2 bbl. carburetor, barrel sizes: 1.437 in. Compression Ratio: 9.0:1. Displacement: 350 cu. in. (5.73 liters). Horsepower: 230 @ 4400 rpm. Torque: Net: 350 lb.-ft. @ 2400 rpm. Oil refill capacity: 5 qt. with filter change. Fuel Requirements: Regular.

CHASSIS FEATURES: Separate body and frame. Deep web frame, wide flange, lightweight pressed steel with five cross members. Dimensions: 2406W: 183.75 in. x 44.50 in. Section modulus: 3.610 in. 3. 3408W: 195.75 in. x 44.50 in. Section modulus: 3.610 in. 3. 3408X and 3408Y 195.75 in. x 44.50 in. Section modulus: 7.530 in. 3. 3407Z: 195.75 in. x 44.50 in. Section modulus: 8.000 in. 3.

SUSPENSION AND RUNNING GEAR: Front Suspension: 2406W, 3408W with 6-cyl. engine: 6-leaf, semi-elliptical springs, 44 in. x 2.00 in. Spring rate: 216 lb./in. Capacity at Pad: 1275 lb. Capacity at ground: 1470 lb. 2406W, 3408W with V-8: 5000 lb. GVW: 6-leaf, semi-elliptical springs, 44 in. x 2.00 in. Spring rate: 216 lb./in. Capacity at Pad: 1390 lb. Capacity at ground: 1585 lb. 3408X, 3408Y with 6-cyl. engine: 8-leaf, semi-elliptical springs, 44 in. x 2.00 in. Spring rate: 240 lb./in. Capacity at pad: 1330 lb. Capacity at ground: 1575 lb. 3408X, 3408Y, 3407Z with V-8 engine: 8-leaf, semi-elliptical springs, 44 in. x 2.00 in. Spring rate: 240 lb./in. Capacity at pad: 1561 lb. Capacity at ground: 1826 lb. Optional: 2406W, 3408W, 3408X: 6-leaf, semi-elliptical springs, 44 in. x 2.00 in. Spring rate: 271 lb./in. Capacity at pad: 1380 lb. Capacity at ground: 1575 lb. Rear Suspension: 2406W: 8 semi-elliptical leaf springs, 52 in. x 2.50 in. Spring rate: 160-295 lb./in. Capacity at pad: 1500 lb. Capacity at ground: 1680 lb. 3408W: 6-semi-elliptical leaf springs, 57 in. x 2.50 in. Spring rate: 185-375 lb./in. Capacity at pad: 1720 lb. Capacity at ground: 1900 lb. 3408X: 6 semi-elliptical leaf springs, 52 in. x 2.50 in. Spring rate: 185-375 lb./in. Capacity at pad: 2060 lb. Capacity at ground: 2285 lb. 3408Y: 7 semi-elliptical leaf springs, 52 in. x 2.60 in. Spring rate: 375 lb./in. Capacity at pad: 2450 lb. Capacity at ground: 2700 lb. 3407Z: 7 semi-elliptical leaf springs, 52 in. x 2.60 in. Spring rate: 270-450 lb./ in. Capacity at pad: 2735 lb. Capacity at ground: 3085 lb. Optional: 2406W: 10 semi-elliptical leaf springs, 52 in. x 2.50 in. Spring rate: 238-400 lb./in. Capacity at pad: 2620 lb. Capacity at ground: 2800 lb. 3408W: 7 semi-elliptical leaf springs, 57 in. x 2.50 in. Spring rate: 270-450 lb./in. Capacity at pad: 2735 lb. Capacity at ground: 2965 lb. 3408X: 7 semi-elliptical leaf springs, 52 in. x 2.50 in. Spring rate: 240-432 lb./in. Capacity at pad: 2735 lb. Capacity at ground: 2965 lb. 3408Y: 7 semi-elliptical leaf springs, 52 in. x 2.50 in. Spring rate: 270-450 lb./ in. Capacity at pad: 2735 lb. Capacity at ground: 2975 lb. Front Axle Type and Capacity: Spicer 44-1F, 3000 lb. capacity. Rear Axle Type and Capacity: 2406W, 3408W: Spicer model 44. Capacity: 3500 lb. 3408X, 3408Y: Spicer model 60-2. Capacity: 5000 lb. 3407Z: Spicer 60FF. Capacity: 5000 lb. Optional: Powr-Lok differential.

Final Drive Ratio:

Hi-Torque 6 cyl.	Transmission		
	3-spd.	4-spd.	Auto
2406W	4.09:1 4.88:1*	3.92:1 4.88:1*	3.54:1 4.88:1
3408W	4.09:1 4.89:1*	4.09:1 4.89:1*	4.09:1 4.89:1*
3408X, 3408Y	4.10:1 4.89:1*	4.10:1 4.89:1*	4.10:1 4.89:1*

* Optional at no extra cost.

Dauntless V-8	Transmission		
	3-spd.	4-spd.	Auto
2406W	4.09:1 4.27:1*	3.92:1 4.27:1*	3.54:1 3.92:1*
3408W	4.09:1 4.89:1*	4.09:1 4.89:1*	4.09:1 N.A.
3408X, 3408Y	4.10:1 4.89:1*	4.10:1 4.89:1*	4.10:1 N.A.
3407Z	4.10:1	4.10:1	4.10:1

* Optional at no extra cost.

Transfer Case: All models: 2-speed Dana model 20, 2.03:1, 1.0:1. Brakes: Type: Hydraulic, front and rear drums. Dimensions: 2406W, 3408W: Front and rear: 11.0 in. x 2.00 in. Total effective area: 180.86 sq. in. 3408Y, 3408X: Front and rear: 12 in. x 2.00 in. Total effective area: 195.6 sq. in. 3407Z: 12.125 in. x 2.00 in. front and rear. Total effective area: 209.6 in. Optional: Power brakes. Wheels: Full drop center. 2406W and 3408W: 15 x 6K, 5 studs on 5.5 in. circle. 3408X and 3408Y: 16 x 6L, 5 studs on 5.5 in. circle. 3407Z: 16 x 5.5F, 8 studs on 6.5 in. circle. Tires: 2406W and 3408W: 8.55 x 15 in., 4-ply Suburbanite, black sidewall. 3408X and 3408Y: 7.00 x 16 in., 8-ply Super Hi-Miler, black sidewall. 3407Z: 7.50 x 16 in., 10-ply Super Hi-Miler, black sidewall. Optional: 2606W and 3408W: 8.55 x 15 in. 4-ply Power Cushion, black sidewall, 8.5 x 15 8-ply Suburbanite black sidewall, 7.00 x 15 in. 4-ply All-Service, black sidewall. 8.75 x 16.5 6-ply Super Hi-Miler, black sidewall (3408W only). 3408X: 7.00 x 16 in. 8 ply All-Service, black sidewall, 8.75 x 16.5 in. 6-ply Super Hi-Miler, black sidewall, 7.00 x 16 in. 8-ply Hi-Miler Xtra Grip, black sidewall. 3408Y: 7.00 x 16 in. All-Service 8-ply, black sidewall, 8.75 x 16.5 8-ply Super Hi-Miler, black sidewall, 7.50 x 16 in. 8-ply Hi-Miler Xtra Grip, black sidewall. Steering: Worm and Roller. Ratio: 24:1. Turns Lock-to-Lock: 5.6. Turning Circle: J-2000: 49.5 ft., J-4000: 52.0 ft. Optional: Saginaw power steering. Ratios: 22.8:1. Standard: Transmission: 3408W, 3408X, 3408Y with 6-cyl. engine, and all models with V-8 engine: Warner T15A 3-speed manual, all synchromesh. Ratios: 2.997, 1.8332, 1.0:1. Reverse: 2.997:1. Optional: 4-speed Warner T18 4-speed manual, synchromesh on top three gears (standard for 3407Z). Ratios: 4.020, 3.092, 1.686, 1.00:1. Reverse: 7.439:1. Optional: 3-spd. Turbo Hydra-Matic 400 automatic transmission. Ratios: 2.4815, 1.4815, 1.0:1. Reverse: 2.0769:1. Clutch: V-8 models: 11 in. Single dry plate. Total lining area: 123.7 sq. in. 6-cyl. models: 10.0 in single dry plate. Total lining area: 106.8 sq. in.

VEHICLE DIMENSIONS: Wheelbase: J-2000: 120 in.; J-4000: 132 in. Overall Length: J-2000: Cab and Chassis: 188.56 in.; J-4000: 200.56 in. Townside 7 ft. box (120 in. wheelbase): 193.64 in., Thriftside 7 ft. box (120 in. wheelbase), Townside 8 ft. box (132 in. wheelbase): 205.64 in. Front/Rear Tread: J-2000: 63.5/63.81 in.; J-4000: 63.87 in. /64.38 in. Overall Height: J-2000: 69.50 in.; J-4000: 3408W: 69.50 in., 3408X: 71.32 in., 3408Y and 3407Z: 72.37 in. Width: 78.90 in. Front/Rear Overhang: 28.56 in./40.0 in. Tailgate: Width and Height: Townside: 55.74 in. x 20.20 in. Thriftside: 48.60 in. x 15.60 in. Approach/Departure Degrees: 45/26 (27 for 4000). Ground Clearance: Lowest point: 8.75 in. Load space: Townside 7 ft.: 84.34 in. x 71 in. x 20.20 in. Thriftside 7 ft.: 84.34 in. x 48.60 in. x 15.60 in. Townside 8 ft.: 96.34 in. x 71.0 in. x 20.20 in. Front legroom: 45.00 in. Headroom: 38.25 in. Hip room: 60.62 in.

CAPACITIES: Fuel Tank: 20.0 gal. Coolant System: 6-cyl.: 9.5 qt., V-8: 15 qt.

ACCOMMODATIONS: Seating Capacity: Three.

INSTRUMENTATION: Speedometer, odometer, gauges for fuel level and engine coolant temperature, indicator lights for alternator charging and oil pressure, transfer case indicator lights,

OPTIONS AND PRICES: J-2000: 350 Dauntless V-8: $222.37. Tires (these tires became available on January 2, 1970 and thus some have different specifications that those previously noted): All J-200 and J-4500 3408W: 8.55 x 15 Power Cushion: $40.12. H-78 x 15 Polyglas Suburbanite: $68.06. H-78 x15 Polyglas Power Cushion white sidewall: $100.48. 8.55 x15 Suburbanite (4-ply): $40.16. 8.55 x15 Suburbanite (8-ply rating): $74.21. Locking rear differential: $49.43. J-4600 3408X 6000 lb. GVW: 7.00 x 16 Hi-Miler X-grip: $95.89. 7.00 x 16 Super Hi-Miler: $65.70. J-4700 3408Y 7000 lb. GVW: 7.50 x 16 Hi-Miler X-grip: $109.25. 7.50 x 16 Super Hi-Miler: 75.06. J-4800 3407Z: 7.50 x 16 10-ply Super Hi-Miler: $80.28. Custom Accessory Group: $101.32. Two-tone paint (with Custom Accessory Group): $67.55. Power brakes: 47.44. E-Z Eye glass (all windows): $26.27. Power steering: $134.03. 4-speed transmission: $105.18. Heavy-duty 70 amp battery: $7.34. Cigarette lighter: $3.43. Heavy-duty cooling system (V-8 only): $52.80. Air conditioning (heavy-duty cooling included with V-8): $463.59. Turbo Hydra-Matic with oil cooler: $280.43. Bucket seats with center console: $112.74. 55 amp alternator: $28.15. Dealer installed options: Push button radio: $71.06. Antenna: $6.41. Inside mirror: $5.67. Outside rearview mirror, cowl mount: $10.68. Outside rearview mirror, belt mount: $6.12. Cigarette lighter: $4.13. Power brakes: $82.00. Deluxe horn ring: $4.32. Courtesy lights: $8.97. Parking brake warning light: $5.38. Electric clock: $20.01. Glove box lock: $2.10.Window vent shades: $9.48. Spare tire lock: $3.98. Locking gas cap (with Thriftside body only): $2.72. Front mud flaps: $5.38. Pintle hook: $37.90.

HISTORICAL FOOTNOTES: The restyled 1970 Gladiators were introduced in the fall of 1969.

1971 GLADIATOR

In 1971, when all Gladiators were fitted with AMC engines, the J-4800 (model 3407Z) was equipped with a standard 360 cu. in. V-8 as standard equipment. The 258 cu. in. six was standard in all other models with the 304 and 360 cu. in. V-8's optional. Whereas a three-speed manual, all-synchromesh transmission with a floor-mounted shifter was standard for all other models, the J-4800 had a standard four-speed heavy-duty manual transmission. The Gladiator's standard equipment and color selection was unchanged from 1970. Eliminated from the Gladiator lineup were several series of trucks including the J-2600, J-2700, J-3500, J-3600, and J-3700.

I.D. DATA: The serial number was located on the left-hand hinge pillar. The V.I.N. indicated the model as follows: Vehicles produced prior to January 4, 1971: Cab & Chassis: J-2500: 2406W17-204,698 and up; J-4500: 3408W17-201,403; J-4600: 3408X17-201,498 and up; J-4700: 3408Y17-202,136. J-2500: 2406W19-302,423 and up; J-4500: 3408W19-302,561 and up; J-4600: 3408X19-304,680 and up; J-4700: 3408Y19-300,802 and up; J-4800: 3407Z19-300,692 and up. Vehicles produced after January 4, 1971: J-2500: 2406W17-400000 and up; J-3800: 3407Z19-300692 and up. J-4500: 3408W17-400000 and up; J-4600: 3408X17-40000 and up; J-4700: 3408Y17-40000 and up; J-4800: 3407Z19-60000 and up.

Model Number	Body Type	Factory Price	GVW	Shipping Weight	Prod. Total
J-2000, 120 in. wheelbase, 7 ft. box. (J-2500:1/2 ton)					
J-2500	Chassis/Cab	$3251	5000	3125	—
J-2500	Pickup Thriftside	$3406	5000	3420	—
J-2500	Pickup Townside	$3406	5000	3528	—
J-3000, 132 in. wheelbase, 8 ft. box. (J-3800: 3/4 ton)					
J-3800	Chassis/Cab	$4113	8000	3792	—
J-3800	Pickup Townside	$4264	8000	4220	—
J-4000, 132 in. wheelbase. 8 ft. box. (J-4500 & J-4600: 1/2 ton; J-4700 & J-4800: 3/4 ton)					
J-4500	Chassis & Cab	$3281	5000	3151	—
J-4500	Pickup Townside	$3443	5000	3579	—
J-4600	Chassis & Cab	$3405	6000	3289	—
J-4600	Pickup Townside	$3567	6000	3717	—
J-4700	Chassis & Cab	$3567	7000	3378	—
J-4700	Pickup Townside	$3729	7000	3806	—
J-4800	Chassis & Cab	$4218	8000	3866	—
J-4800	Pickup Townside	$4370	8000	4294	—

STANDARD ENGINE: All models except J-4800: Engine Type: OHV, In-line-6. Cast iron block and cylinder head. Bore x Stroke: 3.75 in. x 3.90 in. Lifters: Hydraulic. Number of main bearings-7. Fuel Induction: 1 bbl. Carter Type RTBS or Holley model 1931C-3705. Barrel size: 1.69 in. Compression Ratio: 8.5:1. Displacement: 258 cu. in. (4.22 liters). Horsepower: 150 @ 3800 rpm. Torque: 240 lb.-ft. @ 1800 rpm. Oil refill capacity: 5 qt. with filter change. Fuel Requirements: Regular.

OPTIONAL ENGINE: (Except for J-4800): Engine Type: OHV, V-8. Cast iron block and cylinder head. Bore x Stroke: 3.75 in. x 3.44 in. Lifters: Hydraulic. Number of main bearings-5. Fuel Induction: 2 bbl. carburetor. Barrel size: 1.562 in. Compression Ratio: 8.4:1. Displacement: 304 cu. in. (4.98 liters). Horsepower: Net: 210 @ 4400 rpm. Torque: Net: 300 lb.-ft. @ 2600 rpm. Oil refill capacity: 5 qt. with filter change. Fuel Requirements: Regular.

OPTIONAL ENGINE: (Standard J-4800): Engine Type: OHV, V-8. Cast iron block and cylinder head. Bore x Stroke: 4.08 in. x 3.44 in. Lifters: Hydraulic. Number of main bearings-5. Fuel Induction: 2 bbl. carburetor. Barrel size: 1.562 in. Compression Ratio: 8.5:1. Displacement: 360 cu. in. (5.89 liters) Horsepower: 245 @ 4400 rpm. Torque: 365 lb.-ft. @ 2600 rpm.

CHASSIS FEATURES: Separate body and frame. Deep web frame, wide flange, lightweight pressed steel with five cross members. Dimensions: 2406W: 183.75 in. x 44.50 in. Section modulus: 3.610 in. 3. 3408W: 195.75 in. x 44.50 in. Section modulus: 3.610 in. 3. 3408X and 3408Y 195.75 in. x 44.50 in. Section modulus: 7.530 in. 3. 3407Z: 195.75 in. x 44.50 in. Section modulus: 8.000 in. 3.

SUSPENSION AND RUNNING GEAR: Front Suspension: 2406W, 3408W with 6-cyl. engine: 6-leaf, semi-elliptical springs, 44. in. x 2.00 in. Spring rate: 216 lb./in. Capacity at Pad: 1275 lb. Capacity at ground: 1470 lb. 2406W, 3408W with V-8 engine: 6-leaf, semi-elliptical springs, 44 in. x 2.00 in. Spring rate: 216 lb./in. Capacity at Pad: 1390 lb. Capacity at ground: 1585 lb. 3408X, 3408Y with 6-cyl. engine: 8-leaf, semi-elliptical springs, 44 in. x 2.00 in. Spring rate: 240 lb./in. Capacity at pad: 1330 lb. Capacity at ground: 1575 lb. 3408X, 3408Y, 3407Z with V-8 engine: 8-leaf, semi-elliptical springs, 44 in. x 2.00 in. Spring rate: 240 lb./in. Capacity at pad: 1561 lb. Capacity at ground: 1826 lb. Optional: 2406W, 3408W: 8-leaf, semi-elliptical springs, 44 in. x 2.00 in. Spring rate: 240 lb./in. Capacity at pad: 1330 lb. Capacity at ground: 1575 lb. 2406W and 3408W with V-8 engine: 8-leaf, semi-elliptical springs, 44 in. x 2.00 in. Spring rate: 240 lb./in. Capacity at pad: 1561 lb. Capacity at ground: 1826 lb. Rear Suspension: 2406W: 8 semi-elliptical leaf springs, 52 in. x 2.50 in. Spring rate: 160-295 lb./in. Capacity at pad: 1500 lb. Capacity at ground: 1680 lb. 3408W: 6 semi-elliptical leaf springs, 57 in. x 2.50 in. Spring rate: 185-375 lb./in. Capacity at pad: 2060 lb. Capacity at ground: 2285 lb. 3408X: 6 semi-elliptical leaf springs, 52 in. x 2.50 in. Spring rate: 185-375 lb./in. Capacity at pad: 2060 lb. Capacity at ground: 2285 lb. 3408Y: 7 semi-elliptical leaf springs, 52 in. x 2.60 in. Spring rate: 375 lb./in. Capacity at pad: 2450 lb. Capacity at ground: 2700 lb. 3407Z: 7-semi-elliptical leaf springs, 52 in. x 2.60 in. Spring rate: 270-450 lb./in. Capacity at pad: 2735 lb. Capacity at ground: 3085 lb. Optional: 2406W: 10 semi-elliptical leaf springs, 52 in. x 2.50 in. Spring rate: 238-400 lb./in. Capacity at pad: 2620 lb. Capacity at ground: 2800 lb. 3408W: 7 semi-elliptical leaf springs, 57 in. x 2.50 in. Spring rate: 270-450 lb./in. Capacity at pad: 2735 lb. Capacity at ground: 2965 lb. 3408Y: 7 semi-elliptical leaf springs, 52 in. x 2.50 in. Spring rate: 270-450 lb./in. Capacity at pad: 2735 lb. Capacity at ground: 2975 lb. Front Axle Type and Capacity: Spicer 44-1F, 3000 lb. capacity. Rear Axle Type and Capacity: 2406W, 3408W: Spicer model 44. Capacity: 3500 lb. 3408X, 3408Y: Spicer model 60-2. Capacity: 5000 lb. 3407Z: Spicer 60FF. Capacity: 5000 lb. Optional: Powr-Lok differential.

Final Drive Ratio:

5000, 6000 and 7000 lb. GVW:

258 6-cyl.

	3-spd.	4-spd.	Auto. trans.
Standard:	4.09:1	4.09:1	4.09:1
Optional:	4.88:1	4.88:1	4.88:1

304 V-8

	3-spd.	4-spd.	Auto. trans.
Standard:	4.09:1	4.09:1	4.09:1
Optional:	4.88:1	4.88:1	N.A.

360 V-8

	3-spd.	4-spd.	Auto. trans.
Standard:	4.09:1	4.09:1	4.09:1
Optional:	4.88:1	4.88:1	N.A.

8000 lb. GVW:

360 V-8

	3-spd.	4-spd.	Auto. trans.
Standard:	N.A.	4.09:1	4.09:1
Optional:	—	N.A.	N.A.

Transfer Case: All models: 2-speed Dana model 20, 2.03:1, 1.0:1. Brakes: Type: Hydraulic, front and rear drums. Dimensions: 2406W, 3408W: Front: 11.0 in. x 2.00 in. front and rear. Total effective area: 180.0 sq. in. 3408Y, 3408X: 12 in. x 2.00 in. front and rear. Total effective area: 195.6 sq. in. 3407Z: 12.125 in. x 2.00 in. front and rear. Total effective area: 209.6 in. Optional: Power brakes. Wheels: Full drop center. 2406W and 3408W: 15 x 6K, 5 studs on 5.5 in. circle. 3408X and 3408Y: 16 x 6L, 5 studs on 5.5 in. circle. 3407Z: 16 x 5.5F, 8 studs on 6.5 in. circle. Tires: 2406W and 3408W: 8.25 x 15 in., 4-ply Power Cushion, black sidewall. 3408X: 7.00 x 16 in., 8-ply Super Hi-Miler, black sidewall. 3408Y: 7.50 x16, 8-ply Supreme Hi-Miler. 3407Z: 7.50 x 16 in., 10-ply Super Hi-Miler, black sidewall. Optional: 2606W and 3408W: 8.25 x 15 in. 4-ply Power Cushion, black sidewall, 8.55 x 15 in. 4-ply Power Cushion, black sidewall, 8.55 x 15 4-ply Suburbanite black sidewall (2406W only), 8.55 x 15 8-ply Suburbanite black sidewall (2406W only), 7.00 x 15 in., 8-ply Super Hi-Miler black sidewall (2406W only). 7.00 x 16, 8-ply Hi-Miler Xtra Grip black sidewall (2406W only), H-78 x 15 in. Polyglas Power Cushion white sidewall, H-78 x 15 in. Polyglas Suburbanite black sidewall.

3408X: 7.00 x 16 in. 8 ply All-Service, black sidewall, 7.00 x 16 in., 8-ply Hi-Miler Xtra Grip black sidewall. 3408Y: 7.50 x 16 in. All-Service 8-ply, black sidewall, 7.50 x 16 in. 8-ply Hi-Miler Xtra Grip, black sidewall. Steering: Left-hand drive models: Worm and roller. Right-hand drive models: Worm and Roller. Ratio: Recirculating ball and Worm and Roller: 24:1. Turns Lock-to-Lock: 5.6. Turning Circle: J-2000: 49.5 ft., J-4000: 52.0 ft. Optional: Saginaw power steering. Ratios: 22.8:1. Standard: Transmission: 3408W, 3408X, 3408Y with 6-cyl. engine, and all models with V-8 engine: Warner T15A 3-speed manual, all synchromesh. Ratios: 2.997, 1.8332, 1.0:1. Reverse: 2.997:1. Optional: 4-speed Warner T18 4-speed manual, synchromesh on top three gears (standard for 3407Z). Ratios: 4.020, 3.092, 1.686, 1.00:1. Reverse: 7.439:1. Optional: 3-spd. Turbo Hydra-Matic 400 automatic transmission. Ratios: 2.4815, 1.4815, 1.0:1. Reverse: 2.0769:1. Clutch: V-8 models: 11 in. Single dry plate. Total lining area: 123.7 sq. in. 6-cyl. models: 10.0 in single dry plate. Total lining area: 106.8 sq. in.

VEHICLE DIMENSIONS: Wheelbase: J-2000: 120 in.; J-4000: 132 in. Overall Length: J-2000: Cab and Chassis: 188.56 in.; J-4000: 200.56 in. Townside 7 ft. box (120 in. wheelbase): 193.64 in., Thriftside 7 ft. box (120 in. wheelbase), Townside 8 ft. box (132 in. wheelbase): 205.64 in. Front/Rear Tread: J-2000: 63.5/63.81 in.; J-4000: 63.87 in. /64.38 in. Overall Height: J-2000: 69.50 in.; J-4000: 69.50 in., 3408X: 71.32 in., 3408Y and 3407Z: 72.37 in. Width: 78.90 in. Front/Rear Overhang: 28.56 in./40.0 in. Tailgate: Width and Height: Townside: 55.74 in. x 20.20 in. Thriftside: 48.60 in. x 15.60 in. Approach/Departure Degrees: 45/26 (27 for 4000). Ground Clearance: Lowest point: 8.75 in. Load space: Townside 7 ft.: 84.34 in. x 71 in. x 20.20 in. Thriftside 7 ft.: 84.34 in. x 48.60 in. x 15.60 in. Townside 8 ft.: 96.34 in. x 71.0 in. x 20.20 in. Front legroom: 45.00 in. Headroom: 38.25 in. Hip room: 60.62 in.

CAPACITIES: Fuel Tank: 20.0 gal. Coolant System: 6-cyl.: 9.5 qt., V-8: 15 qt.

ACCOMMODATIONS: Seating Capacity: Three.

INSTRUMENTATION: Speedometer, odometer, gauges for fuel level and engine coolant temperature, indicator lights for alternator charging and oil pressure, transfer case indicator lights.

OPTIONS AND PRICES: 304 V-8: $173.55. 360 V-8: $222.50. 4-spd. manual trans.: $112.45. Turbo Hydra-Matic: $280.45. Optional axle ratios: $12.95. Rear Trac-Lok differential: $62.70. Power brakes: $47.45. Power steering: $150.80. AM radio with antenna: $73.85. Cigarette lighter: $6.65. Tinted glass: $26.20. Air conditioning (V-8 only, includes heavy-duty cooling system): $464.90. Custom Cab: $101.25. Heavy-duty battery: $11.95. 55 amp alternator: $28.20. Heavy-duty front and rear shock absorbers: $15.70. Heavy-duty front springs: $20.50. Heavy-duty rear springs: $20.50. Heavy-duty cooling system: $28.35. Tires: 7.50 x 16 8-ply Hi-Miler: $107.50. 7.50 x 16 7.00 x 16 8-ply Hi-Miler: Price varies from $51.35 to $230.40, depending on truck model ordered. 8.55 x 15 4-ply Power Cushion: $39.90. H78 x 15 Polyglas Suburbanite black sidewall: $65.65. H78 x 15 Polyglas Power Cushion white sidewall: $97.85. 8.55 x 15 4-ply Suburbanite: $39.90. 8.55 x 15 4-ply/8 ply rating Suburbanite: $73.65. 7.00 x 16 8-ply Hi-Miler: Prices varies from $64.90 to $166.05 depending on truck model ordered. 7.50 x 16 8-ply Super Hi-Miler: $74.15. 7.50 x 16 10-ply Super Hi-Miler: $79.30. Warn semi-automatic front hubs: $66.15. California fuel vaporization system: $37.85. Two-tone paint for standard cab: $83.65. Two-tone for Custom Cab: $57.95. Bucket seats with center armrest: $118.30.

HISTORICAL FOOTNOTES: The first of the AMC-built Jeep trucks were introduced in the fall of 1970.

1972 TRUCKS

The Gladiator name was dropped in 1972. Instead, AMC referred to these models simply as Jeep trucks. Appearance and design changes were very minor. Shared with the Wagoneer was a wider day/night mirror in place of the older day-only unit as well as a new Saginaw power steering pump. A new series of J-2600 models with a 6000 GVW were introduced. All J-3000 models were dropped.

1972 Jeep J4000 Townside pickup

I.D. DATA: The serial number was located on the left-hand hinge pillar. The V.I.N. indicated the model as follows: J-2500: 2406W; J-2600: 2406X; J-4600: 3408X; J-4700: 3408Y; J-4800: 3407Z.

Model Number	Body Type	Factory Price	GVW	Shipping Weight	Prod. Total
J-2000, 120 in. wheelbase, 7 ft. box. (J-2500: 1/2 ton)					
J-2500	Chassis/Cab	$3181	5000	3272	—
J-2500	Pickup Thriftside	$3328	5000	3567	—
J-2500	Pickup Townside	$3328	5000	3675	—
J-2600	Chassis & Cab	$3302	6000	3394	—
J-2600	Pickup Thriftside	$3449	6000	3689	—
J-2600	Pickup Townside	$3449	6000	3797	—

J-4000, 132 in. wheelbase. 8 ft. box. (J-4500 &J-4600: 1/2 ton; J-4700 & J-4800: 3/4 ton)

J-4500	Chassis & Cab	$3210	5000	3298	—
J-4500	Pickup Townside	$3365	5000	3726	—
J-4600	Chassis & Cab	$3331	6000	3436	—
J-4600	Pickup Townside	$3486	6000	3864	—
J-4700	Chassis & Cab	$3698	7000	3732	—
J-4700	Pickup Townside	$3853	7000	4160	—
J-4800	Chassis & Cab	$4107	8000	4013	—
J-4800	Pickup Townside	$4262	8000	4441	—

STANDARD ENGINE: All models except J-4800: Engine Type: OHV, In-line-6. Cast iron block and cylinder head. Bore x Stroke: 3.75 in. x 3.90 in. Lifters: Hydraulic. Number of main bearings-7. Fuel Induction: 1 bbl. Carter Type RTBS or Holley model 1931C-3705. Barrel size: 1.69 in. Compression Ratio: 8.0:1. Displacement: 258 cu. in. (4.22 liters). Horsepower: Net 110 @ 3600 rpm. Torque: Net 195 lb.-ft. @ 2000 rpm. Oil refill capacity: 5 qt. with filter change. Fuel Requirements: Regular.

OPTIONAL ENGINE: (Except for J-4800): Engine Type: OHV, V-8. Cast iron block and cylinder head. Bore x Stroke: 3.75 in. x 3.44 in. Lifters: Hydraulic. Number of main bearings-5. Fuel Induction: 2 bbl. carburetor. Barrel size: 1.562 in. Compression Ratio: 8.4:1. Displacement: 304 cu. in. (4.98 liters). Horsepower: Net: 150 @ 4200 rpm. Torque: Net: 245 lb.-ft. @ 2500 rpm. Oil refill capacity: 5 qt. with filter change. Fuel Requirements: Regular.

OPTIONAL ENGINE: (Standard J-4800: Engine Type: OHV, V-8. Cast iron block and cylinder head. Bore x Stroke: 4.08 in. x 3.44 in. Lifters: Hydraulic. Number of main bearings-5. Fuel Induction: 2 bbl. carburetor. Barrel size: 1.562 in. Compression Ratio: 8.5:1. Displacement: 360 cu. in. (5.89 liters). Horsepower: Net 175 @ 4000 rpm. Torque: Net 285 lb.-ft. @ 2400 rpm.

CHASSIS FEATURES: Separate body and frame. Deep web frame, wide flange, lightweight pressed steel with five cross members. Dimensions: 2406W: 183.75 in. x 44.50 in. Section modulus: 3.610 in. 3. 3408W: 195.75 in. x 44.50 in. Section modulus: 3.610 in. 3. 3408X and 3408Y 195.75 in. x 44.50 in. Section modulus: 7.530 in. 3. 3407Z: 195.75 in. x 44.50 in. Section modulus: 8.000 in. 3.

SUSPENSION AND RUNNING GEAR: Front Suspension: 2406W, 3408W with 6-cyl. engine: 6-leaf, semi-elliptical springs, 44 in. x 2.00 in. Spring rate: 216 lb./in. Capacity at Pad: 1275 lb. Capacity at ground: 1470 lb. 2406W, 3408W with V-8: 5000 lb. GVW: 6-leaf, semi-elliptical springs, 44 in. x 2.00 in. Spring rate: 216 lb./in. Capacity at Pad: 1390 lb. Capacity at ground: 1585 lb. 3408X, 3408Y with 6-cyl. engine: 8-leaf, semi-elliptical springs, 44 in. x 2.00 in. Spring rate: 240 lb./in. Capacity at pad: 1330 lb. Capacity at ground: 1575 lb. 3408X, 3408Y, 3407Z with V-8 engine: 8-leaf, semi-elliptical springs, 44 in. x 2.00 in. Spring rate: 240 lb./in. Capacity at pad: 1561 lb. Capacity at ground: 1826 lb. Optional: 2406W, 3408W: 8-leaf, semi-elliptical springs, 44 in. x 2.00 in. Spring rate: 240 lb./in. Capacity at pad: 1330 lb. Capacity at ground: 1575 lb. 2406W and 3408W with V-8 engine: 8-leaf, semi-elliptical springs, 44 in. x 2.00 in. Spring rate: 240 lb./in. Capacity at pad: 1561 lb. Capacity at ground: 1826 lb. Rear Suspension: 2406W: 8 semi-elliptical leaf springs, 52 in. x 2.50 in. Spring rate: 160-295 lb./in. Capacity at pad: 1500 lb. Capacity at ground: 1680 lb. 3408W: 6 semi-elliptical leaf springs, 57 in. x 2.50 in. Spring rate: 185-375 lb./in. Capacity at pad: 2060 lb. Capacity at ground: 2285 lb. 3408X: 6 semi-elliptical leaf springs, 52 in. x 2.50 in. Spring rate: 185-375 lb./in. Capacity at pad: 2060 lb. Capacity at ground: 2285 lb. 3408Y: 7 semi-elliptical leaf springs, 52 in. x 2.60 in. Spring rate: 375 lb./in. Capacity at pad: 2450 lb. Capacity at ground: 2700 lb. 3407Z: 7 semi-elliptical leaf springs, 52 in. x 2.60 in. Spring rate: 270-450 lb./in. Capacity at pad: 2735 lb. Capacity at ground: 3085 lb. Optional: 2406W: 10 semi-elliptical leaf springs, 52 in. x 2.50 in. Spring rate: 238-400 lb./in. Capacity at pad: 2620 lb. Capacity at ground: 2800 lb. 3408W: 7 semi-elliptical leaf springs, 57 in. x 2.50 in. Spring rate: 270-450 lb./in. Capacity at pad: 2735 lb. Capacity at ground: 2965 lb. 3408Y: 7 semi-elliptical leaf springs, 52 in. x 2.50 in. Spring rate: 270-450 lb./in. Capacity at pad: 2735 lb. Capacity at ground: 2975 lb. Front Axle Type and Capacity: Spicer 44-1F, 3000 lb. capacity. Rear Axle Type and Capacity: 2406W, 3408W: Spicer model 44. Capacity: 3500 lb. 3408X, 3408Y: Spicer model 60-2. Capacity: 5000 lb. 3407Z: Spicer 60FF. Capacity: 5000 lb. Optional: Powr-Lok differential.

Final Drive Ratio:

5000, 6000 and 7000 lb. GVW:

	3-spd.	4-spd.	Auto. trans.
258 6-cyl.			
Standard:	4.09:1	4.09:1	4.09:1
Optional:	4.88:1	4.88:1	4.88:1
304 V-8			
Standard:	4.09:1	4.09:1	4.09:1
Optional:	4.88:1	4.88:1	N.A.
360 V-8			
Standard:	4.09:1	4.09:1	4.09:1
Optional:	4.88:1	4.88:1	N.A.

8000 lb. GVW:

	3-spd.	4-spd.	Auto. trans.
360 V-8			
Standard:	N.A.	4.09:1	4.09:1
Optional:	—	N.A.	N.A.

Transfer Case: All models: 2-speed Dana model 20, 2.03:1, 1.0:1. Brakes: Type: Hydraulic, front and rear drums. Dimensions: 2406W, 3408W: Front: 11.0 in. x 2.00 in. front and rear. Total effective area: 180.0 sq. in. 3408Y, 3408X: 12 in. x 2.00 in. front and rear. Total effective area: 195.6 sq. in. 3407Z: 12.125 in. x 2.00 in. front and rear. Total effective area: 209.6 in. Optional: Power brakes. Wheels: Full drop center. 2406W and 3408W: 15 x 6K, 5 studs on 5.5 in. circle. 3408X and 3408Y: 16 x 6L, 5 studs on 5.5 in. circle. 3407Z: 16 x 5.5F, 8 studs on 6.5 in. circle. Tires: 2406W and 3408W: 8.25 x 15 in., 4-ply Power Cushion, black sidewall. 3408X: 7.00 x 16 in., 8-ply Super Hi-Miler, black sidewall. 3408Y: 7.50 x16, 8-ply Supreme Hi-Miler. 3407Z: 7.50 x 16 in., 10-ply Super Hi-Miler, black sidewall. Optional: 2606W and 3408W: 8.25 x 15 in. 4-ply Power Cushion, black sidewall, 8.55 x 15 in. 4-ply Power Cushion, black sidewall, 8.55 x 15 4-ply Suburbanite black sidewall (2406W only), 8.55 x 15 8-ply Suburbanite black sidewall (2406W only), 7.00 x 16 in., 8-ply Super Hi-Miler black sidewall (2406W only). 7.00 x 16, 8-ply Hi-Miler Xtra Grip black sidewall (2406W only), H-78 x 15 in. Polyglas Power Cushion white sidewall, H-78 x 15 in. Polyglas Suburbanite black sidewall. 3408X: 7.00 x 16 in. 8 ply All-Service, black sidewall, 7.00 x 16 in., 8-ply Hi-Miler Xtra Grip black sidewall. 3408Y: 7.50 x 16 in. All-Service 8-ply, black sidewall, 7.50 x 16 in. 8-ply Hi-Miler Xtra Grip, black sidewall. Steering: Left-hand drive models: Recirculating ball. Right-hand drive models: Worm and Roller. Ratio: Recirculating ball and Worm and Roller: 24:1. Turns Lock-to-Lock: 5.6. Turning Circle: J-2000: 49.5 ft., J-4000: 52.0 ft. Optional: Saginaw power steering. Ratios: 22.8:1. Standard: Transmission: 3408W, 3408X, 3408Y with 6-cyl. engine, and all models with V-8 engine: Warner T15A 3-speed manual, all synchromesh. Ratios: 2.997, 1.8332, 1.0:1. Reverse: 2.997:1. Optional: 4-speed Warner T18 4-speed manual, synchromesh on top three gears (standard for 3407Z). Ratios: 4.020, 3.092, 1.686, 1.00:1. Reverse: 7.439:1. Optional: 3-spd. Turbo Hydra-Matic 400 automatic transmission. Ratios: 2.4815, 1.4815, 1.0:1. Reverse: 2.0769:1. Clutch: V-8 models: 11 in. Single dry plate. Total lining area: 123.7 sq. in. 6-cyl. models: 10.0 in single dry plate. Total lining area: 106.8 sq. in.

VEHICLE DIMENSIONS: Wheelbase: J-2000: 120 in.; J-4000: 132 in. Overall Length: J-2000: Cab and Chassis: 188.56 in.; J-4000: 200.56 in. Townside 7 ft. box (120 in. wheelbase): 193.64 in., Thriftside 7 ft. box (120 in. wheelbase), Townside 8 ft. box (132 in. wheelbase): 205.64 in. Front/Rear Tread: J-2000: 63.5/63.81 in.; J-4000: 63.87 in. /64.38 in. Overall Height: J-2000: 69.50 in.; J-4000: 3408W: 69.50 in., 3408X: 71.32 in., 3408Y and 3407Z: 72.37 in. Width: 78.90 in. Front/Rear Overhang: 28.56 in./40.0 in. Tailgate: Width and Height: Townside: 55.74 in. x 20.20 in. Thriftside: 48.60 in. x 15.60 in. Approach/Departure Degrees: 45/26 (27 for 4000). Ground Clearance: Lowest point: 8.75 in. Load space: Townside 7 ft.: 84.34 in. x 71 in. x 20.20 in. Thriftside 7 ft.: 84.34 in. x 48.60 in. x 15.60 in. Townside 8 ft.: 96.34 in. x 71.0 in. x 20.20 in. Front legroom: 45.00 in. Headroom: 38.25 in. Hip room: 60.62 in.

CAPACITIES: Fuel Tank: 20.0 gal. Coolant System: 6-cyl.: 9.5 qt., V-8: 15 qt.

ACCOMMODATIONS: Seating Capacity: Three.

INSTRUMENTATION: Speedometer, odometer, gauges for fuel level and engine coolant temperature, indicator lights for alternator charging and oil pressure, transfer case indicator lights.

OPTIONS AND PRICES: Prices of popular options for 1972 were as follows: 304 cid V-8 (2-bbl. carb.): $165. 360 cid V-8 (2 bbl. carb.): $223. Automatic transmission: $280 ($161.75: J-4000). Air conditioning: $464.90. Power brakes: $47.45. Power steering: $150.80. Free-running front hubs: $66. AM radio and antenna: $73.85. E-Z Eye glass: $26.20. Auxiliary fuel tank: $79.05. Brake warning light: $6.65. Custom Trim Package: $99.40. Bucket seats with center armrest: $118.30. Two-tone exterior paint: $57.95. Powr-Lok rear differential: $62.70. 7.50 x 16-109-ply Super-Hi Miler tires: $79.30.

HISTORICAL FOOTNOTES: This was a year of transition in which the J-truck's original design began to exhibit the influence of American Motors.

1973 TRUCKS

Along with the other Jeep products, the 1973 model trucks reflected the impact of American Motors' redesign efforts. Leading the list of changes was Quadra-Trac which was available in limited quantity for the trucks during the model year. As with the Wagoneer, the Quadra-Trac equipped Jeep truck was powered by the 360 cu. in. V-8 and used the Turbo Hydra-Matic transmission. Models with manual transmission had a new mechanical clutch linkage in place of the cables used on earlier models. The new arrangement provided easier operation, required less maintenance and had a longer service life. Additional refinements included new higher quality wiring, upgraded standard and optional 15 in. passenger-type tires, more durable extended-life front axle and prop shaft joints, and an upgraded exhaust system.

The Townside models had a redesigned tail/back-up light assembly. Both the woodgrain trim and body side moldings were new for 1973. In addition, the trucks now used new double-wall side panels on their pickup beds, a wider by nearly three inches tailgate that opened with one hand and had new folding support straps in place of the previously used chains, and a completely new instrument panel. This last item was shared with the Wagoneer and featured easier-to-read circular gauges for all instruments including oil pressure and ammeter, and increased padding. Park brake and brake failure warning lights were standard. The dash, steering column and new floor mats were all color-coordinated to create what Jeep depicted as a "car-like interior." The color-keyed vinyl floor mat replaced the black rubber mats previously used for the standard truck cab. The crash pad was redesigned. A new energy-absorbing steering column with anti-theft ignition, steering lock and transmission lock was introduced as was a new 16 in. x 15.5 in. steering wheel with pad. Added to the optional Custom Cab Package were these items: Woodgrain cluster trim, glove box door light, courtesy lights and bright overlays for the door armrests. The bucket seat option for the custom cab had Houndstooth check fabric inserts in place of the Scorpio fabric insert used in 1972. A new manual lane-changer feature was incorporated into the turn signals. A new ball bearing ashtray was featured and a clock was now optional. The Jeep trucks were offered in the same selection of nine colors, five of which were new for 1973, as the Wagoneer models. Both the Wagoneer and Jeep trucks were also available in six fleet colors: Raven black, forest green, Omaha orange, transport yellow, metallic marlin blue and federal grey. The standard cab interior was an embossed "Rio Grande" perforated vinyl. The custom models had a "Leo" pleated fabric. Optional for the custom models was a "Uganda" perforated pleated vinyl. A new green seat trim color joined buff and black choices for 1973. The 304 V-8 was discontinued. The 6-cylinder engine had new induction-hardening of the exhaust valve seats and operated on any type of normal fuel. New simplified sales reference numbers were used for model identification as follows: 25: 120 in. wheelbase, 5000 lb. GVW; 26: 120 in. wheelbase, 6000 GVW; 46: 132 in. wheelbase, 6000 lb. GVW; 47: 132 in. wheelbase, 7000 lb. GVW and 48: 132 in. wheelbase, 8000 lb. GVW.

1973 Jeep Truck with 8000 lb. Camper Package

I.D. DATA: The serial number was located on the left-hand hinge pillar. The V.I.N. arrangement consisted of 13 symbols. The first letter identified the Jeep Corporation. Next was a letter identifying the year of manufacture. The third letter identified the transmission, drivetrain and assembly plant. The next two numbers identified the vehicle series or model. The sixth entry, a letter, identified the body type. Then followed another letter for the model type and GVW. A letter then identified the engine type. The last five numbers were the sequential production number.

Model Number	Body Type	Factory Price	GVW	Shipping Weight	Prod. Total
J-2000, 120 in. wheelbase. 7 ft. box. (J-2500:1/2 ton)					
J-2500	Chassis/Cab	$3206	5000	3275	—
J-2500	Pickup Thriftside	$3353	5000	3570	—
J-2500	Pickup Townside	$3353	5000	3715	—
J-2600	Chassis & Cab	$3327	6000	3390	—
J-2600	Pickup Thriftside	$3474	6000	3690	—
J-2600	Pickup Townside	$3474	6000	3835	—
J-4000, 132 in. wheelbase. 8 ft. box. (J-4500 &J-4600: 1/2 ton; J-4700 & J-4800: 3/4 ton)					
J-4500	Chassis & Cab	$3235	5000	3300	—
J-4500	Pickup Townside	$3390	5000	3760	—
J-4600	Chassis & Cab	$3356	6000	3435	—
J-4600	Pickup Townside	$3511	6000	3895	—
J-4700	Chassis & Cab	$3723	7000	3730	—
J-4700	Pickup Townside	$3878	7000	4190	—
J-4800	Chassis & Cab	$4132	8000	4015	—
J-4800	Pickup Townside	$4287	8000	4475	—

STANDARD ENGINE: Engine Type: OHV, In-line-6. Cast iron block and cylinder head. Bore x Stroke: 3.75 in. x 3.90 in. Lifters: Hydraulic. Number of main bearings-7. Fuel Induction: 1-bbl. Carter Type RTBS or Holley model 1931C-3705. Barrel size: 1.69 in. Compression Ratio: 8.0:1. Displacement: 258 cu. in. (4.22 liters). Horsepower: Net 110 @ 3600 rpm. Torque: Net 195 lb.-ft. @ 2000 rpm. Oil refill capacity: 5 qt. with filter change. Fuel Requirements: Regular.

OPTIONAL ENGINE: Engine Type: OHV, V-8. Cast iron block and cylinder head. Bore x Stroke: 4.08 in. x 3.44 in. Lifters: Hydraulic. Number of main bearings-5. Fuel Induction: 2 bbl. carburetor. Barrel size: 1.562 in. Compression Ratio: 8.5:1. Displacement: 360 cu. in. (5.89 liters). Horsepower: Net 175 @ 4000 rpm. Torque: Net 285 lb.-ft. @ 2400 rpm.

OPTIONAL ENGINE: Engine Type: OHV, V-8. Cast iron block and cylinder head. Bore x Stroke: 4.08 in. x 3.44 in. Lifters: Hydraulic. Number of main bearings-5. Fuel Induction: 4 bbl. downdraft carburetor. Compression Ratio: 8.5:1. Displacement: 360 cu. in. (5.89 liters). Horsepower: Net 195 @ 4400 rpm. Torque: Net 295 lb.-ft. @ 2900 rpm.

CHASSIS FEATURES: Separate body and frame. Deep web frame, wide flange, lightweight pressed steel with five cross members. Dimensions: Model 25 and 26: 183.75 in. x 44.50 in. Section modulus: 3.610 in. 3. 3408W: 195.75 in. x 44.50 in. Section modulus: 3.610 in. 3. Model 46 and 47: 195.75 in. x 44.50 in. Section modulus: 7.530 in. 3. Model 48: 195.75 in. x 44.50 in. Section modulus: 8.000 in. 3.

SUSPENSION AND RUNNING GEAR: Front Suspension: 2500 with 6 cyl.: 6-leaf, semi-elliptical springs, 44 in. x 2.00 in. Spring rate: 216 lb./in. Capacity at Pad: 1275 lb. Capacity at ground: 1470 lb. 2500 with V-8: 5000 lb. GVW: 6-leaf, semi-elliptical springs, 44 in. x 2.00 in. Spring rate: 216 lb./in. Capacity at Pad: 1390 lb. Capacity at ground: 1585 lb. 2600 and 4600 with 6-cyl. engine: 8-leaf, semi-elliptical springs, 44 in. x 2.00 in. Spring rate: 240 lb./in. Capacity at pad: 1330 lb. Capacity at ground: 1575 lb. 2600 and 4600 with V-8 engine: 8-leaf, semi-elliptical springs, 44 in. x 2.00 in. Spring rate: 240 lb./in. Capacity at pad: 1561 lb. Capacity at ground: 1826 lb. Optional: 2600 and 4600: 8-leaf, semi-elliptical springs, 44 in. x 2.00 in. Spring rate: 240 lb./in. Capacity at pad: 1330 lb. Capacity at ground: 1575 lb. 2600 and 4600 with V-8 engine: 8-leaf, semi-elliptical springs, 44 in. x 2.00 in. Spring rate: 240 lb./in. Capacity at pad: 1561 lb. Capacity at ground: 1826 lb. Rear Suspension: 2500, 2600: 8 semi-elliptical leaf springs, 52 in. x 2.50 in. Spring rate: 160-295 lb./in. Capacity at pad: 1500 lb. Capacity at ground: 1680 lb. 4600: 6 semi-elliptical leaf springs, 57 in. x 2.50 in. Spring rate: 190-375 lb./in. Capacity at pad: 2060 lb. Capacity at ground: 2285 lb. 4700: 7 semi-elliptical leaf springs, 52 in. x 2.60 in. Spring rate: 375 lb./in. Capacity at pad: 2450 lb. Capacity at ground: 2700 lb. 4800: 7 semi-elliptical leaf springs, 52 in. x 2.60 in. Spring rate: 275-450 lb./in. Capacity at pad: 2735 lb. Capacity at ground: 3085 lb. Optional: 2600: 10 semi-elliptical leaf springs, 52 in. x 2.50 in. Spring rate: 238-400 lb./in. Capacity at pad: 2620 lb. Capacity at ground: 2800 lb. 4700: 7 semi-elliptical leaf springs, 57 in. x 2.50 in. Spring rate: 270-450 lb./in. Capacity at pad: 2735 lb. Capacity at ground: 2965 lb. Front Axle Type and Capacity: Dana 44, 2850 lb. capacity. 8000 lb. GVW: 4000 lb. Rear Axle Type and Capacity: J-2500, J-4500: Dana model 44, Semi-floating. Capacity: 3500 lb. J-2600, J-4600, J-4700: Dana model 60SF, Semi-floating. Capacity: 5000 lb. J-4800: Dana model 60FF, full-floating. Capacity: 5500 lb. Optional: Powr-Lok differential. Final Drive Ratio: 258 6-cyl., 360 2 bbl. and 4 bbl.: 4.88:1. 360 2 bbl. with 8000 lb. GVW, automatic or 4-spd manual trans.: 4.09:1. All Quadra-Trac models: 4.09:1. Optional: 258 6-cyl., 360 2 bbl. and 4 bbl.: 4.09:1. Transfer Case: All models: 2-speed Dana model 20, 2.03:1, 1.0:1. Brakes: Type: Hydraulic, front and rear drums. Dimensions: J-2500, J-2600, J-4600, J-4700: 12 in. x 2.00 in. front and rear. Total effective area: 195.6 sq. in. J-4800: 12.125 in. x 2.00 in. front and rear. Total effective area: 209.6 in. Optional: Power brakes. Wheels: Full drop center. J-2500:15 x 6L, J-2600: 16 x 6L, J-4500: 15 x 6L, J-4600: 16 x 6L, J-4700: 16 x 5.5F, J-4800: 16 x 6L. Tires: J-2500: F78 x 15B, J-2600: 7.00 x 16D, J-4500: F78 x 15B, J-4600: 7.00 x 16D, J-4700: 7.50 x 16D, J-4800: 7.50 x 16E. Optional: 6000 lb. GVW: 7.50 x 16D 8-ply All-Service, 7.50 x 16D 8-ply Custom Grip. 7000 lb. GVW: 7.50 x 16D 8-ply All-Service, 7.50 x 16D 8-ply Custom X-Grip: 8000 lb. GVW: 7.50 x 16E Custom X-Grip. All tires have black sidewalls. Steering: Left-hand drive models: Recirculating ball. Right-hand drive models: Worm and Roller. Ratio: Recirculating ball and Worm and Roller: 24:1. Turns Lock-to-Lock: 5.6. Turning Circle: J-2000: 49.5 ft., J-4000: 52.0 ft. Optional: Saginaw power steering. Ratios: 22.8:1. Standard: Transmission: Warner T15A 3-speed manual, all synchromesh. Ratios: 2.997, 1.8332, 1.0:1. Reverse: 2.997:1. Optional: 4-speed Warner T18 4-speed manual, synchromesh on top three gears (standard for 8000 lb. GVW). Ratios: 4.020, 3.092, 1.686, 1.00:1. Reverse: 7.439:1. Optional: 3-spd. Turbo Hydra-Matic 400 automatic transmission. Ratios: 2.4815, 1.4815, 1.0:1. Reverse: 2.0769:1. Clutch: V-8 models: 11 in. Single dry plate. Total lining area: 123.7 sq. in. 6-cyl. models: 10.0 in single dry plate. Total lining area: 106.8 sq. in.

VEHICLE DIMENSIONS: Wheelbase: J-2500, J-2600: 120 in.; J-4500, J-4600, J-4700, J-4800: 132 in. wheelbase. Overall Length: J-2500, J-2600: 193.6 in.; J-4500, J-4600, J-4700: 205.64 in. (200.6 in. for Chassis & Cab models). Front/Rear Tread: J-2500: 63.5/63.8 in.; All other models: 63.90/64.4 in. Overall Height: 69.5 in. to 72.4 in., depending on model and tire size. Width: 78.9 in. Front/Rear Overhang: 28.6 in./40.0 in. Tailgate: Width and Height: Townside: 59 in. x 24 in. Thriftside: 48.60 in. x 13.75 in. Approach/Departure Degrees: 132 in. wheelbase: 45/26. Ground Clearance: J-4500 with Quadra-Trac: Front axle: 7.7 in. Rear axle: 7.9 in. Oil pan: 16.0 in. Transfer case: 12.5 in. Load space: 120 in. wheelbase. Townside: 84 in. x 51 in. x 20 in.; 132 in. wheelbase. Townside: 96 in. x 51 in. x 20 in. Front headroom: 36.5 in. Front legroom: 45.00 in. Front hip room: 60.0 in. Pedal to seat back (max.): 43.0 in. Steering wheel to seat back (max.): 25.0 in. Seat to ground: 35.0 in. Floor to ground: 20.0 in.

CAPACITIES: Fuel Tank: 20.0 gal. Coolant System: 6-cyl.: 9.5 qt., V-8: 15 qt.

ACCOMMODATIONS: Seating Capacity: Three.

INSTRUMENTATION: 0-120 mph speedometer, 0-99,999.9 mi. odometer, gauges for fuel level, engine coolant temperature, alternator charging and oil pressure. Transfer case indicator lights.

OPTIONS AND PRICES: Quadra-Trac (high and low range): $149.50. Power brakes: $45.10. Power steering: $143.50. Air conditioning: $442.80. Heavy-duty 70 amp battery: $11.30. Custom cab: $94.60. AM radio: $70.25. Front bumper guards: $16.10. E-Z Eye glass: $24.90. Fuel tank skid plate: $36.70. Dual horns: $7.00. 360 4 bbl. V-8: $257.85. 4-spd. heavy-duty manual trans.: $107. Turbo Hydra-Matic: $267. Free-wheeling front hubs: $63. Optional axle ratios: $12. Limited slip rear differential: $60. Heavy-duty front and rear shock absorbers: $15. Heavy-duty front and rear springs: $20. Bucket seat without center armrest: $95, with armrest: $112.55. Electric clock: $17.55. Tinted glass: $24.90.

HISTORICAL FOOTNOTES: The Jeep truck was the only pickup available in the U.S. with full-time four wheel drive.

1974 TRUCKS

Exterior appearance of the Jeep trucks was little changed for 1974. A change in model designation took place in which the 1/2 ton models were known as the J-10 series and the 3/4 ton models as the J-20 series. The J-10 trucks were offered in either 119 or 131 in. wheelbase versions, the J-20 was limited to the 131 in. wheelbase chassis. Model availability was also reduced for 1974. Not to be quickly discounted was the use of heavier gauge side members for the Jeep truck chassis. The Jeep trucks also shared several engineering advancements with the Wagoneer and Cherokee models. These included a new open-end front axle, tapered leaf front springs, higher load ratings and a reduced turning circle. Other improvements for 1974 included a new articulated windshield wiper mechanism, a new tilt steering wheel option, 6-stud wheels and an improved air conditioning system. A new Pioneer Package for 1974 was offered consisting of woodgrain side body trim, bucket seats finished in "Tru-Knit" vinyl, "Adjust-O-Tilt" steering wheel, tinted glass, two-tone exterior paint and Pioneer lettering, air conditioning, chrome front bumper, cigarette lighter, floor carpeting, door trim panel carpeting, woodgrain trim, courtesy lights, dual horns and a cargo light. For the first time the Truck was also offered with optional aluminum alloy wheels.

Although drum brakes were still standard on the J-10, the J-20 was fitted with front disc brakes as standard equipment. The model 26 J-10 had 12.0 in. discs, the model 46 had 12.5 in. units. The 12.0 in. discs were now available for the J-10 as part of the optional Power Brake Package, retailing for $65. The use of the new front axle resulted in a much smaller turning circle for all models. That of the J-10s was now 41.9 feet; the J-20s was 45.4 feet. Also a consequence of the adoption of the new axle was a one-inch reduction in the wheelbase of all models. This change also accompanied a revised and considerably scaled down model/series listing for 1974.

Except for models fitted with Quadra-Trac, which continued to use the 360 cu. in. V-8, the J-10 Trucks had the 258 cu. in. 6-cylinder as their base engine. For the first time the trucks were available with AMC's 401 cu. in. V-8.

Standard Jeep truck equipment included these items: 50 amp battery (258 engine), 60 amp battery (all V-8 engines), front painted bumper, color-keyed vinyl floor covering, oil and ammeter gauges, 2-speed windshield wipers, electric windshield wipers, inside day/night mirror, outside left side rearview mirrors, padded instrument panel, padded sun visors, dual armrests, chrome grille and single horn.

The color selection for 1974 consisted of eight colors: Champagne white, mellow yellow, Trans-Am red, fawn beige, golden tan metallic, copper metallic, silver green metallic, fairway green metallic, and jetset blue metallic.

1974 Jeep J-10 Townside pickup

I.D. DATA: The serial number was located on the left-hand hinge pillar. The V.I.N. arrangement consisted of 13 symbols. The first letter identified the Jeep Corporation. Next was a letter identifying the year of manufacture. The third letter identified the transmission, drivetrain and assembly plant. The next two numbers identified the vehicle series or model. The sixth entry, a letter, identified the body type. Then followed another letter for the model type and GVW. A letter then identified the engine type. The last five numbers were the sequential production number.

Model Number	Body Type	Factory Price	GVW	Shipping Weight	Prod. Total
J-10, 6-cyl. 119 in. wheelbase: 7 ft. box, 131 in. wheelbase: 8 ft. box (J-10: 1/2 ton) 119 in.: Model 25, 131 in. Model 45					
J-10	Pickup Townside, 120 in. wb.	$3776	5200	3770	—
J-10	Pickup Townside, 131 in. wb	$3474	5200	3820	—
J-20, 360 V-8. 131 in. wheelbase. 8 ft. box: Model 46. (J-20: 3/4 ton)					
J-20	Pickup Townside	$4375	6500*	4390	—

* 7200 lb. and 8000 lb. GVW optional.

STANDARD ENGINE: J-10. Not avail. for California. Engine Type: OHV, In-line-6. Cast iron block and cylinder head. Bore x Stroke: 3.75 in. x 3.90 in. Lifters: Hydraulic. Number of main bearings-7. Fuel Induction: 1 bbl. carburetor. Compression Ratio: 8.0:1. Displacement: 258 cu. in. (4.2 liters). Horsepower: Net: 110 @ 3500 rpm. Torque: Net: 195 lb.-ft. @ 2000 rpm. Oil refill capacity: 5 qt. with filter change. Fuel Requirements: 91 octane.

STANDARD ENGINE: J-20, optional J-10. Engine Type: OHV, V-8. Cast iron block and cylinder head. Bore x Stroke: 4.08 in. x 3.44 in. Lifters: Hydraulic. Number of main bearings-5. Fuel Induction: 2 bbl. carburetor. Compression Ratio: 8.25:1. Displacement: 360 cu. in. (5.89 liters). Horsepower: Net: 175 @ 4000 rpm. Torque: Net: 285 lb.-ft. @ 2400 rpm. Oil refill capacity: 5 qt. with filter change. Fuel Requirements: 91 octane.

OPTIONAL ENGINE: J-10 and J-20. Engine Type: OHV, 360 V-8. Cast iron block and cylinder head. Bore x Stroke: 4.08 in. x 3.44 in. Lifters: Hydraulic. Number of main bearings-5. Fuel Induction: 4 bbl. carburetor. Compression Ratio: 8.5:1. Displacement: 360 cu. in. (5.89 liters). Horsepower: Net: 195 @ 4400 rpm. Torque: Net: 295 lb.-ft. @ 2900 rpm. Oil refill capacity: 5 qt. with filter change. Fuel Requirements: 91 octane.

OPTIONAL ENGINE: J-10 and J-20. Engine Type: OHV, 401 V-8. Cast iron block and cylinder head. Bore x Stroke: 4.165 in. x 3.68 in. Lifters: Hydraulic. Number of main bearings-5. Fuel Induction: 4 bbl. carburetor. Compression Ratio: 8.35:1. Displacement: 401 cu. in. (6.57 liters). Horsepower: Net: 215 @ 4400 rpm. Torque: Net: 320 lb.-ft. @ 2800 rpm. Oil refill capacity: 5 qt. with filter change. Fuel Requirements: 91 octane.

CHASSIS FEATURES: Separate body and frame. Deep web frame, wide flange, lightweight pressed steel with five cross members.

SUSPENSION AND RUNNING GEAR: Front Suspension: Dual leaf semi-elliptical springs. Spring rate: 220 lb./in. Hydraulic double-action shock absorbers, 1.19 in. piston dia. (J-10), 1.38 in. (J-20). Optional: Heavy-duty front springs and heavy-duty shock absorbers. Rear Suspension: Semi-elliptical 5-leaf springs. Spring rate: 230 lb./in. (model 25), dual-leaf spring rate: 340 lb./in. (model) 45 and 46). Hydraulic double-action shock absorbers, 1.38 in. piston dia. Optional: Heavy-duty springs and shock absorbers. Front Axle Type and Capacity: Dana 44, full floating, Hypoid, open end. Capacity: 2940 lb. (J-10), 3500 lb. (J-20). Rear Axle Type and Capacity: Semi-floating-J-10 models and J-20 model 26 (model 26 was for export only. It had a 6000 lb. GVW and the 119 in. wheelbase). Full-floating-J-20 model 46. Capacity: 2940 lb. (J-10), 4090 lb. (J-20). Optional: Powr-Lok differential. Final Drive Ratio: 3.54:1 or 4.09:1 (J-10), 3.73:1 or 4.09:1 (J-20). Transfer Case: All models with manual trans.: 2-speed Dana model 20, 2.03:1, 1.0:1. Quadra-Trac: 2.57:1, 1.00:1. Brakes: Type: J-20: Hydraulic, front discs and rear drums. J-10: Hydraulic drums front and rear. Dimensions: J-20: Front: 12.5 in. dia. (model 46), 12.0 in. (model 26) disc, rear: 11.0 in. x 2.00 in drums. Total brake swept area: 376 sq. in. J-10: 11.0 in. x 2.00 in. front and rear. Total effective area: 181.0 sq. in. Optional: Power front disc brakes for J-10. Wheels: Full drop center. J-10: 15 x 6, 6-bolt; J-20, model 26: 16 x 6, 8-bolt, model 46: 16.5 x 6, 8-bolt. Tires: J-10: G78 x 15B; J-20, model 26: 7.50 x 16D, model 46: 8.00 x 16.5D. Optional: J-10: H78 x 15B, H78 x 15D, 7.00 x 15D. Steering: Recirculating ball. Ratio: 24:1. Turns Lock-to-Lock: 4.0. Turning Circle: J-10, model 25 and J-20 model 26: 41.9 ft., J-10 model 45 and J-20 model 46: 45.4 ft. Optional: Variable ratio power steering. Ratios: 20/16.4:1. Standard: Transmission: 3-spd. man. trans. except for vehicles with 8000 lb. GVW (J-4800) which have 4-spd. manual standard. Ratios: 3.00:1, 1.83:1, 1.00:1. Optional: 3-spd. Turbo Hydra-Matic. Not avail. for 8000 lb. GVW vehicles. Ratios: 2.48:1, 1.48:1, 1.00:1. Optional: 4-speed manual trans (synchromesh on top three gears). Ratios: 4.02:1, 3.09:1, 1.68:1, 1.00:1. Clutch: V-8 models: 11 in. Single dry plate. Total lining area: 123.7 sq. in. 6-cyl. models: 10.0 in single dry plate. Total lining area: 106.8 sq. in. Optional: Heavy-duty clutch.

VEHICLE DIMENSIONS: Wheelbase: Model 25 & 26: 119 in.; model 45 & 46: 131 in. Overall Length: Model 25 & 26: 193.6 in. Models 45 & 46: 205.6 in. Front/Rear Tread: Model 25: 62.9/63.8 in. Model 26 & 45: 62.9/64.4 in. Model 46 and all models with disc brakes: 63.0/64.4 in. Overall Height: Model 25, 26, 45, 46: 69.5 in. Model 25 with 5600 lb. GVW, model 45 with 5600 lb. GVW, model 46 with 7200 lb. GVW: 71.3 in. Model 46 with 8000 lb. GVW: 72.4 in. Width: 78.9 in. Front/Rear Overhang: 28.6 in./40.0 in. Tailgate: Width and Height: 59.3 in. x 20.8 in. Approach/Departure Degrees: 119 in. wheelbase: 45/26.Ground Clearance: J-10 with manual trans.: Front axle: 7.8 in. Rear axle: 8.2 in. Oil pan: 15.2 in. Transfer case: 11.2 in. Fuel tank: 12.0 in. Load space: 119 in. wheelbase: 84 in. x 50 in. x 20.8 in.; 131 in. wheelbase. 96 in. x 50 in. x 20.8 in. Front headroom: 36.5 in. Front legroom: 45.00 in. Front hip room: 60.0 in. Pedal to seat back (max.): 43.0 in. Steering wheel to seat back (max.): 25.0 in. Seat to ground: 35.0 in. Floor to ground: 20.0 in.

CAPACITIES: Fuel Tank: 19.0 gal. Coolant System: 6-cyl.: 9.5 qt., V-8: 15 qt.

ACCOMMODATIONS: Seating Capacity: Three.

INSTRUMENTATION: 110 mph speedometer, 0-99,999.9 mi. odometer, gauges for fuel level, engine coolant temperature, oil pressure and ammeter; Transfer case indicator lights.

OPTIONS AND PRICES: 360 cid 2 bbl. V-8: $201. 360 cid 4 bbl. V-8: $245. 401 cid V-8: $295 ($94 for J-20). 4-speed manual trans.: $102. Quadra-Trac (high range): $38. Quadra-Trac (high and low range): $142. Turbo Hydra-Matic: $254. Free-running front hubs (not avail. with Quadra-Trac): $60. Rear Trac-Lok differential (not avail. with Quadra-Trac): $57. Power brakes (front discs): $65 (for J-10 only). Power steering: $138. Heavy-duty shock absorbers: $14. Front stabilizer bar: $33. Bucket seats with center armrest: $107. Tinted glass: $24. Air conditioning: $421. Dual Junior West Coast mirrors. Wheelcovers. Courtesy lights. Rear step bumper. Chrome front bumper. Sliding rear window. AM radio. AM/FM radio. Custom Package. Pioneer Package. Two-tone paint. Convenience Package. Tilt steering wheel. Auxiliary fuel tank. Locking gas cap. Tinted glass. 51 amp alternator. Dual horns. Electric clock. Aluminum styled wheels. Side-mounted spare tire carrier. Pintle hook with lock pin. Fuel tank skid plate.

HISTORICAL FOOTNOTES: The 1974 Jeep trucks were introduced in the fall of 1973.

1975 TRUCKS

Numerous mechanical improvements and refinements as well as a broader choice of options, trim and body colors highlighted the 1975 Jeep trucks. Standard engine in the J-10 series remained the 258 cu. in. 6-cylinder. In the J-20 series the 360 cu. in. V-8 was continued. Both versions has a standard 3-speed manual transmission and Dana 20 manual-shift four-wheel drive.

The Jeep truck's fuel economy was improved by the use of new carburetors for the 4-barrel V-8 engines with smaller primary and larger secondary metering valves; new insulation to reduce heat input from engine to carburetor, new optional cruise control, and new optional HR-78 white sidewall tires for J-10 models.

Mechanical and functional improvements for 1975 began with a new electronic ignition system. Other revisions included new springs and shock absorbers for a somewhat smoother ride; heat shields for the muffler and exhaust pipe; stronger engine supports; a more efficient defroster; a new power steering gear for improved road "feel"; a new three-belt accessory drive system for V-8 engines that provided a more efficient power transfer to engine accessories and a new stainless steel whip-type radio antenna.

A wider choice of options was provided for the 1975 models, including a new stereo AM/FM radio with two speakers; new two-tone paint treatment; new Pioneer woodgrain body trim; new Sport steering wheel; new hubcaps for the J-20 series; 70 amp battery and 62 amp alternator and a new convenience group with dual low profile mirrors, visor vanity mirror and electric clock, courtesy light, glove box light and ashtray light. All 131 in. wheelbase models could now be fitted with a 20 gallon auxiliary fuel tank (standard fuel tank capacity was 19 gallons).

The number of interior trim color combinations was increased from three to four. Two new colors, blue and green, joined two carryover colors, black and buff. Standard seat trim in the base model was Vinyl Laramie. A new standard trim for the Custom and Pioneer Packages, Derby Check fabric (similar to Houndstooth), was introduced with the 1975 models. Optional for these two packages was a "Sport Knit" vinyl. The Pioneer Package included woodgrain inserts for the instrument panel cluster, door trim panels that matched the exterior trim, deep pile carpeting, chrome front bumper, bright exterior window moldings, bright wheelcovers (J-10) or bright hubcaps (J-20), dual horns, locking glove box, cigarette lighter and bright armrest overlays. Bucket seats continued to be a Jeep truck option. Primary standard equipment features included these items: 50 amp battery, vinyl covered headliner, vinyl floor covering, 12 in. day/night rearview mirror, padded instrument panel, dual padded sun visors, and oil and ammeter gauges.

1975 Jeep J-20 Pioneer

I.D. DATA: The serial number was located on the left-hand hinge pillar. The V.I.N. arrangement consisted of 13 symbols. The first letter identified the Jeep Corporation. Next was a letter identifying the year of manufacture. The third letter identified the transmission, drivetrain and assembly plant. The next two numbers identified the vehicle series or model. The sixth entry, a letter, identified the code model and GVW. The seventh entry, a letter, identified the engine. The last six numbers were the sequential production number.

Model Number	Body Type	Factory Price	GVW	Shipping Weight	Prod. Total
J-10, 6-cyl. 119 in. wheelbase: 7 ft. box, 131 in. wheelbase: 8 ft. box (J-10:1/2 ton) 119 in.: Model 25, 131 in. Model 45					
J-10	Pickup Townside, 120 in. wb.	$4228	6025	3712	—
J-10	Pickup Townside, 131 in. wb.	$4289	6025	3770	—
J-20, 360 V-8. 131 in. wheelbase. 8 ft. box: Model 46. (J-20: 3/4 ton)					
J-20	Pickup Townside	$4975	6500*	4333	—

* 7200 lb. and 8000 lb. GVW optional.

STANDARD ENGINE: J-10: Not avail. for California. Engine Type: OHV, In-line-6. Cast iron block and cylinder head. The 4 bbl.360 V-8 is standard for all Jeep trucks in California. Bore x Stroke: 3.75 in. x 3.90 in. Lifters: Hydraulic. Number of main bearings-7. Fuel Induction: 1 bbl. carburetor. Compression Ratio: 8.0:1. Displacement: 258 cu. in. (4.2 liters). Horsepower: Net: 110 @ 3500 rpm. Torque: Net: 195 lb.-ft. @ 2000 rpm. Oil refill capacity: 5 qt. with filter change. Fuel Requirements: Regular, low-lead or no-lead.

STANDARD ENGINE: J-20, optional J-10: Engine Type: OHV, V-8. Cast iron block and cylinder head. Not avail. for California. Bore x Stroke: 4.08 in. x 3.44 in. Lifters: Hydraulic. Number of main bearings-5. Fuel Induction: 2 bbl. carburetor. Compression Ratio: 8.25:1. Displacement: 360 cu. in. (5.89 liters). Horsepower: Net: 175 @ 4000 rpm. Torque: Net: 285 lb.-ft. Oil refill capacity: 5 qt. with filter change. Fuel Requirements: 91 octane.

OPTIONAL ENGINE: J-10 and J-20: Engine Type: OHV, 360 V-8. Cast iron block and cylinder head. Bore x Stroke: 4.08 in. x 3.44 in. Lifters: Hydraulic. Number of main bearings-5. Fuel Induction: 4 bbl. carburetor. Compression Ratio: 8.25:1. Displacement: 360 cu. in. (5.89 liters). Horsepower: Net: 195 @ 4400 rpm. Torque: Net: 295 lb.-ft. @ 2900 rpm. Oil refill capacity: 5 qt. with filter change. Fuel Requirements: 91 octane.

OPTIONAL ENGINE: J-10 and J-20: Engine Type: OHV, 401 V-8. Cast iron block and cylinder head. Bore x Stroke: 4.165 in. x 3.68 in. Lifters: Hydraulic. Number of main bearings-5. Fuel Induction: 4 bbl. carburetor. Compression Ratio: 8.35:1. Displacement: 401 cu. in. (6.57 liters). Horsepower: Net: 215 @ 4400 rpm. Torque: Net: 320 lb.-ft. @ 2800 rpm. Oil refill capacity: 5 qt. with filter change. Fuel Requirements: 91 octane.

CHASSIS FEATURES: Separate body and frame. Deep web frame, wide flange, lightweight pressed steel with five cross members. Section modulus. Standard Engine: J-10, 119 in. wheelbase: 3.61 in., 131 in. wheelbase: 3.82 in. J-20: 3.82 in.

SUSPENSION AND RUNNING GEAR: Front Suspension: J-10 & J-20: 5-leaf semi-elliptical springs. Hydraulic double-action shock absorbers. Optional: Heavy-duty front springs and heavy-duty shock absorbers. Rear Suspension: J-10 119 in. wheelbase: 5-leaf semi-elliptical springs; J-10, 131 in. wheelbase and J-20: 2 tapered leaf springs. Hydraulic double-action shock absorbers. Optional: Heavy-duty springs and shock absorbers. Front Axle Type and Capacity: Dana 44, full floating, Hypoid, open end. Capacity: 3200 lb. (J-10), 3500 lb. (J-20). Rear Axle Type and Capacity: J-10: Semi-floating, J-20: Full-floating. Capacity: J-10: 3200 lb. J-20/6500 lb. GVW: 4090 lb., J-20/7200 lb. GVW: 4700 lb.; J-20/8000 lb. GVW: 5500 lb. Optional: Powr-Lok differential. Final Drive Ratio: J-10: 4.09:1 (258-6 cyl.); 3.54:1 (all V-8 engines). J-20: 3.73:1 (all engines). Optional: J-10: 3.54:1 (360 V-8 engines only). J-20: 4.09:1 (360 V-8 engines only). Transfer Case: All models with manual trans.: 2-speed Dana model 20, 2.03:1, 1.0:1. Quadra-Trac: 2.57:1, 1.00:1. Brakes: Type: J-20: Hydraulic, front discs and rear drums. J-10: Hydraulic drums front and rear. Dimensions: J-20: Front: 12.5 in. dia. disc, rear: 11.0 in. x 2.00 in drums. Total brake swept area: 429 sq. in. J-10: 11.0 in. x 2.00 in. front and rear. Total effective area: 181.0 sq. in. Optional: Power front disc brakes for J-10. Wheels: Full drop center. J-10: 15 x 6, 6-bolt; J-20, model 26: 16 x 6, 8-bolt, model 46: 16.5 x 6, 8-bolt. Tires: J-10: H78 x 15B; J-20: 8.00 x 16.5D. Optional: J-10: H78 x 15B, H78 x 15D, 7.00 x 15D. Steering: Recirculating ball. Ratio: 24:1. Turns Lock-to-Lock: 4.0. Turning Circle: J-10, model 25 and J-20 model 26: 41.9 ft., J-10 model 45 and J-20 model 46: 45.4 ft. Optional: Variable ratio power steering. Ratios: 20/16.4:1. Standard: Transmission: 3-spd. man. trans. except for vehicles with 8000 lb. GVW (J-4800) which have 4-spd. manual standard. Ratios: 3.00:1, 1.83:1, 1.00:1. Optional: 3-spd. Turbo Hydra-Matic. Not avail. for 8000 lb. GVW vehicles. Ratios: 2.48:1, 1.48:1, 1.00:1. Optional: 4-speed manual trans (synchromesh on top three gears). Ratios: 4.02:1, 3.09:1, 1.68:1, 1.00:1. Clutch: V-8 models: 11 in. Single dry plate. Total lining area: 123.7 sq. in. 6-cyl. models: 10.0 in single dry plate. Total lining area: 106.8 sq. in. Optional: Heavy-duty clutch.

VEHICLE DIMENSIONS: Wheelbase: Model 25 & 26: 119 in.; model 45 & 46: 131 in. Overall Length: Model 25 & 26: 193.6 in. Models 45 & 46: 205.6 in. Front/Rear Tread: Model 25: 62.9/63.8 in. Model 26 & 45: 62.9/64.4 in. Model 46 and all models with disc brakes: 63.0/64.4 in. Overall Height: Model 25, 26, 45, 46: 69.5 in. Model 25 with 5600 lb. GVW, model 45 with 5600 lb. GVW, model 46 with 7200 lb. GVW: 71.3 in. Model 46 with 8000 lb. GVW: 72.4 in. Width: 78.9 in. Front/Rear Overhang: 28.6 in./40.0 in. Tailgate: Width and Height: 59.3 in. x 20.8 in. Approach/Departure Degrees: 119 in. wheelbase: 45/26. Ground Clearance: J-10 with manual trans.: Front axle: 7.8 in. Rear axle: 8.2 in. Oil pan: 15.2 in. Transfer case: 11.2 in. Fuel tank: 12.0 in. Load space: 119 in. wheelbase: 84 in. x 50 in. x 20.8 in.; 131 in. wheelbase. 96 in. x 50 in. x 20.8 in. Front headroom: 36.5 in. Front legroom: 45.00 in. Front hip room: 60.0 in. Pedal to seat back (max.): 43.0 in. Steering wheel to seat back (max.): 25.0 in. Seat to ground: 35.0 in. Floor to ground: 20.0 in.

CAPACITIES: Fuel Tank: 19.0 gal. Coolant System: 6-cyl.: 9.5 qt., V-8: 15 qt.

ACCOMMODATIONS: Seating Capacity: Three.

INSTRUMENTATION: 0-110 mph speedometer, 0-99,999.9 mi. odometer, gauges for fuel level, engine coolant temperature, oil pressure and ammeter; Transfer case indicator lights.

OPTIONS AND PRICES: 360 cid 2 bbl. V-8 (J-10): $201.25. 360 cid 4 bbl. V-8 (J-10): $245. 401 cid 4 bbl. V-8: $295 ($94 for J-20). 4-speed manual trans (J-10): $129. Turbo Hydra-Matic with Quadra-Trac: $291. Turbo Hydra-Matic with Quadra-Trac and low range: $395.80. Free-running front hubs: $85. Limited slip rear differential: $69 Heavy-duty shock absorbers: $14.10. Heavy-duty front springs: $35. Heavy-duty rear springs: $30. Front stabilizer bar: $33. Power front disc brakes (J-10 only): $65. Power steering: $138.10. Tinted glass: $23.65. Hubcaps: $10.40. Fuel tank skid plate: $34.85. Air conditioning: $420.65. Pioneer Package: $283.25.

HISTORICAL FOOTNOTES: *Four Wheeler* magazine, December, 1974, reported that "the 1/2 ton Jeep pickup may be one of the best kept secrets in the four-wheel drive world...it is amazing that American Motors doesn't sell more of them." *Four Wheeler*, September, 1975 praised its ride noting that "of all 4x4 pickups this J-10 1/2 ton was one of the smoothest riding...The J-10 is nearly as comfortable as a passenger car and as comfortable as a two-wheel drive pickup....We think it is sad that more people aren't buying the 1/2 ton Jeep pickup. It is a great all-around 4-wheel-drive truck with great performance and with excellent comfort and luxury." *Pickup Van &4WD*, September, 1975 declared that "In terms of all-around four-wheel drive performance this truck remains King of the Hill."

1976 TRUCKS

For 1976, there were many numerous mechanical improvements and refinements as well as new choices in options, trim and body colors offered for the Jeep trucks.

All models had upgraded frames with splayed side rails, stronger cross members and box section side rails. Besides allowing wider spaced springs to be used this frame design also made a direct steering mounting possible. Also introduced were new multi-leaf springs and new shock absorbers for a smoother ride.

The three-speed manual transmission previously teamed with the V-8 engine was now also used with the J-10's standard 258 cu. in. 6-cylinder engine. Its torque capacity was 325 lb.-ft. compared to the 230 lb.-ft. of the older transmission.

Other mechanical and functional improvements included a dual-nozzle windshield washer system; a new standard seat-belt warning system with a three-point lap and shoulder harness assembly; a new optional front stabilizer bar; more attractive 15 in. wheelcovers for the J-10; new graphics for the instrument panel, radio, clock, heater and other controls.

1976 Jeep J-10 pickup

All models had new seat and door trim designs available in a choice of color-keyed black, blue, green and buff. The base model's bench seat was finished in a simulated knit "Fairway" vinyl. The interior was color-keyed. The custom and Pioneer models had a "Potomac Stripe" pleated fabric upholstery. The Pioneer had color-keyed cut-pile carpets and woodgrain trim. Both the bench seat and optional bucket seats were also offered in a "Sof-Touch" vinyl. Additional features of the Pioneer pickup included woodgrain exterior trim, chrome front bumper, bright exterior moldings, bright wheelcovers (J-10 only), bright hubcaps (J-20 only), dual horns, glove box lock, cigarette lighter, woodgrain instrument cluster trim and bright armrest overlays.

For the first time Jeep pickups were offered with a factory installed "Snow Boss" Plowing Package consisting of a 90 in. Moldboard plow and complete mounting elements, hydraulic cylinders for power angling and lifting, electric control, switches and wiring, plow lights and body decals. This package joined the "Camper Special Package" which had made J-20 pickups popular with campers. For 1976 it included heavy-duty shocks, large capacity radiator, 70 amp battery and 62 amp alternator, West Coast mirrors, sliding rear window and 9.50 x 16.5 Goodyear Cushion tires with a D load range.

In early 1976 Jeep introduced a Sporty Honcho pickup to compete with similar models from Ford and Chevrolet. The Honcho Package listed for $699 and required purchase of the $69 power front disc brakes and the $179 power steering option. This brought the price of a Honcho pickup to $5680.

The Honcho had a body side tape treatment of gold with accents of black and white. Its grille also had black accents. The fender lip strips were gold and white and the tailgate striping was gold finished. A rear step bumper was installed along with a chrome front bumper. Stainless steel window molding were also included in the Honcho Package. A blue Sport steering wheel was installed. The Honcho interior was finished in a blue Levi's denim. Body color availability was alpine white, firecracker red, brilliant blue, black, nautical blue and medium blue. Bold "Honcho" lettering was applied to the door panels. Goodyear Tracker AT 10 x 15 tubeless 4-ply polyester tires were mounted on slot-style 15 x 8 inch steel wheels.

The Honcho interior consisted of a bench seat with blue "Levi's" fabric and door panels with a "Levi's" insert. A blue Sport steering wheel was used along with an engine turned instrument panel cluster overlay. Standard equipment included a cigarette lighter, floor carpeting in either blue or tan, glove box lock, bright armrest overlays. Also found on Honcho pickups were dual horns and hood insulation.

Standard Jeep truck equipment consisted of the following: 3-speed floor-mounted transmission, power front disc brakes (J-20 only), oil, amp and engine coolant temperature gauges, 50 amp battery (J-10 only), 60 amp battery (J-20 only), 37 amp alternator (J-10 only), 40 amp alternator (J-20 only), vinyl covered headliner, 12 in. day/night rearview mirror, padded instrument panel, and heavy-duty air cleaner.

The color selection for the standard J-10 and J-20 consisted of twelve choices. New for 1976 were these colors: Sand tan, dark cocoa metallic (not available for Honcho), sunshine yellow, firecracker red, brilliant blue (not available for Pioneer pickup), and nautical blue. Carried over from 1975 were: Alpine white, Renegade orange, pewter grey, reef green metallic, medium blue metallic, and classic black.

1976 Jeep J-20 pickup

I.D. DATA: The serial number was located on the left-hand hinge pillar. The V.I.N. arrangement consisted of 13 symbols. The first letter identified the Jeep Corporation. Next was a letter identifying the year of manufacture. The third letter identified the transmission, drivetrain and assembly plant. The next two numbers identified the vehicle series or model. The sixth entry, a letter, identified the code model and GVW. The seventh entry, a letter, identified the engine. The last six numbers were the sequential production number.

Model Number	Body Type	Factory Price	GVW	Shipping Weight	Prod. Total
J-10, 6-cyl. 119 in. wheelbase: 7 ft. box, 131 in. wheelbase: 8 ft. box (J-10:1/2 ton) 119 in.: Model 25, 131 in. Model 45					
J-10	Pickup Townside, 120 in. wb.	$4643	6025	3773	—
J-10	Pickup Townside, 131 in. wb.	$4704	6025	3873	—
J-20, 360 V-8. 131 in. wheelbase. 8 ft. box: Model 46. (J-20: 3/4 ton)					
J-20	Pickup Townside	$5290	6500*	4285	—

* 7200 lb. and 8000 lb. GVW optional.

STANDARD ENGINE: J-10: Not avail. for California. For California, the 360 cu. in. V-8 with a 4-barrel carburetor and 4-speed transmission was standard. The only optional engine was the 401 cu. in. V-8 with the 4-barrel carburetor. Engine Type: OHV, In-line-6. Cast iron block and cylinder head. The 4 bbl. 360 V-8 is standard for all Jeep trucks in California. Bore x Stroke: 3.75 in. x 3.90 in. Lifters: Hydraulic. Number of main bearings-7. Fuel Induction: 1 bbl. carburetor. Compression Ratio: 8.0:1. Displacement: 258 cu. in. (4.22 liters). Horsepower: Net: 110 @ 3500 rpm. Torque: Net: 195 lb.-ft. @ 2000 rpm. Oil refill capacity: 5 qt. with filter change. Fuel Requirements: Regular, low-lead or no-lead.

STANDARD ENGINE: J-20, optional J-10: Type: OHV, V-8. Cast iron block and cylinder head. Not avail. for California. Bore x Stroke: 4.08 in. x 3.44 in. Lifters: Hydraulic. Number of main bearings-5. Fuel Induction: 2 bbl. carburetor. Compression Ratio: 8.25:1. Displacement: 360 cu. in. (5.89 liters). Horsepower: Net: 175 @ 4000 rpm. Torque: Net: 285 lb.-ft. Oil refill capacity: 5 qt. with filter change. Fuel Requirements: 91 octane.

OPTIONAL ENGINE: J-10 and J-20: Engine Type: OHV, 360 V-8. Cast iron block and cylinder head. Bore x Stroke: 4.08 in. x 3.44 in. Lifters: Hydraulic. Number of main bearings-5. Fuel Induction: 4 bbl. carburetor. Compression Ratio: 8.25:1. Displacement: 360 cu. in. (5.89 liters). Horsepower: Net: 195 @ 4400 rpm. Torque: Net: 295 lb.-ft. @ 2900 rpm. Oil refill capacity: 5 qt. with filter change. Fuel Requirements: 91 octane.

OPTIONAL ENGINE: J-10 and J-20. Engine Type: OHV, 401 V-8. Cast iron block and cylinder head. Bore x Stroke: 4.165 in. x 3.68 in. Lifters: Hydraulic. Number of main bearings-5. Fuel Induction: 4 bbl. carburetor. Compression Ratio: 8.35:1. Displacement: 401 cu. in. (6.57 liters). Horsepower: Net: 215 @ 4400 rpm. Torque: Net: 320 lb.-ft. @ 2800 rpm. Oil refill capacity: 5 qt. with filter change. Fuel Requirements: 91 octane.

CHASSIS FEATURES: Separate body and frame. Deep web frame, splayed box section side rails, wide flange, lightweight pressed steel with five cross members.

SUSPENSION AND RUNNING GEAR: Front Suspension: J-10: semi-elliptical leaf springs. Hydraulic double-action shock absorbers, J-20: 2-leaf semi-elliptical, 3500 lb. capacity. Optional: Heavy-duty front springs and heavy-duty shock absorbers. Rear Suspension: J-10 119 in. wheelbase: semi-elliptical springs; J-20: 3 semi-elliptical leaf springs, 5500 lb. capacity. Hydraulic double-action shock absorbers. Optional: Heavy-duty springs and shock absorbers. Front Axle Type and Capacity: Dana 44, full floating, Hypoid, open end. Capacity: 3200 lb. (J-10), 3500 lb. (J-20). Rear Axle Type and Capacity: J-10: Semi-floating. J-20: Full-floating. Capacity: J-10: 3200 lb. J-20/6500 lb. GVW: 4090 lb., J-20/7200 lb. GVW: 4700 lb.; J-20/8000 lb. GVW: 5500 lb. Optional: Powr-Lok differential.

Engines, axle ratios and transmissions for 1976

	Engine	Axle Ratios		Dana 20 4-WD		Quadra-Trac 4-WD
		Std.	Opt.	3-spd.	4-spd.	
J-10	258/1 bbl.	4.09	N.A.	Std.	Opt.	Opt.
	360/2 bbl.	3.54	4.09	Std.	Opt.	Opt.
	360/4 bbl.	3.54	4.09	N.A.	Std.	Opt.
	401/4 bbl.	3.54	N.A.	N.A.	N.A.	Std.
J-20	360/2 bbl.	3.73	4.09	Std.	Opt.	Opt.
	360/4 bbl.	3.73	4.09	N.A.	Std.	Opt.
	401/4 bbl.	3.73	N.A.	N.A	N.A.	Std.

Transfer Case: All models with manual trans.: 2-speed Dana model 20, 2.03:1, 1.0:1. Quadra-Trac: 2.57:1, 1.00:1. Brakes: Type: J-20: Hydraulic, front discs and rear drums. J-10: Hydraulic drums front and rear. Dimensions: J-20: Front: 12.5 in. dia. disc, rear: 11.0 in. x 2.00 in. drums. Total brake swept area: 429 sq. in. J-10: 11.0 in. x 2.00 in. front and rear. Total effective area: 181.0 sq. in. Optional: Power front disc brakes for J-10. Wheels: Full drop center. J-10: 15 x 6, 6-bolt; J-20, model 26: 16 x 6, 8-bolt, model 46: 16.5 x 6, 8-bolt. Optional: J-10: 15 x 7.00 (aluminum); J-20: 16.5 x 6.75, 16 x 5.0. Tires: J-10: H78 x 15B steel belted radial, J-20: 8.00 x 16.5 (6500 lb. GVW), 9.50 x 16.5 (7200 and 8000 lb. GVW). Optional: J-10: HR78 x 15 steel belted radial, H78 x 15D 4-ply Custom Power Cushion & Power Cushion "78", HR78 x 15 steel belted radial Mud and Snow, H78 x 15 Suburbanite Polyglas and Suburbanite XG Polyglas,10 x 15 Tracker A-T (short wheelbase J-10 only; included as part of the Honcho Package). J-20: 8.00 x 16.5 8-ply Cushion Miler White sidewall, 9.50 x 16.5 8-ply Cushion Miler, 7.50 x 16 6, 8 or 10 ply Cushion Xtra Grip Hi-Miler. Steering: Recirculating ball. Ratio: 24:1. Turns Lock-to-Lock: 4.0. Turning Circle: J-10, model 25: 40.6 ft., Honcho: 41.2 ft., J-10 model 45 and J-20 model 46: 44.5 ft. Optional: Variable ratio power steering. Ratios: 20/16.4:1. Standard: Transmission: 3-spd. man. trans. except for vehicles with 8000 lb. GVW (J-4800) which have 4-spd. manual standard. Ratios: 3.00:1, 1.83:1, 1.00:1. Optional: 3-spd. Turbo Hydra-Matic. Not avail. for 8000 lb. GVW vehicles. Ratios: 2.48:1, 1.48:1, 1.00:1. Optional: 4-speed manual trans (synchromesh on top three gears). Ratios: 4.02:1, 3.09:1, 1.68:1, 1.00:1. Clutch: V-8 models: 11 in. Single dry plate. Total lining area: 123.7 sq. in. 6-cyl. models: 10.0 in single dry plate. Total lining area: 106.8 sq. in. Optional: Heavy-duty clutch.

VEHICLE DIMENSIONS: Wheelbase: Model 25: 118.7 in.; model 45 & 46: 130.7 in. Overall Length: Model 25: 192.5 in. Models 45 & 46: 204.5 in. Front/Rear Tread: Model 25 and model 45: 63.3/63.8 in. Model 46 and all models with disc brakes: 64.6/65.9 in. Overall Height: Model 25: 69.3 in., model 45: 69.1 in., model 46: 70.7 in. Width: 78.9 in. Front/Rear Overhang: 29.9 in./43.9 in. Tailgate: Width and Height: 57.2 in. x 20.5 in. Approach/Departure Degrees: 119 in. wheelbase: 45/26.Ground Clearance: Minimum ground clearance: J-10: 7.7 in.; J-20: 8.1 in. Load space: 118.7 in. wheelbase: 83.6 in. x 50 in. x 20.5 in.; 130.7 in. wheelbase. 95.6 in. x 50 in. x 20.5 in. Maximum capacity: Model 25: 67.0 cu. ft.; model 45 and model 46: 76.6 cu. ft. Front headroom: 40.2 in. Front legroom: 45.00 in. Front shoulder room: 58.3 in. Front hip room: 60.5 in. Pedal to seat back (max.): 43.0 in. Steering wheel to seat back (max.): 25.0 in. Seat to ground: 35.0 in. Floor to ground: Model 25: 20.7 in.; model 45: 20.5 in.; model 46: 22.1 in.

CAPACITIES: Fuel Tank: 19.0 gal. 20 gal. tank optional. Coolant System capacity: 6-cyl.: 9.5 qt. V-8: 15 qt.

ACCOMMODATIONS: Seating Capacity: Three.

INSTRUMENTATION: 0-110 mph speedometer, 0-99,999.9 mi. odometer, gauges for fuel level, engine coolant temperature, oil pressure and ammeter; Transfer case indicator lights.

OPTIONS AND PRICES: 360 cid 2 bbl. V-8 (J-10). 360 cid 4 bbl. V-8 (J-20): $44. 401 cid 4-bbl. V-8: $295 ($94 for J-20). 4-speed manual trans (J-10). Turbo Hydra-Matic with Quadra-Trac: $325. Turbo Hydra-Matic with Quadra-Trac and low range: $455. Free-running front hubs: $90. Rear Trac-Lok differential: $73. Heavy-duty shock absorbers: $18. Heavy-duty front springs: $37. Heavy-duty rear springs: $32. Front stabilizer bar: $35. Power front disc brakes (J-10 only. Power steering: $179. Tinted glass. Hubcaps. Fuel tank skid plate: $42. Air conditioning. Pioneer Package. Camper Special Package. Includes 8000 lb. GVW rating, heavy-duty shock absorbers, large capacity radiator, 70 amp battery, 62 amp alternator, West Coast style left and right side mirrors, sliding rear window: $199. Front bucket seats with center arm rest (custom, Pioneer and Honcho only): $157. Forged, 7 in. aluminum styled wheels (J-10 only). AM radio. AM/FM radio. Citizen's Band radio. Snow Boss Package. 15 in. Sport steering wheel. Leather-wrapped steering wheel. Tilt steering wheel. Cruise control. Sliding rear window. Aluminum cargo cap. Wheelcovers. Includes special covers for vehicles equipped with Quadra-Trac. Auxiliary fuel tank. Available for 130.7 in. wheelbase. only. Not available in California. Rear step bumper. Custom Trim Package. Includes chrome bumpers, bright exterior window and body side moldings, cigarette lighter, glove box lock and pleated seat fabric. Light Group. Includes electric clock, visor vanity mirror and dual low-profile mirrors. Cold Climate Group. Includes engine block heater, 70 amp battery and heavy-duty alternator. Front bumper guards with nerf strips. Locking front hubs. Not available with Quadra-Trac: $90.

HISTORICAL FOOTNOTES: The Honcho Package was announced in January, 1976. The 1976 line had been introduced in the fall of 1975.

1977 TRUCKS

A more powerful 6-cylinder engine (the 2 bbl. 258 cu. in. engine) and standard front disc brakes were among the major improvements found in the 1977 J-10 pickup trucks. A heavier tube frame section was now standard for all J-10 models. All J trucks had a new standard hinged back for bench seats and a new rear window reinforcement design. These changes resulted in a more comfortable seat-back angle and easier access to the storage area behind the seat. The exterior woodgrain trim included in the 1976 Pioneer Trim Package was now listed as a separate option for the long wheelbase J-10 and J-20 trucks. The balance of the Pioneer Trim Package was, for 1977, combined with the 1976 custom option to form a new single package which included "Sport Knit" vinyl bench seat, chrome front bumper, bright exterior moldings, Deluxe door trim pads, dual horns, glove box lock, cigarette lighter, bright armrest overlays and special instrument cluster trim. Interior trim on all trucks was new for 1977. A new paint break stripe for two-tone trucks was optional.

In the J -20 series, the GVW ratings were increased for heavier payloads. The standard rating was moved up to 6800 lb. while the optional ratings were each increased by 400 pounds. The Honcho Package, introduced early in 1976 continued as an option for the J-10, 118.7 in. wheelbase model only. It continued to include such features as blue "Levi's" fabric bench seat and "Levi's" inserts in the door panels, a chrome front bumper, a rear step bumper, stainless steel moldings, blue steering wheel, engine-turned instrument cluster overlay, cigarette lighter, blue floor carpeting, glove box lock, dual horns and special stripes and accents. Its exterior was now offered in either gold with brown and orange accents or dark blue with gold and orange accents. New spoke-style 15 x 8 in. steel wheels were now included in the Honcho Package. They were also optional for all J-10 models.

Mid-way through 1977 another new Trim Package, the Golden Eagle, joined the Honcho Package (which was priced at $749 for 1977). Many items from the Honcho Package such as its chrome front bumper, rear step bumper, 10-15 tracker OWL tires, bright window frames, bright armrest overlays and hood insulation were included in the $999 Golden Eagle Package. In addition, it featured 8 inch spoked wheels painted gold with black accent stripes, pickup box roll bar, steel grille guard, off-road driving lamps mounted on the roll bar, beige "Levi's" bucket seats and custom interior and a "engine-turned" instrument panel cluster. The Golden Eagle Package also included bold exterior body accents. The hood sported a large eagle decal with dual belt-line stripes on the door, cab and upper box sides. The gold, black and orange theme of these graphics was carried over to the lower body side, tailgate and wheel-lip stripes. Golden Eagle lettering was located on the lower door panel.

Twelve body colors were available, including five new colors: Autumn red metallic, loden green metallic, midnight blue metallic, mocha brown metallic and tawny orange. Other colors included alpine white, brilliant blue, classic black, firecracker red, pewter grey metallic, sand tan and sunshine yellow.

I.D. DATA: The V.I.N. consisted of 13 symbols. The first (a letter) identified the Jeep Corporation. The second (a number) indicated the model year. The third entry (a letter) identified the transmission/drivetrain/assembly plant. The fourth and fifth symbols (both numbers) identified the model. The sixth symbol (a letter) indicated the code model and GVW. The seventh entry (a letter) indicated the engine. The last six number served as the sequential production number. The serial number was located on the left-hand hinge pillar.

1977 Jeep J-10 Golden Eagle pickup

Model Number	Body Type	Factory Price	GVW	Shipping Weight	Prod. Total
J-10, 6-cyl. 118.7 in. wheelbase: 7 ft. box, 130.7 in. wheelbase: 8 ft. box (J-10:1/2 ton) 118.7 in.: Model 25, 130.7 in. Model 45					
J-10	Pickup Townside, 118.7 in. wb.	$4995	6025	3826	—
J-10	Pickup Townside, 130.7 in. wb.	$5059	6025	3926	—
J-20, 360 V-8. 130.7 in. wheelbase. 8 ft. box: Model 46. (J-20: 3/4 ton)					
J-20	Pickup Townside	$5607	6800	4285	—

* 7600 lb. and 8400 lb. GVW optional.

STANDARD ENGINE: J-10: Not avail. for California. For California, the 360 cu. in. V-8 with a 4-barrel carburetor and 4-speed transmission was standard. The only optional engine was the 401 cu. in. V-8 with the 4-barrel carburetor. Engine Type: OHV, In-line-6. Cast iron block and cylinder head. The 4 bbl.360 V-8 is standard for all Jeep trucks in California. Bore x Stroke: 3.75 in. x 3.90 in. Lifters: Hydraulic. Number of main bearings-7. Fuel Induction: 2 bbl. carburetor. Compression Ratio: 8.0:1. Displacement: 258 cu. in. (4.2 liters). Horsepower: Net: 110 @ 3500 rpm. Torque: Net: 195 lb.-ft. @ 2000 rpm. Oil refill capacity: 5 qt. with filter change. Fuel Requirements: Leaded or unleaded.

STANDARD ENGINE: J-20, optional J-10: Engine Type: OHV, V-8. Cast iron block and cylinder head. Not avail. for California. Bore x Stroke: 4.08 in. x 3.44 in. Lifters: Hydraulic. Number of main bearings-5. Fuel Induction: 2 bbl. carburetor. Compression Ratio: 8.25:1. Displacement: 360 cu. in. (5.89 liters). Horsepower: Net: 175 @ 4000 rpm. Torque: Net: 285 lb.-ft. Oil refill capacity: 5 qt. with filter change. Fuel Requirements: Leaded or unleaded.

OPTIONAL ENGINE: J-10 and J-20: Engine Type: OHV, 360 V-8. Cast iron block and cylinder head. Bore x Stroke: 4.08 in. x 3.44 in. Lifters: Hydraulic. Number of main bearings-5. Fuel Induction: 4 bbl. carburetor. Compression Ratio: 8.25:1. Displacement: 360 cu. in. (5.89 liters). Horsepower: Net: 195 @ 4400 rpm. Torque: Net: 295 lb.-ft. @ 2900 rpm. Oil refill capacity: 5 qt. with filter change. Fuel Requirements: Leaded.

OPTIONAL ENGINE: J-10 and J-20: Engine Type: OHV, 401 V-8. Cast iron block and cylinder head. Bore x Stroke: 4.165 in. x 3.68 in. Lifters: Hydraulic. Number of main bearings-5. Fuel Induction: 4 bbl. carburetor. Compression Ratio: 8.35:1. Displacement: 401 cu. in. (6.57 liters). Horsepower: Net: 215 @ 4400 rpm. Torque: Net: 320 lb.-ft. @ 2800 rpm. Oil refill capacity: 5 qt. with filter change. Fuel Requirements: Leaded or unleaded.

CHASSIS FEATURES: Separate body and frame. Deep web frame, splayed box section side rails, wide flange, lightweight pressed steel with five cross members.

SUSPENSION AND RUNNING GEAR: Front Suspension: J-10: 5-leaf semi-elliptical; Spring rate: 195 lb./in. Hydraulic double-action shock absorbers, J-20: 2-leaf semi-elliptical, Spring rate: 260 lb./in. Optional: J-10: Heavy-duty front springs with rates of 215, 260 or 330 lb./in., and heavy-duty shock absorbers. J-20: Heavy-duty front springs with 330 lb/in. rate, and heavy-duty shock absorbers. Rear Suspension: J-10 118.7 in. wheelbase: 5-leaf semi-elliptical springs; Spring rate: 118.7 in. wheelbase: 165 lb./in.; 130.7 in. wheelbase: 285 lb./in. J-20: 3 semi-elliptical leaf springs. Spring rate: 340 lb./in. Hydraulic double-action shock absorbers. Optional: J-10, 118.7 in. wheelbase: Heavy-duty springs and shock absorbers. Spring rate: 165/265 lb./in., 130.7 in. wheelbase: 340 lb./in/spring rate. J-20: Heavy-duty springs and shock absorbers. Spring rate: 510 lb/in. Front Axle Type and Capacity: Dana 44, full floating, hypoid, open end. Capacity: 3200 lb. (J-10), 3500 lb. (J-20). Rear Axle Type and Capacity: J-10: Semi-floating, full-floating-J-20. Capacity: J-10: 3200 lb. J-20/6800 lb. GVW: 4090 lb., J-20/7600 lb. GVW: 4700 lb.; J-20/8400 lb. GVW: 5500 lb. Optional: Powr-Lok differential.

Engines, axle ratios and transmissions for 1977

	Engine	Axle Ratios		Dana 20 4-WD		Quadra-Trac 4-WD
		Std.	Opt.	3-spd.	4-spd.	
J-10	258/2 bbl.	3.54	4.09	Std.	Opt.	Opt.
	360/2 bbl.	3.54	4.09	Std.	Opt.	Opt.
	360/4 bbl.	3.54	4.09	N.A.	Std.	Opt.
	401/4 bbl.	3.54	N.A.	N.A.	N.A.	Std.
J-20	360/2 bbl.	3.73	4.09	Std.	Opt.	Opt.
	360/4 bbl.	3.73	4.09	N.A.	Std.	Opt.
	401/4 bbl.	3.73	N.A.	N.A.	N.A.	Std.

Transfer Case: All models with manual trans.: 2-speed Dana model 20, 2.03:1, 1.0:1. Quadra-Trac: 2.57:1, 1.00:1. Brakes: Type: J-10 & J-20: Hydraulic, front discs and rear drums. Dimensions: Front: J-10: 12.0 in.; J-20: 12.5 in. dia. disc, rear: J-10: 11.0 in. x 2.00 in. drums, J-20: 12 in. x 2.00 in. drums. Total brake swept area: J-10: 364 sq. in. J-20: 429 sq. in. Wheels: Full drop center. J-10: 15 x 6, 6-bolt; J-20, model 26: 16 x 6, 8-bolt, model 46: 16.5 x 6, 8-bolt. Optional: J-10: 15 x 7.00 (aluminum), 15 x 8 in. (spoke-style steel); J-20: 16.5 x 6.75, 16 x 5.0. Tires: J-10: H78 x 15B steel belted radial, J-20: 8.00 x 16.5 (6800 lb. GVW), 9.50 x 16.5 (7600 and 8400 lb. GVW). Optional: J-10: HR78 x 15 steel belted radial, H78 x 15D 4-ply Custom Power Cushion & Power Cushion "78", HR78 x 15 steel belted radial Mud and Snow, H78 x 15 Suburbanite Polyglas and Suburbanite XG Polyglas,10 x 15 Tracker A-T (short wheelbase J-10 only; included as part of the Honcho Package). J-20: 8.00 x 16.5 8-ply Cushion Miler White sidewall, 9.50 x 16.5 8-ply Cushion Miler, 7.50 x 16 6, 8 or 10 ply Cushion Xtra Grip Hi-Miler. Steering: Recirculating ball. Ratio: 24:1. Turns Lock-to-Lock: 4.0. Turning Circle: J-10, model 25: 40.6 ft., Honcho: 41.2 ft., J-10 model 45 and J-20 model 46: 44.5 ft. Optional: Variable ratio power steering. Ratios: 20/16.4:1. Standard: Transmission: 3-spd. man. trans. except for vehicles with 8000 lb. GVW (J-4800) which have 4-spd. manual standard. Ratios: 3.00:1, 1.83:1, 1.00:1. Optional: 3-spd. Turbo Hydra-Matic. Not avail. for 8000 lb. GVW vehicles. Ratios: 2.48:1, 1.48:1, 1.00:1. Optional: 4-speed manual trans (synchromesh on top three gears). Ratios: 4.02:1, 3.09:1, 1.68:1, 1.00:1. Clutch: V-8 models: 11 in. Single dry plate. Total lining area: 123.7 sq. in. 6-cyl. models: 10.0 in single dry plate. Total lining area: 106.8 sq. in. Optional: Heavy-duty clutch.

VEHICLE DIMENSIONS: Wheelbase: Model 25: 118.7 in.; model 45 & 46: 130.7 in. Overall Length: Model 25: 192.5 in. Models 45 & 46: 204.5 in. Front/Rear Tread: Model 25 and model 45: 63.3/63.8 in. Model 46: 64.6/65.9 in. Overall Height: Model 25: 69.3 in., model 45: 69.1 in., model 46: 70.7 in. Width: 78.9 in. Front/Rear Overhang: 29.9 in./43.9 in. Tailgate: Width and Height: 57.2 in. x 20.5 in. Approach/Departure Degrees: 119 in. wheelbase: 45/26. Ground Clearance: Minimum ground clearance: J-10: 7.7 in.; J-20: 8.1 in. Load space: 118.7 in. wheelbase: 83.6 in. x 50 in. x 20.5 in.; 130.7 in. wheelbase. 95.6 in. x 50 in. x 20.5 in. Maximum capacity (Volume Index): Model 25: 67.0 cu. ft.; model 45 and model 46: 76.6 cu. ft. Front headroom: 40.2 in. Front legroom: 45.00 in. Front shoulder room: 58.3 in. Front hip room: 60.5 in. Pedal to seat back (max.): 43.0 in. Steering wheel to seat back (max.): 25.0 in. Seat to ground: 35.0 in. Floor to ground: Model 25: 20.7 in.; model 45: 20.5 in.; model 46: 22.1 in.

CAPACITIES: Fuel Tank: 19.0 gal. 20 gal. tank optional. Not available for 118.7 in. wheelbase. Coolant System: 6-cyl.: 9.5 qt. V-8: 15 qt.

ACCOMMODATIONS: Seating Capacity: Three.

INSTRUMENTATION: 0-110 mph speedometer, 0-99,999.9 mi. odometer, gauges for fuel level, engine coolant temperature, oil pressure and ammeter; Transfer case indicator lights. Quadra-Trac lockout indicator.

OPTIONS AND PRICES: 360 cid 2 bbl. V-8 (J-10): $214. 360 cid 4 bbl. V-8 (J-10): $361 (standard for California). 401 cid 4 bbl. V-8: $314. 4-speed manual trans (J-10): $144 (not available for California). Turbo Hydra-Matic with Quadra-Trac: $345. Turbo Hydra-Matic with Quadra-Trac and low range: $482. Free-running front hubs: $95. Rear Trac-Lok differential: $77. Heavy-duty front and rear shock absorbers: $21. Heavy-duty front springs: $39. Heavy-duty rear springs: $34. Front stabilizer bar: $37. Power steering. Required with Quadra-Trac, air conditioning or V-8 engine: $200. Fuel tank skid plate. Air conditioning: $509. Pioneer Package. Camper Special Package. Includes 8400 lb. GVW rating, heavy-duty shock absorbers, large capacity radiator, 70 amp battery, 62 amp alternator, West Coast style left and right side mirrors, sliding rear window. Front bucket seats with center arm rest: $146. Forged, 15 x 7 in. aluminum styled wheels (J-10 only). 15 x 8 in. spoke-style steel wheels (J-10 only). AM radio. AM/FM radio. Citizen's Band radio. Snow Boss Package. 15 in. Sport steering wheel. Leather-wrapped steering wheel. Tilt steering wheel. Cruise Control. Sliding rear window. Aluminum cargo cap. Wheelcovers. Includes special covers for vehicles equipped with Quadra-Trac. Auxiliary fuel tank. Available for 130.7 in. wheelbase. only. Not available in California. Rear step bumper. Cold Climate Group. Includes engine block heater, 70 amp battery and heavy-duty alternator. Front bumper guards with nerf strips. Locking front hubs. Not available with Quadra-Trac. Golden Eagle Package: $999.

HISTORICAL FOOTNOTES: During 1977 Jeep production was increased at the Toledo, Ohio plant for the 12th time since AMC had assumed ownership of Jeep.

1978 TRUCKS

Both the Honcho and Golden Eagle Packages were continued for 1978. A third package, the 10-4, was introduced. Like the Honcho and Golden Eagle Packages, it was limited to installation on the J-10 with the 119 in. wheelbase. It was offered in a choice of 10 body colors and was highlighted by body side striping in two-tone orange with black accent. A two-tone orange "10-4" decal was mounted on the body side panel. Also standard with the 10-4 were 10-15 Tracker OWL tires, 15 x 8 styled wheels (white with red pinstripe), a truck bed-mounted roll bar and a rear step bumper. The Honcho Package included 8 inch white painted styled steel wheels, rear step bumper, chrome front bumper, 10-15 Tracker A-T OWL tires, bright door window frames, fender lip extensions, Sport steering wheel, bright armrest overlays and hood insulation. Eleven exterior body colors were available, with body side tape striping in gold with brown and orange accents, or dark blue with gold and orange accents. Bench seats trimmed in Levi's door trim were standard, with Levi's cloth bucket seats optional. Levi's door trim panel inserts were also included in the Honcho Package. Floor carpeting was either blue or tan. The Golden Eagle Package had a broader choice of body colors — Mocha brown metallic, oakleaf brown, loden green, sand tan, alpine white, golden ginger metallic and classic black. Among the features in the Golden Eagle Package were chrome front bumper, rear step bumper, 8 in. spoked steel wheels painted gold with black accent stripe, 10-15 Tracker A-T OWL tires, bright door window frames, roll bar for the pickup box, steel grille guard, off-road driving lamps mounted on the roll bar, beige Levi's bucket seats and custom interior, Tan carpeting, tan Sport steering wheel, "engine turned" instrument panel, bright armrest overlays and hood insulation. Exterior features were dominated by a large Golden Eagle decal on the hood. Other exterior items included double belt-line stripes on the doors, cab and upper box sides, and wheel-lip stripes. The Golden Eagle name also appears on the lower door panel.

The 10-4 Package was available for the short wheelbase J-10 truck. It was offered in any of the following body colors: Mocha brown metallic, oakleaf brown, autumn red metallic, alpine white, sand tan, pewter grey metallic, firecracker red, classic black and brilliant blue. It also included a unique body side striping in two-tone orange with black accent. Mounted on the body side panel was a two-tone orange "10-4" Package identifier decal. The 10-4 could be ordered with or without factory-installed CB radio with AM/FM or AM, or without. Standard with the 10-4 was 10-15 Tracker OWL tires, 15 x 8 in. styled wheels (white with red pin stripe), truck bed roll bar and rear step bumper.

1978 Jeep Honcho pickup

The Honcho Package included 8 in. white painted spoked style steel wheels, rear step bumper, chrome front bumper, 10-15 Tracker A-T OWL tires, bright door window frames, fender lip accents, Sport steering wheel, bright armrest overlays and hood insulation. Eleven body colors were offered, with body side tape striping in gold with brown and orange accents, or dark blue with gold and orange accents. A bench seat trimmed in Levi's cloth was standard, with Levi's cloth bucket seats optional. Levi's door trim panel inserts are also included in the Honcho Package. The floor carpeting was in either blue or tan.

Like the 1978 Cherokee and Wagoneer models, all Jeep trucks had increased, by 2.5 inches, driver legroom due to a modified toe board and relocated accelerator pedal. Also shared with those models was the truck's new ambient air intake system which lowered engine temperature thus increasing engine efficiency. Gross vehicle weight rating of the J-10 series was increased from 6025 to 6200 pounds.

New options for 1978 included a factory-installed CB radio, offered in conjunction with AM/FM Stereo or with AM; a new AM/FM Multi-Plex 8-Track tape system, 7 inch chrome-plated spoked steel wheels for the J-10 models; grille guard, and a pickup bed-mounted roll bar.

Noting the limited color selection for the Golden Eagle and 10-4 Packages, the 1978 J-truck body selection was as follows for 1978: Loden green metallic (not available for Honcho), mocha brown metallic, oakleaf brown, autumn red metallic, alpine white, sand tan, pewter grey metallic (not available for Honcho), sunshine yellow, firecracker red (not available for Honcho), Classic Black, golden ginger metallic, captain blue metallic, sun orange. The last three colors listed were new for 1978.

1978 Jeep J-20 pickup

I.D. DATA: The V.I.N. consisted of 13 symbols. The first (a letter) identified the Jeep Corporation. The second (a number) indicated the model year. The third entry (a letter) identified the transmission/drivetrain/assembly plant. The fourth and fifth symbols (both numbers) identified the model. The sixth symbol (a letter) indicated the code model and GVW. The seventh entry (a letter) indicated the engine. The last six number indicated the sequential production number. The serial number was located on the left-hand hinge pillar.

Model Number	Body Type	Factory Price	GVW	Shipping Weight	Prod. Total
J-10, 6-cyl. 118.7 in. wheelbase: 7 ft. box, 130.7 in. wheelbase: 8 ft. box (J-10:1/2 ton) 118.7 in.: Model 25, 130.7 in. Model 45					
J-10	Pickup Townside, 118.7 in. wb.	$5675	6200	3831	—
J-10	Pickup Townside, 130.7 in. wb.	$5743	6200	3898	—
J-20, 360 V-8. 130.7 in. wheelbase. 8 ft. box: Model 46. (J-20: 3/4 ton)					
J-20	Pickup Townside	$6324	6800	4269	—

* 7600 lb. and 8400 lb. GVW optional.

STANDARD ENGINE: J-10: Not avail. for California. For California, the 360 cu. in. V-8 with a 4-barrel carburetor and 4-speed transmission was standard. The only optional engine was the 401 cu. in. V-8 with the 4-barrel carburetor. Engine Type: OHV, In-line-6. Cast iron block and cylinder head. The 4 bbl.360 V-8 is standard for all Jeep trucks in California. Bore x Stroke: 3.75 in. x 3.90 in. Lifters: Hydraulic. Number of main bearings-7. Fuel Induction: 2 bbl. carburetor. Compression Ratio: 8.0:1. Displacement: 258 cu. in. (4.2 liters). Horsepower: Net: 110 @ 3500 rpm. Torque: Net: 195 lb.-ft. @ 2000 rpm. Oil refill capacity: 5 qt. with filter change. Fuel Requirements: Leaded or unleaded.

STANDARD ENGINE: J-20, optional J-10: Engine Type: OHV, V-8. Cast iron block and cylinder head. Not avail. for California. Bore x Stroke: 4.08 in. x 3.44 in. Lifters: Hydraulic. Number of main bearings-5. Fuel Induction: 2 bbl. carburetor. Compression Ratio: 8.25:1. Displacement: 360 cu. in. (5.89 liters). Horsepower: Net: 175 @ 4000 rpm. Torque: Net: 285 lb.-ft. Oil refill capacity: 5 qt. with filter change. Fuel Requirements: Leaded or unleaded.

OPTIONAL ENGINE: J-10 and J-20: Engine Type: OHV, 360 V-8. Cast iron block and cylinder head. Bore x Stroke: 4.08 in. x 3.44 in. Lifters: Hydraulic. Number of main bearings-5. Fuel Induction: 4 bbl. carburetor. Compression Ratio: 8.25:1. Displacement: 360 cu. in. (5.89 liters). Horsepower: Net: 195 @ 4400 rpm. Torque: Net: 295 lb.-ft. @ 2900 rpm. Oil refill capacity: 5 qt. with filter change. Fuel Requirements: Leaded.

OPTIONAL ENGINE: J-10 and J-20. Engine Type: OHV, 401 V-8. Cast iron block and cylinder head. Bore x Stroke: 4.165 in. x 3.68 in. Lifters: Hydraulic. Number of main bearings-5. Fuel Induction: 4 bbl. carburetor. Compression Ratio: 8.35:1. Displacement: 401 cu. in. (6.57 liters). Horsepower: Net: 215 @ 4400 rpm. Torque: Net: 320 lb.-ft. @ 2800 rpm. Oil refill capacity: 5 qt. with filter change. Fuel Requirements: Leaded or unleaded.

CHASSIS FEATURES: Separate body and frame. Deep web frame, splayed box section side rails, wide flange, lightweight pressed steel with five cross members.

SUSPENSION AND RUNNING GEAR: Front Suspension: J-10: 5-leaf semi-elliptical; Spring rate: 195 lb./in. Hydraulic double-action shock absorbers, J-20: 2-leaf semi-elliptical, Spring rate: 260 lb./in. Optional: J-10: Heavy-duty front springs with rates of 215, 260 or 330 lb./in., and heavy-duty shock absorbers. J-20: Heavy-duty front springs with 330 lb/in. rate, and heavy-duty shock absorbers. Rear Suspension: J-10 118.7 in. wheelbase: 5-leaf semi-elliptical springs; Spring rate: 118.7 in. wheelbase: 165 lb./in.; 130.7 in. wheelbase: 285 lb./in. J-20: 3 semi-elliptical leaf springs. Spring rate: 340 lb./in. Hydraulic double-action shock absorbers. Optional: J-10, 118.7 in. wheelbase: Heavy-duty springs and shock absorbers. Spring rate: 165/265 lb./in., 130.7 in. wheelbase: 340 lb./in/spring rate. J-20: Heavy-duty springs and shock absorbers. Spring rate: 510 lb/in. Front Axle Type and Capacity: Dana 44, full floating, hypoid, open end. Capacity: 3200 lb. (J-10), 3500 lb. (J-20). Rear Axle Type and Capacity: J-10: Semi-floating, full-floating-J-20. Capacity: J-10: 3200 lb. J-20/6800 lb. GVW: 4090 lb., J-20/7600 lb. GVW: 4700 lb.; J-20/8400 lb. GVW: 5500 lb. Optional: Powr-Lok differential.

Engines, axle ratios and transmissions for 1978

	Engine	Axle Ratios		Dana 20 4-WD		Quadra-Trac 4-WD
		Std.	Opt.	3-spd.	4-spd.	
J-10	258/2 bbl.	3.54	4.09	Std.	Opt.	Opt.
	360/2 bbl.	3.54	4.09	Std.	Opt.	Opt.
	360/4 bbl.	3.54	4.09	N.A.	Std.	Opt.
	401/4 bbl.	3.54	N.A.	N.A.	N.A.	Std.
J-20	360/2 bbl.	3.73	4.09	Std.	Opt.	
	360/4 bbl.	3.73	4.09	N.A.	Std.	Opt.
	401/4 bbl.	3.73	N.A.	N.A.	N.A.	Std.

Transfer Case: All models with manual trans.: 2-speed Dana model 20, 2.03:1, 1.0:1. Quadra-Trac: 2.57:1, 1.00:1. Brakes: Type: J-10 & J-20: Hydraulic, front discs and rear drums. Dimensions: Front: J-10: 12.0 in.; J-20: 12.5 in. dia. disc, rear: J-10: 11.0 in. x 2.00 in. drums, J-20: 12 in. x 2.00 in. drums. Total brake swept area: J-10: 364 sq. in. J-20: 429 sq. in. Wheels: Full drop center. J-10: 15 x 6, 6-bolt; J-20, model 26: 16 x 6, 8-bolt, model 46: 16.5 x 6, 8-bolt. Optional: J-10: 15 x 7.00 (aluminum), 15 x 8 in. (spoke-style steel); J-20: 16.5 x 6.75, 16 x 5.0. Tires: J-10: H78 x 15B steel belted radial, J-20: 8.00 x 16.5 (6800 lb. GVW), 9.50 x 16.5 (7600 and 8400 lb. GVW). Optional: J-10: HR78 x 15 steel belted radial, H78 x 15D 4-ply Custom Power Cushion & Power Cushion "78", HR78 x 15 steel belted radial Mud and Snow, H78 x 15 Suburbanite Polyglas and Suburbanite XG Polyglas,10 x 15 Tracker A-T (short wheelbase J-10 only; included as part of the Honcho Package). J-20: 8.00 x 16.5 8-ply Cushion Miler white sidewall, 9.50 x 16.5 8-ply Cushion Miler, 7.50 x 16 6, 8 or 10 ply Cushion Xtra Grip Hi-Miler. Steering: Recirculating ball. Ratio: 24:1. Turns Lock-to-Lock: 4.0. Turning Circle: J-10, model 25: 40.6 ft., Honcho: 41.2 ft., J-10 model 45 and J-20 model 46: 44.5 ft. Optional: Variable ratio power steering. Ratios: 20/16.4:1. Standard: Transmission: 3-spd. man. trans. except for vehicles with 8000 lb. GVW (J-4800) which have 4-spd. manual standard. Ratios: 3.00:1, 1.83:1, 1.00:1. Optional: 3-spd. Turbo Hydra-Matic. Not avail. for 8000 lb. GVW vehicles. Ratios: 2.48:1, 1.48:1, 1.00:1. Optional: 4-speed manual trans (synchromesh on top three gears). Ratios: 4.02:1, 3.09:1, 1.68:1, 1.00:1. Clutch: V-8 models: 11 in. Single dry plate. Total lining area: 123.7 sq. in. 6-cyl. models: 10.0 in single dry plate. Total lining area: 106.8 sq. in. Optional: Heavy-duty clutch.

VEHICLE DIMENSIONS: Wheelbase: Model 25: 118.7 in.; model 45 & 46: 130.7 in. Overall Length: Model 25: 192.5 in. Models 45 & 46: 204.5 in. Front/Rear Tread: Model 25 and model 45: 63.3/63.8 in. Model 46: 64.6/65.9 in. Overall Height: Model 25: 69.3 in., model 45: 69.1 in., model 46: 70.7 in. Width: 78.9 in. Front/Rear Overhang: 29.9 in./43.9 in. Tailgate: Width and Height: 57.2 in. x 20.5 in. Approach/Departure Degrees: 119 in. wheelbase: 45/26. Ground Clearance: Minimum ground clearance: J-10: 7.7 in.; J-20: 8.1 in. Load space: 118.7 in. wheelbase: 83.6 in. x 50 in. x 20.5 in.; 130.7 in. wheelbase. 95.6 in. x 50 in. x 20.5 in. Maximum capacity (Volume Index): Model 25: 67.0 cu. ft.; model 45 and model 46: 76.6 cu. ft. Front headroom: 40.2 in. Front legroom: 45.00 in. Front shoulder room: 58.3 in. Front hip room: 60.5 in. Pedal to seat back (max.): 43.0 in. Steering wheel to seat back (max.): 25.0 in. Seat to ground: 35.0 in. Floor to ground: Model 25: 20.7 in.; model 45: 20.5 in.; model 46: 22.1 in.

CAPACITIES: Fuel Tank: 19.0 gal. 20 gal. tank optional. Not available for 118.7 in. wheelbase. Coolant System: 6-cyl.: 9.5 qt. V-8: 15 qt.

ACCOMMODATIONS: Seating Capacity: Three.

INSTRUMENTATION: 0-110 mph speedometer, 0-99,999.9 mi. odometer, gauges for fuel level, engine coolant temperature, oil pressure and ammeter; Transfer case indicator lights. Quadra-Trac lockout indicator.

OPTIONS AND PRICES: 360 cid 2 bbl. V-8 (J-10): $260. 360 cid 4 bbl. V-8 (J-10), standard for California. 401 cid 4 bbl. V-8. 4-speed manual trans (J-10): $153 (not available for California). Turbo Hydra-Matic with Quadra-Trac. Turbo Hydra-Matic with Quadra-Trac and low range. Free-running front hubs. Rear Trac-Lok differential. Heavy-duty front and rear shock absorbers. Heavy-duty front springs. Heavy-duty rear springs. Front stabilizer bar. Power steering. Required with Quadra-Trac, air conditioning or V-8 engine. Tinted glass. Hubcaps. Fuel tank skid plate. Air conditioning. Camper Special Package. Includes 8400 lb. GVW rating, heavy-duty shock absorbers, large capacity radiator, 70 amp battery, 62 amp alternator, West Coast style left and right side mirrors, sliding rear window. Front bucket seats with center arm rest. Forged, 15 x 7 in. aluminum styled wheels (J-10 only). 15 x8 in. spoke-style steel wheels (J-10 only). AM radio. AM/FM radio. Citizen's Band radio. Snow Boss Package: $1165. 15 in. Sport steering wheel. Leather-wrapped steering wheel. Tilt steering wheel. Cruise Control. Sliding rear window. Aluminum cargo cap. Wheelcovers. Includes special covers for vehicles equipped with Quadra-Trac. Auxiliary fuel tank. Available for 130.7 in. wheelbase. only. Not available in California. Rear step bumper. Cold Climate Group. Includes engine block heater, 70 amp battery and heavy-duty alternator. Front bumper guards with nerf strips. Locking front hubs. Not available with Quadra-Trac. Golden Eagle Package: $999. Honcho Package: $749.

HISTORICAL FOOTNOTES: American Motors converted its Brampton, Ontario plant to Jeep truck production during 1978.

1979 TRUCKS

All 1979 model trucks had standard power brakes with front discs. Previously only the J-20 had them as standard equipment. For the first time since 1970 the Jeep truck had a new front end design. Identical to that used on the Cherokee Chief, it was an attractive one-piece item with single rectangular headlights and bright center bars. A new one-piece stamped aluminum front bumper was available with optional rubber bumper guards.

Interior trim of the 1979 base model was elevated to approximately the level of the 1978 custom standard. Thus it had a custom steering wheel and higher grade door panels. Its seats were covered in a Cara vinyl with accent striping.

New options included an Extra-Quiet Insulation Package, intermittent windshield wipers as part of the Convenience Group, a "high style" pickup box enclosure for both long and short wheelbase models, a lighted visor vanity mirror in the light group and a passenger assist handle for the Honcho and 10-4 Packages. The Honcho Package had bolder multi-color, graduated body striping. Full content of the Honcho Package, which was limited to the short wheelbase J-10, consisted of denim fabric bench seat (bucket seats were optional), denim door inserts, carpeting, engine turned instrument cluster overlay, Soft-Feel Sport steering wheel, hood insulation, bright moldings on door window frames, body side tape and tailgate striping (orange or blue), Honcho lettering on doors, unique grille, rear step bumper, 10 x 15 outline white letter Tracker A-T tires, white styled steel wheels and passenger assist handle.

1979 Jeep Honcho pickup

The Golden Eagle Package, also limited to the 118.7 in. wheelbase J-10 offered these features: Bucket seats with center armrest, custom beige denim door panels, carpeting, Soft-Feel Sport steering wheel, engine turned instrument panel cluster overlay, Golden Eagle hood decal and lettering in black and gold, body and hood striping, bright door window frames, roll bar (mounted in pickup box), brush guard, off-road driving lights, 15 x 8 in. styled steel wheels with gold and black stripes, 10 x 15 outline white letter tracker A-T tires, and hood insulation.

The 10-4 Package, also a J-10/117.8 in. wheelbase-only option, had this content: Two-tone orange with black accent bodystriping, 10-4 decal on body sides, rear step bumper, 15 x 8 in. styled steel wheels (white with red stripes), 10 x 15 outline white letter Tracker A-T tires, roll bar, and passenger assist handle.

With both the 401 cu. in. V-8 and 4-barrel carburetor version of the 360 cu. in. V-8 no longer offered the Jeep truck engine lineup was limited to just the 258 cu. in. six (standard in the J-10) and the 360 cu. in. V-8 which was standard for the J-20 and optional for the J-10.

Standard interior equipment for the J-10 and J-20 trucks consisted of these items: Ashtray, left and right side armrests, color-keyed vinyl floor covering, gauges for oil pressure, voltmeter, engine coolant temperature, and fuel level; glove box lock, heater and defroster, lap and shoulder belt restraint system, 12 in. inside rearview mirror, padded instrument panel, padded sun visors, and bench seat with seat belts and retractors. Standard exterior features were as follows: Front chrome-plated aluminum bumper, side safety markers, outside left side mirror, bright trim moldings for vent window and windshield, and high impact windshield glass. The standard functional features included these components: 45 amp battery (6-cyl. engine), 60 amp battery (V-8 engine), foot lever parking brake, dual horns, and electric windshield washers and 2-speed windshield wipers.

I.D. DATA: The V.I.N. consisted of 13 symbols. The first (a letter) identified the Jeep Corporation. The second (a number) indicated the model year. The third entry (a letter) identified the transmission/drivetrain/assembly plant. The fourth and fifth symbols (both numbers) identified the model. The sixth symbol (a letter) indicated the code model and GVW. The seventh entry (a letter) indicated the engine. The last six numbers indicated the sequential production number. The serial number was located on the left-hand hinge pillar.

1979 Jeep J-20 pickup

Model Number	Body Type	Factory Price	GVW	Shipping Weight	Prod. Total
J-10, 6-cyl. 118.7 in. wheelbase: 7 ft. box, 130.7 in. wheelbase: 8 ft. box (J-10:1/2 ton) 118.7 in.: Model 25, 130.7 in. Model 45					
J-10	Pickup Townside, 118.7 in. wb.	$6172	6200	3693	—
J-10	Pickup Townside, 130.7 in. wb.	$6245	6200	3760	—
J-20, 360 V-8. 130.7 in. wheelbase. 8 ft. box: Model 46. (J-20: 3/4 ton)					
J-20	Pickup Townside	$6872	6800	4167	—

* 7600 lb. and 8400 lb. GVW optional.

STANDARD ENGINE: J-10: Not avail. for California. For California, the 360 cu. in. V-8 with a 2-barrel carburetor was standard. for all models. Power steering was a required option. Engine Type: OHV, In-line-6. Cast iron block and cylinder head. Bore x Stroke: 3.75 in. x 3.90 in. Lifters: Hydraulic. Number of main bearings-7. Fuel Induction: 2 bbl. carburetor. Compression Ratio: 8.0:1. Displacement: 258 cu. in. (4.2 liters). Horsepower: Net: 110 @ 3500 rpm. Torque: Net: 195 lb.-ft. @ 2000 rpm. Oil refill capacity: 5 qt. with filter change. Fuel Requirements: Unleaded.

STANDARD ENGINE: J-20, optional J-10: Type: OHV, V-8. Cast iron block and cylinder head. Bore x Stroke: 4.08 in. x 3.44 in. Lifters: Hydraulic. Number of main bearings-5. Fuel Induction: 2 bbl. carburetor. Compression Ratio: 8.25:1. Displacement: 360 cu. in. (5.89 liters). Horsepower: Net: 129 @ 3700 rpm. Torque: Net: 245 lb.-ft. @ 1600 rpm. Oil refill capacity: 5 qt. with filter change. Fuel Requirements: Unleaded.

CHASSIS FEATURES: Separate body and frame. Deep web frame, splayed box section side rails, wide flange, lightweight pressed steel with five cross members.

SUSPENSION AND RUNNING GEAR: Front Suspension: J-10: 5-leaf semi-elliptical; Spring rate: 215 lb./in. Hydraulic double-action shock absorbers, J-20: 7-leaf semi-elliptical, Spring rate: 260 lb./in. Optional: J-10 and J-20: Extra-Duty Suspension Package, Heavy-duty front and rear shock absorbers, front stabilizer bar. Rear Suspension: J-10 118.7 in. wheelbase: 5-leaf semi-elliptical springs; Spring rate: 165 lb./in.; J-10 130.7 in. wheelbase: 4-leaf semi-elliptical springs, spring rate: 245 lb./in. J-20: 2-leaf tapered springs, spring rate: 340 lb./in. Hydraulic double-action shock absorbers,. Optional: J-10, 118.7 in. wheelbase: Heavy-duty springs and shock absorbers. Spring rate: 165/265 lb./in., 130.7 in. wheelbase: 340 lb./in/ spring rate. J-20: Heavy-duty springs and shock absorbers. Spring rate: 510 lb/in. Front Axle Type and Capacity: Dana 44, full floating, hypoid, open end. Capacity: 3200 lb. (J-10), 3500 lb. (J-20). Rear Axle Type and Capacity: J-10: Semi-floating, full-floating-J-20. Capacity: J-10: 3200 lb. J-20/6800 lb. GVW: 4090 lb., J-20/7600 lb. GVW: 4700 lb.; J-20/8400 lb. GVW: 5500 lb. Optional: Powr-Lok differential.

Standard and optional engines, axle ratios and transmissions for 1979

	Engine	Axle Ratios		Dana 20 4-WD		Quadra-Trac 4-WD
		Std.	Opt.	3-spd.	4-spd.	
J-10	258/2 bbl.	3.54	4.09	Std.	Opt.	Opt.
J-20	360/2 bbl.	3.73	4.09	Std.	Opt.	Opt.

Transfer Case: All models with manual trans.: 2-speed Dana model 20, 2.03:1, 1.0:1. Quadra-Trac: 2.57:1, 1.00:1. Brakes: Type: J-10 & J-20: Hydraulic, front discs and rear drums. Dimensions: Front: J-10: 12.0 in.; J-20: 12.5 in. dia. disc, rear: J-10: 11.0 in. x 2.00 in drums, J-20: 12 in. x 2.50 in. drums. Total brake swept area: J-10: 364 sq. in. J-20: 429 sq. in. Wheels: Full drop center. J-10: 15 x 6, 6-bolt, 5.5 in. circle; J-20: 16.5 x 6, 8-bol, 6.5 in. circle. Optional: J-10: 15 x 7.00 (aluminum). Tires: J-10: H78 x 15 black polyester Highway, unbelted. J-20: 8.75 x 16.5 black polyester Cushion Miler R.V. Optional: J-10: H78 x 15B white sidewall polyester Highway Cruiser unbelted), H78 x15B white or black sidewall Town & Country, H78 x 15 black sidewall Viva with two fiberglass cord belts, P225/75R15 white sidewall Tiempo double steel belted radials, HR78 x 15 white sidewall American Eagle with two Flexten cord belts, and HR78 x 15 white sidewall F32 All-Weather Flexten radials. J-20: 9.50 x 16.5 black sidewall Goodyear Tufsyn Cushion Miler, 8.75 x 16.5 and 9.50 x 16.5 black sidewall Custom Xtra Grip. Steering: Recirculating ball. Ratio: 24:1. Turns Lock-to-Lock: 4.0. Turning Circle: J-10, model 25: 40.6 ft., Honcho: 41.2 ft., J-10 model 45 and J-20 model 46: 44.5 ft. Optional: Variable ratio power steering. Ratios: 16.0/13.0:1. Standard: Transmission: 3-spd. man. trans. except for vehicles with 8000 lb. GVW (J-4800) which have 4-spd. manual standard. Ratios: 3.00:1, 1.83:1, 1.00:1. Optional: 3-spd. Turbo Hydra-Matic. Not avail. for 8000 lb. GVW vehicles. Ratios: 2.48:1, 1.48:1, 1.00:1. Optional: 4-speed manual trans (synchromesh on top three gears). Ratios: 4.02:1, 3.09:1, 1.68:1, 1.00:1. Clutch: 11 in. Single dry plate. Total lining area: 123.7 sq. in.

VEHICLE DIMENSIONS: Wheelbase: Model 25: 118.7 in.; model 45 & 46: 130.7 in. Overall Length: Model 25: 192.5 in. Models 45 & 46: 204.5 in. Front/Rear Tread: Model 25 and model 45: 63.3/63.8 in. Model 46: 64.6/65.9 in. Overall Height: Model 25: 69.3 in., model 45: 69.1 in., model 46: 70.7 in. Width: 78.9 in. Front/Rear Overhang: 29.9 in./43.9 in. Tailgate: Width and Height: 57.2 in. x 20.5 in. Approach/Departure Degrees: 119 in. wheelbase: 45/26. Ground Clearance: Minimum ground clearance: J-10: 7.7 in.; J-20: 8.1 in. J-20: Front and differential: 8.1 in. Load space: 118.7 in. wheelbase: 83.6 in. x 50 in. x 20.5 in.; 130.7 in. wheelbase. 95.6 in. x 50 in. x 20.5 in. Maximum capacity (Volume Index): Model 25: 67.0 cu. ft.; model 45 and model 46: 76.6 cu. ft. Front headroom: 40.2 in. Front legroom: 45.00 in. Front shoulder room: 58.3 in. Front hip room: 60.5 in. Pedal to seat back (max.): 43.0 in. Steering wheel to seat back (max.): 25.0 in. Seat to ground: 35.0 in. Floor to ground: Model 25: 20.7 in.; model 45: 20.5 in.; model 46: 22.1 in.

CAPACITIES: Fuel Tank: 19.0 gal. Coolant System: 6-cyl.: 9.5 gal. V-8: 15 qt.

ACCOMMODATIONS: Seating Capacity: Three with bench seat, two with bucket seats.

INSTRUMENTATION: 0-110 mph speedometer, 0-99,999.9 mi. odometer, gauges for fuel level, engine coolant temperature, oil pressure and ammeter; Transfer case indicator lights. Quadra-Trac lockout indicator.

OPTIONS AND PRICES: Custom Miler tires: $228. Custom Package. Includes Custom bench seat in vinyl trim, Custom door trim panels, passenger assist handle, engine turned instrument panel cluster overlay, hood insulation, bright moldings on door window frames and body sides: $126. Honcho Package: $749. Golden Eagle Package: $999. 10-4 Package. Soft-Feel Sport steering wheel. Leather-wrapped Sport steering wheel. Aluminum wheels (not available for J-20). 15 in. wheelcovers (not available for J-20). Hubcaps (J-20): $41. Convenience Group: $83. Air conditioning: $596. Tinted glass: $34. Tilt steering wheel. Cruise control. Light Group. Includes lights for cargo box, glove box, ashtray, engine compartment, plus lighted visor vanity mirror, dome/map light and courtesy lights: $63. Electric clock. Passenger side outside mirror. Low profile dual outside mirrors: $38. Bucket seats with center cushion and folding armrest. AM push-button radio. AM/FM stereo radio. AM/CB 40-channel radio. AM/FM/CB stereo radio: $367. AM/FM/Tape stereo radio. Rear step bumper: $76. Sliding rear window: $83. Cargo Cap: $589. 360 V-8: $260. 4-spd. manual transmission (floor shift): $153. Turbo Hydra-Matic with Quadra-Trac. Turbo Hydra-Matic with Quadra-Trac and low range: $549. Rear Trac-Lok differential. Free wheeling front hubs. Heavy-duty cooling system. Extra-duty Suspension Package. Heavy-duty front and rear shock absorbers. Front stabilizer bar: $41. Heavy-duty 70 amp battery. Heavy-duty 53 amp alternator. Cold Climate group. Includes heavy-duty battery, heavy-duty alternator and engine block heater. Roll bar. Fuel tank skid plate: $56. Front bumper guards. Brush guard. Protective floor mats. Floor carpeting: $28. Snow Boss Package: $1165. Power steering: $226.

HISTORICAL FOOTNOTES: The 1979. Jeep trucks were introduced in the fall of 1978.

1980 TRUCKS

The content of the 1980 Jeep trucks was altered to make them more fuel efficient. The list of changes for the new model year were among the most extensive made in the truck's design since their introduction as 1963 models. Both the part-time and Quadra-Trac four-wheel drive systems were all-new and lighter in weight. The part-time system was available with Chrysler's TorqueFlite automatic or with a new standard 4-speed manual transmission. This latter gearbox had lighter weight aluminum parts, close-spaced gear ratios and full forward gear synchronization. For the first time, Jeep pickups with automatic transmission could be equipped with either the part-time or Quadra-Trac four-wheel drive systems. The J-20 continued to use the same 4-speed manual transmission with a "creeper" first gear as in 1979. Manual free wheeling hubs were included in the four-wheel drive system on models with 4-speed manual transmissions. Both the part-time and full-time four-wheel drive units used by Jeep in the pickup, Cherokee and Wagoneer models were supplied by New Process, a wholly owned subsidiary of Chrysler. However, their use was a Jeep exclusive. The Quadra-Trac, or New Process 219 system was very similar to the New Process 119 model which was introduced in the 1980 Eagle. The main difference between them was that the 119 was a single-speed transfer case whereas the 219 had a high and low range. The Quadra-Trac control was located just below and forward of the driver's seat. The control for the part-time NP 208 was mounted on the floor tunnel to the right of the driver's seat. When used with automatic transmission it was located just below and forward of the driver's seat. These locations also apply to the 1980 Cherokee and Wagoneer models.

Added to the changes made in the J-truck drivetrain components were numerous trim, standard or optional features for 1980. New options included power windows, power door locks, an electronic digital clock, dual remote controlled outside mirrors, a new cassette tape AM/FM radio combination, body side scuff moldings, a chrome step bumper and, for the J-10 only, chrome-plated styled wheels. The previously optional front stabilizer bar was now standard on all pickups. Also standard on models with V-8 or automatic transmission was power steering. All trucks had a new single loop seat belt system and a new high density blow molded fuel tank.

For the first time since 1973 Jeep offered a stepside body style for the J-10. Previously identified as the Thriftside the new stepside was known as the Sportside. Included in the Sportside model were all the custom features including bright finish moldings on the door window frames, body side scuff moldings, deluxe door trim panels, engine turned instrument cluster trim, armrest overlays with a brushed insert, hood insulation and a passenger assist handle. The Sportside was also equipped with a flareside box with a metal floor, "balloon" fenders, 15 x 8 OWL Tracker A-T tires, rear step bumper, black and chrome grille (the custom had a chrome plated grille with grey and black accent paint), vinyl bucket seats and floor carpeting. When the Honcho Package was installed on a Sportside truck it differed from its form on the Townside models due to its unique pickup box fender decals, wood box side and front panel rails, contoured roll bar and denim bucket seats.

A new top-of-the-line Trim Package, the Laredo, was offered for 1980. Included in its $1600 price were features such as special painted hubcaps, 15 x 8 chrome styled wheels, 10R x 15 Wrangler radial tires, black and chrome grille, chrome rear step bumper, chrome exterior remote control mirrors, body striping in either silver or gold tones, full carpeting, high back bucket seats, door pull straps, leather-wrapped steering wheel, center armrest, instrument panel and glove box striping, extra quiet insulation, Convenience Group, Light Group, bumper guards, front and rear nerf bars and the Visibility Group.

The 1980 color selection was as follows: Smoke grey metallic, dark brown metallic, Saxon yellow, navy blue, cardinal red, olympic white, caramel, cameo tan, alpaca brown metallic, dark green metallic, medium teal blue, russet red metallic, bordeaux metallic, and classic black, which was the only color carried over from 1979. The Laredo Package was available in olympic white, cameo tan, dark brown metallic, bordeaux metallic, Saxon yellow, classic black, and navy blue.

1980 Jeep J-10 Honcho Pickup

I.D. DATA: The V.I.N. consisted of 13 symbols. The first (a letter) identified the Jeep Corporation. The second (a number) indicated the model year. The third entry (a letter) identifies the transmission/drivetrain/assembly Plant. The fourth and fifth symbols (both numbers) identified the model. The sixth symbol (a letter) indicates the code model and GVW. The seventh entry (a letter) indicated the engine. The last six numbers indicated the sequential production number. The serial number was located on the left-hand hinge pillar.

Model Number	Body Type	Factory Price	GVW	Shipping Weight	Prod. Total
J-10, 6-cyl. 118.7 in. wheelbase: 7 ft. box, 130.7 in. wheelbase: 8 ft. box (J-10:1/2 ton) 118.7 in.: Model 25, 130.7 in. Model 45					
J-10	Pickup Townside, 118.7 in. wb	$6874	6200	3714	8636[1]
J-10	Pickup Townside, 130.7 in. wb.	$6972	6200	3776	—

J-20, 360 V-8. 130.7 in. wheelbase. 8 ft. box: Model 46. (J-20: 3/4 ton)

J-20	Pickup Townside	$7837	6800[2]	4246	—

NOTE 1: All J series trucks.
NOTE 2: 7600 lb. and 8400 lb. GVW optional.

STANDARD ENGINE: J-10: Not avail. for California. Engine Type: OHV, In-line-6. Cast iron block and cylinder head. The 2 bbl. 360 V-8 is standard for all Jeep trucks in California. Bore x Stroke: 3.75 in. x 3.90 in. Lifters: Hydraulic. Number of main bearings-7. Fuel Induction: 2 bbl. carburetor. Compression Ratio: 8.0:1. Displacement: 258 cu. in. (4.2 liters). Horsepower: Net: 110 @ 3500 rpm. Torque: Net: 195 lb.-ft. @ 2000 rpm. Oil refill capacity: 5 qt. with filter change. Fuel Requirements: Unleaded.

STANDARD ENGINE: J-20, optional J-10: Engine Type: OHV, V-8. Cast iron block and cylinder head. Bore x Stroke: 4.08 in. x 3.44 in. Lifters: Hydraulic. Number of main bearings-5. Fuel Induction: 2 bbl. carburetor. Compression Ratio: 8.25:1. Displacement: 360 cu. in. (5.89 liters). Horsepower: Net: 129 @ 3700 rpm. Torque: Net: 245 lb.-ft. @ 1600 rpm. Oil refill capacity: 5 qt. with filter change. Fuel Requirements: Unleaded.

CHASSIS FEATURES: Separate body and frame. Deep web frame, splayed box section side rails, wide flange, lightweight pressed steel with five cross members.

SUSPENSION AND RUNNING GEAR: Front Suspension: J-10: 5-leaf semi-elliptical; Spring rate: 215 lb./in. Hydraulic double-action shock absorbers, J-20: 7-leaf semi-elliptical, Spring rate: 260 lb./in. Optional: Spring Rates: J-10: 210, 230 and 260 lb./in. J-20: 330 lb./in. Heavy-duty front and rear shock absorbers. Rear Suspension: J-10 118.7 in. wheelbase: 5-leaf semi-elliptical springs; Spring rate: 165 lb./in.; J-10 130.7 in. wheelbase: 4-leaf semi-elliptical springs, spring rate: 245 lb./in. J-20: 2-leaf tapered springs, spring rate: 340 lb./in. Hydraulic double-action shock absorbers. Optional: J-10, 118.7 in. wheelbase: Heavy-duty springs and shock absorbers. Spring rate: 165/265 lb./in., 130.7 in. wheelbase: 340 lb./in/spring rate. J-20: Heavy-duty springs and shock absorbers. Spring rate: 510 lb/in. Front Axle Type and Capacity: Dana 44, full floating, Hypoid, open end. Capacity: 3200 lb. (J-10), 3500 lb. (J-20). Rear Axle Type and Capacity: J-10: Semi-floating, full-floating-J-20. Capacity: J-10: 3200 lb. J-20/6800 lb. GVW: 3980 lb., J-20/7600 lb. GVW: 4700 lb.; J-20/8400 lb. GVW: 5500 lb. Optional: Powr-Lok differential. Axle Ratios: J-10 (6-cyl.): 3.31:1, J-10 (V-8, 4-spd.): 3.31:1, J-10 (V-8, automatic trans.): 2.73:1. J-20 (4-spd. and automatic trans.): 3.73:1. Transfer Case: All models with manual trans.: 2-speed NP 219:. Brakes: Type: J-10 & J-20: Hydraulic, front discs and rear drums. Dimensions: Front: J-10: 12.0 in.; J-20: 12.5 in. dia. disc, rear: J-10: 11.0 in. x 2.00 in drums, J-20: 12 in. x 2.50 in. drums. Total brake swept area: J-10: 364 sq. in. J-20: 429 sq. in. Wheels: Full drop center. J-10: 15 x 6, 6-bolt, 5.5 in. circle; J-20: 16.5 x 6, 8-bol, 6.5 in. circle. Optional: J-10: 15 x 7.00 (aluminum). Tires: J-10: H78 x 15 black polyester Highway, unbelted, J-20 with 6800 lb. GVW: 8.75 x 16.5 black polyester Cushion Miler R.V., J-20 with 7600 and 8400 lb. GVW: 9.50 x 16.5D. Optional: J-10: H78 x15B white sidewall polyester Highway Cruiser unbelted), H78 x15B white or black sidewall Town & Country, H78 x 15 black sidewall Viva with two fiberglass cord belts, P225/75R15 white sidewall Tiempo double steel belted radials, HR78 x 15 white sidewall American Eagle with two Flexten cord belts, and HR78 x 15 Wwhite sidewall F32 All-Weather Flexten radials. J-20: 9.50 x 16.5 black sidewall Goodyear Tufsyn Cushion Miler, 8.75 x 16.5 and 9.50 x 16.5 black sidewall Custom Xtra Grip. Steering: Recirculating ball. Ratio: 24:1. Turns Lock-to-Lock: 4.0. Turning Circle: J-10, model 25: 40.6 ft., Honcho: 41.2 ft., J-10 model 45 and J-20 model 46: 44.5 ft. Optional: Variable ratio power steering. Ratios: 16.0/13.0:1. Standard: Transmission: 4-spd. man. transmission. J-20 models have carry-over 4-spd. manual transmission with creeper first gear. Optional: 3-spd. TorqueFlite. Clutch: 11 in. Single dry plate. Total lining area: 111 sq. in.

VEHICLE DIMENSIONS: Wheelbase: Model 25: 118.7 in.; model 45 & 46: 130.7 in. Overall Length: Model 25: 192.5 in. Models 45 & 46: 204.5 in. Front/Rear Tread: Model 25 and model 45: 63.3/63.8 in. Model 46: 64.6/65.9 in. Overall Height: Model 25: 69.3 in., model 45: 69.1 in., model 46: 70.7 in. Width: 78.9 in. Front/Rear Overhang: 29.9 in./43.9 in. Tailgate: Width and Height: 57.2 in. x 20.5 in. Approach/Departure Degrees: 118.7 in. wheelbase: 45/26.Ground Clearance: Minimum ground clearance: J-10: 7.7 in.; J-20: 8.1 in. J-20: Front and differential: 8.1 in. Load space: 118.7 in. wheelbase: 83.6 in. x 50 in. x 20.5 in.; 130.7 in. wheelbase. 95.6 in. x 50 in. x 20.5 in. Maximum capacity (Volume Index): Model 25: 67.0 cu. ft.; model 45 and model 46: 76.6 cu. ft. Front headroom: 40.2 in. Front legroom: 45.00 in. Front shoulder room: 58.3 in. Front hip room: 60.5 in. Pedal to seat back (max.): 43.0 in. Steering wheel to seat back (max.): 25.0 in. Seat to ground: 35.0 in. Floor to ground: Model 25: 20.7 in.; model 45: 20.5 in.; model 46: 22.1 in.

CAPACITIES: Fuel Tank: 19.7 gal. with skid plate. Coolant System: 6-cyl.: 9.5 qt. V-8: 15 qt.

ACCOMMODATIONS: Seating Capacity: Three with bench seat, two with bucket seats.

INSTRUMENTATION: 0-110 mph speedometer, 0-99,999.9 mi. odometer, gauges for fuel level, engine coolant temperature, oil pressure and ammeter; Transfer case indicator lights. Quadra-Trac lockout indicator.

OPTIONS AND PRICES: Custom Package: $149. Honcho Package: $849. Laredo Package: $1600. Sportside Package: $899. Honcho Sportside Package: $1325. Power steering: $233. AM radio. Premium Sound Group. Includes power amplifier and higher fidelity speakers: $95. AM/FM stereo radio: $245. AM/FM stereo with tape player: $355. AM/FM stereo CB radio: $495. 360 cu. in. V-8: $420. Heavy-duty battery: $40. Air conditioning: $614. Visibility Group. Includes dual remote control mirrors, and intermittent windshield wipers. Convenience Group. Includes lights-on buzzer, digital clock, and engine compartment light. Light Group includes cargo box light, glove box light, ashtray light, map/dome light, and lighted visor vanity mirror. Power windows. Power door locks. Soft-Feel steering wheel. Leather-wrapped Sport steering wheel. Heavy-duty cooling system. Tilt steering wheel. Painted or chrome rear bumper. Extra-duty Suspension Package. Heavy-duty front and rear shock absorbers. Heavy-duty battery. Heavy-duty alternator. Cool Climate group. Includes heavy-duty alternator and battery, and engine block heater. Snow Boss Package: $1260. Trailer Towing Packages.

HISTORICAL FOOTNOTES: The 1980 Jeep trucks were introduced in the fall of 1979.

1981 TRUCKS

The 1981 Jeep Trucks shared many of the technical developments and styling revisions of the 1981 Cherokee and Wagoneer models. Thus its 6-cylinder engine was 90 pounds lighter and all models had a vertically slotted grille, low-drag front power disc brakes, power steering and a lock-up torque converter for the automatic transmission. The front roof-lip was removed for 1981 and a new drag reducing front air dam was added. All models also had new upper windshield, end caps and drip moldings.

The 4-speed manual transmission for the V-8 powered J-10 now had a 3.82:1 instead of 3.52:1 first gear ratio. This change was accompanied by a drop in standard axle ratio for the J-10 from 3.31: To 2.73:1.

All pickup trim options except the 10-4 Package were carried over from 1980. The Honcho featured new body side tape striping in red, blue, or yellow, depending on exterior color. Added to the Honcho Package was striping on the tailgate. The Laredo Package was revised to include Laredo nameplates on the body and instrument panel, and body striping in silver and grey or nutmeg and bronze, depending on body color.

The 1981 Jeep pickup trucks had one-side galvanized steel for their top front-cowl and inner panels, gussets running from rocker panels to cowl side panels, body rear lower panels and reinforcements, support and extension toe risers and front floor seat belt anchor reinforcements. One-side galvanized steel was also used for the truck's outer front end panels, inner side panels, front and rear floor extensions and pick-up box posts. Hot wax was applied to the truck's inner door panels, tailgates and rear quarter panels. Aluminum wax was sprayed inside of the rocker panels.

Primary standard equipment included these items: Ashtray, left and right side armrests, cigarette lighter, color-keyed vinyl floor covering, heater and defroster, 12 in. inside day/night mirror, glove box lock, padded instrument panel, bench seat, electric 2-speed windshield wipers and windshield washers, bright moldings for vent window and windshield with new windshield upper moldings, end cap and drip rails, new front air dam, 42 amp alternator, 55-580 battery, front stabilizer bar, new inside hood release, rear fender stone protection, and power steering.

The 1981Jeep Trucks were offered in these colors: Cameo tan, vintage red metallic, classic black, autumn gold, moonlight blue, steel grey metallic, dark brown metallic, deep maroon metallic, olympic white, copper brown metallic, oriental red, Montana blue, sherwood green metallic, and chestnut brown metallic.

1981 Jeep J-10 Honcho pickup

I.D. DATA: The serial number was located on the left-hand hinge pillar. The V.I.N. had 17 symbols. The first three entries identified the manufacturer, make and type of vehicle. The fourth unit, a letter, designated the engine. The fifth character, a letter, identified the transmission. The sixth and seventh characters identified the series and body style. The eighth character identified the GVW rating. Next followed a check digit. The eleventh character was the manufacturing plant identification. The final six digits were the sequential production number.

Model Number	Body Type	Factory Price	GVW	Shipping Weight	Prod. Total
J-10, 6-cyl. 118.7 in. wheelbase: 7 ft. box, 130.7 in. wheelbase: 8 ft. box (J-10:1/2 ton) 118.7 in.: Model 25, 130.7 in. Model 26					
J-10	Pickup Townside, 118.7 in. wb.	$7960	6200	3702	6516[1]
J-10	Pickup Townside, 130.7 in. wb.	$8056	6200	3764	—
J-20, 360 V-8. 130.7 in. wheelbase. 8 ft. box: Model 27. (J-20: 3/4 ton)					
J-20	Pickup Townside	$8766	6800[2]	4308	—

NOTE 1: All J series trucks.
NOTE 2: 7600 lb. and 8400 lb. GVW optional.

STANDARD ENGINE: J-10: Engine Type: OHV, In-line-6. Cast iron block and cylinder head. Bore x Stroke: 3.75 in. x 3.90 in. Lifters: Hydraulic. Number of main bearings-7. Fuel Induction: 2 bbl. carburetor. Compression Ratio: 8.0:1. Displacement: 258 cu. in. (4.2 liters). Horsepower: Net: 115 @ 3200 rpm. Torque: Net: 210 lb.-ft. @ 1800 rpm. Oil refill capacity: 5 qt. with filter change. Fuel Requirements: Unleaded.

OPTIONAL ENGINE: J-10, standard for J-20: Not available for California. Engine Type: OHV, V-8. Cast iron block and cylinder head. Bore x Stroke: 4.08 in. x 3.44 in. Lifters: Hydraulic. Number of main bearings-5. Fuel Induction: 2 bbl. carburetor. Compression Ratio: 8.25:1. Displacement: 360 cu. in. (5.89 liters). Horsepower: Net: 129 @ 3700 rpm. Torque: Net: 245 lb.-ft. @ 1600 rpm. Oil refill capacity: 5 qt. with filter change. Fuel Requirements: Unleaded.

CHASSIS FEATURES: Separate body and frame. Deep web frame, splayed box section side rails, wide flange, lightweight pressed steel with five cross members.

SUSPENSION AND RUNNING GEAR: Front Suspension: J-10: 5-leaf semi-elliptical; Spring rate: 215 lb./in. Hydraulic double-action shock absorbers, J-20: 7-leaf semi-elliptical, Spring rate: 260 lb./in. Optional: Spring rates: J-10: 210, 230 and 260 lb./in. J-20: 330 lb./in. Heavy-duty front and rear shock absorbers. Rear Suspension: J-10 118.7 in. wheelbase: 5-leaf semi-elliptical springs; Spring rate: 165 lb./in.; J-10 130.7 in. wheelbase: 4-leaf semi-elliptical springs, spring rate: 245 lb./in. J-20: 2-leaf tapered springs, spring rate: 340 lb./in. Hydraulic double-action shock absorbers,. Optional: J-10, 118.7 in. wheelbase: Heavy-duty springs and shock absorbers. Spring rate: 165/265 lb./in., 130.7 in. wheelbase: 340 lb./in/spring rate. J-20: Heavy-duty springs and shock absorbers. Spring rate: 510 lb/in. Front Axle Type and Capacity: Dana 44, full floating, Hypoid, open end. Capacity: 3200 lb. (J-10), 3500 lb. (J-20). Rear Axle Type and Capacity: J-10: Semi-floating, full-floating-J-20. Capacity: J-10: 3200 lb. J-20/6800 lb. GVW: 3980 lb., J-20/7600 lb. GVW: 4700 lb.; J-20/8400 lb. GVW: 5500 lb. Optional: Powr-Lok differential. Axle Ratios: J-10 2.73:1. J-20 (4-spd. and automatic trans.): 3.73:1. Transfer Case: All models with manual trans. Ratios: 2.60:1, 1.0:1. Brakes: Type: J-10 & J-20: Hydraulic, front discs and rear drums. Dimensions: Front: J-10: 12.0 in.; J-20: 12.5 in. dia. disc, rear: J-10: 11.0 in. x 2.00 in drums, J-20: 12 in. x 2.50 in. drums. Total brake swept area: J-10: 364 sq. in. J-20: 429 sq. in. Wheels: Full drop center. J-10: 15 x 6, 6-bolt, 5.5 in. circle; J-20: 16.5 x 6, 8-bolt, 6.5 in. circle. Optional: J-10: 15 x 7.00 (aluminum). Tires: J-10: H78 x 15 black sidewall polyester Cruiser 78, unbelted. J-20: 8.75 x 16.5 black sidewall polyester Cushion Miler R.V., J-20 with 7600 and 8400 lb. GVW: 9.50 x 16.5D. Optional: J-10: Wrangler 10R-15 outlined white letters steel radial, Tiempo P225/75R15 white sidewall double steel belted radial, Tracker A-T 10-15 outlined white letters wide all-terrain-all-weather, Suburbanite XG polyglas L78 x 15 black sidewall, Suburbanite belted fiberglass, H78 x 15 black sidewall, Viva P225/75R15 black or white sidewall fiberglass radial. J-20: Goodyear Tufsyn Cushion Miler, 8.75 x 16.5 and 9.50 x 16.5 black sidewall. Custom Xtra Grip, 8.75 x 16.5 in. and 9.50 x 16.5 in. black sidewall. Steering: Variable ratio power steering. Ratios: 16.0/13.0:1. Turns Lock-to-Lock: 4.0. Turning Circle: J-10, model 25: 40.6 ft., Honcho: 41.2 ft., J-10 model 26 and J-20 model 27: 44.5 ft. Standard: Transmission: all-synchromesh 4-speed Tremec model T-176. J-20 models have carry over 4-spd. manual transmission with creeper first gear. Ratios: Transmission ratios: 3.52:1, 2.27:1, 1.46:1, 1.00:1. The 4-speed manual transmission for the V-8 powered J-10 now had a 3.82:1 instead of 3.52:1 first gear ratio. Optional: 3-spd. TorqueFlite. Ratios: 2.45:1, 1.45:1, 1.0:1 . Clutch: 11 in. Single dry plate. Total lining area: 111 sq. in.

VEHICLE DIMENSIONS: Wheelbase: Model 25: 118.7 in.; model 26 & 27: 130.7 in. Overall Length: Model 25: 192.5 in. Models 26 & 27: 204.5 in. J-10 Sportside: 196.9 in. Front/Rear Tread: Model 25 and model 26: 63.3/63.8 in. Model 27: 64.6/65.9 in. J-10 with wide wheels: 65.1/64.9 in. Overall Height: Model 25: 69.3 in., model 26: 69.1 in., model 27: 70.7 in. J-10 Sportside: 69.1 in. Width: 78.9 in. Front/Rear Overhang: 29.9 in./43.9 in. Tailgate: Width and Height: 57.2 in. x 20.5 in. Approach/Departure Degrees: 118.7 in. wheelbase: 45/26. Ground Clearance: Minimum ground clearance: J-10: 7.7 in.; J-20: 8.1 in. J-10 Sportside and J-10 with wide wheels: 8.6 in. J-20: Front and differential: 8.1 in. Load space: 118.7 in. wheelbase: 83.6 in. x 50 in. x 20.5 in.; 130.7 in. wheelbase. 95.6 in. x 50 in. x 20.5 in. Maximum capacity (Volume Index): Model 25: 67.0 cu. ft.; model 26 and model 27: 76.6 cu. ft. Front headroom: 40.2 in. Front legroom: 45.00 in. Front shoulder room: 58.3 in. Front hip room: 60.5 in. Pedal to seat back (max.): 43.0 in. Steering wheel to seat back (max.): 25.0 in. Seat to ground: 35.0 in. Floor to ground: Model 25: 20.7 in.; model 26: 20.5 in.; model 27: 22.1 in.

CAPACITIES: Fuel Tank: 18.2 gal. with skid plate. Coolant System: 6-cyl.: 9.5 qt. V-8: 15 qt.

ACCOMMODATIONS: Seating Capacity: Three with bench seat, two with bucket seats.

INSTRUMENTATION: 110 mph speedometer, 0-99,999.9 mi. odometer, gauges for fuel level, engine coolant temperature, oil pressure and ammeter; Transfer case indicator lights. Quadra-Trac lockout indicator.

OPTIONS AND PRICES: Automatic transmission: $350. Air conditioning: $591. AM/FM/CB radio: $420. FM radio: $224. Premium sound system: $100. Tilt steering wheel: $81. Limited slip rear differential: $179. Roll bar: $121. Heavy-duty battery: $42. Heavy-duty front suspension: $58. Heavy-duty rear suspension: $47. Heavy-duty shock absorbers: $30. Dual front shock absorbers. Heavy-duty cooling. Goodyear Wrangler 10R-15LT radial tires: $158. 15 x 8 in. Chrome wheels (J-10): $118. Convenience Group. Includes underhood light, lights-on buzzer and digital clock (included with Laredo): $71. Trac-Lok rear differential: $179. Air conditioning: $591. Tinted glass: $38. Aluminum wheels (J-10): $360. Interior Group: $71. Cruise control: $132. Floor mats: $17. Grille guard/Winch Mount: $80. Visibility Group: $143. Light Group. Includes cargo box light, courtesy lights, glove box light, ashtray light, map/dome light, and lighted visor vanity mirror (included with Laredo): $45. Off-road driving lights: $83. Dual exterior mirrors: $13. Front bumper guards: $56. Extra-Quiet Insulation Package: $39. Honcho Package: $1392. Stepside Package: $944. Laredo Package: $1680. Snow Boss Package: $1323. Two-tone paint. Soft-Feel Sport steering wheel (standard with Honcho). Leather-wrapped Sport steering wheel (standard with Laredo). 15 x 8 in. painted styled wheels. Clear lens fog lights. Quartz halogen headlights. Pickup box cap (Townside only). Cold Climate Group. Includes heavy-duty battery and alternator and engine block heater. Roll bar. Chrome rear step bumper. Brush guard.

HISTORICAL FOOTNOTES: In spite of the age of their basic design, the Jeep trucks remained competitive in a time of increased awareness of fuel efficiency.

1982 TRUCKS

The 1982 Jeep trucks were available with the new Warner Gear 5-speed overdrive transmission as an option. Standard equipment for the J-10 and J-20 models included these items: Front air dam, 63 amp alternator, front armrests, bright anodized aluminum bumpers, front cigarette lighter and ashtray, color-keyed vinyl floor covering, lockable glove box, heater and defroster, electronic ignition, inside hood release, 12 in. day/night inside mirror, outside driver side rearview mirror, bright moldings for vent window, windshield and tailgate, padded instrument panel, padded sun visors, front bench seat, skidplates for fuel tank and transfer case, rear fender stone protection, electric windshield washers and 2-speed windshield wipers.

The J-10/J-20 Custom Townside standard equipment list follows: Deluxe grain vinyl bench seat in beige, blue or black, upper body side molding, bright door and window moldings, deluxe door trim panels, instrument panel cluster trim, hood insulation, and passenger assist handle. The custom Sportside J-10 was equipped with all items found in the Custom Package plus the following: Sportside pickup box, 15 x 8 in. white spoked styled wheels and 10-15 Tracker A-T tires, painted rear step bumper, bright door frame moldings, vinyl bucket seats in beige, blue or black, and carpeted cab doors.

Debuting for 1982 was a new Pioneer Package for the Townside J-10 and J-20 trucks. It included all items of the Custom Package plus these features: Upper body side scuff molding, tailgate stripes, Pioneer decals, dark argent painted grille, carpeted cab floor, Western Weave cloth and vinyl bench seat, matching door trim panels, woodgrain inserts for armrests and instrument panel, Soft-Feel Sport steering wheel, painted rear step bumper, front bumper guards, full wheelcovers (J-10 only), extra-quiet insulation, and Light Group.

The Honcho Sportside Package for the J-10 included everything in the Custom Packages plus special decals on the box fenders, Honcho striping, roll bar, front panel rails, Cara vinyl bucket seats in beige, blue or black with fixed center armrest, and Soft-Feel steering wheel.

1982 Jeep J-10 Honcho Sportside pickup

The J-10 short wheelbase Honcho Townside included all of the features of the Custom Townside Package plus three-color tailgate striping, tailgate striping, Honcho decals, 15 x 8 in. white styled steel wheels and 10-15 Tracker A-T OWL tires, painted rear step bumper, Western Weave cloth and vinyl bench seat in beige, blue or black (bucket seats with center armrest in beige, blue, black or nutmeg available), matching door trim panels, and carpeted cab area.

The Laredo Package for the J-10 Townside added the following to the content of the Custom Package: Special Trim Package and Laredo black and silver nameplates, 15 x 8 in. chrome styled wheels, 10R15 Goodyear Wrangler radial tires, special painted hubs, chrome rear step bumper, bright door frame moldings, front bumper guards and nerf stripes, special vinyl back bucket seats with center armrest trimmed in black with grey accent straps or nutmeg with honey accent straps, matching door trim panels with door pull straps, special instrument panel striping, Laredo nameplates and cluster decoration, special color-keyed interior molding, leather-wrapped steering wheel, carpeted full cab floor, extra-quiet insulation, Convenience Group, Light Group, and Visibility Group.

I.D. DATA: The serial number was located on the left-hand hinge pillar. The V.I.N. had 17 symbols. The first three entries identified the manufacturer, make and type of vehicle. The fourth unit, a letter, designated the engine. The fifth character, a letter, identified the transmission. The sixth and seventh characters identified the series and body style. The eighth character identified the GVW rating. Next followed a check digit. The eleventh character was the manufacturing plant identification. The final six digits were the sequential production number.

Model Number	Body Type	Factory Price	GVW	Shipping Weight	Prod. Total
J-10, 6-cyl. 118.7 in. wheelbase: 7 ft. box, 130.7 in. wheelbase: 8 ft. box (J-10:1/2 ton) 118.7 in.: Model 25, 130.7 in. Model 26					
J-10	Pickup Townside, 118.7 in. wb.	$8610	6200	3656	6113[1]
J-10	Pickup Townside, 130.7 in. wb.	$8756	6200	3708	—
J-20, 360 V-8. 130.7 in. wheelbase. 8 ft. box: Model 27. (J-20: 3/4 ton)					
J-20	Pickup Townside	$9766	6800[2]	4270	—

NOTE 1: Calendar year production, all J series trucks.
NOTE 2: 7600 lb. and 8400 lb. GVW optional.

STANDARD ENGINE: J-10: Engine Type: OHV, In-line-6. Cast iron block and cylinder head. Bore x Stroke: 3.75 in. x 3.90 in. Lifters: Hydraulic. Number of main bearings-7. Fuel Induction: 2 bbl. carburetor. Compression Ratio: 8.0:1. Displacement: 258 cu. in. (4.2 liters). Horsepower: Net: 115 @ 3200 rpm. Torque: Net: 210 lb.-ft. @ 1800 rpm. Oil refill capacity: 5 qt. with filter change. Fuel Requirements: Unleaded.

OPTIONAL ENGINE: J-10, standard for J-20: Not available for California. Engine Type: OHV, V-8. Cast iron block and cylinder head. Bore x Stroke: 4.08 in. x 3.44 in. Lifters: Hydraulic. Number of main bearings-5. Fuel Induction: 2 bbl. carburetor. Compression Ratio: 8.25:1. Displacement: 360 cu. in. (5.89 liters). Horsepower: Net: 150 @ 3400 rpm. Torque: Net: 265 lb.-ft. @ 1500 rpm. Oil refill capacity: 5 qt. with filter change. Fuel Requirements: Unleaded.

CHASSIS FEATURES: Separate body and frame. Deep web frame, splayed box section side rails, wide flange, lightweight pressed steel with five cross members.

SUSPENSION AND RUNNING GEAR: Front Suspension: J-10: 5-leaf semi-elliptical; Spring rate: 215 lb./in. Hydraulic double-action shock absorbers, J-20: 7-leaf semi-elliptical, Spring rate: 260 lb./in. Optional: J-10: Spring rates: 210, 230 and 260 lb./in. Spring rates. J-20: Spring rates: 330 lb./in. Heavy-duty front and rear shock absorbers. Rear Suspension: J-10 118.7 in. wheelbase: 5-leaf semi-elliptical springs; Spring rate: 165 lb./in.; J-10 130.7 in. wheelbase: 4-leaf semi-elliptical springs, spring rate: 245 lb./in. J-20: 2-leaf tapered springs, spring rate: 340 lb./in. Hydraulic double-action shock absorbers,. Optional: J-10, 118.7 in. wheelbase: Heavy-duty springs and shock absorbers. Spring rate: 165/265 lb./in., 130.7 in. wheelbase: 340 lb./in/spring rate. J-20: Heavy-duty springs and shock absorbers. Spring rate: 510 lb/in. Front Axle Type and Capacity: Dana 44, full floating, hypoid, open end. Capacity: 3200 lb. (J-10), 3500 lb. (J-20). Rear Axle Type and Capacity: J-10: Semi-floating, full-floating-J-20. Capacity: J-10: 3200 lb. J-20/6800 lb. GVW: 3980 lb., J-20/7600 lb. GVW: 4700 lb.; J-20/8400 lb. GVW: 5500 lb. Optional: Powr-Lok differential. Axle Ratios: J-10 2.73:1. Optional: 3.31:1. J-20 (4-spd. and automatic trans.): 3.73:1. Transfer Case: New Process 208 part-time transfer case. Ratios: 2.61:1, 1.00:1. Optional: Quadra Trac with New Process 219 transfer case. Brakes: Type: J-10 & J-20: Hydraulic, front discs and rear drums. Dimensions: Front: J-10: 12.0 in.; J-20: 12.5 in. dia. disc, rear: J-10: 11.0 in. x 2.00 in. drums, J-20: 12 in. x 2.50 in. drums. Total brake swept area: J-10: 364 sq. in. J-20: 429 sq. in. Wheels: Full drop center. J-10: 15 x 6, 6-bolt, 5.5 in. circle; J-20: 16.5 x 6, 8-bolt, 6.5 in. circle. Optional: J-10: 15 x 7.00 (aluminum). Tires: J-10: H78 x 15 black polyester Cruiser 78, unbelted. J-20 8.75 x 16.5 black sidewall polyester Cushion Miler RV polyester. Optional: Suburbanite XG H78 x 15 black sidewall, fiberglass belted. Not available for J-20. Tiempo P225/75R15 white sidewall double steel belted radial. Not available for J-20. F-32 Flexten HR78 x 15 white sidewall winter radial. Not available for J-20. Arriva P225/75R15 steel radial white sidewall. Wrangler 10R-15 outlined white letters steel radial. Not available for J-20. Tracker AT 10-15 OWL wide all-terrain-all-weather. Not available for J-20. Goodyear Tufsyn Cushion Miler 7.50 x 16.5 black sidewall. Available for J-20 only. Custom Xtra Grip, 8.75 x 16.5 or 7.50 x 16.5 black sidewall. Available for J-20 only. Steering: Recirculating ball. Ratio: 24:1. Turns Lock-to-Lock: 4.0. Turning Circle: J-10, model 25: 40.6 ft., Honcho: 41.2 ft., J-10 model 26 and J-20 model 27: 44.5 ft. Optional: Variable ratio power steering. Ratios: 16.1/13.0:1. Standard: Transmission: all-synchromesh 4-speed Warner Gear. Ratios: Transmission ratios: 4.03:1, 2.37:1, 1.50:1, 1.00:1. J-20 models have 4-spd. manual transmission with creeper first gear. Optional: Warner gear 5-speed manual with overdrive. ratios: 4.03:1, 2.37:1, 1.50:1, 1.0:1, 0.76 or 0.86:1 depending on engine/axle ratio combination. Optional: 3-spd. TorqueFlite. Ratios: 2.45:1, 1.45:1, 1.0:1 . Clutch: 11 in. Single dry plate. Total lining area: 111 sq. in.

VEHICLE DIMENSIONS: Wheelbase: J-10 short wheelbase model 25: 118.8 in.; J-10 model 26 and J-20 model 27 long wheelbase: 130.8 in. Overall Length: Model 25: 194.0 in. Models 26 & 27: 206.0 in. Front/Rear Tread: Model 25 and model 26: 63.3/63.8 in. Model 27: 64.9/65.9 in. Overall Height: Model 25: 68.5 in., model 26: 68.3 in., model 27: 70.1 in. Width: 78.9 in. Front/Rear Overhang: 31.3 in./43.9 in. Tailgate: Width and Height: 57.2 in. x 20.5 in. Approach/Departure Degrees: 118.7 in. wheelbase: 45/26. Ground Clearance: Minimum ground clearance: J-10: 7.7 in.; J-20: 8.1 in. J-20: Front and differential: 8.1 in. Load space: 118.7 in. wheelbase: 83.6 in. x 50 in. x 20.5 in.; 130.7 in. wheelbase. 95.6 in. x 50 in. x 20.5 in. Maximum capacity (Volume Index): Model 25: 67.0 cu. ft.; model 26 and model 27: 76.6 cu. ft. Front headroom: 40.2 in. Front legroom: 41.60 in. Front shoulder room: 58.3 in. Front hip room: 60.5 in. Pedal to seat back (max.): 43.0 in. Steering wheel to seat back (max.): 25.0 in. Seat to ground: 35.0 in. Floor to ground: Model 25: 20.7 in.; model 26: 20.5 in.; model 27: 22.1 in.

CAPACITIES: Fuel Tank: 19.7 gal. with skid plate. Coolant System: 6-cyl.: 9.5 qt. V-8: 15 qt.

ACCOMMODATIONS: Seating Capacity: Three with bench seat, two with bucket seats.

INSTRUMENTATION: 0-110 mph speedometer, 0-99,999.9 mi. odometer, gauges for fuel level, engine coolant temperature, oil pressure and ammeter; Transfer case indicator lights. Quadra-Trac lockout indicator.

OPTIONS AND PRICES: Air conditioning. Tinted glass. Tilt steering wheel. Extra-quiet insulation. Soft-Feel steering wheel. Leather-wrapped steering wheel. Custom Package: $169. Sportside Package. Pioneer Package: $599. Honcho Package: $949. Honcho Sportside Package: $470. Laredo Package: $1749. Snow Boss Package: $1399. 360 V-8: $200. Painted styled steel wheels. Chrome styled wheels (J-10 only). Forged aluminum wheels (J-10 only). Bumper guards. Rear step bumper. Upper body side scuff molding. AM radio. AM/FM stereo radio. AM/FM radio and cassette tape player. AM/FM/CB stereo radio. Electronic tuned stereo AM/FM radio and cassette tape player. Automatic transmission. Cruise control. Power front bucket seats. Power remote control outside rearview mirrors. Rear Trac-Lok differential. Quadra Trac. 5-spd. manual overdrive transmission. Quartz halogen headlights. Clear lens fog lamps. Heavy-duty shock absorbers. Dual front shock absorbers. Heavy-duty battery and alternator. Cold Climate Group. Convenience Group. Light Group. Visibility Group. Trailer Towing Packages.

HISTORICAL FOOTNOTES: *Pickup Van & 4WD*, December, 1981, tested a J-10 Honcho Sportside and depicted it as "an appealing machine with a hunkered down look."

1983 TRUCKS

The 1983 J-10 was available with the Selec-Trac two-/four-wheel drive system which was standard on the 1983 Wagoneer and also optional for the Cherokee. Its standard 258 cu. in. 6-cylinder engine had a higher 9.2:1 compression ratio and the same fuel feedback and knock sensor as used in other installations of this engine in 1983 Jeeps. Except in California, the J-20 continued to have the 360 cu. in. V-8 with a 2-barrel carburetor as its standard engine.

1983 Jeep J-10 Laredo pickup

I.D. DATA: The serial number was located on the left-hand hinge pillar. The V.I.N. had 17 symbols. The first three entries identified the manufacturer, make and type of vehicle. The fourth unit, a letter, designated the engine. The fifth character, a letter, identified the transmission. The sixth and seventh characters identified the series and body style. The eighth character identified the GVW rating. Next followed a check digit. The eleventh character was the manufacturing plant identification. The final six digits were the sequential production number.

Model Number	Body Type	Factory Price	GVW	Shipping Weight	Prod. Total
J-10, 6-cyl. 118.7 in. wheelbase: 7 ft. box, 130.7 in. wheelbase: 8 ft. box (J-10:1/2 ton)) 118.7 in.: Model 25, 130.7 in. Model 26					
J-10	Pickup Townside, 118.7 in. wb.	$9082	6200	3728	4261[1]
J-10	Pickup Townside, 130.7 in. wb.	$9227	6200	3790	—
J-20, 360 V-8. 130.7 in. wheelbase. 8 ft. box: Model 27. (J-20: 3/4 ton)					
J-20	Pickup Townside	$10,117	6800[2]	4336	—

NOTE 1: 1983 calendar year sales, all J series trucks.
NOTE 2: 7600 lb. and 8400 lb. GVW optional.

STANDARD ENGINE: J-10: Engine Type: OHV, In-line-6. Cast iron block and cylinder head. Bore x Stroke: 3.75 in. x 3.90 in. Lifters: Hydraulic. Number of main bearings-7. Fuel Induction: 2 bbl. carburetor. Compression Ratio: 9.2:1. Displacement: 258 cu. in. (4.2 liters). Horsepower: Net: 115 @ 3200 rpm. Torque: Net: 210 lb.-ft. @ 1800 rpm. Oil refill capacity: 5 qt. with filter change. Fuel Requirements: Unleaded.

OPTIONAL ENGINE: J-10, standard for J-20: Not available for California. Type: OHV, V-8. Cast iron block and cylinder head. Bore x Stroke: 4.08 in. x 3.44 in. Lifters: Hydraulic. Number of main bearings-5. Fuel Induction: 2 bbl. carburetor. Compression Ratio: 8.25:1. Displacement: 360 cu. in. (5.89 liters). Horsepower: Net: 150 @ 3400 rpm. Torque: Net: 265 lb.-ft. @ 1500 rpm. Oil refill capacity: 5 qt. with filter change. Fuel Requirements: Unleaded.

CHASSIS FEATURES: Separate body and frame. Deep web frame, splayed box section side rails, wide flange, lightweight pressed steel with five cross members.

SUSPENSION AND RUNNING GEAR: Front Suspension: J-10: 5-leaf semi-elliptical; Spring rate: 215 lb./in. Hydraulic double-action shock absorbers, J-20: 7-leaf semi-elliptical, Spring rate: 260 lb./in. Optional: J-10: Spring rates: 210, 230 and 260 lb./in. Spring rates. and J-20: Spring rates: 330 lb./in. Heavy-duty front and rear shock absorbers. Rear Suspension: J-10 118.7 in. wheelbase: 5-leaf semi-elliptical springs; Spring rate: 165 lb./in.; J-10 130.7 in. wheelbase: 4-leaf semi-elliptical springs, spring rate: 245 lb./in. J-20: 2-leaf tapered springs, spring rate: 340 lb./in. Hydraulic double-action shock absorbers,. Optional: J-10, 118.7 in. wheelbase: Heavy-duty springs and shock absorbers. Spring rate: 165/265 lb./in., 130.7 in. wheelbase: 340 lb./in/spring rate. J-20: Heavy-duty springs and shock absorbers. Spring rate: 510 lb/in. Front Axle Type and Capacity: Dana 44, full floating, hypoid, open end. Capacity: 3200 lb. (J-10), 3500 lb. (J-20). Rear Axle Type and Capacity: J-10: Semi-floating, full-floating-J-20. Capacity: J-10: 3200 lb. J-20/6800 lb. GVW: 3980 lb., J-20/7600 lb. GVW: 4700 lb.; J-20/8400 lb. GVW: 5500 lb. Optional: Powr-Lok differential. Axle Ratios: J-10 2.73:1. Optional: 3.31:1. J-20 (4-spd. and automatic trans.): 3.73:1. Transfer Case: New Process 208 part-time transfer case. Ratios: 2.61:1, 1.00:1. Optional: Select-Trac 2-wheel/four-wheel drive (J-10 only). Ratios: 2.60:1, 1.00:1. Brakes: Type: J-10 & J-20: Hydraulic, front discs and rear drums. Dimensions: Front: J-10: 12.0 in.; J-20: 12.5 in. dia. disc, rear: J-10: 11.0 in. x 2.00 in drums, J-20: 12 in. x 2.50 in. drums. Total brake swept area: J-10: 364 sq. in. J-20: 429 sq. in. Wheels: Full drop center. J-10: 15 x 6, 6-bolt, 5.5 in. circle; J-20: 16.5 x 6, 8-bolt, 6.5 in. circle. Optional: J-10: 15 x 7.00 (aluminum). Tires: J-10:P225/75R15 glass belted radial black sidewall. J-20:8.75 x 16.5 black sidewall polyester Cushion Miler RV polyester. Optional: Suburbanite XG H78 x 15 black sidewall, fiberglass belted. Not available for J-20. Tiempo P225/75R15 white sidewall double steel belted radial. Not available for J-20. F-32 Flexten HR78 x 15 white sidewall winter radial. Not available for J-20. Arriva P225/75R15 steel radial white sidewall. Wrangler 10R-15 outlined White letters steel radial. Not available for J-20. Tracker AT 10-15 OWL wide all-terrain-all-weather. Not available for J-20. Goodyear Tufsyn Cushion Miler 7.50 x 16.5 black sidewall. Available for J-20 only. Custom Xtra Grip, 8.75 x 16.5 or 7.50 x 16.5 black sidewall. Available for J-20 only. Steering: Recirculating ball. Ratio: 24:1. Turns Lock-to-Lock: 4.0. Turning Circle: J-10, model 25: 40.6 ft., Honcho: 41.2 ft., J-10 model 26 and J-20 model 27: 44.5 ft. Optional: Variable ratio power steering. Ratios: 16.1/13.0:1. Standard: Transmission: all-synchromesh 4-speed Warner Gear. Ratios: Transmission ratios: 4.03:1, 2.37:1, 1.50:1, 1.00:1. J-20 models have 4-spd. manual transmission with creeper first gear. Optional: Warner gear 5-speed manual with overdrive (J-10 only). Ratios: 4.03:1, 2.37:1, 1.50:1,1.0:1,0.76 or 0.86:1 depending on engine/axle ratio combination. Optional: 3-spd. TorqueFlite. Ratios: 2.45:1, 1.45:1, 1.0:1 . Clutch: 11 in. Single dry plate. Total lining area: 111 sq. in.

VEHICLE DIMENSIONS: Wheelbase: J-10 short wheelbase model 25: 118.8 in.; J-10 model 26 and J-20 model 27 long wheelbase: 130.8 in. Overall Length: Model 25: 194.0 in. Models 26 & 27: 206.0 in. Front/Rear Tread: Model 25 and model 26: 63.3/63.8 in. Model 27: 64.9/65.9 in. Overall Height: Model 25: 68.5 in., model 26: 68.3 in., model 27: 70.1 in. Width: 78.9 in. Front/Rear Overhang: 31.3 in./43.9 in. Tailgate: Width and Height: 57.2 in. x 20.5 in. Approach/Departure Degrees: 118.7 in. wheelbase: 45/26. Ground Clearance: Minimum ground clearance: J-10: 7.7 in.; J-20: 8.1 in. J-20: Front and differential: 8.1 in. Load space: 118.7 in. wheelbase: 83.6 in. x 50 in. x 20.5 in.; 130.7 in. wheelbase. 95.6 in. x 50 in. x 20.5 in. Maximum capacity (Volume Index): Model 25: 67.0 cu. ft.; model 26 and model 27: 76.6 cu. ft. Front headroom: 40.2 in. Front legroom: 41.60 in. Front shoulder room: 58.3 in. Front hip room: 60.5 in. Pedal to seat back (max.): 43.0 in. Steering wheel to seat back (max.): 25.0 in. Seat to ground: 35.0 in. Floor to ground: Model 25: 20.7 in.; model 26: 20.5 in.; model 27: 22.1 in.

CAPACITIES: Fuel Tank: 18.2 gal. with skid plate. Coolant System: 6-cyl.: 9.5 qt. V-8: 15 qt.

ACCOMMODATIONS: Seating Capacity: Three with bench seat, two with bucket seats. Instrumentation: 0-110 mph speedometer, 0-99,999.9 mi. odometer, gauges for fuel level, engine coolant temperature, oil pressure and ammeter; Transfer case indicator lights.

OPTIONS AND PRICES: Halogen fog lamps replaced the clear lens fog lamp option for 1983. Other options were carried over for 1983. The trim option prices follow: Custom Package: $175. Pioneer Package: $619. Laredo Package (for Model 25 only): $1807.

HISTORICAL FOOTNOTES: The 1983 models were introduced in the fall of 1982.

1984 TRUCKS

There were virtually no changes made in the Jeep pickups in 1984. The only Trim Packages offered were the Pioneer and Laredo priced respectively at $456 and $2129.

1984 Jeep J-10 pickup

I.D. DATA: The serial number was located on the left-hand hinge pillar. The V.I.N. had 17 symbols. The first three entries identified the manufacturer, make and type of vehicle. The fourth unit, a letter, designated the engine. The fifth character, a letter, identified the transmission. The sixth and seventh characters identified the series and body style. The eighth character identified the GVW rating. Next followed a check digit. The eleventh character was the manufacturing plant identification. The final six digits were the sequential production number.

Model Number	Body Type	Factory Price	GVW	Shipping Weight	Prod. Total
J-10, 6-cyl. 118.7 in. wheelbase: 7 ft. box, 130.7 in. wheelbase: 8 ft. box (J-10:1/2 ton) 118.7 in.: Model 25, 130.7 in. Model 26					
J-10	Pickup Townside, 118.7 in. wb.	$9967	6200	3724	3404[1]
J-10	Pickup Townside, 130.7 in. wb.	$10,117	6200	3811	—
J-20, 360 V-8. 130.7 in. wheelbase. 8 ft. box: Model 27. (J-20: 3/4 ton)					
J-20	Pickup Townside	$11,043	6800[2]	4323	—

NOTE 1: 1984 calendar year sales, all J series trucks.
NOTE 2: 7600 lb. and 8400 lb. GVW optional.

STANDARD ENGINE: J-10. Engine Type: OHV, In-line-6. Cast iron block and cylinder head. Bore x Stroke: 3.75 in. x 3.90 in. Lifters: Hydraulic. Number of main bearings-7. Fuel Induction: 2 bbl. carburetor. Compression Ratio: 9.2:1. Displacement: 258 cu. in. (4.2 liters). Horsepower: Net: 115 @ 3200 rpm. Torque: Net: 210 lb.-ft. @ 1800 rpm. Oil refill capacity: 5 qt. with filter change. Fuel Requirements: Unleaded.

OPTIONAL ENGINE: J-10, standard for J-20. Not available for California. Type: OHV, V-8. Cast iron block and cylinder head. Bore x Stroke: 4.08 in. x 3.44 in. Lifters: Hydraulic. Number of main bearings-5. Fuel Induction: 2 bbl. carburetor. Compression Ratio: 8.25:1. Displacement: 360 cu. in. (5.89 liters). Horsepower: Net: 150 @ 3400 rpm. Torque: Net: 265 lb.-ft. @ 1500 rpm. Oil refill capacity: 5 qt. with filter change. Fuel Requirements: Unleaded.

CHASSIS FEATURES: Separate body and frame. Deep web frame, splayed box section side rails, wide flange, lightweight pressed steel with five cross members.

SUSPENSION AND RUNNING GEAR: Front Suspension: J-10: 5-leaf semi-elliptical; Spring rate: 215 lb./in. Hydraulic double-action shock absorbers, J-20: 7-leaf semi-elliptical, Spring rate: 260 lb./in. Optional: J-10: Spring rates: 210, 230 and 260 lb./in. Spring rates. and J-20: Spring rates: 330 lb./in. Heavy-duty front and rear shock absorbers. Rear Suspension: J-10 118.7 in. wheelbase: 5-leaf semi-elliptical springs; Spring rate: 165 lb./in.; J-10 130.7 in. wheelbase: 4-leaf semi-elliptical springs, spring rate: 245 lb./in. J-20: 2-leaf tapered springs, spring rate: 340 lb./in. Hydraulic double-action shock absorbers,. Optional: J-10, 118.7 in. wheelbase: Heavy-duty springs and shock absorbers. Spring rate: 165/265 lb./in., 130.7 in. wheelbase: 340 lb./in/spring rate. J-20: Heavy-duty springs and shock absorbers. Spring rate: 510 lb/in. Front Axle Type and Capacity: Dana 44, full floating, hypoid, open end. Capacity: 3200 lb. (J-10), 3500 lb. (J-20). Rear Axle Type and Capacity: J-10: Semi-floating, full-floating-J-20. Capacity: J-10: 3200 lb. J-20/6800 lb. GVW: 3980 lb., J-20/7600 lb. GVW: 4700 lb.; J-20/8400 lb. GVW: 5500 lb. Optional: Powr-Lok differential. Axle Ratios: J-10 2.73:1. Optional: 3.31:1. J-20 (4-spd. and automatic trans.): 3.73:1. Transfer Case: New Process 208 part-time transfer case. Ratios: 2.61:1, 1.00:1. Optional: Select-Trac 2-wheel/four-wheel drive (J-10 only). Ratios: 2.60:1, 1.00:1. Brakes: Type: J-10 & J-20: Hydraulic, front discs and rear drums. Dimensions: Front: J-10: 12.0 in.; J-20: 12.5 in. dia. disc, rear: J-10: 11.0 in. x 2.00 in drums, J-20: 12 in. x 2.50 in. drums. Total brake swept area: J-10: 364 sq. in. J-20: 429 sq. in. Wheels: Full drop center. J-10: 15 x 6, 6-bolt, 5.5 in. circle; J-20: 16.5 x 6, 8-bolt, 6.5 in. circle. Optional: J-10: 15 x 7.00 (aluminum). Tires: J-10:P225/75R15 glass belted radial black sidewall. J-20:8.75 x 16.5 black sidewall polyester Cushion Miler RV polyester. Optional: Suburbanite XG H78 x 15 black sidewall, fiberglass belted. Not available for J-20. Tiempo P225/75R15 white sidewall double steel belted radial. Not available for J-20. F-32 Flexten HR78 x 15 white sidewall winter radial. Not available for J-20. Arriva P225/75R15 steel radial white sidewall. Wrangler 10R-15 outlined White letters steel radial. Not available for J-20. Tracker AT 10-15 OWL wide all-terrain-all-weather. Not available for J-20. Goodyear Tufsyn Cushion Miler 7.50 x 16.5 black sidewall. Available for J-20 only. Custom Xtra Grip, 8.75 x 16.5 or 7.50 x 16.5 black sidewall. Available for J-20 only. Steering: Recirculating ball. Ratio: 24:1. Turns Lock-to-Lock: 4.0. Turning Circle: J-10, model 25: 40.6 ft., Honcho: 41.2 ft., J-10 model 26 and J-20 model 27: 44.5 ft. Optional: Variable ratio power steering. Ratios: 16.1/13.0:1. Standard: Transmission: all-synchromesh 4-speed Warner Gear. Ratios: Transmission ratios: 4.03:1, 2.37:1, 1.50:1, 1.00:1. J-20 models have 4-spd. manual transmission with creeper first gear. Optional: Warner gear 5-speed manual with overdrive (J-10 only). Ratios: 4.03:1, 2.37:1, 1.50:1,1.0:1,0.76 or 0.86:1 depending on engine/axle ratio combination. Optional: 3-spd. TorqueFlite. Ratios: 2.45:1, 1.45:1, 1.0:1 . Clutch: 11 in. Single dry plate. Total lining area: 111 sq. in.

VEHICLE DIMENSIONS: Wheelbase: J-10 short wheelbase model 25: 118.8 in.; J-10 model 26 and J-20 model 27 long wheelbase: 130.8 in. Overall Length: Model 25: 194.0 in. Models 26 & 27: 206.0 in. Front/Rear Tread: Model 25 and model 26: 63.3/63.8 in. Model 27: 64.9/65.9 in. Overall Height: Model 25: 68.5 in., model 26: 68.3 in., model 27: 70.1 in. Width: 78.9 in. Front/Rear Overhang: 31.3 in./43.9 in. Tailgate: Width and Height: 57.2 in. x 20.5 in. Approach/Departure Degrees: 118.7 in. wheelbase: 45/26. Ground Clearance: Minimum ground clearance: J-10: 7.7 in.; J-20: 8.1 in. J-20: Front and differential: 8.1 in. Load space: 118.7 in. wheelbase: 83.6 in. x 50 in. x 20.5 in.; 130.7 in. wheelbase. 95.6 in. x 50 in. x 20.5 in. Maximum capacity (Volume Index): Model 25: 67.0 cu. ft.; model 26 and model 27: 76.6 cu. ft. Front headroom: 40.2 in. Front legroom: 41.60 in. Front shoulder room: 58.3 in. Front hip room: 60.5 in. Pedal to seat back (max.): 43.0 in. Steering wheel to seat back (max.): 25.0 in. Seat to ground: 35.0 in. Floor to ground: Model 25: 20.7 in.; model 26: 20.5 in.; model 27: 22.1 in.

CAPACITIES: Fuel Tank: 18.2 gal. with skid plate. Coolant System: 6-cyl.: 9.5 qt. V-8: 15 qt.

ACCOMMODATIONS: Seating Capacity: Three with bench seat, two with bucket seats. Instrumentation: 0-110 mph speedometer, 0-99,999.9 mi. odometer, gauges for fuel level, engine coolant temperature, oil pressure and ammeter; Transfer case indicator lights.

OPTIONS AND PRICES: Major options from 1983 were carried over for 1984. The trim option prices follow: Custom Package. Pioneer Package: $456. Laredo Package (for model 25 only): $2129.

HISTORICAL FOOTNOTES: Introduction of the 1984 models took place in the fall of 1983.

1985 TRUCKS

In 1985 the 118.7 inch wheelbase J-10 model was dropped and all models had the 131 inch wheelbase and 8 foot Townside box. The only two trim levels were base and the $475 Pioneer. Standard equipment for the J-10 included the 258 engine, 4-speed manual transmission with floor shift, P225/75R15 black Arriva All-Weather steel-belted radial tires, front stabilizer bar. The base J-20 was equipped with the 360 V-8 engine, 3-speed automatic transmission, and 9.50 x 16.5 in. black nylon custom XG tubeless tires.

The following items were standard for both the base J-10 and J-20 trucks: Left and right side armrests, front ashtray, cigarette lighter, color-keyed vinyl floor covering, oil, ammeter, fuel level and engine coolant temperature gauges, glove box lock, heater and defroster, inside hood release, padded instrument panel, 12 in. day/night rearview mirror, lap and shoulder belts restraint system, bench seat with seat belts and retractors, 3-spoke steering wheel, padded sun visors, tinted glass, bright metal front bumper, black grille insert, outside left side mirror, bright vent window and windshield moldings, bright rear roof molding, 42 amp alternator, dual horns, fuel tank skid plate, power steering, white painted steel 15 x 6 in. L rim wheels, white painted 16.5 x 6.0 in. for J-20, and electric windshield washers and 2-speed wipers.

Included in the Pioneer Package were these features: Floor carpeting, fabric door panel inserts, woodgrain instrument cluster overlay, Extra-Quiet Insulation Package (includes custom headliner, under dash insulation and special sound deadening materials in passenger compartment), wheelcovers (J-10 only), armrest overlays, bench seat in deluxe grain vinyl, Soft-Feel Sport steering wheel, exterior Pioneer decals, chrome grille, bright finish door window frames, upper body side scuff moldings, tailgate stripes, and wheelcovers (J-10 only). The standard exterior color selection for 1985 consisted of olympic white, classic black, almond beige, sebring red and deep night blue. The standard truck's front seat was finished in Celtic vinyl. The Pioneer Package provided a Deluxe vinyl seat. Both were available in a single color, honey.

I.D. DATA: The serial number was located on the left-hand hinge pillar. The V.I.N. had 17 symbols. The first three entries identified the manufacturer, make and type of vehicle. The fourth unit, a letter, designated the engine. The fifth character, a letter, identified the transmission. The sixth and seventh characters identified the series and body style. The eighth character identified the GVW rating. Next followed a check digit. The eleventh character was the manufacturing plant identification. The final six digits were the sequential production number.

Model Number	Body Type	Factory Price	GVW	Shipping Weight	Prod. Total
J-10, 130.7 in.					
J-10	Pickup Townside, Model 26	$10,331	5975[1]	3799	1953[2]

NOTE 1: 6200 lb. GVW optional.
NOTE 2: 1985 calendar year sales, all J series trucks.

Model Number	Body Type	Factory Price	GVW	Shipping Weight	Prod. Total
J-20, 360 V-8. 130.7 in. wheelbase					
J-20	Pickup Townside, Model 27	$11,275	7600[3]	4353	—

NOTE 3: 7600 lb. and 8400 lb. GVW optional.

STANDARD ENGINE: J-10: Engine Type: OHV, In-line-6. Cast iron block and cylinder head. Bore x Stroke: 3.75 in. x 3.90 in. Lifters: Hydraulic. Number of main bearings-7. Fuel Induction: 2 bbl. carburetor. Compression Ratio: 9.2:1. Displacement: 258 cu. in. (4.2 liters). Horsepower: Net: 115 @ 3200 rpm. Torque: Net: 210 lb.-ft. @ 1800 rpm. Oil refill capacity: 5 qt. with filter change. Fuel Requirements: Unleaded.

OPTIONAL ENGINE: J-10, standard for J-20: Not available for California. Type: OHV, V-8. Cast iron block and cylinder head. Bore x Stroke: 4.08 in. x 3.44 in. Lifters: Hydraulic. Number of main bearings-5. Fuel Induction: 2 bbl. carburetor. Compression Ratio: 8.25:1. Displacement: 360 cu. in. (5.89 liters). Horsepower: Net: 150 @ 3400 rpm. Torque: Net: 265 lb.-ft. @ 1500 rpm. Oil refill capacity: 5 qt. with filter change. Fuel Requirements: Unleaded.

CHASSIS FEATURES: Separate body and frame. Deep web frame, splayed box section side rails, wide flange, lightweight pressed steel with five cross members.

SUSPENSION AND RUNNING GEAR: Front Suspension: J-10: 5-leaf semi-elliptical; Spring rate: 215 lb./in. Hydraulic double-action shock absorbers, J-20: 7-leaf semi-elliptical, Spring rate: 260 lb./in. Hydraulic double-action shock absorbers. Optional: J-10: 230 Spring rates. Heavy-duty front and rear shock absorbers. J-20: 330 lb./in. Rear Suspension: J-10: 4-leaf semi-elliptical springs, spring rate: 245 lb./in. J-20: 2-leaf tapered springs, spring rate: 340 lb./in. Hydraulic double-action shock absorbers. Optional: J-10: 340 lb./in/spring rate. J-20: Heavy-duty springs and shock absorbers. Spring rate: 510 lb/in. Front Axle Type and Capacity: Dana 44, full floating, Hypoid, open end. Capacity: 3200 lb. (J-10), 3500 lb. (J-20). Rear Axle Type and Capacity: J-10: Semi-floating, AMC/Jeep. J-20: Full-floating Dana model 60. Capacity: J-10: 3200 lb. J-20/7600 lb. GVW: 4700 lb.; J-20/8400 lb. GVW: 5500 lb. Optional: Power-Lok differential. Axle ratios: J-10 2.73:1 with 4-speed manual transmission, 3.31:1 with automatic transmission. J-20: 3.73:1. Transfer Case: J-10: Manual transmission: New Process 228 part-time transfer case. Ratios: 2.62:1, 1.00:1. J-10 and J-20: Automatic transmission: New Process 208 full-time transfer case. Ratios: 2.62:1, 1.00:1. Brakes: Type: J-10 & J-20: Hydraulic, front discs and rear drums. Dimensions: Front: J-10: 12.0 in.; J-20: 12.5 in. dia. disc, rear: J-10: 11.0 in. x 2.00 in. drums, J-20: 12.52 in. x 2.50 in. drums. Wheels: Full drop center. J-10: 15 x 6, 6-bolt, 5.5 in. circle; white painted. J-20: 16.5 x 6L, 8-bolt, 6.5 in. circle, white painted. Optional: J-10: 15 x 8 painted style wheel. Tires: J-10: P225/75R15 black sidewall Arriva all-weather steel belted radial. J-20: 9.50 x 16.5 black sidewall nylon custom XG tubeless. Optional: J-10: P2325/75R15 Vector all weather, P235/75R15(B) RBL Wrangler steel radial Mud and Snow. Steering: Power recirculating ball. Ratio: 13-16:1. Turns Lock-to-Lock: 4.0. Turning Circle: 44.5 ft. Standard Transmission: J-10: all-synchromesh 4-speed. Ratios: Transmission ratios: 4.03:1, 2.37:1, 1.50:1, 1.00:1. Standard: J-20 (Optional for J-10): 3-spd. automatic transmission. Ratios: 2.74:1, 1.55:1, 1.0:1 . Clutch: 11 in. Single dry plate. Total lining area: 111 sq. in. Optional: None.

VEHICLE DIMENSIONS: Wheelbase: 130.8 in. Overall Length: 206.0 in. Front/Rear Tread: 63.3/63.8 in. Wide wheel option: 64.6/64.6 in. Overall Height: J-10: 68.3 in. J-20: 70.17 in. Width: 78.9 in. Front/Rear Overhang: 29.9 in./43.9 in. Tailgate: Width and Height: 57.2 in. x 20.5 in. Load space: 95.6 in. x 50 in. x 20.5 in. Maximum capacity (Volume Index): 76.6 cu. ft. Front headroom: 40.2 in. Front legroom: 41.60 in. Front shoulder room: 58.3 in. Front hip room: 60.5 in. Pedal to seat back (max.): 43.0 in. Steering wheel to seat back (max.): 25.0 in. Seat to ground: 35.0 in. Floor to ground: Model 26: 20.5 in.; model 27: 22.1 in.

CAPACITIES: Fuel Tank: 18.2 gal. with skid plate. Coolant System: 6-cyl.: 9.5 qat. V-8: 15 qt.

ACCOMMODATIONS: Seating Capacity: Three.

INSTRUMENTATION: 0-110 mph speedometer, 0-99,999.9 mi. odometer, gauges for fuel level, engine coolant temperature, oil pressure and ammeter; Transfer case indicator lights.

OPTIONS AND PRICES: Pioneer Package: $554. Protective floor mats with carpeting. Deluxe grain bench seat. Soft-Feel Sport steering wheel. Leather-wrapped steering wheel. Chrome grille. Dual low profile type mirrors. Dual low profile type mirrors with Visibility Group (replaces remote control). Sliding rear window (clear glass only). Air conditioning. Includes heavy-duty cooling system. Heavy-duty 63 amp alternator. Heavy-duty battery. Cold Climate group. Includes heavy-duty battery, heavy-duty alternator and engine block heater. Convenience Group. Includes electric digital clock, lights-on buzzer, engine compartment light. Heavy-duty cooling system. Included with air conditioning. Includes extra-capacity radiator, fan shoud, coolant recovery and viscous fan (6-cyl. only). California emissions system. High altitude emissions system. 8400 lb. GVW option (J-20 only). Includes heavy-duty springs and shock absorbers, not available for California. 6200 lb. GVW option (J-10 only). Includes heavy-duty springs and shock absorbers, not available for California. Extra-Quiet Insulation Package. Includes custom headliner, under dash insulation and special sound deadening materials in passenger compartment (included in Pioneer Package). Light Group. Includes cargo box light, courtesy lights, glove box light, ashtray light and visor vanity mirror lights. Rear axle Trac-Lok differential.

HISTORICAL FOOTNOTES: The 1985 Jeep trucks debuted in the fall of 1984.

1986 TRUCKS

For 1986 both the J-10 and J-20 received an interior face-lift that was shared with the Grand Wagoneer. The instrument panel was totally re-designed, with new gauges, a climate control panel and a steering wheel with column-mounted controls for the high and low beam headlight operation and windshield wipers.

The base engine/transmission combination for the J-10 continued to be the 258 cu. in. 6-cylinder and a manual 4-speed transmission. The 360 cu. in. V-8 and automatic transmission were standard for the J-20 and optional for the J-10. The automatic transmission was available only with the V-8 engine. Both the J-10 and J-20 continued to have a standard part-time four-wheel drive system with the Selec-Trac full-time four-wheel drive option for the J -10 only. For 1986 Selec-Trac was available with a Trac-Loc rear differential. The J-10 and J-20

were available in either base or Pioneer form. Standard equipment for each vehicle included power front disc brakes, electronic ignition system, free-wheeling front hubs, power steering, front stabilizer bar and padded instrument panel. The J-20, with its greater load-carrying capacity, offered as standard larger front disc brakes, heavy-duty engine cooling, larger front and rear springs, as well as larger wheels and tires. Pioneer models continued to offer such features as extra-quiet insulation, chrome grille, wheelcovers, tailgate stripes and Pioneer name decals. Exterior colors available for the J-10 and J-20 were white, beige, red, classic black, dark brown, garnet and deep night blue.

1986 Jeep J-10 pickup

I.D. DATA: The serial number was located on the left-hand hinge pillar. The V.I.N. had 17 symbols. The first three entries identified the manufacturer, make and type of vehicle. The fourth unit, a letter, designated the engine. The fifth character, a letter, identified the transmission. The sixth and seventh characters identified the series and body style. The eighth character identified the GVW rating. Next followed a check digit. The eleventh character was the manufacturing plant identification. The final six digits were the sequential production number.

Model Number	Body Type	Factory Price	GVW	Shipping Weight	Prod. Total
J-10, 130.7 in.					
J-10	Pickup Townside, Model 26	$10,870	6001[1]	3808	1515[2]

NOTE 1: 7000 lb. GVW optional.
NOTE 2: 1986 calendar year production, all J series trucks.

Model Number	Body Type	Factory Price	GVW	Shipping Weight	Prod. Total
J-20, 360 V-8. 130.7 in. wheelbase.					
J-20	Pickup Townside, Model 27	$12160	70013	4388	—

NOTE 3: 7600 lb. and 8400 lb. GVW optional.

STANDARD ENGINE: J-10: Engine Type: OHV, In-line-6. Cast iron block and cylinder head. Bore x Stroke: 3.75 in. x 3.90 in. Lifters: Hydraulic. Number of main bearings-7. Fuel Induction: 2 bbl. carburetor. Compression Ratio: 9.2:1. Displacement: 258 cu. in. (4.2 liters). Horsepower: Net: 115 @ 3200 rpm. Torque: Net: 210 lb.-ft. @ 1800 rpm. Oil refill capacity: 5 qt. with filter change. Fuel Requirements: Unleaded.

OPTIONAL ENGINE: J-10, standard for J-20: Type: OHV, V-8. Cast iron block and cylinder head. Bore x Stroke: 4.08 in. x 3.44 in. Lifters: Hydraulic. Number of main bearings-5. Fuel Induction: 2 bbl. carburetor. Compression Ratio: 8.25:1. Displacement: 360 cu. in. (5.89 liters). Horsepower: Net: 150 @ 3400 rpm. Torque: Net: 265 lb.-ft. @ 1500 rpm. Oil refill capacity: 5 qt. with filter change. Fuel Requirements: Unleaded.

CHASSIS FEATURES: Separate body and frame. Deep web frame, splayed box section side rails, wide flange, lightweight pressed steel with five cross members.

SUSPENSION AND RUNNING GEAR: Front Suspension: J-10: 5-leaf semi-elliptical; Spring rate: 210 lb./in. Hydraulic double-action shock absorbers, 0.87 in. stabilizer bar. J-20: 7-leaf semi-elliptical, Spring rate: 260 lb./in. Hydraulic shock absorbers, 1.06 in. stabilizer bar. Optional: J-10: Spring rate: 230 lb./in. J-20: Spring rate: 330 lb./in. Heavy-duty front and rear shock absorbers. Rear Suspension: J-10: 4-leaf semi-elliptical springs, spring rate: 245 lb./in. J-20: 2-leaf tapered springs, spring rate: 240 lb./in. Hydraulic double-action shock absorbers. Optional: J-10: 340 lb./in/spring rate. J-20: Heavy-duty springs and shock absorbers. Spring rate: 510 lb/in. Front Axle Type and Capacity: Dana 44, full floating, Hypoid, open end. Capacity: 3200 lb. (J-10), 3500 lb. (J-20). Rear Axle Type and Capacity: J-10: Semi-floating, AMC/Jeep. J-20: Full-floating Dana model 60. Capacity: J-10: 3200 lb. J-20/7600 lb. GVW: 4700 lb.; J-20/8400 lb. GVW: 5500 lb. Optional: Power-Lok differential. Axle Ratios:. J-10 2.73:1 with 4-speed manual transmission, 3.31:1 with automatic transmission. Optional: None. J-20: 3.73:1. Transfer Case: J-10: Manual transmission: New Process 208 part-time transfer case. Ratios: 2.62:1, 1.00:1. J-10 and J-20: Automatic transmission: New Process 208 full-time transfer case. Ratios: 2.61:1, 1.00:1. Brakes: Type: J-10 & J-20: Hydraulic, front discs and rear drums. Dimensions: Front: J-10: 12.0 in.; J-20: 12.5 in. dia. disc, rear: J-10: 11.0 in. x 2.00 in drums, J-20: 12.52 in. x 2.50 in. drums. Wheels: Full drop center. J-10: 15 x 6JJ, 6-bolt, 5.5 in. circle, white painted. J-20: 16.5 x 6L, 8-bolt, 6.5 in. circle, white painted. Optional: J-10: 15 x 77JJ, 15 x 8 painted style wheel. J-20: 16.5 x 6.75. Tires: J-10: P225/75R15 black sidewall Arriva all-weather steel belted radial. J-20: 8.75 x 16.5C black sidewall nylon custom XG tubeless. Optional: J-10: 10R-15 LT. J-20: 9.50 x 16.5D. Steering: Saginaw power recirculating ball-type. Ratio: 13-16:1. Turns Lock-to-Lock: 3.7. Turning Circle: 44.5 ft. Standard Transmission: J-10: Tremec T-176 all-synchromesh 4-speed. Ratios: Transmission ratios: 6-cyl.: 3.82:1, 2.291, 1.46:1, 1.00:1. V-8: 3.52:1, 2.27:1, 1.46:1, 1.00:1. Standard: J-20 (Optional for J-10): Chrysler model 727 3-spd. automatic transmission. Ratios: 2.45:1, 1.55:1, 1.0:1 . Clutch: 11 in. Single dry plate. Total lining area: 111 sq. in. Optional: None.

VEHICLE DIMENSIONS: Wheelbase: J-10: 130.7 in. J-20: 130.8 in. Overall Length: 206.0 in. Front/Rear Tread: 63.3/63.8 in. Wide wheel option: 64.6/64.6 in. Overall Height: J-10: 69.0 in. J-20: 70.0 in. Width: 78.9 in. Front/Rear Overhang: 31.3 in./43.9 in. Tailgate: Width and Height: 57.2 in. x 20.5 in. Approach/Departure Degrees: 35/25. Ground Clearance: Rear axle: J-10: 7.5 in.; J-20: 8.2 in. Load space: 95.6 in. x 50 in. x 20.5 in. Maximum capacity (Volume Index): 76.6 cu. ft. Front headroom: 40.2 in. Front legroom: 41.60 in. Front shoulder room: 58.3 in. Front hip room: 60.5 in. Pedal to seat back (max.): 43.0 in. Steering wheel to seat back (max.): 25.0 in. Seat to ground: 35.0 in. Floor to ground: Model 26: 20.5 in.; model 27: 22.1 in.

CAPACITIES: Fuel Tank: 18.2 gal. with skid plate. Coolant System: 6-cyl.: 9.5 qt. V-8: 15 qt.

ACCOMMODATIONS: Seating Capacity: Three, two with bucket seats.

INSTRUMENTATION: 110 mph speedometer, 0-99,999.9 mi. odometer, gauges for fuel level, engine coolant temperature, oil pressure and ammeter; Transfer case indicator lights.

OPTIONS AND PRICES: Pioneer Package: $554. Protective floor mats with carpeting. Deluxe grain bench seat. Soft-Feel Sport steering wheel. Leather-wrapped steering wheel. Chrome grille. Dual low profile type mirrors. Dual low profile type mirrors with Visibility Group (replaces remote control). Sliding rear window (clear glass only). Air conditioning. Includes heavy-duty cooling system. Heavy-duty 63 amp alternator. Heavy-duty battery. Cold Climate group. Includes heavy-duty battery, heavy-duty alternator and engine block heater. Convenience Group. Includes electric digital clock, lights-on buzzer, engine compartment light. Heavy-duty cooling system. Included with air conditioning. Includes extra-capacity radiator, fan shroud, coolant recovery and viscous fan (6-cyl. only). California emissions system. High altitude emissions system. 8400 lb. GVW option (J-20 only). Includes heavy-duty springs and shock absorbers, not available for California. 6200 lb. GVW option (J-10 only). Includes heavy-duty springs and shock absorbers, not available for California. Extra-Quiet Insulation Package. Includes custom headliner, under dash insulation and special sound deadening materials in passenger compartment (included in Pioneer Package). Light Group. Includes cargo box light, courtesy lights, glove box light, ashtray light and visor vanity mirror lights. Rear axle Trac-Lok differential.

HISTORICAL FOOTNOTES: Introduction of the 1986 Jeep trucks took place in the fall of 1985.

1987 TRUCKS

The Jeep full-size pickup trucks were again offered in J-10 and J-20 form for 1987. No changes were made in their drivetrain/engine/transmission choices. Both versions received three new exterior colors for 1987 — Colorado red, grenadine metallic and briarwood metallic. Carry-over colors were: Olympic white, beige, classic black, and deep night blue. The Pioneer Trim Package received a new tan stripe color. A tan interior trim color was also new for 1987. A new "4x4" badge, similar to those found on the Cherokee, Wagoneer and Comanche models was affixed to the upper rear of the cargo box on all J-10 and J-20 models.

Both the J-10 and J-20 were offered in Base or Pioneer trim levels. Standard equipment included power front disc brakes, electronic ignition system, free-wheeling front hubs, power steering, front stabilizer bar and padded instrument panel. The J-20, with its greater load-carrying capacity had as standard larger front disc brakes, heavy-duty engine cooling, larger front and rear springs, larger wheels and tires. Features found on Pioneer models included extra-quiet insulation, carpet, chrome grille, wheelcovers, tailgate stripes and Pioneer name decals.

1987 Jeep J-10 pickup

I.D. DATA: The V.I.N. had 17 symbols. The first three entries identified the manufacturer, make and type of vehicle. The fourth unit, a letter, designated the engine. The fifth character, a letter, identified the transmission. The sixth and seventh characters identified the series and body style. The eighth character identified the GVW rating. Next followed a check digit. The eleventh character was the manufacturing plant identification. The final six digits were the sequential production number.

Model Number	Body Type	Factory Price	GVW	Shipping Weight	Prod. Total
J-10, 130.7 in.					
J-10	Pickup Townside, Model 26	$11,544	6001[1]	3790	1153[2]

NOTE 1: 7000 lb. GVW optional.
NOTE 2: Sales for the 1987 calendar year were 1,327.

Model Number	Body Type	Factory Price	GVW	Shipping Weight	Prod. Total
J-20, 360 V-8. 130.7 in. wheelbase					
J-20	Pickup Townside, Model 27	$12,941	7001[3]	4386	—

NOTE 3: 7600 lb. and 9000 lb. GVW optional.

STANDARD ENGINE: J-10: Engine Type: OHV, In-line-6. Cast iron block and cylinder head. Bore x Stroke: 3.75 in. x 3.90 in. Lifters: Hydraulic. Number of main bearings-7. Fuel Induction: 2 bbl. carburetor. Compression Ratio: 9.2:1. Displacement: 258 cu. in. (4.2 liters). Horsepower: Net: 115 @ 3200 rpm. Torque: Net: 210 lb.-ft. @ 1800 rpm. Oil refill capacity: 5 qt. with filter change. Fuel Requirements: Unleaded.

OPTIONAL ENGINE: J-10, standard for J-20: Type: OHV, V-8. Cast iron block and cylinder head. Bore x Stroke: 4.08 in. x 3.44 in. Lifters: Hydraulic. Number of main bearings-5. Fuel Induction: 2 bbl. carburetor. Compression Ratio: 8.25:1. Displacement: 360 cu. in. (5.89 liters). Horsepower: Net: 150 @ 3400 rpm. Torque: Net: 265 lb.-ft. @ 1500 rpm. Oil refill capacity: 5 qt. with filter change. Fuel Requirements: Unleaded.

CHASSIS FEATURES: Separate body and frame. Deep web frame, splayed box section side rails, wide flange, lightweight pressed steel with five cross members.

SUSPENSION AND RUNNING GEAR: Front Suspension: J-10: 5-leaf semi-elliptical; Spring rate: 210 lb./in. Hydraulic double-action shock absorbers, 0.87 in. stabilizer bar. J-20: 7-leaf semi-elliptical, Spring rate: 260 lb./in. Hydraulic shock absorbers, 1.06 in. stabilizer bar. Optional: J-10: Spring rate: 230 lb./in. J-20: Spring rate: 330 lb./in. Heavy-duty front and rear shock absorbers. Rear Suspension: J-10: 4-leaf semi-elliptical springs, spring rate: 245 lb./in. J-20: 2-leaf tapered springs, spring rate: 240 lb./in. Hydraulic double-action shock absorbers. Optional: J-10: 340 lb./in/spring rate. J-20: Heavy-duty springs and shock absorbers. Spring rate: 510 lb/in. Front Axle Type and Capacity: Dana 44, full floating, Hypoid, open end. Capacity: 3200 lb. (J-10), 3500 lb. (J-20). Rear Axle Type and Capacity: J-10: Semi-floating, AMC/Jeep. J-20: Full-floating Dana model 60. Capacity: J-10: 3200 lb. J-20/7600 lb. GVW: 4700 lb.; J-20/8400 lb. GVW: 5500 lb. Optional: Power-Lok differential. Axle Ratios:. J-10 2.73:1 with 4-speed manual transmission, 3.31:1 with automatic transmission. Optional: None. J-20: 3.73:1. Transfer Case: J-10: Manual transmission: New Process 208 part-time transfer case. Ratios: 2.62:1, 1.00:1. J-10 and J-20: Automatic transmission: New Process 208 full-time transfer case. Ratios: 2.61:1, 1.00:1. Brakes: Type: J-10 & J-20: Hydraulic, front discs and rear drums. Dimensions: Front: J-10: 12.0 in.; J-20: 12.5 in. dia. disc, rear: J-10: 11.0 in. x 2.00 in drums, J-20: 12.52 in. x 2.50 in. drums. Wheels: Full drop center. J-10: 15 x 6JJ, 6-bolt, 5.5 in. circle; white painted. J-20: 16.5 x 6L, 8-bolt, 6.5 in. circle, White painted. Optional: J-10: 15 x 77JJ, 15 x 8 painted style wheel. J-20: 16.5 x 6.75. Tires: J-10: P225/75R15 black sidewall Arriva all-weather steel belted radial. J-20: 8.75 x 16.5C black sidewall nylon custom XG tubeless. Optional: J-10: 10R-15 LT. J-20: 9.50 x 16.5D. Steering: Saginaw power recirculating ball-type. Ratio: 13-16:1. Turns Lock-to-Lock: 3.7. Turning Circle: 44.5 ft. Standard Transmission: J-10: Tremec T-176 all-synchromesh 4-speed. Ratios: Transmission ratios: 6-cyl.: 3.82:1, 2.291, 1.46:1, 1.00:1. V-8: 3.52:1, 2.27:1, 1.46:1, 1.00:1. Standard: J-20 (Optional for J-10): Chrysler model 727 3-spd. automatic transmission. Ratios: 2.45:1, 1.55:1, 1.0:1 . Clutch: 11 in. Single dry plate. Total lining area: 111 sq. in. Optional: None.

VEHICLE DIMENSIONS: Wheelbase: J-10: 130.7 in. J-20: 130.8 in. Overall Length: 206.0 in. Front/Rear Tread: 63.3/63.8 in. Wide wheel option: 64.6/64.6 in. Overall Height: J-10: 69.0 in. J-20: 70.0 in. Width: 78.9 in. Front/Rear Overhang: 31.3 in./43.9 in. Tailgate: Width and Height: 57.2 in. x 20.5 in. Approach/Departure Degrees: 35/25. Ground Clearance: Rear axle: J-10: 7.5 in.; J-20: 8.2 in. Load space: 95.6 in. x 50 in. x 20.5 in. Maximum capacity (Volume Index): 76.6 cu. ft. Front headroom: 40.2 in. Front legroom: 41.60 in. Front shoulder room: 58.3 in. Front hip room: 60.5 in. Pedal to seat back (max.): 43.0 in. Steering wheel to seat back (max.): 25.0 in. Seat to ground: 35.0 in. Floor to ground: Model 26: 20.5 in.; model 27: 22.1 in.

CAPACITIES: Fuel Tank: 18.2 gal. with skid plate. Coolant System: 6-cyl.: 9.5 qt. V-8: 15 qt.

ACCOMMODATIONS: Seating Capacity: Three, two with bucket seats.

INSTRUMENTATION: 110 mph speedometer, 0-99,999.9 mi. odometer, gauges for fuel level, engine coolant temperature, oil pressure and ammeter; Transfer case indicator lights.

OPTIONS AND PRICES: Pioneer Package: $581. Protective floor mats with carpeting. Deluxe Grain bench seat. Soft-Feel Sport steering wheel. Leather-wrapped steering wheel. Chrome grille. Dual low profile type mirrors. Dual low profile type mirrors with Visibility Group (replaces remote control). Sliding rear window (clear glass only). Air conditioning. Includes heavy-duty cooling system. Heavy-duty 63 amp alternator. Heavy-duty battery. Cold Climate group. Includes heavy-duty battery, heavy-duty alternator and engine block heater. Convenience Group. Includes electric digital clock, lights-on buzzer, engine compartment light. Heavy-duty cooling system. Included with air conditioning. Includes extra-capacity radiator, fan shoud, coolant recovery and viscous fan (6-cyl. only). California emissions system. High altitude emissions system. 8400 lb. GVW option (J-20 only). Includes heavy-duty springs and shock absorbers, not available for California. 7000 lb. GVW option (J-10 only). Includes heavy-duty springs and shock absorbers, not available for California. Extra-Quiet Insulation Package. Includes custom headliner, under dash insulation and special sound deadening materials in passenger compartment (included in Pioneer Package). Light Group. Includes cargo box light, courtesy lights, glove box light, ashtray light and visor vanity mirror lights. Rear axle Trac-Lok differential.

HISTORICAL FOOTNOTES: This was the final year the J trucks were produced. Although a price schedule was released for 1988 models, none were manufactured.

JEEP WAGONEER & CHEROKEE
1963-1993

1963 WAGONEER

After the cessation of passenger car production on 1955, Willys Motors began an extensive research and engineering program geared towards the development of utilitarian four-wheel drive models for the mass-market. A major result of this program was the introduction on November 14, 1962 of the Jeep Wagoneer. Completely new in virtually every aspect, the Wagoneer introduced the automotive industry's first automatic transmission in combination with four-wheel drive. Obviously proud of the new Wagoneer, KAISER Jeep Corporation, (this name change took place in March, 1963) noted that the Wagoneer was "the first station wagon to provide complete passenger car styling, comfort and convenience in combination with the advantages of four-wheel drive. The Wagoneer, said Willys was "All new, all Jeep." It was most definitely, emphasized Willys, "not a converted passenger car with a tailgate thrown in, nor a modified truck with windows...The all new 'Jeep' was conceived and designed as a wagon from its wheels to its reinforced roof."

Since Willys wasn't in the habit of frequently changing body styles, the appearance of the Wagoneer avoided a dependence upon styling features likely to quickly become dated. While the new Wagoneer was, in comparison with earlier Jeep models, a far sleeker vehicle, a strong visual connection with the CJ models was retained. The Wagoneer's angular wheelwell cutouts were suggestive of Jeep "styling" as was the simple grille format consisting of vertical dividers. The outer edge of the fenders and hood was extended slightly forward of the grille and front lights. Mounted inboard of the single headlamps were air-intakes for the interior. Rectangular parking/directional lights were positioned directly below the headlights. A Jeep logo with the Jeep name spelled out in broad gold letters and fitted with an outer ring of turbine vanes surrounding quadrants of alternating gold and red fields was mounted in the lower right side of the grille. The Wagoneer's large windows were called "pano-scopic" by Willys. At the rear simple uncomplicated square taillights and circular backup lamps were used. The Wagoneer's practical nature was found in numerous small but worthwhile features such as doors that opened 82 degrees (wider than those of any other station wagon).

Standard equipment for the base models included all vinyl plastic interior trim with rubberized floor mats, dual sun visors, electric windshield wipers, cigarette lighter and compass. Custom models (initially they were referred to as Deluxe models) were identified by their chrome grille, stainless steel door frame trim and windshield molding and wheel rings. Interior custom features included front and rear carpeting, covered cargo floor area, fabric seat inserts, higher grade headliner and door trim panels, interior wheelhouse covers, front and rear chrome-trimmed armrests and rearview mirror, chrome control knobs, rear seat chrome ashtray, courtesy lights, chrome molding for instrument panel and radio speaker, chrome cigarette lighter, foam seat cushions and Deluxe horn ring.

The only body style available was a station wagon with two or four doors in either two or four-wheel drive. The two door version was also offered as a panel delivery vehicle with its rear quarter panel windows replaced by sheet metal. In this form only a front seat was installed. This model also had two vertically hung rear doors instead of the conventional tailgate-upwardly hinged rear window arrangement found on other Wagoneers.

1963 Jeep Wagoneer

Development and design of the Wagoneer and its derivatives took place over a three year time span and cost $20 million. Much of this time and treasure was committed to the creation of a new engine, which Willys identified as the Tornado OHC, by its chief engineer, A.C. Sampietro. The most interesting feature of the Tornado engine was its overhead cam, (with six cam lobes, each operating one intake and one exhaust valve) which was operated by a silent-type Morse chain. The timing for both the intake and exhaust valves was 250 degrees with 30 degrees of overlap. The valves were inclined and respective intake and exhaust valve head measurements were 1.895 and 1.618 in. Hemispherical combustion chambers (that Willys preferred to call "spheroidal") were used.

Attracting nearly as much attention as the overhead cam engine were the new front suspension systems Willys offered for the J series wagons. There were two different four-wheel drive versions available with independent suspension or solid front axles for heavy-duty use. The independent unit with torsion bars and a swing axle. The axle (a Dana model 27DFS0), articulated near its center, served as the lower suspension wishbones. A strut bar was used for lateral axle control and for caster adjustment. The upper suspension components consisted of short A-arms and ball joints linked to the 0.78 in. diameter torsion bars. This suspension was offered as $160 option for the four-wheel drive versions.

For heavier duty operation the J-164 models were available with a solid front axle with longitudinal leaf springs. As applied to the J series this arrangement used four leaf, semi-elliptical springs measuring 44 in. x 2.5 in.

Ten exterior colors were offered for the Wagoneer: White cap, sprucetip green, parkway green, president red, nordic blue, Sierra blue, parade blue, jet line grey, tree bark brown and amber metallic. Interior finishes were available in three low gloss paints: Sylvan green for cars with exterior green paint, nordic blue for those with exterior blues and amber metallic for all others.

I.D. DATA: The serial number was located on the left-hand hinge pillar. The first four digits indicated the model as follows: 1412-Two-door station wagon, 1414-Four-door station wagon, 1413-Panel delivery. The fifth symbol was a letter. The sequential production number followed. The starting number for each series was 10001. The engine number was located on the right-hand corner of the block. The engine codes were ND60C and TD60C.

Model Number	Body Type	Factory Price	GVW	Shipping Weight	Prod. Total
Series J-100 Wagoneer Station Wagon					
1414	4-dr.	$3332	4500	3623	—
1412	2-dr.	$3278	4500	3596	—
1414C	Custom 4-dr.	$3526	4500	3658	—
1412C	Custom 2-dr.	$3472	4500	3631	—
1413	Panel Del.	$2996	4500	3396	—

STANDARD ENGINE: Engine Type: OHV, OHC, In-line-6. Cast iron block and cylinder head. Bore x Stroke: 3.4375 in. x 4.375 in. Lifters: Hydraulic. Number of main bearings-4. Fuel Induction: 1-bbl. Holley model 1920 (manual trans. models); 2-bbl. Holley model 2415 (auto. trans.). Compression Ratio: 8.5:1. Displacement: 230 cu. in. (3.77 liters). Horsepower: Net:140 @ 4000 rpm. Torque: Net: 210 lb.-ft. @ 1750 rpm. Oil refill capacity: 6 qt. with filter change. Fuel Requirements: Regular.

OPTIONAL ENGINE: None

CHASSIS FEATURES: Separate body and frame. Deep web frame, wide flange, lightweight pressed steel with five cross members.

SUSPENSION AND RUNNING GEAR: Front Suspension: 4-Leaf semi-elliptical springs, 44 in. x 2.5 in. Rating: 1500 lb./in. Hydraulic double-action shock absorbers: 12.75 in. on solid front axle, 12.18 in. dia. for torsion bar suspension. Optional Torsion bar. Rear Suspension: Semi-elliptical 4-leaf springs with anti-windup top half spring, 52 in. x 2.5 in. Hydraulic double-action, 10.75 in. dia. shock absorbers. Optional: 6-leaf semi-elliptical springs, 52 in. x 2.5 in. Front Axle Type and Capacity: Dana model 27AF, 2500 lb. capacity. Rear Axle Type and Capacity: Dana model 44 semi-floating, 3000 lb. capacity. Optional: None. Final Drive Ratio: 4.89:1. Optional: 3.73,4.27:1. Transfer Case: Man. trans. models: 2-speed Spicer model 20, 2.03:1, 1.0:1. Auto. trans. models: Spicer model 21, single speed (1.00:1). Brakes: Type: Hydraulic, front and rear drums. Dimensions: Front: 11.0 in. x 2.00 in. front and rear. Total effective area: 161.16 sq. in. Optional: Power brakes. Models with auto. trans. had a Bendix system with a wide and low-positioned pedal. Models with manual trans. have a Midland system with a narrower and lower positioned pedal. Wheels: Kelsey-Hayes 15 x 5.5K, disc type, full-drop center 5-stud. Tires: 6.70 x 15, subsequently changed to 7.10 x 15, 4 ply rating. Optional: other sizes available. Steering: Ross Cam lever. Ratio: 24:1. Turns Lock-to-Lock: 5.6. Turning Circle: 38.3 ft. With the front torsion bar suspension, the turning radius was reduced by 16 in. Optional: Thompson Power steering. Ratios: 20:1 (later revised to 24:1). Standard: Transmission: Warner Gear T-90, 3-speed synchromesh manual. Transmission ratios: 2.798:1, 1.551:1, 1.00:1. Reverse: 3.798:1. Optional: Borg-Warner model AS-8F, three speed torque converter automatic transmission: Ratios: 2.4:1, 1.467:1, 1.00:1. Reverse: 2.01:1. Clutch: Borg & Beck single dry plate. Clutch diameter: 9.25 in. dia. Optional: Borg & Beck single dry plate. Clutch Diameter: 10.0 in.

VEHICLE DIMENSIONS: Wheelbase: 110 in. Overall Length: 183.66 in. Front/Rear Tread: 57 in./57 in. Overall Height: 64.2 in. Width: 75.6 in. Tailgate: Width: 55 in. Ground Clearance: Lowest point: 7.75 in. Load space: 111 in. x 55 in. x 39.5 in. Maximum capacity: 107 cu. ft. (2-door model). Front legroom: 45.25 in. Rear legroom: 38.25 in.

CAPACITIES: Fuel Tank: 20.0 gal. Coolant System: 12 qt., 13 qt. with heater.

ACCOMMODATIONS: Seating Capacity: Six passengers.

INSTRUMENTATION: Speedometer, odometer, gauges for fuel level, engine coolant temperature, battery charge and oil pressure, transfer case indicator lights.

OPTIONS: 40-60 amp alternator. Power steering. Power brakes. Drive line brake. Powr-Lok differential (rear axle only). Oil bath air cleaner. Front-mounted winch. Power take-off (rear-mounted). Warn free-wheeling front hubs. Engine governors. Locking gas cap. Magnetic drain plug. Speedometer reading in kilometers. Electric-operated tailgate. Dual-speed wipers. Windshield washers. Fresh-air heater and defroster. Electric clock. Back-up lights. Push-button AM radio. Parking light indicator. Compass. Transfer case indicator lights (four). Chrome exterior mirror. Padded dash panel. Seat belts. E-Z Eye windshield glass. Glove box light.

HISTORICAL FOOTNOTES: The new Wagoneer model debuted on November 14, 1962. It was destined for a long production life.

1964 WAGONEER

No changes were made in the Wagoneer's design or specifications for 1964. Air conditioning was added to its optional equipment list and a lower compression version of the OHC 6-cylinder engine was now available.

I.D. DATA: The serial number was located on the left-hand hinge pillar. The first four digits indicated the model as follows: 1412-Two-door station wagon, 1414-Four-door station wagon, 1413-Panel delivery. The fifth symbol was a letter. The sequential production number followed. The starting number for each series was 10001. The engine number was located on the right-hand corner of the block. The engine codes were ND60C and TD60C.

Model Number	Body Type	Factory Price	GVW	Shipping Weight	Prod. Total
Series J-100 Wagoneer Station Wagon					
1414	4-dr.	$3434	4500	3623	—
1412	2-dr.	$3379	4500	3596	—
1414C	Custom 4-dr.	$3633	4500	3658	—
1412C	Custom 2-dr.	$3578	4500	3631	—
1413	Panel Del.	$3082	4500	3396	—

STANDARD ENGINE: Engine Type: OHV, OHC, In-line-6. Cast iron block and cylinder head. Bore x Stroke: 3.4375 in. x 4.375 in. Lifters: Hydraulic. Number of main bearings-4. Fuel Induction: 1-bbl. Holley model 1920 (manual trans. models); 2-bbl. Holley model 2415 (auto. trans.). Compression Ratio: 8.5:1. Displacement: 230 cu. in. (3.77 liters). Horsepower: Net:140 @ 4000 rpm. Torque: Net: 210 lb.-ft. @ 1750 rpm. Oil refill capacity: 6 qt. with filter change. Fuel Requirements: Regular.

OPTIONAL ENGINE: Engine Type: OHV, OHC In-line-6. Cast iron block and cylinder head. Bore x Stroke: 3.4375 in. x 4.375 in. Lifters: Hydraulic. Number of main bearings-4. Fuel Induction: 1-bbl. Holley model 1920 (manual trans. models); 2-bbl. Holley model 2415 (auto. trans.). Compression Ratio: 7.5:1. Displacement: 230 cu. in. (3.77 liters). Horsepower: Net:133 @ 4000 rpm. Torque: Net: 199 lb.-ft. @ 2400 rpm. Tach redline: NA. Oil refill capacity: 6 qt. with filter change. Fuel Requirements: Regular.

CHASSIS FEATURES: Separate body and frame. Deep web frame, wide flange, lightweight pressed steel with five cross members.

SUSPENSION AND RUNNING GEAR: Front Suspension: 4-Leaf semi-elliptical springs, 44 in. x 2.5 in. Rating: 1500 lb./in. Hydraulic double-action shock absorbers: 12.75 in. on solid front axle, 12.18 in. dia. for torsion bar suspension). Optional Torsion bar. Rear Suspension: Semi-elliptical 4-leaf springs with anti-windup top half spring, 52 in. x 2.5 in. Hydraulic double-action, 10.75 in. dia. shock absorbers. Optional: 6-leaf semi-elliptical springs, 52 in. x 2.5 in. Front Axle Type and Capacity: Dana model 27AF, 2500 lb. capacity. Rear Axle Type and Capacity: Dana model 44 semi-floating, 3000 lb. capacity. Optional: None. Final Drive Ratio: 4.89:1. Optional: 3.73,4.27:1. Transfer Case: Man. trans. models: 2-speed Spicer model 20, 2.03:1, 1.0:1. Auto. trans. models: Spicer model 21, single speed (1.00:1). Brakes: Type: Hydraulic, front and rear drums. Dimensions: Front: 11.0 in. x 2.00 in. front and rear. Total effective area: 161.16 sq. in. Optional: Power brakes. Models with auto. trans. had a Bendix system with a wide and low-positioned pedal. Models with manual trans. have a Midland system with a narrower and lower positioned pedal. Wheels: Kelsey-Hayes 15 x 5.5K, disc type, full-drop center 5-stud. Tires: 6.70 x 15, subsequently changed to 7.10 x 15, 4 ply rating. Optional: other sizes available. Steering: Ross Cam lever. Ratio: 24:1. Turns Lock-to-Lock: 5.6. Turning Circle: 38.3 ft. With the front torsion bar suspension, the turning radius was reduced by 16 in. Optional: Thompson Power steering. Ratios: 20:1 (later revised to 24:1). Standard: Transmission: Warner Gear T-90, 3-speed synchromesh manual. Transmission ratios: 2.798:1, 1.551:1, 1.00:1. Reverse: 3.798:1. Optional: Borg-Warner model AS-8F, three speed torque converter automatic transmission: Ratios: 2.4:1, 1.467:1, 1.00:1. Reverse: 2.01:1. Clutch: Borg & Beck single dry plate. Clutch diameter: 9.25 in. dia. Optional: Borg & Beck single dry plate. Clutch Diameter: 10.0 in.

VEHICLE DIMENSIONS: Wheelbase: 110 in. Overall Length: 183.66 in. Front/Rear Tread: 57 in./57 in. Overall Height: 64.2 in. Width: 75.6 in. Tailgate: Width: 55 in. Ground Clearance: Lowest point: 7.75 in. Load space: 111 in. x 55 in. x 39.5 in. Maximum capacity: 107 cu. ft. (2-door model). Front legroom: 45.25 in. Rear legroom: 38.25 in.

CAPACITIES: Fuel Tank: 20.0 gal. Coolant System: 12 qt., 13 qt. with heater.

ACCOMMODATIONS: Seating Capacity: Six passengers.

INSTRUMENTATION: Speedometer, odometer, gauges for fuel level, engine coolant temperature, battery charge and oil pressure, transfer case indicator lights.

OPTIONS: Air conditioning. 40-60 amp alternator. Power steering. Power brakes. Drive line brake. Powr-Lok differential (rear axle only). Oil bath air cleaner. Front-mounted winch. Power take-off (rear-mounted). Warn free-wheeling front hubs. Engine governors. Locking gas cap. Magnetic drain plug. Speedometer reading in kilometers. Electric-operated tailgate. Dual-speed wipers. Windshield washers. Fresh-air heater and defroster. Electric clock. Back-up lights. Push-button AM radio. Parking light indicator. Compass. Transfer case indicator lights (four). Chrome exterior mirror. Padded dash panel. Seat belts. E-Z Eye windshield glass. Glove box light.

HISTORICAL FOOTNOTES: The 1964 Wagoneers were introduced in the fall of 1963.

1965 WAGONEER

The early 1965 models continued to have the same styling as found on the 1963-64 models. In April, 1965 the Wagoneer became the first Jeep vehicle to be offered with a V-8 engine when the American Motors' 327 cu. in. V-8 became available as an option. This move was announced by James Beattie, Kaiser Jeep Corporation's vice-president-marketing who explained that rather than wait for the new model year to begin, Kaiser's policy was to announce product improvements as they became available. The overhead cam six was still

the standard engine, but this "Vigilante" V-8 was, at $190.83, an attractive alternative. With a 2-barrel carburetor the V-8 developed 250 horsepower at 4700 rpm and 340 lb.-ft. of torque at 2600 rpm.

This engine was originally introduced in 1956 for the Nash Ambassador Special line. At that time it displaced 250 cu. in. with a bore and stroke of 3.50 x 3.25 in. Four main bearings were used and with all accessories, but minus its flywheel and clutch this V-8 weighed 601 pounds. Thin wall construction was used for all iron castings and with good-sized valves (1.79 in. intake and 1.41 in. exhaust) plus a 4.75 in. bore center-to-bore center measurement that was easily expanded to 327 cu. in. with a 4 in. bore and 3.25 in. stroke in 1957.

In conjunction with use of this V-8 Kaiser, Jeep also made available General Motors' Turbo Hydra-Matic 3-speed torque converter automatic transmission. This engine-transmission did not replace any of the J series existing standard or optional engine-transmission choices. A 3-speed manual transmission was standard with the V-8. Overdrive was also available.

The 2-speed transfer case used in conjunction with Hydra-Matic was a Spicer 20 unit with a 2.03:1 ratio. Other Wagoneers with automatic transmissions did not have this extra low set of gears since a manual clutch was required to shift them. General Motors, through its Saginaw division, also supplied the Wagoneer's full-time power steering which was of a recirculating ball worm design. Also phased in during 1965 as a replacement for the short-lived OHC 6-cylinder engine (which was still used in the 6-230 models for this, their final year of production) was another engine purchased from American Motors, the Hi-Torque 6, a conventional OHV 6-cylinder engine.

All Wagoneer models for 1965 had a new standard Safety Package consisting of front and rear seat belts, padded sun visors, high-impact windshield glass, chrome outside mirror, dual brake system, 4-way warning flashers, backup lights, and dual-speed wipers and windshield wipers. Exterior colors for 1965 consisted of prairie gold, bronze mist, sprucetip green, gold beige, empire blue, glacier white and president red.

I.D. DATA: The serial number was located on the left-hand hinge pillar. The first four digits indicated the model as follows: 1412-Two-door station wagon, 1414-Four-door station wagon, 1413-Panel delivery. The fifth symbol was a letter. The sequential production number followed. The starting number for each series was 10001. The engine number was located on the right-hand corner of the block. The engine codes were ND60C and TD60C.

Model Number	Body Type	Factory Price	GVW	Shipping Weight	Prod. Total
Series J-100 Wagoneer Station Wagon (with OHC 6-cyl. engine)					
1414	4-dr.	$3449	4500	3623	—
1412	2-dr.	$3395	4500	3596	—
1414C	Custom 4-dr.	$3644	4500	3658	—
1412C	Custom 2-dr.	$3590	4500	3631	—
1413	Panel Del.	$3396	4500	3396	—

STANDARD ENGINE: During the 1965 model year this engine was phased out. Engine Type: OHV, OHC, L-6. Cast iron block and cylinder head. Bore x Stroke: 3.4375 in. x 4.375 in. Lifters: Hydraulic. Number of main bearings-4. Fuel Induction: 1-bbl. Holley modelHolley model 1920 (manual trans. models); 2-bbl. Holley model 2415 (auto. trans.). Compression Ratio: 8.5:1. Displacement: 230 cu. in. (3.77 liters). Horsepower: Net:140 @ 4000 rpm. Torque: Net: 210 lb.-ft. @ 1750 rpm. Oil refill capacity: 6 qt. with filter change. Fuel Requirements: Regular.

STANDARD ENGINE: Engine Type: OHV, L-6. Cast iron block and cylinder head. Bore x Stroke: 3.75 in. x 3.50 in. Lifters: Hydraulic. Number of main bearings-7. Fuel Induction: 1-bbl. Carter Type RTBS or Holley model 1931C-3705. Compression Ratio: 8.5:1. Displacement: 232 cu. in. (3.8 liters). Horsepower: 145 @ 4300 rpm. Torque: 215 lb.-ft. @ 1600 rpm. Oil refill capacity: 5 qt. with filter change. Fuel Requirements: Regular.

OPTIONAL ENGINE: Engine Type: OHV, "Vigilante" V-8. Cast iron block and cylinder head. Bore x Stroke: 4.00 in. x 3.25 in. Lifters: Hydraulic. Number of main bearings-4. Fuel Induction: 2-bbl. downdraft carburetor. Compression Ratio: 8.7:1. Displacement: 327 cu. in. (5.36 liters). Horsepower: 250 @ 4700 rpm. Torque: Net: 340 lb.-ft. @ 2600 rpm. Oil refill capacity: 5 qt. with filter change. Fuel Requirements: Regular.

CHASSIS FEATURES: Separate body and frame. Deep web frame, wide flange, lightweight pressed steel with five cross members.

SUSPENSION AND RUNNING GEAR: Front Suspension: 7-leaf semi-elliptical springs, 44 in. x 2.5 in. Rating: 160 lb./in. 12.75 in. Hydraulic double-action shock absorbers. Optional: Torsion bar, independent. Rear Suspension: Variable rate, 4-leaf springs, 52 in. x 2.5 in. Rating: 133/215 lb./in. with hydraulic double-action, 10.75 in. dia. shock absorbers. Optional: None. Front Axle Type and Capacity: Dana model 27AF, 2500 lb. capacity. Rear Axle Type and Capacity: Dana model 44 semi-floating, 3000 lb. capacity. Optional: None. Final Drive Ratio: 6-cyl.: Manual trans.: 4.09:1. Auto. trans.: 3.73:1.V-8: Man. trans.: 3.73:1. Auto. trans.: 3.31:1. Optional: 6-cyl.: Man. trans.: 4.27:1. Auto. trans.: 4.09:1 V-8: Man. trans.: 4.09:1. Auto. trans.: 3.73:1. Transfer Case: Man. trans. and Turbo Hydra-Matic models: 2-speed Spicer model 20, 2.03:1, 1.0:1. Brakes: Type: Hydraulic, front and rear drums. Dimensions: Front: 11.0 in. x 2.00 in. front and rear. Total effective area: 161.16 sq. in. Optional: Power brakes. Wheels: Kelsey-Hayes 15 x 5.5K, disc type, full-drop center 5-stud. Tires: 7.75 x 15. Steering: Recirculating ball. Ratio: 24:1. Turns Lock-to-Lock: 5.6. Turning Circle: 44.5 ft. Optional: Saginaw Power steering. Ratios: 17.5:1. Turns Lock-to-Lock: 4.0. Standard: Transmission: 3-speed synchromesh manual. Transmission ratios: 6-cyl.: 2.798:1, 1.687:1, 1.00:1. Reverse: 3.798:1.V-8: 2.490:1, 1.5871, 1.00:1. Reverse: 3.154:1. Optional: Turbo Hydra-Matic 3-spd. Ratios: 2.48:1, 1.48:1, 1.0:1. Reverse: 2.08:1. Clutch: Borg & Beck single dry plate. Clutch diameter: 6-cyl.: 10.0 in. dia. V-8:10.5 in. Total lining area: 6-cyl.: 100.5 sq. in., V-8: 106.8 sq. in. Total plate pressure: 6-cyl.: 1350 lb., V-8: 1858 lb.

VEHICLE DIMENSIONS: Wheelbase: 110 in. Overall Length: 183.66 in. Front/Rear Tread: 57 in./57 in. Overall Height: 64.2 in. Width: 75.6 in. Tailgate: Width and Height: 55 in. Ground Clearance: Lowest point: 7.75 in. Load space: 111 in. x 55 in. x 39.5 in. Maximum capacity: 107 cu. ft. (two-door model). Front legroom: 45.25 in. Rear legroom: 38.25 in.

CAPACITIES: Fuel Tank: 20.0 gal. Coolant System: 230 6-cyl.: 11 qt., 12 qt. with heater, 232 6-cyl.: 9.5 qt., 10.5 qt. with heater, V-8: 18.5 qt., 19.5 qt. with heater.

ACCOMMODATIONS: Seating Capacity: Six passengers.

INSTRUMENTATION: Speedometer, odometer, gauges for oil pressure, engine coolant temperature, battery charge, fuel level, Transfer case indicator lights.

OPTIONS AND PRICES: Heavy-duty alternator. Air conditioning. Drawbar. Power brakes. Transmission brakes. Locking gas cap. Electric clock. Heavy-duty clutch. Vigilante V-8: $190.83. E-Z Eye glass. Fresh-air heater and defroster. Heavy-duty springs and shock absorbers. Selective drive hubs. Parking brake warning light. Spare tire lock. Right-side outside rearview mirror. Fuel tank skid plate. Power take-offs. Push-button transistor radio. Power steering: $96.78. Turbo Hydra-Matic. Snowplow. Push plate. Winches. Power tailgate. Rear Powr-Lok differential. Mud flap. Luggage rack. Pleated vinyl seats.

HISTORICAL FOOTNOTES: The Wagoneer was the first V-8 powered Jeep.

1966 WAGONEER

The Wagoneer was essentially unchanged for 1966. The change-over to the 1966 models began with those registered on or after August 23, 1965. This would make 1966 a year of minor consequence to the Jeep enthusiast if not for the introduction of an important new model, the Super Wagoneer. Beyond depicting the Super Wagoneer as "a new dimension in motoring", Kaiser Jeep noted that: "No matter the number of automobiles possessed in a lifetime, there is little else of a material nature as exciting as the first hours and days of ownership of a truly fine car."

The Super Wagoneer's exterior featured two side trim panels, that widened from front to rear. The top panel contained an "antiqued gold" insert while the lower and narrower panel was painted black to match the color of the standard padded roof. The Super Wagoneer's rear deck had similar detailing consisting of a wide upper panel with a vertically-ribbed gold insert and a much narrower black panel. A gold "Super" trim plate was added to the Wagoneer script on the rear fender panel. Bull's-eye-shaped ornaments were positioned on the front fender tops. The Super Wagoneer was also equipped with mag-styled wheelcovers with simulated knock-off hubs. The Super Wagoneer's color selection consisted of empire blue, Indian ceramic, glacier white or prairie gold.

1966 Jeep Super Wagoneer

Interior appointments of the Super Wagoneer substantiated Kaiser Jeep's claim that it was "the most elegant 4-wheeler auto ever crafted." Courtesy lights were mounted in the ceiling and near the floor and an adjustable steering wheel tilting to any of seven positions was installed. The seats (front buckets and rear bench) had foam cushions and were finished in pleated knit back British calf grain and Cranstone. Door panels were trimmed in soft vinyl with simulated walnut woodgrain and chrome accents. The scuff panel was covered in a color-coordinated carpet. The Super Wagoneer's seats were machine stitched. Both the dashboard and sun visors were padded and a vanity mirror was attached to the back of the passenger's sun visor. The rearview mirror was equipped with a prismatic lenses with day and night positions. When not in use the front seat belts automatically retracted into belt retainers. Rear seat belts were also standard.

The Super Wagoneer was also fitted with many other standard features including air conditioning, Turbo Hydra-Matic, power steering and brakes, power tailgate window, tinted safety glass in all windows, white sidewall 8.45 x 15 Power Cushion tires with a 4-ply rating, luggage carrier chrome outside rearview mirror, and a push-button transistor radio equipped with an automatic volume control which kept the audio amplitude constant.

Powering the Super Wagoneer was the 4-barrel version of the 327 cu. in. Vigilante V-8 with a 9.7:1 compression ratio. Its ratings were 270 horsepower at 4700 rpm and 360 lb.-ft. of torque at 2600 rpm.

All Wagoneer models were fitted with a wider selection of interior color selections.

I.D. DATA: The serial number was located on the left-hand hinge pillar. The first four digits indicated the model as follows: 1412-Two-door station wagon, 1414-Four-door station wagon, 1413-Panel delivery. The fifth symbol was a letter. The sequential production number followed. The engine number was located on the right-hand corner of the block. The engine codes were ND60C and TD60C.

Serial number data: Model 1414: 1414-22501 and up; model 1412: 1412-11606 and up; model 1414C: 1414C-15519 and up; model 1412C: 1412C-10368, Model 1413: 1413-10250 and up, Model 1414D: 1414D-10368 and up

Model Number	Body Type	Factory Price	GVW	Shipping Weight	Prod. Total
Series J-100 Wagoneer Station Wagon (with 6-cyl. engine)					
1414	4-dr.	$3585	4500	3623	—
1412	2-dr.	$3531	4500	3596	—
1414C	Custom 4-dr.	$3780	4500	3658	—
1412C	Custom 2-dr.	$3725	4500	3631	—
1413	Panel Del.	$3223	4500	3396	—
1414D	Super	$5943	4500	4241	—

STANDARD ENGINE: (Except for Super Wagoneer): Engine Type: OHV, L-6. Cast iron block and cylinder head. Bore x Stroke: 3.75 in. x 3.50 in. Lifters: Hydraulic. Number of main bearings-7. Fuel Induction: 1-bbl. Carter Type RTBS or Holley model 1931C-3705. Compression Ratio: 8.5:1. Displacement: 232 cu. in. (3.8 liters). Horsepower: 145 @ 4300 rpm. Torque: 215 lb.-ft. @ 1600 rpm. Oil refill capacity: 5 qt. with filter change. Fuel Requirements: Regular. Standard: Super Wagoneer. Engine Type: OHV, "Vigilante" V-8. Cast iron block and cylinder head. Bore x Stroke: 4.00 in. x 3.25 in. Lifters: Hydraulic. Number of main bearings-4. Fuel Induction: 4-bbl. downdraft carburetor. Compression Ratio: 9.7:1. Displacement: 327 cu. in. (5.36 liters). Horsepower: 270 @ 4700 rpm. Torque: Net: 360 lb.-ft. @ 2600 rpm. Oil refill capacity: 5 qt. with filter change. Fuel Requirements: Regular.

OPTIONAL ENGINE: (For all models except Super Wagoneer): Engine Type: OHV, "Vigilante" V-8. Cast iron block and cylinder head. Bore x Stroke: 4.00 in. x 3.25 in. Lifters: Hydraulic. Number of main bearings-4. Fuel Induction: 2-bbl. downdraft carburetor. Compression Ratio: 8.7:1. Displacement: 327 cu. in. (5.36 liters). Horsepower: 250 @ 4700 rpm. Torque: Net: 340 lb.-ft. @ 2600 rpm. Oil refill capacity: 5 qt. with filter change. Fuel Requirements: Regular.

CHASSIS FEATURES: Separate body and frame. Deep web frame, wide flange, lightweight pressed steel with five cross members.

SUSPENSION AND RUNNING GEAR: Front Suspension: 7-leaf semi-elliptical springs, 44 in. x 2.5 in. Rating: 160 lb./in. 12.75 in. Hydraulic double-action shock absorbers. Optional. Torsion bar, independent. Rear Suspension: Variable rate, 4-leaf springs, 52 in. x 2.5 in. Rating: 133/215 lb./in. with Hydraulic double-action, 10.75 in. dia. shock absorbers. Optional: None. Front Axle Type and Capacity: Dana model 27AF, 2500 lb. capacity. Rear Axle Type and Capacity: Dana model 44 semi-floating, 3000 lb. capacity. Optional: None. Final Drive Ratio: 6-cyl.: Manual trans.: 4.09:1. Auto. trans.: 3.73:1.V-8: Man. trans.: 3.73:1. Auto. trans.: 3.31:1. Optional: 6-cyl.: Man. trans.: 4.27:1. Auto. trans.: 4.09:1 V-8: Man. trans.: 4.09:1. Auto. trans.: 3.73:1. Transfer Case: Man. trans. and Turbo Hydra-Matic models: 2-speed Spicer model 20, 2.03:1, 1.0:1. Brakes: Type: Hydraulic, front and rear drums. Dimensions: Front: 11.0 in. x 2.00 in. front and rear. Total effective area: 161.16 sq. in. Optional: Power brakes. Wheels: Kelsey-Hayes 15 x 5.5K, disc type, full-drop center 5-stud. Tires: 7.75 x 15. Super Wagoneer: 8.45 x 15 Super Cushion white sidewall. Steering: Recirculating ball. Ratio: 24:1. Turns Lock-to-Lock: 5.6. Turning Circle: 44.5 ft. Optional: Saginaw Power steering. Ratios: 17.5:1. Turns Lock-to-Lock: 4.0. Standard for Super Wagoneer. Standard: Transmission: 3-speed synchromesh manual. Transmission ratios: 6-cyl.: 2.798:1, 1.687:1. 1.00:1. Reverse: 3.798:1. V-8: 2.490:1, 1.5871, 1.00:1. Reverse: 3.154:1. Optional: Turbo Hydra-Matic 3-spd. Ratios: 2.48:1, 1.48:1, 1.0:1. Reverse: 2.08:1. Standard for Super Wagoneer. Clutch: Borg & Beck single dry plate. Clutch diameter: 6-cyl.: 10.0 in. dia. V-8:10.5 in. Total lining area: 6-cyl.: 100.5 sq. in., V-8: 106.8 sq. in. Total plate pressure: 6-cyl.: 1350 lb., V-8: 1858 lb.

VEHICLE DIMENSIONS: Wheelbase: 110 in. Overall Length: 183.66 in. Front/Rear Tread: 57 in./57 in. Overall Height: 64.2 in. Width: 75.6 in. Tailgate: Width and Height: 55 in. Ground Clearance: Lowest point: 7.75 in. Load space: 111 in. x 55 in. x 39.5 in. Maximum capacity: 107 cu. ft. (two-door model). Front legroom: 45.25 in. Rear legroom: 38.25 in.

CAPACITIES: Fuel Tank: 20.0 gal. Coolant System: 230 6-cyl.: 11 qt., 12 qt. with heater, 232 6-cyl.: 9.5 qt., 10.5 qt. with heater, V-8: 18.5 qt., 19.5 qt. with heater.

ACCOMMODATIONS: Seating Capacity: Six passengers.

INSTRUMENTATION: Speedometer, odometer, gauges for oil pressure, engine coolant temperature, battery charge, fuel level, Transfer case indicator lights,

OPTIONS: Heavy-duty alternator. Air conditioning. Drawbar. Power brakes. Transmission brakes. Locking gas cap. Electric clock. Heavy-duty clutch. Vigilante V-8E-Z Eye glass. Fresh-air heater and defroster. Heavy-duty springs and shock absorbers. Selective drive hubs. Parking brake warning light. Spare tire lock. Right-side outside rearview mirror. Fuel tank skid plate. Power take-offs. Push-button transistor radio. Power steering Turbo Hydra-Matic. Snowplow. Push plate. Winches. Power tailgate. Rear Powr-Lok differential. Mud flap. Luggage rack. Pleated vinyl seats.

HISTORICAL FOOTNOTES: The Super Wagoneer was the first of the American luxury-oriented four-wheel drive vehicles.

1967 WAGONEER

Except for minor changes in the axle ratio availability, no major design changes were made for 1967.

1967 Jeep Wagoneer

I.D. DATA: The serial number was located on the left-hand hinge pillar. The first four digits indicated the model as follows: 1414-Four-door station wagon, 1412-Two-door station wagon, 1414C-Four-door custom station wagon, 1412C-Two-door custom station wagon, 1414D-Four-door super station wagon. The fifth symbol was a letter. The sequential production number for all models except the super station wagon was 200001 and up. The sequential production number for the super station wagon was 100002 and up.

Model Number	Body Type	Factory Price	GVW	Shipping Weight	Prod. Total
Series J-100 Wagoneer Station Wagon (with 6-cyl. engine)					
1414	4-dr.	$3702	4500	3654	—
1412	2-dr.	$3648	4500	3627	—
1414C	Custom 4-dr.	$3898	4500	3689	—
1412C	Custom 2-dr.	$3844	4500	3662	—
1413	Panel Del.	$3357	4500	3424	—
1414D	Super	$6048	4500	4241	—

STANDARD ENGINE: (Except for Super Wagoneer): Engine Type: OHV, L-6. Cast iron block and cylinder head. Bore x Stroke: 3.75 in. x 3.50 in. Lifters: Hydraulic. Number of main bearings-7. Fuel Induction: 1-bbl. Carter Type RTBS or Holley model 1931C-3705.

Compression Ratio: 8.5:1. Displacement: 232 cu. in. (3.8 liters). Horsepower: 145 @ 4300 rpm. Torque: 215 lb.-ft. @ 1600 rpm. Oil refill capacity: 5 qt. with filter change. Fuel Requirements: Regular. Standard: Super Wagoneer. Engine Type: OHV, "Vigilante" V-8. Cast iron block and cylinder head. Bore x Stroke: 4.00 in. x 3.25 in. Lifters: Hydraulic. Number of main bearings-4. Fuel Induction: 4-bbl. downdraft carburetor. Compression Ratio: 9.7:1. Displacement: 327 cu. in. (5.36 liters). Horsepower: 270 @ 4700 rpm. Torque: Net: 360 lb.-ft. @ 2600 rpm. Oil refill capacity: 5 qt. with filter change. Fuel Requirements: Regular.

OPTIONAL ENGINE: (For all models except Super Wagoneer): Engine Type: OHV, "Vigilante" V-8. Cast iron block and cylinder head. Bore x Stroke: 4.00 in. x 3.25 in. Lifters: Hydraulic. Number of main bearings-4. Fuel Induction: 2-bbl. downdraft carburetor. Compression Ratio: 8.7:1. Displacement: 327 cu. in. (5.36liters). Horsepower: 250 @ 4700 rpm. Torque: Net: 340 lb.-ft. @ 2600 rpm. Oil refill capacity: 5 qt. with filter change. Fuel Requirements: Regular.

CHASSIS FEATURES: Separate body and frame. Deep web frame, wide flange, lightweight pressed steel with five cross members.

SUSPENSION AND RUNNING GEAR: Front Suspension: 7-leaf semi-elliptical springs, 44 in. x 2.5 in. Rating: 160 lb./in. 12.75 in. Hydraulic double-action shock absorbers. Optional. Torsion bar, independent. Rear Suspension: Variable rate, 4-leaf springs, 52 in. x 2.5 in. Rating: 133/215 lb./in. with Hydraulic double-action, 10.75 in. dia. shock absorbers. Optional: None. Front Axle Type and Capacity: Dana model 27AF, 2500 lb. capacity. Rear Axle Type and Capacity: Dana model 44 semi-floating, 3000 lb. capacity. Optional: None.

Final Drive Ratio:

	3-spd. Manual	4-spd. Manual	Auto. Trans.
Hi-Torque6	4.09:1	N.A.	3.73:1
	4.27:1*, 4.88:1*	—	4.09:1*
Vigilante V-8	3.73:1	N.A.	3.31:1
	4.09:1*	—	3.73:1*

* Optional at no extra cost.

Transfer Case: Man. trans. and Turbo Hydra-Matic models: 2-speed Spicer model 20, 2.03:1, 1.0:1. Brakes: Type: Hydraulic, front and rear drums. Dimensions: Front: 11.0 in. x 2.00 in. front and rear. Total effective area: 161.16 sq. in. Optional: Power brakes. Wheels: Kelsey-Hayes 15 x 5.5K, disc type, full-drop center 5-stud. Tires: 7.75 x 15. Super Wagoneer: 8.45 x 15 Super Cushion white sidewall. Steering: Recirculating ball. Ratio: 24:1. Turns Lock-to-Lock: 5.6. Turning Circle: 44.5 ft. Optional: Saginaw power steering. Ratios: 17.5:1. Turns Lock-to-Lock: 4.0. Standard for Super Wagoneer. Standard: Transmission: 3-speed synchromesh manual. Transmission ratios: 6-cyl.: 2.798:1, 1.687:1. 1.00:1. Reverse: 3.798:1. V-8: 2.490:1, 1.5871, 1.00:1. Reverse: 3.154:1. Optional: Turbo Hydra-Matic 3-spd. Ratios: 2.48:1, 1.48:1, 1.0:1. Reverse: 2.08:1. Standard for Super Wagoneer. Clutch: Borg & Beck single dry plate. Clutch diameter: 6-cyl.: 10.0 in. dia. V-8:10.5 in. Total lining area: 6-cyl.: 100.5 sq. in., V-8: 106.8 sq. in. Total plate pressure: 6-cyl.: 1350 lb., V-8: 1858 lb.

VEHICLE DIMENSIONS: Wheelbase: 110 in. Overall Length: 183.66 in. Front/Rear Tread: 57 in./57 in. Overall Height: 64.2 in. Width: 75.6 in. Tailgate: Width and Height: 55 in. Ground Clearance: Lowest point: 7.75 in. Load space: 111 in. x 55 in. x 39.5 in. Maximum capacity: 107 cu. ft. (two-door model). Front legroom: 45.25 in. Rear legroom: 38.25 in.

CAPACITIES: Fuel Tank: 20.0 gal. Coolant System: 230 6-cyl.: 11 qt., 12 qt. with heater, 232 6-cyl.: 9.5 qt., 10.5 qt. with heater, V-8: 18.5 qt., 19.5 qt. with heater.

ACCOMMODATIONS: Seating Capacity: Six passengers.

INSTRUMENTATION: Speedometer, odometer, gauges for oil pressure, engine coolant temperature, battery charge, fuel level, transfer case indicator lights.

OPTIONS: Heavy-duty alternator. Air conditioning. Drawbar. Power brakes. Transmission brakes. Locking gas cap. Electric clock. Heavy-duty clutch. Vigilante V-8. E-Z Eye glass. Fresh-air heater and defroster. Heavy-duty springs and shock absorbers. Selective drive hubs. Parking brake warning light. Spare tire lock. Right-side outside rearview mirror. Fuel tank skid plate. Power take-offs. Push-button transistor radio. Power steering Turbo Hydra-Matic. Snowplow. Push plate. Winches. Power tailgate. Rear Powr-Lok differential. Mud flap. Luggage rack. Pleated vinyl seats.

HISTORICAL FOOTNOTES: The 1967 models were introduced in the fall of 1966.

1968 WAGONEER

A new model, the Custom V-8 four-door Wagoneer was introduced. No other changes were made for 1968.

1968 Jeep Wagoneer

I.D. DATA: The serial number was located on the left-hand hinge pillar. The vehicle identification indicated the model as follows: 1414017-Four-door station wagon, 1412017-Two-door station wagon, 1414C17-Four-door custom station wagon, 1412C17-Two-door custom station wagon, 1414D19-Four-door super station wagon, 1414x 19-Four-door custom V-8 station wagon. The fifth symbol was a letter. Vehicle identification was as follows: 1414017 or 1414S-20568 and up; four-door station wagon, 1412017 or 1412S-200358-Two-door station wagon, 1414C17 or 1414C-200621-Four-door custom station wagon, 1412C17 or 1412CS-200015 and up; two-door custom station wagon, 1414D19 or 1414DS-101078 and up; four-door super station wagon, 1414X19300001 and up: Four-door custom V-8 station wagon, 1413S-200583 and up: Panel delivery.

Model Number	Body Type	Factory Price	GVW	Shipping Weight	Prod. Total
Series J-100 Wagoneer Station Wagon (with 6-cyl. engine)					
1414017	4-dr.	$3869	4500	3710	—
1412017	2-dr.	$3815	4500	3683	—
1414C17	Custom 4-dr.	$4065	4500	3745	—
1412C17	Custom 2-dr.	$4011	4500	3718	—
1413S	Panel Del.	$3457	4500	3483	—
1414D19	Super	$6163	4500	4263	—
1414X19	Custom V-8 4-dr.	$5671	4500	3907	—

STANDARD ENGINE: (Except for Super Wagoneer): Engine Type: OHV, L-6. Cast iron block and cylinder head. Bore x Stroke: 3.75 in. x 3.50 in. Lifters: Hydraulic. Number of main bearings-7. Fuel Induction: 1-bbl. Carter Type RTBS or Holley model 1931C-3705. Compression Ratio: 8.5:1. Displacement: 232 cu. in. (3.8 liters). Horsepower: 145 @ 4300 rpm. Torque: 215 lb.-ft. @ 1600 rpm. Oil refill capacity: 5 qt. with filter change. Fuel Requirements: Regular. Standard: Super Wagoneer. Engine Type: OHV, "Vigilante" V-8. Cast iron block and cylinder head. Bore x Stroke: 4.00 in. x 3.25 in. Lifters: Hydraulic. Number of main bearings-4. Fuel Induction: 4-bbl. downdraft carburetor. Compression Ratio: 9.7:1. Displacement: 327 cu. in. (5.36 liters). Horsepower: 270 @ 4700 rpm. Torque: Net: 360 lb.-ft. @ 2600 rpm. Oil refill capacity: 5 qt. with filter change. Fuel Requirements: Regular.

OPTIONAL ENGINE: (For all models except Super Wagoneer): Engine Type: OHV, "Vigilante" V-8. Cast iron block and cylinder head. Bore x Stroke: 4.00 in. x 3.25 in. Lifters: Hydraulic. Number of main bearings-4. Fuel Induction: 2-bbl. downdraft carburetor. Compression Ratio: 8.7:1. Displacement: 327 cu. in. (5.36 liters). Horsepower: 250 @ 4700 rpm. Torque: Net: 340 lb.-ft. @ 2600 rpm. Oil refill capacity: 5 qt. with filter change. Fuel Requirements: Regular.

CHASSIS FEATURES: Separate body and frame. Deep web frame, wide flange, lightweight pressed steel with five cross members.

SUSPENSION AND RUNNING GEAR: Front Suspension: 7-leaf semi-elliptical springs, 44 in. x 2.5 in. Rating: 160 lb./in. 12.75 in. Hydraulic double-action shock absorbers. Optional. Torsion bar, independent. Rear Suspension: Variable rate, 4-leaf springs, 52 in. x 2.5 in. Rating: 133/215 lb./in. with Hydraulic double-action, 10.75 in. dia. shock absorbers. Optional: None. Front Axle Type and Capacity: Spicer model 27AF, 2500 lb. capacity. Rear Axle Type and Capacity: Spicer model 44 semi-floating, 3000 lb. capacity. Optional: None.

Final Drive Ratio

	3-spd. Manual	4-spd. Manual	Auto. Trans.
Hi-Torque 6	4.09:1	N.A.	3.73:1
	4.27:1*, 4.88:1*	—	4.09:1*
Vigilante V-8	3.73:1	N.A.	3.31:1
	4.09:1*	—	3.73:1*

* Optional at no extra cost.

Transfer Case: Man. trans. and Turbo Hydra-Matic models: 2-speed Spicer model 20, 2.03:1, 1.0:1. Brakes: Type: Hydraulic, front and rear drums. Dimensions: Front: 11.0 in. x 2.00 in. front and rear. Total effective area: 161.16 sq. in. Optional: Power brakes. Wheels: Kelsey-Hayes 15 x 5.5K, disc type, full-drop center 5-stud. Tires: 7.75 x 15. Super Wagoneer: 8.45 x 15 Super Cushion white sidewall. Steering: Recirculating ball. Ratio: 24:1. Turns Lock-to-Lock: 5.6. Turning Circle: 44.5 ft. Optional: Saginaw power steering. Ratios: 17.5:1. Turns Lock-to-Lock: 4.0. Standard for Super Wagoneer. Standard: Transmission: 3-speed synchromesh manual. Transmission ratios: 6-cyl.: 2.798:1, 1.687:1, 1.00:1. Reverse: 3.798:1.V-8: 2.490:1, 1.5871, 1.00:1. Reverse: 3.154:1. Optional: Turbo Hydra-Matic 3-spd. Ratios: 2.48:1, 1.48:1, 1.0:1. Reverse: 2.08:1. Standard for Super Wagoneer. Clutch: Borg & Beck single dry plate. Clutch diameter: 6-cyl.: 10.0 in. dia. V-8:10.5 in. Total lining area: 6-cyl.: 100.5 sq. in., V-8: 106.8 sq. in. Total plate pressure: 6-cyl.: 1350 lb., V-8: 1858 lb.

VEHICLE DIMENSIONS: Wheelbase: 110 in. Overall Length: 183.66 in. Front/Rear Tread: 57 in./57 in. Overall Height: 64.2 in. Width: 75.6 in. Tailgate: Width and Height: 55 in. Ground Clearance: Lowest point: 7.75 in. Load space: 111 in. x 55 in. x 39.5 in. Maximum capacity: 107 cu. ft. (two-door model). Front legroom: 45.25 in. Rear legroom: 38.25 in.

CAPACITIES: Fuel Tank: 20.0 gal. Coolant System: 230 6-cyl.: 11 qt., 12 qt. with heater, 232 6-cyl.: 9.5 qt., 10.5 qt. with heater, V-8: 18.5 qt., 19.5 qt. with heater.

ACCOMMODATIONS: Seating Capacity: Six passengers.

INSTRUMENTATION: Speedometer, odometer, gauges for oil pressure, engine coolant temperature, battery charge, fuel level, transfer case indicator lights,

OPTIONS: Heavy-duty alternator. Air conditioning. Drawbar. Power brakes. Transmission brakes. Locking gas cap. Electric clock. Heavy-duty clutch. Vigilante V-8 E-Z Eye glass. Fresh-air heater and defroster. Heavy-duty springs and shock absorbers. Selective drive hubs. Parking brake warning light. Spare tire lock. Right-side outside rearview mirror. Fuel tank skid plate. Power take-offs. Push-button transistor radio. Power steering Turbo Hydra-Matic. Snowplow. Push plate. Winches. Power tailgate. Rear Powr-Lok differential. Mud flap. Luggage rack. Pleated vinyl seats.

HISTORICAL FOOTNOTES: The 1968 models were introduced in the fall of 1967.

1969 WAGONEER

All two-door models as well as the Panel delivery and Super Wagoneer (which was phased out during the model year) were dropped for 1969. An all-synchronized 3-speed manual transmission was now standard. The 145 horsepower "Hi-Torque" 6-cylinder engine remained the Wagoneer's standard engine but replacing the AMC 327 cu. in. V-8 was a 350 cu. in. "Dauntless" V-8 supplied by Buick.

The standard Wagoneer interior offered foam-padded seats with three simulated leather grain vinyl coverings. Vertical grain panels in the seat and seat back were separated by a horizontal saddle-stitch grain. The seat bolsters were covered with calf grain vinyl. Embossed vinyl door panels accented by mylar were also included. Color-keyed appointments included the headliner, padded instrument panel, padded sun visors, front and rear seat belts and retainers, and textured floor mats. The Custom Wagoneer was also fitted with foam-padded seats. The custom upholstery consisted of rayon-nylon fabrics and soft expanded vinyl. It also had a vinyl headliner and upgraded door panels. The Custom Wagoneer also featured high-pile carpeting, chrome instrument panel control knobs, color-keyed steering wheel with Deluxe horn ring, courtesy lights, vinyl floor covering in cargo area, stainless steel exterior moldings and chrome wheelcovers. Both the standard and custom interiors were offered in rawhide, charcoal or marlin blue. An optional Custom Wagoneer interior of pleated vinyl was available in either president red or charcoal.

These models were offered in a choice of nine colors: Avocado mist, spring green, empire blue, burnished bronze, prairie gold, sprucetip green, vintage gold, champagne white and president red. All painted surfaces were first treated with a zinc-phosphate coating and primer. After painting was completed and inspected each Wagoneer was undercoated and sprayed with a wax coating for protection during shipping.

1969 Jeep Wagoneer

I.D. DATA: The serial number was located on the left-hand hinge pillar. The vehicle identification indicated the model as follows: 1414017-207515 and up: Four-door station wagon 1414C17-200792: Four-door custom station wagon; 1414X19-30001 and up: V-8 four-door custom station wagon. 1414D19-300001 and up: Four-door super station wagon. The fifth symbol was a letter. Vehicle identification was as follows: 1414: Four-door station wagon, 1414C: Four-door custom station wagon, 1414X: Four-door custom V-8 station wagon, 1414D: Super station wagon.

Model Number	Body Type	Factory Price	GVW	Shipping Weight	Prod. Total
Series J-100 Wagoneer Station Wagon (with 6-cyl. engine)					
1414	4-dr.	$4145	4500	3710	—
1414C	Custom 4-dr.	$4342	4500	3745	—
1414D	Super	$6163	4500	4263	—
1414X	Custom V-8 4-dr.	$5671	4500	3907	—

STANDARD ENGINE: (Except for Super Wagoneer) Engine Type: OHV, In-line-6. Cast iron block and cylinder head. Bore x Stroke: 3.75 in. x 3.50 in. Lifters: Hydraulic. Number of main bearings-7. Fuel Induction: 1-bbl. Carter Type RTBS or Holley model 1931C-3705. Compression Ratio: 8.5:1. Displacement: 232 cu. in. (3.8 liters). Horsepower: 145 @ 4300 rpm. Torque: 215 lb.-ft. @ 1600 rpm. Oil refill capacity: 5 qt. with filter change. Fuel Requirements: Regular.

STANDARD ENGINE: Super Wagoneer; optional for all other Wagoneers. Engine Type: OHV, "Dauntless" V-8. Cast iron block and cylinder head. Bore x Stroke: 3.80 in. x 3.85 in. Lifters: Hydraulic. Number of main bearings-5. Fuel Induction: 2-bbl. carburetor, 1,437 in. barrels. Compression Ratio: 9.0:1. Displacement: 350 cu. in. (5.7 liters). Horsepower: 230 @ 4400 rpm. Torque: Net: 350 lb.-ft. @ 2400 rpm. Oil refill capacity: 5 qt. with filter change. Fuel Requirements: Regular.

CHASSIS FEATURES: Separate body and frame. Deep web frame, 173.96 in. x 38.0 in. Section modulus: 2.050 in. 3, wide flange, lightweight pressed steel with five cross members.

SUSPENSION AND RUNNING GEAR: Front Suspension: 7-leaf, semi-elliptical springs, 44 in. x 2.5 in. Rating: 160 lb./in. Capacity (at pad): 1150 lb. Capacity (at ground): 1320 lb. 12.75 in. Hydraulic double-action shock absorbers. Optional: 5-leaf, semi-elliptical springs, 44 in. x 2.50 in. Rating: 230 lb./in. Capacity (at pad): 1500 lb. Capacity at ground): 1670 lb. Rear Suspension: Variable rate, 5-leaf semi-elliptical springs, 52.0 in. x 2.50 in. Rating: 144-256 lb./in. Capacity (at pad): 1260 lb. Capacity (at ground): 1430 lb. Hydraulic double-action, 10.75 in. dia. shock absorbers. Optional: 6-leaf semi-elliptical springs, 52.0 in. x 2.50 in. Rating: 230 lb./in. Capacity (at pad): 1585 lb. Capacity (at ground): 1735 lb. Hydraulic double-action, 10.75 in. dia. shock absorbers. Front Axle Type and Capacity: Full-floating Spicer model 27AF, 2500 lb. capacity. Rear Axle Type and Capacity: Full-floating Spicer model 44 semi-floating, 3000 lb. capacity. Optional: None.

Final Drive Ratio:

	3-spd. Manual	4-spd.	Auto. Trans.
Hi-Torque 6	4.09:1	4.09:1	3.73:1.
	4.27:1*	—	4.09:1*
Dauntless V-8	3.31:1	3.31:1	3.31:1
	3.73:1*	—	3.73:1*

* Optional at no extra cost.

Transfer Case: Man. trans. and Turbo Hydra-Matic models: 2-speed Dana model 20, 2.03:1, 1.0:1. Brakes: Type: Hydraulic, front and rear drums. Dimensions: Front: 11.0 in. x 2.00 in. front and rear. Total effective area: 180.8 sq. in. Optional: Power brakes. Wheels: Kelsey-Hayes 15 x 5.5K, disc type, full-drop center 5-stud. Tires: 7.75 x 15, 4-ply rating. Optional: Other types and sizes available in both black and white sidewall. Steering: Recirculating ball type. Ratio: 24:1. Turns Lock-to-Lock: 5.6. Turning Circle: 44.5 ft. Optional: Saginaw Power steering. Ratios 17.5:1. Turns Lock-to-Lock: 4.0. Standard: Transmission: 6-cyl.: Warner T14A, 3-speed all-synchromesh manual. Transmission ratios: 3.10, 1.612, 1.00:1. Reverse: 3.1:1. V-8: Warner T15A, 3-speed all-synchromesh manual. Transmission ratios: 2.997, 1.832, 1.00:1. Reverse: 2.997:1. Optional: Turbo Hydra-Matic 3-spd. automatic. Ratios: 2.48:1, 1.48:1, 1.0:1. Reverse: 2.08:1. Optional: Heavy-duty Warner T18 4-speed manual transmission, synchromesh on top three gears. Transmission ratios: 4.02, 3.092, 1.686, 1.00:1. Reverse: 7.439:1. Clutch: Single dry plate. Clutch diameter: 6-cyl.: 10.5 in., V-8: 11.0 in. Total lining area: 6-cyl.: 106.75 in., V-8: 123.7 sq. in. Total plate pressure: 6-cyl.: 1640 lb., V-8: 2450-2750 lb.

VEHICLE DIMENSIONS: Wheelbase: 110 in. Overall Length: 183.66 in. Front/Rear Tread: 57 in./57 in. Overall Height: 65.30 in. Width: 75.6 in. Front/Rear Overhang: 28.70 in./44.96 in. Tailgate: Width and Height: 55 in. Approach/Departure Degrees: 39/20. Ground Clearance: Front axle: 8.54 in. Rear axle: 7.75 in. Load space: 111 in. x 55 in. x 39.5 in. Maximum capacity: 91.03 cu. ft. Front headroom: 35.12 in. Front legroom: 45.00 in. Front hip room: 58-12 in. Rear headroom: 36.56 in. Rear legroom: 36.0 in. Rear hip room: 58.35 in. Seat to floor: 12.58 in.

CAPACITIES: Fuel Tank: 22.0 gal. Coolant System: 6-cyl.: 10.5 qt. V-8: 15 qt.

ACCOMMODATIONS: Seating Capacity: Six passengers.

INSTRUMENTATION: 0-110 mph speedometer, odometer, gauges for engine coolant temperature and fuel level, warning lights for oil pressure and battery charge.

OPTIONS: Factory installed options: V-8 engine. Cigarette lighter. Locking rear differential. Radio and antenna. Heavy-duty rear springs. Power brakes. E-Z Eye glass. Power steering. Heavy-duty cooling system (V-8 only). Air conditioner with heavy-duty cooling (V-8 only). 4-speed manual transmission. Heavy-duty 70 amp battery. Turbo Hydra-Matic. Pleated vinyl trim in lieu of Deluxe trim (model 1414C only). Power tailgate window. Dealer installed options: Bumper guards. Push-button radio. Antenna. Inside mirror. Outside rearview mirror, cowl mount. Outside rearview mirror, belt mount. Cigarette lighter, chrome knob. Power brakes. Deluxe horn ring. Courtesy lights, parking brake warning light. Electric clock. Helper air rear springs. Luggage rack. Ski rack adapter. Car pak kit. Spare tire lock. Locking gas cap. Window vent shades.

HISTORICAL FOOTNOTES: The 1969 Wagoneer was introduced in the fall of 1968.

1970 WAGONEER

With the old Wagoneer grille transferred to the Gladiator trucks the 1970 version of the Wagoneer (the last produced under Kaiser management) Jeep retained its identification among Jeep models thanks to its new egg-crate grille and front fender mounted side lights. The old grille-mounted circular Jeep logo was replaced by more contemporary-looking JEEP block lettering mounted in the grille's right portion. New side body trim consisted of Jeep lettering positioned lower on the front fenders than was similar identification on 1969 models and revised four-wheel drive/model identification located just in back of the front wheel cutout. The Wagoneer script located on the rear panel of the 1969 models was no longer used. The rear panel of custom models was fitted with a checkered patterned insert bracketing the license plate panel.

1970 Jeep Wagoneer

The exterior body color selection for 1970 consisted of island blue, candlelight yellow, burnished bronze, sprucetip green, president red, champagne white, vintage gold, avocado mist and spring green. Both the standard and custom interiors were offered in charcoal, marlin blue or buckskin. The Custom Wagoneer was also available in an optional pleated vinyl upholstery in the same color selection. The clutch in standard transmission models offered smoother operation thanks to a new mechanical linkage.

American Motors acquired the Kaiser Jeep assets in January, 1970. In June, 1970 it announced a new power operated sun roof option for the Wagoneer priced at $490.50. Included in this price was a vinyl-covered roof and side body trim similar to that of the discontinued Super Wagoneer offered in a choice of four colors: White, black, brown or saddle. It was available for any Custom Wagoneer, Wagoneer custom special or the regional model, Western Wagoneer.

Standard equipment included oil filter, oil bath air cleaner, directional signals, front seat belts with retractor boots, hubcaps, chrome grille, padded sun visors, padded instrument panel, rear seat belts, outside left rearview mirror, 2-speed electric windshield wipers and washers, back up lights, 4-way flasher, and heater and defroster.

I.D. DATA: The serial number was located on the left-hand hinge pillar. The vehicle identification indicated the model as follows: 1414017-209588 and up: 6-cyl. four-door station wagon, 1414019-305118 and up: V-8 station wagon, 1414C17-200948: 6-cyl. four-door custom station wagon; 1414C19-30914 and up: VB-8 four-door custom station wagon; 1414X19-301242 and up: V-8 four-door special station wagon. The fifth symbol was a letter. Vehicle identification was as follows: 1414: Four-door station wagon, 1414C: Four-door custom station wagon, 1414X: Four-door special V-8 station wagon.

Model Number	Body Type	Factory Price	GVW	Shipping Weight	Prod. Total
Series J-100 Wagoneer Station Wagon (with 6-cyl. engine)					
1414	4-dr.	$4284	4500	3710	—
1414C	Custom 4-dr.	$4526	4500	3745	—
1414X	Custom V-8 4-dr.	$5876	4500	3907	—

STANDARD ENGINE: Engine Type: OHV, In-line-6. Cast iron block and cylinder head. Bore x Stroke: 3.75 in. x 3.50 in. Lifters: Hydraulic. Number of main bearings-7. Fuel Induction: 1-bbl. Carter Type RTBS or Holley model 1931C-3705. Compression Ratio: 8.5:1. Displacement: 232 cu. in. (3.8 liters). Horsepower: 145 @ 4300 rpm. Torque: 215 lb.-ft. @ 1600 rpm. Oil refill capacity: 5 qt. with filter change. Fuel Requirements: Regular.

OPTIONAL ENGINE: Engine Type: OHV, "Dauntless" V-8. Cast iron block and cylinder head. Bore x Stroke: 3.80 in. x 3.85 in. Lifters: Hydraulic. Number of main bearings-5. Fuel Induction: 2-bbl. carburetor, 1,437 in. barrels. Compression Ratio: 9.0:1. Displacement: 350 cu. in. (5.7 liters). Horsepower: 230 @ 4400 rpm. Torque: Net: 350 lb.-ft. @ 2400 rpm. Oil refill capacity: 5 qt. with filter change. Fuel Requirements: Regular.

CHASSIS FEATURES: Separate body and frame. Deep web frame, 173.96 in. x 38.0 in. Section modulus: 2.050 in. 3, wide flange, lightweight pressed steel with five cross members.

SUSPENSION AND RUNNING GEAR: Front Suspension: 7-leaf, semi-elliptical springs, 44 in. x 2.5 in. Rating: 160 lb./in. Capacity (at pad): 1150 lb. Capacity (at ground): 1320 lb. 12.75 in. Hydraulic double-action shock absorbers. Optional. 5-leaf, semi-elliptical springs, 44 in. x 2.50 in. Rating: 230 lb./in. Capacity (at pad): 1500 lb. Capacity at ground): 1670 lb. Rear Suspension: Variable rate, 5-leaf semi-elliptical springs, 52.0 in. x 2.50 in. Rating: 144-256 lb./ in. Capacity (at pad): 1260 lb. Capacity (at ground): 1430 lb. Hydraulic double-action, 10.75 in. dia. shock absorbers. Optional: 6-leaf semi-elliptical springs, 52.0 in. x 2.50 in. Rating: 230 lb./in. Capacity (at pad): 1585 lb. Capacity (at ground): 1735 lb. Hydraulic double-action, 10.75 in. dia. shock absorbers. Front Axle Type and Capacity: Full-floating Spicer model 27AF, 2500 lb. capacity. Rear Axle Type and Capacity: Full-floating Spicer model 44 semi-floating, 3000 lb. capacity. Optional: None.

Final Drive Ratio:

	3-spd. Manual	4-spd.	Auto. Trans.
Hi-Torque 6	4.09:1	4.09:1	3.73:1
	4.27:1*	—	4.09:1*
Dauntless V-8	3.31:1	3.31:1	3.31:1
	3.73:1*	—	3.73:1*

* Optional at no extra cost.

Transfer Case: Man. trans. and Turbo Hydra-Matic models: 2-speed Dana model 20, 2.03:1, 1.0:1. Brakes: Type: Hydraulic, front and rear drums. Dimensions: Front: 11.0 in. x 2.00 in. front and rear. Total effective area: 180.8 sq. in. Optional: Power brakes. Wheels: Kelsey-Hayes 15 x 5.5K, disc type, full-drop center 5-stud. Tires: 7.75 x 15, 4-ply rating. Optional: Other types and sizes available in both black and white sidewall. Steering: Recirculating ball type. Ratio: 24:1. Turns Lock-to-Lock: 5.6. Turning Circle: 44.5 ft. Optional: Saginaw Power steering. Ratios 17.5:1. Turns Lock-to-Lock: 4.0. Standard: Transmission: 6-cyl.: Warner T14A, 3-speed all-synchromesh manual. Transmission ratios: 3.10, 1.612, 1.00:1. Reverse: 3.1:1. V-8: Warner T15A, 3-speed all-synchromesh manual. Transmission ratios: 2.997, 1.832, 1.00:1. Reverse: 2.997:1. Optional: Turbo Hydra-Matic 3-spd. automatic. Ratios: 2.48:1, 1.48:1, 1.0:1. Reverse: 2.08:1. Optional: Heavy-duty Warner T18 4-speed manual transmission, synchromesh on top three gears. Transmission ratios: 4.02, 3.092, 1.686, 1.00:1. Reverse: 7.439:1. Clutch: Single dry plate. Clutch diameter: 6-cyl.: 10.5 in., V-8: 11.0 in. Total lining area: 6-cyl.: 106.75 in., V-8: 123.7 sq. in. Total plate pressure: 6-cyl.: 1640 lb., V-8: 2450-2750 lb.

VEHICLE DIMENSIONS: Wheelbase: 110 in. Overall Length: 183.66 in. Front/Rear Tread: 57 in./57 in. Overall Height: 65.30 in. Width: 75.6 in. Front/Rear Overhang: 28.70 in./44.96 in. Tailgate: Width and Height: 55 in. Approach/Departure Degrees: 39/20. Ground Clearance: Front axle: 8.54 in. Rear axle: 7.75 in. Load space: 111 in. x 55 in. x 39.5 in. Maximum capacity: 91.03 cu. ft. Front headroom: 35.12 in. Front legroom: 45.00 in. Front hip room: 58-12 in. Rear headroom: 36.56 in. Rear legroom: 36.0 in. Rear hip room: 58.35 in. Seat to floor: 12.58 in.

CAPACITIES: Fuel Tank: 22.0 gal. Coolant System: 6-cyl.: 10.5 qt. V-8: 15 qt.

ACCOMMODATIONS: Seating Capacity: Six passengers.

INSTRUMENTATION: 0-110 mph speedometer, odometer, gauges for engine coolant temperature and fuel level, warning lights for oil pressure and battery charge.

OPTIONS: Factory installed options: V-8 engine: $217.88. 8.55 x 15 Power Cushion tires: $55.54. 8.55 x 15 Suburbanite tires: $55.54. 7.75 x 15 Power Cushion white sidewall: $46.56. 8.55 x 15 Suburbanite white sidewall tires: $87.12. 8.55 x 15 Power Cushion white sidewall: $87.12. H-78 x 15 Polyglas Suburbanite: $82.21. H-78 x 15 Polyglas Power Cushion white sidewall: $114.01. Cigarette lighter: $3.43. Locking rear differential: $48.43. Radio and antenna: $66.19. Heavy-duty rear springs: $14.97. Power brakes: $46.48. E-Z Eye Glass: $41.29. Power steering: $131.22. Heavy-duty cooling system (V-8 only): $51.74. Air conditioner with Heavy-duty cooling (V-8 only): $454.41. 4-speed manual transmission: $130.37 (V-8), $209.11 (6-cyl.). Heavy-duty 70 amp battery: $7.19. Turbo Hydra-Matic: $274.76. Pleated vinyl trim in lieu of Deluxe trim (model 1414C only): 75.79. Power tailgate window: $46.69. Dealer installed options: Bumper guards: $15.56. Push-button radio: $71.06. Antenna: $6.41. Inside mirror: $5.67. Outside rearview mirror, cowl mount: $10.68. Outside rearview mirror, belt mount: $6.12 Cigarette lighter, chrome knob: $4.13. Power brakes: $82. Deluxe horn ring: $4.31. Courtesy lights: $8.97 Parking brake warning light: $5.38. Electric clock: $20.01. Helper air rear springs: $47.89. Luggage rack: $82.21. Ski rack adapter: $43.33. Car pak kit: $45.08. Spare tire lock: $3.98. Locking gas cap: $3.35. Window vent shades: $14.83.

HISTORICAL FOOTNOTES: The Wagoneer was promoted as "The 2-Car car" in 1970. Ownership of Jeep was acquired by American Motors in January, 1970.

1971 WAGONEER

No changes were made in the 1971 Wagoneers until American Motors, on January 4, 1971 began producing Wagoneers with a standard 258 cu. in. 6-cylinder engine. This was a derivative of the 232 cu. in. 6-cylinder and had a 3.75 in. bore and a 3.90 in. stroke. Peak horsepower was 150. As options American Motors now offered its V-8 engines in either 304 or 360 cu. in. displacements. Their respective horsepower ratings were 210 at 4400 rpm and 245 at 4400 rpm. Maximum torque for the 360 cu. in. V-8 was 365 lb.-ft. at 2600 rpm. The Custom Wagoneer Package consisted of these interior items: Floor carpeting, cargo area floor covering, Deluxe headlining, Deluxe door trim panels, full wheelcovers, Deluxe trim on seat back, front and rear door armrests with Deluxe trim, Deluxe control knobs, rear seat Deluxe ashtray, Deluxe inside rearview mirror, Deluxe cigarette lighter, Deluxe horn ring, and courtesy lights. Exterior features consisted of stainless steel door frame moldings, windshield moldings and rear body moldings. A new Woodgrain Accessory Package (optional when the Custom Wagoneer Package was ordered) added these features: Woodgrain exterior trim and moldings, luggage rack, outside passenger side rearview mirror, inside day/night mirror and parking brake warning light.

AMC also offered a model 1414 X, Wagoneer Special for 1971 as a "Limited-Quality Vehicle, For Sales Promotion Only". This Wagoneer had the following standard equipment: 350 cu. in, 230 horsepower V-8, automatic transmission, column mount, console with armrest and electric clock, front bucket seats, AM radio with antenna, power brakes, power steering, power tailgate window, tinted glass, courtesy lights, golden lime metallic paint, Custom Wagoneer Package, Woodgrain Accessory Package, air deflector with Di-Noc trim, 8.55 x 15 4-ply Polyester Power Cushion white sidewall tires, plus all other standard Wagoneer equipment. The only options for this "Special-Built" Wagoneer were the rear Trac-Lok differential and air conditioning which included heavy-duty cooling.

Standard colors for 1971 were: Sprucetip green metallic, president red, avocado mist metallic, champagne white, spring green, vintage gold metallic, island blue metallic and candlelight yellow. Reissued on January 4, 1971 was burnished bronze metallic. The interior color selection consisted of buckskin, marlin blue and charcoal.

I.D. DATA: The serial number was located on the left-hand hinge pillar. The vehicle identification indicated the model as follows: Prior to January 4,1971: 1414017-212612 and up: 6-cyl. four-door standard station wagon, 1414C17-201, 123: 6-cyl. custom station wagon, 1414019-311015 and up: V-8 four-door station wagon, 1414C19-312, 275: V-8. Four-door custom station wagon. Models produced on or after January 4, 1971: 1414017-400,000 and up: 6-cyl. standard station wagon, 1414C17-400,00 and up: 6-cyl. custom station wagon, 141401-500,000 and up: 304 V-8 standard station wagon, 1414C19-500,000 and up: 304 V-8 custom station wagon, 14144019-600,000 and up: 360 V-8 standard station wagon, 1414C19-600,000 and up: 360 V-8 custom station wagon.

Model Number	Body Type	Factory Price	GVW	Shipping Weight	Prod. Total
Series J-100 Wagoneer Station Wagon (with 6-cyl. engine)					
1414	4-dr.	$4284	4500	3710	—
1414C	Custom 4-dr.	$4526	4500	3745	—
1414X	Special V-8 4-dr.	$6114	4500	3907	—

STANDARD ENGINE: Engine Type: OHV, In-line-6. Cast iron block and cylinder head. Bore x Stroke: 3.75 in. x 3.50 in. Lifters: Hydraulic. Number of main bearings-7. Fuel Induction: 1-bbl. Carter Type RTBS or Holley model 1931C-3705. Compression Ratio: 8.5:1. Displacement: 232 cu. in. (3.8 liters). Horsepower: 145 @ 4300 rpm. Torque: 215 lb.-ft. @ 1600 rpm. Oil refill capacity: 5 qt. with filter change. Fuel Requirements: Regular.

STANDARD ENGINE: After January 4, 1971: Engine Type: OHV, In-line-6. Cast iron block and cylinder head. Bore x Stroke: 3.75 in. x 3.90 in. Lifters: Hydraulic. Number of main bearings-7. Fuel Induction: 1-bbl. Carter Type RTBS or Holley model 1931C-3705. Compression Ratio: 8.0:1. Displacement: 258 cu. in. (4.22 liters). Horsepower: 150 @ 3800 rpm. Torque: 240 lb.-ft. @ 1800 rpm. Oil refill capacity: 5 qt. with filter change. Fuel Requirements: Regular.

OPTIONAL ENGINE: Engine Type: OHV, V-8. Cast iron block and cylinder head. Bore x Stroke: 3.75 in. x 3.44 in. Lifters: Hydraulic. Number of main bearings-5. Fuel Induction: 2-bbl. downdraft carburetor, 1.562 in. barrels. Compression Ratio: 8.4:1. Displacement: 304 cu. in. (4.98 liters). Horsepower: 210 @ 4400 rpm. Torque: Net: 300 lb.-ft. @ 2600 rpm. Oil refill capacity: 5 qt. with filter change. Fuel Requirements: Regular.

OPTIONAL ENGINE: Engine Type: OHV, 360 V-8. Cast iron block and cylinder head. Bore x Stroke: 4.08 in. x 3.44 in. Lifters: Hydraulic. Number of main bearings-5. Fuel Induction: 2-bbl. downdraft carburetor. 1.562 in. barrel size. Compression Ratio: 8.5:1. Displacement: 360 cu. in. (5.89 liters). Horsepower: 245 @ 4400 rpm. Torque: 365 lb.-ft. @ 2400 rpm. Oil refill capacity: 5 qt. with filter change. Fuel Requirements: Regular.

CHASSIS FEATURES: Separate body and frame. Deep web frame, 173.96 in. x 38.0 in. Section modulus: 2.050 in. 3, wide flange, lightweight pressed steel with five cross members.

SUSPENSION AND RUNNING GEAR: Front Suspension: 7-leaf, semi-elliptical springs, 44 in. x 2.5 in. Rating: 160 lb./in. Capacity (at pad): 1150 lb. Capacity (at ground): 1320 lb. 12.75 in. Hydraulic double-action shock absorbers. Optional. 5-leaf, semi-elliptical springs, 44 in. x 2.50 in. Rating: 230 lb./in. Capacity (at pad): 1500 lb. Capacity at ground): 1670 lb. Rear Suspension: Variable rate, 5-leaf semi-elliptical springs, 52.0 in. x 2.50 in. Rating: 144-256 lb./ in. Capacity (at pad): 1260 lb. Capacity (at ground): 1430 lb. Hydraulic double-action, 10.75 in. dia. shock absorbers. Optional: 6-leaf semi-elliptical springs, 52.0 in. x 2.50 in. Rating: 230 lb./in. Capacity (at pad): 1585 lb. Capacity (at ground): 1735 lb. Hydraulic double-action, 10.75 in. dia. shock absorbers. Front Axle Type and Capacity: Full-floating Spicer model 27AF, 2500 lb. capacity. Rear Axle Type and Capacity: Full-floating Spicer model 44 semi-floating, 3000 lb. capacity. Optional: None.

Final Drive Ratio

	3-spd. Manual	4-spd.	Auto. Trans.
Hi-Torque 6	4.09:1	4.09:1	3.73:1.
	4.27:1*	—	4.09:1*
Dauntless V-8	3.31:1	3.31:1	3.31:1
	3.73:1*	—	3.73:1*

* Optional at no extra cost.

Transfer Case: Man. trans. and Turbo Hydra-Matic models: 2-speed Dana model 20, 2.03:1, 1.0:1. Brakes: Type: Hydraulic, front and rear drums. Dimensions: Front: 11.0 in. x 2.00 in. front and rear. Total effective area: 180.8 sq. in. Optional: Power brakes. Wheels: Kelsey-Hayes 15 x 5.5K, disc type, full-drop center 5-stud. Tires: 7.75 x 15, 4-ply rating. Optional: Other types and sizes available in both black and white sidewall. Steering: Recirculating ball type. Ratio: 24:1. Turns Lock-to-Lock: 5.6. Turning Circle: 44.5 ft. Optional: Saginaw Power steering. Ratios: 17.5:1. Turns Lock-to-Lock: 4.0. Standard: Transmission: 6-cyl.: Warner T14A, 3-speed all-synchromesh manual. Transmission ratios: 3.10, 1.612, 1.00:1. Reverse: 3.1:1. V-8: Warner T15A, 3-speed all-synchromesh manual. Transmission ratios: 2.997, 1.832, 1.00:1. Reverse: 2.997:1. Optional: Turbo Hydra-Matic 3-spd. automatic. Ratios: 2.48:1, 1.48:1, 1.0:1. Reverse: 2.08:1. Optional: Heavy-duty Warner T18 4-speed manual transmission, synchromesh on top three gears. Transmission ratios: 4.02, 3.092, 1.686, 1.00:1. Reverse: 7.439:1. Clutch: Single dry plate. Clutch diameter: 6-cyl.: 10.5 in., V-8: 11.0 in. Total lining area: 6-cyl.: 106.75 in., V-8: 123.7 sq. in. Total plate pressure: 6-cyl.: 1640 lb., V-8: 2450-2750 lb.

VEHICLE DIMENSIONS: Wheelbase: 110 in. Overall Length: 183.66 in. Front/Rear Tread: 57 in./57 in. Overall Height: 65.30 in. Width: 75.6 in. Front/Rear Overhang: 28.70 in./44.96 in. Tailgate: Width and Height: 55 in. Approach/Departure Degrees: 39/20. Ground Clearance: Front axle: 8.54 in. Rear axle: 7.75 in. Load space: 111 in. x 55 in. x 39.5 in. Maximum capacity: 91.03 cu. ft. Front headroom: 35.12 in. Front legroom: 45.00 in. Front hip room: 58 12 in. Rear headroom: 36.56 in. Rear legroom: 36.0 in. Rear hip room: 58.35 in. Seat to floor: 12.58 in.

CAPACITIES: Fuel Tank: 22.0 gal. Coolant System: 6-cyl.: 10.5 qt. V-8: 15 qt.

ACCOMMODATIONS: Seating Capacity: Six passengers.

INSTRUMENTATION: 0-110 mph speedometer, odometer, gauges for engine coolant temperature and fuel level, warning lights for oil pressure and battery charge.

OPTIONS AND PRICES: 210 hp. V-8: $169.95. 245 hp. V-8: $217.75. 4-spd. man. trans.: $110.10. Auto. trans.: $274.50. Optional axle ratios: $12.65. Rear Trac-Lok differential: $61.35. Power brakes: $46.45. Power steering: $147.65. Power tailgate window: $46.65. AM radio with antenna: $72.30. Cigarette lighter: $6.50. Tinted glass: $41.25. Air conditioning with Heavy-duty cooling: $455.05. Park brake warning light: $6.50. Luggage rack: $77.75. Custom Wagoneer Package. Not available for model 1414, standard for 1414C: No charge. Woodgrain Accessory Package. (Not available for model 1414): $178.75. Wheelcovers: $429.75. Heavy-duty 70 amp battery: $11.70. 55 amp alternator: $27.60. Heavy-duty cooling system: $27.75. Heavy-duty shock absorbers: $15.35. Heavy-duty front springs: $20.10. Heavy-duty rear springs: $20.10. 8.55 x 15 Power Cushion tires: $55.54. 8.55 x 15 Suburbanite tires: $55.54. 8.55 x 15 Suburbanite black sidewall tires: $54.60. 8.55 x 15 Power Cushion white sidewall tires: $87.00. 8.55 x 15 Suburbanite black sidewall tires: $54.60. 8.55 x 15 Polyglas Suburbanite black sidewall tires: $80.50. H78 x 15 Polyglas Power Cushion white sidewall tires: $112.90. Warn semi-automatic front hubs: $64.75. Fuel vaporization system. Mandatory for California: $37.05. Pleated vinyl trim. Not available for model 1414: $75.70.

HISTORICAL FOOTNOTES: Introduction of the 1971 models took place in the fall of 1970.

1972 WAGONEER

Although the Wagoneer was the least-changed model in the Jeep lineup for 1972, there were a few examples of AMC's influence to be found besides the all-AMC engine lineup which was carried over from 1971. The standard interior now had an embossed vinyl seat trim while buyers of the custom model could choose from either houndstooth fabric or perforated-pleated vinyl seats. A new door trim scheme was also used on the Custom Wagoneers. A large, 9 inch day/night rearview mirror was adopted as was a quieter Saginaw power steering pump. Front bucket

seats were now listed as a Wagoneer option. The custom special model was dropped for 1972 although al its features were still available as individual options.

I.D. DATA: The serial number was located on the left-hand hinge pillar. The vehicle identification indicated the model as follows: J2( )144( )A00001 and up: All models. Vehicle identification was as follows: 1414: Four-door station wagon, 1414C: Four-door custom station wagon.

Model Number	Body Type	Factory Price	GVW	Shipping Weight	Prod. Total
Series J-100 Wagoneer Station Wagon (with 6-cyl. engine)					
1414	4-dr.	$4398	4500	3808	—
1414C	Custom 4-dr.	$4640	4500	3843	—

STANDARD ENGINE: Engine Type: OHV, In-line-6. Cast iron block and cylinder head. Bore x Stroke: 3.75 in. x 3.90 in. Lifters: Hydraulic. Number of main bearings-7. Fuel Induction: 1-bbl. Carter Type RTBS or Holley model 1931C-3705. Compression Ratio: 8.0:1. Displacement: 258 cu. in. (4.22 liters). Horsepower: 150 @ 3800 rpm. Torque: 240 lb.-ft. @ 1800 rpm. Oil refill capacity: 5 qt. with filter change. Fuel Requirements: Regular.

OPTIONAL ENGINE: Engine Type: OHV, V-8. Cast iron block and cylinder head. Bore x Stroke: 3.75 in. x 3.44 in. Lifters: Hydraulic. Number of main bearings-5. Fuel Induction: 2-bbl. downdraft carburetor, 1.562 in. barrels. Compression Ratio: 8.4:1. Displacement: 304 cu. in. (4.98 liters). Horsepower: 210 @ 4400 rpm. Torque: Net: 300 lb.-ft. @ 2600 rpm. Oil refill capacity: 5 qt. with filter change. Fuel Requirements: Regular.

OPTIONAL ENGINE: Engine Type: OHV, 360 V-8. Cast iron block and cylinder head. Bore x Stroke: 4.08 in. x 3.44 in. Lifters: Hydraulic. Number of main bearings-5. Fuel Induction: 2-bbl. downdraft carburetor. 1.562 in. barrel size. Compression Ratio: 8.5:1. Displacement: 360 cu. in. (5.89 liters). Horsepower: 245 @ 4400 rpm. Torque: 365 lb.-ft. @ 2400 rpm. Oil refill capacity: 5 qt. with filter change. Fuel Requirements: Regular.

CHASSIS FEATURES: Separate body and frame. Deep web frame, 173.96 in. x 38.0 in. Section modulus: 2.050 in. 3, wide flange, lightweight pressed steel with five cross members.

SUSPENSION AND RUNNING GEAR: Front Suspension: 7-leaf, semi-elliptical springs, 44 in. x 2.5 in. Rating: 160 lb./in. Capacity (at pad): 1150 lb. Capacity (at ground): 1320 lb. 12.75 in. Hydraulic double-action shock absorbers. Optional. 5-leaf, semi-elliptical springs, 44 in. x 2.50 in. Rating: 230 lb./in. Capacity (at pad): 1500 lb. Capacity at ground): 1670 lb. Rear Suspension: Variable rate, 5-leaf semi-elliptical springs, 52.0 in. x 2.50 in. Rating: 144-256 lb./in. Capacity (at pad): 1260 lb. Capacity (at ground): 1430 lb. Hydraulic double-action, 10.75 in. dia. shock absorbers. Optional: 6-leaf semi-elliptical springs, 52.0 in. x 2.50 in. Rating: 230 lb./in. Capacity (at pad): 1585 lb. Capacity (at ground): 1735 lb. Hydraulic double-action, 10.75 in. dia. shock absorbers. Front Axle Type and Capacity: Full-floating Spicer model 27AF, 2500 lb. capacity. Rear Axle Type and Capacity: Full-floating Spicer model 44 semi-floating, 3000 lb. capacity. Optional: None.

Final Drive Ratio:

	3-spd. Manual	4-spd.	Auto. Trans.
Hi-Torque 6	4.09:1	4.09:1	3.73:1
	4.27:1*	—	4.09:1*
Dauntless V-8	3.31:1	3.31:1	3.31:1
	3.73:1*	—	3.73:1*

* Optional at no extra cost.

Transfer Case: Man. trans. and Turbo Hydra-Matic models: 2-speed Dana model 20, 2.03:1, 1.0:1. Brakes: Type: Hydraulic, front and rear drums. Dimensions: Front: 11.0 in. x 2.00 in. front and rear. Total effective area: 180.8 sq. in. Optional: Power brakes. Wheels: Kelsey-Hayes 15 x 5.5K, disc type, full-drop center 5-stud. Tires: 7.75 x 15, 4-ply rating. Optional: Other types and sizes available in both black and white sidewall. Steering: Recirculating ball type. Ratio: 24:1. Turns Lock-to-Lock: 5.6. Turning Circle: 44.5 ft. Optional: Saginaw Power steering. Ratios 17.5:1. Turns Lock-to-Lock: 4.0. Standard: Transmission: 6-cyl.: Warner T14A, 3-speed all-synchromesh manual. Transmission ratios: 3.10, 1.612, 1.00:1. Reverse: 3.1:1. V-8: Warner T15A, 3-speed all-synchromesh manual. Transmission ratios: 2.997, 1.832, 1.00:1. Reverse: 2.997:1. Optional: Turbo Hydra-Matic 3-spd. automatic. Ratios: 2.48:1, 1.48:1, 1.0:1. Reverse: 2.08:1. Optional: Heavy-duty Warner T18 4-speed manual transmission, synchromesh on top three gears. Transmission ratios: 4.02, 3.092, 1.686, 1.00:1. Reverse: 7.439:1. Clutch: Single dry plate. Clutch diameter: 6-cyl.: 10.5 in., V-8: 11.0 in. Total lining area: 6-cyl.: 106.75 in., V-8: 123.7 sq. in. Total plate pressure: 6-cyl.: 1640 lb., V-8: 2450-2750 lb.

VEHICLE DIMENSIONS: Wheelbase: 110 in. Overall Length: 183.66 in. Front/Rear Tread: 57 in./57 in. Overall Height: 65.30 in. Width: 75.6 in. Front/Rear Overhang: 28.70 in./44.96 in. Tailgate: Width and Height: 55 in. Approach/Departure Degrees: 39/20. Ground Clearance: Front axle: 8.54 in. Rear axle: 7.75 in. Load space: 111 in. x 55 in. x 39.5 in. Maximum capacity: 91.03 cu. ft. Front headroom: 35.12 in. Front legroom: 45.00 in. Front hip room: 58-12 in. Rear headroom: 36.56 in. Rear legroom: 36.0 in. Rear hip room: 58.35 in. Seat to floor: 12.58 in.

CAPACITIES: Fuel Tank: 22.0 gal. Coolant System: 6-cyl.: 10.5 qt. V-8: 15 qt.

ACCOMMODATIONS: Seating Capacity: Six passengers.

INSTRUMENTATION: 0-110 mph speedometer, odometer, gauges for engine coolant temperature and fuel level, warning lights for oil pressure and battery charge.

OPTIONS: 210 hp. V-8. 245 hp. V-8:. 4-spd. man. trans. Auto. trans. Optional axle ratios. Rear Trac-Lok differential. Power brakes. Power steering. Power tailgate window. AM radio with antenna. Cigarette lighter. Tinted glass. Air conditioning with heavy-duty cooling. Park brake warning light. Luggage rack. Custom Wagoneer Package. Not available for model 1414, standard for 1414C: No charge. Woodgrain Accessory Package. Not available for model 1414. Wheelcovers. Heavy-duty 70 amp battery. 55 amp alternator. Heavy-duty cooling system. Heavy-duty shock absorbers. Heavy-duty front springs. Heavy-duty rear springs. 8.55 x 15 Power Cushion tires. 8.55 x 15 Suburbanite tires. 8.55 x 15 Suburbanite black sidewall tire. 8.55 x 15 Power Cushion white sidewall tires. 8.55 x 15 Suburbanite black sidewall tires. 8.55 x 15 Polyglas Suburbanite black sidewall tires. H78 x 15 Polyglas Power Cushion white sidewall tires. Warn semi-automatic front hubs. Fuel vaporization system. Mandatory for California. Pleated vinyl trim. Not available for model 1414.

HISTORICAL FOOTNOTES: Total production of Jeep vehicles for 1972 was 71,204 vehicles.

1973 WAGONEER

For 1973 the big news from Jeep was the availability of the Quadra-Trac four-wheel drive system supplied by Borg-Warner. Supporting the comment made by Marvin Stucky, American Motors vice-president in charge of Jeep product development, that "The Quadra-Trac system, which has been under development for more than four years, represents an advance which is as significant to the four-wheel drive vehicle as the first automatic transmission was to the automobile" was American Motors' observation that "the revolution in four-wheel drive begins...." The basic philosophy of Quadra-Trac was simple; regardless of the driving conditions the front and rear differentials automatically adjusted the power and speed of the wheels they controlled, thus, each wheel received the correct proportion of driving power required.

In a similar fashion, a unique limited slip third differential (which received power from the rear of the transmission via a duplex chain) mounted mid-way on the drivetrain had a cone clutch setup with a torque biasing ability which enabled it to transmit power to the front and rear differentials in the proportion required by road conditions. As a result, Strucky noted that the new system gives "maximum handling response on and off the road at all times and under all driving conditions."

Aside from the improved control and handling that resulted, Quadra-Trac also was quieter in operation than competing systems, reduced tire wear and, of course, eliminated the need for selective drive hubs. Included with Quadra-Trac was Turbo Hydra-Matic and the 360 cu. in. engine with a single 2-barrel carburetor and an 8.5:1 compression ratio. Its net ratings for 1973 were 175 horsepower at 4000 rpm and 285 lb.-ft. of torque at 2400 rpm. A 4-barrel carburetor version with 195 horsepower at 4400 rpm and 295 lb.-ft. of torque at 2900 rpm was a new engine option. The 304 V-8 was not offered for 1973. The 6-cylinder engine had new induction-hardening exhaust valve seats.

1973 Jeep Wagoneer

As either a dealer-installed or factory option, a separate, self-contained low range was available for Quadra-Trac that provided a 2.57:1 ratio in addition to the standard 1.0:1 ratio. It mounted directly to the transfer case at the end of the transmission main shaft. Low range was operated by a control knob located on the dash board to the right of the steering column. The Wagoneer could be either stopped or be moving no faster than five miles per hour when low range was to be engaged. To accomplish this the transmission was placed in neutral and the handle pulled out. To cope with extreme or unusual conditions the third differential could be deactivated by a control knob located in the glove box. When this was turned counter-clockwise the lockout was engaged and a light on the dash indicated this condition. When the knob was turned in the opposite direction the light did not function.

Quadra-Trac Wagoneers were initially in limited supply since the Quadra-Trac system was gradually fed into Wagoneer production as AMC determined the extent of demand.

Aside from the introduction of Quadra-Trac, there were many other changes made in the Wagoneer for 1973. The clutch linkage for manual transmissions was redesigned for easier operation, less maintenance an longer service life. Both the front axle and prop shaft were equipped with stronger, longer lasting joints. A floor shift for the standard 3-speed, all-synchromesh manual transmission was now used. The optional 4-speed manual continued to have a floor-mounted shift lever while Turbo Hydra-Matic once again used a column-mounted control lever. Also apparent was a new instrument panel with a three-section cluster housing the speedometer/odometer in the center with the fuel and temperature gauges along with warning lights for the parking brake and brake failure to their left. The third unit, with new oil and ammeter gauges, (in place of the former warning lights) was positioned to the right of the center pod. Standard parking brake and brake-failure warnings lights were located in the upper left cluster pod. All control knobs were of a "Soft-Feel" construction and were marked with international code symbols in white lettering. Also distinguishing the new dash was a much wider brow and an ashtray mounted on ball-bearings. All models also had a new energy absorbing steering column, a restyled steering wheel, new armrests, new standard rear armrest for standard Wagoneer, new optional clock, locking column ignition switch and a hazard warning light control.

The Wagoneer continued to be offered in both standard and custom form. The latter model had woodgrain trim for the instrument cluster and a color-keyed instrument panel, steering column and steering wheel as well as "double needle" switching for the seat inserts. A "Rio Grande" embossed vinyl upholstery was standard on the Wagoneer. Custom models had a "Leo" pleated fabric interior with "Uganda" perforated vinyl optional.

The 1973 color selection consisted of nine colors. Five colors were new for 1973: Fawn beige, fairway green metallic, copper tan metallic, daisy yellow and Trans-Am red. Carried over from 1972 were champagne white, jetset blue metallic, avocado mist metallic and butterscotch gold. A new green color replaced blue in the choice of interior colors. Also available was buff and black.

Primary standard equipment features included back-up lights, electric windshield wipers and washers, interior day/night rearview mirror outside rearview mirror, dual horns, chrome grille, padded instrument panel and padded sun visors.

I.D. DATA: The serial number was located on the left-hand hinge pillar. The vehicle identification indicated the model as follows: J3( )144( )A00001 and up: All models. Vehicle identification was as follows: 14: Four-door station wagon, 15: Four-door custom station wagon.

Model Number	Body Type	Factory Price	GVW	Shipping Weight	Prod.
Series J-100 Wagoneer Station Wagon (with 6-cyl. engine)					
14	4-dr.	$4501	5600	3810	—
14	Custom 4-dr.	$4739	5600*	3850	—

* GVW for both models with 360 V-8: 5810 lb.

STANDARD ENGINE: Engine Type: OHV, In-line-6. Cast iron block and cylinder head. Bore x Stroke: 3.75 in. x 3.90 in. Lifters: Hydraulic. Number of main bearings-7. Fuel Induction: 1-bbl. carburetor. Compression Ratio: 8.0:1. Displacement: 258 cu. in. (4.22 liters). Horsepower: Net: 110 @ 3500 rpm. Torque: Net: 195 lb.-ft. @ 2000 rpm. Oil refill capacity: 5 qt. with filter change. Fuel Requirements: Regular, low-lead or no-lead.

OPTIONAL ENGINE: Engine Type: OHV, V-8. Cast iron block and cylinder head. Bore x Stroke: 4.08 in. x 3.44 in. Lifters: Hydraulic. Number of main bearings-5. Fuel Induction: 2-bbl. carburetor. Compression Ratio: 8.5:1. Displacement: 360 cu. in. (5.89 liters). Horsepower: Net: 175 @ 4000 rpm. Torque: Net: 285 lb.-ft. @ 2400 rpm. Oil refill capacity: 5 qt. with filter change. Fuel Requirements: Regular, low-lead or no-lead.

OPTIONAL ENGINE: Engine Type: OHV, 360 V-8. Cast iron block and cylinder head. Bore x Stroke: 4.08 in. x 3.44 in. Lifters: Hydraulic. Number of main bearings-5. Fuel Induction: 4-bbl. carburetor. Compression Ratio: 8.5:1. Displacement: 360 cu. in. (5.89 liters). Horsepower: Net: 195 @ 4400 rpm. Torque: Net: 295 lb.-ft. @ 2900 rpm. Oil refill capacity: 5 qt. with filter change. Fuel Requirements: Regular, low-lead or no-lead.

CHASSIS FEATURES: Separate body and frame. Deep web frame, wide flange, lightweight pressed steel with five cross members, 173.96 in. x 38.0 in. Section modulus: 2.06 in.

CHASSIS FEATURES: Separate body and frame. Deep web frame, 173.96 in. x 38.0 in. Section modulus: 2.050 in. 3, wide flange, lightweight pressed steel with five cross members.

SUSPENSION AND RUNNING GEAR: Front Suspension: 7-leaf, semi-elliptical springs, 44 in. x 2.5 in. Rating: 160 lb./in. Capacity (at pad): 6-cyl.: 1150 lb., V-8: 1216 lb. Capacity (at ground): 6-cyl.: 1320 lb., V-8: 1380 lb. 12.75 in. Hydraulic double-action shock absorbers. Optional. 5-leaf, semi-elliptical springs, 44 in. x 2.50 in. Rating: 230 lb./in. Capacity (at pad): 1500 lb. Capacity at ground): 1670 lb. Rear Suspension: Variable rate, 5-leaf semi-elliptical springs, 52.0 in. x 2.50 in. Rating: 140-250 lb./in. Capacity (at pad): 1260 lb. Capacity (at ground): 1430 lb. Hydraulic double-action, 10.75 in. dia. shock absorbers. Optional: 6-leaf semi-elliptical springs, 52.0 in. x 2.50 in. Rating: 230 lb./in. Capacity (at pad): 1585 lb. Capacity (at ground): 1735 lb. Hydraulic double-action, 10.75 in. dia. shock absorbers. Front Axle Type and Capacity: Full-floating Dana model 30, 2790 lb. capacity. Rear Axle Type and Capacity: Full-floating Dana model 44 semi-floating, 3500 lb. capacity. Optional: None. Final Drive Ratio: Standard: 258 engine: 4.27:1, all transmissions. 360 V-8: 3.73:1 all transmissions. Optional: 258 engine: 3.73:1, all transmissions. 360 V-8: 3.31:1, all transmissions. Transfer Case: Man. trans. and Turbo Hydra-Matic models: 2-speed Dana model 20, 2.03:1, 1.0:1. Brakes: Type: Hydraulic, front and rear drums. Dimensions: Front: 11.0 in. x 2.00 in. front and rear. Total effective area: 180.8 sq. in. Optional: Power brakes. Wheels: Kelsey-Hayes 15 x 5.5K, disc type, full-drop center 5-stud. Tires: F-78 x 15 Power Cushion black sidewall, 4-ply rating. Optional: Other types and sizes available in both black and white sidewall. Steering: Recirculating ball type. Ratio: 24:1. Turns Lock-to-Lock: 5.6. Turning Circle: 44.5 ft. Optional: Saginaw power steering. Ratios 17.5:1. Turns Lock-to-Lock: 4.0. Standard Transmission: 6-cyl.: Warner T14A, 3-speed all-synchromesh manual. Transmission ratios: 3.10, 1.612, 1.00:1. Reverse: 3.1:1. V-8: Warner T15A, 3-speed all-synchromesh manual. Transmission ratios: 2.997, 1.832, 1.00:1. Reverse: 2.997:1. Optional: Turbo Hydra-Matic 3-spd. automatic. Ratios: 2.48:1, 1.48:1, 1.0:1. Reverse: 2.08:1. Optional: Heavy-duty Warner T18 4-speed manual transmission, synchromesh on top three gears. Transmission ratios: 4.02, 3.092, 1.686, 1.00:1. Reverse: 7.439:1. Clutch: Single dry plate. Clutch diameter: 6-cyl.: 10.5 in., V-8: 11.0 in. Total lining area: 6-cyl.: 106.75 in., V-8: 123.7 sq. in. Total plate pressure: 6-cyl.: 1640 lb., V-8: 2450-2750 lb.

VEHICLE DIMENSIONS: Wheelbase: 110 in. Overall Length: 183.7 in. Front/Rear Tread: 57.3 in./57.5 in. Overall Height: 65.30 in. Width: 75.6 in. Front/Rear Overhang: 28.70 in./44.96 in. Tailgate: Width and Height: 55 in. Approach/Departure Degrees: 39/20. Ground Clearance: Front axle: 8.6 in. Rear axle: 7.8 in. Load space: 111 in. x 55 in. x 39.5 in. Maximum capacity: 91.03 cu. ft. Front headroom: 35.12 in. Front legroom: 45.00 in. Front hip room: 58-12 in. Rear headroom: 36.56 in. Rear legroom: 36.0 in. Rear hip room: 58.35 in. Seat to floor: 12.58 in.

CAPACITIES: Fuel Tank: 22.0 gal. Coolant System: 6-cyl.: 10.5 qt. V-8: 15 qt.

ACCOMMODATIONS: Seating Capacity: Six passengers.

INSTRUMENTATION: 0-110 mph speedometer, odometer, gauges for engine coolant temperature, fuel level, oil pressure and ammeter.

OPTIONS: 360 2-bbl. V-8. 360 4-bbl. V-8. Heavy-duty cooling system. Included heavy-duty radiator, 7-blade fan/Tempatrol (V-8 only) and fan shroud. Heavy-duty front and rear springs and shock absorbers. Heavy-duty 55 amp alternator. 70 amp battery. Air conditioning. Includes heavy-duty cooling system and 55 amp alternator. AM radio with antenna. Courtesy lights. Pleated perforated vinyl seat trim (custom only). Bucket seats with center armrest (custom only). Electric clock. Power tailgate window. Luggage rack. Tinted glass (all windows). Air deflector with woodgrain insert. Custom wheelcovers. Outside passenger mirror. Rear shoulder belts. Rear Trac-Lok differential (not available with Quadra-Trac). Selective drive front hubs (not available with Quadra-Trac). Fuel tank skid plate. Front bumper guards. Quadra-Trac. Power steering. Turbo Hydra-Matic. Four-speed manual trans. Woodgrain Accessory Package (available for Custom Wagoneer only). Includes woodgrain exterior trim and moldings, luggage rack, outside passenger mirror and air deflector with woodgrain. Woodgrain trim and body side moldings (available for Custom Wagoneer only). Includes the following color-keyed interior components: Passenger area carpeting, vinyl cargo-area floor covering, full-foam seats with custom trim, Deluxe door trim panels, armrests, headlining and control knobs. Additional features were: Cigarette lighter, courtesy lights and rear-seat ashtray. Comprising the exterior trim features were custom wheelcovers, trim moldings for the windshield, roof rail, door frames, body side and rear body and a textured tailgate panel.

HISTORICAL FOOTNOTES: The introduction of Quadra-Trac was recognized as a turning point in four-wheel drive technology.

1974 WAGONEER & CHEROKEE

The introduction of the new Cherokee in 1974 positioned Jeep in a very important and growing section of the four-wheel drive field. It was accompanied by an equally dramatic elevation of the Wagoneer into a fully equipped, prestige four-wheel drive vehicle. Giving the Wagoneer a fresh face was a new grille featuring a gridwork with wider subdivisions and housing the parking/directional lights in rectangular pods. Also reshaped and repositioned were the front fender side markers. The rear license plate light was also new. A roof rack continued to be offered but for 1974 it had adjustable cross bars and side rails with woodgrain trim. It had a load capacity of 300 pounds. New options included a set of aluminum alloy wheels, 5-mph bumpers and a tilt steering wheel.

The equipment content of the standard and Custom Wagoneer models was expanded for 1974. Powering all Wagoneers was the 360 cu. in. V-8 with a 2-barrel carburetor. Joining the optional 4-barrel 360 cu. in. V-8 was AMC's 401 cu. in. V-8 fitted with a single 4-barrel carburetor. The Wagoneer exhaust system now had 2.5 in. instead of 2.0 in. pipes as well as a new muffler. Turbo Hydra-Matic was the only transmission available for the Wagoneer. It was joined to Quadra-Trac. The 1974 Wagoneer was equipped with standard power brakes (the front units were new 12 in. disc units while 11 in. rear drums were carried over from 1973). A new Saginaw variable-ratio power steering system with increased road feel replaced the older version. The Wagoneer and Cherokee was also equipped with a new articulated windshield wiper system with articulated arms that cleaned a larger glass area than did the older system. The Wagoneer and Cherokee could be fitted with optional 5 mph front and rear bumpers, a tilt steering wheel and aluminum alloy wheels.

The use of a Dana model 44 open-end front axle reduced the Wagoneer's turning circle from 44.5 feet to 38.4 feet. This axle was snubbed at the differential instead of at the springs which increased the amount of spring travel. The old multi-leaf front springs were replaced with low-friction tapered units that were 1.5 in. longer. Use of the new axle reduced the Wagoneer and Cherokee wheelbase from 110.0 in. to 109.0 in. Also new 1974 was the use of 6 instead of 5-stud wheels.

1974 Jeep Cherokee

In terms of its physical dimensions and basic sheet metal, the new 1974 Cherokee was identical to the 1974 Wagoneer. But there were important differences between the two vehicles. The Cherokee was a two-door wagon fitted with a grille identical to that used by the Jeep trucks since 1970. At the rear the Cherokee used vertically positioned taillights rather than the wraparound units found on the Wagoneer.

The Cherokee's standard engine was the AMC 258 cu. in. overhead valve 6-cylinder engine. With a single one-barrel carburetor and 8.0:1 compression ratio it developed 110 horsepower at 3500 rpm and 195 lb.-ft. of torque at 2000 rpm. Three V-8's were also available, beginning with the two and four-barrel versions of the 360 V-8 and including the 401 cu. in. V-8 with a 4-barrel carburetor.

The Warner Gear supplied Quadra-Trac full-time four-wheel drive system was standard with both the 360 engine with 4-barrel carburetor and the 401 engine. Although it was optional for the 2-barrel 360 engine Quadra-Trac was not available for the 6-cylinder engine. The basic Quadra-Trac system had a single high range. A unit with both high and low ranges was optional.

The four-wheel drive unit for Cherokees with the base engine used a Dana 20 transfer case with a conventional in-and-out format. It could be fitted with free-wheeling front hubs. A 4-speed heavy-duty manual transmission was available for the 360 V-8 with a 2-barrel carburetor when used in conjunction with the Dana 20 transfer case. The standard transmission offered for the 6-cylinder engine was a 3-speed manual gearbox. Turbo Hydra-Matic was optional.

As was the case with the Wagoneer, the Cherokee used a Dana 44 open end front axle with a 6-stud wheel pattern. The semi-floating hypoid rear axle (also a Dana 44) for V-8 Cherokees had a standard 3.07:1 ratio. A 3.54:1 ratio was optional. For the 6-cylinder version a 3.54:1 ratio was standard with 4.09:1 optional. Front and rear suspension, like the Wagoneer's, consisted of leaf springs.

This was the first year power discs as well as variable ratio power steering were offered for Jeep vehicles. The latter unit was supplied by Saginaw.

The Cherokee was offered in two models, the base model 16 and model 17 or S (for Sport) version. It was not difficult to distinguish the two versions from each other. The base model had black window moldings, painted bumpers, rubber floor mats and full-width front and rear seats. The S Cherokee had fancy side body and lower tape striping, bright window reveals, chrome bumpers, flipper quarter windows, aluminum styled 15 x 7 wheels (model 16 had small hubcaps), roof rack and an "S" medallion on the rear side panel.

The Cherokee shared its interior format with the Wagoneer. Instrumentation included gauges for the ammeter and oil pressure. The S model had embossed vinyl seat trim, cigarette lighter, an instrument panel overlay, dash-mounted "S" medallion, custom door and rear side panel trim, a locking glove box, dual horns, armrest overlays, vinyl cargo mat, courtesy lights and two rear seat ashtrays. A number of the features included on the model 17 were available as options for model 16. These included the tape trim, flipper quarter windows, courtesy lights and cigarette lighter.

I.D. DATA: The serial number was located on the left-hand hinge pillar. The vehicle identification indicated the model as follows: Wagoneer: J4( )(model)4( )( )00001 and up. Cherokee: J4( )(model)( )( )( )00001 and up. Vehicle identification was as follows: 14: Four-door Wagoneer station wagon, 15: Four-door Wagoneer custom station wagon, 16: Cherokee station wagon, 17: Cherokee "S" station wagon.

Model Number	Body Type	Factory Price	GVW	Shipping Weight	Prod. Total
Wagoneer Station Wagon V-8					
14	4-dr.	$5466	5600	4270	—
15	Custom 4-dr.	$4739	5600	3850	—
Cherokee Station Wagon 6-cyl.					
16	2-dr.	$4161	5600	3870	—
17	"S" 2-dr.	$4724	5600	3870	—

STANDARD ENGINE: Cherokee: Engine Type: OHV, In-line-6. Cast iron block and cylinder head. Bore x Stroke: 3.75 in. x 3.90 in. Lifters: Hydraulic. Number of main bearings-7. Fuel Induction: 1-bbl. carburetor. Compression Ratio: 8.0:1. Displacement: 258 cu. in. (4.22 liters). Horsepower: Net: 110 @ 3500 rpm. Torque: Net: 195 lb.-ft. @ 2000 rpm. Oil refill capacity: 5 qt. with filter change. Fuel Requirements: Regular, low-lead or no-lead.

STANDARD ENGINE: Wagoneer, optional Cherokee: Engine Type: OHV, V-8. Cast iron block and cylinder head. Bore x Stroke: 4.08 in. x 3.44 in. Lifters: Hydraulic. Number of main bearings-5. Fuel Induction: 2-bbl. carburetor. Compression Ratio: 8.25:1. Displacement: 360 cu. in. (5.89 liters). Horsepower: Net: 175 @ 4000 rpm. Torque: Net: 285 lb.-ft. @ 2400rpm. Oil refill capacity: 5 qt. with filter change. Fuel Requirements: 91 octane.

OPTIONAL ENGINE: Wagoneer and Cherokee: Engine Type: OHV, 360 V-8. Cast iron block and cylinder head. Bore x Stroke: 4.08 in. x 3.44 in. Lifters: Hydraulic. Number of main bearings-5. Fuel Induction: 4-bbl. carburetor. Compression Ratio: 8.25:1. Displacement: 360 cu. in. (5.89 liters). Horsepower: Net: 195 @ 4400 rpm. Torque: Net: 295 lb.-ft. @ 2900 rpm. Oil refill capacity: 5 qt. with filter change. Fuel Requirements: 91 octane.

OPTIONAL ENGINE: Wagoneer and Cherokee: Engine Type: OHV, 401 V-8. Cast iron block and cylinder head. Bore x Stroke: 4.165 in. x 3.68 in. Lifters: Hydraulic. Number of main bearings-5. Fuel Induction: 4-bbl. carburetor. Compression Ratio: 8.35:1. Displacement: 401 cu. in. (6.57 liters). Horsepower: Net: 215 @ 4400 rpm. Torque: Net: 320 lb.-ft. @ 2800 rpm. Oil refill capacity: 5 qt. with filter change. Fuel Requirements: 91 octane.

CHASSIS FEATURES: Separate body and frame. Deep web frame, wide flange, lightweight pressed steel with five cross members, 173.96 in. x 38.0 in. Section modulus: 2.06 in.

SUSPENSION AND RUNNING GEAR: Front Suspension: Low-friction tapered, semi-elliptical springs, 44 in. x 2.5 in. Rating: 1475 lb./in. 12.75 in. Hydraulic double-action shock absorbers. Optional. 1615 lb. rated springs. Rear Suspension: Semi-elliptical springs. Rating: 1735 lb. with Hydraulic double-action, 1.19 in. piston dia. shock absorbers. Optional: None. Front Axle Type and Capacity: Wagoneer & Cherokee: Dana 44, full-floating, hypoid, open end, 3000 lb. capacity. Rear Axle Type and Capacity: Wagoneer & Cherokee: Dana 44, semi-floating, 3000 lb. capacity. Optional: None. Final Drive Ratio: V-8 Cherokees: 3.07:1, 6-cylinder: 3.54:1., Wagoneer: 3.07:1. Optional: Cherokee 6-cyl.: 4.09:1, V-8: 3.54:1. Wagoneer: 3.54:1. Transfer Case: Cherokee standard transmission models: Dana 20: ratios: 2.03:1, 1.00:1. Standard for Wagoneer and optional for Cherokee: Quadra Trac (with V-8 engine and Turbo Hydra-Matic only): Standard 1.00:1. Optional: 2.57:1 ratio in addition to the standard 1.00:1 ratio. Brakes: Type: Wagoneer: Hydraulic, front discs and rear drums. Cherokee: Hydraulic drums front and rear. Dimensions: Wagoneer: Front: 12.0 in. dia. disc. Rear: 11.0 in. x 2.00 in. drums. Total brake swept area: 376 sq. in. Cherokee: 11.0 in. x 2.00 in. front and rear. Total effective area: 181.0 sq. in. Optional: Power front disc brakes for Cherokee. Wheels: Wagoneer and Cherokee: 15 x 6L, disc type, full-drop center 6-stud on 5.5 in. circle. Optional: Wagoneer & Cherokee: 15 x 7 aluminum alloy wheels. Tires: Wagoneer & Cherokee: F78 x 15B Power Cushion black sidewall. Optional: Wagoneer & Cherokee: H78 x 15B, H78 x 15D. Steering: Wagoneer: Power Saginaw recirculating ball type. Ratio: 20/16:1. Turns Lock-to-Lock: 4.0. Turning Circle: 38.4 ft. Cherokee: Saginaw recirculating ball. Ratio: 24: 1. Turns Lock-to-Lock: 4.0. Optional: Power Saginaw recirculating ball type. Required with combination of 258 engine and air conditioning. Ratio: 20/16:1. Turns Lock-to-Lock: 4.0. Turning Circle: 38.4 ft. Standard Transmission: Wagoneer: Turbo Hydra-Matic 3-spd. automatic. Ratios: 2.48:1, 1.48:1, 1.0:1. Optional: None. Cherokee: 3-speed all-synchromesh manual. Transmission ratios: 3.00:1, 1.83:1, 1.00:1. Optional: Turbo Hydra-Matic 3-spd. automatic. Ratios: 2.48:1, 1.48:1, 1.0:1. Reverse: 2.08:1. 4-spd. manual (synchromesh on top three gears). Ratios: 6.32:1, 3.09:1, 1.68:1, 1.0:1. Clutch: Cherokee: Single dry plate. Clutch diameter: 10.5 in. dia. (6-cyl.); 11.0 in. (V-8). Total lining area: 107 sq. in. (6-cyl.), 112 sq. in. (V-8).

VEHICLE DIMENSIONS: Wagoneer & Cherokee (except as noted) Wheelbase: 109 in. Overall Length: 183.70 in. Front/Rear Tread: Wagoneer: 59.0/57.5 in. Cherokee: 58.8/57.5 in. Overall Height: 65.3 in. Width: 75.6 in. Front/Rear Overhang: 27.0 in./43.0 in. Tailgate: Width and Height: 57.5 in. x 26.5 in. Approach/Departure Degrees: 28/21. Ground Clearance: Front axle: 8.3 in. Rear axle: 8.3 in. Oil pan: 16.2 in. Transfer case: 11.5 in. Load space: With rear seat in position: 39 in. x 44 in. x 39.0 in. With rear seat folded or removed: 58 in. x 44 in. x 39.0 in. Maximum capacity: 91.03 cu. ft. Front headroom: 38.6 in. Front legroom: 45.00 in. Front shoulder room: 60.1 in. Front hip room: 60.6 in. Rear headroom: 37.0 in. Rear legroom: 38.25 in. Rear hip room: 61.0 in. Pedal to seat back (max.): 41.5 in. Steering wheel to seat back (max.): 18.5 in. Seat to ground: 31.5 in.

CAPACITIES: Fuel Tank: 22.0 gal. Coolant System: 6-cyl.: 10.5 qt. V-8: 15 qt.

ACCOMMODATIONS: Seating Capacity: Six passengers.

INSTRUMENTATION: Oil and Ammeter gauges, speedometer, odometer, warning lights for brake system warning, hazard lights operation, Quadra-Trac lockout indicator (if equipped with Quadra-Trac).

OPTIONS AND PRICES: 360 2-bbl. V-8 (Cherokee only): $212. 360 4-bbl. V-8: $258 (Cherokee), $44 (Wagoneer). 401 V-8: $295 (Cherokee), $94 (Wagoneer). 4-spd. manual transmission (Cherokee only): $107. Turbo Hydra-Matic: $267 (Cherokee only, standard for Wagoneer). Quadra-Trac (high range only): $40 (Cherokee). Quadra-Trac (high and low range): $150 (Cherokee), $105 (Wagoneer). Free-running front hubs (Cherokee only): $65. Limited slip rear differential (Cherokee only): $60. Power brakes, front discs (Cherokee only): $65. Power steering (Cherokee only): $144. 15 x 7 aluminum wheels: $200. Heavy-duty front and rear shock absorbers: $14. Heavy-duty front and rear springs: $39. Front bucket seats (standard on Cherokee S): $107. Center armrest (available with bucket seats only): $39.00 Tinted glass: $40. Air conditioning: $443. H78-15 Polyglas whitewall tires: $107. Aluminum styled 15 x 7 wheels. $200. AM radio. AM/FM radio: $137.75. Front bumper guards: $15.30 Electric clock: $16.65. Fuel tank skid plate: $51.50. Power tailgate window: $43.00. Tilt steering wheel: $45.10. Roof luggage rack: $71.80. Dual front shoulder belts: $29.85. Rear window air deflector: $22.80. Convenience Group. Includes remote control mirror, visor vanity mirror and glove box light: $19.65. Locking gas cap. Rear quarter vent windows (Cherokee model 16, standard for model 17).

HISTORICAL FOOTNOTES: Introduction of the Cherokee to the press took place in October, 1973 on the Cherokee Indian Reservation in Cherokee, North Carolina. *Pickup, Van and Four-Wheel Drive* magazine depicted the 1974 Quadra-Trac Wagoneer as "the best four-wheel drive vehicle in the world." *Four Wheeler* magazine presented its first annual Achievement Award to American Motors for "making the most significant advancement in the field of four wheeling" with the introduction of the Cherokee.

1975 WAGONEER & CHEROKEE

The 1975 Wagoneer and Cherokee engines, like those for other Jeep lines, featured a new electronic ignition system, new insulation intended to reduce heat transfer from the engine to carburetor, and on V-8's, new carburetors with smaller primary and larger secondary metering valves. The latest Wagoneer and Cherokee models had new front and rear 5-leaf springs (a progressive type was used at the rear), longer shock absorbers mounted in a staggered position at the rear, heat shields for the muffler and exhaust pipes, a new power steering gear for improved road feel, a 3-belt accessory drive system on V-8 engines and a new stainless steel whip-type radio antenna. The standard Cherokee 6-cylinder engine was fitted with quieter mufflers for 1975. Like the Cherokee, the Wagoneer could now be ordered with optional HR-78 x 15 white sidewall radial tires.

The top-of-the-line Custom Wagoneer was available with a new optional woodgrain trim panel that was much wider than the older version. Content of the Wagoneer custom included pleated fabric seat trim, custom door trim panels with woodgrain trim and carpet on floor and wheel-housings, exterior bright window molding and wheelcovers. Added to the custom's standard equipment was a new Light Group consisting of cargo, courtesy, glove box and ashtray lights. This latter feature was just one of several new or revised Wagoneer and Cherokee options that also included a stereo AM/FM radio with four speakers, electrically-heated rear-window defogger, cruise command speed control system, leather-wrapped 15 in. Sport steering wheel, cargo area carpeting and insulation pad, engine block heater, 70 amp alternator and a new Convenience Group consisting of remote outside mirror, visor vanity mirror and electric clock.

1975 Jeep Wagoneer

Standard equipment for the Wagoneer included variable ratio power steering, front and rear chrome bumpers, 12 in. day/night rearview mirror, padded instrument panel, padded sun visors, heavy-duty 60 amp battery, roll-up tailgate window, dual electric horns, heavy-duty air cleaner and under-hood insulation.

Both the standard and Custom Wagoneer interiors were available in four colors: Blue, green, black and buff. The latter two colors were carries over from 1974. The standard model had Laramie vinyl bench seats with the custom equipped with Derby Check fabric bench seats with matching woodgrain trim installed on the door panels. The Custom Wagoneer was also available with an optional Sports knit vinyl upholstery. Bucket seats also continued to be an option for the Custom Wagoneer. For increased heat and insulation in the cargo area, new color-keyed carpeting with a rubber insulation pad and protective skid strips were optional on all Wagoneers. Both the Wagoneer and Cherokee had higher base GVW ratings of 6025 lb. for 1975. A total of ten exterior colors were offered for the Wagoneer and Cherokee: Alpine white, raven black, fawn beige, mellow yellow, red, copper metallic, green apple, reef green metallic, pewter grey metallic and medium blue metallic.

The Cherokee's marketplace competitiveness was strengthened with the introduction of the Cherokee Chief which made its world debut at the Detroit Automobile Show in January, 1975. The Chief Package retailed for $349 over the price of a model 17 and $649 above that of a model 16. Its exterior trim features consisted of low gloss black and a black tape for the rear deck plus "Cherokee Chief" lettering on the tailgate and lower body region. Interior attractions included a leather-wrapped Sport steering wheel and bright trim. The Chief was available in all 1975 Jeep colors as well as special Renegade orange and blue. The interior could be appointed in any of the four standard colors or "Levi's" vinyl.

1975 Jeep Cherokee

Wider front and rear axles plus special slot-type wheels carrying 10 x 15 Goodyear Tracker A-T tires were also part of the Chief option. To accommodate these tires the Chief had larger front and rear wheel openings and fender extensions. The standard Cherokee interior was finished in Laramie vinyl. The Cherokee S had a standard Desert Flower upholstery. Both were offered in blue, green, black and buff. Key standard features of the Cherokee S consisted of "Cherokee 'S'" side body stripes, 15 x 7 in. forged aluminum wheels, chrome front and rear bumpers, flipper rear quarter windows, Sport steering wheel, 'S' medallion identification, bright windshield reveal moldings and vent window moldings, rear quarter window trim, foam-cushioned front bucket seats in Desert Flower vinyl, matching front and rear quarter trim pads, color-keyed carpet, and engine turned instrument panel.

Standard Cherokee equipment included a roll-up tailgate window, front bucket seats with rear bench seat, 12 in. day/night mirror, color-keyed vinyl floor covering, color-keyed cargo area covering, padded vinyl instrument panel, padded sun visors, and folding rear seat.

I.D. DATA: The serial number was located on the left-hand hinge pillar. The vehicle identification indicated the model as follows: Wagoneer: J5( )(model)( )( )00001 and up. Cherokee: J5( )(model)( )( )( )00001 and up. Vehicle identification was as follows: 14: Four-door Wagoneer station wagon, 15: Four-door Wagoneer custom station wagon, 16: Cherokee station wagon, 17: Cherokee "S" station wagon.

Model Number	Body Type	Factory Price	GVW	Shipping Weight	Prod. Total
Wagoneer Station Wagon V-8					
14	4-dr.	$6013	6025	4240	—
15	Custom 4-dr.	$6246	6025	4256	—
Cherokee Station Wagon 6-cyl.					
16	2-dr.	$4851	5600	3657	—
17	"S" 2-dr.	$5399	5600	3677	—

STANDARD ENGINE: Cherokee: Not available for California. Standard for California is 360 V-8 with 4-bbl. carburetor. Engine Type: OHV, In-line-6. Cast iron block and cylinder head. Bore x Stroke: 3.75 in. x 3.90 in. Lifters: Hydraulic. Number of main bearings-7. Fuel Induction: 1-bbl. carburetor. Compression Ratio: 8.0:1. Displacement: 258 cu. in. (4.22 liters). Horsepower: Net: 110 @ 3500 rpm. Torque: Net: 195 lb.-ft. @ 2000 rpm. Oil refill capacity: 5 qt. with filter change. Fuel Requirements: Regular, low-lead or no-lead.

STANDARD ENGINE: Wagoneer, optional Cherokee: Engine Type: OHV, V-8. Cast iron block and cylinder head. Bore x Stroke: 4.08 in. x 3.44 in. Lifters: Hydraulic. Number of main bearings-5. Fuel Induction: 2-bbl. carburetor. Compression Ratio: 8.25:1. Displacement: 360 cu. in. (5.89 liters). Horsepower: Net: 175 @ 4000 rpm. Torque: Net: 285 lb.-ft. @ 2900 rpm. Oil refill capacity: 5 qt. with filter change. Fuel Requirements: 91 octane.

OPTIONAL ENGINE: Wagoneer and Cherokee: Engine Type: OHV, 360 V-8. Cast iron block and cylinder head. Bore x Stroke: 4.08 in. x 3.44 in. Lifters: Hydraulic. Number of main bearings-5. Fuel Induction: 4-bbl. carburetor. Compression Ratio: 8.25:1. Displacement: 360 cu. in. (5.89 liters). Horsepower: Net: 195 @ 4400 rpm. Torque: Net: 295 lb.-ft. @ 2900 rpm. Oil refill capacity: 5 qt. with filter change. Fuel Requirements: 91 octane.

OPTIONAL ENGINE: Wagoneer and Cherokee: Engine Type: OHV, 401 V-8. Cast iron block and cylinder head. Bore x Stroke: 4.165 in. x 3.68 in. Lifters: Hydraulic. Number of main bearings-5. Fuel Induction: 4-bbl. carburetor. Compression Ratio: 8.35:1. Displacement: 401 cu. in. (6.57 liters). Horsepower: Net: 215 @ 4400 rpm. Torque: Net: 320 lb.-ft. @ 2800 rpm. Oil refill capacity: 5 qt. with filter change. Fuel Requirements: 91 octane.

CHASSIS FEATURES: Separate body and frame. Deep web frame, wide flange, lightweight pressed steel with five cross members. Section modulus: 2.06 in.

SUSPENSION AND RUNNING GEAR: Front Suspension: 5-leaf semi-elliptical springs front and rear, Front: 47 in. x 2.5 in. Rear: 52 in. x 2.5 in. Deflection rate: 200 lb./in. Hydraulic double-action shock absorbers. Optional. Heavy-duty springs with 260 lb./in. deflection rate. Rear Suspension: 5-leaf semi-elliptical, progressive design. Deflection rate: 160/260 lb./in. Hydraulic double-action shock absorbers. Optional: Heavy-duty with deflection rate of 230 lb./in. Front Axle Type and Capacity: Wagoneer & Cherokee: Dana 44, full-floating, hypoid, open end, 3500 lb. capacity. Rear Axle Type and Capacity: Wagoneer & Cherokee: Dana 44, semi-floating, 3500 lb. capacity, 3540 lb. rating. Optional: None. Final Drive Ratio: All engines 3.07:1, Optional: All engines: 3.54:1. Transfer Case: Cherokee standard transmission models: Dana 20: ratios: 2.03:1, 1.00:1. Standard for Wagoneer and optional for Cherokee: Quadra Trac (with V-8 engine and Turbo Hydra-Matic only): Standard 1.00:1. Optional: 2.57:1 ratio in addition to the standard 1.0:1 ratio. Brakes: Type: Wagoneer: Hydraulic, front discs and rear drums. Cherokee: Hydraulic drums front and rear. Dimensions: Wagoneer: Front: 12.0 in. dia. disc. Rear: 11.0 in. x 2.00 in. drums. Total brake swept area: 376 sq. in. Cherokee: 11.0 in. x 2.00 in. front and rear. Total effective area: 181.0 sq. in. Optional: Power front disc brakes for Cherokee. Wheels: Wagoneer and Cherokee: 15 x 6L, disc type, full-drop center 6-stud on 5.5 in. circle. Optional: Wagoneer & Cherokee: 15 x 7 aluminum alloy wheels. Tires: Wagoneer & Cherokee: H78 x 15B Power Cushion black sidewall. Optional: Wagoneer & Cherokee: HR78 x 15 steel belted radial 1/2 ply, white sidewall, H78 x 15 custom Cushion Power Polyglas, 4-ply black sidewall or Power Cushion "78" 4-ply white sidewall, H78 x 15 Suburbanite Polyglas 2/6 ply black sidewall (not available with aluminum wheels), H78 x 15 Suburbanite XG Polyglas 2/4 ply. Steering: Wagoneer: Power Saginaw recirculating ball type. Ratio: 20/16:1. Turns Lock-to-Lock: 4.0. Turning Circle: 38.4 ft. Cherokee: Saginaw recirculating ball. Ratio: 24: 1. Turns Lock-to-Lock: 4.0. Optional: Power Saginaw recirculating ball type. Required with combination of 258 engine and air conditioning. Ratio: 20/16:1. Turns Lock-to-Lock: 4.0. Turning Circle: 38.4 ft. Standard Transmission: Wagoneer: Turbo Hydra-Matic 3-spd. automatic. Ratios: 2.48:1, 1.48:1, 1.0:1. Optional: None. Cherokee: 3-speed all-synchromesh manual. Transmission ratios: 3.00:1, 1.83:1, 1.00:1. Optional: Turbo Hydra-Matic 3-spd. automatic. Ratios: 2.48:1, 1.48:1, 1.0:1. Reverse: 2.08:1. 4-spd. manual (synchromesh on top three gears). Ratios: 6.32:1, 3.09:1, 1.68:1, 1.0:1. Clutch: Cherokee: Single dry plate. Clutch diameter: 10.5 in. dia. (6-cyl.); 11.0 in. (V-8). Total lining area: 107 sq. in. (6-cyl.), 112 sq. in. (V-8). Optional: None.

VEHICLE DIMENSIONS: Wagoneer & Cherokee (except as noted) Wheelbase: 109 in. Overall Length: 183.70 in. Front/Rear Tread: Wagoneer: 59.0/57.5 in. Cherokee: 58.8/57.5 in. Overall Height: 65.3 in. Width: 75.6 in. Front/Rear Overhang: 27.0 in./43.0 in. Tailgate: Width and Height: 57.5 in. x 26.5 in. Approach/Departure Degrees: 28/21. Ground Clearance: Front axle: 8.3 in. Rear axle: 8.3 in. Oil pan: 16.2 in. Transfer case: 11.5 in. Load space: With rear seat in position: 39 in. x 44 in. x 39.0 in. With rear seat folded or removed: 58 in. x 44 in. x 39.0 in. Maximum capacity: 91.03 cu. ft. Front headroom: 38.6 in. Front legroom: 45.00 in. Front shoulder room: 60.1 in. Front hip room: 60.6 in. Rear headroom: 37.0 in. Rear legroom: 38.25 in. Rear hip room: 60.6 in. Pedal to seat back (max.): 41.5 in. Steering wheel to seat back (max.): 18.5 in. Seat to ground: 31.5 in.

CAPACITIES: Fuel Tank: 22.0 gal. Coolant System: 6-cyl.: 10.5 qt. V-8: 15 qt.

ACCOMMODATIONS: Seating Capacity: Six passengers.

INSTRUMENTATION: Oil and Ammeter gauges, speedometer, odometer, warning lights for brake system warning, hazard lights operation, Quadra-Trac lockout indicator (if equipped with Quadra-Trac).

OPTIONS AND PRICES: Cherokee: 360 cu. in., 2-bbl. V-8 (Cherokee only): $201. 360 cu. in. 4-bbl. V-8: $245 (for Cherokee). 401 cu. in. V-8: $295 (for Cherokee). 4-speed manual trans.: $129 (Cherokee only). Turbo Hydra-Matic with Quadra-Trac: $291 (for Cherokee). Turbo Hydra-Matic with Quadra-Trac and low range: $395.80 (for Cherokee). Free-wheeling front hubs: $85 (Cherokee only). Limited slip differential: $69 (Cherokee only). Power front disc brakes: $65 (Cherokee only). Power steering: $169 (standard for Wagoneer). Heavy-duty front shock absorbers: $17. Heavy-duty front and rear shock absorbers: $29.95. Heavy-duty front springs: $35. Heavy-duty rear springs: $30. Air conditioning: $457. AM radio: $69. AM/FM radio with 4 speakers. Citizen's Band radio. Cruise control. 15 in. Sport steering wheel. Leather-wrapped steering wheel: $13.50. Tilt steering wheel. Electric rear window defogger. Luggage rack: $75. Bucket seats with center armrest (Wagoneer only). Center cushion and folding armrest (Cherokee only): $49. Trailer Towing Package. Front bumper guards with rear nerf strips: $39. Forged aluminum styled wheels. Woodgrain side trim (for Custom Wagoneer only). Power rear window: $49. Cargo area carpeting and insulation pad: $59. Protective floor mats (Cherokee only): $15. Heavy-duty cooling. AM radio. Convenience Group. Includes left outside remote control mirror, visor vanity mirror and electric clock. Light Group: $24. Fuel tank skid plate: $51.50. Dual low-profile mirrors. Tinted glass: $39.95. Cold Climate Group. Spare tire lock. Cigarette lighter (standard on Custom Wagoneer). Heavy-duty 62 amp alternator (Cherokee only): $34. Heavy-duty 70 amp battery: $18. Free-wheeling front hubs (Cherokee only, not avail. with Quadra-Trac). Decor Group (Cherokee only). Includes chrome bumpers, wheelcovers, bright windshield and vent window moldings, two-tone paint: $39.95. Outside passenger mirror (Cherokee only): $7.50. Wheelcovers (Cherokee only). Locking gas cap. Dual horns (Cherokee only, standard on S model). Cigarette lighter (base Cherokee and Wagoneer only). Dealer installed accessories: Electric and mechanical winches. Trailer hitch. Inside-mounted spare tire. Snowplow. Front push bumper.

HISTORICAL FOOTNOTES: The 1975 Wagoneer and Cherokee models debuted in the fall of 1974.

1976 WAGONEER & CHEROKEE

The most important changes for the 1976 Wagoneer (which AMC described as "the ultimate four-wheel drive experience") and Cherokee were their more rugged frame with stronger cross members and box section side rail construction. At the rear the side rails were slightly splayed to allow the rear springs to be wider spaced than in 1975. New rear springs of a new asymmetrical design provided a smoother ride. The front springs were unchanged in form but had increased up-and-down clearance. The new frame's design made possible the use of a direct steering gear mounting eliminating the need for adapter subassemblies. Available for the first time for the Cherokee and Wagoneer was an optional front stabilizer bar. The Cherokee was offered with new optional heavy-duty springs that offered better handling, comfort and suspension clearance than the 1975 heavy-duty springs. The Wagoneer was available with a new optional heavy-duty suspension.

Detail changes found on all 1976 Cherokee and Wagoneer models included a more efficient dual-nozzle windshield washer system and a new seat-belt warning system with a three-way lap and shoulder harness assembly. Both Jeeps had new graphics for the instrument panel, radio clock, heater and other controls.

The standard Cherokee interior included front bucket seats and a rear bench seat finished in a new Fairway vinyl available in black, blue, green or buff. Other features included color-keyed floor and cargo area covering and armrests.

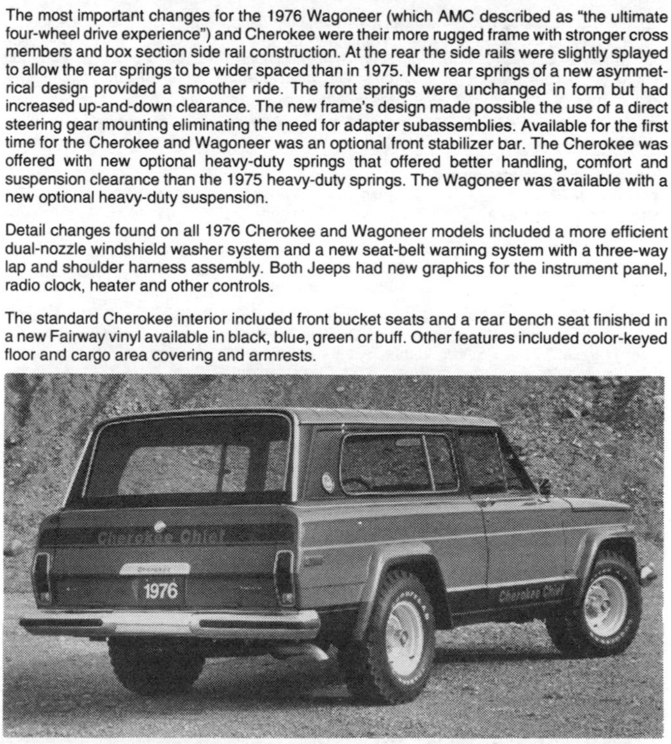

1976 Jeep Cherokee Chief

Basic Cherokee standard equipment a new forward pivoting front passenger bucket seat, roll-up tailgate window, padded instrument panel, padded sun visors, oil and amp gauges, heavy-duty air cleaner, 37 amp alternator, folding rear seat, and 50 amp battery. Cherokees with Quadra-Trac also had new 15 in. wheelcovers.

The S interior featured a Diamond Stripe vinyl with matching door and rear quarter trim panels, color-keyed carpeting, an engine turned instrument cluster and a forward pivoting driver's seat for easier rear seat access.

Two Cherokee Chief Packages were offered. The Chief Package included 10 x 15 "Tracker A-T" Goodyear tires with raised white lettering, mounted on special 8 in. slot-style wheels, 3.54:1 axle ratio, flared fenders, upper and lower body two-tone paint in low gloss black and lower body accent striping with "Cherokee Chief" lettering. A tailgate stripe also carried the Cherokee Chief name. Other appearance items were a leather-wrapped steering wheel and bright trim. The Chief wide-wheel and Tire Package included the 10 x 15 tires, special wheels, 3.54:1 axle ratio and flared fenders. Standard on the Chief were power disc brakes, power steering, fuel tank skid plate.

Except for a new floor-mounted lever to operate the Quadra-Trac low range, no changes were made in either model's standard or optional drivetrain-engine combinations. Added to the list of factory installed equipment for the Cherokee was the "Snow Boss" Plow Package which included complete mounting for an 84 in. Mold-board plow, hydraulic cylinders, electrical control switches and wiring, plow lights and special decals.

Although both the standard and Custom Wagoneer interiors were revamped they remained available in the same selection of blue, green, black and buff colors seats as were offered in 1975. The standard version used Fairway vinyl covered front and rear bench seats. Custom models now had a "Potomac Stripe" fabric with pleated patterned inserts. The custom's standard and optional bucket seats were offered in a new "Sof-Touch" vinyl.

The woodgrain side body trim available only for the custom reverted back to its more conservative pre-1975 form. Also revised were the 15 in. wheelcovers that were standard on the custom model and optional for the base Wagoneer. For 1976 the center cap carrying Jeep identification was more rounded while the surrounding vaned portion was enlarged. Twelve standard body colors were offered for the Wagoneer and Cherokee. New for 1976 were these colors: Sand tan, dark cocoa metallic (not available for Cherokee Chief), sunshine yellow, firecracker red, brilliant blue (not available for Wagoneer), and nautical blue (not available for Cherokee Chief). Carried over from 1975 were these six colors: Alpine white, Renegade orange, pewter grey, reef green metallic, medium blue metallic, and classic black (not available for Cherokee Chief).

Late in the model year, the Cherokee was equipped with standard power front disc brakes. They had the same specifications as those used on the Wagoneer.

1976 Jeep Wagoneer

I.D. DATA: The serial number was located on the left-hand hinge pillar. The vehicle identification indicated the model as follows: Wagoneer: J6( )(model)( )( )00001 and up. Cherokee: J6( )(model)( )( )( )00001 and up. Vehicle identification was as follows: 14: Four-door Wagoneer station wagon, 15: Four-door Wagoneer custom station wagon, 16: Cherokee station wagon, 17: Cherokee "S" station wagon.

Model Number	Body Type	Factory Price	GVW	Shipping Weight	Prod. Total
Wagoneer Station Wagon V-8					
14	4-dr.	$6339	6025	4329	—
15	Custom 4-dr.	$6572	6025	4345	—
Cherokee Station Wagon 6-cyl.					
16	2-dr.	$5258	5600	3918	—
17	"S" 2-dr.	$5806	5600	3938	—

STANDARD ENGINE: Cherokee: Not available for California. Standard for California is 360 V-8 with 4-bbl. carburetor. Engine Type: OHV, In-line-6. Cast iron block and cylinder head. Bore x Stroke: 3.75 in. x 3.90 in. Lifters: Hydraulic. Number of main bearings-7. Fuel Induction: 1-bbl. carburetor. Compression Ratio: 8.0:1. Displacement: 258 cu. in. (4.22 liters). Horsepower: Net: 110 @ 3500 rpm. Torque: Net: 195 lb.-ft. @ 2000 rpm. Oil refill capacity: 5 qt. with filter change. Fuel Requirements: Regular, low-lead or no-lead.

STANDARD ENGINE: Wagoneer, optional Cherokee: Engine Type: OHV, V-8. Cast iron block and cylinder head. Bore x Stroke: 4.08 in. x 3.44 in. Lifters: Hydraulic. Number of main bearings-5. Fuel Induction: 2-bbl. carburetor. Compression Ratio: 8.25:1. Displacement: 360 cu. in. (5.89 liters). Horsepower: Net: 175 @ 4000 rpm. Torque: Net: 285 lb.-ft. @ 2900 rpm. Oil refill capacity: 5 qt. with filter change. Fuel Requirements: 91 octane.

OPTIONAL ENGINE: Wagoneer and Cherokee: Engine Type: OHV, 360 V-8. Cast iron block and cylinder head. Bore x Stroke: 4.08 in. x 3.44 in. Lifters: Hydraulic. Number of main bearings-5. Fuel Induction: 4-bbl. carburetor. Compression Ratio: 8.25:1. Displacement: 360 cu. in. (5.89 liters). Horsepower: Net: 195 @ 4400 rpm. Torque: Net: 295 lb.-ft. @ 2900 rpm. Oil refill capacity: 5 qt. with filter change. Fuel Requirements: 91 octane.

OPTIONAL ENGINE: Wagoneer and Cherokee: Engine Type: OHV, 401 V-8. Cast iron block and cylinder head. Bore x Stroke: 4.165 in. x 3.68 in. Lifters: Hydraulic. Number of main bearings-5. Fuel Induction: 4-bbl. carburetor. Compression Ratio: 8.35:1. Displacement: 401 cu. in. (6.57 liters). Horsepower: Net: 215 @ 4400 rpm. Torque: Net: 320 lb.-ft. @ 2800 rpm. Oil refill capacity: 5 qt. with filter change. Fuel Requirements: 91 octane.

CHASSIS FEATURES: Separate body and frame. Box section side rails, deep web frame, wide flange, lightweight pressed steel with five cross members.

SUSPENSION AND RUNNING GEAR: Front Suspension: 5-leaf semi-elliptical springs front and rear, Front: 47 in. x 2.5 in. Rear: 52 in. x 2.5 in. Deflection rate: Front: 6-cyl.: 195 lb./in.; V-8: 215 lb./in. Hydraulic double-action shock absorbers. Optional. Heavy-duty springs: 6-cyl.: 215 lb./in., V-8: 260 lb./in. deflection rate. Rear Suspension: 5-leaf semi-elliptical, asymmetrical design. Deflection rate: 165 lb./in. Hydraulic double-action shock absorbers. Optional: Heavy-duty with deflection rate of 165-245 lb./in. Front Axle Type and Capacity: Wagoneer & Cherokee: Dana 44, full-floating, hypoid, open end, 3215 lb. rating. Rear Axle Type and Capacity: Wagoneer & Cherokee: Dana 44, semi-floating, 3215 lb. rating. Optional: None. Final Drive Ratio: All engines 3.07:1, Optional: All engines: 3.54:1. Transfer Case: Cherokee standard transmission models: Dana 20: ratios: 2.03:1, 1.00:1. Standard for Wagoneer and optional for Cherokee: Quadra Trac (with V-8 engine and Turbo Hydra-Matic only): Standard 1.00:1. Optional: 2.57:1 ratio in addition to the standard 1.0:1 ratio. Brakes: Type: Wagoneer: Hydraulic, front discs and rear drums. Cherokee: Hydraulic drums front and rear. Dimensions: Wagoneer: Front: 12.0 in. dia. disc. Rear: 11.0 in. x 2.00 in. drums. Total brake swept area: 376 sq. in. Cherokee: 11.0 in. x 2.00 in. front and rear. Total effective area: 181.0 sq. in. Optional: Power front disc brakes for Cherokee. Wheels: Wagoneer and Cherokee: 15 x 6L, disc type, full-drop center 6-stud on 5.5 in. circle. Optional: Wagoneer & Cherokee: 15 x 7 aluminum alloy wheels. Tires: Wagoneer & Cherokee: H78 x 15B Power Cushion black sidewall. Optional: Wagoneer & Cherokee: HR78 x 15 steel belted radial 1/2 ply, white sidewall, H78 x 15 custom Cushion Power Polyglas, 4-ply black sidewall or Power Cushion "78" 4-ply white sidewall, H78 x 15 Steel belted radial Mud and Snow, H78 x 15 Suburbanite Polyglas and Suburbanite XG Polyglas, 2/4 ply. Steering: Wagoneer: Power Saginaw recirculating ball type. Ratio: 20/16:1. Turns Lock-to-Lock: 4.0. Turning Circle: 38.4 ft. Cherokee: Saginaw recirculating ball. Ratio: 24:1. Turns Lock-to-Lock: 4.0. Optional: Power Saginaw recirculating ball type. Required with combination of 258 engine and air conditioning. Ratio: 20/16:1. Turns Lock-to-Lock: 4.0. Turning Circle: 38.4 ft. Standard Transmission: Wagoneer: Turbo Hydra-Matic 3-spd. automatic. Ratios: 2.48:1, 1.48:1, 1.0:1. Optional: None. Cherokee: 3-speed all-synchromesh manual. Transmission ratios: 3.00:1, 1.83:1, 1.00:1. Optional: Turbo Hydra-Matic 3-spd. automatic. Ratios: 2.48:1, 1.48:1, 1.0:1. Reverse: 2.08:1. 4-spd. manual (synchromesh on top three gears). Ratios: 6.32:1, 3.09:1, 1.68:1, 1.0:1. Clutch: Cherokee: Single dry plate. Clutch diameter: 10.5 in. dia. (6-cyl.); 11.0 in. (V-8). Total lining area: 107 sq. in. (6-cyl.), 112 sq. in. (V-8). Optional: None.

VEHICLE DIMENSIONS: Wagoneer & Cherokee (except as noted) Wheelbase: 109 in. Overall Length: 183.70 in. Front/Rear Tread: Wagoneer: 59.4/57.8 in. Cherokee: 59.2/57.8 in. Cherokee S: 59.9/58.5 in. Cherokee Chief: 65.4/62.3 in. Overall Height: Wagoneer: 66.7 in. Cherokee: 66.9 in. Cherokee Chief: 67.6 in. Width: 75.6 in. Cherokee Chief: 78.9 in. Front/Rear Overhang: 27.0 in./43.0 in. Tailgate: Width and Height: 57.5 in. x 26.5 in. Approach/Departure Degrees: 28/21. Ground Clearance: Front axle: 8.3 in. Rear axle: 8.3 in. Oil pan: 16.2 in. Transfer case: 11.5 in. Load space: With rear seat in position: 39 in. x 44 in. x 39.0 in. With rear seat folded or removed: 58 in. x 44 in. x 39.0 in. Maximum capacity: 95.1 cu. ft. (with rear seat removed). Front headroom: 38.0 in. Front legroom: 38.8 in. Front shoulder room: 60.1 in. Front hip room: 60.5 in. Rear headroom: Wagoneer: 37.2 in. Cherokee: 38.0 in. Rear legroom: Wagoneer: 38.25 in. Cherokee: 37.0 in. Rear hip room: Wagoneer: 60.6 in. Cherokee: 60.9 in. Pedal to seat back (max.): 41.5 in. Steering wheel to seat back (max.): 18.5 in. Seat to ground: 31.5 in.

CAPACITIES: Fuel Tank: 22.0 gal. Coolant System: 6-cyl.: 10.5 qt. V-8: 15 qt.

ACCOMMODATIONS: Seating Capacity: Six passengers.

INSTRUMENTATION: Oil and Ammeter gauges, speedometer, odometer, warning lights for brake system warning, hazard lights operation, Quadra-Trac lockout indicator (if equipped with Quadra-Trac).

OPTIONS: 360 cu. in., 2-bbl. V-8 (Cherokee only). 360 cu. in. 4-bbl. V-8. 401 cu. in. V-8. Air conditioning. Citizen's Band radio. Quadra-Trac and automatic transmission (Cherokee only). Power front disc brakes (Cherokee only). AM/FM stereo radio. Cruise control. Tilt steering wheel. 15 in. Sport steering wheel. Leather-wrapped Sport steering wheel. Bucket seats with center armrest. Center armrest (Cherokee only). 4-speed manual transmission (Cherokee only, available with 360 V-8 engines only). 6.5 in. x 9.5 in., low profile mirrors. Mechanical winch. Electrical winch. Forged 7.0 in. aluminum styled wheels (standard on Cherokee S). Forward pivoting driver bucket seat (Cherokee only, standard with Cherokee S). Cargo area carpeting and insulation pad. Fuel tank skid plate. Front bumper guards and front and rear bumper nerf strips. Trailer Towing Package. Luggage rack. Power rear window. Woodgrain trim. Electric rear window defogger. Front stabilizer bar. Heavy-duty cooling system. Extra-duty suspension system. Low range for Quadra-Trac. Front and rear heavy-duty shock absorbers. Convenience Group. Contains left outside remote control mirror, visor vanity mirror and electric clock. Tinted glass-all windows. Cold Climate Group. Includes engine block heater, 70 amp battery and 60 amp alternator. Light Group (standard on Custom Wagoneer). Provided illumination for cargo area, under dash, glove box and ashtray. AM transistor radio. Heavy-duty alternator. Heavy-duty 70 amp battery. Outside passenger mirror. Snow Boss Package. Includes plow mountings, 84 in. Moldboard plow, hydraulic cylinders for plowing and lifting, electric control switches and wiring, plow lights and special decals.

HISTORICAL FOOTNOTES: Total United States and Canadian Jeep retail sales in 1976 established a new record of 95,718 units. Jeep had 16 percent of the total U.S. four-wheel drive market. But in the recreational-utility segment which included the Cherokee, Jeep held almost 40 percent. Ever since AMC had acquired Jeep one of its priorities had been the strengthening of the Jeep dealer force. During 1976 the number of Jeep dealers increased from 1531 to 1608. The number selling both AMC and Jeep products climbed from 910 to 1049. AMC reported to stockholders that "the four-wheel drive market picture continues bright in the United States and Canada. The U.S. market climbed from 390,000 units in 1975 to more than 580,000 in 1976. It is expected to reach about 630,000 in 1977. Four-wheel drive vehicles are becoming a second or third family car. In some cases they are purchased as the only tranSportation by people who previously owned passenger cars."

1977 WAGONEER & CHEROKEE

Only one model of the Wagoneer was available in 1977. Priced at $6,966, it was the equivalent of the 1976 custom model but did not carry the custom designation. Changes from 1976 were extremely limited consisting of a new vertical-mount interior spare tire carrier (also offered for the Cherokee) as an alternative to the standard under-the-rear tire mount and a new interior trim scheme. Now standard for the Wagoneers with bench seats was a Rallye perforated vinyl. A new option for Wagoneers with either bucket and bench seats was a Brampton plaid fabric. Both seat trims were available in tan, blue, black or a new berry color.

1977 Jeep Wagoneer

The Wagoneer, and Cherokee were available in twelve body colors, including five that were new — Autumn red metallic, loden green metallic, mocha brown metallic and tawny orange. The carry-over colors were alpine white, brilliant blue, classic black, firecracker red, pewter grey metallic, sand tan and sunshine yellow.

The power front disc brakes that had been standard for the Wagoneer and J-20 trucks were now standard for the Cherokee. Replacing the single-barrel carburetor version of the 258 cu. in. 6-cylinder engine as the standard Cherokee engine was a two-barrel model.

Expanding the Cherokee's sales potential was the addition of a four-door model 18 version to its lineup. Its price of $5736 was just $100 more than that of the two-door model 16. Both were available with the $599 S Package. The S Package was also available for both the base two-door Cherokee and the Chief wide-wheel and Tire Package, which AMC also identified as the wide track version. The latter had new 15 x 8 in. styled steel wheels and 10 x 15 raised white letter tires plus wider axles and flared front and rear wheel openings. The Cherokee Chief exterior trim continued as an option for the wide track model only. It included unique upper body two-tone paint and lower body blackout with Cherokee Chief name, tailgate stripe with Cherokee Chief name, bright windshield molding, chrome bumpers, flipper rear windows, "S" medallion, and all interior appointments included in the S Package. All Cherokee interiors were new for 1977.

The S Package, available as an option for all Cherokee models, included chrome front and rear bumpers, bright windshield and vent window moldings, 15 x 7 in. aluminum wheels (except for wide-wheel model), new body side and tailgate tape stripes, "S" medallion, flipper quarter window trim on two-door models, cigarette lighter, glove box lock, bright armrest overlays, dual horns, carpeted wheelhouse covers, rear seat ashtrays, high-line trim all-vinyl bucket seats with folding center armrest, custom door and rear quarter trim panels, engine-turned instrument panel cluster, interior pillar covers for the four-door model, and folding driver seat-back for two-door Cherokees.

The most important technical change for 1977 was a new ambient air-intake system for V-8 engines.

1977 Jeep Cherokee four-door

I.D. DATA: The serial number was located on the left-hand hinge pillar. The vehicle identification indicated the model as follows: Wagoneer: J7( )(15)( )( )00001 and up. Cherokee: J7( )(model)( )( )( )00001 and up. Vehicle identification was as follows: 15: Four-door Wagoneer station wagon, 16: Cherokee station wagon, 17: Cherokee wide-wheel station wagon, 18: Cherokee Four-door station wagon.

Model Number	Body Type	Factory Price	GVW	Shipping Weight	Prod. Total
Wagoneer Station Wagon V-8					
15	4-dr.	$6996	6025	4345	—
Cherokee Station Wagon 6-cyl.					
16	2-dr.	$5636	6025	3971	—
17	Wide-wheel 2-dr.	$6059	6025	3991	—
18	4-dr.	$5736	6025	4106	—

STANDARD ENGINE: Cherokee: Not available for California. Standard for California is 360 V-8 with 4-bbl. carburetor. Engine Type: OHV, In-line-6. Cast iron block and cylinder head. Bore x Stroke: 3.75 in. x 3.90 in. Lifters: Hydraulic. Number of main bearings-7. Fuel Induction: 1-bbl. carburetor. Compression Ratio: 8.0:1. Displacement: 258 cu. in. (4.22 liters). Horsepower: Net: 110 @ 3500 rpm. Torque: Net: 195 lb.-ft. @ 2000 rpm. Oil refill capacity: 5 qt. with filter change. Fuel Requirements: Regular, low-lead or no-lead.

STANDARD ENGINE: Wagoneer, optional Cherokee: Engine Type: OHV, V-8. Cast iron block and cylinder head. Bore x Stroke: 4.08 in. x 3.44 in. Lifters: Hydraulic. Number of main bearings-5. Fuel Induction: 2-bbl. carburetor. Compression Ratio: 8.25:1. Displacement: 360 cu. in. (5.89 liters). Horsepower: Net: 175 @ 4000 rpm. Torque: Net: 285 lb.-ft. @ 2900 rpm. Oil refill capacity: 5 qt. with filter change. Fuel Requirements: 91 octane.

OPTIONAL ENGINE: Wagoneer and Cherokee: Engine Type: OHV, 360 V-8. Cast iron block and cylinder head. Bore x Stroke: 4.08 in. x 3.44 in. Lifters: Hydraulic. Number of main bearings-5. Fuel Induction: 4-bbl. carburetor. Compression Ratio: 8.25:1. Displacement: 360 cu. in. (5.89 liters). Horsepower: Net: 195 @ 4400 rpm. Torque: Net: 295 lb.-ft. @ 2900 rpm. Oil refill capacity: 5 qt. with filter change. Fuel Requirements: 91 octane.

OPTIONAL ENGINE: Wagoneer and Cherokee: Engine Type: OHV, 401 V-8. Cast iron block and cylinder head. Bore x Stroke: 4.165 in. x 3.68 in. Lifters: Hydraulic. Number of main bearings-5. Fuel Induction: 4-bbl. carburetor. Compression Ratio: 8.35:1. Displacement: 401 cu. in. (6.57 liters). Horsepower: Net: 215 @ 4400 rpm. Torque: Net: 320 lb.-ft. @ 2800 rpm. Oil refill capacity: 5 qt. with filter change. Fuel Requirements: 91 octane.

CHASSIS FEATURES: Separate body and frame. Box section side rails, deep web frame, wide flange, lightweight pressed steel with five cross members.

SUSPENSION AND RUNNING GEAR: Front Suspension: 5-leaf semi-elliptical springs front and rear, Front: 47 in. x 2.5 in. Rear: 52 in. x 2.5 in. Deflection rate: Front: 6-cyl.: 195 lb./in.; V-8: 215 lb./in. Hydraulic double-action shock absorbers. Optional. Heavy-duty springs: Deflection rate: 215, 260, 300 lb./in. Rear Suspension: 5-leaf semi-elliptical, asymmetrical design. Deflection rate: 165 lb./in. Hydraulic double-action shock absorbers. Optional: Heavy-duty with deflection rate of 165-245 lb./in. Front Axle Type and Capacity: Wagoneer & Cherokee: Dana 44, full-floating, hypoid, open end, 3215 lb. rating. Rear Axle Type and Capacity: Wagoneer & Cherokee: Dana 44, semi-floating, 3215 lb. rating. Optional: None. Final Drive Ratio: All engines 3.07:1, Optional: All engines: 3.54:1. Transfer Case: Cherokee standard transmission models: Dana 20: ratios: 2.03:1, 1.00:1. Standard for Wagoneer and optional for Cherokee: Quadra Trac (with V-8 engine and Turbo Hydra-Matic only): Standard 1.00:1. Optional: 2.57:1 ratio in addition to the standard 1.0:1 ratio. Brakes: Type: Wagoneer and Cherokee: Hydraulic, front discs and rear drums. Cherokee: Hydraulic drums front and rear. Dimensions: Wagoneer and Cherokee: Front: 12.0 in. dia. disc. Rear: 11.0 in. x 2.00 in. drums. Total brake swept area: 376 sq. in. Wheels: Wagoneer and Cherokee: 15 x 6, disc type, full-drop center 6-stud on 5.5 in. circle. Wide-wheel model: 15 x 8, 6-bolt. Tires: Wagoneer & Cherokee: H78 x 15B Power Cushion black sidewall. Optional: Wagoneer & Cherokee: HR78 x 15 steel belted radial 1/2 ply, white sidewall, H78 x 15 custom Cushion Power Polyglas, 4-ply black sidewall or Power Cushion "78" 4-ply white sidewall, H78 x 15 Steel belted radial Mud and Snow, H78 x 15 Suburbanite Polyglas and Suburbanite XG Polyglas, 2/4 ply. Steering: Wagoneer: Power Saginaw recirculating ball type. Ratio: 20/16:1. Turns Lock-to-Lock: 4.0. Turning Circle: 38.4 ft. Cherokee: Saginaw recirculating ball. Ratio: 24: 1. Turns Lock-to-Lock: 4.0. Optional: Power Saginaw recirculating ball type. Required with combination of 258 engine and air conditioning. Ratio: 20/16:1. Turns Lock-to-Lock: 4.0. Turning Circle: 38.4 ft. Standard Transmission: Wagoneer: Turbo Hydra-Matic 3-spd. automatic. Ratios: 2.48:1, 1.48:1, 1.0:1. Optional: None. Cherokee: 3-speed all-synchromesh manual. Transmission ratios: 3.00:1, 1.83:1, 1.00:1. Optional: Turbo Hydra-Matic 3-spd. automatic. Ratios: 2.48:1, 1.48:1, 1.0:1. Reverse: 2.08:1. 4-spd. manual (synchromesh on top three gears). Ratios: 6.32:1, 3.09:1, 1.68:1, 1.0:1. Clutch: Cherokee: Single dry plate. Clutch diameter: 10.5 in. dia. (6-cyl.); 11.0 in. (V-8). Total lining area: 107 sq. in. (6-cyl.), 112 sq. in. (V-8). Optional: None.

VEHICLE DIMENSIONS: Wagoneer & Cherokee (except as noted): Wheelbase: 109 in. Overall Length: 183.70 in. Front/Rear Tread: Wagoneer: 59.4/57.8 in. Cherokee: 59.2/57.8 in. Cherokee S: 59.9/58.5 in. Cherokee Chief: 65.4/62.3 in. Overall Height: Wagoneer: 66.7 in. Cherokee: 66.9 in. Cherokee Chief: 67.6 in. Width: 75.6 in. Cherokee Chief: 78.9 in. Front/Rear Overhang: 27.0 in./43.0 in. Tailgate: Width and Height: 57.5 in. x 26.5 in. Approach/Departure Degrees: 28/21. Ground Clearance: All models except Cherokee model 17: 7.7 in.; model 17: 8.6 in. 1976 data: Front axle: 8.3 in. Rear axle: 8.3 in. Oil pan: 16.2 in. Transfer case: 11.5 in. Load space: With rear seat in position: 39 in. x 44 in. x 39.0 in. With rear seat folded or removed: 58 in. x 44 in. x 39.0 in. Maximum capacity: 95.1 cu. ft. (with rear seat removed). Front headroom: 38.0 in. Front legroom: 38.8 in. Front shoulder room: 60.1 in. Front hip room: 60.5 in. Rear headroom: Wagoneer: 37.2 in. Cherokee: 38.0 in. Rear legroom: Wagoneer: 38.25 in. Cherokee: 37.0 in. Rear hip room: Wagoneer: 60.6 in. Cherokee: 60.9 in. Pedal to seat back (max.): 41.5 in. Steering wheel to seat back (max.): 18.5 in. Seat to ground: 31.5 in.

CAPACITIES: Fuel Tank: 22.0 gal. Coolant System: 6-cyl.: 10.5 qt. V-8: 15 qt.

ACCOMMODATIONS: Seating Capacity: Six passengers.

INSTRUMENTATION: Oil and Ammeter gauges, speedometer, odometer, warning lights for brake system warning, hazard lights operation, Quadra-Trac lockout indicator (if equipped with Quadra-Trac).

OPTIONS AND PRICES: Power steering (standard for Wagoneer): $190. Automatic transmission with Quadra-Trac (standard for Wagoneer): $345. 4-speed manual trans. (for Cherokee only): $144. AM/FM stereo radio: $22. Roof rack: $85. Aluminum styled wheels: $223. Cherokee S Package. Cherokee Chief Package (model 17): $469. Air conditioning: $509. Cruise control: $80. 360 cu. in., 2-bbl. V-8 (Cherokee only): 360 cu. in. 4-bbl. V-8: 401 cu. in. V-8. Air conditioning. Citizen's Band radio. Quadra-Trac and automatic transmission (Cherokee only). AM/FM stereo radio. Cruise control. Tilt steering wheel. 15 in. Sport steering wheel. Leather-wrapped Sport steering wheel. Bucket seats with center armrest. Center armrest (Cherokee only). 4-speed manual transmission (Cherokee only, available with 360 V-8 engine only). 6.5 in. x 9.5 in., low profile mirrors. Mechanical winch. Electrical winch. Forged 7.0 in. aluminum styled wheels (standard on Cherokee S). Forward pivoting driver bucket seat (Cherokee only, standard with Cherokee S). Cargo area carpeting and insulation pad. Fuel tank skid plate. Front bumper guards and front and rear bumper nerf strips. Trailer Towing Package. Luggage rack. Power rear window. Woodgrain trim. Electric rear window defogger. Front stabilizer bar. Heavy-duty cooling system. Extra-duty suspension system. Low range for Quadra-Trac. Front and rear heavy-duty shock absorbers. Convenience Group. Contains left outside remote control mirror, visor vanity mirror and electric clock. Tinted glass-all windows. Cold Climate Group. Includes engine block heater, 70 amp battery and 60 amp alternator. Light Group (standard on Custom Wagoneer). Provided illumination for cargo area, under dash, glove box and ashtray. AM transistor radio. Heavy-duty alternator. Heavy-duty 70 amp battery. Outside passenger mirror. Snow Boss Package. Includes plow mountings, 84 in. Moldboard plow, hydraulic cylinders for plowing and lifting, electric control switches and wiring, plow lights and special decals.

HISTORICAL FOOTNOTES: Total Jeep sales in the U.S. and Canada reached 117,077, which for the third consecutive year represented a new record. AMC stockholders were informed that "Jeep is successful because the company had developed a range of choices for customers-not just vehicle types, but a growing list of comfort conveniences and appearance options. Jeep buyers increasingly want style and individuality to go with toughness and durability. Their vehicles are used for recreation and work, and for multi-purpose family tranSportation."

1978 WAGONEER & CHEROKEE

Although for 1978 the Wagoneer's appearance changes were held to a minimum, there were numerous detail revisions. Leading the list were color-keyed seat belts and shoulder harnesses, a new horn bar pad for the standard steering wheel, a "Soft-Feel" pleated vinyl seat trim, chrome-plated armrest bases and a relocated fuel filler cap. Joining the forged aluminum-styled wheels as an alternative to the standard wheels were 7 inch chrome-plated spoked steel wheels. Shared with the Cherokee was the addition of 2.5 in. of driver legroom due to an extended toe board and relocation of the accelerator as well as a new ambient air-intake system that resulted in a lower engine operating temperature.

No changes were made in the Wagoneer's engine lineup but unlike 1977 when the standard engine for California-bound Wagoneers was the 360 cu. in. V-8 with a 4-barrel carburetor, all 1978's had the 2-barrel version standard with the 4-barrel carburetor 360 V-8 as well as the 401 cu. in. V-8 fitted with a 4-barrel carburetor available in all states except California as options.

1978 Jeep Cherokee two-door

The price of the Wagoneer, at $7695, was given an extra boost upward mid-way during 1978 when AMC introduced the Limited model whose sticker price moved up an additional $3120 to $10,715. Jeep depicted the Limited as "a cut above excellence...built for the man who demands the ultimate in four-wheel drive performance without compromising on luxury." Beyond the already high content of the standard Wagoneer was added a long list of features to create the Limited model. These items included air conditioning, tinted glass, power tailgate window, cruise control, tilt steering wheel, AM/FM/CB radio (or AM/FM 8-track), front sway bar, stabilizer bar, front bumper guards, Extra-Quiet Insulation Package, headlights-on warning buzzer, intermittent windshield wipers, remote control driver's side mirror, leather seats, leather-wrapped steering wheel, extra thick carpeting in the seating and cargo area, special interior and exterior nameplates wide woodgrain side and rear trim, roof rack, special forged aluminum styled wheels and American Eagle Flexten white sidewall tires.

No engine changes were made for the Cherokee but the ambient air-intake used for V-8 engines in1977 was now standard for all models.

The seat belts and shoulder harnesses were now color-keyed to the interior and the optional "Levi's" cloth bucket seats were available in a new beige color as well as in traditional blue.

A number of items previously listed as options were now included as standard equipment on all Cherokees. These included bright windshield and vent moldings, cigarette lighter, glove box lock and dual horns. Offered for the first time as options were factory-installed AM/FM/CB and AM/CB radios, plus a AM/FM/Multi-Plex 8-track tape system. Gross vehicle weight ratings for 1978 were increased from 6025 to 6200 pounds.

The S Package, available for all Cherokee models, included chrome front and rear bumpers, new 15 x 7 in. chrome-plated wheels except in the window wheel model, body side and tailgate tape stripes, S medallion, flipper quarter windows with bright trim on two-door models, Sport steering wheel, instrument panel medallion, rear seat ashtrays, bright armrest overlays, carpeted wheelhouse covers, color keyed carpeting, high-line trim all-vinyl bucket seats and door and rear quarter trim panels, engine-turned instrument panel cluster overlay, interior pillar covers for the four-door, and folding center armrest with folding driver and passenger seat backs for the two-door Cherokees.

The Cherokee Chief Package (available on the wide track model) included unique upper body two-tone paint and lower body blackout with Cherokee Chief name, tailgate stripe with Cherokee Chief name, bright drip and roof rear moldings, chrome bumpers, flipper quarter windows with bright trim, an S medallion and all interior appointments of the S Package. Two new exterior colors were offered for 1978: Captain blue metallic, and sun orange (not available for the Wagoneer). Additional colors for 1978 consisted of loden green metallic (not available for the Cherokee Chief), mocha brown metallic (not available for the Cherokee Chief), oakleaf brown (not available for the Cherokee Chief and Wagoneer), autumn red metallic, alpine white, sand tan, pewter grey metallic, sunshine yellow, firecracker red, classic black (not available for the Cherokee Chief), and brilliant blue (not available for the Wagoneer).

I.D. DATA: The serial number was located on the left-hand hinge pillar. The vehicle identification indicated the model as follows: Wagoneer: J8( )(15)N( )00001 and up. Cherokee: J8( )(model)N( )00001 and up. Vehicle identification was as follows: 15: Four-door Wagoneer station wagon, 16: Cherokee station wagon, 17: Cherokee wide-wheel station wagon, 18: Cherokee Four-door station wagon.

Model Number	Body Type	Factory Price	GVW	Shipping Weight	Prod. Total
Wagoneer Station Wagon V-8					
15	4-dr.	$7695	6200	4345	—
Cherokee Station Wagon 6-cyl.					
16	2-dr.	$6229	6200	3971	—
17	Wide-wheel 2-dr.	$6675	6200	3991	—
18	4-dr.	$6335	6200	4106	—

STANDARD ENGINE: Cherokee: Not available for California. Standard for California is 360 V-8 with 4-bbl. carburetor in conjunction with automatic transmission and Quadra-trac. Engine Type: OHV, In-line-6. Cast iron block and cylinder head. Bore x Stroke: 3.75 in. x 3.90 in. Lifters: Hydraulic. Number of main bearings-7. Fuel Induction: 2-bbl. carburetor. Compression Ratio: 8.0:1. Displacement: 258 cu. in. (4.22 liters). Horsepower: Net: 110 @ 3500 rpm. Torque: Net: 195 lb.-ft. @ 2000 rpm. Oil refill capacity: 5 qt. with filter change. Fuel Requirements: Regular, low-lead or no-lead.

STANDARD ENGINE: Wagoneer, optional Cherokee: Engine Type: OHV, V-8. Cast iron block and cylinder head. Not available for California. Standard for California is 360 V-8 with 4-bbl. carburetor. Bore x Stroke: 4.08 in. x 3.44 in. Lifters: Hydraulic. Number of main bearings-5. Fuel Induction: 2-bbl. carburetor. Compression Ratio: 8.25:1. Displacement: 360 cu. in. (5.89 liters). Horsepower: Net: 175 @ 4000 rpm. Torque: Net: 285 lb.-ft. @ 2900 rpm. Oil refill capacity: 5 qt. with filter change. Fuel Requirements: 91 octane. Optional: Engine: Wagoneer and Cherokee. Engine Type: OHV, 360 V-8. Cast iron block and cylinder head. Bore x Stroke: 4.08 in. x 3.44 in. Lifters: Hydraulic. Number of main bearings-5. Fuel Induction: 4-bbl. carburetor. Compression Ratio: 8.25:1. Displacement: 360 cu. in. (5.89 liters). Horsepower: Net: 195 @ 4400 rpm. Torque: Net: 295 lb.-ft. @ 2900 rpm. Oil refill capacity: 5 qt. with filter change. Fuel Requirements: 91 octane.

OPTIONAL ENGINE: Wagoneer and Cherokee: Engine Type: OHV, 401 V-8. Cast iron block and cylinder head. Bore x Stroke: 4.165 in. x 3.68 in. Lifters: Hydraulic. Number of main bearings-5. Fuel Induction: 4-bbl. carburetor. Compression Ratio: 8.35:1. Displacement: 401 cu. in. (6.57 liters). Horsepower: Net: 215 @ 4400 rpm. Torque: Net: 320 lb.-ft. @ 2800 rpm. Oil refill capacity: 5 qt. with filter change. Fuel Requirements: 91 octane.

CHASSIS FEATURES: Separate body and frame. Box section side rails, deep web frame, wide flange, lightweight pressed steel with five cross members.

SUSPENSION AND RUNNING GEAR: Front Suspension: 5-leaf semi-elliptical springs front and rear, Front: 47 in. x 2.5 in. Rear: 52 in. x 2.5 in. Deflection rate: Front: 6-cyl.: 195 lb./in.; V-8: 215 lb./in. Hydraulic double-action shock absorbers. Optional. Heavy-duty springs: Deflection rate: 215, 260, 300 lb./in. Rear Suspension: 5-leaf semi-elliptical, asymmetrical design. Deflection rate: 165 lb./in. Hydraulic double-action shock absorbers. Optional: Heavy-duty with deflection rate of 165-245 lb./in. Front Axle Type and Capacity: Wagoneer & Cherokee: Dana 44, full-floating, hypoid, open end, 3215 lb. rating. Rear Axle Type and Capacity: Wagoneer & Cherokee: Dana 44, semi-floating, 3215 lb. rating. Optional: None. Final Drive Ratio: All engines 3.07:1, Optional: All engines: 3.54:1. Transfer Case: Cherokee standard transmission models: Dana 20: ratios: 2.03:1, 1.00:1. Standard for Wagoneer and optional for Cherokee: Quadra Trac (with V-8 engine and Turbo Hydra-Matic only): Standard 1.00:1. Optional: 2.57:1 ratio in addition to the standard 1.0:1 ratio. Brakes: Type: Wagoneer and Cherokee: Hydraulic, front discs and rear drums. Cherokee: Hydraulic drums front and rear. Dimensions: Wagoneer and Cherokee: Front: 12.0 in. dia. disc. Rear: 11.0 in. x 2.00 in. drums. Total brake swept area: 376 sq. in. Wheels: Wagoneer and Cherokee: 15 x 6, disc type, full-drop center 6-stud on 5.5 in. circle. Wide-wheel model: 15 x 8, 6-bolt. Tires: Wagoneer & Cherokee: H78 x 15B Power Cushion black sidewall. Optional: Wagoneer & Cherokee: HR78 x 15 steel belted radial 1/2 ply, white sidewall, H78 x 15 custom Cushion Power Polyglas, 4-ply black sidewall or Power Cushion "78" 4-ply white sidewall, H78 x 15 steel belted radial Mud and Snow, H78 x 15 Suburbanite Polyglas and Suburbanite XG Polyglas, 2/4 ply. Steering: Wagoneer: Power Saginaw recirculating ball type. Ratio: 20/16:1. Turns Lock-to-Lock: 4.0. Turning Circle: 38.4 ft. Cherokee: Saginaw recirculating ball. Ratio: 24: 1. Turns Lock-to-Lock: 4.0. Optional: Power Saginaw recirculating ball type. Required with combination of 258 engine and air conditioning. Ratio: 20/16:1. Turns Lock-to-Lock: 4.0. Turning Circle: 38.4 ft. Standard Transmission: Wagoneer: Turbo Hydra-Matic 3-spd. automatic. Ratios: 2.48:1, 1.48:1, 1.0:1. Optional: None. Cherokee: 3-speed all-synchromesh manual. Transmission ratios: 3.00:1, 1.83:1, 1.00:1. Optional: Turbo Hydra-Matic 3-spd. automatic. Ratios: 2.48:1, 1.48:1, 1.0:1. Reverse: 2.08:1. 4-spd. manual (synchromesh on top three gears). Ratios: 6.32:1, 3.09:1, 1.68:1, 1.0:1. Clutch: Cherokee: Single dry plate. Clutch diameter: 10.5 in. dia. (6-cyl.); 11.0 in. (V-8). Total lining area: 107 sq. in. (6-cyl.), 112 sq. in. (V-8). Optional: None.

VEHICLE DIMENSIONS: Wagoneer & Cherokee (except as noted): Wheelbase: 109 in. Overall Length: 183.70 in. Front/Rear Tread: Wagoneer: 59.4/57.8 in. Cherokee: 59.2/57.8 in. Cherokee S: 59.9/58.5 in. Cherokee Chief: 65.4/62.3 in. Overall Height: Wagoneer: 66.7 in. Cherokee: 66.9 in. Cherokee Chief: 67.6 in. Width: 75.6 in. Cherokee Chief: 78.9 in. Front/ Rear Overhang: 27.0 in./43.0 in. Tailgate: Width and Height: 57.5 in. x 26.5 in. Approach/ Departure Degrees: 28/21. Ground Clearance: All models except Cherokee model 17: 7.7 in.; model 17: 8.6 in. 1976 data: Front axle: 8.3 in. Rear axle: 8.3 in. Oil pan: 16.2 in. Transfer case: 11.5 in. Load space: With rear seat in position: 39 in. x 44 in. x 39.0 in. With rear seat folded or removed: 58 in. x 44 in. x 39.0 in. Maximum capacity: 95.1 cu. ft. (with rear seat removed). Front headroom: 38.0 in. Front legroom: 38.8 in. Front shoulder room: 60.1 in. Front hip room: 60.5 in. Rear headroom: Wagoneer: 37.2 in. Cherokee: 38.0 in. Rear legroom: Wagoneer: 38.25 in. Cherokee: 37.0 in. Rear hip room: Wagoneer: 60.6 in. Cherokee: 60.9 in. Pedal to seat back (max.): 41.5 in. Steering wheel to seat back (max.): 18.5 in. Seat to ground: 31.5 in.

CAPACITIES: Fuel Tank: 22.0 gal. Coolant System: 6-cyl.: 10.5 qt. V-8: 15 qt.

ACCOMMODATIONS: Seating Capacity: Six passengers.

INSTRUMENTATION: Oil and Ammeter gauges, speedometer, odometer, warning lights for brake system warning, hazard lights operation, Quadra-Trac lockout indicator (if equipped with Quadra-Trac).

OPTIONS AND PRICES: Cherokee S Package: $375 (wide-wheel version), $475 for all other applications. Wagoneer Limited Package: $3120. 360 cu. in. 2-bbl. V-8: $250. 360 cu. in. 4-bbl. V-8: $300. 401 cu. in. V-8: $475. 4-speed manual transmission (Cherokee): $153. Turbo Hydra-Matic/Quadra-Trac (high range only): $366 (standard for Wagoneer). Turbo Hydra-Matic/Quadra-Trac (high/low range): $511 (for Cherokee). Air conditioning: $577. 63 amp alternator: $45. Locking rear axle: $82. Optional axle ratio: $17. Heavy-duty battery: $36. Brush guard: $69. Cold Climate Group (without AC): $91. Cold Climate Package (with AC): $46. Convenience Group: $49. Heavy-duty cooling: $39. Cruise control: $100. Rear window defroster: $94. Free wheeling front hubs: $101 (Cherokee only). Aluminum styled wheels: $211. Woodgrain trim (Wagoneer only). Light Group: $34. AM radio: $86. AM/FM radio: $229. AM/FM stereo with tape player: $329. AM/FM/Citizens Band: $349. Fuel tank skid plate: $60. Snow Boss Package: $1165. Power steering: $212 (Cherokee only). Suspension Package: $115. Tinted glass: $48. Towing Package "A": $75. Towing Package "B": $125. Power tailgate: $69. Rear quarter vent windows: $47.

HISTORICAL FOOTNOTES: Jeep sales accounted for 34 percent of the Sports-utility market in 1978. Total sales for the U.S. and Canada market moved up to a record 153,000 which was 31 percent above the 1977 total. AMC reported that "at year's end Jeep vehicle sales had risen over year-ago periods for 37 consecutive months."

1979 WAGONEER & CHEROKEE

The latest Wagoneers were easy to spot with their new single piece grille of vertical bars and single rectangular headlights. Also debuting were one-piece aluminum bumpers. The only engine available for the Wagoneer was the 2-barrel 360 cu. in. V-8.

The standard equipment interior content for all Wagoneer models for 1979 included these items — Front ashtray, front and rear armrests, cigarette lighter, carpeting for the front and rear floor areas and wheel house covers, vinyl cargo area mat, gauges for oil, voltmeter, engine coolant temperature and fuel, glove box lock, heater and defroster, lap and shoulder belt restraint system, Light Group included courtesy lights, glove box light, ashtray light, cargo area light, engine compartment light, lighted visor vanity mirror, and dome/map light; 12 in. inside day/night rearview mirror, padded instrument panel, padded sun visors, variable ratio power steering, front and rear bench seats with seat belts (outboard retractor in front and rear), custom interior including custom seats and door trim panels and rear seat ashtray. Standard exterior equipment consisted of front and rear chrome plated aluminum bumpers, side safety markers, outside left-side mirror, moldings for windshield, doors, quarter window frames, rear roof rail and tail gate, and high impact resistant windshield glass. Additional standard components included cellulose-fiber air cleaner, 37 amp alternator, 60 amp battery, foot-lever parking brake, electronic ignition system, dual horns, electric 2-speed windshield wipers, and 15 in. wheelcovers.

The Wagoneer Limited included in addition to the items just listed, these additional interior features or variations: Bucket seat with tan leather/cord trim, center armrest and special door panels, tan, leather-wrapped steering wheel, 22 oz. tan carpeting in seating area, 18 oz. carpeting in cargo area, dome/reading light, woodgrain overlay on lower instrument section, "Limited" nameplate on instrument panel, and protective floor mats. Exterior aspects of the Limited were as follows: Wide woodgrain side and rear trim with wide moldings or special two-tone paint, roof rack with woodgrain inserts, bright drip rail overlays, front bumper guards, forged aluminum 15 x 7 in. wheels, HR78 "American Eagle" radial tires, and Limited nameplates. The Wagoneer Limited also had a variety of standard special equipment features consisting of air conditioning with tinted glass, power tailgate window, tilt steering wheel, AM/FM/CB stereo radio (an AM/FM/cassette tape player was a no-cost option), extra-quiet insulation, Convenience Group, and stabilizer bar.

An Extra-Quiet Insulation Package was a new option for the regular Wagoneer model in 1979. Additional new options included a smooth ride suspension, lighted visor vanity mirror and dome/reading lamp as part of the Convenience Group, Caberfae corduroy fabric trim, all vinyl seats body side scuff molding with woodgrain insert and a new two-tone paint scheme (including three special two-tone exteriors for the Wagoneer Limited).

In 1979, for the first time in its five years of production the Cherokee received a new grille. Highlights of the new Cherokee "face" included rectangular headlights set within a one-piece grille of bright chrome in combination with dark argent and low gloss paint. The grille design consisted of thin horizontal and vertical dividers and an extruded center section. Also easily noticed were the Cherokee's new one-piece chrome bumpers that were much more substantial-appearing than the previous units.

The Cherokee's standard equipment interior content was as follows: Front ashtray, front and rear armrests, color-keyed vinyl front and rear seat floor covering, vinyl cargo area mat, oil, voltmeter, engine coolant and fuel level gauges, glove box lock, heater and defroster, lap and shoulder belt restraint system, 12 in. inside day/night rearview mirror, padded instrument panel padded sun visors, and front and rear bench seats with seat belts (outboard front and rear). Standard exterior features consisted of front and rear chrome plated aluminum bumpers, side safety markers, outside left side mirror, bright moldings for vent window, windshield and tailgate, and high impact resistent glass for windshield. Additional standard features included 37 amp alternator, 45 amp battery for 6-cyl. and 60 amp for V-8 engines, foot lever parking brake, dual horns, electric washers and 2-speed windshield wipers, hubcaps and, for wide-wheel Cherokees, wide-wheels and ties plus wider axles and flared fenders.

1979 Jeep Cherokee

Adding to the appeal of the Cherokee was the introduction of the Golden Eagle Package as an option for the wide-wheel two-door Cherokee. The Package comprised beige denim fabric bucket seats with center armrest, passenger assist handle, tan carpets, tan Soft-Feel Sport steering wheel, engine turned instrument panel overlay, driver's folding seat, carpeted wheel-house covers, rear seat ashtray, bright door frame moldings, Golden Eagle decal on hood, special tape striping on hood, cowl, body sides, and tailgate, Golden Eagle lettering on lower door panels, flipper quarter windows, bronze tone tinted rear quarter windows, black brush guard, 15 x 8 in. styled steel wheels painted gold with black striping, outline white 10 x 15 Tracker A-T tires (available for wide-wheel Cherokees only), and two-tone paint.

The popular S model was spruced up with a new side body Indian graphic theme with either a black or white background. The Chief Package had new body striping, trim and ornamentation. It also included custom vinyl bucket seats, center armrest, and cushion, driver's folding seat back, assist handle, interior pillar covers on four-door models, engine turned instrument panel overlay, custom door and rear quarter trim panels, color-keyed carpeting and carpeted wheel house covers, rear seat ashtrays, Soft-Feel Sport steering wheel, body side and tailgate tape stripe, bright trim in rear window of two-door model, flipper rear quarter windows on two-door, interior and exterior S medallions, and 15 x 7 in. aluminum wheels.

The Chief Package for the wide-wheel model included most of the interior features of the S Package plus these exterior items: Unique body side two-tone paint in low gloss black in place of tape striping, Cherokee Chief lettering on lower body sides and tailgate, bright drip and rear roof moldings, and 10 x 15 outline white letter Tracker A-T tires. White styled steel wheels and flared fenders replaced the wheel/tires offerings of the S Package.

Interior changes found on all Cherokees included a 4-spoke custom steering wheel, new armrest design and a new dome light. The interior of the base model, which was upgraded to approximately the level of the 1978 S model, featured Cara vinyl with accent striping. Both the S and Chief Packages used a printed "Stripe" vinyl with a coarse material known as "Western Weave" optional. This upholstery, having vertical striping and trimmed in the Cara vinyl, was praised both for its breathing ability and its tendency to prevent the seat occupant from sliding around when the going got rough.

No longer available for any Jeep product was the 401 cu. in. V-8. Also pruned from the optional engine list was the 4-barrel version of the 360 cu. in. V-8. This left the standard 258 cu. in. 6-cylinder and the 360 cu. in. V-8 with a 2-barrel carburetor as the only engines offered for the Cherokee. The V-8 was substantially redesigned for 1979. Primary changes included a larger carburetor, revised distributor and a redesigned ERG system which AMC claimed provided for an over 20 percent increase in horsepower at higher speed and 100 percent compensation for higher performance at higher altitudes.

New Cherokee options for 1979 included an Extra-Quiet Insulation Package, intermittent windshield wipers as part of the Convenience Group, a lighted visor vanity mirror as part of the Light Group, and for the high-line S, Chief and Golden Eagle Trim Packages a new dome/reading lamp and a soft material passenger assist handle.

For the first time all Cherokees except the wide-wheel model were available with a smooth ride suspension system. This was not recommended for extended off-road use and consisted of special front springs and rear shocks plus a front stabilizer bar. This package was the direct opposite of the extra-duty suspension which included heavy-duty springs and shock absorbers. Midway between them was the standard suspension with its 5-leaf front and rear springs with respective ratings of 215 lb./ft. and 165 lb./ft.

Fourteen exterior colors, twelve of which were new, were offered for 1979. This selection and its availability for Wagoneer and Cherokee models was as follows: Olympic white (all models), arrowhead silver metallic (not available for Golden Eagle, Wagoneer Limited and 10-4 models), classic black (not available for Cherokee Chief), Morocco buff (all models), alpaca brown metallic (all models), sable brown metallic (not available for Cherokee Chief), Cumberland green metallic (not available for Cherokee Chief), saxon yellow (not available for Golden Eagle models), wedgewood blue (not available for Golden Eagle, Wagoneer Limited and 10-4 models), ensign blue (not available for Golden Eagle, Chief and Wagoneer Limited models), mandarin orange (Not available for Wagoneer, Wagoneer Limited and Golden eagle), firecracker red (not available for Golden Eagle and Wagoneer Limited), russet metallic (all models), and bordeaux metallic (not available for Cherokee Chief). firecracker red and classic black were carry-over colors from 1978.

I.D. DATA: The serial number was located on the left-hand hinge pillar. The vehicle identification indicated the model as follows: Wagoneer: J9( )(15)N( )00001 and up. Cherokee: J9( )(model)N( )00001 and up. Vehicle identification was as follows: 15: Four-door Wagoneer station wagon, 16: Cherokee station wagon, 17: Cherokee wide-wheel station wagon, 18: Cherokee four-door station wagon.

Model Number	Body Type	Factory Price	GVW	Shipping Weight	Prod. Total
Wagoneer Station Wagon V-8					
15	4-dr.	$9065	6200	4034	22,566*
15	4-dr. Limited	$12,485	6200	4181	—

* Includes all Wagoneer models.

Model Number	Body Type	Factory Price	GVW	Shipping Weight	Prod. Total
Cherokee Station Wagon 6-cyl.					
16	2-dr.	$7328	6200	3653	27,568*
17	Wide-wheel 2-dr.	$7671	6200	3774	—
18	4-dr.	$7441	6200	3761	—

* Includes all Cherokee models.

STANDARD ENGINE: Cherokee: Not available for California. Standard for California is 360 V-8 with 2-bbl. carburetor, with automatic transmission and Quadra-Trac, requires power steering. Engine Type: OHV, In-line-6. Cast iron block and cylinder head. Bore x Stroke: 3.75 in. x 3.90 in. Lifters: Hydraulic. Number of main bearings-7. Fuel Induction: 2-bbl. carburetor. Compression Ratio: 8.0:1. Displacement: 258 cu. in. (4.22 liters). Horsepower: Net: 114 @ 3200 rpm. Torque: Net: 210 lb.-ft. @ 2000 rpm. Oil refill capacity: 5 qt. with filter change. Fuel Requirements: Unleaded.

STANDARD ENGINE: Wagoneer, optional Cherokee: Type: OHV, V-8. Cast iron block and cylinder head. Bore x Stroke: 4.08 in. x 3.44 in. Lifters: Hydraulic. Number of main bearings-5. Fuel Induction: 2-bbl. carburetor. Compression Ratio: 8.25:1. Displacement: 360 cu. in. (5.89 liters). Horsepower: Net: 155 @ 3200 rpm. Torque: Net: 280 lb.-ft. @ 1500 rpm. Oil refill capacity: 5 qt. with filter change. Fuel Requirements: Unleaded.

CHASSIS FEATURES: Separate body and frame. Box section side rails, deep web frame, wide flange, lightweight pressed steel with five cross members.

SUSPENSION AND RUNNING GEAR: Front Suspension: 5-leaf semi-elliptical springs front and rear, Front: 47 in. x 2.5 in. Rear: 52 in. x 2.5 in. Deflection rate: Front: 6-cyl.: 195 lb./in.; V-8: 215 lb./in. Hydraulic double-action shock absorbers. Optional: Cherokee and Wagoneer: Extra-Duty Suspension Package, front and rear heavy-duty shock absorbers, Smooth-Ride Suspension (tuned for off-road usage on Cherokee), Front stabilizer bar. Rear Suspension: 5-leaf semi-elliptical, asymmetrical design. Deflection rate: 165 lb./in. Hydraulic double-action shock absorbers. Optional: Heavy-duty with deflection rate of 165-245 lb./in. Front Axle Type and Capacity: Wagoneer & Cherokee: Dana 44, full-floating, hypoid, open end, 3215 lb. rating. Rear Axle Type and Capacity: Wagoneer & Cherokee: Dana 44, semi-floating, 3215 lb. rating. Optional: None. Final Drive Ratio: All engines 3.54:1, Optional: 3.07:1. Transfer Case: Cherokee standard transmission models: Dana 20: ratios: 2.03:1, 1.00:1. Standard for Wagoneer and optional for Cherokee: Quadra Trac (with V-8 engine and Turbo Hydra-Matic only): Standard 1.00:1. Optional: 2.57:1 ratio in addition to the standard 1.0:1 ratio. Brakes: Type: Wagoneer and Cherokee: Hydraulic, front discs and rear drums. Cherokee: Hydraulic drums front and rear. Dimensions: Wagoneer and Cherokee: Front: 12.0 in. dia. disc. Rear: 11.0 in. x 2.00 in. drums. Total brake swept area: 376 sq. in. Wheels: Wagoneer and Cherokee: 15 x 6, disc type, full-drop center 6-stud on 5.5 in. circle. Wide-wheel Cherokee model: 15 x 8, 5.5 circle white painted spoke steel. 15 x 7 6-bolt 5.5 in. circle aluminum wheels included in Cherokee S Package. 15 x 7 6-bolt on 5.5 in. circle forged aluminum wheels optional for Wagoneer. Tires: Wagoneer & Cherokee: H78 x 15B black sidewall polyester Highway Cruiser (unbelted). Wide-wheel Cherokee model: L78-15 black sidewall fiberglass Mud and Snow. Optional: Wagoneer & Cherokee (not including wide-wheel model): H78 x 15B white sidewall polyester Highway Cruise (unbelted), H78x 15 white or black sidewall Town & Country, H78 x 15 black sidewall Viva with two fiberglass cord belts, P225/756R15 white sidewall Tiempo double steel belted radial, HR78 x 15 white sidewall American Eagle with two Flexten cord belts (standard for Wagoneer Limited), HR78 x 15 white sidewall F32 All-Weather radials. Wide-wheel Cherokee: 10 x 15 OWL Tracker All-Terrain, All-Weather. Steering: Wagoneer: Power Saginaw recirculating ball type. Ratio: 20/16:1. Turns Lock-to-Lock: 4.0. Turning Circle: Wagoneer, Cherokee model 16 & 18: 37.7 ft.; model 17: 39.4 ft. Cherokee: Saginaw recirculating ball. Ratio: 24: 1. Turns Lock-to-Lock: 4.0. Optional: Power Saginaw recirculating ball type. Required with combination of 258 engine and air conditioning. Ratio: 20/16:1. Turns Lock-to-Lock: 4.0. Turning Circle: 38.4 ft. Standard Transmission: Wagoneer: Turbo Hydra-Matic 3-spd. automatic. Ratios: 2.48:1, 1.48:1, 1.0:1. Optional: None. Cherokee: 3-speed all-synchromesh manual. Transmission ratios: 3.00:1, 1.83:1, 1.00:1. Optional: Turbo Hydra-Matic 3-spd. automatic. Ratios: 2.48:1, 1.48:1, 1.0:1. Reverse: 2.08:1. 4-spd. manual (synchromesh on top three gears). Ratios: 6.32:1, 3.09:1, 1.68:1, 1.0:1. Clutch: Cherokee: Single dry plate. Clutch diameter: 10.5 in. dia. (6-cyl.); 11.0 in. (V-8). Total lining area: 107 sq. in. (6-cyl.), 112 sq. in. (V-8). Optional: None.

VEHICLE DIMENSIONS: Wagoneer & Cherokee (except as noted) Wheelbase: 109 in. Overall Length: 183.70 in. Front/Rear Tread: Wagoneer: 59.4/57.8 in. Cherokee: 59.2/57.8 in. Cherokee S: 59.9/58.5 in. Cherokee Chief: 65.4/62.3 in. Overall Height: Wagoneer: 66.7 in. Cherokee: 66.9 in. Cherokee Chief: 67.6 in. Width: 75.6 in. Cherokee Chief: 78.9 in. Front/Rear Overhang: 27.0 in./43.0 in. Tailgate: Width and Height: 57.5 in. x 26.5 in. Approach/Departure Degrees: 28/21. Ground Clearance: All models except Cherokee model 17: 7.7 in.; model 17: 8.6 in. Cherokee Chief: Front axle: 9.0 in. Rear axle: 9.0 in. Oil pan: 18.3 in. Transfer case: 13.3 in. Load space: With rear seat in position: 39 in. x 44 in. x 39.0 in. With rear seat folded or removed: 58 in. x 44 in. x 39.0 in. Maximum capacity: 95.1 cu. ft. (with rear seat removed). Front headroom: 38.0 in. Front legroom: 38.8 in. Front shoulder room: 60.1 in. Front hip room: 60.5 in. Rear headroom: Wagoneer: 37.2 in. Cherokee: 38.0 in. Rear legroom: Wagoneer: 38.25 in. Cherokee: 37.0 in. Rear hip room: Wagoneer: 60.6 in. Cherokee: 60.9 in. Pedal to seat back (max.): 41.5 in. Steering wheel to seat back (max.): 18.5 in. Seat to ground: 31.5 in.

CAPACITIES: Fuel Tank: 21.5 gal. Coolant System: 6-cyl.: 10.5 qt. V-8: 15 qt.

ACCOMMODATIONS: Seating Capacity: Six passengers.

INSTRUMENTATION: Oil and Ammeter gauges, speedometer, odometer, warning lights for brake system warning, hazard lights operation, Quadra-Trac lockout indicator (if equipped with Quadra-Trac).

OPTIONS AND PRICES: Cherokee S Package (model 16 and 18): $699. Cherokee Chief Package (model 17): $624. Cherokee Golden Eagle Package: $970. 360 cu. in. V-8: $273 (Cherokee) Turbo Hydra-Matic/Quadra-Trac (high range): $396 (Cherokee). Turbo Hydra-Matic/Quadra-Trac (low/high range): $549 (price for Cherokee). Four-speed manual transmission: $165. Free-wheeling front hubs (Cherokee only): $105. Limited slip rear differential: $85. Bucket seats with armrests: $48 (Cherokee). Convenience Group. Includes remote control left exterior rearview mirror, electric clock, lights-on buzzer and intermittent windshield wipers: $83. Air conditioning: $586. Power steering: $226 (Cherokee). Power tailgate window: $73. Tinted glass: $51. Roof rack: $100. Fuel tank skid plate: $69. Tilt steering wheel: $76. Cruise control: $105. AM/FM stereo radio: $241. AM/FM/CB stereo radio with tape player: $367. Heavy-duty 70 amp battery: $38. Carpeted and insulated cargo floor area: $74. Front stabilizer bar: $31. Light Group: $69. Front bumper guards: $25. Floor mats: $19. Additional Wagoneer options: Two-tone paint. Leather-wrapped Sport steering wheel. Woodgrain body side panels. Bucket seats with center cushion (Wagoneer). Aluminum wheels. Dual low profile exterior mirrors. Inside spare tire mount. Heavy-duty cooling system. Extra-Duty Suspension Package. Smooth-Ride suspension. Heavy-duty front and rear shock absorbers. Front stabilizer bar. Heavy-duty 70 amp battery. Heavy-duty 63 amp alternator. Cold Climate Group. Included heavy-duty battery, heavy-duty alternator and engine block heater. Front bumper guards. Brush guard. Carpeted cargo floor and insulation. Protective floor mats. Side scuff moldings with woodgrain inserts. Snow Boss Package. Trailer Towing Package. Bucket seats in fabric or vinyl (four-door Cherokee). Flipper rear quarter vent windows (Cherokee). Bronze-tone tinted glass for flipper windows (Cherokee).

HISTORICAL FOOTNOTES: In late 1979 when sales began to drop off due to external economic conditions, output of the Cherokee and Wagoneer at the main Jeep plant in Toledo was reduced in July.

1980 WAGONEER & CHEROKEE

Numerous changes, intended to improve both fuel economy and performance highlighted the Cherokee and Wagoneer lines for 1980. Replacing both the standard Borg-Warner 3-speed transmission and optional 4-speed transmission with their cast iron cases was an all-synchromesh 4-speed Tremec model T-176 with an all-aluminum case. Joined to this transmission was a New Process 208 part-time transfer case in place of the Dana 20 unit previously used. This 2-speed case could also be used with an automatic transmission which for 1980 was a Chrysler TorqueFlite unit. This move wasn't greeted with overwhelming enthusiasm by Jeep enthusiasts. But in TorqueFlite's favor was its more efficient design and lighter weight. For the first time in seven years, the Wagoneer was, in 1980, offered with either a full or part-time four-wheel drive system. A new Quadra-Trac system had a viscous coupling limited slip differential in place of the cone-clutch friction system used in 1979. In 1980 a low range was an integral part of Quadra-Trac.

The Wagoneer was also available with either the new Quadra-Trac or the new part-time four-wheel drive system. Automatic transmission and Quadra-Trac were standard on all Wagoneers, but the 258 cu. in. 6-cyl. engine was offered as a delete option for the Wagoneer with either 4-speed manual transmission, automatic transmission, part-time four-wheel drive, or Quadra-Trac. The last time a 6-cylinder Wagoneer had been available had been 1973. Fuel economy was improved by the use of a new Fuel Feedback System (FFB) in which the air/fuel mixture was maintained at a constant 14.7:1.

1980 Jeep Cherokee Laredo

Beyond these significant developments the 1980 Wagoneers were offered with several new options including a pop-up sun roof and a cassette tape/AM/FM radio combination. The Wagoneer Limited had a new quartz electronic digital clock and new style aluminum wheels. Additional features of the Limited Option Package consisted of tinted glass, nerf strips, cruise control, air conditioning, tilt steering wheel, Convenience Group, power tailgate window, extra-quiet insulation, Visibility Group, AM/FM/CB or AM/FM/8-track tape player, power windows and door locks, front and rear bumper guards, protective floor mats, full body side and tailgate woodgrain treatment or two-tone paint version, special roof rack, bright drip rail overlay, Limited nameplates, special 15 x 7 in. forged aluminum wheels, P225/75R15 Goodyear American Eagle Flexten radial white sidewall tires, special interior trim with leather and corduroy bucket seats and center armrest, Cara vinyl door trim panel, fully carpeted passenger compartment and cargo area, leather-wrapped steering wheel, lower instrument panel woodgrain overlay, armrest overlays with woodgrain insert, woodgrained door garnish molding overlays, and Limited nameplate on instrument panel. All Wagoneers now were fitted with the previously optional front stabilizer bar as standard equipment.

The 1980 Cherokee had a number of important running gear changes. As standard equipment Cherokees with the part-time four-wheel drive system had manual free-wheeling front hubs. Used on all Cherokees was a new propeller shaft that was in a direct line with the engine crankshaft rather than being offset as on older models. Included in the base price for V-8 or automatic transmission equipped models was a front stabilizer bar and power steering. Both of these had previously been optional. Deflection rates for the Cherokee's front and rear springs were unchanged for 1980.

A small number of changes were made in the $784 S Package including an Indian head medallion, new "High Line" door and rear quarter trim panels and print strip vinyl front bucket seats.

The Chief Package, available only for the wide-wheel model 17 Cherokee retailed for $799. It contained all S Package features plus upper body 2-tone paint, lower body blackout striping with Cherokee Chief lettering, black and chrome grille and color-keyed carpeting. Also continued for 1980 was the Golden Eagle Package.

The Cherokee's version of the new top-of-the-line. $1600, Laredo Package (available only for the wide-wheel model) consisted of all S features plus bright drip moldings, special painted hubcaps, 15 x 8 chrome styled wheels, 10R15 Goodyear Wrangler radial tires, black and chrome grille, dual exterior remote control mirrors, full interior carpeting, special vinyl bucket seats with front folding seat backs, special door trim panels, door pullstraps, leather-wrapped steering wheel, center armrest, instrument, and glove box striping, Extra-Quiet Insulation Package, Convenience Group, nerf bars and Visibility Group.

Among the new Cherokee options available for 1980 were power window and door locks, quartz digital clock and a premium audio system with a power amplifier and upgraded high fidelity speakers.

The 1980 color selection was as follows: Smoke grey metallic (not available for Laredo, Limited or Golden Eagle models), dark brown metallic (not available for Cherokee Chief), Saxon yellow (not available for Golden Eagle), navy blue (not available for Cherokee Chief and Golden Eagle), cardinal red (not available for Laredo, Limited or Golden Eagle models), olympic white, caramel (not available for Laredo or Limited models), cameo tan, alpaca brown metallic (not available for Laredo), dark green metallic (not available for Laredo), medium teal blue (not available for Laredo, Limited or Golden Eagle models), russet red metallic (not available for Laredo), bordeaux metallic (not available for Cherokee Chief), and classic black (not available for Cherokee Chief). The only color carried over from 1979 was classic black.

1980 Jeep Wagoneer Limited

I.D. DATA: The serial number was located on the left-hand hinge pillar. The vehicle identification indicated the model as follows: Wagoneer: J0( )15NC00001 and up. Cherokee: J0( )(model)N( )00001 and up. Vehicle identification was as follows: 15: Four-door Wagoneer station wagon, 16: Cherokee station wagon, 17: Cherokee wide-wheel station wagon, 18: Cherokee four-door station wagon.

Model Number	Body Type	Factory Price	GVW	Shipping Weight	Prod. Total
Wagoneer Station Wagon V-8					
15	4-dr.	$9732	6200	3964	10,402 *
15	4-dr. Limited	$13,653	6200	4111	—

* Includes all Wagoneer models.

Model Number	Body Type	Factory Price	GVW	Shipping Weight	Prod. Total
Cherokee Station Wagon 6-cyl.					
16	2-dr.	$8180	6200	3780	11,490 *
17	Wide-wheel 2-dr.	$8823	6200	3868	—
18	4-dr.	$8380	6200	3849	—

* Includes all Cherokee models

STANDARD ENGINE: Cherokee: Not available for California. Standard for California is 360 V-8 with 2-bbl. carburetor, with automatic transmission and Quadra-Trac, requires power steering. Engine Type: OHV, In-line-6. Cast iron block and cylinder head. Bore x Stroke: 3.75 in. x 3.90 in. Lifters: Hydraulic. Number of main bearings-7. Fuel Induction: 2-bbl. carburetor. Compression Ratio: 8.3:1. Displacement: 258 cu. in. (4.22 liters). Horsepower: Net: 118 @ 3200 rpm. Torque: Net: 205 lb.-ft. @ 1800 rpm. Oil refill capacity: 5 qt. with filter change. Fuel Requirements: Unleaded.

STANDARD ENGINE: Wagoneer, optional Cherokee: Engine Type: OHV, V-8. Cast iron block and cylinder head. Bore x Stroke: 4.08 in. x 3.44 in. Lifters: Hydraulic. Number of main bearings-5. Fuel Induction: 2-bbl. carburetor. Compression Ratio: 8.25:1. Displacement: 360 cu. in. (5.89 liters). Horsepower: Net: 160 @ 3400 rpm. Torque: Net: 280 lb.-ft. @ 1500 rpm. Oil refill capacity: 5 qt. with filter change. Fuel Requirements: Unleaded.

CHASSIS FEATURES: Separate body and frame. Box section side rails, deep web frame, wide flange, lightweight pressed steel with five cross members.

SUSPENSION AND RUNNING GEAR: Front Suspension: Cherokee: 5-leaf semi-elliptical springs 47 in. x 2.5 in. Rear: 52 in. x 2.5 in. Deflection rate: 215 lb./in.; Wagoneer: 6-leaf semi-elliptical springs. Deflection rate: 210 lb./in. Hydraulic double-action shock absorbers. Optional: Cherokee and Wagoneer: Extra-Duty Suspension Package, Front and rear heavy-duty shock absorbers, Smooth-Ride suspension (tuned for off-road usage on Cherokee), Front stabilizer bar. Rear suspension: Cherokee and Wagoneer: 5-leaf semi-elliptical, asymmetrical design. Deflection rate: 165 lb./in. Hydraulic double-action shock absorbers. Optional: 165/265 lb./in. Front Axle Type and Capacity: Wagoneer & Cherokee: Dana 44, full-floating, hypoid, open end, 3200 lb. rating. Rear Axle Type and Capacity: Wagoneer & Cherokee: Dana 44, semi-floating, 3200 lb. rating. Optional: None. Final Drive Ratio: Cherokee: 3.31:1 for both the 6-cylinder and V-8 engines with manual transmission. The combination of a V-8 and automatic transmission used a 2.73:1 ratio. Wide-wheel model 17 V-8: 3.31:1 ratio. Wagoneer: 2.73:1. Transfer Case: Cherokee standard transmission models: New Process 208 part-time transfer case. Ratios: 2.61:1, 1.00:1. Standard for Wagoneer and optional for Cherokee: Quadra Trac with New Process 219 transfer case. Ratios: 2.60:1, 1.00:1. Brakes: Type: Wagoneer and Cherokee: Hydraulic, front discs and rear drums. Dimensions: Wagoneer and Cherokee: Front: 12.0 in. dia. disc. Rear: 11.0 in. x 2.00 in. drums. Total brake swept area: 376 sq. in. Wheels: Wagoneer and Cherokee: 15 x 6, disc type, full-drop center 6-stud on 5.5 in. circle. Wide-wheel Cherokee model: 15 x 8, 5.5 circle white painted spoke steel. 15 x 7 6-bolt 5.5 in. circle aluminum wheels included in Cherokee S Package. 15 x 7 6-bolt on 5.5 in. circle forged aluminum wheels optional for Wagoneer. Tires: Wagoneer & Cherokee: H78 x 15B black sidewall polyester Highway Cruiser 78 (unbelted). Wide-wheel Cherokee model: L78-15 black sidewall fiberglass Mud and Snow. Optional: Wagoneer & Cherokee (not including wide-wheel model): H78 x 15B white sidewall polyester Highway Cruise (unbelted), H78x 15 white or black sidewall Town & Country, H78 x 15 black sidewall Viva with two fiberglass cord belts, P225/756R15 white sidewall Tiempo double steel belted radial, HR78 x 15 white sidewall American Eagle with two Flexten cord belts (standard for

Wagoneer Limited), HR78 x 15 white sidewall F32 All-Weather radials. Wide-wheel Cherokee: 10 x 15 OWL Tracker All-Terrain, All-Weather. Steering: Wagoneer: Power Saginaw recirculating ball type. Ratio: 20/16:1. Turns Lock-to-Lock: 4.0. Turning Circle: Wagoneer, Cherokee model 16 & 18: 37.7 ft.; model 17: 39.4 ft. Cherokee: Saginaw recirculating ball. Ratio: 24:1. Turns Lock-to-Lock: 4.0. Optional: Power Saginaw recirculating ball type. Required with combination of 258 engine and air conditioning. Standard for Wagoneer. Ratio: 13/16:1. Turns Lock-to-Lock: 4.0. Standard Transmission: Wagoneer: Chrysler TorqueFlite A-727, 3-spd. automatic. Ratios: 2.45:1, 1.45:1, 1.0:1. Cherokee: All-synchromesh 4-speed Tremec model T-176. Cherokee: All-synchromesh 4-speed Tremec model T-176. Transmission ratios: 3.52:1, 2.27:1, 1.46:1, 1.00:1. Optional: Chrysler TorqueFlite A-727, 3-spd. automatic. Ratios: 2.45:1, 1.45:1, 1.0:1. Clutch: Cherokee: Single dry plate. Clutch diameter: 11.0 Total lining area: 112 sq. in. Optional: None.

VEHICLE DIMENSIONS: Wagoneer & Cherokee (except as noted) Wheelbase: 108.7 in. Overall Length: 183.50 in. Front/Rear Tread: Wagoneer: 59.4/57.8 in. Cherokee model 16 & 18: 59.4/57.8 in. Model 17: 65.4/62.3 in. Overall Height: Wagoneer: 66.7 in. Cherokee model 16 & 18: 66.9 in. Model 17: 67.6 in. Width: All models except Cherokee model 17: 75.6 in. Cherokee model 17: 78.9 in. Front/Rear Overhang: 27.9 in./44.9 in. Tailgate: Width and Height: 54.9 in. x 26.5 in. Approach/Departure Degrees: 30/21. Ground Clearance: Cherokee: Front axle: 8.25 in. Rear axle: 8.25 in. Oil pan: 15.25 in. Transfer case: 13.0 in. Load space: With rear seat in position: 45.75 in. x 43.1 in. x 39.0 in. With rear seat folded: 66.25 in. x 43.1 in. x 39.0 in. With rear seat removed: 81.25 in. x 43.1 in. x 39.0 in. Maximum capacity: 95.1 cu. ft. (with rear seat removed). Front headroom: 38.0 in. Front legroom: 38.8 in. Front shoulder room: 58.3 in. Front hip room: 60.5 in. Rear headroom: 37.2 in. Rear legroom: Wagoneer: 38.25 in. Cherokee: 37.0 in. Rear shoulder room: 58.3 in. Rear hip room: Wagoneer: 60.6 in. Cherokee: 60.9 in. Pedal to seat back (max.): 41.5 in. Steering wheel to seat back (max.): 18.5 in. Seat to ground: 31.5 in.

CAPACITIES: Fuel Tank: 21.3 gal. with standard skid plate. Coolant System: 6-cyl.: 10.5 qt. V-8: 15 qt.

ACCOMMODATIONS: Seating Capacity: Six passengers.

INSTRUMENTATION: Oil pressure, engine coolant temperature and voltmeter gauges, speedometer, odometer, warning lights for brake system warning, hazard lights operation, Quadra-Trac lockout indicator (if equipped with Quadra-Trac).

OPTIONS AND PRICES: Power steering: $233 (Cherokee). Automatic transmission: $333. (Cherokee). Limited slip rear differential (not available for Quadra-Trac): $120. AM radio. Premium Sound Group. Includes power amplifier and higher fidelity speakers: $95. AM/FM stereo radio: $245. AM/FM stereo with tape player: $355. AM/FM stereo CB radio: $495. Moon roof: $300. S Package (Cherokee models 16 and 17): $784. Cherokee Chief Package: $799. Cherokee Laredo Package: $1600. 360 cu. in. V-8: $420. Heavy-duty battery: $40. Rear window defroster: $102. Air conditioning: $614. Power tailgate window: $786. Luggage rack. Inside spare tire mount and cover. Visibility Group. Includes dual remote control mirrors, and intermittent windshield wipers. Convenience Group. Digital clock: $52. Convenience Group. Includes lights-on buzzer, digital clock, and engine compartment light. Light Group for Cherokee. Includes cargo area light, glove box light, ashtray light, map/dome light, and lighted visor vanity mirror. Full wheelcovers. Carpeted passenger and cargo areas. Soft-Feel steering wheel. Leather-wrapped Sport steering wheel. Painted styled steel wheels. Painted or chrome rear step bumper, two-tone paint. Scuff molding. Heavy-duty cooling system. Extra-Duty Suspension Package: $137. Heavy-duty front and rear shock absorbers: $28. Heavy-duty battery. Heavy-duty alternator. Cold Climate Group. Includes heavy-duty alternator and battery, and engine block heater. Snow Boss Package (not available for Wagoneer Limited). Trailer Towing Packages.

HISTORICAL FOOTNOTES: The 1980 models were introduced in the fall of 1979.

1981 WAGONEER & CHEROKEE

The Wagoneer line was expanded to include three levels: Custom, Brougham and Limited for 1981. Both the Cherokee and the Wagoneer (as well as the J trucks) had a front air dam beneath the front bumper that by funneling air downward, reduced wind resistance. Redesigned front and rear springs reduced the height of both the Wagoneer and Cherokee. The Cherokee and Wagoneer had a new front brake system with drag-free calipers without the constant brake pad-rotor contact of earlier versions. This system also had many lighter weight parts, among them a quick-take-up master cylinder with aluminum body and glass-filled nylon reservoir, new power booster and proportioning valve.

The 360 cu. in. V-8 became optional for the 1981 Wagoneer. Replacing it as the standard powerplant was the 258 cu. in. 6-cylinder engine which was available in combination with either a 4-speed manual or 3-speed automatic transmission. This engine was redesigned for substantially better fuel economy than its predecessor, improved reliability and lower levels of maintenance and noise.

A significant weight reduction of 90 pounds for the 258 engine was achieved through the redesign of its primary componentry and the use of alternate materials including aluminum as well as adoption of an engine block 30 pounds lighter than its 1980 model counterpart. This weight reduction was achieved by reducing the wall thickness, web reduction and miscellaneous flange reductions. The redesigned cylinder head was 12 pounds lighter than the 1980 version. A straighter and reshaped rocker cover flange eliminated excess cast iron and allowed for a simpler geometric shape for the application of RTV sealer to the rocker arm. Contributing a net weight reduction of two pounds was a redesigned rocker cover fabricated of glass-filled nylon in place of the older A stamped steel cover. Aluminum housings, instead of cast iron, were used for the oil pump and water pump. The exhaust manifold was now separated from the intake manifold and did not have a heat valve. The intake manifold was also completely redesigned and was now aluminum rather than cast iron. It now included an electrically heated warm-up device and a water heated circuit to replace the exhaust heat valve. Use of a new cam with an altered profile provided a lower idle speed and increased low speed torque. A new idle speed control system contributed to a reduction in idle speed without compromise to idle quality. Whereas the older engine weighed 535 lbs, its successor reported in at only 445 lbs. The old multi-belt system was replaced by a single, six groove serpentine drive beltline.

1981 Jeep Cherokee

All 258 cu. in. engines had a new emissions control system. This advance wasn't at the expense of power output. A new cam with slightly higher lift was also used. Unlike 1980 when the 6-cylinder engine wasn't available in California, the 1981 version was the only engine installed in California bound Cherokees and Wagoneers. The California engines used a closed-loop pollution control with a microprocessor that sampled the exhaust gases and made appropriate adjustments to the engine's air/fuel mixture.

A new lockup converter for the TorqueFlite automatic transmission both improved fuel economy and reduced engine wear as well as lowering engine temperature. This was accomplished by a lessening of the friction that occurred in a conventional torque converter. With the new lockup torque converter, a clutch within the transmission engaged automatically when the output shaft reached approximately 1,100 rpm. When this took place the engine speed and transmission output shaft speed were the same, enabling smoother, more efficient transfer of engine power to the drivetrain as well as less engine wear, a lower transmission operating temperature and a marginal improvement in fuel economy.

Both the Wagoneer and Cherokee had lower numerical axle ratios and higher first gear ratios for their manual transmissions.

Standard equipment for the Cherokee consisted of front ashtray, front and rear armrests, cigarette lighter, color-keyed vinyl front and rear floor area, vinyl cargo area mat, gauges for oil, engine coolant temperature, and fuel level, 12 in. inside day/night mirror, padded instrument panel, padded sun visors, front bucket seats, rear bench seat, electric windshield washers and 2-speed wipers, chrome plated aluminum bumpers, outside left side mirror, bright moldings for vent window and windshield and tailgate, front air dam, 63 amp alternator, 55-380 battery, front stabilizer bar, new inside hood release, power steering, and wheelcovers (base two-door model).

Standard Wagoneer equipment consisted of these items: Front and rear ashtray, front and rear armrests, carpeting for front and rear seat floor area and wheelhousing, gauges for oil, voltmeter, engine coolant temperature, and fuel level, glove box lock, heater and defroster, electric windshield washers and 2-speed wipers, chrome plated aluminum bumpers, outside left side mirror, bright moldings for vent window and windshield with new windshield upper moldings, end cap and drip rails, front air dam, 63 amp alternator, 55-380 battery, front stabilizer bar, new inside hood release, and power steering.

The seats of the Custom Wagoneer were trimmed in a Cara grain vinyl in black, blue or beige.

The use of one and two-sided galvanized steel in the manufacture of the Wagoneer and Cherokee was expanded for 1981. One-side galvanized steel was now used for the top front-cowl and inner panels, gussets running from rocker panels to cowl side panels, body rear lower pillars and reinforcements, support and extension toe risers and front floor seat belt anchor reinforcements. The tailgate inner panel lower supports on Wagoneers and Cherokees also utilized one-side galvanized, while two-side galvanized steel was used for extension panels between the rear wheelhousings and quarter panels. Hot wax was also sprayed on the inside of doors, tailgates and rear quarter panels of the Wagoneer and Cherokee bodies. An aluminum wax was sprayed inside the rocker panels.

The new Wagoneer Brougham model had all the appointments and equipment of the custom plus a Coventry Check fabric upholstery for the standard bench or optional bucket seats. Also available was a Deluxe grain vinyl trim. Both were offered in black, blue, beige or nutmeg. Other Brougham's appointments included premium door trim panels, a soft headliner and woodgrain trim for the instrument cluster and horn cover. Exterior identification included bright door and quarter window frames, lower tailgate moldings, and a thin body side scuff molding with a narrow woodgrain insert. The custom used a wider body side trim. All 1981 Wagoneers had standard P225/75R15 Goodyear Viva radial tires. The Brougham's were installed on 15 x 7 in.chrome styled wheels.

Included in the Brougham's base equipment price of $11,434, which was $970 above that of the $10,464 Custom, was extra-quiet insulation, Convenience Group (consisting of underhood light, lights-on buzzer and digital clock), Light Group (consisting of interior cargo light and tailgate switch, lighted visor vanity mirror, courtesy, map/dome, glove box and ashtray lights), a roof rack, floor mats and a power tailgate window.

1981 Jeep Wagoneer

The Wagoneer Limited, priced at $15,164 had a long list of standard features, including those of the Brougham. Other items consisted of bucket seats with leather/cord trim, center armrest, unique door panels in either nutmeg or beige, leather-wrapped steering wheel, extra thick 22 oz. carpeting in the seating area (20 oz. carpeting was used in the cargo area with insulation), retractable cargo cover and woodgrain trim on the lower instrument panel. The Limited's wide woodgrain side and rear trim was set off with wide moldings. The roof rack had woodgrain inserts, bright drip rails were used as were 15 x 7 in. forged aluminum wheels and Limited nameplates.

Additional technical and convenience features of the Limited included Quadra-Trac, automatic transmission, air conditioning, tinted glass, power windows/door locks, power tailgate window, cruise control, AM/FM stereo radio, premium audio system, Convenience Group, Visibility Group, bumper guard and nerf strips, floor mats, extra-quiet insulation and power six-way driver and passenger seats.

The Cherokee's standard engine was the new lighter weight 258 cu. in. engine. Exterior changes for 1981 began with a new lightweight plastic grille. Both the S and Golden Eagle Packages were dropped for 1981. The Chief Package was now standard for the four-door Cherokee. The four-door version used 15 x 7 white styled wheels and P235/75R Wrangler steel radial tires instead of the 15 x 8 wheels and 10-15 Tracker A/T OWL tires found on the wide-wheel two-door. Slightly revised exterior graphics for the Chief were used. The circular Indian Chief emblem previously found just ahead of the front doors was no longer used. The rear panel tape strip now angled upward and over the rear wheel cutout.

The Laredo Package was offered for both the wide-wheel two-door and four-door Cherokees. The two-door used 15 x 8 wheels and 10R15 Wrangler steel belted radial tires while the four-door had 15 x 7 wheels and P235/75R Wrangler tires. The four-door model also lacked the wide axle and flared wheel wells found on the two-door version. A new double shock absorber option was also exclusive to the wide-wheel models.

The following colors were offered for 1981: Cameo tan, vintage red metallic, classic black, autumn gold, moonlight blue, steel grey metallic, dark brown metallic, deep maroon metallic, olympic white, copper brown metallic, oriental red, Montana blue, sherwood green metallic, and chestnut brown metallic.

I.D. DATA: The serial number was located on the left-hand hinge pillar. The V.I.N. had 17 symbols. The first three entries identified the manufacturer, make and type of vehicle. The fourth unit, a letter, designated the engine. The fifth character, a letter, identified the transmission. The sixth and seventh characters identified the series and body style. The eighth character identified the GVW rating. Next followed a check digit. The eleventh character was the manufacturing plant identification. The final six digits were the sequential production number. The vehicle identification indicated the model as follows: Wagoneer: 1J( )C( )15N( )BT00001 and up. Cherokee: 1J( )C(model)( )( )BT00001 and up. Vehicle identification was as follows: 15: Four-door Wagoneer station wagon, 16: Cherokee station wagon, 17: Cherokee wide-wheel station wagon, 18: Cherokee four-door station wagon.

Model Number	Body Type	Factory Price	GVW	Shipping Weight	Prod. Total
Wagoneer Station Wagon 6-cyl.					
15	4-dr.	$10,464	6200	3779	12,554*
15	4-dr. Limited	$15,164	6200	—	—

* Includes all Wagoneer models.

Model Number	Body Type	Factory Price	GVW	Shipping Weight	Prod. Total
Cherokee Station Wagon 6-cyl.					
16	2-dr.	$9574	6200	3699	5801*
17	Wide-wheel 2-dr.	$9837	6200	3748	—
18	4-dr. Chief	$10,722	6200	3822	—

* Includes all Cherokee models.

STANDARD ENGINE: Wagoneer and Cherokee: Not available for California. Standard for California is 360 V-8 with 2-bbl. carburetor, with automatic transmission and Quadra-Trac, requires power steering. Engine Type: OHV, In-line-6. Cast iron block and cylinder head. Bore x Stroke: 3.75 in. x 3.90 in. Lifters: Hydraulic. Number of main bearings-7. Fuel Induction: 2-bbl. carburetor. Compression Ratio: 8.0:1. Displacement: 258 cu. in. (4.22 liters). Horsepower: Net: 110 @ 3500 rpm. Torque: Net: 195 lb.-ft. @ 2000 rpm. Oil refill capacity: 5 qt. with filter change. Fuel Requirements: Unleaded.

OPTIONAL ENGINE: Wagoneer and Cherokee: Not available for California. Type: OHV, V-8. Cast iron block and cylinder head. Bore x Stroke: 4.08 in. x 3.44 in. Lifters: Hydraulic. Number of main bearings-5. Fuel Induction: 2-bbl. carburetor. Compression Ratio: 8.25:1. Displacement: 360 cu. in. (5.89 liters). Horsepower: Net: 129 @ 3700 rpm. Torque: Net: 245 lb.-ft. @ 1600 rpm. Oil refill capacity: 5 qt. with filter change. Fuel Requirements: Unleaded.

CHASSIS FEATURES: Separate body and frame. Box section side rails, deep web frame, wide flange, lightweight pressed steel with five cross members.

SUSPENSION AND RUNNING GEAR: Front Suspension: Cherokee: 5-leaf semi-elliptical springs 47 in. x 2.5 in. Rear: 52 in. x 2.5 in. Deflection rate: 215 lb./in.; Wagoneer: 6-leaf semi-elliptical springs. Deflection rate: 210 lb./in. Hydraulic double-action shock absorbers. Optional: Cherokee and Wagoneer: Extra-Duty Suspension Package, front and rear heavy-duty shock absorbers, Smooth-Ride Suspension (tuned for off-road usage on Cherokee), Front stabilizer bar. Rear Suspension: Cherokee and Wagoneer: 5-leaf semi-elliptical, asymmetrical design. Deflection rate: 165 lb./in. Hydraulic double-action shock absorbers. Optional: 165/265 lb./in. Front Axle Type and Capacity: Wagoneer & Cherokee: Dana 44, full-floating, hypoid, open end, 3200 lb. rating. Rear Axle Type and Capacity: Wagoneer & Cherokee: Dana 44, semi-floating, 3200 lb. rating. Optional: None. Final Drive Ratio: The Wagoneer with automatic transmission and 6-cylinder engine was available with an optional 3.31:1 axle ratio. The Cherokee's optional 3.31:1 ratio offered for the manual transmission model with the 360 cu. in. V-8 was not available for a similarly equipped Wagoneer. Transfer Case: Cherokee and Wagoneer (except for Wagoneer Limited): New Process 208 part-time transfer case. Ratios: 2.61:1, 1.00:1. Standard for Wagoneer Limited and optional for Cherokee and other Wagoneer models: Quadra Trac with New Process 219 transfer case. Ratios: Brakes: Type: Wagoneer and Cherokee: Hydraulic, front discs and rear drums. Dimensions: Wagoneer and Cherokee: Front: 12.0 in. dia. discdisc. Rear: 11.0 in. x 2.00 in. drums. Total brake swept area: 376 sq. in. Wheels: Wagoneer and Cherokee: 15 x 6, disc type, full-drop center 6-stud on 5.5 in. circle. Wagoneer Limited: 15 x 7 in. forged aluminum wheels (optional for other Wagoneer models). Wide-wheel Cherokee model: 15 x 7, white painted spoke steel, 5.5 circle on four-door model). 15 x 8 in. white painted spoke steel, 5.5 in. circle on two-door model. Tires: Wagoneer custom: P225/75R15 black sidewall radial. Wagoneer Limited: P225/75R15 white sidewall Arriva steel radials. Cherokee: P225/75R15 black sidewall Goodyear Viva radials; wide-wheel model: P225/75R15 Suburbanite XG Polyglas. Optional: Wagoneer: Tiempo P225/75R15 white sidewall double steel belted radial, Arriva P225/75R15 steel radial, F-32 Flexten HR78 x 15 white sidewall winter radial, Viva P225/75R15 black or white sidewall fiberglass radial. Cherokee: Wrangler 10R-15 outlined white letters steel radial, Tiempo P225/75R15 white sidewall double steel belted radial, Arriva P225/75R15 steel radial, F-32 Flexten HR78 x 15 white sidewall winter radial, Tracker A-T 10-15 outlined white letters wide All-Terrain All-Weather, Suburbanite XG Polyglas L78 x 15 black sidewall, Viva P225/75R15 black or white sidewall fiberglass radial. Steering: Wagoneer and Cherokee: Power Saginaw recirculating ball type. Ratio: 20/16:1. Turns Lock-to-Lock: 4.0. Turning Circle: Wagoneer, Cherokee model 16 & 18: 37.7 ft.; model 17: 39.4 ft. Standard Transmission: Wagoneer Limited (optional for Wagoneer custom and Cherokee): Chrysler TorqueFlite 3-spd. automatic. Ratios: 2.45:1, 1.45:1, 1.0:1. Wagoneer custom and Cherokee: All-synchromesh 4-speed Tremec model T-176. Transmission ratios: 3.52:1, 2.27:1, 1.46:1, 1.00:1. Clutch: Wagoneer and Cherokee: Single dry plate. Clutch diameter: 10.5 in. dia. (6-cyl.); 11.0 in. (V-8). Total lining area: 107 sq. in. (6-cyl.), 112 sq. in. (V-8). Optional: None.

VEHICLE DIMENSIONS: Wagoneer & Cherokee (except as noted): Wheelbase: 108.7 in. Overall Length: 186.40 in. Front/Rear Tread: Wagoneer: 59.4/57.8 in. Cherokee: 59.4/57.8 in. Cherokee two-door wide-wheel: 65.3/62.3 in. Overall Height: Wagoneer: 65.9 in. Cherokee 66.1. Wide-wheel two-door model: 66.8 in. Width: All models except Cherokee two-door wide-wheel: 75.6 in. Cherokee two-door wide-wheel: 78.9 in. Front/Rear Overhang: 31.3 in./46.4 in. Tailgate: Width and Height: 54.9 in. x 26.5 in. Approach/Departure Degrees: 31/21. Ground Clearance: All models except Cherokee wide-wheel: 7.7 in.; wide-wheel: 8.6 in. Load space: With rear seat in position: 39 in. x 44 in. x 39.0 in. With rear seat folded or removed: 58 in. x 44 in. x 39.0 in. Maximum capacity: 95.1 cu. ft. (with rear seat removed). Front headroom: 38.0 in. Front legroom: 41.6 in. Front shoulder room: 58.3 in. Front hip room: 60.5 in. Rear headroom: 37.2 in. Rear legroom: 37.0 in. Rear shoulder room: 58.3 in. Rear hip room: 60.9 in. Pedal to seat back (max.): 41.5 in. Steering wheel to seat back (max.): 18.5 in. Seat to ground: 31.5 in.

CAPACITIES: Fuel Tank: 21.3 gal. with standard skid plate. Coolant System: 6-cyl.: 10.5 qt. V-8: 15 qt.

ACCOMMODATIONS: Seating Capacity: Six passengers.

INSTRUMENTATION: Oil pressure, engine coolant temperature and voltmeter gauges, speedometer, odometer, warning lights for brake system warning, hazard lights operation

OPTIONS AND PRICES: Automatic transmission: $409. AM/FM radio (included with Limited): $224. AM/FM stereo CB: $420. Sun roof: $369. Cruise control: $147. Power sun roof: $1549 (Wagoneer Limited only). Cherokee Chief Package: $879. Cherokee Laredo Package (model17): $1733. Cherokee Laredo Package (model 18): $950. Power seats: $275. 360 cu. in. V-8: $345. Snow Boss Package: $1399. Wagoneer Brougham Package: $970. Power seats: $275. Power 6-way bucket seats: $250. Power tailgate window: $76. Auxiliary automatic transmission oil cooler: $45. Two-tone paint (Wagoneer). Leather-wrapped Sport steering wheel. Tilt steering wheel: $83. Soft-Feel steering wheel for Cherokee (included with Cherokee Chief). Painted styled wheels for Cherokee. Carpeted passenger and cargo areas. Cargo Area cover: $59. Scuff molding. Convenience Group (included with Limited, Brougham and Laredo). Includes underhood light, lights-on buzzer and digital clock. Visibility Group. (included with Limited and Laredo). Includes right and left matching remote outside mirrors, intermittent windshield wipers, halogen headlights. Light Group (included with Limited, Brougham and Laredo). Includes interior cargo light and tailgate switch, courtesy lights, glove box light, ashtray light, map/dome light, and lighted vanity mirror. Tinted glass (included with Limited). Rear window defroster. Vinyl roof (with Sun roof only). Dual front shock absorbers (wide-wheel two-door Cherokee). Inside spare tire mount and cover. Clear lens fog lamps (included with Limited): $70. Premium audio system (included with Limited): $95. Heavy-duty cooling. Extra-duty suspension system. Heavy-duty front and rear shock absorbers. Heavy-duty 70 amp battery: $40. Heavy-duty 70 amp alternator. Cold Climate Group. Front and rear bumper guards (included with Limited). Brush guard. Protective floor mats (included with Limited and Brougham). Trailer Towing Package: $300.

HISTORICAL FOOTNOTES: AMC reported a loss of $160.9 million for 1981.

1982 WAGONEER & CHEROKEE

Except for use of halogen headlights, the availability of an electronically tuned AM/FM cassette radio and the offering of a tilt steering wheel with the manual transmission (previously it was available only with automatic transmission), the Wagoneer line was unchanged for 1982.

Visual changes in the 1982 Cherokee were virtually nonexistent. The most important technical development was the availability of a 5-speed Warner Gear T5 manual transmission. Its fifth gear was an overdrive with either a 0.76:1 or 0.86:1 ratio, depending on the engine and final drive ratio selected. Also new for 1982 was a tilt steering wheel option for Cherokees with manual transmissions. Previously, this feature was offered only on Cherokees with automatic transmission.

1982 Jeep Cherokee Laredo two-door

Basic standard equipment for the Cherokee and Wagoneer included these features: Front air dam, 63 amp alternator, front and rear armrests, bright anodized aluminum bumpers, front cigarette lighter and ashtray, color-keyed vinyl floor covering (Cherokee), front, rear and cargo area carpeting (Cherokee four-door and Wagoneer), lockable glove box, heater and defroster, electronic ignition, inside hood release, 12 in. day/night inside mirror, outside driver side rearview mirror, bright moldings for vent window, windshield and tailgate, padded instrument panel, padded sun visors, front bucket seats and rear bench seat (Cherokee), front and rear bench seat (Wagoneer), skid plates for fuel tank and transfer case, rear fender stone protection (two-door wide-wheel Cherokee), electric windshield washers and 2-speed windshield wipers.

The Chief Package was, as in 1981, standard on the four-door Cherokee and optional for the two-door wide-wheel model. The package included: Upper and lower body blackout treatment and special body side and tailgate striping (this could be deleted or replaced by vinyl upper body side molding), bright drip rails, 15 x 7 in. white styled wheels, P235/75R15 Arriva black sidewall tires (four-door), 10 x 15 Tracker A/T OWL tires (wide-wheel two-door), blackout grille, Sun Valley vinyl front bucket seats and rear bench seat in beige, blue, black or nutmeg (an optional Western weave fabric in beige, blue, black or nutmeg with tri-tone accent straps was also available), matching door and front quarter trim panels, folding driver seat back (wide-wheel two-door), Soft-Feel Sport steering wheel, color-keyed carpeting on floor and wheelhousings, instrument panel cluster overlay, front center armrest, passenger assist handle, and rear ashtray.

The Laredo Package was available for either the four-door Cherokee or the two-door wide-wheel model. It included: Special silver and grey or nutmeg and bronze exterior striping, 15 x 8 in. chrome styled wheels with black hubcaps and 10R15 Goodyear Wrangler radial tires (wide-wheel two-door) or 15 x 7 in. argent styled wheels with bright trim rings and hubcaps and P235/75R15 Arriva black sidewall radial (four-door model), black and silver Laredo nameplates, chrome grille insert, flipper quarter windows with grey or bronze-tone glass, depending on interior (wide-wheel two-door), bright roof drip and door frame moldings, luggage rack, special folding driver and passenger front bucket seats with center armrest and rear bench seat trimmed in a choice of Cara vinyl black and grey, or nutmeg and light nutmeg, or Western weave fabric in black or nutmeg with tri-tone accent straps, black or nutmeg carpeting on floor, wheelhousing and side panels to beltline, leather-wrapped steering wheel, passenger assist handle and door-mounted pull straps, special door trim panels, instrument panel overlay, instrument panel striping, Laredo nameplate for instrument panel, rear seat ashtrays, extra-quiet insulation, Convenience Group, underhood light, lights-on buzzer, digital clock, Light Group, and Visibility Group.

The Custom Wagoneer had the following standard equipment content: Power steering and brakes, 15 x 7 in. P225/75R15 Goodyear Viva tires, full wheelcovers, full width front and rear bench seats trimmed in Cara grain vinyl, full carpeting in passenger and cargo areas, protective cargo area mat, color-keyed front and rear seat belts, body side molding and bright window and tailgate trim, chrome grille insert, front stabilizer bar and steering damper, and fuel tank and transfer case skid plate.

The Wagoneer Brougham was equipped with all features of the Custom Wagoneer plus these items: Coventry grain or Deluxe grain vinyl front and rear bench seats in beige, blue, black or nutmeg, custom door trim panels, woodgrain instrument cluster and steering wheel trim, soft headliner, power tailgate window, extra-quiet insulation, argent painted styled steel wheels with stainless steel trim rings, bright door and quarter window frames, bright lower tailgate molding, woodgrain body side rub strip, Light Group, Convenience Group and Visibility Group.

1982 Jeep Wagoneer Limited

The Wagoneer Limited, described by AMC as "America's most completely equipped, elegantly appointed four-wheel drive wagon", had, in addition to the content of the Custom Wagoneer, these features: Full body side and tailgate woodgrain treatment with vinyl surround moldings, special luggage rack with woodgrain side rail inserts, bright drip rails, Limited nameplates, 15 x 7 in. forged aluminum wheel, P225/75R15 Goodyear Arriva white sidewall steel radial tires, available special two-tone paint treatment, front bucket seats and rear bench seats trimmed in beige or nutmeg leather, matching leather trimmed armrest, door panels in beige or nutmeg Cara grained vinyl, woodgrain trim on doors, steering wheel, lower instrument panel and armrests, special carpeting in the passenger and load areas, leather-wrapped steering wheel, air conditioning, tinted glass, cruise control, tilt steering wheel, AM/FM stereo radio and premium audio system, power windows and door locks, power driver and front passenger seat, power tailgate, electric remote control outside mirrors, retractable cargo area cover, front and rear bumper guards and nerf stripes, Convenience Group, Light Group, and Visibility Group.

The 1982 color selection consisted of fourteen colors: Olympic white, mist silver metallic, classic black, sherwood green metallic, Jamaica meige, topaz gold metallic (available for Wagoneer only), copper brown metallic, slate blue metallic, deep night blue, oriental red (not available for Wagoneer), deep maroon metallic (available for Wagoneer only), sun yellow (not available for Wagoneer), and chestnut brown metallic.

I.D. DATA: The serial number was located on the left-hand hinge pillar. The V.I.N. had 17 symbols. The first three entries identified the manufacturer, make and type of vehicle. The fourth unit, a letter, designated the engine. The fifth character, a letter, identified the transmission. The sixth and seventh characters identified the series and body style. The eighth character identified the GVW rating. Next followed a check digit. The eleventh character was the manufacturing plant identification. The final six digits were the sequential production number. The vehicle identification indicated the model as follows: Wagoneer: 1J( )C( )15N( )CT00001 and up. Cherokee: 1J( )C(model)( )( )CT00001 and up. Vehicle identification was as follows: 15: Four-door Wagoneer station wagon, 16: Cherokee station wagon, 17: Cherokee wide-wheel station wagon, 18: Cherokee Four-door station wagon.

Model Number	Body Type	Factory Price	GVW	Shipping Weight	Prod. Total
Wagoneer Station Wagon 6-cyl.					
15	4-dr.	$11,114	6200	3797	15,547*
15	4-dr. Brougham	$12,084	6200	—	—
15	4-dr. Limited	$15,964	6200	—	—

* Includes all Wagoneer models.

Cherokee Station Wagon 6-cyl.

Model Number	Body Type	Factory Price	GVW	Shipping Weight	Prod. Total
16	2-dr.	$9849	6200	3692	4165 *
17	Wide-wheel 2-dr.	$10,812	6200	3741	—
18	4-dr. Chief	$11,647	6200	3296	—

* Includes all Cherokee models.

CHASSIS FEATURES: Separate body and frame. Box section side rails, deep web frame, wide flange, lightweight pressed steel with five cross members.

SUSPENSION AND RUNNING GEAR: Front Suspension: Cherokee: 5-leaf semi-elliptical springs 47 in. x 2.5 in. Rear: 52 in. x 2.5 in. Deflection rate: 215 lb./in.; Wagoneer: 6-leaf semi-elliptical springs. Deflection rate: 210 lb./in. Hydraulic double-action shock absorbers. Optional: Cherokee and Wagoneer: Extra-Duty Suspension Package, Front and rear heavy-duty shock absorbers, Smooth-Ride suspension (tuned for off-road usage on Cherokee), Front stabilizer bar. Rear Suspension: Cherokee and Wagoneer: 5-leaf semi-elliptical, asymmetrical design. Deflection rate: 165 lb./in. Hydraulic double-action shock absorbers. Optional: 165/265 lb./in. Front Axle Type and Capacity: Wagoneer & Cherokee: Dana 44, full-floating, hypoid, open end, 3200 lb. rating. Rear Axle Type and Capacity: Wagoneer & Cherokee: Dana 44, semi-floating, 3200 lb. rating. Optional: None. Final Drive Ratio: The Wagoneer with automatic transmission and 6-cylinder engine was available with an optional 3.31:1 axle ratio. The Cherokee's optional 3.31:1 ratio offered for the manual transmission model with the 360 cu. in. V-8 was not available for a similarly equipped Wagoneer. Transfer Case: Cherokee and Wagoneer (except for Wagoneer Limited): New Process 208 part-time transfer case. Ratios: 2.61:1, 1.00:1. Standard for Wagoneer Limited and optional for Cherokee and other Wagoneer models: Quadra Trac with New Process 219 transfer case. Ratios: Brakes: Type: Wagoneer and Cherokee: Hydraulic, front discs and rear drums. Dimensions: Wagoneer and Cherokee: Front: 12.0 in. dia. disc. Rear: 11.0 in. x 2.00 in. drums. Total brake swept area: 376 sq. in. Wheels: Wagoneer and Cherokee: 15 x 6, disc type, full-drop center 6-stud on 5.5 in. circle. Wagoneer Limited: 15 x 7 in. forged aluminum wheels (optional for other Wagoneer models). Wide-wheel Cherokee model: 15 x 7, white painted spoke steel, 5.5 circle on four-door model). 15 x 8 in. white painted spoke steel, 5.5 in. circle on two-door model. Tires: Wagoneer custom: P225/75R15 black sidewall radial. Wagoneer Limited: P225/75R15 white sidewall Arriva steel radials. Cherokee: P225/75R15 black sidewall Goodyear Viva radials; wide-wheel model: P225/75R15 Suburbanite XG Polyglas. Optional: Wagoneer: Tiempo P225/75R15 white sidewall double steel belted radial, Arriva P225/75R15 steel radial, F-32 Flexten HR78 x 15 white sidewall winter radial, Viva P225/75R15 black or white sidewall fiberglass radial. Cherokee: Wrangler 10R-15 outlined white letters steel radial, Tiempo P225/75R15 white sidewall double steel belted radial, Arriva P225/75R15 steel radial, F-32 Flexten HR78 x 15 white sidewall winter radial, Tracker A-T 10-15 outlined white letters wide All-Terrain All-Weather, Suburbanite XG Polyglas L78 x 15 black sidewall, Viva P225/75R15 black or white sidewall fiberglass radial. Steering: Wagoneer and Cherokee: Power Saginaw recirculating ball type. Ratio: 20/16:1. Turns Lock-to-Lock: 4.0. Turning Circle: Wagoneer, Cherokee model 16 & 18: 37.7 ft.; model 17: 39.4 ft. Standard Transmission: Wagoneer Limited (optional for Wagoneer custom and Cherokee): Chrysler TorqueFlite 3-spd. automatic. Ratios: 2.45:1, 1.45:1, 1.0:1. Wagoneer custom and Cherokee: All-synchromesh 4-speed Tremec model T-176. Transmission ratios: 3.52:1, 2.27:1, 1.46:1, 1.00:1. Clutch: Wagoneer and Cherokee: Single dry plate. Clutch diameter: 10.5 in. dia. (6-cyl.); 11.0 in. (V-8). Total lining area: 107 sq. in. (6-cyl.), 112 sq. in. (V-8). Optional: 5-speed Warner Gear T5 manual transmission with floor shifter. Available with part-time four-wheel drive only. Ratios: 4.03:1, 2.37:1, 1.50:1, 1.00:1, 0.76:1 or 0.86:1, depending on engine size and axle ratio. Reverse: 3.76:1.

VEHICLE DIMENSIONS: Wagoneer & Cherokee (except as noted) Wheelbase: 108.7 in. Overall Length: 186.40 in. Front/Rear Tread: Wagoneer: 59.4/57.8 in. Cherokee: 59.4/57.8 in. Cherokee two-door wide-wheel: 65.3/62.3 in. Overall Height: Wagoneer: 65.9 in. Cherokee 66.1. Wide-wheel two-door model: 66.8 in. Width: All models except Cherokee two-door wide-wheel: 75.6 in. Cherokee two-door wide-wheel: 78.9 in. Front/Rear Overhang: 31.3 in./46.4 in. Tailgate: Width and Height: 54.9 in. x 26.5 in. Approach/Departure Degrees: 31/21. Ground Clearance: All models except Cherokee wide-wheel: 7.7 in.; wide-wheel: 8.6 in. Load space: With rear seat in position: 39 in. x 44 in. x 39.0 in. With rear seat folded or removed: 58 in. x 44 in. x 39.0 in. Maximum capacity: 95.1 cu. ft. (with rear seat removed). Front headroom: 38.0 in. Front legroom: 41.6 in. Front shoulder room: 58.3 in. Front hip room: 60.5 in. Rear headroom: 37.2 in. Rear legroom: 37.0 in. Rear shoulder room: 58.3 in. Rear hip room: 60.9 in. Pedal to seat back (max.): 41.5 in. Steering wheel to seat back (max.): 18.5 in. Seat to ground: 31.5 in.

CAPACITIES: Fuel Tank: 21.3 gal. with standard skid plate. Coolant System: 6-cyl.: 10.5 qt. V-8: 15 qt.

ACCOMMODATIONS: Seating Capacity: Six passengers.

INSTRUMENTATION: Oil pressure, engine coolant temperature and voltmeter gauges, speedometer, odometer, warning lights for brake system warning, hazard lights operation.

OPTIONS AND PRICES: AM radio, AM/FM stereo (Standard for Wagoneer Limited): $249. AM/FM stereo/tape: $359. AM/FM stereo CB: $456. Electronically tuned AM/FM stereo radio: with cassette tape player: $499. Cruise control (Standard for Wagoneer Limited): $159. Rear window defroster: $125. Luggage rack (Standard for Wagoneer Limited): $118. Sun roof: $377. Air conditioning: $650. Power sun roof (Wagoneer Limited and Cherokee Laredo only): $1585. Power seats (Standard for Wagoneer Limited): $169. 360 V-8: $351. Extra-quiet insulation. Soft-Feel steering wheel. Leather-wrapped Sport steering wheel. Painted style steel wheels (standard for wide-wheel two-door Cherokee). Chrome styled steel wheels (Cherokee wide-wheel two-door only). Forged aluminum wheels (not available for Cherokee wide-wheel two-door). Retractable cargo area cover. Bumper guards. Upper body side scuff molding (not available for Wagoneer). Carpeting (standard for Wagoneer). Power windows and door locks (not available for two-door Cherokee): $410. Power tailgate. 6-way power driver and passenger seat: $281. Tinted glass: $89. Cruise control: $159. Luggage rack. Tilt steering wheel. Extra-quiet insulation. Power front bucket seats. Soft-Feel steering wheel. Power remote control outside rearview mirrors. Rear Trac-Lok differential. Quartz halogen headlights. Clear lens fog lamps: $90. Heavy-duty shock absorbers. Dual front shock absorbers. Soft-Ride suspension (Wagoneer, Cherokee two-door and four-door only): $48. Heavy-duty battery and alternator: $45. Inside spare tire carrier and cover: $74. Cold Climate Group. Includes heavy-duty battery and alternator, and engine block heater. Convenience Group. Includes underhood light, lights-on buzzer, digital clock. Light Group. Includes cargo ashtray, glove box, courtesy, visor vanity and map lights. Visibility Group. Includes right and left side remote mirrors, intermittent windshield wipers, and halogen headlights: $142. Trailer Towing Packages. Chief Package: $899. Laredo Package: $1749.

HISTORICAL FOOTNOTES: Commenting on the Wagoneer's improved sales for 1982, Joseph E. Cappy, then American Motors' vice-president-marketing group, noted, "Wagoneer sales increased 24 percent in 1982 over 1981 and we expect them to continue strong for a long time to come."

1983 WAGONEER & CHEROKEE

Model Number	Body Type	Factory Price	GVW	Shipping Weight	Prod. Total
Wagoneer Station Wagon V-8					
15	4-dr. Brougham	$13,173	6200	3869	19,155*
15	4-dr. Limited	$16,889	6200	—	

* Calendar year 1983 sales, includes all Wagoneer models.

Model Number	Body Type	Factory Price	GVW	Shipping Weight	Prod. Total
Cherokee Station Wagon 6-cyl.					
16	2-dr.	$10,315	6200	3764	4165 *
17	2-dr. W-W Chief	$12,022	6200	3903	—
18	4-dr. Pioneer	$12,006	6200	3868	—

* Calendar year 1983 sales, includes all Cherokee models.

Standard equipment for the 1983 Wagoneer and optional for Cherokees with automatic transmission, was a new Selec-Trac two/four-wheel drive system. The Selec-Trac low range mode was activated only when the vehicle was in four-wheel drive since a sequential lockout system within the transfer case prevented low range operation when the vehicle was in two-wheel drive. The low range was made operational by a floor-mounted lever positioned next to the driver's seat.

In order to engage a Selec-Trac Cherokee for either two or four-wheel drive the vehicle was first brought to a stop. The driver then moved a dash-mounted lever to either its "two-wheel drive" or "four-wheel drive" position. To prevent accidental movement of the lever, a safety switch had to be first pulled to engage the system.

1983 Wagoneer Limited

When the transfer case was shifted into two-wheel drive the front drivetrain was released from the freely turning front wheels by a vacuum-activated spline clutch built into the front axle assembly. This device, which was connected in four-wheel drive mode, released torque to the left axle shaft in its two-wheel drive mode. Since the axle differential equalized torque between the right and left axle shafts, the release of the left axle shaft and its subsequent free-wheeling also disconnected the right axle shaft. The process to move into full-time four-wheel drive was opposite of this procedure. Also included in the Selec-Trac system, which was available with either the 6-cylinder or V-8 engine, was a viscous coupling providing a front-torque biasing.

The 258 6-cyl. engine's compression ratio was increased from 8.3:1 to 9.2:1. A fuel feedback system and knock sensor were added to improve performance and fuel efficiency. Aside from this major development and the reduction of the Wagoneer line to the Brougham and Limited models, there were no significant changes found in the latest Wagoneers.

Appearance-wise, the 1983 Cherokee was unchanged from the 1982 version. A major revision did take place in the Cherokee's Trim Package offering. Standard for the four-door model and optional for the two-door was a new Pioneer Package consisting of the following items: Sun Valley vinyl bucket seats with center armrests (Western weave cloth optional), custom door and rear quarter trim panels, color-keyed carpeting including wheel wells and cargo area, Soft-Feel 3-spoke color keyed Sport steering wheel, engine turned instrument panel cluster overlay, bright armrest overlays with argent insert, passenger assist handle, dual rear seat ashtrays, driver's folding seat back (two-door model), black vinyl body side moldings, exterior body "Pioneer" decals, chrome grille, extra-quiet insulation, and P235/75R15 Arriva radial tires mounted on argent styled steel wheels with trim rings and bright hub covers.

The Chief and Laredo Packages were continued but were restricted to installation on the wide-wheel model only.

1983 Jeep Cherokee

I.D. DATA: The serial number was located on the left-hand hinge pillar. The V.I.N. had 17 symbols. The first three entries identified the manufacturer, make and type of vehicle. The fourth unit, a letter, designated the engine. The fifth character, a letter, identified the transmission. The sixth and seventh characters identified the series and body style. The eighth character identified the GVW rating. Next followed a check digit. The eleventh character was the manufacturing plant identification. The final six digits were the sequential production number. The vehicle identification indicated the model as follows: Wagoneer: 1JCC( )15N( )DT00001 and up. Cherokee: 1JCC( )( )( )( )DT00001 and up. Vehicle identification was as follows: 15: Four-door Wagoneer station wagon, 16: Cherokee station wagon, 17: Cherokee Chief station wagon, 18: Cherokee Pioneer four-door station wagon.

STANDARD ENGINE: Wagoneer and Cherokee: Engine Type: OHV, In-line-6. Cast iron block and cylinder head. Bore x Stroke: 3.75 in. x 3.90 in. Lifters: Hydraulic. Number of main bearings-7. Fuel Induction: 2-bbl. carburetor. Compression Ratio: 9.2:1. Displacement: 258 cu. in. (4.22 liters). Horsepower: Net: 115 @ 3200 rpm. Torque: Net: 210 lb.-ft. @ 1800 rpm. Oil refill capacity: 6 qt. with filter change. Fuel Requirements: Unleaded.

OPTIONAL ENGINE: Wagoneer and Cherokee: Not available for California. Type: OHV, V-8. Cast iron block and cylinder head. Bore x Stroke: 4.08 in. x 3.44 in. Lifters: Hydraulic. Number of main bearings-5. Fuel Induction: 2-bbl. carburetor. Compression Ratio: 8.25:1. Displacement: 360 cu. in. (5.89 liters). Horsepower: Net: 129 @ 3700 rpm. Torque: Net: 245 lb.-ft. @ 1600 rpm. Oil refill capacity: 5 qt. with filter change. Fuel Requirements: Unleaded.

CHASSIS FEATURES: Separate body and frame. Box section side rails, deep web frame, wide flange, lightweight pressed steel with five cross members.

SUSPENSION AND RUNNING GEAR: Front Suspension: Cherokee: 5-leaf semi-elliptical springs 47 in. x 2.5 in. Rear: 52 in. x 2.5 in. Deflection rate: 215 lb./in.; Wagoneer: 6-leaf semi-elliptical springs. Deflection rate: 210 lb./in. Hydraulic double-action shock absorbers. Optional: Cherokee and Wagoneer: Extra-Duty Suspension Package. Spring rate: 210, 260, 330 lb./in., Front and rear heavy-duty shock absorbers, Soft-Ride suspension (includes special front springs and front and rear shock absorbers). Spring rate: 160 lb./in. Rear Suspension: Cherokee and Wagoneer: 5-leaf semi-elliptical, asymmetrical design. Deflection rate: 165 lb./in. Hydraulic double-action shock absorbers. Optional: 165/265 lb./in. Front Axle Type and Capacity: Wagoneer & Cherokee: Dana 44, full-floating, hypoid, open end, 3200 lb. rating. Rear Axle Type and Capacity: Wagoneer & Cherokee: Dana 44, semi-floating, 3200 lb. rating. Optional: None. Final Drive Ratio: 2.73:1. Optional: 3.31:1. Transfer Case: Cherokee and Wagoneer: New Process 208 part-time transfer case. Ratios: 2.61:1, 1.00:1. Optional for Cherokee and other Wagoneer models: Selec-Trac two-wheel/four-wheel drive. Ratios: 2.6:1, 1.00:1. Brakes: Type: Wagoneer and Cherokee: Hydraulic, front discs and rear drums. Dimensions: Wagoneer and Cherokee: Front: 12.0 in. dia. disc. Rear: 11.0 in. x 2.00 in. drums. Total brake swept area: 376 sq. in. Wheels: Wagoneer and Cherokee: 15 x 6, disc type, full-drop center 6-stud on 5.5 in. circle. Wagoneer Limited: 15 x 7 in. forged aluminum wheels (optional for other Wagoneer models). Wide-wheel Cherokee model: 15 x 7, white painted spoke steel, 5.5 circle on four-door model). 15 x 8 in. chrome styled wheel, 5.5 in. circle on Laredo wide-wheel two-door model. Tires: Wagoneer Brougham: P225/75R15 Polyglas radial white sidewall highway, Wagoneer Limited: P225/75R15 white sidewall Arriva steel radials. Cherokee: P225/75R15 glass belted radial black sidewall highway, Cherokee wide-wheel two-door: Tracker A/T 10 x 15 in. OWL. Cherokee Laredo wide-wheel two-door: 10R-15 Goodyear Wrangler steel-belted radial, Cherokee Pioneer: P235/75R15 black Arriva radial. Optional: Wagoneer and Cherokee: Suburbanite XG H78 x 15 black sidewall, fiberglass belted. Not available for two-door wide-wheel Cherokee. Tiempo P225/75R15 white sidewall double steel belted radial. Not available for four-door Cherokee. F-32 Flexten HR78 x 15 white sidewall winter radial. Not available for four-door Cherokee. Arriva P225/75R15 steel radial white sidewall. Not available for four-door Cherokee. Standard for Wagoneer Limited. Wrangler 10R-15 outlined white letters steel radial. Available for two-door wide-wheel Cherokee only. Tracker AT 10-15 OWL wide All-Terrain All-Weather. Available for two-door wide-wheel Cherokee only. Steering: Power Saginaw recirculating ball type. Ratio: 20/16:1. Turns Lock-to-Lock: 4.0. Turning Circle: Wagoneer, Cherokee model 16 & 18: 37.7 ft.; model 17: 39.4 ft. Standard Transmission: Wagoneer Brougham and Limited (optional for Cherokee): Chrysler TorqueFlite 3-spd. automatic. Ratios: 2.45:1, 1.45:1, 1.0:1. Cherokee: All-synchromesh 4-speed Tremec model T-176. Transmission ratios: 3.52:1, 2.27:1, 1.46:1, 1.00:1. Clutch: Cherokee: Single dry plate. Clutch diameter: 11.0 in. dia. Total lining area: 112 sq. in. Optional: None.

VEHICLE DIMENSIONS: Wagoneer & Cherokee (except as noted) Wheelbase: 108.7 in. Overall Length: 186.40 in. Front/Rear Tread: Wagoneer: 59.4/57.8 in. Cherokee: 59.4/57.8 in. Cherokee two-door wide-wheel: 65.3 in./62.3 in. Overall Height: Wagoneer: 65.9 in. Cherokee 66.1 in. Width: All models except Cherokee two-door wide-wheel: 75.6 in. Cherokee two-door wide-wheel: 78.9 in. Front/Rear Overhang: 31.3 in./46.4 in. Tailgate: Width and Height: 54.9 in. x 26.5 in. Approach/Departure Degrees: 31/21. Ground Clearance: All models except Cherokee two-door wide-wheel: 7.7 in.; wide-wheel: 8.6 in. Load space: With rear seat in position: 39 in. x 44 in. x 39.0 in. With rear seat folded or removed: 58 in. x 44 in. x 39.0 in. Maximum capacity: 95.1 cu. ft. (with rear seat removed). Front headroom: 38.0 in. Front legroom: 41.5 in. Front shoulder room: 58.3 in. Front hip room: 60.5 in. Rear headroom: 37.2 in. Rear legroom: 37.0 in. Rear shoulder room: 58.3 in. Rear hip room: 60.9 in. Pedal to seat back (max.): 41.5 in. Steering wheel to seat back (max.): 18.5 in. Seat to ground: 31.5 in.

CAPACITIES: Fuel Tank: 20.3 gal. with standard skid plate. Coolant System: 10.5 qt. (6-cyl.), 15 qt. (V-8).

ACCOMMODATIONS: Seating Capacity: Six passengers.

INSTRUMENTATION: Oil pressure, engine coolant temperature and voltmeter gauges, speedometer, odometer, warning lights for brake system warning, hazard lights operation.

OPTIONS AND PRICES: Except for the addition of halogen fog lamps (and the concurrent elimination of the clear fog lamps option), the Wagoneer and Cherokee option selection was unchanged for 1983. A selection of Cherokee options and their prices follow: AM/FM stereo: $199. AM/FM stereo with cassette tape player: $329. Cruise control: $184. Rear window defroster: $134. Tilt steering wheel: $106. Luggage rack: $122. Sun roof: $389. Power sun roof: $1637. Power seats: $290. Cherokee Laredo Package: $1128. Cherokee Pioneer Package (wide-wheel model): $1131.

HISTORICAL FOOTNOTES: The 1983 models debuted in the fall of 1982.

1984 WAGONEER & CHEROKEE

For 1984, a new down-sized series of Wagoneers and Cherokees were introduced. Five years in development, these new models weighed nearly 1000 pounds less, were more compact and offered superior fuel economy when compared to their predecessors. While the Cherokee and Wagoneer retained a distinctively Jeep appearance, each had an distinctive styling personality with unique grille treatments, taillamps, exterior trim and moldings, as well as interior design, fabric and trim. Referred to as "Sportwagons" by AMC, the new Cherokee/Wagoneers were 21 in. shorter, 6 in. narrower and four in. shorter in height than the 1983 versions. The new models retained the crisp, angular body lines, squared-off front and rear wheel openings and the slotted grille characteristics of the older models while clearly being more aerodynamic and contemporary than the older body shell.

The familiar Jeep grille was used with several major changes. The hood opening was recessed from the top of the grille which was slightly racked back. A one-piece fiberglass rear liftgate was used. Two audio speakers were built into the liftgate. A completely new instrument panel with a fully integrated air conditioning option, exposed storage bin as well as a full-size glove box was featured. For the first time a tachometer was included as was an upshift light option. Initially, this latter feature was offered only in combination with a 4-speed manual and 4-cylinder engine.

The steering wheels were redesigned and the windshield wiper controls were transferred to the steering column form the instrument panel. All transmission controls, manual or automatic were floor-mounted. A pedestal seat design, similar to that used in the Renault Alliance was used for front seat passengers. The rear compartment was designed to allow a full-size spare to be stowed in a vertical position. The rear seat cushion tipped forward to a vertical position behind the rear of the front seats, allowing the rear seat back to be folded flush with the cargo floor. The rear seat also had a quick-release feature that allowed it to be completely removed to accommodate extra-long cargo loads. A one-piece vinyl headliner was used that reduced potential wrinkles while providing additional headroom.

1984 Jeep Grand Wagoneer

The new model's front suspension, dubbed "Quadra-Link" by AMC combined coil springs with four locating arms. An anti-roll bar, constant velocity joints and hydraulic shock absorbers were also used. At the rear semi-elliptical springs and an anti-roll bar were joined by gas-filled shock absorbers. A part-time, "Command-Trac" system was standard for the Wagoneer and Cherokee. It used a New Process 207 transfer case which had an all-aluminum, two-piece casting. Optional was Selec-Trac utilizing a viscous clutch and a New Process 239 limited slip center differential (a differential lock in low range was also included). Three transmissions were offered for the new Wagoneer and Cherokee. Standard for the Cherokee was an all-synchromesh 4-speed manual. Standard for the base Wagoneer and optional for the Cherokee was a 5-speed overdrive manual transmission. Standard for the Wagoneer Limited and optional for all the models was a Chrysler model 904, 3-speed automatic transmission.

A new AMC-designed 4-cylinder "Hurricane" engine was standard for all models. Although this engine shared some components with the 258 6-cyl. engine, it was essentially an all-new design with computer-controlled electronic ignition, single-barrel carburetor with electronic fuel feedback and an aluminum intake manifold. All models were available with a 2.8 liter V-6 engine supplied by Chevrolet.

The Cherokee was available with either Chief or Pioneer Packages. The Wagoneer was produced in Brougham and Limited Packages. The base Cherokee model was identified by its black bumpers, end caps and fender flares. The base grille had Jeep lettering on the hood and rear license visor, black tailgate surround, a black background with an argent insert of narrow, wide-spaced bars. Other standard features included black and argent headlight bezels, black hubcaps, 15 x 6 in. argent colored styled steel wheels, P195/75R15 black sidewall tires, driver's side black-finish mirror, and black molding for the door window frame, vend window divider and drip rail and 2-speed electric windshield wipers and washers.

Interior features of the base Cherokee included a 2-spoke polypropylene black steering wheel, a mini color-keyed console, black plastic door opening scuff plates, vinyl covered straight armrests, color-keyed textured vinyl trim for the passenger and cargo areas and rear seat back, color-keyed grained vinyl covered sun visors, black instrument panel cluster overlay, and a painted molded board liftgate panel. The front bucket and rear bench seat were finished in a Celtic grain vinyl in either almond or slate blue.

The upscale Pioneer and Cherokee Chief models had these features: Three-spoke steering wheel, "hockey-style" front armrests, 12 oz. nylon passenger area carpeting with heat and noise insulation, 14 oz. needled polypropylene carpeting for the cargo, wheelhouse covers, and rear seat backs, four cargo area tie-down hooks, full-length color-keyed console with armseat and rear ashtray (the ashtray on four-door models was located in the door handles; on two-door models it was located in the trim panel), rear heat ducts, cloth headliner and sun visors, bright instrument panel accent surround, electronic digital clock, gauges for voltmeter and engine coolant temperature, low fuel indicator, trip odometer, rear seat cup holders for

two-door models, front bucket seats finished in Deluxe grain vinyl, deep tinted glass for rear quarter windows on two-door models, tinted glass onfour-door models, Light Group, AM radio with two speakers, rear window wiper and 2-speed windshield wipers, halogen headlights and color-keyed vinyl spare tire cover. The Cherokee Chief had these additional or unique features: Black headlight bezels, and 15 x 7 in. white styled spoke wheels (available as options for the base model and the Pioneer) with bright hub covers, Goodyear Wrangler P215/7515 OWL steel belted radial, All-Terrain tires, special hood striping and rocker panel trim with Cherokee Chief lettering.

The Wagoneer was offered in either base or Limited trim level. The Wagoneer's standard equipment included vinyl covered door panels with carpeted lower map pocket, Westchester cloth seat trim in a choice of four colors, halogen headlights, front door "hockey-style" armrests with bright upper and lower surrounds, four cargo area tie down hooks, 14 oz. polypropylene carpet cover for the liftgate panel, cloth headliner, color-keyed instrument panel with bright surrounds, black plastic door opening scuff moldings, dual rear and single front passenger assist handles, flat-folding rear seats with quick-release removable bottom cushion, color-keyed vinyl spare tire cover, bright bumpers with black end caps, bright door handles, color-keyed fender flares, special exterior body graphics, bright grille and headlight bezels, Jeep logo on driver's side of GVOP and lower right corner of liftgate, rear quarter panel-mounted identification for either four-wheel drive or Selec-Trac, Wagoneer lettering on front fenders and rear license visor, bright door frames, drip rails, liftgate surround, black lower body side trim with bright insert, bright quarter window and windshield surrounds, rear seat ashtrays, cigarette lighter, electronic clock with digital display, Gauge Group, glove box light, Light Group, power brakes and steering, and tinted glass.

1984 Jeep Cherokee Chief

The Wagoneer Limited had full-length, color-keyed console with armrest, rear ashtray and heating ducts, exclusive woodgrain side body panels, swing-out front vent windows, a unique interior design combination of woodgrain, leather and fabric. Country Cord upholstery with leather inserts with embroidered Limited lettering on the front seats, air conditioning, heavy-duty battery, Protection Group, AM/FM stereo radio, roof rack, leather-wrapped Sport steering wheel with tilt feature, and Soft-Ride suspension.

With the introduction of the new down-sized Cherokee and Wagoneer models there was speculation that AMC might bring the curtain down on Wagoneer production just as it did with its Cherokee derivative. This did not take place, instead the Wagoneer returned as the Grand Wagoneer. AMC unashamedly described the Grand Wagoneer as the "Grand Daddy in four-wheel drive."

But its advanced age and the strong sales of the new Wagoneer and Cherokee didn't seem to affect the popularity of the Grand Wagoneer whose sales of 19,081 were virtually unchanged from the 1983 level of 19,155. The Grand Wagoneer's base equipment content included virtually every option including a clearcoat metallic paint that AMC offered. Among the few options available were the 360 cu. in. V-8, a power-operated sun roof (by the early eighties this feature was increasingly depicted as a moonroof) and a 5,000 lb. Towing Package.

A total of ten colors were offered for the Cherokee, Wagoneer and Grand Wagoneer: Olympic white, deep night blue, classic black, almond beige, silver metallic clearcoat, chestnut brown metallic clearcoat, and garnet metallic clearcoat. Exclusive to the Cherokee were sebring red and ice blue metallic clearcoat. Available only for the Wagoneer were nordic green and cinnamon clearcoat metallic. The Cherokee was also offered in a variety of two-tone color combinations: Olympic white/deep night blue, olympic white/sebring red, olympic white/almond beige, champagne metallic/classic black and ice blue metallic/deep night blue.

I.D. DATA: The serial number was located on the left-hand hinge pillar. The V.I.N. had 17 symbols. The first three entries identified the manufacturer, make and type of vehicle. The fourth unit, a letter, designated the engine. The fifth character, a letter, identified the transmission. The sixth and seventh characters identified the series and body style. The eighth character identified the GVW rating. Next followed a check digit. The eleventh character was the manufacturing plant identification. The final six digits were the sequential production number. The vehicle identification indicated the model as follows: Grand Wagoneer: 1JCC( )15N( )DT00001 and up. Wagoneer (4-cyl.): IJCU( )75( )ET000001 and up; Wagoneer (6-cyl.): 1JCW( )75( )( )ET000001 and up, Cherokee (4-cyl.): 1JCU( )(model)( )( )ET000001 and up, Cherokee (6-cyl.): 1JCW( )(model)( )( )ET000001 and up. Cherokee: 1JCC( )15( )( )ET00001 and up. Vehicle identification was as follows: 15: Grand Wagoneer station wagon, 75: Wagoneer, 77: Two-door Cherokee, 78: Four-door Cherokee.

Model Number	Body Type	Factory Price	GVW	Shipping Weight	Prod. Total
Grand Wagoneer Station Wagon V-8					
15	4-dr.	$19,306	6200	4221	19,081
Wagoneer Station Wagon 4-cyl.					
75	4-dr.	$12,444	4549	3047	24728*
75	2-dr. Limited	$17,076	4549	3222	—
Wagoneer Station Wagon 6-cyl.					
75	4-dr.	$12,749	4598	3065	—
75	4-dr. Limited	$17,381	4598	3240	—
* 1984 model year-all models.					
Cherokee Station Wagon 4-cyl.					
77	2-dr.	$9995	4549	2917	77786*
78	4-dr.	$10,295	4549	2979	—

Cherokee Station Wagon 6-cyl.

77	2-dr.	$10,300	4598	2963	—
78	4-dr.	$10,600	4598	3023	—

* 1984 model year production-includes all Cherokee models.

STANDARD ENGINE: Grand Wagoneer: Engine Type: OHV, In-line-6. Cast iron block and cylinder head. Bore x Stroke: 3.75 in. x 3.90 in. Lifters: Hydraulic. Number of main bearings-7. Fuel Induction: 2-bbl. carburetor. Compression Ratio: 9.2:1. Displacement: 258 cu. in. Horsepower: Net: 115 @ 3200 rpm. Torque: Net: 210 lb.-ft. @ 1800 rpm. Oil refill capacity: 6 qt. with filter change. Fuel Requirements: Unleaded.

OPTIONAL ENGINE: Grand Wagoneer: Engine Type: OHV, V-8. Cast iron block and cylinder head. Bore x Stroke: 4.08 in. x 3.44 in. Lifters: Hydraulic. Number of main bearings-5. Fuel Induction: 2-bbl. carburetor. Compression Ratio: 8.25:1. Displacement: 360 cu. in. (5.89 liters). Horsepower: Net: 129 @ 3700 rpm. Torque: Net: 245 lb.-ft. @ 1600 rpm. Oil refill capacity: 5 qt. with filter change. Fuel Requirements: Unleaded.

STANDARD ENGINE: Cherokee and Wagoneer: Engine Type: OHV, In-line-4. Cast iron block and cylinder head. Bore x Stroke: 3.88 in. x 3.19 in. Lifters: Hydraulic. Number of main bearings-5. Fuel Induction: 1-bbl. carburetor. Compression Ratio: 9.2:1. Displacement: 150.45 cu. in. (2.4 liters). Horsepower: Net: 105 @ 5000 rpm. Torque: Net: 132 lb.-ft. @ 2800 rpm. Oil refill capacity: 5 qt. with filter change. Fuel Requirements: Unleaded.

OPTIONAL ENGINE: Cherokee and Wagoneer: Engine Type: OHV, V-6. Cast iron block and cylinder head. Bore x Stroke: 3.50 in. x 2.99 in. Lifters: Hydraulic. Number of main bearings-4. Fuel Induction: 2-bbl. Rochester 2SE carburetor. Compression Ratio: 8.5:1. Displacement: 173 cu. in. (2.8 liters). Horsepower: Net: 115 @ 4800 rpm. Torque: Net: 145 lb.-ft. @ 2400 rpm. Oil refill capacity: 5 qt. with filter change. Fuel Requirements: Unleaded. Note: All Grand Wagoneer technical data was unchanged from 1983. The following material relates to the Cherokee and Wagoneer models.

CHASSIS FEATURES: "Uniframe" full-length boxed steel frame welded to unitized body.

SUSPENSION AND RUNNING GEAR: Front Suspension: Coil springs with leading links and track bar, link-type 0.87 in. dia. stabilizer bar. Spring rate at wheel: 120 lb./in. Rear Suspension: Semi-elliptical leaf springs, link type 0.55 in. dia. stabilizer bar. Optional: Heavy-duty front and rear suspension, Soft-Ride suspension. Front Axle Type: Dana model 30 Hypoid. Rear Axle Type: Hotchkiss. Optional: None. Final Drive Ratio: Cherokee: 3.31:1, Wagoneer: 3.73:1. Optional: None. Transfer Case: Automatic transmission (also available with 5-speed manual transmission): Selec-Trac New Process 229. Ratios: 2.61:1, 1.00:1. 4-speed and 5-speed manual transmission: Command-Trac New Process 207. Ratios: 2.61:1, 1.00:1. Brakes: Type: Hydraulic, front discs and rear drums. Dimensions: Front: 10.98 in. dia. disc. Rear: 10.0.0 in. x 1.750 in. drums. Wheels: 15 x 6.0JJ Optional: 15 x 7.0JJ. aluminum wheels. Tires: Cherokee: P195/75R15 steel belted All-Weather black sidewall radial. Wagoneer: P205/75R15 white sidewall radials. Optional: P215/75R15. OWL radials. Steering: Manual Saginaw recirculating ball type. Ratio: 26:1. Turns Lock-to-Lock: 4.8. Optional: Power Saginaw recirculating ball type. Ratio: 19:1. Turns Lock-to-Lock: 3.5:1. Turning Circle: 36.1 ft. Standard Transmission: 4-speed manual. Ratios: 3.93:1, 2.33:1, 1.45:1, 1.00:1. Reverse: 3.76:1. Optional: 5-speed manual (standard for Wagoneer). Ratios: 3.93:1, 2.33:1, 1.45:1, 1.00:1, 0.85:1. Reverse: 3.76:1. Optional Chrysler model 904 3-speed automatic. Ratios: 2.74:1, 1.55:1, 1.00:1. Reverse: 2.2:1. Clutch: Clutch diameter: 9.7 in. dia. Optional: None.

VEHICLE DIMENSIONS: Wheelbase: 101.4 in. Overall Length: 165.3 in. Front/Rear Tread: 58.0 in./58.0 in. Overall Height: 64.1 in. Width: 70.5 in. Front/Rear Overhang: 27.5 in./36.4 in. Approach/Departure Degrees: 39.7/31.1. Ground Clearance: Minimum clearance: 8.7 in. Maximum capacity: 71.2 cu. ft. (with rear seat folded). Front headroom: 38.3 in. Front legroom: 41.6 in. Front shoulder room: 55.3 in. Front hip room: 55.3 in. Rear headroom: 38.0 in. Rear legroom: 35.3 in. Rear shoulder room: 55.3 in. Rear hip room: 44.5 in.

CAPACITIES: Fuel Tank: 13.5 gal. Optional: 20.3 gal.

ACCOMMODATIONS: Seating Capacity: Six passengers.

INSTRUMENTATION: Speedometer, odometer, warning lights for alternator, oil pressure, and engine coolant temperature. Brake system warning, hazard lights operation. Cherokee Pioneer and Chief models have standard voltmeter, oil pressure and engine coolant temperature gauges.

OPTIONS AND PRICES: Cherokee and Wagoneer: Color-keyed passenger area carpeting. Electronic clock with digital display. Tunnel-mounted console with armrest and rear ashtray. Sentinel headlamp switch. Color-keyed floor mats. Color-keyed vinyl spare tire cover. Front and rear bumper guards. Locking gas cap. Bright Sport grille. Black lower body side protection. Roof rack: $119. Spare tire carrier. Tinted glass (two-door base model). Front and rear tow hooks. Air conditioning. Air conditioning Prep Package. Includes heavy-duty cooling, heavy-duty battery, heavy-duty alternator. Heavy-duty battery. Cold Climate Group. Includes engine block heater, heavy-duty battery and alternator. Heavy-duty cooling. Includes 7.0 in. radiator wall thickness. Included with air conditioning. Maximum Cooling Package. Includes 1.25 in. radiator wall thickness available with V-6 engine only. Cruise control: $191. Electric rear window defroster: $140. Included in Visibility Group. Requires heavy-duty alternator and tinted glass. Diesel Cold Start Package. Includes engine coolant heater and battery blanket heater. California emissions system. High Altitudes Emissions Package. 2.8 liter V-6. Not available with 4-speed manual transmission, required automatic transmission for California. Fog lamps, required bumper guards. Extra capacity fuel tank. Extra-Quiet Insulation Package. Light Group. Includes glove box lamp, ashtray lamp, illuminated ring around cigarette lighter, dome/map lamp, cargo area lamp with on-off switch, under IP courtesy lamps, lighted visor mirror (not available for two-door base Cherokee), door switches for dome/courtesy lights added to rear doors. Dual low profile swing-away truck style mirrors. Dual manual remote mirrors. Power remote control exterior mirrors, required power windows, door locks and full length console. Power door locks (four-door models only). Six-way power driver's seat. Passenger and driver 6-way power seats. Power steering. Power windows and locks, required tinted glass. Automatic actuating antenna, required stereo radio. Protection Group. Included front and rear bumper guards, floor mats, door edge guards, cargo area skid strips. AM radio with two speakers. AM/FM/MPX high output radio with four speakers. Electronically tuned AM/FM/MPX/cassette high output stereo radio with Dolby noise reduction, coaxial front and rear speakers, and digital clock display. Pre-stereo kit with four speakers, stereo wiring harness and antenna (standard when AM radio is deleted on Cherokee Pioneer and Chief). Automatic actuating rear load leveling. Not available with Trailer Tow B Package). Rear Trac-Lok differential. Not available with Selec-Trac. Skid Plate Package. Includes protection for transfer case, fuel tank and front suspension. Tilt steering wheel, requires intermittent windshield wipers. Three-spoke steering wheel. Leather-wrapped steering wheel. Heavy-duty suspension. Soft-Ride suspension (not available with Trailer Tow B Package). Tachometer. Trailer A Package (2000 lb.). Included dead weight hitch, 5-wire harness. Trailer B Package (4200 lb.). Includes load leveling hitch, 7-wire harness, not available with diesel engine. Automatic 3-speed transmission. Requires power steering. Selec-Trac. Not available with manual transmission. Visibility Group. Includes dual manual remote mirrors, intermittent windshield wipers, rear window defroster. 15 x 7 in. Sport style aluminum wheels. 15 x 7 in. white styled steel wheels. Bright trim rings, available for base 15 x 6 in. wheels only. Front door vent, swing-out design, requires tinted glass. Deep tinted two-door quarter glass. Includes tinted windshield, door windows and liftgate window. Intermittent windshield wipers: $110. Retractable underhood worklight. Grand Wagoneer: Straight shade non-clearcoat paint. Power sun roof with full vinyl roof: $1694. California emissions. High altitude emissions. 360 V-8. Engine block heater. Auxiliary transmission oil cooler, required with Trailer Towing B Package. Heavy-Duty Suspension Package. Includes heavy-duty front and rear shock absorbers. Trailer Towing A Package (3500 lb. capacity). Trailer Towing B Package (5000 lb. capacity). Cherokee Chief Package: $1310. Cherokee Pioneer Package: $1000.

HISTORICAL FOOTNOTES: *4 Wheel & Off-Road* magazine named the Jeep Cherokee the "4x4 of the Year."

1985 WAGONEER & CHEROKEE

The 1985 Cherokee carried forward the award-winning design introduced for 1984. Available for 1985 was the Cherokee base, the Pioneer, the Chief and the new top of the line, Cherokee Laredo. Standard equipment included the 2.5 liter 4-cyl. engine, 4-speed manual transmission, 2-speed Command-Trac transfer case. New standard equipment for most models included front seat headrests, a rocker/recliner capability with front bucket seats (included as standard for Pioneer, Chief and Laredo), cargo area tie-down hooks (not included in Base model), and passenger assist handles. New optional equipment for 1985 included a 2.1 liter 4-cylinder turbo diesel a new shift-on-the-fly capability with Selec-Trac, Sentry, a keyless entry system, and a swing-away spare tire carrier for four-door models. The new optional offerings were also available for the Wagoneer which continued to be produced as a base or Limited model. New standard equipment included the addition of headrests and rocker/recliner capability to the front seats on the base Wagoneer. The Limited model had standard power seats with seat back recliner. Cargo area tie-down hooks were added along with three J-rail-mounted passenger assist handles.

1985 Jeep Wagoneer Limited

In place of or in addition to the content of the Chief Package, the new Cherokee Laredo was equipped with these features: 18 oz. nylon passenger area carpeting with extra-quiet insulation, 18 oz. needled polypropylene cargo floor/wheelhouse/rear seat back carpeting, carpeted liftgate trim panel, full length, color-keyed console with armrest, rear ashtray and rear heating ducts, upgraded vinyl door panels with cloth insert and 18 oz. nylon carpeted lower section, vinyl door trim with cloth insert and 18 oz. nylon carpeted lower area, instrument panel with brushed pewter overlay, front rocker/recliner wing back bucket seats with headrests in Highland check fabric, color-keyed vinyl spare tire cover with cloth insert, vinyl storage pockets located on back of front seat, bumper guards, bright door handles, color-keyed fender flares (also installed on Pioneer), dual upper body side stripes, dual hood, cowl, and G.O.P. stripes, flare stripe, bright grille insert, bright headlight bezels, Laredo lettering located below Cherokee lettering on front fenders, black right and left rearview remote mirrors, body side scuff lower molding with bright insert, bright liftgate window surround (also found on Pioneer), bright drip rail (also found on Pioneer), bright windshield surround (also found on Pioneer), 15 x 7 in. cast aluminum wheels with bright hub covers, Insulation Package, Protection Group, roof rack, leather-wrapped Sport steering wheel, P215/75R15 OWL steel-belted radial All-Terrain Michelin tires, Visibility Group, and swing-out front vent windows.

The standard exterior color selection for the Cherokee consisted of olympic white, almond beige, sebring red, classic black and deep night blue. The last two colors listed were not available with the Chief Package. Extra cost metallic-clearcoat colors available were: Sterling, ice blue, champagne, dark honey, charcoal, and garnet. The Chief Package was not available with the last two colors listed. The Wagoneer color selection differed slightly from that of the Cherokee. These colors were standard for the Wagoneer: Olympic white, classic black, almond beige and deep night blue. The extra-cost metallic-clearcoat colors were: Charcoal, sterling, champagne, dark honey, dark brown and garnet.

The Grand Wagoneer for 1985 was fitted with a special "Handling Package" that offered a smoother, more comfortable ride, and Selec-Trac with shift-on-the-fly capability. Also new for 1985 was a moveable center armrest that allowed for the seating of three adults in the front, and front bucket seats with moveable headrests. The Grand Wagoneer's standard 15 x 7 in. forged aluminum wheels now had new gold hub cover inserts. Three new exterior clearcoat colors — Medium green, dark honey and dark brown joined these colors carried over from 1984: Olympic white, classic black, almond beige, deep night blue, charcoal clearcoat metallic, sterling clearcoat metallic, and champagne clearcoat metallic. Two new interiors colors were offered: Honey and garnet.

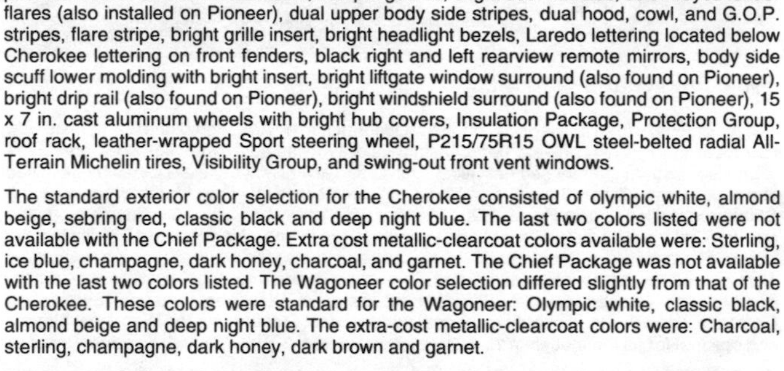

1985 Jeep Grand Wagoneer

I.D. DATA: The serial number was located on the left-hand hinge pillar. The V.I.N. had 17 symbols. The first three entries identified the manufacturer, make and type of vehicle. The fourth unit, a letter, designated the engine. The fifth character, a letter, identified the transmission. The sixth and seventh characters identified the series and body style. The eighth character identified the GVW rating. Next followed a check digit. The eleventh character was the manufacturing plant identification. The final six digits were the sequential production number. The vehicle identification indicated the model as follows: Grand Wagoneer: 1JCC( )15( )( )FT00001 and up. Wagoneer (4-cyl.): IJCU( )75( )( )FT000001 and up; Wagoneer (6-cyl.): 1JCW( )75( )( )FT000001 and up, Cherokee (4-cyl.): 1JCU( )(model)( )( )FT000001 and up, Cherokee (6-cyl.): 1JCW( )(model)( )( )FT000001 and up. Vehicle identification was as follows: 15: Grand Wagoneer station wagon, 75: Wagoneer, 77: Two-door Cherokee, 78: Four-door Cherokee.

Model Number	Body Type	Factory Price	GVW	Shipping Weight	Prod. Total
Grand Wagoneer Station Wagon V-8					
15	4-dr.	$20,462	6200	4228	—
Wagoneer Station Wagon 4-cyl.					
75	4-dr.	$13,255	4549	3063	—
75	2-dr. Limited	$17,953	4549	3222	—
Wagoneer Station Wagon 6-cyl.					
75	4-dr.	$13,604	4598	3106	—
75	4-dr. Limited	$18,302	4598	3265	—
Cherokee Station Wagon 4-cyl.					
77	2-dr.	$10,405	4549	2923	—
78	4-dr.	$10,976	4549	2984	—
Cherokee Station Wagon 6-cyl.					
77	2-dr.	$10,754	4598	2998	—
78	4-dr.	$11,325	4598	3059	—

STANDARD ENGINE: Grand Wagoneer: Engine Type: OHV, In-line-6. Cast iron block and cylinder head. Bore x Stroke: 3.75 in. x 3.90 in. Lifters: Hydraulic. Number of main bearings-7. Fuel Induction: 2-bbl. carburetor. Compression Ratio: 9.2:1. Displacement: 258 cu. in. (4.22 liters). Horsepower: Net: 115 @ 3200 rpm. Torque: Net: 210 lb.-ft. @ 1800 rpm. Oil refill capacity: 5 qt. with filter change. Fuel Requirements: Unleaded.

OPTIONAL ENGINE: Grand Wagoneer: Type: OHV, V-8. Cast iron block and cylinder head. Bore x Stroke: 4.08 in. x 3.44 in. Lifters: Hydraulic. Number of main bearings-5. Fuel Induction: 2-bbl. carburetor. Compression Ratio: 8.25:1. Displacement: 360 cu. in. (5.89 liters). Horsepower: Net: 129 @ 3700 rpm. Torque: Net: 245 lb.-ft. @ 1600 rpm. Oil refill capacity: 5 qt. with filter change. Fuel Requirements: Unleaded.

STANDARD ENGINE: Cherokee and Wagoneer: Engine Type: OHV, In-line-4. Cast iron block and cylinder head. Bore x Stroke: 3.88 in. x 3.19 in. Lifters: Hydraulic. Number of main bearings-5. Fuel Induction: 1-bbl. carburetor. Compression Ratio: 9.2:1. Displacement: 150.45 cu. in. (2.4 liters). Horsepower: Net: 105 @ 5000 rpm. Torque: Net: 132 lb.-ft. @ 2800 rpm. Tach redline: NA. Oil refill capacity: 4 qt. with filter change. Fuel Requirements: Unleaded.

OPTIONAL ENGINE: Cherokee and Wagoneer: Requires power steering and 5-speed manual or automatic transmission on Cherokee. Engine Type: OHV, V-6. Cast iron block and cylinder head. Bore x Stroke: 3.50 in. x 2.99 in. Lifters: Hydraulic. Number of main bearings-4. Fuel Induction: 2-bbl. Rochester 2SE carburetor. Compression Ratio: 8.5:1. Displacement: 173 cu. in. (2.8 liters). Horsepower: Net: 115 @ 4800 rpm. Torque: Net: 145 lb.-ft. @ 2400 rpm. Oil refill capacity: 4qt. with filter change. Fuel Requirements: Unleaded.

OPTIONAL ENGINE: Cherokee and Wagoneer. Requires power steering and 5-speed manual or automatic transmission on Cherokee. Not available for base Cherokee. Engine Type: OHV, Renault 4-cyl. Turbo-charged diesel. Cast aluminum block and cylinder head. Not available for California. Bore x Stroke: 3.49 in. x 3.51 in. Lifters: Hydraulic. Number of main bearings-5. Fuel Induction: Bosch Injection. Compression Ratio: 21.5:1. Displacement: 126 cu. in. (2.1 liters). Horsepower: Net: 85 @ 3250 rpm. Torque: Net: 132 lb.-ft. @ 3000 rpm. Oil refill capacity: 5 qt. with filter change. Fuel Requirements: #1, #2D diesel fuel. Note: All Grand Wagoneer, technical data was unchanged from 1984. The following material, except where noted, relates to the Cherokee and Wagoneer models.

CHASSIS FEATURES: "Uniframe" full-length boxed steel frame welded to unitized body.

SUSPENSION AND RUNNING GEAR: Front Suspension: Coil springs with leading links and track bar, link-type 0.87 in. dia. stabilizer bar. Spring rate at wheel: 120 lb./in. Rear Suspension: Semi-elliptical leaf springs, link type 0.55 in. dia. stabilizer bar. Optional: Heavy-duty front and rear suspension, Soft-Ride suspension. Front Axle Type and Capacity: Dana model 30 Hypoid. Rear Axle Type and Capacity: Hotchkiss. Optional: None. Final Drive Ratio: Cherokee: 3.31:1, Wagoneer: 3.73:1. Optional: None. Transfer Case: Automatic transmission (also available with 5-speed manual transmission): Selec-Trac New Process 229. Ratios: 2.61:1, 1.00:1. 4-speed and 5-speed Manual transmission: Command-Trac New Process 207. Ratios: 2.61:1, 1.00:1. Brakes: Type: Hydraulic, front discs and rear drums. Dimensions: Front: 10.98 in. dia. disc. Rear: 10.0.0 in. x 1.750 in. drums. Wheels: Base Cherokee: 15 x 6 in., 5-bolt argent styled steel wheels with black hub covers. Cherokee Pioneer: 15 x 6 in. 5-bolt, argent styled steel wheels with bright trim rings and black hub covers. Cherokee Chief: 15 x 7 in. 5-bolt, white styled steel spoke wheel. Cherokee Laredo: 15 x 7 in. 5-bolt, Sport aluminum wheels. Base Wagoneer: 15 x 6 in. 5-bolt, steel wheels with argent styled covers. Wagoneer Limited: 15 x 6 in. 5-bolt luxury aluminum wheels. Tires: Base Cherokee: P195/75R15 steel belted All-Weather black sidewall radial. Cherokee Pioneer: P205/75R15 black sidewall steel-belted radial All-Weather. Cherokee Chief and Laredo: P215/75R15 OWL steel-belted radial Wrangler or Michelin XMS-1. Base and Limited Wagoneer: P205/75R15 white sidewall radials. Grand Wagoneer: P235/75R15 white steel-belted radial. Optional: Base Cherokee only: P205/75R15 black sidewall steel-belted radial All-Weather. Base and Pioneer Cherokee: P205/75R15 white sidewall All-Weather steel radial, P215/75R15 OWL steel-belted radial Michelin XMS-1 (requires 15 x 7 in. wheels). Base and Limited Wagoneer: P205/75R black sidewall steel All-Weather radial. Steering: Manual Saginaw recirculating ball type. Ratio: 26:1. Turns Lock-to-Lock: 4.8. Optional: Power Saginaw recirculating ball type. Ratio: 19:1. Turns Lock-to-Lock: 3.5:1. Turning Circle: 36.1 ft. Standard Transmission: Cherokee: 4-speed manual. Ratios: 3.93:1, 2.33:1, 1.45:1, 1.00:1. Reverse: 3.76:1. Optional: 5-speed manual (standard for Wagoneer). Ratios: 3.93:1, 2.33:1, 1.45:1, 1.00:1, 0.85:1. Reverse: 3.76:1. Optional Chrysler model 904 3-speed automatic. Ratios: 2.74:1, 1.55:1, 1.00:1. Reverse: 2.2:1. Standard for Wagoneer Limited. Clutch: Clutch diameter: 9.7 in. dia. Optional: None.

VEHICLE DIMENSIONS: Wheelbase: 101.4 in. Overall Length: 165.3 in. Front/Rear Tread: 58.0/58.0 in. Overall Height: 64.1 in. Width: 70.5 in. Front/Rear Overhang: 27.5 in./36.4 in. Approach/Departure Degrees: 39.7/31.1. Ground Clearance: Minimum clearance: 8.7 in. Maximum capacity: 71.2 cu. ft. (with rear seat folded). Front headroom: 38.3 in. Front legroom: 41.6 in. Front shoulder room: 55.3 in. Front hip room: 55.3 in. Rear headroom: 38.0 in. Rear legroom: 35.3 in. Rear shoulder room: 55.3 in. Rear hip room: 44.5 in.

CAPACITIES: Fuel Tank: 13.5 gal. Optional: 20.3 gal.

ACCOMMODATIONS: Seating Capacity: Six passengers.

INSTRUMENTATION: Speedometer, odometer, warning lights for alternator, oil pressure, and engine coolant temperature. Brake system warning, hazard lights operation. Cherokee Pioneer, Chief and Laredo models have standard voltmeter, oil pressure and engine coolant temperature gauges.

OPTIONS AND PRICES: Cherokee and Wagoneer: Color-keyed passenger area carpeting. Electronic clock with digital display. Tunnel-mounted console with armrest and rear ashtray. Sentinel headlamp switch. Color-keyed floor mats. Color-keyed vinyl spare tire cover. Front and rear bumper guards. Locking gas cap. Bright Sport grille. Black lower body side protection. Roof rack: $124. Spare tire carrier. Tinted glass (two-door base model). Front and rear tow hooks. Air conditioning. Air conditioning Prep Package. Includes heavy-duty cooling, heavy-duty battery, heavy-duty alternator. Heavy-duty battery. Cold Climate Group. Includes engine block heater, heavy-duty battery and alternator. Standard on 2.1 liter Turbo diesel. Heavy-duty cooling. Includes 7.0 in. radiator wall thickness. Included with air conditioning. Maximum Cooling Package. Includes 1.25 in. radiator wall thickness Available with V-6 engine only. Cruise Control: $199. Electric rear window defroster. Included in Visibility Group. Requires heavy-duty alternator and tinted glass: $146. Diesel Cold Start Package. Includes engine coolant heater and battery blanket heater. California emissions system. High Altitudes Emissions Package. 2.8 liter V-6. Not available with 4-speed manual transmission, required automatic transmission for California. 2.1 liter Turbo diesel engine. Fog lamps, required bumper guards. Extra capacity fuel tank. Extra-Quiet Insulation Package. Keyless entry system, required power door locks. Light Group. Includes glove box lamp, ashtray lamp, illuminated ring around cigarette lighter, dome/map lamp, cargo area lamp with on-off switch, under IP courtesy lamps, lighted visor mirror (not available for two-door base Cherokee), door switches for dome/courtesy lights added to rear doors. Dual low profile swing-away truck style mirrors. Dual manual remote mirrors. Power remote control exterior mirrors. Required power windows, door locks and full length console. Power door locks (four-door models only). Six-way power driver's seat. Passenger and driver 6-way power seats. Power steering. Power windows and locks. Required tinted glass: $188. Automatic actuating antenna. Required stereo radio. Protection Group. Included front and rear bumper guards. floor mats, door edge guards, cargo area skid strips. AM radio with two speakers. AM/FM/MPX high output radio with four speakers. Electronically tuned AM/FM/MPX/cassette high output stereo radio with Dolby noise reduction, coaxial front and rear speakers, and digital clock display. Pre-stereo kit with four speakers, stereo wiring harness and antenna (standard when AM radio is deleted on Cherokee Pioneer and Chief). Automatic actuating rear load leveling. (Not available with Trailer Tow B Package or diesel engine). Rear Trac-Lok differential. Not available with Selec-Trac or Systems Entry. Skid Plate Package. Includes protection for transfer case, fuel tank and front suspension. Tilt steering wheel, requires intermittent windshield wipers: $115. Three-spoke steering wheel. Leather-wrapped steering wheel. Heavy-duty suspension. Soft-Ride suspension (not available with Trailer Tow B Package). Systems Sentry. requires power steering, not available with diesel engine. Tachometer. Trailer A Package (2000 lb.). Included dead weight hitch, 5-wire harness. Trailer B Package (4200 lb.). Includes load leveling hitch, 7-wire harness, not available with diesel engine. Automatic 3-speed transmission. Requires power steering. Selec-Trac. Not available with manual transmission. Visibility Group. Includes dual manual remote mirrors, intermittent windshield wipers, rear window defroster. 15 x 7 in. Sport style aluminum wheels. 15 x 7 in. white styled steel wheels. Bright trim rings, available for base 15 x 6 in. wheels only. Front door vent, swing-out design. Requires tinted glass. Deep tinted two-door quarter glass. Includes tinted windshield, door windows and liftgate window. Intermittent windshield wipers. retractable underhood worklight. Not available with diesel engine. Grand Wagoneer: Straight shade non-clearcoat paint. Power sun roof with full vinyl roof: $1763. California emissions. High altitude emissions. 360 V-8. Engine block heater. Auxiliary transmission oil cooler, required with Trailer Towing B Package. Heavy-Duty Suspension Package. Includes heavy-duty front and rear shock absorbers. Trailer Towing A Package (3500 lb. capacity). Trailer Towing B Package (5000 lb. capacity).

HISTORICAL FOOTNOTES: The popularity of the Cherokee and Wagoneer continued to soar in 1985. During the first half of the model year they captured 28 percent of the sports utility vehicle market. Sales for that period reached 51,470 units, approximately 5,000 ahead of their nearest rival, the Ford Bronco II.

1986 WAGONEER & CHEROKEE

The Jeep Grand Wagoneer received significant appearance and additional convenience features for 1986. A new grille was adopted along with a stand-up Jeep hood ornament. Changes to the instrument panel included integrated controls for the heater/defroster and air conditioning systems. Both systems were modified for improved efficiency. The dash was redesigned to feature new gauges and a woodgrain overlay along with a full-face radio with a premium stereo sound system (Accusound by Jensen) with four speakers. The steering column and steering wheel were also redesigned to include column-mounted control functions for the light dimmer switch, windshield wipers and windshield washer. The Grand Wagoneer's leather seats now had Cumberland Cord fabric inserts. The standard Grand Wagoneer full-time four-wheel drive Selec-Trac driveline had a new Trac-Lok limited slip differential for 1986. This differential shifted the engine power to the wheel with the best traction. The Grand Wagoneer's extensive standard equipment content was continued for 1986. The Grand Wagoneer color section included a new beige paint color.

All Cherokee and Wagoneer models were powered by a redesigned version of AMC's 2.5 liter 4-cylinder engine which was equipped with throttle body fuel injection. This engine had both higher horsepower and torque outputs for 1986. The Cherokee had revised graphics for 1986. A special new Off-Highway Vehicle Package was introduced that consisted of premium high-pressure gas shock absorbers (painted yellow), five P225/75R15 OWL Wrangler tires, five 15 x 7 in. white styled "spoker" wheels, the Skid Plate Package, 4.10:1 axle ratio, tow hooks (two front, one rear), and a high ground clearance suspension consisting of unique front and rear springs and jounce bumpers providing a one in. higher ride height. Power steering and the air conditioning Prep Package were minimum equipment requirements with this Package. Recommended equipment included the Trac-Lok differential, brushguard and winch. Due to conflicting components, the heavy-duty suspension and rear load leveling options were not available with the Off-Road Suspension Package.

1986 Jeep Grand Wagoneer

The Trac-Lok limited slip rear differential, previously offered only in combination with the standard Command-Trac four-wheel drive system, was now available for the Cherokee and Wagoneer models fitted with the optional Selec-Trac four-wheel drive system.

The Cherokee continued to be offered in base, Pioneer, Chief and Laredo Trim Packages. The Wagoneer was available as a base or Limited model.

The Cherokee Laredo, available in either two-door or four-door body styles was highlighted by its unique exterior graphics that included bright door handles, grille, moldings, special striping, color-keyed fender flares and Laredo nameplates. Interior features included wing back rocker/recliner front seats with headrests, special trim, leather-wrapped Sport steering wheel, console, extra-pile carpeting and special storage pockets. Also included under the Laredo umbrella was power steering, roof rack, swing-out front vent windows, swing-out rear quarter vents windows and privacy glass (two-door only), rear window wiper/washer and rear seat beverage holders (two-door only). The Cherokee Chief continued to share many features of the Laredo along with unique exterior blackout graphics. The Wagoneer's extensive list of standard features was continued for 1986.

Clearcoat exterior colors available for the Cherokee and Wagoneer were white, beige, classic black, deep night blue and sebring red (Cherokee only). Metallic clearcoat paint colors consisted of medium blue (Cherokee only), garnet, sterling, dark honey, dark brown, champagne and charcoal.

1986 Jeep Cherokee

I.D. DATA: The serial number was located on the left-hand hinge pillar. The V.I.N. had 17 symbols. The first three entries identified the manufacturer, make and type of vehicle. The fourth unit, a letter, designated the engine. The fifth character, a letter, identified the transmission. The sixth and seventh characters identified the series and body style. The eighth character identified the GVW rating. Next followed a check digit. The eleventh character was the manufacturing plant identification. The final six digits were the sequential production number. The vehicle identification indicated the model as follows: Grand Wagoneer: 1JCC( )15U( )GT00001 and up. Wagoneer (4-cyl.): IJCH( )75( )( )GT000001 and up; Wagoneer (6-cyl.): 1JCW( )75( )( )GT000001 and up, Cherokee (4-cyl.): 1JC( )( )(model)( )( )GT000001 and up, Cherokee (6-cyl.): 1JCW( )(model)( )( )GT000001 and up. Vehicle identification was as follows: 15: Grand Wagoneer station wagon, 75: Wagoneer, 77: Two-door Cherokee, 78: Four-door Cherokee.

Model Number	Body Type	Factory Price	GVW	Shipping Weight	Prod. Total
Grand Wagoneer Station Wagon V-8					
15	4-dr.	$21,350	6200	4252	—
Wagoneer Station Wagon 4-cyl.					
75	4-dr.	$13,630	4549	3039	—
75	2-dr. Limited	$18,600	4549	3234	—
Wagoneer Station Wagon 6-cyl.					
75	4-dr.	$14,067	4598	3104	—
75	4-dr. Limited	$19,037	4598	3299	—
Cherokee Station Wagon 4-cyl.					
77	2-dr.	$10,695	4549	2917	—
78	4-dr.	$11,320	4549	2968	—
Cherokee Station Wagon 6-cyl.					
77	2-dr.	$11,132	4598	3013	—
78	4-dr.	$11,757	4598	3064	—

STANDARD ENGINE: Grand Wagoneer: Engine Type: OHV, In-line-6. Cast iron block and cylinder head. Bore x Stroke: 3.75 in. x 3.90 in. Lifters: Hydraulic. Number of main bearings-7. Fuel Induction: 2-bbl. carburetor. Compression Ratio: 9.2:1. Displacement: 258 cu. in. (4.2 liters). Horsepower: Net: 115 @ 3200 rpm. Torque: Net: 210 lb.-ft. @ 1800 rpm. Oil refill capacity: 5 qt. with filter change. Fuel Requirements: Unleaded. The two-

OPTIONAL ENGINE: Grand Wagoneer: Type: OHV, V-8. Cast iron block and cylinder head. Bore x Stroke: 4.08 in. x 3.44 in. Lifters: Hydraulic. Number of main bearings-5. Fuel Induction: 2-bbl. carburetor. Compression Ratio: 8.25:1. Displacement: 360 cu. in. (5.89 liters). Horsepower: Net: 129 @ 3700 rpm. Torque: Net: 245 lb.-ft. @ 1600 rpm. Oil refill capacity: 5 qt. with filter change. Fuel Requirements: Unleaded.

STANDARD ENGINE: Cherokee and Wagoneer: Engine Type: OHV, In-line-4. Cast iron block and cylinder head. Bore x Stroke: 3.88 in. x 3.19 in. Lifters: Hydraulic. Number of main bearings-5. Fuel Induction: Throttle body single point fuel injection. Compression Ratio: 9.2:1. Displacement: 150.45 cu. in. (2.4 liters). Horsepower: Net: 117 @ 5000 rpm. Torque: Net: 135 lb.-ft. @ 3500 rpm. Oil refill capacity: 4 qt. with filter change. Fuel Requirements: Unleaded.

OPTIONAL ENGINE: Cherokee and Wagoneer: Requires power steering and 5-speed manual or automatic transmission on Cherokee. Engine Type: OHV, V-6. Cast iron block and cylinder head. Bore x Stroke: 3.50 in. x 2.99 in. Lifters: Hydraulic. Number of main bearings-4. Fuel Induction: 2-bbl. Rochester 2SE carburetor. Compression Ratio: 8.5:1. Displacement: 173 cu. in. (2.8 liters). Horsepower: Net: 115 @ 4800 rpm. Torque: Net: 145 lb.-ft. @ 2400 rpm. Oil refill capacity: 5 qt. with filter change. Fuel Requirements: Unleaded.

OPTIONAL ENGINE: Cherokee and Wagoneer: Requires power steering and 5-speed manual or automatic transmission on Cherokee. Not available for base Cherokee. Engine Type: OHV, Renault 4-cyl. Turbo-charged diesel. Cast aluminum block and cylinder head. Not available for California. Bore x Stroke: 3.49 in. x 3.51 in. Lifters: Hydraulic. Number of main bearings-5. Fuel Induction: Bosch Injection. Compression Ratio: 21.5:1. Displacement: 126 cu. in. (2.1 liters). Horsepower: Net: 85 @ 3250 rpm. Torque: Net: 132 lb.-ft. @ 3000 rpm. Oil refill capacity: 5 qt. with filter change. Fuel Requirements: #1, #2D diesel fuel. Note: All Grand Wagoneer, Cherokee and Wagoneer technical data was unchanged from 1985. The following material, except where noted, relates to the Cherokee and Wagoneer models.

CHASSIS FEATURES: "Uniframe" full-length boxed steel frame welded to unitized body.

SUSPENSION AND RUNNING GEAR: Front Suspension: Coil springs with leading links and track bar, link-type 0.87 in. dia. stabilizer bar. Spring rate at wheel: 120 lb./in. Rear Suspension: Semi-elliptical leaf springs, link type 0.55 in. dia. stabilizer bar. Optional: Heavy-duty front and rear suspension, Soft-Ride suspension. Front Axle Type and Capacity: Dana model 30 Hypoid. Rear Axle Type and Capacity: Hotchkiss. Optional: None. Final Drive Ratio: Cherokee: 3.31:1, Wagoneer: 3.73:1. Optional: None. Transfer Case: Automatic transmission (also available with 5-speed manual transmission): Selec-Trac New Process 229. Ratios: 2.61:1, 1.00:1. 4-speed and 5-speed Manual transmission; Command-Trac New Process 207. Ratios: 2.61:1, 1.00:1. Brakes: Type: Hydraulic, front discs and rear drums. Dimensions: Front: 10.98 in. dia. disc. Rear: 10.0.0 in. x 1.750 in. drums. Wheels: Base Cherokee: 15 x 6 in., 5-bolt argent styled steel wheels with black hub covers. Cherokee Pioneer: 15 x 6 in. 5-bolt, argent styled steel wheels with bright trim rings and black hub covers. Cherokee Chief: 15 x 7 in. 5-bolt, white styled steel spoke wheel. Cherokee Laredo: 15 x 7 in. 5-bolt, Sport aluminum wheels. Base Wagoneer: 15 x 6 in. 5-bolt, steel wheels with argent styled covers. Wagoneer Limited: 15 x 6 in. 5-bolt luxury aluminum wheels. Tires: Base Cherokee: P195/75R15 steel belted All-Weather black sidewall radial. Cherokee Pioneer: P205/75R15 black sidewall steel-belted radial All-Weather. Cherokee Chief and Laredo: P215/75R15 OWL steel-belted radial Wrangler or Michelin XMS-1. Base and Limited Wagoneer: P205/75R15 white sidewall radials. Grand Wagoneer: P235/75R15 white steel-belted radial. Optional: Base Cherokee only: P205/75R15 black sidewall steel-belted radial All-Weather. Base and Pioneer Cherokee: P205/75R15 white sidewall All-Weather steel radial, P215/75R15 OWL steel-belted radial Michelin XMS-1 (requires 15 x 7 in. wheels). Base and Limited Wagoneer: P205/75R black sidewall steel All-Weather radial. Steering: Manual Saginaw recirculating ball type. Ratio: 26:1. Turns Lock-to-Lock: 4.8. Optional: Power Saginaw recirculating ball type. Ratio: 19:1. Turns Lock-to-Lock: 3.5:1. Turning Circle: 36.1 ft. Standard Transmission: Cherokee: 4-speed manual. Ratios: 3.93:1, 2.33:1, 1.45:1, 1.00:1. Reverse: 3.76:1. Optional: 5-speed manual (standard for Wagoneer). Ratios: 3.93:1, 2.33:1, 1.45:1, 1.00:1, 0.85:1. Reverse: 3.76:1. Optional Chrysler model 904 3-speed automatic. Ratios: 2.74:1, 1.55:1, 1.00:1. Reverse: 2.2:1. Standard for Wagoneer Limited. Clutch: Clutch diameter: 9.7 in. dia. Optional: None.

VEHICLE DIMENSIONS: Wheelbase: 101.4 in. Overall Length: 165.3 in. Front/Rear Tread: 58.0/58.0 in. Overall Height: 64.1 in. Width: 70.5 in. Front/Rear Overhang: 27.5 in./36.4 in. Approach/Departure Degrees: 39.7/31.1. Ground Clearance: Minimum clearance: 8.7 in. Maximum capacity: 71.2 cu. ft. (with rear seat folded). Front headroom: 38.3 in. Front legroom: 41.6 in. Front shoulder room: 55.3 in. Front hip room: 55.3 in. Rear headroom: 38.0 in. Rear legroom: 35.3 in. Rear shoulder room: 55.3 in. Rear hip room: 44.5 in.

CAPACITIES: Fuel Tank: 13.5 gal. Optional: 20.3 gal.

ACCOMMODATIONS: Seating Capacity: Six passengers.

INSTRUMENTATION: Speedometer, odometer, warning lights for alternator, oil pressure, and engine coolant temperature. Brake system warning, hazard lights operation. Cherokee Pioneer, Chief and Laredo models have standard voltmeter, oil pressure and engine coolant temperature gauges.

OPTIONS AND PRICES: With the exception of the new Jensen stereo system and Off-Highway Vehicle Package, the options for the Grand Wagoneer, Cherokee and Wagoneer were unchanged for 1986.

HISTORICAL FOOTNOTES: All 1986 Jeep vehicles were covered by a Jeep New Vehicle Limited Warranty which provided 12 month/12,000 mile coverage for the entire vehicle (except tires) as well as a three year corrosion protection. The major engine, transmission and power-train components were covered for 24 months/24,000 miles. The 1986 EPA rating estimate for the Cherokee and Wagoneer with 5-speed manual transmission was 21 mpg city and 25 mpg highway.

1987 WAGONEER & CHEROKEE

All versions of the 1987 Wagoneer and Cherokee were available with a new optional 4.0 liter 6-cylinder engine that gave them a zero to 60 mph capability of less than ten seconds and increased their maximum trailering capacity to 5,000 lbs. Optional for the Cherokee and standard for the Wagoneer was a new wide-ratio 4 speed automatic transmission. This transmission was electronically controlled and had an overdrive 4th gear and a lock-up converter. It also featured dual shift modes for either power or comfort settings. In the power mode, under hard acceleration, the transmission upshifted at a higher engine rpm, downshifted more rapidly and was more sensitive to the throttle setting. The comfort mode provided normal operating conditions with a more conservative and economical shifting schedule. The optional Selec-Trac featured a new New Process 242 full-time four-wheel drive transfer case in which all shift modes were controlled by a single lever. Five shift positions were provided. The two-wheel drive/four-wheel drive vacuum control switch employed on previous year Cherokee and Wagoneer models was eliminated with the NP 242 transfer case. The standard transfer case for the Cherokee and Wagoneer remained the NP 231 part-time four-wheel drive system.

1987 Jeep Grand Wagoneer

The latest Cherokee had revised exterior graphics. A new option for the Cherokee base and Laredo two-door models was a two-tone paint configuration. This was standard on base Wagoneer models. New door trim panels with stowage bins were also standard for all 1987 Cherokees. Initially, four trim levels were offered for the Cherokee: Base, Pioneer, Chief and Laredo. At mid-year a new Limited model was offered for the four-door Cherokee. It was offered in a choice of three monochromatic exterior colors: Charcoal metallic, grenadine metallic and classic black. The Cherokee Limited also featured a low gloss black and body-color grille, body-color bumpers, body-color fender flares and a front air dam. Black nerf stripes with gold inserts were installed in the front and rear bumpers. Gold color cast aluminum wheels with P225/70HR 15 Goodyear Eagle GT+4 tires were also standard. The wheels were emblazoned with Jeep lettering. The Limited special body graphics included dual, upper body side and liftgate gold stripes and a Limited logo integrated with the body side striping. The Limited interior had unique leather wingback front bucket seats with perforated leather inserts and recessed seat back panels, recliners, adjustable headrests and leather facing. A six-way power adjustment was also standard. Carpeting was installed in the passenger and cargo area. Other appointments included a full-length console with armrest, rear ashtray, rear heating/cooling ducts, leather-wrapped steering wheel and special instrument panel cluster graphics. The Limited was powered by the 4.0 liter engine and was equipped with Selec-Trac. Additional standard features consisted of Gauge Package, tachometer, power steering, air conditioning, power windows and locks, tinted glass, tilt wheel, cruise control, extra-quiet insulation, extra-capacity fuel tank, remote control door locks, premium sound system with AM/FM/MPX cassette electronically-tuned stereo radio with eight "Accusound by Jensen" speakers, power antenna, front vent windows, front sway bar and unique, tuned shock absorbers. The Laredo Package had a new standard Hunter's Plaid fabric offered in either cordovan or tan. The Cherokee Chief had new blackout graphics for 1987. A new English walnut exterior body side molding was introduced for the latest Wagoneer Limited. The equipment content of the base Wagoneer was revised to include new door trim panels and stowage bins, fabric wingback bucket seats with headrests, woodgrain instrument panel overlay, leather-wrapped Sport steering wheel, swing-out front door vent windows and the new 4-speed automatic transmission. Both the Cherokee and Wagoneer were offered with a new 5-spoke aluminum wheel option. The 10-spoke aluminum wheel remained available. The Wagoneer Limited had new Michelin "Tru-Seal" P205/75R15 self-sealing tires as standard equipment. They were also offered as an option for the base Wagoneer.

The Grand Wagoneer's standard engine was the 5.9 liter V-8. The Grand Wagoneer was also fitted with standard Michelin "Tru Seal" P235/75R15 white sidewall steel radial tires. The Grand Wagoneer's exterior received a new English Walnut woodgrain color, and new Grand Wagoneer and V-8 nameplates. Two new exterior clearcoat metallic colors were offered: Grenadine and briarwood. Two new interior colors were also offered: Tan and cordovan. As in the past, the Grand Wagoneer had a long list of standard features including power steering, power front disc brakes, leather seats, air conditioning, power door locks, six-way power seat, cruise control, dual electric remote outside mirrors, halogen fog lamps, tilt steering wheel, rear defroster, quartz electronic digital clock, roof rack, tinted glass and electronically-tuned AM/FM radio with four Jensen speakers.

Clearcoated solid colors available on the Cherokee and Wagoneer were classic black, Colorado red (not available for Wagoneer), olympic white, deep night blue and beige. Extra cost clearcoat metallic colors were briarwood, grenadine, charcoal, medium blue (not available for Wagoneer), dark pewter (Wagoneer only), sterling silver and champagne. The two-tone color selection consisted of beige/briarwood, olympic white/medium blue, sterling silver/charcoal and sterling silver/grenadine.

1987 Jeep Wagoneer Limited

I.D. DATA: The serial number was located on the left-hand hinge pillar. The V.I.N. had 17 symbols. The first three entries identified the manufacturer, make and type of vehicle. The fourth unit, a letter, designated the engine (C-4.2 liter 6-cyl., H-2.5 liter 4-cyl., M-4.0 liter 6-cyl., N-5.9 liter V-8). The fifth character, a letter, identified the transmission. The sixth and seventh characters identified the series and body style. The eighth character identified the GVW rating. Next followed a check digit. The eleventh character was the manufacturing plant identification. The final six digits were the sequential production number. The vehicle identification indicated the model as follows: Grand Wagoneer: ( )( )CN( )15(U)HT000001 and up. Wagoneer (4-cyl.): ( )( )CH( )75( )( )HT000001 and up; Wagoneer (6-cyl.): ( )( )CM( )75( )( )HT000001 and up, Cherokee (4-cyl.): 1JC( )( )(model)( )( )HT000001 and up, Cherokee (6-cyl.): 1JCM( )(model)( )( )HT000001 and up. Vehicle identification was as follows: 15: Grand Wagoneer Station Wagon, 75: Wagoneer, 77: Two-door Cherokee, 78: Four-door Cherokee.

Model Number	Body Type	Factory Price	GVW	Shipping Weight	Prod. Total
Grand Wagoneer Station Wagon V-8					
15	4-dr.	$23,560	6200	4509	14,265*

* Calendar year production. Calendar sales were 14,079 units.

Model Number	Body Type	Factory Price	GVW	Shipping Weight	Prod. Total
Wagoneer Station Wagon 4-cyl.					
75	4-dr.	$15,126	4549	3083	15,033*
75	2-dr. Limited	$19,995	4549	3278	—
Wagoneer Station Wagon 6-cyl.					
75	4-dr.	$15,634	4598	3216	—
75	4-dr. Limited	$20,503	4598	3411	—

* 1987 calendar year production-all Wagoneer models. Calender year sales totalled 12,305 units.

Model Number	Body Type	Factory Price	GVW	Shipping Weight	Prod. Total
Cherokee Station Wagon 4-cyl.					
77	2-dr.	$11,753	4549	2936	139,295*
78	4-dr.	$12,298	4549	2983	—
Cherokee Station Wagon 6-cyl.					
77	2-dr.	$12,261	4598	3079	—
78	4-dr.	$12,806	4598	3126	—
78	4-dr. Limited	$22,104	4598	3294	—

* 1987 calendar year production-includes all Cherokee models. 1987 calendar year sales totalled 112,005 units.

STANDARD ENGINE: Grand Wagoneer: Engine Type: OHV, V-8. Cast iron block and cylinder head. Bore x Stroke: 4.08 in. x 3.44 in. Lifters: Hydraulic. Number of main bearings-5. Fuel Induction: 2-bbl. carburetor. Compression Ratio: 8.25:1. Displacement: 360 cu. in. (5.89 liters). Horsepower: Net: 175 @ 4000 rpm. Torque: Net: 285 lb.-ft. @ 2400 rpm. Oil refill capacity: 5 qt. with filter change. Fuel Requirements: Unleaded.

STANDARD ENGINE: Cherokee and Wagoneer: Engine Type: OHV, In-line-4. Cast iron block and cylinder head. Bore x Stroke: 3.88 in. x 3.19 in. Lifters: Hydraulic. Number of main bearings-5. Fuel Induction: Throttle body single point fuel injection. Compression Ratio: 9.2:1. Displacement: 150.45 cu. in. (2.4 liters). Horsepower: Net: 121 @ 5000 rpm. Torque: Net: 141 lb.-ft. @ 3500 rpm. Oil refill capacity: 5 qt. with filter change. Fuel Requirements: Unleaded.

OPTIONAL ENGINE: Cherokee and Wagoneer: Engine Type: OHV, 6-cyl. Cast iron block and cylinder head. Bore x Stroke: 3.88 in. x 3.14 in. Lifters: Hydraulic. Number of main bearings-7. Fuel Induction: Multi-point high pressure fuel injection. Compression Ratio: 9.2:1. Displacement: 241.6 cu. in. (3.96 liters). Horsepower: Net: 173 @ 4500 rpm. Torque: Net: 220 lb.-ft. @ 2500 rpm. Oil refill capacity: 5 qt. with filter change. Fuel Requirements: Unleaded.

OPTIONAL ENGINE: Cherokee and Wagoneer: Requires power steering and 5-speed manual or automatic transmission on Cherokee. Not available for base Cherokee. Engine Type: OHV, Renault 4-cyl. Turbo-charged diesel. Cast aluminum block and cylinder head. Not available for California or high altitude areas. Bore x Stroke: 3.49 in. x 3.51 in. Lifters: Hydraulic. Number of main bearings-5. Fuel Induction: Bosch Injection. Compression Ratio: 21.5:1. Displacement: 126 cu. in. (2.1 liters). Horsepower: Net: 85 @ 3250 rpm. Torque: Net: 132 lb.-ft. @ 3000 rpm. Oil refill capacity: 5 qt. with filter change. Fuel Requirements: #1, #2D diesel fuel.

CHASSIS FEATURES: Cherokee and Wagoneer: "Uniframe" full-length boxed steel frame welded to unitized body. Grand Wagoneer: Separate body and frame.

SUSPENSION AND RUNNING GEAR: Cherokee and Wagoneer: Front Suspension: Coil springs with leading links and track bar, link-type 0.95 in. dia. stabilizer bar. Spring rate at wheel: 120 lb./in. Grand Wagoneer: Leaf spring mounted below axle. 1.00 in. link type stabilizer bar. Spring rate at wheel: 160 lb./in. Rear Suspension: Cherokee and Wagoneer: Semi-elliptical leaf springs, link type 0.63 in. dia. stabilizer bar Spring rate at wheel: 165 lb./in. Grand Wagoneer: Leaf spring mounted below axle. Optional: Cherokee and Wagoneer (available for 4.0 liter only): Heavy-duty front and rear suspension, heavy-duty rear axle. Front Axle Type and Capacity: Cherokee and Wagoneer: Dana model 30 Hypoid. Grand Wagoneer: Dana model 44 full-floating. Rear Axle Type and Capacity: Cherokee and Wagoneer: Dana HOL 35C or Dana MO4 44. Grand Wagoneer: AMC Hypoid semi-floating. Final Drive Ratio: Cherokee and Wagoneer: Turbo diesel/4-spd. man. trans.: 3.07:1; 4-cyl./5-spd. man. trans.: 3.08:1; 6-cyl./4-spd. auto. trans.: 3.54:1. Grand Wagoneer: 2.73:1 (New Process 228 transfer case), 3.31:1 (New Process 208 transfer case). Optional: Cherokee and Wagoneer: For 6-cyl.: 3.55:1, 4.11:1, 4.56:1. Transfer Case: Cherokee and Wagoneer: Standard: Command-Trac New Process 231. Ratios: 2.61:1, 1.00:1: Optional: Selec-Trac New Process 242 transfers case. Ratios: 2.61:1, 1.00:1. Grand Wagoneer: Selec-Trac New Process 242. Ratios: 2.61:1, 1.0:1. Brakes: Type: Cherokee, Wagoneer and Grand Wagoneer: Hydraulic, front discs and rear drums. Dimensions: Cherokee and Wagoneer: Front: 10.98 in. dia. disc. Rear: 10.0.0 in. x 1.750 in. drums. Grand Wagoneer: Front: 12.0 in. dia. disc. Rear: 11.0 x 2.00 in. drums. Wheels: Base Cherokee: 15 x 6 in., 5-bolt argent styled steel wheels with black hub covers. Cherokee Pioneer: 15 x 6 in. 5-bolt, argent styled steel wheels with bright trim rings and black hub covers. Cherokee Chief: 15 x 7 in. 5-bolt, white styled steel spoke wheel with bright hub covers. Cherokee Laredo: 15 x 7 in. 5-bolt, cast aluminum 10 spoke wheels with bright hubs. Base Wagoneer: 15 x 6 in. 5-bolt, steel wheels with argent styled covers. Wagoneer Limited: 15 x 6 in. 5-bolt cast aluminum 5-spoke wheels. Tires: Base Cherokee: P195/75R15 steel belted All-Weather black sidewall radial. Cherokee Pioneer: P205/75R15 black sidewall steel-belted radial All-Weather with 15 x 6 or 15 x 7 in. wheels. Cherokee Chief and Laredo: P215/75R15 Michelin OWL steel-belted radial All-Terrain. Requires 15 x 7 in. wheels. Not available with 2.5 liter engine with 4-spd. trans. Base Wagoneer: P205/75R15 white sidewall All-Weather radials with either 15 x 6 in. or 15 x 7 in. wheels. Wagoneer Limited: P205/75R15 white sidewall Michelin Tru-Seal puncture resistant steel radial with 15 x 6 in. or 15 x 7 in. wheels. Grand Wagoneer: P235/75R15 Michelin white sidewall Tru-Seal puncture resistant radial. Optional: Base Cherokee only: P205/75R15 black sidewall steel-belted radial All-Weather. Base and Pioneer Cherokee: P205/75R15 white sidewall All-Weather steel radial with 15 x 6 in. or 15 x 7 in. wheels, P215/75R15 black sidewall Goodyear Wrangler steel-belted radial All-Terrain (requires 15 x 7 in. wheels), P215/75R15 Michelin OWL steel belted radial All-Terrain (requires 15 x 7 in. wheel, not available with 2.5 liter engine with 4-spd. trans). Wagoneer: P205/75R15 white sidewall Michelin Tru-Seal steel belted radial (with 15 x

6 or 15 x 7 in. wheels). Wagoneer and Wagoneer Limited: P205/75R15 black steel belted radial All-Weather (with 15 x 6 or 15 x 7 in. wheels). Steering: Cherokee: Manual recirculating ball type. Ratio: 24:1. Turns Lock-to-Lock: 4.8. Wagoneer (optional for Cherokee): Power Saginaw recirculating ball type. Ratio: 14:1. Turns Lock-to-Lock: 3.5:1. Grand Wagoneer: Power Saginaw recirculating ball type, variable ratio. Ratio: 16:1, 13:1. Turns Lock-to-Lock: 3.5. Turning Circle: Cherokee and Wagoneer: 35.7 ft. Grand Wagoneer: 37.7 ft. Standard Transmission: Base and Pioneer Cherokee: 4-speed manual. Ratios: 3.93:1, 2.33:1, 1.45:1, 1.00:1. Reverse: 3.76:1. Standard for Cherokee Chief and Laredo (optional for Cherokee base, Cherokee Pioneer and Wagoneer). 5-speed manual. (A-S 5-spd. for 4-cyl. engines, Peugeot 5-spd. for 6-cyl.) Ratios: A-S: 3.93:1, 2.33:1, 1.45:1, 1.00:1, 0.85:1. Reverse: 4.74:1. Peugeot: 4.03:1, 2.39:1, 1.52:1, 1.0:1, 0.72:1. Reverse: 3.76:1. Optional for all Cherokee models and standard for Wagoneer: Aisin-Warner 30-40 LE 4-speed automatic. Ratios: 2.80:1, 1.53:1, 1.00:1, 0.71:1. Reverse: 2.39:1. Grand Wagoneer: Chrysler model 727 3-speed automatic. Ratios: 2.45:1, 1.55:1, 1.0:1. Reverse: 2.20:1. Clutch: Cherokee and Wagoneer: Clutch diameter: 9.1 in. dia. Hydraulic actuation. Optional: None.

VEHICLE DIMENSIONS: Wagoneer and Cherokee. Wheelbase: 101.4 in. Overall Length: 165.3 in. Front/Rear Tread: 57.0 in./57.0 in. Overall Height: 63.33 in. Width: 70.5 in. Front/Rear Overhang: 27.5 in./36.4 in. Approach/Departure Degrees: 39.7/31.0. Ground Clearance: Minimum clearance: 7.4 in. (rear axle to ground). Minimum Running Clearance: 8.8 in. Maximum capacity: 71.8 cu. ft. (with rear seat folded). Front headroom: 38.3 in. Front legroom: 39.9 in. Front shoulder room: 55.3 in. Front hip room: 55.3 in. Rear headroom: 38.0 in. Rear legroom: 35.3 in. Rear shoulder room: 55.3 in. Rear hip room: 44.5 in. Grand Wagoneer. Wheelbase: 108.7 in. Overall Length: 186.4 in. Front/Rear Tread: 59.4 in./57.8 in. Overall Height: 66.4 in. Width: 74.8 in. Front/Rear Overhang: 31.3 in./46.4 in. Approach/Departure Degrees: 39/20. Ground Clearance: Minimum clearance: 7.2 in. (rear axle to ground). Minimum Running Clearance: 10.1 in. Maximum capacity: 95.1 cu. ft. (with rear seat folded). Front headroom: 37.1 in. Front legroom: 40.5 in. Front shoulder room: 58.3 in. Front hip room: 60.5 in. Rear headroom: 36.8 in. Rear legroom: 37.0 in. Rear shoulder room: 58.3 in. Rear hip room: 60.9 in.

CAPACITIES: Fuel Tank: Cherokee and Wagoneer: 13.5 gal. Optional: 20.2 gal. Grand Wagoneer: 20.3 gal.

ACCOMMODATIONS: Seating Capacity: Cherokee and Wagoneer: Five passengers, Grand Wagoneer: Six passengers.

INSTRUMENTATION: Cherokee: Speedometer, odometer, warning lights for alternator, oil pressure, and engine coolant temperature. Brake system warning, high beam/hazard lights operation. Wagoneer, Cherokee Pioneer, Chief and Laredo models have the previously listed items plus standard trip odometer, digital clock, and voltmeter, oil pressure and engine coolant temperature gauges. Grand Wagoneer: Speedometer, fuel gauge, gauges for voltmeter, oil pressure and engine coolant temperature, warning lights for seat belts, parking brake and four-wheel drive, indicator lights for directional/4-way hazard, high beam.

OPTIONS: Cherokee and Wagoneer: Color-keyed passenger area carpeting. Sun roof. Electronic clock with digital display (standard for Wagoneer). Console with armrest, storage box, rear ashtray and rear heating ducts. Color-keyed floor mats. Rear quarter flipper window (two-door only). Color-keyed inside-mounted vinyl spare tire cover. Front and rear bumper guards. Roof rack. Outside spare tire carrier. Requires full-size spare. Front and rear tow hooks. Air conditioning. Heavy-duty battery. Intermittent wipers. Rear window washer and wiper. Cold Climate Group. Includes engine block heater, heavy-duty battery and alternator. Standard on 2.1 liter Turbo diesel. Heavy-duty cooling. Includes 7.0 in. radiator wall thickness. Included with air conditioning. Cruise control. Halogen fog lamps. Requires bumper guards. Extended-range 20.2 gal. fuel tank. Keyless entry system. Requires power door locks and windows. Electric rear window defroster. Included in Visibility Group. Requires heavy-duty alternator and tinted glass. California emissions system. High Altitudes Emissions Package. 2.8 liter V-6. Not available with 4-speed manual transmission, required automatic transmission for California. 2.1 liter Turbo diesel engine. Extra-Quiet Insulation Package. Keyless entry system, required power door locks. Light Group. Includes ashtray light, dome/map light, cargo area light with tailgate switch, courtesy lights, retractable underhood work light, door switches, visor mirror light, Sentinel headlight switch (not available for base Cherokee, standard for Wagoneer). Dual low profile swing-away truck style mirrors. Dual manual remote mirrors. Power remote control exterior mirrors. Required power windows, door locks. Power door locks. Six-way power driver and passenger seat. Power steering. Required with air conditioning, 4 liter and diesel engines, or automatic transmission. Protection Group. Included front and rear bumper guards, floor mats, door edge guards, cargo area skid strips and locking gas cap. AM radio with two speakers. AM/FM monaural radio with two speakers. Electronically tuned AM/FM stereo radio with four speakers. Electronically tuned AM/FM stereo radio with cassette tape player and dynamic noise reduction. Electronically tuned high-output AM/FM stereo radio with Dolby system and six premium "Accusound by Jensen" speakers (requires power windows and door locks). Power antenna. Skid Plate Package. Includes protection for transfer case, fuel tank and front suspension. Tilt steering column, requires intermittent windshield wipers. Leather-wrapped 3-spoke steering wheel. Custom two-tone paint with high-break. Heavy-duty suspension. Includes heavy-duty springs and shock absorbers, heavy-duty rear axle. Available for 4 liter engine only. Off-Road Package. Includes heavy-duty rear axle, high-pressure gas shock absorbers, 15 x 7 in. white styled spoker P225/75R15 OWL All-Terrain tires, full-size spare, Skid Plate Package, tow hooks (2 front, 1 rear), unique front and rear springs and jounce bumpers. Requires power windows, heavy-duty battery and heavy-duty cooling. Not available with 2.5 liter with 4-spd. manual trans. or diesel engine or Wagoneer) Tachometer. Included with diesel engine. Trailer A Package (2000 lb.). Included dead weight hitch, 5-wire harness. Trailer B Package (4200 lb.). Includes load leveling hitch, 7-wire harness, not available with diesel engine. Automatic 4-speed overdrive transmission. Requires power steering. Five-speed manual overdrive transmission with floor shift. Four-speed automatic overdrive transmission with Selec-Trac. Requires 4 liter engine and power steering. Visibility Group. Includes dual manual remote mirrors, intermittent windshield wipers, rear window defroster. 15 x 6 in. styled steel wheels with bright trim rings (not available for Wagoneer). 15 x 7 in. cast aluminum 10 spoke wheels (not available for Wagoneer). 15 x 7 in. cast aluminum 5-spoke wheels. Front door vent, swing-out design (standard for Wagoneer). Deep tinted two-door quarter glass. Includes tinted windshield, door windows and liftgate window. Light-Duty Trailer Package A. Heavy-Duty Trailer Package B. Grand Wagoneer: Power sun roof with vinyl roof. Power sun roof without vinyl roof. Rear Trac-Lok differential. Includes 3.31:1 axle ratio, requires full-size spare. Auxiliary automatic transmission oil cooler. Required with Trailer Towing Package A and B. Cold Climate Group. Includes engine block heater. Heavy-duty shock absorbers. Full-size spare tire. Trailer Towing A Package 3500 lb. capacity). Trailer Towing B Package (5000 lb. capacity). Cherokee Chief Package. Cherokee Laredo Package. Cherokee Pioneer Package:

HISTORICAL FOOTNOTES: Jeep was the world's first vehicle manufacturer to offer the Michelin "Tru Seal" tires as standard equipment. In 1987, Jeep dealers sold 208,440 Jeep vehicles, an all-time U.S. sales record. This was the third year of consecutive sales records for Jeep.

1988 WAGONEER & CHEROKEE

Jeep expanded the Cherokee Limited series to include a two-door model for 1988. The Wagoneer was available only in Limited form for 1988. The electronically fuel injected 4 liter 6-cylinder "Power Tech Six" engine was standard for the Jeep Wagoneer and Cherokee Limited models for 1988. The turbo-charged diesel was not available in 1988.

1988 Jeep Cherokee Pioneer

All Cherokee models had a new eight-slot grille for 1988. The Cherokee Laredo had new exterior trim, including bright door handles, grille, moldings, special pin striping, and new, lower body side moldings. The Laredo interior was revised by the use of new trim colors. Early in 1988, Jeep expanded the market spread of the Cherokee with the introduction of the Sport Package for the two-door model. Positioned below the Pioneer and Laredo versions, the Sport was fitted with 10-hole aluminum wheels, 5-speed manual transmission, unique exterior graphics and floor carpeting.

A new optional feature for the Grand Wagoneer was an electric sun roof with integral air deflector and venting capability. Also new was the Grand Wagoneer's standard sound system, an AM/FM/MPX electronically-tuned stereo cassette with four premium "Accusound by Jensen" speakers.

1988 Jeep Cherokee Chief

I.D. DATA: The serial number was located on the left-hand hinge pillar. The V.I.N. had 17 symbols. The first three entries identified the manufacturer, make and type of vehicle. The fourth unit, a letter, designated the engine (C-4.2 liter 6-cyl., H-2.5 liter 4-cyl., M-4.0 liter 6-cyl., N-5.9 liter V-8). The fifth character, a letter, identified the transmission. The sixth and seventh characters identified the series and body style. The eighth character identified the GVW rating. Next followed a check digit. The eleventh character was the manufacturing plant identification. The final six digits were the sequential production number. The vehicle identification indicated the model as follows: Grand Wagoneer: ( )( )N( )15U( )J000001 and up. Wagoneer (6-cyl.): ( )( )CM( )754( )J( )000001 and up, Cherokee (4-cyl.): ( )( )CH( )(model)( )( )J000001 and up, Cherokee (6-cyl.): ( )( )CM(model)( )( )J( )000001 and up. Vehicle identification was as follows: 15: Grand Wagoneer station wagon, 75: Wagoneer, 77: Two-door Cherokee, 78: Four-door Cherokee.

Model Number	Body Type	Factory Price	GVW	Shipping Weight	Prod. Total
Grand Wagoneer Station Wagon V-8					
15	4-dr.	$24,623	6200	4488	14,177*
*Calendar year production					
Wagoneer Station Wagon 6-cyl.					
75	4-dr. Limited	$21,926	4797	3409	10,902*
*Calendar year production					
Cherokee Station Wagon 4-cyl.					
77	2-dr.	$12,415	4657	2972	187,136*
78	4-dr.	$13,027	4657	3008	—
Cherokee Station Wagon 6-cyl.					
77	2-dr.	$12,942	4797	3105	—
78	4-dr.	$13,554	4797	3141	—
77	2-dr. Limited	$22,260	4797	3590	—
78	4-dr. Limited	$23,153	4797	3626	—

* 1988 calendar year production-includes all Cherokee models.

STANDARD ENGINE: Grand Wagoneer: Engine Type: OHV, V-8. Cast iron block and cylinder head. Bore x Stroke: 4.08 in. x 3.44 in. Lifters: Hydraulic. Number of main bearings-5. Fuel Induction: 2-bbl. carburetor. Compression Ratio: 8.25:1. Displacement: 360 cu. in. (5.89 liters). Horsepower: Net: 175 @ 4000 rpm. Torque: Net: 285 lb.-ft. @ 2400 rpm. Oil refill capacity: 5 qt. with filter change. Fuel Requirements: Unleaded.

STANDARD ENGINE: Cherokee: Engine Type: OHV, In-line-4. Cast iron block and cylinder head. Bore x Stroke: 3.88 in. x 3.19 in. Lifters: Hydraulic. Number of main bearings-5. Fuel Induction: Throttle body single point fuel injection. Compression Ratio: 9.2:1. Displacement: 150.45 cu. in. (2.4 liters). Horsepower: Net: 121 @ 5000 rpm. Torque: Net: 141 lb.-ft. @ 3500 rpm. Oil refill capacity: 5 qt. with filter change. Fuel Requirements: Unleaded.

OPTIONAL ENGINE: Cherokee: Standard for Cherokee Limited and Wagoneer Limited. Engine Type: OHV, 6-cyl. Cast iron block and cylinder head. Bore x Stroke: 3.88 in. x 3.14 in. Lifters: Hydraulic. Number of main bearings-7. Fuel Induction: Multi-point, electronic fuel injection. Compression Ratio: 9.2:1. Displacement: 241.6 cu. in. (3.96 liters). Horsepower: Net: 177 @ 4500 rpm. Torque: Net: 224 lb.-ft. @ 2500 rpm. Oil refill capacity: 5 qt. with filter change. Fuel Requirements: Unleaded. All chassis features, suspension, dimensions, etc. were unchanged for 1988.

CHASSIS FEATURES: Cherokee and Wagoneer: "Uniframe" full-length boxed steel frame welded to unitized body. Grand Wagoneer: Separate body and frame.

SUSPENSION AND RUNNING GEAR: Cherokee and Wagoneer: Front Suspension: Coil springs with leading links and track bar, link-type 0.95 in. dia. stabilizer bar. Spring rate at wheel: 120 lb./in. Grand Wagoneer: Leaf spring mounted below axle. 1.00 in. link type stabilizer bar. Spring rate at wheel: 160 lb./in. Rear Suspension: Cherokee and Wagoneer: Semi-elliptical leaf springs, link type 0.63 in. dia. stabilizer bar Spring rate at wheel: 165 lb./in. Grand Wagoneer: Leaf spring mounted below axle. Optional: Cherokee and Wagoneer (available for 4.0 liter only): Heavy-duty front and rear suspension, heavy-duty rear axle. Front Axle Type and Capacity: Cherokee and Wagoneer: Dana model 30 Hypoid. Grand Wagoneer: Dana model 44 full-floating. Rear Axle Type and Capacity: Cherokee and Wagoneer: Dana HOL 35C or Dana MO4 44. Grand Wagoneer: AMC Hypoid semi-floating. Final Drive Ratio: Cherokee and Wagoneer: Turbo diesel/4-spd. man. trans.: 3.07:1; 4-cyl./5-spd. man. trans.: 3.08:1; 6-cyl./4-spd. auto. trans.: 3.54:1. Grand Wagoneer: 2.73:1 (New Process 228 transfer case), 3.31:1 (New Process 208 transfer case). Optional: Cherokee and Wagoneer: For 6-cyl.: 3.55:1, 4.11:1, 4.56:1. Transfer Case: Cherokee and Wagoneer: Standard: Command-Trac New Process 231. Ratios: 2.61:1, 1.00:1: Optional: Selec-Trac New Process 242 transfers case. Ratios: 2.61:1, 1.00:1. Grand Wagoneer: Selec-Trac New Process 242. Ratios: 2.61:1, 1.0:1. Brakes: Type: Cherokee, Wagoneer and Grand Wagoneer: Hydraulic, front discs and rear drums. Dimensions: Cherokee and Wagoneer: Front: 10.98 in. dia. disc. Rear: 10.0.0 in. x 1.750 in. drums. Grand Wagoneer: Front: 12.0 in. dia. disc. Rear: 11.0 x 2.00 in. drums. Wheels: Base Cherokee: 15 x 6 in., 5-bolt argent styled steel wheels with black hub covers. Cherokee Pioneer: 15 x 6 in. 5-bolt, argent styled steel wheels with bright trim rings and black hub covers. Cherokee Chief: 15 x 7 in. 5-bolt, white styled steel spoke wheel with bright hub covers. Cherokee Laredo: 15 x 7 in. 5-bolt, cast aluminum 10 spoke wheels with bright hubs. Base Wagoneer: 15 x 6 in. 5-bolt, steel wheels with argent styled covers. Wagoneer Limited: 15 x 6 in. 5-bolt cast aluminum 5-spoke wheels. Tires: Base Cherokee: P195/75R15 steel belted All-Weather black sidewall radial. Cherokee Pioneer: P205/75R15 black sidewall steel-belted radial All-Weather with 15 x 6 or 15 x 7 in. wheels. Cherokee Chief and Laredo: P215/75R15 Michelin OWL steel-belted radial All-Terrain. Requires 15 x 7 in. wheels. Not available with 2.5 liter engine with 4-spd. trans. Base Wagoneer: P205/75R15 white sidewall All-Weather radials with either 15 x 6 in. or 15 x 7 in. wheels. Wagoneer Limited: P205/75R15 white sidewall Michelin Tru-Seal puncture resistant steel radial with 15 x 6 in. or 15 x 7 in. wheels. Grand Wagoneer: P235/75R15 Michelin white sidewall Tru-Seal puncture resistant radial. Optional: Base Cherokee only: P205/75R15 black sidewall steel-belted radial All-Weather. Base and Pioneer Cherokee: P205/75R15 white sidewall All-Weather steel radial with 15 x 6 in. or 15 x 7 in. wheels, P215/75R15 black sidewall Goodyear Wrangler steel-belted radial All-Terrain (requires 15 x 7 in. wheels), P215/75R15 Michelin OWL steel belted radial All-Terrain (requires 15 x 7 in. wheel, not available with 2.5 liter engine with 4-spd. trans). Wagoneer: P205/75R15 white sidewall Michelin Tru-Seal steel belted radial (with 15 x 6 or 15 x 7 in. wheels). Wagoneer and Wagoneer Limited: P205/75R15 black steel belted radial All-Weather (with 15 x 6 or 15 x 7 in. wheels). Steering: Cherokee: Manual recirculating ball type. Ratio: 24:1. Turns Lock-to-Lock: 4.8. Wagoneer (optional for Cherokee): Power Saginaw recirculating ball type. Ratio: 14:1. Turns Lock-to-Lock: 3.5:1. Grand Wagoneer: Power Saginaw recirculating ball type, variable ratio. Ratio: 16:1, 13:1. Turns Lock-to-Lock: 3.5. Turning Circle: Cherokee and Wagoneer: 35.7 ft. Grand Wagoneer: 37.7 ft. Standard Transmission: Base and Pioneer Cherokee: 4-speed manual. Ratios: 3.93:1, 2.33:1, 1.45:1, 1.00:1. Reverse: 3.76:1. Standard for Cherokee Chief and Laredo (optional for Cherokee base, Cherokee Pioneer and Wagoneer). 5-speed manual. (A-S 5-spd. for 4-cyl. engines, Peugeot 5-spd. for 6-cyl.) Ratios: A-S: 3.93:1, 2.33:1, 1.45:1, 1.00:1, 0.85:1. Reverse: 4.74:1. Peugeot: 4.03:1, 2.39:1, 1.52:1, 1.0:1, 0.72:1. Reverse: 3.76:1. Optional for all Cherokee models and standard for Wagoneer: Aisin-Warner 30-40 LE 4-speed automatic. Ratios: 2.80:1, 1.53:1, 1.00:1, 0.71:1. Reverse: 2.39:1. Grand Wagoneer: Chrysler model 727 3-speed automatic. Ratios: 2.45:1, 1.55:1, 1.0:1. Reverse: 2.20:1. Clutch: Cherokee and Wagoneer: Clutch diameter: 9.1 in. dia. Hydraulic actuation. Optional: None.

1988 Jeep Wagoneer Limited

VEHICLE DIMENSIONS: Wagoneer and Cherokee: Wheelbase: 101.4 in. Overall Length: 165.3 in. Front/Rear Tread: 57.0 in./57.0 in. Overall Height: 63.33 in. Width: 70.5 in. Front/Rear Overhang: 27.5 in./36.4 in. Approach/Departure Degrees: 39.7/31.0. Ground Clearance: Minimum clearance: 7.4 in. (rear axle to ground). Minimum Running Clearance: 8.8 in. Maximum capacity: 71.8 cu. ft. (with rear seat folded). Front headroom: 38.3 in. Front legroom: 39.9 in. Front shoulder room: 55.3 in. Front hip room: 55.3 in. Rear headroom: 38.0 in. Rear legroom: 35.3 in. Rear shoulder room: 55.3 in. Rear hip room: 44.5 in. Grand Wagoneer. Wheelbase: 108.7 in. Overall Length: 186.4 in. Front/Rear Tread: 59.4 in./57.8 in. Overall Height: 66.4 in. Width: 74.8 in. Front/Rear Overhang: 31.3 in./46.4 in. Approach/Departure Degrees: 39/20. Ground Clearance: Minimum clearance: 7.2 in. (rear axle to ground). Minimum Running Clearance: 10.1 in. Maximum capacity: 95.1 cu. ft. (with rear seat folded). Front headroom: 37.1 in. Front legroom: 40.5 in. Front shoulder room: 58.3 in. Front hip room: 60.5 in. Rear headroom: 36.8 in. Rear legroom: 37.0 in. Rear shoulder room: 58.3 in. Rear hip room: 60.9 in.

CAPACITIES: Fuel Tank: Cherokee and Wagoneer: 13.5 gal. Optional: 20.2 gal. Grand Wagoneer: 20.3 gal.

ACCOMMODATIONS: Seating Capacity: Cherokee and Wagoneer: Five passengers, Grand Wagoneer: Six passengers.

INSTRUMENTATION: Cherokee: Speedometer, odometer, warning lights for alternator, oil pressure, and engine coolant temperature. Brake system warning, high beam/hazard lights operation. Wagoneer, Cherokee Pioneer, Chief and Laredo models have the previously listed items plus standard trip odometer, digital clock, and voltmeter, oil pressure and engine coolant temperature gauges. Grand Wagoneer: Speedometer, fuel gauge, gauges for voltmeter, oil pressure and engine coolant temperature, warning lights for seat belts, parking brake and four-wheel drive, indicator lights for directional/4-way hazard, high beam.

OPTIONS: Color-keyed passenger area carpeting. Sun roof. Electronic clock with digital display (standard for Wagoneer Limited). Console with armrest, storage box, rear ashtray and rear heating ducts. Color-keyed floor mats. Rear quarter flipper window (two-door only). Color-keyed inside-mounted vinyl spare tire cover. Front and rear bumper guards. Roof rack. Outside spare tire carrier. Requires full-size spare. Front and rear tow hooks. Air conditioning. Heavy-duty battery. Intermittent wipers. Rear window washer and wiper. Cold Climate Group. Includes engine block heater, heavy-duty battery and alternator. Heavy-duty cooling. Includes 7.0 in. radiator wall thickness. Included with air conditioning. Cruise control. Halogen fog lamps. Requires bumper guards. Extended-range 20.2 gal. fuel tank. Keyless entry system. Requires power door locks and windows. Electric rear window defroster. Included in Visibility Group. Requires heavy-duty alternator and tinted glass. California emissions system. High Altitudes Emissions Package. 2.8 liter V-6. Not available with 4-speed manual transmission, required automatic transmission for California. 2.1 liter Turbo diesel engine. Extra-Quiet insulation Package. Keyless entry system, required power door locks. Light Group. Includes ashtray light, dome/map light, cargo area light with tailgate switch, courtesy lights, retractable underhood work light, door switches, visor mirror light, Sentinel headlight switch (not available for base Cherokee, standard for Wagoneer). Dual low profile swing-away truck style mirrors. Dual manual remote mirrors. Power remote control exterior mirrors. Required power windows, door locks. Power door locks. Six-way power driver and passenger seat. Power steering. Required with air conditioning, 4.0 liter engines, or automatic transmission. Protection Group. Included front and rear bumper guards, floor mats, door edge guards, cargo area skid strips and locking gas cap. AM radio with two speakers. AM/FM monaural radio with two speakers. Electronically tuned AM/FM stereo radio with four speakers. Electronically tuned AM/FM stereo radio with cassette tape player and dynamic noise reduction. Electronically tuned high-output AM/FM stereo radio with Dolby system and six premium "Accusound by Jensen" speakers (requires power windows and door locks). Power antenna. Skid Plate Package. Includes protection for transfer case, fuel tank and front suspension. Tilt steering column, requires intermittent windshield wipers. Leather-wrapped 3-spoke steering wheel. Custom two-tone paint with high-break. Heavy-duty suspension. Includes heavy-duty springs and shock absorbers, heavy-duty rear axle. Available for 4 liter engine only. Off-Road Package. Includes heavy-duty rear axle, high-pressure gas shock absorbers, 15 x 7 in. White styled spoker P225/75R15 OWL All-Terrain tires, full-size spare, Skid Plate Package, tow hooks (2 front, 1 rear), unique front and rear springs and jounce bumpers. Requires power steering, heavy-duty battery and heavy-duty cooling. Not available with 2.5 liter with 4-spd. manual trans. or Wagoneer) Tachometer. Included with diesel engine. Trailer A Package (2000 lb.). Included dead weight hitch, 5-wire harness. Trailer B Package (4200 lb.). Includes load leveling hitch, 7-wire harness, not available with diesel engine. Automatic 4-speed overdrive transmission. Requires power steering. Five-speed manual overdrive transmission with floor shift. Four-speed automatic overdrive transmission with Selec-Trac. Requires 4 liter engine and power steering. Visibility Group. Includes dual manual remote mirrors, intermittent windshield wipers, rear window defroster. 15 x 6 in. styled steel wheels with bright trim rings (not available for Wagoneer). 15 x 7 in. cast aluminum 10 spoke wheels (not available for Wagoneer). 15 x 7 in. cast aluminum 5-spoke wheels. Front door vent, swing-out design (standard for Wagoneer). Deep tinted two-door quarter glass. Includes tinted windshield, door windows and liftgate window. Light-Duty Trailer Package A. Heavy-Duty Trailer Package B. Cherokee Chief Package. Cherokee Laredo Package. Cherokee Pioneer Package: $1158. Grand Wagoneer: Power sun roof with vinyl roof. Power sun roof without vinyl roof. Rear Trac-Lok differential. Includes 3.31:1 axle ratio, requires full-size spare. Auxiliary automatic transmission oil cooler. Required with Trailer Towing Package A and B. Cold Climate Group. Includes engine block heater. Heavy-duty shock absorbers. Full-size spare tire. Trailer Towing A Package (3500 lb. capacity). Trailer Towing B Package (5000 lb. capacity).

HISTORICAL FOOTNOTES: The best selling Jeep model of the top ten Jeep-Eagle dealers in the United States was the Cherokee.

1988 Jeep Grand Wagoneer

1989 WAGONEER & CHEROKEE

For 1989 Cherokee and Wagoneer models fitted with the 4.0 liter engine, automatic transmission and Selec-Trac were available with a four-wheel anti-lock braking system which operated in both two and four-wheel drive. For 1989 power steering was made standard for the base Cherokee model. All Cherokees and Wagoneers had a larger 20 gal. capacity fuel tank. Standard for the Cherokee Limited and Wagoneer Limited was a new Power Equipment Group which was optional for other Cherokee models. It included power windows, power door locks and a keyless entry system. Bright dual power outside mirrors, fog lamps and a tachometer were added to the standard equipment of the Wagoneer Limited. The Cherokee front end was slightly revised for 1989.

I.D. DATA: The serial number was located on the left-hand hinge pillar. The V.I.N. had 17 symbols. The first three entries identified the manufacturer, make and type of vehicle. The fourth unit, a letter, designated the engine (C-4.2 liter 6-cyl., H-2.5 liter 4-cyl., M-4.0 liter 6-cyl., N-5.9 liter V-8). The fifth character, a letter, identified the transmission. The sixth and seventh characters identified the series and body style. The eighth character identified the GVW rating. Next followed a check digit. The eleventh character was the manufacturing plant identification. The final six digits were the sequential production number. The vehicle identification indicated the model as follows: Grand Wagoneer: ( )J4( )S587( )K( )000001 and up. Wagoneer (6-cyl.): ( )J4( )N78L( )K( )000001 and up, Cherokee (4-cyl.): ( )J4( )(model)E( )K000001 and up, Cherokee (6-cyl.): ( )J4( )(model)L( )K( )000001 and up. Vehicle identification was as follows: S58: Grand Wagoneer Station Wagon, N78: Wagoneer, J27: Two-door Cherokee, J28: Four-door Cherokee, J77: Two-door Cherokee Limited, J78: Four-door Cherokee Limited.

Model Number	Body Type	Factory Price	GVW	Shipping Weight	Prod. Total
Grand Wagoneer Station Wagon V-8					
S58	4-dr.	$26,395	6200	4498	17,057
Wagoneer Station Wagon 6-cyl.					
N78	4-dr. Limited	$23,220	4797	3444	7673*
* Model year sales					
Cherokee Station Wagon 4-cyl.					
J27	2-dr.	$13,657	4657	2974	207,216*
J28	4-dr.	$14,293	4657	3012	—
Cherokee Station Wagon 6-cyl.					
J27	2-dr.	$14,270	4797	3161	—
J28	4-dr.	$14,906	4797	3199	—
J77	2-dr. Limited	$23,130	4797	—	—
J78	4-dr. Limited	$24,958	4797	—	—

* 1989 model year production-includes all Cherokee models.

STANDARD ENGINE: Grand Wagoneer: Engine Type: OHV, V-8. Cast iron block and cylinder head. Bore x Stroke: 4.08 in. x 3.44 in. Lifters: Hydraulic. Number of main bearings-5. Fuel Induction: 2-bbl. carburetor. Compression Ratio: 8.25:1. Displacement: 360 cu. in. (5.89 liters). Horsepower: Net: 175 @ 4000 rpm. Torque: Net: 285 lb.-ft. @ 2400 rpm. Oil refill capacity: 5 qt. with filter change. Fuel Requirements: Unleaded.

STANDARD ENGINE: Cherokee: Engine Type: OHV, In-line-4. Cast iron block and cylinder head. Bore x Stroke: 3.88 in. x 3.19 in. Lifters: Hydraulic. Number of main bearings-5. Fuel Induction: Throttle body single point fuel injection. Compression Ratio: 9.2:1. Displacement: 150.45 cu. in. (2.4 liters). Horsepower: Net: 121 @ 5000 rpm. Torque: Net: 141 lb.-ft. @ 3500 rpm. Oil refill capacity: 5 qt. with filter change. Fuel Requirements: Unleaded.

OPTIONAL ENGINE: Cherokee: Standard for Cherokee Limited and Wagoneer Limited. Engine Type: OHV, 6-cyl. Cast iron block and cylinder head. Bore x Stroke: 3.88 in. x 3.14 in. Lifters: Hydraulic. Number of main bearings-7. Fuel Induction: Multi-point, electronic fuel injection. Compression Ratio: 9.2:1. Displacement: 241.6 cu. in. (3.96 liters). Horsepower: Net: 177 @ 4500 rpm. Torque: Net: 224 lb.-ft. @ 2500 rpm. Oil refill capacity: 5 qt. with filter change. Fuel Requirements: Unleaded. All chassis features, suspension, dimensions, etc. were unchanged for 1989.

CHASSIS FEATURES: Cherokee and Wagoneer: "Uniframe" full-length boxed steel frame welded to unitized body. Grand Wagoneer: Separate body and frame.

SUSPENSION AND RUNNING GEAR: Cherokee and Wagoneer: Front Suspension: Coil springs with leading links and track bar, link-type 0.95 in. dia. stabilizer bar. Spring rate at wheel: 120 lb./in. Grand Wagoneer: Leaf spring mounted below axle. 1.00 in. link type stabilizer bar. Spring rate at wheel: 160 lb./in. Rear Suspension: Cherokee and Wagoneer: Semi-elliptical leaf springs, link type 0.63 in. dia. stabilizer bar Spring rate at wheel: 165 lb./in. Grand Wagoneer: Leaf spring mounted below axle. Optional: Cherokee and Wagoneer (available for 4.0 liter only): Heavy-duty front and rear suspension, heavy-duty rear axle. Front Axle Type and Capacity: Cherokee and Wagoneer: Dana model 30 Hypoid. Grand Wagoneer: Dana model 44 full-floating. Rear Axle Type and Capacity: Cherokee and Wagoneer: Dana HOL 35C or Dana MO4 44. Grand Wagoneer: AMC Hypoid semi-floating. Final Drive Ratio: Cherokee and Wagoneer: Turbo diesel/4-spd. man. trans.: 3.07:1; 4-cyl./5-spd. man. trans.: 3.08:1; 6-cyl./4-spd. auto. trans.: 3.54:1. Grand Wagoneer: 2.73:1 (New Process 228 transfer case), 3.31:1 (New Process 208 transfer case). Optional: Cherokee and Wagoneer: For 6-cyl.: 3.55:1, 4.11:1, 4.56:1. Transfer Case: Cherokee and Wagoneer: Standard: Command-Trac New Process 231. Ratios: 2.61:1, 1.00:1. Optional: Selec-Trac New Process 242 transfers case. Ratios: 2.61:1, 1.00:1. Grand Wagoneer: Selec-Trac New Process 242. Ratios: 2.61:1, 1.0:1. Brakes: Type: Cherokee, Wagoneer and Grand Wagoneer: Hydraulic, front discs and rear drums. Dimensions: Cherokee and Wagoneer: Front: 10.98 in. dia. disc. Rear: 10.0 in. x 1.750 in. drums. Grand Wagoneer: Front: 12.0 in. dia. disc. Rear: 11.0 x 2.00 in. drums. Wheels: Base Cherokee: 15 x 6 in., 5-bolt argent styled steel wheels with black hub covers. Cherokee Pioneer: 15 x 6 in. 5-bolt, argent styled steel wheels with bright trim rings and black hub covers. Cherokee Chief: 15 x 7 in. 5-bolt, white styled steel spoke wheel with bright hub covers. Cherokee Laredo: 15 x 7 in. 5-bolt, cast aluminum 10 spoke wheels with bright hubs. Base Wagoneer: 15 x 6 in. 5-bolt, steel wheels with argent styled covers. Wagoneer Limited: 15 x 6 in. 5-bolt cast aluminum 5-spoke wheels. Tires: Base Cherokee: P195/75R15 steel belted All-Weather black sidewall radial. Cherokee Pioneer: P205/75R15 black sidewall steel-belted radial All-Weather with 15 x 6 or 15 x 7 in. wheels. Cherokee Chief and Laredo: P215/75R15 Michelin OWL steel-belted radial All-Terrain. Requires 15 x 7 in. wheels. Not available with 2.5 liter engine with 4-spd. trans. Base Wagoneer: P205/75R15 white sidewall All-Weather radials with either 15 x 6 in. or 15 x 7 in. wheels. Wagoneer Limited: P205/75R15 white sidewall Michelin Tru-Seal puncture resistant steel radial with 15 x 6 in. or 15 x 7 in. wheels. Grand Wagoneer: P235/75R15 Michelin white sidewall Tru-Seal puncture resistant radial. Optional: Base Cherokee only: P205/75R15 black sidewall steel-belted radial All-Weather. Base and Pioneer Cherokee: P205/75R15 white sidewall All-Weather steel radial with 15 x 6 in. or 15 x 7 in. wheels, P215/75R15 black sidewall Goodyear Wrangler steel-belted radial All-Terrain (requires 15 x 7 in. wheels), P215/75R15 Michelin OWL steel belted radial All-Terrain (requires 15 x 7 in. wheel, not available with 2.5 liter engine with 4-spd. trans.). Wagoneer: P205/75R15 white sidewall Michelin Tru-Seal steel belted radial (with 15 x 6 or 15 x 7 in. wheels). Wagoneer and Wagoneer Limited: P205/75R15 black steel belted radial All-Weather (with 15 x 6 or 15 x 7 in. wheels). Steering: Cherokee: Manual recirculating ball type. Ratio: 24:1. Turns Lock-to-Lock: 4.8. Wagoneer (optional for Cherokee): Power Saginaw recirculating ball type. Ratio: 14:1. Turns Lock-to-Lock: 3.5:1. Grand Wagoneer: Power Saginaw recirculating ball type, variable ratio. Ratio: 16:1, 13:1. Turns Lock-to-Lock: 3.5. Turning Circle: Cherokee and Wagoneer: 35.7 ft. Grand Wagoneer: 37.7 ft. Standard Transmission: Base and Pioneer Cherokee: 4-speed manual. Ratios: 3.93:1, 2.33:1, 1.45:1, 1.00:1. Reverse: 3.76:1. Standard for Cherokee Chief and Laredo (optional for Cherokee base, Cherokee Pioneer and Wagoneer). 5-speed manual. (A-S 5-spd. for 4-cyl. engines, Peugeot 5-spd. for 6-cyl.). Ratios: A-S: 3.93:1, 2.33:1, 1.45:1, 1.00:1, 0.85:1. Reverse: 4.74:1. Peugeot: 4.03:1, 2.39:1, 1.52:1, 1.0:1, 0.72:1. Reverse: 3.76:1. Optional for all Cherokee models and standard for Wagoneer: Aisin-Warner 30-40 LE 4-speed automatic. Ratios: 2.80:1, 1.53:1, 1.00:1, 0.71:1. Reverse: 2.39:1. Grand Wagoneer: Chrysler model 727 3-speed automatic. Ratios: 2.45:1, 1.55:1, 1.0:1. Reverse: 2.20:1. Clutch: Cherokee and Wagoneer: Clutch diameter: 9.1 in. dia. Hydraulic actuation. Optional: None.

VEHICLE DIMENSIONS: Wagoneer and Cherokee. Wheelbase: 101.4 in. Overall Length: 165.3 in. Front/Rear Tread: 57.0 in./57.0 in. Overall Height: 63.33 in. Width: 70.5 in. Front/Rear Overhang: 27.5 in./36.4 in. Approach/Departure Degrees: 39.7/31.0. Ground Clearance: Minimum clearance: 7.4 in. (rear axle to ground). Minimum Running Clearance: 8.8 in. Maximum capacity: 71.8 cu. ft. (with rear seat folded). Front headroom: 38.3 in. Front legroom: 39.9 in. Front shoulder room: 55.3 in. Front hip room: 55.3 in. Rear headroom: 38.0 in. Rear legroom: 35.3 in. Rear shoulder room: 55.3 in. Rear hip room: 44.5 in. Grand Wagoneer. Wheelbase: 108.7 in. Overall Length: 186.4 in. Front/Rear Tread: 59.4 in./57.8 in. Overall Height: 66.4 in. Width: 74.8 in. Front/Rear Overhang: 31.3 in./46.4 in. Approach/Departure Degrees: 39/20. Ground Clearance: Minimum clearance: 7.2 in. (rear axle to ground). Minimum Running Clearance: 10.1 in. Maximum capacity: 95.1 cu. ft. (with rear seat folded). Front headroom: 37.1 in. Front legroom: 40.5 in. Front shoulder room: 58.3 in. Front hip room: 60.5 in. Rear headroom: 36.8 in. Rear legroom: 37.0 in. Rear shoulder room: 58.3 in. Rear hip room: 60.9 in.

CAPACITIES: Fuel Tank: Cherokee and Wagoneer: 13.5 gal. Optional: 20.2 gal. Grand Wagoneer: 20.3 gal.

ACCOMMODATIONS: Seating Capacity: Cherokee and Wagoneer: Five passengers, Grand Wagoneer: Six passengers.

INSTRUMENTATION: Cherokee: Speedometer, odometer, warning lights for alternator, oil pressure, and engine coolant temperature. Brake system warning, high beam/hazard lights operation. Wagoneer, Cherokee Pioneer, Chief and Laredo models have the previously listed items plus standard trip odometer, digital clock, and voltmeter, oil pressure and engine coolant temperature gauges. Grand Wagoneer: Speedometer, fuel gauge, gauges for voltmeter, oil pressure and engine coolant temperature, warning lights for seat belts, parking brake and four-wheel drive, indicator lights for directional/4-way hazard, high beam.

OPTIONS AND PRICES: 4.0 liter engine: $595. Anti-lock brakes (Cherokee Laredo and Limited, Wagoneer Limited): $852. Automatic transmission: $795. Selec-Trac (requires 4.0 liter engine and auto. trans.): $386. Rear Trac-Lok differential (requires 4.0 liter engine and conventional spare): $279. Air conditioning: $820. Pioneer Package: $1217. Laredo Package: $2937. Sport Package (two-door Cherokee). Includes 4.0 liter engine, carpeting, body side stripes, exterior body moldings, 225/75R15 OWL tires, aluminum wheels: $945. Sport Option Group (two-door Cherokee). Includes Sport Package content plus console with armrest, Gauge Group with tachometer, AM/FM electronically tuned stereo radio, spare tire cover: $1450. Option Group 1 (base two-door Cherokee). Includes floor carpeting, spare tire cover, 205/75R15 tires, and wheel trim rings: $259. Option Group 1 (base four-door Cherokee). Includes floor carpeting, spare tire cover, 205/75R15 tires, wheel trim rings, air conditioning, console with armrest, AM/FM electronically tuned stereo radio, roof rack and rear window wiper and washer: $1464. Pioneer Package Option Group 1 (two-door Cherokee only). Includes content of Pioneer Package plus air conditioning, console with armrest, extra-quiet insulation, Protection Group, roof rack, tilt steering column, remote control exterior mirrors, intermittent windshield wipers and rear defogger: $2415. Pioneer Package Option Group 2 (two-door Cherokee only). Includes content of Group 1 plus cruise control, power windows and locks, keyless entry system, AM/FM/ET radio and cassette player: $3047. Laredo Package Option Group. Contains Laredo Package, air conditioning, cruise control, fog lamps, power windows and locks, keyless entry system, AM/FM/ET radio and cassette player: $3597. Fabric bucket seats (base and Sport Cherokee): $134. Carpeting (base Cherokee): $205. Console with armrest (requires carpeting option): $118. Cruise control (requires Visibility Group, not available with 4-cyl. engine and manual transmission): $217. Deep tinted glass (Cherokee base and Sport two-door): $301. Deep tinted glass (Cherokee Pioneer): $143. Rear window defogger: $158. Heavy-duty alternator and battery: $132, $71 with air conditioning. Extra-Quiet Insulation Package: $124. Gauge Package (Cherokee Sport). Includes tachometer, digital clock, gauges for engine coolant temperature and oil pressure, low fuel level warning and trip odometer. Tachometer (Cherokee Pioneer): $62. Remote mirrors (Cherokee base, Sport and Pioneer): $75. Power Windows and Locks Group (Cherokee base, Pioneer and Laredo two-door): $418. Power Windows and Locks Group. Includes power windows and locks, keyless entry system (four-door Cherokee Pioneer and Laredo): $561. Power front seats (Cherokee Laredo): $408. Protection Group (Cherokee base, Sport and Pioneer): $195. Skid Plate Group: $141. AM/FM stereo extended range radio (Cherokee base and Sport): $187. AM/FM stereo extended range radio and cassette player (Cherokee base and Sport): $384. AM/FM stereo extended range radio and cassette player (Cherokee Pioneer and Laredo, Wagoneer Limited): $197. Premium Speakers and power antenna (Cherokee Pioneer and Laredo, Wagoneer Limited). Requires power windows, and Locks Group, and stereo radio: $171. Roof rack (Cherokee base and Sport and Pioneer): $136. Rear quarter flipper windows (Cherokee base and Sport): $158. Outside spare tire carrier (not available for Cherokee Limited): $170. Spare tire cover (Cherokee base and Sport): $45. Leather-wrapped steering wheel (Cherokee Sport): $47. Manual sun roof. Requires roof rack (Cherokee Pioneer and Laredo, and Wagoneer Limited): $350. Off-Road Suspension Package. Includes high pressure gas shock absorbers, 225/75R15 OWL tires, styled steel wheels (aluminum alloy on Laredo), front and rear tow hooks, Skid Plate Package, heavy-duty cooling. Cherokee base with 4.0 liter engine and auto. trans.: $963, Cherokee base with 5-spd. man. trans.: $922, Cherokee Sport with auto. trans.: $582, Cherokee Sport with 5-spd. man. trans.: $541. Cherokee Pioneer with 4.0 liter engine and auto. trans.: $865. Cherokee Pioneer with 5-spd. man. trans.: $824, Cherokee Laredo with 4.0 liter engine and auto. trans.: $606, Cherokee Laredo with 5-spd. man. trans.: $565. Tilt steering column (requires Visibility Group): $124. Trailer Towing Package A (2000 lb. rating): $117. Trailer Towing Package B (5000 lb. rating): $351. Front vent windows (Cherokee base, Sport and Pioneer) $89. Visibility Group. Includes remote exterior mirrors, intermittent windshield wipers, rear window defogger, and rear window wiper and washer. (Cherokee base and Sport): $144. California Emissions Package: $122. Grand Wagoneer: Power sun roof with vinyl roof. Power sun roof without vinyl roof. Rear Trac-Lok differential. Includes 3.31:1 axle ratio, requires full-size spare. Auxiliary automatic transmission oil cooler. Required with Trailer Towing Package A and B. Cold Climate Group. Includes engine block heater. Heavy-duty shock absorbers. Full-size spare tire. Trailer Towing A Package 3500 lb. capacity). Trailer Towing B Package (5000 lb. capacity).

HISTORICAL FOOTNOTES: The Grand Wagoneer was described by *Automotive News* as "a favorite of gentlemen, farmers, car armorers, political security forces, bodyguards."

1990 WAGONEER & CHEROKEE

New for 1990 were three-point lap and shoulder belts for all out-board passengers (front and rear). Redesigned for 1990 was the Cherokee's optional exterior-mounted swing-away spare tire carrier. For 1990 it was entirely bumper-mounted to reduce the potential for body corrosion. The Cherokee Limited and Wagoneer Limited had a new standard overhead console housing holders for garage door opener and sun glasses, outside temperature display, compass, lights for front and rear seating areas, and remote-control door lock receiver. This feature was optional for the Cherokee Laredo. All Cherokees for 1990 had a standard AM/FM electronically tuned radio with four speakers. The exterior color selection for the 1990 Cherokee models consisted of bright white, black, Colorado red, black cherry pearlcoat, sand metallic, midnight blue metallic, sterling metallic, dover grey metallic, dark baltic metallic and spinnaker blue metallic. All paints were clearcoat except for black cherry. The metallic paints were extra cost. The color selection for the Wagoneer Limited was restricted to bright white, black, black cherry pearlcoat, midnight blue metallic, and dover grey metallic. As with the Cherokee models, the metallic paints were extra-cost items for the Wagoneer Limited. The Grand Wagoneer's color selection consisted of bright white, black, black cherry pearlcoat, sand metallic, sterling metallic, dover grey metallic, and dark baltic metallic. The interiors of the Wagoneer Limited and Grand Wagoneer were upholstered in leather/Country cord fabric and offered in either cordovan or sand.

I.D. DATA: The serial number was located on the left-hand hinge pillar. The V.I.N. had 17 symbols. The first three entries identified the manufacturer, make and type of vehicle. The fourth unit, a letter, designated the engine (C-4.2 liter 6-cyl., H-2.5 liter 4-cyl., M-4.0 liter 6-cyl., N-5.9 liter V-8). The fifth character, a letter, identified the transmission. The sixth and seventh characters identified the series and body style. The eighth character identified the GVW rating. Next followed a check digit. The eleventh character was the manufacturing plant identification. The final six digits were the sequential production number. The vehicle identification indicated the model as follows: Grand Wagoneer: ( )J4( )S587( )L( )000001 and up. Wagoneer (6-cyl.): ( )J4( )N78L( )L( )000001 and up, Cherokee (4-cyl.): ( )J4( )(model)E( )L000001 and up, Cherokee (6-cyl.): ( )J4( )(model)L( )L( )000001 and up. Vehicle identification was as follows: S58: Grand Wagoneer station wagon, N78: Wagoneer, J27: Two-door Cherokee, J28: Four-door Cherokee, J77:Two-door Cherokee Limited, J78: Four-door Cherokee Limited.

Model Number	Body Type	Factory Price	GVW	Shipping Weight	Prod. Total
Grand Wagoneer Station Wagon V-8					
S58	4-dr.	$27,795	5980	4499	6449*
* Calendar year production.					
Wagoneer Station Wagon 6-cyl.					
N78	4-dr. Limited	$24,795	4900	3453	3888*
* Calendar year production					
Cherokee Station Wagon 4-cyl.					
J27	2-dr.	$14,695	4850	3033	151,230*
J28	4-dr.	$15,545	4900	3076	—
Cherokee Station Wagon 6-cyl.					
J27	2-dr.	$15,295	4850	3157	—
J28	4-dr.	$16,145	4900	3200	—
J77	2-dr. Limited	$24,650	4850	—	—
J78	4-dr. Limited	$25,775	4900	—	—

* Calendar year production-includes all Cherokee models.

STANDARD ENGINE: Grand Wagoneer: Engine Type: OHV, V-8. Cast iron block and cylinder head. Bore x Stroke: 4.08 in. x 3.44 in. Lifters: Hydraulic. Number of main bearings-5. Fuel Induction: 2-bbl. carburetor. Compression Ratio: 8.25:1. Displacement: 360 cu. in. (5.89 liters). Horsepower: Net: 144 @ 3200 rpm. Torque: Net: 280 lb.-ft. @ 1500 rpm. Oil refill capacity: 5 qt. with filter change. Fuel Requirements: Unleaded.

STANDARD ENGINE: Cherokee: Engine Type: OHV, In-line-4. Cast iron block and cylinder head. Bore x Stroke: 3.88 in. x 3.19 in. Lifters: Hydraulic. Number of main bearings-5. Fuel Induction: Throttle body single point fuel injection. Compression Ratio: 9.2:1. Displacement: 150.45 cu. in. (2.4 liters). Horsepower: Net: 121 @ 5000 rpm. Torque: Net: 141 lb.-ft. @ 3500 rpm. Oil refill capacity: 5 qt. with filter change. Fuel Requirements: Unleaded.

OPTIONAL ENGINE: Cherokee: Standard for Cherokee Limited and Wagoneer Limited. Engine Type: OHV, 6-cyl. Cast iron block and cylinder head. Bore x Stroke: 3.88 in. x 3.14 in. Lifters: Hydraulic. Number of main bearings-7. Fuel Induction: Multi-point, electronic fuel injection. Compression Ratio: 9.2:1. Displacement: 241.6 cu. in. (3.96 liters). Horsepower: Net: 177 @ 4500 rpm. Torque: Net: 224 lb.-ft. @ 2500 rpm. Oil refill capacity: 5 qt. with filter change. Fuel Requirements: Unleaded.

CHASSIS FEATURES: Cherokee and Wagoneer: "Uniframe" full-length boxed steel frame welded to unitized body. Grand Wagoneer: Separate body and frame.

SUSPENSION AND RUNNING GEAR: Cherokee and Wagoneer: Front Suspension: Coil springs with leading links and track bar, link-type 0.95 in. dia. stabilizer bar. Spring rate at wheel: 120 lb./in. Grand Wagoneer: Leaf spring mounted below axle. 1.00 in. link type stabilizer bar. Spring rate at wheel: 160 lb./in. Rear Suspension: Cherokee and Wagoneer: Semi-elliptical leaf springs, link type 0.63 in. dia. stabilizer bar Spring rate at wheel: 165 lb./in. Grand Wagoneer: Leaf spring mounted below axle. Optional: Cherokee and Wagoneer (available for 4.0 liter only): Heavy-duty front and rear suspension, heavy-duty rear axle. Front Axle Type and Capacity: Cherokee and Wagoneer: Dana model 30 Hypoid. Grand Wagoneer: Dana model 44 full-floating. Rear Axle Type and Capacity: Cherokee and Wagoneer: Dana HOL 35C or Dana MO4 44. Grand Wagoneer: AMC Hypoid semi-floating. Final Drive Ratio: Cherokee and Wagoneer: Turbo diesel/4-spd. man. trans.: 3.07:1; 4-cyl./5-spd. man. trans.: 3.08:1; 6-cyl./4-spd. auto. trans.: 3.54:1. Grand Wagoneer: 2.73:1 (New Process 228 transfer case), 3.31:1 (New Process 208 transfer case). Optional: Cherokee and Wagoneer: For 6-cyl.: 3.55:1, 4.11:1, 4.56:1. Transfer Case: Cherokee and Wagoneer: Standard: Command-Trac New Process 231. Ratios: 2.61:1, 1.00:1: Optional: Selec-Trac New Process 242 transfers case. Ratios: 2.61:1, 1.00:1. Grand Wagoneer: Selec-Trac New Process 242. Ratios: 2.61:1, 1.0:1. Brakes: Type: Cherokee, Wagoneer and Grand Wagoneer: Hydraulic, front discs and rear drums. Dimensions: Cherokee and Wagoneer: Front: 10.98 in. dia. disc. Rear: 10.0.0 in. x 1.750 in. drums. Grand Wagoneer: Front: 12.0 in. dia. disc. Rear: 11.0 x 2.00 in. drums. Wheels: Base Cherokee: 15 x 6 in., 5-bolt argent styled steel wheels with black hub covers. Cherokee Pioneer: 15 x 6 in. 5-bolt, argent styled steel wheels with bright trim rings and black hub covers. Cherokee Chief: 15 x 7 in. 5-bolt, white styled steel spoke wheel with bright hub covers. Cherokee Laredo: 15 x 7 in. 5-bolt, cast aluminum 10 spoke wheels with bright hubs. Base Wagoneer: 15 x 6 in. 5-bolt, steel wheels with argent styled covers. Wagoneer Limited: 15 x 6 in. 5-bolt cast aluminum 5-spoke wheels. Tires: Base Cherokee: P195/75R15 steel belted All-Weather black sidewall radial. Cherokee Pioneer: P205/75R15 black sidewall steel-belted radial All-Weather with 15 x 6 or 15 x 7 in. wheels. Cherokee Chief and Laredo: P215/75R15 Michelin OWL steel-belted radial All-Terrain. Requires 15 x 7 in. wheels. Not available with 2.5 liter engine with 4-spd. trans. Wagoneer Limited: P205/75R15 white sidewall Michelin Tru-Seal puncture resistant steel radial with 15 x 6 in. or 15 x 7 in. wheels. Grand Wagoneer: P235/75R15 Michelin white sidewall Tru-Seal puncture resistant radial. Optional: Base Cherokee only: P205/75R15 black sidewall steel-belted radial All-Weather. Base and Pioneer Cherokee: P205/75R15 white sidewall All-Weather steel radial with 15 x 6 in. or 15 x 7 in. wheels, P215/75R15 black sidewall Goodyear Wrangler steel-belted radial All-Terrain (requires 15 x 7 in. wheels), P215/75R15 Michelin OWL steel belted radial All-Terrain (requires 15 x 7 in. wheel, not available with 2.5 liter engine with 4-spd. trans). Wagoneer Limited: P205/75R15 black steel belted radial All-Weather (with 15 x 6 or 15 x 7 in. wheels). Steering: Cherokee: Manual recirculating ball type. Ratio: 24:1. Turns Lock-to-Lock: 4.8. Wagoneer (optional for Cherokee): Power Saginaw recirculating ball type. Ratio: 14:1. Turns Lock-to-Lock: 3.5:1. Grand Wagoneer: Power Saginaw recirculating ball type, variable ratio. Ratio: 16:1, 13:1. Turns Lock-to-Lock: 3.5. Turning Circle: Cherokee and Wagoneer: 35.7 ft. Grand Wagoneer: 37.7 ft. Standard Transmission: Base and Pioneer Cherokee: 4-speed manual. Ratios: 3.93:1, 2.33:1, 1.45:1, 1.00:1. Reverse: 3.76:1. Standard for Cherokee Chief and Laredo (optional for Cherokee base, Cherokee Pioneer and Wagoneer). 5-speed manual. (A-S 5-spd. for 4-cyl. engines, Peugeot 5-spd. for 6-cyl.) Ratios: A-S: 3.93:1, 2.33:1, 1.45:1, 1.00:1, 0.85:1. Reverse: 4.74:1. Peugeot: 4.03:1, 2.39:1, 1.52:1, 1.0:1, 0.72:1. Reverse: 3.76:1. Optional for all Cherokee models and standard for Wagoneer: Aisin-Warner 30-40 LE 4-speed automatic. Ratios: 2.80:1, 1.53:1, 1.00:1, 0.71:1. Reverse: 2.39:1. Grand Wagoneer: Chrysler model 727 3-speed automatic. Ratios: 2.45:1, 1.55:1, 1.0:1. Reverse: 2.20:1. Clutch: Cherokee and Wagoneer: Clutch diameter: 9.1 in. dia. Hydraulic actuation. Optional: None.

VEHICLE DIMENSIONS: Wagoneer and Cherokee. Wheelbase: 101.4 in. Overall Length: 165.3 in. Front/Rear Tread: 57.0 in./57.0 in. Overall Height: 63.33 in. Width: 70.5 in. Front/Rear Overhang: 27.5 in./36.4 in. Approach/Departure Degrees: 39.7/31.0. Ground Clearance: Minimum clearance: 7.4 in. (rear axle to ground). Minimum Running Clearance: 8.8 in. Maximum capacity: 71.8 cu. ft. (with rear seat folded). Front headroom: 38.3 in. Front legroom: 39.9 in. Front shoulder room: 55.3 in. Front hip room: 55.3 in. Rear headroom: 38.0 in. Rear legroom: 35.3 in. Rear shoulder room: 55.3 in. Rear hip room: 44.5 in. Grand Wagoneer. Wheelbase: 108.7 in. Overall Length: 186.4 in. Front/Rear Tread: 59.4 in./57.8 in. Overall Height: 66.4 in. Width: 74.8 in. Front/Rear Overhang: 31.3 in./46.4 in. Approach/Departure Degrees: 39/20. Ground Clearance: Minimum clearance: 7.2 in. (rear axle to ground). Minimum Running Clearance: 10.1 in. Maximum capacity: 95.1 cu. ft. (with rear seat folded). Front headroom: 37.1 in. Front legroom: 40.5 in. Front shoulder room: 58.3 in. Front hip room: 60.5 in. Rear headroom: 36.8 in. Rear legroom: 37.0 in. Rear shoulder room: 58.3 in. Rear hip room: 60.9 in.

CAPACITIES: Fuel Tank: Cherokee and Wagoneer: 13.5 gal. Optional: 20.2 gal. Grand Wagoneer: 20.3 gal.

ACCOMMODATIONS: Seating Capacity: Cherokee and Wagoneer: Five passengers, Grand Wagoneer: Six passengers.

INSTRUMENTATION: Cherokee: Speedometer, odometer, warning lights for alternator, oil pressure, and engine coolant temperature. Brake system warning, high beam/hazard lights operation. Wagoneer, Cherokee Pioneer, Chief and Laredo models have the previously listed items plus standard trip odometer, digital clock, and voltmeter, oil pressure and engine coolant temperature gauges. Grand Wagoneer: Speedometer, fuel gauge, gauges for voltmeter, oil pressure and engine coolant temperature, warning lights for seat belts, parking brake and four-wheel drive, indicator lights for directional/4-way hazard, high beam.

OPTIONS: 4.0 liter engine: Anti-lock brakes (Cherokee Laredo and Limited, Wagoneer Limited). Automatic transmission. Selec-Trac (requires 4.0 liter engine and auto. trans.). Rear Trac-Lok differential (requires 4.0 liter engine and conventional spare. Air conditioning. Pioneer Package. Laredo Package. Sport Package (two-door Cherokee). Includes 4.0 liter engine, carpeting, body side stripes, exterior body moldings, 225/75R15 OWL tires, aluminum wheels. Sport Option Group (two-door Cherokee). Includes Sport Package content plus console with armrest, Gauge Group with tachometer, AM/FM electronically tuned stereo radio, spare tire cover. Option Group 1 (base two-door Cherokee). Includes floor carpeting, spare tire cover, 205/75R15 tires, and wheel trim rings. Option Group 1 (base four-door Cherokee). Includes floor carpeting, spare tire cover, 205/75R15 tires, wheel trim rings, air conditioning, console with armrest, AM/FM electronically tuned stereo radio, roof rack and rear window wiper and washer. Pioneer Package Option Group 1 (two-door Cherokee only). Includes content of Pioneer Package plus air conditioning, console with armrest, extra-quiet insulation, Protection Group, roof rack, tilt steering column, remote control exterior mirrors, intermittent windshield wipers and rear defogger. Pioneer Package Option Group 2 (two-door Cherokee only). Includes content of Group 1 plus cruise control, power windows and locks, keyless entry system, AM/FM/ET radio and cassette player. Laredo Package Option Group. Contains Laredo Package, air conditioning, cruise control, fog lamps, power windows and locks, keyless entry system, AM/FM/ET radio and cassette player. Fabric bucket seats (base and Sport Cherokee. Carpeting (base Cherokee). Console with armrest (requires carpeting option). Cruise control (requires Visibility Group, not available with 4-cyl. engine and manual transmission). Deep tinted glass (Cherokee base and Sport two-door). Deep tinted glass (Cherokee Pioneer). Rear window defogger. Heavy-duty alternator and battery. Extra-Quiet Insulation Package. Gauge Package (Cherokee Sport). Includes tachometer, digital clock, gauges for engine coolant temperature and oil pressure, low fuel level warning and trip odometer. Tachometer (Cherokee Pioneer). Remote mirrors (Cherokee base, Sport and Pioneer). Power Windows and Locks Group (Cherokee base, Pioneer and Laredo two-door): Power Windows and Locks Group. Includes power windows and locks, keyless entry system (four-door Cherokee Pioneer and Laredo) Power front seats (Cherokee Laredo). Protection Group (Cherokee base, Sport and Pioneer). Skid Plate Group. AM/FM stereo extended range radio and cassette player (Cherokee base and Sport). AM/FM stereo extended range radio and cassette player (Cherokee Pioneer and Laredo, and Wagoneer Limited). Premium speakers and power antenna (Cherokee Pioneer and Laredo, Wagoneer Limited). Requires power windows, and Locks Group, and stereo radio. Roof rack (Cherokee base and Sport and Pioneer). Rear quarter flipper windows (Cherokee base and Sport). Outside spare tire carrier (not available for Cherokee Limited. Spare tire cover (Cherokee base and Sport). Leather-wrapped steering wheel (Cherokee Sport). Manual sun roof. Requires roof rack (Cherokee Pioneer and Laredo, and Wagoneer Limited). Off-Road Suspension Package. Includes high pressure gas shock absorbers, 225/75R15 OWL tires, styled steel wheels (aluminum alloy on Laredo), front and rear tow hooks, Skid Plate Package, heavy-duty cooling. Tilt steering column (requires Visibility Group). Trailer Towing Package A (2000 lb. rating). Trailer Towing Package B (5000 lb. rating). Front vent windows (Cherokee base, Sport and Pioneer). Visibility Group. Includes remote exterior mirrors, intermittent windshield wipers, rear window defogger, and rear window wiper and washer. (Cherokee base and Sport). California Emissions Package. Grand Wagoneer: Power sun roof with vinyl roof. Power sun roof without vinyl roof. Overhead console and driver's lighted vanity mirror omitted with power sun roof. Rear Trac-Lok differential. Includes 3.31:1 axle ratio, requires full-size spare. Auxiliary automatic transmission oil cooler. Required with Trailer Towing Package A and B. Cold Climate Group. Includes engine block heater. Heavy-duty shock absorbers. Full-size spare tire. Trailer Towing A Package 3500 lb. capacity). Trailer Towing B Package (5000 lb. capacity).

HISTORICAL FOOTNOTES: In 1990, as in earlier years, the Jeep Cherokee's production exceeded the previous year's total.

1991 WAGONEER & CHEROKEE

The Power-Tech Six engine standard on all Cherokees except the base model was now rated at 190 horsepower and 225 lb.-ft. of torque. The 2.5 liter 4-cylinder was fitted with multi-point electronic fuel injection for 1991. This development, along with other refinements increased its output to 130 horsepower and 149 lb.-ft. of torque. No longer offered was Pioneer version of the Cherokee. The Cherokee Briarwood with new wheels and teak woodgrain exterior accents replaced the Wagoneer Limited. A new four-door Sport model was introduced. The Cherokee Limited model was updated with new body color wheels, bumpers and cladding. A factory-installed anti-theft alarm system was standard for the Briarwood and Limited models, and optional for the Laredo. The rear window/washer system now included a pulse feature. The rear doors on four-door models were now fitted with childproof locks. A single board engine control computer was new 1991. It monitored all engine functions. New underhood identification labels highlighted maintenance points. A new option, an illuminated entry system was introduced for 1991. Double-bitted keys were now standard on all models. New exterior colors for the Cherokees were: Hunter green metallic (available for base and Briarwood), grey mist metallic (not available for Briarwood), silver star metallic (not available for Laredo, Limited and Briarwood) and dark cordovan pearlcoat (not available for Briarwood). They joined spinnaker blue (not available for Sport, Limited and Briarwood models), midnight blue metallic (not available for Sport and Limited), bright white, Colorado red (not available for Limited and Briarwood), black cherry pearlcoat (not available for Limited and Briarwood), and black. Both the base and Sport models had a standard Jayne vinyl seating trim available in either charcoal or dark sand. The standard Laredo upholstery was a luggage fabric in charcoal, cordovan or dark sand. The Limited model's standard leather seating was offered in charcoal or dark sand. The Briarwood standard leather seats were available in cordovan or dark sand.

The only change for the Grand Wagoneer was the availability of these new exterior colors: Hunter green metallic, grey mist metallic, silver star metallic, dark cordovan pearlcoat and spinnaker blue metallic.

I.D. DATA: The serial number was located on the left-hand hinge pillar. The V.I.N. had 17 symbols. The first entry was a number (1-U.S., 2-Canada). The second entry was the letter J identifying the manufacturer as Jeep. The third unit was a letter indicating GVWR as follows: E-3003-4000 lb., F-4001-5000 lb., G-5001-6000 lb., H-6001-7000 lb. The next entry, a letter identifying the product model line as follows: J-Cherokee, N-Briarwood, S-Grand Wagoneer. The next item was a number identifying the series as follows: 2-Base, 3-Pioneer, 5-Laredo, 7-Limited/Briarwood. A number followed to identify the body as follows; 7-Two-door wagon, 8-Four-door wagon. The engine identification followed according to this format: P-2.5 liter, 4-cyl., S-4.0 liter, 6-cyl., 7-5.9 liter, V-8. A check digit was next. The letter M followed to indicate the 1991 model year. Identification of the assembly plant location followed according to this scheme: J-Brampton, L-Toledo #1, Toledo #2. The sequential series number was next beginning with 000001 and up.

Model Number	Body Type	Factory Price	GVW	Shipping Weight	Prod. Total
Grand Wagoneer Station Wagon V-8					
SJJP74	4-dr.	$29,189	6025	4499	1560
* Calendar year production					
Cherokee base Station Wagon 4-cyl.					
XJJL72	2-dr.	$14,454	4550	3033	151,578*
XJJL74	4-dr.	$15,437	4900	3076	—
Cherokee Sport Station Wagon 6-cyl.					
XJJL72	2-dr.	$14,963	4550	3157	—
XJJL74	4-dr.	$15,946	4900	3200	—
Cherokee Laredo Station Wagon 6-cyl.					
XJJL72	2-dr.	$16,996	4550	—	—
XJJL74	4-dr.	$17,379	4900	—	—
Cherokee Limited Station Wagon 6-cyl.					
XJJL74	4-dr.	$24,699	4900	—	—
Cherokee Briarwood Station Wagon 6-cyl.					
XJJL74	4-dr.	$24,178	4900	—	—

* Calendar year production, all models.

STANDARD ENGINE: Grand Wagoneer: Engine Type: OHV, V-8. Cast iron block and cylinder head. Bore x Stroke: 4.08 in. x 3.44 in. Lifters: Hydraulic. Number of main bearings-5. Fuel Induction: 2-bbl. carburetor. Compression Ratio: 8.25:1. Displacement: 360 cu. in. (5.89 liters). Horsepower: Net: 144 @ 3200 rpm. Torque: Net: 280 lb.-ft. @ 1500 rpm. Oil refill capacity: 5 qt. with filter change. Fuel Requirements: Unleaded.

STANDARD ENGINE: Cherokee base: Engine Type: OHV, In-line-4. Cast iron block and cylinder head. Bore x Stroke: 3.88 in. x 3.19 in. Lifters: Hydraulic. Number of main bearings-5. Fuel Induction: Sequential multipoint fuel injection. Compression Ratio: 9.1:1. Displacement: 150.45 cu. in. (2.4 liters). Horsepower: Net: 130 @ 5250 rpm. Torque: Net: 149 lb.-ft. @ 3250 rpm. Oil refill capacity: 5 qt. with filter change. Fuel Requirements: Unleaded.

OPTIONAL ENGINE: Cherokee base: Standard for Cherokee Sport, Laredo Limited, and Briarwood. Engine Type: OHV, 6-cyl. Cast iron block and cylinder head. Bore x Stroke: 3.88 in. x 3.14 in. Lifters: Hydraulic. Number of main bearings-7. Fuel Induction: Multi-point, electronic fuel injection. Compression Ratio: 8.8:1. Displacement: 241.6 cu. in. (3.96 liters). Horsepower: Net: 190 @ 4750 rpm. Torque: Net: 225 lb.-ft. @ 4000 rpm. Oil refill capacity: 5 qt. with filter change. Fuel Requirements: Unleaded.

CHASSIS FEATURES: Cherokee: "Uniframe" full-length boxed steel frame welded to unitized body. Grand Wagoneer: Separate body and frame.

SUSPENSION AND RUNNING GEAR: Front Suspension: Cherokee: Coil springs with leading links and track bar, link-type 0.95 in. dia. stabilizer bar. Spring rate at wheel: 120 lb./in. Grand Wagoneer: Leaf spring mounted below axle. 1.00 in. link type stabilizer bar. Spring rate at wheel: 160 lb./in. Rear Suspension: Cherokee: Semi-elliptical leaf springs, link type 0.63 in. dia. stabilizer bar. Spring rate at wheel: 165 lb./in. Grand Wagoneer: Leaf spring mounted below axle. Optional: Off-road suspension, for base, Sport and Laredo. Front Axle Type and Capacity: Cherokee: Dana model 30 Hypoid. Grand Wagoneer: Dana model 44 full-floating. Rear Axle Type and Capacity: Cherokee: Dana HOL 35C or Dana MO4 44. Grand Wagoneer: AMC Hypoid semi-floating. Final Drive Ratio: Cherokee base: 4-cyl./5-spd. man. trans.: 4.11:1; 6-cyl./5-spd. man. trans.: 3.08:1; 6-cyl./4-spd. auto. trans.: 3.55:1. Wagoneer Limited: 3.55:1. Grand Wagoneer: 2.73:1. Optional: Grand Wagoneer: 3.31:1 with optional Trac-Lok rear differential. Transfer Case: Standard for Cherokee models except Limited and Briarwood: Command-Trac New Process 231. Ratios: 2.72:1, 1.00:1: Optional and standard for the Cherokee Limited and Briarwood: Selec-Trac New Process 242 transfer case. Ratios: 2.72:1, 1.00:1. Grand Wagoneer: Selec-Trac New Process 229 Ratios: 2.62:1, 1.0:1. Brakes: Type: Cherokee and Grand Wagoneer: Hydraulic, front discs and rear drums. Dimensions: Cherokee: Front: 10.98 in. dia. disc. Rear: 10.0.0 in. x 1.750 in. drums. Grand Wagoneer: Front: 12.0 in. dia. disc. Rear: 11.0 x 2.00 in. drums. Wheels: Base Cherokee: 15 x 6 in., 5-bolt argent styled steel wheels with black hub covers. Cherokee Sport: 15 x 7 in. 10-hole, cast aluminum wheels. Cherokee Laredo: 15 x 7 in., 5-spoke cast aluminum. Cherokee Limited and Briarwood: 15 x 7 in. Crosswire cast aluminum wheels, color-keyed on Limited, dark silver on Briarwood. Grand Wagoneer: 15 x 7 in. cast aluminum. Optional: Cherokee base: 15 x 7 in. 6-spoke silver styled wheels with black hub cover, 15 x 6 in. argent steel wheels with black hub cover and bright trim ring. Tires: Cherokee base: P195/75R15 steel belted All-Season black sidewall radial. Cherokee Sport: P225/75R15 Goodyear Wrangler outline white letter steel-belted radial, All-Terrain. Cherokee Laredo: P215/75R15 outline white letter steel-belted radial All-Terrain. Cherokee Limited: P225/75R15 Goodyear Eagle GT+4. Cherokee Briarwood: P215/75R15 black steel-belted radial All-Season. Grand Wagoneer: P235/75R15 white sidewall radial. Optional: Cherokee base: P205/75R15 black sidewall steel-belted radial All-Season, P215/75R15 outline white letter steel-belted radial All-Terrain (requires 15 x 7 in. wheels). Cherokee base and Laredo: P25/75R15 Goodyear Wrangler outline white letter steel-belted radial (requires 15 x 7 in. wheels). Steering: Cherokee: Power recirculating ball type. Ratio: 14:1. Turns Lock-to-Lock: 3.5. Grand Wagoneer: Power recirculating ball type. Ratio: 13:1. Turns Lock-to-Lock: 3.5. Turning Circle: Cherokee: 35.7 ft. Grand Wagoneer: 37.7 ft. Standard Transmission: Cherokee base, Laredo and Sport: 5-speed manual overdrive, all-synchromesh transmission. Ratios: 3.93, 2.33, 1.45, 1.00, 0.85:1. Reverse: 4.74:1. Standard transmission: Cherokee Briarwood and Limited: 4-speed automatic overdrive transmission. with NP 242 transfer case. Optional for Cherokee base, Sport and Laredo with 4.0 liter engine and either NP 231 or NP 242 transfer case. Ratios: 2.80, 1.53, 1.00, 0.75. Reverse: 2.39:1. Standard: Grand Wagoneer: Chrysler model 727 3-speed automatic. Ratios: 2.45, 1.45, 1.00:1. Reverse: 2.20:1. Clutch: Cherokee: Clutch diameter: 9.1 in. dia. (2.5 liter engine); 10.5 in. dia. (4.0 liter engine). Hydraulic actuation. Optional: None.

VEHICLE DIMENSIONS: Cherokee. Wheelbase: 101.4 in. Overall Length: 167.0 in. Front/Rear Tread: 57.0 in./57.0 in. (58 in./58 in. when equipped with 15 x 7 in. wheels). Overall Height: 63.20 in. Width: 70.5 in. Front/Rear Overhang: 29.1 in./36.4 in. Approach/Departure Degrees: 39.8/30.5. Ground Clearance: Minimum running ground clearance: Cherokee: 8.8 in. Maximum capacity: 71.8 cu. ft. (with rear seat folded). Front headroom: 38.3 in. Front legroom: 39.9 in. Front shoulder room: 55.3 in. Front hip room: 55.3 in. Rear headroom: 38.0 in. Rear legroom: 35.3 in. Rear shoulder room: 55.3 in. Rear hip room: 44.5 in. Grand Wagoneer. Wheelbase: 108.7 in. Overall Length: 186.5 in. Front/Rear Tread: 58.5 in./58.5 in. Overall Height: 68.8 in. Width: 73.9 in. Front/Rear Overhang: 32.4 in./46.9 in. Approach/Departure Degrees: 29.8/20.8. Ground Clearance: Minimum clearance: 7.2 in. (rear axle to ground). Minimum Running Clearance: 10.1 in. Maximum capacity: 76.4 cu. ft. (with rear seat folded). Front headroom: 36.8 in. Front legroom: 40.6 in. Front shoulder room: 58.3 in. Front hip room: 56.3 in. Rear headroom: 36.8 in. Rear legroom: 37.7 in. Rear shoulder room: 58.7 in. Rear hip room: 60.9 in.

CAPACITIES: Fuel Tank: Cherokee: 2.2 gal. Grand Wagoneer: 20.3 gal. Coolant System: 2.5 liter engine: 9 qt.

ACCOMMODATIONS: Seating Capacity: Cherokee: Five passengers, Grand Wagoneer: Six passengers.

INSTRUMENTATION: Cherokee base and Sport: Speedometer, odometer, warning lights for alternator, oil pressure, and engine coolant temperature, brake system warning, high beam/hazard lights operation. Cherokee Laredo, Limited and Briarwood models have the previously listed items plus standard trip odometer, LCD clock, and voltmeter, oil pressure and engine coolant temperature gauges, plus low fuel warning light. Grand Wagoneer: Speedometer, fuel gauge, gauges for voltmeter, oil pressure and engine coolant temperature, warning lights for seat belts, parking brake and four-wheel drive, indicator lights for directional/4-way hazard, high beam. The overhead console contains a compass and outside temperature gauge.

OPTIONS AND PRICES: Cherokee base and Sport: Metallic paint: $173. Jamaica fabric seats: $137. Air conditioning: $836. Carpeting for passenger and cargo area: $209. Floor console with armrest: $142. Rear window defroster: $161. Dual remote mirrors: $77. AM/FM stereo radio with cassette: $201. Roof rack: $139. Tilt steering column: $132. P205/75R15 black sidewall tires: $46. Conventional spare tire (TNC): $46. Conventional spare tire (TPF): $59. Visibility Group: $138. Bright wheel trim rings: $65. Styled steel wheels: $38. Rear window wiper/washer: $147. California emissions: $124. Gauge Group with tachometer (Sport only): $158. Spare tire cover (Sport only): $46. Deep tint quarter windows-Two-door: $333. Rear Trac-Lok differential: $285. Heavy-Duty Alternator/Battery Group: $135, (with air conditioning: $72). Leather seats (Cherokee Laredo): $535. Selec-Trac transfer case: $394. Air conditioning: $836. Anti-locking brakes: $799. Overhead console, requires Power Window/Lock Group: $203. Fog lamps: $110. Illuminated entry system: $78. Power mirrors: $100. Power Window/Lock Group: $437 (two-door), $582 (four-door). Power seats: $416. AM/FM radio with cassette tape player: $201. Premium radio speakers (six): $174. Security alarm system: $226. Skid Plate Group: $144. Speed control: $230. Tilt steering wheel: $132. P225/785R15 OWL tires: $46. Conventional spare: $189 (TMW), $201 (TRN). Trailer Tow Package B: $358, with Off-Road Package: $242. Front door vent windows: $91. California emissions: $124. Protection Group: $164. Outside spare tire carrier: $173. Leather-wrapped steering wheel (Sport only): $48. Manual sun roof $154 (Limited and Briarwood), $357 (Sport and Laredo). Off-Road Suspension Package: $982 (base), $552 (Sport), $359 (Laredo). Ten spoke aluminum wheels: $432 (base). Rear quarter vent windows (base and Sport): $161.

HISTORICAL FOOTNOTES: This was the final year the Grand Wagoneer was produced. Jeep reported that the average income of Grand Wagoneer purchasers was $102,000.

1992 WAGONEER & CHEROKEE

The Wagoneer series was not offered for 1992. The Cherokee remained available in base, Sport, Laredo, Limited and Briarwood versions. For 1992 two new exterior colors — Midnight blue and hunter green were added to the colors available for the Cherokee Limited. The base and Sport models were now available with the Light Group option. Carpeting was now standard for the base Cherokee. The base model could also be ordered with the sun roof option. A new radio was available with an integral clock function. Now standard with the full-length center console was a detachable cupholder. Standard for the 1992 Laredo, Limited and Briarwood were front vent windows. A new leather seat option in either sand or cordovan was offered for the Laredo four-door model.

1992 Jeep Cherokee Sport

I.D. DATA: The serial number was located on the left-hand hinge pillar. The V.I.N. had 17 symbols. The first entry was a number (1-U.S., 2-Canada). The second entry was the letter J identifying the manufacturer as Jeep. The third unit was a letter indicating GVWR as follows: E-3003-4000 lb., F-4001-5000 lb., G-5001-6000 lb., H-6001-7000 lb. The next entry, a letter identifying the product model line as follows: J-Cherokee, N-Briarwood. The next item was a number identifying the series as follows: 2-Base, 3-Pioneer, 5-Laredo, 7-Limited/Briarwood. A number followed to identify the body as follows: 7-Two-door wagon, 8-Four-door wagon. The engine identification followed according to this format: P-2.5 liter, 4-cyl., S-4.0 liter, 6-cyl. A check digit was next. The letter N followed to indicate the 1992 model year. Identification of the assembly plant location followed according to this scheme: J-Brampton, L-Toledo #1, Toledo #2. The sequential series number was next beginning with 000001 and up.

Model Number	Body Type	Factory Price	GVW	Shipping Weight	Prod. Total
Cherokee base Station Wagon 4-cyl.					
XJJL72	2-dr.	$15,832	4550	3033	—
XJJL74	4-dr.	$16,842	4900	3076	—
Cherokee Sport Station Wagon 6-cyl.					
XJJL72	2-dr.	$—	4550	3157	—
XJJL74	4-dr.	$—	4900	3200	—
Cherokee Laredo Station Wagon 6-cyl.					
XJJL72	2-dr.	$—	4550	—	—
XJJL74	4-dr.	$—	4900	—	—
Cherokee Limited Station Wagon 6-cyl.					
XJJL74	4-dr.	$25,484	4900	—	—
Cherokee Briarwood Station Wagon 6-cyl.					
XJJL74	4-dr.	$24,949	4900	—	—

STANDARD ENGINE: Cherokee base: Engine Type: OHV, In-line-4. Cast iron block and cylinder head. Bore x Stroke: 3.88 in. x 3.19 in. Lifters: Hydraulic. Number of main bearings-5. Fuel Induction: Sequential multipoint fuel injection. Compression Ratio: 9.1:1. Displacement: 150.45 cu. in. (2.4 liters). Horsepower: Net: 130 @ 5250 rpm. Torque: Net: 149 lb.-ft. @ 3250 rpm. Oil refill capacity: 5 qt. with filter change. Fuel Requirements: Unleaded.

OPTIONAL ENGINE: Cherokee base: Standard for Cherokee Sport, Laredo Limited, and Briarwood. Engine Type: OHV, 6-cyl. Cast iron block and cylinder head. Bore x Stroke: 3.88 in. x 3.14 in. Lifters: Hydraulic. Number of main bearings-7. Fuel Induction: Multi-point, electronic fuel injection. Compression Ratio: 8.8:1. Displacement: 241.6 cu. in. (3.96 liters). Horsepower: Net: 190 @ 4750 rpm. Torque: Net: 225 lb.-ft. @ 4000 rpm. Oil refill capacity: 5 qt. with filter change. Fuel Requirements: Unleaded.

CHASSIS FEATURES: Cherokee: "Uniframe" full-length boxed steel frame welded to unitized body.

SUSPENSION AND RUNNING GEAR: Front Suspension: Cherokee: Coil springs with leading links and track bar, link-type 0.95 in. dia. stabilizer bar. Spring rate at wheel: 120 lb./in. Rear Suspension: Cherokee: Semi-elliptical leaf springs, link type 0.63 in. dia. stabilizer bar. Spring rate at wheel: 165 lb./in. Optional: Off-road suspension, for base, Sport and Laredo. Front Axle Type and Capacity: Cherokee: Dana model 30 Hypoid. Rear Axle Type and Capacity: Cherokee: Dana HOL 35C or Dana MO4 44. Final Drive Ratio: Cherokee base: 4-cyl./5-spd. man. trans.: 4.11:1; 6-cyl./5-spd. man. trans.: 3.08:1; 6-cyl./4-spd. auto. trans.: 3.55:1. Wagoneer Limited: 3.55:1. Transfer Case: Standard for Cherokee models except Limited and Briarwood: Command-Trac New Process 231. Ratios: 2.72:1, 1.00:1. Optional and standard for the Cherokee Limited and Briarwood: Selec-Trac New Process 242 transfer case. Ratios: 2.72:1, 1.00:1. Brakes: Type: Hydraulic, front discs and rear drums. Dimensions: Front: 10.98 in. dia. disc. Rear: 10.0 in. x 1.750 in. drums. Wheels: Base Cherokee: 15 x 6 in., 5-bolt argent styled steel wheels with black hub covers. Cherokee Sport: 15 x 7 in. 10-hole, cast aluminum wheels. Cherokee Laredo: 15 x 7 in., 5-spoke cast aluminum. Cherokee Limited and Laredo: 15 x 7 in. Crosswise cast aluminum wheels, color-keyed on Limited, dark silver on Briarwood. Optional: Cherokee base: 15 x 7 in. 6-spoke silver styled wheels with black hub cover, 15 x 6 in. argent steel wheels with black hub cover and bright trim ring. Tires: Cherokee base: P195/75R15 steel belted All-Season black radial. Cherokee Sport: P225/75R15 Goodyear Wrangler outline white letter steel-belted radial, All-Terrain. Cherokee Laredo: P215/75R15 outline white letter steel-belted radial All-Terrain. Cherokee Limited: P225/75R15 Goodyear Eagle GT+4. Cherokee Briarwood: P215/75R15 black steel-belted radial All-Season. Optional: Cherokee base: P205/75R15 black sidewall steel-belted radial All-Season, P215/75R15 outline white letter steel-belted radial All-Terrain (requires 15 x 7 in. wheels). Cherokee base and Laredo: P25/75R15 Goodyear Wrangler outline white letter steel-belted radial (requires 15 x 7 in. wheels). Steering: Power recirculating ball type. Ratio: 14:1. Turns Lock-to-Lock: 3.5. Turning Circle: Cherokee: 35.7 ft. Standard Transmission: Cherokee base, Laredo and Sport: 5-speed manual overdrive, all-synchromesh transmission. Ratios: 3.93, 2.33, 1.45, 1.00, 0.85:1. Reverse: 4.74:1. Standard transmission: Cherokee Briarwood and Limited: 4-speed automatic overdrive transmission. with NP 242 transfer case. Optional for Cherokee base, Sport and Laredo with 4.0 liter engine and either NP 231 or NP 242 transfer case. Ratios: 2.80, 1.53, 1.00, 0.75. Reverse: 2.39:1. Clutch: Clutch diameter: 9.1 in. dia. (2.5 liter engine); 10.5 in. dia. (4.0 liter engine). Hydraulic actuation. Optional: None.

VEHICLE DIMENSIONS: Wheelbase: 101.4 in. Overall Length: 167.0 in. Front/Rear Tread: 57.0 in./57.0 in. (58 in./58 in. when equipped with 15 x 7 in. wheels). Overall Height: 63.20 in. Width: 70.5 in. Front/Rear Overhang: 29.1 in./36.4 in. Approach/Departure Degrees: 39.8/

30.5. Ground Clearance: Minimum running ground clearance: Cherokee: 8.8 in. Maximum capacity: 71.8 cu. ft. (with rear seat folded). Front headroom: 38.3 in. Front legroom: 39.9 in. Front shoulder room: 55.3 in. Front hip room: 55.3 in. Rear headroom: 38.0 in. Rear legroom: 35.3 in. Rear shoulder room: 55.3 in. Rear hip room: 44.5 in.

CAPACITIES: Fuel Tank: Cherokee: 20.2 gal. Coolant System: 2.5 liter engine: 9 qt.

ACCOMMODATIONS: Seating Capacity: Five passengers.

INSTRUMENTATION: Cherokee base and Sport: Speedometer, odometer, warning lights for alternator, oil pressure, and engine coolant temperature, brake system warning, high beam/hazard lights operation. Cherokee Laredo, Limited and Briarwood models have the previously listed items plus standard trip odometer, LCD clock, and voltmeter, oil pressure and engine coolant temperature gauges, plus low fuel warning light.

OPTIONS: Air conditioning. Anti-lock brake system. Body side moldings. Cargo area cover. Cloth seats. Console with armrests. Overhead console. Cruise control. Rear window defroster. Bright dual electric mirrors. California emissions. 4.0 liter 6-cyl. engine. Fog lamps. Gauge Group. Gold lattice aluminum wheels (no-cost option for Limited). Heavy-Duty Alternator/Battery Group. Illuminated entry. Leather seats (four-door Laredo only). Light Group. Dual remote mirrors. Power Equipment Package. Includes keyless entry, power door locks, and power windows. Power seats. Premium Audio Package. Includes six premium speakers and power antenna. AM/FM cassette tape player, extended range stereo. Roof rack. Selec-Trac transfer case. Security alarm system. Skid Plate Group. Spare tire cover. Sun roof. Off-Road Suspension Package. Trac-Lok rear differential. Tilt steering wheel. Conventional spare tire. Trailer Towing Package. Aluminum wheels. Front door window vent. Rear window wiper/washer. Intermittent windshield wipers.

HISTORICAL FOOTNOTES: The Jeep dealership with the highest new-unit sales for 1992 was Don-A-Vee Jeep-Eagle.

1992 Jeep Cherokee Limited

1993 WAGONEER & CHEROKEE

1993 Jeep Grand Wagoneer

The Cherokee's model line-up was repositioned for 1993 to consist of base, Sport and Country models in both two-door and four-door form. Aside from this developments, there were many new features for 1993. A stainless steel exhaust system was now standard. A unique exterior appearance was provided for the Country. It began with a champagne lower body side treatment with cladding, fender flares, bumpers and endcaps. In addition, this feature contained a body color grille and headlight bezels, and a champagne "Country" body side and liftgate tape treatment.

1993 Jeep Grand Cherokee Limited

The Country interior featured a woodgrain instrument panel applique and door trim with an upper woodgrain and vinyl lower door trim.

1993 Jeep Grand Cherokee Laredo V-8

The special exterior appearance for the Sport consisted of full-face styled steel wheels, a black lower body side two-tone treatment, black lower body side two-tone treatment with a black with red insert lower body side scuff molding. The base Cherokee had a black lower body side scuff molding. A new Visibility Package was introduced. The Trac-Lok limited-slip differential was now available with the 2.6 liter engine.

1993 Jeep Cherokee Country

New exterior colors for 1993 were flame red, canyon blue, light champagne, deep blue pearlcoat, and Navajo turquoise.

1993 Jeep Cherokee Sport

I.D. DATA: The serial number was located on the left-hand hinge pillar. The V.I.N. had 17 symbols.

Model Number	Body Type	Factory Price	GVW	Shipping Weight	Prod. Total

Prices of the 1993 models were not available at press time.

STANDARD ENGINE: Base Cherokee: Engine Type: OHV, In-line-4. Cast iron block and cylinder head. Bore x Stroke: 3.88 in. x 3.19 in. Lifters: Hydraulic. Number of main bearings:5. Fuel Induction: Throttle body single point fuel injection. Compression Ratio: 9.2:1. Displacement: 150.45 cu. in. (2.4 liters). Horsepower: Net: 130 @ 5250 rpm. Torque: Net: 149 lb.-ft. @ 3250 rpm. Fuel Requirements: Unleaded.

STANDARD ENGINE: Sport and Country, optional for Base: Engine Type: OHV, 4-cyl. Cast iron block and cylinder head. Bore x Stroke: 3.88 in. x 3.14 in. Lifters: Hydraulic. Fuel Induction: Multi-point, electronic fuel injection. Compression Ratio: 8.8:1. Displacement: 241.6 cu. in. (3.96 liters). Horsepower: Net: 190 @ 4750 rpm. Torque: Net: 225 lb.-ft. @ 4000 rpm. Fuel Requirements: Unleaded.

CHASSIS FEATURES: "Uniframe" full-length boxed steel frame welded to unitized body.

SUSPENSION AND RUNNING GEAR: Front Suspension: Coil springs with leading links and track bar, link-type 0.95 in. dia. stabilizer bar. Low pressure gas charged twin tube shock absorbers. Spring rate at wheel: 120 lb./in. Rear Suspension: Semi-elliptical leaf springs, link type 0.63 in. dia. stabilizer bar. Twin tube low pressure gas charged shock absorbers. Spring rate at wheel: 165 lb./in. Front Axle Type and Capacity: Dana model 30 Hypoid. Rear Axle Type and Capacity: Dana HOL 35C or Dana MO4 44. Final Drive Ratio: 2.5 liter engine/5-spd. manual trans.: 4.11:1; 4.0 liter/5-spd. man. trans. and part-time four-wheel drive: 3.08:1; 4.0 liter engine/4-spd. auto. trans. and either part-time or full-time four-wheel drive: 3.55:1. Transfer Case: Standard Command-Trac New Process 231. Ratios: 2.72:1, 1.00:1. Optional: Selec-Trac New Process 242 transfer case. Ratios: 2.72:1, 1.00:1. Brakes: Type: hydraulic, front discs and rear drums. Dimensions: Front: 11.02 in. dia. disc. Rear: 90 in. dia. drums. Wheels: Cherokee base: 15 x 7 in. styled steel. Cherokee Sport: Full face steel, 15 x 7 in. Cherokee Country: 15 x 7 in. machined face lattice. Tires: Base Cherokee: P195/75R15 steel belted All-Weather black sidewall radial. Cherokee Sport: P225/75R15 OWL steel radial. Cherokee Country: P215/75ROWL steel radial. Optional: P225/75R15 OWL (base). Steering: Power recirculating ball type. Ratio: 14.0:1. Turns Lock-to-Lock: 3.4. Turning Circle: 35.9 ft. Standard Transmission:. 5-speed manual. (A-S 5-spd. for 4-cyl. engines, Peugeot 5-spd. for 6-cyl.). Ratios: A-S: 3.93:1, 2.33:1, 1.45:1, 1.00:1, 0.85:1. Reverse: 4.74:1. Peugeot: 4.03:1, 2.39:1, 1.52:1, 1.0:1, 0.72:1. Reverse: 3.76:1. Optional: Aisin-Warner 30-40 LE 4-speed automatic. Ratios: 2.80:1, 1.53:1, 1.00:1, 0.71:1. Reverse: 2.39:1. Clutch: Clutch diameter: 9.1 in. dia. (2.5 liter engine); 10.5 in. dia. (4.0 liter engine). Hydraulic actuation. Optional: None.

VEHICLE DIMENSIONS: Wheelbase: 101.4 in. Overall Length: 165.3 in. Front/Rear Tread: 58.0 in./58.0 in. Overall Height: 63.33 in. Width: 70.5 in. Front/Rear Overhang: 27.5 in./36.4 in.. Approach/Departure Degrees: 39.8/30.5. Ground Clearance: Minimum clearance: Front/Rear Axle: with 215 tires: 8.0 in./8.0 in.; P225 tires: 8.4 in./8.3 in. Minimum running ground clearance: 8.8 in. Maximum capacity: 71.8 cu. ft. (with rear seat folded). Front head room: 38.3 in. Front leg room: 41.0 in. Front shoulder room: 55.3 in. Front hip room: 55.3 in. Rear head room: 38.0 in. Rear leg room: 35.3 in. Rear shoulder room: 55.3 in. Rear hip room: 44.5 in.

CAPACITIES: Fuel Tank: 20 gal.

ACCOMMODATIONS: Seating Capacity: Five passengers.

INSTRUMENTATION: Base Cherokee: speedometer, odometer, fuel level and warning lights for alternator, oil pressure, and engine coolant temperature. Brake system warning, high beam/hazard lights operation. Sport and Country models have the previously listed items plus tamper resistant odometer, tachometer, voltmeter, oil pressure and engine coolant temperature gauges, (fuel gauge has low fuel warning).

OPTIONS: Air conditioning. Anti-lock brake system. Body side moldings. Cargo area cover. Cloth seats. Console with armrests. Overhead console. Cruise control. Rear window defroster. Bright dual electric mirrors. California emissions. 4.0 liter 6-cyl. engine. Fog lamps. Gauge Group. Heavy-duty alternator/battery Group. Illuminated entry. Leather seats (Country only). 6-way power driver seat (Country only). Light Group. Dual remote mirrors. Power Equipment Package. Includes Keyless Entry, power door locks, and power windows. Power seats. Premium Audio Package. Includes six premium speakers and power antenna. AM/FM cassette tape player, extended range stereo. Roof rack. Selec-Trac transfer case. Security Alarm System. Skid Plate Group. Spare tire cover. Sun roof. Off-Road Suspension Package. Trac-Lok rear differential. Tilt steering wheel. Conventional spare tire. Trailer Towing Package. Aluminum wheels. Front door window vent. Rear window wiper/washer. Intermittent windshield wipers.

HISTORICAL FOOTNOTES: The market repositioning of the Cherokee resulted in very strong demand for a vehicle first introduced for the 1984 model year.

1993 Jeep Cherokee

JEEP JEEPSTER/ COMMANDO
1967-1973

1967 JEEPSTER/ COMMANDO

Model Number	Body Type	Factory Price	GVW	Shipping Weight	Prod. Total
8701	Convertible	$3186	3550*	2724	—
8705F	St. Wagon	$2749	3550	2673	—
8705	Roadster	$2466	3550	2461	—
8705H	Pickup	$2548	3550	2610	—

* 4200 lb. GVW with optional heavy-duty suspension or overload springs-air bag combination.

Sixteen years after the original Jeepster was discontinued, a second generation version debuted in January, 1967. The Jeepster had a CJ type grille with seven vertical openings and close-set headlights extending into the outer grille bars. The Jeepster front fenders were simple, squared-off affairs. Compared to the CJ Jeep the Jeepster's front parking lights were set higher and further apart. The Jeepster's hood was wider than the CJ's. A short rear deck ended in a sharply angled panel with vertically-mounted, rectangular-shaped taillights, a recessed center section and a continental tire mount. The front passenger bucket seat hinged forward to provide access to the rear.

The Jeepster Sports convertible was offered in both standard and custom versions. Basic equipment for the standard model included foam-molded seats, front armrests, front and rear floor mats and door-side panels color-keyed to the exterior finish, chrome bumpers, hood latches and hinges; hubcaps, manual convertible top with a glass rear window, padded instrument panel and sun visors, 2-speed electric wipers with non-glare arms, seat belts and an exterior-mounted rearview mirror. The custom model was equipped with vinyl-pleated seats, rear armrests, front and rear thick-pile carpeting, rear seat rise cover, courtesy lights, wheel trim rings and a convertible top boot.

1967 Jeepster convertible

In addition to the Jeepster, Kaiser Jeep offered four other models: The Jeepster Commando station wagon, convertible, pickup truck and roadster. All shared the Jeepster Sports convertible's basic structure but each also had its own unique functions and appeal. They did not have the Sport convertible's upper body chrome trim. A Commando identification plate on their hood panels. A similar arrangement was found on their deck. Unlike the Sports convertible, the Commandos had fold-down rear tailgates.

The station wagon was outfitted with a steel top, a top-hinged rear window casing and a standard rear seat. All models were available with the Deluxe Trim Group A option which consisted of the cigarette lighter, front armrests, door scuff plates, front and rear floor mats, chrome bumpers, hubcaps and trim rings. A station wagon-only option was the Deluxe Trim Group B. This included deluxe seats, headliner and door trim, front and rear carpeting and armrests, cigarette lighter, courtesy lights, rear quarter side-open windows, chrome outside mirror and bumpers, hubcaps and wheel trim rings.

Both the Commando station wagon and convertible had a spare tire mounted flat on the cargo door behind the rear seat. The convertible's top had a zippered rear window insert and roadster-type installation.

The 2 passenger roadster version of the Commando was offered with either a soft full or half top, or with no top at all. A full station wagon top with non-yellowing vinyl rear and tailgate windows as well as a rear seat was available.

A wide choice of exterior colors were listed for the Jeepsters. The top for both the roadster and Sports convertible was offered in glacier white, empire blue or charcoal. The top for the station wagon and pickup was available only in glacier white. Body color selections for the Sports convertible consisted of prairie white, president red, glacier white and empire blue. These colors plus spruce tip green and gold beige were available for the remaining Jeepster models.

I.D. DATA: The serial number was located on a plate found on the left door hinge pillar post and the left firewall. The V.I.N. consisted of nine to eleven symbols. The engine number was stamped on top of the cylinder block water pump boss.

STANDARD ENGINE: Engine Type: 4-cyl., F-head, cast iron block and cylinder head. Bore x Stroke: 3.125 in. x 4.375 in. Lifters: Solid. Number of main bearings-3. Fuel Induction: Carter single barrel carburetor. Compression Ratio: 6.9:1 (7.4:1 optional). Displacement: 134.2 cu. in. (2.19 liters). Horsepower: 75 @ 4000 rpm. Torque: 114 lb.-ft. @ 2000 rpm. Oil refill capacity: 4 qt. Fuel Requirements: Regular.

OPTIONAL ENGINE: Engine Type: 6-cyl., 90 degree V-6, iron alloy block and cylinder head. Bore x Stroke: 3.75 in. x 3.40 in. Lifters: Hydraulic. Number of main bearings-4. Fuel Induction: Two barrel, 1.4375 in. barrel size, downdraft carburetor. Compression Ratio: 9.0:1. Displacement: 225 cu. in. (3.68 liters). Horsepower: 160 @ 4200 rpm. Torque: 235 lb.-ft. @ 2400 rpm. Oil refill capacity: 5 qt. Fuel Requirements: Regular.

CHASSIS FEATURES: Separate body and chassis. Ladder-type frame, five cross members with front reinforcements. Overall length: 159.0 in. Overall width: 29.75 in. Section modulus: 2.247. Yield strength: 35,000 p.s.i.

SUSPENSION AND RUNNING GEAR: Front Suspension: 4-cyl.: 5-leaf longitudinal springs, 46.0 in. x 1.75 in. Spring rate: 160 lb./in. Capacity at ground: 1005 lb. double action, 1.1875 in. diameter telescopic shock absorbers and stabilizer bar. V-6: 4-leaf longitudinal springs, 46.0 in. x 2.00 in. Spring rate: 135 lb./in. Capacity at ground: 945 lb. Optional: 4-cyl.: 6-leaf springs, 46.0 in. x 1.75 in. Spring rate: 183 lb./in. Capacity at ground: 1055 lb. V-6: 5-leaf springs, 46.0 in. x 2.0 in. Spring rate: 183 lb./in. Capacity at ground: 1055 lb. Rear Suspension: Single leaf, semi-elliptical springs asymmetrically mounted. Front Axle Type and Capacity: Spicer model 27-AF full-floating. Capacity: 2,000 lb. Axle ratio: 4-cyl.: 4.27:1. V-6 with Hydra-Matic: V-6 with 3-speed manual trans.: 3.73:1. No extra cost was involved for any optional ratio to be installed. Optional: 4-cyl.: 5.38:1. V-6-cyl. with manual trans.: 4.88:1. V-6 with auto. trans.: 3.73:1. Rear Axle Type and Capacity: Spicer model 44, full-floating. Capacity: 2500 lb. Transfer Case: Dana 20. Ratios: 2.03, 1.0:1. Brakes: Type: Hydraulic, front and rear cast iron drums, dual master cylinder, double hydraulic circuit. Dimensions: Front and rear: 10.00 in. x 2.0 in. Total effective lining area: 156-sq. in. Wheels: 15 x 5.5K. Tires: Low-profile 7.35 x 16 black sidewall. Optional: 8.45 x 15 Power Cushion whitewalls or Suburbanite Mud and Snow tires. Steering: Worm and lever. Ratio: 24.01:1. Turns Lock-to-Lock: 4.5. Turning Circle: 43.6-ft. Optional None. Standard Transmission: 4-cyl.: Warner T86 CC 3-speed manual, all-synchromesh transmission with floor-mounted shifter. Transmission ratios: 3.39, 1.851, 1.0:1 Reverse: 4.531:1. V-6: Warner T14A 3-speed manual, all-synchromesh. Transmission ratios: 3.1, 1.612, 1.0:1. Reverse: 3.1:1. Optional: Model 400 Turbo Hydra-Matic with floor-mounted shift levers. Torque converter ratio of 2.30:1, overall ratio of 38.32:1. Four-cylinder models could not be ordered with the automatic transmission. Transmission ratios: 2.4815, 1.4815, 1.00:1. Reverse: 2.0769: 1. Clutch: Four cyl.: 9.25 in. dia., V-6: 10.4 in. dia. Optional: None.

VEHICLE DIMENSIONS: Wheelbase: 101 in. Overall Length: Sport Convertible:168.4 in. All other models:168.40 in. Front/Rear Tread: 50.0 in./50.0 in. Overall Height: 64.2 in. Width: 65.2 in. Front/Rear Overhang: 23 in./44.38 in. Tailgate: Width and Height: 48.50 in. x 15.75 in. Approach/Departure Degrees: 46/23. Ground Clearance: Front axle: 7.5 in. Rear axle: 7.5 in. Load space: Pickup: 63.5 in. x 59.0 in. x 16.19 in. Maximum capacity (Volume Index): 16.14 cu. ft. Front headroom: Conv.: 38.56 in. Station wagon: 39.28 in. Pickup: 39.18 in. Front legroom: 39.75 in. Front hip room: 51.88 in.

CAPACITIES: Fuel Tank: 15 gallon capacity. Optional: Auxiliary 9.5 gal. capacity unit.

ACCOMMODATIONS: Seating Capacity: Three. (Station wagon: Five).

INSTRUMENTATION: Speedometer, odometer, gauges for fuel and engine coolant temperature, warning lights for oil pressure and alternator.

OPTIONS AND PRICES: Model 1400 Turbo Hydra-Matic: $208. Wheel discs. 8.45 x 15 Power Cushion whitewalls or Suburbanite Mud and Snow tires: $60. Power top (the Jeepster was the only four-wheel drive vehicle available with this feature). Power brakes. Console (standard with Hydra-Matic). Air conditioning. Heater-defroster. E-Z Eye tinted glass. A transmission brake (for Hydra-Matic). Heavy-duty cooling system (V-6 only). Deluxe Trim Group A. Deluxe Trim Group B. Roof rack. Heavy-duty suspension. Overload springs-air bag combination. Commando-only options: Pindle hook. Drawbar. Push plate. Power take-off. Roof rack (station wagon only). Dealer options included wheel covers, transistor radio, selective drive, free-wheeling front hubs; locks for the gas filler and spare tire, electric clock (available only with the console shifter); overload springs and air bags; convertible top boot (standard models), snowplow, front-mounted winch, and for 4-cylinder models a ceramic fuel filter and oil pan magnetic drainplug.

HISTORICAL FOOTNOTES: The second-generation Jeepster was introduced in January, 1967. The Jeepster was the only four-wheel drive vehicle available with a power top.

1968 JEEPSTER/ COMMANDO

Jeepster changes for 1968 were limited to a new top design and a hinged tailgate for the Sports convertible.

I.D. DATA: The serial number was located on a plate found on the left door hinge pillar post and the left firewall. The V.I.N. consisted of nine to eleven symbols. The engine number was stamped on top of the cylinder block water pump boss.

Model Number	Body Type	Factory Price	GVW	Shipping Weight	Prod. Total
8702	Convertible	$3442	3550*	2853	—
8705F	St. Wagon	$3005	3550	2722	—
8705	Roadster	$2730	3550	2510	—
8705H	Pickup	$2817	3550	2659	—

* 4200 lb. GVW with optional heavy-duty suspension or overload springs-air bag combination.

STANDARD ENGINE: Engine Type: 4-cyl., F-head, cast iron block and cylinder head. Bore x Stroke: 3.125 in. x 4.375 in. Lifters: Solid. Number of main bearings-3. Fuel Induction: Carter single barrel carburetor. Compression Ratio: 6.9:1 (7.4:1 optional). Displacement: 134.2 cu. in. (2.19 liters). Horsepower: 75 @ 4000 rpm. Torque: 114 lb.-ft. @ 2000 rpm. Oil refill capacity: 4 qt. Fuel Requirements: Regular.

OPTIONAL ENGINE: Engine Type: 6-cyl., 90 degree V-6, iron alloy block and cylinder head. Bore x Stroke: 3.75 in. x 3.40 in. Lifters: Hydraulic. Number of main bearings-4. Fuel Induction: Two barrel, 1.4375 in. barrel size, downdraft carburetor. Compression Ratio: 9.0:1. Displacement: 225 cu. in. (3.68 liters). Horsepower: 160 @ 4200 rpm. Torque: 235 lb.-ft. @ 2400 rpm. Oil refill capacity: 5 qt. Fuel Requirements: Regular.

CHASSIS FEATURES: Separate body and chassis. Ladder-type frame, five cross members with front reinforcements. Overall length: 159.0 in. Overall width: 29.75 in. Section modulus: 2.247. Yield strength: 35,000 p.s.i.

SUSPENSION AND RUNNING GEAR: Front Suspension: 4-cyl.: 5-leaf longitudinal springs, 46.0 in. x 1.75 in. Spring rate: 160 lb./in. Capacity at ground: 1005 lb. double action, 1.1875 in. diameter telescopic shock absorbers and stabilizer bar. V-6: 4-leaf longitudinal springs, 46.0 in. x 2.00 in. Spring rate: 135 lb./in. Capacity at ground: 945 lb. Optional: 4-cyl.: 6-leaf springs, 46.0 in. x 1.75 in. Spring rate: 183 lb./in. Capacity at ground: 1055 lb. V-6: 5-leaf springs, 46.0 in. x 2.0 in. Spring rate: 183 lb./in. Capacity at ground: 1055 lb. Rear Suspension: Single leaf, semi-elliptical springs asymmetrically mounted. Front Axle Type and Capacity: Spicer model 27-AF full-floating. Capacity: 2,000 lb. Axle ratio: 4-cyl.: 4.27:1. V-6 with Hydra-Matic: V-6 with 3-speed manual trans.: 3.73:1. No extra cost was involved for any optional ratio to be installed. Optional: 4-cyl.: 5.38:1. V-6-cyl. with manual trans.: 4.88:1, V-6 with auto. trans.: 3.73:1. Rear Axle Type and Capacity: Spicer model 44, full-floating. Capacity: 2500 lb. Transfer Case: Dana 20. Ratios: 2.03, 1.0:1. Brakes: Type: Hydraulic, front and rear cast iron drums, dual master cylinder, double hydraulic circuit. Dimensions: Front and rear: 10.00 in. x 2.0 in. Total effective lining area: 156 sq. in. Wheels: 15 x 5.5K. Tires: Low-profile 7.35 x 16 black sidewall. Optional: 8.45 x 15 Power Cushion whitewalls or Suburbanite Mud and Snow tires. Steering: Worm and lever. Ratio: 24.01:1. Turns Lock-to-Lock: 4.5. Turning Circle: 43.6-ft. Optional: None. Standard Transmission: 4-cyl.: Warner T86 CC 3-speed manual, all-synchromesh transmission with floor-mounted shifter. Transmission ratios: 3.39, 1.851, 1.0:1 Reverse: 4.531:1. V-6: Warner T14A 3-speed manual, all-synchromesh. Transmission ratios: 3.1, 1.612, 1.0:1. Reverse: 3.1:1. Optional: Model 400 Turbo Hydra-Matic with floor-mounted shift levers. Torque converter ratio of 2.30:1, overall ratio of 38.32:1. Four-cylinder models could not be ordered with the automatic transmission. Transmission ratios: 2.4815, 1.4815, 1.00:1. Reverse: 2.0769: 1. Clutch: Four cyl.: 9.25 in. dia., V-6: 10.4 in. dia. Optional: None.

VEHICLE DIMENSIONS: Wheelbase: 101 in. Overall Length: Sport convertible:168.4 in. All other models: 168.40 in. Front/Rear Tread: 50.0 in./50.0 in. Overall Height: 64.2 in. Width: 65.2 in. Front/Rear Overhang: 23 in./44.38 in. Tailgate: Width and Height: 48.50 in. x 15.75 in. Approach/Departure Degrees: 46/23. Ground Clearance: Front axle: 7.5 in. Rear axle: 7.5 in. Load space: Pickup: 63.5 in. x 59.0 in. x 16.19 in. Maximum capacity (Volume Index): 16.14 cu. ft. Front headroom: Conv.: 38.56 in. Station wagon: 39.28 in. Pickup: 39.18 in. Front legroom: 39.75 in. Front hip room: 51.88 in.

CAPACITIES: Fuel Tank: 15 gallon capacity. Optional: Auxiliary 9.5 gal. capacity unit.

ACCOMMODATIONS: Seating Capacity: Three. Station Wagon: Five.

INSTRUMENTATION: Speedometer, odometer, gauges for fuel and engine coolant temperature, warning lights for oil pressure and alternator.

OPTIONS Model 1400 Turbo Hydra-Matic. Wheel discs. 8.45 x 15 Power Cushion whitewalls or Suburbanite Mud and Snow tires. Power top (the Jeepster was the only four-wheel drive vehicle available with this feature). Power brakes. Console (standard with Hydra-Matic). Air conditioning. Heater-defroster. E-Z Eye tinted glass. A transmission brake (for Hydra-Matic). Heavy-duty cooling system (V-6 only). Deluxe Trim Group A. Deluxe Trim Group B. Roof rack. Heavy-duty suspension. Overload springs-air bag combination. Commando-only options: Pindle hook. Drawbar. Push plate. Power take-off. Roof rack (station wagon only). Dealer options include wheelcovers, transistor radio, selective drive, free-wheeling front hubs; locks for the gas filler and spare tire, electric clock (available only with the console shifter), overload springs and air bags; convertible top boot (standard models), snowplow, front-mounted winch, and for 4-cylinder models a ceramic fuel filter and oil pan magnetic drainplug.

HISTORICAL FOOTNOTES: The 1968 Jeepster models were announced in the fall of 1967.

1969 JEEPSTER/ COMMANDO

Jeepster changes for 1969 were limited to new side body markers.

I.D. DATA: The serial number was located on a plate found on the left door hinge pillar post and the left firewall. The V.I.N. consisted of nine to eleven symbols. The engine number was stamped on top of the cylinder block water pump boss. Serial number range: Conv.: 8701015-12545. Pickup: 8705H-28002 and up.

Model Number	Body Type	Factory Price	GVW	Shipping Weight	Prod. Total
8702	Convertible	$3005	3550*	2707	—
8705F	St. Wagon	$3113	3550	2722	—
8705	Roadster	$2824	3550	2510	—
8705H	Pickup	$2914	3550	2659	—

* 4200 lb. GVW with optional heavy-duty suspension or overload springs-air bag combination.

STANDARD ENGINE: Engine Type: 4-cyl., F-head, cast iron block and cylinder head. Bore x Stroke: 3.125 in. x 4.375 in. Lifters: Solid. Number of main bearings-3. Fuel Induction: Carter single barrel carburetor. Compression Ratio: 6.9:1 (7.4:1 optional). Displacement: 134.2 cu. in. (2.19 liters). Horsepower: 75 @ 4000 rpm. Torque: 114 lb.-ft. @ 2000 rpm. Oil refill capacity: 4 qt. Fuel Requirements: Regular.

OPTIONAL ENGINE: Engine Type: 6-cyl., 90 degree V-6, iron alloy block and cylinder head. Bore x Stroke: 3.75 in. x 3.40 in. Lifters: Hydraulic. Number of main bearings-4. Fuel Induction: Two barrel, 1.4375 in. barrel size, downdraft carburetor. Compression Ratio: 9.0:1. Displacement: 225 cu. in. (3.68 liters). Horsepower: 160 @ 4200 rpm. Torque: 235 lb.-ft. @ 2400 rpm. Oil refill capacity: 5 qt. Fuel Requirements: Regular.

CHASSIS FEATURES: Separate body and chassis. Ladder-type frame, five cross members with front reinforcements. Overall length: 159.0 in. Overall width: 29.75 in. Section modulus: 2.247. Yield strength: 35,000 p.s.i.

SUSPENSION AND RUNNING GEAR: Front Suspension: 4-cyl.: 5-leaf longitudinal springs, 46.0 in. x 1.75 in. Spring rate: 160 lb./in. Capacity at ground: 1005 lb. double action, 1.1875 in. diameter telescopic shock absorbers and stabilizer bar. V-6: 4-leaf longitudinal springs, 46.0 in. x 2.00 in. Spring rate: 135 lb./in. Capacity at ground: 945 lb. Optional: 4-cyl.: 6-leaf springs, 46.0 in. x 1.75 in. Spring rate: 183 lb./in. Capacity at ground: 1055 lb. V-6: 5-leaf springs, 46.0 in. x 2.0 in. Spring rate: 183 lb./in. Capacity at ground: 1055 lb. Rear Suspension: Single leaf, semi-elliptical springs asymmetrically mounted. Front Axle Type and Capacity: Spicer model 27-AF full-floating. Capacity: 2,000 lb. Axle ratio: 4-cyl.: 4.27:1. V-6 with Hydra-Matic: V-6 with 3-speed manual trans.: 3.73:1. No extra cost was involved for any optional ratio to be installed. Optional: 4-cyl.: 5.38:1. V-6-cyl. with manual trans.: 4.88:1, V-6 with auto. trans.: 3.73:1. Rear Axle Type and Capacity: Spicer model 44, full-floating. Capacity: 2500 lb. Transfer Case: Dana 20. Ratios: 2.03, 1.0:1. Brakes: Type: Hydraulic, front and rear cast iron drums, dual master cylinder, double hydraulic circuit. Dimensions: Front and rear: 10.00 in. x 2.0 in. Total effective lining area: 156-sq. in. Wheels: 15 x 5.5K. Tires: Low-profile 7.35 x 16 black sidewall. Optional: 8.45 x 15 Power Cushion whitewalls or Suburbanite Mud and Snow tires. Steering: Worm and lever. Ratio: 24.01:1. Turns Lock-to-Lock: 4.5. Turning Circle: 43.6-ft. Optional: None. Standard Transmission: 4-cyl.: Warner T86 CC 3-speed manual, all-synchromesh transmission with floor-mounted shifter. Transmission ratios: 3.39, 1.851, 1.0:1 Reverse: 4.531:1. V-6: Warner T14A 3-speed manual, all-synchromesh. Transmission ratios: 3.1, 1.612, 1.0:1. Reverse: 3.1:1. Optional: Model 400 Turbo Hydra-Matic with floor-mounted shift levers. Torque converter ratio of 2.30:1, overall ratio of 38.32:1. Four-cylinder models could not be ordered with the automatic transmission. Transmission ratios: 2.4815, 1.4815, 1.00:1. Reverse: 2.0769: 1. Clutch: Four cyl.: 9.25 in. dia., V-6: 10.4 in. dia. Optional: None.

VEHICLE DIMENSIONS: Wheelbase: 101 in. Overall Length: Sport convertible:168.4 in. All other models: 168.40 in. Front/Rear Tread: 50.0 in./50.0 in. Overall Height: 64.2 in. Width: 65.2 in. Front/Rear Overhang: 23 in./44.38 in. Tailgate: Width and Height: 48.50 in. x 15.75 in. Approach/Departure Degrees: 46/23. Ground Clearance: Front axle: 7.5 in. Rear axle: 7.5 in. Load space: Pickup: 63.5 in. x 59.0 in. x 16.19 in. Maximum capacity (Volume Index): 16.14 cu. ft. Front headroom: Conv.: 38.56 in. Station wagon: 39.28 in. Pickup: 39.18 in. Front legroom: 39.75 in. Front hip room: 51.88 in.

CAPACITIES: Fuel Tank: 15 gallon capacity. Optional: Auxiliary 9.5 gal. capacity unit.

ACCOMMODATIONS: Seating Capacity: Three. (Station wagon: Five).

INSTRUMENTATION: Speedometer, odometer, gauges for fuel and engine coolant temperature, warning lights for oil pressure and alternator.

OPTIONS AND PRICES: Model 1400 Turbo Hydra-Matic: $208. Wheel discs. 8.45 x 15 Power Cushion whitewalls or Suburbanite Mud and Snow tires: $60. Power top (the Jeepster was the only four-wheel drive vehicle available with this feature). Power brakes. Console (standard with Hydra-Matic). Air conditioning. Heater-defroster. E-Z Eye tinted glass. A transmission brake (for Hydra-Matic). Heavy-duty cooling system (V-6 only). Deluxe Trim Group A. Deluxe Trim Group B. Roof rack. Heavy-duty suspension. Overload springs-air bag combination. Commando-only options: Pindle hook. Drawbar. Push plate Power take-off. Roof rack (station wagon only). Dealer options include wheelcovers, transistor radio, selective drive, free-wheeling front hubs; locks for the gas filler and spare tire, electric clock (available only with the console shifter), overload springs and air bags; convertible top boot (standard models), snowplow, front-mounted winch, and for 4-cylinder models a ceramic fuel filter and oil pan magnetic drainplug.

HISTORICAL FOOTNOTES: The 1969 models were introduced in the fall of 1968.

1970 JEEPSTER/ COMMANDO

Except for the introduction of power steering as an option for models with the V-6 engine, no changes were made in the Jeepster/Commando line for 1970. Standard equipment consisted of oil filter, directional signals, back-up lights, 4-way flasher, driver, padded sun visor, padded instrument panel, driver's side exterior mirror, 2-speed electric windshield wipers and washers, exhaust emission control, heater and defroster, power cushion, scuff plates and front floor mat.

Standard equipment unique to the convertible was a convertible top passenger, and rear seats with seat belts. The station wagon had standard headlining, full metal cab, driver and passenger adjustable bucket seats with seat belts and rear seat with seat belts. The pickup had a standard half metal cab and front driver and passenger adjustable bucket seats with seat belts. The roadster had standard driver and passenger adjustable bucket seats with seat belts.

1970 Jeepster Commando station wagon

I.D. DATA: The serial number was located on a plate found on the left door hinge pillar post and the left firewall. The V.I.N. consisted of nine to eleven symbols. The engine number was stamped on top of the cylinder block water pump boss. Serial number range: Station wagon: 4-cyl.: 8705F15-32389 and up; V-6: 8705F17-56466 and up. Pickup: 8705H15-28002 and up. Roadster: 4-cyl.: 8705015-32389 and up; V-6: 8705017-56466 and up. Convertible: 4-cyl.: 870215-50081 and up; V-6: 870217-50631 and up.

Model Number	Body Type	Factory Price	GVW	Shipping Weight	Prod. Total
8702	Convertible	$3116.58	3550*	2707	—
8705F	St. Wagon	$3207.82	3550	2722	—
8705	Roadster	$2916.87	3550	2510	—
8705H	Pickup	$3013.66	3550	2659	—

* 4200 lb. GVW with optional heavy-duty suspension or overload springs-air bag combination.

STANDARD ENGINE: Engine Type: 4-cyl., F-head, cast iron block and cylinder head. Bore x Stroke: 3.125 in. x 4.375 in. Lifters: Solid. Number of main bearings-3. Fuel Induction: Carter single barrel carburetor. Compression Ratio: 6.9:1 (7.4:1 optional). Displacement: 134.2 cu. in. (2.19 liters). Horsepower: 75 @ 4000 rpm. Torque: 114 lb.-ft. @ 2000 rpm. Oil refill capacity: 4 qt. Fuel Requirements: Regular.

OPTIONAL ENGINE: Engine Type: 6-cyl., 90 degree V-6, iron alloy block and cylinder head. Bore x Stroke: 3.75 in. x 3.40 in. Lifters: Hydraulic. Number of main bearings-4. Fuel Induction: Two barrel, 1.4375 in. barrel size, downdraft carburetor. Compression Ratio: 9.0:1. Displacement: 225 cu. in. (3.68 liters). Horsepower: 160 @ 4200 rpm. Torque: 235 lb.-ft. @ 2400 rpm. Oil refill capacity: 5 qt. Fuel Requirements: Regular.

CHASSIS FEATURES: Separate body and chassis. Ladder-type frame, five cross members with front reinforcements. Overall length: 159.0 in. Overall width: 29.75 in. Section modulus: 2.247. Yield strength: 35,000 p.s.i.

SUSPENSION AND RUNNING GEAR: Front Suspension: 4-cyl.: 5-leaf longitudinal springs, 46.0 in. x 1.75 in. Spring rate: 160 lb./in. Capacity at ground: 1005 lb. double action, 1.1875 in. diameter telescopic shock absorbers and stabilizer bar. V-6: 4-leaf longitudinal springs, 46.0 in. x 2.00 in. Spring rate: 135 lb./in. Capacity at ground: 945 lb. Optional: 4-cyl.: 6-leaf springs, 46.0 in. x 1.75 in. Spring rate: 183 lb./in. Capacity at ground: 1055 lb. V-6: 5-leaf springs, 46.0 in. x 2.0 in. Spring rate: 183 lb./in. Capacity at ground: 1055 lb. Rear Suspension: Longitudinal, 3-leaf, semi-elliptical springs asymmetrically mounted. Spring rate: 200 lb./in. Front Axle Type and Capacity: Spicer model 27-AF full-floating. Capacity: 2,000 lb. Axle ratio: 4-cyl.: 4.27:1. V-6 with Hydra-Matic: V-6 with 3-speed manual trans.: 3.73:1. No extra cost was involved for any optional ratio to be installed. Optional: 4-cyl.: 5.38:1. V-6-cyl. with manual trans.: 4.88:1, V-6 with auto. trans.: 3.73:1. Rear Axle Type and Capacity: Spicer model 44, full-floating. Capacity: 2500 lb. Transfer Case: Dana 20. Ratios: 2.03, 1.0:1. Brakes: Type: Hydraulic, front and rear cast iron drums, dual master cylinder, double hydraulic circuit. Dimensions: Front and rear: 10.00 in. x 2.0 in. Total effective lining area: 156 sq. in. Wheels: 15 x 5.5K. Tires: Low-profile 7.35 x 16 black sidewall. Optional: 8.45 x 15 Power Cushion whitewalls or Suburbanite Mud and Snow tires. Steering: Worm and lever. Ratio: 24.01:1. Turns Lock-to-Lock: 4.5. Turning Circle: 43.6 ft. Standard Transmission: 4-cyl.: Warner T86 CC 3-speed manual, all-synchromesh transmission with floor-mounted shifter. Transmission ratios: 3.39, 1.851, 1.0:1. Reverse: 4.531:1. V-6: Warner T14A 3-speed manual, all-synchromesh. Transmission ratios: 3.1, 1.612, 1.0:1. Reverse: 3.1:1. Optional: Model 400 Turbo Hydra-Matic with floor-mounted shift levers. Torque converter ratio of 2.30:1, overall ratio of 38.32:1. Four-cylinder models could not be ordered with the automatic transmission. Transmission ratios: 2.4815, 1.4815, 1.00:1. Reverse: 2.0769. Clutch: Four cyl.: 9.25 in. dia., V-6: 10.4 in. dia. Optional: None.

VEHICLE DIMENSIONS: Wheelbase: 101 in. Overall Length: Sport convertible: 168.4 in. All other models: 168.40 in. Front/Rear Tread: 50.0 in./50.0 in. Overall Height: 64.2 in. Width: 65.2 in. Front/Rear Overhang: 23 in./44.38 in. Tailgate: Width and Height: 48.50 in. x 15.75 in. Approach/Departure Degrees: 46/23. Ground Clearance: Front axle: 7.5 in. Rear axle: 7.5 in. Load space: Pickup: 63.5 in. x 59.0 in.x 16.19 in. Maximum capacity (Volume Index): 16.14 cu. ft. Front headroom: Conv.: 38.56 in. Station wagon: 39.28, Pickup: 39.18 in. Front legroom: 39.75 in. Front hip room: 51.88 in.

CAPACITIES: Fuel Tank: 15 gallon capacity. Optional: Auxiliary 9.5 gal. capacity unit.

ACCOMMODATIONS: Seating Capacity: Three. Station Wagon: Five.

INSTRUMENTATION: Speedometer, odometer, gauges for fuel and engine coolant temperature, warning lights for oil pressure and alternator.

OPTIONS AND PRICES: Dauntless V-6: $210.95. Power Cushion 8.55 x 15 4-ply tires: $55.05. H78 x 15 Polyglas Suburbanite tires: $81.72. H78 x 15 Polyglas Power Cushion white sidewall: $113.52. Suburbanite 8.55 x 15 4-ply: $55.05. Suburbanite 8.55 x 15 4-ply white sidewall: $86.63. Power Cushion 8.55 x 15 4-ply white sidewall: $86.60. Power Cushion 7.35 x 15 white sidewall: $43.56. Cigarette lighter: $4.99. Locking rear differential (available axle ratios: 4-cyl.: 4.27, 5.38; V-6: 3.31, 3.73. 4.27, 4.88:1): $48.43. Radio and antenna: $66.19. Heavy-duty cooling system (V-6 only): $17.80. Heavy-duty springs and shock absorbers (V-6 only): $25.74. Power brakes: $46.48. Power steering (V-6 only): $131.32. Automatic transmission with console (V-6 only): $325.60. Console: $50.84. Trim Package A. Includes front armrests, cigarette lighter, front and rear chrome bumpers, scuff plates, wheelcovers, and front and rear rubber floor mats (front only for pickup): Convertible, station wagon, roadster: $121.65, pickup: $124.16. Power-activated convertible top (convertible only): $67.92. 55 amp alternator: $27.58. Trim Package B (station wagon only). Includes all of Package A plus deluxe seats, courtesy lights, front and rear carpets, vinyl door trim panels, sliding rear quarter windows, rear luggage platform, rear seat riser cover and chrome inside rearview mirror: $349.72. Dealer installed accessories: Locking gas cap: $3.25. Magnetic drain plug (4-cyl. only): $1.63. Air bag type helper front springs: $46.19. Right outside rearview mirror: $6.12. Cigarette lighter: $3.67. Courtesy lights: $4.13. Electric clock: $27.76. Push button radio: $73.98. Antenna: $6.41. Mag-type wheelcovers: $103.50.

HISTORICAL FOOTNOTES: The latest Jeepsters debuted in the fall of 1969.

1971 JEEPSTER/ COMMANDO

Initially, the convertible was dropped for 1971. However, on January 4, 1971 it was again made available. Neither the Dauntless nor the Hurricane name was used for the Jeepster engines in 1971. Several new options, including air conditioning and tinted glass were offered for 1971. The 1971 Jeepster Commando color selection was as follows: Sprucetip green metallic, president red, avocado mist metallic, champagne white, spring green, vintage gold metallic, burnished bronze metallic, island blue metallic, candlelight yellow. Three interior colors were available: Buckskin, marlin blue and charcoal.

During the model year two special Commando models were introduced. The Commando SC-1, based on the station wagon, was introduced as a 1971-1/2 model. Its features included a butterscotch gold body, a white top and black Rallye striping incorporating "SC-1" identification on its hood and body sides. Additional standard equipment included the V-6 engine, luggage rack and radio.

The Hurst/Jeepster Special was also based on the Commando wagon This vehicle was an enterprise of American Motors and the Hurst Performance Company. Initially 500 units of the Hurst/Jeepster Special were to be built. Of these, 300 were to have automatic transmissions controlled by a Hurst dual gate shifter. The remaining 200 units were to have three-speed manual transmissions with Hurst T-Handle shifters. Eventually, less than 100 were built. All had a white exterior with blue and red Rallye striping running down the hood's center line and across the front cowl and rear tailgate.

A special ABS plastic hood-mounted scoop containing a 0-8000 rpm tachometer was another unique feature. Other features included a roof rack, Goodyear Polyglas F70 x15 tires with raised white lettering, a 15 inch foam steering wheel with brushed chrome spokes, and bucket seats offered in charcoal, blue or buckskin. Power brakes were standard.

I.D. DATA: The serial number was located on a plate found on the left door hinge pillar post and the left firewall. The V.I.N. consisted of nine to eleven symbols. The engine number was stamped on top of the cylinder block water pump boss. Serial number range: Station wagon: 4-cyl.: 8705F15-32671 and up; V-6: 8705F17-68585 and up. Pickup: 8705H15-32671 and up. Roadster: 4-cyl.: 8705015-32671 and up; V-6: 8705017-68585 and up. Convertible: 8702015-51123

Model Number	Body Type	Factory Price	GVW	Shipping Weight	Prod. Total
87020	Convertible	$3465	3550*	2787	—
8705F	St. Wagon	$3446	3550	2802	—
8705	Roadster	$3197	3550	2590	—
8705H	Pickup	$3291	3550	2659	—

* 4200 lb. GVW with optional heavy-duty suspension or overload springs-air bag combination.

STANDARD ENGINE: Engine Type: 4-cyl., F-head, cast iron block and cylinder head. Bore x Stroke: 3.125 in. x 4.375 in. Lifters: Solid. Number of main bearings-3. Fuel Induction: Carter single barrel carburetor. Compression Ratio: 6.9:1 (7.4:1 optional). Displacement: 134.2 cu. in. (2.19 liters). Horsepower: 75 @ 4000 rpm. Torque: 114 lb.-ft. @ 2000 rpm. Oil refill capacity: 4 qt. Fuel Requirements: Regular.

OPTIONAL ENGINE: Engine Type: 6-cyl., 90 degree V-6, iron alloy block and cylinder head. Bore x Stroke: 3.75 in. x 3.40 in. Lifters: Hydraulic. Number of main bearings-4. Fuel Induction: Two barrel, 1.4375 in. barrel size, downdraft carburetor. Compression Ratio: 9.0:1. Displacement: 225 cu. in. (3.68 liters). Horsepower: 160 @ 4200 rpm. Torque: 235 lb.-ft. @ 2400 rpm. Oil refill capacity: 5 qt. Fuel Requirements: Regular.

CHASSIS FEATURES: Separate body and chassis. Ladder-type frame, five cross members with front reinforcements. Overall length: 159.0 in. Overall width: 29.75 in. Section modulus: 2.247. Yield strength: 35,000 p.s.i.

SUSPENSION AND RUNNING GEAR: Front Suspension: 4-cyl.: 5-leaf longitudinal springs, 46.0 in. x 1.75 in. Spring rate: 160 lb./in. Capacity at ground: 1005-lb. double action, 1.1875 in. diameter telescopic shock absorbers and stabilizer bar. V-6: 4-leaf longitudinal springs, 46.0 in. x 2.00 in. Spring rate: 135 lb./in. Capacity at ground: 945 lb. Optional: 4-cyl.: 6-leaf springs, 46.0 in. x 1.75 in. Spring rate: 183 lb./in. Capacity at ground: 1055 lb. V-6: 5-leaf springs, 46.0 in. x 2.0 in. Spring rate: 183 lb./in. Capacity at ground: 1055 lb. Rear Suspension: Longitudinal, 3-leaf, semi-elliptical springs asymmetrically mounted. Spring rate: 200 lb./in.

Front Axle Type and Capacity: Spicer model 27-AF full-floating. Capacity: 2,000 lb. Axle ratio: 4-cyl.: 4.27:1. V-6 with Hydra-Matic. V-6 with 3-speed manual trans.: 3.73:1. No extra cost was involved for any optional ratio to be installed. Optional: 4-cyl.: 5.38:1. V-6-cyl. with manual trans.: 4.88:1, V-6 with auto. trans.: 3.73:1. Rear Axle Type and Capacity: Spicer model 44, full-floating. Capacity: 2500 lb. Transfer Case: Dana 20. Ratios: 2.03, 1.0:1. Brakes: Type: Hydraulic, front and rear cast iron drums, dual master cylinder, double hydraulic circuit. Dimensions: Front and rear: 10.00 in. x 2.0 in. Total effective lining area: 156 sq. in. Wheels: 15 x 5.5K. Tires: Low-profile 7.35 x 16 black sidewall. Optional: 8.45 x 15 Power Cushion whitewalls or Suburbanite Mud and Snow tires. Steering: Worm and lever. Ratio: 24.01:1. Turns Lock-to-Lock: 4.5. Turning Circle: 43.6 ft. Standard Transmission: 4-cyl.: Warner T86 CC 3-speed manual, all-synchromesh transmission with floor-mounted shifter. Transmission ratios: 3.39, 1.851, 1.0:1 Reverse: 4.531:1. V-6: Warner T14A 3-speed manual, all-synchromesh. Transmission ratios: 3.1, 1.612, 1.0:1. Reverse: 3.1:1. Optional: Model 400 Turbo Hydra-Matic with floor-mounted shift levers. Torque converter ratio of 2.30:1, overall ratio of 38.32:1. Four-cylinder models could not be ordered with the automatic transmission. Transmission ratios: 2.4815, 1.4815, 1.00:1. Reverse: 2.0769. Clutch: Four cyl.: 9.25 in. dia., V-6: 10.4 in. dia. Optional: None.

VEHICLE DIMENSIONS: Wheelbase: 101 in. Overall Length: Sport convertible:168.4 in. All other models: 168.40 in. Front/Rear Tread: 50.0 in./50.0 in. Overall Height: 64.2 in. Width: 65.2 in. Front/Rear Overhang: 23 in./44.38 in. Tailgate: Width and Height: 48.50 in. x 15.75 in. Approach/Departure Degrees: 46/23. Ground Clearance: Front axle: 7.5 in. Rear axle: 7.5 in. Load space: Pickup: 63.5 in. x 59.0 in. x 16.19 in. Maximum capacity (Volume Index): 16.14 cu. ft. Front headroom: Conv.: 38.56 in. Station wagon: 39.28 Pickup: 39.18 in. Front legroom: 39.75 in. Front hip room: 51.88 in.

CAPACITIES: Fuel Tank: 15 gallon capacity. Optional: Auxiliary 9.5 gal. capacity unit.

ACCOMMODATIONS: Seating Capacity: Three. Station Wagon: Five.

INSTRUMENTATION: Speedometer, odometer, gauges for fuel and engine coolant temperature, warning lights for oil pressure and alternator.

OPTIONS AND PRICES: Excluding pickup: 225 engine: $100. Pickup: $102.25. 4-speed manual trans. (V-6 only): $174.65. Automatic trans. (V-6 only): $325.30. Pickup: $332.35. Rear axle ratios: 5.38:1 (4-cyl., 3-spd. only), 4.27:1 (V-6, 3 or 4-spd.), 4.88:1 (V-6, 3 or 4-spd.), 3.73:1 (V-6, auto. trans.): $12.65. Pickup: $12.95. Rear axle Trac-Lok: $61.35. Pickup: $62.70. Power brakes (V-6 only): $46.45. Pickup: $47.45. Power steering (V-6 only): $147.65. Pickup: $150.80. AM radio with antenna: $72.30. Pickup: $73.85. Cigarette lighter: $6.50. Pickup: $6.65. Tinted glass (all windows): $34.80. Pickup: $35.55. Air conditioning (includes heavy-duty cooling system): $410.60. Pickup: $419.50. Courtesy lights: $10.30. Pickup: $10.50. Luggage rack: $72.30. Luggage platform: $29.95. Sliding rear quarter windows: 109.25. Trim Package A. Includes cigarette lighter, wheelcovers, front door armrests, chrome front and rear bumpers, front and rear floor mats (front mats on roadster and pickup), and scuff mats (scuff plates on pickup): $121.55. Pickup: $124.20. Trim Package B. Includes contents of Package A except that carpets replace mats. Other items include custom seats, door trim panels, courtesy lights, rear luggage platform, rear seat riser cover, sliding rear windows and chrome inside rearview mirror. Not available for pickup: $349.50. Heavy-duty 70 amp-hr. battery: $11.70. Pickup: $11.95. 55 amp alternator: $27.60. Pickup: $28.20. Heavy-duty cooling system (V-6 only): $23.35. Pickup: $23.85. Heavy-duty front and rear springs and shock absorbers (V-6 only): $38.85. Pickup: $39.65. 7.35 x 15 white sidewall Power Cushion 4-ply tires: $43.40. Pickup: $44.35. Power Cushion black sidewall 8.55 x 15 4-ply tires: $54.60. Pickup: $55.75. 8.55 x 15 white sidewall Power Cushion 4-ply tires: $87. Pickup: $88.90. 8.55 x 15 black sidewall Suburbanite 4-ply tires: $54.60. Pickup: $55.75. 8.55 x 15 white sidewall Suburbanite 4-ply tires: $87. Pickup: $88.90. H78 x 15 white sidewall Polyglas Power Cushion: $112.90. Pickup: $115.30. Warn semi-automatic front hubs: $64.70. Pickup: $66.15. Fuel vaporization system: $37. Pickup: $37.85. Rear seat with dual seat belts (standard for station wagon): $92.10.

HISTORICAL FOOTNOTES: Introduction of the 1971 Jeepsters took place in the fall of 1970.

1972 JEEPSTER/ COMMANDO

Replacing the Jeepster name in 1972 was the Commando title. The Sports convertible model was not offered. Numerous substantial changes took place for the 1972 model year. Both the F-head (except for export models) and V-6 engines were dropped. The standard Jeep Commando engine was the 100 horsepower AMC 232 cu. in. 6-cylinder engine. Two AMC engines were optional, the 258 cu. in. 6-cylinder and the 304 cu. in. V-8. Along with these engines came a revamping of the Commando's transmission lineup. Joining the list of available transmissions was a heavy-duty 4-speed manual transmission. Its availability was limited to the 6-cylinder engine. The automatic was optional for either the 258 or 304 cu. in. engines.

Use of the new engines necessitated a stretching out of the Commando chassis which now had a 104 in. wheelbase. The front shock absorbers were now anchored ahead of the axle rather than behind as had been the case on the 1967-71 models.

Also optional (with the V-8 engine only) were power brakes. A self-balancing hood replaced the older side hook-latch setup.

A longer hood extended into a new mesh-insert grille incorporating directional/parking lights. Single headlights were used. The tailgate had an extruded center section to provide room for the spare tire to be mounted flat behind the optional rear seat or directly behind the bulkhead.

Full-foam front bucket seats were now standard. The front seats were positioned 1.5 in. further to the rear. The rear seat was set back an additional 4.8 inches. Rear seat passengers appreciated the smaller wheel housings. Additional interior revisions included use of an elliptically shape rather than circular steering wheel and a white instead of black headliner. Standard equipment for 1972 included directional signals, 4-way hazard flashers, side safety marker lights, back-up lights, electric windshield washer and 2-speed windshield wipers, dual horns, interior and exterior mirrors, padded instrument panel, sound absorbing headlining (Station Wagon only), 37 amp alternator, and 50 amp-hr. battery. The standard driver and passenger bucket seats were finished in Wellington vinyl in either buff or black color. The bucket seats for the optional Custom Decor Group was finished in a striped Uganda perforated vinyl in a blue color. A split bench seats was optional for the Custom Decor Group.

I.D. DATA: The V.I.N. contained 13 symbols. The first entry, a letter, designated the manufacturer (Jeep Corporation). The next unit was a number indicating the model year. Then followed a letter identifying the transmission, drivetrain and plant. Next were two numbers identifying the vehicle line or model. Then came either a number or letter representing the body style. Next came the seventh unit, a letter indicating the model type and GVW. The eighth character, a letter, identified the engine. The final five numbers were the sequential production numbers. For all series the production sequence was: J2( )87( )UA00001 and up

Model Number	Body Type	Factory Price	GVW	Shipping Weight	Prod. Total
8705F	St. Wag.	$3408	3900*	3002	—
8705	Roadster	$3257	3900	2790	—
8705H	Pickup	$3284	3900	2639	—

* 4700 lb. GVW Package optional.

STANDARD ENGINE: Engine Type: 6-cyl., OHV, cast iron block and cylinder head. Bore x Stroke: 3.75 in. x 3.50 in. Lifters: Hydraulic. Number of main bearings-7. Fuel Induction: Single barrel carburetor. Compression Ratio: 8.0:1. Displacement: 232 cu. in. (3.8 liters). Horsepower: Net 100 @ 3600 rpm. Torque: Net 185 lb.-ft. @ 1800 rpm. Tach redline: NA. Oil refill capacity: 5 qt. Fuel Requirements: Regular, low-lead or no-lead.

OPTIONAL ENGINE: Engine Type: 6-cyl., OHV, iron alloy block and cylinder head. Bore x Stroke: 3.75 in. x 3.90 in. Lifters: Hydraulic. Number of main bearings-7. Fuel Induction: Single barrel carburetor. Compression Ratio: 8.0:1. Displacement: 258 cu. in. (4.2 liters). Horsepower: Net 110 @ 3500 rpm. Torque: Net 195 lb.-ft. @ 2000 rpm. Oil refill capacity: 5 qt. Fuel Requirements: Regular, low-lead or no-lead.

OPTIONAL ENGINE: Engine Type: V-8., OHV, iron alloy block and cylinder head. Bore x Stroke: 3.75 in. x 3.44 in. Lifters: Hydraulic. Number of main bearings-5. Fuel Induction: Two barrel carburetor. Compression Ratio: 8.4:1. Displacement: 304 cu. in. (4.98 liters). Horsepower: Net 150 @ 4200 rpm. Torque: Net 245 lb.-ft. @ 2500 rpm. Oil refill capacity: 5 qt. Fuel Requirements: Regular, low-lead or no-lead.

CHASSIS FEATURES: Separate body and chassis. Heavy-channeled and boxed side rails with five cross members. Overall length: 164.88 in. Overall width: 29.25 in. Section modulus: 1.493. Yield strength: 35,000 p.s.i.

SUSPENSION AND RUNNING GEAR: Front Suspension: 5-leaf longitudinal springs, 46.0 in. x 2.0 in. Spring rate: 158 lb./in. Capacity at ground: 1080 lb. double action, 1.1875 in. diameter telescopic shock absorbers and stabilizer bar. Optional: 6-leaf springs, 46.0 in. x 2.0 in. Spring rate: 205 lb./in. Capacity at ground: 1120 lb. Rear Suspension: Longitudinal, 3-leaf, semi-elliptical springs asymmetrically mounted, 56 in. x 2.50 in. Spring rate: 200 lb./in. Capacity at ground: 1185 lb. Longitudinal, 6-leaf, semi-elliptical springs asymmetrically mounted, 56 in. x 2.50 in. Spring rate: 266 lb. Capacity at ground: 1524 lb. The 4700 lb. GVW Package also includes 16 x 4.5E wheels and 6.00 x 16 tires. Front Axle Type and Capacity: Dana model 30 full-floating. Capacity: 2,300 lb. Axle ratio: 4.27:1. Optional: 3.73:1. Rear Axle Type and Capacity: Dana model 44, semi-floating. Capacity: 3500 lb. Transfer Case: Dana 20. Ratios: 2.03, 1.0:1. Brakes: Type: Hydraulic, front and rear cast iron drums, dual master cylinder, double hydraulic circuit. Dimensions: Front and rear: 10.00 in. x 2.0 in. Total effective lining area: 156 sq. in. Optional: V-8 only: Power brakes. Wheels: 15 x 6K. Optional: 16 x 4.5E. Tires: 7.35 x 15 4-ply. Black sidewall. Optional: Various sizes available. Ratio: 24.01:1. Turns Lock-to-Lock: 4.5. Turning Circle: 37.8 ft. Optional V-8 only. Power steering. Ratio: 17.5:1. Standard Transmission: 6-cyl.: Warner T14A 3-speed manual, all-synchromesh transmission. Transmission ratios: 3.10, 1.612, 1.0:1 Reverse: 3.1:1. V-8: Warner T15A 3-speed manual, all-synchromesh. Transmission ratios: 2.997, 1.832, 1.0:1. Reverse: 2.997:1. Optional: Warner T-18 4-speed manual transmission with synchromesh on top three gears and floor-mounted cane-type shift lever. For 6-cyl. only. Transmission ratios: 4.02, 2.41, 1.41, 1.00:1. Reverse: 4.73:1. Optional: Turbo Hydra-Matic 400 3-speed automatic transmission. For 258 and 304 engines only. Transmission ratios: 2.4815, 1.4815, 1.0:1. Reverse: 2.0769:1. Clutch: 10.5 in. dia. Optional: None.

VEHICLE DIMENSIONS: Wheelbase: 104 in. Overall Length: 174.5 in. Front/Rear Tread: 51.5 in./50.0 in. Overall Height: 62.4 in. (varies according to type of enclosure). Width: 65.2 in. Front/Rear Overhang: 26.1 in./44.4 in. Tailgate: Width and Height: 48.50 in. x 15.75 in. Approach/Departure Degrees: 44/24. Ground Clearance: Front axle: 7.5 in. Rear axle: 7.5 in. Load space: Pickup: 62.3 in. x 59.0 in. x 16.2 in. Maximum capacity (Volume Index): 16.14 cu. ft. Front headroom: Station wagon and pickup: 39.3 in. Front legroom: 45.0 in. Front shoulder room: 51.1 in. Front hip room: 51.9 in.

CAPACITIES: Fuel Tank: 16.5 gallon capacity. Optional: None. Coolant system: 6-cyl.: 9.5 qt. V-8: 15 qt.

ACCOMMODATIONS: Seating Capacity: Two. Station wagon: Four with rear seat.

INSTRUMENTATION: 0-110 mph speedometer, odometer, gauges for fuel and engine coolant temperature, warning lights for oil pressure and alternator.

OPTIONS AND PRICES: 258 engine: $56. 304 cu. in. V-8: $130. Turbo Hydra-Matic: $262. Air conditioning: $411. Power steering: $148. Power brakes: $46. Free running front hubs: $98. Rear Trac-Loc limited slip rear differential: $61. Decor Group: $121. Custom Decor Group: $225. Rear seat with seat belts and flat floor-mounted spare tire (Station Wagon and roadster models): $92. Front full-foam 2/3-1/3 split front bench seat: $89. AM radio: $74. Heavy-duty springs and shock absorbers: $39. Heavy-duty 4-speed manual trans.: $175. Heavy-duty cooling system: $24. 55 amp alternator: $25. 70 amp battery: $12. Cigarette lighter: $7. Luggage rack (station wagon only): $72. Heavy-duty cooling system. 15 in. wheelcovers. Cigarette lighter. Tinted glass. Courtesy lights. 4700 lb. GVW Package. Includes heavy-duty front and rear springs and shock absorbers, 6.00 x 16C X-Grip tires and 16 x 4.5 in. E rims. Drawbar. Four-speed manual trans. Decor Group. Includes cigarette lighter, 15 in. wheelcovers, front door armrests, chrome front and rear bumpers and black vinyl floor mats. Custom Decor Group (station wagon only). Includes cigarette lighter, 15 in. custom wheel covers, chrome front and rear bumpers, color-keyed custom interior, full vinyl floor mats, custom seat trim, door trim panels, front door armrests, rear quarter soft trim (rear seat models only), B-pillar hardboard cover and vinyl spare tire cover, custom exterior bright moldings for side windows and vent frames, mylar moldings for windshield, quarter windows and tailgate window.

HISTORICAL FOOTNOTES: The new Commando Jeeps were indicative of American Motors' commitment to Jeep product development.

1973 JEEPSTER/ COMMANDO

Three models of the Commando were again offered for 1973. New simplified model numbers were used. The engine/transmission combinations were the same as 1972. New induction-hardening of exhaust valves seats was credited with improving the service life of the 6-cylinder engines. Or 1973 the 6-cylinder engines could operate with any type of normal fuel — regular grade, low-lead or no-lead fuels (at least 0.5 grams lead per gallon) of 91 Research Octane or higher. A new mechanical clutch linkage replaced the previously used cables for easier operation, less maintenance and longer life. The standard and optional 15 inch tires were upgraded. A new green seat trim replaced blue for the station wagon with the optional Decor Group which was also available in black or buff. New lettering was used for the heater control panel for improved identification.

The color selection for 1973 consisted of nine colors, five of which were new: Champagne white, fawn blue, jetset blue metallic, fairway green metallic, avocado mist metallic, copper tan metallic, butterscotch gold, daisy yellow and Trans-Am red. If three or more vehicles were ordered, the following fleet colors were available: Raven black, Omaha orange, transport yellow, marlin blue metallic, federal gray and forest green.

1973 Jeep Commando station wagon

I.D. DATA: The V.I.N. contained 13 symbols. The first entry, a letter, designated the manufacturer (Jeep Corporation). The next unit was a number indicating the model year. Then followed a letter identifying the transmission, drivetrain and plant. Next were two numbers identifying the vehicle line or model. Then came either a number or letter representing the body style. Next came the seventh unit, a letter indicating the model type and GVW. The eighth character, a letter, identified the engine. The final five numbers were the sequential production numbers. For all series the production sequence was: J3( )model( )( )00001 and up

Model Number	Body Type	Factory Price	GVW	Shipping Weight	Prod. Total
89	St. Wagon	$3506	3900*	3010	—
87	Roadster	$3355	3900	2800	—
88	Pickup	$3382	3900	2650	—

* 4700 lb. GVW Package optional.

STANDARD ENGINE: Engine Type: 6-cyl., OHV, cast iron block and cylinder head. Bore x Stroke: 3.75 in. x 3.50 in. Lifters: Hydraulic. Number of main bearings-7. Fuel Induction: Single barrel carburetor. Compression Ratio: 8.0:1. Displacement: 232 cu. in. (3.8 liters). Horsepower: Net 100 @ 3600 rpm. Torque: Net 185 lb.-ft. @ 1800 rpm. Tach redline: NA. Oil refill capacity: 5 qt. Fuel Requirements: Regular, low-lead or no-lead.

OPTIONAL ENGINE: Engine Type: 6-cyl., OHV, iron alloy block and cylinder head. Bore x Stroke: 3.75 in. x 3.90 in. Lifters: Hydraulic. Number of main bearings-7. Fuel Induction: Single barrel carburetor. Compression Ratio: 8.0:1. Displacement: 258 cu. in. (4.2 liters). Horsepower: Net 110 @ 3500 rpm. Torque: Net 195 lb.-ft. @ 2000 rpm. Oil refill capacity: 5qt. Fuel Requirements: Regular, low-lead or no-lead.

OPTIONAL ENGINE: Engine Type: V-8, OHV, iron alloy block and cylinder head. Bore x Stroke: 3.75 in. x 3.44 in. Lifters: Hydraulic. Number of main bearings-5. Fuel Induction: Two barrel carburetor. Compression Ratio: 8.4:1. Displacement: 304 cu. in. (4.98 liters). Horsepower: Net 150 @ 4200 rpm. Torque: Net 245 lb.-ft. @ 2500 rpm. Oil refill capacity: 5 qt. Fuel Requirements: Regular, low-lead or no-lead.

CHASSIS FEATURES: Separate body and chassis. Heavy-channeled and boxed side rails with five cross members. Overall length: 164.88 in. Overall width: 29.25 in. Section modulus: 1.493. Yield strength: 35,000 p.s.i.

SUSPENSION AND RUNNING GEAR: Front Suspension: 5-leaf longitudinal springs, 46.0 in. x 2.0 in. Spring rate: 158 lb./in. Capacity at ground: 1080 lb. double action, 1.1875 in. diameter telescopic shock absorbers and stabilizer bar. Optional: 6-leaf springs, 46.0 in. x 2.0 in. Spring rate: 205 lb./in. Capacity at ground: 1120 lb. Rear Suspension: Longitudinal, 3-leaf, semi-elliptical springs asymmetrically mounted, 56 in. x 2.50 in. Spring rate: 200 lb./in. Capacity at ground: 1185 lb. Longitudinal, 6-leaf, semi-elliptical springs asymmetrically mounted, 56 in. x 2.50 in. Spring rate: 266 lb. Capacity at ground: 1524 lb. The 4700 lb. GVW Package also includes 16 x 4.5E wheels and 6.00 x 16 tires. Front Axle Type and Capacity: Dana model 30 full-floating. Capacity: 2,300 lb. Axle ratio: 4.27:1. Optional: 3.73:1. Rear Axle Type and Capacity: Dana model 44, semi-floating. Capacity: 3500 lb. Transfer Case: Dana 20. Ratios: 2.03, 1.0:1. Brakes: Type: Hydraulic, front and rear cast iron drums, dual master cylinder, double hydraulic circuit. Dimensions: Front and rear: 10.00 in. x 2.0 in. Total effective lining area: 156 sq. in. Optional: V-8 only: Power brakes. Wheels: 15 x 6K. Optional: 16 x 4.5E. Tires: F78 x 15B Power Cushion black sidewall. Optional: H78 x 15 Power Cushion black or white sidewall, 7.35 x 15B Suburbanite XG black or white sidewall, 6.00 x 16-C All-Service black sidewall, 6.00 x 16C Custom X-Grip black sidewall, H78 x 15 Power Cushion Polyglas white sidewall, H78 x 15-B Suburbanite Polyglas black sidewall, H78 x 15D Suburbanite black sidewall. Ratio: 24.01:1. Turns Lock-to-Lock: 4.5. Turning Circle: 37.8 ft. Optional V-8 only. Power steering. Ratio: 17.5:1. Standard Transmission: 6-cyl.: Warner T14A 3-speed manual, all-synchromesh transmission. Transmission ratios: 3.10, 1.612, 1.0:1 Reverse: 3.1:1. V-8: Warner T15A 3-speed manual, all-synchromesh. Transmission ratios: 2.997, 1.832, 1.0:1. Reverse: 2.997:1. Optional: Warner T-18 4-speed manual transmission with synchromesh on top three gears and floor-mounted cane-type shift lever. For 6-cyl. only. Transmission ratios: 4.02, 2.41, 1.41, 1.00:1. Reverse: 4.73:1. Optional: Turbo Hydra-Matic 400 3-speed automatic transmission. For 258 and 304 engines only. Transmission ratios: 2.4815, 1.4815, 1.0:1. Reverse: 2.0769:1. Clutch: 10.5 in. dia. Optional: None.

VEHICLE DIMENSIONS: Wheelbase: 104 in. Overall Length: 174.5 in. Front/Rear Tread: 51.5 in./50.0 in. Overall Height: 62.4 in. (varies according to type of enclosure). Width: 65.2 in. Front/Rear Overhang: 26.1 in./44.4 in. Tailgate: Width and Height: 48.50 in. x 15.75 in. Approach/Departure Degrees: 44/24. Ground Clearance: Front axle: 7.5 in. Rear axle: 7.5 in. Load space: Pickup: 62.3 in. x 59.0 in. x 16.2 in. Maximum capacity (Volume Index): 16.14 cu. ft. Front headroom: Station wagon and pickup: 39.3 in. Front legroom: 45.0 in. Front shoulder room:-51.1 in. Front hip room: 51.9 in.

CAPACITIES: Fuel Tank: 16.5 gallon capacity. Optional: None. Coolant system: 6-cyl.: 9.5 qt. V-8: 15 qt.

ACCOMMODATIONS: Seating Capacity: Two. Station wagon: Four with rear seat.

INSTRUMENTATION: 0-110 mph Speedometer, odometer, gauges for fuel and engine coolant temperature, warning lights for oil pressure and alternator.

OPTIONS: 258 engine. 304 cu. in. V-8. Turbo Hydra-Matic. Air conditioning. Power steering. Power brakes. Free running front hubs. Rear Trac-Loc limited slip rear differential. Decor Group. Custom Decor Group. Rear seat with seat belts and flat floor-mounted spare tire (station wagon and roadster models). Front full-foam 2/3-1/3 split front bench seat. AM radio. Heavy-duty springs and shock absorbers. Heavy-duty 4-speed manual trans. Heavy-duty cooling system. 55 amp alternator. 70 amp battery. Cigarette lighter. Luggage rack (station wagon only). Heavy-duty cooling system. 15 in. wheelcovers. Cigarette lighter. Tinted glass. Courtesy lights. 4700 lb. GVW Package. Includes heavy-duty front and rear springs and shock absorbers, 6.00 x 16C X-Grip tires and 16 x 4.5 in. E rims. Drawbar. Four speed manual trans. Decor Group. Includes cigarette lighter, 15 in. wheelcovers, front door armrests, chrome front and rear bumpers and black vinyl floor mats. Custom Decor Group (station wagon only). Includes cigarette lighter, 15 in. custom wheelcovers, chrome front and rear bumpers, color-keyed custom interior, full vinyl floor mats, custom seat trim, door trim panels, front door armrests, rear quarter soft trim (rear seat models only), B-pillar hardboard cover and vinyl spare tire cover, custom exterior bright moldings for side windows and vent frames, mylar moldings for windshield, quarter windows and tailgate window.

HISTORICAL FOOTNOTES: This was the final year the Commando was offered.

JEEP SCRAMBLER

1981-1985

1981 SCRAMBLER

The Jeep Scrambler pickup program was approved by management in September, 1979. The first Jeep Scrambler model came off the assembly line in January, 1981 and, on March 25, 1981 sales began. The Scrambler was fitted with a five-foot pickup box. The spare tire mount was attached to the tailgate which, when lowered, was supported by plastic covered cables. As an option, a swing-away spare tire mount was available allowing the tailgate to form a flat surface with the box bed.

From the windshield forward the Scrambler was all Jeep in appearance. In soft top form it was America's only roadster pickup. In most of its essential mechanical components, the Scrambler was a twin to both the CJ-5 and CJ-7. The Scrambler's standard engine was the Pontiac-built 82 horsepower 4-cylinder 151 cubic inch engine. In soft top form it was America's only roadster pickup. Both a soft half top/steel door model and a version with a removable hardtop with metal doors were offered.

Standard features of the base Scrambler model included 2-speed windshield wipers and washers, heater-defroster, painted front bumper, dual exterior mirrors and a folding windshield. Front bucket seats were finished in linen grain black or beige vinyl. Two appearance options were offered. the SR and SL Sport Packages. The SR Sport Package included high-back bucket seats trimmed in blue, black or nutmeg denim-look vinyl (which was also available as a separate option), the Convenience Group (consisting of 8-inch day/night mirror, underhood light, courtesy light and spare tire lock) and the Decor Group (rocker panel molding, Sport steering wheel, front frame cover and instrument panel overlay), L78 x 15 Goodyear Tracker P/G OWL tires, white styled steel wheels, wheel-lip extensions and special Scrambler hood lettering. The SR exterior graphics consisted of hood and body striping in gradations of yellow, blue or red, depending on the exterior color.

The SL Sport Package included bucket seats finished in either black cara with light gray accents or nutmeg vinyl with honey accents, black leather-wrapped steering wheel and passenger assist bar, console, clock and tachometer. The pin-striped instrument panel, along with the indoor/outdoor carpeting was available in either black or nutmeg. The front grille panel, wheels, front and rear bumpers and mirror heads and arms were chrome trimmed. Goodyear P235/75R15 Wrangler radial tires were installed as were wheel-lip extensions. Exterior SL graphics in combinations of either silver and gray or nutmeg and bronze included double pinstriping for the beltline, fenders and hood. The SL option also included Convenience Group, heavy-duty shocks, hood insulation and black rocker molding.

1981 Jeep Scrambler

I.D. DATA: The V.I.N. contained 17 symbols. The first three characters identified the manufacturer, make and type of vehicle. The next entry, a letter, designated the engine. The fifth unit, another letter, identified the transmission. The sixth and seventh characters identified the series and body style. The GVW rating was identified by the eighth character. The ninth character was the check digit. The tenth character, a letter, represented the model year. The eleventh character identified the assembly plant. The last six digits were the sequential production number.

Model Number	Body Type	Factory Price	GVW	Shipping Weight	Prod. Total
88	Soft Top Pickup	$7288	4150	2650	7840*
88	Steel Dr. Pickup	$7588	4150	N.A.	—
88	Hardtop Pickup	$7922	4150	N.A.	—

* All variations

STANDARD ENGINE: Engine Type: 4-cyl., In-line, OHV, cast iron block and cylinder head. Bore x Stroke: 4.00 in. x 3.00 in. Lifters: Hydraulic. Number of main bearings-5. Fuel Induction: Rochester staged 2-bbl. carburetor. Compression Ratio: 8.2:1. Displacement: 151 cu. in. (2.45 liters). Horsepower: Net 82 @ 4000 rpm. Torque: Net 125 lb.-ft. @ 2600 rpm. Oil refill capacity: 4 qt. Fuel Requirements: Regular.

OPTIONAL ENGINE: Engine Type: 6-cyl., OHV, iron alloy block and cylinder head. Bore x Stroke: 3.75 in. x 3.90 in. Lifters: Hydraulic. Number of main bearings-7. Fuel Induction: Two barrel carburetor. Compression Ratio: 8.3:1. Displacement: 258 cu. in. (4.2 liters). Horsepower: Net 110 @ 3500 rpm. Torque: Net 205 lb.-ft. @ 1800 rpm. Oil refill capacity: 5 qt. with filter change. Fuel Requirements: Regular, low-lead or no-lead.

CHASSIS FEATURES: Body on frame construction. Fully boxed, reinforced frame.

SUSPENSION AND RUNNING GEAR: Front Suspension: Four-leaf semi-elliptic springs. Spring rate: 170 lb./in. Tubular shock absorbers, free-running hubs and anti-roll bar. Optional: Extra-duty suspension option with heavy-duty springs and shock absorbers. Rear Suspension: Four-leaf semi-elliptic springs. Spring rate: 185 lb./in. Scramblers ordered with the fiberglass hardtop were fitted with 5-leaf springs. Optional: See above. Front Axle Type and Capacity: Dana Model 30 full-floating 2200 pound capacity. Rear Axle Type and Capacity: AMC/Jeep semi- floating. Capacity: 2700 lb. Transfer Case: Dana 300, 2-speed transfer case, 2.62:1, 1.00:1. Brakes: Type: Front disc brakes, Rear drum brakes. Dimensions: Front: 10.4 in. dia. disc. Rear: 10.00 in. x 1.75 in. Optional: Power brakes. Wheels: 15 x 5.5 in. Optional: 15 x 7 in. Tires: H78 x 15B black sidewall. Optional: 9.00 x 15, P235/75R x 15 tires. Steering: Manual reciprocating ball. Ratio: 24.0:1. Turns Lock-to-Lock: 4.5. Turning Circle: 37.6-ft. Optional Power steering. Ratio: 17.6:1. Standard Transmission: Warner SR4, all-synchromesh 4-speed manual transmission. Transmission ratios: 4.07, 2.39, 1.49 and 1.1:1. Optional: Tremac T-176 all-synchromesh 4-speed manual transmission. For 6-cyl. only. Transmission ratios: 3.52, 2.27, 1.46, 1.0:1. Optional: 4-cyl.: Chrysler Model 904 6-cyl.: Chrysler Model 999. Transmission ratios: Model 904: 2.74, 1.55, 1.0:1. Model 999: 2.45, 1.45, 1.0:1. Clutch: 4-cyl.: 9.125 in. dia. (71.78 sq. in.). 6-cyl.: 10.5 in. dia. (106.75 sq. in.). Optional: None.

VEHICLE DIMENSIONS: Wheelbase: 103.5 in. Overall Length: 177.3 in. Front/Rear Tread: 51.5 in./50.0 in. Overall Height: 67.6 in. (Hardtop: 70.5 in.). Width: 68.6 in. Front/Rear Overhang: 23.5 in./50.3 in. Tailgate: Width and Height: 34.5 in. x 16.4 in. Ground Clearance: 6.9 in. Load space: Pickup: 61.5 in. x 55.8 in. x 16.4 in. Maximum capacity (Volume Index): 30.4 cu. ft. Front headroom: Hardtop: 39.9 in. Soft top: 40.9 in. Front legroom: 39.1 in. Front shoulder room: Hardtop: 53.8 in. Front hip room: 53.8 in.

CAPACITIES: Fuel Tank: 15.0 gallon capacity. Optional: None.

ACCOMMODATIONS: Seating Capacity: Two.

INSTRUMENTATION: Speedometer calibrated in mph and km/h. fuel level, voltmeter, oil pressure and engine coolant temperature gauges, and indicator light for partial brake failure.

OPTIONS AND PRICES: Swing-away spare tire mount. Lockable metal doors: $190. Extra-duty suspension: $98 (for base model). Limited slip rear differential: $179. Heavy-duty shock absorbers: $30. 258 cu. in. 6-cylinder engine: $136. Power steering: $206. Tonneau cover. Wood side rails. Halogen fog lamps. Tilt wheel. Door steps. AM radio. AM/FM radio. Lockable metal doors: $190. SR Sport Package: $775. SL Sport Package: $1975.

HISTORICAL FOOTNOTES: The Scrambler reached its all-time best sales volume in 1981.

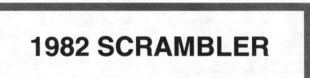

1982 SCRAMBLER

Both a 20 gallon fuel tank and a 5-speed, overdrive transmission were offered as options for the 1982. Scrambler. No other changes took place. The SR Package price was increased to $799 with the SL moving up to $1999. The 1982 exterior color consisted of olympic white, mist silver metallic, classic black, Sherwood green metallic, Jamaica beige, copper brown metallic, slate blue metallic, deep night blue, oriental red, sun yellow, vintage red metallic and chestnut brown metallic.

1982 Jeep Scrambler SR Sport

I.D. DATA: The V.I.N. contained 17 symbols. The first three characters identified the manufacturer, make and type of vehicle. The next entry, a letter, designated the engine. The fifth unit, another letter, identified the transmission. The sixth and seventh characters identified the series and body style. The GVW rating was identified by the eighth character. The ninth character was the check digit. The tenth character, a letter, represented the model year. The eleventh character identified the assembly plant. The last six digits were the sequential production number.

Model Number	Body Type	Factory Price	GVW	Shipping Weight	Prod. Total
88	Soft Top Pickup	$7588	4150	2650	7138*
88	Steel Dr. Pickup	$7888	4150	N.A.	—
88	Hardtop Pickup	$8222	4150	N.A.	—

* All variations.

STANDARD ENGINE: Engine Type: 4-cyl., In-line, OHV, cast iron block and cylinder head. Bore x Stroke: 4.00 in. x 3.00 in. Lifters: Hydraulic. Number of main bearings-5. Fuel Induction: Rochester staged 2-bbl. carburetor. Compression Ratio: 8.2:1. Displacement: 151 cu. in. (2.45 liters). Horsepower: Net 82 @ 4000 rpm. Torque: Net 125 lb.-ft. @ 2600 rpm. Oil refill capacity: 4 qt. Fuel Requirements: Regular.

OPTIONAL ENGINE: Engine Type: 6-cyl., OHV, iron alloy block and cylinder head. Bore x Stroke: 3.75 in. x 3.90 in. Lifters: Hydraulic. Number of main bearings-7. Fuel Induction: Two barrel carburetor. Compression Ratio: 8.3:1. Displacement: 258 cu. in. (4.2 liters). Horsepower: Net 110 @ 3500 rpm. Torque: Net 205 lb.-ft. @ 1800 rpm. Oil refill capacity: 5 qt. with filter change. Fuel Requirements: Regular, low-lead or no-lead.

CHASSIS FEATURES: Body on frame construction. Fully boxed, reinforced frame.

SUSPENSION AND RUNNING GEAR: Front Suspension: 4-leaf semi-elliptical springs. Spring rate: 170 lb./in. Tubular shock absorbers, free-running hubs and anti-roll bar. Optional: Extra-duty suspension option with heavy-duty springs and shock absorbers. Rear Suspension: 4-leaf semi-elliptical springs. Spring rate: 185 lb./in. Scramblers ordered with the fiberglass hardtop were fitted with 5-leaf springs. Optional: See above. Front Axle Type and Capacity: Dana model 30 full-floating 2200 pound capacity. Rear Axle Type and Capacity: AMC/Jeep semi-floating. Capacity: 2700 lb. Transfer Case: Dana 300, 2-speed transfer case, 2.62:1, 1.00:1. Brakes: Type: Front: Disc brakes. Rear: Drum brakes. Dimensions: Front: 10.4 in. dia. disc. Rear: 10.00 in. x 1.75 in. Optional: Power brakes. Wheels: 15 x 5.5 in. Optional: 15 x 7 in. Tires: H78 x 15B black sidewall. Optional: 9.00 x 15, P235/75R x 15 tires. Steering: Manual reciprocating ball. Ratio: 24.0:1. Turns Lock-to-Lock: 4.5. Turning Circle: 37.6 ft. Optional power steering. Ratio: 17.6:1. Standard Transmission: Warner SR4, all-synchromesh 4-speed manual transmission. Transmission ratios: 4.07, 2.39, 1.49 and 1.1:1. Optional: Tremac T-176 all-synchromesh 4-speed manual transmission. For 6-cyl. only. Transmission ratios: 3.52, 2.27, 1.46, 1.0:1. Optional: 4-cyl.: Chrysler model 904 6-cyl.: Chrysler model 999. Transmission ratios: Model 904: 2.74, 1.55, 1.0:1. Model 999: 2.45, 1.45, 1.0:1. Clutch: 4-cyl.: 9.125 in. dia. (71.78 sq. in.). 6-cyl.: 10.5 in. dia. (106.75 sq. in.). Optional: None.

VEHICLE DIMENSIONS: Wheelbase: 103.5 in. Overall Length: 177.3 in. Front/Rear Tread: 51.5 in./50.0 in. Overall Height: 67.6 in. (Hardtop: 70.5 in.). Width: 68.6 in. Front/Rear Overhang: 23.5 in./50.3 in. Tailgate: Width and Height: 34.5 in. x 16.4 in. Ground Clearance: 6.9 in. Load space: Pickup: 61.5 in. x 55.8 in. x 16.4 in. Maximum capacity (Volume Index): 30.4 cu. ft. Front headroom: Hardtop: 39.9 in. Soft top: 40.9 in. Front legroom: 39.1 in. Front shoulder room: Hardtop: 53.8 in. Front hip room: 53.8 in.

CAPACITIES: Fuel Tank: 15.0 gallon capacity. Optional: 20 gal.

ACCOMMODATIONS: Seating Capacity: Two.

INSTRUMENTATION: Speedometer calibrated in mph and km/h. fuel level, voltmeter, oil pressure and engine coolant temperature gauges, and indicator light for partial brake failure.

OPTIONS AND PRICES: Swing-away spare tire mount. Lockable metal doors. Extra-duty suspension. Limited slip rear differential. Heavy-duty shock absorbers. 258 cu. in. 6-cylinder engine. Power steering. Tonneau cover. Wood side rails. Halogen fog lamps. Tilt wheel. Door steps. AM radio. AM/FM radio. Lockable metal doors. SR Sport Package: $799. SL Sport Package: $1999.

HISTORICAL FOOTNOTES: The 1982 Scrambler was introduced in the fall of 1981.

1983 SCRAMBLER

For 1983 the standard mounting for the Scrambler's spare tire was relocated to the roll bar. The side graphics of the SR Package were revised to resemble the form of an over-sized hockey stick. The SR Package listed for $825 with the SL priced at $2065. Content of the SR Sport Package consisted of high-back denim vinyl bucket seats (available in blue, black or nutmeg), Sof-Feel 3-spoke steering wheel, 8.0. in. day/night mirror, courtesy lights, instrument panel overlay, rocker panel protection overlay, front frame cover, Scrambler hood decal and lower side stripes in yellow, blue or red, L78 x 15 Tracker P/G fiberglass white letter tires, 15 x 7 in. white styled steel wheels, underhood light, spare tire lock, polyspare tire with vinyl cover.

The SL Sport Package contained these items: Cara grain vinyl high-back bucket seats, leather-wrapped black 3-spoke steering wheel, leather-wrapped passenger assist bar in either black or nutmeg, pin-striped instrument panel with black or nutmeg instrument panel pad and Laredo nameplate, console, indoor/outdoor carpeting in black or nutmeg, courtesy lights, 8 in. day/night mirror, Scrambler hood decal, special striping in silver and gray or nutmeg and bronze on hood, rocker panels, all wheel openings and around rear corners, half cab soft top in black or nutmeg (includes textured overlay in door inset and door trim panels with garnish pads), chrome front bumper, chrome grille overlay, chrome mirror heads and arms, front frame cover, black rocker moldings, chrome footman loops, P235/75R15 OWL Wrangler outline white tires, 15 x 7 in. styled chrome plated wheels, tachometer and clock, hood insulation, underhood light, die cast chrome plated hub cover, and polyspare tire with vinyl cover.

1983 Jeep Scrambler SL Sport

I.D. DATA: The V.I.N. contained 17 symbols. The first three characters identified the manufacturer, make and type of vehicle. The next entry, a letter, designated the engine. The fifth unit, another letter, identified the transmission. The sixth and seventh characters identified the series and body style. The GVW rating was identified by the eighth character. The ninth

character was the check digit. The tenth character, a letter, represented the model year. The eleventh character identified the assembly plant. The last six digits were the sequential production number.

Model Number	Body Type	Factory Price	GVW	Shipping Weight	Prod. Total
88	Soft Top Pickup	$7563[1]	4150	2650	4678[2]
88	Steel Dr. Pickup	$7888	4150	N.A.	—
88	Hardtop Pickup	$8392	4150	N.A.	—

NOTE 1: During the 1983 model year the Scrambler's base price was reduced to $6765.
NOTE 2: All variations.

STANDARD ENGINE: Engine Type: 4-cyl., In-line, OHV, cast iron block and cylinder head. Bore x Stroke: 4.00 in. x 3.00 in. Lifters: Hydraulic. Number of main bearings-5. Fuel Induction: Rochester staged 2-bbl. carburetor. Compression Ratio: 8.2:1. Displacement: 151 cu. in. (2.45 liters). Horsepower: Net 82 @ 4000 rpm. Torque: Net 125 lb.-ft. @ 2600 rpm. Oil refill capacity: 4 qt. Fuel Requirements: Regular.

OPTIONAL ENGINE: Engine Type: 6-cyl., OHV, iron alloy block and cylinder head. Bore x Stroke: 3.75 in. x 3.90 in. Lifters: Hydraulic. Number of main bearings-7. Fuel Induction: Two barrel carburetor. Compression Ratio: 8.3:1. Displacement: 258 cu. in. (4.2 liters). Horsepower: Net 110 @ 3500 rpm. Torque: Net 205 lb.-ft. @ 1800 rpm. Oil refill capacity: 5 qt. with filter change. Fuel Requirements: Regular, low-lead or no-lead.

CHASSIS FEATURES: Body on frame construction. Fully boxed, reinforced frame.

SUSPENSION AND RUNNING GEAR: Front Suspension: 4-leaf semi-elliptical springs. Spring rate: 170 lb./in. Tubular shock absorbers, free-running hubs and anti-roll bar. Optional: Extra-duty suspension option with heavy-duty springs and shock absorbers. Rear Suspension: 4-leaf semi-elliptical springs. Spring rate: 185 lb./in. Scramblers ordered with the fiberglass hardtop were fitted with 5-leaf springs. Optional: See above. Front Axle Type and Capacity: Dana model 30 full-floating 2200 pound capacity. Rear Axle Type and Capacity: AMC/Jeep semi- floating. Capacity: 2700 lb. Transfer Case: Dana 300, 2-speed transfer case, 2.62:1, 1.00:1. Brakes: Type: Front: Disc brakes. Rear: Drum brakes. Dimensions: Front: 10.4 in. dia. disc. Rear: 10.00 in. x 1.75 in. Optional: Power brakes. Wheels: 15 x 5.5 in. Optional: 15 x 7 in. Tires: H78 x 15B black sidewall. Optional: 9.00 x 15, P235/75R x 15 tires. Steering: Manual reciprocating ball. Ratio: 24.0:1. Turns Lock-to-Lock: 4.5. Turning Circle: 37.6 ft. Optional power steering. Ratio: 17.6:1. Standard Transmission: Warner SR4, all-synchromesh 4-speed manual transmission. Transmission ratios: 4.07, 2.39, 1.49 and 1.1:1. Optional: Tremac T-176 all-synchromesh 4-speed manual transmission. For 6-cyl. only. Transmission ratios: 3.52, 2.27, 1.46, 1.0:1. Optional: 4-cyl.: Chrysler model 904 6-cyl.: Chrysler model 999. Transmission ratios: Model 904: 2.74, 1.55, 1.0:1. Model 999: 2.45, 1.45, 1.0:1. Clutch: 4-cyl.: 9.125 in. dia. (71.78 sq. in.). 6-cyl.: 10.5 in. dia. (106.75 sq. in.). Optional: None.

VEHICLE DIMENSIONS: Wheelbase: 103.5 in. Overall Length: 177.3 in. Front/Rear Tread: 51.5 in./50.0 in. Overall Height: 67.6 in. (Hardtop: 70.5 in.). Width: 68.6 in. Front/Rear Overhang: 23.5 in./50.3 in. Tailgate: Width and Height: 34.5 in. x 16.4 in. Ground Clearance: 6.9 in. Load space: Pickup: 61.5 in. x 55.8 in. x 16.4 in. Maximum capacity (Volume Index): 30.4 cu. ft. Front headroom: Hardtop: 39.9 in. Soft top: 40.9 in. Front legroom: 39.1 in. Front shoulder room: Hardtop: 53.8 in. Front hip room: 53.8 in.

CAPACITIES: Fuel Tank: 15.0 gallon capacity. Optional: None.

ACCOMMODATIONS: Seating Capacity: Two.

INSTRUMENTATION: Speedometer calibrated in mph and km/h. fuel level, voltmeter, oil pressure and engine coolant temperature gauges, and indicator light for partial brake failure.

OPTIONS AND PRICES: Swing-away spare tire mount. Lockable metal doors. Extra-duty suspension. Limited-slip rear differential. Heavy-duty shock absorbers. 258 cu. in. 6-cylinder engine. Power steering. Tonneau cover. Wood side rails. Halogen fog lamps. Tilt wheel. Door steps. AM radio. AM/FM radio. Lockable metal doors. SR Sport Package: $825. SL Sport Package: $2065.

HISTORICAL FOOTNOTES: The 1983 Scrambler was introduced in the fall of 1982.

1984 SCRAMBLER

The Scrambler's standard engine for 1984 was AMC's 2.5 liter 4-cylinder. No other changes took place in its design.

1984 Jeep Scrambler

I.D. DATA: The V.I.N. contained 17 symbols. The first three characters identified the manufacturer, make and type of vehicle. The next entry, a letter, designated the engine. The fifth unit, an other letter, identified the transmission. The sixth and seventh characters identified the series and body style. The GVW rating was identified by the eighth character. The ninth character was the check digit. The tenth character, a letter, represented the model year. The eleventh character identified the assembly plant. The last six digits were the sequential production number.

Model Number	Body Type	Factory Price	GVW	Shipping Weight	Prod. Total
88	Soft Top Pickup	$7282	4150	2701	2826*
88	Steel Dr. Pickup	$N.A.	4150	N.A.	—
88	Hardtop Pickup	$N.A.	4150	N.A.	—

* 1984 model year sales of all versions.

STANDARD ENGINE: Engine Type: 4-cyl., In-line, OHV, cast iron block and cylinder head. Bore x Stroke: 3.88 in. x 3.19 in. Lifters: Hydraulic. Number of main bearings-5. Fuel Induction: 1-bbl. carburetor. Compression Ratio: 8.2:1. Displacement: 150.4 cu. in. (2.5 liters). Horsepower: Net 86 @ 3650 rpm. Torque: Net 132 lb.-ft. @ 3200 rpm. Oil refill capacity: 4 qt. Fuel Requirements: Regular.

OPTIONAL ENGINE: Engine Type: 6-cyl., OHV, iron alloy block and cylinder head. Bore x Stroke: 3.75 in. x 3.90 in. Lifters: Hydraulic. Number of main bearings-7. Fuel Induction: Two barrel carburetor. Compression Ratio: 8.3:1. Displacement: 258 cu. in. (4.2 liters). Horsepower: Net 110 @ 3500 rpm. Torque: Net 205 lb.-ft. @ 1800 rpm. Oil refill capacity: 5 qt. with filter change. Fuel Requirements: Regular.

CHASSIS FEATURES: Body on frame construction. Fully boxed, reinforced frame.

SUSPENSION AND RUNNING GEAR: Front Suspension: 4-leaf semi-elliptical springs. Spring rate: 170 lb./in. Tubular shock absorbers, free-running hubs and anti-roll bar. Optional: Extra-duty suspension option with heavy-duty springs and shock absorbers. Rear Suspension: 4-leaf semi-elliptical springs. Spring rate: 185 lb./in. Scramblers ordered with the fiberglass hardtop were fitted with 5-leaf springs. Optional: See above. Front Axle Type and Capacity: Dana model 30 full-floating 2200 pound capacity. Rear Axle Type and Capacity: AMC/Jeep semi-floating. Capacity: 2700 lb. Transfer Case: Dana 300, 2-speed transfer case, 2.62:1, 1.00:1. Brakes: Type: Front: Disc brakes. Rear: Drum brakes. Dimensions: Front: 10.4 in. dia. disc. Rear: 10.00 in. x 1.75 in. Optional: Power brakes. Wheels: 15 x 5.5 in. Optional: 15 x 7 in. Tires: H78 x 15B black sidewall. Optional: 9.00 x 15, P235/75R x 15 tires. Steering: Manual reciprocating ball. Ratio: 24.0:1. Turns Lock-to-Lock: 4.5. Turning Circle: 37.6 ft. Optional power steering. Ratio: 17.6:1. Standard Transmission: Warner SR4, all-synchromesh 4-speed manual transmission. Transmission ratios: 4.07, 2.39, 1.49 and 1.1:1. Optional: Tremac T-176 all-synchromesh 4-speed manual transmission. For 6-cyl. only. Transmission ratios: 3.52, 2.27, 1.46, 1.0:1. Optional: 4-cyl.: Chrysler model 904 6-cyl.: Chrysler model 999. Transmission ratios: Model 904: 2.74, 1.55, 1.0:1. Model 999: 2.45, 1.45, 1.0:1. Clutch: 4-cyl.: 9.125 in. dia. (71.78 sq. in.). 6-cyl.: 10.5 in. dia. (106.75 sq. in.). Optional: None.

VEHICLE DIMENSIONS: Wheelbase: 103.5 in. Overall Length: 177.3 in. Front/Rear Tread: 51.5 in./50.0 in. Overall Height: 67.6 in. (Hardtop: 70.5 in.). Width: 68.6 in. Front/Rear Overhang: 23.5 in./50.3 in. Tailgate: Width and Height: 34.5 in. x 16.4 in. Ground Clearance: 6.9 in. Load space: Pickup: 61.5 in. x 55.8 in. x 16.4 in. Maximum capacity (Volume Index): 30.4 cu. ft. Front headroom: Hardtop: 39.9 in. Soft top: 40.9 in. Front legroom: 39.1 in. Front shoulder room: Hardtop: 53.8 in. Front hip room: 53.8 in.

CAPACITIES: Fuel Tank: 15.0 gallon capacity. Optional: 20 gal.

ACCOMMODATIONS: Seating Capacity: Two.

INSTRUMENTATION: Speedometer calibrated in mph and km/h. fuel level, voltmeter, oil pressure and engine coolant temperature gauges, and indicator light for partial brake failure.

OPTIONS: Front floor carpet. Center console. Convenience Group. AM radio. AM/FM stereo radio with two speakers. AM/FM stereo radio with cassette tape player and two speakers (requires factory hard or soft top). Roll Bar Accessory Package. Includes padded roll bar and roll bar saddle bags. High-back bucket seats in denim vinyl. Sof-Feel Sport steering wheel. Leather-wrapped Sport steering wheel. Rear lockable storage box. Tachometer and rallye clock. Tilt steering wheel. Bright front chrome bumper. Bumper Accessory Package. Includes front tow hooks, bumper extensions, and rear bumperettes. Chrome rear step bumper. Painted rear step bumper. Steel doors with black and honey soft top. Outside passenger mirror. Included with hardtop. Body side step. Vinyl sift top. Hardtop. Air conditioning. Heavy-duty alternator. Heavy-duty battery. Power front disc brakes, Cold Climate Group. Includes heavy-duty battery and alternator, engine block heater. Heavy-duty cooling system. Includes extra capacity radiator, 7 blade fan (6-cyl.), Tempatrol viscous fan drive, fan shroud (6-cyl.) and coolant recovery. Coolant recovery system. Cruise control. Drawbar. Not available with step bumper. 5-speed manual overdrive transmission. Automatic transmission. Rear Trac-Lok differential. California emission system. High altitude emission system. 4.2 liter engine. Fog lights with clear lens. 20 gal. fuel tank. Halogen headlights. Extra quiet insulation (hardtop). Front and rear heavy-duty shock absorbers. Rear swing-away spare tire carrier and tailgate. Spare tire lock. Included with 7 in. wheel. Power steering. Extra-Duty Suspension Package. Includes Heavy-duty front and rear springs and shock absorbers. Soft-Ride suspension. 15 x 7 in. styled steel chrome wheels. 15 x 7 in. steel painted wheels. SR Sport Package. SL Sport Package.

HISTORICAL FOOTNOTES: The latest Jeep Scrambler was introduced in the fall of 1983.

1985 SCRAMBLER

Revisions for 1985, began with chrome Scrambler lettering on the rear fender in place of the old hood identification. Both the SR and SL Packages were dropped. The Base Scrambler seats were covered in either black or almond linen grain vinyl). The SR Sport was replaced by the Renegade. The Laredo replaced the SL Sport.

Interior features of the Renegade Package included black, garnet or honey denim-look vinyl high-back bucket seats courtesy lights, day/night rearview mirror, glove box lock, intermittent wipers and a Sof-Feel Sport steering wheel. Exterior features and identification consisted of P235/75R15 black Wrangler steel radial tires, a "Polyspare" spare tire with cover, rocker panel molding, body graphics with yellow, blue or red striping and 15 x 7 white styled steel wheels with chrome hub covers.

The Scrambler Laredo had Celtic grain vinyl high-back bucket seats in combinations of black and gray or honey and dark honey; a center console, color-keyed interior with removable indoor/outdoor carpeting, courtesy lights day/night mirror, glove box lock, intermittent wipers, leather-wrapped steering wheel and passenger assist bar, pinstriped instrument panel, tachometer and clock. The Laredo's exterior continued to have many features of the old SL including chromed body parts, body and hood graphics in either silver and gray or brown and Gold, and P235/75R15 white letter Wrangler tires on 15 x 7 inch styled wheels. The soft top was available in either black or honey. The hardtop color choices were black, white or honey.

The 1985 Scramblers were available in four standard colors: Olympic white, classic black, almond beige and sebring red. Six extra cost metallic clearcoat paints were offered: Sterling, ice blue, charcoal, dark honey, dark brown and garnet.

Scrambler

1985 Jeep Scrambler

I.D. DATA: The V.I.N. contained 17 symbols. The first three characters identified the manufacturer, make and type of vehicle. The next entry, a letter, designated the engine. The fifth unit, an other letter, identified the transmission. The sixth and seventh characters identified the series and body style. The GVW rating was identified by the eighth character. The ninth character was the check digit. The tenth character, a letter, represented the model year. The eleventh character identified the assembly plant. The last six digits were the sequential production number.

Model Number	Body Type	Factory Price	GVW	Shipping Weight	Prod. Total
88	Soft Top Pickup	$7282	4150	2701	2826*
88	Steel Dr. Pickup	N.A.	4150	N.A.	—
88	Hardtop Pickup	N.A.	4150	N.A.	—

* 1984 model year sales of all versions.

STANDARD ENGINE: Engine Type: 4-cyl., In-line, OHV, cast iron block and cylinder head. Bore x Stroke: 3.88 in. x 3.19 in. Lifters: Hydraulic. Number of main bearings-5. Fuel Induction: 1-bbl. carburetor. Compression Ratio: 8.2:1. Displacement: 150.4 cu. in. (2.5 liters). Horsepower: Net 86 @ 3650 rpm. Torque: Net 132 lb.-ft. @ 3200 rpm. Oil refill capacity: 4 qt. Fuel Requirements: Regular.

OPTIONAL ENGINE: Engine Type: 6-cyl., OHV, iron alloy block and cylinder head. Bore x Stroke: 3.75 in. x 3.90 in. Lifters: Hydraulic. Number of main bearings-7. Fuel Induction: Two barrel carburetor. Compression Ratio: 8.3:1. Displacement: 258 cu. in. (4.2 liters). Horsepower: Net 110 @ 3500 rpm. Torque: Net 205 lb.-ft. @ 1800 rpm. Oil refill capacity: 5 qt. with filter change. Fuel Requirements: Regular.

CHASSIS FEATURES: Body on frame construction. Fully boxed, reinforced frame.

SUSPENSION AND RUNNING GEAR: Front Suspension: 4-leaf semi-elliptical springs. Spring rate: 170 lb./in. Tubular shock absorbers, free-running hubs and anti-roll bar. Optional: Extra-duty suspension option with heavy-duty springs and shock absorbers. Rear Suspension: 4-leaf semi-elliptical springs. Spring rate: 185 lb./in. Scramblers ordered with the fiberglass hardtop were fitted with 5-leaf springs. Optional: See above. Front Axle Type and Capacity: Dana model 30 full-floating 2200 pound capacity. Rear Axle Type and Capacity: AMC/Jeep semi-floating. Capacity: 2700 lb. Transfer Case: Dana 300, 2-speed transfer case, 2.62:1, 1.00:1. Brakes: Type: Front: Disc brakes. Rear: Drum brakes. Dimensions: Front: 10.4 in. dia. disc. Rear: 10.00 in. x 1.75 in. Optional: Power brakes. Wheels: 15 x 5.5 inch. Optional: 15 x 7 in. styled steel chrome and painted. Tires: H78 x 15B black sidewall. Optional: P215/75R15 black sidewall Wrangler radial Mud and Snow. P235/75R15 OWL Wrangler radial Mud and Snow. P235/75R15 RBL Wrangler Mud and Snow. Steering: Manual recirculating ball. Ratio: 24.0:1. Turns Lock-to-Lock: 4.5. Turning Circle: 37.6 ft. Optional Power steering. Ratio: 17.6:1. Standard Transmission: Warner SR4, all-synchromesh 4-speed manual transmission. Transmission ratios: 4.07, 2.39, 1.49 and 1.1:1. Optional: Tremac T-176 all-synchromesh 4-speed manual transmission. For 6-cyl. only. Transmission ratios: 3.52, 2.27, 1.46, 1.0:1. Optional: 5-speed overdrive manual transmission. Ratios: 3.93, 2.33, 1.45, 1.00, 0.85:1. Reverse: 3.76:1. Optional: Automatic trans. 4-cyl.: Chrysler model 904 6-cyl.: Chrysler model 999. Transmission ratios: Model 904: 2.74, 1.55, 1.0:1. Model 999: 2.45, 1.45, 1.0:1. Clutch: 4-cyl.: 9.125 in. dia. (71.78 sq. in.). 6-cyl.: 10.5 in. dia. (106.75 sq. in.).

VEHICLE DIMENSIONS: Wheelbase: 103.5 in. Overall Length: 177.3 in. Front/Rear Tread: 51.5 in./50.0 in. Overall Height: 67.6 in. (Hardtop: 70.5 in.). Width: 68.6 in. Front/Rear Overhang: 23.5 in./50.3 in. Tailgate: Width and Height: 34.5 in. x 16.4 in. Ground Clearance: 6.9 in. Load space: Pickup: 61.5 in. x 55.8 in. x 16.4 in. Maximum capacity (Volume Index): 30.4 cu. ft. Front headroom: Hardtop: 39.9 in. Soft top: 40.9 in. Front legroom: 39.1 in. Front shoulder room: Hardtop: 53.8 in. Front hip room: 53.8 in.

CAPACITIES: Fuel Tank: 15.0 gallon capacity. Optional: 20 gal.

ACCOMMODATIONS: Seating Capacity: Two.

INSTRUMENTATION: Speedometer calibrated in mph and km/h. Fuel level, voltmeter, oil pressure and engine coolant temperature gauges, and indicator light for partial brake failure.

OPTIONS: Front floor carpet. Center console. Convenience Group. AM radio. AM/FM stereo radio with two speakers. AM/FM stereo radio with cassette tape player and two speakers (requires factory hard or soft top). Roll Bar Accessory Package. Includes padded roll bar and roll bar saddle bags. High-back bucket seats in denim vinyl. Sof-Feel Sport steering wheel. Leather-wrapped Sport steering wheel. Rear lockable storage box. Tachometer and rallye clock. Tilt steering wheel. Bright front chrome bumper. Bumper Accessory Package. Includes front tow hooks, bumper extensions, and rear bumperettes. Chrome rear step bumper. Painted rear step bumper. Steel doors with black and honey soft top. Outside passenger mirror. Included with hardtop. Body side step. Vinyl sift top. Hardtop. Air conditioning. Heavy-duty alternator. Heavy-duty battery. Power front disc brakes. Cold Climate Group. Includes heavy-duty battery and alternator, engine block heater. Heavy-duty cooling system. Includes extra capacity radiator, 7 blade fan (6-cyl.), Tempatrol viscous fan drive, fan shroud (6-cyl.) and coolant recovery. Coolant recovery system. Cruise control. Draw bar. Not available with step bumper. 5-speed manual overdrive transmission. Automatic transmission. Rear Trac-Lok differential. California emission system. High altitude emission system. 4.2 liter engine. Fog lights with clear lens. 20 gal. fuel tank. Halogen headlights. Extra quiet insulation (hardtop). Front and rear heavy-duty shock absorbers. Rear swing-away spare tire carrier and tailgate. Spare tire lock. Included with 7 in. wheel. Power steering. Extra-Duty Suspension Package. Includes heavy-duty front and rear springs and shock absorbers. Soft-Ride suspension. 15 x 7 in. Styled steel chrome wheels. 15 x 7 in. steel painted wheels.

HISTORICAL FOOTNOTES: This was the final year of Scrambler production.

JEEP COMANCHE

1986-1992

1986 COMANCHE

The Comanche four-wheel drive compact pickup truck was derived form the Cherokee sport utility vehicle. As such, it reached the market with time-proven features as uniframe body construction and the Quadralink front suspension. The Comanche also featured the longest wheelbase (119.7 in.) of any U.S. or import entry in its field, a 7 ft., 4 in. long pickup box, a payload capacity of up to 2,205 lbs., and a double-walled pickup box. The Comanche also offered buyers a choice of two four-wheel drive systems. the Command-Trac part-time transfer case or the Selec-Trac full-time transfer case. Both had shift-on-the fly capability. Either system was available with three engine selections. The throttle body fuel injected 2.5 liter 4-cyl. was standard. Optional were the 2.8 liter V-6 and the 2.1 liter turbo-charged diesel. Three transmissions were available-a standard 4-speed manual or optional 5-speed manual and 3-speed automatic transmissions.

The Comanche was offered in three trim levels — the base custom, the mid-range X and the high-line XLS. Standard equipment interior content of the custom consisted of these items: Straight armrest, ashtray, cigarette lighter, mini console, B-pillar-mounted dome lights, color-keyed vinyl door panels, black textured vinyl floor covering, glove box light, heater and defroster, molded vinyl covered headliner, lap and shoulder belt restraint system, 9.5 in. day/night rearview mirror, passenger assist handles, vinyl-covered bench seat, 2-spoke black steering wheel and vinyl covered sun visor. The standard exterior features of the custom Comanche consisted of black front bumper with black end caps, black door and tailgate handles, black fender flares and front air dam, black grille with argent insert, black and argent headlight bezels, black dual rearview exterior mirrors, black moldings for windshield surround, door window frames, drip rails, and rear window weather strip, and black hub covers. The custom models also had electric 2-speed windshield wipers, dual horns, halogen headlights, and a buzzer warning system.

Equipment for the X Package in addition to, or in place of that of the Comanche custom was as follows: Hockey stick style armrests, custom trim door panels, color-keyed vinyl floor covering, instrument panel bright accents on black cluster overlay and ventlouver, AM radio, premium custom vinyl bench seat, color-keyed sport 3-spoke steering wheel, bright front bumper with black end caps, bright grille with bright surround moldings and headlight bezels, bright moldings for windshield surround, rear windows and drip rail, black taillamp trim, dual pin upper body side stripes in bright orange/red or light blue/medium blue, and bright wheel trim rings.

The XLS Package had the following interior equipment in addition to or in place of that of the Custom Package: Hockey stick armrest with custom trim, carpeted floor covering, color-keyed fabric headliner and sun visors, bright surround for instrument panel with color-keyed insert, "Luggage" fabric covered bench seat, color-keyed 2-spoke steering wheel, Gauge Group, Light Group and AM radio. The XLS exterior was identified by these items: Bright front bumper with black end caps, color-keyed fender flares and air dam, bright grille with bright surround moldings and headlamp bezels, bright dual rearview exterior mirrors, bright moldings for door window frame, rear window, windshield and drip rail, dual pin stripes in gold, dark red or dark blue for body side, hood and tailgate, bright taillight trim and wheeltrim rings with bright hub covers.

1986 Jeep Comanche XLS

Two optional equipment groups were limited to installation on Comanches with either the X or XLS Packages. The Interior Decor Group consisted of reclining wing-back bucket seats with headrests in Highland Check fabric, upgraded door panels with fabric inserts and carpeted lower area, color-keyed carpeted passenger area and rear cab trim panel, fabric-covered sun visors and headliner, color-keyed full length center console with armrest and stowage compartment, leather-wrapped Sport steering wheel and upgraded instrument panel with brushed pewter overlay.

The Sport Decor Group included black grille and headlight bezels, black front bumper, black fender flares and front air dam, lower body side blackout,15 x 7 in. white style steel wheels with bright hub covers, Sport body side, hood and tailgate decals color-keyed to body color (silver, bronze or orange/red), and black taillamp trim (not available with 633 tires, delete lower body side protective moldings). If the optional rear step bumper or pickup box side rails were ordered along with the Sport Decor group, they were black.

Available only for the custom Comanche was an optional Fuel Saver Package consisting of the 2.5 liter engine, 4-speed manual transmission, shift indicator light, 3.31:1 axle ratio. The following items were deleted as part of this package: Compact high pressure spare tire, tailgate, spare tire4 wrench, jack and handle. The vinyl floor covering was replaced by black carpeting. No other options could be ordered with this package. It was not available in California, high altitude, or the states of Maryland, Illinois and Tennessee.

Five standard clearcoat and six extra cost clearcoat metallic exterior colors were offered for the Comanche. The standard colors were olympic white, beige, sebring red, deep night blue and classic black. The optional colors were medium blue, champagne, dark honey, garnet, sterling and charcoal. During the model year a number of two-tone paint combinations were available.

I.D. DATA: The serial number was located on the left-hand hinge pillar. The V.I.N. had 17 symbols. The first three entries identified the manufacturer, make and type of vehicle. The fourth unit, a letter, designated the engine. The fifth character, a letter, identified the transmission. The sixth and seventh characters identified the series and body style. The eighth character identified the GVW rating. Next followed a check digit. The eleventh character was the manufacturing plant identification. The final six digits were the sequential production number.

Model Number	Body Type	Factory Price	GVW	Shipping Weight	Prod. Total
Comanche, 119.9 in. wheelbase, 2.8 liter V-6					
Model 65	Pickup	$7049	4001	3098	33,386[1]

NOTE 1: Calendar year production.

STANDARD ENGINE: Engine Type: OHV, In-line-4. Cast iron block and cylinder head. Bore x Stroke: 3.88 in. x 3.19 in. Lifters: Hydraulic. Number of main bearings-5. Fuel Induction: Throttle body single point fuel injection. Compression Ratio: 9.2:1. Displacement: 150.45 cu. in. (2.46 liters). Horsepower: Net: 117 @ 3500 rpm. Torque: Net: 135 lb.-ft. @ 3500 rpm. Oil refill capacity: 5 qt. with filter change. Fuel Requirements: Unleaded.

OPTIONAL ENGINE: Requires power steering and 5-speed manual transmission and Gauge Group. Engine Type: OHV, Renault 4-cyl. Turbo-charged diesel. Cast aluminum block and cylinder head. Not available for California or high altitude areas. Bore x Stroke: 3.49 in. x 3.51 in. Lifters: Hydraulic. Number of main bearings-5. Fuel Induction: Bosch Injection. Compression Ratio: 21.5:1. Displacement: 126 cu. in. (2.1 liters). Horsepower: Net: 85 @ 3250 rpm. Torque: Net: 132 lb.-ft. @ 3000 rpm. Oil refill capacity: 5 qt. with filter change. Fuel Requirements: #1, #2D diesel fuel.

OPTIONAL ENGINE: Requires power steering and 5-spd. manual or automatic transmission. Engine Type: OHV, V-6. Cast iron block and cylinder head. Bore x Stroke: 3.50 in. x 2.99 in. Lifters: Hydraulic. Fuel Induction: 2-bbl. carburetor. Compression Ratio: 8.5:1. Displacement: 173.0 cu. in. (2.8 liters). Horsepower: Net: 115 @ 4800 rpm. Torque: Net: 150 lb.-ft. @ 2100 rpm. Oil refill capacity: 5 qt. with filter change. Fuel Requirements: Unleaded.

CHASSIS FEATURES: Uniframe body construction.

SUSPENSION AND RUNNING GEAR: Front Suspension: Coil springs, live axle with leading links and track bar. Spring rate: 140 lb./in., link type 0.95 in. stabilizer bar. Rear Suspension: Hotchkiss, leaf-springs. Spring rates (at wheel): First stage: 130 lb./in. Second stage: 230 lb./in. Optional: Off-highway suspension. Front Axle Type and Capacity: Dana model 30 Hypoid. Rear Axle Type and Capacity: AMC Hypoid. Axle Ratios: 3.54:1. Optional: 3.31:1, 4.10:1. Transfer Case: New Process 228 Selec-Trac (automatic trans. only). Ratios: 2.61;1, 1.00:1. New Process Command-Trac. Ratios: 2.61;1, 1.00:1. Brakes: Type: Hydraulic, front disc type vented cast iron rotor, rear cast iron drums. Dimensions: Front: 10.98 in. x 0.88 in.; rear: 10.0 in. x 1.75 in. Wheels: Full drop center, 5-stud 15 x 6JJ, argent color. Optional: 15 x 7JJ painted white, 15 x 7JJ styled steel wheels, 15 x 7JJ sport aluminum wheels. Tires: P195/75R15 black sidewall, steel radial All-Weather. Optional: P205/75R 15 black sidewall, steel radial All-Weather, P205/75R15 white sidewall, steel radial Goodyear All-Weather, P205/75R15 white sidewall, steel radial Michelin All-Weather, P215/75R15 black sidewall, steel radial All-Terrain (requires 15 x 7 in. wheels, includes 4.10:1 axle ratio), P215/75R15 OWL, steel radial Wrangler All-Terrain (requires 15 x 7 in. wheels, includes 4.10:1 axle ratio), P215/75R15 OWL, steel radial Michelin All-Terrain (requires 15 x 7 in. wheels, includes 4.10:1 axle ratio), P225/75R15 black sidewall, steel radial All-Terrain (requires 15 x 7 in. wheels, includes 4.10:1 axle ratio), P225/75R15 OWL, steel radial Wrangler All-Terrain (requires 15 x 7 in. wheels, includes 4.10:1 axle ratio), P225/75R15 OWL, steel radial Michelin All-Terrain (requires 15 x 7 in. wheels, includes 4.10:1 axle ratio). Steering: Saginaw recirculating ball-type. Ratio: 26:1. Turns Lock-to-Lock: 4.8. Turning Circle: 41.3 ft. Optional Saginaw ratio power recirculating ball-type. Ratio: 15:2:1. Standard Transmission: 4-speed manual. Ratios: Transmission ratios: 3.93:1, 2.33:1, 1.45:1, 1.00:1. Reverse: 4.74:1. Optional: 5-speed manual. Ratios: 3.93:1, 2.33:1, 1.45:1, 1.00:1, 0.85:1. Reverse: 4.74:1. Optional: Chrysler Model 904 3-speed automatic. Ratios: 2.74:1, 1.55:1, 1.0:1. Reverse: 2.20:1. Clutch: 9.1 in. Single dry plate. Optional: None.

VEHICLE DIMENSIONS: Wheelbase: 119.9 in. Overall Length: 195.5 in. Front/Rear Tread: 57.0 in./57.0 in. Overall Height: 64.7 in. Width: 71.7 in. Front/Rear Overhang: 27.5 in./47.1 in. Tailgate: Width and Height: 52.3 in. x 16.4 in. Approach/Departure Degrees: 38/26. Ground Clearance: Rear axle: 7.5 in. Minimum running clearance: 10.3 in. Load space: 88.5 in. x 60.0 in. x 43.8 in. Maximum capacity (Volume Index): 46.4 cu. ft. Front headroom: 39.2 in. Front legroom: 39.9 in. Front shoulder room: 55.3 in. Front hip room: 55.3 in.

CAPACITIES: Fuel Tank: 16.0 gal. Optional: 23.5 gal.

ACCOMMODATIONS: Seating Capacity: Three, two with bucket seats.

INSTRUMENTATION: speedometer, 0-99,999.9 mi. odometer, fuel level gauge, warning lights for engine coolant temperature, oil pressure and alternator; transfer case indicator lights.

OPTIONS AND PRICES: Metallic paint. Mesa II fabric bench seat. Deluxe grain vinyl reclining bucket seats. 2.8 liter V-6 engine: $437. 2.1 liter turbo diesel: $1258. 5-spd. manual overdrive transmission: $175. 3-spd. automatic transmission: $670. Trac-Lok rear differential: $225. Selec-Trac (with automatic transmission): $932. California Emissions Package. High Altitude Emissions Package. X Package: $588. XLS Package: $905. Fuel Saver Package. Interior Decor Package: $434. Sport Decor Package: $235. Metric Ton Package (2205 lbs.) Includes heavy-duty rear axle, 15 x 7 in. white styled steel wheels. Front and rear heavy-duty springs and shock absorbers, requires P225 tires. Not available with 4-cylinder engine or automatic transmission: $201. Air conditioning. Air conditioning prep kit. Axle ratio (4.10:1). Heavy-duty battery. Front bumper guards. Passenger floor carpeting. Cold Climate Group. Console with armrest, maximum cooling system. Cruise control. Extra capacity 23.5 gal. fuel tank. Extra-Quiet Insulation Package. Includes Amberlite padding on back of cab, underhood insulation, fabric covered sun visors and headliner, and additional sound deadening materials. Color-keyed floor mats. Halogen fog lamps. Gauge Group. Includes digital clock, oil pressure gauge, voltmeter, engine coolant temperature gauge, low fuel indicator and trip odometer. Light Group. Includes ashtray light, cargo box light, courtesy lights, lighted visor mirror, fabric-covered sun visors and headliner, underhood light, headlights-on warning buzzer and Sentinel headlamp switch. Left and right side remote control mirrors. Left and right low-profile mirrors. Power door locks and windows. Power steering. Protection group. Includes front bumper guards, floor mats, door edge guards, and locking gas cap. Black lower body side protection moldings. AM radio. AM/FM monaural radio. AM/FM/Cassette tape player with dynamic noise reduction. Radio Prep Package. Black pickup box siderails. Bright pickup box siderails (black with Sport Decor Group). Skid Plate Package. Includes skid plates for transfer case, fuel tank, and front suspension. Sliding rear window. Sport steering wheel. Leather-wrapped Sport steering wheel. Black rear step bumper. Bright rear step bumper (black with Sport Decor Group). Flat black Sport bar. Off-highway vehicle suspension. Includes front and rear high pressure gas shock absorbers, P225/75R124 OWL radial tires, conventional full-size spare tire, white styled 15 x 7 in. steel wheels, 4.10:1 axle ratio, and Skid Plate Package. Tachometer. Tilt steering wheel. Tinted glass (all windows). Front door vent windows. Visibility Group. Includes right and left remote control mirrors, and intermittent windshield wipers. Bright trim wheel rings. White painted 15 x 7 in. styled steel wheels. Sport 15 x 7 in. aluminum wheels. Intermittent windshield wipers. Retractable under hood work light. Not available with diesel engine. Front license plate bracket. Clearcoat metallic paint: $161. P205/765R15 black sidewall steel belted tires: $43. P205/765R15 white sidewall steel belted tires: $128. P205/75R15 OWL tires: $332. P215/75R15 OWL tires: $375.

HISTORICAL FOOTNOTES: The new Comanche widened Jeep's market stance into yet another niche.

1987 COMANCHE

A new 113 in. wheelbase version of the Comanche with a 6 foot pickup box joined the original 119.6 in. 7 foot pickup box model for 1987. Introduced as an extra cost alternative to the Comanche's standard 2.5 liter engine was a new 4.0 liter In-line 6-cylinder engine with electronic multi-port, sequential fuel injection. The diesel engine was not offered for four-wheel drive models. Another significant new option for 1987 was a 4-speed automatic transmission with both power and comfort modes. In the power mode under hard acceleration, the transmission shifted at a higher engine RPM, downshifted more rapidly and was more sensitive to throttle position. The automatic transmission gear position indicator was relocated to the instrument panel display cluster. Previously, it was mounted on the steering column.

The 1987 Comanche was offered in four trim series. The Base and the Pioneer were available in both wheelbase forms. A new Sporty Comanche Chief Package was offered only on the short wheelbase platform. A premium Laredo Trim Package was exclusive to the 119.7 in. wheelbase models. Highlights of the base model included black finish for the grille, front bumper, window trim and fender flares. A bright surround was used for the grille. Functional equipment standard on the Base included the 2.5 liter engine, 4-speed manual transmission (short wheelbase models only), power brakes, P195/75R15 blackwall tires (P205/75R15 on long-box models), Command-Trac part-time four-wheel drive, 16 gal. fuel tank and halogen headlights. Highlights of the Comanche Pioneer included bright trim moldings, premium vinyl bench seat, new and upgraded door trim panels with stowage bins, AM monaural radio, bright and black instrument panel applique and a Sport steering wheel. The Comanche Chief offered lower body side and tailgate stripes, with graduated lower door tape and a "Comanche Chief" lettering cutout that permitted the vehicle body side to show through. The Chief interior had a premium grain vinyl notched bench seat, upgraded instrument panel with bright accent surrounds, passenger area carpeting, upgraded door trim panels with stowage bins, hockey-stick style armrests and a Soft-Feel Sport steering wheel. The Chief also had a 5-speed full-synchromesh floor shift manual transmission, P225/75R15 OWL Goodyear Wrangler All-Terrain tires, 15 x 7 in. white styled steel wheels and an AM monaural radio with two speakers.

1987 Jeep Comanche Chief shortbed

The Comanche Laredo had all the content of the base model plus the following items and features: Hunter's Plaid cloth and vinyl-backed wingback bucket seats with recliners, adjustable headrests, upgraded door trim with stowage bins, upgraded instrument panel trim with bright surrounds and a brushed pewter finish applique, hockey-stick style armrests, passenger area carpeting, carpeted trim panel on the back of the cab, passenger assist handle, and Soft-Feel Sport steering wheel. The Laredo exterior made extensive use of bright trim for the grille, front bumper, door window frame moldings, windshield surround molding, door and tailgate handles, wheel trim rings and hub covers, drip rail moldings and tailgate trim. A Jeep decal was installed on the tailgate, color-keyed to the pinstriped on the body side. The Laredo model also had the 5-speed manual transmission with floor shift standard, as well as the Light Group, Gauge Package and AM monaural radio with two speakers.

All Comanches except for the short box versions and the Comanche Chief were available with a new 4x4 Sport Graphics Package that included Sport body side, hood and tailgate decals available in three color configurations, each consisting of three-color tape, 4x4 Sport tape decal on the body side, and a Jeep decal on the tailgate that was color-keyed to the body side decal.

Standard clearcoat paint colors for the Comanche were olympic white, beige, Colorado red, deep night blue and classic black. Extra cost metallic clearcoat colors were medium blue, champagne, briarwood, grenadine, sterling and charcoal. A wide variety of two-tone paint combinations using the foregoing colors was also available.

I.D. DATA: The serial number was located on the left-hand hinge pillar. The V.I.N. had 17 symbols. The first three entries identified the manufacturer, make and type of vehicle. The fourth unit, a letter, designated the engine. The fifth character, a letter, identified the transmission. The sixth and seventh characters identified the series and body style. The eighth character identified the GVW rating. Next followed a check digit. The eleventh character was the manufacturing plant identification. The final six digits were the sequential production number.

Model Number	Body Type	Factory Price	GVW	Shipping Weight	Prod. Total
Comanche, 4.0 liter engine					
Model 66	Pickup, 119.9 in. wb.	$7860	4001	2955	43,070[1]
Model 64	Pickup, 113 in. wb.	$6495	4001	2897	—

NOTE 1: Calendar year production, all models. Calendar year sales totalled 38,094.

STANDARD ENGINE: Engine Type: OHV, In-line-4. Cast iron block and cylinder head. Bore x Stroke: 3.88 in. x 3.19 in. Lifters: Hydraulic. Number of main bearings-5. Fuel Induction: Throttle body single point fuel injection. Compression Ratio: 9.2:1. Displacement: 150.45 cu. in. (2.46 liters). Horsepower: Net: 121 @ 5000 rpm. Torque: Net: 141 lb.-ft. @ 3500 rpm. Oil refill capacity: 5 qt. with filter change. Fuel Requirements: Unleaded.

OPTIONAL ENGINE: Engine Type: OHV, In-line 6-cyl. Cast iron block and cylinder head. Bore x Stroke: 3.88 in. x 3.41 in. Lifters: Hydraulic. Fuel Induction: Electronic multi-port, sequential fuel injection. Compression Ratio: 9.2:1. Displacement: 241.6 cu. in. (3.966 liters). Horsepower: Net: 173 @ 4500 rpm. Torque: Net: 220 lb.-ft. @ 2500 rpm. Oil refill capacity: 5 qt. with filter change. Fuel Requirements: Unleaded.

CHASSIS FEATURES: Uniframe body construction.

SUSPENSION AND RUNNING GEAR: Front Suspension: Coil springs, live axle with leading links and track bar. Spring rate: 140 lb./in., link type 0.95 in. stabilizer bar. Rear Suspension: Hotchkiss, leaf-springs. Spring rates (at wheel): First stage: 130 lb/in., Second stage: 230 lb./in. Optional: Off Highway Suspension. Front Axle Type and Capacity: Dana model 30 Hypoid. Rear Axle Type and Capacity: AMC Hypoid. Axle Ratios: 4.56, 3.55, 4.1, 4.09, 3.54, 3.08, 3.07:1. Transfer Case: New Process 228 Selec-Trac (automatic trans. only). Ratios: 2.61;1, 1.00:1. New Process Command-Trac. Ratios: 2.61;1, 1.00:1. Brakes: Type: Hydraulic, front disc type vented cast iron rotor, rear cast iron drums. Dimensions: Front: 10.98 in. x 0.88 in.; rear: 10.0 in. x 1.75 in. Wheels: Full drop center, 5-stud 15 x 6JJ, argent color. Optional: 15 x 77JJ painted white, 15 x 7JJ styled steel wheels, 15 x 7JJ sport aluminum wheels. Tires: P195/75R15 black sidewall, steel radial All-Weather. Optional: P205/75R 15 black sidewall, steel radial All-Weather, P205/75R15 white sidewall, steel radial Goodyear All-Weather, P205/75R15 white sidewall, steel radial Michelin All-Weather, P215/75R15 black sidewall, steel radial All-Terrain (requires 15 x 7 in. wheels, includes 4.10:1 axle ratio), P215/75R15 OWL, steel radial Wrangler All-Terrain (requires 15 x 7 in. wheels, includes 4.10:1 axle ratio), P215/75R15 OWL, steel radial Michelin All-Terrain (requires 15 x 7 in. wheels, includes 4.10:1 axle ratio), P225/75R15 black sidewall, steel radial All-Terrain (requires 15 x 7 in. wheels, includes 4.10:1 axle ratio), P225/75R15 OWL, steel radial Wrangler All-Terrain (requires 15 x 7 in. wheels, includes 4.10:1 axle ratio), P225/75R15 OWL, steel radial Michelin All-Terrain (requires 15 x 7 in. wheels, includes 4.10:1 axle ratio). Steering: Saginaw recirculating ball-type. Ratio: 26:1. Turns Lock-to-Lock: 4.8. Turning Circle: 41.3 ft. Optional Saginaw ratio power recirculating ball-type. Ratio: 15:2:1. Turns Lock-to-Lock: 3.5. Standard Transmission: 4-speed manual. Ratios: 3.93:1, 2.33:1, 1.45:1, 1.00:1. Reverse: 4.74:1. Optional: 5-speed manual. Ratios: A-S (4-cyl. models): 3.93:1, 2.33:1, 1.45:1, 1.00:1, 0.85:1. Reverse: 4.74:1. Peugeot (6-cyl. models): 4.03:1, 2.39:1, 1.52:1, 1.00:1, 0.72:1. Reverse: 3.76:1. Optional: 4-speed automatic. Ratios: 2.80:1, 1.53:1, 1.0:1. 0.71:1. Reverse: 2.39:1. Clutch: 4-cyl.: 9.1 in. 6-cyl.: 10.1 in. Single dry plate. Optional: None.

VEHICLE DIMENSIONS: Wheelbase: 113/119.9 in. Overall Length: 179.2 in./195.5 in. Front/Rear Tread: 57.0 in./57.0 in. Overall Height: 63.7 in. Width: 71.7 in. Front/Rear Overhang: 113 in. wheelbase: 27.5 in./38.7 in. 119 in. wheelbase: 27.5 in./47.1 in. Tailgate: Width and Height: 52.3 in. x 16.4 in. Approach/Departure Degrees: 113 in. wheelbase: 39.9/30.1. 119 in. wheelbase: 39.8/24.8. Ground Clearance: Rear axle: 7.5 in. Minimum running clearance: 9.4 in. Load space: 88.5 in. x 60.0 in. x 43.8 in. Maximum capacity (Volume Index): 38.6 cu. ft. (113 in. wheelbase); 46.4 cu. ft. (119 in. wheelbase). Front headroom: 39.2 in. Front legroom: 39.9 in. Front shoulder room: 55.3 in. Front hip room: 55.3 in.

CAPACITIES: Fuel Tank: 16.0 gal. Optional: 23.5 gal.

ACCOMMODATIONS: Seating Capacity: Three, two with bucket seats.

INSTRUMENTATION: Speedometer, 0-99,999.9 mi. odometer, warning lights for engine coolant temperature, oil pressure and ammeter, fuel level gauge, Transfer case indicator lights.

OPTIONS AND PRICES: The Comanche was offered with essentially the same options as in 1987. Among the highlights were these items: Pioneer Trim Package: $544. Chief Trim Package: $1237. Laredo Trim Package: $1187. 4.0 liter 6-cyl. engine. Trac-Lok limited slip rear axle. Power steering. Larger tires. Full-size spare tire. Off-Road Package. Extra-capacity fuel tank. Metric-ton Payload Package. Skid Plate Package. Gauge Group. Tachometer. Visibility Group. Console with armrest. Power windows and door locks. Cruise control. Air conditioning. Tilt steering column. Sliding rear window. Swing-out front vent windows. Halogen fog lamps. Tinted glass. Intermittent windshield wipers. Extra-Quiet Insulation Package. Sport Graphics Package. Bumper guards. Metallic clearcoat paint. Protection Group. Black or bright rear step bumper. Bright pickup box side rails. Sport bar. AM radio. AM/FM monaural radio. AM/FM MPX stereo radio with four speakers. Electronically-tuned AM/FM/MPX radio with DNR and four speakers, and cassette tape player

HISTORICAL FOOTNOTES: The Archer Brothers racing team won the Manufacturers Championship with their 2.5 liter Comanche trucks. The Jeep Comanche was also the winner of the Manufacturers Championship in the HDRA/SCORE Off-Road Racing Series.

1988 COMANCHE

The 1988 Jeep Comanche was identified by its new eight-slot grille. A Sportruck model with the same basic equipment as the base model was available on the shortbed chassis. The base model was available only as a longbed model. The base model's essentially utilitarian character was emphasized by its black painted grille and the use of black moldings, front bumper, window trim and fender flares. A door-mounted, black exterior driver's side mirror replaced the sail-mounted unit used on previous Comanches. The Comanche cab's standard bench seat was revamped to provide improved legroom. The base Comanche had an improved 1475 lb. payload capacity. The shortbed models continued to have a standard 4-speed manual transmission while the longbed used the standard 5-speed manual. A 16 gal. fuel tank was fitted to the shortbeds with an 18 gal. unit on the longbed Comanches. Highlights of the base model's standard equipment were power brakes, Command-Trac part-time four-wheel drive and Halogen headlights. The step-up Comanche Pioneer received a new body side decal that included the Pioneer name, black front bumper, black body side scuff moldings, black windshield and drip rail moldings, and new 6-spoke 15 x 7 in. steel wheels with bright hub cover.

The Comanche Chief, again available only as a shortbed version had the new eight-slot grille in black, the new 6-spoke 15 x 7 in. steel wheels with bright hub cover, lower body side and tailgate strips with graduated lower door tape and Comanche Chief lettering cut-out to permit the vehicle body color to show through. The Chief's interior had premium grade vinyl notched bench seat, upgraded instrument panel trim with accent surrounds, passenger area carpeting, upgraded door trim panels with stowage bins, hockey-stick style armrests, AM monaural radio with two speakers, and a Soft-Feel Sport steering wheel.

1988 Jeep Comanche Chief

The Comanche Laredo, still offered only in the 7 foot box version, was updated with unique exterior lower body side moldings, a black and bright grille and additional new trim features. The Laredo interior featured Hunter's Plaid cloth and vinyl wingback bucket seats with recliners and see-thru headrests.

All Comanches except the base model were available with new "special value" Option Packages that offered substantial savings when compared to the prices of the options if purchased separately.

I.D. DATA: The serial number was located on the left-hand hinge pillar. The V.I.N. had 17 symbols. The first three entries identified the manufacturer, make and type of vehicle. The fourth unit, a letter, designated the engine. The fifth character, a letter, identified the transmission. The sixth and seventh characters identified the series and body style. The eighth character identified the GVW rating. Next followed a check digit. The tenth entry, a letter, represented the model year. The eleventh character was the manufacturing plant identification. The final six digits were the sequential production number.

Model Number	Body Type	Factory Price	GVW	Shipping Weight	Prod. Total
Comanche, 4.0 liter engine					
Model 66	Pickup, 119.9 in. wb.	$7787	4001[1]	3069	43,718[2]
Model 64	Pickup, 113 in. wb.	$6995	4001	2914	—

NOTE 1: 6000 lb. GVW optional for both models.
NOTE 2: 1988 calendar year production.

STANDARD ENGINE: Engine Type: OHV, In-line-4. Cast iron block and cylinder head. Bore x Stroke: 3.88 in. x 3.19 in. Lifters: Hydraulic. Number of main bearings-5. Fuel Induction: Throttle body single point fuel injection. Compression Ratio: 9.2:1. Displacement: 150.45 cu. in. (2.46 liters). Horsepower: Net: 121 @ 5000 rpm. Torque: Net: 141 lb.-ft. @ 3500 rpm. Oil refill capacity: 5 qt. with filter change. Fuel Requirements: Unleaded.

OPTIONAL ENGINE: Engine Type: OHV, In-line 6-cyl. Cast iron block and cylinder head. Bore x Stroke: 3.88 in. x 3.41 in. Lifters: Hydraulic. Fuel Induction: Electronic multi-port, sequential fuel injection. Compression Ratio: 9.2:1. Displacement: 241.6 cu. in. (3.966 liters). Horsepower: Net: 173 @ 4500 rpm. Torque: Net: 220 lb.-ft. @ 2500 rpm. Oil refill capacity: 5 qt. with filter change. Fuel Requirements: Unleaded.

CHASSIS FEATURES: Uniframe body construction.

SUSPENSION AND RUNNING GEAR: Front Suspension: Coil springs, live axle with leading links and track bar. Spring rate: 140 lb./in., link type 0.95 in. stabilizer bar. Rear Suspension: Hotchkiss, leaf-springs. Spring rates (at wheel): First stage: 130 lb/in., Second stage: 230 lb./ in. Optional: Off Highway Suspension. Front Axle Type and Capacity: Dana model 30 Hypoid. Rear Axle Type and Capacity: Dana model 35c, semi-floating. Axle Ratios: 4.56, 3.55, 4.11, 4.09, 3.54, 3.08, 3.07:1. Transfer Case: New Process 242 Selec-Trac (automatic trans. only). Ratios: 2.61;1, 1.00:1. New Process 231 Command-Trac. Ratios: 2.61;1, 1.00:1. Brakes: Type: Hydraulic, front disc type vented cast iron rotor, rear cast iron drums. Dimensions: Front: 10.98 in. x 0.88 in.; rear: 10.0 in. x 1.75 in. Wheels: Full drop center, 5-stud 15 x 6JJ, argent color. Optional: 15 x 77JJ painted white, 15 x 7JJ styled steel wheels, 15 x 7JJ sport aluminum wheels. Tires: P195/75R15 black sidewall, steel radial All-Weather. Optional: P205/75R 15 black sidewall, steel radial All-Weather, P205/75R15 white sidewall, steel radial Goodyear All-Weather, P205/75R15 white sidewall, steel radial Michelin All-Weather, P215/75R15 black sidewall, steel radial All-Terrain (requires 15 x 7 in. wheels, includes 4.10:1 axle ratio), P215/ 75R15 OWL, steel radial Wrangler All-Terrain (requires 15 x 7 in. wheels, includes 4.10:1 axle ratio), P215/75R15 OWL, steel radial Michelin All-Terrain (requires 15 x 7 in. wheels, includes 4.10:1 axle ratio), P225/75R15 black sidewall, steel radial All-Terrain (requires 15 x 7 in. wheels, includes 4.10:1 axle ratio), P225/75R15 OWL, steel radial Wrangler All-Terrain (requires 15 x 7 in. wheels, includes 4.10:1 axle ratio), P225/75R15 OWL, steel radial Michelin All-Terrain (requires 15 x 7 in. wheels, includes 4.10:1 axle ratio). Steering: Saginaw recirculating ball-type. Ratio: 26:1. Turns Lock-to-Lock: 4.8. Turning Circle: 41.3 ft. Optional Saginaw ratio power recirculating ball-type. Ratio: 15:2:1. Turns Lock-to-Lock: 3.5. Standard Transmission: 4-speed manual. Ratios: Transmission ratios: 3.93:1, 2.33:1, 1.45:1, 1.00:1. Reverse: 4.74:1. Optional: 5-speed manual. Ratios: A-S (4-cyl. models): 3.93:1, 2.33:1, 1.45:1, 1.00:1, 0.85:1. Reverse: 4.74:1. Peugeot (6-cyl. models): 4.03:1, 2.39:1, 1.52:1, 1.00:1, 0.72:1. Reverse: 3.76:1. Optional: 4-speed automatic. Ratios: 2.80:1, 1.53:1, 1.0:1. 0.71:1. Reverse: 2.39:1. Clutch: 4-cyl.: 9.1 in. 6-cyl.: 10.1 in. Single dry plate. Optional: None.

VEHICLE DIMENSIONS: Wheelbase: 113/119.9 in. Overall Length: 179.2 in./195.5 in. Front/ Rear Tread: 57.0 in./57.0 in. Overall Height: 63.7 in. Width: 71.7 in. Front/Rear Overhang: 113 in. wheelbase: 27.5 in./38.7 in. 119 in. wheelbase: 27.5 in./47.1 in. Tailgate: Width and Height: 52.3 in. x 16.4 in. Approach/Departure Degrees: 113 in. wheelbase: 39.9/30.1. 119 in. wheelbase: 39.8/24.8. Ground Clearance: Rear axle: 7.5 in. Minimum running clearance: 9.4 in. Load space: Shortbed: 73.7 in. x 60.0 in. x 43.8 in. Longbed: 88.5 in. x 60.0 in. x 43.8 in. Maximum capacity (Volume Index). 38.6 cu. ft. (113 in. wheelbase); 46.4 cu. ft. (119 in. wheelbase). Front headroom: 39.4 in. Front legroom: 43.0 in. Front shoulder room: 55.3 in. Front hip room: 55.3 in.

CAPACITIES: Fuel Tank: 16.0 gal. (113 in. wheelbase), 18.0 gal. (119 in. wheelbase). Optional: 23.5 gal.

ACCOMMODATIONS: Seating Capacity: Three (bench seat), two with bucket seats.

INSTRUMENTATION: Speedometer, 0-99,999.9 mi. odometer, fuel level gauge, warning lights for engine coolant temperature, oil pressure and ammeter; transfer case indicator lights.

OPTIONS AND PRICES: Pioneer Trim Package ($767). Chief Trim Package. Laredo Trim Package. 4.0 liter 6-cyl. engine. Trac-Lok limited slip rear axle. Power steering. Three larger tires sizes. Full-sized spare tire. Jeep Off-Road Package. 23.5 gal. fuel tank. 2205 lb. Payload Package (longbed models only). Skid Plate Package. Gauge Group. Tachometer. Visibility Group. Console with armrest. Power windows and door locks. Cruise control. Air conditioning. Tilt steering column. Sliding rear window. Swing-out front vent windows. Halogen fig lamps. Tinted glass. Intermittent windshield wipers. Extra-Quiet Insulation Package. Bumper guards. Metallic clearcoat paint. Protection Group. Rear step bumper in either bright or black to match the front bumper. Bright pickup box rails Sport bar. Rear tubular black bumper. AM monaural radio with two speakers. Electronically tuned AM/FM MPX stereo radio with four speakers. Electronically tuned AM/FM radio with Dolby, four speakers and cassette tape player.

HISTORICAL FOOTNOTES: The Archer Brothers racing team once again won the Manufacturers Championship with their 2.5 liter Comanche trucks. The Comanche also had the best record of any domestic model in the Mickey Thompson Stadium Racing Series. The Jeep Comanche was also the winner of the Manufacturers Championship in the HDRA/SCORE Off-Road Racing Series.

1989 COMANCHE

The latest Comanches on the longbed chassis had standard 23.5 gal. fuel tanks. The fuel capacity of the tank on the 113 in. chassis Comanche was increased to 18 gal. The Laredo and Chief models were not offered for 1989. Standard equipment for the shortbed SporTruck (1989's spelling style!) and the base longbed model was as follows: 61 amp alternator, 58-390 cold cranking amps battery, compact limited-duty high-pressure spare tire, electric two-speed windshield wipers and washer, black molded plastic B-pillar applique, black front bumper with black end caps, black fender flares and air dam, tinted glass for all windows, body side decal graphics (SporTruck only), halogen headlights, left-mounted manual exterior mirror, bright windshield surround and drip moldings, black door window frames and division bars, color-keyed straight-type armrests, AM monaural radio with two speakers, mini console, dome lights mounted on left and right B-pillars, color-keyed vinyl door trim panels, black textured rubber floor covering, heater and defroster, color-keyed molded fabric-covered headliner and sun visors, inside hood release, instrument panel cluster overlay (black with bright accents on vent louvers), color-keyed energy-absorbing instrument panel pad, glove box with lock and light, utility bin below glove box, day/night rearview mirror, bench seat and seat belts in grain vinyl, lap and shoulder belt restraint system, and black plastic 2-spoke steering wheel.

The Pioneer trim level was offered in either the113 in. or 119 in, wheelbase form. Content of the Pioneer in place of or in addition to that of the base/SporTruck consisted of these items: Variable ratio power steering, color-keyed fender flares and air dam, body side graphics decal, black and argent grille, black windshield surround and drip rails, black body side scuff molding, black rear step bumper with black end caps, color-keyed hockey-style armrests, color-keyed carpeting for back of cab, color-keyed custom vinyl door trim panels with lower nylon carpeting and stowage bin, roof-mounted, passenger side grab handle, instrument panel cluster overlay-black with bright accents on gauge surrounds and vent louvers, bench seat and seat belts in Canyon fabric, and color-keyed Soft-Feel three-spoke steering wheel. The Selec-Trac transfer case was not offered for 1989.

The exterior colors offered for 1989 were: Pearl white, classic black, Colorado red, sand, dark vivid red metallic, dover grey metallic, sterling metallic, dark baltic metallic, spinmaker blue metallic and sand metallic. The metallic colors were extra cost options.

I.D. DATA: The serial number was located on the left-hand hinge pillar. The V.I.N. had 17 symbols. The first three entries identified the manufacturer, make and type of vehicle. The fourth unit, a letter, designated the GVW range. The fifth sixth and seventh characters identified the series and body style. The eighth character identified the engine. Next followed a check digit. The tenth entry, a letter, identified the model year. The eleventh character was the manufacturing plant identification. The final six digits were the sequential production number.

Model Number	Body Type	Factory Price	GVW	Shipping Weight	Prod. Total
Comanche, 4.0 liter engine					
Model T26	Pickup, 119.9 in. wb.	$9076	4001[1]	3098	25,311[2]
Model T26	Pickup, 113 in. wb.	$8259	4001	3040	—

NOTE 1: 6000 lb. GVW optional for both models.
NOTE 2: Calendar year production, all models.

STANDARD ENGINE: Engine Type: OHV, In-line-4. Cast iron block and cylinder head. Bore x Stroke: 3.88 in. x 3.19 in. Lifters: Hydraulic. Number of main bearings-5. Fuel Induction: Throttle body single point fuel injection. Compression Ratio: 9.2:1. Displacement: 150.45 cu. in. (2.46 liters). Horsepower: Net: 121 @ 5000 rpm. Torque: Net: 141 lb.-ft. @ 3500 rpm. Oil refill capacity: 5 qt. with filter change. Fuel Requirements: Unleaded.

OPTIONAL ENGINE: Engine Type: OHV, In-line 6-cyl. Cast iron block and cylinder head. Bore x Stroke: 3.88 in. x 3.41 in. Lifters: Hydraulic. Fuel Induction: Electronic multi-port, sequential fuel injection. Compression Ratio: 9.2:1. Displacement: 241.6 cu. in. (3.966 liters). Horsepower: Net: 177 @ 4500 rpm. Torque: Net: 224 lb.-ft. @ 2500 rpm. Oil refill capacity: 5 qt. with filter change. Fuel Requirements: Unleaded.

CHASSIS FEATURES: Uniframe body construction.

SUSPENSION AND RUNNING GEAR: Front Suspension: Coil springs, live axle with leading links and track bar. Spring rate: 140 lb./in., link type 0.95 in. stabilizer bar. Rear Suspension: Hotchkiss, leaf-springs. Spring rates (at wheel): First stage: 130 lb/in., Second stage: 230 lb./ in. Optional: Off-Road Package, Big-Ton Payload Package. Front Axle Type and Capacity: Dana model 30 Hypoid. Rear Axle Type and Capacity: Dana model 35c, semi-floating. Axle Ratios: Standard with 2.5 liter engine: 3.55:1, with 4.0 liter engine: 3.08:1. Transfer Case: New Process 231 Command-Trac. Ratios: 2.72;1, 1.00:1. Brakes: Type: Hydraulic, front disc type vented cast iron rotor, rear cast iron drums. Dimensions: Front: 10.98 in. x 0.88 in.; rear: 10.0

in. x 1.75 in. Wheels: Full drop center, 5-stud. SporTruck shortbed: 15 x 6 in. argent styled steel wheels with small black hub covers and bright trim rings. Base longbed: 15 x 6 in. argent styled steel wheels with small black hub covers. Pioneer: 15 x 7 in. silver styled steel wheels with bright hub covers. Optional: Base longbed: 15 x 6 in. argent styled steel wheels with small black hub covers and bright trim rings. Base longbed and SporTruck shortbed: 15 x 7 in. silver styled steel wheels with bright hub covers. All models except those with P195 tires or Big-Ton Package: 15 x 7 in. 10-hole cast aluminum wheels with bright hub covers. Tires: SporTruck shortbed and base longbed: P195/75R15 black sidewall, steel radial All-Weather. Pioneer: P205/75R15 black sidewall, steel radial All-Weather. Optional: SporTruck shortbed and base longbed: P205/75R15 black sidewall, steel radial All-Weather. All models: P215/75R15 Michelin or Goodyear Wrangler OWL steel radial All-Terrain. Requires 15 x 7 in. wheels, not available with 2.5 liter engine and 4-spd. manual trans. P225/75R15 Goodyear Wrangler OWL steel radial All-Terrain. Requires 15 x 7 in. wheels, not available with 2.5 liter engine and 4--spd. manual trans. Steering: Saginaw recirculating ball-type. Ratio: 24:1. Turns Lock-to-Lock: 4.8. Turning Circle: 41.3 ft. Optional Saginaw ratio power recirculating ball-type. Standard for Pioneer. Ratio: 14:1. Turns Lock-to-Lock: 3.5. Standard Transmission: Sportruck shortbed: 4-speed, al-synchromesh manual with floor shift. Not available with 4.0 liter engine. Ratios: Transmission ratios: 3.93:1, 2.33:1, 1.45:1, 1.00:1. Reverse: 4.74:1. Standard Transmission: Base longbed and Pioneer: 5-speed manual overdrive with floor shift. Ratios: A-S (4-cyl. models): 3.93:1, 2.33:1, 1.45:1, 1.00:1, 0.85:1. Reverse: 4.74:1. Peugeot (6-cyl. models): 4.03:1, 2.39:1, 1.52:1, 1.00:1, 0.72:1. Reverse: 3.76:1. Optional: 4-speed automatic overdrive floor shift with lockup torque converter. Requires bucket seats; not available on Longbed models with 2.5 liter engine. Ratios: 2.80:1, 1.53:1, 1.0:1. 0.71:1. Reverse: 2.39:1. Clutch: 4-cyl.: 9.1 in. 6-cyl.: 10.1 in. Single dry plate with hydraulic actuation. Optional: None.

VEHICLE DIMENSIONS: Wheelbase: 112.9/119.4 in. Overall Length: 179.3 in./194.0 in. Front/Rear Tread: 57.0 in./57.0 in. Overall Height: 64.7 in. Width: 71.7 in. Front/Rear Overhang: 112.9 in. wheelbase: 27.5 in./38.8 in. 119.4 in. wheelbase: 27.5 in./47.1 in. Tailgate: Width and Height: 52.3 in. x 16.4 in. Approach/Departure Degrees: 112.9 in. wheelbase: 41.7/31.5. 119.4 in. wheelbase: 41.5/26.1.

Ground Clearance:

	Front Axle: Shortbed	Longbed
P195 tires:	7.7 in.	7.6 in.
P205 tires:	7.9 in.	7.9 in.
P215 tires:	8.3 in.	8.3 in.
P225 tires:	8.5 in.	8.5 in.

	Rear Axle: Shortbed	Longbed
P195 tires:	7.5 in.	7.5 in.
P205 tires:	7.8 in.	7.8 in.
P215 tires:	8.2 in.	8.2 in.
P225 tires:	8.4 in.	8.4 in.

Running ground clearance: 9.4 in. Load space: Shortbed: 73.7 in. x 60.0 in. x 43.8 in. Longbed: 88.5 in. x 60.0 in. x 43.8 in. Maximum capacity (Volume Index): 38.6 cu. ft. (shortbed); 46.4 cu. ft. (longbed). Front headroom: 39.4 in. Front legroom: 43.0 in. Front shoulder room: 55.3 in. Front hip room: 55.3 in.

CAPACITIES: Fuel Tank: 16.0 gal. (113 in. wheelbase), 18.0 gal. (119 in. wheelbase). Optional: 23.5 gal.

ACCOMMODATIONS: Seating Capacity: Three (bench seat), two with bucket seats.

INSTRUMENTATION: Speedometer, fuel gauge, warning lights for alternator, oil pressure, engine coolant temperature, seat belts and parking brake.

OPTIONS: Pioneer Trim Package 4.0 liter 6-cyl. engine. Requires power steering and 5-speed manual or auto. trans. Air conditioning. Heavy-duty 58-475 cold crank battery (requires Heavy-Duty Alternator and Battery Group). Cruise control. Requires intermittent windshield wipers. Heavy-Duty Alternator and Battery Group. Includes 74 amp alternator with 2.5 liter engine; 100 amp with 4.0 liter engine, 58-475 cold crank battery. Off-Road Package. Includes front and rear high-pressure gas shock absorbers, 15 x 7 in. silver styled steel wheels, P225/75R15 Goodyear Wrangler OWL radial tires, full-size spare, Skid Plate Group, front tow hooks, heavy-duty radiator, auxiliary electric fan (on 4.0 liter engine), auxiliary transmission air cooler (on 4.0 liter engine with auto. trans.). Requires power steering and Heavy-Duty Alternator and Battery Group; not available with 2.5 liter engine and 4-spd. man. trans. or Big-Ton Payload Package. Variable ratio power steering (SporTruck and Base only). Skid Plate Package. Includes transfer case, fuel tank and front suspension skid plates. Big-Ton Payload Package. Available for longbed models only. Includes 2205 lb. heavy-duty rear axle (Dana 44), 15 x 7 in. silver styled steel wheels, full-size wheels, heavy-duty front and rear springs and shock absorbers, and P225/75R15 tires (not available with 2.5 liter engine and 4-speed man. or auto. trans.). Trac-Lok limited slip rear axle. Requires 4.0 liter engine and full-size spare tire. Trailer Towing Package. Includes Heavy-duty Dana 44 rear axle, heavy-duty radiator, auxiliary electric fan, auxiliary transmission cooler. Package A rated at 2000 lb., Package B rated at 5000 lb. Package B requires the following equipment: 4.0 liter engine, automatic transmission, full-size spare tire, and Heavy-Duty Alternator and Battery Group. Both packages require 205 or larger tires. 5-speed man. trans. (SporTruck only). 4-spd. overdrive auto. trans. Electric windshield wipers with intermittent feature. Front bumper guards. Requires Protection Group. Not available for base and SporTruck models. Dual exterior manual remote control mirrors. Metallic paint. Protection Group. Includes front bumper guards, floor mats, and door edge guards; requires carpeting. Not available for base and SporTruck models. Black rear step bumper with black end caps (for base and SporTruck models). Sliding rear window. Front door, swing-out design vent windows. AM/FM electronically tuned stereo radio with4 dual-cone speakers. AM/FM electronically tuned stereo radio with Dolby system and cassette tape player and 4 dual-cone speakers. Full console with armrest storage box. Requires bucket seats and floorshift transmission. Not available for base and SporTruck models. Extra-Quiet Insulation Package. Not available for base and SporTruck models. Includes Amberlite padding on cab back, underhood insulation, and additional sound-deadening material. Color-keyed carpeting (for base and SporTruck models). Instrument panel cluster. Includes tachometer, voltmeter, oil pressure and engine coolant temperature gauges, low-fuel indicator light, trip odometer, and liquid crystal display clock. Not available with automatic trans. column shift. Cigarette lighter (base and SporTruck models). Light Group. Includes ashtray light, cargo box light, courtesy lights, retractable underhood work light, headlights-on warning buzzer, visor mirror light and Sentinel headlamp switch. Canyon fabric bench seat (base and SporTruck models). Recliner wingback bucket seats with adjustable headrest in tooled grain vinyl (for Pioneer only). Tilt steering column. Requires intermittent windshield wipers.

HISTORICAL FOOTNOTES: 1989 model year sales of the Comanche were 27,399.

1990 COMANCHE

Joining the four-wheel drive Comanche lineup for 1990 was the Eliminator model. Previously it had been offered only as a two-wheel drive model. Now standard for both the Pioneer and Eliminator was an AM/FM electronically tuned stereo radio. The Eliminator featured the following items in place of or in addition to the content of the Pioneer Package: P225/75R15 Goodyear Wrangler or Michelin OWL steel radial all-terrain tires, 15 x 7 in. 10-hole cast aluminum wheels with bright hub covers, front bumper guards, halogen fog lamps, color-keyed grille, body side decal graphics, and black body side scuff moldings with bright insert. The 1990 exterior color selection consisted of bright white, black, Colorado red, dover grey metallic, sterling metallic, dark baltic metallic, spinmaker blue metallic and sand metallic. All colors were available in clearcoat form at extra cost.

A Premium vinyl interior was standard for the base and SporTruck models with a bench seat. It was also standard for the Pioneer when optional bucket seats were ordered. It was offered in charcoal, sand or cordovan. Standard for the Pioneer with a bench seat was a Canyon fabric in charcoal, sand or cordovan. It was optional for the base and SporTruck with bench seat. A luggage fabric was standard for the Eliminator's wingback bucket seats. It was offered only in charcoal.

I.D. DATA: The serial number was located on the left-hand hinge pillar. The V.I.N. had 17 symbols. The first three entries identified the manufacturer, make and type of vehicle. The fourth unit, a letter, designated the GVW range. The fifth, sixth and seventh characters identified the series and body style. The eighth character identified the engine. Next followed a check digit. The tenth entry, a letter, identified the model year. The eleventh character was the manufacturing plant identification. The final six digits were the sequential production number.

Model Number	Body Type	Factory Price	GVW	Shipping Weight	Prod Total
Comanche, 4.0 liter engine					
Model T26	Pickup, 119.9 in. wb.	$8975	4001[1]	3127	9576[2]
Model T26	Pickup, 113 in. wb.	$8095	4001	3042	—

NOTE 1: 6000 lb. GVW optional for both models.
NOTE 2: 1990 calendar year production, all models.

STANDARD ENGINE: Engine Type: OHV, In-line-4. Cast iron block and cylinder head. Bore x Stroke: 3.88 in. x 3.19 in. Lifters: Hydraulic. Number of main bearings-5. Fuel Induction: Throttle body single point fuel injection. Compression Ratio: 9.2:1. Displacement: 150.45 cu. in. (2.46 liters). Horsepower: Net: 121 @ 5000 rpm. Torque: Net: 141 lb.-ft. @ 3500 rpm. Oil refill capacity: 5 qt. with filter change. Fuel Requirements: Unleaded.

OPTIONAL ENGINE: (Standard for Eliminator): Requires power steering and 5-spd. man. or auto. trans. Engine Type: OHV, In-line 6-cyl. Cast iron block and cylinder head. Bore x Stroke: 3.88 in. x 3.41 in. Lifters: Hydraulic. Fuel Induction: Electronic multi-port, sequential fuel injection. Compression Ratio: 9.2:1. Displacement: 241.6 cu. in. (3.966 liters). Horsepower: Net: 177 @ 4500 rpm. Torque: Net: 224 lb.-ft. @ 2500 rpm. Oil refill capacity: 5 qt. with filter change. Fuel Requirements: Unleaded.

CHASSIS FEATURES: Uniframe body construction.

SUSPENSION AND RUNNING GEAR: Front Suspension: Coil springs, live axle with leading links and track bar. Spring rate: 140 lb./in., link type 0.95 in. stabilizer bar. Rear Suspension: Hotchkiss, leaf-springs. Spring rates (at wheel): First stage: 130 lb/in., Second stage: 230 lb./in. Optional: Off-Road Package, Big-Ton Payload Package. Front Axle Type and Capacity: Dana model 30 Hypoid. Rear Axle Type and Capacity: Dana model 35c, semi-floating. Axle Ratios: Standard and available only for SporTruck and base models with 2.5 liter engine and 4-spd. man. trans.: 3.55:1, with 2.5 liter engine and 5-spd. man. trans.: 4.11:1(standard for Pioneer and Eliminator, optional for SporTruck and base models), optional for SporTruck and Pioneer shortbed with 2.5 liter engine and auto. trans.: 4.56:1, standard for Eliminator and optional for all others with 4.0 liter engine and 5-spd. man. trans.: 3.08:1, optional for all models with 4.0 liter engine and auto. trans.: 3.55:1. Transfer Case: New Process 231 Command-Trac. Ratios: 2.72;1, 1.00:1. Brakes: Type: Hydraulic, front disc type vented cast iron rotor, rear cast iron drums. Dimensions: Front: 10.98 in. x 0.88 in.; rear: 10.0 in. x 1.75 in. Wheels: Full drop center, 5-stud. SporTruck shortbed: 15 x 6 in. argent styled steel wheels with small black hub covers and bright trim rings. Base longbed: 15 x 6 in. argent styled steel wheels with small black hub covers. Pioneer: 15 x 7 in. silver styled steel wheels with bright hub covers. 15 x7 in. 10-hole cast aluminum. Optional: Base longbed and SporTruck shortbed: 15 x 7 in. silver styled steel wheels with bright hub covers. All models except those with P195 tires or Big-Ton Package: 15 x 7 in. 10-hole cast aluminum wheels with bright hub covers. Tires: SporTruck shortbed and base longbed: P195/75R15 black sidewall, steel radial All-Weather. Pioneer: P205/75R15 black sidewall, steel radial All-Weather. Eliminator: P225/75R15 Goodyear Wrangler OWL steel radial all-terrain. Optional: SporTruck shortbed and base longbed: P205/75R15 black sidewall, steel radial All-Weather. All models except Eliminator: P215/75R15 Michelin or Goodyear Wrangler OWL steel radial All-Terrain. Requires 15 x 7 in. wheels, not available with 2.5 liter engine and 4-spd. manual trans., P225/75R15 Goodyear Wrangler OWL steel radial All-Terrain. Requires 15 x 7 in. wheels, not available with 2.5 liter engine and 4-spd. manual trans. Steering: Saginaw recirculating ball-type. Ratio: 24:1. Turns Lock-to-Lock: 4.8. Turning Circle: 41.3 ft. Optional Saginaw ratio power recirculating ball-type. Standard for base, Pioneer and Eliminator. Ratio: 14:1. Turns Lock-to-Lock: 3.5. Standard Transmission: SporTruck shortbed: 4-speed, all-synchromesh manual with floor shift. Not available with 4.0 liter engine. Ratios: Transmission ratios: 3.93:1, 2.33:1, 1.45:1, 1.00:1. Reverse: 4.74:1. Standard Transmission: Base longbed, Pioneer and Eliminator: 5-speed manual overdrive with floor shift. Ratios: A-S (4-cyl. models): 3.93:1, 2.33:1, 1.45:1, 1.00:1, 0.85:1. Reverse: 4.74:1. Peugeot (6-cyl. models): 4.03:1, 2.39:1, 1.52:1, 1.00:1, 0.72:1. Reverse: 3.76:1. Optional: All models except Eliminator: 4-speed automatic overdrive column shift with lockup torque converter. Requires bench seat; not available on longbed models with 2.5 liter engine. All models except SporTruck and Base: 4-speed automatic overdrive floor shift with lockup torque converter. Requires bucket seats; not available with 2.5 liter engine. Ratios: 2.80:1, 1.53:1, 1.0:1. 0.71:1. Reverse: 2.39:1. Clutch: 4-cyl.: 9.1 in. 6-cyl.: 10.1 in. Single dry plate with hydraulic actuation. Optional: None.

VEHICLE DIMENSIONS: Wheelbase: 112.9/119.4 in. Overall Length: 179.3 in./194.0 in. Front/Rear Tread: 57.0 in./57.0 in. 58.0 in./58.0 in. when equipped with 15 x 7 in. wheels (standard for Pioneer and Eliminator). Overall Height: 64.7 in. Width: 71.7 in. Front/Rear Overhang: 112.9 in. wheelbase: 27.5 in./38.8 in. 119.4 in. wheelbase: 27.5 in./47.1 in. Tailgate: Width and Height: 52.3 in. x 16.4 in. Approach/Departure Degrees: 112.9 in. wheelbase: 41.7/31.5. 119.4 in. wheelbase: 41.5/26.1.

Ground Clearance:

	Front Axle: Shortbed	Longbed
P195 tires:	7.7 in.	7.6 in.
P205 tires:	7.9 in.	7.9 in.
P215 tires:	8.3 in.	8.3 in.
P225 tires:	8.5 in.	8.5 in.
	Rear Axle: Shortbed	Longbed
P195 tires:	7.5 in.	7.5 in.
P205 tires:	7.8 in.	7.8 in.
P215 tires:	8.2 in.	8.2 in.
P225 tires:	8.4 in.	8.4 in.

Running ground clearance: 9.4 in. Load space: Shortbed: 73.7 in. x 60.0 in. x 43.8 in. Longbed: 88.5 in. x 60.0 in. x 43.8 in. Maximum capacity (Volume Index). 38.6 cu. ft. (shortbed); 46.4 cu. ft. (longbed). Front headroom: 39.4 in. Front legroom: 43.0 in. Front shoulder room: 55.3 in. Front hip room: 55.3 in.

CAPACITIES: Fuel Tank: 16.0 gal. (113 in. wheelbase), 18.0 gal. (119 in. wheelbase). Optional: 23.5 gal.

ACCOMMODATIONS: Seating Capacity: Three (bench seat), two with bucket seats.

INSTRUMENTATION: Speedometer, fuel gauge, warning lights for alternator, oil pressure, engine coolant temperature, seat belts and parking brake.

OPTIONS: Pioneer Trim Package Eliminator Trim Package. 4.0 liter 6-cyl. engine. Requires power steering and 5-speed manual or auto. trans. Air conditioning. Heavy-duty 58-475 cold crank battery (requires Heavy-Duty Alternator and Battery Group). Cruise control. Requires intermittent windshield wipers. Heavy-Duty Alternator and Battery Group. Includes 74 amp alternator with 2.5 liter engine; 100 amp with 4.0 liter engine, 58-475 cold crank battery. Off-Road Package. Includes front and rear high-pressure gas shock absorbers, 15 x 7 in. silver styled steel wheels, P225/75R15 Goodyear Wrangler OWL radial tires, full-size spare, Skid Plate Group, front tow hooks, heavy-duty radiator, auxiliary electric fan (on 4.0 liter engine), auxiliary transmission air cooler (on 4.0 liter engine with auto. trans.). Requires power steering and Heavy-Duty Alternator and Battery Group; not available with 2.5 liter engine and 4-spd. man. trans. or Big-Ton Payload Package. Variable ratio power steering (SporTruck and base only). Skid Plate Package. Includes transfer case, fuel tank and front suspension skid plates. Big-Ton Payload Package. Available for longbed models only. Includes 2205 lb. heavy-duty rear axle (Dana 44), 15 x 7 in. silver styled steel wheels, full-size wheels, heavy-duty front and rear springs and shock absorbers, and P225/75R15 tires (not available with 2.5 liter engine and 4-speed man. or auto. trans.). Trac-Lok limited slip rear axle. Requires 4.0 liter engine and full-size spare tire. Trailer Towing Package. Includes heavy-duty Dana 44 rear axle, heavy-duty radiator, auxiliary electric fan, auxiliary transmission cooler. Package A rated at 2000 lb., Package B rated at 5000 lb. Package B requires the following equipment: 4.0 liter engine, automatic transmission, full-size spare tire, and Heavy-Duty Alternator and Battery Group. Both packages require 205 or larger tires. 5-speed man. trans. (SporTruck only). 4-spd. overdrive auto. trans. Electric windshield wipers with intermittent feature. Front bumper guards. Requires Protection Group. Not available for base and SporTruck models. Dual exterior manual remote control mirrors. Metallic paint. Protection Group. Includes front bumper guards, floor mats, and door edge guards; requires carpeting. Not available for base and SporTruck models. Black rear step bumper with black end caps (for base and SporTruck models). Sliding rear window. Front door, swing-out design vent windows. AM/FM electronically tuned stereo radio with 4 dual-cone speakers. AM/FM electronically tuned stereo radio with Dolby system and cassette tape player and 4 dual-cone speakers. Full console with armrest storage box. Requires bucket seats and floorshift transmission. Not available for base and SporTruck models. Extra-Quiet Insulation Package. Not available for base and SporTruck models. Includes Amberlite padding on cab back, underhood insulation, and additional sound-deadening material. Color-keyed carpeting (for base and SporTruck models). Instrument panel cluster. Includes tachometer, voltmeter, oil pressure and engine coolant temperature gauges, low-fuel indicator light, trip odometer, and liquid crystal display clock. Not available with automatic trans. column shift. Cigarette lighter (base and SporTruck models). Light Group. Includes ashtray light, cargo box light, courtesy lights, retractable underhood work light, headlights-on warning buzzer, visor mirror light and Sentinel headlamp switch. Canyon fabric bench seat (base and SporTruck models). Recliner wingback bucket seats with adjustable headrest in tooled grain vinyl (for Pioneer only). Tilt steering column requires intermittent windshield wipers.

HISTORICAL FOOTNOTES: The Comanche won the 1989 HDRA/SCORE desert truck series. A Jeep Comanche driven by Rob MacCachren won the 7S championship with wins in the Mojave 250, Nevada 500 and Baja 1000.

1991 COMANCHE

Heading the list of changes for 1991 was a more powerful 4-cylinder engine for the Comanche with sequential multi-point electronic fuel injection in place of the throttle body unit used in 1990. This engine was standard for the base, SporTruck and Pioneer models. It was not available with automatic transmission. The 4.0 liter Power Tech engine was revised to provide a new output of 190 horsepower. It continued to be standard for the Eliminator and optional for other Comanches. New exterior stripe graphics were offered for the SporTruck, Pioneer and Eliminator. Other changes included the use of a more accurate electric speedometer, the replacement of the LCD clock display by a blue-green vacuum fluorescent clock, and the addition of "Check Engine" and "Maintenance Required" to the instrument cluster. A single board engine computer monitored the engine functions on all models. New underhood identification labels highlighted maintenance points. Optional 5-spoke aluminum wheels replaced the older 10 hole units. Double-bitted keys were now standard on al models. A new dark sand color along with two new fabrics — Jayne vinyl and Jamaica fabric was offered for the interior. Five new exterior colors were introduced: Silver star metallic, grey mist metallic, dark cordovan pearlcoat, black cherry pearlcoat and hunter green metallic. Retained from 1990 were bright white, black, Colorado red, midnight blue metallic, and spinmaker blue metallic. The standard upholstery for the bench seat in the base, SporTruck and for the Pioneer when fitted with optional bucket seats was the Jayne vinyl in charcoal, cordovan or dark sand. Standard for the Pioneer with bench seat and optional for the base and SporTruck with bench seat was Jamaica fabric in charcoal, cordovan or dark sand. Standard for the Eliminator were wingback bucket seats in a charcoal color luggage fabric.

I.D. DATA: The serial number was located on the left-hand hinge pillar. The V.I.N. had 17 symbols. The first entry, a number identified the country of manufacture (1=U.S., 2=Canada). The second entry, the letter J identified the manufacturer as Jeep. The next character, a letter identified the vehicle type (4=MPV, 6=Incomplete, 7=Truck). A letter followed identifying the GVWR (E=3001-4000 lb., F=4001-5000 lb., G=5001-6000 lb., H=6001-7000 lb.). The next entry, a letter identified the line (T=Comanche). The series identification, a number, followed (2=Base, 3=Pioneer, 6=Eliminator, 8=Sport). The body identification was via a letter (6=Two-door pickup). The ninth entry, a letter identified the engine (P=2.5 liter 4-cyl., S=4.0 liter 6-cyl.). A check digit followed. The 1991 model year wa identified by the letter M. The plant location followed (J=Brampton, L=Toledo #1, P=Toledo #2). The last six numbers were the sequential serial numbers.

Model Number	Body Type	Factory Price	GVW	Shipping Weight	Prod. Total
Comanche, Base 2.5 liter engine					
MJJL61	Pickup, 6 ft. box	$11,775[1]	4850	3081	5188[3]
MJJL62	Pickup, 7 ft. box	$12,484	4850[2]	3178	—

6 ft. box-13.1 in. wheelbase. 7 ft. box-119.6 in. wheelbase.

NOTE 1: Jeep revised the Comanche prices effective June 13, 1991 as follows: MJJL61: $11,953, MJJL62: $12,661.
NOTE 2: Longbed Big-Ton option-5550 lb.
NOTE 3: 1991 calendar year production, all models.

STANDARD ENGINE: Engine Type: OHV, In-line-4. Cast iron block and cylinder head. Bore x Stroke: 3.88 in. x 3.19 in. Lifters: Hydraulic. Number of main bearings-5. Fuel Induction: sequential multi-point electronic fuel injection. Compression Ratio: 9.2:1. Displacement: 150.45 cu. in. (2.46 liters). Horsepower: Net: 130 @ 5250 rpm. Torque: Net: 149 lb.-ft. @ 3250 rpm. Oil refill capacity: 5 qt. with filter change. Fuel Requirements: Unleaded.

OPTIONAL ENGINE: (Standard for Eliminator): Requires power steering and 5-spd. man. or auto. trans. Engine Type: OHV, In-line 6-cyl. Cast iron block and cylinder head. Bore x Stroke: 3.88 in. x 3.41 in. Lifters: Hydraulic. Fuel Induction: Electronic multi-port, sequential fuel injection. Compression Ratio: 8.8:1. Displacement: 241.6 cu. in. (3.966 liters). Horsepower: Net: 190 @ 4750 rpm. Torque: Net: 225 lb.-ft. @ 4000 rpm. Oil refill capacity: 5 qt. with filter change. Fuel Requirements: Unleaded.

CHASSIS FEATURES: Uniframe body construction.

SUSPENSION AND RUNNING GEAR: Front Suspension: Coil springs, live axle with leading links and track bar. Spring rate: 140 lb./in., link type 0.95 in. stabilizer bar. Rear Suspension: Hotchkiss, leaf-springs. Spring rates (at wheel): First stage: 130 lb/in., Second stage: 230 lb./in. Optional: Off-Road Package, Big-Ton Payload Package. Front Axle Type and Capacity: Dana model 30 Hypoid. Rear Axle Type and Capacity: Dana model 35c, semi-floating. Axle Ratios: Standard and available only for SporTruck models with 2.5 liter engine and 4-spd. man. trans.: 3.55:1; with 2.5 liter engine and 5-spd. man. trans.: 4.11:1 (standard for base, Pioneer and Eliminator, optional for SporTruck); optional for all models with 4.0 liter engine and auto. trans.: 3.55:1. Transfer Case: New Process 231 Command-Trac. Ratios: 2.72;1, 1.00:1. Brakes: Type: Hydraulic, front disc type vented cast iron rotor, rear cast iron drums. Dimensions: Front: 10.98 in. x 0.88 in.; rear: 10.0 in. x 1.75 in. Wheels: Full drop center, 5-stud. SporTruck shortbed and base longbed: 15 x 6 in. argent styled steel wheels with small black hub covers (bright trim rings optional for SporTruck only). Pioneer: 15 x 7 in. silver styled steel wheels with bright hub covers. Eliminator: 15 x 7 in. 10-hole aluminum with bright hub covers. Optional: Base longbed and SporTruck shortbed: 15 x 7 in. silver styled steel wheels with bright hub cover. Eliminator: 15 x 7 in. 10-hole aluminum with bright hub covers. Optional: Base longbed and SporTruck shortbed: 15 x 7 in. silver styled steel wheels with bright hub covers. All models except thos with P195 tires or Big-Ton Package and Eliminator: 15 x 7 in 5-spoke cast aluminum wheels. Tires: SporTruck shortbed and base longbed: P195/75R15 black sidewall, steel radial All-Weather. Pioneer: P205/75R15 black sidewall, steel radial All-Weather. Eliminator: P225/75R15 Goodyear Wrangler or Michelin OWL steel radial all-terrain. Optional: SporTruck shortbed and Base Longbbed: P205/75R15 black sidewall, steel radial All-Weather. All models except Eliminator: P215/75R15 Michelin or Goodyear Wrangler OWL steel radial All-Terrain. Requires 15 x 7 in. wheels, not available with 2.5 liter engine and 4-spd. manual trans., P225/75R15 Goodyear Wrangler OWL steel radial All-Terrain. Requires 15 x 7 in. wheels, not available with 2.5 liter engine and 4-spd. manual trans. Steering: Saginaw recirculating ball-type. Ratio: 24:1. Turns Lock-to-Lock: 4.8. Turning Circle: 41.3 ft. Optional: Saginaw ratio power recirculating ball-type.Ratio: 14:1. Turns Lock-to-Lock: 3.5. Standard Transmission: SporTruck shortbed: 4-speed, all synchromesh manual with floor shift. Not available with 4.0 liter engine. Ratios: Transmission ratios: 3.93:1, 2.33:1, 1.45:1, 1.00:1. Reverse: 4.74:1. Standard Transmission: Base longbed, Pioneer and Eliminator: 5-speed manual overdrive with floor shift. Ratios: A-S (4-cyl. models): 3.93:1, 2.33:1, 1.45:1, 1.00:1, 0.85:1. Reverse: 4.74:1. (6-cyl. models): 3.83:1, 2.33:1, 1.44:1, 1.00:1, 0.79:1. Reverse: 4.22:1. Optional: All models with 4.0 liter engine. 4-speed automatic overdrive column shift with lockup torque converter. The transmission shift lever is mounted on either steering column or the floor center console depending on the model and transer case. Ratios: 2.80:1, 1.53:1, 1.0:1, 0.71:1. Reverse: 2.39:1. Clutch: 4-cyl.: 9.1 in. 6-cyl.: 10.1 in. Single dry plate with hydraulic actuation. Optional: None.

VEHICLE DIMENSIONS: Wheelbase: 112.9/119.4 in. Overall Length: 184.5 in (with rear step bumper)/199.3 in (with rear step bumper), 194.0 in. (without rear step bumper). Front/Rear Tread: 57.0 in/57.0 in. 58.0 in/58.0 in when equipped with 15 x 7 in. wheels (standard for Pioneer and Eliminator). Overall Height: 64.7 in. Width: 71.7 in. Front/Rear Overhang: 112.9 in. wheelbase: 27.5 in/38.8 in. 119.4 in. wheel base: 27.5 in/47.1 in. Tailgate: Width and Height: 52.3 in. x 16.4 in. Approach/Departure Degrees: 112.9 in wheelbase: 41.7/31.5. 119.4 in. wheelbase: 41.5/26.1.

Ground Clearance:

	Front Axle: Shortbed	Longbed
P195 tires:	7.7 in.	7.6 in.
P205 tires:	7.9 in.	7.9 in.
P215 tires:	8.3 in.	8.3 in.
P225 tires:	8.5 in.	8.5 in.
	Rear Axle: Shortbed	Longbed
P195 tires:	7.5 in.	7.5 in.
P205 tires:	7.8 in.	7.8 in.
P215 tires:	8.2 in.	8.2 in.
P225 tires:	8.4 in.	8.4 in.

Running ground clearance: 9.4 in. Load space: Shortbed: 73.7 in. x 60.0 in. x 43.8 in. Longbed: 88.5 in. x 60.0 in. x 43.8 in. Maximum capacity (Volume Index): 38.6 cu. ft. (shortbed); 46.4 cu. ft. (longbed). Front headroom: 39.4 in. Front legroom: 43.0 in. Front shoulder room: 55.3 in. Front hip room: 55.3 in.

CAPACITIES: Fuel Tank: 18.0 gal. (112.9 in. wheelbase), 23.5 gal. (119 in. wheelbase).

ACCOMMODATIONS: Seating Capacity: Three (bench seat), two with bucket seats.

INSTRUMENTATION: Speedomoter, fuel gauge, warning lights for alternator, oil pressure, engine coolant temperature, seat belts, check engine, maintenance required and parking brake.

OPTIONS AND PRICES: Metallic paint: $173. Bench seat with Jamaica fabric and headrests: $84. Recliner vinyl bench seats: $144. 4.0 liter engine (requires power steering): $612. 5-spd. manual trans. (includes Command-Trac, standard on Longbed with 4.0 liter engine): $201. Automatic overdrive transmission (includes Command-Trac, requires 6-cyl. engine): $1002 (shortbed), $801 (longbed and all Pioneer). Rear Trak-Lok differential: $285. California emission system: $124. Pioneer Group: $1635 (shortbed), $1138 (longbed). Eliminator Decor Group: $3452. Air conditioning: $836. Passenger floor carpeting: $58. Cigarette lighter: $28. Console with armrest: $142. Speed control: $230. Heavy-Duty Alternator Battery Group: $135, $78 (with air conditioning). Extra-Quiet Insulation Package: $106. Gauge Group: $158. Light Group: $147. Left and right side remote mirrors: $77. Power steering (standard on longbed, required with air conditioning or 6-cyl. engine or automatic transmission): $296. AM/FM E.T. stereo radio: $312. AM/FM cassette E.T. stereo radio $512 (with Dolby system), $201 (with digital display and 4-speakers). Skid Plate Group: $144. Sliding rear window: $119. Rear step bumper (black): $135. Off-Road Suspension Package: $970 (base), $822 (Pioneer). Big-Ton Package: $754 (base), $577 (Pioneer). Tilt steering wheel: $132. P205/75R15 black radial All-Weather tires: $46. P215/75R15 OWL radial All-Terrain (requires 15 x 7 in. wheels: $359 (base), $313 (Pioneer). Front door vent windows: $91. Bright wheel trim rings: $65. Styled steel wheels: $103, $129 (with 5-spoke styled steel wheels). Five-spoke aluminum wheels: $348 (base), $245 (Pioneer). Ten-hole aluminum wheels: $432 (base), $329 (Pioneer). Intermittent windshield wipers: $61.

HISTORICAL FOOTNOTES: Jeep reported that the typical Comanche buyer had a medium age of 35, and a median income of $35,000. Sixty percent were married and 86 percent were male.

1992 COMANCHE

Limited changes were made in the Comanche for 1992. They consisted of a new radio with a clock function, a Sport model with new tape treatment that replaced the SporTruck model, and a detachable double cupholder that was standard with the full length center console.

1992 Jeep Comanche Eliminator

I.D. DATA: The serial number was located on the left-hand hinge pillar. The V.I.N. had 17 symbols. The first entry, a number identified the country of manufacture (1=U.S., 2=Canada). The second entry, the letter J identified the manufacturer as Jeep. The next character, a letter identified the vehicle type (4=MPV, 6=Incomplete, 7=Truck). A letter followed identifying the GVWR (E=3001-4000 lb., F=4001-5000 lb., G=5001-6000 lb., H=6001-7000 lb.). The next entry, a letter identified the Line (T=Comanche). The Series identification, a number, followed (2=Base, 3=Pioneer, 6=Eliminator, 8=Sport). The Body identification was via a letter (6=Two-door pickup). The ninth entry, a letter identified the engine (P=2.5 liter 4-cyl., S=4.0 liter 6-cyl.). A check digit followed. The 1991 model year was identified by the letter N. The plant location followed (J=Brampton, L=Toledo #1, P=Toledo #2). The last six numbers were the sequential serial numbers.

Model Number	Body Type	Factory Price	GVW	Shipping Weight	Prod. Total
Comanche, Base 2.5 liter engine					
MJJL61	Pickup, 6 ft. box	$12,246	4850	3081	3142[2]
MJJL62	Pickup, 7 ft. box	$12,977	4850[1]	3178	—

NOTE 1: Big-Ton 5550 lb. GVW optional.
NOTE 2: 1992 model year sales to June, 1992.

STANDARD ENGINE: Engine Type: OHV, In-line-4. Cast iron block and cylinder head. Bore x Stroke: 3.88 in. x 3.19 in. Lifters: Hydraulic. Number of main bearings-5. Fuel Induction: sequential multi-point electronic fuel injection. Compression Ratio: 9.2:1. Displacement: 150.45 cu. in. (2.46 liters). Horsepower: Net: 130 @ 5250 rpm. Torque: Net: 149 lb.-ft. @ 3250 rpm. Oil refill capacity: 5 qt. with filter change. Fuel Requirements: Unleaded.

OPTIONAL ENGINE: (Standard for Eliminator). Requires power steering and 5-spd. man. or auto. trans. Engine Type: OHV, In-line 6-cyl. Cast iron block and cylinder head. Bore x Stroke: 3.88 in. x 3.41 in. Lifters: Hydraulic. Fuel Induction: Electronic multi-port, sequential fuel injection. Compression Ratio: 8.8:1. Displacement: 241.6 cu. in. (3.966 liters). Horsepower: Net: 190 @ 4750 rpm. Torque: Net: 225 lb.-ft. @ 4000 rpm. Oil refill capacity: 5 qt. with filter change. Fuel Requirements: Unleaded.

CHASSIS FEATURES: Uniframe body construction.

SUSPENSION AND RUNNING GEAR: Front Suspension: Coil springs, live axle with leading links and track bar. Spring rate: 140 lb./in., link type 0.95 in. stabilizer bar. Rear Suspension: Hotchkiss, leaf-springs. Spring rates (at wheel): First stage: 130 lb/in., Second stage: 230 lb./in. Optional: Off-Road Package, Big-Ton Payload Package. Front Axle Type and Capacity: Dana model 30 Hypoid. Rear Axle Type and Capacity: Dana model 35c, semi-floating. Axle Ratios: Standard and available only for SporTruck models with 2.5 liter engine and 4-spd. man. trans.: 3.55:1; with 2.5 liter engine and 5-spd. man. trans.: 4.11:1 (standard for base, Pioneer and Eliminator, optional for SporTruck); optional for all models with 4.0 liter engine and auto. trans.: 3.55:1. Transfer Case: New Process 231 Command-Trac. Ratios: 2.72;1, 1.00:1. Brakes: Type: Hydraulic, front disc type vented cast iron rotor, rear cast iron drums. Dimensions: Front: 10.98 in. x 0.88 in.; rear: 10.0 in. x 1.75 in. Wheels: Full drop center, 5-stud. SporTruck shortbed and base longbed: 15 x 6 in. argent styled steel wheels with small black hub covers (bright trim rings optional for SporTruck only). Pioneer: 15 x 7 in. silver styled steel wheels with bright hub covers. Eliminator: 15 x 7 in. 10-hole aluminum with bright hub covers. Optional: Base longbed and SporTruck shortbed: 15 x 7 in. silver styled steel wheels with bright hub covers. All models except those with P195 tires or Big-Ton Package and Eliminator: 15 x 7 in. 5-spoke cast aluminum wheels. Tires: SporTruck shortbed and base longbed: P195/75R15 black sidewall, steel radial All-Weather. Pioneer: P205/75R15 black sidewall, steel radial All-Weather. Eliminator: P225/75R15 Goodyear Wrangler or Michelin OWL steel radial all-terrain. Optional: SporTruck shortbed and base longbed: P205/75R15 black sidewall, steel radial All-Weather. All models except Eliminator: P215/75R15 Michelin or Goodyear Wrangler OWL steel radial All-Terrain. Requires 15 x 7 in. wheels, not available with 2.5 liter engine and 4-spd. manual trans., P225/75R15 Goodyear Wrangler OWL steel radial All-Terrain. Requires 15 x 7 in. wheels, not available with 2.5 liter engine and 4-spd. manual trans. Steering: Saginaw recirculating ball-type. Ratio: 24:1. Turns Lock-to-Lock: 4.8. Turning Circle: 41.3 ft. Optional: Saginaw ratio power recirculating ball-type. Ratio: 14:1. Turns Lock-to-Lock: 3.5. Standard Transmission: SporTruck shortbed: 4-speed, all-synchromesh manual with floor shift. Not available with 4.0 liter engine. Ratios: Transmission ratios: 3.93:1, 2.33:1, 1.45:1, 1.00:1. Reverse: 4.74:1. Standard Transmission: Base longbed, Pioneer and Eliminator: 5-speed manual overdrive with floor shift. Ratios: A-S (4-cyl. models): 3.93:1, 2.33:1, 1.45:1, 1.00:1, 0.85:1. Reverse: 4.74:1. (6-cyl. models): 3.83:1, 2.33:1, 1.44:1, 1.00:1, 0.79:1. Reverse: 4.22:1. Optional: All models with 4.0 liter engine. 4-speed automatic overdrive column shift with lockup torque converter. The transmission shift lever is mounted on either the steering column or the floor center console depending on the model and transfer case. Ratios: 2.80:1, 1.53:1, 1.0:1. 0.71:1. Reverse: 2.39:1. Clutch: 4-cyl.: 9.1 in. 6-cyl.: 10.1 in. Single dry plate with hydraulic actuation. Optional: None.

VEHICLE DIMENSIONS: Wheelbase: 112.9/119.4 in. Overall Length: 184.5 in. (with rear step bumper), 179.3 in. (without rear step bumper)/199.3 in. (with rear step bumper),194.0 in. (without rear step bumper). Front/Rear Tread: 57.0 in./57.0 in. 58.0 in./58.0 in. when equipped with 15 x 7 in. wheels (standard for Pioneer and Eliminator). Overall Height: 64.7 in. Width: 71.7 in. Front/Rear Overhang: 112.9 in. wheelbase: 27.5 in./38.8 in. 119.4 in. wheelbase: 27.5 in./47.1 in. Tailgate: Width and Height: 52.3 in. x 16.4 in. Approach/Departure Degrees: 112.9 in. wheelbase: 41.7/31.5. 119.4 in. wheelbase: 41.5/26.1.

Ground Clearance:

	Front Axle: Shortbed	Longbed
P195 tires:	7.7 in.	7.6 in.
P205 tires:	7.9 in.	7.9 in.
P215 tires:	8.3 in.	8.3 in.
P225 tires:	8.5 in.	8.5 in.

	Rear Axle: Shortbed	Longbed
P195 tires:	7.5 in.	7.5 in.
P205 tires:	7.8 in.	7.8 in.
P215 tires:	8.2 in.	8.2 in.
P225 tires:	8.4 in.	8.4 in.

Running ground clearance: 9.4 in. Load space: Shortbed: 73.7 in. x 60.0 in. x 43.8 in. Longbed: 88.5 in. x 60.0 in. x 43.8 in. Maximum capacity (Volume Index): 38.6 cu. ft. (shortbed); 46.4 cu. ft. (longbed). Front headroom: 39.4 in. Front legroom: 43.0 in. Front shoulder room: 55.3 in. Front hip room: 55.3 in.

CAPACITIES: Fuel Tank: 18.0 gal. (112.9 in. wheelbase), 23.5 gal. (119 in. wheelbase).

ACCOMMODATIONS: Seating Capacity: Three (bench seat), two with bucket seats.

INSTRUMENTATION: Speedometer, fuel gauge, warning lights for alternator, oil pressure, engine coolant temperature, seat belts, Check Engine, Maintenance Required and parking brake.

OPTIONS: Pioneer Trim Package. Eliminator Trim Package. 4.0 liter 6-cyl. engine. Requires power steering and 5-speed manual or auto. trans. Air conditioning. Heavy-duty 58-475 cold crank battery (requires Heavy-Duty Alternator and Battery Group). Cruise control. Requires intermittent windshield wipers. Heavy-Duty Alternator and Battery Group. Includes 74 amp alternator with 2.5 liter engine; 100 amp with 4.0 liter engine, 58-475 cold crank battery. Off-Road Package. Includes front and rear high-pressure gas shock absorbers, 15 x 7 in. silver styled steel wheels, P225/75R15 Goodyear Wrangler OWL radial tires, full-size spare, Skid Plate Group, front tow hooks, heavy-duty radiator, auxiliary electric fan (on 4.0 liter engine), auxiliary transmission air cooler (on 4.0 liter engine with auto. trans.). Requires power steering and Heavy-Duty Alternator and Battery Group; not available with 2.5 liter engine and 4-spd. man. trans. or Big-Ton Payload Package. Variable ratio power steering (SporTruck and Base only). Skid Plate Package. Includes transfer case, fuel tank and front suspension skid plates. Big-Ton Payload Package. Available for longbed models only. Includes 2205 lb. heavy-duty rear axle (Dana 44), 15 x 7 in. silver styled steel wheels, full-size wheels, heavy-duty front and rear springs and shock absorbers, and P225/75R15 tires (not available with 2.5 liter engine and 4-speed man. or auto. trans.). Trac-Lok limited slip rear axle. Requires 4.0 liter engine and full-size spare tire. Trailer Towing Packages. 5-speed man. trans. 4-spd. overdrive auto. trans. Electric windshield wipers with intermittent feature. Dual exterior manual remote control mirrors. Metallic paint. Black rear step bumper with black end caps (for base and SporTruck models). Sliding rear window (standard for Eliminator). Front door, swing-out design vent windows. AM/FM electronically tuned stereo radio with 4 dual-cone speakers (standard for Pioneer and Eliminator). AM/FM electronically tuned stereo radio with Dolby system and cassette tape player and 4 dual-cone speakers. Full console with armrest storage box. Requires bucket seats and floorshift transmission. Not available for base models. Extra-Quiet Insulation Package. Not available for base models. Includes Amberlite padding on cab back, underhood insulation, and additional sound-deadening material. Color-keyed carpeting (for base and Sport models). Instrument panel cluster. Includes tachometer, voltmeter, oil pressure and engine coolant temperature gauges, low-fuel indicator light, trip odometer, and digital clock. Not available with automatic trans. column shift. Cigarette lighter (Sport models). Light Group. Includes ashtray light, cargo box light, courtesy lights, retractable underhood work light, headlights-on warning buzzer, visor mirror light and Sentinel headlamp switch. Jamaica fabric bench seat (base and Sport models). Recliner wingback bucket seats with adjustable headrest in Jamaica fabric (for Pioneer only). Tilt steering column requires intermittent windshield wipers.

HISTORICAL FOOTNOTES: The Comanche had the longest warranty in its class — a 7/70 extended powertrain warranty. In June, 1992, Chrysler announced it would drop the Comanche at the end of the 1992 model year. Total sales to that point had been 164,458.

OLDSMOBILE BRAVADA
1991-1993

1991 BRAVADA

Oldsmobile's entry into the four-wheel drive market, the Bravada, is admittedly an effort to help a once prosperous GM division return to a position of strong sales. This reality aside, the Bravada represents a major effort by GM and Oldsmobile to provide up-scale buyers with a sophisticated four-wheel drive vehicle.

The Oldsmobile Bravada, while based upon the Chevrolet Blazer, was a 4x4 vehicle with its own high level of trim and performance features. Exterior identification was provided by a front end with a two-piece grille with thin vertical inserts. Narrow fog lights were integrated into the front air dam. Only a four-door version was offered. The Bravada's powertrain combined the 4.3 liter Vortex engine and Smartrak, a system consisting of full-time all-wheel drive and full-time four-wheel anti-lock braking. A four-speed automatic transmission was standard. Additional standard equipment included the following: Limited slip differential, viscous clutch with internal differential, power steering, aluminum wheels, rooftop luggage carrier with adjustable crossbar, remote lock controls, composite halogen headlights, gold metallic body side accent stripes, exterior dual power mirrors, pulse windshield wipers, tailgate wiper/washer, air conditioning, cruise control, reclining front bucket seats, folding rear bench seat with center armrest, side/rear window defoggers, Rallye instrument cluster, day/night rearview mirror with built-in compass and reading lamps, AM/FM stereo with Seek-Scan, auto-reverse cassette tape player with music search, graphic equalizer and digital clock; leather-wrapped steering wheel, tilt-wheel steering, flo-thru ventilation, power windows, inside power tailgate lock release, swing-up rear window with gas struts, Soft-Ray tinted windows (deep tint in rear), front and rear lap/shoulder safety belts, outboard positions plus center passenger lap belt; assist handles for all passenger seating positions, carpeted floor and lower door panels, front and rear carpeted floor mats, protective rear cargo mat, console with cupholders and dual 12-volt electrical accessory outlets, 15 in. aluminum styled wheels, and a heavy-duty, high capacity battery. Available exterior colors were white, dark red, dark blue metallic, medium gray metallic and black.

1991 Oldsmobile Bravada

I.D. DATA: The vehicle identification number was located on a V.I.N. plate attached to the driver's side door body latch post. The V.I.N. consisted of 17 elements.

Body Type	Factory Price	GVW	Shipping Weight	Prod. Total
Oldsmobile Bravada				
Sports Utility	$23,795	5100	4,000	14,440

STANDARD ENGINE: Engine Type: OHV, V-6. Bore x Stroke: 4.00 in. x 3.48 in. Lifters: Hydraulic. Fuel Induction: Electronic fuel injection. Compression Ratio: 9.3:1. Displacement: 262 cu. in. (4.3 liters). Horsepower: Net: 160 @ 4000 rpm. Torque: Net: 230 lb.-ft. @ 2800 rpm. Oil refill capacity: 5 qt. with filter change. Fuel Requirements: Unleaded.

CHASSIS FEATURES: Frame: Unitized body on full-frame chassis. Front Suspension: Independent with upper and lower control arms, high pressure Bilstein gas shock absorbers, torsion bars and anti-roll bar. Rear Suspension: Semi-elliptical leaf springs and high pressure Bilstein gas shock absorbers. Axle ratio: 3.42:1. Brakes: Type: Power, hydraulic. Front: Discs. Rear: Drums. Wheels: 15 x 7.0 in. Cast aluminum. Tires: P235/75R15. Steering: Integral power steering. Ratio: 17.5:1. Turning Circle: 37.1 ft. Transmission: 4-speed overdrive automatic. Ratios: 3.06, 1.62, 1.00, 0.70:1. Transfer Case: Borg Warner, model 2030N-M, chain-driven full time, single speed.

VEHICLE DIMENSIONS: Wheelbase: 107 in. Overall Length: 178.9 in. Front/Rear Tread: 55.6 in./54.1 in. Overall Height: 65.5 in. Width: 65.2 in. Ground clearance: 7.7 in. (at exhaust). Front headroom: 39.1 in. Rear headroom: 38.8 in. Front legroom: 42.5 in. Rear legroom: 36.5 in. Front shoulder room: 54.2 in. Rear shoulder room: 55.6 in. Cargo area: With rear seat folded down: 68.6 in. x 38.4 in. x 35.0 in. With rear seat raised: 35.5 in. x 38.4 in. x 35.0 in. Cargo capacity: With rear seat folded down: 74.3 cu. ft. With rear seat raised: 35.2 cu. ft.

CAPACITIES: Fuel Tank: 20.0 gal. Engine coolant system capacity: 11.9 qt.

ACCOMMODATIONS: Seating Capacity: 5 passenger.

INSTRUMENTATION: 0-100 mph speedometer, 99,999.9 mile odometer, trip odometer, gauges for fuel level, voltmeter and engine coolant temperature. Anti-lock brake monitor light.

OPTIONS: Electronic instrument panel cluster. Cold Climate Package. Leather seating areas. Heavy-Duty Towing Package. Mud and Snow tires.

HISTORICAL FOOTNOTES: The Bravada was the first four-wheel drive vehicle offered by Oldsmobile.

1992 BRAVADA

New for 1992 was an optional high performance version of the Vortex V-6 that developed 200 horsepower. Exterior colors for 1992 were white, bright red, dark red, dark blue metallic, medium gray metallic and black.

Whatever your destination, the Bravada is intelligently engineered to get you there.

1992 Oldsmobile Bravada

I.D. DATA: The vehicle identification number was located on a V.I.N. plate attached to the driver's side door body latch post. The V.I.N. consisted of 17 elements.

Body Type	Factory Price	GVW	Shipping Weight	Prod. Total
Oldsmobile Bravada				
Sports Utility	$24,855	5100	4,000	—

STANDARD ENGINE: Engine Type: OHV, V-6. Bore x Stroke: 4.00 in. x 3.48 in. Lifters: Hydraulic. Fuel Induction: Electronic fuel injection. Compression Ratio: 9.3:1. Displacement: 262 cu. in. (4.3 liters). Horsepower: Net: 160 @ 4000 rpm. Torque: Net: 230 lb.-ft. @ 2800 rpm. Oil refill capacity: 5 qt. with filter change. Fuel Requirements: Unleaded.

OPTIONAL ENGINE: Engine Type: OHV, V-6. Bore x Stroke: 4.00 in. x 3.48 in. Lifters: Hydraulic. Fuel Induction: Electronic fuel injection. Compression Ratio: 9.3:1. Displacement: 262 cu. in. (4.3 liters). Horsepower: Net: 200 @ 4500 rpm. Torque: Net: 260 lb.-ft. @ 3600 rpm. Oil refill capacity: 5 qt. with filter change. Fuel Requirements: Unleaded.

CHASSIS FEATURES: Frame: Unitized body on full-frame chassis. Front Suspension: Independent with upper and lower control arms, high pressure Bilstein gas shock absorbers, torsion bars and anti-roll bar. Rear Suspension: Semi-elliptical leaf springs and high pressure Bilstein gas shock absorbers. Axle ratio: 3.42:1. Brakes: Type: Power, hydraulic. Front: Discs; Rear: Drums. Wheels: 15 x 7.0 in. Cast aluminum. Tires: P235/75R15. Steering: Integral power steering. Ratio: 17.5:1. Turning Circle: 37.1 ft. Transmission: 4-speed overdrive automatic. Transfer Case: Borg Warner, model 4472, chain-driven full time, single speed.

VEHICLE DIMENSIONS: Wheelbase: 107 in. Overall Length: 178.9 in. Front/Rear Tread: 55.6 in./54.1 in. Overall Height: 65.5 in. Width: 65.2 in. Ground clearance: 7.7 in. (at exhaust). Front headroom: 39.1 in. Rear headroom: 38.8 in. Front legroom: 42.5 in. Rear legroom: 36.5 in. Front shoulder room: 54.2 in. Rear shoulder room: 55.6 in. Cargo area: With rear seat folded down: 68.6 in. x 38.4 in. x 35.0 in. With rear seat raised: 35.5 in. x 38.4 in. x 35.0 in. Cargo capacity: With rear seat folded down: 74.3 cu. ft. With rear seat raised: 35.2 cu. ft.

CAPACITIES: Fuel Tank: 20.0 gal. Engine coolant system capacity: 11.9 qt.

ACCOMMODATIONS: Seating Capacity: 5 passenger.

INSTRUMENTATION: 0-100 mph speedometer, 99,999.9 mile odometer, trip odometer, gauges for fuel level, voltmeter and engine coolant temperature. Anti-lock brake monitor light.

OPTIONS: Electronic instrument panel cluster. Exterior spare tire carrier. Engine block heater. Leather seating areas. Heavy-Duty Towing Package. Mud and Snow tires.

HISTORICAL FOOTNOTES: Oldsmobile reported that the Bravada was "designed to provide the rugged performance characteristics of a truck along with the ride and comforts of a luxury sedan."

1993 BRAVADA

The 200 horsepower L35 central port electronic fuel injection V-6 was standard for the 1993 Bravada. Features of this engine included Vortex II cylinder heads, dual-tuned aluminum intake manifold, counter-rotating balance shaft, linear EGR control, roller-type hydraulic valve lifters, and single serpentine belt accessory drive. Backing up the L35 V-6 was a new 4L60-E Hydra-Matic transmission. This was the fifth electronically-controlled automatic engineered by GM's powertrain division and the second for trucks. Four shift solenoids were governed by a powertrain control module. The 4L60-E had four-speeds forward and an electronically controlled lockup torque converter.

Refinements for 1993 included a package of powertrain brace rods that reduced driveline vibration above 1700 rpm. An electronic fuel shut-off insured that vehicle speed would not exceed the tire's maximum velocity rating. New shock absorber calibrations provided an improved ride. Dual-note horns were now used. Solar-Ray windshield and front door glass provided a cooler interior and a diminished work load for the air conditioner. The tailgate handle was larger for easier operation. A new Gold Package option provided the exterior with special gold and black aluminum wheels and gold-toned nameplates. Interior changes included a new overhead console with an exterior temperature thermometer and a compass. The driver's seat now had a 6-way power adjuster. Power lumbar adjusters were standard on both front bucket seats. New dual action sun visors had extender panels. The cargo hold had two new coat hooks and an optional convenience net. For 1993 a new interior blue color was offered.

1993 Oldsmobile Bravada

I.D. DATA: The vehicle identification number was located on a V.I.N. plate attached to the driver's side door body latch post. The V.I.N. consisted of 17 elements.

Body Type	Factory Price	GVW	Shipping Weight	Prod. Total
Oldsmobile Bravada				
Sports Utility	$N.A.	5100	4,002	—

STANDARD ENGINE: Engine Type: OHV, V-6. Bore x Stroke: 4.00 in. x 3.48 in. Lifters: Hydraulic. Fuel Induction: Electronic fuel injection. Compression Ratio: 9.3:1. Displacement: 262 cu. in. (4.3 liters). Horsepower: Net: 200 @ 4500 rpm. Torque: Net: 260 lb.-ft. @ 3600 rpm. Oil refill capacity: 5 qt. with filter change. Fuel Requirements: Unleaded.

CHASSIS FEATURES: Frame: Unitized body on full-frame chassis. Front Suspension: Independent with upper and lower control arms, high pressure Bilstein gas shock absorbers, torsion bars and anti-roll bar. Rear Suspension: Semi-elliptical leaf springs and high pressure Bilstein gas shock absorbers. Axle ratio: 3.42:1. Optional: 3.73:1. Brakes: Type: Power, hydraulic. Front: Discs. Rear: Drums. Wheels: 15 x 7.0 in. Cast aluminum. Tires: P235/75R15 All-Season radial blackwall. Steering: Integral power steering. Ratio: 17.5:1. Turning Circle: 37.1 ft. Transmission: 4-speed overdrive automatic. Ratios: 3.06, 1.62, 1.00, 0.70:1. Transfer Case: Borg Warner, model 4472, chain-driven full time, single speed.

VEHICLE DIMENSIONS: Wheelbase: 107 in. Overall Length: 178.9 in. Front/Rear Tread: 55.6 in./54.1 in. Overall Height: 65.5 in. Width: 65.2 in. Ground clearance: 7.7 in. (at exhaust). Front headroom: 39.1 in. Rear headroom: 38.8 in. Front legroom: 42.5 in. Rear legroom: 36.5 in. Front shoulder room: 54.2 in. Rear shoulder room: 55.6 in. Cargo area: With rear seat folded down: 68.6 in. x 38.4 in. x 35.0 in. With rear seat raised: 35.5 in. x 38.4 in. x 35.0 in. Cargo capacity: With rear seat folded down: 74.3 cu. ft. With rear seat raised: 35.2 cu. ft.

CAPACITIES: Fuel Tank: 20.0 gal. Engine coolant system capacity: 11.9 qt.

ACCOMMODATIONS: Seating Capacity: 5 passenger.

INSTRUMENTATION: 0-100 mph speedometer, 99,999.9 mile odometer, trip odometer, gauges for fuel level, voltmeter and engine coolant temperature. Anti-lock brake monitor light.

OPTIONS: Electronic instrument panel cluster. Exterior spare tire carrier. Engine block heater. Gold Package. Convenience net. Leather seating areas. Heavy-Duty Towing Package. Mud and Snow tires.

HISTORICAL FOOTNOTES Oldsmobile reported that "with two model years under its belt, Bravada is gaining a strong reputation in the sport utility segment."

PONTIAC
1988-1990

1988 6000 STE AWD

Pontiac's short-lived venture into the four-wheel drive market belied its long tenure as a major player in the American automobile industry. Debuting just after the demise of the AMC Eagle, the four-wheel drive Pontiac STE appeared tailor-made for a market that AMC's new owner, Chrysler, apparently found of little interest. Unfortunately, the All-Wheel-Drive Pontiac, like the AWD Ford Tempo, failed to generate sufficient interest to warrant develop of second generation models.

During the 1988 model year Pontiac introduced a full-time All-Wheel Drive (AWD) option for the 6000 STE sedan. The AWD system used Pontiac's all-new 3.1 liter multi-port fuel injected V-6 and a THM-125C 3-speed automatic transmission. The transaxle case was modified to accept the bolt-on AWD transfer case and allowed the use of equal-length half shafts. In order to accommodate the tailshaft and locate the power steering rack, a redesigned cross member was adapted to the front cradle which was otherwise of conventional layout. Except for the outersteering links and a revised 27mm (3mm larger than the standard STE bar) stabilizer bar, the remaining front suspension components were the same as those used on the standard front-wheel drive STE models. The floor pan was widened at both front and rear for clearance. A two-piece, equal-length prop shaft with a center bearing carrier was used. The standard catalytic converter was rotated from a horizontal position so as not to interfere with the driveline components. The STE AWD Pontiac used an all-new independent rear-drive module, fitted with insulating rubber pads, and a stamped steel carrier mounted to reinforced underbody frame rails. Housed within the carrier was a Saginaw Division-produced front axle unit that was also used on General Motors T series trucks. An additional housing piece was also utilized to provide for the usage of equal-length axle shafts which essentially eliminated torque steer tendencies.

The AWD independent rear suspension used a transversely-mounted composite single-leaf spring similar to that used on the 1988 Pontiac Grand Prix. It was mounted in the rear cradle and protected by the lateral suspension pads. Pads on each end of the spring free-rode on the lower A-arm. The hub knuckles attached to the lower arms and to the MacPherson struts. A 16mm stabilizer bar was incorporated into the rear suspension system. Minor relocation of the fuel tank to clear the rear driveline had, as a by-product, an increased capacity of 18 gals. vs. 15.7 gals. as found on the standard 6000 and STE. The AWD STE had four-wheel disc brakes and an anti-lock brake system. It used new P195/70R15 Eagle GT+4 All-Season tires.

Torque distribution was 60/40 front-to-rear, which was also the same ratio for the weight of the vehicle at rest and with two people aboard. A hydro-mechanical differential system locking system could be activated by the driver by means of a rocker switch on the center console. This improved traction under adverse road conditions. By locking the front and rear systems together, drive power was assured to at least one front and one rear wheel. Standard equipment of the STE AWD included acoustical insulation, black-finished door window frames, carpeted lower door panels, center high-mounted stop lamp, color-keyed seat belts, compact spare tire, composite headlights, cut-pile carpeting, left and right side door map pockets, map pockets on front seat backs, fluidic windshield washer system with two nozzles, front air dam, glove compartment with lock, GM computer command control, inside hood release, warm red instrument panel lighting, locking fuel-filler door, lower accent two-tone paint, accessory kit (flare, rain coat, first-aid kit), anti-lock power four-wheel disc brakes, controlled cycle windshield wipers, deluxe carpeted floor mats, driver information center, dual-outlet Sport exhaust, electrically-operated sideview mirrors, electronic ride control, General Motors Protection Plan, illuminated visor vanity mirror, power door locks, Delco ETR touch control, AM/FM stereo radio with cassette tape player and anti-theft Delco-Loc, rear seat with fold-down center armrest, four-spoke leather-wrapped steering wheel with integral radio controls, tilt steering wheel, STE aluminum wheels and windshield sunshade with pockets.

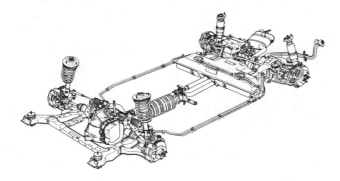

Drivetrain for 1988 Pontiac STE All-Wheel Drive

I.D. DATA: The V.I.N. plate was located on the top left hand surface of the instrument panel. The V.I.N. contained 17 symbols.

Body Type	Factory Price	GVW	Shipping Weight	Prod. Total
Pontiac 6000 STE AWD				
4-door Sedan	$21,879	N.A.	3381	—

STANDARD ENGINE: Engine Type: OHV 60 degree V-6, cast iron cylinder block, aluminum cylinder head. Bore x Stroke: 3.50 in. x 3.31 in. Lifters: Hydraulic. Fuel Induction: Multi-port fuel injection. Compression Ratio: 8.8:1. Displacement: 191 cu. in. (3.1 liters). Horsepower: 135 @ 4800 rpm. Torque: 180 lb.-ft. @ 3600 rpm. Fuel Requirements: 87 octane unleaded.

OPTIONAL ENGINE: None.

CHASSIS FEATURES: Unitized body/chassis.

SUSPENSION AND RUNNING GEAR: Front Suspension: Independent, MacPherson struts, 27mm stabilizer bar. Rear Suspension: Independent, composite single-leaf, transversely-mounted spring, lateral suspension arms, 16mm stabilizer bar and MacPherson struts. Final Drive Ratio: 3.18:1. Transfer Case: 1.0:1. Brakes: Type: Hydraulic power assisted. Front: Vented discs. Rear: Solid discs. Dimensions: Front: 10.2 in. dia. Rear: 10.3 in. dia. Total swept area: 270.6 sq. in. Wheels: 15 x 6.0 in. Aluminum. Optional: None. Tires: P195/70R15 Eagle GT+4 steel belted radial. Steering: Power assisted, rack and pinion. Ratio: 16:1. Turns Lock-to-Lock: 3.05. Turning Circle: 38.5 ft. Optional: None. Transmission: THM-125C 3-speed automatic. Transmission Ratios: 2.92, 1.56, 1.00:1. Stall torque ratio: 1.95:1. Optional: None.

VEHICLE DIMENSIONS: Wheelbase: 104.9 in. Overall Length: 188.8 in. Overall Height: 53.7 in. Width: 72.0 in. Front headroom: 38.6 in. Front legroom: 42.1 in. Front shoulder room: 56.2 in. Front hip room: 52.7 in. Rear headroom: 38.0 in. Rear legroom: 35.8 in. Rear shoulder room: 56.2 in. Rear hip room: 53.0 in.

CAPACITIES: Fuel Tank: 18.0 gal.

ACCOMMODATIONS: Seating Capacity: 5 passenger. Optional: None.

OPTIONS: Power glass sun roof (includes dual reading lamps).

HISTORICAL FOOTNOTES: Among GM products the STE's all-wheel drive system was exclusive to Pontiac and represented the first mass-production usage of a high-torque, transverse-mounted V-6 engine and automatic transmission combination in a full-time, all-wheel drive vehicle.

1989 6000 STE AWD

Pontiac repositioned its AWD model for 1989 making it standard equipment for the top-of-the-6000-line STE model. The latest STE had a new rear roof line as well as a standard rear deck spoiler. The side body STE identification was both reformatted and relocated for 1989. From its 1988 location just ahead of the front wheel cutouts it was moved to a position just ahead of the front door's leading edge. Also identifying the latest STE were its new side body trim and upswept rear body "aero-skirt." The front end was distinguished by new rectangular fog lights mounted in the front air dam and standard high intensity halogen headlights. The STE steering wheel was of a new 4-spoke. leather-wrapped "ergonomic" design. Both the front and rear suspension of the STE AWD were redesigned for 1989. A smaller, 22mm (instead of 27mm) stabilizer bar was used at the front. Replacing the 16mm stabilizer bar of 1988 was a 22mm unit. The standard equipment content of the STE was extensive, consisting of cruise control, rear window defogger, power door locks, left and right side door map pockets, dual horns, Rallye gauges including tachometer, accessory kit (containing flare, raincoat, first-aid kit), anti-lock brake system, controlled-cycle windshield wipers, deluxe carpeted floor mats, driver information center, dual-outlet sport exhaust, electronically operated side view mirrors, electronic ride control, fog lamps, locking fuel-filler door, right side illuminated vanity visor mirror, Delco ETR AM/FM stereo radio with Seek-Scan, cassette tape player, and anti-theft Delco-Lok, rear seat with fold-down center armrest, specific STE four-spoke, leather-wrapped tilt steering wheel with duplicate integral radio controls and specific 15 x 6 in. aluminum STE wheels.

1990 Pontiac 6000 SE AWD

I.D. DATA: The V.I.N. plate was located on the top left hand surface of the instrument panel. The V.I.N. contained 17 symbols.

Body Type	Fact. Price	GVW	Shipping Weight	Prod. Total
Pontiac 6000 STE AWD				
Model AH5				
4-dr. Sedan	$22,599	—	3381	—

STANDARD ENGINE: Engine Type: OHV 60 degree V-6, cast iron cylinder block, aluminum cylinder head. Bore x Stroke: 3.50 in. x 3.31 in. Lifters: Hydraulic. Fuel Induction: Multi-port fuel injection. Compression Ratio: 8.8:1. Displacement: 191 cu. in. (3.1 liters). Horsepower: 140 @ 4800 rpm. Torque: 180 lb.-ft. @ 3200 rpm. Fuel Requirements: 87 octane unleaded.

OPTIONAL ENGINE: None.

CHASSIS FEATURES: Unitized body/chassis.

SUSPENSION AND RUNNING GEAR: Front Suspension: Independent, MacPherson struts, 27mm stabilizer bar. Rear Suspension: Independent, composite single-leaf, transversely-mounted spring, lateral suspension arms, 16mm stabilizer bar and MacPherson struts. Final Drive Ratio: 3.18:1. Transfer Case: 1.0:1. Brakes: Type: Hydraulic power assisted. Front: Vented discs. Rear: Solid discs. Dimensions: Front: 10.2 in. dia. Rear: 10.3 in. dia. Total swept area: 270.6 sq. in. Wheels: 15 x 6.0 in. Aluminum. Optional: None. Tires: P195/70R15 Eagle GT+4 steel belted radial. Steering: Power assisted, rack and pinion. Ratio: 16:1. Turns Lock-to-Lock: 3.05. Turning Circle: 38.5 ft. Optional: None. Transmission: THM-125C 3-speed automatic. Transmission Ratios: 2.92, 1.56, 1.00:1. Stall torque ratio: 1.95:1. Optional: None.

VEHICLE DIMENSIONS: Wheelbase: 104.9 in. Overall Length: 188.8 in. Overall Height: 53.7 in. Width: 72.0 in. Front headroom: 38.6 in. Front legroom: 42.1 in. Front shoulder room: 56.2 in. Front hip room: 52.7 in. Rear headroom: 38.0 in. Rear legroom: 35.8 in. Rear shoulder room: 56.2 in. Rear hip room: 53.0 in.

CAPACITIES: Fuel Tank: 18.0 gal.

ACCOMMODATIONS: Seating Capacity: 5 passenger. Optional: None.

INSTRUMENTATION: Speedometer, tachometer trip odometer, gauges for voltmeter, engine coolant temperature and oil pressure.

OPTIONS: California emissions system (NB2). Front license bracket (VK3). Delco ETR AM/FM stereo radio with Seek-Scan, auto reverse cassette tape player with search and replay feature, graphic equalizer, digital clock and steering wheel controls (U1A).

HISTORICAL FOOTNOTES: The top Pontiac dealer in 1989 had sales totalling $233 million.

1990 6000 STE AWD

For 1990 the all-wheel drive system was an option (RPO F73) for the S/E sedan. It included ABS anti-lock disc brakes at all four wheels, P195/70R15 Goodyear Eagle GT+4 tire and electronic ride control. The 6000 S/E AWD remained unique among the 6000 models in having all-independent suspension. THe AWD was offered in two exterior colors: Medium red metallic or dark blue metallic. Identification of the AWD, which had the same ride height as a two-wheel drive 6000 S/E, was aided by its gold accents and emblems, S/E AWD badges, unique rear deck spoiler and specific fog lights. As the top 6000 series model, the S/E AWD had a long list of standard equipment features including power windows, power door locks, cruise control, controlled-cycle windshield wipers, AM/FM stereo radio with cassette tape player, front seat back map pockets, and body color aero moldings.

I.D. DATA: The V.I.N. plate was located on the top left hand surface of the instrument panel. The V.I.N. contained 17 symbols.

Body Type	Fact. Price	GVW	Shipping Weight	Prod. Total
Model J69				
4-dr. Sedan	$16,909	—	3381	—
RPO F73	$3,635	—	—	—

STANDARD ENGINE: Engine Type: OHV 60 degree V-6, cast iron cylinder block, aluminum cylinder head. Bore x Stroke: 3.50 in. x 3.31 in. Lifters: Hydraulic. Fuel Induction: Multi-port fuel injection. Compression Ratio: 8.8:1. Displacement: 191 cu. in. (3.1 liters). Horsepower: 140 @ 4800 rpm. Torque: 180 lb.-ft. @ 3200 rpm. Fuel Requirements: 87 octane unleaded.

OPTIONAL ENGINE: None.

CHASSIS FEATURES: Unitized body/chassis.

SUSPENSION AND RUNNING GEAR: Front Suspension: Independent, MacPherson struts, 27mm stabilizer bar. Rear Suspension: Independent, composite single-leaf, transversely-mounted spring, lateral suspension arms, 16mm stabilizer bar and MacPherson struts. Final Drive Ratio: 3.18:1. Transfer Case: 1.0:1. Brakes: Type: Hydraulic power assisted. Front: Vented discs. Rear: Solid discs. Dimensions: Front: 10.2 in. dia. Rear: 10.3 in. dia. Total swept area: 270.6 sq. in. Wheels: 15 x 6.0 in. Aluminum. Optional: None. Tires: P195/70R15 Eagle GT+4 steel belted radial. Steering: Power assisted, rack and pinion. Ratio: 16:1. Turns Lock-to-Lock: 3.05. Turning Circle: 38.5 ft. Optional: None. Transmission: THM-125C 3-speed automatic. Transmission Ratios: 2.92, 1.56, 1.00:1. Stall torque ratio: 1.95:1. Optional: None.

VEHICLE DIMENSIONS: Wheelbase: 104.9 in. Overall Length: 188.8 in. Overall Height: 53.7 in. Width: 72.0 in. Front headroom: 38.6 in. Front legroom: 42.1 in. Front shoulder room: 56.2 in. Front hip room: 52.7 in. Rear headroom: 38.0 in. Rear legroom: 35.8 in. Rear shoulder room: 56.2 in. Rear hip room: 53.0 in.

CAPACITIES: Fuel Tank: 15.7 gal.

ACCOMMODATIONS: Seating Capacity: 5 passenger. Optional: None.

INSTRUMENTATION: Speedometer, tachometer trip odometer, gauges for voltmeter, engine coolant temperature and oil pressure.

OPTIONS AND PRICES: California emissions system (NB2). Front license bracket (VK3). Delco ETR AM/FM stereo radio with Seek-Scan, auto reverse cassette tape player with search and replay feature, graphic equalizer, digital clock and steering wheel controls (U1A): $501.

HISTORICAL FOOTNOTES: This was the final year Pontiac offered the 6000 sedan with four-wheel drive.

PRICING

CHEVROLET

1957

Series 3100	6	5	4	3	2	1
PU	450	1500	2500	5000	8800	12,600
Panel Dly	350	900	1550	3100	6000	8600
Suburban	450	1500	2500	5000	8800	12,600
Series 3200						
PU (LBx)	350	900	1550	3100	6000	8600
Series 3600						
PU	350	850	1500	2900	5700	8200
Cus Cab PU	350	950	1600	3200	6050	8700
Platform	350	750	1250	2400	5050	7200
Platform & Stake	350	750	1300	2500	5300	7600
Series 3800						
PU	350	900	1550	3000	5850	8400
Panel Dly	450	1000	1600	3300	6250	8900
Platform	350	725	1200	2350	4800	6800
Platform & Stake	350	750	1250	2350	5000	7100

NOTE: 1955-up prices based on top of the line models. Deduct 20 percent for 6-cyl.

1958

Series 3100	6	5	4	3	2	1
Stepside PU	350	900	1550	3100	6000	8600
Fleetside PU	450	1000	1650	3400	6350	9100
Panel	350	800	1450	2750	5600	8000
Suburban	350	850	1500	2950	5800	8300
Series 3200						
Stepside (LBx)	350	900	1550	3100	6000	8600
Fleetside (LBx)	450	950	1600	3250	6150	8800
Series 3600						
Stepside PU	350	900	1550	3000	5850	8400
Fleetside PU	350	950	1600	3200	6050	8700
Stake	350	750	1300	2400	5200	7400
Series 3800						
PU	450	950	1600	3250	6150	8800
Panel	350	750	1300	2500	5300	7600
Stake	350	750	1300	2400	5200	7400

NOTE: 1955-up prices based on top of the line models. Deduct 20 percent for 6-cyl.

1959

Series 3100	6	5	4	3	2	1
Stepside PU	350	900	1550	3100	6000	8600
Fleetside PU	450	1000	1650	3400	6350	9100
Panel	350	800	1450	2750	5600	8000
Suburban	350	850	1500	2900	5700	8200
Series 3200						
Stepside PU	350	900	1550	3100	6000	8600
Fleetside PU	450	950	1600	3250	6150	8800
Series 3600						
Stepside PU	350	850	1500	2900	5700	8200
Fleetside PU	350	900	1550	3000	5850	8400
Series 3800						
PU	350	750	1350	2650	5450	7800
Panel	350	750	1300	2400	5200	7400
Stake	350	750	1250	2400	5100	7300

NOTE: 1955-up prices based on top of the line models. Deduct 20 percent for 6-cyl.

1960

Series C14 - (1/2-Ton)	6	5	4	3	2	1
Stepside PU	350	900	1550	3100	6000	8600
Fleetside PU	450	1000	1650	3400	6350	9100
Panel	350	800	1450	2750	5600	8000
Suburban	350	850	1500	2950	5800	8300
Series C15 "Long Box" - (1/2-Ton)						
Stepside PU	350	800	1450	2750	5600	8000
Fleetside PU	350	850	1500	2900	5700	8200
Series C25 - (3/4-Ton)						
Stepside PU	350	900	1550	3100	6000	8600
Fleetside PU	450	950	1600	3250	6150	8800
8-ft. Stake	350	750	1250	2350	5000	7100
Series C36 - (1-Ton)						
Stepside	350	750	1350	2650	5450	7800
Panel	350	750	1300	2400	5200	7400
9-ft. Stake	350	750	1250	2400	5100	7300

NOTE: 1955-up prices based on top of the line models. Deduct 20 percent for 6-cyl.

1961

Fleetside Pickups	6	5	4	3	2	1
K10 PU (SBx)	450	1100	1800	3700	6700	9600
K10 PU (LBx)	450	1100	1700	3650	6650	9500
K20 PU (LBx)	350	850	1500	2800	5650	8100
Stepside Pickups						
K10 PU (SBx)	450	1100	1700	3650	6650	9500
K10 PU (LBx)	450	1050	1700	3600	6600	9400
K20 PU (LBx)	350	800	1450	2750	5600	8000
Panel/Suburban/Stake-Bed						
K10 Panel	200	550	900	2100	3700	5300
K10 Suburban	350	700	1150	2300	4550	6500
K20 Panel	200	600	950	2200	3900	5600
K20 Suburban	350	725	1200	2350	4850	6900
K20 Stake	200	650	1000	2200	4100	5900
K30 Panel (10-1/2 ft. bed)	200	650	1000	2200	4150	5900
K30 Stake	200	650	1000	2200	4150	5900

NOTE: 1955-up prices based on top of the line models. 10 is the 1/2-Ton series, 20 is 3/4-Ton series, 30 is the 1-Ton series. Short box has 6-1/2 ft. bed. Long box has 8-ft. bed.

1962

Fleetside Pickups	6	5	4	3	2	1
K10 PU (SBx)	450	1100	1800	3700	6700	9600

1961 (continued)

	6	5	4	3	2	1
K10 PU (LBx)	450	1100	1700	3650	6650	9500
K20 PU (LBx)	350	850	1500	2800	5650	8100
Stepside Pickups						
K10 PU (SBx)	450	1100	1700	3650	6650	9500
K10 PU (LBx)	450	1050	1700	3600	6600	9400
K20 PU (LBx)	350	800	1450	2750	5600	8000
Panel/Suburban/Stake-Bed						
K10 Panel	200	550	900	2150	3800	5400
K10 Suburban	350	725	1150	2300	4700	6700
K20 Stake	200	600	950	2200	3900	5600
K30 Panel (10-1/2 ft. bed)	200	600	1000	2200	4000	5700
K30 Stake	200	650	1000	2200	4150	5900

NOTE: 1955-up prices based on top of the line models. 10 is 1/2-Ton series. 20 is 3/4-Ton series. 30 is 1-Ton series. Short box has 6-1/2 ft. bed. Long box has 8-ft. bed.

1963

Fleetside Pickups	6	5	4	3	2	1
K10 PU (SBx)	450	1100	1800	3700	6700	9600
K10 PU (LBx)	450	1100	1650	3650	6650	9500
K20 PU (LBx)	350	850	1500	2800	5650	8100
Stepside Pickups						
K10 PU (SBx)	450	1100	1700	3650	6650	9500
K10 PU (LBx)	450	1050	1700	3600	6600	9400
K20 PU (LBx)	350	800	1450	2750	5600	8000
Panel/Suburban/Stake-Bed						
K10 Panel	200	550	900	2150	3800	5400
K10 Suburban	350	725	1150	2300	4700	6700
K20 Stake	200	650	1000	2200	4100	5800
K30 Panel (10-1/2 ft. bed)	200	650	1000	2200	4150	5900
K30 Stake	200	650	1000	2200	4150	5900

NOTE: 1955-up prices based on top of the line models. 10 is 1/2-Ton series. 20 is 3/4-Ton series. 30 is the 1-Ton series. Short box has 6-1/2 ft. bed. Long box has 8-ft. bed.

1964

Fleetside Pickups	6	5	4	3	2	1
K10 PU (SBx)	450	1100	1800	3700	6700	9600
K10 PU (LBx)	450	1100	1700	3650	6650	9500
K20 PU (LBx)	350	850	1500	2800	5650	8100
Stepside Pickups						
K10 PU (SBx)	450	1100	1700	3650	6650	9500
K10 PU (LBx)	450	1050	1700	3600	6600	9400
Panel/Suburban/Stake-Bed						
K10 Panel	200	550	900	2150	3800	5400
K10 Suburban	350	725	1150	2300	4700	6700
K20 Stake	200	600	950	2200	3900	5600
K30 Panel (10-1/2 ft. bed)	200	600	1000	2200	4000	5700
K30 Stake	200	600	1000	2200	4000	5700

NOTE: 1955-up prices based on top of the line models. 10 is 1/2-Ton series. 20 is 3/4-Ton series. 30 is 1-Ton series. Short box has 6-1/2 ft. bed. Long box has 8-ft. bed.

1965

Fleetside Pickups	6	5	4	3	2	1
K10 PU (SBx)	450	1100	1800	3700	6700	9600
K10 PU (LBx)	450	1100	1700	3650	6650	9500
K20 PU (LBx)	350	850	1500	2800	5650	8100
Stepside Pickups						
K10 PU (SBx)	450	1100	1700	3650	6650	9500
K10 PU (LBx)	450	1050	1700	3600	6600	9400
K30 PU (8-1/2 ft. bed)	350	850	1500	2950	5800	8300
Panel/Suburban/Stake-Bed						
K10 Panel	200	550	900	2150	3800	5400
K10 Suburban	350	725	1150	2300	4700	6700
K20 Stake	200	600	950	2200	3900	5600
K30 Panel	200	650	1000	2200	4150	5900
K30 Stake	200	650	1000	2200	4150	5900

NOTE: 1955-up prices based on top of the line models. C is conventional drive model. K is 4-wheel drive (4WD) 10 is 1/2-Ton series. 20 is 3/4-Ton series. 30 is 1-Ton series. Short box has 6-1/2 ft. bed. Long box has 8-ft. bed.

1966

Fleetside Pickup Series	6	5	4	3	2	1
K14 PU (SBx)	450	1100	1800	3700	6700	9600
K15 PU (LBx)	450	1100	1700	3650	6650	9500
K25 PU (LBx)	350	850	1500	2800	5650	8100
Stepside Pickup Series						
K14 PU (SBx)	450	1100	1700	3650	6650	9500
K15 PU (LBx)	450	1050	1700	3600	6600	9400
K25 PU (LBx)	350	800	1450	2750	5600	8000
Panel/Suburban/Stake-Bed						
K14 Panel	125	250	700	1150	2450	3500
K14 Suburban	150	450	800	1800	3300	4800
K25 Stake	150	300	700	1250	2600	3700
K36 Panel	150	350	750	1350	2800	4000
K36 Stake	150	350	750	1350	2800	4000

NOTE: 14 is 1/2-Ton Short box (6-1/2 ft. bed). 15 is 1/2-Ton Long box (8-ft. bed). 25 is 3/4-Ton. 36 is 1-Ton.

1967

Fleetside Pickups	6	5	4	3	2	1
K10 PU (SBx)	450	1150	1800	3800	6800	9700
K10 PU (LBx)	450	1100	1700	3650	6650	9500
K20 PU (LBx)	350	950	1600	3200	6050	8700
K20 PU (8-1/2 ft. bed)	350	900	1550	3100	6000	8600
K30 PU (8-1/2 ft. bed)	350	850	1500	2900	5700	8200
Stepside Pickups						
K20 PU (LBx)	350	900	1550	3100	6000	8600
Panel/Suburbans/Stakes						
K10 Panel	200	600	950	2200	3900	5600
K10 Suburban	350	725	1200	2350	4850	6900
K20 Stake	350	700	1100	2300	4500	6400
K20 Panel	200	650	1050	2250	4200	6000
K20 Suburban	350	725	1150	2300	4700	6700
K30 Stake	350	700	1150	2300	4600	6600

NOTE: 1955-up prices based on top of the line models. 10 is 1/2-Ton series. 20 is 3/4-Ton series. 30 is 1-Ton series. Short box has 6-1/2 ft. bed. Long box has 8-ft. bed.

1968

	6	5	4	3	2	1
Fleetside PU						
K10 PU (SBx)	450	1150	1800	3800	6800	9700
K10 PU (LBx)	450	1100	1700	3650	6650	9500
K20 PU (LBx)	350	950	1600	3200	6050	8700
K20 PU (8-1/2 ft. bed)	350	900	1550	3100	6000	8600
Stepside Pickups						
K10 PU (SBx)	450	1100	1700	3650	6650	9500
K10 PU (LBx)	450	1050	1700	3600	6600	9400
K20 PU (LBx)	350	900	1550	3100	6000	8600
Panel/Suburban/Stake-Bed						
K10 Panel	200	600	950	2200	3900	5600
K10 Suburban	350	725	1200	2350	4850	6900
K20 Stake	200	650	1050	2250	4200	6000

NOTE: 1955-up prices based on top of the line models.

1969

	6	5	4	3	2	1
Blazer Series						
Blazer	400	1300	2200	4400	7700	11,000
Fleetside Series						
K10 PU (SBx)	400	1200	2000	3950	7000	10,000
K10 PU (LBx)	450	1150	1900	3850	6850	9800
K20 PU (LBx)	450	1100	1800	3700	6700	9600
K20 PU (long horn)	450	1150	1800	3800	6800	9700
Stepside Series						
K10 PU (SBx)	450	1150	1900	3900	6900	9900
K10 PU (LBx)	450	1150	1800	3800	6800	9700
K20 PU (LBx)	450	1150	1800	3800	6800	9700
K20 PU (long horn)	450	1100	1800	3700	6700	9600
Panel/Suburban Series - (115" wb)						
K10 Panel	350	750	1300	2500	5300	7600
K10 Suburban	450	1000	1650	3400	6350	9100
Panel/Suburban Series - (127" wb)						
K20 Panel	350	750	1300	2400	5200	7400
K20 Suburban	350	850	1500	2800	5650	8100

NOTE: 1955-up prices based on top of the line models. 10 is 1/2-Ton series. 20 is 3/4-Ton series. 30 is 1-Ton series. Short box pickup has 6-1/2 ft. bed and 115" wb. Long box pickup has 8-ft. bed and 127" wb. Long horn pickup has 8-1/2 to 9-ft. bed and 133" wb.

1970

	6	5	4	3	2	1
Blazer Series K10						
Blazer	400	1200	2000	3950	7000	10,000
Fleetside Pickups						
K10 PU (SBx)	400	1200	2000	3950	7000	10,000
K10 PU (LBx)	450	1150	1900	3850	6850	9800
K20 PU (LBx)	450	1100	1800	3700	6700	9600
K20 PU (long horn)	450	1150	1800	3800	6800	9700
Stepside Pickups						
K10 PU (SBx)	450	1150	1900	3900	6900	9900
K10 PU (LBx)	450	1150	1800	3800	6800	9700
K20 PU (LBx)	450	1150	1800	3800	6800	9700
Panel/Suburban Series - (115" wb)						
K10 Panel	200	650	1000	2200	4100	5800
K10 Suburban	350	750	1250	2400	5100	7300
Panel/Suburban Series - (127" wb)						
K20 Panel	200	600	950	2200	3900	5600
K20 Suburban	200	675	1100	2250	4400	6300
Series C30 - (133" wb)						
1-Ton Stake (9-ft. bed)	200	500	850	1900	3500	5000

10 is 1/2-Ton series. 20 is 3/4-Ton series. 30 is 1-Ton series. Short box pickup has 6-1/2 ft. bed and 115" wb. Long box pickup has 8-ft. bed and 127" wb. Long horn pickup has 8-1/2 to 9-ft. bed and 133" wb.

1971

	6	5	4	3	2	1
Blazer Series K10						
Blazer	400	1250	2100	4200	7400	10,500
Fleetside Pickups						
K10 PU (SBx)	400	1250	2100	4200	7400	10,500
K10 PU (LBx)	400	1250	2050	4100	7200	10,300
K20 PU (LBx)	450	1100	1800	3700	6700	9600
K20 PU (long horn)	450	1150	1800	3800	6800	9700
K30 PU (long horn)	350	850	1500	2900	5700	8200
Stepside Pickups						
K10 PU (SBx)	450	1100	1800	3700	6700	9600
K10 PU (LBx)	450	1050	1700	3550	6500	9300
K20 PU (LBx)	450	1050	1650	3500	6400	9200
K30 PU (long horn)	450	1100	1700	3650	6650	9500
Panels/Suburbans/Stakes						
K10 Suburban	450	1100	1800	3700	6700	9600
K20 Suburban	350	850	1500	2900	5700	8200
K20 Stake	350	750	1250	2400	5050	7200
K30 Stake	350	750	1250	2400	5050	7200

NOTE: 1955-up prices based on top of the line models.
See previous notes for 1969-1970 explaining "model" information.

1972

	6	5	4	3	2	1
Blazer						
K10 Blazer	400	1300	2200	4400	7700	11,000
Fleetside Pickups						
K10 PU (SBx)	400	1300	2150	4300	7600	10,800
K10 PU (LBx)	400	1250	2100	4200	7400	10,500
K20 PU (SBx)	450	1100	1800	3700	6700	9600
K20 PU (LBx)	450	1150	1800	3800	6800	9700
K30 PU (long horn)	350	850	1500	2900	5700	8200
Stepside Pickups						
K10 PU (SBx)	450	1150	1900	3850	6850	9800
K10 PU (LBx)	450	1100	1700	3650	6650	9500
K10 PU (LBx)	450	1150	1900	3850	6850	9800
K20 PU (LBx)	450	1050	1700	3550	6500	9300
K30 PU (long horn)	450	1100	1700	3650	6650	9500
Suburban						
K10 Suburban	450	1100	1800	3700	6700	9600
K20 Suburban	350	850	1500	2900	5700	8200
Stake Bed						
K20 Stake	350	750	1250	2400	5050	7200
K30 Stake	350	750	1250	2400	5050	7200

NOTE: 1955-up prices based on top of the line models.

1973

	6	5	4	3	2	1
Blazer K10						
Blazer	350	900	1550	3050	5900	8500
K10 - (1/2-Ton)						
Stepside (SBx)	200	600	1000	2200	4000	5700
Stepside (LBx)	200	650	1000	2200	4100	5800
Fleetside (SBx)	200	650	1000	2200	4150	5900
Fleetside (LBx)	200	650	1050	2250	4200	6000
Suburban	200	650	1050	2250	4200	6000
K20 - (3/4-Ton)						
Stepside (LBx)	200	650	1000	2200	4100	5800
Fleetside (LBx)	200	650	1000	2200	4150	5900
6P (LBx)	200	600	950	2150	3850	5500
Suburban	200	675	1050	2250	4350	6200
K30 - (1-Ton)						
Stepside (LBx)	200	600	1000	2200	4000	5700
Fleetside (LBx)	200	650	1000	2200	4150	5900
6P (LBx)	200	600	950	2200	3900	5600

NOTE: 1955-up prices based on top of the line models.

1974

	6	5	4	3	2	1
Blazer K10						
Blazer	350	900	1550	3050	5900	8500
K10 - (1/2-Ton)						
Stepside (SBx)	200	600	1000	2200	4000	5700
Stepside (LBx)	200	650	1000	2200	4100	5800
Fleetside (SBx)	200	650	1000	2200	4150	5900
Fleetside (LBx)	200	650	1050	2250	4200	6000
Suburban	200	650	1050	2250	4200	6000
K20 - (3/4-Ton)						
Stepside (LBx)	200	650	1000	2200	4100	5800
Fleetside (LBx)	200	650	1000	2200	4150	5900
6P (LBx)	200	600	950	2150	3850	5500
Suburban	200	675	1050	2250	4350	6200
K30 - (1-Ton)						
Stepside (LBx)	200	600	1000	2200	4000	5700
Fleetside (LBx)	200	650	1000	2200	4150	5900
6P (LBx)	200	600	950	2200	3900	5600

NOTE: 1955-up prices based on top of the line models.

1975

	6	5	4	3	2	1
Blazer K10						
Blazer	350	900	1550	3050	5900	8500
K10 - (1/2-Ton)						
Stepside (SBx)	200	600	1000	2200	4000	5700
Stepside (LBx)	200	650	1000	2200	4100	5800
Fleetside (SBx)	200	650	1000	2200	4150	5900
Fleetside (LBx)	200	650	1050	2250	4200	6000
Suburban	200	650	1050	2250	4200	6000
K20 - (3/4-Ton)						
Stepside (LBx)	200	650	1000	2200	4100	5800
Fleetside (LBx)	200	650	1000	2200	4150	5900
6P (LBx)	200	600	950	2150	3850	5500
Suburban	200	675	1050	2250	4350	6200
K30 (1-Ton)						
Stepside (LBx)	200	600	1000	2200	4000	5700
Fleetside (LBx)	200	650	1000	2200	4150	5900
6P (LBx)	200	600	950	2200	3900	5600

NOTE: 1955-up prices based on top of the line models.

1976

	6	5	4	3	2	1
Blazer K10						
Blazer	350	750	1200	2350	4900	7000
K10 - (1/2-Ton)						
Stepside (SBx)	200	600	1000	2200	4000	5700
Stepside (LBx)	200	650	1000	2200	4100	5800
Fleetside (SBx)	200	650	1000	2200	4150	5900
Fleetside (LBx)	200	650	1050	2250	4200	6000
Suburban	200	650	1000	2200	4100	5800
K20 - (3/4-Ton)						
Stepside (LBx)	200	650	1000	2200	4100	5800
Fleetside (LBx)	200	650	1000	2200	4150	5900
6P (LBx)	200	600	950	2150	3850	5500
Suburban	200	650	1000	2200	4100	5800
K30 (1-Ton)						
Stepside (LBx)	200	600	1000	2200	4000	5700
Fleetside (LBx)	200	650	1000	2200	4150	5900
6P (LBx)	200	600	950	2200	3900	5600

NOTE: 1955-up prices based on top of the line models.

1977

	6	5	4	3	2	1
Blazer K10						
Blazer	350	725	1150	2300	4700	6700
K10 (1/2-Ton)						
Stepside (SBx)	200	500	850	1950	3600	5100
Stepside (LBx)	200	550	900	2000	3600	5200
Fleetside (SBx)	200	550	900	2000	3600	5200
Fleetside (LBx)	200	550	900	2100	3700	5300
Suburban	200	550	900	2150	3800	5400
K20 (3/4-Ton)						
Stepside PU	200	550	900	2150	3800	5400
Fleetside PU	200	600	950	2200	3900	5600
Bonus Cab PU	200	600	950	2150	3850	5500
Crew Cab PU	200	550	900	2150	3800	5400
Suburban	200	600	950	2200	3900	5600
K30 (1-Ton)						
Stepside PU	200	550	900	2150	3800	5400
Fleetside PU	200	600	950	2200	3900	5600
Bonus Cab PU	200	600	950	2150	3850	5500
Crew Cab PU	200	550	900	2150	3800	5400

NOTE: 1955-up prices based on top of the line models.

1978

	6	5	4	3	2	1
Blazer - K10 - (V-8)						
Blazer	350	725	1150	2300	4700	6700
K10 (1/2-Ton)						
Stepside (SBx)	200	500	850	1950	3600	5100
Stepside (LBx)	200	550	900	2000	3600	5200
Fleetside (SBx)	200	550	900	2000	3600	5200
Fleetside (LBx)	200	550	900	2100	3700	5300
Suburban	200	550	900	2150	3800	5400
K20 (3/4-Ton)						
Stepside PU	200	550	900	2150	3800	5400
Fleetside PU	200	600	950	2200	3900	5600
Bonus Cab PU	200	600	950	2150	3850	5500
Crew Cab PU	200	550	900	2150	3800	5400
Suburban	200	600	950	2200	3900	5600
K30 (1-Ton)						
Stepside PU	200	550	900	2150	3800	5400
Fleetside PU	200	600	950	2200	3900	5600
Bonus Cab PU	200	600	950	2150	3850	5500
Crew Cab PU	200	550	900	2150	3800	5400
"Big Dooley"	200	675	1050	2250	4300	6100

NOTE: 1955-up prices based on top of the line models.

1979

	6	5	4	3	2	1
LUV						
PU	125	200	600	1100	2200	3100
LBx	125	200	600	1100	2250	3200
Blazer - K10 - (V-8)						
Blazer	350	725	1150	2300	4700	6700
K10 - (V-8)						
Stepside (SBx)	200	500	850	1950	3600	5100
Stepside (LBx)	200	550	900	2000	3600	5200
Fleetside (SBx)	200	550	900	2000	3600	5200
Fleetside (LBx)	200	550	900	2100	3700	5300
Suburban	200	550	900	2150	3800	5400

	6	5	4	3	2	1
K20 - (V-8)						
Stepside PU	200	550	900	2150	3800	5400
Fleetside PU	200	600	950	2200	3900	5600
Bonus Cab PU	200	600	950	2150	3850	5500
Crew Cab PU	200	550	900	2150	3800	5400
Suburban	200	600	950	2200	3900	5600
K30 - (V-8)						
Stepside PU	200	550	900	2150	3800	5400
Fleetside PU	200	600	950	2200	3900	5600
Bonus Cab PU	200	600	950	2150	3850	5500
Crew Cab PU	200	550	900	2150	3800	5400
"Big Dooley"	200	675	1050	2250	4350	6200

NOTE: 1955-up prices based on top of the line models.

1980

	6	5	4	3	2	1
LUV						
PU	125	200	600	1100	2250	3200
LBx PU	125	200	600	1100	2300	3300
Blazer - K10						
Blazer	350	725	1200	2350	4800	6800
K10 - (1/2-Ton) - (117" or 131" wb)						
Stepside SBx PU	200	550	900	2000	3600	5200
Stepside LBx PU	200	550	900	2100	3700	5300
Fleetside SBx PU	200	550	900	2100	3700	5300
Fleetside LBx PU	200	550	900	2150	3800	5400
Suburban	200	600	950	2150	3850	5500
K20 - (3/4-Ton) - (131" or 164" wb)						
Stepside PU	200	600	950	2150	3850	5500
Fleetside PU	200	600	1000	2200	4000	5700
Bonus Cab PU	200	600	950	2200	3900	5600
Crew Cab PU	200	600	950	2150	3850	5500
Suburban	200	600	1000	2200	4000	5700
K30 - (1-Ton) - (131" or 164" wb)						
Stepside PU	200	550	900	2150	3800	5400
Fleetside PU	200	600	950	2200	3900	5600
Bonus Cab PU	200	600	950	2150	3850	5500
Crew Cab PU	200	550	900	2150	3800	5400
"Big Dooley	200	650	1000	2200	4150	5900

1981

	6	5	4	3	2	1
LUV - (1/2-Ton) - (104.3" or 117.9" wb)						
PU SBx	125	200	600	1100	2300	3300
PU LBx	125	250	700	1150	2400	3400
Blazer K10 - (1/2-Ton) - (106.5" wb)						
Blazer	350	750	1200	2350	4900	7000
K10 - (1/2-Ton) - (117" or 131" wb)						
Stepside PU SBx	200	550	900	2150	3800	5400
Stepside PU LBx	200	550	900	2100	3700	5300
Fleetside PU SBx	200	600	950	2150	3850	5500
Fleetside PU LBx	200	600	950	2200	3900	5600
Suburban	200	650	1000	2200	4100	5800
K20 - (3/4-Ton) - (131" or 164" wb)						
Stepside PU LBx	200	650	1000	2200	4150	5900
Fleetside PU LBx	200	650	1050	2250	4200	6000
Fleetside PU Bonus Cab LBx	200	675	1050	2250	4350	6200
Fleetside PU Crew Cab LBx	200	675	1050	2250	4300	6100
Suburban	350	700	1100	2300	4500	6400
K30 - (1-Ton) - (131" or 164" wb)						
Stepside PU LBx	200	650	1050	2250	4200	6000
Fleetside PU LBx	200	675	1050	2250	4300	6100
Fleetside PU Bonus Cab LBx	200	675	1050	2250	4350	6200
Fleetside PU Crew Cab LBx	200	675	1050	2250	4300	6100

1982

	6	5	4	3	2	1
LUV - (1/2-Ton) - (104.3" or 117.9" wb)						
PU SBx	100	125	500	950	1700	2400
PU LBx	100	150	450	1000	1750	2500
Blazer K10 - (1/2-Ton) - (106.5" wb)						
HdTp	200	650	1050	2250	4200	6000
K10 - (1/2-Ton) - (117" or 131" wb)						
Stepside PU SBx	150	400	750	1650	3150	4500
Fleetside PU SBx	150	450	750	1700	3200	4600
Fleetside PU LBx	150	400	750	1550	3050	4300
Suburban	200	500	850	1900	3500	5000
K20 - (3/4-Ton) - (131" or 164" wb)						
Stepside PU LBx	200	500	850	1850	3350	4900
Fleetside PU LBx	200	500	850	1900	3500	5000
Fleetside PU Bonus Cab LBx	200	550	900	2100	3700	5300
Fleetside PU Crew Cab LBx	200	500	850	1850	3350	4900
Suburban	200	600	950	2150	3850	5500
K30 - (1-Ton) - (131" or 164" wb)						
Stepside PU LBx	150	450	800	1800	3300	4800
Fleetside PU LBx	200	500	850	1850	3350	4900
Fleetside PU Bonus Cab LBx	200	550	900	2000	3600	5200
Fleetside PU Crew Cab LBx	200	500	850	1900	3500	5000

1983

	6	5	4	3	2	1
S10 - (1/2-Ton) - (100.5" wb)						
Blazer	150	400	750	1600	3100	4400
Blazer K10 - (1/2-Ton) - (106.5" wb)						
Blazer	200	650	1050	2250	4200	6000
S10 - (1/2-Ton) - (108" or 122" wb)						
Fleetside PU SBx	125	250	700	1150	2450	3500
Fleetside PU LBx	125	250	700	1150	2500	3600
Fleetside PU Ext Cab	150	300	700	1250	2650	3800
K10 - (1/2-Ton) - (117" or 131" wb)						
Stepside PU SBx	150	450	750	1700	3200	4600
Fleetside PU SBx	150	450	800	1750	3250	4700
Fleetside PU LBx	150	400	750	1600	3100	4400
Suburban	200	500	850	1950	3600	5100
K20 - (3/4-Ton) - (131" or 164" wb)						
Stepside PU LBx	200	500	850	1850	3350	4900
Fleetside PU LBx	200	500	850	1900	3500	5000
Fleetside PU Bonus Cab LBx	200	550	900	2100	3700	5300
Fleetside PU Crew Cab LBx	150	450	800	1800	3300	4800
Suburban	200	600	950	2150	3850	5500
K30 - (1-Ton) - (131" or 164" wb)						
Stepside PU LBx	150	450	800	1750	3250	4700
Fleetside PU LBx	150	450	800	1800	3300	4800
Fleetside PU Bonus Cab LBx	200	500	850	1900	3500	5000
Fleetside PU Crew Cab LBx	200	500	850	1850	3350	4900

1984

	6	5	4	3	2	1
S10 - (1/2-Ton) - (100.5" wb)						
Blazer	200	550	900	2000	3600	5200
K10 Blazer - (1/2-Ton) - (106.5" wb)						
Blazer	350	700	1150	2300	4600	6600
S10 - (1/2-Ton) - (108" or 118" wb)						
Fleetside PU SBx	150	350	750	1450	2900	4100
Fleetside PU LBx	150	350	750	1450	3000	4200
Fleetside PU Ext Cab	150	400	750	1600	3100	4400
K10 - (1/2-Ton) - (117" or 131" wb)						
Stepside PU SBx	200	550	900	2000	3600	5200
Stepside PU LBx	200	550	900	2100	3700	5300
Fleetside PU LBx	200	500	850	1950	3600	5100
Suburban	200	600	1000	2200	4000	5700
K20 - (3/4-Ton) - (131" or 164" wb)						
Stepside PU LBx	200	600	950	2150	3850	5500
Fleetside PU LBx	200	600	950	2200	3900	5600
Fleetside PU Bonus Cab LBx	200	650	1000	2200	4150	5900
Fleetside PU Crew Cab LBx	200	650	1000	2200	4100	5800
Suburban	200	675	1050	2250	4300	6100
K30 - (1-Ton) - (131" or 164" wb)						
Stepside PU LBX	200	550	900	2100	3700	5300
FLeetside PU LBx	200	550	900	2150	3800	5400
FLeetside PU Bonus Cab LBx	200	600	950	2150	3850	5500
Fleetside PU Crew Cab LBx	200	550	900	2150	3800	5400

1985

	6	5	4	3	2	1
S10 Blazer - (1/2-Ton) - (100.5" wb)						
Blazer	200	675	1050	2250	4350	6200
K10 Blazer - (1/2-Ton) - (106.5" wb)						
Blazer	350	750	1250	2400	5050	7200
S10 - (1/2-Ton) - (108.3" or 123" wb)						
Fleetside PU SBx	150	350	750	1350	2800	4000
Fleetside PU LBx	150	300	750	1350	2700	3900
Fleetside PU Ext Cab	150	400	750	1550	3050	4300
K10 - (1/2-Ton) - (117" or 131" wb)						
Stepside PU SBx	200	500	850	1850	3350	4900
Fleetside PU SBx	200	500	850	1900	3500	5000
Fleetside PU LBx	150	450	800	1800	3300	4800
Suburban	200	675	1050	2250	4300	6100
K20 - (3/4-Ton) - (131" or 164" wb)						
Stepside PU LBx	200	550	900	2100	3700	5300
Fleetside PU LBx	200	550	900	2150	3800	5400
Fleetside PU Bonus Cab LBx	200	650	1000	2200	4150	5900
Fleetside PU Crew Cab LBx	200	675	1050	2250	4300	6100
Suburban	350	700	1150	2300	4600	6600
K30 - (1-Ton) - (131" or 164" wb)						
Stepside PU LBx	200	550	900	2000	3600	5200
Fleetside PU LBx	200	550	900	2100	3700	5300
Fleetside PU Bonus Cab LBx	200	550	900	2100	3700	5300
Fleetside PU Crew Cab LBx	200	650	1050	2250	4200	6000

DODGE

1946

	6	5	4	3	2	1
Power Wag WDX - (1-Ton) - (126" wb)						
Chassis & Cab	200	650	1050	2250	4200	6000
PU	450	1000	1650	3350	6300	9000

1947

	6	5	4	3	2	1
Power-Wagon WDX - (1-Ton)						
PU	450	1000	1650	3350	6300	9000

1948-1949

	6	5	4	3	2	1
Series B-1-Power Wag - (1-Ton) - (126" wb)						
PU	450	1000	1650	3350	6300	9000

1950

	6	5	4	3	2	1
Series B-2-PW Power-Wagon - (1-Ton) - (126" wb)						
PU	450	1000	1650	3350	6300	9000

1951

	6	5	4	3	2	1
Series B-3-PW Power-Wagon - (1-Ton) - (126" wb)						
PU	450	1000	1650	3350	6300	9000

1952

	6	5	4	3	2	1
Series B-3-PW Power-Wagon - (1-Ton) - (126" wb)						
PU	450	1000	1650	3350	6300	9000

1953

	6	5	4	3	2	1
Series B-4-PW Power-Wagon - (1-Ton) - (126" wb)						
PU	450	1000	1650	3350	6300	9000

1954

	6	5	4	3	2	1
Series C-1-PW Power-Wagon - (1-Ton) - (126" wb)						
PU	350	800	1450	2750	5600	8000

NOTE: Add 15 percent for V-8 engine.

1955

	6	5	4	3	2	1
Series C-3-PW Power-Wag - (1-Ton) - (126" wb)						
PU	350	800	1450	2750	5600	8000

NOTE: Add 15 percent for V-8 engine.

1956

	6	5	4	3	2	1
Series C-4-PW Power-Wagon - (1-Ton) - (126" wb)						
PU	350	800	1450	2750	5600	8000

NOTE: Add 15 percent for V-8 engine.

1957

	6	5	4	3	2	1
Series K6-D100 - (1/2-Ton) - (108" wb)						
PU	350	700	1150	2300	4550	6500
Panel	200	650	1050	2250	4200	6000
6P Wag	200	675	1050	2250	4300	6100
8P Wag	200	675	1050	2250	4300	6100
Series K6-W100 - (1/2-Ton) - (116" wb)						
PU	350	700	1100	2300	4500	6400
Platform	200	550	900	2150	3800	5400
Stake	200	600	950	2150	3850	5500
Series K6-W200 - (3/4-Ton) - (116" wb)						
PU	200	675	1050	2250	4350	6200
Platform	200	550	900	2100	3700	5300
Stake	200	550	900	2150	3800	5400
Series K6-W300 - (1-Ton) - (126" wb)						
PU	350	750	1300	2450	5250	7500

NOTE: Add 10 percent for V-8 engine.

1958

	6	5	4	3	2	1
Series L6-W100 - (1/2-Ton) - (108" wb)						
PU	350	700	1150	2300	4550	6500
Twn Panel	200	650	1050	2250	4200	6000
6P Wag	200	675	1050	2250	4300	6100
8P Wag	200	675	1050	2250	4300	6100
Series L6-W100 - (1/2-Ton) - (116" wb)						
PU	350	700	1100	2300	4500	6400
Platform	200	550	900	2150	3800	5400
Stake	200	600	950	2150	3850	5500
Series L6-W200 - (3/4-Ton) - (116" wb)						
PU	200	675	1050	2250	4350	6200
Platform	200	550	900	2100	3700	5300
Stake	200	550	900	2150	3800	5400
Series L6-W300 - (1-Ton) - (129" wb)						
PU	200	650	1050	2250	4200	6000
Platform	200	500	850	1950	3600	5100
Stake	200	550	900	2000	3600	5200

	6	5	4	3	2	1
L6-W300M Power-Wagon - (1-Ton) - (126" wb)						
PU	350	750	1300	2450	5250	7500

NOTE: Add 10 percent for V-8 engine.

1959

	6	5	4	3	2	1
Series M6-W100 - (1/2-Ton) - (108" wb)						
Utiline PU	350	700	1150	2300	4550	6500
Twn Panel	200	650	1050	2250	4200	6000
6P Wag	200	675	1050	2250	4300	6100
8P Wag	200	675	1050	2250	4300	6100
Series M6-W100 - (1/2-Ton) - (116" wb)						
Utiline PU	350	700	1100	2300	4500	6400
Platform	200	550	900	2150	3800	5400
Stake	200	600	950	2150	3850	5500
Series M6-W200 - (3/4-Ton) - (116" wb)						
Utiline PU	200	675	1050	2250	4350	6200
Platform	200	550	900	2100	3700	5300
Stake	200	550	900	2150	3800	5400
Series M6-W300 - (1-Ton) - (129" wb)						
Utiline PU	200	650	1050	2250	4200	6000
Platform	200	500	850	1950	3600	5100
Stake	200	550	900	2000	3600	5200
Series M6-W300M Power-Wagon - (1-Ton) - (126" wb)						
PU	350	750	1300	2450	5250	7500

NOTE: Add 10 percent for V-8 engine.

1960

	6	5	4	3	2	1
Series P6-W100 - (1/2-Ton) - (108" wb)						
Utiline PU	350	700	1150	2300	4550	6500
Sweptline PU	350	725	1150	2300	4700	6700
Twn Panel	200	650	1050	2250	4200	6000
6P Wag	200	675	1050	2250	4300	6100
8P Wag	200	675	1050	2250	4300	6100
Series P6-W100 - (1/2-Ton) - (116" wb)						
Utiline PU	350	700	1100	2300	4500	6400
Sweptline PU	350	700	1150	2300	4600	6600
Platform	200	550	900	2150	3800	5400
Stake	200	600	950	2150	3850	5500
Series P6-W200 - (3/4-Ton) - (116" wb)						
Utiline PU	200	675	1050	2250	4350	6200
Sweptline PU	350	700	1100	2300	4500	6400
Platform	200	550	900	2100	3700	5300
Stake	200	550	900	2150	3800	5400
Series P6-W300 - (1-Ton) - (129" wb)						
Utiline PU	200	650	1050	2250	4200	6000
Sweptline PU	200	675	1050	2250	4350	6200
Platform	200	500	850	1950	3600	5100
Stake	200	550	900	2000	3600	5200
Series P6-WM300 Power-Wagon - (1-Ton) - (126" wb)						
Utiline PU	350	750	1300	2450	5250	7500

NOTE: Add 10 percent for V-8 engine.

1961

	6	5	4	3	2	1
Series R6-W100 - (1/2-Ton) - (114" wb)						
Utiline PU	200	650	1000	2200	4100	5800
Sweptline PU	200	600	1000	2200	4000	5700
Twn Panel	200	650	1000	2200	4150	5900
6P Wag	200	675	1050	2250	4350	6200
8P Wag	200	675	1050	2250	4350	6200
Series R6-W200 - (3/4-Ton) - (122" wb)						
Utiline PU	200	600	950	2150	3850	5500
Sweptline PU	200	600	1000	2200	4000	5700
Platform	200	500	850	1950	3600	5100
Stake	200	550	900	2000	3600	5200
Series R6-W200 - (1-Ton) - (133" wb)						
Utiline PU	200	550	900	2000	3600	5200
Platform	200	500	850	1850	3350	4900
Stake	200	500	850	1950	3600	5100
Series R6-WM300 - (1-Ton) - (126" wb)						
PU	350	900	1550	3050	5900	8500

NOTE: Add 10 percent for V-8 engine.

1962

	6	5	4	3	2	1
Series S6-W100 - (1/2-Ton) - (114" wb)						
Utiline PU	200	650	1000	2200	4100	5800
Sweptline PU	200	600	1000	2200	4000	5700
Twn Panel	200	650	1000	2200	4150	5900
6P Wag	200	675	1050	2250	4350	6200
8P Wag	200	675	1050	2250	4350	6200
Series S6-W200 - (3/4-Ton) - (122" wb)						
Utiline PU	200	600	950	2150	3850	5500
Sweptline PU	200	600	1000	2200	4000	5700
Platform	200	500	850	1950	3600	5100
Stake	200	550	900	2000	3600	5200
Series S6-W300 - (1-Ton) - (133" wb)						
Utiline PU	200	550	900	2000	3600	5200
Platform	200	500	850	1850	3350	4900
Stake	200	500	850	1950	3600	5100
S6-WM300 Power-Wagon - (1-Ton) - (126" wb)						
PU	350	900	1550	3050	5900	8500

NOTE: Add 10 percent for V-8 engine.

1963

	6	5	4	3	2	1
Series T6-W100 - (1/2-Ton) - (114" wb)						
Utiline PU	200	650	1000	2200	4100	5800
Sweptline PU	200	600	1000	2200	4000	5700
Twn Panel	200	650	1000	2200	4150	5900
6P Wag	200	675	1050	2250	4350	6200
8P Wag	200	675	1050	2250	4350	6200
Series T6-W200 - (3/4-Ton) - (122" wb)						
Utiline PU	200	600	950	2150	3850	5500
Sweptline PU	200	600	1000	2200	4000	5700
Platform	200	500	850	1950	3600	5100
Stake	200	550	900	2000	3600	5200
T6-W200 Crew Cab - (3/4-Ton) - (146" wb)						
Utiline PU	200	500	850	1900	3500	5000
Sweptline PU	200	500	850	1950	3600	5100
Series T6-W300 - (1-Ton) - (133" wb)						
Utiline PU	200	550	900	2000	3600	5200
Platform	200	500	850	1850	3350	4900
Stake	200	500	850	1950	3600	5100
T6-WM300 Power-Wagon - (1-Ton) - (126" wb)						
Utiline PU	350	900	1550	3050	5900	8500

NOTE: Add 10 percent for V-8 engine.

1964

	6	5	4	3	2	1
Series V6-W100 - (1/2-Ton) - (114" wb)						
Utiline PU	200	650	1000	2200	4100	5800
Sweptline PU	200	600	1000	2200	4000	5700
Twn Panel	200	650	1000	2200	4150	5900
6P Wag	200	675	1050	2250	4350	6200
8P Wag	200	675	1050	2250	4350	6200
Series V6-W200 - (3/4-Ton) - (122" wb)						
Utiline PU	200	600	950	2150	3850	5500
Sweptline PU	200	600	1000	2200	4000	5700
Platform	200	500	850	1950	3600	5100
Stake	200	550	900	2000	3600	5200
V6-W200 Crew Cab - (3/4-Ton) - (146" wb)						
Utiline PU	200	500	850	1900	3500	5000
Sweptline PU	200	500	850	1950	3600	5100
Series V6-W300 - (1-Ton) - (133" wb)						
Utiline PU	200	550	900	2000	3600	5200
Platform	200	500	850	1850	3350	4900
Stake	200	500	850	1950	3600	5100
V6-WM300 Power-Wagon - (1-Ton) - (126" wb)						
Utiline PU	350	900	1550	3050	5900	8500

NOTES: Add 10 percent for V-8 engine.
Add 4 percent for power winch.

1965

	6	5	4	3	2	1
Series A6-W100 - (1/2-Ton) - (114" wb)						
Utiline PU	200	650	1000	2200	4100	5800
Sweptline PU	200	600	1000	2200	4000	5700
Twn Panel	200	650	1000	2200	4150	5900
6P Wag	200	675	1050	2250	4350	6200
8P Wag	200	675	1050	2250	4350	6200
Series A6-W200 - (3/4-Ton) - (122" or 128" wb)						
Utiline PU	200	600	950	2150	3850	5500
Sweptline PU	200	600	1000	2200	4000	5700
Platform	200	500	850	1950	3600	5100
Stake	200	550	900	2000	3600	5200
A6-W200 Crew Cab - (3/4-Ton) - (146" wb)						
Utiline PU	200	500	850	1900	3500	5000
Sweptline PU	200	500	850	1950	3600	5100
Series A6-W300 - (1-Ton) - (133" wb)						
Utiline PU	200	550	900	2000	3600	5200
Platform	200	500	850	1850	3350	4900
Stake	200	500	850	1950	3600	5100
A6-WM300 Power-Wagon - (1-Ton) - (126" wb)						
Utiline PU	350	900	1550	3050	5900	8500

NOTES: Add 10 percent for V-8 engine.
Add 4 percent for power winch.

1966

	6	5	4	3	2	1
Series B6-W100 - (1/2-Ton) - (114" wb)						
Utiline PU	200	650	1000	2200	4100	5800
Sweptline PU	200	600	1000	2200	4000	5700
Twn Panel	200	650	1000	2200	4150	5900
6P Wag	200	675	1050	2250	4350	6200
8P Wag	200	675	1050	2250	4350	6200
Series B6-W200 - (3/4-Ton) - (122" or 128" wb)						
Utiline PU	200	600	950	2150	3850	5500
Sweptline PU	200	600	1000	2200	4000	5700
Platform	200	500	850	1950	3600	5100
Stake	200	550	900	2000	3600	5200
B6-W200 Crew Cab - (3/4-Ton) - (146" wb)						
Utiline PU	200	500	850	1900	3500	5000
Sweptline PU	200	500	850	1950	3600	5100
Series B6-W300 - (1-Ton) - (133" wb)						
Utiline PU	200	550	900	2000	3600	5200
Platform	200	500	850	1850	3350	4900
Stake	200	500	850	1950	3600	5100
B6-WM300 Power-Wagon - (1-Ton) - (126" wb)						
Utiline PU	350	900	1550	3050	5900	8500

NOTES: Add 10 percent for V-8 engine.
Add 4 percent for power winch.

1967

	6	5	4	3	2	1
Series W100 - (1/2-Ton) - (114" wb)						
Utiline PU	200	650	1000	2200	4150	5900
Sweptline PU	200	650	1050	2250	4200	6000
Series W200 - (3/4-Ton) - (128" wb)						
Utiline PU	200	600	1000	2200	4000	5700
Sweptline PU	200	650	1000	2200	4100	5800
Platform	200	500	850	1900	3500	5000
Stake	200	500	850	1950	3600	5100
W200 Crew Cab - (3/4-Ton) - (146" wb)						
Utiline PU	200	500	850	1950	3600	5100
Sweptline PU	200	550	900	2000	3600	5200
Series W300 - (1-Ton) - (133" wb)						
Utiline PU	200	500	850	1950	3600	5100
Platform	200	500	850	1850	3350	4900
Stake	200	500	850	1900	3500	5000
WM300 Power-Wagon - (1-Ton) - (126" wb)						
Utiline PU	350	900	1550	3050	5900	8500

NOTES: Add 10 percent for V-8 engine.
Add 4 percent for power winch.

1968

	6	5	4	3	2	1
Series W100 - (1/2-Ton) - (114" wb)						
Utiline PU	200	650	1000	2200	4150	5900
Sweptline PU	200	650	1050	2250	4200	6000
Series W200 - (3/4-Ton) - (128" wb)						
Utiline PU	200	600	1000	2200	4000	5700
Sweptline PU	200	650	1000	2200	4100	5800
Platform	200	500	850	1900	3500	5000
Stake	200	500	850	1950	3600	5100
W200 Crew Cab - (3/4-Ton) - (146" wb)						
Utiline PU	200	500	850	1950	3600	5100
Sweptline PU	200	550	900	2000	3600	5200
Series W300 - (1-Ton) - (133" wb)						
Utiline PU	200	500	850	1950	3600	5100
Platform	200	500	850	1850	3350	4900
Stake	200	500	850	1900	3500	5000
WM300 Power-Wagon - (1-Ton) - (126" wb)						
Utiline PU	350	900	1550	3050	5900	8500

NOTES: Add 10 percent for V-8 engine.
Add 4 percent for power winch.

1969

	6	5	4	3	2	1
Series W100 - (1/2-Ton) - (114" wb)						
Utiline PU	200	650	1000	2200	4150	5900
Sweptline PU	200	650	1050	2250	4200	6000
Series W200 - (3/4-Ton) - (128" wb)						
Utiline PU	200	500	850	1950	3600	5100
Sweptline PU	200	550	900	2000	3600	5200
Platform	200	500	850	1850	3350	4900
Stake	200	500	850	1900	3500	5000
W200 Crew Cab - (3/4-Ton) - (146" wb)						
Utiline PU	200	500	850	1900	3500	5000
Sweptline PU	200	500	850	1950	3600	5100
Series W300 - (1-Ton) - (133" wb)						
Utiline PU	200	500	850	1950	3600	5100

	6	5	4	3	2	1
Platform	150	450	800	1800	3300	4800
Stake	200	500	850	1850	3350	4900

1970

Series W100 - (1/2-Ton) - (114" wb)						
Utiline PU	200	650	1000	2200	4150	5900
Sweptline PU	200	650	1050	2250	4200	6000
Series W100 - (1/2-Ton) - (128" wb)						
Utiline PU	200	650	1050	2250	4200	6000
Sweptline PU	200	675	1050	2250	4300	6100
Series W200 - (3/4-Ton) - (128" wb)						
Utiline PU	200	500	850	1950	3600	5100
Sweptline PU	200	550	900	2000	3600	5200
Platform	200	500	850	1850	3350	4900
Stake	200	500	850	1900	3500	5000
W200 Crew Cab - (3/4-Ton) - (146" wb)						
Utiline PU	200	500	850	1900	3500	5000
Sweptline PU	200	500	850	1950	3600	5100
Series W300 - (1-Ton) - (133" wb)						
Utiline PU	200	500	850	1950	3600	5100
Platform	150	450	800	1800	3300	4800
Stake	200	500	850	1850	3350	4900

NOTE: Add 10 percent for V-8 engine.

1971

Series W100 - (1/2-Ton)						
Utiline PU (114" wb)	200	650	1000	2200	4150	5900
Sweptline PU (114" wb)	200	650	1050	2250	4200	6000
Utiline PU (128" wb)	200	650	1050	2250	4200	6000
Sweptline PU (128" wb)	200	675	1050	2250	4300	6100
Series W200 - (3/4-Ton) - (128" wb)						
Utiline PU	200	500	850	1950	3600	5100
Sweptline PU	200	550	900	2000	3600	5200
W200 Crew Cab - (3/4-Ton) - (146" wb)						
Utiline PU	200	500	850	1900	3500	5000
Sweptline PU	200	500	850	1950	3600	5100
Series W300 - (1-Ton) - (133" wb)						
Utiline PU	200	500	850	1950	3600	5100
Platform	150	450	800	1800	3300	4800
Stake	200	500	850	1850	3350	4900

NOTE: Add 10 percent for V-8 engine.

1972

Series W100 - (1/2-Ton)						
Utiline PU (115" wb)	200	550	900	2150	3800	5400
Sweptline PU (115" wb)	200	600	950	2150	3850	5500
Utiline PU (131" wb)	200	550	900	2100	3700	5300
Sweptline PU (131" wb)	200	550	900	2150	3800	5400
Series W200 - (3/4-Ton) - (131" wb)						
Utiline PU	200	500	850	1950	3600	5100
Sweptline PU	200	550	900	2000	3600	5200
W200 Crew Cab - (3/4-Ton) - (149" wb)						
Utiline PU	200	500	850	1900	3500	5000
Sweptline PU	200	500	850	1950	3600	5100
Series W300 - (1-Ton) - (135" wb)						
Utiline PU	200	500	850	1850	3350	4900
Platform	150	450	750	1700	3200	4600
Stake	150	450	800	1750	3250	4700

NOTE: Add 10 percent for V-8 engine.

1973

Series W100 - (1/2-Ton)						
Utiline PU (115" wb)	200	550	900	2150	3800	5400
Sweptline PU (115" wb)	200	600	950	2150	3850	5500
Utiline PU (131" wb)	200	550	900	2100	3700	5300
Sweptline PU (131" wb)	200	550	900	2150	3800	5400
Series W200 - (3/4-Ton) - (131" wb)						
Utiline PU	200	500	850	1950	3600	5100
Sweptline PU	200	550	900	2000	3600	5200
W200 Crew Cab - (3/4-Ton) - (149" wb)						
Utiline PU	200	500	850	1900	3500	5000
Sweptline PU	200	500	850	1950	3600	5100
Series W300 - (1-Ton) - (135" wb)						
Utiline PU	200	500	850	1850	3350	4900
Platform	150	450	750	1700	3200	4600
Stake	150	450	800	1750	3250	4700

NOTE: Add 10 percent for V-8 engine.

1974

AW100 Ramcharger - (1/2-Ton) - (106" wb)						
Spt	200	650	1000	2200	4100	5800
Series W100 - (1/2-Ton)						
Utiline PU (115" wb)	200	550	900	2150	3800	5400
Sweptline PU (115" wb)	200	600	950	2150	3850	5500
Utiline PU (131" wb)	200	550	900	2100	3700	5300
Sweptline PU (131" wb)	200	550	900	2150	3800	5400
Series W100 Club Cab - (1/2-Ton)						
Sweptline PU (133" wb)	200	550	900	2100	3700	5300
Sweptline PU (149" wb)	200	500	850	1950	3600	5100
Series W200 - (3/4-Ton)						
Utiline PU (131" wb)	200	500	850	1950	3600	5100
Sweptline PU (131" wb)	200	550	900	2000	3600	5200
Sweptline Clb Cab (149" wb)	200	550	900	2100	3700	5300
Series W200 Crew Cab - (3/4-Ton) - (149" wb)						
Utiline PU	200	500	850	1900	3500	5000
Sweptline PU	200	500	850	1950	3600	5100
Series W300 - (1-Ton) - (135" wb)						
Utiline PU	200	500	850	1850	3350	4900

NOTES: Add 10 percent for V-8 engine.
Add 12 percent for 440 CID V-8.

1975

Ramcharger - (1/2-Ton) - (106" wb)						
AW100	200	650	1000	2200	4100	5800
Series W100 - (1/2-Ton)						
Utiline PU (115" wb)	200	550	900	2150	3800	5400
Sweptline PU (115" wb)	200	600	950	2150	3850	5500
Utiline PU (131" wb)	200	550	900	2100	3700	5300
Sweptline PU (131" wb)	200	550	900	2150	3800	5400
Series W100 Club Cab - (1/2-Ton)						
Sweptline PU (133" wb)	200	550	900	2100	3700	5300
Sweptline PU (149" wb)	200	500	850	1950	3600	5100
Series W200 - (3/4-Ton)						
Utiline PU (131" wb)	200	500	850	1950	3600	5100
Sweptline PU (131" wb)	200	550	900	2000	3600	5200
Sweptline Clb Cab (149" wb)	200	550	900	2100	3700	5300
Series W200 Crew Cab - (3/4-Ton) - (149" wb)						
Utiline PU	200	500	850	1900	3500	5000
Sweptline PU	200	500	850	1950	3600	5100
Series W300 - (1-Ton) - (135" wb)						
Utiline PU	200	500	850	1850	3350	4900

NOTES: Add 10 percent for V-8 engine.
Add 12 percent for 440 CID V-8.

1976

Ramcharger - (1/2-Ton) - (106" wb)

	6	5	4	3	2	1
AW100	200	600	950	2200	3900	5600
Series W100 - (1/2-Ton)						
Utiline PU (115" wb)	200	550	900	2100	3700	5300
Sweptline PU (115" wb)	200	600	950	2150	3850	5500
Utiline PU (131" wb)	200	550	900	2150	3800	5400
Sweptline PU (131" wb)	200	600	950	2200	3900	5600
W100 Club Cab - (1/2-Ton)						
Sweptline PU (133" wb)	200	500	850	1850	3350	4900
Sweptline PU (149" wb)	150	450	800	1800	3300	4800
Series W200 - (3/4-Ton)						
Utiline PU (131" wb)	150	450	800	1750	3250	4700
Sweptline PU (131" wb)	150	450	800	1800	3300	4800
Sweptline Clb (149" wb)	200	500	850	1850	3350	4900
W200 Crew Cab - (3/4-Ton) - (149" wb)						
Utiline PU	150	450	800	1800	3300	4800
Sweptline PU	200	500	850	1850	3350	4900

NOTES: Add 10 percent for V-8 engine.
Add 12 percent for 440 CID V-8 engine.

1977

Ramcharger - (1/2-Ton) - (106" wb)						
AW100	200	600	950	2200	3900	5600
Series W100 - (1/2-Ton)						
Utiline PU (115" wb)	200	550	900	2100	3700	5300
Sweptline PU (115" wb)	200	600	950	2150	3850	5500
Utiline PU (131" wb)	200	550	900	2150	3800	5400
Sweptline PU (131" wb)	200	600	950	2200	3900	5600
Series W100 Club Cab - (1/2-Ton)						
Sweptline PU (133" wb)	200	500	850	1850	3350	4900
Sweptline PU (149" wb)	150	450	800	1800	3300	4800
Series W150 - (1/2-Ton)						
Utiline PU (115" wb)	150	450	800	1750	3250	4700
Sweptline PU (115" wb)	150	450	800	1800	3300	4800
Utiline PU (131" wb)	150	450	800	1800	3300	4800
Sweptline PU (131" wb)	200	500	850	1850	3350	4900
W150 Club Cab - (1/2-Ton)						
Sweptline PU (133" wb)	150	450	750	1700	3200	4600
Sweptline PU (149" wb)	150	400	750	1650	3150	4500
Series W200 - (3/4-Ton) - (131" wb)						
Utiline PU	150	450	800	1800	3300	4800
Sweptline PU	200	500	850	1850	3350	4900
W200 Club or Crew Cab - (3/4-Ton) - (149" wb)						
Sweptline Clb	200	500	850	1900	3500	5000
Utiline Crew	150	450	800	1800	3300	4800
Sweptline Crew	200	500	850	1850	3350	4900

NOTE: Add 10 percent for V-8 engine.

1978

Ramcharger - (1/2-Ton) - (106" wb)						
AW100	200	600	950	2200	3900	5600
Series W150 - (1/2-Ton)						
Utiline PU (115" wb)	200	550	900	2100	3700	5300
Sweptline PU (115" wb)	200	600	950	2150	3850	5500
Utiline PU (131" wb)	200	550	900	2150	3800	5400
Sweptline PU (131" wb)	200	600	950	2200	3900	5600
W150 Club Cab						
Sweptline PU (133" wb)	200	550	900	2000	3600	5200
Sweptline PU (149" wb)	200	500	850	1900	3500	5000
Series W200 - (3/4-Ton) - (131" wb)						
Utiline PU	150	450	800	1800	3300	4800
Sweptline PU	200	500	850	1850	3350	4900
W200 Club or Crew Cab - (3/4-Ton) - (149" wb)						
Clb Sweptline	200	500	850	1900	3500	5000
Crew Sweptline	150	450	800	1800	3300	4800

NOTE: Add 10 percent for V-8 engine.

1979

Ramcharger - (1/2-Ton) - (106" wb)						
AW100	200	600	950	2200	3900	5600
Series W150 - (1/2-Ton)						
Utiline PU (115" wb)	200	550	900	2100	3700	5300
Sweptline PU (115" wb)	200	600	950	2150	3850	5500
Utiline PU (131" wb)	200	550	900	2150	3800	5400
Sweptline PU (131" wb)	200	600	950	2200	3900	5600
W150 Club Cab						
Sweptline PU (133" wb)	200	550	900	2000	3600	5200
Sweptline PU (149" wb)	200	500	850	1900	3500	5000
Series W200 - (3/4-Ton) - (131" wb)						
Utiline PU	150	450	800	1800	3300	4800
Sweptline PU	200	500	850	1850	3350	4900
W200 Club or Crew Cab - (3/4-Ton) - (149" wb)						
Sweptline Clb	200	500	850	1900	3500	5000
Sweptline Crew	150	450	800	1800	3300	4800

NOTE: Add 10 percent for V-8 engine.

1980

Ramcharger HdTp - (1-Ton) - (106" wb)						
AW100	200	650	1000	2200	4100	5800
Series W150 - (1/2-Ton)						
Utiline PU (115" wb)	200	550	900	2150	3800	5400
Sweptline PU (115" wb)	200	600	950	2200	3900	5600
Utiline PU (131" wb)	200	600	950	2150	3850	5500
Sweptline PU (131" wb)	200	650	1000	2200	4100	5800
Series W150 Club Cab - (1/2-Ton)						
Sweptline PU (133" wb)	200	600	1000	2200	4000	5700
Sweptline PU (149" wb)	200	600	950	2200	3900	5600
Series W200 - (3/4-Ton) - (131" wb)						
Utiline PU	200	600	950	2150	3850	5500
Sweptline PU	200	600	1000	2200	4000	5700
W200 Club or Crew Cab - (3/4-Ton)						
Sweptline Clb (149" wb)	200	500	850	1900	3500	5000
Sweptline Crew (149" wb)	150	450	800	1800	3300	4800

1981

Ramcharger						
Wag	200	650	1050	2250	4200	6000

1982

Power Ram 50						
PU	100	125	500	950	1700	2400
Cus PU	100	150	450	1000	1750	2500
Royal PU	100	150	450	1000	1800	2600
Spt PU	100	150	450	1000	1900	2700
Ramcharger						
Wag	200	650	1050	2250	4200	6000

1983

Power Ram 50						
PU	100	150	450	1000	1800	2600
Cus PU	100	150	450	1000	1900	2700

	6	5	4	3	2	1
Royal PU	100	175	525	1050	1950	2800
Spt PU	100	175	525	1050	2050	2900
Ramcharger						
Wag	350	700	1150	2300	4550	6500

1984

	6	5	4	3	2	1
Power Ram 50						
Cus PU	100	175	525	1050	2100	3000
Royal PU	125	200	600	1100	2200	3100
Spt PU	125	200	600	1100	2250	3200
Ramcharger						
Wag	350	750	1200	2350	4900	7000

1985

	6	5	4	3	2	1
Power Ram 50						
Cus PU	150	350	750	1350	2800	4000
Royal PU	150	350	750	1450	3000	4200
Spt PU	150	400	750	1550	3050	4300
Ramcharger						
Wag	350	750	1200	2350	4900	7000
Colt Vista, 103.5" wb, 4-cyl.						
Wag	150	400	750	1650	3150	4500

FORD

1959

	6	5	4	3	2	1
F-100 Series, 1/2-Ton, 6-cyl, 110" wb						
Styleside PU, 6-1/2'	350	850	1500	2800	5650	8100
Flareside PU, 6-1/2'	350	900	1550	3100	6000	8600
F-100 Series, 1/2-Ton, 6-cyl, 118" wb						
Styleside PU, 8'	350	800	1450	2750	5600	8000
Flareside PU, 8'	350	850	1500	2900	5700	8200
F-250 Series, 3/4-Ton, 6-cyl, 118" wb						
Styleside PU	350	850	1500	2950	5800	8300
Flareside PU	350	850	1500	2800	5650	8100

NOTE: Add 5 percent for 292 cid/172 hp V-8, (all models).

1960

	6	5	4	3	2	1
F-100 Series, 1/2-Ton, 6-cyl, 110" wb						
Styleside PU, 6-1/2'	350	850	1500	2800	5650	8100
Flareside PU, 6-1/2'	350	900	1550	3100	6000	8600
F-100 Series, 1/2-Ton, 6-cyl, 118" wb						
Styleside PU, 8'	350	800	1450	2750	5600	8000
Flareside PU, 8'	350	850	1500	2900	5700	8200
F-250 Series, 3/4-Ton, 6-cyl, 118" wb						
Styleside PU	350	850	1500	2950	5800	8300
Flareside PU	350	850	1500	2800	5650	8100
Stake	200	650	1050	2250	4200	6000

NOTE: Add 5 percent for 292 cid/172 hp, V-8.

1961

	6	5	4	3	2	1
F-100 Series, 1/2-Ton, 6-cyl, 110" wb						
Styleside PU, 6-1/2'	350	750	1350	2650	5450	7800
Flareside PU, 6-1/2'	350	750	1300	2500	5300	7600
F-100 Series, 1/2-Ton, 6-cyl, 118" wb						
Styleside PU, 8'	350	750	1300	2500	5300	7600
Flareside PU, 8'	350	750	1300	2400	5200	7400
F-250 Series, 3/4-Ton, 6-cyl, 118" wb						
Styleside PU	350	850	1500	2950	5800	8300
Flareside PU	350	850	1500	2800	5650	8100
Stake	200	650	1050	2250	4200	6000

NOTE: Add 10 percent for 292 cid/160 hp, V-8.

1962

	6	5	4	3	2	1
F-100 Series, 1/2-Ton, 6-cyl, 114" wb						
Styleside PU, 6-1/2' unit	350	750	1300	2500	5300	7600
Flareside PU, 6-1/2'	350	750	1350	2650	5450	7800
Styleside PU, 6-1/2', Sep.	350	850	1500	2800	5650	8100
F-100 Series, 1/2-Ton, 6-cyl, 122" wb						
Styleside PU, 8', unit	350	750	1300	2400	5200	7400
Flareside PU, 8'	350	750	1300	2500	5300	7600
Styleside PU, 8', Sep.	350	800	1350	2700	5500	7900
F-250 Series, 3/4-Ton, 6-cyl, 122" wb						
Styleside PU, 8', unit	350	800	1350	2700	5500	7900
Flareside PU, 8'	350	850	1500	2800	5650	8100
Styleside PU, 8', Sep.	350	900	1550	3000	5850	8400
Stake	200	600	950	2150	3850	5500

NOTE: Add 5 percent for V-8.

1963

	6	5	4	3	2	1
F-100 Series, 1/2-Ton, 6-cyl, 114" wb						
Styleside PU, 6-1/2' unit	350	750	1350	2600	5400	7700
Flareside PU, 6-1/2'	350	800	1350	2700	5500	7900
Styleside PU, 6-1/2', Sep.	350	850	1500	2900	5700	8200
F-100 Series, 1/2-Ton, 6-cyl, 122" wb						
Styleside PU, 8', unit	350	750	1300	2450	5250	7500
Flareside PU, 8'	350	750	1350	2600	5400	7700
Styleside PU, 8', Sep.	350	800	1450	2750	5600	8000
F-250 Series, 3/4-Ton, 6-cyl, 122" wb						
Styleside PU, 8', unit	350	750	1300	2450	5250	7500
Flareside PU, 8'	350	850	1500	2800	5650	8100
Styleside PU, 8', Sep.	350	900	1550	3000	5850	8400

NOTE: Add 5 percent for V-8.

1964

	6	5	4	3	2	1
F-100/Model F-101, 1/2-Ton, 6-cyl, 114" wb						
Flareside PU	350	750	1350	2600	5400	7700
Styleside PU	350	800	1350	2700	5500	7900
F-100/Model F-102, 1/2-Ton, 6-cyl, 128" wb						
Flareside PU LBx	350	750	1300	2450	5250	7500
Styleside PU LBx	350	750	1350	2600	5400	7700
F-250, 3/4-Ton, 6-cyl, 128" wb						
Flareside PU LBx	350	750	1300	2450	5250	7500
Styleside PU LBx	350	750	1350	2600	5400	7700

NOTE: Add 5 percent for F-Series 202 cid/160 hp, V-8.

1965

	6	5	4	3	2	1
F-100/Model F-101, 1/2-Ton, 6-cyl, 115" wb						
Flareside PU	350	750	1350	2600	5400	7700
Styleside PU	350	800	1350	2700	5500	7900
F-100/Model F-102, 1/2-Ton, 6-cyl, 129" wb						
Flareside PU LBx	350	750	1300	2450	5250	7500
Styleside PU LBx	350	750	1350	2600	5400	7700
F-250, 3/4-Ton, 6-cyl, 129" wb						
Flareside PU LBx	350	750	1300	2450	5250	7500
Styleside PU LBx	350	750	1350	2650	5450	7800

NOTE: Add 5 percent for V-8.

1966

	6	5	4	3	2	1
Bronco U-100, 1/2-Ton, 6-cyl, 90" wb						
Rds	350	750	1250	2400	5100	7300
Spt Utl	350	750	1350	2600	5400	7700
Wag	350	750	1300	2500	5300	7600
F-100/Model F-101, 1/2-Ton, 115" wb						
Flareside PU	350	750	1350	2600	5400	7700
Styleside PU	350	800	1350	2700	5500	7900
F-100/Model F-102, 1/2-Ton, 129" wb						
Flareside PU	350	750	1300	2450	5250	7500
Styleside PU	350	750	1350	2600	5400	7700
F-250, 3/4-Ton, 129" wb						
Flareside PU	350	750	1300	2450	5250	7500
Styleside PU	350	750	1350	2600	5400	7700
Platform	200	500	850	1950	3600	5100
Stake	200	550	900	2100	3700	5300

NOTE: Add 5 percent for V-8.

1967

	6	5	4	3	2	1
Bronco U-100, 1/2-Ton, 6-cyl						
Rds	350	750	1250	2400	5100	7300
Spt Utl	350	750	1300	2500	5300	7600
Wag	350	750	1350	2600	5400	7700
F-100/Model F-101, 1/2-Ton, 6-cyl						
Flareside PU 6-1/2'	350	750	1350	2650	5450	7800
Styleside PU 6-1/2'	350	750	1350	2650	5450	7800
Flareside 8'	350	750	1300	2500	5300	7600
Styleside 8'	350	750	1350	2650	5450	7800
F-250, 3/4-Ton, 6-cyl						
Flareside PU 8'	350	750	1300	2500	5300	7600
Styleside PU 8'	350	800	1350	2700	5500	7900
Platform	200	550	900	2000	3600	5200
Stake	200	550	900	2150	3800	5400

NOTE: Add 5 percent for V-8.

1968

	6	5	4	3	2	1
Bronco U-100, 1/2-Ton, 6-cyl						
Rds	350	750	1300	2400	5200	7400
Spt Utl	350	750	1350	2600	5400	7700
Wag	350	750	1350	2650	5450	7800
F-100/Model F-101, 1/2-Ton, 6-cyl						
Flareside PU	350	750	1350	2650	5450	7800
Styleside PU	350	800	1450	2750	5600	8000
F-100/Model F-102, 1/2-Ton, 6-cyl						
Flareside PU LBx	350	750	1300	2500	5300	7600
Styleside PU LBx	350	750	1350	2650	5450	7800
F-250, 3/4-Ton, 6-cyl						
Flareside PU LBx	350	750	1300	2500	5300	7600
Styleside PU LBx	350	800	1350	2700	5500	7900
Platform	200	550	900	2000	3600	5200
Stake	200	550	900	2150	3800	5400

NOTE: Add 5 percent for V-8.

1969

	6	5	4	3	2	1
Bronco U-100, 1/2-Ton, 6-cyl						
PU	350	750	1300	2450	5250	7500
Wag	350	750	1350	2650	5450	7800
F-100, 1/2-Ton, 6-cyl						
Flareside PU 6-1/2'	350	750	1300	2500	5300	7600
Styleside PU 6-1/2'	350	750	1300	2450	5250	7500
Flareside PU 8'	350	750	1300	2400	5200	7400
Styleside PU 8'	350	750	1250	2400	5100	7300
F-250, 3/4-Ton, 6-cyl						
Flareside PU 8'	350	750	1350	2650	5450	7800
Styleside PU 8'	350	750	1350	2600	5400	7700
Platform 7-1/2'	200	550	900	2150	3800	5400
Stake 7-1/2'	200	600	950	2200	3900	5600

NOTE: Add 5 percent for V-8.

1970

	6	5	4	3	2	1
Bronco U-100, 1/2-Ton, 6-cyl						
PU	350	750	1300	2450	5250	7500
Wag	350	750	1350	2650	5450	7800
F-100, 1/2-Ton, 6-cyl						
Flareside PU 6-1/2'	350	750	1350	2650	5450	7800
Styleside PU 6-1/2'	350	750	1350	2600	5400	7700
Flareside PU 8'	350	750	1300	2400	5200	7400
Styleside PU 8'	350	750	1250	2400	5100	7300
F-250, 3/4-Ton, 6-cyl						
Flareside PU	350	750	1350	2650	5450	7800
Styleside PU	350	750	1350	2600	5400	7700
Platform	200	550	900	2150	3800	5400
Stake	200	600	950	2200	3900	5600

NOTE: Add 5 percent for V-8.

1971

	6	5	4	3	2	1
Bronco U-100, 1/2-Ton, 6-cyl						
PU	350	750	1300	2450	5250	7500
Wag	350	750	1350	2650	5450	7800
Cargo Van	125	200	600	1100	2300	3300
F-100, 1/2-Ton, 6-cyl						
Flareside PU 6-1/2'	350	750	1300	2500	5300	7600
Styleside PU 6-1/2'	350	750	1300	2450	5250	7500
Flareside PU 8'	350	750	1300	2400	5200	7400
Styleside PU 8'	350	750	1250	2400	5100	7300
F-250, 3/4-Ton, 6-cyl						
Flareside PU	350	750	1350	2650	5450	7800
Styleside PU	350	750	1350	2600	5400	7700
Platform	200	550	900	2150	3800	5400
Stake	200	600	950	2200	3900	5600

NOTE: Add 5 percent for V-8.

1972

	6	5	4	3	2	1
Bronco U-100, 1/2-Ton, 6-cyl						
PU	350	750	1300	2450	5250	7500
Wag	350	750	1350	2650	5450	7800
F-100, 1/2-Ton, 6-cyl						
Flareside PU 6-1/2'	350	800	1350	2700	5500	7900
Styleside PU 6-1/2'	350	750	1350	2650	5450	7800
Flareside PU 8'	350	750	1300	2500	5300	7600
Styleside PU 8'	350	750	1300	2450	5250	7500
F-250, 3/4-Ton, 6-cyl						
Flareside PU	350	750	1350	2650	5450	7800
Styleside PU	350	750	1350	2600	5400	7700
Platform	200	550	900	2150	3800	5400
Stake	200	600	950	2150	3850	5500

NOTE: Add 5 percent for V-8.

1973

	6	5	4	3	2	1
Bronco U-100, 1/2-Ton, 6-cyl						
Wag	350	750	1350	2650	5450	7800
F-100, 1/2-Ton, 6-cyl						
Flareside PU 6-1/2'	350	750	1350	2650	5450	7800
Styleside PU 6-1/2'	350	800	1350	2700	5500	7900
Flareside PU 8'	350	750	1350	2600	5400	7700
Styleside PU 8'	350	750	1350	2650	5450	7800
F-250, 3/4-Ton, 6-cyl						
Flareside PU	350	750	1350	2650	5450	7800

	6	5	4	3	2	1
Styleside PU	350	750	1350	2600	5400	7700
Platform	200	550	900	2150	3800	5400
Stake	200	600	950	2200	3900	5600

NOTE: Add 5 percent for V-8.

1974

Bronco						
Wag	350	750	1250	2400	5100	7300
F-100 - (1/2-Ton)						
Flareside PU	200	650	1050	2250	4200	6000
Styleside PU	200	675	1050	2250	4300	6100
Sup Cab PU	200	650	1000	2200	4100	5800
F-250 - (3/4-Ton)						
Flareside PU	200	600	1000	2200	4000	5700
Styleside PU	200	650	1000	2200	4100	5800
Sup Cab	200	600	950	2150	3850	5500
Platform	200	550	900	2150	3800	5400
Stake	200	600	950	2150	3850	5500

1975

Bronco						
Wag	350	750	1300	2400	5200	7400
F-100 - (1/2-Ton)						
Flareside PU	200	550	900	2100	3700	5300
Styleside PU	200	550	900	2150	3800	5400
Sup Cab PU	200	500	850	1900	3500	5000
F-250 - (3/4-Ton)						
Flareside PU	200	550	900	2150	3800	5400
Styleside PU	200	600	950	2150	3850	5500
Sup Cab	200	550	900	2150	3800	5400
Platform	200	500	850	1950	3600	5100
Stake	200	550	900	2000	3600	5200

1976

Bronco						
Wag	350	750	1300	2400	5200	7400
F-100 - (1/2-Ton)						
Flareside PU	200	500	850	1900	3500	5000
Styleside PU	200	500	850	1950	3600	5100
Sup Cab PU	200	500	850	1850	3350	4900
F-250 - (3/4-Ton)						
Flareside PU	200	550	900	2000	3600	5200
Styleside PU	200	550	900	2100	3700	5300
Sup Cab	200	500	850	1950	3600	5100
Platform	150	450	800	1800	3300	4800
Stake	200	500	850	1850	3350	4900

1977

Bronco						
Wag	350	750	1300	2400	5200	7400
F-100 - (1/2-Ton)						
Flareside PU	200	500	850	1900	3500	5000
Styleside PU	200	500	850	1950	3600	5100
Sup Cab PU	200	500	850	1900	3500	5000
F-250 - (3/4-Ton)						
Flareside PU	200	500	850	1950	3600	5100
Styleside PU	200	550	900	2000	3600	5200
Sup Cab	200	500	850	1950	3600	5100
Platform	150	450	800	1800	3300	4800
Stake	200	500	850	1850	3350	4900

1978

Bronco						
Wag	350	725	1200	2350	4850	6900
F-100 - (1/2-Ton)						
Flareside PU	200	500	850	1900	3500	5000
Styleside PU	200	500	850	1950	3600	5100
Sup Cab PU	200	500	850	1950	3600	5100
F-250 - (3/4-Ton)						
Flareside PU	200	500	850	1950	3600	5100
Styleside PU	200	550	900	2000	3600	5200
Sup Cab PU	200	550	900	2100	3700	5300

1979

Bronco						
Wag	350	725	1200	2350	4850	6900
F-100 - (1/2-Ton)						
Flareside PU	200	500	850	1900	3500	5000
Styleside PU	200	500	850	1950	3600	5100
Sup Cab	200	500	850	1950	3600	5100
F-250 - (3/4-Ton)						
Flareside PU	200	500	850	1950	3600	5100
Styleside PU	200	550	900	2000	3600	5200
Sup Cab	200	550	900	2100	3700	5300

1980

Bronco						
Wag	350	725	1200	2350	4850	6900
F-100 - (1/2-Ton)						
Flareside PU	200	500	850	1900	3500	5000
Styleside PU	200	500	850	1950	3600	5100
Sup Cab	200	500	850	1950	3600	5100
F-250 - (3/4-Ton)						
Flareside PU	200	500	850	1950	3600	5100
Styleside PU	200	550	900	2000	3600	5200
Sup Cab	200	550	900	2000	3600	5200

1981

Bronco						
Wag	350	725	1200	2350	4800	6800
F-150						
Flareside PU SBx	200	500	850	1900	3500	5000
Styleside PU SBx	200	500	850	1950	3600	5100
Styleside PU LBx	200	500	850	1850	3350	4900
Styleside Sup Cab PU	200	500	850	1900	3500	5000
F-250						
Styleside PU LBx	200	500	850	1950	3600	5100
Styleside Sup Cab PU	200	550	900	2100	3700	5300
F-350						
Styleside PU LBx	200	550	900	2000	3600	5200
Styleside Crew Cab PU	200	500	850	1950	3600	5100

1982

Bronco						
Wag	200	650	1000	2200	4150	5900
Econoline E-150						
F-150						
Flareside PU SBx	200	500	850	1900	3500	5000
Styleside PU SBx	200	500	850	1950	3600	5100
Styleside PU LBx	200	500	850	1900	3500	5000
Styleside PU Sup Cab	200	550	900	2100	3700	5300
F-250						
Styleside PU LBx	200	550	900	2000	3600	5200
Styleside Sup Cab	200	600	950	2150	3850	5500

	6	5	4	3	2	1
F-350						
Styleside PU LBx	200	550	900	2100	3700	5300

1983

Bronco						
Wag	350	700	1150	2300	4550	6500
Ranger						
Styleside PU SBx	150	350	750	1450	3000	4200
Styleside PU LBx	150	400	750	1650	3150	4500
F-150						
Flareside PU SBx	200	500	850	1900	3500	5000
Styleside PU SBx	200	500	850	1950	3600	5100
Styleside PU LBx	200	500	850	1900	3500	5000
Styleside Sup Cab PU	200	550	900	2000	3600	5200
F-250						
Styleside PU LBx	200	550	900	2150	3800	5400
Styleside Sup Cab PU	200	600	950	2150	3850	5500
F-350						
Styleside PU LBx	200	550	900	2150	3800	5400
Styleside Crew Cab PU	200	550	900	2100	3700	5300

1984

Bronco II						
Wag	200	600	950	2200	3900	5600
Bronco						
Wag	350	750	1200	2350	4900	7000
Ranger						
Styleside PU SBx	150	350	750	1450	3000	4200
Styleside PU LBx	150	400	750	1650	3150	4500
Styleside Sup Cab PU	150	450	750	1700	3200	4600
F-150						
Flareside PU SBx	200	500	850	1900	3500	5000
Styleside PU SBx	200	500	850	1950	3600	5100
Styleside PU LBx	200	500	850	1900	3500	5000
Styleside Sup Cab SBx	200	550	900	2100	3700	5300
Styleside Sup Cab LBx	200	550	900	2150	3800	5400
F-250						
Styleside PU LBx	200	600	950	2150	3850	5500
Styleside Sup Cab PU LBx	200	600	1000	2200	4000	5700
Styleside PU LBx	200	550	900	2100	3700	5300
Styleside Sup Cab PU LBx	200	600	950	2150	3850	5500
F-350						
Styleside PU LBx	200	675	1050	2250	4300	6100
Styleside Sup Cab PU LBx	200	675	1050	2250	4350	6200

1985

Bronco II						
Wag	200	600	950	2200	3900	5600
Bronco						
Wag	350	750	1250	2400	5050	7200
Ranger						
Styleside PU SBx	150	400	750	1600	3100	4400
Styleside PU LBx	150	400	750	1650	3150	4500
Styleside Sup Cab PU	150	450	750	1700	3200	4600
F-150						
Flareside PU SBx	200	600	1000	2200	4000	5700
Styleside PU SBx	200	650	1000	2200	4100	5800
Styleside PU LBx	200	600	1000	2200	4000	5700
Styleside Sup Cab PU SBx	200	650	1000	2200	4150	5900
Styleside Sup Cab PU LBx	200	650	1050	2250	4200	6000
F-250						
Styleside PU LBx	200	675	1050	2250	4300	6100
Styleside Sup Cab PU LBx	200	675	1050	2250	4350	6200
F-350						
Styleside PU LBx	200	675	1050	2250	4350	6200
Styleside Sup Cab PU LBx	200	675	1100	2250	4400	6300

GMC

1956

	6	5	4	3	2	1
Series 100						
PU	400	1300	2150	4300	7500	10,700
Panel	350	850	1500	2800	5650	8100
Suburban	350	850	1500	2800	5650	8100
Series 150						
PU	350	900	1550	3050	5900	8500
Stake Rack	100	150	450	1000	1800	2600
Series 250						
PU	350	800	1450	2750	5600	8000
Panel	350	950	1600	3200	6050	8700
Dly Panel	450	1000	1600	3300	6250	8900
Stake Rack	350	725	1200	2350	4800	6800

1957

Series 100						
PU	450	1400	2350	4700	8200	11,700
Panel	350	850	1500	2800	5650	8100
Suburban	450	1150	1800	3800	6800	9700
Series 150						
PU	350	900	1550	3050	5900	8500
Stake Rack	350	750	1300	2500	5300	7600
Series 250						
PU	350	800	1450	2750	5600	8000
Panel	350	950	1600	3200	6050	8700
Dly Panel	450	1000	1600	3300	6250	8900
Stake Rack	350	725	1200	2350	4800	6800

1958

Series 100						
PU	350	850	1500	2950	5800	8300
Wide-Side PU	350	900	1550	3000	5850	8400
PU (LWB)	350	800	1450	2750	5600	8000
Wide-Side PU (LWB)	350	850	1500	2800	5650	8100
Panel	350	850	1500	2900	5700	8200
Panel DeL	350	900	1550	3000	5850	8400
Suburban	350	900	1550	3050	5900	8500
Series 150						
PU	350	750	1250	2400	5100	7300
Wide-Side PU	350	750	1300	2450	5250	7500
Stake Rack	200	675	1100	2250	4400	6300
Series PM-150						
Panel (8-ft.)	350	750	1300	2500	5300	7600
Panel (10-ft.)	350	750	1300	2400	5200	7400
Panel (12-ft.)	350	750	1250	2400	5050	7200
Series 250						
PU	350	750	1300	2450	5250	7500
Panel	350	725	1200	2350	4850	6900
Panel DeL	350	750	1200	2350	4900	7000
Stake Rack	200	675	1050	2250	4350	6200

	6	5	4	3	2	1
Series PM-250						
Panel (8-ft.)	350	750	1300	2450	5250	7500
Panel (10-ft.)	350	750	1300	2400	5200	7400
1959						
Series 100						
PU	350	850	1500	2950	5800	8300
Wide-Side PU	350	900	1550	3000	5850	8400
PU (LWB)	350	800	1450	2750	5600	8000
Wide-Side PU (LWB)	350	850	1500	2800	5650	8100
Panel	350	850	1500	2900	5700	8200
Panel DeL	350	900	1550	3000	5850	8400
Suburban	350	900	1550	3050	5900	8500
Series 150						
PU	350	750	1250	2400	5050	7200
Wide-Side PU	350	750	1300	2400	5200	7400
Stake Rack	200	675	1050	2250	4350	6200
Series PM-150						
Panel (8-ft.)	350	750	1300	2450	5250	7500
Panel (10-ft.)	350	750	1250	2400	5100	7300
Panel (12-ft.)	350	750	1250	2350	5000	7100
Series 250						
PU	350	750	1300	2400	5200	7400
Panel	350	725	1200	2350	4800	6800
Panel DeL	350	725	1200	2350	4850	6900
Stake Rack	200	675	1050	2250	4300	6100
Series PM-250						
Panel (8-ft.)	350	750	1300	2400	5200	7400
Panel (10-ft.)	350	750	1250	2400	5100	7300
1960						
(1/2-Ton) - (115" wb)						
Fender-Side PU	350	750	1350	2600	5400	7700
Wide-Side PU	350	850	1500	2900	5700	8200
(1/2-Ton) - (127" wb)						
Fender-Side PU	350	750	1250	2400	5050	7200
Wide-Side PU	350	800	1350	2700	5500	7900
Panel	200	500	850	1850	3350	4900
Suburban	200	500	850	1950	3600	5100
(3/4-Ton) - (127" wb)						
Fender-Side PU	200	500	850	1850	3350	4900
Wide-Side PU	200	500	850	1900	3500	5000
Stake	150	450	800	1800	3300	4800
(1-Ton) - (121" or 133" wb)						
PU	150	450	800	1800	3300	4800
Panel	150	450	750	1700	3200	4600
Stake	150	400	750	1650	3150	4500
1961						
(1/2-Ton) - (115" wb)						
Fender-Side PU	350	850	1500	2900	5700	8200
Wide-Side PU	350	950	1600	3200	6050	8700
(1/2-Ton) - (127" wb)						
Fender-Side PU	350	750	1350	2600	5400	7700
Wide-Side PU	350	850	1500	2900	5700	8200
Panel	200	500	850	1850	3350	4900
Suburban	200	500	850	1950	3600	5100
(3/4-Ton) - (127" wb)						
Fender-Side PU	200	500	850	1900	3500	5000
Wide-Side PU	200	500	850	1950	3600	5100
Stake	200	500	850	1850	3350	4900
1962						
(1/2-Ton) - (115" wb)						
Fender-Side PU	350	750	1350	2600	5400	7700
Wide-Side PU	350	850	1500	2900	5700	8200
(1/2-Ton) - (127" wb)						
Fender-Side PU	350	750	1250	2400	5050	7200
Wide-Side PU	350	750	1350	2600	5400	7700
Panel	200	500	850	1900	3500	5000
Suburban	200	550	900	2000	3600	5200
(3/4-Ton) - (127" wb)						
Fender-Side PU	200	500	850	1950	3600	5100
Wide-Side PU	200	550	900	2000	3600	5200
Stake	200	500	850	1850	3350	4900
1963						
(1/2-Ton) - (115" wb)						
Fender-Side PU	350	850	1500	2900	5700	8200
Wide-Side PU	350	950	1600	3200	6050	8700
(1/2-Ton) - (127" wb)						
Fender-Side PU	350	750	1350	2600	5400	7700
Wide-Side PU	350	850	1500	2900	5700	8200
Panel	200	500	850	1900	3500	5000
Suburban	200	550	900	2000	3600	5200
(3/4-Ton) - (127" wb)						
Fender-Side PU	200	500	850	1950	3600	5100
Wide-Side PU	200	550	900	2000	3600	5200
Stake	200	500	850	1850	3350	4900
1964						
(1/2-Ton) - (115" wb)						
Fender-Side PU	350	850	1500	2950	5800	8300
Wide-Side PU	350	900	1550	3000	5850	8400
(1/2-Ton) - (127" wb)						
Fender-Side PU	350	850	1500	2900	5700	8200
Wide-Side PU	350	850	1500	2950	5800	8300
Panel	200	500	850	1900	3500	5000
Suburban	200	550	900	2000	3600	5200
(3/4-Ton) - (127" wb)						
Fender-Side PU	200	500	850	1950	3600	5100
Wide-Side PU	200	550	900	2000	3600	5200
Stake	200	500	850	1850	3350	4900
1965						
(1/2-Ton) - (115" wb)						
Fender-Side PU	350	850	1500	2900	5700	8200
Wide-Side PU	350	850	1500	2950	5800	8300
(1/2-Ton) - (127" wb)						
Fender-Side PU	350	850	1500	2800	5650	8100
Wide-Side PU	350	850	1500	2900	5700	8200
Panel	200	500	850	1900	3500	5000
Suburban	200	550	900	2000	3600	5200
(3/4-Ton) - (127" wb)						
Fender-Side PU	200	500	850	1900	3500	5000
Wide-Side PU	200	500	850	1950	3600	5100
Stake	200	500	850	1850	3350	4900
1966						
(1/2-Ton) - (115" wb)						
Fender-Side PU	350	850	1500	2900	5700	8200
Wide-Side PU	350	850	1500	2950	5800	8300
(1/2-Ton) - (127" wb)						
Fender-Side PU	350	850	1500	2800	5650	8100
Wide-Side PU	350	850	1500	2900	5700	8200
Panel	200	500	850	1900	3500	5000
Suburban	200	500	850	1950	3600	5100
(3/4-Ton) - (127" wb)						
Fender-Side PU	200	500	850	1950	3600	5100
Wide-Side PU	200	550	900	2000	3600	5200
Stake	200	500	850	1850	3350	4900
1967						
(1/2-Ton) - (115" wb)						
Fender-Side PU	450	1050	1700	3600	6600	9400
Wide-Side PU	450	1150	1800	3800	6800	9700
(1/2-Ton) - (127" wb)						
Fender-Side PU	350	950	1600	3200	6050	8700
Wide-Side PU	450	1050	1650	3500	6400	9200
Panel	150	450	800	1750	3250	4700
Suburban	200	675	1050	2250	4350	6200
(3/4-Ton) - (127" wb)						
Fender-Side PU	350	900	1550	3000	5850	8400
Wide-Side PU	450	1000	1600	3300	6250	8900
Panel	200	500	850	1850	3350	4900
Suburban	350	700	1100	2300	4500	6400
Stake	150	450	800	1800	3300	4800
1968						
(1/2-Ton) - (115" wb)						
Fender-Side PU	450	1050	1700	3600	6600	9400
Wide-Side PU	450	1150	1800	3800	6800	9700
(1/2-Ton) - (127" wb)						
Fender-Side PU	450	1000	1600	3300	6250	8900
Wide-Side PU	450	1050	1650	3500	6400	9200
Panel	150	450	800	1750	3250	4700
Suburban	200	675	1050	2250	4350	6200
(3/4-Ton) - (127" wb)						
Fender-Side PU	350	900	1550	3000	5850	8400
Wide-Side PU	450	1000	1600	3300	6250	8900
Panel	200	500	850	1850	3350	4900
Suburban	350	700	1100	2300	4500	6400
Stake	150	450	800	1800	3300	4800
1969						
(1/2-Ton) - (115" wb)						
Fender-Side PU	400	1300	2150	4300	7500	10,700
Wide-Side PU	400	1350	2250	4500	7800	11,200
(1/2-Ton) - (127" wb)						
Fender-Side PU	400	1200	2050	4100	7100	10,200
Wide-Side PU	400	1300	2150	4300	7500	10,700
Panel	150	450	800	1750	3250	4700
Suburban	200	675	1050	2250	4350	6200
(3/4-Ton) - (127" wb)						
Fender-Side PU	450	1000	1600	3300	6250	8900
Wide-Side PU	450	1050	1700	3600	6600	9400
Panel	200	500	850	1850	3350	4900
Suburban	350	700	1100	2300	4500	6400
Stake	150	450	800	1800	3300	4800
1970						
Jimmy (104" wb)						
Jimmy	450	1100	1700	3650	6650	9500
(1/2-Ton) - (115" wb)						
Fender-Side PU	400	1300	2150	4300	7500	10,700
Wide-Side PU	400	1350	2250	4500	7800	11,200
(1/2-Ton) - (127" wb)						
Fender-Side PU	400	1200	2050	4100	7100	10,200
Wide-Side PU	400	1300	2150	4300	7500	10,700
Panel	150	450	800	1750	3250	4700
Suburban	200	675	1050	2250	4350	6200
(3/4-Ton) - (127" wb)						
Fender-Side PU	450	1000	1600	3300	6250	8900
Wide-Side PU	450	1050	1700	3600	6600	9400
Panel	200	500	850	1850	3350	4900
Suburban	350	700	1100	2300	4500	6400
Stake	150	450	800	1800	3300	4800
1971						
Jimmy (104" wb)						
Jimmy	400	1200	2000	3950	7000	10,000
(1/2-Ton) - (115" wb)						
Fender-Side PU	400	1200	2050	4100	7100	10,200
Wide-Side PU	400	1350	2250	4500	7800	11,200
(1/2-Ton) - (127" wb)						
Fender-Side PU	450	1150	1800	3800	6800	9700
Wide-Side PU	400	1300	2150	4300	7500	10,700
Panel	200	500	850	1900	3500	5000
Suburban	350	850	1500	2900	5700	8200
(3/4-Ton) - (127" wb)						
Fender-Side PU	450	1050	1700	3600	6600	9400
Wide-Side PU	450	1150	1900	3900	6900	9900
Panel	200	600	950	2200	3900	5600
Suburban	350	900	1550	3000	5850	8400
Stake	200	500	850	1900	3500	5000
1972						
Jimmy (104" wb)						
Jimmy	400	1200	2000	3950	7000	10,000
(1/2-Ton) - (115" wb)						
Fender-Side PU	400	1200	2050	4100	7100	10,200
Wide-Side PU	400	1350	2250	4500	7800	11,200
(1/2-Ton) - (127" wb)						
Fender-Side PU	450	1150	1800	3800	6800	9700
Wide-Side PU	400	1300	2150	4300	7500	10,700
Panel	200	500	850	1900	3500	5000
Suburban	350	850	1500	2900	5700	8200
(3/4-Ton) - (127" wb)						
Fender-Side PU	450	1050	1700	3600	6600	9400
Wide-Side PU	450	1150	1900	3900	6900	9900
Panel	200	600	950	2200	3900	5600
Suburban	350	900	1550	3000	5850	8400
Stake	200	500	850	1900	3500	5000
1973						
Jimmy - (1/2-Ton) - (106" wb)						
Jimmy	350	750	1300	2450	5250	7500
(1/2-Ton) - (117" wb)						
Fender-Side PU	350	750	1350	2600	5400	7700
Wide-Side PU	350	850	1500	2900	5700	8200
(1/2-Ton) - (125" wb)						
Fender-Side PU	350	750	1250	2350	5000	7100
Wide-Side PU	350	750	1350	2600	5400	7700
Suburban	200	675	1050	2250	4350	6200
(3/4-Ton) - (125" wb)						
Fender-Side PU	350	700	1100	2300	4500	6400
Wide-Side PU	350	700	1150	2300	4600	6600
Suburban	350	700	1150	2300	4550	6500

1974

Jimmy - (1/2-Ton) - (106" wb)	6	5	4	3	2	1
Jimmy	350	750	1300	2450	5250	7500
(1/2-Ton) - (117" wb)						
Fender-Side PU	350	750	1350	2600	5400	7700
Wide-Side PU	350	850	1500	2900	5700	8200
(1/2-Ton) - (125" wb)						
Fender-Side PU	350	750	1250	2400	5050	7200
Wide-Side PU	350	750	1350	2600	5400	7700
Suburban	200	675	1050	2250	4350	6200
(3/4-Ton) - (125" wb)						
Fender-Side PU	350	700	1100	2300	4500	6400
Wide-Side PU	350	700	1150	2300	4600	6600
Suburban	350	700	1150	2300	4550	6500

1975

Jimmy - (1/2-Ton) - (106" wb)	6	5	4	3	2	1
Jimmy	350	750	1300	2450	5250	7500
(1/2-Ton) - (117" wb)						
Fender-Side PU	350	750	1350	2600	5400	7700
Wide-Side PU	350	850	1500	2900	5700	8200
(1/2-Ton) - (125" wb)						
Fender-Side PU	350	750	1250	2400	5050	7200
Wide-Side PU	350	750	1350	2600	5400	7700
Suburban	200	675	1050	2250	4350	6200
(3/4-Ton) - (125" wb)						
Fender-Side PU	350	700	1100	2300	4500	6400
Wide-Side PU	350	700	1150	2300	4600	6600
Suburban	350	700	1150	2300	4550	6500

1976

Jimmy - (1/2-Ton) - (106" wb)	6	5	4	3	2	1
Jimmy	350	750	1300	2450	5250	7500
(1/2-Ton) - (117" wb)						
Fender-Side PU	350	750	1350	2600	5400	7700
Wide-Side PU	350	850	1500	2900	5700	8200
(1/2-Ton) - (125" wb)						
Fender-Side PU	350	750	1250	2400	5050	7200
Wide-Side PU	350	750	1350	2600	5400	7700
Suburban	200	675	1050	2250	4350	6200
(3/4-Ton) - (125" wb)						
Fender-Side PU	350	700	1100	2300	4500	6400
Wide-Side PU	350	700	1150	2300	4600	6600
Suburban	200	650	1000	2200	4100	5800

1977

Jimmy - V-8 - (106" wb)	6	5	4	3	2	1
Jimmy	350	750	1300	2450	5250	7500
C1500 - (1/2-Ton)						
Fender-Side PU SBx	200	600	950	2200	3900	5600
Wide-Side PU SBx	200	600	1000	2200	4000	5700
Fender-Side PU LBx	200	600	950	2150	3850	5500
Wide-Side PU LBx	200	600	950	2200	3900	5600
Suburban	200	600	950	2150	3850	5500
C2500 - (3/4-Ton)						
Fender-Side PU	200	600	950	2150	3850	5500
Wide-Side PU	200	600	1000	2200	4000	5700
Bonus Cab PU	200	600	950	2200	3900	5600
Crew Cab PU	200	600	950	2150	3850	5500
Stake	200	550	900	2000	3600	5200
Suburban	200	600	1000	2200	4000	5700

1978

Jimmy - V-8 - (106" wb)	6	5	4	3	2	1
Jimmy	350	700	1150	2300	4600	6600
C1500 - (1/2-Ton)						
Fender-Side PU SBx	200	500	850	1950	3600	5100
Wide-Side PU SBx	200	550	900	2000	3600	5200
Fender-Side PU LBx	200	550	900	2000	3600	5200
Wide-Side PU LBx	200	550	900	2100	3700	5300
Suburban	200	550	900	2150	3800	5400
C2500 - (3/4-Ton)						
Fender-Side PU	200	600	950	2150	3850	5500
Wide-Side PU	200	600	1000	2200	4000	5700
Bonus Cab PU	200	600	950	2200	3900	5600
Crew Cab PU	200	600	950	2150	3850	5500
Stake	200	550	900	2000	3600	5200
Suburban	200	600	1000	2200	4000	5700

1979

Jimmy - V-8 - (106" wb)	6	5	4	3	2	1
Jimmy	350	700	1150	2300	4600	6600
C1500 - (1/2-Ton)						
Fender-Side PU SBx	200	500	850	1950	3600	5100
Wide-Side PU SBx	200	550	900	2000	3600	5200
Fender-Side PU LBx	200	550	900	2000	3600	5200
Wide-Side PU LBx	200	550	900	2100	3700	5300
Suburban	200	550	900	2150	3800	5400
C2500 - (3/4-Ton)						
Fender-Side PU	200	550	900	2150	3800	5400
Wide-Side PU	200	600	1000	2200	4000	5700
Bonus Cab PU	200	600	950	2200	3900	5600
Crew Cab PU	200	600	950	2150	3850	5500
Stake	200	550	900	2000	3600	5200
Suburban	200	600	1000	2200	4000	5700

1980

Jimmy - V-8 - (106" wb)	6	5	4	3	2	1
Jimmy	350	700	1150	2300	4600	6600
C1500 - (1/2-Ton)						
Fender-Side PU SBx	200	500	850	1950	3600	5100
Wide-Side PU SBx	200	550	900	2000	3600	5200
Fender-Side PU LBx	200	550	900	2000	3600	5200
Wide-Side PU LBx	200	550	900	2100	3700	5300
Suburban	200	550	900	2150	3800	5400
C2500 - (3/4-Ton)						
Fender-Side PU	200	600	950	2150	3850	5500
Wide-Side PU	200	600	1000	2200	4000	5700
Bonus Cab PU	200	600	950	2200	3900	5600
Crew Cab PU	200	600	950	2150	3850	5500
Stake	200	550	900	2000	3600	5200
Suburban	200	600	1000	2200	4000	5700

1981

K1500 - (1/2-Ton) - (106.5" wb)	6	5	4	3	2	1
Jimmy	350	750	1200	2350	4900	7000
Jimmy Conv. Top	350	750	1250	2400	5050	7200
C1500 - (1/2-Ton) - (117.5" or 131.5" wb)						
Fender-Side PU SBx	200	600	950	2150	3850	5500
Wide-Side PU SBx	200	600	950	2200	3900	5600
Wide-Side PU LBx	200	550	900	2150	3800	5400
Suburban 4d	200	650	1000	2200	4150	5900
C2500 - (3/4-Ton) - (131" wb)						
Fender-Side PU LBx	200	675	1050	2250	4300	6100
Wide-Side PU LBx	200	675	1050	2250	4350	6200
Bonus Cab 2d PU LBx	350	700	1100	2300	4500	6400
Crew Cab 4d PU LBx	200	675	1100	2250	4400	6300
Suburban 4d	350	700	1150	2300	4600	6600

1982

K1500 - (1/2-Ton) - (106.5" wb)	6	5	4	3	2	1
Jimmy	200	650	1050	2250	4200	6000
S15 - (1/2-Ton) - (108.3" or 122.9" wb)						
Wide-Side PU SBx	100	150	450	1000	1900	2700
Wide-Side PU LBx	100	175	525	1050	1950	2800
C1500 - (1/2-Ton) - (117.5" or 131.5" wb)						
Fender-Side PU SBx	150	400	750	1650	3150	4500
Wide-Side PU SBx	150	450	750	1700	3200	4600
Wide-Side PU LBx	150	400	750	1550	3050	4300
Suburban 4d	200	500	850	1900	3500	5000
C2500 - (3/4-Ton) - (131" wb)						
Fender-Side PU LBx	200	500	850	1950	3600	5100
Wide-Side PU LBx	200	550	900	2000	3600	5200
Bonus Cab 2d PU LBx	200	600	950	2150	3850	5500
Crew Cab 4d PU LBx	200	500	850	1950	3600	5100
Suburban 4d	200	600	950	2200	3900	5600

1983

S15 - (1/2-Ton) - (100.5" wb)	6	5	4	3	2	1
Jimmy	150	350	750	1350	2800	4000
K1500 - (1/2-Ton) - (106.5" wb)						
Jimmy	200	675	1050	2250	4300	6100
S15 - (1/2-Ton) - (108.3" or 122.9" wb)						
Wide-Side PU SBx	100	150	450	1000	1900	2700
Wide-Side PU LBx	100	175	525	1050	1950	2800
Wide-Side Ext Cab PU	100	175	525	1050	2100	3000
C1500 - (1/2-Ton) - (117.5" or 131.5" wb)						
Fender-Side PU SBx	150	450	750	1700	3200	4600
Wide-Side PU SBx	150	450	800	1750	3250	4700
Wide-Side PU LBx	150	400	750	1600	3100	4400
Suburban 4d	200	500	850	1950	3600	5100
C2500 - (3/4-Ton) - (131" wb)						
Fender-Side PU LBx	200	550	900	2000	3600	5200
Wide-Side PU LBx	200	550	900	2100	3700	5300
Bonus Cab 2d PU LBx	200	600	950	2200	3900	5600
Crew Cab 4d PU LBx	200	500	850	1950	3600	5100
Suburban 4d	200	650	1000	2200	4100	5800

1984

S15 - (1/2-Ton) - (100.5" wb)	6	5	4	3	2	1
Jimmy	150	450	800	1750	3250	4700
K1500 - (1/2-Ton) - (106.5" wb)						
Jimmy	350	725	1150	2300	4700	6700
S15 - (1/2-Ton) - (108.3" or 122.9" wb)						
Wide-Side PU SBx	125	200	600	1100	2300	3300
Wide-Side PU LBx	125	250	700	1150	2400	3400
Wide-Side Ext Cab PU	125	250	700	1150	2500	3600
C1500 - (1/2-Ton) - (117.5" or 131.5" wb)						
Fender-Side PU SBx	200	500	850	1850	3350	4900
Wide-Side PU SBx	200	500	850	1900	3500	5000
Wide-Side PU LBx	150	450	800	1750	3250	4700
Suburban 4d	200	600	1000	2200	4000	5700
C2500 - (3/4-Ton) - (131" wb)						
Fender-Side PU LBx	200	600	950	2150	3850	5500
Wide-Side PU LBx	200	600	950	2200	3900	5600
Bonus Cab 2d PU LBx	200	650	1050	2250	4200	6000
Crew Cab 4d PU LBx	200	650	1000	2200	4150	5900
Suburban 4d	200	675	1050	2250	4350	6200

1985

S15 - (1/2-Ton) - (100.5" wb)	6	5	4	3	2	1
Jimmy	350	700	1150	2300	4550	6500
K1500 - (1/2-Ton) - (106.5" wb)						
Jimmy	350	750	1300	2450	5250	7500
S15 - (1/2-Ton) - (108.3" or 122.9" wb)						
Wide-Side PU SBx	150	350	750	1350	2800	4000
Wide-Side PU LBx	150	350	750	1450	2900	4100
Wide-Side Ext Cab PU	150	400	750	1550	3050	4300
C1500 - (1/2-Ton) - (117.5" or 131.5" wb)						
Fender-Side PU SBx	200	500	850	1850	3350	4900
Wide-Side PU SBx	200	500	850	1900	3500	5000
Wide-Side PU LBx	150	450	800	1800	3300	4800
Suburban 4d	200	650	1050	2250	4200	6000
C2500 - (3/4-Ton) - (131" wb)						
Fender-Side PU LBx	200	600	950	2200	3900	5600
Wide-Side PU LBx	200	600	1000	2200	4000	5700
Bonus Cab 2d PU LBx	200	675	1050	2250	4350	6200
Crew Cab 4d PU LBx	350	700	1100	2300	4500	6400
Suburban 4d	350	725	1200	2350	4800	6800

IHC

1953-1955

Series R-120 - (3/4-Ton) - (115" or 127" wb)	6	5	4	3	2	1
PU (6-1/2 ft.)	200	675	1100	2250	4400	6300
Panel (7-1/2 ft.)	200	675	1050	2250	4350	6200
PU (8-ft.)	200	650	1000	2200	4100	5800
Stake	200	600	950	2200	3900	5600

1956-1957

Series S-120 - (3/4-Ton) - (115" or 127" wb)	6	5	4	3	2	1
PU (6-1/2 ft.)	350	700	1150	2300	4550	6500
Panel	150	400	750	1550	3050	4300
Travelall	200	650	1000	2200	4100	5800
PU (8-ft.)	200	675	1100	2250	4400	6300
Stake	200	550	900	2100	3700	5300
Platform	200	550	900	2000	3600	5200

1957-1/2 - 1958

Series A-120 - (3/4-Ton)	6	5	4	3	2	1
PU (7-ft.)	200	675	1100	2250	4400	6300
Cus PU (7-ft.)	350	700	1150	2300	4550	6500
Panel (7-ft.)	150	450	750	1700	3200	4600
Travelall (7-ft.)	200	675	1050	2250	4300	6100
PU (8-1/2 ft.)	200	675	1050	2250	4300	6100
Utl PU (6-ft.)	200	650	1000	2200	4150	5900
Cus Utl PU (6-ft.)	200	650	1050	2250	4200	6000

1959

Series B-120/B-122 - (3/4-Ton)	6	5	4	3	2	1
PU (7-ft.)	200	650	1000	2200	4100	5800
Panel (7-ft.)	200	600	1000	2200	4000	5700
Travelall	200	650	1000	2200	4100	5800
PU (8-1/2 ft.)	200	550	900	2150	3800	5400
Travelette (6-ft.)	200	550	900	2000	3600	5200

NOTE: Add 5 percent for V-8 engines.

1960
Series B-120/B-122 - (3/4-Ton)

	6	5	4	3	2	1
PU (7-ft.)	200	675	1100	2250	4400	6300
Panel (7-ft.)	150	400	750	1650	3150	4500
Travelall	200	650	1000	2200	4100	5800
PU (8-1/2 ft.)	200	650	1000	2200	4100	5800
Travelette (6-ft.)	200	550	900	2150	3800	5400

NOTE: Deduct 5 percent for 6-cyl. engines.

1961
Series Scout 80 - (1/4-Ton) - (5-ft.)

PU	200	650	1000	2200	4100	5800

NOTE: Add 5 percent for vinyl Sport-Top (full enclosure).
Add 4 percent for steel Travel-Top.

Series C-120 - (3/4-Ton)

PU (7-ft.)	200	550	900	2150	3800	5400
Panel (7-ft.)	150	400	750	1600	3100	4400
Travelall	200	650	1000	2200	4100	5800
Cus Travelall	200	675	1050	2250	4350	6200
PU (8-1/2 ft.)	200	550	900	2100	3700	5300
Travelette PU	200	500	850	1950	3600	5100

NOTE: Deduct 5 percent for 6-cyl. engine (all series "C").

1962
Scout 80 - (1/4-Ton) - (5-ft.)

PU	200	675	1050	2250	4350	6200

NOTE: Add 5 percent for vinyl Sport-Top (full enclosure).
Add 4 percent for steel Travel-Top.

Series C-120 - (3/4-Ton)

PU (7-ft.)	200	550	900	2150	3800	5400
Bonus PU (7-ft.)	200	600	950	2150	3850	5500
Panel (7-ft.)	150	400	750	1600	3100	4400
Travelall	200	650	1000	2200	4100	5800
Cus Travelall	200	675	1050	2250	4350	6200
PU (8-1/2 ft.)	200	550	900	2100	3700	5300
Bonus PU (8-1/2 ft.)	200	550	900	2100	3700	5300
Travelette PU	200	600	1000	2200	4000	5700

NOTE: Deduct 5 percent for 6-cyl. engine (all series "C").

1963
Scout Series - (1/4-Ton)

PU	200	650	1000	2200	4100	5800

NOTE: Add 5 percent for vinyl Sport-Top (full-length).
Add 10 percent for steel Travel-Top.

Series C-1200 - (Heavy Duty) - (1/2-Ton)

PU (7-ft.)	200	650	1000	2200	4100	5800
Bonus Load PU (7-ft.)	200	650	1000	2200	4150	5900
PU (8-ft.)	200	600	1000	2200	4000	5700
Bonus Load PU (8-ft.)	200	650	1000	2200	4100	5800
Panel	200	500	850	1950	3600	5100
Travelall	200	675	1050	2250	4300	6100
Travelette PU	200	550	900	2100	3700	5300
Bonus Load Travelette PU	200	550	900	2150	3800	5400

NOTE: Add 5 percent for V-8 (all "C" series).

1964
Scout Series

PU	200	650	1000	2200	4100	5800

NOTE: Add 5 percent for full-length vinyl Sport-Top. Add 10 percent for steel Travel-Top. Add 15 percent for "Champagne Edition" Scout.

Series C-1100 - (Heavy Duty) - (1/2-Ton)

PU	200	600	1000	2200	4000	5700
Bonus Load PU	200	650	1000	2200	4100	5800
Travelette PU	200	500	850	1900	3500	5000
Panel	150	450	800	1800	3300	4800
Cus Travelall	200	650	1050	2250	4200	6000

Series C-1200 - (3/4-Ton)

PU	200	650	1000	2200	4100	5800
Bonus Load PU	200	650	1000	2200	4150	5900
Travelette PU	200	500	850	1950	3600	5100
Travelette Camper	200	600	1000	2200	4000	5700
Panel	200	500	850	1850	3350	4900
Cus Travelall	200	550	900	2000	3600	5200

Series C-1300 - (1-Ton)

PU	200	600	950	2150	3850	5500
Bonus Load PU	200	600	950	2200	3900	5600

1965
Scout 800 Series

PU	200	650	1050	2250	4200	6000

NOTE: Add 5 percent for full-length Sport-Top.
Add 7 percent for steel Travel-Top.

Series D-1100

PU	200	650	1000	2200	4150	5900
Bonus Load PU	200	650	1050	2250	4200	6000
Travelette PU	200	550	900	2150	3800	5400
Panel	200	550	900	2000	3600	5200
Cus Travelall	200	600	950	2150	3850	5500

Series D-1200

PU	200	650	1000	2200	4150	5900
Bonus Load PU	200	650	1050	2250	4200	6000
Travelette PU	200	550	900	2000	3600	5200
Travelette Camper	200	675	1050	2250	4350	6200
Panel	200	550	900	2000	3600	5200
Cus Travelall	200	550	900	2150	3800	5400

Series C-1300

PU	200	600	950	2200	3900	5600
Bonus Load PU	200	600	1000	2200	4000	5700

1966
Scout 800 Series

Utl PU	200	650	1000	2200	4150	5900
Cus PU	200	650	1050	2250	4200	6000
Utl Rds	200	650	1000	2200	4100	5800
Cus Rds	200	650	1000	2200	4150	5900
Utl Travel-Top	200	675	1100	2250	4400	6300
Cus Travel-Top	350	700	1100	2300	4500	6400
Soft Sport-Top	350	700	1150	2300	4550	6500
Hard Sport-Top	350	725	1150	2300	4700	6700

NOTE: Add 3 percent for Turbo-charged models.
Add 2 percent for V-8.

1967
Scout 800 Series

Utl PU	200	650	1000	2200	4150	5900
Cus PU	200	650	1050	2250	4200	6000
Utl Rds	200	650	1000	2200	4100	5800
Cus Rds	200	650	1000	2200	4150	5900
Utl Travel-Top	200	675	1100	2250	4400	6300
Cus Travel-Top	350	700	1100	2300	4500	6400
Spt Soft-Top	350	700	1150	2300	4550	6500
Spt HdTp	350	725	1150	2300	4700	6700

NOTE: Add 5 percent for soft Travel-Top. Add 4 percent for all steel Travel-Top. Add 2 percent for V-8 model. Add 3 percent for Turbo-charged 4-cyl.

1966-67 Series 1100B

	6	5	4	3	2	1
PU (6-ft. 8")	200	650	1050	2250	4200	6000
Bonus Load PU (6-ft. 8")	200	675	1050	2250	4300	6100
PU (8-1/2 ft.)	200	650	1000	2200	4150	5900
Bonus Load PU (8-ft.)	200	650	1050	2250	4200	6000
Panel (7-ft.)	200	550	900	2100	3700	5300
Travelette Cab	200	600	950	2150	3850	5500
B.L. Travelette PU (6-ft.)	200	600	950	2200	3900	5600

Series 1200B

PU (7-ft.)	200	650	1050	2250	4200	6000
Bonus Load PU (7-ft.)	200	675	1050	2250	4300	6100
PU (8-1/2 ft.)	200	650	1000	2200	4100	5800
Panel (7-ft.)	200	550	900	2100	3700	5300
Travelette PU	200	550	900	2100	3700	5300
B.L. Travelette PU (6-ft.)	200	550	900	2150	3800	5400

Series 1300B

PU (8-1/2 ft.)	200	600	1000	2200	4000	5700
Travelette	200	500	850	1900	3500	5000
B.L. Travelette PU (6-ft.)	200	500	850	1950	3600	5100

1968
Scout 800 Series

Utl PU	200	650	1000	2200	4150	5900
Cus PU	200	650	1050	2250	4200	6000
Utl Rds	200	650	1000	2200	4100	5800
Cus Rds	200	650	1000	2200	4150	5900
Utl Travel-Top	200	675	1100	2250	4400	6300
Cus Travel-Top	350	700	1100	2300	4500	6400
Spt Soft-Top	350	700	1150	2300	4550	6500
Spt HdTp	350	725	1150	2300	4700	6700

NOTE: Add 5 percent for soft Travel-Top. Add 4 percent for all steel Travel-Top. Add 2 percent for V-8 model. Add 3 percent for Turbo-charged 4-cyl.

Series 1100B

PU (6-ft. 8")	200	650	1050	2250	4200	6000
Bonus Load PU (6-ft. 8")	200	675	1050	2250	4300	6100
PU (8-1/2 ft.)	200	650	1000	2200	4150	5900
Bonus Load PU (8-ft.)	200	650	1050	2250	4200	6000
Panel (7-ft.)	200	550	900	2100	3700	5300
Travelette Cab	200	600	950	2150	3850	5500
B.L. Travelette PU (6-ft.)	200	600	950	2200	3900	5600

Series 1200B

PU (7-ft.)	200	650	1050	2250	4200	6000
Bonus Load PU (7-ft.)	200	675	1050	2250	4300	6100
PU (8-1/2 ft.)	200	650	1000	2200	4100	5800
Bonus Load PU (8-ft.)	200	650	1000	2200	4150	5900
Panel (7-ft.)	200	550	900	2000	3600	5200
Travelette PU	200	550	900	2000	3600	5200
B.L. Travelette PU (6-ft.)	200	550	900	2150	3800	5400

Series 1300B

PU (8-1/2 ft.)	200	600	1000	2200	4000	5700
Travelette	200	500	850	1900	3500	5000
B.L. Travelette PU (6-ft.)	200	500	850	1950	3600	5100

NOTE: See 1967 for percent additions for special equipment and optional engines (all series).

1969-1970
Scout 800A Series

PU	350	700	1100	2300	4500	6400
Rds	200	650	1000	2200	4150	5900
Travel-Top	350	700	1150	2300	4550	6500
Aristocrat	350	750	1200	2350	4900	7000

Series 1100D

PU (6-1/2 ft.)	200	675	1050	2250	4300	6100
Bonus Load PU (6-1/2 ft.)	200	675	1050	2250	4350	6200
PU (8-ft.)	200	600	950	2200	3900	5600
Bonus Load PU (8-ft.)	200	600	1000	2200	4000	5700
Panel	200	550	900	2150	3800	5400

Series 1200D

PU (6-1/2 ft.)	200	675	1050	2250	4300	6100
Bonus Load PU (6-1/2 ft.)	200	675	1050	2250	4350	6200
PU (8-ft.)	200	650	1000	2200	4150	5900
Bonus Load PU (8-ft.)	200	650	1050	2250	4200	6000
Panel	200	550	900	2150	3800	5400
Travelette (6-1/2 ft.)	200	550	900	2150	3800	5400
B.L. Travelette PU (8-ft.)	200	600	950	2150	3850	5500

Series 1300D

PU (9-ft.)	200	650	1000	2200	4100	5800
Travelette	200	550	900	2000	3600	5200
B.L. Travelette (6-1/2 ft.)	200	500	850	1950	3600	5100

NOTE: See 1967 for percent additions for special equipment and optional engines (all series).

1971
Scout II Series

PU	350	700	1150	2300	4550	6500
Travel-Top	350	725	1150	2300	4700	6700

NOTE: Add 5 percent for Custom trim package. Add 3 percent for V-8.

Series 1110

PU (6-1/2 ft.)	200	675	1050	2250	4300	6100
Bonus Load PU (6-1/2 ft.)	200	675	1050	2250	4350	6200
PU (8-ft.)	200	600	950	2200	3900	5600
Bonus Load PU (8-ft.)	200	600	1000	2200	4000	5700
Panel	200	550	900	2150	3800	5400
Travelall	200	675	1050	2250	4300	6100

Series 1210

PU (6-1/2 ft.)	200	675	1050	2250	4300	6100
Bonus Load PU (6-1/2 ft.)	200	675	1050	2250	4350	6200
PU (8-ft.)	200	650	1000	2200	4150	5900
Bonus Load PU (8-ft.)	200	650	1050	2250	4200	6000
Panel	200	550	900	2150	3800	5400
Travelette PU (6-1/2 ft.)	200	550	900	2150	3800	5400
B.L. Travelette PU (8-ft.)	200	600	950	2150	3850	5500

NOTE: Add 3 percent for V-8. Add 1 percent for 5-speed.

Series 1310

PU (9-ft.)	200	650	1000	2200	4100	5800
Travelette PU	200	550	900	2000	3600	5200
Bonus Load Travelette PU	200	500	850	1950	3600	5100

NOTE: Add 3 percent for V-8.
Add 1 percent for 5-speed.

1972
Scout II

PU	350	700	1150	2300	4600	6600
Travel-Top	350	725	1200	2350	4800	6800

Travelall Series

1110 Sta Wag	200	650	1000	2200	4100	5800
1210 Sta Wag	200	600	1000	2200	4000	5700

Light Truck Series 1110

PU	200	600	1000	2200	4000	5700
Bonus Load PU	200	650	1000	2200	4100	5800

Light Truck Series 1210	6	5	4	3	2	1
PU	200	500	850	1850	3350	4900
Bonus Load PU	200	500	850	1900	3500	5000
Travelette	200	500	850	1900	3500	5000

NOTE: Add 3 percent for V-8 engine (all series). Add 1 percent for 5-speed transmission. Add 5 percent for Custom trim packages.

1973

Scout II						
Travel-Top	350	725	1200	2350	4800	6800
Cab Top	350	700	1150	2300	4600	6600
Travelall Series 1110						
Sta Wag	200	650	1000	2200	4100	5800
Travelall Series 1210						
Sta Wag (4WD)	200	600	1000	2200	4000	5700
Light Truck Series 1110						
PU (6-1/2 ft.)	200	600	1000	2200	4000	5700
Bonus Load PU (6-1/2 ft.)	200	650	1000	2200	4100	5800
PU (8-ft.)	200	600	950	2150	3850	5500
Bonus Load PU (8-ft.)	200	550	900	2150	3800	5400
Light Truck Series 1210						
PU (6-1/2 ft.)	200	500	850	1850	3350	4900
Bonus Load PU (6-1/2 ft.)	200	500	850	1900	3500	5000
PU (8-ft.)	150	450	750	1700	3200	4600
Bonus Load PU (8-ft.)	150	450	800	1750	3250	4700
Travelette PU (6-1/2 ft.)	200	500	850	1900	3500	5000
B.L. Travelette PU (6-1/2 ft.)	200	500	850	1950	3600	5100
Travelette PU (8-ft.)	200	500	850	1900	3500	5000
B.L. Travelette PU (8-ft.)	200	500	850	1950	3600	5100
Light Truck Series 1310						
PU (9-ft.)	150	450	800	1800	3300	4800

NOTE: Add 3 percent for 304 CID V-8. Add 4 percent for 345 CID V-8. Add 5 percent for 392 CID V-8. Add 5 percent for Custom trim package. Add 1 percent for 5-speed transmission.

1974

Scout II						
Travel-Top	350	725	1200	2350	4800	6800
Cab Top	350	700	1150	2300	4600	6600
Travelall Series 100						
Sta Wag	200	650	1000	2200	4100	5800
Travelall Series 200						
Sta Wag	200	600	1000	2200	4000	5700
Series 100						
Fender PU (115" wb)	200	600	1000	2200	4000	5700
Fender PU (132" wb)	200	600	950	2150	3850	5500
Bonus Load PU (115" wb)	200	650	1000	2200	4100	5800
Bonus Load PU (132" wb)	200	600	950	2200	3900	5600
Series 200						
Fender PU (132" wb)	200	500	850	1850	3350	4900
Bonus Load PU (132" wb)	200	500	850	2200	3500	5000

NOTE: Add 2 percent for Deluxe exterior trim. Add 5 percent for Custom exterior trim. Add 4 percent for 345 or 392 CID V-8. Add 10 percent for Camper Special.

1975

Scout Series XLC						
Travel-Top	350	725	1200	2350	4800	6800
Cab Top	350	700	1150	2300	4600	6600
Travelall Series 150						
Sta Wag	200	650	1000	2200	4100	5800
Travelall Series 200						
Sta Wag	200	600	1000	2200	4000	5700
Series 150						
Bonus Load PU (115" wb)	200	650	1000	2200	4100	5800
Bonus Load PU (132" wb)	200	600	950	2200	3900	5600
Series 200						
Bonus Load PU	200	500	850	1900	3500	5000

NOTE: Add 2 percent for Deluxe exterior trim. Add 5 percent for Custom exterior trim. Add 4 percent for optional V-8. Add 10 percent for Camper Special.

1976

Scout II						
Travel-Top	200	675	1050	2250	4350	6200
Scout II Diesel						
Travel-Top	200	650	1000	2200	4150	5900
Terra						
PU	200	650	1050	2250	4200	6000
Terra Diesel						
PU	200	600	1000	2200	4000	5700
Traveler						
Sta Wag	350	700	1100	2300	4500	6400

NOTE: Add 3 percent for V-8 engines. Add 3 percent for 4-speed transmission. Add 6 percent for Rally package. Add 4 percent for Custom trim. Add 2 percent for Deluxe trim.

1977

Scout II						
Travel-Top	200	675	1050	2250	4300	6100
Scout II Diesel						
Travel-Top	200	650	1000	2200	4100	5800
Terra						
PU	200	650	1000	2200	4150	5900
Terra Diesel						
PU	200	600	950	2200	3900	5600
Traveler						
Sta Wag	200	675	1100	2250	4400	6300
Traveler Diesel						
Sta Wag	200	650	1050	2250	4200	6000

NOTE: Add 3 percent for V-8 engine. Add 3 percent for 4-speed transmission. Add 6 percent for Rally package. Add 8 percent for SSII. Add 2 percent for Deluxe trim. Add 4 percent for Custom trim.

1978

Scout Series						
Scout II	200	675	1050	2250	4350	6200
SS II	350	700	1100	2300	4500	6400
Terra PU	200	675	1050	2250	4300	6100
Traveler Sta Wag	350	700	1150	2300	4550	6500

NOTE: Add 3 percent for V-8 engine. Deduct 4 percent for diesel engine. Add 6 percent for Rally package. Add 4 percent for Custom trim package. Add 2 percent for 4WD running gear.

1979

Scout Series						
Scout II	200	675	1050	2250	4300	6100
SS II	200	675	1100	2250	4400	6300
Terra PU	200	650	1050	2250	4200	6000
Traveler Sta Wag	350	700	1100	2300	4500	6400

NOTE: Add 3 percent for V-8 engine. Deduct 4 percent for 6-cyl. diesel engine. Add 6 percent for Rally package. Add 4 percent for Custom trim package.

1980

Scout Series						
Scout II	200	600	1000	2200	4000	5700
Terra PU	200	600	950	2200	3900	5600
Traveler Sta Wag	200	650	1050	2200	4200	6000

NOTE: Add 3 percent for V-8 engines. Add 5 percent for Turbo-charged diesel engine. Add 4 percent for Custom trim package. Add 6 percent for Rally trim.

JEEP

WILLYS-OVERLAND - JEEP

1945

Jeep Series	6	5	4	3	2	1
CJ-2 Jeep	400	1300	2150	4300	7500	10,700

NOTE: All Jeep prices in this catalog are for civilian models unless noted otherwise. Military Jeeps may sell for higher prices.

1946

Jeep Series						
CJ-2 Jeep	400	1300	2150	4300	7500	10,700

1947

Willys Jeep						
CJ-2 Jeep	400	1300	2150	4300	7500	10,700
Willys Truck						
1-Ton PU	200	600	950	2150	3850	5500
1-Ton Platform	200	500	850	1900	3500	5000

1948

Jeep Series						
CJ-2 Jeep	400	1300	2150	4300	7500	10,700
Willys Truck						
PU	200	600	950	2150	3850	5500
Platform	200	500	850	1900	3500	5000

1949

Jeep Series						
CJ-2 Jeep	400	1300	2150	4300	7500	10,700
CJ-3 Jeep	400	1250	2100	4200	7400	10,500
Willys Truck						
PU	200	600	950	2150	3850	5500
Platform	200	500	850	1900	3500	5000

1950

Jeep Series						
CJ-3 Jeep	400	1300	2150	4300	7500	10,700
Jeep Truck						
PU	200	600	950	2150	3850	5500
Utl Wag	200	650	1000	2200	4100	5800
Stake	200	500	850	1900	3500	5000

1951

Jeep Series						
Farm Jeep	400	1250	2050	4100	7200	10,300
CJ-3 Jeep	400	1250	2100	4200	7400	10,500
Jeep Trucks						
PU	200	600	950	2150	3850	5500
Utl Wag	200	650	1000	2200	4100	5800
Stake	200	500	850	1900	3500	5000

1952

Jeep Series						
CJ-3 Open	400	1250	2100	4200	7400	10,500
Jeep Trucks						
PU	200	600	950	2200	3900	5600
Utl Wag	200	650	1000	2200	4150	5900
Stake	200	500	850	1900	3500	5000

1953

Jeep Series						
CJ-3B Jeep	400	1300	2200	4400	7700	11,000
CJ-3B Farm Jeep	400	1300	2150	4300	7500	10,700
CJ-3A Jeep	400	1300	2150	4300	7500	10,700
Jeep Trucks						
Sed Dly	200	675	1100	2250	4400	6300
PU	200	600	1000	2200	4000	5700
Utl Wag	200	650	1050	2250	4200	6000
Stake	200	500	850	1900	3500	5000

1954

Jeep Series						
Open Jeep	400	1300	2200	4400	7700	11,000
Farm Jeep	400	1300	2150	4300	7500	10,700
Jeep Trucks						
PU	350	700	1100	2300	4500	6400
Stake	200	500	850	1950	3600	5100
Sed Dly	350	700	1100	2300	4500	6400
Utl Wag	350	725	1150	2300	4700	6700
1-Ton PU	200	600	950	2150	3850	5500
1-Ton Stake	200	500	850	1900	3500	5000

1955

Jeep Series						
CJ-3B	400	1300	2200	4400	7700	11,000
CJ-5	400	1300	2200	4400	7700	11,000
Jeep Trucks						
Sed Dly	350	700	1150	2300	4550	6500
1-Ton PU	200	600	950	2200	3900	5600
Utl Wag	350	725	1200	2350	4800	6800
1-Ton Stake	200	500	850	1950	3600	5100

1956

Jeep Series						
CJ-3B	400	1300	2200	4400	7700	11,000
CJ-5	400	1300	2200	4400	7700	11,000
CJ-6	400	1250	2100	4200	7400	10,500
Jeep Trucks						
Sed Dly	350	700	1150	2300	4600	6600
Sta Wag	350	725	1200	2350	4800	6800
PU	200	650	1050	2250	4200	6000
1-Ton PU	200	600	950	2200	3900	5600
1-Ton Stake	200	500	850	1950	3600	5100

1957

Jeep Series						
CJ-3B	400	1300	2200	4400	7700	11,000
CJ-5	400	1300	2200	4400	7700	11,000
CJ-6	400	1250	2100	4200	7400	10,500
Jeep Trucks						
Dly	350	700	1150	2300	4600	6600
PU	200	650	1050	2250	4200	6000
Utl Wag	350	725	1200	2350	4800	6800
1-Ton PU	200	600	950	2200	3900	5600
1-Ton Stake	200	500	850	1950	3600	5100
Forward Control						
3/4-Ton PU	200	650	1050	2250	4200	6000
3/4-Ton Stake	200	650	1000	2200	4100	5800
1-Ton PU	200	600	950	2200	3900	5600
1-Ton Stake	200	550	900	2150	3800	5400

1958

Jeep Series						
CJ-3B	400	1250	2100	4200	7400	10,500
CJ-5	400	1300	2200	4400	7700	11,000
CJ-6	400	1250	2100	4200	7400	10,500

Jeep Trucks	6	5	4	3	2	1
Dly	200	600	950	2200	3900	5600
Utl Wag	200	600	1000	2200	4000	5700
1-Ton PU	150	450	750	1700	3200	4600
1-Ton Stake	150	350	750	1450	2900	4100
Forward Control						
3/4-Ton PU	200	650	1050	2250	4200	6000
3/4-Ton Stake	200	650	1000	2200	4100	5800
1-Ton PU	200	600	950	2200	3900	5600
1-Ton Stake	200	550	900	2150	3800	5400

1959

Jeep Series						
CJ-3	400	1300	2150	4300	7500	10,700
CJ-5	400	1300	2200	4400	7700	11,000
CJ-6	400	1250	2100	4200	7400	10,600
Jeep Trucks						
Utl Dly	200	600	1000	2200	4000	5700
PU	200	500	850	1900	3500	5000
Utl Wag	200	650	1000	2200	4150	5900
1-Ton PU	150	450	800	1750	3250	4700
1-Ton Stake	150	400	750	1650	3150	4500
Forward Control						
3/4-Ton PU	200	675	1050	2250	4300	6100
3/4-Ton Stake	200	650	1000	2200	4150	5900
1-Ton PU	200	600	1000	2200	4000	5700
1-Ton Stake	200	600	950	2150	3850	5500

1960

Jeep Series						
CJ-3	400	1300	2150	4300	7500	10,700
CJ-5	400	1300	2200	4400	7700	11,000
CJ-6	400	1250	2100	4200	7400	10,600
Jeep Trucks						
Utl Wag	200	600	1000	2200	4000	5700
Utl Dly	200	600	950	2150	3850	5500
1-Ton PU	200	550	900	2150	3800	5400
1-Ton Stake	200	500	850	1900	3500	5000
Forward Control						
3/4-Ton PU	200	600	950	2200	3900	5600
3/4-Ton Stake	200	550	900	2150	3800	5400
1-Ton PU	200	550	900	2000	3600	5200
1-Ton Stake	200	500	850	1900	3500	5000

1961

Jeep Series						
CJ-3	400	1300	2150	4300	7600	10,800
CJ-5	400	1350	2250	4500	7800	11,200
CJ-6	400	1300	2150	4300	7500	10,700
Jeep Trucks						
Utl Wag	200	600	950	2150	3850	5500
Utl Dly	200	500	850	1900	3500	5000
1-Ton PU	150	450	800	1800	3300	4800
1-Ton Stake	150	400	750	1550	3050	4300
Forward Control						
3/4-Ton PU	200	550	900	2000	3600	5200
3/4-Ton Stake	200	500	850	1900	3500	5000
1-Ton PU	150	450	800	1800	3300	4800
1-Ton Stake	150	450	750	1700	3200	4600

1962

Jeep Series						
CJ-3	400	1300	2150	4300	7600	10,800
CJ-5	400	1350	2250	4500	7800	11,200
CJ-6	400	1300	2150	4300	7500	10,700
Jeep Trucks						
Utl Wag	200	600	950	2150	3850	5500
Utl Dly	200	500	850	1900	3500	5000
1-Ton PU	150	450	800	1800	3300	4800
1-Ton Stake	150	400	750	1550	3050	4300
Forward Control						
3/4-Ton PU	200	550	900	2000	3600	5200
3/4-Ton Stake	200	500	850	1900	3500	5000
1-Ton PU	150	450	800	1800	3300	4800
1-Ton Stake	150	450	750	1700	3200	4600

KAISER - JEEP

1963

Jeep Universal	6	5	4	3	2	1
CJ-3B Jeep	400	1300	2200	4400	7700	11,000
CJ-5 Jeep	450	1450	2400	4800	8400	12,000
CJ-6 Jeep	450	1400	2300	4600	8100	11,500
"Jeep" Wagons and Trucks - (1/2-Ton)						
Sta Wag	200	650	1050	2250	4200	6000
Traveller	200	675	1050	2250	4350	6200
Utl	200	650	1050	2250	4200	6000
Panel	200	650	1000	2200	4100	5800
"Jeep" Wagons and Truck - (1-Ton)						
PU	150	450	800	1800	3300	4800
Stake	200	500	850	1900	3500	5000

NOTE: Add 3 percent for L-Head 6-cyl.
Add 4 percent for OHC 6-cyl.

Forward-Control - (3/4-Ton)						
PU	200	550	900	2000	3600	5200
Stake	200	650	1000	2200	4150	5900
Forward-Control - (1-Ton)						
PU	200	500	850	1950	3600	5100
Stake	200	650	1000	2200	4100	5800
HD PU	200	550	900	2000	3600	5200
HD Stake	200	500	850	1850	3350	4900
Fire Truck	350	700	1150	2300	4550	6500
Gladiator/Wagoneer - (1/2-Ton)						
2d Wag	200	650	1000	2200	4150	5900
4d Wag	200	650	1050	2250	4200	6000
2d Cus Wag	200	650	1050	2250	4200	6000
4d Cus Wag	200	675	1050	2250	4300	6100
Panel Dly	200	550	900	2100	3700	5300
Gladiator - (1/2-Ton) - (120" wb)						
Thriftside PU	200	600	950	2150	3850	5500
Townside PU	200	600	1000	2200	4000	5700
Gladiator - (1/2-Ton) - (126" wb)						
Thriftside PU	200	550	900	2100	3700	5300
Townside PU	200	600	950	2150	3850	5500
Gladiator - (3/4-Ton) - (120" wb)						
Thriftside PU	200	500	850	1950	3600	5100
Townside PU	200	550	900	2100	3700	5300
Stake	150	450	800	1750	3250	4700
Gladiator - (3/4-Ton) - (126" wb)						
Thriftside PU	200	500	850	1900	3500	5000
Townside PU	200	550	900	2000	3600	5200

	6	5	4	3	2	1
Stake	150	450	750	1700	3200	4600
Gladiator - (1-Ton) - (120" wb)						
Stake	150	400	750	1650	3150	4500
Wrecker	200	550	900	2000	3600	5200
Fire Truck	200	675	1050	2250	4350	6200
Gladiator - (1-Ton) - (126" wb)						
Stake	150	400	750	1650	3150	4500
Wrecker	200	550	900	2100	3700	5300
Fire Truck	350	700	1150	2300	4550	6500

1964

Jeep Universal						
CJ-3B Jeep	400	1300	2200	4400	7700	11,000
CJ-5 Jeep	450	1450	2400	4800	8400	12,000
CJ-5A Tuxedo Park	450	1500	2500	5000	8800	12,500
CJ-6 Jeep	450	1450	2450	4900	8500	12,200
CJ-6A Jeep Park	450	1500	2500	5000	8700	12,400
"Jeep" Wagons and Trucks - (1/2-Ton)						
Sta Wag	200	600	950	2150	3850	5500
Utl	200	650	1000	2200	4100	5800
Traveler	200	675	1050	2250	4350	6200
Panel	200	600	950	2200	3900	5600
"Jeep" Wagons and Trucks - (1-Ton) - (4WD)						
PU	200	550	900	2100	3700	5300
Stake	200	500	850	1900	3500	5000

NOTE: Add 3 percent for L-Head 6-cyl.
Add 4 percent for OHC 6-cyl.

Forward-Control - (3/4-Ton)						
PU	150	450	800	1750	3250	4700
Stake	150	400	750	1600	3100	4400
Forward-Control - (1-Ton)						
PU	150	450	750	1700	3200	4600
Stake	150	400	750	1550	3050	4300
HD PU	150	450	800	1750	3250	4700
HD Stake	150	400	750	1600	3100	4400
Fire Truck	200	675	1050	2250	4350	6200
Fleetvan						
FJ-3 Step-in Dly	150	400	750	1650	3150	4500
FJ-3A Step-in Dly	150	450	750	1700	3200	4600
Gladiator/Wagoneer - (1/2-Ton)						
2d Wag	200	650	1000	2200	4150	5900
4d Wag	200	650	1050	2250	4200	6000
2d Cus Wag	200	650	1050	2250	4200	6000
4d Cus Wag	200	675	1050	2250	4300	6100
Panel Dly	200	550	900	2100	3700	5300
Gladiator Pickup/Truck - (1/2-Ton) - (120" wb)						
Thriftside PU	200	500	850	1900	3500	5000
Townside PU	200	550	900	2000	3600	5200
Gladiator Pickup/Truck - (1/2-Ton) - (126" wb)						
Thriftside PU	200	550	900	2000	3600	5200
Townside PU	200	550	900	2150	3800	5400
Gladiator Pickup/Truck - (3/4-Ton) - (120" wb)						
Thriftside PU	200	500	850	1900	3500	5000
Townside PU	200	550	900	2000	3600	5200
Platform Stake	150	450	750	1700	3200	4600
Gladiator Pickup/Truck - (3/4-Ton) - (126" wb)						
Thriftside PU	200	500	850	1850	3350	4900
Townside PU	200	500	850	1950	3600	5100
Platform Stake	150	400	750	1650	3150	4500
Gladiator Pickup/Truck - (1-Ton) - (120" wb)						
Platform Stake	150	400	750	1600	3100	4400
Wrecker	200	500	850	1950	3600	5100
Fire Truck	350	700	1100	2300	4500	6400
Gladiator Pickup/Truck - (1-Ton) - (126" wb)						
Stake	150	400	750	1600	3100	4400
Wrecker	200	550	900	2000	3600	5200
Fire Truck	350	700	1150	2300	4600	6600

1965

Jeep Universal						
CJ-3B Jeep	400	1300	2200	4400	7700	11,000
CJ-5 Jeep	450	1400	2300	4600	8100	11,500
CJ-5A Tuxedo Park	450	1450	2400	4800	8400	12,000
CJ-6 Jeep	450	1400	2300	4600	8100	11,600
CJ-6A Tuxedo Park	450	1400	2350	4700	8300	11,800
"Jeep" Wagons and Trucks - (1/2-Ton)						
Sta Wag	200	600	950	2150	3850	5500
Utl Wag	200	650	1000	2200	4100	5800
Traveler	200	675	1050	2250	4350	6200
Panel	200	600	950	2200	3900	5600
"Jeep" Wagons and Trucks - (1-Ton)						
PU	200	550	900	2100	3700	5300
Stake	200	500	850	1900	3500	5000

NOTE: Add 3 percent for L-Head 6-cyl. engine.

Forward-Control - (3/4-Ton)						
PU	150	450	800	1750	3250	4700
Stake	150	400	750	1600	3100	4400
Forward-Control - (1-Ton)						
PU	150	450	750	1700	3200	4600
Stake	150	400	750	1550	3050	4300
HD PU	150	450	800	1750	3250	4700
HD Stake	150	400	750	1600	3100	4400
Fire Truck	200	675	1050	2250	4350	6200
Gladiator/Wagoneer - (1/2-Ton)						
2d Wag	200	675	1100	2250	4400	6300
4d Wag	350	700	1100	2300	4500	6400
2d Cus Wag	350	700	1100	2300	4500	6400
4d Cus Wag	350	700	1150	2300	4550	6500
Panel Dly	200	600	1000	2200	4000	5700
Gladiator Pickup/Truck - (1/2-Ton) - (120" wb)						
Thriftside PU	200	550	900	2150	3800	5400
Townside PU	200	600	950	2200	3900	5600
Stake	150	450	800	1800	3300	4800
Gladiator Pickup/Truck - (1/2-Ton) - (126" wb)						
Thriftside PU	200	550	900	2000	3600	5200
Townside PU	200	550	900	2150	3800	5400
Stake	150	450	800	1750	3250	4700
Gladiator Pickup/Truck - (3/4-Ton) - (120" wb)						
Thriftside PU	200	500	850	1900	3500	5000
Townside PU	200	550	900	2000	3600	5200
Stake	150	450	750	1700	3200	4600
Gladiator Pickup/Truck - (3/4-Ton) - (126" wb)						
Thriftside PU	200	500	850	1850	3350	4900
Townside PU	200	500	850	1950	3600	5100
Stake	150	400	750	1650	3150	4500
Gladiator Pickup/Truck - (1-Ton) - (120" wb)						
Stake	150	400	750	1600	3100	4400
Wrecker	200	500	850	1950	3600	5100
Fire Truck	350	700	1150	2300	4600	6600

Gladiator Pickup/Truck - (1-Ton) - (126" wb)

	6	5	4	3	2	1
Stake	150	400	750	1600	3100	4400
Wrecker	200	550	900	2000	3600	5200
Fire Truck	350	725	1150	2300	4700	6700

NOTE: Add 5 percent for V-8.

1966

Jeep Universal						
CJ-3B Jeep	400	1300	2200	4400	7700	11,000
CJ-5 Jeep	450	1400	2300	4600	8100	11,500
CJ-5A Tuxedo Park	450	1450	2400	4800	8400	12,000
CJ-6 Jeep	450	1400	2300	4600	8100	11,600
CJ-6A Tuxedo Park	450	1400	2350	4700	8300	11,800
Forward-Control - (3/4-Ton)						
PU	150	450	800	1750	3250	4700
Stake	150	400	750	1600	3100	4400
Forward-Control - (1-Ton)						
PU	150	450	750	1700	3200	4600
Stake	150	400	750	1550	3050	4300
HD PU	150	450	800	1750	3250	4700
HD Stake	150	400	750	1600	3100	4400
Fire Truck	200	650	1050	2250	4200	6000
Wagoneer - (1/2-Ton)						
2d Wag	200	550	900	2150	3800	5400
4d Wag	200	600	950	2150	3850	5500
2d Cus Sta Wag	200	600	950	2150	3850	5500
4d Cus Sta Wag	200	600	950	2200	3900	5600
Panel Dly	150	450	800	1800	3300	4800
4d Super Wag	200	675	1100	2250	4400	6300
Gladiator - (1/2-Ton) - (120" wb)						
Thriftside PU	200	550	900	2150	3800	5400
Townside PU	200	600	950	2200	3900	5600
Stake	150	450	800	1800	3300	4800
Gladiator - (1/2-Ton) - (126" wb)						
Thriftside PU	200	550	900	2000	3600	5200
Townside PU	200	550	900	2150	3800	5400
Stake	150	450	800	1750	3250	4700
Gladiator - (3/4-Ton) - (120" wb)						
Thriftside PU	200	500	850	1900	3500	5000
Townside PU	200	550	900	2000	3600	5200
Stake	150	450	750	1700	3200	4600
Gladiator - (3/4-Ton) - (126" wb)						
Thriftside PU	200	500	850	1850	3350	4900
Townside PU	200	500	850	1950	3600	5100
Stake	150	400	750	1650	3150	4500
Gladiator - (1-Ton) - (120" wb)						
Stake	150	400	750	1600	3100	4400
Wrecker	200	500	850	1950	3600	5100
Fire Truck	350	700	1100	2300	4500	6400
Gladiator - (1-Ton) - (126" wb)						
Stake	150	400	750	1600	3100	4400
Wrecker	200	500	850	1950	3600	5100
Fire Truck	350	700	1150	2300	4550	6500

NOTE: Add 5 percent for V-8.

1967

Jeep Universal						
CJ-5 Jeep	400	1300	2200	4400	7700	11,000
CJ-5A Jeep	450	1400	2300	4600	8100	11,500
CJ-6 Jeep	450	1450	2400	4800	8400	12,000
CJ-6A Jeep	450	1500	2500	5000	8800	12,500
Jeepster Commando						
Conv	350	700	1150	2300	4600	6600
Sta Wag	200	650	1000	2200	4150	5900
Cpe-Rds	350	725	1200	2350	4800	6800
PU	200	600	950	2150	3850	5500
Wagoneer						
2d Wag	200	550	900	2150	3800	5400
4d Wag	200	600	950	2150	3850	5500
2d Cus Sta Wag	200	600	950	2150	3850	5500
4d Cus Sta Wag	200	600	950	2200	3900	5600
Panel Dly	150	450	800	1800	3300	4800
4d Sup Wag	200	650	1000	2200	4100	5800
Gladiator - (1/2-Ton) - (120" wb)						
Thriftside PU	200	500	850	1950	3600	5100
Townside PU	200	550	900	2000	3600	5200
Stake	150	400	750	1600	3100	4400
Gladiator - (3/4-Ton) - (120" wb)						
Thriftside PU	200	500	850	1900	3500	5000
Townside PU	200	500	850	1950	3600	5100
Stake	150	450	750	1700	3200	4600
Gladiator - (1-Ton) - (120" wb)						
Stake	150	400	750	1650	3150	4500
Gladiator - (1/2-Ton) - (126" wb)						
Thriftside PU	200	550	900	2000	3600	5200
Townside PU	200	550	900	2100	3700	5300
Stake	150	400	750	1600	3100	4400
Gladiator - (3/4-Ton) - (126" wb)						
Thriftside PU	200	500	850	1900	3500	5000
Townside PU	200	500	850	1950	3600	5100
Stake	150	400	750	1600	3100	4400
Gladiator - (1-Ton) - (126" wb)						
Stake	150	400	750	1550	3050	4300

NOTE: Add 5 percent for V-8 (except Super V-8).

1968

Jeep Universal						
CJ-5 Jeep	400	1300	2200	4400	7700	11,000
CJ-5A Jeep	450	1400	2300	4600	8100	11,500
CJ-6 Jeep	450	1450	2400	4800	8400	12,000
CJ-6A Jeep	450	1500	2500	5000	8800	12,500

NOTE: Add 4 percent for V-6 engine.
Add 5 percent for diesel engine.

Wagoneer - (V-8) - (4x4)						
4d Sta Wag	200	600	1000	2200	4000	5700
4d Sta Wag Cus	200	650	1000	2200	4100	5800
4d Sta Wag Sup	200	650	1000	2200	4150	5900
Jeepster Commando						
Conv	350	700	1150	2300	4600	6600
Sta Wag	200	650	1000	2200	4150	5900
Cpe-Rds	350	725	1200	2350	4800	6800
PU	200	600	950	2150	3850	5500

NOTE: Add 4 percent for V-6 engine.

1969

	6	5	4	3	2	1
Jeep						
CJ-5 Jeep	400	1300	2200	4400	7700	11,000
CJ-6 Jeep	450	1400	2300	4600	8100	11,500
DJ-5 Courier	200	600	950	2150	3850	5500
Jeepster Commando						
Conv	350	700	1150	2300	4600	6600
Sta Wag	200	650	1000	2200	4150	5900
Cpe-Rds	350	725	1200	2350	4800	6800
PU	200	600	950	2150	3850	5500
Conv	350	725	1200	2350	4850	6900
Wagoneer						
4d Wag	200	650	1000	2200	4100	5800
4d Cus Wag	200	650	1000	2200	4150	5900
Gladiator - (1/2-Ton) - (120" wb)						
Thriftside PU	200	600	950	2150	3850	5500
Townside PU	200	600	950	2200	3900	5600
Stake	150	400	750	1650	3150	4500
Gladiator - (3/4-Ton) - (120" wb)						
Thriftside PU	200	550	900	2100	3700	5300
Townside PU	200	550	900	2150	3800	5400
Stake	150	450	800	1800	3300	4800
Gladiator - (1/2-Ton) - (126" wb)						
Townside	200	550	900	2100	3700	5300
Stake	150	450	800	1750	3250	4700
Gladiator - (3/4-Ton) - (126" wb)						
Townside	200	500	850	1950	3600	5100
Stake	150	450	800	1750	3250	4700

NOTE: Add 4 percent for V-6 engine. Add 5 percent for V-8 engine. Add 10 percent for factory Camper Package.

AMC - JEEP

1970

	6	5	4	3	2	1
Model J-100, 110" wb						
4d Sta Wag	350	725	1200	2350	4800	6800
4d Cus Sta Wag	350	725	1200	2350	4850	6900
Model J-100, 101" wb						
4d Cus Sta Wag	350	700	1150	2300	4600	6600
Jeepster Commando, 101" wb						
Sta Wag	350	725	1200	2350	4850	6900
Rds	350	750	1350	2600	5400	7700
Jeepster						
Conv	350	750	1350	2650	5450	7800
Conv Commando	350	800	1350	2700	5500	7900
CJ-5, 1/4-Ton, 81" wb						
Jeep	400	1200	2000	3950	7000	10,000
CJ-6, 101" wb						
Jeep	450	1100	1700	3650	6650	9500
DJ-5, 1/4-Ton, 81" wb						
Jeep	350	750	1200	2350	4900	7000
Jeepster, 1/4-Ton, 101" wb						
PU	350	750	1200	2350	4900	7000
Wagoneer V-8						
4d Cus Sta Wag	350	750	1250	2400	5050	7200

NOTE: Deduct 10 percent for 6-cyl.

Series J-2500						
Thriftside PU	200	650	1000	2200	4150	5900
Townside PU	200	650	1050	2250	4200	6000
Series J-2600						
Thriftside PU	200	600	1000	2200	4000	5700
Townside PU	200	650	1000	2200	4100	5800
Platform Stake	200	600	950	2150	3850	5500
Series J-2700, 3/4-Ton						
Thriftside PU	200	550	900	2000	3600	5200
Townside PU	200	550	900	2100	3700	5300
Platform Stake	200	500	850	1950	3600	5100
Series J-3500, 1/2-Ton						
Townside PU	200	550	900	2000	3600	5200
Series J-3600, 1/2-Ton						
Townside PU	200	550	900	2000	3600	5200
Platform Stake	200	500	850	1900	3500	5000
Series J-3700, 3/4-Ton						
Townside PU	200	500	850	1950	3600	5100
Platform Stake	200	500	850	1850	3350	4900
Series J-4500						
Townside PU	200	500	850	1900	3500	5000
Series J-4600						
Townside PU	200	500	850	1850	3350	4900
Series J-4700						
Townside PU						

1971

Model J-100, 110" wb						
4d Sta Wag	350	725	1150	2300	4700	6700
4d Cus Sta Wag	350	725	1200	2350	4850	6900
4d Spl Sta Wag	350	725	1200	2350	4800	6800
Jeepster Commando, 101" wb						
Sta Wag	350	725	1200	2350	4850	6900
Rds	350	750	1350	2600	5400	7700
Jeepster Commando Six						
Sta Wag	350	750	1250	2350	5000	7100
Rds	350	750	1350	2650	5450	7800
Conv	350	800	1350	2700	5500	7900
CJ-5, 1/4-Ton						
Jeep	400	1200	2000	3950	7000	10,000
CJ-6, 1/2-Ton						
Jeep	450	1100	1700	3650	6650	9500
DJ-5, 1/4-Ton						
Open	350	900	1550	3050	5900	8500
Jeepster, 1/2-Ton						
PU	350	750	1200	2350	4900	7000
Wagoneer V-8						
4d Sta Wag Cus	350	725	1200	2350	4850	6900

NOTE: Deduct 10 percent for 6-cyl.

Series J-2500						
Thriftside PU	200	650	1000	2200	4150	5900
Townside PU	200	650	1000	2200	4100	5800
Series J-3800						
Townside PU	200	600	1000	2200	4000	5700
Series J-4500						
Townside PU	200	600	950	2200	3900	5600
Series J-4600						
Townside PU	200	600	950	2150	3850	5500
Series J-4700						
Townside PU	200	550	900	2150	3800	5400
Series J-4800						
Townside PU	200	550	900	2100	3700	5300

1972

Wagoneer, 6-cyl.						
4d Sta Wag	350	725	1200	2350	4800	6800
4d Cus Sta Wag	350	750	1200	2350	4900	7000
Commando, 1/2-Ton, 6-cyl, 101" wb						
4d Sta Wag	350	750	1250	2350	5000	7100
Rds	350	750	1350	2650	5450	7800

	6	5	4	3	2	1
CJ-5, 1/4-Ton						
Jeep	400	1200	2000	3950	7000	10,000
CJ-6, 1/4-Ton						
Jeep	450	1100	1700	3650	6650	9500
Series J-2500, 1/2-Ton						
Thriftside PU	200	650	1000	2200	4150	5900
Townside PU	200	650	1000	2200	4100	5800
Series J-2600, 1/2-Ton						
Thriftside PU	200	650	1000	2200	4100	5800
Townside PU	200	600	1000	2200	4000	5700
Series J-4500, 3/4-Ton						
Townside PU	200	600	950	2200	3900	5600
Series J-4600, 3/4-Ton						
Townside PU	200	600	950	2150	3850	5500
Series J-4700, 3/4-Ton						
Townside PU	200	550	900	2150	3800	5400
Series J-4800, 3/4-Ton						
Townside PU	200	550	900	2100	3700	5300
1973						
Wagoneer, 6-cyl, 110" wb						
4d Sta Wag	350	725	1200	2350	4800	6800
4d Cus Sta Wag	350	750	1200	2350	4900	7000
Jeep Commando, 6-cyl						
2d Sta Wag	350	725	1150	2300	4700	6700
Rds	350	750	1350	2600	5400	7700
CJ-5, 1/4-Ton						
Jeep	400	1200	2000	3950	7000	10,000
CJ-6, 1/4-Ton						
Jeep	450	1100	1700	3650	6650	9500
Commando, 1/2-Ton, 104" wb						
PU	200	675	1100	2250	4400	6300
Series J-2500, 1/2-Ton						
Thriftside PU	200	650	1050	2250	4200	6000
Townside PU	200	675	1050	2250	4300	6100
Series J-2600, 1/2-Ton						
Thriftside PU	200	650	1000	2200	4150	5900
Townside PU	200	650	1050	2250	4200	6000
Series J-4500, 3/4-Ton						
Townside PU	200	650	1000	2200	4100	5800
Series J-4600, 3/4-Ton						
Townside PU	200	600	1000	2200	4000	5700
Series J-4800, 3/4-Ton						
Townside PU	200	600	950	2200	3900	5600
1974						
Wagoneer, V-8, 109" wb						
4d Sta Wag	350	725	1200	2350	4850	6900
4d Cus Sta Wag	350	750	1250	2350	5000	7100
Cherokee, 6-cyl, 109" wb						
2d Sta Wag	350	725	1200	2350	4800	6800
2d "S" Sta Wag	350	725	1200	2350	4850	6900
CJ-5, 1/4-Ton, 84" wb						
Jeep	400	1200	2000	3950	7000	10,000
CJ-6, 1/4-Ton, 104" wb						
Jeep	450	1100	1700	3650	6650	9500
Series J-10, 1/2-Ton, 110"-131" wb						
Townside PU, SWB	200	650	1000	2200	4100	5800
Townside PU, LWB	200	600	1000	2200	4000	5700
Series J-20, 3/4-Ton						
Townside PU, LWB	200	600	950	2200	3900	5600
1975						
Wagoneer, V-8						
4d Sta Wag	350	725	1200	2350	4850	6900
4d Cus Sta Wag	350	750	1250	2350	5000	7100
Cherokee, 6-cyl						
2d Sta Wag	350	725	1200	2350	4800	6800
2d "S" Sta Wag	350	725	1200	2350	4850	6900
CJ-5, 1/4-Ton, 84" wb						
Jeep	400	1200	2000	3950	7000	10,000
CJ-6, 1/4-Ton, 104" wb						
Jeep	450	1100	1700	3650	6650	9500
Series J-10, 1/2-Ton, 119" or 131" wb						
Townside PU, SWB	200	650	1000	2200	4100	5800
Townside PU LWB	200	600	1000	2200	4000	5700
Series J-20, 3/4-Ton, 131" wb						
Townside PU	200	600	950	2200	3900	5600
1976						
Wagoneer, V-8						
4d Sta Wag	350	725	1200	2350	4850	6900
4d Cus Sta Wag	350	750	1250	2400	5050	7200
Cherokee, 6-cyl.						
2d Sta Wag	350	725	1200	2350	4800	6800
2d "S" Sta Wag	350	725	1200	2350	4850	6900
CJ-5, 1/4-Ton, 84" wb						
Jeep	400	1200	2000	3950	7000	10,000
CJ-7, 1/4-Ton, 94" wb						
Jeep	450	1100	1700	3650	6650	9500
Series J-10, 1/2-Ton, 119" or 131" wb						
Townside PU, SWB	200	600	1000	2200	4000	5700
Townside PU, LWB	200	600	950	2200	3900	5600
Series J-20, 3/4-Ton, 131" wb						
Townside PU, LWB	200	600	950	2150	3850	5500
1977						
Wagoneer, V-8						
4d Sta Wag	350	750	1250	2350	5000	7100
Cherokee, 6-cyl						
2d Sta Wag	350	725	1200	2350	4800	6800
2d "S" Sta Wag	350	725	1200	2350	4850	6900
4d Sta Wag	350	725	1200	2350	4800	6800
CJ-5, 1/4-Ton, 84" wb						
Jeep	450	1050	1650	3500	6400	9200
CJ-7, 1/4-Ton, 94" wb						
Jeep	450	1000	1650	3350	6300	9000
Series J-10, 1/2-Ton, 119" or 131" wb						
Townside PU, SWB	200	600	950	2200	3900	5600
Townside PU, LWB	200	600	950	2150	3850	5500
Series J-20, 3/4-Ton, 131" wb						
Townside PU	200	550	900	2150	3800	5400
1978						
Wagoneer, 108.7" wb						
4d Sta Wag	350	750	1250	2350	5000	7100
Cherokee, 6-cyl						
2d Sta Wag	350	725	1200	2350	4800	6800
2d "S" Sta Wag	350	725	1200	2350	4850	6900
4d Sta Wag	350	725	1200	2350	4800	6800
CJ-5, 1/4-Ton, 84" wb						
Jeep	450	1050	1650	3500	6400	9200

	6	5	4	3	2	1
CJ-7, 1/4-Ton, 94" wb						
Jeep	450	1000	1650	3350	6300	9000
Series J-10, 1/2-Ton, 119" or 131" wb						
Townside PU, SWB	200	600	950	2200	3900	5600
Townside PU, LWB	200	600	950	2150	3850	5500
Series J-20, 3/4-Ton, 131" wb						
Townside PU	200	550	900	2150	3800	5400
1979						
Wagoneer, V-8, 108.7" wb						
4d Sta Wag	350	750	1200	2350	4900	7000
4d Ltd Sta Wag	350	750	1250	2400	5050	7200
Cherokee, 6-cyl						
2d Sta Wag	350	725	1200	2350	4800	6800
2d "S" Sta Wag	350	725	1200	2350	4850	6900
4d Sta Wag	350	725	1200	2350	4800	6800
CJ-5, 1/4-Ton, 84" wb						
Jeep	450	1000	1600	3300	6250	8900
CJ-7, 1/4-Ton, 94" wb						
Jeep	350	900	1550	3050	5900	8500
Series J-10, 1/2-Ton, 119" or 131" wb						
Townside PU, SWB	200	600	950	2200	3900	5600
Townside PU, LWB	200	600	950	2150	3850	5500
Series J-20, 3/4-Ton, 131" wb						
Townside PU	200	550	900	2150	3800	5400
1980						
Wagoneer, 6-cyl, 108.7" wb						
4d Sta Wag	350	750	1200	2350	4900	7000
4d Ltd Sta Wag	350	750	1250	2400	5050	7200
Cherokee, 6-cyl						
2d Sta Wag	350	700	1150	2300	4550	6500
2d "S" Sta Wag	350	725	1150	2300	4700	6700
4d Sta Wag	350	725	1200	2350	4850	6900
CJ-5, 1/4-Ton, 84" wb						
Jeep	350	900	1550	3050	5900	8500
CJ-7, 1/4-Ton, 94" wb						
Jeep	350	800	1450	2750	5600	8000
Series J-10, 1/2-Ton, 119" or 131" wb						
Townside PU, SWB	200	600	950	2200	3900	5600
Townside PU, LWB	200	600	950	2150	3850	5500
Series J-20, 3/4-Ton, 131" wb						
Townside PU	200	550	900	2150	3800	5400
1981						
Wagoneer, 108.7" wb						
4d Sta Wag	350	750	1200	2350	4900	7000
4d Brgm Sta Wag	350	750	1250	2400	5050	7200
4d Ltd Sta Wag	350	750	1300	2400	5200	7400
Cherokee						
2d Sta Wag	200	650	1000	2200	4150	5900
2d Sta Wag, Wide Wheels	200	650	1050	2250	4200	6000
4d Sta Wag	200	675	1050	2250	4300	6100
Scrambler, 1/2-Ton, 104" wb						
PU	200	500	850	1950	3600	5100
CJ-5, 1/4-Ton, 84" wb						
Jeep	200	550	900	2000	3600	5200
CJ-7, 1/4-Ton, 94" wb						
Jeep	200	550	900	2000	3600	5200
Series J-10, 1/2-Ton, 119" or 131" wb						
Townside PU, SWB	200	600	950	2150	3850	5500
Townside PU, LWB	200	550	900	2150	3800	5400
Series J-20, 3/4-Ton, 131" wb						
Townside PU	200	550	900	2100	3700	5300
1982						
Wagoneer, 6-cyl						
4d Sta Wag	350	725	1200	2350	4850	6900
4d Brgm Sta Wag	350	750	1250	2400	5100	7300
4d Ltd Sta Wag	350	750	1350	2600	5400	7700
Cherokee, 6-cyl						
2d Sta Wag	200	650	1000	2200	4150	5900
4d Sta Wag	200	675	1050	2250	4300	6100
Scrambler, 1/2-Ton, 103.4" wb						
PU	200	550	900	2100	3700	5300
CJ-5, 1/4-Ton, 84" wb						
Jeep	350	800	1450	2750	5600	8000
CJ-7, 1/4-Ton, 93.4" wb						
Jeep	350	750	1300	2450	5250	7500
Series J-10, 1/2-Ton, 119" or 131" wb						
Townside PU, SWB	200	600	950	2150	3850	5500
Townside PU, LWB	200	550	900	2150	3800	5400
Series J-20, 3/4-Ton, 131" wb						
Townside PU	200	550	900	2100	3700	5300
Series J-10, 1/2-Ton, 119" wb						
Sportside PU	200	600	950	2200	3900	5600
1983						
Wagoneer, 6-cyl						
4d Brgm Sta Wag	350	800	1450	2750	5600	8000
4d Ltd Sta Wag	350	900	1550	3050	5900	8500
Cherokee, 6-cyl						
2d Sta Wag	350	750	1200	2350	4900	7000
Scrambler, 1/2-Ton, 103.4" wb						
PU	200	550	900	2150	3800	5400
CJ-5, 1/4-Ton, 83.4" wb						
Jeep	350	800	1450	2750	5600	8000
CJ-7, 1/4-Ton, 93.4" wb						
Townside Pickup						
Jeep	350	750	1300	2450	5250	7500
Series J-10, 1/2-Ton, 119" or 131" wb						
Townside PU, SWB	200	550	900	2150	3800	5400
Townside PU, LWB	200	550	900	2100	3700	5300
Series J-10, 1/2-Ton						
Sportside PU	200	600	950	2150	3850	5500
Series J-20, 3/4-Ton, 131" wb						
Townside PU	200	550	900	2000	3600	5200
1984						
Wagoneer, 4-cyl						
4d Sta Wag	350	750	1250	2400	5050	7200
4d Ltd Sta Wag	350	750	1200	2350	4900	7000
Wagoneer, 6-cyl						
4d Sta Wag	350	750	1300	2400	5200	7400
4d Ltd Sta Wag	350	750	1300	2450	5250	7500
Grand Wagoneer, V-8						
4d Sta Wag	350	750	1350	2650	5450	7800
Cherokee, 4-cyl						
2d Sta Wag	350	750	1250	2350	5000	7100
4d Sta Wag	350	750	1200	2350	4900	7000
Cherokee, 6-cyl						
2d Sta Wag	350	750	1250	2400	5100	7300
4d Sta Wag	350	750	1250	2400	5050	7200

Scrambler, 1/2-Ton, 103.4" wb	6	5	4	3	2	1
PU	200	550	900	2150	3800	5400
CJ-7, 1/4-Ton, 93.4" wb						
Jeep	350	750	1350	2650	5450	7800
Series J-10, 1/2-Ton, 119" or 131" wb						
Townside PU	200	675	1050	2250	4350	6200
Series J-20, 3/4-Ton, 131" wb						
Townside PU	200	675	1100	2250	4400	6300

1985

Wagoneer, 4-cyl, 101.4" wb	6	5	4	3	2	1
4d Sta Wag	350	750	1200	2350	4900	7000
4d Ltd Sta Wag	350	750	1300	2450	5250	7500
Wagoneer, 8-cyl, 101.4" wb						
4d Sta Wag	350	750	1300	2450	5250	7500
4d Ltd Sta Wag	350	800	1450	2750	5600	8000
Grand Wagoneer, 108.7" wb						
4d Sta Wag	350	750	1200	2350	4900	7000
Cherokee, 4-cyl, 101.4" wb						
2d Sta Wag	350	700	1150	2300	4550	6500
4d Sta Wag	350	725	1150	2300	4700	6700
Cherokee, 6-cyl, 101.4" wb						
2d Sta Wag	350	725	1150	2300	4700	6700
4d Sta Wag	350	725	1200	2350	4850	6900
Scrambler, 1/2-Ton, 103.5" wb						
PU	200	675	1050	2250	4350	6200
CJ-7, 1/4-Ton, 93.5" wb						
Jeep	350	800	1450	2750	5600	8000
Series J-10, 1/2-Ton, 131" wb						
Townside PU	200	650	1050	2250	4200	6000
Series J-20, 3/4-Ton, 131" wb						
Townside PU	350	700	1150	2300	4550	6500

AMC - EAGLE

1980

Eagle, 6-cyl	6	5	4	3	2	1
4 dr Sed	200	500	850	1900	3500	5000
2 dr Cpe	200	500	850	1850	3350	4900
4 dr Sta Wag	200	550	900	2000	3600	5200
4 dr Sed Ltd	200	550	900	2000	3600	5200
2 dr Cpe Ltd	200	500	850	1950	3600	5100
4 dr Sta Wag Ltd	200	550	900	2150	3800	5400

1981

Eagle 50, 4-cyl	6	5	4	3	2	1
2 dr HBk SX4	150	450	800	1800	3300	4800
2 dr HBk	150	450	800	1750	3250	4700
2 dr HBk SX4 DL	200	500	850	1900	3500	5000
2 dr HBk DL	200	500	850	1850	3350	4900
Eagle 50, 6-cyl						
2 dr HBk SX4	200	550	900	2000	3600	5200
2 dr HBk	200	500	850	1950	3600	5100
2 dr HBk SX4 DL	200	550	900	2150	3800	5400
2 dr HBk DL	200	550	900	2100	3700	5300

1982

Eagle 50, 4-cyl	6	5	4	3	2	1
2 dr HBk SX4	200	500	850	1900	3500	5000
2 dr HBk	200	500	850	1850	3350	4900
2 dr HBk SX4 DL	200	550	900	2000	3600	5200
2 dr HBk DL	200	500	850	1950	3600	5100
Eagle 50, 6-cyl						
2 dr HBk SX4	200	550	900	2150	3800	5400
2 dr HBk	200	550	900	2100	3700	5300
2 dr HBk SX4 DL	200	600	950	2200	3900	5600
2 dr HBk DL	200	600	950	2150	3850	5500
Eagle 30, 4-cyl						
4 dr Sed	150	450	800	1750	3250	4700
2 dr Cpe	150	450	750	1700	3200	4600
4 dr Sta Wag	150	450	800	1800	3300	4800
4 dr Sed Ltd	150	450	800	1800	3300	4800
2 dr Cpe Ltd	150	450	800	1750	3250	4700
4 dr Sta Wag Ltd	200	500	850	1900	3500	5000
Eagle 30, 6-cyl						
4 dr Sed	200	500	850	1950	3600	5100
2 dr Cpe	200	500	850	1900	3500	5000
4 dr Sta Wag	200	550	900	2100	3700	5300
4 dr Sed Ltd	200	550	900	2100	3700	5300
2 dr Cpe Ltd	200	550	900	2000	3600	5200
4 dr Sta Wag Ltd	200	600	950	2150	3850	5500

1983

Eagle 50, 4-cyl	6	5	4	3	2	1
2 dr HBk SX4	200	500	850	1950	3600	5100
2 dr HBk SX4 DL	200	550	900	2100	3700	5300
Eagle 50, 6-cyl						
2 dr HBk SX4	200	600	950	2150	3850	5500
2 dr HBk SX4 DL	200	600	1000	2200	4000	5700
Eagle 30, 4-cyl						
4 dr Sed	200	500	850	1850	3350	4900
4 dr Sta Wag	200	500	850	1950	3600	5100
4 dr Sta Wag Ltd	200	550	900	2100	3700	5300
Eagle 30, 6-cyl						
4 dr Sed	200	550	900	2100	3700	5300
4 dr Sta Wag	200	600	950	2150	3850	5500
4 dr Sta Wag Ltd	200	600	1000	2200	4000	5700

1984

Eagle, 4-cyl	6	5	4	3	2	1
4 dr Sed	200	500	850	1900	3500	5000
4 dr Sta Wag	200	550	900	2000	3600	5200
4 dr Sta Wag Ltd	200	550	900	2150	3800	5400
Eagle, 6-cyl						
4 dr Sed	200	550	900	2150	3800	5400
4 dr Sta Wag	200	600	950	2200	3900	5600
4 dr Sta Wag Ltd	200	650	1000	2200	4100	5800

1985

Eagle	6	5	4	3	2	1
4 dr Sed	200	600	950	2150	3850	5500
4 dr Sta Wag	200	600	1000	2200	4000	5700
4 dr Sta Wag Ltd	200	650	1000	2200	4150	5900

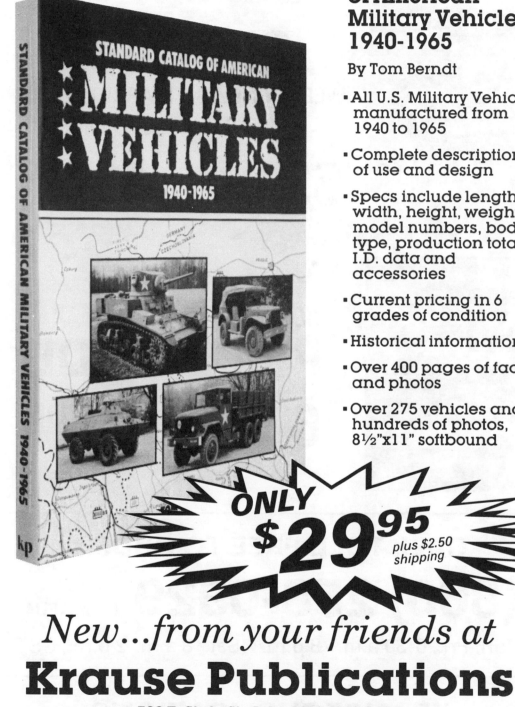

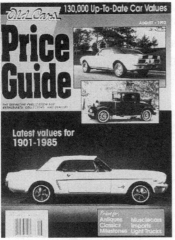